2022 STANDARD POSTAGE STAMP CATALOGUE

ONE HUNDRED AND SEVENTY-EIGHTH EDITION IN SIX VOLUMES

Volume 2A

C-Cur

EDITOR-IN-CHIEF	Jay Bigalke
EDITOR-AT-LARGE	Donna Houseman
CONTRIBUTING EDITOR	Charles Snee
EDITOR EMERITUS	James E. Kloetzel
SENIOR EDITOR /NEW ISSUES AND VALUING	Martin J. Frankevicz
ADMINISTRATIVE ASSISTANT/CATALOGUE LAYOUT	Eric Wiessinger
PRINTING AND IMAGE COORDINATOR	Stacey Mahan
SENIOR GRAPHIC DESIGNER	Cinda McAlexander
SALES DIRECTOR	David Pistello
SALES DIRECTOR	Eric Roth

Released May 2021
Includes New Stamp Listings through the March 2021 Linn's Stamp News Monthly Catalogue Update

AMOS MEDIA
1660 Campbell Road, Suite A, Sidney, OH 45365
Publishers of *Linn's Stamp News, Linn's Stamp News Monthly, Coin World* and *Coin World Monthly.*

Table of contents

See the following volumes for other country listings:
Volume 1A: United States, United Nations, Abu Dhabi-Australia; Volume 1B: Austria-B
Volume 2B: Cyp-F
Volume 3A: G; Volume 3B: H-I
Volume 4A: J-L; Volume 4B: M
Volume 5A: N-Phil; Volume 5B: Pit-Sam
Volume 6A: San-Tete; Volume 6B: Thai-Z

Scott Catalogue Mission Statement

The Scott Catalogue Team exists to serve the recreational, educational and commercial hobby needs of stamp collectors and dealers.

We strive to set the industry standard for philatelic information and products by developing and providing goods that help collectors identify, value, organize and present their collections.

Quality customer service is, and will continue to be, our highest priority.
We aspire toward achieving total customer satisfaction.

Copyright Notice

Trademark Notice

ISBN 978-0-89487-604-2

Library of Congress Card No. 2-3301

What's new for 2022 Scott Standard Volume 2?

Another catalog season is upon us as we continue the journey of the 153-year history of the Scott catalogs. The 2022 volumes are the 178th edition of the Scott *Standard Postage Stamp Catalogue*. Volume 2A includes listings for countries of the world Cambodia through Curacao. Listings for Cyprus through F countries of the world can be found in Vol. 2B.

This year's covers feature the Newfoundland 1937 15¢ King George VI and Harp Seal Pup stamp (Scott 239) on the Vol. 2A catalog and the Denmark 1935 10-ore The Little Mermaid stamp (248) from a set of stamps honoring Hans Christian Andersen's *Fairy Tales* on Vol. 2B.

Because Vol. 2B is a continuation of the first part of the Vol. 2 catalog, the introduction pages are not repeated in each volume this year.

Much of the review for this year's catalog took place throughout 2020 and into 2021. The world was interrupted by the COVID-19 pandemic, and the effects of that hit the stamp world in multiple ways. Some collectors returned to collecting, auction houses saw increases in realizations, traditional in-person stamp shows took a pause, and collectors shifted to purchasing more online. Some of these situations impacted valuing decisions this year and could lead to more changes as we continue our reviews.

One of the significant updates to this volume is the addition of the stamps of Carpatho-Ukraine. A total of 110 new major Scott numbers were added. Carpatho-Ukraine was an autonomous region established in December 1938 within the Second Czechoslovak Republic and proclaimed an independent republic in March 1939. The Czechoslovak government-in-exile was established in Khust in late 1944 and began issuing overprinted and surcharged Hungary stamps in February 1945. The Soviet National Council of Carpatho-Ukraine (NZRU) issued three sets of definitive stamps in 1945. Carpatho-Ukraine was ceded to the Ukrainian Soviet Socialist Republic in 1946.

For the Carpatho-Ukraine section, we would like to acknowledge the contributions of Jay T. Carrigan (1939-2015) and thank Ingert Kuzych and Mark Stelmacovich for their research and assistance with this section that was years in the making.

Canada and provinces were reviewed closely, and approximately 100 changes were made. Because of the pandemic, fewer auctions of Canadian material took place compared to previous years. For Newfoundland, two new listings (Scott 26a and 48c) were added for cover values where the major-number stamp was used as a half (bisect) on cover.

Chile received a review, and approximately 300 value changes, largely increases, were made. One of the increases was for the Flora and Fauna issue of February 1985. This block of 12 10-peso stamps (Scott 686) increased in used condition from $12.50 to $20. Values for similar stamps issued in later years also increased slightly.

China, Republic of China (Taiwan) and the People's Republic of China were looked at closely for this volume with 80, 1,300 and 700 value changes made, respectively. For the People's Republic of China, a number of post-2000 stamp issues with miniature sheets were footnoted and valued for the first time.

There were 75 value changes for the stamps of Colombia, many of which were increases. Some more modern material is proving difficult to find as collectors work to complete collections.

Costa Rica saw approximately 750 changes. Many of the value changes for post-1996 issues were slight increases. For example, the 2017 Insects sheet of four (Scott 687) moved from $8.75 to $9.75 in unused condition.

For Denmark, approximately 75 value changes were made. One of the important updates to this country was the addition of phosphor tagging varieties as minor listings. Around 60 new minor-letter listings were added for stamps that were issued with and without tagging. Some values were also changed to reflect the distinction between ordinary and fluorescent papers. A complete listing of the numbers added is found on the Number Additions, Deletions and Changes page in this volume.

A thorough review of Ecuador resulted in more than 1,500 value changes, with a mix of decreases and increases throughout. New overprint varieties were added for an Official and two postal tax issues: Scott O137a, RA1a and RA31b. Additionally, values were added for the Coat of Arms overprints (Scott 113 and 114). These two stamps are each valued at $100 in used condition, and Scott 113 is valued at $100 in mint condition. A dash remains for the mint value of Scott 114. These new values are in italics to indicated that the stamps trade infrequently.

Many other countries received reviews that are not noted in this letter. We encourage you to pay special attention to the Number Additions, Deletions and Changes listing in this volume. We also suggest reading the catalog introduction, which includes an abundance of useful information.

Lastly, the new Scott *Stamp Illustrated Identifier,* formerly included as the Illustrated Identifier in each Scott Standard catalog volume, is now a separate publication. The softcover 6-inch-by-9-inch booklet will make it easier to identify stamps while consulting listings in the Scott catalog without having to flip back and forth. To purchase a copy, visit online at www.amosadvantage.com.

Best wishes in your stamp collecting pursuits!

Jay Bigalke, Scott catalog editor-in-chief

Acknowledgments

Our appreciation and gratitude go to the following individuals who have assisted us in preparing information included in this year's Scott catalogues. Some helpers prefer anonymity. These individuals have generously shared their stamp knowledge with others through the medium of the Scott catalogue.

Those who follow provided information that is in addition to the hundreds of dealer price lists and advertisements and scores of auction catalogues and realizations that were used in producing the catalogue values. It is from those noted here that we have been able to obtain information on items not normally seen in published lists and advertisements. Support from these people goes beyond data leading to catalogue values, for they also are key to editorial changes.

A special acknowledgment to Liane and Sergio Sismondo of The Classic Collector for their assistance and knowledge sharing that have aided in the preparation of this year's Standard and Classic Specialized Catalogues.

Clifford J. Alexander
(Carriers and Locals Society)
Roland Austin
Michael & Cecilia Ball (A To Z Stamps)
Jim Bardo (Bardo Stamps)
John Birkinbine II
Brian M. Bleckwenn
(The Philatelic Foundation)
Les Bootman
Roger S. Brody
Tom Brougham
(Canal Zone Study Group)
Paul and Josh Buchsbayew
(Cherrystone Auctions, Inc.)
Timothy Bryan Burgess
Tina and John Carlson (JET Stamps)
Jay T. Carrigan
Carlson Chambliss
Bob Coale
Tony L. Crumbley
(Carolina Coin and Stamp, Inc.)
Christopher Dahle
Charles Deaton
Bob and Rita Dumaine
(Sam Houston Duck Co.)
Charles Epting (H.R. Harmer)
Mike Farrell
David Feldman International Auctioneers
Robert A. Fisher
Jeffrey M. Forster
Robert S. Freeman
Henry L. Gitner
(Henry Gitner Philatelists, Inc.)
Stan Goldfarb

Marc E. Gonzales
Daniel E. Grau
Bruce Hecht (Bruce L. Hecht Co.)
Eric Jackson
Michael Jaffe (Michael Jaffe Stamps, Inc.)
William A. (Bill) Jones
Allan Katz (Ventura Stamp Co.)
Patricia A. Kaufmann
(Civil War Philatelic Society)
Jon Kawaguchi
(Ryukyu Philatelic Specialist Society)
Han Ki Kim
Ingert Kuzych
Ulf Lindahl (Ethiopian Philatelic Society)
Ignacio Llach (Filatelia Llach, S.L.)
William K. McDaniel
Pat McElroy
Brian Metz
Mark S. Miller (India Study Circle)
Gary Morris (Pacific Midwest Co.)
Peter Mosiondz Jr.
Bruce M. Moyer
(Moyer Stamps & Collectables)
Scott Murphy
Dr. Tiong Tak Ngo
Nik & Lisa Oquist
Don Peterson
(International Philippine Philatelic Society)
Stanley M. Piller
(Stanley M. Piller & Associates)
Dr. Charles Posner
Peter W. W. Powell
Ed Reiser (Century Stamp Co.)

Ghassan D. Riachi
Robert G. Rufe
Theodosios D. Sampson Ph.D.
Dennis W. Schmidt
Joyce & Chuck Schmidt
Guy Shaw
(Mexico-Elmhurst Philatelic Society International)
J. Randall Shoemaker
(Philatelic Stamp Authentication and Grading, Inc.)
Sergio and Liane Sismondo
(The Classic Collector)
Jay Smith
Telah Smith
Mark Stelmacovich
Scott R. Trepel
(Siegel Auction Galleries, Inc.)
Dan Undersander
Steven Unkrich
Herbert R. Volin
Philip T. Wall
Val Zabijaka (Zabijaka Auctions)

Addresses, telephone numbers, web sites, email addresses of general and specialized philatelic societies

Collectors can contact the following groups for information about the philately of the areas within the scope of these societies, or inquire about membership in these groups. Aside from the general societies, we limit this list to groups that specialize in particular fields of philately, particular areas covered by the Scott *Standard Postage Stamp Catalogue*, and topical groups. Many more specialized philatelic society exist than those listed below. These addresses are updated yearly, and they are, to the best of our knowledge, correct and current. Groups should inform the editors of address changes whenever they occur. The editors also want to hear from other such specialized groups not listed.

Unless otherwise noted all website addresses begin with http://

General Societies

American Philatelic Society, 100 Match Factory Place, Bellefonte, PA 16823-1367; (814) 933-3803; https://stamps.org; apsinfo@stamps.org

International Society of Worldwide Stamp Collectors, Joanne Murphy, M.D., P.O. Box 19006, Sacramento, CA 95819; www.iswsc.org; executivedirector@iswsc.org

Royal Philatelic Society of Canada, P.O. Box 69080, St. Clair Post Office, Toronto, ON M4T 3A1 Canada; (888) 285-4143; www.rpsc.org; info@rpsc.org

Royal Philatelic Society London, 15 Abchurch Lane, London EX4N 7BW, United Kingdom; +44 (0) 20 7486 1044; www.rpsl.org.uk; secretary@rpsl.org.uk

Libraries, Museums, and Research Groups

American Philatelic Research Library, 100 Match Factory Place, Bellefonte, PA 16823; (814) 933-3803; www.stamplibrary.org; library@stamps.org.

V. G. Greene Philatelic Research Foundation, P.O. Box 69100, St. Clair Post Office, Toronto, ON M4T 3A1, Canada; (416) 921-2073; info@greenefoundation.ca

Aero/Astro Philately

American Air Mail Society, Stephen Reinhard, P.O. Box 110, Mineola, NY 11501; www.americanairmailsociety.org; sreinhard1@optonline.net

Postal History

Auxiliary Markings Club, Jerry Johnson, 6621 W. Victoria Ave., Kennewick, WA 99336; www.postal-markings.org; membership-2010@postal-markings.org

Postage Due Mail Study Group, Bob Medland, Camway Cottage, Nanny Hurn's Lane, Cameley, Bristol BS39 5AJ, United Kingdom; 01761 45959; www.postageduemail.org.uk; secretary.pdmsg@gmail.com

Postal History Society, Yamil Kouri, 405 Waltham St. #347, Lexington, MA 02421; www.postalhistorysociety.org; yhkouri@massmed.org

Post Mark Collectors Club, Bob Milligan, 7014 Woodland Oaks Drive, Magnolia, TX 77354; (281) 259-2735; www.postmarks.org; bob.milligan0@gmail.com

U.S. Cancellation Club, Roger Curran, 18 Tressler Blvd., Lewisburg, PA 17837; rdcnrc@ptd.net

Revenues and Cinderellas

American Revenue Association, Lyman Hensley, 473 E. Elm St., Sycamore, IL 60178-1934; www.revenuer.org; ilrno2@netzero.net

Christmas Seal and Charity Stamp Society, John Denune Jr., 234 E. Broadway, Granville, OH 43023; (740) 814-6031; www.seal-society.org

National Duck Stamp Collectors Society, Anthony J. Monico, P.O. Box 43, Harleysville, PA 19438-0043; www.ndscs.org; ndscs@ndscs.org

State Revenue Society, Kent Gray, P.O. Box 67842, Albuquerque, NM 87193; www.staterevenue.org; srssecretary@comcast.net

Thematic Philately

Americana Unit, Dennis Dengel, 17 Peckham Road, Poughkeepsie, NY 12603-2018; www.americanaunit.org; ddengel@americanaunit.org

American Topical Association, Jennifer Miller, P.O. Box 2143, Greer, SC 29652-2143; (618) 985-5100; americantopical.org; ata@americantopical.org

Astronomy Study Unit, Leonard Zehr, 1411 Chateau Ave., Windsor, ON N8P 1M2, Canada; (416) 833-9317; www.astronomystudyunit.net; lenzehr@gmail.com

Bicycle Stamps Club, Corey Hjalseth, 1102 Broadway, Suite 200, Tacoma, WA 98402; (253) 318-6222; www.bicyclestampsclub.org; coreyh@evergreenhomeloans.com

Biology Unit, Chris Dahle, 1401 Linmar Drive NE, Cedar Rapids, IA 52402-3724; www.biophilately.org; chris-dahle@biophilately.org

Bird Stamp Society, Mr. S. A. H. (Tony) Statham, Ashlyns Lodge, Chesham Road, Berkhamsted, Herts HP4 2ST United Kingdom; www.bird-stamps.org/bss; tony.statham@sky.com

Captain Cook Society, Jerry Yucht, 8427 Leale Ave., Stockton, CA 95212, www.captaincooksociety.com; us@captaincooksociety.com

The CartoPhilatelic Society, Marybeth Sulkowski, 2885 Sanford Ave., SW, #32361, Grandville, MI 49418-1342; www.mapsonstamps.org; secretary@mapsonstamps.org

Casey Jones Railroad Unit, Jeff Lough, 2612 Redbud Land, Apt. C, Lawrence, KS 66046; www.uqp.de/cjr; jeffydplaugh@gmail.com

Cats on Stamps Study Unit, Robert D. Jarvis, 2731 Teton Lane, Fairfield, CA 94533; www.catstamps.info; catmews1@yahoo.com

Chemistry and Physics on Stamps Study Unit, Dr. Roland Hirsch, 13830 Metcalf Ave., Apt. 15218, Overland Park, KS 66223-8017; (301) 792-6296; www.cpossu.org; rfhirsch@cpossu.org

Chess on Stamps Study Unit, Barry Keith, 511 First St. N., Apt. 106; Charlottesville, VA 22902; www.chessonstamps.org; keithfam@embarqmail.com

Cricket Philatelic Society, A. Melville-Brown, 11 Weppons, Ravens Road, Shoreham-by-Sea, West Sussex BN43 5AW, United Kingdom; www.cricketstamp.net; mel.cricket.100@googlemail.com

Earth's Physical Features Study Group, Fred Klein, 515 Magdalena Ave., Los Altos, CA 94024; http://epfsu.jeffhayward.com; epfsu@jeffhayward.com

Ebony Society of Philatelic Events and Reflections (ESPER); Don Neal, P.O. Box 5245, Somerset, NJ 08875-5245; www.esperstamps.org; esperdon@verizon.net

Europa Study Unit, Tonny E. Van Loij, 3002 S. Xanthia St.; Denver, CO 80231-4237; (303) 752-0189; www.europastudyunit.org; tvanloij@gmail.com

Fire Service in Philately, John Zaranek, 81 Hillpine Road, Cheektowaga, NY 14227-2259; (716) 668-3352; jczaranek@roadrunner.com

Gastronomy on Stamps Study Unit, David Wolfersburger, 5062 NW 35th Lane Road, Ocala, FL 34482; (314) 494-3795; www.gastronomystamps.org

Gay and Lesbian History on Stamps Club, Joe Petronie, P.O. Box 190842, Dallas, TX 75219-0842; www.glhsonline.org; glhsc@aol.com

Gems, Minerals and Jewelry Study Unit, Fred Haynes, 10 Country Club Drive, Rochester, NY 14618-3720; fredmhaynes55@gmail.com

Graphics Philately Association, Larry Rosenblum. 1030 E. El Camino Real, PMB 107, Sunnyvale, CA 94087-3759; www.graphics-stamps.org; larry@graphics-stamps.org

Journalists, Authors and Poets on Stamps, Christopher D. Cook, 7222 Hollywood Road, Berrien Springs, MI 49103; cdcook2@gmail.com

Lighthouse Stamp Society; www.lighthousestampsociety.org; dalene@lighthousestampsociety.org

Lions International Stamp Club, David McKirdy, s-Gravenwetering 248, 3062 SJ Rotterdam, Netherlands; 31(0) 10 212 0313; www.lisc.nl; davidmckirdy@aol.com

Masonic Study Unit, Gene Fricks, 25 Murray Way, Blackwood, NJ 08012-4400; genefricks@comcast.net

Medical Subjects Unit, Dr. Frederick C. Skvara, P.O. Box 6228, Bridgewater, NJ 08807; fcskvara@optonline.net

Napoleonic Age Philatelists, Ken Berry, 4117 NW 146th St., Oklahoma City, OK 73134-1746; (405) 748-8646; www.nap-stamps.org; krb4117@att.net

Old World Archaeological Study Unit, Caroline Scannell, 14 Dawn Drive, Smithtown, NY 11787-176; www.owasu.org; editor@owasu.org

Petroleum Philatelic Society International, Feitze Papa, 922 Meander Drive, Walnut Creek, CA 94598-4239; www.ppsi.org.uk; oildad@astound.net

Rotary on Stamps Fellowship, Gerald L. Fitzsimmons, 105 Calle Ricardo, Victoria, TX 77904; www.rotaryonstamps.org; glfitz@suddenlink.net

Scouts on Stamps Society International, Woodrow (Woody) Brooks, 498 Baldwin Road, Akron, OH 44312; (330) 612-1294; www.sossi.org; secretary@sossi.org

Ships on Stamps Unit, Erik Th. Matzinger, Voorste Havervelden 30, 4822 AL Breda, Netherlands; www.shipsonstamps.org; erikships@gmail.com

Space Topic Study Unit, David Blog, P.O. Box 174, Bergenfield, NJ 07621; www.space-unit.com; davidblognj@gmail.com

Stamps on Stamps Collectors Club, Michael Merritt, 73 Mountainside Road, Mendham, NJ 07945; www.stampsonstamps.org; michael@mischu.me

Windmill Study Unit, Walter J. Hallien, 607 N. Porter St., Watkins Glenn, NY 14891-1345; (607) 229-3541; www.windmillworld.com

Wine On Stamps Study Unit, David Wolfersburger, 5062 NW 35th Lane Road, Ocala, FL 34482; (314) 494-3795; www.wine-on-stamps.org;

United States

American Air Mail Society, Stephen Reinhard, P.O. Box 110, Mineola, NY 11501; www.americanairmailsociety.org; sreinhard1@optonline.net

American First Day Cover Society, P.O. Box 246, Colonial Beach VA 22443-0246; (520) 321-0880; www.afdcs.org; afdcs@afdcs.org

Auxiliary Markings Club, Jerry Johnson, 6621 W. Victoria Ave., Kennewick, WA 99336; www.postal-markings.org; membership-2010@postal-markings.org

American Plate Number Single Society, Rick Burdsall, APNSS Secretary, P.O. BOX 1023, Palatine, IL 60078-1023; www.apnss.org; apnss.sec@gmail.com

American Revenue Association, Lyman Hensley, 473 E. Elm St., Sycamore, IL 60178-1934; www.revenuer.org; ilrno2@netzero.net

American Society for Philatelic Pages and Panels, Ron Walenciak, P.O. Box 1042, Washington Township, NJ 07676; www.asppp.org; ron.walenciak@asppp.org

Canal Zone Study Group, Mike Drabik, P.O. Box 281, Bolton, MA 01740, www.canalzonestudygroup.com; czsgsecretary@gmail.com

Carriers and Locals Society, John Bowman, 14409 Pentridge Drive, Corpus Christi, TX 78410; (361) 933-0757; www.pennypost.org; jbowman@stx.rr.com

Christmas Seal & Charity Stamp Society, John Denune Jr., 234 E. Broadway, Granville, OH 43023; (740) 814-6031; www.seal-society.org; john@christmasseals.net

Civil War Philatelic Society, Patricia A. Kaufmann, 10194 N. Old State Road, Lincoln, DE 19960-3644; (302) 422-2656; www.civilwarphilatelicsociety.org; trishkauf@comcast.net

Error, Freaks, and Oddities Collectors Club, Scott Shaulis, P.O. Box 549, Murrysville, PA 15668-0549; (724) 733-4134; www.efocc.org; scott@shaulisstamps.com

National Duck Stamp Collectors Society, Anthony J. Monico, P.O. Box 43, Harleysville, PA 19438-0043; www.ndscs.org; ndscs@ndscs.org

Plate Number Coil Collectors Club (PNC3), Gene Trinks, 16415 W. Desert Wren Court, Surprise, AZ 85374; (623) 322-4619; www.pnc3.org; gctrinks@cox.net

Post Mark Collectors Club, Bob Milligan, 7014 Woodland Oaks Drive, Magnolia, TX 77354; (281) 259-2735; www.postmarks.org; bob.milligan0@gmail.com

Souvenir Card Collectors Society, William V. Kriebel, www.souvenircards.org; kriebewv@drexel.edu

United Postal Stationery Society, Dave Kandziolka, 404 Sundown Drive, Knoxville, TN 37934; www.upss.org; membership@upss.org

U.S. Cancellation Club, Roger Curran, 18 Tressler Blvd., Lewisburg, PA 17837; rdcnrc@ptd.net

U.S. Philatelic Classics Society, Rob Lund, 2913 Fulton St., Everett, WA 98201-3733; www.uspcs.org; membershipchairman@uspcs.org

US Possessions Philatelic Society, Daniel F. Ring, P.O. Box 113, Woodstock, IL 60098; http://uspps.tripod.com; danielfring@hotmail.com

United States Stamp Society, Rod Juell, P.O. Box 3508, Joliet, IL 60434-3508; www.usstamps.org; execsecretary@usstamps.org

Africa

Bechuanalands and Botswana Society, Otto Peetoom, Roos, East Yorkshire HU12 0LD, United Kingdom; 44(0)1964 670239; www.bechuanalandphilately.com; info@bechuanalandphilately.com

Egypt Study Circle, Mike Murphy, 11 Waterbank Road, Bellingham, London SE6 3DJ United Kingdom; (44) 0203 6737051; www.egyptstudycircle.org.uk; secretary@egyptstudycircle.org.uk

Ethiopian Philatelic Society, Ulf Lindahl, 21 Westview Place, Riverside, CT 06878; (203) 722-0769; https://ethiopianphilatelicsociety.weebly.com; ulindahl@optonline.net

Liberian Philatelic Society, P.O. Box 1570, Parker, CO 80134; www.liberiastamps.org; liberiastamps@comcast.net

Orange Free State Study Circle, J. R. Stroud, RDPSA, 24 Hooper Close, Burnham-on-sea, Somerset TA8 1JQ United Kingdom; 44 1278 782235; www.orangefreestatephilately.org.uk; richard@richardstroud.plus.com

Philatelic Society for Greater Southern Africa, David McNamee, 15 Woodland Drive, Alamo, CA 94507; www.psgsa.org; alan.hanks@sympatico.ca

Rhodesian Study Circle, William R. Wallace, P.O. Box 16381, San Francisco, CA 94116; (415) 564-6069; www.rhodesianstudycircle.org.uk; bwall8rscr@earthlink.net

Society for Moroccan and Tunisian Philately, S.P.L.M., 206, Bld Pereire, 75017 Paris, France; http://splm-philatelie.org; splm206@aol.com

South Sudan Philatelic Society, William Barclay, 1370 Spring Hill Road, South Londonderry, VT 05155; barclayphilatelics@gmail.com

Sudan Study Group, Andy Neal, Bank House, Coedway, Shrewsbury SY5 9AR United Kingdom; www.sudanstamps.org; andywneal@gmail.com

Transvaal Study Circle, c/o 9 Meadow Road, Gravesend, Kent DA11 7LR United Kingdom; www.transvaalstamps.org.uk; transvaalstudycircle@aol.co.uk

West Africa Study Circle, Martin Bratzel, 1233 Virginia Ave., Windsor, ON N8S 2Z1 Canada; www.wasc.org.uk; marty_bratzel@yahoo.ca

Asia

Aden & Somaliland Study Group, Malcom Lacey, 108 Dalestorth Road, Sutton-in-Ashfield, Nottinghamshire NG17 3AA, United Kingdom; www.stampdomain.com/aden; neil53williams@yahoo.co.uk

Burma (Myanmar) Philatelic Study Circle, Michael Whittaker, 1, Ecton Leys, Hillside, Rugby, Warwickshire CV22 5SL United Kingdom; https://burmamyanmarphilately.wordpress.com/burma-myanmar-philatelic-study-circle; manningham8@mypostoffice.co.uk

Ceylon Study Circle, Rodney W. P. Frost, 42 Lonsdale Road, Cannington, Bridgwater, Somerset TA5 2JS United Kingdom; 01278 652592; www.ceylonsc.org; rodney.frost@tiscali.co.uk

China Stamp Society, H. James Maxwell, 1050 W. Blue Ridge Blvd., Kansas City, MO 64145-1216; www.chinastampsociety.org; president@chinastampsociety.org

Hong Kong Philatelic Society, John Tang, G.P.O. Box 446, Hong Kong; www.hkpsociety.com; hkpsociety@outlook.com

Hong Kong Study Circle, Robert Newton, www.hongkongstudycircle.com/index.html; newtons100@gmail.com

India Study Circle, John Warren, P.O. Box 7326, Washington, DC 20044; (202) 488-7443; https://indiastudycircle.org; jw-kbw@earthlink.net

International Philippine Philatelic Society, James R. Larot, Jr., 4990 Bayleaf Court, Martinez, CA 94553; (925) 260-5425; www.theipps.info; jlarot@ccwater.com

International Society for Japanese Philately, P.O. Box 1283, Haddonfield NJ 08033; www.isjp.org; secretary@isjp.org

Iran Philatelic Study Circle, Nigel Gooch, Marchwood, 56, Wickham Ave., Bexhill-on-Sea, East Sussex TN39 3ER United Kingdom; www.iranphilately.org; nigelmgooch@gmail.com

Korea Stamp Society, Peter Corson, 1109 Gunnison Place, Raleigh, NC 27609; (919) 787-7611; koreastampsociety.org; pbcorson@aol.com

Nepal & Tibet Philatelic Study Circle, Colin Hepper, 12 Charnwood Close, Peterborough, Cambs PE2 9BZ United Kingdom; http://fuchs-online.com/ntpsc; ntpsc@fuchs-online.com

Pakistan Philatelic Study Circle, Jeff Siddiqui, P.O. Box 7002, Lynnwood, WA 98046; jeffsiddiqui@msn.com

Society of Indo-China Philatelists, Ron Bentley, 2600 N. 24th St., Arlington, VA 22207; (703) 524-1652; www.sicp-online.org; ron.bentley@verizon.net

Society of Israel Philatelists, Inc., Sarah Berezenko, 100 Match Factory Place, Bellefonte, PA 16823-1367; (814) 933-3803 ext. 212; www.israelstamps.com; israelstamps@gmail.com

Australasia and Oceania

Australian States Study Circle of the Royal Sydney Philatelic Club, Ben Palmer, G.P.O. 1751, Sydney, NSW 2001 Australia; http://club.philas.org.au/states

Fellowship of Samoa Specialists, Trevor Shimell, 18 Aspen Drive, Newton Abbot, Devon TQ12 4TN United Kingdom; www.samoaexpress.org; trevor.shimell@gmail.com

Malaya Study Group, Michael Waugh, 151 Roker Lane, Pudsey, Leeds LS28 9ND United Kingdom; http://malayastudygroup.com; mawpud43@gmail.com

New Zealand Society of Great Britain, Michael Wilkinson, 121 London Road, Sevenoaks, Kent TN13 1BH United Kingdom; 01732 456997; www.nzsgb.org.uk; mwilkin799@aol.com

Pacific Islands Study Circle, John Ray, 24 Woodvale Ave., London SE25 4AE United Kingdom; www.pisc.org.uk; secretary@pisc.org.uk

Papuan Philatelic Society, Steven Zirinsky, P.O. Box 49, Ansonia Station, New York, NY 10023; (718) 706-0616; www.papuanphilatelicsociety.com; szirinsky@cs.com

Pitcairn Islands Study Group, Dr. Everett L. Parker, 207 Corinth Road, Hudson, ME 04449-3057; (207) 573-1686; www.pisg.net; eparker@hughes.net

Ryukyu Philatelic Specialist Society, Laura Edmonds, P.O. Box 240177, Charlotte, NC 28224-0177; (336) 509-3739; www.ryukyustamps.org; secretary@ryukyustamps.org

Society of Australasian Specialists / Oceania, Steve Zirinsky, P.O. Box 230049, New York, NY 10023-0049; www.sasoceania.org; president@sosoceania.org

Sarawak Specialists' Society, Stephen Schumann, 2417 Cabrallo Drive, Hayward, CA 94545; (510) 785-4794; www.britborneostamps.org.uk; vpnam@s-s-s.org.uk

Western Australia Study Group, Brian Pope, P.O. Box 423, Claremont, WA 6910 Australia; (61) 419 843 943; www.wastudygroup.com; wastudygroup@hotmail.com

Europe

American Helvetia Philatelic Society, Richard T. Hall, P.O. Box 15053, Asheville, NC 28813-0053; www.swiss-stamps.org; secretary2@swiss-stamps.org

American Society for Netherlands Philately, Hans Kremer, 50 Rockport Court, Danville, CA 94526; (925) 820-5841; www.asnp1975.com; hkremer@usa.net

Andorran Philatelic Study Circle, David Hope, 17 Hawthorn Drive, Stalybridge, Cheshire SK15 1UE United Kingdom; www.andorranpsc.org.uk; andorranpsc@btinternet.com

Austria Philatelic Society, Ralph Schneider, P.O. Box 978, Iowa Park, TX 76376; (940) 213-5004; www.austriaphilatelicsociety.com; rschneiderstamps@gmail.com

Channel Islands Specialists Society, Richard Flemming, Burbage, 64 Falconers Green, Hinckley, Leicestershire, LE102SX, United Kingdom; www.ciss.uk; secretary@ciss.uk

Cyprus Study Circle, Rob Wheeler, 47 Drayton Ave., London W13 0LE United Kingdom; www.cyprusstudycircle.org; robwheeler47@aol.com

Danish West Indies Study Unit of Scandinavian Collectors Club, Arnold Sorensen, 7666 Edgedale Drive, Newburgh, IN 47630; (812) 480-6532; www.scc-online.org; valbydwi@hotmail.com

Eire Philatelic Association, John B. Sharkey, 1559 Grouse Lane, Mountainside, NJ 07092-1340; www.eirephilatelicassoc.org; jsharkeyepa@me.com

Faroe Islands Study Circle, Norman Hudson, 40 Queen's Road, Vicar's Cross, Chester CH3 5HB United Kingdom; www.faroeislandssc.org; jntropics@hotmail.com

France & Colonies Philatelic Society, Edward Grabowski, 111 Prospect St., 4C, Westfield, NJ 07090; (908) 233-9318; www.franceandcolsps.org; edjjg@alum.mit.edu

Germany Philatelic Society, P.O. Box 6547, Chesterfield, MO 63006-6547; www.germanyphilatelicusa.org; info@germanyphilatelicsocietyusa.org

Gibraltar Study Circle, Susan Dare, 22, Byways Park, Strode Road, Clevedon, North Somerset BS21 6UR United Kingdom; www.gibraltarstudycircle.wordpress.com; smldare@yahoo.co.uk

International Society for Portuguese Philately, Clyde Homen, 1491 Bonnie View Road, Hollister, CA 95023-5117; www.portugalstamps.com; ispp1962@sbcglobal.net

Italy and Colonies Study Circle, Richard Harlow, 7 Duncombe House, 8 Manor Road, Teddington, Middlesex TW118BE United Kingdom; 44 208 977 8737; www.icsc-uk.com; richardharlow@outlook.com

Liechtenstudy USA, Paul Tremaine, 410 SW Ninth St., Dundee, OR 97115-9731; (503) 538-4500; www.liechtenstudy.org; tremaine@liechtenstudy.org

Lithuania Philatelic Society, Audrius Brazdeikis, 9915 Murray Landing, Missouri City, TX 77459; (281) 450-6224; www.lithuanianphilately.com/lps; audrius@lithuanianphilately.com

Luxembourg Collectors Club, Gary B. Little, 7319 Beau Road, Sechelt, BC V0N 3A8 Canada; (604) 885-7241; http://lcc.luxcentral.com; gary@luxcentral.com

Plebiscite-Memel-Saar Study Group of the German Philatelic Society, Clayton Wallace, 100 Lark Court, Alamo, CA 94507; claytonwallace@comcast.net

Polonus Polish Philatelic Society, Daniel Lubelski, P.O. Box 2212, Benicia, CA 94510; (419) 410-9115; www.polonus.org; info@polonus.org

Rossica Society of Russian Philately, Alexander Kolchinsky, 1506 Country Lake Drive, Champaign, IL 61821-6428; www.rossica.org; alexander.kolchinsky@rossica.org

Scandinavian Collectors Club, Alan Warren, Scandinavian Collectors Club, P.O. Box 39, Exton PA 19341-0039; (612) 810-8640; www.scc-online.org; alanwar@att.net

Society for Czechoslovak Philately, Tom Cossaboom, P.O. Box 4124, Prescott, AZ 86302; (928) 771-9097; www.csphilately.org; klfck1@aol.com

Society for Hungarian Philately, Alan Bauer, P.O. Box 4028, Vineyard Haven, MA 02568; (617) 645-4045; www.hungarianphilately.org; alan@hungarianstamps.com

Spanish Study Circle, Edith Knight, www.spaincircle.wixsite.com/spainstudycircle; spaincircle@gmail.com

Ukrainian Philatelic & Numismatic Society, Martin B. Tatuch, 5117 8th Road N., Arlington, VA 22205-1201; www.upns.org; treasurer@upns.org

Vatican Philatelic Society, Dennis Brady, 4897 Ledyard Drive, Manlius NY 13104-1514; www.vaticanphilately.org; dbrady7534@gmail.com

Yugoslavia Study Group, Michael Chant, 1514 N. Third Ave., Wausau, WI 54401; 208-748-9919; www.yugosg.org; membership@yugosg.org

Interregional Societies

American Society of Polar Philatelists, Alan Warren, P.O. Box 39, Exton, PA 19341-0039; (610) 321-0740; www.polarphilatelists.org; alanwar@att.net

First Issues Collector's Club, Kurt Streepy, 3128 E. Mattatha Drive, Bloomington, IN 47401; www.firstissues.org; secretary@firstissues.org

Former French Colonies Specialist Society, Col.fra, BP 628, 75367 Paris, France; www.colfra.org; postmaster@colfra.org

France & Colonies Philatelic Society, Edward Grabowski, 111 Prospect St., 4C, Westfield, NJ 07090; (908) 233-9318, www.franceandcolsps.org; edjjg@alum.mit.edu

Joint Stamp Issues Society, Richard Zimmermann, 29A, Rue Des Eviats, 67220 Lalaye, France; www.philarz.net; richard.zimmermann@club-internet.fr

The King George VI Collectors Society, Brian Livingstone, 21 York Mansions, Prince of Wales Drive, London SW11 4DL United Kingdom; www.kg6.info; livingstone484@btinternet.com

International Society of Reply Coupon Collectors, Peter Robin, P.O. Box 353, Bala Cynwyd, PA 19004; peterrobin@verizon.net

Italy and Colonies Study Circle, Richard Harlow, 7 Duncombe House, 8 Manor Road, Teddington, Middlesex TW118BE United Kingdom; 44 208 977 8737; www.icsc-uk.com; richardharlow@outlook.com

St. Helena, Ascension & Tristan Da Cunha Philatelic Society, Dr. Everett L. Parker, 207 Corinth Road, Hudson, ME 04449-3057; (207) 573-1686; www.shatps.org; eparker@hughes.net

United Nations Philatelists, Blanton Clement, Jr., P.O. Box 146, Morrisville, PA 19067-0146; www.unpi.com; bclemjunior@gmail.com

Latin America

Asociación Filatélica de Panamá, Edward D. Vianna B. ASOFILPA, 0819-03400, El Dorado, Panama; http://asociacionfilatelicadepanama.blogspot.com; asofilpa@gmail.com

Asociacion Mexicana de Filatelia (AMEXFIL), Alejandro Grossmann, Jose Maria Rico, 129, Col. Del Valle, 3100 Mexico City, DF Mexico; www.amexfil.mx; amexfil@gmail.com

Associated Collectors of El Salvador, Pierre Cahen, Vipsal 1342, P.O. Box 02-5364, Miami FL 33102; www.elsalvadorphilately.org; sfes-aces@elsalvadorphilately.org

Association Filatelic de Costa Rica, Giana Wayman (McCarty), #SJO 4935, P.O. Box 025723, Miami, FL 33102-5723; 011-506-2-228-1947; scotland@racsa.co.cr

Brazil Philatelic Association, William V. Kriebel, www.brazilphilatelic.org, info@brazilphilatelic.org

Canal Zone Study Group, Mike Drabik, P.O. Box 281, Bolton, MA 01740; www.canalzonestudygroup.com; czsgsecretary@gmail.com

Colombia-Panama Philatelic Study Group, Allan Harris, 26997 Hemmingway Ct, Hayward CA 94542-2349; www.copaphil.org; copaphilusa@aol.com

Falkland Islands Philatelic Study Groups, Morva White, 42 Colton Road, Shrivenham, Swindon SN6 8AZ United Kingdom; 44(0) 1793 783245; www.fipsg.org.uk; morawhite@supanet.com

Federacion Filatelica de la Republica de Honduras, Mauricio Mejia, Apartado Postal 1465, Tegucigalpa, D.C. Honduras; 504 3399-7227; www.facebook.com/filateliadehonduras; ffrh@hotmail.com

International Cuban Philatelic Society (ICPS), Ernesto Cuesta, P.O. Box 34434, Bethesda, MD 20827; (301) 564-3099; www.cubafil.org; ecuesta@philat.com

International Society of Guatemala Collectors, Jaime Marckwordt, 449 St. Francis Blvd., Daly City, CA 94015-2136; (415) 997-0295; www.guatemalastamps.com; president@guatamalastamps.com

Mexico-Elmhurst Philatelic Society International, Eric Stovner, P.O. Box 10097, Santa Ana, CA 92711-0097; www.mepsi.org; treasurer@mepsi.org

Nicaragua Study Group, Erick Rodriguez, 11817 S. W. 11th St., Miami, FL 33184-2501; nsgsec@yahoo.com

North America (excluding United States)

British Caribbean Philatelic Study Group, Bob Stewart, 7 West Dune Lane, Long Beach Township, NJ 08008; (941) 379-4108; www.bcpsg.com; bcpsg@comcast.net

British North America Philatelic Society, Andy Ellwood, 10 Doris Ave., Gloucester, ON K1T 3W8 Canada; www.bnaps.org; secretary@bnaps.org

British West Indies Study Circle, Steve Jarvis, 5 Redbridge Drive, Andover, Hants SP10 2LF United Kingdom; 01264 358065; www.bwisc.org; info@bwisc.org

Bermuda Collectors Society, John Pare, 405 Perimeter St., Mount Horeb, WI 53572; (608) 852-7358; www.bermudacollectorssociety.com; pare16@mhtc.net

Haiti Philatelic Society, Ubaldo Del Toro, 5709 Marble Archway, Alexandria, VA 22315; www.haitiphilately.org; u007ubi@aol.com

Hawaiian Philatelic Society, Gannon Sugimura, P.O. Box 10115, Honolulu, HI 96816-0115, www.hpshawaii.com; hiphilsoc@gmail.com

Stamp Dealer Associations

American Stamp Dealers Association, Inc., P.O. Box 513, Centre Hall PA 16828; (800) 369-8207; www.americanstampdealer.com; asda@americanstampdealer.com

National Stamp Dealers Association, Sheldon Ruckens, President, 3643 Private Road 18, Pinckneyville, IL 62274-3426; (618) 357-5497; www.nsdainc.org; nsda@nsdainc.org

Youth Philately

Young Stamp Collectors of America, 100 Match Factory Place, Bellefonte, PA 16823; (814) 933-3803; https://stamps.org/learn/youth-in-philately; ysca@stamps.org

SHOWGARD MOUNTS

Showgard mounts are manufactured with the highest archival qualities in mind. The foil used to produce the mounts is acid free and stronger than other mounts for maximum protection and durability. Selecting the right size mount for your stamp is easy. Simply use a millimeter ruler to measure the stamps' width then the height. Showgard incorporates these measurements into their product numbers to insure you get the right size. Mounts available with clear (c) or black (b) backgrounds, with a few exceptions. Please specify background preference when ordering.

Item	*Description*	*Mounts*	*Retail*	*AA**
SGC50X31	50/31 U.S. Jumbo Singles - Horizontal	40	$3.95	**$2.85**
SGCV31X50	31/50 U.S. Jumbo Singles - Vertical	40	$3.95	**$2.85**
SGJ40X25	40/25 U.S. Commem. - Horizontal	40	$3.95	**$2.85**
SGJV25X40	25/40 U.S. Commem. - Vertical	40	$3.95	**$2.85**
SGE22X25	22/25 U.S. Regular Issues - Vertical	40	$3.95	**$2.85**
SGEH25X22	25/22 U.S. Regular Issues - Horizontal	40	$3.95	**$2.85**
SGT25X27	25/27 U.S. Famous Americans	40	$3.95	**$2.85**
SGU33X27	33/27 U.N., Germany	40	$3.95	**$2.85**
SGN40X27	40/27 United Nations	40	$3.95	**$2.85**
SGAH41X31	41/31 U.S. Semi Jumbo - Horizontal	40	$3.95	**$2.85**
SGAV31X41	31/41 U.S. Semi Jumbo - Vertical	40	$3.95	**$2.85**
SGDH52X36	52/36 U.S. Duck Stamps	30	$3.95	**$2.85**
SGS31X31	31/31 U.S. Celebrate the Century	30	$3.95	**$2.85**
SGUS2	Cut Style with Tray-8 Sizes	320	$32.95	**$23.50**
SGUS3	Strip Style w/Tray-No. 22 thru No. 52	75	$49.95	**$35.75**
SGUS1	U.S. Strip Sizes No. 22 thru No. 52	50	$24.50	**$17.50**
SG67X25	67/25 U.S. Coil Strips of 3	40	$8.35	**$5.95**
SG57X55	57/55 U.S. Regular Issue	25	$8.35	**$5.95**
SG106X55	106/55 U.S. 3¢, 4¢ Commemoratives	20	$8.35	**$5.95**
SG105X57	105/57 U.S. Giori Press Issues	20	$8.35	**$5.95**
SG127X70	127/70 U.S. Jumbo Issues	10	$8.35	**$5.95**
SG140X89	140/89 Postcards, Souvenir Sheets	10	$8.35	**$5.95**
SG165X94	165/94 First Day Covers	10	$8.35	**$5.95**
SG20	215/20 U.S. Mini Stamps, etc.	22	$9.75	**$6.95**
SG22	215/22 Narrow U.S. Airs	22	$9.75	**$6.95**
SG24	215/24 U.K. and Canada, early U.S.	22	$9.75	**$6.95**
SG25	215/25 U.S. Commem. & Regular Issues	22	$9.75	**$6.95**
SG27	215/27 U.S. Famous Americans, U.N.	22	$9.75	**$6.95**
SG28	215/28 Switzerland, Liechtenstein	22	$9.75	**$6.95**
SG30	215/30 U.S. Special Stamps, Jamestown	22	$9.75	**$6.95**
SG31	315/31 U.S. Squares & Semi Jumbo	22	$9.75	**$6.95**
SG33	215/33 U.K. Issues, Misc. Foreign	22	$9.75	**$6.95**
SG36	215/36 Duck Stamps, Misc. Foreign	15	$9.75	**$6.95**
SG39	215/39 U.S. Magsaysay, Misc. Foreign	15	$9.75	**$6.95**
SG41	215/41 U.S. Vertical Commem. Israel Tabs	15	$9.75	**$6.95**
SG44	215/44 Booklet Panes, Hatteras Quartet	15	$9.75	**$6.95**
SG48	215/48 Canada Reg. Issue & Comm Blocks	15	$9.75	**$6.95**
SG50	215/50 U.S. Plain Blocks of 4	15	$9.75	**$6.95**
SG52	215/52 France Paintings, Misc. Foreign	15	$9.75	**$6.95**
SG57	215/57 U.S. Commem. Plate Blocks	15	$9.75	**$6.95**
SG61	215/61 Souvenir Sheets, Tab Singles, etc.	15	$9.75	**$6.95**
SG63	240/63 U.S. Semi Jumbo Blocks	10	$11.95	**$8.75**
SG66	240/66 U.S. ATM Panes, SA Duck Panes	10	$11.95	**$8.75**
SG68	240/68 Canadian Plate Blocks, etc.	10	$11.95	**$8.75**
SG74	240/74 U.N. Inscription Blocks of 4	10	$11.95	**$8.75**
SG80	240/80 U.S. Commem. Blocks	10	$11.95	**$8.75**
SG82	240/82 U.N. Chagall SS, Canada Plate Blocks	10	$11.95	**$8.75**
SG84	240/84 Israel Plate Blocks, etc.	10	$11.95	**$8.75**
SG89	240/89 U.N. Inscription Blocks of 6	10	$11.95	**$8.75**
SG100	240/100 U.S. Squares Plate Blocks	7	$11.95	**$8.75**
SG120	240/120 Miniature Sheets	7	$11.95	**$8.75**
SG70	264/70 U.S. Jumbo Plate Blocks	10	$16.25	**$11.50**
SG91	264/91 U.K. Souvenir Sheets	10	$16.25	**$11.50**
SG105	264/105 U.K. Blocks, Covers, etc.	10	$16.25	**$11.50**
SG107	264/107 U.S. Plate No. Strip of 20	10	$16.25	**$11.50**
SG111	264/111 U.S. Floating Plate No. Strips of 20	5	$10.75	**$7.75**
SG127	264/127 Modern U.S. Definitive Sheets of 20	5	$11.95	**$8.50**
SG137	264/137 U.N. SS, U.K. Coronation	5	$12.95	**$9.50**
SG158	264/158 Miniature Sheets, Apollo Soyuz PB	5	$14.50	**$10.50**
SG175	264/175 U.S. Sheets-Pan American Reissues	5	$15.95	**$11.75**
SG188	264/188 U.S. Miniature Sheets-Hollywood, etc.	5	$16.95	**$11.95**
SG198	264/198 U.S. Miniature Sheets	5	$17.25	**$12.50**
SGMPK	Assortment No. 22 thru No. 41	12	$7.50	**$5.50**
SGMPK2	Assortment No. 76 thru No. 171	15	$32.75	**$23.75**
SGAB	U.S. SS to 1975-except White Plains	11	$8.75	**$6.50**
SGWSE	World Stamp Expo Souvenir Sheets	3	$2.75	**$1.95**
SGRP94	U.S. 1994 Souvenir Sheets (*Black Only*)	5	$10.25	**$7.50**
SGRPAC97	Pacific 97 Issues	7	$5.75	**$4.25**
SGDC2006	Washington 2006 Souvenir Sheets (*Black Only*)	4	$7.95	**$5.75**
SGTM	Trans-Mississippi Issues	11	$5.75	**$4.25**
SGSPC	Space Exploration Sheets	5	$7.25	**$5.25**
SGNY2016	New York 2016 WWS Releases		$12.50	**$10.00**
SG265X231	265/231 U.S. Full Sheets & Souvenir Cards	5	$21.25	**$15.25**
SG260X25	260/25 U.S. Coil Strips of up to 11 stamps	25	$12.75	**$8.95**
SG293X30	293/30 U.S. American Eagle Coil Strips of up to 11 stamps	5	$4.25	**$3.25**

Item	*Description*	*Mounts*	*Retail*	*AA**
SG260X40	260/40 U.S. Postal People Full Strip	10	$10.50	**$7.50**
SG260X46	260/46 U.S. Vending Booklets	10	$10.50	**$7.50**
SG260X55	260/55 U.S. 13¢ Eagle Full Strip	10	$10.50	**$7.50**
SG260X59	260/59 U.S. Double Press Reg. Iss. Strips of 20	10	$10.50	**$7.50**
SG111X91	111/91 U.S. Columbian Souvenir Sheets	6	$5.50	**$3.95**
SG229X131	229/131 U.S. WWII Sheets, Looney Tunes	5	$10.75	**$7.75**
SG187X144	187/144 U.N. Flag Sheetlets	10	$18.50	**$12.95**
SG204X153	204/153 U.S. Commem. Sheets, Bicentennial	5	$11.25	**$8.25**
SG120X207	120/207 U.S. Ameripex Presidential Sheetlets	4	$7.75	**$5.75**
SG192X201	192/201 U.S. Classics Mini-Sheets	5	$13.50	**$9.75**
SG280X228	280/228 U.S. Greetings From America Sheets	5	$20.50	**$14.75**
SG191X229	191/229 U.S. Celebrate The Century Sheets	5	$15.25	**$11.25**
SG146X84	146/84 Distinguished Americans, Cycling Souvenir Sheet and other miniature panes	3	$3.75	**$2.75**
SG203X146	203/146 Hanukkah, Kwanzaa, Eid, Wedding Cake Series, Ronald Reagan, Dogs at Work, Jose Ferrer, Samuel de Champlain SS, etc.	3	$7.50	**$5.50**
SG178X181	178/181 Butterfly Series, Carmel Mission Express Mail, Celebrate Scouting, Cranes, etc.	3	$7.50	**$5.50**
SG148X196	148/196 $5.00 Waves of Color, Moon Landing 25th Anniversary, etc.	3	$7.50	**$5.50**
SG76	264/76 BEP SS, Booklets, Plate Blocks	5	$11.95	**$8.75**
SG96	264/96 Souvenir Sheets, Panes	5	$11.95	**$8.75**
SG109	264/109 Foreign Miniature Sheets	5	$11.95	**$8.75**
SG115	264/115 Foreign Miniature Sheets	5	$11.95	**$8.75**
SG117	264/117 Foreign Miniature Sheets	5	$11.95	**$8.75**
SG121	264/121 Foreign Miniature Sheets	5	$11.95	**$8.75**
SG131	264/131 Looney Toons, Misc. Sheetlets	5	$11.95	**$8.75**
SG135	264/135 Foreign Miniature Sheets	5	$11.95	**$8.75**
SG139	264/139 White House Pane, etc.	5	$11.95	**$8.75**
SG143	264/143 Victorian Love, Misc. Sheets	5	$11.95	**$8.75**
SG147	264/147 Cinco de Mayo, etc.	5	$14.95	**$10.75**
SG151	264/151 Antique Auto, Communication, etc.	5	$15.50	**$11.08**
SG163	264/163 Tropical Flowers, UN Human Rights	5	$14.95	**$10.75**
SG167	264/167 Misc. U.S. Sheetlets	5	$14.95	**$10.75**
SG171	264/171 Helping Children Learn, etc.	5	$14.95	**$10.75**
SG181	264/181 U.S. Sheets–Calder, All Aboard, etc.	5	$18.50	**$13.25**
SG201	264/201 Dinosaurs, etc.	5	$18.50	**$13.25**
SG215	264/215 U.S. Sheets–Arctic Animals, Ballet, etc.	5	$18.50	**$13.25**

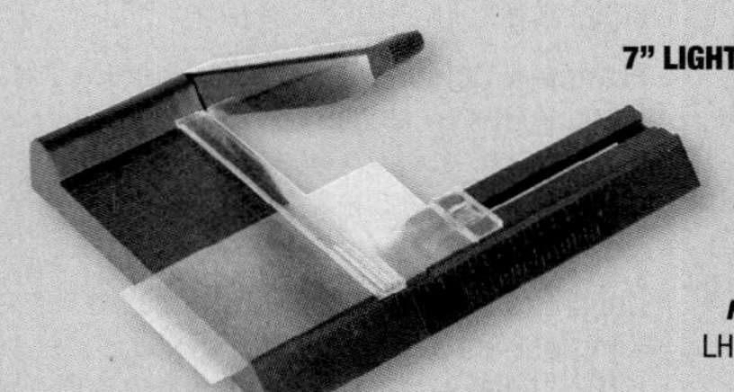

7" LIGHTHOUSE STAMP MOUNT CUTTER

This affordable and versatile mount cutter features an attachable measuring scale up to 7" (180mm) with an adjustable stop for accurate and clean cuts every time.

Item	*Retail*	*AA**
LH180MC	$24.95	**$19.95**

AMOS ADVANTAGE

Call **1-800-572-6885**

Outside U.S. & Canada: (937) 498-0800

Visit **www.AmosAdvantage.com**

Mail orders to: P.O. Box 4129, Sidney, OH 45365

ORDERING INFORMATION: *AA prices apply to paid subscribers of Amos Media titles, or orders placed online. Prices, terms and product availability subject to change. Taxes will apply in CA, OH, & IL. Shipping and handling rates will apply.

SHIPPING & HANDLING: United States: Order total $0-$10.00 charged $3.99 shipping; Order total $10.01-$79.99 charged $7.99 shipping; Order total $80.00 or more charged 10% of order total for shipping. Maximum Freight Charge $45.00. **Canada:** 20% of order total. Minimum charge $19.99; maximum charge $200.00. **Foreign:** Orders are shipped via FedEx Int'l. or USPS and billed actual freight.

Expertizing services

The following organizations will, for a fee, provide expert opinions about stamps submitted to them. Collectors should contact these organizations to find out about their fees and requirements before submitting philatelic material to them. The listing of these groups here is not intended as an endorsement by Amos Media Co.

General Expertizing Services

American Philatelic Expertizing Service (a service of the American Philatelic Society)
100 Match Factory Place
Bellefonte PA 16823-1367
(814) 237-3803
www.stamps.org/stamp-authentication
apex@stamps.org
Areas of Expertise: Worldwide

BPA Expertising, Ltd.
P.O. Box 1141
Guildford, Surrey, GU5 0WR
United Kingdom
www.bpaexpertising.com
sec@bpaexpertising.org
Areas of Expertise: British Commonwealth, Great Britain, Classics of Europe, South America and the Far East

Philatelic Foundation
22 E. 35th St., 4th Floor
New York NY 10016
(212) 221-6555
www.philatelicfoundation.org
philatelicfoundation@verizon.net
Areas of Expertise: U.S. & Worldwide

Philatelic Stamp Authentication and Grading, Inc.
P.O. Box 41-0880
Melbourne FL 32941-0880
(305) 345-9864
www.psaginc.com
info@psaginc.com
Areas of Expertise: U.S., Canal Zone, Hawaii, Philippines, Canada & Provinces

Professional Stamp Experts
P.O. Box 539309
Henderson NV 89053-9309
(702) 776-6522
www.gradingmatters.com
www.psestamp.com
info@gradingmatters.com
Areas of Expertise: Stamps and Covers of U.S., U.S. Possessions, British Commonwealth

Royal Philatelic Society London Expert Committee
15 Abchurch Lane
London, EX4N 7BW
United Kingdom
www.rpsl.limited/experts.aspx
experts@rpsl.limited
Areas of Expertise: Worldwide

Expertizing Services Covering Specific Fields or Countries

China Stamp Society Expertizing Service
1050 W. Blue Ridge Blvd.
Kansas City MO 64145
(816) 942-6300
hjmesq@aol.com
Areas of Expertise: China

Civil War Philatelic Society Authentication Service
C/O Stefan T. Jaronski
P.O. Box 232
Sidney, MT 59270-0232
www.civilwarphilatelicsociety.org/authentication/
authentication@civilwarphilatelicsociety.org
Areas of Expertise: Confederate stamps and postal history

Errors, Freaks and Oddities Collectors Club Expertizing Service
138 East Lakemont Drive
Kingsland GA 31548
(912) 729-1573
Areas of Expertise: U.S. errors, freaks and oddities

Hawaiian Philatelic Society Expertizing Service
P.O. Box 10115
Honolulu HI 96816-0115
www.stampshows.com/hps.html
hiphilsoc@gmail.com
Areas of Expertise: Hawaii

Hong Kong Stamp Society Expertizing Service
P.O. Box 206
Glenside PA 19038
Areas of Expertise: Hong Kong

International Association of Philatelic Experts United States Associate members:

Paul Buchsbayew
119 W. 57th St.
New York NY 10019
(212) 977-7734
Areas of Expertise: Russia, Soviet Union

William T. Crowe
P.O. Box 2090
Danbury CT 06813-2090
wtcrowe@aol.com
Areas of Expertise: United States

John Lievsay
(see American Philatelic Expertizing Service and Philatelic Foundation)
Areas of Expertise: France

Robert W. Lyman
P.O. Box 348
Irvington on Hudson NY 10533
(914) 591-6937
Areas of Expertise: British North America, New Zealand

Robert Odenweller
P.O. Box 401
Bernardsville NJ 07924-0401
(908) 766-5460
Areas of Expertise: New Zealand, Samoa to 1900

Sergio Sismondo
The Regency Tower, Suite 1109
770 James St.
Syracuse NY 13203
(315) 422-2331
Areas of Expertise: British East Africa, Cameroons, Cape of Good Hope, Canada, British North America

International Society for Japanese Philately Expertizing Committee
132 North Pine Terrace
Staten Island NY 10312-4052
(718) 227-5229
Areas of Expertise: Japan and related areas, except WWII Japanese Occupation issues

International Society for Portuguese Philately Expertizing Service
P.O. Box 43146
Philadelphia PA 19129-3146
(215) 843-2106
s.s.washburne@worldnet.att.net
Areas of Expertise: Portugal and Colonies

Mexico-Elmhurst Philatelic Society International Expert Committee
Expert Committee Administrator
Marc E. Gonzales
P.O. Box 29040
Denver CO 80229-0040
www.mepsi.org/expert_committeee.htm
expertizations@mepsi.org
Areas of Expertise: Mexico

Ukrainian Philatelic & Numismatic Society Expertizing Service
30552 Dell Lane
Warren MI 48092-1862
Areas of Expertise: Ukraine, Western Ukraine

V. G. Greene Philatelic Research Foundation
P.O. Box 69100
St. Clair Post Office
Toronto, ON M4T 3A1
Canada
(416) 921-2073
www.greenefoundation.ca
info@greenefoundation.ca
Areas of Expertise: British North America

Information on catalogue values, grade and condition

Catalogue value

The Scott Catalogue value is a retail value; that is, an amount you could expect to pay for a stamp in the grade of Very Fine with no faults. Any exceptions to the grade valued will be noted in the text. The general introduction on the following pages and the individual section introductions further explain the type of material that is valued. The value listed for any given stamp is a reference that reflects recent actual dealer selling prices for that item.

Dealer retail price lists, public auction results, published prices in advertising and individual solicitation of retail prices from dealers, collectors and specialty organizations have been used in establishing the values found in this catalogue. Amos Media Co. values stamps, but Amos Media is not a company engaged in the business of buying and selling stamps as a dealer.

Use this catalogue as a guide for buying and selling. The actual price you pay for a stamp may be higher or lower than the catalogue value because of many different factors, including the amount of personal service a dealer offers, or increased or decreased interest in the country or topic represented by a stamp or set. An item may occasionally be offered at a lower price as a "loss leader," or as part of a special sale. You also may obtain an item inexpensively at public auction because of little interest at that time or as part of a large lot.

Stamps that are of a lesser grade than Very Fine, or those with condition problems, generally trade at lower prices than those given in this catalogue. Stamps of exceptional quality in both grade and condition often command higher prices than those listed.

Values for pre-1900 unused issues are for stamps with approximately half or more of their original gum. Stamps with most or all of their original gum may be expected to sell for more, and stamps with less than half of their original gum may be expected to sell for somewhat less than the values listed. On rarer stamps, it may be expected that the original gum will be somewhat more disturbed than it will be on more common issues. Post-1900 unused issues are assumed to have full original gum. From breakpoints in most countries' listings, stamps are valued as never hinged, due to the wide availability of stamps in that condition. These notations are prominently placed in the listings and in the country information preceding the listings. Some countries also feature listings with dual values for hinged and never-hinged stamps.

Grade

A stamp's grade and condition are crucial to its value. The accompanying illustrations show examples of Very Fine stamps from different time periods, along with examples of stamps in Fine to Very Fine and Extremely Fine grades as points of reference. When a stamp seller offers a stamp in any grade from fine to superb without further qualifying statements, that stamp should not only have the centering grade as defined, but it also should be free of faults or other condition problems.

FINE stamps (illustrations not shown) have designs that are quite off center, with the perforations on one or two sides very close to the design but not quite touching it. There is white space between the perforations and the design that is minimal but evident to the unaided eye. Imperforate stamps may have small margins, and earlier issues may show the design just touching one edge of the stamp design. Very early perforated issues normally will have the perforations slightly cutting into the design. Used stamps may have heavier than usual cancellations.

FINE-VERY FINE stamps will be somewhat off center on one side, or slightly off center on two sides. Imperforate stamps will have two margins of at least normal size, and the design will not touch any edge. For perforated stamps, the perfs are well clear of the design, but are still noticeably off center. *However, early issues of a country may be printed in such a way that the design naturally is very close to the edges. In these cases, the perforations may cut into the design very slightly.* Used stamps will not have a cancellation that detracts from the design.

VERY FINE stamps will be just slightly off center on one or two sides, but the design will be well clear of the edge. The stamp will present a nice, balanced appearance. Imperforate stamps will be well centered within normal-sized margins. *However, early issues of many countries may be printed in such a way that the perforations may touch the design on one or more sides. Where this is the case, a boxed note will be found defining the centering and margins of the stamps being valued.* Used stamps will have light or otherwise neat cancellations. This is the grade used to establish Scott Catalogue values.

EXTREMELY FINE stamps are close to being perfectly centered. Imperforate stamps will have even margins that are slightly larger than normal. Even the earliest perforated issues will have perforations clear of the design on all sides.

Amos Media Co. recognizes that there is no formally enforced grading scheme for postage stamps, and that the final price you pay or obtain for a stamp will be determined by individual agreement at the time of transaction.

Condition

Grade addresses only centering and (for used stamps) cancellation. *Condition* refers to factors other than grade that affect a stamp's desirability.

Factors that can increase the value of a stamp include exceptionally wide margins, particularly fresh color, the presence of selvage, and plate or die varieties. Unusual cancels on used stamps (particularly those of the 19th century) can greatly enhance their value as well.

Factors other than faults that decrease the value of a stamp include loss of original gum, regumming, a hinge remnant or foreign object adhering to the gum, natural inclusions, straight edges, and markings or notations applied by collectors or dealers.

Faults include missing pieces, tears, pin or other holes, surface scuffs, thin spots, creases, toning, short or pulled perforations, clipped perforations, oxidation or other forms of color changelings, soiling, stains, and such man-made changes as reperforations or the chemical removal or lightening of a cancellation.

Grading illustrations

On the following two pages are illustrations of various stamps from countries appearing in this volume. These stamps are arranged by country, and they represent early or important issues that are often found in widely different grades in the marketplace. The editors believe the illustrations will prove useful in showing the margin size and centering that will be seen on the various issues.

In addition to the matters of margin size and centering, collectors are reminded that the very fine stamps valued in the Scott catalogues also will possess fresh color and intact perforations, and they will be free from defects.

Examples shown are computer-manipulated images made from single digitized master illustrations.

Stamp illustrations used in the catalogue

It is important to note that the stamp images used for identification purposes in this catalogue may not be indicative of the grade of stamp being valued. Refer to the written discussion of grades on this page and to the grading illustrations on the following two pages for grading information.

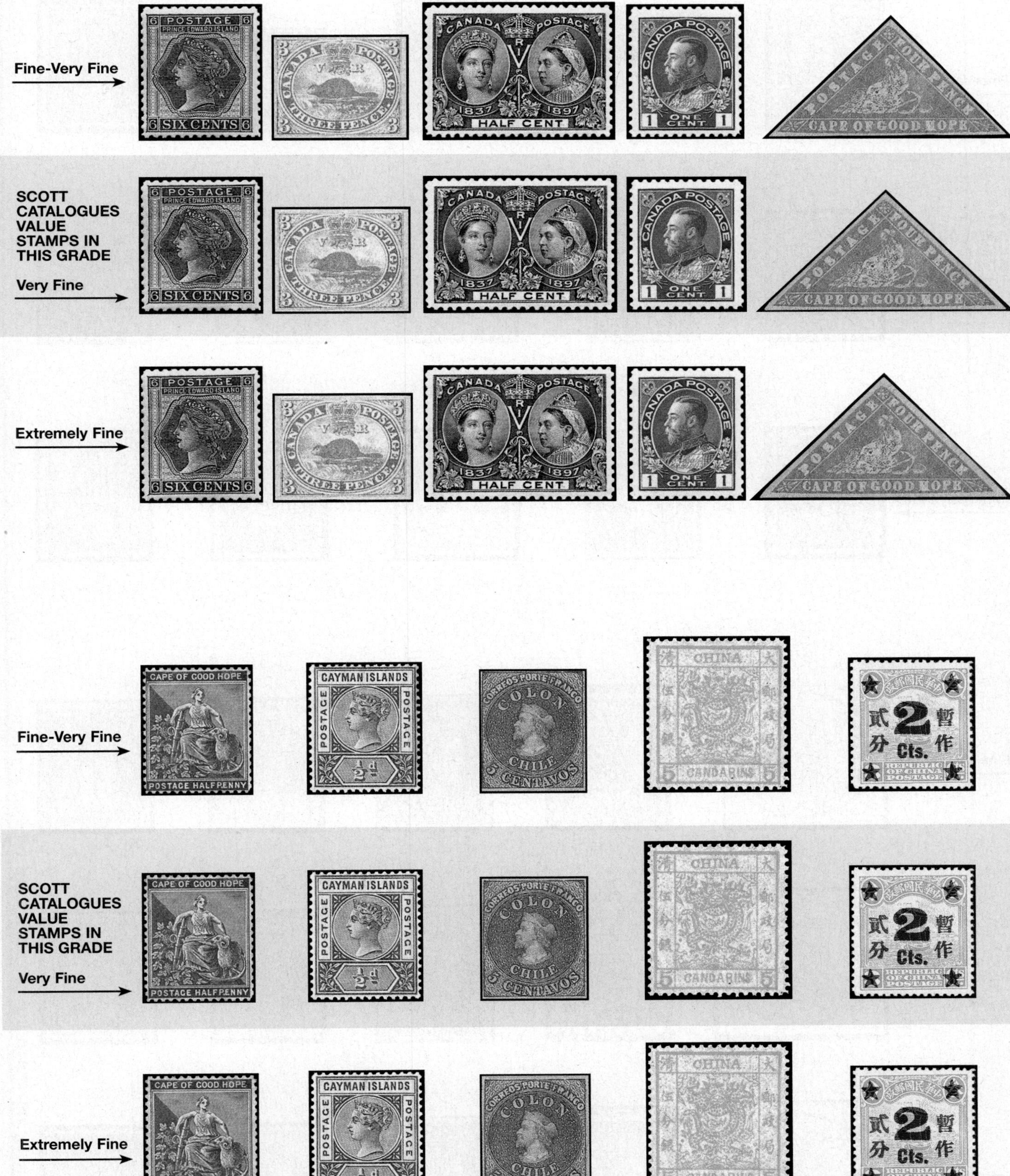
Fine-Very Fine
SCOTT CATALOGUES VALUE STAMPS IN THIS GRADE
Very Fine
Extremely Fine
Fine-Very Fine
SCOTT CATALOGUES VALUE STAMPS IN THIS GRADE
Very Fine
Extremely Fine

Fine-Very Fine

SCOTT CATALOGUES VALUE STAMPS IN THIS GRADE

Very Fine

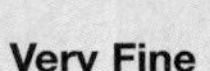

Extremely Fine

Fine-Very Fine

SCOTT CATALOGUES VALUE STAMPS IN THIS GRADE

Very Fine

Extremely Fine

Gum Conditions

For purposes of helping to determine the gum condition and value of an unused stamp, Scott presents the following chart which details different gum conditions and indicates how the conditions correlate with the Scott values for unused stamps. Used together, the Illustrated Grading Chart on the previous pages and this Illustrated Gum Chart should allow catalogue users to better understand the grade and gum condition of stamps valued in the Scott catalogues.

Never Hinged (NH; ★★): A never-hinged stamp will have full original gum that will have no hinge mark or disturbance. The presence of an expertizer's mark does not disqualify a stamp from this designation.

Original Gum (OG; ★): Pre-1900 stamps should have approximately half or more of their original gum. On rarer stamps, it may be expected that the original gum will be somewhat more disturbed than it will be on more common issues. Post-1900 stamps should have full original gum. Original gum will show some disturbance caused by a previous hinge(s) which may be present or entirely removed. The actual value of a post-1900 stamp will be affected by the degree of hinging of the full original gum.

Disturbed Original Gum: Gum showing noticeable effects of humidity, climate or hinging over more than half of the gum. The significance of gum disturbance in valuing a stamp in any of the Original Gum categories depends on the degree of disturbance, the rarity and normal gum condition of the issue and other variables affecting quality.

Regummed (RG; (★)): A regummed stamp is a stamp without gum that has had some type of gum privately applied at a time after it was issued. This normally is done to deceive collectors and/or dealers into thinking that the stamp has original gum and therefore has a higher value. A regummed stamp is considered the same as a stamp with none of its original gum for purposes of grading.

Gum Categories:	**MINT N.H.**	**ORIGINAL GUM (O.G.)**				**NO GUM**
	 **Mint Never Hinged** *Free from any disturbance*	 **Lightly Hinged** *Faint impression of a removed hinge over a small area*	 **Hinge Mark or Remnant** *Prominent hinged spot with part or all of the hinge remaining*	 **Large part o.g.** *Approximately half or more of the gum intact*	**Small part o.g.** Approximately less than half of the gum intact	**No gum** *Only if issued with gum*
Commonly Used Symbol:	★★	★	★	★	★	(★)
Pre-1900 Issues (Pre-1881 for U.S.)	*Very fine pre-1900 stamps in these categories trade at a premium over Scott value*			Scott Value for "Unused"		Scott "No Gum" listings for selected unused classic stamps
From 1900 to breakpoints for listings of never-hinged stamps	Scott "Never Hinged" listings for selected unused stamps	Scott Value for "Unused" (Actual value will be affected by the degree of hinging of the full o.g.)				
From breakpoints noted for many countries	Scott Value for "Unused"					

Understanding the listings

On the opposite page is an enlarged "typical" listing from this catalogue. Below are detailed explanations of each of the highlighted parts of the listing.

1 Scott number — Scott catalogue numbers are used to identify specific items when buying, selling or trading stamps. Each listed postage stamp from every country has a unique Scott catalogue number. Therefore, Germany Scott 99, for example, can only refer to a single stamp. Although the Scott catalogue usually lists stamps in chronological order by date of issue, there are exceptions. When a country has issued a set of stamps over a period of time, those stamps within the set are kept together without regard to date of issue. This follows the normal collecting approach of keeping stamps in their natural sets.

When a country issues a set of stamps over a period of time, a group of consecutive catalogue numbers is reserved for the stamps in that set, as issued. If that group of numbers proves to be too few, capital-letter suffixes, such as "A" or "B," may be added to existing numbers to create enough catalogue numbers to cover all items in the set. A capital-letter suffix indicates a major Scott catalogue number listing. Scott generally uses a suffix letter only once. Therefore, a catalogue number listing with a capital-letter suffix will seldom be found with the same letter (lower case) used as a minor-letter listing. If there is a Scott 16A in a set, for example, there will seldom be a Scott 16a. However, a minor-letter "a" listing may be added to a major number containing an "A" suffix (Scott 16Aa, for example).

Suffix letters are cumulative. A minor "b" variety of Scott 16A would be Scott 16Ab, not Scott 16b.

There are times when a reserved block of Scott catalogue numbers is too large for a set, leaving some numbers unused. Such gaps in the numbering sequence also occur when the catalogue editors move an item's listing elsewhere or have removed it entirely from the catalogue. Scott does not attempt to account for every possible number, but rather attempts to assure that each stamp is assigned its own number.

Scott numbers designating regular postage normally are only numerals. Scott numbers for other types of stamps, such as air post, semi-postal, postal tax, postage due, occupation and others have a prefix consisting of one or more capital letters or a combination of numerals and capital letters.

2 Illustration number — Illustration or design-type numbers are used to identify each catalogue illustration. For most sets, the lowest face-value stamp is shown. It then serves as an example of the basic design approach for other stamps not illustrated. Where more than one stamp use the same illustration number, but have differences in design, the design paragraph or the description line clearly indicates the design on each stamp not illustrated. Where there are both vertical and horizontal designs in a set, a single illustration may be used, with the exceptions noted in the design paragraph or description line.

When an illustration is followed by a lower-case letter in parentheses, such as "A2(b)," the trailing letter indicates which overprint or surcharge illustration applies.

Illustrations normally are 70 percent of the original size of the stamp. Oversized stamps, blocks and souvenir sheets are reduced even more. Overprints and surcharges are shown at 100 percent of their original size if shown alone, but are 70 percent of original size if shown on stamps. In some cases, the illustration will be placed above the set, between listings or omitted completely. Overprint and surcharge illustrations are not placed in this catalogue for purposes of expertizing stamps.

3 Paper color — The color of a stamp's paper is noted in italic type when the paper used is not white.

4 Listing styles — There are two principal types of catalogue listings: major and minor.

Major listings are in a larger type style than minor listings. The catalogue number is a numeral that can be found with or without a capital-letter suffix, and with or without a prefix.

Minor listings are in a smaller type style and have a small-letter suffix or (if the listing immediately follows that of the major number) may show only the letter. These listings identify a variety of the major item. Examples include perforation and shade differences, multiples (some souvenir sheets, booklet panes and se-tenant combinations), and singles of multiples.

Examples of major number listings include 16, 28A, B97, C13A, 10N5, and 10N6A. Examples of minor numbers are 16a and C13Ab.

5 Basic information about a stamp or set — Introducing each stamp issue is a small section (usually a line listing) of basic information about a stamp or set. This section normally includes the date of issue, method of printing, perforation, watermark and, sometimes, some additional information of note. *Printing method, perforation and watermark apply to the following sets until a change is noted.* Stamps created by overprinting or surcharging previous issues are assumed to have the same perforation, watermark, printing method and other production characteristics as the original. Dates of issue are as precise as Scott is able to confirm and often reflect the dates on first-day covers, rather than the actual date of release.

6 Denomination — This normally refers to the face value of the stamp; that is, the cost of the unused stamp at the post office at the time of issue. When a denomination is shown in parentheses, it does not appear on the stamp. This includes the nondenominated stamps of the United States, Brazil and Great Britain, for example.

7 Color or other description — This area provides information to solidify identification of a stamp. In many recent cases, a description of the stamp design appears in this space, rather than a listing of colors.

8 Year of issue — In stamp sets that have been released in a period that spans more than a year, the number shown in parentheses is the year that stamp first appeared. Stamps without a date appeared during the first year of the issue. Dates are not always given for minor varieties.

9 Value unused and Value used — The Scott catalogue values are based on stamps that are in a grade of Very Fine unless stated otherwise. Unused values refer to items that have not seen postal, revenue or any other duty for which they were intended. Pre-1900 unused stamps that were issued with gum must have at least most of their original gum. Later issues are assumed to have full original gum. From breakpoints specified in most countries' listings, stamps are valued as never hinged. Stamps issued without gum are noted. Modern issues with PVA or other synthetic adhesives may appear ungummed. Unused self-adhesive stamps are valued as appearing undisturbed on their original backing paper. Values for used self-adhesive stamps are for examples either on piece or off piece. For a more detailed explanation of these values, please see the "Catalogue Value," "Condition" and "Understanding Valuing Notations" sections elsewhere in this introduction.

In some cases, where used stamps are more valuable than unused stamps, the value is for an example with a contemporaneous cancel, rather than a modern cancel or a smudge or other unclear marking. For those stamps that were released for postal and fiscal purposes, the used value represents a postally used stamp. Stamps with revenue cancels generally sell for less.

Stamps separated from a complete se-tenant multiple usually will be worth less than a pro-rated portion of the se-tenant multiple, and stamps lacking the attached labels that are noted in the listings will be worth less than the values shown.

10 Changes in basic set information — Bold type is used to show any changes in the basic data given for a set of stamps. These basic data categories include perforation gauge measurement, paper type, printing method and watermark.

11 Total value of a set — The total value of sets of three or more stamps issued after 1900 are shown. The set line also notes the range of Scott numbers and total number of stamps included in the grouping. The actual value of a set consisting predominantly of stamps having the minimum value of 25 cents may be less than the total value shown. Similarly, the actual value or catalogue value of se-tenant pairs or of blocks consisting of stamps having the minimum value of 25 cents may be less than the catalogue values of the component parts.

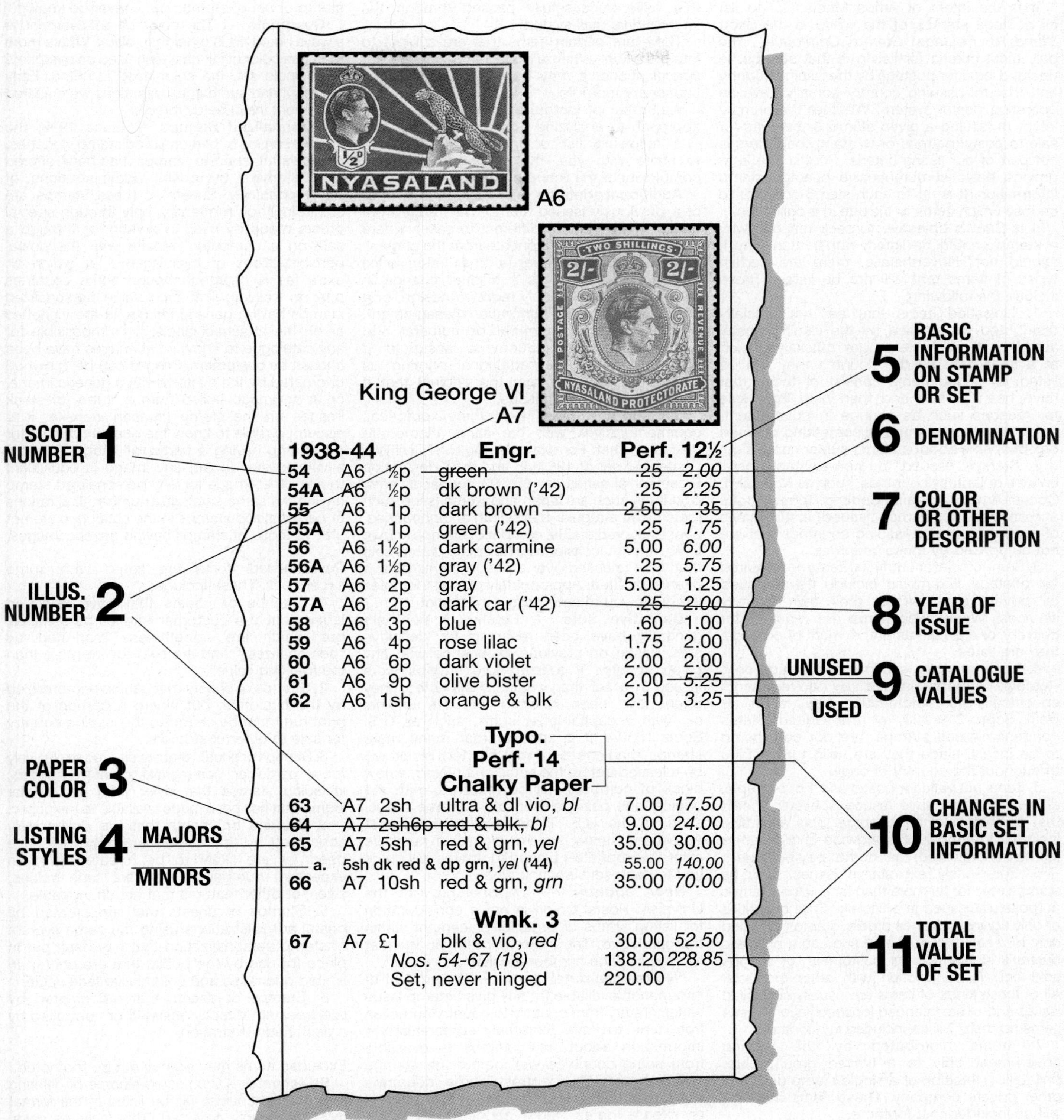
NYASALAND
A6
TWO SHILLINGS
2/- 2/-
POSTAGE REVENUE
NYASALAND PROTECTORATE
King George VI
A7
SCOTT NUMBER 1
ILLUS. NUMBER 2
PAPER COLOR 3
LISTING STYLES 4 MAJORS MINORS
5 BASIC INFORMATION ON STAMP OR SET
6 DENOMINATION
7 COLOR OR OTHER DESCRIPTION
8 YEAR OF ISSUE
UNUSED 9 CATALOGUE VALUES USED
10 CHANGES IN BASIC SET INFORMATION
11 TOTAL VALUE OF SET
1938-44 Engr. Perf. 12½
54 A6 ½p green .25 2.00
54A A6 ½p dk brown ('42) .25 2.25
55 A6 1p dark brown 2.50 .35
55A A6 1p green ('42) .25 1.75
56 A6 1½p dark carmine 5.00 6.00
56A A6 1½p gray ('42) .25 5.75
57 A6 2p gray 5.00 1.25
57A A6 2p dark car ('42) .25 2.00
58 A6 3p blue .60 1.00
59 A6 4p rose lilac 1.75 2.00
60 A6 6p dark violet 2.00 2.00
61 A6 9p olive bister 2.00 5.25
62 A6 1sh orange & blk 2.10 3.25
Typo.
Perf. 14
Chalky Paper
63 A7 2sh ultra & dl vio, bl 7.00 17.50
64 A7 2sh6p red & blk, bl 9.00 24.00
65 A7 5sh red & grn, yel 35.00 30.00
a. 5sh dk red & dp grn, yel ('44) 55.00 140.00
66 A7 10sh red & grn, grn 35.00 70.00
Wmk. 3
67 A7 £1 blk & vio, red 30.00 52.50
Nos. 54-67 (18) 138.20 228.85
Set, never hinged 220.00

Catalogue listing policy

It is the intent of Amos Media Co. to list all postage stamps of the world in the Scott *Standard Postage Stamp Catalogue*. The only strict criteria for listing is that stamps be decreed legal for postage by the issuing country and that the issuing country actually have an operating postal system. Whether the primary intent of issuing a given stamp or set was for sale to postal patrons or to stamp collectors is not part of our listing criteria. Scott's role is to provide basic comprehensive postage stamp information. It is up to each stamp collector to choose which items to include in a collection.

It is Scott's objective to seek reasons why a stamp should be listed, rather than why it should not. Nevertheless, there are certain types of items that will not be listed. These include the following:

1. Unissued items that are not officially distributed or released by the issuing postal authority. If such items are officially issued at a later date by the country, they will be listed. Unissued items consist of those that have been printed and then held from sale for reasons such as change in government, errors found on stamps or something deemed objectionable about a stamp subject or design.

2. Stamps "issued" by non-existent postal entities or fantasy countries, such as Nagaland, Occusi-Ambeno, Staffa, Sedang, Torres Straits and others. Also, stamps "issued" in the names of legitimate, stamp-issuing countries that are not authorized by those countries.

3. Semi-official or unofficial items not required for postage. Examples include items issued by private agencies for their own express services. When such items are required for delivery, or are valid as prepayment of postage, they are listed.

4. Local stamps issued for local use only. Postage stamps issued by governments specifically for "domestic" use, such as Haiti Scott 219-228, or the United States nondenominated stamps, are not considered to be locals, since they are valid for postage throughout the country of origin.

5. Items not valid for postal use. For example, a few countries have issued souvenir sheets that are not valid for postage. This area also includes a number of worldwide charity labels (some denominated) that do not pay postage.

6. Egregiously exploitative issues such as stamps sold for far more than face value, stamps purposefully issued in artificially small quantities or only against advance orders, stamps awarded only to a selected audience such as a philatelic bureau's standing order customers, or stamps sold only in conjunction with other products. All of these kinds of items are usually controlled issues and/or are intended for speculation. These items normally will be included in a footnote.

7. Items distributed by the issuing government only to a limited group, club, philatelic exhibition or a single stamp dealer or other private company. These items normally will be included in a footnote.

8. Stamps not available to collectors. These generally are rare items, all of which are held by public institutions such as museums. The existence of such items often will be cited in footnotes.

The fact that a stamp has been used successfully as postage, even on international mail, is not in itself sufficient proof that it was legitimately issued. Numerous examples of so-called stamps from non-existent countries are known to have been used to post letters that have successfully passed through the international mail system.

There are certain items that are subject to interpretation. When a stamp falls outside our specifications, it may be listed along with a cautionary footnote.

A number of factors are considered in our approach to analyzing how a stamp is listed. The following list of factors is presented to share with you, the catalogue user, the complexity of the listing process.

Additional printings — "Additional printings" of a previously issued stamp may range from an item that is totally different to cases where it is impossible to differentiate from the original. At least a minor number (a small-letter suffix) is assigned if there is a distinct change in stamp shade, noticeably redrawn design, or a significantly different perforation measurement. A major number (numeral or numeral and capital-letter combination) is assigned if the editors feel the "additional printing" is sufficiently different from the original that it constitutes a different issue.

Commemoratives — Where practical, commemoratives with the same theme are placed in a set. For example, the U.S. Civil War Centennial set of 1961-65 and the Constitution Bicentennial series of 1989-90 appear as sets. Countries such as Japan and Korea issue such material on a regular basis, with an announced, or at least predictable, number of stamps known in advance. Occasionally, however, stamp sets that were released over a period of years have been separated. Appropriately placed footnotes will guide you to each set's continuation.

Definitive sets — Blocks of numbers generally have been reserved for definitive sets, based on previous experience with any given country. If a few more stamps were issued in a set than originally expected, they often have been inserted into the original set with a capital-letter suffix, such as U.S. Scott 1059A. If it appears that many more stamps than the originally allotted block will be released before the set is completed, a new block of numbers will be reserved, with the original one being closed off. In some cases, such as the U.S. Transportation and Great Americans series, several blocks of numbers exist. Appropriately placed footnotes will guide you to each set's continuation.

New country — Membership in the Universal Postal Union is not a consideration for listing status or order of placement within the catalogue. The index will tell you in what volume or page number the listings begin.

"No release date" items — The amount of information available for any given stamp issue varies greatly from country to country and even from time to time. Extremely comprehensive information about new stamps is available from some countries well before the stamps are released. By contrast some countries do not provide information about stamps or release dates. Most countries, however, fall between these extremes. A country may provide denominations or subjects of stamps from upcoming issues that are not issued as planned. Sometimes, philatelic agencies, those private firms hired to represent countries, add these later-issued items to sets well after the formal release date. This time period can range from weeks to years. If these items were officially released by the country, they will be added to the appropriate spot in the set. In many cases, the specific release date of a stamp or set of stamps may never be known.

Overprints — The color of an overprint is always noted if it is other than black. Where more than one color of ink has been used on overprints of a single set, the color used is noted. Early overprint and surcharge illustrations were altered to prevent their use by forgers.

Personalized Stamps — Since 1999, the special service of personalizing stamp vignettes, or labels attached to stamps, has been offered to customers by postal administrations of many countries. Sheets of these stamps are sold, singly or in quantity, only through special orders made by mail, in person, or through a sale on a computer website with the postal administrations or their agents for which an extra fee is charged, though some countries offer to collectors at face value personalized stamps having generic images in the vignettes or on the attached labels. It is impossible for any catalogue to know what images have been chosen by customers. Images can be 1) owned or created by the customer, 2) a generic image, or 3) an image pulled from a library of stock images on the stamp creation website. It is also impossible to know the quantity printed for any stamp having a particular image. So from a valuing standpoint, any image is equivalent to any other image for any personalized stamp having the same catalogue number. Illustrations of personalized stamps in the catalogue are not always those of stamps having generic images.

Personalized items are listed with some exceptions. These include:

1. Stamps or sheets that have attached labels that the customer cannot personalize, but which are nonetheless marketed as "personalized," and are sold for far more than the franking value.

2. Stamps or sheets that can be personalized by the customer, but where a portion of the print run must be ceded to the issuing country for sale to other customers.

3. Stamps or sheets that are created exclusively for a particular commercial client, or clients, including stamps that differ from any similar stamp that has been made available to the public.

4. Stamps or sheets that are deliberately conceived by the issuing authority that have been, or are likely to be, created with an excessive number of different face values, sizes, or other features that are changeable.

5. Stamps or sheets that are created by postal administrations using the same system of stamp personalization that has been put in place for use by the public that are printed in limited quantities and sold above face value.

6. Stamps or sheets that are created by licensees not directly affiliated or controlled by a postal administration.

Excluded items may or may not be footnoted.

Se-tenants — Connected stamps of differing features (se-tenants) will be listed in the format most commonly collected. This includes pairs, blocks or larger multiples. Se-tenant units are not always symmetrical. An example is Australia Scott 508, which is a block of seven stamps. If the stamps are primarily collected as a unit, the major number may be assigned to the multiple, with minors going to each component stamp. In cases where continuous-design or other unit se-tenants will receive significant postal use, each stamp is given a major Scott number listing. This includes issues from the United States, Canada, Germany and Great Britain, for example.

Special notices

Classification of stamps

The Scott Standard Postage Stamp Catalogue lists stamps by country of issue. The next level of organization is a listing by section on the basis of the function of the stamps. The principal sections cover regular postage, semi-postal, air post, special delivery, registration, postage due and other categories. Except for regular postage, catalogue numbers for all sections include a prefix letter (or number-letter combination) denoting the class to which a given stamp belongs. When some countries issue sets containing stamps from more than one category, the catalogue will at times list all of the stamps in one category (such as air post stamps listed as part of a postage set).

The following is a listing of the most commonly used catalogue prefixes.

Prefix.......Category
C..........Air Post
M.........Military
P..........Newspaper
N..........Occupation - Regular Issues
O..........Official
Q..........Parcel Post
J..........Postage Due
RA.......Postal Tax
B..........Semi-Postal
E..........Special Delivery
MR.......War Tax

Other prefixes used by more than one country include the following:
H..........Acknowledgment of Receipt
I...........Late Fee
CO.......Air Post Official
CQ.......Air Post Parcel Post
RAC.....Air Post Postal Tax
CF........Air Post Registration
CB.......Air Post Semi-Postal
CBO....Air Post Semi-Postal Official
CE.......Air Post Special Delivery
EY.......Authorized Delivery
S..........Franchise
G..........Insured Letter
GY.......Marine Insurance
MC.......Military Air Post
MQ......Military Parcel Post
NC.......Occupation - Air Post
NO.......Occupation - Official
NJ........Occupation - Postage Due
NRA.....Occupation - Postal Tax
NB.......Occupation - Semi-Postal
NE.......Occupation - Special Delivery
QY.......Parcel Post Authorized Delivery
AR.......Postal-fiscal
RAJ......Postal Tax Due
RAB.....Postal Tax Semi-Postal
F..........Registration
EB........Semi-Postal Special Delivery
EO.......Special Delivery Official
QE.......Special Handling

New issue listings

Updates to this catalogue appear each month in the *Linn's Stamp News* monthly magazine. Included in this update are additions to the listings of countries found in the Scott *Standard Postage Stamp Catalogue* and the *Specialized Catalogue of United States Stamps and Covers,* as well as corrections and updates to current editions of this catalogue.

From time to time there will be changes in the final listings of stamps from the *Linn's Stamp News* magazine to the next edition of the catalogue. This occurs as more information about certain stamps or sets becomes available.

The catalogue update section of the *Linn's Stamp News* magazine is the most timely presentation of this material available. Annual subscriptions to *Linn's Stamp News* are available from Linn's Stamp News, Box 4129, Sidney, OH 45365-4129.

Number additions, deletions and changes

A listing of catalogue number additions, deletions and changes from the previous edition of the catalogue appears in each volume. See Catalogue Number Additions, Deletions & Changes in the table of contents for the location of this list.

Understanding valuing notations

The *minimum catalogue value* of an individual stamp or set is 25 cents. This represents a portion of the cost incurred by a dealer when he prepares an individual stamp for resale. As a point of philatelic-economic fact, the lower the value shown for an item in this catalogue, the greater the percentage of that value is attributed to dealer mark up and profit margin. In many cases, such as the 25-cent minimum value, that price does not cover the labor or other costs involved with stocking it as an individual stamp. The sum of minimum values in a set does not properly represent the value of a complete set primarily composed of a number of minimum-value stamps, nor does the sum represent the actual value of a packet made up of minimum-value stamps. Thus a packet of 1,000 different common stamps — each of which has a catalogue value of 25 cents — normally sells for considerably less than $250!

The *absence of a retail value* for a stamp does not necessarily suggest that a stamp is scarce or rare. A dash in the value column means that the stamp is known in a stated form or variety, but information is either lacking or insufficient for purposes of establishing a usable catalogue value.

Stamp values in *italics* generally refer to items that are difficult to value accurately. For expensive items, such as those priced at $1,000 or higher, a value in italics indicates that the affected item trades very seldom. For inexpensive items, a value in italics represents a warning. One example is a "blocked" issue where the issuing postal administration may have controlled one stamp in a set in an attempt to make the whole set more valuable. Another example is an item that sold at an extreme multiple of face value in the marketplace at the time of its issue.

One type of warning to collectors that appears in the catalogue is illustrated by a stamp that is valued considerably higher in used condition than it is as unused. In this case, collectors are cautioned to be certain the used version has a genuine and contemporaneous cancellation. The type of cancellation on a stamp can be an important factor in determining its sale price. Catalogue values do not apply to fiscal, telegraph or non-contemporaneous postal cancels, unless otherwise noted.

Some countries have released back issues of stamps in canceled-to-order form, sometimes covering as much as a 10-year period. The Scott Catalogue values for used stamps reflect canceled-to-order material when such stamps are found to predominate in the marketplace for the issue involved. Notes frequently appear in the stamp listings to specify which items are valued as canceled-to-order, or if there is a premium for postally used examples.

Many countries sell canceled-to-order stamps at a marked reduction of face value. Countries that sell or have sold canceled-to-order stamps at *full* face value include United Nations, Australia, Netherlands, France and Switzerland. It may be almost impossible to identify such stamps if the gum has been removed, because official government canceling devices are used. Postally used examples of these items on cover, however, are usually worth more than the canceled-to-order stamps with original gum.

Abbreviations

Scott uses a consistent set of abbreviations throughout this catalogue to conserve space, while still providing necessary information.

Color Abbreviations

amb.......... amber
anil.......... aniline
ap..............apple
aqua..aquamarine
az...............azure
bis............ bister
bl..................blue
bld............ blood
blk..............black
bril...........brilliant
brn............ brown
brnsh ....brownish
brnz.......... bronze
brt .... bright
brnt .... burnt
car..........carmine
cer.............cerise
chlky .... chalky
cham......chamois
chnt........chestnut
choc.....chocolate
chr.......... chrome
cit.............. citron
cl...............claret
cob........... cobalt
cop.......... copper
crim.........crimson
cr.............. cream
dk................ dark
dl....................dull
dp .... deep
db ....drab
emer....... emerald
gldn.......... golden
grysh........grayish
grn .... green
grnsh.......greenish
hel....... heliotrope
hn..............henna
ind.............indigo
int............intense
lav ....lavender
lem ....lemon
lil .... lilac
lt...................light
mag....... magenta
man...........manila
mar .... maroon
mv.............mauve
multi..multicolored
mlky .... milky
myr............myrtle
ol................. olive
olvn .... olivine
org .... orange
pck.........peacock
pnksh ....pinkish
Prus ....Prussian
pur .... purple
redsh........reddish
res............reseda
ros.............rosine
ryl................royal
sal ....salmon
saph.......sapphire
scar...........scarlet
sep.............sepia
sien .... sienna
sil .... silver
sl...................slate
stl.................steel
turq ...... turquoise
ultra... ultramarine
Ven.........Venetian
ver.......... vermilion
vio.................violet
yel .... yellow
yelsh .....yellowish

When no color is given for an overprint or surcharge, black is the color used. Abbreviations for colors used for overprints and surcharges include: "(B)" or "(Blk)," black; "(Bl)," blue; "(R)," red; and "(G)," green.

Additional abbreviations in this catalogue are shown below:

Adm. ....Administration
AFL ....American Federation of Labor
Anniv. ....Anniversary
APS...............American Philatelic Society
Assoc............Association
ASSR. ....Autonomous Soviet Socialist Republic
b....................Born
BEP...............Bureau of Engraving and Printing
Bicent. ....Bicentennial
Bklt. ....Booklet
Brit. ....British
btwn.............Between
Bur. ....Bureau
c. or ca. ....Circa
Cat. ....Catalogue
Cent. ....Centennial, century, centenary
CIO ....Congress of Industrial Organizations
Conf. ....Conference
Cong. ....Congress
Cpl. ....Corporal
CTO ....Canceled to order
d....................Died
Dbl. ....Double
EDU ....Earliest documented use
Engr..............Engraved
Exhib............Exhibition
Expo. ....Exposition
Fed................Federation
GB ....Great Britain
Gen. ....General
GPO.............General post office
Horiz. ....Horizontal
Imperf. ....Imperforate
Impt. ....Imprint
Intl.................International
Invtd.............Inverted
L....................Left
Lieut., lt.........Lieutenant
Litho..............Lithographed
LL..................Lower left
LR ....Lower right
mm ....Millimeter
Ms.................Manuscript
Natl. ....National
No. ....Number
NY..................New York
NYC ....New York City
Ovpt. ....Overprint
Ovptd............Overprinted
P ....Plate number
Perf. ....Perforated, perforation
Phil. ....Philatelic
Photo. ....Photogravure
PO..................Post office
Pr. ....Pair
P.R. ....Puerto Rico
Prec. ....Precancel, precanceled
Pres. ....President
PTT ....Post, Telephone and Telegraph
R ....Right
Rio ....Rio de Janeiro
Sgt. ....Sergeant
Soc. ....Society
Souv..............Souvenir
SSR...............Soviet Socialist Republic, see ASSR
St. ....Saint, street
Surch. ....Surcharge
Typo. ....Typographed
UL ....Upper left
Unwmkd. ......Unwatermarked
UPU ....Universal Postal Union
UR.................Upper Right
US.................United States
USPOD ....United States Post Office Department
USSR............Union of Soviet Socialist Republics
Vert. ....Vertical
VP ....Vice president
Wmk. ....Watermark
Wmkd. ....Watermarked
WWI ....World War I
WWII ....World War II

Examination

Amos Media Co. will not comment upon the genuineness, grade or condition of stamps, because of the time and responsibility involved. Rather, there are several expertizing groups that undertake this work for both collectors and dealers. Neither will Amos Media Co. appraise or identify philatelic material. The company cannot take responsibility for unsolicited stamps or covers sent by individuals.

All letters, emails, etc. are read attentively, but they are not always answered because of time considerations.

How to order from your dealer

When ordering stamps from a dealer, it is not necessary to write the full description of a stamp as listed in this catalogue. All you need is the name of the country, the Scott catalogue number and whether the desired item is unused or used. For example, "Japan Scott 422 unused" is sufficient to identify the unused stamp of Japan listed as "422 A206 5y brown."

Basic stamp information

A stamp collector's knowledge of the combined elements that make a given stamp issue unique determines his or her ability to identify stamps. These elements include paper, watermark, method of separation, printing, design and gum. On the following pages each of these important areas is briefly described.

Paper

Paper is an organic material composed of a compacted weave of cellulose fibers and generally formed into sheets. Paper used to print stamps may be manufactured in sheets, or it may have been part of a large roll (called a web) before being cut to size. The fibers most often used to create paper on which stamps are printed include bark, wood, straw and certain grasses. In many cases, linen or cotton rags have been added for greater strength and durability. Grinding, bleaching, cooking and rinsing these raw fibers reduces them to a slushy pulp, referred to by paper makers as "stuff." Sizing and, sometimes, coloring matter is added to the pulp to make different types of finished paper.

After the stuff is prepared, it is poured onto sieve-like frames that allow the water to run off, while retaining the matted pulp. As fibers fall onto the screen and are held by gravity, they form a natural weave that will later hold the paper together. If the screen has metal bits that are formed into letters or images attached, it leaves slightly thinned areas on the paper. These are called watermarks.

When the stuff is almost dry, it is passed under pressure through smooth or engraved rollers — dandy rolls — or placed between cloth in a press to be flattened and dried.

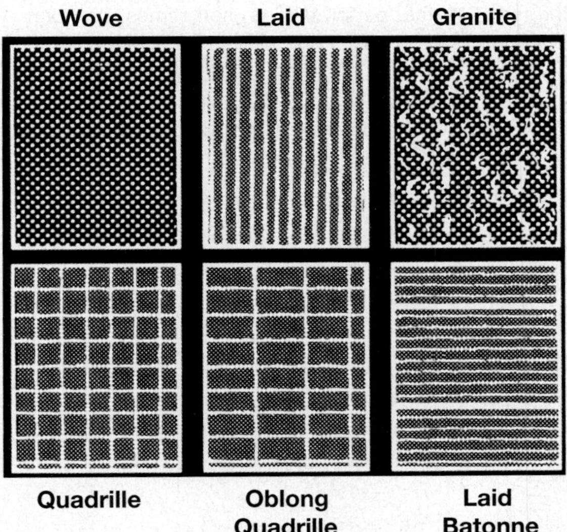

Stamp paper falls broadly into two types: wove and laid. The nature of the surface of the frame onto which the pulp is first deposited causes the differences in appearance between the two. If the surface is smooth and even, the paper will be of fairly uniform texture throughout. This is known as wove paper. Early papermaking machines poured the pulp onto a continuously circulating web of felt, but modern machines feed the pulp onto a cloth-like screen made of closely interwoven fine wires. This paper, when held to a light, will show little dots or points very close together. The proper name for this is "wire wove," but the type is still considered wove. Any U.S. or British stamp printed after 1880 will serve as an example of wire wove paper.

Closely spaced parallel wires, with cross wires at wider intervals, make up the frames used for what is known as laid paper. A greater thickness of the pulp will settle between the wires. The paper, when held to a light, will show alternate light and dark lines. The spacing and the thickness of the lines may vary, but on any one sheet of paper they are all alike. See Russia Scott 31-38 for examples of laid paper.

Batonne, from the French word meaning "a staff," is a term used if the lines in the paper are spaced quite far apart, like the printed ruling on a writing tablet. Batonne paper may be either wove or laid. If laid, fine laid lines can be seen between the batons.

Quadrille is the term used when the lines in the paper form little squares. Oblong quadrille is the term used when rectangles, rather than squares, are formed. Grid patterns vary from distinct to extremely faint. See Mexico-Guadalajara Scott 35-37 for examples of oblong quadrille paper.

Paper also is classified as thick or thin, hard or soft, and by color. Such colors may include yellowish, greenish, bluish and reddish.

Brief explanations of other types of paper used for printing stamps, as well as examples, follow.

Colored — Colored paper is created by the addition of dye in the paper-making process. Such colors may include shades of yellow, green, blue and red. Surface-colored papers, most commonly used for British colonial issues in 1913-14, are created when coloring is added only to the surface during the finishing process. Stamps printed on surface-colored paper have white or uncolored backs, while true colored papers are colored through. See Jamaica Scott 71-73.

Pelure — Pelure paper is a very thin, hard and often brittle paper that is sometimes bluish or grayish in appearance. See Serbia Scott 169-170.

Native — This is a term applied to handmade papers used to produce some of the early stamps of the Indian states. Stamps printed on native paper may be expected to display various natural inclusions that are normal and do not negatively affect value. Japanese paper, originally made of mulberry fibers and rice flour, is part of this group. See Japan Scott 1-18.

Manila — This type of paper is often used to make stamped envelopes and wrappers. It is a coarse-textured stock, usually smooth on one side and rough on the other. A variety of colors of manila paper exist, but the most common range is yellowish-brown.

Silk — Introduced by the British in 1847 as a safeguard against counterfeiting, silk paper contains bits of colored silk thread scattered throughout. The density of these fibers varies greatly and can include as few as one fiber per stamp or hundreds. U.S. revenue Scott R152 is a good example of an easy-to-identify silk paper stamp.

Silk-thread paper has uninterrupted threads of colored silk arranged so that one or more threads run through the stamp or postal stationery. See Great Britain Scott 5-6 and Switzerland Scott 14-19.

Granite — Filled with minute cloth or colored paper fibers of various colors and lengths, granite paper should not be confused with either type of silk paper. Austria Scott 172-175 and a number of Swiss stamps are examples of granite paper.

Chalky — A chalk-like substance coats the surface of chalky paper to discourage the cleaning and reuse of canceled stamps, as well as to provide a smoother, more acceptable printing surface. Because the designs of stamps printed on chalky paper are imprinted on what is often a water-soluble coating, any attempt to remove a cancellation will destroy the stamp. Do not soak these stamps in any fluid. To remove a stamp printed on chalky paper from an envelope, wet the paper from underneath the stamp until the gum dissolves enough to release the stamp from the paper. See St. Kitts-Nevis Scott 89-90 for examples of stamps printed on this type of chalky paper.

India — Another name for this paper, originally introduced from China about 1750, is "China Paper." It is a thin, opaque paper often used for plate and die proofs by many countries.

Double — In philately, the term double paper has two distinct meanings. The first is a two-ply paper, usually a combination of a thick and a thin sheet, joined during manufacture. This type was used experimentally as a means to discourage the reuse of stamps.

The design is printed on the thin paper. Any attempt to remove a cancellation would destroy the design. U.S. Scott 158 and other Banknote-era stamps exist on this form of double paper.

The second type of double paper occurs on a rotary press, when the end of one paper roll, or web, is affixed to the next roll to save time feeding the paper through the press. Stamp designs are printed over the joined paper and, if overlooked by inspectors, may get into post office stocks.

Goldbeater's Skin — This type of paper was used for the 1866 issue of Prussia, and was a tough, translucent paper. The design was printed in reverse on the back of the stamp, and the gum applied over the printing. It is impossible to remove stamps printed on this type of paper from the paper to which they are affixed without destroying the design.

Ribbed — Ribbed paper has an uneven, corrugated surface made by passing the paper through ridged rollers. This type exists on some copies of U.S. Scott 156-165.

Various other substances, or substrates, have been used for stamp manufacture, including wood, aluminum, copper, silver and gold foil, plastic, and silk and cotton fabrics.

Watermarks

Watermarks are an integral part of some papers. They are formed in the process of paper manufacture. Watermarks consist of small designs, formed of wire or cut from metal and soldered to the surface of the mold or, sometimes, on the dandy roll. The designs may be in the form of crowns, stars, anchors, letters or other characters or symbols. These pieces of metal — known in the paper-making industry as "bits" — impress a design into the paper. The design sometimes may be seen by holding the stamp to the light. Some are more easily seen with a watermark detector. This important tool is a small black tray into which a stamp is placed face down and dampened with a fast-evaporating watermark detection fluid that brings up the watermark image in the form of dark lines against a lighter background. These dark lines are the thinner areas of the paper known as the watermark. Some watermarks are extremely difficult to locate, due to either a faint impression, watermark location or the color of the stamp. There also are electric watermark detectors that come with plastic filter disks of various colors. The disks neutralize the color of the stamp, permitting the watermark to be seen more easily.

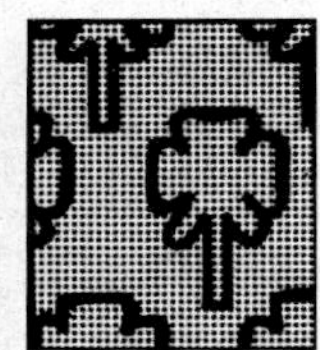

Multiple watermarks of Crown Agents and Burma

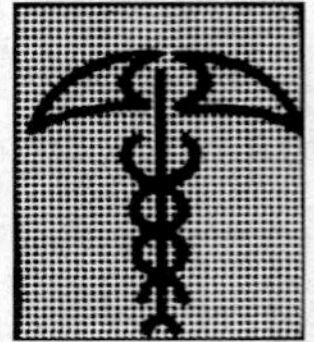

Watermarks of Uruguay, Vatican City and Jamaica

WARNING: Some inks used in the photogravure process dissolve in watermark fluids (Please see the section on Soluble Printing Inks). Also, see "chalky paper."

Watermarks may be found normal, reversed, inverted, reversed and inverted, sideways or diagonal, as seen from the back of the stamp. The relationship of watermark to stamp design depends on the position of the printing plates or how paper is fed through the press. On machine-made paper, watermarks normally are read from right to left. The design is repeated closely throughout the sheet in a "multiple-watermark design." In a "sheet watermark," the design appears only once on the sheet, but extends over many stamps. Individual stamps may carry only a small fraction or none of the watermark.

"Marginal watermarks" occur in the margins of sheets or panes of stamps. They occur on the outside border of paper (ostensibly outside the area where stamps are to be printed). A large row of letters may spell the name of the country or the manufacturer of the paper, or a border of lines may appear. Careless press feeding may cause parts of these letters and/or lines to show on stamps of the outer row of a pane.

Soluble printing inks

WARNING: Most stamp colors are permanent; that is, they are not seriously affected by short-term exposure to light or water. Many colors, especially of modern inks, fade from excessive exposure to light. There are stamps printed with inks that dissolve easily in water or in fluids used to detect watermarks. Use of these inks was intentional to prevent the removal of cancellations. Water affects all aniline inks, those on so-called safety paper and some photogravure printings - all such inks are known as fugitive colors. Removal from paper of such stamps requires care and alternatives to traditional soaking.

Separation

"Separation" is the general term used to describe methods used to separate stamps. The three standard forms currently in use are perforating, rouletting and die-cutting. These methods are done during the stamp production process, after printing. Sometimes these methods are done on-press or sometimes as a separate step. The earliest issues, such as the 1840 Penny Black of Great Britain (Scott 1), did not have any means provided for separation. It was expected the stamps would be cut apart with scissors or folded and torn. These are examples of imperforate stamps. Many stamps were first issued in imperforate formats and were later issued with perforations. Therefore, care must be observed in buying single imperforate stamps to be certain they were issued imperforate and are not perforated copies that have been altered by having the perforations trimmed away. Stamps issued imperforate usually are valued as singles. However, imperforate varieties of normally perforated stamps should be collected in pairs or larger pieces as indisputable evidence of their imperforate character.

PERFORATION

The chief style of separation of stamps, and the one that is in almost universal use today, is perforating. By this process, paper between the stamps is cut away in a line of holes, usually round, leaving little bridges of paper between the stamps to hold them together. Some types of perforation, such as hyphen-hole perfs, can be confused with roulettes, but a close visual inspection reveals that paper has been removed. The little perforation bridges, which project from the stamp when it is torn from the pane, are called the teeth of the perforation.

As the size of the perforation is sometimes the only way to differentiate between two otherwise identical stamps, it is necessary to be able to accurately measure and describe them. This is done with a perforation gauge, usually a ruler-like device that has dots or graduated lines to show how many perforations may be counted in the space of two centimeters. Two centimeters is the space universally adopted in which to measure perforations.

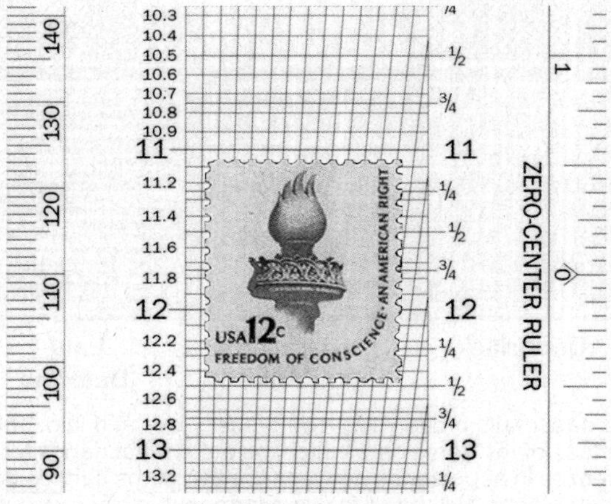

Perforation gauge

To measure a stamp, run it along the gauge until the dots on it fit exactly into the perforations of the stamp. If you are using a graduated-line perforation gauge, simply slide the stamp along the surface until the lines on the gauge perfectly project from the center of the bridges or holes. The number to the side of the line of dots or lines that fit the stamp's perforation is the measurement. For example, an "11" means that 11 perforations fit between two centimeters. The description of the stamp therefore is "perf. 11." If the gauge of the perforations on the top and bottom of a stamp differs from that on the sides, the result is what is known as compound perforations. In measuring compound perforations, the gauge at top and bottom is always given first, then the sides. Thus, a stamp that measures 11 at top and bottom and 10½ at the sides is "perf. 11 x 10½." See U.S. Scott 632-642 for examples of compound perforations.

Stamps also are known with perforations different on three or all four sides. Descriptions of such items are clockwise, beginning with the top of the stamp.

A perforation with small holes and teeth close together is a "fine perforation." One with large holes and teeth far apart is a "coarse perforation." Holes that are jagged, rather than clean-cut, are "rough perforations." *Blind perforations* are the slight impressions left by the perforating pins if they fail to puncture the paper. Multiples of stamps showing blind perforations may command a slight premium over normally perforated stamps.

The term *syncopated perfs* describes intentional irregularities in the perforations. The earliest form was used by the Netherlands from 1925-33, where holes were omitted to create distinctive patterns. Beginning in 1992, Great Britain has used an oval perforation to help prevent counterfeiting. Several other countries have started using the oval perfs or other syncopated perf patterns.

A new type of perforation, still primarily used for postal stationery, is known as microperfs. Microperfs are tiny perforations (in some cases hundreds of holes per two centimeters) that allows items to be intentionally separated very easily, while not accidentally breaking apart as easily as standard perforations. These are not currently measured or differentiated by size, as are standard perforations.

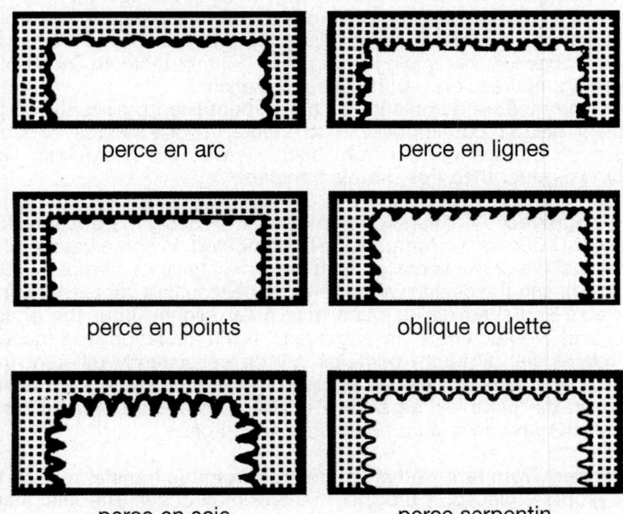

ROULETTING

In rouletting, the stamp paper is cut partly or wholly through, with no paper removed. In perforating, some paper is removed. Rouletting derives its name from the French roulette, a spur-like wheel. As the wheel is rolled over the paper, each point makes a small cut. The number of cuts made in a two-centimeter space determines the gauge of the roulette, just as the number of perforations in two centimeters determines the gauge of the perforation.

The shape and arrangement of the teeth on the wheels varies. Various roulette types generally carry French names:

Perce en lignes — rouletted in lines. The paper receives short, straight cuts in lines. This is the most common type of rouletting. See Mexico Scott 500.

Perce en points — pin-rouletted or pin-perfed. This differs from a small perforation because no paper is removed, although round, equidistant holes are pricked through the paper. See Mexico Scott 242-256.

Perce en arc and perce en scie — pierced in an arc or saw-toothed designs, forming half circles or small triangles. See Hanover (German States) Scott 25-29.

Perce en serpentin — serpentine roulettes. The cuts form a serpentine or wavy line. See Brunswick (German States) Scott 13-18.

Once again, no paper is removed by these processes, leaving the stamps easily separated, but closely attached.

DIE-CUTTING

The third major form of stamp separation is die-cutting. This is a method where a die in the pattern of separation is created that later cuts the stamp paper in a stroke motion. Although some standard stamps bear die-cut perforations, this process is primarily used for self-adhesive postage stamps. Die-cutting can appear in straight lines, such as U.S. Scott 2522, shapes, such as U.S. Scott 1551, or imitating the appearance of perforations, such as New Zealand Scott 935A and 935B.

Printing processes

ENGRAVING (Intaglio, Line-engraving, Etching)

Master die — The initial operation in the process of line engraving is making the master die. The die is a small, flat block of softened steel upon which the stamp design is recess engraved in reverse.

Photographic reduction of the original art is made to the appropriate size. It then serves as a tracing guide for the initial outline of the design. The engraver lightly traces the design on the steel with his graver, then slowly works the design until it is completed. At various points during the engraving process, the engraver hand-inks the die and makes an impression to check his progress. These are known as progressive die proofs. After completion of the engraving, the die is hardened to withstand the stress and pressures of later transfer operations.

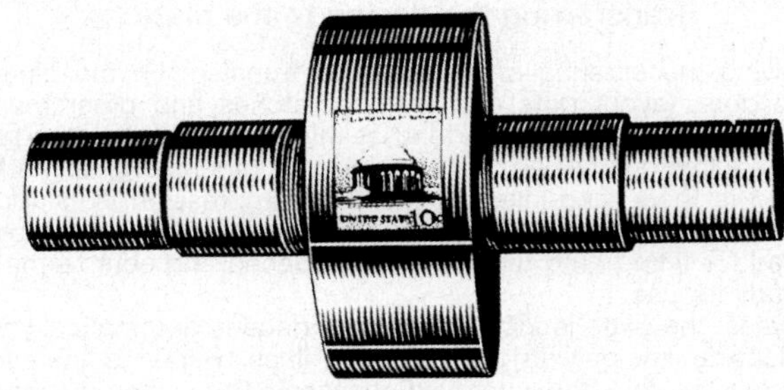

Transfer roll

Transfer roll — Next is production of the transfer roll that, as the name implies, is the medium used to transfer the subject from the master die to the printing plate. A blank roll of soft steel, mounted on a mandrel, is placed under the bearers of the transfer press to allow it to roll freely on its axis. The hardened die is placed on the bed of the press and the face of the transfer roll is applied to the die, under pressure. The bed or the roll is then rocked back and forth under increasing pressure, until the soft steel of the roll is forced into every engraved line of the die. The resulting impression on the roll is known as a "relief" or a "relief transfer." The engraved image is now positive in appearance and stands out from the steel. After the required number of reliefs are "rocked in," the soft steel transfer roll is hardened.

Different flaws may occur during the relief process. A defective relief may occur during the rocking in process because of a minute piece of foreign material lodging on the die, or some other cause. Imperfections in the steel of the transfer roll may result in a breaking away of parts of the design. This is known as a relief break, which will show up on finished stamps as small, unprinted areas. If a damaged relief remains in use, it will transfer a repeating defect to the plate. Deliberate alterations of reliefs sometimes occur. "Altered reliefs" designate these changed conditions.

Plate — The final step in pre-printing production is the making of the printing plate. A flat piece of soft steel replaces the die on the bed of the transfer press. One of the reliefs on the transfer roll is positioned over this soft steel. Position, or layout, dots determine the correct position on the plate. The dots have been lightly marked on the plate in advance. After the correct position of the relief is determined, the design is rocked in by following the same method used in making the transfer roll. The difference is that this time the image is being transferred from the transfer roll, rather than to it. Once the design is entered on the plate, it appears in reverse and is recessed. There are as many transfers entered on the plate as there are subjects printed on the sheet of stamps. It is during this process that double and shifted transfers occur, as well as re-entries. These are the result of improperly entered images that have not been properly burnished out prior to rocking in a new image.

Modern siderography processes, such as those used by the U.S. Bureau of Engraving and Printing, involve an automated form of rocking designs in on preformed cylindrical printing sleeves. The same process also allows for easier removal and re-entry of worn images right on the sleeve.

Transferring the design to the plate

Following the entering of the required transfers on the plate, the position dots, layout dots and lines, scratches and other markings generally are burnished out. Added at this time by the siderographer are any required guide lines, plate numbers or other marginal markings. The plate is then hand-inked and a proof impression is taken. This is known as a plate proof. If the impression is approved, the plate is machined for fitting onto the press, is hardened and sent to the plate vault ready for use.

On press, the plate is inked and the surface is automatically wiped clean, leaving ink only in the recessed lines. Paper is then forced under pressure into the engraved recessed lines, thereby receiving the ink. Thus, the ink lines on engraved stamps are slightly raised, and slight depressions (debossing) occur on the back of the stamp. Prior to the advent of modern high-speed presses and more advanced ink formulations, paper had to be dampened before receiving the ink. This sometimes led to uneven shrinkage by the time the stamps were perforated, resulting in improperly perforated stamps, or misperfs. Newer presses use drier paper, thus both *wet and dry printings* exist on some stamps.

Rotary Press — Until 1914, only flat plates were used to print engraved stamps. Rotary press printing was introduced in 1914, and slowly spread. Some countries still use flat-plate printing.

After approval of the plate proof, older rotary press plates require additional machining. They are curved to fit the press cylinder. "Gripper slots" are cut into the back of each plate to receive the "grippers," which hold the plate securely on the press. The plate is then hardened. Stamps printed from these bent rotary press plates are longer or wider than the same stamps printed from flat-plate presses. The stretching of the plate during the curving process is what causes this distortion.

Re-entry — To execute a re-entry on a flat plate, the transfer roll is re-applied to the plate, often at some time after its first use on the press. Worn-out designs can be resharpened by carefully burnishing out the original image and re-entering it from the transfer roll. If the original impression has not been sufficiently removed and the transfer roll is not precisely in line with the remaining impression, the resulting double transfer will make the re-entry obvious. If the registration is true, a re-entry may be difficult or impossible to distinguish. Sometimes a stamp printed from a successful re-entry is identified by having a much sharper and clearer impression than its neighbors. With the advent of rotary presses, post-press re-entries were not possible. After a plate was curved for the rotary press, it was impossible to make a re-entry. This is because the plate had already been bent once (with the design distorted).

However, with the introduction of the previously mentioned modern-style siderography machines, entries are made to the preformed cylindrical printing sleeve. Such sleeves are dechromed and softened. This allows individual images to be burnished out and re-entered on the curved sleeve. The sleeve is then rechromed, resulting in longer press life.

Double Transfer — This is a description of the condition of a transfer on a plate that shows evidence of a duplication of all, or a portion of the design. It usually is the result of the changing of the registration between the transfer roll and the plate during the rocking in of the original entry. Double transfers also occur when only a portion of the design has been rocked in and improper positioning is noted. If the worker elected not to burnish out the partial or completed design, a strong double transfer will occur for part or all of the design.

It sometimes is necessary to remove the original transfer from a plate and repeat the process a second time. If the finished re-worked image shows traces of the original impression, attributable to incomplete burnishing, the result is a partial double transfer.

With the modern automatic machines mentioned previously, double transfers are all but impossible to create. Those partially doubled images on stamps printed from such sleeves are more than likely re-entries, rather than true double transfers.

Re-engraved — Alterations to a stamp design are sometimes necessary after some stamps have been printed. In some cases, either the original die or the actual printing plate may have its "temper" drawn (softened), and the design will be re-cut. The resulting impressions from such a re-engraved die or plate may differ slightly from the original issue, and are known as "re-engraved." If the alteration was made to the master die, all future printings will be consistently different from the original. If alterations were made to the printing plate, each altered stamp on the plate will be slightly different from each other, allowing specialists to reconstruct a complete printing plate.

Dropped Transfers — If an impression from the transfer roll has not been properly placed, a dropped transfer may occur. The final stamp image will appear obviously out of line with its neighbors.

Short Transfer — Sometimes a transfer roll is not rocked its entire length when entering a transfer onto a plate. As a result, the finished transfer on the plate fails to show the complete design, and the finished stamp will have an incomplete design printed. This is known as a "short transfer." U.S. Scott No. 8 is a good example of a short transfer.

TYPOGRAPHY (Letterpress, Surface Printing, Flexography, Dry Offset, High Etch)

Although the word "Typography" is obsolete as a term describing a printing method, it was the accepted term throughout the first century of postage stamps. Therefore, appropriate Scott listings in this catalogue refer to typographed stamps. The current term for this form of printing, however, is "letterpress."

As it relates to the production of postage stamps, letterpress printing is the reverse of engraving. Rather than having recessed areas trap the ink and deposit it on paper, only the raised areas of the design are inked. This is comparable to the type of printing seen by inking and using an ordinary rubber stamp. Letterpress includes all printing where the design is above the surface area, whether it is wood, metal or, in some instances, hardened rubber or polymer plastic.

For most letterpress-printed stamps, the engraved master is made in much the same manner as for engraved stamps. In this instance, however, an additional step is needed. The design is transferred to another surface before being transferred to the transfer roll. In this way, the transfer roll has a recessed stamp design, rather than one done in relief. This makes the printing areas on the final plate raised, or relief areas.

For less-detailed stamps of the 19th century, the area on the die not used as a printing surface was cut away, leaving the surface area raised. The original die was then reproduced by stereotyping or electrotyping. The resulting electrotypes were assembled in the required number and format of the desired sheet of stamps. The plate used in printing the stamps was an electroplate of these assembled electrotypes.

Once the final letterpress plates are created, ink is applied to the raised surface and the pressure of the press transfers the ink impression to the paper. In contrast to engraving, the fine lines of letterpress are impressed on the surface of the stamp, leaving a debossed surface. When viewed from the back (as on a typewritten page), the corresponding line work on the stamp will be raised slightly (embossed) above the surface.

PHOTOGRAVURE (Gravure, Rotogravure, Heliogravure)

In this process, the basic principles of photography are applied to a chemically sensitized metal plate, rather than photographic paper. The design is transferred photographically to the plate through a halftone, or dot-matrix screen, breaking the reproduction into tiny dots. The plate is treated chemically and the dots form depressions, called cells, of varying depths and diameters, depending on the degrees of shade in the design. Then, like engraving, ink is applied to the plate and the surface is wiped clean. This leaves ink in the tiny cells that is lifted out and deposited on the paper when it is pressed against the plate.

Gravure is most often used for multicolored stamps, generally using the three primary colors (red, yellow and blue) and black. By varying the dot matrix pattern and density of these colors, virtually any color can be reproduced. A typical full-color gravure stamp will be created from four printing cylinders (one for each color). The original multicolored image will have been photographically separated into its component colors.

Modern gravure printing may use computer-generated dot-matrix screens, and modern plates may be of various types including metal-coated plastic. The catalogue designation of Photogravure (or "Photo") covers any of these older and more modern gravure methods of printing.

For examples of the first photogravure stamps printed (1914), see Bavaria Scott 94-114.

LITHOGRAPHY (Offset Lithography, Stone Lithography, Dilitho, Planography, Collotype)

The principle that oil and water do not mix is the basis for lithography. The stamp design is drawn by hand or transferred from engraving to the surface of a lithographic stone or metal plate in a greasy (oily) substance. This oily substance holds the ink, which will later be transferred to the paper. The stone (or plate) is wet with an acid fluid, causing it to repel the printing ink in all areas not covered by the greasy substance.

Transfer paper is used to transfer the design from the original stone or plate. A series of duplicate transfers are grouped and, in turn, transferred to the final printing plate.

Photolithography — The application of photographic processes to lithography. This process allows greater flexibility of design, related to use of halftone screens combined with line work. Unlike photogravure or engraving, this process can allow large, solid areas to be printed.

Offset — A refinement of the lithographic process. A rubber-covered blanket cylinder takes the impression from the inked lithographic plate. From the "blanket" the impression is offset or transferred to the paper. Greater flexibility and speed are the principal reasons offset printing has largely displaced lithography. The term "lithography" covers both processes, and results are almost identical.

EMBOSSED (Relief) Printing

Embossing, not considered one of the four main printing types, is a method in which the design first is sunk into the metal of the die. Printing is done against a yielding platen, such as leather or linoleum. The platen is forced into the depression of the die, thus forming the design on the paper in relief. This process is often used for metallic inks.

Embossing may be done without color (see Sardinia Scott 4-6); with color printed around the embossed area (see Great Britain Scott 5 and most U.S. envelopes); and with color in exact registration with the embossed subject (see Canada Scott 656-657).

HOLOGRAMS

For objects to appear as holograms on stamps, a model exactly the same size as it is to appear on the hologram must be created. Rather than using photographic film to capture the image, holography records an image on a photoresist material. In processing, chemicals eat away at certain exposed areas, leaving a pattern of constructive and destructive interference. When the photoresist is developed, the result is a pattern of uneven ridges that acts as a mold. This mold is then coated with metal, and the resulting form is used to press copies in much the same way phonograph records are produced.

A typical reflective hologram used for stamps consists of a reproduction of the uneven patterns on a plastic film that is applied to a reflective background, usually a silver or gold foil. Light is reflected off the background through the film, making the pattern present on the film visible. Because of the uneven pattern of the film, the viewer will perceive the objects in their proper three-dimensional relationships with appropriate brightness. The first hologram on a stamp was produced by Austria in 1988 (Scott 1441).

FOIL APPLICATION

A modern technique of applying color to stamps involves the application of metallic foil to the stamp paper. A pattern of foil is applied to the stamp paper by use of a stamping die. The foil usually is flat, but it may be textured. Canada Scott 1735 has three different foil applications in pearl, bronze and gold. The gold foil was textured using a chemical-etch copper embossing die. The printing of this stamp also involved two-color offset lithography plus embossing.

THERMOGRAPHY

In the 1990s stamps began to be enhanced with thermographic printing. In this process, a powdered polymer is applied over a sheet that has just been printed. The powder adheres to ink that lacks drying or hardening agents and does not adhere to areas where the ink has these agents. The excess powder is removed and the sheet is briefly heated to melt the powder. The melted powder solidifies after cooling, producing a raised, shiny effect on the stamps. See Scott New Caledonia C239-C240.

COMBINATION PRINTINGS

Sometimes two or even three printing methods are combined in producing stamps. In these cases, such as Austria Scott 933 or Canada 1735 (described in the preceding paragraph), the multiple-printing technique can be determined by studying the individual characteristics of each printing type. A few stamps, such as Singapore Scott 684-684A, combine as many as three of the four major printing types (lithography, engraving and typography). When this is done it often indicates the incorporation of security devices against counterfeiting.

INK COLORS

Inks or colored papers used in stamp printing often are of mineral origin, although there are numerous examples of organic-based pigments. As a general rule, organic-based pigments are far more subject to varieties and change than those of mineral-based origin.

The appearance of any given color on a stamp may be affected by many aspects, including printing variations, light, color of paper, aging and chemical alterations.

Numerous printing variations may be observed. Heavier pressure or inking will cause a more intense color, while slight interruptions in the ink feed or lighter impressions will cause a lighter appearance. Stamps printed in the same color by water-based and solvent-based inks can differ significantly in appearance. This affects several stamps in the U.S. Prominent Americans series. Hand-mixed ink formulas (primarily from the 19th century) produced under different conditions (humidity and temperature) account for notable color variations in early printings of the same stamp (see U.S. Scott 248-250, 279B, for example). Different sources of pigment can also result in significant differences in color.

Light exposure and aging are closely related in the way they affect stamp color. Both eventually break down the ink and fade colors, so that a carefully kept stamp may differ significantly in color from an identical copy that has been exposed to light. If stamps are exposed to light either intentionally or accidentally, their colors can be faded or completely changed in some cases.

Papers of different quality and consistency used for the same stamp printing may affect color appearance. Most pelure papers, for example, show a richer color when compared with wove or laid papers. See Russia Scott 181a, for an example of this effect.

The very nature of the printing processes can cause a variety of differences in shades or hues of the same stamp. Some of these shades are scarcer than others, and are of particular interest to the advanced collector.

Luminescence

All forms of tagged stamps fall under the general category of luminescence. Within this broad category is fluorescence, dealing with forms of tagging visible under longwave ultraviolet light, and phosphorescence, which deals with tagging visible only under shortwave light. Phosphorescence leaves an afterglow and fluorescence does not. These treated stamps show up in a range of different colors when exposed to UV light. The differing wavelengths of the light activates the tagging material, making it glow in various colors that usually serve different mail processing purposes.

Intentional tagging is a post-World War II phenomenon, brought about by the increased literacy rate and rapidly growing mail volume. It was one of several answers to the problem of the need for more automated mail processes. Early tagged stamps served the purpose of triggering machines to separate different types of mail. A natural outgrowth was to also use the signal to trigger machines that faced all envelopes the same way and canceled them.

Tagged stamps come in many different forms. Some tagged stamps have luminescent shapes or images imprinted on them as a form of security device. Others have blocks (United States), stripes, frames (South Africa and Canada), overall coatings (United States), bars (Great Britain and Canada) and many other types. Some types of tagging are even mixed in with the pigmented printing ink (Australia Scott 366, Netherlands Scott 478 and U.S. Scott 1359 and 2443).

The means of applying taggant to stamps differs as much as the intended purposes for the stamps. The most common form of tagging is a coating applied to the surface of the printed stamp. Since the taggant ink is frequently invisible except under UV light, it does not interfere with the appearance of the stamp. Another common application is the use of phosphored papers. In this case the paper itself either has a coating of taggant applied before the stamp is printed, has taggant applied during the papermaking process (incorporating it into the fibers), or has the taggant mixed into the coating of the paper. The latter method, among others, is currently in use in the United States.

Many countries now use tagging in various forms to either expedite mail handling or to serve as a printing security device against counterfeiting. Following the introduction of tagged stamps for public use in 1959 by Great Britain, other countries have steadily joined the parade. Among those are Germany (1961); Canada and Denmark (1962); United States, Australia, France and Switzerland (1963); Belgium and Japan (1966); Sweden and Norway (1967); Italy (1968); and Russia (1969). Since then, many other countries have begun using forms of tagging, including Brazil, China, Czechoslovakia, Hong Kong, Guatemala, Indonesia, Israel, Lithuania, Luxembourg, Netherlands, Penrhyn Islands, Portugal, St. Vincent, Singapore, South Africa, Spain and Sweden to name a few.

In some cases, including United States, Canada, Great Britain and Switzerland, stamps were released both with and without tagging. Many of these were released during each country's experimental period. Tagged and untagged versions are listed for the aforementioned countries and are noted in some other countries' listings. For at least a few stamps, the experimentally tagged version is worth far more than its untagged counterpart, such as the 1963 experimental tagged version of France Scott 1024.

In some cases, luminescent varieties of stamps were inadvertently created. Several Russian stamps, for example, sport highly fluorescent ink that was not intended as a form of tagging. Older stamps, such as early U.S. postage dues, can be positively identified by the use of UV light, since the organic ink used has become slightly fluorescent over time. Other stamps, such as Austria Scott 70a-82a (varnish bars) and Obock Scott 46-64 (printed quadrille lines), have become fluorescent over time.

Various fluorescent substances have been added to paper to make it appear brighter. These optical brightners, as they are known, greatly affect the appearance of the stamp under UV light. The brightest of these is known as Hi-Brite paper. These paper varieties are beyond the scope of the Scott Catalogue.

Shortwave UV light also is used extensively in expertizing, since each form of paper has its own fluorescent characteristics that are impossible to perfectly match. It is therefore a simple matter to detect filled thins, added perforation teeth and other alterations that involve the addition of paper. UV light also is used to examine stamps that have had cancels chemically removed and for other purposes as well.

Gum

The Illustrated Gum Chart in the first part of this introduction shows and defines various types of gum condition. Because gum condition has an important impact on the value of unused stamps, we recommend studying this chart and the accompanying text carefully.

The gum on the back of a stamp may be shiny, dull, smooth, rough, dark, white, colored or tinted. Most stamp gumming adhesives use gum arabic or dextrine as a base. Certain polymers such as polyvinyl alcohol (PVA) have been used extensively since World War II.

The *Scott Standard Postage Stamp Catalogue* does not list items by types of gum. The *Scott Specialized Catalogue of United States Stamps and Covers* does differentiate among some types of gum for certain issues.

Reprints of stamps may have gum differing from the original issues. In addition, some countries have used different gum formulas for different seasons. These adhesives have different properties that may become more apparent over time.

Many stamps have been issued without gum, and the catalogue will note this fact. See, for example, United States Scott 40-47. Sometimes, gum may have been removed to preserve the stamp. Germany Scott B68, for example, has a highly acidic gum that eventually destroys the stamps. This item is valued in the catalogue with gum removed.

Reprints and reissues

These are impressions of stamps (usually obsolete) made from the original plates or stones. If they are valid for postage and reproduce obsolete issues (such as U.S. Scott 102-111), the stamps are reissues. If they are from current issues, they are designated as *second, third*, etc., *printing*. If designated for a particular purpose, they are called *special printings*.

When special printings are not valid for postage, but are made from original dies and plates by authorized persons, they are *official reprints*. *Private reprints* are made from the original plates and dies by private hands. An example of a private reprint is that of the 1871-1932 reprints made from the original die of the 1845 New Haven, Conn., postmaster's provisional. *Official reproductions* or imitations are made from new dies and plates by government authorization. Scott will list those reissues that are valid for postage if they differ significantly from the original printing.

The U.S. government made special printings of its first postage stamps in 1875. Produced were official imitations of the first two stamps (listed as Scott 3-4), reprints of the demonetized pre-1861 issues (Scott 40-47) and reissues of the 1861 stamps, the 1869 stamps and the then-current 1875 denominations. Even though the official imitations and the reprints were not valid for postage, Scott lists all of these U.S. special printings.

Most reprints or reissues differ slightly from the original stamp in some characteristic, such as gum, paper, perforation, color or watermark. Sometimes the details are followed so meticulously that only a student of that specific stamp is able to distinguish the reprint or reissue from the original.

Remainders and canceled to order

Some countries sell their stock of old stamps when a new issue replaces them. To avoid postal use, the remainders usually are canceled with a punch hole, a heavy line or bar, or a more-or-less regular-looking cancellation. The most famous merchant of remainders was Nicholas F. Seebeck. In the 1880s and 1890s, he arranged printing contracts between the Hamilton Bank Note Co., of which he was a director, and several Central and South American countries. The contracts provided that the plates and all remainders of the yearly issues became the property of Hamilton. Seebeck saw to it that ample stock remained. The "Seebecks," both remainders and reprints, were standard packet fillers for decades.

Some countries also issue stamps *canceled-to-order (CTO)*, either in sheets with original gum or stuck onto pieces of paper or envelopes and canceled. Such CTO items generally are worth less than postally used stamps. In cases where the CTO material is far more prevalent in the marketplace than postally used examples, the catalogue value relates to the CTO examples, with postally used examples noted as premium items. Most CTOs can be detected by the presence of gum. However, as the CTO practice goes back at least to 1885, the gum inevitably has been soaked off some stamps so they could pass as postally used. The normally applied postmarks usually differ slightly from standard postmarks, and specialists are able to tell the difference. When applied individually to envelopes by philatelically minded persons, CTO material is known as *favor canceled* and generally sells at large discounts.

Cinderellas and facsimiles

Cinderella is a catch-all term used by stamp collectors to describe phantoms, fantasies, bogus items, municipal issues, exhibition seals, local revenues, transportation stamps, labels, poster stamps and many other types of items. Some cinderella collectors include in their collections local postage issues, telegraph stamps, essays and proofs, forgeries and counterfeits.

A *fantasy* is an adhesive created for a nonexistent stamp-issuing authority. Fantasy items range from imaginary countries (Occusi-Ambeno, Kingdom of Sedang, Principality of Trinidad or Torres Straits), to non-existent locals (Winans City Post), or nonexistent transportation lines (McRobish & Co.'s Acapulco-San Francisco Line).

On the other hand, if the entity exists and could have issued stamps (but did not) or was known to have issued other stamps, the items are considered bogus stamps. These would include the Mormon postage stamps of Utah, S. Allan Taylor's Guatemala and Paraguay inventions, the propaganda issues for the South Moluccas and the adhesives of the Page & Keyes local post of Boston.

Phantoms is another term for both fantasy and bogus issues.

Facsimiles are copies or imitations made to represent original stamps, but which do not pretend to be originals. A catalogue illustration is such a facsimile. Illustrations from the Moens catalogue of the last century were occasionally colored and passed off as stamps. Since the beginning of stamp collecting, facsimiles have been made for collectors as space fillers or for reference. They often carry the word "facsimile," "falsch" (German), "sanko" or "mozo" (Japanese), or "faux" (French) overprinted on the face or stamped on the back. Unfortunately, over the years a number of these items have had fake cancels applied over the facsimile notation and have been passed off as genuine.

Forgeries and counterfeits

Forgeries and counterfeits have been with philately virtually from the beginning of stamp production. Over time, the terminology for the two has been used interchangeably. Although both forgeries and counterfeits are reproductions of stamps, the purposes behind their creation differ considerably.

Among specialists there is an increasing movement to more specifically define such items. Although there is no universally accepted terminology, we feel the following definitions most closely mirror the items and their purposes as they are currently defined.

Forgeries (also often referred to as Counterfeits) are reproductions of genuine stamps that have been created to defraud collectors. Such spurious items first appeared on the market around 1860, and most old-time collections contain one or more. Many are crude and easily spotted, but some can deceive experts.

An important supplier of these early philatelic forgeries was the Hamburg printer Gebruder Spiro. Many others with reputations in this craft included S. Allan Taylor, George Hussey, James Chute, George Forune, Benjamin & Sarpy, Julius Goldner, E. Oneglia and L.H. Mercier. Among the noted 20th-century forgers were Francois Fournier, Jean Sperati and the prolific Raoul DeThuin.

Forgeries may be complete replications, or they may be genuine stamps altered to resemble a scarcer (and more valuable) type. Most forgeries, particularly those of rare stamps, are worth only a small fraction of the value of a genuine example, but a few types, created by some of the most notable forgers, such as Sperati, can be worth as much or more than the genuine. Fraudulently produced copies are known of most classic rarities and many medium-priced stamps.

In addition to rare stamps, large numbers of common 19th- and early 20th-century stamps were forged to supply stamps to the early packet trade. Many can still be easily found. Few new philatelic forgeries have appeared in recent decades. Successful imitation of well-engraved work is virtually impossible. It has proven far easier to produce a fake by altering a genuine stamp than to duplicate a stamp completely.

Counterfeit (also often referred to as Postal Counterfeit or Postal Forgery) is the term generally applied to reproductions of stamps that have been created to defraud the government of revenue. Such items usually are created at the time a stamp is current and, in some cases, are hard to detect. Because most counterfeits are seized when the perpetrator is captured, postal counterfeits, particularly used on cover, are usually worth much more than a genuine example to specialists. The first postal counterfeit was of Spain's 4-cuarto carmine of 1854 (the real one is Scott 25). Apparently, the counterfeiters were not satisfied with their first version, which is now very scarce, and they soon created an engraved counterfeit, which is common. Postal counterfeits quickly followed in Austria, Naples, Sardinia and the Roman States. They have since been created in many other countries as well, including the United States.

An infamous counterfeit to defraud the government is the 1-shilling Great Britain "Stock Exchange" forgery of 1872, used on telegraph forms at the exchange that year. The stamp escaped detection until a stamp dealer noticed it in 1898.

Fakes

Fakes are genuine stamps altered in some way to make them more desirable. One student of this part of stamp collecting has estimated that by the 1950s more than 30,000 varieties of fakes were known. That number has grown greatly since then. The widespread existence of fakes makes it important for stamp collectors to study their philatelic holdings and use relevant literature. Likewise, collectors should buy from reputable dealers who guarantee their stamps and make full and prompt refunds should a purchased item be declared faked or altered by some mutually agreed-upon authority. Because fakes always have some genuine characteristics, it is not always possible to obtain unanimous agreement among experts regarding specific items. These students may change their opinions as philatelic knowledge increases. More than 80 percent of all fakes on the philatelic market today are regummed, reperforated (or perforated for the first time), or bear forged overprints, surcharges or cancellations.

Stamps can be chemically treated to alter or eliminate colors. For example, a pale rose stamp can be re-colored to resemble a blue shade of high market value. In other cases, treated stamps can be made to resemble missing color varieties. Designs may be changed by painting, or a stroke or a dot added or bleached out to turn an ordinary variety into a seemingly scarcer stamp. Part of a stamp can be bleached and reprinted in a different version, achieving an inverted center or frame. Margins can be added or repairs done so deceptively that the stamps move from the "repaired" into the "fake" category.

Fakers have not left the backs of the stamps untouched either. They may create false watermarks, add fake grills or press out genuine grills. A thin India paper proof may be glued onto a thicker backing to create the appearance an issued stamp, or a proof printed on cardboard may be shaved down and perforated to resemble a stamp. Silk threads are impressed into paper and stamps have been split so that a rare paper variety is added to an otherwise inexpensive stamp. The most common treatment to the back of a stamp, however, is regumming.

Some in the business of faking stamps have openly advertised fool-proof application of "original gum" to stamps that lack it, although most publications now ban such ads from their pages. It is believed that very few early stamps have survived without being hinged. The large number of never-hinged examples of such earlier material offered for sale thus suggests the widespread extent of regumming activity. Regumming also may be used to hide repairs or thin spots. Dipping the stamp into watermark fluid, or examining it under longwave ultraviolet light often will reveal these flaws.

Fakers also tamper with separations. Ingenious ways to add margins are known. Perforated wide-margin stamps may be falsely represented as imperforate when trimmed. Reperforating is commonly done to create scarce coil or perforation varieties, and to eliminate the naturally occurring straight-edge stamps found in sheet margin positions of many earlier issues. Custom has made straight-edged stamps less desirable. Fakers have obliged by perforating straight-edged stamps so that many are now uncommon, if not rare.

Another fertile field for the faker is that of overprints, surcharges and cancellations. The forging of rare surcharges or overprints began in the 1880s or 1890s. These forgeries are sometimes difficult to detect, but experts have identified almost all. Occasionally, overprints or cancellations are removed to create non-overprinted stamps or seemingly unused items. This is most commonly done by removing a manuscript cancel to make a stamp resemble an unused example. "SPECIMEN" overprints may be removed by scraping and repainting to create non-overprinted varieties. Fakers use inexpensive revenues or pen-canceled stamps to generate unused stamps for further faking by adding other markings. The quartz lamp or UV lamp and a high-powered magnifying glass help to easily detect removed cancellations.

The bigger problem, however, is the addition of overprints, surcharges or cancellations — many with such precision that they are very difficult to ascertain. Plating of the stamps or the overprint can be an important method of detection.

Fake postmarks may range from many spurious fancy cancellations to a host of markings applied to transatlantic covers, to adding normally appearing postmarks to definitives of some countries with stamps that are valued far higher used than unused. With the increased popularity of cover collecting, and the widespread interest in postal history, a fertile new field for fakers has come about. Some have tried to create entire covers. Others specialize in adding stamps, tied by fake cancellations, to genuine stampless covers, or replacing less expensive or damaged stamps with more valuable ones. Detailed study of postal rates in effect at the time a cover in question was mailed, including the analysis of each handstamp used during the period, ink analysis and similar techniques, usually will unmask the fraud.

Restoration and repairs

Scott bases its catalogue values on stamps that are free of defects and otherwise meet the standards set forth earlier in this introduction. Most stamp collectors desire to have the finest copy of an item possible. Even within given grading categories there are variances. This leads to a controversial practice that is not defined in any universal manner: stamp *restoration*.

There are broad differences of opinion about what is permissible when it comes to restoration. Carefully applying a soft eraser to a stamp or cover to remove light soiling is one form of restoration, as is washing a stamp in mild soap and water to clean it. These are fairly accepted forms of restoration. More severe forms of restoration include pressing out creases or removing stains caused by tape. To what degree each of these is acceptable is dependent upon the individual situation. Further along the spectrum is the freshening of a stamp's color by removing oxide build-up or the effects of wax paper left next to stamps shipped to the tropics.

At some point in this spectrum the concept of *repair* replaces that of restoration. Repairs include filling thin spots, mending tears by reweaving or adding a missing perforation tooth. Regumming stamps may have been acceptable as a restoration or repair technique many decades ago, but today it is considered a form of fakery.

Restored stamps may or may not sell at a discount, and it is possible that the value of individual restored items may be enhanced over that of their pre-restoration state. Specific situations dictate the resultant value of such an item. Repaired stamps sell at substantial discounts from the value of sound stamps.

Terminology

Booklets — Many countries have issued stamps in small booklets for the convenience of users. This idea continues to become increasingly popular in many countries. Booklets have been issued in many sizes and forms, often with advertising on the covers, the panes of stamps or on the interleaving.

The panes used in booklets may be printed from special plates or made from regular sheets. All panes from booklets issued by the United States and many from those of other countries contain stamps that are straight edged on the sides, but perforated between. Others are distinguished by orientation of watermark or other identifying features. Any stamp-like unit in the pane, either printed or blank, that is not a postage stamp, is considered to be a *label* in the catalogue listings.

Scott lists and values booklet panes. Modern complete booklets also are listed and valued. Individual booklet panes are listed only when they are not fashioned from existing sheet stamps and, therefore, are identifiable from their sheet stamp counterparts.

Panes usually do not have a used value assigned to them because there is little market activity for used booklet panes, even though many exist used and there is some demand for them.

Cancellations — The marks or obliterations put on stamps by postal authorities to show that they have performed service and to prevent their reuse are known as cancellations. If the marking is made with a pen, it is considered a "pen cancel." When the location of the post office appears in the marking, it is a "town cancellation." A "postmark" is technically any postal marking, but in practice the term generally is applied to a town cancellation with a date. When calling attention to a cause or celebration, the marking is known as a "slogan cancellation." Many other types and styles of cancellations exist, such as duplex, numerals, targets, fancy and others. See also "precancels," below.

Coil Stamps — These are stamps that are issued in rolls for use in dispensers, affixing and vending machines. Those coils of the United States, Canada, Sweden and some other countries are perforated horizontally or vertically only, with the outer edges imperforate. Coil stamps of some countries, such as Great Britain and Germany, are perforated on all four sides and may in some cases be distinguished from their sheet stamp counterparts by watermarks, counting numbers on the reverse or other means.

Covers — Entire envelopes, with or without adhesive postage stamps, that have passed through the mail and bear postal or other markings of philatelic interest are known as covers. Before the introduction of envelopes in about 1840, people folded letters and wrote the address on the outside. Some people covered their letters with an extra sheet of paper on the outside for the address, producing the term "cover." Used airletter sheets, stamped envelopes and other items of postal stationery also are considered covers.

Errors — Stamps that have some major, consistent, unintentional deviation from the normal are considered errors. Errors include, but are not limited to, missing or wrong colors, wrong paper, wrong watermarks, inverted centers or frames on multicolor printing, inverted or missing surcharges or overprints, double impressions, missing perforations, unintentionally omitted tagging and others. Factually wrong or misspelled information, if it appears on all examples of a stamp, are not considered errors in the true sense of the word. They are errors of design. Inconsistent or randomly appearing items, such as misperfs or color shifts, are classified as freaks.

Color-Omitted Errors — This term refers to stamps where a missing color is caused by the complete failure of the printing plate to deliver ink to the stamp paper or any other paper. Generally, this is caused by the printing plate not being engaged on the press or the ink station running dry of ink during printing.

Color-Missing Errors — This term refers to stamps where a color or colors were printed somewhere but do not appear on the finished stamp. There are four different classes of color-missing errors, and the catalog indicates with a two-letter code appended to each such listing what caused the color to be missing. These codes are used only for the United States' color-missing error listings.

FO = A *foldover* of the stamp sheet during printing may block ink from appearing on the face of a stamp. Instead, the color will appear on the back of the foldover (where it might fall on the back of the selvage or perhaps a bit on the back of the stamp or on the back of another stamp. FO also will be used in the case of foldunders, where the paper may fold underneath the other stamp paper and the color will print on the platen.

EP = When the extraneous paper is removed, an unprinted area of stamp paper remains and may show a color or colors to be totally missing on the finished stamp.

CM = A misregistration of the printing plates during printing will result in a *color misregistration*, and such a misregistraion may result in a color not appearing on the finished stamp.

PS = *A perforation shift* after printing may remove a color from the finished stamp. Normally, this will occur on a row of stamps at the edge of the stamp pane.

Measurements – When measurements are given in the Scott catalogues for stamp size, grill size or any other reason, the first measurement given is always for the top and bottom dimension, while the second measurement will be for the sides (just as perforation gauges are measured). Thus, a stamp size of 15mm x 21mm will indicate a vertically oriented stamp 15mm wide at top and bottom, and 21mm tall at the sides. The same principle holds for measuring or counting items such as U.S. grills. A grill count of 22x18 points (B grill) indicates that there are 22 grill points across by 18 grill points down.

Overprints and Surcharges — Overprinting involves applying wording or design elements over an already existing stamp. Overprints can be used to alter the place of use (such as "Canal Zone" on U.S. stamps), to adapt them for a special purpose ("Porto" on Denmark's 1913-20 regular issues for use as postage due stamps, Scott J1-J7) or to commemorate a special occasion (United States Scott 647-648).

A *surcharge* is a form of overprint that changes or restates the face value of a stamp or piece of postal stationery.

Surcharges and overprints may be handstamped, typeset or, occasionally, lithographed or engraved. A few hand-written overprints and surcharges are known.

Personalized Stamps — In 1999, Australia issued stamps with se-tenant labels that could be personalized with pictures of the customer's choice. Other countries quickly followed suit, with some offering to print the selected picture on the stamp itself within a frame that was used exclusively for personalized issues. As the picture used on these stamps or labels vary, listings for such stamps are for any picture within the common frame (or any picture on a se-tenant label), be it a "generic" image or one produced especially for a customer, almost invariably at a premium price.

Precancels — Stamps that are canceled before they are placed in the mail are known as precancels. Precanceling usually is done to expedite the handling of large mailings and generally allow the affected mail pieces to skip certain phases of mail handling.

In the United States, precancellations generally identified the point of origin; that is, the city and state. This information appeared across the face of the stamp, usually centered between parallel lines. More recently, bureau precancels retained the parallel lines, but the city and state designations were dropped. Recent coils have a service inscription that is present on the original printing plate. These show the mail service paid for by the stamp. Since these stamps are not intended to receive further cancellations when used as intended, they are considered precancels. Such items often do not have parallel lines as part of the precancellation.

In France, the abbreviation *Affranchts* in a semicircle together with the word *Postes* is the general form of precancel in use. Belgian precancellations usually appear in a box in which the name of the city appears. Netherlands precancels have the name of the city enclosed between concentric circles, sometimes called a "lifesaver." Precancellations of other countries usually follow these patterns, but may be any arrangement of bars, boxes and city names.

Precancels are listed in the Scott catalogues only if the precancel changes the denomination (Belgium Scott 477-478); if the precanceled stamp is different from the non-precanceled version (such as untagged U.S. precancels); or if the stamp exists only precanceled (France Scott 1096-1099, U.S. Scott 2265).

Proofs and Essays — Proofs are impressions taken from an approved die, plate or stone in which the design and color are the same as the stamp issued to the public. Trial color proofs are impressions taken from approved dies, plates or stones in colors that vary from the final version. An essay is the impression of a design that differs in some way from the issued stamp. "Progressive die proofs" generally are considered to be essays.

Provisionals — These are stamps that are issued on short notice and intended for temporary use pending the arrival of regular issues. They usually are issued to meet such contingencies as changes in government or currency, shortage of necessary postage values or military occupation.

During the 1840s, postmasters in certain American cities issued stamps that were valid only at specific post offices. In 1861, postmasters of the Confederate States also issued stamps with limited validity. Both of these examples are known as "postmaster's provisionals."

Se-tenant — This term refers to an unsevered pair, strip or block of stamps that differ in design, denomination or overprint.

Unless the se-tenant item has a continuous design (see U.S. Scott 1451a, 1694a) the stamps do not have to be in the same order as shown in the catalogue (see U.S. Scott 2158a).

Specimens — The Universal Postal Union required member nations to send samples of all stamps they released into service to the International Bureau in Switzerland. Member nations of the UPU received these specimens as samples of what stamps were valid for postage. Many are overprinted, handstamped or initial-perforated "Specimen," "Canceled" or "Muestra." Some are marked with bars across the denominations (China-Taiwan), punched holes (Czechoslovakia) or back inscriptions (Mongolia).

Stamps distributed to government officials or for publicity purposes, and stamps submitted by private security printers for official approval, also may receive such defacements.

The previously described defacement markings prevent postal use, and all such items generally are known as "specimens."

Tete-Beche — This term describes a pair of stamps in which one is upside down in relation to the other. Some of these are the result of intentional sheet arrangements, such as Morocco Scott B10-B11. Others occurred when one or more electrotypes accidentally were placed upside down on the plate, such as Colombia Scott 57a. Separation of the tete-beche stamps, of course, destroys the tete beche variety.

Vols. 2A-2B number additions, deletions and changes

Number in 2021 Catalogue	Number in 2022 Catalogue
Canada	
Newfoundland	
new	26a
new	48c
Cape of Good Hope - Mafeking	
new	172E
Carpatho-Ukraine	
new	1-110
Chile	
794a	794b
794b	794a
new	814a
new	816a
China	
new	224a
China, Republic of	
new	C61a
Czechoslovakia	
254B	deleted
Denmark	
new	220a
new	224d
new	297a
new	298a
new	299a
new	318a
new	333a
new	380a
new	382a
new	383a
new	384a
new	385a
new	386a
new	387a
new	389a
new	390a
new	399a
new	400a
new	401a
new	402a
new	403a
new	404a
new	405a
new	406a
new	407a
new	408a
new	409a
new	410a
new	411a
new	412a
new	413a
new	414a
new	415a
new	416a
new	417a
new	418a
new	419a
new	420a
new	421a
new	422a
new	423a

Number in 2021 Catalogue	Number in 2022 Catalogue
Denmark	
new	424a
new	425a
new	426a
new	427a
new	429a
new	430a
new	431a
new	432a
new	433a
new	434a
new	435a
new	438a
new	439a
new	543a
new	B30a
Dominican Republic	
new	RA78a
Ecuador	
new	O137a
new	RA1a
new	RA31b
France	
new	109b
new	110b
new	111c
new	121b
new	122b
new	123b
new	125b
new	139b
new	159c
new	162g
new	166c
new	168d
new	170b
new	J29a-J32a
new	J34a
new	J38b

Currency conversion

Country	Dollar	Pound	S Franc	Yen	HK $	Euro	Cdn $	Aus $
Australia	1.2958	1.7662	1.4737	0.0126	0.1671	1.5925	1.0202	—
Canada	1.2702	1.7313	1.4446	0.0123	0.1638	1.5610	—	0.9802
European Union	0.8137	1.1091	0.9254	0.0079	0.1049	—	0.6406	0.6280
Hong Kong	7.7533	10.568	8.8176	0.0753	—	9.5285	6.1040	5.9834
Japan	102.98	140.36	117.12	—	13.282	126.56	81.074	79.472
Switzerland	0.8793	1.1985	—	0.0085	0.1134	1.0806	0.6923	0.6766
United Kingdom	0.7337	—	0.8344	0.0071	0.0946	0.9017	0.5776	0.5662
United States	—	1.3630	1.1373	0.0097	0.1290	1.2290	0.7673	0.7717

Country	Currency	U.S. $ Equiv.
Cambodia	riel	.0002
Cameroun	Community of French Africa (CFA) franc	.0019
Canada	dollar	.7673
Cape Verde	escudo	.0112
Caribbean Netherlands	US dollar	1.0000
Cayman Islands	dollar	1.2195
Central African Republic	CFA franc	.0019
Chad	CFA franc	.0019
Chile	peso	.0014
China (Taiwan)	dollar	.0356
China (People's Republic)	yuan	.1547
Christmas Island	Australian dollar	.7717
Cocos Island	Australian dollar	.7717
Colombia	peso	.0003
Comoro Islands	franc	.0025
Congo Republic	CFA franc	.0019
Cook Islands	New Zealand dollar	.7207
Costa Rica	colon	.0016
Croatia	kuna	.1627
Curacao	guilder	.5587
Cyprus	euro	1.2290
Czech Republic	koruna	.0470
Denmark	krone	.1652
Djibouti	franc	.0056
Dominica	East Caribbean dollar	.3704
Dominican Republic	peso	.0172
Ecuador	US dollar	1.0000
Egypt	pound	.0636
Equatorial Guinea	CFA franc	.0019
Eritrea	nakfa	.0667
Estonia	euro	1.2290
Ethiopia	birr	.0254
Falkland Islands	pound	1.3630
Faroe Islands	krone	.1652
Fiji	dollar	.4906
Finland	euro	1.2290
Aland Islands	euro	1.2290
France	euro	1.2290
French Polynesia	Community of French Pacific (CFP) franc	.0103
French So. & Antarctic Terr.	euro	1.2290

Source: xe.com Jan. 4, 2021. Figures reflect values as of Jan. 4, 2021.

COMMON DESIGN TYPES

Pictured in this section are issues where one illustration has been used for a number of countries in the Catalogue. Not included in this section are overprinted stamps or those issues which are illustrated in each country. Because the location of Never Hinged breakpoints varies from country to country, some of the values in the listings below will be for unused stamps that were previously hinged.

EUROPA

Europa, 1956

The design symbolizing the cooperation among the six countries comprising the Coal and Steel Community is illustrated in each country.

Belgium	*496-497*
France	*805-806*
Germany	*748-749*
Italy	*715-716*
Luxembourg	*318-320*
Netherlands	*368-369*

Nos. 496-497 (2)	9.00	.50
Nos. 805-806 (2)	5.25	1.00
Nos. 748-749 (2)	7.40	1.10
Nos. 715-716 (2)	9.25	1.25
Nos. 318-320 (3)	65.50	42.00
Nos. 368-369 (2)	25.75	1.50
Set total (13) Stamps	122.15	47.35

Europa, 1958

"E" and Dove — CD1

European Postal Union at the service of European integration.

1958, Sept. 13

Belgium	527-528
France	889-890
Germany	790-791
Italy	750-751
Luxembourg	341-343
Netherlands	375-376
Saar	317-318

Nos. 527-528 (2)	3.75	.60
Nos. 889-890 (2)	1.65	.55
Nos. 790-791 (2)	2.95	.60
Nos. 750-751 (2)	1.05	.60
Nos. 341-343 (3)	1.35	.90
Nos. 375-376 (2)	1.25	.75
Nos. 317-318 (2)	1.05	2.30
Set total (15) Stamps	13.05	6.30

Europa, 1959

6-Link Enless Chain — CD2

1959, Sept. 19

Belgium	536-537
France	929-930
Germany	805-806
Italy	791-792
Luxembourg	354-355
Netherlands	379-380

Nos. 536-537 (2)	1.55	.60
Nos. 929-930 (2)	1.40	.80
Nos. 805-806 (2)	1.35	.60
Nos. 791-792 (2)	.80	.50
Nos. 354-355 (2)	2.65	1.00
Nos. 379-380 (2)	2.10	1.85
Set total (12) Stamps	9.85	5.35

Europa, 1960

19-Spoke Wheel CD3

First anniverary of the establishment of C.E.P.T. (Conference Europeenne des Administrations des Postes et des Telecommunications.) The spokes symbolize the 19 founding members of the Conference.

1960, Sept.

Belgium	553-554
Denmark	379
Finland	376-377
France	970-971
Germany	818-820
Great Britain	377-378
Greece	688
Iceland	327-328
Ireland	175-176
Italy	809-810
Luxembourg	374-375
Netherlands	385-386
Norway	387
Portugal	866-867
Spain	941-942
Sweden	562-563
Switzerland	400-401
Turkey	1493-1494

Nos. 553-554 (2)	1.25	.55
No. 379 (1)	.55	.50
Nos. 376-377 (2)	1.70	1.80
Nos. 970-971 (2)	.50	.50
Nos. 818-820 (3)	1.90	1.35
Nos. 377-378 (2)	8.00	5.00
No. 688 (1)	4.25	1.75
Nos. 327-328 (2)	1.30	1.85
Nos. 175-176 (2)	47.50	27.50
Nos. 809-810 (2)	.50	.50
Nos. 374-375 (2)	1.00	.80
Nos. 385-386 (2)	2.00	2.00
No. 387 (1)	1.00	.80
Nos. 866-867 (2)	3.00	1.75
Nos. 941-942 (2)	1.50	.75
Nos. 562-563 (2)	1.05	.55
Nos. 400-401 (2)	1.75	.75
Nos. 1493-1494 (2)	2.10	1.35
Set total (34) Stamps	80.85	50.05

Europa, 1961

19 Doves Flying as One — CD4

The 19 doves represent the 19 members of the Conference of European Postal and Telecommunications Administrations C.E.P.T.

1961-62

Belgium	572-573
Cyprus	201-203
France	1005-1006
Germany	844-845
Great Britain	382-384
Greece	718-719
Iceland	340-341
Italy	845-846
Luxembourg	382-383
Netherlands	387-388
Spain	1010-1011
Switzerland	410-411
Turkey	1518-1520

Nos. 572-573 (2)	.75	.50
Nos. 201-203 (3)	2.10	1.20
Nos. 1005-1006 (2)	.50	.50
Nos. 844-845 (2)	.60	.75
Nos. 382-384 (3)	.75	.75
Nos. 718-719 (2)	.80	.50
Nos. 340-341 (2)	1.10	1.60
Nos. 845-846 (2)	.50	.50
Nos. 382-383 (2)	.55	.55
Nos. 387-388 (2)	.50	.50
Nos. 1010-1011 (2)	.60	.50
Nos. 410-411 (2)	1.90	.60
Nos. 1518-1520 (3)	1.55	.90
Set total (29) Stamps	12.20	9.35

Europa, 1962

Young Tree with 19 Leaves CD5

The 19 leaves represent the 19 original members of C.E.P.T.

1962-63

Belgium	582-583
Cyprus	219-221
France	1045-1046
Germany	852-853
Greece	739-740
Iceland	348-349
Ireland	184-185
Italy	860-861
Luxembourg	386-387
Netherlands	394-395
Norway	414-415
Switzerland	416-417
Turkey	1553-1555

Nos. 582-583 (2)	.65	.65
Nos. 219-221 (3)	76.25	6.75
Nos. 1045-1046 (2)	.60	.50
Nos. 852-853 (2)	.65	.75
Nos. 739-740 (2)	2.00	1.15
Nos. 348-349 (2)	.85	.85
Nos. 184-185 (2)	2.00	.50
Nos. 860-861 (2)	1.00	.55
Nos. 386-387 (2)	.75	.55
Nos. 394-395 (2)	1.35	.90
Nos. 414-415 (2)	1.75	1.70
Nos. 416-417 (2)	1.65	1.00
Nos. 1553-1555 (3)	2.05	1.10
Set total (28) Stamps	91.55	16.95

Europa, 1963

Stylized Links, Symbolizing Unity — CD6

1963, Sept.

Belgium	598-599
Cyprus	229-231
Finland	419
France	1074-1075
Germany	867-868
Greece	768-769
Iceland	357-358
Ireland	188-189
Italy	880-881
Luxembourg	403-404
Netherlands	416-417
Norway	441-442
Switzerland	429
Turkey	1602-1603

Nos. 598-599 (2)	1.60	.55
Nos. 229-231 (3)	64.00	9.40
No. 419 (1)	1.25	.55
Nos. 1074-1075 (2)	.60	.50
Nos. 867-868 (2)	.50	.55
Nos. 768-769 (2)	4.65	1.65
Nos. 357-358 (2)	1.20	1.20
Nos. 188-189 (2)	4.75	3.25
Nos. 880-881 (2)	.50	.50
Nos. 403-404 (2)	.75	.55
Nos. 416-417 (2)	1.30	1.00
Nos. 441-442 (2)	2.60	2.40
No. 429 (1)	.90	.60
Nos. 1602-1603 (2)	1.20	.50
Set total (27) Stamps	85.80	23.20

Europa, 1964

Symbolic Daisy — CD7

5th anniversary of the establishment of C.E.P.T. The 22 petals of the flower symbolize the 22 members of the Conference.

1964, Sept.

Austria	738
Belgium	614-615
Cyprus	244-246
France	1109-1110
Germany	897-898
Greece	801-802
Iceland	367-368
Ireland	196-197
Italy	894-895
Luxembourg	411-412
Monaco	590-591
Netherlands	428-429
Norway	458
Portugal	931-933
Spain	1262-1263
Switzerland	438-439
Turkey	1628-1629

No. 738 (1)	1.10	.25
Nos. 614-615 (2)	1.40	.60
Nos. 244-246 (3)	32.25	5.10
Nos. 1109-1110 (2)	.50	.50
Nos. 897-898 (2)	.50	.50
Nos. 801-802 (2)	4.15	1.55
Nos. 367-368 (2)	1.40	1.15
Nos. 196-197 (2)	17.00	4.25
Nos. 894-895 (2)	.50	.50
Nos. 411-412 (2)	.75	.55
Nos. 590-591 (2)	2.50	.70
Nos. 428-429 (2)	.75	.60
No. 458 (1)	3.50	3.50
Nos. 931-933 (3)	10.00	2.00
Nos. 1262-1263 (2)	1.15	.80
Nos. 438-439 (2)	1.65	.50
Nos. 1628-1629 (2)	2.00	.80
Set total (34) Stamps	81.10	23.85

Europa, 1965

Leaves and "Fruit" CD8

1965

Belgium	636-637
Cyprus	262-264
Finland	437
France	1131-1132
Germany	934-935
Greece	833-834
Iceland	375-376
Ireland	204-205
Italy	915-916
Luxembourg	432-433
Monaco	616-617
Netherlands	438-439
Norway	475-476
Portugal	958-960
Switzerland	469
Turkey	1665-1666

Nos. 636-637 (2)	.50	.50
Nos. 262-264 (3)	25.35	6.00
No. 437 (1)	1.25	.55
Nos. 1131-1132 (2)	.70	.55
Nos. 934-935 (2)	.50	.50
Nos. 833-834 (2)	2.25	1.15
Nos. 375-376 (2)	2.50	1.75
Nos. 204-205 (2)	16.00	3.35
Nos. 915-916 (2)	.50	.50
Nos. 432-433 (2)	.75	.55
Nos. 616-617 (2)	3.25	1.65
Nos. 438-439 (2)	.55	.50
Nos. 475-476 (2)	2.40	1.90
Nos. 958-960 (3)	10.00	2.75
No. 469 (1)	1.15	.50
Nos. 1665-1666 (2)	2.00	1.25
Set total (32) Stamps	69.65	23.95

Europa, 1966

Symbolic Sailboat — CD9

1966, Sept.

Andorra, French	172
Belgium	675-676
Cyprus	275-277
France	1163-1164
Germany	963-964

Greece....................862-863
Iceland....................384-385
Ireland....................216-217
Italy....................942-943
Liechtenstein....................415
Luxembourg....................440-441
Monaco....................639-640
Netherlands....................441-442
Norway....................496-497
Portugal....................980-982
Switzerland....................477-478
Turkey....................1718-1719

No. 172 (1)	3.00	3.00
Nos. 675-676 (2)	.80	.50
Nos. 275-277 (3)	*4.75*	*2.75*
Nos. 1163-1164 (2)	.55	.50
Nos. 963-964 (2)	.50	.55
Nos. 862-863 (2)	2.10	1.05
Nos. 384-385 (2)	4.50	3.50
Nos. 216-217 (2)	6.75	2.00
Nos. 942-943 (2)	.50	.50
No. 415 (1)	.40	.35
Nos. 440-441 (2)	.70	.55
Nos. 639-640 (2)	2.00	.65
Nos. 441-442 (2)	.85	.50
Nos. 496-497 (2)	2.35	2.15
Nos. 980-982 (3)	*9.75*	2.25
Nos. 477-478 (2)	1.40	.60
Nos. 1718-1719 (2)	3.35	1.75
Set total (34) Stamps	44.25	23.15

Europa, 1967

Cogwheels
CD10

1967

Andorra, French....................174-175
Belgium....................688-689
Cyprus....................297-299
France....................1178-1179
Germany....................969-970
Greece....................891-892
Iceland....................389-390
Ireland....................232-233
Italy....................951-952
Liechtenstein....................420
Luxembourg....................449-450
Monaco....................669-670
Netherlands....................444-447
Norway....................504-505
Portugal....................994-996
Spain....................1465-1466
Switzerland....................482
Turkey....................B120-B121

Nos. 174-175 (2)	10.75	6.25
Nos. 688-689 (2)	1.05	.55
Nos. 297-299 (3)	*4.25*	*2.50*
Nos. 1178-1179 (2)	.55	.50
Nos. 969-970 (2)	.55	.55
Nos. 891-892 (2)	3.05	.85
Nos. 389-390 (2)	3.00	2.00
Nos. 232-233 (2)	5.90	2.30
Nos. 951-952 (2)	.60	.50
No. 420 (1)	.45	.40
Nos. 449-450 (2)	1.00	.70
Nos. 669-670 (2)	2.75	.70
Nos. 444-447 (4)	2.70	2.05
Nos. 504-505 (2)	2.00	1.80
Nos. 994-996 (3)	*9.50*	1.85
Nos. 1465-1466 (2)	.50	.50
No. 482 (1)	.60	.30
Nos. B120-B121 (2)	2.50	2.00
Set total (38) Stamps	51.70	26.30

Europa, 1968

Golden Key with C.E.P.T. Emblem
CD11

1968

Andorra, French....................182-183
Belgium....................705-706
Cyprus....................314-316
France....................1209-1210
Germany....................983-984
Greece....................916-917
Iceland....................395-396
Ireland....................242-243
Italy....................979-980
Liechtenstein....................442
Luxembourg....................466-467
Monaco....................689-691
Netherlands....................452-453
Portugal....................1019-1021
San Marino....................687
Spain....................1526
Switzerland....................488
Turkey....................1775-1776

Nos. 182-183 (2)	16.50	10.00
Nos. 705-706 (2)	1.25	.50
Nos. 314-316 (3)	*2.90*	*2.50*
Nos. 1209-1210 (2)	.85	.55
Nos. 983-984 (2)	.50	.55
Nos. 916-917 (2)	3.10	1.45
Nos. 395-396 (2)	3.00	2.20
Nos. 242-243 (2)	3.30	2.25
Nos. 979-980 (2)	.50	.50
No. 442 (1)	.45	.40
Nos. 466-467 (2)	.80	.70
Nos. 689-691 (3)	*5.40*	.95
Nos. 452-453 (2)	1.05	.70
Nos. 1019-1021 (3)	*9.75*	2.10
No. 687 (1)	.55	.35
No. 1526 (1)	.25	.25
No. 488 (1)	.40	.25
Nos. 1775-1776 (2)	2.50	1.25
Set total (35) Stamps	53.05	27.45

Europa, 1969

"EUROPA" and "CEPT"
CD12

Tenth anniversary of C.E.P.T.

1969

Andorra, French....................188-189
Austria....................837
Belgium....................718-719
Cyprus....................326-328
Denmark....................458
Finland....................483
France....................1245-1246
Germany....................996-997
Great Britain....................585
Greece....................947-948
Iceland....................406-407
Ireland....................270-271
Italy....................1000-1001
Liechtenstein....................453
Luxembourg....................475-476
Monaco....................722-724
Netherlands....................475-476
Norway....................533-534
Portugal....................1038-1040
San Marino....................701-702
Spain....................1567
Sweden....................814-816
Switzerland....................500-501
Turkey....................1799-1800
Vatican....................470-472
Yugoslavia....................1003-1004

Nos. 188-189 (2)	18.50	12.00
No. 837 (1)	.55	.25
Nos. 718-719 (2)	.75	.50
Nos. 326-328 (3)	*3.00*	*2.25*
No. 458 (1)	.75	.75
No. 483 (1)	3.50	.75
Nos. 1245-1246 (2)	.55	.50
Nos. 996-997 (2)	.70	.50
No. 585 (1)	.25	.25
Nos. 947-948 (2)	4.00	1.25
Nos. 406-407 (2)	4.20	2.40
Nos. 270-271 (2)	3.50	2.00
Nos. 1000-1001 (2)	.50	.50
No. 453 (1)	.45	.45
Nos. 475-476 (2)	.95	.50
Nos. 722-724 (3)	*10.50*	2.00
Nos. 475-476 (2)	1.35	1.00
Nos. 533-534 (2)	2.20	1.95
Nos. 1038-1040 (3)	17.75	2.40
Nos. 701-702 (2)	.90	.90
No. 1567 (1)	.25	.25
Nos. 814-816 (3)	4.00	2.85
Nos. 500-501 (2)	1.85	1.00
Nos. 1799-1800 (2)	2.50	1.65
Nos. 470-472 (3)	.75	.75
Nos. 1003-1004 (2)	4.00	4.00
Set total (51) Stamps	88.20	43.60

Europa, 1970

Interwoven Threads
CD13

1970

Andorra, French....................196-197
Belgium....................741-742
Cyprus....................340-342
France....................1271-1272
Germany....................1018-1019
Greece.................... 985, 987
Iceland....................420-421
Ireland....................279-281
Italy....................1013-1014
Liechtenstein....................470
Luxembourg....................489-490
Monaco....................768-770
Netherlands....................483-484
Portugal....................1060-1062
San Marino....................729-730
Spain....................1607
Switzerland....................515-516
Turkey....................1848-1849
Yugoslavia....................1024-1025

Nos. 196-197 (2)	20.00	8.50
Nos. 741-742 (2)	1.10	.55
Nos. 340-342 (3)	*2.70*	*2.75*
Nos. 1271-1272 (2)	.65	.50
Nos. 1018-1019 (2)	.60	.50
Nos. 985,987 (2)	*6.35*	1.60
Nos. 420-421 (2)	6.00	4.00
Nos. 279-281 (3)	7.50	2.50
Nos. 1013-1014 (2)	.50	.50
No. 470 (1)	.45	.45
Nos. 489-490 (2)	.80	.55
Nos. 768-770 (3)	*6.35*	2.10
Nos. 483-484 (2)	1.30	1.15
Nos. 1060-1062 (3)	*9.75*	2.35
Nos. 729-730 (2)	.90	.55
No. 1607 (1)	.25	.25
Nos. 515-516 (2)	1.85	.70
Nos. 1848-1849 (2)	2.50	1.50
Nos. 1024-1025 (2)	.80	.80
Set total (40) Stamps	70.35	31.80

Europa, 1971

"Fraternity, Cooperation, Common Effort"
CD14

1971

Andorra, French....................205-206
Belgium....................803-804
Cyprus....................365-367
Finland....................504
France....................1304
Germany....................1064-1065
Greece....................1029-1030
Iceland....................429-430
Ireland....................305-306
Italy....................1038-1039
Liechtenstein....................485
Luxembourg....................500-501
Malta....................425-427
Monaco....................797-799
Netherlands....................488-489
Portugal....................1094-1096
San Marino....................749-750
Spain....................1675-1676
Switzerland....................531-532
Turkey....................1876-1877
Yugoslavia....................1052-1053

Nos. 205-206 (2)	20.00	7.75
Nos. 803-804 (2)	1.30	.55
Nos. 365-367 (3)	*2.60*	*3.25*
No. 504 (1)	5.00	.75
No. 1304 (1)	.45	.40
Nos. 1064-1065 (2)	.60	.50
Nos. 1029-1030 (2)	4.00	1.80
Nos. 429-430 (2)	5.00	3.75
Nos. 305-306 (2)	4.50	1.50
Nos. 1038-1039 (2)	.65	.50
No. 485 (1)	.45	.45
Nos. 500-501 (2)	1.00	.65
Nos. 425-427 (3)	*.80*	*.80*
Nos. 797-799 (3)	*15.00*	2.80
Nos. 488-489 (2)	1.20	.95
Nos. 1094-1096 (3)	*9.75*	1.75
Nos. 749-750 (2)	.65	.55
Nos. 1675-1676 (2)	.75	.55
Nos. 531-532 (2)	1.85	.65
Nos. 1876-1877 (2)	2.50	1.25
Nos. 1052-1053 (2)	.50	.50
Set total (43) Stamps	78.55	31.65

Europa, 1972

Sparkles, Symbolic of Communications
CD15

1972

Andorra, French....................210-211
Andorra, Spanish....................62
Belgium....................825-826
Cyprus....................380-382
Finland....................512-513
France....................1341
Germany....................1089-1090
Greece....................1049-1050
Iceland....................439-440
Ireland....................316-317
Italy....................1065-1066
Liechtenstein....................504
Luxembourg....................512-513
Malta....................450-453
Monaco....................831-832
Netherlands....................494-495
Portugal....................1141-1143
San Marino....................771-772
Spain....................1718
Switzerland....................544-545
Turkey....................1907-1908
Yugoslavia....................1100-1101

Nos. 210-211 (2)	21.00	7.00
No. 62 (1)	60.00	60.00
Nos. 825-826 (2)	.95	.55
Nos. 380-382 (3)	*5.95*	*4.25*
Nos. 512-513 (2)	7.00	1.40
No. 1341 (1)	.50	.35
Nos. 1089-1090 (2)	1.10	.50
Nos. 1049-1050 (2)	2.00	1.55
Nos. 439-440 (2)	2.90	2.65
Nos. 316-317 (2)	13.00	4.50
Nos. 1065-1066 (2)	.55	.50
No. 504 (1)	.45	.45
Nos. 512-513 (2)	.95	.65
Nos. 450-453 (4)	1.05	1.40
Nos. 831-832 (2)	5.00	1.40
Nos. 494-495 (2)	1.20	.90
Nos. 1141-1143 (3)	*9.75*	1.50
Nos. 771-772 (2)	.70	.50
No. 1718 (1)	.50	.40
Nos. 544-545 (2)	1.65	.60
Nos. 1907-1908 (2)	4.00	2.00
Nos. 1100-1101 (2)	1.20	1.20
Set total (44) Stamps	141.40	94.25

Europa, 1973

Post Horn and Arrows
CD16

1973

Andorra, French....................219-220
Andorra, Spanish....................76
Belgium....................839-840
Cyprus....................396-398
Finland....................526
France....................1367
Germany....................1114-1115
Greece....................1090-1092
Iceland....................447-448
Ireland....................329-330
Italy....................1108-1109
Liechtenstein....................528-529
Luxembourg....................523-524
Malta....................469-471
Monaco....................866-867
Netherlands....................504-505
Norway....................604-605
Portugal....................1170-1172
San Marino....................802-803
Spain....................1753
Switzerland....................580-581
Turkey....................1935-1936
Yugoslavia....................1138-1139

Nos. 219-220 (2)	20.00	11.00
No. 76 (1)	1.25	.85
Nos. 839-840 (2)	1.00	.65
Nos. 396-398 (3)	*4.25*	*3.85*
No. 526 (1)	1.25	.55
No. 1367 (1)	1.25	.75
Nos. 1114-1115 (2)	.85	.50
Nos. 1090-1092 (3)	2.10	1.40
Nos. 447-448 (2)	6.65	3.35

Nos. 329-330 (2)	5.25	2.00
Nos. 1108-1109 (2)	.50	.50
Nos. 528-529 (2)	.60	.60
Nos. 523-524 (2)	.90	.75
Nos. 469-471 (3)	.90	1.20
Nos. 866-867 (2)	15.00	2.40
Nos. 504-505 (2)	1.20	.95
Nos. 604-605 (2)	4.00	1.80
Nos. 1170-1172 (3)	*13.00*	2.15
Nos. 802-803 (2)	*1.00*	.60
No. 1753 (1)	.35	.25
Nos. 580-581 (2)	1.55	.60
Nos. 1935-1936 (2)	4.15	2.25
Nos. 1138-1139 (2)	1.15	1.10
Set total (46) Stamps	88.15	40.05

Europa, 2000

CD17

2000

Albania....2621-2622
Andorra, French....522
Andorra, Spanish....262
Armenia....610-611
Austria....1814
Azerbaijan....698-699
Belarus....350
Belgium....1818
Bosnia & Herzegovina (Moslem)....358
Bosnia & Herzegovina (Serb)....111-112
Croatia....428-429
Cyprus....959
Czech Republic....3120
Denmark....1189
Estonia....394
Faroe Islands....376
Finland....1129
Aland Islands....166
France....2771
Georgia....228-229
Germany....2086-2087
Gibraltar....837-840
Great Britain (Jersey)....935-936
Great Britain (Isle of Man)....883
Greece....1959
Greenland....363
Hungary....3699-3700
Iceland....910
Ireland....1230-1231
Italy....2349
Latvia....504
Liechtenstein....1178
Lithuania....668
Luxembourg....1035
Macedonia....187
Malta....1011-1012
Moldova....355
Monaco....2161-2162
Poland....3519
Portugal....2358
Portugal (Azores)....455
Portugal (Madeira)....208
Romania....4370
Russia....6589
San Marino....1480
Slovakia....355
Slovenia....424
Spain....3036
Sweden....2394
Switzerland....1074
Turkey....2762
Turkish Rep. of Northern Cyprus....500
Ukraine....379
Vatican City....1152

Nos. 2621-2622 (2)	11.00	11.00
No. 522 (1)	2.00	1.00
No. 262 (1)	1.75	.80
Nos. 610-611 (2)	4.75	4.75
No. 1814 (1)	1.25	1.25
Nos. 698-699 (2)	6.00	6.00
No. 350 (1)	1.75	1.75
No. 1818 (1)	1.40	.60
No. 358 (1)	4.75	4.75
Nos. 111-112 (2)	110.00	110.00
Nos. 428-429 (2)	6.25	6.25
No. 959 (1)	2.10	1.40
No. 3120 (1)	1.20	.40
No. 1189 (1)	3.50	2.25
No. 394 (1)	1.25	1.25
No. 376 (1)	2.40	2.40
No. 1129 (1)	2.00	.60
No. 166 (1)	2.00	1.10
No. 2771 (1)	1.25	.40
Nos. 228-229 (2)	9.00	9.00
Nos. 2086-2087 (2)	4.35	2.10
Nos. 837-840 (4)	5.50	5.30
Nos. 935-936 (2)	2.40	2.40
No. 883 (1)	1.75	1.75
No. 363 (1)	1.90	1.90
Nos. 3699-3700 (2)	6.50	2.50
No. 910 (1)	1.60	1.60
Nos. 1230-1231 (2)	4.35	4.35
No. 2349 (1)	1.50	.40
No. 504 (1)	5.00	2.40
No. 1178 (1)	2.25	1.75
No. 668 (1)	1.50	1.50
No. 1035 (1)	1.40	.85
No. 187 (1)	3.00	3.00
Nos. 1011-1012 (2)	4.35	4.35
No. 355 (1)	3.50	3.50
Nos. 2161-2162 (2)	2.80	1.40
No. 3519 (1)	1.25	.75
No. 2358 (1)	1.25	.65
No. 455 (1)	1.25	.50
No. 208 (1)	1.25	.50
No. 4370 (1)	2.50	1.25
No. 6589 (1)	4.00	.85
No. 1480 (1)	1.00	1.00
No. 355 (1)	1.60	.80
No. 424 (1)	3.25	3.25
No. 3036 (1)	1.00	.40
No. 2394 (1)	3.00	1.50
No. 1074 (1)	2.10	1.05
No. 2762 (1)	2.75	2.00
No. 500 (1)	2.50	2.50
No. 379 (1)	4.50	3.00
No. 1152 (1)	1.25	1.25
Set total (68) Stamps	263.70	229.25

The Gibraltar stamps are similar to the stamp illustrated, but none have the design shown above. All other sets listed above include at least one stamp with the design shown, but some include stamps with entirely different designs. Bulgaria Nos. 4131-4132, Guernsey Nos. 802-803 and Yugoslavia Nos. 2485-2486 are Europa stamps with completely different designs.

PORTUGAL & COLONIES
Vasco da Gama

Fleet Departing CD20

Fleet Arriving at Calicut — CD21

Embarking at Rastello CD22

Muse of History CD23

San Gabriel, da Gama and Camoens CD24

Archangel Gabriel, the Patron Saint CD25

Flagship San Gabriel — CD26

Vasco da Gama — CD27

Fourth centenary of Vasco da Gama's discovery of the route to India.

1898

Azores....93-100
Macao....67-74
Madeira....37-44
Portugal....147-154
Port. Africa....1-8
Port. Congo....75-98
Port. India....189-196
St. Thomas & Prince Islands....170-193
Timor....45-52

Nos. 93-100 (8)	113.50	73.50
Nos. 67-74 (8)	138.75	91.75
Nos. 37-44 (8)	60.55	37.25
Nos. 147-154 (8)	155.00	50.25
Nos. 1-8 (8)	35.00	23.50
Nos. 75-98 (24)	52.15	41.65
Nos. 189-196 (8)	25.25	15.50
Nos. 170-193 (24)	56.30	43.00
Nos. 45-52 (8)	39.75	27.25
Set total (104) Stamps	676.25	403.65

Pombal
POSTAL TAX
POSTAL TAX DUES

Marquis de Pombal — CD28

Planning Reconstruction of Lisbon, 1755 — CD29

Pombal Monument, Lisbon — CD30

Sebastiao Jose de Carvalho e Mello, Marquis de Pombal (1699-1782), statesman, rebuilt Lisbon after earthquake of 1755. Tax was for the erection of Pombal monument. Obligatory on all mail on certain days throughout the year. Postal Tax Dues are inscribed "Multa."

1925

Angola.... RA1-RA3, RAJ1-RAJ3
Azores.... RA9-RA11, RAJ2-RAJ4
Cape Verde.... RA1-RA3, RAJ1-RAJ3
Macao.... RA1-RA3, RAJ1-RAJ3
Madeira.... RA1-RA3, RAJ1-RAJ3
Mozambique.... RA1-RA3, RAJ1-RAJ3
Nyassa.... RA1-RA3, RAJ1-RAJ3
Portugal.... RA11-RA13, RAJ2-RAJ4
Port. Guinea.... RA1-RA3, RAJ1-RAJ3
Port. India.... RA1-RA3, RAJ1-RAJ3
St. Thomas & Prince Islands.... RA1-RA3, RAJ1-RAJ3
Timor.... RA1-RA3, RAJ1-RAJ3

Nos. RA1-RA3,RAJ1-RAJ3 (6)	6.60	6.60
Nos. RA9-RA11,RAJ2-RAJ4 (6)	6.60	6.60
Nos. RA1-RA3,RAJ1-RAJ3 (6)	4.50	3.90
Nos. RA1-RA3,RAJ1-RAJ3 (6)	21.25	13.20
Nos. RA1-RA3,RAJ1-RAJ3 (6)	7.95	*14.70*
Nos. RA1-RA3,RAJ1-RAJ3 (6)	2.40	2.55
Nos. RA1-RA3,RAJ1-RAJ3 (6)	63.00	63.00
Nos. RA11-RA13,RAJ2-RAJ4 (6)	5.95	5.20
Nos. RA1-RA3,RAJ1-RAJ3 (6)	5.10	4.65
Nos. RA1-RA3,RAJ1-RAJ3 (6)	3.45	3.45
Nos. RA1-RA3,RAJ1-RAJ3 (6)	4.50	4.50
Nos. RA1-RA3,RAJ1-RAJ3 (6)	2.10	3.90
Set total (72) Stamps	133.40	132.25

Vasco da Gama CD34

Mousinho de Albuquerque CD35

Dam CD36

Prince Henry the Navigator CD37

Affonso de Albuquerque CD38

Plane over Globe CD39

1938-39

Angola....274-291, C1-C9
Cape Verde....234-251, C1-C9
Macao....289-305, C7-C15
Mozambique....270-287, C1-C9
Port. Guinea....233-250, C1-C9
Port. India....439-453, C1-C8
St. Thomas & Prince Islands... 302-319, 323-340, C1-C18
Timor....223-239, C1-C9

Nos. 274-291,C1-C9 (27)	129.40	22.85
Nos. 234-251,C1-C9 (27)	87.00	27.15
Nos. 289-305,C7-C15 (26)	495.70	149.20
Nos. 270-287,C1-C9 (27)	63.45	11.20
Nos. 233-250,C1-C9 (27)	130.20	49.15
Nos. 439-453,C1-C8 (23)	82.75	30.95
Nos. 302-319,323-340,C1-C18 (54)	467.70	244.80
Nos. 223-239,C1-C9 (26)	193.55	94.50
Set total (237) Stamps	1,650.	629.80

Lady of Fatima

Our Lady of the Rosary, Fatima, Portugal — CD40

1948-49

Angola....315-318
Cape Verde....266
Macao....336
Mozambique....325-328
Port. Guinea....271
Port. India....480
St. Thomas & Prince Islands....351
Timor....254

Nos. 315-318 (4)	68.00	17.25
No. 266 (1)	8.50	4.50
No. 336 (1)	42.50	12.00
Nos. 325-328 (4)	73.25	16.85
No. 271 (1)	6.50	3.50
No. 480 (1)	4.50	3.00
No. 351 (1)	8.50	7.00
No. 254 (1)	6.00	6.00
Set total (14) Stamps	217.75	70.10

A souvenir sheet of 9 stamps was issued in 1951 to mark the extension of the 1950 Holy Year. The sheet contains: Angola No. 316, Cape Verde No. 266, Macao No. 336, Mozambique No. 325, Portuguese Guinea No. 271, Portuguese India Nos. 480, 485, St. Thomas & Prince Islands No. 351, Timor No. 254. The sheet also contains a portrait of Pope Pius XII and is inscribed "Encerramento do

Ano Santo, Fatima 1951." It was sold for 11 escudos.

Holy Year

Church Bells and Dove CD41

Angel Holding Candelabra CD42

Holy Year, 1950.

1950-51

Angola 331-332
Cape Verde 268-269
Macao 339-340
Mozambique 330-331
Port. Guinea 273-274
Port. India 490-491, 496-503
St. Thomas & Prince Islands ...353-354
Timor 258-259

Nos. 331-332 (2)	7.60	1.35
Nos. 268-269 (2)	5.50	3.50
Nos. 339-340 (2)	60.00	14.00
Nos. 330-331 (2)	3.00	1.10
Nos. 273-274 (2)	11.25	3.50
Nos. 490-491,496-503 (10)	10.40	4.95
Nos. 353-354 (2)	7.75	4.90
Nos. 258-259 (2)	8.00	4.00
Set total (24) Stamps	113.50	37.30

A souvenir sheet of 8 stamps was issued in 1951 to mark the extension of the Holy Year. The sheet contains: Angola No. 331, Cape Verde No. 269, Macao No. 340, Mozambique No. 331, Portuguese Guinea No. 275, Portuguese India No. 490, St. Thomas & Prince Islands No. 354, Timor No. 258, some with colors changed. The sheet contains doves and is inscribed 'Encerramento do Ano Santo, Fatima 1951.' It was sold for 17 escudos.

Holy Year Conclusion

Our Lady of Fatima — CD43

Conclusion of Holy Year. Sheets contain alternate vertical rows of stamps and labels bearing quotation from Pope Pius XII, different for each colony.

1951

Angola 357
Cape Verde 270
Macao 352
Mozambique 356
Port. Guinea 275
Port. India 506
St. Thomas & Prince Islands 355
Timor 270

No. 357 (1)	5.25	1.50
No. 270 (1)	1.50	1.25
No. 352 (1)	45.00	10.00
No. 356 (1)	2.25	1.00
No. 275 (1)	1.75	.90
No. 506 (1)	2.50	1.00
No. 355 (1)	3.00	2.00
No. 270 (1)	5.75	2.40
Set total (8) Stamps	67.00	20.05

Medical Congress

CD44

First National Congress of Tropical Medicine, Lisbon, 1952. Each stamp has a different design.

1952

Angola 358
Cape Verde 287
Macao 364
Mozambique 359
Port. Guinea 276
Port. India 516
St. Thomas & Prince Islands 356
Timor 271

No. 358 (1)	1.50	.50
No. 287 (1)	.75	.60
No. 364 (1)	10.00	6.00
No. 359 (1)	1.25	.55
No. 276 (1)	1.00	.45
No. 516 (1)	5.50	2.00
No. 356 (1)	.35	.30
No. 271 (1)	2.50	1.30
Set total (8) Stamps	22.85	11.70

Postage Due Stamps

CD45

1952

Angola J37-J42
Cape Verde J31-J36
Macao J53-J58
Mozambique J51-J56
Port. Guinea J40-J45
Port. India J47-J52
St. Thomas & Prince Islands ...J52-J57
Timor J31-J36

Nos. J37-J42 (6)	4.30	2.55
Nos. J31-J36 (6)	2.80	2.30
Nos. J53-J58 (6)	17.45	6.85
Nos. J51-J56 (6)	1.80	1.55
Nos. J40-J45 (6)	2.55	2.55
Nos. J47-J52 (6)	6.10	6.10
Nos. J52-J57 (6)	3.85	3.85
Nos. J31-J36 (6)	6.20	3.50
Set total (48) Stamps	45.05	29.25

Sao Paulo

Father Manuel da Nobrega and View of Sao Paulo — CD46

Founding of Sao Paulo, Brazil, 400th anniv.

1954

Angola 385
Cape Verde 297
Macao 382
Mozambique 395
Port. Guinea 291
Port. India 530
St. Thomas & Prince Islands 369
Timor 279

No. 385 (1)	.80	.50
No. 297 (1)	.70	.60
No. 382 (1)	15.00	6.00
No. 395 (1)	.40	.30
No. 291 (1)	.35	.25
No. 530 (1)	.80	.40
No. 369 (1)	.70	.50
No. 279 (1)	3.00	1.25
Set total (8) Stamps	21.75	9.80

Tropical Medicine Congress

CD47

Sixth International Congress for Tropical Medicine and Malaria, Lisbon, Sept. 1958. Each stamp shows a different plant.

1958

Angola 409
Cape Verde 303
Macao 392
Mozambique 404
Port. Guinea 295
Port. India 569
St. Thomas & Prince Islands 371
Timor 289

No. 409 (1)	3.50	1.10
No. 303 (1)	5.50	2.10
No. 392 (1)	10.00	5.00
No. 404 (1)	2.50	.85
No. 295 (1)	3.00	1.10
No. 569 (1)	1.75	.75
No. 371 (1)	2.75	2.00
No. 289 (1)	3.50	2.75
Set total (8) Stamps	32.50	15.65

Sports

CD48

Each stamp shows a different sport.

1962

Angola 433-438
Cape Verde 320-325
Macao 394-399
Mozambique 424-429
Port. Guinea 299-304
St. Thomas & Prince Islands ...374-379
Timor 313-318

Nos. 433-438 (6)	5.50	3.20
Nos. 320-325 (6)	15.25	5.20
Nos. 394-399 (6)	68.65	14.60
Nos. 424-429 (6)	5.70	2.45
Nos. 299-304 (6)	6.00	3.00
Nos. 374-379 (6)	6.75	3.20
Nos. 313-318 (6)	9.15	5.05
Set total (42) Stamps	117.00	36.70

Anti-Malaria

Anopheles Funestus and Malaria Eradication Symbol — CD49

World Health Organization drive to eradicate malaria.

1962

Angola 439
Cape Verde 326
Macao 400
Mozambique 430
Port. Guinea 305
St. Thomas & Prince Islands 380
Timor 319

No. 439 (1)	1.75	.90
No. 326 (1)	1.40	.90
No. 400 (1)	7.00	2.25
No. 430 (1)	1.40	.40
No. 305 (1)	1.25	.45
No. 380 (1)	2.25	1.25
No. 319 (1)	1.50	1.00
Set total (7) Stamps	16.55	7.15

Airline Anniversary

Map of Africa, Super Constellation and Jet Liner — CD50

Tenth anniversary of Transportes Aereos Portugueses (TAP).

1963

Angola 490
Cape Verde 327
Mozambique 434
Port. Guinea 318
St. Thomas & Prince Islands 381

No. 490 (1)	1.00	.35
No. 327 (1)	1.10	.70
No. 434 (1)	.40	.25
No. 318 (1)	.65	.35
No. 381 (1)	.80	.50
Set total (5) Stamps	3.95	2.15

National Overseas Bank

Antonio Teixeira de Sousa — CD51

Centenary of the National Overseas Bank of Portugal.

1964, May 16

Angola 509
Cape Verde 328
Port. Guinea 319
St. Thomas & Prince Islands 382
Timor 320

No. 509 (1)	.90	.30
No. 328 (1)	1.10	.75
No. 319 (1)	.65	.40
No. 382 (1)	.70	.50
No. 320 (1)	1.50	.85
Set total (5) Stamps	4.85	2.80

ITU

ITU Emblem and the Archangel Gabriel — CD52

International Communications Union, Cent.

1965, May 17

Angola 511
Cape Verde 329
Macao 402
Mozambique 464
Port. Guinea 320
St. Thomas & Prince Islands 383
Timor 321

No. 511 (1)	1.25	.65
No. 329 (1)	2.10	1.40
No. 402 (1)	6.00	2.25
No. 464 (1)	.45	.25
No. 320 (1)	1.90	.75
No. 383 (1)	2.00	1.00
No. 321 (1)	1.50	.90
Set total (7) Stamps	15.20	7.20

National Revolution

CD53

40th anniv. of the National Revolution. Different buildings on each stamp.

1966, May 28

Angola 525
Cape Verde 338
Macao 403
Mozambique 465
Port. Guinea 329
St. Thomas & Prince Islands 392
Timor 322

No. 525 (1)	.50	.25
No. 338 (1)	.60	.45
No. 403 (1)	9.00	2.25
No. 465 (1)	.50	.30
No. 329 (1)	.55	.35
No. 392 (1)	.80	.50
No. 322 (1)	1.75	.95
Set total (7) Stamps	13.70	5.05

Navy Club

CD54

Centenary of Portugal's Navy Club. Each stamp has a different design.

1967, Jan. 31

Angola 527-528
Cape Verde 339-340
Macao 412-413
Mozambique 478-479
Port. Guinea 330-331
St. Thomas & Prince Islands ... 393-394
Timor 323-324

Nos. 527-528 (2)	1.75	.75
Nos. 339-340 (2)	2.00	1.40
Nos. 412-413 (2)	11.25	4.00
Nos. 478-479 (2)	1.40	.65
Nos. 330-331 (2)	1.20	.90
Nos. 393-394 (2)	3.30	1.30
Nos. 323-324 (2)	4.65	1.90
Set total (14) Stamps	25.55	10.90

Admiral Coutinho

CD55

Centenary of the birth of Admiral Carlos Viegas Gago Coutinho (1869-1959), explorer and aviation pioneer. Each stamp has a different design.

1969, Feb. 17

Angola 547
Cape Verde 355
Macao 417
Mozambique 484
Port. Guinea 335
St. Thomas & Prince Islands 397
Timor 335

No. 547 (1)	.85	.35
No. 355 (1)	.50	.25
No. 417 (1)	5.00	1.75
No. 484 (1)	.25	.25
No. 335 (1)	.35	.25
No. 397 (1)	.60	.35
No. 335 (1)	2.50	1.05
Set total (7) Stamps	10.05	4.25

Administration Reform

Luiz Augusto Rebello da Silva — CD56

Centenary of the administration reforms of the overseas territories.

1969, Sept. 25

Angola 549
Cape Verde 357
Macao 419
Mozambique 491
Port. Guinea 337
St. Thomas & Prince Islands 399
Timor 338

No. 549 (1)	.35	.25
No. 357 (1)	.50	.25
No. 419 (1)	6.00	1.00
No. 491 (1)	.25	.25
No. 337 (1)	.25	.25
No. 399 (1)	.45	.45
No. 338 (1)	1.25	.50
Set total (7) Stamps	9.05	2.95

Marshal Carmona

CD57

Birth centenary of Marshal Antonio Oscar Carmona de Fragoso (1869-1951), President of Portugal. Each stamp has a different design.

1970, Nov. 15

Angola 563
Cape Verde 359
Macao 422
Mozambique 493
Port. Guinea 340
St. Thomas & Prince Islands 403
Timor 341

No. 563 (1)	.45	.25
No. 359 (1)	.55	.35
No. 422 (1)	2.00	1.00
No. 493 (1)	.40	.25
No. 340 (1)	.35	.25
No. 403 (1)	.75	.40
No. 341 (1)	1.00	.35
Set total (7) Stamps	5.50	2.85

Olympic Games

CD59

20th Olympic Games, Munich, Aug. 26-Sept. 11. Each stamp shows a different sport.

1972, June 20

Angola 569
Cape Verde 361
Macao 426
Mozambique 504
Port. Guinea 342
St. Thomas & Prince Islands 408
Timor 343

No. 569 (1)	.65	.25
No. 361 (1)	.85	.30
No. 426 (1)	4.25	1.00
No. 504 (1)	.30	.25
No. 342 (1)	.45	.25
No. 408 (1)	.45	.25
No. 343 (1)	1.60	.80
Set total (7) Stamps	8.55	3.10

Lisbon-Rio de Janeiro Flight

CD60

50th anniversary of the Lisbon to Rio de Janeiro flight by Arturo de Sacadura and Coutinho, March 30-June 5, 1922. Each stamp shows a different stage of the flight.

1972, Sept. 20

Angola 570
Cape Verde 362
Macao 427
Mozambique 505
Port. Guinea 343
St. Thomas & Prince Islands 409
Timor 344

No. 570 (1)	.35	.25
No. 362 (1)	1.50	.30
No. 427 (1)	22.50	8.50
No. 505 (1)	.25	.25
No. 343 (1)	.25	.25
No. 409 (1)	.50	.25
No. 344 (1)	1.40	.60
Set total (7) Stamps	26.75	10.40

WMO Centenary

WMO Emblem — CD61

Centenary of international meterological cooperation.

1973, Dec. 15

Angola 571
Cape Verde 363
Macao 429
Mozambique 509
Port. Guinea 344
St. Thomas & Prince Islands 410
Timor 345

No. 571 (1)	.45	.25
No. 363 (1)	.65	.30
No. 429 (1)	6.00	1.75
No. 509 (1)	.30	.25
No. 344 (1)	.45	.35
No. 410 (1)	.60	.50
No. 345 (1)	4.25	2.50
Set total (7) Stamps	12.70	5.90

FRENCH COMMUNITY

Upper Volta can be found under Burkina Faso in Vol. 1
Madagascar can be found under Malagasy in Vol. 3

Colonial Exposition

People of French Empire CD70

Women's Heads CD71

France Showing Way to Civilization CD72

"Colonial Commerce" CD73

International Colonial Exposition, Paris.

1931

Cameroun 213-216
Chad 60-63
Dahomey 97-100
Fr. Guiana 152-155
Fr. Guinea 116-119
Fr. India 100-103
Fr. Polynesia 76-79
Fr. Sudan 102-105
Gabon 120-123
Guadeloupe 138-141
Indo-China 140-142
Ivory Coast 92-95
Madagascar 169-172
Martinique 129-132
Mauritania 65-68
Middle Congo 61-64
New Caledonia 176-179
Niger 73-76
Reunion 122-125
St. Pierre & Miquelon 132-135
Senegal 138-141
Somali Coast 135-138
Togo 254-257
Ubangi-Shari 82-85
Upper Volta 66-69
Wallis & Futuna Isls. 85-88

Nos. 213-216 (4)	23.00	18.25
Nos. 60-63 (4)	22.00	22.00
Nos. 97-100 (4)	26.00	26.00
Nos. 152-155 (4)	22.00	22.00
Nos. 116-119 (4)	19.75	19.75
Nos. 100-103 (4)	18.00	*18.00*
Nos. 76-79 (4)	30.00	30.00
Nos. 102-105 (4)	19.00	19.00
Nos. 120-123 (4)	17.50	17.50
Nos. 138-141 (4)	19.00	19.00
Nos. 140-142 (3)	12.00	11.50
Nos. 92-95 (4)	22.50	22.50
Nos. 169-172 (4)	9.25	6.50
Nos. 129-132 (4)	21.00	21.00
Nos. 65-68 (4)	22.00	22.00
Nos. 61-64 (4)	20.00	18.50
Nos. 176-179 (4)	24.00	24.00
Nos. 73-76 (4)	20.50	20.50
Nos. 122-125 (4)	22.00	22.00
Nos. 132-135 (4)	24.00	24.00
Nos. 138-141 (4)	20.00	20.00
Nos. 135-138 (4)	22.00	22.00
Nos. 254-257 (4)	22.00	22.00
Nos. 82-85 (4)	21.00	21.00
Nos. 66-69 (4)	19.00	19.00
Nos. 85-88 (4)	31.00	35.00
Set total (103) Stamps	548.50	543.00

Paris International Exposition
Colonial Arts Exposition

"Colonial Resources"
CD74 CD77

Overseas Commerce CD75

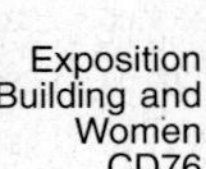

Exposition Building and Women CD76

"France and the Empire" CD78

Cultural Treasures of the Colonies CD79

Souvenir sheets contain one imperf. stamp.

1937

Cameroun 217-222A
Dahomey 101-107
Fr. Equatorial Africa 27-32, 73
Fr. Guiana 162-168
Fr. Guinea 120-126
Fr. India 104-110
Fr. Polynesia 117-123
Fr. Sudan 106-112
Guadeloupe 148-154
Indo-China 193-199
Inini 41
Ivory Coast 152-158
Kwangchowan 132
Madagascar 191-197
Martinique 179-185
Mauritania 69-75
New Caledonia 208-214
Niger 77-83
Reunion 167-173
St. Pierre & Miquelon 165-171
Senegal 172-178
Somali Coast 139-145
Togo 258-264
Wallis & Futuna Isls. 89

Nos. 217-222A (7)	18.80	20.30
Nos. 101-107 (7)	23.60	27.60
Nos. 27-32, 73 (7)	28.10	32.10
Nos. 162-168 (7)	22.50	24.50
Nos. 120-126 (7)	24.00	28.00
Nos. 104-110 (7)	21.15	36.50
Nos. 117-123 (7)	58.50	75.00
Nos. 106-112 (7)	23.60	27.60
Nos. 148-154 (7)	19.55	21.05
Nos. 193-199 (7)	17.70	19.70
No. 41 (1)	21.00	27.50
Nos. 152-158 (7)	22.20	26.20
No. 132 (1)	9.25	11.00
Nos. 191-197 (7)	19.25	21.75
Nos. 179-185 (7)	19.95	21.70
Nos. 69-75 (7)	20.50	24.50
Nos. 208-214 (7)	39.00	50.50
Nos. 73-83 (11)	40.60	45.10
Nos. 167-173 (7)	21.70	23.20
Nos. 165-171 (7)	49.60	64.00
Nos. 172-178 (7)	21.00	23.80
Nos. 139-145 (7)	25.60	32.60
Nos. 258-264 (7)	20.40	20.40
No. 89 (1)	19.00	37.50
Set total (154) Stamps	606.55	742.10

Curie

Pierre and Marie Curie CD80

40th anniversary of the discovery of radium. The surtax was for the benefit of the Intl. Union for the Control of Cancer.

1938

Cameroun	B1
Cuba	B1-B2
Dahomey	B2
France	B76
Fr. Equatorial Africa	B1
Fr. Guiana	B3
Fr. Guinea	B2
Fr. India	B6
Fr. Polynesia	B5
Fr. Sudan	B1
Guadeloupe	B3
Indo-China	B14
Ivory Coast	B2
Madagascar	B2
Martinique	B2
Mauritania	B3
New Caledonia	B4
Niger	B1
Reunion	B4
St. Pierre & Miquelon	B3
Senegal	B3
Somali Coast	B2
Togo	B1

No. B1 (1)	10.00	10.00
Nos. B1-B2 (2)	12.00	3.35
No. B2 (1)	9.50	9.50
No. B76 (1)	21.00	12.50
No. B1 (1)	24.00	24.00
No. B3 (1)	13.50	13.50
No. B2 (1)	8.75	8.75
No. B6 (1)	10.00	10.00
No. B5 (1)	20.00	20.00
No. B1 (1)	12.50	12.50
No. B3 (1)	11.00	10.50
No. B14 (1)	12.00	12.00
No. B2 (1)	11.00	7.50
No. B2 (1)	11.00	11.00
No. B2 (1)	13.00	13.00
No. B3 (1)	7.75	7.75
No. B4 (1)	16.50	17.50
No. B1 (1)	16.50	16.50
No. B4 (1)	14.00	14.00
No. B3 (1)	21.00	22.50
No. B3 (1)	10.50	10.50
No. B2 (1)	7.75	7.75
No. B1 (1)	20.00	20.00
Set total (24) Stamps	313.25	294.60

Caillie

Rene Caillie and Map of Northwestern Africa — CD81

Death centenary of Rene Caillie (1799-1838), French explorer. All three denominations exist with colony name omitted.

1939

Dahomey	108-110
Fr. Guinea	161-163
Fr. Sudan	113-115
Ivory Coast	160-162
Mauritania	109-111
Niger	84-86
Senegal	188-190
Togo	265-267

Nos. 108-110 (3)	1.20	3.60
Nos. 161-163 (3)	1.20	3.20
Nos. 113-115 (3)	1.20	3.20
Nos. 160-162 (3)	1.05	2.55
Nos. 109-111 (3)	1.05	3.80
Nos. 84-86 (3)	2.35	2.35
Nos. 188-190 (3)	1.05	2.90
Nos. 265-267 (3)	1.05	3.30
Set total (24) Stamps	10.15	24.90

New York World's Fair

Natives and New York Skyline CD82

1939

Cameroun	223-224
Dahomey	111-112
Fr. Equatorial Africa	78-79
Fr. Guiana	169-170
Fr. Guinea	164-165
Fr. India	111-112
Fr. Polynesia	124-125
Fr. Sudan	116-117
Guadeloupe	155-156
Indo-China	203-204
Inini	42-43
Ivory Coast	163-164
Kwangchowan	133-134
Madagascar	209-210
Martinique	186-187
Mauritania	112-113
New Caledonia	215-216
Niger	87-88
Reunion	174-175
St. Pierre & Miquelon	205-206
Senegal	191-192
Somali Coast	179-180
Togo	268-269
Wallis & Futuna Isls.	90-91

Nos. 223-224 (2)	2.80	2.40
Nos. 111-112 (2)	1.60	3.20
Nos. 78-79 (2)	1.60	3.20
Nos. 169-170 (2)	2.60	2.60
Nos. 164-165 (2)	1.60	3.20
Nos. 111-112 (2)	3.00	*8.00*
Nos. 124-125 (2)	4.80	4.80
Nos. 116-117 (2)	1.60	3.20
Nos. 155-156 (2)	2.50	2.50
Nos. 203-204 (2)	2.05	2.05
Nos. 42-43 (2)	7.50	9.00
Nos. 163-164 (2)	1.50	3.00
Nos. 133-134 (2)	2.50	2.50
Nos. 209-210 (2)	1.50	2.50
Nos. 186-187 (2)	2.35	2.35
Nos. 112-113 (2)	1.40	2.80
Nos. 215-216 (2)	3.35	3.35
Nos. 87-88 (2)	1.60	2.80
Nos. 174-175 (2)	2.80	2.80
Nos. 205-206 (2)	4.80	6.00
Nos. 191-192 (2)	1.40	2.80
Nos. 179-180 (2)	1.40	2.80
Nos. 268-269 (2)	1.40	2.80
Nos. 90-91 (2)	5.00	6.00
Set total (48) Stamps	62.65	86.65

French Revolution

Storming of the Bastille CD83

French Revolution, 150th anniv. The surtax was for the defense of the colonies.

1939

Cameroun	B2-B6
Dahomey	B3-B7
Fr. Equatorial Africa	B4-B8, CB1
Fr. Guiana	B4-B8, CB1
Fr. Guinea	B3-B7
Fr. India	B7-B11
Fr. Polynesia	B6-B10, CB1
Fr. Sudan	B2-B6
Guadeloupe	B4-B8
Indo-China	B15-B19, CB1
Inini	B1-B5
Ivory Coast	B3-B7
Kwangchowan	B1-B5
Madagascar	B3-B7, CB1
Martinique	B3-B7
Mauritania	B4-B8
New Caledonia	B5-B9, CB1
Niger	B2-B6
Reunion	B5-B9, CB1
St. Pierre & Miquelon	B4-B8
Senegal	B4-B8, CB1
Somali Coast	B3-B7
Togo	B2-B6
Wallis & Futuna Isls.	B1-B5

Nos. B2-B6 (5)	60.00	60.00
Nos. B3-B7 (5)	47.50	47.50
Nos. B4-B8,CB1 (6)	120.00	120.00
Nos. B4-B8,CB1 (6)	79.50	79.50
Nos. B3-B7 (5)	47.50	47.50
Nos. B7-B11 (5)	28.75	*32.50*
Nos. B6-B10,CB1 (6)	122.50	122.50
Nos. B2-B6 (5)	50.00	50.00
Nos. B4-B8 (5)	50.00	50.00
Nos. B15-B19,CB1 (6)	85.00	85.00
Nos. B1-B5 (5)	80.00	100.00
Nos. B3-B7 (5)	43.75	43.75
Nos. B1-B5 (5)	46.25	46.25
Nos. B3-B7,CB1 (6)	65.50	65.50
Nos. B3-B7 (5)	52.50	52.50
Nos. B4-B8 (5)	42.50	42.50
Nos. B5-B9,CB1 (6)	101.50	101.50
Nos. B2-B6 (5)	60.00	60.00
Nos. B5-B9,CB1 (6)	87.50	87.50
Nos. B4-B8 (5)	67.50	72.50
Nos. B4-B8,CB1 (6)	56.50	56.50
Nos. B3-B7 (5)	45.00	45.00
Nos. B2-B6 (5)	42.50	42.50
Nos. B1-B5 (5)	80.00	110.00
Set total (128) Stamps	1,562.	1,621.

Plane over Coastal Area CD85

All five denominations exist with colony name omitted.

1940

Dahomey	C1-C5
Fr. Guinea	C1-C5
Fr. Sudan	C1-C5
Ivory Coast	C1-C5
Mauritania	C1-C5
Niger	C1-C5
Senegal	C12-C16
Togo	C1-C5

Nos. C1-C5 (5)	4.00	4.00
Nos. C1-C5 (5)	4.00	4.00
Nos. C1-C5 (5)	4.00	4.00
Nos. C1-C5 (5)	3.80	3.80
Nos. C1-C5 (5)	3.50	3.50
Nos. C1-C5 (5)	3.50	3.50
Nos. C12-C16 (5)	3.50	3.50
Nos. C1-C5 (5)	3.15	3.15
Set total (40) Stamps	29.45	29.45

Defense of the Empire

Colonial Infantryman — CD86

1941

Cameroun	B13B
Dahomey	B13
Fr. Equatorial Africa	B8B
Fr. Guiana	B10
Fr. Guinea	B13
Fr. India	B13
Fr. Polynesia	B12
Fr. Sudan	B12
Guadeloupe	B10
Indo-China	B19B
Inini	B7
Ivory Coast	B13
Kwangchowan	B7
Madagascar	B9
Martinique	B9
Mauritania	B14
New Caledonia	B11
Niger	B12
Reunion	B11
St. Pierre & Miquelon	B8B
Senegal	B14
Somali Coast	B9
Togo	B10B
Wallis & Futuna Isls.	B7

No. B13B (1)	1.60
No. B13 (1)	1.20
No. B8B (1)	3.50
No. B10 (1)	1.40
No. B13 (1)	1.40
No. B13 (1)	1.25
No. B12 (1)	3.50
No. B12 (1)	1.40
No. B10 (1)	1.00
No. B19B (1)	3.00
No. B7 (1)	1.75
No. B13 (1)	1.25
No. B7 (1)	.85
No. B9 (1)	1.50
No. B9 (1)	1.40
No. B14 (1)	.95
No. B12 (1)	1.40
No. B11 (1)	1.60
No. B8B (1)	4.50
No. B14 (1)	1.25
No. B9 (1)	1.60
No. B10B (1)	1.10
No. B7 (1)	1.75
Set total (23) Stamps	40.15

Each of the CD86 stamps listed above is part of a set of three stamps. The designs of the other two stamps in the set vary from country to country. Only the values of the Common Design stamps are listed here.

Colonial Education Fund

CD86a

1942

Cameroun	CB3
Dahomey	CB4
Fr. Equatorial Africa	CB5
Fr. Guiana	CB4
Fr. Guinea	CB4
Fr. India	CB3
Fr. Polynesia	CB4
Fr. Sudan	CB4
Guadeloupe	CB3
Indo-China	CB5
Inini	CB3
Ivory Coast	CB4
Kwangchowan	CB4
Malagasy	CB5
Martinique	CB3
Mauritania	CB4
New Caledonia	CB4
Niger	CB4
Reunion	CB4
St. Pierre & Miquelon	CB3
Senegal	CB5
Somali Coast	CB3
Togo	CB3
Wallis & Futuna	CB3

No. CB3 (1)	1.10	
No. CB4 (1)	.80	5.50
No. CB5 (1)	.80	
No. CB4 (1)	1.10	
No. CB4 (1)	.40	5.50
No. CB3 (1)	.90	
No. CB4 (1)	2.00	
No. CB4 (1)	.40	5.50
No. CB3 (1)	1.10	
No. CB5 (1)	2.00	
No. CB3 (1)	1.25	
No. CB4 (1)	1.00	5.50
No. CB4 (1)	1.00	
No. CB5 (1)	.65	
No. CB3 (1)	1.00	
No. CB4 (1)	.80	
No. CB4 (1)	2.25	
No. CB4 (1)	.35	
No. CB4 (1)	.90	
No. CB3 (1)	7.00	
No. CB5 (1)	.80	6.50
No. CB3 (1)	.70	
No. CB3 (1)	.35	
No. CB3 (1)	2.00	
Set total (24) Stamps	30.65	28.50

Cross of Lorraine & Four-motor Plane CD87

1941-5

Cameroun	C1-C7
Fr. Equatorial Africa	C17-C23
Fr. Guiana	C9-C10
Fr. India	C1-C6
Fr. Polynesia	C3-C9
Fr. West Africa	C1-C3
Guadeloupe	C1-C2
Madagascar	C37-C43

Martinique.................................. C1-C2
New Caledonia......................... C7-C13
Reunion................................. C18-C24
St. Pierre & Miquelon................ C1-C7
Somali Coast............................. C1-C7

Nos. C1-C7 (7)	6.30	6.30
Nos. C17-C23 (7)	10.40	6.35
Nos. C9-C10 (2)	3.80	3.10
Nos. C1-C6 (6)	9.30	*15.00*
Nos. C3-C9 (7)	13.75	10.00
Nos. C1-C3 (3)	9.50	3.90
Nos. C1-C2 (2)	3.75	2.50
Nos. C37-C43 (7)	5.60	3.80
Nos. C1-C2 (2)	3.00	1.60
Nos. C7-C13 (7)	8.85	7.30
Nos. C18-C24 (7)	7.05	5.00
Nos. C1-C7 (7)	11.60	9.40
Nos. C1-C7 (7)	13.95	11.10
Set total (71) Stamps	106.85	85.35

Somali Coast stamps are inscribed "Djibouti".

Transport Plane CD88

Caravan and Plane CD89

1942

Dahomey.................................. C6-C13
Fr. Guinea................................ C6-C13
Fr. Sudan................................. C6-C13
Ivory Coast.............................. C6-C13
Mauritania............................... C6-C13
Niger....................................... C6-C13
Senegal.................................. C17-C25
Togo.. C6-C13

Nos. C6-C13 (8)	7.15
Nos. C6-C13 (8)	5.75
Nos. C6-C13 (8)	8.00
Nos. C6-C13 (8)	11.15
Nos. C6-C13 (8)	9.75
Nos. C6-C13 (8)	6.20
Nos. C17-C25 (9)	9.45
Nos. C6-C13 (8)	6.75
Set total (65) Stamps	64.20

Red Cross

Marianne CD90

The surtax was for the French Red Cross and national relief.

1944

Cameroun................................. B28
Fr. Equatorial Africa.................. B38
Fr. Guiana................................ B12
Fr. India................................... B14
Fr. Polynesia............................. B13
Fr. West Africa............................ B1
Guadeloupe.............................. B12
Madagascar.............................. B15
Martinique................................ B11
New Caledonia.......................... B13
Reunion.................................... B15
St. Pierre & Miquelon................ B13
Somali Coast............................ B13
Wallis & Futuna Isls. B9

No. B28 (1)	2.00	1.60
No. B38 (1)	1.60	1.20
No. B12 (1)	1.75	1.25
No. B14 (1)	1.50	1.25
No. B13 (1)	2.00	1.60
No. B1 (1)	6.50	4.75
No. B12 (1)	1.40	1.00
No. B15 (1)	.90	.90
No. B11 (1)	1.20	1.20
No. B13 (1)	1.50	1.50
No. B15 (1)	1.60	1.10
No. B13 (1)	2.60	2.60
No. B13 (1)	1.75	2.00
No. B9 (1)	3.00	3.00
Set total (14) Stamps	29.30	24.95

Eboue

CD91

Felix Eboue, first French colonial administrator to proclaim resistance to Germany after French surrender in World War II.

1945

Cameroun................................296-297
Fr. Equatorial Africa.................156-157
Fr. Guiana................................171-172
Fr. India..................................210-211
Fr. Polynesia.............................150-151
Fr. West Africa............................15-16
Guadeloupe...............................187-188
Madagascar...............................259-260
Martinique.................................196-197
New Caledonia...........................274-275
Reunion.....................................238-239
St. Pierre & Miquelon.................322-323
Somali Coast..............................238-239

Nos. 296-297 (2)	2.40	1.95
Nos. 156-157 (2)	2.55	2.00
Nos. 171-172 (2)	2.45	2.00
Nos. 210-211 (2)	2.20	1.95
Nos. 150-151 (2)	3.60	2.85
Nos. 15-16 (2)	2.40	2.40
Nos. 187-188 (2)	2.05	1.60
Nos. 259-260 (2)	2.00	1.45
Nos. 196-197 (2)	2.05	1.55
Nos. 274-275 (2)	3.40	3.00
Nos. 238-239 (2)	2.40	2.00
Nos. 322-323 (2)	4.40	3.45
Nos. 238-239 (2)	2.45	2.10
Set total (26) Stamps	34.35	28.30

Victory

Victory — CD92

European victory of the Allied Nations in World War II.

1946, May 8

Cameroun.. C8
Fr. Equatorial Africa...................... C24
Fr. Guiana...................................... C11
Fr. India... C7
Fr. Polynesia.................................. C10
Fr. West Africa.................................. C4
Guadeloupe....................................... C3
Indo-China...................................... C19
Madagascar..................................... C44
Martinique... C3
New Caledonia................................. C14
Reunion.. C25
St. Pierre & Miquelon......................... C8
Somali Coast...................................... C8
Wallis & Futuna Isls. C1

No. C8 (1)	1.60	1.20
No. C24 (1)	1.60	1.25
No. C11 (1)	1.75	1.25
No. C7 (1)	1.00	4.00
No. C10 (1)	2.75	2.00
No. C4 (1)	1.60	1.20
No. C3 (1)	1.25	1.00
No. C19 (1)	1.00	.55
No. C44 (1)	1.00	.35
No. C3 (1)	1.30	1.00
No. C14 (1)	1.50	1.25
No. C25 (1)	1.10	.90
No. C8 (1)	2.10	2.10
No. C8 (1)	1.75	1.40
No. C1 (1)	2.25	1.90
Set total (15) Stamps	23.55	21.35

Chad to Rhine

Leclerc's Departure from Chad — CD93

Battle at Cufra Oasis — CD94

Tanks in Action, Mareth — CD95

Normandy Invasion — CD96

Entering Paris — CD97

Liberation of Strasbourg — CD98

"Chad to the Rhine" march, 1942-44, by Gen. Jacques Leclerc's column, later French 2nd Armored Division.

1946, June 6

Cameroun.................................. C9-C14
Fr. Equatorial Africa.............. C25-C30
Fr. Guiana............................. C12-C17
Fr. India.................................. C8-C13
Fr. Polynesia.......................... C11-C16
Fr. West Africa........................ C5-C10
Guadeloupe............................... C4-C9
Indo-China............................. C20-C25
Madagascar............................ C45-C50
Martinique................................. C4-C9
New Caledonia........................ C15-C20
Reunion.................................. C26-C31
St. Pierre & Miquelon.............. C9-C14
Somali Coast........................... C9-C14
Wallis & Futuna Isls. C2-C7

Nos. C9-C14 (6)	12.05	9.70
Nos. C25-C30 (6)	14.70	10.80
Nos. C12-C17 (6)	12.65	10.35
Nos. C8-C13 (6)	12.80	*15.00*
Nos. C11-C16 (6)	17.55	13.40
Nos. C5-C10 (6)	16.05	11.95
Nos. C4-C9 (6)	12.00	9.60
Nos. C20-C25 (6)	6.40	6.40
Nos. C45-C50 (6)	10.30	8.40
Nos. C4-C9 (6)	8.85	7.30
Nos. C15-C20 (6)	13.40	11.90
Nos. C26-C31 (6)	10.25	6.55
Nos. C9-C14 (6)	17.30	14.35
Nos. C9-C14 (6)	18.10	12.65
Nos. C2-C7 (6)	13.75	10.45
Set total (90) Stamps	196.15	158.80

UPU

French Colonials, Globe and Plane — CD99

Universal Postal Union, 75th anniv.

1949, July 4

Cameroun.. C29
Fr. Equatorial Africa...................... C34
Fr. India.. C17
Fr. Polynesia.................................. C20
Fr. West Africa................................ C15
Indo-China...................................... C26
Madagascar.................................... C55
New Caledonia................................ C24
St. Pierre & Miquelon...................... C18
Somali Coast................................... C18
Togo... C18
Wallis & Futuna Isls. C10

No. C29 (1)	8.00	4.75
No. C34 (1)	16.00	12.00
No. C17 (1)	11.50	8.75
No. C20 (1)	20.00	15.00
No. C15 (1)	12.00	8.75
No. C26 (1)	4.75	4.00
No. C55 (1)	4.00	2.75
No. C24 (1)	7.50	5.00
No. C18 (1)	20.00	12.00
No. C18 (1)	14.00	10.50
No. C18 (1)	8.50	7.00
No. C10 (1)	11.00	8.25
Set total (12) Stamps	137.25	98.75

Tropical Medicine

Doctor Treating Infant CD100

The surtax was for charitable work.

1950

Cameroun.. B29
Fr. Equatorial Africa...................... B39
Fr. India.. B15
Fr. Polynesia.................................. B14
Fr. West Africa.................................. B3
Madagascar.................................... B17
New Caledonia................................ B14
St. Pierre & Miquelon...................... B14
Somali Coast................................... B14
Togo... B11

No. B29 (1)	7.25	5.50
No. B39 (1)	7.25	5.50
No. B15 (1)	6.00	4.00
No. B14 (1)	10.50	8.00
No. B3 (1)	9.50	7.25
No. B17 (1)	5.50	5.50
No. B14 (1)	6.75	5.25
No. B14 (1)	16.00	15.00
No. B14 (1)	7.75	6.25
No. B11 (1)	5.00	3.50
Set total (10) Stamps	81.50	65.75

Military Medal

Medal, Early Marine and Colonial Soldier — CD101

Centenary of the creation of the French Military Medal.

1952

Cameroun..322
Comoro Isls. 39
Fr. Equatorial Africa.......................186

Fr. India....................................233
Fr. Polynesia....................................179
Fr. West Africa....................................57
Madagascar....................................286
New Caledonia....................................295
St. Pierre & Miquelon....................................345
Somali Coast....................................267
Togo....................................327
Wallis & Futuna Isls....................................149

No. 322 (1)	7.25	3.25
No. 39 (1)	45.00	37.50
No. 186 (1)	8.00	5.50
No. 233 (1)	5.50	7.00
No. 179 (1)	13.50	10.00
No. 57 (1)	8.75	6.50
No. 286 (1)	3.75	2.50
No. 295 (1)	6.50	6.00
No. 345 (1)	16.00	15.00
No. 267 (1)	9.00	8.00
No. 327 (1)	5.50	4.75
No. 149 (1)	7.25	7.25
Set total (12) Stamps	136.00	113.25

Liberation

Allied Landing, Victory Sign and Cross of Lorraine — CD102

Liberation of France, 10th anniv.

1954, June 6

Cameroun.................................... C32
Comoro Isls.................................... C4
Fr. Equatorial Africa.................................... C38
Fr. India.................................... C18
Fr. Polynesia.................................... C22
Fr. West Africa.................................... C17
Madagascar.................................... C57
New Caledonia.................................... C25
St. Pierre & Miquelon.................................... C19
Somali Coast.................................... C19
Togo.................................... C19
Wallis & Futuna Isls.................................... C11

No. C32 (1)	7.25	4.75
No. C4 (1)	32.50	19.00
No. C38 (1)	12.00	8.00
No. C18 (1)	11.00	8.00
No. C22 (1)	10.00	8.00
No. C17 (1)	12.00	5.50
No. C57 (1)	3.25	2.00
No. C25 (1)	7.50	5.00
No. C19 (1)	19.00	12.00
No. C19 (1)	10.50	8.50
No. C19 (1)	7.00	5.50
No. C11 (1)	11.00	8.25
Set total (12) Stamps	143.00	94.50

FIDES

Plowmen CD103

Efforts of FIDES, the Economic and Social Development Fund for Overseas Possessions (Fonds d' Investissement pour le Developpement Economique et Social). Each stamp has a different design.

1956

Cameroun....................................326-329
Comoro Isls....................................43
Fr. Equatorial Africa....................................189-192
Fr. Polynesia....................................181
Fr. West Africa....................................65-72
Madagascar....................................292-295
New Caledonia....................................303
St. Pierre & Miquelon....................................350
Somali Coast....................................268-269
Togo....................................331

Nos. 326-329 (4)	6.90	3.20
No. 43 (1)	2.25	1.60
Nos. 189-192 (4)	3.20	1.65
No. 181 (1)	4.00	2.00
Nos. 65-72 (8)	16.00	6.35
Nos. 292-295 (4)	2.25	1.20
No. 303 (1)	1.90	1.10
No. 350 (1)	6.00	4.00
Nos. 268-269 (2)	5.35	3.15
No. 331 (1)	4.25	2.10
Set total (27) Stamps	52.10	26.35

Flower

CD104

Each stamp shows a different flower.

1958-9

Cameroun....................................333
Comoro Isls....................................45
Fr. Equatorial Africa....................................200-201
Fr. Polynesia....................................192
Fr. So. & Antarctic Terr....................................11
Fr. West Africa....................................79-83
Madagascar....................................301-302
New Caledonia....................................304-305
St. Pierre & Miquelon....................................357
Somali Coast....................................270
Togo....................................348-349
Wallis & Futuna Isls....................................152

No. 333 (1)	1.60	.80
No. 45 (1)	5.25	4.25
Nos. 200-201 (2)	3.60	1.60
No. 192 (1)	6.50	4.00
No. 11 (1)	8.75	7.50
Nos. 79-83 (5)	10.45	5.60
Nos. 301-302 (2)	1.60	.60
Nos. 304-305 (2)	8.00	3.00
No. 357 (1)	4.50	2.25
No. 270 (1)	4.25	1.40
Nos. 348-349 (2)	1.10	.50
No. 152 (1)	3.25	3.25
Set total (20) Stamps	58.85	34.75

Human Rights

Sun, Dove and U.N. Emblem CD105

10th anniversary of the signing of the Universal Declaration of Human Rights.

1958

Comoro Isls....................................44
Fr. Equatorial Africa....................................202
Fr. Polynesia....................................191
Fr. West Africa....................................85
Madagascar....................................300
New Caledonia....................................306
St. Pierre & Miquelon....................................356
Somali Coast....................................274
Wallis & Futuna Isls....................................153

No. 44 (1)	9.00	9.00
No. 202 (1)	2.40	1.25
No. 191 (1)	13.00	8.75
No. 85 (1)	2.40	2.00
No. 300 (1)	.80	.40
No. 306 (1)	2.00	1.50
No. 356 (1)	3.50	2.50
No. 274 (1)	3.50	2.10
No. 153 (1)	4.50	4.50
Set total (9) Stamps	41.10	32.00

C.C.T.A.

CD106

Commission for Technical Cooperation in Africa south of the Sahara, 10th anniv.

1960

Cameroun....................................339
Cent. Africa....................................3
Chad....................................66
Congo, P.R....................................90
Dahomey....................................138
Gabon....................................150
Ivory Coast....................................180
Madagascar....................................317
Mali....................................9
Mauritania....................................117
Niger....................................104
Upper Volta....................................89

No. 339 (1)	1.60	.75
No. 3 (1)	1.60	.75
No. 66 (1)	1.75	.50
No. 90 (1)	1.00	1.00
No. 138 (1)	.50	.25
No. 150 (1)	1.25	1.10
No. 180 (1)	1.10	.50
No. 317 (1)	.60	.30
No. 9 (1)	1.20	.50
No. 117 (1)	.75	.40
No. 104 (1)	.85	.45
No. 89 (1)	.65	.40
Set total (12) Stamps	12.85	6.90

Air Afrique, 1961

Modern and Ancient Africa, Map and Planes — CD107

Founding of Air Afrique (African Airlines).

1961-62

Cameroun.................................... C37
Cent. Africa.................................... C5
Chad.................................... C7
Congo, P.R.................................... C5
Dahomey.................................... C17
Gabon.................................... C5
Ivory Coast.................................... C18
Mauritania.................................... C17
Niger.................................... C22
Senegal.................................... C31
Upper Volta.................................... C4

No. C37 (1)	1.00	.50
No. C5 (1)	1.00	.65
No. C7 (1)	1.00	.25
No. C5 (1)	1.75	.90
No. C17 (1)	.80	.40
No. C5 (1)	11.00	6.00
No. C18 (1)	2.00	1.25
No. C17 (1)	2.40	1.25
No. C22 (1)	1.75	.90
No. C31 (1)	.80	.30
No. C4 (1)	3.50	1.75
Set total (11) Stamps	27.00	14.15

Anti-Malaria

CD108

World Health Organization drive to eradicate malaria.

1962, Apr. 7

Cameroun.................................... B36
Cent. Africa.................................... B1
Chad.................................... B1
Comoro Isls.................................... B1
Congo, P.R.................................... B3
Dahomey.................................... B15
Gabon.................................... B4
Ivory Coast.................................... B15
Madagascar.................................... B19
Mali.................................... B1
Mauritania.................................... B16
Niger.................................... B14
Senegal.................................... B16
Somali Coast.................................... B15
Upper Volta.................................... B1

No. B36 (1)	1.00	.45
No. B1 (1)	1.40	1.40
No. B1 (1)	1.00	.50
No. B1 (1)	3.50	3.50
No. B3 (1)	1.40	1.00
No. B15 (1)	.75	.75
No. B4 (1)	1.00	1.00
No. B15 (1)	1.25	1.25
No. B19 (1)	.75	.50
No. B1 (1)	1.25	.60
No. B16 (1)	.50	.50
No. B14 (1)	.75	.75
No. B16 (1)	1.10	.65
No. B15 (1)	7.00	7.00
No. B1 (1)	.75	.70
Set total (15) Stamps	23.40	20.55

Abidjan Games

CD109

Abidjan Games, Ivory Coast, Dec. 24-31, 1961. Each stamp shows a different sport.

1962

Cent. Africa....................................19-20, C6
Chad....................................83-84, C8
Congo, P.R....................................103-104, C7
Gabon....................................163-164, C6
Niger....................................109-111
Upper Volta....................................103-105

Nos. 19-20,C6 (3)	4.15	2.85
Nos. 83-84,C8 (3)	5.80	1.55
Nos. 103-104,C7 (3)	3.85	1.80
Nos. 163-164,C6 (3)	5.00	3.00
Nos. 109-111 (3)	2.60	1.25
Nos. 103-105 (3)	2.80	1.75
Set total (18) Stamps	24.20	12.20

African and Malagasy Union

Flag of Union CD110

First anniversary of the Union.

1962, Sept. 8

Cameroun....................................373
Cent. Africa....................................21
Chad....................................85
Congo, P.R....................................105
Dahomey....................................155
Gabon....................................165
Ivory Coast....................................198
Madagascar....................................332
Mauritania....................................170
Niger....................................112
Senegal....................................211
Upper Volta....................................106

No. 373 (1)	2.00	.75
No. 21 (1)	1.25	.75
No. 85 (1)	1.25	.25
No. 105 (1)	1.50	.50
No. 155 (1)	1.25	.90
No. 165 (1)	1.60	1.25
No. 198 (1)	2.10	.75
No. 332 (1)	.80	.80
No. 170 (1)	.75	.50
No. 112 (1)	.80	.50
No. 211 (1)	.80	.50
No. 106 (1)	1.10	.75
Set total (12) Stamps	15.20	8.20

Telstar

Telstar and Globe Showing Andover and Pleumeur-Bodou — CD111

First television connection of the United States and Europe through the Telstar satellite, July 11-12, 1962.

1962-63

Andorra, French....................................154
Comoro Isls.................................... C7
Fr. Polynesia.................................... C29
Fr. So. & Antarctic Terr.................................... C5
New Caledonia.................................... C33
St. Pierre & Miquelon.................................... C26
Somali Coast.................................... C31
Wallis & Futuna Isls.................................... C17

No. 154 (1)	2.00	1.60
No. C7 (1)	4.50	2.75
No. C29 (1)	11.50	8.00

No. C5 (1)	29.00	21.00
No. C33 (1)	25.00	18.50
No. C26 (1)	7.25	4.50
No. C31 (1)	1.00	1.00
No. C17 (1)	3.75	3.75
Set total (8) Stamps	84.00	61.10

Freedom From Hunger

World Map and Wheat Emblem CD112

U.N. Food and Agriculture Organization's "Freedom from Hunger" campaign.

1963, Mar. 21

Cameroun	B37-B38
Cent. Africa	B2
Chad	B2
Congo, P.R.	B4
Dahomey	B16
Gabon	B5
Ivory Coast	B16
Madagascar	B21
Mauritania	B17
Niger	B15
Senegal	B17
Upper Volta	B2

Nos. B37-B38 (2)	2.25	.75
No. B2 (1)	1.25	1.25
No. B2 (1)	1.10	.50
No. B4 (1)	1.40	1.00
No. B16 (1)	.80	.80
No. B5 (1)	1.00	1.00
No. B16 (1)	1.50	1.50
No. B21 (1)	.60	.45
No. B17 (1)	.60	.60
No. B15 (1)	.75	.75
No. B17 (1)	.80	.50
No. B2 (1)	.75	.70
Set total (13) Stamps	12.80	9.80

Red Cross Centenary

CD113

Centenary of the International Red Cross.

1963, Sept. 2

Comoro Isls.	55
Fr. Polynesia	205
New Caledonia	328
St. Pierre & Miquelon	367
Somali Coast	297
Wallis & Futuna Isls.	165

No. 55 (1)	7.50	6.00
No. 205 (1)	15.00	12.00
No. 328 (1)	8.00	6.75
No. 367 (1)	12.00	5.50
No. 297 (1)	6.25	6.25
No. 165 (1)	4.00	4.00
Set total (6) Stamps	52.75	40.50

African Postal Union, 1963

UAMPT Emblem, Radio Masts, Plane and Mail CD114

Establishment of the African and Malagasy Posts and Telecommunications Union.

1963, Sept. 8

Cameroun	C47
Cent. Africa	C10
Chad	C9
Congo, P.R.	C13
Dahomey	C19
Gabon	C13
Ivory Coast	C25
Madagascar	C75
Mauritania	C22
Niger	C27
Rwanda	36
Senegal	C32
Upper Volta	C9

No. C47 (1)	2.25	1.00
No. C10 (1)	1.90	.90
No. C9 (1)	1.80	.60
No. C13 (1)	1.40	.75
No. C19 (1)	.75	.25
No. C13 (1)	1.90	.80
No. C25 (1)	2.50	1.50
No. C75 (1)	1.25	.80
No. C22 (1)	1.50	.60
No. C27 (1)	1.25	.60
No. 36 (1)	1.00	.75
No. C32 (1)	1.75	.50
No. C9 (1)	1.50	.75
Set total (13) Stamps	20.75	9.80

Air Afrique, 1963

Symbols of Flight — CD115

First anniversary of Air Afrique and inauguration of DC-8 service.

1963, Nov. 19

Cameroun	C48
Chad	C10
Congo, P.R.	C14
Gabon	C18
Ivory Coast	C26
Mauritania	C26
Niger	C35
Senegal	C33

No. C48 (1)	1.25	.40
No. C10 (1)	1.80	.60
No. C14 (1)	1.60	.60
No. C18 (1)	1.25	.65
No. C26 (1)	1.00	.50
No. C26 (1)	.70	.25
No. C35 (1)	1.00	.55
No. C33 (1)	2.00	.65
Set total (8) Stamps	10.60	4.20

Europafrica

Europe and Africa Linked — CD116

Signing of an economic agreement between the European Economic Community and the African and Malagasy Union, Yaounde, Cameroun, July 20, 1963.

1963-64

Cameroun	402
Cent. Africa	C12
Chad	C11
Congo, P.R.	C16
Gabon	C19
Ivory Coast	217
Niger	C43
Upper Volta	C11

No. 402 (1)	2.25	.60
No. C12 (1)	2.50	1.75
No. C11 (1)	1.60	.50
No. C16 (1)	1.60	1.00
No. C19 (1)	1.25	.75
No. 217 (1)	1.10	.35
No. C43 (1)	.85	.50
No. C11 (1)	1.50	.80
Set total (8) Stamps	12.65	6.25

Human Rights

Scales of Justice and Globe CD117

15th anniversary of the Universal Declaration of Human Rights.

1963, Dec. 10

Comoro Isls.	56
Fr. Polynesia	206
New Caledonia	329
St. Pierre & Miquelon	368
Somali Coast	300
Wallis & Futuna Isls.	166

No. 56 (1)	7.50	6.00
No. 205 (1)	15.00	12.00
No. 329 (1)	7.00	6.00
No. 368 (1)	7.00	3.50
No. 300 (1)	8.50	8.50
No. 166 (1)	7.00	7.00
Set total (6) Stamps	52.00	43.00

PHILATEC

Stamp Album, Champs Elysees Palace and Horses of Marly CD118

Intl. Philatelic and Postal Techniques Exhibition, Paris, June 5-21, 1964.

1963-64

Comoro Isls.	60
France	1078
Fr. Polynesia	207
New Caledonia	341
St. Pierre & Miquelon	369
Somali Coast	301
Wallis & Futuna Isls.	167

No. 60 (1)	4.00	3.50
No. 1078 (1)	.25	.25
No. 206 (1)	15.00	10.00
No. 341 (1)	6.50	6.50
No. 369 (1)	11.00	8.00
No. 301 (1)	7.75	7.75
No. 167 (1)	3.00	3.00
Set total (7) Stamps	47.50	39.00

Cooperation

CD119

Cooperation between France and the French-speaking countries of Africa and Madagascar.

1964

Cameroun	409-410
Cent. Africa	39
Chad	103
Congo, P.R.	121
Dahomey	193
France	1111
Gabon	175
Ivory Coast	221
Madagascar	360
Mauritania	181
Niger	143
Senegal	236
Togo	495

Nos. 409-410 (2)	2.50	.50
No. 39 (1)	.90	.50
No. 103 (1)	1.00	.25
No. 121 (1)	.90	.35
No. 193 (1)	.80	.35
No. 1111 (1)	.25	.25
No. 175 (1)	.90	.60
No. 221 (1)	1.10	.35
No. 360 (1)	.60	.25
No. 181 (1)	.60	.35
No. 143 (1)	.80	.40
No. 236 (1)	1.60	.85
No. 495 (1)	.70	.25
Set total (14) Stamps	12.65	5.25

ITU

Telegraph, Syncom Satellite and ITU Emblem CD120

Intl. Telecommunication Union, Cent.

1965, May 17

Comoro Isls.	C14
Fr. Polynesia	C33
Fr. So. & Antarctic Terr.	C8
New Caledonia	C40
New Hebrides	124-125
St. Pierre & Miquelon	C29
Somali Coast	C36
Wallis & Futuna Isls.	C20

No. C14 (1)	18.00	9.00
No. C33 (1)	80.00	52.50
No. C8 (1)	200.00	160.00
No. C40 (1)	10.00	8.00
Nos. 124-125 (2)	32.25	27.25
No. C29 (1)	24.00	11.50
No. C36 (1)	15.00	9.00
No. C20 (1)	16.00	16.00
Set total (9) Stamps	395.25	293.25

French Satellite A-1

Diamant Rocket and Launching Installation — CD121

Launching of France's first satellite, Nov. 26, 1965.

1965-66

Comoro Isls.	C16a
France	1138a
Reunion	359a
Fr. Polynesia	C41a
Fr. So. & Antarctic Terr.	C10a
New Caledonia	C45a
St. Pierre & Miquelon	C31a
Somali Coast	C40a
Wallis & Futuna Isls.	C23a

No. C16a (1)	9.00	9.00
No. 1138a (1)	.65	.65
No. 359a (1)	3.50	3.00
No. C41a (1)	14.00	14.00
No. C10a (1)	29.00	24.00
No. C45a (1)	7.00	7.00
No. C31a (1)	14.50	14.50
No. C40a (1)	7.00	7.00
No. C23a (1)	8.50	8.50
Set total (9) Stamps	93.15	87.65

French Satellite D-1

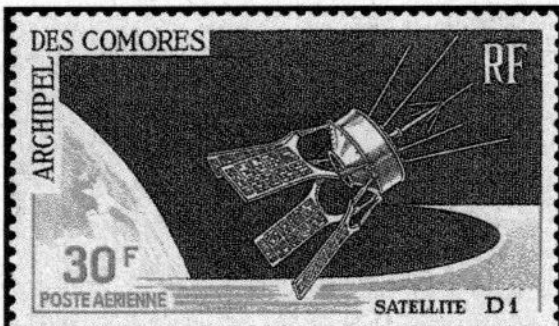

D-1 Satellite in Orbit — CD122

Launching of the D-1 satellite at Hammaguir, Algeria, Feb. 17, 1966.

1966

Comoro Isls.	C17
France	1148

Fr. Polynesia C42
Fr. So. & Antarctic Terr. C11
New Caledonia C46
St. Pierre & Miquelon C32
Somali Coast C49
Wallis & Futuna Isls. C24

No. C17 (1)	4.00	4.00
No. 1148 (1)	.25	.25
No. C42 (1)	7.00	4.75
No. C11 (1)	57.50	40.00
No. C46 (1)	2.25	2.00
No. C32 (1)	9.00	6.00
No. C49 (1)	4.25	2.75
No. C24 (1)	3.50	3.50
Set total (8) Stamps	87.75	63.25

Air Afrique, 1966

Planes and Air Afrique Emblem — CD123

Introduction of DC-8F planes by Air Afrique.

1966

Cameroun C79
Cent. Africa C35
Chad C26
Congo, P.R. C42
Dahomey C42
Gabon C47
Ivory Coast C32
Mauritania C57
Niger C63
Senegal C47
Togo C54
Upper Volta C31

No. C79 (1)	.80	.25
No. C35 (1)	1.00	.50
No. C26 (1)	.85	.25
No. C42 (1)	1.00	.25
No. C42 (1)	.75	.25
No. C47 (1)	.90	.35
No. C32 (1)	1.00	.60
No. C57 (1)	.60	.30
No. C63 (1)	.70	.35
No. C47 (1)	.80	.30
No. C54 (1)	.80	.25
No. C31 (1)	.75	.50
Set total (12) Stamps	9.95	4.15

African Postal Union, 1967

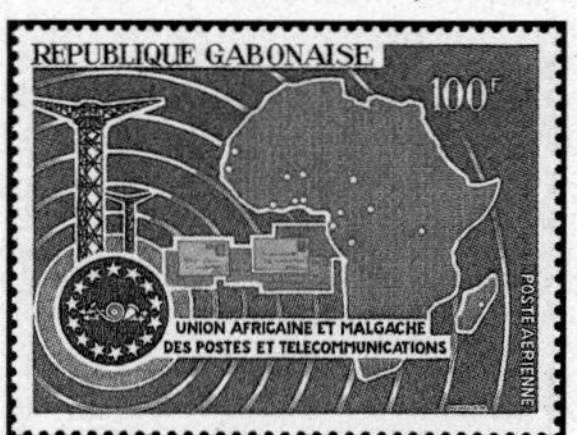

Telecommunications Symbols and Map of Africa — CD124

Fifth anniversary of the establishment of the African and Malagasy Union of Posts and Telecommunications, UAMPT.

1967

Cameroun C90
Cent. Africa C46
Chad C37
Congo, P.R. C57
Dahomey C61
Gabon C58
Ivory Coast C34
Madagascar C85
Mauritania C65
Niger C75
Rwanda C1-C3
Senegal C60
Togo C81
Upper Volta C50

No. C90 (1)	2.40	.65
No. C46 (1)	2.25	.85
No. C37 (1)	2.00	.60
No. C57 (1)	1.60	.60
No. C61 (1)	1.75	.95
No. C58 (1)	2.00	.85
No. C34 (1)	3.50	1.50
No. C85 (1)	1.25	.60
No. C65 (1)	1.25	.60
No. C75 (1)	1.40	.60
Nos. C1-C3 (3)	2.30	1.25
No. C60 (1)	1.75	.50
No. C81 (1)	1.90	.30
No. C50 (1)	1.80	.70
Set total (16) Stamps	27.15	10.55

Monetary Union

Gold Token of the Ashantis, 17-18th Centuries — CD125

West African Monetary Union, 5th anniv.

1967, Nov. 4

Dahomey 244
Ivory Coast 259
Mauritania 238
Niger 204
Senegal 294
Togo 623
Upper Volta 181

No. 244 (1)	.65	.65
No. 259 (1)	.85	.40
No. 238 (1)	.45	.25
No. 204 (1)	.55	.25
No. 294 (1)	.60	.25
No. 623 (1)	.60	.25
No. 181 (1)	.65	.35
Set total (7) Stamps	4.35	2.40

WHO Anniversary

Sun, Flowers and WHO Emblem CD126

World Health Organization, 20th anniv.

1968, May 4

Afars & Issas 317
Comoro Isls. 73
Fr. Polynesia 241-242
Fr. So. & Antarctic Terr. 31
New Caledonia 367
St. Pierre & Miquelon 377
Wallis & Futuna Isls. 169

No. 317 (1)	3.00	3.00
No. 73 (1)	2.40	1.75
Nos. 241-242 (2)	22.00	12.75
No. 31 (1)	62.50	47.50
No. 367 (1)	4.00	2.25
No. 377 (1)	12.00	9.00
No. 169 (1)	5.75	5.75
Set total (8) Stamps	111.65	82.00

Human Rights Year

Human Rights Flame — CD127

1968, Aug. 10

Afars & Issas 322-323
Comoro Isls. 76
Fr. Polynesia 243-244
Fr. So. & Antarctic Terr. 32
New Caledonia 369
St. Pierre & Miquelon 382
Wallis & Futuna Isls. 170

Nos. 322-323 (2)	6.75	4.00
No. 76 (1)	3.25	3.25
Nos. 243-244 (2)	24.00	14.00
No. 32 (1)	55.00	47.50
No. 369 (1)	2.75	1.50
No. 382 (1)	8.00	5.50
No. 170 (1)	3.25	3.25
Set total (9) Stamps	103.00	79.00

2nd PHILEXAFRIQUE

CD128

Opening of PHILEXAFRIQUE, Abidjan, Feb. 14. Each stamp shows a local scene and stamp.

1969, Feb. 14

Cameroun C118
Cent. Africa C65
Chad C48
Congo, P.R. C77
Dahomey C94
Gabon C82
Ivory Coast C38-C40
Madagascar C92
Mali C65
Mauritania C80
Niger C104
Senegal C68
Togo C104
Upper Volta C62

No. C118 (1)	3.25	1.25
No. C65 (1)	1.75	1.75
No. C48 (1)	2.40	1.00
No. C77 (1)	2.00	1.75
No. C94 (1)	2.25	2.25
No. C82 (1)	2.00	2.00
Nos. C38-C40 (3)	14.50	14.50
No. C92 (1)	1.75	.85
No. C65 (1)	1.75	1.00
No. C80 (1)	1.90	.75
No. C104 (1)	3.00	1.90
No. C68 (1)	2.00	1.40
No. C104 (1)	2.25	.45
No. C62 (1)	4.00	3.25
Set total (16) Stamps	44.80	34.10

Concorde

Concorde in Flight CD129

First flight of the prototype Concorde supersonic plane at Toulouse, Mar. 1, 1969.

1969

Afars & Issas C56
Comoro Isls. C29
France C42
Fr. Polynesia C50
Fr. So. & Antarctic Terr. C18
New Caledonia C63
St. Pierre & Miquelon C40
Wallis & Futuna Isls. C30

No. C56 (1)	26.00	16.00
No. C29 (1)	18.00	12.00
No. C42 (1)	.75	.35
No. C50 (1)	55.00	35.00
No. C18 (1)	55.00	37.50
No. C63 (1)	27.50	20.00
No. C40 (1)	32.50	11.00
No. C30 (1)	15.00	10.00
Set total (8) Stamps	229.75	141.85

Development Bank

Bank Emblem — CD130

African Development Bank, fifth anniv.

1969

Cameroun 499
Chad 217
Congo, P.R. 181-182
Ivory Coast 281
Mali 127-128
Mauritania 267
Niger 220
Senegal 317-318
Upper Volta 201

No. 499 (1)	.80	.25
No. 217 (1)	.90	.25
Nos. 181-182 (2)	1.00	.50
No. 281 (1)	.70	.40
Nos. 127-128 (2)	1.00	.50
No. 267 (1)	.60	.25
No. 220 (1)	.70	.30
Nos. 317-318 (2)	1.55	.50
No. 201 (1)	.65	.30
Set total (12) Stamps	7.90	3.25

ILO

ILO Headquarters, Geneva, and Emblem — CD131

Intl. Labor Organization, 50th anniv.

1969-70

Afars & Issas 337
Comoro Isls. 83
Fr. Polynesia 251-252
Fr. So. & Antarctic Terr. 35
New Caledonia 379
St. Pierre & Miquelon 396
Wallis & Futuna Isls. 172

No. 337 (1)	2.75	2.00
No. 83 (1)	1.25	.75
Nos. 251-252 (2)	24.00	12.50
No. 35 (1)	15.00	10.00
No. 379 (1)	2.25	1.10
No. 396 (1)	10.00	5.50
No. 172 (1)	2.75	2.75
Set total (8) Stamps	58.00	34.60

ASECNA

Map of Africa, Plane and Airport CD132

10th anniversary of the Agency for the Security of Aerial Navigation in Africa and Madagascar (ASECNA, Agence pour la Securite de la Navigation Aerienne en Afrique et a Madagascar).

1969-70

Cameroun 500
Cent. Africa 119
Chad 222
Congo, P.R. 197
Dahomey 269
Gabon 260
Ivory Coast 287
Mali 130
Niger 221
Senegal 321
Upper Volta 204

No. 500 (1)	2.00	.60
No. 119 (1)	2.00	.80
No. 222 (1)	1.00	.25
No. 197 (1)	2.00	.40
No. 269 (1)	.90	.55
No. 260 (1)	1.75	.75
No. 287 (1)	.90	.40
No. 130 (1)	.90	.40
No. 221 (1)	1.40	.70
No. 321 (1)	1.60	.50
No. 204 (1)	1.75	1.00
Set total (11) Stamps	16.20	6.35

U.P.U. Headquarters

CD133

New Universal Postal Union headquarters, Bern, Switzerland.

1970

Afars & Issas....342
Algeria....443
Cameroun....503-504
Cent. Africa....125
Chad....225
Comoro Isls.....84
Congo, P.R.....216
Fr. Polynesia....261-262
Fr. So. & Antarctic Terr.....36
Gabon....258
Ivory Coast....295
Madagascar....444
Mali....134-135
Mauritania....283
New Caledonia....382
Niger....231-232
St. Pierre & Miquelon....397-398
Senegal....328-329
Tunisia....535
Wallis & Futuna Isls.....173

No. 342 (1)	2.50	1.40
No. 443 (1)	1.10	.40
Nos. 503-504 (2)	2.60	.55
No. 125 (1)	1.75	.70
No. 225 (1)	1.20	.25
No. 84 (1)	5.50	2.00
No. 216 (1)	1.00	.25
Nos. 261-262 (2)	20.00	10.00
No. 36 (1)	40.00	27.50
No. 258 (1)	.90	.55
No. 295 (1)	1.10	.50
No. 444 (1)	.55	.25
Nos. 134-135 (2)	1.05	.50
No. 283 (1)	.60	.30
No. 382 (1)	3.00	1.50
Nos. 231-232 (2)	1.50	.60
Nos. 397-398 (2)	34.00	16.25
Nos. 328-329 (2)	1.55	.55
No. 535 (1)	.60	.25
No. 173 (1)	3.25	3.25
Set total (26) Stamps	123.75	67.55

De Gaulle

CD134

First anniversary of the death of Charles de Gaulle, (1890-1970), President of France.

1971-72

Afars & Issas....356-357
Comoro Isls.....104-105
France....1325a
Fr. Polynesia....270-271
Fr. So. & Antarctic Terr.....52-53
New Caledonia....393-394
Reunion....380a
St. Pierre & Miquelon....417-418
Wallis & Futuna Isls.....177-178

Nos. 356-357 (2)	12.50	7.50
Nos. 104-105 (2)	9.00	5.75
No. 1325a (1)	3.00	2.50
Nos. 270-271 (2)	51.50	29.50
Nos. 52-53 (2)	40.00	29.50
Nos. 393-394 (2)	23.00	11.75
No. 380a (1)	9.25	8.00
Nos. 417-418 (2)	56.50	31.00
Nos. 177-178 (2)	20.00	16.25
Set total (16) Stamps	224.75	141.75

African Postal Union, 1971

UAMPT Building, Brazzaville, Congo — CD135

10th anniversary of the establishment of the African and Malagasy Posts and Telecommunications Union, UAMPT. Each stamp has a different native design.

1971, Nov. 13

Cameroun....C177
Cent. Africa....C89
Chad....C94
Congo, P.R.....C136
Dahomey....C146
Gabon....C120
Ivory Coast....C47
Mauritania....C113
Niger....C164
Rwanda....C8
Senegal....C105
Togo....C166
Upper Volta....C97

No. C177 (1)	2.00	.50
No. C89 (1)	2.25	.85
No. C94 (1)	1.50	.50
No. C136 (1)	1.60	.75
No. C146 (1)	1.75	.80
No. C120 (1)	1.75	.70
No. C47 (1)	2.00	1.00
No. C113 (1)	1.10	.65
No. C164 (1)	1.25	.60
No. C8 (1)	2.75	2.50
No. C105 (1)	1.60	.50
No. C166 (1)	1.25	.40
No. C97 (1)	1.50	.70
Set total (13) Stamps	22.30	10.45

West African Monetary Union

African Couple, City, Village and Commemorative Coin — CD136

West African Monetary Union, 10th anniv.

1972, Nov. 2

Dahomey....300
Ivory Coast....331
Mauritania....299
Niger....258
Senegal....374
Togo....825
Upper Volta....280

No. 300 (1)	.65	.25
No. 331 (1)	1.00	.50
No. 299 (1)	.75	.25
No. 258 (1)	.65	.30
No. 374 (1)	.50	.30
No. 825 (1)	.60	.25
No. 280 (1)	.60	.25
Set total (7) Stamps	4.75	2.10

African Postal Union, 1973

Telecommunications Symbols and Map of Africa — CD137

11th anniversary of the African and Malagasy Posts and Telecommunications Union (UAMPT).

1973, Sept. 12

Cameroun....574
Cent. Africa....194
Chad....294
Congo, P.R.....289
Dahomey....311
Gabon....320
Ivory Coast....361
Madagascar....500
Mauritania....304
Niger....287
Rwanda....540
Senegal....393
Togo....849
Upper Volta....297

No. 574 (1)	1.75	.40
No. 194 (1)	1.25	.75
No. 294 (1)	1.75	.40
No. 289 (1)	1.60	.50
No. 311 (1)	1.25	.55
No. 320 (1)	1.40	.75
No. 361 (1)	2.50	1.00
No. 500 (1)	1.10	.35
No. 304 (1)	1.10	.40
No. 287 (1)	.90	.60
No. 540 (1)	4.00	2.00
No. 393 (1)	1.60	.50
No. 849 (1)	1.00	.35
No. 297 (1)	1.25	.70
Set total (14) Stamps	22.45	9.25

Philexafrique II — Essen

CD138

CD139

Designs: Indigenous fauna, local and German stamps. Types CD138-CD139 printed horizontally and vertically se-tenant in sheets of 10 (2x5). Label between horizontal pairs alternately commemoratives Philexafrique II, Libreville, Gabon, June 1978, and 2nd International Stamp Fair, Essen, Germany, Nov. 1-5.

1978-1979

Benin....C286a
Central Africa....C201a
Chad....C239a
Congo Republic....C246a
Djibouti....C122a
Gabon....C216a
Ivory Coast....C65a
Mali....C357a
Mauritania....C186a
Niger....C292a
Rwanda....C13a
Senegal....C147a
Togo....C364a

No. C286a (1)	9.00	8.50
No. C201a (1)	7.50	7.50
No. C239a (1)	7.50	4.00
No. C246a (1)	7.00	7.00
No. C122a (1)	6.50	6.50
No. C216a (1)	6.50	4.00
No. C65a (1)	9.00	9.00
No. C357a (1)	5.00	3.00
No. C186a (1)	5.50	5.00
No. C292a (1)	6.00	6.00
No. C13a (1)	4.00	4.00
No. C147a (1)	10.00	4.00
No. C364a (1)	3.00	1.50
Set total (13) Stamps	86.50	70.00

BRITISH COMMONWEALTH OF NATIONS

The listings follow established trade practices when these issues are offered as units by dealers. The Peace issue, for example, includes only one stamp from the Indian state of Hyderabad. The U.P.U. issue includes the Egypt set. Pairs are included for those varieties issued with bilingual designs se-tenant.

Silver Jubilee

Windsor Castle and King George V CD301

Reign of King George V, 25th anniv.

1935

Antigua....77-80
Ascension....33-36
Bahamas....92-95
Barbados....186-189
Basutoland....11-14
Bechuanaland Protectorate....117-120
Bermuda....100-103
British Guiana....223-226
British Honduras....108-111
Cayman Islands....81-84
Ceylon....260-263
Cyprus....136-139
Dominica....90-93
Falkland Islands....77-80
Fiji....110-113
Gambia....125-128
Gibraltar....100-103
Gilbert & Ellice Islands....33-36
Gold Coast....108-111
Grenada....124-127
Hong Kong....147-150
Jamaica....109-112
Kenya, Uganda, Tanzania....42-45
Leeward Islands....96-99
Malta....184-187
Mauritius....204-207
Montserrat....85-88
Newfoundland....226-229
Nigeria....34-37
Northern Rhodesia....18-21
Nyasaland Protectorate....47-50
St. Helena....111-114
St. Kitts-Nevis....72-75
St. Lucia....91-94
St. Vincent....134-137
Seychelles....118-121
Sierra Leone....166-169
Solomon Islands....60-63
Somaliland Protectorate....77-80
Straits Settlements....213-216
Swaziland....20-23
Trinidad & Tobago....43-46
Turks & Caicos Islands....71-74
Virgin Islands....69-72

The following have different designs but are included in the omnibus set:

Great Britain....226-229
Offices in Morocco (Sp. Curr.)....67-70
Offices in Morocco (Br. Curr.)....226-229
Offices in Morocco (Fr. Curr.)....422-425
Offices in Morocco (Tangier)....508-510
Australia....152-154
Canada....211-216
Cook Islands....98-100
India....142-148
Nauru....31-34
New Guinea....46-47
New Zealand....199-201
Niue....67-69
Papua....114-117
Samoa....163-165
South Africa....68-71
Southern Rhodesia....33-36
South-West Africa....121-124

Nos. 77-80 (4)	20.25	*23.25*
Nos. 33-36 (4)	58.50	*127.50*
Nos. 92-95 (4)	25.00	*46.00*
Nos. 186-189 (4)	30.00	50.30
Nos. 11-14 (4)	11.60	*21.25*
Nos. 117-120 (4)	15.75	*36.00*
Nos. 100-103 (4)	16.80	*58.50*
Nos. 223-226 (4)	22.35	35.50
Nos. 108-111 (4)	15.25	*16.35*
Nos. 81-84 (4)	21.60	*24.50*
Nos. 260-263 (4)	10.40	21.60
Nos. 136-139 (4)	39.75	*34.40*
Nos. 90-93 (4)	18.85	19.85
Nos. 77-80 (4)	55.00	14.75
Nos. 110-113 (4)	20.25	34.00
Nos. 125-128 (4)	13.05	*25.25*
Nos. 100-103 (4)	28.75	42.75
Nos. 33-36 (4)	36.80	*67.00*
Nos. 108-111 (4)	25.75	*78.10*
Nos. 124-127 (4)	16.70	*40.60*
Nos. 147-150 (4)	59.00	18.75
Nos. 109-112 (4)	17.00	39.00
Nos. 42-45 (4)	8.75	*11.00*
Nos. 96-99 (4)	35.75	49.60
Nos. 184-187 (4)	22.00	33.70
Nos. 204-207 (4)	44.60	58.25
Nos. 85-88 (4)	10.25	*30.25*
Nos. 226-229 (4)	17.50	12.05
Nos. 34-37 (4)	17.50	*70.00*
Nos. 18-21 (4)	17.00	15.00
Nos. 47-50 (4)	39.75	*80.25*
Nos. 111-114 (4)	31.15	*36.50*
Nos. 72-75 (4)	10.80	*18.65*
Nos. 91-94 (4)	16.00	*20.80*
Nos. 134-137 (4)	9.45	*21.25*
Nos. 118-121 (4)	15.75	*40.00*
Nos. 166-169 (4)	23.60	*50.35*
Nos. 60-63 (4)	29.00	38.00
Nos. 77-80 (4)	17.00	*48.25*
Nos. 213-216 (4)	15.00	*25.10*
Nos. 20-23 (4)	6.80	18.25
Nos. 43-46 (4)	14.05	27.75
Nos. 71-74 (4)	9.90	14.50
Nos. 69-72 (4)	25.00	55.25
Nos. 226-229 (4)	5.15	*4.40*

Nos. 67-70 (4)	13.60	*30.70*
Nos. 226-229 (4)	16.30	*56.00*
Nos. 422-425 (4)	6.35	3.10
Nos. 508-510 (3)	26.00	*33.50*
Nos. 152-154 (3)	49.50	45.35
Nos. 211-216 (6)	23.85	13.35
Nos. 98-100 (3)	9.65	*12.00*
Nos. 142-148 (7)	28.85	14.00
Nos. 31-34 (4)	9.90	*9.90*
Nos. 46-47 (2)	4.35	1.70
Nos. 199-201 (3)	23.00	*28.50*
Nos. 67-69 (3)	11.80	*26.50*
Nos. 114-117 (4)	9.20	*17.50*
Nos. 163-165 (3)	4.40	6.50
Nos. 68-71 (4)	57.50	*153.00*
Nos. 33-36 (4)	27.75	*45.25*
Nos. 121-124 (4)	13.00	*36.10*
Set total (245) Stamps	1,355.	2,187.

Coronation

Queen Elizabeth and King George VI
CD302

1937

Aden....13-15
Antigua....81-83
Ascension....37-39
Bahamas....97-99
Barbados....190-192
Basutoland....15-17
Bechuanaland Protectorate....121-123
Bermuda....115-117
British Guiana....227-229
British Honduras....112-114
Cayman Islands....97-99
Ceylon....275-277
Cyprus....140-142
Dominica....94-96
Falkland Islands....81-83
Fiji....114-116
Gambia....129-131
Gibraltar....104-106
Gilbert & Ellice Islands....37-39
Gold Coast....112-114
Grenada....128-130
Hong Kong....151-153
Jamaica....113-115
Kenya, Uganda, Tanzania....60-62
Leeward Islands....100-102
Malta....188-190
Mauritius....208-210
Montserrat....89-91
Newfoundland....230-232
Nigeria....50-52
Northern Rhodesia....22-24
Nyasaland Protectorate....51-53
St. Helena....115-117
St. Kitts-Nevis....76-78
St. Lucia....107-109
St. Vincent....138-140
Seychelles....122-124
Sierra Leone....170-172
Solomon Islands....64-66
Somaliland Protectorate....81-83
Straits Settlements....235-237
Swaziland....24-26
Trinidad & Tobago....47-49
Turks & Caicos Islands....75-77
Virgin Islands....73-75

The following have different designs but are included in the omnibus set:

Great Britain....234
Offices in Morocco (Sp. Curr.)....82
Offices in Morocco (Fr. Curr.)....439
Offices in Morocco (Tangier)....514
Canada....237
Cook Islands....109-111
Nauru....35-38
Newfoundland....233-243
New Guinea....48-51
New Zealand....223-225
Niue....70-72
Papua....118-121
South Africa....74-78
Southern Rhodesia....38-41
South-West Africa....125-132

Nos. 13-15 (3)	2.70	*5.65*
Nos. 81-83 (3)	1.85	*8.00*
Nos. 37-39 (3)	2.75	*2.75*
Nos. 97-99 (3)	1.05	*3.05*
Nos. 190-192 (3)	1.10	1.95
Nos. 15-17 (3)	1.15	*3.00*
Nos. 121-123 (3)	.95	3.35
Nos. 115-117 (3)	1.25	5.00
Nos. 227-229 (3)	1.45	3.05
Nos. 112-114 (3)	1.20	2.40
Nos. 97-99 (3)	1.10	2.70
Nos. 275-277 (3)	8.25	10.35
Nos. 140-142 (3)	3.75	6.50
Nos. 94-96 (3)	.85	2.40
Nos. 81-83 (3)	2.90	*2.30*
Nos. 114-116 (3)	1.35	*5.75*
Nos. 129-131 (3)	.85	3.95
Nos. 104-106 (3)	2.25	6.45
Nos. 37-39 (3)	.85	*2.15*
Nos. 112-114 (3)	3.10	*10.00*
Nos. 128-130 (3)	1.00	.85
Nos. 151-153 (3)	23.00	12.50
Nos. 113-115 (3)	1.25	1.25
Nos. 60-62 (3)	1.00	2.35
Nos. 100-102 (3)	1.55	4.00
Nos. 188-190 (3)	1.25	1.60
Nos. 208-210 (3)	1.75	3.50
Nos. 89-91 (3)	1.00	3.35
Nos. 230-232 (3)	7.00	2.80
Nos. 50-52 (3)	3.25	8.50
Nos. 22-24 (3)	.95	2.25
Nos. 51-53 (3)	1.05	1.30
Nos. 115-117 (3)	1.45	2.05
Nos. 76-78 (3)	.95	2.15
Nos. 107-109 (3)	1.05	2.05
Nos. 138-140 (3)	.80	*4.75*
Nos. 122-124 (3)	1.20	*1.90*
Nos. 170-172 (3)	1.95	5.65
Nos. 64-66 (3)	.90	2.00
Nos. 81-83 (3)	1.10	*3.50*
Nos. 235-237 (3)	3.25	1.60
Nos. 24-26 (3)	.75	2.70
Nos. 47-49 (3)	1.00	1.00
Nos. 75-77 (3)	2.25	1.55
Nos. 73-75 (3)	2.20	6.90
No. 234 (1)	.25	.25
No. 82 (1)	.80	.60
No. 439 (1)	.35	.25
No. 514 (1)	1.25	.40
No. 237 (1)	.35	.25
Nos. 109-111 (3)	.85	.80
Nos. 35-38 (4)	1.10	*5.50*
Nos. 233-243 (11)	41.90	30.40
Nos. 48-51 (4)	1.40	*7.90*
Nos. 223-225 (3)	1.75	*2.25*
Nos. 70-72 (3)	.80	*2.05*
Nos. 118-121 (4)	1.60	*5.25*
Nos. 74-78 (5)	7.60	9.35
Nos. 38-41 (4)	3.55	15.50
Nos. 125-132 (8)	5.00	8.40
Set total (189) Stamps	172.15	261.95

Peace

King George VI and Parliament Buildings, London
CD303

Return to peace at the close of World War II.

1945-46

Aden....28-29
Antigua....96-97
Ascension....50-51
Bahamas....130-131
Barbados....207-208
Bermuda....131-132
British Guiana....242-243
British Honduras....127-128
Cayman Islands....112-113
Ceylon....293-294
Cyprus....156-157
Dominica....112-113
Falkland Islands....97-98
Falkland Islands Dep....1L9-1L10
Fiji....137-138
Gambia....144-145
Gibraltar....119-120
Gilbert & Ellice Islands....52-53
Gold Coast....128-129
Grenada....143-144
Jamaica....136-137
Kenya, Uganda, Tanzania....90-91
Leeward Islands....116-117
Malta....206-207
Mauritius....223-224
Montserrat....104-105
Nigeria....71-72
Northern Rhodesia....46-47
Nyasaland Protectorate....82-83
Pitcairn Islands....9-10
St. Helena....128-129
St. Kitts-Nevis....91-92
St. Lucia....127-128
St. Vincent....152-153
Seychelles....149-150
Sierra Leone....186-187
Solomon Islands....80-81
Somaliland Protectorate....108-109
Trinidad & Tobago....62-63
Turks & Caicos Islands....90-91
Virgin Islands....88-89

The following have different designs but are included in the omnibus set:

Great Britain....264-265
Offices in Morocco (Tangier)....523-524
Aden
  Kathiri State of Seiyun....12-13
  Qu'aiti State of Shihr and Mukalla....12-13
Australia....200-202
Basutoland....29-31
Bechuanaland Protectorate....137-139
Burma....66-69
Cook Islands....127-130
Hong Kong....174-175
India....195-198
  Hyderabad....51-53
New Zealand....247-257
Niue....90-93
Pakistan-Bahawalpur....O16
Samoa....191-194
South Africa....100-102
Southern Rhodesia....67-70
South-West Africa....153-155
Swaziland....38-40
Zanzibar....222-223

Nos. 28-29 (2)	.95	2.50
Nos. 96-97 (2)	.50	*.80*
Nos. 50-51 (2)	.80	*2.00*
Nos. 130-131 (2)	.50	1.40
Nos. 207-208 (2)	.50	1.10
Nos. 131-132 (2)	.55	*.55*
Nos. 242-243 (2)	1.05	*1.40*
Nos. 127-128 (2)	.50	.50
Nos. 112-113 (2)	.80	.80
Nos. 293-294 (2)	.60	*2.10*
Nos. 156-157 (2)	.90	.70
Nos. 112-113 (2)	.50	.50
Nos. 97-98 (2)	.90	1.35
Nos. 1L9-1L10 (2)	1.30	1.00
Nos. 137-138 (2)	.75	*1.75*
Nos. 144-145 (2)	.50	.95
Nos. 119-120 (2)	.75	*1.00*
Nos. 52-53 (2)	.50	*1.10*
Nos. 128-129 (2)	1.85	*3.75*
Nos. 143-144 (2)	.50	*.95*
Nos. 136-137 (2)	.80	*12.50*
Nos. 90-91 (2)	.65	.65
Nos. 116-117 (2)	.50	1.50
Nos. 206-207 (2)	.65	2.00
Nos. 223-224 (2)	.50	1.05
Nos. 104-105 (2)	.50	.50
Nos. 71-72 (2)	.70	*2.75*
Nos. 46-47 (2)	1.25	*2.00*
Nos. 82-83 (2)	.50	.50
Nos. 9-10 (2)	1.40	1.40
Nos. 128-129 (2)	.65	.70
Nos. 91-92 (2)	.50	.50
Nos. 127-128 (2)	.50	.60
Nos. 152-153 (2)	.50	.50
Nos. 149-150 (2)	.55	.50
Nos. 186-187 (2)	.50	.50
Nos. 80-81 (2)	.50	1.50
Nos. 108-109 (2)	.70	.50
Nos. 62-63 (2)	.50	.50
Nos. 90-91 (2)	.50	.50
Nos. 88-89 (2)	.50	.50
Nos. 264-265 (2)	.50	.50
Nos. 523-524 (2)	1.60	2.30
Nos. 12-13 (2)	.50	.90
Nos. 12-13 (2)	.50	*1.25*
Nos. 200-202 (3)	1.60	*1.25*
Nos. 29-31 (3)	2.10	2.60
Nos. 137-139 (3)	2.05	*4.75*
Nos. 66-69 (4)	1.50	1.25
Nos. 127-130 (4)	2.00	1.85
Nos. 174-175 (2)	6.75	3.15
Nos. 195-198 (4)	5.60	5.50
Nos. 51-53 (3)	1.50	1.70
Nos. 247-257 (11)	3.35	3.65
Nos. 90-93 (4)	1.70	*2.20*
No. O16 (1)	5.50	*7.00*
Nos. 191-194 (4)	2.05	1.00
Nos. 100-102 (3)	1.00	3.25
Nos. 67-70 (4)	1.40	1.75
Nos. 153-155 (3)	1.85	3.25
Nos. 38-40 (3)	2.40	*5.50*
Nos. 222-223 (2)	.65	1.00
Set total (151) Stamps	74.65	113.45

Silver Wedding

King George VI and Queen Elizabeth
CD304 CD305

1948-49

Aden....30-31
  Kathiri State of Seiyun....14-15
  Qu'aiti State of Shihr and Mukalla....14-15
Antigua....98-99
Ascension....52-53
Bahamas....148-149
Barbados....210-211
Basutoland....39-40
Bechuanaland Protectorate....147-148
Bermuda....133-134
British Guiana....244-245
British Honduras....129-130
Cayman Islands....116-117
Cyprus....158-159
Dominica....114-115
Falkland Islands....99-100
Falkland Islands Dep....1L11-1L12
Fiji....139-140
Gambia....146-147
Gibraltar....121-122
Gilbert & Ellice Islands....54-55
Gold Coast....142-143
Grenada....145-146
Hong Kong....178-179
Jamaica....138-139
Kenya, Uganda, Tanzania....92-93
Leeward Islands....118-119
Malaya
  Johore....128-129
  Kedah....55-56
  Kelantan....44-45
  Malacca....1-2
  Negri Sembilan....36-37
  Pahang....44-45
  Penang....1-2
  Perak....99-100
  Perlis....1-2
  Selangor....74-75
  Trengganu....47-48
Malta....223-224
Mauritius....229-230
Montserrat....106-107
Nigeria....73-74
North Borneo....238-239
Northern Rhodesia....48-49
Nyasaland Protectorate....85-86
Pitcairn Islands....11-12
St. Helena....130-131
St. Kitts-Nevis....93-94
St. Lucia....129-130
St. Vincent....154-155
Sarawak....174-175
Seychelles....151-152
Sierra Leone....188-189
Singapore....21-22
Solomon Islands....82-83
Somaliland Protectorate....110-111
Swaziland....48-49
Trinidad & Tobago....64-65
Turks & Caicos Islands....92-93
Virgin Islands....90-91
Zanzibar....224-225

The following have different designs but are included in the omnibus set:

Great Britain....267-268
  Offices in Morocco (Sp. Curr.)....93-94
  Offices in Morocco (Tangier)....525-526
Bahrain....62-63
Kuwait....82-83
Oman....25-26
South Africa....106
South-West Africa....159

Nos. 30-31 (2)	40.40	56.50
Nos. 14-15 (2)	17.85	*16.00*
Nos. 14-15 (2)	18.55	*12.50*
Nos. 98-99 (2)	13.55	*15.75*
Nos. 52-53 (2)	55.55	50.45
Nos. 148-149 (2)	45.25	40.30
Nos. 210-211 (2)	18.35	13.55
Nos. 39-40 (2)	52.80	*55.25*
Nos. 147-148 (2)	42.85	*47.75*
Nos. 133-134 (2)	47.75	*55.25*
Nos. 244-245 (2)	24.25	*28.45*
Nos. 129-130 (2)	25.25	*53.20*
Nos. 116-117 (2)	25.25	*33.50*
Nos. 158-159 (2)	58.50	*78.05*
Nos. 114-115 (2)	25.25	*32.75*
Nos. 99-100 (2)	112.10	76.10
Nos. 1L11-1L12 (2)	4.25	6.00
Nos. 139-140 (2)	18.20	11.50
Nos. 146-147 (2)	21.25	21.25
Nos. 121-122 (2)	61.00	*78.00*
Nos. 54-55 (2)	14.25	*26.25*
Nos. 142-143 (2)	35.25	48.20
Nos. 145-146 (2)	21.75	21.75
Nos. 178-179 (2)	283.50	96.50
Nos. 138-139 (2)	27.85	*60.25*
Nos. 92-93 (2)	50.25	*67.75*
Nos. 118-119 (2)	7.00	8.25
Nos. 128-129 (2)	29.25	*53.25*
Nos. 55-56 (2)	35.25	*50.25*
Nos. 44-45 (2)	35.75	*62.75*
Nos. 1-2 (2)	35.40	*49.75*
Nos. 36-37 (2)	28.10	*38.20*
Nos. 44-45 (2)	28.00	*38.05*
Nos. 1-2 (2)	40.50	37.80

Nos. 99-100 (2)	27.80	37.75
Nos. 1-2 (2)	33.50	58.00
Nos. 74-75 (2)	30.25	25.30
Nos. 47-48 (2)	32.75	61.75
Nos. 223-224 (2)	40.55	45.25
Nos. 229-230 (2)	19.25	45.25
Nos. 106-107 (2)	8.75	17.25
Nos. 73-74 (2)	17.85	22.80
Nos. 238-239 (2)	35.30	45.75
Nos. 48-49 (2)	100.30	90.25
Nos. 85-86 (2)	18.25	30.25
Nos. 11-12 (2)	44.75	48.50
Nos. 130-131 (2)	32.80	42.80
Nos. 93-94 (2)	11.25	10.50
Nos. 129-130 (2)	22.25	40.25
Nos. 154-155 (2)	27.75	30.25
Nos. 174-175 (2)	50.40	52.90
Nos. 151-152 (2)	16.25	48.25
Nos. 188-189 (2)	25.25	29.75
Nos. 21-22 (2)	116.00	45.40
Nos. 82-83 (2)	13.40	13.40
Nos. 110-111 (2)	8.40	8.75
Nos. 48-49 (2)	40.30	47.75
Nos. 64-65 (2)	32.75	38.25
Nos. 92-93 (2)	14.25	20.25
Nos. 90-91 (2)	16.25	22.25
Nos. 224-225 (2)	29.60	38.00
Nos. 267-268 (2)	30.40	25.25
Nos. 93-94 (2)	17.10	25.75
Nos. 525-526 (2)	18.40	23.25
Nos. 62-63 (2)	38.50	57.75
Nos. 82-83 (2)	69.50	45.50
Nos. 25-26 (2)	41.00	42.50
No. 106 (1)	.80	1.00
No. 159 (1)	1.10	.35
Set total (136) Stamps	2,483.	2,679.

U.P.U.

Mercury and Symbols of Communications — CD306

Plane, Ship and Hemispheres — CD307

Mercury Scattering Letters over Globe CD308

U.P.U. Monument, Bern CD309

Universal Postal Union, 75th anniversary.

1949

Aden 32-35
Kathiri State of Seiyun....................16-19
Qu'aiti State of Shihr and Mukalla 16-19
Antigua 100-103
Ascension 57-60
Bahamas 150-153
Barbados 212-215
Basutoland 41-44
Bechuanaland Protectorate 149-152
Bermuda 138-141
British Guiana 246-249
British Honduras 137-140
Brunei 79-82
Cayman Islands 118-121
Cyprus 160-163
Dominica 116-119
Falkland Islands 103-106
Falkland Islands Dep....................1L14-1L17
Fiji 141-144
Gambia 148-151
Gibraltar 123-126
Gilbert & Ellice Islands 56-59
Gold Coast 144-147
Grenada 147-150
Hong Kong 180-183
Jamaica 142-145
Kenya, Uganda, Tanzania 94-97
Leeward Islands 126-129
Malaya
Johore 151-154
Kedah 57-60
Kelantan 46-49
Malacca 18-21
Negri Sembilan 59-62
Pahang 46-49
Penang 23-26
Perak 101-104
Perlis 3-6
Selangor 76-79
Trengganu 49-52
Malta 225-228
Mauritius 231-234
Montserrat 108-111
New Hebrides, British 62-65
New Hebrides, French 79-82
Nigeria 75-78
North Borneo 240-243
Northern Rhodesia 50-53
Nyasaland Protectorate 87-90
Pitcairn Islands 13-16
St. Helena 132-135
St. Kitts-Nevis 95-98
St. Lucia 131-134
St. Vincent 170-173
Sarawak 176-179
Seychelles 153-156
Sierra Leone 190-193
Singapore 23-26
Solomon Islands 84-87
Somaliland Protectorate 112-115
Southern Rhodesia 71-72
Swaziland 50-53
Tonga 87-90
Trinidad & Tobago 66-69
Turks & Caicos Islands 101-104
Virgin Islands 92-95
Zanzibar 226-229

The following have different designs but are included in the omnibus set:

Great Britain 276-279
Offices in Morocco (Tangier) 546-549
Australia 223
Bahrain 68-71
Burma 116-121
Ceylon 304-306
Egypt 281-283
India 223-226
Kuwait 89-92
Oman 31-34
Pakistan-Bahawalpur 26-29, O25-O28
South Africa 109-111
South-West Africa 160-162

Nos. 32-35 (4)	5.85	8.45
Nos. 16-19 (4)	2.75	16.00
Nos. 16-19 (4)	2.60	8.00
Nos. 100-103 (4)	3.60	7.70
Nos. 57-60 (4)	11.10	9.00
Nos. 150-153 (4)	5.35	9.30
Nos. 212-215 (4)	4.40	14.85
Nos. 41-44 (4)	4.75	10.00
Nos. 149-152 (4)	3.35	7.25
Nos. 138-141 (4)	4.75	6.15
Nos. 246-249 (4)	2.75	4.20
Nos. 137-140 (4)	3.30	6.35
Nos. 79-82 (4)	9.50	8.45
Nos. 118-121 (4)	3.60	7.25
Nos. 160-163 (4)	4.60	10.70
Nos. 116-119 (4)	2.30	5.65
Nos. 103-106 (4)	14.00	17.10
Nos. 1L14-1L17 (4)	14.60	14.50
Nos. 141-144 (4)	3.35	15.75
Nos. 148-151 (4)	2.75	7.10
Nos. 123-126 (4)	5.90	8.75
Nos. 56-59 (4)	4.30	13.00
Nos. 144-147 (4)	2.55	10.35
Nos. 147-150 (4)	2.15	3.55
Nos. 180-183 (4)	57.25	18.25
Nos. 142-145 (4)	2.25	2.45
Nos. 94-97 (4)	2.90	3.40
Nos. 126-129 (4)	3.05	9.60
Nos. 151-154 (4)	4.70	8.90
Nos. 57-60 (4)	4.80	12.00
Nos. 46-49 (4)	4.25	12.65
Nos. 18-21 (4)	4.25	17.30
Nos. 59-62 (4)	3.50	10.75
Nos. 46-49 (4)	3.00	7.25
Nos. 23-26 (4)	5.10	11.75
Nos. 101-104 (4)	3.65	10.75
Nos. 3-6 (4)	3.95	14.25
Nos. 76-79 (4)	4.90	12.30
Nos. 49-52 (4)	5.55	12.25
Nos. 225-228 (4)	4.50	4.85
Nos. 231-234 (4)	3.70	7.05
Nos. 108-111 (4)	3.30	4.35
Nos. 62-65 (4)	1.60	4.25
Nos. 79-82 (4)	15.40	22.00
Nos. 75-78 (4)	2.80	9.25
Nos. 240-243 (4)	7.15	6.50
Nos. 50-53 (4)	5.00	6.50
Nos. 87-90 (4)	4.05	4.05
Nos. 13-16 (4)	18.50	16.50
Nos. 132-135 (4)	4.85	7.10
Nos. 95-98 (4)	3.35	5.55
Nos. 131-134 (4)	2.55	3.85
Nos. 170-173 (4)	2.20	5.05
Nos. 176-179 (4)	8.15	10.85
Nos. 153-156 (4)	3.00	5.15
Nos. 190-193 (4)	2.90	9.15
Nos. 23-26 (4)	19.00	13.70
Nos. 84-87 (4)	4.05	4.90
Nos. 112-115 (4)	3.95	8.70
Nos. 71-72 (2)	1.95	2.25
Nos. 50-53 (4)	2.80	4.65
Nos. 87-90 (4)	3.00	5.25
Nos. 66-69 (4)	3.15	3.15
Nos. 101-104 (4)	3.05	8.90
Nos. 92-95 (4)	2.60	5.90
Nos. 226-229 (4)	5.45	13.50
Nos. 276-279 (4)	1.35	1.00
Nos. 546-549 (4)	2.60	16.00
No. 223 (1)	.40	.40
Nos. 68-71 (4)	4.75	16.50
Nos. 116-121 (6)	7.30	5.35
Nos. 304-306 (3)	3.35	4.25
Nos. 281-283 (3)	5.75	2.70
Nos. 223-226 (4)	27.25	10.50
Nos. 89-92 (4)	6.10	10.25
Nos. 31-34 (4)	8.00	15.75
Nos. 26-29,O25-O28 (8)	2.00	42.00
Nos. 109-111 (3)	2.00	2.70
Nos. 160-162 (3)	3.00	5.50
Set total (313) Stamps	453.10	729.05

University

Arms of University College CD310

Alice, Princess of Athlone CD311

1948 opening of University College of the West Indies at Jamaica.

1951

Antigua 104-105
Barbados 228-229
British Guiana 250-251
British Honduras 141-142
Dominica 120-121
Grenada 164-165
Jamaica 146-147
Leeward Islands 130-131
Montserrat 112-113
St. Kitts-Nevis 105-106
St. Lucia 149-150
St. Vincent 174-175
Trinidad & Tobago 70-71
Virgin Islands 96-97

Nos. 104-105 (2)	1.35	3.75
Nos. 228-229 (2)	1.75	2.65
Nos. 250-251 (2)	1.10	1.25
Nos. 141-142 (2)	1.40	2.20
Nos. 120-121 (2)	1.40	1.75
Nos. 164-165 (2)	1.20	1.60
Nos. 146-147 (2)	.90	.70
Nos. 130-131 (2)	1.35	4.00
Nos. 112-113 (2)	.85	2.00
Nos. 105-106 (2)	.90	2.25
Nos. 149-150 (2)	1.40	1.50
Nos. 174-175 (2)	1.00	2.15
Nos. 70-71 (2)	.75	.75
Nos. 96-97 (2)	1.50	3.75
Set total (28) Stamps	16.85	30.30

Coronation

Queen Elizabeth II — CD312

1953

Aden 47
Kathiri State of Seiyun....................28
Qu'aiti State of Shihr and Mukalla 28
Antigua 106
Ascension 61
Bahamas 157
Barbados 234
Basutoland 45
Bechuanaland Protectorate 153
Bermuda 142
British Guiana 252
British Honduras 143
Cayman Islands 150
Cyprus 167
Dominica 141
Falkland Islands 121
Falkland Islands Dependencies 1L18
Fiji 145
Gambia 152
Gibraltar 131
Gilbert & Ellice Islands 60
Gold Coast 160
Grenada 170
Hong Kong 184
Jamaica 153
Kenya, Uganda, Tanzania 101
Leeward Islands 132
Malaya
Johore 155
Kedah 82
Kelantan 71
Malacca 27
Negri Sembilan 63
Pahang 71
Penang 27
Perak 126
Perlis 28
Selangor 101
Trengganu 74
Malta 241
Mauritius 250
Montserrat 127
New Hebrides, British 77
Nigeria 79
North Borneo 260
Northern Rhodesia 60
Nyasaland Protectorate 96
Pitcairn Islands 19
St. Helena 139
St. Kitts-Nevis 119
St. Lucia 156
St. Vincent 185
Sarawak 196
Seychelles 172
Sierra Leone 194
Singapore 27
Solomon Islands 88
Somaliland Protectorate 127
Swaziland 54
Trinidad & Tobago 84
Tristan da Cunha 13
Turks & Caicos Islands 118
Virgin Islands 114

The following have different designs but are included in the omnibus set:

Great Britain 313-316
Offices in Morocco (Tangier) 579-582
Australia 259-261
Bahrain 92-95
Canada 330
Ceylon 317
Cook Islands 145-146
Kuwait 113-116
New Zealand 280-284
Niue 104-105
Oman 52-55
Samoa 214-215
South Africa 192
Southern Rhodesia 80
South-West Africa 244-248
Tokelau Islands 4

No. 47 (1)	1.25	1.25
No. 28 (1)	.75	1.50
No. 28 (1)	1.10	.60
No. 106 (1)	.40	.75
No. 61 (1)	1.25	2.75
No. 157 (1)	1.40	.75
No. 234 (1)	1.00	.25
No. 45 (1)	.50	.60
No. 153 (1)	.75	.35
No. 142 (1)	.85	.50
No. 252 (1)	.45	.25
No. 143 (1)	.60	.40
No. 150 (1)	.40	1.75
No. 167 (1)	1.60	.75
No. 141 (1)	.40	.40
No. 121 (1)	.90	1.50
No. 1L18 (1)	1.80	1.40
No. 145 (1)	1.00	.60
No. 152 (1)	.50	.50
No. 131 (1)	.50	.50
No. 60 (1)	.65	2.25
No. 160 (1)	1.00	.25

No. 170 (1)	.30	.25
No. 184 (1)	6.00	.35
No. 153 (1)	.70	.25
No. 101 (1)	.40	.25
No. 132 (1)	1.00	*2.25*
No. 155 (1)	1.40	.30
No. 82 (1)	2.25	.60
No. 71 (1)	1.60	1.60
No. 27 (1)	1.10	*1.50*
No. 63 (1)	1.40	.65
No. 71 (1)	2.25	.25
No. 27 (1)	1.75	.30
No. 126 (1)	1.60	.25
No. 28 (1)	1.75	*4.00*
No. 101 (1)	1.75	.25
No. 74 (1)	1.50	1.00
No. 241 (1)	.50	.25
No. 250 (1)	1.10	.25
No. 127 (1)	.60	.45
No. 77 (1)	.75	.60
No. 79 (1)	.45	.25
No. 260 (1)	1.75	1.00
No. 60 (1)	.70	.25
No. 96 (1)	.75	.75
No. 19 (1)	2.25	2.25
No. 139 (1)	1.25	1.25
No. 119 (1)	.35	.25
No. 156 (1)	.70	.35
No. 185 (1)	.50	.30
No. 196 (1)	2.00	*1.75*
No. 172 (1)	.80	.80
No. 194 (1)	.40	.40
No. 27 (1)	2.50	.40
No. 88 (1)	1.00	1.00
No. 127 (1)	.40	.25
No. 54 (1)	.30	.25
No. 84 (1)	.25	.25
No. 13 (1)	1.00	1.75
No. 118 (1)	.40	*1.10*
No. 114 (1)	.40	*1.00*
Nos. 313-316 (4)	16.35	5.95
Nos. 579-582 (4)	8.15	5.30
Nos. 259-261 (3)	3.60	2.75
Nos. 92-95 (4)	15.25	12.75
No. 330 (1)	.25	.25
No. 317 (1)	1.40	.25
Nos. 145-146 (2)	2.65	2.65
Nos. 113-116 (4)	16.00	8.50
Nos. 280-284 (5)	3.30	*4.55*
Nos. 104-105 (2)	1.60	1.60
Nos. 52-55 (4)	14.25	6.50
Nos. 214-215 (2)	2.50	.80
No. 192 (1)	.45	.30
No. 80 (1)	7.25	7.25
Nos. 244-248 (5)	3.00	2.35
No. 4 (1)	2.75	2.75
Set total (106) Stamps	165.65	115.55

Separate designs for each country for the visit of Queen Elizabeth II and the Duke of Edinburgh.

Royal Visit 1953

1953

Aden	62
Australia	267-269
Bermuda	163
Ceylon	318
Fiji	146
Gibraltar	146
Jamaica	154
Kenya, Uganda, Tanzania	102
Malta	242
New Zealand	286-287

No. 62 (1)	.65	4.00
Nos. 267-269 (3)	2.75	2.05
No. 163 (1)	.50	.25
No. 318 (1)	1.00	.25
No. 146 (1)	.65	.35
No. 146 (1)	.50	.30
No. 154 (1)	.50	.25
No. 102 (1)	.50	.25
No. 242 (1)	.35	.25
Nos. 286-287 (2)	.50	.50
Set total (13) Stamps	7.90	8.45

West Indies Federation

Map of the Caribbean CD313

Federation of the West Indies, April 22, 1958.

1958

Antigua	122-124
Barbados	248-250
Dominica	161-163
Grenada	184-186
Jamaica	175-177
Montserrat	143-145
St. Kitts-Nevis	136-138
St. Lucia	170-172
St. Vincent	198-200
Trinidad & Tobago	86-88

Nos. 122-124 (3)	5.80	3.80
Nos. 248-250 (3)	1.60	*2.90*
Nos. 161-163 (3)	1.95	1.85
Nos. 184-186 (3)	1.50	1.20
Nos. 175-177 (3)	2.65	3.45
Nos. 143-145 (3)	2.35	1.35
Nos. 136-138 (3)	3.00	3.10
Nos. 170-172 (3)	2.05	2.80
Nos. 198-200 (3)	1.50	1.75
Nos. 86-88 (3)	.75	.90
Set total (30) Stamps	23.15	23.10

Freedom from Hunger

Protein Food CD314

U.N. Food and Agricultural Organization's "Freedom from Hunger" campaign.

1963

Aden	65
Antigua	133
Ascension	89
Bahamas	180
Basutoland	83
Bechuanaland Protectorate	194
Bermuda	192
British Guiana	271
British Honduras	179
Brunei	100
Cayman Islands	168
Dominica	181
Falkland Islands	146
Fiji	198
Gambia	172
Gibraltar	161
Gilbert & Ellice Islands	76
Grenada	190
Hong Kong	218
Malta	291
Mauritius	270
Montserrat	150
New Hebrides, British	93
North Borneo	296
Pitcairn Islands	35
St. Helena	173
St. Lucia	179
St. Vincent	201
Sarawak	212
Seychelles	213
Solomon Islands	109
Swaziland	108
Tonga	127
Tristan da Cunha	68
Turks & Caicos Islands	138
Virgin Islands	140
Zanzibar	280

No. 65 (1)	1.50	1.75
No. 133 (1)	.35	.35
No. 89 (1)	1.00	.50
No. 180 (1)	.65	.65
No. 83 (1)	.50	.25
No. 194 (1)	.50	.50
No. 192 (1)	1.00	.50
No. 271 (1)	.45	.25
No. 179 (1)	.60	.25
No. 100 (1)	3.25	2.25
No. 168 (1)	.55	.30
No. 181 (1)	.30	.30
No. 146 (1)	10.50	2.50
No. 198 (1)	3.50	2.25
No. 172 (1)	.50	.25
No. 161 (1)	4.00	2.25
No. 76 (1)	1.40	.40
No. 190 (1)	.30	.25
No. 218 (1)	47.50	7.50
No. 291 (1)	2.00	2.00
No. 270 (1)	.45	.25
No. 150 (1)	.55	.35
No. 93 (1)	.60	.25
No. 296 (1)	1.90	.75
No. 35 (1)	10.00	4.50
No. 173 (1)	2.25	1.10
No. 179 (1)	.40	.40
No. 201 (1)	.90	.50
No. 212 (1)	1.60	*1.75*
No. 213 (1)	.85	.35
No. 109 (1)	3.00	.85
No. 108 (1)	.50	.50
No. 127 (1)	.60	.35
No. 68 (1)	.75	.35
No. 138 (1)	.50	.25
No. 140 (1)	.50	.50
No. 280 (1)	1.50	.80
Set total (37) Stamps	107.20	39.05

Red Cross Centenary

Red Cross and Elizabeth II CD315

1963

Antigua	134-135
Ascension	90-91
Bahamas	183-184
Basutoland	84-85
Bechuanaland Protectorate	195-196
Bermuda	193-194
British Guiana	272-273
British Honduras	180-181
Cayman Islands	169-170
Dominica	182-183
Falkland Islands	147-148
Fiji	203-204
Gambia	173-174
Gibraltar	162-163
Gilbert & Ellice Islands	77-78
Grenada	191-192
Hong Kong	219-220
Jamaica	203-204
Malta	292-293
Mauritius	271-272
Montserrat	151-152
New Hebrides, British	94-95
Pitcairn Islands	36-37
St. Helena	174-175
St. Kitts-Nevis	143-144
St. Lucia	180-181
St. Vincent	202-203
Seychelles	214-215
Solomon Islands	110-111
South Arabia	1-2
Swaziland	109-110
Tonga	134-135
Tristan da Cunha	69-70
Turks & Caicos Islands	139-140
Virgin Islands	141-142

Nos. 134-135 (2)	1.00	*2.00*
Nos. 90-91 (2)	6.75	3.35
Nos. 183-184 (2)	2.30	2.80
Nos. 84-85 (2)	1.20	.90
Nos. 195-196 (2)	.95	.85
Nos. 193-194 (2)	3.00	2.80
Nos. 272-273 (2)	.85	.60
Nos. 180-181 (2)	1.00	2.50
Nos. 169-170 (2)	1.10	*3.00*
Nos. 182-183 (2)	.70	*1.05*
Nos. 147-148 (2)	18.00	5.50
Nos. 203-204 (2)	3.25	2.80
Nos. 173-174 (2)	.75	1.00
Nos. 162-163 (2)	6.25	5.40
Nos. 77-78 (2)	2.00	*3.50*
Nos. 191-192 (2)	.80	.50
Nos. 219-220 (2)	35.00	7.35
Nos. 203-204 (2)	.75	*1.65*
Nos. 292-293 (2)	2.50	4.75
Nos. 271-272 (2)	.85	.50
Nos. 151-152 (2)	1.00	.75
Nos. 94-95 (2)	1.00	.50
Nos. 36-37 (2)	6.50	5.50
Nos. 174-175 (2)	1.70	2.30
Nos. 143-144 (2)	.90	.90
Nos. 180-181 (2)	1.25	1.25
Nos. 202-203 (2)	.90	.90
Nos. 214-215 (2)	1.00	1.50
Nos. 110-111 (2)	1.25	1.15
Nos. 1-2 (2)	1.25	1.25
Nos. 109-110 (2)	1.10	1.10
Nos. 134-135 (2)	1.00	1.25
Nos. 69-70 (2)	1.15	.80
Nos. 139-140 (2)	.85	.75
Nos. 141-142 (2)	.80	1.25
Set total (70) Stamps	110.65	73.95

Shakespeare

Shakespeare Memorial Theatre, Stratford-on-Avon — CD316

400th anniversary of the birth of William Shakespeare.

1964

Antigua	151
Bahamas	201
Bechuanaland Protectorate	197
Cayman Islands	171
Dominica	184
Falkland Islands	149
Gambia	192
Gibraltar	164
Montserrat	153
St. Lucia	196
Turks & Caicos Islands	141
Virgin Islands	143

No. 151 (1)	.35	.25
No. 201 (1)	.60	.35
No. 197 (1)	.35	.35
No. 171 (1)	.35	.30
No. 184 (1)	.35	.35
No. 149 (1)	1.60	.50
No. 192 (1)	.35	.25
No. 164 (1)	.65	.55
No. 153 (1)	.35	.25
No. 196 (1)	.45	.25
No. 141 (1)	.40	.25
No. 143 (1)	.45	.45
Set total (12) Stamps	6.25	4.10

ITU

ITU Emblem CD317

Intl. Telecommunication Union, cent.

1965

Antigua	153-154
Ascension	92-93
Bahamas	219-220
Barbados	265-266
Basutoland	101-102
Bechuanaland Protectorate	202-203
Bermuda	196-197
British Guiana	293-294
British Honduras	187-188
Brunei	116-117
Cayman Islands	172-173
Dominica	185-186
Falkland Islands	154-155
Fiji	211-212
Gibraltar	167-168
Gilbert & Ellice Islands	87-88
Grenada	205-206
Hong Kong	221-222
Mauritius	291-292
Montserrat	157-158
New Hebrides, British	108-109
Pitcairn Islands	52-53
St. Helena	180-181
St. Kitts-Nevis	163-164
St. Lucia	197-198
St. Vincent	224-225
Seychelles	218-219
Solomon Islands	126-127
Swaziland	115-116
Tristan da Cunha	85-86
Turks & Caicos Islands	142-143
Virgin Islands	159-160

Nos. 153-154 (2)	1.45	1.35
Nos. 92-93 (2)	1.90	1.30
Nos. 219-220 (2)	1.35	1.50
Nos. 265-266 (2)	1.50	1.25
Nos. 101-102 (2)	.85	.65
Nos. 202-203 (2)	1.10	.75
Nos. 196-197 (2)	2.15	*2.25*
Nos. 293-294 (2)	.50	.50
Nos. 187-188 (2)	.75	.75
Nos. 116-117 (2)	1.75	1.75
Nos. 172-173 (2)	1.00	.85
Nos. 185-186 (2)	.55	.55
Nos. 154-155 (2)	6.75	3.15
Nos. 211-212 (2)	2.00	1.05
Nos. 167-168 (2)	9.00	5.95
Nos. 87-88 (2)	.85	.60
Nos. 205-206 (2)	.50	.50
Nos. 221-222 (2)	24.50	3.80
Nos. 291-292 (2)	1.10	.50
Nos. 157-158 (2)	1.05	1.15
Nos. 108-109 (2)	.65	.50
Nos. 52-53 (2)	6.25	4.30
Nos. 180-181 (2)	.80	.60
Nos. 163-164 (2)	.60	.60
Nos. 197-198 (2)	1.25	1.25
Nos. 224-225 (2)	.80	.90
Nos. 218-219 (2)	.75	.60
Nos. 126-127 (2)	.70	.55
Nos. 115-116 (2)	.70	.70
Nos. 85-86 (2)	1.00	.65
Nos. 142-143 (2)	.75	.50
Nos. 159-160 (2)	.85	.85
Set total (64) Stamps	75.70	42.15

Intl. Cooperation Year

ICY Emblem CD318

1965

Antigua	155-156
Ascension	94-95
Bahamas	222-223
Basutoland	103-104
Bechuanaland Protectorate	204-205
Bermuda	199-200
British Guiana	295-296
British Honduras	189-190
Brunei	118-119
Cayman Islands	174-175
Dominica	187-188
Falkland Islands	156-157
Fiji	213-214
Gibraltar	169-170
Gilbert & Ellice Islands	104-105
Grenada	207-208
Hong Kong	223-224
Mauritius	293-294
Montserrat	176-177
New Hebrides, British	110-111
New Hebrides, French	126-127
Pitcairn Islands	54-55
St. Helena	182-183
St. Kitts-Nevis	165-166
St. Lucia	199-200
Seychelles	220-221
Solomon Islands	143-144
South Arabia	17-18
Swaziland	117-118
Tristan da Cunha	87-88
Turks & Caicos Islands	144-145
Virgin Islands	161-162

Nos. 155-156 (2)	.55	.50
Nos. 94-95 (2)	1.30	1.40
Nos. 222-223 (2)	.65	1.90
Nos. 103-104 (2)	.75	.85
Nos. 204-205 (2)	.85	1.00
Nos. 199-200 (2)	2.05	1.25
Nos. 295-296 (2)	.55	.50
Nos. 189-190 (2)	.60	.55
Nos. 118-119 (2)	.85	.85
Nos. 174-175 (2)	1.00	.75
Nos. 187-188 (2)	.55	.55
Nos. 156-157 (2)	6.00	1.65
Nos. 213-214 (2)	1.95	1.25
Nos. 169-170 (2)	1.25	*2.75*
Nos. 104-105 (2)	.85	.60
Nos. 207-208 (2)	.50	.50
Nos. 223-224 (2)	22.00	3.10
Nos. 293-294 (2)	.65	.50
Nos. 176-177 (2)	.80	.65
Nos. 110-111 (2)	.50	.50
Nos. 126-127 (2)	12.00	12.00
Nos. 54-55 (2)	6.35	4.50
Nos. 182-183 (2)	.95	.50
Nos. 165-166 (2)	.80	.60
Nos. 199-200 (2)	.55	.55
Nos. 220-221 (2)	.80	.60
Nos. 143-144 (2)	.70	.60
Nos. 17-18 (2)	1.20	.50
Nos. 117-118 (2)	.75	.75
Nos. 87-88 (2)	1.05	.65
Nos. 144-145 (2)	.65	.50
Nos. 161-162 (2)	.65	.50
Set total (64) Stamps	70.65	43.85

Churchill Memorial

Winston Churchill and St. Paul's, London, During Air Attack CD319

1966

Antigua	157-160
Ascension	96-99
Bahamas	224-227
Barbados	281-284
Basutoland	105-108
Bechuanaland Protectorate	206-209
Bermuda	201-204
British Antarctic Territory	16-19
British Honduras	191-194
Brunei	120-123
Cayman Islands	176-179
Dominica	189-192
Falkland Islands	158-161
Fiji	215-218
Gibraltar	171-174
Gilbert & Ellice Islands	106-109
Grenada	209-212
Hong Kong	225-228
Mauritius	295-298
Montserrat	178-181
New Hebrides, British	112-115
New Hebrides, French	128-131
Pitcairn Islands	56-59
St. Helena	184-187
St. Kitts-Nevis	167-170
St. Lucia	201-204
St. Vincent	241-244
Seychelles	222-225
Solomon Islands	145-148
South Arabia	19-22
Swaziland	119-122
Tristan da Cunha	89-92
Turks & Caicos Islands	146-149
Virgin Islands	163-166

Nos. 157-160 (4)	3.05	3.05
Nos. 96-99 (4)	10.00	6.40
Nos. 224-227 (4)	2.30	*3.20*
Nos. 281-284 (4)	3.00	4.95
Nos. 105-108 (4)	2.80	3.25
Nos. 206-209 (4)	2.50	2.50
Nos. 201-204 (4)	4.00	*4.75*
Nos. 16-19 (4)	41.20	18.00
Nos. 191-194 (4)	2.45	1.30
Nos. 120-123 (4)	7.65	6.55
Nos. 176-179 (4)	3.10	3.65
Nos. 189-192 (4)	1.15	1.15
Nos. 158-161 (4)	12.75	9.55
Nos. 215-218 (4)	4.40	3.00
Nos. 171-174 (4)	3.05	5.30
Nos. 106-109 (4)	1.50	1.30
Nos. 209-212 (4)	1.10	1.10
Nos. 225-228 (4)	52.50	11.40
Nos. 295-298 (4)	3.70	3.75
Nos. 178-181 (4)	1.60	1.55
Nos. 112-115 (4)	2.30	1.00
Nos. 128-131 (4)	8.35	8.35
Nos. 56-59 (4)	11.00	6.75
Nos. 184-187 (4)	1.85	1.95
Nos. 167-170 (4)	1.50	1.70
Nos. 201-204 (4)	1.50	1.50
Nos. 241-244 (4)	1.50	1.75
Nos. 222-225 (4)	3.20	4.35
Nos. 145-148 (4)	1.50	1.60
Nos. 19-22 (4)	2.95	2.20
Nos. 119-122 (4)	1.70	2.55
Nos. 89-92 (4)	5.95	2.70
Nos. 146-149 (4)	1.60	1.75
Nos. 163-166 (4)	1.90	1.90
Set total (136) Stamps	210.60	135.75

Royal Visit, 1966

Queen Elizabeth II and Prince Philip CD320

Caribbean visit, Feb. 4 - Mar. 6, 1966.

1966

Antigua	161-162
Bahamas	228-229
Barbados	285-286
British Guiana	299-300
Cayman Islands	180-181
Dominica	193-194
Grenada	213-214
Montserrat	182-183
St. Kitts-Nevis	171-172
St. Lucia	205-206
St. Vincent	245-246
Turks & Caicos Islands	150-151
Virgin Islands	167-168

Nos. 161-162 (2)	3.50	2.60
Nos. 228-229 (2)	3.05	3.05
Nos. 285-286 (2)	3.00	2.00
Nos. 299-300 (2)	2.35	.85
Nos. 180-181 (2)	3.45	1.80
Nos. 193-194 (2)	3.00	.60
Nos. 213-214 (2)	.80	.50
Nos. 182-183 (2)	2.00	1.00
Nos. 171-172 (2)	.90	.75
Nos. 205-206 (2)	1.50	1.35
Nos. 245-246 (2)	2.75	1.35
Nos. 150-151 (2)	1.20	.55
Nos. 167-168 (2)	1.75	1.75
Set total (26) Stamps	29.25	18.15

World Cup Soccer

Soccer Player and Jules Rimet Cup CD321

World Cup Soccer Championship, Wembley, England, July 11-30.

1966

Antigua	163-164
Ascension	100-101
Bahamas	245-246
Bermuda	205-206
Brunei	124-125
Cayman Islands	182-183
Dominica	195-196
Fiji	219-220
Gibraltar	175-176
Gilbert & Ellice Islands	125-126
Grenada	230-231
New Hebrides, British	116-117
New Hebrides, French	132-133
Pitcairn Islands	60-61
St. Helena	188-189
St. Kitts-Nevis	173-174
St. Lucia	207-208
Seychelles	226-227
Solomon Islands	167-168
South Arabia	23-24
Tristan da Cunha	93-94

Nos. 163-164 (2)	.80	.85
Nos. 100-101 (2)	2.50	2.00
Nos. 245-246 (2)	.65	.65
Nos. 205-206 (2)	1.75	1.75
Nos. 124-125 (2)	1.30	1.25
Nos. 182-183 (2)	.75	.65
Nos. 195-196 (2)	1.20	.75
Nos. 219-220 (2)	1.70	.60
Nos. 175-176 (2)	1.85	1.75
Nos. 125-126 (2)	.70	.60
Nos. 230-231 (2)	.65	*.95*
Nos. 116-117 (2)	1.00	1.00
Nos. 132-133 (2)	7.00	7.00
Nos. 60-61 (2)	5.50	5.00
Nos. 188-189 (2)	1.25	.60
Nos. 173-174 (2)	.85	.80
Nos. 207-208 (2)	1.15	.90
Nos. 226-227 (2)	.85	.75
Nos. 167-168 (2)	1.10	1.10
Nos. 23-24 (2)	1.90	.55
Nos. 93-94 (2)	1.25	.80
Set total (42) Stamps	35.70	30.30

WHO Headquarters

World Health Organization Headquarters, Geneva — CD322

1966

Antigua	165-166
Ascension	102-103
Bahamas	247-248
Brunei	126-127
Cayman Islands	184-185
Dominica	197-198
Fiji	224-225
Gibraltar	180-181
Gilbert & Ellice Islands	127-128
Grenada	232-233
Hong Kong	229-230
Montserrat	184-185
New Hebrides, British	118-119
New Hebrides, French	134-135
Pitcairn Islands	62-63
St. Helena	190-191
St. Kitts-Nevis	177-178
St. Lucia	209-210
St. Vincent	247-248
Seychelles	228-229
Solomon Islands	169-170
South Arabia	25-26
Tristan da Cunha	99-100

Nos. 165-166 (2)	1.15	.55
Nos. 102-103 (2)	6.60	3.35
Nos. 247-248 (2)	.80	.80
Nos. 126-127 (2)	1.35	1.35
Nos. 184-185 (2)	2.25	1.20
Nos. 197-198 (2)	.75	.75
Nos. 224-225 (2)	4.70	3.30
Nos. 180-181 (2)	6.50	4.50
Nos. 127-128 (2)	.80	.70
Nos. 232-233 (2)	.80	.50
Nos. 229-230 (2)	11.25	2.30
Nos. 184-185 (2)	1.00	1.00
Nos. 118-119 (2)	.75	.50
Nos. 134-135 (2)	8.50	8.50
Nos. 62-63 (2)	7.25	6.50
Nos. 190-191 (2)	3.50	1.50
Nos. 177-178 (2)	.60	.60
Nos. 209-210 (2)	.80	.80
Nos. 247-248 (2)	1.15	1.05
Nos. 228-229 (2)	1.25	.65
Nos. 169-170 (2)	.95	.80
Nos. 25-26 (2)	2.10	.70
Nos. 99-100 (2)	1.90	1.25
Set total (46) Stamps	66.70	43.15

UNESCO Anniversary

"Education" — CD323

"Science" (Wheat ears & flask enclosing globe). "Culture" (lyre & columns). 20th anniversary of the UNESCO.

1966-67

Antigua	183-185
Ascension	108-110
Bahamas	249-251
Barbados	287-289
Bermuda	207-209
Brunei	128-130
Cayman Islands	186-188
Dominica	199-201
Gibraltar	183-185
Gilbert & Ellice Islands	129-131
Grenada	234-236
Hong Kong	231-233
Mauritius	299-301
Montserrat	186-188
New Hebrides, British	120-122
New Hebrides, French	136-138
Pitcairn Islands	64-66
St. Helena	192-194
St. Kitts-Nevis	179-181
St. Lucia	211-213
St. Vincent	249-251
Seychelles	230-232
Solomon Islands	171-173
South Arabia	27-29
Swaziland	123-125
Tristan da Cunha	101-103
Turks & Caicos Islands	155-157
Virgin Islands	176-178

Nos. 183-185 (3)	1.90	*2.50*
Nos. 108-110 (3)	11.00	5.80
Nos. 249-251 (3)	2.35	2.35
Nos. 287-289 (3)	2.35	2.15
Nos. 207-209 (3)	3.80	*3.90*
Nos. 128-130 (3)	4.65	5.40
Nos. 186-188 (3)	2.50	1.50
Nos. 199-201 (3)	1.60	.75
Nos. 183-185 (3)	6.50	3.25
Nos. 129-131 (3)	2.50	*2.45*
Nos. 234-236 (3)	1.10	1.20
Nos. 231-233 (3)	69.50	17.50
Nos. 299-301 (3)	2.10	1.50
Nos. 186-188 (3)	2.40	2.40
Nos. 120-122 (3)	1.90	1.90
Nos. 136-138 (3)	7.75	7.75
Nos. 64-66 (3)	7.10	4.75
Nos. 192-194 (3)	5.25	3.65
Nos. 179-181 (3)	.90	.90
Nos. 211-213 (3)	1.15	1.15
Nos. 249-251 (3)	2.30	1.35
Nos. 230-232 (3)	2.40	2.40
Nos. 171-173 (3)	2.00	1.50
Nos. 27-29 (3)	5.50	5.50
Nos. 123-125 (3)	1.40	1.40
Nos. 101-103 (3)	2.00	1.40
Nos. 155-157 (3)	1.05	.90
Nos. 176-178 (3)	1.40	1.30
Set total (84) Stamps	156.35	88.50

Silver Wedding, 1972

Queen Elizabeth II and Prince Philip — CD324

Designs: borders differ for each country.

1972

Anguilla	161-162
Antigua	295-296
Ascension	164-165
Bahamas	344-345
Bermuda	296-297
British Antarctic Territory	43-44
British Honduras	306-307
British Indian Ocean Territory	48-49

Brunei....................................186-187
Cayman Islands........................304-305
Dominica.................................352-353
Falkland Islands 223-224
Fiji 328-329
Gibraltar..................................292-293
Gilbert & Ellice Islands............206-207
Grenada...................................466-467
Hong Kong 271-272
Montserrat 286-287
New Hebrides, British 169-170
New Hebrides, French 188-189
Pitcairn Islands........................127-128
St. Helena 271-272
St. Kitts-Nevis..........................257-258
St. Lucia 328-329
St.Vincent................................344-345
Seychelles...............................309-310
Solomon Islands......................248-249
South Georgia 35-36
Tristan da Cunha.....................178-179
Turks & Caicos Islands 257-258
Virgin Islands..........................241-242

Nos. 161-162 (2)	1.10	*1.50*
Nos. 295-296 (2)	.50	.50
Nos. 164-165 (2)	.70	.70
Nos. 344-345 (2)	.60	.60
Nos. 296-297 (2)	.50	*.65*
Nos. 43-44 (2)	6.50	5.65
Nos. 306-307 (2)	.80	.80
Nos. 48-49 (2)	2.00	1.00
Nos. 186-187 (2)	.70	.70
Nos. 304-305 (2)	.75	.75
Nos. 352-353 (2)	.65	.65
Nos. 223-224 (2)	1.00	1.15
Nos. 328-329 (2)	.70	.70
Nos. 292-293 (2)	.50	.50
Nos. 206-207 (2)	.50	.50
Nos. 466-467 (2)	.70	.70
Nos. 271-272 (2)	1.70	1.50
Nos. 286-287 (2)	.50	.50
Nos. 169-170 (2)	.50	.50
Nos. 188-189 (2)	1.25	1.25
Nos. 127-128 (2)	.90	.85
Nos. 271-272 (2)	.60	1.20
Nos. 257-258 (2)	.65	.50
Nos. 328-329 (2)	.75	.75
Nos. 344-345 (2)	.55	.55
Nos. 309-310 (2)	.90	.90
Nos. 248-249 (2)	.50	.50
Nos. 35-36 (2)	1.40	1.40
Nos. 178-179 (2)	.70	.70
Nos. 257-258 (2)	.50	.50
Nos. 241-242 (2)	.50	.50
Set total (62) Stamps	30.10	29.15

Princess Anne's Wedding

Princess Anne and Mark Phillips — CD325

Wedding of Princess Anne and Mark Phillips, Nov. 14, 1973.

1973

Anguilla...................................179-180
Ascension................................177-178
Belize.......................................325-326
Bermuda...................................302-303
British Antarctic Territory.............60-61
Cayman Islands.......................320-321
Falkland Islands 225-226
Gibraltar...................................305-306
Gilbert & Ellice Islands............216-217
Hong Kong 289-290
Montserrat 300-301
Pitcairn Islands........................135-136
St. Helena 277-278
St. Kitts-Nevis..........................274-275
St. Lucia 349-350
St. Vincent................................358-359
St. Vincent Grenadines.....................1-2
Seychelles................................311-312
Solomon Islands......................259-260
South Georgia 37-38
Tristan da Cunha.....................189-190
Turks & Caicos Islands 286-287
Virgin Islands..........................260-261

Nos. 179-180 (2)	.55	.55
Nos. 177-178 (2)	.60	.60
Nos. 325-326 (2)	.50	.50
Nos. 302-303 (2)	.50	.50
Nos. 60-61 (2)	1.10	1.10
Nos. 320-321 (2)	.50	.50
Nos. 225-226 (2)	.70	.60
Nos. 305-306 (2)	.55	.55
Nos. 216-217 (2)	.50	.50
Nos. 289-290 (2)	2.65	2.00
Nos. 300-301 (2)	.55	.55
Nos. 135-136 (2)	.70	.60
Nos. 277-278 (2)	.50	.50
Nos. 274-275 (2)	.50	.50
Nos. 349-350 (2)	.50	.50
Nos. 358-359 (2)	.50	.50
Nos. 1-2 (2)	.50	.50
Nos. 311-312 (2)	.65	.65
Nos. 259-260 (2)	.70	.70
Nos. 37-38 (2)	.75	.75
Nos. 189-190 (2)	.50	.50
Nos. 286-287 (2)	.50	.50
Nos. 260-261 (2)	.50	.50
Set total (46) Stamps	15.50	14.65

Elizabeth II Coronation Anniv.

CD326

CD327

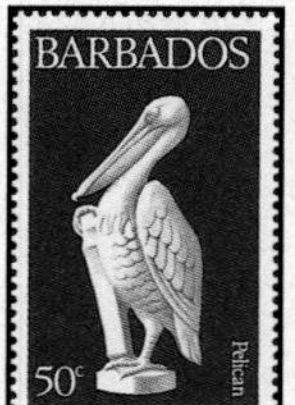

CD328

Designs: Royal and local beasts in heraldic form and simulated stonework. Portrait of Elizabeth II by Peter Grugeon. 25th anniversary of coronation of Queen Elizabeth II.

1978

Ascension..229
Barbados 474
Belize..397
British Antarctic Territory..................71
Cayman Islands...............................404
Christmas Island 87
Falkland Islands 275
Fiji 384
Gambia..380
Gilbert Islands 312
Mauritius...464
New Hebrides, British 258
New Hebrides, French 278
St. Helena 317
St. Kitts-Nevis.................................354
Samoa 472
Solomon Islands.............................368
South Georgia 51
Swaziland 302
Tristan da Cunha.............................238
Virgin Islands..................................337

No. 229 (1)	2.00	2.00
No. 474 (1)	1.35	1.35
No. 397 (1)	1.40	1.75
No. 71 (1)	6.00	6.00
No. 404 (1)	2.00	2.00
No. 87 (1)	3.50	*4.00*
No. 275 (1)	4.00	5.50
No. 384 (1)	1.75	1.75
No. 380 (1)	1.50	1.50
No. 312 (1)	1.25	1.25
No. 464 (1)	2.10	2.10
No. 258 (1)	1.75	1.75
No. 278 (1)	3.50	3.50
No. 317 (1)	1.75	1.75
No. 354 (1)	1.00	1.00
No. 472 (1)	2.10	2.10
No. 368 (1)	2.50	2.50
No. 51 (1)	3.00	3.00
No. 302 (1)	1.60	1.60
No. 238 (1)	1.50	1.50
No. 337 (1)	1.80	1.80
Set total (21) Stamps	47.35	49.70

Queen Mother Elizabeth's 80th Birthday

CD330

Designs: Photographs of Queen Mother Elizabeth. Falkland Islands issued in sheets of 50; others in sheets of 9.

1980

Ascension..261
Bermuda...401
Cayman Islands...............................443
Falkland Islands 305
Gambia..412
Gibraltar..393
Hong Kong 364
Pitcairn Islands...............................193
St. Helena 341
Samoa 532
Solomon Islands.............................426
Tristan da Cunha.............................277

No. 261 (1)	.40	.40
No. 401 (1)	.45	.75
No. 443 (1)	.40	.40
No. 305 (1)	.40	.40
No. 412 (1)	.40	.50
No. 393 (1)	.35	.35
No. 364 (1)	1.10	1.25
No. 193 (1)	.60	.60
No. 341 (1)	.50	.50
No. 532 (1)	.55	.55
No. 426 (1)	.50	.50
No. 277 (1)	.45	.45
Set total (12) Stamps	6.10	6.65

Royal Wedding, 1981

Prince Charles and Lady Diana — CD331

CD331a

Wedding of Charles, Prince of Wales, and Lady Diana Spencer, St. Paul's Cathedral, London, July 29, 1981.

1981

Antigua 623-627
Ascension................................294-296
Barbados 547-549
Barbuda...................................497-501
Bermuda..................................412-414
Brunei......................................268-270
Cayman Islands.......................471-473
Dominica.................................701-705
Falkland Islands 324-326
Falkland Islands Dep............1L59-1L61
Fiji 442-444
Gambia....................................426-428
Ghana......................................759-764
Grenada................................1051-1055
Grenada Grenadines...............440-443
Hong Kong 373-375
Jamaica 500-503
Lesotho....................................335-337
Maldive Islands.......................906-909
Mauritius.................................520-522
Norfolk Island 280-282
Pitcairn Islands........................206-208
St. Helena 353-355
St. Lucia 543-549
Samoa 558-560
Sierra Leone............................509-518
Solomon Islands......................450-452
Swaziland................................382-384
Tristan da Cunha.....................294-296
Turks & Caicos Islands 486-489
Caicos Island.................................8-11
Uganda 314-317
Vanuatu 308-310
Virgin Islands..........................406-408

Nos. 623-627 (5)	6.55	2.55
Nos. 294-296 (3)	1.00	1.00
Nos. 547-549 (3)	.90	.90
Nos. 497-501 (5)	10.95	10.95
Nos. 412-414 (3)	2.00	2.00
Nos. 268-270 (3)	2.15	*4.50*
Nos. 471-473 (3)	1.20	1.30
Nos. 701-705 (5)	8.35	2.35
Nos. 324-326 (3)	1.65	1.70
Nos. 1L59-1L61 (3)	1.45	1.45
Nos. 442-444 (3)	1.35	1.35
Nos. 426-428 (3)	.80	.80
Nos. 759-764 (9)	6.20	6.20
Nos. 1051-1055 (5)	9.85	1.85
Nos. 440-443 (4)	2.35	2.35
Nos. 373-375 (3)	3.05	2.85
Nos. 500-503 (4)	1.45	1.35
Nos. 335-337 (3)	.90	.90
Nos. 906-909 (4)	1.55	1.55
Nos. 520-522 (3)	2.15	2.15
Nos. 280-282 (3)	1.75	1.75
Nos. 206-208 (3)	1.10	1.10
Nos. 353-355 (3)	.85	.85
Nos. 543-549 (5)	7.00	7.00
Nos. 558-560 (3)	.85	.85
Nos. 509-518 (10)	15.50	15.50
Nos. 450-452 (3)	1.25	1.25
Nos. 382-384 (3)	1.30	1.25
Nos. 294-296 (3)	.90	.90
Nos. 486-489 (4)	2.20	2.20
Nos. 8-11 (4)	5.00	5.00
Nos. 314-317 (4)	3.30	3.00
Nos. 308-310 (3)	1.15	1.15
Nos. 406-408 (3)	1.10	1.10
Set total (131) Stamps	109.10	92.95

Princess Diana

CD332

CD333

Designs: Photographs and portrait of Princess Diana, wedding or honeymoon photographs, royal residences, arms of issuing country. Portrait photograph by Clive Friend. Souvenir sheet margins show family tree, various people related to the princess. 21st birthday of Princess Diana of Wales, July 1.

1982

Antigua 663-666
Ascension................................313-316
Bahamas 510-513
Barbados 585-588
Barbuda...................................544-547
British Antarctic Territory.............92-95
Cayman Islands.......................486-489
Dominica.................................773-776
Falkland Islands 348-351
Falkland Islands Dep............1L72-1L75
Fiji 470-473
Gambia....................................447-450
Grenada...............................1101A-1105
Grenada Grenadines...............485-491
Lesotho....................................372-375
Maldive Islands.......................952-955
Mauritius.................................548-551
Pitcairn Islands........................213-216
St. Helena 372-375
St. Lucia 591-594
Sierra Leone............................531-534
Solomon Islands......................471-474
Swaziland................................406-409
Tristan da Cunha.....................310-313
Turks and Caicos Islands 531-534
Virgin Islands..........................430-433

Nos. 663-666 (4)	8.25	7.35
Nos. 313-316 (4)	3.50	3.50
Nos. 510-513 (4)	6.00	3.85
Nos. 585-588 (4)	3.40	3.25
Nos. 544-547 (4)	9.75	7.70
Nos. 92-95 (4)	4.25	3.45
Nos. 486-489 (4)	*4.75*	*2.70*
Nos. 773-776 (4)	7.05	7.05
Nos. 348-351 (4)	2.95	2.95
Nos. 1L72-1L75 (4)	2.50	2.60
Nos. 470-473 (4)	3.25	2.95
Nos. 447-450 (4)	2.85	2.85
Nos. 1101A-1105 (7)	16.05	15.55

Nos. 485-491 (7)	17.65	17.65
Nos. 372-375 (4)	4.00	4.00
Nos. 952-955 (4)	5.50	3.90
Nos. 548-551 (4)	5.00	5.00
Nos. 213-216 (4)	2.15	2.15
Nos. 372-375 (4)	2.00	2.00
Nos. 591-594 (4)	8.70	8.70
Nos. 531-534 (4)	7.20	7.20
Nos. 471-474 (4)	2.90	2.90
Nos. 406-409 (4)	3.85	2.25
Nos. 310-313 (4)	3.65	1.45
Nos. 486-489 (4)	2.20	2.20
Nos. 430-433 (4)	3.00	3.00
Set total (110) Stamps	142.35	128.15

250th anniv. of first edition of Lloyd's List (shipping news publication) & of Lloyd's marine insurance.

CD335

Designs: First page of early edition of the list; historical ships, modern transportation or harbor scenes.

1984

Ascension 351-354
Bahamas 555-558
Barbados 627-630
Cayes of Belize 10-13
Cayman Islands 522-526
Falkland Islands 404-407
Fiji 509-512
Gambia 519-522
Mauritius 587-590
Nauru 280-283
St. Helena 412-415
Samoa 624-627
Seychelles 538-541
Solomon Islands 521-524
Vanuatu 368-371
Virgin Islands 466-469

Nos. 351-354 (4)	2.90	2.55
Nos. 555-558 (4)	4.15	2.95
Nos. 627-630 (4)	6.10	5.15
Nos. 10-13 (4)	2.65	2.65
Nos. 522-526 (5)	9.30	8.45
Nos. 404-407 (4)	3.50	3.65
Nos. 509-512 (4)	5.30	4.90
Nos. 519-522 (4)	4.20	4.30
Nos. 587-590 (4)	9.40	9.40
Nos. 280-283 (4)	2.40	2.35
Nos. 412-415 (4)	2.40	2.40
Nos. 624-627 (4)	2.55	2.35
Nos. 538-541 (4)	5.00	5.00
Nos. 521-524 (4)	4.65	3.95
Nos. 368-371 (4)	2.40	2.40
Nos. 466-469 (4)	4.25	4.25
Set total (65) Stamps	71.15	66.70

Queen Mother 85th Birthday

CD336

Designs: Photographs tracing the life of the Queen Mother, Elizabeth. The high value in each set pictures the same photograph taken of the Queen Mother holding the infant Prince Henry.

1985

Ascension 372-376
Bahamas 580-584
Barbados 660-664
Bermuda 469-473
Falkland Islands 420-424
Falkland Islands Dep. 1L92-1L96
Fiji 531-535
Hong Kong 447-450
Jamaica 599-603
Mauritius 604-608
Norfolk Island 364-368
Pitcairn Islands 253-257
St. Helena 428-432
Samoa 649-653
Seychelles 567-571
Zil Elwannyen Sesel 101-105
Solomon Islands 543-547
Swaziland 476-480
Tristan da Cunha 372-376
Vanuatu 392-396

Nos. 372-376 (5)	4.65	4.65
Nos. 580-584 (5)	7.70	6.45
Nos. 660-664 (5)	8.00	6.70
Nos. 469-473 (5)	9.40	9.40
Nos. 420-424 (5)	7.35	6.65
Nos. 1L92-1L96 (5)	8.00	8.00
Nos. 531-535 (5)	6.15	6.15
Nos. 447-450 (4)	9.50	8.50
Nos. 599-603 (5)	6.15	7.00
Nos. 604-608 (5)	11.30	11.30
Nos. 364-368 (5)	5.00	5.00
Nos. 253-257 (5)	5.25	5.95
Nos. 428-432 (5)	5.25	5.25
Nos. 649-653 (5)	8.40	7.55
Nos. 567-571 (5)	8.70	8.70
Nos. 101-105 (5)	6.60	6.60
Nos. 543-547 (5)	3.95	3.95
Nos. 476-480 (5)	7.75	7.25
Nos. 372-376 (5)	5.40	5.40
Nos. 392-396 (5)	5.25	5.25
Set total (99) Stamps	139.75	135.70

Queen Elizabeth II, 60th Birthday

CD337

1986, April 21

Ascension 389-393
Bahamas 592-596
Barbados 675-679
Bermuda 499-503
Cayman Islands 555-559
Falkland Islands 441-445
Fiji 544-548
Hong Kong 465-469
Jamaica 620-624
Kiribati 470-474
Mauritius 629-633
Papua New Guinea 640-644
Pitcairn Islands 270-274
St. Helena 451-455
Samoa 670-674
Seychelles 592-596
Zil Elwannyen Sesel 114-118
Solomon Islands 562-566
South Georgia 101-105
Swaziland 490-494
Tristan da Cunha 388-392
Vanuatu 414-418
Zambia 343-347

Nos. 389-393 (5)	2.80	3.30
Nos. 592-596 (5)	2.75	*3.70*
Nos. 675-679 (5)	3.25	3.10
Nos. 499-503 (5)	4.65	*5.15*
Nos. 555-559 (5)	4.55	5.60
Nos. 441-445 (5)	3.95	*4.95*
Nos. 544-548 (5)	3.00	3.00
Nos. 465-469 (5)	8.75	6.75
Nos. 620-624 (5)	2.75	2.70
Nos. 470-474 (5)	2.10	2.10
Nos. 629-633 (5)	3.50	3.50
Nos. 640-644 (5)	4.10	4.10
Nos. 270-274 (5)	2.70	2.70
Nos. 451-455 (5)	2.50	3.05
Nos. 670-674 (5)	2.55	2.55
Nos. 592-596 (5)	2.70	2.70
Nos. 114-118 (5)	2.15	2.15
Nos. 562-566 (5)	2.90	2.90
Nos. 101-105 (5)	3.30	3.65
Nos. 490-494 (5)	2.15	2.15
Nos. 388-392 (5)	3.00	3.00
Nos. 414-418 (5)	3.10	3.10
Nos. 343-347 (5)	1.75	1.75
Set total (115) Stamps	74.95	77.65

Royal Wedding

Marriage of Prince Andrew and Sarah Ferguson
CD338

1986, July 23

Ascension 399-400
Bahamas 602-603
Barbados 687-688
Cayman Islands 560-561
Jamaica 629-630
Pitcairn Islands 275-276
St. Helena 460-461
St. Kitts 181-182
Seychelles 602-603
Zil Elwannyen Sesel 119-120
Solomon Islands 567-568
Tristan da Cunha 397-398
Zambia 348-349

Nos. 399-400 (2)	1.60	1.60
Nos. 602-603 (2)	2.75	2.75
Nos. 687-688 (2)	2.00	1.25
Nos. 560-561 (2)	1.70	*2.35*
Nos. 629-630 (2)	1.35	1.35
Nos. 275-276 (2)	2.40	2.40
Nos. 460-461 (2)	1.05	1.05
Nos. 181-182 (2)	1.50	2.25
Nos. 602-603 (2)	2.50	2.50
Nos. 119-120 (2)	2.30	2.30
Nos. 567-568 (2)	1.00	1.00
Nos. 397-398 (2)	1.40	1.40
Nos. 348-349 (2)	1.10	1.30
Set total (26) Stamps	22.65	23.50

Queen Elizabeth II, 60th Birthday

Queen Elizabeth II & Prince Philip, 1947 Wedding Portrait — CD339

Designs: Photographs tracing the life of Queen Elizabeth II.

1986

Anguilla 674-677
Antigua 925-928
Barbuda 783-786
Dominica 950-953
Gambia 611-614
Grenada 1371-1374
Grenada Grenadines 749-752
Lesotho 531-534
Maldive Islands 1172-1175
Sierra Leone 760-763
Uganda 495-498

Nos. 674-677 (4)	8.00	8.00
Nos. 925-928 (4)	5.50	6.20
Nos. 783-786 (4)	23.15	23.15
Nos. 950-953 (4)	7.25	7.25
Nos. 611-614 (4)	8.25	7.90
Nos. 1371-1374 (4)	6.80	6.80
Nos. 749-752 (4)	6.75	6.75
Nos. 531-534 (4)	5.25	5.25
Nos. 1172-1175 (4)	6.25	6.25
Nos. 760-763 (4)	5.25	5.25
Nos. 495-498 (4)	8.50	8.50
Set total (44) Stamps	90.95	91.30

Royal Wedding, 1986

CD340

Designs: Photographs of Prince Andrew and Sarah Ferguson during courtship, engagement and marriage.

1986

Antigua 939-942
Barbuda 809-812
Dominica 970-973
Gambia 635-638
Grenada 1385-1388
Grenada Grenadines 758-761
Lesotho 545-548
Maldive Islands 1181-1184
Sierra Leone 769-772
Uganda 510-513

Nos. 939-942 (4)	7.00	*8.75*
Nos. 809-812 (4)	14.55	14.55
Nos. 970-973 (4)	7.25	7.25
Nos. 635-638 (4)	7.80	7.80
Nos. 1385-1388 (4)	8.30	8.30
Nos. 758-761 (4)	9.00	9.00
Nos. 545-548 (4)	7.45	7.45
Nos. 1181-1184 (4)	8.45	8.45
Nos. 769-772 (4)	5.35	5.35
Nos. 510-513 (4)	9.25	10.00
Set total (40) Stamps	84.40	86.90

Lloyds of London, 300th Anniv.

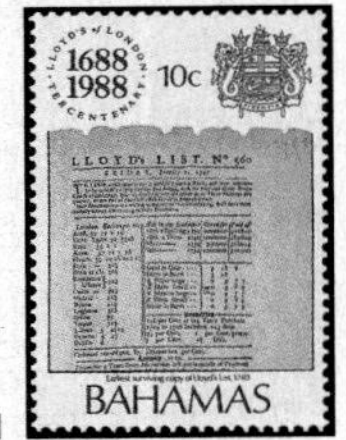

CD341

Designs: 17th century aspects of Lloyds, representations of each country's individual connections with Lloyds and publicized disasters insured by the organization.

1986

Ascension 454-457
Bahamas 655-658
Barbados 731-734
Bermuda 541-544
Falkland Islands 481-484
Liberia 1101-1104
Malawi 534-537
Nevis 571-574
St. Helena 501-504
St. Lucia 923-926
Seychelles 649-652
Zil Elwannyen Sesel 146-149
Solomon Islands 627-630
South Georgia 131-134
Trinidad & Tobago 484-487
Tristan da Cunha 439-442
Vanuatu 485-488

Nos. 454-457 (4)	5.00	5.00
Nos. 655-658 (4)	8.90	4.95
Nos. 731-734 (4)	12.50	8.35
Nos. 541-544 (4)	8.00	*6.60*
Nos. 481-484 (4)	5.45	3.85
Nos. 1101-1104 (4)	4.25	4.25
Nos. 534-537 (4)	11.00	7.85
Nos. 571-574 (4)	8.35	8.35
Nos. 501-504 (4)	8.70	7.15
Nos. 923-926 (4)	8.80	8.80
Nos. 649-652 (4)	12.85	12.85
Nos. 146-149 (4)	11.25	11.25
Nos. 627-630 (4)	7.00	4.45
Nos. 131-134 (4)	6.30	3.70
Nos. 484-487 (4)	10.25	6.35
Nos. 439-442 (4)	7.60	7.60
Nos. 485-488 (4)	5.90	5.90
Set total (68) Stamps	142.10	117.25

Moon Landing, 20th Anniv.

CD342

Designs: Equipment, crew photographs, spacecraft, official emblems and report profiles created for the Apollo Missions. Two stamps in each set are square in format rather than like the stamp shown; see individual country listings for more information.

1989

Ascension 468-472
Bahamas 674-678
Belize 916-920
Kiribati 517-521
Liberia 1125-1129
Nevis 586-590
St. Kitts 248-252
Samoa 760-764
Seychelles 676-680
Zil Elwannyen Sesel 154-158
Solomon Islands 643-647
Vanuatu 507-511

Nos. 468-472 (5)	9.40	8.60
Nos. 674-678 (5)	23.00	19.70
Nos. 916-920 (5)	22.85	18.10
Nos. 517-521 (5)	12.50	12.50
Nos. 1125-1129 (5)	8.50	8.50
Nos. 586-590 (5)	7.50	7.50

Nos. 248-252 (5)	8.00	8.25
Nos. 760-764 (5)	9.85	9.30
Nos. 676-680 (5)	16.05	16.05
Nos. 154-158 (5)	26.85	26.85
Nos. 643-647 (5)	9.00	6.75
Nos. 507-511 (5)	9.90	9.90
Set total (60) Stamps	163.40	152.00

Queen Mother, 90th Birthday

CD343

CD344

Designs: Portraits of Queen Elizabeth, the Queen Mother. See individual country listings for more information.

1990

Ascension....................491-492
Bahamas....................698-699
Barbados....................782-783
British Antarctic Territory....................170-171
British Indian Ocean Territory....................106-107
Cayman Islands....................622-623
Falkland Islands....................524-525
Kenya....................527-528
Kiribati....................555-556
Liberia....................1145-1146
Pitcairn Islands....................336-337
St. Helena....................532-533
St. Lucia....................969-970
Seychelles....................710-711
Zil Elwannyen Sesel....................171-172
Solomon Islands....................671-672
South Georgia....................143-144
Swaziland....................565-566
Tristan da Cunha....................480-481

Nos. 491-492 (2)	4.75	4.75
Nos. 698-699 (2)	5.25	5.25
Nos. 782-783 (2)	4.00	3.70
Nos. 170-171 (2)	6.00	6.00
Nos. 106-107 (2)	18.00	18.50
Nos. 622-623 (2)	4.00	*5.50*
Nos. 524-525 (2)	4.75	4.75
Nos. 527-528 (2)	7.00	7.00
Nos. 555-556 (2)	4.75	4.75
Nos. 1145-1146 (2)	3.25	3.25
Nos. 336-337 (2)	4.25	4.25
Nos. 532-533 (2)	5.25	5.25
Nos. 969-970 (2)	4.60	4.60
Nos. 710-711 (2)	6.60	6.60
Nos. 171-172 (2)	8.25	8.25
Nos. 671-672 (2)	5.00	*5.30*
Nos. 143-144 (2)	5.50	6.50
Nos. 565-566 (2)	4.10	4.10
Nos. 480-481 (2)	5.60	5.60
Set total (38) Stamps	110.90	113.90

Queen Elizabeth II, 65th Birthday, and Prince Philip, 70th Birthday

CD345

CD346

Designs: Portraits of Queen Elizabeth II and Prince Philip differ for each country. Printed in sheets of 10 + 5 labels (3 different) between. Stamps alternate, producing 5 different triptychs.

1991

Ascension....................506a
Bahamas....................731a
Belize....................970a
Bermuda....................618a
Kiribati....................572a
Mauritius....................734a
Pitcairn Islands....................349a
St. Helena....................555a
St. Kitts....................319a
Samoa....................791a
Seychelles....................724a
Zil Elwannyen Sesel....................178a
Solomon Islands....................689a
South Georgia....................150a
Swaziland....................587a
Vanuatu....................541a

No. 506a (1)	3.50	3.75
No. 731a (1)	4.00	4.00
No. 970a (1)	3.75	3.75
No. 618a (1)	3.50	*4.00*
No. 572a (1)	4.00	4.00
No. 734a (1)	4.00	4.00
No. 349a (1)	3.25	3.25
No. 555a (1)	2.75	2.75
No. 319a (1)	3.00	3.00
No. 791a (1)	3.75	3.75
No. 724a (1)	5.00	5.00
No. 178a (1)	6.25	6.25
No. 689a (1)	3.75	3.75
No. 150a (1)	4.75	7.00
No. 587a (1)	4.00	4.00
No. 541a (1)	2.50	2.50
Set total (16) Stamps	61.75	64.75

Royal Family Birthday, Anniversary

CD347

Queen Elizabeth II, 65th birthday, Charles and Diana, 10th wedding anniversary: Various photographs of Queen Elizabeth II, Prince Philip, Prince Charles, Princess Diana and their sons William and Henry.

1991

Antigua....................1446-1455
Barbuda....................1229-1238
Dominica....................1328-1337
Gambia....................1080-1089
Grenada....................2006-2015
Grenada Grenadines....................1331-1340
Guyana....................2440-2451
Lesotho....................871-875
Maldive Islands....................1533-1542
Nevis....................666-675
St. Vincent....................1485-1494
St. Vincent Grenadines....................769-778
Sierra Leone....................1387-1396
Turks & Caicos Islands....................913-922
Uganda....................918-927

Nos. 1446-1455 (10)	21.70	20.05
Nos. 1229-1238 (10)	125.00	119.50
Nos. 1328-1337 (10)	30.20	30.20
Nos. 1080-1089 (10)	24.65	24.40
Nos. 2006-2015 (10)	25.45	22.10
Nos. 1331-1340 (10)	23.85	23.35
Nos. 2440-2451 (12)	21.40	21.15
Nos. 871-875 (5)	13.55	13.55
Nos. 1533-1542 (10)	28.10	28.10
Nos. 666-675 (10)	23.65	23.65
Nos. 1485-1494 (10)	26.75	25.90
Nos. 769-778 (10)	25.40	25.40
Nos. 1387-1396 (10)	26.35	26.35
Nos. 913-922 (10)	27.50	25.30
Nos. 918-927 (10)	26.60	26.60
Set total (147) Stamps	470.15	455.60

Queen Elizabeth II's Accession to the Throne, 40th Anniv.

CD348

Various photographs of Queen Elizabeth II with local Scenes.

1992

Antigua....................1513-1518
Barbuda....................1306-1311
Dominica....................1414-1419
Gambia....................1172-1177
Grenada....................2047-2052
Grenada Grenadines....................1368-1373
Lesotho....................881-885
Maldive Islands....................1637-1642
Nevis....................702-707
St. Vincent....................1582-1587
St. Vincent Grenadines....................829-834
Sierra Leone....................1482-1487
Turks and Caicos Islands....................978-987
Uganda....................990-995
Virgin Islands....................742-746

Nos. 1513-1518 (6)	15.00	*15.10*
Nos. 1306-1311 (6)	125.25	83.65
Nos. 1414-1419 (6)	12.50	12.50
Nos. 1172-1177 (6)	14.95	14.85
Nos. 2047-2052 (6)	15.95	15.95
Nos. 1368-1373 (6)	17.00	15.35
Nos. 881-885 (5)	11.90	11.90
Nos. 1637-1642 (6)	17.55	17.55
Nos. 702-707 (6)	13.55	13.55
Nos. 1582-1587 (6)	14.40	14.40
Nos. 829-834 (6)	19.65	19.65
Nos. 1482-1487 (6)	22.50	22.50
Nos. 913-922 (10)	27.50	25.30
Nos. 990-995 (6)	19.50	19.50
Nos. 742-746 (5)	15.50	15.50
Set total (92) Stamps	362.70	317.25

CD349

1992

Ascension....................531-535
Bahamas....................744-748
Bermuda....................623-627
British Indian Ocean Territory....................119-123
Cayman Islands....................648-652
Falkland Islands....................549-553
Gibraltar....................605-609
Hong Kong....................619-623
Kenya....................563-567
Kiribati....................582-586
Pitcairn Islands....................362-366
St. Helena....................570-574
St. Kitts....................332-336
Samoa....................805-809
Seychelles....................734-738
Zil Elwannyen Sesel....................183-187
Solomon Islands....................708-712
South Georgia....................157-161
Tristan da Cunha....................508-512
Vanuatu....................555-559
Zambia....................561-565

Nos. 531-535 (5)	6.10	6.10
Nos. 744-748 (5)	6.90	4.70
Nos. 623-627 (5)	7.40	*7.55*
Nos. 119-123 (5)	22.75	19.25
Nos. 648-652 (5)	7.60	6.60
Nos. 549-553 (5)	5.95	5.90
Nos. 605-609 (5)	5.15	*5.50*
Nos. 619-623 (5)	5.10	5.25
Nos. 563-567 (5)	9.10	9.10
Nos. 582-586 (5)	3.85	3.85
Nos. 362-366 (5)	5.35	5.35
Nos. 570-574 (5)	5.70	5.70
Nos. 332-336 (5)	6.60	5.50
Nos. 805-809 (5)	7.85	5.90
Nos. 734-738 (5)	10.55	10.55
Nos. 183-187 (5)	9.40	9.40
Nos. 708-712 (5)	5.00	5.30
Nos. 157-161 (5)	5.60	5.90
Nos. 508-512 (5)	8.75	8.30
Nos. 555-559 (5)	3.65	3.65
Nos. 561-565 (5)	5.60	5.60
Set total (105) Stamps	153.95	144.95

Royal Air Force, 75th Anniversary

CD350

1993

Ascension....................557-561
Bahamas....................771-775
Barbados....................842-846
Belize....................1003-1008
Bermuda....................648-651
British Indian Ocean Territory....................136-140
Falkland Is....................573-577
Fiji....................687-691
Montserrat....................830-834
St. Kitts....................351-355

Nos. 557-561 (5)	15.60	14.60
Nos. 771-775 (5)	24.65	21.45
Nos. 842-846 (5)	14.15	12.85
Nos. 1003-1008 (6)	16.55	16.50
Nos. 648-651 (4)	9.65	*10.45*
Nos. 136-140 (5)	16.10	16.10
Nos. 573-577 (5)	10.85	10.85
Nos. 687-691 (5)	17.75	17.40
Nos. 830-834 (5)	14.10	14.10
Nos. 351-355 (5)	22.80	23.55
Set total (50) Stamps	162.20	157.85

Royal Air Force, 80th Anniv.

Design CD350 Re-inscribed

1998

Ascension....................697-701
Bahamas....................907-911
British Indian Ocean Terr....................198-202
Cayman Islands....................754-758
Fiji....................814-818
Gibraltar....................755-759
Samoa....................957-961
Turks & Caicos Islands....................1258-1265
Tuvalu....................763-767
Virgin Islands.................... 879-883

Nos. 697-701 (5)	16.10	16.10
Nos. 907-911 (5)	13.60	12.65
Nos. 136-140 (5)	16.10	16.10
Nos. 754-758 (5)	15.25	15.25
Nos. 814-818 (5)	14.00	12.75
Nos. 755-759 (5)	9.70	9.70
Nos. 957-961 (5)	15.70	14.90
Nos. 1258-1265 (2)	27.50	27.50
Nos. 763-767 (5)	9.75	9.75
Nos. 879-883 (5)	15.00	15.00
Set total (47) Stamps	152.70	149.70

End of World War II, 50th Anniv.

CD351

CD352

1995

Ascension....................613-617
Bahamas....................824-828
Barbados....................891-895
Belize....................1047-1050
British Indian Ocean Territory....................163-167
Cayman Islands....................704-708
Falkland Islands....................634-638
Fiji....................720-724
Kiribati....................662-668
Liberia....................1175-1179
Mauritius....................803-805
St. Helena....................646-654
St. Kitts....................389-393
St. Lucia....................1018-1022
Samoa....................890-894
Solomon Islands....................799-803
South Georgia....................198-200
Tristan da Cunha....................562-566

Nos. 613-617 (5)	21.50	21.50

Nos. 824-828 (5)	22.00	18.70
Nos. 891-895 (5)	14.20	11.90
Nos. 1047-1050 (4)	6.05	5.90
Nos. 163-167 (5)	16.25	16.25
Nos. 704-708 (5)	17.65	13.95
Nos. 634-638 (5)	18.65	17.15
Nos. 720-724 (5)	17.50	14.50
Nos. 662-668 (7)	16.30	16.30
Nos. 1175-1179 (5)	15.25	11.15
Nos. 803-805 (3)	7.50	7.50
Nos. 646-654 (9)	26.10	26.10
Nos. 389-393 (5)	16.40	16.40
Nos. 1018-1022 (5)	12.25	10.15
Nos. 890-894 (5)	15.25	14.50
Nos. 799-803 (5)	14.75	14.75
Nos. 198-200 (3)	14.50	15.50
Nos. 562-566 (5)	20.10	20.10
Set total (91) Stamps	292.20	272.30

UN, 50th Anniv.

CD353

1995

Bahamas 839-842
Barbados 901-904
Belize 1055-1058
Jamaica 847-851
Liberia 1187-1190
Mauritius 813-816
Pitcairn Islands 436-439
St. Kitts 398-401
St. Lucia 1023-1026
Samoa 900-903
Tristan da Cunha 568-571
Virgin Islands 807-810

Nos. 839-842 (4)	7.15	6.40
Nos. 901-904 (4)	7.00	5.75
Nos. 1055-1058 (4)	4.70	4.70
Nos. 847-851 (5)	5.40	5.45
Nos. 1187-1190 (4)	9.65	9.65
Nos. 813-816 (4)	4.55	4.55
Nos. 436-439 (4)	8.15	8.15
Nos. 398-401 (4)	6.15	7.15
Nos. 1023-1026 (4)	7.50	7.25
Nos. 900-903 (4)	9.35	8.20
Nos. 568-571 (4)	13.50	13.50
Nos. 807-810 (4)	7.45	7.45
Set total (49) Stamps	90.55	88.20

Queen Elizabeth, 70th Birthday

CD354

1996

Ascension 632-635
British Antarctic Territory 240-243
British Indian Ocean Territory 176-180
Falkland Islands 653-657
Pitcairn Islands 446-449
St. Helena 672-676
Samoa 912-916
Tokelau 223-227
Tristan da Cunha 576-579
Virgin Islands 824-828

Nos. 632-635 (4)	5.30	5.30
Nos. 240-243 (4)	9.45	8.15
Nos. 176-180 (5)	11.50	11.50
Nos. 653-657 (5)	13.55	11.20
Nos. 446-449 (4)	8.60	8.60
Nos. 672-676 (5)	12.45	12.70
Nos. 912-916 (5)	10.50	10.50
Nos. 223-227 (5)	10.50	10.50
Nos. 576-579 (4)	8.35	8.35
Nos. 824-828 (5)	11.30	11.30
Set total (46) Stamps	101.50	98.10

Diana, Princess of Wales (1961-97)

CD355

1998

Ascension 696
Bahamas 901A-902
Barbados 950
Belize 1091
Bermuda 753
Botswana 659-663
British Antarctic Territory 258
British Indian Ocean Terr. 197
Cayman Islands 752A-753
Falkland Islands 694
Fiji 819-820
Gibraltar 754
Kiribati 719A-720
Namibia 909
Niue 706
Norfolk Island 644-645
Papua New Guinea 937
Pitcairn Islands 487
St. Helena 711
St. Kitts 437A-438
Samoa 955A-956
Seycelles 802
Solomon Islands 866-867
South Georgia 220
Tokelau 252B-253
Tonga 980
  Niuafo'ou 201
Tristan da Cunha 618
Tuvalu 762
Vanuatu 718A-719
Virgin Islands 878

No. 696 (1)	5.25	5.25
Nos. 901A-902 (2)	5.30	5.30
No. 950 (1)	6.25	6.25
No. 1091 (1)	5.00	5.00
No. 753 (1)	5.00	5.00
Nos. 659-663 (5)	8.25	8.80
No. 258 (1)	5.50	5.50
No. 197 (1)	5.50	5.50
Nos. 752A-753 (3)	7.40	7.40
No. 694 (1)	5.00	5.00
Nos. 819-820 (2)	5.25	5.25
No. 754 (1)	4.75	4.75
Nos. 719A-720 (2)	4.85	4.85
No. 909 (1)	1.75	1.75
No. 706 (1)	5.50	5.50
Nos. 644-645 (2)	5.60	5.60
No. 937 (1)	6.25	6.25
No. 487 (1)	4.75	4.75
No. 711 (1)	4.25	4.25
Nos. 437A-438 (2)	5.15	5.15
Nos. 955A-956 (2)	7.00	7.00
No. 802 (1)	6.25	6.25
Nos. 866-867 (2)	5.40	5.40
No. 220 (1)	4.50	5.00
Nos. 252B-253 (2)	6.00	6.00
No. 980 (1)	5.75	5.75
No. 201 (1)	6.50	6.50
No. 618 (1)	5.00	5.00
No. 762 (1)	4.00	4.00
Nos. 718A-719 (2)	8.00	8.00
No. 878 (1)	4.50	4.50
Set total (46) Stamps	169.45	170.50

Wedding of Prince Edward and Sophie Rhys-Jones

CD356

1999

Ascension 729-730
Cayman Islands 775-776
Falkland Islands 729-730
Pitcairn Islands 505-506
St. Helena 733-734
Samoa 971-972
Tristan da Cunha 636-637
Virgin Islands 908-909

Nos. 729-730 (2)	4.50	4.50
Nos. 775-776 (2)	4.95	4.95
Nos. 729-730 (2)	14.00	14.00
Nos. 505-506 (2)	7.00	7.00
Nos. 733-734 (2)	5.00	5.00
Nos. 971-972 (2)	5.00	5.00
Nos. 636-637 (2)	7.50	7.50
Nos. 908-909 (2)	7.50	7.50
Set total (16) Stamps	55.45	55.45

1st Manned Moon Landing, 30th Anniv.

CD357

1999

Ascension 731-735
Bahamas 942-946
Barbados 967-971
Bermuda 778
Cayman Islands 777-781
Fiji 853-857
Jamaica 889-893
Kirbati 746-750
Nauru 465-469
St. Kitts 460-464
Samoa 973-977
Solomon Islands 875-879
Tuvalu 800-804
Virgin Islands 910-914

Nos. 731-735 (5)	12.80	12.80
Nos. 942-946 (5)	14.10	14.10
Nos. 967-971 (5)	9.45	8.25
No. 778 (1)	9.00	9.00
Nos. 777-781 (5)	9.25	9.25
Nos. 853-857 (5)	9.25	8.45
Nos. 889-893 (5)	8.30	7.18
Nos. 746-750 (5)	8.85	8.85
Nos. 465-469 (5)	9.25	8.00
Nos. 460-464 (5)	11.35	11.65
Nos. 973-977 (5)	12.60	12.45
Nos. 875-879 (5)	7.50	7.50
Nos. 800-804 (5)	7.45	7.45
Nos. 910-914 (5)	11.75	11.75
Set total (66) Stamps	140.90	136.68

Queen Mother's Century

CD358

1999

Ascension 736-740
Bahamas 951-955
Cayman Islands 782-786
Falkland Islands 734-738
Fiji 858-862
Norfolk Island 688-692
St. Helena 740-744
Samoa 978-982
Solomon Islands 880-884
South Georgia 231-235
Tristan da Cunha 638-642
Tuvalu 805-809

Nos. 736-740 (5)	15.50	15.50
Nos. 951-955 (5)	13.75	12.65
Nos. 782-786 (5)	8.35	8.35
Nos. 734-738 (5)	30.00	28.25
Nos. 858-862 (5)	12.80	13.25
Nos. 688-692 (5)	9.50	9.50
Nos. 740-744 (5)	16.15	16.15
Nos. 978-982 (5)	12.50	12.10
Nos. 880-884 (5)	7.50	7.00
Nos. 231-235 (5)	29.75	30.00
Nos. 638-642 (5)	18.00	18.00
Nos. 805-809 (5)	8.65	8.65
Set total (60) Stamps	182.45	179.40

Prince William, 18th Birthday

CD359

2000

Ascension 755-759
Cayman Islands 797-801
Falkland Islands 762-766
Fiji 889-893
South Georgia 257-261
Tristan da Cunha 664-668
Virgin Islands 925-929

Nos. 755-759 (5)	15.50	15.50
Nos. 797-801 (5)	11.15	10.90
Nos. 762-766 (5)	24.60	22.50
Nos. 889-893 (5)	12.90	12.90
Nos. 257-261 (5)	29.00	28.75
Nos. 664-668 (5)	21.50	21.50
Nos. 925-929 (5)	14.50	14.50
Set total (35) Stamps	129.15	126.55

Reign of Queen Elizabeth II, 50th Anniv.

CD360

2002

Ascension 790-794
Bahamas 1033-1037
Barbados 1019-1023
Belize 1152-1156
Bermuda 822-826
British Antarctic Territory 307-311
British Indian Ocean Territory 239-243
Cayman Islands 844-848
Falkland Islands 804-808
Gibraltar 896-900
Jamaica 952-956
Nauru 491-495
Norfolk Island 758-762
Papua New Guinea 1019-1023
Pitcairn Islands 552
St. Helena 788-792
St. Lucia 1146-1150
Solomon Islands 931-935
South Georgia 274-278
Swaziland 706-710
Tokelau 302-306
Tonga 1059
  Niuafo'ou 239
Tristan da Cunha 706-710
Virgin Islands 967-971

Nos. 790-794 (5)	14.10	14.10
Nos. 1033-1037 (5)	15.25	15.25
Nos. 1019-1023 (5)	12.90	12.90
Nos. 1152-1156 (5)	12.65	12.25
Nos. 822-826 (5)	18.00	18.00
Nos. 307-311 (5)	23.00	23.00
Nos. 239-243 (5)	19.40	19.40
Nos. 844-848 (5)	13.25	13.25
Nos. 804-808 (5)	23.00	22.00
Nos. 896-900 (5)	6.65	6.65
Nos. 952-956 (5)	16.65	16.65
Nos. 491-495 (5)	17.75	17.75
Nos. 758-762 (5)	15.90	15.90
Nos. 1019-1023 (5)	14.50	14.50
No. 552 (1)	9.25	9.25
Nos. 788-792 (5)	19.75	19.75
Nos. 1146-1150 (5)	12.25	12.25
Nos. 931-935 (5)	12.40	12.40
Nos. 274-278 (5)	28.00	28.50
Nos. 706-710 (5)	12.50	12.50
Nos. 302-306 (5)	14.50	14.50
No. 1059 (1)	8.50	8.50
No. 239 (1)	8.75	8.75
Nos. 706-710 (5)	18.50	18.50
Nos. 967-971 (5)	16.50	16.50
Set total (113) Stamps	383.90	383.00

Queen Mother Elizabeth (1900-2002)

CD361

2002

Ascension 799-801
Bahamas 1044-1046
Bermuda.................................834-836
British Antarctic Territory..........312-314
British Indian Ocean Territory 245-247
Cayman Islands.......................857-861
Falkland Islands 812-816
Nauru.....................................499-501
Pitcairn Islands........................561-565
St. Helena 808-812
St. Lucia 1155-1159
Seychelles 830
Solomon Islands......................945-947
South Georgia 281-285
Tokelau 312-314
Tristan da Cunha.....................715-717
Virgin Islands..........................979-983

Nos. 799-801 (3)	8.85	8.85
Nos. 1044-1046 (3)	9.10	9.10
Nos. 834-836 (3)	12.25	12.25
Nos. 312-314 (3)	18.75	18.75
Nos. 245-247 (3)	17.35	17.35
Nos. 857-861 (5)	15.00	15.00
Nos. 812-816 (5)	28.50	28.50
Nos. 499-501 (3)	14.00	14.00
Nos. 561-565 (5)	15.25	15.25
Nos. 808-812 (5)	12.00	12.00
Nos. 1155-1159 (5)	12.00	12.00
No. 830 (1)	6.50	6.50
Nos. 945-947 (3)	9.25	9.25
Nos. 281-285 (5)	19.50	19.50
Nos. 312-314 (3)	11.85	11.85
Nos. 715-717 (3)	16.25	16.25
Nos. 979-983 (5)	23.50	23.50
Set total (63) Stamps	249.90	249.90

Head of Queen Elizabeth II

CD362

2003

Ascension 822
Bermuda..865
British Antarctic Territory.................322
British Indian Ocean Territory 261
Cayman Islands...............................878
Falkland Islands 828
St. Helena 820
South Georgia 294
Tristan da Cunha.............................731
Virgin Islands................................1003

No. 822 (1)	12.50	12.50
No. 865 (1)	50.00	50.00
No. 322 (1)	9.50	9.50
No. 261 (1)	11.00	11.00
No. 878 (1)	14.00	14.00
No. 828 (1)	9.00	9.00
No. 820 (1)	9.00	9.00
No. 294 (1)	8.50	8.50
No. 731 (1)	10.00	10.00
No. 1003 (1)	10.00	10.00
Set total (10) Stamps	143.50	143.50

Coronation of Queen Elizabeth II, 50th Anniv.

CD363

2003

Ascension 823-825
Bahamas 1073-1075
Bermuda.................................866-868
British Antarctic Territory..........323-325
British Indian Ocean Territory 262-264
Cayman Islands.......................879-881
Jamaica 970-972
Kiribati 825-827
Pitcairn Islands........................577-581
St. Helena 821-823
St. Lucia 1171-1173
Tokelau 320-322
Tristan da Cunha.....................732-734
Virgin Islands.......................1004-1006

Nos. 823-825 (3)	12.50	12.50
Nos. 1073-1075 (3)	13.00	13.00
Nos. 866-868 (2)	14.25	14.25
Nos. 323-325 (3)	23.00	23.00
Nos. 262-264 (3)	28.00	28.00
Nos. 879-881 (3)	19.25	19.25
Nos. 970-972 (3)	10.00	10.00
Nos. 825-827 (3)	13.50	13.50
Nos. 577-581 (5)	14.40	14.40
Nos. 821-823 (3)	7.25	7.25
Nos. 1171-1173 (3)	8.75	8.75
Nos. 320-322 (3)	17.25	17.25
Nos. 732-734 (3)	16.75	16.75
Nos. 1004-1006 (3)	25.00	25.00
Set total (43) Stamps	222.90	222.90

Prince William, 21st Birthday

CD364

2003

Ascension 826
British Indian Ocean Territory 265
Cayman Islands.......................882-884
Falkland Islands 829
South Georgia 295
Tokelau 323
Tristan da Cunha.............................735
Virgin Islands.......................1007-1009

No. 826 (1)	7.25	7.25
No. 265 (1)	8.00	8.00
Nos. 882-884 (3)	6.95	6.95
No. 829 (1)	13.50	13.50
No. 295 (1)	8.50	8.50
No. 323 (1)	7.25	7.25
No. 735 (1)	6.00	6.00
Nos. 1007-1009 (3)	10.00	10.00
Set total (12) Stamps	67.45	67.45

British Commonwealth of Nations

Dominions, Colonies, Territories, Offices and Independent Members

Comprising stamps of the British Commonwealth and associated nations.

A strict observance of technicalities would bar some or all of the stamps listed under Burma, Ireland, Kuwait, Nepal, New Republic, Orange Free State, Samoa, South Africa, South-West Africa, Stellaland, Sudan, Swaziland, the two Transvaal Republics and others but these are included for the convenience of collectors.

1. Great Britain

Great Britain: Including England, Scotland, Wales and Northern Ireland.

2. The Dominions, Present and Past

AUSTRALIA

The Commonwealth of Australia was proclaimed on Jan. 1, 1901. It consists of six former colonies as follows:

New South Wales
Queensland
South Australia
Victoria
Tasmania
Western Australia

The following islands and territories are, or have been, administered by Australia: Australian Antarctic Territory, Christmas Island, Cocos (Keeling) Islands, Nauru, New Guinea, Norfolk Island, Papua.

CANADA

The Dominion of Canada was created by the British North America Act in 1867. The following provinces were former separate colonies and issued postage stamps:

British Columbia and Vancouver Island
New Brunswick
Newfoundland
Nova Scotia
Prince Edward Island

FIJI

The colony of Fiji became an independent nation with dominion status on Oct. 10, 1970.

GHANA

This state came into existence March 6, 1957, with dominion status. It consists of the former colony of the Gold Coast and the Trusteeship Territory of Togoland. Ghana became a republic July 1, 1960.

INDIA

The Republic of India was inaugurated on Jan. 26, 1950. It succeeded the Dominion of India which was proclaimed Aug. 15, 1947, when the former Empire of India was divided into Pakistan and the Union of India. The Republic is composed of about 40 predominantly Hindu states of three classes: governor's provinces, chief commissioner's provinces and princely states. India also has various territories, such as the Andaman and Nicobar Islands.

The old Empire of India was a federation of British India and the native states. The more important princely states were autonomous. Of the more than 700 Indian states, these 43 are familiar names to philatelists because of their postage stamps.

CONVENTION STATES

Chamba
Faridkot
Gwalior
Jhind
Nabha
Patiala

FEUDATORY STATES

Alwar
Bahawalpur
Bamra
Barwani
Bhopal
Bhor
Bijawar
Bundi
Bussahir
Charkhari
Cochin
Dhar
Dungarpur
Duttia
Faridkot (1879-85)
Hyderabad
Idar
Indore
Jaipur
Jammu
Jammu and Kashmir
Jasdan
Jhalawar
Jhind (1875-76)
Kashmir
Kishangarh
Kotah
Las Bela
Morvi
Nandgaon
Nowanuggur
Orchha
Poonch
Rajasthan
Rajpeepla
Sirmur
Soruth
Tonk
Travancore
Wadhwan

NEW ZEALAND

Became a dominion on Sept. 26, 1907. The following islands and territories are, or have been, administered by New Zealand:

Aitutaki
Cook Islands (Rarotonga)
Niue
Penrhyn
Ross Dependency
Samoa (Western Samoa)
Tokelau Islands

PAKISTAN

The Republic of Pakistan was proclaimed March 23, 1956. It succeeded the Dominion which was proclaimed Aug. 15, 1947. It is made up of all or part of several Moslem provinces and various districts of the former Empire of India, including Bahawalpur and Las Bela. Pakistan withdrew from the Commonwealth in 1972.

SOUTH AFRICA

Under the terms of the South African Act (1909) the self-governing colonies of Cape of Good Hope, Natal, Orange River Colony and Transvaal united on May 31, 1910, to form the Union of South Africa. It became an independent republic May 3, 1961.

Under the terms of the Treaty of Versailles, South-West Africa, formerly German South-West Africa, was mandated to the Union of South Africa.

SRI LANKA (CEYLON)

The Dominion of Ceylon was proclaimed Feb. 4, 1948. The island had been a Crown Colony from 1802 until then. On May 22, 1972, Ceylon became the Republic of Sri Lanka.

3. Colonies, Past and Present; Controlled Territory and Independent Members of the Commonwealth

Abu Dhabi
Aden
Aitutaki
Alderney
Anguilla
Antigua
Ascension
Australia
Bahamas
Bahrain
Bangladesh
Barbados
Barbuda
Basutoland
Batum
Bechuanaland
Bechuanaland Prot.
Belize
Bermuda
Botswana
British Antarctic Territory
British Central Africa
British Columbia and Vancouver Island

British East Africa
British Guiana
British Honduras
British Indian Ocean Territory
British New Guinea
British Solomon Islands
British Somaliland
Brunei
Burma
Bushire
Cameroons
Canada
Cape of Good Hope
Cayman Islands
Christmas Island
Cocos (Keeling) Islands
Cook Islands
Crete,
  British Administration
Cyprus
Dominica
East Africa & Uganda
  Protectorates
Egypt
Falkland Islands
Fiji
Gambia
German East Africa
Ghana
Gibraltar
Gilbert Islands
Gilbert & Ellice Islands
Gold Coast
Grenada
Griqualand West
Guernsey
Guyana
Heligoland
Hong Kong
Indian Native States
  (see India)
Ionian Islands
Jamaica
Jersey
Jordan
Kenya
Kenya, Uganda & Tanzania
Kiribati
Kuwait
Labuan
Lagos
Leeward Islands
Lesotho
Madagascar
Malawi
Malaya
  Federated Malay States
  Johore
  Kedah
  Kelantan
  Malacca
  Negri Sembilan
  Pahang
  Penang
  Perak
  Perlis
  Selangor
  Singapore
  Sungei Ujong
  Trengganu
Malaysia
Maldive Islands
Malta
Man, Isle of
Mauritius
Mesopotamia
Montserrat
Mozambique
Muscat
Namibia
Natal
Nauru
Nevis
New Britain
New Brunswick
Newfoundland
New Guinea
New Hebrides
New Republic
New South Wales
New Zealand
Niger Coast Protectorate
Nigeria
Niue
Norfolk Island
North Borneo
Northern Nigeria
Northern Rhodesia
North West Pacific Islands
Nova Scotia
Nyasaland Protectorate
Oman
Orange River Colony
Pakistan
Palestine
Papua New Guinea
Penrhyn Island
Pitcairn Islands
Prince Edward Island
Qatar
Queensland
Rhodesia
Rhodesia & Nyasaland
Ross Dependency
Rwanda
Sabah
St. Christopher
St. Helena
St. Kitts
St. Kitts-Nevis-Anguilla
St. Lucia
St. Vincent
Samoa
Sarawak
Seychelles
Sierra Leone
Singapore
Solomon Islands
Somaliland Protectorate
South Africa
South Arabia
South Australia
South Georgia
Southern Nigeria
Southern Rhodesia
South-West Africa
Sri Lanka
Stellaland
Straits Settlements
Sudan
Swaziland
Tanganyika
Tanzania
Tasmania
Tobago
Togo
Tokelau Islands
Tonga
Transvaal
Trinidad
Trinidad and Tobago
Tristan da Cunha
Trucial States
Turks and Caicos
Turks Islands
Tuvalu
Uganda
United Arab Emirates
Vanuatu
Victoria
Virgin Islands
Western Australia
Zambia
Zanzibar
Zimbabwe
Zululand

POST OFFICES IN FOREIGN COUNTRIES

Africa
  East Africa Forces
  Middle East Forces
Bangkok
China
Morocco
Turkish Empire

Colonies, former colonies, offices, territories controlled by parent states

Belgium

Belgian Congo
Ruanda-Urundi

Denmark

Danish West Indies
Faroe Islands
Greenland
Iceland

Finland

Aland Islands

France

COLONIES PAST AND PRESENT, CONTROLLED TERRITORIES

Afars & Issas, Territory of
Alaouites
Alexandretta
Algeria
Alsace & Lorraine
Anjouan
Annam & Tonkin
Benin
Cambodia (Khmer)
Cameroun
Castellorizo
Chad
Cilicia
Cochin China
Comoro Islands
Dahomey
Diego Suarez
Djibouti (Somali Coast)
Fezzan
French Congo
French Equatorial Africa
French Guiana
French Guinea
French India
French Morocco
French Polynesia (Oceania)
French Southern & Antarctic Territories
French Sudan
French West Africa
Gabon
Germany
Ghadames
Grand Comoro
Guadeloupe
Indo-China
Inini
Ivory Coast
Laos
Latakia
Lebanon
Madagascar
Martinique
Mauritania
Mayotte
Memel
Middle Congo
Moheli
New Caledonia
New Hebrides
Niger Territory
Nossi-Be
Obock
Reunion
Rouad, Ile
Ste.-Marie de Madagascar
St. Pierre & Miquelon
Senegal
Senegambia & Niger
Somali Coast
Syria
Tahiti
Togo
Tunisia
Ubangi-Shari
Upper Senegal & Niger
Upper Volta
Viet Nam
Wallis & Futuna Islands

POST OFFICES IN FOREIGN COUNTRIES

China
Crete
Egypt
Turkish Empire
Zanzibar

Germany

EARLY STATES

Baden
Bavaria
Bergedorf
Bremen
Brunswick
Hamburg
Hanover
Lubeck
Mecklenburg-Schwerin
Mecklenburg-Strelitz
Oldenburg
Prussia
Saxony
Schleswig-Holstein
Wurttemberg

FORMER COLONIES

Cameroun (Kamerun)
Caroline Islands
German East Africa
German New Guinea
German South-West Africa
Kiauchau
Mariana Islands
Marshall Islands
Samoa
Togo

Italy

EARLY STATES

Modena
Parma
Romagna
Roman States
Sardinia
Tuscany
Two Sicilies
Naples
Neapolitan Provinces
Sicily

FORMER COLONIES, CONTROLLED TERRITORIES, OCCUPATION AREAS

Aegean Islands
Calimno (Calino)
Caso
Cos (Coo)
Karki (Carchi)
Leros (Lero)
Lipso
Nisiros (Nisiro)
Patmos (Patmo)
Piscopi
Rodi (Rhodes)
Scarpanto
Simi
Stampalia
Castellorizo
Corfu
Cyrenaica
Eritrea
Ethiopia (Abyssinia)
Fiume
Ionian Islands
Cephalonia
Ithaca
Paxos
Italian East Africa
Libya
Oltre Giuba
Saseno
Somalia (Italian Somaliland)
Tripolitania

POST OFFICES IN FOREIGN COUNTRIES

"ESTERO"*
Austria
China
Peking
Tientsin
Crete
Tripoli
Turkish Empire
Constantinople
Durazzo
Janina
Jerusalem
Salonika
Scutari
Smyrna
Valona

**Stamps overprinted "ESTERO" were used in various parts of the world.*

Netherlands

Aruba
Caribbean Netherlands
Curacao
Netherlands Antilles (Curacao)
Netherlands Indies
Netherlands New Guinea
St. Martin
Surinam (Dutch Guiana)

Portugal

COLONIES PAST AND PRESENT, CONTROLLED TERRITORIES

Angola
Angra
Azores
Cape Verde
Funchal
Horta
Inhambane
Kionga
Lourenco Marques
Macao
Madeira
Mozambique
Mozambique Co.
Nyassa
Ponta Delgada
Portuguese Africa
Portuguese Congo
Portuguese Guinea
Portuguese India
Quelimane
St. Thomas & Prince Islands
Tete
Timor
Zambezia

Russia

ALLIED TERRITORIES AND REPUBLICS, OCCUPATION AREAS

Armenia
Aunus (Olonets)
Azerbaijan
Batum
Estonia
Far Eastern Republic
Georgia
Karelia
Latvia
Lithuania
North Ingermanland
Ostland
Russian Turkestan
Siberia
South Russia
Tannu Tuva
Transcaucasian Fed. Republics
Ukraine
Wenden (Livonia)
Western Ukraine

Spain

COLONIES PAST AND PRESENT, CONTROLLED TERRITORIES

Aguera, La
Cape Juby
Cuba
Elobey, Annobon & Corisco
Fernando Po
Ifni
Mariana Islands
Philippines
Puerto Rico
Rio de Oro
Rio Muni
Spanish Guinea
Spanish Morocco
Spanish Sahara
Spanish West Africa

POST OFFICES IN FOREIGN COUNTRIES

Morocco
Tangier
Tetuan

Dies of British colonial stamps

DIE A:

1. The lines in the groundwork vary in thickness and are not uniformly straight.

2. The seventh and eighth lines from the top, in the groundwork, converge where they meet the head.

3. There is a small dash in the upper part of the second jewel in the band of the crown.

4. The vertical color line in front of the throat stops at the sixth line of shading on the neck.

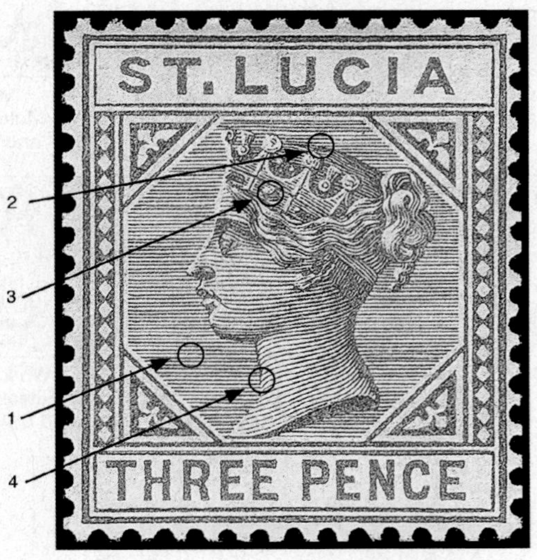

DIE B:

1. The lines in the groundwork are all thin and straight.

2. All the lines of the background are parallel.

3. There is no dash in the upper part of the second jewel in the band of the crown.

4. The vertical color line in front of the throat stops at the eighth line of shading on the neck.

DIE I:

1. The base of the crown is well below the level of the inner white line around the vignette.

2. The labels inscribed "POSTAGE" and "REVENUE" are cut square at the top.

3. There is a white "bud" on the outer side of the main stem of the curved ornaments in each lower corner.

4. The second (thick) line below the country name has the ends next to the crown cut diagonally.

DIE Ia.	DIE Ib.
1 as die II.	1 and 3 as die II.
2 and 3 as die I.	2 as die I.

DIE II:

1. The base of the crown is aligned with the underside of the white line around the vignette.

2. The labels curve inward at the top inner corners.

3. The "bud" has been removed from the outer curve of the ornaments in each corner.

4. The second line below the country name has the ends next to the crown cut vertically.

Wmk. 1
Crown and C C

Wmk. 2
Crown and C A

Wmk. 3
Multiple Crown and C A

Wmk. 4
Multiple Crown and Script C A

Wmk. 4a

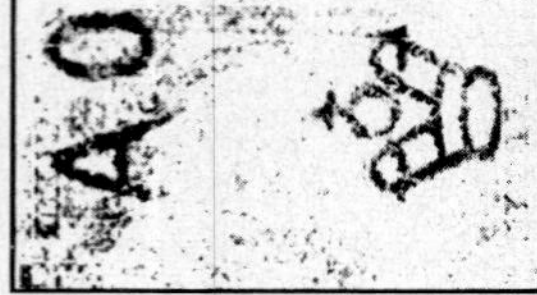
Wmk. 46

Wmk. 314
St. Edward's Crown and C A Multiple

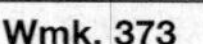
Wmk. 373

Wmk. 384

Wmk. 406

British Colonial and Crown Agents watermarks

Watermarks 1 to 4, 314, 373, 384 and 406, common to many British territories, are illustrated here to avoid duplication.

The letters "CC" of Wmk. 1 identify the paper as having been made for the use of the Crown Colonies, while the letters "CA" of the others stand for "Crown Agents." Both Wmks. 1 and 2 were used on stamps printed by De La Rue & Co.

Wmk. 3 was adopted in 1904; Wmk. 4 in 1921; Wmk. 46 in 1879; Wmk. 314 in 1957; Wmk. 373 in 1974; Wmk. 384 in 1985; Wmk 406 in 2008.

In Wmk. 4a, a non-matching crown of the general St. Edwards type (bulging on both sides at top) was substituted for one of the Wmk. 4 crowns which fell off the dandy roll. The non-matching crown occurs in 1950-52 printings in a horizontal row of crowns on certain regular stamps of Johore and Seychelles, and on various postage due stamps of Barbados, Basutoland, British Guiana, Gold Coast, Grenada, Northern Rhodesia, St. Lucia, Swaziland and Trinidad and Tobago. A variation of Wmk. 4a, with the non-matching crown in a horizontal row of crown-CA-crown, occurs on regular stamps of Bahamas, St. Kitts-Nevis and Singapore.

Wmk. 314 was intentionally used sideways, starting in 1966. When a stamp was issued with Wmk. 314 both upright and sideways, the sideways varieties usually are listed also — with minor numbers. In many of the later issues, Wmk. 314 is slightly visible.

Wmk. 373 is usually only faintly visible.

CAMBODIA

kam-'bō-dē-ə

(Kampuchea)

(Khmer Republic)

LOCATION — Southern Indo-China
GOVT. — Republic
AREA — 69,898 sq. mi.
POP. — 11,626,520 (1999 est.)
CAPITAL — Phnom Penh

Before 1951, Cambodia used stamps of Indo-China. In October, 1970, the Kingdom of Cambodia became the Khmer Republic.

From 1978 to 1980 money was abolished.

100 Cents = 1 Piaster
100 Cents = 1 Riel (1955)

Imperforates

Most Cambodia stamps exist imperforate in issued and trial colors, and also in small presentation sheets in issued colors.

Catalogue values for all unused stamps in this country are for Never Hinged items.

Apsaras — A1

King Norodom Sihanouk — A3

Enthronement Hall — A2

1951-52 Unwmk. Engr. *Perf. 13*

No.	Type	Denomination / Color	Unused	Used
1	A1	10c dk blue green	.90	*3.00*
2	A1	20c cl & org brn	.60	*1.25*
3	A1	30c pur & indigo	.60	.50
4	A1	40c ultra & brt bl grn	.80	.80
5	A2	50c dk grn & dk ol grn	.70	.70
6	A3	80c bl blk & dk bl grn	1.50	*2.50*
7	A2	1pi indigo & purple	1.40	1.00
8	A3	1.10pi dp car & brt red	1.75	*2.50*
9	A3	1.50pi blk brn & red brn ('51)	1.75	1.25
10	A1	1.50pi dp car & cerise	1.75	1.75
11	A2	1.50pi indigo & dp ultra	1.75	1.25
12	A3	1.90pi indigo & dp ultra	3.50	*5.75*
13	A2	2pi dp car & org brn	2.50	1.00
14	A3	3pi dp car & org brn	3.75	2.00
15	A1	5pi indigo & purple	12.00	6.50
a.		Souvenir sheet of 1	52.50	
16	A2	10pi purple & indigo	14.00	11.00
a.		Souvenir sheet of 1	52.50	
17	A3	15pi dk pur & pur	32.50	22.50
a.		Souvenir sheet of 1	52.50	
		Nos. 1-17 (17)	81.75	65.25

Nos. 15a, 16a, 17a sold in a booklet. Value, $300.

Stamps with completely white gum and no toning sell for a premium.

For surcharges see Nos. B1-B4.

Phnom Daun Penh — A4

East Gate, Angkor Thom — A5

Arms of Cambodia — A6

Methods of Mail Transport — A7

1954-55 Unwmk. *Perf. 13*

No.	Type	Denomination / Color	Unused	Used
18	A4	10c rose carmine	1.25	*1.75*
a.		Souvenir sheet of 5 ('55)	45.00	45.00
19	A4	20c dark green	1.50	.45
20	A4	30c indigo	1.40	*2.10*
21	A4	40c dark purple	1.60	.70
22	A4	50c dk violet brn	1.50	.30
23	A5	70c chocolate	2.00	*3.00*
a.		Souvenir sheet of 5 ('55)	45.00	45.00
24	A5	1pi red violet	2.00	1.60
25	A5	1.50pi red	2.00	.50
26	A6	2pi rose red	2.00	.40
a.		Souvenir sheet of 5 ('55)	45.00	45.00
27	A6	2.50pi green	2.00	.55
28	A7	2.50pi blue green	2.00	.50
a.		Souvenir sheet of 5 ('55)	45.00	45.00
29	A6	3pi ultra	2.10	1.50
30	A7	4pi black brown	3.00	2.75
31	A6	4.50pi purple	2.75	2.75
32	A7	5pi rose red	3.50	1.60
33	A6	6pi chocolate	3.00	2.25
34	A7	10pi purple	3.75	2.50
35	A7	15pi deep blue	4.50	4.50
36	A5	20pi ultra	10.00	4.75
37	A5	30pi blue green	16.00	7.50
		Nos. 18-37 (20)	67.85	41.95
		Nos. 18a//28a, Set of 4	160.00	

The 4 souvenir sheets each contain 5 stamps: No. 18a (10c, 20c, 30c, 40c, 50c); #23a (70c, 1pi, 1.50pi, 20pi, 30pi); No. 26a (2pi, 2.50pi green, 3pi, 4.50pi, 6pi); No. 28a (2.50pi blue green, 4pi, 5pi. 10pi, 15pi). Size of No. 18a, 26a and 28a: 120x120mm. Size of No. 23a: 160x92mm. Values are for very fine, unblemished sheets. Examples with toning and/or gum bends sell for less.

For overprints see Nos. 99-100.

King Norodom Suramarit — A8

King Norodom Suramarit and Queen Kossamak Nearirat Serey Vathana A9

Portraits: 50c (No. 39), 2.50r, 4r, 6r, 15r, Queen Kossamak Nearirat Serey Vathana.

Perf. 14x13(A8), 13(A9)

1955, Nov. 24 Engr. Unwmk.

No.	Type	Denomination / Color	Unused	Used
38	A8	50c violet	.40	.40
39	A8	50c indigo	.40	.40
40	A8	1r car lake	.50	.45
41	A9	1.50r dk brown	.80	.50
42	A9	2r black & indigo	.70	.45
43	A8	2r dp ultra	.80	.60
44	A8	2.50r dk vio brn	1.10	.60
45	A9	3r brn org & car	1.00	.60
46	A8	4r dark green	1.40	.90
47	A9	5r blk & dk grn	1.50	1.10
48	A8	6r deep plum	1.75	1.10
49	A8	7r dark brown	2.00	1.10
50	A9	10r brn car & vio	2.50	1.25
51	A8	15r purple	3.00	2.00
52	A8	20r deep green	4.75	2.75
		Nos. 38-52 (15)	22.60	14.20

Coronation of King Norodom Suramarit and Queen Kossamak Nearirat Serey Vathana.

See Nos. 74-75. For surcharge see No. 122.

Queen Kossamak Nearirat Serey Vathana — A10

Portrait: 2r, 10r, 30r, King Norodom Suramarit.

1956, Mar. 8 *Perf. 13*

No.	Type	Denomination / Color	Unused	Used
53	A10	2r dark red	2.25	2.00
54	A10	3r dark blue	3.25	2.75
55	A10	5r yellow green	4.50	3.75
56	A10	10r dark green	9.00	7.50
57	A10	30r dark violet	19.00	15.00
58	A10	50r rose lilac	35.00	35.00
		Nos. 53-58 (6)	73.00	66.00

Coronation of King Norodom Suramarit and Queen Kossamak Nearirat Serey Vathana.

Prince Sihanouk, Globe and Flags — A11

1957, Mar. 1

No.	Type	Denomination / Color	Unused	Used
59	A11	2r grn, ultra & car	1.50	1.10
60	A11	4.50r ultra	1.50	1.10
61	A11	8.50r carmine	1.50	1.10
		Nos. 59-61 (3)	4.50	3.30

Admission to the UN, 1st anniv. (in 1956).

Type of Semi-Postal Stamps, 1957

1957, May 12 Unwmk. *Perf. 13*

No.	Type	Denomination / Color	Unused	Used
62	SP1	1.50r vermilion	1.00	1.00
63	SP1	6.50r bluish violet	1.25	1.25
64	SP1	8r dark green	1.50	1.50
		Nos. 62-64 (3)	3.75	3.75

2500th anniv. of the birth of Buddha.

King Ang Duong A12

1958, Mar. 4

No.	Type	Denomination / Color	Unused	Used
65	A12	1.50r purple & brown	.60	.60
66	A12	5r olive gray & olive	.80	.80
67	A12	10r claret & dull brn	1.50	1.50
a.		Souvenir sheet of 3, #65-67	6.50	6.00
		Nos. 65-67 (3)	2.90	2.90

King Ang Duong (1795-1860).

No. 67a sold for 25r.

King Norodom I — A13

1958-59 Engr. *Perf. 12½x13*

No.	Type	Denomination / Color	Unused	Used
68	A13	2r ultra & olive	.70	.50
69	A13	6r orange & sl grn	1.00	.70
70	A13	15r green & ol gray	2.00	1.40
a.		Souv. sheet of 3, #68-70 ('59)	6.50	6.00
		Nos. 68-70 (3)	3.70	2.60

King Norodom I (1835-1904).

No. 70a sold for 32r.

Issued: Nos. 68-70, 11/3/58; No. 70a, 1/31/59.

For surcharge see No. 184.

Children of the World — A14

1959, Dec. 9 Unwmk. *Perf. 13*

No.	Type	Denomination / Color	Unused	Used
71	A14	20c rose violet	.30	.30
72	A14	50c blue	.55	.55
73	A14	80c rose carmine	1.10	1.10
		Nos. 71-73 (3)	1.95	1.95

Issued to promote friendship among the children of the world.

For surcharges see Nos. 115, B8-B10.

Nos. 49 and 52 with Black Border

1960 *Perf. 14x13*

No.	Type	Denomination / Color	Unused	Used
74	A8	7r dk brown & blk	4.50	4.50
75	A8	20r dp green & blk	4.50	4.50

Death of King Norodom Suramarit.

Port of Sihanoukville, Prince Sihanouk and Serpent Naga — A15

20r (double size)

1960, Apr. *Perf. 13x12½*

No.	Type	Denomination / Color	Unused	Used
76	A15	2r carmine & sepia	.65	.65
a.		Cambodian 20r	3.50	3.50
77	A15	5r ultra & dp brown	.65	.65
a.		Cambodian 20r	4.00	4.00
78	A15	20r lilac & dk blue	2.40	2.40
		Nos. 76-78 (3)	3.70	3.70

Opening of the port of Sihanoukville. By error the denomination in Cambodian on the 2r and 5r was engraved as 20r; it was corrected later.

Ceremonial Plow — A16

1960 *Perf. 12*

No.	Type	Denomination / Color	Unused	Used
79	A16	1r magenta	.65	.65
80	A16	2r brown	.90	.90
81	A16	3r bluish green	1.25	1.25
		Nos. 79-81 (3)	2.80	2.80

Feast of the Sacred Furrow.

Fight Against Illiteracy A17

Water Conservation, Dam at Chhouksar — A18

Dove, Factory and Books A19

Buddhist Ceremony A20

Works of Sangkum: 6r, Workman and house. 10r, Woman in rice field.

1960, Sept. 1 Engr. *Perf. 13*

82	A17	2r dk grn, brn & dk bl	.65	.40
a.		Souvenir sheet of 3	8.00	8.00
83	A18	3r brown & green	.80	.40
a.		Souvenir sheet of 3	8.00	8.00
84	A19	4r rose car, vio & grn	.80	.55
85	A17	6r brown, org & grn	.90	.70
86	A17	10r ultra, grn & bis	2.25	1.40
87	A20	25r dk car, red & mag	4.50	2.75
		Nos. 82-87 (6)	9.90	6.20

No. 82a contains one each of Nos. 82, 85 and 87, and sold for 42r. No. 83a contains one each of Nos. 83, 84 and 86, and sold for 23r. Nos. 82a-83a were issued Dec. 5, 1960.

Cambodian Flag and Dove — A21

1960, Dec. 24 Engr. *Perf. 13*

Flag in Ultramarine and Red

88	A21	1.50r brown & green	.40	.25
89	A21	5r orange red	.60	.35
90	A21	7r green & ultra	1.25	1.00
a.		Souvenir sheet of 3, #88-90	14.00	14.00
b.		Souv. sheet of 3 (colors changed)	9.50	9.50
		Nos. 88-90 (3)	2.25	1.60

Peace propaganda. No. 90a sold for 16r. No. 90b contains one of each denomination with colors changed to: 1.50r orange red, 5r green & ultramarine, 7r brown & green and sold for 20r.

Frangipani — A22

1961, July 1 Unwmk. *Perf. 13*

91	A22	2r shown	.65	.65
92	A22	5r Oleander	1.10	1.10
93	A22	10r Amaryllis	2.75	2.75
a.		Souvenir sheet of 3, #91-93	8.50	8.50
		Nos. 91-93 (3)	4.50	4.50

No. 93a sold for 20r.

Krishna in Chariot, Khmer Frieze — A23

1961-63 Typo. *Perf. 14x13½*

94	A23	1r lilac	.40	.25
94A	A23	2r blue ('63)	3.25	1.60
95	A23	3r emerald	.90	.40
96	A23	6r orange	.90	.40
a.		Souvenir sheet of 3	6.50	6.50
		Nos. 94-96 (4)	5.45	2.65

Issued to honor Cambodian armed forces. No. 94A issued in coils. No. 96a contains one each of Nos. 94, 95, 96. Sold for 12r.

Independence Monument — A24

1961, Nov. 9 Engr. *Perf. 13x12½*

97	A24	2r green	.50	.50
98	A24	4r gray brown	.50	.50
a.		Souvenir sheet of 2, #97-98	5.00	5.00
		Nos. 97-98,C15-C17 (5)	9.40	7.05

10th anniv. of Independence.

For surcharge see No. 116.

Nos. 27 and 31 Overprinted in Red

1961, Nov. 11 *Perf. 13*

99	A6	2.50pi green	1.10	.65
100	A6	4.50pi purple	1.75	1.00

Sixth World Conference of Buddhism.

Highway (American Aid) — A25

Foreign Aid: 2r, Power station (Czech aid). 4r, Textile factory (Chinese aid). 5r, Hospital (Russian aid). 6r, Airport (French aid).

1961, Dec. Engr. *Perf. 13*

101	A25	2r org & rose car	.45	.30
102	A25	3r bl, grn & org brn	.45	.30
103	A25	4r dl bl, org brn & mag	.45	.40
104	A25	5r dl grn & lil rose	.65	.40
105	A25	6r dk bl & org brn	1.25	.55
a.		Souvenir sheet of 5, #101-105	7.00	7.00
		Nos. 101-105 (5)	3.25	1.95

Malaria Eradication Emblem — A26

1962, Apr. 7 Unwmk. *Perf. 13*

106	A26	2r magenta & brown	.50	.40
107	A26	4r green & dk brown	.50	.40
108	A26	6r violet & olive bister	.75	.45
		Nos. 106-108 (3)	1.75	1.25

WHO drive to eradicate malaria.

For surcharges see Nos. B11-B12.

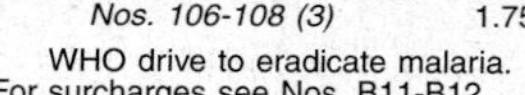

Fruits A27

1962, June 4 Engr.

109	A27	2r Cardamom	.60	.45
110	A27	4r Sugar apple	1.10	.75
111	A27	6r Mangosteens	1.10	.75
a.		Souvenir sheet of 3, #109-111	5.50	5.50
		Nos. 109-111 (3)	2.80	1.95

Nos. 111a sold for 15r.

Pineapples — A28

1962 Unwmk. *Perf. 13*

112	A28	2r shown	.80	.50
113	A28	5r Sugar cane	1.25	.75
114	A28	9r Sugar palms	1.50	.70
		Nos. 112-114 (3)	3.55	1.95

No. 73 Surcharged

1962, Nov. 9 *Perf. 13*

115	A14	50c on 80c rose car	.70	.40

No. 97 Srchd. in Red and Ovptd. in Black

1962

116	A24	3r on 2r green	1.00	.40

Dedication of Independence Monument. See No. C18.

Corn, Rice and FAO Emblem A29

1963, Mar. 21 Engr. *Perf. 13*

117	A29	3r multicolored	.70	.55
118	A29	6r org red, vio bl & ocher	.70	.55

FAO "Freedom from Hunger" campaign.

Preah Vihear, Ancient Temple — A30

1963, June 15 *Perf. 12½x13*

119	A30	3r clar, brn & sl grn	.45	.40
120	A30	6r org, sl grn & grnsh blk	.80	.65
121	A30	15r blue, choc & green	1.25	1.10
		Nos. 119-121 (3)	2.50	2.15

Return by Thailand of Preah Vihear on the Mekong River.

For overprint see No. 176.

No. 44 Surcharged

1963 Engr. *Perf. 14x13*

122	A8	3r on 2½r dk violet brn	.90	.55

Tonsay Lake — A31

7r, Popokvil Falls. 20r, Beach, horiz.

Perf. 12x12½, 12½x12

1963, Aug. 1 Photo.

123	A31	3r multicolored	.50	.50
124	A31	7r multicolored	.80	.70
125	A31	20r multicolored	2.50	1.10
		Nos. 123-125 (3)	3.80	2.30

UNESCO Emblem, Scales and Globe A32

1963, Dec. 10 Engr. *Perf. 13*

126	A32	1r vio bl, rose cl & grn	.50	.50
127	A32	3r yel grn, vio bl & rose cl	.90	.90
128	A32	12r rose cl, yel grn & vio bl	1.60	1.60
		Nos. 126-128 (3)	3.00	3.00

15th anniversary of the Universal Declaration of Human Rights.

For surcharge see No. 183.

Kouprey A33

1964, Mar. 3 Unwmk. *Perf. 13*

129	A33	50c grn, dk brn & org brn	.95	.55
130	A33	3r org, brn, dk brn & grn	1.40	.70
131	A33	6r blue, dk brn & grn	2.10	1.40
		Nos. 129-131 (3)	4.45	2.65

Black-billed Magpie — A34

1964, May 2 Engr. *Perf. 13*

132	A34	3r shown	1.40	.65
133	A34	6r Kingfisher	2.10	1.00
134	A34	12r Gray heron	3.75	2.00
		Nos. 132-134 (3)	7.25	3.65

For overprint & surcharge see Nos. 303, B16.

Emblem of Royal Cambodian Airline A35

1964 Unwmk. *Perf. 13x12½*

135 A35 1.50r rose car & purple .40 .25
136 A35 3r ver & dk blue .55 .40
137 A35 7.50r ultra & car 1.25 .60
Nos. 135-137 (3) 2.20 1.25

8th anniv. of the Royal Cambodian Airline.

Prince Norodom Sihanouk — A36

1964 Engr. *Perf. 12½x13*

138 A36 2r purple .50 .40
139 A36 3r red brown .70 .50
140 A36 10r dark blue 1.35 .90
Nos. 138-140 (3) 2.55 1.80

10th anniv. of the Sangkum (political party).
For overprints see Nos. 144-145.

A set of three stamps, imperf, showing clasped hands, was prepared for International Cooperation Year but were never issued. Value, $200.

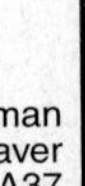

Woman Weaver A37

Khmer Handicrafts: 3r, Metal worker. 5r, Basket maker.

1965, Feb. 1 *Perf. 13x12½*

141 A37 1r multicolored .40 .40
142 A37 3r red lil, red brn & gray ol .65 .40
143 A37 5r green, dk brn & car 1.10 .85
Nos. 141-143 (3) 2.15 1.65

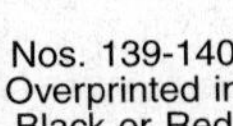

Nos. 139-140 Overprinted in Black or Red

1965, Mar. 1 *Perf. 12½x13*

144 A36 3r red brown .70 .40
145 A36 10r dark blue (R) 1.00 .55

Conference of the people of Indo-China.

ITU Emblem, Old and New Communication Equipment — A38

1965, May 17 Engr. *Perf. 13*

146 A38 3r green & olive bister .40 .30
147 A38 4r red & blue .70 .40
148 A38 10r violet & rose lilac 1.00 .70
Nos. 146-148 (3) 2.10 1.40

Centenary of the ITU.

Cotton Plant — A39

3r, Peanut plant. 7.50r, Coconut palm.

1965, Aug. 2 *Perf. 12½x13*

149 A39 1.50r org, sl grn & pur .50 .40
150 A39 3r blue, yel, grn & brn .80 .60
151 A39 7.50r org brn & sl grn 1.35 1.00
Nos. 149-151 (3) 2.65 2.00

Preah Ko Temple, Rolouoh — A40

Temples at Angkor: 5r, Baksei Chamkrong, Rolouoh. 7r, Banteay Srei (Citadel of Women). 9r, Angkor Wat. 12r, Bayon, Angkor Thom.

1966, Feb. 1 Engr. *Perf. 13*

152 A40 3r gray ol, sal & dl grn 1.25 .80
153 A40 5r lil, dk grn & redsh brn 1.50 .85
154 A40 7r dk grn, redsh brn & bis 1.75 1.60
155 A40 9r vio bl, pur & dk grn 2.50 2.10
156 A40 12r dk grn, rose car & ver 3.00 2.75
Nos. 152-156 (5) 10.00 8.10

For overprints see Nos. 172-175, 177.

WHO Headquarters, Geneva — A41

1966, July 1 Photo. *Perf. 12½x13*
WHO Emblem in Blue and Yellow

157 A41 2r black & pale rose .40 .25
158 A41 3r black & yel grn .50 .40
159 A41 5r black & lt bl .80 .55
Nos. 157-159 (3) 1.70 1.20

Inauguration of WHO Headquarters, Geneva.

Tree Planting — A42

1966, July 22 Engr. *Perf. 12½x13*

160 A42 1r brn, dull brn & brt grn .30 .25
161 A42 3r org, dull brn & brt grn .55 .30
162 A42 7r gray, dull brn & brt grn .85 .40
Nos. 160-162 (3) 1.70 .95

Issued for Arbor Day.

UNESCO Emblem — A43

1966 Photo. *Perf. 13*

163 A43 3r multicolored .50 .40
164 A43 7r multicolored .75 .55

20th anniv. of UNESCO.

Wrestlers and Games' Emblem A44

GANEFO Games (Games Emblem and): 3r, Stadium, Phnom Penh. 7r, Swordsmen. 10r, Indian club swingers. Bas-reliefs from Angkor Wat.

1966, Nov. 25 Engr. *Perf. 13*

165 A44 3r violet blue .40 .25
166 A44 4r green .45 .30
167 A44 7r dk car rose .70 .50
168 A44 10r dark brown 1.10 .65
Nos. 165-168 (4) 2.65 1.70

Indian Wild Boar A45

Perf. 13x12½, 12½x13

1967, Feb. 20 Engr.

169 A45 3r shown 1.40 .40
170 A45 5r Muntjac, vert. 1.75 .65
171 A45 7r Elephant 2.40 .95
Nos. 169-171 (3) 5.55 2.00

Nos. 152-153, 155-156 and 121 Overprinted in Red

1967, Apr. 27 Engr. *Perf. 13*

172 A40 3r multicolored .75 .75
173 A40 5r multicolored .80 .75
174 A40 9r multicolored 1.25 1.25
175 A40 12r multicolored 1.50 1.50
176 A30 15r multicolored 1.75 1.75
Nos. 172-176 (5) 6.05 6.00

International Tourist Year, 1967.

No. 154 Overprinted in Red

1967, Apr. 27

177 A40 7r multicolored 1.50 .60

Banteay Srei Temple at Angkor, millennium.

Royal Ballet Dancer — A46

Various Dancers

1967, June Engr. *Perf. 13*

178 A46 1r orange .40 .40
179 A46 3r Prus blue .75 .60
180 A46 5r ultra 1.25 .55
181 A46 7r carmine rose 1.50 .80
182 A46 10r multicolored 1.75 1.00
Nos. 178-182 (5) 5.65 3.35

Cambodian Royal Ballet.

Nos. 128 and 70 Srchd. in Red

1967, Sept. 8 Engr.

183 A32 6r on 12r multi 1.00 .50
184 A13 7r on 15r grn & olive gray 1.25 .70

Intl. Literacy Day, Sept. 8. The surcharge on No. 184 is adapted to fit the shape of the stamp.

Symbolic Water Cycle — A47

1967, Nov. 1 Typo. *Perf. 13x14*

185 A47 1r black, bl & org .30 .25
186 A47 6r lilac, lt bl & org .60 .30
187 A47 10r dk blue, emer & org .90 .50
Nos. 185-187 (3) 1.80 1.05

Hydrological Decade (UNESCO), 1965-74.

Royal University, Kompong Cham A48

6r, Engineering School, Phnom Penh. 9r, University Center, Sangkum Reastr Niyum.

1968, Mar. 1 Engr. *Perf. 13*

188 A48 4r violet bl & multi .50 .40
189 A48 6r slate & multi .65 .40
190 A48 9r Prus blue & multi .90 .55
Nos. 188-190 (3) 2.05 1.35

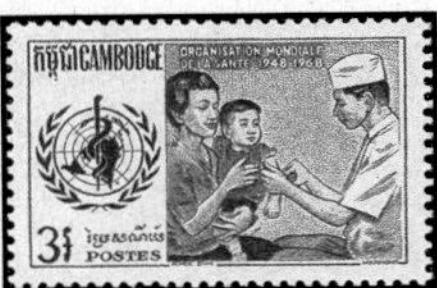

Vaccination and WHO Emblem A49

WHO, 20th Anniv.: 7r, Malaria control and WHO emblem (man spraying DDT).

1968, July 8 Engr. *Perf. 13*

191 A49 3r ultramarine .60 .40
192 A49 7r deep blue .90 .55

Stadium, Mexico City — A50

1968, Oct. 12 Engr. *Perf. 13*

193 A50 1r shown .55 .55
194 A50 2r Wrestling .70 .55
195 A50 3r Bicycling .75 .55
196 A50 5r Boxing, vert. .95 .55
197 A50 7.50r Torch bearer, vert. 1.25 .75
Nos. 193-197 (5) 4.20 2.95

19th Olympic Games, Mexico City, 12/12-27.

Red Cross Team A51

1968, Nov. 1 Engr. *Perf. 13*
198 A51 3r Prus bl, grn & red 1.50 .50

Issued to honor the Cambodian Red Cross.

Prince Norodom Sihanouk A52

8r, Soldiers wading through swamp.

1968, Nov. 9
199 A52 7r emer, ultra & pur .50 .40
200 A52 8r bl, grn & dp brn .75 .55

15th anniversary of independence.

Human Rights Flame and Prince Sihanouk A53

1968, Dec. 10 Engr. *Perf. 13*
201 A53 3r blue .45 .25
202 A53 5r bright plum .80 .35
203 A53 7r multicolored 1.10 .55
Nos. 201-203 (3) 2.35 1.15

International Human Rights Year.

ILO Emblem A54

1969, May 1 Engr. *Perf. 13*
204 A54 3r ultra .50 .25
205 A54 6r dp carmine .70 .40
206 A54 9r blue green 1.00 .55
Nos. 204-206 (3) 2.20 1.20

ILO, 50th anniversary.

Globe, Red Cross, Crescent, Lion and Sun Emblems A55

1969, May 8
207 A55 1r blue, red & yel .40 .25
208 A55 3r sl grn, red & vio brn .65 .40
209 A55 10r brt lil, red & brn 1.40 .60
Nos. 207-209 (3) 2.45 1.25

50th anniv. of the League of Red Cross Societies.

Papilio Oeacus A56

Butterflies: 4r, Papilio agamenon. 8r, Danaus plexippus.

1969, Oct. 10 Engr. *Perf. 13*
210 A56 3r lilac, blk & yel 3.25 1.00
211 A56 4r ver, blk & grn 4.00 2.00
212 A56 8r yel grn, dk brn & org 5.75 3.00
Nos. 210-212 (3) 13.00 6.00

Map of Cambodia and Diesel Engine A57

Various railroad stations and trains.

1969, Nov. 27 Engr. *Perf. 13*
213 A57 3r multicolored 1.00 .75
214 A57 6r slate grn & lt brn 2.00 1.50
215 A57 8r black 3.25 2.25
216 A57 9r dk green & blue 3.75 2.40
Nos. 213-216 (4) 10.00 6.90

Issued to publicize the new rail link between Phnom Penh and Sihanoukville.

Fish — A58

1970, Jan. 29 Photo. *Perf. 13*
217 A58 3r Tripletail 1.75 .90
218 A58 7r Sleeper goby 3.75 1.50
219 A58 9r Snakehead 5.50 2.00
Nos. 217-219 (3) 11.00 4.40

Wat Maniratanaram — A59

Monasteries: 2r, Wat Tepthidaram, vert. 6r, Wat Patumavati. 8r, Wat Unnalom.

1970, Apr. 29 Photo. *Perf. 13*
220 A59 2r multicolored .35 .40
221 A59 3r multicolored .40 .40
222 A59 6r multicolored .85 .40
223 A59 8r multicolored 1.60 .55
Nos. 220-223 (4) 3.20 1.75

UPU Headquarters and Monument, Bern — A60

1970, May 20
224 A60 1r green & multi .35 .25
225 A60 3r scarlet & multi .50 .30
226 A60 4r dp blue & multi .65 .30
227 A60 10r brown & multi 1.00 .60
Nos. 224-227 (4) 2.50 1.45

New UPU Headquarters in Bern.

Open Book and Satellite Earth Receiving Station — A61

1970, May 17 Photo. *Perf. 13*
228 A61 3r dk vio bl & multi .30 .25
229 A61 4r sl grn & multi .40 .25
230 A61 9r brn ol & multi .85 .35
Nos. 228-230 (3) 1.55 .85

World Telecommunications Day.

Nelumbium Speciosum A62

Flowers: 4r, Eichhornia crassipes. 13r, Nymphea lotus.

1970, Aug. 17 Photo. *Perf. 13*
231 A62 3r multicolored .70 .30
a. Cambodian and Arabic 3's transposed 35.00 35.00
232 A62 4r multicolored 1.40 .45
233 A62 13r multicolored 3.00 .70
Nos. 231-233 (3) 5.10 1.45

Elephant God, Bas relief at Banteay Srei — A63

1970, Sept. 21 Engr. *Perf. 13*
234 A63 3r lil rose & dp grn .35 .25
235 A63 4r bl grn, grn & lil rose .55 .25
236 A63 7r bl grn, dk brn & grn .85 .40
Nos. 234-236 (3) 1.75 .90

Issued for World Meteorological Day.

Khmer Republic

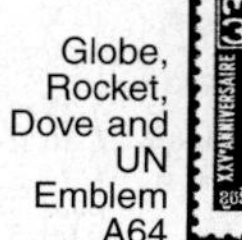

Globe, Rocket, Dove and UN Emblem A64

1970, Nov. 9 Photo. *Perf. 12½x12*
237 A64 3r black & multi .30 .25
238 A64 5r brown red & multi .45 .25
239 A64 10r dp violet & multi .90 .50
Nos. 237-239 (3) 1.65 1.00

25th anniversary of the United Nations.

Education Year Emblem A65

1970, Nov. 9 Engr. *Perf. 13x12½*
240 A65 1r blue .25 .25
241 A65 3r brt rose lilac .35 .25
242 A65 8r blue green .75 .45
Nos. 240-242 (3) 1.35 .95

Issued for International Education Year.

Chuon-Nath — A66

1971, Jan. 27 Photo. *Perf. 13*
243 A66 3r ol grn & multi .35 .25
244 A66 8r purple & multi .75 .35
245 A66 9r violet & multi 1.00 .55
Nos. 243-245 (3) 2.10 1.15

In memory of Chuon-Nath (1883-1969), Cambodian language expert.

For surcharge see No. 322.

Soldiers in Battle A67

1971, Mar. 18 Photo. *Perf. 13*
246 A67 1r gray & multi .35 .25
247 A67 3r bister & multi .55 .40
248 A67 10r blue & multi 1.40 .75
Nos. 246-248 (3) 2.30 1.40

National territorial defense.

For overprint see No. 321.

UN Emblem, Men of Four Races A68

1971, Mar. 21
249 A68 3r blue & multi .65 .25
250 A68 7r green & multi 1.25 .40
251 A68 8r brt rose & multi 2.00 .55
Nos. 249-251 (3) 3.90 1.20

Intl. year against racial discrimination.

General Post Office, Phnom Penh — A69

1971, Apr. 19
252 A69 3r blue & multi .35 .25
253 A69 9r lilac rose & multi .65 .35
254 A69 10r black & multi 1.05 .40
Nos. 252-254 (3) 2.05 1.00

Symbolic Globe and Waves A70

Design: 7r, 8r, ITU emblem and waves.

1971, May 17 Photo. *Perf. 13*
255 A70 3r green, blk & bl .25 .25
256 A70 4r yellow & multi .40 .25
257 A70 7r lilac, blk & red .50 .25
258 A70 8r sal pink, blk & red .60 .30
Nos. 255-258 (4) 1.75 1.05

3rd World Telecommunications Day.

Erythrina Indica A71

Wild Flowers: 3r, Bauhinia variegata. 6r, Butea frondosa. 10r, Lagerstroemia floribunda, vert.

1971, July 5 *Perf. 13x12½, 12½x13*
259 A71 2r lt ultra & multi .55 .45
260 A71 3r yel grn & multi .65 .55
261 A71 6r blue & multi 1.40 1.10
262 A71 10r brown & multi 1.75 1.40
Nos. 259-262 (4) 4.35 3.50

Khmer Coat of Arms — A72

Flag and Square of the Republic — A73

1971, Oct. 9 **Engr.** ***Perf. 13***

263	A72	3r brt grn & bis	.25	.25
264	A73	3r purple & multi	.30	.25
265	A73	4r dp claret & multi	.40	.25
266	A72	8r orange & bis	.50	.25
267	A72	10r lt brn & bis	.80	.30
a.		Souv. sheet of 3, #263, 266-267	3.25	3.25
268	A73	10r slate grn & multi	.80	.35
a.		Souv. sheet of 3, #264-265, 268	3.25	3.25
		Nos. 263-268 (6)	3.05	1.65

Republic, 1st anniv.

No. 267a sold for 25r, No. 268a for 20r.

For overprints and surcharges see Nos. 301-302, B13-B14.

UNICEF Emblem — A74

1971, Dec. 11

269	A74	3r black brown	.35	.25
270	A74	5r ultra	.50	.25
271	A74	9r dk pur & brn red	1.00	.45
		Nos. 269-271 (3)	1.85	.95

25th anniv. of UNICEF.

This set and others exist with overprint "RPK," both with and without frame. Status has not been determined.

Book Year Emblem A75

1972, Feb. 7

272	A75	3r blue, grn & vio	.40	.25
273	A75	8r violet, grn & bl	.60	.30
274	A75	9r emerald & multi	1.00	.50
a.		Souvenir sheet of 3, #272-274	3.00	3.00
		Nos. 272-274 (3)	2.00	1.05

Intl. Book Year. No. 274a sold for 23r.

Lion of St. Mark A76

Designs: 5r, Waves engulfing St. Mark's Basilica. 10r, Bridge of Sighs, vert.

1972, Feb. 7 **Engr.** ***Perf. 13***

275	A76	3r lil rose & org brn	.50	.25
276	A76	5r yel grn & org brn	1.00	.40
277	A76	10r org brn, bl & yel grn	1.25	.50
a.		Souvenir sheet of 3, #275-277	3.00	3.00
		Nos. 275-277 (3)	2.75	1.15

UNESCO campaign to save Venice. No. 277a sold for 23r.

UN Emblem A77

1972, Mar. 28

278	A77	3r deep carmine	.50	.25
279	A77	6r deep blue	.75	.35
280	A77	9r deep orange	.90	.50
a.		Souvenir sheet of 3, #278-280	2.75	2.75
		Nos. 278-280 (3)	2.15	1.10

25th anniv. UN Economic Commission for Asia and the Far East (ECAFE). No. 280a sold for 23r.

Dancing Apsarases — A78

1972, May 5 **Engr.** ***Perf. 13***

281	A78	1r golden brn	.25	.25
282	A78	3r violet	.30	.25
283	A78	7r rose claret	.40	.30
284	A78	8r olive brn	.55	.30
285	A78	9r blue grn	.60	.30
286	A78	10r ultra	.90	.30
287	A78	12r purple	1.00	.30
288	A78	14r Prus blue	1.25	.45
		Nos. 281-288 (8)	5.25	2.45

"UIT" A79

1972, May 17 **Litho.**

289	A79	3r blk, yel & grnsh bl	.40	.25
290	A79	9r blk, dp lil rose & bl grn	.75	.30
291	A79	14r blk, brn & bl grn	1.10	.45
		Nos. 289-291 (3)	2.25	1.00

4th World Telecommunications Day.

"Human Environment" — A80

1972, June 5 **Engr.**

292	A80	3r org, plum & grn	.50	.25
293	A80	12r brt grn & plum	.75	.30
294	A80	15r plum & brt grn	1.25	.50
a.		Souvenir sheet of 3, #292-294	3.00	3.00
		Nos. 292-294 (3)	2.50	1.05

UN Conf. on Human Environment, Stockholm, June 5-16. No. 294a sold for 35r.

For overprints and surcharges see Nos. 304-305, B15, B17.

Javan Rhinoceros A81

1972, Aug. 1 **Engr.** ***Perf. 13***

295	A81	3r shown	.55	.25
296	A81	4r Serow	.65	.25
297	A81	6r Malayan sambar	1.25	.30
298	A81	7r Banteng	1.75	.30
299	A81	8r Water buffalo	2.00	.50
300	A81	10r Gaur	2.25	.60
		Nos. 295-300 (6)	8.45	2.20

Nos. 263, 267, 134, 293, 294 Overprinted in Red

1972, Sept. 9 **Engr.** ***Perf. 13***

301	A72	3r brt grn & bister	.60	.30
302	A72	10r orange & bister	1.20	.65
303	A34	12r multicolored	1.20	.80
304	A80	12r brt grn & plum	1.30	.80
305	A80	15r plum & brt grn	1.75	1.00
		Nos. 301-305 (5)	6.05	3.55

20th Olympic Games, Munich, 8/26-9/11.

Raising Khmer Flag — A82

1972, Oct. 9 **Photo.** ***Perf. 12½x13***

306	A82	3r multicolored	.25	.25
307	A82	5r brt rose & multi	.40	.30
308	A82	9r yel grn & multi	.90	.50
		Nos. 306-308 (3)	1.55	1.05

2nd anniversary of the establishment of the Khmer Republic.

For surcharge see No. 323.

Stupa and Crest — A83

1973, May 12 **Engr.** ***Perf. 13***

309	A83	3r ocher & multi	.45	.25
310	A83	12r yel grn & multi	.45	.25
311	A83	14r blue & multi	.75	.50
a.		Souvenir sheet of 3, #309-311	3.25	3.25
		Nos. 309-311 (3)	1.65	1.00

New Constitution. No. 311a sold for 34r.

Apsaras — A84

Sculptures from Angkor Wat: 8r, 10r, Devata, diff.

1973, July 23 **Engr.** ***Perf. 13***

312	A84	3r brown black	.50	.25
313	A84	8r Prus green	.65	.30
314	A84	10r olive bister	1.60	.50
a.		Souvenir sheet of 3, #312-314	3.00	3.00
		Nos. 312-314 (3)	2.75	1.05

No. 314a sold for 25r.

INTERPOL Emblem — A85

1973, Oct. 2 **Engr.** ***Perf. 13***

315	A85	3r green & multi	.45	.25
316	A85	7r red brn & multi	.55	.30
317	A85	10r olive & multi	.75	.45
a.		Souvenir sheet of 3, #315-317	4.50	4.50
		Nos. 315-317 (3)	1.75	1.00

50th anniv. of the Intl. Criminal Police Org. No. 317a sold for 30r.

Marshal Lon Nol — A86

1973, Oct. 9

318	A86	3r lt grn, blk & brn	.40	.25
319	A86	8r brown, ol & blk	.60	.30
320	A86	14r black & brn	1.00	.40
a.		Souvenir sheet of 3	5.00	5.00
		Nos. 318-320 (3)	2.00	.95

Marshal Lon Nol, 1st pres. of the Republic. No. 320a contains stamps similar to Nos. 318-320 in changed colors. Sold for 50r.

Nos. 248, 243 and 307 Srchd. & Ovptd. in Red or Silver

1974 **Photo.** ***Perf. 13, 12½x13***

321	A67	10r multi (R)	*4.50*	2.50
322	A66	50r on 3r multi	*9.50*	4.00
323	A82	100r on 5r multi	*22.50*	6.50
		Nos. 321-323 (3)	*36.50*	13.00

4th anniversary of the Republic.

Copernicus and "Nerva" — A87

Copernicus, various spacecraft and events: 5r, Mariner II. 10r, Apollo. 25r, Telstar. 50r, Space walk. 100r, Moon landing. 150r, Separation of spaceship and module.

1974, Sept. 10 **Litho.** ***Perf. 13***

324	A87	1r shown	.35	.30
325	A87	5r multicolored	.40	.30
326	A87	10r multicolored	.65	.40
327	A87	25r multicolored	1.50	.75
328	A87	50r multicolored	2.50	1.50
329	A87	100r multicolored	6.00	3.75
330	A87	150r multicolored	8.00	5.50
		Nos. 324-330 (7)	19.40	12.50
		Nos. 324-330,C46-C47 (9)	44.40	28.00

500th anniversary of the birth of Nicolaus Copernicus (1473-1543), Polish astronomer.

Carrier Pigeon and UPU Emblem — A88

Design: 60r, Sailing ship and UPU emblem.

1974, Nov. 2

331	A88	10r multicolored	*1.50*	*1.50*
332	A88	60r multicolored	*4.50*	*4.50*
		Nos. 331-332,C50 (3)	*17.50*	*17.50*

Cent. of UPU. Souvenir sheets of one exist, both imperf. and simulated perfs for Nos. 331 and 332. Value, set of 3, $30 each. Also, set of 2 souvenirs sheets of one each No. 332 and

No. C50 with silver borders, perf. and imperf. (simulated perfs.) Value, set $9 perf., $40 imperf.

A set of 8 stamps picturing musical instruments, overprinted and surcharged for use by the Khmer Republic just before the fall of the government in Apr. 1975, exists. Value, $1,100. Value for same set without surcharge, $500.

A89

1976 Summer Olympic Games, Montreal — A90

1r, 18th cent. swordsmen. 5r, Modern fencers. 10r, Ancient Olympic runner. 25r, Modern runner. 50r, Ancient rowers. 100r, Modern kayakers. 150r, Ancient horseman. 200r, Modern equestrian competitor. 250r, Buildings, Olympic flame. No. 345, Buildings, runner.

1975, Jan. 2 Litho. *Perf. 13½*
333-341 A89 Set of 9 11.00

Litho. & Embossed

342 A90 1200r gold & multi *20.00*

Souvenir Sheets

343 A89 200r silver & multi *9.00*
344 A89 250r silver & multi *9.00*
345 A90 1,200r gold & multi *20.00*

Nos. 337-345 are airmail.

Nos. 333-341 exist imperf. Value, set $47.50. Nos. 333-341 exist in souvenir sheets of one.

Nos. 342-345 exist imperf. Value, set $175.

A91

1974 World Cup Soccer Championships — A92

Soccer players and arms of: 1r, Hamburg. 5r, Gelsenkirchen. 10r, Dortmund. 25r, Stuttgart. 50r, Dusseldorf. 100r, Hannover. 150r, Frankfurt. 200r, Munich. 250r, Berlin.

Litho. (#346-354, 356-357)
Litho. & Embossed (#355, 358)

1975, Feb. 13
346-354 A91 Set of 9 12.00
355 A92 1200r gold & multi *16.00*

Souvenir Sheets

356 A91 200r gold & multi *6.50*
357 A91 250r gold & multi *6.50*
358 A92 1200r gold & multi *14.00*

Nos. 350-358 are airmail. Nos. 346-354 exist in imperforate souvenir sheets.

UPU, Cent. — A93

Designs: 15r, Letter carrier, pack mule. 20r, Biplane. 70r, Post coach. 160r, Biplane, Concorde. 180r, Steam-powered wagon. 235r, Postrider, tail of mailplane. 500r, Railway mail car. 1000r, Airship. 2000r, Caravel.

1975, Apr. 12
359-367 A93 Set of 9 9.00
366a Souvenir sheet of 1 *4.75*
367a Souvenir sheet of 1 *4.75*

Nos. 365-367 are airmail. Nos. 366a and 367a exist imperf. Values, each $25.

Nos. 359-367 exist in imperf souvenir sheets of 1 with simulated perforations. Value, set of 9 sheets $22.50.

People's Republic of Kampuchea

Soldiers — A94

Designs, horiz.: 20c, People, flag. 50c, Fishermen. 1r, Soldiers passing flag.

1980, Apr. 10 Litho. *Perf. 11*
368-371 A94 Set of 4 *57.50 57.50*

Soviet Union, 60th Anniv. — A95

Designs: 50c, Globe, Kremlin. 1r, Buildings, map of USSR.

1982, Dec. 30 *Perf. 12x12½*
372-373 A95 Set of 2 1.60 .55

People's Republic of Kampuchea, 4th Anniv. — A96

Designs: 50c, Natl. arms, vert. 1r, shown. 3r, Map, stylized figures, vert. 6r, Temple, vert.

1983, Jan. 7 Litho. *Perf. 13*
374-376 A96 Set of 3 4.75 1.25

Souvenir Sheet

377 A96 6r multicolored 6.00 2.25

1984 Summer Olympic Games, Los Angeles A97

Designs: 20c, Runner with torch. 50c, Javelin. 80c, Pole vault. 1r, Discus. 1.50r, Relay race. 2r, Swimming. 3r, Basketball.

20c-1r, 3r are vert.

1983, Jan. 20 Litho. *Perf. 13*
378-384 A97 Set of 7 7.00 1.50

Souvenir Sheet

385 A97 6r Soccer 5.75 3.25

No. 385 contains one 32x40mm stamp.

Butterflies — A98

20c, Salatura genutia. 50c, Euploea althaea. 80c, Byasa polyeuctes. 1r, Stichophthalma howqua. 1.50r, Kallima inachus. 2r, Precis orithya. 3r, Catopsilia pomona.

20c, 50c, 1.50r, 2r, 3r are vert.

1983, Feb. 18 Litho. *Perf. 13*
386-392 A98 Set of 7 8.50 2.00

Khmer Culture A99

Designs: 20c, Ruins, Srah Srang. 50c, Temple, Bakong. 80c, Ta Son. 1r, North Gate, Angkor Thom. 1.50r, Two winged figures. 2r, Apsara, Angkor. 3r, Statue of Banteai Srei.

80c-3r are vert.

1983, Mar. 15
393-399 A99 Set of 7 6.00 1.75

Folk Dances A100

Various dances. Denominations 50c, 1r, 3r.

1983, Apr. 17 Litho. *Perf. 13*
400-402 A100 Set of 3 4.00 1.25

Souvenir Sheet

403 A100 6r Native, "buffalo" 6.50 1.40

No. 403 contains one 32x40mm stamp.

Raphael (1483-1520) — A101

Parnassus (details): No. 404, 20c, Dante, Ennius, Homer. No. 406, 80c, Horace, Ovid, others. No. 409, 2r, The Muses. No. 410, 3r, Alcaeus, Petrarch, others.

School at Athens (details): No. 407, 1r, Euclid, disciples. No. 408, 1.50r, Telange, Pythagoras.

Details from: No. 405, 50c, Mass of Bolsena). 6r, Angels from Dispute of the Holy Sacrament, horiz.

1983, May 10 Litho. *Perf. 12½x13*
404-410 A101 Set of 7 6.00 2.25

Souvenir Sheet

Perf. 13

411 A101 6r multicolored 7.25 2.75

No. 411 contains one 40x32mm stamp.

1st Hot Air Balloon Ascension, Bicent. A102

Designs: 20c, Montgolfier. 30c, Ville d'Orleans. 50c, Hydrogen balloon. 1r, Blanchard & Jeffries, 1785. 1.50r, Ascension in Arctic. 2r, Stratosphere balloon. 3r, Balloon race. 6r, Balloons over town.

1983, June 3 *Perf. 12½*
412-418 A102 Set of 7 6.00 2.00

Souvenir Sheet

Perf. 13

419 A102 6r multicolored 7.25 1.75

Reptiles — A103

Designs: 20c, Iguana. 30c, Cobra. 80c, Trionyx turtle. 1r, Chameleon. 1.50r, Boa constrictor. 2r, Crocodile. 3r, Turtle.

30c, 1r, 1.50r are vert.

1983, June 28
420-426 A103 Set of 7 8.00 2.50

Birds A104

Designs: 20c, Lorikeet. 50c, Swallow. 80c, Eagle. 1r, Vulture. 1.50r, Turtle dove. 2r, Magpie. 3r, Hornbill.
20c-50c, 2r-3r are vert.

1983, Sept. 20
427-433 A104 Set of 7 11.00 3.00

Flowers — A105

20c, Sunflower. 50c, Caprifoliacae. 80c, Bougainvillea. 1r, Renonculacae. 1.50r, Nyctaginaceae. 2r, Cockscomb. 3r, Roses.

1983, Oct. 18 ***Perf. 13***
434-440 A105 Set of 7 6.00 1.75

1984 Winter Olympic Games, Sarajevo — A106

Designs: 1r, Luge. 2r, Biathlon. 4r, Ski jumping. 5r, Two-man bobsled. 7r, Hockey.
6r, Cross-country skiing.

1983, Nov. 10 ***Perf. 12½***
441-445 A106 Set of 5 14.00 2.75

Souvenir Sheet

446 A106 6r multicolored 5.50 3.25

No. 446 contains one 40x32mm stamp.

Fish A107

20c, 1.50r, 2r, 3r, Various Cyprinidae. 50c, Trout. 80c, Catfish. 1r, Moray eel.

1983, Nov. 16 ***Perf. 13***
447-453 A107 Set of 7 8.00 2.00

Festival of Rebirth — A108

50c, Factory. 1r, Bull, tractor. 3r, Bridge, ship, train. 6r, Radio antenna. 50c, 3r, 6r vert.

Perf. 12½x13, 13x12½

1983, Dec. 2 **Litho.**
454-456 A108 Set of 3 3.50 1.00

Souvenir Sheet

457 A108 6r multicolored 6.50 1.75

No. 457 contains one 32x40mm stamp.

People's Republic of Kampuchea, 5th Anniv. — A109

Designs: 50c, Red Cross. 1r, Soldiers. 3r, People celebrating. 6r, Man carrying water.

1984, Jan. 7 **Litho.** ***Perf. 13***
458-460 A109 Set of 3 3.75 1.25

Souvenir Sheet

461 A109 6r multicolored 6.50 1.75

No. 461 contains one 32x40mm stamp.
For surcharges see No. 776.

1984 Winter Olympics, Sarajevo A110

Designs: 20c, Speed skating. 50c, Hockey. 80c, Slalom skiing. 1r, Ski jumping. 1.50r, Biathlon. 2r, Cross-country skiing. 3r, Pairs figure skating. 6r, Women's figure skating.

1984, Jan. 6 **Litho.** ***Perf. 13***
462-468 A110 Set of 7 6.50 2.50

Souvenir Sheet

469 A110 6r multicolored 5.00 3.00

No. 469 contains one 32x40mm stamp.
For surcharges see No. 775.

Birds — A111

Designs: 10c, Bubulcus ibis. 40c, Lanius schach. 80c, Psittacula himalayana. 1r, Chloropsis aurifrons. 1.20r, Clamator coromandus. 2r, Motacilla cinerea. 2.50r, Dendronanthus indicus.

1984, Feb. 2
470-476 A111 Set of 7 15.00 4.00

Intl. Peace in Southeast Asia Forum — A112

Background color: 50c, Green. 1r, Blue. 3r, Violet.

1984, Feb. 25 ***Perf. 13x12½***
477-479 A112 Set of 3 3.75 1.00

Space Exploration — A113

Designs: 10c, Luna 1. 40c, Luna 2. 80c, Luna 3. 1r, Soyuz 6. 1.20r, Soyuz 7. 2r, Soyuz 8. 2.50r, Book, rocket, S.P. Koralev. 6r, Salyut space station.
1r-2.50r are vert.

1984, Mar. 8 ***Perf. 12½***
480-486 A113 Set of 7 6.00 2.00

Souvenir Sheet

487 A113 6r multicolored 6.50 1.75

No. 487 contains one 40x32mm stamp.

1984 Summer Olympic Games, Los Angeles A114

Designs: 20c, Discus. 50c, Long jump. 80c, Hurdles. 1r, Relay race. 1.50r, Pole vault. 2r, Javelin. 3r, High jump. 6r, Sprint race.

1984, Apr. 20 ***Perf. 13***
488-494 A114 Set of 7 7.00 2.50

Souvenir Sheet

495 A114 6r multicolored 5.00 2.50

No. 495 contains one 32x40mm stamp.

Souvenir Sheet

ESPAÑA '84, Madrid — A115

5r, 1933 Hispano-Suiza K6.

1984, Apr. 24 ***Perf. 12½***
496 A115 5r multicolored 5.75 2.25

Wild Animals A116

Designs: 10c, Canis latrans. 40c, Canis dingo. 80c, Lycaon pictus. 1r, Canis aureus. 1.20r, Vulpes vulpes. 2r, Chrysocyon brachyurus, vert. 2.50r, Canis lupus.

1984, May 5 ***Perf. 13***
497-503 A116 Set of 7 9.00 1.75

Locomotives — A117

Designs: 10c, BB-1002, France, 1966. 40c, BB-1052, France, 1966. 80c, Franco-Belgian, 1945. 1r, #231-505, Franco-Belgian, 1929. 1.20r, #803, Germany, 1968. 2r, BDE-405, France, 1957. 2.50r, DS-01, France, 1979.

1984, June 15 **Litho.** ***Perf. 12½***
504-510 A117 Set of 7 7.75 1.75

Flowers A118

Designs: 10c, Magnolia. 40c, Plumeria. 80c, Himenoballis. 1r, Peltophorum roxburghii. 1.20r, Couroupita guianensis. 2r, Lagerstroemia. 2.50r, Thevetia perubiana.

1984, July 10 **Litho.** ***Perf. 13***
511-517 A118 Set of 7 6.00 2.25

Classic Automobiles — A119

Designs: 20c, Mercedes-Benz. 50c, Bugatti. 80c, Alfa Romeo. 1r, Franklin. 1.50r, Hispano-Suiza. 2r, Rolls Royce. 3r, Tatra. 6r, Mercedes Benz, diff.

1984, Sept. 15 ***Perf. 13x12½***
518-524 A119 Set of 7 6.00 2.00

Souvenir Sheet

Perf. 12½

525 A119 6r multicolored 5.00 1.75

No. 525 contains one 40x32mm stamp.

Musical Instruments — A120

Designs: 10c, Sra Lai. 40c, Skor drum. 80c, Skor thom. 1r, Thro khmer. 1.20r, Raneat ek. 2r, Raneat kong. 2.50r, Thro khe.
10c, 80c are vert.

1984, Oct. 10 ***Perf. 13***
526-532 A120 Set of 7 5.00 1.75

Wild Animals A121

Designs: 10c, Gazelle. 40c, Capreolus capreolus. 80c, Lepus. 1r, Cervus elaphus. 1.20r, Elephas maximus. 2r, Genet. 2.50r, Bibos sauveli.
10c-40c, 1r-1.20r are vert.

1984, Nov. 11 ***Perf. 13***
533-539 A121 Set of 7 7.50 1.75

Correggio (1489-1534) — A122

Details from paintings: 20c, Rest on Flight into Egypt. 50c, Martyrdom of the Four Saints. 80c, Mystic Marriage of St. Catherine with Saints Francis and Dominic. 1r, Madonna & Child with Saints John the Baptist, Geminian, Peter Martyr and George. 1.50r, Mystic Marriage of St. Catherine. 2r, The Deposition. 2.50r, The Deposition, diff. 6r, Virgin Crowned by Christ.

1984, Dec. 10 ***Perf. 12½x13***
540-546 A122 Set of 7 4.25 1.00

Souvenir Sheet
Perf. 12½

547 A122 6r multicolored 5.00 1.00

No. 547 contains one 40x32mm stamp.

Natl. Festival — A123

50c, Oxcart. 1r, Horse-drawn cart. 3r, Elephants. 6r, Oxcart with passengers, vert.

1985, Jan. 5 ***Perf. 12½x12***
548-550 A123 Set of 3 4.00 1.00

Souvenir Sheet
Perf. 12½

551 A123 6r multicolored 6.00 1.00

No. 551 contains one 32x40mm stamp.

1986 World Cup Soccer Championships, Mexico — A124

Various soccer players; 20c, vert. 50c, vert. 80c, vert. 1r. 1.50r. 2r, vert. 3r, vert.

1985, Feb. 4 ***Perf. 13***
552-558 A124 Set of 7 4.50 1.25

Souvenir Sheet

559 A124 6r multicolored 5.50 1.00

No. 559 contains one 40x32mm stamp.

Motorcycles — A125

20c, 1939 Eska-Mofa. 50c, 1939 Wanderer. 80c, 1929 Premier. 1r, 1939 Ardie. 1.50r, 1932 Jawa. 2r, 1983 Simson. 3r, 1984 CZ-125.

1985, Mar. 8 **Litho.** ***Perf. 13***
560-566 A125 Set of 7 5.00 1.75

Souvenir Sheet

567 A125 6r 1984 MBA 6.00 1.50

No. 567 contains one 40x32mm stamp.

Mushrooms — A126

Designs: 20c, Gymnopilus spectabilis. 50c, Coprinus micaceus. 80c, Amanita panterina. 1r, Hebelona crustuliniforme. 1.50r, Amanita muscaria. 2r, Coprinus comatus. 3r, Amanita caesarea.

Nos. 569-574 are vert.

1985, Apr. 4 ***Perf. 13***
568-574 A126 Set of 7 6.00 1.40

Soviet Space Achievements — A127

Designs: 20c, Sputnik. 50c, Yuri Gagarin, rocket. 80c, Valentina Tereshkova, Vostok 6. 1r, Cosmonaut walking in space. 1.50r, Soyuz 4 docked with Soyuz 5. 2r, Lunar rover. 3r, Apollo-Soyuz mission. 6r, Soyuz capsule.

1985, Apr. 12 ***Perf. 13***
575-581 A127 Set of 7 4.50 1.25

Souvenir Sheet

582 A127 6r multicolored 5.00 1.00

No. 582 contains one 40x32mm stamp.

Traditional Dances — A128

Designs: 50c, Four dancers. 1r, Three dancers. 3r, One dancer, vert.

1985, Apr. 13 **Litho.** ***Perf. 12½***
583-585 A128 Set of 3 3.00 1.25

End of World War II, 40th Anniv. A129

Designs: 50c, Soldiers celebrating. 1r, Victory parade, Moscow. 3r, Tank battle.

1985, May 9 **Litho.** ***Perf. 12x12½***
586-588 A129 Set of 3 4.25 1.50

Cats — A130

Various cats: 20c, 50c, 80c, 1r, 1.50r, 2r, 3r.

1985, May 16 **Litho.** ***Perf. 12x12½***
589-595 A130 Set of 7 5.50 2.50

Flowers — A131

20c, Lilium Black Dragon. 50c, Iris delavayi. 80c, Crocus aureus. 1r, Cyclamen persicum, wild form. 1.50r, Primula malacoides. 2r, Viola tricolor. 3r, Crocus purpureus.

1985, June 5 **Litho.** ***Perf. 13***
596-602 A131 Set of 7 4.75 1.25

Intl. Music Year — A132

Paintings: 20c, Mezzetin, by Watteau. 50c, St. Cecilia and the Angel, by Saraceni. 80c, Still Life with Violin, Flute and Guitar, by Oudry, horiz. 1r, Three Musicians, by F. Leger. 1.50r, Opera Orchestra, by Degas. 2r, St. Cecilia, by Schedoni. 3r, Young Harlequin with Violin, by Caillard. 6r, The Fifer, by Manet.

1985, June 13 ***Perf. 13***
603-609 A132 Set of 7 4.00 1.25

Souvenir Sheet

610 A132 6r multicolored 4.00 1.25

No. 610 contains one 32x40mm stamp.

Lenin (1870-1924) A133

1r, Portrait. 3r, Lenin standing, map of Soviet Union.

1985, June 20 **Litho.** ***Perf. 13***
611-612 A133 Set of 2 3.25 1.00

ARGENTINA '85 — A134

Birds: 20c, Xanthopsar flavus. 50c, Sicalis flaveola. 80c, Thraupis bonariensis. 1r, Amblyramphus holosericeus. 1.50r, Chiloroceryle amazona. 2r, Ramphastos toco. 3r, Turdus rufiventris.

20c-80c, 1.50r-2r are vert.

1985, July 5 **Litho.** ***Perf. 12½***
613-619 A134 Set of 7 8.50 2.00

Ships A135

Designs: 10c, River boat, 1942. 40c, River boat, 1948. 80c, Tugboat, Japan, 1913. 1r, Dredge. 1.20r, Tugboat, US. 2r, Freighter. 2.50r, Tanker, Panama.

1985, Aug. 8
620-626 A135 Set of 7 4.00 1.40

ITALIA 85 — A136

Paintings: 20c, The Flood, by Michelangelo. 50c, Virgin & St. Margaret, by Il Parmigianino (Filippo Mazzola). 80c, Martyrdom of St. Peter Martyr, by Domenichino. 1r, Spring, by Botticelli. 1.50r, Sacrifice of Abraham, by Veronese. 2r, Meeting of St. Joachim and St. Anne, by Giotto. 3r, Bacchus, by Caravaggio.

6r, Early train.

1985, Oct. 25
627-633 A136 Set of 7 5.00 1.10

Souvenir Sheet

634 A136 6r multicolored 4.00 1.25

No. 634 contains one 32x40mm stamp.

Son Ngoc Minh — A137

1985, Dec. 2 **Litho.** ***Perf. 12x12½***
635-637 A137 Set of 3, 50c, 1r, 3r 2.50 1.25

Fish A138

20c, Barbus tetrazona. 50c, Ophiocephalus micropeltes. 80c, Carassius auratus. 1r, Trichogaster leeri. 1.50r, Puntius hexazona. 2r, Betta splendens. 3r, Datnioides microlepis.

1985, Dec. 28 **Litho.** ***Perf. 13***
638-644 A138 Set of 7 5.50 1.50

1986 World Cup Soccer Championships, Mexico — A139

Various soccer players: 20c, 50c, 80c, 1r, 1.50r, 2r, 3r.

1986, Jan. 29
645-651 A139 Set of 7 4.25 1.25

Souvenir Sheet

652 A139 6r multicolored 4.50 2.50

No. 652 contains one 32x40mm stamp.

Horses A140

Designs: 20c, Cob. 50c, Arabian. 80c, Australian pony. 1r, Appaloosa. 1.50r, Quarter horse. 2r, Vladimir heavy draft. 3r, Andalusian.

1986, Feb. 15
653-659 A140 Set of 7 5.00 1.50

27th Soviet Communist Party Congress A141

Designs: 50c, Space capsules. 1r, Lenin. 5r, Statue, rocket lift-off.

1986, Feb. 25 ***Perf. 12x12½***
660-662 A141 Set of 3 4.25 1.25

Prehistoric Animals — A142

Designs: 20c, Edaphosaurus, horiz. 50c, Sauroctonus, horiz. 80c, Mastodonsaurus, horiz. 1r, Rhamphorhynchus. 1.50r, Brachiosaurus. 2r, Tarbosaurus. 3r, Indricotherium.

1986, Mar. 20 ***Perf. 12½***
663-669 A142 Set of 7 9.00 3.00

Manned Space Flight, 25th Anniv. — A143

10c, Luna 16. 40c, Luna 3. 80c, Vostok. 1r, Alexei Leonov walking in space. 1.20r, Apollo-Soyuz mission. 2r, Soyuz capsule docking with Salyut station. 2.50r, Yuri Gagarin.

1986, Apr. 12 ***Perf. 12½***
670-676 A143 Set of 7 5.75 1.50

Khmer Culture — A144

20c, Temple. 50c, Head of Buddha. 80c, Temple entrance. 1r, 1.50r, 2r, 3r, Various fans.

1986, Apr. 12 ***Perf. 13***
677-683 A144 Set of 7 4.00 1.60

Mercedes-Benz Automobiles — A145

20c, 1885 3-wheel. 50c, 1935 sedan. 80c, 1907 open touring car. 1r, 1920 convertible. 1.50r, 1932 cabriolet. 2r, 1938 2-door. 3r, 1985 sedan.

1986, May 14 ***Perf. 13x12½***
684-690 A145 Set of 7 4.25 1.50

Butterflies A146

Designs: 20c, Danaus genutia. 50c, Graphium amtiphates. 80c, Papilio demoleus. 1r, Danaus sita. 1.50r, Idea blanchardi. 2r, Papilio polytes. 3r, Dabasa payeni.

1986, June 19 ***Perf. 13***
691-697 A146 Set of 7 5.50 1.75

Ships A147

20c, English cog. 50c, Cog. 80c, Nile barge. 1r, Galley. 1.50r, Viking long ship. 2r, Two-masted lateen-rigged ship. 3r, Cog, diff.

1986, July 7 ***Perf. 13***
698-704 A147 Set of 7 4.25 1.50

Halley's Comet — A148

Designs: 10c, Solar system, Copernicus, Galileo, Brahe. 20c, Comet above Adoration of the Magi in painting by Giotto. 50c, Comet, observatory. 80c, Edmond Halley. 1.20r, Giotto probe. 1.50r, Vega probe. 2r, Computer-enhanced images of comet. 6r, Vega probe, diff.

1986, July 21 **Litho.** ***Perf. 12x12½***
705-711 A148 Set of 7 3.25 1.40

Souvenir Sheet

Perf. 13

712 A148 6r multicolored 4.25 1.25

No. 712 contains one 32x40mm stamp.

STOCKHOLMIA 86 — A149

Chess masters: 20c, Ruy Lopez. 50c, Francois Philador. 80c, Adolph Anderssen. 1r, Wilhelm Steinetz. 1.50r, Emanuel Lasker. 2r, José Capablanca. 3r, Alexander Alekhine. 6r, Chess pieces.

1986, Aug. 28 **Litho.** ***Perf. 12½***
713-719 A149 Set of 7 5.00 1.60

Souvenir Sheet

Perf. 13

720 A149 6r multicolored 6.00 1.60

No. 720 contains one 40x32mm stamp.

Cactus — A150

20c, Parodia maasii. 50c, Rebutia marsoneri. 80c, Melocactus evae. 1r, Gymnocalycium valnicekianum. 1.50r, Discocactus silichromus. 2r, Neochilenia simulans. 3r, Weingartia chiqichuquensis.

1986, Sept. 25 ***Perf. 13***
721-727 A150 Set of 7 4.25 1.40

Fruit — A151

Designs: 10c, Bananas. 40c, Papayas. 80c, Mangos. 1r, Breadfruit. 1.20r, Litchi. 2r, Pineapple. 2.50r, Grapefruit, horiz.

1986, Oct. 4 ***Perf. 12½***
728-734 A151 Set of 7 3.00 1.50

Aircraft — A152

20c, Concorde. 50c, DC-10. 80c, 747. 1r, IL-62. 1.50r, IL-86. 2r, AN-124. 3r, A-300.

1986, Nov. 21
735-741 A152 Set of 7 4.25 1.60

Silverware — A153

Designs: 50c, Elephant, containers. 1r, Covered bowl. 3r, Serving dish.

1986, Dec. 2 ***Perf. 13***
742-744 A153 Set of 3 3.75 1.40

World Wildlife Fund A154

Designs: No. 745, 20c, Kouprey. No. 746, 20c, Gaur. 80c, Banteng. 1.50r, Buffalo.

1986, Dec. 30 **Litho.** ***Perf. 13***
745-748 A154 Set of 4 *14.00* 4.00

Tou Samouth A155

Denominations and background colors: 50c, green. 1r, blue, 3r, yellow.

1987, Jan. 7 **Litho.** ***Perf. 13***
749-751 A155 Set of 3 2.75 1.00

1988 Winter Olympic Games, Calgary — A156

Designs: 20c, Biathlon. 50c, Women's figure skating. 80c, Speed skating. 1r, Hockey. 1.50r, Luge. 2r, Two-man bobsled. 3r, Cross-country skiing. 6r, Slalom skiing.

1987, Jan. 14 ***Perf. 13x12½***
752-758 A156 Set of 7 4.25 1.25

Souvenir Sheet

Perf. 12½

759 A156 6r multicolored 4.25 1.10

No. 759 contains one 40x32mm stamp.

1988 Summer Olympic Games, Seoul — A157

Designs: 20c, Weight lifting, vert. 50c, Archery. 80c, Fencing. 1r, Gymnastics, vert. 1.50r, Discus. 2r, Javelin, vert. 3r, Hurdles. 6r, Wrestling.

1987, Feb. 2 *Perf. 12½x13, 13x12½*
760-766 A157 Set of 7 4.25 1.25

Souvenir Sheet
Perf. 13

767 A157 6r multicolored 4.25 1.25

No. 767 contains one 40x32mm stamp.

Dogs A158

Designs: 20c, shown. 50c, Greyhound. 80c, Great Dane. 1r, Doberman pinscher. 1.50r, Samoyed. 2r, Borzoi. 3r, Collie.

1987, Mar. 3 *Perf. 13*
768-774 A158 Set of 7 6.50 1.50

Nos. 458, 463 Surcharged

1987, Mar. **Litho.** *Perf. 13*
775 A110 35r on 50c #463 5.00
776 A109 50r on 50c #458 5.00

Soviet Spacecraft A159

Designs: 20c, Sputnik. 50c, Weather satellite. 80c, Proton. 1r, Vostok 1. 1.50r, Electron-2. 2r, Kosmos. 3r, Luna 2. 6r, Electron-4.

1987, Apr. 12 **Litho.** *Perf. 13*
777-783 A159 Set of 7 4.25 1.60

Souvenir Sheet

784 A159 6r multicolored 4.25 1.25

No. 784 contains one 40x32mm stamp.

Silverware — A159a

Designs: 50c, Long-necked pot, vert. 1r, Box. 1.50r, Tea set. 3r, Sword.

1987, Apr. 13 *Perf. 13*
785-788 A159a Set of 4 3.00 1.00

CAPEX 87 — A160

Birds: 20c, Merops nubicus. 50c, Upupa epops. 80c, Balearica pavonina. 1r, Tyto alba. 1.50r, Halcyon leucocephala. 2r, Pycnonotus jocosus. 3r, Ardea purpurea. 6r, Terpsiphone paradisi.

50c-1.50r, 3r are vert.

1987, May 5 *Perf. 13*
789-795 A160 Set of 7 4.75 1.25

Souvenir Sheet

796 A160 6r multicolored 5.25 2.50

No. 796 contains one 32x40mm stamp.

Early Aircraft Designs A161

Designs by: 20c, Horatio F. Phillips, 1893. 50c, John Stringfellow, 1848. 80c, Thomas Moy, 1875. 1r, Leonardo da Vinci, 1490. 1.50r, Sir George Cayley, 1840. 2r, Sir Hiram Maxim, 1894. 3r, William S. Henson, 1842. 6r, Da Vinci, diff.

1987, Aug. 7 *Perf. 13*
797-803 A161 Set of 7 5.25 1.40

Souvenir Sheet
Perf. 12½

804 A161 6r multicolored 5.00 1.00

No. 804 contains one 32x40mm stamp.

Reptiles A162

Designs: 20c, Testudo gigantea. 50c, Uromastix acanthinuros. 80c, Cyclura macleayi. 1r, Phrynosoma coronatum. 1.50r, Sauromalus obesus. 2r, Ophisaurus apodus. 3r, Thamnophis sirtalis.

1987, Sept. 9 *Perf. 13*
805-811 A162 Set of 7 4.75 1.75

HAFNIA 87 — A163

Helicopters: 20c, Kamov KA-15. 50c, Kamov KA-18. 80c, Westland Lynx WG-13. 1r, Sud Aviation Gazelle. 1.50r, Sud Aviation Puma. 2r, Boeing CH-47 Chinook. 3r, Boeing UTTAS. 6r, Fairey Rotodyne.

1987, Oct. 16 *Perf. 12½x12*
812-818 A163 Set of 7 4.00 1.40

Souvenir Sheet
Perf. 13

819 A163 6r multicolored 4.25 1.50

No. 819 contains one 40x32mm stamp.

Russian October Revolution, 70th Anniv. — A164

1987 **Litho.** *Perf. 12x12¼*
820 A164 2r Soldiers, horse 1.25 .30
821 A164 3r Soldiers 1.75 .50
822 A164 5r Lenin, aides 3.50 .80

Two additional stamps were issued in this set. The editors would like to examine them.

Fire Trucks A165

1987, Nov. 24 **Litho.** *Perf. 13*
823-829 A165 20c, 50c, 80c, 1r, 1.50r, 2r, 3r, set of 7 5.50 2.25

Telecommunications — A166

50c, Dish antenna, vert. 1r, Broadcast center, vert. 3r, Dish antenna, broadcast center.

Perf. 13x12½, 12x12½, 12½x12

1987, Dec. 2
830-832 A166 Set of 3 3.00 1.10

No. 830 is 29x40mm. No. 831 is 28x44mm. No. 832 printed with se-tenant label.

1988 Winter Olympic Games, Calgary A167

Designs: 20c, Speed skating. 50c, Hockey. 80c, Downhill skiing. 1r, Ski jumping. 1.50r, Biathlon. 2r, Pairs figure skating. 3r, Cross-country skiing. 6r, Four-man bobsled.

1988, Jan. 7 *Perf. 12½*
833-839 A167 Set of 7 4.00 1.00

Souvenir Sheet
Perf. 13

840 A167 6r multicolored 2.75 1.10

No. 840 contains one 32x40mm stamp.

Water Projects A168

Designs: 50c, Canal. 1r, Dam under construction. 3r, Dam, bridge.

1988, Jan. 7 **Litho.** *Perf. 13*
841-843 A168 Set of 3 3.00 1.25

1988 Summer Olympic Games, Seoul — A169

Designs: 20c, Balance beam, vert. 50c, Uneven bars. 80c, Rhythmic gymnastics ribbon, vert. 1r, Rhythmic gymnastics hoop, vert. 1.50r, Rhythmic gymnastics clubs, vert. 2r, Rhythmic gymnastics ball. 3r, Floor exercise. 6r, Rhythmic gymnastics, diff.

Perf. 12½x13, 13x12½

1988, Feb. 2 **Litho.**
844-850 A169 Set of 7 4.00 1.50

Souvenir Sheet
Perf. 12½

851 A169 6r multicolored 5.00 2.50

No. 851 contains one 32x40mm stamp.

JUVALUX 88 A170

Various cats. Denominations: 20c, 50c, 80c, 1r, 1.50r, 2r, 3r. Nos. 853-854, 856-858 are vert.

1988, Mar. 15 *Perf. 12½*
852-858 A170 Set of 7 4.75 1.25

Souvenir Sheet
Perf. 13

859 A170 6r multicolored 5.25 2.50

No. 859 contains one 40x32mm stamp.

ESSEN 88 — A171

Ships: 20c, Passenger liner. 50c, Passenger liner, diff. 80c, Research ship. 1r, Communications ship. 1.50r, Tanker. 2r, Hydrofoil. 3r, Hovercraft.

1988, Apr. 14 **Litho.** *Perf. 12½*
860-866 A171 Set of 7 4.00 1.50

Souvenir Sheet
Perf. 13

867 A171 6r Hydrofoil 3.25 1.10

Satellites — A172

Various satellites. Denominations: 20c, 50c, 80c, 1r, 1.50r, 2r, 3r. Nos. 868-870 are vert.

1988, Apr. 24 *Perf. 12½x13, 13x12½*
868-874 A172 Set of 7 4.00 1.50

Souvenir Sheet
Perf. 13

875 A172 6r multicolored 4.75 1.50

No. 875 contains one 40x32mm stamp.

FINLANDIA 88 — A173

Fish: 20c, Xiphophorus helleri. 50c, Hemigrammus ocellifer. 80c, Macropodus opercularis. 1r, Carassius auratus. 1.50r, Hyphessobrycon inesi. 2r, Corynopoma riisei. 3r, Mollienisia latipinna.

6r, Pterophyllum scalare.

1988, Jun 10 **Litho.** *Perf. 13x12½*
876-882 A173 Set of 7 5.75 1.50

Souvenir Sheet
Perf. 12½

883 A173 6r multicolored 5.00 1.50

No. 883 contains one 32x40mm stamp.

Shells — A174

Designs: 20c, Helicostyla florida. 50c, Helicostyla marinduquensis. 80c, Helicostyla fulgens. 1r, Helicostyla woodiana. 1.50r, Chloraea sirena. 2r, Helicostyla mirabilis. 3r, Helicostyla limansauensis.

1988, Aug. 5 Litho. ***Perf. 13x12½***
884-890 A174 Set of 7 5.25 1.50

Insects — A175

Designs: 20c, Coccinellidae. 50c, Zonabride geminata. 80c, Carabus auronitens. 1r, Apis mellifera. 1.50r, Praying mantis. 2r, Odonata. 3r, Malachius aeneus.

1988, Sept. 6 ***Perf. 13x12½***
891-897 A175 Set of 7 6.00 1.50

Orchids A176

Designs: 20c, Cattleya aclandiae. 50c, Odontoglossum Royal Sovereign. 80c, Cattleya labiata. 1r, Ophrys apifera. 1.50r, Laelia anceps. 2r, Laelia pumila. 3r, Stanhopea tigrina, horiz.

1988, Oct. 10 ***Perf. 12½x13, 13x12½***
898-904 A176 Set of 7 5.00 2.00

Reptiles — A177

Designs: 20c, Naja haje, vert. 50c, Iguana iguana, vert. 80c, Dryophis nasuta. 1r, Terrapene carolina. 1.50r, Cyclura macleayi. 2r, Bothrops bicolor. 3r, Naja naja, with hood spread, vert.

1988, Nov. 7 ***Perf. 12x12½, 12½x12***
905-911 A177 Set of 7 6.00 1.75

Dance of the Peacock A178

50c, Trott dance (3 dancers), vert. 1r, Paons dance. 3r, Kantere dance (2 dancers).

1988, Dec. 2 ***Perf. 13***
912-914 A178 Set of 3 3.50 1.25

For surcharges see Nos. 1195-1196.

Bridges — A179

Various Bridges. Denominations: 50c, 1r, 3r.

1989 ***Perf. 13x12½***
915-917 A179 Set of 3 3.25 1.40

Decade of Progress — A180

3r, Telecommunications station. 12r, Central Electrical Plant No. 4. 30r, Cement plant, vert.

1989
918-920 A180 Set of 3 2.75 1.50

1990 World Cup Soccer Championships, Italy — A181

Various soccer players. Denominations: 2r, 3r, 5r, 10r, 15r, 20r, 35r.

1989 ***Perf. 12½x13***
921-927 A181 Set of 7 5.50 1.50

Souvenir Sheet
Perf. 13

928 A181 45r multicolored 4.00 2.00

No. 928 contains one 32x40mm stamp.

Trains A182

Various locomotives. Denominations: 2r, 3r, 5r, 10r, 15r, 20r, 35r.

1989 ***Perf. 13***
929-935 A182 Set of 7 5.75 1.50

Souvenir Sheet
Perf. 12½

936 A182 45r multicolored 5.00 2.00

No. 936 contains one 40x32mm stamp.

A183

1989 ***Perf. 13***
937 A183 12r red & black 1.10 .55

Cuban Revolution, 30th anniv.

Birds — A184

20c, Ara macao. 80c, Kakatoe galerita. 3r, Psittacula krameri. 6r, Ara ararauna. 10r, Poicephalus robustus. 15r, Amazona aestiva. 25r, Pionus senilis, horiz.
45r, Cyanoramphus novaezelandiae.

1989
938-944 A184 Set of 7 6.25 1.25

Souvenir Sheet
Perf. 12½

945 A184 45r multicolored 5.25 2.00

No. 945 contains one 40x32mm stamp.

1992 Winter Olympic Games, Albertville A185

2r, Slalom skiing. 3r, Biathlon. 5r, Cross-country skiing. 10r, Ski jumping. 15r, Speed skating. 20r, Hockey. 35r, Bobsled.
45r, Pairs figure skating.

1989, Mar. 30 ***Perf. 13***
946-952 A185 Set of 7 5.50 1.50

Souvenir Sheet
Perf. 12½

953 A185 45r multicolored 5.00 2.00

No. 953 contains one 32x40mm stamp.

Water Lilies A186

20c, Nymphaea capensis (pink). 80c, Nymphaea capensis (purple). 3r, Nymphaea lotus. 6r, Nymphaea Dir. Geo. T. Moore. 10r, Nymphaea Sunrise. 15r, Nymphaea Escarboncie. 25r, Nymphaea Cladstoniana.
45r, Nymphaea Paul Hariot.

1989 ***Perf. 12½x13***
954-960 A186 Set of 7 4.25 1.25

Souvenir Sheet
Perf. 12½

961 A186 45r multicolored 4.00 2.00

No. 961 contains one 32x40mm stamp.

1992 Summer Olympic Games, Barcelona — A187

Designs: 2r, Wrestling. 3r, Pommel horse, vert. 5r, Shot put. 10r, Running, vert. 15r, Fencing. 20r, Canoeing, vert. 35r, Steeplechase, vert.
45r, Weight lifting, vert.

1989 ***Perf. 13***
962-968 A187 Set of 7 5.50 1.50

Souvenir Sheet
Perf. 12½

969 A187 45r multicolored 5.00 2.50

No. 969 contains one 32x40mm stamp.

Mushrooms A188

Designs: 20c, Xerocomus subtomentosus. 80c, Inocybe patouillardii. 3r, Armillaria mellea. 6r, Agaricus campestris. 10r, Paxillus involutus. 15r, Coprinus comatus. 25r, Lepiota procera.

1989 ***Perf. 12½x13***
970-976 A188 Set of 7 4.50 2.50

Horses — A189

Designs: 2r, Shire. 3r, Brabant. 5r, Bolounais. 10r, Breton. 15r, Vladimir heavy draft. 20r, Italian heavy draft. 35r, Freiberger.
45r, Horse-drawn cart.

1989 ***Perf. 12½***
977-983 A189 Set of 7 4.50 1.50

Souvenir Sheet

984 A189 45r multicolored 4.50 2.50

Nos. 977-983 printed with se-tenant label. No. 984 contains one 40x32mm stamp.

Angkor Wat — A190

Denominations: 35r, 50r, 80r, 100r.

1989, May 15 Litho. ***Perf. 13¼***
985-988 A190 Set of 4 *175.00 175.00*

Cambodia

PHILEXFRANCE 89 — A191

Mail coaches: 2r, 17th cent. 3r, Paris-Lyon, 1720. 5r, 1793. 10r, 1805. 15r, Royal Mail. 20r, 1843. 35r, Paris-Lille, 1837, vert.
45r, 1815, vert.

1989 Litho. *Perf. 13*
989-995 A191 Set of 7 4.75 1.50

Souvenir Sheet
Perf. 12½
996 A191 45r multicolored 4.00 2.50

No. 996 contains one 23x40mm stamp.

BRASILIANA 89 — A192

Butterflies: 2r, Papilio zagreus. 3r, Morpho catenarius. 5r, Morpho aega. 10r, Callithea sapphira. 15r, Catagramma sorana. 20r, Pierella nereis. 35r, Papilio brasiliensis.
45r, Thacia marsyas, horiz.

1989 *Perf. 13*
997-1003 A192 Set of 7 8.00 1.50

Souvenir Sheet
1004 A192 45r multicolored 7.00 2.00

No. 1004 contains one 40x32mm stamp.

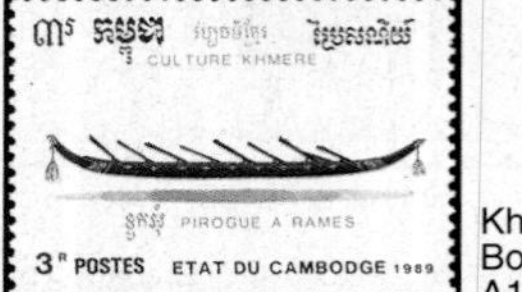

Khmer Boats A193

Various pirogues. Denominations: 3r, 12r, 30r.

1989, Dec. 2 Litho. *Perf. 12½*
1005-1007 A193 Set of 3 3.00 1.25

Natl. Organizations — A194

3r, Youth, vert. 12r, Labor. 30r, Natl. Front.

1990, Jan. 7 Litho. *Perf. 13*
1008-1010 A194 Set of 3 3.50 1.25

1990 World Cup Soccer Championships, Italy — A195

Various soccer players. Denominations: 2r, 3r, 5r, 10r, 15r, 20r, 35r.

1990, Jan. 5 Litho. *Perf. 13*
1011-1017 A195 Set of 7 4.00 1.50

Souvenir Sheet
1018 A195 45r multicolored 3.00 2.00

No. 1018 contains one 32x40mm stamp.
For surcharges see Nos. 1072-1076A.

STAMPWORLD LONDON 90 — A196

Various mail coaches. Denominations: 2r, 3r, 5r, 10r, 15r, 20r, 35r.
45r, Single horse van for rural deliveries.

1990 *Perf. 12½x12*
1019-1025 A196 Set of 7 4.00 1.25

Souvenir Sheet
Perf. 13
1026 A196 45r multicolored 4.25 1.50

Nos. 1019-1025 are printed with se-tenant label. No. 1026 contains one 40x32mm stamp.

Rice — A197

Designs: 3r, Woman, rice. 12r, People hauling rice, horiz. 30r, Women threshing rice.

1990, June 19 Litho. *Perf. 13*
1027-1029 A197 Set of 3 3.25 1.25

1992 Winter Olympic Games, Albertville A198

2r, 4-man bobsled. 3r, Speed skating. 5r, Pairs figure skating. 10r, Hockey. 15r, Biathlon. 20r, Luge. 35r, Ski jumping.
45r, Hockey goalie.

1990 Litho. *Perf. 13*
1030-1036 A198 Set of 7 4.50 1.50

Souvenir Sheet
1037 A198 45r multicolored 3.25 1.50

No. 1037 contains one 32x40mm stamp.

1992 Summer Olympic Games, Barcelona A199

Designs: 2r, Shooting. 3r, Shot put. 5r, Weight lifting. 10r, Boxing. 15r, Pole vault. 20r, Basketball. 35r, Fencing.
45r, Rhythmic gymnastics.

1990
1038-1044 A199 Set of 7 4.50 1.50

Souvenir Sheet
1045 A199 45r multicolored 3.00 1.50

No. 1045 contains one 32x40mm stamp.

Khmer Culture A200

Designs: 3r, Facade, Bantey Srei. 12r, Relief. 30r, Ruins, Banon.

Perf. 12½, 12½x13 (#1048)
1990, Dec. 2 Litho.
1046-1048 A200 Set of 3 3.25 1.25

No. 1048 is 36x21mm.

Dogs A201

20c, Poodle. 80c, Shetland. 3r, Samoyed. 6r, Springer spaniel. 10r, Fox terrier. 15r, Afghan. 25r, Dalmatian.
45r, Bernese.

1990 Litho. *Perf. 13*
1049-1055 A201 Set of 7 5.25 1.25

Souvenir Sheet
1056 A201 45r multicolored 4.00 1.50

No. 1056 contains one 40x32mm stamp.

Cacti — A202

Designs: 20c, Cereus hexagonus. 80c, Arthrocereus rondonianus. 3r, Matucana multicolor. 6r, Hildewintera aureispina. 10r, Opuntia retrosa. 15r, Erdisia tenuicula. 25r, Mamillaria yaquensis.

1990
1057-1063 A202 Set of 7 4.50 1.50

NEW ZEALAND 90 — A203

Butterflies: 2r, Zizina oxleyi. 3r, Cupha prosope. 5r, Heteronympha merope. 10r, Dodonidia helmsi. 15r, Argirophenga antipodum. 20r, Tysonotis danis. 35r, Pyrameis gonnarilla.
45r, Pyrameis itea.

1990 *Perf. 13*
1064-1070 A203 Set of 7 8.00 1.50

Souvenir Sheet
Perf. 12½
1071 A203 45r multicolored 5.50 1.25

No. 1071 contains one 40x32mm stamp.

Nos. 1012-1017 Surcharged in Red

1990 Litho. *Perf. 13*

1072	A195	200r on 3r #1012	
1073	A195	300r on 5r #1013	
1074	A195	500r on 10r #1014	
1075	A195	800r on 15r #1015	
1076	A195	1000r on 20r #1016	
1076A	A195	2000r on 35r #1017	

Intl. Literacy Year — A204

Denominations: 3r, 12r, 30r.

1990 Litho. *Perf. 13*
1077-1079 A204 Set of 3 4.25 1.50

Ships A205

Designs: 20c, English, 1200. 80c, Spanish galleon, 16th cent. 3r, Dutch ship, 1627. 6r, La Couronne, 1638. 10r, L'Astrolabe, 1826. 15r, French packet, Louisiana, 1864. 25r, Clipper ship, 1900, vert.
45r, Merchant ship, 1800.

1990 Litho. *Perf. 13*
1080-1086 A205 Set of 7 6.00 1.50

Souvenir Sheet
Perf. 12½
1087 A205 45r multicolored 3.50 1.50

No. 1087 contains one 32x40mm stamp.

Natl. Building Campaign — A206

3r, Railroad. 12r, Cargo ship, Kampong Som. 30r, Fishing boats, Kampong Som.

1990 Litho. *Perf. 13*
1088-1090 A206 Set of 3 4.50 1.25

PARIS 90 — A207

Chess pieces and: 2r, Sacré Coeur. 3r, Equestrian statue. 5r, Winged Victory of Samothrace. 10r, Chateau, Azay le Riddeau. 15r,

Sculpture, "The Dance." 20r, Eiffel Tower. 35r, Arc de Triomphe.
45r, Chess pieces, horiz.

1990, Nov. 15 Litho. *Perf. 13*
1091-1097 A207 Set of 7 5.75 2.00

Souvenir Sheet

1098 A207 45r multicolored 4.75 1.50

No. 1098 contains one 40x32mm stamp.

Space Day — A208

Designs: 2r, Vostok. 3r, Soyuz. 5r, Artificial satellite. 10r, Luna 10. 15r, Mars 1. 20r, Venera 3. 35r, Mir.
45r, Energia, Buran.

1990 Litho. *Perf. 13*
1099-1105 A208 Set of 7 5.00 1.50

Souvenir Sheet

1106 A208 45r multicolored 3.50 1.50

No. 1106 contains one 32x40mm stamp.
For surcharges see Nos. 1145-1151.

Discovery of America, 500th Anniv. (in 1992) — A209

Designs: 2r, Columbus. 3r, Queen Isabella's jewelry chest. 5r, Queen Isabella. 10r, Santa Maria. 15r, Juan de la Cosa. 20r, Columbus Monument. 35r, Pyramid, Yucatan.
45r, Columbus, diff.

1990, Oct. 12 Litho. *Perf. 13*
1107-1113 A209 Set of 7 6.75 2.00

Souvenir Sheet

1114 A209 45r multicolored 4.00 1.25

No. 1114 contains one 32x40mm stamp.

Natl. Festival A210

Designs: 100r, Tire production. 300r, Rural infirmary. 500r, Fisherman, vert.

Perf. 12½, 13 (#1117)

1991, Jan. 7 Litho.
1115-1117 A210 Set of 3 4.00 1.75

No. 1117 is 28x40mm.

1994 World Cup Soccer Championships, US — A211

Various soccer players. Denominations: 5r, 25r, 70r, 100r, 200r, 400r, 1000r.

1991, Feb. 15 Litho. *Perf. 13*
1118-1124 A211 Set of 7 5.00 1.75

Souvenir Sheet

1125 A211 900r multicolored 2.75 1.25

No. 1125 contains one 32x40mm stamp.

1992 Winter Olympic Games, Albertville A212

Designs: 5r, Speed skating. 25r, Slalom skiing. 70r, Hockey. 100r, Bobsled. 200r, Freestyle skiing. 400r, Pairs figure skating. 1000r, Downhill skiing.
900r, Ski jumping.

1991, Mar. 30 Litho. *Perf. 12½*
1126-1132 A212 Set of 7 5.00 2.00

Souvenir Sheet

Perf. 13

1133 A212 900r multicolored 4.25 1.25

No. 1133 contains one 32x40mm stamp.

Khmer Culture A213

Statues: 100r, Garuda, 10th cent. 300r, Torso of Vishnu reclining, 11th cent. 500r, Reclining Nandin, 7th cent.

1991, Apr. 13 Litho. *Perf. 12½*
1134-1136 A213 Set of 3 3.25 2.00

1992 Summer Olympic Games, Barcelona A214

Designs: 5r, Pole vault. 25r, Table tennis. 70r, Women's running. 100r, Wrestling. 200r, Women's gymnastics. 400r, Tennis. 1000r, Boxing.
900r, Balance beam.

1991, Apr. 25 Litho. *Perf. 12½x13*
1137-1143 A214 Set of 7 4.75 1.50

Souvenir Sheet

Perf. 13

1144 A214 900r multicolored 3.25 1.25

No. 1144 contains one 32x40mm stamp.

Nos. 1099-1105 Surcharged in Red

1991 Litho. *Perf. 13*

1145 A208 100r on 2r #1099 —
1146 A208 150r on 3r #1100 *75.00*
1147 A208 200r on 5r #1101 *75.00*
1148 A208 300r on 10r #1102 *75.00*
1149 A208 500r on 15r #1103 *75.00*
1150 A208 1500r on 20r #1104 — —
1151 A208 2000r on 35r #1105 *75.00*

Aircraft — A215

Designs: 5r, DC-10-30. 25r, MD-11. 70r, IL-96-300. 100r, A-310. 200r, YAK-42. 400r, TU-154. 1000r, DC-9

1991, June 15 Litho. *Perf. 13x12½*
1152-1158 A215 Set of 7 5.00 1.75

ESPAMER 91 — A216

Pre-Columbian pottery: 5r, Catamarca. 25r, Catamarca, vert. 70r, Tucuman, vert. 100r, Santiago del Estero. 200r, Santiago del Estero, diff. 400r, Tucuman, diff., vert. 1000r, Catamarca, diff.
900r, Catamarca, diff.

1991, July 10 *Perf. 13*
1159-1165 A216 Set of 7 5.50 2.00

Souvenir Sheet

Perf. 12½

1166 A216 900r multicolored 3.75 1.25

No. 1166 contains one 40x32mm stamp.

Discovery of America, 500th Anniv. (in 1992) — A217

Designs: 5r, Pinta, vert. 25r, Niña, vert. 70r, Santa Maria, vert. 100r, Landing of Columbus. 200r, Encountering new cultures. 400r, First European settlement in Americas. 1000r, Native village.
900r, Columbus.

1991, Oct. 12 *Perf. 12½x13, 13x12½*
1167-1173 A217 Set of 7 6.00 2.00

Souvenir Sheet

Perf. 12½

1174 A217 900r multicolored 3.25 1.10

No. 1174 contains one 40x32mm stamp.

PHILANIPPON 91 — A218

Butterflies: 5r, Neptis pryeri. 25r, Papilio xuthus. 70r, Cyrestis thyodamas. 100r, Argynnis anadiomene. 200r, Lethe marginalis. 400r, Artopoetes pryeri. 1000r, Danaus chrysippus.
900r, Ochlodes subhyalina.

1991, Nov. 16 *Perf. 13*
1175-1181 A218 Set of 7 7.50 2.00

Souvenir Sheet

Perf. 12½

1182 A218 900r multicolored 6.00 2.50

No. 1182 contains one 40x32mm stamp.

Natl. Building Campaign A219

Designs: 100r, Fishing port. 300r, Preparing palm sugar, vert. 500r, Harvesting peppers.

1991, Dec. 2 Litho. *Perf. 12½*
1183-1185 A219 Set of 3 4.25 2.40

Natl. Festival — A220

Traditional costumes: 150r, Chakdomuk. 350r, Longvek. 1000r, Angkor.

1992, Jan. 7 *Perf. 13*
1186-1188 A220 Set of 3 3.50 1.25

1992 Summer Olympic Games, Barcelona A221

5r, Wrestling. 15r, Soccer. 80r, Weight lifting. 400r, Archery. 1500r, Balance beam.
1000r, Equestrian.

1992, Jan. Litho. *Perf. 13*
1189-1193 A221 Set of 5 3.50 1.25

Souvenir Sheet

Perf. 12½

1194 A221 1000r multicolored 3.25 1.25

No. 1194 contains one 32x40mm stamp.

Nos. 913-914 Surcharged in Red

1992, Jan. Litho. *Perf. 13*

1195 A178 200r on 3r #914
1196 A178 300r on 1r #913

Fish A222

Designs: 5r, Hyphessobrycon innesi. 15r, Betta splendens. 80r, Nematobrycon palmen. 400r, Colisa lalia. 1500r, Hoplosternum thoracatum.
1000r, Pterophyllum scalare.

1992, Feb. 8 Litho. *Perf. 12½*
1197-1201 A222 Set of 5 5.00 1.50

Souvenir Sheet

1202 A222 1000r multicolored 3.75 1.25

No. 1202 contains one 40x32mm stamp.

1994 World Cup Soccer Championships, US — A223

Various soccer plays. Denominations: 5r, 15r, 80r, 400r, 1500r. Nos. 1203, 1205-1207 are vert.

1992, Mar. 6 Litho. *Perf. 12½*
1203-1207 A223 Set of 5 3.75 1.50

Souvenir Sheet

1208 A223 1000r multicolored 2.75 1.25

No. 1208 contains one 40x32mm stamp.

Khmer Culture — A224

19th cent. structures: 150r, Monument. 350r, Stupa. 1000r, Library of Mandapa.

1992, Apr. 13 Litho. *Perf. 12½*
1209-1211 A224 Set of 3 4.75 2.75

Leonardo da Vinci (1452-1519) — A225

Designs: 5r, Automobile. 15r, Container ship. 80r, Helicopter. 400r, Scuba gear. 1500r, Parachute, vert.
1000r, Portrait.

1992, Apr. 15 Litho. *Perf. 12x12½*
1212-1216 A225 Set of 5 7.00 1.50

Souvenir Sheet

Perf. 13

1217 A225 1000r multicolored 4.25 1.25

Nos. 1212-1216 each printed with se-tenant labels showing Da Vinci's conceptions of the items shown on the stamps. No. 1217 contains one 32x40mm stamp.

EXPO 92, Seville A226

Inventors, builders: 5r, De la Cierva, autogyro. 15r, Edison, electric light bulb. 80r, Morse, telegraph. 400r, Monturiol, submarine. No. 1222, 1500r, Bell, telephone.
No. 1223, 1500r, Fulton, steamship.

1992, Apr. 23 *Perf. 12½*
1218-1222 A226 Set of 5 4.75 1.25

Souvenir Sheet

Perf. 13

1223 A226 1000r pink & black 3.25 1.25

No. 1223 contains one 32x40mm stamp.

1992 Summer Olympic Games, Barcelona — A227

Designs: 5r, Weight lifting. 15r, Boxing. 80r, Basketball. 400r, Sprints. 1500r, Water polo.
1000r, Women's gymnastics.

1992, May 15 *Perf. 13*
1224-1228 A227 Set of 5 7.00 1.50

Souvenir Sheet

Perf. 12½

1229 A227 1000r multicolored 4.50 1.25

No. 1229 contains one 40x32mm stamp.

Environmental Protection — A228

Designs: 5r, Women filling water jars. 15r, Pagoda. 80r, Palm trees. 400r, Boy riding water buffalo. 1500r, Lake, swimmers.
1000r, Angkor Wat.

1992, June 16 Litho. *Perf. 12½*
1230-1234 A228 Set of 5 5.00 1.75

Souvenir Sheet

Perf. 13

1235 A228 1000r multicolored 3.75 1.25

No. 1235 contains one 42x32mm stamp.

GENOA 92 — A229

Explorers, ship: 5r, Bougainville, Boudeuse. 15r, Cook, Endeavour. 80r, Darwin, Beagle. 400r, Cousteau, Calypso. 1500r, Heyerdahl, Kon Tiki.
1000r, Columbus.

1992, Aug. 1 Litho. *Perf. 12x12½*
1236-1240 A229 Set of 5 4.25 1.50

Souvenir Sheet

Perf. 12½

1241 A229 1000r multicolored 3.00 1.25

No. 1241 contains one 32x40mm stamp.

Mushrooms A230

Designs: 5r, Albatrellus confluens. 15r, Boletus calopus. 80r, Stropharia aeruginosa. 400r, Telamonia armillata. 1500r, Cortinarius traganus.

1992, Sept. 25 *Perf. 13*
1242-1246 A230 Set of 5 4.50 1.50

Seaplanes — A231

Designs: 5r, Bellanca Pacemaker, 1930. 15r, Canadair CL-215, 1965. 80r, G-21A Goose, 1937. 400r, Sealand SA-6, 1947. 1500r, Short S-23, 1936.
1000r, G-44 Widgeon, 1940.

1992, Oct. 16 *Perf. 12½x12*
1247-1251 A231 Set of 5 4.00 1.25

Souvenir Sheet

Perf. 13

1252 A231 1000r multicolored 3.00 1.25

No. 1252 contains one 32x40mm stamp.

Natl. Development A232

Designs: 150r, Dish antenna. 350r, Dish antenna, flags. 1000r, Hotel Cambodiana.

1992, Dec. 2 Litho. *Perf. 12½*
1253-1255 A232 Set of 3 4.25 1.25

Natl. Festival A233

Designs: 50r, Sociological Institute. 450r, Motel Cambodiana. 1000r, Theater.

1993, Jan. 7 Litho. *Perf. 12½*
1256-1258 A233 Set of 3 4.25 1.25

Dolphin, Bathyscaph — A234

Fauna, machine: 150r, shown. 200r, Falcon, jet fighter. 250r, Beaver, dam. 500r, Bat, satellite. 900r, Hummingbird, helicopter.

1993, Feb. 5 Litho. *Perf. 13*

Without Gum

1259-1263 A234 Set of 5 4.50 1.25

Flowers — A235

Designs: 150r, Datura suaveolens. 200r, Convolvulus tricolor. 250r, Hippeastrum hybrid. 500r, Camellia hybrid. 900r, Lilium speciosum.
1000r, Datura suaveolens, camellia, lilium speciosum.

1993, Mar. 15 *Perf. 13*

Without Gum

1264-1268 A235 Set of 5 5.75 1.25

Souvenir Sheet

Perf. 12½

1269 A235 1000r multicolored 3.75 1.25

No. 1269 contains one 40x32mm stamp.

Khmer Culture A236

Designs: 50r, Statue of a Nandin. 450r, Temple Vihear. 1000r, Man with offerings.

1993, Apr. 13 Litho. *Perf. 12½*
1270-1272 A236 Set of 3 5.00 2.75

Wildlife — A237

150r, Cynocephalus volans. 200r, Petuarista petuarista. 250r, Ptychozoon homalocephalum. 500r, Rhacophorus nigropalmatus. 900r, Draco volans.

1993, May 4 Litho. *Perf. 12½x12*

Without Gum

1273-1277 A237 Set of 5 4.50 1.50

BRASILIANA 93 — A238

Butterflies: 250r, Symbrenthia hypselis. 350r, Sithon nedymond. 600r, Geitoneura minyas. 800r, Argyreus hyperbius. 1000r, Argyrophenga antipodum.
1500r, Pararge schakra.

1993, June 15 *Perf. 12½x12*

Without Gum

1278-1282 A238 Set of 5 8.25 1.50

Souvenir Sheet

Perf. 12½

1283 A238 1500r multicolored 5.00 2.50

No. 1283 contains one 40x32mm stamp.

UN Transitional Authority in Cambodia (UNTAC) Pacification Program A239

150r, Cambodian soldiers approaching UN base. 200r, Cambodians entering camp. 250r, Cambodians surrendering weapons to UN. 500r, Vocational training. 900r, Cambodians re-entering society.
1000r, Returning to homes and family.

1993, Aug. 4 Litho. *Perf. 12½*
1284-1288 A239 Set of 5 5.00 1.50

Souvenir Sheet

Perf. 13

1289 A239 1000r blue & black 4.50 2.00

No. 1289 contains one 32x40mm stamp.

Ships A240

150r, Venetian caravel. 200r, Phoenician galley. 250r, Egyptian merchantman. 500r, Genoese merchantman. 900r, English merchantman.

1993, Aug. 27 Litho. *Perf. 13*
Without Gum
1290-1294 A240 Set of 5 4.00 1.25

Alberto Santos-Dumont (1873-1932) — A241

Designs: 150r, Portrait, Balloon, Eiffel Tower, vert. 200r, 14-bis, 1906. 250r, Demoiselle. 500r, EMB-201A. 900r, EMB-111.

1993, Sept. 10 *Perf. 13*
Without Gum
1295-1299 A241 Set of 5 4.00 1.25

1994 World Cup Soccer Championships, US — A242

Various soccer plays. Denominations: 250r, 350r, 600r, 800r, 1000r, vert.

1993, Sept. 23 Litho. *Perf. 12½*
1300-1304 A242 Set of 5 5.00 1.75
Souvenir Sheet
1305 A242 1500r multicolored 4.00 1.50

No. 1305 contains one 40x32mm stamp.

BANGKOK 93 — A243

Ducks: 250r, Anas penelope. 350r, Anas formosa. 600r, Aix galericulata. 800r, Aix sponsa. 1000r, Histrionicus histrionicus.
1500r, Head of Air galericulata.

1993, Oct. 1 Litho. *Perf. 13*
Without Gum
1306-1310 A243 Set of 5 5.00 1.75
Souvenir Sheet
1311 A243 1500r multicolored 5.00 2.50

No. 1311 contains one 40x32mm stamp.

Vertical Take-Off Aircraft — A244

Designs: 150r, First helicopter model, France, 1784, vert. 200r, Steam helicopter model, 1863, vert. 250r, New York-Atlanta-Miami autogyro flight, 1927. 500r, Sikorsky helicopter, 1943. 900r, French VTOL jet.
1000r, Juan de la Cierva's autogyro C-4, 1923.

Perf. 12x12½, 12½x12
1993, Nov. 6 Without Gum
1312-1316 A244 Set of 5 4.00 1.25
Souvenir Sheet
Perf. 12½
1317 A244 1000r multicolored 3.00 1.25

No. 1317 contains one 40x32mm stamp.

Insects — A245

Designs: 50r, Cnaphalocrosis medinalis. 450r, Cicadelle brune. 500r, Scirpophaga incertulas. No. 1321, 1000r, Diopsis macrophthlalma.
No. 1322, Leptocorisa oratorius.

1993, Dec. 2 *Perf. 13*
1318-1321 A245 Set of 4 5.00 1.25
Souvenir Sheet
Perf. 12½
1322 A245 1000r multicolored 4.00 1.25

Issued without gum.
No. 1322 contains one 32x40mm stamp.

Independence, 40th Anniv. — A246

Designs: 300r, Ministry of Posts and Telecommunications. 500r, Independence Monument, 1953, vert. 700r, Natl. flag.

1993 Litho. *Perf. 12½*
1323-1325 A246 Set of 3 5.25 2.00

Hummel Figurines A247

Designs: 50r, Boy riding pony. 100r, Girl with baby carriage. 150r, Girl bathing doll. 200r, Girl holding doll. 250r, Boys playing. 300r, Girls pulling boy in cart. 350r, Girls playing ring-around-the-rosie. 600r, Boys with stick and drum.

1993 Litho. *Perf. 12½*
1326-1333 A247 Set of 8 6.25 1.75

1994 Winter Olympic Games, Lillehammer — A248

150r, Women's figure skating, vert. 250r, Two-man luge. 400r, Downhill skiing. 700r, Biathlon. 1000r, Speed skating, vert.
1500r, Curling, vert.

1994, Jan. 23 *Perf. 13*
1334-1338 A248 Set of 5 5.00 1.50
Souvenir Sheet
1339 A248 1500r multicolored 3.25 1.25

No. 1339 contains one 32x40mm stamp.

Classic Automobiles — A249

Designs: 150r, 1924 Opel. 200r, 1901 Mercedes. 250r, 1927 Model T Ford. 500r, 1907 Rolls Royce. 900r, 1908 Hutton.
1000r, 1931 Duesenberg.

1994, Feb. 20 *Perf. 13*
1340-1344 A249 Set of 5 5.00 1.25
Souvenir Sheet
1345 A249 1000r multicolored 4.00 1.25

No. 1345 contains one 32x40mm stamp.

1996 Summer Olympic Games, Atlanta — A250

Designs: 150r, Women's gymnastics. 200r, Soccer. 250r, Javelin. 300r, Canoeing. 600r, Running. 1000r, Diving, horiz.
1500r, Equestrian.

1994, Mar. 20 *Perf. 13*
1346-1351 A250 Set of 6 4.50 1.50
Souvenir Sheet
1352 A250 1500r multicolored 4.00 1.25

No. 1352 contains one 32x40mm stamp.

Khmer Statues — A251

Designs: 300r, Siva and Uma. 500r, Vishnu. 700r, King Jayavarman VII.

1994, Apr. 13
1353-1355 A251 Set of 3 5.00 2.75

Intl. Olympic Committee, Cent. — A252

Designs: 100r, Olympic Flag. 300r, Flag, Torch. 600r, Flag, Baron de Coubertin.

1994, Apr. 23 *Perf. 12½*
1356-1358 A252 Set of 3 3.25 1.40

Prehistoric Animals — A253

150r, Mesonyx. 250r, Doedicurus. 400r, Mylodon. 700r, Uintatherium. 1000r, Hyrachyus.

1994, May 10 *Perf. 12½*
1359-1363 A253 Set of 5 6.00 2.00

1994 World Cup Soccer Championships, U.S. — A254

Various soccer plays. Denominations: 150r, 250r, 400r, 700r, 1000r.
1500r, Player in long sleeved green shirt and black shorts with "1" holding ball.

1994, June 17 *Perf. 12½*
1364-1368 A254 Set of 5 5.00 1.50
Souvenir Sheet
1369 A254 1500r multicolored 4.00 1.25

No. 1369 contains one 32x40mm stamp.

Statues A255

Designs: 300r, shown. 500r, Soldiers in combat, vert. 700r, Lions, vert.

1994 *Perf. 13*
1370-1372 A255 Set of 3 4.50 2.75

Beetles A256

Designs: 150r, Chlorophanus viridis. 200r, Chrysochroa fulgidissima. 250r, Lytta vesicatoria. 500r, Purpuricenus kaehleri. 900r, Dynastes hercules.
1000r, Timarcha tenebricosa.

1994, July 7 *Perf. 12½*
1373-1377 A256 Set of 5 5.50 1.50
Souvenir Sheet
1378 A256 1000r multicolored 3.75 1.00

No. 1378 contains one 40x32mm stamp.

Submarines — A257

Designs: 150r, Halley's diving bell, 1690, vert. 200r, Gimnote, 1886. 250r, Peral, 1888. 500r, Nuclear-powered Nautilus, 1954. 900r, Bathyscaphe Trieste, 1953.
1000r, Ictineo, 1885.

1994, Aug. 12 ***Perf. 13***
1379-1383 A257 Set of 5 5.25 1.50

Souvenir Sheet

Perf. 12½

1384 A257 1000r multicolored 3.75 1.00

No. 1384 contains one 40x32mm stamp.

Chess Champions — A258

Designs: 150r, Francois-André Philador, 1795. 200r, Louis de la Bourdonnais, 1821. 250r, Adolph Anderssen, 1851. 500r, Paul Morphy, 1858. 900r, Wilhelm Steinitz, 1866. 1000r, Emanuel Lasker, 1894.

1994, Sept. 20 ***Perf. 13***
1385-1389 A258 Set of 5 4.75 1.50

Souvenir Sheet

1390 A258 1000r multicolored 3.00 1.00

No. 1390 contains one 32x40mm stamp.

Aircraft A259

Designs: 150r, Sikorsky S-42 flying boat. 200r, Vought-Sikorsky VS-300A helicopter. 250r, Sikorsky S-37 biplane. 500r, Sikorsky S-35 biplane. 900r, Sikorsky S-43 amphibian. 1000r, 1st 4-engine bomber, Ilya Mourometz.

1994, Oct. 6 ***Perf. 13***
1391-1395 A259 Set of 5 4.25 1.50

Souvenir Sheet

Perf. 12½

1396 A259 1000r multicolored 3.25 1.00

No. 1396 contains one 40x32mm stamp.

Birds A260

Designs: 150r, Remiz pendulinus, vert. 250r, Panurus biarmicus. 400r, Emberiza rustica. 700r, Emberiza schoeniclus. 1000r, Regulus regulus. 1500r, Pitta angolensis.

1994, Nov. 20 ***Perf. 12½***
1397-1401 A260 Set of 5 5.50 1.50

Souvenir Sheet

Perf. 13

1402 A260 1500r multicolored 4.00 1.40

No. 1402 contains one 32x40mm stamp.

Independence Festival — A261

Designs: 300r, Postal Service float. 500r, Soldiers marching. 700r, Army unit marching.

1994, Dec. 9 ***Perf. 13***
1403-1405 A261 Set of 3 4.50 1.75

Natl. Development — A262

Designs: 300r, Chruoi Changwar Bridge. 500r, Olympic Commercial Center. 700r, Sakamony Chedei Temple.

1994, Dec. 10
1406-1408 A262 Set of 3 4.50 1.50

Prehistoric Animals — A263

100r, Psittacosaurus. 200r, Protoceratops. 300r, Montanoceraptors. 400r, Centrosaurus. 700r, Styracosaurus. 800r, Triceratops.

1995, Jan. 10
1409-1414 A263 Set of 6 6.50 1.50

Butterflies A264

100r, Anthocharis cardamines. 200r, Iphiclides podalirius. 300r, Mesoacidalia aglaja. 600r, Vanessa atalanta. 800r, Inachis io.

1995, Feb. 12
1415-1419 A264 Set of 5 7.00 1.50

1996 Summer Olympic Games, Atlanta A265

Designs: 100r, Swimming. 200r, Rhythmic gymnastics. 400r, Basketball. 800r, Soccer. 1000r, Cycling. 1500r, Running. 200r-1500r are vert.

1995, Mar. 9
1420-1424 A265 Set of 5 5.50 1.50

Souvenir Sheet

1425 A265 1500r multicolored 3.50 1.25

No. 1425 contains one 32x40mm stamp.

Mushrooms A266

Designs: 100r, Amanita phalloides. 200r, Cantharellus cibarius. 300r, Armillaria mellea. 600r, Agaricus campestris. 800r, Amanita muscaria.

1995, Mar. 23
1426-1430 A266 Set of 5 5.25 1.50

Statues — A267

Designs: 300r, Kneeling ascetic. 500r, Parasurama. 700r, Siva.

1995, Apr. 13 ***Perf. 12½***
1431-1433 A267 Set of 3 4.00 1.40

Protected Wildlife — A268

Designs: 300r, Bos gaurus. 500r, Bos sauveli, vert. 700r, Grus antigone, vert.

1995, May 5 ***Perf. 13***
1434-1436 A268 Set of 3 4.00 1.25

Parrots — A269

Designs: 100r, Lorus lory. 200r, Polytelis alexandrae. 400r, Eclectus voratus. 800r, Ara macao. 1000r, Melopsittacus undulatus. 1500r, Amazona ochrocephala.

1995, May 23 ***Perf. 13***
1437-1441 A269 Set of 5 6.50 1.50

Souvenir Sheet

Perf. 12½

1442 A269 1500r multicolored 5.00 2.50

No. 1442 contains one 32x40mm stamp.

Tourism A270

Public gardens: 300r, Sculpture of Garuda. 500r, Fountain. 700r, Sculpture of mythological figures.

1995, July 15 ***Perf. 12½***
1443-1445 A270 Set of 3 4.00 1.50

Locomotives — A271

100r, Richard Trevithick's steam locomotive, 1804. 200r, George Stephenson's Rocket, 1830. 300r, Stephenson's Locomotion, 1825. 600r, Lafayette, 1837. 800r, Best Friend of Charleston, 1830. 1000r, Stephenson, vert.

1995, Aug. 17
1446-1450 A271 Set of 5 4.50 1.50

Souvenir Sheet

1451 A271 1000r multicolored 3.50 1.25

No. 1451 contains one 32x40mm stamp.

World War II Aircraft A272

100r, Bristol Blenheim II, vert. 200r, North American B-25. 300r, Avro Anson. 600r, Avro Manchester. 800r, Consolidated B-24. 1000r, Boeing B-17E.

Perf. 12x12½, 12½x12

1995, Sept. 15
1452-1456 A272 Set of 5 4.50 1.50

Souvenir Sheet

Perf. 12½

1457 A272 1000r multicolored 3.25 1.25

No. 1457 contains one 32x40mm stamp.

FAO, 50th Anniv. A273

Designs: 300r, Separating rice plants. 500r, Transplanting rice. 700r, Model rice farm.

1995, Oct. 24 ***Perf. 13***
1458-1460 A273 Set of 3 3.50 1.00

UN, 50th Anniv. A274

Designs: 300r, Bridge. 500r, People on bridge. 700r, Central spans of bridge.

1995, Oct. 24 ***Perf. 12½***
1461-1463 A274 Set of 3 4.00 1.50

Queen Monineath A275

700r, shown. 800r, King Norodom Sihanouk.

1995, Nov. 9 ***Perf. 12½x13***
1464-1465 A275 Set of 2 4.75 1.50

Fish A276

100r, Heniochus acuminatus. 200r, Chelmon rostratus. 400r, Amphiprion percula. 800r, Paracanthurus hepatus. 1000r, Holocanthus ciliaris. 1500r, Coris angulata, vert.

1995, Nov. 19 ***Perf. 12½***
1466-1470 A276 Set of 5 5.75 1.50

Souvenir Sheet

1471 A276 1500r multicolored 4.75 1.25

Main Post Office, Cent. A277

Denominations: 300r, 500r, 700r.

1995, Dec. 2 ***Perf. 12½***
1472-1474 A277 Set of 3 5.50 1.40

Admission to UN, 40th Anniv. — A278

300r, Independence Monument. 400r, Angkor Wat. 800r, Natl. flag, vert.

Perf. 12½x13, 13x12½

1995, Dec. 14 **Litho.**
1475-1477 A278 Set of 3 5.50 1.25

1996 Summer Olympic Games, Atlanta — A279

Designs: 100r, Tennis. 200r, Volleyball. 300r, Soccer. No. 1480A, 500r, Running. 900r, Baseball. 1000r, Basketball.
1500r, Windsurfing.

1996, Jan. 10 **Litho.** ***Perf. 12½x13***
1478-1482 A279 Set of 6 5.50 1.50

Souvenir Sheet

Perf. 12½

1483 A279 1500r multicolored 3.50 1.25

No. 1483 contains one 32x40mm stamp.

Tourism — A280

50r, Kep State Chalet. 100r, Power station. 200r, Wheelchair. 500r, Wheelchair basketball. 800r, Making crutches, vert. 1000r, Kep beach. 1500r, Serpent Island.

1996, Jan. 30 ***Perf. 12½***

1484	A280	50r multi	.25	.25
1485	A280	100r multi	.25	.25
1486	A280	200r multi	.25	.25
1487	A280	500r multi	.55	.25
1488	A280	800r multi	.90	.25
1489	A280	1000r multi	1.25	.35
1490	A280	1500r multi	1.75	.45
		Nos. 1484-1490 (7)	5.20	2.05

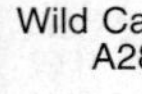

Wild Cats A281

100r, Felis libyca, vert. 200r, Felis silvestris. 300r, Felis caracal. 500r, Felis geoffroyi. 900r, Felis nigripes. 1000r, Felis planiceps.

1996, Feb. 8 ***Perf. 13***
1491-1496 A281 Set of 6 5.75 2.00

1998 World Cup Soccer Championships, France — A282

Various soccer players. Denominations: 100r, 200r, 300r, 500r, 900r, 1000r. No. 1502 is horiz.

1996, Mar. 15 ***Perf. 13***
1497-1502 A282 Set of 6 5.50 1.50

Souvenir Sheet

1503 A282 1500r multicolored 3.50 1.25

No. 1503 contains one 32x40mm stamp.

Khmer Culture — A283

100r, Tusmukh. 500r, Ream Iso. 900r, Isei.

1996, Apr. 13 **Litho.** ***Perf. 12½x13***
1504-1506 A283 Set of 3 3.75 1.50

Locomotives — A284

100r, Pacific Type. 200r, Unidentified, 1902. 300r, Unidentified, 1930. 500r, Unidentified, 1914. 900r, LMS #6202, 1930. 1000r, Snake, 1864.
1500r, Canadian Pacific.

1996, Apr. 20
1507-1512 A284 Set of 6 4.25 1.50

Souvenir Sheet

1513 A284 1500r multicolored 2.75 1.25

No. 1513 contains one 40x32mm stamp.
CAPEX 96 (No. 1513).

Birds A285

Designs: 100r, Kittacinela malabarica, vert. 200r, Leiothrix lutea. 300r, Parus varius, vert. 500r, Oriolus chinensis. 900r, Cettia diphone. 1000r, Cyanoptila cyanomelana, vert.

1996, May 7
1514-1519 A285 Set of 6 5.00 1.50

Olymphilex '96 — A286

Designs: 100r, Rhythmic gymnastics. 200r, Judo. 300r, High jump. 500r, Wrestling. 900r, Weight lifting. 1000r, Soccer.
1500r, Diving.

1996, June 14 **Litho.** ***Perf. 13x12½***
1520-1525 A286 Set of 6 5.00 1.25

Souvenir Sheet

Perf. 12½

1526 A286 1500r multicolored 4.00 1.25

No. 1526 contains one 32x40mm stamp.

Early Aircraft — A287

100r, Douglas M-2, 1926. 200r, Pitcairn PA-5 Mailwing, 1928. 300r, Boeing 40 B, 1928. 500r, Potez 25, 1925. 900r, Stearman C-3MB, 1927. 1000r, De Havilland DH4, 1918.
1500r, Standard JR-1B, 1918.

1996, July 5 ***Perf. 12½x12***
1527-1532 A287 Set of 6 4.25 1.50

Souvenir Sheet

Perf. 13

1533 A287 1500r multicolored 3.00 1.00

No. 1533 contains one 40x32mm stamp.

Historic Sites — A288

50r, 100r, 200r, Diff. Apsaras, Tonle Bati. No. 1537, Statue, Angkor Wat. No. 1538, Statue of a Goddess. 500r, Carved wall, Tonle Bati. No. 1540, 1000r, No. 1543, Various structures, Tonle Bati. No. 1541, No. 1544, 1700r, 2500r, 3000r, Various views of Angkor Wat.
Nos. 1539, 1543, 1545-1547 are horiz.

1996-97 **Litho.** ***Perf. 12½***

1534	A288	50r blk & yel org	.25	.25
1535	A288	100r black & blue	.25	.25
1536	A288	200r black & tan	.40	.25
1537	A288	300r blk & light bl	.30	.25
1538	A288	300r black & red	.30	.25
1539	A288	500r blk & bright bl	.80	.25
1540	A288	800r blk & yel grn	1.00	.25
1541	A288	800r blk & yel grn	.60	.25
1542	A288	1000r black & green	1.10	.40
1543	A288	1500r black & bister	1.40	.50
1544	A288	1500r black & brown	1.40	.25
1545	A288	1700r black & org brn	1.50	.30
1546	A288	2500r black & blue	2.00	.40
1547	A288	3000r black & dk grn	3.50	.50
		Nos. 1534-1547 (14)	14.80	4.35

Issued: 50r, 100r, 200r, 500r, No. 1540, 1000r, No. 1543, 7/30/96; others, 3/26/97.
See Nos. 1686-1692, 1846-1852.

Dinosaurs — A289

No. 1548: a, 50r, Coelophysis. b, 100r, Euparkeria. c, 150r, Plateosaurus. d, 200r, Herrerasaurus.

No. 1549: a, 250r, Dilophosaurus. b, 300r, Tuojiangosaurus. c, 350r, Camarasaurs. d, 400r, Ceratosaurus.

No. 1550: a, 500r, Spinosaurus. b, 700r, Ouranosaurus. c, 800r, Avimimus. d, 1200r, Deinonychus.

1996, Aug. 8 **Litho.** ***Perf. 13***
1548 A289 Sheet of 4, #a.-d. 1.00 .25
1549 A289 Sheet of 4, #a.-d. 2.75 .60
1550 A289 Sheet of 4, #a.-d. 6.25 1.50

Chess Champions A290

100r, José Raul Capablanca. 200r, Alexander Alekhine. 300r, Vassily Smyslov. 500r, Mikhail Tal. 900r, Bobby Fischer. 1000r, Anatoly Karpov.
1500r, Garry Kasparov.

1996, Sept. 10 ***Perf. 13***
1551-1556 A290 Set of 6 4.50 1.50

Souvenir Sheet

Perf. 12½

1557 A290 1500r multicolored 3.00 1.25

No. 1557 contains one 32x40mm stamp.

Wild Animals A291

Designs: 100r, Ursus arctos. 200r, Panthera leo. 300r, Tapirus indicus. 500r, Camelus ferus. 900r, Capra ibex. 1000r, Zalophus californianus.

1996, Oct. 3 ***Perf. 13x12½***
1558-1563 A291 Set of 6 4.50 1.25

Dogs — A292

Designs: 200r, Collie. 300r, Labrador retriever. 500r, Doberman pinscher. 900r, German shepherd. 1000r, Boxer.

1996, Nov. 8 ***Perf. 12½x13***
1564-1568 A292 Set of 5 4.75 1.25

Independence — A293

100, 500, 900r, Various water treatment plants.

1996, Nov. 9 ***Perf. 13***
1569-1571 A293 Set of 3 3.00 1.50

Ships A294

Designs: 200r, Chinese junk. 300r, Galley. 500r, Roman galley. 900r, Clipper ship, 19th cent. 1000r, Paddle steamer Sirius, 1838. 1500r, Great Eastern, 1858.

1996, Dec. 15 ***Perf. 12½x13***
1572-1576 A294 Set of 5 4.00 1.25

Souvenir Sheet
Perf. 12½

1577 A294 1500r multicolored 2.75 1.00

No. 1577 contains one 40x32mm stamp.

Cambodia's Admission to UPU, 45th Anniv. — A295

Denominations: 200r, 400r, 900r.

1996, Dec. 21 ***Perf. 12½***
1578-1580 A295 Set of 3 3.50 1.50

New Year 1997 (Year of the Ox) — A296

Paintings of oxen, attributed to Han Huang 723-87): a, Facing left. b, Looking right. c, Brown & white spotted. d, Facing left, head down.

1996, Dec. 28 ***Perf. 13x12½***
1581 A296 500r Strip of 4, #a.-d. + label 3.00 1.00

UN Intl. Day of Volunteers — A297

Designs: 100r, Phnom Kaun Sat Dam. 900r, Chrey Krem Dam. 1500r, Angkrung Canal.

1996, Dec. 30
1582-1584 A297 Set of 3 3.50 1.50

Greenpeace, 25th Anniv. — A298

Helicopter: 200r, Hovering over cargo. 300r, Hovering over ship. 500r, On helipad. 900r, Lifting cargo.
1000r, Close-up of helicopter.

1996, Dec. 30 ***Perf. 12½x13***
1585-1588 A298 Set of 4 5.00 1.75

Souvenir Sheet
Perf. 12½

1589 A298 1000r multicolored 5.25 1.00

No. 1589 contains one 32x40mm stamp.

1998 World Cup Soccer Championships, France — A299

Various soccer plays. Denominations: 100r, 200r, 300r, 500r, 900r, 1000r.

1997, Jan. 6 Litho. ***Perf. 12½x13***
1590-1595 A299 Set of 6 4.25 1.50

Souvenir Sheet
Perf. 13

1596 A299 2000r multicolored 2.75 1.25

No. 1596 contains one 40x32mm stamp.

Elephas Maximus — A300

World Wildlife Fund: a, 300r, Two walking. b, 500r, Three standing. c, 900r, Two fighting. d, 1000r, Adult, calf.

1997, Feb. 12 ***Perf. 12½x12***
1597 A300 Strip of 4, #a.-d. 7.00 3.00

Birds — A301

600r, Bombycilla garrulus. 900r, Lanius excubitor. 1000r, Passer montanus. 2000r, Phoenicurus phoenicurus. 2500r, Emberiza schoeniclus. 3000r, Emberiza hortulana.

1997, Feb. 20 ***Perf. 13x12½***
1598-1603 A301 Set of 6 13.00 4.50

Express mail service.

Fire Fighting Vehicles A302

Designs: 200r, English, 1731. 500r, Putnam, 1863. 900r, Merryweather, 1894. 1000r, Shand Mason Co., 1901. 1500r, Maxim Motor Co., Ford, 1949. 4000r, Merryweather, 1950.
5400r, Mack Truck Co., 1953.

1997, Mar. 11 ***Perf. 12½x13***
1604-1609 A302 Set of 6 7.00 1.50

Souvenir Sheet
Perf. 13

1610 A302 5400r multicolored 4.75 1.25

No. 1610 contains one 40x32mm stamp.

Ducks A303

Designs: 200r, Polystieta stelleri. 500r, Alopochen aegyptiacus. 900r, Anas americana. 1000r, Anas falcata. 1500r, Melanitta perspicillata. 4000r, Anas discors.
5400r, Anas formosa, vert.

1997, Apr. 7 ***Perf. 12½x13***
1611-1616 A303 Set of 6 4.50 1.50

Souvenir Sheet
Perf. 12½

1617 A303 5400r multicolored 3.25 1.75

No. 1617 contains one 32x40mm stamp.

Heinrich Von Stephan (1831-1897), Founder of UPU — A304

Denominations: 500r, 1500r, 2000r.

1997, Apr. 8 ***Perf. 12½x13***
1618-1620 A304 Set of 3 3.00 1.00

Khmer Culture — A305

Various views of Bantea Srei Temple. Denominations: 500r, 1500r, 2000r.

1997, Apr. 13 ***Perf. 13x12½***
1621-1623 A305 Set of 3 3.50 1.00

Cats — A306

Designs: 200r, Birman. 500r, Exotic shorthair. 900r, Persian. 1000r, Turkish. 1500r, American short-hair. 4000r, Scottish fold.
5400r, Sphinx.

1997, May 8 ***Perf. 13x12½***
1624-1629 A306 Set of 6 9.00 1.75

Souvenir Sheet
Perf. 13

1630 A306 5400r multicolored 4.00 1.25

No. 1630 contains one 32x40mm stamp.

Trains A307

200r, 4-4-2T, #488. 500r, Frederick Smith 4-6-0. 900r, 0-8-0, #3131. 1000r, Transport #1, London #L44, 0-4-4. 1500r, 0-6-2, #1711. 4000r, 4-6-2, #60523.
5400r, North Yorkshire Moor (K1), 2-6-0, #2005.

1997, Jun 9 ***Perf. 12½x12***
1631-1636 A307 Set of 6 4.25 1.50

Souvenir Sheet
Perf. 13

1637 A307 5400r multicolored 3.25 1.75

No. 1637 contains one 40x32mm stamp.

Dogs A308

Designs: 200r, Shar-pei. 500r, Tchin-tchin. 900r, Pekinese. 1000r, Chow-chow, vert. 1500r, Pug, vert. 4000r, Akita, vert.
5400r, Tufted Chinese, vert.

1997, July 4 ***Perf. 12½x13, 13x12½***
1638-1643 A308 Set of 6 4.25 1.50

Souvenir Sheet
Perf. 12½

1644 A308 5400r multicolored 3.00 1.50

No. 1644 contains one 32x40mm stamp.

ASEAN, 30th Anniv. A309

Designs: 500r, Dunalom Wat. 1500r, Royal Palace. 2000r, Natl. Museum.

1997, Aug. 5 ***Perf. 12½x13***
1645-1647 A309 Set of 3 4.00 1.00

Ships A310

Designs: 200r, Caravelle, 15th cent. 500r, Spanish galleon, 16th cent. 900r, Galleon "Great Harry," 16th cent. 1000r, Galleon "Le Couronne," 17th cent. 1500r, Cargo ship, 18th cent. 4000r, Clipper ship, 19th cent.
5400r, HMS Victory.

1997, Sept. 10 ***Perf. 12½x12***
1648-1653 A310 Set of 6 5.50 1.50

Souvenir Sheet
Perf. 13

1654 A310 5400r multicolored 4.00 1.10

No. 1654 contains one 40x32mm stamp.

A311

Nos. 1655-1658, Various public gardens. Nos. 1659-1661, Various dams. No. 1657 is vert.

1997, Sept. 30 ***Perf. 12½***

1655	A311	300r black & yel grn	.25	.25
1656	A311	300r black & red	.25	.25
1657	A311	800r black & citron	.50	.25
1658	A311	1500r black & org brn	.95	.30
1659	A311	1700r blk & red brn	1.05	.35
1660	A311	2500r blk & grn bl	1.20	.50
1661	A311	3000r black & blue	1.50	.65
		Nos. 1655-1661 (7)	5.70	2.55

Mushrooms A312

Designs: 200r, Boletus satanas. 500r, Amanita regalis. 900r, Morchella semilibera. 1000r,

Gomphus clavatus. 1500r, Hygrophorus hypothejus. 4000r, Albatrellus confluens.
5400r, Boletus chrysenteron.

1997, Oct. 5 ***Perf. 12½x13***
1662-1667 A312 Set of 6 6.00 1.50

Souvenir Sheet
Perf. 12½

1668 A312 5400r multicolored 4.00 1.25

No. 1668 contains one 32x40mm stamp.

Fish A313

200r, Betta imbellis. 500r, Colisa fasciata. 900r, Puntius conchonius. 1000r, Macropodus concolor. 1500r, Epalzeorhynchos frenatus. 4000r, Capoeta tetrazona.
5400r, Rasbora heteromorpha.

1997, Nov. 8 ***Perf. 12½x13***
1669-1674 A313 Set of 6 5.25 1.50

Souvenir Sheet
Perf. 13

1675 A313 5400r multicolored 3.50 1.25

No. 1675 contains one 40x32mm stamp.

Independence, 44th Anniv. — A314

Post Offices: 1000r, Kampot. 3000r, Prey Veng.

1997, Nov. 9 ***Perf. 13***
1676-1677 A314 Set of 2 2.75 1.00

Orchids — A315

200r, Orchis milicaris. 500r, Orchiaceras bivonae. 900r, Orchiaceras spuria. 1000r, Gymnadenia conopsea. 1500r, Serapias neglecta. 4000r, Pseudorhiza bruniana.
5400r, Dactylodenia wintonii.

1997, Dec. 12 ***Perf. 13***
1678-1683 A315 Set of 6 9.00 1.75

Souvenir Sheet

1684 A315 5400r multicolored 6.75 1.10

No. 1684 contains one 32x40mm stamp.

Princess Diana (1961-97) — A316

Designs: a, 100r, In dark blue jacket. b, 200r, In black dress. c, 300r, Holding hand to throat. d, 500r, Wearing face shield. e, 1000r, Watching mine clearing operation. f, 1500r, With Elizabeth Dole. g, 2000r, Holding land mine. h, 2500r, With members of Mother Teresa's Order.

1997, Dec. 30 ***Perf. 12x12½***
1685 A316 Sheet of 8, #a.-h. + label 6.00 1.75

Historic Sites Type of 1996-97

Temples: 300r, Prasat Suorprat. 500r, Preah Kumlung, horiz. 1200r, Prasat Bapuon, horiz. 1500r, Palilai. 1700r, Prasat Prerup, horiz. 2000r, Prasat Preah Khan, horiz. 3000r, Prasat Bayon.

1998 **Litho.** ***Perf. 12½***

1686	A288	300r black & orange	.25	.25
1687	A288	500r black & pink	.30	.25
1688	A288	1200r black & buff	.70	.25
1689	A288	1500r black & buff	.90	.30
1690	A288	1700r black & blue	1.00	.35
1691	A288	2000r black & green	1.25	.45
1692	A288	3000r black & violet	1.75	.65
		Nos. 1686-1692 (7)	6.15	2.50

New Year 1998 (Year of the Tiger) A317

Various pictures of panthera tigris: 200r, vert., 500r, vert., 900r, vert., 1000r, 1500r, 4000r.
5400r, Tiger, vert.

1998 ***Perf. 13***
1693-1698 A317 Set of 6 4.75 1.50

Souvenir Sheet
Perf. 12½

1699 A317 5400r multicolored 4.00 1.50

No. 1699 contains one 32x40mm stamp.

1998 World Cup Soccer Championships, France — A318

Designs showing portion of soccer player at left, various plays at right, stadium: 200r, 500r, 900r, 1000r, 1500r, 4000r.
5400r, Two players kicking ball.

1998 ***Perf. 13***
1700-1705 A318 Set of 6 4.25 1.50

Souvenir Sheet

1706 A318 5400r multicolored 3.00 1.50

No. 1706 contains one 40x32mm stamp.

Domestic Cats A319

Designs: 200r, Scottish fold. 500r, Ragdoll. 900r, Welsh. 1000r, Devon rex. 1500r, American curl. 4000r, Sphinx.
5400r, Japanese bobtail.

1998
1707-1712 A319 Set of 6 4.00 1.50

Souvenir Sheet

1713 A319 5400r multi 3.00 1.50

No. 1713 contains one 40x32mm stamp.

Italia '98, Intl. Philatelic Exhibition A320

Paintings: 200r, Baptism of Christ from triptych, Jean de Trompes, by Gerard David. 500r, The Virgin of Martin van Niuwenhoven, by Hans Memling. 900r, Baptism of Christ, by Hendrich Goltzius. 1000r, Christ Carrying the Cross, by Luis de Morales. 1500r, Angel in the Desert, by Dirk Bouts. 4000r, The Virgin, by Petrus Christus.
5400r, The Immaculate Conception, by Bartolomé Esteban Murillo.

1998 **Litho.** ***Perf. 12½x13***
1714-1719 A320 Set of 6 5.00 1.50

Souvenir Sheet
Perf. 12½

1720 A320 5400r multicolored 4.00 1.50

No. 1720 contains one 40x32mm stamp.

Butterflies — A321

200r, Phyciodes tharos. 500r, Pararge mergera. 900r, Danaus plexippus. 1000r, Parnassius apollo. 1500r, Papilio machaon. 4000r, Eumenis semele.
5400r, Morpho rhetenor.

1998 ***Perf. 12½***
1721-1726 A321 Set of 6 5.25 1.50

Souvenir Sheet

1727 A321 5400r multicolored 5.25 1.50

No. 1727 contains one 40x32mm stamp.

Mail Boxes — A322

Designs: 1000r, 1997. 3000r, 1951.

1998 **Litho.** ***Perf. 13***
1728-1729 A322 Set of 2 2.25 1.00

Trains — A323

No. 1730a, 200r, Oakland, Antioch & Eastern. No. 1730b, 500r, New York, Westchester & Boston. No. 1731a, 900r, Spokane & Inland. No. 1731b, 1000r, International Railway. No. 1732a, 1500r, British columbia Electric Railway. No. 1732b, 4000r, Southern Pacific.
5400r, Storage battery locomotive.

1998, Mar. 2 **Litho.** ***Perf. 12½***

Pairs, #a.-b.

1730-1732 A323 Set of 3 5.00 1.50

Souvenir Sheet

1733 A323 5400r multicolored 4.00 1.50

Dogs — A324

200r, Rottweiler. 500r, Beauceron. 900r, Boxer. 1000r, Siberian husky. 1500r, Welsh corgi (Pembroke). 4000r, Basset hound.
5400r, Schnauzer.

1998, Mar. 30 **Litho.** ***Perf. 12¼***
1734-1739 A324 Set of 6 4.75 1.50

Souvenir Sheet
Perf. 12½

1740 A324 5400r multicolored 3.25 1.50

Insects A325

200r, Lucanus cervus. 500r, Carabus auronitens. 900r, Rosalia alpina. 1000r, Geotrupes. 1500r, Megasoma elephas. 4000r, Chalcosoma.
5400r, Leptura rubra.

1998, Apr. 10 **Litho.** ***Perf. 12½***
1741-1746 A325 Set of 6 5.00 1.50

Souvenir Sheet

1747 A325 5400r multicolored 4.00 1.75

Khmer Culture A326

Designs: 500r, Prasat Prerup. 1500r, Prasat Bayon. 2000r, Angkor Wat.

1998, Apr. 13 **Litho.** ***Perf. 12¾***
1748-1750 A326 Set of 3 3.25 1.10

Historic Ships A327

200r, Cutter. 500r, Steamship "Britannia." 900r, Viking ship. 1000r, Steamship "Great Britain." 1500r, Coaster. 4000r, Frigate.
5400r, Tartan.

1998, May 7 Litho. *Perf. 12¾*
1751-1756 A327 Set of 6 5.75 1.50

Souvenir Sheet
Perf. 13

1757 A327 5400r multicolored 3.50 1.75

No. 1757 contains one 40x32mm stamp.

Flowers — A328

200r, Petasites japonica. 500r, Gentiana triflora. 900r, Doronicum cordatum. 1000r, Scabiosa japonica. 1500r, Magnolia sieboldii. 4000r, Erythronium japonica.
5400r, Callistephus chinensis.

1998 Litho. *Perf. 12¾*
1758-1763 A328 Set of 6 4.75 1.50

Souvenir Sheet
Perf. 13

1764 A328 5400r multicolored 3.25 1.50

No. 1764 contains one 32x40mm stamp.

Turtles A329

200r, Platysternon megacephalum. 500r, Chelonia mydas. 900r, Trionyx spiniferus. 1000r, Eretmochelys imbricata. 1500r, Megalochelys gigantea. 4000r, Dermochelys coriacea.
5400r, Chelus fimbriatus.

1998, Nov. 8 Litho. *Perf. 12¾*
1765-1770 A329 Set of 6 5.00 1.50

Souvenir Sheet
Perf. 13x13¼

1771 A329 5400r multi 4.75 1.50

No. 1771 contains one 40x32mm stamp.

Independence, 45th Anniv. — A330

Various dancers: 500r, 1500r, 2000r.

1998, Nov. 9 Litho. *Perf. 12½x12¼*
1772-1774 A330 Set of 3 2.50 1.00

Gemstones A331

Designs: 200r, Aquamarine. 500r, Cat's eye. 900r, Malachite. 1000r, Emerald. 1500r, Turquoise. 4000r, Ruby.
5400r, Diamond, horiz.

1998, Dec. 28 Litho. *Perf. 12¾*
1775-1780 A331 Set of 6 4.50 1.50

Souvenir Sheet
Perf. 13

1781 A331 5400r multi 3.50 1.50

No. 1781 contains one 40x32mm stamp.

Wild Cats A332

Designs: 200r, Acinonyx juabatus. 500r, Panthera uncia. 900r, Felis pardalis. 1000r, Panthera pardus. 1500r, Felis serval. 4000r, Panthera onca.
5400r, Panthera tigris.

1998 Litho. *Perf. 12½x12¼*
1782-1787 A332 Set of 6 5.00 1.50

Souvenir Sheet
Perf. 13

1788 A332 5400r multi 4.00 1.50

No. 1788 contains one 32x40mm stamp.

New Year 1999 (Year of the Rabbit) A333

Various rabbits: 200r, 500r, 900r, 1000r, 1500r, 4000r. 4000r is vert.

1999, Jan. 5 Litho. *Perf. 12¾*
1790-1795 A333 Set of 6 6.75 1.50

Souvenir Sheet
Perf. 13

1796 A333 5400r Rabbit, diff. 5.00 1.50

No. 1796 contains one 40x32mm stamp.

Trains — A334

Designs: 200r, Stourbridge Lion. 500r, Atlantic. 900r, 035. 100r, Iron Duke. 1500r, 4-6-0. 4000r, 4-4-2.

Perf. 12½x12¼
1999, Nov. 20 Litho.
1797-1802 A334 Set of 6 5.25 1.50

Souvenir Sheet
Perf. 12½

1803 A334 5400r Firefly 3.25 1.50

No. 1803 contains one 40x32mm stamp.

Dogs A335

Designs: 200r, Shiba inu, vert. 500r, Shih tzu. 900r, Tibetan spaniel. 1000r, Ainu, vert. 1500r, Lhasa apso. 4000r, Tibetan terrier.

Perf. 12¼x12½ (200, 1000r), 12¾
1999, Feb. 3 Litho.
1804-1809 A335 Set of 6 5.00 1.50

Souvenir Sheet
Perf. 12½

1810 A335 5400r Tosa inu, vert. 3.00 1.50

Size of Nos. 1804, 1807: 48x30mm. No. 1810 contains one 32x40mm stamp.

Antique Automobiles — A336

Designs: 200r, 1881 La Rapide. 500r, 1895 Duryea. 900r, 1898 Barbarou. 1000r, 1898 Panhard. 1500r, 1901 Mercedes-Benz. 4000r, 1915 Ford.
5400r, 1875 Siegfried Marcus.

1999, Mar. 5 Litho. *Perf. 13x12¾*
1811-1816 A336 Set of 6 4.75 1.50

Souvenir Sheet
Perf. 13

1817 A336 5400r multi 3.75 1.50

No. 1817 contains one 40x32mm stamp.

Cats — A337

Designs: 200r, Ragdoll. 500r, Russian blue. 900r, Bombay. 1000r, Snowshoe. 1500r, Oriental. 4000r, Somali.

1999, Mar. 30 Litho. *Perf. 13*
1818-1823 A337 Set of 6 5.25 1.50

Souvenir Sheet

1824 A337 5400r Egyptian mau 3.00 1.50

No. 1824 contains one 32x40mm stamp.

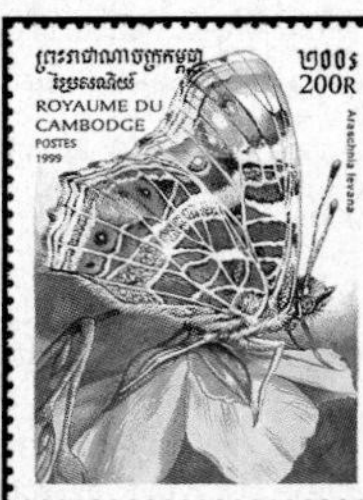

Butterflies A338

Designs: 200r, Araschnia levana. 500r, Vanessa cardui, horiz. 900r, Clossiana euphrosyne. 1000r, Coenonympha hero. 1500r, Parnassius apollo, horiz. 4000r, Plebejus argus.
5400r, Palaeochrysophanus hippothoe.

1999, Apr. 25 *Perf. 12¾*
1825-1830 A338 Set of 6 6.00 1.50

Souvenir Sheet
Perf. 12½

1831 A338 5400r multi 4.00 2.00

No. 1831 contains one 32x40mm stamp.

Dinosaurs — A339

Designs: 200r, Saurornitholestes. 500r, Prenocephalus. 900r, Wuerhosaurus. 1000r, Muttaburrasaurus. 1500r, Shantungosaurus. 4000r, Microceratops.
5400r, Daspletosaurus.

1999, May 10 Litho. *Perf. 12¾*
1832-1837 A339 Set of 6 4.75 1.50

Souvenir Sheet
Perf. 13

1838 A339 5400r multi 3.25 1.50

No. 1838 contains one 40x32mm stamp.

Molluscs A340

Designs: 200r, Flabellina affinis. 500r, Octopus macropus. 900r, Helix hortensis. 1000r, Lima hians. 1500r, Arion empiricorum. 4000r, Anodonta cygnaea.
5400r, Eledone aldrovandii.

1999, May 31 Litho. *Perf. 12¾*
1839-1844 A340 Set of 6 5.00 1.50

Souvenir Sheet
Perf. 12½

1845 A340 5400r multi 3.50 1.00

No. 1845 contains one 32x40mm stamp.

Historic Sites Type of 1996-97

Designs: 100r, Prasat Neak Poan, horiz. 300r, Statue, Prasat Neak Poan, horiz. 500r, Prasat Banteay Srey. 1400r, Prasat Banteay Samré, horiz. 1600r, Prasat Banteay Srey, horiz. 1800r, Bas-relief, Angkor Wat. 1900r, Prasat Takeo, horiz.

1999 Litho. *Perf. 12½*
Vignette Colors

1846	A288	100r blue	.30	.25
1847	A288	300r red	.30	.25
1848	A288	500r olive green	.40	.25
1849	A288	1400r bright green	1.00	.30
1850	A288	1600r pink	1.10	.30
1851	A288	1800r violet	1.25	.35
1852	A288	1900r brown	1.50	.45
		Nos. 1846-1852 (7)	5.85	2.15

Khmer Culture A341

Designs: 500r, Dragon Bridge. 1500r, Temple with 100 columns, Kratie. 2000r, Krapum Chhouk stupa, Kratie.

1999, Apr. 13 *Perf. 13*
1853-1855 A341 Set of 3 3.00 .85

UPU, 125th Anniv. A342

1999 Litho. *Perf. 12½x12¼*
1856 A342 1600r multi 1.50 .85

Independence — A343

People and: 500r, Map. 1500r, Ship, airplane, dove, public works. 2000r, Buildings.

1999, Nov. 9 ***Perf. 12½***
1857-1859 A343 Set of 3 2.75 1.00

Snakes A344

Designs: 200r, Aspidelaps lubricus. 500r, Epicrates cenchria. 900r, Eunectes notaeus. 1000r, Diadophus punctatus. 1500r, Micrurus fulvius. 4000r, Telescopus semiannulatus.
5400r, Chondropython viridis.

1999, Dec. 6 ***Perf. 12¾***
1860-1865 A344 Set of 6 5.75 1.50

Souvenir Sheet

Perf. 13

1866 A344 5400r multi 3.25 1.50

No. 1866 contains one 39x31mm stamp.

Birds of Prey A345

Designs: 200r, Harpia harpyja. 500r, Terthopius ecaudatus, vert. 900r, Neophron pernopterus, vert. 1000r, Falco peregrinus, vert. 1500r, Buteo jamaicensis, vert. 4000r, Haliaetus leucocephalus.
5400r, Milvus milvus.

1999, Oct. 5 **Litho.** ***Perf. 12¾***
1867-1872 A345 Set of 6 6.00 1.50

Souvenir Sheet

Perf. 12½

1873 A345 5400r multi 3.75 1.50

No. 1873 contains one 31x39mm stamp.

Philex France 99 — A346

Still life paintings by: 200r, Henri Fantin-Latour. 500r, Paul Cézanne. 900r, André Derain. 1000r, Henri Matisse. 1500r, Othon Friesz. 4000r, Matisse, diff.
5400r, Cézanne, diff.

1999, June 10 **Litho.** ***Perf. 12½***
1874-1879 A346 Set of 6 6.00 1.50

Souvenir Sheet

Perf. 13

1880 A346 5400r multi 5.00 2.50

Souvenir Sheet

China 1999 World Philatelic Exhibition — A347

Pagodas: a, 200r, Tongzhou. b, 500r, Tianing Temple. c, 900r, Summer Palace. d, 900r, Temple of the Clouds. e, 1000r, Bei Hai. f, 1000r, Perfumed Hill. g, 1500r, Yunju. h, 4000r, Miaoying Temple.

Perf. 12¼x12½

1999, Aug. 12 **Litho.**
1881 A347 Sheet of 8, #a-h, + label 6.25 3.00

Orchids A348

Designs: 200r, Cymbidium insigne. 500r, Papillonanthe teres. 900r, Panisea uniflora. 1000r, Euanthe sanderiana. 1500r, Dendrobium trigonopus. 4000r, Vanda coerulea.
5400r, Paphiopedilum callosum.

1999, Aug. 5 **Litho.** ***Perf. 12¾***
1889-1894 A348 Set of 6 5.75 1.50

Souvenir Sheet

Perf. 12½

1895 A348 5400r multi 5.50 2.00

No. 1895 contains one 32x40mm stamp.

Birds A349

Designs: 200r, Pyrrhula pyrrhula. 500r, Coccothraustes coccothraustes. 900r, Carduelis chloris. 1000r, Dendroica petechia. 1500r, Lanius excubitor. 4000r, Parus caeruleus.
5400r, Erithacus rubecula.

1999, Sept. 5 **Litho.** ***Perf. 12¾***
1896-1901 A349 Set of 6 6.00 1.50

Souvenir Sheet

Perf. 13

1902 A349 5400r multi 5.00 2.50

No. 1902 contains one 40x32mm stamp.

Fish A350

Designs: 200r, Capoeta tetrazona. 500r, Epalzeorhynchus frenatus. 900r, Rasbora kalochroma. 1000r, Etroplus maculatus. 1500r, Betta imbellis. 4000r, Colisa sota.
5400r, Tetraodon biocellatus.

Perf. 12½x12¼

1999, Sept. 20 **Litho.**
1903-1908 A350 Set of 6 6.00 1.50

Souvenir Sheet

Perf. 13

1909 A350 5400r multi 5.00 2.00

No. 1909 contains one 40x32mm stamp.

Wildlife — A351

Designs: 200r, Ailuropada melanoleuca. 500r, Bos mutus. 900r, Hydropotes inermis. 1000r, Neomys fodiens, horiz. 1500r, Lutra lutra, horiz. 4000r, Panthera tigris, horiz.
5400r, Elaphurus davidianus, vert.

1999, Nov. 20 **Litho.** ***Perf. 12¾***
1910-1915 A351 Set of 6 6.00 1.50

Souvenir Sheet

Perf. 12½

1916 A351 5400r multi 5.00 2.50

No. 1916 contains one 32x40mm stamp.

Bangkok 2000 Stamp Exhibition — A352

Turtle-shaped objects and turtles: 200r, Cuora amboinensis, vert. 500r, Cuora flavomarginata, vert. 900r, Geoemyda spengleri. 1000r, Manouria impressa. 1500r, Chinemys reevesi. 4000r, Heosemys spinosa.
4500r, Hieremys annandalei.

2000, Feb. 27 ***Perf. 12¾***
1917-1922 A352 Set of 6 7.00 1.50

Souvenir Sheet

Perf. 13

1923 A352 4500r multi 5.00 2.00

No. 1923 contains one 40x32mm stamp.

Dinosaurs — A353

Designs: 200r, Iguanodon. 500r, Euoplocephalus. 900r, Dilophosaurus. 1000r, Diplodocus. 1500r, Stegoceras. 4000r, Stegosaurus.
4500r, Brachiosaurus, vert.

2000, Jan. 30 **Litho.** ***Perf. 12½x12¼***
1924-1929 A353 Set of 6 4.50 1.50

Souvenir Sheet

Perf. 12½

1930 A353 4500r multi 3.00 1.50

No. 1930 contains one 32x40mm stamp.

Beetles A354

Designs: 200r, Calosoma sycophanta. 500r, Oryctes nasicornis. 900r, Diochrysa fastuosa. 1000r, Blaps gigas. 1500r, Cincindela campestris. 4000r, Cissistes cephalotes.
4500r, Scarabeus aegyptiorum.

2000, Feb. 5 **Litho.** ***Perf. 12¾***
1931-1936 A354 Set of 6 5.50 1.50

Souvenir Sheet

Perf. 13

1937 A354 4500r multi 2.75 1.50

No. 1937 contains one 40x32mm stamp.

New Year 2000 (Year of the Dragon) — A355

Various dragons. Denominations: 200r, 500r, 900r, 1000r, 1500r, 4000r.

2000, Jan. 20 **Litho.** ***Perf. 12¼x12½***
1938-1943 A355 Set of 6 6.00 1.50

Souvenir Sheet

Perf. 13

1944 A355 4500r multi 3.25 1.50

No. 1944 contains one 32x40mm stamp.

Bettas — A356

Designs: 200r, Unimaculata, Pugnax. 500r, Macrostoma, Taeniata. 900r, Foerschi, Imbellis. 1000r, Tessyae, Picta. 1500r, Edithae, Belica. 4000r, Smaragdina.
4500r, Splendens.

2000, Apr. 10 **Litho.** ***Perf. 12½x12¼***
1945-1950 A356 Set of 6 4.00 1.50

Souvenir Sheet

Perf. 13

1951 A356 4500r multi 3.25 1.50

No. 1951 contains one 40x32mm stamp.

Mushrooms A357

Designs: 200r, Amanita muscaria. 500r, Amanita pantherina. 900r, Clitocybe oleana. 1000r, Lactarius scrobiculatus. 1500r, Scleroderma vulgare. 4000r, Amanita verna.
4500r, Amanita phalloides.

2000, Mar. 20 Litho. *Perf. 12¾*
1952-1957 A357 Set of 6 4.50 1.50

Souvenir Sheet
Perf. 13

1958 A357 4500r multi 2.75 1.50

No. 1958 contains one 32x40mm stamp.

Khmer Culture — A358

Designs: 500r, Srei Snam. 1500r, Srei Snam, diff. 2000r, Srei Krub Lakhna,

2000, Apr. 13 Litho. *Perf. 13*
1959-1961 A358 Set of 3 2.75 1.10

Growing Rice — A359

Designs: 100r, Transporting seedlings. 300r, Harrowing. 500r, Threshing. 1400r, Winnowing. 1600r, Transplanting. 1900r, Plowing. 2200r, Harvesting.

2000, Mar. 1 *Perf. 12¼x12½*
Vignette Color

1962 A359 100r brt yel grn .25 .25
1963 A359 300r brt blue .25 .25
1964 A359 500r brt pink .35 .25
1965 A359 1400r brn orange .95 .25
1966 A359 1600r dull blue 1.05 .30
1967 A359 1900r bister brn 1.30 .35
1968 A359 2200r red 1.50 .40
Nos. 1962-1968 (7) 5.65 2.05

Locomotives — A360

Designs: 200r, Jules Petiet. 500r, Longue Chaudiere. 900r, Les Grand Chocolats. 1000r, Glehn du Bousquet. 1500r, Le Pendule Français. 4000r, TGV 001.
4500r, Le Shuttle.

2000, Mar. 5 Litho. *Perf. 12½x12¼*
1969-1974 A360 Set of 6 6.75 1.50

Souvenir Sheet
Perf. 13

1975 A360 4500r multi 3.00 1.50

WIPA 2000 Philatelic Exhibition, Vienna (No. 1975). No. 1975 contains one 80x32mm stamp.

Birds A361

Designs: 200r, Diomedea irrorata. 500r, Charadrius alexandrinus, vert. 900r, Sula nebouxii. 1000r, Sterna hirundo. 1500r, Larus argentatus, vert. 4000r, Chlidonia hybrida.
4500r, Sula bassana.

2000, May 8 *Perf. 12¾*
1976-1981 A361 Set of 6 5.00 1.50

Souvenir Sheet
Perf. 13

1982 A361 4500r multi 3.00 1.50

No. 1982 contains one 40x32mm stamp.

Orchids — A362

Designs: 200r, Cypripedium macranthum. 500r, Vandopsis gigantea. 900r, Calypso bulbosa. 1000r, Vanda luzonica. 1500r, Paphiopedilum villosum. 4000r, Vanda merrillii.
4500r, Paphiopedilum victoria.

2000, May 30 *Perf. 12¾*
1983-1988 A362 Set of 6 6.00 1.50

Souvenir Sheet
Perf. 13

1989 A362 4500r multi 4.00 1.50

No. 1989 contains one 32x40mm stamp.

Children's Stories — A363

Designs: 200r, The Courageous Little Tailor, vert. 500r, Tom Thumb, vert. 900r, Thumbelina, vert. 1000r, Pinocchio. 1500r, The Crayfish. 4000r, Peter Pan.
4500r, The Pied Piper, vert.

2000, Nov. 20 Litho. *Perf. 12¾*
1990-1995 A363 Set of 6 4.75 4.00

Souvenir Sheet
Perf. 12½

1996 A363 4500r multi 3.00 3.00

No. 1996 contains one 32x40mm stamp.

Water Festival and Tourism A364

Designs: 500r, Men rowing canoe. 1500r, Men at canoe prow. 2000r, Temples, elephant, woman.

2000, June 1 Litho. *Perf. 13*
1997-1999 A364 Set of 3 4.25 2.75

Fire Trucks A365

Designs: 200r, Metz DLK 23-6. 500r, Iveco-Magirus SLF24/100. 900r, Metz SLF 7000 WS. 1000r, Iveco-Magirus TLF 24/50. 1500r, Saval-Kronenburg RFF 11000. 4000r, Metz TLF 24/50.
4500r, Metz TLF 16/25.

2000, July 30 *Perf. 12¾*
2000-2005 A365 Set of 6 5.25 5.25

Souvenir Sheet
Perf. 13

2006 A365 4500r multi 3.50 3.50

No. 2006 contains one 40x32mm stamp.

Independence, 47th Anniv. — A366

Flag, temple and: 500r, Flowers. 1500r, Dove. 2000r, People carrying torch.

2000, Oct. 9 *Perf. 12¾*
2007-2009 A366 Set of 3 4.25 2.75

Antique Automobiles — A367

Designs: 200r, 1912 Rover 12C. 500r, 1907, Austin 30CV. 900r, 1909 Rolls-Royce Silver Ghost. 1000r, 1929 Graham Paige Phaeton DC. 1500r, 1937 Austin 12. 4000r, 1957 Mercedes-Benz 300SL.
4500r, 1936 MG.

2000, Sept. 30 *Perf. 12¾*
2010-2015 A367 Set of 6 5.00 2.50

Souvenir Sheet
Perf. 13

2016 A367 4500r multi 3.50 2.00

España 2000 Intl. Philatelic Exhibition (No. 2016). No. 2016 contains one 40x32mm stamp.

Dachshunds — A368

Designs: 200r, Smooth-haired dachshund. 500r, Wire-haired dachshund. 900r, Long-haired dachshund. 1000r, Two dachshunds. 1500r, Dachshund with pups. 4000r, Dachshunds resting.
4500r, Wire-haired dachshund, vert.

2000, Aug. 30 *Perf. 13*
2017-2022 A368 Set of 6 5.75 2.50

Souvenir Sheet
Perf. 12½

2023 A368 4500r multi 2.75 2.00

No. 2023 contains one 32x40mm stamp.

Cats and Art A369

Cat or cats and: 200r, Korean silk painting, 18th cent. 500r, Portuguese tile, 18th cent. 900r, Japanese ceramic cat. 1000r, Egyptian metallic cat. 1500r, Scandinavian engraving. 4000r, Japanese painting.
4500r, Cat on hind legs.

2000, Oct. 5 *Perf. 12½x12¼*
2024-2029 A369 Set of 6 5.75 2.50

Souvenir Sheet
Perf. 13x13¼

2030 A369 4500r multi 3.00 1.50

No. 2030 contains one 40x32mm stamp.

Birds A370

Designs: 200r, Creatophora cinerea. 500r, Sturnus vulgaris. 900r, Leiothrix lutea. 1000r, Rupicola rupicola. 1500r, Prunella collaris. 4000r, Panurus biarnicus.
4500r, Muscicapula pallipes, vert.

2000, Dec. 10 *Perf. 13*
2031-2036 A370 Set of 6 5.00 3.50

Souvenir Sheet

2037 A370 4500r multi 3.25 2.00

No. 2037 contains one 32x40mm stamp.

Sports — A371

Designs: 200r, Weight lifting. 500r, Rhythmic gymnastics. 900r, Baseball. 1000r, Women's tennis. 1500r, Basketball. 4000r, Women's high jump.

Perf. 12¾, 12½ (#2044)

2000, June 30 Litho.
2038-2043 A371 Set of 6 5.75 2.75

Souvenir Sheet

2044 A371 4500r Runners 2.75 1.75

No. 2044 contains one 32x40mm stamp.

New Year 2001 (Year of the Snake) — A372

Various stylized snakes with background colors of: 200r, Beige. 500r, Dull bister. 900r, Light blue. 1000r, Greenish blue. 1500r, Dull green. 4000r, Blue.
5400r, Blue, horiz.

2001, Jan. 15 Litho. *Perf. 12¼x12½*
2045-2050 A372 Set of 6 5.25 3.50

Souvenir Sheet
Perf. 13x13¼

2051 A372 5400r multi 4.00 2.75

No. 2051 contains one 40x32mm stamp.

Millennium — A373

Designs: 200r, Johannes Gutenberg, printers. 500r, Michael Faraday, electric motor. 900r, Samuel F. B. Morse, telegraph. 1000r, Alexander Graham Bell, telephone. 1500r, Enrico Fermi, nuclear energy. 4000r, Edward Roberts, computer.
No. 2058: a, Christopher Columbus, ships. b, Neil Armstrong, lunar module.

2001, Jan. 5 **Litho.** ***Perf. 12¾***
2052-2057 A373 Set of 6 7.00 4.00

Souvenir Sheet
Perf. 12½

2058 A373 5400r Sheet of 2, #a-b + label 8.00 8.00

No. 2058 contains two 40x32mm stamps.

Fire and Rescue Equipment A374

Designs: 200r, 1910 Sandou ladder wagon. 500r, 1899 Gallo cart. 900r, Merryweather pumper, 1950s. 1000r, 1940 Merryweather ambulance. 1500r, 1972 Man-Metz pumper. 4000r, Roman Diesel pumper, 1970s.
5400r, 1898 Metropolitan steam pumper.

2001, Feb. 5 ***Perf. 12¾***
2059-2064 A374 Set of 6 7.00 4.00

Souvenir Sheet
Perf. 13x13¼

2065 A374 5400r multi 4.00 4.00

No. 2065 contains one 40x32mm stamp.

Mushrooms — A375

Designs: 200r, Lycoperdon perlatum. 500r, Trametes versicolor. 900r, Hipholoma sublateritium. 1000r, Amanita muscaria. 1500r, Lycoperdon umbrinum. 4000r, Cortinarius orellanus.
5400r Amanita phalloides, vert.

2001, Feb. 25 ***Perf. 12¾***
2066-2071 A375 Set of 6 6.00 4.00

Souvenir Sheet
Perf. 12½

2072 A375 5400r multi 4.00 4.00

No. 2072 contains one 32x40mm stamp.

Belgica 2001 Intl. Stamp Exhibition, Brussels — A376

Butterflies: 200r, Nymphalis polychloros. 500r, Cethosia hypsea. 900r, Papilio palinurus. 1000r, Apatura ilia. 1500r, Parthenos sylvia. 4000r, Morpho grandensis.
5400r, Heliconius melpomene.

2001, Apr. 5 ***Perf. 12¾***
2073-2078 A376 Set of 6 6.25 4.00

Souvenir Sheet
Perf. 13x13¼

2079 A376 5400r multi 4.00 2.50

Film Personalities A377

Designs: 200r, Gary Cooper. 500r, Marlene Dietrich. 900r, Walt Disney. 1000r, Clark Gable. 1500r, Jeanette MacDonald. 4000r, Melvyn Douglas.
No. 2086: a, Rudolph Valentino. b, Marilyn Monroe.

2001, Apr. 25 **Litho.** ***Perf. 12¾***

2080	A377	200r multi	.25	.25
2081	A377	500r multi	.50	.30
2082	A377	900r multi	.70	.40
2083	A377	1000r multi	.90	.50
2084	A377	1500r multi	1.25	.75
2085	A377	4000r multi	3.25	1.75
		Nos. 2080-2085 (6)	6.85	3.95

Souvenir Sheet
Perf. 13

2086 A377 5400r Sheet of 2, #a-b 9.00 7.00

Natl. Culture Day A378

Sculptures: 500r, Angkor. 1500r, Bayon. 2000r, Bayon, diff.

2001, Apr. 3 **Litho.** ***Perf. 12¾***
2087-2089 A378 Set of 3 3.50 2.00

Temples — A379

Designs: 200r, Preah Vihear. 300r, Thonmanom. 600r, Tasom. 1000r, Kravan. 1500r, Takeo. 1700r, Mebon. 2200r, Banteay Kdei.

2001, Mar. 15 ***Perf. 12¼x12½***
2090-2096 A379 Set of 7 6.00 3.50

Automobiles — A380

Designs: 200r, 1972 TVR Series M. 500r, 1958 Ferrari 410. 900r, 1995 Peugeot 405. 1000r, 1953 Fiat 8VZ. 1500r, 1997 Citroen Xsara. 4000r, 1997 Renault Espace.
5400r, 1963 Ferrari 250 GT SWB.

2001, June 5 **Litho.** ***Perf. 12¾***
2097-2102 A380 Set of 6 7.00 4.00

Souvenir Sheet
Perf. 13x13¼

2103 A380 5400r multi 3.50 2.50

No. 2103 contains one 40x32mm stamp.

Tourism A381

Designs: 500r, Sourire de Bayon. 1500r, Bayon. 2000r, Bayon, diff.

2001, June 5 ***Perf. 12¾***
2104-2106 A381 Set of 3 3.25 2.50

Philanippon '01 — A382

Locomotives: 200r, 4-6-0. 500r, 4-6-4. 900r, 4-4-0. 1000r, 4-6-4, diff. 1500r, 4-6-2. 4000r, 4-8-2.
5400r, Undescribed locomotive.

2001, July 5 ***Perf. 12½x12¼***
2107-2112 A382 Set of 6 7.50 5.00

Souvenir Sheet
Perf. 13x13¼

2113 A382 5400r multi 5.50 4.50

No. 2113 contains one 40x32mm stamp.

Penguins A383

Designs: 200r, Aptenodytes forsteri. 500r, Spheniscus demersus. 900r, Spheniscus humboldti. 1000r, Eudypes cristatus. 1500r, Aptenodytes patagonica. 4000r, Pygoscelis antarctica.
5400r, Pygoscelis papua.

2001, Aug. 5 ***Perf. 12¾***
2114-2119 A383 Set of 6 8.00 5.50

Souvenir Sheet
Perf. 13x13¼

2120 A383 5400r multi 5.00 5.00

No. 2120 contains one 40x32mm stamp.

Cats A384

Designs: 200r, Singapura. 500r, Cymric. 900r, Exotic shorthair. 1000r, Ragdoll. 1500r, Manx. 4000r, Somali.
5400r, Egyptian Mau.

2001, Aug. 25 ***Perf. 12½x12¼***
2121-2126 A384 Set of 6 7.00 5.00

Souvenir Sheet
Perf. 13x13¼

2127 A384 5400r multi 5.75 4.75

No. 2127 contains one 40x32mm stamp.

Kites A385

Designs: 300r, Khleng Chak. 500r, Khleng Kanton. 1000r, Khleng Phnong. 1500r, Khleng Kaun Morn. 3000r, Khleng Me Ambao.

2001, Sept. 7 ***Perf. 12¾***
2128-2132 A385 Set of 5 6.50 5.50

Cacti — A386

Designs: 200r, Parodia cintiensis. 500r, Astrophytum astenas. 900r, Parodia faustiana. 1000r, Coryphantha sulcolanata. 1500r, Neochilenia hankena. 4000r, Mammilaria boolii.
5400r, Mammilaria swinglei.

2001, Sept. 15 ***Perf. 12¾***
2133-2138 A386 Set of 6 7.00 5.00

Souvenir Sheet
Perf. 12½

2139 A386 5400r multi 6.25 5.00

No. 2139 contains one 32x40mm stamp.

Khmer Culture A387

Designs: 500r, Fish Dance. 1500r, Red Fish Ballet. 2000r, Apsara Ballet.

2001, Oct. 9 ***Perf. 12¾***
2140-2142 A387 Set of 3 4.25 3.50

Wolves and Foxes A388

Designs: 200r, Canis lupus occidentalis. 500r, Canis lupus tundrorum, vert. 900r, Vulpes fulvas. 1000r, Canis latrans. 1500r, Vulpes zerda, vert. 4000r, Alopex lagopus.
5400r, Canis lupus signatus, vert.

2001, Oct. 15 ***Perf. 12¾***
2143-2148 A388 Set of 6 7.00 5.00

Souvenir Sheet
Perf. 12½

2149 A388 5400r multi 3.00 3.00

No. 2103 contains one 32x40mm stamp.

Human Evolution — A389

Designs: 100r, Australopithecus anamensis. 200r, Australopithecus afarensis. 300r, Australopithecus africanus. No. 2153, 500r, Australopithecus rudolfensis. No. 2154, 500r, Australopithecus boisei. 1000r, Homo habilis. 1500r, Homo erectus. 4000r, Homo sapiens neanderthalensis.
5400r, Homo sapiens sapiens.

2001, Oct. 25 ***Perf. 13***
2150-2157 A389 Set of 8 9.50 6.00

Souvenir Sheet

2158 A389 5400r multi 6.50 5.00

No. 2158 contains one 40x32mm stamp.

King Norodom Sihanouk, 80th Birthday (in 2002) A389a

Various photos: 100r, 200r, 300r, 400r, 500r, 600r, 700r, 800r, 900r, 1000r, 1500r, 2000r, 3000r.

2001, Oct. 31 **Litho.** ***Perf. 13***
2158A-2158M A389a Set of 13 *17.00 10.00*

Chess A390

Designs: 200r, Rook. 500r, Pawn. 900r, King. 1000r, Bishop. 1500r, Queen. 4000r, Knight.
5400r, Pieces of Oriental chess-like game.

2001, Dec. 25 ***Perf. 12¾***
2159-2164 A390 Set of 6 7.00 6.00

Souvenir Sheet

Perf. 13

2165 A390 5400r multi 5.50 4.00

No. 2165 contains one 40x32mm stamp.

Italian Soccer A391

Designs: 200r, 1934 World Cup championship team. 500r, 1938 World Cup championship team. 900r, 1968 European Cup championship team. 1000r, 1982 World Cup championship team. 1500r, 2002 World Cup team. 4000r, Italian soccer federation emblem.

2001 ***Perf. 12¾***
2166-2171 A391 Set of 6 7.00 7.00

ASEAN Post, 10th Anniv A392

Temples: 500r, Prasat Preah Vihear. 1000r, Prasat Preah Ko. 1500r, Prasat Banteay Srei. 2500r, Prasat Bayon. 3500r, Prasat Angkor Wat.

2002, July 9 ***Perf. 13***
2172-2176 A392 Set of 5 11.00 10.00

Sugar Palm — A393

Designs: 300r, Tree. 500r, Female flower. 700r, Male flower. 1500r, Fruit.

2003, June 20 **Litho.**
2177-2180 A393 Set of 4 7.50 7.00

Japanese Grant Aid — A394

Designs: 100r, Drawing of Bridge No. 26, Highway 6A. 200r, Bridge No. 26, Highway 6A. 400r, Chroy Changvar Bridge. 800r, Kizuna Bridge. 3500r, Monument, vert.

2003, Apr. 25
2181-2185 A394 Set of 5 7.50 6.00

Cambodian Red Cross — A395

Designs: 100r, Ox cart. 200r, Woman carrying rice bag, vert. 300r, Queen with Red Cross volunteers. 400r, Queen and women. 500r, Queen and elderly people. 700r, Queen and women, diff. 800r, Queen and Prime Minister's wife giving items to people. 1000r, Like 800r, diff. 1900r, Like 800r, diff., vert. 2100r, Like 800r, diff., vert. 4000r, Queen and Prime Minister's wife with baby.

2003, May 8
2186-2196 A395 Set of 11 12.00 12.00

Cambodia/People's Republic of China Diplomatic Relations, 50th Anniv. — A396

No. 2197: a, Angkor Wat. b, Great Wall of China.

2003, July 19 ***Perf. 12¼x12***
2197 A396 2000r Horiz. pair, #a-b 5.00 4.00

Association of South East Asian Nations, 36th Anniv. — A397

Designs: 400r, Conference emblem. 500r, Apsara dancer. 600r, Apsara dancer, diff. 1600r, Apsara dancers. 1900r, Temonorom dancers.

2003, Aug. 8 ***Perf. 13***
2198-2202 A397 Set of 5 8.00 6.50

King Norodom Sihanouk — A398

Designs: 200r, Pointing at map. 400r, Meeting rural Cambodians, vert. 500r, Sitting in forest, vert. 800r, Pointing in forest, vert. 1000r, Saluting, vert. 2000r, Saluting, with flag and Independence Monument, vert. 5000r, With handicapped people.

2003, Nov. 9
2203-2209 A398 Set of 7 10.00 7.00

Khmer Culture A399

Sculptures: 100r, Bayon. 200r, Banteay Srei. 400r, Banteay Srei, diff. 800r, Bayon, vert. 3500r, Banteay Srei, vert.
2000r, Unattributed sculpture, vert.

2004, Apr. 3
2210-2214 A399 Set of 5 5.00 4.00

Souvenir Sheet

2215 A399 2000r multi 3.25 2.00

Rural Areas A400

Designs: 600r, Mill. 900r, House, field and cattle. 2000r, House and trees.
2000r, Ox cart and driver.

2004, Apr. 13
2216-2218 A400 Set of 3 6.00 4.00

Souvenir Sheet

2219 A400 2000r multi 3.00 2.25

Tepmonorum Dancers — A401

Dancers with: 400r, Yellow costumes. 1000r, Blue costumes. 2100r, Blue and yellow costumes.
2100r, Blue and yellow costumes, diff.

2004, May 5
2220-2222 A401 Set of 3 5.00 4.00

Souvenir Sheet

2223 A401 2000r multi 3.00 2.50

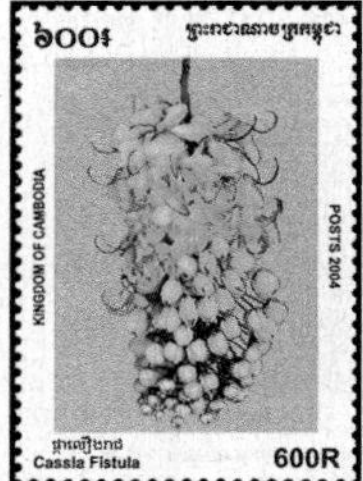

Flowers — A402

Designs: 600r, Cassia fistula. 700r, Butea monosperma. 900r, Couroupita quianensis. 1000r, Delonix regia, horiz. 1800r, Lagerstroemia floribunda.
2000r, Lagerstroemia floribunda, horiz.

2004, Aug. 25 **Litho.** ***Perf. 13***
2224-2228 A402 Set of 5 5.50 4.00

Souvenir Sheet

2229 A402 2000r multi 3.25 1.75

Tourism — A403

Designs: 200r, Prasat Preah Khan. 500r, Prasat Preup. 600r, PrasatBanteay Samre. 1600r, Prasat Bayon. 1900r, Angkor Wat.
2000r, Prasat Bayon, vert.

2004, Sept. 27 **Litho.** ***Perf. 13***
2230-2234 A403 Set of 5 5.00 3.50

Souvenir Sheet

2235 A403 2000r multi 3.25 2.00

Coronation of King Norodom Shiamoni A404

Various photos: 100r, 400r, 500r, 600r, 700r, 900r, 2100r, 2200r, 4000r. 700r-4000r are horiz.

2004, Oct. 29
2236-2244 A404 Set of 9 8.00 8.00

Ancient Fishing Tools A405

Various scoops and baskets: 100r, 200r, 800r, 1700r, 2200r. 1700r and 2200r are vert.
2000r, Child with basket, vert.

2004, Dec. 5
2245-2249 A405 Set of 5 5.50 4.00

Souvenir Sheet

2250 A405 2000r multi 4.25 2.50

Cambodian Red Cross, 50th Anniv. — A406

Designs: 400r, Emblem. 700r, Volunteers, horiz. 800r, Volunteers, diff., horiz. 1900r, Volunteers, diff., horiz. 2100r, Volunteers, diff. horiz. 2200r, Royalty on dais, horiz.

2005, Feb. 18
2251-2256 A406 Set of 6 7.25 7.25

Apsaras Dance — A407

Dancer with background color of: 800r, Pink. 900r, Light blue. 1400r, Green. 1600r, Rose. 2000r, Blue.
4000r, Brown.

2005, Apr. 12
2257-2261 A407 Set of 5 6.50 5.00
Souvenir Sheet
2262 A407 4000r multi 4.25 3.00

Khmer Culture A408

Designs: 500r, Banteay Kdei. 700r, Elephant Terrace. 1000r, Thommanon. 2000r, Ta Prohm. 2500r, Angkor Wat.
4000r, Ta Reach, vert.

2005, May 16
2263-2267 A408 Set of 5 6.25 5.00
Souvenir Sheet
2268 A408 4000r multi 4.25 3.00

Flowers — A409

Nymphaea lotus in: 100r, Purple. 500r, White. 1200r, Blue. 2000r, Yellow. 2500r, Red.
4000r, Red flowers in canoe, horiz.

2005, July 25 Litho. ***Perf. 13***
2269-2273 A409 Set of 5 6.00 4.50
Souvenir Sheet
2274 A409 4000r multi 4.25 3.00

Fish A410

Designs: 700r, Pangasionodon gigas. 800r, Catlocarpio siamensis. 1000r, Mekongina erythrospila. 1900r, Probarbus labeaminor, vert. 2200r, Wallago leeri, vert.
4000r, Scleropages formosus.

2005, Sept. 5 ***Perf. 13***
2275-2279 A410 Set of 5 6.25 5.50
Souvenir Sheet
2280 A410 4000r multi 4.25 3.75

Coronation of King Norodom Sihamoni, 1st Anniv. — A411

Frame colors: 500r, Green. 1500r, Blue. 2200r, Red.

2005, Oct. 29 Litho. ***Perf. 13***
2281-2283 A411 Set of 3 3.25 3.25

Miniature Sheet

Birds — A412

No. 2284: a, 200r, Great egret. b, 400r, Great-billed heron. c, 1000r, Painted stork. d, 1200r, Spot-billed pelican. e, 1800r, Sarus crane, horiz. f, 3500r, Greater adjutant, horiz.

2005, Dec. 5
2284 A412 Sheet of 6, #a-f 8.00 8.00

Khmer Culture A413

Women at work: 100r, Scooping dyes. 800r, Washing clothes. 1500r, Weaving. 2200r, Spinning thread. 3500r, Weaving, diff.
5400r, Weaving, diff.

2006, Jan. 26
2285-2289 A413 Set of 5 6.75 6.00
Souvenir Sheet
2290 A413 5400r multi 4.00 3.00

Marine Mammals — A414

Designs: 500r, Sousa chinensis. 900r, Neophocaena phocaenoides. 1400r, Dolphinus capensis tropicalis. 2100r, Stenella longirostris roseinventris. 3500r, Tursiops aduncus.
5400r, Neophocaena phocaenoides and boat.

2006, Mar. 9
2291-2295 A414 Set of 5 7.50 6.50
Souvenir Sheet
2296 A414 5400r multi 4.00 3.00

Reamker Legend — A415

Designs: 1000r, Jup Leak and Ream Leak. 1400r, Preah Ream, vert. 1600r, Neang Seda, vert. 1900r, Krong Reap, vert. 2100r, Hanuman, vert.
5400r, Two characters in water.

2006, Apr. 13
2297-2301 A415 Set of 5 6.50 5.50
Souvenir Sheet
2302 A415 5400r multi 4.25 3.25

Elephants — A416

Designs: 400r, Adult and juvenile elephant. 700r, Elephants in water. 1600r, Elephant, vert. 2200r, Elephant facing right. 3500r, Elephant facing left.
5400r, Elephants in water, diff.

2006, June 15 Litho. ***Perf. 13***
2303-2307 A416 Set of 5 7.00 5.50
Souvenir Sheet
2308 A416 5400r multi 4.25 3.50

Dances — A417

Designs: 600r, Chhai Yaim dance. 1900r, Sacrifice of Buffalo dance. 2200r, Mouth Organ dance. 3500r, Rice Harvest dance.

2006, Aug. 17
2309-2312 A417 Set of 4 6.50 5.50

Birds A418

Designs: 600r, Threskionis melanocephalus. 800r, Plegadis facinellus. 1500r, Houbaropsis bengalensis. 2100r, Pseudibis gigantea. 3500r, Pseudibis davisoni.
5400r, Pseudibis gigantea, vert.

2006, Nov. 8 Litho. ***Perf. 13***
2313-2317 A418 Set of 5 7.50 6.00
Souvenir Sheet
2318 A418 5400r multi 7.00 5.50

Condom Use Program — A419

Designs: 300r, Man, woman, program emblem. 500r, Man, motorcycle, program emblem. 2200r, Men on boat, flag with program emblem.

2006, Dec. 1 Litho. ***Perf. 13***
2319-2321 A419 Set of 3 2.25 2.25
World AIDS Day.

Cambodian Red Cross HIV/AIDS Campaign — A420

Campaign leader Bun Rany, wife of Prime Minister Hun Sen and captions: 1500r, Caring. 1900r, Stop discrimination, vert. 2000r, Give hope to families. 2100r, National and Asia-Pacific Leadership Forum Champion. 2200r, National and Asia-Pacific Leadership Forum Champion, diff.

2007 Litho. ***Perf. 13***
2322-2326 A420 Set of 5 6.50 6.50

Sculpture A421

Flags of Viet Nam and Cambodia A422

2007, June 24
2327 A421 500r shown .45 .45
2328 A421 800r Sculpture, diff. .65 .65
2329 A421 1000r Sculpture, diff. .75 .75
2330 A421 1500r Sculpture, diff. 1.25 1.25
2331 A422 1900r shown 1.50 1.50
Nos. 2327-2331 (5) 4.60 4.60

Diplomatic relations between Cambodia and Viet Nam, 40th anniv.

Handicap International, 25th Anniv. — A423

Denominations: 1000r, 1500r.

2007, July 25
2332-2333 A423 Set of 2 2.00 2.00

Dancers — A424

Architecture — A425

Various dancers with denominations of: 800r, 900r, 1400r, 1600r, 2000r.

No. 2339: a, Secretariat Building, Bandar Seri Begawan, Brunei. b, National Museum of Cambodia. c, Fatahillah Museum, Jakarta, Indonesia. d, Typical house, Laos. e, Malayan Railway Headquarters Building, Kuala Lumpur, Malaysia. f, Yangon Post Office, Myanmar (Burma). g, Malacañang Palace, Philippines. h, National Museum of Singapore. i, Vimanmek Mansion, Bangkok, Thailand. j, Presidential Palace, Hanoi, Viet Nam.

2007, Aug. 8

2334-2338 A424 Set of 5 5.00 5.00
2339 A425 1000r Sheet of 10, #a-j 10.00 10.00

Association of South East Asian Nations (ASEAN), 40th anniv. See Brunei No. 607, Burma No. 370, Indonesia Nos. 2120-2121, Laos Nos. 1717-1718, Malaysia No. 1170, Philippines Nos. 3103-3105, Singapore No. 1265, Thailand No. 2315, and Viet Nam Nos. 3302-3311.

Flowers — A426

Designs: 100r, Monochoria vaginalis. 600r, Alternanthera sessilis. 1900r, Nymphoides hydrophylla. 2000r, Limnophila geoffrayi. 2200r, Xyris indica.

6000r, Eichhornia crassipes.

2008, June 30 Litho. *Perf. 13*

2340-2344 A426 Set of 5 — —

Souvenir Sheet

Perf. 13¾x13½

2345 A426 6000r multi — —

No. 2345 contains one 32x43mm stamp.

Friendship Between Cambodia and People's Republic of China, 50th Anniv. — A427

No. 2346: a, Tian An Men Rostrum, flag of People's Republic of China. b, Royal Palace, flag of Cambodia.

2008, July 25 Litho. *Perf. 12*

2346 A427 2000r Horiz. pair, #a-b 2.00 2.00

Best Wishes Dancers — A428

Various dancers with background color of: 600r, Yellow green. 1000r, Lilac. 1700r, Green. 1800r, Dark blue. 1900r, Dark blue.

6000r, Best Wishes dancer with temple in background.

2008, Aug. 8 Litho. *Perf. 13*

2347 A428 600r multi — —
2348 A428 1000r multi — —
2349 A428 1700r multi — —
2350 A428 1800r multi — —
2351 A428 1900r multi — —

Souvenir Sheet

Perf. 13¾x13½

2352 A428 6000r multi — —

No. 2352 contains one 32x43mm stamp.

Addition of Preah Vihear to UNESCO World Heritage List — A429

Designs: 600r, Gopura I. 700r, Gopura II. 1000r, Gopura III. 2000r, Gopura IV. 3000r, Gopura V.

6000r, Temple of Preah Vihear.

2008, Nov. 9 Litho. *Perf. 13*

2353 A429 600r multi — —
2354 A429 700r multi — —
2355 A429 1000r multi — —
2356 A429 2000r multi — —
2357 A429 3000r multi — —

Souvenir Sheet

Perf. 13½x13¾

2358 A429 6000r multi — —

No. 2358 contains one 43x32mm stamp.

A430

Pottery Making — A431

Various women making pottery: 100r, 700r, 1900r, 2000r, 2200r.

6000r, Oxcart with pottery.

2008, Dec. 5 Litho. *Perf. 13*

2359-2363 A430 Set of 5 3.50 3.50

Souvenir Sheet

Perf. 13¾x13½

2364 A431 6000r multi 3.00 3.00

Buildings, School Children, Athletes A432

30th Anniversary Emblem — A432a

Designs: 200r, Agriculture. 1500r, Factory, power line towers, dam. 2200r, Mail truck and telecommunications. 2500r, Trucks, bridge and cranes at port. 2800r, Temple, dancers, elephant and boats.

2009, Jan. 7 Litho. *Perf. 13*

2365-2370 A432 Set of 6 — —
2371 A432a 3000r multi — —

Victory Day, 30th anniv.

Preah Vihear as UNESCO World Heritage Site, 1st Anniv. A433

UNESCO World Heritage emblem and various sites at Preah Vihear: 300r, 800r, 1600r, 1800r, 2800r.

2009, July 7 Litho. *Perf. 13*

2372-2376 A433 Set of 5 — —

Ancient Agricultural Tools — A434

Designs: 300r, Plow. 1200r, Harrow. 1700r, Spiked roller. 1800r, Water wheel. 2800r, Cart.

6000r, Farmer operating water wheel, vert.

2010, Mar. 30 Litho. *Perf. 13*

2377-2381 A434 Set of 5 3.75 3.75

Souvenir Sheet

Perf. 13¾x13½

2382 A434 6000r multi 3.00 3.00

Environmental Protection A435

Designs: 200r, Filled trash can, face on Earth. 800r, Watering can pouring water on Earth, cars in flood. 1400r, Tree inside split Earth. 1700r, Buildings in hourglass. 3000r, Tree in hands.

6000r, Cars in flood, palm trees.

2010, May 25 Litho. *Perf. 13*

2383-2387 A435 Set of 5 3.50 3.50

Souvenir Sheet

Perf. 13¾x13½

2388 A435 6000r multi 3.00 3.00

Diplomatic Relations Between Cambodia and the United States, 60th Anniv. — A436

2010, July 11 Litho. *Perf. 13*

2389 A436 2800r multi 1.40 1.40

Campaign Against AIDS — A437

Red AIDS ribbon and: 1000r, Wrapped and unwrapped condoms, condom with face. 1500r, Man, woman and child. 2800r, Men and woman at night club. 4000r, Two birds.

2011, June 29 Litho. *Perf. 13*

2390-2393 A437 Set of 4 4.75 4.75

First day cancels show a June 5 date, but the stamps were not sold until June 29.

Fish A438

Designs: 500r, Barbonymus schwanenfeldii. 1500r, Hypsibarbus lagleri. 2800r, Puntioplites falcifer. 3000r, Osteochilus melanopleurus. 3500r, Hampala macrolepidota.

6000r, Fish, fishermen and nets.

2011, Aug. 8 Litho. *Perf. 13*

2394-2398 A438 Set of 5 5.25 5.25

Souvenir Sheet

Perf. 13½x13¾

2399 A438 6000r multi 3.00 3.00

A439

King Norodom Sihanouk (1922-2012) A440

2011, Nov. 14 Litho. *Perf. 13*

2400 A439 2800r multi — —
2401 A440 3000r multi — —

Return of King Norodom Sihanouk to Cambodia, 20th anniv.

Temples — A441

Designs: 500r, Prasat Ta Moan Thom. 2800r, Prasat Nokor Bachey. 3500r, Prasat Ta Krabey. 5000r, Prasat Ta Moan Thom, horiz.

6000r, Prasat Phnom Banan.

2012, July 27 Litho. *Perf. 13*

2402 A441 500r multi — —
2403 A441 2800r multi — —
2404 A441 3500r multi — —
2405 A441 5000r multi — —

Souvenir Sheet

Perf. 13¾x13½

2406 A441 6000r multi — —

Banteay Srei Temple Statues — A442

Statue of: 2000r, Ascetic. 2500r, Apsara. 2800r, Apsara, diff. 3000r, Apsara, diff. 6000r, Dancer.

2012, Sept. 18 Litho. *Perf. 13*
2407-2410 A442 Set of 4 — —

Souvenir Sheet
Perf. 13¾x13½
2411 A442 6000r multi — —

60th Birthday of King Norodom Sihamoni A443

2013, May 14 Litho. *Perf. 13*
2412 A443 5000r multi 6.25 6.25

Banteay Srei Temple — A444

Various temple details.

2013, July 17 Litho. *Perf. 13*
2413 A444 1500r multi 1.90 1.90
2414 A444 2500r multi 3.25 3.25
2415 A444 2800r multi 3.50 3.50
2416 A444 3000r multi 3.75 3.75
Nos. 2413-2416 (4) 12.40 12.40

Nos. 2413-2416 exist in perforated and imperforate sheets of 4. Value, $16 and $42.50, respectively.

Rice Growing A445

Designs: 1800r, Three planters in paddy. 2200r, Four transplanters in paddy. 3000r, Farmer and oxen plowing in paddy. 3500r, Farmers and oxen in paddy.
6000r, Farmers harvesting crops.

2013, Sept. 19 Litho. *Perf. 13*
2417-2420 A445 Set of 4 13.00 13.00

Souvenir Sheet
Perf. 13¾x13½
2421 A445 6000r multi 8.75 8.75

Nos. 2417-2420 exist in perforated and imperforate sheets of 4. Value, $16 and $42.50, respectively.

Friendship Between Cambodia and People's Republic of China, 55th Anniv. (in 2013) — A446

No. 2422: a, Wat Phnom, Phnom Penh, Cambodia. b, Kaiyuan Temple, Quanzhou, People's Republic of China.

2014, May 14 Litho. *Perf. 12*
2422 A446 3000r Horiz. pair, #a-b 7.75 7.75
c. Souvenir sheet of 2, #2422a-2422b 8.75 8.75

Dated 2013.

Traditional Dances — A447

Various dancers: 1000r, 2000r, 3000r, 3500r.
6000r, Dancers, diff.

2014, Oct. 10 Litho. *Perf. 13*
2423-2426 A447 Set of 4 11.00 11.00

Souvenir Sheet
Perf. 13x13¼
2427 A447 6000r multi 8.25 8.25

No. 2427 contains one 31x46mm stamp.
Nos. 2423-2426 exist in perforated and imperforate sheets of 4. Value, $16 and $42.50, respectively.

Flags and Emblem of Association of Southeast Asian Nations A448

2015, Aug. 8 Litho. *Perf. 13½*
2428 A448 1200r multi 1.60 1.60

See Brunei No. 656, Burma Nos. 417-418, Indonesia No. 2428, Laos No. , Malaysia No. 1562, Philippines No. 3619, Singapore No. 1742, Thailand No. 2875, Viet Nam No. 3529.

Banteay Chhmar A449

Various views of Banteay Chhmar: 500r, 2000r, 2800r, 3000r.
6000r, Banteay Chhmar, vert.

2015, Oct. 9 Litho. *Perf. 13*
2429-2432 A449 Set of 4 9.25 9.25

Souvenir Sheet
2433 A449 6000r multi 13.00 13.00

No. 2433 contains one 31x46mm stamp.
Nos. 2429-2432 exist in perforated and imperforate sheets of 4. Value, $16 and $42.50, respectively.

United Nations Mine Sweeping A450

Various soldiers sweeping for mines: 2000r, 3000r, 3500r.
6000r, Soldier sweeping for mines, diff.

2016, Aug. 8 Litho. *Perf. 13*
2434-2436 A450 Set of 3 9.25 9.25

Souvenir Sheet
2437 A450 6000r multi 7.75 7.75

No. 2437 contains one 31x46mm stamp.
Nos. 2434-2436 exist in perforated and imperforate sheets of 3. Value, $16 and $42.50, respectively.

Statues — A451

Designs: 500r, Tevi. 2000r, Buddha. 2500r, Harihara. 3000r, Vishnu, facing left. 3500r, Vishnu, facing forward.
6000r, Shiva statues.

2016, Nov. 11 Litho. *Perf. 13*
2438-2442 A451 Set of 5 12.50 12.50
2442a Souvenir sheet of 5, #2438-2442, + label *21.00 21.00*

Souvenir Sheet
2443 A451 6000r multi 7.75 7.75

No. 2442a exists imperforate. Value, $45.
No. 2443 contains one 31x46mm stamp.

Rumdul A452

2017, Aug. 8 Litho. *Perf. 13*
2444 A452 3000r multi 3.25 3.25

Souvenir Sheet
2445 A452 6000r Rumdul, vert. 15.00 15.00

Association of Southeast Asian Nations, 50th anniv. No. 2445 contains one 31x41mm stamp.

International Year of Sustainable Tourism for Development — A453

Tourist attractions: 500r, Koh Rong Sanloem. 1000r, Ream National Park. 2000r, Wat Phnom. 3000r, Angkor Wat at sunset. 4000r, Angkor Wat and 3 men.
6000r, Angkor Wat, vert.

2017, Sept. 19 Litho. *Perf. 13*
2446-2450 A453 Set of 5 11.00 11.00

Souvenir Sheet
2451 A453 6000r multi 22.00 22.00

No. 2451 contains one 31x46mm stamp.

Lighthouses A454

Designs: 500r, Chong Khneas Lighthouse. 800r, Croachamar Lighthouse. 2100r, Chhlong Lighthouse. 3000r, Koh Dach Lighthouse. 4000r, Kohrongsamloem Lighthouse.
6000r, Kampong Cham Lighthouse.

2017, Oct. 10 Litho. *Perf. 13*
2452-2456 A454 Set of 5 11.00 11.00
2456a Souvenir sheet of 5, #2452-2456, perf. 13¾ *27.50 27.50*

Souvenir Sheet
2457 A454 6000r multi 11.00 11.00

No. 2456a exists imperforate. Value, $40.
No. 2457 contains one 31x46mm stamp.

Friendship Between Cambodia and People's Republic of China — A455

Designs: No. 2458, 3000r, Iron Lion of Cangzhou, People's Republic of China. No. 2459, 3000r, Stone Lion, Temple Phnom Bakheng, Cambodia, vert.

2017, Nov. 16 Litho. *Perf. 13*
2458-2459 A455 Set of 2 6.75 6.75

See People's Republic of China Nos. 4496-4497.

Sculptures of Apsaras — A456

Various sculptures of Apsaras: 500r, 800r, 2000r, 3000r, 4000r.
6000r, Apsaras, diff.

2017, Dec. 12 Litho. *Perf. 13*
2460-2464 A456 Set of 5 11.50 11.50

Souvenir Sheet
2465 A456 6000r multi 22.00 22.00

No. 2465 contains one 46x31mm stamp.

Soccer A457

Soccer Federation of Cambodia emblem and: 500r, Cambodian flag, crowd at soccer match. 900r, Three soccer players. 2000r, Six soccer players. 3000r, Four soccer players, vert. 4000r, Crowd at soccer match, vert.
6000r, Emblem and Phnom Penh Olympic Stadium, vert.

2018, June 14 Litho. *Perf. 13*
2466-2470 A457 Set of 5 11.00 11.00

Souvenir Sheet
2471 A457 6000r multi 13.50 13.50

No. 2471 contains one 31x46mm stamp.
No. 2471 exists imperforate. Value, $16.50.

A458

Baha'i House of Worship, Battambang A459

2018, June 22 Litho. *Perf. 13*
2472 A458 2000r multi 2.75 2.75
2473 A459 2100r multi 2.75 2.75

Bahá'u'lláh (1817-92), founder of Baha'i Faith.

Sambor Prei Kuk Temple A460

Various sculptures and buildings: 2000r, 3000r, 4000r.
6000r, Temple, vert.

2018, July 8 Litho. *Perf. 13*
2474-2476 A460 Set of 3 12.00 12.00

Souvenir Sheet

2477 A460 6000r multi 13.50 13.50

No. 2477 contains one 31x46mm stamp.

Carved Stone Heads of Angkor Wat — A461

Stamps with white frames depicting various heads: 500r, 1200r, 2100r, 3000r, 4000r.
No. 2483: a, Head, small area of blue sky at UR, denomination below chin. b, Head, diff, larger area of blue sky at UR, denomination touching chin.

2018, Aug. 13 Litho. *Perf. 13*
2478-2482 A461 Set of 5 12.00 12.00

Souvenir Sheet

2483 A461 3000r Sheet of 2, #a-b 14.50 14.50

No. 2483 contains two 31x46mm stamps.
No. 2483 exists imperforate. Value, $15.

National Museum A462

Designs: 500r, Vessel for Prahok fermented fish. 800r, Statue of King Jayavarman VII. 2000r, Statue of Buddhist Trial. No. 2487, 3000r, Kinnari box, horiz. 4000r, Statue of reclining Vishnu, horiz.
No. 2489, 3000r, National Museum, vert.

2018, Sept. 7 Litho. *Perf. 13*
2484-2488 A462 Set of 5 11.00 11.00

Souvenir Sheet

2489 A462 3000r multi 6.75 6.75

No. 2489 contains one 31x46mm stamp.
No. 2489 exists imperforate. Value, $8.75.

Birds A463

Designs: 500r, Giant ibis. 900r, Red-headed vulture. 2000r, White-shouldered ibis. 3000r, Sarus crane, vert. 4000r, Greater adjutant, vert.
6000r, Juvenile painted stork, (Mycteria leucocephala), vert.

2018, Nov. 16 Litho. *Perf. 13*
2490-2494 A463 Set of 5 11.00 11.00

Souvenir Sheet

2495 A463 6000r multi 13.50 13.50

No. 2495 contains one 31x46mm stamp.

A464

Prionailurus Viverrinus — A465

Various depictions of Prionailurus viverrinus: 500r, 900r, 1000r, 2000r, 2500r, 3000r, 4000r. 3000r and 4000r are vert.
6000r, Prionailurus viverrinus, vert.

2019, Feb. 22 Litho. *Perf. 13*
2496-2502 A464 Set of 7 15.50 15.50

Souvenir Sheet

2503 A465 6000r multi 13.50 13.50

An imperforate 6000r souvenir sheet with a different illustration was produced in limited quantities. Value, $15.
Nos. 2496-2502 were issued individually in sheets of 10 with a gutter between two rows of five stamps.

Angkor Wat A466

Various sites at Angkor Wat: 500r, 900r, 1400r, 3000r, 4000r.
6000r, Stupa.

2019, Mar. 13 Litho. *Perf. 13*
2504-2508 A466 Set of 5 10.50 10.50

Souvenir Sheet

2509 A466 6000r multi 14.00 14.00

No. 2509 contains one 46x31mm stamp.
No. 2509 exists imperforate. Value, $14.
Nos. 2404-2508 were issued individually in sheets of 10 with a gutter between two rows of five stamps.

New Year 2019 (Year of the Pig) — A467

2019, Mar. 13 Litho. *Perf. 13*
2510 A467 3000r multi 4.00 4.00

No. 2510 was issued in sheets of 10: two vertical strips of five with a gutter.

Tonle Sap A468

Designs: 500r, Shelter with thatched roof. 900r, Birds. 1000r, Houses on stilts above water, boats. 1200r, Aerial view of village and boats. 2000r, Water level view of village and boats. 3000r, Fisherman casting net. 3500r, Boat near jungle.
6000r, Bird facing left.

2019, Apr. 24 Litho. *Perf. 13*
2511-2517 A468 Set of 7 13.50 13.50

Souvenir Sheet

2518 A468 6000r multi 14.00 14.00

No. 2518 contains one 46x31mm stamp. An imperforate 6000r souvenir sheet with a different bird illustration was produced in limited quantities. Value, $14.
Nos. 2511-2517 were issued individually in sheets of 10 with a gutter between two rows of five stamps.

Angkor Era Gold Jewelry A469

Various pieces of jewelry: 500r, 800r, 2000r, 3000r, 4000r.
6000r, Statue with jewelry, vert.

2019, May 15 Litho. *Perf. 13*
2519-2523 A469 Set of 5 11.00 11.00

Souvenir Sheet

2524 A469 6000r multi 8.75 8.75

No. 2524 contains one 31x46mm stamp.
No. 2524 exists imperforate. Value, $14.
Nos. 2519-2523 were issued individually in sheets of 10 with a gutter between two rows of five stamps.

Traditional Costumes for Cambodian Men and Women — A470

2019, Aug. 8 Litho. *Perf. 13*
2525 A470 3000r multi 2.75 2.75

No. 2525 was issued in sheets of 10: two vertical strips of five with a gutter.

SEMI-POSTAL STAMPS

Nos. 8, 12, 14 and 15 Surcharged in Black

1952, Oct. 20 Unwmk. *Perf. 13*
B1 A3 1.10pi + 40c 4.25 *8.50*
B2 A3 1.90pi + 60c 4.25 *8.50*
B3 A3 3pi + 1pi 4.25 *8.50*
B4 A1 5pi + 2pi 4.25 *8.50*
Nos. B1-B4 (4) 17.00 *34.00*

For students assistance.

Preah Stupa — SP1

1957, Mar. 15 Engr. *Perf. 13*
B5 SP1 1.50r + 50c ind, ol & red 2.00 2.00
B6 SP1 6.50r + 1.50r red lil, ol & red 3.00 3.00
B7 SP1 8r + 2r bl, ol & red 5.00 5.00
Nos. B5-B7 (3) 10.00 10.00

Birth of Buddha, 2,500th anniv. See #62-64.

Regular Issue, 1959, with Red Typographed Surcharge

1959, Dec. 9
B8 A14 20c + 20c rose vio .50 .50
B9 A14 50c + 30c blue .80 .80
B10 A14 80c + 50c rose car 1.75 1.75
Nos. B8-B10 (3) 3.05 3.05

The surtax was for the Red Cross.

Nos. 107-108 Surcharged and Overprinted in Red

1963, Oct. 1 Unwmk. *Perf. 13*
B11 A26 4r + 40c grn & dk brn 1.00 1.00
B12 A26 6r + 60c vio & ol bis 1.50 1.50

Centenary of International Red Cross.

Nos. 263, 267, 293-294, 134 Surcharged in Red

1972, Nov. 15 Engr. *Perf. 13*
B13 A72 3r + 2r multi .60 .40
B14 A72 10r + 6r multi .90 .80
B15 A80 12r + 7r multi 1.00 .90

B16 A34 12r + 7r multi 1.00 .90
B17 A80 15r + 8r multi 1.50 1.50
Nos. B13-B17 (5) 5.00 4.50

Surtax was for war victims. Surcharge arranged differently on Nos. B15-B17.

AIR POST STAMPS

Kinnari — AP1

Unwmk.

1953, Apr. 16 Engr. *Perf. 13*

C1 AP1 50c deep green 2.00 1.00
a. Souv. sheet of 4, #C1, C3, C5, C9 75.00 75.00
C2 AP1 3pi red brown 2.00 1.25
a. Souv. sheet of 3, #C2, C4, C8 75.00 75.00
C3 AP1 3.30pi rose violet 3.00 2.00
C4 AP1 4pi dk brn & dp bl 2.00 2.00
C5 AP1 5.10pi brn, red & org 3.75 3.00
C6 AP1 6.50pi dk brn & lil rose 3.75 3.25
a. Souv. sheet of 2, #C6-C7 75.00 75.00
C7 AP1 9pi lil rose & dp grn 4.50 5.00
C8 AP1 11.50pi multi 9.00 7.00
C9 AP1 30pi dk brn, bl grn & org 17.50 12.00
Nos. C1-C9 (9) 47.50 36.50

No. C1a sold for 50pi, No. C2a for 25pi, No. C6a for 20pi.

Souvenir sheets with completely white gum, no toning and no gum bends sell for a premium.

AP2

1957, Dec. 11

C10 AP2 50c maroon .40 .25
C11 AP2 1r emerald .70 .25
C12 AP2 4r ultra 2.25 .75
C13 AP2 50r carmine rose 8.75 4.00
C14 AP2 100r grn, bl & car 16.00 6.00
a. Souv. sheet of 5, #C10-C14 32.50 32.50
Nos. C10-C14 (5) 28.10 11.25

No. C14a sold for 160r.
See note after No. C9.

Independence Type of 1961

1961, Nov. 9 *Perf. 13x12½*

C15 A24 7r multicolored .90 .80
C16 A24 30r grn, car & ultra 3.00 2.25
C17 A24 50r ind, grn & ol 4.50 3.00
a. Souv. sheet of 3, #C15-C17 11.00 11.00
Nos. C15-C17 (3) 7.55 7.55

No. C15 Srchd. in Red and Ovptd. in Black

1962, Nov. 9

C18 A24 12r on 7r multi 2.25 1.25

Dedication of Independence Monument.

Hanuman, Monkey God — AP3

1964, Sept. 1 Engr. *Perf. 13*

C19 AP3 5r multicolored 1.00 .50
C20 AP3 10r ol bis, lil rose & grn 1.50 .60
C21 AP3 20r vio, bl & ol bis 2.25 1.25
C22 AP3 40r bl, ol bis & dk bl 5.50 2.00
C23 AP3 80r multicolored 9.50 5.50
Nos. C19-C23 (5) 19.75 9.85

Nos. C19-C22 Surcharged in Red

1964, Oct.

C24 AP3 3r on 5r multi .90 .55
C25 AP3 6r on 10r multi 1.40 .85
C26 AP3 9r on 20r multi 1.75 1.10
C27 AP3 12r on 40r multi 3.50 2.00
Nos. C24-C27 (4) 7.55 4.50

18th Olympic Games, Tokyo, Oct. 10-25.

1972 Summer Olympic Games, Munich — AP4

Designs: No. C28, shown. No. C29, Munich churches, Olympic emblem, vert.

Litho. & Embossed

1972, Sept. 28 *Perf. 13½*

C28 AP4 900r gold & multi *42.50 42.50*
C29 AP4 900r gold & multi *42.50 42.50*
a. Souvenir sheet of 2, #C28-C29 *80.00*

No. C29a exists imperf. Value, $110.

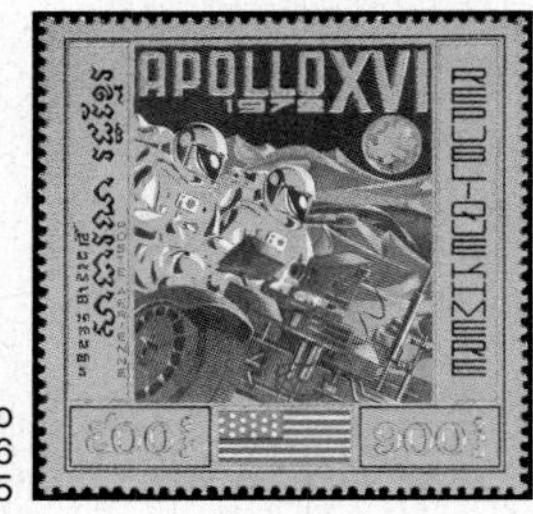

Apollo 16 AP5

Designs: No. C30, Astronauts in Lunar Rover. No. C31, Astronaut walking on moon.

1972, Sept. 28

C30 AP5 900r gold & multi *45.00 45.00*
C31 AP5 900r gold & multi *45.00 45.00*
a. Souvenir sheet of 2, #C30-C31 *70.00*

No. C31a exists imperf. Value, $130.

Pres. Nixon's Visit to the People's Republic of China — AP6

Nixon, Mao Zedong: No. C32, Large portraits (shown). No. C33, Small portraits.

1972, Sept. 28 *Perf. 12½*

C32 AP6 900r gold & multi *80.00 80.00*
C33 AP6 900r gold & multi *80.00 80.00*

Garuda, 12th Century, Angkor Thom — AP7

1973, Jan. 18 Engr. *Perf. 13*

C34 AP7 3r carmine .35 .25
C35 AP7 30r violet blue 2.00 1.00
C36 AP7 50r dull purple 3.75 2.00
C37 AP7 100r dull green 5.25 3.00
Nos. C34-C37 (4) 11.35 6.25

1972 Summer Olympic Games, Munich AP8

Gold medalists: No. C38, Heide Rosendahl. No. C39, Mark Spitz.

Litho. & Embossed

1973, May 18 *Perf. 13½*

C38 AP8 900r gold & multi *35.00 35.00*
C39 AP8 900r gold & multi *35.00 35.00*
a. Souvenir sheet, #C38-C39 *60.00*

No. C39a exists imperf. Value $100.

Nos. C38-C39 Overprinted

1973, Nov. 19

C40 AP8 900r on C38 *40.00 40.00*
C41 AP8 900r on C39 *40.00 40.00*
a. Souvenir sheet, #C40-C41 *80.00*

No. C41a exists imperf. Value, $160.

1974 World Cup Soccer Championships, Munich — AP9

Designs: No. C42, Trophy, players. No. C43, Trophy, players, vert.

1973, Nov. 19 Litho. & Embossed

C42 AP9 900r gold & multi *35.00 35.00*
C43 AP9 900r gold & multi *35.00 35.00*
a. Souvenir sheet, #C42-C43 *55.00*

No. C43a exists imperf. Value, $100.

John F. Kennedy, Apollo 11 — AP10

No. C44, shown. No. C45, Kennedy, Apollo 17.

1974, Feb. 18

C44 AP10 1100r gold & multi *95.00 95.00*
C45 AP10 1100r gold & multi *95.00 95.00*
a. Souv. sheet of 2, #C44-C45 *200.00*

Nos. C44-C45a exist imperf. Values slightly higher.

Copernicus Type of 1974 and

Copernicus, Sun — AP11

200r, Copernicus and Skylab III. 250r, Copernicus, Concorde and solar eclipse. No. C48, shown. No. C49, Moon, Skylab, hand holding symbol of sun.

1974, Sept. 10 Litho. *Perf. 13*

C46 A87 200r multi 10.00 5.50
C47 A87 250r multi 15.00 10.00

Litho. & Engraved

Perf. 13½

C48 AP11 1200r gold & multi *30.00 30.00*

Souvenir Sheet of 1

C49 AP11 1200r gold & multi *30.00 30.00*

Nos. C46-C47 exist in perf or imperf souvenir sheets of 1. Values, $25 perf., $50 imperf. Nos. C48-C49 exist imperf. Values, each $55.

UPU Type of 1974 and

AP12

700r, Rocket, globe and UPU emblem. No. C51, UPU Headquarters. No. C52, US #1434-1435.

1974, Nov. 2 Litho. *Perf. 13*

C50 A88 700r gold & multi *11.50 11.50*

Litho. & Embossed

Perf. 13½

C51 AP12 1200r gold & multi *20.00 20.00*

Souvenir Sheet

C52 AP12 1200r gold & multi *30.00*

Nos. C50-C51 exist in souvenir sheets of one. Nos. C51-C52 exist imperf.

UPU, Cent. (in 1974) AP13

UPU emblem and: No. C53, Biplane, train. No. C54, Satellite, sailboat.

Litho. & Embossed

1975, Apr. 12 *Perf. 13¼*

C53 AP13 2000r gold & multi *13.50* —

Souvenir Sheet

C54 AP13 2000r gold & multi *40.00* —

No. C53 exists in a souvenir sheet of 1.

Post Aerienne at Right — AP14

Denominations: 5r, 10r, 15r, 25r.

1984, Feb. 1 Litho. *Perf. 12x12½*

C55-C58 AP14 Set of 4 45.00 8.50

Post Aerienne at Left — AP15

Denominations: 5r, 10r, 15r, 25r.

1986, Mar. 4 Litho. *Perf. 12x12½*

C59-C62 AP15 Set of 4 40.00 8.00

POSTAGE DUE STAMPS

D1

1957 Unwmk. Typo. *Perf. 13½*

Denomination in Black

J1 D1 10c ver & pale blue .30 .30
J2 D1 50c ver & pale blue .55 .55
J3 D1 1r ver & pale blue .85 .85
J4 D1 3r ver & pale blue 1.25 1.25
J5 D1 5r ver & pale blue 2.00 2.00
Nos. J1-J5 (5) 4.95 4.95

Frieze, Angkor Wat — D2

1974, Feb. 18 Engr. *Perf. 12½x13*

J6 D2 2r ocher .30 .30
J7 D2 6r green .45 .45
J8 D2 8r deep carmine .70 .70
J9 D2 10r violet blue 1.00 1.00
Nos. J6-J9 (4) 2.45 2.45

CAMEROONS

ˌka-mə-ˈrüns

LOCATION — West coast of Africa, north of equator
GOVT. — British Trust Territory
AREA — 34,081 sq. mi.
POP. — 868,637 (estimated)
CAPITAL — Buea

Prior to World War I, Cameroons (Kamerun) was a German Protectorate. It was occupied during the War by Great Britain and France and in 1922 was mandated to these countries by the League of Nations. Stamps of Nigeria were used in the British part until 1960. The northern section of the British Cameroons became part of the independent state of Nigeria in 1960, and the southern section became a United Kingdom Trust Territory. After a referendum, this U.K.T.T. joined the independent State of Cameroun to form the Federal Republic of Cameroun, Oct. 1; 1961.

Stamps of the German Protectorate, the French Mandate, the independent state and the Cameroun Federal Republic are listed under Cameroun.

Catalogue values for unused stamps in this country are for Never Hinged items.

United Kingdom Trust Territory

Stamps and Type of Nigeria, 1953, Ovptd. in Red

Perf. 13½, 14

1960, Oct. 1 Wmk. 4 Engr.

Size: 35½x22½mm

66 A17 ½p red org & black .25 *1.75*
67 A17 1p ol gray & black .25 *.60*
68 A17 1½p blue green .25 .25
69 A17 2p gray .65 *2.00*
70 A17 3p purple & black .25 .25
71 A17 4p ultra & black .25 *2.25*
72 A18 6p blk & org brn, perf. 14 .40 .25
a. Perf. 13x13½ ('61) .35 *2.25*
73 A17 1sh brown vio & blk .35 .25

Size: 40½x24½mm

74 A17 2sh6p green & black 2.00 .80
75 A17 5sh ver & black 3.00 *3.00*
76 A17 10sh red brn & blk 3.75 *6.50*

Size: 42x31½mm

77 A17 £1 violet & black 18.50 *27.50*
Nos. 66-77 (12) 29.90 *45.40*

Nos. 66-77 were withdrawn in Northern Cameroons on May 31, 1961, when that territory joined Nigeria and in Southern Cameroons Sept. 30, 1961, when that territory joined the Cameroun Federal Republic.

CAMEROUN

ˌka-mə-ˈrün

(Kamerun)

LOCATION — On the west coast of Africa, north of the equator
GOVT. — Republic
AREA — 183,520 sq. mi.
POP. — 15,456,092 (1999 est.)
CAPITAL — Yaounde

Before World War I, Cameroun (Kamerun) was a German Protectorate. It was occupied during the war by Great Britain and France and in 1922 was mandated to these countries by the League of Nations. The French-mandated part became the independent State of Cameroun on January 1, 1960. The Southern Cameroons, a United Kingdom Trust Territory, joined this state to form the Federal Republic of Cameroun on October 1, 1961. The name was changed to United Republic of Cameroon on May 20, 1972.

Stamps of Southern Cameroons are listed under Cameroons.

100 Pfennig = 1 Mark
12 Pence = 1 Shilling
100 Centimes = 1 Franc

Catalogue values for unused stamps in this country are for Never Hinged items, beginning with Scott 296 in the regular postage section, Scott B29 in the semi-postal section, Scott C8 in the air-post section, Scott J24 in the postage due section, and Scott M1 in the military stamp section.

Watermark

Wmk. 125 — Lozenges

Wmk. 385

Issued under German Dominion

Stamps of Germany Overprinted in Black

1897 Unwmk. *Perf. 13½x14½*

1 A9 3pf yel brn 11.00 *15.00*
a. 3pf red brown 55.00 *200.00*
b. 3pf dark brown 15.00 *37.50*
c. 3pf olive brown 8.75 *37.50*
2 A9 5pf green 7.00 *7.00*
3 A10 10pf carmine 5.00 *4.50*
4 A10 20pf ultra 5.00 *7.00*
a. Diagonal half used as 10pf on cover 18,750.
5 A10 25pf orange 20.00 *37.50*
6 A10 50pf red brn 15.00 *24.00*
Nos. 1-6 (6) 63.00 *95.00*

A3

Kaiser's Yacht "Hohenzollern" — A4

1900 Unwmk. Typo. *Perf. 14*

7 A3 3pf brown 1.25 *1.50*
8 A3 5pf green 10.50 1.20
9 A3 10pf carmine 35.00 1.25
10 A3 20pf ultra 22.50 1.75
a. Vertical half used as 10pf on cover (Longii, '11) 6,750.
11 A3 25pf org & blk, *yel* 1.50 *5.00*
12 A3 30pf org & blk, *sal* 2.00 *4.00*
13 A3 40pf lake & blk 2.00 *4.00*
14 A3 50pf pur & blk, *sal* 2.00 *6.00*
15 A3 80pf lake & blk, *rose* 2.25 *10.00*

Engr. *Perf. 14½x14*

16 A4 1m carmine 67.50 *67.50*
17 A4 2m blue 5.25 *65.00*
18 A4 3m blk vio 5.25 *105.00*
19 A4 5m slate & car 150.00 *450.00*
Nos. 7-19 (13) 307.00 *722.20*

1905-18 Wmk. 125 Typo.

20 A3 3pf brown ('18) .70
21 A3 5pf green .70 *1.60*
a. Bklt. pane of 6 15.00
b. Bklt. pane of 6, 2 #21 + 4 #22 62.50
c. Booklet pane of 5 + label 375.00
22 A3 10pf carmine ('06) 2.25 *1.50*
a. Bklt pane of 6 17.50
b. Booklet pane of 5 + label *500.00*
23 A3 20pf ultra ('14) 3.50 *125.00*
24 A4 1m carmine ('15) 12.00
25 A4 5m slate & car ('13) 40.00 *4,000.*
Nos. 20-25 (6) 68.35

The 3pf and 1m were not placed in use.

Nos. 21a, 22a were made from sheet stamps.

Issued under British Occupation

Stamps of German Cameroun Surcharged

No. 53

No. 62

Wmk. Lozenges (125) (#54-56, 65); Unwmk. (Other Values)

1915 *Perf. 14, 14½*

Blue Surcharge

53 A3 ½p on 3pf brn 15.00 *60.00*
54 A3 ½p on 5pf grn 7.75 *11.00*
a. Double surcharge *1,100.*
b. Black surcharge — —
55 A3 1p on 10pf car 1.45 *11.00*
a. "1" with thin serifs 15.00 *75.00*
b. Double surcharge 475.00
c. Black surcharge 18.00 *65.00*
d. As "c," "1" with thin serifs 300.00

Black Surcharge

56 A3 2p on 20pf ultra 4.00 *24.00*
57 A3 2½p on 25pf org & blk, *yel* 21.00 *60.00*
a. Double surcharge *15,000.*
58 A3 3p on 30pf org & blk, *sal* 15.00 *65.00*
59 A3 4p on 40pf lake & blk 15.00 *65.00*
60 A3 6p on 50pf pur & blk, *sal* 15.00 *65.00*

No.	Type	Description	Unused	Used
61	A3	8p on 80pf lake & blk, *rose*	15.00	*65.00*
62	A4	1sh on 1m car	220.00	*1,000.*
a.		"S" inverted	1,100.	*4,000.*
63	A4	2sh on 2m bl	250.00	*1,050.*
a.		"S" inverted	1,100.	*4,000.*
64	A4	3sh on 3m blk vio	250.00	*1,050.*
a.		"S" inverted	1,100.	*4,400.*
b.		Double surcharge	*16,500.*	
65	A4	5sh on 5m sl & car	300.00	*1,100.*
a.		"S" inverted	1,425.	*4,750.*
		Nos. 53-65 (13)	1,129.	*4,626.*

The letters "C. E. F." are the initials of "Cameroons Expeditionary Force."

Numerous overprint varieties exist for Nos. 53-65.

Counterfeits exist of Nos. 54a, 54b.

See Cameroons for Nos. 66-77.

Issued under French Occupation

Gabon Nos. 37, 49-52, 54, 57-58, 60, 62-64, 66, 69-70 Overprinted

1915 Unwmk. *Perf. 13½x14*

Inscribed "Congo Français"

No.	Type	Description	Unused	Used
101	A10	10c red & car	32.50	24.00

Inscribed "Afrique Equatoriale"

No.	Type	Description	Unused	Used
102	A10	1c choc & org	110.00	47.50
103	A10	2c blk & choc	200.00	150.00
104	A10	4c vio & dp bl	200.00	150.00
105	A10	5c ol gray & grn	40.00	24.00
105A	A10	10c red & car	*21,500.*	*24,000.*
106	A10	20c ol brn & dk vio	210.00	210.00
107	A11	25c dp bl & choc	60.00	47.50
108	A11	30c gray blk & red	200.00	200.00
109	A11	35c dk vio & grn	67.50	45.00
a.		Double overprint	1,900.	
110	A11	40c choc & ultra	200.00	200.00
111	A11	45c car & vio	225.00	225.00
112	A11	50c bl grn & gray	225.00	225.00
113	A11	75c org & choc	275.00	225.00
114	A12	1fr dk brn & bis	260.00	225.00
115	A12	2fr car & brn	300.00	260.00
		Nos. 101-105,106-115 (15)	2,605.	2,258.

The overprint is vertical, reading up, on Nos. 101-106, 114-115, and horizontal on Nos. 107-113.

Stamps of Middle Congo, Issue of 1907, Overprinted

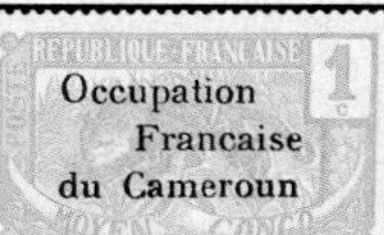

1916 Unwmk.

No.	Type	Description	Unused	Used
116	A1	1c ol gray & brn	110.00	110.00
117	A1	2c violet & brn	110.00	110.00
118	A1	4c blue & brown	120.00	120.00
119	A1	5c dk green & blue	32.50	32.50
120	A2	35c violet brn & bl	110.00	75.00
121	A2	45c violet & red	87.50	75.00

The overprint is vert., reading down, on Nos. 120-121.

Same Overprint On Stamps of French Congo, 1900

Wmk. Branch of Thistle (122)

No.	Type	Description	Unused	Used
122	A4	15c dull vio & ol grn	120.00	120.00
a.		Inverted overprint	200.00	180.00

Wmk. Branch of Rose Tree (123)

No.	Type	Description	Unused	Used
123	A5	20c yellow grn & org	140.00	92.50
124	A5	30c car rose & org	110.00	87.50
125	A5	40c org brn & brt grn	105.00	80.00
126	A5	50c gray vio & lil	110.00	87.50
127	A5	75c red vio & org	110.00	85.00

Wmk. Branch of Olive (124)

No.	Type	Description	Unused	Used
128	A6	1fr gray lilac & ol	125.00	120.00
129	A6	2fr carmine & brn	160.00	120.00
		Nos. 116-129 (14)	1,550.	1,315.

The overprint is horiz. on No. 122. The overprint is vert., reading down or up, on Nos. 123-129. Values are for the cheaper variety. See the *Scott Classic Specialized Catalogue of Stamps & Covers* for detailed listings.

Values are for stamps centered in the grade of fine.

Counterfeits exist of Nos. 101-129.

Stamps of Middle Congo, Issue of 1907 Overprinted

1916-17 Unwmk.

No.	Type	Description	Unused	Used
130	A1	1c ol gray & brn	.40	.40
131	A1	2c violet & brn	.50	.50
132	A1	4c blue & brn	.75	.75
133	A1	5c dk green & bl	.50	.40
134	A1	10c carmine & bl	1.10	.80
135	A1	15c brn vio & rose ('17)	2.00	.80
136	A1	20c brown & bl	.80	.80
137	A2	25c blue & grn	.80	.80
a.		Triple overprint	550.00	*700.00*
138	A2	30c scarlet & grn	1.25	.80
a.		Double overprint	400.00	*575.00*
139	A2	35c vio brn & bl	.80	.80
140	A2	40c dull grn & brn	2.40	1.60
141	A2	45c violet & red	2.40	1.60
142	A2	50c blue grn & red	2.40	1.60
143	A2	75c brown & blue	2.40	1.60
144	A3	1fr dp grn & vio	2.00	1.60
145	A3	2fr vio & gray grn	8.00	6.75
146	A3	5fr blue & rose	13.50	11.00
		Nos. 130-146 (17)	42.00	32.60

Nos. 130-146 exist on ordinary paper and, with the exception of No. 135, on chalk surfaced paper. Nos. 137-146 are known with inverted 'S' in 'Francaise' and without period after 'Francaise.' See the *Scott Classic Specialized Catalogue of Stamps & Covers* for detailed listings.

On Nos. 137-146 there is 7mm between "Cameroun" and "Occupation."

Provisional French Mandate

Types of Middle Congo, 1907, Overprinted

1921

No.	Type	Description	Unused	Used
147	A1	1c ol grn & org	.35	.30
148	A1	2c brown & rose	.35	.30
149	A1	4c gray & lt grn	.55	.55
150	A1	5c dl red & org	.55	.55
a.		Double overprint	1,200.	
151	A1	10c bl grn & lt grn	1.25	.90
152	A1	15c blue & org	.55	.55
153	A1	20c red brn & ol	.80	.80
154	A2	25c slate & org	1.20	.80
155	A2	30c rose & ver	1.25	.80
156	A2	35c gray & ultra	.80	.80
157	A2	40c ol grn & org	1.25	.80
158	A2	45c brown & rose	.80	.80
159	A2	50c blue & ultra	1.25	.80
160	A2	75c red brn & lt grn	1.25	.80
161	A3	1fr slate & org	2.40	2.40
162	A3	2fr ol grn & rose	6.50	5.50
163	A3	5fr dull red & gray	9.50	8.00
		Nos. 147-163 (17)	30.60	25.45

The 1c, 2c, 4c, 15c, 20c, 25c and 50c exist with overprint omitted. For listings, see the *Scott Specialized Catalogue of Stamps & Covers.*

No. 152 Surcharged

Nos. 162-163 Surcharged

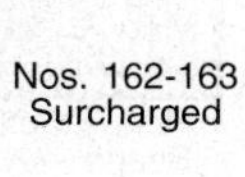

Nos. 158, 160 Surcharged

1924-25

No.	Type	Description	Unused	Used
164	A1	25c on 15c bl & org ('25)	1.25	1.25
165	A3	25c on 2fr ol grn & rose	1.25	1.60
166	A3	25c on 5fr red & gray	1.25	1.60
a.		Pair, one without new value and bars		
167	A2	65c on 45c brn & rose ('25)	2.00	2.00
168	A2	85c on 75c red brn & lt grn ('25)	2.40	2.40
		Nos. 164-168 (5)	8.15	8.85

French Mandate

Herder and Cattle Crossing Sanaga River — A5

Tapping Rubber Tree — A6

Rope Suspension Bridge A7

1925-38 Typo. *Perf. 14x13½*

No.	Type	Description	Unused	Used
170	A5	1c ol grn & brn vio, *lav*	.25	.25
171	A5	2c rose & grn, *grnsh*	.25	.25
172	A5	4c blue & blk	.25	.25
173	A5	5c org & red vio, *lav*	.25	.25
174	A5	10c red brn & org, *yel*	.45	.40
175	A5	15c sl grn & grn	.45	.40
176	A5	15c lilac & red ('27)	1.00	.80

Perf. 13½x14

No.	Type	Description	Unused	Used
177	A6	20c ol brn & red brn	.70	.40
178	A6	20c green ('26)	.65	.50
179	A6	20c brn red & ol brn ('27)	.65	.65
180	A6	25c lt green & blk	.95	.50
181	A6	30c bluish grn & ver	.50	.30
182	A6	30c dk grn & grn ('27)	.90	.65
183	A6	35c brown & black	1.10	.50
184	A6	35c dl grn & grn ('38)	1.90	1.20
185	A6	40c orange & vio	2.00	1.20
186	A6	45c dp rose & cer	.80	.50
187	A6	45c vio & org brn ('27)	2.25	1.60
188	A6	50c lt green & cer	.80	.30
189	A6	55c ultra & car ('38)	1.60	1.60
190	A6	60c red vio & blk	.80	.55
191	A6	60c brown red ('26)	.95	.55
192	A6	65c indigo & brn	1.20	1.20
193	A6	75c indigo & dp bl	.80	.80
194	A6	75c org brn & red vio ('27)	1.40	1.10
195	A6	80c car & brn ('38)	1.40	1.20
196	A6	85c dp rose & bl	1.60	1.20
197	A6	90c brn red & cer ('27)	2.75	1.20

Perf. 14x13½

No.	Type	Description	Unused	Used
198	A7	1fr indigo & brn	1.20	1.20
199	A7	1fr dull bl ('26)	.80	.55
200	A7	1fr ol brn & red vio ('27)	1.10	.80
201	A7	1fr grn & dk brn ('29)	2.40	1.20
202	A7	1.10fr rose red & dk brn ('28)	4.75	*6.50*
203	A7	1.25fr gray & dp bl ('33)	4.75	3.50
204	A7	1.50fr dull bl ('27)	1.20	.80
205	A7	1.75fr brn & org ('33)	1.60	1.20
206	A7	1.75fr dk bl & lt bl ('38)	2.40	1.60
207	A7	2fr dl grn & brn org	2.00	1.20
208	A7	3fr ol brn & red vio ('27)	8.00	2.75
209	A7	5fr brn & blk, *bluish*	3.50	2.00
a.		Cliché of 2fr in plate of 5fr	1,450.	
b.		As "a," in pair with #209	1,700.	
210	A7	10fr org & vio ('27)	14.50	7.25
211	A7	20fr rose & ol grn ('27)	21.00	15.00
		Nos. 170-211 (42)	97.80	65.85

Shades exist for several values.

For overprints and surcharge see Nos. 212, 264, 276, 278, 279, B7-B9, B21.

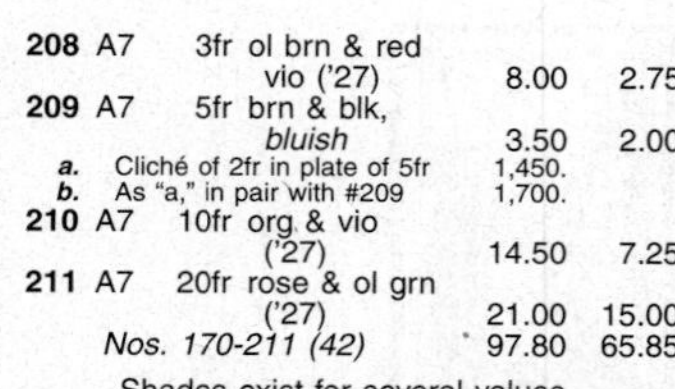

No. 199 Surcharged in Red

1926

No.	Type	Description	Unused	Used
212	A7	1.25fr on 1fr dull blue	1.20	.80

Common Design Types pictured following the introduction.

Colonial Exposition Issue

Common Design Types

Name of Country in Black

1931 Engr. *Perf. 12½*

No.	Type	Description	Unused	Used
213	CD70	40c deep green	5.50	4.00
214	CD71	50c violet	5.50	4.75
215	CD72	90c red orange	5.50	4.75
216	CD73	1.50fr dull blue	6.50	4.75
		Nos. 213-216 (4)	23.00	18.25

Paris International Exposition Issue

Common Design Types

1937 *Perf. 13*

No.	Type	Description	Unused	Used
217	CD74	20c deep violet	1.75	1.75
218	CD75	30c dark green	1.75	1.75
219	CD76	40c car rose	1.75	1.75
220	CD77	50c dark brown	1.75	1.75
221	CD78	90c red	1.90	1.90
222	CD79	1.50fr ultramarine	1.90	1.90
		Nos. 217-222 (6)	10.80	10.80

French Colonial Art Exhibition

Common Design Type

Souvenir Sheet

1937 *Imperf.*

No.	Type	Description	Unused	Used
222A	CD77	3fr org red & blk	8.00	*9.50*

New York World's Fair Issue

Common Design Type

1939 *Perf. 12½x12*

No.	Type	Description	Unused	Used
223	CD82	1.25fr carmine lake	1.40	1.20
224	CD82	2.25fr ultra	1.40	1.20

For overprints and surcharges see Nos. 280-281, B14-B17, B23, B25.

Mandara Woman — A19

Falls on M'bam River near Banyo — A20

Elephants A21

Man in Yaré — A22

1939-40 Engr. *Perf. 13*

225	A19	2c	black brn	.25	.25
226	A19	3c	magenta ('40)	.25	.25
227	A19	4c	deep ultra	.25	.25
228	A19	5c	red brown	.25	.25
229	A19	10c	dp bl grn	.25	.25
230	A19	15c	rose red	.30	.30
231	A19	20c	plum	.30	.30
232	A20	25c	black brn	.65	.65
233	A20	30c	dk red	.80	.70
234	A20	40c	ultra ('40)	.80	.80
235	A20	45c	sl grn ('40)	2.60	2.25
236	A20	50c	brown car	.90	.70
237	A20	60c	pck blue ('40)	.75	.65
238	A20	70c	plum ('40)	3.25	2.90
239	A21	80c	Prus blue	2.60	2.10
240	A21	90c	Prus blue	.95	.75
241	A21	1fr	car rose	1.90	.95
242	A21	1fr	choc ('40)	1.40	.80
243	A21	1.25fr	car rose	4.00	3.25
244	A21	1.40fr	org red ('40)	1.25	.95
245	A21	1.50fr	chocolate	1.20	.95
246	A21	1.60fr	black brn ('40)	2.50	2.25
247	A21	1.75fr	dk blue	1.40	.95
248	A21	2fr	dk green	.90	.90
249	A21	2.25fr	dk blue	1.40	.90
250	A21	2.50fr	brt red vio ('40)	1.20	1.00
251	A21	3fr	dk violet	1.40	.80
252	A22	5fr	black brn	1.40	.95
253	A22	10fr	brt red vio	2.00	1.60
254	A22	20fr	dk green	4.00	3.25
			Nos. 225-254 (30)	41.10	32.85

For overprints and surcharges see Nos. 255-263, 265-275, 277, 278A, 279A, B10-B13, B22, B24.

Stamps of 1925-40 Overprinted in Black or Orange

1940 *Perf. 14x13½, 13½x14, 13*

255	A19	2c	blk brn (O)	1.60	1.60
256	A19	3c	magenta	2.40	2.40
257	A19	4c	dp ultra (O)	1.60	1.60
258	A19	5c	red brn	5.50	5.50
259	A19	10c	dp bl grn (O)	1.60	1.60
260	A19	15c	rose red	2.40	2.40
260A	A19	20c	plum (O)	13.50	13.50
261	A20	25c	blk brn	1.60	1.60
b.			Inverted overprint	260.00	260.00
261A	A20	30c	dk red	14.50	14.50
262	A20	40c	ultra	5.50	5.50
263	A20	45c	slate green	4.00	4.00
264	A6	50c	lt grn & cer	2.40	1.60
a.			Inverted overprint	225.00	
265	A20	60c	pck bl	6.50	6.50
266	A20	70c	plum	3.25	3.25
267	A21	80c	Prus bl (O)	5.50	5.50
268	A21	90c	Prus bl (O)	1.60	1.60
269	A21	1.25fr	car rose	1.60	1.60
270	A21	1.40fr	org red	4.75	4.75
271	A21	1.50fr	chocolate	1.60	1.60
272	A21	1.60fr	blk brn (O)	3.25	3.25
273	A21	1.75fr	dk bl (O)	2.40	2.40
274	A21	2.25fr	dk bl (O)	1.60	1.60
275	A21	2.50fr	brt red vio	1.60	1.60
276	A7	5fr	brn & blk, *bluish*	24.00	24.00
277	A22	5fr	black brn	24.00	16.00
278	A7	10fr	org & vio	32.50	32.50
278A	A22	10fr	brt red vio	65.00	45.00
279	A7	20fr	rose & ol grn	55.00	55.00
279A	A22	20fr	dk green	190.00	190.00

Overprint on Stamps of 1939

Perf. 12½x12

280	CD82	1.25fr	car lake	12.00	12.00
281	CD82	2.25fr	ultra	12.00	12.00
			Nos. 255-281 (31)	504.75	475.95

Issued to note Cameroun's affiliation with General de Gaulle's "Free France" movement. Numerous overprint varieties exist.

Cattle Fording Sanaga River and Marshal Petain A22a

1941 Engr. *Perf. 12½x12*

281A	A22a	1fr	green	.40
281B	A22a	2.50fr	dark blue	.40
			Set, never hinged	1.60

Nos. 281A-281B were issued by the Vichy government in France, but were not placed on sale in Cameroun.

For surcharges, see Nos. B25A-B25B.

Lorraine Cross and Joan of Arc Shield — A23

1941 Photo. *Perf. 14x14½*

282	A23	5c	brown	.25	.25
283	A23	10c	dk blue	.25	.25
284	A23	25c	emerald	.25	.25
285	A23	30c	dp orange	.25	.25
286	A23	40c	dk slate green	.25	.25
287	A23	80c	red brown	.50	.25
288	A23	1fr	dp red lilac	.50	.50
289	A23	1.50fr	brt red	.50	.50
290	A23	2fr	gray black	.75	.50
291	A23	2.50fr	brt ultra	.80	.50
292	A23	4fr	dull violet	.90	.75
293	A23	5fr	bister	.95	.90
294	A23	10fr	dp brown	.95	.90
295	A23	20fr	dp green	1.90	1.40
			Nos. 282-295 (14)	9.00	7.45

For surcharges see Nos. 297A-303.

Catalogue values for unused stamps in this section, from this point to the end of the section, are for Never Hinged items.

Eboue Issue

Common Design Type

1945 Unwmk. Engr. *Perf. 13*

296	CD91	2fr	black	.80	.55
297	CD91	25fr	Prus green	1.60	1.40

Nos. 282, 284, 291 Surcharged with New Values and Bars in Red, Carmine or Black

1946 *Perf. 14x14½*

297A	A23	50c	on 5c (R)	.65	.50
298	A23	60c	on 5c (R)	.75	.55
a.			Inverted surcharge	200.00	
299	A23	70c	on 5c (R)	1.00	.75
300	A23	1.20fr	on 5c (C)	1.00	.75
301	A23	2.40fr	on 25c	.95	.75
302	A23	3fr	on 25c	1.40	1.00
302A	A23	4.50fr	on 25c	1.90	1.40
303	A23	15fr	on 2.50fr (C)	2.00	1.50
			Nos. 297A-303 (8)	9.65	7.20

Zebu and Herder A25

Tikar Women — A26

Porters Carrying Bananas — A27

Bowman A28

Lamido Horsemen A29

Farmer — A30

1946 Engr. *Perf. 12½x12, 12x12½*

304	A25	10c	blue grn	.50	.30
305	A25	30c	brown org	.50	.30
306	A25	40c	brt ultra	.50	.30
307	A26	50c	olive brn	.50	.30
308	A26	60c	dp plum	.65	.30
309	A26	80c	chnt brn	.80	.50
310	A27	1fr	org red	.50	.25
311	A27	1.20fr	dp green	.90	.50
312	A27	1.50fr	dk car	2.25	1.40
313	A28	2fr	black	.50	.25
314	A28	3fr	dk carmine	.65	.30
314A	A28	3.60fr	red brn	1.60	1.10
315	A28	4fr	dp blue	.90	.40
316	A29	5fr	brown car	1.00	.65
317	A29	6fr	ultra	1.00	.55
318	A29	10fr	slate green	1.75	.50
319	A30	15fr	grnsh blue	2.40	.90
320	A30	20fr	dk green	3.25	.90
321	A30	25fr	black	3.25	1.40
			Nos. 304-321 (19)	23.40	11.10

Shades exist for most values.

For surcharges see Nos. 343-344, 346.

Imperforates

Most Cameroun stamps from 1952 onward exist imperforate in issued and trial colors, and also in small presentation sheets in issued colors.

Military Medal Issue

Common Design Type

Engraved and Typographed

1952 Unwmk. *Perf. 13*

322	CD101	15fr	multicolored	7.25	3.25

Porters Carrying Bananas — A32

Picking Coffee Beans — A33

1954 Engr.

323	A32	8fr	red vio, org brn & vio bl	1.20	.80
324	A32	15fr	brn red, yel & blk brn	1.60	.80
325	A33	40fr	blk brn, org brn & lil rose	2.00	.80
			Nos. 323-325 (3)	4.80	2.40

FIDES Issue

Common Design Type

Designs: 5fr, Plowmen. 15fr, Wouri bridge. 20fr, Technical instruction. 25fr, Mobile medical station.

1956 Unwmk. *Perf. 13*

326	CD103	5fr	org brn & dk brn	1.20	.50
327	CD103	15fr	aqua, slate & blk	1.60	.80
328	CD103	20fr	grnsh bl & dp ultra	1.60	.80
329	CD103	25fr	dp ultra	2.50	1.10
			Nos. 326-329 (4)	6.90	3.20

For surcharges see Nos. 345, 347.

Coffee Issue

Coffee A35

1956 Engr. *Perf. 13*

330	A35	15fr	car & brt red	1.60	.80

For surcharge see No. 348.

Autonomous Government

Flag and Woman Holding Child A36

1958

331	A36	20fr	multicolored	1.60	.80

Anniv. of the installation of the 1st autonomous government of Cameroun.

Men Looking to the Sun — A37

1958

332	A37	20fr	sepia & brn red	1.60	.80

10th anniv. of the signing of the Universal Declaration of Human Rights.

Flower Issue

Common Design Type

Design: 20fr, Randia malleifera.

1959 Photo. *Perf. 12½x12*

333	CD104	20fr	dp grn, yel & rose	1.60	.80

Loading Bananas A38

Harvesting Bananas — A39

1959 Engr. *Perf. 13*

334	A38	20fr	dk grn & org	1.20	.40
335	A39	25fr	maroon & slate grn	1.60	.80

For surcharge see No. 349.

Independent State

Map and Flag of Cameroun — A40

Prime Minister Ahmadou Ahidjo — A41

1960 Unwmk. Engr. *Perf. 13*

336 A40 20fr multicolored .80 .25

337 A41 25fr blk, grn & pale lem .85 .25

Declaration of independence, Jan. 1, 1960.

For surcharge see No. 350.

Uprooted Oak Emblem A42

1960

338 A42 30fr red brn, ultra & yel grn 1.10 .45

World Refugee Year, 7/1/59-6/30/60.

For surcharge see No. 351.

C.C.T.A. Issue

Common Design Type

1960

339 CD106 50fr dull claret & slate 1.60 .75

UN Headquarters, NYC, and Flag — A43

1961, May 20 *Perf. 13*

Flag in Green, Red and Yellow

340 A43 15fr grn, dk bl & brn .60 .30

341 A43 25fr dk blue & grn .75 .30

342 A43 85fr red, dk bl & vio brn 2.40 1.20

Nos. 340-342 (3) 3.75 1.80

Cameroun's admission to the UN, Sept. 20, 1960.

Federal Republic

Stamps of 1946-60 Surcharged in Red or Black

Type I

Type II

Two types of 2sh6p:

I — Large figures. "2/6" measures 8x3¾mm.

II — Small figures. "2/6" measures 6x2½mm.

Perf. 12x12½, 13

1961, Oct. 1 Engr.

343 A27 ½p on 1fr (#310) .35 .25

344 A28 1p on 2fr (#313) .45 .30

345 CD103 1½p on 5fr (#326) .55 .35

346 A29 2p on 10fr (#318) 1.00 .45

347 CD103 3p on 15fr (#327) 1.40 .60

348 A35 4p on 15fr (Bk) (#330) 1.10 .70

349 A38 6p on 20fr (#334) 2.40 1.00

350 A41 1sh on 25fr (#337) 2.75 1.50

351 A42 2sh6p on 30fr (#338) (I) 5.00 5.00

a. Type II 21.00 21.00

Nos. 343-351 (9) 15.00 10.15

Issued for use in the former United Kingdom Trust Territory of Southern Cameroons.

The "Republique Federale" overprint is in one line on Nos. 345, 347-349, in two vertical lines on No. 350. See Nos. C38-C40.

President Ahidjo and Prime Minister Foncha A45

Unwmk.

1962, Jan. 1 Engr. *Perf. 13*

352 A45 20fr vio & choc 8.00 7.00

353 A45 25fr dk grn & brn 14.00 11.00

354 A45 60fr car & dl grn 40.00 32.50

Nos. 352-354 (3) 62.00 50.50

Surcharged for Use in Southern Cameroons

355 A45 3p on 20fr 175.00 160.00

356 A45 6p on 25fr 175.00 160.00

357 A45 2sh6p on 60fr 175.00 160.00

Nos. 355-357 (3) 525.00 480.00

Reunification of the former French and British Sections of Cameroun. It is reported that Nos. 352-357 were withdrawn after a few days and destroyed.

Mustache Monkey A46

Designs: 1fr, 4fr, Elephant, Ntem Falls. 1.50fr, 3fr, Buffon's kob, Dschang. 2fr, 5fr, Hippopotamus. 6fr, 15fr, Mustache monkey. 8fr, 30fr, Manatee, Lake Ossa. 10fr, 25fr, Buffalo, Batouri. 20fr, 40fr, Giraffes, Waza Reservation, vert.

1962 Unwmk. Engr. *Perf. 12*

358 A46 50c brn, brt grn & bl .25 .25

359 A46 1fr gray brn, bl grn & org .25 .25

360 A46 1.50fr brn, lt grn & sl grn .25 .25

361 A46 2fr dk gray, grnsh bl & grn .25 .25

362 A46 3fr brn, org & lil rose .25 .25

363 A46 4fr brn, yel grn & bl grn .25 .25

364 A46 5fr gray brn, grn & sal .25 .25

365 A46 6fr brn, yel & bl .45 .25

366 A46 8fr dk bl, red & grn .90 .50

367 A46 10fr ol blk, org & brt bl .75 .25

368 A46 15fr brn, Prus bl & bl 1.00 .40

369 A46 20fr brn & gray 1.25 .40

370 A46 25fr red brn, grn & yel 3.25 1.00

371 A46 30fr blk, org & bl 4.50 1.10

372 A46 40fr dp cl, yel grn & blk 7.50 1.50

Nos. 358-372 (15) 21.35 7.15

See Nos. 396-397.

African and Malagasy Union Issue

Common Design Type

1962, Sept. 8 Photo. *Perf. 12½x12*

373 CD110 30fr multicolored 2.00 .75

Village and Map of Cameroun A48

Designs: 20fr, 25fr, Sun rising over city. 50fr, Hands holding scroll.

1962, Oct. 1 Engr. *Perf. 13*

374 A48 9fr pur, olive & dk brn .40 .25

375 A48 18fr grn, org brn & dk bl .50 .25

376 A48 20fr lil rose, ol bis & ind .50 .25

377 A48 25fr bl, red org & sep .60 .25

378 A48 50fr dk red, sepia & bl 1.75 .50

Nos. 374-378 (5) 3.75 1.50

1st anniv. of the reunification of Cameroun.

"School under the Trees" — A49

1962, Nov. 5 Photo. *Perf. 12x12½*

379 A49 20fr ver, emerald & yel 1.00 .35

Literacy and popular education campaign.

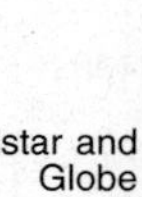

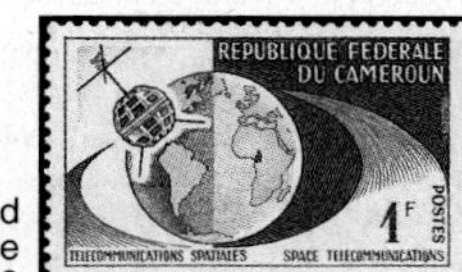

Telstar and Globe A50

1963, Feb. 9 Engr. *Perf. 13*

Size: 36x22mm

380 A50 1fr dk bl, olive & pur .25 .25

381 A50 2fr dk bl, claret & grn .25 .25

382 A50 3fr dk grn, ol & dp cl .25 .25

383 A50 25fr grn, dp cl & brt bl .75 .40

Nos. 380-383,C45 (5) 4.00 1.80

1st TV connection of the US and Europe through the Telstar satellite, July 11-12, 1962.

High Frequency Transmission Station, Mt. Bankolo — A51

Design: 20fr, Station and wiring plan.

1963, May 18 Photo. *Perf. 12x12½*

384 A51 15fr multicolored .45 .25

385 A51 20fr multicolored .60 .25

Nos. 384-385,C46 (3) 3.55 1.15

Issued to publicize the high frequency telegraph connection Douala-Yaounde.

"Yaoundé-Regional Center of Textbook Production" — A52

1963, Aug. 10 Unwmk. *Perf. 12½*

386 A52 20fr emer, blk & red .45 .25

387 A52 25fr org, blk & red .55 .25

388 A52 100fr gold, blk & red 2.10 .60

Nos. 386-388 (3) 3.10 1.10

UNESCO regional center for the production of school books at Yaounde.

Pres. Ahmadou Ahidjo and Flag — A53

Design: 18fr, Flag and map of Cameroun.

1963, Oct. 1 *Perf. 12x12½*

Flag in Green, Red and Yellow

389 A53 9fr grn, bl & dk brn .45 .25

390 A53 18fr grn, bl & lil .65 .25

391 A53 20fr grn, blk & yel grn .70 .25

Nos. 389-391 (3) 1.80 .75

Second anniversary of reunification.

Scales, Globe, UNESCO Emblem A54

1963, Dec. 10 Photo. *Perf. 12½x12*

392 A54 9fr ultra, blk & sal .40 .25

393 A54 18fr brt yel grn, blk & rose red .50 .25

394 A54 25fr rose red, blk & brt yel grn .70 .25

395 A54 75fr yel, blk & ultra 2.00 .50

Nos. 392-395 (4) 3.60 1.25

Universal Declaration of Human Rights, 15th anniv.

Animal Type of 1962

Design: 10fr, 25fr, Lion, Waza National Park, North Cameroun.

1964, June 20 Engr. *Perf. 13*

396 A46 10fr red brn, bis & grn 1.25 .40

397 A46 25fr green & bister 3.00 1.25

Soccer Game in Stadium A55

18fr, Pile of sports equipment. 30fr, Stadium (outside), flags and map of Africa.

1964, July 11 Engr. *Perf. 13*

398 A55 10fr grn, bl & red brn .50 .25

399 A55 18fr car, grn & vio .60 .35

400 A55 30fr blk, dk bl & org brn 1.00 .50

Nos. 398-400 (3) 2.10 1.10

Tropics Cup Games, Yaounde, July 11-19.

Europafrica Issue
Common Design Type and

Palace of Justice, Yaounde — A56

40fr, Emblems of Science, Agriculture, Industry and Education and two sunbursts.

1964, July 20 Photo. ***Perf. 12x13***
401 A56 15fr multicolored 1.25 .25
402 CD116 40fr multicolored 2.25 .60

1st anniv. of the economic agreement between the European Economic Community and the African and Malgache Union.

Hurdling and Olympic Flame — A57

Design: 10fr, Runners, vert.

1964, Oct. 10 Engr. ***Perf. 13***
403 A57 9fr red, yel grn & blk 1.50 .40
404 A57 10fr red, vio & ol gray 2.25 .40
Nos. 403-404,C49 (3) 11.25 2.80

18th Olympic Games, Tokyo, Oct. 10-25.

Bamileke Dance Dress — A58

Ntem Falls, Ebolowa Region — A59

Designs: 18fr, Dance mask, Bamenda region. 25fr, Fulani horseman, North Cameroun, horiz.

1964 Unwmk. ***Perf. 13***
405 A58 9fr red, yel grn & bl .55 .25
406 A58 18fr bl, red & brn .70 .25
407 A59 20fr dk car, grn & ol .90 .25
408 A58 25fr dk brn, org & car 1.40 .25
Nos. 405-408,C50 (5) 4.55 1.35

Cooperation Issue
Common Design Type

1964, Nov. 7 Engr.
409 CD119 18fr dk bl, yel grn & dk brn 1.00 .25
410 CD119 30fr red brn, bl grn & dk brn 1.50 .25

Memorial Stone — A60

1965, Jan. 1 Engr. ***Perf. 13***
411 A60 12fr bl, indigo & grn 1.00 .25

Diesel Train A61

Typo. ***Perf. 14x13***
412 A61 20fr rose car, yel & grn 2.50 .25

Laying of the 1st rail of the Mbanga-Kumba Railroad, Mar. 28, 1964.

Red Cross Station and Ambulance A62

50fr, Red Cross nurse and infant, vert.

1965, May 8 Engr. ***Perf. 13***
413 A62 25fr car, slate grn & ocher .95 .25
414 A62 50fr gray, red & red brn 2.25 .30

Issued for the Cameroun Red Cross.

Coins Inserted in Map of Cameroun, and Bankbook — A63

Savings Bank Building — A64

Design: 20fr, Bankbook and coins inserted in cacao pod-shaped bank, vert.

1965, June 10 **Size: 22x37mm**
415 A63 9fr grn, red & org .45 .25

Size: 48x27mm, 27x48mm
416 A64 15fr choc, ultra & grn .55 .25
417 A63 20fr ocher, brt grn & brn .65 .25
Nos. 415-417 (3) 1.65 .75

Federal Postal Savings Banks.

Soccer Players and Africa Cup — A65

Unwmk.
1965, June 26 Engr. ***Perf. 13***
418 A65 9fr car, brn & yel .55 .25
419 A65 20fr car, slate bl & yel 1.40 .25

Cameroun Oryx Club, winner of the club champions' Africa Cup, February 1965.

Symbolic Map of Europe and Africa — A66

40fr, Delegates around conference table.

1965, July 20 Photo. ***Perf. 12x12½***
420 A66 5fr car, blk & lilac .30 .25
421 A66 40fr brn, buff, grn & ultra 1.50 .35

2nd, anniv. of the economic agreement between the European Economic Community and the African and Malgache Union.

UPU Monument, Bern A67

1965, July 26 Engr. ***Perf. 13***
422 A67 30fr black & red .80 .25

Cameroun's admission to the UPU, 5th anniv.

ICY Emblem — A68

1965, Sept. 11 Unwmk. ***Perf. 13***
423 A68 10fr dk bl & car rose .45 .25

Issued for the International Cooperation Year, 1964-65. See No. C57.

Pres. Ahidjo and Government House — A69

Design: 9fr, 20fr, Pres. Ahidjo and Government House, vert.

Perf. 12x12½, 12½x12
1965, Oct. 1 Photo. Unwmk.
424 A69 9fr multicolored .25 .25
425 A69 18fr multicolored .55 .25
426 A69 20fr multicolored .65 .25
427 A69 25fr multicolored .80 .25
Nos. 424-427 (4) 2.25 1.00

Reelection of Pres. Ahmadou Ahidjo.

National Tourist Office, Yaoundé A70

Designs: 9fr, Pouss Musgum houses. 18fr, Great Calao's dance (North Cameroun). 20fr, Gate of Sultan's Palace, Foumban, vert.

1965 Engr. ***Perf. 13***
428 A70 9fr brn, rose red & grn .45 .25
429 A70 18fr brt bl, brn & grn .65 .25
430 A70 20fr bl, brn & choc 1.00 .25
431 A70 25fr mar, emer & gray .90 .25
Nos. 428-431 (4) 3.00 1.00

See No. C58.

Mountain Hotel, Buea — A71

Designs: 20fr, Hotel of the Deputies, Yaoundé. 35fr, Dschang Health Center.

1966
432 A71 9fr sl grn, rose cl & brn .35 .25
433 A71 20fr brt bl, sl grn & blk .45 .25
434 A71 35fr brn, sl grn & car .80 .30
Nos. 432-434,C63-C69 (10) 15.10 4.90

Bas-relief, Foumban A72

Designs: 18fr, Ekoi mask, vert. 20fr, Mother and child, carving, Bamiléké, vert. 25fr, Ceremonial stool, Bamoun.

1966, Apr. 15 Unwmk.
435 A72 9fr red & blk .60 .25
436 A72 18fr brt grn, org brn & choc .75 .25
437 A72 20fr brt bl, red brn & pur 1.15 .25
438 A72 25fr pur & dk brn 1.25 .25
Nos. 435-438 (4) 3.75 1.00

Intl. Negro Arts Festival, Dakar, Senegal, 4/1-24.

New WHO Headquarters, Geneva — A73

1966, May 3 Photo. ***Perf. 12½x13***
439 A73 50fr ultra, red brn & yel 1.25 .50

ITU Headquarters, Geneva — A74

1966, May 3 Photo. ***Perf. 12½x13***
440 A74 50fr ultra & yellow 1.25 .50

Phaeomeria Magnifica — A75

Flowers: 18fr, Hibiscus (rose of China). 20fr, Mountain rose.

1966, May 20 ***Perf. 12x12½***
Flowers in Natural Colors
Size: 22x36mm
441 A75 9fr red brown .55 .25
442 A75 18fr green .70 .25
443 A75 20fr dark green .70 .25
Nos. 441-443,C70-C72 (6) 7.55 1.50

See No. 469.

"6" and Men Dancing around UN Emblem — A76

Design: 50fr, UN General Assembly, horiz.

1966, Sept. 20 **Engr.** ***Perf. 13***

444 A76 50fr ultra, grn & vio brn .90 .25
445 A76 100fr red brn, grn & ultra 2.00 .50

6th anniv. of Cameroun's admission to the UN.

Prime Minister's Residence, Buea — A77

Designs (Prime Minister's Residences): 18fr, at Yaoundé, front view. 20fr, at Yaoundé, side view. 25fr, at Buea, front view.

1966, Oct. 1 **Photo.**

446 A77 9fr multicolored .45 .25
447 A77 18fr multicolored .65 .25
448 A77 20fr multicolored .60 .35
449 A77 25fr multicolored .80 .35
Nos. 446-449 (4) 2.50 1.20

5th anniversary of re-unification.

Learning to Write and UNESCO Emblem A78

No. 451, Children's heads & UNICEF emblem.

1966, Nov. 24 **Engr.** ***Perf. 13***

450 A78 50fr red lil, bl & brn 1.40 .30
451 A78 50fr red lil, blk & brt bl 1.40 .30

20th anniv. of UNESCO, 20th anniv. of UNICEF.

Independence Proclamation — A79

1967, Jan. 1 **Engr.** ***Perf. 13***

452 A79 20fr grn, red & yel 2.25 .60

7th anniversary of independence.

Map of Africa and Madagascar, Railroad Tracks and Symbols — A80

25fr, Map of Africa and Madagascar and train.

1967, Feb. 21 **Photo.** ***Perf. 13***

453 A80 20fr multicolored 3.50 1.50
454 A80 25fr multicolored 5.00 2.00

5th Conf. of African and Madagascan Railroad Technicians.

Lions Emblem and Forest — A81

Design: 100fr, Lions emblem and palms.

1967, Mar. 3

455 A81 50fr multicolored .90 .35
456 A81 100fr multicolored 2.10 .65

Lions International, 50th anniversary.

Jet and I.C.A.O. Emblem — A82

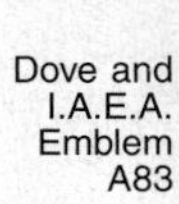

Dove and I.A.E.A. Emblem A83

Perf. 13x12½, 12½x13

1967, Mar. 15 **Photo.**

457 A82 50fr ultra, lt bl, brn & gold 1.40 .35
458 A83 50fr ultra & emer 1.40 .35

UN agencies: No. 457, the ICAO; No. 458, the Intl. Atomic Energy Agency.

Rotary International Emblem — A84

1967, Apr. 17 **Photo.** ***Perf. 12½***

459 A84 25fr crim, vio bl & gold 1.25 .25

10th anniversary of the Douala, Cameroun, branch of Rotary International.

Grapefruit — A85

1967, May 10 **Photo.** ***Perf. 12x12½***

460 A85 1fr shown .25 .25
461 A85 2fr Papaya .25 .25
462 A85 3fr Custard apple .25 .25
463 A85 4fr Breadfruit .25 .25
464 A85 5fr Coconut .35 .25
465 A85 6fr Mango .45 .25
466 A85 8fr Avacado .90 .25
467 A85 10fr Pineapple 1.40 .25
468 A85 30fr Bananas 3.50 .25
Nos. 460-468 (9) 7.60 2.25

For surcharges see Nos. 550, 593.

Bird of Paradise Flower — A86

1967, June 22 **Photo.** ***Perf. 12x12½***

Size: 22x36mm

469 A86 15fr lt blue & multi .90 .25

Sanaga Falls and ITY Emblem — A87

1967, Aug. 14 **Photo.** ***Perf. 13x12½***

470 A87 30fr multicolored .85 .25

Issued for International Tourist Year 1967.

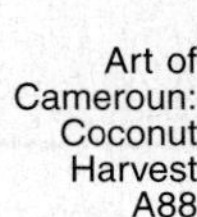

Art of Cameroun: Coconut Harvest A88

Carved Bas-relief: 20fr, Lion hunt. 30fr, Women carrying baskets. 100fr, Carved chest.

1967, Sept. 22 ***Perf. 12½x13***

471 A88 10fr brn, bl & car .35 .25
472 A88 20fr brn, yel & grn .55 .25
473 A88 30fr emer, brn & car .90 .25
474 A88 100fr red org, brn & emer 2.25 .40
Nos. 471-474 (4) 4.05 1.15

Coat of Arms A89

1968, Jan. 1 **Litho.** ***Perf. 12½x13***

475 A89 30fr gold & multi 1.00 .25

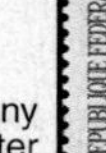

Spiny Lobster A90

Designs (Fish and Crustaceans): 10fr, River crayfish. 15fr, Nile mouth-breeder. 20fr, Sole. 25fr, Common pike. 30fr, Crab. 40fr, Spadefish, vert. 50fr, Shrimp, vert. 55fr, African snakehead. 60fr, Threadfin.

1968, July 25 **Engr.** ***Perf. 13***

476 A90 5fr brn, vio bl & dl grn .30 .25
477 A90 10fr ultra, brn ol & slate .30 .25
478 A90 15fr sal, red lil & sepia .85 .25
479 A90 20fr red brn, dp bl & sep 1.00 .25
480 A90 25fr lt brn, emer & slate 1.10 .25
481 A90 30fr mag, dk bl & dk brn 1.50 .25
482 A90 40fr slate bl & org 2.25 .25
483 A90 50fr emer, gray & rose car 3.00 .25
484 A90 55fr lt brn, Prus bl & dk brn 4.50 .25
485 A90 60fr brn, bl grn & indigo 6.75 .35
Nos. 476-485 (10) 21.55 2.60

Tanker, Refinery and Map of Area Served — A91

1968, July 30 **Photo.** ***Perf. 12½***

486 A91 30fr multicolored 1.60 .25

Port Gentil (Gabon) Refinery opening, 6/12/68.

Human Rights Flame A92

1968, Sept. 14 **Photo.** ***Perf. 12½x13***

487 A92 15fr blue & salmon .65 .25

Intl. Human Rights Year. See No. C110.

Pres. Ahmadou Ahidjo A93

1969, Apr. 10 **Photo.** ***Perf. 12½x12***

488 A93 30fr carmine & multi .80 .25

Chocolate Vat — A94

Designs: 30fr, Chocolate factory. 50fr, Candy making, vert.

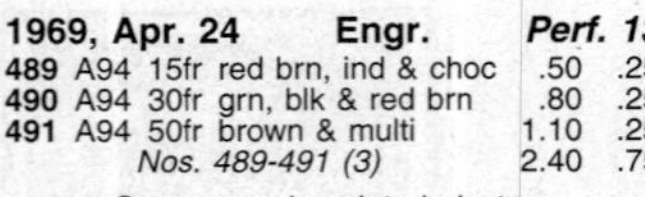

1969, Apr. 24 **Engr.** ***Perf. 13***

489 A94 15fr red brn, ind & choc .50 .25
490 A94 30fr grn, blk & red brn .80 .25
491 A94 50fr brown & multi 1.10 .25
Nos. 489-491 (3) 2.40 .75

Cameroun chocolate industry.

Fertility Symbol, Abbia — A95

Art and Folklore from Abbia: 10fr, Two toucans, horiz. 15fr, Forest symbol. 30fr, Vulture attacking monkey, horiz. 70fr, Oliphant player.

1969, May 30 **Engr.** ***Perf. 13***

492 A95 5fr ultra, Prus bl & brt rose lil .25 .25
493 A95 10fr bl, ol gray & org .35 .25
494 A95 15fr ultra, dk red & blk .50 .25
495 A95 30fr brt bl, lem & grn .90 .25
496 A95 70fr brt bl, dk grn & ver 1.90 .50
Nos. 492-496 (5) 3.90 1.50

Diesel Train on Bridge — A96

Design: 30fr, Kumba Railroad station, horiz.

Perf. 12½x13, 13x12½

1969, July 11 **Photo.**

497 A96 30fr blue & multi 1.25 .30
498 A96 50fr black & multi 3.25 .60

Opening of Mbanga-Kumba Railroad.

Development Bank Issue
Common Design Type

1969, Sept. 10 **Engr.** ***Perf. 13***

499 CD130 30fr vio bl, grn & ocher .80 .25

African Development Bank, 5th anniv.

ASECNA Issue
Common Design Type

1969, Dec. 12 **Engr.** ***Perf. 13***

500 CD132 100fr slate green 2.00 .60

Red Sage — A99

Design: 30fr, Passionflower.

1970, Mar. 24 **Photo.** ***Perf. 12x12½***
Size: 22x36½mm

501 A99 15fr yel grn & multi .45 .25
502 A99 30fr multicolored 1.00 .25
Nos. 501-502,C140-C141 (4) 5.60 1.75

UPU Headquarters Issue
Common Design Type

1970, May 20 **Engr.** ***Perf. 13***

503 CD133 30fr blue, pur & grn 1.00 .25
504 CD133 50fr gray, red & bl 1.60 .30

Brewery A100

Design: 30fr, Cellar with barrels.

1970, July 9 **Engr.** ***Perf. 13***

505 A100 15fr brn, gray & dk grn .50 .25
506 A100 30fr bl grn, dk brn & brn red 1.00 .30

Cameroun brewing industry.

Ozila Dancers — A101

Design: 50fr, Ozila dancer and drummer.

1970, Oct. 19 **Engr.** ***Perf. 13***

507 A101 30fr multicolored 1.00 .35
508 A101 50fr red & multi 1.25 .75

Cameroun Doll — A102

Designs: 15fr, Doll in short skirt. 30fr, Doll with basket on back.

1970, Nov. 2

509 A102 10fr car & multi .60 .25
510 A102 15fr dk grn & multi .70 .25
511 A102 30fr brn red & multi 1.90 .30
Nos. 509-511 (3) 3.20 .80

Cogwheels and Grain A103

1970, Feb. 9 **Photo.** ***Perf. 13***

512 A103 30fr multicolored .85 .25

Europafrica Economic Conference.

Federal University, Yaoundé A104

1971, Jan. 19 **Engr.**

513 A104 50fr multicolored 1.00 .25

Inauguration of Federal University at Yaoundé.

Presidents Ahidjo and Pompidou, Flags of Cameroun and France — A105

1971, Feb. 9 **Photo.** ***Perf. 13***

514 A105 30fr multicolored 1.50 .35

Visit of Georges Pompidou, Pres. of France.

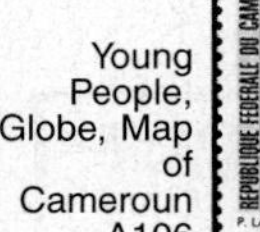

Young People, Globe, Map of Cameroun A106

1971, Feb. 11

515 A106 30fr blue & multi .90 .30

Fifth National Youth Festival, Feb. 11.

Gerbera Hybrida — A107

Designs: 40fr, Opuntia polyantha (cactus). 50fr, Hemerocallis hybrida (lily).

1971, Mar. 14 **Photo.**

516 A107 20fr multicolored .60 .25
517 A107 40fr green & multi 1.50 .25
518 A107 50fr blue & multi 2.10 .25
Nos. 516-518 (3) 4.20 .75

Men of Four Races — A108

Design: 30fr, Hands and globe.

1971, Mar. 21 ***Perf. 13x12½***

519 A108 20fr green & multi .55 .25
520 A108 30fr ultra & multi .75 .25

Intl. year against racial discrimination.

Crowned Cranes at Waza Camp A109

20fr, Canoe on Sanaga River. 30fr, Sanaga River.

1971, Apr. 9. **Engr.** ***Perf. 13***

521 A109 10fr red, grn & blk 1.50 .25
522 A109 20fr dk grn, brn & red 1.00 .25
523 A109 30fr red, dk grn & brt bl 1.50 .25
Nos. 521-523 (3) 4.00 .75

International Court, The Hague — A110

1971, June 14 **Engr.** ***Perf. 13***

524 A110 50fr ultra, org brn & sl grn 1.25 .35

25th anniversary of the International Court in The Hague, Netherlands.

Liana Bridge — A111

Local Market A112

1971, Aug. 16 **Photo.** ***Perf. 13***

525 A111 40fr multicolored 1.60 .25
526 A112 45fr multicolored 1.60 .25

Bamoun Horseman A113

African Art: 15fr, Animal fetish statuette.

1971, Sept. 18

527 A113 10fr brown & yellow .50 .50
528 A113 15fr dp brn & org yel .50 .50

Communications Satellite and Globe — A114

1971, Oct. 14 ***Perf. 13x12½***

529 A114 40fr Prus bl, sl grn & org .80 .25

Pan-African telecommunications system.

UNICEF Emblem A115

50fr, UNICEF emblem and grain, vert.

1971, Dec. 11 **Engr.** ***Perf. 13***

530 A115 40fr sl grn, bl grn & plum .95 .25
531 A115 50fr dp bl, dk red & lt grn 1.25 .25

25th anniv. of UNICEF.

Houses from South-Central Region — A116

Design: 15fr, Adamaua round houses.

1972, Jan. 15 Photo. *Perf. 13*

532 A116 10fr dk blue & multi .25 .25

533 A116 15fr black & multi .55 .25

Giraffe — A117

Designs: 5fr, Home industries. 10fr, Smith, horiz. 15fr, Women carrying burdens.

Perf. 13x13½, 13½x13

1972, Feb. 18 Litho.

534 A117 2fr multicolored .30 .25

535 A117 5fr black, org & red .30 .25

536 A117 10fr multicolored .30 .25

537 A117 15fr multicolored .30 .25

Nos. 534-537 (4) 1.20 1.00

Youth Day 1972.

Soccer Players and Field — A118

Designs: 20fr, African Soccer Cup, vert. 45fr, Team captains shaking hands, vert.

1972, Feb. 22 *Perf. 13½*

538 A118 20fr gray & multi .55 .25

539 A118 40fr gray & multi .95 .25

540 A118 45fr yellow & multi 1.50 .25

Nos. 538-540 (3) 3.00 .75

African Soccer Cup, Yaoundé, 2/23-3/5.

Government Building, Yaoundé, and Laurel — A119

1972, Apr. 6 Photo. *Perf. 12½x12*

541 A119 40fr multicolored .80 .25

110th session of Inter-Parliamentary Council, Yaoundé, Apr. 1972.

"Fantasia," North Cameroun A120

Bororo Woman — A121

40fr, Boat on Wouri River & Mt. Cameroun.

1972, Apr. 24 *Perf. 13x12½, 12½x13*

542 A120 15fr dk vio & multi .35 .25

543 A121 20fr multicolored .45 .25

544 A120 40fr multicolored 1.50 .25

Nos. 542-544 (3) 2.30 .75

Chemical Apparatus A122

1972, May 15 Engr. *Perf. 13*

545 A122 40fr lilac, red & green .80 .25

President Ahmadou Ahidjo Prize.

United Republic

Solanum Macranthum A123

Design: 45fr, Wax plant.

1972, July 20 Photo. *Perf. 13*

546 A123 40fr multicolored .95 .25

547 A123 45fr yellow & multi 1.25 .25

Charaxes Ameliae A124

Design: 45fr, Papilio tynderaeus.

1972, Aug. 20 Photo. *Perf. 13*

548 A124 40fr bl, dk bl & gold 4.00 .40

549 A124 45fr lt grn, blk & gold 5.50 .60

No. 468 Surcharged

1972, Aug. 30 Photo. *Perf. 12x12½*

550 A85 40fr on 30fr multicolored 1.00 .25

Resurrection Lily — A125

Flowers: 45fr, Candlestick cassia. 50fr, Amaryllis.

1972, Sept. 16 *Perf. 13*

551 A125 40fr lt green & multi 1.00 .25

552 A125 45fr multicolored 1.25 .25

553 A125 50fr lt blue & multi 1.50 .35

Nos. 551-553 (3) 3.75 .85

Great Blue Touraco — A126

Design: 45fr, Red-faced lovebirds, horiz.

Perf. 12½x13, 13x12½

1972, Nov. 20 Litho.

554 A126 10fr yellow & multi 1.75 .25

555 A126 45fr yellow & multi 3.75 .25

Cotton (North) — A127

10fr, Cacao (south central). 15fr, Logging (southeast & southern coast). 20fr, Coffee (west). 45fr, Tea (northwest & southwest).

1973, Mar. 26 Photo. *Perf. 12½x13*

556 A127 5fr black & multi .25 .25

557 A127 10fr black & multi .25 .25

558 A127 15fr black & multi .75 .25

559 A127 20fr black & multi 1.50 .25

560 A127 45fr black & multi 2.50 .40

Nos. 556-560 (5) 5.25 1.40

Third 5-Year Plan.

For surcharge see No. 568.

Flag and Map of Cameroun, Pres. Ahidjo and No. 331 — A128

Design: 20fr, Proclamation of independence, Pres. Ahidjo and No. 336.

1973, May 20 Engr. *Perf. 13*

561 A128 10fr ultra & multi .65 .25

562 A128 20fr multicolored 1.00 .25

Nos. 561-562,C200-C201 (4) 3.45 1.15

United Republic of Cameroun, 1st anniv.

Bamoun Mask — A129

Designs: Various Bamoun masks.

1973, July 10 Engr. *Perf. 13*

563 A129 5fr green, brn & blk .25 .25

564 A129 10fr lilac, brn & blk .25 .25

565 A129 45fr red, brn & blk .75 .25

566 A129 100fr ultra, brn & blk 2.00 .40

Nos. 563-566 (4) 3.25 1.15

Dr. Hansen — A130

1973, July 25 Engr. *Perf. 13*

567 A130 45fr multicolored 2.00 .25

Centenary of the discovery by Dr. Armauer G. Hansen of the Hansen bacillus, the cause of leprosy.

No. 556 Surcharged

1973, Aug. 16 Photo. *Perf. 12½x13*

568 A127 100fr on 5fr 1.75 .40

African solidarity in drought emergency.

Dancers, South West Africa — A131

Designs: Southwest African dances.

1973, Aug. 17 *Perf. 13*

569 A131 10fr multicolored .25 .25

570 A131 25fr multicolored .55 .25

571 A131 45fr multicolored 1.10 .25

Nos. 569-571 (3) 1.90 .75

WMO Emblem — A132

1973, Sept. 1 Engr. *Perf. 13*

572 A132 45fr green & ultra 1.60 .25

Cent. of intl. meteorological cooperation.

Garoua Party Headquarters — A133

1973, Sept. 1 Photo.

573 A133 40fr multicolored .80 .25

7th anniv. of Cameroun National Union.

African Postal Union Issue, 1973

Common Design Type

1973, Sept. 12 Engr.

574 CD137 100fr brt bl, bl & sl grn 1.75 .40

Avocados — A135

1973, Sept. 20

575	A135	10fr shown	.70	.25
576	A135	20fr Mangos	.80	.25
577	A135	45fr Plums	2.00	.25
578	A135	50fr Custard apple	2.50	.25
		Nos. 575-578 (4)	6.00	1.00

Kirdi Village A136

45fr, Mabas village. 50fr, Fishing village.

1973, Oct. 25 **Engr.** ***Perf. 13***

579	A136	15fr black, bis & grn	.25	.25
580	A136	45fr mag, brn & org	.90	.25
581	A136	50fr green, blk & org	1.25	.25
		Nos. 579-581 (3)	2.40	.75

Handshake on Map of Africa — A137

1974, May 15 **Engr.** ***Perf. 12½x13***

582	A137	40fr carmine & multi	.55	.25
583	A137	45fr indigo & multi	.70	.25

Organization for African Unity, 10th anniv.

Spinning Mill — A138

1974, May 25 **Engr.** ***Perf. 13x12½***

584	A138	45fr multicolored	.80	.25

CICAM Industrial Complex.

Carved Panel from Bilinga A139

Cameroun Art (Carvings): 40fr, Detail from Bubinga chair. 45fr, Detail Acajou Ngollon panel.

1974, May 30

585	A139	10fr brt grn & ocher	.25	.25
586	A139	40fr red & brown	.80	.25
587	A139	45fr blue & rose brn	1.10	.25
		Nos. 585-587 (3)	2.15	.75

Zebu — A140

1974, June 1 ***Perf. 13½***

588	A140	40fr multicolored	1.40	.25

North Cameroun cattle raising. See No. C210.

Laying Rail Section A141

Designs: 5fr, Map showing line Yaoundé to Ngaoundéré, vert. 40fr, Welding rail joint, vert. 100fr, Train on Djerem River Bridge.

Perf. 12½x13, 13x12½

1974, June 10 **Engr.**

589	A141	5fr multicolored	.65	.25
590	A141	20fr multicolored	1.25	.30
591	A141	40fr multicolored	2.00	.60
592	A141	100fr multicolored	3.25	.90
		Nos. 589-592 (4)	7.15	2.05

Opening of Yaoundé-Ngaoundéré railroad line.

For surcharge see No. 596.

No. 466 Surcharged

1974, June 1 **Photo.** ***Perf. 12x12½***

593	A85	40fr on 8fr multi	.80	.25

UPU Emblem, Hands Holding Letters A142

1974, Oct. 8 **Engr.** ***Perf. 13***

594	A142	40fr multicolored	.90	.25
		Nos. 594,C218-C219 (3)	5.90	1.75

Cent. of the UPU.

Presidents and Flags of Cameroun, CAR, Congo, Gabon and Meeting Center — A143

1974, Dec. 8 **Photo.** ***Perf. 13***

595	A143	40fr gold & multi	1.50	.25

10th anniversary of Central African Customs and Economic Union (Union Douanière et Economique de l'Afrique Centrale, UDEAC). See No. C223.

No. 589 Surcharged in Violet Blue

1974, Dec. 10 **Engr.** ***Perf. 12½x13***

596	A141	100fr on 5fr multi	2.50	.85

Virgin of Autun, 15th Century Sculpture A144

Christmas: 45fr, Virgin and Child, by Luis de Morales (c. 1509-1586).

1974, Dec. 20 **Photo.** ***Perf. 13***

597	A144	40fr gold & multi	.95	.25
598	A144	45fr gold & multi	1.25	.25

Tropical Plants — A145

5fr, Cockscomb. 40fr, Costus spectabilis. 45fr, Mussaenda erythrophylla.

1975, Mar. 10 **Photo.** ***Perf. 13***

599	A145	5fr multicolored	.30	.25
600	A145	40fr multicolored	1.50	.25
601	A145	45fr multicolored	1.90	.35
		Nos. 599-601 (3)	3.70	.85

Fishing by Night — A146

1975, Apr. 1 **Engr.** ***Perf. 13***

602	A146	40fr shown	1.75	.40
603	A146	45fr Fishing by day	1.75	.40

Afo Akom Statue and Chief's Stool — A147

1975, Apr. 1 **Photo.**

604	A147	40fr multicolored	.65	.25
605	A147	45fr multicolored	.85	.25
606	A147	200fr multicolored	2.50	.75
		Nos. 604-606 (3)	4.00	1.25

Tree Fungus — A148

1975, Apr. 14

607	A148	15fr shown	125.00	2.00
608	A148	40fr Chrysalis	85.00	1.00

Ministry of Posts and Telecommunications — A149

1975, July 21 **Engr.** ***Perf. 13***

609	A149	40fr brn, grn & Prus bl	.65	.25
610	A149	45fr Prus bl, brn & grn	.90	.25

Presbyterian Church, Elat — A150

Designs: No. 612, Foumban Mosque. 45fr, Catholic Church, Ngaoundere.

1975, Aug. 20 **Engr.** ***Perf. 13***

611	A150	40fr multicolored	.45	.25
612	A150	40fr multicolored	.45	.25
613	A150	45fr multicolored	.65	.25
		Nos. 611-613 (3)	1.55	.75

Plowing A151

Design: No. 615, Corn harvest, vert.

Perf. 13x12½, 12½x13

1975, Dec. 15 **Photo.**

614	A151	40fr deep grn & multi	.70	.25
615	A151	40fr deep grn & multi	.70	.25

Green revolution.

Zamengoe Satellite Monitoring Station — A152

1976, May 20 **Litho.** ***Perf. 13***

616	A152	40fr shown	.50	.25
617	A152	100fr Radar, vert.	1.25	.40

Porcelain Rose — A153

Design: 50fr, Flower of North Cameroun.

1976, July 20 Litho. *Perf. 12½*

618 A153 40fr multicolored 1.00 .25
619 A153 50fr multicolored 1.40 .35

Leopard Dance — A154

1976, Sept. 15 Litho. *Perf. 12*

620 A154 40fr gray & multi .80 .25
Nos. 620,C233-C234 (3) 2.55 .85

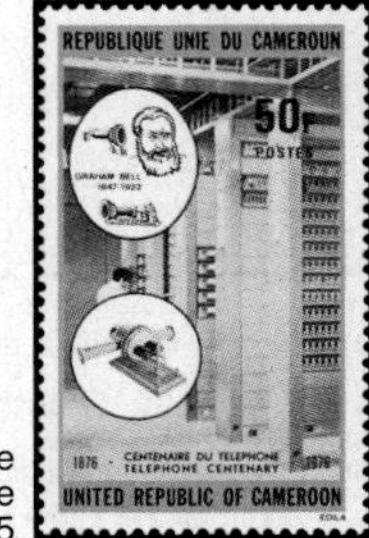

Telephone Exchange A155

1976, Oct. 5 *Perf. 13*

621 A155 50fr multicolored .80 .25

Centenary of first telephone call by Alexander Graham Bell, Mar. 10, 1876.

Young Men Building House — A156

Design: 45fr, Young women working in field.

1976, Oct. 10 Litho. *Perf. 12*

622 A156 40fr multicolored .35 .25
623 A156 45fr multicolored .60 .25

10th National Youth Day.

Konrad Adenauer (1876-1967), German Chancellor, Cologne Cathedral A157

1976, Oct. 20

624 A157 100fr multicolored .95 .40

Party Headquarters, Douala — A158

No. 626, Party Headquarters, Yaoundé.

1976, Dec. 28 Litho. *Perf. 12*

625 A158 50fr orange & multi .45 .25
626 A158 50fr blue & multi .45 .25

10th anniv. of the Cameroun National Union.

Bamoun Copper Pipe — A159

1977, Feb. 4 Litho. *Perf. 12½*

627 A159 50fr multicolored .70 .25

2nd World Black and African Festival, Lagos, Nigeria, 1/15-2/12. See No. C239.

Ostrich — A160

1977, Mar. 20 Litho. *Perf. 12*

628 A160 30fr shown 2.50 .40
629 A160 50fr Crowned cranes 3.00 .75

Cameroun No. 609 and Switzerland No. 3L1 — A161

1977, June 5 Litho. *Perf. 12*

630 A161 50fr multicolored 1.00 .30
Nos. 630,C252-C253 (3) 4.35 1.25

Jufilex Philatelic Exhibition, Bern, Switzerland. See Nos. C252-C253.

Winter Olympics 1976, set of five, 40, 50fr, airmail 140, 200, 350fr, and airmail souv. sheet, 500fr, issued Aug. 10, 1977. Nos. 7701-7706. Value, set $7.50, souvenir sheet $5.

Apollo-Soyuz — A163

Designs: 40fr, Astronaut Thomas P. Stafford, Apollo lifting off. 60fr, Cosmonaut Alexei Leonov, Soyuz lifting off.

1977, Aug. 10 Litho. *Perf. 14x13½*

633 A163 40fr multicolored *.45 .25*
634 A163 60fr multicolored *.70 .50*
Nos. 633-634,C256-C258 (5) *7.55 2.60*

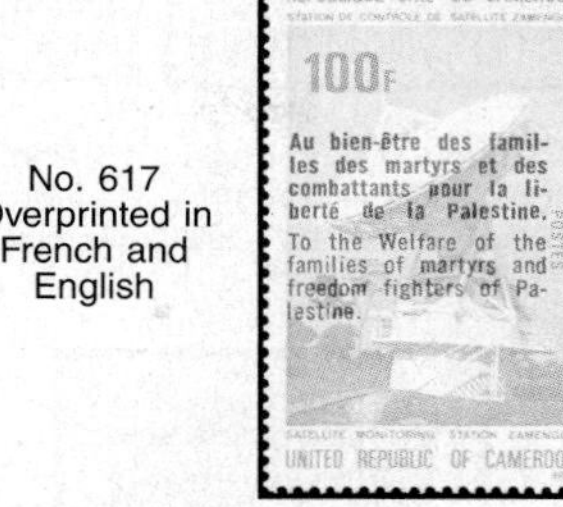

No. 617 Overprinted in French and English

1977, Aug. 22 Litho. *Perf. 13*

635 A152 100fr multicolored .90 .40

Palestinian fighters and their families.

Chairman Mao and Great Wall A164

1977, Sept. 9 Engr. *Perf. 13*

636 A164 100fr olive & brown 4.25 .55

Mao Tse-tung (1893-1976), Chinese communist leader, first death anniversary.

Nativity, by Albrecht Altdorfer A165

50fr, Madonna of the Grand Duke, by Raphael.

1977, Dec. 15 Litho. *Perf. 12½x12*

637 A165 30fr multicolored .55 .25
638 A165 50fr multicolored 1.10 .25
Nos. 637-638,C264-C265 (4) 7.65 2.50

Christmas 1977.

Gazelle and Rotary Emblem — A166

1978, Feb. 11 Litho. *Perf. 12*

639 A166 50fr orange & multi .70 .25

Rotary Club of Yaounde, 20th anniversary.

Pres. Ahidjo, Flag and Map of Cameroun A167

1978, Apr. 3 Litho. *Perf. 12½*

640 A167 50fr multicolored .90 .25

New flag of Cameroun. See No. C266.

Cardioglossa Escalerae — A168

Design: 60fr, Cardioglossa elegans.

1978, Apr. 5

641 A168 50fr multicolored 1.75 .25
642 A168 60fr multicolored 3.00 .25
Nos. 641-642,C267 (3) 8.50 1.25

Jules Verne and "From Earth to Moon" — A169

1978, Oct. 10 Litho. *Perf. 12*

643 A169 250fr multicolored 2.25 1.40

Jules Verne (1828-1905), science fiction writer, birth sesquicentennial. See No. C276.

Hypolimnas Salmacis Drury — A170

Butterflies: 25fr, Euxanthe trajanus ward. 30fr, Euphaedra cyparissa cramer.

1978, Oct. 15

644 A170 20fr multicolored 2.00 .60
645 A170 25fr multicolored 2.25 .60
646 A170 30fr multicolored 3.75 .60
Nos. 644-646 (3) 8.00 1.80

Men Planting Seedlings — A171

1978, Oct. 30 *Perf. 12½*

647 A171 10fr multicolored .25 .25
648 A171 15fr multicolored .35 .25

Green barrier against the desert.

Carved Bamun Drum — A172

60fr, String instrument (Gueguerou), horiz.

1978, Nov. 20 Litho. *Perf. 12½*

649 A172 50fr multicolored .45 .25
650 A172 60fr multicolored .90 .25
Nos. 649-650,C277 (3) 2.60 .90

Pres. Ahidjo, Giscard D'Estaing, Flags of Cameroun and France — A173

1979, Feb. 8 Photo. *Perf. 13*

651 A173 60fr multicolored 1.50 .60

Visit of Pres. Valery Giscard D'Estaing of France to Cameroun.

Human Rights Emblem, Globe, Scroll and African — A174

1979, Feb. 11 Litho. *Perf. 12x12½*

652 A174 5fr multicolored .25 .25

Universal Declaration of Human Rights, 30th anniversary (in 1978).
See Nos. 803, C278.

Boy and Girl Greeting Sun — A175

1979, Aug. 15 Litho. *Perf. 12*

653 A175 50fr multicolored .80 .25

International Year of the Child.

Protected Animals A176

Nos. 655, 658 vert.

1979, Sept. 20 *Perf. 12½*

654 A176 50fr Rhinoceros 1.40 .30
655 A176 60fr Giraffe 1.90 .40
656 A176 60fr Gorilla 1.90 .40
657 A176 100fr Leopard 2.90 .60
658 A176 100fr Elephant 2.90 .60
Nos. 654-658 (5) 11.00 2.30

Eugene Jamot, Map of Cameroun, Tsetse Fly — A177

1979, Nov. 5 Engr. *Perf. 13*

659 A177 50fr multicolored 3.00 .40

Eugene Jamot (1879-1937), discoverer of sleeping sickness cure.

Annunciation, by Fra Filippo Lippi — A178

Paintings; 50fr, Rest During the Flight to Egypt, c. 1620. No. 622, Flight into Egypt, by Jan Joest, No. 663, Nativity, by Joest. 100fr, Nativity, by Botticelli.

1979, Dec. 6 Litho. *Perf. 12½x12*

660 A178 10fr multicolored .25 .25
661 A178 50fr multicolored .60 .25
662 A178 60fr multicolored .75 .30
663 A178 60fr multicolored .75 .30
a. Pair, #662-663 1.50 1.50
664 A178 100fr multicolored 1.50 .40
Nos. 660-664 (5) 3.85 1.50

Christmas 1979.

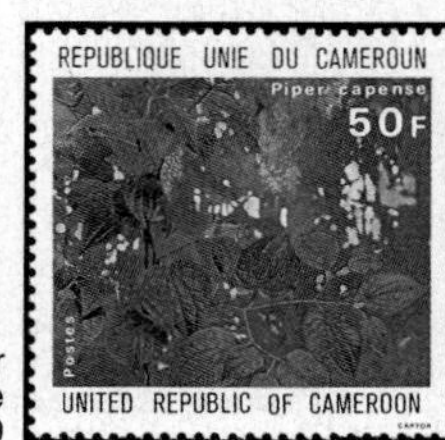

Piper Capense A179

Medicinal Plants: 60fr, Bracken fern.

1979, Dec. 15 Litho. *Perf. 12½*

665 A179 50fr multicolored 1.25 .30
666 A179 60fr multicolored 1.50 .40

Pres. Ahidjo, Cameroun Map, Arms and No. 331 A180

1980, Feb. 12 Litho. *Perf. 12½*

667 A180 50fr multicolored .65 .25

Independence, 20th anniversary.

Congress Building, Bafoussam A181

1980, Feb. 12

668 A181 50fr multicolored .65 .25

Cameroun National Union, 3rd Ordinary Congress, Bafoussam, Feb. 12-17.

Rotary Emblem, Map of Cameroun A182

Rotary Intl., 75th Anniv.: No. 670, Anniv. emblem.

1980, Mar. 15 Litho. *Perf. 12½*

669 A182 200fr multicolored 2.00 .80
670 A182 200fr multicolored 2.00 .80
a. Souvenir sheet of 2, #669-670 5.25 4.00

Voacanga Medicinal Beans A183

60fr, Voacanga tree, vert. 100fr, Voacanga flower, vert.

1980, Dec. 3 Litho. *Perf. 12½*

671 A183 50fr shown 1.00 .25
672 A183 60fr multicolored 1.25 .25
673 A183 100fr multicolored 1.75 .40
Nos. 671-673 (3) 4.00 .90

Violet Mellowstone A184

60fr, Patula. 100fr, Cashmere bouquet.

1980, Dec. 5

674 A184 50fr shown .70 .25
675 A184 60fr multicolored 1.00 .25
676 A184 100fr multicolored 1.60 .40
Nos. 674-676 (3) 3.30 .90

Occupation of Mecca by Mohammed, 1350th Anniversary — A185

1980, Dec. 9

677 A185 50fr multicolored 1.00 .30

African Slender-snouted Crocodile (Endangered Species) — A186

300fr, Buffon's antelope, vert.

1980, Dec. 24

678 A186 200fr shown 3.25 .80
679 A186 300fr multicolored 4.00 1.20

See Nos. 888-889.

Bororo Girls and Roumsiki Peaks — A187

60fr, Dschang tourist center.

1980, Dec. 29

680 A187 50fr shown .55 .25
681 A187 60fr multicolored .55 .25

Banana Tree A188

1981, Feb. 5

682 A188 50fr shown .65 .30
683 A188 60fr Cattle, vert. .80 .40

Girl on Crutches — A189

150fr, Boy in motorized wheelchair.

1981, Feb. 20 Litho. *Perf. 12½*

684 A189 60fr shown .55 .25
685 A189 150fr multicolored 1.25 .65

International Year of the Disabled.

Air Terminal, Douala Airport — A190

200fr, Boeing 747. 300fr, Douala Intl. Airport.

1981, Apr. 4 Litho. *Perf. 12½*

686 A190 100fr shown 1.00 .55
687 A190 200fr multi 2.00 1.10
688 A190 300fr multi 3.00 1.60
Nos. 686-688 (3) 6.00 3.25

Cameroun Airlines, 10th anniv.

Pres. Ahidjo Presenting Trophy to Canon Soccer Team — A191

No. 690, Union team captain.

1981, Apr. 20

689 A191 60fr shown .90 .40
690 A191 60fr multicolored .90 .40

1979 African Soccer Cup champions.

Scaly Anteater A192

Designs: Endangered species.

1981, July 20 **Litho.** ***Perf. 12½***
691 A192 50fr Moutourou 1.50 .25
692 A192 50fr Tortoise 1.50 .25
693 A192 100fr shown 3.25 .40
Nos. 691-693 (3) 6.25 .90

Prince Charles and Lady Diana, St. Paul's Cathedral A193

No. 695, Couple, royal coach.

1981, July 29 **Litho.** ***Perf. 12½***
694 A193 500fr shown 4.50 2.00
695 A193 500fr multicolored 4.50 2.00
a. Souvenir sheet of 2, #694-695 10.00 4.00

Royal wedding.

Bafoussam-Bamenda Highway — A194

1981, Sept. 10 **Litho.** ***Perf. 12½***
696 A194 50fr multicolored .55 .25

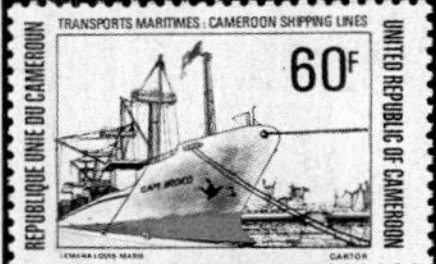

Freighter Cam Iroko (Cameroun Shipping Line) A195

1981, Sept. 25
697 A195 60fr multicolored 1.00 .40

20th Anniv. of Reunification — A196

1981, Oct. 10 ***Perf. 12½x13***
698 A196 50fr multicolored .70 .25

Medicinal Plants — A197

60fr, Voacanga thouarsii. 70fr, Cassia alata.

1981, Dec. 31 **Litho.** ***Perf. 12½***
699 A197 60fr multicolored 1.10 .30
700 A197 70fr multicolored 1.40 .40

Easter 1982 — A198

Paintings: 100fr, Christ in the Garden of Olives, by Delacroix. 200fr, Descent from the Cross, by Giotto. 250fr, Pieta in the Countryside, by Bellini.

1982, Apr. 10 **Litho.** ***Perf. 13***
701 A198 100fr multicolored .90 .35
702 A198 200fr multicolored 1.75 .65
703 A198 250fr multicolored 2.25 .90
Nos. 701-703 (3) 4.90 1.90

PHILEXFRANCE '82 Stamp Exhibition, Paris, June 11-21 — A199

1982, Apr. 25 ***Perf. 12***
704 A199 90fr multicolored 1.90 .40

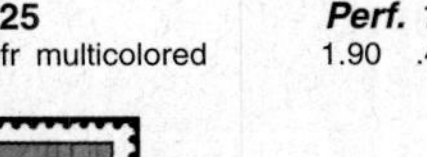

Snakeskin Handbag — A200

1982, Apr. 30 ***Perf. 12½***
705 A200 60fr shown .70 .25
706 A200 70fr Clay water jug .80 .35

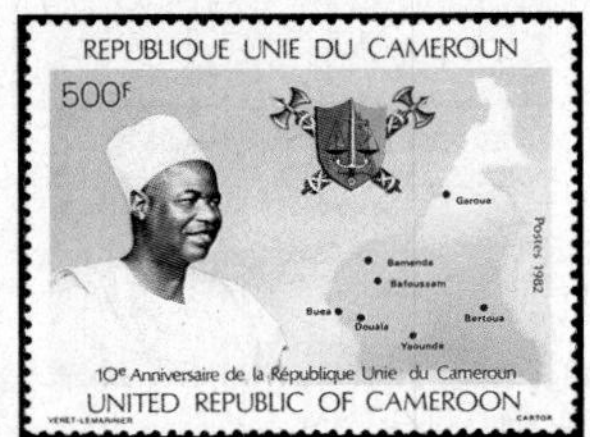

10th Anniv. of Republic — A201

1982, May 20 ***Perf. 13***
707 A201 500fr multicolored 4.50 2.00

Town Hall, Douala — A202

1982, June 15 **Litho.** ***Perf. 12½***
708 A202 40fr shown .45 .25
709 A202 60fr Yaounde .65 .25

See Nos. 730-731, 757-758, 790-791, 867.

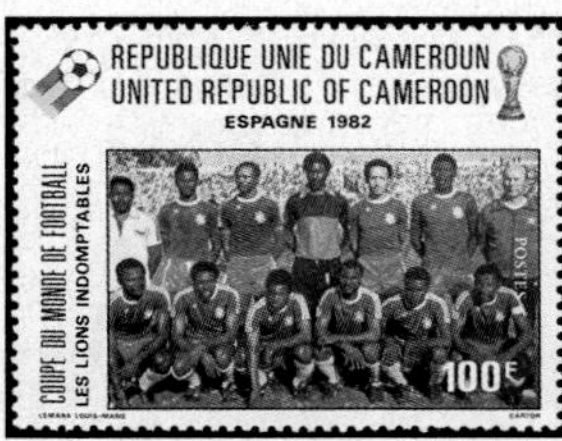

1982 World Cup — A203

100fr, National team. 200fr, Semi-finalists. 300fr, Players, vert. 400fr, National team 2nd lineup.

1982, July 10 ***Perf. 13***
710 A203 100fr multi 1.40 .40
711 A203 200fr multi 2.75 .75
712 A203 300fr multi 4.50 1.25
713 A203 400fr multi 5.75 1.60
a. Souvenir sheet of 2, #713 14.50 3.50
Nos. 710-713 (4) 14.40 4.00

Partridge — A204

Bongo Antelope — A204a

15fr, Turtle dove. 20fr, Swallow. 300fr, Black colobus.

1982 ***Perf. 12½x13***
714 A204 10fr shown 2.50 .40
715 A204 15fr multi 3.00 .85
716 A204 20fr multi 5.50 1.10
717 A204a 200fr shown 3.00 .80
718 A204a 300fr multi 4.00 1.25
Nos. 714-718 (5) 18.00 4.40

Issued: 200fr, 300fr, July 20; others Aug. 10.
See No. 804.

Scouting Year A205

1982, Sept. 30 **Litho.** ***Perf. 13x12½***
719 A205 200fr Campfire 2.50 .80
720 A205 400fr Baden-Powell 4.50 1.60

25th Anniv. of the Presbyterian Church in Cameroun — A206

45fr, Buea Chapel. 60fr, Nyasoso Chapel, vert.

1982, Oct. 30 ***Perf. 13x12½, 12½x13***
721 A206 45fr multi .55 .25
722 A206 60fr multi .65 .25

ITU Plenipotentiaries Conference, Nairobi, Sept. — A207

1982, Oct. 5 **Litho.** ***Perf. 12½x13***
723 A207 70fr multicolored .70 .25

Italy's Victory in 1982 World Cup — A208

1982, Nov. ***Perf. 13***
724 A208 500fr multicolored 5.50 2.00
725 A208 1000fr multicolored 10.50 4.00

30th Anniv. of Customs Cooperation Council — A209

No. 726, Emblem. No. 727, Headquarters, Brussels.

1983, Jan. 10 ***Perf. 12½x13***
726 A209 250fr multicolored 2.25 .80
727 A209 250fr multicolored 2.25 .80

2nd Yaoundé Medical Conference — A210

1983, Jan. 23 **Litho.** ***Perf. 13***
728 A210 60fr grn & multi .70 .25
729 A210 70fr brn & multi .90 .25

City Hall Type of 1982

1983, Feb. 25 **Litho.** ***Perf. 12½***
730 A202 60fr Bafoussam .60 .25
731 A202 70fr Garoua .70 .30

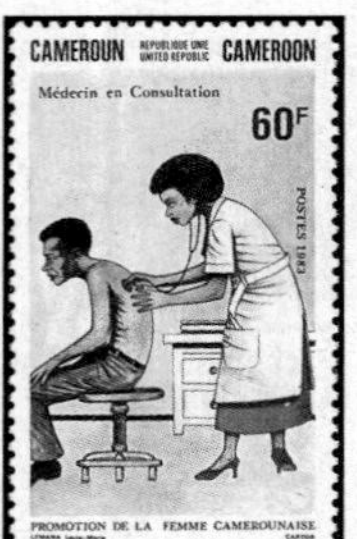

Homage to Women — A211

1983, Apr. 25 Litho. *Perf. 12½*
733 A211 60fr Nurse .75 .25
734 A211 70fr Lawyer .75 .25

11th Anniv. of Independence — A212

Flag and Pres. Paul Biya.

1983, May 18 Litho. *Perf. 13*
735 A212 60fr dk grn & multi .55 .25
736 A212 70fr dk bl & multi .70 .30

25th Anniv. of Intl. Maritime Org. A213

1983, May 23 *Perf. 13x12½*
737 A213 500fr multicolored 5.50 1.50

Eagle — A214

1983, June 15 Litho. *Perf. 12½x13*
738 A214 25fr shown 1.50 .40
739 A214 30fr Sparrowhawk 2.50 .75
740 A214 50fr Purple heron 4.50 1.00
Nos. 738-740 (3) 8.50 2.15

See Nos. 798-800, 873, 882, 886.

A215

60fr, Pearl mask, by Wery-Nwen-Nto, 1899. 70fr, Basket with lid.

1983, July 25 Litho. *Perf. 12*
741 A215 60fr multicolored .70 .25
742 A215 70fr multicolored .90 .30

A216

90fr, Mobile Post Office, horiz. 150fr, Telegraph Operator. 250fr, Tom-tom.

1983, Aug. 20 Litho. *Perf. 12*
743 A216 90fr multicolored .90 .25
744 A216 150fr multicolored 1.40 .35
745 A216 250fr multicolored 2.75 .55
Nos. 743-745 (3) 5.05 1.15

World Communications Year.

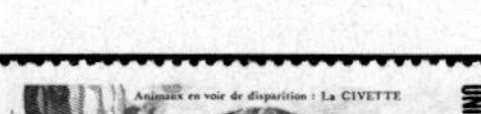

Endangered Species — A217

1983, Sept. 22 *Perf. 12*
746 A217 200fr Civet Cat 2.75 .50
747 A217 200fr Gorilla, vert 2.75 .50
748 A217 350fr Cobaya, vert 4.50 1.25
Nos. 746-748 (3) 10.00 2.25

See No. 887.

Lake Tizon — A218

1983, Nov. 25 Litho. *Perf. 13*
749 A218 60fr shown .55 .25
750 A218 70fr Mt. Cameroon .70 .25

Human Rights Declaration, 35th Anniv — A219

1983, Dec. 20 Litho. *Perf. 12½x13*
751 A219 60fr multicolored .55 .25
752 A219 70fr multicolored .70 .25

Christmas 1983 — A220

60fr, Christmas tree. 200fr, Stained glass window, Yaoundé Cathedral. No. 755, Rest during Flight into Egypt, by Philipp Otto Runge. No. 756, Angel of the Annunciation. 60fr, 200fr, No. 756 vert.

1983, Dec. 20 Litho. *Perf. 12½*
753 A220 60fr multicolored .45 .25
754 A220 200fr multicolored 1.75 .50
755 A220 500fr multicolored 4.50 1.25
756 A220 500fr multicolored 4.50 1.25
  a. Souvenir sheet of 3, #754-756 12.50 12.50
Nos. 753-756 (4) 11.20 3.25

City Hall Type of 1982

1984, Apr. 20 Litho. *Perf. 12½*
757 A202 60fr Bamenda .55 .25
758 A202 70fr Mbalmayo .70 .25

Catholic Church, Zoetele — A221

70fr, Protestant Church, Yaounde.

1984, July 25 Litho. *Perf. 13*
759 A221 60fr shown .55 .25
760 A221 70fr multicolored .70 .25

Endangered Species — A222

1984, Aug. 15
761 A222 250fr Wild pig 3.50 .75
762 A222 250fr Deer 3.50 .75

1984, Oct. 10 Litho. *Perf. 13½*
763 A222 60fr Nightingale 4.50 1.00
764 A222 60fr Vultures 4.50 1.00

See No. 883.

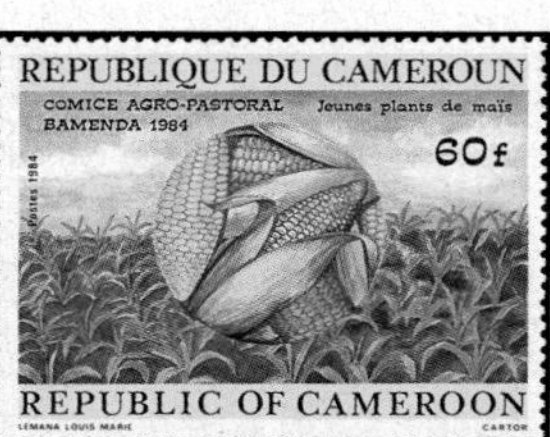

Bamenda Farming Fair — A223

1984, Dec. 10 Litho. *Perf. 13*
765 A223 60fr Corn .60 .25
766 A223 70fr Cattle .90 .25
767 A223 300fr Potatoes 3.50 .90
Nos. 765-767 (3) 5.00 1.40

International Civil Aviation Organization, 40th Anniv. — A224

No. 768, Icarus. No. 769, ICAO emblem, vert. No. 770, Boeing 747. No. 771, Solar Princess painting.

1984, Dec. 20 Litho. *Perf. 12½*
768 A224 200fr multi 1.75 .60
769 A224 200fr multi 1.75 .60
770 A224 300fr multi 2.75 .90
771 A224 300fr multi 3.25 .90
Nos. 768-771 (4) 9.50 3.00

Olymphilex '85, Lausanne — A225

150fr, Wrestlers, exhibition emblem.

Wmk. 385

1985, Apr. 5 Photo. *Perf. 13*
772 A225 150fr multicolored 1.50 .40

Domestic Musical Instruments A226

60fr, Balafons (xylophone). 70fr, Guitar. 100fr, Flute.

1985, Apr. 23 *Perf. 13½*
773 A226 60fr multicolored .65 .25
774 A226 70fr multicolored .80 .25
775 A226 100fr multicolored 1.10 .30
Nos. 773-775 (3) 2.55 .80

INTELSAT Org., 20th Anniv. — A227

125fr, Intelsat V. 200fr, Intelcam, Yaounde.

1985, May 8 *Perf. 13*
776 A227 125fr multicolored 1.60 .35
777 A227 200fr multicolored 2.10 .60

New York Headquarters — A228

1985, May 30
778 A228 250fr multicolored 2.40 1.10
779 A228 500fr multicolored 4.50 2.25

UN, 40th anniv.

Pres. Mitterand, Biya — A229

1985, June 20

780	A229	60fr multicolored	2.25	.25
781	A229	70fr multicolored	2.50	.25

Visit of Pres. Mitterand of France.

UNICEF A230

UN Infant Survival Campaign A231

1985, July 15

782	A230	60fr multicolored	.55	.25
783	A231	300fr multicolored	2.75	1.00

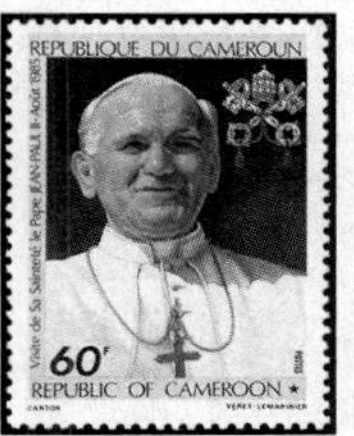

Visit of Pope John Paul II, Aug. 10-14 — A232

60fr, Pope, papal arms. 70fr, Pope, crosier. 200fr, Pres. Biya, John Paul II.

1985, Aug. 9 ***Perf. 13x12½***

784	A232	60fr multi	1.10	.40
785	A232	70fr multi	1.25	.55

Size: 55x38mm

786	A232	200fr multi	4.00	2.25
a.		Souv. sheet of 3, #784-786	8.00	8.00
		Nos. 784-786 (3)	6.35	3.20

Landscapes — A233

60fr, Lake Barumbi, Kumba. 70fr, Bonando Pygmy Village, Doume. 150fr, Cameroun River.

1985, July 25 **Litho.** ***Perf. 12½***

787	A233	60fr multicolored	.70	.25
788	A233	70fr multicolored	.70	.25
789	A233	150fr multicolored	1.40	.40
		Nos. 787-789 (3)	2.80	.90

City Hall Type of 1982

1985, July 30

790	A202	60fr Ngaoundere	.55	.25
791	A202	60fr D'Ebolowa	.55	.25

Wildlife — A234

1985, Aug. 20 ***Perf. 13½***

792	A234	125fr Porcupine	1.50	.40
793	A234	200fr Squirrel	2.50	.60
794	A234	350fr Hedgehog	4.00	1.10
		Nos. 792-794 (3)	8.00	2.10

Wood Sculptures A235

60fr, Mask. 70fr, Mask, diff. 100fr, Wood bas-relief, horiz.

1985, Sept. 15

795	A235	60fr multicolored	.65	.25
796	A235	70fr multicolored	.90	.25
797	A235	100fr multicolored	1.25	.30
		Nos. 795-797 (3)	2.80	.80

Bird Type of 1983 Redrawn

140fr, Toucans. 150fr, Rooster. 200fr, Red-throated bee-eater.

1985, Nov. 10

798	A214	140fr multicolored	2.25	.50
799	A214	150fr multicolored	2.25	.55
800	A214	200fr multicolored	3.25	.70
		Nos. 798-800 (3)	7.75	1.75

Nos. 798-800 inscribed "Republic of Cameroon".

See No. 873. For surcharge see No. 871.

American Peace Corps in Cameroun, 25th Anniv. — A237

1986, Jan. 1 **Litho.** ***Perf. 12½***

801	A237	70fr multicolored	.70	.25
802	A237	100fr multicolored	1.00	.30

Stamps of 1979-1982 Redrawn

1986, Mar. ***Perf. 13, 13½***

803	A174	5fr multicolored	.35	.35
804	A204	10fr multicolored	.35	.35

Nos. 803-804 inscribed "Republic of Cameroon" instead of "United Republic of Cameroon."

Easter — A238

Paintings: 210fr, Head of the Virgin, by Pierre-Paul Prud'Hon (1758-1823). 350fr, The Stoning of St. Steven, by Van Scorel (1495-1562).

1986, Apr. 15 ***Perf. 13½***

805	A238	210fr multicolored	1.75	.60
806	A238	350fr multicolored	3.00	1.00

Insects — A239

1986, Apr. 20

807	A239	70fr Honeybee	1.75	.40
808	A239	70fr Dragonfly	1.75	.40
809	A239	100fr Grasshopper	2.50	.65
		Nos. 807-809 (3)	6.00	1.45

Nos. 808-809 horiz.

Flags, Conference Center — A240

1986, Apr. 25 **Litho.** ***Perf. 13***

810	A240	100fr Map, vert.	1.00	.30
811	A240	175fr shown	2.00	.60

Conference of Ministers of the Economic Commission for Africa, Apr. 9-29.

Statues — A241

70fr, Bronze earth mother. 100fr, Wood funerary figure. 130fr, Wood equestrian figure.

1986, July 5 **Litho.** ***Perf. 13½***

812	A241	70fr multicolored	.85	.25
813	A241	100fr multicolored	.95	.30
814	A241	130fr multicolored	1.60	.40
		Nos. 812-814 (3)	3.40	.95

Queen Elizabeth II, 60th Birthday — A242

100fr, Elizabeth. 175fr, Elizabeth, Pres. Biya. 210fr, Elizabeth, diff.

1986, July 15 **Litho.** ***Perf. 13***

815	A242	100fr multicolored	1.00	.40
816	A242	175fr multicolored	1.40	.60
817	A242	210fr multicolored	2.00	.75
		Nos. 815-817 (3)	4.40	1.75

Natl. Democratic Party, 1st Anniv. — A243

No. 818, Party headquarters, Bamenda. No. 819, Pres. Biya, vert. No. 820, Presidential address, vert.

1986, July 25 ***Perf. 12½***

818	A243	70fr multicolored	.70	.25
819	A243	70fr multicolored	.70	.25
820	A243	100fr multicolored	1.00	.35
		Nos. 818-820 (3)	2.40	.85

Kwem Mask Dancers of the Northeast — A244

1986, Aug. 1 ***Perf. 13½***

821	A244	100fr multicolored	1.00	.35
822	A244	130fr multicolored	1.25	.45

Endangered Species — A245

1986, Aug. 20

823		300fr Varanus niloticus	3.50	1.00
824		300fr Panthera pardus	3.50	1.00

For surcharge see No. 872.

A246

Intl. Peace Year: 175fr, 200fr, Desmond Tutu, South Africa, Nobel Peace Prize winner. 250fr, UN and IPY emblems.

1986, Sept. 7 **Litho.** ***Perf. 13½***

825	A246	175fr multicolored	1.75	1.10
826	A246	200fr multicolored	2.00	1.25
827	A246	250fr multicolored	2.50	1.50
		Nos. 825-827 (3)	6.25	3.85

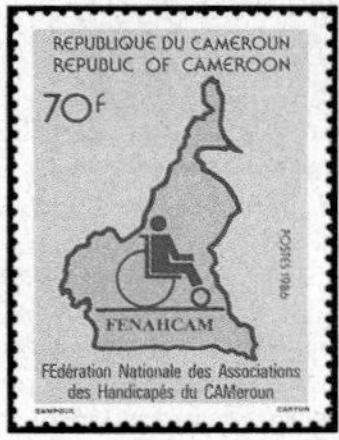

A247

1986, Oct. 30 **Litho.** ***Perf. 13½***

828	A247	70fr multicolored	.65	.25

Natl. Fed. of Associations for the Handicapped.

African Vaccination Year — A248

70fr, Family under umbrella. 100fr, Child immunization.

1986, Nov. 9

829 A248 70fr multicolored .90 .25
830 A248 100fr multicolored 1.10 .35

Arbor Day — A249

70fr, Afforestation map. 100fr, Hands, seedling.

1986, Dec. 20 Litho. ***Perf. 13½***

831 A249 70fr multicolored .90 .25
832 A249 100fr multicolored 1.10 .35

Agricultural Development — A250

No. 833, ONCPB seminar. No. 834, Coconut farming, Dibombari. No. 835, Pineapple farm.

1986, Dec. 24

833 A250 70fr multicolored .75 .40
834 A250 70fr multicolored .75 .40
835 A250 200fr multicolored 2.00 1.10
Nos. 833-835 (3) 3.50 1.90

Insects Destructive to Agriculture A251

70fr, Antestiopsis lineaticollis intricata. 100fr, Distantiella theobroma.

1987, Sept. 25 Litho. ***Perf. 13½***

836 A251 70fr multicolored 1.50 .50
837 A251 100fr multicolored 2.00 .70

4th African Games, Nairobi — A252

1987, Oct. 1 ***Perf. 12½***

838 A252 100fr Shot put .90 .70
839 A252 140fr Pole vault 1.25 1.00

Maroua Agricultural Show — A253

1988, Jan. 6

840 A253 70fr Millet field .90 .50
841 A253 100fr Cotton 1.10 .70
842 A253 150fr Cattle 1.60 1.10
Nos. 840-842 (3) 3.60 2.30

World Wildlife Fund — A254

Baboons, Papio leucophaeus: 30fr, Adult. 40fr, Adult grooming young. 70fr, Baboon on branch. 100fr, Adult carrying young.

1988, Apr. 25 Litho. ***Perf. 13***

843 A254 30fr multicolored 1.75 .75
844 A254 40fr multicolored 2.25 .75
845 A254 70fr multicolored 3.50 1.25
846 A254 100fr multicolored 6.00 1.75
Nos. 843-846 (4) 13.50 4.50

Interparliamentary Union, Cent. — A255

1989 Litho. ***Perf. 13½***

847 A255 50fr Natl. Assembly .60 .30

World Cup Soccer Championships, Italy — A256

No. 849, Players, diff. No. 850, Goalkeeper, flags. No. 851, Team.

1990, Oct. 27 Litho. ***Perf. 11½***
Granite Paper

848 A256 200fr shown 1.75 1.00
849 A256 250fr multicolored 2.25 1.25
850 A256 250fr multicolored 2.25 1.25
851 A256 300fr multicolored 3.00 1.50
a. Souv. sheet of 4, #848-851 9.00 6.50
Nos. 848-851 (4) 9.25 5.00

Roger Milla, World Cup Soccer Player A257

1990, July 4 Litho. ***Perf. 11½***
Granite Paper

852 A257 500fr multicolored 6.50 3.50
a. Souv. sheet of 1 9.00 6.00

Agriculture A258

70fr, Treating cacao plants. 100fr, Sheep.

1990, Dec. 1 Litho. ***Perf. 13½***

853 A258 70fr multicolored 1.25 .55
854 A258 100fr multicolored 1.75 .80
a. Sheet of 2, #853-854, perf. 12½ 8.00 8.00

For surcharges see Nos. 894-895.

UN Development Program, 40th Anniv. — A259

1990, Dec. 31 Litho. ***Perf. 13½***

855 A259 50fr multicolored .60 .40

Intl. Literacy Year A260

1990, Dec. 31

856 A260 200fr bl, blk, & lt bl 2.00 .75

Independence, 30th Anniv. — A261

1000fr, Flag, Palace, #336.

1991, Jan. 1 ***Perf. 13***

857 A261 150fr shown 1.75 1.25
858 A261 1000fr multi 9.00 8.00
a. Souv. sheet. of 2, #857-858 12.50 12.50

A262

Fight Against AIDS — A262a

1991, Jan. 15

859 A262 15fr Hearts, map, vert. .25 .25
860 A262a 25fr shown .35 .25

See Nos. 884-885.

Birds A263

Designs: Nos. 861, 864, Pie grieche, vert. Nos. 862, 863, Picathartes chauve.

1991, May 3 Litho. ***Perf. 13½***

861 A263 70fr grn & multi .75 .35
862 A263 70fr bl & multi .75 .40
863 A263 300fr blk & multi 3.25 2.00
864 A263 350fr blk & multi 3.50 2.25
a. Souv. sheet of 2, #863-864 9.00 5.50
Nos. 861-864 (4) 8.25 5.00

Wild Animals A264

1991, May 8 ***Perf. 13½***

865 A264 125fr Elephant 1.60 1.00
866 A264 250fr Water buffalo 3.00 2.00
a. Souvenir sheet of 2, #865-866, perf. 12½ 9.00 3.50

City Hall Type of 1982 Redrawn

1991 ***Perf. 13***

867 A202 40fr multicolored .60 .25

No. 867 inscribed "Republic of Cameroon" instead of "United Republic of Cameroon."

Cameroun Catholic Church, Cent. (in 1990) A265

125fr, Mvolye church. 250fr, Akono church.

1991, Dec. 8 Litho. ***Perf. 13½***

868 A265 125fr multicolored 1.25 .75
a. Booklet pane of 4 7.00 —
Complete booklet, #868a 7.00
869 A265 250fr multicolored 2.25 1.75
a. Souvenir sheet of 2, #868-869 perf. 12½x13 4.00 3.00
b. Booklet pane of 4 10.00 —
Complete booklet, #869a 10.00

Issued: Nos. 868a, 869b, 1993.

Intl. Savings Banks Institute, 7th Meeting of the African Group A266

1991, Dec. 9

870 A266 250fr multicolored 2.40 1.60
a. Souv. sheet of 1, perf. 12½x13 3.00 2.00

No. 799 Surcharged

No. 824 Surcharged

1992 ***Perf. 13½***

871 A214 20fr on 150fr #799 1.75 .25
872 A245 70fr on 300fr #824 5.75 .55

Bird Type of 1983

1992 Litho. ***Perf. 13½***

873 A214 125fr like #800 1.50 .95

Dated 1985.

Cameroun Soccer League A267

125fr, Mbappe Mbappe Samuel (1936-85), soccer player, vert. 250fr, Linafoote League emblem, vert. 400fr, Linafoote emblem, diff. 500fr, Stadium.

1992, Aug. ***Perf. 11½***

874 A267 125fr multicolored	1.25	.75
875 A267 250fr multicolored	2.40	1.75
876 A267 400fr multicolored	3.50	2.75
877 A267 500fr multicolored	5.50	3.50
Nos. 874-877 (4)	12.65	8.75

See Nos. 896-896B.

Discovery of America, 500th Anniv. A268

Columbus and: 125fr, Fleet of ships. 250fr, Landing in New World. 400fr, Meeting with natives. 500fr, Map, ships.

1992, Aug.

878 A268 125fr multicolored	1.40	.75
879 A268 250fr multicolored	2.10	1.75
880 A268 400fr multicolored	3.50	2.75
881 A268 500fr multicolored	5.00	3.50
Nos. 878-881 (4)	12.00	8.75

Types of 1983-84 Redrawn

1992 Litho. ***Perf. 13½***

882 A214 200fr like #739	2.25	1.40
a. Booklet pane of 5		
Complete booklet, #882a		
883 A222 350fr like #763	3.75	2.50

Nos. 882-883 inscribed "Republic of Cameroon".

AIDS Type of 1991

1993 Litho. ***Perf. 13½***

884 A262 100fr like #859	1.10	.70
885 A262 175fr like #860	1.90	1.25

Types of 1983 Redrawn

886 A214 370fr like #738	3.50	2.50

Perf. 13

887 A217 410fr like #746	4.50	2.90

Nos. 886-887 inscribed "Republic of Cameroon".

Wild Animal Type of 1980 Redrawn

125fr, Crocodile. 250fr, Buffon's antelope, vert.

1993 Litho. ***Serpentine Die Cut 9½***

Booklet Stamps

Self-Adhesive

888 A186 125fr multicolored	1.40	.65
a. Booklet pane of 4	5.75	
889 A186 250fr multicolored	2.75	1.25
a. Booklet pane of 4	11.50	

Nos. 888-889 inscribed "Republic of Cameroon".

By their nature, Nos. 888a, 889a are complete booklets. The peelable backing serves as a booklet cover.

1994 World Cup Soccer Championships, US — A270

Designs: 125fr, Pres. Paul Biya holding soccer ball, lion. 250fr, Logo, lion, player, map. 450fr, Players, globe, World Cup, flag. 500fr, US eagle, Cameroun lion, soccer ball.

1994, Mar. 28 Litho. ***Perf. 13***

890 A270 125fr multicolored	.75	.40
891 A270 250fr multicolored	1.50	.75
892 A270 450fr multicolored	2.75	1.50
893 A270 500fr multicolored	3.00	1.75
a. Min. sheet of 4, #890-893	55.00	40.00
Nos. 890-893 (4)	8.00	4.40

Nos. 853-854 Srchd. in Gold and Black

1993 Litho. ***Perf. 13½***

894 A258 125fr on 70fr #853	—	6.00
895 A258 125fr on 100fr #854	—	—
a. With gold obliterator, new denomination in black omitted	65.00	—

Cameroun Soccer League Type of 1992

1992-93 Litho. ***Perf. 11½***

896 A267 10fr like #876	—	—
896A A267 25fr like #875	—	—
896B A267 50fr like #874	—	—

Nos. 896-896A dated 1993.

Issued: 50fr, 8/1/92; others, 1993.

Psittacus Erithacus — A271

1995 Litho. ***Perf. 11½***

Granite Paper

897 A271 125fr multicolored	3.00	1.00

Visit of Pope John Paul II A272

125fr, Pope, open text, cross.

1995, Sept. 14 ***Perf. 12½***

898 A272 55fr shown	.35	.25
a. Souvenir sheet of 1	—	
899 A272 125fr multicolored	.95	.50
a. Souvenir sheet of 1	—	

UN, 50th Anniv. A273

1995, Oct. 24 ***Perf. 11½***

900 A273 200fr shown	1.25	.60
901 A273 250fr "50," people	1.50	.80

Conf. of Heads of State & Govt., Yaounde A274

Perf. 12½, 14¾x14 (200fr, 250fr)

1996-97 Litho.

902 A274 125fr blue & multi	1.00	.50
c. A274 125fr Perf. 14¾x14	—	.75
902A A274 200fr lt grn & multi ('97)	1.50	.75
902B A274 250fr yel & multi ('97)	2.00	1.00
903 A274 410fr pink & multi, vert.	3.00	2.00

No. 902c is dated "1997."

World Records Set at 1996 Summer Olympic Games, Atlanta A275

125fr, Baily, M. Johnson. 250fr, Harrison, Galfione, Perec, vert.

1996 ***Perf. 11½***

904 A275 125fr multi	—	1.50
905 A275 250fr multi	—	2.00

Universal Declaration of Human Rights, 50th Anniv. — A279

1998 Litho. ***Perf. 14x14¾***

918 A279 370fr multicolored	6.00	2.00

1998 World Cup Soccer Championships, France — A280

Design: 125fr, Flag of Cameroun, World Cup trophy, vert.

1998 Litho. ***Perf. 13***

922 A280 125fr multicolored	—	2.00
923 A280 250fr multicolored	7.00	2.50

Shrike A281

1998 Litho. ***Perf. 13x13½***

926 A281 125fr multicolored	22.50	2.00

Economic and Monetary Community of Central Africa Week — A281a

Design: 125fr, Flags surrounding map of Africa. 225fr, Flags above map of Africa.

1999 Litho. ***Perf. 14½***

927 A281a 125fr multi	—	—
928 A281a 225fr multi	—	—

Flora & Fauna — A282

2000 Litho. ***Perf. 14x14½***

929 A282 100fr Pineapple	11.00	2.00
930 A282 125fr Pineapple	—	2.00
930A A282 150fr Coffee beans	12.00	3.00
930B A282 175fr Crowned crane	—	—
931 A282 200fr Baboon	20.00	2.00
932 A282 250fr Coffee beans	12.00	2.00
934 A282 410fr Crowned crane	20.00	2.00

Dated 1998.

Peace, Work, Country A283

Map and Scenes — A284

Airplane and Wildlife — A285

2000 Litho. ***Perf. 11¾***

935 A283 125fr multi	20.00	2.00
936 A284 200fr multi	20.00	2.00
937 A285 250fr multi	20.00	2.00

Palais des Congrés, Yaounde A286

Perf. 11¾x11½

2001, Mar. 26 **Litho.**

938 A286 125fr multi	—	—

Cooperation between Cameroun and People's Republic of China, 30th anniv.

Campaign Against AIDS — A287

Design: 125fr, Woman vaccinating child, Chantal Biya Foundation emblem. 250fr, Chantal Biya Foundation emblem, globe, ribbon, woman with fetus.

2001 Litho. ***Perf. 13¼x13***

939 A287 125fr multi	12.50	4.00
941 A287 250fr multi	12.50	4.00
a. Souvenir sheet, #939, 941	150.00	—

2002 World Cup Soccer Championships, Japan and Korea — A287a

Indomitable Lions Soccer Team, 20th Anniv. of Success A288

2002, June 20 Litho. ***Perf. 13¾***

943 A287a 125fr multi	50.00	3.00

Perf. 13x13¼

944 A288 250fr multi	50.00	3.00

Souvenir Sheet

945 Sheet of 2, #943, 945a	100.00	—
a. As #944, 40x44mm, perf. 13½	—	—

71st Interpol General Assembly, Yaounde — A289

2002 Litho. *Perf. 13¼x13*

946 A289 125fr multi *11.00* —
a. Souvenir sheet of 1 *27.50* —

Cooperation Between Cameroun and Japan — A290

2005 Litho. *Perf. 13*

948 A290 100fr multi *20.00 1.50*
a. "Postes 2005" *12.00 1.00*
949 A290 125fr multi *20.00 1.50*
a. "Postes 2005" *12.00 1.00*
950 A290 200fr multi *20.00 1.50*
a. "Postes 2005" *12.00 1.00*
951 A290 250fr multi *15.00 1.50*
a. "Postes 2005" *12.00 1.00*
952 A290 370fr multi — —
953 A290 410fr multi *12.00 2.00*
954 A290 500fr multi *21.00 3.50*
a. "Postes 2005" *12.00 2.00*
955 A290 1000fr multi *28.00 6.50*
a. "Postes 2005" *12.00 4.00*

Cameroun postal officials have declared as illegal a stamp inscribed "Republic of Cameroon" dated "2005" marking the 70th birthday of Elvis Presley.

Postal Savings Bank — A291

2006 Litho. *Perf. 15x14*

956 A291 500fr multi — —

No. 956 was issued in 1997 as a stamp to pay fees for opening an account with the Postal Savings Bank. It was made available for postal use in 2006.

Visit of Pope Benedict XVI to Cameroun A292

Flags of Vatican City and Cameroun, Pope Benedict XVI, Pres. Paul Biya and background color of: 200fr, Yellow. 250fr, Bright pink.

2009 Litho. *Perf. 13x13¼*

957-958 A292 Set of 2 6.00 3.00

New Challenges for Africa Conference, Yaounde — A293

Colors: 125fr, Black & gray. 250fr, Multicolored.

2010 Litho. *Perf. 13½*

959-960 A293 Set of 2 *5.75* —

Reunification and Independence, 50th Anniv. — A294

Designs: 125fr, Cameroun flag shown rotated 90 degrees clockwise. 200fr, 50th anniversary emblem. 250fr, Arms of Cameroun. 500fr, Pres. Paul Biya in black.
1000fr, Pres. Biya in color.

2010

961-964 A294 Set of 4 *20.00 9.00*
964a Horiz. strip of 4, #961-964 *20.00* —
964b Booklet pane of 8, 2 each #961-964 *40.00* —
Complete booklet, #964b *40.00*

Souvenir Sheet

965 A294 1000fr multi *20.00* —

No. 965 sold for 1500fr.

A295

Designs: 125fr, Workers digging trenches for optical fibers. 200fr, Gynecological, Obstetrics and Pediatric Hospital, Yaoundé. 250fr, Multi-purpose Sports Complex, Yaounde. 500fr, Cameroun Pres. Paul Biya and Chinese Pres. Hu Jintao shaking hands.

2011, Mar. 26 *Perf. 12*

966-969 A295 Set of 4 *20.00 8.00*
968a Souvenir sheet of 3, #966-968 *15.00* —

Diplomatic Relations Between Cameroun and People's Republic of China, 25th Anniv.
See Nos. 975-976.

First Douala-Paris Camair-Co Flight — A296

Litho. & Embossed

2011, Mar. 28 *Perf. 13x13¼*

Denomination Color

970 A296 250fr green *8.00 3.00*
971 A296 500fr white *8.00 3.00*
a. Souvenir sheet of 2, #970-971 20.00 —

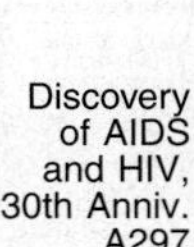

Discovery of AIDS and HIV, 30th Anniv. A297

Designs: 100fr, Emblem of Cameroun National Committee for the Campaign Against AIDS. 250fr, AIDS ribbon, map of Africa. 500fr, Chantal Biya, First Lady of Cameroun and founder of Synergies Africaines charity.

2011, June 3 Litho.

972-974 A297 Set of 3 *11.00 6.00*

Diplomatic Relations Type of 2011

Souvenir Sheets

Design as before.

2011, Sept. 14 Litho. *Perf. 12*

975 A295 500fr multi *15.00* —

Litho. With Three-Dimensional Plastic Affixed

Without Gum

976 A295 500fr multi *30.00* —

No. 975 contains one 60x40mm stamp. No. 976 contains one 76x50mm stamp.

E-Post Data Center A298

2014, July 21 Litho. *Perf. 13x13¼*

Panel Color

977 A298 70fr yellow *1.50 1.50*
978 A298 250fr black *1.50 1.50*

EMS Emblem, Sprinter, Cameroun Post Office, Pyramid, Eiffel Tower and Statue of Liberty A299

2014, Aug. 18 Litho. *Perf. 13x13¼*

Panel Color

979 A299 50fr white *1.50 1.50*
980 A299 200fr dark blue *1.50 1.50*

A300

Reunification Monument, Buéa — A301

2015 Litho. *Perf. 13*

981 A300 100fr multi *6.00 3.00*

Perf. 13x13¼

982 A301 125fr multi *6.00 3.00*

Values for No. 981 are for stamps with surrounding selvage.

Deep Water Port, Kribi A302

2015 Litho. *Perf. 13¼x13*

983 A302 500fr multi *6.00 3.00*

SEMI-POSTAL STAMPS

Curie Issue

Common Design Type

1938 Unwmk. *Perf. 13*

B1 CD80 1.75fr + 50c brt ultra 10.00 10.00

French Revolution Issue

Common Design Type

Photogravure; Name and Value Typographed in Black

1939

B2 CD83 45c + 25c green 11.50 11.50
B3 CD83 70c + 30c brown 11.50 11.50
B4 CD83 90c + 35c red org 11.50 11.50
B5 CD83 1.25fr + 1fr rose pink 11.50 11.50
B6 CD83 2.25fr + 2fr blue 14.00 14.00
Nos. B2-B6 (5) 60.00 60.00

Stamps of 1925-33 Srchd. in Black

1940 *Perf. 14x13½*

B7 A7 1.25fr + 2fr gray & dp bl 32.50 24.00
B8 A7 1.75fr + 3fr brn & org 32.50 24.00
B9 A7 2fr + 5fr dl grn & brn org 32.50 24.00
Nos. B7-B9 (3) 97.50 72.00

The surtax was used for war relief work.

Regular Stamps of 1939 Surcharged in Black

1940 *Perf. 13*

B10 A20 25c + 5fr blk brn 130.00 110.00
B11 A20 45c + 5fr slate grn 130.00 110.00
B12 A20 60c + 5fr peacock bl 130.00 120.00
B13 A20 70c + 5fr plum 130.00 120.00
Nos. B10-B13 (4) 520.00 460.00

The surtax was used to purchase Spitfire planes for the Free French army.

Common Design Type and

Military Doctor SP2

Cameroun Militiaman — SP4

1941 Photo. *Perf. 13½*

B13A SP2 1fr + 1fr red 1.60
B13B CD86 1.50fr + 3fr maroon 1.60
B13C SP4 2.50fr + 1fr dk bl 1.60
Nos. B13A-B13C (3) 4.80

Nos. B13A-B13C were issued by the Vichy government in France, but were not placed on sale in Cameroun.

Nos. 223-224 Surcharged in Black or Blue

1941 *Perf. 12½x12*

B14 CD82 1.25fr + 10fr car lake 120.00 120.00
B15 CD82 2.25fr + 10fr ultra 120.00 120.00

Nos. 223-224 Surcharged in Black or Blue

1941

B16 CD82 1.25fr + 10fr car lake (Bl) 40.00 40.00
B17 CD82 2.25fr + 10fr ultra (Bk) 40.00 40.00

The surtax was used to purchase ambulances for the Free French army.

Regular Stamps of 1933-39 Surcharged in Black

1943 ***Perf. 14x13½, 13, 12½x12***

B21 A7 1.25fr + 100 gray & dp bl 27.50 27.50
B22 A21 1.25fr + 100fr car rose 27.50 27.50
B23 CD82 1.25fr + 100fr car lake 27.50 27.50
B24 A21 1.50fr + 100fr choc 27.50 27.50
B25 CD82 2.25fr + 100fr ultra 27.50 27.50
Nos. B21-B25 (5) 137.50 137.50

Nos. 281A-281B Surcharged in Black or Red

1944 **Engr.** ***Perf. 12½x12***

B25A 50c + 1.50fr on 2.50fr deep blue (R) .40
B25B + 2.50fr on 1fr green .40

Colonial Development Fund.

Nos. B25A-B25B were issued by the Vichy government in France, but were not placed on sale in Cameroun.

Red Cross Issue

Common Design Type

1944 **Photo.** ***Perf. 14½x14***

B28 CD90 5fr + 20fr rose 2.00 1.60

The surtax was for the French Red Cross and national relief.

Catalogue values for unused stamps in this section, from this point to the end of the section, are for Never Hinged items.

Tropical Medicine Issue

Common Design Type

1950 **Engr.** ***Perf. 13***

B29 CD100 10fr + 2fr dk bl grn & dk grn 7.25 5.50

The surtax was for charitable work.

Independent State

Map and Flag — SP7

Unwmk.

1961, Mar. 25 **Engr.** ***Perf. 13***

B30 SP7 20fr + 5fr grn, car & yel 1.10 1.00
B31 SP7 25fr + 10fr multi 1.40 1.25
B32 SP7 30fr + 15fr car, yel & grn 2.00 1.75
Nos. B30-B32 (3) 4.50 4.00

The surtax was for the Red Cross.

Federal Republic

Map of Cameroun, Lions Emblem and Physician Helping Leper
SP8

1962, Jan. 28

B33 SP8 20fr + 5fr multi .70 .40
B34 SP8 25fr + 10fr multi .90 .50
B35 SP8 50fr + 15fr multi 1.75 .85
Nos. B33-B35 (3) 3.35 1.75

Issued for leprosy relief work.

Anti-Malaria Issue

Common Design Type

1962, Apr. 7 ***Perf. 12½x12***

B36 CD108 25fr + 5fr rose lilac 1.00 .45

WHO drive to eradicate malaria.

Freedom from Hunger Issue

Common Design Type

1963, Mar. 21 **Engr.** ***Perf. 13***

B37 CD112 18fr + 5fr multi 1.00 .35
B38 CD112 25fr + 5fr multi 1.25 .40

Antelopes — SP9

Designs: 125fr+10fr, Ourebia ourebi. 250fr+20fr, Kobus defassa.

1991, Apr. 30 **Litho.** ***Perf. 13½x13***

B39 SP9 125fr + 10fr multi 2.00 1.10
B40 SP9 250fr + 20fr multi 3.00 2.25
a. Souvenir sheet of 2, #B39-B40, perf. 12½ 8.00 8.00

AIR POST STAMPS

Common Design Type

1942 **Unwmk.** **Photo.** ***Perf. 14½x14***

C1 CD87 1fr dk orange .30 .30
C2 CD87 1.50fr brt red .30 .30
C3 CD87 5fr brown red .65 .65
C4 CD87 10fr black .80 .80
C5 CD87 25fr ultra 1.10 1.10
C6 CD87 50fr dk green 1.40 1.40
C7 CD87 100fr plum 1.75 1.75
Nos. C1-C7 (7) 6.30 6.30

Types AP9 and AP10 without "RF" and

Plane Over Coast
AP3

1943-44 **Photo.** ***Perf. 13, 13½***

C7A AP9 25c brown red .25
C7B AP9 50c green .25
C7C AP9 1fr brt violet .30
C7D AP10 5fr red brown .55
C7E AP10 10fr black .65
C7F AP10 12fr orange .70
C7G AP10 20fr crimson .95
C7H AP10 50fr blue 1.10
C7I AP3 100fr lilac brown 1.25
Nos. C7A-C7I (9) 6.00

Nos. C7A to C7I were issued by the Vichy Government in France, but were not placed on sale in Cameroun.

For Types AP9 and AP10 inscribed RF, see Nos. C15-C24.

Catalogue values for unused stamps in this section, from this point to the end of the section, are for Never Hinged items.

Victory Issue

Common Design Type

1946, May 8 **Engr.** ***Perf. 12½***

C8 CD92 8fr dk violet brn 1.60 1.20

European victory of the Allied Nations in WWII.

Chad to Rhine Issue

Common Design Types

1946, June 6

C9 CD93 5fr dk blue grn 1.60 1.25
C10 CD94 10fr dk rose vio 1.60 1.25
C11 CD95 15fr red 2.00 1.60
C12 CD96 20fr brt blue 2.00 1.60
C13 CD97 25fr orange red 2.10 1.75
C14 CD98 50fr gray 2.75 2.25
Nos. C9-C14 (6) 12.05 9.70

Plane and Map — AP9

Seaplane Alighting
AP10

Plane and Freighters
AP11

1946 **Photo.** ***Perf. 13, 13½***

C15 AP9 25c brown red .40 .25
C16 AP9 50c green .40 .25
C17 AP9 1fr brt violet .50 .30
C18 AP10 2fr olive grn .65 .50
C19 AP10 3fr chocolate .65 .50
C20 AP10 4fr deep ultra .65 .50
C21 AP10 6fr blue grn .65 .50
C22 AP10 7fr brt violet 1.10 .80
C23 AP10 12fr orange 5.50 3.50
C24 AP10 20fr crimson 1.90 1.40
C25 AP11 50fr dk ultra 2.75 1.90
Nos. C15-C25 (11) 15.15 10.40

Nos. C15 to C25 were issued in 1941 in France by the Vichy Government, but were not sold in Cameroun until 1946.

See Nos. C7A-C7H for stamps without "RF."

Birds over Mountains — AP12

Cavalry and Plane — AP13

Warrior, Dance Mask and Nose of Plane — AP14

Perf. 12½

1947, Feb. 10 **Unwmk.** **Engr.**

C26 AP12 50fr dk green 3.25 1.20
C27 AP13 100fr brn red 4.75 1.20
C28 AP14 200fr black 7.25 2.40
Nos. C26-C28 (3) 15.25 4.80

UPU Issue

Common Design Type

1949, July ***Perf. 13***

C29 CD99 25fr multicolored 8.00 4.75

Rhumsiki Peak — AP16

1953, Feb. 16

C30 AP16 500fr grnsh blk, dk vio & vio bl 26.00 4.00

For surcharge see No. C40.

Edéa Dam and Sacred Ibis — AP17

1953, Nov. 18

C31 AP17 15fr choc, brn lake & ultra 5.50 1.60

Dedication of Edea Dam on the Sanaga River.

Liberation Issue

Common Design Type

1954, June 6

C32 CD102 15fr dk grnsh bl & bl grn 7.25 4.75

Dr. Eugene Jamot, Research Laboratory and Tsetse Flies — AP19

1954, Nov. 29

C33 AP19 15fr dk grn, ind & dk brn 4.75 2.75

75th anniv. of the birth of Dr. Eugene Jamot.

Logging — AP20

100fr, Giraffes. 200fr, Port of Douala.

1955, Jan. 24

C34 AP20 50fr ol grn, brn & vio brn 4.00 .80
C35 AP20 100fr grnsh bl, brn & dk brn 8.00 1.60
C36 AP20 200fr dk grn, choc & dp ultra 10.50 2.40
Nos. C34-C36 (3) 22.50 4.80

For surcharges see Nos. C38-C39.

Federal Republic
Air Afrique Issue
Common Design Type
Unwmk.

1962, Feb. 17 Engr. *Perf. 13*
C37 CD107 25fr mar, pur & lt grn 1.00 .50

Nos. C35-C36 and C30 Surcharged in Red

Type I

Two types of 5sh:
I — "5/-" measures 6½x4mm.
II — "5/" measures 3¾x3mm, No dash after diagonal line.

Three types of 10sh:
I — "10/-" measures 9x3¾mm.
II — "10/-" measures 7x2½-3mm.
III — "1" of "10/" vertically in line with last "E" of "FEDERALE".

Two types of £1:
I — "REPUBLIQUE / FEDERALE" 17¼mm wide.
II — "REPUBLIQUE / FEDERALE" 22mm wide.

1961, Oct. 1 Engr. *Perf. 13*
C38 AP20 5sh on 100fr (I) 10.00 6.00
a. Type II 32.50 18.00
C39 AP20 10sh on 200fr (I) 22.00 13.00
a. Type II 77.50 42.50
b. Type III 32.50 30.00
C40 AP16 £1 on 500fr (I) 35.00 22.00
a. Type II 60.00 35.00
Nos. C38-C40 (3) 67.00 41.00

Issued for use in the former United Kingdom Trust Territory of Southern Cameroons.

Kapsikis Mokolo — AP21

Designs: 50fr, Cocotieres Hotel, Douala. 100fr, Cymothoe sangaris butterflies. 200fr, Ostriches, Waza Reservation.

1962, June 15
C41 AP21 50fr sl grn, bl & dl red .90 .25
C42 AP21 100fr multicolored 5.75 .60
C43 AP21 200fr dk grn, blk & bis 8.00 1.40
C44 AP21 500fr vio brn, bl & ocher 9.00 2.25
Nos. C41-C44 (4) 23.65 4.50

Telstar Type of Regular Issue

1963, Feb. 9 Size: 48x27mm
C45 A50 100fr dk grn & red brn 2.50 .65

Edéa Relay Station — AP22

1963, May 18 Photo. *Perf. 12x12½*
C46 AP22 100fr multicolored 2.50 .65

Issued to publicize the high frequency telegraph connection Douala-Yaoundé.

African Postal Union Issue
Common Design Type

1963, Sept. 8 Unwmk. *Perf. 12½*
C47 CD114 85fr ultra, ocher & red 2.25 1.00

Air Afrique Issue, 1963
Common Design Type

1963, Nov. 19 *Perf. 13x12*
C48 CD115 50fr pink, gray, blk & grn 1.25 .40

Olympic Games Type of 1964

300fr, Greco-Roman wrestlers (ancient).

1964, Oct. 10 Engr. *Perf. 13*
C49 A57 300fr red, dk brn & dl grn 7.50 2.00
a. Sheet of 3, #403-404, C49 13.50 4.25

Kribi Port — AP25

1964, Oct. 26 Unwmk. *Perf. 13*
C50 AP25 50fr red brn, ultra & grn 1.00 .35

Black Rhinoceros — AP26

1964, Dec. 15 Engr. *Perf. 13*
C51 AP26 250fr brn red, grn & dk brn 10.00 3.00

Pres. John F. Kennedy — AP27

1964, Dec. 8 Photo. *Perf. 12½*
C52 AP27 100fr grn, yel grn & brn 2.50 1.10
a. Souvenir sheet of 4 10.00 4.50

Pres. John F. Kennedy (1917-63).

Abraham Lincoln — AP28

1965, Apr. 20 Unwmk. *Perf. 13*
C53 AP28 100fr multicolored 2.50 .80

Abraham Lincoln, death centenary.

Syncom Satellite and ITU Emblem — AP29

1965, May 17 Engr.
C54 AP29 70fr red, dk bl, & blk 1.60 .60

Cent. of the ITU.

Sir Winston Spencer Churchill, Statesman and World War II Leader — AP30

Designs: 12fr, Churchill giving V sign. 18fr, Churchill, battleship and oak leaves with acorns.

Perf. 13x12½

1965, May 28 Photo. Unwmk.
C55 12fr multicolored 1.00 .50
C56 18fr multicolored 1.00 .50
a. AP40 Strip of 2, #C55-C56 + label 2.75 1.40

ICY Type of Regular Issue

1965, Sept. 11 Engr. *Perf. 13*
C57 A68 100fr dk red & dk bl 2.25 .70

Racing Boat, Sanaga River, Edéa — AP31

1965, Oct. 27 Unwmk. *Perf. 13*
C58 AP31 50fr brn, dk grn & sl 2.25 .35

Edward H. White Floating in Space and Gemini IV — AP32

Designs: 50fr, Vostok 6. 200fr, Gemini V and REP (rendezvous evaluation pod). 500fr, Gemini VI & VII rendezvous.

1966, Mar. 30 Engr. *Perf. 13*
C59 AP32 50fr car rose & dk sl grn .90 .35
C60 AP32 100fr red lil & vio bl 2.10 .65
C61 AP32 200fr ultra & dk pur 3.75 1.40
C62 AP32 500fr brt bl & indigo 9.00 3.00
Nos. C59-C62 (4) 15.75 5.40

Man's conquest of space.

Hotel Type of Regular Issue

18fr, Mountain Hotel, Buea. 25fr, Hotel Akwa Palace, Douala. 50fr, Terminus Hotel, Yaoundé. 60fr, Imperial Hotel, Yaoundé. 85fr, Independence Hotel, Yaoundé. 100fr, Hunting Lodge, Mora, vert. 150fr, Boukarous (round huts), Waza Camp.

1966
C63 A71 18fr sl grn, brt bl & blk .45 .25
C64 A71 25fr car, ultra & sl .65 .25
C65 A71 50fr choc, grn & ocher 2.50 .90
C66 A71 60fr choc, grn & brt bl 1.50 .50
C67 A71 85fr dk car rose, dl bl & grn 1.90 .60
C68 A71 100fr brn, grn & sl 2.75 .70
C69 A71 150fr brn, dl bl & ocher 3.75 .90
Nos. C63-C69 (7) 13.50 4.05

Issued: Nos. C63-C64, 4/6; Nos. C65-C69, 6/4.

Flower Type of Regular Issue

Flowers: 25fr, Hibiscus mutabilis. 50fr, Delonix regia. 100fr, Bougainvillea.

1966, May 20 Photo. *Perf. 12½*
Flowers in Natural Colors
Size: 26x45mm
C70 A75 25fr slate green .75 .25
C71 A75 50fr brt grnsh bl 1.60 .25
C72 A75 100fr gold 3.25 .25
Nos. C70-C72 (3) 5.60 .65

Military Police — AP33

25fr, "Army," soldier, tanks & parachutes. 60fr, "Navy," & "Vigilante." 100fr, "Air Force," plane.

1966, June 21 Engr. *Perf. 13*
C73 AP33 20fr vio bl, org brn & dl pur .55 .25
C74 AP33 25fr dk grn, dl pur & brn .55 .25
C75 AP33 60fr bl grn, bl & ind 1.60 .30
C76 AP33 100fr brn, Prus bl & car rose 2.75 .65
Nos. C73-C76 (4) 5.45 1.45

Issued to honor Cameroun's armed forces.

Wembley Stadium, London — AP34

1966, July 20
C77 AP34 50fr shown 1.40 .25
C78 AP34 200fr Soccer 4.75 1.10

8th World Cup Soccer Championship, Wembley, England, July 11-30.

Air Afrique Issue, 1966
Common Design Type

1966, Aug. 31 Photo. *Perf. 13*
C79 CD123 25fr red lil, blk & gray .80 .25

Yaoundé Cathedral — AP35

18fr, Buea Cathedral. 30fr, Orthodox Church, Yaoundé. 60fr, Mosque, Garoua.

1966, Dec. 19 Engr. *Perf. 13*
C80 AP35 18fr choc, bl & grn .45 .25
C81 AP35 25fr brn, grn & brt vio .55 .25
C82 AP35 30fr lil, grn & dl red .70 .25
C83 AP35 60fr mar, brt grn & grn 1.40 .35
Nos. C80-C83 (4) 3.10 1.10

Pioneer A and Moon — AP36

1967, Apr. 30 Engr. *Perf. 13*

C84 AP36 25fr shown .50 .25
C85 AP36 50fr Ranger 6 .90 .35
C86 AP36 100fr Luna 9 2.25 .65
C87 AP36 250fr Luna 10 4.75 2.00
Nos. C84-C87 (4) 8.40 3.25

"Conquest of the Moon."

Flower Type of Regular Issue

200fr, Thevetia Peruviana. 250fr, Amaryllis.

1967, June 22 Photo. *Perf. 12½*
Size: 26x46mm

C88 A86 200fr multi 4.50 .90
C89 A86 250fr multi 5.50 1.10

African Postal Union Issue, 1967
Common Design Type

1967, Sept. 9 Engr. *Perf. 13*

C90 CD124 100fr red brn, Prus bl & brt lil 2.40 .65

Skis, Ice Skates, Olympic Flame and Emblem — AP38

1967, Oct. 11 Engr. *Perf. 13*

C91 AP38 30fr ultra & sepia 1.60 .25

Issued to publicize the 10th Winter Olympic Games, Grenoble, Feb. 6-8, 1968.

Cameroun Exhibit, EXPO '67 — AP39

100fr, Bangwa house poles carved with ancestor figures. 200fr, Canadian Pavilions.

1967, Oct. 18

C92 AP39 50fr mag, ol & mar 1.00 .25
C93 AP39 100fr dk grn, mar & dk brn 3.25 .70
C94 AP39 200fr brn, lil rose & sl grn 4.25 1.25
Nos. C92-C94 (3) 8.50 2.20

EXPO '67, International Exhibition, Montreal, Apr. 28-Oct. 27, 1967.
See note after No. C116 regarding 1969 moon overprint.

Konrad Adenauer (1876-1967), Chancellor of West Germany (1949-63) and Cologne Cathedral AP40

70fr, Adenauer and Chancellery, Bonn.

1967, Dec. 1 Photo. *Perf. 12½*

C95 AP40 30fr multi .90 .25
C96 AP40 70fr multi 1.50 .40
a. Pair, #C95-C96 + label 3.50 2.50

Pres. Ahidjo, King Faisal and View of Mecca — AP41

60fr, Pres. Ahidjo, Pope Paul VI & view of Rome.

1968, Feb. 18 Photo. *Perf. 12½*

C97 AP41 30fr multi .90 .25
C98 AP41 60fr multi 2.10 .30

Issued to commemorate President Ahidjo's Pilgrimage to Mecca and visit to Rome.

Earth on Television Transmitted by Explorer VI — AP42

30fr, Molniya spacecraft. 40fr, Earth on television screen transmitted by Molniya.

1968, Apr. 20 Engr. *Perf. 13*

C99 AP42 20fr multi .55 .25
C100 AP42 30fr multi .80 .25
C101 AP42 40fr multi 1.10 .25
Nos. C99-C101 (3) 2.45 .75

Telecommunication by satellite.

Forge — AP43

No. C103, Tea harvest. No. C104, Trans-Cameroun railroad (diesel train emerging from tunnel). 40fr, Rubber harvest. 60fr, Douala Harbor, horiz.

1968, June 5 Engr. *Perf. 13*

C102 AP43 20fr red brn, dk grn & ind .60 .25
C103 AP43 30fr dk brn, grn & ultra 1.10 .35
C104 AP43 30fr ind, sl grn & bis brn 7.50 2.50
C105 AP43 40fr ol bis, dk grn & bl grn 1.10 .35
C106 AP43 60fr ultra, dk brn & sl 3.00 1.00
Nos. C102-C106 (5) 13.30 4.45

Second Economic Development Five-Year Plan.

Boxing — AP44

50fr, Long jump. 60fr, Athlete on rings.

1968, Aug. 19 Engr. *Perf. 13*

C107 AP44 30fr brt grn, dk grn & choc .65 .25
C108 AP44 50fr brt grn, brn red & choc 1.25 .30
C109 AP44 60fr brt grn, ultra & choc 1.50 .35
a. Min. sheet of 3, #C107-C109 4.00 4.00
Nos. C107-C109 (3) 3.40 .90

19th Olympic Games, Mexico City, 10/12-27.

Human Rights Type of Regular Issue

1968, Sept. 14 Photo. *Perf. 12½x13*

C110 A92 30fr grn & brt pink .80 .25

Martin Luther King, Jr. — AP45

Portraits: No. C112, Mahatma Gandhi and map of India. 40fr, John F. Kennedy. 60fr, Robert F. Kennedy. No. C115, Rev. Martin Luther King, Jr. No. C116, Mahatma Gandhi.

1968, Dec. 5 Photo. *Perf. 12½*

C111 AP45 30fr bl & blk .60 .25
C112 AP45 30fr multi .60 .25
C113 AP45 40fr pink & blk 1.00 .50
C114 AP45 60fr bluish lil & blk 1.25 .50
C115 AP45 70fr yel grn & blk 1.40 .60
a. Souvenir sheet of 4, #C112-C115 8.00 8.00
C116 AP45 70fr multi 1.40 .60
Nos. C111-C116 (6) 6.25 2.70

Issued to honor exponents of non-violence. The 2 King stamps (Nos. C111 and C115), the 2 Gandhi stamps (Nos. C112 and C116) and the 2 Kennedy stamps (Nos. C113-C114) are each printed as triptychs with a descriptive label between.

In 1969 Nos. C111-C116 and C94 were overprinted in carmine capitals: "Premier Homme / sur la Lune / 20 Juillet 1969" and "First Man / Landing on Moon / 20 July 1969". Two types of overprints were used: Type I - English and French text 25mm apart; Type II - English and French text close together. Values: on No. C94, $50; on Nos. C111-C116, $325; on No. C115a (2 different souvenir sheets, with both overprint types on different stamps), each $300.

PHILEXAFRIQUE Issue

The Letter, by Armand Cambon AP46

1968, Dec. 10

C117 AP46 100fr multi 3.25 1.25

PHILEXAFRIQUE, Philatelic Exhibition in Abidjan, Feb. 14-23, 1969. Printed with alternating light green label.

2nd PHILEXAFRIQUE Issue
Common Design Type

Design: Cameroun #199 and Wouri Bridge.

1969, Feb. 14 Engr. *Perf. 13*

C118 CD128 50fr multi 3.25 1.25

Caladium Bicolor — AP47

Flowers: 50fr, Aristolochia elegans. 100fr, Gloriosa simplex.

1969, May 14 Photo. *Perf. 12½*

C119 AP47 30fr lil & multi .75 .25
C120 AP47 50fr grn & multi 1.50 .40
C121 AP47 100fr brn & multi 3.50 1.00
Nos. C119-C121 (3) 5.75 1.65

3rd Intl. Flower Show, Paris, Apr. 23-Oct. 5.

Douala Post Office — AP48

50fr, Buèa P.O. 100fr, Bafoussam P.O.

1969, June 19 Engr. *Perf. 13*

C122 AP48 30fr grn, vio bl & brn .55 .25
C123 AP48 50fr sl, emer & red brn .90 .25
C124 AP48 100fr dk brn, brt grn & brn 1.75 .50
Nos. C122-C124 (3) 3.20 1.00

Coronation of Napoleon I, by Jacques Louis David — AP49

Napoleon Crossing Saint Bernard, after J. L. David — AP50

1969, July 4 Photo. *Perf. 12x12½*

C125 AP49 30fr vio bl & multi 1.00 .40

Die-cut Perf. 10
Embossed on Gold Foil

C126 AP50 1000fr gold 45.00 45.00

Bicentenary of birth of Napoleon I.

William E. B. Du Bois (1868-1963), American Writer — AP51

15fr, Dr. Price Mars, Haiti (1876-1969). No. C128, Aimé Cesaire, Martinique (1913-). No. C130, Langston Hughes, US (1902-67). No. C131, Marcus Garvey, Jamaica (1887-1940). 100fr, René Maran, Martinique (1887-1960).

1969, Sept. 25 Photo. *Perf. 12½*

C127 AP51 15fr lt bl & blk .45 .25
C128 AP51 30fr lem & blk .55 .25
C129 AP51 30fr rose brn & blk .55 .25
C130 AP51 50fr gray & blk .80 .25
C131 AP51 50fr emer & blk .80 .25
C132 AP51 100fr yel & blk 2.00 .60
a. Min. sheet of 6, #C127-C132 6.75 4.50
Nos. C127-C132 (6) 5.15 1.85

Issued to honor Negro writers.

ILO Emblem — AP52

1969, Oct. 29 Photo. *Perf. 13*

C133 AP52 30fr blk, bl grn & gray .80 .25
C134 AP52 50fr blk, dp lil rose & gray 1.40 .35

50th anniv. of the ILO.

Armstrong, Collins and Aldrin Splashdown in the Pacific — AP53

Design: 500fr, Landing module and Nell A. Armstrong's first step on moon.

1969, Nov. 29 Photo. *Perf. 12½*

C135 AP53 200fr multi 5.00 1.25
C136 AP53 500fr multi 12.00 3.00

See note after Algeria No. 427.

Pres. Ahidjo, Arms and Map of Cameroun — AP54

Embossed on Gold Foil

1970, Jan. 1 *Die-cut Perf. 10*

C137 AP54 1000fr gold & multi 26.00 25.00

10th anniversary of independence.

Hotel Mont Fébé, Yaoundé — AP55

1970, Jan. 15 Engr. *Perf. 13*

C138 AP55 30fr lt brn, sl grn & gray .80 .25

Lenin — AP56

1970, Jan. 25 Photo. *Perf. 12½*

C139 AP56 50fr org & blk 2.00 .55

Plant Type of Regular Issue

Designs: 50fr, Cleome speciosa (caper). 100fr, Mussaenda erythrophylla (madder).

1970, Mar. 24 Photo. *Perf. 12½*

Size: 26x46mm

C140 A99 50fr blk & multi 1.40 .35
C141 A99 100fr multi 2.75 .90

Map of Africa and Lions Emblem Pinpointing Yaoundé — AP57

1970, May 2 Photo. *Perf. 12½*

C142 AP57 100fr multi 2.25 .75

13th Lions International Congress of District 13, Yaoundé, May 2, 1970.

UN Emblem and Doves — AP58

Design: 50fr, UN emblem and dove, vert.

1970, June 26 Engr. *Perf. 13*

C143 AP58 30fr brn & org 1.00 .25
C144 AP58 50fr Prus bl & sl bl 1.25 .40

25th anniversary of the United Nations.

Japanese Pavilion and EXPO Emblem — AP59

Designs (EXPO Emblem and): 100fr, Map of Japan, vert. 150fr, Australian pavilion.

1970, Aug. 1 Engr. *Perf. 13*

C145 AP59 50fr ind, lt grn & ver .90 .30
C146 AP59 100fr bl, lt grn & red 2.00 .55
C147 AP59 150fr choc, bl & gray 3.25 .65
Nos. C145-C147 (3) 6.15 1.50

EXPO '70 International Exhibition, Osaka, Japan, Mar. 15-Sept. 13.

Charles de Gaulle — AP60

Design: 200fr, de Gaulle in unifrom.

1970, Aug. 27

C148 100fr grn, vio bl & ol brn 2.25 .80
C149 200fr ol brn, vio bl & grn 4.50 1.40
a. AP60 Pair, #C148-C149 + label 8.00 8.00

Rallying of the Free French, 30th anniv. For overprints see Nos. C159-C160.

Pelé and Team — AP61

Designs: 50fr, Aztec Stadium, Mexico City, horiz. 100fr, Mexican soccer team, horiz.

1970, Oct. 14 Photo. *Perf. 12½*

C150 AP61 50fr multi .90 .30
C151 AP61 100fr multi 2.00 .65
C152 AP61 200fr multi 3.50 1.00
Nos. C150-C152 (3) 6.40 1.95

9th World Soccer Championships for the Jules Rimet Cup, Mexico City, May 30-June 21, and the final victory of Brazil over Italy.

Ludwig van Beethoven (1770-1827), Composer AP62

1970, Nov. 23 Engr. *Perf. 13*

C153 AP62 250fr multi 5.75 1.75

Christ at Emmaus, by Rembrandt — AP63

150fr, The Anatomy Lesson, by Rembrandt.

1970, Dec. 5 Photo. *Perf. 12x12½*

C154 AP63 70fr grn & multi 1.40 .35
C155 AP63 150fr multi 2.75 .75

Charles Dickens — AP64

Designs: 50fr, Scenes from David Copperfield. 100fr, Dickens holding quill.

1970, Dec. 22 *Perf. 13*

C156 AP64 40fr blk & rose .95 .25
C157 AP64 50fr bis & multi 1.00 .30
C158 AP64 100fr rose & multi 2.00 .65
a. Strip of 3, #C156-C158 5.00 2.00

Charles Dickens (1812-1870), English novelist.

De Gaulle Type of 1970 Overprinted

1971, Jan. 15 Engr. *Perf. 13*

C159 100fr vio bl, emer & brn red 2.75 .75
C160 200fr brn red, emer & vio bl 5.00 1.25
a. AP60 Pair, #C159-C160 + label 8.00 8.00

In memory of Gen. Charles de Gaulle (1890-1970), President of France.

Timber Storage, Douala — AP65

Industrialization: 70fr, ALUCAM aluminum plant, Edea, vert. 100fr, Mbakaou Dam.

1971, Feb. 14 Engr. *Perf. 13*

C161 AP65 40fr dk red, bl grn & ol brn .55 .25
C162 AP65 70fr ol brn, sl grn & brt bl 1.10 .30
C163 AP65 100fr Prus bl, yel grn & red brn 1.75 .40
Nos. C161-C163 (3) 3.40 .95

Relay Race — AP66

50fr, Torch bearer, vert. 100fr, Discus.

1971, Apr. 24 Engr. *Perf. 13*

C164 AP66 30fr dk brn, ver & ind .65 .25
C165 AP66 50fr blk, bl & choc .80 .25
C166 AP66 100fr multi 1.75 .40
Nos. C164-C166 (3) 3.20 .90

75th anniv. of revival of Olympic Games.

Fishing Trawler — AP67

Designs: 40fr, Local fishermen, Northern Cameroun. 70fr, Fishing harbor, Douala. 150fr, Shrimp boats, Douala.

1971, May 14 Engr. *Perf. 13*

C167 AP67 30fr lt brn, bl & grn .70 .30
C168 AP67 40fr sl grn, bl & dk brn .90 .30
C169 AP67 70fr dk brn, bl & red org 2.00 .40
C170 AP67 150fr multi 4.25 1.00
Nos. C167-C170 (4) 7.85 2.00

Cameroun fishing industry.

Cameroun No. 123 and War Memorial, Yaoundé — AP68

Designs (Cameroun Stamps): 25fr, No. C33 and Jamot memorial. 40fr, No. 431 and government buildings, Yaoundé. 50fr, No. 19 and Imperial German postal emblem. 100fr, No. 101 and World War II memorial.

1971, Aug. 1 Engr. *Perf. 13*

C171	AP68	20fr grn, ocher & dk brn	.45	.25
C172	AP68	25fr dk brn, vio bl & sl grn	.65	.25
C173	AP68	40fr grn, mar & sl	.80	.25
C174	AP68	50fr dk brn, blk & ver	1.25	.25
C175	AP68	100fr mar, sl grn & org	1.75	.50
		Nos. C171-C175 (5)	4.90	1.50

PHILATECAM 1971 Philatelic Exhibition.

Cameroun Flag, Pres. Ahidjo and Reunification Highway — AP69

Typographed, Silk Screen, Embossed

1971, Oct. 1 *Perf. 12½*

C176 AP69 250fr gold & multi 6.00 4.50

PHILATECAM Philatelic Exhibition, Yaoundé-Douala.

African Postal Union Issue, 1971

Common Design Type

1971, Nov. 13 Photo. *Perf. 13x13½*

C177 CD135 100fr bl & multi 2.00 .50

Annunciation, by Fra Angelico — AP71

Christmmas (Paintings): 45fr, Virgin and Child, by Andrea del Sarto. 150fr, Christ Child with Lamb, detail from Holy Family, by Raphael, vert.

1971, Dec. 19 *Perf. 13x13½, 13½x13*

C178	AP71	40fr multi	.55	.25
C179	AP71	45fr multi	.70	.25
C180	AP71	150fr multi	3.25	.75
		Nos. C178-C180 (3)	4.50	1.25

Cameroun Airlines Emblem AP72

1972, Feb. 2 Photo. *Perf. 12½x12*

C181 AP72 50fr lt bl & multi .80 .25

Inauguration of Cameroun Airlines.

Doge's Palace, by Ippolito Caffi AP73

100fr, 200fr, Details from "Regatta on the Grand Canal," by School of Canaletto.

1972, Mar. 19 Photo. *Perf. 13*

C182	AP73	40fr gold & multi	.70	.25
C183	AP73	100fr gold & multi	1.75	.40
C184	AP73	200fr gold & multi	4.00	.80
		Nos. C182-C184 (3)	6.45	1.45

UNESCO campaign to save Venice.

Cosmonauts Patsayev, Dobrovolsky and Volkov — AP74

1972, May 1 Photo. *Perf. 13x13½*

C185 AP74 50fr multi 1.00 .30

Salute-Soyuz 11 space mission, and in memory of the Russian cosmonauts Victor I. Patsayev, Georgi T. Dobrovolsky and Vladislav N. Volkov, who died during Soyuz 11 space mission, June 6-30, 1971.

UN Headquarters, Chinese Flag and Gate of Heavenly Peace — AP75

1972, May 19 *Perf. 13*

C186 AP75 50fr blk, scar & gold 3.25 .35

Admission of People's Republic of China to UN.

United Republic

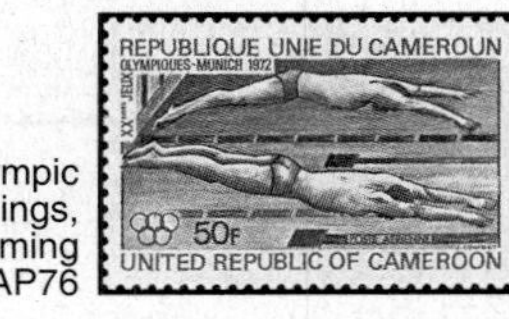

Olympic Rings, Swimming AP76

Designs (Olympic Rings and): No. C188, Boxing, vert. 200fr, Equestrian.

1972, Aug. 1 Engr. *Perf. 13*

C187	AP76	50fr lake & slate grn	.90	.25
C188	AP76	50fr choc & slate	.90	.25
C189	AP76	200fr cl, gray & dk brn	3.50	1.00
a.		Min. sheet of 3	5.75	5.75
		Nos. C187-C189 (3)	5.30	1.50

20th Olympic Games, Munich, Aug. 26-Sept. 11. No. C189a contains stamps similar to Nos. C187-C189, but in changed colors. The 50fr (swimming) is Prussian blue, violet & brown; the 50c (boxing) lilac, Prussian blue & brown; the 200fr, Prussian blue & brown.

Nos. C187-C189 Overprinted in Red or Black

a

b

c

1972, Oct. 23 Engr. *Perf. 13*

C190	AP76(a)	50fr (R)	.90	.25
C191	AP76(b)	50fr	.90	.25
C192	AP76(c)	200fr	3.50	1.00
		Nos. C190-C192 (3)	5.30	1.50

Gold Medal Winners in 20th Olympic Games: Mark Spitz, US, swimming (No. C190); Dieter Kottysch, West Germany, light middleweight boxing (No. C191); Richard Meade, Great Britain, 3-day equestrian (No. C192).

Madonna with Angels, by Cimabue AP77

Christmas: 140fr, Madonna of the Rose Arbor, by Stefan Lochner.

1972, Dec. 21 Photo. *Perf. 13*

C193	AP77	45fr gold & multi	1.00	.25
C194	AP77	140fr gold & multi	2.75	1.00

St. Teresa, the Little Flower — AP78

100fr, Lisieux Cathedral and St. Teresa.

1973, Jan. 2 Engr.

C195	AP78	45fr vio bl, pur & mar	.70	.25
C196	AP78	100fr mag, ultra & brn	1.75	.40

Centenary of the birth of St. Teresa of Lisieux (1873-1897), Carmelite nun.

African Unity Hall, Addis Ababa and Emperor Haile Selassie — AP79

1973, Mar. 14 Photo. *Perf. 13*

C197 AP79 45fr yellow & multi 1.00 .25

80th birthday of Emperor Haile Selassie of Ethiopia.

Corn, Grain, Healthy and Starving People — AP80

1973, Apr. 10 Typo. *Perf. 13*

C198 AP80 45fr multi .80 .25

World Food Program, 10th anniversary.

Hearts and Blood Vessels — AP81

1973, May 5 Engr.

C199 AP81 50fr dk car rose & dk vio bl 1.00 .25

"Your Heart is Your Health" and for the 25th anniv. of the WHO.

Type of Regular Issue

Designs: 45fr, Map of Cameroun, Pres. Ahidjo and No. C176. 70fr, National colors and commemorative inscriptions.

1973, May 20 Engr. *Perf. 13*

C200	A128	45fr grn & multi	.80	.25
C201	A128	70fr red & multi	1.00	.40

Scout Emblem and Flags — AP82

1973, July 31 Typo. *Perf. 13*

C202	AP82	40fr multi	1.00	.25
C203	AP82	45fr multi	1.25	.35
C204	AP82	100fr multi	3.25	.60
		Nos. C202-C204 (3)	5.50	1.20

Cameroun's admission to the World Scout Conference, Mar. 26, 1971.

African Weeks Issue

Head and City Hall, Brussels — AP83

1973, Sept. 17 Engr. *Perf. 13*

C205 AP83 40fr dp brn & rose claret .80 .25

African Weeks, Brussels, Sept. 15-30.

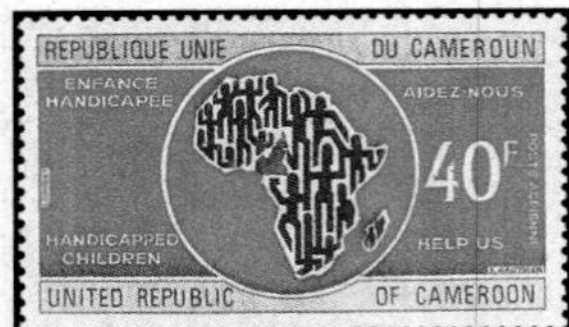

Map of Africa with Cameroun — AP84

1973, Sept. 29 Engr. *Perf. 13*

C206	AP84 40fr blk, red & grn	.80	.25

Help for handicapped children.

Zamengoe Radar Station AP85

1973, Dec. 8 Engr. *Perf. 13*

C207	AP85 100fr bl, lt brn & grn	1.50	.45

Chancellor Rolin Madonna, by Van Eyck AP86

Christmas: 140fr, Nativity, by Federigo Barocei.

1973, Dec. 11 Photo. *Perf. 13*

C208	AP86 45fr gold & multi	1.00	.30
C209	AP86 140fr gold & multi	2.75	1.00

Zebu Type of 1974

1974, June 1 Litho. *Perf. 13*

C210	A140 45fr Zebu herd	1.40	.35

Churchill and Union Jack AP87

1974, July 10 Engr. *Perf. 13*

C211	AP87 100fr blk, bl & red	1.60	.45

Winston Churchill (1874-1965).

Soccer, Arms of Frankfurt, Dortmund, Gelsenkirchen and Stuttgart — AP88

100fr, Soccer & arms of Berlin, Hamburg, Hanover & Düsseldorf. 200fr, Soccer cup & game.

1974, Aug. 5 Photo. *Perf. 13*

C212	AP88 45fr gray, sl & org	.70	.25
C213	AP88 100fr gray, sl & org	1.25	.40
C214	AP88 200fr org, slate & bl	2.75	1.00
a.	Strip of 3, Nos. C212-C214	5.00	5.00

World Cup Soccer Championship, Munich, June 13-July 7.

Nos. C212-C214 Overprinted in Dark Blue

1974, Sept. 16 Photo. *Perf. 13*

C215	AP88 45fr multi	.65	.25
C216	AP88 100fr multi	1.25	.40
C217	AP88 200fr multi	2.40	1.00
a.	Strip of 3, Nos. C215-C217	5.00	5.00

World Cup Soccer Championship, 1974, victory of German Federal Republic.

UPU Type of 1974

100fr, Cameroun #503. 200fr, Cameroun #C29.

1974, Oct. 8 Engr. *Perf. 13*

C218	A142 100fr blue & multi	1.75	.50
C219	A142 200fr red & multi	3.25	1.00

Copernicus and Planets Circling Sun — AP89

1974, Oct. 15 Engr. *Perf. 13*

C220	AP89 250fr multi	3.50	1.25

500th anniversary of the birth of Nicolaus Copernicus (1473-1543), Polish astronomer.

21st Chess Olympiad, Nice, France, June 6-30 — AP90

1974, Nov. 3 Photo. *Perf. 13x12½*

C221	AP90 100fr Chess pieces	5.25	1.00

Mask and ARPHILA Emblem — AP91

1974, Nov. 30 Engr. *Perf. 13*

C222	AP91 50fr choc & magenta	.80	.25

ARPHILA 75, Paris, June 6-16, 1975.

Presidents and Flags of Cameroun, CAR, Gabon and Congo — AP92

1974, Dec. 8 Photo.

C223	AP92 100fr gold & multi	2.25	.45

See note after No. 595.

Man Landing on Moon — AP93

1974, Dec. 15 Engr.

C224	AP93 200fr brn, bl & car	3.25	1.00

5th anniv. of man's 1st landing on the moon.

Charles de Gaulle and Félix Eboué — AP94

1975, Feb. 24 Typo. *Perf. 13*

C225	AP94 45fr multi	1.50	.35
C226	AP94 200fr multi	5.00	1.50

Felix A. Eboué (1884-1944), Governor of Chad, first colonial governor to join Free French in WWII, 30th death anniversary.

Marquis de Lafayette AP95

American Bicentennial: 140fr, Washington and soldiers. 500fr, Franklin and Independence Hall.

1975, Oct. 20 Engr. *Perf. 13*

C227	AP95 100fr vio bl & multi	2.25	.60
C228	AP95 140fr brn & multi	2.40	.65
C229	AP95 500fr grn & multi	7.25	2.00
	Nos. C227-C229 (3)	11.90	3.25

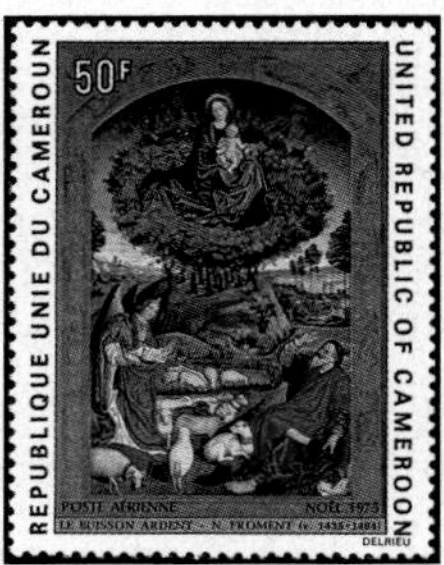

The Burning Bush, by Nicolas Froment AP96

Painting: 500fr, Adoration of the Kings, by Gentile da Fabriano, horiz.

1975, Dec. 25 Photo. *Perf. 13*

C230	AP96 50fr gold & multi	.90	.30
C231	AP96 500fr gold & multi	7.25	3.00

Christmas 1975.

Concorde and Route: Paris-Dakar-Rio de Janeiro — AP97

1976, July 20 Litho. *Perf. 13*

C232	AP97 500fr lt bl & multi	6.50	1.60
a.	Souvenir sheet of 1	9.00	9.00

1st commercial flight of supersonic jet Concorde from Paris to Rio de Janeiro, Jan. 21. No. C232a sold for 600fr.

For overprint see No. C263.

Dance Type of 1976

50fr, Dancers & drummer. 100fr, Woman dancer.

1976, Sept. 15 Litho. *Perf. 12*

C233	A154 50fr gray & multi	.65	.25
C234	A154 100fr gray & multi	1.10	.35

Virgin and Child, by Giovanni Bellini — AP98

Paintings: 30fr, Adoration of the Shepherds, by Le Brun. 60fr, Adoration of the Kings, by Rubens. 500fr, The Newborn, by Georges de la Tour.

1976, Dec. 15 Litho. *Perf. 12½*

C235	AP98 30fr gold & multi	.70	.25
C236	AP98 60fr gold & multi	.90	.25
C237	AP98 70fr gold & multi	1.25	.35
C238	AP98 500fr gold & multi	9.00	3.00
a.	Souv. sheet of 4, #C235-C238	12.50	12.00
	Nos. C235-C238 (4)	11.85	3.85

Christmas 1976.

Festival Type of 1977

Traditional Chief on his throne, sculpture.

1977, Feb. 4 Litho. *Perf. 12½*

C239	A159 60fr multi	1.10	.25

Easter — AP99

75fr, Crucifixion, by Matthias Grunewald. 125fr, Christ on the Cross, by Velazquez, vert. 150fr, The Deposition, by Titian.

1977, Apr. 2 Litho. *Perf. 12½*

C240	50fr gold & multi	.90	.25
C241	125fr gold & multi	1.75	.45
C242	150fr gold & multi	2.50	.65
a.	AP99 Souv. sheet of 3, #C240-C242, perf. 12	6.75	1.75
	Nos. C240-C242 (3)	5.15	1.35

No. C242a sold for 350fr.

Lions Emblem, Map of Africa — AP100

1977, Apr. 29 Litho. *Perf. 12½*

C243	AP100	250fr multi	3.00	1.00

Lions Club of Douala, 19th Cong., 4/29-30.

Rotary Emblem AP101

1977, May 18

C244	AP101	60fr multi	.70	.25

Rotary Club of Douala, 20th anniversary.

Antoine de Saint-Exupéry AP102

Charles Lindbergh and Spirit of St. Louis — AP103

Designs: 50fr, Jean Mermoz and his plane. 80fr, Maryse Bastié and her plane. 100fr, Sikorsky S-43. 300fr, Concorde.

1977, May 20 Engr. *Perf. 13*

C245	AP103	50fr org & bl	.90	.25
C246	AP102	60fr dp car & org	.95	.25
C247	AP103	80fr mag & bl	1.25	.30
a.		Souv. sheet, #C245-C247	3.25	3.25
C248	AP103	100fr grn & yel	1.50	.40
C249	AP103	300fr multi	5.50	1.25
C250	AP103	500fr multi	8.00	2.50
a.		Souv. sheet, #C248-C250	14.50	14.50
		Nos. C245-C250 (6)	18.10	4.95

Aviation pioneers and events. No. C247a sold for 200fr. No. C250a sold for 1000fr.

For overprint see No. C262.

Sassenage Castle, Grenoble — AP104

1977, May 21 Litho. *Perf. 12½*

C251	AP104	70fr multi	1.60	1.00

10th anniv. of Intl. French Language Council.

Jufilex Type of 1977

Designs: 70fr, Switzerland (Zurich) No. 1L1 and Cameroun No. 16. 100fr, Switzerland (Geneva) No. 2L1 and Cameroun No. 254.

1977, June 5 Litho. *Perf. 12*

C252	A161	70fr multi	1.25	.35
C253	A161	100fr multi	2.10	.60

Apollo-Soyuz Type

100fr, Astronaut Vance Brand, Apollo in orbit. 250fr, Apollo and Soyuz docking. 350fr, Cosmonaut Valery Kubasov, Soyuz in orbit. 500fr, Astronaut Donald Slayton, handshake.

1977, Aug. 10 Litho. *Perf. 14x13½*

C256	A163	100fr multicolored	.90	.25
C257	A163	250fr multicolored	2.25	.60
C258	A163	350fr multicolored	3.25	1.00
		Nos. C256-C258 (3)	6.40	5.85

Souvenir Sheet

C259	A163	500fr multicolored	5.00	5.00

Diseased Knee, WHO Emblem AP105

1977, Oct. 15 Engr. *Perf. 13*

C260	AP105	70fr multi	.70	.25

World Rheumatism Year.

Nos. C249 and C232 Overprinted in Red

Engraved, Lithographed

1977, Nov. 22 *Perf. 13*

C262	AP103	300fr multi	3.25	1.25
C263	AP97	500fr multi	5.00	2.00

Concorde, 1st commercial flight Paris to NY.

Christmas Type of 1977

Paintings: 60fr, Virgin and Child with 4 Saints, by Bellini, horiz. 400fr, Adoration of the Shepherds, by George de la Tour, horiz.

1977, Dec. 15 Litho. *Perf. 12x12½*

C264	A165	60fr multi	1.00	.25
C265	A165	400fr multi	5.00	1.75

Flag Type of 1978

60fr, New flag, Pres. Ahidjo and spear.

1978, Apr. 3 Litho. *Perf. 12½*

C266	A167	60fr multi	.55	.25

Frog Type of 1978

Design: 100fr, Cardioglossa trifasciata.

1978, Apr. 5

C267	A168	100fr multi	3.75	.75

L'Arlesienne, by Van Gogh — AP106

No. C269, Burial of Christ, by Albrecht Dürer.

1978, May 15 Litho. *Perf. 12½*

C268	AP106	200fr multi	4.25	1.10
C269	AP106	200fr multi	5.75	1.10

Leprosy Distribution on World Map, Raoul Follereau — AP107

1978, June 6 Litho. *Perf. 12*

C270	AP107	100fr multi	1.10	.55

25th World Leprosy Day.

Capt. Cook and Siege of Quebec — AP108

Design: 250fr, Capt. Cook, Adventure and Resolution, map of voyages.

1978, July 26 Engr. *Perf. 13*

C271	AP108	100fr multi	2.10	.55
C272	AP108	250fr multi	5.00	1.40

Capt. James Cook (1728-1779), explorer.

Argentine Soccer Team, Coat of Arms and Rimet Cup — AP109

200fr, Two soccer players, vert. 1000fr, Soccer ball illuminating world map, vert.

1978, Sept. 1 Litho. *Perf. 13*

C273	AP109	100fr multi	1.00	.55
C274	AP109	200fr multi	1.75	1.10
C275	AP109	1000fr multi	10.00	5.50
		Nos. C273-C275 (3)	12.75	7.15

11th World Cup Soccer Championship, Argentina, June 1-25.

Jules Verne Type of 1978

Design: 400fr, Jules Verne and "20,000 Leagues Under the Sea," horiz.

1978, Oct. 10 Litho. *Perf. 12*

C276	A169	400fr multi	4.00	2.00

Musical Instrument Type of 1978

Design: 100fr, Man playing Mvet zither.

1978, Nov. 20 Litho. *Perf. 12½*

C277	A172	100fr multi	1.25	.40

Human Rights Type of 1979

1979, Feb. 11 Litho. *Perf. 12x12½*

C278	A174	500fr multi	5.50	2.50

Lions Emblem, Map of District 403 — AP110

1979, Apr. 26 Litho. *Perf. 12½*

C279	AP110	60fr multi	.70	.25

21st Congress of Lions Club of Yaoundé.

Penny Black, Hill, Cameroun No. 9 — AP111

1979, Oct. 10 Engr. *Perf. 13*

C280	AP111	100fr multi	1.00	.40

Sir Rowland Hill (1795-1879), originator of penny postage.

"TELECOM 79" — AP112

1979, Sept. 26 Litho. *Perf. 13x12½*

C281	AP112	100fr multi	1.10	.40

3rd World Telecommunications Exhibition, Geneva, Sept. 20-26.

Pope Paul VI — AP113

1979, Oct. 23 Engr. *Perf. 12½x13*

C282	AP113	100fr shown	2.25	.50
C283	AP113	100fr John Paul I	2.25	.50
C284	AP113	100fr John Paul II	2.25	.50
		Nos. C282-C284 (3)	6.75	1.50

"Double Eagle" over French Coastline AP114

Design: No. C286, Balloonists and balloon.

1979, Dec. 15 Litho. *Perf. 12½*

C285	AP114	500fr multi	5.00	2.25
C286	AP114	500fr multi	5.00	2.25

First Transatlantic balloon crossing.

100-Meter Race — AP115

Designs: 150fr, Figure skating pairs. 200fr, Javelin. 300fr, Wrestling.

1980, Dec. 18 Litho. *Perf. 12½*

C287 AP115 100fr yel brn & brn .90 .50
C288 AP115 150fr bl & brn 1.25 .70
C289 AP115 200fr grn & brn 1.75 1.00
C290 AP115 300fr red & brn 2.50 1.40
Nos. C287-C290 (4) 6.40 3.60

22nd Summer Olympic Games, Moscow, July 19-Aug. 3; 13th Winter Olympic Games, Lake Placid, Feb. 12-24 (150fr).

Alan Shepard and Freedom 7 — AP116

No. C292, Yuri Gagarin, Vostok I.

1981, Sept. 15 Litho. *Perf. 12½*

C291 AP116 500fr shown 5.00 2.25
C292 AP116 500fr multi 5.00 2.25

Manned space flight, 20th anniv.

4th African Scouting Conference, Abidjan, June — AP117

100fr, Emblem, salute, badge. 500fr, Scout saluting.

1981, Oct. 5

C293 AP117 100fr multi .70 .40
C294 AP117 500fr multi 4.50 2.00

Guernica (detail), by Pablo Picasso (1881-1973) — AP118

No. C296, Landscape, by Paul Cezanne (1839-1906).

1981, Nov. 10 Litho. *Perf. 12½*

C295 AP118 500fr multi 6.00 2.00
C296 AP118 500fr multi 6.00 2.00

Christmas 1981 — AP119

Designs: 50fr, Virgin and Child, by Froment, vert. 60f, San Zeno Altarpiece, by Mantegna, vert. 400fr, Flight into Egypt, by Giotto.

1981, Dec. 1 Litho. *Perf. 12½*

C297 AP119 50fr multi .45 .25
C298 AP119 60fr multi .65 .30
C299 AP119 400fr multi 3.50 2.00
a. Souv. sheet of 3, #C297-C299, perf. 13x13½ 9.00 9.00
Nos. C297-C299 (3) 4.60 2.55

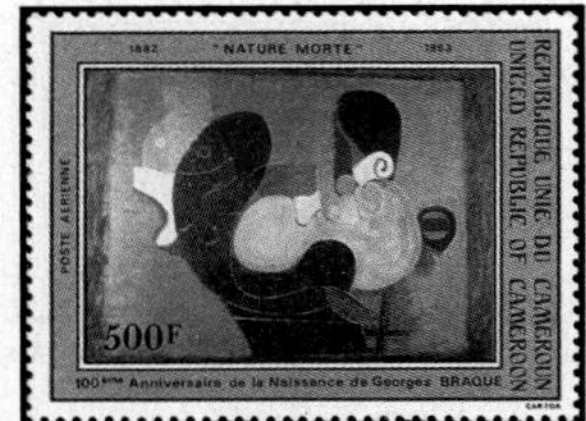

Still Life, by Georges Braque (1882-1963) — AP120

Paintings: No. C301, Olympia, by Edouard Manet (1832-1883).

1982, Dec. 5 Litho. *Perf. 13*

C300 AP120 500fr multi 5.00 2.00
C301 AP120 500fr multi 5.00 2.00

Pres. John F. Kennedy (1917-63) AP121

1983, Mar. 15 Litho. *Perf. 13*

C302 AP121 500fr multi 4.50 2.00

Lions District 403 (Douala), 2nd Convention, May — AP122

1983, May 5 Litho. *Perf. 12½*

C303 AP122 70fr multi .55 .30
C304 AP122 150fr multi 1.25 .65

Jeanne of Aragon by Raphael AP123

No. C306, Massacre of Scio by Delacroix.

1983, Oct. 15 Litho. *Perf. 13*

C305 AP123 500fr multi 5.00 1.00
C306 AP123 500fr multi 5.00 1.00

Easter 1984 — AP124

200fr, Pieta, by G. Hernandez. 500fr, Martyrdom of St. John the Evangelist, by C. Le Brun.

1984, Mar. 30 Litho. *Perf. 13*

C307 AP124 200fr multi 1.75 .50
C308 AP124 500fr multi 4.50 1.40
a. Souv. sheet of 2, #C307-C308 7.25 7.25

1984 Summer Olympics AP125

1984, Apr. 30 *Perf. 12½*

C309 AP125 100fr High jump .90 .25
C310 AP125 150fr Volleyball 1.25 .35
C311 AP125 250fr Handball 2.25 .55
C312 AP125 500fr Bicycling 4.50 1.10
Nos. C309-C312 (4) 8.90 2.25

See Nos. C321-C324.

European Soccer Championship, June 12-27 — AP126

No. C313, Player in red shorts. No. C314, Yellow shorts. No. C315, Players.

1984, June 5 Litho. *Perf. 12½*

C313 AP126 250fr multicolored 2.25 .65
C314 AP126 250fr multicolored 2.25 .65
C315 AP126 500fr multicolored 4.50 1.25
a. Souvenir sheet of 3 10.00 10.00
Nos. C313-C315 (3) 9.00 2.55

No. C315a contains Nos. C313-C315 in changed panel colors.

Presidential Oath — AP127

1984 Litho. *Perf. 13*

C316 AP127 60fr French inscription .55 .25
a. English inscription .55 .25
C317 AP127 70fr French inscription .55 .25
a. English inscription .55 .25
C318 AP127 200fr French inscription 1.75 .40
a. English inscription 1.75 .40
Nos. C316-C318 (3) 2.85 .90

Issue dates: French, Sept. 15; English, Nov.

Paintings — AP128

No. C319, Diana in the Bath, by Watteau (1684-1721). No. C320, Portrait of Diderot (1713-1784).

1984, Sept. 20 Litho. *Perf. 13*

C319 AP128 500fr Watteau 5.00 1.00
C320 AP128 500fr Diderot, vert. 5.00 1.00

Nos. C309-C312 in Changed Colors with Added Inscriptions

MOEGENBURG (R.F.A.) 11-08-84

U.S.A. 11-08-84

YOUGOSLAVIE 9-08-84

GORSKI (U.S.A.) 3-08-84

1984, Sept. 25 Litho. *Perf. 12½*

C321 AP125 100fr multi .90 .25
C322 AP125 150fr multi 1.25 .30
C323 AP125 250fr multi 2.25 .50
C324 AP125 500fr multi 4.50 1.00
Nos. C321-C324 (4) 8.90 2.05

Moon Landing, 15th Anniv. — AP129

No. C325, Neil Armstrong. No. C326, Apollo 12 launching.

1984, Nov. 15 Litho. *Perf. 12½*

C325 AP129 500fr multi 4.50 1.50
C326 AP129 500fr multi 4.50 1.50

Louis Pasteur (1822-1895), Chemist, Microbiologist — AP130

No. C328, Mourning Woman (detail), Mausoleum of Henri Claude d'Harcourt, by sculptor Jean Baptiste Pigalle (1714-1785).

1985, Oct. 10 Litho. *Perf. 13*

C327 AP130 500fr multi 6.00 1.75
C328 AP130 500fr multi 6.00 1.75

Christmas AP131

250fr, Children's gifts. 300fr, Akono Church. 400fr, Holy Family & drummer boy. 500fr, The Virgin with the Blue Diadem, by Raphael.

1985, Dec. 20 Litho. *Perf. 13*

C329 AP131 250fr multi 2.25 .90
C330 AP131 300fr multi 2.50 1.10
C331 AP131 400fr multi 3.25 1.50
C332 AP131 500fr multi 5.00 2.00
Nos. C329-C332 (4) 13.00 5.50

1986 World Cup Soccer Championships, Mexico — AP132

250fr, Argentina, winner. 300fr, Stadium. 400fr, Mexican team.

1986 *Perf. 13½*

C333 AP132 250fr multi 2.75 1.40
C334 AP132 300fr multi 2.75 1.60
C335 AP132 400fr multi 3.50 2.25
Nos. C333-C335 (3) 9.00 5.25

Issued: 300fr, 400fr, 5/15; 250fr, 7/26.

Famous Men — AP133

No. C336, Pierre Curie (1859-1906), chemist, atom, and elements. No. C337, Jean Mermoz (1901-1936), aviator, and aircraft.

1986, Sept. 10 Litho. *Perf. 12½*

C336 AP133 500fr multi 6.25 2.00
C337 AP133 500fr multi 6.25 2.00

AIR POST SEMI-POSTAL STAMPS

Doctor Examining Child — SPAP1

Unwmk.

1942, June 22 Engr. *Perf. 13*

CB1 SPAP1 1.50fr + 50c green 1.00
CB2 SPAP1 2fr + 6fr brn & red brn 1.00

Native children's welfare fund.

Nos. CB1-CB2 were issued by the Vichy government in France, but were not placed on sale in Cameroun.

Colonial Education Fund
Common Design Type

1942, June 22

CB3 CD86a 1.20fr + 1.80fr blue & red 1.10

No. CB3 was issued by the Vichy government in France, but was not placed on sale in Cameroun.

POSTAGE DUE STAMPS

Man Felling Tree — D1

Perf. 14x13½

1925-27 Unwmk. Typo.

J1 D1 2c lt bl & blk .30 .50
J2 D1 4c ol bis & red vio .30 .50
J3 D1 5c vio & blk .65 .80
J4 D1 10c red & blk .65 .80
J5 D1 15c gray & blk .75 .95
J6 D1 20c olive grn & blk .75 .95
J7 D1 25c yel & blk 1.40 1.60
J8 D1 30c blue & org 1.60 1.90
J9 D1 50c brn & blk 2.00 2.40
J10 D1 60c bl grn & rose red 2.00 2.40
J11 D1 1fr dl red & grn, *grnsh* 2.40 3.25
J12 D1 2fr red & vio ('27) 4.75 5.50
J13 D1 3fr org brn & ultra ('27) 7.25 8.00
Nos. J1-J13 (13) 24.80 29.55

Shades occur for several values.

Carved Figures — D2

1939 Engr. *Perf. 14x13*

J14 D2 5c brt red vio .25 .80
J15 D2 10c Prus blue .75 .90
J16 D2 15c car rose .25 .40
J17 D2 20c blk brn .25 .40
J18 D2 30c ultra .50 .65
J19 D2 50c dk grn .50 .65
J20 D2 60c brn vio .85 1.00
J21 D2 1fr dk vio 1.10 1.20
J22 D2 2fr org red 1.60 1.60
J23 D2 3fr dark blue 2.25 2.40
Nos. J14-J23 (10) 8.30 10.00

1944 Type D2 without "RF"

J23A D2 10c Prussian blue .80

No. J23A was issued by the Vichy government in France, but was not placed on sale in Cameroun.

Catalogue values for unused stamps in this section, from this point to the end of the section, are for Never Hinged items.

D3

1947 Unwmk. *Perf. 13*

J24 D3 10c dark red .40 .30
J25 D3 30c dp org .40 .30
J26 D3 50c grnsh blk .40 .30
J27 D3 1fr dark car .50 .40
J28 D3 2fr dp yel grn .65 .55
J29 D3 3fr dp red lil .65 .55
J30 D3 4fr dp ultra .90 .70
J31 D3 5fr red brn 1.00 .90
J32 D3 10fr peacock bl 1.90 1.60
J33 D3 20fr sepia 2.75 2.25
Nos. J24-J33 (10) 9.55 7.85

Federal Republic

Hibiscus — D4

Flowers: No. J35, Erythrina. No. J36, Plumeria lutea. No. J37, Ipomoea. No. J38, Hoodia gordonii. No. J39, Crinum. No. J40, Ochna. No. J41, Gloriosa. No. J42, Costus spectabilis. No. J43, Bougainvillea spectabilis. No. J44, Delonix regia. No. J45, Haemanthus. No. J46, Ophthalmophyllum. No. J47, Titanopsis. No. J48, Amorphophallus. No. J49, Zingiberacee.

Unwmk.

1963, Apr. 10 Engr. *Perf. 11*

J34 D4 50c car, bl, grn & yel .25 .25
J35 D4 50c car, bl, grn & yel .25 .25
a. Pair, #J34-J35 .55 .45
J36 D4 1fr mag, grn & yel .25 .25
J37 D4 1fr mag, grn & yel .25 .25
a. Pair, #J36-J37 .55 .45
J38 D4 1.50fr dk grn, lil & yel .25 .25
J39 D4 1.50fr dk grn, lil & yel .25 .25
a. Pair, #J38-J39 .55 .45
J40 D4 2fr org ver, yel & grn .25 .25
J41 D4 2fr org ver, yel & grn .25 .25
a. Pair, #J40-J41 .55 .45
J42 D4 5fr mag, grn & yel .25 .25
J43 D4 5fr mag, grn & yel .25 .25
a. Pair, #J42-J43 .55 .45
J44 D4 10fr crim, grn & yel .50 .25
J45 D4 10fr crim, grn & yel .50 .25
a. Pair, #J44-J45 1.20 .45
J46 D4 20fr grn, yel & lil 1.10 .45
J47 D4 20fr grn, yel & lil 1.10 .45
a. Pair, #J46-J47 2.40 1.00
J48 D4 40fr lilac & yel 2.00 .80
J49 D4 40fr lilac & yel 2.00 .80
a. Pair, #J48-J49 4.25 1.75
Nos. J34-J49 (16) 9.70 5.50

The pairs are se-tenant at the base.

MILITARY STAMPS

Catalogue values for unused stamps in this section are for Never Hinged items.

M1

Unwmk.

1963, July 1 Typo. *Perf. 13*

M1 M1 rose claret 3.00 3.00

Type of 1963 Inscribed
"REPUBLIC UNIE DU CAMEROUN / UNITED REPUBLIC OF CAMEROUN"

1976? Litho. *Perf. 13x13½*

M2 M1 rose claret

CANADIAN PROVINCES

BRITISH COLUMBIA & VANCOUVER IS.

'bri-tish kə-'ləm-bē-ə
and van-'kü-vər 'ī-lənd

LOCATION — On the northwest coast of North America
GOVT. — British Colony
AREA — 355,900 sq. mi.
POP. — 694,300

In 1871 the colony became a part of the Canadian Confederation and the postage stamps of Canada have since been used.

12 Pence = 1 Shilling
20 Shillings = 1 Pound
100 Cents = 1 Dollar (1865)

Values for unused stamps are for examples with original gum as defined in the catalogue introduction. Very fine examples of Nos. 2 and 5-18 will have perforations touching the design on at least one side due to the narrow spacing of the stamps on the plates. Stamps with perfs clear of the design on all four sides are extremely scarce and will command much higher prices.

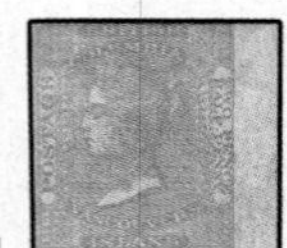

Queen Victoria — A1

1860 Unwmk. Typo. *Imperf.*

1	A1	2½p dull rose	*27,500.*	

No. 1 was not placed in use and may be a proof or reprint. Most examples are without gum. Value without gum, $18,000.

Perf. 14

2	A1	2½p dull rose	*450.*	240.

VANCOUVER ISLAND

A2

A3

1865 Wmk. 1 *Imperf.*

3	A2	5c rose	*70,000.*	*11,000.*
		No gum	*40,000.*	
4	A3	10c blue	3,500.	1,100.

Perf. 14

5	A2	5c rose	500.	300.
6	A3	10c blue	500.	300.

BRITISH COLUMBIA

Seal of British Columbia — A4

1865, Nov. 1

7	A4	3p blue	160.00	110.00

Type A4 of 1865 Surcharged in Various Colors

1867-69 *Perf. 14*

8	2c on 3p brown (Bk)	160.00	150.00
9	5c on 3p brt red (Bk) ('69)	300.00	250.00
10	10c on 3p lilac rose (Bl)	2,000.	
11	25c on 3p orange (V) ('69)	400.00	325.00
12	50c on 3p violet (R)	900.00	*1,050.*
13	$1 on 3p green (G)	2,000.	

Nos. 10 and 13 were not placed in use.

1869 *Perf. 12½*

14	5c on 3p brt red (Bk)	2,250.	1,300.
15	10c on 3p lilac rose (Bl)	1,300.	1,000.
16	25c on 3p orange (V)	1,100.	800.00
17	50c on 3p violet (R)	1,600.	1,000.
18	$1 on 3p green (G)	2,500.	1,750.

NEW BRUNSWICK

'nü 'brənz-ˌwik

LOCATION — Eastern Canada, bordering on the Bay of Fundy and the Gulf of St. Lawrence.
GOVT. — British Province
AREA — 27,985 sq. mi.
POP. — 285,594 (1871)
CAPITAL — Fredericton

At one time a part of Nova Scotia, New Brunswick became a separate province in 1784. Upon joining the Canadian Confederation in 1867 its postage stamps were superseded by those of Canada.

12 Pence = 1 Shilling
100 Cents = 1 Dollar (1860)

Crown of Great Britain and Heraldic Flowers of the United Kingdom
A1

1851 Unwmk. Engr. *Imperf.*
Blue Paper

1	A1	3p red	5,500.	575.
a.		3p dark red	5,750.	600.
b.		Half used as 1½p on cover		*4,750.*
2	A1	6p olive yellow	7,500.	1,200.
a.		6p orange yellow	7,500.	1,200.
b.		Half used as 3p on cover		3,000.
c.		Quarter used as 1½p on cover		*35,000.*
d.		6p mustard yellow	10,000.	1,400.
3	A1	1sh brt red violet	*30,000.*	*6,250.*
a.		Half used as 6p on cover		*22,500.*
b.		Quarter used as 3p on cover		*45,000.*
4	A1	1sh dull violet	35,000.	*7,500.*
a.		Half used as 6p on cover		*22,500.*
b.		Quarter used as 3p on cover		*45,000.*

The reprints are on stout white paper. The 3p is printed in orange and the 6p and 1sh in violet black. Value about $275 per set of 3.

Charles Connell — A2

1860 *Perf. 12*

5	A2	5c brown	*14,000.*	

No. 5 was prepared for use but not issued. Most examples of No. 5 have creases or other faults. Value of an average example is about half that shown here.

Locomotive
A3

Victoria
A4

A5

A6

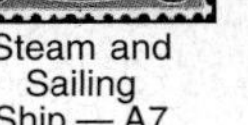

Steam and Sailing Ship — A7

Edward VII as Prince of Wales — A8

1860-63 White Paper *Perf. 12*

6	A3	1c red lilac	42.50	37.50
a.		1c brown violet	90.00	70.00
b.		Horiz. pair, imperf. vert., no gum	700.00	
7	A4	2c orange ('63)	20.00	17.50
a.		Vertical pair, imperf. horiz., no gum	775.00	
8	A5	5c yellow green	27.50	22.50
a.		5c blue green	32.50	22.50
b.		5c olive green	175.00	37.50
9	A6	10c vermilion	55.00	47.50
a.		Half used as 5c on cover		1,000.
b.		Double impression	*400.00*	200.00
10	A7	12½c blue	90.00	75.00
11	A8	17c black	55.00	*65.00*
		Nos. 6-11 (6)	290.00	265.00
		Set, never hinged	645.00	

NEWFOUNDLAND

'nü-fən-d-lənd

LOCATION — Island in the Atlantic Ocean off the coast of Canada, and Labrador, a part of the mainland
GOVT. — British Dominion
AREA — 42,734 sq. mi.
POP. — 321,177 (1945)
CAPITAL — St. John's

Newfoundland was a self-governing Dominion of the British Empire from 1855 to 1933, when it became a Crown Colony. In 1949 it united with Canada.

12 Pence = 1 Shilling
100 Cents = 1 Dollar (1866)

Values for unused stamps are for examples with original gum as defined in the catalogue introduction. However, very fine examples of Nos. 2-7, 9, 11, 12, 13 and 15 without gum are often traded at values very close to those for examples with original gum.

Watermark

Wmk. 224 Coat of Arms

As the watermark 224 does not show on every stamp in the sheet, pairs are found one with and one without watermark. This applies to all stamps with watermark 224.

Crown of Great Britain and Heraldic Flowers of the United Kingdom — A1

Rose, Thistle and Shamrock — A3

A2

A4

A5

A6

A7

A8

1857 Unwmk. Engr. *Imperf.*
Thick Porous Wove Paper with Mesh

1	A1	1p brn vio	125.00	*225.00*
a.		Half used as ½p on cover		*37,500.*
2	A2	2p scar ver	*17,500.*	7,000.
a.		Vert. half used as 1p on cover		*27,500.*
3	A3	3p green	800.00	575.00
4	A4	4p scar ver	*12,500.*	4,250.
a.		Half used as 2p on cover		*27,500.*
5	A1	5p brn vio	325.00	*600.00*
6	A5	6p scar ver	*27,500.*	5,000.
7	A6	6½p scar ver	5,000.	*4,000.*
8	A7	8p scar ver	400.00	*475.00*
a.		Half used as 4p on cover		4,500.
9	A8	1sh scar ver	*42,500.*	*9,500.*
a.		Half used as 6p on cover		*20,000.*

1860
Thin to Thick Wove Paper, No Mesh

11	A2	2p orange	500.00	*525.00*
11A	A3	3p green	85.00	*110.00*
12	A4	4p orange	5,500.	1,350.
b.		Half used as 2p on cover		*22,500.*
12A	A1	5p vio brown	85.00	*150.00*
13	A5	6p orange	5,250.	1,100.
15	A8	1sh orange	*37,500.*	12,000.
b.		Half used as 6p on cover		*37,500.*

A 6½p orange exists as a souvenir item.

A 1sh exists in orange on horizontally or vertically laid paper. Most authorities consider these to be proofs. Value, $27,500.

1861-62

No.	Type	Description	Unused	Used
15A	A1	1p vio brown	175.00	*250.00*
16	A1	1p reddish brown	*13,000.*	
17	A2	2p rose	175.00	*175.00*
18	A4	4p rose	37.50	*70.00*
a.		Half used as 2p on cover		—
19	A1	5p reddish brown	75.00	*77.50*
20	A5	6p rose	22.50	*62.50*
a.		Half used as 3p on cover		*18,000.*
21	A6	6½p rose	85.00	*275.00*
22	A7	8p rose	85.00	*300.00*
23	A8	1sh rose	42.50	*250.00*
a.		Half used as 6p on cover		*18,000.*

Some sheets of Nos. 11-23 are known with the papermaker's watermark "STACEY WISE 1858" in large capitals. Values unused and used about 25% more than values shown, except about 50% more for unused Nos. 12 and 13, and 75% more for unused No. 16.

No. 16 was prepared but not issued.

False cancellations are found on Nos. 1, 3, 5, 8, 11, 11A, 12A and 17-23.

Forgeries exist of most or all of Nos. 1-23.

Codfish — A9

Harp Seal — A10

Prince Albert — A11

Victoria — A12

Fishing Ship — A13

Victoria — A14

1865-94 ***Perf. 12***

White Paper(#24, 27, 28)

Thin Yellowish Paper (#25-26, 29-31)

No.	Type	Description	Unused	Used
24	A9	2c green	125.00	35.00
a.		Thin yellowish paper	165.00	70.00
b.		Half used as 1c on cover		*8,000.*
25	A10	5c brown	600.00	450.00
a.		Half used as 2c on cover		*10,000.*
26	A10	5c black ('68)	375.00	275.00
a.		Half used as 2p on cover		6,750.
27	A11	10c black	375.00	60.00
a.		Thin yellowish paper	450.00	115.00
b.		Half used as 5c on cover		*9,000.*
28	A12	12c pale red brn	85.00	47.50
a.		Thin yellowish paper	600.00	190.00
b.		Half used as 6c on cover		*4,500.*
29	A12	12c brn, *white* ('94)	70.00	55.00
30	A13	13c orange	250.00	115.00
31	A14	24c blue, thin transluscent paper	75.00	35.00
a.		Thicker white paper ('70)	375.00	300.00

See Nos. 38, 40.

Edward VII as Prince of Wales — A15

Queen Victoria — A16

1868-94

No.	Type	Description	Unused	Used
32	A15	1c violet	75.00	60.00
32A	A15	1c brn lil (re-engr. '71)	115.00	75.00
33	A16	3c ver ('70)	425.00	190.00
34	A16	3c blue ('73)	375.00	75.00
35	A16	6c dull rose ('70)	37.50	17.50
36	A16	6c car lake ('94)	50.00	22.50
		Nos. 32-36 (6)	1,078.	440.00

In the re-engraved 1c the top of the letters "N" and "F" are about ½mm from the ribbon with "ONE CENT." In No. 32 they are fully 1mm away. There are many small differences in the engraving.

1876-79 ***Rouletted***

No.	Type	Description	Unused	Used
37	A15	1c brn lilac ('77)	160.00	52.50
38	A9	2c green ('79)	200.00	52.50
39	A16	3c blue ('77)	425.00	15.00
40	A10	5c blue	275.00	15.00
		Nos. 37-40 (4)	1,060.	135.00

A17

A19

A18

A20

1880-96 ***Perf. 12***

No.	Type	Description	Unused	Used
41	A17	1c violet brown	60.00	11.50
42	A17	1c gray brown	60.00	11.50
43	A17	1c brown ('96)	130.00	70.00
44	A17	1c deep green ('87)	30.00	4.25
45	A17	1c green ('97)	30.00	4.25
46	A19	2c yellow green	75.00	14.00
47	A19	2c green ('96)	125.00	27.50
48	A19	2c red org ('87)	37.50	9.50
a.		Imperf., pair, no gum	500.00	
c.		Half used as 1c on cover		*450.00*
49	A18	3c blue ('96)	70.00	7.00
51	A18	3c umber brn ('87)	80.00	4.75
52	A18	3c vio brown ('96)	120.00	90.00
53	A20	5c pale blue	425.00	14.00
54	A20	5c dark blue ('87)	225.00	10.00
55	A20	5c bright bl ('94)	75.00	6.50
		Nos. 41-55 (14)	1,543.	284.75

Newfoundland Dog — A21

Schooner — A22

1887-96

No.	Type	Description	Unused	Used
56	A21	½c rose red	12.50	7.50
57	A21	½c org red ('96)	80.00	45.00
58	A21	½c black ('94)	14.00	7.25
59	A22	10c black	145.00	67.50
		Nos. 56-59 (4)	251.50	127.25
		Set, never hinged	505.00	

Queen Victoria — A23

1890

No.	Type	Description	Unused	Used
60	A23	3c slate	30.00	1.60
a.		3c gray lilac	30.00	1.60
b.		3c brown lilac	50.00	1.60
c.		3c lilac	35.00	1.60
d.		3c slate violet	70.00	3.00
e.		Vert. pair, imperf. horiz.	750.00	

For surcharges see Nos. 75-77.

Victoria — A24

Cabot (John?) — A25

Cape Bonavista A26

Caribou Hunting A27

Mining — A28

Logging — A29

Fishing — A30

Cabot's Ship "Matthew" A31

Willow Ptarmigan A32

Seals — A33

Salmon Fishing — A34

Colony Seal — A35

Iceberg off St. John's — A36

Henry VII — A37

1897, June 24

No.	Type	Description	Unused	Used
61	A24	1c deep green	1.60	1.75
62	A25	2c carmine lake	2.10	1.40
63	A26	3c ultramarine	4.25	1.40
64	A27	4c olive green	6.00	2.75
65	A28	5c violet	11.00	2.75
66	A29	6c red brown	5.50	3.25
67	A30	8c red orange	22.50	15.00
68	A31	10c black brown	22.50	7.50
69	A32	12c dark blue	25.00	15.00
70	A33	15c scarlet	20.00	13.00
71	A34	24c gray violet	25.00	12.00
72	A35	30c slate	60.00	55.00
73	A36	35c red	110.00	60.00
74	A37	60c black	16.00	11.50
		Nos. 61-74 (14)	331.45	202.30
		Set, never hinged	662.50	

400th anniv. of John Cabot's discovery of Newfoundland; 60th year of Victoria's reign. The ship on the 10c was previously used by the American Bank Note Co. as the "Flagship of Columbus" on US No. 232. The portrait on the 2c, intended to be of John Cabot, is said to be a Holbein painting of his son, Sebastian.

For surcharges and overprints see Nos. 127-130, C2-C4.

No. 60a Surcharged

No. 75

No. 76

No. 77

Available Oct. 19 through Dec. 3, 1897

No.	Type	Description	Unused	Used
75	A23	1c on 3c gray lil	85.00	50.00
a.		Dbl. surch., one diagonal	*2,000.*	
b.		Vert. pair, "ONE CENT" and lower bar omitted on bottom stamp	*4,250.*	
76	A23	1c on 3c gray lil	275.00	225.00
77	A23	1c on 3c gray lil	825.00	700.00
		Nos. 75-77 (3)	1,185.	975.00
		Set, never hinged	3,065.	

Most examples of Nos. 75-77 are poorly centered. Fine examples sell for about 60% of the values given. No. 75b is valued in the grade of fine.

Trial surcharges of Nos. 75-77 exist with red surcharge and with double surcharge, one in red and one in black, but these were not issued.

Edward VIII as a Child — A38

Victoria — A39

Edward VII as Prince of Wales — A40

Queen Alexandra as Princess of Wales — A41

Queen Mary as Duchess of York — A42

George V as Duke of York — A43

1897-1901 **Engr.**

No.	Type	Description	Unused	Used
78	A38	½c olive green ('98)	4.25	2.75
79	A39	1c carmine rose ('97)	5.25	5.00
80	A39	1c yel grn ('98)	5.25	.35
b.		Vert. pair, imperf. horiz.	400.00	
81	A40	2c orange ('97)	6.50	4.25
82	A40	2c ver ('98)	11.50	.75
b.		Pair, imperf. between	575.00	
83	A41	3c orange ('98)	30.00	.75
a.		Vert. pair, imperf. horiz.	450.00	
84	A42	4c violet ('01)	40.00	4.50
85	A43	5c blue ('99)	45.00	3.00
		Nos. 78-85 (8)	147.75	21.35
		Set, never hinged	295.50	

No. 80b is valued in the grade of fine.

Imperf., Pairs

78a	A38	½c	600.00	*800.00*
81a	A40	2c		*425.00*
82a	A40	2c	375.00	*950.00*
83b	A41	3c	425.00	
84a	A42	4c	650.00	

No. 82a used is valued on cover. Three such covers are recorded.

Imperf., Pairs

Newfoundland imperforates virtually always are proofs on stamp paper or "postmaster's perquisites." Most part-perforate varieties also are "postmaster's perquisites." These items were not regularly issued, but rather were sold or given to favored persons.

Map of Newfoundland — A44

1908, Sept.

86	A44	2c rose carmine	60.00	3.50
		Never hinged	120.00	

Guy Issue

James I — A45

Arms of the London and Bristol Co. — A46

John Guy A47

Guy's Ship, the "Endeavour" A48

View of Cupids — A49

Lord Bacon — A50

View of Mosquito — A51

Logging Camp — A52

Paper Mills — A53

Edward VII — A54

George V — A55

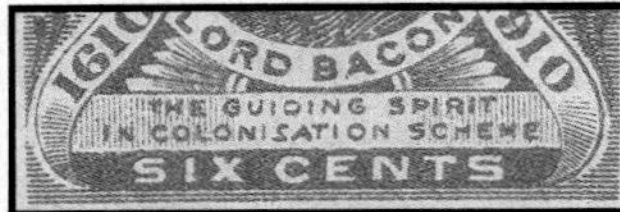

Type I

Type II

SIX CENT TYPES
I — "Z" of "COLONIZATION" reversed.
II — "Z" of normal.

1910, Aug. 15 Litho. *Perf. 12*

87	A45	1c deep green, perf. 12x11	2.00	1.10
a.		Perf. 12	4.25	1.90
b.		Perf. 12x14	7.50	2.25
c.		Horiz. pair, imperf. btwn.	400.00	—
d.		Vert. pair, imperf. btwn.	450.00	
h.		Perf. 12x12x12x11		—
88	A46	2c carmine	11.00	1.15
a.		Perf. 12x14	8.50	.85
b.		As "a," horiz. pair, imperf. between	900.00	
c.		Perf. 12x11½	725.00	350.00
89	A47	3c brown olive	25.00	14.00
90	A48	4c dull violet	25.00	14.00
91	A49	5c ultramarine, perf. 14x12	27.50	4.50
a.		Perf. 12	32.50	7.50
92	A50	6c claret, type I	90.00	70.00
92A	A50	6c claret, type II	50.00	37.50
b.		Imperf., pair	425.00	
93	A51	8c pale brown	75.00	55.00
94	A52	9c olive green	75.00	55.00
95	A53	10c vio black	75.00	55.00
96	A54	12c lilac brown	75.00	55.00
a.		Imperf., pair	375.00	
97	A55	15c gray black	80.00	65.00
		Nos. 87-97 (12)	610.50	427.25
		Set, never hinged	1,211.	

Tercentenary of the Colonization of Newfoundland.

On No. 87 printing flaws such as "NFW" and "JANES" exist.

1911 Engr. *Perf. 14*

98	A50	6c brown vio	37.50	25.00
b.		Horiz. pair, imperf. btwn.	*1,150.*	
99	A51	8c bister brn	75.00	67.50
b.		Horiz. pair, imperf. btwn.	*1,500.*	
100	A52	9c olive grn	70.00	60.00
b.		Horiz. pair, imperf. btwn.	*1,250.*	
101	A53	10c violet blk	95.00	95.00
b.		Horiz. pair, imperf. btwn.	*1,250.*	
102	A54	12c red brown	70.00	75.00
b.		Horiz. pair, imperf. btwn.	—	
103	A55	15c slate grn	70.00	75.00
b.		Horiz. pair, imperf. btwn.	*1,250.*	
		Nos. 98-103 (6)	417.50	*397.50*
		Set, never hinged	805.00	

Nos. 100 and 103 are known with papermaker's watermark "E. TOWGOOD FINE." Values, unused or used: No. 100, $800; No. 103, $1,000.

Imperf., Pairs

98a	A50	6c	325.00
99a	A51	8c	325.00
100a	A52	9c	325.00
101a	A53	10c	325.00
102a	A54	12c	325.00
103a	A55	15c	325.00

Nos. 98a-103a were made with and without gum. Values the same.

Royal Family Issue

Queen Mary — A56

George V — A57

Prince of Wales (Edward VIII) — A58

Prince Albert (George VI) — A59

Princess Mary — A60

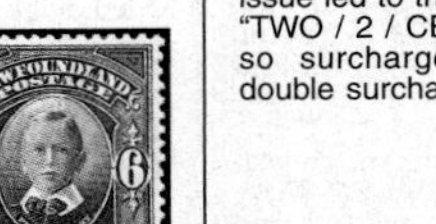
Prince Henry — A61

Prince George A62

Prince John A63

Queen Alexandra A64

Duke of Connaught A65

Seal of Colony — A66

1911, June 19 *Perf. 13½x14, 14*

104	A56	1c yellow grn	3.00	.25
105	A57	2c carmine	2.75	1.00
106	A58	3c red brown	35.00	19.00
107	A59	4c violet	35.00	13.50
108	A60	5c ultra	22.50	1.90
109	A61	6c black	32.50	22.50
110	A62	8c blue (paper colored through)	80.00	65.00
a.		8c peacock blue	90.00	70.00
111	A63	9c bl violet	35.00	20.00
112	A64	10c dark green	50.00	37.50
113	A65	12c plum	40.00	37.50
114	A66	15c magenta	32.50	*37.50*
		Nos. 104-114 (11)	368.25	255.65
		Set, never hinged	744.00	

Coronation of King George V.

Imperf., Pairs
Without Gum

104a	A56	1c	325.00
105a	A57	2c	325.00
108a	A60	5c	325.00
113a	A65	12c	425.00
114a	A66	15c	140.00

Trail of the Caribou Issue

Caribou
A67 A68

1919, Jan. 2 *Perf. 14*

115	A67	1c green	2.75	.35
116	A68	2c scarlet	3.00	.50
117	A67	3c red brown	3.50	.30
118	A67	4c violet	5.00	1.40
119	A68	5c ultramarine	9.00	1.40
120	A67	6c gray	22.50	22.50
121	A68	8c magenta	25.00	19.00
122	A67	10c dark green	22.50	5.50
123	A68	12c orange	75.00	45.00
124	A67	15c dark blue	42.50	42.50
125	A67	24c bister	45.00	42.50
126	A67	36c olive green	37.50	35.00
		Nos. 115-126 (12)	293.25	215.95
		Set, never hinged	616.50	

Services of the Newfoundland contingent in WWI.

Each denomination of type A67 is inscribed with the name of a different action in which Newfoundland troops took part.

For overprint and surcharge see Nos. C1, C5.

A shipment delay of the Trail of the Caribou issue led to trial surcharges of No. 74 reading "TWO / 2 / CENTS" in red. Fifty stamps were so surcharged, including examples with double surcharge. Value, $1,500.

Imperf., Pairs
Without Gum

115a	A67	1c		290.00
116a	A68	2c		290.00
117a	A67	3c	red brown	290.00
118a	A67	4c		290.00
119a	A68	5c		290.00
120a	A67	6c		290.00
121a	A68	8c		290.00
122a	A67	10c		290.00
123a	A68	12c		290.00
124a	A67	15c		290.00
125a	A67	24c		290.00
126a	A67	36c		290.00

No. 72 Surcharged in Black

Available Sept. 24 through Sept. 27, 1920

127	A35	2c on 30c slate	5.25	5.50
		Never hinged	8.00	
a.		Inverted surcharge	1,100.	

No. 127 with red surcharge is an unissued color trial. 25 examples are known. Value, $1,250.

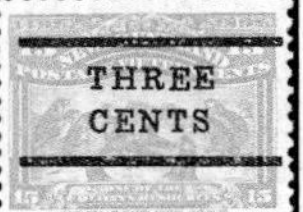

Nos. 70 and 73 Surcharged in Black

THREE CENTS
Type I — Bars 10½mm apart.
Type II — Bars 13½mm apart.

Available Sept. 13 through Oct. 3, 1920

128	A33	3c on 15c scar (I)	220.00	240.00
		Never hinged	350.00	
a.		Inverted surcharge	*2,750.*	
129	A33	3c on 15c scar (II)	17.50	11.00
		Never hinged	35.00	
130	A36	3c on 35c red	11.00	9.50
		Never hinged	20.00	
a.		Lower bar omitted	140.00	140.00

Trial surcharges of "THREE CENTS" between bars on No. 66 in red or brown are known. Twenty-five of each were produced, Value, $1,000.

Twin Hills, Tor's Cove — A70

South West Arm, Trinity — A71

War Memorial, St. John's A72

Humber River A73

Coast of Trinity — A74

Upper Steadies, Humber River — A75

Quidi Vidi, near St. John's — A76

Caribou Crossing Lake — A77

Humber River Canyon A78

Shell Bird Island A79

Mt. Moriah, Bay of Islands A80

Humber River near Little Rapids A81

Placentia, from Mt. Pleasant A82

Topsail Falls near St. John's A83

1923-24 Engr. *Perf. 14, 13½x14*

131	A70	1c gray green	1.75	.30
a.		Booklet pane of 8	500.00	
132	A71	2c carmine	1.75	.30
a.		Booklet pane of 8	310.00	
		Complete booklet, #131a, 2 #132a	*2,750.*	
133	A72	3c brown	2.25	.30
134	A73	4c brn violet	2.60	1.80
135	A74	5c ultramarine	6.50	2.25
136	A75	6c gray black	6.50	6.00
137	A76	8c dull violet	4.75	4.50
138	A77	9c slate green	42.50	27.50
139	A78	10c dark violet	4.25	2.50
140	A79	11c olive green	7.00	7.00
141	A80	12c lake	7.00	7.50
142	A81	15c deep blue	8.50	8.00
143	A82	20c red brn ('24)	12.00	7.50
144	A83	24c blk brn ('24)	80.00	50.00
		Nos. 131-144 (14)	187.35	125.45
		Set, never hinged	315.50	

For surcharge see No. 160.

Imperf., Pairs

131b	A70	1c	200.00
132b	A71	2c	200.00
133a	A72	3c	325.00
134a	A73	4c	250.00
135a	A74	5c	250.00
136a	A75	6c	250.00
137a	A76	8c	250.00
138a	A77	9c	250.00
139a	A78	10c	250.00
140a	A79	11c	250.00
141a	A80	12c	250.00
142a	A81	15c	185.00

Nos. 133a-139a, 141a-142a are without gum. Others are either with or without gum; values about the same.

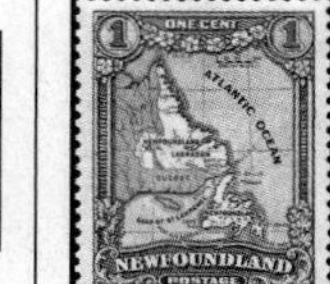
Map of Newfoundland A84

Steamship "Caribou" A85

Queen Mary, George V — A86

Prince of Wales — A87

Express Train — A88

Newfoundland Hotel, St. John's — A89

Heart's Content — A90

Cabot Tower, St. John's — A91

War Memorial, St. John's — A92

GPO, St. John's — A93

First Nonstop Transatlantic Flight, 1919 — A94

Colonial Building, St. John's — A95

Grand Falls, Labrador — A96

Perf. 14, 13½x13, 13x13½

1928, Jan. 3

145	A84	1c deep green	1.85	.75
146	A85	2c deep carmine	2.50	.70
a.		Imperf., pair	300.00	
147	A86	3c brown	2.75	.50
148	A87	4c lilac rose	3.50	1.80
149	A88	5c slate green	10.00	4.25
150	A89	6c ultramarine	5.75	5.00
151	A90	8c lt red brown	7.25	4.50
152	A91	9c myrtle green	7.00	7.00
153	A92	10c dark violet	9.00	4.25
154	A93	12c brn carmine	5.50	5.00
155	A91	14c red brown	10.50	7.00
156	A94	15c dark blue	9.25	7.00
157	A95	20c gray black	12.50	6.50
158	A93	28c gray green	35.00	27.50
159	A96	30c olive brown	17.50	7.50
		Nos. 145-159 (15)	139.85	89.25
		Set, never hinged	280.25	

See Nos. 163-182.

No. 136 Surcharged in Red or Black

Type I — 5mm between "CENTS" and bar.
Type II — 3mm between "CENTS" and bar.

Available Aug. 23-Aug. 30, 1929

160	A75	3c on 6c gray black (II) (R)	4.25	*5.50*
		Never hinged	6.75	
a.		Inverted surcharge (II)	1,000.	

The stamps with black surcharge, type I and II, were trial surcharges, and were not issued. There were 50 examples of each. Value, each $1,750.

Types of 1928 Issue Re-engraved

1c — On No. 145 the lines of the engraving are thinner and the impression is clearer than on No. 163. On the former "C. BAULD" is above "C. NORMAN." On the latter these words are transposed.

2c — On the 1928 stamp the "D" of "NEWFOUNDLAND" is 1mm from the scroll at the right; the flag at the stern is lower than the top of the boat davit. On the 1929 stamp the "D" is ½mm from the scroll and the flag rises above the davits.

3c — On the 1928 stamp the pearls at the top of the crown, the jewels of the tiara and the pillars flanking the portraits are all unshaded. On the reengraved stamp there are small curved lines inside the pearls, the jewels of the tiara have vertical shading lines. On the 1928 stamps the tablets with "THREE" and "CENTS" have a background of crossed lines (vertical and horizontal). On the 1929 stamp the background is of horizontal lines only.

4c — On the 1928 stamp the figures "4" have shading of horizontal and diagonal crossed lines. There are six circles at each side of the portrait.

On the 1929 stamp the "4s" have shading of horizontal lines only. There are five roses at each side of the portrait.

5c — The crossbars of the telegraph pole touch the frame at the left on the 1929 stamp but just clear it on the 1928 stamp. In the 1928 issue the foliate ornaments beside and below the figures "5" end in small scrolls and a small spur. These spurs are omitted on the 1929 stamp.

6c — On the re-engraved stamp the columns at right and left of the picture have heavy wavy outlines on the inner sides. There is no period after "JOHNS." The numerals in the lower corners are 1½mm wide instead of 1¼mm.

8c — The impression of the 1928 stamp is clear, that of 1931 is slightly blurred. The 1928 stamp has three horizontal lines above "EIGHT CENTS" and four berries on the laurel branch at the right side. On the 1931 stamp there are two horizontal lines and three berries.

10c — On the re-engraved stamp there is no period after "ST. JOHN'S." The letters of "TEN CENTS" are slightly larger and the numerals "10" slightly smaller than in 1928. Inside the "0" of "10" at the right there are two vertical lines instead of three. The clouds are fainter in 1929 and the cross upheld by the figure on the monument is more distinct. On the 1928 stamp the torch at the left side terminates in a single tongue of flame. On the 1929-30 stamp it terminates in two tongues.

15c — On the 1928 stamp the "N" of "NEWFOUNDLAND" is 1½mm from the left frame, the "L" of "LEAVING" is under the first "A" of "AIRPLANE" and the apostrophe in "JOHN'S" breaks the first line above it.

On the 1929 stamp the "N" of "NEWFOUNDLAND" is 1mm from the left frame, the "L" of "LEAVING" is below the "T" of "FIRST" and the apostrophe in "JOHN'S" does not touch the line above it.

20c — On the 1928 stamp the points of the "W" of "NEWFOUNDLAND" are truncated. The "O" is wide and nearly round. The columns that form the sides of the frame have a shading of evenly spaced horizontal lines at their inner sides.

On the 1929-31 stamp the points of the "W" form sharp angles. The "O" is narrow and has a small opening. Many lines have been added to the shading on the inner sides of the columns, making it almost solid.

30c — 1928 stamp. Size: 19¼x24½mm. At the outer side of the right column there are three strong and two faint vertical lines. Faint period after "FALLS."

1931 stamp. Size: 19x25mm. At the outer side of the right column there are two strong vertical lines and a fragment of the lower end of a faint one. Clear period after "FALLS." A great many of the small lines of the design have been deepened making the whole stamp appear darker.

1929-31 Unwmk. *Perf. 13½ to 14*

163	A84	1c green	2.00	.65
a.		Double impression	*425.00*	
b.		Vert. pair, imperf. btwn.	210.00	
164	A85	2c deep carmine	2.00	.70
165	A86	3c dp red brown	2.00	.70
166	A87	4c magenta	3.50	1.25
167	A88	5c slate green	7.00	2.50
168	A89	6c ultramarine	9.00	9.00
169	A92	10c dark violet	8.00	2.25
170	A94	15c deep blue ('30)	45.00	37.50
171	A95	20c gray blk ('31)	70.00	27.50
		Nos. 163-171 (9)	148.50	82.05
		Set, never hinged	297.00	

Imperf., Pairs

163c	A84	1c	120.00
164a	A85	2c pale carmine, *cream*	145.00
b.		2c dark carmine	145.00
165a	A86	3c	145.00
166a	A87	4c	160.00

No. 164b is without gum, others with gum.

Types of 1928 Issue Re-engraved

1931 Wmk. 224 *Perf. 13½x14*

172	A84	1c green, perf. 13½	2.25	1.30
a.		Horiz. pair, imperf. btwn.	450.00	
173	A85	2c red	7.00	1.30
174	A86	3c red brown	3.50	1.30
175	A87	4c rose	4.25	2.75
176	A88	5c grnsh gray	12.50	7.00
177	A89	6c ultramarine	17.50	17.50
178	A90	8c lt red brn	22.50	17.50
179	A92	10c dk violet	15.00	9.00
180	A94	15c deep blue	45.00	27.50
181	A95	20c gray black	55.00	17.50
182	A96	30c olive brown	45.00	25.00
		Nos. 172-182 (11)	229.50	127.65
		Set, never hinged	459.00	

Codfish — A97

George V — A98

Queen Mary — A99

Prince of Wales — A100

Caribou A101

Princess Elizabeth A102

Salmon Leaping Falls — A103

Newfoundland Dog — A104

Harp Seal Pup — A105

Cape Race — A106

Sealing Fleet — A107

Fishing Fleet Leaving for "The Banks" — A108

Type I Type II

FIVE CENT
Die I — Antlers even, or equal in height.
Die II — Antler under "T" higher.

1932-38 Engr. ***Perf. 13½, 14***

No.	Type	Description	Unused	Used
183	A97	1c green	2.75	.50
a.		Booklet pane of 4, perf. 13	75.00	
c.		Vert. pair, imperf. btwn.	200.00	
184	A97	1c gray black	.60	.25
a.		Bklt. pane of 4, perf. 13½	57.50	
b.		Booklet pane of 4, perf. 14	72.50	
185	A98	2c rose	2.25	.35
a.		Booklet pane of 4, perf. 13½	35.00	
b.		Booklet pane of 4, perf. 13	47.50	
186	A98	2c green	1.10	.25
a.		Bklt. pane of 4, perf. 13½	25.00	
b.		Booklet pane of 4, perf. 14	35.00	
d.		Horiz. pair, imperf. btwn.	150.00	
187	A99	3c orange brn	1.10	.35
a.		Bklt. pane of 4, perf. 13½	55.00	
		Complete booklet, #184a, 3 #186a, #187a	*525.00*	
b.		Booklet pane of 4, perf. 14	67.50	
		Complete booklet, #184b, 3 #186b, #187b	*575.00*	
c.		Booklet pane of 4, perf. 13	75.00	
		Complete booklet, #183a, 3 #185b, #187c	*900.00*	
		Complete booklet, #183a, 3 #185a, #187c	*900.00*	
e.		Vert. pair, imperf. btwn.	300.00	
188	A100	4c deep violet	7.00	2.00
189	A100	4c rose lake	.75	.50
b.		Vert. pair, imperf. btwn.	120.00	
c.		Horiz. pair, imperf. btwn.	120.00	
190	A101	5c vio brn, perf. 13½ (Die I)	9.50	2.00
191	A101	5c dp vio, perf. 13½ (Die II)	1.10	.40
a.		5c dp vio, perf. 13½ (Die I)	14.00	1.25
c.		Horiz. pair, imperf. btwn. (I)	240.00	
g.		Horiz. pair, imperf. btwn. (II)	240.00	
192	A102	6c dull blue	10.00	11.00
193	A103	10c olive black	1.40	.85
194	A104	14c int black	3.25	2.75
195	A105	15c magenta	2.50	2.25
196	A106	20c gray green	2.50	1.00
197	A107	25c gray	2.75	2.00
b.		Horiz. pair, imperf. btwn.	500.00	
c.		Vert. pair, imperf. btwn.	500.00	
198	A108	30c ultra	32.50	24.00
b.		Vert. pair, imperf. btwn.	1,000.	
199	A108	48c red brn ('38)	10.00	5.25
		Nos. 183-199 (17)	91.05	55.70
		Set, never hinged	133.05	

Two dies were used for 2c green, one for 2c rose.

See Nos. 253-266.

Imperf., Pairs

No.	Type	Value		
183b	A97	1c		240.00
184c	A97	1c		47.50
185c	A98	2c		250.00
186c	A98	2c		47.50
187d	A99	3c		95.00
189a	A100	4c		60.00
190a	A101	5c		200.00
191b	A101	5c	(II)	75.00
191d	A101	5c	(I)	100.00
192a	A102	6c		175.00
193a	A103	10c		110.00
194a	A103	14c		130.00
195a	A103	15c		130.00
196a	A106	20c		225.00
197a	A107	25c		225.00
198a	A108	30c		800.00
199a	A108	48c		125.00

All with gum. Nos. 186c, 187d, 192a, 193a and 196a also made without gum; values about 10% less.

Queen Elizabeth when Duchess of York — A109

Corner Brook Paper Mills — A110

Loading Iron Ore at Bell Island — A111

1932

No.	Type	Description	Unused	Used
208	A109	7c red brown	1.40	1.25
a.		Imperf., pair	160.00	
b.		Horiz. pair, imperf. between	575.00	
209	A110	8c orange red	1.40	1.10
a.		Imperf., pair	140.00	
210	A111	24c light blue	2.75	2.75
a.		Imperf., pair	200.00	
b.		Double impression	1,900.	
		Nos. 208-210 (3)	5.55	5.10
		Set, never hinged	7.75	

No. 208a was made both with and without gum. Values about the same.

See Nos. 259, 264.

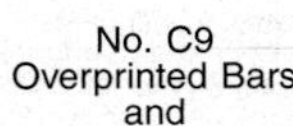
No. C9 Overprinted Bars and

1933, Feb. 9 Wmk. 224 ***Perf. 14***

No.	Type	Description	Unused	Used
211	AP6	15c brown	11.00	9.50
		Never hinged	17.00	
a.		Vert. pair, one without overprint	8,000.	
b.		Overprint reading up	5,000.	

The end of the period of use and availability of No. 211 is unknown.

"L. & S." stands for "Land and Sea."

Sir Humphrey Gilbert Issue

Sir Humphrey Gilbert — A112

Compton Castle, Home of the Gilbert Family — A113

Gilbert Coat of Arms — A114

Eton College — A115

Token from Queen Elizabeth I — A116

Sir Humphrey Receiving Royal Patents for Colonization A117

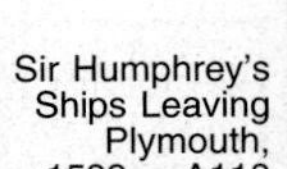
Sir Humphrey's Ships Leaving Plymouth, 1583 — A118

The Ships Arriving at St. John's — A119

Annexation of Newfoundland, Aug. 5, 1583 — A120

Coat of Arms of England A121

Sir Humphrey on the Deck of the "Squirrel" A122

Capt. John Mason's Map of Newfoundland, 1626 — A123

Queen Elizabeth I A124

Gilbert Statue at Truro A125

Wmk. 224

1933, Aug. 3 Engr. ***Perf. 13½***

No.	Type	Description	Unused	Used
212	A112	1c gray black	1.30	.75
213	A113	2c green	1.30	.75
b.		Double impression	*600.00*	
214	A114	3c yellow brn	2.75	.75
215	A115	4c carmine	2.00	.75
216	A116	5c dull violet	3.25	1.10
217	A117	7c blue	17.50	12.50
218	A118	8c orange red	8.50	7.00
219	A119	9c ultramarine	10.00	7.50
220	A120	10c red brown	8.50	6.25
221	A121	14c black	17.50	15.00
222	A122	15c claret	17.50	15.00
223	A123	20c deep green	15.00	10.00
224	A124	24c vio brown	27.50	22.50
225	A125	32c gray	27.50	22.50
		Nos. 212-225 (14)	160.10	122.35
		Set, never hinged	229.90	

350th anniv. of annexation of Newfoundland to England, Aug. 5, 1583, by authority of Letters Patent issued by Queen Elizabeth I to Sir Humphrey Gilbert.

Imperf., Pairs

No.	Type	Value	
212a	A112	1c	45.00
213a	A113	2c	45.00
214a	A114	3c	375.00
215a	A115	4c	50.00
216a	A116	5c	375.00
219a	A119	9c	500.00
220a	A120	10c	500.00
221a	A120	14c	400.00
222a	A120	15c	240.00
224a	A124	24c	225.00

No. 212a was made both with and without gum. Value of pair without gum about 10% less.

Common Design Types pictured following the introduction.

Silver Jubilee Issue

Common Design Type

1935, May 6 Wmk. 4 ***Perf. 11x12***

No.	Type	Description	Unused	Used
226	CD301	4c bright rose	2.25	.70
227	CD301	5c violet	2.25	.85
228	CD301	7c dark blue	4.00	3.50
229	CD301	24c olive green	9.00	7.00
		Nos. 226-229 (4)	17.50	12.05
		Set, never hinged	25.35	

Coronation Issue

Common Design Type

1937, May 12 ***Perf. 11x11½***

No.	Type	Description	Unused	Used
230	CD302	2c deep green	1.75	.70
231	CD302	4c carmine rose	1.75	.70
232	CD302	5c dark violet	3.50	1.40
		Nos. 230-232 (3)	7.00	2.80
		Set, never hinged	9.80	

Codfish A126

Map of Newfoundland — A127

Caribou A128

Corner Brook Paper Mills A129

Salmon A130

Newfoundland Dog — A131

Harp Seal Pup A132

Cape Race A133

Loading Iron Ore at Bell Island A134

Sealing Fleet A135

Fishing Fleet Leaving for "The Banks" A136

Type I

Type II

Two types of the 3c
Type I — Fine impression; no lines on bridge of nose.
Type II — Coarse impression; lines on bridge of nose.

Perf. 13½, 14 (#234-235)

1937, May 12 Wmk. 224

233 A126 1c gray black .65 .30
234 A127 3c org brn, die I 2.75 1.10
a. Die II 2.25 1.10
b. Vert. pair, imperf. btwn. (I) 850.00
c. Vert. pair, imperf. btwn. (II) 850.00
d. Horiz. pair, imperf. btwn. (I) 575.00
e. Horiz. pair, imperf. btwn. (II) 575.00
f. Imperf., pair (II) 240.00
i. Horiz. pair, imperf. vert., never hinged *1,600.*
j. Imperf., pair (I) *750.00*
235 A128 7c blue 3.00 2.50
236 A129 8c orange red 3.00 2.50
a. Imperf., pair 450.00
b. Vert. pair, imperf. between 1,500.
c. Horiz. pair, imperf. vert. *1,900.*
237 A130 10c olive gray 4.25 4.25
a. Double impression 280.00
238 A131 14c black 4.25 3.50
a. Imperf., pair 400.00
239 A132 15c rose lake 4.25 3.50
a. Vert. pair, imperf. between 1,500.
240 A133 20c green 4.25 2.25
a. Vert. pair, imperf. between 2,250.
241 A134 24c turq blue 4.25 3.25
a. Vert. pair, imperf. between 3,500.
242 A135 25c gray 4.25 3.25
a. Imperf., pair 250.00
243 A136 48c dark violet 7.00 4.00
a. Vert. pair, imperf. between 3,000.
b. Imperf., pair 275.00
Nos. 233-243 (11) 41.90 30.40
Set, never hinged 64.50

Imperfs are with gum. No. 238a, 242a issued without gum. No. 234f and 243b also made without gum; value the same.

Princess Elizabeth — A139

Designs: 2c, King George VI. 3c, Queen Elizabeth. 7c, Queen Mother Mary.

1938, May 12 ***Perf. 13½***

245 A139 2c green 1.75 .25
246 A139 3c dark carmine 1.75 .25
247 A139 4c light blue 2.30 .25
248 A139 7c dark ultra 1.60 1.10
b. Vert. pair, imperf. between *1,100.*
Nos. 245-248 (4) 7.40 1.85
Set, never hinged 9.40

See Nos. 254-256, 258, 269.

Imperf., Pairs

245a A139 2c 120.00
246a A139 3c 120.00
247a A139 4c 120.00
248a A139 7c 120.00
Set, never hinged 700.00

Nos. 245a-248a issued with or without gum; values the same.

George VI and Queen Elizabeth A141

1939, June 17 Unwmk.

249 A141 5c violet blue 1.25 1.10
Never hinged 1.75

Visit of King George and Queen Elizabeth.

No. 249 Surcharged in Brown or Red

Available Nov. 21 and exhausted by Dec. 16, 1939

250 A141 2c on 5c vio blue (Br) 1.40 1.00
251 A141 4c on 5c vio blue (R) 1.00 1.00
Set, never hinged 3.20

There are many varieties of broken letters and figures in the settings of the surcharges.

Sir Wilfred Grenfell and "Strathcona II" — A142

1941, Dec. 1 ***Perf. 12***

252 A142 5c dull blue .40 .30
Never hinged .50

Grenfell Mission, 50th anniv.

Types of 1931-38

1941-43 Wmk. 224 ***Perf. 12½***

253 A97 1c dark gray ('42) .35 .25
a. Imperf., pair 140.00
254 A139 2c deep green .35 .25
255 A139 3c rose carmine .50 .25
a. Imperf., pair 275.00
256 A139 4c blue .70 .30
257 A101 5c violet (Die I) 1.00 .25
a. Imperf., pair 180.00
b. Horiz. pair, imperf. vert. 450.00
c. Double impression 400.00
258 A139 7c vio blue ('42) 1.20 1.00
259 A110 8c red ('42) 1.40 .65
260 A103 10c brownish blk 1.40 .60
261 A104 14c black ('43) 2.00 1.75
a. Imperf., pair 240.00
c. Vert. pair, imperf. horiz. 500.00
262 A105 15c pale rose vio ('43) 2.00 1.40
263 A106 20c green ('43) 2.00 1.10
264 A111 24c deep blue ('43) 2.25 2.00
265 A107 25c slate ('43) 2.25 2.00
266 A108 48c red brown ('43) 3.25 1.75
Nos. 253-266 (14) 20.65 13.55
Set, never hinged 26.35

Nos. 254 and 255 are re-engraved.

Memorial University College A143

1943, Jan. 2 Unwmk. ***Perf. 12***

267 A143 30c carmine 1.40 1.00
Never hinged 1.85

No. 267 Surcharged in Black

Available Mar. 21 through April 1, 1946

268 A143 2c on 30c carmine .30 .30
Never hinged .40

Princess Elizabeth — A144

Wmk. 224

1947, Apr. 21 Engr. ***Perf. 12½***

269 A144 4c light blue .30 .25
Never hinged .40
a. Imperf., pair 225.00
b. Horiz. pair, imperf. vert. 400.00

Princess Elizabeth's 21st birthday.

Deck of the Matthew A145

1947, June 24

270 A145 5c rose violet .30 .25
Never hinged .40
a. Horiz. pair, imperf. between 1,350.
b. Imperf., pair 240.00

Cabot's arrival off Cape Bonavista, 450th anniv.

AIR POST STAMPS

No. 117 Overprinted in Black

Manuscript "Aerial Atlantic Mail JAR"

1919, Apr. 12 Unwmk. ***Perf. 14***

C1 A67 3c red brown *25,000. 15,000.*
Never hinged *40,000.*
a. Manuscript "Aerial Atlantic Mail JAR" *75,000. 25,000.*

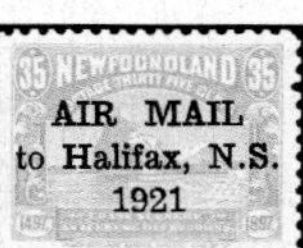
No. 70 Surcharged in Black on Block of 25 with Selvage Removed

1919, June 9 ***Perf. 12***

C2 A33 $1 on 15c scarlet 210.00 210.00
Never hinged 325.00
a. Without comma after "Post" 240.00 *275.00*
b. As "a," without period after "1919" 450.00 450.00

No. 73 Overprinted in Black on Block of 25 with Selvage Removed

1921, Nov. 7

C3 A36 35c red, 2½mm between "AIR" and "MAIL" 140.00 *190.00*
a. Inverted overprint 5,750.
b. With period after "1921" 160.00 *200.00*
c. As "b," inverted overprint *6,500.*

No. 74 Overprinted in Red on Block of 50 with Selvage

1927, May 21

C4 A37 60c black *45,000. 17,500.*
Never hinged *60,000.*

No. 126 Surcharged in Black on Block of 4

1930, Sept. 25 ***Perf. 14***

C5 A67 50c on 36c ol grn *9,000. 9,000.*
Never hinged *13,000.*

Dog Sled and Airplane — AP6

First Transatlantic Mail Airplane and Packet Ship — AP7

Routes of Historic Transatlantic Flights — AP8

1931, Jan. 2 Engr. Unwmk.

C6 AP6 15c brown 10.00 7.00
a. Horiz. pair, imperf. between 950.00
b. Vert. pair, imperf. between 1,050.
c. Imperf., pair 625.00
C7 AP7 50c green 32.50 25.00
a. Horiz. pair, imperf. between 1,250. 850.00
b. Vert. pair, imperf. between 1,350. 850.00
c. Imperf., pair 725.00
C8 AP8 $1 blue 70.00 55.00
a. Horiz. pair, imperf. between 1,200.
b. Vert. pair, imperf. between 1,200.
c. Imperf., pair 725.00
Nos. C6-C8 (3) 112.50 87.00
Set, never hinged 190.00

1931 Wmk. 224 Sideways

C9 AP6 15c brown 10.00 7.00
a. Horiz. pair, imperf. between 1,000.
b. Vert. pair, imperf. between 1,300.
c. Imperf., pair 600.00
C10 AP7 50c green 35.00 35.00
a. Horiz. pair, imperf. between 1,100.
b. Vert. pair, imperf. between 1,250.
c. Horiz. pair, Imperf. vert. 950.00
C11 AP8 $1 blue 95.00 90.00
a. Vert. pair, imperf. between 1,200.
c. Horiz. pair, imperf. between 1,200.
d. Vert. pair, imperf. horiz. 1,100.
e. Imperf., pair 700.00
Nos. C9-C11 (3) 140.00 132.00
Set, never hinged 260.00

As the watermark 224 does not show on every stamp in the sheet, pairs are found one with and one without watermark.

For overprint and surcharge see Nos. 211, C12.

No. C11 Surcharged in Red on Block of 4

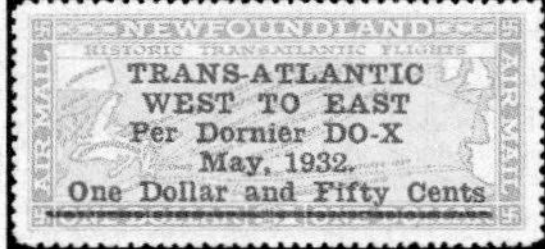

1932, May 19

C12 AP8 $1.50 on $1 blue 275.00 275.00
Never hinged 350.00
a. Inverted surcharge *20,000.*
Never hinged *25,000.*

A stamp of this design was produced in the US in 1932 by a private company under contract with Newfoundland authorities. The government canceled the contract and the stamp was not valid for prepayment of postage. Value, $35.

"Put to Flight" — AP9

"Land of Heart's Delight" AP10

"Spotting the Herd" AP11

"News from Home" AP12

"Labrador, The Land of Gold" AP13

Perf. 11½ (10, 60c), 14 (5, 30, 75c)

1933, June 9 **Engr.**

C13 AP9 5c lt brown 9.50 11.00
- *b.* Horiz. pair, imperf. between *1,100.*
- *c.* Vert. pair, imperf. between *1,250.*

C14 AP10 10c yellow 17.00 17.50
C15 AP11 30c blue 29.00 30.00
C16 AP12 60c green 62.50 57.50
C17 AP13 75c bister, perf. 14.3 57.50 57.50
- *b.* Horiz. pair, imperf. between *3,500.*
- *c.* Vert. pair, imperf. between *3,500.*

Nos. C13-C17 (5) 175.50 173.50
Set, never hinged 270.00

Beware of clever forgeries of Nos. C13b, C13c, C17b and C17c. Certificates of authenticity are highly recommended.

Imperf., Pairs

C13a	AP9	5c	250.00
C14a	AP10	10c	180.00
C15a	AP11	30c	700.00
C16a	AP12	60c	700.00
C17a	AP13	75c	700.00
Set, never hinged			3,150.

No. C17 Surcharged in Black

1933, July 24 ***Perf. 14.3***

C18 AP13 $4.50 on 75c bister 325.00 350.00
Never hinged 450.00
- *a.* Inverted surcharge *120,000.*
  Never hinged *150,000.*

On return from the Chicago World Fair "Century of Progress" with his "armada" of 24 seaplanes, Gen. Italo Balbo made a stopover in Shoal Harbour and accepted mail to Italy of about 1,150 covers.

No. C18a was not regularly issued.

The $4.50 on No. C14, 10c yellow, is a proof. Value, $62,500.

View of St. John's AP14

1943, June 1 **Unwmk.** ***Perf. 12***

C19 AP14 7c bright ultra .35 .30
Never hinged .45

POSTAGE DUE STAMPS

D1

Perf. 10-10½, Compound

1939-49 **Litho.** **Unwmk.**

J1 D1 1c yellow green, perf. 11 ('49) 4.25 *5.50*
- *a.* Perf. 10-10½ 7.00 5.50

J2 D1 2c vermilion 7.00 5.50
- *a.* Perf. 11x9 ('46) 7.00 5.50

J3 D1 3c ultramarine 7.00 5.50
- *a.* Perf. 11x9 ('49) 7.50 7.50
- *b.* Perf. 9 *3,750.*

J4 D1 4c yel org, perf. 11x9 ('49) 9.50 9.50
- *a.* Perf 10-10½ 15.00 15.00

J5 D1 5c pale brown 15.00 4.25
J6 D1 10c dark violet 7.00 6.50
Nos. J1-J6 (6) 49.75 36.75
Set, never hinged 78.75

1949 **Wmk. 224** ***Perf. 11***

J7 D1 10c dark violet 10.00 *15.00*
Never hinged 17.50
- *a.* Vert. pair, imperf. between *1,000.*

For used examples of Nos. J1-J7 with dated cancels from 1939-49, triple the values shown.

NOVA SCOTIA

ˌnō-və-ˈskō-shə

LOCATION — Eastern coast of Canada between the Gulf of St. Lawrence and the Atlantic Ocean
GOVT. — British Crown Colony
AREA — 21,428 sq. mi.
POP. — 386,500 (1871)
CAPITAL — Halifax

Nova Scotia joined the Canadian Confederation in 1867 and is now a province of the Dominion. Postage stamps of Canada are used.

12 Pence = 1 Shilling
100 Cents = 1 Dollar (1860)

Values for unused stamps are for examples with original gum as defined in the catalogue introduction except for Nos. 4-7, which are rarely found with any remaining original gum.

Queen Victoria — A1

Crown of Great Britain and Heraldic Flowers of the Empire — A2

Blue Paper

1851-57 **Unwmk.** **Engr.** ***Imperf.***

1 A1 1p red brown ('53) 2,500. 500.
- *a.* Half used as ½p on cover —

2 A2 3p bright blue 1,750. 225.
- *a.* Half used as 1½p on cover *3,750.*
- *b.* 3p pale blue ('57) 1,750. 275.
- *c.* As "b," half used as 1½p on cover *3,750.*

3 A2 3p dark blue 2,250. 300.
- *a.* Half used as 1½p on cover *4,500.*

4 A2 6p yellow green 5,500. 825.
- *a.* Half used as 3p on cover *4,500.*

5 A2 6p dark green ('57) 10,000. 2,250.
- *a.* Half used as 3p on cover *5,000.*
- *b.* Quarter used as 1½p on cover *47,500.*

6 A2 1sh reddish pur ('57) 22,500. 5,000.
- *a.* Half used as 6p on cover *35,000.*
- *b.* 1sh deep purple *25,000.* 6,000.
- *c.* As "6," quarter used as 3p on cover *90,000.*

7 A2 1sh dull violet 25,000. 6,000.
- *a.* Half used as 6p on cover *47,500.*

Reprints are on thin hard white paper. 1p in brown, 3p in blue, 6p dark green. 1sh violet black. Value about $300 per set.

No. 6 was reproduced by the collotype process in a souvenir sheet distributed at the London International Stamp Exhibition 1950.

Queen Victoria — A3

A5

A6

White or Yellowish Paper

1860-63 ***Perf. 12***

8 A3 1c black 15.00 7.50
- *a.* White paper 15.00 7.50
- *b.* Half used as ½c on cover *8,500.*
- *c.* Horiz. pair, imperf. vert. 350.00

9 A3 2c lilac 15.00 12.50
- *a.* Yellowish paper 15.00 12.50
- *b.* Half used as 1c on cover *3,500.*

10 A3 5c blue 425.00 12.00
- *a.* Yellowish paper 425.00 12.00
- *b.* Half used as 2½c on cover *5,000.*

11 A5 8½c green 15.00 *22.00*
- *a.* White paper 15.00 *22.00*

12 A5 10c vermilion 15.00 12.00
- *a.* Yellowish paper 15.00 12.00
- *b.* Half used as 5c on cover *1,200.*

13 A6 12½c black 42.50 37.50
- *a.* White paper 42.50 37.50

Nos. 8-13 (6) 527.50 103.50
Set, never hinged 1,460.

The stamps of Nova Scotia were replaced by those of Canada.

PRINCE EDWARD ISLAND

ˈprinˌtˌs ˈed-wərd ˈī-lənd

LOCATION — In the Gulf of St. Lawrence, opposite the provinces of New Brunswick and Nova Scotia
GOVT. — British Crown Colony
AREA — 2,184 sq. mi.
POP. — 92,000 (estimated)
CAPITAL — Charlottetown

Originally annexed to Nova Scotia, Prince Edward Island was a separate colony from 1769 to 1873, when it became a part of the Canadian Confederation. Postage stamps of Canada are now used.

12 Pence = 1 Shilling
100 Cents = 1 Dollar (1872)

A1 A2

Queen Victoria — A3

1861, Jan. 1 **Unwmk.** **Typo.** ***Perf. 9***

1 A1 2p dull rose 1,100. 325.
- *a.* 2p deep rose 1,350. 350.
- *b.* Rouletted *27,500.*
- *c.* Horiz. pair, imperf. between *6,750.*
- *d.* Diagonal half used as 1p on cover *7,000.*

2 A2 3p blue 2,250. 750.
- *a.* Diagonal half used as 1½p on cover *7,500.*
- *b.* Double impression 4,750.

No. 2b is valued with very small faults.

3 A3 6p yellow green 2,750. 1,200.

A4

A5

White or Yellowish Paper

1862-65 ***Perf. 11½-12***

4 A4 1p yellow orange 42.50 35.00
- *a.* 1p brown orange, perf. 11 50.00 35.00
- *b.* Imperf., pair 200.00
- *c.* Half used as ½p on cover *3,500.*

5 A1 2p rose 8.50 7.50
- *a.* Yellowish paper 22.50 7.50
- *b.* Imperf., pair 100.00
- *c.* Horiz. pair, imperf. vert. 275.00
- *d.* Vert. pair, imperf. horiz. 400.00
- *e.* Diagonal half used as 1p on cover *2,750.*
- *f.* "TWC" for "TWO" 75.00 60.00

6 A2 3p blue 16.00 15.00
- *a.* Yellowish paper 35.00 15.00
- *b.* Imperf., pair 150.00
- *c.* Vert. pair, imperf. horiz. 400.00
- *d.* Horiz. pair, imperf. vert. 400.00
- *e.* Diagonal half used as 1½p on cover 250.00
- *g.* Imperf. pair with gutter btwn. 950.00
- *h.* Imperf. tete-beche pair with gutter btwn. *3,000.*

7 A3 6p yellow green 125.00 95.00
- *a.* 6p blue green 125.00 95.00
- *c.* Diagonal half used as 3p on cover 5,500.

8 A5 9p mauve 95.00 80.00
- *a.* Imperf., pair 375.00
- *b.* Horiz. pair, imperf. vert. 450.00
- *c.* Diagonal half used as 4½p on cover 4,250.

Nos. 4-8 (5) 287.00 232.50
Set, never hinged 465.00

Queen Victoria — A6

1868

9 A6 4p black 9.00 19.00
- *a.* Yellowish paper 15.00 20.00
- *b.* Horiz. pair, imperf. vert. 190.00
- *c.* Diagonal half used as 2p on cover *2,250.*
- *d.* Imperf., pair 140.00
- *e.* Horiz. pair, imperf. between 160.00
- *g.* Horiz. strip of 3, imperf. btwn. *1,100.*

Queen Victoria — A7

1870, June 1 **Engr.** ***Perf. 12***

10 A7 4½p brown 90.00 75.00

A8

A9

A10

A11

A12

A13

1872, Jan. 1 Typo. *Perf. 12, 12½*

No.	Type	Description	Unused	Used
11	A8	1c brown orange	7.00	*7.50*
a.		Imperf., pair	240.00	
12	A9	2c ultra	35.00	*42.50*
a.		Imperf., pair	450.00	
b.		Diagonal half used as 1c on cover		*3,250.*
13	A10	3c rose	30.00	22.50
a.		Imperf., pair	475.00	
b.		Diagonal half used as 1½c on cover		—
c.		Horiz. or vert. pair, imperf. between	275.00	
14	A11	4c green	11.50	*16.00*
a.		Imperf., pair	475.00	
b.		Diagonal half used as 2c on cover		5,500.
15	A12	6c black	7.50	*13.00*
a.		Horiz. pair, imperf. btwn.	250.00	
b.		Half used as 3c on cover		*1,750.*
16	A13	12c violet	7.50	*30.00*
a.		Imperf., pair	450.00	
b.		Half used as 6c on cover		—
		Nos. 11-16 (6)	98.50	*131.50*
		Set, never hinged	138.50	

Scott 14b is unique and used in combination with No. 11.

CANADA

ˈka-nə-də

LOCATION — Northern part of North American continent, except for Alaska
GOVT. — Self-governing dominion in the British Commonwealth of Nations
AREA — 3,851,809 sq. mi.
POP. — 28,846,761 (1996)
CAPITAL — Ottawa

Included in the dominion are British Columbia, Vancouver Island, Prince Edward Island, Nova Scotia, New Brunswick and Newfoundland, all of which formerly issued stamps.

12 Pence = 1 Shilling
100 Cents = 1 Dollar (1859)

Catalogue values for unused stamps in this country are for Never Hinged items, beginning with Scott 268 in the regular postage section, Scott B1 in the semi-postal section, Scott C9 in the air post section, Scott CE3 in the air post special delivery section, Scott CO1 in the air post official section, Scott E11 in the special delivery section, Scott EO1 in the special delivery official section, Scott J15 in the postage due section, and Scott O1 in the official section.

Values for unused stamps of Nos. 1-33 are for examples with partial original gum. Stamps without gum often trade at prices very close to those of stamps with partial gum. Examples with full original gum and lightly hinged are extremely scarce and generally sell for substantially more than the values listed.

Very fine examples of the perforated issues between Nos. 11-20 will have perforations touching the design or frameline on at least one side due to the narrow spacing of the stamps on the plates. Stamps with perfs clear of the designs on all four sides are extremely scarce and will command much higher prices.

Province of Canada

Beaver — A1

Prince Albert — A2

Queen Victoria — A3

1851 Unwmk. Engr. *Imperf.*
Laid Paper

No.	Type	Description	Unused	Used
1	A1	3p red	*45,000.*	1,000.
2	A2	6p slate violet	*40,000.*	1,500.
a.		Diagonal half used as 3p on cover		*32,500.*
3	A3	12p black	*175,000.*	*135,000.*

On some stamps the laid lines of Nos. 1-3 are practically invisible.

1852-57 Wove Paper

No.	Type	Description	Unused	Used
4	A1	3p red	1,500.	225.
a.		3p brown red ('53)	1,600.	250.
b.		Diagonal half used as 1½p on cover		*32,500.*
c.		Ribbed paper	4,500.	525.
d.		Thin paper	1,500.	225.
5	A2	6p slate gray ('55)	30,000.	1,150.
a.		6p brownish gray	40,000.	1,700.
b.		6p greenish gray	30,000.	1,150.
c.		Diagonal half used as 3p on cover		20,000.
d.		Thick hard paper (gray vio) ('57)	30,000.	2,750.

Re-entries of the 3p are numerous. The main re-entry is distinguishable most easily by the line through "EE" and "PEN".

Most authorities believe the 12p black does not exist on wove paper.

Jacques Cartier — A4

1855

No.	Type	Description	Unused	Used
7	A4	10p blue	12,000.	1,600.
a.		Thick paper	12,000.	2,000.

Queen Victoria
A5 A6

1857

No.	Type	Description	Unused	Used
8	A5	½p rose	1,100.	700.
a.		Horizontally ribbed paper	10,000.	2,500.
b.		Vertically ribbed paper	10,000.	3,750.
9	A6	7½p green	10,000.	3,500.

Very Thick Soft Wove Paper

No.	Type	Description	Unused	Used
10	A2	6p reddish pur	32,500.	6,750.
a.		Half used as 3p on cover		*25,000.*

1858-59 Wove Paper *Perf. 12*

No.	Type	Description	Unused	Used
11	A5	½p rose	4,250.	1,500.
12	A1	3p red	17,500.	1,400.
13	A2	6p brown vio ('59)	25,000.	7,500.
a.		6p gray violet	25,000.	7,500.
b.		Diagonal half used as 3p on cover		*20,000.*

Nos. 11-13 values are for examples with perfs touching the design.

A7

A8

A9

A10

A11

1859

No.	Type	Description	Unused	Used
14	A7	1c rose	425.00	90.00
a.		Imperf., pair	5,500.	
b.		1c deep rose	575.00	150.00
15	A8	5c ver	575.00	37.50
		On cover		47.50
a.		Imperf., pair	*17,500.*	—
b.		Diagonal half used as 2½c on cover		*6,250.*
c.		5c brick red	625.00	42.50
16	A9	10c blk brn, perf. 11¾	25,000.	6,500.
a.		Half used as 5c on cover		*12,500.*
17	A9	10c red lil	1,500.	175.00
a.		10c violet	2,000.	160.00
b.		10c brown	1,500.	140.00
c.		Imperf., pair	15,000.	
d.		Diagonal half used as 5c on cover		*7,000.*
e.		10c deep red purple	3,250.	900.00
18	A10	12½c yel grn	850.00	150.00
a.		12½c blue green	1,050.	135.00
b.		Imperf., pair	5,750.	
19	A11	17c blue	1,250.	200.00
a.		17c slate blue	1,300.	225.00
b.		Imperf., pair	5,500.	

Values for Nos. 14-19 are for examples with perfs touching the design.

No. 15b was used with a 10c for a 12½c rate.

No. 16 should be accompanied by a certificate of authenticity issued by a recognized expertizing authority. Less expensive dark brown shades of the 10c often are offered as the rare black brown.

Imperfs. are without gum.

Re-entries of the 5c are numerous. Many of them are slight and have only small premium value. The major re-entry has many lines of the design double, especially the outlines of the ovals and frame at left. Value, used, about $800.

A12

1864

20 A12 2c rose 675.00 300.00
- *a.* 2c deep claret rose 750.00 350.00
- *b.* Imperf., pair 3,500.

Imperfs. are without gum.

Values are for examples with perfs touching the design.

Dominion of Canada

Queen Victoria
A13 A14

A15 A16

A17 A18

A19 A20

1868-76 ***Perf. 12, 11½x12 (5c)***

21 A13 ½c black 110.00 80.00
- *a.* Perf. 11½x12 ('73) 150.00 90.00
- *b.* Watermarked *25,000.* *11,000.*
- *c.* Thin paper 150.00 80.00

22 A14 1c brn red 800.00 160.00
- *a.* Watermarked *3,250.* 500.00
- *b.* Thin paper 950.00 150.00

23 A14 1c yell org 1,750. 250.00
- *a.* 1c deep orange 2,500. 225.00

24 A15 2c green 1,000. 100.00
- *a.* Watermarked 3,250. 400.00
- *b.* Thin paper 950.00 120.00
- *c.* Diagonal half used as 1c on cover *4,000.*

25 A16 3c red 2,250. 40.00
- *a.* Watermarked 5,250. 475.00
- *b.* Thin paper 2,500. 55.00

26 A17 5c ol grn ('75) 2,000. 225.00
- *a.* Perf. 12 *8,000.* 1,000.
- *b.* Imperf., pair *32,500.*

27 A18 6c dk brn 2,750. 140.00
- *a.* 6c yellow brown 2,500. 125.00
- *b.* Watermarked *22,500.* *2,500.*
- *c.* Thin paper 2,350. 160.00
- *d.* Diagonal half used as 3c on cover *3,000.*
- *e.* Vert. half used as 3c on cover *3,500.*
- *f.* 6c black brown, thin paper (Mar. '68, 1st printing) 3,250. 250.00

28 A19 12½c blue 1,200. 125.00
- *a.* Watermarked *7,000.* 425.00
- *b.* Thin paper 1,150. 150.00
- *c.* Horiz. pair, imperf. vert. —
- *d.* Vert. pair, imperf. horiz. *16,000.*

29 A20 15c gray vio 90.00 65.00
- *a.* Perf. 11½x12 ('74) 1,800. 475.00
- *b.* 15c red lilac 1,400. 125.00
- *c.* Watermarked *12,500.* 1,000.
- *d.* Imperf., pair 1,150.
- *e.* Thin paper 1,100. 150.00

30 A20 15c gray 90.00 65.00
- *a.* Perf. 11½x12 ('73) 2,000. 475.00
- *b.* 15c blue gray ('75) 135.00 75.00
- *c.* Very thick paper (dp vio) *5,250.* 1,200.
- *d.* Script wmk., Perf. 11½x12, ('76) *25,000.* *7,500.*
- *e.* 15c deep blue 1,850. 425.00

The watermark on Nos. 21b, 22a, 24a, 25a, 27b, 28a and 29c consists of double-lined letters reading: "E. & G. BOTHWELL CLUTHA MILLS." The script watermark on No. 30d reads in full: "Alexr. Pirie & Sons." Values for all these watermarked stamps are for fine examples. Very fine examples are rare, seldom traded, and generally command premiums of about 100% over the values listed.

No. 21b unused and used, and Nos. 26a and 26b unused are valued in the grade of fine. No. 26b is a unique pair.

The existence of No. 28c has been questioned.

1868 **Laid Paper**

31 A14 1c brown red *45,000.* *8,500.*
32 A15 2c green *250,000.*
33 A16 3c bright red *30,000.* 2,000.

Only three examples of No. 32 are recorded, none being very fine.

Montreal and Ottawa Printings

A21 A22

A23

A24 A25

A26 A27

1870-89 **Wove Paper** ***Perf. 12***

34 A21 ½c black ('82) 22.50 10.00
- *a.* Imperf., pair 600.00 400.00
- *b.* Horiz. pair, imperf. between 1,000.

35 A22 1c yellow 50.00 1.25
- *a.* 1c orange ('70) 300.00 11.00
- *b.* Imperf., pair 450.00
- *c.* Diagonal half used as ½c on circular 4,750.

36 A23 2c green ('72) 85.00 2.50
- *a.* Imperf., pair 675.00
- *b.* Diagonal half used as 1c on cover 2,100.
- *c.* Vertical half used as 1c on cover 2,100.
- *d.* 2c blue green ('89) 110.00 5.00
- *f.* Double impression *6,000.* —

37 A24 3c org red ('73) 175.00 1.50
- *a.* 3c rose ('71) 625.00 17.50
- *b.* 3c copper red ('70) 1,750. 65.00
- *c.* 3c dull red ('72) 175.00 3.25

38 A25 5c sl green ('76) 800.00 27.50
39 A26 6c yel brn ('72) 600.00 27.50
- *a.* Diagonal half used as 3c on cover 3,500.
- *c.* Imperf., pair 3,500.

40 A27 10c dull rose lil ('77) 1,600. 90.00
- *a.* 10c magenta ('80) 1,600. 90.00
- *b.* 10c deep lilac rose 1,600. 90.00

No. 34a was made with and without gum; values the same.

Examples of Nos. 36b and 36c postmarked "Halifax" are a private speculation.

No. 39c is unique and in the form of a strip of three.

1870 ***Perf. 12½***

37d A24 3c copper red (Ottawa) 11,000. 1,500.

1873-79 ***Perf. 11½x12***

35d A22 1c orange 500.00 20.00
36e A23 2c green 750.00 25.00
37e A24 3c red 575.00 12.50
38a A25 5c slate green 1,250. 52.50
39b A26 6c yellow brown 1,000. 60.00
40c A27 10c dull rose lilac 1,750. 250.00

The gum on Nos. 35d-40c is always dull and usually blotchy or streaky. It is distinct from the earlier clear, smooth gum and from the bright shiny gums of the later periods.

Nos. 38 and 40 were printed at Montreal. Printings of Nos. 34 to 37, and 39 were made at Ottawa or Montreal and can be separated only by differences in paper and gum.

Ottawa Printing

A28 A29

1888-97 ***Perf. 12***

41 A24 3c brt vermilion 65.00 .80
- *a.* 3c rose carmine 525.00 16.00

42 A25 5c gray 230.00 5.00
43 A26 6c red brown 225.00 12.50
- *a.* 6c chocolate ('90) 550.00 35.00

44 A28 8c viol blk ('93) 260.00 7.00
- *a.* 8c blue gray 425.00 8.50
- *b.* 8c slate 300.00 7.00
- *c.* 8c gray 300.00 7.00

45 A27 10c brn red ('97) 675.00 65.00
- *a.* 10c dull rose 625.00 55.00
- *b.* 10c pink 725.00 65.00

46 A29 20c ver ('93) 400.00 125.00
47 A29 50c dp blue ('93) 400.00 85.00

Stamps of the 1870-93 issues are found on paper varying from very thin to thick, also occasionally on paper showing a distinctly ribbed surface.

The gum on Nos. 41-47 appears bright and shiny, often with a yellowish tint.

Imperf., Pairs

41b	A24	3c	450.
42a	A25	5c	675.
43b	A26	6c	550.
44d	A28	8c	725.
45c	A27	10c	550.
46a	A29	20c	1,350.
47a	A29	50c	1,350.

Nos. 41b-45c made with and without gum. Without gum sell for the same as the unused hinged price.

Imperforates and Part-Perforates

From 1859 through 1943 (Nos. 14a/262a), imperforate stamps were printed. The earliest imperforates through perhaps 1917 most likely were from imprimatur sheets (i.e. the first sheets from the approved plates, normally kept in government files) or proof sheets on stamp paper that once were in the post office archives. The imperforates from approximately 1927 to 1943 (often made both with and without gum) were specially created and traded for classic stamps needed for the post office museum, given as gifts to governmental or other dignitaries, or sold or given to favored persons.

The only imperforates from this entire period that were issued to the public were Nos. 90A and 136-138.

Similarly, almost all stamps that are known part-perforate (i.e., horizontal pairs imperforate vertically and vertical pairs imperforate horizontally) were specially made for trading purposes or as presentation items to be given to favored persons. These part-perforates are not listed here, but they are listed in *Scott Classic Specialized Catalogue of Stamps & Covers.* Part-perforate error stamps that are believed to have been actually issued to the public are listed in this catalogue.

See the similar imperforates in the air post, Nos. CE1a and CE2a, special delivery, No. F2c (but not No. F1c which was an issued error), postage dues, and Nos. MR4b and MR4c.

Jubilee Issue

Queen Victoria, "1837" and "1897" — A30

1897, June 19 **Unwmk.** ***Perf. 12***

50 A30 ½c black 110.00 110.00
Never hinged 275.00
51 A30 1c orange 30.00 8.00
Never hinged 75.00
52 A30 2c green 37.50 15.00
Never hinged 92.50
53 A30 3c bright rose 30.00 2.50
Never hinged 75.00
54 A30 5c deep blue 60.00 45.00
Never hinged 170.00
55 A30 6c yell brn 220.00 175.00
Never hinged 575.00
56 A30 8c dark violet 130.00 70.00
Never hinged 300.00
57 A30 10c brown violet 160.00 120.00
Never hinged 400.00
58 A30 15c steel blue 275.00 190.00
Never hinged 675.00
59 A30 20c vermilion 275.00 190.00
Never hinged 650.00
60 A30 50c ultra 375.00 190.00
Never hinged 775.00
61 A30 $1 lake 850.00 650.00
Never hinged 2,750.
62 A30 $2 dk purple 1,300. 450.00
Never hinged 3,750.
63 A30 $3 yel bister 1,300. 1,000.
Never hinged 3,750.
64 A30 $4 purple 1,300. 1,000.
Never hinged 3,750.
65 A30 $5 olive green 1,300. 1,000.
Never hinged 3,750.
Nos. 50-60 (11) 1,703. 1,116.
Set, never hinged 4,062.50

60th year of Queen Victoria's reign.

Roller and smudged cancels on Nos. 61-65 sell for less.

A31

1897-98

66 A31 ½c black 15.00 8.50
Never hinged 37.50
67 A31 1c blue green 50.00 2.00
Never hinged 115.00
68 A31 2c purple 50.00 2.25
Never hinged 125.00
69 A31 3c car ('98) 90.00 2.00
Never hinged 225.00
70 A31 5c dk bl, *bluish* 175.00 10.00
Never hinged 500.00
71 A31 6c brown 140.00 45.00
Never hinged 350.00
72 A31 8c orange 325.00 21.00
Never hinged 850.00
73 A31 10c brn vio ('98) 600.00 100.00
Never hinged 1,500.
Nos. 66-73 (8) 1,445. 190.75
Set, never hinged 3,702.50

For surcharge see No. 87.

Imperf., Pairs

66a	A31	½c	500.
		Never hinged	950.
67a	A31	1c	400.
		Never hinged	750.
68a	A31	2c	500.
		Never hinged	950.
69a	A31	3c	800.
		Never hinged	1,450.
70a	A31	5c	525.
		Never hinged	800.
71a	A31	6c	700.
		Never hinged	1,450.
72a	A31	8c	700.
		Never hinged	1,300.
73a	A31	10c	700.
		Never hinged	1,300.

Nos. 66a, 67a, 68a and 70a made with and without gum. Specialists can distinguish printings made with and without gum by shade and paper quality. Without gum sell for about 80% of the unused hinged price.

A32

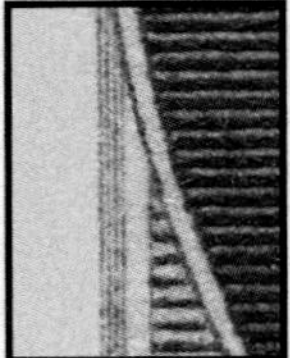

Type I

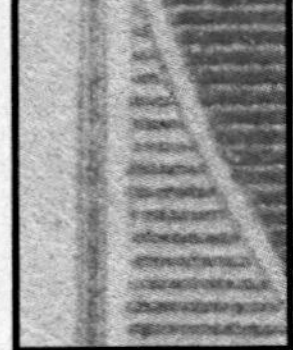

Type II

TWO CENTS:
Type I — Frame of four very thin lines.
Type II — Frame of a thick line between two thin ones.

1898-1902

74 A32 ½c black 12.50 2.75
Never hinged 25.00
75 A32 1c gray green 50.00 .75
Never hinged 100.00
76 A32 2c purple (I) 50.00 .75
Never hinged 80.00
a. Thick paper ('99) 175.00 15.00
Never hinged 350.00
77 A32 2c car (I) ('99) 55.00 .75
Never hinged 110.00
a. 2c carmine (II) ('99) 70.00 .60
Never hinged 140.00
b. Booklet pane of 6 (II) ('00) 1,600. —
Never hinged 3,000.
Complete booklet, 2 #77b *3,250.*
78 A32 3c carmine 110.00 1.10
Never hinged 250.00
79 A32 5c blue, *bluish* ('99) 250.00 3.00
Never hinged 500.00
80 A32 6c brown 200.00 57.50
Never hinged 400.00
81 A32 7c ol yel ('02) 140.00 22.50
Never hinged 280.00
82 A32 8c orange 350.00 27.50
Never hinged 700.00
83 A32 10c brown vio 450.00 30.00
Never hinged 1,000.
84 A32 20c ol grn ('00) 650.00 110.00
Never hinged 1,300.
Nos. 74-84 (11) 2,318. 256.60
Set, never hinged 4,615.

For surcharges see Nos. 88-88C.

Imperf., Pairs

74a A32 ½c 500.
Never hinged 800.
75a A32 1c 1,100.
Never hinged 2,100.
77c A32 2c (I) 550.
Never hinged 875.
77d A32 2c (II) *1,150.*
e. As No. 77b, imperf., 2 panes tete beche ('00) *15,000.*
79a A32 5c 1,100.
Never hinged 1,750.
80a A32 6c 1,100.
Never hinged 1,750.
81a A32 7c 600.
82a A32 8c 1,100.
Never hinged 2,000.
83a A32 10c 1,100.
Never hinged 2,000.
84a A32 20c 5,500.

Nos. 77d, 77e, 81a and 84a were made only without gum. No. 80a was made only with gum. Others either with or without gum and of these those without gum sell for about ⅔ of the values shown for unused hinged. Specialists can distinguish printings made with and without gum by shade and paper quality.

Values for complete booklets from No. 77b to No. 306b are for booklets with uncreased and very fine covers containing never-hinged panes with normal centering, which is fine. Booklets with very fine panes will sell for more. Booklet values from No. 325a to the present are for booklets with panes that are very fine. Values are for the most common booklet covers; other cover types exist for some booklets from No. 104a to 341a, and these may sell for more.

Imperial Penny Postage Issue

Map of British Empire on Mercator Projection A33

No. 86

1898, Dec. 7 **Engr. & Typo.**

85 A33 2c black, lav & car 40.00 9.00
Never hinged 100.00
a. Imperf., pair 450.00
86 A33 2c black, bl & car 40.00 9.00
Never hinged 100.00
a. Imperf., pair 450.00

Imperfs. are without gum.

Nos. 69 and 78 Surcharged in Black

1899, July

87 A31 2c on 3c carmine 17.50 7.50
Never hinged 45.00
88 A32 2c on 3c carmine 32.50 6.00
Never hinged 82.50

No. 78 Surcharged in Blue or Violet

A32a A32b

1899, Jan. 5

88B A32a 1(c) on ⅓ of 3c, on cover (Bl) *7,500.*
88C A32b 2(c) on ⅔ of 3c, on cover (V) *7,000.*

Nos. 88B-88C were prepared and used on Jan. 5 only at Port Hood, Nova Scotia, without official authorization.

Nos. 88B-88C must be accompanied by certificates from recognized expertizing organizations. Covers reported to date were backdated and never saw postal use.

King Edward VII — A34

Type I

Type II

Two types of 2c carmine.
Type I — Has breaks in the upper left shading lines above "DA" in Canada.
Type II — Has solid lines, no breaks.

1903-08 **Engr.**

89 A34 1c green 45.00 .40
Never hinged 115.00
90 A34 2c carmine, type II 55.00 .40
Never hinged 135.00
b. Booklet pane of 6 1,600. *1,100.*
Never hinged *2,750.*
Complete booklet, 2 #90b *3,500.*
e. 2c carmine, type I 150.00 2.00
Never hinged 375.00
f. Vert. pair, imperf. btwn and at either top or bottom *5,000.*
91 A34 5c blue, *blue* 250.00 5.75
Never hinged 600.00
92 A34 7c olive bister 225.00 6.25
Never hinged 550.00
93 A34 10c brown lilac 400.00 15.00
Never hinged 1,000.
94 A34 20c ol grn ('04) 750.00 50.00
Never hinged 1,875.
95 A34 50c purple ('08) 850.00 175.00
Never hinged 2,100.
Nos. 89-95 (7) 2,575. 252.80
Set, never hinged 6,275.

Values for Nos. 94 and 95 used are for examples with contemporaneous circular datestamps. Stamps with heavy cancellations or parcel cancellations sell for much less.

Issued: 1c-10c, 7/1/03; 20c, 9/27/04; 50c, 11/19/08.

Imperf., Type II

90A A34 2c carmine 40.00 40.00
Never hinged 80.00

No. 90A is the only imperforate Canada stamp besides Nos. 136-138 regularly issued to the public. 100,000 were issued.

Imperf., Pairs, Without Gum

89a A34 1c 675.00
90c A34 2c Type I 825.00
d. As No. 90c, imperf, 2 panes tete beche *20,000.*
91a A34 5c 1,100.
92a A34 7c 750.
93a A34 10c 1,100.

Quebec Tercentenary Issue

Prince and Princess of Wales, 1908 — A35

Jacques Cartier and Samuel de Champlain A36

Queen Alexandra and King Edward A37

Champlain's Home in Quebec A38

Generals Montcalm and Wolfe — A39

View of Quebec in 1700 — A40

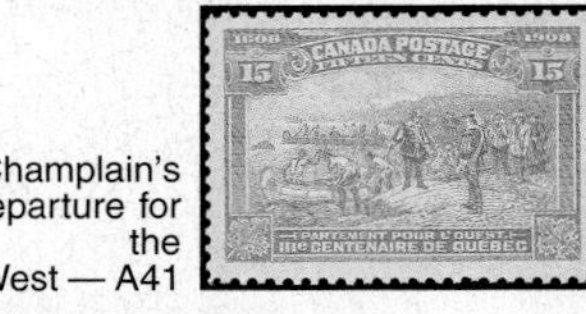

Champlain's Departure for the West — A41

Arrival of Cartier at Quebec A42

1908, July 16 ***Perf. 12***

96 A35 ½c black brown 8.00 5.00
Never hinged 19.00
97 A36 1c blue green 30.00 6.00
Never hinged 75.00
98 A37 2c carmine 40.00 3.00
Never hinged 100.00
99 A38 5c dark blue 85.00 70.00
Never hinged 210.00
100 A39 7c olive green 140.00 100.00
Never hinged 350.00
101 A40 10c dark violet 200.00 125.00
Never hinged 500.00
102 A41 15c red orange 225.00 160.00
Never hinged 550.00
103 A42 20c yellow brown 250.00 225.00
Never hinged 625.00
Nos. 96-103 (8) 978.00 694.00
Set, never hinged 2,429.

Imperf., Pairs

96a A35 ½c 750.
Never hinged 1,400.
97a A36 1c 750.
Never hinged 1,400.
98a A37 2c 750.
Never hinged 1,400.
99a A38 5c 750.
Never hinged 1,400.
100a A39 7c 750.
Never hinged 1,400.
101a A40 10c 750.
Never hinged 1,400.
102a A41 15c 750.
Never hinged 1,400.
103a A42 20c 750.
Never hinged 1,400.

100 pairs of imperfs made, 50 with gum and 50 without. Due to demand, pairs without gum generally sell for 90-95% of the unused hinged price.

King George V — A43

Type I

Type II

Two types of 1c.
Type I — The "N" of "ONE" is separated from the oval above it.
Type II — The "N" of "ONE" almost touches the oval above it.

Type I

Type II

Two types of 3c carmine.
Type I — The "R" of "THREE" is separated from the oval above it. The bottom line of the vignette does not touch the heavy diagonal stroke at right.
Type II — The "R" of "THREE" almost touches the oval above it. The bottom horizontal line of the vignette touches the heavy diagonal stroke at right.

Note that the values for Nos. 104-122 are for sheet stamps with perforations on four sides. Single stamps from booklet panes Nos. 104a, 105a, 105b, 106a, 106d, 107b, 107c, 108a and 109a all have natural straight edges on one or two sides, and (except for No. 107d singles) they are worth much less than the listed sheet stamps.

See note on booklet panes and complete booklets after Nos. 74-84. Values for listed booklet panes throughout this catalog are for very fine panes.

1911-25

104 A43 1c dark green 25.00 .25
Never hinged 60.00
a. As "b," booklet pane of 6 30.00 30.00
Never hinged 70.00
Complete booklet, 4 #104a 200.00
d. As "c," booklet pane of 6 180.00 180.00
Never hinged 325.00
Complete booklet, 4 #104d *875.00*
e. 1c yellow green 25.00 .25
Never hinged 60.00
f. As "e," booklet pane of 6 35.00 35.00

Never hinged 70.00
Complete booklet, 4 #104f 180.00

105 A43 1c org yell (I) ('22) 25.00 .25
Never hinged 60.00
a. Booklet pane of 4 + 2 labels 55.00 55.00
Never hinged 110.00
b. Booklet pane of 6 62.50 62.50
Never hinged 125.00
Complete booklet, 4 #105b *375.00*
d. 1c org yellow (II) 20.00 .25
Never hinged 50.00

106 A43 2c carmine 25.00 .25
Never hinged 60.00
a. Booklet pane of 6 35.00 35.00
Never hinged 80.00
Complete booklet, 2 #106a 140.00
b. 2c pink 150.00 18.00
Never hinged 350.00
c. 2c rose carmine 25.00 .25
Never hinged 60.00
d. As "c," booklet pane of 6 160.00 160.00
Never hinged 320.00

107 A43 2c yel grn ('22) 27.50 .25
Never hinged 65.00
a. Thin paper ('24) 20.00 2.50
Never hinged 50.00
b. Booklet pane of 4 + 2 labels ('22) 70.00 *80.00*
Never hinged 140.00
c. Booklet pane of 6 ('22) 325.00 *325.00*
Never hinged 575.00
Complete booklet, 2 #107c 800.00

108 A43 3c brown ('18) 30.00 .40
Never hinged 70.00
a. Booklet pane of 4 + 2 labels 90.00 *95.00*
Never hinged 180.00
Complete booklet, 2 #108a 550.00
Complete booklet, #105a, 107b, 108a *475.00*

109 A43 3c car (I) ('23) 20.00 .25
Never hinged 47.50
a. Booklet pane of 4 + 2 labels 70.00 *75.00*
Never hinged 140.00
Complete booklet, 2 #109a 325.00
Complete booklet, #105a, 107b, 109a *350.00*
c. Die II ('24) 50.00 .25
Never hinged 125.00

110 A43 4c ol bis ('22) 55.00 4.50
Never hinged 120.00

111 A43 5c dark blue ('12) 200.00 1.75
Never hinged 450.00

112 A43 5c violet ('22) 40.00 1.00
Never hinged 100.00
a. Thin paper ('24) 35.00 7.50
Never hinged 87.50

113 A43 7c yel ocher ('12) 55.00 3.50
Never hinged 130.00

114 A43 7c red brn ('24) 22.50 10.00
Never hinged 55.00

115 A43 8c blue ('25) 37.50 10.00
Never hinged 92.50

116 A43 10c plum ('12) 275.00 4.00
Never hinged 700.00

117 A43 10c blue ('22) 47.50 2.00
Never hinged 115.00

118 A43 10c bis brn ('25) 40.00 2.00
Never hinged 100.00

119 A43 20c ol grn ('25) 100.00 1.75
Never hinged 275.00

120 A43 50c blk brn ('25) 70.00 3.75
Never hinged 200.00
a. 50c black ('12) 300.00 12.00
Never hinged 700.00

122 A43 $1 orange ('23) 85.00 10.00
Never hinged 215.00
Nos. 104-122 (18) 1,180. 55.90
Set, never hinged 2,915.

For type A43 perforated 12x8 see No. 184.
For surcharges see Nos. 139-140.
Issued: Nos. 104, 106, 12/22/11; No. 105, 6/7/22; No. 108, 8/6/18; No. 109, 12/18/23; 4c, 7/7/22; No. 111, 1/17/12; No. 112, 2/2/22; Nos. 113, 116, 1/12/12; No. 114, 12/12/24; 8c, 9/1/25; No. 117, 2/20/22; No. 118, 8/1/25; 20c, 1/23/12; 50c, 1/26/12; $1, 7/22/23.

Imperf., Panes

105c As No. 105b, imperf, 2 panes tete beche *15,000.*
107d As No. 107c, imperf, 2 panes tete beche *15,000.*
109b As No. 109a, imperf, 2 panes tete beche *15,000.*

Imperf., Pairs

110a A43 4c 2,250.
Never hinged 4,250.
112b A43 5c 2,250.
Never hinged 4,250.
114a A43 7c 2,250.
Never hinged 4,250.
115a A43 8c 2,250.
Never hinged 4,250.
118a A43 10c 2,250.
Never hinged 4,250.
119a A43 20c 2,250.
Never hinged 4,250.
120b A43 50c 2,750.
Never hinged 5,500.
122a A43 $1 2,250.
Never hinged 4,250.

Nos. 105c and 109b made without gum, others with gum. About half of the No. 120b pairs have creases; value thus $500.

Coil Stamps

1913 *Perf. 8 Horizontally*

123 A43 1c dark green 110.00 65.00
Never hinged 275.00
124 A43 2c carmine 110.00 65.00
Never hinged 275.00

1912-24 *Perf. 8 Vertically*

125 A43 1c green 25.00 2.00
Never hinged 50.00
126 A43 1c org yell (II) ('23) 11.00 7.50
Never hinged 22.00
a. As #126, block of 4 (II) 55.00 50.00
Never hinged 85.00
b. 1c org yellow (I) 30.00 11.00
Never hinged 60.00
c. As "b," block of 4 (I) 700.00
Never hinged 1,200.
127 A43 2c carmine 40.00 2.00
Never hinged 80.00
128 A43 2c green ('22) 25.00 1.10
Never hinged 50.00
a. Block of 4 65.00 60.00
Never hinged 100.00
129 A43 3c brown ('18) 30.00 1.30
Never hinged 60.00
130 A43 3c carmine (I) ('24) 70.00 9.00
Never hinged 140.00
a. Block of 4 (I) 1,050. 750.00
Never hinged 1,650.
b. Die II 100.00 10.00
Never hinged 200.00
Nos. 125-130 (6) 201.00 22.90
Set, never hinged 402.00

Nos. 126a and 128a were issued to the public. Nos. 126c and 130a were issued "by favor" as were the various other imperf and part-perfs of this era.
Beware of fakes of No. 130a made from No. 138.

1915-24 *Perf. 12 Horizontally*

131 A43 1c dark green 7.00 6.50
Never hinged 14.00
132 A43 2c carmine 40.00 10.00
Never hinged 80.00
133 A43 2c yell grn ('24) 85.00 70.00
Never hinged 170.00
134 A43 3c brown ('21) 12.50 6.50
Never hinged 25.00
Nos. 131-134 (4) 144.50 93.00
Set, never hinged 289.00

"The Fathers of Confederation" — A44

1917, Sept. 15 *Perf. 12*

135 A44 3c brown 45.00 2.25
Never hinged 115.00
a. Imperf., pair 500.00

50th anniv. of the Canadian Confederation. Imperfs. are without gum.

1924 *Imperf.*

136 A43 1c orange yellow (I) 35.00 35.00
Never hinged 65.00
Pair 70.00 70.00
Never hinged 130.00
137 A43 2c green 35.00 35.00
Never hinged 65.00
Pair 70.00 70.00
Never hinged 130.00
138 A43 3c carmine (I) 17.50 17.50
Never hinged 32.50
Pair 35.00 35.00
Never hinged 70.00
Nos. 136-138 (3) 87.50 87.50
Set, never hinged 162.50

No. 109 Surcharged

a

b

1926 *Perf. 12*

139 A43(a) 2c on 3c carmine (I) 55.00 55.00
Never hinged 90.00
a. Pair, one without surcharge 700.00
Never hinged 1,150.
b. Double surcharge 275.00
Never hinged 425.00
c. Die II 850.00
Never hinged 1,700.
140 A43(b) 2c on 3c carmine 25.00 25.00
Never hinged 47.50
a. Double surcharge 250.00 *250.00*
Never hinged 390.00
b. Triple surcharge 250.00 *275.00*
Never hinged 390.00
c. Double surch., one invtd. 525.00
Never hinged 775.00

Sir John A. Macdonald A45

Sir Wilfrid Laurier A48

"The Fathers of Confederation" — A46

Parliament Building at Ottawa A47

Map of Canada A49

1927, June 29

141 A45 1c orange 2.75 1.30
Never hinged 5.00
142 A46 2c green 2.00 .25
Never hinged 3.75
143 A47 3c brown carmine 8.50 4.25
Never hinged 15.00
144 A48 5c violet 4.25 2.10
Never hinged 8.00

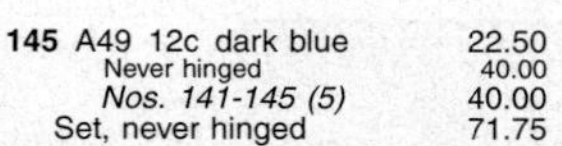
145 A49 12c dark blue 22.50 5.75
Never hinged 40.00
Nos. 141-145 (5) 40.00 13.65
Set, never hinged 71.75

60th year of the Canadian Confederation. Nos. 141-145 exist partly perforated.

Imperf., Pairs

141a A45 1c 120.00
Never hinged 180.00
142a A46 2c 120.00
Never hinged 180.00
143a A47 3c 120.00
Never hinged 180.00
144a A48 5c 120.00
Never hinged 180.00
145a A49 12c 120.00
Never hinged 180.00

Thomas d'Arcy McGee — A50

Laurier and Macdonald A51

Robert Baldwin and Sir Louis Hypolyte Lafontaine A52

1927, June 29

146 A50 5c violet 4.00 3.00
Never hinged 7.25
147 A51 12c green 10.00 5.50
Never hinged 18.00
148 A52 20c brown carmine 27.50 6.50
Never hinged 50.00
Nos. 146-148 (3) 41.50 15.00
Set, never hinged 75.25

Nos. 146-148 were to have been issued in July, 1926, as a commemorative series, but were withheld and issued June 29, 1927.

Imperf., Pairs

146a A50 5c 120.00
Never hinged 180.00
147a A51 12c 120.00
Never hinged 180.00
148a A52 20c 120.00
Never hinged 180.00

King George V — A53

Mt. Hurd from Bell-Smith's Painting "The Ice-crowned Monarch of the Rockies" A54

Quebec Bridge A55

Harvesting Wheat A56

Schooner "Bluenose" A57

Parliament Building A58

1928-29

149 A53 1c orange 3.25 .30
Never hinged 6.00
a. Booklet pane of 6 27.50 20.00
Never hinged 40.00
Complete booklet, 4 #149a 140.00
150 A53 2c green 1.90 .25
Never hinged 3.50
a. Booklet pane of 6 27.50 20.00
Never hinged 40.00
Complete booklet, 2 #150a 85.00
151 A53 3c dk carmine 27.50 12.50
Never hinged 50.00
152 A53 4c bister ('29) 22.50 5.00
Never hinged 40.00
153 A53 5c dp violet 15.00 2.50
Never hinged 30.00
a. Booklet pane of 6 220.00 220.00
Never hinged 300.00
Complete booklet, 3 #149a, 2 #150a, 1 #153a *600.00*

154 A53 8c blue 18.00 9.00
Never hinged 32.50
155 A54 10c green 20.00 2.50
Never hinged 37.50
156 A55 12c gray ('29) 45.00 8.00
Never hinged 85.00
157 A56 20c dk car ('29) 65.00 11.00
Never hinged 120.00
158 A57 50c dk blue ('29) 225.00 65.00
Never hinged 425.00
159 A58 $1 ol grn ('29) 300.00 80.00
Never hinged 575.00
Nos. 149-159 (11) 743.15 196.05
Set, never hinged 1,405.

Imperf., Panes

149c As No. 149a, imperf, 2 panes tete beche 950.
Never hinged 1,350.
150c As No. 150a, imperf, 2 panes tete beche 950.
Never hinged 1,350.
153c As No. 153a, imperf, 2 panes tete beche 950.
Never hinged 1,350.

Imperf., Pairs

149b A53 1c 90.00
Never hinged 125.00
150b A53 2c 90.00
Never hinged 125.00
151a A53 3c 110.00
Never hinged 160.00
152a A53 4c 110.00
Never hinged 160.00
153b A53 5c 110.00
Never hinged 160.00
154a A53 8c 110.00
Never hinged 160.00
155a A54 10c 180.00
Never hinged 270.00
156a A55 12c 180.00
Never hinged 270.00
157a A56 20c 180.00
Never hinged 270.00
158a A57 50c 750.00
Never hinged 1,125.
159a A58 $1 675.00
Never hinged 975.00

Coil Stamps

1929 ***Perf. 8 Vertically***

160 A53 1c orange 40.00 22.50
Never hinged 75.00
Precanceled 17.50
161 A53 2c green 40.00 3.50
Never hinged 75.00

King George V A59

Library of Parliament A60

The Citadel at Quebec A61

Harvesting Wheat A62

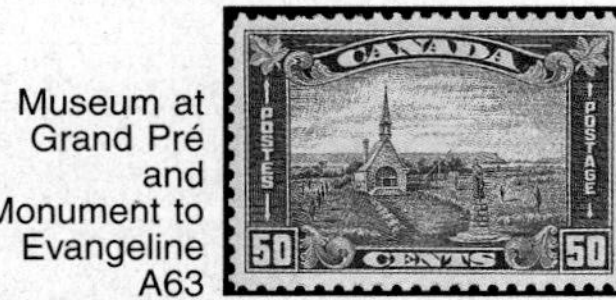

Museum at Grand Pré and Monument to Evangeline A63

Mt. Edith Cavell A64

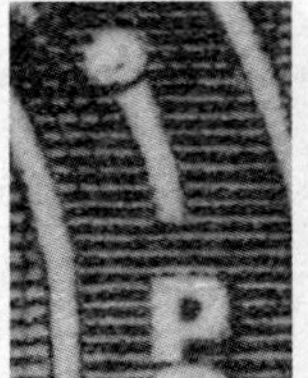

Type I

Type II

Two types of 1c.
Type I — Three thick and one thin colored lines between "P" at right and ornament above it.
Type II — Four thick colored lines. Curved line in ball of ornament at right is longer than in die I.

Type I

Type II

Two types of 2c.
Type I — The top of the letter "P" encloses a tiny dot of color.
Type II — The top of the "P" encloses a larger spot of color than in die I. The "P" appears almost like a "D."

1930-31 ***Perf. 11***

162 A59 1c orange 1.25 .70
Never hinged 2.50
163 A59 1c dp grn (II) 2.00 .25
Never hinged 4.00
a. Booklet pane of 4 + 2 labels (II) 120.00 100.00
Never hinged 180.00
b. Die I 2.00 .25
Never hinged 4.00
c. Booklet pane of 6 (I) 22.50 20.00
Never hinged 35.00
Complete booklet, 4 #163c 180.00
164 A59 2c dull green (I) 1.75 .25
Never hinged 3.50
a. Booklet pane of 6 32.50 32.50
Never hinged 47.50
Complete booklet, 2 #164a 170.00
165 A59 2c deep red (I) 1.75 .30
Never hinged 3.50
a. Die II 1.90 .25
Never hinged 3.75
b. Booklet pane of 6 (I) 25.00 22.50
Never hinged 37.50
Complete booklet, 2 #165b 80.00
166 A59 2c dk brn (II) ('31) 1.75 .25
Never hinged 3.50
a. Booklet pane of 4 + 2 labels (II) 130.00 115.00
Never hinged 200.00
b. Die I 5.00 4.00
Never hinged 10.00
c. Booklet pane of 6 (I) 57.50 57.50
Never hinged 87.50
Complete booklet, 2 #166c 225.00
167 A59 3c deep red ('31) 2.75 .25
Never hinged 5.50
a. Booklet pane of 4 + 2 labels 40.00 32.50
Never hinged 60.00
Complete booklet, 2 #167a 110.00
Complete booklet, #163a, 166a, 167a *450.00*
168 A59 4c yel bister 15.00 6.00
Never hinged 30.00
169 A59 5c dull violet 7.00 5.00
Never hinged 14.00
170 A59 5c dull blue 8.50 1.25
Never hinged 17.00
171 A59 8c dark blue 20.00 13.50
Never hinged 55.00
172 A59 8c red orange 8.50 5.50
Never hinged 17.00
173 A60 10c olive green 10.00 1.30
Never hinged 20.00
174 A61 12c gray black 25.00 4.50
Never hinged 50.00
175 A62 20c brown red 47.50 1.40
Never hinged 95.00
176 A63 50c dull blue 175.00 14.00
Never hinged 350.00
177 A64 $1 dk ol green 175.00 27.50
Never hinged 350.00
Nos. 162-177 (16) 502.75 81.95
Set, never hinged 1,020.50

See No. 201. For surcharge see No. 191. For overprint see No. 203.

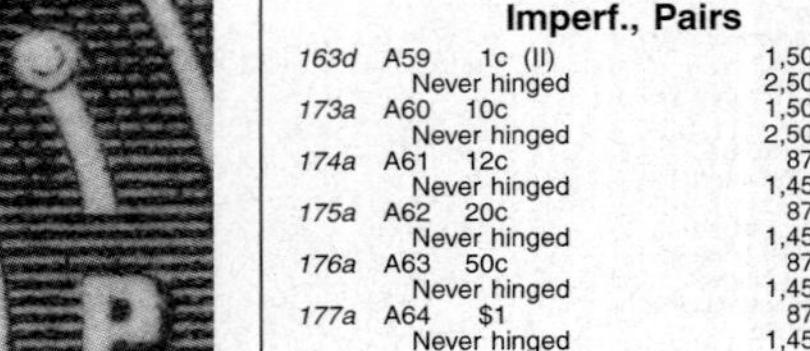

Imperf., Pairs

163d A59 1c (II) 1,500.
Never hinged 2,500.
173a A60 10c 1,500.
Never hinged 2,500.
174a A61 12c 875.
Never hinged 1,450.
175a A62 20c 875.
Never hinged 1,450.
176a A63 50c 875.
Never hinged 1,450.
177a A64 $1 875.
Never hinged 1,450.

Coil Stamps

1930-31 ***Perf. 8½ Vertically***

178 A59 1c orange 12.50 8.00
Never hinged 25.00
179 A59 1c deep green 9.00 5.25
Never hinged 18.00
180 A59 2c dull green 5.00 2.50
Never hinged 10.00
181 A59 2c deep red 20.00 2.00
Never hinged 40.00
182 A59 2c dark brown ('31) 12.50 .65
Never hinged 25.00
183 A59 3c deep red ('31) 18.00 .65
Never hinged 36.00
Nos. 178-183 (6) 77.00 19.05
Set, never hinged 154.00

George V Type of 1912-25

1931, June 24 ***Perf. 12x8***

184 A43 3c carmine 8.00 4.00
Never hinged 20.00

Sir Georges Etienne Cartier — A65

1931, Sept. 30 ***Perf. 11***

190 A65 10c dark green 12.50 .25
Never hinged 27.50
a. Imperf., pair 375.00
Never hinged 750.00

Nos. 165, 165a Surcharged

1932, June 21

191 A59 3c on 2c dp red (II) 1.25 .25
Never hinged 2.00
a. Die I 3.00 1.90
Never hinged 5.00

King George V — A66

Edward, Prince of Wales — A67

Allegory of British Empire A68

1932, July 12

192 A66 3c deep red 1.25 .25
Never hinged 2.50
193 A67 5c dull blue 7.00 2.50
Never hinged 14.00
194 A68 13c deep green 9.00 6.00
Never hinged 18.00
Nos. 192-194 (3) 17.25 8.75
Set, never hinged 34.50

Imperial Economic Conference, Ottawa.

Type of 1930 and

King George V — A69

Type I

Type II

Two types of 3c.

Type I — Upper left tip of "3" level with horizontal line to its left.

Type II — Raised "3"; upper left tip of "3" is above horizontal line.

1932, Dec. 1

No.	Type	Description	Unused	Used
195	A69	1c dk green	1.25	.25
		Never hinged	2.25	
a.		Booklet pane of 4 + 2 labels ('33)	90.00	85.00
		Never hinged	135.00	
b.		Booklet pane of 6 ('33)	50.00	47.50
		Never hinged	75.00	
		Complete booklet, 4 #195b	225.00	
196	A69	2c black brown	1.30	.25
		Never hinged	2.50	
a.		Booklet pane of 4 + 2 labels ('33)	120.00	110.00
		Never hinged	180.00	
b.		Booklet pane of 6 ('33)	90.00	70.00
		Never hinged	135.00	
		Complete booklet, 2 #196b	*375.00*	
c.		Inverted surcharge	—	
d.		Rotary press dry printing, perf. 11¼x12	*37.50*	*5.50*
197	A69	3c deep red (I)	1.40	.25
		Never hinged	2.75	
c.		Die II	1.50	.25
		Never hinged	2.75	
d.		Booklet pane of 4 + 2 labels, die II ('33)	42.50	37.50
		Never hinged	85.00	
		Complete booklet, 2 #197d	125.00	
		Complete booklet, #195a, 196a, 197d	250.00	
198	A69	4c ocher	50.00	7.00
		Never hinged	95.00	
199	A69	5c dark blue	12.00	.50
		Never hinged	21.00	
a.		Horiz. pair, imperf. vert.	1,350.	
		Never hinged	1,900.	
200	A69	8c red orange	35.00	3.50
		Never hinged	65.00	
201	A61	13c dull violet	40.00	3.50
		Never hinged	75.00	
		Nos. 195-201 (7)	140.95	15.25
		Set, never hinged	263.50	

Type A66 has at the foot of the stamp "OTTAWA-CONFERENCE 1932". This inscription does not appear on the stamps of type A69.

Imperf., Pairs

No.	Type	Description	Value
195c	A69	1c	225.00
		Never hinged	375.00
196c	A69	2c	225.00
		Never hinged	375.00
197b	A69	3c (I)	225.00
		Never hinged	375.00
197e	A69	3c (II)	*3,500.*
198a	A69	4c	225.00
		Never hinged	375.00
199b	A69	5c	225.00
		Never hinged	375.00
200a	A69	8c	225.00
		Never hinged	375.00
201a	A69	13c	750.00
		Never hinged	1,200.

No. 197e exists as one unused block of 4.

Government Buildings, Ottawa — A70

1933, May 18 *Perf. 11*

No.	Type	Description	Unused	Used
202	A70	5c dark blue	10.00	3.00
		Never hinged	18.50	
a.		Imperf., pair	575.00	
		Never hinged	950.00	

Meeting of the Executive Committee of the UPU at Ottawa, May and June, 1933.

No. 175 Overprinted in Blue

1933, July 24

No.	Type	Description	Unused	Used
203	A62	20c brown red	40.00	14.00
		Never hinged	70.00	
a.		Imperf., pair	575.00	
		Never hinged	950.00	

World's Grain Exhibition and Conference at Regina.

Steamship Royal William — A71

1933, Aug. 17

No.	Type	Description	Unused	Used
204	A71	5c dark blue	11.00	3.75
		Never hinged	20.00	
a.		Imperf., pair	575.00	
		Never hinged	950.00	

Centenary of the linking by steam of the Dominion, then a colony, with Great Britain, the mother country. The Royal William's 1833 voyage was the first Trans-Atlantic passage under steam all the way.

George V Type of 1932
Coil Stamps

1933 *Perf. 8½ Vertically*

No.	Type	Description	Unused	Used
205	A69	1c dark green	12.50	2.50
		Never hinged	22.50	
206	A69	2c black brown	17.50	1.10
		Never hinged	32.50	
207	A69	3c deep red	17.50	.40
		Never hinged	32.50	
		Nos. 205-207 (3)	47.50	4.00
		Set, never hinged	87.50	

Cartier's Arrival at Quebec — A72

1934, July 1 *Perf. 11*

No.	Type	Description	Unused	Used
208	A72	3c blue	4.00	1.40
		Never hinged	7.50	
a.		Imperf., pair	525.00	
		Never hinged	850.00	

Landing of Jacques Cartier, 400th anniv.

Group from Loyalists Monument, Hamilton, Ontario A73

1934, July 1

No.	Type	Description	Unused	Used
209	A73	10c olive green	28.00	7.50
		Never hinged	52.50	
a.		Imperf., pair	1,400.	
		Never hinged	2,250.	

Emigration of the United Empire Loyalists from the US to Canada, 150th anniv.

Seal of New Brunswick — A74

1934, Aug. 16

No.	Type	Description	Unused	Used
210	A74	2c red brown	2.50	2.00
		Never hinged	4.75	
a.		Imperf., pair	600.00	
		Never hinged	1,050.	

150th anniv. of the founding of the Province of New Brunswick.

Princess Elizabeth A75

Duke of York A76

King George V and Queen Mary — A77

Prince of Wales — A78

Windsor Castle A79

Royal Yacht Britannia A80

1935, May 4 *Perf. 12*

No.	Type	Description	Unused	Used
211	A75	1c green	.65	.35
		Never hinged	1.00	
212	A76	2c brown	.70	.25
		Never hinged	1.10	
213	A77	3c carmine	2.00	.25
		Never hinged	3.00	
214	A78	5c blue	4.00	3.00
		Never hinged	6.00	
215	A79	10c green	8.00	3.00
		Never hinged	12.75	
216	A80	13c dark blue	8.50	6.50
		Never hinged	13.25	
		Nos. 211-216 (6)	23.85	13.35
		Set, never hinged	37.10	

25th anniv. of the accession to the throne of George V.

Imperf., Pairs

No.	Type	Description	Value
211a	A75	1c	275.00
		Never hinged	425.00
212a	A76	2c	275.00
		Never hinged	425.00
213a	A77	3c	275.00
		Never hinged	425.00
214a	A78	5c	275.00
		Never hinged	425.00
215a	A79	10c	275.00
		Never hinged	425.00
216b	A80	13c	275.00
		Never hinged	425.00

King George V — A81

Royal Canadian Mounted Police — A82

Confederation Conference at Charlottetown, 1864 — A83

Niagara Falls — A84

Parliament Buildings, Victoria, B.C. — A85

Champlain Monument, Quebec A86

1935, June 1 *Perf. 12*

217 A81 1c green .30 .25
Never hinged .45
a. Bklt. pane of 4 + 2 labels 70.00 70.00
Never hinged 105.00
b. Booklet pane of 6 50.00 50.00
Never hinged 80.00
Complete booklet, 4 #217b 125.00
218 A81 2c brown .30 .25
Never hinged .45
a. Bklt. pane of 4 + 2 labels 70.00 70.00
Never hinged 105.00
b. Booklet pane of 6 60.00 60.00
Never hinged 75.00
Complete booklet, 2 #218b 130.00
219 A81 3c dk carmine .65 .25
Never hinged .90
a. Bklt. pane of 4 + 2 labels 40.00 40.00
Never hinged 60.00
Complete booklet, 2 #219a 100.00
Complete booklet, #217a, 218a, 219a 225.00
c. Printed on gummed side 600.00
220 A81 4c yellowish org 2.50 .55
Never hinged 3.75
221 A81 5c blue 3.25 .35
Never hinged 5.00
a. Horiz. pair, imperf. vert. 200.00
Never hinged 300.00
222 A81 8c dp orange 2.50 2.25
Never hinged 3.75
223 A82 10c car rose 8.00 .25
Never hinged 12.50
224 A83 13c violet 8.00 .75
Never hinged 12.50
225 A84 20c olive green 14.00 .75
Never hinged 21.00
226 A85 50c dull violet 25.00 6.00
Never hinged 37.50
227 A86 $1 deep blue 55.00 11.00
Never hinged 82.50
Nos. 217-227 (11) 119.50 22.65
Set, never hinged 180.30

No. 219c is valued in the grade of fine. Very fine examples are rare and sell for much more.

Imperf., Pairs

217c A81 1c 200.00
Never hinged 290.00
218c A81 2c 200.00
Never hinged 290.00
219b A81 3c 200.00
Never hinged 290.00
220a A81 4c 200.00
Never hinged 290.00
221b A81 5c 200.00
Never hinged 290.00
222a A81 8c 200.00
Never hinged 290.00
223a A82 10c 200.00
Never hinged 290.00
224a A83 13c 200.00
Never hinged 290.00
225a A84 20c 200.00
Never hinged 290.00
226a A85 50c 200.00
Never hinged 290.00
227a A86 $1 325.00
Never hinged 475.00

Coil Stamps

1935 *Perf. 8 Vertically*

228 A81 1c green 12.50 3.00
Never hinged 19.00
229 A81 2c brown 15.50 1.00
Never hinged 30.00
230 A81 3c dark carmine 12.50 .60
Never hinged 19.00
Nos. 228-230 (3) 40.50 4.60
Set, never hinged 68.00

George VI — A87

1937 *Perf. 12*

231 A87 1c green .30 .25
Never hinged .45
a. Booklet pane of 4 + 2 labels 15.00 *22.50*
Never hinged 22.50
b. Booklet pane of 6 7.50 *20.00*
Never hinged 11.50
Complete booklet, 4 #231b *37.50*
232 A87 2c brown .65 .25
Never hinged 1.00
a. Booklet pane of 4 + 2 labels 20.00 *22.50*
Never hinged 30.00
b. Booklet pane of 6 12.00 *16.00*
Never hinged 18.00
Complete booklet, 2 #232b *40.00*
233 A87 3c carmine .65 .25
Never hinged 1.00
a. Booklet pane of 4 + 2 labels 7.00 *12.50*
Never hinged 10.50
Complete booklet, 2 #233a *17.50*
Complete booklet, #231a, 232a, 233a *47.50*
234 A87 4c yellow 2.75 .25
Never hinged 4.00
235 A87 5c blue 3.50 .25
Never hinged 5.00
236 A87 8c orange 2.75 .45
Never hinged 4.00
Nos. 231-236 (6) 10.60 1.70
Set, never hinged 15.45

Imperf., Pairs

231c A87 1c 300.00
Never hinged 425.00
232c A87 2c 300.00
Never hinged 425.00
233b A87 3c 300.00
Never hinged 425.00
234a A87 4c 300.00
Never hinged 425.00
235a A87 5c 300.00
Never hinged 425.00
236a A87 8c 300.00
Never hinged 425.00

George VI and Queen Elizabeth A88

1937, May 10

237 A88 3c carmine .35 .25
Never hinged .40
a. Imperf., pair 550.00
Never hinged 800.00

Coronation of King George VI and Queen Elizabeth.

George VI Types of 1937 Coil Stamps

1937 *Perf. 8 Vertically*

238 A87 1c green 2.75 1.00
Never hinged 4.00
239 A87 2c brown 5.00 .35
Never hinged 7.50
240 A87 3c carmine 8.00 .25
Never hinged 12.00
Nos. 238-240 (3) 15.75 1.60
Set, never hinged 23.50

Memorial Chamber, Parliament Building, Ottawa — A89

Entrance to Halifax Harbor A90

Fort Garry Gate, Winnipeg A91

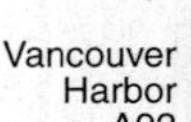

Vancouver Harbor A92

Chateau de Ramezay, Montreal A93

1938 *Perf. 12*

241 A89 10c dk carmine 10.00 .25
Never hinged 13.00
a. 10c carmine rose 8.00 .25
Never hinged 12.00
242 A90 13c deep blue 12.00 .60
Never hinged 18.00
243 A91 20c red brown 16.00 .45
Never hinged 24.00
244 A92 50c green 35.00 6.00
Never hinged 50.00
245 A93 $1 dull violet 70.00 7.00
Never hinged 110.00
a. Vert. pair, imperf. horiz. *4,250.*
Never hinged *6,500.*
Nos. 241-245 (5) 143.00 14.30
Set, never hinged 215.00

Imperf., Pairs

241b A89 10c dark carmine 500.00
Never hinged 750.00
241c A89 10c carmine rose 500.00
Never hinged 750.00
242a A90 13c 500.00
Never hinged 750.00
243a A91 20c 500.00
Never hinged 750.00
244a A92 50c 500.00
Never hinged 750.00
245b A93 $1 675.00
Never hinged 1,000.

Princess Elizabeth and Princess Margaret Rose — A94

War Memorial, Ottawa — A95

King George VI and Queen Elizabeth A96

Unwmk.

1939, May 15 **Engr.** *Perf. 12*

246 A94 1c green & black .35 .25
Never hinged .40
247 A95 2c brown & black .35 .25
Never hinged .40
248 A96 3c dk car & black .35 .25
Never hinged .40
Nos. 246-248 (3) 1.05 .75
Set, never hinged 1.20

Visit of George VI and Queen Elizabeth to Canada and the US.

Imperf., Pairs

246a A94 1c 500.00
Never hinged 725.00
247a A95 2c 500.00
Never hinged 725.00
248a A96 3c 500.00
Never hinged 725.00

A97

A98

King George VI — A99

Grain Elevators A100

Farm Scene A101

Parliament Buildings — A102

"Ram" Tank — A103

Corvette A104

Munitions Factory A105

Destroyer A106

1942-43 **Engr.** *Perf. 12*

249 A97 1c green .35 .25
Never hinged .45
a. Booklet pane of 4 + 2 labels 3.50 *3.50*
Never hinged 5.25
b. Booklet pane of 6 5.00 *5.00*
Never hinged 7.50
Complete booklet, 4 #249b *21.00*
c. Booklet pane of 3 ('43) 2.50 *5.00*
Never hinged 3.75
250 A98 2c brown .40 .25
Never hinged .60
a. Booklet pane of 4 + 2 labels ('43) 7.00 *7.00*
Never hinged 10.50
b. Booklet pane of 6 10.50 *11.50*
Never hinged 16.00
Complete booklet, 2 #250b *32.50*
d. Vert. strip of 3, imperf. horiz. *5,500.*
251 A99 3c dk carmine .60 .25
Never hinged .90
a. Booklet pane of 4 + 2 labels 4.25 *5.25*
Never hinged 6.50
Complete booklet, 2 #251a *10.00*
Complete booklet, #249a, 250a, 251a *22.50*
252 A99 3c rose violet ('43) .50 .25
Never hinged .70
a. Booklet pane of 4 + 2 labels 3.25 4.50
Never hinged 5.00
Complete booklet, 2 #252a *5.50*
b. Booklet pane of 3 3.25 *4.50*
Never hinged 4.75
c. Booklet pane of 6 ('47) 3.75 *3.75*
Never hinged 5.50
253 A100 4c greenish black 1.25 .60
Never hinged 1.90
254 A98 4c dk car ('43) .65 .25
Never hinged .95
a. Booklet pane of 6 5.25 *10.50*

No.	Type	Description	Unused	Used
		Never hinged	8.00	
		Complete booklet, #254a	*6.50*	
		Complete booklet, #252c, 254a, 2 #C9a	*30.00*	
b.		Booklet pane of 3	3.25	*4.50*
		Never hinged	4.75	
		Complete booklet, #249c, 252b, 254b	*11.25*	
255	A97	5c deep blue	1.20	.25
		Never hinged	1.80	
256	A101	8c red brown	1.60	.50
		Never hinged	2.40	
257	A102	10c brown	4.75	.25
		Never hinged	7.00	
258	A103	13c dull green	4.75	3.60
		Never hinged	7.00	
259	A103	14c dull grn ('43)	7.50	.35
		Never hinged	11.25	
260	A104	20c chocolate	9.00	.25
		Never hinged	13.50	
261	A105	50c violet	27.50	1.75
		Never hinged	40.00	
262	A106	$1 deep blue	55.00	7.50
		Never hinged	85.00	
		Nos. 249-262 (14)	115.05	16.30
		Set, never hinged	173.45	

Canada's contribution to the war effort of the Allied Nations.

No. 250d totally imperf horiz. is unique and is valued in the grade of fine. Beware of strips with blind perfs; these sell for much less.

For overprints see Nos. O1-O4.

For valuing information concerning complete booklets, see lined note before No. 85.

Imperf., Pairs

No.	Type	Description	Value
249d	A97	1c	275.00
		Never hinged	400.00
250c	A98	2c	275.00
		Never hinged	400.00
251b	A99	3c	275.00
		Never hinged	400.00
252d	A99	3c	275.00
		Never hinged	400.00
253a	A100	4c	275.00
		Never hinged	400.00
254c	A98	4c	275.00
		Never hinged	400.00
255a	A97	5c	275.00
		Never hinged	400.00
256a	A100	8c	275.00
		Never hinged	400.00
257a	A102	10c	400.00
		Never hinged	600.00
258a	A103	13c	400.00
		Never hinged	600.00
259a	A103	14c	400.00
		Never hinged	600.00
260a	A104	20c	400.00
		Never hinged	600.00
261a	A105	50c	400.00
		Never hinged	600.00
262a	A106	$1	575.00
		Never hinged	850.00

Types of 1942 Coil Stamps

1942-43 ***Perf. 8 Vertically***

No.	Type	Description	Unused	Used
263	A97	1c green ('43)	1.40	.55
		Never hinged	2.25	
264	A98	2c brown	2.10	1.10
		Never hinged	3.00	
265	A99	3c dark carmine	2.10	1.10
		Never hinged	3.00	
266	A99	3c rose violet ('43)	4.25	.35
		Never hinged	6.00	
267	A98	4c dk carmine ('43)	7.00	.30
		Never hinged	9.00	
		Nos. 263-267 (5)	16.85	3.40
		Set, never hinged	23.25	

See Nos. 278-281.

Catalogue values for unused stamps in this section, from this point to the end of the section, are for Never Hinged items.

Farm Scene, Ontario A107

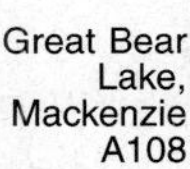

Great Bear Lake, Mackenzie A108

Hydroelectric Station, Saint Maurice River A109

Combine A110

Logging, British Columbia A111

Train Ferry, Prince Edward Island A112

1946, Sept. 16 **Engr.** ***Perf. 12***

No.	Type	Description	Unused	Used
268	A107	8c red brown	2.00	.70
269	A108	10c olive	2.50	.25
270	A109	14c black brown	4.00	.25
271	A110	20c slate black	4.50	.25
272	A111	50c dk blue green	17.50	1.75
273	A112	$1 red violet	42.50	3.00
		Nos. 268-273 (6)	73.00	6.20

For overprints see Nos. O6-O10, O21-O23, O25.

Alexander Graham Bell — A113

1947, Mar. 3

274 A113 4c deep blue .25 .25

Birth centenary of Alexander Graham Bell.

Citizen of Canada — A114

1947, July 1

275 A114 4c deep blue .25 .25

Issued on the 80th anniv. of the Canadian Confederation, to mark the advent of Canadian Citizenship.

Princess Elizabeth — A115

1948, Feb. 16

276 A115 4c deep blue .25 .25

Marriage of Princess Elizabeth to Lieut. Philip Mountbatten, R. N., on Nov. 20, 1947.

Parliament Buildings Ottawa A116

1948, Oct. 1

277 A116 4c gray .25 .25

Centenary of Responsible Government.

George VI Types of 1942 Coil Stamps

1948 ***Perf. 9½ Vertically***

No.	Type	Description	Unused	Used
278	A97	1c green	6.50	3.25
279	A98	2c brown	21.00	8.50
280	A99	3c rose violet	15.00	3.00
281	A98	4c dark carmine	21.00	2.25
		Nos. 278-281 (4)	63.50	17.00

John Cabot's Ship "Matthew" A117

1949, Apr. 1 **Engr.** ***Perf. 12***

282 A117 4c deep green .25 .25

Entry of Newfoundland into confederation with Canada.

"Founding of Halifax, 1749" A118

1949, June 21 **Unwmk.**

283 A118 4c purple .25 .25

200th anniv. of the founding of Halifax, Nova Scotia.

A119

A120

A121

A122

A123

1949, Nov. 15

No.	Type	Description	Unused	Used
284	A119	1c green	.25	.25
a.		Booklet pane of 3 ('50)	.75	*3.00*
285	A120	2c sepia	.25	.25
286	A121	3c rose violet	.35	.25
a.		Booklet pane of 3 ('50)	2.50	*6.50*
b.		Booklet pane of 4 + 2 labels ('50)	3.25	*3.75*
		Complete booklet, 2 #286b	*7.00*	

287 A122 4c dk carmine .55 .25
a. Booklet pane of 3 ('50) 12.50 12.50
Complete booklet, #284a, 286a, 287a *21.00*
b. Booklet pane of 6 ('50) 18.00 18.00
Complete booklet, #287b *22.50*
288 A123 5c deep blue 1.25 .65
Nos. 284-288 (5) 2.65 1.65

Stamps from booklet panes of 3 are imperf. on 2 or 3 sides.

"POSTES POSTAGE" Omitted

1950, Jan. 19
289 A119 1c green .25 .25
290 A120 2c sepia .35 .25
291 A121 3c rose violet .35 .25
292 A122 4c dark carmine .35 .25
293 A123 5c deep blue 1.25 1.00
Nos. 289-293 (5) 2.55 2.00

See Nos. 295-300, 305-306, 309-310. For overprints see Nos. O12-O20.

Oil Wells, Alberta A124

1950, Mar. 1 Engr. *Perf. 12*
294 A124 50c dull green 8.50 1.30

Development of oil wells in Canada. For overprints see Nos. O11, O24.

Types of 1949 "POSTES POSTAGE" Omitted Coil Stamps

1950 ***Perf. 9½ Vertically***
295 A119 1c green .75 .30
296 A121 3c rose violet 1.10 .55

With "POSTES POSTAGE" *Perf. 9½ Vertically*

297 A119 1c green .40 .25
298 A120 2c sepia 3.50 1.50
299 A121 3c rose violet 2.10 .25
300 A122 4c dark carmine 19.00 .75
Nos. 297-300 (4) 25.00 2.75

Indians Drying Skins on Stretchers A125

1950, Oct. 2 ***Perf. 12***
301 A125 10c black brown .90 .25

Canada's fur resources. For overprint see No. O26.

Fishing A126

1951, Feb. 1 Unwmk.
302 A126 $1 bright ultra 35.00 10.00

Canada's fish resources. For overprint see No. O27.

Sir Robert Laird Borden A127

William L. Mackenzie King A128

1951, June 25 ***Perf. 12***
303 A127 3c dp turq green .25 .25
304 A128 4c rose pink .25 .25

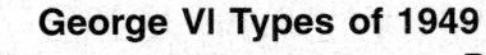

George VI Types of 1949

1951 ***Perf. 12***
305 A120 2c olive green .25 .25
306 A122 4c orange vermilion .35 .25
a. Booklet pane of 3 5.25 2.75
Complete booklet, #284a, 286a, 306a *13.00*
b. Booklet pane of 6 5.00 5.00
Complete booklet, #306b *6.75*

For overprints see Nos. O28-O29.

Coil Stamps *Perf. 9½ Vertically*

309 A120 2c olive green 1.40 .60
310 A122 4c orange vermilion 2.75 .70

Trains of 1851 and 1951 — A129

"Threepenny Beaver" of 1851 — A130

Designs: 5c, Steamships City of Toronto and Prince George. 7c, Stagecoach and Plane.

1951, Sept. 24 Unwmk. *Perf. 12*
311 A129 4c dark gray .60 .25
312 A129 5c purple 1.80 1.25
313 A129 7c deep blue 1.10 .30
314 A130 15c bright red 1.20 .30
Nos. 311-314 (4) 4.70 2.10

Centenary of British North American postal administration.

Princess Elizabeth and Duke of Edinburgh A131

1951, Oct. 26 Engr.
315 A131 4c violet .25 .25

Visit of Princess Elizabeth, Duchess of Edinburgh and the Duke of Edinburgh to Canada and the US.

Symbols of Newsprint Paper Production A132

1952, Apr. 1 Unwmk. *Perf. 12*
316 A132 20c gray 1.50 .25

Canada's paper production. For overprint see No. O30.

Red Cross on Sun — A133

1952, July 26 Engr. and Litho.
317 A133 4c blue & red .25 .25

18th Intl. Red Cross Conf., Toronto, July 1952.

Sir John J. C. Abbott A134

Alexander Mackenzie A135

1952, Nov. 3 Engr.
318 A134 3c rose lilac .25 .25
319 A135 4c orange vermilion .25 .25

Canada Goose A136

1952, Nov. 3
320 A136 7c blue .40 .25

For overprint see No. O31.

Pacific Coast Indian House and Totem Pole — A137

1953, Feb. 2
321 A137 $1 gray 5.75 .90

For overprint see No. O32.

Natl. Wildlife Week — A138

1953, Apr. 1
322 A138 2c Polar bear .25 .25
323 A138 3c Moose .25 .25
324 A138 4c Bighorn sheep .25 .25
Nos. 322-324 (3) .75 .75

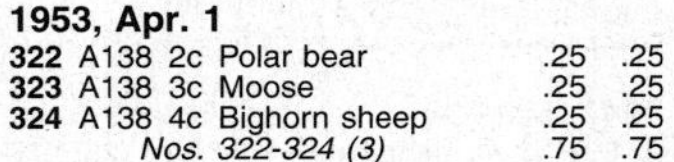

Elizabeth II — A139

1953, May 1
325 A139 1c violet brown .25 .25
a. Booklet pane of 3 1.40 1.40
326 A139 2c green .25 .25
327 A139 3c carmine rose .25 .25
a. Booklet pane of 3 1.90 1.40
b. Booklet pane of 4 + 2 labels 1.30 *1.75*
Complete booklet, 2 #327b 3.00
328 A139 4c violet .25 .25
a. Booklet pane of 3 1.90 1.75
Complete booklet, #325a, 327a, 328a 9.00
b. Booklet pane of 6 1.40 1.40
Complete booklet, #328b 2.00
329 A139 5c ultramarine .35 .25
Nos. 325-329 (5) 1.35 1.25

Stamps from booklet panes of 3 are imperf. on 2 or 3 sides.
See Nos. 331-333. For overprints see Nos. O33-O37.

Coronation Issue

Queen Elizabeth II — A140

1953, June 1
330 A140 4c violet .25 .25

Coil Stamps

1953 ***Perf. 9½ Vertically***
331 A139 2c green 1.50 1.00
332 A139 3c carmine rose 1.50 1.00
333 A139 4c violet 3.50 1.50
Nos. 331-333 (3) 6.50 3.50

See note after No. 329.
Issued: 2c, 7/30; 3c, 7/27; 4c, 9/3.

Bobbin, Cloth and Spinning Wheel A141

1953, Nov. 2 ***Perf. 12***
334 A141 50c light green 2.75 .25

For overprint see No. O38.

Walrus A142

Beaver A143

1954, Apr. 1
335 A142 4c gray .30 .25
336 A143 5c ultramarine .35 .25
a. Booklet pane of 5 + label 1.75 1.40
Complete booklet, #336a 2.25

National Wildlife Week, 1954.

Elizabeth II A144

Gannet A145

1954-61
337 A144 1c violet brn .25 .25
a. Booklet pane of 5 + label ('56) 1.10 1.10
338 A144 2c green .25 .25
a. Pane of 25 ('61) 3.75 3.75
b. Vert. pair, imperf. between, 5 pairs in a block of 10 *25,000.*
339 A144 3c carmine rose .25 .25
a. Horiz. pair, imperf. vert. *1,400.*
340 A144 4c violet .25 .25
a. Booklet pane of 5 + label ('56) 1.40 1.40
Complete booklet, #337a, 340a 3.00
b. Booklet pane of 6 ('55) 3.00 3.00
Complete booklet, #340b 3.50
341 A144 5c bright blue .25 .25
a. Booklet pane of 5 + label 1.10 1.10
Complete booklet, #341a 2.00
b. Pane of 20 (5 x 4) ('61) 6.50 6.50
c. Horiz. pair, imperf. vert. *5,500.*
342 A144 6c orange .50 .25
343 A145 15c gray 1.50 .25
Nos. 337-343 (7) 3.25 1.75

Panes of 20 and 25 are imperf. on 4 sides.
Issued: 5c, 15c, 4/1; others, 6/10.
At this time, No. 338b is known only as a unique block of 10, as listed.
For overprints see Nos. O40-O44.

Luminescence

The overprinting of regular stamps with vertical luminescent bands began experimentally in 1962 when Nos. 337p-341p were released at Winnipeg. The bands are of varying number, position and chemical content.

Tagged varieties of stamps which were issued both untagged and with luminescent overprint are listed with suffix letter "p".

1962, Jan. 13 **Tagged**
337p A144 1c violet brown 1.30 .95
338p A144 2c green 1.30 .95
339p A144 3c carmine rose 1.30 .95
340p A144 4c violet 3.75 3.25
341p A144 5c bright blue 4.00 2.25
Nos. 337p-341p (5) 11.65 8.35

Coil Stamps

1954 ***Perf. 9½ Vertically***
345 A144 2c green .55 .25
347 A144 4c violet 1.50 .25
348 A144 5c bright blue 2.25 .25
Nos. 345-348 (3) 4.30 .75

Issued: 2c, 9/9; 3c, 8/23; 4c, 7/6.

Sir John Sparrow David Thompson A146

Sir Mackenzie Bowell A147

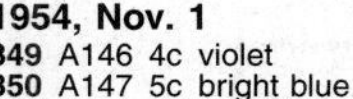

1954, Nov. 1 ***Perf. 12***

349 A146 4c violet .35 .25
350 A147 5c bright blue .35 .25

Eskimo and Kayak A148

1955, Feb. 21

351 A148 10c violet brown .40 .25

For overprint see No. O39.

Musk Ox — A149

Whooping Cranes A150

1955, Apr. 4

352 A149 4c purple .35 .25
353 A150 5c blue .40 .25

National Wildlife Week, April 10-16.

Torch, Dove and Maple Leaves — A151

1955, June 1 **Unwmk.**

354 A151 5c brt blue & dk blue .40 .25

ICAO, 10th anniversary.

Pioneer Settlers A152

1955, June 30 ***Perf. 12***

355 A152 5c ultramarine .40 .25

50th anniv. of the founding of the provinces of Alberta and Saskatchewan.

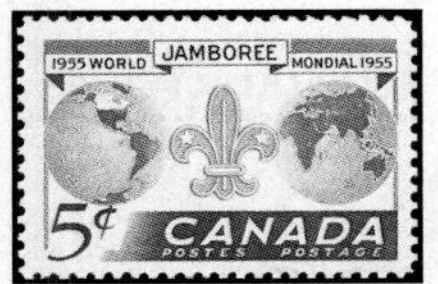

Globe and Scout Emblem A153

1955, Aug. 20 **Engr.**

356 A153 5c green & org brown .40 .25

8th Boy Scout World Jamboree, Niagara-on-the-Lake, Ont.

Richard Bedford Bennett A154

Sir Charles Tupper A155

1955, Nov. 8

357 A154 4c violet .35 .25
358 A155 5c ultramarine .35 .25

Ice Hockey Players A156

1956, Jan. 23

359 A156 5c ultramarine .35 .25

Issued to publicize Canada's most popular winter sport.

Caribou A157

Mountain Goat A158

1956, Apr. 12

360 A157 4c violet .40 .25
361 A158 5c ultramarine .40 .25

National Wildlife Week, 1956.

"Paper Industry" A159

"Chemical Industry" — A160

1956, June 7 **Engr.**

362 A159 20c green 1.50 .25
363 A160 25c red 1.60 .25

For overprint see No. O45.

House on Fire — A161

1956, Oct. 9 **Unwmk.** ***Perf. 12***

364 A161 5c gray & red .35 .25

Issued to emphasize the needless waste caused by preventable fires.

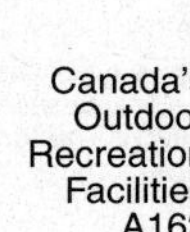

Canada's Outdoor Recreation Facilities A162

No. 365, Fishing. No. 366, Swimming. No. 367, Hunter and dog. No. 368, Skiing.

1957, Mar. 7

365 A162 5c blue .40 .25
366 A162 5c blue .40 .25
367 A162 5c blue .40 .25
368 A162 5c blue .40 .25
a. Block of 4, #365-368 1.60 1.10

All four designs are printed alternating in sheet of 50, with various combinations possible.

Loon — A163

1957, Apr. 10 ***Perf. 12***

369 A163 5c black .35 .25

David Thompson and Map of Western Canada A164

1957, June 5 **Unwmk.**

370 A164 5c ultramarine .35 .25

David Thompson (1770-1857), explorer and geographer.

Parliament Building, Ottawa — A165

Post Horn and Globe A166

1957, Aug. 14 ***Perf. 12***

371 A165 5c deep dull blue .35 .25
372 A166 15c deep dull blue 2.25 2.00

UPU, 14th Congress, Ottawa, Aug. 1957.

Miner With Pneumatic Drill — A167

1957, Sept. 5

373 A167 5c black .30 .25

Canada's mining industry; 6th Commonwealth Mining and Metallurgical Congress, Vancouver, Sept. 8-Oct. 8.

Elizabeth II and Prince Philip — A168

1957, Oct. 10 **Unwmk.**

374 A168 5c black .30 .25

Visit of Queen Elizabeth II and Prince Philip to Canada, Oct. 12-16.

Newspapers and Symbols of Industry A169

1958, Jan. 22 **Engr.**

375 A169 5c black .35 .25

Canadian press; the importance of a free press.

Microscope and Globe — A170

1958, Mar. 5 ***Perf. 12***

376 A170 5c blue .35 .25

Intl. Geophysical Year, 1957-1958.

Miner Panning Gold — A171

1958, May 8
377 A171 5c bluish green .35 .25

Province of British Columbia, cent.

La Verendrye A172

1958, June 4
378 A172 5c bright ultra .35 .25

Pierre Gaultier de Varenne, Sieur de la Verendrye, 18th century French explorer of Western Canada.

Champlain and View of Quebec A173

1958, June 26
379 A173 5c dk green & bis brn .35 .25

Founding of Quebec, 350th anniv.

Nurse — A174

1958, July 30 **Engr.**
380 A174 5c rose lilac .35 .25

Importance of health, both to the individual and to the nation.

Kerosene Lamp and Refinery — A175

1958, Sept. 10 ***Perf. 12***
381 A175 5c olive & red .35 .25

Centennial of Canada's oil industry.

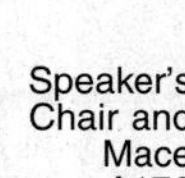
Speaker's Chair and Mace A176

1958, Oct. 2
382 A176 5c slate blue .35 .25

Bicentennial of the meeting of the first House of Representatives in Canada, Halifax, Oct. 2, 1758.

"Silver Dart" and Delta Wing Planes A177

1959, Feb. 23
383 A177 5c blue & black .35 .25

50th anniv. of the 1st airplane flight in Canada near Baddeck, N. S., with J. A. D. McCurdy as pilot.

Globe and Dove — A178

1959, Apr. 2
384 A178 5c violet blue .35 .25

NATO, 10th anniversary.

Woman Tending Tree — A179

1959, May 13
385 A179 5c olive yell & blk .35 .25

Associated Country Women of the World.

Elizabeth II — A180

1959, June 18
386 A180 5c dark carmine .35 .25

Visit of Queen Elizabeth and Prince Philip to Canada, June 18-Aug. 1.

Great Lakes, Maple Leaf and Eagle Emblems A181

1959, June 26 **Engr.**
387 A181 5c red & blue .35 .25
a. Center inverted *9,000.* *7,500.*

Opening of the St. Lawrence Seaway, June 26, 1959.
See United States No. 1131.

British Lion, Fleur-de-Lis and Maple Leaves A182

1959, Sept. 10 ***Perf. 12***
388 A182 5c crim rose & dk green .35 .25

Bicentenary of the Battle of the Plains of Abraham.

Girl Guide Emblem — A183

1960, Apr. 20 **Unwmk.**
389 A183 5c brn org & dp blue .35 .25

Canadian Girl Guides Assoc., 50th anniv.

Dollard des Ormeaux and Battle Scene — A184

1960, May 19
390 A184 5c ultra & bis brown .35 .25

Battle of the Long Sault, 300th anniv.

Compass Rose, Earth Mover and Surveyor — A185

1961, Feb. 8 **Engr.**
391 A185 5c green & vermilion .35 .25

Development of Canada's Northland.

Emily Pauline Johnson — A186

1961, Mar. 10
392 A186 5c green & red .35 .25

Emily Pauline Johnson (1861-1913), Mohawk princess and poet.

Arthur Meighen — A187

1961, Apr. 19
393 A187 5c ultramarine .35 .25

Arthur Meighen, Prime Minister of Canada, (1920-21, 1926).

Power Plant and Men Holding Blueprint A188

1961, June 28 **Unwmk.**
394 A188 5c lt red brn & blue .35 .25

10th anniv. of the Colombo Plan, initiated to assist underdeveloped countries by providing trained manpower and resources.

Natural Resources and Hands Holding Cogwheel — A189

1961, Oct. 12 **Engr.**
395 A189 5c brown & blue grn .35 .25

Canada's "Resources for Tomorrow Program" and to publicize the close link between industry and the country's renewable natural resources.

Young Adults and Education Symbols — A190

1962, Feb. 28
396 A190 5c black & lt red brn .35 .25

Issued to stimulate public awareness of the importance of education.

Scottish Settler and Lord Selkirk A191

1962, May 3
397 A191 5c lt green & vio brn .35 .25

150th anniv. of the Red River Settlement in Western Canada (Prairie Provinces).

Jean Talon Presenting Gifts to Young Farm Couple — A192

1962, June 13 **Unwmk.**
398 A192 5c dark blue .35 .25

Jean Talon, administrator of New France (Canada), 1665-1668.

British Columbia Legislative Building and Stamp of 1860 — A193

1962, Aug. 22 **Engr.**
399 A193 5c black & reddish org .35 .25

Centenary of Victoria as incorporated city.

In middle to late 1962, Canadian Bank Note Co. changed their perforation equipment from a gauge of 11.95 to gauge 11.85. The gauge 11.85 perforation holes are slightly larger than those of the 11.95 gauge.

This change affected some of the reprintings of then-current low- and medium-value Wilding definitives (including Nos. 320, 321, 334, 338, 340, 343, 351, 362, 363, 411), at least one commemorative (No. 399), low-value Cameo definitives (Nos. 401a, 402a, 404a, 405b, 405p), a low-value Centennial booklet (No. 458a) and several postage dues (Nos. J15-J20). Other issues may be affected and the editors would like to hear of any new discoveries.

Arms of the Provinces A194

1962, Aug. 31
400 A194 5c brown orange & black .35 .25

Official opening of the Trans-Canada Highway, Rogers Pass, Glacier National Park, Sept. 4.

Queen Elizabeth II and Wheat — A195

Designs (Symbol in upper left corner): 1c, Mineral crystals. 2c, Tree. 3c, Fish. 4c, Electric high tension tower.

1962-63	**Engr.**	***Perf. 12***	
401	A195 1c dp brn ('63)	.25	.25
a.	Booklet pane of 5 + label ('63)	3.00	3.00
402	A195 2c green ('63)	.25	.25
a.	Pane of 25 ('63)	7.50	7.50
403	A195 3c purple ('63)	.25	.25
404	A195 4c carmine ('63)	.25	.25
a.	Booklet pane of 5 + label ('63)	3.00	3.00
	Complete booklet, #401a, 404a	6.75	
b.	Pane of 25 ('63)	11.00	11.00
405	A195 5c violet blue	.25	.25
a.	Booklet pane of 5 + label ('63)	3.00	3.00
	Complete booklet, #405a	3.75	
b.	Pane of 20 ('63)	13.00	13.00
c.	Imperf., pair (#405b)	*4,500.*	
d.	Vert. pair, imperf. horiz.	*4,250.*	*575.00*
	Nos. 401-405 (5)	1.25	1.25

Nos. 402a, 404b, and 405b are imperf. on four sides.

Used examples of No. 405d are canceled "Gonor, MB." Beware of examples with traces of blind perfs; a certificate of authenticity is recommended.

Issued: 5c, 10/3; 1c, 4c, 2/4/63; 2c, 3c, 5/2/63.

For overprints see Nos. O46-O49.

1963		**Tagged**	
401p	A195 1c deep brown	.25	.25
402p	A195 2c green	.25	.25
403p	A195 3c purple	.25	.25
404p	A195 4c carmine	.75	.50
405p	A195 5c violet blue	.45	.25
q.	Pane of 20	42.50	42.50
	Nos. 401p-405p (5)	1.95	1.50

See note after No. 343.

Coil Stamps

1962-63		***Perf. 9½ Horiz.***	
406	A195 2c green	4.75	2.25
407	A195 3c purple	3.50	1.75
408	A195 4c carmine	4.75	2.25
a.	Pair, imperf between	*3,000.*	
409	A195 5c violet blue	4.75	1.00
	Nos. 406-409 (4)	17.75	7.25

No. 408a is valued in the grade of fine. Beware of dangerous fakes; a certificate of authenticity is necessary.

Issued: 5c, 10/3; 4c, 2/4/63; 2c, 3c, 5/2/63.

Sir Casimir Stanislaus Gzowski (1813-98), Engineer, Soldier and Educator — A196

1963, Mar. 5	**Unwmk.**	***Perf. 12***	
410	A196 5c rose lilac	.30	.25

Export Crate and Mercator Map — A197

1963, June 14			
411	A197 $1 rose carmine	8.00	2.25

Sir Martin Frobisher (1535-1594), Explorer and Discoverer of Frobisher Bay — A198

1963, Aug. 21			
412	A198 5c ultramarine	.30	.25

Postrider and First Land Mail Routes A199

1963, Sept. 25			
413	A199 5c green & red brn	.30	.25

Bicentennial of the 1st regular postal service between Quebec, Three Rivers & Montreal.

Jet at Ottawa Airport — A200

Canada Geese — A201

1963-64			
414	A200 7c blue ('64)	.50	.40
415	A201 15c deep ultra	1.80	.25

See No. 436. For surcharge see No. 430.

"Peace on Earth" — A202

1964, Apr. 8	**Engr. & Litho.**		
416	A202 5c grnsh blue, Prus bl & ocher	.30	.25

Issued to promote world peace.

Three-Maple-Leaf Emblem (Canadian Unity) — A203

White Trillium and Arms of Ontario A204

No. 419, White garden lily and arms of Quebec. No. 420, Mayflower (trailing arbutus) and arms of Nova Scotia. No. 421, Purple violet and arms of New Brunswick. No. 422, Prairie crocus and arms of Manitoba. No. 423, Dogwood and arms of British Columbia. No. 424, Lady's slipper and arms of Prince Edward Island. No. 425, Prairie lily and arms of Saskatchewan. No. 426, Wild rose and arms of Alberta. No. 427, Pitcher plant and arms of Newfoundland. No. 428, Fireweed and arms of Yukon. No. 429, Mountain avens and arms of Northwest Territories. No. 429A, Maple leaf and arms of Canada.

1964-66	**Engr. & Litho.**	***Perf. 12***	
417	A203 5c lt blue & dk car	.25	.25
418	A204 5c red brn, buff & green	.25	.25
419	A204 5c grn, yel & org	.25	.25
420	A204 5c blue, pink & grn	.25	.25
421	A204 5c car, green & vio	.25	.25
422	A204 5c red brn, lil & dl grn	.25	.25
423	A204 5c lilac, grn & bis	.25	.25
424	A204 5c vio, grn & dp rose	.25	.25
425	A204 5c sepia, org & grn	.25	.25
426	A204 5c dl grn, yel & car	.25	.25
427	A204 5c black, grn & car	.25	.25
428	A204 5c dk bl, rose & grn	.25	.25
429	A204 5c ol, yel & green	.25	.25
429A	A204 5c dk blue & dp red	.25	.25
	Nos. 417-429A (14)	3.50	3.50

Issued: No. 417, 5/14/64; Nos. 418-419, 6/30/64; Nos. 420-421, 2/3/65; Nos. 422-423, 4/28/65; No. 424, 7/21/65; Nos. 425-426, 1/19/66; No. 427, 2/23/66; Nos. 428-429, 3/23/66; No. 429A, 6/30/66.

No. 414 Surcharged

1964, July 15		**Engr.**	
430	A200 8c on 7c blue	.45	.25
a.	Pair, one without surcharge	*11,500.*	
b.	Surcharge on reverse, inverted		*3,750.*

Nos. 430a and 430b are each unique.

Fathers of Confederation Memorial, Charlottetown — A205

1964, July 29			
431	A205 5c black	.30	.25

Centenary of the Charlottetown, P.E.I., Conference, Sept. 1-9, 1864, which led to the creation of the Canadian nation in 1867.

Maple Leaf and Hand Holding Quill Pen — A206

1964, Sept. 9			
432	A206 5c dark brown & rose	.25	.25

Centenary of the Quebec Conference, Oct. 10-27, 1864, which led to the creation of the Canadian nation.

Elizabeth II — A207

1964, Oct. 5			
433	A207 5c claret	.25	.25

Queen Elizabeth's visit, Oct. 6-13.

Family and Star of Bethlehem — A208

1964, Oct. 14 ***Perf. 12***

434 A208 3c red .25 .25
a. Pane of 25 7.50 7.50
p. Tagged .65 .35
q. As "a," tagged 11.00 11.00
435 A208 5c blue .25 .25
p. Tagged 1.10 .35

Panes of 25 are imperf. on four sides.

Jet Type of 1964

1964, Nov. 18 **Unwmk.**

436 A200 8c blue .40 .25

Maple Leaf and ICY Emblem A209

1965, Mar. 3

437 A209 5c slate green .25 .25

International Cooperation Year.

Sir Wilfred Grenfell at Wheel of Hospital Ship Strathcona II A210

1965, June 9

438 A210 5c Prussian blue .25 .25

Sir Wilfred Grenfell, author, medical missionary and founder of the Grenfell Mission, birth cent.

Canada's Maple Leaf Flag, 1965 A211

1965, June 30

439 A211 5c blue & red .25 .25

Winston Churchill — A212

1965, Aug. 12 **Litho.** ***Perf. 12***

440 A212 5c brown .25 .25

Sir Winston Spencer Churchill (1874-1965).

Peace Tower, Ottawa — A213

1965, Sept. 8 **Engr.**

441 A213 5c slate green .25 .25

Meeting of the Inter-Parliamentary Union, Ottawa, Sept. 8-17.

Parliament and Ottawa River A214

1965, Sept. 8

442 A214 5c brown .25 .25

Centenary of the final selection of Ottawa as national capital.

Gifts of the Wise Men — A215

1965, Oct. 13

443 A215 3c olive .25 .25
a. Pane of 25 6.25 6.25
p. Tagged .25 .25
q. As "a," tagged 8.50 8.50
444 A215 5c violet blue .25 .25
p. Tagged .35 .25

Christmas. Panes of 25 are imperf. on four sides.

Alouette II Orbiting Globe — A216

1966, Jan. 5

445 A216 5c dark violet blue .25 .25

Launching (in California) of the Canadian satellite Alouette II, Nov. 28, 1965, as part of the Canadian-American program of space research.

La Salle, Map of 17th Century Canada, Ship, Canoe, Spyglass and Compass — A217

1966, Apr. 13

446 A217 5c blue green .25 .25

Tercentenary of the arrival in Canada of Rene Robert Cavelier, Sieur de La Salle (1643-1687).

Traffic Signs — A218

1966, May 2

447 A218 5c black, lt blue & yel .25 .25

Issued to publicize traffic safety.

House of Commons, Thames River and Canadian Delegates A219

1966, May 26

448 A219 5c brown .25 .25

Centenary of the London Conf., Dec. 4, 1866, which resulted in the British North America Act.

Atomic Reactor, Heavy Water Atom Symbol and Microscope A220

1966, July 27

449 A220 5c deep ultra .25 .25

Peaceful uses of atomic power. The design shows a stylized view of the Douglas Point Nuclear Power Station, Lake Huron, Ontario.

Parliamentary Library, Ottawa — A221

1966, Sept. 8

450 A221 5c plum .25 .25

12th General Conf. of the Commonwealth Parliamentary Assoc., Ottawa, Sept. 8-Oct. 5.

Praying Hands, by Albrecht Dürer — A222

1966, Oct. 12

451 A222 3c carmine rose .25 .25
a. Pane of 25 3.75 3.75
p. Tagged .25 .25
q. As "a," tagged 5.00 5.00
452 A222 5c orange .25 .25
p. Tagged .45 .25

Christmas. Panes of 25 are imperf. on four sides.

Canadian Flag over Globe and Centennial Emblem — A223

1967, Jan. 11

453 A223 5c blue & red .25 .25
p. Tagged .40 .30

Canada's centenary as a nation.

Northern Lights and Dog Team — A224

"Alaska Highway" by A. Y. Jackson A225

Two Types of 6c Black

Type I Type II

Designs: 2c, Totem pole (Pacific Area). 3c, Combine and oil rig (Prairie Region). 4c, Ship in lock (Central Canada). 5c, Lobster traps and boat (Atlantic Provinces). 6c, Transportation means. 10c, "The Jack Pine" by Tom Thomson. 15c, "Bylot Island" by Lawren Harris. 20c, "The Ferry, Quebec" by James Wilson Morrice. 25c, "The Solemn Land" by J. E. H. MacDonald. 50c, "Summer's Stores" by John Ensor (grain elevators). $1, Oilfield near Edmonton, by H. G. Glyde.

1967-72 **Engr.** ***Perf. 12***

454 A224 1c brown .25 .25
a. Booklet pane of 5 + label .45 .35
b. Bklt. pane, 1 #454d, 4 #459 + label, perf. 10 ('68) 3.00 2.50
c. Bklt. pane, 5 #454d + 5 #457d, perf. 10 ('68) 1.40 1.40
d. Perf. 10 ('68) .25 .25
e. Perf. 12½x12 ('71) .25 .25
f. Printed on gummed side *1,000.*
455 A224 2c green .25 .25
a. Bklt. pane, 4 #455, 4 #456 with gutter btwn. ('70) 1.50 1.50
456 A224 3c dull purple .25 .25
a. Perf. 12½x12 ('71) .75 .30
457 A224 4c car rose .25 .25
a. Booklet pane of 5 + label 1.25 1.25
b. Pane of 25 (5x5) 25.00 20.00
c. Booklet pane of 25 + 2 labels, perf. 10 ('68) 7.50 7.00
d. Perf. 10 .50 .25
458 A224 5c blue .25 .25
a. Booklet pane of 5 + label 5.25 5.25
b. Pane of 20 30.00 27.50
c. Bklt. pane of 20, perf. 10 ('68) 7.50 7.50
d. Perf. 10 .60 .25
459 A224 6c org, perf. 10 .25 .25
a. Bklt. pane of 25 + 2 labels, perf. 10 ('68) 7.50 7.50
b. Perf. 12½x12 ('69) .25 .25
460 A224 6c black (I), perf. 12½x12 .25 .25
a. Bklt. pane of 25 + 2 labels (I), perf. 10 ('70) 11.00 7.50
b. As "a," perf. 12½x12 15.00 13.00
c. Type II, perf. 12½x12 .25 .25
d. As "c," booklet pane of 4 3.50 3.25
e. As "d," perf. 10 ('70) 10.00 6.00
f. Type II, perf. 12 ('72) .35 .25
g. Type I, perf. 10 1.50 .30
h. Type II, perf. 10 2.00 .65
i. As "f," printed on gummed side 18.00
461 A225 8c violet brown .25 .25
462 A225 10c olive green .25 .25
463 A225 15c dull purple .45 .25
464 A225 20c dark blue .55 .25
465 A225 25c slate green 1.50 .25
465A A225 50c brown org 3.75 .25
465B A225 $1 carmine rose 6.00 .75
Nos. 454-465B (14) 14.50 4.00

Nos. 454d, 454e, 456a, 457d, 458d, 460c, 460g and 460h are from booklet panes.

Issued: No. 459, 11/1/68; No. 460, 1/7/70; others, 2/8/67.

See Nos. 543-544, 549-550.

Tagged

454p A224 1c brown .25 .25
ep. Perf. 12½x12 ('71) .25 .25
455p A224 2c green .25 .25
456p A224 3c dull purple .25 .25
457p A224 4c car rose .60 .25
458p A224 5c blue .60 .25
bp. Pane of 20 55.00 47.50
459p A224 6c org, perf. 10 .70 .25
bp. Perf. 12½x12 ('69) .75 .30
460p A224 6c black (I), perf. 12½x12 .35 .25
cp. Type II ('70) .45 .50
fp. As "cp," perf. 12 ('72) .25 .25
462p A225 10c olive green .90 .35
463p A225 15c dull purple .90 .35
464p A225 20c dark blue 1.50 .55
465p A225 25c slate green 7.50 2.25
Nos. 454p-465p (11) 13.80 5.25

Nos. 454ep and 460cp are from booklet panes Nos. 544q-544s.

Issued: 1c-5c, 2/8/67; No. 459p, 11/1/68; No. 460p, 1/7/70; others, 12/9/69.

See note after No. 343.

Coil Stamps

1967-70 ***Perf. 9½ Horiz.***

466 A224 3c dull purple 3.75 .85
467 A224 4c carmine rose 1.10 .50
468 A224 5c blue 2.25 .65

Perf. 10 Horiz.

468A A224 6c orange .45 .25
c. Imperf., pair 275.00
468B A224 6c black, die II .35 .25
d. Imperf., pair 2,500.
Nos. 466-468B (5) 7.90 2.50

Horizontal pairs or blocks of Nos. 468A and 468B may be found with a fine vertical score line between the stamps. These sell for little more than vertical pairs or strips.

Issued: No. 468A, 1/69; No. 468B, 8/70; others, 2/8/67.

EXPO '67 Emblem and Canadian Pavilion A226

1967, Apr. 28 **Engr.** ***Perf. 12***

469 A226 5c blue & red .25 .25

EXPO '67, Intl. Exhib., Montreal, Apr. 28-Oct. 27.

Symbolic Woman and Ballot — A227

1967, May 24 **Litho.**
470 A227 5c black & rose lilac .25 .25

50th anniversary of woman suffrage.

Elizabeth II — A228

1967, June 30 **Engr.**
471 A228 5c deep org & purple .25 .25

Centennial Year visit of Queen Elizabeth II and the Duke of Edinburgh.

Runner A229

1967, July 19
472 A229 5c red .25 .25

Pan-American Games, Winnipeg, Manitoba, July 22-Aug. 7.

Globe and Flash A230

1967, Aug. 31
473 A230 5c deep ultra .25 .25

50th anniv. of the Canadian Press, news gathering and distributing service.

Georges Philias Vanier A231

1967, Sept. 15 **Engr. & Litho.**
474 A231 5c black .25 .25

Georges Philias Vanier (1888-1967), Governor General of Canada, 1959-1967.

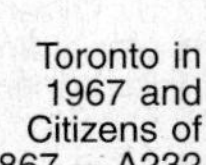

Toronto in 1967 and Citizens of 1867 — A232

1967, Sept. 28
475 A232 5c sl grn & sal pink .25 .25

Centenary of Toronto as capital of Ontario.

Singing Children and Peace Tower, Ottawa — A233

1967, Oct. 11
476 A233 3c carmine .25 .25
a. Pane of 25 3.25 3.25
p. Tagged .25 .25
q. As "a" tagged 4.50 4.50
477 A233 5c green .25 .25
p. Tagged .30 .25

Christmas. Panes of 25 are imperf. on four sides.

Gray Jays — A234

1968, Feb. 15 **Litho.**
478 A234 5c grn, blk & pink .45 .25

Weather Map and Composite of Instruments A235

1968, Mar. 13 ***Perf. 11***
479 A235 5c dk & lt blue, yel & red .25 .25

200th anniv. of Canada's first long-term fixed point weather observations at Fort Prince of Wales, Churchill, by William Wales and Joseph Dymond.

Male Narwhal A236

1968, Apr. 10
480 A236 5c multicolored .25 .25

Weighing Rain Gauge, World Map and Maple Leaf A237

1968, May 8
481 A237 5c multicolored .25 .25

Intl. Hydrological Decade, 1965-74.

The Nonsuch A238

Photo. & Engr.

1968, June 5 ***Perf. 10***
482 A238 5c dk blue & multi .25 .25

300th anniv. of the voyage of the Nonsuch which opened the way to Canada's West through the fur trade.

Contemporary and Indian Lacrosse Players — A239

1968, July 3
483 A239 5c yel, black & red .25 .25

A240

Design: George Brown, "Globe" Front Page and Legislature, Prince Edward Island.

1968, Aug. 21
484 A240 5c multicolored .25 .25

George Brown (1818-1880), founder of Toronto "Globe" and political leader.

Henri Bourassa and Newspaper Page — A241

Litho. & Engr.

1968, Sept. 4 ***Perf. 12***
485 A241 5c ver, buff & black .25 .25

Henri Bourassa (1868-1952), jounalist and statesman.

Canadian Memorial, Near Vimy, France — A242

1968, Oct. 15 **Engr.**
486 A242 15c slate 2.00 1.25

50th anniv. of the Armistice which ended WWI. The stamp shows "The Defenders and the Breaking of the Sword," a detail from the memorial designed by W. S. Allward.

John McCrae and "Flanders Fields" A243

1968, Oct. 15 **Litho. & Engr.**
487 A243 5c multicolored .25 .25

50th death anniv. of Lt. Col. John McCrae (1872-1918), author of "In Flanders Fields."

Eskimo Family, Carving — A244

Eskimo soapstone carving: 6c, Mother and infant, by Munamee of Cape Dorset.

1968, Nov. **Photo.**

488 A244 5c brt blue & black .25 .25
a. Booklet pane of 10 3.00 3.00
p. Tagged .25 .25
q. As "a," tagged 3.75 3.75
489 A244 6c dp bister & black .25 .25
p. Tagged .25 .25

Christmas. Issued: 5c, Nov. 1; 6c, Nov. 15.

Curling A245

Photo. & Engr.

1969, Jan. 15 ***Perf. 10***

490 A245 6c black, brt blue & car .25 .25

Vincent Massey — A246

Litho. & Engr.

1969, Feb. 20 ***Perf. 12***

491 A246 6c yel olive & dk brn .25 .25

Vincent Massey (1887-1967), 1st Canadian-born Gov. General of Canada, 1952-59.

Return from the Harvest Field, by Aurele de Foy Suzor-Cote A247

1969, Mar. 14 **Photo.**

492 A247 50c multicolored 3.50 2.50

Aurele de Foy Suzor-Cote (1869-1937), painter.

Globe and Tools of Various Trades A248

1969, May 21 **Engr.** ***Perf. 12x12½***

493 A248 6c dk olive green .25 .25

50th anniv. of the ILO.

Vickers Vimy, 1919, and Map of the Atlantic A249

1969, June 13 **Photo. and Engr.**

494 A249 15c red brn, yel grn & lt ultra 1.90 1.50

50th anniv. of the first non-stop Atlantic flight from Newfoundland to Ireland of Capt. John Alcock and Lt. Arthur Whitten Brown.

Sir William Osler — A250

1969, June 23 ***Perf. 12½x12***

495 A250 6c dk blue & lt red brn .25 .25

Osler (1849-1919), physician, professor of physiology and pathology in Canada, US and England.

Ipswich Sparrow A251

Birds: 6c, White-throated sparrows, vert. 25c, Hermit thrush.

1969, July 23 **Litho.** ***Perf. 12***

496 A251 6c multicolored .35 .25
497 A251 10c ultra & multi .75 .40
498 A251 25c black & multi 1.90 1.50
Nos. 496-498 (3) 3.00 2.15

Map of Prince Edward Island A252

Photo. & Engr.

1969, Aug. 15 ***Perf. 12x12½***

499 A252 6c ultra, org brn & black .25 .25

Bicentenary of Charlottetown as capital of Prince Edward Island.

Flags of Summer and Winter Canada Games — A253

Litho. & Engr.

1969, Aug. 15 ***Perf. 12***

500 A253 6c ultra, brt green & red .25 .25

1st Canada Summer Games, Halifax and Dartmouth, N.S., Aug. 16-24.

Sir Isaac Brock and Memorial Queenston Heights — A254

1969, Sept. 12

501 A254 6c yel brn, brn & pale sal .25 .25

Major General Sir Isaac Brock (1769-1812), administrator of Upper Canada and leader in the war of 1812.

Children of Various Races — A255

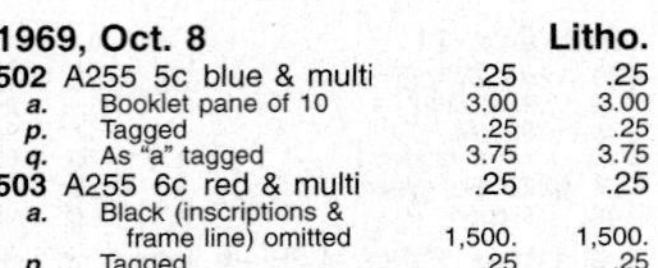

1969, Oct. 8 **Litho.**

502 A255 5c blue & multi .25 .25
a. Booklet pane of 10 3.00 3.00
p. Tagged .25 .25
q. As "a" tagged 3.75 3.75
503 A255 6c red & multi .25 .25
a. Black (inscriptions & frame line) omitted 1,500. 1,500.
p. Tagged .25 .25

Christmas.

Stephen Leacock, Comedy Mask and Mariposa View A256

Photo. & Engr.

1969, Nov. 12 ***Perf. 12x12½***

504 A256 6c multicolored .25 .25

Stephen Butler Leacock (1869-1944), humorist, historian and economist.

Manitoba, Crossroads of Canada A257

1970, Jan. 27 **Litho.** ***Perf. 12***

505 A257 6c blue, yel & red .25 .25
p. Tagged .30 .25

Centenary of the province of Manitoba.

Enchanted Owl, by Kenojuak — A258

1970, Jan. 27 **Engr.**

506 A258 6c dark red & black .25 .25

Centenary of Nortwest Territories.

Microscopic View of Inside of Leaf A259

1970, Feb. 18 **Photo. & Engr.**

507 A259 6c green, lt org & blue .25 .25

Canada's participation in the Intl. Biological Program, 1967-1972.

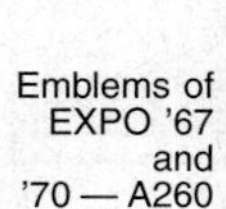

Emblems of EXPO '67 and '70 — A260

EXPO '70 Emblem and Dogwood, British Columbia A261

Designs: No. 510, EXPO '70 emblem and white garden lily, Quebec. No. 511, EXPO '70 emblem and white trillium, Ontario.

1970, Mar. 18 **Litho.**

508 A260 25c red emblem 2.00 2.00
p. Tagged 2.50 2.50
509 A261 25c violet emblem 2.00 2.00
p. Tagged 2.50 2.50
510 A261 25c green emblem 2.00 2.00
p. Tagged 2.50 2.50
511 A261 25c blue emblem 2.00 2.00
p. Tagged 2.50 2.50
a. Block of 4, #508-511 8.00 8.00
b. As "a," tagged 10.00 10.00
Nos. 508-511 (4) 8.00 8.00

EXPO '70 Intl. Exhibition, Osaka, Japan, Mar. 15-Sept. 13. Nos. 508-511 printed se-tenant in panes of 50 (5x10), with various combinations possible.

Henry Kelsey A262

Photo. & Engr.

1970, Apr. 15 ***Perf. 12x12½***

512 A262 6c multicolored .25 .25

300th birth anniv. of Henry Kelsey, explorer of Canada's western plains.

"A Divided World, with Energy Focused on Unification..." — A263

1970, May 13 **Litho.** ***Perf. 11***

513 A263 10c blue .75 .60
p. Tagged .95 .95
514 A263 15c lilac & dk red 1.20 .75
p. Tagged 1.60 1.60

25th anniversary of the United Nations.

Louis Riel — A264

1970, June 19 **Photo.** ***Perf. 12½x12***

515 A264 6c red & brt blue .25 .25

Louis Riel (1844-1885), Metis leader who became president of the Council of Assiniboin in 1870.

Mackenzie Rock, Dean Channel — A265

1970, June 25 **Engr.** ***Perf. 12***

516 A265 6c brown .25 .25

Sir Alexander Mackenzie (1764-1820), Scottish explorer who in 1793 completed the first crossing of the North American continent north of Mexico.

Sir Oliver Mowat and Parliament, Ottawa A266

Photo. & Engr.

1970, Aug. 12 ***Perf. 12x12½***

517 A266 6c red & black .25 .25

Sir Oliver Mowat (1820-1903), government leader and a Father of Confederation.

Isle of Spruce, by Arthur Lismer A267

1970, Sept. 18 Litho. *Perf. 11*

518 A267 6c multicolored .25 .25

50th anniv. of "The Group of Seven," Canadian landscape artists.

Santa Claus — A268

Christ Child — A269

Child in the Manger and Star-studded Sky — A270

Christmas, Designs by Canadian School Children: No. 519, 527 Santa Claus. No. 520, Horse-drawn Sleigh. No. 521, Nativity. No. 522, Children Skiing. No. 523, Snowmen and Christmas Tree. No. 524, 529 Christ Child. No. 525, Christmas Tree and Children. No. 526, Toy Store. . No. 528, Church. No. 530, Snowmobile and Trees.

1970, Oct. 7 Litho. *Perf. 12*

519	A268 5c multicolored		.30	.25
520	A268 5c multicolored		.30	.25
521	A268 5c multicolored		.30	.25
522	A268 5c multicolored		.30	.25
523	A268 5c multicolored		.30	.25
a.	Strip of 5, #519-523		2.75	2.25
b.	As "a," triple impression of black		*550.00*	
524	A269 6c multicolored		.35	.25
525	A269 6c multicolored		.35	.25
526	A269 6c multicolored		.35	.25
527	A269 6c multicolored		.35	.25
528	A269 6c multicolored		.35	.25
a.	Strip of 5, #524-528		3.00	2.50
529	A270 10c multicolored		.40	.35
530	A270 15c multicolored		.90	.90
	Nos. 519-530 (12)		4.55	3.75

Tagged

519p	A268 5c multicolored		.35	.25
520p	A268 5c multicolored		.35	.25
521p	A268 5c multicolored		.35	.25
522p	A268 5c multicolored		.35	.25
523p	A268 5c multicolored		.35	.25
ap.	Strip of 5, #519p-523p		3.25	2.75
524p	A269 6c multicolored		.40	.25
525p	A269 6c multicolored		.40	.25
526p	A269 6c multicolored		.40	.25
527p	A269 6c multicolored		.40	.25
528p	A269 6c multicolored		.40	.25
ap.	Strip of 5, #524p-528p		4.50	3.00
529p	A270 10c multicolored		.50	.50
530p	A270 15c multicolored		1.10	1.10
	Nos. 519p-530p (12)		5.35	4.10

Christmas.

The sheets of 100 of both 5c and 6c contain all 5 designs, generally alternating, and arranged to permit vertical and horizontal pairs of each design in the two center vertical and horizontal rows. The center block of 4 is entirely of No. 522 (5c) and 525 (6c). The sheet may also be broken to provide 20 strips of 5, each stamp of different design.

Sir Donald Alexander Smith — A271

1970, Nov. 4

531 A271 6c dk grn, yel & black .25 .25

Smith (1820-1914), railroad builder and Canadian High Commissioner, 1896-1914.

Big Raven, by Emily Carr — A272

1971, Feb. 12

532 A272 6c multicolored .25 .25

Emily Carr (1871-1945), painter and writer.

Laboratory Equipment Used for Insulin Discovery — A273

1971, Mar. 3 *Perf. 11*

533 A273 6c multicolored .25 .25

Discovery of insulin by Dr. Frederick G. Banting and Dr. Charles H. Best, 50th anniversary.

A274

1971, Mar. 24

534 A274 6c red, org & black .25 .25

Sir Ernest Rutherford (1871-1937), physicist, developer of theory of spontaneous disintegration of the atom.

Spring, Winged Maple Seed — A275

1971

535 A275 6c shown .30 .25
a. Imperf., pair *800.00* *1,400.*
536 A275 6c Summer .30 .25
537 A275 7c Autumn .30 .25
538 A275 7c Winter .30 .25
Nos. 535-538 (4) 1.20 1.00

Issue dates: No. 535, Apr. 14; No. 536, June 16; No. 537, Sept. 3; No. 538, Nov. 19.

Louis Joseph Papineau — A276

Litho. & Engr.

1971, May 7 ***Perf. 12½x12***

539 A276 6c multicolored .25 .25

Louis Joseph Papineau (1786-1871), member of Legislative Assembly and leader of French Canadian Patriote party.

Map of Copper Mine River Basin A277

1971, May 7 ***Perf. 12x12½***

540 A277 6c buff, red & brown .25 .25

Bicentenary of Samuel Hearne's expedition to the Copper Mine River.

Maple Leaves A278

1971, June 1

541 A278 15c blk, red org & yel 1.75 1.10
p. Tagged 2.50 2.25

Inauguration of new transmitters for Radio Canada International.

Computer Tape and Reels — A279

1971, June 1

542 A279 6c black, ultra & red .25 .25

Centenary of measured progress through census.

Migrating Phosphor

Canada's "Ottawa/General" tagging of engraved stamps printed March-October, 1972, used a phosphor which migrates onto or through other stamps, booklet covers and album pages. It fluoresces yellow under ultraviolet light.

This bleeding, contaminating "OP4" phosphor can be somewhat contained in mounts or envelopes of acetate, glassine or polyethylene, but it may leak or penetrate.

The migrating phosphor is found on all examples of Nos. 560p-561p, and on some of Nos. 544p, 544q, 544r, 544s, 562p-565p and 594-598.

Transportation Means — A280

Design: 8c, Library of Parliament.

1971-72 **Engr.** ***Perf. 12½x12***

543 A280 7c slate green .35 .25
a. Booklet pane of 5 + label (#454e, #456a + 3#543) 7.50 4.50
b. Booklet pane of 20 (4 #454e, 4 #456a, 12 #543) 8.00 6.50
p. Tagged .60 .25
544 A280 8c slate .25 .25
a. Booklet pane of 6 (3 #454e, 1 #460c, 2 #544) 3.50 1.75
b. Booklet pane of 18 (6 #454e, 1 #460c, 11 #544) 5.25 3.00
c. Booklet pane of 10 (4 #454e, 1 #460c, 5 #544 ('72) 2.25 2.25
p. Tagged .30 .25
q. As "a," tagged 1.75 1.75
r. As "b," tagged 3.25 3.25
s. As "c," tagged 2.00 2.00

Coil Stamps

1971 ***Perf. 10 Horiz.***

549 A280 7c slate green .40 .25
a. Imperf, pair 1,050.
550 A280 8c slate .30 .25
a. Imperf, pair 600.00
p. Tagged .25 .25
q. As "p," imperf, pair 850.00

See note below No. 468B.
Issued: 7c, 6/30/71; 8c, 12/30/71.

Abstract "BC" A282

1971, July 20 **Litho.** ***Perf. 12***

552 A282 7c multicolored .25 .25

Centenary of British Columbia's entry into Canadian Confederation.

Indian Encampment on Lake Huron, by Kane — A283

1971, Aug. 11 ***Perf. 12½***

553 A283 7c multicolored .40 .25

Paul Kane (1810-1871), painter.

Snowflake — A284

1971, Oct. 6 **Engr.** ***Perf. 12***

Size: 24x30mm

554 A284 6c dark blue .25 .25
p. Tagged .25 .25
a. All color omitted (from foldover) *2,000.*
b. Printed on gummed side (from foldover) *1,200.*
555 A284 7c bright green .25 .25
p. Tagged .30 .25

Litho. and Engr.

Size: 30x30mm

556 A284 10c dp car & silver .35 .30
p. Tagged .45 .30
557 A284 15c lt ultra, dp car & silver .70 .65
p. Tagged .90 .75
Nos. 554-557 (4) 1.55 1.45

Christmas.

Pierre Laporte — A285

1971, Oct. 20 ***Perf. 12½x12***

558 A285 7c black .25 .25

Pierre Laporte (1921-1970), Minister of Labor, kidnapped and killed.

Figure Skating — A286

1972, Mar. 1 **Litho.** ***Perf. 12***

559 A286 8c deep red lilac .25 .25

World Figure Skating Championships, Calgary, Alberta, Mar. 6-12.

"Your Heart is your Health" A287

1972, Apr. 7 **Engr.** ***Perf. 12x12½***

560 A287 8c red .30 .25
p. Tagged .55 .35

World Health Day, Apr. 7.

Frontenac, by Philippe Hébert and Fort Saint Louis, Quebec A288

1972, May 17 **Photo. and Engr.**

561 A288 8c red brown & multi .25 .25
p. Tagged .75 .75

Tercentenary of the appointment of Louis de Buade, Count of Frontenac and Palluau (1622-1698), as Governor of New France.

Indians of Canada

Buffalo Chase, by George Catlin A289

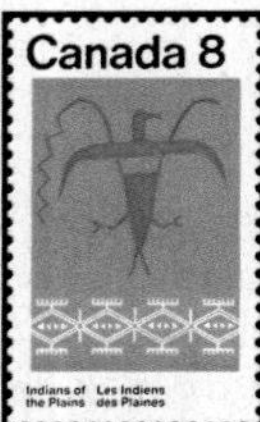

Thunderbird, Assiniboin Pattern — A290

No. 563, Plains Indian artifacts. No. 565, Ceremonial sun dance costume.

In Nos. 562-581, the first two and last two stamps of each annual set are printed checkerwise in same sheet of 50.

1972 **Litho.** ***Perf. 12x12½***

562 A289 8c shown .40 .25
p. Tagged .55 .30
563 A289 8c multicolored .40 .25
p. Tagged .55 .30
a. Pair, #562-563 .80 .50
b. As "a," tagged 1.10 .75

Perf. 12½x12

Photo. & Engr.

564 A290 8c shown .35 .25
p. Tagged .55 .30
565 A290 8c multicolored .35 .25
p. Tagged .55 .30
a. Pair, #564-565 .70 .50
b. As "a," tagged 1.10 .75

Plains Indians of Canada.

Issued: Nos. 562-563, 7/6; Nos. 564-565, 10/4.

Tagged (Nos. 566-581)

No. 566, Algonkian artifacts. No. 567, "Micmac Indians." No. 568, Thunderbird and belt. No. 569, Algonkian man and woman.

1973 **Litho.** ***Perf. 12x12½***

566 A289 8c multicolored .35 .25
567 A289 8c multicolored .35 .25
a. Pair, #566-567 .70 .50

Perf. 12½x12

Photo. & Engr.

568 A290 8c multicolored .30 .25
569 A290 8c multicolored .30 .25
a. Pair, #568-569 .60 .50

Algonkian-speaking Indians of Canada (Malecite, Micmac, Montagnais, Algonquin and Ojibwa).

Issued: Nos. 566-567, 2/21; Nos. 568-569, 11/28.

1974 **Litho.** ***Perf. 12x12½***

No. 570, Nootka Sound, house, inside. No. 571, Artifacts. No. 572, Chief wearing Chilkat blanket. No. 573, Thunderbird from Kwakiutl house.

570 A289 8c multicolored .30 .25
571 A289 8c multicolored .30 .25
a. Pair, #570-571 .60 .50

Perf. 12½x12

Photo. & Engr.

572 A290 8c multicolored .30 .25
573 A290 8c multicolored .30 .25
a. Pair, #572-573 .60 .50

Pacific Coast Indians of Canada (Haida, Salish, Tsimshian, Chilkat and Kwakiutl).

Issued: Nos. 570-571, 1/16; Nos. 572-573, 2/22.

1975, Apr. 4 **Litho.** ***Perf. 13½***

No. 574, Montagnais-Naskapi artifacts. No. 575, Dance of the Kutcha-Kutchin. No. 576, Kutchin ceremonial costume. No. 577, Ojibwa thunderbird and Naskapi pattern.

574 A289 8c multicolored .25 .25
575 A289 8c multicolored .25 .25
a. Pair, #574-575 .50 .50

Perf. 12½

576 A290 8c multicolored .25 .25

Litho. and Embossed

577 A290 8c multicolored .25 .25
a. Pair, #576-577 .50 .50

Subarctic Indians.

1976, Sept. 17 **Litho.** ***Perf. 13½***

No. 578, Cornhusk mask, artifacts. No. 579, Iroquoian Encampment, by George Heriot. No. 580, Iroquoian thunderbird. No. 581, Iroquoian man, woman.

578 A289 10c multicolored .25 .25
579 A289 10c multicolored .25 .25
a. Pair, #578-579 .50 .50

Perf. 12½

Litho. & Embossed

580 A290 10c multicolored .25 .25

Litho.

581 A290 10c multicolored .25 .25
a. Pair, #580-581 .50 .50
Nos. 562-581 (20) 6.00 5.00

Iroquois (Mohawk, Cayuga, Seneca, Oneida, Onondaga and Tuscarora).

Geological Fault — A291

No. 583, Bird's eye view of town. No. 584, Aerial map photography. No. 585, Contour lines.

1972, Aug. 2 ***Perf. 12***
582 A291 15c shown 1.50 1.10
p. Tagged 2.00 1.50
583 A291 15c multicolored 1.50 1.10
p. Tagged 2.00 1.50
584 A291 15c multicolored 1.50 1.10
p. Tagged 2.00 1.50
585 A291 15c multicolored 1.50 1.10
p. Tagged 2.00 1.50
a. Block of 4, #582-585 6.00 5.50
b. As "a," tagged 8.00 *11.00*
Nos. 582-585 (4) 6.00 4.40

Earth sciences: 24th Intl. Geological Cong. (No. 582); 22nd Intl. Geographical Cong. (No. 583); 12th Cong. of Intl. Soc. of Photogrammetry (No. 584); 6th Cong. of Intl. Cartographic Assoc. (No. 585).

Sir John A. Macdonald A292

Elizabeth II A292a

Forest, Central Canada — A293

Vancouver, B.C. — A294

Designs: 2c, Sir Wilfrid Laurier. 3c, Sir Robert L. Borden. 4c, William Lyon Mackenzie King. 5c Richard Bedford Bennett. 6c, Lester B. Pearson. 7c, Louis St. Laurent. 15c, Mountain sheep, Western Canada. 20c, Grain fields, Prairie. 25c, Polar bears, North. 50c, Seashore. $2, Quebec.

1972-76 **Engr.** ***Perf. 12x12½***
Tagged
586 A292 1c orange ('73) .25 .25
a. Booklet pane, 3 #586, 1 #591, 2 #593 ('74) 1.25 1.10
b. Bklt. pane, 6 #586, 1 #591, 11 #593 ('75) 1.50 1.50
c. Bklt. pane, 2 #586, 4 #587, 4 #593Ac ('76) 1.25 1.10
d. Printed on gummed side 850.00
587 A292 2c green ('73) .25 .25
588 A292 3c brown ('73) .25 .25
589 A292 4c black ('73) .25 .25
590 A292 5c lilac ('73) .25 .25
591 A292 6c dk red ('73) .25 .25
a. Printed on gummed side 180.00
592 A292 7c dk brn ('74) .25 .25
593 A292a 8c ultra ('73) .25 .25
b. Perf. 13x13½ ('76) .75 .25

Perf. 13x13½
593A A292a 10c dk car ('76) .25 .25
c. Perf. 12x12½ .35 .25

Perf. 12½x12
Photo. & Engr.
594 A293 10c multicolored .30 .25
595 A293 15c multicolored .50 .25
596 A293 20c multicolored .50 .25
597 A293 25c multicolored .55 .25
598 A293 50c multicolored 1.20 .25
599 A294 $1 multi ('73) 2.50 .50

Perf. 11
Litho. & Engraved
600 A294 $1 multicolored 6.00 1.60
601 A294 $2 multicolored 4.50 2.25
Nos. 586-601 (17) 18.30 7.85

No. 599 has engraved shading added in some areas.

Plates 1 and 2 of the scenic 10c differ in impression and colors. Plate 1 has distinct crosshatching of "Canada" background. On plate 2, released in 1974, this area appears solidly inked.

A 1976 printing of the 15c shows the blue trees on the hillside as solid color, while the 1972 printing shows clear detail on the trees.

A 1974 printing of the 50c has darker shading and a deeper tone for the dark blue areas of the photogravure impression.

Nos. 600 and 601 are untagged.

1976-77 **Photo. & Engr.** ***Perf. 13½***
594a A293 10c multicolored .30 .25
595a A293 15c multicolored .45 .25
596a A293 20c multicolored .60 .25
597a A293 25c multicolored .65 .25
598a A293 50c multicolored 1.75 .25
599a A294 $1 multi ('77) 2.50 .30
Nos. 594a-599a (6) 6.25 1.55

Coil Stamps
1974-76 **Engr.** ***Perf. 10 Vert.***
604 A292a 8c ultramarine .25 .25
a. Imperf., horiz. pair 150.00
605 A292a 10c dk carmine ('76) .30 .25
a. Imperf., horiz. pair 160.00

See note below No. 468B. No. 604 also exists in vertical multiples without score line.

Candles — A295

Candles and Fruit A296

Christmas: 8c, Like 6c. 15c, Candles, 15th century prayer book, boxes and brass vase.

1972, Nov. 1 **Litho.** ***Perf. 12½x12***
606 A295 6c red & multi .25 .25
p. Tagged .30 .25
607 A295 8c vio blue & multi .25 .25
p. Tagged .35 .25

Perf. 11
608 A296 10c green & multi .45 .35
p. Tagged .65 .55
609 A296 15c yel bister & multi .75 .75
p. Tagged 1.25 1.20
Nos. 606-609 (4) 1.70 1.60

"The Blacksmith's Shop," by Krieghoff — A297

1972, Nov. 29 ***Perf. 12½***
610 A297 8c multicolored .30 .25
p. Tagged .35 .25

Cornelius Krieghoff (1815-1872), painter.

Tagged

From No. 611 onward, all stamps are tagged unless otherwise noted.

Monsignor de Laval — A298

1973, Jan. 31 ***Perf. 11***
611 A298 8c silver, ultra & gold .25 .25

Francois-Xavier de Montmorency-Laval de Montigny (1623-1708), 1st Bishop of Quebec and founder of many educational institutions; one of the builders of New France.

Commissioner G. A. French and Map of 1874 Trek — A299

10c, Spectrograph. 15c, R.C.M.P. Musical Ride.

1973, Mar. 9
612 A299 8c dk brn, org & red .25 .25
613 A299 10c dk blue & multi .35 .30
614 A299 15c yel grn & multi .75 .50
a. Imperf., pair 375.00
Nos. 612-614 (3) 1.35 1.05

Royal Canadian Mounted Police, cent.

Imperfs of No. 614 with a double impression and examples with 15c printed on 10c are from printer's waste.

Jeanne Mance A300

1973, Apr. 18
615 A300 8c multicolored .25 .25
a. Printed on gummed side *750.00*

Jeanne Mance (1606-1673), first secular nurse in North America and founder of first hospital, the Hôtel-Dieu in Montreal settlement.

Joseph Howe — A301

1973, May 16
616 A301 8c gold & black .25 .25

Joseph Howe (1804-1873), journalist, poet and Lieutenant-Governor of Nova Scotia.

Mist Fantasy, by James MacDonald A302

1973, June 8 ***Perf. 12½***
617 A302 15c multicolored .60 .50

Centenary of the birth of James E. H. MacDonald (1873-1932), painter.

Oaks on Shore A303

Photo. & Engr.
1973, June 22 ***Perf. 12x12½***
618 A303 8c orange & red brn .25 .25

Centenary of Prince Edward Island's entry into Confederation.

Scottish Settlers and "Hector" A304

1973, July 20
619 A304 8c multicolored .25 .25

Bicentenary of arrival of Scottish settlers at Pictou, N.S.

Queen Elizabeth II — A305

1973, Aug. 2 **Photo. and Engr.**
620 A305 8c silver & multi .25 .25
621 A305 15c gold & multi .70 .60

Visit to Ottawa of Elizabeth II and the Duke of Edinburgh, July 31-Aug. 4, and meeting of Commonwealth Heads of Government, Ottawa, Aug. 2-10.

Nellie McClung — A306

1973, Aug. 29 **Litho.** ***Perf. 10½x11***
622 A306 8c multicolored .25 .25

Nellie McClung (1873-1951), leader of women's suffrage movement, social reformer and writer.

Montreal Olympic Games — A307

1973, Sept. 20 ***Perf. 12x12½***
Size: 26x44mm
623 A307 8c silver & multi .25 .25
624 A307 15c gold & multi .60 .50

21st Olympic Games, Montreal, 1976. See Nos. B1-B3.

Ice Skate — A308

Santa Claus — A309

8c, Dove. 15c, Shepherd and star.

1973, Nov. 7 ***Perf. 12½x12***

625	A308 6c multicolored	.25	.25
a.	Double impression of black	100.00	
626	A308 8c multicolored	.25	.25

Perf. 10½

627	A309 10c multicolored	.30	.30
628	A309 15c multicolored	.60	.60
	Nos. 625-628 (4)	1.40	1.40

Christmas.

Children Diving from Dock — A310

1974, Mar. 22 **Engr.** ***Perf. 12***

629	A310 8c shown	.35	.25
630	A310 8c Joggers	.35	.25
631	A310 8c Bicycling family	.35	.25
632	A310 8c Hikers	.35	.25
a.	Block of 4, #629-632	1.40	1.00

"Keep Fit." 21st Summer Olympic Games, Montreal, 1976. When stamps are observed at an angle the Montreal Olympic Games' emblem can be seen.

Main St. and Portage Ave., Winnipeg, 1872 — A311

Litho. & Engr.

1974, May 3 ***Perf. 12x12½***

633	A311 8c multicolored	.25	.25

Winnipeg's incorporation as a city, cent.

Postmaster A312

No. 635, Mail collector and truck. No. 636, Mail handler. No. 637, Mail sorters. No. 638, Mailman. No. 639, Rural mail delivery.

1974, June 11 **Litho.** ***Perf. 13½x13***

634	A312 8c shown	.35	.30
635	A312 8c multicolored	.35	.30
636	A312 8c multicolored	.35	.30
637	A312 8c multicolored	.35	.30
638	A312 8c multicolored	.35	.30
639	A312 8c multicolored	.35	.30
a.	Block of 6, #634-639	2.25	2.25

Centenary of letter carrier delivery service. Printed in sheets of 50 (5x10).

Agricultural Education A313

1974, July 12 ***Perf. 12½x12***

640	A313 8c multicolored	.25	.25

Ontario Agricultural College centenary.

Pedestal, Gallows Frame and Contempra Telephones A314

1974, July 26 ***Perf. 12½***

641	A314 8c multicolored	.25	.25
a.	Imperf., pair	*1,250.*	

Centenary of the idea for the telephone by Alexander Graham Bell while visiting Brantford, Canada.

Bicycle Wheel and Cycling Emblem A315

Photo. & Engr.

1974, Aug. 7 ***Perf. 12x12½***

642	A315 8c black, red & silver	.25	.25

World Cycling Championships, Montreal, Aug. 14-25.

Mennonite Settlers A316

1974, Aug. 28 **Litho.** ***Perf. 12x12½***

643	A316 8c multicolored	.25	.25

Centenary of arrival of Mennonite settlers in Manitoba.

Snowshoeing A317

1974, Sept. 23 **Engr.** ***Perf. 13½***

644	A317 8c shown	.35	.25
645	A317 8c Skiing	.35	.25
646	A317 8c Skating	.35	.25
647	A317 8c Curling	.35	.25
a.	Block of 4, #644-647	1.40	1.40
b.	Block or strip of 4, printed on gummed side	*3,000.*	

"Keep Fit." 1976 Winter Olympic Games. When the stamps are observed at an angle the Montreal Olympic Games' emblem can be seen.

Warning: No. 647b must show each design; blocks exist that contain 2 No. 645 but no example of No. 647. Value thus, $1,500.

Mercury with Winged Horses, UPU Emblem A318

Photo. & Engr.

1974, Oct. 9 ***Perf. 12x12½***

648	A318 8c violet, red & blue	.25	.25
649	A318 15c violet, red & blue	.90	.75

Centenary of Universal Postal Union.

Nativity, by Jean Paul Lemieux A319

Skaters at Hull, by Henri Masson — A320

Christmas (Paintings): 10c, The Ice Cone, Montmorency Falls, by Robert C. Todd. 15c, Village in the Laurentian Mountains, by Clarence A. Gagnon.

1974, Nov. 1 **Litho.** ***Perf. 13½***

650	A319 6c multicolored	.25	.25
651	A320 8c multicolored	.25	.25
652	A319 10c multicolored	.35	.30
653	A319 15c multicolored	.60	.55
	Nos. 650-653 (4)	1.45	1.35

Marconi and St. John's, Newfoundland, from Signal Hill — A321

1974, Nov. 15 ***Perf. 13***

654	A321 8c multicolored	.25	.25

Guglielmo Marconi (1874-1937), Italian electrical engineer and inventor.

Merritt and Welland Canal A322

Litho. & Engr.

1974, Nov. 29 ***Perf. 13x13½***

655	A322 8c multicolored	.25	.25

Sesquicentennial of the start of construction of the Welland Canal between Lakes Ontario and Erie, a project conceived and supervised by William Hamilton Merritt (1793-1862). Portrait by Robert Whale.

The Sprinter — A323

The Plunger — A324

Designs: Sculptures by Robert Tait McKenzie, M.D. (1867-1938), and Montreal Olympic Games' emblem.

Perf. 12½x12, 12x12½

1975, Mar. 14 **Litho.; Embossed**

656	A323 $1 multicolored	2.25	2.25
657	A324 $2 multicolored	4.50	4.50

21st Olympic Games, Montreal, July 17-Aug. 1, 1976.

A325

No. 658, Anne of Green Gables. No. 659, Maria Chapdelaine.

1975, May 15 **Litho.** ***Perf. 13***

658	8c blue & multi	.25	.25
659	8c brown & multi	.25	.25
a.	A325 Pair, #658-659	.50	.50

Birth centenary of Lucy Maud Montgomery (1874-1942), writer and author of "Anne of Green Gables"; Louis Hémon (1880-1913), writer and author of "Maria Chapdelaine." Nos. 658-659 printed checkerwise.

Marguerite Bourgeoys A327

Alphonse Desjardins A328

1975, May 30 **Litho.** ***Perf. 12½x12***

660	A327 8c red & multi	.25	.25
661	A328 8c red & multi	.25	.25

Marguerite Bourgeoys (1620-1700), founder of the Congrégation de Notre-Dame, Montreal, first girls' school in New France; Alphonse Desjardins (1854-1920), journalist, founder of first credit union in North America.

A329

No. 662, Samuel Dwight Chown (1853-1933), Methodist minister, leader of temperance movement, founder of United Church. No. 663, Dr. John Cook (1805-92), 1st Moderator of the United Presbyterian Church in Canada.

Nos. 662-663 printed checkerwise.

Photo. & Engr.

1975, May 30 ***Perf. 12x12½***

662	8c dk brown, yel & buff	.25	.25
663	8c dk brown, buff & yel	.25	.25
a.	A329 Pair, #662-663	.50	.50

Pole Vaulting — A331

Hurdling — A332

Design: 25c, Marathon running and Montreal Olympic Games' emblem.

1975, June 11 Litho. *Perf. 12x12½*

No.	Type	Description	Unused	Used
664	A331	20c dk blue & multi	.60	.45
665	A331	25c maroon & multi	.75	.50
666	A332	50c green & multi	1.50	1.00
		Nos. 664-666 (3)	2.85	1.95

21st Olympic Games, Montreal, July 17-Aug. 1, 1976.

"Untamed" (Wild Horse Race) A333

1975, July 3

No.	Type	Description	Unused	Used
667	A333	8c gray & multi	.25	.25

Centenary of the founding of Calgary.

Female Symbol — A334

Photo. & Engr.

1975, July 14 *Perf. 13*

No.	Type	Description	Unused	Used
668	A334	8c dp yel, gray & black	.25	.25

International Women's Year.

"Justice," by Walter S. Allward — A335

1975, Sept. 2 Litho. *Perf. 12½*

No.	Type	Description	Unused	Used
669	A335	8c multicolored	.25	.25

Supreme Court of Canada, centenary.

"Wm. D. Lawrence" A336

Photo. & Engr.

1975, Sept. 24 *Perf. 13*

No.	Type	Description	Unused	Used
670	A336	8c shown	.35	.30
671	A336	8c "Beaver"	.35	.30
672	A336	8c "Neptune"	.35	.30
673	A336	8c "Quadra"	.35	.30
a.		Block of 4, #670-673	1.40	1.40

Coastal ships.

Santa Claus — A337

Child — A338

Trees — A339

Designs by Canadian School Children: "What Christmas Means to Me" — No. 675, Skater. No. 677, Family and Christmas tree. No. 678, Gift box.

1975, Oct. 22 Litho. *Perf. 13½*

No.	Type	Description	Unused	Used
674	A337	6c shown	.25	.25
675	A337	6c multicolored	.25	.25
a.		Pair, #674-675	.50	.50
676	A338	8c shown	.25	.25
677	A338	8c multicolored	.25	.25
a.		Pair, #676-677	.50	.50
b.		Double impression of black	90.00	
c.		As "a," triple impression of black	300.00	
678	A338	10c multicolored	.25	.25
679	A339	15c shown	.45	.45
		Nos. 674-679 (6)	1.70	1.70

Christmas. Stamps of same denomination printed checkerwise.

Legion Emblem and Bugle A340

Photo. & Engr.

1975, Nov. 10 *Perf. 13*

No.	Type	Description	Unused	Used
680	A340	8c gray & multi	.25	.25

Royal Canadian Legion, 50th anniversary.

Olympic Torch Ignited by Satellite in Canada A341

Montreal Olympic Games' Emblem and: 20c, Canadian athletes carrying Olympic flag. 25c, Women athletes receiving Olympic medals.

1976, June 18 Litho. *Perf. 13*

No.	Type	Description	Unused	Used
681	A341	8c black & multi	.25	.25
682	A341	20c black & multi	.70	.55
683	A341	25c black & multi	.90	.60
		Nos. 681-683 (3)	1.85	1.40

1976 Olympic Games ceremonies.

Communication Arts — A342

25c, Handicraft tools. 50c, Performing arts.

1976, Feb. 6 Photo. *Perf. 12x12½*

No.	Type	Description	Unused	Used
684	A342	20c gray & multi	1.25	.60
685	A342	25c ocher & multi	1.50	.75
686	A342	50c blue & multi	2.50	1.25
		Nos. 684-686 (3)	5.25	2.60

Olympic Fine Arts and Cultural Program.

High-rise Tower, Notre Dame Church, Montreal, and Games' Emblem — A343

Design: $2, Olympic Stadium, Velodrome, flags and emblem.

Photo. & Engr.

1976, Mar. 12 *Perf. 13*

No.	Type	Description	Unused	Used
687	A343	$1 silver & multi	3.25	2.25
688	A343	$2 gold & multi	5.25	4.50

Nos. 681-688 were issued in commemoration of, or in connection with the 21st Olympic Games, Montreal, July 17-Aug. 1. Nos. 687-688 were issued in panes of 8.

Snowflake, Winter Olympics' Emblem — A344

Photo. and Embossed

1976, Feb. 6 *Perf. 12½*

No.	Type	Description	Unused	Used
689	A344	20c multicolored	.90	.65

12th Winter Olympic Games, Innsbruck, Austria, Feb. 4-15.

Flower Growing from City — A345

1976, May 12 Litho. *Perf. 12x12½*

No.	Type	Description	Unused	Used
690	A345	20c multicolored	.60	.45

Habitat, UN Conference on Human Settlements, Vancouver, May 31-June 11.

Franklin and Map of North America, 1776 A346

Litho. & Engr.

1976, June 1 *Perf. 13*

No.	Type	Description	Unused	Used
691	A346	10c multicolored	.35	.25

American Bicentennial; Benjamin Franklin (1706-1790), deputy postmaster general for the colonies (1753-1774).

See US No. 1690.

Royal Military College, Kingston, Ont., Cent. — A347

No. 692, Color Parade, Memorial Arch. No. 693, Wing Parade, Mackenzie Building.

1976, June 1 Litho. *Perf. 12*

No.	Type	Description	Unused	Used
692		8c red & multi	.25	.25
693		8c red & multi	.25	.25
a.		A347 Pair, #692-693	.50	.50
b.		As "a," imperf.	*1,700.*	
c.		Block of 4, imperf. horiz.	*650.00*	
d.		As "a," double impression	*3,250.*	

A few used singles exist of Nos. 692-693 with double impression. Very rare.

Archer in Wheelchair A349

1976, Aug. 3 *Perf. 12x12½*

No.	Type	Description	Unused	Used
694	A349	20c green & multi	.60	.50

Olympiad for the Physically Disabled (25th Stoke Mandeville Games), Toronto, Aug. 3-11.

A350

No. 695, The Cremation of Sam McGee. No. 696, The Outlander.

1976, Aug. 17 *Perf. 13½*

No.	Type	Description	Unused	Used
695		8c multicolored	.25	.25
696		8c multicolored	.25	.25
a.		A350 Pair, #695-696	.50	.50

Robert W. Service (1874-1958), author of poem "The Cremation of Sam McGee"; Germaine Guevremont, author of "Le Survenant" (The Outlander).

Nativity, St. Michael's, Toronto — A352

Stained-glass windows: 10c, Nativity, St. Jude, London, Ontario. 20c, Nativity, by Yvonne Williams.

1976, Nov. 3 *Perf. 13½*

No.	Type	Description	Unused	Used
697	A352	8c multicolored	.25	.25
698	A352	10c multicolored	.25	.25
699	A352	20c multicolored	.40	.40
		Nos. 697-699 (3)	.90	.90

Christmas.

Inland Vessels A353

Litho. & Engr.

1976, Nov. 19 *Perf. 12*

700 A353 10c Northcote .35 .30
701 A353 10c Passport .35 .30
a. Double impression of purple 275.00
702 A353 10c Chicora .35 .30
a. Double impression of blue 275.00
703 A353 10c Athabasca .35 .30
a. Block of 4, #700-703 1.40 1.25

Elizabeth II A354

Litho. and Typo.

1977, Feb. 4 *Perf. 12½x12*

704 A354 25c silver & multi .70 .50
a. Silver omitted 1,100.

25th anniv. of the reign of Elizabeth II.

Authentication strongly recommended for No. 704a. Fakes exist.

Bottle Gentian A355

Elizabeth II A356

Parliament, Ottawa A357

Trembling Aspen A358

Main Street, Prairie Town — A359

Fundy National Park — A359a

Designs: 2c, Western columbine. 3c, Canada lily. 4c, Hepatica. 5c, Shooting star. 10c, Franklin's lady's-slipper. No. 712, Jewelweed. No. 715, Parliament, Ottawa. No. 716, Queen Elizabeth II. 20c, Douglas fir. 25c, Maple. 30c, Red oak. 35c, White pine. 60c, Street scene, Ontario City. 75c, Old houses, eastern City Street. 80c, Street leading to the sea, Eastern Maritime Provinces. $2 Kluane National Park.

Litho. & Engr.

1977-82 *Perf. 12x12½*

705 A355 1c multicolored .25 .25
a. Printed on gummed side, precanceled 1,200.
707 A355 2c multicolored .25 .25
a. Printed on gummed side 850.00
708 A355 3c multicolored .25 .25
709 A355 4c multicolored .25 .25
a. Printed on gummed side 275.00
710 A355 5c multicolored .25 .25
711 A355 10c multicolored .25 .25
a. Perf. 13x13½ ('78) .25 .25

Photo. & Engr.

Perf. 13x13½

712 A355 12c multi ('78) .30 .25
713 A356 12c blue & multi .25 .25
a. Perf. 12x12½ .30 .25

Engraved

Perf. 13x13½

714 A357 12c blue .25 .25
a. Printed on gummed side 300.00
715 A357 14c red ('78) .25 .25
a. Printed on gummed side 37.50
b. All color omitted 375.00

Photo. & Engr.

Perf. 13x13½

716 A356 14c red & blk ('78) .25 .25
a. Perf. 12x12½ .25 .25
b. As "a," booklet pane of 25 + 2 labels ('78) 5.50 6.00
c. Red omitted *1,000.*

Perf. 13½

717 A358 15c multi .50 .25
718 A358 20c multi .35 .25
a. Black (denomination) omitted *750.00*
719 A358 25c multi .50 .25
720 A358 30c multi ('78) .60 .25
721 A358 35c multi ('79) .60 .25
723 A359 50c multi ('78) 1.10 .25
723A A359 50c multi, litho. & engr. ('78) .90 .25
b. Dark brown (engr., all inscriptions, etc.) omitted *1,800.*
c. Magenta (litho.) and dark brown (engr.) missing (from foldover) *15,000.*
723C A359 60c multi, litho. ('82) 1.25 .25
724 A359 75c multi ('78) 1.30 .30
725 A359 80c multi ('78) 1.50 .35

Lithographed and Engraved

726 A359a $1 multi ('79) 1.50 .55
a. Untagged 2.50 .70
b. As "a," blk inscriptions omitted 450.00 450.00
727 A359a $2 multi ('79) 3.60 1.40
a. Silver inscriptions omitted 300.00
b. Double impression of silver inscriptions *750.00*
Nos. 705-727 (23) 16.50 7.35

On No. 715b, a strong embossed impression from the plate, without color, is evident.

On No. 723A license plate on yellow car reads "1978."

No. 723Ac is unique.

Certificate of authenticity recommended for No. 727b. "Kiss prints" also exist that are not true double impressions.

See Nos. 781-806, 934-937, 1084.

Coil Stamps

1977-78 **Engr.** *Perf. 10 Vert.*

729 A357 12c blue .25 .25
a. Imperf., pair 140.00
730 A357 14c red ('78) .30 .25
a. Imperf., pair 160.00

See note below No. 468B.

Eastern Cougar A360

1977, Mar. 30 **Litho.** *Perf. 12½*

732 A360 12c multicolored .25 .25

Wildlife protection.

April in Algonquin Park, by Thomson — A361

No. 734, Autumn Birches, by Tom Thomson.

1977, May 26 *Perf. 12*

733 A361 12c black & multi .25 .25
734 A361 12c ocher & multi .25 .25
a. Pair, #733-734 .50 .50

Tom Thomson (1877-1917), landscape painter, birth centenary. Nos. 733-734 printed checkerwise.

Names of Governors General and Standard A362

1977, June 30 *Perf. 12½*

735 A362 12c vio blue & multi .25 .25

Honoring Canadian-born Governors General: Vincent Massey, Georges Philias Vanier, Daniel Roland Michener and Jules Léger.

Order of Canada A363

Litho. & Embossed

1977, June 30

736 A363 12c multicolored .25 .25

Order of Canada, 10th anniversary.

Peace Bridge, Canadian, US and UN Flags A364

1977, Aug. 4 **Litho.**

737 A364 12c blue & multi .25 .25

50th anniversary of the Peace Bridge, connecting Fort Erie, Ontario, with Buffalo, N.Y.

Joseph E. Bernier, CGS Arctic A365

Sandford Fleming, Railroad Bridge A366

1977, Sept. 16 **Engr.** *Perf. 13*

738 A365 12c dark blue .25 .25
739 A366 12c brown .25 .25
a. Pair, #738-739 .50 .50

Joseph-Elzéar Bernier (1852-1934), explorer; Sandford Fleming (1827-1915), mapped route for Intercolonial Railway and designed Canada's first stamp.

Nos. 738-739 printed checkerwise.

Peace Tower, Parliament, Ottawa A367

1977, Sept. 19 **Litho.** *Perf. 12½*

740 A367 25c multicolored .75 .65

23rd Commonwealth Parliamentary Conference, Ottawa, Sept. 19-25.

Hunters Following Star — A368

Christmas: 12c, Angelic choir in northern light. 25c, Christ Child in Ring of Glory blessing chiefs from afar. Illustrations for Canada's first Christmas carol, written by Father Brébeuf, 1649.

1977, Oct. 26 *Perf. 13½*

741 A368 10c multicolored .25 .25
a. Horiz. pair, imperf between *900.00*
b. Printed on gummed side 650.00
c. Imperf., pair *1,150.*
742 A368 12c multicolored .25 .25
a. Left margin block of 4, left vert. pair imperf, right pair part perf *1,750.*
b. Double impression of purple, blue, green; quadruple impression of black (inscriptions) 650.00
743 A368 25c multicolored .45 .35
Nos. 741-743 (3) .95 .85

Pinky A369

Canadian sailing ships — No. 745, Tern schooner. No. 746, 5-masted schooner. No. 747, Mackinaw boat.

Litho. and Engr.

1977, Nov. 18 *Perf. 12x12½*

744 A369 12c shown .25 .25
745 A369 12c multicolored .25 .25
746 A369 12c multicolored .25 .25
747 A369 12c multicolored .25 .25
a. Block of 4, #744-747 1.00 1.00
b. As "a," #745, 747 imperf; #744, 746 part perf *3,000.*

See Nos. 776-779.

Seal Hunter, Soapstone Sculpture A370

Disguised Caribou Hunter, Print — A371

Inuit Art: No. 749, Spear fishing. No. 751, Walrus hunt. Nos. 749-751 are after stonecut prints.

1977, Nov. 18 **Litho.**

748 A370 12c multicolored .25 .25
749 A371 12c multicolored .25 .25
a. Pair, #748-749 .50 .50
b. As "a," gray (inscriptions) omitted on No. 749 *2,250.*
750 A371 12c multicolored .25 .25
751 A371 12c multicolored .25 .25
a. Pair, #750-751 .50 .50
Nos. 748-751 (4) 1.00 1.00

Inuit hunting. Nos. 748-749 and Nos. 750-751 printed se-tenant checkerwise.

Peregrine Falcon A372

1978, Jan. 18

752 A372 12c multicolored .25 .25

Endangered wildlife.

Canada No. 3, 1851 — A373

1978 **Photo. & Engr.** *Perf. 13½*

753 A373 12c shown .25 .25
754 A373 14c No. 7 .25 .25
755 A373 30c No. 8 .55 .30

756 A373 $1.25 No. 2 2.00 1.00
a. Souvenir sheet of 3 3.25 3.25
Nos. 753-756 (4) 3.05 1.80

CAPEX '78, Canadian Intl. Phil. Exhib., Toronto, June 9-18 (cent. of Canada's admission to UPU).

No. 756a contains one each of Nos. 754-756 ($1.25 untagged). Value of No. 756 untagged, $2.75.

Issue dates: 12c, Jan. 18; others, June 10.

Games' Emblem A374

Design: 30c, Badminton.

1978, Mar. 31 Litho. *Perf. 12½*
757 A374 14c silver & multi .25 .25
758 A374 30c silver & multi .55 .45

Stadium A375

No. 760, Running. No. 761, Alberta Legislature building, Edmonton. No. 762, Lawn bowling.

1978, Aug. 3
759 A375 14c silver & multi .30 .25
760 A375 14c silver & multi .30 .25
a. Pair, #759-760 .60 .50
b. Imperf., pair *650.00*
761 A375 30c silver & multi .55 .50
762 A375 30c silver & multi .55 .50
a. Pair, #761-762 1.10 1.00
Nos. 759-762 (4) 1.70 1.50

Nos. 757-762 commemorate 11th Commonwealth Games, Edmonton, Aug. 3-12.

Nos. 760a, 762a printed checkerwise.

All known examples of No. 760b have slight wrinkling from mishandling. Value is for a pair with only minimal wrinkling.

A376

No. 763, Capt. Cook, by Nathaniel Dance. No. 764, Nootka Sound, by John Webber.

1978, Apr. 26 *Perf. 13*
763 14c multicolored .25 .25
764 14c multicolored .25 .25
a. A376 Pair, #763-764 .60 .50

Capt. James Cook (1728-1779), explorer of Canada's East and West Coasts and bicentenary of his anchorage near Anchorage, June 1, 1778. Nos. 763-764 printed checkerwise.

Silver Mine, Cobalt Lake A378

Stripmining, Athabasca Tar Sands A379

1978, May 19 *Perf. 12½*
765 A378 14c multicolored .25 .25
766 A379 14c multicolored .25 .25
a. Pair, #765-766 .50 .50
b. As "a," No. 766 with double impression of brown (inscriptions) 600.00

Development of national resources. Nos. 765-766 printed checkerwise.

Prince's Gate A380

1978, Aug. 16
767 A380 14c multicolored .25 .25

Canadian National Exhibition, centenary.

Mère d'Youville and Miracle of Food — A381

1978, Sept. 21 *Perf. 13x13½*
768 A381 14c multicolored .25 .25

Marguerite d'Youville (1701-1771), founder of the Gray Nuns, beatified 1959.

Woman Walking, by Pitseolak A382

Migration, Soapstone by Joe Talurinili A383

Works by Eskimo Artists: No. 771, Plane over village, stonecut and stencil print by Pudlo. No. 772, Dogteam and sled, ivory sculpture by Abraham Kingmeatook.

1978, Sept. 27 *Perf. 13½*
769 A382 14c multicolored .25 .25
770 A383 14c multicolored .25 .25
a. Pair, #769-770 .50 .50
771 A382 14c multicolored .25 .25
772 A383 14c multicolored .25 .25
a. Pair, #771-772 .50 .50
Nos. 769-772 (4) 1.00 1.00

Travels of the Inuit. Printed checkerwise.

Madonna of the Flowering Pea, Cologne School — A384

Renaissance Paintings in National Gallery of Canada: 14c, Virgin and Child, by Hans Memling. 30c, Virgin and Child, by Jacopo Di Cione.

1978, Oct. 20 *Perf. 12½*
773 A384 12c multicolored .25 .25
774 A384 14c multicolored .25 .25
a. Black omitted 1,000.
775 A384 30c multicolored .55 .25
Nos. 773-775 (3) 1.05 .75

Christmas.

Sailing Ships Type of 1977

No. 776, "Chief Justice Robinson," 1842. No. 777, "St. Roch," 1928. No. 778, "Northern Light," 1928. No. 779, "Labrador," 1954.

Litho. & Engr.

1978, Nov. 15 *Perf. 13*
776 A369 14c multicolored .30 .25
777 A369 14c multicolored .30 .25
778 A369 14c multicolored .30 .25
779 A369 14c multicolored .30 .25
a. Block of 4, #776-779 1.25 1.10

Ice vessels.

Quebec Carnival — A386

1979, Feb. 1 Litho. *Perf. 13½*
780 A386 14c multicolored .25 .25

Flower, Queen & Parliament Types

1c, Bottle gentian. 2c, Western columbine. 3c, Canada lily. 4c, Hepatica. 5c, Shooting star. 10c, Franklin's lady's-slipper. 15c, Canada violet. No. 789, Elizabeth II. No. 790, Parliament, Ottawa.

Photo. & Engr., Engr. (#790)

1977-83 *Perf. 13x13½*
781 A355 1c multi ('79) .25 .25
a. Perf. 12x12½ ('77) .25 .25
b. Bklt. pane, 2 #781a, 4 #713a 1.00 1.00
782 A355 2c multi ('79) .25 .25
a. Bklt. pane, 4 #782b, 3 #716a + label 1.00 1.00
b. Perf. 12x12½ ('78) .25 .25
783 A355 3c multi ('79) .25 .25
784 A355 4c multi ('79) .25 .25
785 A355 5c multi ('79) .25 .25
786 A355 10c multi ('79) .25 .25
787 A355 15c multi ('79) .30 .25
789 A356 17c green & blk ('79) .30 .25
a. Perf. 12x12½ .35 .25
b. Bklt. pane of 25 #789a + 2 labels 6.50 *7.50*
c. Horiz. pair, imperf. btwn. and at left and bottom *1,800.*
d. Black inscriptions omitted *750.00*
790 A357 17c slate green ('79) .25 .25
a. Printed on gummed side 37.50
791 A356 30c multi ('82) .45 .25
a. Black (engr.) omitted *2,250.*
792 A356 32c multi ('83) .50 .25
Nos. 781-792 (11) 3.30 2.75

Nos. 781a, 782b, 789a are from booklet panes. No. 782b has one straight edge, others one or two.

Beware of examples purported to be No. 791a that actually have tiny amounts of black present. Only two examples have been confirmed with 100% omission. Certification strongly recommended.

No. 789d also shows the horiz. perfs. shifted.

Parliament Type of 1977
Booklet Stamps

1979, Mar. 28 Engr. *Perf. 12x12½*
797 A357 1c slate blue .40 .25
a. Bklt. pane, 1 #797, 3 #800, 2 #789a 1.40
800 A357 5c violet brown .30 .25

No. 797 has one straight edge, No. 800 has one or two.

Coil Stamps

1979, Mar. 8 *Perf. 10 Vert.*
806 A357 17c slate green .25 .25
a. Imperf., pair 150.00

Endangered Wildlife A392

1979, Apr. 10 Litho. *Perf. 12½*
813 A392 17c Soft-shelled turtle .30 .25
814 A392 35c Bowhead whale .75 .40

Ribbon Around Woman's Finger — A393

No. 816, String around man's finger.

1979, Apr. 10
815 A393 17c multicolored .25 .25
816 A393 17c multicolored .25 .25
a. Pair, #815-816 .50 .50
b. As "a," double impression of black 110.00
c. As "a," triple impression of black 225.00
d. As "a," double impression of red 110.00

Use postal code. Printed checkerwise.

Fruits of the Earth, by F. P. Grove A394

The Golden Vessel, by Emile Nelligan A395

1979, May 3 *Perf. 13x13½*
817 A394 17c multicolored .25 .25
a. Double impression of brown 375.00
818 A395 17c multicolored .25 .25
a. Double impression of blue 375.00
b. Pair, #817-818 .50 .55
c. As "b," left margin block of 4, left vert. pair imperf, right pair part perf *1,500.*

Frederick Philip Grove (1879-1948), teacher and writer; Emile Nelligan (1879-1941), French-Canadian poet. Nos. 817-818 printed checkerwise.

Warning: horizontal pairs exist of No. 818a that appear to be imperforate. These actually are pairs made from No. 818c with normal perforations trimmed off the right edge.

A396

1979, May 11 *Perf. 13½*
819 17c De Salaberry .25 .25
820 17c John By .25 .25
a. A396 Pair, #819-820 .50 .50

Charles-Michel d'Irumberry de Salaberry (1778-1829), and John By (1779-1836), Canadian colonels. Printed checkerwise.

Flag of Ontario A398

Provincial and Territorial flags: No. 822, Quebec. No. 823, Nova Scotia. No. 824, New Brunswick. No. 825, Manitoba. No. 826, British Columbia. No. 827, Prince Edward Island. No. 828, Saskatchewan. No. 829, Alberta. No. 830, Newfoundland. No. 831, Northwest Territories. No. 832, Yukon Territory.

1979, June 15 *Perf. 13½*

821 A398 17c shown .30 .25
822 A398 17c multicolored .30 .25
823 A398 17c multicolored .30 .25
824 A398 17c multicolored .30 .25
825 A398 17c multicolored .30 .25
826 A398 17c multicolored .30 .25
827 A398 17c multicolored .30 .25
828 A398 17c multicolored .30 .25
829 A398 17c multicolored .30 .25
830 A398 17c multicolored .30 .25
831 A398 17c multicolored .30 .25
832 A398 17c multicolored .30 .25
a. Pane of 12, #821-832 4.00 3.75

White Water Kayak Race A399

1979, July 3 *Perf. 12½*

833 A399 17c multicolored .30 .25

Canoe-Kayak (Slalom and Wild Water) World Championships, Jonquière and Desbiens, Quebec, June 30-July 8.

Women's Field Hockey A400

1979, Aug. 16

834 A400 17c multicolored .30 .25

Women's Field Hockey Championship, Vancouver, B.C., Aug. 16-30.

Summer Tent, Print by Kiakshuk A401

Eskimos Building Igloo, by Abraham of Povungnituk A402

Works by Eskimo Artists: No. 837, The Dance, print by Kalvak of Holman Island. No. 838, Two soapstone figures from Repulse Bay, by Madeleine Isserkut and Jean Mapsalak.

1979, Sept. 13 *Perf. 13½*

835 A401 17c multicolored .25 .25
836 A402 17c multicolored .25 .25
a. Pair, #835-836 .50 .50
837 A401 17c multicolored .25 .25
838 A402 17c multicolored .25 .25
a. Pair, #837-838 .50 .50
Nos. 835-838 (4) 1.00 1.00

Inuit shelters and community. Printed checkerwise.

Painted Wooden Train A403

Antique Toys: 17c, Horse, pull toy. 35c, Knitted doll, vert.

1979, Oct. 17 *Perf. 13*

839 A403 15c multicolored .25 .25
840 A403 17c multicolored .30 .25
841 A403 35c multicolored .60 .30
a. Gold (and tagging) omitted *1,000. 700.00*
Nos. 839-841 (3) 1.15 .80

Christmas.

Girl Watering Tree of Life — A404

1979, Oct. 24

842 A404 17c multicolored .25 .25

International Year of the Child.

Curtiss HS-2L A405

No. 844, Canadair CL-215. No. 845, Vickers Vedette. No. 846, Consolidated Canso.

1979, Nov. 15 *Perf. 12½*

843 A405 17c shown .30 .25
844 A405 17c multicolored .30 .25
a. Pair, #843-844 .65 .55
845 A405 35c multicolored .65 .50
846 A405 35c multicolored .65 .50
a. Pair, #845-846 1.30 1.25
Nos. 843-846 (4) 1.90 1.50

Map of Canada Showing Arctic Islands A406

1980, Jan. 23 *Perf. 13½*

847 A406 17c multicolored .25 .25

Acquisition of the Arctic Islands, centenary.

Downhill Skiing A407

1980, Jan. 23

848 A407 35c multicolored .65 .45

13th Winter Olympic Games, Lake Placid, NY, Feb. 12-24.

Meeting of the School Trustees, by Robert Harris A408

Royal Canadian Academy of Arts Centenary: No. 850, Inspiration, bronze sculpture, by Louis-Philippe Hebert (1850-1917). No. 851, Parliament Buildings, by Thomas Fuller (1822-1919). No. 852, Sunrise on the Saguenay, by Lucius O'Brien (1832-99).

1980, Mar. 6

849 A408 17c multicolored .30 .25
850 A408 17c multicolored .30 .25
a. Pair, #849-850 .60 .55
851 A408 35c multicolored .65 .50
852 A408 35c multicolored .65 .50
a. Pair, #851-852 1.30 1.25
Nos. 849-852 (4) 1.90 1.50

Printed checkerwise.

Atlantic Whitefish A409

Endangered wildlife. No. 854, Greater prairie chicken.

1980, May 6 *Perf. 12½*

853 A409 17c multicolored .35 .25
854 A409 17c multicolored .35 .25

Garden — A410

1980, May 29 *Perf. 13½*

855 A410 17c multicolored .25 .25

Intl. Flower Show, Montreal, May 17-Sept. 1.

Helping Hands — A411

Litho. & Embossed

1980, May 29 *Perf. 12½*

856 A411 17c ultra & gold .25 .25

14th World Congress of Rehabilitation International, Winnipeg, June 22-27.

"O Canada" Opening Bars A412

Composers Lavallee, Routhier, Weir A413

1980, June 6 **Litho.**

857 A412 17c multicolored .25 .25
858 A413 17c multicolored .25 .25
a. Pair, #857-858 .50 .50

"O Canada" centenary. Printed checkerwise in sheets of 16.

John George Diefenbaker (1895-1979), Prime Minister, 1956-63 — A414

1980, June 20 **Engr.** *Perf. 13½*

859 A414 17c dark blue .25 .25

Emma Albani (1847-1930), Soprano — A415

No. 861, Healey Willan (1880-1968), organist, composer. Printed checkerwise.

1980, July 4 **Litho.**

860 A415 17c multicolored .25 .25
861 A415 17c multicolored .25 .25
a. Pair, #860-861 .50 .50

Ned Hanlan (1855-1908), Oarsman A416

1980, July 4

862 A416 17c multicolored .25 .25

Wheat Fields, Saskatchewan A417

No. 864, Strip farming and town, Alberta.

1980, Aug. 27

863 A417 17c multicolored .25 .25
864 A417 17c multicolored .25 .25

75th anniversary of Saskatchewan's and Alberta's creation as Provinces.

Uraninite Molecular Structure A418

1980, Sept. 3

865 A418 35c multicolored .65 .50
a. Printed on gummed side 850.00

Discovery of uranium in Canada, 80th anniversary.

Sedna, by Ashoona Kiawak A419

Return of the Sun, Print by Kenojouak A420

Works by Eskimo Artists: No. 868, Bird Spirit, by Doris Hagiolok. No. 869, Shaman, print by Simon Tookoome.

1980, Sept. 25

866 A419 17c multicolored .25 .25
867 A420 17c multicolored .25 .25
a. Pair, #866-867 .50 .50
868 A419 35c multicolored .55 .55
869 A420 35c multicolored .55 .55
a. Pair, #868-869 1.10 1.10
b. As No. 869, double impression of gray 625.00
Nos. 866-869 (4) 1.60 1.60

Inuit spirits. Printed checkerwise.

Christmas Morning, by Frank Charles Hennessey — A421

Christmas (Greeting Cards, 1931): 17c, Sleigh Ride, by Joseph Sydney Hallam. 35c, McGill Cab Stand, by Kathleen Morris.

1980, Oct. 22 *Perf. 12½x12*

870 A421 15c multicolored .25 .25
871 A421 17c multicolored .25 .25
872 A421 35c multicolored .55 .45
Nos. 870-872 (3) 1.05 .95

Avro Canada CF-100, 1950 A422

Military Aircraft: No. 874, Avro Lancaster, 1941. No. 875, Curtiss JN-4 Canuck. No. 876, Hawker Hurricane, 1935.

1980, Nov. 10 ***Perf. 13x13½***

873 A422 17c multicolored	.30	.25
874 A422 17c multicolored	.30	.25
a. Pair, #873-874	.60	.55
875 A422 35c multicolored	.65	.55
876 A422 35c multicolored	.65	.55
a. Pair, #875-876	1.30	1.25
Nos. 873-876 (4)	1.90	1.60

Printed checkerwise.

Emmanuel-Persillier Lachapelle, Caduceus — A423

1980, Dec. 5 ***Perf. 13½***

877 A423 17c multicolored .25 .25

Lachapelle (1845-1918), physician, founded Notre Dame Hospital, Montreal, 1880.

Mandora, 18th Century A424

1981, Jan. 19 ***Perf. 12½***

878 A424 17c multicolored .25 .25

"The Look of Music" rare musical instrument exhibition, Vancouver, Nov. 2, 1980-Apr. 5, 1981.

No. 878 exists printed on gummed side with gold color and tagging omitted, from printer's waste.

Emily Stowe (1831-1903) and Toronto General Hospital — A425

Designs: No. 880, Louise McKinney, (1868-1931) Alberta legislative building. No. 881, Idola Saint-Jean, (1875-1945) Quebec legislative building. No. 882, Henrietta Edwards, (1849-1931) clubwomen.

1981, Mar. 4 ***Perf. 13x13½***

879 A425 17c multicolored	.35	.25
880 A425 17c multicolored	.35	.25
881 A425 17c multicolored	.35	.25
882 A425 17c multicolored	.35	.25
a. Block of 4, #879-882	1.40	1.25

Vancouver Island Marmot, by Michael Dumas A426

Endangered Wildlife: 35c, Wood bison, by Robert Bateman.

1981, Apr. 6

883 A426 17c multicolored	.30	.25
884 A426 35c multicolored	.70	.60

Kateri Tekakwitha ("Lily of the Mohawks"), by Emile Brunet — A427

Brunet Sculpture: No. 886, Marie de L'Incarnation.

1981, Apr. 24 ***Perf. 12½***

885 A427 17c brown & pale grn	.25	.25
886 A427 17c dark blue & lt blue	.25	.25
a. Pair, #885-886	.50	.50

Beatification of Kateri Tekakwitha (1656-1680), first North American Indian saint, and Marie De L'Incarnation (1599-1672), founder of Ursuline Order.

At Baie Saint-Paul, by Marc-Aurele Fortin (1888-1970) — A428

Paintings: No. 888, Self-portrait, by Frederick H. Varley (1881-1969). 35c, Untitled No. 6, by Paul-Emile Borduas (1905-60).

1981, May 22

887 A428 17c multi	.25	.25
888 A428 17c multi, vert.	.25	.25
a. Imperf, pair	*1,500.*	

Photo.

Perf. 13

889 A428 35c multi, vert.	.60	.60
Nos. 887-889 (3)	1.10	1.10

Map of Canada Showing Provincial Boundaries, 1867 — A429

1981, June 30 **Litho.** ***Perf. 13½***

890 A429 17c shown	.30	.25
891 A429 17c 1873	.30	.25
892 A429 17c 1905	.30	.25
893 A429 17c 1949	.30	.25
a. Strip of 4, #890-893	1.20	1.20

Canada Day.

Montreal Rose — A431

1981, July 22 ***Perf. 13½***

896 A431 17c multicolored .25 .25

A432

1981, July 31 **Photo. & Engr.**

897 A432 17c multicolored .25 .25

Niagara-on-the-Lake (1st capital of Upper Canada).

A433

1981, Aug. 14 **Litho.**

898 A433 17c multicolored .25 .25

Acadian Congress centenary.

A434

1981, Sept. 8

899 A434 17c multicolored .25 .25

Aaron Mosher (1881-1959), Labor Congress founder.

A435

1981, Nov. 16 **Litho.**

900 A435 15c 1781	.25	.25
901 A435 15c 1881	.25	.25
902 A435 15c 1981	.25	.25
Nos. 900-902 (3)	.75	.75

Christmas; bicentenary of 1st illuminated Christmas tree in Canada.

Frere Marie-Victorin (1885-1944) Botanist — A430

Botanists: No. 895, John Macoun (1831-1920).

1981, July 22 ***Perf. 12½***

894 A430 17c multicolored	.25	.25
895 A430 17c multicolored	.25	.25
a. Pair, #894-895	.50	.50

Canadair CL-41 Tutor A436

No. 904, de Havilland Tiger Moth. No. 905, Avro Canada C-102. No. 906, de Havilland Canada Dash-7.

1981, Nov. 24 ***Perf. 12½***

903 A436 17c shown	.30	.25
904 A436 17c multicolored	.30	.25
a. Pair, #903-904	.60	.55
905 A436 35c multicolored	.60	.55
906 A436 35c multicolored	.60	.55
a. Pair, #905-906	1.20	1.10
Nos. 903-906 (4)	1.80	1.60

A437

1981, Dec. 29 **Engr.** ***Perf. 13x13½***

907 A437 (30c) red	.90	.25
a. Printed on gummed side	*750.00*	

Coil Stamp

Perf. 10 Vert.

908 A437 (30c) red	.75	.25
a. Imperf., pair	*275.00*	*225.00*

See Nos. 923-924, 940, 943-946, 950-951.

CANADA '82 Intl. Philatelic Youth Exhibition, Toronto, May 20-24 — A438

1982 **Litho.** ***Perf. 13½***

909 A438 30c No. 1	.50	.25
910 A438 30c No. 102	.50	.25
911 A438 35c No. 223	.60	.50
912 A438 35c No. 155	.60	.50
913 A438 60c No. 158	1.20	.75
a. Souvenir sheet of 5, #909-913	3.75	3.75
b. As No. 913, triple impression of reddish brown	*1,400.*	
Nos. 909-913 (5)	3.40	2.25

Issued: Nos. 909, 911, 3/11; others, 5/20.

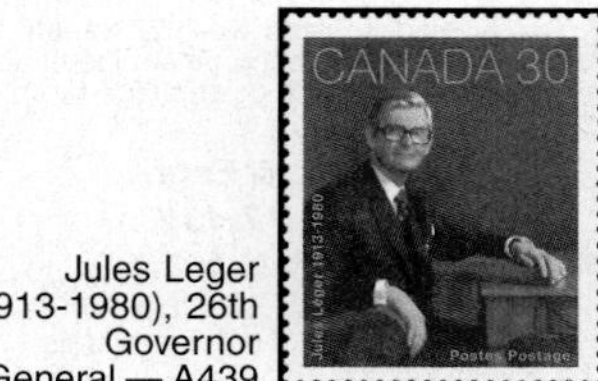

Jules Leger (1913-1980), 26th Governor General — A439

1982, Apr. 2

914 A439 30c multicolored .45 .25

Terry Fox (1958-1981), Marathon of Hope — A440

1982, Apr. 13 ***Perf. 12½***

915 A440 30c multicolored .50 .25

1982 Constitution — A441

1982, Apr. 16 ***Perf. 12x12½***

916 A441 30c multicolored .50 .25

Types of 1979-81 and

18th-19th Cent. Artifacts A442

Parliament (Library) A443

Parliament (West Block) — A444

Parliament (East Block) — A445

Elizabeth II — A446

Designs: 1c, Duck decoy. 2c, Fishing spear. 3c, Stable lantern. 5c, Bucket. 10c, Weather-cock. 20c, Ice skates. 37c, Wooden plow. 39c, Settle-bed. 48c, Cradle. 50c, Sleigh. 64c, Wood stove. 68c, Spinning wheel. $1, Glacier National Park. $1.50, Waterton Lakes National Park. $2, Moraine Lake, Banff National Park. $5, Point Pelee National Park.

1982-87 Litho. *Perf. 14x13½*

917 A442 1c multicolored .25 .25
a. Perf. 13x13½ ('85) .25 .25
918 A442 2c multicolored .25 .25
a. Perf. 13x13½ ('84) .25 .25
b. Bottom margin block of 4, bottom pair imperf, top pair part perf 1,750.
c. As "a," printed on gummed side 60.00
919 A442 3c multicolored .25 .25
a. Perf. 13x13½ ('85) .25 .25
920 A442 5c multicolored .25 .25
a. Perf. 13x13½ ('84) .25 .25
921 A442 10c multicolored .25 .25
a. Perf. 13x13½ ('85) .25 .25
922 A442 20c multicolored .30 .25

The previously listed No. 922 variety with "brown omitted" has been determined to be a normal No. 922 with a color shade or a color changeling.

Photo. & Engr.
Perf. 13x13½

923 A437 30c lt blue, bl, & red .50 .25
a. Bklt. pane of 20, perf. 12x12½ 10.00
b. Perf. 12x12½ 1.40 .45
924 A437 32c beige, red & brn .50 .25
a. Bklt. pane of 25, perf. 12x12½ 12.50 *13.50*
b. Perf. 12x12½ 1.00 .70
c. As #924, beige (and tagging) omitted 750.00

Litho.
Perf. 13½x13

925 A443 34c multicolored .55 .25
a. Booklet pane of 25 13.75
b. Perf. 13½x14 ('86) .75 .25
c. Bklt. pane of 25, perf. 13½x14 14.00 *16.50*

Photo. & Engr.
Perf. 13x13½

926 A446 34c lt bl & int bl .55 .25
926A A446 36c plum 3.00 2.25

Perf. 13½x13

926B A443 36c multicolored .55 .25
c. Booklet pane of 10 #926Be 5.50
d. Booklet pane of 25 #926Be 17.50
e. Perf. 13½x14 ('87) .70 .25
f. Left margin block of 4, left vert. pair imperf, right pair part perf *1,500.*
g. Imperf., horiz. pair 600.00
h. All color missing *1,500.*

No. 926Bh was caused by an extraneous piece of paper overlaying the pane during printing. Two such panes are recorded, one with two color-missing stamps and the other with 16 color-missing stamps. All adjoining stamps have some to most color missing, and if the panes are broken, the color-missing variety must be left se-tenant with a partially printed stamp.

Litho. *Perf. 12x12½*
Size A442: 26x20mm

927 A442 37c multi .55 .25
928 A442 39c multi .65 .25
929 A442 48c multi .75 .30
930 A442 50c multi .75 .25
932 A442 64c multi .95 .35
933 A442 68c multi 1.10 .35

Litho. & Engr.
Perf. 13½

934 A359a $1 multi 1.60 .50
a. Blue inscriptions omitted *750.00*
b. Imperf., pair *3,000.*
935 A359a $1.50 multi 3.25 .55
a. Black omitted *3,000.*
936 A359a $2 multi 3.25 1.10
a. Bluish green inscriptions omitted *1,000.*
937 A359a $5 multi 9.00 2.00
Nos. 917-937 (22) 29.05 10.90

Issued:1c-20c, 10/19; 30c, 5/11; $1.50, 6/18; $5, 1/10/83; 32c, 2/10/83; 37c, 48c, 64c, 4/8/83; $1, 8/15/84; No. 925, $2, 6/21/85; No. 926, 7/12/85; 39c, 50c, 68c, 8/1/85; No. 926B, 3/30/87; No. 926A, 10/1/87.

For former No. 931, see new No. 723C.

Booklet Stamps
Perf. 12x12½ (A437), 12½x12
Engr.

938 A445 1c sage green ('87) .25 .25
939 A444 2c myrtle grn ('85) .25 .25
a. 2c slate green ('89) .25 .25
940 A437 5c deep claret .25 .25
941 A445 5c dp brown ('85) .25 .25
942 A444 6c henna brn ('87) .25 .25
943 A437 8c dk blue ('83) .50 .25
944 A437 10c dark green .45 .25
945 A437 30c red .75 .30
a. Bklt. pane of 4 + 2 labels (2 #940, 944, 945) 1.20 *1.40*
946 A437 32c brown ('83) .60 .25
b. Bklt. pane of 4 + 2 labels (2 #940, 943, 946) 1.10 *1.30*
947 A443 34c dp slate bl ('85) 1.15 .70
a. Bklt. pane of 6 (3 #939, 2 #941, #947) 1.70 *1.25*
948 A443 36c dark lil rose ('87) 1.35 .70
a. Bklt. pane of 5 + label (2 #938, 2 #942, #948) 2.25 *1.40*

Issued: No. 940, 10c, 30c, 3/1; 8c, 32c, 2/15/83; No. 941, 30c, 6/21/85; 1c, 6c, 36c, 3/30/87.

Coil Stamps
Engr. *Perf. 10 Vert.*

950 A437 30c red .90 .25
a. Imperf., pair 300.00
951 A437 32c brown ('83) .75 .25
a. Imperf., pair 160.00

Perf. 10 Horiz.

952 A443 34c dull red brn ('85) .75 .25
a. Imperf., pair 135.00
953 A443 36c dark red ('87) .75 .25
a. Imperf., pair 250.00

Issued: 30c, 5/11; 32c, 2/10/83; 34c, 8/1/85; 36c, 5/19/87.

See Nos. 1080-1083, 1186-1188, 1194-1194A.

Centenary of Salvation Army in Canada A457

1982, June 25 Litho. *Perf. 13*

954 A457 30c multicolored .50 .25

Canada Day A458

Paintings: No. 955, The Highway near Kluana Lake, by A.Y. Jackson. No. 956, Montreal Street Scene, by Adrien Hebert. No. 957, Breakwater, by Christopher Pratt. No. 958, Along Great Slave Lake, by Rene Richard. No. 959, Tea Hill, by Molly Lamb. No. 960, Family and Rainstorm, by Alex Colville. No. 961, Brown Shadows, by Dorothy Knowles. No. 962, The Red Brick House, by David Milne. No. 963, Campus Gates, by Bruno Bobak. No. 964, Prairie Town—Early Morning, by Illingworth Kerr. No. 965, Totems at Ninstints, by Joe Plaskett. No. 966, Doc Snider's House, by Lionel LeMoine FitzGerald.

1982, June 30 *Perf. 12½x12*

955 A458 30c multicolored .65 .65
956 A458 30c multicolored .65 .65
957 A458 30c multicolored .65 .65
958 A458 30c multicolored .65 .65
959 A458 30c multicolored .65 .65
960 A458 30c multicolored .65 .65
961 A458 30c multicolored .65 .65
962 A458 30c multicolored .65 .65
963 A458 30c multicolored .65 .65
964 A458 30c multicolored .65 .65
965 A458 30c multicolored .65 .65
966 A458 30c multicolored .65 .65
a. Min. pane of 12, #955-966 8.00 8.00

Regina Centenary A459

1982, Aug. 3 *Perf. 13½x13*

967 A459 30c multicolored .50 .25

Centenary of Royal Canadian Henley Regatta, St. Catharines, Aug. 4-8 — A460

1982, Aug. 4

968 A460 30c multicolored .50 .25

Fairchild FC-2W1 A461

No. 970, De Havilland Canada Beaver. No. 971, Noorduyn Norseman. No. 972, Fokker Super Universal.

1982, Oct. 5 Litho. *Perf. 12½*

969 A461 30c shown .75 .25
970 A461 30c multicolored .75 .25
a. Pair, #969-970 1.50 1.10
971 A461 60c multicolored 1.10 .75
972 A461 60c multicolored 1.10 .75
a. Pair, #971-972 2.20 1.75
Nos. 969-972 (4) 3.70 2.00

Christmas A462

Designs: Creche figures.

1982, Nov. 3 *Perf. 13½*

973 A462 30c Holy Family .45 .25
a. All colors except black omitted *11,000.*
b. Printed on gummed side, black omitted *11,000.*
974 A462 35c Shepherds .55 .45
975 A462 60c Three Kings .90 .75
Nos. 973-975 (3) 1.90 1.45

Nos. 973a and 973b were caused by a paper foldover.

World Communications Year — A463

1983, Mar. 10 Litho. *Perf. 12x12½*

976 A463 32c multicolored .50 .25
a. Double impression of central multicolored globe 750.00

Commonwealth Day — A464

1983, Mar. 14

977 A464 $2 multicolored 9.00 3.75

Scene from Angeline de Montbrun, by Laure Conan (1845-1924), Painted by Rene Milot — A465

Design: No. 979, Sea Gulls, by Edwin John Pratt (1882-1966), woodcut by Claire Pratt.

1983, Apr. 22 Litho. *Perf. 13½*

978 A465 32c multicolored .50 .25
979 A465 32c multicolored .50 .25
a. Pair, #978-979 1.00 .90
b. As "a," all color missing *4,000.*

No. 979b resulted from an extraneous piece of paper receiving the colors. After removal, the issued pane shows two horizontal pairs without color plus six other stamps with only partial color.

St. John Ambulance Centenary A466

1983, June 3 *Perf. 13½*

980 A466 32c Emblem .50 .25

World University Games, Edmonton, July 1-11 — A467

1983, June 28 *Perf. 13½*

981 A467 32c multicolored .50 .25
a. Printed on gummed side 900.00
982 A467 64c multicolored 1.10 .75

Canada Day — A468

No. 983, Fort Henry, Ontario. No. 984, Fort William, Ontario. No. 985, Fort Rodd Hill, British Columbia. No. 986, Fort Wellington, Ontario. No. 987, Fort Prince of Wales, Manitoba. No. 988, Halifax Citadel, Nova Scotia. No. 989, Fort Chambly, Quebec. No. 990, Fort No. 1, Point Levis, Quebec. No. 991, Fort at Coteau-du-Lac, Quebec. No. 992, Fort Beausejour, New Brunswick. Sizes: Nos. 983, 988: 44x22mm; Nos. 984-985, 989-990, 36x22mm; Nos. 986-987, 991-992, 28x22mm.

Booklet Stamps

1983, June 30 *Perf. 12½x13*

983 A468 32c multicolored .75 .75
984 A468 32c multicolored .75 .75
985 A468 32c multicolored .75 .75
986 A468 32c multicolored .75 .75
987 A468 32c multicolored .75 .75
988 A468 32c multicolored .75 .75
989 A468 32c multicolored .75 .75
990 A468 32c multicolored .75 .75

991	A468	32c multicolored	.75	.75
992	A468	32c multicolored	.75	.75
a.		Booklet pane of 10, #983-992	7.50	7.50

Scouting Year — A469

1983, July 6 ***Perf. 13½***

993	A469	32c multicolored	.50	.25
a.		Red omitted		—

Church Council Emblem — A470

1983, July 22 **Litho.**

994	A470	32c tan & green	.50	.25

6th World Council of Churches Assembly, Vancouver, July 24-Aug. 10.

Humphrey Gilbert — A471

1983, Aug. 3 **Litho.**

995	A471	32c multicolored	.50	.25

400th anniv. of discovery of Newfoundland by Sir Humphrey Gilbert (1537-1583).

Centenary of Discovery of Nickel, Sudbury, Ontario A472

Litho. & Typo.

1983, Aug. 12 ***Perf. 13***

996	A472	32c multicolored	.55	.25
a.		Silver (and tagging) omitted	*625.00*	

Beware of forgeries of No. 996a. A certificate of authenticity is mandatory.

Josiah Henson (1789-1883), Preacher — A473

1983, Sept. 16 **Litho.** ***Perf. 13x13½***

997	A473	32c multicolored	.50	.25

Antoine Labelle (1833-1891), Deputy Minister for Settlement A474

1983, Sept. 16 ***Perf. 13½***

998	A474	32c multicolored	.50	.25

Locomotives — A475

No. 999, Toronto 4-4-0, 1853. No. 1000, Dorchester 0-4-0, 1836. No. 1001, Samson 0-6-0, 1838. No. 1002, Adam Brown 4-4-0, 1860.

1983, Oct. 3 ***Perf. 12½x13***

999	A475	32c multicolored	.50	.25
1000	A475	32c multicolored	.50	.25
a.		Pair, #999-1000	1.00	.90
1001	A475	37c multicolored	.60	.60
1002	A475	64c multicolored	1.10	.90
		Nos. 999-1002 (4)	2.70	2.00

Dalhousie Law School Centenary A476

1983, Oct. 28 ***Perf. 13***

1003	A476	32c Arms	.50	.25

Christmas A477

32c, Urban church. 37c, Family going to church. 64c, Rural church.

1983, Nov. 3 ***Perf. 13½***

1004	A477	32c multicolored	.50	.25
1005	A477	37c multicolored	.55	.45
1006	A477	64c multicolored	1.00	.75
		Nos. 1004-1006 (3)	2.05	1.45

Army Regiments, Centenaries A478

19th Cent. Uniforms: No. 1007, Royal Canadian Regiment, British Columbia Regiment. No. 1008, Royal Winnipeg Rifles, Royal Canadian Dragoons.

1983, Nov. 10 ***Perf. 13½x13***

1007	A478	32c shown	.50	.25
1008	A478	32c multicolored	.50	.25
a.		Pair, #1007-1008	1.00	.90

Yellowknife, 50th Anniv. — A479

1984, Mar. 15 ***Perf. 13½***

1009	A479	32c Gold mine	.50	.25

50th Anniv. of Montreal Symphony Orchestra A480

1984, Mar. 24 ***Perf. 12½***

1010	A480	32c multicolored	.50	.25

450th Anniv. of Cartier's Landing in Quebec A481

1984, Apr. 20 **Photo. & Engr.**

1011	A481	32c multicolored	.50	.25

See France No. 1923.

Voyage of Tall Ships, Saint-Malo, France, to Quebec City — A482

1984, May 18 **Litho.** ***Perf. 12x12½***

1012	A482	32c multicolored	.50	.25

450th anniv. of Cartier's landing in Quebec.

Canadian Red Cross Society, 75th Anniv. — A483

32c, Meritorious Service Medal.

1984, May 28 ***Perf. 13***

1013	A483	32c multicolored	.50	.25

New Brunswick, Bicentenary A484

1984, June 18 **Photo. & Engr.**

1014	A484	32c Galleys	.50	.25

St. Lawrence Seaway, 25th Anniv. — A485

32c, Seaway, Lake Superior.

1984, June 26 **Litho.**

1015	A485	32c multicolored	.50	.25

Canada Day A486

Provincial Landscapes by Jean Paul Lemieux (b. 1904): No. 1016, New Brunswick. No. 1017, British Columbia. No. 1018, Yukon Territory. No. 1019, Quebec. No. 1020, Manitoba. No. 1021, Alberta. No. 1022, Prince Edward Island. No. 1023, Saskatchewan. No. 1024, Nova Scotia, vert. No. 1025, Northwest Territories. No. 1026, Newfoundland. No. 1027, Ontario, vert.

1984, June 29

1016	A486	32c multicolored	.55	.40
1017	A486	32c multicolored	.55	.40
1018	A486	32c multicolored	.55	.40
1019	A486	32c multicolored	.55	.40
1020	A486	32c multicolored	.55	.40
1021	A486	32c multicolored	.55	.40
1022	A486	32c multicolored	.55	.40
1023	A486	32c multicolored	.55	.40
1024	A486	32c multicolored	.55	.40
1025	A486	32c multicolored	.55	.40
1026	A486	32c multicolored	.55	.40
1027	A486	32c multicolored	.55	.40
a.		Min. pane of 12, #1016-1027	6.75	6.25

Nos. 1018 and 1025 incorrectly inscribed. No. 1018 shows Northwest Territories landscape; No. 1025, Yukon Territory church.

Loyalists, British Flag (1606-1801) — A487

1984, July 3

1028	A487	32c multicolored	.50	.25

United Empire Loyalists, American colonists who remained loyal to British throne and emigrated to Canada during American Revolution.

Roman Catholic Church in Newfoundland A488

32c, St. John's Basilica.

1984, Aug. 17 ***Perf. 13½***

1029	A488	32c multicolored	.50	.25

Papal Visit A489

1984, Aug. 31 ***Perf. 12½***

1030	A489	32c multicolored	.50	.25
1031	A489	64c multicolored	1.10	.65

Lighthouses — A490

No. 1032, Louisbourg, 1734. No. 1033, Fisgard, 1860. No. 1034, Ile Verte, 1809. No. 1035, Gibraltar Point, 1808.

1984, Sept. 21

1032	A490	32c multicolored	.55	.25
1033	A490	32c multicolored	.55	.25
1034	A490	32c multicolored	.55	.25
1035	A490	32c multicolored	.55	.25
a.		Block of 4, #1032-1035	2.20	1.20

Steam Locomotives — A491

No. 1036, Scotia. No. 1037, Countess of Dufferin. No. 1038, Grand Trunk Class E3. No. 1039, Canadian Pacific D10a.

1984, Oct. 25 ***Perf. 12½x13***

1036	A491	32c multicolored	.50	.25
1037	A491	32c multicolored	.50	.25
a.		Pair, #1036-1037	1.00	.90
1038	A491	37c multicolored	.75	.65
1039	A491	64c multicolored	1.30	.90
a.		Souvenir sheet	3.00	3.00
		Nos. 1036-1039 (4)	3.05	2.05

No. 1039a contains Nos. 1036-1039 in changed colors.

See Nos. 1071-1074, 1118-1121.

Christmas A492

Paintings: 32c, The Annunciation, by Jean Dallaire. 37c, The Three Kings, by Simone Mary Bouchard. 64c, Snow in Bethlehem, by David Milne.

1984, Nov. 2 ***Perf. 13***

1040 A492 32c multicolored .50 .25
1041 A492 37c multicolored .55 .55
1042 A492 64c multicolored 1.00 .75
Nos. 1040-1042 (3) 2.05 1.55

Royal Canadian Air Force — A493

1984, Nov. 9 ***Perf. 12x12½***

1043 A493 32c Pilots .50 .25

Cent. of La Presse — A494

32c, Treffle Berthiaume.

1984, Nov. 16 ***Perf. 13x13½***

1044 A494 32c multicolored .50 .25

Heart, Arrow, Jeans A495

1985, Feb. 8 ***Perf. 12½***

1045 A495 32c multicolored .50 .25

International Youth Year.

Canadians in Space — A496

1985, Mar. 15 ***Perf. 13½***

1046 A496 32c Astronaut .55 .25

Therese Casgrain (1896-1981), Suffragist A497

Emily Murphy (1868-1933), Writer A498

1985, Apr. 17

1047 A497 32c multicolored .50 .25
1048 A498 32c multicolored .50 .25
a. Pair, #1047-1048 1.00 .90

Gabriel Dumont (1837-1906), Metis Leader — A499

1985, May 6 ***Perf. 13***

1049 A499 32c multicolored .50 .25

Centenary of the Northwest Rebellion.

Canada Day — A500

No. 1050, Lower Ft. Garry, Manitoba. No. 1051, Ft. Anne, Nova Scotia. No. 1052, Ft. York, Ontario. No. 1053, Castle Hill, Newfoundland. No. 1054, Ft. Whoop Up, Alberta. No. 1055, Ft. Erie, Ontario. No. 1056, Ft. Walsh, Saskatchewan. No. 1057, Ft. Lennox, Quebec. No. 1058, York Redoubt, Nova Scotia. No. 1059, Ft. Frederick, Ontario.

Sizes: Nos. 1050, 1055: 48x26mm. Nos. 1051-1052, 1056-1057: 40x26mm. Nos. 1053-1054, 1058-1059, 32x26mm.

Booklet Stamps

1985, June 28 ***Perf. 12½x13***

1050 A500 34c multicolored .95 .65
1051 A500 34c multicolored .95 .65
1052 A500 34c multicolored .95 .65
1053 A500 34c multicolored .95 .65
1054 A500 34c multicolored .95 .65
1055 A500 34c multicolored .95 .65
1056 A500 34c multicolored .95 .65
1057 A500 34c multicolored .95 .65
1058 A500 34c multicolored .95 .65
1059 A500 34c multicolored .95 .65
a. Bklt. pane of 10, #1050-1059 9.50 *12.50*

Intl. Pharmaceutical Federation Congress — A501

Design: Louis Hebert (1575-1627), 1st French Apothecary in North America.

1985, Aug. 30 ***Perf. 12½***

1060 A501 34c multicolored .55 .25

Interparliamentary Union '85, Ottawa — A502

1985, Sept. 3 ***Perf. 13½***

1061 A502 34c multicolored .55 .25

Guide, Brownie Saluting — A503

1985, Sept. 12 Photo. ***Perf. 13½x13***

1062 A503 34c multicolored .55 .25

Natl. Girl Guides movement, cent.

Lighthouses A504

1985, Oct. 3 Litho. ***Perf. 13½***

1063 A504 34c Sisters Islets .75 .25
1064 A504 34c Pelee Passage .75 .25
1065 A504 34c Haut-fond Prince .75 .25
1066 A504 34c Rose Blanche .75 .25
a. Block of 4, #1063-1066 3.00 2.50
b. Souv. sheet of 4, #1063-1066 4.75 4.75

Santa Claus Parade A505

Paintings by Barbara Carroll: 34c, Santa Claus. 39c, Horse-drawn coach. 68c, Christmas tree. No. 1070, 32c, Polar float.

1985, Oct. 23

1067 A505 34c multicolored .55 .25
1068 A505 39c multicolored .65 .55
1069 A505 68c multicolored 1.25 .90

Perf. 13½ on 3 Sides

1070 A505 32c multicolored 1.10 .50
a. Booklet pane of 10 11.00 10.00
Nos. 1067-1070 (4) 3.55 2.20

No. 1070 printed in booklets only.

Locomotives Type of 1984

No. 1071, Grand Trunk K2. No. 1072, Canadian Pacific P2a. No. 1073, Canadian Northern O10a. No. 1074, Canadian Govt. Railways H4D.

1985, Nov. 7 ***Perf. 12½x13***

1071 A491 34c multicolored .75 .25
1072 A491 34c multicolored .75 .25
a. Pair, #1071-1072 1.50 1.10
1073 A491 39c multicolored .75 .70
1074 A491 68c multicolored 1.30 1.00
Nos. 1071-1074 (4) 3.55 2.20

1910 Gunner's Mate, World War II Officer, 1985 Woman Recruit — A507

1985, Nov. 8 ***Perf. 13½x13***

1075 A507 34c multicolored .55 .25

Royal Canadian Navy, 75th anniv.

A508

Design: 34c, Old Holton House, Sherbrooke Street, Montreal, by James Wilson Morrice (1865-1924).

1985, Nov. 15 ***Perf. 13½***

1076 A508 34c multicolored .55 .25

Montreal Museum of Fine Arts, 120th anniv.

Southwestern Alberta, Computer Design Map — A509

1986, Feb. 13 Litho. ***Perf. 12½x13***

1077 A509 34c multicolored .55 .25

1988 Winter Olympics, Calgary, Alberta, Feb. 13-28.

EXPO '86, Vancouver, May 2-Oct. 13 — A510

1986, Mar. 7 **Photo. & Engr.**

1078 A510 34c Canada Pavilion .55 .25
1079 A510 39c Communications .65 .55

Artifacts Type of 1982

Designs: 25c Butter stamp. 42c, Linen chest. 55c, Iron kettle. 72c, Hand-drawn cart.

1987, May 6 Litho. ***Perf. 14x13½***

1080 A442 25c multicolored .55 .30

Size: 20x26mm

Perf. 12x12½

1081 A442 42c multicolored 1.10 .25
1082 A442 55c multicolored 1.40 .30
1083 A442 72c multicolored 1.75 .35
a. Imperf., pair 900.00
Nos. 1080-1083 (4) 4.80 1.20

Park Type of 1979

Design: La Mauricie National Park.

Litho. & Engr.

1986, Mar. 14 ***Perf. 13½***

1084 A359a $5 multi 9.00 2.00
a. Dark blue inscriptions omitted *2,500.* *1,500.*

No. 1084a is valued in the grade of fine as all known examples are centered thus.

Philippe Aubert de Gaspe (1786-1871), Novelist A511

Molly Brant (1736-1796), Iroquois Leader and Loyalist A512

1986, Apr. 14 Litho. ***Perf. 12½***

1090 A511 34c multicolored .55 .25

Perf. 13½

1091 A512 34c multicolored .55 .25

EXPO '86 — A513

34c, Expo Center, Vancouver. 68c, Transportation, horiz.

Photo. & Engr.

1986, Apr. 28 ***Perf. 13x13½***
1092 A513 34c multicolored .55 .25
1093 A513 68c multicolored 1.10 .70

Canadian Forces Postal Service, 75th Anniv. A514

1986, May 9 **Litho.** ***Perf. 13½***
1094 A514 34c multicolored .55 .25

Indigenous Birds — A515

1986, May 22
1095 A515 34c Great blue heron .70 .30
1096 A515 34c Snow goose .70 .30
1097 A515 34c Great horned owl .70 .30
1098 A515 34c Spruce grouse .70 .30
a. Block of 4, #1095-1098 2.80 2.50

19th Intl. Ornithological Congress, Ottawa, June 22-29.

Canada Day — A516

Invention blueprints: No. 1099, Rotary snowplow, 1869. No. 1100, Canadarm, 1986. No. 1101, Anti-gravity flight suit, 1938. No. 1102, Variable pitch propeller, 1923.

1986, June 27
1099 A516 34c multicolored .75 .25
1100 A516 34c multicolored .75 .25
1101 A516 34c multicolored .75 .25
1102 A516 34c multicolored .75 .25
a. Block of 4, #1099-1102 3.00 2.50

Canadian Broadcasting Corp., 50th Anniv. — A517

1986, July 23 ***Perf. 12½***
1103 A517 34c Emblem, map .55 .25

Exploration of Canada A518

No. 1104, Siberian Indians discover and inhabit America, 10,000 B.C. No. 1105, Viking settlement, A.D. 1000. No. 1106, John Cabot lands, 1498. No. 1107, Henry Hudson pioneers Hudson Strait and Bay, 1610.

1986, Aug. 29 ***Perf. 12½x13***
1104 A518 34c multicolored .55 .30
1105 A518 34c multicolored .55 .30
1106 A518 34c multicolored .55 .30
1107 A518 34c multicolored .55 .30
a. Block of 4, #1104-1107 2.20 2.00
b. Souv. sheet of 4, #1104-1107 3.00 2.50

No. 1107b issued Oct. 1 for CAPEX '87.

See Nos. 1126-1129, 1199-1202, 1233-1236.

Peacemakers of the Frontier, 1870s — A519

Designs: No. 1108, Crowfoot (1830-1890), Blackfoot Indian chief. No. 1109, James F. Macleod (1836-1894), asst. commissioner of Northwest Mounted Police.

1986, Sept. 5 ***Perf. 13x13½***
1108 A519 34c scar, gray & ind .55 .25
1109 A519 34c ind, gray & scar .55 .25
a. Pair, #1108-1109 1.10 .90

Intl. Peace Year — A520

Litho. & Embossed

1986, Sept. 16 ***Perf. 13½***
1110 A520 34c multicolored .55 .25

1988 Calgary Winter Olympics — A521

1986, Oct. 15 ***Perf. 13½x13***
1111 A521 34c Ice hockey .55 .25
1112 A521 34c Biathlon .55 .25
a. Pair, #1111-1112 1.10 .90

See Nos. 1130-1131, 1152-1153, 1195-1198.

Christmas Angels — A522

1986, Oct. 29 ***Perf. 12½***
1113 A522 34c multicolored .55 .25
1114 A522 39c multicolored .65 .55
1115 A522 68c multicolored 1.10 .80

Booklet Stamps

Size: 72x26mm

Perf. 13½ Horiz.

1116 A522 29c multicolored 1.40 1.10
a. Booklet pane of 10 14.00 13.00
b. Perf. 12½ horiz. 6.00 2.25
c. Bklt. pane of 10, #1116b 60.00 52.50
Nos. 1113-1116 (4) 3.70 2.70

No. 1116 has bar code at left, for use on covers with printed postal code matrix.

John Molson (1763-1836), Entrepreneur — A523

1986, Nov. 4
1117 A523 34c multicolored .55 .25

Locomotives Type of 1984

Locomotives, 1925-1945.

1986, Nov. 21 ***Perf. 12½x13***
1118 A491 34c CN V1a .75 .30
1119 A491 34c CP T1a .75 .30
a. Pair, #1118-1119 1.50 1.10
1120 A491 39c CN U2a .90 .75
1121 A491 68c CP H1c 1.30 1.10
Nos. 1118-1121 (4) 3.70 2.45

CAPEX '87 — A524

34c, 1st Toronto P.O. 36c, Nelson-Miramichi P.O. 42c, Saint Ours P.O. 72c, Battleford P.O.

1987 **Litho. & Engr.** ***Perf. 13x13½***
1122 A524 34c multicolored .55 .25
1123 A524 36c multicolored .60 .25
1124 A524 42c multicolored .75 .65
1125 A524 72c multicolored 1.30 1.10
Nos. 1122-1125 (4) 3.20 2.25

Souvenir Sheet

Yellow Green Inscription

1125A Sheet of 4 3.25 3.25
b. A524 36c like #1122 .65 .65
c. A524 36c like #1123 .65 .65
d. A524 42c like #1124 .75 .75
e. A524 72c like #1125 1.20 1.20

Issue dates: 34c, Feb. 16; others, June 12.

Exploration Type of 1986

Pioneers of New France: No. 1126, Etienne Brule (c. 1592-1633), 1st European to see the Great Lakes. No. 1127, Pierre Esprit Radisson (c. 1636-1710) & Medard Chouart des Groseilliers 1625-98), British expedition to Hudson Bay, 1668. No. 1128, Louis Jolliet (1645-1700) & Fr. Jacques Marquette (1637-75) discovering the Mississippi River, 1673. No. 1129, Recollet wilderness mission, 1615.

1987, Mar. 13 **Litho.** ***Perf. 12½x13***
1126 A518 34c multicolored .55 .30
1127 A518 34c multicolored .55 .30
1128 A518 34c multicolored .55 .30
1129 A518 34c multicolored .55 .30
a. Block of 4, #1126-1129 2.20 2.00

Olympics Type of 1986

1987, Apr. 3 ***Perf. 13½x13***
1130 A521 36c Speed skating .60 .25
1131 A521 42c Bobsledding .75 .65

Volunteers Week — A525

1987, Apr. 13 ***Perf. 12½x13***
1132 A525 36c multicolored .60 .25

Law Day — A526

1987, Apr. 15 ***Perf. 14x13½***
1133 A526 36c Coat of arms .60 .25
a. Imperf, pair *1,350.*

Canadian Charter of Rights and Freedoms, 5th anniv.

Engineering Institute of Canada, Cent. — A527

1987, May 19 ***Perf. 12½x13***
1134 A527 36c multicolored .60 .25

Canada Day — A528

Inventors & communications innovations: No. 1135, Reginald Aubrey Fessenden (1866-1932), AM radio, 1900. No. 1136, Charles Fenerty, newsprint, 1838. No. 1137, Georges-Edouard Desbarats and William Leggo, halftone engraving, 1869. No. 1138, Frederick Newton Gisborne, No. America's 1st undersea cable, 1852, New Brunswick-Prince Edward Island.

1987, June 25 ***Perf. 13½***
1135 A528 36c multicolored .65 .30
1136 A528 36c multicolored .65 .30
1137 A528 36c multicolored .65 .30
1138 A528 36c multicolored .65 .30
a. Block of 4, #1135-1138 2.60 2.40

Steamships A529

No. 1139, Segwun, 1887. No. 1140, Princess Marguerite, 1948.

1987, July 20 ***Perf. 13½x13***
1139 A529 36c multicolored .60 .30

51x22mm

1140 A529 36c multicolored .60 .30
a. Pair, #1139-1140 1.20 1.00

Shipwrecks A530

No. 1141, Hamilton & Scourge, 1813. No. 1142, San Juan, 1565. No. 1143, Breadalbane, 1853. No. 1144, Ericsson, 1892.

1987, Aug. 7
1141 A530 36c multicolored .60 .30
1142 A530 36c multicolored .60 .30
1143 A530 36c multicolored .60 .30
1144 A530 36c multicolored .60 .30
a. Block of 4, #1141-1144 2.40 2.20

Air Canada, 50th Anniv. — A531

1987, Sept. 1 ***Perf. 13½***
1145 A531 36c multicolored .60 .25

2nd Intl. Francophone Summit, Quebec, 9/2-4 — A532

1987, Sept. 2 ***Perf. 13x12½***
1146 A532 36c multicolored .60 .25

9th Commonwealth Meeting, Vancouver, Oct. 13-17 — A533

1987, Oct. 13
1147 A533 36c multicolored .60 .25

Christmas A534

36c, Poinsettia. 42c, Holly wreath. 72c, Mistletoe, Christmas tree. 31c, Gifts, Christmas tree.

1987, Nov. 2 Litho. *Perf. 13½*
1148 A534 36c multicolored .65 .25
1149 A534 42c multicolored .75 .65
1150 A534 72c multicolored 1.20 .90

Size: 39x25mm

1151 A534 31c multicolored .75 .75
a. Booklet pane of 10 7.50 *10.00*
b. Imperf. btwn., pair, from miscut bklt. pane *2,600.*
Nos. 1148-1151 (4) 3.35 2.55

No. 1151 has bar code at left, for use on covers with printed postal code matrix. Issued in booklets only.

Olympics Type of 1986

No. 1152, Cross-country skiing. No. 1153, Ski jumping.

1987, Nov. 13 *Perf. 13½x13*
1152 A521 36c multicolored .60 .25
1153 A521 36c multicolored .60 .25
a. Pair, #1152-1153 1.20 .90

75th Grey Cup, Vancouver, Nov. 29 — A535

1987, Nov. 20 *Perf. 12½*
1154 A535 36c multicolored .60 .25

Types of 1982 and

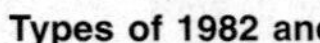

Queen Elizabeth II A536

Mammals A538

Parliament (Center Block) A537 A539

Architecture — A540

Flag and Clouds A541

Flag A542

Natl. Flag, Deciduous Forest A543

Flag and Mountains A544

Designs: No. 1155, Flying squirrel. 2c, Prickly porcupine. 3c, Muskrat. No. 1158, Varying hare. No. 1159, Red fox. 10c, Skunk. 25c, Beaver. 43c, Lynx. 44c, Walrus. 45c, Pronghorn. 46c, Wolverine. 57c, Killer whale. 59c, Musk-ox. 61c, Timber wolf. 63c, Harbor porpoise. 74c, Wapiti. 76c, Grizzly bear. 78c, Beluga whale. 80c, Peary caribou. $1, Runnymede Library, Toronto. $2, McAdam Railway Station, New Brunswick. $5, Bonsecours Market, Montreal. No. 1192, Flag and field. No. 1193, Flag and seacoast.

Sizes Vary on A536, A538

1987-91 Litho. *Perf. 13x13½*
1155 A538 1c multicolored .25 .25
a. Perf. 13x12½ *4.00* .85
b. Imperf, pair *700.00*
1156 A538 2c multicolored .25 .25
a. Imperf, pair *700.00*
1157 A538 3c multicolored .25 .25
a. Imperf, pair *850.00*
1158 A538 5c multicolored .25 .25
a. Imperf, pair *1,500.*
1159 A538 6c multicolored .25 .25
a. Horiz. pair, imperf *2,250.*
1160 A538 10c multicolored .25 .25
a. Perf. 13x12½ 6.00 .40
b. Imperf., pair *700.00*
1161 A538 25c multicolored .40 .25

Perf. 13½x13

1162 A536 37c multicolored .75 .25
1163 A537 37c multicolored .75 .25
a. Bklt. pane of 10, #1163c 7.50 7.50
b. Bklt. pane of 25, #1163c 19.00 17.50
c. Perf. 13½x14 1.40 .40

Perf. 13x12½

1164 A536 38c multicolored .75 .25
a. Perf. 13x13½ .75 .35
b. As "a," bklt. pane of 10 + 2 labels 7.50 7.00
c. Vert. block of 10, middle pair imperf, 2nd and 4th pairs part perf *900.00*
d. As "a," horiz. pair, imperf btwn. *850.00*
e. Bottom margin horiz. pair, imperf —

Perf. 13x13½ on 3 or 4 Sides

1165 A539 38c multicolored .75 .25
a. Bklt. pane of 10 + 2 labels 7.50 7.50
b. Bklt. pane of 25 + 2 labels 19.00 19.00
c. Printed on gummed side 90.00
d. Double impression of all litho colors except black 225.00

Perf. 13½x13

1166 A541 39c multicolored .75 .25
a. Bklt. pane of 10 + 2 labels 7.50
b. Bklt. pane of 25 + 2 labels 19.00
c. Perf. 12½x13 18.00 .75
d. Imperf, pair *525.00*

Perf. 13x13½

1167 A536 39c multicolored .75 .25
a. Bklt. pane of 10 + 2 labels 7.50 7.50
b. Perf. 13 15.00 .85
c. Imperf, pair *500.00*
d. Horiz. pair, imperf btwn. *325.00*
1168 A536 40c multicolored .75 .25
a. Bklt. pane of 10 + 2 labels 7.50 7.00

Perf. 13½x13

1169 A544 40c multicolored .75 .25
a. Bklt. pane of 25 + 2 labels 25.00
b. Bklt. pane of 10 + 2 labels 7.50

Perf. 12x12½

1170 A538 43c multicolored 1.10 .40

Perf. 14½x14

1171 A538 44c multicolored 1.40 .25
a. Perf. 12½x13 2.75 1.75
b. As "a," bklt. pane of 5 + label 12.50 11.50
c. Perf. 13½x13 400.00 400.00
1172 A538 45c multicolored .90 .25
b. As "f," bklt. pane of 5 + label 13.00 14.00
d. Perf. 13 20.00 1.20
f. Perf. 12½x13 2.60 .50
h. Imperf., pair *750.00*

Perf. 13

1172A A538 46c multicolored .90 .25
c. Perf. 12½x13 1.25 .50
e. As "c," bklt. pane of 5 + label 6.25 5.50
g. Perf. 14½x14 5.25 .40

Perf. 12x12½

1173 A538 57c multicolored 1.10 .35

Perf. 14½x14

1174 A538 59c multicolored 1.20 .30
a. Perf. 13 10.00 2.50
1175 A538 61c multicolored 1.20 .35
a. Perf. 13 80.00 6.50
1176 A538 63c multicolored 3.00 .40
a. Perf. 13 6.50 3.00

Perf. 12x12½

1177 A538 74c multicolored 1.90 .75

Perf. 14½x14

1178 A538 76c multicolored 1.90 .75
a. Perf. 12½x13 3.00 2.50
b. As "a," bklt. pane of 5 + label 15.00 15.00
c. Perf. 13 37.50 14.00
1179 A538 78c multicolored 2.20 .75
a. As "c," bklt. pane of 5 15.00 15.00
b. Perf. 13 35.00 6.00
c. Perf. 12½x13 3.50 2.00
d. Imperf, pair *900.00*

Perf. 13

1180 A538 80c multicolored 1.80 .75
a. Perf. 12½x13 3.00 1.10
b. As "a," bklt. pane of 5 + label 15.00 15.00
c. Perf. 14½x14 5.50 2.25
d. Imperf, pair *1,100.*

Perf. 13½

Litho. & Engr.

1181 A540 $1 multicolored 1.50 .55
a. Engr. inscriptions inverted *12,000.*
b. Imperf, pair *1,100.*
c. "CANADA $1" inscription omitted *1,850.*
d. Vert. block of 6, top pair imperf., middle pair perf. at bottom, bottom pair normal *1,750.*
1182 A540 $2 multicolored 3.75 1.00
a. Imperf., pair *850.00*
b. Vert. strip of 5, stamps 3 and 4 imperf vert., horiz. imperf btwn. stamps 2 and 3, and btwn. stamps 3 and 4 *1,500.*
1183 A540 $5 multicolored 7.50 2.25
a. Vert. strip of 5, top stamp imperf on 3 sides, stamp 4 imperf at top and sides *2,600.*
Nos. 1155-1183 (30) 39.25 13.10

A later printing of No. 1182 has more intense and clearly defined green shading on the roofline and the deep orange background extends closer to the roofline.

Imperfs exist of Nos. 1155-1157 and 1160, from printer's waste.

Issued: 1c, 2c, 3c, 5c, 6c, 10c, 25c, 10/3/88; 37c, 12/30/87; 38c, 12/29/88; 43c, 57c, 74c, 1/18/88; 44c, 59c, 76c, 1/18/89; $1, $2, 5/5/89; No. 1166, 12/28/89; 45c, 61c, 78c, No. 1167, 1/12/90; $5, 5/28/90; 40c, 46c, 63c, 80c, 12/28/90.

Booklet Stamps

Perf. 13½x14 on 3 Sides

Litho.

1184 A542 1c multicolored .25 .25
a. Perf. 12½x13 11.00 11.00
1185 A542 5c multicolored .25 .25
a. Perf. 12½x13 7.50 7.50

Perf. 12½x12 on 2 or 3 sides

Engr.

1186 A445 6c dark purple .70 .30
1187 A443 37c dark blue .90 .70
a. Bklt. pane of 4 + 2 labels (#938, 2 #942, #1187) 1.40 1.40
1188 A443 38c dark blue .90 .40
a. Bklt. pane of 5 (3 #939a, #1186, #1188) 1.40 1.40

Perf. 13½x14 on 3 Sides

Litho.

1189 A542 39c multicolored .90 .40
a. Bklt. pane of 4 (#1184, 2 #1185, #1189) 1.65 .65
b. Perf. 12½x13 12.00 12.00
c. Bklt. pane of 4 (#1184a, 2 #1185a, 1189b) 37.50 37.50
1190 A542 40c multicolored 1.50 .55
a. Bklt. pane of 4 (2 #1184, #1185, #1190) 2.40 1.20
b. As "a," imperf *1,000.*

Nos. 1190a, 1190c sold for 50c.

Issued: No. 1187, 2/3/88; No. 1188, 1/18/89; No. 1186, 1989; Nos. 1184-1185, 1189, 1/12/90; No. 1190, 12/28/90.

Self-Adhesives

Die Cut

Booklet Stamps

1191 A543 38c multicolored 1.50 .75
a. Booklet of 12 18.00
b. Blue omitted *1,900.*
c. Yellow omitted *900.00*
1192 A543 39c multicolored 1.40 .75
a. Booklet of 12 17.00
1193 A543 40c multicolored 1.40 .75
a. Booklet of 12 17.00

Issued: 38c, 6/30/89; 39c, 2/8/90; 40c, 1/11/91.

Issued on peelable paper backing serving as booklet cover. Nos. 1191a, 1192a sold for $5, No. 1193a for $5.25.

Coil Stamps

Perf. 10 Horiz.

Engr.

1194 A443 37c dark blue .75 .25
d. Imperf., pair 170.00
1194A A443 38c dark green 1.10 .25
e. Imperf., pair 375.00
1194B A542 39c violet .75 .25
f. Imperf., pair 150.00
1194C A542 40c blue gray .75 .25
g. Imperf., pair 275.00
h. All color omitted (tagged) 375.00

Issued: 37c, 2/22/88; 38c, 2/1/89; 39c, 2/8/90; 40c, 12/28/90.

No. 1194Ch must be collected in a pair with normal or misperfed stamp or (more often) in a strip of four with a pair of normal (or misperfed) stamps and a pair of the color-omitted stamps.

See Nos. 1356-1362, 1375-1376, 1388, 1394-1396, 1682-1683, 1687, 1695, 1698.

Olympics Type of 1986

1988, Feb. 12 Litho. *Perf. 12x12½*
1195 A521 37c Alpine skiing .60 .25
1196 A521 37c Curling .60 .25
a. Pair, #1195-1196 1.20 .90
1197 A521 43c Figure skating .70 .70
1198 A521 74c Luge 1.20 .90
Nos. 1195-1198 (4) 3.10 2.10

Exploration Type of 1986

18th Cent. explorers of the western territories: No. 1199, Anthony Henday, who traveled the Prairies in 1754 from the Hayes River to Red Deer, Alberta. No. 1200, George Vancouver (1757-1798), who circumnavigated Vancouver Is. and explored the Pacific Coast, 1792-94. No. 1201, Simon Fraser (1776-1862), fur trader who discovered and navigated the Fraser River. No. 1202, John Palliser (1807-1887), geographer who determined the topographical boundary between Canada and the US from Lake Superior to the Pacific Coast.

1988, Mar. 17 Litho. *Perf. 12½x13*
1199 A518 37c multicolored .60 .35
1200 A518 37c multicolored .60 .35
1201 A518 37c multicolored .60 .35
1202 A518 37c multicolored .60 .35
a. Block of 4, #1199-1202 2.40 2.00

The Young Reader, by Ozias Leduc A546

Photo. & Engr. with Foil Application

1988, May 20 *Perf. 13x13½*
1203 A546 50c multicolored 1.10 .90

Masterpieces of Canadian art. Printed in sheets of 16.

See Nos. 1241, 1271, 1310, 1419, 1466, 1516, 1545, 1602, 1635, 1754, 1800, 1863, 1916, 1945.

Wildlife and Habitat Conservation A547

1988, June 1 Litho. *Perf. 13x13½*

1204 A547 37c Duck landing .60 .35
1205 A547 37c Moose at water hole .60 .35
a. Pair, #1204-1205 1.20 .90

Grey Owl, born Archibald Belaney, (b. 1888), conservationist; Ducks Unlimited Canada, 50th anniv.

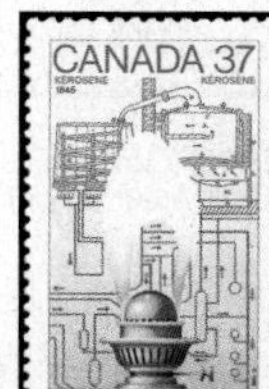

Science and Technology — A548

Inventions: No. 1206, Kerosene, invented by Abraham Gesner (1797-1864), patented in 1854. No. 1207, Marquis wheat, developed in 1908 by Charles Saunders. No. 1208, Electron microscope, developed in 1938 at the University of Toronto by James Hillier and Albert Prebus under the supervision of Eli Burton. No. 1209, Cobalt cancer therapy, introduced by Dr. Harold Johns and Atomic Energy of Canada, Ltd., in 1951.

1988, June 17 *Perf. 12½x13*

1206 A548 37c multicolored .60 .30
1207 A548 37c multicolored .60 .30
1208 A548 37c multicolored .60 .30
1209 A548 37c multicolored .60 .30
a. Block of 4, #1206-1209 2.40 2.00

Intl. Entomology Congress, Vancouver A549

No. 1210, Short-tailed swallowtail. No. 1211, Northern blue. No. 1212, Macoun's Arctic. No. 1213, Canadian tiger swallowtail.

1988, July 4 *Perf. 12*

1210 A549 37c multicolored .60 .35
1211 A549 37c multicolored .60 .35
1212 A549 37c multicolored .60 .35
1213 A549 37c multicolored .60 .35
a. Block of 4, #1210-1213 2.40 2.10

St. John's, Newfoundland, Cent. of Incorporation — A550

37c, Harbor entrance, skyline.

1988, July 22 *Perf. 13½x13*

1214 A550 37c multicolored .60 .25

Canadian 4-H Council, 75th Anniv. A551

37c, Motto, farm, young scientists.

1988, Aug. 5

1215 A551 37c multicolored .60 .25

Les Forges Du St. Maurice (1738-1883), Canada's 1st Industrial Complex — A552

Litho. & Engr.

1988, Aug. 19 *Perf. 13½*

1216 A552 37c multicolored .60 .25

Canadian Kennel Club, Cent. A553

No. 1217, Tahltan bear dog. No. 1218, Nova Scotia duck-tolling retriever. No. 1219, Canadian Eskimo dog. No. 1220, Newfoundland.

1988, Aug. 26 *Perf. 12½x12*

1217 A553 37c multicolored .90 .40
1218 A553 37c multicolored .90 .40
1219 A553 37c multicolored .90 .40
1220 A553 37c multicolored .90 .40
a. Block of 4, #1217-1220 3.60 2.75

A554

1988, Sept. 14 Litho. *Perf. 13½x13*

1221 A554 37c multicolored .60 .25

Sesquicentennial of the 1st baseball game played in Canada, June 4, 1838 at Beachville, Upper Canada.

A555

Christmas (Icons of the Eastern Church): 32c, Nativity. 37c, Conception. 43c, Virgin and Child. 74c, Virgin and Child, diff.

1988, Oct. 27 *Perf. 13½*

1222 A555 37c multicolored .60 .25
1223 A555 43c multicolored .75 .65
1224 A555 74c multicolored 1.50 .90

Booklet Stamp

Size: 35½x21mm

Perf. 12½x13½

1225 A555 32c multicolored .90 .75
a. Booklet pane of 10 9.00 9.00
Nos. 1222-1225 (4) 3.75 2.55

Millennium of Christianity in the Ukraine. No. 1225 has bar code at left; for use on covers with printed postal code matrix.

Inglis and Anglican Church A556

1988, Nov. 1 *Perf. 12½x12*

1226 A556 37c multicolored .60 .25

Charles Inglis (1734-1816), Canada's 1st Anglican bishop and founder of the Kings-Edgehill School, Nova Scotia, and the University of King's College at Halifax, bicent.

Hopkins and *Canoe Manned by Voyageurs* A557

1988, Nov. 18 *Perf. 13½x13*

1227 A557 37c multicolored .60 .25

Frances Ann Hopkins (1838-1918), painter.

The Bluenose and Capt. Walters — A558

1988, Nov. 18 *Perf. 13½*

1228 A558 37c multicolored .60 .25

Angus Walters (1882-1968), mariner.

Small Craft A559

1989, Feb. 1 *Perf. 13½x13*

1229 A559 38c Chipewyan canoe .60 .35
1230 A559 38c Haida canoe .60 .35
1231 A559 38c Inuit kayak .60 .35
1232 A559 38c Micmac canoe .60 .35
a. Block of 4, #1229-1232 2.40 2.20

See Nos. 1266-1269, 1317-1320.

Exploration Type of 1986

Explorers of the North: No. 1233, Matonabbee (c. 1737-1782), Indian guide who led 1st overland European expedition to the Arctic Ocean. No. 1234, Relics of expedition led by Sir John Franklin (1786-1847) that proved the existence of the Northwest Passage. No. 1235, Relics of the discovery of the Alberta fossil bed by geologist Joseph Burr Tyrrell (1858-1957). No. 1236, Vilhjalmur Stefansson (1879-1962), American ethnologist who discovered the last uncharted islands in the Arctic Archipelago.

1989, Mar. 22 *Perf. 12½x13*

1233 A518 38c multicolored .60 .35
1234 A518 38c multicolored .60 .35
1235 A518 38c multicolored .60 .35
1236 A518 38c multicolored .60 .35
a. Block of 4, #1233-1236 2.40 2.20

Photography in Canada, Sesquicentennial — A560

Photographers and their work: No. 1237, William Notman (1826-1891). No. 1238, W. Hanson Boorne (1859-1945). No. 1239, Alexander Henderson (1831-1913). No. 1240, Jules-Ernest Livernois (1851-1933).

1989, June 23 *Perf. 12½x12*

1237 A560 38c multicolored .60 .35
1238 A560 38c multicolored .60 .35
1239 A560 38c multicolored .60 .35
1240 A560 38c multicolored .60 .35
a. Block of 4, #1237-1240 2.40 2.20

Art Type of 1988

Design: Ceremonial Frontlet (headpiece) Worn by Tsimshian Indian Chiefs, Early 20th Cent.

Litho. with Foil Application

1989, June 29 *Perf. 12½x13*

1241 A546 50c multicolored 1.10 .90

Masterpieces of Canadian Art and opening of the Museum of Civilization.

Poets — A562

No. 1243, Louis Frechette (1839-1908). No. 1244, Archibald Lampman (1861-1899).

1989, July 7 Litho. *Perf. 13½*

1243 A562 38c multicolored .60 .35
1244 A562 38c multicolored .60 .35
a. Pair, #1243-1244 1.20 .90

Mushrooms A563

No. 1245, Clavulinopsis fusiformis. No. 1246, Boletus mirabilis. No. 1247, Cantharellus cinnabarinus. No. 1248, Morchella esculenta.

1989, Aug. 4

1245 A563 38c multicolored .60 .35
1246 A563 38c multicolored .60 .35
1247 A563 38c multicolored .60 .35
1248 A563 38c multicolored .60 .35
a. Block of 4, #1245-1248 2.40 2.20

Infantry Regiments, 75th Annivs. A564

No. 1249, Princess Patricia's Canadian Light Infantry. No. 1250, Royal 22nd Regiment.

Litho. & Engr.

1989, Sept. 8 *Perf. 13*

1249 A564 38c multicolored .75 .40
1250 A564 38c multicolored .75 .40
a. Pair, #1249-1250 1.50 1.25

Intl. Trade A565

1989, Oct. 2 Litho. *Perf. 13½x13*

1251 A565 38c multicolored .60 .25

Performing Arts — A566

No. 1252, Dancers. No. 1253, Musicians. No. 1254, Camera, director. No. 1255, Youth and adult entertainers.

1989, Oct. 4 *Perf. 13x13½*

1252 A566 38c multicolored .60 .35
1253 A566 38c multicolored .60 .35
1254 A566 38c multicolored .60 .35
1255 A566 38c multicolored .60 .35
a. Block of 4, #1252-1255 2.40 2.00

Royal Winnipeg Ballet 50th anniv. (No. 1252), Vancouver Opera 30th anniv. (No. 1253), Natl. Film Board 50th anniv. (No. 1254), and Confederation Center of the Arts, Charlottetown, P.E.I., 25th anniv. (No. 1255).

A566a

A567

Winter landscapes: 33c, *Champ-de-Mars, Winter*, 1892, by William Brymner (1855-1925). 38c, *Bend in the Gosselin River, Arthabaska*, c. 1906, by Marc-Aurele de Foy Suzor-Cote (1869-1937). 44c, *Snow II*, 1915, by Lawren S. Harris (1885-1970). 76c, *Ste. Agnes*, c. 1925-30, by Albert H. Robinson (1881-1956). Nos. 1256-1258 vert.

1989, Oct. 26
Size of 44c, 76c: 25x31mm

1256	A566a 38c multi	.60	.25
a.	Bklt. pane of 10, #1256b	45.00	45.00
b.	Perf. 13x12½	4.50	4.50

Perf. 13½

1257	A566a 44c multi	.75	.60
a.	Booklet pane of 5 + label	15.00	15.00
1258	A566a 76c multi	1.30	.90
a.	Booklet pane of 5 + label	27.50	27.50

Booklet Stamp
Size: 35x21mm
Perf. 12½x13½

1259	A567 33c shown	1.50	1.50
a.	Booklet pane of 10	15.00	
b.	Horiz. pair, imperf btwn.	*2,000.*	
c.	As "a," imperf. vert. between	*11,000.*	
	Nos. 1256-1259 (4)	4.15	3.25

Christmas. No. 1259 has bar code at left; for use on covers with printed postal code matrix. Booklet panes separate easily.

Declaration of War, 1939 — A568

Political and military actions taken by Canada at the outbreak of World War II: No. 1261, Army mobilization. No. 1262, Navy convoy system. No. 1263, Commonwealth Air Training Plan.

1989, Nov. 10 ***Perf. 13½***

1260	A568 38c shown	.75	.55
1261	A568 38c multicolored	.75	.55
1262	A568 38c multicolored	.75	.55
1263	A568 38c multicolored	.75	.55
a.	Block of 4, #1260-1263	3.00	2.50

See Nos. 1298-1301, 1345-1348, 1448-1451, 1503-1506, 1537-1544.

Norman Bethune (1890-1939), Surgeon — A569

Litho. & Engr.
1990, Mar. 2 ***Perf. 13x13½***

1264	A569 39c In Canada	.90	.40
1265	A569 39c In China	.90	.40
a.	Pair, #1264-1265	1.80	1.10

See People's Republic of China Nos. 2263-2264.

Small Craft Type of 1989
1990, Mar. 15 Litho. ***Perf. 13½x13***

1266	A559 39c Dory	.70	.35
1267	A559 39c Pointer	.70	.35
1268	A559 39c York boat	.70	.35
1269	A559 39c North canoe	.70	.35
a.	Block of 4, #1266-1269	2.80	2.40

Multicultural Heritage of Canada A570

Litho. & Engr.
1990, Apr. 5 ***Perf. 13***

1270	A570 39c multicolored	.60	.25
a.	Black (inscriptions) omitted	*1,200.*	

Art Type of 1988

Painting: *The West Wind*, by Tom Thomson.

Litho. with Foil Application
1990, May 3 ***Perf. 12½x13***

1271	A546 50c multicolored	1.10	.90

Masterpieces of Canadian Art.

Mail Trucks
A571 A572

1990, May 3 Litho. ***Perf. 13½***
Booklet Stamps

1272	A571 39c multicolored	.75	.55
1273	A572 39c multicolored	.75	.55
a.	Bklt. pane of 8+printed margin (4 each #1272-1273)	6.00	6.00
b.	Bklt. pane of 9+3 labels, printed margin (5 #1272, 4 #1273)	11.50	11.50

Dolls A573

1990, June 8 ***Perf. 12½x12***

1274	A573 39c Native	.65	.35
1275	A573 39c Settlers	.65	.35
1276	A573 39c 4 Commercial	.65	.35
1277	A573 39c 5 Commercial	.65	.35
a.	Block of 4, #1274-1277	2.60	2.40

Natl. Flag, 25th Anniv. — A574

39c, Flag, fireworks.

1990, June 29 ***Perf. 13x12½***

1278	A574 39c multicolored	.65	.25
a.	Silver (inscriptions) omitted	*2,000.*	

Printed in sheets of 16.

Prehistoric Life A575

Litho. & Engr.
1990, July 12 ***Perf. 13x13½***

1279	A575 39c Trilobite	.65	.35
1280	A575 39c Sea scorpion	.65	.35
1281	A575 39c Fossil algae	.65	.35
1282	A575 39c Soft invertebrate	.65	.35
a.	Block of 4, #1279-1282	2.60	2.20

See Nos. 1306-1309.

Canadian Forests A576

No. 1283, Acadian. No. 1284, Great Lakes-St. Lawrence. No. 1285, Coast. No. 1286, Boreal.

1990, Aug. 7 Litho. ***Perf. 12½x13***

1283	A576 39c multicolored	.65	.30
a.	Pane of 4	9.00	7.50
1284	A576 39c multicolored	.65	.30
a.	Pane of 4	9.00	7.50
1285	A576 39c multicolored	.65	.30
a.	Pane of 4	9.00	7.50
1286	A576 39c multicolored	.65	.30
a.	Block of 4, #1283-1286	2.60	2.20
b.	Pane of 4	9.00	7.50

Panes of four sold for $1 each through Petro-Canada gas stations, and for full face value through the philatelic bureau. Issue date: Sept. 7.

Weather Observations in Canada, 150th Anniv. — A577

1990, Sept. 5 ***Perf. 12½x13½***

1287	A577 39c multicolored	.60	.25

The left and right margin singles of No. 1287 differ slightly in design from stamps from columns 2-4, due to the nature of the continuous cloud design across the pane.

Intl. Literacy Year — A578

1990, Sept. 7 ***Perf. 13½x13***

1288	A578 39c multicolored	.60	.25

Legendary Creatures A579

1990, Oct. 1 ***Perf. 12½x13½***

1289	A579 39c Sasquatch	.75	.75
1290	A579 39c Kraken	.75	.75
1291	A579 39c Werewolf	.75	.75
1292	A579 39c Ogopogo	.75	.75
a.	Block of 4, #1289-1292	3.00	3.00
b.	As "a," imperf.	*1,250.*	

Perf. 12½x12

1289a	A579 39c	11.00	3.75
1290a	A579 39c	11.00	3.75
1291a	A579 39c	11.00	3.75
1292c	A579 39c	11.00	3.75
d.	Block of 4, #1289a-1292c	45.00	32.50

Agnes Campbell Macphail (1890-1954), First Woman Member of Parliament — A580

1990, Oct. 9 ***Perf. 13x13½***

1293	A580 39c multicolored	.60	.25

Virgin Mary with Christ Child and St. John the Baptist by Norval Morrisseau A581

Rebirth by Jackson Beardy A582

Indian Art: 45c, Sculpture of Mother and Child by an Inuit artist. 78c, Children of the Raven by Bill Reid.

1990, Oct. 25 ***Perf. 13½***

1294	A581 39c multicolored	.75	.25
a.	Booklet pane of 10	7.50	*9.00*
1295	A581 45c multicolored	.75	.65
a.	Bklt. pane of 5 + label	3.75	4.00
1296	A581 78c multicolored	1.50	1.10
a.	Bklt. pane of 5 + label	7.50	6.50

Booklet Stamp
Perf. 12½x13 on 2 or 3 Sides

1297	A582 34c multicolored	.85	.30
a.	Booklet pane of 10	8.50	*10.00*
	Nos. 1294-1297 (4)	3.85	2.30

Christmas. No. 1297 has bar code at left; for use on covers with printed postal code matrix.

World War II Type of 1989

No. 1298, Home front. No. 1299, Communal war efforts. No. 1300, Food production. No. 1301, Science and war.

1990, Nov. 9 ***Perf. 12½x12***

1298	A568 39c multicolored	.75	.60
1299	A568 39c multicolored	.75	.60
1300	A568 39c multicolored	.75	.60
1301	A568 39c multicolored	.75	.60
a.	Block of 4, #1298-1301	3.00	3.00

A583

Physicians: No. 1302, Jennie Trout (1841-1921), first licensed Canadian woman physician. No. 1303, Wilder Penfield (1891-1976), neurosurgeon. No. 1304, Sir Frederick Banting (1891-1941), discoverer of insulin. No. 1305, Harold Griffith (1894-1985), anesthesiologist.

1991, Mar. 15 ***Perf. 13½***

1302	A583 40c multicolored	.65	.35
1303	A583 40c multicolored	.65	.35
1304	A583 40c multicolored	.65	.35
1305	A583 40c multicolored	.65	.35
a.	Block of 4, #1302-1305	2.60	2.20

Prehistoric Life Type of 1990
1991, Apr. 5 ***Perf. 12½x13½***

1306	A575 40c Microfossils	.65	.35
1307	A575 40c Early tree	.65	.35
1308	A575 40c Early fish	.65	.35
1309	A575 40c Land reptile	.65	.35
a.	Block of 4, #1306-1309	2.60	2.20

Art Type of 1988

Design: Forest, British Columbia by Emily Carr.

Litho. with Foil Application

1991, May 7 *Perf. 12½x13*

1310 A546 50c multicolored 1.10 .90

Masterpieces of Canadian Art.

A584

Public Gardens: No. 1311, Butchart Gardens, Victoria, B.C. No. 1312, Intl. Peace Garden, Boissevain, Manitoba. No. 1313, Royal Botanical Gardens, Hamilton, Ontario. No. 1314, Montreal Botanical Gardens. No. 1315, Halifax Public Gardens, Nova Scotia.

Booklet Stamps

1991, May 22 Litho. *Perf. 13x12½*

1311 A584 40c multicolored .75 .40
1312 A584 40c multicolored .75 .40
1313 A584 40c multicolored .75 .40
1314 A584 40c multicolored .75 .40
1315 A584 40c multicolored .75 .40
a. Strip of 5, #1311-1315 3.75 2.75
b. Bklt. pane, 2 each #1311-1315 7.50 7.00

Canada Day — A585

1991, June 28 *Perf. 13½x13*

1316 A585 40c multicolored .75 .25

Small Craft Type of 1989

1991, July 18

1317 A559 40c Verchere rowboat .65 .35
1318 A559 40c Touring kayak .65 .35
1319 A559 40c Sailing dinghy .65 .35
1320 A559 40c Cedar strip canoe .65 .35
a. Block of 4, #1317-1320 2.60 2.25

Canadian Rivers — A586

No. 1321, South Nahanni. No. 1322, Athabasca. No. 1323, Boundary Waters-Voyageur Waterway. No. 1324, Jacques Cartier. No. 1325, Main.

Booklet Stamps

1991, Aug. 20 *Perf. 13x12½*

1321 A586 40c multicolored .75 .40
1322 A586 40c multicolored .75 .40
1323 A586 40c multicolored .75 .40
1324 A586 40c multicolored .75 .40
1325 A586 40c multicolored .75 .40
a. Strip of 5, #1321-1325 3.75 3.25
b. Bklt. pane, 2 each #1321-1325 7.50 6.75

See Nos. 1408-1412, 1485-1489, 1511-1515.

Arrival of Ukrainians, Cent. — A587

Paintings by William Kurelek: No. 1326, Leaving homeland. No. 1327, Winter in Canada. No. 1328, Clearing land. No. 1329, Growing wheat.

1991, Aug. 29 *Perf. 13½x13*

1326 A587 40c multicolored .65 .35
1327 A587 40c multicolored .65 .35
1328 A587 40c multicolored .65 .35
1329 A587 40c multicolored .65 .35
a. Block of 4, #1326-1329 2.60 2.20

Dangerous Public Service Occupations A588

1991, Sept. 23 *Perf. 13½*

1330 A588 40c Ski Patrol 1.10 .35
1331 A588 40c Police 1.10 .35
1332 A588 40c Fire fighters 1.10 .35
1333 A588 40c Search & Rescue 1.10 .35
a. Block of 4, #1330-1333 4.40 2.60

Folktales A589

1991, Oct. 1 Litho. *Perf. 13½x12½*

1334 A589 40c Witched Canoe .75 .30
1335 A589 40c Orphan Boy .75 .30
1336 A589 40c Chinook Wind .75 .30
1337 A589 40c Buried Treasure .75 .30
a. Block of 4, #1334-1337 3.00 2.50

Queen's University, Kingston, Ont., Sesqui. — A590

1991, Oct. 16

1338 A590 40c multicolored .75 .55
a. Bklt. pane of 10 + 2 labels 7.50 6.00

A591

Santa Claus A592

1991, Oct. 23 *Perf. 13½*

1339 A591 40c At fireplace .75 .25
a. Booklet pane of 10 7.50 6.00
1340 A591 46c With white horse, tree .75 .50
a. Bklt. pane of 5 + label 3.75 3.00
1341 A591 80c Sinterklaas, girl 1.30 .90
a. Bklt. pane of 5 + label 6.50 6.00
b. Imperf., pair 750.00

Booklet Stamp

Perf. 12½x13 on 2 or 3 Sides

1342 A592 35c With punchbowl .75 .25
a. Booklet pane of 10 7.50 4.50
Nos. 1339-1342 (4) 3.55 1.90

Christmas. No. 1342 has bar code at left; for use on covers with printed postal code matrix.

Basketball, Cent. — A593

1991, Oct. 25 *Perf. 13x13½*

1343 A593 40c multicolored .75 .25

Souvenir Sheet

1344 Pane of 3 5.00 5.00
a. A593 40c like #1343 1.10 1.10
b. A593 46c Player shooting, diff. 1.50 1.50
c. A593 80c Player dribbling 2.20 2.20

No. 1344a has 3-line inscription.

World War II Type of 1989

No. 1345, Women's Armed Forces. No. 1346, War industry. No. 1347, Cadets and veterans. No. 1348, Defense of Hong Kong.

1991, Nov. 8 *Perf. 13½*

1345 A568 40c multicolored .75 .55
1346 A568 40c multicolored .75 .55
1347 A568 40c multicolored .75 .55
1348 A568 40c multicolored .75 .55
a. Block or strip of 4, #1345-1348 3.00 2.50

Types of 1987-91 and

Edible Berries — A594

Flag and Hills — A595

Flag and Prairie A596

Flag and Building A597

Trees — A598

Designs: 1c, Blueberry. 2c, Wild strawberry. 3c, Black crowberry. 5c, Rose hip. 6c, Black raspberry. 10c, Kinnikinnick. 25c, Saskatoon berry. 48c, McIntosh apple. 49c, Delicious apple. 50c, Snow apple. 52c, Gravenstein apple. 65c, Black walnut. 67c, Beaked hazelnut. 69c, Shagbark hickory. 71c, American chestnut. 84c, Stanley plum. 86c, Bartlett pear. 88c, Westcot apricot. 90c, Elberta peach. $1, Court House, Yorkton, Saskatchewan. $2, Provincial Normal School, Truro, Nova Scotia. $5, Carnegie Public Library, Victoria, British Columbia. No. 1388, Flag and mountains. No. 1389, Flag and estuary shore.

1991-98 Litho. *Perf. 13x13½*

1349 A594 1c multicolored .25 .25
a. Imperf., pair 650.00
1350 A594 2c multicolored .25 .25
a. Imperf., pair 650.00
1351 A594 3c multicolored .25 .25
a. Imperf., pair 650.00
1352 A594 5c multicolored .25 .25
a. Imperf., pair 650.00
1353 A594 6c multicolored .25 .25
a. Imperf., pair 650.00
1354 A594 10c multicolored .25 .25
a. Horiz. pair, imperf at sides and bottom 1,000.
b. Imperf., pair 650.00
1355 A594 25c multicolored .75 .25
a. Imperf., pair 650.00

Perf. 13½x13

1356 A595 42c multicolored .80 .25
a. Booklet pane of 10 7.50 5.75
b. Bklt. pane of 50 + 2 labels 90.00 75.00
c. Bklt. pane of 25 + 2 labels 17.50 12.50
d. Vert. pair, imperf between 700.00
e. Imperf., pair 700.00

Perf. 13x13½

1357 A536 42c multicolored .75 .25
a. Booklet pane of 10 7.50 6.00
b. Imperf., pair 575.00
1358 A536 43c multicolored .90 .25
a. Booklet pane of 10 9.00 8.50
b. Imperf., pair 900.00

Perf. 13½x13

1359 A596 43c multicolored .90 .25
a. Booklet pane of 10 9.00 7.00
b. Bklt. pane of 25 + 2 labels 22.50 17.50
c. Perf. 14½ 1.10 .25
d. As "c," bklt. pane of 10 9.00 7.50
e. As "c," bklt. pane of 25 + 2 labels 25.00 25.00
f. Vert. pair, imperf between (from #1359e) 600.00
g. Imperf., pair 600.00

Perf. 13x13½

1360 A536 45c multicolored .75 .25
a. Booklet pane of 10 7.50 6.00
Complete booklet, #1360a 7.50

Perf. 14½

1361 A597 45c multicolored .75 .25
a. Booklet pane of 10 7.50 7.00
Complete booklet, #1361a 7.50
b. Bklt. pane of 25 + 2 labels 27.50 22.50
Complete booklet, #1361b 27.50
c. Perf. 13½x13 .75 .25
d. As "c," bklt. pane of 10 7.50 6.75
Complete booklet, #1361d 7.50
e. As "c," bklt. pane of 25 + 2 labels 19.00
Complete booklet, #1361e 19.00

Perf. 13x13½

Size: 16x20mm

1362 A597 45c multicolored .70 .25
a. Booklet pane of 10 7.00 *8.25*
Complete booklet, #1362a 7.00
b. Booklet pane of 30 24.00 24.00
Complete booklet, #1362b 24.00
c. Imperf, pair 450.00

No. 1361 is 17x21mm.

Perf. 13

1363 A598 48c multicolored 1.00 .25
a. Perf. 14½x14 on 3 sides 1.50 .40
b. As "a," bklt. pane of 5 + label 7.50 5.75
c. Imperf., pair 850.00
1364 A598 49c multicolored .90 .25
a. Perf. 14½x14 2.60 .35
b. As "a," bklt. pane of 5 + 1 label 13.00 6.00
c. Booklet pane of 5 + label 12.00 9.50
1365 A598 50c multicolored .90 .30
a. Booklet pane of 5 + label 6.50 5.00
b. Perf. 14½x14 2.25 .45
c. As "b," bklt. pane of 5 + label 13.00 11.50
1366 A598 52c multicolored 1.50 .40
a. Booklet pane of 5 + label 7.50 6.00
Complete booklet, #1366a 8.00
b. Perf. 14½x14 2.25 .55
c. As "b," bklt. pane of 5 + label 11.50 10.00
Complete booklet, #1366c 12.00
1367 A598 65c multicolored 1.10 .40
a. Imperf., pair 1,100.
1368 A598 67c multicolored 1.10 .40
a. Imperf., pair 1,250.
1369 A598 69c multicolored 1.10 .35
1370 A598 71c multicolored 1.10 .35
a. Perf. 14½x14 70.00 7.50
1371 A598 84c multicolored 1.50 .40
a. Perf. 14½x14 on 3 sides 2.25 .60
b. As "a," bklt. pane of 5 + label 11.50 9.00
c. Imperf., pair 1,350.
1372 A598 86c multicolored 1.80 .55
a. Perf. 14½x14 3.00 1.50
b. As "a," bklt. pane of 5 + 1 label 15.00 12.50
c. Booklet pane of 5 + label 17.00 15.00
1373 A598 88c multicolored 1.50 .50
a. Booklet pane of 5 + label 11.00 7.50
b. Perf. 14½x14 4.00 2.25
c. As "b," bklt. pane of 5 + label 20.00 15.00
1374 A598 90c multicolored 1.80 .45
a. Booklet pane of 5 + label 10.00 8.00
Complete booklet, #1374a 10.50
b. Perf. 14½x14 3.75 1.50
c. As "b," bklt. pane of 5+label 19.00 13.00
Complete booklet, #1374c 20.00

Size: 48x40mm

Litho. & Engr.

Perf. 14½x14

1375 A540 $1 multicolored 1.80 .55
a. Dk bl (inscriptions) omitted 1,250.
b. Perf 13½x13 1.80 .55
c. As "b," dk bl (inscriptions) omitted 1,250.
1376 A540 $2 multicolored 3.75 1.00
a. Dk grn (inscriptions) omitted 850.00
b. Engr. inscriptions inverted 8,000.
c. Perf. 13½x13 3.75 1.10

d.	As "c," dk grn (inscriptions) omitted		*1,500.*	

Perf. 13½x13

1378 A540 $5 multicolored 7.50 2.20
Nos. 1349-1378 (29) 36.15 11.85

Self-Adhesive

Die Cut

Imperf

Booklet Stamps

1388 A543 42c multicolored 1.10 .75
a. Booklet of 12 13.50
1389 A543 43c multicolored 1.10 .75
a. Booklet pane of 12 13.50

Nos. 1388a, 1389a issued on peelable paper backing serving as booklet cover and sold for $5.25.

Coil Stamps

Perf. 10 Horiz.

Engr.

1394 A542 42c red .75 .25
a. Imperf., pair 150.00
1395 A542 43c olive green .75 .25
a. Imperf., pair 125.00
1396 A542 45c blue green .75 .25
a. Imperf., pair 125.00
Nos. 1394-1396 (3) 2.25 .75

Nos. 1349-1363 are known imperf from printer's waste. Items exist imperf in wrong colors and with wrong denominations. These may be essays or printer's waste.

Issued: 1c-25c, 8/5/92; Nos. 1356-1357, 1394, 48c, 65c, 84c, 12/27/91; No. 1388, 1/28/92; Nos. 1358-1359, 1364, 1368, 1372, 1395, 12/30/92; No. 1389, 2/15/93; Nos. 1359c-1359e, 1/18/94; Nos. 1364c, 1372c, 1/7/94; 50c, 69c, 88c, 2/25/94; $1, $2, 2/21/94; NOs. 1375b, 1376c, 2/20/95; Nos. 1365c, 1373c, 3/27/95; Nos. 1360-1361, 1396, 52c, 71c, 90c, 7/31/95; $5, 2/29/96; No. 1362, 2/2/98.

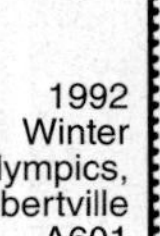

1992 Winter Olympics, Albertville A601

No. 1399, Ski jumping. No. 1400, Pairs figure skating. No. 1401, Hockey. No. 1402, Bobsledding. No. 1403, Alpine skiing.

Booklet Stamps

1992, Feb. 7 Litho. *Perf. 12½x13*

1399 A601 42c multicolored .75 .40
1400 A601 42c multicolored .75 .40
1401 A601 42c multicolored .75 .40
1402 A601 42c multicolored .75 .40
1403 A601 42c multicolored .75 .40
a. Strip of 5, #1399-1403 3.75 3.00
b. Bklt. pane, 2 each #1399-1403 7.50 7.50
Complete booklet, #1403b 8.50

See Nos. 1414-1418.

City of Montreal, 350th Anniv. — A602

Designs: No. 1404, City of Montreal, modern times. No. 1405, Early settlement of Montreal (Ville-Marie). 48c, Jacques Cartier's chart of Canada, snowshoe, ship's mast. 84c, World map, nocturnal and Aztec calendar stone.

1992, Mar. 25 *Perf. 13½*

1404 A602 42c multicolored .65 .30
1405 A602 42c multicolored .65 .30
a. Pair, #1404-1405 1.30 .75
1406 A602 48c multicolored .75 .70
1407 A602 84c multicolored 1.35 .90
a. Souvenir sheet of 4, #1404-1407 4.00 4.00
Nos. 1404-1407 (4) 3.40 2.20

Discovery of America, 500th anniv. (No. 1407).

Nos. 1404-1405 printed checkerwise. No. 1407a with engraved signatures in margin was produced in limited quantities for World Philatelic Youth Exhibition catalogue which sold for $12.

Canadian Rivers Type of 1991

No. 1408, Margaree. No. 1409, West (Eliot). No. 1410, Ottawa. No. 1411, Niagara. No. 1412, South Saskatchewan.

Booklet Stamps

1992, Apr. 22 *Perf. 12½*

1408 A586 42c multicolored .75 .40
1409 A586 42c multicolored .75 .40
1410 A586 42c multicolored .75 .40
1411 A586 42c multicolored .75 .40
1412 A586 42c multicolored .75 .40
a. Strip of 5, #1408-1412 3.75 3.25
b. Bklt. pane, 2 each #1408-1412 7.50
Complete booklet, #1412b 8.50

Nos. 1408-1412 are horiz.

Alaska Highway, 50th Anniv. — A603

1992, May 15 *Perf. 13½*

1413 A603 42c multicolored .65 .25

1992 Olympic Games Type

1992, June 15 *Perf. 12½x13*

1414 A601 42c Gymnastics .75 .40
1415 A601 42c Running .75 .40
1416 A601 42c Diving .75 .40
1417 A601 42c Cycling .75 .40
1418 A601 42c Swimming .75 .40
a. Strip of 5, #1414-1418 3.75 3.75
b. Bklt. pane, 2 each #1414-1418 7.50 7.50
Complete booklet, #1418b 8.50

1992 Summer Olympics, Barcelona.

Stamps in bottom row of No. 1418b are in different sequence than those in No. 1418a.

Art Type of 1988

Painting: Red Nasturtiums, by David Milne.

Litho. with Foil Application

1992, June 29

1419 A546 50c multicolored .90 .75

Masterpieces in Canadian Art.

Miniature Sheet

Canada Day A604

No. 1420, Nova Scotia. No. 1421, Ontario. No. 1422, Prince Edward Island. No. 1423, New Brunswick. No. 1424, Quebec. No. 1425, Saskatchewan. No. 1426, Manitoba. No. 1427, Northwest Territories. No. 1428, Alberta. No. 1429, British Columbia. No. 1430, Yukon. No. 1431, Newfoundland.

1992, June 29

1420 A604 42c multicolored 1.50 1.50
1421 A604 42c multicolored 1.50 1.50
1422 A604 42c multicolored 1.50 1.50
1423 A604 42c multicolored 1.50 1.50
1424 A604 42c multicolored 1.50 1.50
1425 A604 42c multicolored 1.50 1.50
1426 A604 42c multicolored 1.50 1.50
1427 A604 42c multicolored 1.50 1.50
1428 A604 42c multicolored 1.50 1.50
1429 A604 42c multicolored 1.50 1.50
1430 A604 42c multicolored 1.50 1.50
1431 A604 42c multicolored 1.50 1.50
a. Pane of 12, #1420-1431 + 13 labels 18.00 18.00

Canadian Folklore — A605

Legendary heroes: No. 1432, Jerry Potts, guide, interpreter. No. 1433, Captain William Jackman, rescuer. No. 1434, Laura Secord, patriot. No. 1435, Jos Monferrand, lumberjack.

1992, Sept. 8 *Perf. 12½*

1432 A605 42c multicolored .75 .35
1433 A605 42c multicolored .75 .35
1434 A605 42c multicolored .75 .35
1435 A605 42c multicolored .75 .35
a. Block of 4, #1432-1435 3.00 2.50

Minerals A606

1992, Sept. 21

1436 A606 42c Copper .90 .40
1437 A606 42c Sodalite .90 .40
1438 A606 42c Gold .90 .40
1439 A606 42c Galena .90 .40
1440 A606 42c Grossular .90 .40
a. Strip of 5, #1436-1440 4.50 4.50
b. Bklt. pane, 2 each #1436-1440 9.00 9.00
Complete booklet, #1440b 8.50

Canada in Space A607

No. 1441, Anik E2 satellite. No. 1442, Earth, space shuttle.

1992, Oct. 1 *Perf. 13*

1441 A607 42c multicolored .75 .80
a. Silver omitted *2,500.* *2,000.*

Size: 32x26mm

1442 A607 42c multicolored 1.10 1.10
a. Pair, #1441-1442 1.80 *1.80*
b. As "a," hologram omitted on #1442 *1,300.* *1,200.*

No. 1442 has a holographic image. Soaking in water may affect the hologram.

Natl. Hockey League, 75th Anniv. A608

Designs: No. 1443, Skates, stick, puck, photograph from the early years (1917-1942). No. 1444, Photograph, team emblems from the six-team years (1942-1967). No. 1445, Goalie's mask, gloves, photograph from the expansion years (1967-1992).

Booklet Stamps

1992, Oct. 9 *Perf. 13x12½*

1443 A608 42c multicolored .75 .25
a. Bklt. pane of 8 + 4 labels 6.00 5.00
1444 A608 42c multicolored .75 .25
a. Bklt. pane of 8 + 4 labels 6.00 5.00
1445 A608 42c multicolored .75 .25
a. Bklt. pane of 9 + 3 labels 6.75 5.75
Complete booklet, #1443a, 1444a, 1445a 21.00
Nos. 1443-1445 (3) 2.25 .75

A609

No. 1446, Order of Canada, 25th anniv. No. 1447, Daniel Roland Michener (1900-1991), Governor General.

1992, Oct. 21 *Perf. 12½*

1446 42c multicolored .65 .25
1447 42c multicolored .65 .30
a. A609 Pair, #1446-1447 1.30 1.10

Nos. 1446-1447 printed in panes of 25 containing 16 No. 1446 and 9 No. 1447.

World War II Type of 1989

No. 1448, War reporting. No. 1449, Newfoundland air bases. No. 1450, Raid on Dieppe. No. 1451, U-boats offshore.

1992, Nov. 10 *Perf. 13½*

1448 A568 42c multicolored .75 .45
1449 A568 42c multicolored .75 .45
1450 A568 42c multicolored .75 .45
1451 A568 42c multicolored .75 .45
a. Block or strip of 4, #1448-1451 3.00 2.50

A611

Santa Claus A612

1992, Nov. 13 *Perf. 12½*

1452 A611 42c Jouluvana .65 .25
a. Perf. 13½ .90 .25
b. As "a," booklet pane of 10 9.00 5.00
Complete booklet, #1452b 10.00

Perf. 13½

1453 A611 48c La Befana 1.10 .75
a. Booklet pane of 5 + label 5.50 4.75
Complete booklet, #1453a 6.00
1454 A611 84c Weihnachtsmann 1.50 .75
a. Booklet pane of 5 + label 7.50 6.00
Complete booklet, #1454a 8.50

Booklet Stamp

Perf. 12½x13

1455 A612 37c Santa Claus .75 .75
a. Booklet pane of 10 7.50
Complete booklet, #1455a 8.50
Nos. 1452-1455 (4) 4.00 2.50

Christmas. No. 1455 has bar code at left; for use on covers with printed postal code matrix.

A613

Canadian Women: No. 1456, Adelaide Sophia Hoodless (1857-1910), founder of Victorian Order of Nurses. No. 1457, Marie-Josephine Gerin-Lajoie (1890-1971), founder of Notre-Dame du Bon Conseil Institute. No. 1458, Pitseolak Ashoona (c. 1904-83), Inuit graphic artist. No. 1459, Helen Alice Kinnear (1894-1970), first woman appointed King's Counsel and first federally appointed woman judge.

1993, Mar. 8 *Perf. 12½*

1456 A613 43c multicolored .65 .30
1457 A613 43c multicolored .65 .30
1458 A613 43c multicolored .65 .30
1459 A613 43c multicolored .65 .30
a. Block or strip of 4, #1456-1459 2.60 2.25

Natl. Council of Women of Canada (NCWC), and Natl. office of YWCA, cent.

Stanley Cup, Cent. — A614

1993, Apr. 16 ***Perf. 13½***

1460 A614 43c multicolored .75 .25

Handcrafted Textiles — A615

No. 1461, Coverlet, New Brunswick. No. 1462, Pieced quilt, Ontario. No. 1463, Doukhobor bedcover, Saskatchewan. No. 1464, Kwakwaka'wakw ceremonial robe, British Columbia. No. 1465, Boutonne coverlet, Quebec.

Booklet Stamps

Perf. 13x12½ on 3 Sides

1993, Apr. 30

1461 A615 43c multicolored .75 .40
1462 A615 43c multicolored .75 .40
1463 A615 43c multicolored .75 .40
1464 A615 43c multicolored .75 .40
1465 A615 43c multicolored .75 .40
a. Strip of 5, #1461-1465 3.75 3.00
b. Bklt. pane, 2 ea #1461-1465 7.50
Complete booklet, #1465b 8.50

Stamps in bottom row of No. 1465b are in different sequence than those in No. 1465a.

Art Type of 1988

Painting: Drawing for The Owl, by Kenojuak Ashevak.

Litho. with Foil Application

1993, May 17 ***Perf. 12½x13½***

1466 A546 86c multicolored 1.50 1.10

Intl. Year of Indigenous People.

Historic Canadian Pacific Railway Hotels A616

No. 1467, Empress, Victoria, B.C. No. 1468, Banff Springs, Banff, Alberta. No. 1469, Royal York, Toronto, Ont. No. 1470, Chateau Frontenac, Quebec. No. 1471, Algonquin, St. Andrews, N.B.

Booklet Stamps

1993, June 14 ***Perf. 13½ on 3 Sides***

1467 A616 43c multicolored .90 .60
1468 A616 43c multicolored .90 .65
1469 A616 43c multicolored .90 .60
1470 A616 43c multicolored .90 .60
1471 A616 43c multicolored .90 .60
a. Strip of 5, #1467-1471 4.50 3.50
b. Booklet pane, 2 #1471a 9.00
Complete booklet, #1471b 10.00

Opening of Chateau Frontenac, cent.

Miniature Sheet

Canada Day A617

Provincial and Territorial Parks: No. 1472, Algonquin, Ontario. No. 1473, De la Gaspesie, Quebec. No. 1474, Cedar Dunes, Prince Edward Island. No. 1475, Cape St. Mary's Seabird Ecological Reserve, Newfoundland. No. 1476, Mount Robson, British Columbia. No. 1477, Writing-On-Stone, Alberta. No. 1478, Spruce Woods, Manitoba. No. 1479, Herschel Island, Yukon. No. 1480, Cypress Hills, Saskatchewan. No. 1481, The Rocks, New Brunswick, No. 1482, Blomidon, Nova Scotia. No. 1483, Katannilik, Northwest Territories.

1993, June 30 ***Perf. 13***

1472 A617 43c multicolored 1.00 1.00
1473 A617 43c multicolored 1.00 1.00
1474 A617 43c multicolored 1.00 1.00
1475 A617 43c multicolored 1.00 1.00
1476 A617 43c multicolored 1.00 1.00
1477 A617 43c multicolored 1.00 1.00
1478 A617 43c multicolored 1.00 1.00
1479 A617 43c multicolored 1.00 1.00
1480 A617 43c multicolored 1.00 1.00
1481 A617 43c multicolored 1.00 1.00
1482 A617 43c multicolored 1.00 1.00
1483 A617 43c multicolored 1.00 1.00
a. Pane of 12, #1472-1483 12.00 12.00

Algonquin Park, centennial.

City of Toronto, Bicent. — A618

1993, Aug. 6 ***Perf. 13½x13***

1484 A618 43c multicolored .75 .25

Canadian Rivers Type of 1991
Booklet Stamps

1993, Aug. 10 ***Perf. 13x12½***

1485 A586 43c Fraser .75 .40
1486 A586 43c Yukon .75 .40
1487 A586 43c Red .75 .40
1488 A586 43c St. Lawrence .75 .40
1489 A586 43c St. John .75 .40
a. Strip of 5, #1485-1489 3.75 3.50
b. Bklt. pane, 2 each #1485-1489 7.50
Complete booklet, #1489b 8.50
c. As "a," imperf *2,500.*

Miniature Sheet

Historic Automobiles — A619

a, 1867 H.S. Taylor Steam Buggy. b, 1908 Russell Model L Touring Car. c, 1914 Ford Model T Open Touring Car. d, 1950 Studebaker Champion Deluxe Starlight Coupe. e, 1928 McLaughlin-Buick Model 28-496 Special Car. f, 1923-24 Gray-Dort 25-SM Luxury Sedan.

1993, Aug. 23 ***Perf. 12½x13***

1490 A619 Pane of 6 7.50 7.50
a.-b. 43c any single, 35x22mm .75 .75
c.-d. 49c any single, 43x22mm .90 .90
e.-f. 86c any single, 51x22mm 1.50 1.40

See Nos. 1527, 1552, 1604-1605.

Folk Songs A620

Designs: No. 1491, The Alberta Homesteader, Alberta. No. 1492, Les Raftmans, Quebec. No. 1493, I'se the B'y That Builds the Boat, Newfoundland. No. 1494, Onkwa:ri tenhanonniahkwe, Kanien'kehaka (Mohawk).

1993, Sept. 7 ***Perf. 12½***

1491 A620 43c multicolored .65 .30
1492 A620 43c multicolored .65 .30
1493 A620 43c multicolored .65 .30
1494 A620 43c multicolored .65 .30
a. Block of 4, #1491-1494 2.60 2.20

Dinosaurs — A621

No. 1495, Massospondylus. No. 1496, Styracosaurus. No. 1497, Albertosaurus. No. 1498, Platecarpus.

1993, Oct. 1 ***Perf. 13½***

1495 A621 43c multicolored .65 .30
1496 A621 43c multicolored .65 .30
1497 A621 43c multicolored .65 .30
1498 A621 43c multicolored .65 .30
a. Block or strip of 4, #1495-1498 2.60 2.20
b. As "a," imperf. *2,500.*

See Nos. 1529-1532.

A622

Santa Claus A623

43c, Swiety Mikolaj. 49c, Ded Moroz. 86c, Father Christmas, Australia. No. 1502, 38c, Santa Claus.

1993, Nov. 4

1499 A622 43c multicolored .65 .25
a. Booklet pane of 10 6.50 5.00
Complete booklet, #1499a 7.50
b. Horiz. pair, imperf between *1,000.*
1500 A622 49c multicolored .75 .45
a. Booklet pane of 5 + label 3.75 3.25
Complete booklet, #1500a 4.75
1501 A622 86c multicolored 1.50 .55
a. Booklet pane of 5 + label 7.50 6.50
Complete booklet, #1501a 8.50

Booklet Stamp

Perf. 13

1502 A623 38c multicolored .75 .60
a. Booklet pane of 10 7.50 7.00
Complete booklet, #1502a 8.50
Nos. 1499-1502 (4) 3.65 1.85

Christmas. No. 1502 has bar code at left; for use on covers with printed postal code matrix.

World War II Type of 1989

No. 1503, Aid to Allies. No. 1504, Bomber forces. No. 1505, Battle of the Atlantic. No. 1506, Italian campaign.

1993, Nov. 8 ***Perf. 13½***

1503 A568 43c ol grn & blk .75 .45
1504 A568 43c dp turq grn & blk .75 .45
1505 A568 43c blue & black .75 .45
1506 A568 43c org brn & blk .75 .45
a. Block or strip of 4, #1503-1506 3.00 2.50

Greetings — A624

Design: No. 1508, "Canada" at right.

1994, Jan. 28 ***Die Cut***

Self-Adhesive

1507 A624 43c multicolored .90 .70
1508 A624 43c multicolored .90 .70
a. Bklt. pane of 10, 5 each #1507-1508 9.00

No. 1508a also contains 35 self-adhesive greetings labels in seven designs that complete the design when placed in the central circle of Nos. 1507-1508.

See Nos. 1568-1569, 1600-1601.

Jeanne Sauve (1922-93), Governor General — A625

1994, Mar. 8 ***Perf. 12½x13***

1509 A625 43c + label, multi .75 .30
a. Block or horiz. strip of 4 + 4 labels 3.00 2.25

No. 1509 issued se-tenant with label in sheets of 20 + 20 labels in four designs. In alternating rows, labels appear on left or right side of stamp.

T. Eaton Company, 125th Anniv. — A626

1994, Mar. 17 ***Perf. 13½x13***

1510 A626 43c multicolored .75 .30
a. Booklet pane of 10 + 2 labels 7.50 6.25
Complete booklet, #1510a 8.50

Canadian Rivers Type of 1991
Booklet Stamps

1994, Apr. 22 ***Perf. 13½***

1511 A586 43c Saguenay .90 .45
1512 A586 43c French .90 .45
1513 A586 43c Mackenzie .90 .45
1514 A586 43c Churchill .90 .45
1515 A586 43c Columbia .90 .45
a. Strip of 5, #1511-1515 4.50 3.50
b. Bklt. pane, 2 ea #1511-1515 9.00 9.00
Complete booklet, #1515b 10.00

Art Type of 1988

Design: Vera, by Frederick H. Varley (1881-1969).

Litho. with Foil Application

1994, May 6 ***Perf. 14x14½***

1516 A546 88c multicolored 1.50 1.10

XV Commonwealth Games, Victoria, BC — A627

No. 1517, Lawn bowls. No. 1518, Lacrosse. No. 1519, Wheelchair marathon. No. 1520, High jump. No. 1521, Diving. No. 1522, Cycling.

1994 **Litho.** ***Perf. 14***

1517 A627 43c multicolored .75 .25
1518 A627 43c multicolored .75 .25
a. Pair, #1517-1518 1.50 1.10
1519 A627 43c multicolored .75 .25
1520 A627 43c multicolored .75 .25
a. Pair, #1519-1520 1.50 1.10
1521 A627 50c multicolored .90 .75
a. Gold ("CANADA 50") omitted *1,300.*
1522 A627 88c multicolored 1.50 .90
a. Gold ("CANADA 88") omitted *1,600.*
Nos. 1517-1522 (6) 5.40 2.65

Certificates of authenticity recommended for Nos. 1521a and 1522a.

Issued: Nos. 1517-1518, 5/20; Nos. 1519-1522, 8/5.

Souvenir Sheet

Intl. Year of the Family — A628

Designs: a, Mother and infant. b, Adults, children playing. c, Elderly woman, child. d, Adults, children in class. e, Judge, health care worker, child.

1994, June 2

1523 A628 Pane of 5 3.75 3.75
a.-e. 43c any single .75 .75

Canada Day — A629

Maple trees: a, Big leaf. b, Sugar. c, Silver. d, Striped. e, Norway. f, Manitoba. g, Black. h, Douglas. i, Mountain. j, Vine. k, Hedge. l, Red.

1994, June 30 ***Perf. 13x13½***

1524 A629 Pane of 12 9.00 9.00
a.-l. 43c any single .75 .75

A630

No. 1525, Billy Bishop (1894-1956), Fighter Ace. No. 1526, Mary Travers, "La Bolduc" (1894-1941), folk singer.

1994, Aug. 12 ***Perf. 13***

1525 43c multicolored .65 .30
1526 43c multicolored .65 .30
a. A630 Pair, #1525-1526 1.30 .90

Historic Vehicles Type of 1993

Miniature Sheet

Designs: a, 1942 Ford F60L-AMB military ambulance. b, 1925 REO Speed Wagon Police Wagon. c, 1927 Sicard Snow Remover/Snowblower. d, 1936 Bickle Chieftain Fire Engine. e, 1894 Ottawa Car Company Streetcar. f, 1950 Motor Coach Industries Courier 50 Skyview bus.

1994, Aug. 19 ***Perf. 12½x13***

1527 Pane of 6 6.75 6.75
a.-b. A619 43c any single .75 .75
c.-d. A619 50c any single .90 .90
e.-f. A619 88c any single 1.70 1.60

ICAO, 50th Anniv. A632

1994, Sept. 16 ***Perf. 13***

1528 A632 43c multicolored 1.10 .25

Dinosaur Type of 1993

Prehistoric animals: No. 1529, Coryphodon. No. 1530, Megacerops. No. 1531, Short-faced bear. No. 1532, Woolly mammoth.

1994, Sept. 26

1529 A621 43c multicolored .65 .30
1530 A621 43c multicolored .65 .30
1531 A621 43c multicolored .65 .30
1532 A621 43c multicolored .65 .30
a. Block or strip of 4, #1529-1532 2.60 2.20

Family Singing Carols A633

Soloist A634

1994, Nov. 3 ***Perf. 13½***

1533 A633 43c multicolored .65 .25
a. Booklet pane of 10 6.50 6.50
Complete booklet, #1533a 7.00
1534 A633 50c Choir, vert. .75 .55
a. Booklet pane of 5 + label 5.00 4.00
Complete booklet, #1534a 5.50
1535 A633 88c Caroling, vert. 1.50 .90
a. Booklet pane of 5 + label 7.50 7.00
Complete booklet, #1535a 8.00

Booklet Stamp

Perf. 13

1536 A634 38c multicolored .75 .55
a. Booklet pane of 10 7.50 6.00
Complete booklet, #1536a 8.00
Nos. 1533-1536 (4) 3.65 2.25

Christmas. No. 1536 has bar code at left; for use on covers with printed postal code matrix.

Examples exist of 52c and 90c denominations with the same designs as Nos. 1534 (52c) and 1535 (90c). These were prepared in advance in anticipation of a rate increase that was not approved. Virtually all were destroyed, but a small quantity are known in private hands. None were regularly issued or sold at post offices. Values: 52c, $150; 90c, $425.

World War II Type of 1989

No. 1537, D-Day beachhead. No. 1538, Artillery-Normandy. No. 1539, Tactical Air Forces. No. 1540, Walcheren and the Scheldt.

1994, Nov. 7 ***Perf. 13½***

1537 A568 43c multicolored .90 .35
1538 A568 43c multicolored .90 .35
1539 A568 43c multicolored .90 .35
1540 A568 43c multicolored .90 .35
a. Block or strip of 4, #1537-1540 3.60 2.20

World War II Type of 1989

No. 1541, Veterans return home. No. 1542, Freeing the POW. No. 1543, Liberation of civilians. No. 1544, Crossing the Rhine.

1995, Mar. 20

1541 A568 43c multicolored .90 .35
1542 A568 43c multicolored .90 .35
1543 A568 43c multicolored .90 .35
1544 A568 43c multicolored .90 .35
a. Block or strip of 4, #1541-1544 3.60 3.00

Art Type of 1988

Painting: Floraison, by Alfred Pellan (1906-88).

Litho. with Foil Application

1995, Apr. 21 ***Perf. 13***

1545 A546 88c multicolored 1.70 1.10
a. Gold foil omitted *1,400.*

Flag Over Lake — A635

1995, May 1 Litho. ***Perf. 13½x13***

1546 A635 (43c) multicolored .90 .25

No. 1546 was valued at the first class domestic letter rate on day of issue.

Fortress of Louisbourg, 275th Anniv. — A636

No. 1547, Louisbourg Harbor, ships near Dauphin Gate. No. 1548, Walls, streets, buildings of Louisbourg. No. 1549, Museum behind King's Bastion. No. 1550, Drawing of King's Garden, Convent, Hospital and barracks. No. 1551, Partially eroded fortifications.

1995, May 5 ***Perf. 12½x13***

1547 A636 (43c) 48x32mm .75 .40
1548 A636 (43c) 32x32mm .75 .40
1549 A636 (43c) 40x32mm .75 .40
1550 A636 (43c) 56x32mm .75 .40
1551 A636 (43c) 48x32mm .75 .40
a. Strip of 5, #1547-1551 3.75 3.25
b. Booklet pane, 2 #1551a 7.50 6.75
Complete booklet, #1551b 7.75

Nos. 1547-1551 were valued at the first class domestic letter rate on day of issue. No. 1551a is a continuous design.

Historic Vehicles Type of 1993

Miniature Sheet

Farm, frontier vehicles: a, 1950 Cockshutt "30" farm tractor. b, 1970 Bombardier Ski-Doo Olympique 335 snowmobile. c, 1948 Bombardier B-12 CS multi-passenger snowmobile. d, 1924 Gotfredson model 20 farm truck. e, 1962 Robin-Nodwell RN 110 tracked carrier. f, 1942 Massey-Harris No. 21 self-propelled combine.

1995, May 26

1552 Pane of 6 7.00 7.00
a.-b. A619 43c any single, 35x22mm .75 .75
c.-d. A619 50c any single, 43x22mm .95 .95
e.-f. A619 88c any single, 43x22mm 1.80 1.80

Golf in Canada A637

Designs: No. 1553, Banff Springs Golf Club. No. 1554, Riverside Country Club. No. 1555, Glen Abbey Golf Club. No. 1556, Victoria Golf Club. No. 1557, Royal Montreal Golf Club.

Booklet Stamps

Perf. 13½x13 on 3 Sides

1995, June 6

1553 A637 43c multicolored .90 .40
1554 A637 43c multicolored .90 .40
1555 A637 43c multicolored .90 .40
1556 A637 43c multicolored .90 .40
1557 A637 43c multicolored .90 .40
a. Strip of 5, #1553-1557 4.50 3.75
b. Booklet pane, 2 #1557a 9.00 8.00
Complete booklet, #1557b 9.50

Nat. Golf Week. Canadian Amateur Golf Championship, cent. Royal Canadian Golf Assoc., cent.

Lunenburg Academy, Cent. — A638

1995, June 29 ***Perf. 13***

1558 A638 43c multicolored .65 .25

Souvenir Sheets

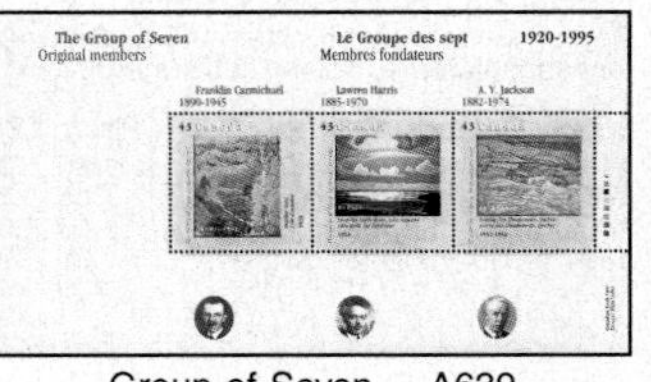

Group of Seven — A639

Painting, original members: No. 1559a, October Gold, by Franklin Carmichael. b, From the North Shore, Lake Superior, by Lawren Harris. c, Evening, Les Eboulements, Quebec, by A.Y. Jackson.

No. 1560a, Serenity, Lake of the Woods, by Frank H. Johnston. b, A September Gale, Georgian Bay, by Arthur Lismer. c, Falls, Montreal River, by J.E.H. MacDonald. d, Open Window, by Frederick Horsman Varley.

Painting, new members: No. 1561a, Mill Houses, by Alfred J. Casson. b, Pembina Valley, by Lionel LeMoine FitzGerald. c, The Lumberjack, by Edwin Headley Holgate.

1995, June 29

1559 A639 Pane of 3 2.75 2.75
a.-c. 43c any single .90 .90
1560 A639 Pane of 4 3.60 3.60
a.-d. 43c any single .90 .90
1561 A639 Pane of 3 2.75 2.75
a.-c. 43c any single .90 .90

Manitoba's Entry Into Confederation, 125th Anniv. — A640

1995, July 14 ***Perf. 13½x13***

1562 A640 43c multicolored .65 .30

Migratory Wildlife — A641

No. 1563, Monarch butterfly. No. 1564, Belted kingfisher. No. 1565, Northern pintail. No. 1566, Hoary bat.

1995, Aug. 15 ***Perf. 13x12½***

1563 A641 45c multicolored .75 .25
1564 A641 45c multicolored .75 .40
1565 A641 45c multicolored .75 .25
1566 A641 45c multicolored .75 .25
a. Block or strip of 4, #1563-1566 3.00 2.50

No. 1564 with Revised Inscription

1995, Sept. 26

1567 A641 45c like #1564 .90 .75
a. Block or strip of 4, #1563, 1565-1567 3.60 3.60

No. 1564 inscribed "aune," No. 1567 "Faune." See Mexico No. 1924.

Greetings Type of 1994

Designs: No. 1568, "Canada" at left. No. 1569, "Canada" at right.

Self-Adhesive

Size: 46x22mm

1995, Sept. 1 ***Die Cut***

1568 A624 45c green & multi .90 .75
1569 A624 45c green & multi .90 .75
a. Bklt. pane, 5 ea #1568-1569 9.00

By its nature, No. 1569a is a complete booklet. The peelable backing serves as a booklet cover.

No. 1569a also contains 15 self-adhesive greetings labels in four designs that complete the design when placed in the central circle of Nos. 1568-1569.

No. 1569a exists with special cover and labels commemorating the Canadian Memorial Chiropractic College, Toronto, 50th anniv.

Bridges A642

No. 1570, Quebec Bridge, Quebec. No. 1571, Highway 403-401-410 interchange, Ontario. No. 1572, Hartland Covered Wooden Bridge, New Brunswick. No. 1573, Alex Fraser Bridge, British Columbia.

1995, Sept. 1 *Perf. 12½x13*

1570 A642 45c multicolored .75 .30
1571 A642 45c multicolored .75 .30
1572 A642 45c multicolored .75 .30
1573 A642 45c multicolored .75 .30
a. Block or strip of 4, #1570-1573 3.00 2.50

Canadian Arctic A643

No. 1574, Polar bear, caribou. No. 1575, Arctic poppy, cargo canoe. No. 1576, Inuk man, igloo, sled dogs. No. 1577, Dog-sled team, ski plane. No. 1578, Children.

Booklet Stamps

1995, Sept. 15 *Perf. 13x12½*

1574 A643 45c multicolored .75 .30
1575 A643 45c multicolored .75 .30
1576 A643 45c multicolored .75 .30
1577 A643 45c multicolored .75 .30
1578 A643 45c multicolored .75 .30
a. Strip of 5, #1574-1578 3.75 3.25
b. Bklt. pane, 2 #1578a 7.50 7.50
Complete booklet, #1578b 8.00

Stamps in bottom row of No. 1578b are in different sequence.

Comic Book Characters A644

No. 1579, Superman. No. 1580, Johnny Canuck. No. 1581, Nelvana. No. 1582, Captain Canuck. No. 1583, Fleur de Lys.

Booklet Stamps

1995, Oct. 2 *Perf. 13x12½*

1579 A644 45c multi 1.10 .40
1580 A644 45c multi 1.10 .40
1581 A644 45c multi 1.10 .40
1582 A644 45c multi 1.10 .40
1583 A644 45c multi 1.10 .40
a. Strip of 5, #1579-1583 5.50 5.00
b. Booklet pane, 2 #1583a 11.00 11.00
Complete booklet, #1583b 11.50

Stamps in the bottom row of No. 1583b are in different sequence.

UN, 50th Anniv. A645

1995, Oct. 24 *Perf. 13½*

1584 A645 45c blue & multi 1.20 .25

No. 1584 printed in panes of 10 with top label equal to 10 stamps. Label shows details of Canadian participation in UN activities. UN emblem on No. 1584 is stamped in blue foil.

Capital Sculptures, by Emile Brunet (1893-1977), Sainte-Anne-de-Deaupre Basilica — A646

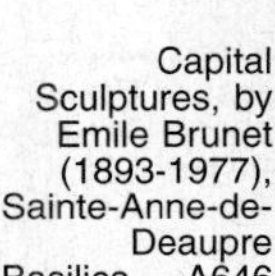

Holly A647

45c, The Nativity. 52c, The Annunciation. 90c, Flight to Egypt.

1995, Nov. 2

1585 A646 45c multicolored .70 .25
a. Booklet pane of 10 7.00 5.50
Complete booklet, #1585a 7.50
1586 A646 52c multicolored .85 .50
a. Booklet pane of 5 + label 4.25 4.25
Complete booklet, #1586a 4.50
1587 A646 90c multicolored 1.40 .60
a. Booklet pane of 5 + label 7.00 7.00
Complete booklet, #1587a 7.50

Booklet Stamp

Perf. 12½x13

1588 A647 40c multicolored .75 .75
a. Booklet pane of 10 7.50 *10.00*
Complete booklet, #1588a 7.75
Nos. 1585-1588 (4) 3.70 2.10

Christmas. No. 1588 has bar code at left; for use on covers with printed postal code matrix.

La Francophonie's Agency for Cultural and Technical Cooperation, 25th Anniv. — A648

1995, Nov. 6 *Perf. 13x13½*

1589 A648 45c multicolored .70 .25

End of the Holocaust, 50th Anniv. — A649

1995, Nov. 9 *Perf. 12½x13*

1590 A649 45c multicolored .70 .25

Birds A650

No. 1591, American kestrel. No. 1592, Atlantic puffin. No. 1593, Pileated woodpecker. No. 1594, Ruby-throated hummingbird.

1996, Jan. 9 *Perf. 13½*

1591 A650 45c multicolored .75 .30
1592 A650 45c multicolored .75 .30
1593 A650 45c multicolored .75 .30
1594 A650 45c multicolored .75 .30
a. Strip of 4, Nos. 1591-1594 3.00 2.75

Issued in panes of 12 stamps, printed checkerwise, and in uncut sheets of 5 panes.

See Nos. 1631-1634, 1710-1713, 1770-1777, 1839-1846, 1886-1893.

High Technology Industries — A651

Designs: No. 1595, Ocean technology. No. 1596, Aerospace technology. No. 1597, Information technology. No. 1598, Biotechnology.

Booklet Stamps

1996, Feb. 15 *Perf. 13½ on 3 Sides*

1595 A651 45c multicolored .90 .35
1596 A651 45c multicolored .90 .35
1597 A651 45c multicolored .90 .35
1598 A651 45c multicolored .90 .35
a. Booklet pane of 12, 3 each Nos. 1595-1598 11.00 7.50
Complete booklet, No. 1598a 11.50
Nos. 1595-1598 (4) 3.60 1.40

Greetings Type of 1994

"Canada": No. 1600, at L. No. 1601, at R.

Self-Adhesive

Size: 51x25mm

1996, Jan. 15 *Die Cut*

1600 A624 45c green & multi 1.50 1.20
1601 A624 45c green & multi 1.50 1.20
a. Booklet pane, 5 ea #1600-1601 15.00
b. As "a," die cutting omitted *3,250.*
c. Imperf., pair *600.00*

By its nature No. 1601a is a complete booklet. The peelable backing serves as a booklet cover.

No. 1601a also contains 35 self-adhesive greetings labels in seven designs that complete the design when placed in the central circle of Nos. 1600-1601.

Art Type of 1988

Sculpture: The Spirit of Haida Gwaii, by Bill Reid.

Litho. with Foil Application

1996, Apr. 30 *Perf. 12½x13*

1602 A546 90c multicolored 1.50 1.00

AIDS Awareness — A652

1996, May 8 **Litho.** *Perf. 13½*

1603 A652 45c multicolored .70 .25

Historic Vehicles Type of 1993

No. 1604: a, 1899 Still Motor Co. Ltd. Electric Van. b, 1914 Waterous Engine Works Road Roller. c, 1938 International D-35 Delivery Truck. d, 1936 Champion Road Grader. e, 1947 White Model WA 122 Tractor Trailer. f, 1975 Hayes HDX 45-115 Logging Truck.

No. 1605: a, like #1490a. b, like #1490b. c, like 1527a. d, like #1527b. e, like #1552b. f, like #1604a. g, like #1604b, h, like #1552a. i, like #1604c. j, like 1604d. k, like #1527e. l, like #1527f. m, like #1604e. n, like #1604f. o, like #1490c. p, like #1490d. q, like #1527d. r, like #1490e. s, like #1490f. t, like #1527c. u, like #1552c. v, like #1552d. w, like #1552e. x, like #1552f. y, 1975 Bricklin SV-1 Sports car.

1996 *Perf. 12½x13*

1604 A619 Pane of 6 6.60 6.60
a.-b. 45c any single .80 .80
c.-d. 52c any single .90 .90
e.-f. 90c any single 1.60 1.60
1605 A619 Pane of 25 9.00 9.00
a.-j. 5c any single .25 .25
k.-n. 10c any single .30 .30
o.-x. 20c any single .45 .45
y. 45c multicolored 1.00 1.00

Nos. 1604e-1604f, 1605k-1605n, 1605y are 51x22mm. Nos. 1605o-1605x are 43x21mm.

Yukon Gold Rush, Cent. — A653

Designs: a, "Skookum" Jim Mason's discovery on Rabbit (Bonanza) Creek, 1896. b, Miners trekking to gold fields, boats on Lake Laberge. c, Supr. Sam Steele, North West Mounted Police, Alaska-Yukon border. d, Dawson, boom town, city of entertainment. e, Klondike gold fields.

1996, June 13 *Perf. 13½*

1606 A653 Strip of 5 5.50 4.75
a.-e. 45c any single 1.10 .60

CAPEX '96. No. 1606 was issued in panes of 10 stamps.

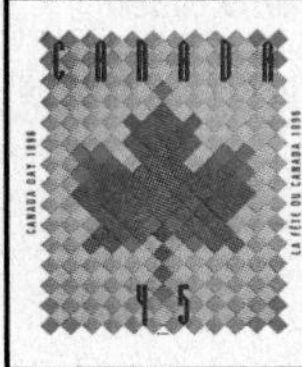

Canada Day — A654

Self-Adhesive

1996, June 28 *Die Cut*

1607 A654 45c multicolored .75 .25
a. Pane of 12 9.00 4.00

Canadian Olympic Gold Medalists A655

No. 1608, Ethel Catherwood, high jump, 1928. No. 1609, Etienne Desmarteau, 56 lb. weight throw, 1904. No. 1610, Fanny Rosenfeld, 100m, 400m relay, 1928. No. 1611, Gerald Ouellette, smallbore rifle, prone, 1956. No. 1612, Percy Williams, 100m, 200m, 1928.

Booklet Stamps

Litho. & Typo.

1996, July 8 *Perf. 13x12½*

1608 A655 45c multicolored 1.10 .60
1609 A655 45c multicolored 1.10 .60
1610 A655 45c multicolored 1.10 .60
1611 A655 45c multicolored 1.10 .60
1612 A655 45c multicolored 1.10 .60
a. Strip of 5, #1608-1612 5.50 4.00
b. Booklet pane, 2 #1612a 11.00
Complete booklet, #1612b 11.50

British Columbia's Entry Into Confederation, 125th Anniv. — A656

1996, July 19

1613 A656 45c multicolored .70 .25

Canadian Heraldry — A657

1996, Aug. 19 **Litho.** *Perf. 12½x12*

1614 A657 45c multicolored .70 .25

Motion Pictures, Cent. — A658

Film strips from motion pictures: No. 1615a, L'arrivée d'un train en gare, Lumière cinematography, 1896. b, Back to God's Country, Nell & Ernest Shipman, 1919. c, Hen Hop, Norman McLaren, 1942. d, Pour la suite du monde, Pierre Perrault, Michel Brault, 1963. e, Goin' Down the Road, Don Shebib, 1970.

No. 1616a, Mon oncle Antoine, Claude Jutra, 1971. b, The Apprenticeship of Duddy Kravitz, Ted Kotcheff, 1974. c, Les Ordres, Michel Brault, 1974. d, Les Bons Débarras, Francis Mankiewiez, 1980. e, The Grey Fox, Philip Borsos, 1982.

Self-Adhesive

1996, Aug. 22 *Die Cut*

1615 Pane of 5 3.50 3.50
a.-e. A658 45c Any single .70 .70
1616 Pane of 5 3.50 3.50
a.-e. A658 45c Any single .70 .70

Edouard Montpetit (1881-1954), Educator A659

1996, Sept. 26 *Perf. 12½*

1617 A659 45c multicolored .70 .25

Winnie the Pooh A660

Designs: No. 1618, Winnie, Lt. Colebourne, 1914. No. 1619, Winnie, Christopher Robin, 1925. No. 1620, Milne and Shepard's Winnie the Pooh, 1926. No. 1621, Winnie the Pooh at Walt Disney World, 1996.

1996, Oct. 1 *Perf. 12½x13*

1618 A660 45c multicolored .75 .40
1619 A660 45c multicolored .75 .40
1620 A660 45c multicolored .75 .40
1621 A660 45c multicolored .75 .40
a. Block of 4, #1618-1621 3.00 2.50
b. Souv. sheet of 4, #1618-1621 7.50 7.50
c. Booklet pane of 16, 4 each #1618-1621 12.00 12.00
Complete booklet, #1621c 12.50

No. 1621c was issued with the halves of the booklet pane printed tete-beche. The booklet pane of 16 was used as a cover for a souvenir story booklet.

Walt Disney World, 25th anniv.

Authors — A661

No. 1622, Margaret Laurence (1926-87). No. 1623, Donald G. Creighton (1902-79). No. 1624, Gabrielle Roy (1909-83). No. 1625, Felix-Antoine Savard (1896-1982). No. 1626, Thomas C. Haliburton (1796-1865).

Booklet Stamps

Perf. 13½x13 on 3 Sides

1996, Oct. 10 **Litho. & Engr.**

1622 A661 45c multicolored 1.10 .40
1623 A661 45c multicolored 1.10 .40
1624 A661 45c multicolored 1.10 .40
1625 A661 45c multicolored 1.10 .40
1626 A661 45c multicolored 1.10 .40
a. Strip of 5, #1622-1626 5.50 5.00
b. Booklet pane, 2 #1626a 11.00 12.00
Complete booklet, #1626b 11.50

A662

Christmas: 45c, Children on snowshoes, sled. 52c, Santa Claus skiing. 90c, Children skating.

Perf. 13½ (#1627, 1629a), 12¾x12¼ (#1628, 1629), 13½x13 (#1627a, 1628a)

1996, Nov. 1 **Litho.**

1627 A662 45c multicolored .70 .25
a. Booklet pane of 10 7.00 7.00
Complete booklet, #1627a 7.50
1628 A662 52c multicolored .85 .25
a. Booklet pane of 5 + label 4.25 4.75
Complete booklet, #1628a 4.50
1629 A662 90c multicolored 1.40 .50
a. Booklet pane of 5 + label 7.00 7.00
Complete booklet, #1629a 7.50

UNICEF, 50th anniv.

New Year 1997 (Year of the Ox) — A663

1997, Jan. 7 *Perf. 13x12½*

1630 A663 45c multicolored .90 .25
a. Souvenir sheet of 2 2.60 2.60
b. As No. 1630, gold omitted *3,750.*
c. As "a," gold omitted *8,000.*

No. 1630a is fan shaped.

No. 1630a with Hong Kong 97 overprint was sold as a limited edition only at the show. Value $7.50.

Bird Type of 1996

No. 1631, Mountain bluebird. No. 1632, Western grebe. No. 1633, Northern gannet. No. 1634, Scarlet tanager.

1997, Jan. 10 *Perf. 12½x13*

1631 A650 45c multicolored .75 .25
1632 A650 45c multicolored .75 .25
1633 A650 45c multicolored .75 .25
1634 A650 45c multicolored .75 .25
a. Block or strip of 4, #1631-1634 3.00 2.50

Nos. 1631-1634 were issued in panes of 20, 5 each, printed checkerwise to contain 4 complete blocks or 5 strips.

Art Type of 1988

Painting: York Boat on Lake Winnipeg, by Walter J. Phillips.

Litho. with Foil Application

1997, Feb. 17

1635 A546 90c gold & multi 1.80 1.10

Canadian Tire, 75th Anniv. A664

1997, Mar. 3 **Litho.** *Perf. 13x13½*

1636 A664 45c multicolored .75 .25

Father Charles-Emile Gadbois (1906-81), Musicologist A665

1997, Mar. 20 *Perf. 13½x13*

1637 A665 45c multicolored .75 .25

Québec en Fleurs 97, Intl. Horticultural Exhibition A666

Booklet Stamps

Perf. 13x12½ on 3 Sides

1997, Apr. 4

1638 A666 45c Blue poppy .75 .25
a. Booklet pane of 12 9.00 10.00
Complete booklet, #1638a 9.50

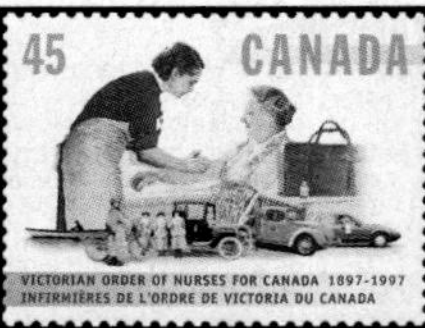

Victorian Order of Nurses for Canada, Cent. A667

1997, May 12 *Perf. 12½x13*

1639 A667 45c multicolored .75 .25

Law Society of Upper Canada, Bicent. — A668

1997, May 23 *Perf. 13½x13*

1640 A668 45c multicolored .75 .25

Salt Water Fish A669

No. 1641, Great white shark. No. 1642, Pacific halibut. No. 1643, Atlantic sturgeon. No. 1644, Bluefin tuna.

1997, May 30 *Perf. 12½x13*

1641 A669 45c multicolored .70 .25
1642 A669 45c multicolored .70 .25
1643 A669 45c multicolored .70 .25
1644 A669 45c multicolored .70 .25
a. Block or strip of 4, #1641-1644 2.80 2.20

Opening of the Confederation Bridge — A670

No. 1645, Lighthouse, bridge. No. 1646, Bridge, bird.

1997, May 31

1645 A670 45c multicolored .70 .25
1646 A670 45c multicolored .70 .25
a. Pair, #1645-1646 + label 1.40 1.10

Gilles Villeneuve (1950-82), Formula One Race Car Driver — A671

45c, Villeneuve winning race in Ferrari T-4. 90c, Close-up, racing in Number 12 Ferrari T-3.

1997, June 12

1647 A671 45c multicolored .75 .25
1648 A671 90c multicolored 1.50 .90
a. Pair, #1647-1648 2.25 2.25
b. Pane of 4 #1648a 9.00 9.00

A672

1997, June 24

1649 A672 45c multicolored .75 .25

John Cabot's Voyage to Canada, 500th Anniv.

See Italy No. 2162.

Scenic Canadian Highways — A673

Designs: No. 1650, Sea to Sky Highway, British Columbia. No. 1651, The Cabot Trail, Nova Scotia. No. 1652, The Wine Route, starting in Ontario. No. 1653, The Big Muddy, Saskatchewan.

1997, June 30

1650 A673 45c multicolored .70 .40
1651 A673 45c multicolored .70 .40
1652 A673 45c multicolored .70 .40
1653 A673 45c multicolored .70 .40
a. Block or strip of 4, #1650-1653 2.80 2.25

See Nos. 1739-1742, 1780-1783.

Canadian Industrial Design — A674

1997, July 23

1654 A674 45c multicolored .70 .25

No. 1654 was issued with se-tenant label in panes of 24 + 24 labels. The 12 different labels each appear twice in different colors. In alternating rows, labels appear on left or right side of stamp.

Association of Canadian Industrial Designers, 50th anniv. and 20th Intl. Congress of Intl. Council of Societies of Industrial Design.

Highland Games, Maxville, Ontario — A675

1997, Aug. 1

1655 A675 45c multicolored .70 .25

Knights of Columbus in Canada, Cent. — A676

1997, Aug. 5 *Perf. 13*

1656 A676 45c multicolored .70 .25

28th World Congress of Postal, Telegraph and Telephone Intl. Labor Union, Montreal A677

1997, Aug. 18

1657 A677 45c multicolored .70 .25

Asia Pacific Year A678

1997, Aug. 25 *Perf. 13½*

1658 A678 45c multicolored .70 .25

Canada-USSR Ice Hockey "Series of the Century," 25th Anniv. — A679

Designs: No. 1659, Canadian players, Paul Henderson, Yvan Cournoyer (No. 12), after scoring winning goal in final game. No. 1660, Canadian team members celebrating victory.

Booklet Stamps

1997, Sept. 20 *Perf. 14x13*

1659 A679 45c multicolored .75 .30
1660 A679 45c multicolored .75 .30
a. Bklt. pane, 5 ea #1659-1660 7.50 8.00
Complete booklet, #1660a 8.00

Famous Politicians A680

No. 1661, Martha Black (1866-1957). No. 1662, Lionel Chevrier (1903-87). No. 1663, Judy LaMarsh (1924-80). No. 1664, Réal Caouette (1917-76).

1997, Sept. 26 *Perf. 13½x13*

1661 A680 45c multicolored .70 .35
1662 A680 45c multicolored .70 .35
1663 A680 45c multicolored .70 .35
a. Double impression of "Canada 45" 55.00
b. Quadruple impression of "Canada 45" 300.00
1664 A680 45c multicolored .70 .35
a. Quintuple impression of "Canada 45" 375.00
b. Block or strip of 4, #1661-1664 2.80 2.25

Supernatural — A681

1997, Oct. 1 *Perf. 13x12½*

1665 A681 45c Vampire .70 .35
1666 A681 45c Werewolf .70 .35
1667 A681 45c Ghost .70 .35
1668 A681 45c Goblin .70 .35
a. Block of 4, #1665-1668 2.80 2.25

Christmas — A682

Stained glass windows: 45c, "Our Lady of the Rosary," Holy Rosary Cathedral, Vancouver. 52c, "Nativity Scene," United Church, Leith, Ontario. 90c, Madonna and Child, St. Stephen's Ukrainian Byzantine Rite Roman Catholic Church, Calgary.

1997, Nov. 3 *Perf. 12½x13*

1669 A682 45c multicolored .70 .25
a. Booklet pane of 10 7.00 7.00
Complete booklet, #1669a 7.50
1670 A682 52c multicolored .80 .35
a. Booklet pane of 5 4.00 4.00
Complete booklet, #1670a 4.25
1671 A682 90c multicolored 1.40 .55
a. Booklet pane of 5 7.00 7.00
Complete booklet, #1671a 7.50
Nos. 1669-1671 (3) 2.90 1.15

75th Royal Agriculture Winter Fair, Toronto A683

1997, Nov. 6

1672 A683 45c multicolored .70 .25

Types of 1987-98 and

Traditional Handiwork A684

Maple Leaf A685

Loon A686

Moose — A687

Flag and Inukshuk — A688

Designs: 1c, Bookbinding. 2c, Ironwork. 3c, Glass blowing. 4c, Oyster farmer. 5c, Weaving. 9c, Quilting. 10c, Artistic woodworking. 25c, Leatherwork. Nos. 1682, 1698, Flag over icebergs. No. 1688, White-tailed deer. No. 1689, Atlantic walrus. No. 1690, Polar bear. No. 1691, Peregrine falcon. No. 1692, Sable Island horses. $8, Grizzly bear.

1997-2005 **Litho.** *Perf. 13¼*

1673 A684 1c multicolored .25 .25
a. Gray (in numeral "1") omitted 300.00 —
1674 A684 2c multicolored .25 .25
1675 A684 3c multicolored .25 .25
1676 A684 4c multicolored .25 .25
a. Imperf., pair 800.00
1677 A684 5c multicolored .25 .25
1678 A684 9c multicolored .25 .25
1679 A684 10c multicolored .25 .25
a. Imperf, single —
b. Block of 4, top two stamps imperf (cut between) 750.00
c. Imperf., vert. pair 1,000.
1680 A684 25c multicolored .40 .25

Perf. 13¼x13

1681 A536 46c multicolored .75 .25

Perf. 13x13¼

1682 A541 46c multicolored .75 .25
a. Booklet pane of 10 7.50 11.00
Complete booklet, #1682a 8.00

Perf. 13¼x13

1683 A536 47c multicolored .75 .25
a. Imperf, pair 600.00
b. Block of 4, bottom pair imperf., top pair part perf. 750.00

Perf. 13x13¼

1684 A685 55c multicolored .90 .25
a. Booklet pane of 5 + label 4.50 3.75
Complete booklet, #1684a 4.75
1685 A685 73c multicolored 1.15 .40
1686 A685 95c multicolored 1.70 .50
a. Booklet pane of 5 + label 8.50 8.00
Complete booklet, #1686a 9.00

Litho. & Engr.

Perf. 13¼x13

1687 A686 $1 multicolored 1.60 .55

Perf. 12½x13

1688 A686 $1 multicolored 1.60 .55
1689 A686 $1 multicolored 1.60 .55
a. Pair, #1688-1689 3.20 2.50
b. Souvenir sheet, 2 each #1688-1689 7.50 7.50

Perf. 13¼x13

1690 A686 $2 multicolored 3.25 1.00

Perf. 12½x13

1691 A686 $2 multicolored 3.25 1.00
1692 A686 $2 multicolored 3.25 1.00
a. Pair, #1691-1692 6.50 4.75
b. Souvenir sheet, 2 each #1691-1692 15.00 15.00

Size 63x48mm

1693 A687 $5 multicolored 8.00 2.00
a. Engraved colors (Moose, etc.) omitted 5,500.
1694 A687 $8 multicolored 12.50 4.50
Nos. 1673-1694 (22) 43.20 15.05

Coil Stamp

Engr.

Perf. 10 Horiz.

1695 A542 46c red .75 .25
a. Imperf, pair 150.00

Photo.

Booklet Stamp

Self-Adhesive

Die Cut

1696 A685 45c multicolored 1.30 2.00
a. Booklet pane of 18 25.00

Typo. & Embossed

Die Cut Perf. 13

Coil Stamp

1697 A685 45c multicolored 1.10 .75

Litho.

Booklet Stamps

Die Cut

1698 A541 46c multicolored .90 .25
a. Booklet pane of 30 27.00
b. Imperf, pair 300.00
c. Vert. strip of 3, die cutting omitted between bottom pair 120.00

Photo.

1699 A685 46c multicolored 2.75 2.75
a. Booklet pane of 18 50.00

Litho.

1700 A688 47c multicolored .75 .25
a. Booklet of 10 7.50
b. Booklet of 30 22.50
c. All colors omitted 225.00
d. As "a," all colors omitted 2,250.
e. As "a," die cutting omitted 1,900.

Nos. 1696a, 1698a-1699a are complete booklets. The peelable backing serves as a booklet cover.

Issued: Nos. 1681, 1682, 1684-1686, 1695, 1698-1700, 12/28/98; No. 1693, 12/19/03; No. 1694, 10/15; No. 1696, 4/14/98. No. 1697, 9/30/98; Nos. 1687, 1690, 10/27/98; Nos. 1673-1680, 4/29/99; No. 1683, 12/28/00; Nos. 1688-1689, 10/20/05; Nos. 1691-1692, 12/19/05.

No. 1697 does not have the "POSTAGE / POSTES" and copyright inscriptions found in No. 1696. The gold on No. 1697 is embossed and brighter than that on No. 1696.

On Nos. 1700c and 1700d, the booklet cover on the reverse side is properly printed, and the tagging is printed as normal.

See Nos. 1928-1930.

New Year 1998 (Year of the Tiger) A690

1998, Jan. 8 **Litho.** *Perf. 13x12½*

1708 A690 45c multicolored .75 .25
a. Souvenir sheet of 2 1.60 1.40

No. 1708a overprinted exists. Value $3.

Provincial Leaders — A691

Designs: a, John P. Robarts (1917-82), Ontario. b, Jean Lesage (1912-80), Quebec. c, John B. McNair (1889-1968), New Brunswick. d, Tommy Douglas (1904-86), Saskatchewan. e, Joseph R. Smallwood (1900-91), Newfoundland. f, Angus L. MacDonald (1890-1954), Nova Scotia. g, W.A.C. Bennett (1900-79), British Columbia. h, Ernest C. Manning (1908-95), Alberta. i, John Bracken (1883-1969), Manitoba. j, J. Walter Jones (1878-1954), Prince Edward Island.

1998, Feb. 18 *Perf. 13½*

1709 A691 Sheet of 10 11.00 9.00
a.-j. 45c any single 1.10 .75

Bird Type of 1996

No. 1710, Hairy woodpecker. No. 1711, Great crested flycatcher. No. 1712, Eastern screech owl. No. 1713, Gray-crowned rosy-finch.

1998, Mar. 13 *Perf. 13x13½*

1710 A650 45c multicolored .75 .30
1711 A650 45c multicolored .75 .30
1712 A650 45c multicolored .75 .30
1713 A650 45c multicolored .75 .30
a. Block or strip of 4, #1710-1713 3.00 2.25

Nos. 1710-1713 were issued in panes of 20, 5 each, printed checkerwise to contain 4 complete blocks or 5 strips.

Fly Fishing in Canada — A693

Lure, type of fish: No. 1715, Coquihalla orange, steelhead trout. No. 1716, Steelhead bee, steelhead trout. No. 1717, Dark Montreal, brook trout. No. 1718, Lady Amherst, Atlantic salmon. No. 1719, Coho blue, coho salmon. No. 1720, Cosseboom special, Atlantic salmon.

1998, Apr. 16 *Perf. 12½x13*

1715 A693 45c multicolored .90 .45
1716 A693 45c multicolored .90 .45
1717 A693 45c multicolored .90 .45
1718 A693 45c multicolored .90 .45
1719 A693 45c multicolored .90 .45
1720 A693 45c multicolored .90 .45
a. Vertical strip of 6, #1715-1720 5.50 4.50
b. Bklt. pane, 2 ea #1715-1720 11.00
Complete booklet, #1720a 11.50

Canadian Institute of Mining, Metallurgy and Petroleum, Cent. — A694

1998, May 4 *Perf. 12½*

1721 A694 45c multicolored .75 .25

Imperial Penny Post, Cent. A695

St. Edward's Crown, #86, Sir William Mulock.

1998, May 29 ***Perf. 12½x13***

1722 A695 45c multicolored .75 .25

No. 1722 was issued in panes of 14 + 1 label.

Sumo Wrestling Tournament, Vancouver — A696

Rising sun, mapleleaf and: No. 1723, Two wrestlers. No. 1724, Sumo champion performing bow twirling ceremony.

1998, June 5 **Litho. & Embossed**

1723 A696 45c multicolored .75 .25
1724 A696 45c multicolored .75 .25
a. Horiz. or Vert. Pair, #1723-1724 + 4 labels 1.50 1.50
b. Souvenir sheet, #1723-1724 3.75 3.75

Nos. 1723-1724 were printed checkerwise in panes of 20, 10 each + 40 labels.

Canals of Canada — A697

No. 1725, St. Peters Canal, Nova Scotia. No. 1726, St. Ours Canal, Quebec. No. 1727, Port Carling Lock, Ontario. No. 1728, Locks, Rideau Canal, Ontario. No. 1729, Peterborough lift lock, Trent-Severn Waterway, Ontario. No. 1730, Chambly Canal, Quebec. No. 1731, Lachine Canal, Quebec. No. 1732, Ice skating on Rideau Canal, Ottawa. No. 1733, Boat on Big Chute Marine Railway, Trent-Severn Waterway. No. 1734, Sault Ste. Marie Canal, Ontario.

Booklet Stamps

1998, June 17 **Litho.** ***Perf. 12½***

1725 A697 45c multicolored 1.10 .75
1726 A697 45c multicolored 1.10 .75
1727 A697 45c multicolored 1.10 .75
1728 A697 45c multicolored 1.10 .75
1729 A697 45c multicolored 1.10 .75
1730 A697 45c multicolored 1.10 .75
1731 A697 45c multicolored 1.10 .75
1732 A697 45c multicolored 1.10 .75
1733 A697 45c multicolored 1.10 .75
1734 A697 45c multicolored 1.10 .75
a. Bklt. pane, #1725-1734 + 10 labels 14.00
Complete booklet, #1734a 15.00

Health Professionals A698

Litho. & Embossed with Foil Application

1998, June 25

1735 A698 45c multicolored .70 .25

Royal Canadian Mounted Police, 125th Anniv. — A699

No. 1736, Male mountie, native, horse. No. 1737, Female mountie, helicopter, cityscape.

1998, July 3 ***Perf. 12½x13***

1736 A699 45c multicolored .70 .25
1737 A699 45c multicolored .70 .25
a. Pair, #1736-1737 + 2 labels 1.40 1.10
b. Souvenir sheet, #1736-1737 + 1 label 1.50 1.50
c. As "b," with signature 3.00 3.00
d. As "b," with Portugal 98 emblem 4.50 4.50
e. As "b," with Italia 98 emblem 4.50 4.50
f. As "d," gold embossed emblem omitted *750.00*

Nos. 1737c-1737e have added inscriptions in gold. Issued: No. 1737c, 7/3; No. 1737d, 9/4; No. 1737e, 10/23.

William James Roué (1879-1970), Naval Architect — A700

Litho. & Engr.

1998, July 24 ***Perf. 13***

1738 A700 45c multicolored .75 .25

Scenic Highway Type of 1997

Designs: No. 1739, Dempster Highway, Yukon. No. 1740, Dinosaur Trail, Alberta. No. 1741, River Valley Scenic Drive, New Brunswick. No. 1742, Blue Heron Route, Prince Edward Island.

1998, July 28 **Litho.** ***Perf. 12½x13***

1739 A673 45c multicolored .70 .35
1740 A673 45c multicolored .70 .35
1741 A673 45c multicolored .70 .35
1742 A673 45c multicolored .70 .35
a. Block or strip of 4, #1739-1742 2.80 2.30

Publication of "Refus Global" by The Automatistes, 50th Anniv. — A701

Painting, artist: No. 1743, "Peinture," Jean-Paul Riopelle. No. 1744, "La dernière campagne de Napoléon," Fernand Leduc. No. 1745, "Jet fuligineux sur noir torturé," Jean-Paul Mousseau. No. 1746, "Le fond du garde-robe," Pierre Gauvreau. No. 1747, "Joie lacustre," Paul-Emile Borduas. No. 1748, "Syndicat des gens de mer," Marcelle Ferron. No. 1749, "Le tumulte á la machoire crispée," Marcel Barbeau.

Self-Adhesive Booklet Stamps

1998, Aug. 7 ***Die Cut***

1743 A701 45c multicolored 1.10 1.10
1744 A701 45c multicolored 1.10 1.10
1745 A701 45c multicolored 1.10 1.10
1746 A701 45c multicolored 1.10 1.10
1747 A701 45c multicolored 1.10 1.10
1748 A701 45c multicolored 1.10 1.10
1749 A701 45c multicolored 1.10 1.10
a. Booklet pane, #1743-1749 7.75

No. 1746 is 34x48mm. No. 1749a is a complete booklet. The peelable paper backing serves as a booklet cover.

Legendary Canadians A702

No. 1750, Napoléon-Alexandre Comeau (1848-1923), outdoorsman, "King of the North Shore." No. 1751, Phyllis Munday (1894-1990), mountaineer, community service worker. No. 1752, Bill Mason (1929-88), film maker, canoe enthusiast. No. 1753, Harry "Red" Foster (1905-1985), founder of Canadian Special Olympics, sports enthusiast.

1998, Aug. 15 ***Perf. 13½***

1750 A702 45c multicolored .70 .25
1751 A702 45c multicolored .70 .25
1752 A702 45c multicolored .70 .25
1753 A702 45c multicolored .70 .25
a. Block or strip of 4, #1750-1753 2.80 2.30

Art Type of 1988

Painting: The Farmer's Family (detail), by Bruno Bobak.

Litho. with Foil Application

1998, Sept. 8 ***Perf. 12½x13***

1754 A546 90c gold & multi 1.50 .90

Housing in Canada A703

a, Native peoples. b, Settler. c, Regional. d, Heritage preservation. e, Multiple unit. f, Prefabricated. g, Veterans. h, Planned community. i, Innovative.

1998, Sept. 23 **Litho.**

1755 Pane of 9 10.00 10.00
a.-i. A703 45c Any single 1.10 1.10

University of Ottawa, 150th Anniv. — A704

1998, Sept. 25 ***Perf. 13***

1756 A704 45c multicolored .70 .25

The Circus — A705

Various circus clowns and: No. 1757, Elephant, bear performing tricks. No. 1758, Woman standing on horse, aerial act. No. 1759, Lion tamer. No. 1760, Contortionists, acrobats.

Booklet Stamps

1998, Oct. 1 ***Perf. 13 on 3 Sides***

1757 A705 45c multicolored .70 .30
1758 A705 45c multicolored .70 .30
1759 A705 45c multicolored .70 .30
1760 A705 45c multicolored .70 .30
a. Bklt. pane, 3 ea #1757-1760 7.00 7.00
Complete booklet, #1760a 7.50
b. Souvenir sheet, #1757-1760 4.50 3.75

Stamps in No. 1760b are perforated on all four sides.

John Peters Humphrey (1905-95), Author of Universal Declaration of Human Rights A706

1998, Oct. 7 ***Perf. 13***

1761 A706 45c multicolored .70 .25

Canadian Naval Reserve, 75th Anniv. — A707

No. 1762, HMCS Sackville. No. 1763, HMCS Shawinigan.

1998, Nov. 4 ***Perf. 12½x13***

1762 A707 45c multicolored .75 .25
1763 A707 45c multicolored .75 .25
a. Pair, #1762-1763 1.50 1.40

Christmas — A708

Sculpted wooden angels: 45c, "Angel of Last Judgment" blowing trumpet. 52c, "Adoring Angel" raising hand. 90c, "Adoring Angel, Kneeling," by Thomas Baillairgé.

1998, Nov. 6 ***Perf. 13***

1764 A708 45c multicolored .75 .25
a. Booklet pane of 10 32.50 32.50
Complete booklet, #1764a 35.00
b. Perf 13x13½ 375.00 16.00
c. As "b," booklet pane of 10 15.00 13.50
Complete booklet, #1764c 16.00

The values for No. 1764b are for singles perfed on all four sides from sheet format. These are extremely scarce. Single stamps from booklet pane No. 1764c have a straight edge on one side. Value, booklet single, unused $1.50, used $.30.

Perf. 13x13½

1765 A708 52c multicolored .85 .40
a. Booklet pane of 5 + label 22.50 22.50
Complete booklet, #1765a 23.50
b. Perf 13 1.10 .60
c. As "b," booklet pane of 5 + label 5.50 5.00
Complete booklet, #1765c 6.00
1766 A708 90c multicolored 1.50 .75
a. Booklet pane of 5 + label 37.50 37.50
Complete booklet, #1766a 40.00
b. Perf 13 1.50 .75
c. As "b," booklet pane of 5 + label 7.50 6.75
Complete booklet, #1766c 8.00
Nos. 1764-1766 (3) 3.10 1.40

New Year 1999 (Year of the Rabbit) A709

1999, Jan. 8 ***Perf. 13½***

1767 A709 46c multicolored .75 .25
a. Red and tagging omitted *650.00*

Souvenir Sheet

Perf. 12½x13

1768 A709 95c Pane of 1 2.25 2.00
a. Single stamp 1.50 1.25
b. Red and tagging omitted *850.00*

No. 1768 with China 99 overprint was sold only at the show. Value same as unoverprinted pane. Also known with red and tagging omitted. Value $1,750.

Le Theatre du Rideau Vert, 50th Anniv. — A710

1999, Feb. 17 ***Perf. 13x12½***

1769	A710	46c multicolored	.75	.25

Bird Type of 1996

Designs: No. 1770, Northern goshawk. No. 1771, Red-winged blackbird. No. 1772, American goldfinch. No. 1773, Sandhill crane.

1999, Feb. 24 ***Perf. 12½x13***

1770	A650	46c multicolored	.75	.30
1771	A650	46c multicolored	.75	.30
1772	A650	46c multicolored	.75	.30
1773	A650	46c multicolored	.75	.30
a.		Block or strip of 4, #1770-1773	3.00	1.50

Booklet Stamps
Self-Adhesive
Die Cut Perf. 11½

1774	A650	46c like #1770	.90	.35
1775	A650	46c like #1771	.90	.35
1776	A650	46c like #1772	.90	.35
1777	A650	46c like #1773	.90	.35
a.		Booklet pane, 2 each #1774-1775, 1 each #1776-1777	5.50	
b.		Booklet pane, 2 each #1776-1777, 1 each #1774-1775	5.50	
		Complete booklet, #1777a, #1777b	11.00	

Nos. 1770-1773 were issued in panes of 20, 5 each, printed checkerwise to contain 4 complete blocks or strips.

The peelable paper backing of Nos. 1777a, 1777b serves as the booklet cover.

Univ. of British Columbia's Museum of Anthropology, 50th Anniv. — A711

1999, Mar. 9 ***Perf. 13½***

1778	A711	46c multicolored	.75	.25

Sailing Ship Marco Polo — A712

1999, Mar. 19 ***Perf. 13x12½***

1779	A712	46c multicolored	.75	.25
a.		Pane of 2, #1779b, Australia #1631 perf. 13½	2.75	2.75
b.		Perf 13 (from No. 1779a)	1.80	1.80

Australia '99 World Stamp Expo. See Australia No. 1631a.

Scenic Highway Type of 1997

No. 1780, Gaspé Peninsula, Highway 132, Quebec. No. 1781, Yellowhead Highway (PTH 16), Manitoba. No. 1782, Dempster Highway 8, Northwest Territories. No. 1783, Discovery Trail, Route 230N, Newfoundland.

1999, Mar. 31 ***Perf. 12½x13***

1780	A673	46c multicolored	.75	.35
1781	A673	46c multicolored	.75	.35
1782	A673	46c multicolored	.75	.35
1783	A673	46c multicolored	.75	.35
a.		Block or strip of 4, #1780-1783	3.00	2.50

Creation of the Nunavut Territory — A713

1999, Apr. 1

1784	A713	46c multicolored	.75	.25

Intl. Year of Older Persons — A714

1999, Apr. 12 ***Perf. 13½***

1785	A714	46c multicolored	.75	.25

A715

1999, Apr. 19 ***Perf. 13***

1786	A715	46c multicolored	1.80	.40

Baisakhi, Religious Holiday of Sikh Canadians, 300th Anniv.

A716

Paintings (Canadian Orchids): No. 1787, Arethusa bulbosa, by Poon-Kuen Chow. No. 1788, Amerorchis rotundifolia, by Yakman Lai. No. 1789, Platanthera psycodes, by Lai. No. 1790, Cypripedium pubescens, by Chow.

Booklet Stamps

1999, Apr. 27 ***Perf. 13x12½***

1787	A716	46c multicolored	.90	.30
1788	A716	46c multicolored	.90	.30
1789	A716	46c multicolored	.90	.30
1790	A716	46c multicolored	.90	.30
a.		Bklt. pane, 3 ea #1787-1790	11.00	
		Complete booklet, #1790a	11.50	
b.		Souvenir sheet, #1787-1790	3.75	3.75

China '99 World Philatelic Exhibition, Beijing. Designs of some stamps contained in No. 1790a extend into selvage of booklet pane.

Issued: No. 1790b, 8/21/99.

Horses A717

No. 1791, Northern Dancer, thoroughbred race horse. No. 1792, Kingsway Skoal, bucking horse. No. 1793, Big Ben, show horse. No. 1794, Armbro Flight, harness race horse.

1999, June 2 ***Perf. 13x13½***

1791	A717	46c multicolored	.90	.40
1792	A717	46c multicolored	.90	.40
1793	A717	46c multicolored	.90	.40
1794	A717	46c multicolored	.90	.40
a.		Block or strip of 4, #1791-1794	3.60	3.00

Booklet Stamps
Self-Adhesive
Serpentine Die Cut 11½

1795	A717	46c like #1791	1.10	.30
1796	A717	46c like #1792	1.10	.30
1797	A717	46c like #1793	1.10	.30
1798	A717	46c like #1794	1.10	.30
a.		Block of 4, #1795-1798	4.40	
b.		Complete booklet, 3 each #1795-1798	13.25	

Nos. 1791-1794 were issued in panes of 16, 4 each, printed checkerwise to contain 4 complete blocks or strips.

Quebec Bar Assoc., 150th Anniv. — A718

1999, June 3 ***Perf. 13½***

1799	A718	46c multicolored	.70	.25

Art Type of 1988

Design: Coq Licorne, by Jean Dallaire (1916-65).

Litho. with Foil Application

1999, July 3 ***Perf. 12½x13¼***

1800	A546	95c Rose gold & multi	1.50	1.10
a.		Silver omitted	*1,250.*	

1999 Pan American Games, Winnipeg A719

Designs: No. 1801, Track & field. No. 1802, Cycling, weight lifting, gymnastics. No. 1803, Swimming, sailboarding, kayaking. No. 1804, Soccer, tennis, medal winners.

1999, July 12 **Litho.** ***Perf. 13¼***

1801	A719	46c multicolored	.75	.35
1802	A719	46c multicolored	.75	.35
1803	A719	46c multicolored	.75	.35
1804	A719	46c multicolored	.75	.35
a.		Block of 4, #1801-1804	3.00	2.50

Issued in panes of 16 stamps.

23rd World Rowing Championships, St. Catharines, Ont. — A720

1999, Aug. 22 ***Perf. 12½x13***

1805	A720	46c multicolored	.75	.25

UPU, 125th Anniv. — A721

1999, Aug. 26

1806	A721	46c multicolored	.75	.25

Airplanes — A722

No. 1807: a, Fokker DR-1, CT-114 Tutors. b, Tutors, H101 Salto sailplane. c, De Havilland DH100 Vampire MKIII. d, Stearman A-75.

No. 1808: a, De Havilland Mosquito FBVI. b, Sopwith F1 Camel. c, De Havilland Canada DHC-3 Otter. d, De Havilland Canada CC-108 Caribou. e, Canadair CL-28 Argus MK 2. f, North American F-86 Sabre 6. g, McDonnell Douglas CF-18 Hornet. h, Sopwith SF-1 Dolphin. i, Armstrong Whitworth Siskin IIIA. j, Canadian Vickers (Northrop) Delta II. k, Sikorsky CH-124A Sea King helicopter. l, Vickers-Armstrong Wellington MKII. m, Avro Anson MKI. n, Canadair (Lockheed) CF-104G Starfighter. o, Burgess-Dunne seaplane. p, Avro 504K.

1999, Sept. 4

1807	A722	Pane of 4	4.40	4.40
a.-d.		46c any single	1.10	.90
1808	A722	Pane of 16	18.00	18.00
a.-p.		46c any single	1.00	1.00

Canadian Intl. Air Show, 50th anniv. (No. 1807). Royal Canadian Air Force, 75th anniv. (No. 1808). Nos. 1808a-1808p are each 56x28mm.

NATO, 50th Anniv. — A723

1999, Sept. 21

1809	A723	46c multicolored	.75	.25

Frontier College, 100th Anniv. A724

1999, Sept. 24 ***Perf. 13x13½***

1810	A724	46c multicolored	.75	.25

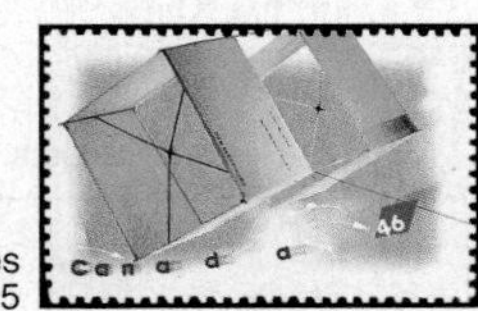

Kites A725

Designs: a, Master Control, sport kite by Lam Hoac (triagular). b, Indian Garden Flying Carpet, edo kite by Skye Morrison (trapezoidal). c, Gibson Girl, manufactured box kite (rectangular). d, Dragon centipede kite by Zhang tian Wei (oval).

Die cut in various patterns

1999, Oct. 1 **Self-Adhesive**

1811		Complete booklet, 2 each #a.-d.	8.00	
a.-d.	A725	46c any single	1.00	.35

A726

A727

Millennium A728

Self-Adhesive (46c)

1999, Oct. 12 Holography *Die Cut*

1812	A726 46c silver	1.00	.40
	Pane of 4	4.75	4.75

Litho.

Perf. 13¼

1813	A727 55c multicolored	1.00	.80
	Pane of 4	4.75	4.75

Engr.

Perf. 12¾

1814	A728 95c brown	1.70	1.50
	Pane of 4	7.00	7.00
	Nos. 1812-1814 (3)	3.70	2.70

Nos. 1812-1814 each exist in souvenir sheets of 1 with decorative border.

Christmas — A729

1999, Nov. 4 Litho. *Perf. 13¼*

1815	A729 46c Angel, drum	.75	.25
a.	Booklet pane of 10	7.50	*8.00*
	Complete booklet	8.00	
b.	Horiz. pair, imperf. btwn.	*1,750.*	
1816	A729 55c Angel, toys	.85	.35
a.	Booklet pane of 5 + label	4.25	*7.50*
	Complete booklet	4.50	
1817	A729 95c Angel, candle	1.50	.75
a.	Booklet pane of 5 + label	8.00	*10.00*
	Complete booklet	8.50	
b.	Horiz. pair, imperf. btwn.	*1,200.*	
	Nos. 1815-1817 (3)	3.10	1.35

Souvenir Sheets

Millennium — A730

No. 1818 — Media Technologies: a, IMAX movies. b, Softimage animation software. c, Ted Rogers, Sr. (1900-39) and radio tube. d, Invention of radio facsimile device for transmission of photographs for publishing by Sir William Stephenson (1896-1989).

No. 1819 — Canadian Entertainment: a, Calgary Stampede. b, Performers from Cirque du Soleil. c, Hockey Night in Canada. d, La Soiree du Hockey.

No. 1820 — Entertainers: a, Portia White (1911-68), singer. b, Glenn Gould (1932-82), pianist. c, Guy Lombardo (1902-77), band leader. d, Félix Leclerc (1914-88), singer, guitarist.

No. 1821 — Fostering Canadian Talent: a, Royal Canadian Academy of Arts (men viewing painting). b, Canada Council (sky, musical staff, "A"). c, National Film Board of Canada. d, Canadian Broadcasting Corporation.

No. 1822 — Medical Innovators: a, Sir Frederick Banting (1891-1941), co-discoverer of insulin, syringe and dog. b, Dr. Armand Frappier (1904-91), microbiologist, holding flask. c, Dr. Hans Selye (1907-82), endocrinologist, and molecular diagram. d, Maude Abbott (1869-1940), pathologist, and roses.

No. 1823 — Social Progress: a, Nun, doctor, hospital. b, Statue of woman holding decree. c, Alphonse Desjardins (1854-1920) and wife Dorimène (1858-1932), credit union founders, and credit union emblem. d, Father Moses Coady (1882-1959), educator of adults.

No. 1824 — Charity: a, Canadian International Development Agency (hands and tools). b, Dr. Lucille Teasdale (1929-96), hospital administrator in Uganda. c, Marathon of Hope inspired by Terry Fox (1958-81). d, Meals on Wheels program.

No. 1825 — Humanitarians and Peacekeepers: a, Raoul Dandurand (1861-1942), b, Pauline Vanier (1898-1991), Red Cross volunteer, and Elizabeth Smellie (1884-1968), head of various nursing services. c, Lester B. Pearson (1897-1972), prime minister, and Nobel Peace Prize winner, and dove. d, Amputee and shadow (Ottawa Convention on Land Mines).

No. 1826 — Canada's First People: a, Chief Pontiac (c. 1720-69). b, Tom Longboat (1887-1949), marathon runner. c, Inuit sculpture of shaman. d, Medicine man.

No. 1827 — Canada's Cultural Fabric: a, Norse boat, L'Anse aux Meadows. b, Immigrants on Halifax's Pier 21. c, Neptune Theater, Halifax (head of Neptune). d, Stratford Festival (actor and theater).

No. 1828 — Literary Legends: a, W. O. Mitchell (1914-98), novelist, and prairie scene. b, Gratien Gélinas (1909-99), actor and playwright, and stars. c, Le Cercle du Livre de France book club. d, Harlequin paperback books.

No. 1829 — Great Thinkers: a, Marshall McLuhan (1911-80), philosopher, and television set. b, Northrop Frye (1912-91), literary critic, and word "code." c, Roger Lemelin (1919-92), novelist, and cast of "The Plouffe Family" TV series. d, Hilda Marion Neatby (1904-75), historian, and farm scene.

No. 1830 — A Tradition of Generosity: a, Hart Massey (1823-96), Hart House, University of Toronto. b, Dorothy (1899-1965) and Izaak Killam (1885-1955), philantropists, and molecular model. c, Eric Lafferty Harvie (1892-1975), philantropist, and mountain scene. d, Macdonald Stewart Foundation.

No. 1831 — Engineering and Technological Marvels: a, Map of Rogers Pass, locomotive, tunnel diggers. b, Manic Dams. c, Canadian satellites, Remote Manipulator Arm. d, CN Tower.

No. 1832 — Fathers of Invention: a, George Klein (1904-92), gearwheels. b, Abraham Gesner (1797-1864), beaker of kerosene and lamp. c, Alexander Graham Bell (1847-1922), passenger-carrying kite, hydrofoil. d, Joseph-Armand Bombardier (1907-64), snowmobile.

No. 1833 — Food: a, Sir Charles Saunders (1867-1937), Marquis wheat. b, Pablum. c, Dr. Archibald Gowanlock Huntsman (1883-1973), marketer of frozen fish. d, Products of McCain Foods, Ltd., tractor.

No. 1834 — Enterprising Giants: a, Hudson's Bay Company (Colonist, Indian, canoe). b, Bell Canada Enterprises (earth, satellite, string of binary digits). c, Vachon Co. snack cakes. d, George Weston Limited (Baked goods, eggs).

1999-2000 Litho. *Perf. 13¼*

1818	A730 Pane of 4	6.50	6.50
a.-d.	46c any single	1.60	1.25
1819	A730 Pane of 4	6.50	6.50
a.-d.	46c any single	1.60	1.25
1820	A730 Pane of 4	6.50	6.50
a.-d.	46c any single	1.60	1.25
1821	A730 Pane of 4	6.50	6.50
a.-d.	46c any single	1.60	1.25
1822	A730 Pane of 4	6.50	6.50
a.-d.	46c any single	1.60	1.25
1823	A730 Pane of 4	6.50	6.50
a.-d.	46c any single	1.60	1.25
1824	A730 Pane of 4	6.50	6.50
a.-d.	46c any single	1.60	1.25
1825	A730 Pane of 4	6.50	6.50
a.-d.	46c any single	1.60	1.25
1826	A730 Pane of 4	6.50	6.50
a.-d.	46c any single	1.60	1.25
1827	A730 Pane of 4	6.50	6.50
a.-d.	46c any single	1.60	1.25
1828	A730 Pane of 4	6.50	6.50
a.-d.	46c any single	1.60	1.25
1829	A730 Pane of 4	6.50	6.50
a.-d.	46c any single	1.60	1.25
1830	A730 Pane of 4	6.50	6.50
a.-d.	46c any single	1.60	1.25
1831	A730 Pane of 4	6.50	6.50
a.-d.	46c any single	1.60	1.25
1832	A730 Pane of 4	6.50	6.50
a.-d.	46c any single	1.60	1.25
1833	A730 Pane of 4	6.50	6.50
a.-d.	46c any single	1.60	1.25
1834	A730 Pane of 4	6.50	6.50
a.-d.	46c any single	1.60	1.25
	Nos. 1818-1834 (17)	110.50	110.50

Issued: Nos. 1818-1821, 12/17; Nos. 1822-1825, 1/17/00; Nos. 1826-1830, 2/17/00; Nos. 1831-1834, 3/17/00.

Stamps similar to these were printed in a hardcover book produced by Canada Post Sept. 15, 1999 that sold for $59.99. Stamps from souvenir panes show a distinct upward turn of the tails of the nines in the small 1999 date at upper left. The tails of the nines on stamps from the book are flat.

Millennium — A731

2000, Jan. 1 *Perf. 13x12½*

1835	A731 46c multicolored	.75	.25

New Year 2000 (Year of the Dragon) — A732

Litho. & Embossed

2000, Jan. 5 *Perf. 12½x12¾*

1836	A732 46c multicolored	.75	.25
a.	Red and tagging omitted	1,100.	

Souvenir Sheet

Perf. 13¾x13¼

1837	A732 95c multicolored	1.70	1.70
a.	Orange and tagging omitted	*1,500.*	

No. 1837 has rounded corners and contains one 56x29mm stamp.

50th National Hockey League All-Star Game A733

Famous NHL players: a, Wayne Gretzky (Oilers jersey No. 99). b, Gordie Howe (Red Wings jersey No. 9). c, Maurice Richard (red, white and blue Canadiens jersey No. 9). d, Doug Harvey (Canadiens jersey No. 2). e, Bobby Orr (Bruins jersey No. 4). f, Jacques Plante (Canadiens jersey No. 1).

2000, Feb. 5 Litho. *Perf. 12¾*

1838	Pane of 6	4.50	4.50
a.-f.	A733 46c any single	.75	.60

Bird Type of 1996

Designs: Nos. 1839, 1843, Canada warbler. Nos. 1840, 1844, Osprey. Nos. 1841, 1845, Pacific loon. Nos. 1842, 1846, Blue jay.

2000, Mar. 1 Litho. *Perf. 12½x13¼*

1839	A650 46c multi	.90	.30
1840	A650 46c multi	.90	.30
1841	A650 46c multi	.90	.30
1842	A650 46c multi	.90	.30
a.	Block or strip of 4	3.60	2.50

Booklet Stamps

Self-Adhesive

Die Cut 11½x11¼

1843	A650 46c multi	.90	.30
1844	A650 46c multi	.90	.30
1845	A650 46c multi	.90	.30
1846	A650 46c multi	.90	.30
a.	Booklet pane, 2 each #1843-1844, 1 each #1845-1846	5.50	
b.	Booklet pane, 2 each #1845-1846, 1 each #1843-1844	5.50	
	Complete bklt., #1846a, 1846b	11.00	

Nos. 1839-1842 were issued in panes of 20, 5 each printed checkerwise to contain 4 complete blocks or strips.

Supreme Court, 125th Anniv. A734

2000, Apr. 10 *Perf. 12½x13¼*

1847	A734 46c multi	.75	.25

Ritual of the Calling of an Engineer, 75th Anniv. — A735

2000, Apr. 25

1848	A735 46c multi	.75	.25
a.	Tete-beche pair	1.50	1.10
b.	Silver ("CANADA 46") omitted	*2,250.*	

Decorated Rural Mailboxes — A736

Mailboxes with: No. 1849, Ship, fish, house designs. No. 1850, Flower, cow and church designs. No. 1851, Tractor design. No. 1852, Goose head, house designs.

Booklet Stamps

Perf. 12½x13¼ on 3 sides

2000, Apr. 28

1849	A736 46c multi	.90	.40
1850	A736 46c multi	.90	.40
1851	A736 46c multi	.90	.40
1852	A736 46c multi	.90	.40
a.	Block of 4, #1849-1852	3.60	2.75
b.	Bklt. pane, 3 ea #1849-1852	11.00	
	Complete booklet, #1852a	11.50	

Picture Frame A737

Self-Adhesive

Serpentine Die Cut 11½

2000, Apr. 28

1853	A737 46c multi	.90	.60
a.	Booklet pane of 5 + 5 different labels	4.50	
	Complete booklet, #1853a	5.00	
b.	Pane of 25 + stickers	*75.00*	

No. 1853b sold for $24.95 each for one or two panes, and $22.95 for three to ten panes. Twenty-five self-adhesive, die cut address labels and reproductions of a photo sent in by the customer are on the reverse of No. 1853b. These panes were not available at post offices or through the philatelic bureau, but special orders from the printer, Ashton-Potter. The front cover of the booklet containing No. 1853a served as the order blank for No. 1853b.

See Nos. 1872, 1882.

A738

A739

A740

A741

A742

A743

A744

A745

A746

Fresh Waters — A747

Self-Adhesive

Serpentine Die Cut 2½ Horiz.

2000, Feb. 23

1854 Complete booklet, #a.-e. 7.50
- *a.* A738 55c multi 1.50 .90
- *b.* A739 55c multi 1.50 .90
- *c.* A740 55c multi 1.50 .90
- *d.* A741 55c multi 1.50 .90
- *e.* A742 55c multi 1.50 .90

1855 Complete booklet, #a.-e. 9.50
- *a.* A743 95c multi 1.90 1.50
- *b.* A744 95c multi 1.90 1.50
- *c.* A745 95c multi 1.90 1.50
- *d.* A746 95c multi 1.90 1.50
- *e.* A747 95c multi 1.90 1.50

Queen Mother (b. 1900) A748

2000, May 23 ***Perf. 13x13¼***

1856 A748 95c multi 1.50 .90
- *a.* Imperf., pair *750.00*

Boys and Girls Clubs of Canada, Cent. — A749

2000, June 1 ***Perf. 13***

1857 A749 46c multi .75 .25

World Session of Seventh Day Adventist Church, Toronto A750

2000, June 29 ***Perf. 13½x13¼***

1858 A750 46c multi .90 .25

Stampin' the Future Children's Stamp Design Contest Winners A751

Designs: No. 1859, Rainbow, space vehicle, astronauts, flag, by Rosalie Anne Nardelli. No. 1860, Three children in space vehicle, three children on ground, by Sarah Lutgen. No. 1861, Children and map of Canada, by Christine Weera. No. 1862, Two astronauts in space vehicle, planets, by Andrew Wright.

2000, July 1 ***Perf. 13¼***

1859 A751 46c multi .75 .35
1860 A751 46c multi .75 .35
1861 A751 46c multi .75 .35
1862 A751 46c multi .75 .35
- *a.* Block or strip, #1859-1862 3.00 2.50
- *b.* Souvenir sheet, #1859-1862 4.75 3.25

Art Type of 1988

Design: The Artist at Niagara, by Cornelius Krieghoff.

Litho. with Foil Application

2000, July 7 ***Perf. 12½x13¼***

1863 A546 95c multi 1.40 .90

Tall Ships in Halifax Harbor — A752

Various ships: No. 1864, Denomination at L. No. 1865, Denomination at R.

Self-Adhesive

Booklet Stamps

Serpentine Die Cut 4¾x5

2000, July 19 **Litho.**

1864 A752 46c multicolored .90 .40
1865 A752 46c multicolored .90 .40
- *a.* Pair, #1864-1865 1.80
- *b.* Booklet, 5 #1864a 9.00

Dept. of Labor, Cent. — A753

2000, Sept. 1 ***Perf. 12½x13¼***

1866 A753 46c multi .75 .25

Petro-Canada, 25th Anniv. — A754

Self-Adhesive

Booklet Stamp

2000, Sept. 13 ***Die Cut***

1867 A754 46c multi .90 .40
- *a.* Booklet pane of 12 11.00
- Booklet, #1867a 11.50
- *b.* Die cutting inverted (2 points jut at T, L) 7.50 7.50

No. 1867a is the cover of an informational booklet about Petro-Canada. No. 1867b was issued in collector packs.

Cetaceans — A755

No. 1868, Monodon monoceros. No. 1869, Balaenoptera musculus. No. 1870, Balaena mysticetus. No. 1871, Delphinapterus leucas.

2000, Oct. 2 ***Perf. 12½x13***

1868 A755 46c multi .75 .30
1869 A755 46c multi .75 .30
1870 A755 46c multi .75 .30
1871 A755 46c multi .75 .30
- *a.* Block of 4, #1868-1871 3.00 2.25

Christmas A756

Self-Adhesive

Booklet Stamp

Serpentine Die Cut 11¾

2000, Oct. 5

1872 A756 46c multi .90 .80
- *a.* Booklet pane of 5 + 5 labels 4.50
- Booklet, #1872a 5.00
- *b.* Pane of 25 + stickers 75.00

See No. 1882f.

Christmas A757

Designs: 46c, Adoration of the shepherds. 55c, Creche. 95c Flight into Egypt.

2000, Nov. 3 ***Perf. 13¼***

1873 A757 46c multi .75 .25
- *a.* Booklet pane of 10 7.50 *9.00*
- Booklet, #1873a 8.00

1874 A757 55c multi .90 .35
- *a.* Booklet pane of 6 5.50 *6.50*
- Booklet, #1874a 6.00

1875 A757 95c multi 1.50 .65
- *a.* Booklet pane of 6 9.00 *10.50*
- Booklet, #1875a 9.50

Nos. 1873-1875 (3) 3.15 1.25

Regiments A758

No. 1876, Lord Strathcona's Horse Regiment. No. 1877, Les Voltigeurs de Quebec.

2000, Nov. 11 ***Perf. 13¼x13***

1876 A758 46c multi .75 .30
1877 A758 46c multi .75 .30
- *a.* Pair, #1876-1877 1.50 .90

Maple Leaves A759

Animals A760

Designs: 60c, Red fox. 75c, Gray wolf. $1.05, White-tailed deer.

Coil Stamps

Serpentine Die Cut 8½ Horiz.

2000, Dec. 28 **Self-Adhesive**

1878 A759 47c multi .75 .25
- *a.* Blue inscriptions omitted *600.00*

1879 A760 60c multi 1.00 .35
- *a.* Booklet pane of 6 10.00

1880 A760 75c multi 1.20 .45
1881 A760 $1.05 multi 1.70 .75
- *a.* Booklet pane of 6 11.00

Nos. 1878-1881 (4) 4.65 1.80

Nos. 1879a and 1881a are complete booklets. See No. 1927.

Frame Type of 2000

No. 1882: a, Silver. b, Like #1853. c, Mahogany. d, Love (roses). e, Christmas.

Booklet Stamps

Serpentine Die Cut 11¾

2000, Dec. 28 **Self-Adhesive**

1882 Bklt. pane of 5 + 5 labels 4.50
- *a.-e.* A737 47c Any single .90 .90
- Booklet, #1882 5.00
- *f.* Pane of 25 + stickers 75.00

No. 1882f was available only by special order.

New Year 2001 (Year of the Snake) A761

Litho. & Embossed

2001, Jan. 5 ***Perf. 13¼***

1883 A761 47c green & multi .75 .25
- *a.* Gold omitted 1,100.

Souvenir Sheet

1884 A761 $1.05 brown & multi 2.25 2.25

National Hockey League Stars A762

No. 1885: a, Jean Beliveau (Montreal Canadiens jersey No. 4). b, Terry Sawchuk (goalie in Detroit Red Wings uniform). c, Eddie Shore (Boston Bruins jersey No. 2). d, Denis Potvin (Islanders jersey No. 5). e, Bobby Hull (Chicago Black Hawks jersey No. 9). f, Syl Apps, Sr. (Toronto Maple Leafs jersey).

Perf. 12½x13 on 3 sides

2001, Jan. 18 **Litho.**

1885 Sheet of 6 + 3 labels 4.50 4.50
a.-f. A762 47c Any single .75 .45
g. Strip of 3 (#1885a, 1885c, 1885e), blue circle and text omitted 5,500.

Bird Type of 1996

Designs: Nos. 1886, 1890, Golden eagle. Nos. 1887, 1891, Arctic tern. Nos. 1888, 1892, Rock ptarmigan. Nos. 1889, 1893, Lapland longspur.

2001, Feb. 1 ***Perf. 12½x13***

1886 A650 47c multi .75 .30
1887 A650 47c multi .75 .30
1888 A650 47c multi .75 .30
1889 A650 47c multi .75 .30
a. Block or strip of 4, #1886-1889 3.00 2.25

Booklet Stamps
Self-Adhesive

Die Cut Perf 11½x11¼

1890 A650 47c multi .90 .35
1891 A650 47c multi .90 .35
1892 A650 47c multi .90 .35
1893 A650 47c multi .90 .35
a. Booklet pane, 2 each #1890-1891, 1 each #1892-1893 5.50
b. Booklet pane, 2 each #1892-1893, 1 each #1890-1891 5.50
Booklet, #1893a, 1893b 11.00

Nos. 1886-1889 were issued in panes of 20, 5 each printed checkerwise to contain 4 complete blocks or strips.

Games of La Francophonie, Ottawa and Hull — A763

2001, Feb. 28 ***Perf. 13¼***

1894 47c High jumper .75 .25
1895 47c Dancer .75 .25
a. A763 Horiz. pair, #1894-1895 1.50 .90

World Figure Skating Championships, Vancouver — A764

Designs: No. 1896, Pairs. No. 1897, Ice dancing. No. 1898, Men's singles. No. 1899, Women's singles.

2001, Mar. 19 ***Perf. 13x12½***

1896 A764 47c shown .75 .30
1897 A764 47c multi .75 .30
1898 A764 47c multi .75 .30
1899 A764 47c multi .75 .30
a. Block of 4, #1896-1899 3.00 2.25

First Canadian Postage Stamps, 150th Anniv. — A765

Litho. & Engr.

2001, Apr. 6 ***Perf. 13***

1900 A765 47c multi .75 .25

Toronto Blue Jays Baseball Team, 25th Anniv. A766

Self-Adhesive

2001, Apr. 9 **Litho.** ***Die Cut***

1901 A766 47c multi .90 .25
a. Booklet pane of 8 7.25

No. 1901a is a complete booklet.

Summit of the Americas, Quebec — A767

2001, Apr. 20 ***Perf. 13¼x13***

1902 A767 47c multi .75 .25

Tourist Attractions — A768

No. 1903: a, Butchart Gardens, British Columbia. b, Apple Blossom Festival, Nova Scotia. c, White Pass and Yukon Route. d, Sugar bushes, Quebec. e, Niagara-on-the-Lake, Ontario.

No. 1904: a, The Forks, Manitoba. b, Barkerville, British Columbia. c, Canadian Tulip Festival, Ontario. d, Auyuittuq National Park, Nunavut. e, Signal Hill National Historic Site, Newfoundland.

Self-Adhesive

2001, May 11 ***Die Cut Perf. 11x11¼***

1903 Booklet of 5 4.50
a.-e. A768 60c Any single .90 .75
1904 Booklet of 5 8.50
a.-e. A768 $1.05 Any single 1.70 1.10

See Nos. 1952-1953, 1989-1990, 2019-2023.

Armenian Church, 1,700th Anniv. — A769

2001, May 16 ***Perf. 13x12½***

1905 A769 47c multi .75 .25

Royal Military College of Canada, 125th Anniv. — A770

2001, June 1 ***Perf. 12½x13***

1906 A770 47c multi .75 .25

Eighth Intl. Amateur Athletic Federation World Championships, Edmonton — A771

2001, June 25 ***Perf. 12¾x12½***

1907 47c Pole vault .75 .25
1908 47c Runner .75 .25
a. A771 Pair, #1907-1908 1.50 .90

Pierre Elliott Trudeau (1919-2000), Prime Minister — A772

2001, July 1 ***Perf. 13x12½***

1909 A772 47c multi .75 .25
a. Souvenir sheet of 4 3.25 3.25

Roses — A773

Designs: Nos. 1910a, 1911, Morden Centennial. Nos. 1910b, 1912, Agnes. Nos. 1910c, 1913, Champlain. Nos. 1910d, 1914, Canadian White Star.

Souvenir Sheet

2001, Aug. 1 ***Perf. 12½x13***

1910 Pane of 4 4.40 4.40
a.-d. A773 47c Any single 1.10 1.10

Booklet Stamps

Die Cut

1911 A773 47c multi .75 .30
1912 A773 47c multi .75 .30
1913 A773 47c multi .75 .30
1914 A773 47c multi .75 .30
a. Booklet pane, #1911-1914 3.00
Booklet, 3 #1914a 9.00

Phila Nippon '01, Japan (No. 1910). Die cutting on Nos. 1911-1914 has "thorn" at the center of each side, pointing outward at top and left and toward the design at bottom and right.

Great Peace of Montreal, 300th Anniv. — A774

2001, Aug. 3 ***Perf. 12½x13***

1915 A774 47c multi .75 .25

Art Type of 1988

Design: The Space Between Columns #21 (Italian), by Jack Shadbolt.

Litho. with Foil Application

2001, Aug. 24 ***Perf. 13x13¼***

1916 A546 $1.05 multi 1.70 .90

Shriners — A775

2001, Sept. 19 **Litho.** ***Perf. 13¼x13***

1917 A775 47c multi .75 .25

Frame Type of 2000 Inscribed "Domestic Lettermail / Poste-lettres du régime intérieur"

No. 1918: a, Like #1882a. b, Like #1882b. c, Baby toys and flowers. d, Like #1882d. e, Like #1882e.

Serpentine Die Cut 11¾

2001, Sept. 21 **Self-Adhesive**

1918 Bklt. pane of 5 + 5 labels 5.00
a.-e. A737 (47c) Any single .90 .90
Booklet, #1918 5.00
f. Pane of 25 + stickers 75.00
g. Pane of 10 + stickers 60.00

Nos. 1918f and 1918g were available only by special order.

Theater Anniversaries — A776

Designs: No. 1919, Théatre du Nouveau Monde, Montreal, 50th anniv. No. 1920, Grand Theater, London, Ont., cent.

2001, Sept. 28 ***Perf. 12½x12¾***

1919 A776 47c multi .70 .25
1920 A776 47c multi .70 .25
a. Horiz. pair, #1919-1920 1.40 .90

Hot Air Balloons A777

Background colors: a, Green. b, Blue violet. c, Red violet. d, Olive.

Self-Adhesive

2001, Oct. 1 ***Die Cut***

1921 Booklet, 2 each #a-d 7.25
a.-d. A777 47c Any single .90 .40

Christmas A778

Illuminated trees and: 47c, Horse-drawn sleigh. 60c, Skaters. $1.05, Children making snowman.

2001, Nov. 1 ***Perf. 12½x13¼***

1922 A778 47c multi .75 .25
a. Booklet pane of 10 7.50 7.50
Booklet, #1922a 8.00
1923 A778 60c multi .95 .40
a. Booklet pane of 6 5.75 5.50
Booklet, #1923a 6.25
1924 A778 $1.05 multi 1.65 .60
a. Booklet pane of 6 10.00 10.00
Booklet, #1924a 10.50

YMCA in Canada, 150th Anniv. — A779

2001, Nov. 8 *Perf. 13¼*
1925 A779 47c multi .75 .25

Royal Canadian Legion, 75th Anniv. — A780

2001, Nov. 11 *Perf. 12½x13*
1926 A780 47c multi .75 .25

Maple Leaves Type of 2000, Traditional Handiwork Type of 1999 and

Flag and Canada Post Headquarters, Ottawa — A781

Designs: 65c, Jewelry making, horiz. 77c, Basket weaving, horiz. $1.25, Sculpture, horiz.

Self-Adhesive
Coil Stamps
Serpentine Die Cut 8½ Horiz.

2002, Jan. 2

1927 A759 48c multi	.75	.25
1928 A684 65c multi	1.00	.30
a. Booklet of 6	6.00	
1929 A684 77c multi	1.10	.40
1930 A684 $1.25 multi	1.80	.65
a. Booklet of 6	11.00	

Booklet Stamp
Serpentine Die Cut 8½

1931 A781 48c multi	.75	.25
a. Booklet of 10	7.50	
b. Booklet of 30	22.50	
c. Blue omitted	350.00	
Nos. 1927-1931 (5)	5.40	1.85

By separating the booklet along the columns of rouletting, No. 1931b could be broken up into three separately obtainable examples of No. 1931a. See No. 1991.

Reign of Queen Elizabeth II, 50th Anniv. A782

2002, Jan. 2 *Perf. 13¼x12½*

1932 A782 48c multi	.70	.25
a. Imperf, pair	*1,100.*	
b. Gold omitted		1,300.

New Year 2002 (Year of the Horse) — A783

Horse and: 48c, Bamboo leaves. $1.25, Peach blossoms.

Litho. & Embossed With Foil Application

2002, Jan. 3 *Perf. 13¼*

1933 A783 48c multi	.75	.25
a. Foil (horse) omitted	*1,100.*	

Souvenir Sheet

1934 A783 $1.25 multi 2.25 2.25

National Hockey League Stars A784

No. 1935: a, Tim Horton (Toronto Maple Leafs jersey No. 7). b, Guy Lafleur (Montreal Canadiens jersey No. 10). c, Howie Morenz (Canadiens jersey, with brown gloves). d, Glenn Hall (Chicago Black Hawks jersey No. 1). e, Red Kelly (Maple Leafs jersey No. 4). f, Phil Esposito (Boston Bruins jersey no. 7).

Perf. 12½x13 on 3 Sides

2002, Jan. 12

1935 Pane of 6 + 3 labels	5.00	5.00
a.-f. A784 48c Any single	.80	.60

2002 Winter Olympics, Salt Lake City — A785

Designs: No. 1936, Short track speed skating. No. 1937, Curling. No. 1938, Freestyle aerial skiing. No. 1939, Women's hockey.

2002, Jan. 25 *Perf. 13¼x13*

1936 A785 48c multi	.75	.35
1937 A785 48c multi	.75	.35
1938 A785 48c multi	.75	.35
1939 A785 48c multi	.75	.35
a. Block or strip of 4, #1936-1939	3.00	2.50

Appointment of First Canadian Governor General, 50th Anniv. — A786

2002, Feb. 1 *Perf. 13¼x12½*
1940 A786 48c multi .75 .25

Universities — A787

Design: No. 1941, University of Manitoba, 125th anniv. No. 1942, Laval University, 150th anniv. No. 1943, University of Trinity College, 150th anniv. No. 1944, Saint Mary's University, Halifax, 200th anniv.

2002 **Booklet Stamp** *Perf. 13½*

1941 A787 48c multi	.75	.25
a. Booklet pane of 8	6.00	6.00
Booklet, #1941a	6.50	
1942 A787 48c multi	.75	.25
a. Booklet pane of 8	6.00	6.00
Booklet, #1942a	6.50	
1943 A787 48c multi	.75	.25
a. Booklet pane of 8	6.00	6.00
Booklet, #1943a	6.50	
1944 A787 48c multi	.75	.25
a. Booklet pane of 8	6.00	6.00
Booklet, #1944a	6.50	
Nos. 1941-1944 (4)	3.00	1.00

Issued: No. 1941, 2/28. No. 1942, 4/4. No. 1943, 4/30. No. 1944, 5/27.

Art Type of 1988

Design: Church and Horse, by Alex Colville.

Litho. with Foil Application

2002, Mar. 22 *Perf. 12½x13*

1945 A546 $1.25 multi	2.00	1.10
a. Foil only (all other colors and tagging omitted)	*1,400.*	
b. Imperf, pair	*1,250.*	

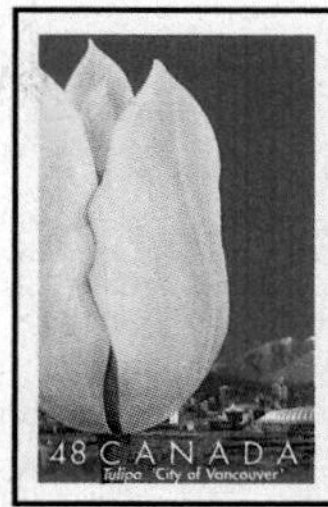
Tulips — A788

Tulip varieties: a, City of Vancouver. b, Monte Carlo. c, Ottawa. d, The Bishop.

No. 1947: a, Like #1946a. b, Like #1946b. c, Like #1946c. d, Like #1946d.

Self-Adhesive

2002, May 3 **Litho.** ***Die Cut***

1946 Booklet pane of 4	3.00	
a.-d. A788 48c Any single	.75	.30
Booklet, 2 #1946	6.00	

Souvenir Sheet
Perf. 13x12½

1947 Pane of 4	3.00	3.00
a.-d. A788 48c Any single	.75	.75

Issued: No. 1946, 5/3; No. 1947, 8/30.

Dendronepthea Giagantea and Dendronepthea Corals — A789

Tubastrea and Echinogorgia Corals — A790

North Atlantic Pink Tree, Pacific Orange Cup and North Pacific Horn Corals — A791

North Atlantic Giant Orange Tree and Black Corals — A792

2002, May 19 *Perf. 12½x13*

1948 A789 48c multi	.75	.30
1949 A790 48c multi	.75	.30
1950 A791 48c multi	.75	.30
1951 A792 48c multi	.75	.30
a. Block of 4, #1948-1951	3.00	2.00
b. Souvenir sheet, #1948-1951, perf. 13¼x13	3.75	3.75

See Hong Kong Nos. 979-982.

Tourist Attractions Type of 2001

No. 1952: a, Yukon Quest, Yukon Territory. b, Icefields Parkway, Alberta. c, Agawa Canyon, Ontario. d, Old Port of Montreal, Quebec. e, Kings Landing, New Brunswick.

No. 1953: a, Northern Lights, Northwest Territories. b, Stanley Park, Vancouver, British Columbia. c, Head-Smashed-In Buffalo Jump, Alberta. d, Saguenay Fjord, Quebec. e, Peggy's Cove, Nova Scotia.

Self-Adhesive

2002, June 1 ***Die Cut Perf. 11x11¼***

1952 Booklet of 5	5.50	
a.-e. A768 65c Any single	1.10	.75
1953 Booklet of 5	10.00	
a.-e. A768 $1.25 Any single	2.00	1.10

Sculpture — A793

Designs: No. 1954, Embacle, by Charles Daudelin. No. 1955, Lumberjacks, by Leo Mol.

2002, June 10 *Perf. 13¼*

1954 A793 48c multi	.75	.25
1955 A793 48c multi	.75	.25
a. Horiz. or vert. pair, #1954-1955	1.50	.90

Canadian Postmasters and Assistants Association, Cent. — A794

2002, July 5 *Perf. 13¼x12½*
1956 A794 48c multi .75 .25

Printed in panes of 16 stamps + 12 labels.

17th World Youth Day, Toronto — A795

Self-Adhesive
Booklet Stamp

2002, July 23 ***Die Cut***

1957 A795 48c multi	.75	.30
a. Booklet of 8	6.00	

Public Services International World Congress, Ottawa — A796

2002, Sept. 4 *Perf. 12½x13*
1958 A796 48c multi .75 .25

Public Pensions, 75th Anniv. — A797

2002, Sept. 10 *Perf. 13¼*
1959 A797 48c multi .75 .25

Souvenir Sheet

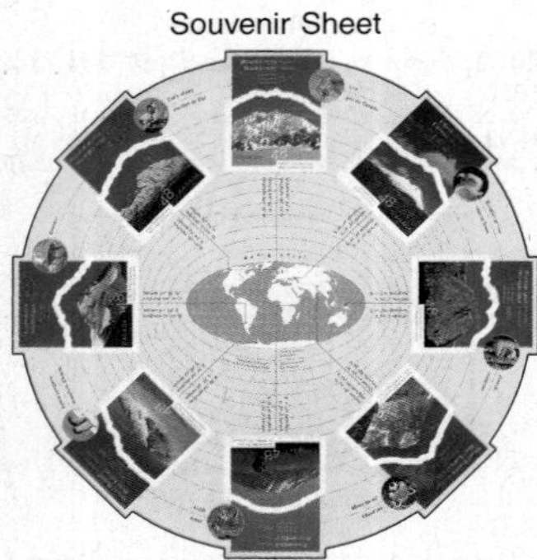

Intl. Year of Mountains — A798

No. 1960: a, Mt. Logan, Canada. b, Mt. Elbrus, Russia. c, Puncak Jaya, Indonesia. d, Mt. Everest, Nepal and China. e, Mt. Kilimanjaro, Tanzania. f, Vinson Massif, Antarctica. g, Mt. Aconcagua, Argentina. h, Mt. McKinley, Alaska.

Self-Adhesive

2002, Oct. 1 ***Die Cut***

1960 A798 Pane of 8 + 8 labels 7.25
a.-h. 48c Any single .90 *1.10*

World Teachers' Day — A799

2002, Oct. 4 ***Perf. 12½x13***

1961 A799 48c multi .75 .25

Toronto Stock Exchange, 150th Anniv. — A800

2002, Oct. 24

1962 A800 48c multi .75 .25

Communication Technology Centenaries — A801

Part of map of North America and: No. 1963, Sir Sandford Fleming (1827-1915), cable-laying ship. No. 1964, Guglielmo Marconi (1874-1937), radio and transmission towers.

2002, Oct. 31 ***Perf. 13x12½***

1963 48c multi .75 .25
1964 48c multi .75 .25
a. A801 Horiz. pair, #1963-1964 1.50 1.10

Cent. of first telegraph message sent over transpacific cable (No. 1963); first transatlantic radio message (No. 1964).

Christmas A802

Art by aboriginals: 48c, Genesis, by Daphne Odjig. 65c, Winter Travel, by Cecil Youngfox. $1.25, Mary and Child, sculpture by Irene Katak Angutitaq.

2002, Nov. 4 ***Perf. 12½x13***

1965 A802 48c multi .75 .25
a. Booklet pane of 10 7.50 7.50
Booklet, #1965a 8.00
1966 A802 65c multi 1.00 .40
a. Booklet pane of 6 6.00 6.00
Booklet, #1966a 6.50
1967 A802 $1.25 multi 2.00 .75
a. Booklet pane of 6 12.00 12.00
Booklet, #1967a 12.50
Nos. 1965-1967 (3) 3.75 1.40

Quebec Symphony Orchestra, Cent. A803

2002, Nov. 7

1968 A803 48c multi .80 .30

New Year 2003 (Year of the Ram) — A804

Litho. & Embossed with Foil Application

2003, Jan. 3 ***Perf. 13***

1969 A804 48c shown .75 .25
a. Gold omitted *200.00*
b. Imperf, pair *1,750.*

Souvenir Sheet

Perf. 13¼

1970 A804 $1.25 Ram, diff. 2.50 2.50

No. 1970 contains one 33x58mm stamp. Slits replace perforations on the vertical sides of the stamps between the point of the acute angle made with the curving perforations and the point perpendicular to where the perforations on the opposite side form the obtuse angle with the curving perforations.

National Hockey League Stars A805

Designs: Nos. 1971a, 1972a, Frank Mahovlich (orange panel). Nos. 1971b, 1972b, Raymond Bourque (lilac panel). Nos. 1971c, 1972c, Serge Savard (blue panel). Nos. 1971d, 1972d, Stan Mikita (red violet panel). Nos. 1971e, 1972e, Mike Bossy (bright pink panel). Nos. 1971f, 1972f, Bill Durnan (green panel).

Perf. 12½x13¼ on 3 Sides

2003, Jan. 18

1971 Pane of 6 + 3 labels 14.00 —
a.-f. A805 48c Any single 2.25 1.50

Self-Adhseive

Die Cut

1972 Pane of 6 60.00 —
a.-f. A805 48c Any single 6.50 1.50

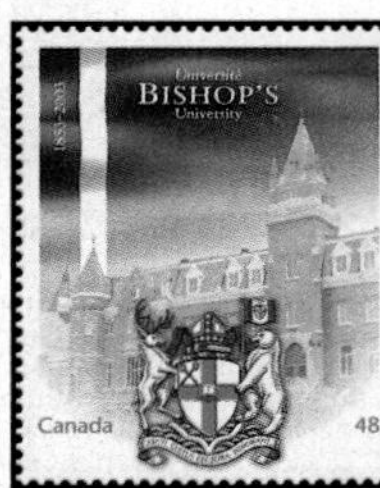

Universities A806

Design: No. 1973, Bishop's University, Lennoxville, Quebec, 150th anniv. No. 1974, University of Western Ontario, London, Ont., 125th anniv. No. 1975, St. Francis Xavier University, Antigonish, N. S., 150th Anniv. No. 1976, Macdonald Institute, Guelph, Ont., cent. No. 1977, University of Montreal, 125th anniv.

Booklet Stamps

2003 ***Perf. 13¼x13½***

1973 A806 48c multi .75 .25
a. Booklet pane of 8 6.00 6.00
Booklet, #1973a 6.50
1974 A806 48c multi .75 .25
a. Booklet pane of 8 6.00 6.00
Booklet, #1974a 6.50
1975 A806 48c multi .75 .25
a. Booklet pane of 8 6.00 6.00
Complete booklet, #1975a 6.50
1976 A806 48c multi .75 .25
a. Booklet pane of 8 6.00 6.00
Complete booklet, #1976a 6.50
1977 A806 48c multi .75 .25
a. Booklet pane of 8 6.00 6.00
Complete booklet, #1977a 6.50

Issued: No. 1973, 1/28. No. 1975, 4/4. No. 1976, 6/20. No. 1977, 9/4. No. 1974, 3/19.

See Nos. 2033-2034, 2089, 2172, 2209-2210.

Bird Paintings by John James Audubon — A807

Designs: No. 1979, Leach's storm petrel. No. 1980, Brant. No. 1981, Great cormorant. No. 1982, Common murre. 65c, Gyrfalcon, vert.

2003, Feb. 21 ***Perf. 13¼x12½***

1979 A807 48c multi .75 .35
1980 A807 48c multi .75 .35
1981 A807 48c multi .75 .35
1982 A807 48c multi .75 .35
a. Block of 4, #1979-1982 3.00 2.25

Booklet Stamp

Self-Adhesive

Die Cut

1983 A807 65c multi 1.10 .75
a. Booklet pane of 6 6.75
Nos. 1979-1983 (5) 4.10 2.15

Canadian Rangers — A808

2003, Mar. 3 ***Perf. 12½x13¼***

1984 A808 48c multi .75 .25

American Hellenic Educational Progressive Association In Canada, 75th Anniv. — A809

2003, Mar. 25

1985 A809 48c multi .75 .25

Volunteer Firefighters — A810

2003, May 30 ***Perf. 13¼***

1986 A810 48c multi .75 .25

Coronation of Queen Elizabeth II, 50th Anniv. A811

2003, June 2 ***Perf. 13x12½***

1987 A811 48c multi .75 .25

Quebec City, Seal of Sovereign Council of New France, Signature of Pedro da Silva — A812

2003, June 6 ***Perf. 13***

1988 A812 48c multi .75 .25

Pedro da Silva, first courier in New France, 50th anniv. of Portuguese immigration to Canada.

Tourist Attractions Type of 2001

No. 1989: a, Wilberforce Falls, Nunavut. b, Inside Passage, B. C. c, Royal Canadian Mounted Police Depot Division, Regina, Sask. d, Casa Loma, Toronto, Ont. e, Gatineau Park, Que.

No. 1990: a, Dragon boat races, Vancouver, B. C. b, Polar bear watching, Man. c, Niagara Falls, Ont. d, Magdalen Islands, Que. e, Charlottestown, P. E. I.

Self-Adhesive

2003, June 12 ***Die Cut Perf. 11¼***

1989 Booklet of 5 5.50
a.-e. A768 65c Any single 1.10 .75
1990 Booklet of 5 10.00
a.-e. A768 $1.25 Any single 2.00 1.10

"Vancouver 2010" Added in Red

Self-Adhesive

Booklet Stamp

Serpentine Die Cut 8½

2003, July 11 **Litho.**

1991 A781 48c multi 1.50 1.20
a. Booklet of 10 15.00
b. Booklet of 30 45.00
e. Die cutting omitted, pair *750.00*

Selection of Vancouver as site of 2010 Winter Olympics. By separating the booklet along the columns of rouletting, No. 1991b could be broken up into three separately obtainable examples of No. 1991a.

Canada-Alaska Cruise Scenes — A813

Mountains and: No. 1991C, Totem pole. No. 1991D, Whale's tail.

Self-Adhesive

2003, July 19 ***Die Cut***
1991C A813 ($1.25) multi 7.50 7.50
1991D A813 ($1.25) multi 7.50 7.50
e. Horiz. pair, #19901C-1991D 15.00

Nos. 1991C-1991D were printed in panes of 10 containing five of each stamp. The blank spaces in each stamp and the three stamp-like vignettes at the left of the pane that lack die cutting and "Postage Paid / Port Payé" inscription could be personalized on cruise ships. Personalized panes sold for $19.95 in US currency, while unpersonalized panes sold for $12.50. Value, unpersonalized complete pane $85.

Lutheran World Federation, 10th Assembly, Winnipeg A814

2003, July 21 ***Perf. 12½x13***
1992 A814 48c multi .75 .25

Korean War Armistice Agreement, 50th Anniv. — A815

2003, July 25 ***Perf. 12¾***
1993 A815 48c multi .75 .25

Authors A816

Designs: No. 1994, Anne Hébert (1916-2000). No. 1995, Hector de Saint-Denys Garneau (1912-43). No. 1996, Morley Callaghan (1903-90). No. 1997, Susanna Moodie (1803-85), and Catharine Parr Traill (1802-99).

Booklet Stamps

2003, Sept. 8 ***Perf. 13¼x12½***
1994 A816 48c multi .75 .35
1995 A816 48c multi .75 .35
1996 A816 48c multi .75 .35
1997 A816 48c multi .75 .35
a. Block of 4, #1994-1997 3.00 2.25
b. Booklet pane, 2 #1997a 6.00 —
Complete booklet, #1997b 6.50

2003 Road Cycling World Championships, Hamilton, Ont. — A817

Booklet Stamp

2003, Sept. 10 ***Perf. 12½x13***
1998 A817 48c multi .75 .55
a. Booklet pane of 8 6.00 —
Complete booklet, #1998a 6.50

Canadian Astronauts A818

No. 1999: a, Marc Garneau. b, Roberta Bondar. c, Steve MacLean. d, Chris Hadfield. e, Robert Thirsk. f, Bjarni Tryggvason. g, Dave Williams. h, Julie Payette.

Self-Adhesive

Litho. With Foil Application

2003, Oct. 1 ***Die Cut***
1999 Pane of 8 8.00
a.-h. A818 48c Any single .90 .90

Trees of Canada and Thailand — A819

Designs: No. 2000, Acer saccharum leaves (Canada). No. 2001, Cassia fistula (Thailand).

2003, Oct. 4 **Litho.** ***Perf. 12¾x12½***
2000 A819 48c multi .75 .25
2001 A819 48c multi .75 .25
a. Pair, #2000-2001 1.50 1.10
b. Souvenir sheet, #2000-2001 7.50 4.00
c. As "a," imperf *900.00*
d. As "b," imperf *1,250.*

Bangkok 2003 Intl. Philatelic Exhibition (No. 2001b).
See Thailand No. 2090.

L'Hommage à Rosa Luxemburg, by Jean-Paul Riopelle — A820

Painting details — No. 2002; a, Red and blue dots between birds at LR. b, Bird with yellow beak at center. c, Three birds in circle at R. d, Sun at UR. e, Birds with purple outlines at L. f, Bird with red outline in circle at R. $1.25, Pink bird in red circle at R.

2003, Oct. 7 ***Perf. 12½x13***
2002 A820 Pane of 6 7.50 7.50
a.-f. 48c Any single 1.25 1.25

Souvenir Sheet

Perf. 12¾

2003 A820 $1.25 multi 3.00 3.00

Christmas A821

Gift boxes and: 48c, Ice skates. 65c, Teddy bear. $1.25, Toy duck.

Self-Adhesive
Booklet Stamps

2003, Nov. 4 ***Die Cut***
2004 A821 48c multi .75 .25
a. Booklet pane of 6 4.50
Complete booklet, 2 #2004a 9.00
b. Pair, die cutting omitted 375.00
2005 A821 65c multi 1.00 .60
a. Booklet pane of 6 6.00
b. As "a," die cutting omitted 1,500.
c. Die cutting omitted, pair *450.00*
2006 A821 $1.25 multi 2.00 1.00
a. Booklet pane of 6 12.00
b. Die cutting omitted, pair 450.00
Nos. 2004-2006 (3) 3.75 1.85

Maple Leaf and Samara A822

Maple Leaf on Twig A823

Flag Over Edmonton, Alberta A824

Queen Elizabeth II A825

Coil Stamps

Serpentine Die Cut 8½ Horiz.

2003, Dec. 19 **Self-Adhesive**
2008 A822 49c multi .75 .25
a. Die cutting omitted, pair 150.00

Serpentine Die Cut 8½ Vert.

2009 A823 80c red & multi 1.20 .40
2010 A823 $1.40 grn & multi 3.00 .55

Booklet Stamps

Die Cut

2011 A824 49c multi .75 .25
a. Booklet pane of 10 7.50
b. Die cutting omitted, pair 150.00
c. As "a," die cutting omitted *750.00*
2012 A825 49c multi .80 .25
a. Booklet pane of 10 8.00
2013 A823 80c red & multi 1.50 .40
a. Booklet pane of 6 9.00
2014 A823 $1.40 grn & multi 2.25 .75
a. Booklet pane of 6 13.50
Nos. 2008-2014 (7) 10.25 2.85

See Nos. 2053-2055, 2075.

New Year 2004 (Year of the Monkey) — A826

Scenes from Chinese story *Journey to the West*: 49c, Monkey King. $1.40, Monkey King, Xuan Zang, Sandy, Pigsy and horse.

Litho. & Embossed with Foil Application

2004, Jan. 8 ***Perf. 13x12½***
2015 A826 49c multi .80 .25

Souvenir Sheet

2016 A826 $1.40 multi 3.00 3.00
a. As No. 2016, with 2004 Hong Kong Stamp Expo ovpt. in margin 3.75 3.75

No. 2016 has rouletted tab at right showing bar code.

National Hockey League Stars A827

Designs: Nos. 2017a, 2018a, Larry Robinson (blue background). Nos. 2017b, 2018b, Marcel Dionne (orange background). Nos. 2017c, 2018c, Ted Lindsay (red background). Nos. 2017d, 2018d, Johnny Bower (green background). Nos. 2017e, 2018e, Brad Park (brown background). Nos. 2017f, 2018f, Milt Schmidt (purple background).

Perf. 12½x13¼ on 3 Sides

2004, Jan. 24 **Litho.**
2017 Pane of 6 + 3 labels 6.00 6.00
a.-f. A827 49c Any single .75 .60

Self-Adhesive

Die Cut

2018 Pane of 6 6.00
a.-f. A827 49c Any single .75 .55

Tourist Attractions Type of 2001

Design: No. 2019, Quebec Winter Carnival; No. 2020, St. Joseph's Oratory, Montreal, Quebec; No. 2021, International Jazz Festival, Montreal. No. 2022, Traversée Internationale du Lac St. Jean Swimming Marathon, Quebec; No. 2023, Canadian National Exhibition, Toronto.

Self-Adhesive
Booklet Stamp

2004, Jan. 29 ***Die Cut***
2019 A768 49c multi .75 .35
a. Booklet of 6 4.50
2020 A768 49c multi .75 .35
a. Booklet of 6 4.50
2021 A768 49c multi .75 .35
a. Booklet of 6 4.50
2022 A768 49c multi .75 .35
a. Booklet of 6 4.50
2023 A768 49c multi .75 .35
a. Booklet of 6 4.50

Issued: No. 2019, 1/29; No. 2020, 4/2; No. 2021, 6/1; No. 2022, 6/18; No. 2023, 7/19.

Governor General Ramon John Hnatyshyn (1934-2002) — A828

2004, Mar. 16 ***Perf. 12½x13***
2024 A828 49c multi .75 .25

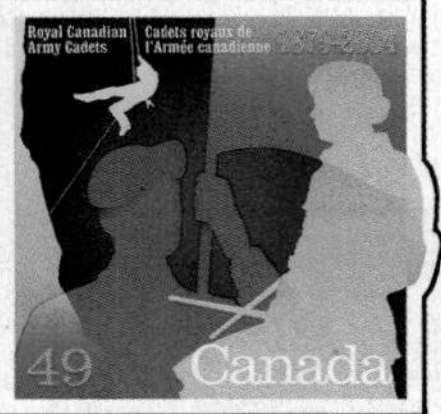

Royal Canadian Army Cadets, 125th Anniv. A829

Self-Adhesive
Booklet Stamp

2004, Mar. 26 ***Die Cut***
2025 A829 49c multi .75 .30
a. Booklet pane of 4 3.00
Complete booklet, 2 #2025a 6.00

The Fram, Ship of Otto Sverdrup (1854-1930), Arctic Explorer — A830

Litho. & Engr.

2004, Mar. 26 *Perf. 13¼*

2026 A830 49c multi .75 .25

Souvenir Sheet

2027 A830 $1.40 multi + 2 labels 3.00 3.00

See Greenland No. 426, Norway Nos. 1398-1399.

Urban Transit and Light Rail Systems — A831

Train cars, station names and system emblems of: No. 2028, Toronto Transit Commission. No. 2029, TransLink SkyTrain, Vancouver. No. 2030, Société de Transport de Montreal. No. 2031, Calgary Transit Light Rail.

2004, Mar. 30 Litho. *Perf. 12½x13*

2028 A831 49c multi .75 .30
2029 A831 49c multi .75 .30
2030 A831 49c multi .75 .30
2031 A831 49c multi .75 .30
a. Vert. strip of 4, #2028-2031 3.00 2.75

Home Hardware, 40th Anniv. — A832

Self-Adhesive

Booklet Stamp

2004, Apr. 19 *Die Cut Perf. 11*

2032 A832 49c multi .75 .30
a. Booklet pane of 10 + label 7.50
Complete booklet, #2032a 8.00

No. 2032a is the inside front cover of the complete booklet. Fifteen self-adhesive seals are on the inside back cover of the complete booklet.

Universities Type of 2003

Designs: No. 2033, Sherbrooke University, Sherbrooke, Quebec, 50th anniv. No. 2034, University of Prince Edward Island, Charlottetown, bicent.

Booklet Stamps

2004 *Perf. 13¼x13½*

2033 A806 49c multi .75 .30
a. Booklet pane of 8 6.00 6.50
Complete booklet, #2033a 6.50
2034 A806 49c multi .75 .30
a. Booklet pane of 8 6.00 6.50
Complete booklet, #2034a 6.50

Issued: No. 2033, 5/4; No. 2034, 5/8.

Montreal Children's Hospital, Cent. — A833

Self-Adhesive

Booklet Stamp

2004, May 6 *Die Cut Perf. 9½x10¾*

2035 A833 49c multi .75 .30
a. Booklet pane of 4 3.00
Complete booklet, 2 #2035a 6.00

Bird Paintings by John James Audubon A834

Designs: No. 2036, Ruby-crowned kinglet. No. 2037, White-winged crossbill. No. 2038, Bohemian waxwing. No. 2039, Boreal chickadee. 80c, Lincoln's sparrow.

2004, May 14 *Perf. 12½x13*

2036 A834 49c multi .75 .35
2037 A834 49c multi .75 .35
2038 A834 49c multi .75 .35
2039 A834 49c multi .75 .35
a. Block of 4, #2036-2039 3.00 2.75

Self-Adhesive

Booklet Stamp

Die Cut

2040 A834 80c multi 1.20 .75
a. Booklet pane of 6 7.25
Nos. 2036-2040 (5) 4.20 2.15

Pioneers of Transatlantic Mail Service — A835

Designs: No. 2041, Sir Samuel Cunard (1787-1865). No. 2042, Sir Hugh Allan (1810-82).

Self-Adhesive

2004, May 28 *Perf. 13¼x12½*

2041 49c multi .75 .30
2042 49c multi .75 .30
a. A835 Horiz. pair, #2041-2042 1.50 1.10

D-Day, 60th Anniv. A836

2004, June 6 *Perf. 13x12½*

2043 A836 49c multi .75 .30

Pierre Dugua de Mons, Leader of First French Settlement in Acadia, and Ship A837

2004, June 26 Litho. & Engr.

2044 A837 49c multi .75 .30

See France No. 3032.

Butterfly and Flower A838

Children on Beach A839

Rose A840

Dog A841

Self-Adhesive

Booklet Stamps

Serpentine Die Cut 11¾

2004, June Litho.

2045 A838 (49c) multi 22.50 *13.00*
a. Booklet pane of 2 55.00
Complete booklet, #2045a + phonecard in greeting card 50.00
2046 A839 (49c) multi 9.00 *13.00*
a. Booklet pane of 2 18.00
Complete booklet, #2046a + phonecard in greeting card 24.00
2047 A840 (49c) multi 9.00 *13.00*
a. Booklet pane of 2 18.00
Complete booklet, #2047a + phonecard in greeting card 24.00
2048 A841 (49c) multi 9.00 *13.00*
a. Booklet pane of 2 18.00
Complete booklet, #2048a + phonecard in greeting card 24.00
Nos. 2045-2048 (4) 49.50 52.00

Nos. 2045-2048, have a frame like No. 1918a, and are similarly inscribed "Domestic Lettermail" and "Poste-lettres du régime intérieur," but Nos. 2045-2048 have the vignettes printed on the stamps, while any vignettes found on No. 1918a are affixed stickers. Nos. 2045a-2048a are affixed to the insides of greeting cards that contain detachable phonecards valid for 15 minutes calling time on any touchtone phone in Canada or the United States. The stamps were available only in the greeting card, which sold for $5.99 along with a blank envelope for sending the greeting card.

2004 Summer Olympics, Athens — A842

Olympic rings and: No. 2049, Spyros Louis, 1896 Marathon gold medalist, diagram of track, "Athens" in Greek, and stylized runner. No. 2050, Soccer net inscribed "Canada," girls playing soccer.

2004, July 28 *Perf. 12½x13¼*

2049 A842 49c multi .75 .30
2050 A842 49c multi .75 .30
a. Horiz. pair, #2049-2050 1.50 1.10

Canadian Open Golf Championship, Cent. — A843

Crowd, trophy and golfer: No. 2051, Finishing swing. No. 2052, Ready to putt.

Self-Adhesive

Litho. & Embossed With Foil Application

2004, Aug. 12 *Serpentine Die Cut*

2051 A843 49c multi .75 .30
2052 A843 49c multi .75 .30
a. Horiz. pair, #2051-2052, silver omitted on both stamps *2,250.*

Nos. 2051-2052 were issued in a sheet containing four of each stamp.

Maple Leaf Types of 2003

Self-Adhesive Coil Stamps

2004, Aug. 18 Litho. *Die Cut*

2053 A822 49c multi .75 .25
a. Die cutting omitted, pair 170.00

Serpentine Die Cut 8¼ Horiz.

2054 A823 80c red & multi 2.00 .50
2055 A823 $1.40 grn & multi 3.75 .90
a. Die cutting omitted, pair —
Nos. 2053-2055 (3) 6.50 1.65

Die cut gauges on Nos. 2054-2055 vary widely within the roll, from 8¼-8¾. Gauge 8¼ is the most common.

Montreal Heart Institute, 50th Anniv. — A844

Self-Adhesive

Booklet Stamp

2004, Sept. 15 *Die Cut Perf. 13½*

2056 A844 49c multi .75 .30
a. Booklet pane of 4 3.00
Complete booklet, 2 #2056 6.00

Pets A845

Self-Adhesive

Booklet Stamps

2004, Oct. 1 *Die Cut*

2057 A845 49c Fish .75 .35
2058 A845 49c Cats .75 .35
2059 A845 49c Rabbit .75 .35
2060 A845 49c Dog .75 .35
a. Booklet pane, #2057-2060 3.00
Complete booklet, 2 #2060a 6.00

Nobel Laureates in Chemistry — A846

Designs: No. 2061, Gerhard Herzberg, 1971 laureate, and molecular structures. No. 2062, Michael Smith, 1993 laureate, and DNA double helix.

2004, Oct. 4 *Perf. 12½x13*

2061 A846 49c multi .75 .30
2062 A846 49c multi .75 .30
a. Pair, #2061-2062 1.50 1.10

Ribbon Frame A847

Picture Album Frame A848

Serpentine Die Cut 12¾x13

2004, Oct. 8 Self-Adhesive

2063 A847 (49c) multi 1.50 1.25
2064 A848 (49c) multi 1.50 1.25

Nos. 2063 and 2064 were each printed in panes of 21 that sold for $9.80. These panes were split by a row of rouletting in the center, with 20 stamps on one side and one on the other side. Panes of 21 with vignettes that could be personalized by the customer were available for $24.95. Panes of 40 stamps with personalized vignettes were also available for $39.95.

Victoria Cross, 150th Anniv. — A849

Designs: No. 2065, Victoria Cross. No. 2066, Design for Canadian Victoria Cross, approved with Queen Elizabeth II's signature.

Litho. & Embossed

2004, Oct. 21 ***Perf. 13x12½***

2065 A849 49c multi .75 .30

Litho.

2066 A849 49c multi .75 .30
a. Pair, #2065-2066 1.50 1.20

Paintings by Jean Paul Lemieux — A850

Designs: 49c, Self-portrait. 80c, A June Wedding, horiz. (53x35mm). $1.40, Summer, horiz. (64x31mm).

2004, Oct. 22 ***Perf. 13x13¼***

2067 A850 49c multi .75 .30
a. Perf. 13 1.50 1.50

Souvenir Sheet

Perf. 13

2068 Sheet, #2067a, 2068a, 2068b 5.25 5.25
a. A850 80c multi 1.50 1.50
b. A850 $1.40 multi 2.25 2.25

Christmas — A851

Santa Claus and: 49c, Sleigh. 80c, Automobile. $1.40, Train.

Booklet Stamps

Serpentine Die Cut 7¼ Horiz.

2004, Nov. 2 Self-Adhesive

2069 A851 49c multi .75 .25
a. Booklet pane of 6 4.50
Complete booklet, 2 #2069a 9.00
b. Printed on gummed side 11.00

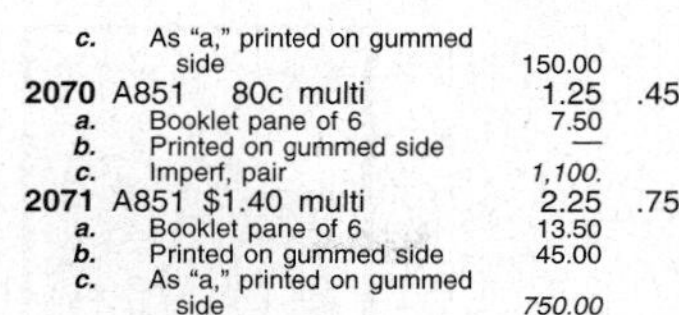

c. As "a," printed on gummed side 150.00
2070 A851 80c multi 1.25 .45
a. Booklet pane of 6 7.50
b. Printed on gummed side —
c. Imperf, pair *1,100.*
2071 A851 $1.40 multi 2.25 .75
a. Booklet pane of 6 13.50
b. Printed on gummed side 45.00
c. As "a," printed on gummed side *750.00*

Queen Type of 2003 and

Red Calla Lilies A852

Flag and Saskatoon, Saskatchewan A853

Flag and Durrell, Newfoundland A854

Flag and Shannon Falls, British Columbia A855

Flag and Mont-Saint-Hilaire, Quebec — A856

Flag and Toronto — A857

Designs: 85c, Yellow calla lily. $1.45, Dutch iris.

Coil Stamps

Serpentine Die Cut 6½-8¾ Horiz.

2004-05 Self-Adhesive

2072 A852 50c multi .75 .25
a. Serpentine die cut 6¾ horiz. ('05) .75 .25
b. Die cutting omitted, pair 75.00
2073 A852 85c multi 1.30 .25
a. Serpentine die cut 6¾ horiz. ('05) 1.50 .25
2074 A852 $1.45 multi 2.25 .60
a. Serpentine die cut 6¾ horiz. ('05) 5.50 2.20

The die cutting gauge on Nos. 2072-2074a will vary between stamps on a roll and between stamps on one roll and other rolls.
Issued: Nos. 2072, 2073, 2074, 12/20/04. Nos. 2072a, 2073a, 2074a, 2/2005. Die cuttings on these issues are variable.

Booklet Stamps

Die Cut

2075 A825 50c multi .75 .25
a. Booklet pane of 10 7.50
2076 A853 50c multi .75 .25
2077 A854 50c multi .75 .25
2078 A855 50c multi .75 .25
2079 A856 50c multi .75 .25
2080 A857 50c multi .75 .25
a. Booklet pane, 2 each #2076-2080 7.50
b. As "a," printed on gummed side 75.00
2081 A852 85c multi 1.40 .40
a. Booklet pane of 6 8.50
b. As "a," black inscriptions omitted *4,000.*
2082 A852 $1.45 multi 2.20 .60
a. Booklet pane of 6 13.25
Nos. 2072-2082 (11) 12.40 3.60

New Year 2005 (Year of the Cock) — A858

Rooster with: 50c, Red tail feathers. $1.45, Gold tail feathers.

Litho. & Embossed with Foil Application

2005, Jan. 7 ***Perf. 13¼***

2083 A858 50c multi .75 .30
a. Red omitted *1,350.*

Souvenir Sheet

Perf. 12½x13

2084 A858 $1.45 multi 2.20 2.20
a. With dates, Canadian and Chinese flags added in sheet margin 3.20 3.20

Canada — People's Republic of China diplomatic relations, 35th anniv. (No. 2084a). No. 2084 contains one 40x40mm stamp.

National Hockey League Stars A859

Designs: Nos. 2085a, 2086a, Henri Richard (blue background). Nos. 2085b, 2086b, Grant Fuhr (orange background). Nos. 2085c, 2086c, Allan Stanley (red background). Nos. 2085d, 2086d, Pierre Pilote (green background). Nos. 2085e, 2086e, Bryan Trottier (purple background). Nos. 2085f, 2086f, John Bucyk (yellow background).

Perf. 12½x13¼ on 3 Sides

2005, Jan. 29 Litho.

2085 Pane of 6 + 3 labels 4.50 4.50
a.-f. A859 50c Any single .75 .55

Self-Adhesive

Die Cut

2086 Pane of 6 4.50
a.-f. A859 50c Any single .75 .55

Fishing Flies — A860

Designs: Nos. 2087a, 2088a, Alevin. Nos. 2087b, 2088b, Jock Scott. Nos. 2087c, 2088d, P. E. I. Fly. Nos. 2087d, 2088c, Mickey Finn.

2005, Feb. 4 ***Perf. 12½x13¼***

2087 A860 Pane of 4 7.50 5.50
a.-d. 50c Any single 1.90 1.10

Self-Adhesive

Serpentine Die Cut 10 Syncopated

2088 A860 Booklet pane of 4 3.60
a.-d. 50c Any single .90 .35
Complete booklet, 2 #2088 7.25

Universities Type of 2003

Design: Nova Scotia Agricultural College, cent.

Booklet Stamp

Die Cut Perf. 12¾x13¼

2005, Feb. 14 Self-Adhesive

2089 A806 50c multi .75 .30
a. Booklet pane of 4 3.00
Complete booklet, 2 #2089a 6.00

Expo 2005, Aichi, Japan — A861

2005, Mar. 4 ***Perf. 13½***

2090 A861 50c multi .75 .30

Daffodils A862

Designs: Nos. 2091a, 2092, Yellow daffodils, green and yellow background. Nos. 2091b, 2093, White daffodils, red orange and yellow background.

Souvenir Sheet

2005, Mar. 10 ***Perf. 13x13¼***

2091 Pane of 2 2.20 2.20
a.-b. A862 50c Either single 1.10 .75

Booklet Stamps

Self-Adhesive

Die Cut Perf. 10

2092 A862 50c multi .75 .30
2093 A862 50c multi .75 .30
a. Booklet pane, 5 each #2092-2093 + 10 stickers 7.50

Pacific Explore 2005 World Stamp Expo, Sydney, Australia (No. 2091).

TD Bank Financial Group, 150th Anniv. — A863

Self-Adhesive

Booklet Stamp

2005, Mar. 18 ***Die Cut Perf. 11¼***

2094 A863 50c multi .75 .35
a. Booklet pane of 10 7.50
Complete booklet, #2094a 10.00

The booklet pane of 10 is the inside front cover of the booklet. Fifteen stickers are on inside back cover.

Bird Paintings by John James Audubon — A864

Designs: No. 2095, Horned lark. No. 2096, Piping plover. No. 2097, Stilt sandpiper. No. 2098, Willow ptarmigan. 85c, Double-crested cormorant.

2005, Mar. 23 ***Perf. 12½x13¼***

2095 A864 50c multi .75 .40
2096 A864 50c multi .75 .40
2097 A864 50c multi .75 .40
2098 A864 50c multi .75 .40
a. Block of 4, #2095-2098 3.00 2.50

Booklet Stamp

Self-Adhesive

Size: 48x39mm

Die Cut

2099 A864 85c multi 1.20 .45
a. Booklet pane of 6 7.25

Bridges — A865

Designs: No. 2100, Jacques Cartier Bridge, Quebec. No. 2101, Souris Swinging Bridge, Manitoba. No. 2102, Angus L. Macdonald Bridge, Nova Scotia. No. 2103, Canso Causeway, Nova Scotia.

Self-Adhesive

2005, Apr. 2 ***Perf. 12½x13***

2100 A865 50c multi .75 .45
2101 A865 50c multi .75 .45
2102 A865 50c multi .75 .45

2103 A865 50c multi .75 .45
a. Block or strip of 4, #2100-2103 3.00 2.75
b. As "a," imperf. 1,500.

Maclean's Magazine, Cent. A866

2005, Apr. 12
2104 A866 50c multi .75 .30

Biosphere Reserves in Canada and Ireland — A867

Designs: No. 2105, Saskatoon berries, Waterton Lakes National Park, Canada. No. 2106, Deer, Killarney National Park, Ireland.

2005, Apr. 22
2105 A867 50c multi .75 .30
2106 A867 50c multi .75 .30
a. Pair, #2105-2106 1.50 1.10
b. Souvenir sheet, #2105-2106 2.00 2.00

See Ireland Nos. 1611-1612.

Battle of the Atlantic, World War II — A868

2005, Apr. 29
2107 A868 50c multi .75 .30

Opening of Canadian War Museum, Ottawa — A869

Booklet Stamp

Serpentine Die Cut 8x8½ Syncopated

2005, May 6 **Self-Adhesive**
2108 A869 50c multi .75 .30
a. Booklet pane of 4 3.00
Complete booklet, 2 #2108a 6.00

Paintings by Homer Watson (1855-1936) — A870

Designs: 50c, Down in the Laurentides. 85c, The Flood Gate (54x40mm)

2005, May 27 ***Perf. 13¼x13***
2109 A870 50c multi .75 .30
a. Perf. 13½x13 1.50 1.50

Souvenir Sheet

Perf. 13½x13

2110 Pane of 2, Nos. 2109a, 2110a 4.50 4.50
a. A870 85c multi 3.00 3.00

Miniature Sheet

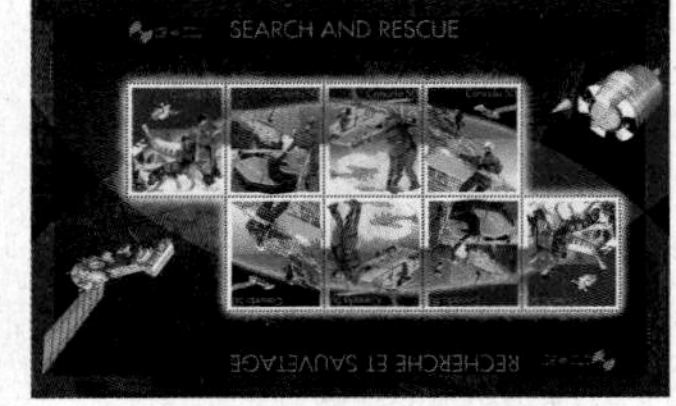

Search and Rescue — A871

No. 2111: a, Rescuer and dog at plane crash. b, Rescuers at shipwreck. c, Helicopter, airplane and rescuers. d, Mountainside rescuers.

2005, June 13 ***Perf. 13x13¼***
2111 A871 Pane of 8, 2 each #a-d 6.00 6.00
a.-d. 50c Any single .75 .55

No. 2111 contains two horizontal strips, one of which is inverted, so that a tete-beche pair of No. 2111c and two tete-beche pairs containing Nos. 2111b and 2111d can be created.

Ellen Fairclough (1905-2004), First Female Cabinet Minister — A872

2005, June 21 ***Perf. 13x12½***
2112 A872 50c multi .75 .30

Diver A873

Swimmer A874

2005, July 5 ***Perf. 13¼***
2113 A873 50c multi .75 .45
2114 A874 50c multi .75 .45
a. Horiz. pair, #2113-2114 1.50 1.00

9th FINA World Championships, Montreal. In No. 2114a, the denomination for one stamp is on the opposite side of the pair from that of the other stamp.

Founding of Port-Royal, Nova Scotia, 400th Anniv. A875

Litho. & Engr.

2005, July 16 ***Perf. 13x12½***
2115 A875 50c multi .75 .30

Province of Alberta, Cent. — A876

Self-Adhesive

2005, July 21 **Litho.** ***Perf. 12½x13***
2116 A876 50c multi .75 .30

Printed in panes of 8 with each stamp having a different design on the backing.

Province of Saskatchewan, Cent. — A877

2005, Aug. 2 ***Perf. 13x12½***
2117 A877 50c multi .75 .30

Oscar Peterson, Pianist, 80th Birthday — A878

2005, Aug. 15
2118 A878 50c multi .75 .30
a. Souvenir sheet of 4 3.00 3.00

No. 176 and Acadian Flag A879

2005, Aug. 15
2119 A879 50c multi .75 .30

Acadian Deportation, 250th anniv.

Children Playing and Leg Braces — A880

2005, Sept. 2 ***Perf. 12½x13***
2120 A880 50c multi .75 .30

Mass polio vaccinations in Canada, 50th anniv.

Youth Sports — A881

No. 2121: a, Wall climbing. b, Skateboarding. c, Mountain biking. d, Snowboarding.

Self-Adhesive

2005, Oct. 1 ***Die Cut***
2121 Complete booklet, 2 each #a-d 6.00
a.-d. A881 50c Any single .75 .35

Wild Cats — A882

Designs: No. 2122, Puma concolor. No. 2123, Panthera pardus orientalis.

Perf. 13½x13¼ Syncopated

2005, Oct. 13
2122 50c multi .75 .35
2123 50c multi .75 .35
a. A882 Horiz. pair, #2122-2123 1.50 .90
b. Souvenir sheet, #2123a 1.70 1.90

Diplomatic relations with People's Republic of China, 35th anniv. (No. 2123b). The perforation column between the two stamps, which gauges perf. 13½, has a maple leaf shaped syncopation.

See People's Republic of China Nos. 3458-3459.

Snowman — A883

Self-Adhesive

Litho. with Hologram Applied

Serpentine Die Cut 8¼ Horiz.

2005, Nov. 2 **Booklet Stamp**
2124 A883 50c multi .75 .30
a. Booklet pane of 6 4.50
Complete booklet, 2 #2124a 9.00

A884

A885

Creche Figures, St. Joseph's Oratory, Montreal — A886

Self-Adhesive

Serpentine Die Cut 6¾ Horiz.

2005, Nov. 2 **Booklet Stamps**
2125 A884 50c multi .75 .30
a. Booklet pane of 6 4.50

Complete booklet, 2 #2125a 9.00

Serpentine Die Cut 6½ Horiz.

2126 A885 85c multi 1.25 .60
a. Booklet pane of 6 7.50

Serpentine Die Cut 6¾ Horiz.

2127 A886 $1.45 multi 2.25 1.10
a. Booklet pane of 6 13.50

Flowers — A887

Designs: 51c, Red bergamot. 89c, Yellow lady's slipper. $1.05, Pink fairy slipper. $1.49, Himalayan blue poppy.

Coil Stamps

Serpentine Die Cut 7 to 9¼ Horiz.

2005, Dec. 19 **Self-Adhesive**

2128 A887 51c multi .75 .25
2129 A887 89c multi 1.40 .45
2130 A887 $1.05 multi 1.70 .60
2131 A887 $1.49 multi 2.20 .90

Booklet Stamps

Die Cut

2132 A887 89c multi 1.40 .40
a. Booklet pane of 6 8.50
2133 A887 $1.05 multi 1.70 .65
a. Booklet pane of 6 10.25
2134 A887 $1.49 multi 2.20 1.00
a. Booklet pane of 6 13.00
Nos. 2128-2134 (7) 11.35 4.25

Flag and Houses, New Glasgow, Prince Edward Island A888

Flag and Bridge, Bouctouche, New Brunswick A889

Flag and Windmills, Pincher Creek, Alberta A890

Flag and Lower Fort Garry, Manitoba A891

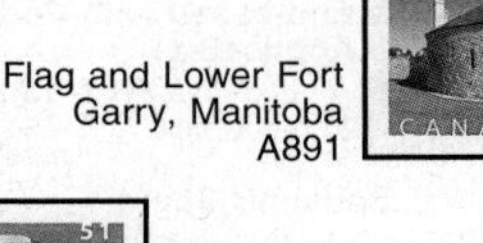

Flag and Dogsled, Yukon Territory — A892

Self-Adhesive

Booklet Stamps

2005, Dec. 19 ***Die Cut***

2135 A888 51c multi .75 .25
2136 A889 51c multi .75 .25
2137 A890 51c multi .75 .25
2138 A891 51c multi .75 .25
2139 A892 51c multi .75 .25
a. Booklet pane, 2 each #2135-2139 7.50
b. As "a," die cutting omitted *1,500.*
Nos. 2135-2139 (5) 3.75 1.25

New Year 2006 (Year of the Dog) — A893

Litho. & Embossed With Foil Application

2006, Jan. 6 ***Perf. 13¼***

2140 A893 51c shown .75 .30

Souvenir Sheet

2141 A893 $1.49 Dog and pup 2.25 2.25

Queen Elizabeth II, 80th Birthday A894

Self-Adhesive

Booklet Stamp

Serpentine Die Cut 10

2006, Jan. 12 **Litho.**

2142 A894 51c multi .75 .30
a. Booklet pane of 10 7.50
b. Die cutting omitted, pair 250.00

See No. 2150.

2006 Winter Olympics, Turin, Italy A895

Designs: No. 2143, Team pursuit speed skating. No. 2144, Skeleton.

2006, Feb. 3 ***Perf. 12½x13***

2143 A895 51c multi .75 .30
2144 A895 51c multi .75 .30
a. Horiz. pair, #2143-2144 1.50 1.00

Gardens — A896

No. 2145: a, Shade garden and black-throated blue warbler. b, Flower garden and American painted lady butterfly. c, Water garden and green darner dragonfly. d, Rock garden and blue-spotted salamander.

Self-Adhesive

2006, Mar. 8 ***Serpentine Die Cut 10***

2145 Complete booklet, 2 each #a-d 6.00
a.-d. A896 51c Any single .75 .45

Party Balloons A897

Booklet Stamp

Serpentine Die Cut 6¾ Horiz.

2006, Apr. 3 **Self-Adhesive**

2146 A897 51c multi .75 .30
a. Booklet pane of 6 6.00

Paintings by Dorothy Knowles — A898

Designs: 51c, The Field of Rapeseed. 89c, North Saskatchewan River, vert. (42x51mm).

2006, Apr. 7 ***Perf. 13¼x12½***

2147 A898 51c multi .75 .30
a. Perf. 12¾x12½ 1.50 1.50

Souvenir Sheet

Perf. 13

2148 Pane, Nos. 2147a, 2148a 3.75 3.75
a. A898 89c multi 2.20 2.20

Canadian Labor Congress, 50th Anniv. — A899

2006, Apr. 20 ***Perf. 13½x13¼***

2149 A899 51c multi .75 .30

Queen Elizabeth II, 80th Birthday Type of 2006

Souvenir Sheet

2006, Apr. 21 ***Perf. 12½x13***

2150 Pane of 2, No. 2150a 4.50 4.50
a. A894 149c multi, 36x28mm 2.40 2.40

McClelland & Stewart Publishing House, Cent. — A900

Self-Adhesive

Booklet Stamp

2006, Apr. 26 ***Die Cut Perf. 11¼x11***

2151 A900 51c slate grn & sil .75 .30
a. Booklet pane of 4 + 4 stickers 3.00
Complete booklet, 2 #2151a 6.00

Northwest Coast Transformation Mask and Northwest Coast Exhibit — A901

Booklet Stamp

Serpentine Die Cut 8 Horiz. Syncopated

2006, May 11 **Self-Adhesive**

2152 A901 89c multi 1.40 .80
a. Booklet pane of 4 3.60
Complete booklet, 2 #2152a 7.50
b. Die cutting omitted, pair *700.00*

Canadian Museum of Civilization, 150th anniv.

Canadians in Hollywood A903

Actors and actresses: Nos. 2153a, 2154a, John Candy (1950-94). Nos. 2153b, 2154c, Fay Wray (1907-2004). Nos. 2153c, 2154d, Lorne Greene (1915-87). Nos. 2153d, 2154b, Mary Pickford (1893-1979).

2006, May 26 ***Perf. 13x12½***

2153 Souvenir sheet of 4 4.50 4.50
a.-d. A903 51c Any single 1.10 1.10

Self-Adhesive

Serpentine Die Cut 9¾x10

2154 Booklet pane of 4 + 4 stickers 3.25
a.-d. A903 51c Any single .75 .45
Complete booklet, 2 #2154 6.00

Complete booklets were issued with four different covers depicting the featured actors or actresses.

See Nos. 2279-2280.

A904

Exploration of Eastern Coast by Samuel de Champlain, 400th Anniv. — A905

Litho. & Engr.

2006, May 28 ***Perf. 13x12½***

2155 A904 51c multi .75 .30

Souvenir Sheet

Perf. 11

2156 A905 Pane of 2 #2156a, 2 US #4074a 7.50 7.00
a. A904 51c multi 1.50 1.10

Washington 2006 World Philatelic Exhibition (No. 2156). No. 2156, sold only by Canada Post for $2, has bar code in pane margin at lower left. United States No. 4074, sold only by the United States Postal Service, lacks this bar code.

Vancouver Aquarium, 50th Anniv. — A906

Self-Adhesive

Booklet Stamp

Serpentine Die Cut 9½

2006, June 15 **Litho.**

2157 A906 51c multi .75 .30
a. Booklet pane of 5 3.75
Complete booklet, 2 #2157a 7.50

Canadian Forces Snowbirds Aerobatics Team — A907

Designs: No. 2158, Pilot in cockpit, two airplanes. No. 2159, Three airplanes, Snowbirds emblem.

2006, June 28 ***Perf. 12½x13¼***

2158 A907 51c multi .75 .30
2159 A907 51c multi .75 .30
a. Horiz. pair, #2158-2159 1.50 1.10
b. Souvenir sheet, #2159a 2.25 2.25

James White, Dividers and Map of Canada
A908

2006, June 30 ***Perf. 13¼x12½***

2160 A908 51c multi .75 .30

Atlas of Canada, cent. Printed in panes of 16 + 4 labels.

World Lacrosse Championships, London, Ontario — A909

Booklet Stamp

Serpentine Die Cut 11¾ Horiz.

2006, July 6 **Self-Adhesive**

2161 A909 51c multi .75 .30
a. Booklet pane of 8 6.00

Alpine Club of Canada, Cent. — A910

Self-Adhesive
Booklet Stamp

2006, July 19 ***Die Cut Perf. 12½x13***

2162 A910 51c multi .75 .30
a. Booklet pane of 8 6.00

Ducks and Duck Decoys
A911

Designs: No. 2163, Barrow's goldeneyes. No. 2164, Mallards. No. 2165, American black ducks. No. 2166, Redbreasted mergansers.

2006, Aug. 3 ***Perf. 13¼x12½***

2163 A911 51c blue & multi .75 .45
2164 A911 51c yel & multi .75 .45
2165 A911 51c red & multi .75 .45
2166 A911 51c grn & multi .75 .45
a. Block of 4, #2163-2166 3.00 2.20
b. Souvenir sheet, #2163-2166 3.75 3.75

Society of Graphic Designers of Canada, 50th Anniv. — A912

2006, Aug. 16 ***Perf. 12½x13***

2167 A912 51c multi .75 .30

Canadian Wines
A913

Canadian Cheeses
A914

Designs: No. 2168, Three glasses of wine. No. 2169, Wine taster, barrels. No. 2170, Various cheeses. No. 2171, Woman with tray of cheeses and fruit.

Self-Adhesive
Booklet Stamps

2006, Aug. 23 ***Die Cut***

2168 A913 51c multi .75 .45
2169 A913 51c multi .75 .45
2170 A914 51c multi .75 .45
2171 A914 51c multi .75 .45
a. Booklet pane, 2 each #2168-2171 6.00
Nos. 2168-2171 (4) 3.00 1.80

Universities Type of 2003

Design: Macdonald College, Sainte-Anne-de-Bellevue, Quebec, cent.

Booklet Stamp

Die Cut Perf. 12¾x13¼

2006, Sept. 26 **Self-Adhesive**

2172 A806 51c multi .75 .30
a. Booklet pane of 4 3.00
Complete booklet, 2 #2172a 6.00

Endangered Animals — A915

Designs: Nos. 2173a, 2174, Newfoundland marten. Nos. 2173b, 2175, Blotched tiger salamander. Nos. 2173c, 2176, Blue racer snake. Nos. 2173d, 2177, Swift fox.

2006, Sept. 29 ***Perf. 13¼***

2173 Pane of 4 + 4 labels 4.50 4.00
a.-d. A915 51c Any single 1.10 .90

Booklet Stamps
Self-Adhesive
Size: 47x24mm
Die Cut

2174 A915 51c multi .75 .45
2175 A915 51c multi .75 .45
2176 A915 51c multi .75 .45
2177 A915 51c multi .75 .45
a. Block of 4, #2174-2177 3.00
b. Booklet pane, 2, #2177a 6.00

See Nos. 2229-2233, 2285-2289.

Opera Singers — A916

Designs: No. 2178, Maureen Forrester. No. 2179, Raoul Jobin (1906-74). No. 2180, Léopold Simoneau (1916-2006) and Pierrette Alarie. No. 2181, Jon Vickers. No. 2182, Edward Johnson (1878-1959).

2006, Oct. 17 ***Perf. 13½x13***

2178 A916 51c multi .75 .45
2179 A916 51c multi .75 .45
2180 A916 51c multi .75 .45
2181 A916 51c multi .75 .45
2182 A916 51c multi .75 .45
a. Vert. strip of 5, #2178-2182 3.75 3.75

Madonna and Child, by Antoine-Sébastien Falardeau
A917

Christmas Card Art
A918

Designs: No. 2184, Snowman, by Yvonne McKague Housser. 89c, Winter Joys, by J. E. Sampson. $1.49, Contemplation, by Edwin Holgate.

Self-Adhesive
Booklet Stamp

2006, Nov. 1 ***Die Cut***

2183 A917 51c multi .75 .25
a. Booklet pane of 12 9.00

Serpentine Die Cut 13¼ Horiz.

2184 A918 51c multi .75 .25
a. Booklet pane of 12 9.00
2185 A918 89c multi 1.35 .55
a. Booklet pane of 6 8.00
2186 A918 $1.49 multi 2.25 .90
a. Booklet pane of 6 13.50
Nos. 2183-2186 (4) 5.10 1.95

Spotted Coralroot
A919

Queen Elizabeth II
A920

Flag and Sirmilik Natl. Park, Nunavut
A921

Flag and Cliff Near Chemainus, British Columbia
A922

Flag and Polar Bears Near Churchill, Manitoba
A923

Flag and Bras d'Or Lake, Nova Scotia
A924

Flag and Tuktut Nogait Natl. Park, Northwest Territories — A925

Self-Adhesive
Coil Stamp

Serpentine Die Cut 7½-9 Horiz.

2006, Nov. 16 **Litho.**

2187 A919 P multi 1.25 .25

Booklet Stamps
Die Cut

2188 A920 P multi 1.30 .25
a. Booklet pane of 10 13.00
b. As "a," die cutting omitted *900.00*
2189 A921 P multi 1.30 .25
2190 A922 P multi 1.30 .25
2191 A923 P multi 1.30 .25
2192 A924 P multi 1.30 .25
2193 A925 P multi 1.30 .25
a. Booklet pane, 2 each #2189-2193 13.00
b. Booklet pane, 6 each #2189-2193 39.00
Nos. 2187-2193 (7) 9.05 1.75

Nos. 2187-2193 each sold for 51c on day of issue. On Nos. 2188a, 2193a and 2193b, adjacent stamps that are on both sides of the booklet fold have rouletting rather than die cutting between them. No. 2193b is sold folded into thirds. Each of the thirds has selvage surrounding the ten stamps on it, unlike No. 2193a. Beware of fake examples of No. 2139b that have been found hand cut from printer's waste.

See No. 2194a.

Spotted Coralroot Type of 2006 and

Flat-leaved Bladderwort — A926

Designs: $1.10, Marsh skullcap. $1.55, Little larkspur.

2006, Dec. 19 ***Perf. 13¼x13***

2194 Souvenir sheet of 4 7.25 7.25
a. A919 P multi 1.30 .75
b. A926 93c multi 1.40 1.10
c. A926 $1.10 multi 1.65 1.25
d. A926 $1.55 multi 2.30 1.90

Self-Adhesive
Coil Stamps

Serpentine Die Cut 7½-9 Horiz.

2195 A926 93c multi 1.40 .40
2196 A926 $1.10 multi 1.65 .60
2197 A926 $1.55 multi 2.30 .60

Booklet Stamps
Die Cut

2198 A926 93c multi 1.40 .60
a. Booklet pane of 6 8.50
2199 A926 $1.10 multi 1.65 .75
a. Booklet pane of 6 10.00
2200 A926 $1.55 multi 2.30 1.10
a. Booklet pane of 6 13.75
Nos. 2195-2200 (6) 10.70 4.05

No. 2194a sold for 51c on day of issue.

See Nos. 2243, 2245-2247, 2254-2256.

New Year 2007 (Year of the Pig)
A927

Pig facing: 52c, Left. $1.55, Right.

Litho. & Embossed with Foil Application

2007, Jan. 5 ***Perf. 13½x13***

2201 A927 52c red & multi .80 .30
a. Gold foil omitted 75.00

Souvenir Sheet

2202 A927 $1.55 grn & multi 2.25 2.25

International Polar Year — A929

Confetti and Streamers
A928

Self-Adhesive
Booklet Stamp

Serpentine Die Cut 6¾ Horiz.

2007, Jan. 15 **Litho.**

2203 A928 52c multi .80 .30
a. Booklet pane of 6 4.75

Designs: No. 2204, Somateria spectabilis. No. 2205, Crossota millsaeare.

Perf. 13½ Syncopated

2007, Feb. 12

2204 52c multi .80 .30
2205 52c multi .80 .30
a. A929 Horiz. pair, #2204-2205 1.60 .90
b. Souvenir sheet, #2205a 2.25 2.25

Lilacs — A930

Color of lilacs: Nos. 2206a, 2207, White. Nos. 2206b, 2208, Purple.

Souvenir Sheet

2007, Mar. 1 ***Perf. 12¾***

2206 A930 Pane of 2 2.20 2.20
a.-b. 52c Either single 1.10 .75
c. Imperf., pane of 2 *2,000.*

Booklet Stamps
Self-Adhesive
Die Cut

2207 A930 52c multi .80 .30
2208 A930 52c multi .80 .30
a. Booklet pane of 10, 5 each #2207-2208 8.00

Universities Type of 2003

Design: No. 2209, HEC Montreal, cent. No. 2210, University of Saskatchewan, cent.

Self-Adhesive
Booklet Stamp

2007 ***Die Cut Perf. 12¾x13¼***

2209 A806 52c multi .80 .30
a. Booklet pane of 4 3.25
Complete booklet, 2 #2209a 6.50
2210 A806 52c multi .80 .30
a. Booklet pane of 4 3.25
Complete booklet, 2 #2210a 6.50

Issued: No. 2209, 3/12. No. 2210, 4/3.

Art by Mary Pratt A931

Designs: 52c, Jelly Shelf. $1.55 Iceberg in the North Atlantic (58x36mm).

2007, Mar. 15 ***Perf. 13x12½***

2211 A931 52c multi .80 .30

Souvenir Sheet

2212 Pane, #2211, 2212a 3.10 3.10
a. A931 $1.55 multi 2.30 2.50

Selection of Ottawa as National Capital, 150th Anniv. — A932

Litho., Litho & Embossed with Foil Application (#2213b)

2007, May 3 ***Perf. 13¼***

2213 Pane of 2, #2213a, 2213b 3.50 3.50
a. A932 52c multi 1.10 1.10
b. A932 $1.55 multi 2.30 2.30

Booklet Stamp
Self-Adhesive
Serpentine Die Cut 7¼ Horiz.

2214 A932 52c multi .80 .30
a. Booklet pane of 4 3.25
Complete booklet, 2 #2214a 6.50

Royal Architectural Institute of Canada, Cent. — A933

Buildings: No. 2215, University of Lethbridge, by Arthur Erickson. No. 2216, St. Mary's Church, by Douglas Cardinal. No. 2217, Ontario Science Centre, by Raymond Moriyama. No. 2218, National Gallery of Canada, by Moshe Safdie.

2007, May 9 **Litho.** ***Perf. 13***

2215 A933 52c multi + label .80 .45
2216 A933 52c multi + label .80 .45
2217 A933 52c multi + label .80 .45
2218 A933 52c multi + label .80 .45
a. Vert. strip of 4, #2215-2218, + 4 labels 3.25 2.50

Nos. 2215-2218 were printed in panes containing two of each stamp. Labels flank the stamps, with labels on the left showing drawings of the buildings and the labels on the right showing the architect.

Capt. George Vancouver (1757-98), Explorer — A934

Litho. & Embossed

2007, June 22 ***Perf. 13x12½***

2219 A934 $1.55 multi 2.25 1.00
a. Souvenir sheet of 1, perf. 13 2.25 2.25

FIFA Under-20 World Soccer Championships, Canada — A935

2007, June 26 **Litho.** ***Perf. 12½x13***

2220 A935 52c multi .80 .30
a. Imperf., pair *950.00*

Popular Singers — A936

Designs: Nos. 2221a, 2222a, Gordon Lightfoot. Nos. 2221b, 2222b, Joni Mitchell. Nos. 2221c, 2222c, Anne Murray. Nos. 2221d, 2222d, Paul Anka.

2007, June 29 ***Perf. 12½x13***

2221 A936 Pane of 4 3.25 3.25
a.-d. 52c Any single .80 .80

Self-Adhesive
Serpentine Die Cut 13½

2222 A936 Booklet pane of 4 3.25
a.-d. 52c Any single .80 .40
Complete booklet, 2 #2222 6.50

Complete booklets were issued with four different covers depicting the featured singers.

National Parks — A937

Designs: No. 2223, Terra Nova National Park, Newfoundland, 50th anniv. No. 2224, Jasper National Park, Alberta, cent.

Self-Adhesive
Booklet Stamps

2007 ***Serpentine Die Cut 13½***

2223 A937 52c multi .80 .30
a. Booklet pane of 5 4.00
Complete booklet, 2 #2223a 8.00
2224 A937 52c multi .80 .30
a. Booklet pane of 5 4.00
Complete booklet, 2 #2224a 8.00
b. Gutter pane, 5 each #2223-2224 11.00

Issued: No. 2223, 7/6; No. 2224, 7/20.

Scouting, Cent. A938

Self-Adhesive
Booklet Stamp

2007, July 25

2225 A938 52c multi .80 .30
a. Booklet pane of 4 + 4 labels 3.25
Complete booklet, 2 #2225a 6.50

Henri Membertou, Grand Chief of Mi'kmaq Tribe — A939

2007, June 26 **Engr.** ***Perf. 13x12½***

2226 A939 52c multi .80 .30

Law Society of Saskatchewan, Cent. — A940

2007, Sept. 13 **Litho.** ***Perf. 13***

2227 A940 52c multi 1.50 .75

Printed in panes of 8 + 8 labels.

Law Society of Alberta, Cent. A941

2007, Sept. 13 ***Perf. 12½x13***

2228 A941 52c multi .80 .30

Endangered Animals Type of 2006

Designs: Nos. 2229a, 2230, North Atlantic right whale. Nos. 2229b, 2231, Northern cricket frog. Nos. 2229c, 2232, White sturgeon. Nos. 2229d, 2233, Leatherback turtle.

2007, Oct. 1 ***Perf. 13¼***

2229 Pane of 4 + 4 labels 3.50 3.50
a.-d. A915 52c Any single .85 .85

Booklet Stamps
Self-Adhesive
Size: 47x24mm
Die Cut

2230 A915 52c multi .80 .30
2231 A915 52c multi .80 .30
2232 A915 52c multi .80 .30
2233 A915 52c multi .80 .30
a. Block of 4, #2230-2233 3.25
b. Booklet pane, 2 #2233a 6.50

Beneficial Insects — A942

No. 2235

No. 2235a

Designs: 1c, Convergent lady beetle (Hippodamia convergens). 3c, Golden-eyed lacewing (Chrysopa oculata). 5c, Northern bumblebee (Bombus polaris). 10c, Canada darner (Aeshna canadensis). 25c, Cecropia moth (Hyalophora cecropia).

2007, Oct. 12 ***Perf. 13¼x13***

2234 A942 1c multi .25 .25
2235 A942 3c multi .25 .25
a. "Canada" shifted to right, touching "Oculata" (pos. 11-14) .40 .25
b. Dated "2012," with added microprinting and small design features (#2409b) .25 .25
2236 A942 5c multi .25 .25
2237 A942 10c multi .25 .25
2238 A942 25c multi .40 .25
a. Souvenir sheet, #2234-2238 1.10 1.00
Nos. 2234-2238 (5) 1.40 1.25

No. 2235a occurs four times on each pane of 50. Panes printed in 2010 correct the errors. See Nos. 2328, 2406-2410, 2708.

Issued: No. 2235b, 10/16/12.

Christmas
A943 A944

Designs: No. 2239, Reindeer and snowflakes. No. 2240, Holy Family. 93c, Angel over town. $1.55, Dove.

Booklet Stamps
Litho. With Hologram Affixed
Serpentine Die Cut 8¼ Horiz.

2007, Nov. 1 **Self-Adhesive**

2239 A943 (52c) multi 1.35 .25
a. Booklet pane of 6 8.00
Complete booklet, 2 #2239a 16.00
b. Die cutting omitted, pair *400.00*

Litho.
Serpentine Die Cut 13½

2240 A944 (52c) multi 1.35 .25
a. Booklet pane of 6 8.00
Complete booklet, 2 #2240a 16.00
2241 A944 93c multi 1.40 .40
a. Booklet pane of 6 8.50
2242 A944 $1.55 multi 2.25 .60
a. Booklet pane of 6 13.50
b. Die cutting omitted, pair *550.00*
Nos. 2239-2242 (4) 6.35 1.50

Flowers Type of 2006 and

Odontioda Island Red Orchid A945

Queen Elizabeth II A946

Flag and Sambro Island Lighthouse, Nova Scotia A947

Flag and Point Clark Lighthouse, Ontario A948

Flag and Cap-des-Rosiers Lighthouse, Quebec — A949

Flag and Warren Landing Lighthouse, Manitoba A950

Flag and Pachena Point Lighthouse, British Columbia A951

Flag and Pachena Point Lighthouse, British Columbia — A951a

Designs: 96c, Potinara Janet Elizabeth "Fire Dancer" orchid. $1.15, Laeliocattleya Memoria Evelyn Light orchid. $1.60, Masdevallia Kaleidoscope "Conni" orchid.

2007, Dec. 27 Litho. *Perf. 13¼x13*

2243	Pane of 4	7.00	7.00
a.	A945 P multi	1.30	.85
b.	A926 96c multi	1.40	1.20
c.	A926 $1.15 multi	1.70	1.30
d.	A926 $1.60 multi	2.40	1.80

Self-Adhesive

Coil Stamps

Serpentine Die Cut 8-9½ Horiz.

2244	A945 P multi	1.30	.25

Serpentine Die Cut 9.2 Horiz.

2244A	A945 P multi	1.45	1.45

Serpentine Die Cut 8-9½

2245	A926 96c multi	1.45	.30
2246	A926 $1.15 multi	1.70	.45
2247	A926 $1.60 multi	2.40	.60
	Nos. 2244-2247 (5)	8.30	3.05

Die cutting is irregular across the stamp (saw tooth tips) on Nos. 2244 and 2245-2247 compared to being consistent across the stamp (rounded tips) on No. 2244A. On No. 2244, stamps are vertically contiguous on the backing paper, while on No. 2244A the stamps are separated on horizontal backing paper that is taller than the stamp.

Booklet Stamps

Serpentine Die Cut 13¼

2248	A946 P multi	1.30	.25
a.	Booklet pane of 10	13.00	
2249	A947 P multi	1.30	.25
2250	A948 P multi	1.30	.25
2251	A949 P multi	1.30	.25
2252	A950 P multi	1.30	.25
2253	A951 P multi	1.30	.25
a.	Booklet pane of 10, 2 each #2249-2253	13.00	

Serpentine Die Cut 13¼

2253B	A951a P multi	1.30	.25
c.	Booklet pane of 10, 2 each #2249-2252, 2253B	13.00	
d.	Booklet pane of 30, 6 each #2249-2252, 2253B	39.00	

Die Cut

2254	A926 96c multi	1.45	.25
a.	Booklet pane of 6	8.75	
2255	A926 $1.15 multi	1.70	.40
a.	Booklet pane of 6	10.25	
2256	A926 $1.60 multi	2.40	.60
a.	Booklet pane of 6	14.50	
	Nos. 2248-2256 (10)	14.65	3.00

Nos. 2243a, 2244, 2248-2253 each sold for 52c on day of issue.

No. 2244A issued 2/21/08.

No. 2253B issued 5/1/08. No. 2253Bd was separated into thirds by two rows of rouletting. The separated thirds of this booklet have the same contents as No. 2253Bc, but have different selvage markings.

New Year 2008 (Year of the Rat) — A952

Designs: 52c, Rat with umbrella. $1.60, Rat with fan.

Litho. & Embossed With Foil Application

2008, Jan. 8 *Perf. 13*

2257	A952 52c multi	.80	.30

Souvenir Sheet

2258	A952 $1.60 multi	3.00	3.00

No. 2257 printed in panes of 25 + 20 labels.

Fireworks A953

Self-Adhesive

Booklet Stamp

Serpentine Die Cut 13½ Horiz.

2008, Jan. 15 Litho.

2259	A953 P multi	1.30	.30
a.	Booklet pane of 6	7.75	

No. 2259 sold for 52c on day of issue.

Peonies — A954

Peony color: Nos. 2260a, 2261, Pink. Nos. 2260b, 2262, Red.

2008, Mar. 3 Litho. *Perf. 13¼*

2260	Pane of 2	2.20	2.20
a.-b.	A954 52c Either single	1.10	.75

Booklet Stamps

Self-Adhesive

Serpentine Die Cut 13¼

2261	A954 52c multi	.80	.30
2262	A954 52c multi	.80	.30
a.	Pair, #2261-2262	1.60	
b.	Booklet pane, 5 each #2261-2262, + 10 stickers	8.50	
c.	Die cutting omitted, pair	*375.00*	

The country name and denomination are closer to the flowers on Nos. 2261-2262 than on Nos. 2260a-2260b.

Universities A955

Designs: No. 2263, University of Alberta, cent. No. 2264, University of British Columbia, cent.

Self-Adhesive

Serpentine Die Cut 13¼

2008, Mar. 7 Booklet Stamps

2263	A955 52c multi	.80	.25
a.	Booklet pane of 8	6.50	
b.	Die cutting omitted, pair	*325.00*	
2264	A955 52c multi	.80	.25
a.	Booklet pane of 8	6.50	
b.	Gutter pane, 4 each #2263-2264	11.00	

2008 Intl. Ice Hockey Federation Championships, Halifax and Quebec — A956

Self-Adhesive

Serpentine Die Cut 13½

2008, Apr. 3 Booklet Stamp

2265	A956 52c multi	.80	.25
a.	Booklet pane of 10	8.00	
b.	Die cutting omitted, pair	*300.00*	

No. 2265a was printed with two different booklet covers.

Guide Dog — A957

Self-Adhesive

Booklet Stamp

Serpentine Die Cut 13½x13

2008, Apr. 21 Litho. & Embossed

2266	A957 52c multi	.80	.25
a.	Booklet pane of 10	8.00	

Montreal Association for the Blind, cent.

Oil and Gas Anniversaries — A958

Designs: No. 2267, Welder welding Trans-Canada Pipeline. No. 2268, James M. Williams, Charles Tripp, Oil Springs, Ontario oil field.

Self-Adhesive

Booklet Stamps

Serpentine Die Cut 13¼

2008, May 2 Litho.

2267	A958 52c multi	.80	.25
a.	Die cutting omitted, pair	750.00	
2268	A958 52c multi	.80	.25
a.	Die cutting omitted, pair	750.00	
b.	Booklet pane of 10, 5 each #2267-2268	8.00	

Trans-Canada Pipeline, 50th anniv., First commercial oil well in Canada, 150th anniv.

Quebec City, 400th Anniv. A959

Litho. & Engr.

2008, May 16 *Perf. 13x12½*

2269	A959 52c multi	.80	.30

See France No. 3437. A souvenir sheet containing No. 2269 and France No. 3437 sold for $4.99.

Photographic Portraits by Yousuf Karsh (1908-2008) A960

Designs: 52c, Self-portrait, 1952. 96c, Audrey Hepburn, 1956. $1.60, Sir Winston Churchill, 1941.

2008, May 21 Litho. *Perf. 13x12½*

2270	A960 52c multi	.80	.30

Souvenir Sheet

2271	Pane of 3, #2270, 2271a, 2271b	4.75	4.75
a.	A960 96c multi	1.45	1.10
b.	A960 $1.60 multi	2.40	2.25

Booklet Stamps

Self-Adhesive

2272	A960 96c multi	1.45	.60
a.	Booklet pane of 4	5.75	
	Complete booklet, 2 #2272a	11.50	
2273	A960 $1.60 multi	2.40	.90
a.	Booklet pane of 4	9.50	
	Complete booklet, 2 #2273a	19.00	
b.	Gutter pane, #2272a, 2273a	16.00	

No. 2270 printed in panes of 16 + 4 labels.

1908 Fifty-cent Coin — A961

Litho. & Embossed

2008, June 4 *Perf. 13x13¼*

2274	A961 52c multi	.80	.30

Royal Canadian Mint, cent. Printed in panes of 16 + 4 labels.

Canadian Nurses Association, Cent. — A962

Self-Adhesive

Booklet Stamp

Serpentine Die Cut 13¼

2008, June 16 Litho.

2275	A962 52c multi	.80	.30
a.	Booklet pane of 10	8.00	

Publication of *Anne of Green Gables,* by Lucy Maud Montgomery, Cent. — A963

Designs: Nos. 2276a, 2277, Anne holding buttercups. Nos. 2276b, 2278, Green Gables House.

Perf. 13½ Syncopated

2008, June 20

Souvenir Sheet

2276	A963 Pane of 2	2.20	2.20
a.-b.	52c Either single	1.10	.90

Booklet Stamps

Self-Adhesive

Serpentine Die Cut 13¼x13

2277	A963 52c multi	.80	.30
2278	A963 52c multi	.80	.30
a.	Booklet pane of 10, 5 each #2277-2278 + 10 stickers	8.00	
b.	Die cutting omitted, pair (#2277-2278)	*375.00*	

See Japan No. 3028.

Canadians in Hollywood Type of 2006

Actors and actresses: Nos. 2279a, 2280c, Norma Shearer (1902?-83). Nos. 2279b, 2280b, Chief Dan George (1899-1981). Nos.

2279c, 2280a, Marie Dressler (1868-1934). Nos. 2279d, 2280d, Raymond Burr (1917-93).

2008, June 30 *Perf. 13x12½*

2279	Souvenir sheet of 4	4.40	4.40
a.-d.	A903 52c Any single	1.10	.90

Self-Adhesive

Serpentine Die Cut 13½x13¼

2280	Booklet pane of 4 + 4 stickers	3.25	
a.-d.	A903 52c Any single	.80	.30
	Complete booklet, 2 #2280	6.50	

Complete booklets were issued with four different covers depicting the featured actors or actresses. The order of the stamps and labels in the booklet pane differed in the four booklets.

2008 Summer Olympics, Beijing — A964

Self-Adhesive

Serpentine Die Cut 13½

2008, July 18 **Booklet Stamp**

2281	A964 52c multi	.80	.30
a.	Booklet pane of 10	8.00	
b.	Die cutting omitted, strip of 3	900.00	

Lifesaving Society, Cent. A965

Self-Adhesive

Serpentine Die Cut 13¼x12¾

2008, July 25 **Booklet Stamp**

2282	A965 52c multi	.80	.25
a.	Booklet pane of 10	8.00	

British Columbia, 150th Anniv. — A966

Self-Adhesive

2008, Aug. 1 *Perf. 12½x13*

2283	A966 52c multi	.80	.30

R. Samuel McLaughlin (1871-1972), Automobile Manufacturer, and Buick Automobile — A967

2008, Sept. 8 *Perf. 12½x13*

2284	A967 52c multi	.80	.30

Endangered Animals Type of 2006

Designs: Nos. 2285a, 2286, Prothonotary warbler. Nos. 2285b, 2287, Taylor's checker-spot butterfly. Nos. 2285c, 2288, Roseate tern. Nos. 2285d, 2289, Burrowing owl.

2008, Oct. 1 *Perf. 13¼*

2285	Pane of 4 + 4 labels	3.25	3.25
a.-d.	A915 52c Any single	.80	.85

Booklet Stamps

Self-Adhesive

Size: 48x24mm

Die Cut

2286	A915 52c multi	.80	.30
2287	A915 52c multi	.80	.30
2288	A915 52c multi	.80	.30
2289	A915 52c multi	.80	.30
a.	Block of 4, #2286-2289	3.20	
b.	Booklet pane, 2 #2289a	6.40	

12th Francophone Summit, Quebec — A968

2008, Oct. 15 *Perf. 12½x13¼*

2290	A968 52c multi	.80	.30

A969

Christmas — A970

Child: Nos. 2291a, 2293, Making snow angel. Nos. 2291b, 2294, Skiing. Nos. 2291c, 2295, Tobogganing.

Souvenir Sheet

2008, Nov. 3 *Perf. 13½*

2291	Pane of 3	5.25	5.25
a.	A969 P multi	1.30	1.00
b.	A969 96c multi	1.45	1.45
c.	A969 $1.60 multi	2.40	2.40

Booklet Stamps

Self-Adhesive

Serpentine Die Cut 13¼

2292	A970 P multi	1.30	.25
a.	Booklet pane of 6	7.75	
	Complete booklet, 2 #2292a	15.50	
b.	Die cutting omitted, pair	600.00	

Serpentine Die Cut 13¾

2293	A969 P multi	1.30	.25
a.	Booklet pane of 6	7.75	
	Complete booklet, 2 #2293a	15.50	
2294	A969 96c multi	1.45	.60
a.	Booklet pane of 6	8.75	
2295	A969 $1.60 multi	2.40	.90
a.	Booklet pane of 6	14.50	
b.	Gutter pane, #2294a, 2295a	26.00	
	Nos. 2292-2295 (4)	6.45	2.00

Nos. 2291a, 2292 and 2293 each sold for 52c on day of issue.

See No. 2343a.

A971

New Year 2009 (Year of the Ox) A972

Litho. & Embossed With Foil Application

2009, Jan. 8 *Perf. 12½*

2296	A971 P multi	1.30	.25

Souvenir Sheet

2297	A972 $1.65 multi	2.50	2.50
a.	With China 2009 emblem overprinted in gold in pane margin	3.40	3.40

No. 2296 sold for 54c on day of issue. See Nos. 3259b, 3260b, 3262.

Queen Elizabeth II — A973

Self-Adhesive

Booklet Stamp

Serpentine Die Cut 13½x13¼

2009, Jan. 12 **Litho.**

2298	A973 P multi	1.30	.25
a.	Booklet pane of 10	13.00	

No. 2298 sold for 54c on day of issue.

Sports of the Winter Olympics and Paralympics

A974 A975

Designs: Nos. 2299a, 2303, Curling. Nos. 2299b, 2302, Bobsledding. Nos. 2299c, 2304, Snowboarding. Nos. 2299d, 2300, Freestyle skiing. Nos. 2299e, 2301, Ice-sled hockey.

2009, Jan. 12 *Perf. 13¼x13*

2299	Pane of 5	6.50	6.50
a.-d.	A974 P Any single	1.30	1.10
e.	A975 P multi	1.30	1.10
f.	As No. 2299, with "Vancouver / 2010" overprinted in sheet margin in silver	17.50	17.50

Booklet Stamps

Self-Adhesive

Serpentine Die Cut 13¼x13½

2300	A974 P multi	1.30	.25
2301	A975 P multi	1.30	.25
2302	A974 P multi	1.30	.25
2303	A974 P multi	1.30	.25
2304	A974 P multi	1.30	.25
a.	Booklet pane of 10, 2 each #2300-2304	13.00	
b.	Booklet pane of 30, 6 each #2300-2304	39.00	

On day of issue, Nos. 2299a-2299e, 2300-2304 each sold for 54c.

No. 2299f was originally sold with a set of coins in 2009. It was made available in 2010 in a set of 3 sheets, Nos. 2299f, 2305f, and 2366c that sold for $8.73.

2010 Vancouver Winter Olympics Emblem A976

2010 Vancouver Winter Paralympics Emblem A977

Miga, Winter Olympics Mascot — A978

Sumi, Paralympics Mascot — A979

Quatchi, Winter Olympics Mascot — A980

2009 *Perf. 13¼x13*

2305	Pane of 5	8.25	8.25
a.	A976 P multi	1.30	1.10
b.	A977 P multi	1.30	1.10
c.	A978 98c multi	1.45	1.55
d.	A979 $1.18 multi	1.75	1.90
e.	A980 $1.65 multi	2.45	2.65
f.	As No. 2305, with "Vancouver / 2010" overprinted in sheet margin in bronze	19.00	19.00

Self-Adhesive

Coil Stamps

Serpentine Die Cut 9¼ (Rounded Tips)

2306	A976 P multi	1.30	1.30
2307	A977 P multi	1.30	1.30

Serpentine Die Cut 7¾-9½ (Sawtooth Tips)

2307A	A976 P multi	1.30	.25
2307B	A977 P multi	1.30	.25
c.	Vert. pair, #2307A-2307B	2.60	
2308	A978 98c multi	1.45	.35
2309	A979 $1.18 multi	1.75	.55
2310	A980 $1.65 multi	2.45	.75

Booklet Stamps

Serpentine Die Cut 9¼ (Rounded Tips)

2311	A978 98c multi	1.40	.25
a.	Booklet pane of 6	8.50	
2312	A979 $1.18 multi	1.80	.40
a.	Booklet pane of 6	11.00	
2313	A980 $1.65 multi	2.40	.55
a.	Booklet pane of 6	14.50	
	Nos. 2306-2313 (10)	16.45	5.95

Issued: Nos. 2305, 2309, 2312, 2/12; Nos. 2306-2308, 2310-2311, 2313, 1/12. On day of issue, Nos. 2305a, 2305b, 2306-2307B each sold for 54c. Rolls of Nos. 2306 and 2307 have horizontal pairs of the same stamp that do not abut each other. Stamps from rolls containing Nos. 2307A and 2307B have pairs of different stamps that abut each other vertically.

No. 2305f was originally sold with a set of coins in 2009. It was made available in 2010 in a set of 3 sheets, Nos. 2299f, 2305f, and 2366c that sold for $8.73.

Celebration A981

Self-Adhesive

Serpentine Die Cut 13½ Horiz.

2009, Feb. 2 **Booklet Stamp**

2314 A981 P multi 1.30 .30
a. Booklet pane of 6 7.75

No. 2314 sold for 54c on day of issue.

Rosemary Brown (1930-2003) A982

Abraham Doras Shadd (1801-82) A983

2009, Feb. 2 ***Perf. 13x12½***

2315 A982 54c multi .80 .30
2316 A983 54c multi .80 .30
a. Pair, #2315-2316 1.60 1.10

Black History Month. Brown and Shadd were the first black woman and man elected to public office in Canada.

First Airplane Flight in Canada, Cent. — A984

Self-Adhesive

2009, Feb. 23 ***Perf. 12½x13***

2317 A984 P multi 1.30 .30

No. 2317 sold for 54c on day of issue.

Rhododendrons — A985

Color of rhododendrons: Nos. 2318a, 2319, White and pink. Nos. 2318b, 2320, Pink.

2009, Mar. 13 ***Perf. 13¼***

2318 A985 Pane of 2 2.20 2.20
a.-b. 54c Either single 1.10 .85

Booklet Stamps

Self-Adhesive

Serpentine Die Cut 13½x12¾

2319 A985 54c multi .80 .30
2320 A985 54c multi .80 .30
a. Booklet pane of 10, 5 each #2319-2320 8.00
b. Die cutting omitted, pair 525.00

Paintings by Jack Bush (1909-77) A986

Designs: 54c, Striped Column. $1.65, Chopsticks, horiz. (57x23mm).

2009, Mar. 20 ***Perf. 13x13¼***

2321 A986 54c multi .80 .30
a. Perf. 12½x13¼ 1.10 1.10

Souvenir Sheet

Perf. 12½x13¼

2322 Pane, #2321a, 2322a 3.75 3.75
a. A986 $1.65 multi 2.25 2.25

Souvenir Sheet

Intl. Year of Astronomy — A987

Designs: Nos. 2323a, 2324, Dominion Astrophysical Observatory, Saanich, British Columbia, and Horsehead Nebula. Nos. 2323b, 2325, Canada-France-Hawaii Telescope, Hawaii, and Eagle Nebula.

2009, Apr. 2 ***Perf. 13¼x13***

2323 A987 Pane of 2 2.20 2.20
a.-b. 54c Either single 1.10 .75
c. As #2323, with buff background behind product code 3.75 3.75

Booklet Stamps

Size: 24x34mm

Self-Adhesive

Serpentine Die Cut 13½

2324 A987 54c multi .80 .30
2325 A987 54c multi .80 .30
a. Booklet pane, 5 each #2324-2325 8.00

The product code on No. 2323 is "063491072031," and on No. 2323c, "063491072024." The background behind the product code on No. 2323 is white. No. 2323c also has a fluorescent overprint in the margin, not found on No. 2323. Nos. 2323a and 2323b are 27x36mm.

Preservation of Polar Regions and Glaciers — A988

2009, Apr. 9 ***Perf. 13x12¾***

2326 A988 54c Polar bear .80 .30
2327 A988 54c Arctic tern .80 .30
a. Pair, #2326-2327 1.60 .90
b. Souvenir sheet, #2326-2327 1.90 1.90

Beneficial Insects Type of 2007

Design: Danaus plexippus caterpillar.

2009, Apr. 22 ***Perf. 13¼x13***

2328 A942 2c multi .25 .25

Horses A989

Designs: No. 2329, Canadian horse. No. 2330, Newfoundland pony.

Self-Adhesive

Serpentine Die Cut 13¼

2009, May 15 **Booklet Stamps**

2329 A989 54c multi .80 .30
2330 A989 54c multi .80 .30
a. Booklet pane of 10, 5 each #2329-2330 8.00

Department of Foreign Affairs and International Trade, Cent. A990

2009, June 1 ***Perf. 13¼x13***

2331 A990 54c multi .80 .30

Boundary Waters Treaty, Cent. A991

2009, June 12 ***Perf. 13¼***

2332 A991 54c multi .80 .30

Popular Singers — A992

Designs: Nos. 2333a, 2334d, Robert Charlebois. Nos. 2333b, 2334c, Edith Butler. Nos. 2333c, 2334b, Stompin' Tom Connors. Nos. 2333d, 2334a, Bryan Adams.

2009, July 2 ***Perf. 12½x13***

2333 A992 Pane of 4 3.25 3.25
a.-d. 54c Any single .80 .80

Self-Adhesive

Serpentine Die Cut 13½

2334 A992 Booklet pane of 4 3.25
a.-d. 54c Any single .80 .40
Complete booklet, 2 #2334 6.50

Complete booklets were issued with four different covers depicting the featured singers. The order of the stamps is different in each booklet.

Roadside Attractions — A993

Designs: Nos. 2335a, 2336a, Mr. PG, Prince George, British Columbia. Nos. 2335b, 2336b, Sign Post Forest, Watson Lake, Yukon Territory. Nos. 2335c, 2336c, Inukshuk, Hay River, Northwest Territories. Nos. 2335d, 2336d, Pysanka, Vegreville, Alberta.

2009, July 6 ***Perf. 13***

2335 A993 Pane of 4 3.25 3.25
a.-d. 54c Any single .80 .80

Self-Adhesive

Serpentine Die Cut 13½

2336 A993 Booklet pane of 4 3.25
a.-d. 54c Any single .80 .40
Complete booklet, 2 #2336 6.50

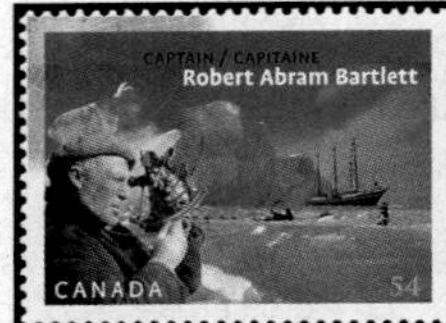

Captain Robert Abram Bartlett (1875-1946), Arctic Explorer — A994

2009, July 10 ***Perf. 13***

2337 A994 54c multi .80 .30

Sports Invented By Canadians — A995

No. 2338: a, Five-pin bowling. b, Ringette. c, Lacrosse. d, Basketball.

Serpentine Die Cut 13¼

2009, Aug. 10

2338 Booklet pane of 4 3.25
a.-d. A995 54c Any single .80 .40
Complete booklet, 2 #2338 6.50

Montreal Canadiens Hockey Jersey — A996

500-Goal Scorers of the Montreal Canadiens — A997

No. 2340 — 500th goal of: a, Maurice Richard. b, Jean Béliveau. c, Guy Lafleur.

Self-Adhesive

Serpentine Die Cut 13½x13¼

2009, Oct. 17 **Booklet Stamp**

2339 A996 P multi 1.30 .30
a. Booklet pane of 10 13.00

Souvenir Sheet

Litho. With Three-Dimensional Plastic Affixed

Serpentine Die Cut 13x13¼

Self-Adhesive

2340 A997 Pane of 3 13.50 13.50
a.-c. $3 Any single 4.50 4.50
d. Die cutting omitted, pane of 3 *1,800.*

Montreal Canadiens hockey team, cent. No. 2339 sold for 54c on day of issue.

Soaking of No. 2340 may cause the stamps to separate into layers. Soaking of used examples also may cause the cancellations to dissolve.

National War Memorial, Ottawa, and Poppy — A998

2009, Oct. 19 **Litho.** ***Perf. 12½***

2341 A998 P multi 1.30 1.10
a. Souvenir sheet of 2 2.60 2.60

Booklet Stamp
Self-Adhesive
Serpentine Die Cut 13¼

2342 A998 P multi 1.30 .30
a. Booklet pane of 10 13.00

End of World War I, 91st anniv. On day of issue, Nos. 2341-2342 each sold for 54c. No. 2341 was issued only in the souvenir sheet of 2.

Christmas Type of 2008 and

Christmas
A999 A1000

Designs: Nos. 2343b, 2345, Madonna and child. 98c, Magus. $1.65, Shepherd and lamb.

2009, Nov. 2 ***Perf. 13x12½***
2343 Pane of 4 + 6 labels 6.50 6.50
a. A970 P multi 1.30 1.10
b. A999 P multi 1.30 1.10
c. A999 98c multi 1.45 1.50
d. A999 $1.65 multi 2.45 2.65

Booklet Stamps
Self-Adhesive
Litho. With Hologram Affixed
Serpentine Die Cut 8¼ Horiz.

2344 A1000 P multi 1.30 .25
a. Booklet pane of 6 7.75
Complete booklet, 2 #2344a 15.50

Litho.
Serpentine Die Cut 13½

2345 A999 P multi 1.30 .25
a. Booklet pane of 6 7.75
Complete booklet, 2 #2345 15.50
2346 A999 98c multi 1.45 .60
a. Booklet pane of 6 8.75
2347 A999 $1.65 multi 2.45 .90
a. Booklet pane of 6 14.75
b. Booklet pane of 12, 6 each #2346-2347 24.00
Nos. 2344-2347 (4) 6.50 2.00

On day of issue, Nos. 2343a, 2343b, 2344, and 2345 each sold for 54c. No. 2347b is Nos. 2346a and 2347a unseparated but with horizontal slits cut in margin between the panes.

New Year 2010 (Year of the Tiger) — A1001

Designs: P, Seal impression of tiger in circle. $1.70, Sculpted tiger seal.

Litho. & Embossed With Foil Application

2010, Jan. 8 ***Perf. 12½***
2348 A1001 P multi 1.30 .45

Souvenir Sheet

2349 A1001 $1.70 multi 2.50 2.50

No. 2348 sold for 57c on day of issue. See Nos. 3259c, 3260c, 3263.

Flag Over Watson's Mill, Manotick, Ont. A1002

Flag Over Keremeos Grist Mill, Keremeos, B.C. A1003

Flag Over Old Stone Mill Natl. Historic Site, Delta, Ont. — A1004

Flag Over Riordon Grist Mill, Caraquet, N. B. — A1005

Flag Over Cornell Mill, Stanbridge East, Que. — A1006

2010, Jan. 11 **Litho.** ***Perf. 13x13¼***
2350 Souvenir sheet of 5 6.50 6.50
a. A1002 P multi 1.30 1.10
b. A1003 P multi 1.30 1.10
c. A1004 P multi 1.30 1.10
d. A1005 P multi 1.30 1.10
e. A1006 P multi 1.30 1.10

Booklet Stamps
Self-Adhesive
Serpentine Die Cut 13¼

2351 A1002 P multi 1.30 .25
2352 A1003 P multi 1.30 .25
2353 A1004 P multi 1.30 .25
2354 A1005 P multi 1.30 .25
2355 A1006 P multi 1.30 .25
a. Booklet pane of 10, 2 each #2351-2355 13.00
b. Booklet pane of 30, 6 each #2351-2355 39.00
Nos. 2351-2355 (5) 6.50 1.25

On day of issue, Nos. 2350a-2350e and 2351-2355 each sold for 57c.

Striped Coralroot Orchid — A1007
Giant Helleborine Orchid — A1008

Rose Pogonia Orchid — A1009
Grass Pink Orchid — A1010

2010, Jan. 11 ***Perf. 13¼x13***
2356 Souvenir sheet of 4 7.00 7.00
a. A1007 P multi 1.30 1.10
b. A1008 $1 multi 1.50 1.25
c. A1009 $1.22 multi 1.80 1.50
d. A1010 $1.70 multi 2.50 2.00

Coil Stamps
Self-Adhesive
Serpentine Die Cut 8 to 9½ (Sawtooth Tips)

2357 A1007 P multi 1.30 .25
2358 A1008 $1 multi 1.50 .30
2359 A1009 $1.22 multi 1.80 .50
2360 A1010 $1.70 multi 2.50 .75

Horiz. pairs, imperf. between, of No. 2357 are from uncut press panels of 100. Value unused, $4.

Serpentine Die Cut 9¼ (Rounded Tips)

2361 A1007 P multi 1.50 1.50
Nos. 2357-2361 (5) 8.60 3.30

Booklet Stamps

2362 A1008 $1 multi 1.50 .35
a. Booklet pane of 6 9.00
2363 A1009 $1.22 multi 1.80 .50
a. Booklet pane of 6 10.75
2364 A1010 $1.70 multi 2.50 .75
a. Booklet pane of 6 15.00
Nos. 2362-2364 (3) 5.80 1.60

On day of issue, Nos. 2356a and 2357 each sold for 57c. No. 2357 was printed in vertical rolls with stamps that are adjacent. No. 2361 was printed in horizontal rolls with stamps that are separated.

Queen Elizabeth II — A1011

Self-Adhesive
Serpentine Die Cut 13¼

2010, Jan. 11 **Booklet Stamp**
2365 A1011 P multi 1.30 .25
a. Booklet pane of 10 13.00

No. 2365 sold for 57c on day of issue.

Venues of the 2010 Winter Olympics — A1012

Designs: Nos. 2366a, 2367, Whistler, B.C. Nos. 2366b, 2368, Vancouver.

2010, Jan. 12 ***Perf. 13½x13¼***
2366 A1012 Souvenir sheet of 2 2.20 2.20
a.-b. 57c Either single 1.10 .75
c. As No. 2366, with "Vancouver / 2010" overprinted in sheet margin in gold 12.00 12.00

Booklet Stamps
Self-Adhesive
Serpentine Die Cut 13¼

2367 A1012 57c multi .85 .30
2368 A1012 57c multi .85 .30
a. Booklet pane of 10, 5 each #2367-2368, + 10 stickers 8.50

No. 2366c was sold in a package of 3 sheets that also contained Nos. 2299f and 2305f.

William Hall (1827-1904), First Black Recipient of Victoria Cross — A1013

2010, Feb. 1 ***Perf. 12¾x12½***
2369 A1013 57c multi .85 .30

Roméo LeBlanc (1927-2009), Governor-General — A1014

2010, Feb. 8 ***Perf. 12½***
2370 A1014 57c multi .85 .30

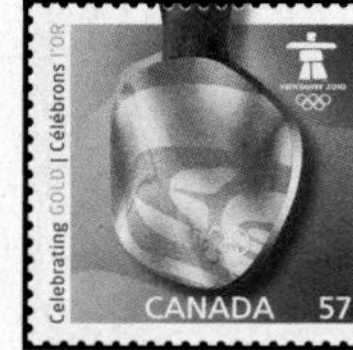

Gold Medal From Vancouver Winter Olympics A1015

2010, Feb. 15 ***Perf. 12½***
2371 Sheet of 2 #2371a 2.20 2.20
a. A1015 57c Single stamp 1.10 .75

First day cancels have a Feb. 14 date, which was the date on which the first gold medal was awarded to a Canadian athlete on home soil, but which also was a Sunday. Post offices in Vancouver had the stamp available for sale on Feb. 15.

Booklet Stamp
Self-Adhesive
Serpentine Die Cut 13½

2372 A1015 57c multi .85 .30
a. Booklet pane of 10 8.50

Awarding of first gold medal to a Canadian on home soil.

Spirit of the Winter Olympics — A1016

Winter Olympic athletes and: Nos. 2373a, 2374, Woman with painted face at left. Nos. 2373b, 2375, Woman with painted face at right.

2010, Feb. 22 ***Perf. 13***
2373 A1016 Souvenir sheet of 2 2.20 2.20
a.-b. 57c Either single 1.10 .75

Booklet Stamps
Self-Adhesive
Serpentine Die Cut 13¼

2374 A1016 57c multi .85 .30
2375 A1016 57c multi .85 .30
a. Booklet pane of 10, 5 each #2374-2375 8.50

African Violet Hybrids — A1017

Flower colors: Nos. 2376a, 2377, Red (Descelles' Avalanche). Nos. 2376b, 2378, Purple (Picasso).

2010, Mar. 3 **Litho.** ***Perf. 13***
2376 A1017 Souvenir sheet of 2 2.60 2.60
a.-b. P Either single 1.30 1.10

Booklet Stamps
Self-Adhesive
Serpentine Die Cut 13½

2377 A1017 P multi 1.30 .30
2378 A1017 P multi 1.30 .30
a. Booklet pane of 10, 5 each #2377-2378 13.00
b. Imperf., pair —
c. As "a," imperf. —

On day of issue, Nos. 2376a, 2376b, 2377 and 2378 each sold for 57c.

Friendship Between Canada and Israel, 60th Anniv. A1018

Booklet Stamp
Self-Adhesive
Serpentine Die Cut 13¼

2010, Apr. 14 **Litho.**
2379 A1018 $1.70 multi 2.60 1.10
a. Booklet pane of 3 + label 7.75
Complete booklet, 2 #2379a 15.50

See Israel No. 1812.

Indian Kings — A1019

Portraits by John Verelst of: No. 2380, Tee Yee Neen Ho Ga Row. No. 2381, Sa Ga Yeath Qua Pieth Tow. No. 2382, Ho Nee Yeath Taw No Row. No. 2383, Etow Oh Koam.

2010, Apr. 19 Litho. *Perf. 12½*

2380 A1019 57c multi .85 .40
2381 A1019 57c multi .85 .40
2382 A1019 57c multi .85 .40
2383 A1019 57c multi .85 .40
a. Block or strip of 4, #2380-2383 3.40 3.40
b. Souvenir sheet of 4, #2380-2383 3.75 3.75
c. As "b," with London 2010 emblem on sheet margin 5.50 5.50
Nos. 2380-2383 (4) 3.40 1.60

Meeting of the four Indian Kings and Queen Anne in London, 300th anniv.

Canadian Navy, Cent. — A1020

Designs: Nos. 2384a, 2385, Male sailor, HMCS Niobe. Nos. 2384b, 2386, Female sailor, HMCS Halifax.

2010, May 4 Litho. *Perf. 12½*

2384 A1020 Sheet of 2 2.20 2.20
a.-b. 57c Either single 1.10 .75

Booklet Stamps
Self-Adhesive
Serpentine Die Cut 13¼x13½

2385 A1020 57c multi .85 .30
2386 A1020 57c multi .85
a. Booklet pane of 10, 5 each #2385-2386 8.50

Sea Mammals — A1021

Designs: No. 2387a, Harbor porpoise. No. 2387b, Sea otter.

Perf. 13x12¼x13x13 Syncopated (#2387a), 13x13x13x12¼ Syncopated (#2387b)

2010, May 13 Litho. & Engr.

2387 A1021 Sheet of 2 2.20 2.20
a.-b. 57c Either single 1.10 .90
c. As "a," perf. 13x12¾ syncopated .75 .35
d. As "b," perf. 13x12¾ syncopated .75 .35
e. Booklet pane of 8, 4 each #2387c-2387d 6.00 6.00
Complete booklet, #2387e 7.00

Nos. 2387a and 2387b have syncopation on left and right side, with the syncopation between the stamps in the shape of a maple leaf. Nos. 2387c and 2387d have syncopation on one side only, with the syncopation between pairs of stamps in the shape of conjoined ovals.

See Sweden No. 2638.

Canadian Geographic's Wildlife Photography of the Year — A1022

Designs: Nos. 2388a, 2393, Ardia herodias, by Martin Cooper. Nos. 2388b, 2392, Vulpes vulpes, by Ben Boulter. Nos. 2388c, 2391, Tettigoniidae, by Julie Bazinet. Nos. 2388d, 2390, Tachycineta bicolor, by Mark Bradley. Nos. 2388e, 2389, Selasphorus rufus, by Wing Yan Tam.

2010, May 22 Litho. *Perf. 12½x13*

2388 A1022 Sheet of 5 5.00 5.00
a.-e. 57c Any single .85 .85

Booklet Stamps
Self-Adhesive
Serpentine Die Cut 13¼

2389 A1022 57c multi .85 .30
2390 A1022 57c multi .85 .30
2391 A1022 57c multi .85 .30
2392 A1022 57c multi .85 .30
2393 A1022 57c multi .85 .30
a. Booklet pane of 10, 2 each #2389-2393 8.50
Nos. 2389-2393 (5) 4.25 1.50

Rotary International in Canada, Cent. A1023

Self-Adhesive
Booklet Stamp
Serpentine Die Cut 13½x12¾

2010, June 18 Litho.

2394 A1023 57c multi .85 .30
a. Booklet pane of 8 6.75

Paintings by Prudence Heward (1896-1947) A1024

Designs: 57c, Rollande. $1.70, At the Theatre, horiz. (42x40mm).

2010, July 2 *Perf. 13¼x13*

2395 A1024 57c multi .85 .30

Souvenir Sheet

2396 Sheet of 2, #2395, 2396a 3.75 3.75
a. A1024 $1.70 multi 2.60 2.60

Roadside Attractions — A1025

Designs: Nos. 2397a, 2398, Coffee Pot, Davidson, Saskatchewan. Nos. 2397b, 2399, Happy Rock, Gladstone, Manitoba. Nos. 2397c, 2400, Wawa Goose, Wawa, Ontario. Nos. 2397d, 2401, Puffin, Longue-Pointe-de-Mingan, Quebec.

2010, July 5 *Perf. 13*

2397 A1025 Sheet of 4 5.25 5.25
a.-d. P Any single 1.30 1.10

Booklet Stamps
Self-Adhesive
Serpentine Die Cut 13½

2398 A1025 P multi 1.30 .40
2399 A1025 P multi 1.30 .40
2400 A1025 P multi 1.30 .40
2401 A1025 P multi 1.30 .40
a. Booklet pane of 4, #2398-2401 5.25
Complete booklet, 2 #2401a 10.50

On day of issue, Nos. 2397a-2397d, 2398-2401 each sold for 57c.

Girl Guides, Cent. — A1026

Self-Adhesive
Serpentine Die Cut 13¾

2010, July 8 Booklet Stamp

2402 A1026 P multi 1.30 .30
a. Booklet pane of 10 13.00

No. 2402 sold for 57c on day of issue.

Founding of Cupids, Newfoundland Settlement, 400th Anniv. — A1027

2010, Aug. 17 *Perf. 12½*

2403 A1027 57c multi .85 .35

Year of British Home Children A1028

2010, Sept. 1

2404 A1028 57c multi .85 .35

Blue Whale — A1029

Litho., Engr. & Silk-screened

2010, Oct. 4 *Perf. 12½x13*

2405 A1029 $10 multi 15.00 5.50

Printed in sheets of 2.

Beneficial Insects Type of 2007

Designs: 4c, Paper wasp (Polistes fuscatus). 6c, Assassin bug (Zelus luridus). 7c, Large milkweed bug (Oncopeltus fasciatus). 8c, Margined leatherwing (Chauliognathus marginatus). 9c, Dogbane beetle (Chrysochus auratus).

2010, Oct. 19 Litho. *Perf. 13¼x13*

2406 A942 4c multi .25 .25
a. With added microprinting and small design features (#2409b) .25 .25
2407 A942 6c multi .25 .25
2408 A942 7c multi .25 .25
2409 A942 8c multi .25 .25
a. With added microprinting and small design features (#2409b) .25 .25
b. Souvenir sheet of 3, #2235b, 2406a, 2409a .25 .25
2410 A942 9c multi .25 .25
a. Souvenir sheet, #2406-2410 2.20 .40
Nos. 2406-2410 (5) 1.25 1.25

Issued: Nos. 2406a, 2409a, 2409b, 10/16/12.

Christmas Ornaments A1030

Madonna and Child, Sculpture by Antonio Caruso A1031

Designs: Nos. 2411a, 2413, Three red ornaments, greenish blue background. $1, Two blue ornaments, purple background. $1.70, Three red ornaments, dull blue background.

2010, Nov. 1 Litho. *Perf. 12½*

2411 Souvenir sheet of 3 5.50 5.50
a. A1030 P multi 1.30 1.10
b. A1030 $1 multi 1.50 1.50
c. A1030 $1.70 multi 2.60 2.60

Booklet Stamps
Self-Adhesive
Serpentine Die Cut 13¼

2412 A1031 P multi 1.30 .25
a. Booklet pane of 6 7.75
Complete booklet, 2 #2412a 15.00

Serpentine Die Cut 13½

2413 A1030 P multi 1.30 .25
a. Booklet pane of 6 7.75
Complete booklet, 2 #2413a 15.50
2414 A1030 $1 multi 1.50 .60
a. Booklet pane of 6 9.00
2415 A1030 $1.70 multi 2.60 1.10
a. Booklet pane of 6 15.50
b. Gutter pane, #2414a, 2415a 27.50
Nos. 2412-2415 (4) 6.70 2.20

Nos. 2411a, 2412 and 2413 each sold for 57c on day of issue.

New Year 2011 (Year of the Rabbit) — A1032

Design: $1.75, Two rabbits in circle.

Litho. & Embossed With Foil Application

2011, Jan. 7 *Perf. 12½*

2416 A1032 P gold & multi 1.30 .40

Souvenir Sheet

2417 A1032 $1.75 multi 2.60 2.60

No. 2416 sold for 59c on day of issue. See Nos. 3259d, 3260d, 3264.

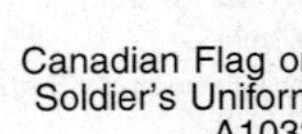

Canadian Flag on Soldier's Uniform A1033

Canadian Flag on Hot-air Balloon A1034

Canadian Flag on Search and Rescue Team's Uniform A1035

Canadian Flag on Canadarm A1036

Canadian Flag on Backpack — A1037

2011, Jan. 17 Litho. *Perf. 13x13¼*

2418 Sheet of 5 6.50 6.50
- a. A1033 P multi 1.30 1.10
- b. A1034 P multi 1.30 1.10
- c. A1035 P multi 1.30 1.10
- d. A1036 P multi 1.30 1.10
- e. A1037 P multi 1.30 1.10

Booklet Stamps
Self-Adhesive
Serpentine Die Cut 13¼

2419 A1033 P multi 1.30 .25
2420 A1034 P multi 1.30 .25
2421 A1035 P multi 1.30 .25
2422 A1036 P multi 1.30 .25
2423 A1037 P multi 1.30 .25
- a. Booklet pane of 10, 2 each #2419-2423 13.00
- b. Booklet pane of 30, 6 each #2419-2423 39.00

Nos. 2419-2423 (5) 6.25 3.00

On day of issue, Nos. 2418a-2418e, 2419-2423 each sold for 59c.

Juvenile Wildlife — A1038

Designs: P, Arctic hare leverets. $1.03, Red fox kit in hollow log. $1.25, Canada goslings. $1.75, Polar bear cub.

2011, Jan. 17 *Perf. 13¼x13*

2424 Sheet of 4 7.25 7.25
- a. A1038 P multi 1.30 1.10
- b. A1038 $1.03 multi 1.50 1.30
- c. A1038 $1.25 multi 1.90 1.65
- d. A1038 $1.75 multi 2.60 2.40

Coil Stamps
Self-Adhesive
Serpentine Die Cut 9¼ Horiz.

2425 A1038 P multi 1.50 1.50

Serpentine Die Cut 8¼ Horiz.

2426 A1038 P multi 1.30 .25
2427 A1038 $1.03 multi 1.55 .30

Horiz. pairs, imperf. between, of No. 2426 are from uncut press panels of 100. Value unused, $3.25.

Serpentine Die Cut 8½ Horiz.

2428 A1038 $1.25 multi 1.90 .55

Serpentine Die Cut 8¼ Horiz.

2429 A1038 $1.75 multi 2.60 .75

Booklet Stamps
Serpentine Die Cut 9¼ Horiz.

2430 A1038 $1.03 multi 1.55 .30
- a. Booklet pane of 6 9.25

2431 A1038 $1.25 multi 1.90 .55
- a. Booklet pane of 6 11.50

2432 A1038 $1.75 multi 2.60 .75
- a. Booklet pane of 6 15.50

Nos. 2425-2432 (8) 18.70 9.40

On day of issue, Nos. 2424a, 2425 and 2426 each sold for 59c. On rolls of No. 2425, stamps do not touch each other and pairs are horizontal. On rolls of No. 2426, stamps touch each other and pairs are vertical.

See Nos. 2504-2512, 2602-2610, 2692, 2692A, 2709-2717.

Black History Month — A1039

Order of Canada recipients: No. 2433, Carrie Best (1903-2001), journalist. No. 2434, Ferguson Jenkins, baseball player.

Self-Adhesive
Serpentine Die Cut 13½x13¾

2011, Feb. 1 Booklet Stamps

2433 A1039 59c multi .90 .30
- a. Booklet pane of 10 9.00

2434 A1039 59c multi .90 .30
- a. Booklet pane of 10 9.00

Gift Box — A1040

Self-Adhesive
Serpentine Die Cut 13½ Horiz.

2011, Feb. 7 Booklet Stamp

2435 A1040 P multi 1.30 .30
- a. Booklet pane of 6 7.75

No. 2435 sold for 59c on day of issue.

Paintings of Daphne Odjig A1041

Paintings: 59c, Pow-wow Dancer. $1.03, Pow-wow (32x39mm). $1.75, Spiritual Renewal (56x39mm).

2011, Feb. 21 *Perf. 12½*

2436 A1041 59c multi .90 .30

Souvenir Sheet

2437 Sheet of 3, #2436, 2437a-2437b 4.00 4.00
- a. A1041 $1.03 multi 1.50 1.50
- b. A1041 $1.75 multi 2.60 2.60

Booklet Stamps
Self-Adhesive
Serpentine Die Cut 13½x13¼

2438 A1041 $1.03 multi 1.55 .65
- a. Booklet pane of 6 9.25

2439 A1041 $1.75 multi 2.60 1.10
- a. Booklet pane of 6 15.50

Sunflower
A1042 A1043

Sunflower varieties: Nos. 2440a, 2441, 2443, Prado Red. Nos. 2440b, 2442, 2444, Sunbright (yellow flower).

2011, Mar. 3 Litho. *Perf. 13¼*

Souvenir Sheet

2440 Sheet of 2 2.60 2.60
- a.-b. A1042 P Either single 1.30 1.10

Coil Stamps
Self-Adhesive
Serpentine Die Cut 8¼ Horiz.

2441 A1043 P multi 1.30 .40
2442 A1043 P multi 1.30 .40
- a. Vert. pair, #2441-2442 2.60

Booklet Stamps
Serpentine Die Cut 13½

2443 A1042 P multi 1.30 .30
2444 A1042 P multi 1.30 .30
- a. Booklet pane of 10, 5 each #2443-2444 13.00

On day of issue, Nos. 2440a-2440b, 2441-2444 each sold for 59c.

Signs of the Zodiac — A1044

No. 2445: a, Aries. b, Taurus. c, Gemini. d, Cancer. No. 2446: a, Leo. b, Virgo. c, Libra. d, Scorpio. No. 2447: a, Sagittarius. b, Capricorn. c, Aquarius. d, Pisces.

No. 2448: a, Aries. b, Taurus. c, Gemini. d, Cancer. e, Leo. f, Virgo. g, Libra. h, Scorpio. i, Sagittarius. j, Capricorn. k, Aquarius. l, Pisces.

No. 2449, Aries. No. 2450, Taurus. No. 2451, Gemini. No. 2452, Cancer. No. 2453, Leo. No. 2454, Virgo. No. 2455, Libra. No. 2456, Scorpio. No. 2457, Sagittarius. No. 2458, Capricorn. No. 2459, Aquarius. No. 2460, Pisces.

2011-13 Litho. *Perf. 12½*

2445 Sheet of 4 5.25 5.25
- a.-d. A1044 P Any single 1.30 1.10

2446 Sheet of 4 5.25 5.25
- a.-d. A1044 P Any single 1.30 1.10

2447 Sheet of 4 5.25 5.25
- a.-d. A1044 P Any single 1.30 1.10

Perf. 12½x13

2448 Sheet of 12 18.00 18.00
- a.-l A1044 P Any single 1.50 1.50

Booklet Stamps
Self-Adhesive
Serpentine Die Cut 13½

2449 A1044 P multi 1.30 .30
- a. Booklet pane of 10 13.00

2450 A1044 P multi 1.30 .30
- a. Booklet pane of 10 12.00
- b. Gutter pane of 12, 6 each #2449-2450 15.00

2451 A1044 P multi 1.30 .30
- a. Booklet pane of 10 13.00

2452 A1044 P multi 1.30 .30
- a. Booklet pane of 10 13.00
- b. Gutter pane of 12, 6 each #2451-2452 15.00

2453 A1044 P multi 1.30 .30
- a. Booklet pane of 10 13.00

2454 A1044 P multi 1.30 .30
- a. Booklet pane of 10 13.00

2455 A1044 P multi 1.30 .30
- a. Booklet pane of 10 13.00

2456 A1044 P multi 1.30 .30
- a. Booklet pane of 10 13.00
- b. Gutter pane of 24, 6 each #2453-2456 30.00

2457 A1044 P multi 1.30 .30
- a. Booklet pane of 10 13.00

2458 A1044 P multi 1.30 .30
- a. Booklet pane of 10 13.00

2459 A1044 P multi 1.30 .30
- a. Booklet pane of 10 13.00

2460 A1044 P multi 1.30 .30
- a. Booklet pane of 10 13.00
- b. Gutter pane of 24, 6 each #2457-2460 30.00

Nos. 2449-2460 (12) 15.60 3.60

Issued: No. 2449, 3/21; Nos. 2450, 2450b, 4/21; No. 2451, 5/20; Nos. 2445, 2452, 2452b, 6/22, Nos. 2446, 2453-2456, 2456b, 7/23/12. Nos. 2447-2448, 2457-2460, 2460b, 2/20/13. Nos. 2445a-2445d, 2449-2452 each sold for 59c on day of issue. Nos. 2446a-2446d, 2453-2456 each sold for 61c on day of issue. Nos. 2447a-2447d, 2448a-2448l, 2457-2460 each sold for 63c on day of issue.

Intl. Year of Forests — A1045

Designs: Nos. 2461a, 2462, Tree. Nos. 2461b, 2463, Mushrooms and plants on forest floor.

2011, Apr. 21 Litho. *Perf. 13½x13*

2461 A1045 Sheet of 2 2.60 2.60
- a.-b. P Either single 1.30 1.10

Booklet Stamps
Self-Adhesive
Serpentine Die Cut 13x13¼

2462 A1045 P multi 1.30 .30
2463 A1045 P multi 1.30 .30
- a. Booklet pane of 8, 4 each #2462-2463 10.50

On day of issue, Nos. 2461a-2461b, 2462-2463 each sold for 59c.

Wedding of Prince William and Catherine Middleton — A1046

Couple with Prince William at: P, Right. $1.75, Left.

2011, Apr. 29 *Perf. 12¾x13¼*

2464 A1046 P multi 1.30 .30
2465 A1046 $1.75 multi 2.60 1.10
- a. Horiz. pair, #2464-2465 4.00 3.00
- b. Souvenir sheet, #2464-2465 4.00 4.00
- c. As "b," with arms of Prince William overprinted in sheet margin in gold 4.50 4.50

Booklet Stamps
Self-Adhesive
Serpentine Die Cut 13¼

2466 A1046 P multi 1.30 .30
- a. Booklet pane of 10 13.00

2467 A1046 $1.75 multi 2.60 1.10
- a. Booklet pane of 10 26.00
- b. Gutter pane, 6 #2466, 4 #2467 55.00

On day of issue, Nos. 2464 and 2468 each sold for 59c.

Methods of Mail Delivery — A1047

Designs: No. 2468, Ponchon. No. 2469, Dog sled.

2011, May 13 *Perf. 12½*

2468 59c multi .85 .30
2469 59c multi .85 .30
- a. A1047 Horiz. pair, #2468-2469 1.70 1.10

Parks Canada, Cent. — A1048

Self-Adhesive
Serpentine Die Cut 13½

2011, May 19 Booklet Stamp

2470 A1048 59c multi .85 .30
- a. Booklet pane of 10 8.50

Details of Art Deco Structures — A1049

Designs: Nos. 2471a, 2472, Burrard Bridge, Vancouver. Nos. 2471b, 2473, Cormier House, Montreal. Nos. 2471c, 2474, R. C. Harris Water Treatment Plant, Toronto. Nos. 2471d, 2475, Supreme Court of Canada,

Ottawa. Nos. 2471e, 2476, Dominion Building, Regina, Saskatchewan.

2011, June 9 Litho. *Perf. 13x12½*

2471 A1049 Sheet of 5 + 5 labels 6.50 6.50
a.-e. P Any single 1.30 1.10

Booklet Stamps
Self-Adhesive

Serpentine Die Cut 13¼x13½

2472 A1049 P multi 1.30 .30
2473 A1049 P multi 1.30 .30
2474 A1049 P multi 1.30 .30
2475 A1049 P multi 1.30 .30
2476 A1049 P multi 1.30 .30
a. Booklet pane of 10, 2 each #2472-2476 13.00
Nos. 2472-2476 (5) 6.50 1.50

On day of issue, Nos. 2471a-2471e, 2472-2476 each sold for 59c.

Duke and Duchess of Cambridge on Their Wedding Day — A1050

2011, June 22 *Perf. 12¾x13¼*

2477 Sheet of 2 #2477a 3.00 2.60
a. A1050 P multi 1.50 .90
b. Sheet similar to #2477, with Royal Tour emblem overprinted in gold in sheet margin 3.75 2.60

Booklet Stamp
Self-Adhesive

Serpentine Die Cut 13¼

2478 A1050 P multi 1.30 .30
a. Booklet pane of 10 13.00

On day of issue, Nos. 2477a and 2478 each sold for 59c. Margin of No. 2477 depicts Westminster Abbey, and that of No. 2477b depicts the Canadian Parliament.

Popular Singers A1051

Designs: Nos. 2479, 2483c, Ginette Reno. Nos. 2480, 2483a, Bruce Cockburn. Nos. 2481, 2483d, Robbie Robertson. Nos. 2482, 2483b, Kate and Anna McGarrigle.

2011 *Perf. 12½*

2479 A1051 P multi 1.80 1.80
a. Perf. 12½x13 1.30 1.10
2480 A1051 P multi 1.80 1.80
a. Perf. 12½x13 1.30 1.10
2481 A1051 P multi 1.80 1.80
a. Perf. 12½x13 1.30 1.10
2482 A1051 P multi 1.80 1.80
a. Perf. 12½x13 1.30 1.10
b. Souvenir sheet of 4, #2479a-2482a 5.25 3.50
Nos. 2479-2482 (4) 7.20 7.20

Self-Adhesive

Serpentine Die Cut 13½

2483 Booklet pane of 4 5.25
a.-d. A1051 P Any single 1.30 .45
Complete booklet, 2 #2483 10.50

Issued: Nos. 2479-2482, 7/30; Nos. 2479a-2482a, 2482b, 2483, 6/30. On day of issue, Nos. 2479a2482, 2479a-2482a and 2483a-2483d each sold for 59c.

Complete booklets were issued with four different covers depicting the featured singers. The order of the stamps is different in each booklet.

Roadside Attractions — A1052

Designs: Nos. 2484a, 2485a, World's Largest Lobster, Shediac, New Brunswick. Nos. 2484b, 2485b, Wild Blueberry, Oxford, Nova Scotia. Nos. 2484c, 2485c, Big Potato, O'Leary, Prince Edward Island. Nos. 2484d, 2485d, Giant Squid, Glover's Harbour, Newfoundland.

2011, July 7 *Perf. 12¾*

2484 A1052 Sheet of 4 5.25 5.25
a.-d. P Any single 1.30 1.10

Self-Adhesive

Serpentine Die Cut13½

2485 A1052 Booklet pane of 4 5.25
a.-d. P Any single 1.30 .45
Complete booklet, 2 #2485 10.50

Third Consecutive Victory of Intl. Harmsworth Trophy by Miss Supertest III Hydroplane — A1053

Designs: P, Miss Supertest III. $1.75, Miss Supertest III, diff.

2011, Aug. 8 Litho. *Perf. 13¼*

2486 A1053 Sheet of 2 4.00 4.00
a. P multi 1.30 1.10
b. $1.75 multi 2.60 2.40

Booklet Stamp
Self-Adhesive

Serpentine Die Cut 13¼ Horiz.

2487 A1053 P multi 1.20 .30
a. Booklet pane of 10 13.00

Nos. 2486a and 2487 each sold for 59c on day of issue.

Canadian Inventions — A1054

No. 2488: a, Pacemaker, developed by Dr. John Hopps. b, BlackBerry, developed by Research in Motion. c, Electric oven, developed by Thomas Ahearn. d, Electric wheelchair, developed by George J. Klein.

Serpentine Die Cut 13¼

2011, Aug. 17 Self-Adhesive

2488 Booklet pane of 4 3.60
a.-d. A1054 59c Any single .90 .45
Complete booklet, 2 #2488 7.25

Dr. John Charles Polanyi, Winner of 1986 Nobel Prize for Chemistry A1055

Self-Adhesive
Booklet Stamp

Serpentine Die Cut 13½

2011, Oct. 3 Litho.

2489 A1055 P multi 1.20 .30
a. Booklet pane of 10 13.00

Intl. Year of Chemistry. No. 2489 sold for 59c on day of issue.

Christmas

A1056 A1057

Stained-glass windows, Cathedral of Saint Mary of the Immaculate Conception, Kingston, Ontario: Nos. 2490a, 2492, Angel. $1.03, Nativity. $1.75, Epiphany.

2011, Nov. 1 Litho. *Perf. 13x12½*

2490 Sheet of 3 5.50 5.50
a. A1056 P multi 1.30 1.10
b. A1056 $1.03 multi 1.50 1.40
c. A1056 $1.75 multi 2.60 2.50

Booklet Stamps
Self-Adhesive

Litho. With Hologram Affixed

Serpentine Die Cut 8¼ Horiz.

2491 A1057 P multi 1.20 .25
a. Booklet pane of 6 7.75
Complete booklet, 2 #2491a 15.50

Litho.

Serpentine Die Cut 13¼

2492 A1056 P multi 1.30 .25
a. Booklet pane of 6 7.75
Complete booklet, 2 #2492a 15.50
2493 A1056 $1.03 multi 1.55 .60
a. Booklet pane of 6 9.25
2494 A1056 $1.75 multi 2.60 1.10
a. Booklet pane of 6 15.50
b. Gutter pane, #2493a, 2494a 26.00
Nos. 2491-2494 (4) 6.65 2.20

On day of issue, Nos. 2490a, 2491 and 2492 each sold for 59c.

New Year 2012 (Year of the Dragon) A1058

Design: $1.80, Dragon's head.

Litho. & Embossed With Foil Application

2012, Jan. 10 *Perf. 12½*

2495 A1058 P gold & multi 1.30 .40

Souvenir Sheet

2496 A1058 $1.80 multi 2.70 2.70
a. Souvenir sheet of 2, #2417, 2496 5.25 5.25

Booklet Stamp
Self-Adhesive

Litho.

Serpentine Die Cut 13½

2497 A1058 $1.80 multi 2.70 1.10
a. Booklet pane of 6 16.25

No. 2495 sold for 61c on day of issue. See Nos. 3259e, 3260e, 3265.

Flag on Coast Guard Ship A1059

Flag in Van Window A1060

Olympic Athlete Carrying Flag A1061

Flag on Bobsled A1062

Inuit Child Waving Flag — A1063

2012, Jan. 16 Litho. *Perf. 13x13¼*

2498 Souvenir sheet of 5 6.50 6.50
a. A1059 P multi 1.30 1.10
b. A1060 P multi 1.30 1.10
c. A1061 P multi 1.30 1.10
d. A1062 P multi 1.30 1.10
e. A1063 P multi 1.30 1.10

Booklet Stamps
Self-Adhesive

Serpentine Die Cut 13¼

2499 A1059 P multi 1.30 .25
a. With "Canada" visible on reverse of stamp 2.25 .35
2500 A1060 P multi 1.30 .25
a. With "Canada" visible on reverse of stamp 2.25 .35
2501 A1061 P multi 1.30 .25
a. With "Canada" visible on reverse of stamp 2.25 .35
2502 A1062 P multi 1.30 .25
a. Microprinting with corrected spelling "Lueders" 1.50 .25
b. As "a," with "Canada" visible on reverse of stamp 2.25 .35
2503 A1063 P multi 1.30 .25
a. Booklet pane of 10, 2 each #2499-2503 13.00
b. Booklet pane of 30, 6 each #2499-2503 39.00
c. Booklet pane of 10, 2 each #2499-2502, 2502a, 2503 19.00
d. With "Canada" visible on reverse of stamp 2.25 .35
e. Booklet pane of 10, 2 each #2499a, 2500a, 2501a, 2502b, 2503d 26.00
Nos. 2499-2503 (5) 6.50 1.25

On day of issue, Nos. 2498a-2498e, 2499-2503 each sold for 61c. The printing on the backing paper on No. 2503a differs from that on the backing paper of any of the component thirds of No. 2503b.

Issued: Nos. 2502a, 2503c, 9/28/12; Nos. 2499a, 2500a, 2501a, 2502b, 2503d, 2013. Nos. 2498d and 2502 have incorrect spelling in microprinting of "Leuders."

Juvenile Wildlife Type of 2011

Designs: P, Three raccoon kits. $1.05, Two caribou calves. $1.29, Adult loon and two chicks. $1.80, Moose calves.

2012, Jan. 16 *Perf. 13¼x13*

2504 Souvenir sheet of 4 8.00 6.50
a. A1038 P multi 1.30 1.10
b. A1038 $1.05 multi 1.60 1.20
c. A1038 $1.29 multi 1.90 1.50
d. A1038 $1.80 multi 2.70 2.40

Self-Adhesive
Coil Stamps

Serpentine Die Cut 9¼ Horiz.

2505 A1038 P multi 1.50 1.50

Serpentine Die Cut 8¼ Horiz.

2506 A1038 P multi 1.30 .25
2507 A1038 $1.05 multi 1.60 .30
2508 A1038 $1.29 multi 1.90 .75
2509 A1038 $1.80 multi 2.70 .90
Nos. 2505-2509 (5) 9.00 3.70

Booklet Stamps

Serpentine Die Cut 9¼ Horiz.

2510 A1038 $1.05 multi 1.60 .30
a. Booklet pane of 6 9.50
2511 A1038 $1.29 multi 1.90 .55
a. Booklet pane of 6 11.50
2512 A1038 $1.80 multi 2.70 .90
a. Booklet pane of 6 16.25
Nos. 2510-2512 (3) 6.20 1.75

On day of issue, Nos. 2504a, 2505 and 2506 each sold for 61c. On rolls of No. 2505, stamps do not touch each other and pairs are horizontal. On rolls of No. 2506, stamps touch each other and pairs are vertical.

A1064

Reign of Queen Elizabeth II, 60th Anniv. — A1065

Designs: No. 2513, Crown, Canada #330. No. 2514, Map of Canada, Canada #471. No. 2515, Document, pen, Canada #704. No. 2516, Jubilee bouquet, Canada #1168. No. 2517, Tiara details, Canada #1932. Nos. 2518, 2519, Queen Elizabeth II wearing robe and tiara.

2012 Litho. *Perf. 13¼*

2513 A1064 P multi 1.30 1.00
2514 A1064 P multi 1.30 1.00
2515 A1064 P multi 1.30 1.00
2516 A1064 P multi 1.30 1.00
2517 A1064 P multi 1.30 1.00

Perf. 13¼x12½

2518 A1065 P multi 1.30 1.10

Booklet Stamp
Self-Adhesive

2519 A1065 P multi 1.30 .30
a. Booklet pane of 10 13.00

Issued: Nos. 2513, 2519, 1/16; No. 2514, 2/6; No. 2515, 3/6; No. 2516, 4/10; No. 2517, 5/7; No. 2518, 6/1. On day of issue, Nos. 2513-2519 each sold for 61c. Nos. 2513-2518 each were printed in sheets of 4.

Black History Month — A1066

Designs: No. 2520, John Ware (c. 1845-1905), cattle driver and rancher. No. 2521, Viola Desmond (1914-65), civil rights activist.

Self-Adhesive
Booklet Stamps

Serpentine Die Cut 13½

2012, Feb. 1 Litho.

2520 A1066 P multi 1.30 .30
a. Booklet pane of 10 13.00
2521 A1066 P multi 1.30 .30
a. Booklet pane of 10 13.00
b. Gutter pane of 12, 6 each #2520-2521 15.00

On day of issue, Nos. 2520-2521 each sold for 61c.

Sculptures by Joe Fafard — A1067

Designs: P, Smoothly She Shifted. $1.05, Dear Vincent, vert. (32x40mm). $1.80, Capilery, horiz. (64x32mm).

2012, Feb. 23 *Perf. 12½*

2522 A1067 P multi 1.30 .30

Souvenir Sheet

2523 Sheet of 3, #2522, 2523a, 2523b 5.00 5.00
a. A1067 $1.05 multi 1.60 1.60
b. A1067 $1.80 multi 1.90 1.90

Booklet Stamps
Self-Adhesive

Serpentine Die Cut 13½

2524 A1067 $1.05 multi 1.60 .65
a. Booklet pane of 6 9.50

Serpentine Die Cut 13¼

2525 A1067 $1.80 multi 2.60 1.10
a. Booklet pane of 6 15.75
b. Gutter pane of 6, 3 each #2524-2525 15.00

No. 2522 sold for 61c on day of issue.

A1068

Daylilies — A1069

Color of daylily: Nos. 2526a, 2527, 2529, Orange. Nos. 2526b, 2528, 2530, Purple.

2012, Mar. 1 *Perf. 13¼*

Souvenir Sheet

2526 Sheet of 2 2.60 2.60
a.-b. A1068 P Either single 1.30 1.10

Coil Stamps
Self-Adhesive

Serpentine Die Cut 8¼ Horiz.

2527 A1069 P multi 1.30 .40
2528 A1069 P multi 1.30 .40
a. Vert. pair, #2527-2528 2.60

Booklet Stamps

Serpentine Die Cut 13½

2529 A1068 P multi 1.30 .30
2530 A1068 P multi 1.30 .30
a. Booklet pane of 10, 5 each #2529-2530 13.00

On day of issue, Nos. 2526a, 2526b, 2527-2530 each sold for 61c.

A1070

Sinking of the Titanic, Cent. — A1071

Flag of the White Star Line and: Nos. 2531, 2536, Bow of Titanic, map showing Halifax, Nova Scotia. Nos. 2532, 2537, Bow of Titanic, map showing Southampton, England. No. 2533, Propellers of Titanic, three men. No. 2534, Propellers of Titanic, six men.

$1.80, Titanic, map of North Atlantic, flag of the White Star Line.

2012, Apr. 5 Litho. *Perf. 12½*

2531 A1070 P multi 1.30 .45
2532 A1070 P multi 1.30 .45
2533 A1070 P multi 1.30 .45
2534 A1070 P multi 1.30 .45
a. Block of 4, #2531-2534 5.25 2.60
Nos. 2531-2534 (4) 5.20 1.80

Souvenir Sheet

Perf. 13

2535 A1071 $1.80 multi 2.60 2.60

Booklet Stamps
Self-Adhesive

Serpentine Die Cut 13½

2536 A1070 P multi 1.30 .30
2537 A1070 P multi 1.30 .30
a. Booklet pane of 10, 5 each #2536-2537 13.00
2538 A1071 $1.80 multi 2.60 1.50
a. Booklet pane of 6 15.75
Nos. 2536-2538 (3) 5.20 2.10

On day of issue, Nos. 2531-2534, 2536-2537 each sold for 61c.

Thomas Douglas, 5th Earl of Selkirk (1771-1820), Founder of Red River Settlement, and Settlers — A1072

2012, May 3 Litho. *Perf. 13¼*

2539 A1072 P multi 1.30 .30

Red River Settlement, bicent. No. 2539 sold for 61c on day of issue.

Reign Of Queen Elizabeth II, 60th Anniv. A1073

2012, May 7 Engr. *Perf. 11½*

2540 A1073 $2 purple 3.00 1.50
a. Souvenir sheet of 1 3.75 3.75

Franklin the Turtle, Children's Book Character by Paulette Bourgeois — A1074

Designs: Nos. 2541a, 2542, Franklin, beaver and teddy bear. Nos. 2541b, 2543, Franklin helping young turtle to read book. Nos. 2541c, 2544, Franklin and snail. Nos. 2541d, 2545, Franklin watching bear feed fish in bowl.

2012, May 11 *Perf. 13x12½*

2541 Miniature sheet of 4 5.25 5.25
a.-d. A1074 P Any single 1.30 1.10

Booklet Stamps
Self-Adhesive

Serpentine Die Cut 13¼

2542 A1074 P multi 1.30 .40
2543 A1074 P multi 1.30 .40
2544 A1074 P multi 1.30 .40
2545 A1074 P multi 1.30 .40
a. Booklet pane of 12, 3 each #2542-2545 15.50
Nos. 2542-2545 (4) 5.20 1.60

Nos. 2541a-2541d, 2542-2545 each sold for 61c on day of issue.

Calgary Stampede, Cent. — A1075

Designs: P, Saddle on rodeo horse. $1.05, Commemorative belt buckle.

2012, May 17 *Perf. 13x13¼*

2546 Souvenir sheet of 2 3.00 3.00
a. A1075 P multi 1.30 1.10
b. A1075 $1.05 multi 1.60 1.60

Booklet Stamps
Self-Adhesive

Serpentine Die Cut 13¼x13

2547 A1075 P multi 1.30 .30
a. Booklet pane of 10 13.00
2548 A1075 $1.05 multi 1.60 .65
a. Booklet pane of 10 16.00
b. Gutter pane of 10, 6 #2547, 4 #2548 15.00

Nos. 2546a and 2547 each sold for 61c on day of issue.

Order of Canada Recipients A1076

Designs: Nos. 2549a, 2550, Louise Arbour, president of International Crisis Group. Nos. 2549b, 2551, Rick Hansen, founder of Rick Hansen Foundation (spinal cord injury research). Nos. 2549c, 2552, Sheila Watt-Cloutier, Inuit rights activist. Nos. 2549d, 2553, Michael J. Fox, actor, founder of Michael J. Fox Foundation for Parkinson's Research.

2012, May 22 Litho. *Perf. 12½*

2549 Miniature sheet of 4 5.25 5.25
a.-d. A1076 P Any single 1.30 1.10

Booklet Stamps
Self-Adhesive

Serpentine Die Cut 13½

2550 A1076 P multi 1.30 .30
a. Booklet pane of 10 13.00
2551 A1076 P multi 1.30 .30
a. Booklet pane of 10 13.00
2552 A1076 P multi 1.30 .30
a. Booklet pane of 10 13.00
2553 A1076 P multi 1.30 .30
a. Booklet pane of 10 13.00
Nos. 2550-2553 (4) 5.20 1.20

On day of issue Nos. 2549a-2549d, 2550-2553 each sold for 61c.

War of 1812, Bicent. — A1077

Designs: No. 2554, Sir Isaac Brock (1769-1812), British Major General. No. 2555, Tecumseh (1768-1813), leader of Indian confederacy.

2012, June 15 *Perf. 13¼x12½*

2554 P multi 1.30 .30
2555 P multi 1.30 .30
a. A1077 Horiz. pair, #2554-2555 2.60 1.10

On day of issue, Nos. 2554-2555 each sold for 61c. See Guernsey No. 1172.

2012 Summer Olympics, London A1078

Self-Adhesive
Booklet Stamp

2012, June 27 *Serpentine Die Cut 8*

2556 A1078 P multi 1.30 .35
a. Booklet pane of 10 13.00

No. 2556 sold for 61c on day of issue.

Tommy Douglas (1904-86), Politician A1079

2012, June 29 *Perf. 12½*

2557 A1079 P multi 1.30 .30

Passage of Saskatchewan's Medical Care Insurance Act, 50th anniv. (start of socialized medicine in Canada). No. 2557 sold for 61c on day of issue.

Canadian Football League Team Emblems — A1080

Designs: Nos. 2558a, 2559, British Columbia Lions. Nos. 2558b, 2560, Edmonton Eskimos. Nos. 2558c, 2561, Calgary Stampeders. Nos. 2558d, 2562, Saskatchewan Roughriders. Nos. 2558e, 2563, Winnipeg Blue Bombers. Nos. 2558f, 2564, Hamilton Tiger-Cats. Nos. 2558g, 2565, Toronto Argonauts. Nos. 2558h, 2566, Montreal Alouettes.

2012, June 29 ***Perf. 13¼x13***

2558 A1080 Sheet of 8 10.50 10.50
a.-h. P Any single 1.30 1.30

Coil Stamps
Self-Adhesive
Serpentine Die Cut 8¼ Horiz.

2559 A1080 P multi 1.30 .45
2560 A1080 P multi 1.30 .45
2561 A1080 P multi 1.30 .45
2562 A1080 P multi 1.30 .45
2563 A1080 P multi 1.30 .45
2564 A1080 P multi 1.30 .45
2565 A1080 P multi 1.30 .45
2566 A1080 P multi 1.30 .45
Nos. 2559-2566 (8) 10.40 3.60

On day of issue, Nos. 2558a-2558h, 2559-2566 each sold for 61c. See No. 2754.

Grey Cup, Cent. — A1081

Grey Cup and: Nos. 2567a, 2568, Two football players, "100." Nos. 2567b, 2569, British Columbia Lions player Geroy Simon, kicker and holder in 1994 game. Nos. 2567c, 2570, Edmonton Eskimos player Tom Wilkinson, quarterback ready to throw pass. Nos. 2567d, 2571, Calgary Stampeders player "Thumper" Wayne Harris, running back and tacklers from 1948 game. Nos. 2567e, 2572, Saskatchewan Roughriders player George Reed, players celebrating in 1989 game. Nos. 2567f, 2573, Winnipeg Blue Bombers player Ken Pipen, players in fog in 1962 game. Nos. 2567g, 2574, Hamilton Tiger-Cats player Danny Mcmanus, player catching ball in 1972 game. Nos. 2567h, 2575, Toronto Argonauts player Michael "Pinball" Clemons, players on muddy field in 1950 game. Nos. 2567i, 2576, Montreal Alouettes player Anthony Calvillo, players at line of scrimmage in 1977 game.

Litho. & Embossed

2012, Aug. 16 ***Perf. 12½***

2567 A1081 Sheet of 9 11.75 11.75
a.-i. P Any single 1.30 1.00

Litho.
Booklet Stamps
Self-Adhesive
Serpentine Die Cut 13¼

2568 A1081 P multi 1.30 .30
a. Booklet pane of 10 13.00
2569 A1081 P multi 1.30 .30
a. Booklet pane of 10 13.00
2570 A1081 P multi 1.30 .30
a. Booklet pane of 10 13.00
2571 A1081 P multi 1.30 .30
a. Booklet pane of 10 13.00
2572 A1081 P multi 1.30 .30
a. Booklet pane of 10 13.00
2573 A1081 P multi 1.30 .30
a. Booklet pane of 10 13.00
2574 A1081 P multi 1.30 .30
a. Booklet pane of 10 13.00
2575 A1081 P multi 1.30 .30
a. Booklet pane of 10 13.00
2576 A1081 P multi 1.30 .30
a. Booklet pane of 10 13.00
Nos. 2568-2576 (9) 11.70 2.70

Nos. 2567a-2567i, 2568-2576 each sold for 61c on day of issue. For overprint, see No. 2598.

Military Regiments, 150th Anniv. A1082

Uniforms of: Nos. 2577a, 2578, Black Watch (Royal Highland) Regiment of Canada. Nos. 2577b, 2579, Royal Hamilton Light Infantry (Wentworth Regiment). Nos. 2577c, 2580, Royal Regiment of Canada

2012, Oct. 11 Litho. ***Perf. 13x13½***

2577 Souvenir sheet of 3 4.00 4.00
a.-c. A1082 P Any single 1.30 1.10

Booklet Stamps
Self-Adhesive
Serpentine Die Cut 13¼x13

2578 A1082 P multi 1.30 .45
a. Booklet pane of 10 13.00
2579 A1082 P multi 1.30 .45
a. Booklet pane of 10 13.00
2580 A1082 P multi 1.30 .45
a. Booklet pane of 10 13.00
Nos. 2578-2580 (3) 3.90 1.35

On day of issue, Nos. 2577a-2577c, 2578-2580 each sold for 61c.

Gingerbread Cookies A1083

Stained Glass Window From St. Mary's of the Immaculate Conception Cathedral, Kingsoton, Ontario A1084

Ribbons on Christmas cookies shaped as: P, Man and woman. $1.05, Five-pointed star. $1.80, Snowflake.

Souvenir Sheet

2012, Oct. 15 ***Perf. 13¾x13¼***

2581 Sheet of 3 5.50 5.50
a. A1083 P multi 1.30 1.10
b. A1083 $1.05 multi 1.60 1.50
c. A1083 $1.80 multi 2.70 2.70

Booklet Stamps
Self-Adhesive
Serpentine Die Cut 13¼

2582 A1084 P multi 1.30 .25
a. Booklet pane of 12 15.50

Serpentine Die Cut 13¼x13

2583 A1083 P multi 1.30 .25
a. Booklet pane of 12 13.00
2584 A1083 $1.05 multi 1.60 .60
a. Booklet pane of 6 9.50
2585 A1083 $1.80 multi 2.70 1.00
a. Booklet pane of 6 16.25
Nos. 2582-2585 (4) 6.90 2.10

Christmas. On day of issue, Nos. 2581a, 2582 and 2583 each sold for 61c.

Dots — A1085

Frame — A1086

Hearts A1087

Creatures A1088

Butterflies A1089

Maple Leaves A1090

Flowers A1091

Snowflakes A1092

Wedding Bells — A1093

Doves and Flowers — A1094

Balloons, Stars, Party Hat — A1095

Holly — A1096

Serpentine Die Cut 13¼

2012, Nov. Self-Adhesive Litho.

2586 A1085 P gray 2.25 2.25
a. Personalized version, any denomination or orientation — —
2587 A1086 P gray 2.25 2.25
a. Personalized version, any denomination or orientation — —
2588 A1087 P gray & red 2.25 2.25
a. Personalized version, any denomination or orientation — —
2589 A1088 P multi 2.25 2.25
a. Personalized version, any denomination or orientation — —
2590 A1089 P multi 2.25 2.25
a. Personalized version, any denomination or orientation — —
2591 A1090 P multi 2.25 2.25
a. Personalized version, any denomination or orientation — —
2592 A1091 P multi 2.25 2.25
a. Personalized version, any denomination or orientation — —
2593 A1092 P multi 2.25 2.25
a. Personalized version, any denomination or orientation — —
2594 A1093 P gray & black 2.25 2.25
a. Personalized version, any denomination or orientation — —
2595 A1094 P gray 2.25 2.25
a. Personalized version, any denomination or orientation — —
2596 A1095 P multi 2.25 2.25
a. Personalized version, any denomination or orientation — —
2597 A1096 P multi 2.25 2.25
a. Personalized version, any denomination or orientation — —
Nos. 2586-2597 (12) 27.00 27.00

Nos. 2586-2597 had a franking value on the day of issue of 61c, and were sold together in a package of single stamps that sold for $7.32. Each vertically-oriented stamp in the package had a gray image area. Horizontally-oriented stamps were not made available in these packages. First day covers of Nos. 2586-2597 are dated 11/5.

Nos. 2586a-2597a have personalized photographs in the image area, and were available with vertical or horizontal orientations and in various denominations. On Nov. 16-24 personalized stamps were offered for sale on iPad and iPhone apps at the P rate (with a franking value of 61c), $1.05, $1.29 and $1.80. It is not known if any personalized stamps of the $1.05, $1.29 and $1.80 denominations were created for customers through these apps during this brief period. On Nov. 24 stamps at the P rate (with a franking value of 61c), $1.10, $1.34 and $1.85 were offered to customers through the Picture Postage page of the Canada Post website, as well as through the apps. Additional stamps with different denominations may be offered for sale later. A $1.29 stamp featuring the image of a Turtle was made available on Nov. 1. It was only available affixed to packages containing a box of Nestle's Turtles candy. A box of candy and affixed stamp sold at post offices for $4.99, and the package could only be sent to Canadian addresses.

Except for the stamp with the turtle's image, the stamps of the various denominations were each made available in sheets of 26, sheets of 50 and booklet panes of 12 (a minimum of three booklet panes needed to be ordered). The selling prices of the personalized sheets and booklets were substantially higher than the face value of the stamps within them.

Vertically oriented stamps have the denomination in the lower right corner of the stamp, with the "C" of "Canada" at the upper left of the stamp, as shown in the illustrations. Horizontally oriented stamps have the denomination in the lower right corner of the stamp, with the "C" of "Canada" at the lower left corner. The dots, frame, hearts, creatures and butterflies images on horizontally-oriented stamps differ from those shown on the vertically-oriented stamps.

No. 2568 Overprinted in Dark Blue, Light Blue, Black and Silver

Booklet Stamp
Serpentine Die Cut 13¼

2012, Nov. 28 **Litho.**

Self-Adhesive

2598 A1081 P multi 1.30 .50
a. Booklet pane of 10 13.00

Grey Cup victory of Toronto Argonauts. No. 2598 sold for 61c on day of issue.

New Year 2013 (Year of the Snake) — A1097

Design: $1.85, Snake's head.

Litho. & Embossed

2013, Jan. 8 ***Perf. 12½***

2599 A1097 P shown 1.30 .40

Souvenir Sheet

Litho. & Embossed With Foil Application

2600 A1097 $1.85 multi 3.00 3.00
a. Souvenir sheet of 2, #2496, 2600 5.50 4.75

Booklet Stamp Self-Adhesive

Litho.

Serpentine Die Cut 13½

2601 A1097 $1.85 multi 3.00 1.20
a. Booklet pane of 6 18.00

No. 2599 sold for 63c on day of issue. See Nos. 2700a, 3259f, 3260f, 3266.

Juvenile Wildlife Type of 2011

Designs: P, Four woodchuck pups. $1.10, Porcupette. $1.34, Fawn. $1.85, Bear cub.

2013, Jan. 14 ***Perf. 13¼x13***

2602 Souvenir sheet of 4 7.75 7.75
a. A1038 P multi 1.30 1.10
b. A1038 $1.10 multi 1.65 1.25
c. A1038 $1.34 multi 2.00 1.60
d. A1038 $1.85 multi 2.80 2.60

Self-Adhesive Coil Stamps

Serpentine Die Cut 9¼ Horiz.

2603 A1038 P multi 1.50 1.50

Serpentine Die Cut 8¼ Horiz.

2604 A1038 P multi 1.30 .25
2605 A1038 $1.10 multi 1.65 .35
2606 A1038 $1.34 multi 2.00 .55
2607 A1038 $1.85 multi 2.80 1.00

Booklet Stamps

Serpentine Die Cut 9¼ Horiz.

2608 A1038 $1.10 multi 1.65 .35
a. Booklet pane of 6 10.00
2609 A1038 $1.34 multi 2.00 .55
a. Booklet pane of 6 12.00
2610 A1038 $1.85 multi 2.80 .90
a. Booklet pane of 6 16.75
Nos. 2603-2610 (8) 15.70 5.45

On day of issue, Nos. 2602a, 2603 and 2604 each sold for 63c. On rolls of No. 2603, stamps do not touch each other and pairs are horizontal. On rolls of No. 2604, stamps touch each other and pairs are vertical.

See No. 2692.

Flag Design on Chairs A1098

Flag on Hay Roll A1099

Flag Design on Spinnaker A1100

Flag in Flower Bed A1101

Flag Design on Hut — A1102

2013, Jan. 14 Litho. ***Perf. 13x13¼***

2611 Souvenir sheet of 5 6.50 6.50
a. A1098 P multi 1.30 1.10
b. A1099 P multi 1.30 1.10
c. A1100 P multi 1.30 1.10
d. A1101 P multi 1.30 1.10
e. A1102 P multi 1.30 1.10

Booklet Stamps Self-Adhesive

Serpentine Die Cut 13¼

2612 A1098 P multi 1.30 .25
a. With "Canada" visible on reverse of stamp 1.30 .25
2613 A1099 P multi 1.30 .25
a. With "Canada" visible on reverse of stamp 1.30 .25
2614 A1100 P multi 1.30 .25
a. With "Canada" visible on reverse of stamp 1.30 .25
2615 A1101 P multi 1.30 .25
a. With "Canada" visible on reverse of stamp 1.30 .25
2616 A1102 P multi 1.30 .25
a. With "Canada" visible on reverse of stamp 1.30 .25
b. Booklet pane of 10, 2 each #2612-2616 13.00
c. Booklet pane of 10, 2 each #2612a-2616a 13.00
d. Booklet pane of 30, 6 each #2612-2616 39.00
e. Booklet pane of 30, 6 each #2612a-2616a 39.00
Nos. 2612-2616 (5) 6.50 1.25

On day of issue, Nos. 2611a-2611e, 2612-2616, 2612a-2616a each sold for 63c. The printing on the backing paper on Nos. 2616b and 2616c differs from that on the backing paper of any of the component thirds of Nos. 2616d and 2616e.

See Nos. 2693-2697.

Queen Elizabeth II — A1103

Booklet Stamp

Serpentine Die Cut 13¼

2013, Jan. 14 **Self-Adhesive**

2617 A1103 P multi 1.30 .25
a. Booklet pane of 10 13.00
b. As #2617,with "Canada" visible on reverse of stamp 1.30 .25
c. Booklet pane of 10 #2617b 13.00

No. 2617 sold for 63c on day of issue. Issued: Nos. 2617b, 2617c, 6/1.

See No. 2698.

A1104

185c, Raoul Wallenberg (1912-47), Swedish Diplomat Who Rescued Jews During World War II.

Booklet Stamp

Serpentine Die Cut 13¼

2013, Jan. 17 **Self-Adhesive**

2618 A1104 185c multi 2.80 1.50
a. Booklet pane of 6 16.75

Oliver Jones, Jazz Musician — A1105

Joe Fortes (1863-1922), First Official Lifeguard of Vancouver — A1106

Booklet Stamps

Serpentine Die Cut 13¼

2013, Feb. 1 **Self-Adhesive**

2619 A1105 P multi 1.30 .35
a. Booklet pane of 10 13.00
2620 A1106 P multi 1.30 .35
a. Booklet pane of 10 13.00

On day of issue, Nos. 2619-2620 each sold for 63c.

Magnolias

A1107 A1108

Magnolia varieties: Nos. 2621a, 2622, 2624, Yellow Bird (yellow flower). Nos. 2621b, 2623, 2625, Eskimo (lilac and white flower).

2013, Mar. 4 Litho. ***Perf. 13¼***

Souvenir Sheet

2621 Sheet of 2 2.60 2.60
a.-b. A1107 P Either single 1.30 1.10

Coil Stamps Self-Adhesive

Serpentine Die Cut 8¼ Horiz.

2622 A1108 P multi 1.30 .40
2623 A1108 P multi 1.30 .40
a. Vert. pair, #2622-2623 2.60

Booklet Stamps

Serpentine Die Cut 13½

2624 A1107 P multi 1.30 .35
2625 A1107 P multi 1.30 .35
a. Booklet pane of 10, 5 each #2624-2625 13.00

On day of issue, Nos. 2621a-2621b, 2622-2625 each sold for 63c.

Photography — A1109

Designs: Nos. 2626a, 2629, Louis-Joseph Papineau, by Thomas Coffin Doane, 1852. Nos. 2626b, 2630, The Kitchen Sink, by Margaret Watkins, 1919. Nos. 2626c, 2632, Kootuck-tuck, by Geraldine Moodie, 1903-05. Nos. 2627a, 2628, Hot Properties #1, by Jim Breukelman, 1987, horiz. Nos. 2627b, 2631, Andor Pasztor, by Gabor Szilasi, 1978, horiz. $1.10, Basement Camera Shop circa 1937, by Rodney Graham, 2011, horiz. $1.85, Yousuf Karsh, by Arnaud Maggs, 1981, horiz.

2013, Mar. 22 ***Perf. 13¼***

2626 A1109 Sheet of 3 4.00 4.00
a.-c. P Any single 1.30 1.10
2627 A1109 Sheet of 4 7.00 7.00
a.-b. P Any single 1.30 1.10
c. $1.10 multi 1.65 1.50
d. $1.85 multi 2.80 2.60

Booklet Stamps Self-Adhesive

Serpentine Die Cut 13½

2628 A1109 P multi 1.30 .35
2629 A1109 P multi 1.30 .35
2630 A1109 P multi 1.30 .35
2631 A1109 P multi 1.30 .35
2632 A1109 P multi 1.30 .35
a. Booklet pane of 10, 2 each #2628-2632 13.00
2633 A1109 $1.10 multi 1.65 .80
a. Booklet pane of 6 10.00
2634 A1109 $1.85 multi 2.80 1.40
a. Booklet pane of 6 16.75
Nos. 2628-2634 (7) 10.95 3.95

On day of issue, Nos. 2626a-2626c, 2627a, 2627b, 2628-2632 each sold for 63c.

See Nos. 2756-2764, 2814-2822, 2902-2910, 3010-3016.

The Prince of Wales' Own Regiment, 150th Anniv. A1110

Serpentine Die Cut 13¼x13

2013, Apr. 9 **Self-Adhesive**

Booklet Stamp

2635 A1110 P multi 1.30 .35
a. Booklet pane of 10 13.00

No. 2635 sold for 63c on day of issue.

Pet Adoption — A1111

Designs: Nos. 2636a, 2637, Cat with bird on branch in background (24x32mm). Nos. 2636b, 2638, Parrot on perch (24x24mm). Nos. 2636c, 2639, Dog with squirrel, butterfly, flower and ball in background (24x40mm). Nos. 2636d, 2640, Dog with fireplace, dog bed and bone in background (40x40mm). Nos. 2636e, 2641, Cat with cat toys in background (24x32mm).

Perf. 12½ (#2636a, 2636e), 13¼ (#2636b), 12½x13¼

2013, Apr. 22

2636 A1111 Sheet of 5 8.00 5.00
a.-e. P Any single 1.30 .45

Booklet Stamps Self-Adhesive

Serpentine Die Cut 13x13¼

2637 A1111 P multi 1.30 .45

Serpentine Die Cut 13

2638 A1111 P multi 1.30 .45

Serpentine Die Cut 13½

2639 A1111 P multi 1.30 .45
2640 A1111 P multi 1.30 .45

Serpentine Die Cut 13x13¼

2641 A1111 P multi 1.30 .45
a. Booklet pane of 10, 2 each #2637-2641 13.00
Nos. 2637-2641 (5) 6.50 2.25

On day of issue, Nos. 2636a-2636e, 2637-2641 each sold for 63c.

Chinatown Gates — A1112

Gates in: Nos. 2642a, 2643a, Toronto. Nos. 2642b, 2643b, Montreal. Nos. 2642c, 2643c, Winnipeg. Nos. 2642d, 2643e, Edmonton. Nos. 2642e, 2643d, Vancouver. Nos. 2642f, 2643f, Ottawa. Nos. 2642g, 2643g, Mississauga, Ontario. Nos. 2642h, 2643h, Victoria.

Litho. With Foil Application

2013, May 1 ***Perf. 12½***

2642 A1112 Miniature sheet of 8 + central label 10.50 10.50
a.-h. P Any single 1.30 1.10

An imperf. pane of 8 exists of No. 2642. Sold only in a "Gates of Chinatown Collection," along with a normal No. 2642 and two coins, for $88.88. Value of imperf. pane, $140.

Litho.

Booklet Stamps Self-Adhesive

Serpentine Die Cut 13½

2643 A1112 Booklet pane of 8 10.50
a.-h. P Any single 1.30 .35

On day of issue Nos. 2642a-2642h, 2643a-2643h each sold for 63c. Label on No. 2642 has a die cut square opening in center.

Coronation of Queen Elizabeth II, 60th Anniv. — A1113

Serpentine Die Cut 13¼

2013, May 8 **Litho.**

Booklet Stamp
Self-Adhesive

2644 A1113 P multi 1.30 .35
a. Booklet pane of 10 13.00

No. 2644 sold for 63c on day of issue.

Big Brothers Big Sisters of Canada, Cent. — A1114

Serpentine Die Cut 13x13½

2013, May 14 **Litho.**

Booklet Stamp
Self-Adhesive

2645 A1114 P multi 1.30 .35
a. Booklet pane of 10 13.00

No. 2645 sold for 63c on day of issue.

Motorcycles — A1115

Designs: Nos. 2646a, 2647, 1908 CCM. Nos. 2646b, 2648, 1914 Indian.

2013, June 5 ***Perf. 12½x13***

Souvenir Sheet

2646 A1115 Sheet of 2 2.60 2.60
a.-b. P Either single 1.30 1.10

Booklet Stamps
Self-Adhesive

Serpentine Die Cut 13¼

2647 A1115 P multi 1.30 .35
2648 A1115 P multi 1.30 .35
a. Booklet pane of 10, 5 each #2647-2648 13.00

On day of issue, Nos. 2646a-2646b, 2647-2648 each sold for 63c.

A1116

Design: Quebec Harbor Scene and Benjamin Franklin (1706-90), British North America Deputy Postmaster.

Booklet Stamp

Serpentine Die Cut 13½

2013, June 10 **Self-Adhesive**

2649 A1116 P multi 1.30 .35
a. Booklet pane of 10 13.00

Mail packet service from Montreal to New York, 250th anniv. No. 2649 sold for 63c on day of issue.

War of 1812 — A1117

Heroic figures of War of 1812: No. 2650, Lieutenant Colonel Charles de Salaberry (1778-1829). No. 2651, Laura Secord (1775-1868).

2013, June 20 ***Perf. 13x12½***

2650 P multi 1.30 .35
2651 P multi 1.30 .35
a. A1117 Horiz. pair, #2650-2651 2.60 1.10

On day of issue, Nos. 2650-2651 each sold for 63c.

Children's Literature — A1118

Characters from series of *Stella* books, by Marie-Louise Gay: Nos. 2652a, 2653, Stella hanging by legs from tree. Nos. 2652b, 2654, Stella, brother Sam, and dog, Fred.

2013, July 5 ***Perf. 12½***

Souvenir Sheet

2652 A1118 Sheet of 2 2.60 2.60
a.-b. P Either single 1.30 1.10

Booklet Stamps
Self-Adhesive

Serpentine Die Cut 13¼

2653 A1118 P multi 1.30 .35
2654 A1118 P multi 1.30 .35
a. Booklet pane of 10, 5 each #2653-2654 13.00

On day of issue, Nos. 2652a-2652b, 2653-2654 each sold for 63c.

Canadian Bands — A1119

Designs: Nos. 2655a, 2656, The Tragically Hip (36x28mm). Nos. 2655b, 2657, Rush (28x28mm). Nos. 2655c, 2658, Beau Dommage (36x28mm). Nos. 2655d, 2659, The Guess Who (28x28mm).

2013, July 19 ***Perf. 12½***

Souvenir Sheet

2655 A1119 Sheet of 4 5.25 5.25
a.-d. P Any single 1.30 1.10

Booklet Stamps
Self-Adhesive

Serpentine Die Cut 13½

2656 A1119 P multi 1.30 .35
a. Booklet pane of 10 13.00
2657 A1119 P multi 1.30 .35
a. Booklet pane of 10 13.00
2658 A1119 P multi 1.30 .35
a. Booklet pane of 10 13.00
2659 A1119 P multi 1.30 .35
a. Booklet pane of 10 13.00
Nos. 2656-2659 (4) 5.20 1.40

On day of issue, Nos. 2655a-2655d, 2656-2659 each sold for 63c.

Robertson Davies (1913-95), Writer — A1120

Booklet Stamp

Serpentine Die Cut 13¼

2013, Aug. 28 **Self-Adhesive**

2660 A1120 63c multi .95 .35
a. Booklet pane of 10 9.50

Pucks With Emblems of Canadian National Hockey League Teams — A1121

Pucks with emblem of: Nos. 2661a, 2662, Vancouver Canucks. Nos. 2661b, 2663, Edmonton Oilers. Nos. 2661c, 2664, Toronto Maple Leafs. Nos. 2661d, 2665, Montreal Canadiens. Nos. 2661e, 2666, Calgary Flames. Nos. 2661f, 2667, Winnipeg Jets. Nos. 2661g, 2668, Ottawa Senators.

2013, Sept. 3 **Litho.** ***Perf. 13¼x13***

2661 A1121 Sheet of 7 6.60 6.60
a.-g. 63c Any single .95 .75

Coil Stamps
Self-Adhesive

Serpentine Die Cut 8¼ Horiz.

2662 A1121 63c multi .95 .40
2663 A1121 63c multi .95 .40
2664 A1121 63c multi .95 .40
2665 A1121 63c multi .95 .40
2666 A1121 63c multi .95 .40
2667 A1121 63c multi .95 .40
2668 A1121 63c multi .95 .40
Nos. 2662-2668 (7) 6.65 2.80

Player and Fans Wearing Home and Away Jerseys A1122

Uniforms of Canadian National Hockey League Teams: Nos. 2669a, 2670, Vancouver Canucks. Nos. 2669b, 2671, Montreal Canadiens. Nos. 2669c, 2672, Edmonton Oilers. Nos. 2669d, 2673, Ottawa Senators. Nos. 2669e, 2674, Calgary Flames. Nos. 2669f, 2675, Winnipeg Jets. Nos. 2669g, 2676, Toronto Maple Leafs.

Serpentine Die Cut 13¼x13½

2013, Sept. 3 **Litho. & Embossed**

2669 Sheet of 7 + 2 labels 6.60 6.60
a.-g. A1122 63c Any single .95 .75

Litho.

Booklet Stamps
Self-Adhesive

2670 A1122 63c multi .95 .35
a. Booklet pane of 10 9.50
2671 A1122 63c multi .95 .35
a. Booklet pane of 10 9.50
2672 A1122 63c multi .95 .35
a. Booklet pane of 10 9.50
2673 A1122 63c multi .95 .35
a. Booklet pane of 10 9.50
2674 A1122 63c multi .95 .35
a. Booklet pane of 10 9.50
2675 A1122 63c multi .95 .35
a. Booklet pane of 10 9.50
2676 A1122 63c multi .95 .35
a. Booklet pane of 10 9.50
Nos. 2670-2676 (7) 6.65 2.45

A1123

A1124

A1125

A1126

A1127

Superman Comics, 75th Anniv. — A1128

2013, Sept. 10 ***Perf. 12½***

2677 Sheet of 5 6.50 6.50
a. A1123 P multi 1.30 1.10
b. A1124 P multi 1.30 1.10
c. A1125 P multi 1.30 1.10
d. A1126 P multi 1.30 1.10
e. A1127 P multi 1.30 1.10

Coil Stamp
Self-Adhesive

Die Cut Perf. 13½

2678 A1128 P multi 1.30 .50

Booklet Stamps

Serpentine Die Cut 13½x13¼

2679 A1123 P multi 1.30 .45
2680 A1124 P multi 1.30 .45
2681 A1125 P multi 1.30 .45
2682 A1126 P multi 1.30 .45
2683 A1127 P multi 1.30 .45
a. Booklet pane of 10, 2 each #2679-2683 13.00
Nos. 2678-2683 (6) 7.80 2.75

Nos. 2677a-2677e, 2678-2683 each sold for 63c on day of issue.

Hastings and Prince Edward Regiment, 150th Anniv. A1129

Serpentine Die Cut 13¼x13

2013, Oct. 18 Litho.

Booklet Stamp Self-Adhesive

2684 A1129 P multi 1.30 .35
a. Booklet pane of 10 13.00

No. 2684 sold for 63c on day of issue.

Birth of Prince George of Cambridge A1130

2013, Oct. 22 Litho. *Perf. 12½*

2685 Sheet of 2 #2685a 2.60 2.60
a. A1130 P Single stamp 1.30 1.10

Booklet Stamp Self-Adhesive

Serpentine Die Cut 13½

2686 A1130 P multi 1.30 .35
a. Booklet pane of 10 13.00

On day of issue, Nos. 2685a and 2686 each sold for 63c.

Christmas
A1131 A1132

Designs: Nos. 2687a, 2689, Cross-stitched horn. $1.10, Cross-stitched reindeer. $1.85, Cross-stitched Christmas tree. No. 2688, St. Anne with the Christ Child, by Georges de La Tour.

2013, Oct. 22 Litho. *Perf. 13½x13¼*

2687 Sheet of 3 5.50 5.50
a. A1131 63c multi .95 .95
b. A1131 $1.10 multi 1.65 1.60
c. A1131 $1.85 multi 2.80 2.60

Booklet Stamps Self-Adhesive

Serpentine Die Cut 13½

2688 A1132 63c multi 1.00 .25
a. Booklet pane of 12 12.00

Serpentine Die Cut 13¼x13

2689 A1131 63c multi .95 .25
a. Booklet pane of 12 11.50
2690 A1131 $1.10 multi 1.65 .60
a. Booklet pane of 6 10.00
2691 A1131 $1.85 multi 2.80 .90
a. Booklet pane of 6 17.00
Nos. 2688-2691 (4) 6.40 2.00

Juvenile Wildlife Type of 2011

Design: 63c, Four woodchuck pups.

Serpentine Die Cut 9¼ Horiz.

2013, Dec. 11 Litho.

Coil Stamps Self-Adhesive

2692 A1038 63c multi .95 .25
b. Without repeating "Canada" underprint on reverse *75.00 7.50*

Serpentine Die Cut 8¼ Horiz.

2692A A1038 63c multi 1.10 1.10

Coils containing No. 2692A are adjacent in vertical strips. Coils containing No. 2692 are in horizontal strips with stamps separated.

Flag Types of 2013

Serpentine Die Cut 13¼

2013, Dec. 11 Litho.

Booklet Stamps Self-Adhesive

2693 A1098 63c multi .95 .25
2694 A1099 63c multi .95 .25
2695 A1100 63c multi .95 .25
2696 A1101 63c multi .95 .25
2697 A1102 63c multi .95 .25
a. Booklet pane of 10, 2 each #2693-2697 9.50
Nos. 2693-2697 (5) 4.75 1.25

Queen Elizabeth II Type of 2013

Serpentine Die Cut 13¼

2013, Dec. 11 Litho.

Booklet Stamp Self-Adhesive

2698 A1103 63c multi .95 .25
a. Booklet pane of 10 9.50

New Year 2014 (Year of the Horse) — A1133

Design: $1.85, Horse, diff.

Litho. & Embossed

2014, Jan. 13 *Perf. 12½*

2699 A1133 63c multi .95 .30

Litho. & Embossed With Foil Application

Souvenir Sheet

2700 A1133 $1.85 multi 2.75 2.75
a. Souvenir sheet of 2, #2600, 2700 5.50 5.50

Litho. With Foil Application

Booklet Stamp Self-Adhesive

Serpentine Die Cut 13½

2701 A1133 $1.85 multi 2.80 1.70
a. Booklet pane of 6 16.75

See Nos. 3259g, 3260g, 3267.

African-Canadian Neighborhoods — A1134

Residents and buildings of: No. 2702, Africville, neighborhood of Halifax, Nova Scotia. No. 2703, Hogan's Alley, neighborhood of Vancouver, British Columbia.

Serpentine Die Cut 13¼

2014, Jan. 30 Litho.

Booklet Stamps Self-Adhesive

2702 A1134 63c multi .95 .35
a. Booklet pane of 10 9.50
2703 A1134 63c multi .95 .35
a. Booklet pane of 10 9.50

Female Athletes — A1135

Designs: Nos. 2704a, 2705, Barbara Ann Scott (1928-2012), figure skater. Nos. 2704b, 2706, Sandra Schmirler (1963-2000), curler. Nos. 2704c, 2707, Sarah Burke (1982-2012), freestyle skier.

2014, Feb. 3 Litho. *Perf. 13*

Souvenir Sheet

2704 Sheet of 3 2.90 2.90
a.-c. A1135 63c Any single .95 .95

Booklet Stamps Self-Adhesive

Serpentine Die Cut 13¼

2705 A1135 63c multi .95 .35
a. Booklet pane of 10 9.50
2706 A1135 63c multi .95 .35
a. Booklet pane of 10 9.50
2707 A1135 63c multi .95 .35
a. Booklet pane of 10 9.50
Nos. 2705-2707 (3) 2.85 1.05

Beneficial Insects Type of 2007

Design: 22c, Monarch butterfly.

2014, Mar. 31 Litho. *Perf. 13¼x13*

2708 A942 22c multi .30 .25

Juvenile Wildlife Type of 2011

Designs: P, Beaver kits. $1, Burrowing owl chicks. $1.20, Mountain goat kid. $1.80, Puffin chicks. $2.50, Newborn wapiti.

2014, Mar. 31 Litho. *Perf. 13¼x13*

2709 Souvenir sheet of 5 11.00 11.00
a. A1038 P multi 1.30 1.10
b. A1038 $1 multi 1.50 1.50
c. A1038 $1.20 multi 1.80 1.80
d. A1038 $1.80 multi 2.70 2.60
e. A1038 $2.50 multi 3.75 3.75

Coil Stamps Self-Adhesive

Die Cut Perf. 13½

2710 A1038 $1 multi 1.50 .25
b. "CANADA $1" inscription omitted *500.00*

Serpentine Die Cut 9¼ Horiz.

2710A A1038 P multi 1.50 1.50

Serpentine Die Cut 8¼ Horiz.

2711 A1038 P multi 1.30 .25
2712 A1038 $1.20 multi 1.80 .35
2713 A1038 $1.80 multi 2.70 .60
2714 A1038 $2.50 multi 3.75 1.10
Nos. 2710-2714 (5) 11.05 2.55

Booklet Stamps

Serpentine Die Cut 9¼ Horiz.

2715 A1038 $1.20 multi 1.80 .35
a. Booklet pane of 6 10.75
2716 A1038 $1.80 multi 2.70 .60
a. Booklet pane of 6 16.25
2717 A1038 $2.50 multi 3.75 1.10
a. Booklet pane of 6 22.50
Nos. 2715-2717 (3) 8.25 2.05

On day of issue, Nos. 2709a, 2710A, 2711 each sold for 85c. On rolls of No. 2710A, stamps do not touch each other and pairs are horizontal. On rolls of No. 2711, stamps touch each other and pairs are vertical.

Gros Morne National Park, Newfoundland and Labrador A1136

Joggins Fossil Cliffs, Nova Scotia A1137

Canadian Rocky Mountain Parks, Alberta and British Columbia A1138

Nahinni National Park, Northwest Territories A1139

Miguasha National Park, Quebec — A1140

2014, Mar. 31 Litho. *Perf. 13¼x13*

2718 Souvenir sheet of 5 6.50 6.50
a. A1136 P multi 1.30 1.10
b. A1137 P multi 1.30 1.10
c. A1138 P multi 1.30 1.10
d. A1139 P multi 1.30 1.10
e. A1140 P multi 1.30 1.10

Booklet Stamps Self-Adhesive

Serpentine Die Cut 13¼

2719 A1136 P multi 1.30 .25
2720 A1139 P multi 1.30 .25
2721 A1137 P multi 1.30 .25
2722 A1140 P multi *1.30* .25
2723 A1138 P multi 1.30 .25
a. Booklet pane of 10, 2 each #2719-2723 13.00
b. Booklet pane of 30, 6 each #2719-2723 37.50
Nos. 2719-2723 (5) 6.50 1.25

UNESCO World Heritage Sites. On day of issue, Nos. 2718a-2718f, 2719-2723 each sold for 85c.

Shiva Natajara Sculpture, Mummified Cat and Bison — A1141

Hadrasaur Skeleton and Luohan Chinese Sculpture A1142

2014, Apr. 14 Litho. *Perf. 12½*

2724 Souvenir sheet of 2 2.60 2.60
a. A1141 P multi 1.30 1.10
b. A1142 P multi 1.30 1.10

Booklet Stamps Self-Adhesive

Serpentine Die Cut 13½x13¼

2725 A1141 P multi 1.30 .35
2726 A1142 P multi 1.30 .35
a. Booklet pane of 10, 5 each #2725-2726 13.00

Royal Ontario Museum, cent. On day of issue, Nos. 2724a-2724b, 2725-2726 each sold for 85c.

Roses
A1143 A1144

Rose varieties: Nos. 2727a, 2729, 2730, Konrad Henkel (red) rose. Nos. 2727b, 2728, 2731, Maid of Honor (white) rose.

2014, Apr. 23 Litho. *Perf. 13*

Souvenir Sheet

2727 Sheet of 2 2.60 2.60
a.-b. A1143 P Either single 1.30 1.10

Coil Stamps Self-Adhesive

Serpentine Die Cut 8¼ Horiz.

2728 A1144 P multi 1.30 .35
2729 A1144 P multi 1.30 .35
a. Vert. pair, #2728-2729 2.60

Booklet Stamps

Serpentine Die Cut 13¼

2730 A1143 P multi 1.30 .35
2731 A1143 P multi 1.30 .35
a. Booklet pane of 10, 5 each #2730-2731 13.00
Nos. 2728-2731 (4) 5.20 1.40

On day of issue, Nos. 2727a-2727b, 2728-2731 each sold for 85c.

Komagata Maru Incident, Cent. — A1145

Serpentine Die Cut 13x12¾

2014, May 1 Litho.

Booklet Stamp Self-Adhesive

2732 A1145 $2.50 multi 3.75 1.90
a. Booklet pane of 6 22.50

National Film Board, 75th Anniv. — A1146

Scenes from Canadian films: Nos. 2733a, 2734, *Flamenco at 5:15,* 1983. Nos. 2733b, 2735, *The Railrodder,* 1965. Nos. 2733c, 2736, *Mon Oncle Antoine,* 1971. Nos. 2733d, 2737, *Log Driver's Waltz,* 1979. Nos. 2733e, 2738, *Neighbours,* 1952.

2014, May 2 Litho. *Perf. 13¼x12½*

2733 A1146 Sheet of 5 + label 6.50 6.50
a.-e. P Any single 1.30 1.10

Booklet Stamps
Self-Adhesive
Serpentine Die Cut 13¼

2734 A1146 P multi 1.30 .35
2735 A1146 P multi 1.30 .35
2736 A1146 P multi 1.30 .35
2737 A1146 P multi 1.30 .35
2738 A1146 P multi 1.30 .35
a. Booklet pane of 10, 2 each #2734-2738 13.00
Nos. 2734-2738 (5) 6.50 1.75

On day of issue, Nos. 2733a-2733e and 2734-2738 each sold for 85c.

UNESCO World Heritage Sites — A1147

Designs: Nos. 2739a, 2741, Head-Smashed-In Buffalo Jump, Alberta. Nos. 2739b, 2740, Old Town Lunenburg, Nova Scotia. Nos. 2739c, 2742, Landscape of Grand Pré, Nova Scotia. Nos. 2739d, 2743, SGang Gwaay, British Columbia. Nos. 2739e, 2744, Rideau Canal, Ontario.

2014, May 16 Litho. *Perf. 12½*
Miniature Sheet

2739 A1147 Sheet of 5 13.00 13.00
a.-c. $1.20 Any single 1.80 1.50
d.-e. $2.50 Either single 3.75 3.50

Booklet Stamps
Self-Adhesive
Serpentine Die Cut 13¼x13½

2740 A1147 $1.20 multi 1.80 1.10
2741 A1147 $1.20 multi 1.80 1.10
2742 A1147 $1.20 multi 1.80 1.10
a. Booklet pane of 6, 2 each #2740-2742 10.75
2743 A1147 $2.50 multi 3.75 2.30
2744 A1147 $2.50 multi 3.75 2.30
a. Booklet pane of 6, 3 each #2743-2744 22.50
Nos. 2740-2744 (5) 12.90 7.90

Sinking of the RMS Empress of Ireland, Cent. — A1148

Designs: P, Empress of Ireland facing right. $2.50, Empress of Ireland facing left, horiz.

2014, May 29 Litho. *Perf. 12½*

2745 A1148 P multi 1.30 .60

Souvenir Sheet
Perf. 12¾

2746 A1148 $2.50 multi 3.75 3.50

Booklet Stamp
Self-Adhesive
Serpentine Die Cut 13½

2747 A1148 P multi 1.30 .35
a. Booklet pane of 10 13.00

On day of issue, Nos. 2745 and 2747 each sold for 85c. No. 2745 was printed in sheets of 16 + 4 labels. No. 2746 contains one 80x32mm stamp.

Haunted Canada A1149

Designs: Nos. 2748a, 2749, Ghost bride, Banff Springs, Alberta. Nos. 2748b, 2751, Ghost train, St. Louis, Saskatchewan. Nos. 2748c, 2753, Apparitions of Fort George, Ontario. Nos. 2748d, 2752, Count of Frontenac Apparition, Château Frontenac Hotel, Quebec. Nos. 2748e, 2750, Phantom ship off Nova Scotia and Prince Edward Island.

2014, June 13 Litho. *Perf. 12½*

2748 Sheet of 5 6.50 6.50
a.-e. A1149 P Any single 1.30 1.10

Booklet Stamps
Self-Adhesive
Serpentine Die Cut 13¼

2749 A1149 P multi 1.30 .45
2750 A1149 P multi 1.30 .45
2751 A1149 P multi 1.30 .45
2752 A1149 P multi 1.30 .45
2753 A1149 P multi 1.30 .45
a. Booklet pane of 10, 2 each #2749-2753 13.00
Nos. 2749-2753 (5) 6.50 2.25

On day of issue, Nos. 2748a-2748e, 2749-2753 each sold for 85c.

Canadian Football League Team Emblems Type of 2012 and

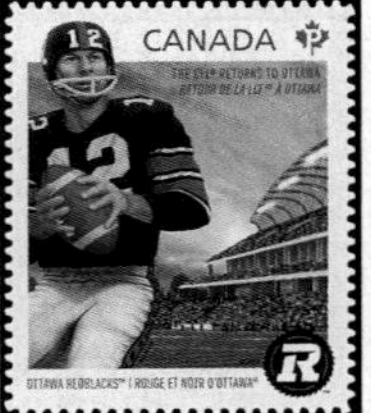

Russ Jackson in Ottawa Rough Riders Uniform, TD Place Stadium, Ottawa Redblacks Emblem A1150

Design: No. 2754, Ottawa Redblacks emblem.

Serpentine Die Cut 8¼ Horiz.
2014, June 19 Litho.

Coil Stamp
Self-Adhesive

2754 A1080 P multi 1.30 .45

Booklet Stamp

2755 A1150 P multi 1.30 .35
a. Booklet pane of 10 13.00

On day of issue, Nos. 2754 and 2755 each sold for 85c.

Photography Type of 2013

Designs: Nos. 2756a, 2762, Unidentified Chinese Man, by C. D. Hoy, c. 1912. Nos. 2756b, 2759, St. Joseph's Convent School, by Michel Lambeth, 1960. Nos. 2756c, 2763, Sitting Bull and Buffalo Bill, Montreal, by William Notman, 1885. Nos. 2757a, 2761, Untitled, by Lynne Cohen, 1970, horiz. Nos. 2757b, 2760, La Ville de Québec en Hiver (Quebec City in Winter), by Louis-Prudent Vallée, 1894, horiz. Nos. 2757c, 2758, Bogner's Grocery, by Fred Herzog, 1960, horiz. Nos. 2757d, 2764, Railcuts: #1, by Edward Burtynsky, 1985, horiz.

2014, July 7 Litho. *Perf. 13¼*

2756 Sheet of 3 4.40 4.40
a.-b. A1109 P Either single 1.30 1.10
c. A1109 $1.20 multi 1.80 1.65
2757 Sheet of 4 7.75 7.75
a.-c. A1109 P Any single 1.30 1.10
d. A1109 $2.50 multi 3.75 4.00

Booklet Stamps
Self-Adhesive
Serpentine Die Cut 13¼

2758 A1109 P multi 1.30 .45
2759 A1109 P multi 1.30 .45
2760 A1109 P multi 1.30 .45
2761 A1109 P multi 1.30 .45
2762 A1109 P multi 1.30 .45
a. Booklet pane of 10, 2 each #2758-2762 13.00
2763 A1109 $1.20 multi 1.80 .90
a. Booklet pane of 6 10.75
2764 A1109 $2.50 multi 3.75 2.00
a. Booklet pane of 6 22.50
Nos. 2758-2764 (7) 12.05 5.15

On day of issue, Nos. 2756a-2756b, 2757a-2757c, 2758-2762 each sold for 85c.

Hank Snow (1914-99), Country Music Recording Artist A1151

Renée Martel, Country Music Recording Artist A1152

Shania Twain, Country Music Recording Artist A1153

Tommy Hunter, Country Music Recording Artist A1154

K. D. Lang, Country Music Recording Artist A1155

2014, July 31 Litho. *Perf. 12½*

2765 Sheet of 5 6.50 6.50
a. A1151 P multi 1.30 1.10
b. A1152 P multi 1.30 1.10
c. A1153 P multi 1.30 1.10
d. A1154 P multi 1.30 1.10
e. A1155 P multi 1.30 1.10

Booklet Stamps
Self-Adhesive
Serpentine Die Cut 13¼

2766 A1151 P multi 1.30 .35
a. Booklet pane of 10 13.00
2767 A1152 P multi 1.30 .35
a. Booklet pane of 10 13.00
2768 A1153 P multi 1.30 .35
a. Booklet pane of 10 13.00
2769 A1154 P multi 1.30 .35
a. Booklet pane of 10 13.00
2770 A1155 P multi 1.30 .35
a. Booklet pane of 10 13.00
Nos. 2766-2770 (5) 6.50 1.75

On day of issue, Nos. 2765a-2765e, 2766-2770 each sold for 85c.

Canadian Museum for Human Rights, Winnipeg A1156

Serpentine Die Cut 13¼
2014, Aug. 20 Litho.

Booklet Stamp
Self-Adhesive

2771 A1156 P multi 1.30 .35
a. Booklet pane of 10 13.00

No. 2771 sold for 85c on day of issue.

Comedians — A1157

Designs: Nos. 2772a, 2773, Mike Myers. Nos. 2772b, 2774, Martin Short. Nos. 2772c, 2775, Catherine O'Hara. Nos. 2772d, 2776, Olivier Guimond (1914-71). Nos. 2772e, 2777, Jim Carrey.

2014, Aug. 29 Litho. *Perf. 12½x13*

2772 Sheet of 5 + label 6.50 6.50
a.-e. A1157 P Any single 1.30 1.10

Booklet Stamps
Self-Adhesive
Serpentine Die Cut 13¼

2773 A1157 P multi 1.30 .35
a. Booklet pane of 10, #2774-2777, 6#2773 13.00
2774 A1157 P multi 1.30 .35
a. Booklet pane of 10, #2773, 2775-2777, 6#2774 13.00
2775 A1157 P multi 1.30 .35
a. Booklet pane of 10, #2773-2774, 2776-2777, 6#2775 13.00
2776 A1157 P multi 1.30 .35
a. Booklet pane of 10, #2773-2775, 2777, 6#2776 13.00
2777 A1157 P multi 1.30 .35
a. Booklet pane of 10, #2773-2776, 6#2777 13.00
Nos. 2773-2777 (5) 6.50 1.75

On day of issue, Nos. 2772a-2772e, 2773-2777 each sold for 85c.

Zamboni With Canadian National Hockey League Team Emblems — A1158

Zamboni with emblem of: Nos. 2778a, 2779, Winnipeg Jets. Nos. 2778b, 2780, Ottawa Senators. Nos. 2778c, 2781, Toronto Maple Leafs. Nos. 2778d, 2782, Montreal Canadiens. Nos. 2778e, 2783, Vancouver Canucks. Nos. 2778f, 2784, Calgary Flames. Nos. 2778g, 2785, Edmonton Oilers.

2014, Oct. 3 Litho. *Perf. 13¼x13*
Miniature Sheet

2778 Sheet of 7 9.00 9.00
a.-g. A1158 P Any single 1.30 1.10

Coil Stamps
Self-Adhesive
Serpentine Die Cut 8¼ Horiz.

2779 A1158 P multi 1.30 .55
2780 A1158 P multi 1.30 .55
2781 A1158 P multi 1.30 .55
2782 A1158 P multi 1.30 .55
2783 A1158 P multi 1.30 .55
2784 A1158 P multi 1.30 .55
2785 A1158 P multi 1.30 .55
Nos. 2779-2785 (7) 9.10 3.85

On day of issue, Nos. 2778a-2778g, 2779-2785 each sold for 85c.

Defensemen in National Hockey League Hall of Fame — A1159

Designs: Nos. 2786a, 2787a, 2788, Tim Horton (1930-74). Nos. 2786b, 2787b, 2789, Doug Harvey. Nos. 2786c, 2787c, 2790, Bobby Orr. Nos. 2786d, 2787d, 2791, Harry Howell. Nos. 2786e, 2787e, 2792, Pierre Pilote. Nos. 2786f, 2787f, 2793, Red Kelly.

Litho., Sheet Margin Litho. & Embossed With Foil Application

2014, Oct. 3 ***Perf. 12½x13***

Miniature Sheet

2786 Sheet of 6 7.75 7.75
a.-f. A1159 P Any single 1.30 1.10

Litho.

Booklet Stamps Self-Adhesive

Serpentine Die Cut 13¼x13½

2787 Booklet pane of 6 8.00
a.-f. A1159 P Any single 1.35 .30

Souvenir Sheets

Serpentine Die Cut 13½x13¼

2788 A1159 $2.50 multi 3.75 3.00
2789 A1159 $2.50 multi 3.75 3.00
2790 A1159 $2.50 multi 3.75 3.00
2791 A1159 $2.50 multi 3.75 3.00
2792 A1159 $2.50 multi 3.75 3.00
2793 A1159 $2.50 multi 3.75 3.00
Nos. 2788-2793 (6) 22.50 18.00

Nos. 2786a-2786f, 2787a-2787f each sold for 85c on day of issue. Nos. 2788-2793 each contain one 52x78mm stamp. Nos, 2788-2793 were sold together in a sealed opaque plastic package. One of every 50 packages contained a souvenir sheet that was autographed by one of the 5 living players depicted.

"Wait for Me Daddy," Photograph by Claude P. Dettloff — A1160

2014, Oct. 4 Litho. ***Perf. 13½x13¼***

2794 A1160 P multi 1.30 .75

Booklet Stamp Self-Adhesive

Serpentine Die Cut 13¼x13½

2795 A1160 P multi 1.30 .35
a. Booklet pane of 10 13.00

Dedication of statue depicting photograph in New Westminster, British Columbia. Nos. 2794 and 2795 each sold for 85c on day of issue. No. 2794 was printed in sheets of 5.

Santa Claus A1161

The Virgin and Child with St. John the Baptist, by Abraham Janssens van Nuyssen A1162

Santa Claus: P, Writing letter. $1.20, Carrying sack. $2.50, With dove.

2014, Oct. 23 Litho. ***Perf. 13½x13¼***

Souvenir Sheet

2796 Sheet of 3 7.00 7.00
a. A1161 P multi 1.30 1.10
b. A1161 $1.20 multi 1.80 1.50
c. A1161 $2.50 multi 3.75 3.25

Booklet Stamps Self-Adhesive

Serpentine Die Cut 13½

2797 A1162 P multi 1.30 .25
a. Booklet pane of 12 15.50

Serpentine Die Cut 13¼x13

2798 A1161 P multi 1.30 .25
a. Booklet pane of 12 15.50
2799 A1161 $1.20 multi 1.80 .75
a. Booklet pane of 6 10.75
2800 A1161 $2.50 multi 3.75 1.30
a. Booklet pane of 6 22.50
Nos. 2797-2800 (4) 8.15 2.55

Christmas. Nos. 2796a, 2797 and 2798 each sold for 85c on day of issue.

New Year 2015 (Year of the Ram) — A1163

Design: $2.50, Ram facing left.

Litho. & Embossed With Foil Application

2015, Jan. 8 ***Perf. 12½***

2801 A1163 P multi 1.30 .55

Souvenir Sheet

2802 A1163 $2.50 multi 3.75 3.75
a. Souvenir sheet of 2, #2700, 2802 6.50 6.50
b. Perf. 13¼ (#2885a) 3.75 3.75

Litho. With Foil Application

Booklet Stamp Self-Adhesive

Serpentine Die Cut 13½

2803 A1163 $2.50 multi 3.75 2.00
a. Booklet pane of 6 22.50

No. 2801 sold for 85c on day of issue.
Issued: No. 2802b, 2/1/16.
See Nos. 3259h, 3260h, 3268.

Sir John A. Macdonald (1815-91), First Prime Minister of Canada A1164

Serpentine Die Cut 13¼

2015, Jan. 11 Litho.

Self-Adhesive

Booklet Stamp

2804 A1164 P multi 1.30 .35
a. Booklet pane of 10 13.00

No. 2804 sold for 85c on day of issue.

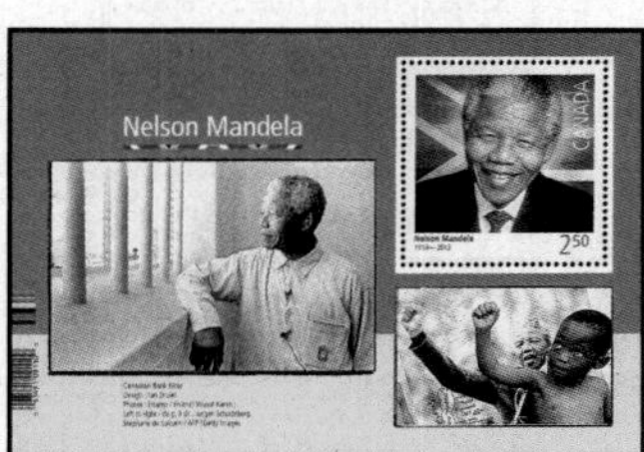

Nelson Mandela (1918-2013), President of South Africa — A1165

2015, Jan. 30 Litho. ***Perf. 12½x13***

Souvenir Sheet

2805 A1165 $2.50 multi 3.75 3.50

Booklet Stamp Self-Adhesive Size: 33x33mm

Serpentine Die Cut 13¼

2806 A1165 P multi 1.30 .35
a. Booklet pane of 10 13.00

No. 2806 sold for 85c on day of issue.

A1166

Canadian Flag, 50th Anniv. — A1167

Serpentine Die Cut 13¼x13½

2015, Feb. 15 Litho.

Booklet Stamp Self-Adhesive

2807 A1166 P multi 1.30 .35
a. Booklet pane of 10 13.00

Souvenir Sheet On Rayon Fabric

Serpentine Die Cut 9½

2808 A1167 $5 multi 7.50 7.50

No. 2807 sold for 85c on day of issue.

Pansies
A1168 A1169

Designs: Nos. 2809a, 2810, 2812, Delta Premium Pure Light Blue pansy (blue and yellow flower). No. 2809b, 2811, 2813, Midnight Glow pansy (purple and yellow flower).

2015, Mar. 2 Litho. ***Perf. 13x13¼***

Souvenir Sheet

2809 Sheet of 2 2.60 2.60
a.-b. A1168 P Either single 1.30 1.10

Coil Stamps Self-Adhesive

Serpentine Die Cut 8¼ Horiz.

2810 A1169 P multi 1.30 .45
2811 A1169 P multi 1.30 .45
a. Vert. pair, #2810-2811 2.60

Booklet Stamps

Serpentine Die Cut 13½

2812 A1168 P multi 1.30 .35
2813 A1168 P multi 1.30 .35
a. Booklet pane of 10, 5 each #2812-2813 13.00

On day of issue Nos. 2809a-2809b, 2810-2813 each sold for 85c.

Photography Type of 2013

Designs: Nos. 2814a, 2820, Shoeshine Stand, by Nina Raginsky, 1974. Nos. 2814b, 2817, Southan Sisters, Montreal, by Harold Mortimer-Lamb, c. 1915-19, horiz. Nos. 2814c, 2822, La Voie Lactée, by Geneviève Cadieux, 1992, horiz. Nos. 2815a, 2816, Angels, Saint-Jean-Baptiste Day, by Sam Tata, 1962, horiz. Nos. 2815b, 2819, Isaac's First Swim, Lambton County, Ontario, Canada, by Larry Towell, 1996, horiz. Nos. 2815c, 2818, Friends and Family and Trips. In Front of Simpsons, by Conrad Poirier, 1936, horiz. Nos. 2815d, 2821, Alex Colville on the Tantramar Marshes, by Geoffrey James, c. 1970, horiz.

2015, Apr. 8 Litho. ***Perf. 12¾***

2814 A1109 Sheet of 3 6.25 6.25
a.-b. P Either single 1.30 1.10
c. $2.50 multi 3.75 3.75
2815 A1109 Sheet of 4 5.75 5.75
a.-c. P Any single 1.30 1.10
d. $1.20 multi 1.80 1.50

Booklet Stamps Self-Adhesive

Serpentine Die Cut 13¼

2816 A1109 P multi 1.30 .55
2817 A1109 P multi 1.30 .55
2818 A1109 P multi 1.30 .55
2819 A1109 P multi 1.30 .55
2820 A1109 P multi 1.30 .55
a. Booklet pane of 10, 2 each #2816-2820 13.00
2821 A1109 $1.20 multi 1.80 1.10
a. Booklet pane of 6 11.00
2822 A1109 $2.50 multi 3.75 2.25
a. Booklet pane of 6 22.50
Nos. 2816-2822 (7) 12.05 6.10

On day of issue, Nos. 2814a-2814b, 2815a-2815c, 2816-2820 each sold for 85c.

Dinosaurs A1170

Designs: Nos. 2823a, 2827, Euplocephalus tutus (33x28mm). Nos. 2823b, 2826, Chasmosaurus belli (28x28mm). Nos. 2823c, 2824, Tyrannosaurus rex. Nos. 2823d, 2828, Ornithomimus edmontonicus. Nos. 2823e, 2825, Tylosaurus pembinensis.

Litho. & Embossed With Foil Application

Serpentine Die Cut 13¼

2015, Apr. 3 Self-Adhesive

2823 Sheet of 5 6.50 6.50
a.-e. A1170 P Any single 1.30 1.10

Booklet Stamps

Litho. With Foil Application

2824 A1170 P multi 1.30 .55
2825 A1170 P multi 1.30 .55
2826 A1170 P multi 1.30 .55
2827 A1170 P multi 1.30 .55
2828 A1170 P multi 1.30 .55
a. Booklet pane of 10, 2 each #2824-2828 13.00

On day of issue, Nos. 2823a-2823e, 2824-2828 each sold for 85c.

Love Your Pet A1171

Designs: Nos. 2829a, 2830, Cat in head cone sniffing flowers. Nos. 2829b, 2831, Dog chasing snowball. Nos. 2829c, 2832, Veterinarian examining cat. Nos. 2829d, 2834, Dog drinking water from bowl. Nos. 2829e, 2833, Cat on leash wearing identification tags.

2015, May 2 Litho. ***Perf. 13***

2829 Sheet of 5 6.50 6.50
a.-e. A1171 P Any single 1.30 1.10

Booklet Stamps Self-Adhesive

Serpentine Die Cut 13¼

2830 A1171 P multi 1.30 .55
2831 A1171 P multi 1.30 .55
2832 A1171 P multi 1.30 .55
2833 A1171 P multi 1.30 .55
2834 A1171 P multi 1.30 .55
a. Booklet pane of 10, 2 each #2830-2834 13.00
Nos. 2830-2834 (5) 6.50 2.75

On day of issue, Nos. 2829a-2829e, 2830-2834 each sold for 85c.

In Flanders Fields, Poem by John McCrae, Cent. A1172

2015, May 3 Litho. ***Perf. 12½***

2835 A1172 P multi 1.30 .75

Booklet Stamp Self-Adhesive

Serpentine Die Cut 13¼x13½

2836 A1172 P multi 1.30 .35
a. Booklet pane of 10 13.00

On day of issue, Nos. 2835-2836 each sold for 85c. No. 2835 was printed in sheets of 5.

2015 Women's World Cup Soccer Championships, Canada — A1173

Serpentine Die Cut 13¼x13½

2015, May 6 **Litho.**

Booklet Stamp
Self-Adhesive

2837 A1173 P multi 1.30 .35
a. Booklet pane of 10 13.00

No. 2837 sold for 85c on day of issue.

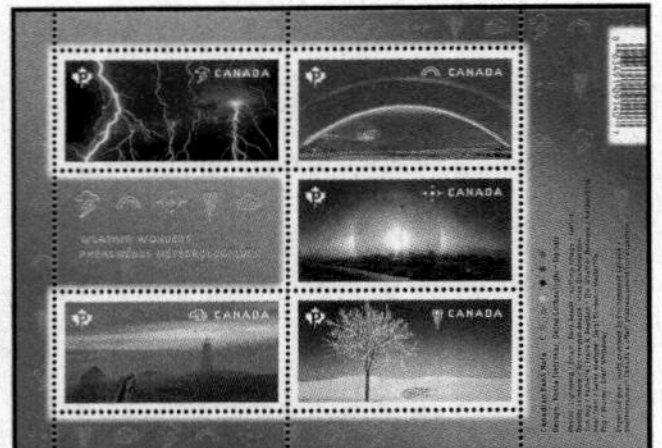

Weather Phenomena — A1174

Designs: Nos. 2838a, 2839, Lightning. Nos. 2838b, 2842, Double rainbow. Nos. 2838c, 2843, Sun dog over Iqaluit, Nunavut. Nos. 2838d, 2841, Fog near Cape Spear Lighthouse. Nos. 2838e, 2840, Hoar frost on tree.

Perf. 12½x13¼

2015, June 18 **Litho.**

2838 A1174 Sheet of 5 + label 6.50 6.50
a.-e. P Any single 1.30 1.10

Booklet Stamps
Self-Adhesive

Serpentine Die Cut 13¼

2839 A1174 P multi 1.30 .55
2840 A1174 P multi 1.30 .55
2841 A1174 P multi 1.30 .55
2842 A1174 P multi 1.30 .55
2843 A1174 P multi 1.30 .55
a. Booklet pane of 10, 2 each #2839-2843 13.00

Nos. 2838a-2838e, 2839-2843 each sold for 85c on day of issue.

Hoodoos, Alberta A1175

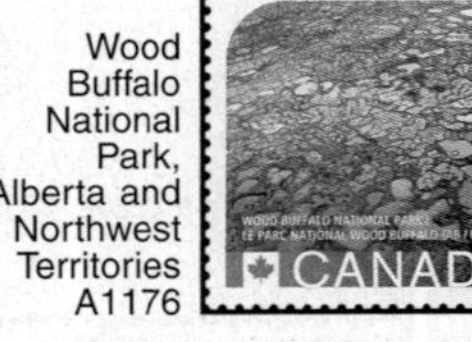

Wood Buffalo National Park, Alberta and Northwest Territories A1176

Red Bay Basque Whaling Station, Newfoundland and Labrador — A1177

Waterton Glacier International Peace Park, Alberta and Montana — A1178

Kluane National Park, Yukon, Wrangell-St. Elias and Glacier Bay National Parks, Alaska, Tatshenshini-Alsek Park, British Columbia — A1179

2015, July 3 **Litho.** ***Perf. 12½***

2844 Sheet of 5 *75.00 75.00*
a. A1175 $1.20 multi *60.00 30.00*
b. A1176 $1.20 multi 1.80 1.25
c. A1177 $1.20 multi 1.80 1.50
d. A1178 $2.50 multi 3.75 3.00
e. A1179 $2.50 multi 3.75 3.00

Booklet Stamps
Self-Adhesive

Serpentine Die Cut 13¼

2845 A1175 $1.20 multi *22.50 19.00*
2846 A1177 $1.20 multi 1.80 1.50
2847 A1176 $1.20 multi 1.80 1.50
a. Booklet pane of 6, 2 each #2845-2847 *55.00*
2848 A1178 $2.50 multi 3.75 2.10
2849 A1179 $2.50 multi 3.75 2.10
a. Booklet pane of 6, 3 each #2848-2849 22.50

UNESCO World Heritage Sites. Nos. 2844 and 2847a were withdrawn from sale on July 6 after it was discovered that illustration A1175 shows hoodoos not located in Dinosaur Provincial Park in Alberta. See Nos. 2857-2858.

Alice Munro, 2013 Nobel Literature Laureate — A1180

Serpentine Die Cut 13¾

2015, July 10 **Litho.**

Booklet Stamp
Self-Adhesive

2850 A1180 P multi 1.30 .35
a. Booklet pane of 10 13.00

No. 2850 sold for 85c on day of issue.

HMS Erebus Trapped in Ice — A1181

Map of Northern Canadian Islands — A1182

Wreckage and Diagram of HMS Erebus — A1183

Litho & Embossed, Litho (A1183)

2015, Aug. 6 ***Perf. 12½***

2851 A1181 P multi 1.30 .60
2852 A1182 P multi 1.30 .60
a. Horiz. pair, #2851-2852 2.60 1.25

Souvenir Sheet

Perf. 13¼

2853 A1183 $2.50 multi 3.75 3.75

Booklet Stamps
Self-Adhesive

Serpentine Die Cut 13½x13¼

2854 A1181 P multi 1.30 .35
2855 A1182 P multi 1.30 .35
a. Booklet pane of 10, 5 each #2854-2855 13.00

Serpentine Die Cut 13¼x13¾

2856 A1183 $2.50 multi 3.75 2.00
a. Booklet pane of 6 22.50
Nos. 2854-2856 (3) 6.35 2.70

Discovery of wreckage of HMS Erebus, 1st anniv. Nos. 2851-2852, 2854-2855 each sold for 85c on day of issue.

Dinosaur Provincial Park, Alberta A1184

2015, Aug. 21 **Litho.** ***Perf. 12½***

2857 Sheet of 5, #2844b-2844e, 2857a 13.00 13.00
a. A1184 $1.20 multi 1.80 .95

Booklet Stamp
Self-Adhesive

2858 A1184 $1.20 multi 1.80 1.10
a. Booklet pane of 6, 2 each #2846, 2847, 2858 11.00

UNESCO World Heritage Sites. Nos. 2857a and 2858 show correct images of landscapes in Dinosaur Provincial Park.

Queen Elizabeth II, Longest-Reigning British Monarch — A1185

Serpentine Die Cut 13¼

2015, Sept. 9 **Litho.**

Booklet Stamp
Self-Adhesive

2859 A1185 P multi 1.30 .35
a. Booklet pane of 10 13.00

No. 2859 sold for 85c on day of issue.

Haunted Canada — A1186

Designs: Nos. 2860a, 2861, Brakeman ghost, Vancouver, British Columbia. Nos. 2860b, 2864, Red River Trail Oxcart, Winnipeg, Manitoba. Nos. 2860c, 2863, Gray Lady of the Citadel, Halifax, Nova Scotia. Nos. 2860d, 2862, Ghost of Marie-Josephte Corriveau, Lévis, Quebec. Nos. 2860e, 2865, Ghost of Caribou Hotel, Carcross, Yukon.

Litho. With Holographic Foil

2015, Sept. 14 ***Perf. 12½x13***

2860 A1186 Sheet of 5 6.50 6.50
a.-e. P Any single 1.30 1.10

Booklet Stamps
Self-Adhesive

Serpentine Die Cut 13¼

2861 A1186 P multi 1.30 .55
2862 A1186 P multi 1.30 .55
2863 A1186 P multi 1.30 .55
2864 A1186 P multi 1.30 .55
2865 A1186 P multi 1.30 .55
a. Booklet pane of 10, 2 each #2861-2865 13.00
Nos. 2861-2865 (5) 6.50 2.75

On day of issue, Nos. 2860a-2860e, 2861-2865 each sold for 85c.

A1187

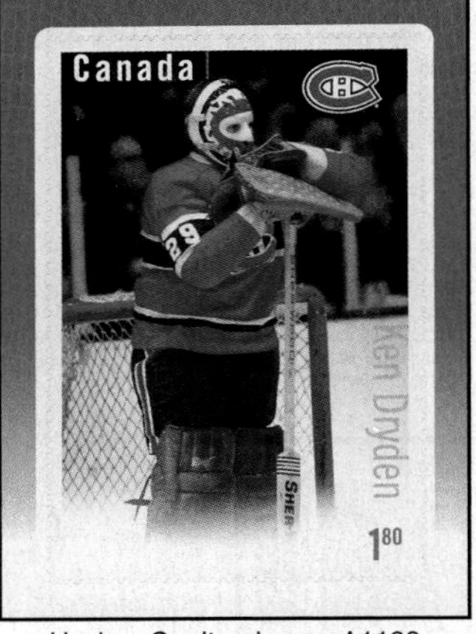

Hockey Goaltenders — A1188

Designs: Nos. 2866a, 2867, 2873, Ken Dryden. Nos. 2866b, 2868, 2874, Tony Esposito. Nos. 2866c, 2869, 2875, Johnny Bower. Nos. 2866d, 2870, 2876, Gump Worsley (1929-2007). Nos. 2866e, 2871, 2877, Bernie Parent. Nos. 2866f, 2872, 2878, Martin Brodeur.

Litho., Sheet Margin Litho. & Embossed With Foil Application

2015, Oct. 2 ***Perf. 12½***

2866 Sheet of 6 + 3 labels 7.75 7.75
a.-f. A1187 P Any single 1.30 1.10

Booklet Stamps
Self-Adhesive
Litho.

Serpentine Die Cut 13¼x13½

2867 A1187 P multi 1.30 .55
2868 A1187 P multi 1.30 .55
2869 A1187 P multi 1.30 .55
2870 A1187 P multi 1.30 .55
2871 A1187 P multi 1.30 .55
2872 A1187 P multi 1.30 .55
a. Booklet pane of 6, #2867-2872 7.75
Nos. 2867-2872 (6) 7.80 3.30

Souvenir Sheets

Serpentine Die Cut 13½x13¼

2873 A1188 $1.80 multi 2.70 2.25
2874 A1188 $1.80 multi 2.70 2.25
2875 A1188 $1.80 multi 2.70 2.25
2876 A1188 $1.80 multi 2.70 2.25
2877 A1188 $1.80 multi 2.70 2.25
2878 A1188 $1.80 multi 2.70 2.25
Nos. 2873-2878 (6) 16.20 13.50

Nos. 2866a-2866f, 2867-2872 each sold for 85c on day of issue. Nos. 2873-2878 each contain one 52x78mm stamp. Nos. 2873-2878 were sold together in a sealed opaque plastic package. One of every 40 packages contained a souvenir sheet signed by Esposito, Bower, Parent or Brodeur.

A1189

Christmas — A1190

Designs: Nos. 2879a, 2881, Moose. Nos. 2879b, 2882, Beaver. Nos. 2879c, 2883, Polar bear. No. 2880, Adoration of the Magi, by Adriaen Isenbrandt.

2015, Nov. 2 Litho. *Perf. 13¾x13¼*

2879 Sheet of 3 6.75 6.75
a. A1189 P multi 1.30 1.10
b. A1189 $1.20 multi 1.80 1.60
c. A1189 $2.50 multi 3.75 3.25

Booklet Stamps
Self-Adhesive

Serpentine Die Cut 13¼x13½

2880 A1190 P multi 1.30 .25
a. Booklet pane of 12 15.50

Serpentine Die Cut 13¼x13

2881 A1189 P multi 1.30 .25
a. Booklet pane of 12 15.50
2882 A1189 $1.20 multi 1.80 .95
a. Booklet pane of 6 11.00
2883 A1189 $2.50 multi 3.75 1.50
a. Booklet pane of 6 22.50
Nos. 2880-2883 (4) 8.15 2.95

Nos. 2879a, 2880 and 2881 each sold for 85c on day of issue.

New Year 2016 (Year of the Monkey) A1191

Design: $2.50, Monkey's head.

Litho. & Embossed With Foil Application

2016 *Perf. 13¼*

2884 A1191 P multi 1.30 .55

Souvenir Sheet

2885 A1191 $2.50 multi 3.75 3.75
a. Souvenir sheet of 2, #2802b, 2885 7.50 7.50
b. Perf. 12½ (#2960a) 3.75 3.50

Litho.

Booklet Stamps
Self-Adhesive

Serpentine Die Cut 13½

2886 A1191 P multi 1.30 .45
a. Booklet pane of 10 13.00
2887 A1191 $2.50 multi 3.75 2.25
a. Booklet pane of 6 22.50

Issued: Nos. 2884, 2886, 1/11; Nos. 2885, 2887, 2/1. No. 2885a, 1/9/17. No. 2885b, 1/9/17. Nos. 2884 and 2886 each sold for 85c on day of issue.

See Nos. 3259i, 3260i, 3269.

Queen Elizabeth II — A1192

Serpentine Die Cut 13½x13¾

2016, Jan. 11 Litho.

Booklet Stamp
Self-Adhesive

2888 A1192 P multi 1.30 .25
a. Booklet pane of 10 13.00

No. 2888 sold for 85c on day of issue.

Landscape of Grand Pré, Nova Scotia A1193

Rideau Canal, Ontario A1194

SGang Gwaay, British Columbia — A1195

Head-Smashed-In Buffalo Jump, Alberta — A1196

Old Town Lunenburg, Nova Scotia — A1197

2016, Jan. 11 Litho. *Perf. 13¼x13*

Souvenir Sheet

2889 Sheet of 5 6.50 6.50
a. A1193 P multi 1.30 1.10
b. A1194 P multi 1.30 1.10
c. A1195 P multi 1.30 1.10
d. A1196 P multi 1.30 1.10
e. A1197 P multi 1.30 1.10

Booklet Stamps
Self-Adhesive

Serpentine Die Cut 13¾x13½

2890 A1193 P multi 1.30 .25
2891 A1195 P multi 1.30 .25
2892 A1197 P multi 1.30 .25
2893 A1194 P multi 1.30 .25
2894 A1196 P multi 1.30 .25
a. Booklet pane of 10, 2 each #2890-2894 13.00
b. Booklet pane of 30, 6 each #2890-2894 37.50

UNESCO World Heritage Sites. On day of issue, Nos. 2889a-2889e, 2890-2894 each sold for 85c.

Organization of No. 2 Construction Battalion (First Black Battalion), Cent. — A1198

Serpentine Die Cut 13½

2016, Feb. 1 Litho.

Booklet Stamp
Self-Adhesive

2895 A1198 P multi 1.30 .50
a. Booklet pane of 10 13.00

No. 2895 sold for 85c on day of issue.

Hydrangeas
A1199 A1200

Designs: Nos. 2896a, 2897, 2899, Hydrangea macrophylla. Nos. 2896b, 2898, 2900, Hydrangea arborescens.

2016, Mar. 1 Litho. *Perf. 13*

Souvenir Sheet

2896 Sheet of 2 2.60 2.60
a.-b. A1199 P Either single 1.30 1.10

Coil Stamps
Self-Adhesive

Serpentine Die Cut 8¼ Vert.

2897 A1200 P multi 1.30 .45
2898 A1200 P multi 1.30 .45
a. Horiz. pair, #2897-2898 2.60

Booklet Stamps

Serpentine Die Cut 13¼

2899 A1199 P multi 1.30 .45
2900 A1199 P multi 1.30 .45
a. Booklet pane of 10, 5 each #2899-2900 13.00
Nos. 2897-2900 (4) 5.20 1.80

On day of issue, Nos. 2896a-2896b, 2897-2900 each sold for 85c.

Woman Suffrage, Cent. — A1201

Serpentine Die Cut 13½x13¾

2016, Mar. 8 Self-Adhesive Litho.

Booklet Stamp

2901 A1201 P gold & black 1.30 .45
a. Booklet pane of 10 13.00

No. 2901 sold for 85c on day of issue.

Photography Type of 2013

Designs: Nos. 2902a, 2904, Toronto, by Lutz Dille, 1960, horiz. Nos. 2902b, 2905, Window, by Angela Grauerholz, 1988, horiz. Nos. 2902c, 2907, Victoria Bridge, Grand Trunk Railway, by Alexander Henderson, c. 1878, horiz. Nos. 2902d, 2906, Freighter's Boat on the Banks of the Red River, Manitoba, by Humphrey Lloyd Hime, 1858, horiz. Nos. 2903a, 2908, Sans Titre 0310/La Chambre Noire, by Michel Campeau, 2005-10, vert. Nos. 2903b, 2909, Climbing Mt. Habel, by Byron Harmon, c. 1909, horiz. Nos. 2903c, 2910, Grey Owl, by Yousuf Karsh, 1936, vert.

2016, Apr. 13 Litho. *Perf. 12¾*

2902 A1109 Sheet of 4 5.25 5.25
a.-d. P Any single 1.30 1.30
2903 A1109 Sheet of 3 7.00 7.00
a. P multi 1.30 1.10
b. $1.20 multi 1.80 1.50
c. $2.50 multi 3.75 3.00

Booklet Stamps
Self-Adhesive

Serpentine Die Cut 13¼

2904 A1109 P sil & multi 1.30 .55
2905 A1109 P sil & multi 1.30 .55
2906 A1109 P sil & multi 1.30 .55
2907 A1109 P sil & multi 1.30 .55
2908 A1109 P sil & multi 1.30 .55
a. Booklet pane of 10, 2 each #2904-2908 13.00
2909 A1109 $1.20 sil & multi 1.80 1.10
a. Booklet pane of 6 10.75
2910 A1109 $2.50 sil & multi 3.75 2.25
a. Booklet pane of 6 22.50
Nos. 2904-2910 (7) 12.05 6.10

On day of issue, Nos. 2902a-2902d, 2903a, 2904-2908 each sold for 85c.

U.S.S. Enterprise NCC-1701 A1202

Klingon Battle Cruiser A1203

Captain James T. Kirk A1204

Klingon Commander Kor — A1205

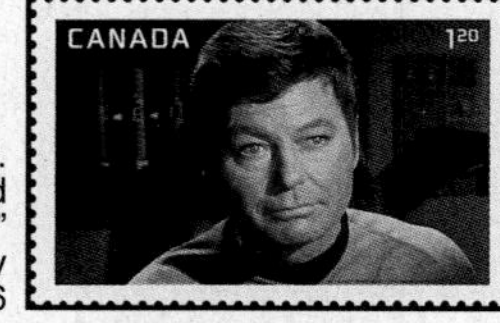
Dr. Leonard "Bones" McCoy A1206

Lieutenant Commander Montgomery "Scotty" Scott — A1207

Commander Spock — A1208

Characters From *Star Trek* Television Series — A1209

No. 2922: a, McCoy, Kirk, Spock and Scott in transporter room. b, Spock, Kirk and planet.

2016, May 5 Litho. *Perf. 13¼x13*

2911 Sheet of 2 2.60 2.60
a. A1202 P multi 1.30 1.10
b. A1203 P multi 1.30 1.10

Perf. 13¼

2912 Sheet of 5 11.00 11.00
a. A1204 P multi 1.30 1.10
b. A1205 $1 multi 1.50 1.30
c. A1206 $1.20 multi 1.80 1.60
d. A1207 $1.80 multi 2.70 2.40
e. A1208 $2.50 multi 3.75 3.50
f. Booklet pane of 4 #2912a 5.25 5.25
g. Booklet pane of 3, #2912c, 2912d, 2912e 8.25 8.25
h. Booklet pane of 1 #2912b 1.50 1.30
i. Booklet pane of 5, #2912a-2912e 11.00 11.00

Coil Stamps
Self-Adhesive

Serpentine Die Cut 8¼ Horiz.

2913 A1202 P multi 1.30 .55
2914 A1203 P multi 1.30 .55
a. Vert. pair, #2913-2914 2.60

Booklet Stamps

Serpentine Die Cut 13¾

2915 A1202 P multi 3.00 3.00
2916 A1203 P multi 3.00 3.00
a. Booklet pane of 2, #2915-2916 6.00
Complete booklet, #2912f, 2912g, 2912h, 2912i, 2916a 30.00

Serpentine Die Cut 13¼x13¼

2917 A1204 P multi 1.30 .55
2918 A1207 P multi 1.30 .55
2919 A1205 P multi 1.30 .55
2920 A1208 P multi 1.30 .55
2921 A1206 P multi 1.30 .55
a. Booklet pane of 10, 2 each #2917-2921 13.00
Nos. 2915-2921 (7) 12.50 8.75

Souvenir Sheet

Litho. With Three-Dimensional Plastic Affixed

Perf. 14¾

2922 A1209 Sheet of 2 15.00 15.00
a.-b. $5 Either single 7.50 7.50

Star Trek television series, 50th anniv. Nos. 2911a, 2911b, 2912a, 2913, 2914, 2917-2921 each sold for 85c on day of issue. Complete booklet sold for $19.95. Nos. 2915-2916 each had a franking value of 85c on day of issue.

Dinosaurs
A1210

Designs: Nos. 2923a, 2924, Troodon inequalis. Nos. 2923b, 2926, Dimetrodon borealis. Nos. 2923c, 2928, Comox Valley elasmosaur. Nos. 2923d, 2925, Cypretherium coarctatum. Nos. 2923e, 2927, Acrotholus audeti.

2016, May 26 Litho. *Perf. 13*

2923		Sheet of 5	6.50	6.50
a.-e.	A1210	P Any single	1.30	1.10

Booklet Stamps
Self-Adhesive

Serpentine Die Cut 13¼

2924	A1210	P multi	1.30	.55
2925	A1210	P multi	1.30	.55
2926	A1210	P multi	1.30	.55
2927	A1210	P multi	1.30	.55
2928	A1210	P multi	1.30	.55
a.		Booklet pane of 10, 2 each #2924-2928	13.00	
		Nos. 2924-2928 (5)	6.50	2.75

On day of issue, Nos. 2923a-2923e, 2924-2928 each sold for 85c.

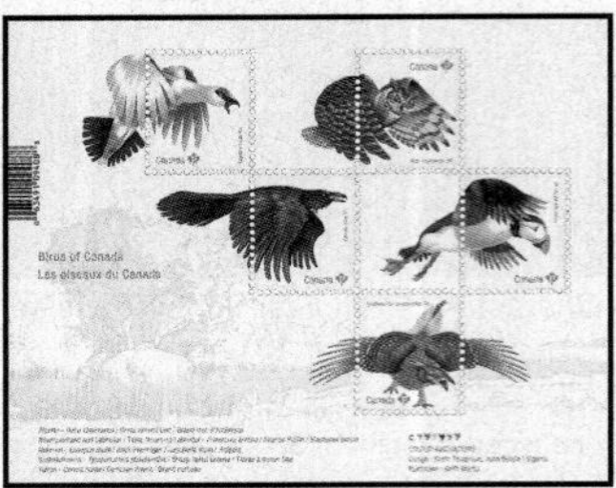

Birds — A1211

Designs: Nos. 2929a, 2934, Lagopus muta. Nos. 2929b, 2931, Bubo virginianus. Nos. 2929c, 2933, Corvus corax. Nos. 2929d, 2932, Fratercula arctica. Nos. 2929e, 2930, Tympanuchus phasianellus.

2016, July 12 Litho. *Perf. 13x13¼*

2929	A1211	Sheet of 5 + label	6.50	6.50
a.-e.		P Any single	1.30	1.10

Booklet Stamps
Self-Adhesive

Serpentine Die Cut 13½x13¾

2930	A1211	P multi	1.30	.55
2931	A1211	P multi	1.30	.55
2932	A1211	P multi	1.30	.55
2933	A1211	P multi	1.30	.55
2934	A1211	P multi	1.30	.55
a.		Booklet pane of 10, 2 each #2930-2934	13.00	
		Nos. 2930-2934 (5)	6.50	2.75

On day of issue, Nos. 2929a-2929e, 2930-2934 each sold for 85c.

Haunted Canada — A1212

Designs: Nos. 2935a, 2936, Bell Island Hag, Newfoundland and Labrador. Nos. 2935b, 2937, Dungarvon Whooper, New Brunswick. Nos. 2935c, 2939, Ghost of the Winter Garden Theater, Toronto, Ontario. Nos. 2935d, 2938, Lady in White of Montmorency Falls, Quebec. Nos. 2935e, 2940, Phantom Bell Ringers of the Kirk of St. James, Charlottetown, Prince Edward Island.

Litho. With Holographic Foil

2016, Sept. 8 *Perf. 13*

2935	A1212	Sheet of 5	6.50	6.50
a.-e.		P Any single	1.30	1.10

Booklet Stamps
Self-Adhesive

Serpentine Die Cut 13½

2936	A1212	P multi	1.30	.55
2937	A1212	P multi	1.30	.55
2938	A1212	P multi	1.30	.55
2939	A1212	P multi	1.30	.55
2940	A1212	P multi	1.30	.55
a.		Booklet pane of 10, 2 each #2936-2940	13.00	
		Nos. 2936-2940 (5)	6.50	2.75

On day of issue, Nos. 2935a-2935e, 2936-2940 each sold for 85c.

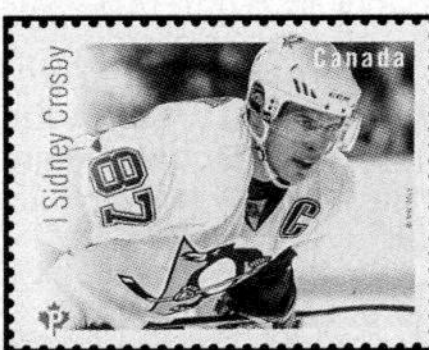

A1213

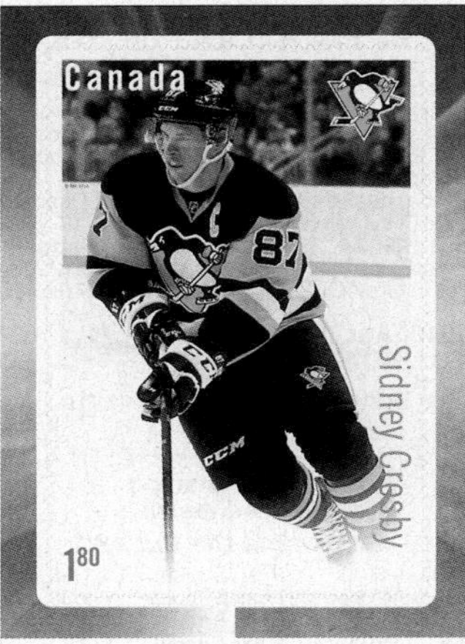

Hockey Forwards — A1214

Designs: Nos. 2941a, 2942, 2948, Sidney Crosby. Nos. 2941b, 2943, 2949, Phil Esposito. Nos. 2941c, 2944, 2950, Guy Lafleur. Nos. 2941d, 2945, 2951, Steve Yzerman. Nos. 2941e, 2946, 2952, Mark Messier. Nos. 2941f, 2947, 2953, Darryl Sittler.

Litho., Sheet Margin Litho. & Embossed With Foil Application

2016, Sept. 23 *Perf. 12½x13*

2941		Sheet of 6 + 3 labels	7.75	7.75
a.-f.	A1213	P Any single	1.30	1.10

Booklet Stamps
Self-Adhesive
Litho.

Serpentine Die Cut 13¼x13½

2942	A1213	P multi	1.30	.55
2943	A1213	P multi	1.30	.55
2944	A1213	P multi	1.30	.55
2945	A1213	P multi	1.30	.55
2946	A1213	P multi	1.30	.55
2947	A1213	P multi	1.30	.55
a.		Booklet pane of 6, #2942-2947	7.75	
		Nos. 2942-2947 (6)	7.80	3.30

Souvenir Sheets

Serpentine Die Cut 13½x13¼

2948	A1214	$1.80 multi	2.70	2.40
2949	A1214	$1.80 multi	2.70	2.40
2950	A1214	$1.80 multi	2.70	2.40
2951	A1214	$1.80 multi	2.70	2.40
2952	A1214	$1.80 multi	2.70	2.40
2953	A1214	$1.80 multi	2.70	2.40
		Nos. 2948-2953 (6)	16.20	14.40

Nos. 2941a-2941f, 2942-2947 each sold for 85c on day of issue. Nos. 2948-2953 each contain one 52x78mm stamp. Nos. 2873-2878 were sold together in a sealed opaque plastic package. One of every 40 packages contained a souvenir sheet signed by Crosby, Esposito, Lafleur, Yzerman, Messier or Sittler.

A1215

Christmas — A1216

Designs: Nos. 2954a, 2956, Santa Claus and Christmas tree. Nos. 2954b, 2957, Stocking cap on Christmas tree. Nos. 2954c, 2958, Dove and Christmas tree. No. 2955, Virgin and Child, by Master of the Castello Nativity.

2016, Nov. 1 Litho. *Perf. 12¾x12½*

2954		Sheet of 3	6.75	6.75
a.	A1215	P multi	1.30	1.10
b.	A1215	$1.20 multi	1.80	1.60
c.	A1215	$2.50 multi	3.75	3.50

Booklet Stamps
Self-Adhesive

Serpentine Die Cut 13¼x13½

2955	A1216	P multi	1.30	.25
a.		Booklet pane of 12	15.50	

Serpentine Die Cut 13

2956	A1215	P multi	1.30	.25
a.		Booklet pane of 12	15.50	
2957	A1215	$1.20 multi	1.80	.90
a.		Booklet pane of 6	10.75	
2958	A1215	$2.50 multi	3.75	1.90
a.		Booklet pane of 6	22.50	
		Nos. 2955-2958 (4)	8.15	3.30

Nos. 2954a, 2955 and 2956 each sold for 85c on day of issue.

New Year 2017 (Year of the Rooster)
A1217

Designs: P, Rooster. $2.50, Head of rooster.

Litho. With Foil Application, Litho. (#2961)

2017, Jan. 9 *Perf. 12½x13¼*

2959	A1217	P gold & multi	1.30	.55
a.		Perf. 13¼x12½	1.30	.55
b.		Pair, #2959, 2959a	2.60	1.90

Souvenir Sheet

Perf. 12½

2960	A1217	$2.50 gold & multi	3.75	3.75
a.		Souvenir sheet of 2, #2885b, 2960	7.50	7.50

Booklet Stamps
Self-Adhesive

Serpentine Die Cut 13½

2961	A1217	P multi	1.30	.55
a.		Booklet pane of 10	13.00	
2962	A1217	$2.50 gold & multi	3.75	2.25
a.		Booklet pane of 6	22.50	

Nos. 2959 and 2961 each sold for 85c on day of issue. On No. 2959b, one stamp of the pair is rotated 90 degrees in relation to the other stamp. Blocks of four contain stamps with four different orientations.

See Nos. 3259j, 3260j, 3270.

The tagging for all Canada stamps issued in 2017 will include the text "Canada 150."

Dinosaur Provincial Park, Alberta
A1218

Mistaken Point, Newfoundland and Labrador
A1219

Historic District of Old Quebec
A1220

L'Anse aux Meadows National Historic Site, Newfoundland and Labrador
A1221

Red Bay Basque Whaling Station, Newfoundland and Labrador — A1222

2017, Jan. 16 Litho. *Perf. 13¼x13*

2963		Sheet of 5	6.50	6.50
a.	A1218	P multi	1.30	1.10
b.	A1219	P multi	1.30	1.10
c.	A1220	P multi	1.30	1.10
d.	A1221	P multi	1.30	1.10
e.	A1222	P multi	1.30	1.10

Booklet Stamps
Self-Adhesive

Serpentine Die Cut 13

2964	A1218	P multi	1.30	.25
2965	A1220	P multi	1.30	.25
2966	A1222	P multi	1.30	.25
2967	A1219	P multi	1.30	.25
2968	A1221	P multi	1.30	.25
a.		Booklet pane of 10, 2 each #2964-2968	13.00	
b.		Booklet pane of 30, 6 each #2964-2968	39.00	
		Nos. 2964-2968 (5)	6.50	1.25

UNESCO World Heritage Sites. Nos. 2963a-2963e, 2964-2968 each sold for 85c on day of issue.

A1223

Design: No. 2969, Mathieu Da Costa, First Recorded Person of African Descent in Canada.

Serpentine Die Cut 13½

2017, Feb. 1 Self-Adhesive Litho.

Booklet Stamp

2969	A1223	P multi	1.30	.45
a.		Booklet pane of 10	13.00	

No. 2969 sold for 85c on day of issue.

Canadian Opera — A1224

Designs: Nos. 2970a, 2971, *Filumena,* by John Estacio and John Murrell. Nos. 2970b, 2972, Gerald Finley, baritone singer. Nos. 2970c, 2973, Adrianne Pieczonka, soprano singer. Nos. 2970d, 2974, Irving Guttman (1928-2014), operatic director. Nos. 2970e, 2975, *Louis Riel,* by Harry Somers, Mavor Moore and Jacques Languirand.

2017, Feb. 4 Litho. *Perf. 13¼*

2970	A1224	Sheet of 5	6.50	6.50
a.-e.		P Any single	1.30	1.10

Booklet Stamps
Self-Adhesive

Serpentine Die Cut 13½

2971	A1224	P multi	1.30	.55
2972	A1224	P multi	1.30	.55
2973	A1224	P multi	1.30	.55
2974	A1224	P multi	1.30	.55
2975	A1224	P multi	1.30	.55
a.		Booklet pane of 10, 2 each #2971-2975	13.00	
		Nos. 2971-2975 (5)	6.50	2.75

On day of issue, Nos. 2970a-2970e, 2971-2975 each sold for 85c.

Daisies
A1225 A1226

Designs: Nos. 2976a, 2977, 2979, Erigeron speciosus (purple petals). Nos. 2976b, 2978, 2980, Tetraneuris herbacea (yellow petals).

2017, Mar. 1 Litho. *Perf. 13*

Souvenir Sheet

2976 Sheet of 2 2.60 2.60
a.-b. A1225 P Either single 1.30 1.10

Self-Adhesive
Coil Stamps
Serpentine Die Cut 8 Vert.

2977 A1226 P multi 1.30 .55
2978 A1226 P multi 1.30 .55
a. Horiz. pair, #2977-2978 2.60

Booklet Stamps
Serpentine Die Cut 13½

2979 A1225 P multi 1.30 .45
2980 A1225 P multi 1.30 .45
a. Booklet pane of 10, 5 each #2979-2980 + 10 stickers 13.00

On day of issue, Nos. 2976a-2976b, 2977-2980 each sold for 85c.

A1227

Battle of Vimy Ridge, Cent. — A1228

No. 2981: a, Pillars and statue. b, Statue of weeping woman.

Litho. & Engr.

2017, Apr. 8 *Perf. 13¼*

2981 A1227 Sheet of 2 7.50 7.50
a.-b. $2.50 Either single 3.75 3.50

Litho.
Booklet Stamp
Self-Adhesive
Serpentine Die Cut 13½

2982 A1228 P multi 1.30 .45
a. Booklet pane of 10 13.00

No. 2982 sold for 85c on day of issue. See France No. 5216.

Admiral James T. Kirk A1229

Captain Jonathan Archer — A1230

Captain Kathryn Janeway A1231

Captain Benjamin Sisko — A1232

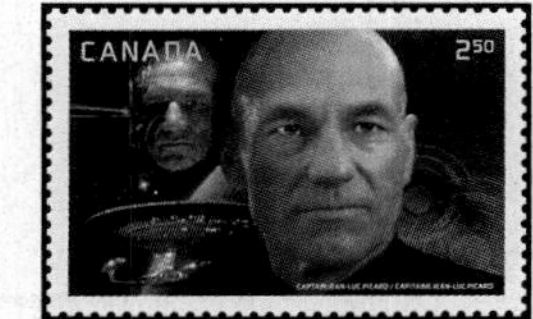

Captain Jean-Luc Picard — A1233

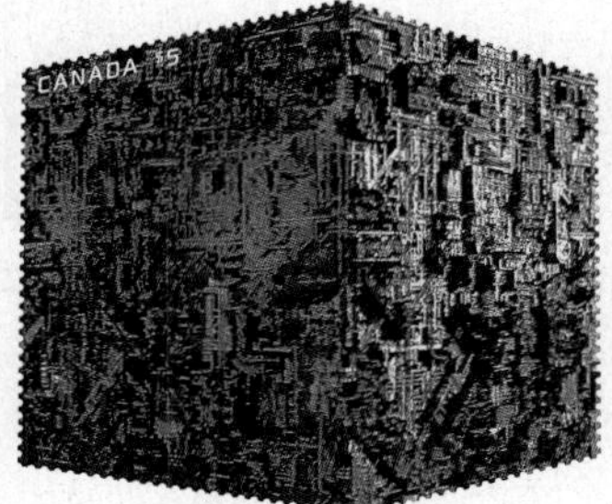

Borg Cube — A1234

Galileo Shuttle — A1235

Litho., Litho & Embossed With Foil Application (#2983)

2017, Apr. 27 *Perf. 13¼*

2983 Miniature sheet of 5 11.00 11.00
a. A1229 P multi 1.30 1.10
b. A1230 $1 multi 1.50 1.30
c. A1231 $1.20 multi 1.80 1.50
d. A1232 $1.80 multi 2.70 2.40
e. A1233 $2.50 multi 3.75 3.50
f. Booklet pane of 3 #2983a 3.90 —
g. Booklet pane of 4, #2983b-2983e 9.75 —
h. Booklet pane of 5, #2983a-2983e 11.25 —

Booklet Stamp
Perf. 13¼ on 2 Sides, 13 on 4 Sides

2984 A1234 $5 blk & silver 7.50 7.50
a. Booklet pane of 1 7.50 —

Coil Stamp
Self-Adhesive
Serpentine Die Cut 8 Horiz.

2985 A1235 P multi 1.30 .55

Booklet Stamps
Serpentine Die Cut 13¼x13¾

2986 A1229 P multi 1.30 .55
2987 A1233 P multi 1.30 .55
2988 A1232 P multi 1.30 .55
2989 A1231 P multi 1.30 .55
2990 A1230 P multi 1.30 .55
a. Booklet pane of 10, 2 each #2986-2990 13.00

Serpentine Die Cut 13¾

2991 A1235 P multi 3.75 3.75
a. Booklet pane of 1 3.75 —
Complete booklet, #2983f, 2983g,2983h, 2984a, 2991a 35.00
Nos. 2986-2991 (6) 10.25 6.50

Lead characters of various *Star Trek* television series. On day of issue, Nos. 2983a, 2985-2991 each sold for 85c. Complete booklet sold for $21.95.

Formula 1 Race Car Drivers — A1236

Race car, checkered flag and: Nos. 2992a, 2993, Sir Jackie Stewart, flag of Great Britain. Nos. 2992b, 2994, Gilles Villeneuve (1950-82), flag of Canada. Nos. 2992c, 2995, Ayrton Senna (1960-94), flag of Brazil. Nos. 2992d, 2996, Michael Schumacher, flag of Germany. Nos. 2992e, 2997, Lewis Hamilton, flag of Great Britain.

2017, May 16 Litho. *Perf. 13*

2992 A1236 Sheet of 5 6.50 6.50
a.-e. P Any single 1.30 1.10

Booklet Stamps
Self-Adhesive
Serpentine Die Cut 16½

2993 A1236 P multi 1.30 .55
2994 A1236 P multi 1.30 .55
2995 A1236 P multi 1.30 .55
2996 A1236 P multi 1.30 .55
2997 A1236 P multi 1.30 .55
a. Booklet pane of 10, 2 each #2993-2997 13.00
Nos. 2993-2997 (5) 6.50 2.75

Canadian Formula 1 Grand Prix, 50th anniv. On day of issue, Nos. 2992a-2992e, 2993-2997 each sold for 85c.

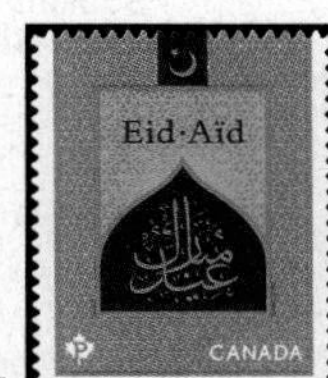

Eid — A1237

Serpentine Die Cut 13½x13¼

2017, May 24 Litho.

Booklet Stamp
Self-Adhesive

2998 A1237 P multi 1.30 .45
a. Booklet pane of 10 13.00

No. 2998 sold for 85c on day of issue.

A1238

Canadian Confederation, 150th Anniv. — A1239

Designs: Nos. 2999a, 3000, Habitat 67 at Expo 67, Montreal, 1967. Nos. 2999b, 3001, Route marker on completed Trans-Canada Highway, 1971. Nos. 2999c, 3002, Summit Series, 1972. Nos. 2999d, 3003, Terry Fox running Marathon of Hope, 1980. Nos. 2999e, 3004, Canadarm in space, 1981. Nos. 2999f, 3005, Canadian Constitution and Charter of Rights and Freedoms, 1982. Nos. 2999g, 3006, Woman from Nunavut, 1999. Nos. 2999h, 3007, Rainbow flag (marriage equality), 2005. Nos. 2999i, 3008, Canadian Olympic athlete (Olympic Games in Canada), 1976, 1988, 2010. Nos. 2999j, 3009, Paralympic skiier (Paralympic Games in Canada), 1976, 2010.

2017, June 1 Litho. *Perf.*

2999 Sheet of 10 + 2 labels 13.00 13.00
a.-j. A1238 P Any single 1.30 1.10

Booklet Stamps
Self-Adhesive
Die Cut

3000 A1239 P multi 1.30 .45
3001 A1239 P multi 1.30 .45
3002 A1239 P multi 1.30 .45
3003 A1239 P multi 1.30 .45
3004 A1239 P multi 1.30 .45
3005 A1239 P multi 1.30 .45
3006 A1239 P multi 1.30 .45
a. Booklet pane of 8 10.50
3007 A1239 P multi 1.30 .45
a. Booklet pane of 8 10.50
3008 A1239 P multi 1.30 .45
3009 A1239 P multi 1.30 .45
a. Booklet pane of 10, #3000-3009 13.00
Nos. 3000-3009 (10) 13.00 4.50

On day of issue, Nos. 2999a-2999j, 3000-3009 each sold for 85c.

Photography Type of 2013

Designs: Nos. 3010a, 3013, Enlacées, by Gilbert Duclos, 1994. Nos. 3010b, 3016, Sir John A. Macdonald, by William James Topley, c. 1883. Nos. 3011a, 3014, Ontario, Canada, by Robert Bourdeau, 1989, horiz. Nos. 3011b, 3015, Construction of the Parliament Buildings, by Samuel McLaughlin, c. 1862, horiz. Nos. 3011c, 3012, Ti-Noir Lajeunesse, the Blind Violinist, Disraeli, Quebec, by Claire Beaugrand-Champagne, 1972, horiz.

2017, July 4 Litho. *Perf. 12¾*

3010 A1109 Sheet of 2 2.60 2.60
a.-b. P Either single 1.30 1.10
3011 A1109 Sheet of 3 4.00 4.00
a.-b. P Any single 1.30 1.10

Booklet Stamps
Self-Adhesive
Serpentine Die Cut 13¼

3012 A1109 P multi 1.30 .45
3013 A1109 P multi 1.30 .45
3014 A1109 P multi 1.30 .45
3015 A1109 P multi 1.30 .45
3016 A1109 P multi 1.30 .45
a. Booklet pane of 10, 2 each #3012-3016 13.00

On day of issue, Nos. 3010a-3010b, 3011a-3011b, 3012-3016 each sold for 85c.

Birds — A1240

Designs: Nos. 3017a, 3020, Cyanocitta cristata. Nos. 3017b, 3019, Falco rusticolus. Nos. 3017c, 3021, Strix nebulosa. Nos. 3017d, 3018, Pandion haliaetus. Nos. 3017e, 3022, Gavia immer.

2017, Aug. 1 Litho. *Perf. 13x13¼*

3017 A1240 Sheet of 5 + label 6.50 6.50
a.-e. P Any single 1.30 1.10

Booklet Stamps
Self-Adhesive
Serpentine Die Cut 13

3018 A1240 P multi 1.30 .55
3019 A1240 P multi 1.30 .55
3020 A1240 P multi 1.30 .55
3021 A1240 P multi 1.30 .55
3022 A1240 P multi 1.30 .55
a. Booklet pane of 10, 2 each #3018-3022 13.00
Nos. 3018-3022 (5) 6.50 2.75

On day of issue, Nos. 3017a-3017e, 3018-3022 each sold for 85c.

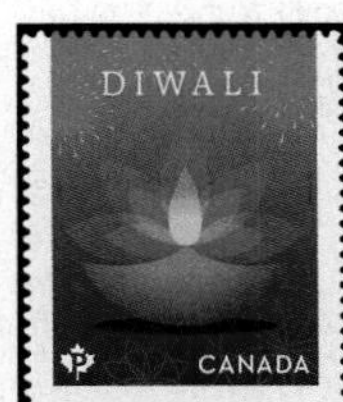

A1241

Diwali — A1242

2017, Sept. 21 Litho. *Perf. 13¼*

Souvenir Sheet

3023 Souvenir sheet of 2, #3023a and Indian stamp 4.50 4.50
a. A1241 $2.50 multi 3.75 3.25

Booklet Stamps
Self-Adhesive

Serpentine Die Cut 13¾x13½

3024 A1241 P multi 1.30 .55
3025 A1242 P multi 1.30 .55
a. Booklet pane of 10, 5 each #3024-3025 13.00

On day of issue, Nos. 3024-3025 each sold for 85c. No. 3023 sold for $3, and contains one 25r Indian stamp similar to type A1242. See India Nos. 2961-2962.

A1243

National Hockey League, Cent. — A1244

French and English versions of National Hockey League emblem and famous players: Nos. 3026a, 3027, 3033, Maurice Richard (1921-2000). Nos. 3026b, 3028, 3034, Jean Béliveau (1931-2014). Nos. 3026c, 3029, 3035, Gordie Howe (1928-2016). Nos. 3026d, 3030, 3036, Bobby Orr. Nos. 3026e, 3031, 3037, Mario Lemieux. Nos. 3026f, 3032, 3038, Wayne Gretzky.

Litho., Sheet Margin Litho. & Embossed With Foil Application

2017, Sept. 28 *Perf. 12½x13*

3026 Sheet of 6 7.75 7.75
a.-f. A1243 P Any single 1.30 .55

Booklet Stamps
Self-Adhesive
Litho.

Serpentine Die Cut 13¼x13½

3027 A1243 P multi 1.30 .55
3028 A1243 P multi 1.30 .55
3029 A1243 P multi 1.30 .55
3030 A1243 P multi 1.30 .55
3031 A1243 P multi 1.30 .55
3032 A1243 P multi 1.30 .55
a. Booklet pane of 6, #3027-3032 7.75
Nos. 3027-3032 (6) 7.80 3.30

Souvenir Sheets

Serpentine Die Cut 13½x13¼

3033 A1244 $1.80 multi 2.70 2.40
3034 A1244 $1.80 multi 2.70 2.40
3035 A1244 $1.80 multi 2.70 2.40
3036 A1244 $1.80 multi 2.70 2.40
3037 A1244 $1.80 multi 2.70 2.40
3038 A1244 $1.80 multi 2.70 2.40
Nos. 3033-3038 (6) 16.20 14.40

Nos. 3026a-3026f, 3027-3032 each sold for 85c on day of issue. Nos. 3033-3038 each contain one 52x78mm stamp. Nos. 3033-3038 were sold together in a sealed opaque plastic package. One of every 40 packages contained a souvenir sheet signed by Orr or Lemieux.

Ice Hockey Player Wearing Helmet and Protective Gear — A1245

Ice Hockey Player Wearing Hat and Scarf — A1246

2017, Oct. 20 Litho. *Perf. 13*

Souvenir Sheet

3039 Sheet of 2 2.60 2.60
a. A1245 P multi 1.30 1.10
b. A1246 P multi 1.30 1.10

Booklet Stamps
Self-Adhesive

3040 A1245 P multi 1.30 .45
3041 A1246 P multi 1.30 .45
a. Booklet pane of 10, 5 each #3040-3041 13.00

History of ice hockey. On day of issue, Nos. 3039a-3039b, 3040-3041 each sold for 85c. See United States Nos. 5252-5253.

Emblem of Toronto Maple Leafs on Jersey — A1247

Emblem of Toronto Maple Leafs on Hockey Puck — A1248

Maple Leaf and "100" — A1249

Litho. With Cloth Patch Affixed

2017, Oct. 24 *Perf. 13x13¼*

Souvenir Sheet

3042 A1247 $5 multi 7.50 7.50

Coil Stamp
Self-Adhesive

Die Cut

3043 A1248 P multi 1.30 .60

Booklet Stamp

Serpentine Die Cut 13¼x13½

3044 A1249 P multi 1.30 .45
a. Booklet pane of 10 13.00

Toronto Maple Leafs hockey team, cent. On day of issue, Nos. 3043-3044 each sold for 85c.

Polar Bear A1250

Cardinal A1251

Caribou A1252

The Adoration of the Shepherds, by Tommaso di Stefano Lunetti (c. 1495-1564) A1253

2017, Nov. 3 Litho. *Perf. 13½x13¼*

Souvenir Sheet

3045 Sheet of 3 6.75 6.75
a. A1250 P multi 1.30 1.10
b. A1251 $1.20 multi 1.50 .95
c. A1252 $2.50 multi 3.75 3.50

Booklet Stamps
Self-Adhesive
Litho. With Foil Application

Serpentine Die Cut 13½

3046 A1253 P multi 1.30 .25
a. Booklet pane of 12 15.50

Litho.

Serpentine Die Cut 13¼x13

3047 A1250 P multi 1.30 .25
a. Booklet pane of 12 15.00
3048 A1251 $1.20 multi 1.80 .90
a. Booklet pane of 6 11.00
3049 A1252 $2.50 multi 3.75 3.50
a. Booklet pane of 6 24.00
Nos. 3046-3049 (4) 8.15 4.90

Christmas. On day of issue, Nos. 3045a, 3046 and 3047 each sold for 85c.

Explosion of the Mont-Blanc in Halifax Harbor, Cent. — A1254

Serpentine Die Cut 13¼x13½

2017, Nov. 6 Litho.

Booklet Stamp
Self-Adhesive

3050 A1254 P multi 1.30 .45
a. Booklet pane of 10 13.00

On day of issue, No. 3050 sold for 85c.

Hanukkah A1255

Serpentine Die Cut 13¼x13½

2017, Nov. 14 Litho.

Booklet Stamp
Self-Adhesive

3051 A1255 P multi 1.30 .45
a. Booklet pane of 10 13.00

On day of issue, No. 3051 sold for 85c.

New Year 2018 (Year of the Dog) — A1256

Dog on Chinese lantern: P, Small dog with bushy tail. $2.50, Large dog with curled tail.

Litho. & Embossed With Foil Application

2018, Jan. 15 *Perf. 12½*

3052 A1256 P gold & multi 1.30 .55

Souvenir Sheet

3053 A1256 $2.50 gold & multi 3.25 3.75
a. Souvenir sheet of 2, #2960, 3053 7.50 7.50
b. Perf. 13¼ (#3162a) 4.00 4.00

Booklet Stamps
Self-Adhesive
Litho.

Serpentine Die Cut 13½

3054 A1256 P multi 1.30 .55
a. Booklet pane of 10 13.00

Litho. With Foil Application

3055 A1256 $2.50 gold & multi 3.75 2.25
a. Booklet pane of 6 222.50

Nos. 3052 and 3054 each sold for 85c on day of issue. Issued: No. 3053b, 1/18/19. See Nos. 3259k, 3260k, 3271.

St. John's, Newfoundland and Labrador A1257

Hopewell Rocks, New Brunswick A1258

MacMillan Provincial Park, British Columbia A1259

Covehead Harbor Lighthouse, Prince Edward Island National Park A1260

Ile-Bonaventure-et-du-Rocher-Percé National Park, Quebec — A1261

Pisew Falls Provincial Park, Manitoba A1262

Point Pelee National Park, Ontario A1263

Náátsʼįhchʼoh National Park Reserve, Northwest Territories A1264

Arctic Bay, Nunavut A1265

2018, Jan. 15 Litho. *Perf. 13¼x13*

3056 Sheet of 9 16.00 16.00
a. A1257 P multi 1.30 1.10
b. A1258 P multi 1.30 1.10
c. A1259 P multi 1.30 1.10
d. A1260 P multi 1.30 1.10
e. A1261 P multi 1.30 1.10
f. A1262 $1 multi 1.50 1.30
g. A1263 $1.20 multi 1.80 1.30
h. A1264 $1.80 multi 2.70 1.70
i. A1265 $2.50 multi 3.75 2.40

Coil Stamps
Self-Adhesive

Serpentine Die Cut 9¼ Horiz.

3057 A1257 P multi 1.50 1.50
3058 A1258 P multi 1.50 1.50
3059 A1259 P multi 1.50 1.50
3060 A1261 P multi 1.50 1.50
3061 A1260 P multi 1.50 1.50
a. Horiz. strip of 5, #3057-3061 7.50

Serpentine Die Cut 8¼ Horiz.

3062 A1257 P multi 1.30 .25
3063 A1258 P multi 1.30 .25
3064 A1259 P multi 1.30 .25
3065 A1261 P multi 1.30 .25
3066 A1260 P multi 1.30 .25
a. Vert. strip of 5, #3062-3066 6.50

3067 A1263 $1.20 multi 1.80 .35
3068 A1264 $1.80 multi 2.70 .65
3069 A1265 $2.50 multi 3.75 .95

Die Cut Perf. 13¼x13

3070 A1262 $1 multi 1.50 .25
Nos. 3057-3070 (14) 23.75 10.95

Booklet Stamps

Serpentine Die Cut 13¼x13½

3071 A1257 P multi 1.30 .25
3072 A1259 P multi 1.30 .25
3073 A1260 P multi 1.30 .25
3074 A1258 P multi 1.30 .25
3075 A1261 P multi 1.30 .25
a. Booklet pane of 10, 2 each #3071-3075 13.00
b. Booklet pane of 30, 6 each #3071-3075 39.00

Serpentine Die Cut 9¼ Horiz.

3076 A1263 $1.20 multi 1.80 .35
a. Booklet pane of 6 10.75
3077 A1264 $1.80 multi 2.70 .65
a. Booklet pane of 6 16.25
3078 A1265 $2.50 multi 3.75 .95
a. Booklet pane of 6 22.50
Nos. 3071-3078 (8) 14.75 3.20

On day of issue, Nos. 3056a-3056e, 3057-3066, 3071-3075 each sold for 85c.

Women in Winter Sports A1266

Designs: Nos. 3079a, 3080, Nancy Greene, alpine skier. Nos. 3079b, 3081, Sharon and Shirley Firth, cross-country skiers. Nos. 3079c, 3082, Danielle Goyette, ice hockey player. Nos. 3079d, 3083, Clara Hughes, speed skater. Nos. 3079e, 3084, Sonja Gaudet, wheelchair curler.

2018, Jan. 24 Litho. *Perf. 13x13¼*

3079 Sheet of 5 6.50 6.50
a.-e. A1266 P Any single 1.30 1.10

Booklet Stamps
Self-Adhesive

Serpentine Die Cut 13¼x13¾

3080 A1266 P multi 1.30 .55
3081 A1266 P multi 1.30 .55
3082 A1266 P multi 1.30 .55
3083 A1266 P multi 1.30 .55
3084 A1266 P multi 1.30 .55
a. Booklet pane of 10, 2 each #3080-3084 13.00
Nos. 3080-3084 (5) 6.50 2.75

On day of issue, Nos. 3079a-3079e, 3080-3084 each sold for 85c.

Black History Month — A1267

Designs: No. 3085, Kay Livingstone (1918-75), founder of Canadian Negro Women's Association. No. 3086, Lincoln M. Alexander (1922-2012), first Black elected to House of Commons.

Serpentine Die Cut 13½x13¼

2018, Feb. 1 Self-Adhesive Litho.

Booklet Stamps

3085 A1267 P multi 1.30 .45
a. Booklet pane of 10 13.00
3086 A1267 P multi 1.30 .45
a. Booklet pane of 10 13.00

On day of issue, Nos. 3085 and 3086 each sold for 85c.

Lotus Flowers
A1268 A1269

Designs: Nos. 3087a, 3088, 3090, Nelumbo nucifera (pink petals). Nos. 3087b, 3089, 3091, Nelumbo lutea (yellow petals).

2018, Mar. 1 Litho. *Perf. 13*

Souvenir Sheet

3087 Sheet of 2 2.60 2.60
a.-b. A1268 P Either single 1.30 1.10

Self-Adhesive
Coil Stamps

Serpentine Die Cut 8 Vert.

3088 A1269 P multi 1.30 .55
3089 A1269 P multi 1.30 .55
a. Horiz. pair, #3088-3089 2.60

Booklet Stamps

Serpentine Die Cut 13½

3090 A1268 P multi 1.30 .45
3091 A1268 P multi 1.30 .45
a. Booklet pane of 10, 5 each #3090-3091 + 10 stickers 13.00

On day of issue, Nos. 3087a-3087b, 3088-3091 each sold for 85c.

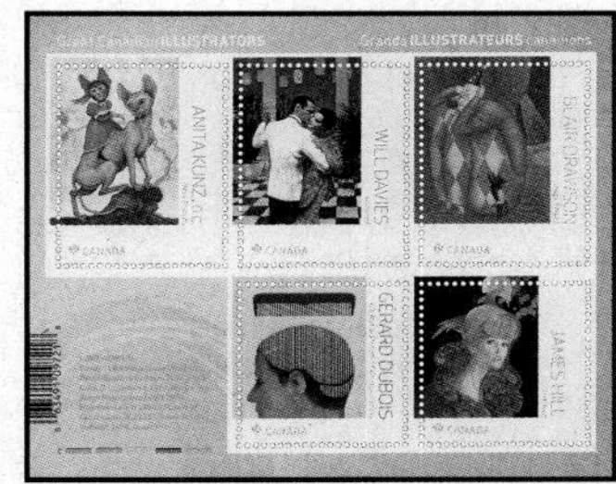
Illustrations — A1270

Designs: Nos. 3092a, 3093, *Best Friends,* by Anita Kunz (32x40mm). Nos. 3092b, 3096, *Untitled,* by Will Davies (1924-2016) (32x40mm). Nos. 3092c, 3094, *Stage Fright,* by Blair Drawson (32x40mm). Nos. 3092d, 3097, *It's Not a Stream of Consciousness,* by Gérard DuBois (32x32mm). Nos. 3092e, 3095, *Untitled,* by James Hill (1930-2004) (32x32mm).

2018, Apr. 5 Litho. *Perf. 12½*

3092 A1270 Sheet of 5 + label 6.50 6.50
a.-e. P Any single 1.30 1.10

Booklet Stamps
Self-Adhesive

Serpentine Die Cut 13½x13¼

3093 A1270 P multi 1.30 .55
3094 A1270 P multi 1.30 .55
3095 A1270 P multi 1.30 .55
3096 A1270 P multi 1.30 .55
3097 A1270 P multi 1.30 .55
a. Booklet pane of 10, 2 each #3093-3097 13.00
Nos. 3093-3097 (5) 6.50 2.75

On day of issue, Nos. 3092a-3092e, 3093-3097 each sold for 85c.

Queen Elizabeth II, 65th Anniv. of Coronation A1271

Serpentine Die Cut 13¼

2018, Apr. 20 Litho.

Booklet Stamp
Self-Adhesive

3098 A1271 P gold & multi 1.30 .45
a. Booklet pane of 10 13.00

No. 3098 sold for 85c on day of issue.

Bees — A1272

Designs: No. 3099, Bombus affinis. No. 3100, Agapostemon virescens.

Serpentine Die Cut 13

2018, May 1 Litho.

Booklet Stamp
Self-Adhesive

3099 A1272 P multi 1.30 .45
3100 A1272 P multi 1.30 .45
a. Booklet pane of 10, 5 each #3099-3100 13.00

Nos. 3099-3100 each sold for 85c on day of issue.

100th Presentation of the Memorial Cup — A1273

Serpentine Die Cut 13¼x13¾

2018, May 18 Litho.

Booklet Stamp
Self-Adhesive

3101 A1273 P sil & multi 1.30 .45
a. Booklet pane of 10 13.00

No. 3101 sold for 85c on day of issue.

Astronomy — A1274

Designs: Nos. 3102a, 3103, Milky Way. No. 3102b, 3104, Northern lights.

2018, June 29 Litho. *Perf. 13¼*

3102 A1274 Sheet of 2 2.60 2.60
a.-b. P Either single 1.30 1.10

Booklet Stamps
Self-Adhesive

Serpentine Die Cut 14x14½

3103 A1274 P multi 1.30 .45
3104 A1274 P multi 1.30 .45
a. Booklet pane of 10, 5 each #3103-3104 13.00

On day of issue, Nos. 3102a-3102b, 3103-3104 each sold for 85c.

Sharks — A1275

Designs: Nos. 3105a, 3110, Isurus oxyrinchus. Nos. 3105b, 3107, Cetorhinus maximus. Nos. 3105c, 3106, Carcharodon carcharias. Nos. 3105d, 3108, Somniosus microcephalus. Nos. 3105e, 3109, Prionace glauca.

2018, July 13 Litho. *Perf. 12½*

3105 A1275 Sheet of 5 6.50 6.50
a.-e. P Any single 1.30 1.10

Booklet Stamps
Self-Adhesive

Serpentine Die Cut 13½

3106 A1275 P multi 1.30 .55
3107 A1275 P multi 1.30 .55
3108 A1275 P multi 1.30 .55
3109 A1275 P multi 1.30 .55
3110 A1275 P multi 1.30 .55
a. Booklet pane of 10, 2 each #3106-3110 13.00
Nos. 3106-3110 (5) 6.50 2.75

On day of issue, Nos. 3105a-3105e, 3106-3110 each sold for 85c.

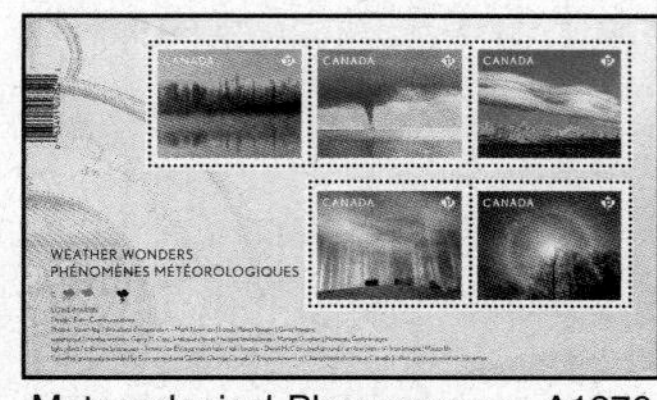

Meteorological Phenomena — A1276

Designs: Nos. 3111a, 3112, Steam fog. Nos. 3111b, 3113, Waterspout. Nos. 3111c, 3114, Lenticular clouds. Nos. 3111d, 3115, Light pillars. Nos. 3111e, 3116, Moon halo.

2018, July 26 Litho. *Perf. 12½*

3111 A1276 Sheet of 5 6.50 6.50
a.-e. P Any single 1.30 1.10

Booklet Stamps
Self-Adhesive

Serpentine Die Cut 13¼x13½

3112 A1276 P multi 1.30 .55
3113 A1276 P multi 1.30 .55
3114 A1276 P multi 1.30 .55
3115 A1276 P multi 1.30 .55
3116 A1276 P multi 1.30 .55
a. Booklet pane of 10, 2 each #3112-3116 13.00
Nos. 3112-3116 (5) 6.50 2.75

On day of issue, Nos. 3111a-3111e, 3112-3116 each sold for 85c.

Birds — A1277

Designs: Nos. 3117a, 3118, Poecile atricapillus. Nos. 3117b, 3121, Bubo scandiacus. Nos. 3117c, 3122, Cyanocitta stelleri. Nos. 3117d, 3120, Branta canadensis. Nos. 3117e, 3119, Grus americana.

2018, Aug. 20 Litho. *Perf. 13x13¼*

3117 A1277 Sheet of 5 + label 7.00 7.00
a.-e. P Any single 1.40 .70
f. As No. 3117, with 2018 International Ornithological Congress emblem added in sheet margin 7.00 7.00

Booklet Stamps
Self-Adhesive

Serpentine Die Cut 13

3118 A1277 P multi 1.40 .70
3119 A1277 P multi 1.40 .70
3120 A1277 P multi 1.40 .70
3121 A1277 P multi 1.40 .70
3122 A1277 P multi 1.40 .70
a. Booklet pane of 10, 2 each #3118-3122 14.00
Nos. 3118-3122 (5) 7.00 3.50

On day of issue, Nos. 3117a-3117e, 3118-3122 each sold for 85c.

Emergency Responders — A1278

Designs: Nos. 3123a, 3124, Members of Canadian Armed Forces and raft. Nos. 3123b, 3126, Paramedics, ambulance and helicopter. Nos. 3123c, 3125, Firefighters and fire. Nos. 3123d, 3127, Police officers, police car and city skyline. Nos. 3123e, 3128, Search and rescue crew members and helicopter in mountains.

2018, Sept. 14 Litho. ***Perf. 13¼x13***

3123 A1278 Sheet of 5 + label 7.00 7.00
a.-e. P Any single 1.40 .70

Booklet Stamps
Self-Adhesive
Serpentine Die Cut 13¾x13½

3124 A1278 P multi 1.40 .70
3125 A1278 P multi 1.40 .70
3126 A1278 P multi 1.40 .70
3127 A1278 P multi 1.40 .70
3128 A1278 P multi 1.40 .70
a. Booklet pane of 10, 2 each #3124-3128 14.00
Nos. 3124-3128 (5) 7.00 3.50

On day of issue, Nos. 3123a-3123e, 3124-3128 each sold for 85c.

Rocky Mountain Bighorn Sheep — A1279

Litho. & Engr.
2018, Oct. 10 ***Perf. 12½x13***

3129 A1279 $4 multi 6.25 3.25

No. 3129 was printed in sheets of 4.

World War I Armistice, Cent. A1280

2018, Oct. 24 Litho. ***Perf. 13¼x13***

3130 A1280 P multi 1.40 .70

Booklet Stamp
Self-Adhesive
Serpentine Die Cut 13¾x14

3131 A1280 P multi 1.40 .70
a. Booklet pane of 10 14.00

On day of issue, Nos. 3130 and 3131 each sold for 85c. No. 3130 was printed in sheets of 5.

Socks A1281

Cap A1282

Mittens A1283

Nativity Scene A1284

2018, Nov. 2 Litho. ***Perf. 13½x13¼***

3132 Sheet of 3 7.50 7.50
a. A1281 P multi 1.40 .70
b. A1282 $1.20 multi 1.90 .95
c. A1283 $2.50 multi 4.00 2.00

Booklet Stamps
Self-Adhesive
Serpentine Die Cut 13¼x13

3133 A1284 P multi 1.40 .70
a. Booklet pane of 12 14.00
3134 A1281 P multi 1.40 .70
a. Booklet pane of 12 14.00
3135 A1282 $1.20 multi 1.90 .95
a. Booklet pane of 6 11.50
3136 A1283 $2.50 multi 4.00 2.00
a. Booklet pane of 6 24.00
Nos. 3133-3136 (4) 8.70 4.35

Christmas. On day of issue, Nos. 3132a, 3133, and 3134 each sold for 85c.

Queen Elizabeth II — A1285

Serpentine Die Cut 13¾x13½
2019, Jan. 14 Litho.
Booklet Stamp
Self-Adhesive

3137 A1285 P multi 1.40 .70
a. Booklet pane of 10 14.00

No. 3137 sold for 90c on day of issue.

Tombstone Territorial Park, Yukon A1286

Athabasca Falls, Jasper National Park, Alberta A1287

Quttinirpaaq National Park, Nunavut A1288

Mahone Bay, Nova Scotia A1289

Little Limestone Lake Provincial Park, Manitoba A1290

Castle Butte, Big Muddy Badlands, Saskatchewan A1291

Algonquin Provincial Park, Ontario A1292

Mingan Archipelago National Park Reserve, Quebec A1293

Iceberg Alley Near Ferryland, Newfoundland and Labrador — A1294

2019, Jan. 14 Litho. ***Perf. 13¼x13***

3138 Sheet of 9 17.50 17.50
a. A1286 P multi 1.40 .70
b. A1287 P multi 1.40 .70
c. A1288 P multi 1.40 .70
d. A1289 P multi 1.40 .70
e. A1290 P multi 1.40 .70
f. A1291 $1.05 multi 1.60 .80
g. A1292 $1.27 multi 1.90 .95
h. A1293 $1.90 multi 3.00 1.50
i. A1294 $2.65 multi 4.00 2.00

Coil Stamps
Self-Adhesive
Serpentine Die Cut 9 Horiz.

3139 A1286 P multi 1.40 .70
3140 A1287 P multi 1.40 .70
3141 A1288 P multi 1.40 .70
3142 A1289 P multi 1.40 .70
3143 A1290 P multi 1.40 .70
a. Horiz. strip of 5, #3139-3143 7.00

Serpentine Die Cut 8 Horiz.

3144 A1286 P multi 1.40 .70
3145 A1287 P multi 1.40 .70
3146 A1288 P multi 1.40 .70
3147 A1289 P multi 1.40 .70
3148 A1290 P multi 1.40 .70
a. Vert. strip of 5, #3144-3148 7.00

Serpentine Die Cut 13¼

3149 A1291 $1.05 multi 1.60 .80

Serpentine Die Cut 8¼ Horiz.

3150 A1292 $1.27 multi 1.90 .95
3151 A1293 $1.90 multi 3.00 1.50
3152 A1294 $2.65 multi 4.00 2.00
Nos. 3139-3152 (14) 24.50 12.25

Booklet Stamps
Serpentine Die Cut 13¾x13½

3153 A1286 P multi 1.40 .70
3154 A1288 P multi 1.40 .70
3155 A1290 P multi 1.40 .70
3156 A1287 P multi 1.40 .70
3157 A1289 P multi 1.40 .70
a. Booklet pane of 10, 2 each #3153-3157 14.00

Serpentine Die Cut 9¼ Horiz.

3158 A1292 $1.27 multi 1.90 .95
a. Booklet pane of 6 11.50
3159 A1293 $1.90 multi 3.00 1.50
a. Booklet pane of 6 18.00
3160 A1294 $2.65 multi 4.00 2.00
a. Booklet pane of 6 24.00
Nos. 3153-3160 (8) 15.90 7.95

On day of issue, Nos. 3138a-3138e, 3139-3148, and 3153-3157 each sold for 90c.

New Year 2019 (Year of the Pig) — A1295

Rake and pig in: P, Armor. $2.65, Robe.

Litho. & Embossed With Foil Application
2019, Jan. 18 ***Perf. 13¼***

3161 A1295 P multi 1.40 .70

Souvenir Sheet

3162 A1295 $2.65 multi 4.00 4.00
a. Souvenir sheet of 2, #3053b, 3162 8.00 8.00
b. Perf. 13 (3230a) 4.00 4.00

Booklet Stamps
Self-Adhesive
Litho.
Serpentine Die Cut 13½

3163 A1295 P multi 1.40 .70
a. Booklet pane of 10 14.00

Litho. With Foil Application

3164 A1295 $2.65 multi 4.00 2.00
a. Booklet pane of 6 24.00

On day of issue, Nos. 3161 and 3163 each sold for 90c. Issued: No. 3162b, 1/17/20.
See Nos. 3259l, 3260lk, 3272.

Albert Jackson (c. 1856-1918), First Black Letter Carrier in Canada — A1296

Serpentine Die Cut 13½x13
2019, Jan. 25 Litho.
Booklet Stamp
Self-Adhesive

3165 A1296 P multi 1.40 .70
a. Booklet pane of 10 14.00

No. 3165 sold for 90c on day of issue.

Gardenia Jasminoides
A1297 A1298

Gardenia with background color of: Nos. 3166a, 3167, 3169, Orange brown. Nos. 3166b, 3168, 3170, Blue green.

2019, Feb. 14 Litho. ***Perf. 13***
Souvenir Sheet

3166 Sheet of 2 2.80 2.80
a.-b. A1297 P Either single 1.40 .70

Self-Adhesive
Coil Stamps
Serpentine Die Cut 8 Vert.

3167 A1298 P multi 1.40 .70
3168 A1298 P multi 1.40 .70
a. Horiz. pair, #3167-3168 2.80

Booklet Stamps
Serpentine Die Cut 13½

3169 A1297 P multi 1.40 .70
3170 A1297 P multi 1.40 .70
a. Booklet pane of 10, 5 each #3169-3170 + 10 stickers 14.00

On day of issue, Nos. 3166a-3166b, 3167-3170 each sold for 90c.

Aviation Pioneers and Airplanes — A1299

Designs: Nos. 3171a, 3172, Elizabeth "Elsie" MacGill (1905-80), first female aeronautical engineer. Nos. 3171b, 3176, Ultraflight Lazair ultralight aircraft. Nos. 3171c, 3175, Avro CF-105 Arrow. Nos. 3171d, 3174, C. H. "Punch" Dickins (1899-1995), bush pilot. Nos. 3171e, 3173, William George Barker (1894-1930), World War I flying ace.

2019, Mar. 27 Litho. ***Perf. 12½***

3171 A1299 Sheet of 5 + label 7.00 7.00
a.-e. P Any single 1.40 .70

Booklet Stamps
Self-Adhesive
Serpentine Die Cut 13¼x13½

3172 A1299 P multi 1.40 .70
3173 A1299 P multi 1.40 .70
3174 A1299 P multi 1.40 .70
3175 A1299 P multi 1.40 .70
3176 A1299 P multi 1.40 .70
a. Booklet pane of 10, 2 each #3172-3176 14.00

On day of issue, Nos. 3171a-3171e, 3172-3176 each sold for 90c.

Sweet Foods — A1300

No. 3177: a, Sugar pie (35x32mm). b, Butter tart (33mm diameter). c, Saskatoon berry pie (43x30mm). d, Nanaimo bar (36x33mm). e, Blueberry grunt (46x26mm).

Serpentine Die Cut 13½

2019, Apr. 17 Litho.

Self-Adhesive

3177 A1300 Sheet of 5 7.00
a.-e. P Any single 1.40 .70
f. Booklet pane of 10, 2 each #3177a-3177e 14.00

Nos. 3177a-3177e each sold for 90c on day of issue.

1940 Vancouver Asahi Baseball Team — A1301

2019, Apr. 25 Litho. *Die Cut*

Booklet Stamp
Self-Adhesive

3178 A1301 P multi 1.40 .70
a. Booklet pane of 10 14.00

No. 3178 sold for 90c on day of issue.

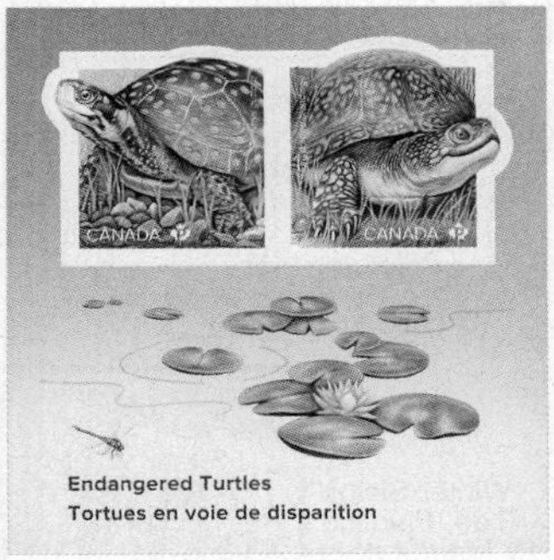

Endangered Turtles — A1302

No. 3179: a, Clemmys guttata (36x33mm). b, Emydoidea blandingii (36x35mm).

Serpentine Die Cut 13½

2019, May 23 Litho.

Self-Adhesive

3179 A1302 Sheet of 2 2.80
a.-b. P Either single 1.40 .70
c. Booklet pane of 10, 5 each #3179a-3179b 14.00

Nos. 3179a-3179b each sold for 90c on day of issue.

Covered Bridges — A1303

Designs: Nos. 3180a, 3181, Hartland Covered Bridge, New Brunswick. Nos. 3180b, 3182, Powerscourt Covered Bridge, Quebec. Nos. 3180c, 3183, Félix-Gabriel-Marchand Covered Bridge, Quebec. Nos. 3180d, 3184, West Montrose Covered Bridge, Ontario. Nos. 3180e, 3185, Ashnola No. 1 Covered Bridge, British Columbia.

2019, June 17 Litho. *Perf. 12¾*

3180 A1303 Sheet of 5 7.00 7.00
a.-e. P Any single 1.40 .70

Booklet Stamps
Self-Adhesive

Serpentine Die Cut 12¾

3181 A1303 P multi 1.40 .70
3182 A1303 P multi 1.40 .70
3183 A1303 P multi 1.40 .70
3184 A1303 P multi 1.40 .70
3185 A1303 P multi 1.40 .70
a. Booklet pane of 10, 2 each #3181-3185 14.00
Nos. 3181-3185 (5) 7.00 3.50

Nos. 3180a-3180e, 3181-3185 each sold for 90c on day of issue.

Flight of Apollo 11, 50th Anniv. — A1304

Designs: Nos. 3186, 3188, Command and Service Modules, Earth. Nos. 3187, 3189, Lunar Module and Moon.

2019, June 27 Litho. *Perf. 13¼*

3186 A1304 P multi 1.40 .70
3187 A1304 P multi 1.40 .70
a. Vert. pair, #3186-3187 2.80 1.40

Booklet Stamps
Self-Adhesive

Serpentine Die Cut 13½

3188 A1304 P multi 1.40 .70
3189 A1304 P multi 1.40 .70
a. Booklet pane of 10, 5 each #3188-3189 14.00

Nos. 3186-3189 each sold for 90c on day of issue. Nos. 3186-3187 were printed in sheets containing three pairs.

Bears — A1305

Designs: Nos. 3190a, 3194, Ursus arctos (grizzly bear). Nos. 3190b, 3192, Ursus maritimus (polar bear). Nos. 3190c, 3191, Ursus americanus with black fur (American black bear). Nos. 3190d, 3193, Ursus americanus with white fur (Kermode bear).

2019, July 24 Litho. *Perf. 13¼*

3190 A1305 Sheet of 4 5.60 5.60
a.-d. P Any single 1.40 .70

Booklet Stamps
Self-Adhesive

Serpentine Die Cut 13½

3191 A1305 P multi 1.40 .70
3192 A1305 P multi 1.40 .70
3193 A1305 P multi 1.40 .70
3194 A1305 P multi 1.40 .70
a. Booklet pane of 8, 2 each #3191-3194 11.50
Nos. 3191-3194 (4) 5.60 2.80

On day of issue, Nos. 3190a-3019d, 3191-3194 each sold for 90c.

Leonard Cohen (1934-2016), Poet and Singer — A1306

Cohen: Nos. 3195a, 3195d, 3196, Squatting. Nos. 3195b, 3195e, 3197, Standing. Nos. 3195c, 3195f, 3198, Sitting and holding eyeglasses.

2019, Sept. 21 Litho. *Perf. 12½*

3195 A1306 Sheet of 6 13.50 13.50
a.-c. P Any single 1.40 .70
d. $1.27 multi 1.90 .95
e. $1.90 multi 3.00 1.50
f. $2.65 multi 4.00 2.00

Booklet Stamps
Self-Adhesive

Serpentine Die Cut 13½x13¼

3196 A1306 P multi 1.40 .70
3197 A1306 P multi 1.40 .70
3198 A1306 P multi 1.40 .70
a. Booklet pane of 9, 3 each #3196-3198 13.00
Nos. 3196-3198 (3) 4.20 2.10

On day of issue, Nos. 3195a-3195c, 3196-3198 each sold for 90c.

Christmas

A1307 A1308

Designs: Nos. 3199a, 3201, Reindeer. Nos. 3199b, 3202, Dancers. Nos. 3199c, 3203, Partridge and pears. No. 3200, Magi on camels.

2019, Nov. 4 Litho. *Perf. 13x12½*

3199 Sheet of 3 7.50 7.50
a. A1307 P multi 1.40 .70
b. A1307 $1.27 multi 2.00 1.00
c. A1307 $2.65 multi 4.00 2.00

Booklet Stamps
Self-Adhesive

Serpentine Die Cut 13¾

3200 A1308 P gold & multi 1.40 .70
a. Booklet pane of 12 17.00

Serpentine Die Cut 13¼x13

3201 A1307 P multi 1.40 .70
a. Booklet pane of 12 17.00
3202 A1307 $1.27 multi 2.00 1.00
a. Booklet pane of 6 12.00
3203 A1307 $2.65 multi 4.00 2.00
a. Booklet pane of 6 24.00
Nos. 3200-3203 (4) 8.80 4.40

On day of issue, Nos. 3199a, 3200 and 3201 each sold for 90c.

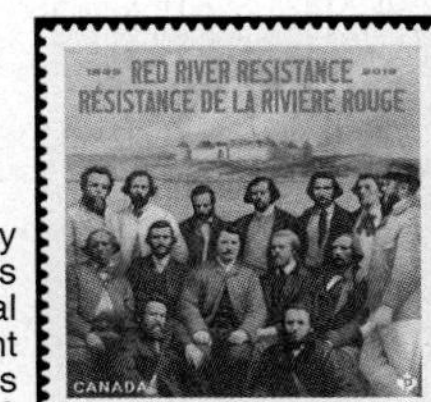

Fort Garry and Métis Provisional Government Members A1309

Serpentine Die Cut 13½

2019, Nov. 6 Litho.

Booklet Stamp
Self-Adhesive

3204 A1309 P multi 1.40 .70
a. Booklet pane of 10 14.00

Red River Resistance, 150th anniv. No. 3204 sold for 90c on day of issue.

Hanukkah A1310

Serpentine Die Cut 13¼x13½

2019, Nov. 14 Litho.

Booklet Stamp
Self-Adhesive

3205 A1310 P multi 1.40 .70
a. Booklet pane of 10 14.00

No. 3205 sold for 90c on day of issue.

Abraham Lake, Alberta A1311

Athabaska Sand Dunes Provincial Park, Saskatchewan A1312

Herschel Island-Qikiqtaruk Territorial Park, Yukon — A1313

French River, Prince Edward Island A1314

Magdalen Islands, Quebec A1315

Carcajou Falls, Northwest Territories A1316

Kootenay National Park, British Columbia A1317

Swallowtail Lighthouse, Grand Manan Island, New Brunswick A1318

Cabot Trail, Cape Breton Island, Nova Scotia A1319

2020, Jan. 13 Litho. *Perf. 13¼x13*

3206 Sheet of 9 18.00 18.00
a. A1311 P multi 1.40 .70
b. A1312 P multi 1.40 .70
c. A1313 P multi 1.40 .70
d. A1314 P multi 1.40 .70
e. A1315 P multi 1.40 .70
f. A1316 $1.07 multi 1.60 .80
g. A1317 $1.30 multi 2.00 1.00
h. A1318 $1.94 multi 3.00 1.50
i. A1319 $2.71 multi 4.25 1.10

Coil Stamps
Self-Adhesive

Serpentine Die Cut 9¼ Horiz.

3207 A1311 P multi 1.40 .70
3208 A1312 P multi 1.40 .70
3209 A1313 P multi 1.40 .70
3210 A1314 P multi 1.40 .70
3211 A1315 P multi 1.40 .70
a. Horiz. strip of 5, #3207-3211 7.00

Serpentine Die Cut 8½ Horiz.

3212 A1311 P multi 1.40 .70
3213 A1312 P multi 1.40 .70
3214 A1313 P multi 1.40 .70
3215 A1314 P multi 1.40 .70

3216 A1315 P multi 1.40 .70
a. Vert. strip of 5, #3212-3216 7.00

Serpentine Die Cut 8¼ Horiz.

3217 A1317 $1.30 multi 2.00 1.00
3218 A1318 $1.94 multi 3.00 1.50
3219 A1319 $2.71 multi 4.25 2.10

Die Cut Perf. 13¼

3220 A1316 $1.07 multi 1.60 .80
Nos. 3207-3220 (14) 24.85 12.40

Booklet Stamps

Serpentine Die Cut 13¾x13½

3221 A1311 P multi 1.40 .70
3222 A1313 P multi 1.40 .70
3223 A1315 P multi 1.40 .70
3224 A1312 P multi 1.40 .70
3225 A1314 P multi 1.40 .70
a. Booklet pane of 10, 2 each #3221-3225 14.00

Serpentine Die Cut 9¼ Horiz.

3226 A1317 $1.30 multi 2.00 1.00
a. Booklet pane of 6 12.00
3227 A1318 $1.94 multi 3.00 1.50
a. Booklet pane of 6 18.00
3228 A1319 $2.71 multi 4.25 2.10
a. Booklet pane of 6 25.50
Nos. 3221-3228 (8) 16.25 8.10

On day of issue, Nos. 3206a-3206e, 3207-3216, and 3221-3225 each sold for 92c.

New Year 2020 (Year of the Rat) — A1320

Designs: P, Rats carrying rat in palinquin. $2.71, Two rats wearing Chinese robes.

Litho. & Embossed With Foil Application

2020, Jan. 17 ***Perf. 13***

3229 A1320 P gold & multi 1.40 .70

Souvenir Sheet

3230 A1320 $2.71 gold & multi 4.25 4.25
a. Souvenir sheet of 2, #3162b, 3230 8.25 8.25

Booklet Stamps
Self-Adhesive
Litho.

Serpentine Die Cut 13½

3231 A1320 P multi 1.40 .70
a. Booklet pane of 10 14.00

Litho. With Foil Application

3232 A1320 $2.71 gold & multi 4.25 4.25
a. Booklet pane of 6 25.50

On day of issue, Nos. 3229 and 3231 each sold for 92c. See Nos. 3259a, 3260a, 3261.

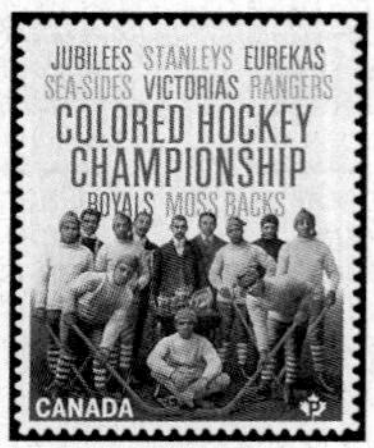

African-Canadian Ice Hockey Players From the Halifax Eurekas 1904 Champions of the Colored Hockey League — A1321

Serpentine Die Cut 13½x13¼

2020, Jan. 24 **Litho.**

Booklet Stamp
Self-Adhesive

3233 A1321 P multi 1.40 .70
a. Booklet pane of 10 14.00

No. 3233 sold for 92c on day of issue.

Dahlias
A1322 A1323

Designs: Nos. 3234a, 3235, 3237, Dahlia without background. Nos. 3234b, 3236, 3238, Dahlias, turquoise green background.

2020, Mar. 2 Litho. ***Perf. 12¼x12½***

Souvenir Sheet

3234 Sheet of 2 2.80 2.80
a.-b. A1322 P Either single 1.40 .70

Self-Adhesive
Coil Stamps

Serpentine Die Cut 8 Vert.

3235 A1323 P multi 1.40 .70
3236 A1323 P multi 1.40 .70
a. Horiz. pair, #3235-3236 2.80

Booklet Stamps

Serpentine Die Cut 13½

3237 A1322 P multi 1.40 .70
3238 A1322 P multi 1.40 .70
a. Booklet pane of 10, 5 each #3237-3238 + 10 stickers 14.00

On day of issue, Nos. 3234a-3234b, 3235-3238 each sold for 92c.

Eid Ul-Fitr — A1324

Serpentine Die Cut 13¼x13½

2020, Apr. 24 **Litho.**

Booklet Stamp
Self-Adhesive

3239 A1324 P multi 1.40 .70
a. Booklet pane of 10 14.00

No. 3239 sold for 92c on day of issue.

Léo Major (1921-2008), Recipient of Distinguished Conduct Medal in World War II and Korean War — A1325

Veronica Foster (1922-2000), Worker on Machine Gun Assembly Line in World War II Popularized on Propaganda Posters — A1326

Serpentine Die Cut 13¼x13½

2020, Apr. 29 **Litho.**

Booklet Stamps
Self-Adhesive

3240 A1325 P gold & multi 1.40 .70
3241 A1326 P gold & multi 1.40 .70
a. Booklet pane of 10, 5 each #3240-3241 14.00

V-E (Victory in Europe) Day, 75th anniv. Nos. 3240-3241 each sold for 92c on day of issue.

Paintings by Group of Seven Artists — A1327

Designs: Nos. 3242a, 3243a, In the Nickel Belt, by Franklin Carmichael (1890-1945). Nos. 3242b, 3243b, Miners' Houses, Glace Bay, by Lawren S. Harris (1887-1970). Nos. 3242c, 3243c, Labrador Coast, by A. Y. Jackson (1882-1974). Nos. 3242d, 3243d, Fire-swept Algoma, by Frank H. Johnston (1888-1949). Nos. 3242e, 3243e, Quebec Village, by Arthur Lismer (1885-1969). Nos. 3242f, 3243f, Church by the Sea, by J. E. H. Macdonald (1873-1932). Nos. 3242g, 3243g, Stormy Weather, Georgian Bay, by Frederick H. Varley (1881-1969).

2020, May 7 Litho. ***Perf. 13x13¼***

3242 A1327 Sheet of 7 10.00 10.00
a.-g. P Any single 1.40 .70

Booklet Stamps
Self-Adhesive

Serpentine Die Cut13¼x13½

3243 A1327 Booklet pane of 7 10.00 10.00
a.-g. P Any single 1.40 .70

Nos. 3242a-3242g, 3243a-3243g each sold for 92c on day of issue.

Microphone of Radio Station XWA and Headphones A1328

Radio Receiver, Speaker and Vacuum Tubes A1329

Serpentine Die Cut 13¼x13½

2020, May 20 **Litho.**

Booklet Stamps
Self-Adhesive

3244 A1328 P multi 1.40 .70
3245 A1329 P multi 1.40 .70
a. Booklet pane of 10, 5 each #3244-3245 14.00

First radio broadcast in Canada, cent. Nos. 3244-3245 each sold for 92c on day of issue.

Medical Researchers A1330

Designs: No. 3246, Dr. James Till and Dr. Ernest McCulloch (1926-2011), stem cell researchers. No. 3247, Dr. M. Vera Peters (1911-93), oncologist. No. 3248, Dr. Julio Montaner, HIV and AIDS researcher. No. 3249, Dr. Balfour Mount, palliative care physician. No. 3250, Dr. Bruce Chown (1893-1986), Rhesus disease researcher.

Serpentine Die Cut 13½

2020, Sept. 10 **Litho.**

Booklet Stamps
Self-Adhesive

3246 A1330 P multi 1.40 .70
3247 A1330 P multi 1.40 .70
3248 A1330 P multi 1.40 .70
3249 A1330 P multi 1.40 .70
3250 A1330 P multi 1.40 .70
a. Booklet pane of 10, 2 each #3246-3250 14.00
Nos. 3246-3250 (5) 7.00 3.50

On day of issue, Nos. 3246-3250 each sold for 92c.

Diwali — A1331

Serpentine Die Cut 15¼x15

2020, Oct. 15 **Litho.**

Booklet Stamp
Self-Adhesive

3251 A1331 P multi 1.40 .70
a. Booklet pane of 10 14.00

No. 3251 sold for 92c on day of issue. No. 3251 was sent to some standing order customers at least ten days in advance of official first day of issue.

Trenches on the Somme, Painting by Mary Riter Hamilton (1867-1954) A1332

Serpentine Die Cut 13

2020, Oct. 28 **Litho.**

Booklet Stamp
Self-Adhesive

3252 A1332 P multi 1.40 .70
a. Booklet pane of 10 14.00

No. 3252 sold for 92c on day of issue.

Winter Sleigh Ride, Painting by Maud Lewis (1901-70) A1333

Team of Oxen in Winter, Painting by Lewis — A1334

Family and Sled, Painting by Lewis — A1335

Holy Family, Ox and Donkey A1336

2020, Nov. 2 Litho. ***Perf. 13½x13¼***

3253 Souvenir sheet of 3 7.75 7.75
a. A1333 P multi 1.40 .70
b. A1334 $1.30 multi 2.00 1.00
c. A1335 $2.71 multi 4.25 2.10

Booklet Stamps
Self-Adhesive

Serpentine Die Cut 13½

3254 A1336 P multi 1.40 .70
a. Booklet pane of 12 17.00

Serpentine Die Cut 13¾x13½

3255 A1333 P multi 1.40 .70
a. Booklet pane of 12 17.00
3256 A1334 $1.30 multi 2.00 1.00
a. Booklet pane of 6 12.00
3257 A1335 $2.71 multi 4.25 2.10
a. Booklet pane of 6 25.50
Nos. 3254-3257 (4) 9.05 4.50

Christmas. On day of issue, Nos. 3253a, 3254 and 3255 each sold for 92c.

Menorah — A1337

Serpentine Die Cut 15½x15¼

2020, Nov. 5 Litho.

Booklet Stamp
Self-Adhesive

3258 A1337 P multi 1.40 .70
a. Booklet pane of 10 14.00

Hanukkah. No. 3258 sold for 92c on day of issue.

SEMI-POSTAL STAMPS

Catalogue values for unused stamps in this section are for Never Hinged items.

Olympic Type of 1973
Size: 20x36mm

1974, Apr. 17 Litho. *Perf. 12½*

B1 A307 8c + 2c multi .35 .35
B2 A307 10c + 5c multi .55 .55
B3 A307 15c + 5c multi .75 .75
Nos. B1-B3 (3) 1.65 1.65

SP1

1975, Feb. 5 *Perf. 13*

B4 SP1 8c + 2c Swimming .35 .35
B5 SP1 10c + 5c Rowing .60 .60
B6 SP1 15c + 5c Sailing .75 .75
Nos. B4-B6 (3) 1.70 1.70

SP2

1975, Aug. 6

B7 SP2 8c + 2c Fencing .35 .35
B8 SP2 10c + 5c Boxing .60 .60
B9 SP2 15c + 5c Judo .75 .75
Nos. B7-B9 (3) 1.70 1.70

1976, Jan. 7

B10 SP2 8c + 2c Basketball .35 .35
B11 SP2 10c + 5c Vaulting .60 .60
B12 SP2 20c + 5c Soccer .90 .90
Nos. B10-B12 (3) 1.85 1.85

21st Olympic Games, Montreal, July 17-Aug. 1. The surtax was for the Canadian Olympic Committee.

Literacy — SP3

1996, Sept. 9 Litho. *Perf. 13x12½*

B13 SP3 45c +5c multi 1.00 .60
a. Booklet pane of 10 10.00
Complete booklet 11.50

No. B13 has die cut opening in center to represent missing puzzle piece.

Surcharge donated to ABC CANADA literacy organization.

Mental Health — SP4

Self-Adhesive
Booklet Stamp

Serpentine Die Cut 13¼

2008, Oct. 6 Litho.

B14 SP4 P +10c multi 1.40 .75
a. Booklet pane of 10 14.00

No. B14 had a franking value of 52c on day of issue. Surtax for Canada Post Foundation for Mental Health.

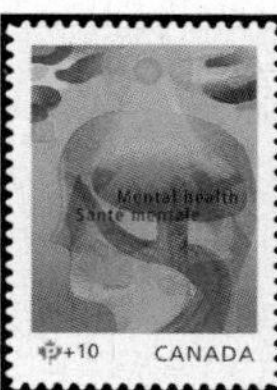

Mental Health — SP5

Self-Adhesive
Booklet Stamp

Serpentine Die Cut 13¼

2009, Sept. 14 Litho.

B15 SP5 P +10c multi 1.40 .75
a. Booklet pane of 10 14.00

No. B15 had a franking value of 54c on day of issue. Surtax for Canada Post Foundation for Mental Health.

Mental Health — SP6

Self-Adhesive
Booklet Stamp

Serpentine Die Cut 13¼

2010, Sept. 7 **Litho.**

B16 SP6 P + 10c multi 1.10 .75
a. Booklet pane of 10 11.00

No. B16 had a franking value of 57c on day of issue. Surtax for Canada Post Foundation for Mental Health.

Mental Health — SP7

2011, Sept. 6 Litho. ***Perf. 12¾x13¼***

B17 Souvenir sheet of 2 #B17a 3.00 3.00
a. SP7 P+10c multi 1.50 1.25

Booklet Stamp
Self-Adhesive

Serpentine Die Cut 13¼

B18 SP7 P+10c multi 1.35 .45
a. Booklet pane of 10 13.50

Nos. B17a and B18 each had a franking value of 59c on day of issue. Surtax was for Canada Post Foundation for Mental Health.

Hands and Heart — SP8

Self-Adhesive

Serpentine Die Cut13x13¼

2012, Sept. 17 **Litho.**

Booklet Stamp

B19 SP8 P +10c multi 1.35 .75
a. Booklet pane of 10 13.50

No. B19 had a franking value of 61c on day of issue. Surtax for Canada Post Community Foundation.

Floating Abroad, Children's Art by Ezra Peters — SP9

Serpentine Die Cut 13x12½

2013, Sept. 30 **Booklet Stamp**

Self-Adhesive

B20 SP9 63c+10c multi 1.10 .75
a. Booklet pane of 10 11.00

Surtax for Canada Post Community Foundation.

Children in Paper Sailboat SP10

Serpentine Die Cut 13½

2014, Sept. 29 **Litho.**

Booklet Stamp
Self-Adhesive

B21 SP10 P+10c multi 1.35 .75
a. Booklet pane of 10 13.50

No. B21 had a franking value of 85c. Surtax for Canada Post Community Foundation.

Children Reading Story Under Tented Bedsheet — SP11

Serpentine Die Cut 13x12½

2015, Sept. 28 **Litho.**

Booklet Stamp
Self-Adhesive

B22 SP11 P+10c multi 1.35 .75
a. Booklet pane of 10 13.50

No. B22 had a franking value of 85c on day of issue. Surtax for Canada Post Community Foundation.

Stylized Bird — SP12

Serpentine Die Cut 13½

2016, Sept. 26 **Litho.**

Booklet Stamps
Self-Adhesive

B23 SP12 P+10c blue & multi 1.35 .75
B24 SP12 P+10c apple grn & multi 1.35 .75
a. Booklet pane of 10, 5 each #B23-B24 13.50

Nos. B23-B24 each had a franking value of 85c on day of issue. Surtax for Canada Post Community Foundation.

Stylized Cats — SP13

Serpentine Die Cut 13½

2017, Sept. 25 **Litho.**

Booklet Stamps
Self-Adhesive

B25 SP13 P+10c red violet & multi 1.35 .75
B26 SP13 P+10c brt grn & multi 1.35 .75
a. Booklet pane of 10, 5 each #B25-B26 13.50

Nos. B25-B26 each had a franking value of 85c on day of issue. Surtax for Canada Post Community Foundation.

Child on Hill Looking at Clouds Shaped Like Animals — SP14

Serpentine Die Cut 13¾x13½

2018, Sept. 24 **Litho.**

Booklet Stamp
Self-Adhesive

B27 SP14 P+10c multi 1.50 1.50
a. Booklet pane of 10 15.00

No. B27 had a franking value of 85c on day of issue. Surtax for Canada Post Community Foundation.

Walking Ice Cream Cones and Ice Pops — SP15

Designs: No. B28, Cone with red ice cream, green pop. No. B29, Cone with blue ice cream, purple pop.

Serpentine Die Cut 13½

2019, Sept. 23 **Litho.**

Booklet Stamps
Self-Adhesive

B28 SP15 P+10c multi 1.50 1.50
B29 SP15 P+10c multi 1.50 1.50
a. Booklet pane of 10, 5 each #B28-B29 15.00

Nos. B28-B28 both had a franking value of 90c on day of issue. Surtax for Canada Post Community Foundation.

Tree and Wildlife SP16

Serpentine Die Cut 13x13¼

2020, Sept. 21 **Litho.**

Booklet Stamp
Self-Adhesive

B30 SP16 P+10c multi 1.60 1.60
a. Booklet pane of 10 16.00

No. B30 had a franking value of 92c on day of issue. Surtax for Canada Post Community Foundation.

AIR POST STAMPS

Allegory of Flight — AP1

Unwmk.

1928, Sept. 21 **Engr.** ***Perf. 12***

C1 AP1 5c brown olive 14.00 5.50
Never hinged 25.00
a. Imperf., pair 260.00
Never hinged 325.00

No. C1 is known imperforate horizontally and imperforate vertically.
For surcharge see No. C3.

For information on imperforate and part-perforate varieties, see note following No. 47a.

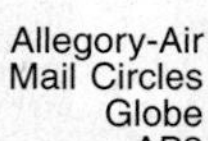

Allegory-Air Mail Circles Globe AP2

1930, Dec. 4 ***Perf. 11***

C2 AP2 5c olive brown 45.00 24.00
Never hinged 75.00

For surcharge see No. C4.

No. C1 Surcharged

1932, Feb. 22 ***Perf. 12***

C3 AP1 6c on 5c brown olive 9.00 4.00
Never hinged 20.00
a. Inverted surcharge 225.00
Never hinged 325.00
b. Double surcharge 650.00
Never hinged 925.00
c. Triple surcharge 400.00
Never hinged 525.00
d. Pair, one without surcharge 950.00
Never hinged 1,350.

Counterfeit surcharges exist.
No. C3b is valued in the grade of fine.

No. C2 Surcharged in Dark Blue

1932, July 12 ***Perf. 11***

C4 AP2 6c on 5c olive brown 32.50 14.00
Never hinged 60.00

Daedalus AP3

1935, June 1 ***Perf. 12***

C5 AP3 6c red brown 4.25 1.25
Never hinged 6.00
a. Horiz. pair, imperf. vert. *10,000.*
b. Imperf., pair 600.00
Never hinged 900.00

No. C5a is unique and is the result of a pre-perforating paper foldover.

Mackenzie River Steamer and Seaplane AP4

1938, June 15

C6 AP4 6c blue 3.75 .40
Never hinged 5.25
a. Imperf., pair 575.00
Never hinged 850.00

Planes and Student Flyers AP5

1942-43

C7 AP5 6c deep blue 5.50 1.30
Never hinged 7.50
a. Imperf., pair 575.00
Never hinged 850.00
C8 AP5 7c deep blue ('43) 1.10 .25
Never hinged 1.60
a. Imperf., pair 575.00
Never hinged 850.00

Canada's contribution to the war effort of the Allied Nations.

Catalogue values for unused stamps in this section, from this point to the end of the section, are for Never Hinged items.

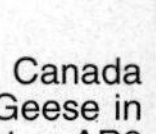

Canada Geese in Flight — AP6

1946, Sept. 16

C9 AP6 7c deep blue 1.25 .25
a. Booklet pane of 4 2.50 2.50

For overprints see Nos. CO1, CO2.
For listing of complete booklet containing No. C9a, see No. 254a.

AIR POST SPECIAL DELIVERY STAMPS

Trans-Canada Airplane and Aerial View of a City — APSD1

1942-43 Unwmk. Engr. *Perf. 12*

CE1 APSD1 16c bright ultra 2.50 2.00
Never hinged 3.50
a. Imperf., pair 575.00
Never hinged 850.00
CE2 APSD1 17c brt ultra ('43) 3.25 3.00
Never hinged 4.75
a. Imperf., pair 575.00
Never hinged 850.00

Canada's contribution to the war effort of the Allied Nations.

Catalogue values for unused stamps in this section, from this point to the end of the section, are for Never Hinged items.

DC-4 Transatlantic Mail Plane Over Quebec — APSD2

1946, Sept. 16

CE3 APSD2 17c bright ultra 7.50 4.75

Circumflex accent on second "E" of "EXPRES."

1946, Dec. 3 Corrected Die

CE4 APSD2 17c bright ultra 7.50 6.00

Grave accent on the 2nd "E" of "EXPRES."

AIR POST OFFICIAL STAMPS

Catalogue values for unused stamps in this section are for Never Hinged items.

No. C9 Overprinted in Black

1949 Unwmk. *Perf. 12*

CO1 AP6 7c deep blue 11.00 4.75
a. No period after "S" 120.00 60.00

Same Overprinted

1950

CO2 AP6 7c deep blue 17.50 13.50

SPECIAL DELIVERY STAMPS

SD1

Unwmk.

1898, June 28 Engr. *Perf. 12*

E1 SD1 10c blue green 150.00 11.00
Never hinged 400.00

SD2

1922, Aug. 21

E2 SD2 20c carmine 100.00 9.00
Never hinged 220.00

Five Stages of Mail Transportation SD3

1927, June 29

E3 SD3 20c orange 35.00 22.50
Never hinged 70.00
a. Imperf., pair 190.00
Never hinged 330.00

No. E3 forms part of the Confederation Commemorative issue. It is known imperforate vertically and imperforate horizontally.

SD4

1930, Sept. 2 *Perf. 11*

E4 SD4 20c henna brown 65.00 17.50
Never hinged 125.00

SD5

1932, Dec. 24

E5 SD5 20c henna brown 60.00 17.50
Never hinged 115.00
a. Imperf., pair 625.00
Never hinged 1,000.

Allegory of Progress — SD6

1935, June 1 *Perf. 12*

E6 SD6 20c dark carmine 11.00 7.50
Never hinged 18.50
a. Imperf., pair 575.00
Never hinged 900.00

Arms of Canada — SD7

1938-39

E7 SD7 10c dk green (4/1/39) 9.00 3.50
Never hinged 15.00
a. Imperf., pair 575.00
Never hinged 850.00
E8 SD7 20c dark carmine (6/15/38) 30.00 25.00
Never hinged 50.00
a. Imperf., pair 575.00
Never hinged 850.00

No. E8 Surcharged in Black

1939, Mar. 1

E9 SD7 10c on 20c dk car 8.00 6.50
Never hinged 12.00

Coat of Arms and Flags SD8

1942, July 1

E10 SD8 10c green 4.00 2.00
Never hinged 5.75
a. Imperf., pair 575.00
Never hinged 850.00

Canada's contribution to the war effort of the Allied Nations.

Catalogue values for unused stamps in this section, from this point to the end of the section, are for Never Hinged items.

Arms of Canada — SD9

1946, Sept. 16

E11 SD9 10c green 4.50 1.25

The laurel and olive branches symbolize Victory and Peace.
For overprints see Nos. EO1, EO2.

SPECIAL DELIVERY OFFICIAL STAMPS

Catalogue values for unused stamps in this section are for Never Hinged items.

No. E11 Overprinted in Black

1950 Unwmk. *Perf. 12*

EO1 SD9 10c green 17.50 12.50

Same Overprinted

EO2 SD9 10c green 30.00 17.50

REGISTRATION STAMPS

R1

1875-88 Unwmk. Engr. *Perf. 12*

F1 R1 2c orange 110.00 6.00
Never hinged 240.00
a. 2c vermilion 160.00 15.00
Never hinged 350.00
b. 2c rose carmine 325.00 110.00
Never hinged 750.00
c. As "a," imperf., pair *3,000.*
d. Perf. 12x11½ 600.00 110.00
Never hinged 1,150.
F2 R1 5c dark green 140.00 5.50
Never hinged 290.00
a. 5c blue green ('88) 160.00 5.50
Never hinged 325.00
b. 5c yellow green 225.00 7.00
Never hinged 450.00
c. Imperf., pair 1,100.
Never hinged *2,100.*
d. Perf. 12x11½ 2,250. 275.00
Never hinged *4,500.*
F3 R1 8c dull blue ('76) 675.00 350.00
Never hinged 2,100.
Nos. F1-F3 (3) 925.00 361.50

The used No. F1c is unique (fine centering).

POSTAGE DUE STAMPS

D1

1906-28 Unwmk. Engr. *Perf. 12*

J1 D1 1c violet 25.00 4.75
Never hinged 45.00
a. Thin paper ('24) 45.00 7.50
Never hinged 80.00
b. Imperf., pair 350.00
J2 D1 2c violet 25.00 1.00
Never hinged 40.00
a. Thin paper ('24) 45.00 11.00
Never hinged 80.00
b. Imperf., pair 350.00
J3 D1 4c violet ('28) 65.00 22.50
Never hinged 120.00
J4 D1 5c violet 25.00 2.00
Never hinged 40.00
a. As "c," thin paper 27.50 7.50
Never hinged 60.00
b. Imperf., pair 350.00
c. 5c reddish violet ('28) 25.00 2.00
Never hinged 40.00

J5 D1 10c violet ('28) 100.00 14.00
Never hinged 180.00
Nos. J1-J5 (5) 240.00 44.25
Set, never hinged 425.00

In 1924 there was a printing of Nos. J1, J2 and J4 on thin semi-transparent paper. Imperf pairs are without gum.

D2

1930-32 ***Perf. 11***

J6 D2 1c dark violet 12.50 4.25
Never hinged 22.50
J7 D2 2c dark violet 7.00 1.10
Never hinged 12.50
J8 D2 4c dark violet 15.00 5.50
Never hinged 25.00
J9 D2 5c dark violet 25.00 6.50
Never hinged 42.50
J10 D2 10c dark violet ('32) 110.00 10.00
Never hinged 200.00
a. Vert. pair, imperf. horiz. 1,750. —
Never hinged 2,750.
Nos. J6-J10 (5) 169.50 27.35
Set, never hinged 302.50

No. J10a is valued in the grade of fine.

D3

1933-34

J11 D3 1c dark violet ('34) 15.00 6.50
Never hinged 27.50
a. Imperf., pair 375.00
Never hinged 600.00
J12 D3 2c dark violet 9.00 1.25
Never hinged 17.50
J13 D3 4c dark violet 15.00 8.00
Never hinged 30.00
J14 D3 10c dark violet 32.50 7.25
Never hinged 57.50
Nos. J11-J14 (4) 71.50 23.00
Set, never hinged 132.50

Catalogue values for unused stamps in this section, from this point to the end of the section, are for Never Hinged items.

D4

1935-65 ***Perf. 12***

J15 D4 1c dark violet .30 .25
a. Imperf., pair 275.00
J16 D4 2c dark violet .30 .25
a. Imperf., pair 275.00
J16B D4 3c dark vio ('65) 2.00 1.50
J17 D4 4c dark violet .35 .25
a. Imperf., pair 275.00
J18 D4 5c dark vio ('48) .40 .35
J19 D4 6c dark vio ('57) 2.25 1.75
J20 D4 10c dark violet .40 .25
a. Imperf., pair 275.00
Nos. J15-J20 (7) 6.00 4.60

D5

Size: 20x17mm

1967, Feb. 8 **Litho.** ***Perf. 12***

J21 D5 1c carmine rose .25 .25
J22 D5 2c carmine rose .25 .25
J23 D5 3c carmine rose .25 .25
J24 D5 4c carmine rose .30 .25
J25 D5 5c carmine rose 1.50 1.50
J26 D5 6c carmine rose .30 .25
J27 D5 10c carmine rose .40 .30
Nos. J21-J27 (7) 3.25 3.05

Size: 20x15¾mm

1969-78 ***Perf. 12***

J28 D5 1c car rose ('70) .45 .30
a. Perf. 12½x12 ('77) .25 .25
J29 D5 2c car rose ('72) .25 .25
J30 D5 3c car rose ('74) .25 .25
J31 D5 4c carmine rose .40 .30
a. Perf. 12½x12 ('77) .25 .25
b. Printed on gummed side 1,400.
J32 D5 5c car rose, perf. 12½x12 ('77) .25 .25
a. Perf. 12 16.00 12.50
J33 D5 6c car rose ('72) .25 .25
J34 D5 8c carmine rose .25 .25
a. Perf. 12½x12 ('78) .40 .30
J35 D5 10c carmine rose .55 .25
a. Perf. 12½x12 ('77) .25 .25
J36 D5 12c carmine rose .75 .60
a. Perf. 12½x12 ('77) 1.50 .70
J37 D5 16c carmine rose ('74) .40 .25

Perf. 12½x12

J38 D5 20c carmine rose ('77) .55 .40
J39 D5 24c carmine rose ('77) .65 .40
J40 D5 50c carmine rose ('77) 1.00 .75
Nos. J28-J40 (13) 6.00 4.50

WAR TAX STAMPS

WT1

Unwmk.

1915, Mar. 25 **Engr.** ***Perf. 12***

MR1 WT1 1c green 27.50 .40
Never hinged 70.00
MR2 WT1 2c carmine 27.50 .40
Never hinged 65.00

In 1915 postage stamps of 5, 20 and 50 cents were overprinted "WAR TAX" in two lines. These stamps were intended for fiscal use, the war tax on postal matter being 1 cent. A few of these stamps were used to pay postage.

WT2

Type I

Type II

TWO TYPES:
Type I — There is a colored line between two white lines below the large letter "T."
Type II — The right half of the colored line is replaced by two short diagonal lines and five small dots.

1916

MR3 WT2 2c + 1c car (I) 40.00 .25
Never hinged 100.00
a. 2c + 1c carmine (II) 275.00 4.50
Never hinged 625.00
b. 2c + 1c rose red (I) 50.00 .40
Never hinged 120.00
MR4 WT2 2c + 1c brn (II) 25.00 .25
Never hinged 65.00
a. 2c + 1c brown (I) 950.00 10.00
Never hinged 1,900.
b. Imperf., pair (I) 175.00
c. Imperf., pair (II) 2,250.

Nos. MR4b and MR4c were made without gum.

Perf. 12x8

MR5 WT2 2c + 1c car (I) 55.00 30.00
Never hinged 140.00

Coil Stamps

Perf. 8 Vertically

MR6 WT2 2c + 1c car (I) 125.00 10.00
Never hinged 400.00
MR7 WT2 2c + 1c brn (II) 50.00 2.25
Never hinged 110.00
a. 2c + 1c brown (I) 200.00 7.50
Never hinged 500.00

OVERPRINTED OFFICIAL STAMPS

Catalogue values for unused stamps in this section are for Never Hinged items.

With Perforated Initials O H M S

On March 28, 1939 the Treasury Board ruled that on and after June 30, 1939 all stamps used by government departments throughout the country should be perforated O H M S (On His Majesty's Service) and that "the Post Office Department is to make arrangements required to provide that all stamps sold to Government Departments are perforated with the letters O H M S." The sale of such perforated stamps was discontinued in 1948.

For listings see the *Scott Classic Specialized Catalogue.*

Nos. 249, 250, 252 and 254 Overprinted in Black

1949-50 **Unwmk.** ***Perf. 12***

O1 A97 1c green 2.75 1.75
a. No period after "S" 250.00 125.00
O2 A98 2c brown 10.00 10.00
a. No period after "S" 375.00 170.00
O3 A99 3c rose violet 2.75 1.25
O4 A98 4c dark carmine 3.00 .75

Nos. 269 to 273 Overprinted in Black

O6 A108 10c olive 3.50 .60
a. No period after "S" 120.00 90.00
O7 A109 14c black brown 6.50 2.25
a. No period after "S" 175.00 80.00
O8 A110 20c slate black 17.50 3.25
a. No period after "S" 200.00 75.00
O9 A111 50c dk blue grn 190.00 110.00
a. No period after "S" 1,000. 600.00
O10 A112 $1 red violet 70.00 35.00
a. No period after "S" 6,000. 3,000.
Nos. O1-O4,O6-O10 (9) 306.00 164.85

It is recommended that a certificate of authenticity be acquired for No. O10a.

Same Overprint on No. 294

1950

O11 A124 50c dull green 45.00 15.00

Nos. 284 to 288 Overprinted in Black

1950

O12 A119 1c green .45 .35
O13 A120 2c sepia 1.10 .80
O14 A121 3c rose violet 1.10 .50
O15 A122 4c dark carmine 1.10 .25
b. No period after "S" 400.00 275.00
O15A A123 5c deep blue 2.25 1.50
c. No period after "S" 110.00 80.00
Nos. O12-O15A (5) 6.00 3.40

It is recommended that a certificate of authenticity be acquired for No. O15b.

Stamps of 1946-50 Overprinted in Black

a

b

1950

O16 A119(a) 1c grn (#284) .65 .25
O17 A120(a) 2c sep (#285) 1.40 .90
O18 A121(a) 3c rose vio (#286) 1.40 .25
O19 A122(a) 4c dk car (#287) 1.40 .25
O20 A123(a) 5c dp bl (#288) 1.75 .90
O21 A108(b) 10c olive 4.25 .50
O22 A109(b) 14c black brn 8.50 2.00
O23 A110(b) 20c slate blk 14.00 1.00
O24 A124(b) 50c dull green 9.00 5.00
O25 A112(b) $1 red violet 90.00 85.00
Nos. O16-O25 (10) 132.35 96.05

Nos. 301-302 Ovptd.

1950-51

O26 A125 10c black brown 1.40 .25
a. Pair, one without "G" 925.00 600.00
O27 A126 $1 brt ultra ('51) 80.00 50.00

It is recommended that a certificate of authenticity be acquired for No. O26a.

Nos. 305-306 Overprinted

1951-52 **Unwmk.** ***Perf. 12***

O28 A120 2c olive green .60 .25
O29 A122 4c orange ver ('52) .95 .25

No. 316 Ovptd.

1952

O30 A132 20c gray 2.50 .25

Nos. 320-321 Ovptd.

1952-53

O31 A136 7c blue 4.00 1.25
O32 A137 $1 gray ('53) 11.00 7.50

Nos. 325-329, 334 Overprinted

1953-61

O33 A139(a) 1c violet brown .40 .25
O34 A139(a) 2c green .40 .25
O35 A139(a) 3c carmine rose .40 .25
O36 A139(a) 4c violet .45 .25
O37 A139(a) 5c ultramarine .45 .25
O38 A141(b) 50c light green 5.00 1.20
a. Overprinted type "c" ('61) 5.00 2.00
Nos. O33-O38 (6) 7.10 2.45

No. 351 Overprinted

No. O39

No. O39a

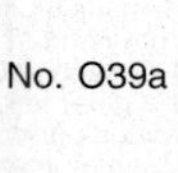

1955-62

O39 A148 10c violet brown 1.00 .25
a. Overprinted type "c" ('62) 1.90 1.25

Nos. 337-338, 340-341 Ovptd.

1955-56

O40 A144 1c vio brown ('56) .40 .30
O41 A144 2c green ('56) .40 .25
O43 A144 4c violet ('56) 1.20 .25
O44 A144 5c bright blue .75 .25
Nos. O40-O44 (4) 2.75 1.05

No. 362 Overprinted

No. O45

No. O45a

1956-62

O45 A159 20c green 1.75 .25
a. Overprinted type "c" ('62) 7.00 .50

Nos. 401-402, 404-405 Overprinted

1963, May 15 Engr. *Perf. 12*

O46 A195 1c deep brown .75 .70
a. Double overprint 750.00
O47 A195 2c green .75 .70
a. Pair, one without "G" 1,000.
O48 A195 4c carmine .80 .70
O49 A195 5c violet blue .70 .50
Nos. O46-O49 (4) 3.00 2.60

CAPE JUBY

'kāp 'jü-bē

LOCATION — Northwest coast of Africa in Spanish Sahara
GOVT. — Spanish administration
AREA — 12,700 sq. mi.
POP. — 9,836
CAPITAL — Villa Bens (Cape Juby)

By agreement with France, Spain's Sahara possessions were extended to include Cape Juby and in 1916 Spanish troops occupied the territory. It was attached for administrative purposes to Spanish Sahara.

100 Centimos = 1 Peseta

Stamps of Rio de Oro, 1914 Surcharged in Violet, Red, Green or Blue

1916 Unwmk. *Perf. 13*

1 A6 5c on 4p rose (V) 200.00 19.00
a. Inverted surcharge 250.00 30.00
d. Double surcharge 325.00 50.00
2 A6 10c on 10p dl vio (R) 50.00 19.00
a. Inverted surcharge 55.00 30.00
d. Double surcharge 75.00 50.00
2E A6 10c on 10p dl vio (V) 100.00 72.50
f. Double surcharge (R, V) 150.00 90.00
2G A6 10c on 10p dl vio (B) 100.00 72.50
3 A6 15c on 50c dk brn (G) 52.50 30.00
a. Inverted surcharge 57.50 30.00
4 A6 15c on 50c dk brn (R) 50.00 19.00
a. Inverted surcharge 55.00 30.00
5 A6 40c on 1p red vio (G) 87.50 35.00
a. Inverted surcharge 75.00 37.50
6 A6 40c on 1p red vio (R) 75.00 26.00
a. Inverted surcharge 75.00 42.50
Nos. 1-6 (8) 715.00 293.00
Set, never hinged 1,150.

Very fine examples of Nos. 1-6 will be somewhat off center. Well centered examples are uncommon and will sell for more.

Stamps of Spain, 1876-1917, Overprinted in Red or Black

1919 *Imperf.*

7 A21 ¼c bl grn (R) .30 .30

Perf. 13x12½, 14

8 A46 2c dk brn (Bk) .30 .30
a. Double overprint 50.00 *60.00*
b. Double overprint (Bk + R) 110.00 110.00
9 A46 5c grn (R) .85 .75
a. Double overprint 50.00 *50.00*
b. Inverted overprint 47.50 *60.00*
10 A46 10c car (Bk) 1.00 .70
a. Double overprint (Bk + R) 110.00 80.00
b. Double overprint (Bk) 40.00 *50.00*
11 A46 15c ocher (Bk) 3.50 3.00
b. Double overprint 50.00 *50.00*
c. Red control # 6.50 3.75
d. As "c," inverted overprint 45.00 45.00
12 A46 20c ol grn (R) 24.00 14.00
13 A46 25c dp bl (R) 3.50 2.50
a. Double overprint 50.00 *52.50*
14 A46 30c bl grn (R) 3.50 3.25
15 A46 40c rose (Bk) 3.50 3.25
16 A46 50c sl bl (R) 4.00 4.00
17 A46 1p lake (Bk) 11.50 9.50
18 A46 4p dp vio (R) 52.50 47.50
19 A46 10p org (Bk) 70.00 65.00
Nos. 7-19 (13) 178.45 154.05
Set, never hinged 355.00

Nos. 8-19 have blue control number on back. For imperfs, see the *Scott Classic Catalogue*.

Same on Stamps of Spain, 1920-21

1922 *Imperf.*

20 A47 1c blue green (R) 25.00 14.00
Never hinged 45.00

Engr. *Perf. 13x12½*

Blue Control Number on Back

23 A46 20c violet 145.00 42.50

A 2c and a 15c exist, values $400 and $10, respectively, for unused, hinged examples, $600 and $15 for never hinged. Overprint on 2c privately applied.

Same on Stamps of Spain, 1922-23

1925 *Perf. 13½x13*

25 A49 5c red vio 5.25 3.50
26 A49 10c bl grn 13.00 3.50
28 A49 20c violet 27.50 10.00
Nos. 25-28 (3) 45.75 17.00
Set, never hinged 72.50

Exists on Spain No. 331, 2c olive green. Value $425 unused hinged and $650 never hinged. Overprint was privately applied.

Seville-Barcelona Exposition Issue

Stamps of Spain, 1929, Overprinted in Red or Blue

1929 *Perf. 11*

29 A52 5c rose lake (Bl) .35 .35
30 A53 10c green (R) .35 .35
31 A50 15c Prus bl (R) .35 .35
32 A51 20c pur (R) .35 .35
33 A50 25c brt rose (Bl) .35 .35
34 A52 30c blk brn (Bl) .35 .35
35 A53 40c dk bl (R) .35 .35
36 A51 50c dp org (Bl) .55 .55
37 A52 1p bl blk (R) 11.00 11.00
38 A53 4p dp rose (Bl) 13.00 13.00
39 A53 10p brn (Bl) 13.00 13.00
Nos. 29-39 (11) 40.00 40.00
Set, never hinged 80.00

Stamps of Spanish Morocco, 1928-33, Overprinted in Black or Red

1934 *Perf. 14*

40 A7 1c brt rose (Bk) .55 .55
41 A2 2c dk vio (R) 5.00 5.00
42 A2 5c dp bl (R) 5.75 5.75
43 A2 10c dk grn (Bk) 14.00 11.50
43A A10 10c dk grn (R) 3.50 3.50
44 A2 15c org brn (Bk) 32.50 29.00
45 A7 20c sl grn (R) 13.00 10.00
46 A3 25c cop red (Bk) 6.00 5.50
47 A10 30c red brn (Bk) 11.00 10.00
48 A13 40c dp bl (R) 40.00 37.50
49 A13 50c red org (Bk) 80.00 70.00
50 A4 1p yel grn (Bk) 57.50 57.50
51 A5 2.50p red vio (Bk) 120.00 115.00
52 A6 4p ultra (R) 160.00 145.00

No. 43A and 1c, 20c, 30c, 40c, 50c, with control numbers.

Same Overprint in Black on Stamp of Spanish Morocco, 1932

53 A2 1c car rose ("Ct") 2.40 2.40
Nos. 40-53 (15) 551.20 508.20
Set, never hinged 900.00

Stamps of Spanish Morocco, 1933-35, Overprinted in Black, Blue or Red

1935-36

54 A8 2c grn (R) 1.25 1.00
55 A9 5c mag (Bk) 3.50 3.50
55A A10 10c dk grn (R) ('36) 21.00 21.00
56 A11 15c yel (Bl) 8.00 8.00
57 A12 25c crim (Bk) 100.00 85.00
58 A8 1p sl blk (R) 13.50 12.50
59 A9 2.50p brn (Bl) 60.00 47.50
60 A11 4p yel grn (R) 100.00 85.00
61 A12 5p blk (R) 85.00 65.00
Nos. 54-61 (9) 392.25 328.50
Set, never hinged 750.00

Same Overprint in Black or Red on Stamps of Spanish Morocco, 1935

1935 *Perf. 13½*

62 A14 25c vio (R) 4.00 4.00
63 A15 30c crim (Bk) 4.00 4.00
64 A14 40c org (Bk) 5.75 5.25
65 A15 50c brt bl (R) 15.00 11.00
66 A14 60c dk bl grn (R) 17.50 14.00
67 A15 2p brn lake (Bk) 95.00 75.00

Same Overprint on Stamps of Spanish Morocco, 1933

Perf. 13½, 14

68 A7 1c brt rose (Bk) .30 .30

Perf. 14

69 A7 20c slate grn (R) 6.75 6.75
Nos. 62-69 (8) 148.30 120.30
Set, never hinged 200.00

Same Overprint on Stamps of Spanish Morocco, 1937

1937 *Perf. 13½*

70 A21 1c dk bl (Bk) .50 .50
71 A21 2c org brn (Bk) .50 .50
72 A21 5c cer (Bk) .50 .50
73 A21 10c emer (Bk) .50 .50
74 A21 15c brt bl (Bk) .50 .50
75 A21 20c red brn (Bk) .50 .50
76 A21 25c mag (Bk) .50 .50
77 A21 30c red org (Bk) .50 .50
78 A21 40c org (Bk) 1.50 1.50
79 A21 50c ultra (R) 1.50 1.50
80 A21 60c yel grn (Bk) 1.50 1.50
81 A21 1p bl vio (Bk) 1.50 1.50
82 A21 2p Prus bl (Bk) 80.00 80.00
83 A21 2.50p gray blk (R) 80.00 80.00
84 A21 4p dk brn (Bk) 80.00 80.00
85 A22 10p vio blk (R) 80.00 80.00
Nos. 70-85 (16) 330.00 330.00
Set, never hinged 550.00

1st Year of the Revolution.

Same Overprint in Black on Types of Spanish Morocco, 1939

Designs: 5c, Spanish quarter. 10c, Moroccan quarter. 15c, Street scene, Larache. 20c, Tetuan.

1939 Photo. *Perf. 13½*

86 A25 5c vermilion .50 .50
87 A25 10c deep green .50 .50
88 A25 15c brown lake .50 .50
89 A25 20c bright blue .50 .50
Nos. 86-89 (4) 2.00 2.00
Set, never hinged 4.00

Same Overprint in Black or Red on Stamps of Spanish Morocco, 1940

1940 *Perf. 11½x11*

90 A26 1c dk brn (Bk) .25 .25
91 A27 2c ol grn (R) .25 .25
92 A28 5c dk bl (R) .25 .25
93 A29 10c dk red lil (Bk) .25 .25
94 A30 15c dk grn (R) .25 .25
95 A31 20c pur (R) .30 .30
96 A32 25c blk brn (R) .30 .30
97 A33 30c brt grn (Bk) .35 .35
98 A34 40c slate grn (R) .85 .75
99 A35 45c org ver (Bk) .85 .75
100 A36 50c brn org (Bk) .90 .90
101 A37 70c saph (R) 2.40 2.25
102 A38 1p ind & brn (Bk) 5.00 5.00
103 A39 2.50p choc & dk grn (Bk) 14.00 12.50
104 A40 5p dk cer & sep (Bk) 14.00 13.00
105 A41 10p dk ol grn & brn org (Bk) 40.00 35.00
Nos. 90-105 (16) 80.20 72.35
Set, never hinged 150.00

Imperfs exist. Value, set $300.

Stamps of Spanish Morocco, 1944. Overprinted in Black or Red

1944, Oct. 2 Unwmk. *Perf. 12½*

106 A47 1c choc & lt bl .25 .25
107 A48 2c slate grn & lt grn .25 .25
108 A49 5c choc & grnsh blk (R) .25 .25
109 A50 10c brt ultra & red org .25 .25
110 A51 15c sl grn & lt grn .25 .25
111 A52 20c dp cl & blk (R) .25 .25
112 A53 25c lt bl & choc .25 .25
113 A47 30c yel grn & brt ultra (R) .25 .25
114 A48 40c choc & red vio .25 .25
115 A49 50c brt ultra, & red brn .25 .25
116 A50 75c yel grn & brt ultra (R) 1.25 1.25
117 A51 1p brt ultra & choc 1.40 1.40
118 A52 2.50p blk & brt ultra (R) 3.25 3.25
119 A53 10p sal & gray blk (R) 25.00 25.00
Nos. 106-119 (14) 33.40 33.40
Set, never hinged 70.00

Nos. 106-119 exist imperf. Value, set $300.

Same Overprint on Stamps of Spanish Morocco, 1946

1946, Mar. *Perf. 10½x10*

120 A54 1c pur & brn .25 .25
121 A55 2c dk Prus grn & vio blk (R) .25 .25
122 A54 10c dp org vio bl .25 .25
123 A55 15c dk bl & bl grn .25 .25
124 A54 25c yel grn & ultra .25 .25
125 A56 40c dk bl & brn (R) .30 .30

126 A55 45c blk & rose .45 .45
127 A57 1p dk Prus grn & dp bl 1.60 1.60
128 A58 2.50p dp org & grnsh gray (R) 4.75 4.75
129 A59 10p dk bl & gray (R) 13.50 13.50
Nos. 120-129 (10) 21.85 21.85
Set, never hinged 40.00

Nos. 120-129 exist imperf. Value, set $200.

Same Overprint in Carmine, Black or Brown on Stamps of Spanish Morocco, 1948

1948, Jan. 1 ***Perf. 10, 10x10½***

130 A64 2c pur & brn .40 *1.00*
131 A65 5c dp claret & vio .25 .25
132 A66 15c brt ultra & bl grn (Bk) .25 .25
133 A67 25c blk & Prus grn .25 .25
134 A65 35c brt ultra & gray blk .25 .25
135 A68 50c red & vio (Br) .25 .25
136 A66 70c dk gray grn & ultra (Bk) .25 .25
137 A67 90c cer & dk gray grn (Bk) .30 .30
138 A68 1p brt ultra & vio (Br) .45 .45
139 A64 2.50p vio brn & sl grn 1.60 1.60
140 A69 10p blk & dp ultra 3.00 3.00
Nos. 130-140 (11) 7.25 7.85
Set, never hinged 12.00

Nos. 130-140 exist imperf. Value, set $200.

SEMI-POSTAL STAMPS

Types of Semi-Postal Stamps of Spain, 1926, Overprinted

1926 **Unwmk.** ***Perf. 12½, 13***

B1 SP1 1c orange 11.50 11.50
B2 SP2 2c rose 11.50 11.50
B3 SP3 5c blk brn 3.00 3.00
B4 SP4 10c dk grn 1.60 1.60
B5 SP1 15c dk vio 1.10 1.10
B6 SP4 20c vio brn 1.10 1.10
B7 SP5 25c dp car 1.10 1.10
B8 SP1 30c ol grn 1.10 1.10
B9 SP3 40c ultra .45 .45
B10 SP2 50c red brn .45 .45
B11 SP4 1p vermilion .45 .45
B12 SP3 4p bister 2.00 2.00
B13 SP5 10p lt vio 3.00 3.00
Nos. B1-B13 (13) 38.35 38.35
Set, never hinged 65.00

Nos. B12-B13 surcharged "Alfonso XIII" and new value are listed as Spain Nos. B68-B69. See Spain No. B6a.

AIR POST STAMPS

Spanish Morocco, Nos. C1 to C10 Overprinted "CABO JUBY" as on #54-61

1938, June 1 **Unwmk.** ***Perf. 13½***

C1 AP1 5c brown .25 .25
C2 AP1 10c brt grn .25 .25
C3 AP1 25c crimson .25 .25
C4 AP1 40c light blue 2.10 2.10
C5 AP2 50c brt mag .25 .25
C6 AP2 75c dk bl .25 .25
C7 AP1 1p sepia .25 .25
C8 AP1 1.50p dp vio 1.90 1.90
C9 AP1 2p dp red brn 2.75 2.75
C10 AP1 3p brn blk 7.25 7.25
Nos. C1-C10 (10) 15.50 15.50
Set, never hinged 45.00

Nos. C1-C10 exist imperf. Value, set $220.

Moroccan Views — AP3

Designs: 5c, Ketama landscape. 10c, Mosque, Tangier. 15c, Velez. 90c, Sanjurjo. 5p, Strait of Gibraltar

1942, Apr. 1 **Photo.** ***Perf. 12½***

C11 AP3 5c deep blue .25 .25
C12 AP3 10c org brn .25 .25
C13 AP3 15c grnsh blk .25 .25
C14 AP3 90c dk rose .50 .50
C15 AP3 5p black 1.75 1.75
Nos. C11-C15 (5) 3.00 3.00
Set, never hinged 4.00

Nos. C11-C15 exist imperf. Value, set $75.

SPECIAL DELIVERY STAMPS

Special Delivery Stamp of Spain Ovptd. "CABO JUBY" as on #7-28

1919 **Unwmk.** ***Perf. 14***

E1 SD1 20c red (Bk) 3.25 3.25
b. Double overprint 27.50 13.00

Spanish Morocco #E4 Overprinted "CABO JUBY" as on #40-52 in Red

1934

E2 SD2 20c black 10.00 10.00

Spanish Morocco No. E5 Overprinted "CABO JUBY" as on Nos. 54-61

1935

E3 SD3 20c vermilion 3.50 3.50

Same Ovpt. on Spanish Morocco #E6

1937 ***Perf. 13½***

E4 SD4 20c bright carmine 1.10 1.10

1st Year of the Revolution.

Same Ovpt. on Spanish Morocco #E8

1940 ***Perf. 11½x11***

E5 SD5 25c scarlet .65 .65

SEMI-POSTAL SPECIAL DELIVERY STAMP

Type of Semi-Postal Special Delivery Stamp of Spain, 1926, Overprinted "CABO-JUBY" as on Nos. B1-B13

1926 **Unwmk.** ***Perf. 12½, 13***

EB1 SPSD1 20c ultra & black 3.50 3.50

CAPE OF GOOD HOPE

'kāp əv 'gud 'hōp

LOCATION — In the extreme southern part of South Africa
GOVT. — Former British Colony
AREA — 276,995 sq mi. (1911)
POP. — 2,564,965 (1911)
CAPITAL — Cape Town

Cape of Good Hope joined with Natal, the Transvaal and the Orange River Colony in 1910, forming the Union of South Africa.

12 Pence = 1 Shilling

Watermarks

Wmk. 15 — Anchor

Wmk. 16 — Anchor

"Hope" Seated A1

Printed by Perkins, Bacon & Co. Wmk. 15

1853, Sept. 1 **Engr.** ***Imperf.***

1 A1 1p brick red, bluish paper 3,500. 400.00
a. 1p pale brick red, deeply blued paper *4,500.* 450.00
b. 1p deep brick red, deeply blued paper *10,500.* 475.00
2 A1 4p deep blue, lightly blued paper 1,750. 170.00
a. 4p deep blue, deeply blued paper 3,500. 375.00
b. 4p blue, bluish paper 3,250. 200.00

Counterfeits exist.

1855-58 **White Paper**

3 A1 1p rose ('57) 850.00 325.00
a. 1p dull red 1,100. 425.00
b. 1p brick red 6,000. 1,050.
4 A1 4p blue 1,000. 85.00
a. Half used as 2p on cover *35,000.*
b. 4p deep blue 1,300. 90.00
e. 4p bright blue 900.00 90.00
5 A1 6p pale lilac ('58) 1,200. 300.00
a. 6p rose lilac 2,500. 400.00
b. 6p grayish lilac on bluish paper 5,000. 540.00
c. 6p slate purple on bluish paper 4,150. 1,200.
d. Half used as 3p on cover —
6 A1 1sh yellow grn ('58) *4,000.* 300.00
a. 1sh dark green 450.00 *600.00*
b. Half used as 6p on cover —

Nos. 3-6 are known rouletted unofficially.
Counterfeits exist.
No. 4 was reproduced by the collotype process in an unwatermarked souvenir sheet distributed at the London Intl. Stamp Exhib. 1950.

A2

Printed by Saul Solomon & Co.

1861 **Laid Paper** **Unwmk.** **Typo.**

7 A2 1p vermilion *17,000.* 2,750.
a. 1p carmine *42,500.* 6,500.
b. 1p red *50,000.* 7,500.
c. 1p milky blue (error) *200,000.* *32,500.*
d. 1p pale blue (error) *36,000.*
9 A2 4p milky blue *40,000.* 2,500.
a. 4p pale blue *42,000.* 3,250.
b. 4p blue *45,000.* 3,500.
c. 4p dark blue *120,000.* 5,750.
d. As #9, right corner retouched 7,750.
e. As #9a, right corner retouched 7,750.
f. 4p vermilion (error) *200,000.* *65,000.*
g. 4p carmine (error) *112,500.*

Nos. 7 and 9 are usually called Wood Blocks. The plates were made locally and composed of clichés mounted on wood. The errors were caused by a cliché of each value being mounted in the plate of the other value.

In 1883 plate proofs of both values on white paper, usually called "reprints," were made. The 1p is in dull orange red; the 4p in dark blue. These are known canceled, as a few were misused as stamps. The proofs do not include the errors.

Counterfeits exist.

Printed by De La Rue & Co.

1863-64 **Wmk. 15** **Engr.**

12 A1 1p dark carmine 350.00 *350.00*
a. 1p reddish brown 650.00 375.00
b. 1p brownish red 650.00 375.00
13 A1 4p dark blue 325.00 135.00
a. 4p slate blue 2,500. 600.00
14 A1 6p purple 450.00 *500.00*
15 A1 1sh emerald 675.00 *725.00*
a. 1sh pale emerald 1,400. —

Nos. 12-15 can be distinguished from Nos. 3-6 not only by colors but because Nos. 12-15 often appear in a granular ink or with the background lightly printed in whole or part.

No. 12a, Wmk. 1, is believed to be a proof. Value, $29,000.

Counterfeits exist.

"Hope" and Symbols of Colony — A3

Frame Line Around Stamp

1864-77 **Typo.** **Wmk. 1** ***Perf. 14***

16 A3 1p rose ('65) 130.00 42.50
17 A3 4p blue ('65) 210.00 4.50
a. 4p pale blue 210.00 4.50
b. 4p dull ultramarine 350.00 50.00
c. 4p deep blue ('72) 275.00 4.50
18 A3 6p bright vio ('77) 235.00 1.50
a. 6p dull violet 375.00 8.25
b. 6p pale lilac 225.00 28.00
19 A3 1sh yellow green 225.00 4.75
a. 1sh blue green 250.00 6.00
Nos. 16-19 (4) 800.00 53.25

Imperf. stamps are believed to be proofs.
For surcharges see Nos. 20-21, N3.
For types A3 and A6 with manuscript surcharge of 1d or overprints "G. W." or "G," see Griqualand West listings.

Stamps of 1864 Surcharged in Red or Black

a

b

1868-74 — Red Surcharge

20 A3(a) 4p on 6p 575.00 17.50
a. "Peuce" for "Pence" 2,400. 750.00
b. "Fonr" for "Four" 775.00
21 A3(b) 1p on 6p ('74) 850.00 140.00
a. "E" of "PENNY" omitted 1,800.

Space between words and bars varies from 12½-16mm on No. 20, and 16½-18mm on No. 21.

1876 — Black Surcharge

22 A3 (b) 1p on 1sh green 150.00 75.00

"Hope" and Symbols of Colony — A6

Without Frame Line Around Stamp

1871-81 — *Perf. 14*

23 A6 ½p gray black ('75) 37.50 17.50
24 A6 1p rose ('72) 55.00 1.25
25 A6 3p lilac rose ('80) 350.00 42.50
26 A6 3p claret ('81) 240.00 4.50
27 A6 4p blue ('76) 210.00 .90
a. 4p ultramarine 350.00 57.50
28 A6 5sh orange 650.00 25.00
Nos. 23-28 (6) 1,543. 91.65

For surcharges see Nos. 29-32, 39, 55.

No. 27 Surcharged in Red

1879

29 A6 3p on 4p blue 200.00 2.50
a. "THE.EE" 3,750. 300.00
b. "PENCB" 3,250. 250.00
c. Double surcharge 12,000. 4,250.
d. As "a," double surcharge — —

Type of 1871 Surcharged in Black

1880

30 A6 3p on 4p lilac rose 145.00 3.25

No. 25 Surcharged in Black

e f

31 A6(e) 3p on 3p lilac rose 400.00 12.00
a. Inverted surcharge 12,500. 1,550.
32 A6(f) 3p on 3p lilac rose 130.00 2.25
a. Inverted surcharge 1,600. 47.50

1882-83 — Wmk. 2

33 A6 ½p gray black 42.50 3.25
34 A6 1p rose 85.00 2.50
35 A6 2p bister 140.00 1.75
36 A6 3p claret 12.50 1.75
37 A3 6p bright violet 160.00 1.00
38 A6 5sh orange ('83) 925.00 300.00

For overprint see Rhodesia No. 49.

Nos. 26 and 36 Surcharged in Black

1882 — Wmk. 1

39 A6 ½p on 3p claret 4,750. 180.00
a. Hyphen omitted 3,750.

Wmk. 2

40 A6 ½p on 3p claret 60.00 8.00
a. "ENNY" 2,300. 775.00
b. "PENN" 1,900. 750.00
c. Hyphen omitted 850.00 400.00

1884-98 — Wmk. 16

41 A6 ½p gray black ('86) 12.00 .25
42 A6 ½p yel green ('96) 1.80 .75
43 A6 1p rose ('85) 15.00 .25
44 A6 2p bister 15.00 .25
45 A6 2p choc brown ('97) 4.75 3.50
46 A6 3p red violet ('98) 25.00 1.40
47 A6 4p blue ('90) 26.00 1.50
48 A6 4p pale ol grn ('97) 12.00 4.25
49 A3 6p violet 22.00 .50
50 A3 1sh dull bluish grn ('89) 180.00 1.25
51 A6 1sh blue grn ('94) 110.00 8.50
52 A6 1sh yel buff ('96) 19.00 3.25
53 A6 5sh orange ('87) 160.00 9.50
54 A6 5sh brown org ('96) 140.00 5.00
Nos. 41-54 (14) 742.55 40.15

For surcharges see Nos. 58, 162, 165-166. For overprints see Rhodesia Nos. 43, 45-48.

Type of 1871 Surcharged in Black

1891, Mar.

55 A6 2½p on 3p deep magenta 8.50 .25
a. "1" of "½" has straight serif 95.00 37.50

Hope Seated — A13

1892-96

56 A13 2½p sage green 26.00 .25
57 A13 2½p ultra ('96) 14.00 .25

For surcharge see No. N4. For overprint see Orange River Colony No. 55.

No. 44 Surcharged in Black

1893, Mar.

58 A6 1p on 2p bister 6.00 .60
a. Double surcharge 600.00
b. No period after "PENNY" 100.00 25.00

Hope Standing — A15

1893-1902

59 A15 ½p green ('98) 11.00 .25
60 A15 1p carmine 4.00 .25
61 A15 3p red violet ('02) 8.00 3.50
Nos. 59-61 (3) 23.00 4.00

For surcharges see Nos. 163-164, N2. For overprints see Orange River Colony Nos. 54, 56, Rhodesia No. 44, Transvaal Nos. 236-236A.

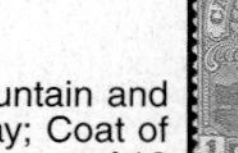

Table Mountain and Bay; Coat of Arms — A16

1900, Jan.

62 A16 1p carmine rose 8.50 .25

King Edward VII — A17

Various frames.

1902-04 — Wmk. 16

63 A17 ½p emerald 4.00 .25
64 A17 1p car rose 3.50 .25
65 A17 2p brown ('04) 24.00 .95
66 A17 2½p ultra ('04) 5.75 13.00
67 A17 3p red violet ('03) 18.50 1.40
68 A17 4p ol green ('03) 20.00 .80
69 A17 6p violet ('03) 30.00 .60
70 A17 1sh bister 20.00 1.25
71 A17 5sh brown org ('03) 160.00 27.50
Nos. 63-71 (9) 285.75 46.00

Imperf. stamps are proofs.

Cape of Good Hope stamps were replaced by those of Union of South Africa.

ISSUED IN MAFEKING

Excellent forgeries of Nos. 162-179 are known.

Stamps of Cape of Good Hope Surcharged

1900, Mar. 24

162 A6 1p on ½p grn 325.00 85.00
163 A15 1p on ½p grn 375.00 125.00
164 A15 3p on 1p rose 325.00 65.00
165 A6 6p on 3p red vio 45,000. 350.00
166 A6 1sh on 4p pale ol grn 8,000. 425.00

Stamps of Bechuanaland Protectorate Surcharged

1900 — Wmk. 30

167 A54 1p on ½p ver 325.00 85.00
a. Inverted surcharge — 8,000.
b. Vert. pair, surcharge tête bêche 40,000.
168 A40 3p on 1p lilac 1,000. 155.00
a. Double surcharge 37,500.
169 A56 6p on 2p grn & car 3,000. 125.00
170 A58 6p on 3p vio, *yel* 7,500. 425.00
a. Inverted surcharge 42,500.
b. Double surcharge — —

The lettering of "Mafeking Besieged" shows varying breaks in various letters, and may have either a period or no punctuation after "Mafeking."

On Stamps of Bechuanaland

Wmk. 29

171 A1 6p on 3p vio & blk 550.00 95.00

Wmk. 30

172 A59 1sh on 4p brn & grn 1,650. 110.00
a. Double surch., one inverted — 30,000.
b. Triple surcharge — 30,000.
c. Inverted surcharge — —
d. Double surcharge — 30,000.
172E A59 2sh on 4p brn & grn 39,000.

Stamps of Bechuanaland Protectorate Surcharged

173 A40 3p on 1p lil 1,100. 100.00
a. Double surcharge — 11,000.
174 A56 6p on 2p grn & car 1,600. 100.00
175 A62 1sh on 6p vio, *rose* 7,500. 130.00

On Stamps of Bechuanaland

176 A62 1sh on 6p vio, *rose* 32,500. 850.00
177 A65 2sh on 1sh green 14,000. 650.00

Sgt. Major Goodyear M1

Gen. Robert S. S. Baden-Powell M2

Wmk. OCEANA FINE

Photographic Print

1900, Apr. — *Perf. 12*

Laid Paper

178 M1 1p blue, *blue* 1,200. 425.00
a. Imperf, pair 25,000.
179 M2 3p blue, *blue,* 18½mm wide 1,750. 450.00
a. Horiz. pair, imperf. between — 100,000.
b. Double impression — 25,000.
c. Reversed design 100,000. 55,000.
180 M2 3p blue, *blue,* 21mm wide 12,000. 1,350.
a. 3p deep blue 13,500. 1,350.
On cover 16,500.

The color of the paper varies from pale to deep blue.

OCEANA FINE is a sheet watermark and does not appear on every stamp.

Imperfs of No. 178 are proofs.

There is one used pair of No. 179a privately owned. A single used, partially imperf. example of No. 179 exists. Value, *$45,000.* There are four used examples of No. 179b reported. There are 2 unused and 6 used examples of No. 179c privately owned.

Issued: No. 179, Apr. 6; Nos. 178 and 180, Apr. 10.

ISSUED IN VRYBURG

Under Boer Occupation

Cape of Good Hope Stamps of 1884-96 Surcharged

Type 1 Type 2

Two Types of Surcharge:

Type I — Surcharge 10mm high. Space between lines 5½mm.

Type II — Surcharge 12mm high. Space between lines 7½mm.

1899, Nov. — Wmk. 16 — *Perf. 14*

N1 A6 ½p on ½p emer (I) 240. 95.
a. Type II 2,250. 825.
N2 A15 1p on 1p rose (I) 275. 120.
a. Double surcharge — —
b. Type II 2,500. 950.
N3 A3 2p on 6p vio (II) 2,250. 750.
N4 A13 2½p on 2½p ultra (I) 1,800. 450.
a. Type II 15,000. 4,500.

Under British Occupation

Transvaal Stamps of 1895-96 Handstamped

1900 **Unwmk.** ***Perf. 12½***

No.	Design	Description	Unused	Used
N5	A13	½p green	—	*3,500.*
N6	A13	1p rose & grn	*14,000.*	*6,000.*
N7	A13	2p brown & grn	—	*45,000.*
N8	A13	2½p ultra & grn	—	*45,000.*

CAPE VERDE

'kāp 'vərd

LOCATION — A group of 10 islands and five islets in the Atlantic Ocean, about 500 miles due west of Senegal.
GOVT. — Republic
AREA — 1,557 sq. mi.
POP. — 405,748 (1999 est.)
CAPITAL — Praia

The Portuguese territory of Cape Verde became independent on July 5, 1975.

1000 Reis = 1 Milreis
100 Centavos = 1 Escudo (1913)

Catalogue values for unused stamps in this country are for Never Hinged items, beginning with Scott 268 in the regular postage section, Scott J31 in the postage due section, and Scott RA6 in the postal tax section.

Crown of Portugal — A1

1877 **Unwmk.** **Typo.** ***Perf. 12½***

No.	Design	Description	Unused	Used
1	A1	5r black	4.25	2.50
2	A1	10r yellow	50.00	11.00
3	A1	20r bister	3.00	2.00
4	A1	25r rose	3.00	2.00
5	A1	40r blue	105.00	55.00
b.		Cliche of Mozambique in Cape Verde plate, in pair with #5	*2,200.*	*1,750.*
6	A1	50r green	170.00	82.50
7	A1	100r lilac	10.00	3.50
8	A1	200r orange	6.00	4.25
9	A1	300r brown	7.00	5.50
		Nos. 1-9 (9)	358.25	168.25

For expanded treatment of Nos. 1-9, see the *Scott Classic Catalogue.*

No.	Description	Unused	Used
c.	100r gray lilac	12.00	5.75
c.	200r redsh orange	17.50	11.50

1881-85 ***Perf. 12½***

No.	Design	Description	Unused	Used
10	A1	10r green	3.50	2.40
11	A1	20r carmine ('85)	6.00	4.00
12	A1	25r violet ('85)	5.00	4.00
13	A1	40r yellow buff	2.75	1.90
a.		Imperf.	40.00	
b.		Cliche of Mozambique in Cape Verde plate, in pair with #13	*150.00*	*140.00*
c.		As "b," imperf.	—	
14	A1	50r blue	8.00	5.00
		Nos. 10-14 (5)	25.25	17.30

Reprints of the 1877-85 issues are on smooth white chalky paper, ungummed, and on thin white paper with shiny white gum. They are perf 13½.

For expanded treatment of nos. 10-14, see the *Scott Classic Catalogue.*

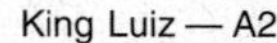

King Luiz — A2

1886 **Embossed** ***Perf. 12½, 13½***
Chalk-Surfaced Paper

No.	Design	Description	Unused	Used
15	A2	5r black	5.25	3.50
16	A2	10r green	6.00	3.50
17	A2	20r carmine	10.50	5.25
18	A2	25r violet	10.00	5.50
19	A2	40r chocolate	10.00	3.75
20	A2	50r blue	10.00	3.75
21	A2	100r yel brown	10.00	5.00
22	A2	200r gray lilac	21.00	11.50
23	A2	300r orange	24.00	6.00
		Nos. 15-23 (9)	106.75	47.75

The 25r, 50r and 100r have been reprinted in aniline colors with clean-cut Perf. 13½.

For expanded treatment of nos. 15-19, see the *Scott Classic Catalogue.*

For surcharges see Nos. 59-67, 184-187.

King Carlos — A3

1894-95 **Typo.** ***Perf. 11½, 12½, 13½***

No.	Design	Description	Unused	Used
24	A3	5r orange	1.75	1.25
25	A3	10r redsh violet	1.75	1.25
26	A3	15r chocolate	4.00	2.60
a.		Perf. 12½	150.00	120.00
27	A3	20r lavender	4.00	2.60
28	A3	25r dp green	3.50	2.25
a.		Perf. 12½	4.00	3.25
29	A3	50r lt blue	3.50	2.25
a.		Perf. 13 1/2	14.00	4.50
30	A3	75r carmine ('95)	11.50	5.75
a.		Perf. 13½	55.00	42.00
31	A3	80r yel grn ('95)	12.00	6.50
a.		Perf. 13½	45.00	35.00
32	A3	100r brn, *buff* ('95)	12.00	5.25
a.		Perf. 12½	125.00	55.00
33	A3	150r car, *rose* ('95)	60.00	50.00
a.		Perf. 12½	450.00	350.00
b.		Perf. 11½	70.00	45.00
34	A3	200r dk blue, *lt blue* ('95)	40.00	27.00
a.		Perf. 12½	150.00	120.00
35	A3	300r dk blue, *sal* ('95)	50.00	17.00
		Nos. 24-35 (12)	204.00	123.70

For surcharges see Nos. 68-78, 137, 189-193, 201-205.

King Carlos — A4

1898-1903 ***Perf. 11½***
Name and Value in Black except 500r

No.	Design	Description	Unused	Used
36	A4	2½r gray	.40	.30
37	A4	5r orange	.50	.30
38	A4	10r lt green	.55	.30
39	A4	15r brown	5.50	2.00
40	A4	15r gray grn ('03)	1.90	1.25
41	A4	20r gray violet	1.60	1.00
42	A4	25r sea green	3.50	1.25
a.		Perf 12½	*275.00*	*140.00*
43	A4	25r carmine ('03)	1.00	.40
44	A4	50r dark blue	3.50	1.50
45	A4	50r brown ('03)	3.75	2.40
46	A4	65r slate blue ('03)	35.00	*25.00*
47	A4	75r rose	10.00	3.50
48	A4	75r lilac ('03)	4.00	2.25
49	A4	80r violet	8.50	3.50
50	A4	100r dk blue, *blue*	3.50	2.00
51	A4	115r org brn, *pink* ('03)	15.00	*10.00*
52	A4	130r brown, *straw* ('03)	15.00	*10.00*
53	A4	150r brown, *straw*	10.00	5.50
54	A4	200r red vio, *pnksh*	4.50	3.00
55	A4	300r dk blue, *rose*	10.00	5.00
56	A4	400r dull blue, *straw* ('03)	15.00	10.00
57	A4	500r blk & red, *blue* ('01)	15.00	5.00
58	A4	700r violet, *yelsh* ('01)	30.00	17.50
		Nos. 36-58 (23)	197.70	112.95

For overprints and suecharges see Nos. 80-99, 139, 200.

Regular Issues Surcharged in Red or Black

Two spacing types of surcharge. See note above Angola No. 61.

On Issue of 1886

1902, Dec. 1 ***Perf. 12½, 13½***

No.	Design	Description	Unused	Used
59	A2	65r on 5r black (R)	7.00	3.75
60	A2	65r on 200r gray lil	7.00	3.75
61	A2	65r on 300r orange	7.00	3.75
62	A2	115r on 10r green	7.00	3.75
63	A2	115r on 20r rose	7.00	3.75
a.		Perf 13½	60.00	35.00
64	A2	130r on 50r blue	7.00	3.75
65	A2	130r on 100r brown	7.00	3.75
66	A2	400r on 25r violet	6.00	2.60
67	A2	400r on 40r choc	12.00	3.75
a.		Perf 13½	50.00	35.00

On Issue of 1894

Perf. 11½, 12½, 13½

No.	Design	Description	Unused	Used
68	A3	65r on 10r red vio	7.00	3.75
69	A3	65r on 20r lavender	7.00	3.75
70	A3	65r on 100r brn, *buff*	8.50	5.25
a.		Perf 12½	26.00	24.00
71	A3	115r on 5r orange	5.00	3.00
a.		Inverted surcharge	60.00	60.00
72	A3	115r on 25r blue grn	4.00	2.10
a.		Perf 11½	55.00	55.00
73	A3	115r on 150r car, *rose*	9.00	6.50
a.		Perf 13½	55.00	25.00
74	A3	130r on 75r car	5.00	3.00
a.		Perf 13½	*250.00*	*200.00*
75	A3	130r on 80r yel grn	4.00	2.00
76	A3	130r on 200r dk blue, *blue*	4.00	2.60
77	A3	400r on 50r lt blue	9.00	3.00
a.		Inverted surcharge	65.00	55.00
b.		Perf 13½	*300.00*	*300.00*
78	A3	400r on 300r dk blue, *sal*	4.00	1.75

On Newspaper Stamp of 1893

No.	Design	Description	Unused	Used
79	N1	400r on 2½r brown	1.60	1.50
a.		Inverted surcharge	30.00	
b.		Perf 12½	*225.00*	*200.00*
		Nos. 59-79 (21)	135.10	70.80

Reprints of Nos. 59, 66, 67, and 77 have shiny white gum and clean-cut perforation 13½.

For overprint and surcharge see Nos. 137, 205-206.

Overprinted in Black On Nos. 39, 42, 44, 47

1902-03 ***Perf. 11½***

No.	Design	Description	Unused	Used
80	A4	15r brown	2.00	1.25
81	A4	25r sea green	2.00	1.25
82	A4	50r blue ('03)	2.00	1.25
83	A4	75r rose ('03)	3.75	2.75
a.		Inverted overprint	42.50	42.50
		Nos. 80-83 (4)	9.75	6.50

For overprint see No. 139.

No. 46 Surcharged in Black

1905, July 1

No.	Design	Description	Unused	Used
84	A4	50r on 65r slate blue	5.00	3.00

Stamps of 1898-1903 Overprinted in Carmine or Green

1911, Aug. 20

No.	Design	Description	Unused	Used
85	A4	2½r gray	.25	.25
86	A4	5r orange	.25	.25
87	A4	10r lt green	1.00	.80
88	A4	15r gray green	.90	.45
89	A4	20r gray violet	1.50	.80
90	A4	25r carmine (G)	.90	.45
91	A4	50r brown	8.50	6.00
92	A4	75r red lilac	1.40	.80
93	A4	100r dk blue, *blue*	1.40	.80
94	A4	115r org brn, *pink*	1.40	.80
95	A4	130r brown, *straw*	1.40	.80
96	A4	200r red vio, *pnksh*	6.50	4.00
97	A4	400r dull bl, *straw*	3.50	1.25
98	A4	500r blk & red, *bl*	3.50	1.25
99	A4	700r violet, *straw*	3.50	1.40
		Nos. 85-99 (15)	35.90	20.10

King Manuel II — A5

Overprinted in Carmine or Green

1912 ***Perf. 11½x12***

No.	Design	Description	Unused	Used
100	A5	2½r violet	.25	.25
101	A5	5r black	.25	.25
102	A5	10r gray grn	.45	.40
103	A5	20r carmine (G)	2.40	1.40
104	A5	25r vio brown	.45	.25
105	A5	50r dk blue	5.00	3.50
106	A5	75r bister brn	1.10	1.00
107	A5	100r brown, *lt grn*	1.10	1.00
108	A5	200r dk green, *sal*	1.75	1.10
109	A5	300r black, *azure*	1.75	1.10

Perf. 14½x15

No.	Design	Description	Unused	Used
110	A5	400r black & blue	3.75	3.00
111	A5	500r ol grn & vio brn	3.75	3.00
		Nos. 100-111 (12)	22.00	16.25

Common Design Types pictured following the introduction.

Vasco da Gama Issue of Various Portuguese Colonies

Common Design Types CD20-CD27 Surcharged

On Stamps of Macao

1913, Feb. 13 ***Perf. 12½ to 16***

No.	Description	Unused	Used
112	¼c on ½a blue grn	1.50	.85
113	½c on 1a red	1.50	.85
114	1c on 2a red violet	1.50	.85
115	2½c on 4a yel grn	1.50	.85
116	5c on 8a dk blue	7.00	6.00
117	7½c on 12a vio brn	5.75	2.40
118	10c on 16a bister brn	2.25	1.60
119	15c on 24a bister	5.75	3.50
	Nos. 112-119 (8)	26.75	16.90

On Stamps of Portuguese Africa
Perf. 14 to 15

No.	Description	Unused	Used
120	¼c on 2½r bl grn	1.50	.60
121	½c on 5r red	1.50	.60
122	1c on 10r red vio	1.50	.60
123	2½c on 25r yel grn	1.50	.60
124	5c on 50r dk blue	1.50	1.50
125	7½c on 75r vio brn	3.75	3.00
126	10c on 100r bis brn	2.00	1.90
127	15c on 150r bister	2.50	2.50
	Nos. 120-127 (8)	15.75	11.30

On Stamps of Timor

No.	Description	Unused	Used
128	¼c on ½a bl grn	1.50	.85
129	½c on 1a red	1.50	.85
130	1c on 2a red vio	1.50	.85
131	2½c on 4a yel grn	1.50	.85
132	5c on 8a dk blue	7.00	5.50
133	7½c On 12a vio brn	5.50	3.00
134	10c on 16a bis brn	2.25	1.90
135	15c on 24a bister	6.00	2.40
	Nos. 128-135 (8)	26.75	16.20
	Nos. 112-135 (24)	*69.25*	*44.40*

For surcharges see Nos. 197-198.

No. 75 Overprinted in Red

1913 ***Perf. 11½, 12½, 13½***

No.	Design	Description	Unused	Used
137	A3	130r on 80r yel grn	6.00	3.75

Nos. 73 and 76 overprinted but not issued. Values, $20, $25.

Same Overprint on No. 83 in Green

1914 ***Perf. 12***

No.	Design	Description	Unused	Used
139	A4	75r rose	6.00	3.75
a.		"PROVISORIO" double (G and R)	80.00	57.50

Ceres — A6

1914 Typo. *Perf. 15x14*
Name and Value in Black
Chalky Paper

144 A6 ¼c olive brn .75 .55
145 A6 ½c black .75 .55
146 A6 1c blue grn .75 .55
147 A6 1½c lilac brown .75 .55
148 A6 2c carmine 1.25 .70
149 A6 2½c lt violet .60 .50
150 A6 5c deep blue 1.00 .80
151 A6 7½c yel brn 1.25 .70
152 A6 8c slate 1.25 .75
153 A6 10c orange brn 2.00 .90
154 A6 15c brn rose ('22) 9.50 5.50
155 A6 20c yel grn 2.00 .90
156 A6 30c brown, *grn* 5.00 3.00
157 A6 40c brown, *pink* 3.00 2.50
158 A6 50c orange, *sal* 3.50 2.50
159 A6 1e green, *blue* 3.50 3.00
Nos. 144-159 (16) 36.85 23.95

1916
Enamel-Surfaced Paper

160 A6 ¼c olive brn .45 .30
161 A6 5c deep blue .75 .45

Ordinary Paper

162 A6 ¼c olive brn .35 .30
163 A6 ½c black .35 .30
164 A6 1c blue grn 5.00 .25
165 A6 1c yel grn ('22) .45 .30
166 A6 1½c lilac brown .45 .30
167 A6 2c carmine .45 .30
168 A6 2½c lt violet .35 .30
169 A6 3c org ('22) .45 .30
170 A6 4c rose ('22) .45 .30
171 A6 12c blue grn ('22) 1.00 .70
172 A6 15c plum 2.50 2.00
Nos. 162-172 (11) 11.80 5.35

1920-26 *Perf. 12x11½*

173 A6 ¼c olive brn .35 .30
174 A6 ½c black .35 .30
175 A6 1c yel grn ('22) .35 .30
176 A6 1½c lilac brown .35 .30
177 A6 2c carmine .35 .30
178 A6 2c gray ('26) .35 .30
179 A6 2½c lt violet .45 .35
180 A6 3c org ('22) 2.40 2.25
181 A6 4c rose ('22) .50 .35
182 A6 4½c gray ('22) .50 .35
183 A6 5c brt blue ('22) .50 .35
183A A6 6c lilac ('22) .50 .35
183B A6 7c ultra ('22) .50 .35
183C A6 7½c yel brn .50 .35
183D A6 8c slate .65 .50
183E A6 10c orange brn .45 .35
183F A6 12c blue grn ('22) 1.00 .70
183G A6 15c plum .45 .35
183H A6 20c yel grn .45 .35
183I A6 24c ultra ('26) 1.50 1.40
183J A6 25c choc ('26) 1.50 1.40
183K A6 30c gray grn ('22) .75 .25
183L A6 40c turq blue ('22) .75 .25
183M A6 50c violet ('26) 1.00 .60
183N A6 60c dk blue ('22) 1.50 .85
183O A6 60c rose ('26) 1.75 .70
183P A6 80c brt rose ('22) 4.00 1.25
Nos. 173-183P (27) 23.70 15.45

For surcharge see No. 214.

Glazed Paper

183Q A6 1e rose ('22) 6.00 2.50
183R A6 1e dp blue ('26) 6.00 3.50
183S A6 2e dk violet ('22) 6.00 2.50
183T A6 5e buff ('26) 12.00 7.00
183U A6 10e pink ('26) 150.00 60.00
183V A6 20e pale turq ('26) 200.00 80.00
Nos. 183Q-183V (6) 380.00 155.50

Provisional Issue of 1902 Overprinted in Carmine

1915 *Perf. 11½, 12½, 13½*

184 A2 115r on 10r green (11½) 2.50 2.00
a. Perf. 13½ 140.00 140.00
185 A2 115r on 20r rose (12½) 2.75 1.75
a. Perf. 13½ 35.00 30.00
186 A2 130r on 50r blue (12½) 2.50 1.25
187 A2 130r on 100r brown (12½) 1.60 1.00
188 A3 115r on 5r org (11½) 1.40 .75
a. Inverted overprint 45.00
189 A3 115r on 25r blue grn (12½) 2.50 1.75
a. Perf. 11½ 70.00 70.00
190 A3 115r on 150r car, *rose* (11½) 1.25 .75
191 A3 130r on 75r car (12½) 2.50 1.00
192 A3 130r on 80r yel grn (11½) 2.50 1.00
a. Inverted overprint 60.00 50.00
193 A3 130r on 200r bl, *bl* (13½) 2.00 1.00
a. Perf. 12½ 125.00 100.00
Nos. 184-193 (10) 21.50 12.25

War Tax Stamps of Portuguese Africa Srchd.

1921, Feb. 3 *Perf. 15x14*

194 WT1 ¼c on 1c green .60 .40
195 WT1 ½c on 1c green .70 .50
a. "1/2" instead of "½" as shown 17.50 15.00
196 WT1 1c green .65 .50

Perf. 12x11½

194B WT1 ¼c on 1c green 1.20 1.00
195B WT1 ½c on 1c green 1.20 1.00
a. "1/2" instead of "½" as shown 25.00 19.00
196B WT1 1c green 1.10 .95

Nos. 194B-196B also exist on enameled paper. The values are the same.

Nos. 127 and 126 Surcharged

Perf. 14 to 15

197 CD27 2c on 15c on 150r 2.25 1.50
198 CD26 4c on 10c on 100r 2.75 2.60
a. On No. 118 (error) 300.00 175.00

The 4c surcharge also exists on No. 134. Value, $500.

No. 50 Surcharged

Perf. 12

200 A4 6c on 100r dk bl, *bl* 3.00 2.25
a. No accent on "U" of surcharge 17.50 15.00
Nos. 194-200 (6) 9.95 7.75

No. 200 has an accent on the "U" of the surcharge.

Stamps of 1913-15 Surcharged

1922, Apr. *Perf. 11½, 12½, 13½*
On No. 137

201 A3 4c on 130r on 80r 1.25 1.25

On Nos. 191-193

202 A3 4c on 130r on 75r 1.60 1.60
203 A3 4c on 130r on 80r 1.25 1.25
204 A3 4c on 130r on 200r 1.00 .80
a. Perf. 12½ 17.50 15.00
Nos. 201-204 (4) 5.10 4.90

Surcharge of Nos. 201-204 with smaller $ occurs once in sheet of 28. Value eight times normal.

Nos. 78-79 Surcharged

1925 *Perf. 13½, 11½*

205 A3 40c on 400r on 300r 1.50 .80
206 N1 40c on 400r on 2½r 1.50 .75

No. 176 Surcharged

1931, Nov. *Perf. 12x11½*

214 A6 70c on 80c brt rose 12.00 5.00

Ceres — A7

1934, May 1 Wmk. 232

215 A7 1c bister .25 .25
216 A7 5c olive brown .25 .25
217 A7 10c violet .25 .25
218 A7 15c black .25 .25
219 A7 20c gray .25 .25
220 A7 30c dk green .25 .25
221 A7 40c red org .25 .25
222 A7 45c brt blue 1.25 .70
223 A7 50c brown .65 .45
224 A7 60c olive grn .65 .45
225 A7 70c brown org .65 .45
226 A7 80c emerald .65 .45
227 A7 85c deep rose 3.00 2.00
228 A7 1e maroon 2.00 .40
229 A7 1.40e dk blue 2.50 2.50
230 A7 2e dk violet 3.50 2.00
231 A7 5e apple green 15.00 4.50
232 A7 10e olive bister 25.00 15.00
233 A7 20e orange 40.00 20.00
Nos. 215-233 (19) 96.60 50.65

For surcharge see No. 256.

Vasco da Gama Issue
Common Design Types

1938 Unwmk. *Perf. 13½x13*
Name and Value in Black

234 CD34 1c gray green .25 .25
235 CD34 5c orange brn .25 .25
236 CD34 10c dk carmine .25 .25
237 CD34 15c dk vio brn .75 .60
238 CD34 20c slate .35 .25
239 CD35 30c rose vio .35 .25
240 CD35 35c brt green .35 .25
241 CD35 40c brown .35 .25
242 CD35 50c brt red vio .35 .25
243 CD36 60c gray blk .35 .25
244 CD36 70c brown vio .35 .25
245 CD36 80c orange .35 .25
246 CD36 1e red .50 .25
247 CD37 1.75e blue 1.40 .55
248 CD37 2e dk blue grn 2.50 1.60
249 CD37 5e ol grn 6.00 1.10
250 CD38 10e blue vio 10.00 1.25
251 CD38 20e red brown 32.50 4.00
Nos. 234-251 (18) 57.20 12.10

For surcharges see Nos. 255, 271-276, 288-292.

Outline Map of Africa — A8

1939, June 23 Litho. *Perf. 11½x12*

252 A8 80c vio, *pale rose* 4.50 2.50
253 A8 1.75e blue, *pale bl* 32.50 25.00
254 A8 20e brown, *buff* 70.00 30.00
Nos. 252-254 (3) 107.00 57.50

Visit of the President of Portugal in 1939.

Nos. 239 and 221 Surcharged with New Value and Bars in Black

1948 Unwmk. *Perf. 13½x13*

255 CD35 10c on 30c rose violet 2.00 1.25

Perf. 12x11½
Wmk. 232

256 A7 25c on 40c red orange 2.00 1.25

Machado Pt., Sao Vicente — A9

Brava Creek, Sao Nicoláo — A10

Designs: 10c, Ribeira Grande. 1e, Harbor, Sao Vicente. 1.75e, Mindelo, distant view. 2e, Joao de Evora Beach. 5e, Mindelo. 10e, Volcano, Fire Island. 20e, Mt. Paul.

Perf. 14½
1948, Oct. 1 Litho. Unwmk.

257 A9 5c vio brn & bis .35 .30
258 A9 10c ol grn & pale grn .35 .30
259 A10 50c mag & lil rose .65 .30
260 A10 1e brn vio & rose lil 2.00 1.25
261 A10 1.75e ultra & grnsh bl 3.00 2.25
262 A10 2e dk brn & buff 6.00 2.00
263 A10 5e ol grn & yel 12.00 5.00
264 A10 10e red & cream 22.50 16.00
265 A10 20e dk vio & bis 50.00 32.00
Nos. 257-265 (9) 96.85 59.40

Lady of Fatima Issue
Common Design Type

1948, Dec.

266 CD40 50c dark blue 8.50 4.50

UPU Symbols — A10a

1949, Oct. *Perf. 14*

267 A10a 1e red vio & pink 7.00 3.00

UPU, 75th anniversary.

Catalogue values for unused stamps in this section, from this point to the end of the section, are for Never Hinged items.

Holy Year Issue
Common Design Types

1950, May *Perf. 13x13½*

268 CD41 1e orange brown 1.00 .75
269 CD42 2e slate 4.50 2.75

Holy Year Conclusion Issue
Common Design Type

1951, Oct. Unwmk. *Perf. 14*

270 CD43 2e pur & lil + label 1.50 1.25

Stamps without labels sell for less.

Nos. 240, 244-245, 247, 250 Surcharged with New Value and Bars

Perf. 13½x13
1951, May 21 Unwmk.

271 CD35 10c on 35c .70 .55
272 CD36 20c on 70c .90 .65
273 CD36 40c on 70c 1.10 .65
274 CD36 50c on 80c 1.10 .65
275 CD37 1e on 1.75e 1.25 .65
276 CD38 2e on 10e 5.75 2.00
a. 1e on 10e 250.00 125.00
Nos. 271-276 (6) 10.80 5.15

Map of Cape Verde Islands, 1502 A11

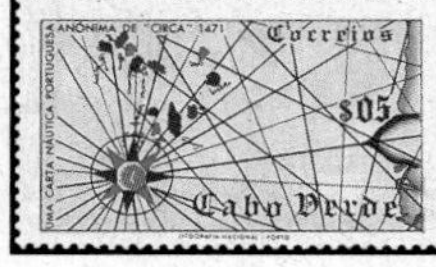

Vicente Dias and Gonçalo de Cintra A12

Portraits: 30c, Diogo Alfonso and Alvaro Fernandes. 50c, Lançarote and Soeiro da Costa. 1e, Diogo Gomes and Antonio da Nola. 2e, Prince Fernando and Prince Henry the Navigator. 3e, Antao Gonçalves and Dinis Dias. 5e, Alfonso Goncalves Baldaia and Joao Fernandes. 10e, Dinis Eanes da Gra and Alvaro de Freitas. 20e, Map of Cape Verde Islands, 1502.

1952, Feb. 24 *Perf. 14*

277	A11	5c	multicolored	.25	.25
278	A12	10c	multicolored	.25	.25
279	A12	30c	multicolored	.25	.25
280	A12	50c	multicolored	.25	.25
281	A12	1e	multicolored	.25	.25
282	A12	2e	multicolored	1.50	.25
283	A12	3e	multicolored	11.50	1.50
284	A12	5e	multicolored	4.00	.70
285	A12	10e	multicolored	8.00	1.75
286	A11	20e	multicolored	14.00	2.40
			Nos. 277-286 (10)	40.25	7.85

Medical Congress Issue
Common Design Type

Design: Hypodermic Injection.

1952, June *Perf. 13½*

287	CD44	20c	ol grn & dk brn	.75	.60

No. 247 Surcharged with New Values and "X" in Black

1952, Jan. 25 *Perf. 13½x13*

288	CD37	10c	on 1.75e	2.00	1.10
289	CD37	20c	on 1.75e	2.00	1.10
290	CD37	50c	on 1.75e	8.00	5.00
291	CD37	1e	on 1.75e	1.50	.25
292	CD37	1.50e	on 1.75e	1.50	.25
			Nos. 288-292 (5)	15.00	7.70

Facade of Jeronymos Convent A13

Perf. 13½

1953, Jan. **Unwmk.** **Litho.**

293	A13	10c	brown & pale olive	.25	.25
294	A13	50c	purple & fawn	.90	.40
295	A13	1e	dark green & fawn	2.10	1.10
			Nos. 293-295 (3)	3.25	1.75

Exhibition of Sacred Missionary Art held at Lisbon in 1951.

Stamp of Portugal and Arms of Colonies — A13a

1953 **Photo.**

296	A13a	50c	multicolored	1.75	1.10

Centenary of Portuguese stamps.

Sao Paulo Issue
Common Design Type

1954 **Litho.** *Perf. 13½*

297	CD46	1e	green, cream & gray	.70	.60

Belem Tower, Lisbon, and Colonial Arms — A14

1955, May 15 **Litho.** *Perf. 13½*

298	A14	1e	multicolored	.50	.25
299	A14	1.60e	buff & multi	.75	.60

Visit of Pres. Francisco H. C. Lopes.

Arms of Praia — A15

1958, June 14 *Perf. 12x11½*

300	A15	1e	multicolored	.65	.45
301	A15	2.50e	pink & multi	1.10	.90

Centenary of city of Praia.

Fair Emblem, Globe and Arms — A15a

1958 *Perf. 12x11½*

302	A15a	2e	multicolored	.90	.40

World's Fair, Brussels, Apr. 17-Oct. 19.

Tropical Medicine Congress Issue
Common Design Type

1958, Sept. 5 *Perf. 13½*

303	CD47	3e	Aloe vera	5.50	2.10

Prince Henry — A16

1960, June 25 **Litho.** *Perf. 13½*

304	A16	2e	multicolored	.50	.25

500th anniv. of the death of Prince Henry the Navigator.

Antonio da Nola — A17

Design: 2.50e, Diogo Gomes.

1960, Oct. **Unwmk.** *Perf. 14½*

305	A17	1e	multicolored	.75	.45
306	A17	2.50e	multicolored	2.50	1.00

Discovery of Cape Verde, 500th anniv.

School Children A18

1960

307	A18	2.50e	multicolored	1.25	.65

10th anniv. of the Commission for Technical Cooperation in Africa South of the Sahara (C.C.T.A.).

Arms of Praia — A19

Arms of various cities & towns of Cape Verde.

1961, July **Litho.** *Perf. 13½*

308	A19	5c	shown	.25	.25
309	A19	15c	Nova Sintra	.25	.25
310	A19	20c	Ribeira Brava	.25	.25
311	A19	30c	Assomada	.25	.25
312	A19	1e	Maio	.65	.25
313	A19	2e	Mindelo	.65	.25
314	A19	2.50e	Santa Maria	1.00	.25
315	A19	3e	Pombas	2.00	.50
316	A19	5e	Sal-Rei	2.00	.50
317	A19	7.50e	Tarrafal	3.00	.90
318	A19	15e	Maria Pia	5.00	.90
319	A19	30e	San Felipe	9.00	2.50
			Nos. 308-319 (12)	24.30	7.05

Sports Issue
Common Design Type

Sports: 50c, Javelin. 1e, Discus. 1.50e, Cricket. 2.50e, Boxing. 4.50e, Hurdling. 12.50e, Golf.

1962, Jan. 18 *Perf. 13½*

320	CD48	50c	lt brown	.25	.25
321	CD48	1e	lt green	.75	.25
322	CD48	1.50e	lt blue grn	10.00	2.00
323	CD48	2.50e	pale vio bl	.75	.35
324	CD48	4.50e	orange	1.10	.75
325	CD48	12.50e	beige	2.40	1.60
			Nos. 320-325 (6)	15.25	5.20

Anti-Malaria Issue
Common Design Type

Design: Anopheles pretoriensis.

1962 **Litho.** *Perf. 13½*

326	CD49	2.50e	multicolored	1.40	.90

Airline Anniversary Issue
Common Design Type

1963, Oct. **Unwmk.** *Perf. 14½*

327	CD50	2.50e	gray & multi	1.10	.70

National Overseas Bank Issue
Common Design Type

Design: 1.50e, Jose da Silva Mendes Leal.

1964, May 16 *Perf. 13½*

328	CD51	1.50e	multicolored	1.10	.75

ITU Issue
Common Design Type

1965, May 17 **Litho.** *Perf. 14½*

329	CD52	2.50e	buff & multi	2.10	1.40

Militia Drummer, 1806 — A20

Designs: 1e, Soldier, Militia, 1806. 1.50e, Grenadier officer, 1833. 2.50e, Grenadier, 1833. 3e, Cavalry officer, 1834. 4e, Grenadier, 1835. 5e, Artillery officer, 1848. 10e, Drum major, infantry, 1856.

1965, Dec. 1 **Litho.** *Perf. 14½*

330	A20	50c	multicolored	.25	.25
331	A20	1e	multicolored	.45	.25
332	A20	1.50e	multicolored	.45	.40
333	A20	2.50e	multicolored	1.25	.35
334	A20	3e	multicolored	2.50	.55
335	A20	4e	multicolored	1.10	.55
336	A20	5e	multicolored	1.25	.55
337	A20	10e	multicolored	2.75	1.75
			Nos. 330-337 (8)	10.00	4.65

National Revolution Issue
Common Design Type

1e, Dr. Adriano Moreira School & Health Center.

1966, May 28 **Litho.** *Perf. 12*

338	CD53	1e	multicolored	.60	.45

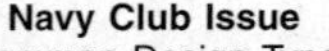

Navy Club Issue
Common Design Type

Designs: 1e, Capt. Fontoura da Costa and gunboat Mandovy. 1.50e, Capt. Carvalho Araujo and minesweeper Augusto Castilho.

1967, Jan. 31 **Litho.** *Perf. 13*

339	CD54	1e	multicolored	.75	.50
340	CD54	1.50e	multicolored	1.25	.90

Virgin Mary Statue — A21

1967, May 13 **Litho.** *Perf. 12½x13*

341	A21	1e	multicolored	.50	.25

50th anniv. of the apparition of the Virgin Mary to 3 shepherd children at Fatima.

Pres. Rodrigues Thomaz — A22

1968, Feb. 9 **Litho.** *Perf. 13½*

342	A22	1e	multicolored	.50	.25

Issued to commemorate the 1968 visit of Pres. Americo de Deus Rodrigues Thomaz.

Cabral Issue

Pedro Alvares Cabral — A23

1e, Cantino's world map, 1502, horiz.

1968, Apr. 22 **Litho.** *Perf. 14*

343	A23	1e	multicolored	.85	.70
344	A23	1.50e	multicolored	1.40	.75

See note after Angola No. 545.
For overprint see No. 365.

Sao Vicente Harbor — A24

Physic Nut — A25

Designs: 1.50e, Peanut plant. 2.50e, Castor-oil plant. 3.50e, Yams. 4e, Date palm. 4.50e, Guavas. 5e, Tamarind. 10e, Bitter cassava. 30e, Woman carrying fruit baskets.

1968, Oct. 15 **Litho.** *Perf. 14*

345	A24	50c	multicolored	.25	.25
346	A25	1e	multicolored	.50	.25
347	A25	1.50e	multicolored	.50	.25
348	A25	2.50e	multicolored	.50	.25
349	A25	3.50e	multicolored	.50	.25
350	A25	4e	multicolored	.50	.25
351	A25	4.50e	multicolored	1.00	.25
352	A25	5	multicolored	2.00	.30
353	A25	10e	multicolored	2.00	.60
354	A25	30e	multicolored	4.00	2.50
			Nos. 345-354 (10)	11.75	5.15

For overprint see No. 372.

Admiral Coutinho Issue

Common Design Type

Adm. Coutinho & map showing route of 1st flight from Lisbon to Rio de Janeiro.

1969, Feb. 17 Litho. *Perf. 14*
355 CD55 30c multi, vert. .50 .25

For surcharge see No. 388.

Vasco da Gama Issue

Vasco da Gama — A26

1969, Aug. 29 Litho. *Perf. 14*
356 A26 1.50e multicolored .50 .25

Vasco da Gama (1469-1524), navigator.

Administration Reform Issue

Common Design Type

1969, Sept. 25 Litho. *Perf. 14*
357 CD56 2e multicolored .50 .25

King Manuel I Issue

King Manuel I — A27

1969, Dec. 1 Litho. *Perf. 14*
358 A27 3e multicolored .55 .35

500th anniv. of the birth of King Manuel I.

Marshal Carmona Issue

Common Design Type

Design: 2.50e, Antonio Oscar Carmona in marshal's uniform.

1970, Nov. 15 Litho. *Perf. 14*
359 CD57 2.50e multi .55 .35

Galleons on Sanaga River — A28

1972, May 25 Litho. *Perf. 13*
360 A28 5e lilac rose & multi 1.00 .30

4th centenary of the publication of The Lusiads by Luiz Camoens.

Olympic Games Issue

Common Design Type

4e, Basketball & boxing, Olympic emblem.

1972, June 20 *Perf. 14x13½*
361 CD59 4e multicolored .85 .30

For surcharge see No. 371.

Lisbon-Rio de Janeiro Flight Issue

Common Design Type

Design: "Lusitania" landing at San Vicente.

1972, Sept. 20 Litho. *Perf. 13½*
362 CD60 3.50e multi 1.50 .30

WMO Centenary Issue

Common Design Type

1973, Dec. 15 Litho. *Perf. 13*
363 CD61 2.50e ultra & multi .65 .30

For overprint see No. 387.

Mindelo Desalination Plant — A29

1974 Litho. *Perf. 13½*
364 A29 4e multicolored 1.25 .85

Opening of the Mindelo desalination plant. For surcharge see No. 371A.

Republic

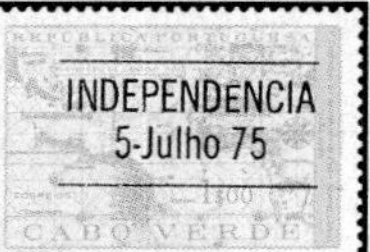

No. 343 Overprinted

1975, Dec. 19 Litho. *Perf. 14*
365 A23 1e multicolored .35 .25

Proclamation of Independence.

Amilcar Cabral, Flag and Crowd — A30

1976, Jan. 20
366 A30 5e multicolored .55 .25

3rd anniv. of the assassination of Amilcar Cabral (1924-73), revolutionary leader.

Rising Sun, Coat of Arms, Liberated People — A31

1976, July 5 Litho. *Perf. 14*
367 A31 50c multicolored .25 .25
368 A31 3e multicolored .90 .25
369 A31 15e multicolored 2.00 .35
370 A31 50e multicolored 6.25 1.25
a. Miniature sheet, #367-370 *15.00 15.00*
Nos. 367-370 (4) 9.40 2.10

First anniversary of independence.

Nos. 351, 361, 364 Overprinted

1976 Litho. *Perf. 14*
371 CD59 4e multi *1,150.* —
371A A29 4e multi *50.00 27.50*
372 A25 4.50e multi 4.25 2.25

Amilcar Cabral, Map and Flag of Cape Verde A32

1976, Sept. 19 *Perf. 14*
373 A32 1e multicolored .45 .25

Party of Intl. Action (PAICC), 20th anniv.

Electronic Tree and ITU Emblem — A33

1977, May 17 Litho. *Perf. 13½x13*
374 A33 5.50e multi .45 .25

World Telecommunications Day.

Ashtray — A34

Carved Coconut Shells: 30c, Bell on stand. 50c, Lamp with Adam and Eve. 1e, Hollow shell with Nativity. 1.50e, Desk lamp. 5e, Jar. 10e, Jar with hinged cover. 20e, Tobacco jar with palms. 30e, Stringed instrument.

1977, July 5 Litho. *Perf. 14*
375 A34 20c lilac & multi .25 .25
376 A34 30c rose & multi .25 .25
377 A34 50c salmon & multi .25 .25
378 A34 1e lt green & multi .35 .25
379 A34 1.50e orange yel & multi .35 .25
380 A34 5e gray & multi .75 .35
381 A34 10e lt blue & multi 1.25 .55
382 A34 20e yellow & multi 2.00 1.25
383 A34 30e rose lilac & multi 3.25 1.40
Nos. 375-383 (9) 8.70 4.80

Cape Verde No. 1 and Coat of Arms — A35

1977, Sept. 12 Litho. *Perf. 13½*
384 A35 4e blue & multi .40 .25
385 A35 8e lilac & multi .80 .35

Centenary of Cape Verde stamps.

Congress Emblem — A36

1977, Nov. 15 *Perf. 14*
386 A36 3.50e multi .60 .25

African Party of Independence of Guinea-Bissau and Cape Verde (PAIGC), 3rd cong., Nov. 15-20.

No. 363 Overprinted

1978, May 1 *Perf. 12*
387 CD61 2.50e ultra & multi .60 .25

No. 355 Surcharged

1978, May 1 *Perf. 14*
388 CD55 3e on 30c multi 2.25 .35

Antenna and ITU Emblem — A37

1978, May 17 Litho. *Perf. 14*
389 A37 3.50e silver & multi .55 .25

10th World Telecommunications Day.

Freighter Cabo Verde — A38

1978, June 25 Litho. *Perf. 14*
391 A38 1e multicolored .70 .25

First ship of Cape Verde merchant marine.

Map of Africa and Equality Emblem — A39

1978, June 21
392 A39 4.50e multicolored .75 .25

Anti-Apartheid Year.

Human Rights Emblem — A40

1978, Dec. 10 Litho. *Perf. 14*
393 A40 1.50e multicolored .35 .25
394 A40 2e multicolored .55 .35

Universal Declaration of Human Rights, 30th anniversary.

Children and Balloons, IYC Emblem — A41

IYC Emblem and Child's Drawing: 3.50e, Children and flowers.

1979, June 1 **Litho.** ***Perf. 14***
395 A41 1.50e multi .65 .25
396 A41 3.50e multi 1.10 .35

International Year of the Child.

Pindjiguiti Massacre Monument — A42

1979, Aug. 3 ***Perf. 13***
397 A42 4.50e multi 3.00 .25

Massacre of Pindjiguiti, 20th anniversary.

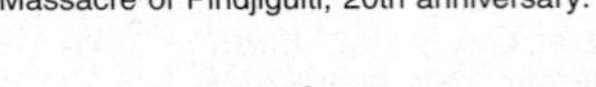

Natl. Youth Week — A42a

1979, Sept. 1 **Litho.** ***Perf. 14***
397A A42a 3.50e Poster 1.25 .25

Centenary of Mindelo — A43

1980, Apr. 23 **Litho.** ***Perf. 12½***
398 A43 4e multicolored .70 .25

Flag of Cape Verde — A44

Stylized Bird, "V" — A45

1980 **Litho.** ***Perf. 12½***
399 A44 4e multicolored 1.25 .25
400 A45 4e multicolored .45 .25
401 A45 7e multicolored .80 .35
402 A45 11e multicolored 1.10 .45
Nos. 399-402 (4) 3.60 1.30

5th anniversary of independence.
Issued: No. 399, June 1; others July 5.

A45a

1980, May 13
402A A45a 3.50e multi .55 .25
402B A45a 4.50e multi .70 .25

1980 Natl. census.

A46

1980, June 6
403 A46 1e Running .25 .25
404 A46 2.50e Boxing .25 .25
405 A46 3e Basketball .35 .25
406 A46 4e Volleyball .50 .30
407 A46 20e Swimming 1.40 .90
408 A46 50e Tennis 4.00 1.75
Nos. 403-408 (6) 6.75 3.70

Souvenir Sheet

Perf. 13

409 A46 30e Soccer, horiz. *18.00 18.00*

22nd Summer Olympic Games, Moscow, July 19-Aug. 3.

Thunnus Alalunga A47

4.50e, Trachurus trachurus. 8e, Muraena helena. 10e, Corvina nigra. 12e, Katsuwonus pelamis. 50e, Prionace glauca.

1980, Nov. 11 **Litho.** ***Perf. 13***
410 A47 50c shown .25 .25
411 A47 4.50e multicolored .50 .25
412 A47 8e multicolored .90 .25
413 A47 10e multicolored 1.50 .35
414 A47 12e multicolored 2.00 .60
415 A47 50e multicolored 5.00 1.90
Nos. 410-415 (6) 10.15 3.60

Lochnera Rosea — A48

4.50e, Poinciana regia-bojer. 8e, Mirabilis jalapa. 10e, Nerium oleander. 12e, Bougainvillia litoralis. 30e, Hibiscus.

1980, Dec. 29
416 A48 50c shown .25 .25
417 A48 4.50e multicolored .30 .25
418 A48 8e multicolored .75 .35
419 A48 10e multicolored .95 .45
420 A48 12e multicolored 1.10 .55
421 A48 30e multicolored 2.60 1.50
Nos. 416-421 (6) 5.95 3.35

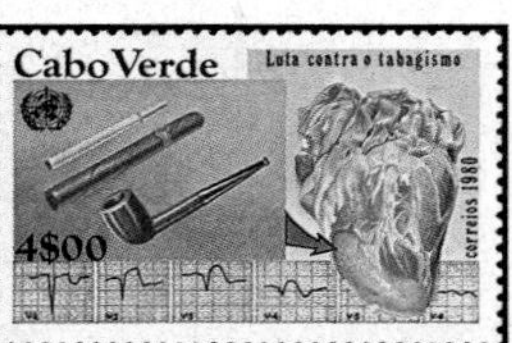

WHO Anti-smoking Campaign — A48a

1980, Sept. 19 ***Perf. 12½***
421A A48a 4e multicolored .50 .25
421B A48a 7e multicolored 1.10 .35

Arca Verde A49

1980, Nov. 30 **Litho.** ***Perf. 12½x12***
422 A49 3e shown .30 .25
423 A49 5.50e Ilha do Maio .50 .25
424 A49 7.50e Ilha de Komo .95 .55
425 A49 9e Boa Vista 1.25 .75
426 A49 12e Santo Antao 1.40 .55
427 A49 30e Santiago 3.25 1.40
Nos. 422-427 (6) 7.65 3.75

Hand-woven Bag, Map — A49a

Various hand-woven articles. 10e, vert.

1978, May 21 **Litho.** ***Perf. 14***
427A A49a 50c multi .25 .25
427B A49a 1.50e multi .25 .25
427C A49a 2e multi .55 .25
427D A49a 3e multi .55 .30
427E A49a 10e multi 1.40 .70
Nos. 427A-427E (5) 3.00 1.75

Desert Erosion Prevention Campaign — A50

1981, Mar. 30 **Litho.** ***Perf. 13***
428 A50 4.50e multi .60 .25
429 A50 10.50e multi 1.25 .50

6th Anniv. of Constitution A51

1981, Apr. 15
430 A51 4.50e multicolored .60 .25

Souvenir Sheet

Austria No. B336 — A52

1981, May 18
431 A52 50e multicolored 6.50 6.50

WIPA '81 Philatelic Exhibition, Vienna, Austria, May 22-31.

Antenna — A53

1981, Aug. 25 **Litho.** ***Perf. 12½***
432 A53 4.50e shown .65 .25
433 A53 8e Dish antenna .95 .40
434 A53 20e Dish antenna, diff. 2.00 .95
Nos. 432-434 (3) 3.60 1.60

Intl. Year of the Disabled A54

1981, Dec. 25 **Litho.** ***Perf. 12½***
435 A54 4.50e multicolored .65 .35

Purple Gallinule A55

1981, Dec. 30
436 A55 1e Egret, vert. .60 .25
437 A55 4.50e Barn owl, vert. 1.25 .40
438 A55 8e Passerine, vert. 2.75 .55
439 A55 10e shown 3.00 .65
440 A55 12e Guinea fowl 3.75 .75
Nos. 436-440 (5) 11.35 2.60

Souvenir Sheet

Perf. 13

441 A55 50e Razo Isld. lark 9.50 9.50

No. 441 contains 31x39mm one stamp.

CILSS Congress, Praia, Jan. 17 — A56

1982, Jan. 17 ***Perf. 13x12½***
442 A56 11.50e multicolored 1.40 .65

Amilcar Cabral Soccer Championship — A57

Designs: Soccer players and flags.

1982, Feb. 10 **Litho.** ***Perf. 12½***
443 A57 4.50e multicolored .55 .25
444 A57 7.50e multicolored .85 .40
445 A57 11.50e multicolored 1.40 .70
Nos. 443-445 (3) 2.80 1.35

1982 World Cup — A58

Designs: Soccer players and ball.

1982, Apr. 25

446 A58 1.50e multi .25 .25
447 A58 4.50e multi .50 .25
448 A58 8e multi .85 .35
449 A58 10.50e multi 1.00 .45
450 A58 12e multi 1.25 .55
451 A58 20e multi 2.25 .90
Nos. 446-451 (6) 6.10 2.75

Souvenir Sheet

452 A58 50e multi 6.25 6.25

First Anniv. of Women's Organization — A59

1982, Apr. 15 Litho. *Perf. 12½x12*

453 A59 4.50e Marching .55 .25
454 A59 8e Farming 1.10 .40
455 A59 12e Child care 1.60 .70
Nos. 453-455 (3) 3.25 1.35

Estaleiros Navais Port, St. Vincent A59a

1982, July 5 Litho. *Perf. 13x12½*

455A A59a 10.50e multi 1.75 .60

Natl. independence, 7th anniv.

Return of Barque Morrissey-Ernestina — A60

1982, July 5 Litho. *Perf. 13*

456 A60 12e multi 2.00 .80

Butterflies — A61

2e, Hypolimnas misippus. 4.50e, Melanitis lede. 8e, Catopsilia florella. 10.50e, Colias electo. 11.50e, Danaus chrysippus. 12e, Papilio demodecus.

1982, July 27 Litho.

457 A61 2e multicolored .35 .25
458 A61 4.50e multicolored .70 .25
459 A61 8e multicolored 1.10 .25
460 A61 10.50e multicolored 1.50 .40
461 A61 11.50e multicolored 1.60 .60
462 A61 12e multicolored 2.75 .70
Nos. 457-462 (6) 8.00 2.45

Francisco Xavier da Cruz (1905-1958), Composer — A62

14e, Eugenio Tavares (1867-1930), poet.

1983, Feb. 20 Litho. *Perf. 13*

463 A62 7e multicolored .45 .30
464 A62 14e multicolored 1.90 .80

World Communications Year — A63

1983, Oct. 10 Litho.

465 A63 13e multicolored 1.60 .80

Local Seashells — A64

1983, Nov. 30 *Perf. 13½*

466 A64 50c Conus ateralbus .25 .25
467 A64 1e Conus decoratus .25 .25
468 A64 3e Conus salreiensis .35 .25
469 A64 10e Conus verdensis 1.50 .55
470 A64 50e Conus cuneolus 5.00 2.75
Nos. 466-470 (5) 7.35 4.05

40th Anniv. of Intl. Civil Aviation Org. A65

Airplanes: 50c, Ogma-Auster D5/160, 1966. 2e, De Havilland DH-104 Dove, 1945. 10e, Hawker Siddeley 748-200, 1972. 13e, De Havilland Dragon Rapide, 1945. 20e, De Havilland Twin Otter, 1977. 50e, Britten-Norman Islander, 1971.

1984, Feb. 15 Litho.

471 A65 50c multicolored .25 .25
472 A65 2e multicolored .30 .25
473 A65 10e multicolored 1.10 .50
474 A65 13e multicolored 1.25 .85
475 A65 20e multicolored 1.90 1.25
476 A65 50e multicolored 4.50 2.50
Nos. 471-476 (6) 9.30 5.60

Amilcar Cabral — A66

1983, Jan. 17 Litho. *Perf. 14½*

477 A66 7e multi 1.00 .50
478 A66 10.50e multi 1.50 .90
a. Souvenir sheet of 2, #477-478 30.00 30.00

Amilcar Cabral Symposium, Jan. 17-20. No. 478a sold for 30e.

Cross Over Islands — A67

1983, Dec. 10 Photo. *Perf. 14½*

479 A67 7e multicolored 1.10 .50

Christianity in Cape Verde, 450th anniv.

Natl. Solidarity Campaign A68

1984, Sept. 12 *Perf. 13½*

480 A68 6.50e multicolored 1.10 .25
481 A68 13.50e multicolored 2.10 .85

2nd Conference of Natl. Women's Orgs., Mar. 23-27 — A69

1985, Mar. 27 Litho. *Perf. 13½*

482 A69 8e multicolored *3.00* 1.50

Miniature Sheet

483 A69 30e multicolored *100.00 100.00*

Natl. Independence, 10th Anniv. — A70

1985, July 5 Litho. *Perf. 14*

484 A70 8c multicolored 1.25 .55
485 A70 12e multicolored 1.90 .80

Intl. Youth Year — A71

1985, Sept. 12 Litho. *Perf. 14*

486 A71 12e multicolored 2.50 .90

Vapor, by Hundertwasser A72

Photogravure and Engraved

1986, Apr. 25 *Perf. 14*

Black Surcharge

487 A72 30e on 10e multi 30.00 4.00

Souvenir Sheets

Background Color

488 Sheet of 4 150.00
a. A72 50e yellow & multi 17.50 17.50
489 Sheet of 4 150.00
a. A72 50e red & multi 17.50 17.50
490 Sheet of 4 150.00
a. A72 50e green & multi 17.50 17.50

No. 487 exists without surcharge.

World Wildlife Fund — A73

8e, Mabuya vaillanti. 10e, Tarentola gigas brancoensis. 15e, Tarentola gigas gigas. 30e, Hemidactylus bouvieri.

No. 495a, Mabuya vaillanti. No. 495b, Hemidactylus bouvieri.

Perf. 13½x14½

1986, June 15 Litho.

491 A73 8e multicolored 6.50 2.50
492 A73 10e multicolored 8.00 3.25
493 A73 15e multicolored 12.00 4.00
494 A73 30e multicolored 24.00 5.00
Nos. 491-494 (4) 50.50 14.75

Souvenir Sheet

495 Sheet of 2 30.00 22.50
a. A73 50e multi 14.00 10.00
b. A73 50e multi 14.00 10.00

No. 495 printed with center label picturing progress union emblem. Nos. 495a-495b printed without WWF emblem.

World Food Day — A74

1986, June 20 *Perf. 14*

496 A74 8e Cauldron .50 .25
497 A74 12e Mortar & pestle .80 .35
498 A74 15e Quern stone 1.40 .50
Nos. 496-498 (3) 2.70 1.10

Intl. Peace Year — A75

1986, Dec. 24 Litho. *Perf. 14*

499 A75 12e multicolored .60 .25
500 A75 30e multicolored 2.10 1.40

Natl. Child Survival Campaign A76

1987, Mar. 27 Litho. *Perf. 14*

501 A76 8e multicolored .45 .25
502 A76 10e multicolored .55 .25
503 A76 12e multicolored .65 .35
504 A76 16e multicolored .95 .50
505 A76 100e multicolored 4.50 2.75
Nos. 501-505 (5) 7.10 4.10

Tourism
A77

1987, May 17

506 A77 1e Bay, Mindelo .25 .25
507 A77 2.50e Hill country .25 .25
508 A77 5e Mountain peak .25 .25
509 A77 8e Monument .45 .25
510 A77 10e Mountain peaks 1.00 .30
511 A77 12e Beached boats 1.00 .40
512 A77 100e Harbor 5.25 3.00
Nos. 506-512 (7) 8.45 4.70

For surcharge see No. 710.

Ships — A78

1987, Aug. 3 ***Perf. 13½x14½***

513 A78 12e Carvalho, 1937 .75 .25
514 A78 16e Nauta, 1943 1.25 .25
515 A78 50e Maria Sony, 1911 3.75 1.25
Nos. 513-515 (3) 5.75 1.75

Souvenir Sheet

516 Sheet of 2 10.00 10.00
a. A78 60e Madalan, 1928 4.00 4.00

Crop
Protection
A80

50c, Identification of insect plague. 2e, Use of insecticides. 9e, Import of parasites. 13e, Import of predators. 16e, Locust. 19e, Estimation of crop loss.
50e, Agricultural Research Institute.

1988, May 9 **Litho.** ***Perf. 13½***

518 A80 50c multicolored .25 .25
519 A80 2e multicolored .25 .25
520 A80 9e multicolored .55 .25
521 A80 13e multicolored .65 .25
522 A80 16e multicolored 1.10 .40
523 A80 19e multicolored 1.40 .60
Nos. 518-523 (6) 4.20 2.00

Souvenir Sheet

524 A80 50e multicolored 5.50 5.50

Maps — A81

1e, Dutch, 17th cent. 2.50e, Belgian, 18th cent. 4.50e, French, 18th cent. 9.50e, English, 18th cent. 19.50e, English, 19th cent. 20e, French, 18th cent., vert.

1988, July 5 **Litho.** ***Perf. 14***

525 A81 1e multicolored .25 .25
526 A81 2.50e multicolored .25 .25
527 A81 4.50e multicolored .30 .25
528 A81 9.50e multicolored .60 .25
529 A81 19.50e multicolored 1.25 .55
530 A81 20e multicolored 1.40 .65
Nos. 525-530 (6) 4.05 2.20

Churches
A82

5e, St. Amaro Abade, Tarrafal, Santiago Is. 8e, Our Lady of the Light, Maio Is. 10e, Nazarene, Praia, Santiago Is. 12e, Our Lady of Rosa'rio, Sao Nicolau Is. 15e, Nazarene, Mindelo, Sao Vicente Is. 20e, Our Lady of Grace, Praia, Santiago Is.

1988, Aug. 15 ***Perf. 13½x14½***

531 A82 5e multicolored .25 .25
532 A82 8e multicolored .45 .25
533 A82 10e multicolored .55 .25
534 A82 12e multicolored .60 .25
535 A82 15e multicolored .85 .35
536 A82 20e multicolored 1.25 .45
Nos. 531-536 (6) 3.95 1.80

Water Conservation — A83

1988, Sept. 26 **Litho.** ***Perf. 14***

537 A83 12e multicolored .75 .35

Intl. Red Cross, 125th Anniv. — A84

1988, Oct. 20

538 A84 7e multi .60 .25

3rd Communist Party (PAICV) Congress — A85

Portrait of Pres. Pereira, PAICV secretary-general, and: 7e, S. Jorginho Vocational Training Center. 10.50e, UN Secretary-General Perez de Cuellar. 30e, 100e, Star and text.

Perf. 14½x13½

1988, Nov. 25 **Litho.**

539 A85 7e multi .40 .25
540 A85 10.50e multi .60 .25
541 A85 30e multi 1.75 .75
Nos. 539-541 (3) 2.75 1.25

Souvenir Sheet

542 A85 100e multi 6.25 6.25

1988 Summer Olympics, Seoul — A86

1988, Dec. 26

543 A86 12e shown .60 .25
544 A86 15e Tennis .90 .35
545 A86 20e Soccer 1.25 .50
546 A86 30e Boxing 1.75 .90
Nos. 543-546 (4) 4.50 2.00

Souvenir Sheet

547 A86 50e Long jump 4.00 4.00

Roberto Duarte Silva (1837-89), Chemist — A86a

1989, May 2 **Litho.** ***Perf. 14¼x14***

547A A86a 12.50e multi .45 .25

2nd JAAC-CV Congress, Sept. 7-12 — A87

1989, Apr. 7 **Litho.** ***Perf. 14***

548 A87 30e Hot air balloon 1.25 .75

Liberty Guiding the People — A88

Relief, Arc de Triomphe — A89

1989, July 7 **Litho.** ***Perf. 14***

549 A88 20e multicolored .85 .45
550 A88 24e multicolored 1.10 .55
551 A88 25e multicolored 1.25 .65
Nos. 549-551 (3) 3.20 1.65

Souvenir Sheet

Perf. 14½x13½

552 A89 100e multicolored 5.50 5.50

French revolution, bicent.

Interparliamentary Union, Cent. — A90

1989, Sept. 18 **Litho.** ***Perf. 14***

553 A90 2e shown .25 .25
554 A90 4e Dove .25 .25
555 A90 13e Natl. Assembly Bldg. .45 .25
Nos. 553-555 (3) .95 .75

Traditional Ceramics A91

1989, Nov. 13 **Litho.** ***Perf. 13½***

Panel Colors

556 A91 13e lilac .50 .25
557 A91 20e red, vert. .70 .40
558 A91 24e brown .90 .50
559 A91 25e orange, vert. 1.00 .55
Nos. 556-559 (4) 3.10 1.70

Outdoor Toys — A92

1989, Dec. 23

560 A92 1e Yellow truck .25 .25
561 A92 6e Car .25 .25
562 A92 8e White truck .35 .25
563 A92 11.50e Trucks .45 .25
564 A92 18e Scooter .75 .45
565 A92 100e Boat 4.00 2.25
Nos. 560-565 (6) 6.05 3.70

Visit of Pope John Paul II — A93

1990, Jan. 25

566 A93 13e blue & multi .50 .25
567 A93 20e purple & multi 1.00 .40

Souvenir Sheet

568 A93 200e multi, diff. 10.00 10.00

Turtles A94

50c, Chelonia mydas. 1e, Dermochelys coriacea. 5e, Lepidochelys olivacea. 10e, Caretta caretta. 42e, Eretmochelys imbricata.

1990, May 17 **Litho.** ***Perf. 13½***

569 A94 50c multicolored .50 .25
570 A94 1e multicolored .50 .25
571 A94 5e multicolored .75 .25
572 A94 10e multicolored 1.00 .25
573 A94 42e multicolored 4.00 .90
Nos. 569-573 (5) 6.75 1.90

Women's Congress A95

1990, Aug. 13

574 A95 9e multicolored .50 .25

A96

Various drawings of soccer players in action.

1990, Aug. 7

575 A96 4e multicolored .25 .25
576 A96 7.50e multicolored .25 .25
577 A96 8e multicolored .25 .25
578 A96 100e multicolored 3.50 2.10
Nos. 575-578 (4) 4.25 2.85

Souvenir Sheet

579 A96 100e multi, diff. 4.50 4.50

World Cup Soccer Championships, Italy.
For surcharges see Nos. 711-712.

A97

Vaccinations: 5e, Emile Roux (1853-1933), diphtheria. 13e, Robert Koch (1843-1910), tuberculosis. 20e, Gaston Ramon (1886-1963), tetanus. 24e, Jonas Salk (1914-95), polio.

Granite Paper

1990, Oct. 15 **Perf. 11½**

580	A97	5e multicolored	.35	.25
581	A97	13e multicolored	1.00	.25
582	A97	20e multicolored	1.40	.40
583	A97	24e multicolored	1.75	.50
		Nos. 580-583 (4)	4.50	1.40

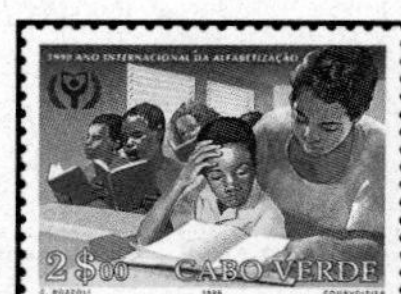

Intl. Literacy Year — A98

Designs: 3e, Adult literacy class. 15e, Teacher holding flash card, children. 19e, Teacher, student at blackboard.

1990, Sept. 28 **Granite Paper**

584	A98	2e shown	.50	.25
585	A98	3e multicolored	.50	.25
586	A98	15e multicolored	.75	.25
587	A98	19e multicolored	1.00	.30
		Nos. 584-587 (4)	2.75	1.05

Traditional Fairy Tales A99

2.50e, Man catching mermaid. 12e, Woman, snake. 25e, Man, eggs, woman.

1990, Dec. 20 **Litho.** **Perf. 12½**

588	A99	50c shown	.25	.25
589	A99	2.50e multicolored	.25	.25
590	A99	12e multicolored	.50	.45
591	A99	25e multicolored	1.00	.40
		Nos. 588-591 (4)	2.00	1.35

Fight Against AIDS A100

1991, Feb. 20 **Litho.** **Perf. 14**

Granite Paper

592	A100	13e multicolored	*.75*	.30
593	A100	24e multi, diff.	*1.25*	.75

Fishing — A101

24e, Man removing hook from fish. 25e, Fishing boats. 50e, Two men long-line fishing.

1991, Apr. 23 **Litho.** **Perf. 11½**

594	A101	10e multicolored	.35	.25
595	A101	24e multicolored	1.10	.60
596	A101	25e multicolored	1.25	.65
597	A101	50e multicolored	2.40	1.50
		Nos. 594-597 (4)	5.10	3.00

Medicinal Plants — A102

10e, Lavandula rotundifolia. 15e, Micromeria forbesii. 21e, Sarcostemma daltonii. 24e, Periploca chevalieri. 30e, Echium hypertropicum. 35e, Erysimum caboverdeanum.

1991, July 5 **Litho.** **Perf. 11½**

598	A102	10e multicolored	.30	.25
599	A102	15e multicolored	.55	.25
600	A102	21e multicolored	1.00	.30
601	A102	24e multicolored	1.25	.35
602	A102	30e multicolored	2.00	.45
603	A102	35e multicolored	3.00	.55
		Nos. 598-603 (6)	8.10	2.15

Landmarks in Old Ribeira Grande on Santiago Island A103

12.50e, Church of Our Lady of the Rosary, 1495. 15e, Ruins of the Cathedral, 1556. 20e, Fortress of San Felipe, 1587. 30e, Ruins of the Convent of St. Francis, 1642. 100e, Pillory, 1520, vert.

1991, June 25 **Litho.** **Perf. 11½**

604	A103	12.50e multicolored	.45	.25
605	A103	15e multicolored	.55	.25
606	A103	20e multicolored	.75	.45
607	A103	30e multicolored	1.10	.75
		Nos. 604-607 (4)	2.85	1.70

Souvenir Sheet

608	A103	100e multicolored	4.00	4.00

Musical Instruments — A104

1991, Oct. 9 **Litho.** **Perf. 11½**

609	A104	10e 6-string guitar	.35	.25
610	A104	20e Violin	.85	.55
611	A104	29e 5-string guitar	1.40	.65
612	A104	47e Cimba	2.00	1.25
		Nos. 609-612 (4)	4.60	2.70

Souvenir Sheet

613	A104	60e Accordion, horiz.	3.00	3.00

Christmas A105

1991, Dec. 20 **Litho.** **Perf. 11½**

614	A105	31e Nativity scene	1.10	.50
615	A105	50e Nativity scene, diff.	1.75	.90

Discovery of America, 500th Anniv. A106

1992, Mar. 31 **Litho.** **Perf. 11½**

616	A106	40e shown	2.50	1.10
617	A106	40e Columbus on ship	2.50	1.10
a.		Pair, #616-617	6.00	6.00

Souvenir Sheet

618	A106	Sheet of 2	9.00	9.00

Stamps in No. 618 are smaller, without white border and "Luis Duran" and "Courvoisier" inscriptions. No. 618 was printed in continuous design and sold for 150e.

Souvenir Sheet

Granada '92 — A107

1992, Apr.24 **Perf. 11½**

619	A107	50e multicolored	8.00	8.00

No. 619 sold for 150e.

Tropical Fruits A108

16e, Syzygium jambos. 25e, Mangifera indica. 31e, Anacardium occidentale. 32e, Persea americana.

1992, Feb. 29 **Perf. 12x11½**

620	A108	16e multicolored	.65	.30
621	A108	25e multicolored	1.10	.50
622	A108	31e multicolored	1.40	.65
623	A108	32e multicolored	1.60	.75
		Nos. 620-623 (4)	4.75	2.20

1992 Summer Olympics, Barcelona A109

16e, Women's javelin. 20e, Weight lifting. 32e, Women's pole vault. 40e, Women's shot put.

100e, Women's gymnastics.

1992, June 30 **Litho.** **Perf. 13½**

624	A109	16e multicolored	.60	.25
625	A109	20e multicolored	.75	.30
626	A109	32e multicolored	1.40	.65
627	A109	40e multicolored	1.60	.85
		Nos. 624-627 (4)	4.35	2.05

Souvenir Sheet

628	A109	100e multicolored	4.25	4.25

Sugar Cane Production — A110

Designs: 19e, Oxen, sugar cane. 20e, Oxen yoked to press. 37e, Man placing cane inside press. 38e, Refining process.

1992, Nov. **Litho.** **Perf. 11**

629	A110	19e multicolored	.65	.30
630	A110	20e multicolored	.65	.30
631	A110	37e multicolored	1.25	.60
632	A110	38e multicolored	1.40	.60
		Nos. 629-632 (4)	3.95	1.80

Domestic Animals A111

1992, Nov. **Perf. 13½**

633	A111	16e Cat	.75	.40
634	A111	31e Chickens	1.40	.80
635	A111	32e Dog, vert.	1.50	.90
636	A111	50e Horse	2.50	1.25
		Nos. 633-636 (4)	6.15	3.35

Corals A112

5e, Tubastrea aurea. 31e, Corallium rubrum. 37e, Porites porites. 50e, Millepora alcicornis.

1993, Apr. 29 **Litho.** **Perf. 11½**

637	A112	5e multicolored	.25	.25
638	A112	31e multicolored	1.25	.80
639	A112	37e multicolored	1.50	1.00
640	A112	50e multicolored	2.00	1.25
		Nos. 637-640 (4)	5.00	3.30

Treaty of Tordesillas, 500th Anniv. (in 1994) — A113

Designs: No. 641, King Ferdinand, Queen Isabella of Spain, Pope Alexander VI. No. 642, Pope Julius II, King John II of Portugal. No. 643, Astrolabe, treaty signing. No. 644, Compass rose, map.

1993, Aug. 1 **Litho.** **Perf. 12x11½**

641		37e multicolored	1.50	.65
642		37e multicolored	1.50	.65
a.	A113	Pair, #641-642	3.50	3.25
643		38e multicolored	1.50	.65
644		38e multicolored	1.50	.65
a.	A113	Pair, #643-644	3.50	3.25
		Nos. 641-644 (4)	6.00	2.60

Souvenir Sheet

Santiago Island, 1806 — A114

1993, July 30 **Perf. 13½**

645	A114	100e multicolored	5.00	5.00

Brasiliana '93.

Lobsters — A115

2e, Palinurus charlestoni. 10e, Panulirus echinatus. 17e, Panulirus regius. 38e, Scyllarides latus.

100e, Panulirus regius, diff.

1993, Sept. 29 Litho. *Perf. 11½*

646 A115 2e multicolored .35 .25
647 A115 10e multicolored .75 .25
648 A115 17e multicolored 1.40 .50
649 A115 38e multicolored 2.90 1.00
Nos. 646-649 (4) 5.40 2.00

Souvenir Sheet

650 A115 100e multicolored 7.50 7.50

No. 650 contains one 51x36mm stamp.

Birds A116

10e, Calonectris edwardsii. 30e, Sula leucogaster. 40e, Fregata magnificens. 41e, Phaeton aethereus.

1993, Oct. 29 Litho. *Perf. 12x11½*

651 A116 10e multicolored .75 .25
652 A116 30e multicolored 3.00 .85
653 A116 40e multicolored 4.00 1.10
a. Souvenir sheet of 1 12.00 11.00
654 A116 41e multicolored 4.00 1.10
Nos. 651-654 (4) 11.75 3.30

Hong Kong '94 (No. 653a). No. 653a sold for 150e.

Flowers A117

1993, Dec. 16 Litho. *Perf. 12x11½*

655 A117 5e Rosa alexandra .25 .25
656 A117 30e Strelitzia reginae 1.10 .80
657 A117 37e Dianthus barbatus 1.60 1.00
a. Souvenir sheet of 1 7.50 7.50
658 A117 50e Dahlia 2.00 1.25
Nos. 655-658 (4) 4.95 3.30

Singapore '95 (No. 657a). Issued 9/1/95. No. 657a sold for 150e.

1994 World Cup Soccer Championships, US — A118

Players, US flag, and: 1e, Giant's Stadium, New Jersey. 20e, Rose Bowl Stadium, Pasadena. 37e, Foxboro Stadium, Boston. 38e, Silverdome, Pontiac. 100e, RFK Stadium, Washington DC.

1994, May 31 Litho. *Perf. 11½*

659 A118 1e multicolored .25 .25
660 A118 20e multicolored .85 .50
661 A118 37e multicolored 1.50 1.00
662 A118 38e multicolored 1.60 1.10
Nos. 659-662 (4) 4.20 2.85

Souvenir Sheet

663 A118 100e multicolored 5.50 5.50

Prince Henry the Navigator (1394-1460) — A119

1994, Mar. 4 Litho. *Perf. 12*

664 A119 37e multicolored 3.00 1.00

See Brazil No. 2463, Macao No. 719, Portugal No. 1987.

Sharks A120

21e, Eugomphodus taurus. 27e, Carcharhinus limbatus. 37e, Rhiniodon typus. 38e, Etmopterus spinax.

1994, June 27 Litho. *Perf. 12x11½*

665 A120 21e multicolored 1.00 .60
666 A120 27e multicolored 1.25 .75
667 A120 37e multicolored 1.75 1.25
668 A120 38e multicolored 2.00 1.40
Nos. 665-668 (4) 6.00 4.00

Bananas A121

1994, Aug. 16 Litho. *Perf. 11½*

669 A121 12e Prata, vert. .50 .25
670 A121 16e Pao .75 .40
671 A121 30e Ana roberta, vert. 1.50 .85
672 A121 40e Roxa, vert. 2.00 1.10
Nos. 669-672 (4) 4.75 2.60

Souvenir Sheet

673 A121 100e Prata, diff., vert. 9.00 9.00

PHILAKOREA '94, SINGPEX '94 (No. 673). No. 673 sold for 150e.

Lighthouses — A122

2e, Fontes Pereira de Melo. 37e, Morro Negro. 38e, Amelia, vert. 50e, Maria Pia, vert.

1994, Oct. 17 *Perf. 12*

674 A122 2e multicolored .25 .25
675 A122 37e multicolored 1.75 1.00
676 A122 38e multicolored 1.75 1.10
677 A122 50e multicolored 2.25 1.40
Nos. 674-677 (4) 6.00 3.75

Wilhelm Roentgen (1845-1923), Discovery of the X-Ray, Cent. — A123

1995, Mar. 31 Litho. *Perf. 12*

678 A123 20e yellow & multi .80 .50
679 A123 37e blue & multi 1.50 1.00
a. Souvenir sheet of 2, #678-679 4.50 4.50

No. 679a sold for 100e.

A124

FAO, 50th Anniv. — A125

1995, May 17 Litho. *Perf. 12*

680 A124 37e multicolored 1.50 .90
681 A125 38e multicolored 1.50 .90

Dogs A126

Dog, scene depicting story of dogs: 1e, Fox terrier, Two foxhounds and fox terrier, by John Emms. 10e, Cavalier King Charles, Shooting over Dogs, by Richard Ansdell. 40e, Rough collie, German shepherd. 50e, Braco, Hounds at Full Cry, by Thomas Blinks.

1995, June 16 Litho. *Perf. 12x11½*

682 A126 1e multicolored .25 .25
683 A126 10e multicolored .55 .25
684 A126 40e multicolored 2.25 1.25
685 A126 50e multicolored 2.75 1.10
Nos. 682-685 (4) 5.80 2.85

Independence, 20th Anniv. — A127

1995, July 20 Litho. *Perf. 12*

686 A127 37e multicolored 1.90 1.25

Traditional Festival A128

Designs: 2e, Horse race. 10e, Horseman leading parade. 37e, People singing, playing drums. 40e, Playing game on horseback.

1995, Oct. 9 *Perf. 12x11½*

687 A128 2e multicolored .25 .25
688 A128 10e multicolored .45 .25
689 A128 37e multicolored 1.50 .85
690 A128 40e multicolored 1.75 1.00
Nos. 687-690 (4) 3.95 2.35

Children's Stories A130

Designs: 10e, The cicadas making music, ants. 25e, Cicada being exposed to light. 38e, Cicada with guitar, ants working. 45e, Ants at table making fun of cicada.

1995, Dec. 15 Litho. *Perf. 11½*

692 A130 10e multicolored .40 .55
693 A130 25e multicolored .85 .85
694 A130 38e multicolored 1.40 1.10
695 A130 45e multicolored 1.60 1.00
Nos. 692-695 (4) 4.25 3.50

Endangered Plants — A131

20e, Sonchus daltonii. 37e, Echium vulcanorum. 38e, Nauplius smithii. 50e, Campanula jacobaea.

1996, Apr. 24 Litho. *Perf. 11½*

696 A131 20e multicolored .65 .40
697 A131 37e multicolored 1.20 .75
698 A131 38e multicolored 1.20 .75
699 A131 50e multicolored 1.60 1.10
Nos. 696-699 (4) 4.65 3.00

1996 Summer Olympic Games, Atlanta A132

1996, June 30 Litho. *Perf. 11½*

700 A132 1e Tennis .25 .25
701 A132 37e Gymnastics 1.10 .75
702 A132 100e Athletics 3.25 2.10
Nos. 700-702 (3) 4.60 3.10

UNICEF, 50th Anniv. — A133

1996, Aug. 1 Litho. *Perf. 12*

703 A133 20e Young girl .90 .40
704 A133 40e Mother, child 1.75 .85

Water Sports — A134

Designs: 2.50e, Fishing. 10e, Windsurfing. 22e, Jet skiing. No. 708, Surfing, horiz. No. 709, Diver's hand, pufferfish, horiz.

1996, Oct. 9 Litho. *Perf. 12*

705 A134 2.50e multicolored .25 .25
706 A134 10e multicolored .35 .25
707 A134 22e multicolored .70 .45
708 A134 100e multicolored 3.25 2.10
Nos. 705-708 (4) 4.55 3.05

Souvenir Sheet

709 A134 100e multicolored 4.50 4.50

No. 709 contains one 80x61mm stamp.

Nos. 507, 575-576 Surcharged

a

b

1997 **Litho.** ***Perf. 14***
710 A77(a) 3e on 2.50e #507 .25 .25

Perf. 13½
711 A96(b) 37e on 4e #575 3.00 .75
712 A96(a) 38e on 7.50e #576 3.00 .75
Nos. 710-712 (3) 6.25 1.75

Natl. Symbols A135

1997 ***Perf. 12***
713 A135 25e Arms .80 .50
714 A135 37e Anthem 1.10 .75
715 A135 50e Flag 1.60 1.00
Nos. 713-715 (3) 3.50 2.25

World Wildlife Fund — A136

Pristis pectinata: a, On seabed. b, Swimming, school of small fish. c, Swimming along seabed, small fish. d, Two near seabed.

1997 **Litho.** ***Perf. 11½***
716 A136 15e Strip of 4, #a.-d. 10.00 10.00

Legends of the Sea — A137

a, Fish, dolphins. b, Merman, mermaid. c, Fish swimming through portal, moray eel.

1997 **Litho.** ***Perf. 11½***
717 A137 45e Strip of 3, #a.-c. 5.00 5.00

Fish A138

Designs: 13e, Thunnus albacares. 21e, Thunnus obesus. 41e, Euthynnus alletteratus. 45e, Katsuwonus pelamis.

1997 **Litho.** ***Perf. 12***
718 A138 13e multicolored .50 .30
719 A138 21e multicolored 1.00 .60
720 A138 41e multicolored 1.75 1.25
721 A138 45e multicolored 2.00 1.50
Nos. 718-721 (4) 5.25 3.65

1998 World Cup Soccer Championships, France — A139

Designs: 30e, Soccer ball in net, vert. 45e, Soccer player, ball, vert. 50e, Globe, ball, World Cup trophy, fans in stadium.

1998 **Litho.** ***Perf. 12x11½, 11½x12***
722 A139 10e shown .40 .25
723 A139 30e multicolored 1.00 .80
724 A139 45e multicolored 1.60 1.25
725 A139 50e multicolored 2.00 1.40
Nos. 722-725 (4) 5.00 3.70

Traditional Cuisine A140

5e, Boiled fish. 25e, Xerém com friginato. 35e, Cachupa. 40e, Molho de Saint-Nicholas.

1998 **Litho.** ***Perf. 12x11½***
726 A140 5e multicolored .25 .25
727 A140 25e multicolored .65 .65
728 A140 35e multicolored 1.00 1.00
729 A140 40e multicolored 1.10 1.10
Nos. 726-729 (4) 3.00 3.00

Early Exploration — A141

a, Quotation from Lusiadas, two men looking at maps. b, Man with sword, man & woman. c, Compass, map, sailing ship, buildings on cliff.

1998 ***Perf. 11½***
730 A141 50e Strip of 3, #a.-c. 6.00 6.00

Women's Traditional Costumes — A142

1998 **Litho.** ***Perf. 12***
731 A142 10e Brava .30 .25
732 A142 18e Fogo .60 .50
733 A142 30e Boa Vista .95 .80
734 A142 50e Santiago 1.60 1.40
Nos. 731-734 (4) 3.45 2.95

Butterflies and Moths A143

Designs: 5e, Byblia ilithyia. 10e, Aganais speciosa. 20e, Utetheisia pulchella. 30e, Vanessa cardui. 50e, Trichoplusia ni. 100e, Grammodes congenita.

1999, Mar. 16 **Litho.** ***Perf. 11¾***
735 A143 5e multi .25 .25
736 A143 10e multi .25 .25
737 A143 20e multi .50 .50
738 A143 30e multi .80 .80
a. Souvenir sheet, #737-738 4.00 4.00
739 A143 50e multi 1.25 1.25
740 A143 100e multi 2.60 2.60
Nos. 735-740 (6) 5.65 5.65

No. 738a sold for 100e.

First Concorde Flight, 30th Anniv. A144

Concorde: 30e, In flight. 50e, On ground.

1999, June 14 **Litho.** ***Perf. 12***
741-742 A144 Set of 2 2.75 2.75

Famous People — A145

Design: 30e, Alain Gerbault (1893-1941), sailor, boats at dock. 50e, Roberto Duarte Silva (1837-89), chemist, Eiffel Tower.

1999, July 2 **Litho.** ***Perf. 14½***
743 A145 30e multi 2.00 2.00
744 A145 50e multi 3.25 3.25
a. Souvenir sheet, #743-744 6.50 6.50

Philex France 99 (No. 744a).

A146

UPU, 125th Anniv. A147

1999, Sept. 15 ***Perf. 12x11¾***
745 A146 30e shown 20.00 20.00
746 A147 50e shown 20.00 20.00

With Country Name Added

No. 747

No. 748

747 A146 30e multi .65 .65
748 A147 50e multi 1.10 1.10
Nos. 745-748 (4) 41.75 41.75

Dance A148

Designs: 10e, Colá Sanjon, vert. 30e, Contradança, vert. 50e, Desfile de tabanca. 100e, Batuque.

Perf. 11¾x12, 12x11¾
1999, Nov. 5 **Litho.**
749-752 A148 Set of 4 5.00 5.00

A149

Millennium — A149a

Designs: 40e, Globe, hourglass and open antique book inscribed "2000," vert. 50e, "2000 Milénio."

2000, Jan. 31 **Litho.** ***Perf. 11¾x11½***
753 A149 40e multicolored 1.75 1.50
754 A149a 50e multicolored 2.00 1.75

SOS Children's Villages A150

Emblem and child: 50e, Seated, vert. 100e, With arms outstretched.

Perf. 11¾x12, 12x11¾
2000, Apr. 28 **Litho.**
755-756 A150 Set of 2 5.00 5.00

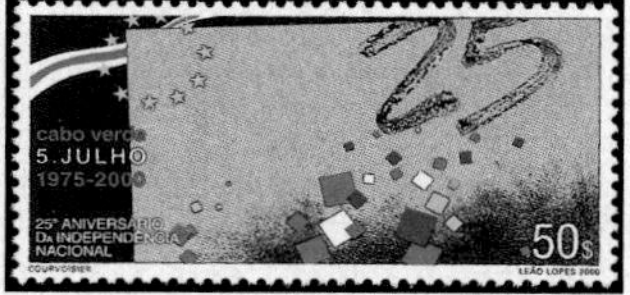

Independence, 25th Anniv. — A151

2000, July 5 ***Perf. 11¾***
757 A151 50e multi 4.00 1.25

2000 Summer Olympics, Sydney A152

Designs: 10e, Women's gymnastics. 40e, Taekwondo. 50e, Women's hurdles.

2000, Sept. 15 **Litho.** ***Perf. 11¾***
758-760 A152 Set of 3 3.50 2.60
760a Souvenir sheet of 3, #758-760 4.00 2.75

Dragoeiro Tree — A153

2000, Oct. 9 **Litho.** ***Perf. 11¾x11½***
761 A153 5e green .25 .25
762 A153 40e red 1.00 1.00
763 A153 60e brown 1.60 1.60

Sao Nicolau Seminary and School — A154

No. 764: a, Seminarians and students (denomination at LR, 27x26mm). b, Seminarians and students (denomination at LL, 29x26mm). c, José Alves Feijo, Dr. Julio Dias and Canon António Bouças (56x26mm).

2000, Dec. 15 **Litho.** ***Perf. 14½***
764 A154 60e Horiz. strip of 3, #a-c 7.50 7.50

Fish A155

Designs: 10e, Diplodus sargus lineatus. 22e, Diplodus prayensis. 28e, Lithognathus mormyrus. 48e, Diplodus fasciatus. 60e, Diplodus puntazzo.

2001, Apr. 24 ***Perf. 12x11¾***
765-769 A155 Set of 5 6.50 6.50

Spiders A156

Designs: 13e, Thomisus onustus. 16e, Scytodes velutina. 40e, Hersiliola simoni. 100e, Loxosceles rufescens.

2001, May 28
770-773 A156 Set of 4 7.50 7.50

Trees — A156a

Designs: 50e, Acacia albida. 60e, Ficus sycomorus.

2001, June 9 Litho. *Perf. 11¾x11½*
773A-773B A156a Set of 2 4.00 4.00

Souvenir Sheet

Belgica 2001 Intl. Stamp Exhibition, Brussels — A157

Perf. 11¾x11½
2001, June 9 Photo.
774 A157 100e multi 4.00 4.00

Medicinal Plants — A157a

Designs: 20e, Artimisia gorgonum. 27e, Globularia amygdalifolia. 47.50e, Sidereoxylon marginata, horiz. 50e, Umbilicus schmidtii, horiz. 60e, Verbascum cystolithicum. 100e, Limonium lobinii.

Perf. 11¾x12, 12x11¾
2001, Sept. 27 Litho.
774A-774F A157a Set of 6 10.00 10.00

Year of Dialogue Among Civilizations — A158

2001, Oct. 9 Litho. *Perf. 11¾x12*
775 A158 60e multi 1.60 1.60

António Aurélio Gonçalves (1901-84), Writer — A159

2001, Dec. 20 *Perf. 12¼*
776 A159 100e multi 2.75 2.75

Medicinal Plants A160

Designs: 10e, Euphorbia tuckeyna. 50e, Limonium sunding, vert. 60e, Aeonium gorgoneum, vert. 100e, Polycarpaea gayi, vert.

Perf. 12x11¾, 11¾x12
2002, Apr. 26 Litho.
777-780 A160 Set of 4 5.75 5.75

2002 World Cup Soccer Championships, Japan and Korea — A161

Designs: 60e, Player heading ball towards goal. 100e, Player kicking ball towards goal.

2002, July 22 *Perf. 12x11¾*
781-782 A161 Set of 2 6.00 4.00

Caretta Caretta A162

Designs: 10e, Pair mating. 20e, Female laying eggs, vert. 30e, Eggs hatching. 60e, Hatchlings heading for sea, vert. No. 787, 100e, Turtle swimming underwater.
No. 788, 100e, Turtle on beach.

2002, Sept. 9 *Perf. 12x11¾, 11¾x12*
783-787 A162 Set of 5 7.50 7.50

Souvenir Sheet

788 A162 100e multi 4.00 4.00

No. 788 contains one 80x60mm stamp.

Basketry A163

Baskets and basket weavers from: 20e, Sao Nicolau Island. 33e, Santo Antao Island. 60e, Santiago Island, 100e, Boa Vista Island.

2002, Oct. 29 *Perf. 12x11¾*
789-792 A163 Set of 4 7.50 7.50

Composers and Poets A164

Designs: 12e, Katcháss (1951-88), composer. 20e, Jorge Monteiro (1913-98), composer. 32e, Luis Rendall (1898-1986), composer. 47.50e, Jorge Barbosa (1902-71), poet. 60e, Januário Leite (1865-1930), poet. 100e, José Lopes (1872-1962), poet.

2003, Feb. 24
793-798 A164 Set of 6 9.00 9.00

Birds — A165

Designs: 10e, Ardea bournei. 27e, Ardea cinerea. 42e, Bubulcus ibis. 60e, Egretta garzeta.

2003, July 9 *Perf. 14x13¾*
799-802 A165 Set of 4 6.00 6.00

Cesaria Evora, Singer A166

Designs: 60e, Evora at left. 100e, Evora at right.
200e, Feet of Evora.

2003, May 26 *Perf. 13¾x14*
803-804 A166 Set of 2 6.00 6.00

Souvenir Sheet

Perf. 12¼x12
805 A166 200e multi + label 7.50 7.50

No. 805 contains one 50x38mm stamp.

Scouting in Cape Verde A167

Emblem and scout of: 60e, Scouts Association of Cape Verde. 100e, Cape Verde Scouts Corps.

2003, Oct. 24 Litho. *Perf. 13¾x14*
806-807 A167 Set of 2 7.50 7.50

Whales A168

Designs: 10e, Balaenoptera musculus. 20e, Physeter macrocephalus. 50e, Megaptera novaeangliae. 60e, Globicephala macrorhynchus.

2003, Nov. 25 *Perf. 12*
808-811 A168 Set of 4 12.00 12.00

First Dakar — Praia Seaplane Flight of Europe — Africa — South America Airmail Service, 75th Anniv. — A169

Seaplane and: 10e, Crew. 42e, Pilot Paulin Paris, map of South America — Africa route. 60e, Map of entire route.
100e, Like 10e.

2003, Dec. 11 *Perf. 14*
812-814 A169 Set of 3 4.00 4.00

Souvenir Sheet

815 A169 100e multi 4.00 4.00

Election of Pope John Paul II, 25th Anniv. — A170

Pope John Paul II and: 30e, Girl. 60e, Boats, horiz.
100e, Censer and crucifix.

2003, Dec. 29 *Perf. 14x13¾, 13¾x14*
816-817 A170 Set of 2 3.50 3.50

Souvenir Sheet

818 A170 100e multi 5.00 5.00

Trees — A171

Designs: 20e, Khaya senegalensis. 27e, Acacia nilotica. 60e, Ceiba pentandra. 100e, Phoenix atlantica.

2004, Jan. 25 *Perf. 14x13¾*
819-822 A171 Set of 4 7.50 7.50

Windmill — A172

Colors: 20e, Blue. 60e, Red. 100e, Green.

2004, June 3 *Perf. 13¼x13*
823-825 A172 Set of 3 9.00 9.00

2004 Summer Olympics, Athens — A173

Designs: 10e, Taekwondo. 60e, Rhythmic gymnastics. 100e, Boxing, horiz.

Perf. 13¼x13, 13x13¼
2004, Aug. 13 Litho.
826-828 A173 Set of 3 6.00 6.00

Lighthouses A174

Designs: 10e, Ponta do Barril Lighthouse, Sao Nicolau Island. 30e, Ponta Jalunga Lighthouse, Brava Island. 40e, D. Luis Lighthouse,

Passaros Islands, horiz. 50e, Ponta Preta Lighthouse, Santiago Island, horiz.

2004, Sept. 7
829-832 A174 Set of 4 6.50 6.50

Houses on Fogo Island A175

Various houses: 20e, 40e, 50e, 60e.

2004, Oct. 9 ***Perf. 13x13¼***
833-836 A175 Set of 4 7.00 7.00

Telephones — A176

Old telephones and: 10e, Switchboard. 40e, Operator. 60e, Telephone directory. 100e, Truck and telephone poles.

2004, Nov. 12
837-840 A176 Set of 4 8.00 8.00

Oral Stories and Legends A177

Designs: 10e, Stória Stória. 20e, Era um Vez! 30e, Sapatinha Ribera Baxu. 60e, Quem ki Sabi Mas, Conta Midjor!, vert.

Perf. 13x13¼, 13¼x13
2005, Feb. 21 **Litho.**
841-844 A177 Set of 4 6.00 6.00

Amilcar Cabral (1924-73), Revolutionary Leader — A178

2005, June 30 Litho. ***Perf. 13¼x13***
845 A178 60e multicolored 3.00 3.00

Independence, 30th anniv.

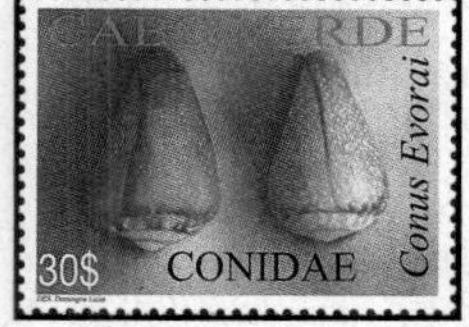

Shells A179

Designs: 30e, Conus evorai. 40e, Harpa doris. 50e, Strombus lotus. 60e, Phyllonotus duplex.

2005, July 18 ***Perf. 13x13¼***
846-849 A179 Set of 4 7.50 7.50

Birds — A180

Designs: 19e, Passer iagoensis. 42e, Estrilda astrild. 44e, Passer domesticus. 55e, Acrocephalus brevipennis.

2005, Aug. 8 ***Perf. 13¼x13***
850-853 A180 Set of 4 6.50 6.50

World Summit on the Information Society, Tunis A181

2005, Nov. 16 Litho. ***Perf. 13x13¼***
854 A181 60e multi 4.00 4.00

Artifacts of the Slave Trade A182

Designs: 5e, Pipe. 10e, Telescope. 30e, Cannon. 60e, Nautical instrument. 100e, Shackles.

2006, Jan. 31
855-858 A182 Set of 4 6.00 6.00

Souvenir Sheet

859 A182 100e multi 6.00 6.00

No. 859 contains one 80x60mm stamp.

Whaling A183

Designs: 10e, Ship and map. 20e, Whalers in ship and longboat chasing whales off shore. 40e, Ship, longboat and whale. 60e, Crew on whaling ship.

2006, May 18 Litho. ***Perf. 13¼x13½***
Granite Paper
860-863 A183 Set of 4 10.00 10.00

2006 World Cup Soccer Championships, Germany — A184

Designs: 30e, Emblem and soccer players. 40e, Emblem, vert. 60e, World Cup trophy and soccer players.

Perf. 13x13¼, 13¼x13
2006, Oct. 18 **Litho.**
Granite Paper
864-866 A184 Set of 3 6.50 6.50

Ribeira Grande and the International Slave Route — A185

Designs: 24e, Ship and buildings. 36e, Ship, slaves, map of Africa, North America and South America. 50e, Ship, slaves, map of Europe, North America, South America and Africa. 60e, Ship, small boat and buildings.

2006, Oct. 30 Litho. ***Perf. 13x13¼***
Granite Paper
867-870 A185 Set of 4 7.50 7.50

An additional stamp was issued in this set. The editors would like to examine any example of it.

Community of Portuguese-Speaking Nations, 10th Anniv. — A186

2006, Nov. 2
872 A186 60e multi 3.50 3.50

Sir Francis Drake (c. 1540-96), Explorer — A187

Drake and: 5e, Sextant. 16e, Ship, map of Cape Verde, compass wheel, horiz. 44e, Ships, horiz. 60e, Old map of Atlantic Ocean, horiz.

2006, Nov. 27 ***Perf. 13¼x13***
Granite Paper (5e, 16e, 60e)

873	A187	5e multi	—	—
874	A187	16e multi	—	—
875	A187	44e multi	—	—
876	A187	60e multi	—	—

Aeronautics — A188

Designs: 10e, Map of Rome-Rio de Janeiro flight via Ilha do Sal, airplane and hangar on Ilha do Sal. 20e, Seaplane, map of Portugal-Brazil flight, monument. 40e, Zeppelin in flight over town. 50e, Ferdinand von Zeppelin, Zeppelins in flight. 60e, Graf Zeppelin in flight, Cape Verde newspaper article.

2006, Dec. 15 Litho. ***Perf. 13x13¼***
Granite Paper
877-881 A188 Set of 5 9.00 9.00

Writers — A189

Designs: No. 882, 60e, Manuel Lopes (1907-2005). No. 883, 60e, Baltasar Lopes da Silva (Osvaldo Alcantara) (1907-89).

2007 ***Perf. 13¼***
882-883 A189 Set of 2 6.50 6.50

Pico do Fogo Volcano A190

Various depictions of erupting volcano: 10e, 50e, 55e, 60e. 50e and 55e are vert.

2007 ***Perf. 13x13¼, 13¼x13***
884-887 A190 Set of 4 9.00 9.00

Luis de Cadamosto (1432-88), Discoverer of Cape Verde Islands — A191

Designs: 16e, Cadamosto and ship. 44e, Ship and compass rose. 60e, Cadamosto. 100e, Cadamosto, ship and astrolabe.

2007 ***Perf. 13¼x13***

888	A191	16e multi	—	—
889	A191	44e multi	—	—
890	A191	60e multi	—	—
891	A191	100e multi	—	—

Whaling A192

Designs: 20e, Whale, map of Cape Verde and world showing whale reproduction sites. 30e, Crew on whaling ship stripping whale. 40e, Whale and ship near shore. 60e, Whale breaching near ship.

2007, June 14 Litho. ***Perf. 13x13¼***
Granite Paper
892-895 A192 Set of 4 10.00 10.00

Aviation A193

Designs: 10e, Airplane, map of South America, Cape Verde, and Africa. 50e, Concorde. 60e, Airplane, map of Africa and Asia. 100e, Airplane over airport.

2007 ***Perf. 13x13¼***
896-899 A193 Set of 4 7.50 7.50

Local Cuisine A194

Designs: 10e, Cozido (stew). 20e, Cuscus com mel (couscous with honey), vert. 60e, Trotxida. 100e, Xerem (cornmeal puree).

2008 ***Perf. 13x13¼, 13¼x13***
900-903 A194 Set of 4 12.00 12.00

Occupations
A195

Designs: 30e, Engraxador (shoe polisher). 40e, Vendedeira de pao (bread seller). 50e, Vendedeira de leite (milk seller), horiz. 100e, Vendedeira de peixe (fish seller).

2008 ***Perf. 13¼x13, 13x13¼***
904-907 A195 Set of 4 *13.00 13.00*

Souvenir Sheet

Praia, 150th Anniv. — A196

2008 ***Perf. 13¼x13***
908 A196 200e multi 12.00 12.00

Peace Corps in Cape Verde, 20th Anniv. — A197

2008
909 A197 60e multi *4.00 4.00*

Birds of Prey — A198

Designs: 5e, Buteo bannermani. 20e, Falco tinnunculus. 40e, Pandion haliaetus. 60e, Falco peregrinus madeus.

2008
910-913 A198 Set of 4 6.50 6.50

Louis Braille (1809-52), Educator of the Blind
A199

Designs: No. 914, 60e, Hands reading Braille text. No. 915, 60e, Blind man with cane. No. 916, 60e, Blind children. No. 917, 60e, Blind man with seeing-eye dog, vert.

2009 ***Perf. 13x13¼, 13¼x13***
Granite Paper
914-917 A199 Set of 4 9.00 9.00

Charles Darwin (1809-82), Naturalist — A200

No. 918 — Map of Darwin's voyages and: a, Darwin, skulls. b, Skull, ship, Darwin's legs. c, Darwin and octopus.

2009 ***Perf. 13½x13¼***
918 A200 Horiz. strip of 3 10.00 10.00
a.-c. 60e Any single 3.00 3.00

Red Cross, 150th Anniv.
A201

2009 **Litho.** ***Perf. 13x13¼***
Granite Paper
919 A201 100e multi 3.50 3.50

Flora and Fauna
A202

Designs: 5e, Chioninia delalandii. 10e, Tornabenea annua. 20e, Tarentola darwini. 30e, Satureja forbesii, vert. 40e, Campylnatus glaber glaber, vert. 60e, Chioninia vailanti.

2009 ***Perf. 13x13¼, 13¼x13***
Granite Paper
920-925 A202 Set of 6 6.00 6.00

Souvenir Sheet

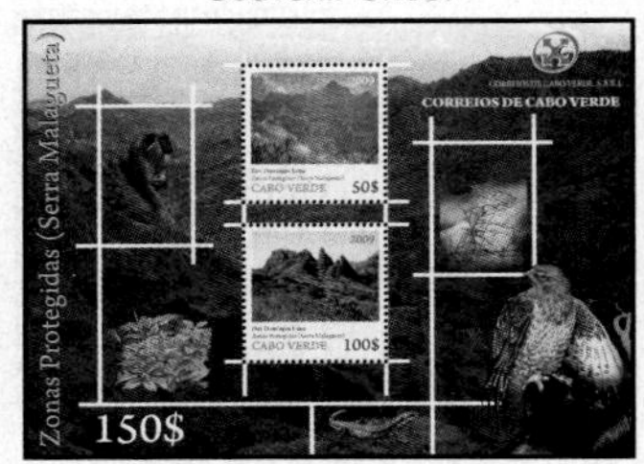

Serra Malagueta Protected Areas — A203

No. 926 — Various views of Serra Malagueta: a, 50e. b, 100e.

2009 **Granite Paper** ***Perf. 13¼***
926 A203 Sheet of 2, #a-b 6.00 6.00

Discovery of Cape Verde Islands, 550th Anniv. — A204

No. 927: a, Two ships. b, Map of Cape Verde and Africa, compass rose, birds, "14." c, Ship, rowboat, map of Africa and Asia, compass rose, "60."

2010 **Granite Paper** ***Perf. 13½x13¼***
927 A204 Horiz. strip of 3 6.00 6.00
a.-c. 60e Any single 1.75 1.75

Monte Gordo Protected Areas — A205

Flora and birds of Monte Gordo Protected Areas: 5e, Diplotaxis gracilis. 20e, Theresia. 30e, Verbascum capitis-viridis. 40e, Coturnix coturnix, horiz. 50e, Corvus ruficollis, horiz. 60e, Columba livia, horiz.
100e, Monte Gordo, horiz.

2010 ***Perf. 13¼x13, 13x13¼***
928-933 A205 Set of 6 7.50 7.50

Souvenir Sheet
934 A205 100e multi 3.50 3.50

2010 World Cup Soccer Championships, South Africa — A206

Designs: 40e, Mascot, silhouettes of players. 50e, Emblem, players, vert. 60e, Mascot, players. 100e, World Cup, silhouettes of players.

2010 ***Perf. 13x13¼, 13¼x13***
935-938 A206 Set of 4 7.50 7.50

Independence, 35th Anniv. — A207

2010, July 5 **Litho.** ***Perf. 13¼***
939 A207 100e multi *6.00 6.00*

Campaigns Against Chronic Diseases
A208

Campaign against: 10e, Alcoholism. 20e, Alcoholism, diff. 30e, Diabetes. 40e, Diabetes, diff. 50e, Tuberculosis. 60e, Tuberculosis, diff.

2010, Aug. 12 ***Perf. 13x13¼***
940-945 A208 Set of 6 *12.00 12.00*

Assoc. of Postal and Telecommunications Operators of Portuguese-Speaking Countries and Territories, 20th Anniv. — A209

2010
946 A209 100e multi *6.50 6.50*

Rebellions — A210

Rebellions at: 40e, Mindelo, 1934. 50e, Paul, 1894. 60e, Rubon Manel, 1910.

2010 ***Perf. 13½***
947-949 A210 Set of 3 *9.00 9.00*

Heart Health
A211

Designs: 20e, Hearts, electrocardiogram waves, mother lifting child. 40e, Heart and stethoscope. 60e, Family, hearts, electrocardiogram waves. 100e, Heart and arteries.

2011 ***Perf. 13x13¼***
950-953 A211 Set of 4 7.50 7.50

Nudibranchs — A212

Designs: 5e, Flabellina arveloi. 10e, Flabellina bulbosa. 20e, Aplysia dactylomela. 40e, Pleurobranchus garciagomezi. 60e, Hypselodoris sp., vert.

2011 ***Perf. 13x13¼, 13¼x13***
954-958 A212 Set of 5 5.00 5.00

Flora and Fauna of Cha das Caldeiras Protected Area — A213

Designs: 5e, Halcion leucocephala. 10e, Verbascum cystolithicum. 20e, Acrocephalus brevipennis. 40e, Echium vulcanorum. 60e, Pterodroma feae. 100e, Erisimum caboverdeanum.
150e, Halcion leucocephala, Acrocephalus brevipennis, horiz.

2011 ***Perf. 13¼x13***
959-964 A213 Set of 6 9.00 9.00

Souvenir Sheet
Perf. 13x13¼
965 A213 150e multi 6.00 6.00

Baltazar Lopes da Silva (1907-89), Writer
A214

2012 ***Perf. 13x13¼***
966 A214 100e multi 4.00 4.00

Old Household Objects — A215

Designs: No. 967, 60e, Oil burner (Fogao a petróleo). No. 968, 60e, Oil lamp (Conddeeiro a petróleo). No. 969, 60e, Washbasin (Lavatório). No. 970, 60e, Iron (Ferro de engomar a carvao), horiz.

2012 ***Perf. 13¼x13, 13x13¼***
967-970 A215 Set of 4 9.00 9.00

Emigration A216

Designs: 30e, Compass rose, man on boat waving to family on dock. 50e, Man writing on envelope. 60e, Agricultural worker, hand picking cacao pod. 100e, Man wheeling suitcase, world map, horiz.

2012 *Perf. 13¼x13, 13x13¼*
971-974 A216 Set of 4 9.00 9.00

Composers and Musicians — A217

Designs: 10e, Ano Nobu (1933-2004), composer. 20e, Ildo Lobo (1953-2004), singer. 30e, Renato Cardoso (1951-89), composer. 40e, Manuel d'Novas (1938-2009), composer. 50e, Codé di Dona (1940-2010), composer. 60e, Orlando Pantera (1967-2001), composer.

2012 Litho. *Perf. 13¼*
975-980 A217 Set of 6 7.50 7.50

Cape Verde National Soccer Team A218

Designs: 40e, Team emblem. 60e, Team jersey, vert.
100e, Like 40e.

2012 *Perf. 13x13¼, 13¼x13*
981-982 A218 Set of 2 3.50 3.50

Souvenir Sheet

983 A218 100e multi 3.50 3.50

Flora and Fauna of Santo Antao Proctected Area — A219

Designs: 10e, Buteo bannermani. 20e, Pterodroma feae. 30e, Sideroxylon marginata. 40e, Carex antolensis, horiz. 50e, Tarentola caboverdiana caboverdiana, horiz. 60e, Papaver gorgoneum, horiz.
100e, Birds in flight over Coza Natural Park, horiz.

2012 *Perf. 13¼x13, 13x13¼*
984-989 A219 Set of 6 7.50 7.50

Souvenir Sheet

990 A219 100e multi 3.50 3.50

Brasiliana 2013 Intl. Philatelic Exhibition, Rio de Janeiro A220

Brasiliana 2013 emblem, Brazil Nos. 1, 2 and 3, and: 60e, Map of Brazil and circle indicating location of Cape Verde. 150e, Cape Verde #1, map of Cape Verde, label without denomination similar to 60e.

2013 Litho. *Perf. 13½*
991 A220 60e multi 2.25 2.25

Size: 145x81mm

Imperf

992 A220 150e multi + label 5.00 5.00

African Union, 50th Anniv. — A221

2013 Litho. *Perf. 13½*
993 A221 60e multi 2.00 2.00

Father Custódio Ferreira de Campos and Church A222

2013, Oct. 9 Litho. *Perf. 13x13¼*
994 A222 60e multi 2.00 2.00

Carnaval — A223

Carnaval participants and animators: No. 995, 60e, Capote (1916-85). No. 996, 60e, Artur Boxe (1910-2004). No. 997, 60e, Negro Sarafe (1924-92).

2014, Feb. 28 Litho. *Perf. 13½*
995-997 A223 Set of 3 6.00 6.00

Portuguese Language, 800th Anniv. A224

2014, May 5 Litho. *Perf. 12x12½*
998 A224 60e multi 2.00 2.00

A225

Intl. Children's Day A226

2014, June 1 Litho. *Perf. 13x13½*
999 A225 60e multi 2.00 2.00
1000 A226 60e multi 2.00 2.00

A227

A228

Corn Processing A229

2014, Oct. 9 Litho. *Perf. 13x13½*
1001 A227 60e multi 3.00 3.00
1002 A228 60e multi 3.00 3.00
1003 A229 60e multi 3.00 3.00
Nos. 1001-1003 (3) 9.00 9.00

Intl. Association of Portuguese-Speaking Countries, 25th Anniv. — A230

2015, Apr. 27 Litho. *Perf. 13¼x13*
1004 A230 60e multi 1.50 1.50

See Angola No. , Brazil No. 3300, Guinea-Bissau No. , Macao No. 1440, Mozambique No. , Portugal Nos. 3694-3695, St. Thomas & Prince Islands No. 2954, and Timor No.

Independence, 40th Anniv. — A231

Perf. 14½x14¼

2015, June 23 Litho.
1005 A231 60e multi 1.50 1.50

Economic Community of West African States, 40th Anniv. A232

2015, July Litho. *Perf. 13x13¼*
1006 A232 60e multi 1.50 1.50

Admission to United Nations, 40th Anniv. A233

2015, Oct. 6 Litho. *Perf. 13x13¼*
1007 A233 60e multi 1.50 1.50

United Nations Food and Agriculture Organization, 70th Anniv. — A234

Designs: No. 1008, 60e, Seeds and peas. No. 1009, 60e, Terraced farmland. No. 1010, 60e, Plate of food.

2015, Oct. 16 Litho. *Perf. 13¼*

Stamp + Label

1008-1010 A234 Set of 3 5.00 5.00

Kriol Jazz Festival, Praia A235

2016, Apr. 8 Litho. *Perf. 13¼*
1011 A235 60e multi 1.50 1.50

Emblem of Atlantic Music Expo — A236

2016, Apr. 12 Litho. *Perf. 13½*
1012 A236 60e multi 1.50 1.50

Values are for stamps with surrounding selvage.

Kavala Fresk Festival — A237

2016, July 9 Litho. *Perf. 14¼x14½*
1013 A237 60e multi 1.50 1.50

Prionace Glauca — A238

No. 1014 — WWF emblem, QR code and: a, Shark swimming left. b, Shark chasing squid. c, Shark swimming right, d, Two sharks, map.

2016, Nov. 15 Litho. *Perf. 13¼*
1014 Horiz. strip of 4 6.00 6.00
a.-d. A238 60e Any single 1.25 1.25

Worldwide Fund for Nature (WWF).

Cesária Evora (1941-2011), Singer — A239

Litho. With Foil Application

2016, Nov. 16 *Perf. 13¾*

1015 A239 60e multi 1.50 1.50

Souvenir Sheet

1016 A239 150e multi 3.50 3.50

Bataclan Terrorist Attack, Paris, 1st anniv. (No. 1016).

National Communications Authority, 10th Anniv. — A240

2016, Nov. 25 **Litho.** *Perf. 14¼*

1017 A240 60e multi 1.50 1.50

National Day Against Sexual Abuse and Exploitation of Minors — A241

2017, Nov. 20 **Litho.** *Perf. 13¼*

1018 A241 60e multi 1.60 1.60

Inforpress (Cape Verdean News Agency), 30th Anniv. — A242

Denominations: 40e, 60e.
100e, Graduates, airplane, map of Cape Verde, crane, bar graph, globe and 30th anniv. emblem.

2018 **Litho.** *Perf. 13½*

1019-1020 A242 Set of 2 2.10 2.10

Size:183x110mm

Imperf

1021 A242 100e multi + label 2.10 2.10

2019 African Beach Games, Sal Island A243

Denominations: 40e, 60e.
150e, Children playing soccer, map of Sal Island, volleyball players, ships and turtle mascot.

2019, June 13 **Litho.** *Perf. 13½*

1022-1023 A243 Set of 2 2.10 2.10

Souvenir Sheet

Size: 141x78mm

Imperf

1024 A243 150e multi 3.25 3.25

AIR POST STAMPS

Common Design Type

Name and Value in Black

Perf. 13½x13

1938, July 26 **Unwmk.**

C1	CD39	10c red orange	.60	.50
C2	CD39	20c purple	.60	.50
C3	CD39	50c orange	.60	.50
C4	CD39	1e ultra	.60	.50
C5	CD39	2e lilac brown	1.40	.80
C6	CD39	3e dk green	1.75	1.40
C7	CD39	5e red brown	5.50	2.10
C8	CD39	9e rose carmine	9.00	3.75
C9	CD39	10e magenta	9.75	5.00
		Nos. C1-C9 (9)	29.80	15.05
		Set, never hinged	50.00	

No. C7 exists with overprint "Exposicao Internacional de Nova York, 1939-1940" and Trylon and Perisphere. Value $200.

POSTAGE DUE STAMPS

D1

1904 **Unwmk.** **Typo.** *Perf. 12*

J1	D1	5r yellow grn	.45	*.25*
J2	D1	10r slate	.45	*.25*
J3	D1	20r yellow brn	.55	*.40*
J4	D1	30r red orange	1.25	*.40*
J5	D1	50r gray brown	.50	*.35*
J6	D1	60r red brown	10.00	4.25
J7	D1	100r lilac	2.00	1.25
J8	D1	130r dull blue	2.00	1.25
J9	D1	200r carmine	1.75	1.60
J10	D1	500r dull violet	5.50	*3.00*
		Nos. J1-J10 (10)	24.45	*13.00*

Overprinted in Carmine or Green

1911

J11	D1	5r yellow grn	.30	.25
J12	D1	10r slate	.30	.25
J13	D1	20r yellow brn	.35	.25
J14	D1	30r orange	.35	.25
J15	D1	50r gray brown	.65	.40
J16	D1	60r red brown	.65	.40
J17	D1	100r lilac	.65	.40
J18	D1	130r dull blue	.75	.65
J19	D1	200r carmine (G)	2.50	1.50
J20	D1	500r dull violet	3.00	2.50
		Nos. J11-J20 (10)	9.50	6.85

D2

1921 *Perf. 11½*

J21	D2	½c yellow grn	.30	.25
J22	D2	1c slate	.30	.25
J23	D2	2c red brown	.30	.25
J24	D2	3c orange	.30	.25
J25	D2	5c gray brown	.30	.25
J26	D2	6c lt brown	.30	.25
J27	D2	10c red violet	.30	.25
J28	D2	13c dull blue	.55	*.40*
J29	D2	20c carmine	.60	*.50*
J30	D2	50c gray	1.75	*1.10*
		Nos. J21-J30 (10)	5.00	*3.75*

Catalogue values for unused stamps in this section, from this point to the end of the section, are for Never Hinged items.

Common Design Type

Photogravure and Typographed

1952 **Unwmk.** *Perf. 14*

Numeral in Red, Frame Multicolored

J31	CD45	10c chocolate	.30	.25
J32	CD45	30c black brown	.30	.25
J33	CD45	50c dark blue	.30	.25
J34	CD45	1e dark blue	.40	.25
J35	CD45	2e red brown	.40	.30
J36	CD45	5e olive green	1.10	1.00
		Nos. J31-J36 (6)	2.80	2.30

NEWSPAPER STAMP

N1

1893 **Typo.** **Unwmk.** *Perf. 11½*

P1	N1	2½r chocolate	1.75	.90
a.		Perf. 12½	3.25	1.75
b.		Perf. 13½	9.00	3.25

For surcharges see Nos. 79, 206.

POSTAL TAX STAMPS

Pombal Issue

Common Design Types

1925 **Unwmk.** **Engr.** *Perf. 12½*

RA1	CD28	15c dull vio & blk	.75	.60
RA2	CD29	15c dull vio & blk	.75	.60
RA3	CD30	15c dull vio & blk	.75	.60
		Nos. RA1-RA3 (3)	2.25	1.80

St. Isabel — PT1

1948 **Litho.** *Perf. 11*

RA4	PT1	50c dark green	3.75	2.40
RA5	PT1	1e henna brown	7.50	3.00

Catalogue values for unused stamps in this section, from this point to the end of the section, are for Never Hinged items.

No. RA5 Surcharged with New Value and Bars

1959

RA6 PT1 50c on 1e henna brown 1.40 1.10

Perf. 14

RA7	PT1	50c carmine rose	2.10	1.00
RA8	PT1	1e blue	2.10	1.00

St. Isabel Type Redrawn

1967-73 **Litho.** *Perf. 14*

RA9	PT1	30c (blue panel)	.50	.50
RA9A	PT1	30c (orange panel)	.50	.50
RA10	PT1	50c (lilac rose panel)	.85	.85
RA11	PT1	50c (red panel) ('72)	*.50*	*.50*
RA12	PT1	1e (brn panel)	1.00	1.00
RA13	PT1	1e (red lilac panel) ('72)	*1.00*	*1.00*
		Nos. RA9-RA13 (6)	*4.35*	*4.35*

Nos. RA9-RA13 are inscribed "ASSISTENCIA" in large letters in bottom panel and "PORTUGAL" and "CABO VERDE" in small letters in upper left corner.

Revenue Stamps Surcharged in Green, Blue or Black — PT2

Black "CABO VERDE" & Value

Pale Green Burelage

1967-72 **Typo.** *Perf. 12*

RA14	PT2	50c on 1c org (Bl) ('71)	1.40	.90
a.		Black surcharge ('68?)	*20.00*	*14.50*
RA15	PT2	50c on 2c org (Bk) ('69)	*25.00*	*14.50*
c.		Inverted surcharge	*50.00*	*35.00*
RA16	PT2	50c on 3c org (G) ('72)	1.10	.60
RA17	PT2	50c on 5c org (G) ('72)	1.10	.60
RA18	PT2	50c on 10c org (G) ('71)	1.25	1.00
RA19	PT2	1e on 1c org (Bk)	2.75	2.10
RA20	PT2	1e on 2c org (G) ('71)	2.00	1.75
a.		Blue surcharge ('71)	3.00	1.10
b.		Black surcharge	4.00	2.10
		Nos. RA14-RA20 (7)	*34.60*	*21.45*

POSTAL TAX DUE STAMPS

Pombal Issue

Common Design Types

1925 **Unwmk.** *Perf. 12½*

RAJ1	CD28	30c dull vio & blk	.75	.70
RAJ2	CD29	30c dull vio & blk	.75	.70
RAJ3	CD30	30c dull vio & blk	.75	.70
		Nos. RAJ1-RAJ3 (3)	2.25	2.10

CARIBBEAN NETHERLANDS

'kar-ē-bbe-ə-n 'ne-thər-lən̦d̦z

LOCATION — The islands of Bonaire (north of Venezuela), Saint Eustatius and Saba (south of Anguilla)
AREA — 125 sq. mi.
POP. — 18,012 (2010)
CAPITAL — Kralendijk, Bonaire; Oranjestad, Saint Eustatius; The Bottom, Saba

On Oct. 10, 2010, Caribbean Netherlands, formerly part of Netherlands Antilles, became special municipalities within the Kingdom of the Netherlands.

100 Cents = 1 Gulden
100 Cents = 1 Dollar (2011)

Catalogue values for all unused stamps in this country are for Never Hinged items.

Map of Islands and West Indies, Arms, Queen Beatrix A1

Perf. 13¾

2010, Oct. 10 Litho. Unwmk.
1 A1 111c multicolored 1.50 1.50

New Constitutional Status — A2

Designs: 63c, Triangle with flags of Bonaire, Saint Eustatius and Saba, Acropora palmata. 81c, Three Glassy sweepers with elements of flags of Bonaire, Saint Eustatius and Saba. 93c, Two Yellowcheek wrasses with elements of Bonaire flag. 96c, Parrotfish with elements of Saint Eustatius flag. 159c, Blue tang surgeonfish with elements of Saba flag.

2011, June 1 ***Perf. 13¼x13***
2-6 A2 Set of 5 10.00 10.00

Greetings — A3

Inscriptions: 33c, Thinking of you. 63c, Always in my prayers. 93c, Celebrate another year. 159c, Love U so much. 226c, For you my cup of tea.

2011, July 11 ***Perf. 13x13¼***
7-11 A3 Set of 5 10.00 10.00

Corals — A4

Designs: 45c, Scolymia wellsi. 63c, Diodogorgia nodulifera, vert. 159c, Eusmilia fastigiata. 226c, Acropora palmata, vert.

Perf. 13¼x13, 13x13¼

2011, Sept. 11
12-15 A4 Set of 4 8.00 7.00

Visit of Queen Beatrix — A5

Queen Beatrix: 81c, Without hat. 159c, Wearing hat.
250c, Queen Beatrix in coach, horiz.

2011, Nov. 4 ***Perf. 14***
16-17 A5 Set of 2 4.50 4.50

Souvenir Sheet

18 A5 250c multi 5.00 5.00

Holiday Light Decorations A6

Designs: 63c, Snowflakes. 81c, Reindeer. 93c, Flowers. 159c, Bells.

2011, Nov. 11 ***Perf. 13½x12¾***
19-22 A6 Set of 4 8.00 8.00

Sailboats A7

Designs: 66c, Catamaran. 99c, Optimist. 101c, Sunfish. 168c, Laser, vert.

Perf. 13½x12¾, 12¾x13½

2012, Feb. 1
23-26 A7 Set of 4 8.50 8.50

Parrots — A8

Designs: 100c, Ara chloropterus. 150c, Aratinga pertinax. 200c, Amazona ochrocephala ochrocephala. 250c, Anodorhynchus hyacinthinus.

2012, June 1 ***Perf. 12¾x13½***
27-30 A8 Set of 4 14.00 14.00

Rafflesia Flower — A9

Mandala — A10

2012, June 18 ***Perf. 13½x12¾***
31 A9 10c multicolored .25 .25

Souvenir Sheet

Perf.

32 A10 200c multicolored 4.00 4.00

Indoensia 2012 World Stamp Exhibition, Jakarta.

Miniature Sheet

Dutch Queens and Heraldry — A11

No. 33: a, Queen Emma. b, Queen Wilhelmina. c, Queen Juliana. d, Queen Beatrix. e, Royal arms.

Litho. & Embossed

2012, Sept. 3 ***Perf. 12¾x13½***
33 A11 300c Sheet of 5, #a-e 30.00 30.00

Arms and Christmas Ornaments A12

Designs: 66c, Arms of Saba, ornament in shape of Saba, ornament with Saba flag elements. 99c, Arms of St. Eustatius, ornament in shape of St. Eustatius, ornament with St. Eustatius flag elements. 101c, Arms of Bonaire, ornament in shape of Bonaire, ornament with Bonaire flag elements. 168c, Arms of Netherlands, ornaments with flag elements of Saba, St. Eustatius and Bonaire.

2012, Nov. 1 Litho. ***Perf. 13¼x13***
34-37 A12 Set of 4 8.25 8.25

Emblem and Flamingo A13

No. 38 — Inscribed: a, Bonaire. b, Saba. c, St, Eustatius. d, Bonaire. e, Saba. f, St. Eustatius.

2014, Oct. 10 Litho. ***Rouletted 6½***
38 Horiz. strip of 6 11.50 11.50
a.-c. A13 88c Any single 1.75 1.75
d.-f. A13 99c Any single 2.00 2.00

Miniature Sheets

Flamingos — A14

Pelicans — A15

Hummingbirds — A16

Various birds, as shown.

Perf. 13¼x13½

2014, Nov. 10 Litho.

Inscribed "Bonaire"

39 A14 99c Sheet of 5, #a-e 10.00 10.00

Inscribed "Saba"

40 A15 99c Sheet of 5, #a-e 10.00 10.00

Inscribed "St. Eustatius"

41 A16 99c Sheet of 5, #a-e 10.00 10.00
Nos. 39-41 (3) 30.00 30.00

Personalized Stamp — A17

Serpentine Die Cut 14¼

2014, Nov. 10 Litho.

Self-Adhesive

42 A17 99c multi + label 2.00 2.00

No. 42 was printed in sheets of 10 + 10 labels. The label shown is a generic label. Two other generic labels, depicting scenes of Saba and St. Eustatius were created. Labels could also be personalized. Sheets containing personalized labels sold for $15.

Miniature Sheet

Flag and King Willem-Alexander — A18

Flag of Bonaire (No. 43), Saba (No. 44) or St. Eustatius (No. 45) with King Willem-Alexander in: a, 99c, Sepia. b, 99c, Full color. c, $1.36, Sepia. d, $1.36, Full color. e, $1.98, Sepia, f, $1.98, Full color. g, $2.82, Sepia, h, $2.82, Full color. i, $4.40, Sepia. j, $4.40, Full color.

2015, Apr. 30 Litho. ***Perf. 14x13½***

Inscribed "Bonaire"

43 A18 Sheet of 10, #a-j 45.00 45.00

Inscribed "Saba"

44 A18 Sheet of 10, #a-j 45.00 45.00

Inscribed "St. Eustatius"

45 A18 Sheet of 10, #a-j 45.00 45.00
Nos. 43-45 (3) 135.00 135.00

A19

A20

A21

Personalized Stamps A22

2016, Jan. 15 Litho. *Perf. 13¼x14*

Inscribed "Bonaire"

46 A19 88c multi 1.90 1.90
47 A20 88c multi 1.90 1.90
48 A21 88c multi 1.90 1.90
49 A22 88c multi 1.90 1.90

Inscribed "Saba"

50 A19 88c multi 1.90 1.90
51 A20 88c multi 1.90 1.90
52 A21 88c multi 1.90 1.90
53 A22 88c multi 1.90 1.90

Inscribed "St. Eustatius"

54 A19 88c multi 1.90 1.90
55 A20 88c multi 1.90 1.90
56 A21 88c multi 1.90 1.90

Inscribed "Sint Eustatius"

57 A22 88c multi 1.90 1.90
Nos. 46-57 (12) 22.80 22.80

Vignette portions of stamps could be personalized. The vignettes shown for types A19-A22 are generic images. Different generic images were created for Nos. 50-57, with colors differing from types A19-A22 being used for frames on these stamps.

Kingdom of the Netherlands, 200th Anniv. — A23

2016, Mar. 30 Litho. *Perf. 14½*

Inscribed "Bonaire"

58 A23 99c purple & pink 2.00 2.00
59 A23 99c deep red & red 2.00 2.00
60 A23 99c grn & pale blue 2.00 2.00

Inscribed "Saba"

61 A23 99c purple & pink 2.00 2.00
a. Souvenir sheet of 2, #60, 61, + central label 4.00 4.00
62 A23 99c deep red & red 2.00 2.00
a. Souvenir sheet of 2, #58, 62, + central label 4.00 4.00
63 A23 99c grn & pale blue 2.00 2.00

Inscribed "St. Eustatius"

64 A23 99c purple & pink 2.00 2.00
a. Souvenir sheet of 2, #59, 64, + central label 4.00 4.00
b. Souvenir sheet of 2, #63, 64, + central label 4.00 4.00
65 A23 99c deep red & red 2.00 2.00
a. Souvenir sheet of 2, #61, 65, + central label 4.00 4.00
66 A23 99c grn & pale blue 2.00 2.00
a. Souvenir sheet of 2, #58, 66, + central label 4.00 4.00
Nos. 58-66 (9) 18.00 18.00

Souvenir Sheets

Inscribed "Bonaire"

67 Sheet of 2 + central label 11.50 11.50
a. A23 282c green & pale blue 5.75 5.75
b. A23 282c orange red & orange 5.75 5.75

Inscribed "Saba"

68 Sheet of 2 + central label 11.50 11.50
a. A23 282c green & pale blue 5.75 5.75
b. A23 282c purple & blue 5.75 5.75

Inscribed "St. Eustatius"

69 Sheet of 2 + central label 11.50 11.50
a. A23 282c green & pale blue 5.75 5.75
b. A23 282c ol bister & yellow 5.75 5.75
Nos. 67-69 (3) 34.50 34.50

Souvenir Sheets

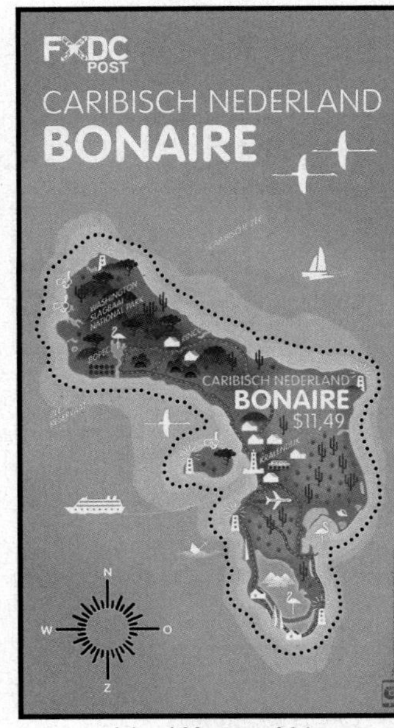

Island Maps — A24

Map of: No. 70, Bonaire. No. 71, Saba. No. 72, St. Eustatius.

2016, Oct. 10 Litho. *Perf.*

Inscribed "Bonaire"

70 A24 $11.49 multi 23.00 23.00

Inscribed "Saba"

71 A24 $11.49 multi 23.00 23.00

Inscribed "St. Eustatius"

72 A24 $11.49 multi 23.00 23.00
Nos. 70-72 (3) 69.00 69.00

No. 70 contains one 68x87mm stamp. No. 71 contains one 68x60mm stamp. No. 72 contains one 68x76mm stamp.

A25

A26

A27

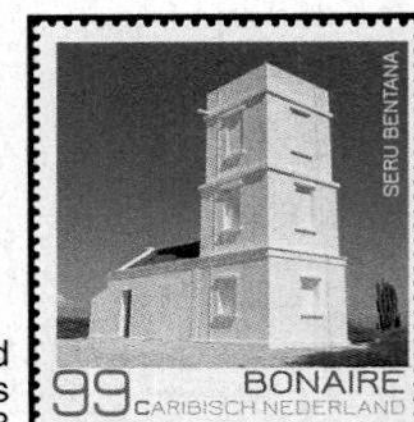

Personalized Stamps A28

2017, Mar. 3 Litho. *Perf. 13¼x13*

Inscribed "Bonaire"

73 A25 99c multi 2.00 2.00
74 A26 99c multi 2.00 2.00
75 A27 99c multi 2.00 2.00
76 A28 99c multi 2.00 2.00

Inscribed "Saba"

77 A25 99c multi 2.00 2.00
78 A26 99c multi 2.00 2.00
79 A27 99c multi 2.00 2.00
80 A28 99c multi 2.00 2.00

Inscribed "St. Eustatius"

81 A25 99c multi 2.00 2.00
82 A26 99c multi 2.00 2.00
83 A27 99c multi 2.00 2.00
84 A28 99c multi 2.00 2.00
Nos. 73-84 (12) 24.00 24.00

Vignette portions of stamps could be personalized. The vignettes shown for types A25-A28 are generic images. Different generic images were created for Nos. 77-84, with colors differing from types A27-A28 being used for frames on these stamps.

Miniature Sheets

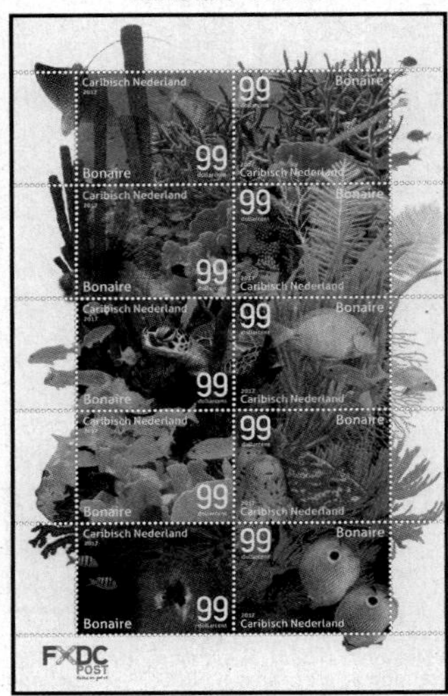

A29

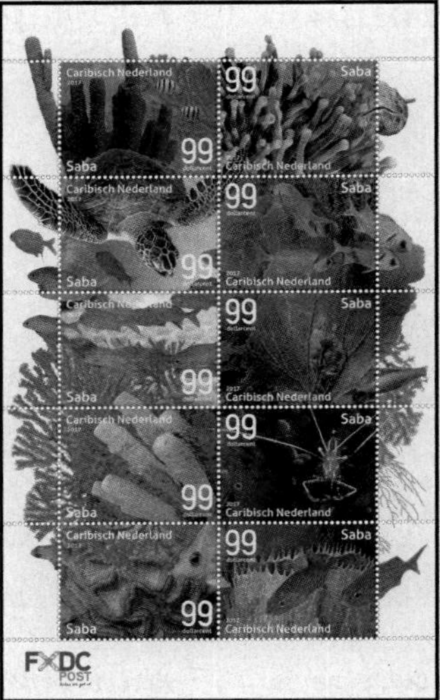

A30

Coral Reef Life — A31

Various marine life, as shown.

2017, July 31 Litho. *Perf. 14x13½*

Inscribed "Bonaire"

85 A29 99c Sheet of 10, #a-j 20.00 20.00

Inscribed "Saba"

86 A30 99c Sheet of 10, #a-j 20.00 20.00

Inscribed "Sint Eustatius"

87 A31 99c Sheet of 10, #a-j 20.00 20.00
Nos. 85-87 (3) 60.00 60.00

Souvenir Sheets

Endangered Animals — A32

Designs: No. 88, Amazona barbadensis. No. 89, Epinephelus striatus. No. 90, Iguana delicatissima.

2017, Nov. 27 Litho. *Perf.*

Inscribed "Bonaire"

88 A32 $11.49 multi 20.00 20.00

Inscribed "Saba"

89 A32 $11.49 multi 20.00 20.00

Inscribed "Sint Eustatius"

90 A32 $11.49 multi 20.00 20.00
Nos. 88-90 (3) 60.00 60.00

Miniature Sheets

Cactus Forest — A33

Cloud Forest — A34

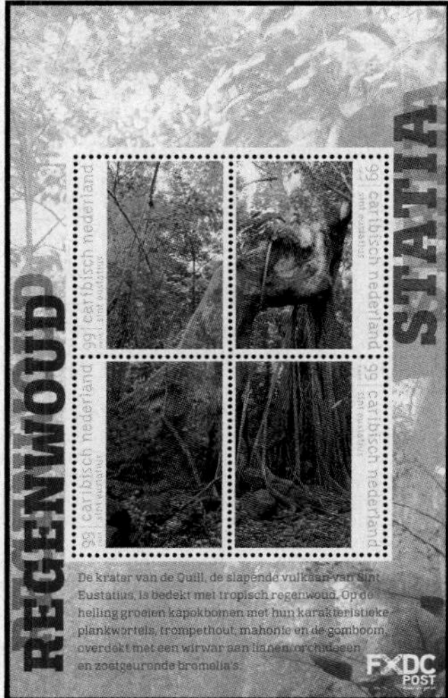

Rain Forest — A35

Various plants, as shown.

2018, Apr. 3 Litho. *Perf. 13½x14*

Inscribed "Bonaire"

91 A33 99c Sheet of 4, #a-d 8.00 8.00

Inscribed "Saba"

92 A34 99c Sheet of 4, #a-d 8.00 8.00

Inscribed "Sint Eustatius"

93 A35 99c Sheet of 4, #a-d 8.00 8.00
Nos. 91-93 (3) 24.00 24.00

Miniature Sheets

Shells — A36

No. 94: a, Nautilus pompilius. b, Strombus gigas. c, Trochus niloticus. d, Phyllonotus erythrostomus.

No. 95: a, Cymatium parthenopeum. b, Cypraea tigris. c, Trochus niloticus, diff. d, Melongena melongena.

No. 96: a, Tonna galea. b, Voluta ebraea. c, Cassis cornuta. d, Mitra papalis.

2018, Apr. 3 Litho. *Perf. 13½x14*

Inscribed "Bonaire"

94 A36 99c Sheet of 4, #a-d 8.00 8.00

Inscribed "Saba"

95 A36 99c Sheet of 4, #a-d 8.00 8.00

Inscribed "Sint Eustatius"

96 A36 99c Sheet of 4, #a-d 8.00 8.00
Nos. 94-96 (3) 24.00 24.00

Miniature Sheets

A37

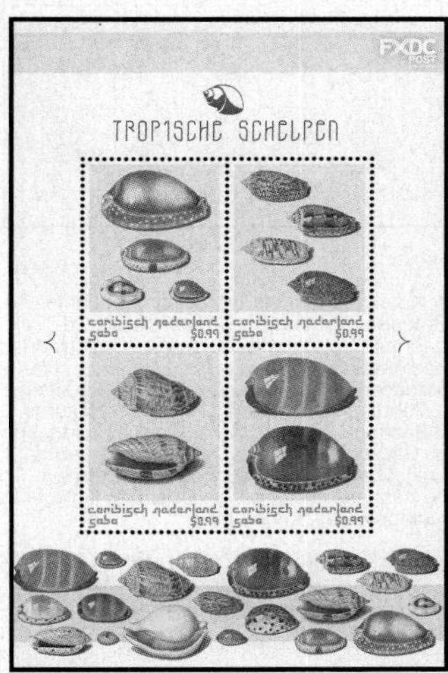

A38

Shells — A39

No. 97: a, Two shells, large shell on top. b, Four shells. c, Three shells. d, Two shells, large shell on bottom.

No. 98: a, Four shells, two on third row. b, Four shells in zigzag pattern. c, Two small shells. d, Two large shells.

No. 99: a, Two shells, large shell on top. b, Three shells. c, Two similarly-sized shells. d, Two shells, large shell on bottom.

2018, Apr. 3 Litho. *Perf. 13¼*

Inscribed "Bonaire"

97 A37 99c Sheet of 4, #a-d 8.00 8.00

Inscribed "Saba"

98 A38 99c Sheet of 4, #a-d 8.00 8.00

Inscribed "Sint Eustatius"

99 A39 99c Sheet of 4, #a-d 8.00 8.00
Nos. 97-99 (3) 24.00 24.00

Miniature Sheets

Marine Life — A40

No. 100 — Inscriptions: a, Slablad Naaktslak op Sterkoraal. b, Boogkrab op Vaasspons. c, Caraibische Poetsvis in Paarse Buisspons. d, Gewone Koraalduivel.

No. 101 — Inscriptions: a, Lucifer-anemoon. b, Kaapersgarnaal op Azuurblauwe Vaasspons. c, Geelneus Koraalgrondel op Steenkoraal. d, Kerstboomworm op Sterkoraal.

No. 102 — Inscriptions: a, Tandbaars in Azuurblauwe Vaasspons. b, Hersenkoraal. c, Hoornkoraal. d, Poetsgarnaal op Een Zeeanemoon.

2018, Apr. 3 Litho. *Perf. 13¼x14*

Inscribed "Bonaire"

100 A40 99c Sheet of 4, #a-d 8.00 8.00

Inscribed "Saba"

101 A40 99c Sheet of 4, #a-d 8.00 8.00

Inscribed "St. Eustatius"

102 A40 99c Sheet of 4, #a-d 8.00 8.00
Nos. 100-102 (3) 24.00 24.00

Miniature Sheets

Surfing and Windsurfing — A41

Butterflies and Flowers — A42

Hummingbirds — A43

No. 103: a, Windsurfer to right of sail. b, Surfer, dark blue wave breaking at right. c, Palm tree and surfboards. d, Surfer on white surfboard, wave breaking at left. e, Surfer with white trunks on yellow surfboard, wave breaking at left. f, Windsurfer to left of sail. g, Surfer on white surfboard, wave breaking at right. h, Windsurfer in front of sail.

No. 104: a, Butterfly in flight. b, Six orange flowers. c, Striped butterfly on flower. d, Yellow and red orchids. e, Three pink orchids. f, Monarch butterfly on flower. g, Pink flower. h, Blue butterfly on foliage.

No. 105: a, Pink hummingbird with bill pointing to UR. b, Green hummingbird with red throat with bill pointing to UL. c, Green hummingbird with bill pointing to UR. d, Hummingbird with red head with bill pointing to LL. e, Hummingbird with orange tail feathers on branch. f, Hummingbird with purple breast with bill pointing to left. g, Hummingbird with red head and wings with bill pointing to LR. h, Blue and black hummingbird with bill pointing to UL.

2018, July 20 Litho. *Perf. 13½x14*

Inscribed "Bonaire"

103 A41 150c Sheet of 8, #a-h, + 2 labels 24.00 24.00

Inscribed "Saba"

104 A42 150c Sheet of 8, #a-h, + 2 labels 24.00 24.00

Inscribed "Sint Eustatius"

105 A43 150c Sheet of 8, #a-h, + 2 labels 24.00 24.00
Nos. 103-105 (3) 72.00 72.00

Miniature Sheet

The Night Watch, by Rembrandt (1606-69) — A44

No. 106 — Painting details: a, Head of woman at left, and head of arquebusier. b, Captain Frans Bannink Cocq and man behind him. c, Lieutenant Willem van Ruytenburch. d, Man with gun. e, Leg of Captain Bannink Cocq at LR. f. Legs of Captain Bannink Cocq. g, Legs of van Ruytenburch. h, Legs of man with gun. i, Man in red with gun. j, Head of woman. k, Gun barrel, extended arm. l, Three men. m, Legs of man in red with gun. n, Stock of gun, chicken, women's legs. o, Back of dog. p, Drum.

2019, Jan. 21 Litho. *Perf. 13½x14*
Stamps Inscribed "Bonaire"

106 A44 99c Sheet of 16, #a-p 32.00 32.00

Miniature Sheet

New Year 2019 (Year of the Pig) — A45

No. 107 — Pig, Chinese lanterns with Chinese inscription and "2019" at: a, LR. b, LL. c, UR. d, UL.

2019, Feb. 5 Litho. *Perf. 13½x14*
Stamps Inscribed "Bonaire"

107 A45 99c Sheet of 4, #a-d 8.00 8.00

Self-Portrait as the Apostle Paul, by Rembrandt (1606-69) — A46

No. 108: a, Headdress and eye, inscriptions at left. b, Headdress, eye and nose, inscriptions at right. c, Cheek, inscriptions at left. d, Cheek, inscriptions at right.

2019, Mar. 18 Litho. *Perf. 13½x14*
Stamps Inscribed "Bonaire"

108 A46 99c Block of 4, #a-d 8.00 8.00

No. 108 was printed in sheets containing four blocks.

The Milkmaid, by Johannes Vermeer (1632-75) — A47

No. 109: a, Baskets on wall, hand of milkmaid, inscriptions at left. b, Head of milkmaid, inscriptions at right. c, Bread basket, milk being poured, inscriptions at left. d, Milkmaid's arm and corner of table, inscriptions at right.

2019, June 24 Litho. *Perf. 13½x14*
Stamps Inscribed "Saba"

109 A47 99c Block of 4, #a-d 8.00 8.00

No. 109 was printed in sheets containing four blocks.

A gold $50 stamp issued July 4, 2019, depicting Rembrandt van Rijn and inscribed "Bonaire" was produced in limited quantities.

Woman Reading a Letter, by Johannes Vermeer (1632-75) — A48

No. 110 — Painting details: a, Side of window shade. b, Woman. c, Chair and desk. d, Legs of woman.

2019, Aug. 20 Litho. *Perf. 13½x14*
Stamps Inscribed "Saba"

110 A48 99c Block of 4, #a-d 8.00 8.00

No. 110 was printed in sheets containing four blocks.

Miniature Sheet

Birds — A49

No. 111: a, Charadrius semipalmatus. b, Setophaga ruticilla. c, Anas discors. d, Pelegasnus occidentalis. e, Onychoprion anaethetus. f, Mniotilta varia. g, Sula sula. h, Megaceryle alcyon. i, Eulampis holosericeus. j, Pandion haliaetus. k, Phaethon lepturus. l, Setophaga americana. m, Quiscalus lugubris. n, Circus cyaneus. o, Sphyrapicus varius. p, Loxigilla noctis. q, Tringa flavipes. r, Nyctanassa violacea. s, Coereba flaveola. t, Leucophaeus atricilla.

2019, Oct. 4 Litho. *Perf. 13½x14*
Stamps Inscribed "Saba" Without "Caribisch Nederland" Inscription

111 A49 150c Sheet of 20, #a-t 60.00 60.00

Miniature Sheet

Butterflies — A50

No. 112: a, Danaus plexippus. b, Strymon acis. c, Ephyriades arcas. d, Cyclargus thomasi. e, Marpesia petreus. f, Ascia monuste. g, Pyrgus oileus. h, Biblis hyperia. i, Eurmea elathea. j, Urbanus proteus. k, Agraulis vanillae. l, Leptotes cassius. m, Junonia coenia. n, Wallengrenia ophites. o, Pheobis sennae. p, Heliconius charitonia. q, Hemiargus hanno. r, Eurema lisa. s, Vanessa cardui. t, Polygonus manueli.

2019, Oct. 4 Litho. *Perf. 13½x14*
Stamps Inscribed "St. Eustatius" Without "Caribisch Nederland" Inscription

112 A50 150c Sheet of 20, #a-t 60.00 60.00

Miniature Sheet

De Magere Compagnie (The Meagre Company), by Frans Hals (c. 1582-1666) — A51

No. 113 — Painting details: a, Flag bearer Nicolaes van Bambeeck. b, Captain Reinier Reael, Lieutenant Cornelis Michielsz Blaeuw and seated man. c, Four men. d, Man with mustache. e, Legs of Bambeeck. f, Shaft of halbard and legs of three men. g, Hand and shaft of halbard. h, Legs of man with mustache. i, Two men, one wearing hat with feather. j, Two men without hats, and arm of third man, two halbard shafts in background. k, Two men without hats. l, Two men, one with hat, two halbard shafts in background. m, Legs of men, one man wearing white stockings. n, Legs of men. o, Legs, two feet pointing in opposite directions. p, Legs of men, diff.

2019, Oct. 21 Litho. *Perf. 13½x14*
Stamps Inscribed "St. Eustatius"

113 A51 99c Sheet of 16, #a-p 32.00 32.00

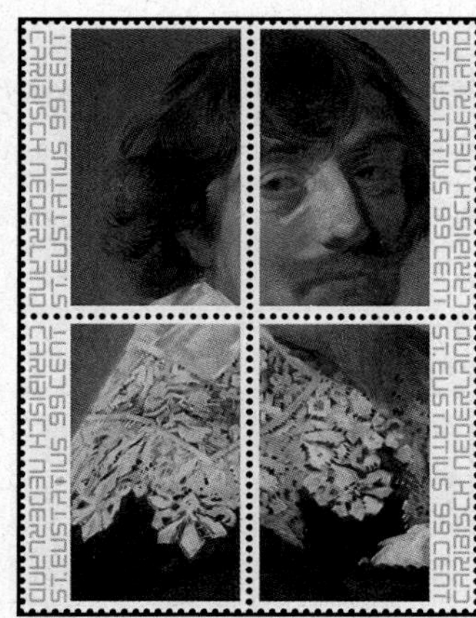

Portrait of a Man, Possibly Nicolaes Hasselaer, by Frans Hals (c. 1582-1666) — A52

No. 114 — Painting details: a, Hair. b, Face. c, Shoulder. d, Chin and chest.

2019, Dec. 16 Litho. *Perf. 13½x14*
Stamps Inscribed "St. Eustatius"

114 A52 99c Block of 4, #a-d 8.00 8.00

No. 114 was printed in sheets containing four blocks.

Dutch Royalty — A53

No. 115: a, King Willem-Alexander, hands visible. b, Close-up of Queen Máxima. c, Queen Máxima, arms visible. d, Close-up of King Willem-Alexander.

2020, Apr. 7 Litho. *Perf. 13¼x14*

115 A53 99c Block of 4, #a-d 8.00 8.00

Birds — A54

No. 116: a, Coerba flaveola. b, Mimus gilvus. c, Quisculus lugubris. d, Eupsittula pertinax. e, Icterus icterus.

No. 117: a, Pelecanus occidentalis. b, Ongchoprion anaethetus. c, Oriolus xanthornus. d, Anous stolidu. e, Pandion haliaetus.

No. 118: a, Pluvialis dominica. b, Numenius phaeopus. c, Chrysolampis mosquitus. d, Caracara. e, Coccyzus americanus.

2020, July 1 Litho. *Perf. 13¼x14*

Inscribed "Bonaire"

116 Horiz. strip of 5 7.50 7.50
a.-e. A54 75c Any single 1.50 1.50

Inscribed "Saba"

117 Horiz. strip of 5 7.50 7.50
a.-e. A54 75c Any single 1.50 1.50

Inscribed "St. Eustatius"

118 Horiz. strip of 5 7.50 7.50
a.-e. A54 75c Any single 1.50 1.50
Nos. 116-118 (3) 22.50 22.50

Butterflies — A55

No. 119: a, Vanessa cardui. b, Danaus plexippus. c, Zerene cesonia. d, Ochlodes sylvanus. e, Calpodes ethlius.

No. 120: a, Leptotes cassius. b, Strymon aciss. c, Ascia monuste. d, Eurema lisa. e, Heliconius charitonia.

No. 121: a, Urbanus dorantes. b, Pyrgus carthami. c, Angerona prunaria. d, Junonia evarete. e, Pyrgus oileus.

2020, July 1 Litho. *Perf. 13¼x14*

Inscribed "Bonaire"

119 Horiz. strip of 5 7.50 7.50
a.-e. A55 75c Any single 1.50 1.50

Inscribed "Saba"

120 Horiz. strip of 5 7.50 7.50
a.-e. A55 75c Any single 1.50 1.50

Inscribed "St. Eustatius"

121 Horiz. strip of 5 7.50 7.50
a.-e. A55 75c Any single 1.50 1.50
Nos. 119-121 (3) 22.50 22.50

Marine Life — A56

No. 122: a, Lobatus gigas. b, Chelonia mydas. c, Pterois. d, Stenella longirostris. e, Scaridae.

No. 123: a, Acanthurus coeruleus. b, Panulirus argus. c, Pomacanthus paru. d, Carcharhinus amblyrhynchos. e, Dermochelys coriacea.

No. 124: a, Dasyatidae. b, Cephalopholis fulva. c, Sphyraena. d, Eretmochelys imbricata. e, Thunnus albacares.

2020, July 1 Litho. *Perf. 13¼x14*

Inscribed "Bonaire"

122 Horiz. strip of 5 7.50 7.50
a.-e. A56 75c Any single 1.50 1.50

Inscribed "Saba"

123 Horiz. strip of 5 7.50 7.50
a.-e. A56 75c Any single 1.50 1.50

Inscribed "St. Eustatius"

124 Horiz. strip of 5 7.50 7.50
a.-e. A56 75c Any single 1.50 1.50
Nos. 122-124 (3) 22.50 22.50

Flowers and Plants — A57

No. 125: a, Agave americana. b, Bougainvillea glabra. c, Hibiscus. d, Tabebuia billbergii. e, Lantana camara.

No. 126: a, Tecoma stans. b, Hippeastrum striatum. c, Orchidacea. d, Rudbeckia hirta. e, Alpinia purpurata.

No. 127: a, Aloe vera. b, Anthurium andreanum. c, Nerium oleander. d, Onagraceae. e, Cattleya luteola.

2020, July 1 Litho. *Perf. 13¼x14*

Inscribed "Bonaire"

125 Horiz. strip of 5 7.50 7.50
a.-e. A57 75c Any single 1.50 1.50

Inscribed "Saba"

126 Horiz. strip of 5 7.50 7.50
a.-e. A57 75c Any single 1.50 1.50

Inscribed "St. Eustatius"

127 Horiz. strip of 5 7.50 7.50
a.-e. A57 75c Any single 1.50 1.50
Nos. 125-127 (3) 22.50 22.50

Miniature Sheets

A58

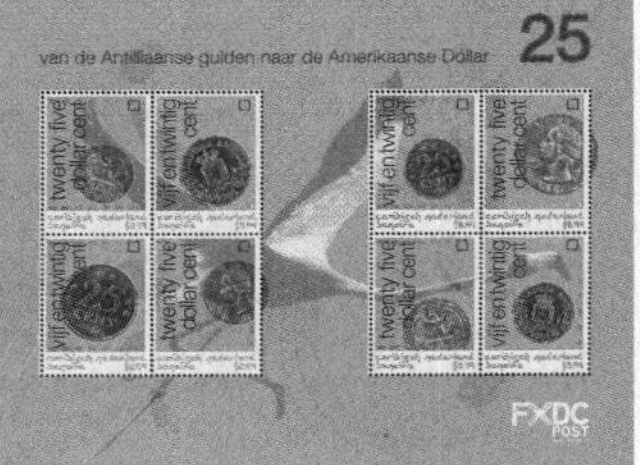
A59

A60

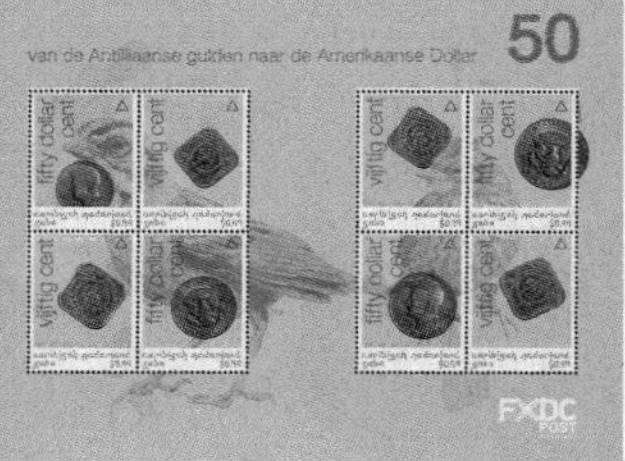
A61

Coins and Birds — A62

No. 128 — Five-cent coin: a, Reverse, from United States, beak of bird. b, Reverse (numeral showing), from Netherlands Antilles, back of bird's head. c, Obverse (arms showing), from Netherlands Antilles, back of bird. d, Obverse, from United States, no part of bird. e, Obverse, from Netherlands Antilles, no part of bird. f, Obverse, from United States, breast of bird. g, Reverse, from United States, leg and tail feathers of bird. h, Reverse, from Netherlands Antilles, tail feathers of bird.

No. 129 — Twenty-five-cent coin: a, Reverse, from United States, wing tip of bird. b, Obverse, from Netherlands Antilles, part of wing of bird. c, Reverse, from Netherlands Antilles, part of wing of bird. d, Obverse, from United States, no part of bird. e, Reverse, from Netherlands Antilles, no part of bird. f, Obverse, from United States, legs and breast of bird. g, Reverse, from United States, neck of bird. h, Obverse, from Netherlands Antilles, head of bird.

No. 130 — Ten-cent coin: a, Obverse, from United States, part of wing of bird at right. b, Obverse, from Netherlands Antilles, part of wing of bird. c, Obverse, from Netherlands Antilles, head of bird. d, Reverse, from United States, beak of bird. e, Reverse, from Netherlands Antilles, part of wing of bird at UR. f, Reverse, from United States, part of wing of bird. g, Obverse, from United States, part of wing of bird at bottom. h, Reverse, from Netherlands Antilles, part of wing of bird at bottom.

No. 131 — Fifty-cent coin: a, Obverse, from United States, head of bird. b, Reverse, from Netherlands Antilles, part of back of bird. c, Obverse (plant showing), from Netherlands Antilles, beak and eye of bird. d, Reverse, from United States, back of head of bird. e, Obverse, from Netherlands Antilles, breast of bird at UR. f, Reverse, from United States, leg and wing of bird. g, Obverse, from United States, part of breast and leg of bird. h, Reverse, from Netherlands Antilles, breast and leg of bird.

No. 132 — One-hundred-cent coin (dollar or gulden): a, Reverse (Statue of Liberty showing), from United States, beak of bird. b, Obverse (Queen showing), from Netherlands Antilles, head of bird. c, Obverse, from Netherlands Antilles, back of bird. d, Obverse (George Washington showing), from United States, tail feathers of bird. e, Reverse (arms showing), from Netherlands Antilles, no part of bird. f, Obverse, from United States, breast of bird. g, Reverse, from United States, part of breast and leg of bird. h, Reverse, from Netherlands Antilles, bird's perch.

2020, Oct. 10 Litho. *Perf. 13¼x14*

Inscribed "Bonaire"

128 A58 99c Sheet of 8, #a-h 16.00 16.00
129 A59 99c Sheet of 8, #a-h 16.00 16.00

Inscribed "Saba"

130 A60 99c Sheet of 8, #a-h 16.00 16.00
131 A61 99c Sheet of 8, #a-h 16.00 16.00

Inscribed "Sint Eustatius"

132 A62 99c Sheet of 8, #a-h 16.00 16.00
Nos. 128-132 (5) 80.00 80.00

SEMI-POSTAL STAMPS

Intl. Year of Cooperatives SP1

2012, Oct. 9 Litho. *Perf. 13½x12¾*

B1 SP1 99c+45c multi 3.00 3.00

CAROLINE ISLANDS

'kar-ə-ˌlīn 'ī-ləndz

LOCATION — A group of about 549 small islands in the West Pacific Ocean, north of the Equator.
GOVT. — German colony
AREA — 550 sq. mi.
POP. — 40,000 (approx. 1915)

100 Pfennig = 1 Mark

Watermark

Wmk. 125 — Lozenges

Stamps of Germany 1889-90 Overprinted in Black

Overprinted at 56 degree Angle

1900	**Unwmk.**	**Perf. 13½x14½**	
1	A9 3pf dk brown	12.00	*13.00*
2	A9 5pf green	15.00	*15.00*
3	A10 10pf carmine	15.00	*16.00*
4	A10 20pf ultra	20.00	*24.00*
5	A10 25pf orange	45.00	*55.00*
6	A10 50pf red brown	45.00	*55.00*
	Nos. 1-6 (6)	152.00	*178.00*

Overprinted at 48 degree Angle

1899

1a	A9 3pf light brown	575.00	*650.00*
2a	A9 5pf green	575.00	*575.00*
3a	A10 10pf carmine	60.00	*125.00*
4a	A10 20pf ultra	60.00	*125.00*
5a	A10 25pf orange	1,400.	*2,500.*
6a	A10 50pf red brown	600.00	*1,400.*

A3

Kaiser's Yacht "Hohenzollern" — A4

1901, Jan.	**Typo.**		**Perf. 14**
7	A3 3pf brown	.90	*1.50*
8	A3 5pf green	.90	*1.75*
9	A3 10pf carmine	.90	*4.25*
a.	Half used as 5pf on cover, back-stamped in Jaluit ('05)		*120.00*
10	A3 20pf ultra	1.10	*7.50*
a.	Half used as 10pf on cover ('10)		*7,500.*
11	A3 25pf org & blk, *yel*	1.40	*12.00*
12	A3 30pf org & blk, *sal*	1.40	*12.00*
13	A3 40pf lake & blk	1.40	*12.00*
14	A3 50pf pur & blk, *sal*	1.75	*19.00*
15	A3 80pf lake & blk, *rose*	2.75	*21.00*

	Engr.		**Perf. 14½x14**
16	A4 1m carmine	3.75	*55.00*
17	A4 2m blue	6.00	*75.00*
18	A4 3m black violet	9.00	*130.00*
19	A4 5m slate & car	160.00	450.00
	Nos. 7-19 (13)	191.25	801.00

No. 9a is known as the "typhoon provisional" the stock of 5pf stamps having been destroyed during a typhoon. Covers (cards) without backstamp, value about $72.50.

Forged cancellations are found on #7-19.

No. 7 Handstamp Surcharged

1910, July 12		
20	A3 5pf on 3pf brown	*4,500.*
a.	Inverted surcharge	*7,750.*
b.	Double surcharge	*11,000.*

Values are for stamps tied to cover. Stamps on piece sell for about 40% less.

1915-19	**Wmk. 125**	**Typo.**
21	A3 3pf brown ('19)	.75
22	A3 5pf green	10.50
	Engr.	
23	A4 5m slate & carmine	35.00
	Nos. 21-23 (3)	46.25

Nos. 21-23 were not placed in use.

CARPATHO-UKRAINE

'kar-pā-thō-yü-'krān

LOCATION — Central Europe within the Czechoslovak Republic
GOVT. — Autonomous region 1938-1939
POP. — 814,000 (1938)
CAPITAL — Khust

An autonomous region established in December 1938 within the Second Czechoslovak Republic and proclaimed an independent republic in March 1939. The Czechoslovak Government-in-Exile was established in Khust in late-1944 and began issuing overprinted and surcharged Hungary stamps in February 1945. The Soviet National Council of Carpatho-Ukraine (NZRU) issued three sets of definitive stamps in 1945. Carpatho-Ukraine was ceded to the Ukrainian Soviet Socialist Republic in 1946.

100 Fillér = 1 Pengö

Catalogue values for unused stamps in this country are for Never Hinged items.

Carpatho-Ukraine No. 1 was previously listed as Czechoslovakia No. 254B. The stamp was initially slated to be issued March 2, 1939, as a regional stamp, with 300,000 stamps sent to the province and more than 600,000 stamps retained in Prague for philatelic sales. The stamp's release was delayed. The Carpatho-Ukrainian diet declared its independence March 14, 1939, and decreed that No. 254B be its first postage stamp, placing it on sale the following day. Stocks in Prague also were placed on sale. It is unlikely that the stamp saw much, if any, postal use either in Carpatho-Ukraine or Czechoslovakia because Germany invaded Czechoslovakia on March 15, and Hungary invaded Carpatho-Ukraine March 16. A few covers, no doubt philatelic, are known from Carpatho-Ukraine.

View of Jasina — A1

Perf. 12½

1939, Mar. 15	**Engr.**	**Unwmk.**	
1	A1 3k ultra, *yelsh*	4.00	40.00

Inauguration of the Carpatho-Ukraine Diet, March 2, 1939.

Printed for use in the province of Carpatho-Ukraine but issued in Prague at the same time.

No. 1 was issued in sheets of 100 stamps with 12 blank labels. Values with attached labels: mint $12, used $80. Used value is for red commemorative cancel.

Uzhhorod Provisional Overprints

The basic Hungarian stamps used for overprinting were issued between 1939 and 1944. All were printed by photogravure. Various comb perforations were used, depending on the size of the stamps. Earlier issues were on paper with Wmk. 210, while later issues have Wmk. 266.

Stamps in used condition command a 50 percent to 100 percent premium, depending on the quality of the cancellation.

Hungary Churches Issue 1939, 1941 Ovptd. and Srchd.

1945, Feb. 1			
2	A75 60f on 3f dark brown	*90.00*	—
3	A75 60f on 16f rose violet	*90.00*	—
4	A76 60f on 24f brown violet	*120.00*	—
5	A82 60f on 30f rose red	*125.00*	—
6	A79 60f on 40f gray black	*130.00*	—
7	A80 2p on 50f bright blue	*130.00*	—
8	A81 2p on 70f gray green	*140.00*	—
9	A78 2p on 80f bister brown	*175.00*	—
	Nos. 2-9 (8)	*1,000.*	

A 40f-on-20f rose red stamp was prepared but not issued.

Nos. 2-5, and 9 exist with overprint and surcharge inverted.

Hungary Nos. 597-599 Ovptd. and Srchd. in Black

1945, Feb.			
10	A92 2p on 1p dk grn & buff	*120.00*	—
11	A92 4p on 2p dk brn & buff	*65.00*	—
12	A92 10p on 5p dk rose vio & buff	*225.00*	—
	Nos. 10-12 (3)	*410.00*	

No. 11 exists with surcharge and overprint inverted.

Varieties of Nos. 11 and 12 include sans-serif letters, broken and missing letters.

Hungary Nos. 570-572 also exist with the same overprints and surcharges. Scott editors are seeking additional information on these overprinted stamps.

Hungary Nos. 573-577 Ovptd. and Srchd. in Black

13	A93 40f on 10f dk ol grn	*130.00*	—
14	A94 60f on 16f ol brn	*140.00*	—
15	A95 1p on 20f car brn	*130.00*	—
16	A96 1.40p on 32f red org	*130.00*	—
17	A97 2p on 40f ryl blue	*130.00*	—
	Nos. 13-17 (5)	*660.00*	

Hungary Nos. 601-616 Ovptd. and Srchd. in Black or Red

18	A99 10f on 1f grnsh blk	*70.00*	—
19	A99 10f on 2f red org	*100.00*	—
20	A99 10f on 3f ultra (R)	*85.00*	—
20A	A99 10f on 3f ultra	—	—
21	A99 40f on 2f red org	*90.00*	—
22	A99 40f on 5f vermilion	*110.00*	—
23	A99 40f on 8f dk ol grn	*125.00*	—
24	A99 40f on 10f brown	*125.00*	—
25	A99 40f on 12f dp bl grn	*125.00*	—
26	A99 40f on 18f dk gray (R)	*150.00*	—
27	A109 40f on 20f chnt brn	*65.00*	—
28	A99 60f on 1f grysh blk	*10.00*	—
29	A99 60f on 2f red org	*15.00*	—
30	A99 60f on 3f ultra	*10.00*	—
30A	A99 60f on 3f ultra (R)	*500.00*	—
31	A99 60f on 4f brown	*10.00*	—
32	A99 60f on 5f vermilion	*25.00*	—
33	A99 60f on 6f slate blue	*10.00*	—
34	A99 60f on 8f dk ol grn	*20.00*	—
35	A99 60f on 10f brown	*5.00*	—
36	A99 60f on 12f dp bl grn	*20.00*	—
37	A99 60f on 18f dk gray (R)	*5.00*	—
37A	A99 60f on 18f dk gray	*500.00*	—
38	A109 60f on 20f chnt brn	*10.00*	—
39	A99 60f on 24f rose vio	*35.00*	—
40	A109 60f on 30f brt car	*10.00*	—
41	A109 2p on 50f blue (R)	*40.00*	—
41A	A109 2p on 50f blue	—	—
42	A109 2p on 80f yel brn	*65.00*	—
43	A109 2p on 1p green	*25.00*	—
	Nos. 18-43 (30)	*2,360.*	

No. 38 exists in vertical tete-beche pairs.

Varieties of Nos. 21, 23, 24 and 26 include sans-serif letters, broken and missing letters.

No. 41 is also known with offset of overprint on reverse.

Hungary Nos. B157-B165 Ovptd. and Srchd. in Black

44	SP92 20f on 1f+1f dk gray	*55.00*	—
45	SP93 40f on 20f+2f dp claret	*125.00*	—
46	SP93 60f on 4f+1f lake	*55.00*	—
47	SP93 60f on 8f+2f green	*90.00*	—
48	SP93 60f on 12f+2f bis brn	*90.00*	—
49	SP93 60f on 40f+4f gray vio	*90.00*	—
50	SP93 1p on 50f+6f org brn	*100.00*	—
51	SP94 1.40p on 70f+8f sl bl	*100.00*	—
	Nos. 44-51 (8)	*705.00*	

Hungary Nos. 617-619 Ovptd. and Srchd. in Black

52	A110 60f on 4f dark green	*25.00*	—
53	A110 60f on 20f dark blue	*35.00*	—
54	A110 60f on 30f brn org	*40.00*	—
	Nos. 52-54 (3)	*100.00*	

Hungary No. 620 Ovptd. and Srchd. in Black

55	A113 60f on 30f dp car	*10.00*	—

No. 55 exists in vertical tete-beche pair, and with overprint and surcharge inverted.

Varieties of No. 55 include sans-serif letters, and broken and missing letters.

Hungary Nos. B171-B174 Ovptd. and Srchd. in Black

56 SP106 1p on 20f+20f brown 140.00 —
57 SP106 1.40p on 30f+30f henna 160.00 —
58 SP106 2p on 50f+50f brn vio 150.00 —
59 SP106 4p on 70f+70f Prus blue 175.00 —
Nos. 56-59 (4) 550.00

Hungary Nos. 621-624 Ovptd. and Srchd. in Black or Red

60 A114 40f on 4f yel brn 65.00 —
61 A115 40f on 30f hen brn 110.00 —
62 A115 60f on 20f dk ol grn 70.00 —
63 A117 1p on 50f slate bl 165.00 —
64 A117 2p on 50f slate bl (R) 80.00 —
Nos. 60-64 (5) 490.00

Nos. 60 and 63 exist with overprints and surcharges inverted. Varieties of both include sans-serif letters, and broken and missing letters.

Hungary Nos. 625-630 Ovptd. and Srchd. in Black or Red

65 A118 40f on 20f brn olive 110.00 —
66 A118 60f on 20f brn olive 30.00 —
67 A118 60f on 24f rose vio 90.00 —
68 A118 60f on 24f rose vio (R) 125.00 —
69 A118 60f on 30f cop red 10.00 —
70 A118 1p on 50f dk bl (R) 65.00 —
71 A118 1.40p on 70f org red 100.00 —
72 A118 2p on 50f dk bl (R) 75.00 —
73 A118 2p on 70f org red 35.00 —
74 A118 2p on 80f brn car 35.00 —
Nos. 65-74 (10) 675.00

Nos. 65, 67, 69, 70, 71 and 74 exist with overprints and surcharges inverted.

Varieties of Nos. 66, 67, 68, 69, 70, 71 and 74 include sans-serif letters, and broken and missing letters.

A 2.40p-on-80f brown carmine stamp was prepared but not issued.

Hungary 1941, 1941-44 Postage Due Issues Surcharged

75 D8 10f on 2f brown red 20.00 —
76 D8 10f on 3f brown red 45.00 —
77 D8 20f on 8f brown red 50.00 —
78 D8 20f on 10f brown red 30.00 —
79 D8 30f on 12f brown red 250.00 —
80 D8 40f on 20f brown red 60.00 —
81 D8 60f on 4f brown red 25.00 —
82 D8 60f on 6f brown red 55.00 —
83 D8 60f on 16f brown red 150.00 —
84 D8 1p on 40f brown red 90.00 —
Nos. 75-84 (10) 775.00

Nos. 77 and 79 exist with overprints and surcharges inverted.

Varieties of Nos. 75, 77, 78, 79, 80 and 84 include sans-serif letters, and broken and missing letters.

A 60f on 2f brown red stamp and 60f on 20f brown red stamp were prepared but not issued.

Hungary 1944 Accounting Revenue Issue (Számolólap Illeték) Overprinted and Surcharged

A2

Surcharge at Left or Right

85 A2 40f on 10f red org (L) 85.00 —
86 A2 40f on 20f ultra (L) 175.00 —
87 A2 60f on 50f dk bl grn (L) 250.00 —
Nos. 85-87 (3) 510.00

A 60f-on-10f red orange was prepared but not issued.

Hungary 1944 Portraits Issue With Khust Overprint in Black or Red

88 A99 60f on 1f grysh blk 100.00 —
89 A99 60f on 2f red org 100.00 —
90 A99 60f on 4f brown 100.00 —
91 A99 60f on 8f dk ol grn 65.00 —
92 A99 60f on 10f brown 65.00 —
93 A99 60f on 12f dp bl grn 175.00 —
94 A99 60f on 18f dk gray (R) 100.00 —
95 A109 60f on 20f chnt brn 175.00 —
96 A109 60f on 30f brt car 100.00 —
97 A114 60f on 4f yel brn 190.00 —
98 A114 60f on 30f copper red 175.00 —
99 A118 2p on 70f orange red 175.00 —
Nos. 88-99 (12) 1,520.

Nos. 88-99 exist with overprints and surcharges inverted.

NRZU Issues

Three separate locally produced definitive stamp sets were issued by National Council of Carpatho-Ukraine (NRZU), all printed by offset lithography at Litografia Lam in Uzhhorod.

Shade varieties (from light to dark) are common, sometimes occurring within the same sheet.

First Definitive Issue

Red Banner, Red Army Soldier, Mountains of Carpatho-Ukraine — A3

Breaking Chain, Mountains — A4

Shackled Hand Breaking Free — A5

Perf. 11½

1945, May 1 Unwmk. Litho.

100 A3 60f red 5.00 —
101 A4 100f dk vio blue 15.00 —
102 A5 200f dark blue & red 20.00 —
Nos. 100-102 (3) 40.00

Values for Nos. 100-102 are for examples with gum (applied by hand). Examples without gum are printer's waste.

Values are for well-centered stamps with intact perforations. Stamps of lesser quality are especially abundant and are often available at substantial discounts.

No. 100 exists in two types. In Type I, the "N" is directly above the "O," while in Type II, the "N" is shifted slightly to the right.

Nos. 100-102 exist imperforate. Value set, $90.

Second Definitive Issue

Star, Hammer and Sickle — A6

1945, June

103 A6 10f dull yellow 5.00 —
104 A6 20f grayish blue 7.50 —
105 A6 40f yellow green 5.00 —
106 A6 60f bright red 5.00 —
107 A6 100f blue, brownish red 10.00 —
108 A6 200f brown, red 12.50 —
Nos. 103-108 (6) 45.00

Nos. 103-108 exist imperforate. Value set, $90.

Third Definitive Issue

Star, Hammer and Sickle — A7

1945, Aug.

109 A7 10f dull yellow 15.00 —
110 A7 20f gray 15.00 —

Nos. 109-110 exist imperforate. Value, $30 each.

CASTELLORIZO

ˌkäs-tə-ˈlor-ə-ˌzō

(Castelrosso)

LOCATION — A Mediterranean island in the Dodecanese group lying close to the coast of Asia Minor and about 60 miles east of Rhodes.
GOVT. — Former Italian Colony
AREA — 4 sq. mi.
POP. — 2,238 (1936)

Formerly a Turkish possession, Castellorizo was occupied by the French in 1915 and ceded to Italy after World War I. In 1945 it became part of Greece.

25 Centimes = 1 Piaster
100 Centimes = 1 Franc

Used values in italics are for postally used copies. Stamps with CTO cancels sell for about the same as hinged, unused stamps.

Issued under French Occupation

Stamps of French Offices in Turkey Overprinted

1920 Unwmk. ***Perf. 14x13½***
1 A2 1c gray 45.00 *65.00*
a. Inverted overprint 175.00 *250.00*
b. Double overprint 175.00 *350.00*
2 A2 2c vio brn 50.00 *70.00*
a. Double overprint 225.00 *300.00*
3 A2 3c red org 45.00 *65.00*
a. Inverted overprint 175.00 *250.00*
4 A2 5c green 75.00 *90.00*
a. Inverted overprint 225.00 *300.00*
5 A3 10c rose 90.00 *125.00*
6 A3 15c pale red 115.00 *150.00*
a. Inverted overprint 450.00 *625.00*
7 A3 20c brn vio 125.00 *150.00*
8 A5 1pi on 25c blue 115.00 125.00
a. Pair, one without overprint 1,150. 800.00
9 A3 30c lilac 125.00 *150.00*
10 A4 40c red & pale bl (down) 200.00 *250.00*
a. Inverted ovpt (reading up) 875.00 950.00
11 A6 2pi on 50c bis brn & lav (down) 225.00 *275.00*
a. Inverted ovpt (reading up) 900.00 1,000.
b. Double overprint 1,250. 1,300.
12 A6 4pi on 1fr cl & ol grn (down) 275.00 *350.00*
a. Double overprint 1,300. 1,350.
b. Inverted ovpt (reading up) 1,050. 1,100.
13 A6 20pi on 5fr dk bl & buff 625.00 *800.00*
a. Double overprint 1,850. *2,000.*
Nos. 1-13 (13) 2,110. 2,665.
Set, never hinged 4,500.

No. 1-9 were overprinted in blocks of 25. Position 4 had "CASTELLORIZO" inverted and Positions 8 and 18 had "CASTELLORISO." The later variety also occurred in the setting of the form for Nos. 10-13.
"B. N. F." are the initials of "Base Navale Francaise".

Overprinted in Black or Red

1920
On Stamps of French Offices in Turkey
14 A2 1c gray 34.00 *40.00*
15 A2 2c vio brn 37.50 *50.00*
16 A2 3c red org 67.50 *80.00*
17 A2 5c green (R) 32.50 *37.50*
19 A3 10c rose 40.00 *47.50*
20 A3 15c pale red 70.00 *80.00*
21 A3 20c brn vio 105.00 *110.00*
22 A5 1pi on 25c bl (R) 67.50 *70.00*
23 A3 30c lilac (R) 77.50 *85.00*
24 A4 40c red & pale bl 75.00 *75.00*
25 A6 2pi on 50c bis brn & lav 72.50 *80.00*
26 A6 4pi on 1fr claret & ol grn 115.00 *140.00*
28 A6 20pi on 5fr dk bl & buff 400.00 450.00
Nos. 14-28 (13) 1,194. 1,345.

On Nos. 25, 26 and 28 the two lines of the overprint are set wider apart than on the lower values.
"O.N.F." are the initials of "Occupation Navale Francaise."
"Casetllorizo" and "astellorizo" varieties are known on Nos. 14-23.
Overprint on 5c in black and on 8pi on 2fr (#37) were prepared but not issued. Values: 5c, $1,300; 8pi on 2fr, $1,450.

On Stamps of France
30 A22 10c red 50.00 *65.00*
a. Inverted overprint 200.00 *250.00*
31 A22 25c blue (R) 50.00 *65.00*
a. Inverted overprint 200.00 *250.00*

This overprint exists on 8 other 1900-1907 denominations of France (5c, 15c, 20c, 30c, 40c, 50c, 1fr, 5fr). These are believed not to have been issued or postally used. Values: 5c, $750; 15c, $750; 20c, $800; 30c, $1,300; 40c, $1,300; 50c, $1,300; 1fr, $1,400; 5fr, $12,500.

Stamps of France, 1900-1907, Handstamped in Black or Violet

1920
33 A22 5c green 175.00 *200.00*
a. Overprint inverted (reading up) 1,300.
b. Double overprint 1,000.
34 A22 10c red 175.00 *200.00*
35 A22 20c vio brn 175.00 *200.00*
a. Overprint inverted (reading up) *1,500.*
b. Double overprint 1,000.
36 A22 25c blue 175.00 *200.00*
37 A18 50c bis brn & lav 1,000. *1,200.*
a. Double overprint *1,700.*
38 A18 1fr cl & ol grn (V) 1,000. 1,200.
Nos. 33-38 (6) 2,700. 3,200.
Set, never hinged 5,400.

French Offices in Turkey Nos. 25//38 were handstamped as Nos. 33-38 locally by the officers in charge of the French Navy postal facilities but were not issued. Values: 5c, 10c, 15c, 20c, 1pi on 25c, each $1,000; 40c, 2pi on 50c, each $2,000; 4pi on 1fr, $2,350; 20pi on 5fr, $10,000.
Covers: Values for covers are for commercial items. Philatelic covers sell for less.
Forgeries of overprints on Nos. 1-38 exist. They abound of Nos. 33-38.

Issued under Italian Dominion

100 Centesimi = 1 Lira

Italian Stamps of 1906-20 Overprinted

1922, July 22 Wmk. 140 ***Perf. 14***
51 A48 5c green 5.00 *30.00*
52 A48 10c claret 3.50 *30.00*
53 A48 15c slate 3.50 *30.00*
54 A50 20c brn org 3.50 *30.00*
a. Double overprint 500.00
b. Vertical pair, one without overprint 2,250.
55 A49 25c blue 3.50 *30.00*
56 A49 40c brown 48.00 35.00
57 A49 50c violet 50.00 37.50
58 A49 60c carmine 50.00 57.50
a. Diagonal overprint 800.00
59 A49 85c chocolate 5.50 *65.00*
Nos. 51-59 (9) 172.50 *345.00*
Set, never hinged 450.00

Map of Castellorizo; Flag of Italy — A1

1923, Jan.
60 A1 5c gray green 7.00 *40.00*
61 A1 10c dull rose 7.00 *40.00*
62 A1 25c dull blue 7.00 *40.00*
63 A1 50c gray lilac 7.00 *40.00*
64 A1 1 l brown 7.00 *40.00*
Nos. 60-64 (5) 35.00 *200.00*
Set, never hinged 65.00

Italian Stamps of 1901-20 Overprinted

1924, March
65 A48 5c green 2.50 *30.00*
66 A48 10c claret 2.50 *30.00*
67 A48 15c slate 2.50 *40.00*
68 A50 20c brn orange 2.50 *40.00*
a. Double overprint 150.00
69 A49 25c blue 2.50 *30.00*
70 A49 40c brown 2.50 *30.00*
71 A49 50c violet 2.50 *40.00*
72 A49 60c carmine 2.50 *50.00*
a. Double overprint 475.00
73 A49 85c red brown 2.50 *60.00*
74 A46 1 l brn & green 2.50 *60.00*
Nos. 65-74 (10) 25.00 *410.00*
Set, never hinged 55.00

Ferrucci Issue

Italian Stamps of 1930, Ovptd. in Red or Blue

1930, Oct. 20 Wmk. Crowns (140)
75 A102 20c violet 10.00 6.00
76 A103 25c dark green 10.00 *25.00*
77 A103 50c black 10.00 6.00
78 A103 1.25 l deep blue 10.00 *25.00*
79 A104 5 l + 2 l dp car (Bl) 10.00 *77.50*
Nos. 75-79 (5) 50.00 *139.50*
Set, never hinged 150.00

Garibaldi Issue

Types of Italian Stamps of 1932, Overprinted like Nos. 75-79 in Red or Blue

1932, Aug. 28
80 A138 10c brown 20.00 *25.00*
81 A138 20c red brn (Bl) 20.00 *25.00*
82 A138 25c dp grn 20.00 *25.00*
83 A138 30c bluish slate 20.00 *25.00*
84 A138 50c red vio (Bl) 20.00 *25.00*
85 A141 75c cop red (Bl) 20.00 *25.00*
86 A141 1.25 l dull blue 20.00 *25.00*
87 A141 1.75 l + 25c brn 20.00 *25.00*
88 A144 2.55 l + 50c org (Bl) 20.00 *25.00*
89 A145 5 l + 1 l dl vio 20.00 *25.00*
Nos. 80-89 (10) 200.00 *250.00*
Set, never hinged 625.00

CAYMAN ISLANDS

ˌkā-ˈman ˈī-ləndz

LOCATION — Three islands in the Caribbean Sea, about 200 miles northwest of Jamaica
GOVT. — British Crown Colony, formerly a dependency of Jamaica
AREA — 100 sq. mi.
POP. — 39,335 (1999 est.)
CAPITAL — George Town, located on Grand Cayman

12 Pence = 1 Shilling
20 Shilling = 1 Pound
100 Cents = 1 Dollar (1969)

Catalogue values for unused stamps in this country are for Never Hinged items, beginning with Scott 112.

Victoria — A1

1900 Typo. Wmk. 2 ***Perf. 14***
1 A1 ½p pale green 15.00 *24.00*
2 A1 1p carmine rose 17.50 5.00

Edward VII — A2

1901-03
3 A2 ½p green ('02) 6.50 *30.00*
4 A2 1p car rose ('03) 12.00 *12.00*
5 A2 2½p ultramarine 12.00 *21.00*
6 A2 6p chocolate 35.00 *70.00*
7 A2 1sh brown orange 67.50 *125.00*
Nos. 3-7 (5) 133.00 *258.00*

1905 Wmk. 3
8 A2 ½p green 12.00 *19.00*
9 A2 1p carmine rose 24.00 *20.00*
10 A2 2½p ultramarine 12.50 6.00
11 A2 6p chocolate 19.00 *45.00*
12 A2 1sh brown orange 35.00 *55.00*
Nos. 8-12 (5) 102.50 *145.00*

For surcharge see No. 17.

1907, Mar. 13
13 A2 4p brown & blue 40.00 *67.50*
14 A2 6p ol green & rose 50.00 *80.00*
15 A2 1sh violet & green 65.00 *95.00*
16 A2 5sh ver & green 225.00 *350.00*
Nos. 13-16 (4) 380.00 *592.50*

Numerals of 4p, 1sh and 5sh of type A2 are in color on colorless tablet.
For surcharges see Nos. 18-20.

Nos. 9, 16, 13 Handstamped

No. 17

No. 18

No. 19

No. 20

1907-08
17 A2 ½p on 1p 60.00 *92.50*
18 A2 ½p on 5sh 325.00 *525.00*
a. Inverted surcharge *100,000.*
b. Double surcharge *12,750.* *12,750.*
c. Double surcharge, one inverted
d. Pair, one without surcharge *100,000.*
19 A2 1p on 5sh 350.00 *525.00*
a. Double surcharge *22,500.* *20,000.*
b. Inverted surcharge *150,000.*
20 A2 2½p on 4p ('08) 2,000. *3,750.*
a. Double surcharge *60,000.* *30,000.*

No. 19b is unique. It exists on the upper left stamp in an upper left corner margin plate no. 1 block of four that is lightly hinged in the top margin only.
The 1p on 4p is a revenue stamp not authorized for postal use, although postally used examples exist. Value for unused is about $300.

A3

1907-09 ***Perf. 14***
21 A3 ½p green 5.25 *5.50*
22 A3 1p carmine rose 2.10 1.10
23 A3 2½p ultramarine 7.50 3.00

Chalky Paper
24 A3 3p violet, *yellow* 4.50 *3.75*
25 A3 4p blk & red, *yel* 67.50 *100.00*
26 A3 6p purple & br pur 27.50 *40.00*
27 A3 1sh black, *grn* 11.00 *30.00*
28 A3 5sh grn & red, *yel* 60.00 *90.00*
Nos. 21-28 (8) 185.35 *273.35*

Issued: ½p, 1p, 12/27/07; 2½p, 3p, 4p, 5sh, 3/30/08; 6d, 10/2/08; 1sh, 4/5/09.
Forged cancellations are found on No. 28.

1908, Mar. 30 **Wmk. 2**

29 A3 1sh black, *green* 80.00 *125.00*
30 A3 10sh grn & red, *grn* 210.00 *350.00*

Numerals of 3p, 4p, 1sh and 5sh of type A3 are in color on plain tablet.

Forged cancellations are found on No. 30.

A4

1908 **Wmk. 3** **Ordinary Paper**

31 A4 ¼p brown 6.00 1.00

King George V — A5

1912-20

32 A5 ¼p brown ('13) 1.25 .50
33 A5 ½p green 3.25 *6.00*
34 A5 1p carmine ('13) 4.00 3.00
35 A5 2p gray 1.25 *12.50*
36 A5 2½p ultra ('14) 8.50 *13.50*

Chalky Paper

37 A5 3p vio, *yel* ('13) 3.00 *22.50*
38 A5 4p blk & red, *yel* ('13) 1.25 *12.50*
39 A5 6p vio & red vio ('13) 5.50 *9.00*
40 A5 1sh blk, *grn* ('13) 4.25 *32.50*
41 A5 2sh vio & ultra, *bl* 16.00 *65.00*
42 A5 3sh green & vio 22.50 *77.50*
43 A5 5sh grn & red, *yel* ('14) 90.00 *190.00*
44 A5 10sh grn & red, *bl grn, olive back* ('18) 125.00 *250.00*
a. 10sh green & red, *grn* ('14) 150.00 *250.00*
Nos. 32-44 (13) 285.75 *694.50*

The first printings of the 3p, 1sh and 10sh have a white back.

For surcharges, see Nos. MR1-MR7.

1913, Nov. 19

Surface-colored Paper

45 A5 3p violet, *yel* 4.25 *9.50*
46 A5 1sh black, *green* 4.25 *4.25*
47 A5 10sh grn & red, *grn* 130.00 *200.00*
Nos. 45-47 (3) 138.50 *213.75*

Numeral of ¼p, 2p, 3p, 4p, 1sh, 2sh, 3sh and 5sh of type A5 are in color on plain tablet.

King George V — A6

1921-26 **Wmk. 4** ***Perf. 14***

50 A6 ¼p yel brown .60 *1.75*
51 A6 ½p gray green .60 .35
52 A6 1p rose red 1.75 1.00
53 A6 1½p orange brn 2.10 .35
54 A6 2p gray 2.10 *4.75*
55 A6 2½p ultramarine ('22) .60 .60
56 A6 3p violet, *yel* 3.25 *5.25*
57 A6 4½p olive grn 4.00 3.75
58 A6 6p claret 6.50 *37.50*
59 A6 1sh black, *grn* ('25) 11.50 *37.50*
60 A6 2sh violet, *blue* 17.00 *32.50*
61 A6 3sh violet 27.50 19.00
62 A6 5sh green, *yel* 30.00 *55.00*
63 A6 10sh car, *green* 72.50 *100.00*
Nos. 50-63 (14) 180.00 *299.30*

Issued: 1½p, 4/4/21; ¼p, ½p, 1p, 2p, 2½p, 6p, 2sh, 3sh, 4/1/22; 3p, 4½p, 6/29/23; 5sh, 2/15/25; 1sh, 5/15/25; 10sh, 9/5/26.

1921-22 **Wmk. 3**

64 A6 3p violet, *org* 1.75 *9.50*
65 A6 4p red, *yel* 1.25 *6.50*
66 A6 1sh black, *green* 1.75 *11.00*
67 A6 5sh green, *yel* 19.00 *80.00*
a. 5sh deep green, *pale yellow* 110.00 *170.00*
68 A6 10sh car, *green* 75.00 *125.00*
Nos. 64-68 (5) 98.75 *232.00*

Issued: 4p, 4/1/22; others, 4/4/21.

King William IV, King George V
A7

Perf. 12½

1932, Dec. 5 **Wmk. 4** **Engr.**

69 A7 ¼p brown 1.90 1.40
70 A7 ½p green 3.25 *11.00*
71 A7 1p carmine 3.25 *15.00*
72 A7 1½p orange 3.25 3.75
73 A7 2p gray 3.25 *4.50*
74 A7 2½p ultramarine 3.25 2.00
75 A7 3p olive green 8.50 *6.75*
76 A7 6p red violet 13.00 *28.00*
77 A7 1sh brn & black 20.00 *40.00*
78 A7 2sh ultra & blk 55.00 *100.00*
79 A7 5sh green & blk 100.00 *160.00*
80 A7 10sh car & black 350.00 *475.00*
Nos. 69-80 (12) 564.65 *847.40*
Set, never hinged 1,250.

Centenary of the formation of the Cayman Islands Assembly.

Common Design Types pictured following the introduction.

Silver Jubilee Issue

Common Design Type

1935, May 6 ***Perf. 13½x14***

81 CD301 ½p green & black .35 *1.50*
82 CD301 2½p blue & brown 6.50 *1.50*
83 CD301 6p ol grn & lt bl 1.75 *10.00*
84 CD301 1sh brt vio & ind 13.00 11.50
Nos. 81-84 (4) 21.60 *24.50*
Set, never hinged 26.00

King George V
A8

Catboat
A9

Red-footed Boobies
A10

Conches and Coconut Palms — A11

Hawksbill Turtles
A12

1935-36 ***Perf. 12½***

85 A8 ¼p brown & blk .60 *1.25*
86 A9 ½p yel grn & ultra 1.25 *1.25*
87 A10 1p car & ultra 5.00 3.00
88 A11 1½p org & black 1.75 *2.25*
89 A9 2p brown vio & ultra 4.50 1.40
90 A12 2½p blue & blk 4.00 1.50
91 A8 3p ol grn & blk 3.00 *3.75*
92 A12 6p red vio & blk 8.50 5.25
93 A9 1sh org & ultra 7.00 *8.00*
94 A10 2sh black & ultra 55.00 45.00
95 A12 5sh green & blk 65.00 65.00
96 A11 10sh car & black 100.00 *110.00*
Nos. 85-96 (12) 255.60 247.65
Set, never hinged 500.00

Issued: No. 86, 2½p, 6p, 1sh, 1/1/36; others, 5/1/35.

Coronation Issue

Common Design Type

1937, May 13 ***Perf. 11x11½***

97 CD302 ½p deep green .25 *1.90*
98 CD302 1p dark carmine .30 .25
99 CD302 2½p deep ultra .55 .55
Nos. 97-99 (3) 1.10 2.70
Set, never hinged 2.25

Beach View, Grand Cayman
A13

Dolphin — A14

Map of the Islands
A15

Hawksbill Turtles — A16

Cayman Schooner
A17

Perf. 12½; 11½x13 or 13x11½ (A14, #111); 14 (#104, 107)

1938-43 **Engr.**

100 A13 ¼p red orange .45 *.75*
a. Perf. 13½x12½ ('43) .25 *1.00*
101 A14 ½p yel green .75 .75
a. Perf. 14 ('43) 1.50 *1.75*
102 A15 1p carmine .25 *1.00*
103 A13 1½p black .25 .25
104 A16 2p dp violet ('43) .40 .35
a. Perf. 11½x13 2.00 .40
105 A17 2½p ultra .25 .25
106 A15 3p orange .25 .25
107 A16 6p dk ol grn ('43) 2.10 1.75
a. Perf. 11½x13 9.00 5.25
108 A14 1sh reddish brown 4.00 2.00
a. Perf. 14 ('43) 4.25 2.50
109 A13 2sh green 17.50 12.00
110 A17 5sh deep rose 24.50 17.00
111 A16 10sh dark brown 20.00 11.00
a. Perf. 14 ('43) 20.00 11.00
Nos. 100-111 (12) 70.70 47.35
Set, never hinged 125.00

See Nos. 114-115.

Catalogue values for unused stamps in this section, from this point to the end of the section, are for Never Hinged items.

Peace Issue

Common Design Type

1946, Aug. 26 **Wmk. 4** ***Perf. 13½***

112 CD303 1½p black .40 .40
113 CD303 3p orange .40 .40

Types of 1938

1947, Aug. 25 ***Perf. 12½***

114 A17 2½p orange 3.50 .65
115 A15 3p ultramarine 3.50 .45

Silver Wedding Issue

Common Design Types

1948, Nov. 29 **Photo.** ***Perf. 14x14½***

116 CD304 ½p dark green .25 *1.00*

Perf. 11½x11

Engr.; Name Typo.

117 CD305 10sh blue violet 25.00 *32.50*

UPU Issue

Common Design Types

Engr.; Name Typo. on #119, 120

1949, Oct. 10 ***Perf. 13½, 11x11½***

118 CD306 2½p orange .35 *1.25*
119 CD307 3p indigo 1.75 *2.75*
120 CD308 6p olive .75 *2.75*
121 CD309 1sh red brown .75 .50
Nos. 118-121 (4) 3.60 *7.25*

Catboat
A18

Designs: ½p, Coconut grove. 1p, Green turtle. 1½p, Thatch rope industry. 2p, Caymanian seamen. 2½p, Map. 3p, Parrot fish. 6p, Bluff, Cayman Brac. 9p, George Town harbor. 1sh, Turtle "crawl". 2sh, Cayman schooner. 5sh, Boat-building. 10sh, Government offices.

Perf. 11½x11

1950, Oct. 2 **Wmk. 4** **Engr.**

122 A18 ¼p rose red & blue .25 *.70*
123 A18 ½p bl grn & red vio .25 *1.50*
124 A18 1p dp blue & olive .65 *.90*
125 A18 1½p choc & bl grn .40 *.90*
126 A18 2p rose car & vio 1.60 *1.75*
127 A18 2½p sepia & aqua 1.90 .75
128 A18 3p bl & blue grn 2.90 1.75
129 A18 6p dp bl & org brn 2.25 1.50
130 A18 9p dk grn & rose red 11.00 2.25
131 A18 1sh red org & brn 4.00 3.25
132 A18 2sh red vio & vio 11.50 *13.00*
133 A18 5sh vio & olive 20.00 8.50
134 A18 10sh rose red & blk 24.50 22.50
Nos. 122-134 (13) 81.20 59.25

Types of 1950 with Portrait of Queen Elizabeth II and

Lighthouse, South Sound — A20

Elizabeth II and Turtles — A21

Perf. 11½x11, 11x11½

1953-59 **Engr.**

135 A18 ¼p rose red & bl 1.40 .70
136 A18 ½p bl grn & red vio 1.10 .65
137 A18 1p dp bl & olive 1.00 .60
138 A18 1½p choc & bl grn .75 .30
139 A18 2p rose car & vio 3.50 1.25
140 A18 2½p black & aqua 4.25 1.10
141 A18 3p blue & bl grn 5.25 .90
142 A20 4p dp blue & blk 2.50 .60
143 A18 6p dp bl & red brn 2.10 .30
144 A18 9p dk grn & rose red 8.50 .40
145 A18 1sh red org & brn 4.75 .40
146 A18 2sh red vio & vio 16.00 10.50
147 A18 5sh violet & olive 17.50 10.00
148 A18 10sh rose red & blk 19.00 10.50
149 A21 £1 bright blue 37.50 15.00
Nos. 135-149 (15) 125.10 53.20

Issued: 4p, 3/2; 2p, 2½p, 9p, 6/2/54; ½p, 1p, 1½p, 6p, 7/7/54; ¼p, 3p, 1sh-10sh, 2/21/55; £1, 1/6/59.

Coronation Issue

Common Design Type

1953, June 2 ***Perf. 13½x13***

150 CD312 1p brt green & black .40 *1.75*

Arms of Cayman Islands A22

Perf. 12

1959, July 4 Wmk. 4 Photo.

151 A22 2½p dull blue & blk .60 *2.25*
152 A22 1sh red orange & blk .65 .50

Granting of a new constitution.

Cayman Parrot — A23

Catboat A24

1½p, Orchid. 2p, Map of Islands. 2½p, Fisherman casting net. 3p, West Bay Beach. 4p, Green turtle. 6p, Cayman schooner. 9p, Angler with kingfish. 1sh, Iguana. 1sh3p, Swimming pool, Cayman Brac. 1sh9p, Girl and sailboat. 5sh, Fort George. 10sh, Coat of Arms. £1, Queen Elizabeth II.

Perf. 11x11½, 11½x11

1962, Nov. 28 Wmk. 314 Engr.

153 A23 ¼p rose red & emer 1.10 *1.60*
154 A24 1p olive & black .95 .40
155 A24 1½p purple & yel 3.75 1.00
156 A24 2p sepia & blue 1.20 .50
157 A24 2½p green & vio .95 *1.25*
158 A24 3p car & blue .45 .40
159 A24 4p pur & green 1.50 .75
160 A24 6p sepia & green 3.50 .45
161 A23 9p pur & vio bl 3.00 .65
162 A24 1sh rose & sepia .95 .25
163 A24 1sh3p brn org & lt grn 4.00 3.50
164 A24 1sh9p vio & bl grn 16.50 1.75
165 A24 5sh grn & dl pur 13.00 14.00
166 A23 10sh blue & olive 20.00 14.00
167 A23 £1 blk & car rose 20.00 *27.50*
Revenue cancel .80
Nos. 153-167 (15) 90.85 68.00

Freedom from Hunger Issue
Common Design Type

1963, June 4 Photo. *Perf. 14x14½*

168 CD314 1sh9p car rose .55 .30

Red Cross Centenary Issue
Common Design Type
Wmk. 314

1963, Sept. 2 Litho. *Perf. 13*

169 CD315 1p black & red .30 *1.25*
170 CD315 1sh9p ultra & red .80 *1.75*

Shakespeare Issue
Common Design Type

1964, Apr. 23 Photo. *Perf. 14x14½*

171 CD316 6p deep lilac rose .35 .30

ITU Issue
Common Design Type

1965, May 17 Litho. Wmk. 314

172 CD317 1p ultra & red lil .25 .25
173 CD317 1sh3p rose lil & grn .75 .60

Intl. Cooperation Year Issue
Common Design Type

1965, Oct. 25 Wmk. 314 *Perf. 14½*

174 CD318 1p blue grn & claret .30 .25
175 CD318 1sh lt vio & green .70 .50

Churchill Memorial Issue
Common Design Type

1966, Jan. 24 Photo. *Perf. 14*
Design in Black, Gold and Carmine Rose

176 CD319 ¼p bright blue .25 *2.00*
177 CD319 1p green .45 .40
178 CD319 1sh brown .80 .40
179 CD319 1sh9p violet 1.60 .85
Nos. 176-179 (4) 3.10 3.65

Royal Visit Issue
Common Design Type

1966, Feb. 4 Litho. *Perf. 11x12*

180 CD320 1p violet blue .70 .30
181 CD320 1sh9p dk car rose 2.75 1.50

World Cup Soccer Issue
Common Design Type

1966, July 1 Litho. *Perf. 14*

182 CD321 1½p multicolored .25 .25
183 CD321 1sh9p multicolored .50 .40

WHO Headquarters Issue
Common Design Type

1966, Sept. 20 Litho. *Perf. 14*

184 CD322 2p multicolored .65 .30
185 CD322 1sh3p multicolored 1.60 .90

UNESCO Anniversary Issue
Common Design Type

1966, Dec. 1 Litho. *Perf. 14*

186 CD323 1p "Education" .25 .25
187 CD323 1sh9p "Science" .75 .35
188 CD323 5sh "Culture" 1.50 .90
Nos. 186-188 (3) 2.50 1.50

Telephone and Map of Caymans — A25

Perf. 14½x14

1966, Dec. 5 Litho. Wmk. 314

189 A25 4p multicolored .25 .25
190 A25 9p multicolored .30 .30

Linking of the Cayman telephone system with the intl. system.

BAC 1-11 Jet Liner over Schooner — A26

1966, Dec. 17

191 A26 1sh blue, ol & black .40 .35
192 A26 1sh9p ultra, grn & sepia .70 .50

Opening of the Grand Cayman Airport jet service.

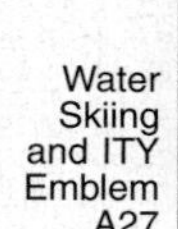

Water Skiing and ITY Emblem A27

ITY Emblem and: 6p, Skin diving. 1sh, Sport fishing. 1sh9p, Sailing.

Perf. 14½x14

1967, Dec. 1 Photo. Wmk. 314

193 A27 4p multi & gold .35 .25
a. Gold omitted *375.00* *325.00*
194 A27 6p multi & gold .35 .25
195 A27 1sh multi & gold .35 .35
196 A27 1sh9p multi & gold .50 *.75*
Nos. 193-196 (4) 1.55 1.60

International Tourist Year.

Human Rights Flame and Freed Slaves A28

1968, June 3 Photo. Wmk. 314

197 A28 3p slate bl, grn & gold .25 .25
198 A28 9p lt brn, grn & gold .25 .25
199 A28 5sh ultra, grn & gold .50 *.80*
Nos. 197-199 (3) 1.00 1.30

International Human Rights Year.

Long Jump A29

1sh3p, High jump. 2sh, Pole vault, vert.

1968, Oct. 1 Litho. *Perf. 13½*

200 A29 1sh multicolored .25 .25
201 A29 1sh3p multicolored .25 .25
202 A29 2sh yellow & multi .30 *.75*
Nos. 200-202 (3) .80 1.25

19th Olympic Games, Mexico City, 10/12-27.

Adoration of Shepherds, by Carel Fabritius — A30

Christmas: 1p, 8p, 2sh, Adoration of the Shepherds, by Rembrandt.

Perf. 14x14½

1968, Nov. 18 Photo. Wmk. 314

203 A30 ¼p brown & multi .25 .25
a. Gold omitted *275.00*
204 A30 1p violet & multi .25 .25
205 A30 6p multicolored .25 .25
206 A30 8p car & multi .25 .25
207 A30 1sh3p multicolored .25 *.30*
208 A30 2sh gray & multi .25 *.30*
Nos. 203-208 (6) 1.50 1.60

1969, Jan. 8 Unwmk.

209 A30 ¼p red lilac & multi .75 .30

Grand Cayman Thrush A31

1p, Brahman cattle. 2p, Blowholes on coast. 2½p, Map of Grand Cayman. 3p, Town scene in George Town. 4p, Royal poinciana. 6p, Map of Cayman Brac and Little Cayman. 8p, Motor vessels at berth. 1sh, Basket making. 1sh3p, Beach scene. 1sh6p, Rope making. 2sh, Barracudas. 4sh, Government House. 10sh, Coat of arms. £1, Queen Elizabeth II.

Unwmk.

1969, June 5 Litho. *Perf. 14*

210 A31 ¼p multi .25 *.85*
211 A31 1p multi .25 .25
212 A31 2p multi .25 .25
213 A31 2½p multi .25 .25
214 A31 3p multi .25 .25
215 A31 4p multi .25 .25
216 A31 6p multi .25 .25
217 A31 8p multi .25 .25
218 A31 1sh multi .25 .25
219 A31 1sh3p multi .30 *1.60*
220 A31 1sh6p multi .35 *1.60*
221 A31 2sh multi 1.25 *1.25*
222 A31 4sh multi .60 *1.25*
223 A31 10sh multi, vert. 1.25 *2.10*
224 A31 £1 multi, vert. 3.00 3.00
Nos. 210-224 (15) 9.00 13.65

See Nos. 262-276. For surcharges see Nos. 227-241.

1969, Aug. 11 Wmk. 314 Sideways

225 A31 ¼p multicolored .70 .70

Type of 1969 Surcharged

1969, Sept. 8 Wmk. 314 *Perf. 14*

227 A31 ¼c on ¼p multi .25 *.85*
228 A31 1c on 1p multi .25 .25
229 A31 2c on 2p multi .25 .25
230 A31 3c on 4p multi .25 .25
231 A31 4c on 2½p multi .25 .25
232 A31 5c on 6p multi .25 .25
233 A31 7c on 8p multi .25 .25
234 A31 8c on 3p multi .25 .25
235 A31 10c on 1s multi .35 .25
236 A31 12c on 1sh3p multi .45 *1.90*
237 A31 15c on 1sh6p multi .55 *1.50*
238 A31 20c on 2sh multi 2.00 *1.90*
239 A31 40c on 4sh multi .55 *1.10*
240 A31 $1 on 10sh multi 1.45 *3.25*
241 A31 $2 on £1 multi 2.25 *4.00*
Nos. 227-241 (15) 9.60 16.50

The surcharge is arranged differently on various denominations.

Madonna and Child, by Alvise Vivarini — A32

Christmas: 1c, 7c, 20c, The Adoration of the Kings, by Jan Gossaert.

1969, Nov. 4 Photo. *Perf. 14*

242 A32 ¼c blue & multi .25 .25
243 A32 ¼c emer & multi .25 .25
244 A32 ¼c red org & multi .25 .25
245 A32 ¼c brt pink & multi .25 .25
246 A32 1c vio blue & multi .25 .25
247 A32 5c red org & multi .25 .25
248 A32 7c dk green & multi .25 .25
249 A32 12c emer & multi .25 .25
250 A32 20c multicolored .25 .25
Nos. 242-250 (9) 2.25 2.25

"Noli me Tangere," by Titian — A33

1970, Mar. 23 Litho. Unwmk.

251 A33 ¼c dull grn & multi .25 .25
252 A33 ¼c dk car & multi .25 .25
253 A33 ¼c violet & multi .25 .25
254 A33 ¼c bister & multi .25 .25
255 A33 10c vio blue & multi .25 .25
256 A33 12c red brn & multi .25 .25
257 A33 40c brn vio & multi .50 *.60*
Nos. 251-257 (7) 2.00 2.10

Easter.

Barnaby from "Barnaby Rudge" by Dickens (1812-70), English Novelist — A34

Characters from Charles Dickens: 12c, Sairey Gamp, from "Martin Chuzzlewit." 20c, Mr. Micawber and David, from "David Copperfield." 40c, The Marchioness from "The Old Curiosity Shop."

1970, June 17 Photo. *Perf. 14½x14*

258 A34 1c ol green, yel & blk .25 .25
259 A34 12c red brn, brick red & black .25 .25
260 A34 20c dk ol bis, gold & black .35 .35
261 A34 40c dp ultra, lt bl & blk .50 .40
Nos. 258-261 (4) 1.35 1.25

Type of Regular Issue 1969 Values in Cents and Dollars

Designs: ¼c, Grand Cayman thrush. 1c, Brahman cattle. 2c, Blowholes on coast. 3c, Royal poinciana. 4c, Map of Grand Cayman. 5c, Map of Cayman Brac and Little Cayman. 7c, Motor vessels at berth. 8c, Town scene in George Town. 10c, Basket making. 12c, Beach scene. 15c, Rope making. 20c, Barracudas. 40c, Government House. $1, Coat of arms, vert. $2, Queen Elizabeth II, vert.

Wmk. 314

1970, Sept. 8 Litho. *Perf. 14*

262 A31 ¼c multicolored .60 .30
263 A31 1c multicolored .25 .25
264 A31 2c multicolored .25 .25
265 A31 3c multicolored .25 .25
266 A31 4c multicolored .25 .25
267 A31 5c multicolored .45 .25
268 A31 7c multicolored .40 .25
269 A31 8c multicolored .40 .25
270 A31 10c multicolored .40 .25
271 A31 12c multicolored 1.00 *1.10*
272 A31 15c multicolored 1.25 *4.00*
273 A31 20c multicolored 3.25 1.75
274 A31 40c multicolored .85 .85
275 A31 $1 multicolored 1.25 *5.75*
276 A31 $2 multicolored 2.00 *5.75*
Nos. 262-276 (15) 12.85 21.50

The Three Wise Men A35

Christmas: 1c, 10c, 20c, Nativity and globe.

1970, Oct. 8 Litho. *Perf. 14*

277 A35 ¼c brt grn & yel grn .25 .25
278 A35 1c bl grn, yel grn & blk .25 .25
279 A35 5c dp claret & org .25 .25
280 A35 10c red org, yel & blk .25 .25
281 A35 12c ultra & lt grnsh bl .25 .25
282 A35 20c grn, yel grn & blk .25 .25
Nos. 277-282 (6) 1.50 1.50

Grand Cayman Terrapin A36

Cayman Islands Turtles: 7c, Green turtle. 12c, Hawksbill turtle. 20c, Turtle farm.

1971, Jan. 28 *Perf. 14x14½*

283 A36 5c multicolored .70 .40
284 A36 7c multicolored .85 .40
285 A36 12c multicolored 1.75 .50
286 A36 20c multicolored 3.00 2.00
Nos. 283-286 (4) 6.30 3.30

Dendrophylax Fawcetii — A37

Wild Orchids of West Indies: 2c, Schomburgkia thomsoniana. 10c, Vanilla claviculata. 40c, Oncidium variegatum.

1971, Apr. 7 Wmk. 314 *Perf. 14*

287 A37 ¼c brown & multi .35 *1.40*
288 A37 2c ol green & multi 1.00 *1.10*
289 A37 10c gray bl & multi 3.25 .65
290 A37 40c lt violet & multi 4.75 4.00
Nos. 287-290 (4) 9.35 7.15

Adoration of the Kings, 15th Century — A38

Christmas: 1c, 15c, Nativity (detail), Paris, 14th cent. 5c, 20c, Adoration of the Kings (detail), Burgundian, 15th cent.

1971, Sept. 27 *Perf. 14*

291 A38 ¼c gold & multi .25 .25
292 A38 1c gold & multi .25 .25
293 A38 5c gold & multi .25 .25
294 A38 12c gold & multi .25 .25
295 A38 15c gold & multi .25 .25
296 A38 20c gold & multi .35 .35
a. Souvenir sheet of 6, #291-296 4.25 4.25
Nos. 291-296 (6) 1.60 1.60

Underwater Cable, Turtle and Telephone — A39

1972, Jan. 10

297 A39 2c multicolored .25 .25
298 A39 10c multicolored .25 .25
299 A39 40c multicolored .75 .75
Nos. 297-299 (3) 1.25 1.25

Coaxial cable for world communications.

Courthouse — A40

Designs: 15c, 40c, Legislative Assembly Building, George Town.

1972, Aug. 15 *Perf. 13½x14*

300 A40 5c dp car & multi .25 .25
301 A40 15c lilac rose & multi .25 .25
302 A40 25c dull grn & multi .25 .25
303 A40 40c dk blue & multi .25 .40
a. Souvenir sheet of 4, #300-303 .90 2.00
Nos. 300-303 (4) 1.00 1.15

New Cayman Islands government buildings.

Silver Wedding Issue, 1972

Common Design Type

Design: Queen Elizabeth II, Prince Philip, hawksbill turtle and conch.

1972, Nov. 20 Photo. *Perf. 14x14½*

304 CD324 12c vio black & multi .25 .25
305 CD324 30c olive & multi .50 .50

$1 Note and 1c Coin A41

6c, $5 note and 5c coin. 15c, $10 note and 10c coin. 25c, $25 note and 25c coin.

1973, Jan. 15

306 A41 3c emerald & multi .25 .25
307 A41 6c yellow & multi .30 .60
308 A41 15c lilac & multi .65 .50
309 A41 25c orange & multi 1.25 .90
a. Souvenir sheet of 4, #306-309 4.00 4.00
Nos. 306-309 (4) 2.45 2.25

First Cayman Islands coinage and bank notes, May 1, 1972.

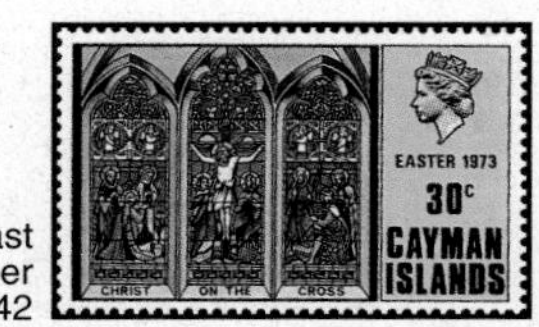

Last Supper A42

Stained Glass Windows: 10c, Christ Carrying Cross, vert. 12c, Resurrection, vert. 30c, Crucifixion.

Perf. 14½x14, 14x14½

1973, Apr. 11 Litho.

310 A42 10c pink & multi .25 .25
311 A42 12c yel green & multi .25 .25
312 A42 20c lt blue & multi .30 .30
313 A42 30c yellow & multi .40 .40
a. Souvenir sheet of 4 1.25 *1.60*
Nos. 310-313 (4) 1.20 1.20

Easter. No. 313a contains 4 stamps similar to Nos. 310-313 with simulated perforations.

Nativity — A43

Christmas: 5c, 12c, 25c, Adoration of the Magi, from Breviary of Queen Isabella. 9c, 15c, Like 3c, Nativity from Sforza Book of Hours.

1973, Oct. 2 *Perf. 14½*

314 A43 3c dull green & multi .25 .25
315 A43 5c dull pur & multi .25 .25
316 A43 9c sepia & multi .25 .25
317 A43 12c dk blue & multi .25 .25
318 A43 15c dp rose & multi .25 .25
319 A43 25c black & multi .25 .25
Nos. 314-319 (6) 1.50 1.50

Princess Anne's Wedding Issue

Common Design Type

1973, Nov. 14 Wmk. 314 *Perf. 14*

320 CD325 10c brt green & multi .25 .25
321 CD325 30c lilac & multi .25 .25

White-winged Dove — A44

10c, Vitelline warblers. 12c, Greater Antillean grackles. 20c, West Indian red-bellied woodpecker. 30c, Stripe-headed tanagers. 50c, Yucatan vireos.

1974, Jan. 2 Litho. *Perf. 14x14½*

322 A44 3c shown 2.50 .40
323 A44 10c multicolored 3.25 .40
324 A44 12c multicolored 3.25 .40
325 A44 20c multicolored 5.25 1.00
326 A44 30c multicolored 6.50 2.00
327 A44 50c multicolored 8.75 6.00
Nos. 322-327 (6) 29.50 10.20

See Nos. 354-359.

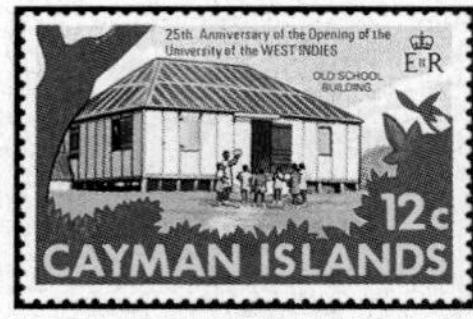

One-room Schoolhouse — A45

Designs: 20c, New comprehensive school. 30c, Creative Arts Center, Mona, Jamaica.

1974, May 1 *Perf. 14*

328 A45 12c multicolored .25 .25
329 A45 20c multicolored .25 .25
330 A45 30c multicolored .35 *.60*
Nos. 328-330 (3) .85 1.10

25th anniv. of the University College of the West Indies.

Hermit Crab and Pirate Gold (#346) A46

Coat of Arms (#344) — A47

Elizabeth II (#348) — A48

Designs: 3c, Pirate, treasure chest and lion's paw. 4c, Spotted scorpionfish and crown. 5c, Flint-lock pistol and brain coral. 6c, Blackbeard on Grand Cayman and green turtle. 8c, 9c, Jeweled pomander and porkfish. 10c, Spiny lobster and gold coins. 12c, Jeweled sword, dagger and sea fan. 15c, Cabrit's murex and jeweled necklace. 20c, Queen conch, pistol and gold cup. 25c, Hogfish and pirate chest. 40c, Gold chalice and sea whip.

Wmk. 314 Upright, Sideways (#331-332, 336, 344-345)

1974-75 Litho. *Perf. 14*

Size: 41x26.5mm

331 A46 1c multi ('75) 4.25 1.75
a. Wmk. upright 3.75 1.25
332 A46 3c multicolored 4.25 1.75
a. Wmk. upright 3.75 .70
333 A46 4c multicolored .70 *.95*
334 A46 5c multicolored 3.50 1.00
335 A46 6c multicolored .50 *2.75*
336 A46 8c multicolored 3.00 *9.50*
337 A46 9c multicolored 5.00 *12.50*
338 A46 10c multicolored 5.50 1.10
339 A46 12c multicolored .50 *2.25*
340 A46 15c multicolored .55 *1.75*
341 A46 20c multicolored 5.00 4.00
342 A46 25c multicolored .60 *.85*
343 A46 40c multicolored 5.00 1.50
344 A47 $1 multicolored 3.25 *3.50*
345 A48 $2 multicolored 9.50 *10.00*
Nos. 331-345 (15) 51.10 *55.15*

Issued: No. 332, 11/12; 8c, 12/16; No. 331, 9/29; others, 8/1.

1976-77 Wmk. 373

332b A46 3c multicolored 1.00 *4.50*
333a A46 4c multi ('77) 1.50 *5.00*
334a A46 5c multi ('77) 7.50 7.50
336b A46 8c multicolored 8.50 6.25
338b A46 10c multicolored 3.75 *5.00*
341b A46 20c multicolored 4.25 3.50
344a A47 $1 multi ('77) 7.50 *11.00*
345b A48 $2 multicolored 8.50 9.25
Nos. 332b-345b (8) 42.50 *52.00*

Issued: 3c, 8c, 10c, 20c, $2, 9/3; 4c, 5c, $1, 10/19.

Design Smaller
Size: 39.5x25mm

Wmk. 373 (Sideways on 1c-40c)

1978-80

346 A46 1c multicolored 1.25 *1.75*
346A A46 3c multicolored 1.00 .75
346B A46 5c multi ('79) 2.75 *3.00*
347 A46 10c multicolored 2.00 1.00
347A A46 20c multicolored 4.00 1.75
347B A46 40c multi ('79) 15.00 22.50
347C A47 $1 multi ('80) 22.50 7.00
348 A48 $2 multi ('80) 6.50 *25.00*
Nos. 346-348 (8) 55.00 *62.75*

Issued: 1c, 3c, 3/16; 10c, 20c, 5/25; 5c, 12/11; $2, 4/3; $1, 7/30.

Sea Captain and Ship — A49

1974, Oct. 7 Wmk. 314 *Perf. 14*

349 A49 8c shown .25 .25
350 A49 12c Thatch weaver .25 .25
351 A49 20c Farmer .50 .50
a. Miniature sheet of 3, #349-351 1.75 *3.00*
Nos. 349-351 (3) 1.00 1.00

Arms of Cinque Ports and Lord Warden's Flag — A50

Churchill Coat of Arms — A51

1974, Nov. 30

352 A50 12c multicolored .25 .25
353 A51 50c multicolored .45 .70
a. Souvenir sheet of 2, #352-353 .95 *1.50*

Sir Winston Churchill (1874-1965).

Bird Type of 1974

3c, Yellow-shafted flicker. 10c, West Indian tree duck. 12c, Yellow warblers. 20c, White-bellied dove. 30c, Magnificent frigate bird. 50c, Cayman amazon.

Wmk. 314

1975, Jan. 1 Litho. *Perf. 14*

354 A44 3c multicolored .70 .45
355 A44 10c multicolored 1.25 .45
356 A44 12c multicolored 1.60 .70
357 A44 20c multicolored 2.50 2.00
358 A44 30c multicolored 3.75 *4.25*
359 A44 50c multicolored 4.50 *12.00*
a. Wmk. 362 (Lesotho) *1,000.*
Nos. 354-359 (6) 14.30 *19.85*

Ivory Crosier with Crucifixion — A52

Design: 35c, Crucifixion, ivory and gilt. Designs show heads of 14th century French pastoral staffs.

Wmk. 314

1975, Mar. 24 Litho. *Perf. 14*

360 A52 15c plum & multi .25 .25
361 A52 35c gray & multi .40 *.55*
a. Souvenir sheet of 2, #360-361 1.10 *2.50*

Easter. No. 361a exists imperf.

See Nos. 366-367.

Israel Hands A53

Designs: Pirates and various scenes.

1975, July 25 Wmk. 314

362 A53 10c shown .50 .25
363 A53 12c John Fenn .50 .25
364 A53 20c Thomas Anstis .85 .50
365 A53 30c Edward Low 1.10 *1.50*
Nos. 362-365 (4) 2.95 2.50

Easter Type of 1975

Designs after ivory carved pastoral staffs showing Virgin and Child with angels, French, 14th century.

Wmk. 373

1975, Oct. 31 Litho. *Perf. 14*

366 A52 12c dk green & multi .25 .25
367 A52 50c multicolored .70 .70
a. Souvenir sheet of 2, #366-367 1.50 *2.75*

Christmas.

Registered Letter with Nos. 1-2; Cayman Brac Government House and Sub Post Office — A54

Cayman Islands 1st postage stamps, 75th anniv.: 20c, Cayman Islands #1 and cancelation used 1890-94; 30c, #2, 20; 50c, #1-2.

1976, Mar. 12 Litho. *Perf. 13½x14*

368 A54 10c lt blue & multi .25 .25
369 A54 20c pink & multi .25 .25
370 A54 30c multicolored .35 .35
371 A54 50c yellow & multi .55 *.65*
a. Souvenir sheet of 4, #368-371 3.50 3.50
Nos. 368-371 (4) 1.40 1.50

Seals of Georgia, Delaware and New Hampshire — A55

15c, Seals of SC, NJ, MD. 20c, Seals of VA, RI, MA. 25c, Seals of NY, CT, NC. 30c, Seal of PA, Liberty Bell and Great Seal of the US.

Wmk. 373

1976, May 29 Litho. *Perf. 14*

372 A55 10c olive & multi .35 .25
373 A55 15c blue & multi .45 .25
374 A55 20c multicolored .60 .30
375 A55 25c blue grn & multi .90 .60
376 A55 30c red brn & multi 1.10 .85
a. Souvenir sheet of 5 + label 5.25 *8.00*
Nos. 372-376 (5) 3.40 2.25

American Bicentennial. Nos. 372-376 printed in sheets of 5. No. 376a contains one each of Nos. 372-376 and corner label inscribed "USA 200."

French Class 470 Racing Dinghies — A56

Design: 50c, One racing dinghy.

1976, Aug. 16 Litho. *Perf. 14*

377 A56 20c multicolored .60 .45
378 A56 50c multicolored 1.10 1.10

21st Olympic Games, Montreal, Canada, July 17-Aug. 1.

Queen Elizabeth II — A57

8c, Prince Charles, 1973 visit. 50c, Preparation for anointing ceremony, horiz.

Perf. 14x13½, 13½x14

1977, Feb. 7 Litho. Wmk. 373

379 A57 8c multicolored .25 .25
380 A57 30c multicolored .25 .25
381 A57 50c multicolored .25 .25
Nos. 379-381 (3) .75 .75

25th anniv. of the reign of Elizabeth II.

Scuba Diving A58

10c, Divers examining underwater wreck. 20c, Fairy basslets (fish). 25c, Sergeant majors (fish).

1977, July 25 *Perf. 13½*

382 A58 5c multicolored .25 .25
383 A58 10c multicolored .25 .25
384 A58 20c multicolored .45 .45
385 A58 25c multicolored .60 .60
a. Souvenir sheet of 4 3.00 *4.00*
Nos. 382-385 (4) 1.55 1.55

Tourist publicity. No. 385a contains one each of Nos. 382-385, perf. 14½.

Composia Fidelissima — A59

Butterflies: 8c, Heliconius charitonius. 10c, Danaus gilippus. 15c, Agraulis vanillae. 20c, Junonia evarete. 30c, Anartia jatrophae.

1977, Dec. 2 Wmk. 373 *Perf. 14x13*

386 A59 5c multicolored 1.10 .25
387 A59 8c multicolored 1.25 .30
388 A59 10c multicolored 1.35 .35
389 A59 15c multicolored 1.60 .55
390 A59 20c multicolored 1.75 .60
391 A59 30c multicolored 2.00 1.10
Nos. 386-391 (6) 9.05 3.15

Cruise Ship "Southward" A60

Designs: 5c, "Renaissance." 30c, New harbor, vert. 50c, "Daphne," vert.

1978, Jan. 23 Litho. *Perf. 14*

392 A60 3c multicolored .45 .25
393 A60 5c multicolored .45 .25
394 A60 30c multicolored 1.25 .40
395 A60 50c multicolored 1.50 .75
Nos. 392-395 (4) 3.65 1.65

New harbor and cruise ships.

Crucifixion, by Dürer — A61

Etchings by Dürer: 15c, Christ at Emmaus. 20c, Entry into Jerusalem. 30c, Christ washing Peter's feet.

1978, Mar. 20 Litho. *Perf. 12*

396 A61 10c multicolored .30 .25
397 A61 15c multicolored .45 .30
398 A61 20c multicolored .55 .40
399 A61 30c multicolored .65 .55
a. Souvenir sheet of 4, #396-399 6.50 6.50
Nos. 396-399 (4) 1.95 1.50

Easter; Albrecht Dürer (1471-1528). Nos. 396-399 issued in sheets of 6.

Explorers, Singing Game — A62

10c, Girls' Brigade presenting flag. 20c, Guides studying Bible, playing guitar, tennis and volleyball. 50c, Guides setting table.

1978, Apr. 25 Litho. *Perf. 14*

400 A62 3c multicolored .25 .25
401 A62 10c multicolored .35 .35
402 A62 20c multicolored .60 .60
403 A62 50c multicolored 1.25 1.25
Nos. 400-403 (4) 2.45 2.45

3rd Intl. Council Meeting of Girls' Brigade.

Elizabeth II Coronation Anniversary Issue

Common Design Types

Souvenir Sheet

1978, June 2 Unwmk. *Perf. 15*

404 Sheet of 6 2.00 2.00
a. CD326 30c Yale of Beaufort .30 .30
b. CD327 30c Elizabeth II .30 .30
c. CD328 30c Screech owl .30 .30

No. 404 contains 2 se-tenant strips of Nos. 404a-404c, separated by horizontal gutter with commemorative and descriptive inscriptions.

A63

A63a

A63: 1c, Trumpetfish. 3c, Nassau grouper. 5c, French angelfish. 10c, Schoolmaster snappers. 20c, Banded butterflyfish. 50c, Black-bar soldierfish.

A63a: 3c, Four-eyed butterflyfish. 5c, Grey angel fish. 10c, Squirrelfish. 15c, Parrotfish. 20c, Spanish hogfish. 30c, Queen angelfish.

1978-79 Wmk. 373 Litho. *Perf. 14*

405 A63 1c multicolored .25 .25
406 A63 3c multicolored .35 .25
407 A63a 3c multicolored .30 .25
408 A63a 5c multicolored .35 .25
409 A63 5c multicolored .30 .25
412 A63a 10c multicolored .55 .25
413 A63 10c multicolored .55 .25
414 A63a 15c multicolored .60 .35
415 A63a 20c multicolored .75 .45

416 A63 20c multicolored .95 .45
417 A63a 30c multicolored 1.50 .70
418 A63 50c multicolored 2.25 1.10
Nos. 405-418 (12) 8.70 4.80

Issued: design A63, 4/20/79; design A63a, 8/28/78.

Lockheed Lodestar — A64

Aircraft: 5c, Consolidated PBY. 10c, Vickers Viking. 15c, BAC1-11. 20c, Piper Cheyenne, HS 125 and Bell 47. 30c, BAC1-11.

1979, Feb. 5 ***Perf. 14½***
420 A64 3c multicolored .40 .25
421 A64 5c multicolored .40 .25
422 A64 10c multicolored .45 .25
423 A64 15c multicolored .75 .40
424 A64 20c multicolored .95 .45
425 A64 30c multicolored 1.10 .55
Nos. 420-425 (6) 4.05 2.15

Opening of Owen Roberts Airport, 25th anniv.

Rowland Hill and No. 2 — A65

Sir Rowland Hill (1795-1879), originator of penny postage, and: 10c, Great Britain #132. 20c, Cayman Islands #149. 50c,Cayman Islands #20.

Perf. 13½x14½
1979, Aug. 15 **Litho.**
426 A65 5c multicolored .25 .25
427 A65 10c multicolored .25 .25
428 A65 20c multicolored .50 .50
Nos. 426-428 (3) 1.00 1.00

Souvenir Sheet

429 A65 50c multicolored 1.40 1.40

Flight into Egypt A66

Christmas: 20c, Shepherds, Star of Bethlehem. 30c, Nativity. 40c, Three Kings, Star of Bethlehem.

1979, Nov. 20 **Litho.** ***Perf. 13½***
430 A66 10c multicolored .25 .25
431 A66 20c multicolored .25 .25
432 A66 30c multicolored .35 .25
433 A66 40c multicolored .55 .30
Nos. 430-433 (4) 1.40 1.05

Bonaventure House, Rotary Emblem — A67

30c, Paul P. Harris, vert. 50c, Anniversary emblem, vert.

Perf. 14x13½, 13½x14
1980, Feb. 14 **Litho.** **Wmk. 373**
434 A67 20c shown .25 .25
435 A67 30c multicolored .45 .25
436 A67 50c multicolored .70 .50
Nos. 434-436 (3) 1.40 1.00

Rotary International, 75th anniversary.

Mailman, London 1980 Emblem A68

1980, May 6 **Litho.** ***Perf. 14***
437 A68 5c shown .25 .25
438 A68 10c Cat boat .25 .25
439 A68 15c Mounted mailman .25 .25
440 A68 30c Mail wagon .40 .35
441 A68 40c Mailman on bicycle .50 .45
442 A68 $1 Mail truck .70 .70
Nos. 437-442 (6) 2.35 2.25

London '80 Intl. Stamp Exhib., May 6-14.

Queen Mother Elizabeth Birthday Issue
Common Design Type

1980, Aug. 4 **Litho.** ***Perf. 14***
443 CD330 20c multicolored .40 .40

Spondylus Americanus A69

10c, Murex brevifrons. 30c, Cymatium femorale. 50c, Vasum muricatum.

1980, Aug. 12 ***Perf. 14½x14***
444 A69 5c shown .80 .25
445 A69 10c multicolored .80 .30
446 A69 30c multicolored 1.60 .65
447 A69 50c multicolored 1.75 1.25
Nos. 444-447 (4) 4.95 2.45

See Nos. 502-505, 518-521.

Lantana — A70

1980, Oct. 21 **Litho.** ***Perf. 14***
448 A70 5c shown .25 .25
449 A70 15c Bauhinia .30 .25
450 A70 30c Hibiscus .55 .30
451 A70 $1 Milk and wine lily 1.45 1.40
Nos. 448-451 (4) 2.55 2.20

See Nos. 478-481.

Juvenile Tarpon and Fire Sponges — A71

5c, Mangrove root oysters. 10c, Mangrove crab. 15c, Lizard, crescent spot butterfly. 20c, Tricolored heron. 30c, Red mangrove flower. 40c, Red mangrove seeds. 50c, Waterhouse's leaf-nosed bat. $1, Black-crowned night heron. $2, Cayman Islands arms. $4, Queen Elizabeth II.

1980, Dec. 9 **Litho.** ***Perf. 13½x13***

Without Imprint

452 A71 3c shown 1.10 *2.25*
453 A71 5c multicolored 1.25 *1.10*
d. Wmk. 384 8.00 8.00
e. Wmk. 384, perf. 14 6.75 7.00
454 A71 10c multicolored .65 *1.10*
d. Wmk. 384, perf. 14 10.00 9.75
455 A71 15c multicolored 1.10 *2.25*
456 A71 20c multicolored 1.50 *2.75*
457 A71 30c multicolored .90 *1.40*
458 A71 40c multicolored .95 *1.25*
459 A71 50c multicolored 1.50 *1.75*
460 A71 $1 multicolored 6.00 *5.50*
461 A71 $2 multicolored 2.25 *3.75*
462 A71 $4 multicolored 4.25 4.25
Nos. 452-462 (11) 21.45 *27.35*

Nos. 453d, 453e and 454d inscribed "1986" below design. Issued: No. 453d, 4/86; Nos. 453e, 454fa, 6/86.

1982, June 14 **Inscribed "1982"**
452a A71 3c shown 5.00 *4.00*
453a A71 5c multicolored 1.25 *.90*
454a A71 10c multicolored 1.25 *.90*
455a A71 15c multicolored 4.50 *2.00*
456a A71 20c multicolored 2.50 *2.25*
457a A71 30c multicolored 1.50 *1.50*
458a A71 40c multicolored 1.50 *1.50*
459a A71 50c multicolored 2.00 *2.00*
460a A71 $1 multicolored 6.00 *5.00*
461a A71 $2 multicolored 4.00 *4.00*
462a A71 $4 multicolored 9.00 *11.00*
Nos. 452a-462a (11) 38.50 *35.05*

Issued: No. 453a, 4/86; No. 454a, 6/86.

1984 **Inscribed "1984"**
453b A71 5c multicolored 2.50 *2.50*

Issued: No. 453b, 6/86.

1985 **Inscribed "1985"**
453c A71 5c multicolored 1.25 *1.25*
454c A71 10c multicolored 1.25 *1.25*
455c A71 15c multicolored 4.50 *4.50*
456c A71 20c multicolored 2.50 *2.50*
457c A71 30c multicolored 1.50 *1.50*
458c A71 40c multicolored 1.50 *1.50*
459c A71 50c multicolored 2.00 *2.00*
460c A71 $1 multicolored 6.00 *5.00*
461c A71 $2 multicolored 5.00 *5.00*
Nos. 453c-461c (9) 25.50 *24.50*

Bread and Wine — A72

1981, Mar. 17 **Wmk. 373** ***Perf. 14***
463 A72 3c shown .25 .25
464 A72 10c Crown of thorns .25 .25
465 A72 20c Crucifix .25 .25
466 A72 $1 Christ .50 *.90*
Nos. 463-466 (4) 1.25 1.65

Easter.

Wood Slave A73

1981, June 16 **Litho.** ***Perf. 13½***
467 A73 20c shown .40 .40
468 A73 30c Cayman iguana .60 .60
469 A73 40c Lion lizard .80 .80
470 A73 50c Freshwater turtle .95 .95
Nos. 467-470 (4) 2.75 2.75

Royal Wedding Issue
Common Design Type

1981, July 22 **Litho.** ***Perf. 14***
471 CD331 20c Bouquet .25 .25
472 CD331 30c Charles .30 .30
473 CD331 $1 Couple .65 *.75*
Nos. 471-473 (3) 1.20 1.30

Intl. Year of the Disabled A74

5c, Scuba divers. 15c, Old School for Handicapped. 20c, New School for Handicapped. $1, Beach scene.

1981, Sept. 29 **Litho.** ***Perf. 14***
474 A74 5c multicolored .25 .25
475 A74 15c multicolored .25 .25
476 A74 20c multicolored .35 .35
477 A74 $1 multicolored 1.40 1.40
Nos. 474-477 (4) 2.25 2.25

Flower Type of 1980

1981, Oct. 20 **Litho.** ***Perf. 14***
478 A70 3c Bougainvillea .25 .25
479 A70 10c Morning glory .25 .25
480 A70 20c Wild amaryllis .55 .55
481 A70 $1 Cordia 2.25 2.25
Nos. 478-481 (4) 3.30 3.30

TB Bacillus Centenary — A75

15c, Koch, horizontal microscope. 30c, Koch, vert. 40c, Microscope, vert. 50c, Koch, diff., vert.

1982, Mar. 24 **Litho.** ***Perf. 14½***
482 A75 15c multicolored .30 .30
483 A75 30c multicolored .65 .65
484 A75 40c multicolored .80 .80
485 A75 50c multicolored 1.10 1.10
Nos. 482-485 (4) 2.85 2.85

Princess Diana Issue
Common Design Type

1982, July 1 **Litho.** ***Perf. 13***
486 CD333 20c Arms *.45* *.40*
487 CD333 30c Diana *.80* *.55*
488 CD333 40c Wedding *.90* *.75*
489 CD333 50c Portrait *2.60* *1.00*
Nos. 486-489 (4) *4.75* *2.70*

Scouting Year A76

1982, Aug. 24 **Wmk. 373** ***Perf. 14***
490 A76 3c Pitching tent .30 .25
491 A76 20c Cooking .65 .65
492 A76 30c Troop 1.10 1.10
493 A76 50c Boating skills 1.50 1.50
Nos. 490-493 (4) 3.55 3.50

Christmas 1982 — A77

Virgin and Child Paintings by Raphael.

1982, Oct. 26 ***Perf. 14½***
494 A77 3c multicolored .25 .25
495 A77 10c multicolored .30 .30
496 A77 20c multicolored .60 .60
497 A77 30c multicolored .85 .85
Nos. 494-497 (4) 2.00 2.00

Representative Govt. Sesquicentennial — A78

3c, Mace. 10c, Old Courthouse. 20c, Commonwealth Parliamentary Assoc. arms. 30c, Legislative Assembley building.

1982, Nov. 9 **Litho.** **Wmk. 373**
498 A78 3c multicolored .25 .25
499 A78 10c multicolored .25 .25
500 A78 20c multicolored .40 .40
501 A78 30c multicolored .60 .60
Nos. 498-501 (4) 1.50 1.50

Shell Type of 1980

5c, Natica canrena. 10c, Cassis tuberosa. 20c, Strombus gallus. $1, Cypraecassis testiculus.

1983, Jan. 11 Litho. *Perf. 13½*
502 A69 5c multicolored .25 .25
503 A69 10c multicolored .40 .40
504 A69 20c multicolored .85 .85
505 A69 $1 multicolored 3.50 *4.00*
Nos. 502-505 (4) 5.00 5.50

Visit of Queen Elizabeth II and Prince Philip A79

20c, Legislative Building, Cayman Brac. 30c, Leg. Bldg., Grand Cayman. 50c, Prince Philip. $1, Queen Elizabeth II.

1983, Feb. 15 Litho. *Perf. 14*
506 A79 20c multicolored .50 .50
507 A79 30c multicolored .85 .75
508 A79 50c multicolored 1.50 1.25
509 A79 $1 multicolored 2.50 2.50
a. Souvenir sheet of 4, #506-509 7.50 7.50
Nos. 506-509 (4) 5.35 5.00

A80

1983, Mar. 14
510 A80 3c Globe .30 .25
511 A80 15c Flags .65 .60
512 A80 20c Fisherman .70 .70
513 A80 40c Elizabeth II 1.10 .95
Nos. 510-513 (4) 2.75 2.50

Commonwealth Day.

Manned Flight Bicentenary and Mosquito Research and Control Unit — A81

Airplanes: 3c, MRCU Cessna. 10c, Consolidated Catalina PBY. 20c, Boeing 727. 40c, Hawker Siddeley HS-748.

1983, Oct. 10 Litho. *Perf. 14½*
514 A81 3c multicolored .95 .70
515 A81 10c multicolored 1.10 .70
516 A81 20c multicolored 1.90 1.90
517 A81 40c multicolored 2.50 *3.75*
Nos. 514-517 (4) 6.45 7.05

Shell Type of 1980

3c, Natica floridana. 10c, Conus austini. 30c, Colubrania obscura. 50c, Turbo cailletii.

1984, Jan. 18 *Perf. 14x14½*
518 A69 3c multicolored 1.25 .40
519 A69 10c multicolored 1.60 .40
520 A69 30c multicolored 4.50 4.50
521 A69 50c multicolored 4.75 4.75
Nos. 518-521 (4) 12.10 10.05

Lloyd's List Issue
Common Design Type

1984, May 16 Litho. *Perf. 14*
522 CD335 5c Cruise ship .65 .25
523 CD335 10c The Old Harbor .75 .30
524 CD335 25c Ridgefield 1.40 1.40
525 CD335 50c Goldfield 3.00 3.00
Nos. 522-525 (4) 5.80 4.95

Souvenir Sheet

526 CD335 $1 Goldfield, diff. 3.50 3.50

No. 525 Overprinted

1984, June 18
527 CD335 50c multicolored 1.60 *2.00*

Local Birds — A82

Perf. 14x14½
1984, Aug. 15 Litho. Wmk. 373
528 A82 5c Snowy egret 1.25 .65
529 A82 10c Bananaquit 1.25 .65
530 A82 35c Kingfisher 4.00 2.50
531 A82 $1 Brown booby 7.50 *11.00*
Nos. 528-531 (4) 14.00 14.80

Christmas — A83

Nos. 532a-532d, evening beach scenes. Nos. 533a-533d, daytime boating and beach scenes.

1984, Oct. 17 Litho. *Perf. 14*
532 A83 Strip of 4 5.00 *5.50*
a.-d. 5c Any single 1.25 *1.35*
533 A83 Strip of 4 6.00 *5.50*
a.-d. 25c Any single 1.50 *1.35*

Souvenir Sheet

534 A83 $1 Bonfire, diff. 6.25 6.25

No. 534 contains one stamp 29x48mm.

Orchids — A84

5c, Schomburgkia thomsoniana var. 10c, Schomburgkia thomsoniana. 25c, Encyclia plicata. 50c, Dendrophylax fawcetti.

1985, Mar. 13 Litho. *Perf. 14x13½*
535 A84 5c multicolored 1.50 .55
536 A84 10c multicolored 1.50 .55
537 A84 25c multicolored 3.75 1.25
538 A84 50c multicolored 4.75 3.50
Nos. 535-538 (4) 11.50 5.85

Shipwrecks A85

Unspecified shipwrecks found in Cayman waters.

1985, May 22 *Perf. 14*
539 A85 5c multicolored 1.25 .55
540 A85 25c multicolored 4.00 1.50
541 A85 35c multicolored 4.25 2.75
542 A85 40c multicolored 4.50 3.75
Nos. 539-542 (4) 14.00 8.55

Intl. Youth Year — A86

5c, Natl. Athletic Assoc. track competition. 15c, High school students studying in Grand Cayman Campus Library. 25c, Amateur League Competition Football. 50c, Natl. Netball Assoc. competition.

1985, Aug. 14 *Perf. 14½*
543 A86 5c multicolored .30 .25
544 A86 15c multicolored .50 .40
545 A86 25c multicolored 1.05 .85
546 A86 50c multicolored 2.10 *3.25*
Nos. 543-546 (4) 3.95 4.75

Telecommunications, 50th Anniv. — A87

Designs: 5c, Morse Code transmitter, 1935. 10c, Hand-cranked telephone, 1935. 25c, Tropospheric scatter dish, 1966. 50c, Earth dish receiver, 1979.

1985, Oct. 25 *Perf. 14*
547 A87 5c multicolored .55 *.70*
548 A87 10c multicolored .60 *.70*
549 A87 25c multicolored 1.75 1.10
550 A87 50c multicolored 3.00 *4.50*
Nos. 547-550 (4) 5.90 7.00

Birds A88

10c, Magnificent frigatebird. 25c, West Indian whistling duck. 35c, La Sagra's flycatcher. 40c, Yellow-faced grassquit.

1986, Mar. 20 Litho. Wmk. 384
551 A88 10c multicolored 2.25 1.00
552 A88 25c multicolored 3.00 1.60
553 A88 35c multicolored 3.50 3.50
554 A88 40c multicolored 4.00 *5.00*
Nos. 551-554 (4) 12.75 11.10

Nos. 552-553 vert.

Queen Elizabeth II 60th Birthday
Common Design Type

Designs: 5c, As bridesmaid at wedding of Lady Mary Cambridge, 1931. 10c, Royal visit to Norway, 1955. 25c, Inspecting West Indian troop, royal tour, 1985. 50c, Gulf tour, 1979. $1, Visiting Crown Agents' offices, 1983.

1986, Apr. 21 *Perf. 14x14½*
555 CD337 5c scar, blk & sil .25 .25
556 CD337 10c ultra, blk & sil .25 .25
557 CD337 25c grn & multi 1.75 .85
558 CD337 50c vio & multi .90 *1.75*
559 CD337 $1 rose vio & multi 1.40 *2.50*
Nos. 555-559 (5) 4.55 5.60

Royal Wedding Issue, 1986
Common Design Type

Designs: 5c, Informal portrait. 50c, Andrew in uniform, helicopter.

Perf. 14½x14
1986, July 23 Litho. Wmk. 384
560 CD338 5c multicolored .30 .25
561 CD338 50c multicolored 1.40 *2.10*

Marine Life — A89

5c, Rhynchocinetes rigeus. 10c, Nemaster rubiginosa. 15c, Calcinus tibicen. 20c, Rhodactis sanctithomae. 25c, Spirobranchus gigantea. 35c, Diodon holacanthus. 50c, Pseudocorynactis aribbeorum. 60c, Astrophyton muricatum. 75c, Cyphoma gibbosum. $1, Conolylactis gigantea. $2, Malacoctenus boehlkei. $4, Lima scabra.

Perf. 13½x13
1986, Sept. 15 Wmk. 373
Inscribed "1986"
562 A89 5c multicolored .80 *1.00*
563 A89 10c multicolored .80 .65
c. Wmk. 384, inscribed "1990" 2.75 3.00
564 A89 15c multicolored .70 *.75*
565 A89 20c multicolored .70 *.95*
566 A89 25c multicolored .45 *3.00*
567 A89 35c multicolored .70 *3.25*
568 A89 50c multicolored .80 *5.00*
569 A89 60c multicolored 3.50 *11.00*
570 A89 75c multicolored 9.50 *13.00*
571 A89 $1 multicolored 2.25 *2.75*
572 A89 $2 multicolored 5.00 *5.25*
573 A89 $4 multicolored 10.00 *7.75*
Nos. 562-573 (12) 35.20 *54.35*

1987 Inscribed "1987"
562a A89 5c multicolored .80 *1.60*
563a A89 10c multicolored .80 *1.25*
564a A89 15c multicolored .70 *1.50*
565a A89 20c multicolored .70 *2.00*
571a A89 $1 multicolored 2.25 *6.50*
572a A89 $2 multicolored 5.00 *10.50*
573a A89 $4 multicolored 10.00 *17.50*
Nos. 562a-573a (7) 20.25 *40.85*

1990 Inscribed "1990"
562b A89 5c multicolored 2.75 *5.00*
563b A89 10c multicolored 2.75 *4.00*
564b A89 15c multicolored 2.50 *5.00*
565b A89 20c multicolored 2.50 *7.00*
566b A89 25c multicolored 1.50 *10.00*
567b A89 35c multicolored —
568b A89 50c multicolored —
571b A89 $1 multicolored 8.00 *10.00*
572b A89 $2 multicolored 17.50 17.50
Nos. 562b-572b (7) 37.50 *58.50*

Tourism A90

Perf. 13x13½
1987, Jan. 26 Wmk. 384
574 A90 10c Golfing 2.50 1.00
575 A90 15c Sailing 2.60 1.00
576 A90 25c Snorkeling 2.60 1.50
577 A90 35c Parasailing 2.60 2.00
578 A90 $1 Fishing 5.75 *11.00*
Nos. 574-578 (5) 16.05 16.50

Fruit — A91

1987, May 20 *Perf. 14½*
579 A91 5c Akee 1.00 *1.25*
580 A91 25c Breadfruit 2.25 .75
581 A91 35c Papaya 2.25 1.00
582 A91 $1 Soursop 6.00 *8.50*
Nos. 579-582 (4) 11.50 *11.50*

Lizards — A92

1987, Aug. 26 Litho. *Perf. 14*

583 A92 10c Lion lizard 2.25 1.00
584 A92 50c Iguana 5.75 4.50
585 A92 $1 Anole 6.75 *8.75*
Nos. 583-585 (3) 14.75 14.25

Flowers — A93

1987, Nov. 18 *Perf. 14½x14*

586 A93 5c Poinsettia 1.25 .55
587 A93 25c Periwinkle 3.00 .90
588 A93 35c Yellow allamanda 3.00 1.25
589 A93 75c Blood lily 5.25 6.00
Nos. 586-589 (4) 12.50 8.70

Butterflies A94

Designs: 5c, Hemiargus ammon erembis and Strymon martialis. 25c, Phocides pigmalion batabano. 50c, Anaea troglodyta cubana. $1, Papilio andraemon andraemon.

1988, Mar. 29 Wmk. 384 *Perf. 14*

590 A94 5c multicolored 1.60 .65
591 A94 25c multicolored 3.50 1.40
592 A94 50c multicolored 5.25 5.25
593 A94 $1 multicolored 6.75 6.75
Nos. 590-593 (4) 17.10 14.05

Herons — A95

5c, Butorides striatus. 25c, Egretta tricolor. 50c, Nycticorax violaceus. $1, Egretta caerulea.

1988, Jan. 26 Litho. *Perf. 14*

594 A95 5c multicolored 2.40 .65
595 A95 25c multicolored 4.50 .90
596 A95 50c multicolored 5.50 5.25
597 A95 $1 multicolored 6.00 5.50
Nos. 594-597 (4) 18.40 12.30

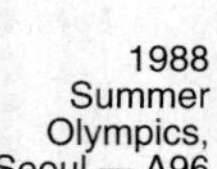

1988 Summer Olympics, Seoul — A96

10c, Cycling. 50c, Natl. team, passenger jet. $1, Yachting.
No. 601, Tennis.

1988, Sept. 21 *Perf. 14½*

598 A96 10c multicolored 2.25 .90
599 A96 50c multicolored 3.75 3.00
600 A96 $1 multicolored 4.00 4.00
Nos. 598-600 (3) 10.00 7.90

Souvenir Sheet

Wmk. 373

601 A96 $1 multicolored 5.75 5.75

No. 601 commemorates the 75th anniv. of the Intl. Tennis Federation.

Visit of Princess Alexandra A97

1988, Nov. 1 Wmk. 373 *Perf. 15*

602 A97 5c Portrait 2.50 1.25
603 A97 $1 Seated in garden 9.00 7.00

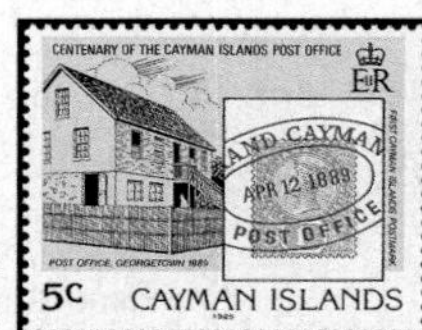

Cayman Islands P.O., Cent. — A98

Designs: 5c, P.O., Georgetown, 1889, and Jamaica #24, canceled. 25c, S.S. Orinoco and Cayman Isls. #1. 35c, Grand Cayman G.P.O. and #442. $1, Cayman Airways mail plane and #191.

1989, Apr. 12 Wmk. 384 *Perf. 14½*

604 A98 5c multicolored 1.10 *1.25*
605 A98 25c multicolored 2.50 1.50
606 A98 35c multicolored 2.75 1.75
607 A98 $1 multicolored 10.00 *11.00*
Nos. 604-607 (4) 16.35 15.50

A99

Mutiny on the Bounty: a, Capt. Bligh. b, HMS Providence, two crewmen. c, HMS Assistant, transplanted breadfruit. d, Moving breadfruit on land, in longboat. e, Midshipman among casks and crates.

1989, May 24 *Perf. 14*

608 Strip of 5 30.00 30.00
a.-e. A99 50c any single 6.00 6.00

A100

5c, Panton House. 10c, Town Hall. 25c, Old Courts House. 35c, Elmslie Memorial Church. $1, Post office.

Perf. 14½x14

1989, Oct. 18 Litho. Wmk. 373

609 A100 5c multicolored .90 *1.00*
610 A100 10c multicolored .90 *1.00*
611 A100 25c multicolored 2.00 .80
612 A100 35c multicolored 2.00 1.25
613 A100 $1 multicolored 5.00 *6.25*
Nos. 609-613 (5) 10.80 *10.30*

Natl. Trust emblem & architecture, George Town.

Island Surveys A101

Maps or survey ships: 5c, Navigational instruments and George Gauld's map of 1773. 25c, Instruments and map created by surveyors aboard HMS *Vidal,* 1956. 50c, *Mutine,* 1914. $1, HMS *Vidal.*

1989, Nov. 15

614 A101 5c multicolored 1.75 1.50
615 A101 25c multicolored 4.50 1.75
616 A101 50c multicolored 7.00 5.50
617 A101 $1 multicolored 11.00 11.00
Nos. 614-617 (4) 24.25 19.75

Angelfish A102

1990, Apr. 25 Wmk. 384 *Perf. 14*

618 A102 10c French 1.60 .65
619 A102 25c Gray 3.00 1.40
620 A102 50c Queen 4.50 1.00
621 A102 $1 Rock beauty 7.25 8.00
Nos. 618-621 (4) 16.35 11.05

Queen Mother, 90th Birthday

Common Design Types

50c, King, Queen Elizabeth, 1948. $1, King, Queen with Churchill, 1940.

1990, Aug. 4 Wmk. 384 *Perf. 14x15*

622 CD343 50c multicolored 1.25 *2.00*

Perf. 14½

623 CD344 $1 multicolored 2.75 *3.50*

Butterflies A103

5c, Soldier. 25c, Pygmy blue. 35c, Cayman crescent spot. $1, Gulf fritillary.

1990, Oct. 24 *Perf. 14½x14*

624 A103 5c multicolored 1.25 1.10
625 A103 25c multicolored 2.75 2.25
626 A103 35c multicolored 3.25 2.50
627 A103 $1 multicolored 7.75 *9.00*
Nos. 624-627 (4) 15.00 14.85

Expo '90, International Garden and Greenery Exposition, Osaka, Japan.

Hurricane Awareness — A104

Designs: 5c, Goes weather satellite. 30c, Meteorologist tracks storm. 40c, Hurricane damage. $1, Lockheed WP-3D Orion flying in hurricane's eye.

1991, Aug. 8 *Perf. 14*

628 A104 5c multicolored 1.40 1.40
629 A104 30c multicolored 3.25 1.75
630 A104 40c multicolored 3.50 2.10
631 A104 $1 multicolored 8.50 8.50
Nos. 628-631 (4) 16.65 13.75

Christmas A105

Local flowers and Christmas scenes: 5c, Angel's trumpet, angels with trumpets. 30c, Golden trumpet, Mary on donkey led by Joseph. 40c, Christmas flower, Adoration of the Magi. 60c, Tree of life, nativity scene.

1991, Nov. 6 Wmk. 373

632 A105 5c multicolored 1.00 1.00
633 A105 30c multicolored 3.00 .85
634 A105 40c multicolored 3.25 1.40
635 A105 60c multicolored 3.75 *6.50*
Nos. 632-635 (4) 11.00 9.75

Island Scenes A106

5c, Coconut tree, vert. 15c, Beach scene. 20c, Poincianas in bloom. 30c, Blowholes. 40c, Police band. 50c, Downtown scene, vert. 60c, The Bluff, Cayman Brac. 80c, Coat of arms, vert. 90c, View of Hell. $1, Sportfishing. $2, Harbor scene, vert. $8, Queen Elizabeth II, vert.

Perf. 12½x13, 13x12½

1991, Dec. 11 Litho. Wmk. 373

636 A106 5c multicolored .65 .50
a. Inscribed "1994" 1.00 .75
637 A106 15c multicolored 1.45 .50
638 A106 20c multicolored .75 .60
639 A106 30c multicolored 2.00 .80
640 A106 40c multicolored 3.25 2.00
641 A106 50c multicolored 2.75 2.00
642 A106 60c multicolored 2.25 3.25
643 A106 80c multicolored 2.00 3.25
644 A106 90c multicolored 2.00 3.25
645 A106 $1 multicolored 4.00 3.25
646 A106 $2 multicolored 8.50 8.00
647 A106 $8 multicolored 20.00 22.50
Nos. 636-647 (12) 49.60 49.90

Queen Elizabeth II's Accession to the Throne, 40th Anniv.

Common Design Type

Wmk. 373, 384 (40c)

1992, Feb. 6 Litho. *Perf. 14*

648 CD349 5c multicolored .45 .45
649 CD349 20c multicolored 1.40 .50
650 CD349 30c multicolored 1.50 .75
651 CD349 40c multicolored 1.50 1.40
652 CD349 $1 multicolored 2.75 *3.50*
Nos. 648-652 (5) 7.60 6.60

1992 Summer Olympics, Barcelona A107

15c, Cyclist. 40c, Two cyclists. 60c, Feet, pedals. $1, Two cyclists, diff.

1992, Aug. 5 Wmk. 373

653 A107 15c multicolored 2.00 .55
654 A107 40c multicolored 3.50 1.50
655 A107 60c multicolored 4.00 4.00
656 A107 $1 multicolored 5.00 5.00
Nos. 653-656 (4) 14.50 11.05

Island Heritage — A108

5c, Lady with donkey. 30c, Making fish nets. 40c, Maypole dancing. 60c, Basket making. $1, Cooking on caboose.

1992, Oct. 21

657 A108 5c multicolored .60 *.70*
658 A108 30c multicolored 1.60 .95
659 A108 40c multicolored 2.75 1.40
660 A108 60c multicolored 3.25 *3.50*
661 A108 $1 multicolored 3.75 *5.00*
Nos. 657-661 (5) 11.95 *11.55*

Rays A109

5c, Yellow stingray. 30c, Southern stingray. 40c, Spotted eagle ray. $1, Manta ray.

Perf. 13½x14

1993, June 16 Litho. Wmk. 373

662	A109	5c multicolored	.95	.75
663	A109	30c multicolored	2.40	1.50
664	A109	40c multicolored	2.75	1.75
665	A109	$1 multicolored	6.25	5.75
		Nos. 662-665 (4)	12.35	9.75

A110

Tourism: No. 666a, Turtle, sailboats. b, Diver, coral, boats. c, Golf. d, Beach, tennis. e, Pirates, sailing ship.

No. 667: a, Cruise ship, boat, sailboat. b, City street scene. c, Submarines. d, Cyclist, scooters. e, Jet planes.

Perf. 14x13½

1993, Sept. 30 Litho. Wmk. 373

666	A110	15c Strip of 5, #a.-e.	11.50	11.50
667	A110	30c Strip of 5, #a.-e.	12.50	12.50
f.		Booklet pane of 10, #666-667	35.00	

A111

Various views of Grand Cayman Parrot.

1993, Oct. 29 *Perf. 14*

668	A111	5c green & multi	1.25	1.25
669	A111	5c red & multi	1.25	1.25
670	A111	30c yellow & multi	3.00	3.00
671	A111	30c blue & multi	3.00	3.00
		Nos. 668-671 (4)	8.50	8.50

Christmas A112

Christmas scenes, orchids: 5c, Manger, Ionopsis utricularioides. 40c, Shepherd, lamb, Encyclia cochleata. 60c, Magi, Vanilla pompona. $1, Virgin in prayer, Oncidium caymanense.

Perf. 13½x14

1993, Dec. 6 Litho. Wmk. 384

672	A112	5c multicolored	1.40	.75
673	A112	40c multicolored	3.75	.95
674	A112	60c multicolored	4.75	4.50
675	A112	$1 multicolored	6.25	*7.00*
		Nos. 672-675 (4)	16.15	13.20

Souvenir Sheet

Reef Life — A113

Designs: a, Holocanthus ciliaris. b, Bodianus pulchellus, anisotremus virginicus. c, Holocanthus tricolor, gramma loreto. d, Pomacanthus paru, chaeton striatus.

Perf. 14½x13

1994, Feb. 18 Litho. Wmk. 373

676	A113	60c Sheet of 4, #a.-d.	13.50	13.50

Hong Kong '94.

Royal Visit — A114

Designs: 5c, Cayman Islands, United Kingdom flags. 15c, Royal yacht Britannia. 30c, Queen Elizabeth II. $2, Queen, Prince Philip.

1994, Feb. 22 *Perf. 14½*

677	A114	5c multicolored	2.00	1.10
678	A114	15c multicolored	3.75	1.25
679	A114	30c multicolored	3.75	1.50
680	A114	$2 multicolored	10.50	*12.00*
		Nos. 677-680 (4)	20.00	15.85

West Indian Whistling Duck A115

5c, One standing. 15c, Landing in water. 20c, Four ducks, various activities. 80c, One raising wings. $1, Adult, chick.

Wmk. 373

1994, Apr. 21 Litho. *Perf. 14*

681	A115	5c multi, vert.	1.75	.90
682	A115	15c multi	2.50	.95
683	A115	20c multi	2.50	1.00
684	A115	80c multi, vert.	5.50	6.00
685	A115	$1 multi, vert.	6.25	6.50
a.		Souvenir sheet of 1	12.00	12.00
		Nos. 681-685 (5)	18.50	15.35

No. 685a has a continuous design and contains Cayman Islands Natl. Trust emblem.

Butterflies A116

No. 686: a, Fulvous hairstreak. b, Atala butterfly.

No. 687: a, Barred sulphur. b, Dorantes skipper.

Wmk. 373

1994, Aug. 16 Litho. *Perf. 13½*

686	A116	10c Pair, #a.-b.	2.75	2.75
687	A116	$1 Pair, #a.-b.	13.00	13.00

Wreck of the Ten Sail, Bicent. — A117

Perf. 13½x14

1994, Oct. 12 Litho. Wmk. 373

688	A117	10c shown	.65	.65
689	A117	10c multicolored	.65	.65
690	A117	15c multicolored	1.10	.55
691	A117	20c multicolored	1.25	.65
692	A117	$2 multicolored	6.75	*7.50*
		Nos. 688-692 (5)	10.40	10.00

Sea Turtles A118

Wmk. 384

1995, Feb. 28 Litho. *Perf. 14*

693	A118	10c Green	.75	.45
694	A118	20c Kemp's ridley	1.10	.55
695	A118	25c Hawksbill	1.25	.65
696	A118	30c Leatherback	1.45	.75
697	A118	$1.30 Loggerhead	5.25	5.25
698	A118	$2 Pacific ridley	6.50	6.50
a.		Souvenir sheet, #693-698	16.50	16.50
		Nos. 693-698 (6)	16.30	14.15

1995 CARIFTA & IAAF Games A119

1995, Apr. 15 Litho. *Perf. 14*

699	A119	10c Running	.90	.50
700	A119	20c Pole vault	1.25	1.00
701	A119	30c Javelin	1.90	1.10
702	A119	$1.30 Sailing	6.50	6.50
		Nos. 699-702 (4)	10.55	9.10

Souvenir Sheet

703	A119	$2 Medal winners	9.00	9.00

End of World War II, 50th Anniv.

Common Design Type

10c, Two soldiers, Cayman Home Guard. 25c, Freighter Comayagua torpedoed off Caymans, 5/14/42. 40c, Type IXc U-Boat U-125. $1, Navy airship L-3 used for U-boat patrol. $1.30, Reverse of War Medal 1939-45.

Wmk. 373

1995, May 8 Litho. *Perf. 13½*

704	CD351	10c multicolored	1.40	.55
705	CD351	25c multicolored	2.75	.90
706	CD351	40c multicolored	3.25	2.25
707	CD351	$1 multicolored	5.75	5.75
		Nos. 704-707 (4)	13.15	9.45

Souvenir Sheet

Perf. 14

708	CD352	$1.30 multicolored	4.50	4.50

Souvenir Sheet

Queen Mother, 95th Birthday — A120

1995, Aug. 25 *Perf. 14½*

709	A120	$4 multicolored	11.50	11.50

Singapore '95.

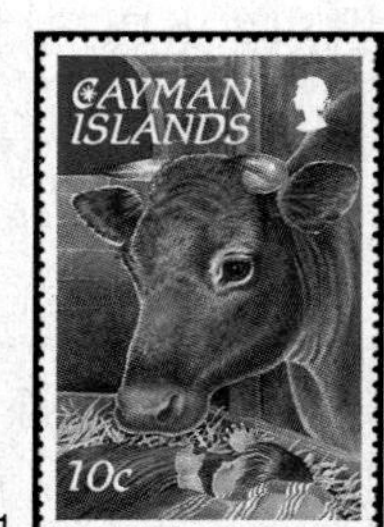

A121

Animals of the Nativity.

1995, Nov. 1 *Perf. 14*

710	A121	10c Ox	.90	.30
711	A121	20c Sheep, lamb	1.40	.50
712	A121	30c Donkey	2.25	.60
713	A121	$2 Camels	8.50	*10.00*
a.		Souvenir sheet of 4, #710-713	14.00	14.00
		Nos. 710-713 (4)	13.05	11.40

Wild Fruit — A122

10c, Sea grape. 25c, Guava. 40c, West Indian cherry. $1, Tamarind.

Wmk. 384

1996, Mar. 21 Litho. *Perf. 14*

714	A122	10c multicolored	.60	.50
715	A122	25c multicolored	1.25	.60
716	A122	40c multicolored	2.00	1.00
717	A122	$1 multicolored	4.00	*5.00*
		Nos. 714-717 (4)	7.85	7.10

Modern Olympic Games, Cent. — A123

Perf. 14x13½

1996, June 19 Litho. Wmk. 384

718	A123	10c Sailing	.65	.45
719	A123	20c Sailboarding	1.25	.55
720	A123	30c Sailing, diff.	1.60	.80
721	A123	$2 Running	6.00	*7.00*
		Nos. 718-721 (4)	9.50	8.80

Symbols of National Identity — A124

Designs: 10c, Guitar, music, natl. song. 20c, Boeing 737. 25c, Queen Elizabeth II opening Legislative Assembly. 30c, Seven Mile Beach. 40c, Scuba diver, stingrays. 60c, School children, Cayman Turtle Farm. 80c, Cayman parrot, natl. bird. 90c, Silver thatch palm, natl. tree. $1, Natl. flag. $2, Wild banana orchid, natl. flower. $4, Natl. arms. $6, Natl. currency.

Wmk. 373

1996, Sept. 26 Litho. *Perf. 14*

Inscribed "1996"

722	A124	10c multicolored	.50	.45
		Complete booklet, 10 #722	5.25	
a.		Inscribed "1997"	.50	.45
723	A124	20c multicolored	1.10	.85
724	A124	25c multicolored	1.25	.80
725	A124	30c multicolored	1.25	.80
		Complete booklet, 10 #725	13.00	
726	A124	40c multicolored	1.60	1.25
		Complete booklet, 10 #726	17.00	
727	A124	60c multicolored	2.25	1.60
728	A124	80c multicolored	3.75	3.00
a.		Souvenir sheet of 1	4.25	4.25
729	A124	90c multicolored	2.50	3.00
730	A124	$1 multicolored	4.00	3.25
731	A124	$2 multicolored	7.25	7.00
732	A124	$4 multicolored	13.00	16.00
733	A124	$6 multicolored	17.00	20.00
		Nos. 722-733 (12)	55.45	58.00

No. 728a for Hong Kong '97. Issued 2/3/97.

1999, Feb. 5 Wmk. 373 Sideways

723a	A124	20c multicolored	1.10	.85
725a	A124	30c multicolored	1.25	.80
727a	A124	60c multicolored	2.25	1.60
		Nos. 723a-727a (3)	4.60	3.25

Christmas
A125

Designs: 10c, Christmas time on North Church Street. 25c, Santa "Gone Fishing." 30c, "Claus Encounters." $2, "Caymanian Christmas."

Wmk. 373

1996, Nov. 12 Litho. *Perf. 14*

734 A125 10c multicolored .65 .35
735 A125 25c multicolored 1.60 .90
736 A125 30c multicolored 2.00 1.25
737 A125 $2 multicolored 4.00 6.00
Nos. 734-737 (4) 8.25 8.50

Queen Elizabeth II and Prince Philip, 50th Wedding Anniv. — A126

No. 738, Queen. No. 739, Royal Guard. No. 740, Young Prince riding horse. No. 741, Queen in blue, Prince in military attire in open carriage. No. 742 Prince holding horse's reins. No. 743, Queen looking at horses.
$1, Queen, Prince in open carriage.

Perf. 14x13½

1997, July 10 Litho. Wmk. 373

738 A126 10c multicolored 1.00 1.00
739 A126 10c multicolored 1.00 1.00
a. Pair, #738-739 2.00 2.00
740 A126 30c multicolored 1.60 1.60
741 A126 30c multicolored 1.60 1.60
a. Pair, #740-741 3.25 3.25
742 A126 40c multicolored 2.00 2.00
743 A126 40c multicolored 2.00 2.00
a. Pair, #742-743 4.00 4.00
Nos. 738-743 (6) 9.20 9.20

Souvenir Sheet

744 A126 $1 multicolored 6.25 6.25

Telecommunications — A127

Designs: 10c, Children using the Internet. 25c, Cable and wireless ship. 30c, Children wearing numbers of new area code, "345." 60c, Cable and wireless satellite communications.

Perf. 14x14½

1997, Oct. 10 Litho. Wmk. 384

745 A127 10c multicolored .45 .30
746 A127 25c multicolored 1.25 .60
747 A127 30c multicolored 1.40 .75
748 A127 60c multicolored 1.90 *2.50*
Nos. 745-748 (4) 5.00 4.15

Christmas
A128

Santa Claus: 10c, Relaxing in hammock, Little Cayman. 30c, With children on bluff, Cayman Brac. 40c, Playing golf. $1, Diving with stingrays.

Wmk. 373

1997, Dec. 3 Litho. *Perf. 13*

749 A128 10c multicolored .35 .25
750 A128 30c multicolored .80 .45
751 A128 40c multicolored 1.75 .80
752 A128 $1 multicolored 2.75 *3.50*
Nos. 749-752 (4) 5.65 5.00

Diana, Princess of Wales (1961-97)

Common Design Type

Portraits: a, 10c. b, 20c. c, 40c. d, $1.

Perf. 14½x14

1998 Litho. Wmk. 373

752A CD355 10c Like #753a .65 .65
752B CD355 20c Like #753b 1.25 1.25

Sheet of 4

753 CD355 #a.-d. 5.50 5.50

No. 753 sold for $1.70 + 30c, with surtax from international sales being donated to the Princess Diana Memorial Fund and surtax from national sales being donated to designated local charity.

Royal Air Force, 80th Anniv.

Common Design Type of 1993 Re-Inscribed

Designs: 10c, Hawker Horsley. 20c, Fairey Hendon. 25c, Hawker Siddeley Gnat. 30c, Hawker Siddeley Dominie.
No. 758: a, 40c, Airco DH-9. b, 60c, Spad 13 Scout. c, 80c, Airspeed Oxford. d, $1, Martin Baltimore.

Wmk. 373

1998, Apr. 1 Litho. *Perf. 14*

754 CD350 10c multicolored 1.00 1.00
755 CD350 20c multicolored 1.25 1.25
756 CD350 25c multicolored 1.60 1.60
757 CD350 30c multicolored 1.90 1.90
Nos. 754-757 (4) 5.75 5.75

Souvenir Sheet

758 CD350 Sheet of 4, #a.-d. 9.50 9.50

Birds — A129

Designs: 10c, West Indian whistling duck. 20c, Magnificent frigatebird. 60c, Red footed booby. $1, Grand Cayman parrot.

1998 Litho. Wmk. 373 *Perf. 13½*

759 A129 10c multicolored 1.10 .60
760 A129 20c multicolored 2.00 .60
761 A129 60c multicolored 3.50 3.50
762 A129 $1 multicolored 4.25 4.25
Nos. 759-762 (4) 10.85 8.95

Christmas
A130

Santa at various island locations: 10c, At Blowholes. 30c, Diving on wreck of MV Capt. Keith Tibbetts. 40c, Visiting Pedro Castle. 60c, Arriving at Little Cayman.

1998 *Perf. 14x14½*

763 A130 10c multicolored .40 .40
764 A130 30c multicolored 1.10 .85
765 A130 40c multicolored 1.50 1.10
766 A130 60c multicolored 2.50 2.50
Nos. 763-766 (4) 5.50 4.85

Easter
A131

Artworks by Miss Lassie (Gladwyn Bush): 10c, "They Rolled the Stone Away." 20c, "Ascension," vert. 30c, "The World Praying for Peace." 40c, "Calvary," vert.

Wmk. 373

1999, Mar. 26 Litho. *Perf. 13*

767 A131 10c multicolored .50 .50
768 A131 20c multicolored .85 .85
769 A131 30c multicolored 1.30 1.30
770 A131 40c multicolored 1.40 1.40
Nos. 767-770 (4) 4.05 4.05

Vision 2008
A132

Children's drawings: 10c, "Cayman House." 30c, "Coral Reef." 40c, "Fisherman on North Sound." $2, "Three Fish and A Turtle."

1999, June *Perf. 13½*

771 A132 10c multicolored .30 .30
772 A132 30c multicolored 1.10 1.10
773 A132 40c multicolored 1.25 1.25
774 A132 $2 multicolored 6.50 6.50
Nos. 771-774 (4) 9.15 9.15

Wedding of Prince Edward and Sophie Rhys-Jones

Common Design Type

Perf. 13¾x14

1999, June 16 Litho. Wmk. 384

775 CD356 10c Separate portraits .45 .45
776 CD356 $2 Couple 4.50 4.50

1st Manned Moon Landing, 30th Anniv.

Common Design Type

Designs: 10c, Coast Guard during launch. 25c, 3rd stage fires and puts rocket in orbit. 30c, Aldrin descends to lunar surface. 60c, Lander module sent back to moon.
$1.50, Looking at earth from moon.

1999, July 20 *Perf. 14x13¾*

777 CD357 10c multicolored .40 .40
778 CD357 25c multicolored 1.00 1.00
779 CD357 30c multicolored 1.10 1.10
780 CD357 60c multicolored 2.25 2.25
Nos. 777-780 (4) 4.75 4.75

Souvenir Sheet

Perf. 14

781 CD357 $1.50 multicolored 4.50 4.50

No. 781 contains one circular stamp 40mm in diameter.

Queen Mother's Century

Common Design Type

Queen Mother: 10c, Looking at London's defenses, 1940. 20c, At Clarence House, 94th birthday. 30c, With Princes Charles and William. 40c, Reviewing the Chelsea Pensioners, 1986.
$1.50, At her wedding.

Wmk. 384

1999, Aug. 18 Litho. *Perf. 13¼*

782 CD358 10c multicolored .40 .40
783 CD358 20c multicolored .70 .70
784 CD358 30c multicolored 1.25 1.25
785 CD358 40c multicolored 1.50 1.50
Nos. 782-785 (4) 3.85 3.85

Souvenir Sheet

786 CD358 $1.50 multicolored 4.50 4.50

Christmas — A133

Wmk. 373

1999, Nov. 17 Litho. *Perf. 13¼*

787 A133 10c #242, vert. .35 .35
788 A133 30c #532d, vert. 1.00 .90
789 A133 40c #749, vert. 1.40 1.25
790 A133 $1 #431 2.75 2.75
a. Souv. sheet, #787-790, perf. 12 5.25 5.25
Nos. 787-790 (4) 5.50 5.25

British Monarchs — A134

No. 792: a, Henry VIII. b, Mary I. c, Charles II. d, Anne. e, George IV. f, George V.

Wmk. 373

2000, Feb. 29 Litho. *Perf. 14*

791 A134 10c Henry VII .70 .70

Sheet of 6

792 A134 40c #a.-f. 9.50 9.50

The Stamp Show 2000, London.

Sesame Street — A135

Designs: 10c, Ernie. 30c, Big Bird.
No. 795: a, Grover. b, Zoe. c, Oscar the Grouch. d, The Count. e, Like 30c. f, Cookie Monster. g, Like 10c. h, Bert. i, Elmo in pond.
No. 796, Elmo collecting stamps.

Perf. 14½x14¾

2000, Mar. 15 Litho. Wmk. 373

793 A135 10c multi .35 .35
794 A135 30c multi 1.00 1.00
795 A135 20c Sheet of 9, #a-i 5.50 5.50

Souvenir Sheet

796 A135 20c multi 1.60 1.60

Prince William, 18th Birthday

Common Design Type

10c, In checked shirt and in sweater and checked shirt. 20c, In white shirt and black bow tie. 30c, In blue casual shirt, vert. 40c, As child, with beret, vert. $1, As infant.

Perf. 14¼x13¾, 13¾x14¼

2000, June 21 Litho. Wmk. 373

Stamps With White Border

797 CD359 10c multi .50 .40
798 CD359 20c multi .80 .75
799 CD359 30c multi 1.10 1.00
800 CD359 40c multi 1.50 1.50
Nos. 797-800 (4) 3.90 3.65

Souvenir Sheet

Stamps Without White Border

Perf. 14¼

801 Sheet of 5 7.25 7.25
a. CD359 10c multi .30 .30
b. CD359 20c multi .65 .65
c. CD359 30c multi .90 .90
d. CD359 40c multi 1.25 1.25
e. CD359 $1 multi 3.50 3.50

Marine Life
A136

10c, Green turtle. 20c, Queen angelfish. 30c, Parrotfish. $1, Green moray eel.

Wmk. 384

2000, Aug. 25 Litho. *Perf. 14*

802-805 A136 Set of 4 7.75 7.75

National Drug Council A137

Various children's drawings. Denominations, 10c, 15c, 30c, $2.

2000, Aug. 25
806-809 A137 Set of 4 10.00 10.00

Christmas A138

10c, Backing sand. 30c, Christmas dinner. 40c, Yard dance. 60c, Conch shell border.

Perf. 14½x14¼
2000, Nov. 14 Wmk. 373
810-813 A138 Set of 4 9.50 9.50

UN Women's Human Rights Campaign — A139

Wmk. 373
2001, Mar. 8 Litho. *Perf. 14*
814 A139 10c multi .80 .80

Cayman Brac A140

Designs: 15c, Red mangrove. 20c, Peter's Cave, vert. 25c, Bight Road stairway, vert. 30c, Westerly Pond. 40c, Aerial view. 60c, Marshes.

2001, Apr. 21
815-820 A140 Set of 6 11.00 11.00

Non-profit Organizations — A141

Designs: Nos. 821, 826a, 15c, National Council of Voluntary Organizations. Nos. 822, 826b, 20c, Cayman Humane Society. Nos. 823, 826c, 25c, Red Cross/Red Crescent. Nos. 824, 826d, 30c, Cayman Islands Cancer Society, vert. Nos. 825, 826e, 40c, Lions Club of Tropical Gardens, vert.

Wmk. 373
2001, Aug. 15 Litho. *Perf. 14*
Stamps With White Margins
821-825 A141 Set of 5 11.00 11.00

Souvenir Sheet
Stamps With Pink Margins
826 A141 Sheet of 5, #a-e 11.00 11.00

No. 826 sold for $1.80, 50c of which went to the various organizations honored.

Transportation — A142

Designs: No. 827, Walking home. No. 828, Boy on donkey. 20c, Bananas by canoe. 25c, Horse and buggy. 30c, Catboats. 40c, Schooner. 60c, Police bicycle, vert. 80c, Lady drivers. 90c, Launcing Cimboco, vert. $1, Seaplane. $4, Freighter. $10, Boeing 767.

Perf. 14¼x14½, 14½x14¼
2001, Sept. 29 Litho. Wmk. 373
827 A142 15c multi .45 .45
828 A142 15c multi .45 .45
829 A142 20c multi .60 .60
830 A142 25c multi .80 .80
831 A142 30c multi .90 .90
832 A142 40c multi 1.25 1.25
833 A142 60c multi 1.75 1.75
834 A142 80c multi 2.60 2.60
835 A142 90c multi 2.75 2.75
836 A142 $1 multi 3.00 3.00
837 A142 $4 multi 12.50 12.50
838 A142 $10 multi 29.00 29.00
Nos. 827-838 (12) 56.05 56.05

Christmas A143

Santa Claus: 15c, With children on dock. 30c, On eagle ray. 40c, In catboat. 60c, Parasailing.

Perf. 14¼x14½
2001, Nov. 21 Litho. Wmk. 373
839-842 A143 Set of 4 7.50 7.50

In Remembrance of Sept. 11, 2001 Terrorist Attacks — A144

Perf. 14x14¾
2002, Jan. 22 Litho. Wmk. 373
843 A144 $1 multi 3.75 3.75

Reign Of Queen Elizabeth II, 50th Anniv. Issue
Common Design Type

Designs: Nos. 844, 848a, 15c, Princess Elizabeth as child. Nos. 845, 848b, 20c, In 1976. Nos. 846, 848c, 30c, With Princess Margaret, 1942. Nos. 847, 848d, 80c, In 1996. No. 848e, $1, 1955 portrait by Annigoni (38x50mm).

Perf. 14¼x14½, 13¾ (#848e)
2002, Feb. 6 Litho. Wmk. 373
With Gold Frames
844 CD360 15c multicolored .45 .45
845 CD360 20c multicolored .65 .65
846 CD360 30c multicolored .90 .90
847 CD360 80c multicolored 2.25 2.25
Nos. 844-847 (4) 4.25 4.25

Souvenir Sheet
Without Gold Frames
848 CD360 Sheet of 5, #a-e 9.00 9.00

Peanuts Comic Strip Characters A145

Designs: 15c, Snoopy painting Woodstock at Cayman Brac Bluff. 20c, Charlie Brown and Sally at Hell Post Office. 25c, Peppermint Patty and Marcie at Little Cayman beach. 30c, Snoopy and Boeing 737-200. 40c, Linus and Snoopy at Point of Sand. 60c, Charlie Brown at Links Golf Course.

Wmk. 373
2002, Mar. 9 Litho. *Perf. 14*
849-854 A145 Set of 6 8.50 8.50
854a Souvenir sheet, #849-854 8.50 8.50

2002 World Cup Soccer Championships, Japan and Korea — A146

Denominations: 30c, 40c.

2002, Apr. 30 *Perf. 13¾*
855-856 A146 Set of 2 4.00 4.00

Queen Mother Elizabeth (1900-2002)
Common Design Type

Designs: 15c, Wearing hat (sepia photograph). 30c, Wearing dark blue hat. Nos. 859, 861a, 40c, Wearing hat (black and white photograph). Nos. 860, 861b, $1, Wearing tiara.

Perf. 13¾x14¼, 14¼ (#859-860)
2002, Aug. 5 Litho. Wmk. 373
With Purple Frames
857 CD361 15c multicolored .65 .65
858 CD361 30c multicolored 1.25 1.25
859 CD361 40c multicolored 1.60 1.60
860 CD361 $1 multicolored 4.00 4.00
Nos. 857-860 (4) 7.50 7.50

Souvenir Sheet
Without Purple Frames
Perf. 14½x14¼
861 CD361 Sheet of 2, #a-b 7.50 7.50

Christmas A147

Designs: 15c, Hail Mary. 20c, Journey to Bethlehem. 30c, Her firstborn Son. 40c, I bring good tidings. 60c Star in the east.

Wmk. 373
2002, Oct. 18 Litho. *Perf. 14*
Stamps + labels
862-866 A147 Set of 5 5.50 5.50
866a Souvenir sheet of 5, #862-866 + 5 labels 6.50 6.50

Aviation in the Cayman Islands, 50th Anniv. A148

Designs: 15c, PBY Catalina Flying Boat. 20c, First landing at Grand Cayman Airport, 1952. 25c, Cayman Brac Airways AC 50. 30c, Cayman Airways B-737. 40c, Concorde at original airport, 1984. $1.30, Island Air DHC6.

2002, Nov. 8
867-872 A148 Set of 6 15.00 15.00

Children's Games A149

Designs: 15c, Rope skipping. 20c, Maypole dancing. 25c, Gig. 30c, Hopscotch. $1, Marbles.

Wmk. 373
2003, May 27 Litho. *Perf. 13¾*
873-877 A149 Set of 5 7.50 7.50

Head of Queen Elizabeth II
Common Design Type

Wmk. 373
2003, June 2 Litho. *Perf. 13¾*
878 CD362 $4 multi 14.00 14.00

Coronation of Queen Elizabeth II, 50th Anniv.
Common Design Type

Designs: Nos. 879, 15c, 881a, 20c, Queen wearing crown. Nos. 880, $2, 881b, $4, Queen holding symbols of office.

Perf. 14¼x14½
2003, June 2 Litho. Wmk. 373
Vignettes Framed, Red Background
879 CD363 15c multicolored .50 .50
880 CD363 $2 multicolored 6.75 6.75

Souvenir Sheet
Vignettes Without Frame, Purple Panel
881 CD363 Sheet of 2, #a-b 12.00 12.00

Prince William, 21st Birthday
Common Design Type

Color photographs: 15c, William with backpack at right. 40c, William in suit and tie at left

No. 884: a, William with hand on chin at right. b, William with white bow tie at left.

Wmk. 373
2003, June 21 Litho. *Perf. 14¼*
882 CD364 15c multi .45 .45
883 CD364 40c multi 1.25 1.25
884 Horiz. pair 5.25 5.25
a. CD364 80c multi 2.25 2.25
b. CD364 $1 multi 3.00 3.00
Nos. 882-884 (3) 6.95 6.95

Discovery of the Cayman Islands, 500th Anniv. A150

Designs: 15c, Turtle hatchlings. No. 886, 20c, Old waterfront. No. 887, 20c, Turtle and ship of Christopher Columbus. 25c, Nassau grouper. 30c, Cayman Brac schooner "Kirk-B." 40c, George Town harbor. 60c, Musical instruments. 80c, Smokewood tree. 90c, Little Cayman Baptist Church. $1, Thatch rope. $1.30, Children's dance troupe. $2, Parliament in session.

Wmk. 373
2003, July 24 Litho. *Perf. 13¾*
885-896 A150 Set of 12 27.50 27.50
896a Souvenir sheet, #885-896 29.00 29.00

Holiday Greetings A151

Various Christmas decorations and inscriptions of: 15c, Merry Christmas. 20c, Celebrate With Family. 30c, Happy New Year. 40c, Happy Holidays. 60c, Seasons Greetings.

Wmk. 373
2003, Nov. 4 Litho. *Perf. 13¼*
897-901 A151 Set of 5 8.00 8.00

Worldwide Fund for Nature (WWF) A152

Short-finned pilot whale: 15c, Adult and calf. 20c, Pod of four whales. 30c, Two whales at surface. 40c, One adult.

2003, Nov. 26 ***Perf. 14***

902-905	A152	Set of 4	8.00	8.00
905a		Sheet, 4 each #902-905	35.00	35.00

Shipping Registry, Cent. — A153

Ships: 15c, Lady Slater. 20c, Seanostrum. 30c, Kirk Pride. $1, Boadicea.

Perf. 14x14¾

2004, Jan. 29 **Litho.** **Wmk. 373**

906-909	A153	Set of 4	11.00	11.00

Easter — A154

Designs: 15c, Jesus Carrying His Cross. 30c, The Ascension.

2004, Mar. 16 ***Perf. 14¾x14***

910-911	A154	Set of 2	3.25	3.25

2004 Summer Olympics, Athens — A155

Designs: 15c, Swimmer. 40c, Runner. 60c, Long jumper. 80c, Swimmers.

Perf. 13½x13¼

2004, Aug. 23 **Litho.** **Wmk. 373**

912-915	A155	Set of 4	6.25	6.25

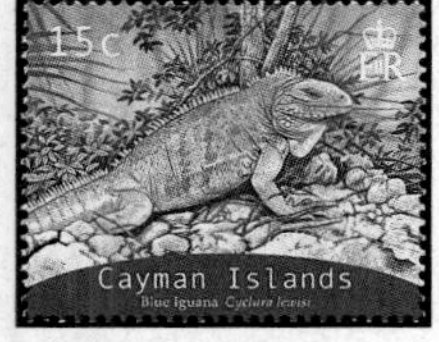

Blue Iguana A156

Designs: 15c, Adult on rocks. 20c, Eggs. 25c, Four juveniles. 30c, Juvenile on finger. 40c, Adult with open mouth. 90c, Eye.

No. 922: a, 60c, On rock facing right. b, 80c, On rock facing left.

2004, Oct. 26 **Litho.** ***Perf. 13¾***

916-921	A156	Set of 6	8.50	8.50

Souvenir Sheet

922	A156	Sheet of 2, #a-b	6.75	6.75

No. 922 sold for $1.90.

Battle of Trafalgar, Bicent. — A157

Designs: 15c, HMS Victory. 20c, HMS Tonnant tangles into the bow of the Algesiras. 25c, Flint cannon lock and linstock. No. 926, 60c, Royal Navy boatswain's mate. $1, Adm. Horatio Nelson, vert. No. 928, $2, HMS Orion in action against the Intrepide.

No. 929, vert.: a, 60c, French gunship Pluton. b, $2, HMS Tonnant.

Wmk. 373, Unwmkd. (15c)

2005, June 8 **Litho.** ***Perf. 13¼***

923-928	A157	Set of 6	14.50	14.50

Souvenir Sheet

929	A157	Sheet of 2, #a-b	8.00	8.00

No. 923 has particles of wood from the HMS Victory embedded in the areas covered by a thermographic process that produces a raised, shiny effect.

Rotary International, Cent. — A158

Designs: 15c, Centennial emblem. 30c, PolioPlus emblem.

2005, June 30 **Wmk. 373** ***Perf. 13¾***

930-931	A158	Set of 2	2.50	2.50

Orchids A159

Designs: 15c, Myrmecophila albopurpurea. 20c, Prosthechea boothiana. 30c, Tolumnia calochila, vert. 40c, Encyclia phoenicia. 80c, Prosthechea cochleata, vert.

$1.50, Encyclia kingsii.

2005, July 28 ***Perf. 14***

932-936	A159	Set of 5	7.75	7.75

Souvenir Sheet

937	A159	$1.50 multi	6.50	6.50

Pope John Paul II (1920-2005) A160

2005, Aug. 18

938	A160	30c multi	1.90	1.90

A161

Butterflies A162

Designs: 15c, Queen. 20c, Mexican fritillary. 25c, Malachite. 30c, Cayman crescent spot. 40c, Cloudless sulphur. 90c, Swallowtail.

Wmk. 373

2005, Sept. 21 **Litho.** ***Perf. 14***

939	A161	15c multi	.65	.65
940	A161	20c multi	.85	.85
941	A161	25c multi	.95	.95
942	A161	30c multi	1.20	1.20
943	A161	40c multi	1.75	1.75
944	A161	90c multi	3.50	3.50
		Nos. 939-944 (6)	8.90	8.90

Booklet Stamps

Self-Adhesive

Unwmk.

Serpentine Die Cut 9½x9

945	A162	15c multi	.80	.80
a.		Booklet pane of 10	8.00	
946	A162	20c multi	1.00	1.00
a.		Booklet pane of 6	6.00	
947	A162	30c multi	1.35	1.35
a.		Booklet pane of 10	13.50	
		Nos. 945-947 (3)	3.15	3.15

Christmas A163

Designs: 15c, Angels. 30c, Magi, horiz. 40c, Holy Family. 60c, Shepherds, horiz.

Perf. 14x14¾, 14¾x14

2005, Oct. 26 **Wmk. 373**

948-951	A163	Set of 4	5.50	5.50
951a		Souvenir sheet, #948-951, perf. 14¾	5.50	5.50

Trees and Blossoms — A164

Designs: 15c, Wash wood. 20c, Red mangrove. 30c, Ironwood. 60c, West Indian cedar. $2, Spanish elm.

Wmk. 373

2006, Feb. 23 **Litho.** ***Perf. 13¼***

Stamp + Label

952-956	A164	Set of 5	12.00	12.00

Queen Elizabeth II, 80th Birthday A165

Designs: 15c, As child. 40c, Wearing uniform and cap. $1, Wearing tiara. $2, Wearing sunglasses.

No. 961: a, 40c, Like #958. b, $1, Like #959.

2006, Apr. 21 ***Perf. 14***

With White Frames

957-960	A165	Set of 4	11.00	11.00

Souvenir Sheet

Without White Frames

961	A165	Sheet of 2, #a-b	11.00	11.00

A166

Marine Life — A167

Designs: Nos. 962, 967a, 968, Hawksbill turtle. Nos. 963, 967b, 969, Gray angelfish. Nos. 964, 967c, 970, Queen angelfish. Nos. 965, 967c, 971, Diamond blenny. Nos. 966, 967e, Juvenile spotted drum, vert. Nos. 964 and 967c are vert.

Wmk. 373

2006, July 18 **Litho.** ***Perf. 14***

With White Margins

962	A166	25c multi	1.00	1.00
963	A166	25c multi	1.00	1.00
964	A166	60c multi	2.50	2.50
965	A166	75c multi	3.25	3.25
966	A166	$1 multi	4.25	4.25
		Nos. 962-966 (5)	12.00	12.00

Souvenir Sheet

Without White Margin

967	A166	Sheet of 5, #a-e	12.00	12.00

Booklet Stamps

Self-Adhesive

Serpentine Die Cut 9½x9

Unwmk.

968	A167	25c multi	.70	.70
a.		Booklet pane of 10	7.00	
969	A167	25c multi	.70	.70
a.		Booklet pane of 10	7.00	
970	A167	60c multi	1.75	1.75
a.		Booklet pane of 10	17.50	
971	A167	75c multi	2.00	2.00
a.		Booklet pane of 10	20.00	
		Nos. 968-971 (4)	5.15	5.15

Birds A168

Designs: 25c, Bananaquit. 50c, Vitelline warbler. 75c, Grand Cayman parrot. 80c, Caribbean dove. $1, Caribbean elaenia. $1.50, West Indian woodpecker. $1.60, Thick-billed vireo. $2, Northern flicker. $4, Cuban bullfinch. $5, Western spindalis. $10, Loggerhead kingbird. $20, Red-legged thrush.

Perf. 13½x13¾

2006, Oct. 9 **Litho.** **Wmk. 373**

972	A168	25c multi	.60	.60
973	A168	50c multi	1.25	1.25
974	A168	75c multi	1.90	1.90
975	A168	80c multi	2.00	2.00
976	A168	$1 multi	2.50	2.50
977	A168	$1.50 multi	3.75	3.75
978	A168	$1.60 multi	4.00	4.00
979	A168	$2 multi	5.00	5.00
980	A168	$4 multi	9.75	9.75
981	A168	$5 multi	12.00	12.00
982	A168	$10 multi	24.00	24.00
983	A168	$20 multi	50.00	50.00
		Nos. 972-983 (12)	116.75	116.75

Booklet Stamps

Self-Adhesive

Unwmk.

Serpentine Die Cut 10x9½

Size:29x24mm

983A	A168	25c multi	.85	.85
d.		Booklet pane of 10	8.50	
983B	A168	75c multi	2.75	2.75
e.		Booklet pane of 10	27.50	
983C	A168	80c multi	2.75	2.75
f.		Booklet pane of 10	27.50	
		Nos. 983A-983C (3)	6.35	6.35

Christmas A169

Designs: 25c, "Faith," Magi. 75c, "Hope," Prophet with scroll. 80c, "Joy," angel. $1, "Love," Madonna and Child.

Perf. 12½x13¼

2006, Oct. 26 **Litho.** **Wmk. 373**

984-987	A169	Set of 4	12.00	12.00

Island Scenes A170

Designs: 20c, Brac Reed dock. 25c, Waterfront buildings, Hog Sty Bay. 30c, East End blowholes, vert. 40c, Man in hammock, vert. 75c, Poinciana blooms. $1, Driftwood on Little Cayman.

Wmk. 373

2007, June 26 Litho. ***Perf. 13¾***
988-993 A170 Set of 6 10.00 10.00

Scouting, Cent. A171

Designs: 25c, Wolf Cubs and leaders, hands lashing rope. 75c, Cub Scouts and leaders, hands with trumpet. 80c, Scouts camping, hand with compass. $1, Scout Drill Team, poppies.
No. 998, vert.: a, 50c, Scouts marching. b, $1.50, Lord Robert Baden-Powell and dog.

2007, July 9
994-997 A171 Set of 4 9.00 9.00

Souvenir Sheet

998 A171 Sheet of 2, #a-b 5.50 5.50

Wedding of Queen Elizabeth II and Prince Philip, 60th Anniv. — A172

Designs: 50c, Couple and wedding coach. 75c, Elizabeth wearing bridal veil. 80c, Princess Elizabeth, Philip, Queen Mother Elizabeth, King George VI, Princess Margaret. $1, Wedding procession, Westminster Abbey.
$2, Couple.

Wmk. 373

2007, Sept. 12 Litho. ***Perf. 13¾***
999-1002 A172 Set of 4 10.50 10.50

Souvenir Sheet

Perf. 14

1003 A172 $2 multi 7.50 7.50

No. 1003 contains one 42x57mm stamp.

Christmas A173

Stained-glass windows from local churches: 25c, Nativity, Wesleyan Holiness Church. 50c, Jesus Praying, Elmslie Memorial Church. 75c, Jesus Calling First Disciples, St. George's Anglican Church. 80c, Dove, East End Adventist Church. $1, Orb, First Baptist Church of Grand Cayman. $1.50, Shepherd, Frank Sound Church of God.

2007, Oct. 22 ***Perf. 15x14***
1004-1009 A173 Set of 6 16.50 16.50

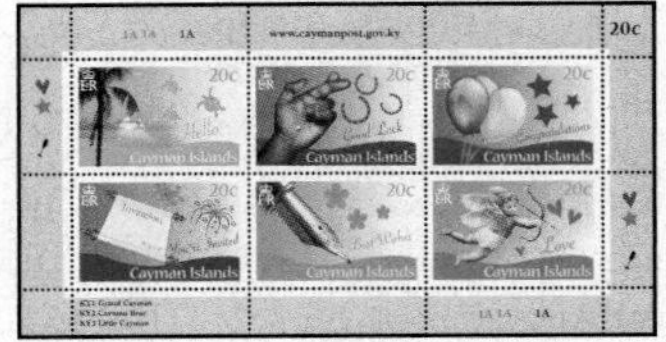
A174

Greetings A175

Nos. 1010-1015: a, Hello. b, Good Luck. c, Congratulations. d, You're Invited. e, Best Wishes. f, Love.
No. 1016, Hello. No. 1017, Congratulations. No. 1018, You're Invited. No. 1019, Love.

Wmk. 373

2008, Feb. 5 Litho. ***Perf. 14¼***
1010 A174 20c Sheet of 6, #a-f 3.00 3.00
1011 A174 25c Sheet of 6, #a-f 3.75 3.75
1012 A174 50c Sheet of 6, #a-f 7.50 7.50
1013 A174 75c Sheet of 6, #a-f 11.00 11.00
1014 A174 80c Sheet of 6, #a-f 12.00 12.00
1015 A174 $1 Sheet of 6, #a-f 15.00 15.00
Nos. 1010-1015 (6) 52.25 52.25

Booklet Stamps
Self-Adhesive

Serpentine Die Cut 9½x9

Unwmk.

1016 A175 20c multi .85 .85
a. Booklet pane of 10 8.50
1017 A175 25c multi 1.00 1.00
a. Booklet pane of 10 10.00
1018 A175 25c multi .85 .85
a. Booklet pane of 10 8.50
1019 A175 25c multi 1.00 1.00
a. Booklet pane of 10 10.00
Nos. 1016-1019 (4) 3.70 3.70

Darwin Initiative A176

Fauna: 20c, Land crab. 25c, Needlecase. 75c, Little Cayman green anole, vert. 80c, Cayman Brac ground boa. $1, White-shouldered bat.
$2, Caribbean reef squid, vert.

Wmk. 373

2008, July 9 Litho. ***Perf. 14***
1020-1024 A176 Set of 5 11.00 11.00

Souvenir Sheet

1025 A176 $2 multi 7.00 7.00

2008 Olympic Games, Beijing A177

Designs: 20c, Lanterns, swimming. 25c, Fish, swimming. 50c, Bamboo, running. 75c, Dragon, hurdles.

Wmk. 373

2008. Aug. 8 Litho. ***Perf. 13¼***
1026-1029 A177 Set of 4 7.00 7.00

Water Authority, 25th Anniv. A178

Children's art: 25c, Stop Water Pollution. 75c, Water droplets. $2, Splash of Life.

Wmk. 373

2008, Oct. 16 Litho. ***Perf. 13¼***
1030-1032 A178 Set of 3 11.00 11.00

Christmas A179

Santa Claus and: 25c, Ship. 75c, Horse-drawn carriage. 80c, Helicopter. $1, Race car.

2008, Nov. 12 ***Perf. 13¾***
1033-1036 A179 Set of 4 11.00 11.00

A180

No. 1037: a, Silver thatch plant. b, People making rope strands. c, Man cobbing rope. d, Thatch products. e, Traditional home.

Wmk. 406

2009, Jan. 28 Litho. ***Perf. 13¾***
1037 A180 Horiz. strip of 5 5.00 5.00
a.-e. 25c Any single 1.00 1.00
Complete booklet, 2 #1037 10.00

Island Scenes A181

Designs: 20c, Hammock, palm trees, boat. 25c, House. 75c, Hammock under shelter at beach, palm trees, vert. 80c, Three cruise liners. $1, Direction signs near bus depot, vert. $1.50, Limestone pinnacles, Hell.
$2, Iguana.

2009, Apr. 9 ***Perf. 12½***
1038-1043 A181 Set of 6 14.00 14.00

Souvenir Sheet

Perf. 13

1044 A181 $2 multi 6.25 6.25

Space Exploration A182

Designs: 20c, Mars Rover, 2004. 25c, Space Shuttle STS-71 launch, 1995. 75c, Hubble Space Telescope. $1, Apollo 11 launch, 1969. $1.50, International Space Station.
$2, Lunar Rover on Moon, painting by Capt. Alan Bean, vert.

Wmk. 406

2009, July 20 Litho. ***Perf. 13¼***
1045-1049 A182 Set of 5 11.00 11.00

Souvenir Sheet

Perf. 13x13¼

1050 A182 $2 multi 6.25 6.25

No. 1050 contains one 40x60mm stamp. Nos. 1045-1049 each were printed in sheets of 6.

Equality Through Democracy A183

Designs: No. 1051, 25c, Hands holding pens signing voting rolls. No. 1052, 25c, George Town Town Hall. 50c, Woman casting ballot.

Wmk. 406

2009, Sept. 23 Litho. ***Perf. 13¾***
1051-1053 A183 Set of 3 3.75 3.75
1053a Sheet of 3, #1051-1053 3.75 3.75

Woman suffrage and Cayman Islands constitution, 50th anniv.

Christmas — A184

Images of Christmas stamps of 1997: 25c, Cayman Islands #749. 75c, Cayman Islands #750. 80c, Cayman Islands #751. $1, Cayman Islands #752.

Wmk. 406

2009, Oct. 22 Litho. ***Perf. 14***
1054-1057 A184 Set of 4 8.00 8.00

Shells A185

Designs: 20c, Hawk-wing conch. 25c, Ornate scallop. 60c, Chestnut turban. 75c Beautiful mitre. 80c, Four-toothed nerite. $1.60, White-spotted marginella.
$3, Queen conch.

Wmk. 406

2010, June 30 Litho. ***Perf. 13¼***
1058-1063 A185 Set of 6 13.50 13.50

Souvenir Sheet

1064 A185 $3 multi 10.50 10.50

Shells — A186

Designs: 25c, Ornate scallop. 75c, Beautiful mitre.

Serpentine Die Cut 9½x9

2010, June 30 Unwmk.

Booklet Stamps
Self-Adhesive

1065 A186 25c multi *1.75 1.75*
a. Booklet pane of 10 *17.50*
1066 A186 75c multi *4.25 4.25*
a. Booklet pane of 10 *42.50*

Girld Guides, Cent. A187

Girl Guides: 20c Uniforms. 25c, Camping. 50c, Parade. 80c, Badges.

Wmk. 406

2010, Dec. 17 Litho. *Perf. 12½*
1067-1070 A187 Set of 4 6.00 6.00

Wedding of Prince William and Catherine Middleton — A188

Designs: 25c, Couple kissing. 75c, Couple in carriage waving, horiz. 80c, Couple holding hands. $2, Couple and father of the bride, horiz.

2011, Aug. 4 *Perf. 14*
1071-1074 A188 Set of 4 8.50 8.50

Catboats A189

Designs: No. 1075, 20c, Men in catboats catching turtles. Nos. 1076, 1081, 25c, Men building catboat. No. 1077, 25c, Catboat sailing around Cayman Brac's Bluff. No. 1078, 50c, Catboats racing regatta style. No. 1079, $1.60, Catboats unloading cargo. No. 1080, $2, Women sewing catboat sail.

2011, Aug. 31 Wmk. 406 *Perf. 14*
1075-1080 A189 Set of 6 12.00 12.00

Booklet Stamp
Self-Adhesive
Size:30x25mm
Serpentine Die Cut 9½x9
Unwmk.

1081 A189 25c multi *1.25 1.25*
a. Booklet pane of 10 *12.50*

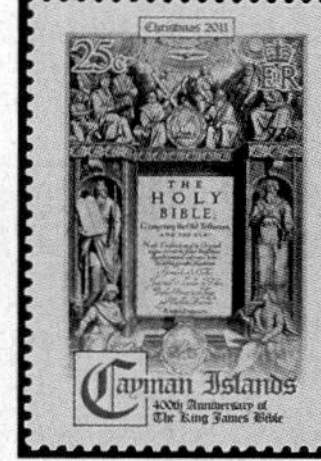

Christmas A190

Designs: 25c, Frontispiece for 1611 edition of the King James Bible. 75c, King James I. 80c, William Tyndale, Bible tanslator. $1, Printers printing the King James Bible. $1.60, Translators in the Jerusalem Chamber.

2011, Nov. 8 Wmk. 406 *Perf. 12½*
1082-1086 A190 Set of 5 12.50 12.50

King James Bible, 400th anniv.

Famous Cayman Islanders A191

Designs: 20c, Almerian Labertha McLaughlin Tomlinson (1882-1974), midwife. 25c, Captain Rayal Brazley Bodden (1885-1976), shipwright and builder. 75c, Irskie Leila Yates (1899-1996), maternity nurse. $1.50, Major Joseph Rodriguez Watler (1890-1965), police inspector.

Perf. 13¼x13¾

2011, Nov. 11 Wmk. 406
1087 A191 20c multi .65 .65
a. Booklet pane of 6 3.90 —
Complete booklet, #1087a 3.90
1088 A191 25c multi .75 .75
a. Booklet pane of 6 4.50 —
Complete booklet, #1088a 4.50
1089 A191 75c multi 2.25 2.25
a. Booklet pane of 6 13.50 —
Complete booklet, #1089a 13.50
1090 A191 $1.50 multi 4.50 4.50
a. Booklet pane of 6 27.00 —
Complete booklet, #1090a 27.00
Nos. 1087-1090 (4) 8.15 8.15

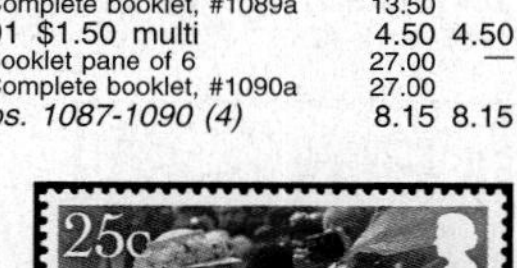

A192

Reign of Queen Elizabeth II, 60th Anniv. — A193

Various photographs of Queen Elizabeth II: 25c, 80c, $1, $1.50.

2012, June 12 Wmk. 406 *Perf. 14*
1091-1094 A192 Set of 4 10.00 10.00

Booklet Stamp
Self-Adhesive
Serpentine Die Cut 9½x9
Unwmk.

1095 A193 25c multi *1.50 1.50*
a. Booklet pane of 10 *15.00*

2012 Summer Olympics, London A194

Designs: 25c, Runner. 50c, Hurdler. 75c, Swimmer. 80c, Two runners. $1.60, Swimmer, diff.

Wmk. 406

2012, Aug. 2 Litho. *Perf. 13¼*
1096-1100 A194 Set of 5 10.50 10.50

A195

A195a

Emergency Services: 20c, Patrol boats. 25c, Ambulance service. 75c, Fire department. $1.50, 911 public safety communications. $2, Police helicopter.

2012, Aug. 30 Wmk. 406 *Perf. 14*
1101-1105 A195 Set of 5 12.00 12.00
1101a Dated "2013" .50 .50

Booklet Stamps
Self-Adhesive
Unwmk.
Serpentine Die Cut 9½x9

1105A A195a 25c multi .75 .75
c. Booklet pane of 10 7.50
1105B A195a 75c multi 2.10 2.10
d. Booklet pane of 10 21.00

A196

A197

Marine Life: 25c, Stoplight parrotfish. 50c, Green sea turtle. 75c, Common sea fan, Yellow tube sponge. 80c, Upside-down jellyfish. $1, Juvenile yellowtail damselfish. $1.50, Spotted trunkfish. $1.60, Caribbean spiny lobster. $2, Giant barrel sponge. $4, Caribbean reef shark. $5, Great barracuda. $10, Southern stingray.$20, West Indian spider crab.

2012, Oct. 9 Wmk. 406 *Perf. 14*
1106 A196 25c multi .60 .60
1107 A196 50c multi 1.25 1.25
1108 A196 75c multi 1.90 1.90
1109 A196 80c multi 2.00 2.00
1110 A196 $1 multi 2.50 2.50
a. Souvenir sheet of 4 10.00 10.00
1111 A196 $1.50 multi 3.75 3.75
1112 A196 $1.60 multi 4.00 4.00
1113 A196 $2 multi 5.00 5.00
1114 A196 $4 multi 9.75 9.75
1115 A196 $5 multi 12.50 12.50
1116 A196 $10 multi 22.50 22.50
1117 A196 $20 multi 45.00 45.00
Nos. 1106-1117 (12) 110.75 110.75

Booklet Stamps
Self-Adhesive
Die Cut Perf. 14x15¼
Unwmk.

1118 A197 25c multi .60 .60
a. Booklet pane of 10 6.00
1119 A197 75c multi 1.90 1.90
a. Booklet pane of 10 19.00
1120 A197 80c multi 2.00 2.00
a. Booklet pane of 10 20.00
Nos. 1118-1120 (3) 4.50 4.50

Christmas A198

Paintings by Gladwyn K. Bush: 25c, Mary and Jesus. 75c, His Name is Jesus. 80c, Every Knee Shall Bow. $1, Nativity.

2012, Dec. 6 Wmk. 406 *Perf. 14*
Stamps + Label
1121-1124 A198 Set of 4 6.50 6.50

A199

Shipwrecks and Anchors — A200

Shipwreck: 20c, Mathusalem. Nos. 1126, 1130, 25c, Inga. No. 1127, 25c, Topsy. $1.50, Tofa. $2, Glamis.

Wmk. 406

2013, Aug. 2 Litho. *Perf. 14*
1125-1129 A199 Set of 5 10.50 10.50

Booklet Stamp
Self-Adhesive
Die Cut Perf. 14x15¼
Unwmk.

1130 A200 25c multi .60 .60
a. Booklet pane of 10 6.00

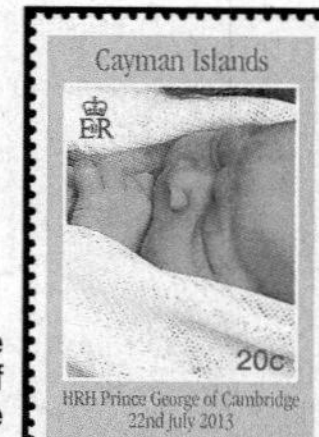

Birth of Prince George of Cambridge A201

Designs: 20c, Prince George. 25c, Duchess of Cambridge holding Prince George. 80c, Duke of Cambridge holding Prince George. $2, Duke and Duchess of Cambridge, Prince George.

Wmk. 406

2013, Oct. 31 Litho. *Perf. 12½*
1131-1134 A201 Set of 4 7.75 7.75

Christmas A202

Santa Claus and: 25c, Old Government House. 75c, Old Homestead. 80c, Bodden Town Mission House. $1, Old District Administration Building.

Wmk. 406

2013, Nov. 5 Litho. *Perf. 13*
1135-1138 A202 Set of 4 6.75 6.75

Houses on Little Cayman and Cayman Brac A203

Designs: 20c, Captain Theo's Villa, Little Cayman. 25c, Carter's House, Cayman Brac. 75c, Captain Charlie's House, Cayman Brac. $1, Foster's House, Cayman Brac.

Wmk. 406

2014, June 10 Litho. *Perf. 13*
1139-1142 A203 Set of 4 5.50 5.50

A204

20th Commonwealth Games, Glasgow, Scotland — A205

Scottish flag and: 20c, Cycling. 25c, Swimming. 55c, Boxing. 80c, Squash. $1, Shooting. $1.60, Gymnastics. $2, Javelin.

Perf. 13¼x13

2014, Oct. 3 Litho. Wmk. 406
1143-1149 A204 Set of 7 16.00 16.00

Booklet Stamp
Self-Adhesive
Serpentine Die Cut 13¾x14
Unwmk.

1150 A205 25c multi .60 .60
a. Booklet pane of 10 6.00

A206

Christmas A207

Christmas ornaments, poinsettia and: Nos. 1151, 1154, 25c, Little Cayman Baptist Church. Nos. 1152, 1155, 25c, South Sound United Church. Nos. 1153, 1156, 25c, Stake Bay Baptist Church.

Wmk. 406

2014, Nov. 15 Litho. *Perf. 13¾*

1151-1153 A206 Set of 3 1.90 1.90

Booklet Stamps
Self-Adhesive

Die Cut Perf. 14x15¼

Unwmk.

1154-1156 A207 Set of 3 1.90 1.90
1156a Booklet pane of 12, 4 each #1154-1156 7.75

Famous Cayman Islanders Type of 2011

Designs: 25c, Timothy E. McField (1928-95), educator. 50c, Annie Huldah Bodden (1908-89), politician. 80c, Ormond L. Panton (1920-92), politician. $1, Captain Keith P. Tibbetts, Sr. (1916-96), politician.

Perf. 13¼x13¾

2015, May 20 Litho. Wmk. 406

1157 A191 25c multi .60 .60
a. Booklet pane of 6 3.75 —
Complete booklet, #1157a 3.75
1158 A191 50c multi 1.25 1.25
a. Booklet pane of 6 7.50 —
Complete booklet, #1158a 7.50
1159 A191 80c multi 2.00 2.00
a. Booklet pane of 6 12.00 —
Complete booklet, #1159a 12.00
1160 A191 $1 multi 2.50 2.50
a. Booklet pane of 6 15.00 —
Complete booklet, #1160a 15.00
Nos. 1157-1160 (4) 6.35 6.35

A208

Christmas A209

Winning designs in children's Christmas stamp design contest depicting: 20c, Christmas tree, presents and crab, by Arianna Anglin. Nos. 1162, 1165, 25c, Parrot, by Clementine Bonnie Lumsden. 75c, Turtle, by Zara Garofolo. 80c, Sun, sailboat, Christmas stockings, by Cerys Martin.

Wmk. 406

2015, Dec. 2 Litho. *Perf. 13*

1161-1164 A208 Set of 4 5.00 5.00

Booklet Stamp
Self-Adhesive

Serpentine Die Cut 13¾x14

Unwmk.

1165 A209 25c multi .60 .60
a. Booklet pane of 10 6.00

Cayman Islands National Museum, 25th Anniv. — A210

Designs: No. 1166, 25c, Ship's sextant, 1960s. No. 1167, 25c, Caymanian Woman, wood carving by Clarice Carter, 1960s. 75c, Coffee grinder, early 1900s. $1.60, Monkey jar, early 1900s.

Wmk. 406

2015, Dec. 3 Litho. *Perf. 14*

1166-1169 A210 Set of 4 7.00 7.00

Ships A211

Designs: 25c, Kirk B. 80c, Nunoca. $1, Rembro. $2, Clara C. Scott. $4, HMS Dragon.

Wmk. 406

2016, May 16 Litho. *Perf. 13*

1170-1173 A211 Set of 4 10.00 10.00

Souvenir Sheet

1174 A211 $4 multi 9.75 9.75

Queen Elizabeth II, 90th Birthday — A212

Various photographs of Queen Elizabeth II: 20c, 25c, 75c, 80c.

2016, Nov. 9 Litho. *Perf. 13½x13¼*

1175-1178 A212 Set of 4 5.00 5.00

Agriculture, 50th Anniv. A213

Designs: 20c, Boer goat. 25c, Fruits and vegetables. 50c, Mixed-breed cow. $2, Peppers. No. 1183 — Farmers: a, Kent Rankin (1946-2016). b, John Bothwell (1920-2006). c, Mercherito Chantilope (1937-2014).

Wmk. 406

2017, Mar. 29 Litho. *Perf. 13¼*

1179-1182 A213 Set of 4 7.25 7.25

Souvenir Sheet

1183 Sheet of 3 7.75 7.75
a. A213 75c multi 1.90 1.90
b. A213 80c multi 2.00 2.00
c. A213 $1.50 multi 3.75 3.75

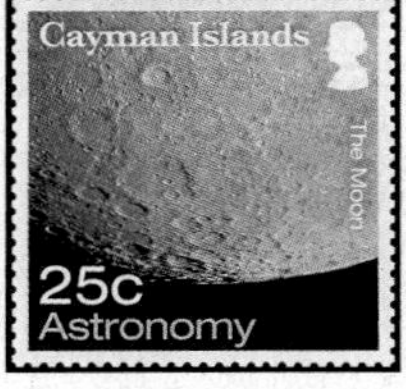
Astronomy A214

Designs: 25c, Moon. 50c, Saturn. 75c, Solar flares. $1.60, Jupiter.

Wmk. 406

2017, June 2 Litho. *Perf. 13¼*

1184-1187 A214 Set of 4 7.75 7.75

Moths A215

Designs: 20c, Faithful beauty moth. 25c, Cayman clearwing wasp moth. $1.60, White-lined sphinx moth. $2, Gaudy sphinx moth.

Wmk. 406

2017, Oct. 12 Litho. *Perf. 13¾*

1188-1191 A215 Set of 4 10.00 10.00

Christmas A216

Christmas decorations at local homes: Nos. 1192, 1196, 25c, Bodden family's nativity scene. 75c, Crighton family's display of Santa Claus and Christmas trees. 80c, Bodden family's carolers. $1, Crighton family's display of Santa Claus and elves.

Perf. 12½x13

2017, Nov. 2 Litho. Wmk. 406

1192-1195 A216 Set of 4 7.00 7.00

Booklet Stamp
Self-Adhesive

Serpentine Die Cut 13¼x13½

Unwmk.

1196 A216 25c multi .60 .60
a. Booklet pane of 10 6.00

70th Wedding Anniversary of Queen Elizabeth II and Prince Philip A217

Map of Cayman Islands and: 20c, Engagement photograph. 25c, Wedding photograph. 75c, Photograph from 1982. 80c, Photograph from 2016.

Perf. 14¼x14½

2017, Dec. Litho. Wmk. 406

1197-1200 A217 Set of 4 5.00 5.00

Nos. 1197-1200 were each printed in sheets of 7 + label.

Wedding of Prince Harry and Meghan Markle — A218

Various photographs of couple: 25c, 75c, 80c, $1.

Perf. 13x13¼

2018, July 18 Litho. Wmk. 406

1201-1204 A218 Set of 4 7.00 7.00

Cayman Airways, 50th Anniv. A219

Designs: Nos. 1205, 1210, 25c, Boeing 737-300. 80c, Boeing 737-800. $1, DeHavilland DHC-6 Twin Otter. $1.50, Saab 340B+. $2, 50th anniversary emblem, vert.

Wmk. 406

2018, Aug. 17 Litho. *Perf. 13½*

1205-1208 A219 Set of 4 8.75 8.75

Souvenir Sheet

Perf. 14

1209 A219 $2 multi 5.00 5.00

Booklet Stamp
Self-Adhesive
Size:39x24mm

Serpentine Die Cut 12¾x13

Unwmk.

1210 A219 25c multi .60 .60
a. Booklet pane of 10 6.00

No. 1209 contains one 33x45mm stamp.

Cayman Islands Coat of Arms, 60th Anniv. A220

Wmk. 406

2018, Oct. 19 Litho. *Perf. 12½*

1211 A220 $2 multi 5.00 5.00
a. Souvenir sheet of 1 5.00 5.00

A221

Christmas A222

Carols: 25c, "We Three Kings of Orient Are." 80c, "O Holy Night." $1.50, "Away in a Manger." $2, "Joy to the World."

Wmk. 406

2018, Nov. 23 Litho. *Perf. 14*

1212-1215 A221 Set of 4 11.00 11.00

Booklet Stamp
Self-Adhesive

Unwmk.

Serpentine Die Cut 10x9¾

1216 A222 25c multi .60 .60
a. Booklet pane of 10 6.00

A223

Christmas A224

Designs: 25c, Santa Claus playing guitar, reindeer playing drum. 75c, Santa Claus playing guitar in hammock, reindeer playing washboard, iguana playing drum. 80c, Santa Claus playing violin in sailboat, reindeer playing drum. $2, Santa Claus and reindeer playing guitars, parrot singing.

Wmk. 406

2019, Nov. 15 Litho. *Perf. 14*

1217-1220 A223 Set of 4 9.25 9.25

Booklet Stamp
Self-Adhesive

Serpentine Die Cut 10x9¾

Unwmk.

1221 A224 25c multi .60 .60
a. Booklet pane of 10 6.00

First Man on the Moon, 500th Anniv. — A225

Designs: 20c, Astronaut's footprint on Moon. 25c, Moon. 75c, Astronaut and U.S. flag on Moon. $1.60, Rocket launch.

Wmk. 406

2019, Dec. 13 Litho. *Perf. 14¼*
1222-1225 A225 Set of 4 7.00 7.00

WAR TAX STAMPS

No. 36 Surcharged

a b

1917, Feb. 26 Wmk. 3 *Perf. 14*
MR1 A5(a) 1½p on 2½p 20.00 *26.00*
a. Fraction bar omitted 275.00 *300.00*
b. Period missing after "STAMP" 900.00
MR2 A5(b) 1½p on 2½p 2.10 *7.25*
a. Fraction bar omitted 85.00 *150.00*

On No. 1 the distance between "WAR STAMP" and "1½" varies.

Surcharged

1917, Sept. 4
MR3 A5 1½p on 2½p ultra 850.00 *2,500.*

Surcharged

1917, Sept. 4
MR4 A5 1½p on 2½p ultra .30 *.65*

No. 33 Overprinted

1919, Feb. 4
MR5 A5 ½p green .70 *3.00*

The "brownish paper" variety comes from the interleaving used for shipment from England.

Type of 1912-16 Surcharged

1919, Feb. 4
MR6 A5 1½p on 2½p orange 1.00 *2.00*

No. 35 Surcharged

1920, Mar. 10
MR7 A5 1½p on 2p gray 5.50 *9.50*

The "rose-tinted paper" variety comes from the interleaving used for shipment from England.
A surcharge in red was not issued.

CENTRAL AFRICAN REPUBLIC

ˈsen-trəl ˈa-fri-kən ri-ˈpə-blik

LOCATION — Western Africa, north of equator
GOVT. — Republic
AREA — 241,243 sq. mi.
POP. — 3,444,951 (1999 est.)
CAPITAL — Bangui

The former French colony of Ubangi-Shari, a unit in French Equatorial Africa, proclaimed itself the Central African Republic Dec. 1, 1958. It became the Central African Empire Dec. 4, 1976. It became the Central African Republic again in 1979.

100 Centimes = 1 Franc

Catalogue values for all unused stamps in this country are for Never Hinged items.

Watermark

Wmk. 385

Premier Barthélemy Boganda and Flag — A1

Design: 25fr, Boganda and flag, horiz.

Unwmk.

1959, Dec. 1 Engr. *Perf. 13*
1 A1 15fr multi .40 .30
2 A1 25fr multi .60 .30

1st anniv. of the Republic and honoring Premier Barthélemy Boganda (1910-59).
For overprints & surcharge see Nos. 12, 59, M1-M2.

Imperforates
Many stamps of Central African Republic exist imperforate in issued and trial colors, and also in small presentation sheets in issued colors.

Common Design Types pictured following the introduction.

C.C.T.A. Issue
Common Design Type

1960, May 21 Unwmk. *Perf. 13*
3 CD106 50fr lt grn & dk bl 1.60 .75

Dactyloceras Widenmanni — A2

Designs: Various butterflies.

1960-61
4 A2 50c bl grn & dk red .25 .25
5 A2 1fr multi .25 .25
6 A2 2fr dk grn & brn .25 .30
7 A2 3fr yel grn & dk red .30 .30
8 A2 5fr multi .35 .30
9 A2 10fr multi .85 .45
10 A2 20fr multi 1.75 .60
11 A2 85fr multi 7.00 1.60
Nos. 4-11 (8) 11.00 4.05

Issued: 50c-3fr, 6/10/61; others, 9/3/60.

No. 2 Overprinted

1960, Dec. 1
12 A1 25fr multi 1.60 1.60

National Holiday, Dec. 1, 1960.

Louis Pasteur and Pasteur Institute, Bangui A3

1961, Feb. 25 Unwmk. *Perf. 13*
13 A3 20fr multi 1.25 .70

Opening of Pasteur Institute at Bangui.

Flag, Map, and UN Emblem A4

1961, Mar. 4 Engr.
14 A4 15fr multi .45 .30
15 A4 25fr multi .45 .30
16 A4 85fr multi 1.50 1.00
Nos. 14-16 (3) 2.40 1.60

Admission to the UN.

No. 15 Overprinted in Green

1961, Dec. 1
17 A4 25fr multi 2.00 2.00

National Holiday, Dec. 1.

No. 16 Srchd. in Red Brown

1962, Mar. 25
18 A4 50fr on 85fr multi 1.90 1.90

Conf. of the African and Malgache Union at Bangui, Mar. 25-27.

Abidjan Games Issue
Common Design Type

1962, July 21 Photo. *Perf. 12½x12*
19 CD109 20fr Hurdling .45 .30
20 CD109 50fr Bicycling 1.20 .80
Nos. 19-20,C6 (3) 4.15 2.85

African-Malgache Union Issue
Common Design Type

1962, Sept. 8 Unwmk.
21 CD110 30fr multi 1.25 .75

African and Malgache Union, 1st anniv.

Pres. David Dacko — A5

1962 *Perf. 12*
22 A5 20fr multi .40 .25
23 A5 25fr multi .60 .30

For surcharge see No. 60.

Soldiers with Flag — A6

1963, Aug. 13 Photo.
24 A6 20fr blk & multi .75 .45

National Army, third anniversary.

Waves Around Globe A6a

Design: 100fr, Orbit patterns around globe.

1963, Sept. 19 Unwmk. *Perf. 12½*
25 A6a 25fr plum & grn .75 .60
26 A6a 100fr org, bl & grn 1.90 1.60

Issued to publicize space communications.

Young Pioneers A7

1963, Oct. 14 Engr. *Perf. 12½*
27 A7 50fr grnsh bl, vio bl & brn .90 .50

Issued to honor Young Pioneers.

Boali Falls — A8

1963, Oct. 28 *Perf. 13*
28 A8 30fr bl, grn & red brn 1.00 .50

Colotis Evippe A9

Designs: Various butterflies.

1963, Nov. 18 Photo. *Perf. 12½x13*

29	A9	1fr multi	.25	.25
30	A9	3fr multi	.75	.25
31	A9	4fr multi	.85	.30
32	A9	60fr multi	6.00	3.00
		Nos. 29-32 (4)	7.85	3.80

For surcharge see No. 58.

UNESCO Emblem, Scales and Tree — A9a

1963, Dec. 10 *Perf. 13*

33	A9a	25fr grn, ol & red brn	1.00	.55

15th anniversary of the Universal Declaration of Human Rights.

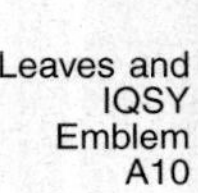

Leaves and IQSY Emblem A10

1964, Apr. 20 Engr. *Perf. 13*

34	A10	25fr org, Prus grn & bis	1.25	.70

International Quiet Sun Year, 1964-65.

Child — A11

Designs: Heads of Children.

1964, Aug. 13 Unwmk. *Perf. 13*

35	A11	20fr multi	.35	.25
36	A11	25fr multi	.40	.30
37	A11	40fr multi	.55	.45
38	A11	50fr multi	.70	.45
a.		Miniature sheet of 4, #35-38	3.00	3.00
		Nos. 35-38 (4)	2.00	1.45

Cooperation Issue

Common Design Type

1964, Nov. 7 Engr.

39	CD119	25fr grn, mag & dk brn	.90	.50

"All Men Are Men" — A12

1964, Dec. 1 Litho. *Perf. 13x12½*

40	A12	25fr multi	1.10	.50

Issued to publicize National Unity.

Putting Yoke on Oxen A13

Designs: 50fr, Ox pulling harrow. 85fr, Team of oxen in field. 100fr, Hay wagon.

1965, Apr. 28 Engr. *Perf. 13*

41	A13	25fr sl grn, sep & rose	.60	.30
42	A13	50fr sl grn, lt bl & brn	1.00	.60
43	A13	85fr bl, grn & red brn	1.40	.80
44	A13	100fr multi	1.90	1.00
		Nos. 41-44 (4)	4.90	2.70

For surcharges see Nos. 63-64.

Telegraph Receiver by Pouget-Maisonneuve — A14

ITU cent.: 30fr, Chappe telegraph, vert. 50fr, Doignon regulator, vert. 85fr, Pouillet telegraph transcriber.

1965, May 17 Unwmk.

45	A14	25fr red, grn & ultra	.60	.40
46	A14	30fr lake & grn	.70	.50
47	A14	50fr car & vio	1.25	.70
48	A14	85fr red lil & slate	1.90	1.10
		Nos. 45-48 (4)	4.45	2.70

"Health" A15

25fr, "Clothes"; shuttle, cloth & women. 60fr, "Teaching"; student & school. 85fr, "Food"; mother feeding child, tractor in wheat field.

1965, June 10 Engr. *Perf. 13*

49	A15	25fr ultra, brt grn & brn	.50	.30
50	A15	50fr ultra, brn & grn	.90	.50
51	A15	60fr grn, ultra & brn	1.00	.60
52	A15	85fr multi	1.40	.80
		Nos. 49-52 (4)	3.80	2.20

Issued to publicize the slogans and aims of "M.E.S.A.N." (Mouvement d'Evolution Sociale de l'Afrique Noire). See No. C30.

Caterpillars and Moth on Coffee Branch — A16

Designs: 3fr, Hawk moth and caterpillar on coffee leaves, horiz. 30fr, Platyedra moth and larvae on cotton plant.

1965, Aug. 25 Engr. *Perf. 13*

53	A16	2fr dk pur, dp org & sl grn	.40	.25
54	A16	3fr blk, sl grn & red	1.00	.25
55	A16	30fr red lil, red & sl grn	6.50	.90
		Nos. 53-55 (3)	7.90	1.40

Issued to publicize plant protection.

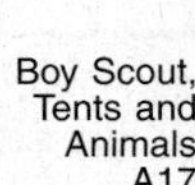

Boy Scout, Tents and Animals A17

Design: 25fr, Campfire and Scout emblem.

1965, Sept. 27 Unwmk. *Perf. 13*

56	A17	25fr red org, bl & red lil	1.00	.25
57	A17	50fr brn & Prus bl	1.25	.60

Issued to honor the Boy Scouts.

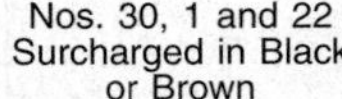

Nos. 30, 1 and 22 Surcharged in Black or Brown

Engraved; Photogravure

Perf. 13, 12, 12½x13

1965, Aug. 26 Unwmk.

58	A9	2fr on 3fr multi	4.25	4.25
59	A1	5fr on 15fr multi	3.50	3.50
60	A5	10fr on 20fr multi (Br)	4.75	4.75
		Nos. 58-60 (3)	12.50	12.50

The surcharges are adjusted to shape of stamps.

UN Emblem and Wheat A18

1965, Oct. 16 Engr. *Perf. 13*

61	A18	50fr ocher, sl grn & brt bl	1.15	.70

FAO "Freedom from Hunger Campaign."

Diamond Cutter A19

1966, Mar. 14 Engr. *Perf. 13*

62	A19	25fr car rose, dk pur & brn	1.25	.45

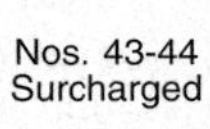

Nos. 43-44 Surcharged

1966, Feb.

63	A13	5fr on 85fr multi	.40	.40
64	A13	10fr on 100fr multi	.65	.65

Issue dates: 5fr, Feb. 17; 10fr, Feb. 15.

Statue of Mbaka Woman Porter — A20

1966, Apr. 9 Photo. *Perf. 13x12½*

65	A20	25fr multi	1.00	.45

Intl. Negro Arts Festival, Dakar, Senegal, Apr. 1-24.

WHO Headquarters, Geneva — A21

1966, May 3 Photo. Unwmk.

66	A21	25fr pur, bl & yel	1.00	.45

Inauguration of the WHO Headquarters, Geneva.

Eulophia Cucullata — A22

Orchids: 5fr, Lissochilus horsfalii. 10fr, Tridactyle bicaudata. 15fr, Polystachya. 20fr, Eulophia alta. 25fr, Microcelia macrorrhynchium.

1966, May 16 Photo. *Perf. 12x12½*

Orchids in Natural Colors

67	A22	2fr dk red	.30	.25
68	A22	5fr brn org & vio	.75	.25
69	A22	10fr bl grn & blk	.90	.40
70	A22	15fr lt grn & dk brn	1.40	.65
71	A22	20fr dk grn	2.00	.70
72	A22	25fr lt ultra & brn	3.00	.80
		Nos. 67-72 (6)	8.35	3.05

For surcharge see No. 78.

Congo Forest Mouse A23

Rodents: 10fr, One-stripe mouse. 20fr, Dollman's tree mouse, vert.

1966, Sept. 15 Photo. *Perf. 12½x12*

73	A23	5fr yel & multi	.60	.30
74	A23	10fr tan & multi	1.15	.45
75	A23	20fr lt grn & multi	2.00	.90
		Nos. 73-75 (3)	3.75	1.65

UNESCO Emblem — A24

1966, Dec. 5 Photo. *Perf. 13*

76	A24	30fr multi	.80	.50

20th anniv. of UNESCO.

Pres. Jean Bedel Bokassa — A25

1967, Jan. 1 *Perf. 12x12½*

77	A25	30fr yel grn, blk & bis brn	.65	.35

No. 72 Surcharged in Black

1967, May 8 Photo. *Perf. 12x12½*

78	A22	10fr on 25fr multi	.70	.30

See No. C43.

Central Market, Bangui A26

1967, Aug. 8 Photo. *Perf. 12½x13*
79 A26 30fr multi 1.00 .50

Safari Hotel, Bangui A27

1967, Sept. 26 Photo. *Perf. 12½x13*
80 A27 30fr multi 1.00 .40

Leucocoprinus Africanus — A28

Various Mushrooms

1967, Oct. 3 Photo. *Perf. 13*
81 A28 5fr dk brn, ol & ocher *9.00 .80*
82 A28 10fr dk brn, ultra & yel *13.50 1.25*
83 A28 15fr dk brn, sl grn & yel *15.50 1.40*
84 A28 30fr multi *45.00 4.00*
85 A28 50fr multi *67.50 6.00*
Nos. 81-85 (5) 150.50 13.45

Map, Radio Tower, Projector and People A29

1967, Oct. 31 Engr.
86 A29 30fr emer, ocher & indigo 1.00 .45

Radiovision service.

African Hair Style — A30

Various African Hair Styles.

1967, Nov. 7 Engr. *Perf. 13*
87 A30 5fr ultra, dk brn & bis brn .30 .25
88 A30 10fr car, dk brn & bis brn .50 .25
89 A30 15fr dp grn, dk brn & bis brn .75 .40
90 A30 20fr org, dk brn & bis brn .75 .50
91 A30 30fr red lil, dk brn & bis brn 1.40 .65
Nos. 87-91 (5) 3.70 2.05

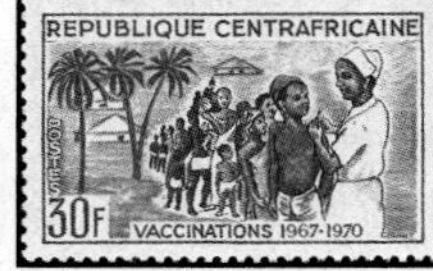

Nurse Vaccinating Children A31

1967, Nov. 14
92 A31 30fr dk red brn & brt grn .90 .50

Vaccination campaign, 1967-70.

Douglas DC-3 A32

1967, Nov. 24
93 A32 1fr shown .35 .25
94 A32 2fr Beechcraft Baron .35 .25
95 A32 5fr Douglas DC-4 .35 .25
Nos. 93-95,C47-C49 (6) 20.80 7.55

Pierced Stone, Kwe Tribe — A33

Designs: 30fr, Primitive dwelling at Toulou, horiz. 100fr, Megaliths, Bouar. 130fr, Rock painting (people), Toulou, horiz.

1967, Dec. 26 Engr. *Perf. 13*
96 A33 30fr crim, ind & mar .85 .45
97 A33 50fr ol brn, ocher & dk grn 1.60 .90
98 A33 100fr dk brn, brt bl & brn 2.75 1.20
99 A33 130fr dk red, brn & dk grn 3.00 1.20
Nos. 96-99 (4) 8.20 3.75

6th Pan-African Prehistoric Cong., Dakar.

Tanker, Refinery and Map of Area Served — A33a

1968, July 30 Photo. *Perf. 12½*
100 A33a 30fr multi 1.00 .40

Issued to commemorate the opening of the Port Gentil (Gabon) Refinery, June 12, 1968.

Bulldozer Clearing Land — A34

Designs: 10fr, Baoule cattle. 20fr, 15,000-spindle spinning machine. No. 104, Automatic Diederichs looms. No. 105, Bulldozer.

1968, Oct. 1 Engr. *Perf. 13*
101 A34 5fr blk, grn & dk brn .40 .25
102 A34 10fr blk, pale grn & bis brn .55 .30
103 A34 20fr grn, red brn & yel .90 .30
104 A34 30fr brn, ol & ultra 1.40 .55
105 A34 30fr ind, red brn & sl grn 1.40 .55
Nos. 101-105 (5) 4.65 1.95

Issued to publicize "Operation Bokassa."

Bangui Mosque A35

1968, Oct. 14
106 A35 30fr grn, bl & ocher .90 .40

Hunting Knife of Baya and Boufi Tribes A36

20fr, Hunting knife of Nzakara tribe. 30fr, Crossbow of Babinga & Babenzele (pygmy) tribes.

1968, Nov. 19 Engr. *Perf. 13*
107 A36 10fr lem, Prus bl & ultra .50 .25
108 A36 20fr ultra, dk ol & sl grn .70 .35
109 A36 30fr sl grn, ultra & brn org 1.25 .65
Nos. 107-109 (3) 2.45 1.25

"Ville de Bangui," 1958 — A37

River Boats: 30fr, "J. B. Gouandjia," 1968. 50fr, "Lamblin," 1944.

1968, Dec. 10 Engr. *Perf. 13*
Size: 36x22mm
110 A37 10fr mag, brt grn & vio bl .65 .40
111 A37 30fr bl, grn & brn 1.25 .50
112 A37 50fr brn, sl & ol grn 2.00 .65
Nos. 110-112,C62-C63 (5) 8.90 3.80

Woman Javelin Thrower — A38

1969, Mar. 18 Photo. *Perf. 13x12½*
113 A38 5fr shown .30 .25
114 A38 10fr Women runners .30 .25
115 A38 15fr Soccer .50 .25
Nos. 113-115,C71-C72 (5) 4.30 1.75

BIT and ILO Emblems and Worker A39

1969, May 20 Photo. *Perf. 12½x13*
116 A39 30fr dp bl, grn & ol brn 1.00 .40
117 A39 50fr dp car, grn & ol brn 1.50 .55

50th anniv. of the ILO.

Pres. Bokassa — A40

1969, Dec. 1 Litho. *Perf. 13x13½*
118 A40 30fr vermilion & multi .75 .30

ASECNA Issue
Common Design Type

1969, Dec. 12 Engr. *Perf. 13*
119 CD132 100fr dp bl 2.00 .80

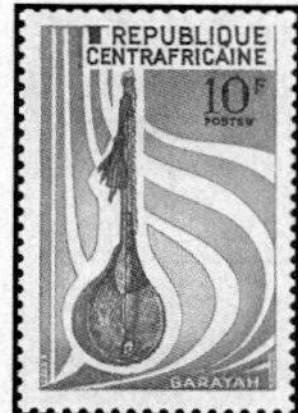

Garayah — A41

Musical Instruments: 15fr, Ngombi (harp) horiz. 30fr, Xylophone, horiz. 50fr, Ndala (lute) horiz. 130fr, Gatta and babyon (drums).

1970, Jan. 6 Engr. *Perf. 13*
120 A41 10fr yel grn, dk grn & ocher .60 .25
121 A41 15fr bl grn, ocher & dk brn .60 .25
122 A41 30fr mar, ocher & dk brn 1.00 .45
123 A41 50fr rose car & ind 1.50 .55
124 A41 130fr brt bl, brn & ol 4.75 1.10
Nos. 120-124 (5) 8.45 2.60

UPU Headquarters Issue
Common Design Type

1970, May 20 Engr. *Perf. 13*
125 CD133 100fr ultra, ver & red brn 1.75 .70

Loading Platform and Flour Storage Bins A42

50fr, Flour milling machinery. 100fr, View of mill.

1970, Feb. 24 Litho. *Perf. 14*
126 A42 25fr sl & multi *11.00 2.00*
127 A42 50fr lil & multi *26.50 3.00*
128 A42 100fr red & multi *37.50 4.00*
Nos. 126-128 (3) 75.00 9.00

Inauguration of SICPAD (Société Industrielle Centrafricaine des Produits Alimentaires et Dérivés), a part of Operation Bokassa, 2/22/68.

Pres. Bokassa — A43

1970, Aug. 13 Litho. *Perf. 14*
129 A43 30fr multi 9.00 5.00
130 A43 40fr multi 10.00 5.00

Cheese Factory, Sarki — A44

Silk Worm — A45

10fr, M'Bali Ranch. 20fr, Zebu, vert.

Perf. 13x13½, 13½x13

1970, Sept. 15

131 A44 5fr red & multi .75 .30
132 A44 10fr red & multi 6.50 4.25
133 A44 20fr red & multi 1.40 .55
134 A45 40fr red & multi 3.00 .85
Nos. 131-134,C83 (5) 15.65 7.20

Issued to publicize Operation Bokassa, a national development plan.

Nos. 131-134 exist perf 10. See No. C83.

Gnathonemus Monteiri — A46

River Fish: 20fr, Mormyrus proboscirostris. 30fr, Marcusenius wilverthi. 40fr, Gnathonemus elephas. 50fr, Gnathonemus curvirostris.

1971, Apr. 6 Photo. *Perf. 12½*

135 A46 10fr multi .40 .25
136 A46 20fr multi .75 .30
137 A46 30fr multi 1.10 .60
138 A46 40fr multi 2.50 .70
139 A46 50fr multi 3.25 1.25
Nos. 135-139 (5) 8.00 3.10

Berberati Cathedral A47

1971, July 20 Litho. *Perf. 13½*

140 A47 5fr grn & multi .55 .25

New Roman Catholic Cathedral at Berberati.

Charles de Gaulle — A48

1971, Aug. 20 *Perf. 13½x13*

141 A48 100fr brt bl & multi 3.25 2.00

In memory of Gen. Charles de Gaulle (1890-1970), president of France.

Gray Galago — A49

Designs: 40fr, Elegant galago. 100fr, Calabar potto, horiz. 150fr, Bosman's potto, horiz. 200fr, Oustalet's colobo, horiz.

1971, Oct. 25 Photo. *Perf. 13*

142 A49 30fr pink & multi .70 .45
143 A49 40fr lt bl & multi .90 .60
144 A49 100fr multi 2.75 1.40
145 A49 150fr multi 4.75 2.25
146 A49 200fr multi 5.75 2.75
Nos. 142-146 (5) 14.85 7.45

Alan B. Shepard — A50

No. 148, Yuri Gagarin. No. 149, Edwin E. Aldrin, Jr. No. 150, Alexei Leonov. No. 151, Neil A. Armstrong on moon. No. 152, Lunokhod I on moon.

1971, Nov. 19 Litho. *Perf. 14*

147 A50 40fr vio & multi .45 .30
148 A50 40fr vio & multi .45 .30
149 A50 100fr multi 1.15 .45
150 A50 100fr multi 1.15 .45
151 A50 200fr red & multi 2.25 1.10
152 A50 200fr red & multi 2.25 1.10
Nos. 147-152 (6) 7.70 3.70

Space achievements of US and Russia.

"Operation Bokassa" and Pres. Bokassa A51

1971, Dec. 1 Photo. *Perf. 13*

153 A51 40fr red & multi .85 .40

12th anniversary of independence.

Racial Equality Emblem A52

1971, Dec. 6 Litho.

154 A52 50fr multi .90 .45

Intl. Year Against Racial Discrimination.

Bokassa School Emblem and Cadets — A53

1972, Jan. 1 Photo.

155 A53 30fr gold & multi .90 .45

J. B. Bokassa Military School.

Book Year Emblem — A54

1972, Mar. 11 Photo. *Perf. 12½x13*

156 A54 100fr red brn, gold & org 3.00 1.25

International Book Year 1972.

"Your Heart is your Health" A55

1972, Apr. 7 Photo. *Perf. 13x12½*

157 A55 100fr yel, blk & car 1.75 .90

World Health Day.

Red Cross Workers in Village — A56

1972, May 8 *Perf. 13*

158 A56 150fr multi 3.00 1.40

25th World Red Cross Day.

Globe A57

1972, May 17 Litho.

159 A57 50fr yel, blk & dp org .90 .55

4th World Telecommunications Day.

Pres. and Mrs. Bokassa and Family — A58

1972, May 28 *Perf. 14*

160 A58 30fr yel & multi .70 .40

Mother's Day. Mothers' gold medal awarded to Catherine Bokassa.

Pres. Bokassa Planting Cotton, Map of Africa — A59

1972, June 5 Photo. *Perf. 13*

161 A59 40fr yel & multi .90 .45

Operation Bokassa, a natl. development plan.

Postal Checking and Savings Center A60

1972, June 21

162 A60 30fr yel org & multi .70 .35

Irrigated Rice Fields — A61

"Le Pacifique" Apartment House A62

25fr, Plowing rice field. No. 166, Swimming pool, Hotel St. Sylvestre. No. 167, Entrance, Hotel St. Sylvestre. No. 168, J. B. Bokassa University.

1972 Litho. *Perf. 13x13½*

163 A61 5fr multi 1.25 .25
164 A61 25fr multi 2.10 .30

Engr. *Perf. 13*

165 A62 30fr multi .40 .25
166 A62 30fr multi .50 .30
167 A62 40fr multi .60 .40
168 A62 40fr multi .65 .40
Nos. 163-168 (6) 5.50 1.90

Operation Bokassa. Issued: 5fr, 25fr, 11/10; No. 165, 6/27; Nos. 166-167, 12/9; No. 168, 8/26.

Bull Chasing Woman on Clock Face — A63

Scenes Painted on Clock Faces: 10fr, Men & open cooking fire. 20fr, Fishermen. 30fr, Palms, monkeys & giraffe. 40fr, Warriors.

1972, July 31 Photo. *Perf. 12½*

169 A63 5fr dk red & multi .30 .30
170 A63 10fr brt bl & multi .30 .30
171 A63 20fr grn & multi .60 .30
172 A63 30fr yel & multi .85 .50
173 A63 40fr vio & multi 1.25 .65
Nos. 169-173 (5) 3.30 2.05

HORCEN Central African clock and watch factory.

Protestant Youth Center — A64

10fr, Postal runner carrying mail in cleft stick.

1972, Aug. 12 *Perf. 13*

174 A64 10fr multi, vert. .30 .30
175 A64 20fr multi .50 .30
Nos. 174-175,C95-C98 (6) 8.35 5.10

Centraphilex 1972, Central African Philatelic Exhibition, Bangui.

Mail Truck
A65

1972, Oct. 23 Photo. *Perf. 13*
176 A65 100fr ocher & multi 2.00 .80

Universal Postal Union Day.

Mother Teaching Child to Write — A66

Central African Mothers: 10fr, Caring for infant. 15fr, Combing child's hair. 20fr, Teaching to read. 180fr, Nursing. 190fr, Teaching to walk.

1972, Dec. 27 *Perf. 13½x13*
177 A66 5fr multi .25 .25
178 A66 10fr lil & multi .30 .25
179 A66 15fr dl org & multi .30 .25
180 A66 20fr yel grn & multi .50 .25
181 A66 180fr multi 2.75 1.25
182 A66 190fr pink & multi 2.75 1.25
Nos. 177-182 (6) 6.85 3.50

Farmer Carrying Sheaf — A67

1973, May 30 Photo. *Perf. 13*
183 A67 50fr vio bl & multi .90 .45

10th anniv. of the World Food Program.

Garcinia Punctata
A68

African Flora: 20fr, Bertiera racemosa. 30fr, Corynanthe pachyceras. 40fr, Combretodendron africanum. 50fr, Xylopia Villosa, vert.

1973, June 8
184 A68 10fr pale bl & multi .50 .25
185 A68 20fr multi .85 .30
186 A68 30fr lt gray & multi 1.00 .45
187 A68 40fr multi 1.60 .60
188 A68 50fr multi 2.00 .80
Nos. 184-188 (5) 5.95 2.40

For surcharge see No. 193.

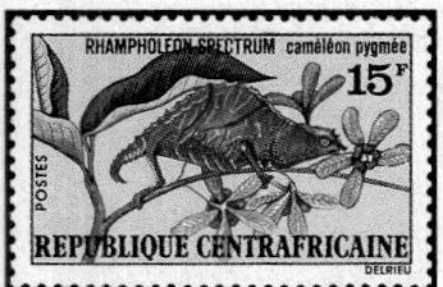

Pygmy Chameleon
A69

1973, June 26 Photo. *Perf. 13*
189 A69 15fr multi 2.25 .40

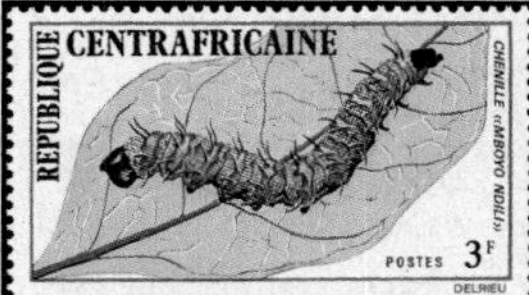

Caterpillar — A70

Designs: Various caterpillars.

1973, Aug. 6 Photo. *Perf. 13*
190 A70 3fr multi 1.25 .30
191 A70 5fr multi 2.00 .40
192 A70 25fr multi 4.00 .80
Nos. 190-192 (3) 7.25 1.50

For surcharge see No. 259.

No. 184 Srchd. and Ovptd. in Red

1973, Aug. 16
193 A68 100fr on 10fr multi 1.75 1.00

African solidarity in drought emergency.

African Postal Union Issue
Common Design Type

1973, Sept. 12 Engr. *Perf. 13*
194 CD137 100fr dk brn, red org & ol 1.25 .75

Pres. Bokassa and CAR Flag — A71

1973, Nov. 30 Photo. *Perf. 12½*
195 A71 1fr brn & multi .25 .25
196 A71 2fr pur & multi .25 .25
197 A71 3fr vio bl & multi .25 .25
198 A71 5fr ocher & multi .25 .25
199 A71 10fr multi .40 .25
200 A71 15fr org & multi .40 .25
201 A71 20fr multi .50 .25
202 A71 30fr dk grn & multi .50 .30
203 A71 40fr dk brn & multi .65 .40
Nos. 195-203,C117-C118 (11) 5.60 3.55

INTERPOL Emblem
A72

1973, Dec. 20 *Perf. 13x12½*
204 A72 50fr yellow & multi 1.00 .60

Intl. Criminal Police Organization, 50th anniv.

Catherine Bokassa Center
A73

40fr, Ambulance in front of Catherine Bokassa Center.

1974, Jan. 24 Engr. *Perf. 13*
205 A73 30fr multi .40 .25
206 A73 40fr multi .55 .35

Catherine Bokassa Center for Mothers and Children.

Cigarette-making Machine — A74

10fr, Cigarette in ashtray, & factory. 30fr, Hand lighting cigarette, & Administration Building.

1974, Jan. 29
207 A74 5fr slate grn & multi .25 .25
208 A74 10fr slate grn & multi .40 .25
209 A74 30fr slate grn & multi .50 .25
Nos. 207-209 (3) 1.15 .75

Publicity for Centra cigarettes.

"Communications"
A75

1974, June 8 Photo. *Perf. 12½x13*
210 A75 100fr multi 1.75 .90

World Telecommunications Day.
For surcharge see No. 280.

People and WPY Emblem
A76

1974, June 20 Engr. *Perf. 13*
211 A76 100fr red, slate grn & brn 1.25 .70

World Population Year.
For surcharge see No. 281.

Mother, Child, WHO Emblem — A77

1974, July 10
212 A77 100fr multi 1.75 .70

26th anniv. of WHO.
For surcharge see No. 282.

Hoeing — A78

Veterans' activities: 10fr, Battle scene ("yesterday"). 15fr, Pastoral scene ("today"). 20fr, Rice planting. 25fr, Storehouse. 40fr, Veterans Headquarters. Borders show tanks and tractors.

1974, Nov. 15 Litho. *Perf. 13*
213 A78 10fr multi .25 .25
214 A78 15fr multi .25 .25
215 A78 20fr multi .25 .25
216 A78 25fr multi .35 .25
217 A78 30fr multi .35 .25
218 A78 40fr multi .55 .25
Nos. 213-218 (6) 2.00 1.50

For surcharges see Nos. 260, 265, 267.

Presidents and Flags of Cameroun, CAR, Congo, Gabon and Meeting Center — A79

1974, Dec. 8 Photo. *Perf. 13*
219 A79 40fr gold & multi .70 .40

See No. C126 and note after Cameroun No. 595.
For surcharge see No. 272.

House in OCAM City — A80

Scenes in housing development, OCAM City.

1975, Feb. 1 Photo. *Perf. 13*
220 A80 30fr multi .35 .25
221 A80 40fr multi .40 .30
222 A80 50fr multi .50 .30
223 A80 100fr multi .75 .55
Nos. 220-223 (4) 2.00 1.40

For surcharges see Nos. 269, 273.

1975, Feb. 22

Cottage scenes in J. B. Bokassa "pilot village."

224 A80 25fr multi .30 .25
225 A80 30fr multi .40 .25
226 A80 40fr multi .50 .40
Nos. 224-226 (3) 1.20 .90

For surcharges see Nos. 268, 270, 274.

Foreign Ministry
A81

Television Station
A82

1975, Feb. 28 *Perf. 13x12½*
227 A81 40fr multi .75 .40

Perf. 13
228 A82 40fr multi .75 .40

Public buildings, Bangui.
For surcharges see Nos. 275-276.

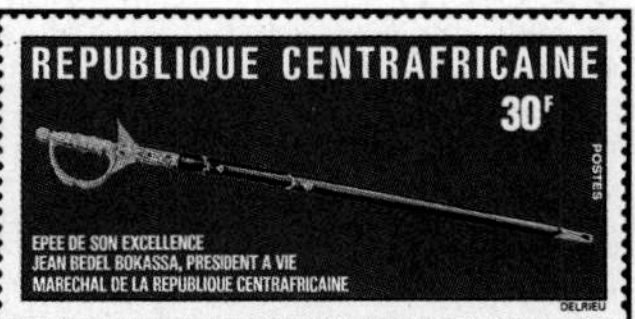

Bokassa's Saber — A83

Design: 40fr, Bokassa's baton.

1975, Feb. 22 Photo. *Perf. 13*
229 A83 30fr dp bl & multi .55 .30
230 A83 40fr vio bl & multi .75 .30

Jean Bedel Bokassa, President for Life and Marshal of the Republic. See Nos. C127-C128. For surcharge see No. 286.

Traffic Signs A84

1975, Mar. 20

231	A84	5fr Do Not Enter	.25	.25
232	A84	10fr Stop	.25	.25
233	A84	20fr No parking	.40	.25
234	A84	30fr School	.60	.25
235	A84	40fr Intersection	.85	.30
		Nos. 231-235 (5)	2.35	1.30

For surcharges see Nos. 261, 277.

Buffon's Kob — A85

1975, June 24 Photo. *Perf. 13*

236	A85	10fr shown	.50	.25
237	A85	15fr Wart hog	1.25	.35
238	A85	20fr Waterbuck	1.75	.35
239	A85	30fr Lion	1.75	.50
		Nos. 236-239 (4)	5.25	1.45

For surcharges see Nos. 262-263, 266, 271.

Crane Lifting Log onto Truck A86

Designs: 10fr, Forest, vert. 15fr, Tree felling, vert. 100fr, Log pile. 150fr, Logs transported by raft. 200fr, Lumberyard.

1975, Nov. 28 Engr. *Perf. 13*

240	A86	10fr multi	.25	.25
241	A86	15fr multi	.30	.25
242	A86	50fr multi	.55	.25
243	A86	100fr multi	1.50	.55
244	A86	150fr multi	1.75	1.00
245	A86	200fr multi	2.25	1.40
		Nos. 240-245 (6)	6.60	3.70

Promotion of Central African wood.
For surcharges see Nos. 264, 279.

Women's Heads and Various Occupations — A87

1975, Dec. 10 Photo.

246	A87	40fr multi	.50	.25
247	A87	100fr multi	1.40	.60

International Women's Year 1975.

Alexander Graham Bell — A88

1976, Mar. 25 Litho. *Perf. 12½x13*

248	A88	100fr yel & blk	2.25	1.00

Centenary of first telephone call by Alexander Graham Bell, Mar. 10, 1876.
For surcharge see No. 283.

Satellite and ITU Emblem — A89

No. 250, UPU emblem, various forms of mail transport.

1976 Engr. *Perf. 13*

249	A89	100fr vio bl, claret & grn	1.90	1.10
250	A89	100fr car, grn & ocher	1.60	.90

World Telecommunications Day (No. 249); Universal Postal Union Day (No. 250).
For surcharges see Nos. 284-285.

Soyuz on Launching Pad — A90

Design: 50fr, Apollo rocket.

1976, June 14 Litho. *Perf. 14x13½*

251	A90	40fr multi	.55	.25
252	A90	50fr multi	1.00	.25
		Nos. 251-252,C135-C137 (5)	6.65	2.25

Apollo Soyuz space test project, Russo-American cooperation, launched July 15, link-up July 17, 1975.
For surcharges see Nos. 287, 290, C161, C168, C173, C177.

Drurya Antimachus — A91

Butterfly: 40fr, Argema mittrei, vert.

1976, Sept. 20 Litho. *Perf. 12½*

253	A91	30fr ocher & multi	7.00	1.10
254	A91	40fr ultra & multi	9.00	1.10
		Nos. 253-254,C145-C146 (4)	31.00	5.70

For surcharge see No. 278.

Slalom, Piero Gros — A92

60fr, Karl Schnabel and Toni Innauer.

1976, Sept. 23 *Perf. 13½*

255	A92	40fr multi	.65	.25
256	A92	60fr multi	1.00	.35
		Nos. 255-256,C147-C149 (5)	7.15	2.75

12th Winter Olympic Games winners, Innsbruck.
For surcharges see Nos. 288, 291, C164, C170, C174, C178.

Viking Components A93

Design: 60fr, Viking take-off.

1976, Dec.

257	A93	40fr multi	.65	.25
258	A93	60fr multi	1.00	.35
		Nos. 257-258,C151-C153 (5)	7.20	2.75

Viking Mars project.
For surcharges and overprints see Nos. 289, 292, 391-392, C165, C171, C175, C179.

Central African Empire

Stamps of 1973-76 Overprinted in Black, Green, Violet Blue, Silver, Carmine, Brown or Red

Nos. 259, 278, 283

Nos. 260, 265, 267, 269, 273, 276, 279

Nos. 261, 277

Nos. 262-263, 266, 271

Nos. 264, 282

Nos. 268, 270, 274, 280, 284-285

Nos. 272, 275

No. 281

Printing and Perforations as Before

1977, Mar.

259	A70	3fr (#190; B)	.50	.45
260	A78	10fr (#213;B)	.35	.35
261	A84	10fr (#232;VB)	.35	.35
262	A85	10fr (#236;C)	.50	.50
263	A85	15fr (#237;C)	.85	.85
264	A86	15fr (#241;B)	.35	.35
265	A78	20fr (#215;B)	.50	.50
266	A85	20fr (#238;C)	.50	.50
267	A78	25fr (#216;B)	.40	.40
268	A80	25fr (#224;B)	.40	.40
269	A80	30fr (#220;VB)	.50	.50
270	A80	30fr (#225;B)	.50	.50
271	A85	30fr (#239;C)	.60	.60
272	A79	40fr (#219;B)	.50	.50
273	A80	40fr (#221;VB)	.50	.50
274	A80	40fr (#226;B)	.50	.50
275	A81	40fr (#227;B & S)	.70	.70
276	A82	40fr (#228;B)	.75	.75
277	A84	40fr (#235;VB)	.75	.75
278	A91	40fr (#254;B)	1.00	1.00
279	A86	50fr (#242;Br)	1.00	1.00
280	A75	100fr (#210;B)	1.90	1.90
281	A76	100fr (#211;B)	1.90	1.90
282	A77	100fr (#212;G)	2.25	2.25
283	A88	100fr (#248;R)	1.90	1.90
284	A89	100fr (#249;B)	2.25	2.25
285	A89	100fr (#250;B)	2.50	2.50
		Nos. 259-285 (27)	24.70	24.65

Stamps of 1975-76 Overprinted in Black on Silver Panel

1977, Apr. 1

286	A83	40fr multi (#230)	.90	.90
287	A90	40fr multi (#251)	.70	.70
288	A92	40fr multi (#255)	.70	.70
289	A93	40fr multi (#257)	.70	.70
290	A90	50fr multi (#252)	1.00	1.00
291	A92	60fr multi (#256)	.90	.90
292	A93	60fr multi (#258)	.90	.90
		Nos. 286-292 (7)	5.80	5.80

Pierre and Marie Curie — A94

Design: 60fr, Wilhelm C. Roentgen.

1977, Apr. 1 Litho. *Perf. 13½*

293	A94	40fr multi	1.25	.40
294	A94	60fr multi	1.00	.40
		Nos. 293-294,C180-C182 (5)	13.25	2.85

Nobel Prize winners.

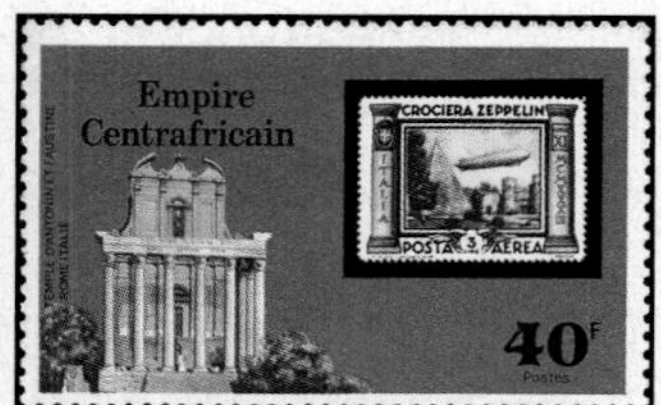

Italy No. C42 and Faustine Temple, Rome — A95

60fr, Russia #C12 & St. Basil's Cathedral, Moscow.

1977, Apr. 11 Litho. *Perf. 11*

295 A95 40fr multi 1.00 .25
296 A95 60fr multi 1.10 .40
Nos. 295-296,C184-C186 (5) 8.70 2.65

75th anniversary of the Zeppelin.

Lindbergh over Paris — A96

Designs: 60fr, Santos Dumont and "14 bis." 100fr, Bleriot and monoplane. 200fr, Roald Amundsen and "N24." 300fr, Concorde. 500fr, Lindbergh and Spirit of St. Louis.

1977, Sept. 30 Litho. *Perf. 13½*

297 A96 50fr multi .60 .25
298 A96 60fr multi .80 .25
299 A96 100fr multi 1.60 .50
300 A96 200fr multi 2.50 .65
301 A96 300fr multi 5.00 1.25
Nos. 297-301 (5) 10.50 2.90

Souvenir Sheet

302 A96 500fr multi 6.00 2.00

History of aviation, famous fliers.

Shot on Goal A97

Designs: 60fr, Heading ball in net. 100fr, Backfield defense. 200fr, Argentina '78 poster. 300fr, Mario Zagalo and stadium. 500fr, Ferenc Puskas.

1977, Nov. 18 Litho. *Perf. 13½*

303 A97 50fr multi .50 .25
304 A97 60fr multi .65 .25
305 A97 100fr multi 1.25 .30
306 A97 200fr multi 2.10 .55
307 A97 300fr multi 3.50 .90
Nos. 303-307 (5) 8.00 2.25

Souvenir Sheet

308 A97 500fr multi 5.50 2.00

World Soccer Championships, Argentina, June 1-25, 1978.
For overprints see Nos. 370-375.

Emperor Bokassa I, Central African Flag — A98

1977, Dec. 4 Litho. *Perf. 13½*

309 A98 40fr multi .40 .25
310 A98 60fr multi .55 .25
311 A98 100fr multi 1.00 .55
312 A98 150fr multi 1.40 .70
Nos. 309-312,C188-C189 (6) 7.60 3.80

Coronation of Emperor Bokassa I, Dec. 4.

Lilium — A99

1977 Litho. *Perf. 13½x14*

313 A99 5fr shown .55 .30
314 A99 10fr Hibiscus 1.10 .65

For overprints see Nos. 408-409.

Electronic Tree, ITU Emblem — A100

1977

315 A100 100fr blk, org & brn 3.00 2.00

World Telecommunications Day.

Bible and People A101

1977 Litho. *Perf. 14x13½*

316 A101 40fr multi 8.00 1.25

Bible Week.

People and Rotary Emblem A102

1977

317 A102 60fr multi 4.25 2.00

Rotary Club of Bangui, 20th anniversary.

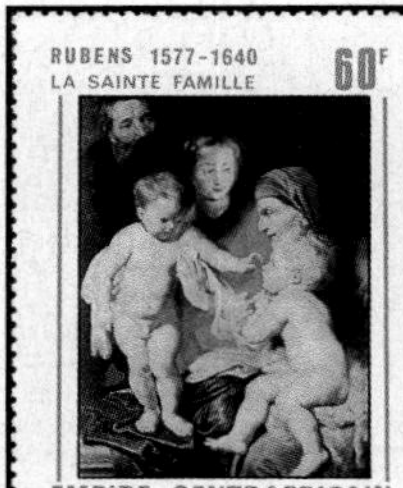

Holy Family, by Rubens A103

Rubens Paintings: 150fr, Marie de Medicis. 200fr, Son of artist. 300fr, Neptune. 500fr, Marie de Medicis, diff.

1978, Jan. 26

318 A103 60fr multi .60 .25
319 A103 150fr multi 1.50 .40
320 A103 200fr multi 2.40 .60
321 A103 300fr multi 3.50 .80
Nos. 318-321 (4) 8.00 2.05

Souvenir Sheet

322 A103 500fr gold & multi 6.00 2.00

Peter Paul Rubens (1577-1640).

Rhinoceros — A104

Endangered Animals and Wildlife Fund Emblem: 50fr, Slender-nosed crocodile. 60fr, Leopard, vert. 100fr, Giraffe, vert. 200fr, Elephant. 300fr, Gorilla, vert.

1978, Feb. 21 Litho. *Perf. 13½*

323 A104 40fr multi *1.60* .30
324 A104 50fr multi *2.25* .35
325 A104 60fr multi *2.50* .55
326 A104 100fr multi *4.25* .90
327 A104 200fr multi *11.00* 1.25
328 A104 300fr multi *12.50* 2.00
Nos. 323-328 (6) *34.10* 5.35

Bokassa Sports Palace A105

Design: 60fr, Sports Palace, side view.

1978 *Perf. 14*

329 A105 40fr multi .50 .25
330 A105 60fr multi .65 .40

Automatic Telephone Exchange, Bangui A106

1978

331 A106 40fr multi .50 .25
332 A106 60fr multi .70 .40

Diligence and Satellite — A107

Designs (UPU Emblem and): 50fr, Steam locomotive and communications via satellite. 60fr, Paddle-wheel steamer and ship-to-shore communication via satellite. 80fr, Old mail truck and satellite.

1978, May 17 *Perf. 13½*

333 A107 40fr multi .50 .25
334 A107 50fr multi 1.50 .65
335 A107 60fr multi .70 .30
336 A107 80fr multi .80 .30
Nos. 333-336,C191-C192 (6) 5.70 2.40

Posts and telecommunications, cent. of progress.

Mask — A108

Designs: 30fr, Mask. 60fr, Women dancers, horiz. 100fr, Men dancers, horiz.

Perf. 13½x14, 14x13½

1978, July 11 Litho.

337 A108 20fr blk & yel .65 .30
338 A108 30fr blk & brt bl .65 .30
339 A108 60fr blk & multi 1.60 .70
340 A108 100fr blk & multi 3.00 .95
Nos. 337-340 (4) 5.90 2.25

Black-African World Arts Festival, Lagos.
For overprints see Nos. 411-412.

Capt. Cook on "Endeavour" A109

60fr, Resolution off Hawaii. 200fr, Hawaiians welcoming Capt. Cook. 350fr, Masked rowers in Hawaiian boat.

1978, Aug. 30 *Perf. 14½*

341 A109 60fr multi, horiz. .60 .25
342 A109 80fr multi 1.00 .35
343 A109 200fr multi, horiz. 2.00 .70
344 A109 350fr multi, horiz. 3.50 1.25
Nos. 341-344 (4) 7.10 2.55

Capt. James Cook (1728-1779), explorer.

Dürer, Self-portrait A110

Dürer Paintings: 80fr, The Four Apostles. 200fr, Virgin and Child. 350fr, Emperor Maximilian I.

1978, Oct. 24 Litho. *Perf. 13½*

345 A110 60fr multi .60 .25
346 A110 80fr multi 1.00 .25
347 A110 200fr multi 2.25 .85
348 A110 350fr multi 4.25 1.60
Nos. 345-348 (4) 8.10 2.95

Albrecht Dürer (1471-1528), German painter.

Tutankhamen's Gold Mask — A111

Treasures of Tutankhamen: 60fr, King and Queen, gold back panel of throne. 80fr, Gilt folding chair. 100fr, King wearing crowns of Upper and Lower Egypt, painted wood sculpture. 120fr, Lion's head. 150fr, Tutankhamen, wood stature. 180fr, Gold throne. 250fr, Gold miniature coffin.

1978, Nov. 22

349	A111	40fr multi	.65	.30
350	A111	60fr multi	.75	.40
351	A111	80fr multi	1.25	.55
352	A111	100fr multi	1.40	.55
353	A111	120fr multi	2.00	.60
354	A111	150fr multi	2.25	.70
355	A111	180fr multi	2.50	.90
356	A111	250fr multi	3.50	1.25
		Nos. 349-356 (8)	14.30	5.25

Tutankhamen, c. 1358 B.C., King of Egypt.

Lenin at Smolny Institute — A112

Soviet Union, 60th anniv.: 60fr, 200fr, 300fr, Various Lenin portraits. 100fr, Ulyanov family, horiz. 150fr, Lenin, Cruiser "Aurora" and flag, horiz. 500fr, "Aurora" and star.

1978, Nov. ***Perf. 14***

357	A112	40fr multi	.50	.30
358	A112	60fr multi	.60	.40
359	A112	100fr blk & gold	1.00	.45
360	A112	150fr blk, gold & red	1.90	.70
361	A112	200fr multi	3.00	1.00
362	A112	300fr multi	4.00	1.40
		Nos. 357-362 (6)	11.00	4.25

Souvenir Sheet

363	A112	500fr multi	6.00	4.00

Catherine Bokassa A113

Design: 60fr, Emperor Bokassa.

1978, Dec. 4 **Litho.** ***Perf. 13***

364	A113	40fr multi	.65	.25
365	A113	60fr multi	.90	.30

1st anniv. of coronation. See No. C202.

Rowland Hill, Letter Scale and G.B. No. 1 — A114

Rowland Hill and: 50fr, US No. 1, mailman on bicycle. 60fr, Austria No. P4, 19th cent. mailman. 80fr, Switzerland No. 2L1, postilion and mailcoach.

1978, Dec. 9 **Litho.** ***Perf. 13½***

366	A114	40fr multi	.65	.30
367	A114	50fr multi	.65	.30
368	A114	60fr multi	.90	.40
369	A114	80fr multi	1.00	.50
		Nos. 366-369,C203-C204 (6)	7.20	2.80

Sir Rowland Hill (1795-1879), originator of penny postage.

Nos. 303-307 Overprinted in Silver

1978, Dec. 27

370	A97	50fr multi	.70	.25
371	A97	60fr multi	.85	.30
372	A97	100fr multi	1.25	.55
373	A97	200fr multi	3.00	1.00
374	A97	300fr multi	4.25	1.40
		Nos. 370-374 (5)	10.05	3.50

Souvenir Sheet

No. 308 Overprinted in Silver

375	A97	500fr multi	5.00	5.00

Argentina's victory in World Cup Soccer Championship 1978.

Balambo Chair — A114a

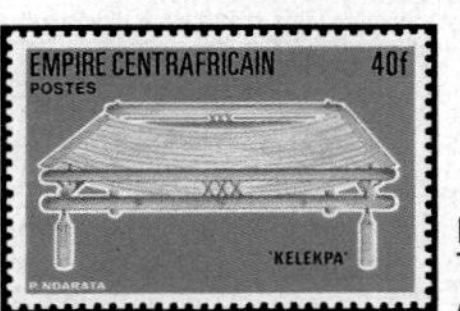

Kelekpa Table — A114b

1978 ? **Litho.** ***Perf. 14x13¼***

375A	A114a	20fr multi	—	—
375B	A114b	40fr multi	—	—

See No. C205A. For overprint, see No. 410.

Children Painting and Dutch Portrait — A115

UNICEF, Eagle Emblems and: 50fr, Eskimo children skiing, ski jump. 60fr, Children with toy racing car, Carl Benz with early car model. 80fr, Children launching rocket, Mariner 5.

1979, Mar. 6 **Litho.** ***Perf. 13½***

376	A115	40fr multi	.65	.25
377	A115	50fr multi	.75	.25
378	A115	60fr multi	.90	.25
379	A115	80fr multi	1.25	.30
		Nos. 376-379,C206-C207 (6)	7.30	2.25

International Year of the Child.

High Jump, Moscow '80 Emblem and "M" — A116

Designs (Moscow '80 Emblem, Various Sports and): 50fr, Bicycling and "O." 60fr, Weight lifting and "C." 80fr, Judo and "K."

1979, Mar. 16 **Litho.** ***Perf. 13***

380	A116	40fr multi	.55	.25
381	A116	50fr multi	.65	.25
382	A116	60fr multi	.75	.25
383	A116	80fr multi	1.10	.30
		Nos. 380-383,C209-C210 (6)	6.25	2.10

22nd Olympic Games, Moscow, July 19-Aug. 3, 1980. Background letters on Nos. 380-383, C209-C210 spell "Mockba." A 1500fr gold embossed stamp showing emblems and Discobolus exists.

Memorial, Bangui, Butterfly, Hibiscus — A117

Design: 150fr, Canoe, truck and letters.

1979, June 8 **Litho.** ***Perf. 12x12½***

384	A117	60fr multi	2.75	1.25
385	A117	150fr multi	5.00	2.50

Philexafrique II, Libreville, Gabon, June 8-17. Nos. 384, 385 each printed in sheets of 10 with 5 labels showing exhibition emblem.

Schoolgirl A118

1979, July 25 **Litho.** ***Perf. 12½x12***

386	A118	70fr multi	.95	.50

Intl. Bureau of Education, Geneva, 50th anniv.

Chicken A119

1979, Aug. ***Perf. 13***

387	A119	10fr shown	1.75	1.10
388	A119	20fr Bull	1.75	1.10
389	A119	40fr Sheep	3.75	2.10
		Nos. 387-389,C211 (4)	12.50	6.30

National Husbandry Assoc.

Souvenir Sheet

Virgin and Child, by Dürer — A120

1979, Aug. ***Perf. 13½***

390	A120	500fr lt grn & dl red	5.25	1.75

Albrecht Dürer (1471-1528), German engraver and printer.

Central African Republic

Nos. 257-258 Overprinted

1979, Nov. 11 **Litho.** ***Perf. 13½***

391	A93	40fr multi	.65	.30
392	A93	60fr multi	.75	.40
		Nos. 391-392,C212-C214 (5)	6.25	3.35

Apollo 11 moon landing, 10th anniversary.

Girl and Rose A121

30fr, Butterfly and girl, vert. 60fr, Hansel and Gretel, vert. 200fr, The Little Match Girl. 250fr, Mermaid, vert.

1979, Dec. 15

393	A121	30fr multicolored	.30	.25
394	A121	40fr shown	.50	.25
395	A121	60fr multicolored	.55	.25
396	A121	200fr multicolored	2.00	.70
397	A121	250fr multicolored	2.50	.80
		Nos. 393-397 (5)	5.85	2.25

International Year of the Child.

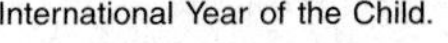

Locomotive, U.S. Type A27, Hill — A122

Locomotives, Hill and Stamps: 100fr, France No. 1. 150fr, Germany type A11. 250fr, Great Britain No. 32. 500fr, CAR No. 2.

1979, Dec. 20

398	A122	60fr multi	.55	.25
399	A122	100fr multi	1.10	.30
400	A122	150fr multi	1.75	.50
401	A122	250fr multi	3.00	1.10
		Nos. 398-401 (4)	6.40	2.15

Souvenir Sheet

402	A122	500fr multi	5.75	2.25

Sir Rowland Hill (1795-1879), originator of penny postage.

Basketball, Moscow '80 Emblem — A123

Pre-Olympic Year: Men's or women's basketball.

1979, Dec. 28 Litho. *Perf. 14½*

403	A123	50fr multi	.45	.25
404	A123	125fr multi	1.00	.40
405	A123	200fr multi	1.75	.65
406	A123	300fr multi	3.00	.90
407	A123	500fr multi	4.50	1.60
		Nos. 403-407 (5)	10.70	3.80

For overprints see Nos. 425-429.

Nos. 313-314 Overprinted in Black on Silver Panel

and

No. 375A Overprinted in Black on Silver Panel

and

Nos. 337-338 Overprinted in Black on Silver Panel

Perf. 13½x14, 14x13½

1980, Mar. 20 Litho.

408	A99	5fr multi	.40	.30
409	A99	10fr multi	.40	.30
410	A114a	20fr multi	.30	.25
411	A108	20fr multi	.30	.25
412	A108	30fr multi	.50	.25
		Nos. 408-412 (5)	1.90	1.35

Apollo-Soyuz — A125

40fr, Viking Satellite. 50fr, Apollo-Soyuz. 60fr, Voyager. 100fr, European Space Agency emblem, flags.

1980, Apr. 8 *Perf. 13½*

413	A125	40fr multicolored	.55	.25
414	A125	50fr multicolored	.65	.25
415	A125	60fr multicolored	.75	.40
416	A125	100fr multicolored	1.25	.60
		Nos. 413-416,C221-C222 (6)	6.35	2.60

Walking, Olympic Medal, Moscow '80 Emblem — A126

1980, July 25 Litho. *Perf. 13½*

417	A126	30fr shown	.50	.25
418	A126	40fr Relay race	.55	.25
419	A126	70fr Running	.75	.25
420	A126	80fr High jump	.90	.25
		Nos. 417-420,C231-C232 (6)	5.30	1.65

For overprints see Nos. 462-465, C248-C250.

Fruit — A126a

1980, Aug. 1 Litho. *Perf. 13½*

420A	A126a	40fr multicolored	—	—
420B	A126a	70fr green & multi	—	—

Agricultural Development A127

40fr, Telecommunications. 70fr, Engineering. 100fr, Civil engineering.

1980, Nov. 4 Litho. *Perf. 13½*

421	A127	30fr shown	.30	.25
422	A127	40fr multicolored	.50	.25
423	A127	70fr multicolored	.90	.25
424	A127	100fr multicolored	1.40	.40
		Nos. 421-424,C234-C235 (6)	6.50	2.25

Europe-Africa cooperation.

Nos. 403-407 Overprinted in Black

1980, Nov. 12 *Perf. 14½*

425	A123	50fr multi	.55	.25
426	A123	125fr multi	1.10	.40
427	A123	200fr multi	1.90	.65
428	A123	300fr multi	3.60	1.10
429	A123	500fr multi	5.00	1.75
		Nos. 425-429 (5)	12.15	4.15

Virgin and Child, by Raphael — A128

Christmas: Paintings by Raphael.

1980, Dec. 20 *Perf. 12½*

430	A128	60fr multi	.65	.25
431	A128	150fr multi	1.60	.60
432	A128	250fr multi	3.00	1.25
		Nos. 430-432 (3)	5.25	2.10

African Postal Union, 5th Anniversary A129

1980, Dec. 24 Photo. *Perf. 13½*

433	A129	70fr multi	.90	.45

Peruvian Soccer Team, Soccer Cup — A130

1981, Jan. 13 Litho. *Perf. 13½*

434	A130	10fr shown	.25	.25
435	A130	15fr Scotland	.35	.25
436	A130	20fr Mexico	.35	.25
437	A130	25fr Sweden	.35	.25
438	A130	30fr Austria	.50	.25
439	A130	40fr Poland	.50	.25
440	A130	50fr France	.90	.25
441	A130	60fr Italy	.90	.25
442	A130	70fr Germany	1.00	.30
443	A130	80fr Brazil	1.00	.35
		Nos. 434-443,C237-C238 (12)	8.85	3.45

ESPANA '82 World Cup Soccer Championship.

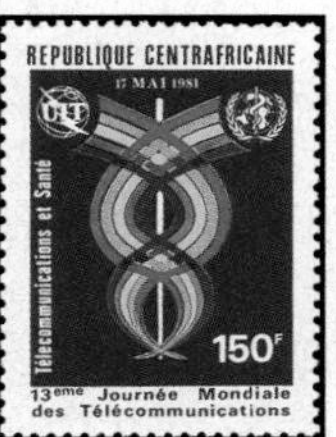

13th World Telecommunications Day — A131

1981, May 17 Litho. *Perf. 12½*

444	A131	150fr multi	1.40	.70

Apollo 15 Crew on Moon — A132

Space Exploration: Columbia space shuttle.

1981, June 10 Litho. *Perf. 14*

445	A132	100fr multi	.80	.30
446	A132	150fr multi	1.35	.40
447	A132	200fr multi	1.90	.60
448	A132	300fr multi	3.25	1.00
		Nos. 445-448 (4)	7.30	2.30

Souvenir Sheet

449	A132	500fr multi	5.00	1.75

Family of Acrobats with Monkey, by Picasso A133

Picasso Birth Cent.: 50fr, The Balcony. 80fr, The Artist's Son as Pierrot. 100fr, The Three Dancers.

1981, June 30 *Perf. 13½*

450	A133	40fr multi	.60	.25
451	A133	50fr multi	.75	.25
452	A133	80fr multi	1.30	.40
453	A133	100fr multi	1.75	.40
		Nos. 450-453,C245-C246 (6)	9.15	2.40

First Anniv. of Zimbabwe's Independence — A134

1981, July 9 Litho. *Perf. 12½*

454	A134	100fr multi	1.10	.45
455	A134	150fr multi	1.50	.55
456	A134	200fr multi	2.25	.80
		Nos. 454-456 (3)	4.85	1.80

Royal Wedding A135

75fr, Charles. 100fr, Diana. 150fr, St. Paul's Cathedral. 175fr, Prince Charles and Lady Diana.

500fr, Couple.

1981, July, 24 *Perf. 14*

457	A135	75fr multicolored	.50	.25
458	A135	100fr multicolored	.70	.25
459	A135	150fr multicolored	1.20	.50
460	A135	175fr multicolored	1.50	.50
		Nos. 457-460 (4)	3.90	1.50

Souvenir Sheet

461	A135	500fr multicolored	5.00	1.75

For overprints see Nos. 529-533.

Nos. 417-420 Overprinted in Gold

1981 Litho. *Perf. 13½*

462 A126 30fr multi .35 .25
463 A126 40fr multi .50 .25
464 A126 70fr multi .90 .35
465 A126 80fr multi .90 .50
Nos. 462-465,C248-C249 (6) 5.05 2.00

Prince Charles and Lady Diana — A136

50fr, Crowned Prince of Wales. 80fr, Diana. 100fr, Naval training.

1981, Aug. 20 Litho. *Perf. 13½*

466 A136 40fr shown .45 .25
467 A136 50fr multicolored .45 .25
468 A136 80fr multicolored .75 .30
469 A136 100fr multicolored 1.00 .40
Nos. 466-469,C251-C252 (6) 6.35 2.15

Royal wedding.

1906 Renault — A137

40fr, Mercedes-Benz, 1937. 50fr, Matra-Ford, 1969. 110fr, Tazio Nuvolari, 1927. 150fr, Jackie Stewart, 1965.
450fr, Finish line, 1914.

1981, Sept. 22 Litho. *Perf. 12½*

470 A137 20fr shown .30 .25
471 A137 40fr multicolored .55 .25
472 A137 50fr multicolored .65 .25
473 A137 110fr multicolored 1.30 .40
474 A137 150fr multicolored 1.90 .70
Nos. 470-474 (5) 4.70 1.85

Souvenir Sheet

Perf. 10

475 A137 450fr multicolored 5.00 5.00

Grand Prix of France, 75th anniv.

World Food Day A138

1981, Oct. 16

476 A138 90fr multi .95 .30
477 A138 110fr multi 1.10 .50

Navigators and their Ships — A139

1981, Sept. 4 Litho. *Perf. 13½*

478 A139 40fr C.V. Rietschoten .50 .30
479 A139 50fr M. Pajot .55 .45
480 A139 60fr K. Jaworski .75 .55
481 A139 80fr M. Birch 1.00 .60
Nos. 478-481,C254-C255 (6) 6.30 4.00

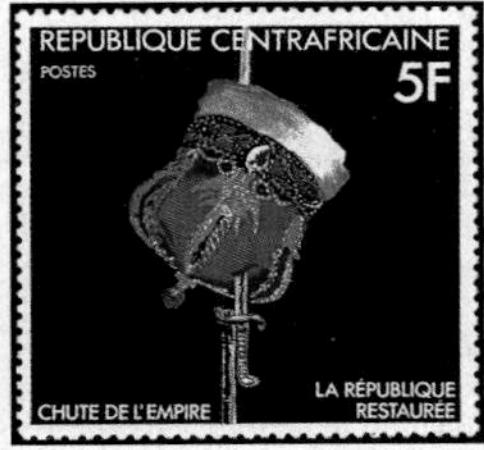

Downfall of Empire A140

5fr, Bayonet through crown. 25fr, Victory holding map. 90fr, Toppled Bokassa statue.

1981, Oct. 6

482 A140 5fr multicolored .25 .25
483 A140 10fr like #482 .25 .25
484 A140 25fr multicolored .30 .25
485 A140 60fr like #484 .65 .25
486 A140 90fr multicolored 1.00 .60
487 A140 500fr like #486 4.25 2.00
Nos. 482-487 (6) 6.70 3.60

Komba — A141

1981, Nov. 17

488 A141 50fr shown .90 .25
489 A141 90fr Dodoro, horiz. 1.75 .30
490 A141 140fr Kaya, horiz. 3.00 .40
Nos. 488-490 (3) 5.65 .95

Central African States Bank A142

1981, Dec. 12 Litho. *Perf. 12½x13*

491 A142 90fr multi .90 .30
492 A142 110fr multi 1.00 .60

Christmas 1981 — A143

Virgin and Child Paintings: 50fr, Fra Angelico, 1430. 60fr, Cosimo Tura, 1484. 90fr, Bramantino. 110fr, Memling.

1981, Dec. 24

493 A143 50fr multicolored .85 .30
494 A143 60fr multicolored .95 .40
495 A143 90fr multicolored 1.50 .55
496 A143 110fr multicolored 1.90 .80
Nos. 493-496,C260-C261 (6) 12.20 3.20

Scouting Year — A144

100fr, Hiking. 150fr, Scouts, horiz. 200fr, Leaning against railing. 300fr, Salute, flag, vert.
500fr, Scout, Baden-Powell, vert.

1982, Jan. 13 *Perf. 12½*

497 A144 100fr multicolored 1.00 .40
498 A144 150fr multicolored 1.50 .55
499 A144 200fr multicolored 2.25 .80
500 A144 300fr multicolored 3.00 1.25
Nos. 497-500 (4) 7.75 3.00

Souvenir Sheet

Perf. 13

501 A144 500fr multicolored 5.75 1.60

Elephant A145

1982, Jan. 22 *Perf. 13½*

502 A145 60fr shown .90 .25
503 A145 90fr Giraffes 1.10 .30
504 A145 100fr Addaxes 1.25 .35
505 A145 110fr Okapi 1.50 .50
Nos. 502-505,C263-C264 (6) 13.50 3.45

Norman Rockwell Illustrations A146

30fr, Grandfather snowman. 60fr, Croquet players. 110fr, Women talking. 150fr, Searching.

1982, Feb. 17 *Perf. 13½x14*

506 A146 30fr multicolored .30 .25
507 A146 60fr multicolored .75 .30
508 A146 110fr multicolored 1.25 .40
509 A146 150fr multicolored 1.75 .55
Nos. 506-509 (4) 4.05 1.50

AT 16 Dirigible A147

10fr, Beyer-Garrat locomotive. 20fr, Bugatti 24 "Royale," 1924. 110fr, Vickers "Valentia," 1928.

1982, Feb. 27 Litho. *Perf. 13½*

510 A147 5fr shown .25 .25
511 A147 10fr multicolored .25 .25
512 A147 20fr multicolored .30 .25
513 A147 110fr multicolored 1.40 .40
Nos. 510-513,C266-C267 (6) 11.45 3.20

Bellvue Garden, by Edouard Manet — A148

Anniversaries: 400fr, Goethe, vert. Nos. 519-520, Princess Diana, 21st birthday, July 1, vert. 300fr, George Washington, vert.

1982, Apr. 6 Litho. *Perf. 13*

517 A148 200fr multi 3.00 1.00
517A A148 300fr multi 2.75 1.00
518 A148 400fr multi 3.50 1.25
519 A148 500fr multi 4.50 2.00
Nos. 517-519 (4) 13.75 5.25

Souvenir Sheet

520 A148 500fr multi 5.50 1.60

23rd Olympic Games, Los Angeles, 1984 — A149

1982, July 24 Litho. *Perf. 13½*

521 A149 5fr Soccer .25 .25
522 A149 10fr Boxing .25 .25
523 A149 20fr Running .30 .25
524 A149 110fr Long jump .90 .30
Nos. 521-524,C269-C270 (6) 9.70 3.25

21st Birthday of Princess Diana — A150

Portraits.

1982, July 20 Litho. *Perf. 13½*

525 A150 5fr multi .25 .25
526 A150 10fr multi .25 .25
527 A150 20fr multi .30 .25
528 A150 110fr multi .90 .30
Nos. 525-528,C272-C273 (6) 10.45 3.25

Nos. 457-461 Overprinted in Blue

1982, Aug. 20 *Perf. 14*

529 A135 75fr multi .55 .25
530 A135 110fr multi .75 .40
531 A135 150fr multi 1.40 .55
532 A135 175fr multi 2.25 .80
Nos. 529-532 (4) 4.95 2.00

Souvenir Sheet

533 A135 500fr multi 5.50 3.50

Birth of Prince William of Wales, June 21.

2nd UN Conference on Peaceful Uses of Outer Space, Vienna, Aug. 9-21 — A151

Various satellites and space scenes.

1982, Aug. 15 Litho. *Perf. 13½*

534 A151 5fr multi .25 .25
535 A151 10fr multi .25 .25
536 A151 20fr multi .30 .25
537 A151 110fr multi .90 .30
Nos. 534-537,C277-C278 (6) 9.70 3.25

Sakpa Basket A152

Baskets and bowls: 25fr, Ngbenda gourd, vert. 120fr, Ta ti ngou jugs. 175fr, Kangu bowls. 300fr, Kolongo bowls, vert.

1982, Sept. 2 *Perf. 13*

538 A152 5fr shown .25 .25
539 A152 10fr like 5fr .25 .25
540 A152 25fr multicolored .30 .25
541 A152 60fr like 25fr .75 .25
542 A152 120fr multicolored 1.60 .40
543 A152 175fr multicolored 1.75 .60
544 A152 300fr multicolored 3.50 1.25
Nos. 538-544 (7) 8.40 3.25

For surcharges see Nos. 792A-792B.

1982 World Cup Soccer Championships, Spain — A152a

Various soccer plays.

1982, Sept. **Litho.** *Perf. 13½x13*

Overprinted in Silver or Gold

545 A152a 60fr Italy, 1st, 2nd .90 .25
546 A152a 150fr Poland, 3rd 1.75 .55
547 A152a 300fr France, 4th 3.50 1.25
Nos. 545-547 (3) 6.15 2.05

Souvenir Sheet

548 A152a 500fr Italy, 1st (G) 5.00 1.60

Not issued without overprint.

13th World UPU Day — A153

1982, Oct. 9

549 A153 60fr multi .55 .35
550 A153 120fr multi 1.20 .55

Comb and Hairpins A154

1982, Oct. 20 *Perf. 13x12½*

551 A154 20fr multi .25 .25
552 A154 30fr multi .40 .25
553 A154 60fr multi .75 .30
554 A154 80fr multi 1.10 .40
555 A154 120fr multi 1.50 .45
Nos. 551-555 (5) 4.00 1.65

Artist Pierre Ndarata and No.69 A155

1982, Oct. *Perf. 13*

556 A155 40fr Jean Tubind at easel, vert. .30 .25
557 A155 70fr shown .55 .25
558 A155 90fr like 70fr .65 .40
559 A155 140fr like 40fr 1.25 .50
Nos. 556-559 (4) 2.75 1.40

TB Bacillus Centenary A156

1982, Nov. 30 *Perf. 13½x13*

560 A156 100fr vio & blk 1.25 .30
561 A156 120fr red org & blk 1.40 .45
562 A156 175fr bl & blk 2.00 .90
Nos. 560-562 (3) 4.65 1.65

10th Anniv. of UN Conference on Human Environment A157

1982, Dec. 8

563 A157 120fr multi 1.20 .40
564 A157 150fr multi 1.30 .55
565 A157 300fr multi 2.50 1.10
Nos. 563-565 (3) 5.00 2.05

Granary A158

1982, Dec. 15 *Perf. 13*

566 A158 60fr multi .55 .25
567 A158 80fr multi .85 .40
568 A158 120fr multi 1.20 .60
569 A158 200fr multi 2.00 1.20
Nos. 566-569 (4) 4.60 2.45

A159

1982, Dec.

570 A159 100fr multi 1.00 .40
571 A159 120fr multi 1.25 .50

ITU Plenipotentiaries Conf., Nairobi, Sept.

A160

5fr, Modes of communication. 120fr, Map, jet.

1983, Jan. 31 **Litho.** *Perf. 13½x13*

572 A160 5fr multicolored .25 .25
573 A160 60fr like 5fr .65 .30
574 A160 120fr multicolored 1.25 .40
575 A160 175fr like 120fr 1.50 .55
Nos. 572-575 (4) 3.65 1.50

UN Decade for African Transportation and Communication, 1978-88.

Chess Champions — A161

Men and Chess Pieces: 5fr, Steinitz, first world champion, 1886. 10fr, Aaron Niemzovitch, castle. 20fr, Alexander Alekhine, knights. 110fr, Botvinnik. 300fr, Boris Spassky, glass pieces. 500fr, Bobby Fischer, king, knight. 600fr, Korchnoi, Karpov, pawn. No. 582A, Bobby Fischer. No. 582B, Reti, Larsen, Petrossian, and Mecking, horiz.

1983, Jan. 15

576 A161 5fr multi .25 .25
577 A161 10fr multi .25 .25
578 A161 20fr multi .35 .25
579 A161 110fr multi 1.10 .25
580 A161 300fr multi 3.00 .75
581 A161 500fr multi 4.25 1.40
Nos. 576-581 (6) 9.20 3.15

Souvenir Sheet

582 A161 600fr multi 5.75 2.00

Litho. & Embossed

Perf. 13½

Size: 35x60mm

582A A161 1500fr gold & multi 25.00 3.50

Souvenir Sheet

582B A161 1500fr gold & multi 10.00 10.00

No. 582 contains one 56x33mm stamp, No. 582B one 35x60mm stamp. 300fr, 500fr, 600fr, Nos. 582A and 582B are airmail.

Marshal Tito (1892-1980) A162

20fr, George Washington.

1983, Jan. 22

583 A162 20fr multicolored .25 .25
a. Souvenir sheet 5.50 —
584 A162 110fr shown 1.25 .30
a. Souvenir sheet 5.50 —

1982 World Cup Soccer Championships, Spain — A162a

Trophy, flags, scores, players: 5fr, Hamilton, Pezzey. 10fr, Borovski, Boniek. 20fr, Littbarski, Zamora. 110fr, Zico, Passarella. 300fr, Rossi, Smolarek. 500fr, Rummenigge, Giresse. 600fr, Rossi, Rummenigge. No. 584I, Platini. No. 584J, Rossi.

1983, Feb. 8 **Litho.** *Perf. 13½*

584B A162a 5fr multi .25 .25
584C A162a 10fr multi .25 .25
584D A162a 20fr multi .40 .25
584E A162a 110fr multi 1.30 .30
584F A162a 300fr multi 2.75 .70
584G A162a 500fr multi 4.75 1.40
Nos. 584B-584G (6) 9.70 3.15

Souvenir Sheet

584H A162a 600fr multi 5.50 4.25

Litho. & Embossed

584I A162a 1500fr gold & multi 21.00 5.50

Souvenir Sheet

584J A162a 1500fr gold & multi 10.00 10.00

Nos. 584F-584J are airmail.

Easter 1983 A163

Rembrandt Paintings: 100fr, Entombment. 300fr, Crucifixion. 400fr, Descent from the Cross.

1983, Apr. 16

585 A163 100fr multicolored .90 .40
586 A163 300fr multicolored 2.75 1.25
587 A163 400fr multicolored 3.50 1.75
Nos. 585-587 (3) 7.15 3.40

Vintage Cars and their Makers A164

A164a

Designs: 10fr, Emile Levassor, Rene Panhard, 1895 car. 20fr, Henry Ford, 1896 car. 30fr, Louis Renault, 1899 car. 80fr, Ettore Bugatti, type 37, 1925. 400fr, Enzo Ferrari, 815 sport, 1940. 500fr, Ferdinand Porsche, 356 coupe, 1951. 600fr, Karl Benz, velocipede, 1886. No. 594A, F.H. Royce and C.S. Rolls, 1911 Rolls-Royce Silver Ghost. No. 594B, G. Daimler, 1900 Mercedes 35CV.

1983, June 3 **Litho.** *Perf. 13½*

588 A164 10fr multi .25 .25
589 A164 20fr multi .25 .25
590 A164 30fr multi .30 .25
591 A164 80fr multi .85 .30
592 A164 400fr multi 4.00 1.10
593 A164 500fr multi 4.75 1.40
Nos. 588-593 (6) 10.40 3.55

Souvenir Sheet

594 A164 600fr multi 5.75 1.60

Litho. & Embossed

594A A164a 1500fr gold & multi 20.00 4.00

Souvenir Sheet

594B A164a 1500fr gold & multi 8.00 6.00

Nos. 592-594B are airmail.

25th Anniv. of Intl. Maritime Org. — A165

1983, July 8 **Litho.** *Perf. 12½x13*

595 A165 40fr multi .50 .25
596 A165 100fr multi 1.00 .40

World Communications Year — A166

1983, July 22
597 A166 50fr multi .45 .25
598 A166 130fr multi 1.25 .45

Pre-Olympics, Los Angeles A167

1984 Summer Olympics, Los Angeles A167a

5fr, Gymnast. 40fr, Javelin throwing. 60fr, Pole vault. 120fr, Fencing. 200fr, Cycling. 300fr, Sailing.
600fr, Handball. No. 605A, 1500fr, Shot put. No. 605B, 1500fr, Dressage, horiz.

1983, Aug. 3 **Litho.** ***Perf. 13***
599 A167 5fr multi .25 .25
600 A167 40fr multi .40 .25
601 A167 60fr multi .65 .25
602 A167 120fr multi 1.40 .30
603 A167 200fr multi 2.25 .40
604 A167 300fr multi 3.25 .80
Nos. 599-604 (6) 8.20 2.25

Souvenir Sheet
605 A167 600fr multi 5.00 1.60

Litho. & Embossed
Perf. 13½
605A A167a 1500fr multi 25.00 3.50

Souvenir Sheet
605B A167a 1500fr multi 9.00 9.00

Nos. 603-605B are airmail.

Namibia Day — A168

1983, Sept. 16 **Litho.** ***Perf. 13***
606 A168 100fr multi 1.00 .50
607 A168 200fr multi 1.75 .80

Manned Flight Bicentenary — A169

A169a

Designs: 50fr, J. Montgolfier and his balloon, 1783. 100fr, J.P. Blanchard, English Channel crossing, 1785. 200fr, L.-J. Gay-Lussac, 4000-meter balloon ascent, 1804. 300fr, Giffard and his dirigible, 1852. 400fr, Santos Dumont, dirigible, Eiffel Tower. 500fr, A. Laquot, captive observation balloon, 1914. 600fr, J.A. Charles, first gas balloon; G. Tissandier, dirigible, 1883. No. 614, Marquis d'Arlandes and Jean Francois Pilatre de Rozier, Montgolfier balloon. No. 614B, Ferdinand von Zeppelin, Graf Zeppelin, horiz.

1983, Sept. 30 **Litho.** ***Perf. 13½***
608 A169 50fr multi .40 .25
609 A169 100fr multi .90 .40
610 A169 200fr multi 2.00 .80
611 A169 300fr multi 2.60 1.10
612 A169 400fr multi 3.50 1.50
613 A169 500fr multi 4.50 1.90
Nos. 608-613 (6) 13.90 5.95

Souvenir Sheet
614 A169 600fr multi 5.50 1.40

Litho. & Embossed
614A A169a 1500fr gold & multi 25.00 4.00

Souvenir Sheet
614B A169a 1500fr gold & multi 9.00 9.00

Nos. 612-614B are airmail.

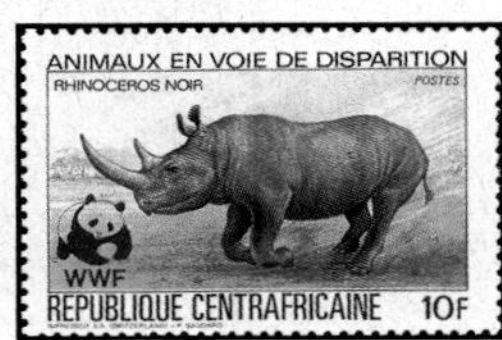

Black Rhinoceros and World Wildlife Emblem — A170

Various black rhinoceroses.

1983, Nov. 14
615 A170 10fr multi 1.00 .40
616 A170 40fr multi 1.20 .60
617 A170 70fr multi 1.75 .80
618 A170 180fr multi 5.25 1.60
Nos. 615-618 (4) 9.20 3.40

Nos. 615-618 were issued in support of the World Wildlife Fund.
See Nos. C291A-C293.

UPU Day, World Communications Year — A171

1983, Nov. 2 **Litho.** ***Perf. 13***
619 A171 205fr multi 2.00 .90

2nd Anniv. of the Natl. Military Committee A172

Gen. Andre Kolingba, head of state.

1983, Sept. 1 ***Perf. 12½***
620 A172 65fr sil & multi .55 .25
621 A172 130fr gold & multi 1.40 .55

Earth Satellite Receiving Station, Bangui M'Poko — A173

1983 ***Perf. 13***
622 A173 130fr multi 1.40 .55

Natl. Day of the Handicapped and the Elderly — A174

1983, Dec. 20 **Engr.** ***Perf. 13x12½***
623 A174 65fr vio & org .55 .30
624 A174 130fr ultra & org 1.10 .55
625 A174 205fr dk grn & org 1.75 .80
Nos. 623-625 (3) 3.40 1.65

Fishing Resources A175

1983, Dec. 31 **Litho.** ***Perf. 12½***
626 A175 25fr Breeding tank .25 .25
627 A175 65fr Net fishing .95 .25
628 A175 100fr Dam fishing 1.05 .40
629 A175 130fr Still life with fish 2.10 .70
630 A175 205fr Basket trap 2.40 .70
Nos. 626-630 (5) 6.75 2.30

Wildlife Protection — A176

1984, Jan. 25 ***Perf. 13***
631 A176 30fr Forest fire 3.25 .40
632 A176 130fr Hunters 4.50 1.10

CC-1500 Locomotive — A177

110fr, CC-1500 locomotive. 240fr, PLM series 210, 1868. 350fr, 231-726 locomotive, 1937. 440fr, Pacific S3/6, 1908. 500fr, Henschel 151 series 45, 1937.

1984, July 16 **Litho.** ***Perf. 12½***
633 A177 110fr multicolored 1.10 .30
634 A177 240fr multicolored 2.40 .85
635 A177 350fr multicolored 3.50 1.10
636 A177 440fr multicolored 4.50 1.25
637 A177 500fr multicolored 5.50 1.60
Nos. 633-637 (5) 17.00 5.10

For overprints see Nos. 702, 704.

Packet Ship Pericles — A177a

120fr, Three-master Pereire. 250fr, Admella. 400fr, Royal William. 500fr, Great Britain.

1984, July 23 **Litho.** ***Perf. 12½***
638 A177a 65fr shown .70 .30
639 A177a 120fr multicolored 1.10 .55
640 A177a 250fr multicolored 2.40 1.10
641 A177a 400fr multicolored 4.50 1.90
642 A177a 500fr multicolored 5.00 2.40
Nos. 638-642 (5) 13.70 6.25

For overprints see Nos. 701, 703.

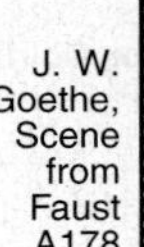

J. W. Goethe, Scene from Faust A178

Designs: 100fr, Henri Dunant, Red Cross Founder, Battle of Solferino, 125th anniv. 200fr, Alfred Nobel, Nobel Foundation headquarters. 300fr, Lord Baden-Powell, World Scouting Jamboree, Alberta, 1983. 400fr, John F. Kennedy, first man on the Moon, 1969. 500fr, 600fr, wedding of Prince and Princess of Wales.

1984, Feb. 25 **Litho.** ***Perf. 13½***
643 A178 50fr multi .45 .25
644 A178 100fr multi .90 .40
645 A178 200fr multi 2.00 .55
646 A178 300fr multi 2.60 1.10
647 A178 400fr multi 3.50 1.10
648 A178 500fr multi 4.50 1.10
Nos. 643-648 (6) 13.95 4.50

Souvenir Sheet
649 A178 600fr multi 4.00 1.40

Nos. 647-649 are airmail.

Old Masters A179

Paintings: 50fr, Madonna and Child, by Raphael. 100fr, Madonna with Pear, by Durer. 200fr, Aldobrandini Madonna, by Raphael. 300fr, Madonna with Carnation, by Durer. 400fr, Virgin and Child, by Correggio. 500fr, La Bohemienne, by Modigliani. 600fr, Madonna and Child on the Throne, by Raphael.

1984, Mar. 30 **Litho.** ***Perf. 13½***
650 A179 50fr multi .50 .25
651 A179 100fr multi .90 .25
652 A179 200fr multi 2.00 .45
653 A179 300fr multi 2.75 .85

654	A179	400fr multi	3.75	1.90
655	A179	500fr multi	4.75	2.50
		Nos. 650-655 (6)	14.65	6.20

Miniature Sheet

656	A179	600fr multi	4.50	1.40

No. 656 contains 1 stamp, size 30x59mm. Nos. 654-656 are airmail.

Space — A180

20fr, Galileo, Ariane rocket. 70fr, Piccard, X-15, balloon. 150fr, Oberth, satellite. 205fr, Einstein, satellites. 300fr, Curie, Viking vehicle. 500fr, Merbold, Spacelab.

600fr, Armstrong, Apollo 11, horiz.

1984, Aug. 6 Litho. *Perf. 13½*

657	A180	20fr multicolored	.30	.25
658	A180	70fr multicolored	.75	.25
659	A180	150fr multicolored	1.50	.45
660	A180	205fr multicolored	2.25	.55
661	A180	300fr multicolored	3.50	.80
662	A180	500fr multicolored	5.00	1.00
		Nos. 657-662 (6)	13.30	3.30

Miniature Sheet

663	A180	600fr multicolored	5.00	1.50

No. 663 contains 1 stamp, size: 42x36mm. 300fr, 500fr and 600fr are airmail.

Forestry Resources A181

1984, Oct. 9 Litho. *Perf. 13x12½*

664	A181	70fr Forest	.90	.30
665	A181	130fr Logging	1.75	.55

UNICEF — A182

1984, Oct. 27 Litho. *Perf. 13x12½*

666	A182	10fr Weighing child	.25	.25
667	A182	30fr Vaccinating child	.50	.30
668	A182	65fr Giving liquids	.60	.40
669	A182	100fr Balancing diet	1.25	.55
		Nos. 666-669 (4)	2.60	1.50

Fishing Traps A183

1984, Nov. 6 Litho. *Perf. 13*

670	A183	50fr Bangui-Kette	.75	.30
671	A183	80fr Mbres	1.00	.55
672	A183	150fr Bangui-Kette	2.25	.90
		Nos. 670-672 (3)	4.00	1.75

Mushrooms A184

5fr, Leptoporus lignosus. 10fr, Phlebopus sudanicus. 40fr, Termitomyces letestui. 130fr, Lepiota esculenta. 300fr, Termitomyces aurantiacus. 500fr, Termitomyces robustus.

600fr, Tricholoma- lobayensis.

1984, Nov. 15 Litho. *Perf. 13½*

673	A184	5fr multicolored	.25	.25
674	A184	10fr multicolored	.25	.25
675	A184	40fr multicolored	.65	.30
676	A184	130fr multicolored	2.00	.30
677	A184	300fr multicolored	3.25	.80
678	A184	500fr multicolored	5.75	1.25
		Nos. 673-678 (6)	12.15	3.15

Souvenir Sheet

679	A184	600fr multicolored	6.00	2.00

Nos. 677-679 are airmail.

1984 Winter Olympics, Sarajevo A184a

Gold medalists, communications satellite and events: 30fr, Gaetan Boucher, Canada, 1000 and 1500-meter speed skating. 90fr, W. Hoppe, R. Wetzig, D. Schauerhammer and A. Kirchner, German Democratic Republic, 4-man bobsled. 140fr, Paoletta Magoni, Italy, women's slalom. 200fr, Jayne Torvill and Christopher Dean, Great Britain, ice dancing. 400fr, Matti Nykaenen, Finland, 90-meter ski jumping. 500fr, USSR, ice hockey. 600fr, Bill Johnson, US, men's downhill.

1984, Nov. 30 Litho. *Perf. 13½*

679A	A184a	30fr multi	.30	.25
679B	A184a	90fr multi	.90	.30
679C	A184a	140fr multi	1.35	.40
679D	A184a	200fr multi	2.00	.55
679E	A184a	400fr multi	3.50	1.00
679F	A184a	500fr multi	4.75	1.25
		Nos. 679A-679F (6)	12.80	3.75

Souvenir Sheet

679G	A184a	600fr multi	5.00	1.60

Nos. 679E-679G are airmail.

Flowers — A185

65fr, Hibiscus. 130fr, Canna Indica. 205fr, Eichlornia Crassipes.

1984, Nov. 22 Litho. *Perf. 13½*

680	A185	65fr multicolored	1.00	.40
681	A185	130fr multicolored	1.75	.50
682	A185	205fr multicolored	2.75	1.00
		Nos. 680-682 (3)	5.50	1.90

Economic Campaign — A186

25fr, Cotton planting. 40fr, Selling cotton crop. 130fr, Cotton market.

1984, Dec. 3 Litho. *Perf. 13½*

683	A186	25fr multicolored	.40	.25
684	A186	40fr multicolored	.65	.40
685	A186	130fr multicolored	1.70	.55
		Nos. 683-685 (3)	2.75	1.20

World Food Day A187

1984, Dec. 10 Litho. *Perf. 13½*

686	A187	205fr Picking corn	2.25	.90

OLYMPHILEX '85 — A188

Publicity posters from previous Games and host city landmarks: 5fr, Stockholm, 1912. 10fr, Paris, 1924. 20fr, London, 1948. 100fr, Tokyo, 1964. 400fr, Mexico. 500fr, Munich, 1972.

600fr, Athens, 1896, Baron Pierre de Coubertin.

1985, Mar 18 Litho. *Perf. 13½*

687	A188	5fr multicolored	.25	.25
688	A188	10fr multicolored	.25	.25
689	A188	20fr multicolored	.30	.25
690	A188	100fr multicolored	4.75	1.00
691	A188	400fr multicolored	2.00	.45
692	A188	500fr multicolored	2.50	.55
		Nos. 687-692 (6)	10.05	2.75

Souvenir Sheet

693	A188	600fr multicolored	5.00	1.50

Nos. 691-693 are airmail. No. 693 contains one 60x30mm stamp.

Anniversaries and Events — A189

Famous men: 50fr, Abraham Lincoln, American Civil War soldiers. 90fr, Auguste Piccard (1884-1962), inventor, bathyscaphe Trieste. 120fr, Gottlieb Daimler (1834-1900), 1938 Mercedes Type 540. 200fr, Louis Bleriot (1872-1936), inventor, plane. 350fr, Anatoly Karpov, world chess champion. 400fr, Jean Henri Dunant (1828-1910), Red Cross founder, worker caring for wounded soldier.

1984, Dec. 22 Litho. *Perf. 13½*

694	A189	50fr multi	.50	.25
695	A189	90fr multi	.90	.30
696	A189	120fr multi	1.40	.40
697	A189	200fr multi	2.00	.55
698	A189	350fr multi	3.50	.80
698A	A189	400fr multi	3.50	.90
		Nos. 694-698A (6)	11.80	3.20

Nos. 698-698A are airmail.

Souvenir Sheet

Queen Mother, 85th Birthday — A189a

1984 Litho. *Perf. 13½*

698B	A189a	600fr multi	5.00	1.60

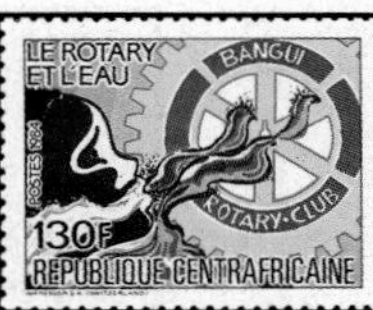

Bangui Rotary Club and Water — A190

1984, Dec. 29

699	A190	130fr multi	1.60	.45
700	A190	205fr multi	2.50	.80

Nos. 635//641, C302A Overprinted with Exhibitions in Red

1985, Mar. 13 Litho. *Perf. 12½*

701	A177	250fr Argentina '85, Buenos Aires (#640)	2.50	1.25
702	A177a	350fr Tsukuba Expo '85 (#635)	3.25	1.60
703	A177	400fr Italia '85, Rome (#641)	4.50	2.25
704	A177a	440fr Mophila '85, Hamburg (#636)	5.00	2.40
		Nos. 701-704 (4)	15.25	7.50

Souvenir Sheet

Perf. 13½x13

705	AP89	500fr Olymphilex '85, Lausanne	5.00	5.00

500fr airmail.

Beetles — A191

15fr, Chelorrhina polyphemus. 20fr, Fornasinius russus. 25fr, Goliathus giganteus. 65fr, Goliathus meleagris.

1985, Mar. Litho. *Perf. 13½*

706	A191	15fr multicolored	*.65*	*.25*
707	A191	20fr multicolored	*1.20*	*.30*
708	A191	25fr multicolored	*1.75*	*.50*
709	A191	65fr multicolored	*4.00*	*1.00*
		Nos. 706-709 (4)	*7.60*	*2.05*

Audubon Birth Bicentenary — A192

Illustrations of North American bird species by John Audubon: 40fr, Cyanocitta cristata. 80fr, Caprimulgus carolinensis. 130fr, Campephilus principales. 250fr, Calocitta formosa. 300fr, Coccizus minor, horiz. 500fr, Hirundo rustica, horiz.
600fr, Dryocopus pileatus, horiz.

1985, Mar. 25 **Litho.** ***Perf. 13½***

710	A192	40fr multicolored	.75	.25
711	A192	80fr multicolored	1.00	.25
712	A192	130fr multicolored	1.90	.25
713	A192	250fr multicolored	2.60	.55
714	A192	300fr multicolored	2.75	.60
715	A192	500fr multicolored	4.75	1.10
		Nos. 710-715 (6)	13.75	3.00

Souvenir Sheet

716 A192 600fr multicolored 7.00 2.50

Nos. 714-716 are airmail.

Intl. Youth Year A193

Famous children's book authors and scenes from their best-known novels: 100fr, The Jungle Book, 1894, by Kipling, vert. 200fr, Les Cavaliers, 1967, by Joseph Kessel (1898-1979). 300fr, Twenty-Thousand Leagues Under the Sea, 1873, by Verne. 400fr, The Adventures of Tom Sawyer, 1876, by Twain.

1985, Apr. **Litho.** ***Perf. 13***

718	A193	100fr multi	1.40	.45
719	A193	200fr multi	2.50	.85
720	A193	300fr multi	3.00	1.25
721	A193	400fr multi	4.50	2.10
		Nos. 718-721 (4)	11.40	4.65

Philexafrica '85, Lome — A194

No. 722, UPU emblem, Postmen unloading parcel post van. No. 723, Exhibition emblem, scout troop.

1985, May 15 ***Perf. 13x12½***

722	A194	200fr multi	2.25	.90
723	A194	200fr multi	2.25	.90
a.		Pair, #722-723 + label	5.50	4.50

Rabies Vaccine Cent., Louis Pasteur (1822-95), Chemist, Microbiologist — A195

Anniversaries and events: 200fr, Battle of Solferino, founding of the Red Cross, 125th Anniv., founder Jean-Henri Dunant (1828-1910), horiz. 300fr, Girl Guides, 75th anniv. 450fr, Elizabeth, the Queen Mother, 85th birthday. 500fr, Statue of Liberty, cent.

1985, June ***Perf. 13***

724	A195	150fr multi	2.25	.50
725	A195	200fr multi	2.75	.60
726	A195	300fr multi	2.25	.90
727	A195	450fr multi	4.00	1.50
728	A195	500fr multi	5.00	1.75
		Nos. 724-728 (5)	16.25	5.25

1986 World Cup Soccer Championships, Mexico — A196

Famous soccer players and match scenes: 5fr, Pele. 10fr, Tony Schumacher. 20fr, Paolo Rossi. 350fr, Kevin Keegan. 400fr, Michel Platini. 500fr, Karl Heinz Rummenigge.
600fr, Diego Armando Maradona.

1985, July 24 **Litho.** ***Perf. 13½***

730	A196	5fr multicolored	.25	.25
731	A196	10fr multicolored	.25	.25
732	A196	20fr multicolored	.25	.25
733	A196	350fr multicolored	3.25	.90
734	A196	400fr multicolored	3.75	.90
735	A196	500fr multicolored	4.75	1.10
		Nos. 730-735 (6)	12.50	3.65

Souvenir Sheet

736 A196 600fr multicolored 5.00 1.40

Nos. 734-736 are airmail.

Kotto Waterfalls A197

1985, July 27 **Litho.** ***Perf. 13½***

737	A197	65fr multi	1.00	.30
738	A197	90fr multi	1.10	.40
739	A197	130fr multi	1.75	.60
		Nos. 737-739 (3)	3.85	1.30

State Visit of Pope John Paul II — A198

Portraits.

1985, Aug. 14

740	A198	65fr multi	1.25	.40
741	A198	130fr multi	2.50	.80

Natl. Economic Development Campaign — A199

Designs: 5fr, Troops plowing. 60fr, Soldier preparing field for planting, vert. 130fr, Planting cotton seeds, vert.

1985, Sept. 1 ***Perf. 13***

742	A199	5fr multi	.25	.25
743	A199	60fr multi	.75	.30
744	A199	130fr multi	1.50	.45
		Nos. 742-744 (3)	2.50	1.00

Queen Mother, 85th Birthday — A200

100fr, Age 4, with brother. 200fr, Duchess of York, 1923. 300fr, Reviewing Irish Guards, 1928. 350fr, Family portrait, 1936. 400fr, George VI coronation, 1937. 500fr, Wedding anniv., 1948.
600fr, Christening Prince Charles, 1948.

1985, Sept. 16 **Litho.** ***Perf. 13½***

745	A200	100fr multicolored	.80	.25
746	A200	200fr multicolored	1.90	.35
747	A200	300fr multicolored	3.00	.70
748	A200	350fr multicolored	3.25	.75
749	A200	400fr multicolored	4.00	.90
750	A200	500fr multicolored	5.00	1.00
		Nos. 745-750 (6)	17.95	3.95

Souvenir Sheet

751 A200 600fr multicolored 4.50 1.40

Nos. 749-751 are airmail.

Dr. Rene Labusquiere (1919-1977), Promoter of Preventive Medicine — A201

1985, Sept. 22 **Litho.** ***Perf. 13½***

752	A201	10fr multi	.25	.25
753	A201	45fr multi	.50	.25
754	A201	110fr multi	.75	.45
		Nos. 752-754 (3)	1.50	.95

Natl. Postal Service — A202

15fr, Loading mail van. 60fr, Bangui P.O., van. 150fr, Hdqtrs, Bangui, and vans.

1985, Oct. 9 ***Perf. 12½***

755	A202	15fr multicolored	.25	.25
756	A202	60fr multicolored	.65	.25
757	A202	150fr multicolored	1.60	.80
		Nos. 755-757 (3)	2.50	1.30

Space Research — A203

Designs: 40fr, Yuri Gagarin, Soviet cosmonaut, and Sergei Korolev, rocket engineer. 110fr, Nicolaus Copernicus, Cassini probe. 240fr, Galileo, Viking orbiter. 300fr, Theodor von Karman (1881-1963), American aeronautical engineer, and space shuttle recovering Palapa B satellite. 450fr, Percival Lowell (1855-1916), American astronomer, and Viking probe. 500fr, Dr. U. Merbold and orbiting space station project Colombo. 600fr, Apollo 11 Project, first step on Moon by Neil Armstrong.

1985, Oct. 31 **Litho.** ***Perf. 13½***

758	A203	40fr multi	.25	.25
759	A203	110fr multi	1.00	.30
760	A203	240fr multi	2.75	.55
761	A203	300fr multi	3.50	.80
762	A203	450fr multi	5.50	1.00
763	A203	500fr multi	6.00	1.10
		Nos. 758-763 (6)	19.00	4.00

Souvenir Sheet

Imperf

764 A203 600fr multi 5.00 1.40

Nos. 762-764 are airmail.

Solar Energy Apparatus, Damara A204

1985, Nov. 4 **Litho.** ***Perf. 13½***

765	A204	65fr multi	.70	.30
766	A204	130fr multi	1.40	.60

Girl Guides Nature Study — A205

No. 768, Quaka Sugar Refinery.

1985, Nov. 16 ***Perf. 13***

767	A205	250fr shown	4.00	1.75
768	A205	250fr multicolored	4.00	1.75
a.		Pair, #767-768 + label	11.50	6.50

PHILEXAFRICA '85, Lome, Togo, 11/16-24.

State Visit of Pres. Mitterand of France, Dec. 12-13 — A206

1985-86 **Litho.** ***Perf. 13x12½***

769	A206	65fr multi	.75	.25
770	A206	130fr multi	1.50	.55
770A	A206	160fr multi ('86)	2.10	.80
		Nos. 769-770A (3)	4.35	1.60

Issued: Nos. 769-770, Dec. 12.

UN 40th Anniv., Central Africa Admission, 25th Anniv. — A207

1985, Dec. 18 *Perf. 13½*

771 A207 140fr multi 1.40 .55

Intl. Youth Year A208

Designs: 40fr, David, by Andrea del Verrocchio; Madonna with the Carnation, 1470, by Leonardo da Vinci. 80fr, Johann Sebastian Bach. 100fr, St. John at Patmos, 1619, by Velazquez. 250fr, The Erl King score, by Franz Schubert. 400fr, Portrait of Vicente Osorio de Moscoso, by Goya. 500fr, The Young Mozart Playing in Paris, 1764. 600fr, Woman in a Plumed Hat, 1901, by Picasso.

1985, Dec. 28

772 A208 40fr multi .40 .25
773 A208 80fr multi .90 .25
774 A208 100fr multi 1.25 .25
775 A208 250fr multi 2.50 .55
776 A208 400fr multi 4.50 .90
777 A208 500fr multi 5.00 1.10
Nos. 772-777 (6) 14.55 3.30

Souvenir Sheet

778 A208 600fr multi 5.25 1.40

Nos. 776-778 are airmail.

Halley's Comet A209

100fr, Edmond Halley, British astronomer. 200fr, Sir Isaac Newton's telescope & comet sighting. 300fr, Halley & Newton observing comet. 350fr, US probe. 400fr, Soviet probe plotting comet's perihelion. 500fr, Isodensity photograph of comet. 600fr, Comet, Earth, Sun & probe.

1985, Dec. 31

779 A209 100fr multi .80 .30
780 A209 200fr multi 1.75 .45
781 A209 300fr multi 2.75 .90
782 A209 350fr multi 3.25 1.10
783 A209 400fr multi 3.75 1.00
784 A209 500fr multi 4.75 1.25
Nos. 779-784 (6) 17.05 5.00

Souvenir Sheet

785 A209 600fr multi 5.25 1.75

Nos. 783-785 are airmail.

Christopher Columbus — A210

Various events leading to the discovery of America and beyond: 90fr, Plotting course. 110fr, Receiving blessing. 240fr, Fleet in port. 300fr, Trade with natives. 400fr, Storm at sea. 500fr, Fleet at sea.
600fr, Portrait.

1986

786 A210 90fr multicolored .90 .30
787 A210 110fr multicolored 1.25 .45
788 A210 240fr multicolored 2.50 .60
789 A210 300fr multicolored 3.25 .90
790 A210 400fr multicolored 4.25 1.00
791 A210 500fr multicolored 5.00 2.40
Nos. 786-791 (6) 17.15 5.65

Souvenir Sheet

792 A210 600fr multicolored 5.75 1.75

Nos. 790-792 are airmail.

Nos. 543-544 Surcharged

No. 792A, Kangu bowls. No. 792B, Kolongo bowls.

1986, Apr. 1 **Litho.** *Perf. 13*

792A A152 30fr on 175fr
792B A152 65fr on 300fr

Hairstyles A211

1986, May 21 **Litho.** *Perf. 12½*

793 A211 20fr multi .40 .25
794 A211 30fr multi .50 .25
795 A211 65fr multi .70 .40
796 A211 160fr multi 2.50 .70
Nos. 793-796 (4) 4.10 1.60

France - Central Africa Week — A212

1986, May 26

797 A212 40fr Communications, horiz. .45 .25
798 A212 60fr Youth, horiz. .60 .30
799 A212 100fr Basket maker 1.25 .45
800 A212 130fr Bicycling 1.75 .60
Nos. 797-800 (4) 4.05 1.60

Centrapalm Palm Oil — A213

25fr, 65fr, Refinery, Bossongo, and palm tree. 120fr, 160fr, Refinery and palm tree.

1986, Aug. 12 **Litho.** *Perf. 13½*

801 A213 25fr multi .30 .25
802 A213 65fr multi .70 .40
803 A213 120fr multi, vert. 1.25 .80
804 A213 160fr multi, vert. 1.75 .60
Nos. 801-804 (4) 4.00 2.05

Dogs and Cats A214

10fr, Pointer. 20fr, Egyptian mau. 200fr, Newfoundland. 300fr, Borzoi. 400fr, Persian red.
500fr, Spaniel, Burmese-Malayan.

1986, Sept. 9

805 A214 10fr multicolored .25 .25
806 A214 20fr multicolored .45 .25
807 A214 200fr multicolored 2.75 .55
808 A214 300fr multicolored 3.50 .60
809 A214 400fr multicolored 5.00 .85
Nos. 805-809 (5) 11.95 2.50

Souvenir Sheet

810 A214 500fr multicolored 6.25 1.75

Nos. 808-810 are airmail.

African Coffee Producers Organization, 25th Anniv. — A215

1986, Sept. 25 **Litho.** *Perf. 13*

811 A215 160fr multi 1.60 .60

1986 World Cup Soccer Championships, Mexico — A216

Satellites, final scores, World Cup and athletes: 30fr, Muller, Socrates. 110fr, Scifo, Ceulemans. 160fr, Stopyra, Platini. 350fr, Brehme, Schumacher. 450fr, Maradona. 500fr, Schumacher, Burruchaga.

1986, Nov. 12 *Perf. 13½*

812 A216 30fr multi .30 .25
813 A216 110fr multi 1.00 .25
814 A216 160fr multi 1.40 .30
815 A216 350fr multi 3.25 .80
816 A216 450fr multi 4.50 1.10
Nos. 812-816 (5) 10.45 2.70

Souvenir Sheet

817 A216 500fr multi 5.50 1.40

Nos. 816-817 are airmail.

US Anniversaries and Events A217

15fr, Judith Resnik. 25fr, Frederic Auguste Bartholdi. 70fr, Elvis Presley. 300fr, Ronald McNair. 450fr, Christa McAuliffe. 500fr, Challenger Astronauts: McAuliffe, Scobee, Smith, Resnik, Onizuka, McNair, Jarvis.

1986, Nov. 19

818 A217 15fr multi .25 .25
819 A217 25fr multi .40 .25
820 A217 70fr multi 1.90 .25
821 A217 300fr multi 3.00 .60
822 A217 450fr multi 4.50 1.10
Nos. 818-822 (5) 10.05 2.45

Souvenir Sheet

823 A217 500fr multi 5.75 1.50

US space shuttle Challenger explosion; Statue of Liberty, cent. Nos. 822-823 are airmail.

For surcharges & overprint see Nos. 851-851B.

Flora and Fauna A218

25fr, Allamanda neriifolia. 65fr, Taurotragus eurycerus. 160fr, Plumieria acuminata. 300fr, Acinonyx jubatus. 400fr, Eulophia erthoplata. 500fr, Leopard.
600fr, Derby's eland, eulophia cucullata.

1986, May 30 **Litho.** *Perf. 13½*

824 A218 25fr multicolored .25 .25
825 A218 65fr multicolored .90 .25
826 A218 160fr multicolored 2.10 .30
827 A218 300fr multicolored 4.50 .80
828 A218 400fr multicolored 4.75 .90
829 A218 500fr multicolored 6.50 1.10
Nos. 824-829 (6) 19.00 3.60

Souvenir Sheet

830 A218 600fr multicolored 5.25 1.75

Nos. 824, 826, 828 vert. Nos. 828-830 are airmail. No. 830 contains one 51x30mm stamp.

Intl. Peace Year — A219

1986, Nov. 29

831 A219 160fr multi 1.75 .75

Air Africa, 25th Anniv. — A220

1986, Dec. 15

832 A220 200fr multi 1.75 .80

UNICEF, 40th Anniv. — A221

130fr, Child immunization. 160fr, Youth, food, map.

1986, Dec. 24

833 A221 15fr shown .25 .25
834 A221 130fr multicolored 1.35 .55
835 A221 160fr multicolored 1.60 .70
Nos. 833-835 (3) 3.20 1.50

German Railways Sesquicentenary — A222

Inventors and locomotives: 40fr, Alfred de Glehn, Prussian Railways DH2 Green Elephant. 70fr, Rudolf Diesel, S3/6 No. 1829 Rheingold. 160fr, Carl Golsdorf, Trans-Europe Express train Type 103. 300fr, Wilhelm Schmidt, Beyer Garratt locomotive. 400fr, Monsieur Du Bousquet, Series 3500 compound locomotive. 500fr, Werner von Siemens, 1980s electric locomotive.

1986, Dec. 31

836 A222 40fr multi .45 .25
837 A222 70fr multi .80 .25
838 A222 160fr multi 1.75 .40
839 A222 300fr multi 3.00 .60
840 A222 400fr multi 3.75 1.10
Nos. 836-840 (5) 9.75 2.60

Souvenir Sheet

841 A222 500fr multi 5.00 1.40

Nos. 840-841 are airmail. No. 841 contains one 42x36mm stamp.

Agriculture Radio Project A223

265fr, Satellite communication.

1986, Dec. 27 Litho. *Perf. 13½*

842 A223 170fr shown 2.25 .90
843 A223 265fr multicolored 3.25 1.40

Pan-African Telecommunications Union congress, Dec. 7, 1986.
No. 842 exists in souvenir sheet of one.

Space A224

Scientists and inventions: 25fr, Sir William Herschel (1738-1822), British astronomer, and Mariner Mark II. 65fr, Wernher von Braun (1912-1977), American engineer, and Mars rover. 160fr, Rudolf Hanel, Mariner Mark II and Titan. 300fr, Patrick Baudry, Hermes shuttle and Eureka platform. 400fr, U. Keller, Halley's Comet and Giotto probe. 500fr, Wubbo Ockels, Ulf Merbold and Columbus European Space Station. 600fr, Wilhelm Obers (1758-1840) and Mariner Mark II surveying asteroids. No. 850 horiz.

1987, Jan. 27

844 A224 25fr multi .35 .25
845 A224 65fr multi .65 .25
846 A224 160fr multi 1.60 .30
847 A224 300fr multi 2.75 .75
848 A224 400fr multi 3.00 .90
849 A224 500fr multi 3.50 1.25
Nos. 844-849 (6) 11.85 3.70

Souvenir Sheet

850 A224 600fr multi 5.75 1.75

Nos. 848-850 are airmail.

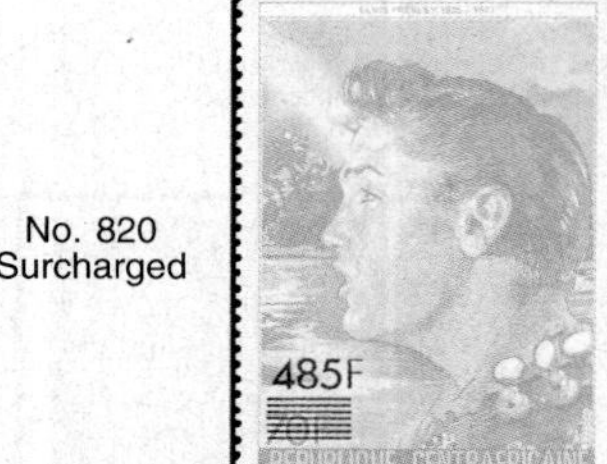

No. 820 Surcharged

1987, Feb. 20 Litho. *Perf. 13½*

851 A217 485fr on 70fr Elvis Presley 7.75 2.00

Nos. 820 and 851 Overprinted in Black

1987, Feb. 20 Litho. *Perf. 13½*

851A A217 70fr multi 1.40 .40
851B A217 485fr on 70fr multi 6.50 2.00

Overprint in red exists.

1992 Barcelona Olympics A225

Athletes and landmarks or sights: 30fr, Soccer player, Lady with Umbrella fountain. 150fr, Judo, Barcelona Cathedral. 265fr, Cyclist, Church of the Holy Family, by Gaudi. 350fr, Gymnast, Tomb of Columbus. 495fr, Runner, human tower. 500fr, Swimmer, Statue of Columbus.

1987, June 4

852 A225 30fr multi .40 .25
853 A225 150fr multi 1.40 .45
854 A225 265fr multi 2.50 .80
855 A225 350fr multi 3.50 1.00
856 A225 495fr multi 5.50 1.40
Nos. 852-856 (5) 13.30 3.90

Souvenir Sheet

857 A225 500fr multi 4.50 1.40

Nos. 855-857 are airmail.

A226

1988 Winter Olympics, Calgary — A227

20fr, Two-man luge. 140fr, Cross-country skiing. 250fr, Women's figure skating. 300fr, Hockey. 400fr, Men's slalom.
500fr, Downhill skiing.

1987, June 26

858 A226 20fr multicolored .30 .25
859 A226 140fr multicolored 1.25 .45
860 A226 250fr multicolored 2.00 .80
861 A226 300fr multicolored 2.75 .90
862 A226 400fr multicolored 3.50 1.10
Nos. 858-862 (5) 9.80 3.50

Souvenir Sheet

863 A227 500fr multicolored 4.50 1.40

Nos. 861-863 are airmail.

Intl. Peace Year — A228

1987, July 20

864 A228 50fr dull ultra, sepia & blk .50 .25
865 A228 160fr lt ol grn, sep & blk 1.40 .60

Intl. Decade of Drinkable Water — A228a

Designs: 5fr, Woman at village pump; 10fr, Two women at village pump; 200fr, Three women at village pump.

1987, Sept. 22 Litho. *Perf. 13½*

865A A228a 5fr multi *30.00* —
865B A228a 10fr multi *30.00* —
865C A228a 200fr multi *35.00* —
Nos. 865A-865C (3) *95.00*

Butterflies A229

100fr, Charaxes candiope. 120fr, Graphium leonidas. 130fr, Charaxes brutus. 160fr, Salamis aetiops.

1987, Oct. 5 Litho. *Perf. 13½*

866 A229 100fr multicolored 2.00 .85
867 A229 120fr multicolored 2.75 .90
868 A229 130fr multicolored 3.00 .90
869 A229 160fr multicolored 3.25 1.10
Nos. 866-869 (4) 11.00 3.75

Pygmy Soccer Team from Nola — A230

1987, Nov. 30 Litho. *Perf. 13*

870 A230 90fr multi 1.35 .75
871 A230 160fr multi 2.00 1.25

Integration of the pygmy people into Central African society.

Dinosaurs — A231

50fr, Brontosaurus. 65fr, Triceratops. 100fr, Ankylosaurus. 160fr, Stegosaurus. 200fr, Tyrannosaurus rex. 240fr, Corythosaurus. 300fr, Allosaurus. 350fr, Brachiosaurus.

Perf. 14x13½, 13½x14

1988, Mar. 19 Litho.

872 A231 50fr multicolored .40 .25
873 A231 65fr multicolored .70 .25
874 A231 100fr multicolored 1.00 .40
875 A231 160fr multicolored 1.75 .60
876 A231 200fr multicolored 1.75 .80
877 A231 240fr multicolored 2.75 .90
878 A231 300fr multicolored 3.25 1.25
879 A231 350fr multicolored 3.75 1.50
Nos. 872-879 (8) 15.35 5.95

Nos. 876-879 vert.

Anniversaries and Events A232

Designs: 40fr, Pres. James Madison and "We the People..." from the US Constitution. 160fr, Elizabeth II and Duke of Edinburgh. 200fr, Steffi Graf, tennis champion. 300fr, Garri Kasparov of Russia, 1985 world chess champion. 400fr, Boris Becker, 1985-86 Wimbledon champion. 500fr, Christoph Willibald Gluck (1714-87), composer. Nos. 880-884 vert.

1988, Feb. 15 *Perf. 13½*

880 A232 40fr multi .40 .25
881 A232 160fr multi 1.50 .25
882 A232 200fr multi 1.90 .45
883 A232 300fr multi 3.00 .80
884 A232 400fr multi 3.50 1.25
Nos. 880-884 (5) 10.30 3.00

Souvenir Sheet

885 A232 500fr multi 6.25 1.75

US Constitution bicentennial (40fr); 40th wedding anniv. of Elizabeth II and Prince Philip (160fr). Nos. 883-885 are airmail.

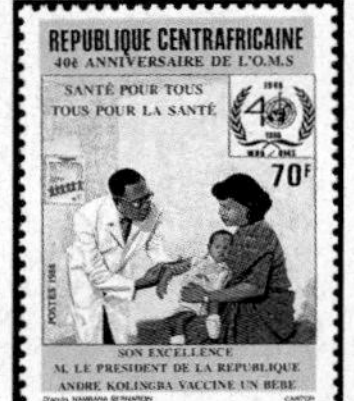

World Health Organization, 40th Anniv. — A233

1988, Apr. 7 Litho. *Perf. 13½*

886 A233 70fr multi .65 .40
887 A233 120fr multi 1.00 .55

Scout Ornithological Activities A234

Scouts and: 25fr, *Merops nubicus.* 170fr, *Euplectes hordeacea.* 300fr, *Ceryle rudis.* 400fr, *Estrilda bengala.* 450fr, *Kaupifalco monogrammicus.* 500fr, *Lamprotornis splendidus.*

1988, July 1 Litho. *Perf. 13½*

888 A234 25fr multi .25 .25
889 A234 170fr multi 1.50 .70
890 A234 300fr multi 3.00 2.00
891 A234 400fr multi 4.25 2.00
892 A234 450fr multi 5.00 2.40
Nos. 888-892 (5) 14.00 7.35

Souvenir Sheet

893 A234 500fr multi 6.00 1.75

Nos. 891-893 are airmail.
For surcharges see Nos. 921-924.

1988 Summer Olympics, Seoul A235

1988, Sept. 30

894 A235 150fr Running, vert. 1.25 .25
895 A235 300fr Judo, vert. 2.75 .70
896 A235 400fr Soccer, vert. 3.00 1.00
897 A235 450fr Tennis, vert. 3.50 1.10
Nos. 894-897 (4) 10.50 3.05

Souvenir Sheet

898 A235 500fr Boxing 5.00 1.50

Nos. 896-898 are airmail.

1988 Winter Olympics, Calgary — A236

170fr, Cross-country skiing. 350fr, Ice hockey. 400fr, Downhill skiing. 450fr, Freestyle.

1988, Sept. 30 Litho. *Perf. 13½*

899 A236 170fr multicolored 1.40 .30
900 A236 350fr multicolored 2.25 .60
901 A236 400fr multicolored 3.00 .90
902 A236 450fr multicolored 3.25 1.00
Nos. 899-902 (4) 9.90 2.80

Souvenir Sheet

903 A236 500fr shown 5.50 1.50

Nos. 899-902 vert. Nos. 901-903 are airmail.

Natl. Arbor Day — A237

50fr, Students planting trees. 130fr, Forest (before and after).

1988, July 16 Litho. *Perf. 13½*

904 A237 50fr multicolored .50 .25
905 A237 100fr like 50fr 1.00 .55
906 A237 130fr multicolored 1.40 .70
Nos. 904-906 (3) 2.90 1.50

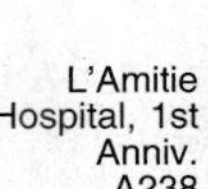

L'Amitie Hospital, 1st Anniv. A238

1988, Nov. 30

907 A238 5fr shown .25 .25
908 A238 60fr Aerial view .65 .40
909 A238 160fr Front gate 1.40 .80
Nos. 907-909 (3) 2.30 1.45

Proclamation of Central African Republic, 30th Anniv. A238a

Design: 65fr, 160fr, Dove, map, flag, people. 240fr, Government buildings, horiz.

1988 (?) Litho. *Perf. 13½*

909A A238a 65fr multi *47.50* —
909B A238b 160fr multi *47.50* —
909C A238a 240fr multi *47.50* —

A239

Olympic Medalists, Seoul, 1988: 150fr, Kristine Otto, DDR, swimming. 240fr, Matt Biondi, US, swimming. 300fr, Florence Griffith-Joyner, US, running. 450fr, Pierre Durand, France, equestrian. 600fr, Carl Lewis, US, running.

1989, Apr. 1

910 A239 150fr multi 2.00 .55
911 A239 240fr multi 3.25 .80
912 A239 300fr multi 4.00 1.10
913 A239 450fr multi 6.75 1.75
a. Souv. sheet of 4, #910-913 16.00
Nos. 910-913 (4) 16.00 4.20

Souvenir Sheet

914 A239 600fr multi 5.25 2.00

Nos. 913-914 airmail. No. 914 contains one 37x43mm stamp.

A240

Transportation Innovations, Inventors: 20fr, Hebmuller and 1953 Volkswagen Beetle. 205fr, Werner von Siemens (1816-1892) and 1879 Locomotive B. 300fr, Dennis Conner, skipper of *Stars and Stripes*, winner of the 1988 America's Cup. 400fr, Andre Citroen (1878-1935) and 1955 Citroen-15 SIX. 450fr, Marc Seguin (1786-1875) and 1895 Decauville-Mallet 020-020. 750fr, Frederick S. Duesenberg (1876-1932), brother August, US flag and 1929 J Phaeton.

1989, Apr. 10 Litho. *Perf. 13½*

915 A240 20fr multi .25 .25
916 A240 205fr multi 1.75 .55
917 A240 300fr multi 2.25 .60
918 A240 400fr multi 3.25 1.10
919 A240 450fr multi 4.00 1.25
Nos. 915-919 (5) 11.50 3.75

Souvenir Sheet

920 A240 750fr multi 5.75 1.50

Nos. 919-920 airmail. No. 920 contains one 43x37mm stamp.

Nos. 915-919 exist in souvenir sheets of 1.

Nos. 889-892 Surcharged in Black or Silver

1988, Oct. 7 Litho. *Perf. 13½*

921 A234 30fr on 170fr (B) .40 .25
922 A234 70fr on 300fr 1.10 .55
923 A234 160fr on 400fr 1.90 .85
924 A234 200fr on 450fr 2.50 1.10
Nos. 921-924 (4) 5.90 2.75

Nos. 923-924 are airmail.

PHILEXFRANCE '89, French Revolution Bicent. — A241

Designs: 200fr, Allegory in Honor of Liberty. 300fr, Declaration of Human Rights and Citizenship. 500fr, The Bastille, horiz.

1989, July 7 Litho. *Perf. 13*

925 A241 200fr multi 1.75 .80
926 A241 300fr multi 3.75 1.25
a. Pair, #925-926 + label 6.50 6.50

Souvenir Sheet

927 A241 500fr multi 5.75 3.75

Souvenir Sheet

Statue of Liberty — A242

Designs: a, Crown and torch observatories lit at night. b, Working on statue's coiffure. c, Face and scaffolding. d, Workman sanding copper sheeting around the crown observatory. e, Re-opening ceremony, 1986. f, Crown observatory at night.

Wmk. 385

1989, July Litho. *Perf. 13*

928 A242 Sheet of 6 11.00 11.00
a.-c. 150fr any single 1.60 .60
d.-f. 200fr any single 1.75 1.00

Statue of Liberty cent. (in 1986). Photograph of the statue is reversed.

M. Champagnat (1789-1840), Founder of the Marist Order — A243

15fr, Madonna and child, map. 50fr, Cross, Earth.

1989 Litho. Unwmk. *Perf. 13½*

929 A243 15fr multicolored .25 .25
930 A243 50fr multicolored .40 .25
931 A243 160fr shown 1.60 1.25
Nos. 929-931 (3) 2.25 1.75

Nos. 929-930 vert.

Harvest Feast, Bambari A244

1989, Oct. 15

932 A244 100fr Produce 1.15 .60
933 A244 160fr Ox plow 1.60 .80

World Food Day A245

60fr, Domestic animals. 240fr, Arresting ivory poachers.

1989, Oct. 16

934 A245 60fr multicolored .60 .40
935 A245 240fr multicolored 2.50 1.20

French Revolution, Bicent. — A246

Battle scenes and leaders: 160fr, Brig.-Gen. Francois-Christophe Kellermann (1735-1820), Battle of Valmy, Sept. 22, 1792. 200fr, Minister of War Charles-Francois du Perier Dumouriez (1739-1823), Battle of Jemappes, Nov. 7, 1792. 500fr, Gen. Jean-Charles Pichegru (1761-1804), capture of the Dutch fleet, Jan. 22, 1795. 600fr, Gen. Louis-Lazare Hoche (1768-97), Battle of Quiberon Bay, July 21, 1795. 1000fr, Napoleon at the Battle of Rivoli Veronese, Jan. 15, 1797. 1500fr, General Jean-Baptiste Jourdan.

1989, Dec. 5 Litho. *Perf. 13½*

936 A246 160fr multicolored 1.40 .40
937 A246 200fr multicolored 1.75 .55
938 A246 500fr multicolored 5.50 1.10
939 A246 600fr multicolored 5.00 1.00
a. Souvenir sheet of 4, #936-939 15.00 15.00
Nos. 936-939 (4) 13.65 3.05

Souvenir Sheet

940 A246 1000fr multicolored 10.00 3.00

Litho. & Embossed

940A A246 1500fr gold & multi — —

PHILEXFRANCE '89. Nos. 938-940A are airmail.

No. 936 is incorrectly inscribed "Francois-Etienne." Jemappes is incorrectly spelled on No. 937. No. 940 is incorrectly inscribed "January 14."

1990 World Cup Soccer Championships, Italy — A247

Various athletes and Italian landmarks: 20fr, Bell tower, Palermo Cathedral. 120fr, Trinity of the Mount, Rome. 160fr, St. Francis Church apse, Bologna. 200fr, Palace, Florence. 1000fr, Milan Cathedral.

1989, Dec. 23

941 A247 20fr multicolored .25 .25
942 A247 120fr multicolored 1.25 .40
943 A247 160fr multicolored 1.40 .40
944 A247 200fr multicolored 1.60 .55
Nos. 941-944 (4) 4.50 1.60

Souvenir Sheet

945 A247 1000fr multicolored 9.25 2.00

Nos. 942 and 945 are airmail.

Save the Forests A247a

1989 Litho. *Perf. 13½*

945A A247a 160fr multicolored 2.00 .75

Town of Bangui, Cent. A247b

Designs: 100fr, Governor's Palace, 1906. 160fr, Outpost. 200fr, A. Dolisie, founder of Bangui, vert. 1000fr, Signing of peace treaty between Michel Dolisie and Chief Gbembo, 1889, vert.

1989 Litho. *Perf. 13½*

945B	A247b	100fr multi		1.25	.40
945C	A247b	160fr multi		1.75	1.00
945D	A247b	200fr multi		2.50	.95
945E	A247b	1000fr multi		10.50	4.25
		Nos. 945B-945E (4)		16.00	6.60

Championship Team from Central Africa, 1987 — A248

1990, Feb. 23 Litho. *Perf. 13½*

946	A248	160fr Flag, players, trophy	1.60	.75
947	A248	240fr shown	2.25	1.00
948	A248	500fr like 160fr	5.50	2.25
		Nos. 946-948 (3)	9.35	4.00

African Basketball Championships. Dated 1988. Nos. 946 and 948 vert.

A249

1990, Feb. 23 Litho. *Perf. 13½*

949	A249	100fr multicolored	1.00	.40
950	A249	130fr multicolored	1.10	.55

Central Africa, winner of the 1987 African Basketball Cup Championships, Tunis. Dated 1989.

A250

1992 Winter Olympics, Albertville: 10fr, Speed skating. 60fr, Cross-country skiing. 500fr, Slalom. 750fr, Figure skating.

1000fr, Downhill skiing. No. 955A, Slalom skier. No. 955B, Pairs figure skating.

1990, Mar. 12 Litho. *Perf. 13½*

951	A250	10fr multi	.25	.25
952	A250	60fr multi	.55	.25
953	A250	500fr multi	4.50	1.00
954	A250	750fr multi	6.25	1.40
		Nos. 951-954 (4)	11.55	2.90

Souvenir Sheet

955	A250	1000fr multi	8.75	2.00

Litho. & Embossed

955A	A250	1500fr gold & multi	12.00	3.50

Souvenir Sheet

955B	A250	1500fr gold & multi	25.00	25.00

Nos. 953-955B are airmail. No. 955 contains one 36x42mm stamp. Nos. 951-954 exist in souvenir sheets of one.

Scout, *Euphaera eusemoides* — A251

Boy scouts and butterflies: 65fr, *Cymothoe beckeri.* 160fr, *Pseudacraea clarki.* 250fr, *Charaxes castor.*300fr, *Euphaedra gausape.* 500fr, *Graphium ridleyanus.* 1000fr, *Euphaedra edwardsi.* No. 962A, Antanartia delius. No. 962B, Spotted flycatcher. No. 962C, Cymothoe sangaris.

1990, Mar. 26

956	A251	25fr multicolored	.30	.25
957	A251	65fr multicolored	.65	.35
958	A251	160fr multicolored	1.60	.45
959	A251	250fr multicolored	2.75	.75
960	A251	300fr multicolored	3.00	.90
961	A251	500fr multicolored	5.25	1.25
		Nos. 956-961 (6)	13.55	3.95

Souvenir Sheet

962	A251	1000fr multicolored	11.00	2.25

Litho. & Embossed

Perf. 12½

962A	A251	1500fr gold & multi	15.00	5.00

Perf. 13½

962B	A251	1500fr gold & multi	45.00	4.00

Souvenir Sheet

962C	A251	1500fr gold & multi	12.00	12.00

Nos. 962A-962C are airmail. No. 962A exists in a souvenir sheet of 1.

1992 Summer Olympics, Barcelona A252

1990, Apr. 1 Litho. *Perf. 13½*

963	A252	10fr Javelin	.25	.25
964	A252	40fr Runner	.40	.25
965	A252	130fr Tennis	1.25	.45
966	A252	240fr Hurdles	2.50	.55
967	A252	400fr Yachting	4.00	1.00
968	A252	500fr Soccer	5.25	1.25
		Nos. 963-968 (6)	13.65	3.75

Souvenir Sheet

969	A252	1000fr Boxing	10.00	2.25

Nos. 963-965 vert. Nos. 967-969 are airmail.

Pres. Gorbachev, Pres. Bush — A253

Pres. Gorbachev, Pope John Paul II — A254

1990, July 27 Litho. *Perf. 13½*

970	A253	120fr multicolored	1.00	.30
971	A254	200fr multicolored	2.00	.45

Pope John Paul II-Gorbachev meeting Dec. 2, 1989. Bush-Gorbachev Summit Meeting Dec. 3, 1989. Nos. 970-971 exist in souvenir sheets of 1. Value, each $20.

Great Britain No. 1, Sir Rowland Hill (1795-1879) — A255

1990, July 27

972	A255	130fr multicolored	1.40	.30

No. 972 exists in a souvenir sheet of 1.

Events and Anniversaries — A256

Designs: 160fr, Galileo Probe to Jupiter. 240fr, Neil Armstrong, 1st man on moon. 250fr, Concorde, rapid-transit train, Rotary Intl. emblem.

1990, July 27 Litho. *Perf. 13½*

973	A256	160fr multicolored	1.50	.40
974	A256	240fr multicolored	2.40	.50
975	A256	250fr multicolored	2.75	.75
		Nos. 973-975 (3)	6.65	1.65

A258

Wildlife Protection — A258a

100fr, Declining elephant population.

1991, Jan. 25 Litho. *Perf. 13½*

976	A258	15fr gold & multi	.75	.25
977	A258	60fr multicolored	2.40	.40
978	A258a	100fr multicolored	3.25	.55
		Nos. 976-978 (3)	6.40	1.20

Eutropius A259

Design: 240fr, Distichodus.

1991, Jan. 26

979	A259	50fr multicolored	1.25	.25
980	A259	160fr gold & multi	2.75	.75
981	A259	240fr multicolored	3.50	.50
		Nos. 979-981 (3)	7.50	1.50

Fight Against AIDS A260

Design: 120fr, Class speaker, vert.

1991, Jan. 24

982	A260	5fr gold & multi	.90	.25
983	A260	70fr multicolored	2.75	.55
984	A260	120fr multicolored	3.50	.80
		Nos. 982-984 (3)	7.15	1.60

Central African Diamonds A260a

Designs: 65fr, Woman polishing diamond, 160fr, Map, diamond.

1991, Feb. 14 Litho. *Perf. 11½*

Granite Paper

984A	A260a	65fr multicolored	—	
984B	A260a	160fr multicolored	—	

Assumption of Power by Pres. Andre Kolingba, 10th Anniv. (in 1991) — A261

1992, Sept. 1 Litho. *Perf. 13x13½*

985	A261	160fr multicolored	3.00	.60

Anniversaries and Events — A262

Designs: 80fr, Maybach Zeppelin, zeppelin airship, Count Ferdinand Zeppelin. 140fr, Child being comforted, Jean-Henri Dunant. 160fr, Benetton-Ford B 192, Michael Schumacher. 350fr, Konrad Adenauer signing Constitution of German Republic. 500fr, Pope John Paul II, mother and child, map. 600fr, Wolfgang Amadeus Mozart. 1000fr, Columbus at La Rabida, sailing ship, and building in Seville, Spain.

1992, Sept. 22 Litho. *Perf. 13½*

986	A262	80fr multicolored	1.00	.25
987	A262	140fr multicolored	1.60	.50
988	A262	160fr multicolored	2.00	.75
989	A262	350fr multicolored	4.50	1.10
990	A262	500fr multicolored	6.25	1.40
991	A262	600fr multicolored	8.25	1.50
		Nos. 986-991 (6)	23.60	5.50

Souvenir Sheet

992	A262	1000fr multicolored	10.00	2.00

Count Zeppelin, 75th anniv. of death (No. 986). Jean-Henri Dunant, first recipient of Nobel Peace Prize, 90th anniv. (in 1991) (No. 987). Grand Prix of Monaco (No. 988). Brandenburg Gate, bicent (No. 989). Visit of Pope John Paul II to Africa (No. 990). Wolfgang Amadeus Mozart, bicent. of death (in 1991) (No. 991). Discovery of America, 500th anniv. and Expo '92, Seville (No. 992).

Nos. 990-992 are airmail. Nos. 986-991 exist in souvenir sheets of 1.

For overprint see No. 1073.

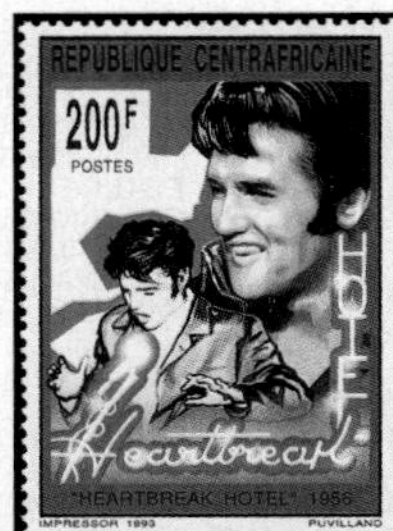

A264

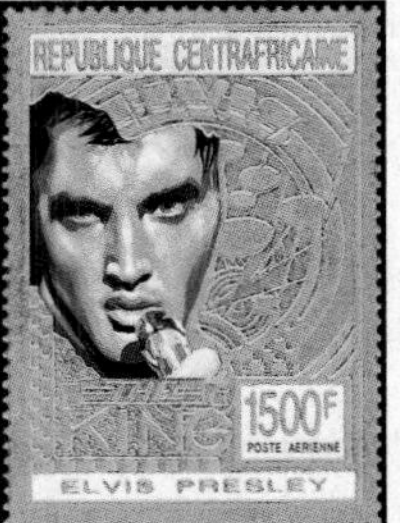

Elvis Presley (1935-1977) — A264a

Portrait of Presley, song or movie: 200fr, Heartbreak Hotel, 1956. 300fr, Love Me Tender, 1957. 400fr, Jailhouse Rock, 1957. 600fr, Harem Scarum, 1965.

1000fr, With guitar, at microphone.

No. 1001A, Holding microphone. No. 1001B, Playing guitar.

1993, July 12 Litho. *Perf. 13½*

997	A264	200fr multi	2.40	.25
998	A264	300fr multi	3.50	.50
999	A264	400fr multi	4.25	.60
1000	A264	600fr multi	6.00	1.00
	Nos. 997-1000 (4)		16.15	2.35

Souvenir Sheet

1001 A264 1000fr multi 9.50 2.40

Litho. & Embossed

1001A A264a 1500fr gold & multi 20.00 7.50

Souvenir Sheet

1001B A264a 1500fr gold & multi 13.00 8.00

Nos. 1000-1001B are airmail. Nos. 997-1000, 1001A exist imperf. and in souvenir sheets of one. Nos. 1001, 1001B exist imperf.

A265

Wedding of Japan's Crown Prince Naruhito and Masako Owada — A265a

Designs: 50fr, Princess Masako, parents. 65fr, Crown Prince Naruhito, parents. 160fr, Princess Masako, Harvard University 450fr, Crown Prince Naruhito, Oxford University. 750fr, Crown Prince, Princess.

1993, July 12 Litho. *Perf. 13½*

1002	A265	50fr multi	.40	.25
1003	A265	65fr multi	.65	.25
1004	A265	160fr multi	1.75	.25
1005	A265	450fr multi	4.50	1.00
	Nos. 1002-1005 (4)		7.30	1.75

Souvenir Sheet

1006 A265 750fr multi 7.75 3.00

Litho. & Embossed

1006A A265a 1500fr gold & multi 26.00 4.00

Nos. 1005-1006A are airmail. Nos. 1002-1005, 1006A exist imperf. and in souvenir sheets of one. No. 1006 exists imperf.

A266

1994 World Cup Soccer Championships, US — A266a

Designs show winning team, scenes from: 40fr, Amsterdam, 1928; Montevideo, 1930. 50fr, Rome, 1934; Paris, 1938. 60fr, Rio, 1950; Berne, 1954. 80fr, Stockholm, 1958; Santiago, 1962. 160fr, London, 1966; Mexico City, 1970. 200fr, Munich, 1974; Buenos Aires, 1978. 400fr, Madrid, 1982; Mexico City, 1986. 500fr, Rome, 1990; emblem for US competition, 1994.

1000fr, 1990 German team; 1994 US team.

No. 1015A, Pele, Brazil. No. 1015B, Gerd Muller, Germany.

1993, Oct. 9 Litho. *Perf. 13½*

1007	A266	40fr multi	.40	.25
1008	A266	50fr multi	.40	.25
1009	A266	60fr multi	.50	.25
1010	A266	80fr multi	.65	.25
1011	A266	160fr multi	1.40	.40
1012	A266	200fr multi	1.90	.70
1013	A266	400fr multi	3.50	.70
1014	A266	500fr multi	5.00	1.00
	Nos. 1007-1014 (8)		13.75	3.80

Souvenir Sheet

1015 A266 1000fr multi 10.00 2.75

Litho. & Embossed

1015A A266a 1500fr gold & multi 26.00

Souvenir Sheet

1015B A266a 1500fr gold & multi 13.50

No. 1015 contains one 60x30mm stamp. No. 1007-1014 exist in souvenir sheets of one. Nos. 1015A-1015B are airmail.

Miniature Sheets

Modern Olympic Games, Cent. (in 1996) — A267

No. 1016: a, Ancient olympian. b, Baron de Coubertin, 1896. c, Charles Bennett, 1900. d, Etienne Desmarteau, 1904. e, Harry Porter, 1908. f, Patrick MacDonald, 1912. g, No games, 1916. h, Frank Loomis, 1920. i, Albert White, 1924.

No. 1017: a, El Ouafi, 1928. b, Eddie Tolan, 1932. c, Jesse Owens, 1936. d, No games, 1940. e, No games, 1944. f, Tapio Rautavaara, 1948. g, Jean Boiteux, 1952. h, Petrus Kasterman, 1956. i, Sante Gaiardoni, 1960.

No. 1018: a, Anton Geesink, 1964. b, Bob Beamon, 1968. c, Mark Spitz, 1972. d, Nadia Comaneci, 1976. e, Aleksandre Dityatin, 1980. f, J.F. Lamour, 1984. g, Pierre Durand, 1988. h, Michael Jordan, 1992. i, Soccer player, 1996.

1993 Litho. *Perf. 13½*

1016	A267	90fr Sheet of 9, #a.-i.	7.50	3.25
1017	A267	100fr Sheet of 9, #a.-i.	9.00	3.75
1018	A267	160fr Sheet of 9, #a.-i.	15.00	5.75

Miniature Sheet

Dinosaurs — A268

Designs: No. 1019a, 25fr, Saltoposuchus. b, 25fr, Rhamphorhynchus. c, 25fr, Dimorphodon. d, 25fr, Archaeopteryx. e, 30fr, Compsognathus longipes. f, 30fr, Cryptocleidus oxoniensis. g, 30fr, Stegosaurus. h, 30fr, Cetiosaurus. i, 50fr, Brontosaurus. j, 50fr, Corythosaurus casuarius. k, 50fr, Styracosaurus. l, 50fr, Gorgosaurus. m, 500fr, Scolosaurus. n, 500fr, Trachodon. o, 500fr, Struthiomimus. p, 500fr, Tarbosaurus.

No. 1020, Tylosaur.

1993, Dec. 3

1019 A268 Sheet of 16, #a.-p. 25.00 25.00

Souvenir Sheet

1020 A268 1000fr multicolored 10.50 2.75

No. 1020 is airmail and contains one 51x60mm stamp.

Biodiversity A269

Various fauna surrounding: 100fr, Man planting tree. 130fr, Man with local fauna, vert.

1993, Oct. 20 Litho. *Perf. 13½*

1021	A269	100fr multicolored	3.75	.75
1022	A269	130fr multicolored	5.50	1.00

M'Bali Dam — A270

200fr, Women, men with fish.

1993, Jan. 14 Litho. *Perf. 13*

1023	A270	160fr shown	1.75	.65
1024	A270	200fr multi	2.40	.90

Cooperation Council, 40th Anniv. — A271

1993, Jan. 26

1025 A271 240fr multicolored 2.75 1.25

Intl. Conference on Nutrition, Rome — A272

1993, Apr. 1

1026	A272	90fr shown	.90	.45
1027	A272	140fr Fresh foods	1.40	.75

University of Bangui A273

1993, Apr. 8

1028 A273 100fr multicolored 1.10 .45

Dated 1992.

Environmental Development A274

Designs: 160fr, Woman with vegetables, fruit. 240fr, Woman cooking food.

1993, Oct. 27 Litho. *Perf. 13½*

1029	A274	160fr multicolored	1.75	.80
1030	A274	240fr multicolored	2.60	1.40

Miniature Sheets

1994 Winter Olympics, Lillehammer — A275

Past Winter Olympic champions: 1031a, Th. Haug, Nordic combined skiing, Chamonix, 1924. b, J. Heaton, 1-man sled, St. Moritz, 1928. c, B. Ruud, ski jumping, Lake Placid, 1932. d, I. Ballangrud, speed skating, Garmisch-Partenkirchen, 1936. e, G. Fraser, women's slalom skiing, St. Moritz, 1948. f, German 4-man bobsled, Oslo, 1952. g, USSR hockey team, Cortina D'Ampezzo, 1956. h, J. Vuarnet, downhill skiing, Squaw Valley, 1960.

No. 1032a, M. Goitschel, giant slalom, Innsbruck, 1964. b, Jean-Claude Killy, slalom skiing, Grenoble, 1968. c, U. Wehling, Nordic combined, Sapporo, 1972. d, Rodnina & Zaitsev, pairs figure skating, Innsbruck, 1976. e, E. Heiden, speed skating, Lake Placid, 1980. f, K. Witt, figure skating, Sarajevo, 1984. g, J. Mueller, luge, Calgary, 1988. h, E. Grospiron, freestyle skiing, Albertville, 1992. i, Speed skiing, Lillehammer, 1994.

1994, Jan. 14 Litho. *Perf. 13½*

1031 A275 100fr Sheet of 8, #a.-h. + label 9.00 9.00
1032 A275 200fr Sheet of 9, #a.-i. 15.00 15.00

1994 Winter Olympics, Lillehammer — A276

Design: 1500fr, Women figure skaters.

1994 Litho. & Embossed *Perf. 13½*

1033 A276 1500fr gold & multi 15.00 5.00

No. 1033 is airmail & exists in a souvenir sheet of 1. Value $24.

Flowers, Vegetables, Fruit, & Mushrooms A277

Flowers: No. 1034a, 25fr, Ansellia africana. b, 60fr, Polystachia bella. c, 90fr, Aerangis rhodosticta. d, 500fr, Angraecum eburneum.

Vegetables: No. 1035a, 30r, Yams. b, 65fr, Manioc. c, 100fr, Corn. d, 400fr, Sweet potato.

Fruits: No. 1036a, 40fr, Orange. b, 70fr, Banana. c, 160fr, Mango. d, 300fr, Coffee.

Mushrooms: No. 1037a, 50fr, Termitomyces schimperi. b, 80fr, Sympodia arborescens. c, 200fr, Phlebopus sudanicus. d, 600fr, Leucocoprinus africanus.

1994, Jan. 21 Litho. *Perf. 13½*

1034 A277 Strip of 4, #a.-d. 5.50 2.50
1035 A277 Strip of 4, #a.-d. 5.00 2.25
1036 A277 Strip of 4, #a.-d. 4.50 2.00
1037 A277 Strip of 4, #a.-d. 8.75 3.75
e. Sheet of 16, #1034-1037 26.00 12.00

Catholic Church in Africa, Cent. — A278

Designs: 130fr, Monsignor Augouard, founder of mission, St. Paul of the Rapids. 160fr, Monsignor Grandin, Abbe Boganda, first sacred ordainment, 1938. 240fr, Father Louis Godart, House of Charity, Bangui.

1994, June 2 Litho. *Perf. 13½*

1038 A278 130fr multicolored .65 .45
1039 A278 160fr multicolored .80 .45
1040 A278 240fr multicolored 1.40 .60
Nos. 1038-1040 (3) 2.85 1.50

Relics from Early Civilizations, Landmarks — A279

Designs: 10fr, Cabin-shaped cinerary urn, Rome. 25fr, Face of the secret denunciation, Venice, vert. 30fr, Statue of the Tetrarchs, Venice, vert. 50fr, Little cube-shaped building, Palermo, vert. 65fr, Frieze, The Alhambra, Granada, vert. 90fr, Grand Chateau, Bellinzona. 100fr, Museum D'Orsay, Paris, vert. 130fr, Granary, Galicia. 140fr, Mural, by Diego Rivera, Mexico, vert. 160fr, Guacamaya mask, Mexico, vert. 200fr, Ivory mask, Western Africa, vert. 240fr, La Sagrada Familia, Barcelona, vert. 260fr, Casbah of Amerhidil. 300fr, Gold aureus of Sulla, Rome, 82 BC. 400fr, Chimborazo volcano.

1994, June 2 *Perf. 13*

1041-1055 A279 Set of 15 12.50 4.50

D-Day, 50th Anniv. — A280

Pegasus Bridge, June 6: No. 1056a, British troops crossing bridge, piper. b, Glider, British and German soldiers. c, German soldiers.

Operation COBRA, July 24: a, Tank, monument, soldiers. b, Bombers, soldiers, gun barrel. c, Tank, soldiers up close.

1994, Oct. 25 Litho. *Perf. 13½*

1056 A280 600fr Strip of 3, #a.-c. 11.00 4.00
1057 A280 600fr Strip of 3, #a.-c. 11.00 4.00

Nos. 1056b, 1057b are 30x46mm. Nos. 1056-1057 are continuous designs. See No. C359.

Anniversaries & Events — A281

No. 1058, 600fr — Characters from "Star Wars:" a, Han Solo, Chewbaca. b, Darth Vader, Princess Leia, Luke Skywalker, R2D2, C3PO. c, Obi Wan Kenobi.

No. 1059 — First manned moon landing, 25th anniv.: a, 400fr, Buzz Aldrin. b, 500fr, Neil Armstrong, Apollo 11 liftoff. c, 600fr, Michael Collins.

No. 1060: a, 400fr, Theodor von Karman. b, 500fr, Apollo 11 command module, Wernher von Braun. c, 600fr, Hermes Rocket, Hermann Oberth.

1994, Oct. 25 Litho. *Perf. 13½*

1058 A281 Strip of 3, #a.-c. 9.50 4.00
1059 A281 Strip of 3, #a.-c. 8.00 3.50
1060 A281 Strip of 3, #a.-c. 7.50 3.00

Motion Pictures, cent. (No. 1058).

Nos. 1058b, 1059b, 1060b are 60x51mm. Nos. 1058-1060 are continuous design and exist in a souvenir sheet of 1.

Natl. Assembly A282

1994, Dec. 8

1061 A282 65fr blue & multi .35 .25
1062 A282 430fr yel brn & multi 1.90 .90

Antoine de Saint-Exupery (1900-44), Aviator, Author — A283

1994, Dec 16

1063 A283 80fr Airplane .60 .30
1064 A283 235fr Portrait, vert. 1.10 .55

Inauguration of Pres. Ange-Felix Patasse, 1st Anniv. — A284

1994, Oct. 22

1065 A284 65fr blue & multi .40 .25
1066 A284 300fr yellow & multi 1.60 .60
1067 A284 385fr green & multi 2.00 .75
Nos. 1065-1067 (3) 4.00 1.60

A285

Intl. Olympic Committee, Cent. — A286

1994, Oct. 25

1068 A285 60fr bl grn & multi .35 .25
1069 A285 405fr yel grn & multi 1.75 .80

Souvenir Sheet

1070 A286 675fr Pierre de Coubertin 3.00 1.40

No. 1070 is airmail.

Nos. 1031-1032 Ovptd. with Medalist & Country Name in Gold

Overprints on No. 1031: No. 1071a, "F.B. LUNDBERG / NORVEGE." b, "G. HACKL / ALLEMAGNE." c, "B. DAEHLIE / NORVEGE." d, "J.O. KOSS / NORVEGE." e, "V. SCHNEIDER / SUISSE." f, "MEDAILLE D'OR / ALLEMAGNE." g, "MEDAILLE D'OR / SUEDE." h, "T. MOE / U.S.A."

Overprints on No. 1032: No. 1072a, "M. WASMEIER / ALLEMAGNE." b, "T. STANGASSINGER / AUTRICHE." c, "MEDAILLE D'OR / PAR EQUIPES / JAPON." d, "Y. GORDEYEVA / S. GRINKOV / RUSSIE." e, "D. JANSEN / U.S.A." f, "O. BAYUL / UKRAINE." g, "G. HACKL / ALLEMAGNE." h, "J.-L. BRASSARO / CANADA." i, "K. SEIZINGER / ALLEMAGNE."

1994

1071 A275 100fr Sheet of 8, #a.-h. + label 7.00 3.00
1072 A275 200fr Sheet of 9, #a.-i. 16.00 7.00

No. 988 Overprinted in Silver

1994, Dec. 28 Litho. *Perf. 13½*

1073 A262 160fr multicolored 10.00 4.50

No. 1073 also exists in souvenir sheet of 1.

1995 Boy Scout Jamboree, Holland — A287

Scout with mushrooms or butterflies: 300fr, Armillariela mellea. 385fr, Charaxes pleione. 405fr, Charaxes candiope. 430fr, Charaxes pollux. 500fr, Volvaria esculenta. 1000fr, Cortinarius.

2000fr, Euphaedra medon.

1995, May 24

1074-1079 A287 Set of 6 15.00 7.00
1077a Sheet, #1075-1077 10.00 2.75
1079a Sheet, #1074, #1078-1079 14.50 4.00

Souvenir Sheet

1080 A287 2000fr multicolored 18.00 4.25

Nos. 1074-1079 exist in souvenir sheets of 1. No. 1080 is airmail and contains one 39x57mm stamp.

1994 World Cup Soccer Championships, US — A288

Stadium: 300fr, Citrus Bowl, Orlando. 385fr, RFK Stadium, Washington, DC. 405fr, Soldier Field, Chicago. 430fr, Cotton Bowl, Dallas. 500fr, Giants Stadium, East Rutherford, NJ. 1000fr, Foxboro Stadium, Foxboro, MA.

2000fr, Rose Bowl, vert.

1995, July 14 Litho. *Perf. 13½*

1081-1086 A288 Set of 6 14.00 6.50

Souvenir Sheet

1087 A288 2000fr multicolored 12.50 5.75

No. 1087 is airmail.

African Development Bank, 30th Anniv. — A289

1995, June 29

1088 A289 70fr multicolored .35 .25
1089 A289 200fr multicolored 1.10 .50

Nos. 1088-1089 also exist in souvenir sheet of 1.

Fish A290

Designs, 25fr, 300fr, Auchenoglanis. 30fr, 50fr, Chrisicntys.

1995, June 22

1090-1093 A290 Set of 4 2.75 .90

Entertainers A291

Designs: 300fr, Freddie Mercury (Queen). 385fr, Jimi Hendrix. 430fr, Marilyn Monroe. 500fr, Michael Jackson. 600fr, Jerry Garcia (Grateful Dead). 800fr, Elvis Presley.
1500fr, Charlton Heston in "Planet of the Apes." 2000fr, Marilyn Monroe, diff.

1995, July 21

1094-1099 A291 Set of 6 15.00 6.50

Souvenir Sheets

1099B A291 1500fr multicolored 8.25 3.25
1100 A291 2000fr multicolored 10.50 4.25

Nos. 1094-1099 exist in souvenir sheets of 1. No. 1100 is airmail. No. 1099B contains one 51x60mm airmail stamp.

Volleyball, Cent. — A292

1995, Oct. 3 Litho. ***Perf. 13½***

1101 A292 300fr multicolored 1.50 .65

No. 1101 exists in a souvenir sheet of 1. Value $10.

Sports Figures A293

400fr, Andre Agassi, tennis. 500fr, Boris Becker, tennis. 700fr, Ayrton Senna (1960-94) race car driver. 800fr, Michael Schumacher, F-1 world driving champion.
2000fr, Michael Schumacher, diff.

1996, June 20 Litho. ***Perf. 13½***

1102-1105 A293 Set of 4 12.00 5.50

Souvenir Sheet

1106 A293 2000fr multicolored 10.00 4.50

No. 1102-1105 exist in souvenir sheets of 1. Value $30.

1996 Summer Olympic Games, Atlanta A294

Olympic athletes, sites in Atlanta: 170fr, Atlanta-Fulton County Stadium. 300fr, Martin Luther King Memorial. 350fr, Alexander H. Stephens Monument. 600fr, High Museum of Art.
2000fr, Pierre de Coubertin, runner.

1996, June 20

1107-1110 A294 Set of 4 7.50 3.25

Souvenir Sheet

1110A A294 2000fr multicolored 9.50 4.00

No. 1110A contains one 42x51mm stamp.

UN, 50th Anniv. (in 1995) A295

1996, July 15 ***Perf. 14***

1111 A295 5fr "50," emblem, vert. .25 .25
1112 A295 430fr shown 2.25 .90

Nos. 1111-1112 each exist in souvenir sheets of 1. Value, set of two sheets $2.75.

1996 Summer Olympic Games, Atlanta A296

1900 Summer Olympics, Paris: 235fr, Alvin Kraenzlein, vert. 300fr, Paris Stadium. 385fr, Irving Baxter. 430fr, British soccer team.
Past Olympic medalists: No. 1117a, Miruts Yifter, 5,000-meters, 1980. b, Germany, team dressage, 1976. c, Bruce Jenner, decathlon, 1976. d, Mark Gorski, 1000-meter match sprint, 1984. e, Randy Williams, long jump, 1972. f, Shinodu Sekine, judo, 1972. g, Kiyomi Kato, wrestling, 1972. h, Mitsuo Tsukahama, gymnastics, 1976. i, Hartwig Steenken, Germany, 1972.
Each 1000fr: No. 1118, Betty Cuthbert, 100-meters, 1956. No. 1119, Gerhard Stock, javelin, 1936.

1996, July 19

1113-1116 A296 Set of 4 6.00 2.75
1117 A296 200fr Sheet of 9, #a.-i. 8.00 3.50

Souvenir Sheets

1118-1119 A296 Set of 2 8.75 4.00

Olymphilex '96 (Nos. 1113-1116, 1118-1119).

Francophonie, 25th Anniv. (in 1995) — A297

300fr, "25 ANS" surrounded by "1970-1995."

1996, July 22

1120 A297 235fr multicolored 1.00 .50
1121 A297 300fr multicolored 1.50 .60

Nos. 1120-1121 each exist in souvenir sheets of 1. Value, set of two sheets $7.50.

FAO, 50th Anniv. (in 1995) A298

Designs: 10fr, Fish being lifted in net, vert. 385fr, Boy drinking water.

1996

1122 A298 10fr multicolored .25 .25
1123 A298 385fr multicolored 2.00 .75

Nos. 1122-1123 each exist in souvenir sheets of 1. Value, set of two sheets $2.75.

Queen Elizabeth II, 70th Birthday — A299

a, Formal portrait. b, In blue suit. c, In red hat.
1000fr, Balmoral Castle.

1996, July 24 ***Perf. 13½x14***

1124 A299 300fr Strip of 3, #a.-c. 3.75 1.75

Souvenir Sheet

1125 A299 1000fr multicolored 4.50 2.00

Nos. 1124 was issued in sheets of 9 stamps.

Pets — A300

1996 Litho. ***Perf. 13½***

1126 A300 250fr Dog 1.25 .60
1127 A300 600fr Cat 3.00 1.40

Nos. 1126-1127 exist in souvenir sheets of 1.

1998 World Cup Soccer Championships, France — A301

Winning country, year, player: No. 1128a, Uruguay 1930, Pedro Cea (Argentina), Italy 1934. b, Italy 1938, Piola (Italy), Uruguay 1950. c, Germany 1954, Brazil 1958, Walter, (Germany). d, Amarildo, (Brazil), Brazil 1962, England 1966.
No. 1129: a, Brazil 1970, Pele (Brazil), Germany 1974. b, Kempes (Argentina), Argentina 1978, Italy 1982. c, Argentina 1986, Mattaus (Germany), Germany 1990. d, Platini (France), Brazil 1994.

1996 Litho. ***Perf. 13½***

1128 A301 375fr Sheet of 4, #a.-d. 7.25 3.25
1129 A301 425fr Sheet of 4, #a.-d. 8.25 3.75

Dinosaur Eggs — A302

Denomination at: a, LR. b, LL.

1996, Apr. 28

1130 A302 140fr Pair, #a.-b. 2.10 .65
c. Souv. Sheet, #1130a-1130b 3.00 .65

CHINA '96 (No. 1130c).

Scouting A303

Raptors, butterflies, mushrooms: 175fr, Buzzard. 200fr, H. misippus. 300fr, Lepiota aspera. 350fr, Raptor with feathers ruffled. 450fr, Amanita caesarea. 500fr, Morpho portis-nymphalidae.

1996 Litho. ***Perf. 13½***

1131-1136 A303 Set of 6 10.00 4.50

Nos. 1132-1133, 1135-1136 exist in souvenir sheets of 1.

Horses — A304

No. 1137, 235fr: a, Appaloosa. b, Arabian. c, Quarter horse. d, Belgian. e, Pure blood English. f, Mustang. g, Haflinger. h, Welsh pony.
No. 1138, 235fr: a, Pinto. b, Palomino. c, Welara. d, Morgan. e, Standard American. f, Norwegian fjord. g, Shetland. h, Shire.
1000fr, Saddlebred.

1996, Nov. 20 *Perf. 14*

Sheets of 8, #a-h

1137-1138 A304 235fr Set of 2 16.00 7.50

Souvenir Sheet

1139 A304 1000fr multicolored 4.50 2.25

Great Nebula, Andromeda — A305

Designs: b, Halley's Comet. c, Jupiter. d, Saturn. e, Moon. f, Mars.

1996, Nov. 22

1140 A305 300fr Sheet of 6, #a.-f. 8.00 3.50

Wildlife — A306

Flowers: a, Bomax costatum. b, Clappertonia flcifolia. c, Canarina abyssinica. d, Kigelia africana. e, Adenium obesum. f, Oncoba spinosa. g, Orinum ornatum. h, Gloriosa simplex. i, Strophanthus gratus.
Bird: 1500fr, Sagittarius serpentarius.

1997, Feb. 6 **Litho.** *Perf. 14*

1141 A306 205fr Sheet of 9, #a.-i. 8.25 3.75

Souvenir Sheet

1142 A306 1500fr multicolored 8.25 3.00

Intl. Express Mail Service A307

300fr, Globe, international express mail routes. 405fr, Emblem of hand holding letter.

1996 **Litho.** *Perf. 13½*

1143 A307 300fr multicolored 1.40 .65
1144 A307 405fr multicolored 1.90 .90

No. 1144 exists in a souvenir sheet of 1.

Human Rights Advocates — A308

Designs: a, Dalai Lama. b, Martin Luther King. c, John F. Kennedy. d, Nelson Mandela. e, Mother Teresa. f, Mahatma Gandhi.

1996

1145 A308 175fr Sheet of 6, #a.-f. + 2 labels 5.00 2.25

Red Cross and Red Crescent Societies — A309

Designs: a, Doctor with patient. b, Man sifting grain. c, Using stethoscope on patient. d, Wounded man. e, Bandaging patient. f, Aiding infant.

1996

1146 A309 250fr Sheet of 6, #a.-f. + 2 labels 7.25 3.25

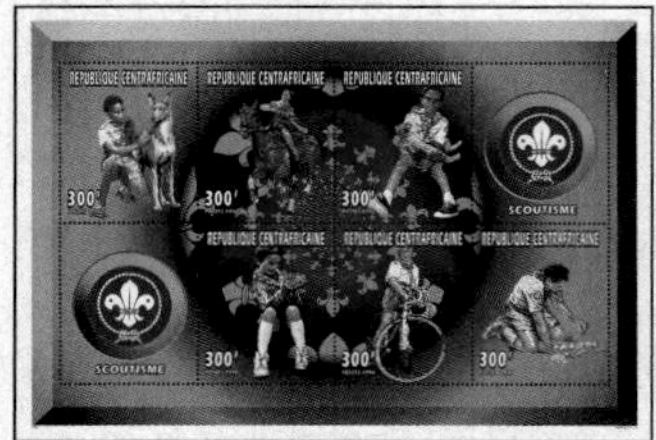

Boy Scouts — A310

Boy scout: a, With dog. b, Riding horse. c, Holding cat. d, Holding butterfly. e, On bicycle. f, Playing game.
Butterfly: 2000fr, Saturnidae, horiz.

1996 **Litho.** *Perf. 13½*

1147 A310 300fr Sheet of 6, #a.-f. + 2 labels 9.00 4.00

Souvenir Sheet

1148 A310 2000fr multicolored 10.00 4.50

No. 1148 contains one 42x36mm stamp.

Lions Intl., Rotary Intl. — A311

Designs: a, Child drinking from cup. b, Child carrying sack. c, Girl holding sheaves of grain. d, Man breaking bread. e, Woman cooking over fire. f, Boy, corn stalk.

1996

1149 A311 500fr Sheet of 6, #a.-f. + 2 labels 14.00 6.50

Flora and Fauna A312

15fr, Cucumis sativus, vert. 20fr, Phyllochistis citrella. 40fr, Cetonia aurata. 65fr, Nomadacris septemfasciata. 100fr, Crocodilus vulgaris. 140fr, Athyrium filix, vert. 405fr, Rhopalo ceres.

1996

1150-1156 A312 Set of 7 5.00 1.75

Nos. 1151, 1156 exist in sourvenir sheets of 1.

UN, UNICEF, 50th Anniv. — A313

Designs: a, Futuristic space vehicle. b, MIR space station. c, US space shuttle, space station. d, Woman carrying food. e, Child receiving vaccination. f, Baby being weighed.

1996

1157 A313 350fr Sheet of 6, #a.-f. + 2 labels 10.00 4.50

Elizabeth Taylor, Actress — A314

Princess Diana — A315

Various portraits.

1997, Apr. 10 **Litho.** *Perf. 14*

1158 A314 300fr Sheet of 6, #a.-f. 8.00 3.50
1159 A315 300fr Sheet of 6, #a.-f. 8.00 3.50

Souvenir Sheets

1160 A314 1500fr multicolored 6.50 3.00
1161 A315 1500fr multicolored 6.50 3.00

For overprints see Nos. 1181-1182.

UNESCO, 50th Anniv. A316

No. 1162, 235fr: a, Fortress ruins, Ethiopia. b, Victoria Falls, Zambia. c, River during dry season, Zimbabwe. d, Nature Reserve, Niger. e, Pelican, Natl. Park, Mauritania. f, Native huts in village, Niokolo-Kobo Natl. Park, Senegal. g, M'Zab Valley, Algeria. h, Mosque, Morocco.

No. 1163, 235fr: a, c, Ruins of Roman Amphitheater, France. b, Split, Croatia. d, e, Quedlinberg, Germany. f, h, Tower of London, England. g, Olympic Natl. Park, US.

No. 1164, 235fr: a, Horyu-Ji, Japan. b, Waterfalls, Amazon River, Los Katios Natl. Park, Colombia. c, Abu Mena Church, Egypt. d, Boat on river, Fortress of Suomenlinna, Finland. e, Venice, Italy. f, Mural, Potala Palace, Lhasa, Tibet, China. g, Cathedral, town of Olinda, Brazil. h, Monastery, Mystras, Greece.

No. 1165, 1000fr, Jiuzhaigou Valley, China. No. 1166, 1000fr, Interior, Pilgrimage Church of Wies, Germany. No. 1167, 1000fr Ruins of Fountains Abbey, Studley Park, England.

1997, Apr. 30 *Perf. 13½x14*

Sheets of 8, #a-h + Label

1162-1164 A316 Set of 3 25.00 12.00

Souvenir Sheets

1165-1167 A316 Set of 3 13.00 6.00

UNICEF, 50th Anniv. — A317

No. 1168: a, 200fr, UN headquarters building. b, 250fr, Baby. c, 500fr, Danny Kaye seated inside vehicle.
1500fr, Child.

1997, Apr. 30 *Perf. 14*

1168 A317 Sheet of 3, #a.-c. 4.00 1.90

Souvenir Sheet

1169 A317 1500fr multicolored 6.50 3.00

US Pres. Bill Clinton and His Cat, "Socks" — A318

Designs: a, b, c, e, g, h, i, Socks in various poses. d, f, Clinton, Socks.

1996

1170 A318 200fr Sheet of 9, #a.-i. 9.00 3.75

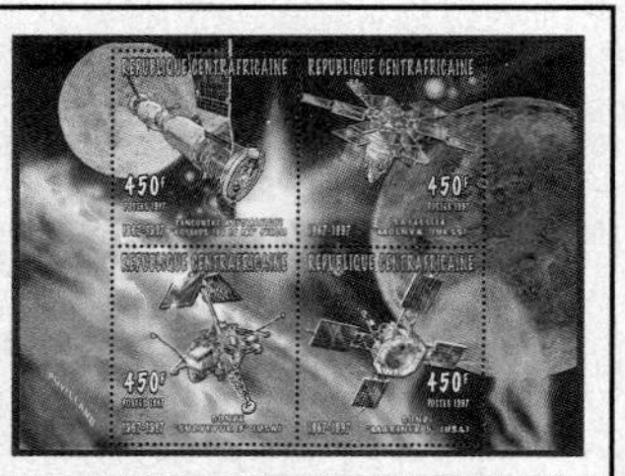

Conquest of Space — A319

Events in 1977: No. 1171: a, Voyager 1, US. b, Space Shuttle Enterprise, US. c, Meteosat 1, US. d, Salyut 6 Space Station, USSR.

Events in 1982: No. 1172: a, Salyut 7 Space Station, USSR. b, Landsat 4 Satellite, US. c, Venera 13, USSR. d, IRAS Infrared Telescope, US.

Events of 1967: No. 1173: a, Cosmos 186 & 188. b, Molniya satellite. c, Surveyor 3. d, Mariner 5.

Events in 1972: No. 1174: a, Copernicus probe, US. b, Pioneer 10, US. c, Apollo 16, US. d, Apollo 17, John F. Kennedy.

Events of 1962: No. 1175: a, Mariner 2, US. b, OSO 1, US. c, John Glenn. d, Mars 1, USSR.

Events of 1957: No. 1176: a, Vostok 1, Yuri Gagarin, USSR. b, Sputnik 2, USSR. c, Sputnik 1, USSR. d, Bell X15, US.

2000fr, Voyager, Pioneer 10, Apollo 11, US.

1997 *Perf. 13½*

1171 A319 250fr Sheet of 4, #a.-d. 5.00 2.00
1172 A319 350fr Sheet of 4, #a.-d. 6.50 3.00
1173 A319 450fr Sheet of 4, #a.-d. 9.00 3.75
1174 A319 500fr Sheet of 4, #a.-d. 10.00 4.00
1175 A319 600fr Sheet of 4, #a.-d. 11.00 5.00

1176 A319 800fr Sheet of 4, #a.-d. 14.50 6.50

Souvenir Sheet

1177 A319 2000fr multicolored 10.00 4.00

No. 1177 contains one 60x30mm stamp.
No. 1173 exists imperf.

Marilyn Monroe (1926-62) — A320

Various portraits.

1997

1178 A320 375fr Sheet of 9, #a.-i. 16.00 6.50

John F. Kennedy (1917-63) — A321

Various portraits.

1997

1179 A321 300fr Sheet of 9, #a.-i. 13.00 5.00

Bruce Lee (1940-73), Actor — A322

Various portraits.

1997 **Litho.** ***Perf. 13½***

1180 A322 200fr Sheet of 9, #a.-i. 9.00 3.25

Nos. 1159, 1161 Ovptd. "In Memoriam"

1997 ***Perf. 14***

1181 A315 300fr Sheet of 6, #a.-f. 8.00 3.50

Souvenir Sheet

1182 A315 1500fr multicolored 7.50 3.00

Nos. 1181-1182 each contain "Diana, Princess of Wales (1961-1997) IN MEMORIAM" in sheet margin and on each stamp in No. 1181.

Dogs & Cats — A323

Dogs: No. 1183: a, Chinese crested. b, King Charles spaniel. c, Dachshund. d, Borzoi. e, Chow chow. f, Welsh springer. g, Rottweiler. h, Keeshond.

Cats: No. 1184: a, Birman. b, Black and white Persian. c, Siamese kitten. d, Red and black. e, American curl. f, Cornish rex. g, Silver shaded. h, White-footed cat.

1500fr, Pekingese. 2000fr, Somali.

1997 **Litho.** ***Perf. 13½***

1183 A323 175fr Sheet of 8, #a.-h. 6.50 2.50
1184 A323 250fr Sheet of 8, #a.-h. 9.00 3.75

Souvenir Sheets

1185 A323 1500fr multicolored 7.50 2.75
1186 A323 2000fr multicolored 10.00 3.75

Nos. 1185-1186 each contain one 42x51mm stamp.

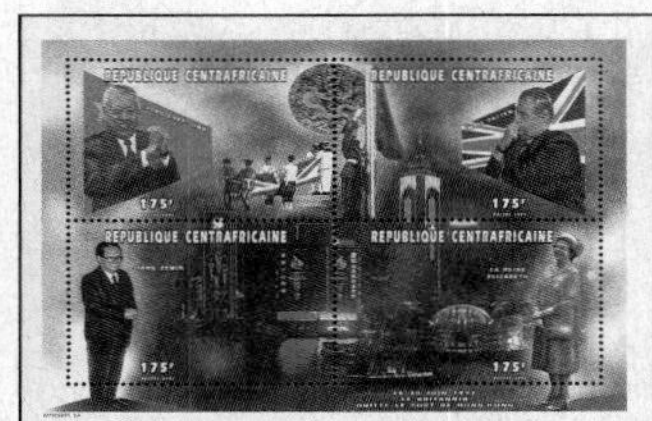

Return of Hong Kong to China — A324

No. 1187: a, Tung Chee-Hwa, taking down British flag. b, Raising Chinese flag, Chris Patten, British flag. c, Jiang Zemin, skyline at night. d, City lights, Queen Elizabeth II.

600fr, Tung Chee-Hwa.

1997

1187 A324 175fr Sheet of 4, #a.-d. 3.25 1.50

Souvenir Sheet

1188 A324 600fr multicolored 3.25 1.25

No. 1188 contains one 38x42mm stamp.

Paintings by Hiroshige (1797-1858) A325

No. 1189: a, Minami-Shinagawa and Samezu Coast. b, Plum Garden, Kamata. c, The Kawaguchi Ferry and Zenkoji Temple. d, Armor-Hanging Pine, Hakkeizaka. e, Robe-Hanging Pine, Senzoku Pond. f, Benten Shrine, Inokashira Pond.

No. 1190: a, A Little Brown Owl on a Pine Branch with a Crescent Moon Behind. b, Sparrows and Camellia in snow. c, Three Wild Geese Flying Downward across the Moon. d, A Blue Bird on a Yellow-flowered Hibiscus. e, Five Swallows in flight.

No. 1191: a, Sparrows and Wild Rose. b, Peonies. c, Morning Glory and Cricket. d, Blossoming Plum Tree. e, Kingfisher above a Yellow-flowered Water Plant.

No. 1192, 1500fr, Haneda Ferry and Benten Shrine. No. 1193, 1500fr, A Bird Clinging to a Tendril of Wisteria. No. 1194, 1500fr, Butterfly and Peony.

1998, Feb. 20 **Litho.** ***Perf. 14***

1189 A325 300fr Sheet of 6, #a.-f. 9.00 3.00
1190 A325 430fr Sheet of 5, #a.-e. 11.00 3.75
1191 A325 500fr Sheet of 5, #a.-e. 9.25 4.25

Souvenir Sheets

1192-1194 A325 Set of 3 18.00 7.50

Nos. 1190-1191 each contain five 26x72mm stamps. Nos. 1192-1194 each contain one 26x72mm stamp.

Chinese Lunar New Year A326

Animals representing lunar year: a, Rat. b, Ox. c, Tiger. d, Hare. e, Dragon. f, Snake. g, Horse. h, Sheep. i, Monkey. j, Rooster. k, Dog. l, Boar.

1000fr, Tiger, diff.

1998 **Litho. & Typo.** ***Perf. 14***

1195 A326 150fr Sheet of 12, #a.-l. 8.00 3.75

Souvenir Sheet

1196 A326 1000fr gold & multi 3.75 1.75

Intl. Scouting, 90th Anniv. — A327

Insects: No. 1196A: b, Apis mellifica. c, Lucanus cervus. d, Oryctes nasicornis. e, Pseudacraea boisduvalii. f, Helictopleurus quadripunctatus, euchroea spininasuta. g, Bombus terrestris. h, Charaxes smaragdalis. i, Euchroea coelestis, mantis religiosa.

Wildlife — No. 1197: a, Coracias caudata, Otocyon megalotis. b, Gnu. c, Milvus aegyptus, pelecanus onocrotalus. d, Panthera leo. e, Loxondonta africana. f, Buffalo. g, Hippopotamus amphibius. h, Acinonyx jubatus.

Raptors — No. 1198: a, Buteo rufinus. b, Circus aeruginosus. c, Aquila verreauxii. d, Circaetus gallicus. e, Terathopius ecaudatus. f, Haliaeetus vocifer. g, Milvus milvus. h, Accipiter badius.

1997(?) **Litho.** ***Perf. 13***

1196A A327 200fr Sheet of 8, #b.-i. 7.00 3.00
1197 A327 300fr Sheet of 8, #a.-h. 10.00 4.50
1198 A327 350fr Sheet of 8, #a.-h. 13.00 5.25

1998 World Cup Soccer Championships, France — A328

Player, country, vert: No. 1199, 300fr, Moore, England. No. 1200, 300fr, Rahn, Germany. No. 1201, 300fr, Paulao, Angola. No. 1202, 300fr, Shearer, England.

No. 1203: a, Seaman, England. b, Schillaci, Italy. c, Romario, Brazil. d, McCoist, Scotland. e, Makanaky, Angola. f, Moore, England. g, Muller, Germany. h, Schmeichel, Denmark.

No. 1204, 1500fr, Moore, England, diff. No. 1205, 1500fr, Pele, Brazil.

1998, June 2 ***Perf. 13½x14, 14x13½***

1199-1202 A328 Set of 4 4.50 2.00
1203 A328 205fr Sheet of 8, #a-h, + label 7.00 7.00

Souvenir Sheets

1204-1205 A328 Set of 2 12.00 12.00

Diana, Princess of Wales (1961-97) — A329

Various portraits.

1998 ***Perf. 13½***

1206 A329 200fr Sheet of 9, #a.-i. 8.00 3.50
1207 A329 250fr Sheet of 9, #a.-i. 10.00 4.50

Diana, Princess of Wales (1961-97) — A330

Diana wearing gowns in one of four seasons: No. 1208, White gown, spring. No. 1209, Blue gown, summer. No. 1210, Bridal gown, fall. No. 1211, High-collared white gown, winter.

1998 **Litho.** ***Perf. 13½***

Souvenir Sheets

1208 A330 1500fr multicolored 7.50 2.50
1209 A330 1500fr multicolored 7.50 2.50
1210 A330 2000fr multicolored 9.00 3.50
1211 A330 2000fr multicolored 9.00 3.50

Nos. 1208-1211 each contain one 50x60mm stamp.

Jacqueline Kennedy Onassis (1929-94) A331

Various portraits.

1997 **Litho.** ***Perf. 13½***

1212 A331 250fr Sheet of 9, #a.-i. 10.50 4.25

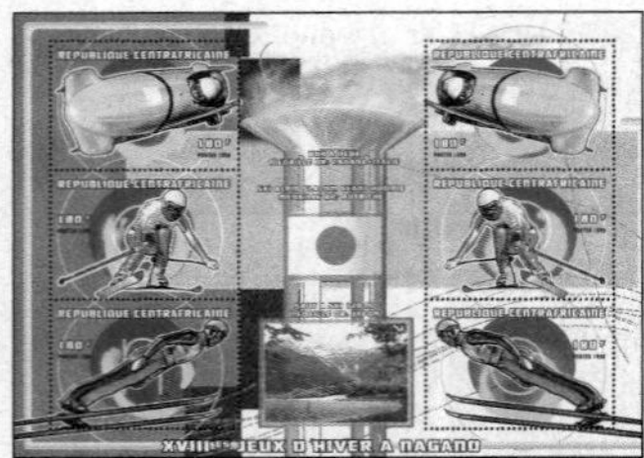

1998 Winter Olympic Games, Nagano — A332

Mirror images of vignette with different backgrounds, denomination at — No. 1213: a, Bobsled, LR. b, Slalom skier, CL. c, Ski jumper, CL. d, Bobsled, LL. e, Slalom skier, CR. f, Ski jumper, CR.

No. 1214: a, Ice hockey, LR. b, Cross-country skier, CR. c, Speed skater, LR. d, Ice hockey, LL. e, Cross-country skier, CL. f, Speed skater, LL.

No. 1215: a, Snow boarding, UR. b, Downhill skier, CR. c, Pairs figure skating, CR. d, Snow boarding, UL. e, Downhill skier, CL. f, Pairs figure skating, CL.

No. 1216, Cross-country, freestyle skiers.

1998

1213 A332 180fr Sheet of 6, #a.-f. 4.00 1.75
1214 A332 300fr Sheet of 6, #a.-f. 7.00 3.00
1215 A332 350fr Sheet of 6, #a.-f. 8.25 3.75

Souvenir Sheet

1216 A332 2000fr multicolored 9.25 3.50

Sports — A333

No. 1217 — Cyclists: a, Woman wearing helmet. b, Woman in pink, white & black outfit. c, Man in black & white outfit. d, Man in yellow & black outfit.

No. 1218 — Female tennis players: a, Holding racket above head. b, Wearing black head band. c, Wearing white head band. d, Wearing dreadlocks.

No. 1219 — Male tennis players: a, Holding racket with his right hand. b, In blue shirt, shorts. c, Holding racket behind head. d, Wearing cap backwards.

No. 1220 — Golfers: a, Completing swing. b, Hitting ball in sand trap. c, In orange knickers, argyle socks. d, Lining up putt.

1998 **Litho.** ***Perf. 13½***

1217 A333 350fr Sheet of 4, #a.-d. 6.50 3.00
1218 A333 375fr Sheet of 4, #a.-d. 7.50 3.50
1219 A333 450fr Sheet of 4, #a.-d. 8.50 3.50
1220 A333 500fr Sheet of 4, #a.-d. 9.00 3.50

Mickey Mouse, 70th Birthday A334

Scenes from various Disney films drawn by Floyd Gottfredson.

No. 1221: a, 10/78. b, 11/78. c, 3/79. d, 7/79. e, 9/79.

No. 1222: a, 10/79. b, 2/80. c, 4/80. d, 6/80. e, 7/80.

No. 1223: a, 11/80. b, 3/81. c, 6/81. d, 9/81. e, 3/82.

No. 1224: a, 5/82. b, 7/82. c, 10/82. d, 3/83. e, 5/83.

No. 1225, 1500fr, Mickey with camera, flashlight. No. 1226, 1500fr, Mickey with pearl in box. No. 1227, 2000fr, Mickey and magic lamp. No. 1228, 2000fr, Floyd Gottfredson.

Perf. 13½x14, 14x13½

1999, Feb. 10 **Litho.**

1221 A334 280fr Sheet of 5, #a.-e., + label 7.00 3.00
1222 A334 365fr Sheet of 5, #a.-e., + label 9.00 3.50
1223 A334 390fr Sheet of 5, #a.-e., + label 10.00 4.00
1224 A334 440fr Sheet of 5, #a.-e., + label 11.00 4.00

Souvenir Sheets

1225-1226 A334 1500fr Set of 2 15.00 5.00
1227-1228 A334 2000fr Set of 2 20.00 6.50

Birds of Africa — A335

Designs: No. 1229, 500fr, Pandion haliaetus. No. 1230, 500fr,Chaetops frenatus. No. 1231, 500fr, Tachymarptis melba. No. 1232, 500fr, Ceratogymna bucinator. No. 1233, 500fr, Laniarius atrococcineus. No. 1234, 500fr, Coturnix coturnix.

No. 1235: a, Lamprotornis superbus. b, Agapornis personatus. c, Coracias spatulata. d, Euplectes jacksoni. e, Nectarinia violacea. f, Emberiza schoeniclus. g, Pica pica. h, Tauraco erythrolophus. i, Sitta europaea.

No. 1236: a, Merops apiaster. b, Coracias garrulus. c, Cuculus canorus. d, Hirundo rustica. e, Motacilla flava. f, Ardea cinerea. g, Falco tinnunculus. h, Tyto alba. i, Charadrius hiaticula.

1500fr, Eremophila alpestris. 2000fr, Delichon urbica.

1999, Mar. 10 **Litho.** ***Perf. 14***

1229-1234 A335 Set of 6 11.00 5.00
1235 A335 280fr Sheet of 9, #a.-i. 9.25 4.25
1236 A335 490fr Sheet of 9, #a.-i. 16.00 7.50

Souvenir Sheets

1237 A335 1500fr multicolored 5.50 2.50
1238 A335 2000fr multicolored 7.50 3.50

World Wildlife Fund — A336

Balaeniceps rex: a, Eating fish. b, Up close. c, Standing. d, One in flight, one up close.

1999

1239 A336 200fr Strip of 4, #a.-d. 5.00 4.00

No. 1239 was issued in sheets of 16 stamps.

Trains A337

No. 1240: a, 40fr, 2-4-0 Steam locomotive. b, 50fr, German Mallat. c, 60fr, Shunting locomotive. d, 260fr, Rhodesian 14A 2-6-2+2-6-2 Garrat. e, 280fr, Steam train. f, 390fr, Engine No. 7, 0-6-0 Baldwin, 1920. g, 440fr, Amtrak passenger train. h, 460fr, German TEE diesel. i, 490fr, "Sir Nigel Gresley."

No. 1241: a, 40fr, Steam train. b, 50fr, 4-4-0, LNWR, 1897. c, 60fr, 2-4-0 locomotive, Midland. d, 260fr, Class XC. e, 280fr, 2-6-0T Sernada and Aveiro, 1910. f, 390fr, East Daggafontein Mines train, Great Britain. g, 440fr, Union Pacific. h, 460fr, Engine No. 6, Baldwin. i, 490fr, 4-4-2 aerodynamic train, Belgium, 1939.

No. 1242, 2000fr, Fairlie, Snake and Auckland, New Zealand, 1874. No. 1243, 2000fr, Steam train arriving at the London-Brighton Depot.

1999, Mar. 11 **Sheets of 9**

1240-1241 A337 Set of 2 25.00 10.00

Souvenir Sheets

1242-1243 A337 Set of 2 18.00 6.50

Prehistoric Animals — A338

No. 1244: a, Archaeopteryx. b, Stegosaurus. c, Placerias. d, Rutiodon. e, Tyrannosaurus rex. f, Lystrosaurus.

No. 1245: a, Spinosaurus. b, Cynognathus. c, Kuehneosaurus. d, Compsognathus. e, Triceratops. f, Euoplocephalus.

2000fr, Desmatosuchus.

1998 **Litho.** ***Perf. 13½***

1244 A338 250fr Sheet of 6, #a.-f. 7.50 2.75
1245 A338 300fr Sheet of 6, #a.-f. 8.50 3.25

Souvenir Sheet

1246 A338 2000fr multicolored 9.00 3.75

No. 1246 contains one 51x36mm stamp.

Transportation — A339

No. 1247 — Antique automobiles: a, 1899 Fiat. b, First Chevrolet. c, Serpolet steam carriage. d, 130HP Fiat.

No. 1248 — Cyclists: a, Swiss rider. b, US rider. c, Miguel Indurain (riding to right). d, Jan. Ullrich (riding to left).

No. 1249 — Sports cars: a, Porsche Boxster. b, Corvette. c, Jaguar S-type. d, Maserati 3200 GT.

No. 1250 — High-speed trains: a, TGV Atlantique. b, Shin Kansen. c, ETR X-500. d, Advanced passenger train.

No. 1251 — Trains: a, Cornish Riviera Express. b, Lancashire and Yorkshire Railway. c, Type 230. d, Pacific Mallard.

No. 1252 — Fire trucks: a, 1916 Seagrave. b, 1927 Ahrens-Fox Model JS-2. c, 1992 Diesel. d, 1958 Mack Bulldog, Type B-95.

No. 1253 — Space flight of John Glenn: a, Portrait in business suit. b, In Project Mercury spacesuit. c, In shuttle launch suit, 1998. d, Orbiting earth, Space Shuttle.

No. 1254 — Supersonic airplanes: a, Boeing 2707. b, Transatmospheric prototype. c, Tupolev 144. d, Project of European Supersonic ESRP.

1998

1247 A339 300fr Sheet of 4, #a.-d. 6.00 3.00
1248 A339 350fr Sheet of 4, #a.-d. 6.50 2.50
1249 A339 400fr Sheet of 4, #a.-d. 8.00 3.00
1250 A339 450fr Sheet of 4, #a.-d. 9.00 3.50
1251 A339 500fr Sheet of 4, #a.-d. 9.00 3.75
1252 A339 600fr Sheet of 4, #a.-d. 11.00 4.50
1253 A339 800fr Sheet of 4, #a.-d. 15.00 6.00
1254 A339 1000fr Sheet of 4, #a.-d. 20.00 7.50

Scouting — A340

No. 1255 — Scouts with flowers: a, Vanilla planifolia. b, Flamboyant. c, Angraecum sesquipedale.

No. 1256 — Scouts with butterflies or bird: a, Hesperie a bande. b, Philepitte souimanga. c, Dryope.

No. 1257 — Scouts with dogs, cats, and their young: a, Basenji. b, Egyptian mau cat. c, White dog.

No. 1258 — Scouts with minerals: a, Tourmaline. b, Jasper. c, Madgascar corundum.

No. 1259 — Scouts administrering Red Cross aid: a, Girl Scout wiping child's tears. b, Scout bandaging child. c, Scout kneeling to help child.

No. 1260 — Scouts in leisure activities: a, Playing table tennis. b, Playing chess. c, Riding horse.

1998 **Litho.** ***Perf. 13½***

1255 A340 400fr Sheet of 3, #a.-c. 6.00 2.25
1256 A340 475fr Sheet of 3, #a.-c. 7.00 2.50
1257 A340 500fr Sheet of 3, #a.-c. 8.00 2.75
1258 A340 600fr Sheet of 3, #a.-c. 9.00 3.25
1259 A340 700fr Sheet of 3, #a.-c. 10.00 3.75
1260 A340 800fr Sheet of 3, #a.-c. 10.00 4.50

Minerals — A341

No. 1261: a, Hematite (red). b, Challophyllite. c, Fer natif. d, Sylvanite. e. Hematite (specularite). f, Spodumene.

No. 1262: a, Amber. b, Opal. c, Struvite. d, Rhodochrosite. e, Polybasite. f, Silver.

1998 **Litho.** ***Perf. 13½***

1261 A341 400fr Sheet of 6, #a.-f. 12.00 4.50
1262 A341 600fr Sheet of 6, #a.-f. 17.00 6.75

A number has been reserved for a souvenir sheet to go with this set.

Mushrooms A342

40fr, Jelly babies. 50fr, Herald of winter. 65fr, Dentate elf cup. 280fr, Pink wax cap. 345fr, Tripe fungus. 465fr, Funnel tooth. 485fr, Common white saddle. 600fr, False morel.

No. 1272: a, Parrot wax cap. b, Orange naval cap. c, Amethyst deceiver. d, Plums and custard. e, Blue legs. f, Tawny funnel cap. g, Goblet. h, Spindle-shank. i, Buttery tough shank.

No. 1273: a, Fetid mummy cap. b, Stainer. c, Lilac bonnet. d, Firm-fleshed brittle gill. e, Fly agaric. f, Arched bonnet. g, King bolete. h, Orange birch bolete. i, Dog stinkhorn.

1500fr, Hedgehog puffball. 2000fr, Striated earth star.

1999, June 11 **Litho.** ***Perf. 14***

1264-1271 A342 Set of 8 9.50 4.25
1272 A342 390fr Sheet of 9, #a.-i. 15.00 6.50

1273 A342 440fr Sheet of 9, #a.-i. 20.00 6.75

Souvenir Sheets

1274 A342 1500fr multicolored 9.00 4.00
1275 A342 2000fr multicolored 11.00 5.00

Birds — A343

No. 1276: a, Psittacula himalayama. b, Anodorhynchus hyacinthinus. c, Trichoglossus haematodus. d, Xipholena punicea. e, Chloebia gouldiae. f, Ramphastos tucanus.
No. 1277: a, Falco sparverius. b, Polyborus plancus. c, Terathopius ecaudatus. d, Tyto alba. e, Glaucidium passerinum. f, Speotyto cunicularia.

1999 Litho. *Perf. 13½*

1276 A343 350fr Sheet of 6, #a.-f. 12.00 5.00
1277 A343 500fr Sheet of 6, #a.-f. 17.50 7.00

Dogs, Cats, & Horses A344

Designs: 60fr, Doberman, vert. 280fr, Domestic cat, vert. No. 1280, 390fr, Korat, vert. No. 1281, 390fr, Hanoverian, vert. 440fr, Ardennais. 490fr, Lhasa apso.
Dogs — No. 1284: a, Alaskan malamute. b, Musterlander. c, German shepherd. d, Borzoi. e, Afghan hound. f, Irish terrier. g, Komondor. h, Finnish spitz.
Cats — No. 1285: a, American bobtail. b, American curl. c, Singapura. d, Burmese. e, Tortoise shell. f, Scottish fold. g, British shorthair blue. h, Turkish van.
Horses — No. 1286: a, Shire. b, Clydesdale. c, Arabian. d, Soviet work horse. e, Finnish work horse. f, Percheron. g, Draco. h, North Swedish.
No. 1287, 2000fr, Beagle. No. 1288, 2000fr, Havana. No. 1289, 2000fr, Hanoverian.

1999, July 9 Litho. *Perf. 14*

1278-1283 A344 Set of 6 9.50 5.00
1284 A344 465fr Sheet of 8, #a.-h. 16.00 9.00
1285 A344 485fr Sheet of 8, #a.-h. 16.00 8.00
1286 A344 515fr Sheet of 8, #a.-h. 16.00 9.00

Souvenir Sheets

1287-1289 A344 Set of 3 24.00 10.50

Nos. 1287-1289 each contain one 44x56mm stamp.

Butterflies A345

Designs: 40fr, Heliconius melpomene. 65fr, Large oak blue. 280fr, Danaus chrysippus. 345fr, Aricia agestis. 485fr, Danis danis. 600fr, Plebejus argus.
No. 1296: a, Delias mysis. b, Ornithoptera priamus. c, Phoebis philea. d, Heliconius doris. e, Thecla coronata f, Lycaena dispar. g, Bematistes aganise. h, Pereute leucodrosime.
No. 1297: a, Colotis danae. b, Eueides isabella. c, Papilio cresphontes. d, Mimacraea marshalli. e, Parathyma nefte. f, Appias nero. g, Uraneis ucubis. h, Eurema brigitta.
No. 1298: a, Heliconius melpomene, diff. b, Mylothris chloris. c, Catopsilia florella. d, Hebomoia glaucippe. e, Palla ussheri. f, Papilio glaucus. g, Colias erytheme. h, Euploea corus.
No. 1299, 1500fr, Unnamed. No. 1300, 1500fr, Papilio, glaucus, vert.

1999, Dec. Litho. *Perf. 14*

1290-1295 A345 Set of 6 9.00 3.25
1296 A345 280fr Sheet of 8, #a.-h. 12.50 5.00
1297 A345 390fr Sheet of 8, #a.-h. 16.00 6.00
1298 A345 465fr Sheet of 8, #a.-h. 19.00 6.50

Souvenir Sheets

1299-1300 A345 Set of 2 15.00 6.00

Trains A346

Designs: No. 1301, 280fr, Le Capitole, France. No. 1302, 390fr, Montreaux-Bern Line, Switzerland. No. 1303, 485fr, Zugspitzbahn, Switzerland. No. 1304, 485fr, Rhatische Bahn, Swizerland.
No. 1305: a, Schwebebahn, Germany. b, Reichsbahn Class 44, Germany. c, Rembrandt, Germany. d, Trans-Europe Express, Germany. e, Inter-city, Germany. f, Steam locomotive, Germany.
No. 1306: a, ETR300, Italy. b, Mistral, France. c, ER200, Russia. d, Pendoline, Italy. e, Class 1100, Netherlands. f, Rheingold Express, Germany.
No. 1307, 1500fr, TGV, France. No. 1308, 1500fr, Austrian train.

2000, Jan. 25

1301-1304 A346 Set of 4 8.50 3.00
1305 A346 280fr Sheet of 6, #a.-f. 9.00 3.00
1306 A346 390fr Sheet of 6, #a.-f. 12.00 4.25

Souvenir Sheets

1307-1308 A346 Set of 2 17.50 5.00

Flowers — A347

No. 1309: a, Orchid, b, Water crinum. c, Flame lily. d, Narcissus poeticus. e, Belladonna lily. f, Table Mountain orchid. g, Upland cotton. h, Narcissus jonquilla.
No. 1310: a, Moore's crinum. b, Cyrtanthus brachyscyphus. c, Namaqualand daisy. d, "Narcissus poeticus," diff. e, Painted homeria. f, Helen O'Connor. g, Pink oxalis. h, Pink oxalis and pink arum.
No. 1311: a, Yellow wild iris. b, White arum lily (mountains in background). c, Blue tulip. d, Osteospermum. e, Table Mountain orchid, diff. f, White arum lily (with stems and leaves). g, Daisy. h, Meadow saffron.
No. 1312, 1500fr, Amaryllis belladonna, horiz. No. 1313, 1500fr, African tulip tree, horiz. No. 1314, 1500fr, Bird of paradise, horiz.

2000, Feb. 24

1309 A347 280fr Sheet of 8, #a.-h. 12.00 3.50
1310 A347 390fr Sheet of 8, #a.-h. 16.00 4.75
1311 A347 515fr Sheet of 8, #a.-h. 20.00 6.00

Souvenir Sheets

1312-1314 A347 Set of 3 22.50 8.00

Inscription on No. 1310d is incorrect.

Birds A348

Designs: 100fr, Dendrocygna bicolor, vert. 150fr, Tockis flavirostris, vert. 200fr, Treron calva. 300fr, Ardeola ralloides. 450fr, Passer melanus, vert. 750fr, Sturnus vulgaris, vert.
No. 1321, vert.: a, Trachyphonus vaillantii. b, Polyhierax semitorquatus. c, Tockus nasutus. d, Estrilda astrild. e, Merops persicus. f, Amandava subflava. g, Guttera pucherani. h, Oriolus oriolus. i, Bycanistes brevis.
No. 1322: a, Butoides striatus. b, Limnocorax flavirostra. c, Terathopius ecaudatus. d, Mycteria ibis. e, Actophilornis africanus. f, Poicephalus rueppellii. g, Alopochen aegyptiacus. h, Morus capensis. i, Sagittarius serpentarius.
No. 1323: a, Gyps africanus. b, Tyto alba. c, Pelecanus onocrotalus. d, Ephippiorhynchus senegalensis. e, Ardea goliath. f, Sylvia communis. g, Buteo rufofuscus. h, Parus caeruleus. i, Dromas ardeola.
No. 1324, 2000fr, Buphagus africanus. No. 1325, 2000fr, Haliaeetus vocifer. No. 1326, 2000fr, Erythropgia coryphaeus, vert.

2000, Feb. 25

1315-1320 A348 Set of 6 8.50 3.00
1321 A348 390fr Sheet of 9, #a.-i. 16.00 5.25
1322 A348 440fr Sheet of 9, #a.-i. 18.00 6.00
1323 A348 485fr Sheet of 9, #a.-i. 18.00 6.50

Souvenir Sheets

1324-1326 A348 Set of 3 27.50 10.00

Aviation A349

Designs: 280fr, Spirit of St. Louis. 345fr, Hindenburg. 465fr, Flight at Kitty Hawk. 485fr, AH-1 Cobra.
No. 1331: a, Fokker triplane. b, Spad XIII. c, Blériot XI. d, Nieuport 12. e, Sopwith Camel. f, 1920s US Mail plane. g, Otto Lilienthal's hang glider. h, Hydrogen-filled balloon of J. A. C. Charles.
No. 1332: a, Mitchell-B25. b, P-38E Lightning. c, Vought F-4U Corsair. d, Mitsubishi Zero. e, B-17 Flying Fortress. f, P-51 Mustang. g, Flying Tiger plane. h, Messerschmitt Bf-109.
No. 1333: a, X-1. b, B-52C. c, Boeing 707. d, F-16C. e, Sabre jet. f, MiG-15. g, F-4 Phantom. h, F-117A Stealth.
No. 1334, 1500fr, Concorde. No. 1335, 1500fr, Space shuttle "Enterprise."

2000, Feb. 28

1327-1330 A349 Set of 4 7.50 2.40
1331 A349 345fr Sheet of 8, #a.-h. 13.00 4.25
1332 A349 390fr Sheet of 8, #a.-h. 14.50 4.75
1333 A349 515fr Sheet of 8, #a.-h. 19.00 6.25

Souvenir Sheets

1334-1335 A349 1500fr Set of 2 13.00 5.00

Chess Players — A350

No. 1336, 280fr: a, Otto IV of Brandenburg. b, Mme. de Verzu and Chevalier de Bourgogne. c, Chess Players by Estienne Porcher. d, Fresco by F. Pella.
No. 1337, 300fr: a, Two Nobles. b, Depiction from book of Jean Wauquelin. c, Girolamo de Cremona. d, Ashtapada.
No. 1338, 390fr: a, Ulysses and Palamedes. b, Christian cavalier and Muslim. c, Two Moorish women. d, Burzurgmikhr and Kannuja.
No. 1339, 465fr: a, Two men, 18th Cent. b, Napoleon and Cornwallis. c, Adolf Anderssen and Wilhelm Steinitz. d, Queen Victoria.
No. 1340, 485fr: a, Two women. b, Chess on an enlarged board. c, Xerxes. d, King Evil-Merodach.
No. 1341, 515fr: a, King Henry VIII of England. b, Queen Elizabeth I of England. c, King Charles I of England. d, Russian czarevitch.

1999 Litho. *Perf. 13½*

Sheets of 4, #a-d

1336-1341 A350 Set of 6 45.00 18.00

Cosmonauts and Astronauts — A351

No. 1342, 485fr: a, Vladimir Soloviev. b, Georgi Beregovoy. c, Alexei Leonov. d, Pavel Popovich. e, Yuri Gagarin. f, Valentina Tereshkova. g, Helena Kondakova. h, Gherman Titov. i, Alexander Volkov.
No. 1343, 515fr: a, Neil Armstrong. b, Edwin Aldrin. c, Michael Collins. d, Alan Bean. e, James Lovell. f, Alan Shepard. g, David Scott. h, John Young. i, Eugene Cernan.
2000fr, Armstrong and Gagarin, horiz.

1999 Sheets of 9, #a-i

1342-1343 A351 Set of 2 35.00 14.00

Souvenir Sheet

1344 A351 2000fr multi 9.00 3.25

No. 1344 contains one 60x51mm stamp.

Millennium — A352

2000, Mar. 31 *Perf. 14*

1345 A352 515fr multicolored 2.50 1.00

Issued in sheets of six.

2000 Summer Olympics, Sydney — A353

No. 1346, 300fr: a, Individual dressage. b, Rhythmic gymnastics. c, Women's 100-meter hurdles. d, Cycling.
No. 1347, 485fr: a, Tennis. b, Diving. c, Soccer. d, Pole vault.
No. 1348, 750fr: a, Long jump. b, Judo. c, Basketball. d, Show jumping.
No. 1349, 800fr: a, Boxing. b, Table tennis. c, Women's 200-meter sprint. d, Individual three-day equestrian event.

2000 *Perf. 13½*

Sheets of 4, #a-d

1346-1349 A353 Set of 4 40.00 15.00

2002 Winter Olympics, Salt Lake City — A354

No. 1350, 280fr: a, Freestyle skiing. b, Cross-country skiing. c, Bobsled. d, Men's slalom.

No. 1351, 390fr: a, Luge. b, Women's ski relay. c, Downhill skiing. d, Short track skating.

No. 1352, 465fr: a, Women's figure skating. b, Hockey. c, Ski jumping. d, Biathlon.

No. 1353, 515fr, a, Pairs figure skating. b, Women's giant slalom. c, Speed skating. d, Nordic combined.

2000 **Sheets of 4, #a-d**

1350-1353 A354 Set of 4 30.00 12.00

UPU, 125th Anniv. — A355

UPU emblem and various men: 280fr, 300fr, 390fr, 465fr, 485fr, 515fr, 750fr, 800fr.

2000, Sept. 8 **Litho.** ***Perf. 13¼***

1354-1361 A355 Set of 8 18.00 6.50

Millennium — A356

No. 1362: a, Roald Amundsen, first polar exploration by dirigible, 1926. b, Vladimir Zworykin, inventor of television camera, 1928. c, Sir Alexander Fleming, discoverer of penicillin, 1928.

No. 1363: a, Henri Dunant, 1901 Nobel Peace prize winner. b, Wilbur and Orville Wright, first airplane, 1903. c, Enrico Caruso, opera singer.

No. 1364: a, Theodore Roosevelt, opening of Panama Canal, 1914. b, Albert Einstein, theory of general relativity, 1916. c, Battle of Verdun, 1916.

No. 1365: a, Auguste Piccard, flight to stratosphere in balloon, 1931. b, Robert Goddard, rocketry pioneer, 1935. c, Ferdinand von Zeppelin and Graf Zeppelin, 1928-37.

No. 1366: a, Felix Eboue, governor of Chad, 1940. b, Mahatma Gandhi, independence of India, 1947. c, Marilyn Monroe (1926-62), actress.

No. 1367: a, Juan Manuel Fangio, race car driver. b, James Dean (1931-55), actor. c, Sputnik 1, 1957.

No. 1368: a, Charles De Gaulle (1890-1970), French general and political leader. b, Yuri Gagarin (1934-68), Soviet Cosmonaut. c, Neil Armstrong (1930-), American Astronaut.

No. 1369: a, Apollo-Soyuz. b, Elvis Presley (1935-77), American entertainer. b, Muhammad Ali (1942-), American boxer.

No. 1370: a, John Young, Space Shuttle, 1981. b, Mikhail Gorbachev, fall of the Berlin Wall, 1989. c, Dalai Lama, 1989 Nobel Peace prize winner.

No. 1371: a, Nelson Mandela, 1993 Nobel Peace prize winner. b, Galileo probe reaches Jupiter, 1995. c, Mars Pathfinder, 1998.

2000, Sept. 28 ***Perf. 13¼***

1362 A356 100fr Sheet of 3, #a-c 1.50 .75
1363 A356 280fr Sheet of 3, #a-c 4.00 1.50
1364 A356 300fr Sheet of 3, #a-c 4.50 2.25
1365 A356 390fr Sheet of 3, #a-c 6.00 2.25
1366 A356 465fr Sheet of 3, #a-c 7.50 3.00
1367 A356 485fr Sheet of 3, #a-c 7.50 3.00
1368 A356 515fr Sheet of 3, #a-c 7.50 3.00
1369 A356 750fr Sheet of 3, #a-c 9.00 4.50
1370 A356 800fr Sheet of 3, #a-c 12.00 4.50
1371 A356 1000fr Sheet of 3, #a-c 15.00 6.50
Nos. 1362-1371 (10) 74.50 31.25

Flora, Dinosaurs and Mushrooms — A357

No. 1372 — Buttlerflies: a, Cymothoe lurida. b, Charaxes lasti. c, Charaxes lactetinctus. d, Charaxes opinatus. e, Charaxes subornatus. f, Coelides hanno.

No. 1373 — Butterflies: a, Charaxes cithaeron. b, Charaxes anticlea. c, Bebearia plistonax. d, Charaxes jahlusa. e, Charaxes acraeoides. f, Bebearia oxione.

No. 1374 — Dinosaurs: a, Compsognathus. b, Kritosaurus. c, Nodosaurus. d, Tuojiangosaurus. e, Homalocephalus. f, Tsintaosaurus.

No. 1375 — Birds: a, Veuve royale. b, Travailleur cardinal. c, Gonolek a ventre rouge. d, Touraco de Schalow. e, Touraco Pauline. f, Souimanga orange.

No. 1376 — Dinosaurs: a, Monoclonius. b, Dryosaurus. c, Anatosaurus. d, Styracosaurus. e, Pinacosaurus. f, Kentrosaurus.

No. 1377 — Birds: a, Bateleur de savanes. b, Corbeau a nuque blanche. c, Corvinelle pie. d, Cordon-bleu violace. e, Fauvette passerinette. f, Crombec a face rousse.

No. 1378 — Mushrooms: a, Lentinus sajorcaju. b, Lentinus velutinus. c, Pleurotus luteoalbus. d, Pluteus congolensis. e, Lentinus crinitus. f, Leucoagaricus ferruginosus.

No. 1379 — Mushrooms: a, Lentinus squarrosulus. b, Phlebopus colossus. c, Lentinus tuberregium. d, Phlebopus sudanicus. e, Phlebopus silvaticus. f, Volvariella congolensis.

No. 1380 — Dogs: a, Briard. b, Pyrenees shepherd. c, Chow chow. d, Cocker spaniel. e, Puli. f, Yorkshire terrier.

No. 1381 — Cats: a, American wirehair. b, California spangled cat. c, Chinchilla. d, Exotic shorthair. e, Selkirk Rex. f, Oriental.

No. 1382 — Dogs: a, Greenland dog. b, Alaskan malamute. c, Samoyed. d, Siberian husky.

2001, May 28 **Litho.** ***Perf. 13¼***

1372 A357 280fr Sheet of 6, #a-f 7.25 3.00
1373 A357 300fr Sheet of 6, #a-f 7.75 3.00
1374 A357 300fr Sheet of 6, #a-f 7.75 3.00
1375 A357 350fr Sheet of 6, #a-f 9.50 3.50
1376 A357 390fr Sheet of 6, #a-f 9.50 4.00
1377 A357 390fr Sheet of 6, #a-f 9.50 4.00
1378 A357 390fr Sheet of 6, #a-f 9.50 4.00
1379 A357 465fr Sheet of 6, #a-f 11.50 4.50
1380 A357 465fr Sheet of 6, #a-f 11.00 4.50
1381 A357 485fr Sheet of 6, #a-f 12.00 4.50
1382 A357 600fr Sheet of 4, #a-d 10.00 4.00
Nos. 1372-1382 (11) 105.25 42.00

Fauna and Fish A358

Designs: 280fr, Salamandra salamandra. No. 1384, 300fr, Epiplatys annualatus. No. 1385, 350fr, Pseudotropheus zebra. 400fr, Trichechus senegalensis. 450fr, Pelomedusa subrufa. 500fr, Xenomystus nigri.

No. 1389, vert.: a, Damaliscus dorcas. b, Manis temmincki. c, Hyaena brunnea. d, Lycaon pictus. e, Diceros bicornis. f, Osteolaemis tetraspis. g, Cercocebus torquatus. h, Bunologus monticularis. i, Myosciurus pumilia.

No. 1390: a, Plotosus lineatus. b, Protopterus dolloi. c, Calamoichthys calabaricus. d, Malapterurus electricus. e, Discoglossus pictus. f, Dugong dugon.

No. 1391, 1500fr, Julidochromis ornatus, vert. No. 1392, 1500fr, Hippopotamus amphibius, vert. No. 1393, 1500fr, Afropavo congensis, vert.

Perf. 13¼x13½, 13½x13¼

2001, July 12

1383-1388 A358 Set of 6 10.00 3.00
1389 A358 300fr Sheet of 9, #a-i 12.50 3.50
1390 A358 350fr Sheet of 6, #a-f 9.50 2.75

Souvenir Sheets

1391-1393 A358 Set of 3 21.00 7.50

Reptiles and Amphibians — A359

No. 1394, 350fr: a, Boa arc-en-ciel. b, Crapaud marine. c, Basilic vert. d, Grenouille taureau. e, Tortue happante. f, Pseudoeurycea leprosa.

No. 1395, 350fr: a, Trionix epinelix. b, Iguane rhinoceros. c, Boa constrictor. d, Boa canin. e, Tortue d'etang. f, Dermophis mexicanus.

No. 1396, 1500fr, Serpent des arbres. No. 1397, 1500fr, Grenouille poison.

2001, July 12 ***Perf. 13¼x13½***

Sheets of 6, #a-f

1394-1395 A359 Set of 2 20.00 5.50

Souvenir Sheets

1396-1397 A359 Set of 2 14.00 6.00

Butterflies — A360

No. 1398, 350fr, vert.: a, Papilio garamus. b, Eunica orphise. c, Parides lysander. d, Julia dryas iulia. e, Adelpha mythra. f, Thecla coronata.

No. 1399, 350fr, vert.: a, Battus polydamas. b, Mesene phareus. c, Anartia jatrophae. d, Siproeta epaphus. e, Uraneis ucubis. f, Pereute leucodrosime.

No. 1400, 1500fr, Prepona meander. No. 1401, 1500fr, Morpho peleides. No. 1402, 1500fr, Pieris rapae. No. 1403, 1500fr, Helconius melpomene.

2001, July 12 ***Perf. 13½x13¼***

Sheets of 6, #a-f

1398-1399 A360 Set of 2 20.00 6.00

Souvenir Sheets

1400-1403 A360 Set of 4 27.50 10.00

Nos. 1398-1399 each contain six 28x42mm stamps.

A361

Birds — A362

Designs: 50fr, Macareux moine. 75fr, Harfang des neiges, vert. 100fr, Manchots, vert. 150fr, Fou à pieds bleus, vert.

No. 1408, 325fr: a, Perruche soleil. b, Toucan de cuvièe. c, Colibri. d, Ara hyacinthe. e, Pione à tete bleue. f, Perruche flavéolée. g, Pelican. h, Flamant rose. i, Toucan toco.

No. 1409, 325fr: a, Touraco à gros bec. b, Martin-chaseur à poitrine bleue. c, Faucon lanier. d, Inséparable masqué. e, Loriquet à tete bleue. f, Perroquet jaco. g, Perenoptere d'Egypte. h, Grue grise couronnée. i, Marabou.

No. 1410, 350fr, vert.: a, Colibri caraibe. b, Jaseur des cèdres. c, Colibri d'abeille. d, Bruant indigo. e, Tourterelle pleureuse. f, Talève pourprée.

No. 1411, 350fr: a, Gros-bec bleu. b, Fauvette à gorge orangée. c, Pic flamboyant. d, Passerin nonpareil. e, Fauvette à capuchon. f, Bananaquit.

No. 1412, 1500fr, Cygne, vert. No. 1413, 1500fr, Pygargue à tete blanche, vert.

No. 1414, 1500fr, shown. No. 1415, 1500fr, Balbuzard, vert.

Perf. 13¼x13½, 13½x13¼

2001, July 19

1404-1407 A361 Set of 4 3.75 1.50

Sheets of 9, #a-i

1408-1409 A361 Set of 2 26.50 8.25

Sheets of 6, #a-f

Perf. 13¼x13, 13x13¼

1410-1411 A362 Set of 2 20.00 6.00

Souvenir Sheets

Perf. 13½x13¼

1412-1413 A361 Set of 2 14.00 5.00

Perf. 13¼

1414-1415 A362 Set of 2 14.00 5.00

No. 1410 contains six 30x40mm stamps; No. 1411 contains six 40x30mm stamps.

Mushrooms
A363

Designs: 550fr, Coltricia montagnei. 600fr, Inocybe fuscodisca. 650fr, Hydnum imbricatum. 700fr, Hygrophorus miniatus.

No. 1420: a, Coprinus picaceus. b, Crinipellis zonata. c, Naematoloma fasciculare. d, Cortinarius caerulescens. e, Amanita muscaria. f, Cortinarius obtusus. g, Entoloma serrulatum. h, Strobilomyces floccopus.

1500fr, Sarcosphaera crassa, horiz.

Perf. 13½x13¼, 13¼x13½

2001, July 26

1416-1419 A363 Set of 4 12.00 3.50
1420 A363 350fr Sheet of 8, #a-h 13.00 4.00

Souvenir Sheet

1421 A363 1500fr multi 7.00 2.50

Prehistoric Animals — A364

Designs: 50fr, Anatasaurus. 100fr, Apatosaurus. 150fr, Allosaurus. 200fr, Velociraptor.

No. 1426, 240fr: a, Rhamphorhynchus. b, Pteranodon. c, Tyrannosaurus rex. d, Deinonychus antirrhopus. e, Parasaurolophus. f, Corythosaurus. g, Patagosaurus. h, Triceratops. i, Brachylophosaurus. j, Europlocephalus. k, Dimetrodon. l, Leptoceratops.

No. 1427, 240fr: a, Perosaur. b, Albertosaurus. c, Dryptosaurus. d, Archaeopteryx. e, Ouranosaurus. f, Myahuera. g, Camptosaurus. h, Ichthyosaurus. i, Geosaurus. j, Trilobita. k, Plesiosaurus. l, Lewisiceras.

No. 1428, 1500fr, Herrerasaurus. No. 1429, 1500fr, Stegosaurus.

2001, July 31 ***Perf. 12½***

1422-1425 A364 Set of 4 2.50 .70

Sheets of 12, #a-l, + 8 labels

1426-1427 A364 Set of 2 27.50 8.25

Souvenir Sheets

1428-1429 A364 Set of 2 14.00 4.25

Dinosaurs
A365

Designs: 250fr, Apatosaurus. 300fr, Baryonyx. 325fr, Albertosaurus. 375fr, Dimetrodon.

No. 1434, 350fr: a, Triceratops. b, Ornithocherius. c, Brachiosaurus. d, Utahraptor. e, Tyrannosaurus rex. f, Stegosaurus.

No. 1435, 350fr: a, Diplodicus. b, Pachycephalosaurus. c, Archaeopteryx. d, Pteranodon. e, Herrerasaurus. f, Struthiomimus.

No. 1436, 1500fr, Rhamphorhynchus. No. 1437, 1500fr, Proleratops and Deinonychus.

2001, July 31 ***Perf. 13¼x13½***

1430-1433 A365 Set of 4 6.00 1.75

Sheets of 6, #a-f

1434-1435 A365 Set of 2 20.00 6.00

Souvenir Sheets

1436-1437 A365 Set of 2 12.00 5.00

Belgica 2001 Intl. Stamp Exhibition, Brussels (Nos. 1434-1437).

2001 Catastrophes — A366

No. 1438: a, Jan. 26 earthquake, India. b, Sept. 11 terrorist attacks, US. c, Dec. 26 fires, Australia. d, Hurricane Michelle, Cuba, Oct. 27. e, July 4 tornado, Canada. f, July 24 eruption of Mt. Etna, Italy.

2002, July 23 ***Perf. 13¼***

1438 A366 390fr Sheet of 6, #a-f 9.00 4.00

Each stamp in sheet exists in a souvenir sheet of 1.

Painters and Paintings — A367

No. 1439, 390fr: a, Claude Monet. b, Woman with an Umbrella, by Monet. c, Argenteuil, by Edouard Manet. d, Manet. e, Joseph Mallord William Turner. f, Mornings Amongst the Conniston Falls, Cumberland, by Turner.

No. 1440, 390fr: a, Girl with a Mandolin, by Pablo Picasso. b, Picasso. c, Georges Braque. d, The Musician, by Braque. e, Woman in Blue, by Fernand Leger. f, Leger.

2002, July 23 **Sheets of 6, #a-f**

1439-1440 A367 Set of 2 17.00 7.00

Chess — A368

No. 1441: a, Board from match between Garry Kasparov and Viswantathan Anand. b, Kasparov. c, Anand. d, Board from match between Anand and Shirov. e, Board from match between Ruslan Ponomariov and Vassily Ivanchuk. f, Ponomariov.

2002, July 23

1441 A368 605fr Sheet of 6, #a-f 13.00 5.50

Each horizontal pair in the sheet exists in a souvenir sheet of 2 stamps.

Cosmonauts — A369

No. 1442: a, Yuri Gagarin, Vostok 1. b, Pavel Vinogradov, Mir 24. c, Valentina Tereshkova, Vostok 6. d, Valeri Kubasov, Apollo-Soyuz. e, Alexei Leonov, Voskhod 2. f, Sergei Treschev, Intl. Space Station.

2002, July 23

1442 A369 605fr Sheet of 6, #a-f 13.00 5.50

Zeppelin NT and Concorde — A370

No. 1443: a, Zeppelin NT over Friedrichshafen, Germany. b, Concorde over Rio de Janeiro. c, Concorde over Alaska. d, Zeppelin NT over Lake Constance. e, Zeppelin NT over Orly Airport, Paris. f, Concorde over New York.

2002, July 23

1443 A370 665fr Sheet of 6, #a-f 15.00 6.00

Each stamp in sheet exists in a souvenir sheet of 1.

Famous People — A371

No. 1444: a, Paul Harris, founder of Rotary International. b, Princess Diana, Intl. Red Cross Ambassador against land mines. c, Pope John Paul II. d, Sir Alexander Fleming. e, Mother Teresa. f, Melvin Jones, founder of Lions Club International.

2002, July 23

1444 A371 665fr Sheet of 6, #a-f 15.00 6.00

Each stamp in sheet exists in a souvenir sheet of 1.

Rotary and Lions Emblems and Animals — A372

No. 1445, 390fr — Turtles: a, Eretmochelys imbricata. b, Lepidochelys olivacea. c, Natator depressa.

No. 1446, 600fr — Dinosaurs: a, Sauropelta. b, Chasmosaurus. c, Herrerasaurus.

2002, Dec. 23 **Sheets of 3, #a-c**
1445-1446 A372 Set of 2 11.00 4.75

Scouts — A373

No. 1447, 605fr — Orchids: a, Dactylorhiza markusii. b, Cephalanthera rubra. c, Neotinea maculata.
No. 1448, 665fr — Mushrooms: a, Agaricus ostreatus. b, Russula virescens. c, Lactarius deliciosus.
No. 1449, 815fr — Dinosaurs: a, Brachiosaurus. b, Sarcosuchus. c, Gigantosaurus carolinii.
No. 1450, 840fr — Minerals: a, Guilleminite. b, Torbernite. c, Bornite.
Nos. 1451-1452A (each 3000fr), Scout playing: Nos. 1451, 1451A, Chess. Nos. 1452, 1452A, Table tennis.

2002, Dec. 23 **Sheets of 3, #a-c**
1447-1450 A373 Set of 4 32.50 14.00

A373a

Litho. & Embossed
Perf. 13½

1451	A373a	gold & multi	9.50	9.50
1451A	A373a	sil & multi	9.50	9.50
1452	A373a	gold & multi	9.50	9.50
1452A	A373a	sil & multi	9.50	9.50
	Nos. 1451-1452A (4)		38.00	38.00

Each stamp in each sheet and Nos. 4151-4152A exists in a souvenir sheet of 1.

Famous People A374

Designs: No. 1453, 485fr, Christopher Columbus (1450-1506), explorer. No. 1454, 485fr, Admiral Horatio Nelson (1758-1805). No. 1455, 605fr, Jacques Cartier (1491-1557), explorer. No. 1456, 605fr, Vladimir Yourkevitch (1885-1964), naval designer. No. 1457, 665fr, Columbus, diff. No. 1458, 665fr, Sir Francis Drake (1540-96), explorer. No. 1459, 815fr, Jean-François Champollion (1790-1832), Egyptologist. No. 1460, 815fr, Queen Mother Elizabeth of England (1900-2002). No. 1461, 840fr, Marilyn Monroe (1926-62), actress. No. 1462, 840fr, Elvis Presley (1935-77), singer. No. 1463, 1000fr, Pres. John F. Kennedy (1917-63). No. 1464, 1000fr, French President Charles de Gaulle (1890-1970).

2003, May 15 **Litho.** ***Perf. 13½***
1453-1464 A374 Set of 12 40.00 16.00

Dated 2002. Each stamp also exists in souvenir sheet of 1.

2004 Summer Olympics, Athens A375

Designs: 390fr, Boxing. 485fr, Basketball. 605fr, Equestrian. 655fr, Tennis. 815fr, Table tennis.

2004, Mar. 3 **Litho.** ***Perf. 13½***
1465-1469 A375 Set of 5 14.00 5.75

Dated 2003. Each stamp also exists in souvenir sheet of 1.

2006 World Cup Soccer Championships, Germany — A376

Various soccer players and stadia: 160fr, 390fr, 485fr, 605fr, 815fr.

2004, Mar. 3 **Litho.** ***Perf. 13½***
1470-1474 A376 Set of 5 9.25 9.25
1474a Horiz. strip of 5, #1470-1474 9.25 9.25

Each stamp also exists in a souvenir sheet of 1.

2004 Summer Olympics, Athens — A376a

Designs: Nos. 1475, 1476, Table tennis. Nos. 1477, 1478, Tennis.

Litho. & Embossed
2004, Mar. 3 ***Perf. 13½***

1475	A376a	3000fr	gold & multi	11.00	11.00
1476	A376a	3000fr	sil & multi	11.00	11.00
1477	A376a	3000fr	gold & multi	11.00	11.00
1478	A376a	3000fr	sil & multi	11.00	11.00
	Nos. 1475-1478 (4)			44.00	44.00

Europa Stamps, 50th Anniv. (in 2006) — A377

Top stamp: 5fr, Netherlands #387. 20fr, Italy #810. 100fr, San Marino #1065. 150fr, Greece #718. 300fr, Italy #1039. 390fr, Italy #916. 465fr, Liechtenstein #368. 485fr, Germany #996. 515fr, Spain #941. 750fr, Finland #419. 800fr, Italy #979. 1500fr, Belgium #840.

2005, Apr. 10 **Litho.** ***Perf. 13½***
1479-1490 A377 Set of 12 22.00 22.00

Gen. François Bozizé, President of Central Africa — A378

2005 ? **Litho.** ***Perf. 13¼***
Frame Color

1491	A378	5fr	olive green	—	—
1492	A378	10fr	reddish purple	—	—
1493	A378	15fr	purple	—	—
1494	A378	20fr	brt blue	—	—
1495	A378	40fr	green	—	—
1497	A378	65fr	olive yellow	—	—
1498	A378	100fr	blue	—	—
1499	A378	150fr	lake brown	—	—
1501	A378	300fr	red	—	—
1502	A378	390fr	yellow green	—	—
1503	A378	485fr	green	—	—
1504	A378	515fr	bister	—	—

Nos. 1498, 1501, 1503 and 1504 are dated 2004. Nos. 1491, 1492, 1493, 1494, 1495, 1497, 1499, 1502 are dated 2006. Two additional stamps were issued in this set. The editors would like to examine any examples.

Pope John Paul II (1920-2005) — A379

Various portraits of Pope John Paul II: 280fr, 1000fr.

2007, Aug. 24 **Litho.** ***Perf. 13¼***
1505-1506 A379 Set of 2 6.00 3.00

Each stamp also exists in a souvenir sheet of 1.

2008 Summer Olympics, Beijing — A380

Designs: 300fr, Chinese female athlete, swimmer. 390fr, Chinese soccer players, stadium. 1000fr, Chinese table tennis players, building.

2007, Apr. 24
1507-1509 A380 Set of 3 7.00 3.50

Each stamp also exists in a souvenir sheet of 1.

Princess Diana (1961-97) — A381

Princess Diana with: No. 1510, 390fr, Mother Teresa. No. 1511, 390fr, Pope John Paul II.

2007, Aug. 24 **Litho.** ***Perf. 13¼***
1510-1511 A381 Set of 2 3.50 3.50

Nos. 1510 and 1511 each exist in souvenir sheets of 1.

Worldwide Fund For Nature (WWF) — A382

Civettictis civetta: 390fr, Standing in grass. 485fr, Adult and juvenile at den. 515fr, Head. 750fr, On branch.

2007, Aug. 24
1512-1515 A382 Set of 4 9.00 9.00

Nos. 1512-1515 exist with printer's inscription at lower left in a souvenir sheet of four. Value, $30.

A386

No. 1522, 650fr — Rhinoceroses: a, Two rhinocersoses facing left. b, Head of rhinoceros facing right, rhinoceros walking left. c, Two rhinoceroses, one facing right, one facing forward. d, Three rhinoceroses.
No. 1523, 650fr — Gorillas: a, Gorilla beringei, adult and juvenile at left, large gorilla at right. b, Gorilla beringei, gorilla in foliage at left, large gorilla at right. c, Gorilla gorilla, large gorilla at left. d, Gorilla beringei, adult and juvenile at left, large gorilla showing teeth at right.
No. 1524, 650fr — Bats: a, Two Rousettus lanosus. b, Three Rousettus lanosus. c, Two Megaloglossus woermanni. d, Two Hipposideros abae.
No. 1525, 650fr — Lions: a, Male and female. b, Two females in tree. c, Three cubs, two playing, one front paws on rock. d, Head of male, cub chewing on stick.
No. 1526, 650fr — Wild cats: a, Felis margarita. b, Pardofelis temminckii. c, Felis silvestris lybica. d, Caracal aurata.
No. 1527, 650fr — Dogs: a, Dogues de Bordeaux. b, Irish terriers. c, Basenjis. d, Boerboels.
No. 1528, 650fr — Elephants: a, Two Loxondonta africana, grass in foreground. b, Two Loxodonta cyclotis, grass in foreground. c, Two Loxodonta africana, elephant with raised trunk at left. d, Loxodonta cyclotis, elephant eating at right..
No. 1529, 650fr — Horses: a, Horse leaping in background. b, Horse running left in background. c, Light brown horses. d, White horse at left, brown horse in background.
No. 1530, 650fr — Dolphins: a, Sousa teuszii, Tursiops truncatus. b,Two Tursiops truncatus, Latin name at LR. c, Two Sousa teuszii. d, Two Tursiops truncatus, latin name at LL.
No. 1531, 650fr — Whales: a, Balaenoptera acutorostrata, Latin name at LL. b, Eubalaena australis. c, Balaenoptera acutorostrata, Latin name at center left. d, Megaptera novaeangliae.
No. 1532, 650fr — Birds of prey: a, Aquila rapax rapax. b, Terathopius ecaudatus. c, Buteo augur. d, Haliaeetus vocifer.
No. 1533, 650fr — Parrots: a, Poicephalus senegalus, Latin name in white. b, Poicephalus rueppellii. c, Psittacus erithacus. d, Poicephalus senegalus, Latin name in black.
No. 1534, 650fr — Peacocks (Afropavo congensis) with Latin name at: a, UR, denomination at LL. b, LL, denomination at top center. c, UR, denomination at right center. d, LR, denomination at UL.
No. 1535, 650fr — Kingfishers: a, Ceryle rudis, Latin name at top. b, Merops apiaster. c, Megaceryle maxima. d, Ceryle rudis, Latin name at right.
No. 1536, 650fr — Owls: a, Asio madagascariensis. b, Asio capensis. c, Bubo africanus. d, Asio flammeus.
No. 1537, 650fr — Owls: a, Scotopelia peli. b, Strix aluco yamadae. c, Scotopelia peli, Strix aluco aluco. d, Strix aluco aluco, denomination at LL.
No. 1538, 650fr — Bees: a, Apis mellifera scutellata and Jean-Henri Fabre (1823-1915), entomologist. b, Apis mellifera monticola and Charles Valentine Riley (1843-95), entomologist. c, Apis mellifera scutellata and Pierre André Latreille (1762-1833), zoologist. d, Apis mellifera scutellata and Léon Provancher (1820-92), naturalist.

No. 1539, 650fr — Beetles: a, Chrysocarabus auronitens, Cleridae. b, Cortodera humeralis, Goliathus goliathus. c, Cleridae. d, Ips typographus, Stictoleptura tripartita.

No. 1540, 650fr — Butterflies: a, Papilio demodocus. b, Phalanta phalantha, Latin name at top center. c, Tarucus thespis. d, Phalanta phalantha, Latin name at left center.

No. 1541, 650fr — Butterflies: a, Tarucus theophrastus, Melanitis leda. b, Catopsilia florella. c, Colotis danae. d, Junonia hierta.

No. 1542, 650fr — Fish: a, Sphyraena barracuda. b, Balistes vetula. c, Pomacanthus imperator. d, Naso elegans.

No. 1543, 650fr — Marine life (Homarus gammarus) and: a, Ostreidae. b, Pecten maximus. c, Tripneustes ventricosus. d, Sepia officinalis.

No. 1544, 650fr — Cacti: a, Opuntia ficus-indica, denomination at UR. b, Opuntia ficus-indica, denomination at LR. c, Brachycereus nesioticus, Rhipsalis baccifera. d, Euphorbia lactea.

No. 1545, 650fr — Orchids: a, Spathoglottis kimballiana and Pierre Marie Auguste Broussonet (1761-1807), naturalist. b, Spathoglottis plicata and Jean-Baptiste de Lamarck (1744-1829), naturalist. c, Eurychone galeandrae and Antoine Gouan (1733-1821), naturalist. d, Eulophia alta and Joseph Pitton de Tournefort (1656-1708), botanist.

No. 1546, 650fr — Minerals: a, Hématite and rutile. b, Limonite, denomination at LL. c, Limonite, denomination at LR. d, Gold.

No. 1547, 650fr — Worldwide Fund for Nature stamps of other countries: a, Botswana #915. b, Niue #730. c, Sierra Leone #588. d, British Antarctic Territory #192.

No. 1548, 2400fr, Two rhinoceroses, diff. No. 1549, 2400fr, Gorilla gorilla and Dian Fossey (1932-85), primatologist. No. 1550, 2400fr, Epomops franqueti. No. 1551, 2400fr, Two male lions. No. 1552, 2400fr, Profelis aurata. No. 1553, 2400fr, Azawakhs. No. 1554, 2400fr, Two elephants, diff. No. 1555, 2400fr, Horse and man. No. 1556, 2400fr, Cephalorhynchus heavisidii. No. 1557, 2400fr, Caperea marginata, Balaenoptera acutorostrata. No. 1558, 2400fr, Aquila nipalensis, Aquila rapax. No. 1559, 2400fr, Poicephalus senegalus, Poicephalus gulielmi. No. 1560, 2400fr, Two Afropavo congensis, diff. No. 1561, 2400fr, Megaceryle maxima, diff. No. 1562, 2400fr, Asio capensis, diff. No. 1563, 2400fr, Strix butleri, Scotopelia peli. No. 1564, 2400fr, Apis mellifera scutellata and Fabre, diff. No. 1565, 2400fr, Phchynoteus, Goliathus goliathus. No. 1566, 2400fr, Belenois aurota and boy with butterfly net. No. 1567, 2400fr, Leptotes pirithous, Eurema hecabe. No. 1568, 2400fr, Ctenochaetus hawaiiensis. No. 1569, 2400fr, Homarus, Venerupis decussata. No. 1570, 2400fr, Opuntia ficus-indica and bat. No. 1571, 2400fr, Eulophia alta and Jean Jules Linden (1817-98), botanist. No. 1572, 2400fr, Quartz and boy. No. 1573, 2400fr, Slovenia #247c.

2011, Dec. 20 Litho. *Perf. 13¼*

Sheets of 4, #a-d

1522-1547 A386 Set of 26 275.00 275.00

Souvenir Sheets

1548-1573 A386 Set of 26 250.00 250.00

A387

No. 1574, 1000fr — Wedding of Prince William and Catherine Middleton: a, Couple. b, Couple and archbishop. c, Couple, vert.

No. 1575, 1000fr — Princess Diana (1961-97): a, Visiting child in Japanese hospital, 1995. b, Visiting child at Mother Teresa Hospice, 1995. c, Holding Camila Fiocco at Northwick Park Hospital, 1997, vert.

No. 1576, 1000fr — Mohandas K. Gandhi (1869-1948), Indian nationalist: a, Leading march, 1931. b, Addressing crowd in Calcutta, 1919. c, With Sarojini Naidu in Salt March, 1930, vert.

No. 1577, 1000fr — Pope John Paul II (1920-2005), papal arms and: a, African animals. b, Map of Africa. c, Tree, vert.

No. 1578, 1000fr — Yuri Gagarin (1934-68), first man in space, and: a, MiG-15. b, His children, monument to Gagarin in Moscow. c, Vostok 1 lifting off, vert.

No. 1579, 1000fr — Marilyn Monroe (1926-62), actress: a, With camera and flag in background. b, With flag stripes in background. c, With mouth open, vert.

No. 1580, 1000fr — Brigitte Bardot, actress, and scene from: a, Viva Maria!, 1965. b, Don Juan, 1973. c, Shalako, 1968, vert.

No. 1581, 1000fr — Romy Schneider (1938-82), actress, and scene from: a, Max and the Junkmen, 1971. b, 10:30 P.M. Summer, 1966. c, Otley, 1968, vert.

No. 1582, 1000fr — Elvis Presley (1935-77), playing guitar, and: a, Denomination at UL. b, Wife, Priscilla, and daughter, Lisa Marie. c, White star in background, vert.

No. 1583, 1000fr — Composers: a, Felix Mendelssohn (1809-47). b, Johann Sebastian Bach (1685-1750). c, Johannes Brahms (1833-97), vert.

No. 1584, 1000fr — Presidents of France: a, Charles de Gaulle (1890-1970). b, Jacques Chirac and Nicolas Sarkozy. c, Georges Pompidou (1911-74), vert.

No. 1585, 1000fr — Nobel Prize winners: a, Ada Yonath, 2009 Chemistry laureate, and ribosome. b, Andre Geim, 2010 Physics laureate, and graphene lattice. c, Elizabeth Blackburn, 2009 Physiology or Medicine laureate, and telomerase, vert.

No. 1586, 1000fr — Impressionist painters and their paintings: a, View of Pontoise: Quai du Pothuis, by Camille Pissarro (1830-1903). b, Flood at Port Marly, by Alfred Sisley (1839-99). c, The Absinthe Drinker, by Edgar Degas (1834-1917), vert.

No. 1587, 1000fr — Entomologists: a, Andrey Avinoff (1884-1949), and Daphnis nerii. b, Eleanor Anne Ormerod (1828-1901), and Junonia orithya. c, Jean-Henri Fabre (1823-1915), and Graphium agamemnon, vert.

No. 1588, 1000fr — Mycologists: a, William Murrill (1869-1957), and Cantharellus aurantiacus. b, Fred Jay Seaver (1877-1970), and Stropharia viridula. c, Arthur Henry Reginald Buller (1874-1944), and Amanita mappa, vert.

No. 1589, 1000fr — Mineralogists: a, Florence Bascom (1862-1945), and kyanite. b, Otto Wilhelm Herrmann von Abich (1806-86), and abichite. c, Auguste Michel-Lévy (1844-1911), and calcaires, vert.

No. 1590, 1000fr — Sports of 2012 Summer Olympics, London: a, Taekwondo. b, Boxing. c, Archery, vert.

No. 1591, 1000fr — Table tennis players: a, Timo Boll. b, Wang Liqin. c, Liu Shiwen, vert.

No. 1592, 1000fr — World chess champions: a, Paul Morphy (1837-84). b, Mikhail Botvinnik (1911-95). c, Alexander Alekhine (1892-1946), vert.

No. 1593, 1000fr — Scouts: a, Five Boy Scouts. b, Boy Scout bugler, Boy Scout with pigeons. c, Boy Scouts adjusting tent, Olave Baden-Powell (1889-1977), vert.

No. 1594, 1000fr — Survivors of the sinking of the Titanic: a, Eva Hart (1905-96). b, Dorothy Gibson (1889-1946). c, Ruth Elizabeth Becker (1899-1990), vert.

No. 1595, 1000fr — New Year 2012 (Year of the Dragon): a, Dragon, denomination at UL. b, Dragon, denomination at UR. c, Dragon, vert.

No. 1596, 1000fr — Indonesia 2012 Intl. Philatelic Exhibition emblem and: a, Rinjani Volcano, Panthera tigris sumatrae. b, Ijen volcanic crater, Pongo abelii, vert. c, Krakatoa Volcano, Elephas maximus borneensis, vert.

No. 1597, 2700fr, Prince William and Catherine Middleton, diff. No. 1598, 2700fr, Princess Diana with child at Hindu temple, London. No. 1599, 2700fr, Gandhi and young girl. No. 1600, 2700fr, Pope John Paul II kissing ground at Bangui Airport. No. 1601, 2700fr, Gagarin and Vostok 1 lifting off, diff. No. 1602, 2700fr, Monroe, diff. No. 1603, 2700fr, Bardot, diff. No. 1604, 2700fr, Schneider, scene from Adorable Sinner, 1959. No. 1605, 2700fr, Presley, diff. No. 1606, 2700fr, Wolfgang Amadeus Mozart (1756-91), composer. No. 1607, 2700fr, French President Nicolas Sarkozy, U.S. President Barack Obama. No. 1608, 2700fr, Robert G. Edwards, 2010 Physiology and Medicine Nobel laureate and in-vitro fertilization. No. 1609, 2700fr, Impression, Soleil Levant, by Clause Monet (1840-1926). No. 1610, 2700fr, Evelyn Cheesman (1881-1969), entomologist, and Phalacrognathus muelleri. No. 1611, 2700fr, Elsie Maud Wakefield (1886-1972), mycologist, and Lactaria vellerea. No. 1612, 2700fr, Ignacy Domeyko (1802-89), mineralogist, and domeykite. No. 1613, 2700fr, Dressage. No. 1614, 2700fr, Table tennis player Ding Ning. No. 1615, 2700fr, World chess champion Anatoly Karpov. No. 1616, 2700fr, Boy Scouts and Lord Robert Baden-Powell (1857-1941). No. 1617, 2700fr, Lolo and Edmond Navratil, survivors of sinking of the Titanic. No. 1618, 2700fr, Dragon, diff. No. 1619, 2700fr, Indonesia 2012 Intl. Philatelic Exhibition emblem and Varanus komodoensis, vert.

2011, Dec. 27 Litho. *Perf. 13¼*

Sheets of 3, #a-c

1574-1596 A387 Set of 23 275.00 275.00

Souvenir Sheets

1597-1619 A387 Set of 23 250.00 250.00

A388

A389

Art — A390

No. 1620, 400fr — Inscriptions: a, Adam et Eve. b, Marie-Madeleine Pénitente. c, La Vierge à L'Enfant.

No. 1621, 400fr — Inscriptions: a, Venus en Devant le Miroir. b, La Flore. c, Le Suicide de Lucrèce.

No. 1622, 400fr — Inscriptions: a, Noli Me Tangere. b, Mater Dolorosa. c, Marie avec L'Enfant et des Saintes.

No. 1623, 400fr, horiz. — Inscriptions: a, La Venus d'Urbino (woman in background). b, La Venus d'Urbino (no woman in background). c, Danaé avec Nourrice.

No. 1624, 3200fr, Like #1620a. No. 1625, 3200fr, Like #1620b. No. 1626, 3200fr, Like #1620c. No. 1627, 3200fr, Like #1621a. No. 1628, 3200fr, Like #1621b. No. 1629, 3200fr, Like #1621c. No. 1630, 3200fr, Like #1622a. No. 1631, 3200fr, Like #1622b. No. 1632, 3200fr, Like #1622c, horiz. No. 1633, 3200fr, Like #1623a (image flipped). No. 1634, 3200fr, Like #1623b. No. 1635, 3200fr, Like #1623c.

No. 1636, 4000fr, Venus et Adonis.

No. 1637, 400fr — Inscriptions: a, La Toilette de Venus. b, Hercule et Omfala. c, Marquise de Pompadour.

No. 1638, 400fr — Inscriptions: a, Venus Consoler Amour. b, Jeune Femme avec un Bouquet de Roses. c, Venus Fin Cupidon.

No. 1639, 400fr — Inscriptions: a, Portrait d'une Femme. b, Putti avec des Oiseaux. c, Diana au Bain.

No. 1640, 400fr, horiz. — Inscriptions: a, Portrait de Marie-Louise O'Murphy. b, L'Odalisque. c, Léda et la Cygne.

No. 1641, 3200fr, Like #1637a. No. 1642, 3200fr, Like #1637b. No. 1643, 3200fr, Like #1637c. No. 1644, 3200fr, Like #1638a. No. 1645, 3200fr, Like #1638b. No. 1646, 3200fr, Like #1638c. No. 1647, 3200fr, Like #1639a. No. 1648, 3200fr, Like #1639b. No. 1649, 3200fr, Like #1639c, horiz. No. 1650, 3200fr, Like #1640a. No. 1651, 3200fr, Like #1640b. No. 1652, 3200fr, Like #1640c.

No. 1653, 4000fr, Renaud et Armide.

No. 1654, 400fr — Inscriptions: a, Portrait de Victor Jaquemont. b, Déjeuner sur l'Herbe de l'Etude. c, Peupliers le Long du Fleuve Epte.

No. 1655, 400fr — Inscriptions: a, Camille avec un Petit Chien. b, Camille Monet en Costume Japonais. c, Femme à l'Ombrelle.

No. 1656, 400fr — Inscriptions: a, Femme à l'Ombrelle Tournée vers la Droite. b, Poly, Pêcheur de Belle-Ile. c, Le Déjeuner.

No. 1657, 400fr, horiz. — Inscriptions: a, Le Pont sur la Seine. b, Le Pont, D'Amsterdam. c, Chambres du Parlement, Coucher de Soleil.

No. 1658, 3200fr, Like #1654a. No. 1659, 3200fr, Like #1654b. No. 1660, 3200fr, Like #1654c. No. 1661, 3200fr, Like #1655a. No. 1662, 3200fr, Like #1655b. No. 1663, 3200fr, Like #1655c. No. 1664, 3200fr, Like #1656a. No. 1665, 3200fr, Like #1656b. No. 1666, 3200fr, Like #1656c. No. 1667, 3200fr, Like #1657a. No. 1668, 3200fr, Like #1657b. No. 1669, 3200fr, Like #1657c.

No. 1670, 4000fr, Camille Monet et un Enfant dans le Jardin de l'Artiste à Argenteuil.

No. 1671, 400fr — Inscriptions: a, Sainte-Anne avec la Vierge et l'Enfant. b, Portrait d'une Jeune Femme Vénitienne. c, Christ comme l'Homme des Douleurs. d, Portrait de Maximilien I. e, Portrait d'Elsbeth Tucher. f, Portrait de Oswolt Krel.

No. 1672, 400fr — Inscriptions: a, Madone et l'Enfant. b, Adam et Eve. c, Lamentations sur le Christ Mort. d, Vierge et l'Enfant avant d'une Arcade. e, Le Vol à Destination de l'Egypte Résineux. f, Jérôme Pénitent.

No. 1673, 3200fr, Like #1671a. No. 1674, 3200fr, Like #1671b. No. 1675, 3200fr, Like #1671c. No. 1676, 3200fr, Like #1671d. No. 1677, 3200fr, Like #1671e. No. 1678, 3200fr, Like #1671f. No. 1679, 3200fr, Like #1672a. No. 1680, 3200fr, Like #1672b. No. 1681, 3200fr, Like #1672c. No. 1682, 3200fr, Like #1672d. No. 1683, 3200fr, Like #1672e. No. 1684, 3200fr, Like #1672f.

No. 1685, 4000fr, Bacchanales avec Silene.

No. 1686, 400fr — Inscriptions: a, David (statue). b, La Pietà (statue). c, Jugement Dernier Christ Juge. d, Le Prophète Zacharie. e, Le Prophète Jérémie. f, La Sibylle de Cumes.

No. 1687, 400fr — Inscriptions: a, Le Prophète Joel. b, Le Prophète Jessaja. c, Le Prophète Ezéchiel. d, La Sibylle d'Erythrée. e, La Sibylle de Delphes. f, La Sibylle de Libye.

No. 1688, 3200fr, Like #1686a. No. 1689, 3200fr, Like #1686b. No. 1690, 3200fr, Like #1686c. No. 1691, 3200fr, Like #1686d. No. 1692, 3200fr, Like #1686e. No. 1693, 3200fr, Like #1686f. No. 1694, 3200fr, Like #1687a. No. 1695, 3200fr, Like #1687b. No. 1696, 3200fr, Like #1687c. No. 1697, 3200fr, Like #1687d. No. 1698, 3200fr, Like #1687e. No. 1699, 3200fr, Like #1687f.

No. 1700, 4000fr, La Chapelle Sixtine.

No. 1701, 400fr — Inscriptions: a, Le Christ Bénissant. b, La Vierge Colonna. c, Saint-George aux Prises avec les Dragons. d, Madone du Chardonneret. e, La Vierge Garvagh. f, La Madone Sixtine.

No. 1702, 400fr — Inscriptions: a, Saint-Michel. b, Le Portrait d'une Jeune Femme. c, Sainte-Catherine d'Alexandrie. d, Madonna del Baldacchio. e, La Sainte Famille avec les Saints Elizabeth et John. f, La Vierge de la Maison d'Orléans.

No. 1703, 3200fr, Like #1701a. No. 1704, 3200fr, Like #1701b. No. 1705, 3200fr, Like #1701c. No. 1706, 3200fr, Like #1701d. No. 1707, 3200fr, Like #1701e. No. 1708, 3200fr, Like #1701f. No. 1709, 3200fr, Like #1702a. No. 1710, 3200fr, Like #1702b. No. 1711, 3200fr, Like #1702c. No. 1712, 3200fr, Like #1702d. No. 1713, 3200fr, Like #1702e. No. 1714, 3200fr, Like #1702f.

No. 1715, 4000fr, La Dispute du Saint Sacrement.

No. 1716, 400fr — Inscriptions: a, Alexandre et de Roxane. b, Viol des Filles de Leucippe. c, Le Débarquement de Marie de Médicis à Marseille. d, Bethsabée à la Fontaine. e, Persée Libératrice Andromède. f, Diane et ses Nymphes Surpris par les Faunes.

No. 1717, 400fr — Inscriptions: a, L'Union de la Terre et de l'Eau. b, Bacchus. c,Vénus à un Miroir. d, Les Trois Grâces. e, Isabelle, Gouverneur des Pays Bas. f, Erection de la Croix.

No. 1718, 3200fr, Like #1716a. No. 1719, 3200fr, Like #1716b. No. 1720, 3200fr, Like #1716c. No. 1721, 3200fr, Like #1716d. No. 1722, 3200fr, Like #1716e. No. 1723, 3200fr, Like #1716f. No. 1724, 3200fr, Like #1717a. No. 1725, 3200fr, Like #1717b. No. 1726, 3200fr, Like #1717c. No. 1727, 3200fr, Like #1717d. No. 1728, 3200fr, Like #1717e. No. 1729, 3200fr, Like #1717f.

No. 1730, 4000fr, Ixion.

No. 1731, 400fr — Inscriptions: a, Philadelphie et Elisabeth Cary. b, Marchesa Durazzo. c, Saint-Pierre. d, Susanna & Aînés. e, Saint Jean le Baptiste dans le Desert. f, St.

Rosalie Intercédant pour les Pestiférés de Palerme.

No. 1732, 400fr — Inscriptions: a, Charles Ier de Chasse. b, Golgotha. c, Silène Ivre. d, L'Homme en Armure avec Foulard Rouge. e, Portrait de Famille. f, Tête d'une Jeune Femme.

No. 1733, 3200fr, Like #1731a. No. 1734, 3200fr, Like #1731b. No. 1735, 3200fr, Like #1731c. No. 1736, 3200fr, Like #1731d. No. 1737, 3200fr, Like #1731e. No. 1738, 3200fr, Like #1731f. No. 1739, 3200fr, Like #1732a. No. 1740, 3200fr, Like #1732b. No. 1741, 3200fr, Like #1732c. No. 1742, 3200fr, Like #1732d. No. 1743, 3200fr, Like #1732e. No. 1744, 3200fr, Like #1732f.

No. 1745, 4000fr, Déploration du Christ.

No. 1746, 400fr — Inscriptions: a, Saskia en Flore. b, Artemis. c, Une Jeune Femme qui Tente sur Boucles d'Oreilles. d, David et Jonathan. e, La Sainte Famille (Jesus in cradle). f, La Sainte Famille (Mary holding Jesus).

No. 1747, 400fr — Inscriptions: a, Abraham le Sacrifice. b, Balaam Ass. c, Tobie Accusant Anna de Voler le Kid. d, La Fête de la Musique. e, Christ dans la Tempête sur le Lac de Galilée. f, Enlèvement de Ganymède.

No. 1748, 3200fr, Like #1746a. No. 1749, 3200fr, Like #1746b. No. 1750, 3200fr, Like #1746c. No. 1751, 3200fr, Like #1746d. No. 1752, 3200fr, Like #1746e. No. 1753, 3200fr, Like #1746f. No. 1754, 3200fr, Like #1747a. No. 1755, 3200fr, Like #1747b. No. 1756, 3200fr, Like #1747c. No. 1757, 3200fr, Like #1747d. No. 1758, 3200fr, Like #1747e. No. 1759, 3200fr, Like #1747f.

No. 1760, 4000fr, La Scène de l'Enfant Prodigue dans la Taverne.

No. 1761, 400fr — Inscriptions: a, Baigneuse Arrangeant ses Cheveux. b, Femme Endormie. c, Baigneuse aux Cheveux Longs. d, La Promenade. e, Une Femme Jouant de la Guitare. f, Femme Arranger ses Cheveux.

No. 1762, 400fr — Inscriptions: a, Femme de Baignade. b, Jeanne Samary. c, Junge Badende. d, La Loge. e, Gabrielle à la Rose. f, Deux Soeurs sur la Terrasse.

No. 1763, 3200fr, Like #1761a. No. 1764, 3200fr, Like #1761b. No. 1765, 3200fr, Like #1761c. No. 1766, 3200fr, Like #1761d. No. 1767, 3200fr, Like #1761e. No. 1768, 3200fr, Like #1761f. No. 1769, 3200fr, Like #1762a. No. 1770, 3200fr, Like #1762b. No. 1771, 3200fr, Like #1762c. No. 1772, 3200fr, Like #1762d. No. 1773, 3200fr, Like #1762e. No. 1774, 3200fr, Like #1762f.

No. 1775, 4000fr, Oarsmen at Chatou.

No. 1776, 400fr — Inscriptions: a, Après le Bain (woman kneeling, striped floral wallpaper in background). b, Les Buveurs d'Absinthe. c, Après le Bain (woman standing with leg lifted). d, La Ballerine. e, Après le Bain (woman kneeling, plain background). f, Petit-Déjeuner Après un Bain.

No. 1777, 400fr — Inscriptions: a, Danseuse Assise. b, Inclinaison Dancer. c, Mademoiselle Malo. d, Femme se Coiffant Devant un Miroir. e, Musiciens de l'Orchestre. f, Six Amis de l'Artiste.

No. 1778, 3200fr, Like #1776a. No. 1779, 3200fr, Like #1776b. No. 1780, 3200fr, Like #1776c. No. 1781, 3200fr, Like #1776d. No. 1782, 3200fr, Like #1776e. No. 1783, 3200fr, Like #1776f. No. 1784, 3200fr, Like #1777a. No. 1785, 3200fr, Like #1777b. No. 1786, 3200fr, Like #1777c. No. 1787, 3200fr, Like #1777d. No. 1788, 3200fr, Like #1777e. No. 1789, 3200fr, Like #1777f.

No. 1790, 4000fr, Filles Spartiates Difficile Garçons.

Illustrations on Nos. 1776a-1776f, 1777a-1777f are flipped in comparison to Nos. 1778-1789.

No. 1791, 400fr — Inscriptions: a, Ange. b, Chef de une Vielle Femme dans un Bonnet Blanc. c, Portrait de Camille Roulin. d, Joseph Etienne Roulin. e, Chef de une Vielle Femme dans un Bonnet Blanc (woman with hand touching her face). f, Le Zouave Assis.

No. 1792, 400fr — Inscriptions: a, Vase avec Douze Tournesols. b, Irisews (Irises). c, Portrait du Père Tanguy. d, Chef de une Paysanne avec un Bonnet de Dentelles Verdatre. e, Van Gogh Chair. f, Berceuse.

No. 1793, 3200fr, Like #1791a. No. 1794, 3200fr, Like #1791b. No. 1795, 3200fr, Like #1791c. No. 1796, 3200fr, Like #1791d. No. 1797, 3200fr, Like #1791e. No. 1798, 3200fr, Like #1791f. No. 1799, 3200fr, Like #1792a. No. 1800, 3200fr, Like #1792b. No. 1801, 3200fr, Like #1792c. No. 1802, 3200fr, Like #1792d. No. 1803, 3200fr, Like #1792e. No. 1804, 3200fr, Like #1792f.

No. 1805, 4000fr, Village de Rue et Escalier avec Chiffres.

No. 1806, 400fr — Inscriptions: a, Nu Assis (blue area at LL). b, Jeanne Hebuterne (head). c, Portrait de Madame Kisling. d, Nu Assise sur un Canapé. e, Portrait de Chaim Soutner. f, Portrait de Celso Lagar.

No. 1807, 400fr — Inscriptions: a, Femme nue. b, Jeanne Hebuterne (seated). c, Nu Assis (seated, dark blue background). d, Nu Assis (seated, blue green background). e, Madame Pompadour. f, Jeune Fille Assise.

No. 1808, 3200fr, Like #1806a. No. 1809, 3200fr, Like #1806b. No. 1810, 3200fr, Like #1806c. No. 1811, 3200fr, Like #1806d. No. 1812, 3200fr, Like #1806e. No. 1813, 3200fr, Like #1806f. No. 1814, 3200fr, Like #1807a. No. 1815, 3200fr, Like #1807b. No. 1816, 3200fr, Like #1807c. No. 1817, 3200fr, Like #1807d. No. 1818, 3200fr, Like #1807e. No. 1819, 3200fr, Like #1807f.

No. 1820, 4000fr, Nu Couché.

No. 1821, 400fr — Inscriptions: a, A. S. Pouchkine. b, Bateau à Voile. c, Mer (Etude). d, Tapez Leandrovoy Tour à Constantinople. e, Navire dans la Mer Orageuse. f, Acropole d'Athènes. g, Portrait de l'Épouse de l'Artiste.

No. 1822, 400fr, horiz. — Inscriptions: a, Brigue "Mercury" Attaque par Deux Navires Turcs. b, L'Arrivée de Flotille Colomb. c, La Bataille dans la Manche Chios. d, Examen de la Flotte de la Mer Noire en 1849. e, Bataille Navale Russo-Turque de Sinop. f, La Bataille de Navarin. g, Bataille près de Sinop.

No. 1823, 400fr, horiz. — Inscriptions: a, Paysage Italien. b, Napoléon. c, La Flotte de la Mer Noire à Feodosiya. d, Vue de Saint-Pétersbourg. e, Vue de Kertch. f, Pêcheurs sur Littoral. g, Pouchkine.

No. 1824, 400fr, horiz — Inscriptions: a, Un Naufrage près du Mont Athos. b, La Tempête. c, Tempête sur la Mer. d, Sur l'île de Crète. e, La Neuvième Vague. f, Signal de la Tempête. g, Le Bulow

No. 1825, 4000fr, Tempête.

2011, Dec. 29 Litho. *Perf. 13¾*

Works of Titian (Tiziano Vecelli)
Sheets of 3, #a-c, + label

1620-1623 A388 Set of 4 19.50 19.50

Souvenir Sheets
Perf. 13x13¼, 13¼x13

1624-1635 A389 Set of 12 155.00 155.00
1636 A390 4000fr multi 16.00 16.00

Works of François Boucher
Sheets of 3, #a-c, + label
Perf. 13¾

1637-1640 A388 Set of 4 19.50 19.50

Souvenir Sheets
Perf. 13x13¼, 13¼x13

1641-1652 A389 Set of 12 155.00 155.00
1653 A390 4000fr multi 16.00 16.00

Works of Claude Monet
Sheets of 3, #a-c, + label
Perf. 13¾

1654-1657 A388 Set of 4 19.50 19.50

Souvenir Sheets
Perf. 13x13¼, 13¼x13

1658-1669 A389 Set of 12 155.00 155.00
1670 A390 4000fr multi 16.00 16.00

Works of Albrecht Dürer
Sheets of 6, #a-f, + 2 labels
Perf. 13¾

1671-1672 A388 Set of 2 19.50 19.50

Souvenir Sheets
Perf. 13x13¼

1673-1684 A389 Set of 12 155.00 155.00
1685 A390 4000fr multi 16.00 16.00

Works of Michelangelo
Sheets of 6, #a-f, + 2 labels
Perf. 13¾

1686-1687 A388 Set of 2 19.50 19.50

Souvenir Sheets
Perf. 13x13¼

1688-1699 A389 Set of 12 155.00 155.00
1700 A390 4000fr multi 16.00 16.00

Works of Raphael (Raffaello Sanzio)
Sheets of 6, #a-f, + 2 labels
Perf. 13¾

1701-1702 A388 Set of 2 19.50 19.50

Souvenir Sheets
Perf. 13x13¼

1703-1714 A389 Set of 12 155.00 155.00
1715 A390 4000fr multi 16.00 16.00

Works of Peter Paul Rubens
Sheets of 6, #a-f, + 2 labels
Perf. 13¾

1716-1717 A388 Set of 2 19.50 19.50

Souvenir Sheets
Perf. 13x13¼

1718-1729 A389 Set of 12 155.00 155.00
1730 A390 4000fr multi 16.00 16.00

Works of Anthony van Dyck
Sheets of 6, #a-f, + 2 labels
Perf. 13¾

1731-1732 A388 Set of 2 19.50 19.50

Souvenir Sheets
Perf. 13x13¼

1733-1744 A389 Set of 12 155.00 155.00
1745 A390 4000fr multi 16.00 16.00

Works of Rembrandt van Rijn
Sheets of 6, #a-f, + 2 labels
Perf. 13¾

1746-1747 A388 Set of 2 19.50 19.50

Souvenir Sheets
Perf. 13x13¼

1748-1759 A389 Set of 12 155.00 155.00
1760 A390 4000fr multi 16.00 16.00

Works of Pierre-Auguste Renoir
Sheets of 6, #a-f, + 2 labels
Perf. 13¾

1761-1762 A388 Set of 2 19.50 19.50

Souvenir Sheets
Perf. 13x13¼

1763-1774 A389 Set of 12 155.00 155.00
1775 A390 4000fr multi 16.00 16.00

Works of Edgar Degas
Sheets of 6, #a-f, + 2 labels
Perf. 13¾

1776-1777 A388 Set of 2 19.50 19.50

Souvenir Sheets
Perf. 13x13¼

1778-1789 A389 Set of 12 155.00 155.00
1790 A390 4000fr multi 16.00 16.00

Works of Vincent van Gogh
Sheets of 6, #a-f, + 2 labels
Perf. 13¾

1791-1792 A388 Set of 2 19.50 19.50

Souvenir Sheets
Perf. 13x13¼

1793-1804 A389 Set of 12 155.00 155.00
1805 A390 4000fr multi 16.00 16.00

Works of Amedeo Modigliani
Sheets of 6, #a-f, + 2 labels
Perf. 13¾

1806-1807 A388 Set of 2 19.50 19.50

Souvenir Sheets
Perf. 13x13¼

1808-1819 A389 Set of 12 155.00 155.00
1820 A390 4000fr multi 16.00 16.00

Works of Ivan Aivazovsky
Sheets of 7, #a-g, + label
Perf. 13¾

1821-1824 A388 Set of 4 45.00 45.00

Souvenir Sheets
Perf. 13x13¼

1825 A390 4000fr multi 16.00 16.00

SEMI-POSTAL STAMPS

Anti-Malaria Issue
Common Design Type
Perf. 12½x12

1962, Apr. 7 Engr. Unwmk.

B1 CD108 25fr + 5fr slate 1.40 1.40

WHO drive to eradicate malaria.

Freedom from Hunger Issue
Common Design Type

1963, Mar. 21 ***Perf. 13***

B2 CD112 25fr + 5fr multi 1.25 1.25

Guinea Fowl and Partridge SP1

Designs: 10fr+5fr, Yellow-backed duiker and snail. 20fr+5fr, Elephant, tortoise and hippopotamus playing tug-of-war. 30fr+10fr, Cuckoo and tortoise. 50fr+20fr, Patas monkey and leopard.

1971, Feb. 9 Photo. ***Perf. 12½x12***

B3 SP1 5fr + 5fr multi 5.25 2.00
B4 SP1 10fr + 5fr multi 6.75 2.50
B5 SP1 20fr + 5fr multi 8.75 2.75
B6 SP1 30fr + 10fr multi 11.50 7.00
B7 SP1 50fr + 20fr multi 18.50 12.00
Nos. B3-B7 (5) 50.75 26.25

Lengué Dancer — SP2

Dancers: 40fr+10fr, Le Lengué. 100fr+40fr, Teke. 140fr+40fr, Englabolo.

1971 Litho. ***Perf. 13***

B8 SP2 20fr + 5fr multi .80 .25
B9 SP2 40fr + 10fr multi 1.40 .40
B10 SP2 100fr + 40fr multi 3.25 1.25
B11 SP2 140fr + 40fr multi 4.25 1.50
Nos. B8-B11 (4) 9.70 3.40

AIR POST STAMPS

Abyssinian Roller — AP1

Birds: 200fr, Gold Coast touraco. 500fr, African fish eagle.

Unwmk.

1960, Sept. 3 Engr. ***Perf. 13***

C1 AP1 100fr vio bl, org brn & emer 2.25 .80
C2 AP1 200fr multi 4.25 2.25
C3 AP1 500fr Prus bl, emer & red brn 13.50 5.25
Nos. C1-C3 (3) 20.00 8.30

French Equatorial Africa No. C37 Surcharged in Red

1960, Dec. 15 ***Perf. 13***

C4 AP8 250fr on 500fr grnsh blk, blk & slate 9.00 8.25

17th Olympic Games, Rome, 8/25-9/11.

Air Afrique Issue
Common Design Type

1962, Feb. 17 Unwmk. ***Perf. 13***

C5 CD107 50fr vio, lt grn & red brn 1.00 .65

Founding of Air Afrique airline.

Pole Vault — AP1a

1962, July 21 Photo. ***Perf. 12x12½***

C6 AP1a 100fr grn, yel, brn & blk 2.50 1.75

Abidjan games.

Red-faced Lovebirds — AP2

1962-63 **Engr.** ***Perf. 13***

C7 AP2 50fr Great blue touraco 2.50 .55
C8 AP2 250fr shown ('63) 7.50 2.50

Issued: 50fr, Nov. 15; 250fr, Mar. 11, 1963.

Runner with Torch and Palm Branch — AP3

1962, Dec. 24

C9 AP3 100fr gray grn, brn & car 2.50 1.50

Tropics Cup Games, Bangui, Dec. 24-31.

African Postal Union Issue
Common Design Type

1963, Sept. 8 **Photo.** ***Perf. 12½***

C10 CD114 85fr emer, ocher & red 1.90 .90

Sun Shining on Africa — AP4

1963, Nov. 9 ***Perf. 13x12***

C11 AP4 25fr bl, yel & vio bl .75 .40

Issued for African unity.

Europafrica Issue
Common Design Type

1963, Nov. 30 ***Perf. 12x13***

C12 CD116 50fr ultra, yel & dk brn 2.50 1.75

Diesel Engine — AP5

Various Locomotives; 25fr, 50fr, vertical.

1963, Dec. 1 **Engr.** ***Perf. 13***

C13 AP5 20fr brn, cl & dk grn .70 .70
C14 AP5 25fr brn, bl & choc .80 .80
C15 AP5 50r brn, red lil & vio 2.75 2.75
C16 AP5 100fr brn, grn & dl red brn 3.75 3.75
a. Min. sheet of 4, #C13-C16 13.00 13.00
Nos. C13-C16 (4) 8.00 8.00

Bangui-Douala railroad project.

Bangui Cathedral — AP6

1964, Jan. 21 **Unwmk.** ***Perf. 13***

C17 AP6 100fr yel grn, org brn & bl 1.90 1.00

Radar Tracking Station and WMO Emblem — AP7

1964, Mar. 23 **Engr.** ***Perf. 13***

C18 AP7 50fr org brn, bl & pur 1.25 1.25

World Meteorological Day.

Map and Presidents of Chad, Congo, Gabon and Central African Republic AP8

1964, June 23 **Photo.** ***Perf. 12½***

C19 AP8 100fr multi 2.00 .90

5th anniversary of the Conference of Chiefs of State of Equatorial Africa.

Javelin Throwers — AP9

Designs: 50fr, Basketball game. 100fr, Four runners. 250fr, Swimmers, one in water.

1964, June 23 **Engr.** ***Perf. 13***

C20 AP9 25fr grn, dk brn & lt vio bl .50 .30
C21 AP9 50fr blk, car & grn 1.00 .50
C22 AP9 100fr grn, vio bl & dk brn 2.00 1.05
C23 AP9 250fr grn, blk & car 5.50 2.75
a. Min. sheet of 4, #C20-C23 13.50 13.50
Nos. C20-C23 (4) 9.00 4.60

18th Olympic Games, Tokyo, 10/10-25/64.

John F. Kennedy — AP10

1964, July 4 **Photo.** ***Perf. 12½***

C24 AP10 100fr lil, brn & blk 2.25 1.75
a. Min. sheet of 4 10.00 10.00

Industrial Symbols, Maps of Africa and Europe — AP11

1964, Dec. 19 **Unwmk.** ***Perf. 13x12***

C25 AP11 50fr yel, org & grn 1.35 .90

See note after Cameroun No. 402.

International Cooperation Year Emblem — AP12

1965, Jan. 2 ***Perf. 13***

C26 AP12 100fr red brn, yel & bl 1.60 .85

International Cooperation Year.

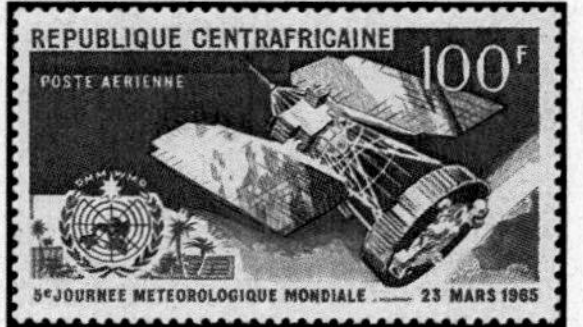

Nimbus Weather Satellite — AP13

1965, Mar. 23 **Engr.** ***Perf. 13***

C27 AP13 100fr org brn, ultra & blk 1.75 .90

Fifth World Meteorological Day.

Lincoln and Statue of Liberty — AP14

1965, Apr. 15 **Photo.** ***Perf. 13***

C28 AP14 100fr bluish grn, ind & bis 1.50 .85

Centenary of death of Abraham Lincoln.

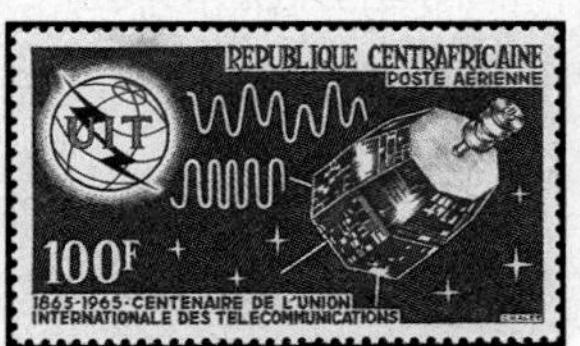

ITU Emblem and Relay Satellite — AP15

1965, May 17 **Engr.** ***Perf. 13***

C29 AP15 100fr dk grn vio bl & brn 1.75 1.00

Centenary of the ITU.

"Housing," New Home in Village — AP16

1965, June 10 **Unwmk.**

C30 AP16 100fr ultra, brn & sl grn 1.40 .80

See note after No. 52.

Europafrica Issue

Tractor, Cotton Picker, Cotton, Sun and Emblem — AP17

1965, Nov. 7 **Photo.** ***Perf. 12x13***

C31 AP17 50fr multi 1.00 .70

See note after Chad No. C11.

Mercury by Antoine Coysevox AP18

1965, Dec. 5 **Engr.** ***Perf. 13***

C32 AP18 100fr red brn, bl & blk 1.75 1.00

5th anniv. of Central African Republic's admission to the UPU.

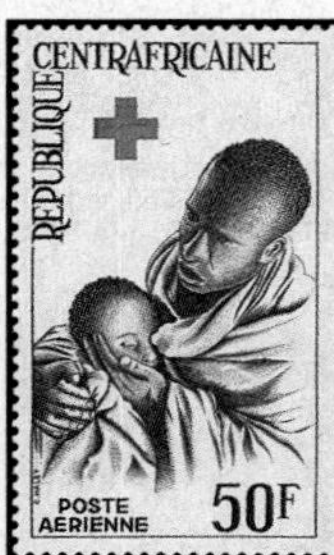

Father Holding Sick Child — AP19

Design: 100fr, Mother and child.

1965, Dec. 12

C33 AP19 50fr dk bl, car & blk 1.10 .55
C34 AP19 100fr red brn, red & brt grn 2.50 1.10

Issued to honor the Red Cross.

Air Afrique Issue
Common Design Type

1966, Aug. 31 **Photo.** ***Perf. 13***

C35 CD123 25fr bl, blk & lem 1.00 .50

For surcharge see No. C43.

Surveyor Spacecraft on Moon — AP20

Designs: No. C37, Luna 9 on Moon and Earth. 200fr, Rocket take-off, Jules Verne's "From the Earth to the Moon."

1966, Oct. 24 Photo. *Perf. 12x12½*

C36 AP20 130fr multi 1.45 1.00
C37 AP20 130fr multi 1.45 1.00
C38 AP20 200fr multi 2.75 1.90
a. Souv. sheet of 3, #C36-C38 8.50 8.50
Nos. C36-C38 (3) 5.65 3.90

Conquest of the Moon.
For surcharges see Nos. C58, C61.

Eugene A. Cernan, Gemini 9 and Agena Rocket — AP21

No. C40, Pavel R. Popovich and rocket.

1966, Nov. 14 Photo. *Perf. 13*

C39 AP21 50fr multi 1.10 .55
C40 AP21 50fr multi 1.10 .55

American and Russian astronauts.

Diamant Rocket, D-1 Satellite and Globe with Map of Africa — AP22

1966, Nov. 14 Engr.

C41 AP22 100fr brt rose lil & brn 1.75 .90

Issued to commemorate the launching of France's first satellite, Nov. 26, 1965, and the launching of the D-1 satellite, Feb. 17, 1966.

Exchange of Agricultural and Industrial Products between Africa and Europe — AP23

1966, Dec. 5 Photo. *Perf. 12x13*

C42 AP23 50fr multi 1.25 .85

See note after Gabon No. C46.

No. C35 Surcharged

1967, May 8 *Perf. 13*

C43 CD123 5fr on 25fr multi .55 .30

The surcharge obliterates the "2" of the original 25fr denomination.

DC-8F Over M'Poko Airport, Bangui — AP24

1967, July 3 Engr. *Perf. 13*

C44 AP24 100fr sl, dk grn & brn 2.25 1.10

View of EXPO '67, Montreal — AP25

1967, July 17

C45 AP25 100fr vio bl, dk red brn & dk grn 2.25 .80

International Exposition. EXPO '67, Montreal, Apr. 28-Oct. 27.

African Postal Union Issue, 1967
Common Design Type

1967, Sept. 9 Engr. *Perf. 13*

C46 CD124 100fr brt grn, dk car rose & plum 2.25 .85

Potez 25 TOE — AP26

1967, Nov. 24 Engr. *Perf. 13*

C47 AP26 100fr shown 1.75 .80
C48 AP26 200fr Junkers 52 4.50 1.75
C49 AP26 500fr Caravelle 11R 13.50 4.25
Nos. C47-C49 (3) 19.75 6.80

For surcharges see Nos. C59-C60.

Presidents Boganda and Bokassa — AP27

1967, Dec. 1 Photo. *Perf. 12½*

C50 AP27 130fr org, red, lt bl & blk 2.00 1.25

9th anniversary of the republic.

Pres. Jean Bedel Bokassa AP28

1968, Jan. 1 *Perf. 12½x12*

C51 AP28 30fr multi .85 .45

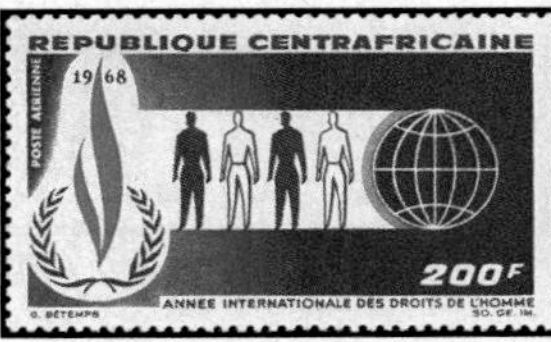

Human Rights Flame, Men and Globe — AP29

1968, Mar. 26 Photo. *Perf. 13*

C52 AP29 200fr brt grn, vio & ver 3.50 1.50

International Human Rights Year.

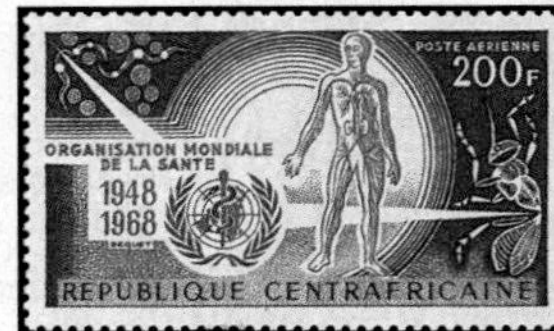

Man, WHO Emblem and Tsetse Fly — AP30

1968, Apr. 8 Engr.

C53 AP30 200fr multi 3.75 1.75

20th anniv. of WHO.

Javelin Thrower — AP31

1968, Apr. 16 Engr. *Perf. 13*

C54 AP31 200fr shown 4.50 3.00
C55 AP31 200fr Downhill skier 4.50 3.00

The 1968 Olympic Games.

Space Probe Landing on Venus — AP32

1968, Apr. 23

C56 AP32 100fr ultra, dk & brt grn 1.75 .95

Venus exploration by Venera 4, 10/18/67.

Marie Curie and "Cancer Destroyed" — AP33

1968, Apr. 30

C57 AP33 100fr vio, brt bl & brn 2.50 1.10

Marie Curie (1867-1934), scientist.

Nos. C36-C37 and C47-C48 Surcharged with New Value

Photogravure; Engraved

1968, Sept. 16 *Perf. 12x12½, 13*

C58 AP20 5fr on 130fr multi .25 .25
C59 AP26 10fr on 100fr multi .30 .25
C60 AP26 20fr on 200fr multi .50 .30
C61 AP20 50fr on 130fr multi 1.10 .55
Nos. C58-C61 (4) 2.15 1.35

On No. C58 the old denomination has been obliterated with "XIX," on No. C61 the obliteration is a rectangular bar. On Nos. C59-C60 the last zero of the old denomination has been obliterated with a black square.

River Boat Type of Regular Issue

Craft: 100fr, "Pie X," Bangui, 1894. 130fr, "Ballay," Bangui, 1891.

1968, Dec. 10 Engr. *Perf. 13*
Size: 48x27mm

C62 A37 100fr bl, dk brn & ol 2.25 1.00
C63 A37 130fr brt pink, sl grn & slate 2.75 1.25

PHILEXAFRIQUE Issue

Mme. de Sévigné, French School, 17th Century AP34

1968, Dec. 17 Photo. *Perf. 12½*

C64 AP34 100fr brn & multi 3.00 2.25

Issued to publicize PHILEXAFRIQUE, Philatelic Exhibition in Abidjan, Feb. 14-23. Printed with alternating brown label.

2nd PHILEXAFRIQUE Issue
Common Design Type

Design: 50fr, Ubangi-Shari No. J16, cotton field and Pres. Bokassa.

1969, Feb. 14 Engr. *Perf. 13*

C65 CD128 50fr bis brn, blk & dk grn 1.75 1.75

Holocerina Angulata Aur. — AP35

Butterflies and Moths: 20fr, Nudaurelia dione fabr. 30fr, Eustera troglophylla hamp., vert. 50fr, Aurivillius aratus west. 100fr, Epiphora albida druce.

1969, Feb. 25 Photo.

C66 AP35 10fr yel & multi 1.10 .35
C67 AP35 20fr vio & multi 1.60 .55
C68 AP35 30fr multi 3.75 1.00
C69 AP35 50fr multi 5.25 2.25
C70 AP35 100fr multi 9.00 3.25
Nos. C66-C70 (5) 20.70 7.40

Boxing — AP36

1969, Mar. 18 **Photo.** ***Perf. 13***

C71	AP36 50fr shown	1.10	.35
C72	AP36 100fr Basketball	2.10	.65

Apollo 8 over Moonscape — AP37

1969, May 27 **Photo.** ***Perf. 13***

C73	AP37 200fr dp bl, gray & yel	3.50	1.75

US Apollo 8 mission, the 1st men in orbit around the moon, Dec. 21-27, 1968.

For overprint see No. C81.

Market Cross, Nuremberg, and Toys — AP38

1969, June 3

C74	AP38 100fr blk, brt rose lil & emer	2.10	1.10

Intl. Toy Fair in Nuremberg, Germany.

Napoleon as First Consul, by Anne-Louis Girodet-Trioson — AP39

Designs: 130fr, Napoleon meeting Emperor Francis II, by Antoine Jean Gros, horiz. 200fr, The Wedding of Napoleon and Marie-Louise, by Georges Rouget, horiz.

1969, Nov. 4 **Photo.** ***Perf. 12½***

C75	AP39 100fr multi	2.00	1.25
C76	AP39 130fr brn & multi	3.00	1.50
C77	AP39 200fr multi	5.00	2.75
	Nos. C75-C77 (3)	10.00	5.50

Napoleon Bonaparte (1769-1821).

Pres. Bokassa, Map of Africa and Flag — AP40

1970, Jan. 1 ***Die-cut; Perf. 10½***

Embossed on Gold Foil

C78	AP40 2000fr gold	*35.00*	*35.00*

Franklin Delano Roosevelt — AP41

1970 **Litho.** ***Perf. 13½x14***

C79	AP41 100fr shown	2.00	1.00
C80	AP41 100fr Lenin	3.00	1.25

Roosevelt, 25th death anniv., Lenin, birth cent.

Issue dates: No. C79, Apr. 29; No. C80. Apr. 22.

No. C73 Overprinted in Red

1970, June 1 **Photo.** ***Perf. 13***

C81	AP37 200fr multi	13.50	9.00

Moon landing mission of Apollo 12, 11/14-24/69.

AP42

1970, Sept. 15 **Litho.** ***Perf. 10***

C82	AP42 Pair + label	4.00	2.75
a.	100fr Dancer	1.75	.65
b.	100fr Still life	1.75	.65

Knokphila 70, 6th Intl. Phil. Exhib. at Knokke, Belgium, July 4-10. Imperf. between stamps and label.

Sericulture Type of Regular Issue

1970, Sept. 15 ***Perf. 10***

C83	A45 140fr multi	4.00	1.25

C.A.R. Flag, EXPO Emblem and Pavilion — AP43

1970, Dec. 18 **Litho.** ***Perf. 13½x13***

C84	AP43 200fr red & multi	3.00	1.50

Intl. Exposition EXPO '70, Osaka, Japan.

Soccer — AP44

1970, Dec. 8 ***Perf. 13x13½***

C85	AP44 200fr multi	3.50	1.50

World Soccer Championships, Mexico, May 30-June 21, 1970.

Dove — AP45

1970, Dec. 31

C86	AP45 200fr bl, yel & blk	3.50	1.50

25th anniversary of the United Nations.

Presidents Mobutu, Bokassa, and Tombalbaye — AP46

1971, Jan. 10

C87	AP46 140fr multi	2.75	.90

Return of Central African Republic to the United States of Central Africa which also includes Congo Democratic Republic and Chad.

Satellite over Globe — AP47

1971, May 17 **Photo.** ***Perf. 12½***

C88	AP47 100fr multi	2.25	.90

3rd World Telecommunications Day.

African Postal Union Issue, 1971

Common Design Type

Design: 100fr, Carved head and UAMPT building, Brazzaville, Congo.

1971, Nov. 13 **Photo.** ***Perf. 13x13½***

C89	CD135 100fr bl & multi	2.25	.85

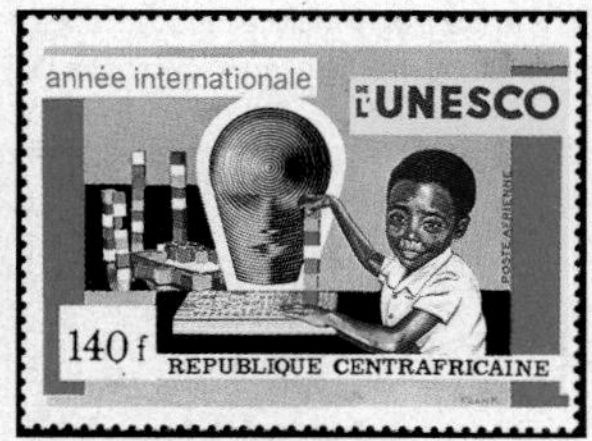

Child and Education Year Emblem — AP48

1971, Nov. 11 **Litho.** ***Perf. 13x13½***

C90	AP48 140fr multi	1.75	.70

25th anniv. of UNESCO.

Fight Against Cancer — AP49

1971, Nov. 20 **Photo.** ***Perf. 12½***

C91	AP49 100fr grn & multi	2.75	1.10

Gamal Abdel Nasser — AP50

1972, Jan. 15

C92	AP50 100fr dk red, blk & bister	2.10	.90

In memory of Gamal Abdel Nasser (1918-1970), president of Egypt.

Olympic Rings and Boxing — AP51

No. C94, Long jumper and Olympic rings, vert.

1972, May 26 **Engr.** ***Perf. 13***

C93	AP51 100fr brn org & sepia	1.50	1.10
C94	AP51 100fr green & violet	1.50	1.10
a.	Miniature sheet of 2	4.25	4.25

20th Olympic Games, Munich, Aug. 26-Sept. 10. No. C94a contains 2 stamps similar to Nos. C93-C94, but in changed colors. The boxing stamp is red lilac and green, the track stamp ocher and red lilac.

For overprints see Nos. C100-C101.

Tiling's Mail Rocket, 1931, and Mailman — AP52

Designs: 50fr, DC-3 and mailman riding camel, vert. 150fr, Sirio satellite and rocket, vert. 200fr, Intelsat 4 and rocket.

1972, Aug. 12

C95	AP52 40fr bl, org & indigo	.65	.45
C96	AP52 50fr bl, brn & org	.90	.55
C97	AP52 150fr brn, org & gray	2.50	1.25
C98	AP52 200fr brn, bl & org	3.50	2.25
a.	Souv. sheet of 4, #C95-C98	8.00	8.00
	Nos. C95-C98 (4)	7.55	4.50

Centraphilex 1972, Central African Philatelic Exhibition, Bangui.

Europafrica Issue

Arrows with Symbols of Agriculture and Industry — AP53

1972, Nov. 17 **Litho.** ***Perf. 13***
C99 AP53 100fr multi 1.75 .90

Nos. C93-C94, C94a Overprinted

(a)

(b)

1972, Nov. 24 **Engr.**
C100 AP51 (a) 100fr 1.60 .95
C101 AP51 (b) 100fr 1.60 .95
a. Miniature sheet of 2 3.75 3.75

Gold Medal Winners in 20th Olympic Games: Viatscheslav Lemechev, USSR, middleweight boxing; Randy Williams, US, broad jump.

Lunar Rover and Module — AP54

1972, Dec. 18 **Engr.** ***Perf. 13***
C102 AP54 100fr slate grn, bl & gray 1.60 .90

Apollo 16 US moon mission, 4/15-27/72.

Virgin and Child, by Francesco Pesellino AP55

Christmas: 150fr, Adoration of the Child with St. John the Baptist and St. Romuald, by Fra Filippo Lippi.

1972, Dec. 25 **Photo.**
C103 AP55 100fr gold & multi 1.40 .90
C104 AP55 150fr gold & multi 2.50 1.40

Parthenon, Athens, Spyridon Louis, Marathon, 1896 — AP56

Olympic Rings and: 40fr, Arc de Triomphe, Paris, H. Barrelet, single scull, 1900. 50fr, Old Courthouse and Western Arch, St. Louis, Myer Prinstein, triple jump, 1904. 100fr, Tower, London, Henry Taylor, swimming, 1908. 150fr, City Hall, Stockholm, Greco-Roman wrestling, 1912.

1972, Dec. 28 **Engr.**
C105 AP56 30fr brt grn, mag & brn .40 .25
C106 AP56 40fr vio bl, emer & brn .50 .25
C107 AP56 50fr car rose, vio bl & Prus bl .55 .40
C108 AP56 100fr sl, red lil & brn 1.00 .50
C109 AP56 150fr red lil, blk & Prus bl 1.60 1.20
Nos. C105-C109 (5) 4.05 2.60

Olympic Games 1896-1912.

WHO Emblem, Surgeon and Nurse — AP57

1973, Apr. 7 **Photo.** ***Perf. 13***
C110 AP57 100fr multi 1.50 .85

WHO, 25th anniv.

World Map, Arrows, Waves — AP58

1973, May 17 **Litho.** ***Perf. 12½***
C111 AP58 200fr multicolored 2.40 1.10

5th International Telecommunications Day.

AP58a

Head and City Hall, Brussels.

1973, Sept. 17 **Engr.** ***Perf. 13***
C112 AP58a 100fr pur, ocher & brn 1.40 .80

African Weeks, Brussels, Sept. 15-30, 1973.

Europafrica Issue

Map of Central African Republic with Industry and Agriculture, Young Man — AP59

1973, Sept. 28 **Engr.** ***Perf. 13***
C113 AP59 100fr sepia, grn & org 1.60 .80

Carrier Pigeon with Letter and UPU Emblem — AP60

1973, Oct. 9 **Photo.**
C114 AP60 200fr multi 2.50 1.10

Universal Postal Union Day.

WMO Emblem, Weather Map — AP61

1973, Oct. 20 **Engr.** ***Perf. 13***
C115 AP61 150fr brt ultra & sl grn 2.50 1.00

Cent. of intl. meteorological cooperation.

Copernicus, Heliocentric System — AP62

1973, Nov. 2 **Photo.**
C116 AP62 100fr gold & multi 3.00 1.75

Copernicus (1473-1543), Polish astronomer.

Pres. Bokassa AP63

Pres. Bokassa — AP64

1973, Nov. 30 **Photo.** ***Perf. 12½***
C117 AP63 50fr multi .75 .40
C118 AP64 100fr multi 1.40 .70

Rocket Launch and Apollo 17 Badge — AP65

65fr, Capsule over moonscape, horiz. 100fr, Moon landing, horiz. 150fr, Astronauts on moon. 200fr, Splashdown with parachutes and badge.

1973, Dec. 15 **Engr.** ***Perf. 13***
C119 AP65 50fr ver, gray grn & brn .50 .30
C120 AP65 65fr dk brn, brn red & sl grn .65 .40
C121 AP65 100fr ver, slate & choc 1.10 .60
C122 AP65 150fr brn, ol & sl grn 1.75 .80
C123 AP65 200fr red, bl & sl grn 2.00 1.10
Nos. C119-C123 (5) 6.00 3.20

Apollo 17 US moon mission, 12/7-19/72.

St. Teresa — AP66

1973, Dec. 25
C124 AP66 500fr vio bl & grnsh bl 5.75 3.50

St. Teresa of the Infant Jesus, the Little Flower (1873-1897), Carmelite nun.

UPU Emblem, Letter — AP67

1974, Oct. 9 **Engr.** ***Perf. 13***
C125 AP67 500fr multi 6.75 4.00

Centenary of Universal Postal Union.
For surcharge see No. C159.

Presidents and Flags of Cameroun, CAR, Gabon and Congo — AP68

1974, Dec. 8 **Photo.** ***Perf. 13***
C126 AP68 100fr gold & multi 1.40 .70

See note after Cameroun No. 595.
For surcharge see No. C155.

Marshal Bokassa AP69

100fr, Bokassa in Marshal's uniform with cape.

1975, Feb. 22 Photo. *Perf. 13*

C127	AP69	50fr tan & multi	.65	.40
C128	AP69	100fr tan & multi	1.40	.45

Jean Bedel Bokassa, President for Life and Marshal of the Republic.

Mask, Map of Africa, Arphila Emblem — AP70

1975, Aug. 25 Engr. *Perf. 13*

C129	AP70	100fr brt bl, red brn & red	1.25	.65

ARPHILA 75 International Philatelic Exhibition, Paris, June 6-16.
For surcharge see No. C156.

Albert Schweitzer and Dugout, Lambarene AP71

1975, Sept. 30 Engr. *Perf. 13*

C130	AP71	200fr blk, ultra & ol	4.50	2.25

Dr. Albert Schweitzer (1875-1965), medical missionary and musician.
For surcharge see No. C158.

Pres. Bokassa's Houseboat, Bow — AP72

40fr, Pres. Bokassa's houseboat, stern.

1976, Feb. 22 Litho. *Perf. 13*

C131	AP72	30fr multi	.60	.30
C132	AP72	40fr multi	.80	.55

Monument to Franco-CAR Cooperation AP73

Presidents and Flags of France and CAR AP74

1976, Mar. 5

C133	AP73	100fr multi	1.40	.90
C134	AP74	200fr multi	2.50	1.35

Official visit of Pres. Valery Giscard d'Estaing to Central African Republic, 3/5-8.
For surcharge see No. C157.

Apollo Soyuz Type, 1976

Designs: 100fr, Soyuz space ship. 200fr, Apollo space ship. 300fr, Astronauts and cosmonauts in cabin. 500fr, Apollo and Soyuz after link-up.

1976, June 14 Litho. *Perf. 14x13½*

C135	A90	100fr multi	.90	.25
C136	A90	200fr multi	1.60	.55
C137	A90	300fr multi	2.60	.95
		Nos. C135-C137 (3)	6.45	1.75

Souvenir Sheet

C138	A90	500fr multi	5.00	1.75

For surcharges see Nos. C161, C168, C173, C177.

French Hussar AP75

Uniforms: 125fr, Scottish "Black Watch." 150fr, German dragoon. 200fr, British grenadier. 250fr, American ranger. 450fr, American dragoon.

1976, July 4 *Perf. 13½*

C139	AP75	100fr multi	.75	.30
C140	AP75	125fr multi	.80	.45
C141	AP75	150fr multi	1.00	.45
C142	AP75	200fr multi	1.50	.55
C143	AP75	250fr multi	2.00	.95
		Nos. C139-C143 (5)	6.05	2.70

Souvenir Sheet

C144	AP75	450fr multi	6.75	2.50

American Bicentennial.
For surcharges see Nos. C162, C166-C167, C169, C172, C176.

Acherontia Atropos — AP76

100fr, Papilio nireus & niocha marnois.

1976, Sept. 20 Litho. *Perf. 12½*

C145	AP76	50fr multi	5.00	1.50
C146	AP76	100fr multi	10.00	2.00

For surcharges see Nos. C160, C163.

Olympic Winners Type, 1976

Designs: 100fr, Women's figure skating, Dorothy Hamill, vert. 200fr, Ice skating, Alexander Gorshkov and Ludmilla Pakhomova. 300fr, Men's figure skating, John Curry, vert. 500fr, Downhill skiing, Rosi Mittermaier, vert.

1976, Sept. 23 Litho. *Perf. 13½*

C147	A92	100fr multi	.65	.35
C148	A92	200fr multi	2.10	.70
C149	A92	300fr multi	2.75	1.10
		Nos. C147-C149 (3)	5.50	2.15

Souvenir Sheet

C150	A92	500fr multi	5.50	1.75

For surcharges see Nos. C164, C170, C174, C178.

Viking Mars Type, 1976

Designs: 100fr, Phases of Mars landing. 200fr, Viking descending on Mars, horiz. 300fr, Viking probe. 500fr, Viking flight to Mars, horiz.

1976, Dec.

C151	A93	100fr multi	.85	.35
C152	A93	200fr multi	2.10	.70
C153	A93	300fr multi	2.60	1.10
		Nos. C151-C153 (3)	5.55	2.15

Souvenir Sheet

C154	A93	500fr multi	5.00	1.75

For surcharges and overprints see Nos. C165, C171, C175, C179, C212-C215.

Central African Empire

Stamps of 1973-76 Overprinted in Black, Violet Blue or Gold

Printing and Perforations as Before

1977, Mar.

C155	AP68	100fr (#C126;B)	1.30	1.30
C156	AP70	100fr (#C129;VB)	1.30	1.30
C157	AP73	100fr (#C133;G)	1.30	1.30
C158	AP71	200fr (#C130;B)	4.00	4.00
C159	AP67	500fr (#C125;B)	12.00	12.00
		Nos. C155-C159 (5)	19.90	19.90

No bar on No. C159.

Stamps of 1976 Overprinted in Black on Silver Panel

1977, Apr. 1

C160	AP76	50fr (#C145)	.55	.55
C161	A90	100fr (#C135)	1.10	1.10
C162	AP75	100fr (#C139)	1.10	1.10
C163	AP76	100fr (#C146)	1.10	1.10
C164	A92	100fr (#C147)	1.10	1.10
C165	A93	100fr (#C151)	1.10	1.10
C166	AP75	125fr (#C140)	1.40	1.40
C167	AP75	150fr (#C141)	1.60	1.60
C168	A90	200fr (#C136)	2.75	2.75
C169	AP75	200fr (#C142)	2.50	2.50
C170	A92	200fr (#C148)	2.25	2.25
C171	A93	200fr (#C152)	2.25	2.25
C172	AP75	250fr (#C143)	2.75	2.75
C173	A90	300fr (#C137)	3.50	3.50
C174	A92	300fr (#C149)	3.50	3.50
C175	A93	300fr (#C153)	3.50	3.50
		Nos. C160-C175 (16)	32.05	32.05

Souvenir Sheets

C176	AP75	450fr (#C144)	5.50	5.50
C177	A90	500fr (#C138)	8.00	8.00
C178	A92	500fr (#C150)	5.50	5.50
C179	A93	500fr (#C154)	5.50	5.50

Overprint on type AP75 is in upper and lower case letters.

Nobel Prize Type, 1977

Designs: 100fr, Rudyard Kipling. 200fr, Ernest Hemingway. 300fr, Luigi Pirandello. 500fr, Rabindranath Tagore.

1977, Apr. 1 Litho. *Perf. 13½*

C180	A94	100fr multi	1.75	.40
C181	A94	200fr multi	3.50	.70
C182	A94	300fr multi	5.75	.95
		Nos. C180-C182 (3)	11.00	2.05

Souvenir Sheet

C183	A94	500fr multi	5.50	1.75

Zeppelin Type of 1977

100fr, Germany No. C42 and North Pole. 200fr, Germany No. C44 and Science and Industry Building, Chicago. 300fr, Germany No. C35 and Brandenburg Gate, Berlin. 500fr, US No. C14 and US Capitol.

1977, Apr. 11 Litho. *Perf. 11*

C184	A95	100fr multi	1.20	.35
C185	A95	200fr multi	2.40	.65
C186	A95	300fr multi	3.00	1.00
		Nos. C184-C186 (3)	6.60	2.00

Souvenir Sheet

C187	A95	500fr multi	5.50	2.00

75th anniversary of Zeppelin.

Bokassa Type of 1977

1977, Dec. 4 Litho. *Perf. 13½*

C188	A98	200fr multi	1.75	.80
C189	A98	300fr multi	2.50	1.25
a.		Souvenir sheet, 500fr	5.50	2.50

Coronation of Emperor Bokassa I, Dec. 4. No. C189a contains a horizontal stamp in similar design. A 2500fr gold embossed horizontal stamp in similar design exists. Value $20.

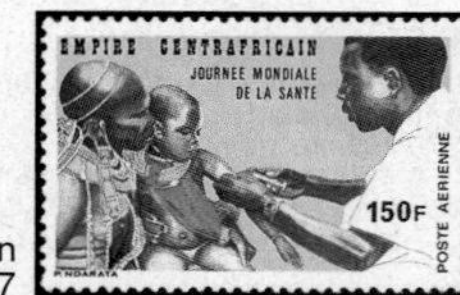

Vaccination AP77

1977 Litho. *Perf. 14x13½*

C190	AP77	150fr multi	3.50	1.50

World Health Day.

Communications Type of 1978

Designs: 100fr, Balloon and spaceships docking in space. 200fr, Hydrofoil and Concorde. 500fr, Tom-tom and Zeppelin. No. C193A, Early postman and rider, UPU emblem, Concorde. No. C193B, Mail coach, dove, satellites.

1978, May 17 Litho. *Perf. 13½*

C191	A107	100fr multi	1.10	.35
C192	A107	200fr multi	1.10	.55

Souvenir Sheet

C193	A107	500fr multi	5.75	2.25

Cent. of progress of posts and telecommunications. No. C193 contains one 53x35mm stamp.

1978, Mar. 21 Litho. & Embossed
Size: 57x39mm

C193A	A107	1500fr gold & multi	*30.00*	5.00

Souvenir Sheet

C193B	A107	1500fr gold & multi	15.00	4.75

Nos. C193A-C193B exist imperf. No. C193A exists in a souvenir sheet of one. No. C193B contains one 57x39mm stamp.

Clement Ader and his Plane — AP78

Designs: 50fr, Wilbur and Orville Wright and plane. 60fr, John W. Alcock, Arthur W. Brown and plane. 100fr, Alan Cobham and plane 150fr, Claude Dornier and hydroplane. 500fr, Wilbur and Orville Wright and plane.

1978, Sept. 19 *Perf. 14*

C194 AP78 40fr multi .50 .25
C195 AP78 50fr multi .50 .25
C196 AP78 60fr multi .60 .35
C197 AP78 100fr multi 1.15 .40
C198 AP78 150fr multi 1.75 .65
Nos. C194-C198 (5) 4.50 1.90

Souvenir Sheet

C199 AP78 500fr multi 5.50 1.75

History of aviation.

Philexafrique II-Essen Issue
Common Design Types

No. C200, Crocodile, No. C3. No. C201, Birds, Mecklenburg-Schwerin No. 1.

1978, Nov. 1 Litho. *Perf. 12½*

C200 CD138 100fr multi 1.90 1.10
C201 CD139 100fr multi 1.90 1.10
a. Pair, #C200-C201 + label 7.50 7.50

Bokassa Type of 1978

150fr, Catherine & Jean Bedel Bokassa.

1978, Dec. 4 Litho. *Perf. 13*

C202 A113 150fr multi, horiz. 1.90 .70

First anniv. of coronation. A 1000fr gold embossed souvenir sheet showing Emperor Bokassa exists. Value $9.

Rowland Hill Type of 1978

Designs (Rowland Hill and): 100fr, Mailman and Tuscany No. 23. 200fr, Balloon and France No. 1. 500fr, Central Africa Nos. 1-2.

1978, Dec. 27

C203 A114 100fr multi 1.75 .60
C204 A114 200fr multi 2.25 .70

Souvenir Sheet

C205 A114 500fr multi 5.00 1.75

Sir Rowland Hill (1795-1879), originator of penny postage. No. C205 contains one 37½x39mm stamp.

A 1500fr gold embossed stamp and souvenir sheet exist. Value, set $27.50.

Rattan Table and Chair — AP76a

1978 ? Litho. *Perf. 14x13¼*

C205A AP76a 60fr multi — —

IYC Type of 1979

Designs (UNICEF, Eagle Emblems and): 100fr, Chinese girl flying kites and German Do-X flying boat, 1929. 200fr, Boys playing leapfrog, hurdler and Olympic emblem. 500fr, Child with abacus and Albert Einstein with his equation.

1979, Mar. 6 *Perf. 13½*

C206 A115 100fr multi 1.25 .40
C207 A115 200fr multi 2.50 .80

Souvenir Sheet

C208 A115 500fr multi 5.00 1.75

International Year of the Child. No. C208 contains one 56x33mm stamp.

A 1500fr gold embossed stamp and souvenir sheet exist. Value, set $27.50.

Olympic Type of 1979

Moscow '80 Emblem, various sports and: 100fr, Hurdles & "B." 200fr, Broad jump & "A." 500fr, Pole vault, horiz.

1979, Mar. 16 Litho. *Perf. 13*

C209 A116 100fr multi 1.10 .40
C210 A116 200fr multi 2.10 .65

Souvenir Sheet

C210A A116 500fr multi — —

22nd Olympic Games, Moscow, July 19-Aug. 3, 1980. No. C210A contains one 57x39mm stamp. A 1500fr gold embossed souvenir sheet exists showing diver, runner and javelin. Value, $12.50.

National Husbandry Association Type

1979, Aug. Litho. *Perf. 13*

C211 A119 60fr Horse 5.25 2.00

Central African Republic

Nos. C151-C154 Overprinted in Black or Silver

1979, Oct. Litho. *Perf. 14x13½*

C212 A93 100fr multi .85 .55
C213 A93 200fr multi 1.60 .85
C214 A93 300fr multi 2.40 1.25
Nos. C212-C214 (3) 4.85 2.65

Souvenir Sheet

C215 A93 500fr multi (S) 5.00 5.00

Apollo 11 moon landing, 10th anniversary.

Ski Jump, Lake Placid '80 Emblem — AP79

1979, Nov. 11 Litho. *Perf. 13½*

C216 AP79 60fr shown .55 .25
C217 AP79 100fr Downhill skiing .90 .40
C218 AP79 200fr Hockey 1.90 .85
C219 AP79 300fr Slalom 2.60 1.25
Nos. C216-C219 (4) 5.95 2.75

Souvenir Sheet

C220 AP79 500fr Bobsledding 5.00 1.75

13th Winter Olympics Games, Lake Placid, NY, Feb. 12-24, 1980.

For overprints see Nos. C224-C228.

Space Type of 1980

150fr, Early satellites. 200fr, Space shuttle. 500fr, Apollo 11, Armstrong. No. C223A, Armstrong, Apollo 11. No. C223B, Space shuttle, horiz.

1980, Apr. 8 Litho. *Perf. 13½*

C221 A125 150fr multi 1.40 .45
C222 A125 200fr multi 1.75 .65

Souvenir Sheet

C223 A125 500fr multi 5.50 1.40

Litho. & Embossed

Size: 51x57mm

C223A A125 1500fr multi *25.00* 5.00

Souvenir Sheet

C223B A125 1500fr multi 8.50

C223A-C223B exist imperf. No. C223A exists in a souvenir sheet of one. Value $40. No. C223B contains one 57x51mm stamp.

Nos. C216-C220 Overprinted

a

b

c

d

e

1980, May 12 Litho. *Perf. 13½*

C224 AP79 (a) 60fr multi .45 .25
C225 AP79 (b) 100fr multi .70 .40
C226 AP79 (c) 200fr multi 1.75 .85
C227 AP79 (d) 300fr multi 2.50 1.25
Nos. C224-C227 (4) 5.40 2.75

Souvenir Sheet

C228 AP79 (e) 500fr multi 5.00 5.00

World Telecommunications Day — AP80

1980, June 26 Litho. *Perf. 12½*

C229 AP80 100fr multi 1.10 .55
C230 AP80 150fr multi, vert. 1.40 .80

Olympic Type of 1980

100fr, Boxing. 150fr, Hurdles.

250fr, Long jump. No. C233A, Relay race, diff. No. C233B, Basketball, vert.

1980, July 25 Litho. *Perf. 13½*

C231 A126 100fr multi 1.00 .25
C232 A126 150fr multi 1.60 .40

Souvenir Sheet

C233 A126 250fr multi 3.00 .65

Litho. & Embossed

C233A A126 1500fr multi 25.00 5.00

Souvenir Sheet

C233B A126 1500fr multi 11.00 4.75

22nd Summer Olympic Games, Moscow, July 19-Aug. 3. No. C233 contains one 39x36mm stamp.

For overprints see Nos. C248-C250B.

Europe-Africa Type of 1980

150fr, Meteorology. 200fr, Aviation.

500fr, Concorde jet. No. C236A, Boy Scouts. No. C236B, Concorde.

1980, Nov. 4 Litho. *Perf. 13½*

C234 A127 150fr multi 1.50 .50
C235 A127 200fr multi 1.90 .60

Souvenir Sheet

C236 A127 500fr multi 5.50 1.60

No. C236 contains one 41½x29mm stamp.

Litho. & Embossed

Size: 42x39mm

C236A A127 1500fr multi 15.00 4.00

Souvenir Sheet

C236B A127 1500fr multi 12.00 4.75

Nos. C236A-C236B exist imperf. No. C236B contains one 42x39mm stamp.

No. C236A exists in a souvenir sheet of one. Value $30.

Soccer Type of 1981

100fr, Netherlands. 200fr, Spain.

500fr, Argentina. No. C239A, Players, trophy. No. C239B, Players, trophy, diff.

1981, Jan. 13 Litho. *Perf. 13½*

C237 A130 100fr multi 1.00 .25
C238 A130 200fr multi 1.75 .55

Souvenir Sheet

C239 A130 500fr multi 6.25 1.75

Litho. & Embossed

Size: 57x39mm

C239A A130 1500fr multi 22.50 5.50

Souvenir Sheet

C239B A130 1500fr multi 10.00 4.00

No. C239A exists with tabs for either Philexafrique II or Essen 78.

Nos. C239A-C239B exist imperf. No. C239A exists in a souvenir sheet of one. Value $38. No. C239B contains one 36x60mm stamp.

Jacob Wrestling with the Angel, by Rembrandt AP81

Rembrandt Paintings: 90fr, Christ during the Storm. 150fr, Jeremiah Mourning the Destruction of Jerusalem. 250fr, Tobit Accusing Anne of Theft of a Goat. 500fr, Belshazzar's Feast, horiz.

1981, Feb. 20 *Perf. 12½*

C240 AP81 60fr multi .55 .25
C241 AP81 90fr multi 1.00 .25
C242 AP81 150fr multi 1.75 .65
C243 AP81 250fr multi 3.00 .80
Nos. C240-C243 (4) 6.30 1.95

Souvenir Sheet

C244 AP81 500fr multi 5.50 1.75

Picasso Type of 1981

Paintings: 150fr, Woman in Mirror with Self-portrait. 200fr, Woman Sleeping, The Dream. 500fr, Portrait of Maia (the Artist's Daughter). No. C247A, Two Women and Glasses, Picasso. No. C247B, Woman with Handbag, statue of standing woman, vert.

1981, June 30 Litho. *Perf. 13½*

C245 A133 150fr multi 2.25 .45
C246 A133 200fr multi 2.50 .65

Souvenir Sheet

C247 A133 500fr multi 5.75 2.25

No. C247 contains one 42x46mm stamp.

Litho. & Embossed

Size: 57x39mm

C247A A133 1500fr gold & multi 17.50 6.00

Souvenir Sheet

C247B A133 1500fr gold & multi 12.00

Nos. C247A-C247B exist imperf. No. C247A exists in a souvenir sheet of one. Value $22.50. No. C247B contains one 39x58mm stamp.

Nos. C231-C233B Overprinted in Gold

1981 **Litho.** ***Perf. 13½***

C248 A126 100fr multi 1.00 .25
C249 A126 150fr multi 1.40 .40

Souvenir Sheet

C250 A126 250fr multi 3.00 .65

Litho. & Embossed

C250A A126 1500fr on #C233A 16.00 6.00

Souvenir Sheet

C250B A126 1500fr on #C233B 15.00

No. C250A exists in a souvenir sheet of 1. Value $35.

Royal Wedding Type of 1981

150fr, Prince of Wales arms. 200fr, Palace. 500fr, St. Paul's Cathedral. No. C253A, Diana, Charles. No. C253B, Charles, Diana, ship.

1981, Aug. 20 **Litho.** ***Perf. 13½***

C251 A136 150fr multi 1.60 .40
C252 A136 200fr multi 2.10 .55

Souvenir Sheet

C253 A136 500fr multi 4.75 1.40

No. C253 contains one 60x32mm stamp.

Litho. & Embossed

Size: 51x42mm

C253A A136 1500fr multi 15.00 4.00

Souvenir Sheet

C253B A136 1500fr multi 12.00

Nos. C253A-C253B exist imperf. No. C253A exists in a souvenir sheet of one. Value $21. No. C253B contains one 51x42mm stamp.

Navigator Type of 1981

100fr, O. Kersauson. 200fr, Chichester. 500fr, A. Colas. No. C256A, Riguidel. No. C256B, Tabarly.

1981, Sept. 4 **Litho.** ***Perf. 13½***

C254 A139 100fr multi 1.10 .70
C255 A139 200fr multi 2.40 1.40

Souvenir Sheet

C256 A139 500fr multi 6.50 1.40

Litho. & Embossed

Size: 51x42mm

C256A A139 1500fr multi 16.00 4.50

Souvenir Sheet

C256B A139 1500fr multi 13.00

Nos. C256A-C256B exist imperf. No. C256A exists in a souvenir sheet of one. Value $40. No. C256B contains one 51x42mm stamp.

Lizard AP82

1981, Oct. 30 ***Perf. 12½x13***

C257 AP82 30fr shown 1.00 .25
C258 AP82 60fr Snake 1.25 .30
C259 AP82 110fr Crocodile 2.50 .45
Nos. C257-C259 (3) 4.75 1.00

Christmas Type of 1981

140fr, Correggio. 200fr, Gentileschi, 1610. 500fr, Holy Family, by Cranach. No. C262A, Hans Memling, c. 1470. No. C262B, Fra Angelico, 1438.

1981, Dec. 24 ***Perf. 13½***

C260 A143 140fr multi 2.50 .45
C261 A143 200fr multi 4.50 .70

Souvenir Sheet

C262 A143 500fr multi 6.75 1.75

No. C262 contains one 41x50mm stamp.

Litho. & Embossed

Size: 30x60mm

C262A A143 1500fr multi 15.00 4.50

Souvenir Sheet

C262B A143 1500fr multi 11.00

Nos. C262A-C262B exist imperf. No. C262A exists in a souvenir sheet of one. Value $25. No. C262B contains one 30x60mm stamp.

Animal Type of 1982

300fr, Mandrill. 500fr, Lion.
600fr, Nile crocodiles. No. C265A, Leopard, Rotary emblem. No. C265B, Emblem, eagle, horiz.

1982, Jan. 22 **Litho.** ***Perf. 13½***

C263 A145 300fr multi 3.25 .65
C264 A145 500fr multi 5.50 1.40

Souvenir Sheet

C265 A145 600fr multi 6.75 1.60

No. C265 contains one 47x38mm stamp.

Litho. & Embossed

Size: 51x57mm

C265A A145 1500fr multi 15.00 4.00

Souvenir Sheet

C265B A145 1500fr multi 13.00

Nos. C265A-C265B exist imperf. No. C265A exists in a souvenir sheet of one. Value $42.50. No. C265B contains one 57x51mm stamp.

Transportation Type of 1982 and

AP82a

Designs: 300fr, Savannah cargo ship. 500fr, Columbia space shuttle. 600fr, Spirit of Locomotion emblem. No. C268A, Space shuttle launch, horiz. No. C268B, Shuttle, space telescope.

1982, Feb. 27 **Litho.** ***Perf. 13½***

C266 A147 300fr multi 3.75 .65
C267 A147 500fr multi 5.50 1.40

Souvenir Sheet

C268 A147 600fr multi 5.50 1.60

Litho. & Embossed

C268A AP82a 1500fr gold & multi 15.00 4.50

Souvenir Sheet

C268B AP82a 1500fr gold & multi 11.50

No. C268 contains one 39x43mm stamp. No. C268B contains one 51x42mm stamp.
No. C268A exists in a souvenir sheet of 1. Value $50.

Olympic Type of 1982

1982, July 24 **Litho.** ***Perf. 13½***

C269 A149 300fr Diving 3.00 .80
C270 A149 500fr Equestrian 5.00 1.40

Souvenir Sheet

C271 A149 600fr Basketball 5.50 1.60

No. C271 contains one 38x56mm stamp.

Diana Type of 1982

1982, July 20 **Litho.** ***Perf. 13½***

C272 A150 300fr multi 3.25 .80
C273 A150 500fr multi 5.50 1.40

Souvenir Sheet

C274 A150 600fr multi 5.75 1.60

No. C274 contains one 56x32mm stamp.

Christmas 1982 AP83

Raphael Paintings: 150fr, Beautiful Gardener. 500fr, Holy Family.

1982, Dec. ***Perf. 13***

C275 AP83 150fr multi 2.00 .50
C276 AP83 500fr multi 5.50 1.40

Space Type of 1982

Designs: Various satellites and space scenes. No. C279A, European communications satellite, controller. No. C279B, Viking on Mars, vert.

1982, Aug. 15 **Litho.** ***Perf. 13½***

C277 A151 300fr multi 3.00 .80
C278 A151 500fr multi 5.00 1.40

Souvenir Sheet

C279 A151 600fr multi 5.00 1.60

Litho. & Embossed

Size: 60x36mm

C279A A151 1500fr gold & multi 15.00 4.50

Souvenir Sheet

C279B A151 1500fr gold & multi 12.00

Nos. C279A-C279B exist imperf. No. C279A exists in a souvenir sheet of one. Value $55. No. C279B contains one 36x60mm stamp.

Birth of Prince William of Wales, June 21, 1982 — AP84

500fr, Diana, William.
600fr, Family. No. C281A, Diana, William, Charles. No. 281B, Diana, William, vert.

1983, Jan. 22

C280 AP84 500fr multi 5.50 1.40

Souvenir Sheet

C281 AP84 600fr multi 5.50 4.00

Litho. & Embossed

C281A AP84 1500fr gold & multi 15.00 3.50

Souvenir Sheet

C281B AP84 1500fr gold & multi 10.00

No. C281A exists in a souvenir sheet of 1. Value $40.

Manned Flight Bicentenary AP85

65fr, Robert's & Hullin's balloon. 130fr, John Wise's, 1859. 350fr, Mail balloon, 1870. 400fr, Dirigible Underberg.
500fr, Montgolfiere, 1783.

1983, Apr.

C282 AP85 65fr multicolored 1.00 .25
C283 AP85 130fr multicolored 1.50 .35
C284 AP85 350fr multicolored 3.25 1.00
C285 AP85 400fr multicolored 4.25 1.25
Nos. C282-C285 (4) 10.00 2.85

Souvenir Sheet

C286 AP85 500fr multicolored 5.75 1.75

Pre-Olympics — AP86

Various equestrian events.

1983, July **Litho.** ***Perf. 13***

C287 AP86 100fr multi 1.00 .50
C288 AP86 200fr multi 2.10 .70
C289 AP86 300fr multi 2.75 .90
C290 AP86 400fr multi 3.50 1.25
Nos. C287-C290 (4) 9.35 3.35

Souvenir Sheet

C291 AP86 500fr multi 5.50 1.40

Animal Type of 1983

Endangered Animals, Rotary Emblem: 400fr, Black rhinoceros, parrot, zebra, scouts. 500fr, Lions, parrot, antelope, elephant, flag, Rotary Int'l emblem. 600fr, Leopard.

1983, Nov. 14 **Litho.** ***Perf. 13½***

C291A A170 400fr multicolored 10.00 3.00
C292 A170 500fr multicolored 12.00 3.50

Souvenir Sheet

C293 A170 600fr multicolored 16.00 4.00

15th World Scout Jamboree, Alberta (400fr). No. C293 contains one 47x32mm stamp.

Christmas 1983 AP88

Paintings: 130fr, Annunciation, by da Vinci. 205fr, Virgin of the Rocks, by da Vinci. 350fr, Adoration of the Shepherds, by Rubens. 500fr, Virgin and Child with Donor, by Rubens.

1984, Jan. 3 **Litho.** ***Perf. 13***

C294 AP88 130fr multi 1.25 .40
C295 AP88 205fr multi 2.00 .55
C296 AP88 350fr multi 3.50 1.10
C297 AP88 500fr multi 5.00 1.35
Nos. C294-C297 (4) 11.75 3.40

1984 Summer Olympics — AP89

Various gymnastic and rhythmic gymnastic events. 65fr, 100fr, 205fr, 350fr vert.
500fr, Rhythmic formation.

1984, Mar. 13 **Litho.** ***Perf. 13***

C298 AP89 65fr multi .55 .25
C299 AP89 100fr multi 1.10 .25
C300 AP89 130fr multi 1.40 .35
C301 AP89 205fr multi 2.25 .65
C302 AP89 350fr multi 4.00 1.10
Nos. C298-C302 (5) 9.30 2.60

Souvenir Sheet

Perf. 13½x13

C302A AP89 500fr multi 5.50 1.75

For overprint see No. 705.

Summer Olympics Winners AP90

60fr, 400 meter relay. 140fr, 400 meter hurdles. 300fr, 5000 meter race. 440fr, Decathlon. 550fr, 800 meter race, horiz.

1985, Jan. 7 Litho. *Perf. 14*
C303 AP90 60fr multicolored .55 .25
C304 AP90 140fr multicolored 1.75 .45
C305 AP90 300fr multicolored 3.50 .90
C306 AP90 440fr multicolored 4.50 1.20
Nos. C303-C306 (4) 10.30 2.80

Souvenir Sheet

C307 AP90 500fr multicolored 5.50 1.75

Christmas 1984 — AP91

Paintings by Titian: 130fr, Virgin and Infant Jesus. 350fr, Virgin with Rabbit. 400fr, Virgin and Child.

1985, Jan. 17 Litho. *Perf. 13*
C308 AP91 130fr multi 1.10 .55
C309 AP91 350fr multi 2.50 1.25
C310 AP91 400fr multi 3.50 1.60
Nos. C308-C310 (3) 7.10 3.40

Audubon Bicentenary — AP92

60fr, Otus asio. 110fr, Coccizus minor, vert. 200fr, Zenaidura macroura, vert. 500fr, Aix sponsa.

1985, Jan. 25 Litho. *Perf. 13*
C311 AP92 60fr multicolored .80 .25
C312 AP92 110fr multicolored 1.20 .45
C313 AP92 200fr multicolored 2.00 1.00
C314 AP92 500fr multicolored 5.00 2.50
Nos. C311-C314 (4) 9.00 4.20

Christmas 1985 AP93

Religious paintings: 100fr, Virgin with Angels, by the Master of Burgo de Osma. 200fr, Nativity, by Louis Le Nain (1593-1648). 400fr, Virgin and Child with Dove, by Piero de Cosimo (1462-1521).

1985, Dec. 24 Litho. *Perf. 13*
C315 AP93 100fr multi 1.00 .45
C316 AP93 200fr multi 2.25 .90
C317 AP93 400fr multi 4.25 1.50
Nos. C315-C317 (3) 7.50 2.85

Halley's Comet — AP94

110fr, Edmond Halley. 130fr, Giotto probe. 200fr, Comet, planet. 300fr, Vega probe. 400fr, Space shuttle.

1986, Mar. 8
C318 AP94 110fr multicolored 1.00 .25
C319 AP94 130fr multicolored 1.40 .25
C320 AP94 200fr multicolored 2.25 .50
C321 AP94 300fr multicolored 3.00 .75
C322 AP94 400fr multicolored 4.50 1.00
Nos. C318-C322 (5) 12.15 2.75

Christmas AP95

Painting details: 250fr, Nativity, by Giotto. 440fr, Adoration of the Magi, by Botticelli, vert. 500fr, Nativity, by Giotto, diff.

1986, Dec. 24 Litho. *Perf. 13½*
C323 AP95 250fr multi 2.10 .90
C324 AP95 440fr multi 3.75 1.35
C325 AP95 500fr multi 4.50 1.90
Nos. C323-C325 (3) 10.35 4.15

Tennis at the 1988 Olympics — AP96

Various plays.

1986, Dec. 31 *Perf. 12½*
C326 AP96 150fr multi 1.40 .60
C327 AP96 250fr multi, vert. 2.75 .70
C328 AP96 440fr multi, vert. 3.25 1.35
C329 AP96 600fr multi 5.75 1.40
Nos. C326-C329 (4) 13.15 3.95

1988 Summer Olympics, Seoul — AP97

100fr, Triple jump, vert. 200fr, High jump. 300fr, Long jump. 400fr, Pole vault, vert. 500fr, High jump, diff.

1987, June 15 Litho. *Perf. 13*
C330 AP97 100fr multicolored .80 .35
C331 AP97 200fr multicolored 1.60 .65
C332 AP97 300fr multicolored 2.40 .90
C333 AP97 400fr multicolored 3.25 1.75
Nos. C330-C333 (4) 8.05 3.65

Souvenir Sheet

C334 AP97 500fr multicolored 4.25 2.50

1988 Summer Olympics, Seoul — AP98

Stamps on stamps and gymnasts: 90fr, No. C94, balance beam, vert. 200fr, No. C21, balance beam, diff. 300fr, No. C22, pommel horse. 400fr, No. C23, parallel bars. 500fr, No. C93, rings.

1988, July 26 Litho. *Perf. 13*
C335 AP98 90fr multi .80 .30
C336 AP98 200fr multi 1.75 .50
C337 AP98 300fr multi 2.75 .90
C338 AP98 400fr multi 3.50 1.40
Nos. C335-C338 (4) 8.80 3.10

Souvenir Sheet

C339 AP98 500fr multi 5.00 2.00

1st Moon Landing, 20th Anniv. AP99

1989, Aug. 4 Litho. *Perf. 13*
C340 AP99 40fr Apollo 11 .30 .25
C341 AP99 80fr Apollo 15 .65 .30
C342 AP99 130fr Apollo 16 1.25 .75
C343 AP99 1000fr Apollo 17 9.00 2.75
Nos. C340-C343 (4) 11.20 4.05

World Cup Soccer Championships, Italy — AP100

1990, July 7 Litho. *Perf. 13*
C344 AP100 5fr multicolored .25 .25
C345 AP100 30fr multi, diff. .30 .25
C346 AP100 500fr multi, diff. 4.50 1.10
C347 AP100 1000fr multi, diff. 8.25 2.00
Nos. C344-C347 (4) 13.30 3.60

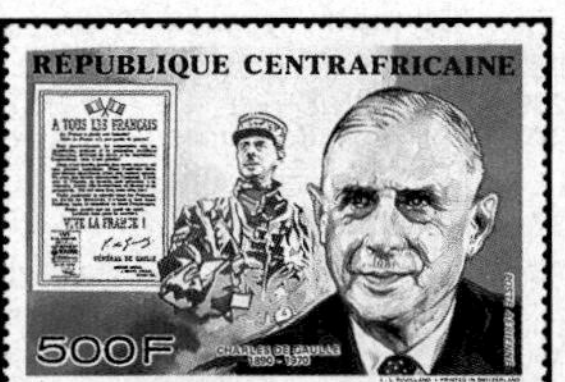

Charles de Gaulle (1890-1979) — AP101

1990, July 27 *Perf. 13½*
C348 AP101 500fr multicolored 3.75 1.10

No. C348 exists in a souvenir sheet of 1.

For overprint see No. C360.

Don Mattingly, Baseball Player — AP102

Saturn V Rocket, Apollo 11 Astronauts — AP103

Charles de Gaulle, Birth Cent. AP104

No. C352, De Gaulle and Cross of Lorraine.

1990, July 27 Litho. *Perf. 13½*
C349 AP102 300fr multicolored 2.75 .80

Souvenir Sheet

C350 AP103 1000fr multicolored 9.00 2.00

Litho. & Embossed

C351 AP104 1500fr gold & multi 16.00 5.50

Souvenir Sheet

C352 AP104 1500fr gold & multi 12.00

No. C351 exists in souvenir sheet of 1. Value $15. This souvenir sheet also exists imperf. and with an overprint in the sheet margin.

For overprints see Nos. C355-C356.

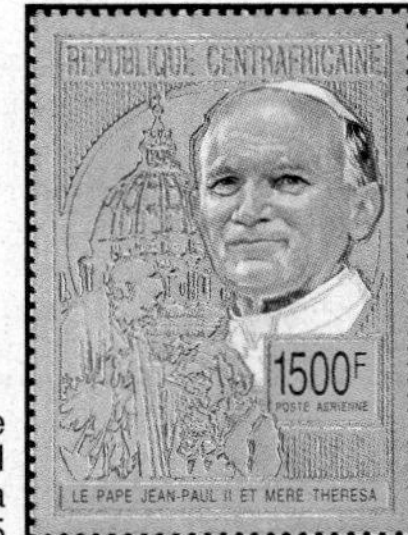

Visit of Pope John Paul II to Africa AP105

Pope John Paul II and: No. C353, Mother Theresa, portrait. No. C354, Papal arms, globe.

1993 Litho. & Embossed *Perf. 13½*
C353 AP105 1500fr gold & multi 15.00 5.00

Souvenir Sheet

C354 AP105 1500fr gold & multi 20.00

No. C353 exists in a souvenir sheet of 1. Value $20.

No. C351 Overprinted

Litho. & Embossed

1994, June 6 ***Perf. 13½***

C355	AP104	1500fr gold & multi	15.00	5.00

No. C352 Ovptd. in Silver in Sheet Margin

Souvenir Sheet

C356	AP104	1500fr gold & multi	15.00	5.00

Overprint on No. C356 contains map, soldiers and "50 eme ANNIVERSAIRE DU /DEBARQUEMENT."

No. C355 exists in souvenir sheet of 1. Value $15.

Souvenir Sheets

Japanese Exploration of Antarctica — AP106

No. C357, Nobu Shirase. No. C358, Schooner Kainman Maru, horiz.

1994, Oct. 25

C357	AP106	1200fr multi	5.50	4.75
C358	AP106	1200fr multi	5.50	4.75

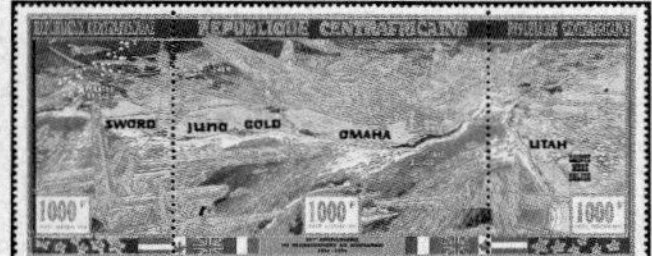

D-Day, 50th Anniv. (in 1994) — AP107

Designs: a, Gliders over Pegasus Bridge, Sword beach. b, Fighter planes over Juno, Gold and Omaha beaches. c, Planes over Utah beach, St. Mere Eglise.

Litho. & Embossed

1995, Oct. 25 ***Perf. 13½***

C359	AP107	1000fr Strip of 3, #a.-c.	13.00	13.00

No. C359b is 60x45mm.

Souvenir Sheet

No. C348 Overprinted

1995, Oct. 10 **Litho.** ***Perf. 13½***

C360	AP101	500fr multicolored	11.50	11.50

AIR POST SEMI-POSTAL STAMPS

Isis of Kalabsha SPAP1

Unwmk.

1964, Mar. 7 **Engr.** ***Perf. 13***

CB1	SPAP1	25fr + 10fr multi	1.25	1.25
CB2	SPAP1	50fr + 10fr multi	2.00	2.00
CB3	SPAP1	100fr + 10fr multi	3.00	3.00
		Nos. CB1-CB3 (3)	6.25	6.25

UNESCO world campaign to save historic monuments in Nubia.

African Infants and Globe — SPAP2

1971, Dec. 11 **Litho.** ***Perf. 13x13½***

CB4	SPAP2	140fr + 50fr multi	3.25	1.75

25th anniv. of UNICEF, and Children's Day.

POSTAGE DUE STAMPS

Sternotomis Virescens — D1

Beetles: No. J2, Sternotomis gama. No. J3, Augosoma centaurus. No. J4, Phosphorus virescens, ceroplesis carabarica. No. J5, Cetoine scaraboidae. No. J6, Ceroplesis S.P. No. J7, Macrorhina S.P. No. J8, Cetoine scaraboidae. No. J9, Phryneta leprosa. No. J10, Taurina longiceps. No. J11, Monohamus griseoplagiatus. No. J12, Jambonus trifasciatus.

Unwmk.

1962, Oct. 15 **Engr.** ***Perf. 11***

J1	D1	50c grn & dp org	.25	.25
J2	D1	50c grn & dp org	.25	.25
a.		Pair, #J1-J2	.45	
J3	D1	1fr blk, brn & lt grn	.30	.30
J4	D1	1fr blk, brn & lt grn	.30	.30
a.		Pair, #J3-J4	.75	
J5	D1	2fr blk, org & yel grn	.40	.40
J6	D1	2fr blk & red org	.40	.40
a.		Pair, #J5-J6	.85	
J7	D1	5fr brn, org & grn	.55	.55
J8	D1	5fr brn, org, grn & red	.55	.55
a.		Pair, #J7-J8	1.25	
J9	D1	10fr blk, grn & brn	1.00	1.00
J10	D1	10fr blk, brn & grn	1.00	1.00
a.		Pair, #J9-J10	2.25	
J11	D1	25fr blk, bl grn & brn	3.00	2.40
J12	D1	25fr blk, brn & bl grn	3.00	2.40
a.		Pair, #J11-J12	6.50	
		Nos. J1-J12 (12)	11.00	9.80

Pairs se-tenant at the base.

Giant Anteater — D2

1985, Jan. 25 **Litho.** ***Perf. 12½***

J13	D2	5fr multi	.50	.50
J14	D2	20fr multi	.90	.90
J15	D2	30fr multi	1.10	1.10
		Nos. J13-J15 (3)	2.50	2.50

MILITARY STAMPS

No. 1 Overprinted

Unwmk.

1962, Jan. 1 **Engr.** ***Perf. 13***

M1	A1	bl, car, grn & yel	14.00	—

No. 1 Overprinted

1963

M2	A1	bl, car, grn & yel	15.00	—

OFFICIAL STAMPS

Coat of Arms — O1

Imprint: "d'après G. RICHER SO.GE.IM."

Perf. 13x12½

1965-69 **Litho.** **Unwmk.**

Arms in Original Colors

O1	O1	1fr blk & brn org	.25	.25
O2	O1	2fr blk & violet	.25	.25
O3	O1	5fr blk & gray	.25	.25
O4	O1	10fr blk & green	.25	.25
O5	O1	20fr blk & red brn	.55	.25
O6	O1	30fr blk & emer ('69)	1.00	.55
O7	O1	50fr blk & dk bl	1.10	.70
O8	O1	100fr blk & bister	2.60	1.10
O9	O1	130fr blk & ver ('69)	4.00	2.25
O10	O1	200fr blk & claret	5.75	2.75
		Nos. O1-O10 (10)	16.00	8.60

Redrawn

Imprint: "d'après G. RICHER DELRIEU"

1971 **Photo.** ***Perf. 12x12½***

Arms in Original Colors

O11	O1	5fr blk & gray	.25	.25
O12	O1	30fr blk & emer	.50	.25
O13	O1	40fr blk & dp claret	.70	.30
O14	O1	100fr blk & bister	1.60	.55
O15	O1	140fr blk & lt bl	3.00	.85
O16	O1	200fr blk & claret	3.75	1.40
		Nos. O11-O16 (6)	9.80	3.60

Empire

Nos. O11, O13-O16 Overprinted in Black

1977 **Litho.** ***Perf. 12x12½***

O17	O1	5fr multi	.35	.25
O18	O1	40fr multi	.50	.30
O19	O1	100fr multi	1.40	.45
O20	O1	140fr multi	1.75	.70
O21	O1	200fr multi	2.75	1.10
		Nos. O17-O21 (5)	6.75	2.80

Type of 1965 Inscribed: "EMPIRE CENTRAFRICAIN"

1978, July **Litho.** ***Perf. 12½***

O22	O1	1fr multi	.25	.25
O23	O1	2fr multi	.25	.25
O24	O1	5fr multi	.25	.25
O25	O1	10fr multi	.25	.25
O26	O1	15fr multi	.25	.25
O27	O1	20fr multi	.25	.25
O28	O1	30fr multi	.30	.25
O29	O1	40fr multi	.40	.25
O30	O1	50fr multi	.55	.30
O31	O1	60fr multi	.75	.40
O32	O1	100fr multi	1.00	.55
O33	O1	130fr multi	1.60	.95
O34	O1	140fr multi	1.75	.95
O35	O1	200fr multi	3.50	1.60
		Nos. O22-O35 (14)	11.35	6.75

CENTRAL LITHUANIA

ˈsen-trəl ˌli-thə-ˈwā-nē-ə

LOCATION — North of Poland and east of Lithuania
CAPITAL — Vilnius

At one time Central Lithuania was a grand duchy of Lithuania but at the end of the 18th Century it fell under Russian rule. After World War I, Lithuania regained her sovereignty but certain areas were occupied by Poland. During the Russo-Polish war this territory was seized by Lithuania whose claim was promptly recognized by the Soviet Government. Under the leadership of the Polish General Zeligowski the territory was recaptured and it was during this occupation the stamps of Central Lithuania came into being. Subsequently the territory became a part of Poland.

100 Fennigi = 1 Markka

Coat of Arms — A1

Perf. 11½, Imperf.

1920-21 Typo. Unwmk.

1	A1	25f red	.40	*.55*
2	A1	25f dark grn ('21)	.40	*.55*
3	A1	1m blue	.40	*.55*
4	A1	1m dark brn ('21)	.40	*.55*
5	A1	2m violet	.40	*.55*
6	A1	2m orange ('21)	.40	*.55*
		Nos. 1-6 (6)	2.40	*3.30*

For surcharges see Nos. B1-B5.

Lithuanian Stamps of 1919 Surcharged in Blue or Black

Perf. 11½x12, 12½x11½, 14

1920, Nov. 23 Wmk. 145

13	A5	2m on 15sk lil	47.50	*55.00*
a.		Inverted surcharge	*200.00*	*900.00*
14	A5	4m on 10sk red	47.50	*52.50*
a.		Inverted surcharge	*150.00*	
15	A5	4m on 20sk dl bl (Bk)	47.50	*52.50*
a.		Inverted surcharge	*150.00*	
16	A5	4m on 30sk buff	75.00	*52.50*
a.		Inverted surcharge	*150.00*	
17	A6	6m on 50sk lt grn	47.50	*52.50*
a.		4m on 50sk (error)	*200.00*	
b.		10m on 50sk (error)	*200.00*	
c.		Surcharge inverted		—
18	A6	6m on 60sk vio & red	47.50	*52.50*
a.		4m on 60sk (error)	*200.00*	
b.		10m on 60sk (error)	*200.00*	
19	A6	6m on 75sk bis & red	47.50	*52.50*
a.		4m on 75sk (error)	*200.00*	
b.		10m on 75sk (error)	*200.00*	
20	A8	10m on 1auk gray & red	95.00	110.00
a.		Inverted surcharge	*210.00*	
21	A8	10m on 3auk lt brn & red	*1,400.*	*1,800.*
22	A8	10m on 5auk bl grn & red	*1,400.*	*1,800.*
		Nos. 13-20 (8)	455.00	*480.00*
		Nos. 13-22 (10)	*3,255.*	*4,080.*

The overprint on Nos. 17-19 is down-reading, i.e., the top of the overprint is at the right of the original design, the bottom at the left. The inverted overprint on No. 17c is up-reading.

Reprints of Nos. 17a, 17b, 18a, 18b, 19a, 19b. Value, each $45.

Counterfeits of Nos. 21-22 exist.

Lithuanian Girl — A2

Warrior — A3

Holy Gate of Vilnius — A4

Tower and Cathedral, Vilnius — A5

Rector's Insignia — A6

Gen. Lucien Zeligowski — A7

Perf. 11½, Imperf.

1920 Litho. Unwmk.

23	A2	25f gray	.25	*.75*
24	A3	1m orange	.25	*.75*
25	A4	2m claret	.45	*1.00*
26	A5	4m gray grn & buff	.60	*1.25*
27	A6	6m rose & gray	2.00	*2.75*
28	A7	10m brown & yellow	3.00	*4.00*
		Nos. 23-28 (6)	6.55	*10.50*

For surcharges see Nos. B13-B14, B17-B19.

St. Anne's Church, Vilnius — A8

St. Stanislas Cathedral, Vilnius — A9

White Eagle, White Knight Vytis — A10

Queen Hedwig and King Ladislas II Jagello — A11

Coat of Arms of Vilnius — A12

Poczobut Astronomical Observatory A13

Union of Lithuania and Poland — A14

Tadeusz Kosciuszko and Adam Mickiewicz A15

1921 ***Perf. 14, Imperf.***

35	A8	1m dk gray & yel	.60	*1.10*
36	A9	2m rose & green	.60	*1.10*
37	A10	3m dark green	.60	*1.10*
38	A11	4m brown & buff	.60	*1.10*
39	A12	5m red brown	.60	*1.10*
40	A13	6m slate & buff	.60	*1.40*
41	A14	10m red vio & buff	.85	*2.25*
42	A15	20m brn ol & buff	.85	*2.25*
		Nos. 35-42 (8)	5.30	*11.40*

Set, perf. 13½, $150.
Stamps perf. 11½ were privately produced.

Peasant Girl Sowing — A16

White Eagle and Vytis — A17

Great Theater at Vilnius — A18

Allegory: Peace and Industry — A19

Gen. Zeligowski Entering Vilnius — A20

Gen. Zeligowski — A21

1921-22 ***Perf. 11½, Imperf.***

53	A16	10m brown ('22)	3.00	*6.00*
54	A17	25m red & yel ('22)	3.25	*7.50*
55	A18	50m dk blue ('22)	4.50	*11.00*
56	A19	75m violet ('22)	4.75	*20.00*
57	A20	100m bl & bister	2.00	*5.25*
58	A21	150m ol grn & brn	3.00	*6.75*
		Nos. 53-58 (6)	20.50	*56.50*

Opening of the Natl. Parliament, Nos. 53-56; anniv. of the entry of General Zeligowski into Vilnius, Nos. 57-58.

SEMI-POSTAL STAMPS

Nos. 1-6 Surcharged in Black or Red

1921 Unwmk. ***Perf. 11½, Imperf.***

B1	A1	25f + 2m red (Bk)	1.00	*1.75*
B2	A1	25f + 2m dk green	1.00	*1.75*
B3	A1	1m + 2m blue	1.00	*1.75*
B4	A1	1m + 2m dk brown	1.00	*1.75*
B5	A1	2m + 2m violet	1.00	*1.75*
B6	A1	2m + 2m orange	1.00	*1.75*
		Nos. B1-B6 (6)	6.00	*10.50*

The surcharge means "For Silesia 2 marks." The stamps were intended to provide a fund to assist the plebiscite in Upper Silesia.

Nos. 25, 26 Surcharged

a

b

Perf. 11½, Imperf.

B13	A4	(a) 2m + 1(m) claret	1.10	*2.00*
B14	A5	(b) 4m + 1m gray green & buff	1.10	*2.00*
a.		Tête-beche pair	25.00	

Nos. 25-26, 28 with inset

Perf. 11½, Imperf.

B17	A4	2m + 1m claret	.85	*1.25*
B18	A5	4m + 1m gray green & buff	.85	*1.25*
B19	A7	10m + 2m brn & yel	1.00	*1.25*
		Nos. B13-B19 (5)	4.90	*7.75*

POSTAGE DUE STAMPS

University, Vilnius — D1

Castle Hill, Vilnius — D2

Castle Ruins, Troki D3

Holy Gate, Vilnius D4

St. Stanislas Cathedral D5

St. Anne's Church, Vilnius D6

1920-21 Unwmk. ***Perf. 11½, Imperf.***

J1	D1	50f red violet	.40	*1.25*
J2	D2	1m green	.40	*1.25*
J3	D3	2m red violet	.50	*1.25*
J4	D4	3m red violet	.85	*1.60*
J5	D5	5m red violet	1.00	*2.50*
J6	D6	20m scarlet	2.00	*3.25*
		Nos. J1-J6 (6)	5.15	*11.10*

CEYLON

si-'lan

LOCATION — An island in the Indian Ocean separated from India by the Gulf of Manaar
GOVT. — Independent republic within the British Commonwealth
AREA — 25,332 sq. mi.
POP. — 12,670,000 (est. 1971)
CAPITAL — Colombo

Ceylon changed its name to Republic of Sri Lanka on May 22, 1972.

12 Pence = 1 Shilling
100 Cents = 1 Rupee (1872)

Values for unused stamps are for examples with original gum as defined in the catalogue introduction except for Nos. 2, 5, 8-9 which seldom have any remaining trace of their original gum. Many unused stamps of Ceylon, especially between Nos. 59 and 274, have toned gum or tropical stains. Values quoted are for stamps with fresh gum. Toned stamps have lower values, and common stamps with toned gum are worth very little.

Very fine examples of Nos. 1-15 will be cut square, will have small margins, but will show an intact design. Inferior examples with the design partly cut away will sell for much less, and examples with large margins will command higher prices. Very fine examples of Nos. 17-58b will have perforations just cutting into the design on one or more sides due to the narrow spacing of the stamps on the plates and to imperfect perforating methods. Stamps with perfs clear on all four sides are extremely scarce and will command substantially higher prices.

Catalogue values for unused stamps in this country are for Never Hinged items, beginning with Scott 290 in the regular postage section and Scott B1 in the semi-postal section.

Watermarks

Wmk. 1a — 22½mm high, Oval Letters

Wmk. 1b — 21mm high, Round Letters

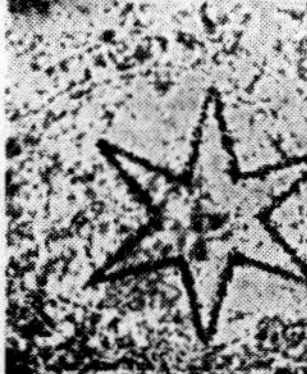

Wmk. 6 — Large Star

Wmk. 290 — Lotus and "Sri" Multiple

Queen Victoria
A1 A2

1857 Engr. Wmk. 6 *Imperf.*
Blued Paper

No.	Type	Description	Unused	Used
1	A1	1p blue	—	300.
2	A1	6p plum	*12,000.*	575.

1857-59 White Paper

No.	Type	Description	Unused	Used
3	A1	1p dp turq	1,100.	45.00
4	A1	2p deep grn	210.00	65.00
a.		2p yellow green	575.00	105.00
5	A2	4p dl rose ('59)	*75,000.*	5,250.
6	A1	5p org brown	1,750.	175.00
6A	A1	6p plum	*2,850.*	170.00
7	A1	6p brown	*10,500.*	700.00
8	A2	8p brown ('59)	*30,000.*	1,750.
9	A2	9p lil brn ('59)	*62,500.*	1,050.
10	A1	10p vermilion	950.00	350.00
11	A1	1sh violet	5,750.	260.00
12	A2	1sh9p green ('59)	1,000.	925.00
a.		1sh9p yellow green	5,500.	3,500.
13	A2	2sh blue ('59)	6,750.	1,400.

Stamps of type A2 frequently have repaired corners.

Nos. 3-4 exist unofficially rouletted. See the *Scott Classic Specialized Catalogue of Stamps & Covers* for listings.

Beware of Nos. 17-57 trimmed to resemble Nos. 3-13. Values are for stamps with clear margins on all sides.

No. 5 was reproduced by the collotype process in a souvenir sheet distributed at the London International Stamp Exhibition 1950. The paper is unwatermarked.

A3

1857-58 Typo. Unwmk.

No.	Type	Description	Unused	Used
14	A3	½p lilac ('58)	200.	*250.*
15	A3	½p lilac, *bluish*	4,250.	650.

Values are for stamps without cracking of the surface, and examples showing cracking should be discounted.

Clean-Cut Perf. 14 to 15½

1861 Wmk. 6 Engr.

No.	Type	Description	Unused	Used
17	A1	1p blue	210.00	18.00
18	A1	2p yel grn	275.00	27.50
b.		Vert. pair, imperf between		—
19	A2	4p dull rose	2,300.	325.00
20	A1	5p org brown	125.00	10.00
20A	A1	6p brown	3,200.	190.00
b.		6p bister brown	2,250.	290.00
21	A2	8p brown	2,600.	575.00
22	A2	9p lilac brown	16,000.	275.00
23	A1	1sh violet	145.00	17.50
24	A2	2sh blue	4,750.	875.00

Rough Perf. 14 to 15½

No.	Type	Description	Unused	Used
25	A1	1p blue	170.00	12.50
b.		Blued paper	850.00	27.50
26	A1	2p yel green	475.00	92.50
27	A2	4p rose red	600.00	130.00
28	A1	6p olive brown	1,250.	120.00
a.		6p deep brown	1,350.	130.00
b.		6p bister brown	2,300.	200.00
29	A2	8p brown	1,775.	675.00
30	A2	8p yel brown	1,800.	425.00
31	A2	9p olive brown	875.00	85.00
32	A2	9p deep brown	160.00	120.00
33	A1	10p vermilion	325.00	30.00
a.		Imperf. vert., pair		—
34	A1	1sh violet	300.00	17.50
35	A2	1sh9p green	825.00	
36	A2	2sh blue	800.00	160.00

The 1sh9p green was never placed in use.

1863 *Perf. 12½*

No.	Type	Description	Unused	Used
37	A1	10p vermilion	340.00	22.50

1864 Typo. Unwmk.

No.	Type	Description	Unused	Used
38	A3	½p lilac	225.00	175.00

See note following No. 15.

1862 Engr. *Perf. 13*

No.	Type	Description	Unused	Used
39	A1	1p blue	180.00	7.00
40	A1	5p car brown	1,850.	175.00
41	A1	6p deep brown	210.00	30.00
42	A2	9p brown	1,400.	120.00
43	A1	1sh grayish violet	2,100.	95.00

Parts of the papermaker's sheet watermark, "T. H. SAUNDERS 1862," may be found on some examples of Nos. 39-43.

Perf. 12

No.	Type	Description	Unused	Used
44	A1	1p blue	1,900.	150.00
a.		Horiz. pair, imperf. btwn.		*18,000.*

Two Types of Watermark Crown and CC (1)

1863-67 Typo. Wmk. 1a *Perf. 12½*

No.	Type	Description	Unused	Used
45	A3	½p lilac	80.00	50.00
a.		½p reddish lilac	90.00	65.00

Engr.

No.	Type	Description	Unused	Used
46	A1	1p blue	180.00	9.00
a.		1p dark blue	180.00	9.00
c.		Perf. 11½	3,400.	350.00
47	A1	2p gray green	100.00	15.00
48	A1	2p emerald	190.00	120.00
48A	A1	2p yel green	*10,000.*	475.00
48B	A1	2p bottle green		*4,250.*
49	A1	2p olive	325.00	275.00
50	A2	4p rose	550.00	130.00
a.		4p carmine rose	900.00	275.00
51	A1	5p car brown	325.00	110.00
52	A1	5p olive green	1,700.	350.00
e.		5p deep sage green	2,000.	425.00
53	A1	6p choc brown	250.00	7.50
a.		Perf. 13	2,750.	250.00
b.		6p black brown	300.00	11.50
c.		As "b," double impression		*4,500.*
d.		6p reddish brown	350.00	14.00
54	A2	8p red brown	150.00	80.00
55	A2	9p brown	360.00	52.50
c.		Perf. 13	6,750.	1,100.
56	A1	10p vermilion	5,000.	70.00
a.		10p orange	7,500.	500.00
58	A2	2sh blue	375.00	45.00

The ½p, 1p blue, 2p olive, 4p and 5p green exist imperf.

Wmk. 1b

No.	Type	Description	Unused	Used
46d	A1	1p blue	325.00	17.50
e.		1p dark blue	275.00	16.00
49d	A1	2p orange yellow	135.00	8.00
e.		2p olive yellow	175.00	14.00
f.		2p olive green	175.00	20.00
50b	A2	4p rose	325.00	65.00
c.		4p carmine rose	80.00	30.00
52b	A1	5p myrtle green	100.00	25.00
c.		5p olive green	150.00	27.50
d.		5p bronze green	60.00	*60.00*
53e	A1	6p chocolate brown	140.00	11.00
f.		6p brown	190.00	9.00
54a	A2	8p red brown	140.00	80.00
55a	A2	9p dark brown	70.00	8.00
b.		9p bister brown	975.00	40.00
56b	A1	10p orange	150.00	18.00
c.		10p orange red	90.00	18.00
d.		10p vermilion	*5,600.*	170.00
57	A1	1sh purple	150.00	12.00
a.		1sh reddish lilac	325.00	32.50
58a	A2	2sh deep blue	160.00	17.50
b.		2sh indigo	300.00	22.50

The 1p blue and 6p brown exist imperf.
For overprints see Nos. O2, O4-O7.

A4

A5

1866 Typo. Wmk. 1 *Perf. 12½*

No.	Type	Description	Unused	Used
59	A5	3p rose	275.00	105.00
a.		Imperf., pair	*1,000.*	

For overprint see No. O3.

1868 *Perf. 14*

No.	Type	Description	Unused	Used
61	A4	1p blue	30.00	12.00
a.		Imperf., pair	—	
62	A5	3p rose	95.00	52.50

For overprint see No. O1.

A6

A7

A8

A9

A10

A11

A12

A13

A14

A15

1872-80 *Perf. 14*

No.	Type	Description	Unused	Used
63	A6	2c brown	37.50	4.50
64	A7	4c gray	50.00	2.00
65	A7	4c lil rose ('80)	82.50	1.60
66	A8	8c orange	62.50	7.25
a.		8c orange yellow	47.50	8.00
67	A9	16c violet	140.00	3.00
68	A10	24c green	80.00	2.25
69	A11	32c slate bl ('77)	175.00	16.00
70	A12	36c blue	190.00	28.00
71	A13	48c rose	110.00	9.50
72	A14	64c red brn ('77)	300.00	80.00
73	A15	96c olive gray	275.00	30.00
		Nos. 63-73 (11)	1,503.	184.10

For surcharges see Nos. 83-84, 94A-110, 112-114. For types surcharged see Nos. 124-129.

1872 *Perf. 12½*

No.	Type	Description	Unused	Used
74	A6	2c brown	*4,200.*	260.00
75	A7	4c gray	*2,750.*	325.00

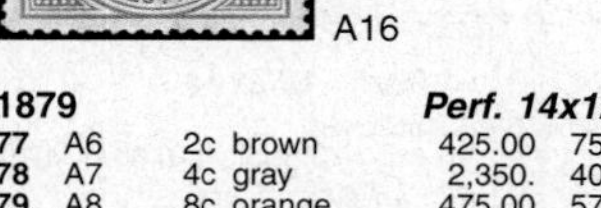

A16

1879 *Perf. 14x12½*

No.	Type	Description	Unused	Used
77	A6	2c brown	425.00	75.00
78	A7	4c gray	2,350.	40.00
79	A8	8c orange	475.00	57.50

Perf. 12½x14

No.	Type	Description	Unused	Used
82	A16	2r50c claret	800.00	425.00

The 32c and 64c are known perf. 14x12½, but were not regularly issued.

No. 82, perf. 12½, was not regularly issued.

See Nos. 142, 158. For surcharges see Nos. 111, 115, 130. For types surcharged see Nos. 160-161.

Nos. 68, 72 Surcharged

1882 *Perf. 14*

83 A10 16c on 24c green 42.50 10.00
a. Inverted surcharge —
84 A14 20c on 64c red brn 14.50 10.00
a. Double surcharge 1,750.

1883-99 **Wmk. 2**

85 A6 2c pale brown 70.00 3.50
86 A6 2c green ('84) 3.25 .25
a. Perf. 12 6,750.
87 A6 2c org brn ('99) 4.75 .40
88 A7 4c lilac rose 6.50 .50
89 A7 4c rose ('84) 7.00 *13.50*
a. Perf. 12 6,750.
90 A7 4c brt rose ('98) 12.00 *15.00*
91 A7 4c yellow ('99) 4.00 3.75
92 A8 8c orange 10.00 *13.00*
93 A9 16c violet 1,900. 175.00
94 A10 24c purple brown 1,600.
b. Perf. 12 *7,250.*

Nos. 86a, 89a, 94 and 94b were never placed in use. A 48c brown, perf. 12, was prepared but not issued.

For surcharges and overprints see Nos.116-123, 143-151D, 155-156. O8-O9.

Issues of 1872-82 Surcharged

a

b

c

d

1885 **Wmk. 1** *Perf. 14*

94A A9 (a) 5c on 16c *3,000.*
95 A10 (a) 5c on 24c *6,000.* 100.00
96 A11 (a) 5c on 32c 67.50 16.00
a. Inverted surcharge 2,700.
97 A12 (a) 5c on 36c 275.00 13.50
a. Inverted surcharge *2,750.*
98 A13 (a) 5c on 48c 2,300. 65.00
99 A14 (a) 5c on 64c 135.00 12.50
a. Double surcharge 3,250.
100 A15 (a) 5c on 96c 525.00 75.00
101 A9 (b) 10c on 16c *11,000.* 3,000.
102 A10 (b) 10c on 24c 475.00 130.00
103 A12 (b) 10c on 36c 450.00 260.00
104 A14 (b) 10c on 64c 425.00 240.00
105 A10 (c) 20c on 24c 80.00 30.00
106 A11 (c) 20c on 32c 87.50 75.00
107 A11 (c) 25c on 32c 26.00 10.00
108 A13 (c) 28c on 48c 40.00 11.50
a. Double surcharge 3,000.
109 A12 (b) 30c on 36c 17.00 13.00
a. Inverted surcharge 300.00 140.00
110 A15 (b) 56c on 96c 35.00 27.50

Perf. 12½

111 A16 (d) 1r12c on 2r50c 700.00 110.00

Perf. 14x12½

112 A11 (a) 5c on 32c 800.00 52.50
113 A14 (a) 5c on 64c 900.00 52.50
114 A14 (b) 10c on 64c 90.00 *160.00*
a. Vert. pair, imperf. btwn. 6,000.

Perf. 12½x14

115 A16 (d) 1r12c on 2r50c 110.00 47.50

Perf. 14
Wmk. 2

117 A7 (a) 5c on 4c rose 25.00 5.50
a. Inverted surcharge *325.00*
118 A8 (a) 5c on 8c org 90.00 12.00
a. Inverted surcharge *4,250.*
b. Double surcharge *3,500.*
119 A9 (a) 5c on 16c vio 175.00 18.00
a. Inverted surcharge *240.00*
120 A10 (a) 5c on 24c pur brn — 540.00
121 A9 (b) 10c on 16c vio 12,000. 1,650.
122 A10 (b) 10c on 24c pur brn 18.00 11.00
123 A9 (b) 15c on 16c vio 15.00 11.50

A 5c on 4c lilac rose and a 5c on 24c green are known to exist and are considered to be a forgeries.

Types of 1872-80 Surcharged

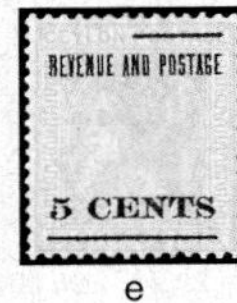

e

f

g

1885-87

124 A 8 (e) 5c on 8c lilac 26.00 1.60
125 A10 (f) 10c on 24c pur brn 14.00 10.00
126 A 9 (f) 15c on 16c org 62.50 16.00
127 A11 (f) 28c on 32c sl bl 28.00 2.75
128 A12 (f) 30c on 36c ol grn 28.00 16.00
129 A15 (f) 56c on 96c ol gray 50.00 16.00

Wmk. 1 Sideways

130 A16 (g) 1r12c on 2r50c cl 60.00 *135.00*
Nos. 124-130 (7) *268.50 197.35*

A23

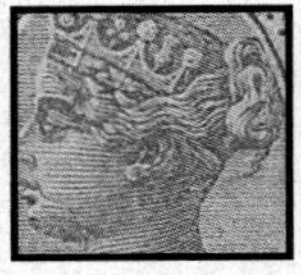
Type I

Type II

FIVE CENTS

Type I — Thin lines in background. Hair and curl clear.

Type II — Thicker lines in background. Heavier shading under chin.

1886 **Wmk. 2**

131 A23 5c lilac, type I 3.75 .25
a. Type II 3.75 .25

For overprint see No. O12.

A24

1886-1900

132 A24 3c org brn & green ('93) 6.50 .50
133 A24 3c green ('00) 4.75 .60
134 A24 6c rose & blk ('99) 3.00 .50
135 A24 12c ol grn & car ('00) 5.50 *10.00*
136 A24 15c olive green 10.00 2.40
137 A24 15c ultra ('00) 8.00 1.50
138 A24 25c yel brn 7.50 2.00
a. 25c yel brn, value in ol yel 155.00 90.00
139 A24 28c slate 27.00 1.50
140 A24 30c vio & org brown ('93) 4.75 3.50
141 A24 75c blk & org brown ('00) 11.00 10.00
Nos. 132-141 (10) 88.00 *32.50*

Numeral tablet of 3c, 12c and 75c has lined background with colorless value and "c."

For surcharges & overprints see Nos. 152-154, 157, 159, O10-O11, O13-O17.

1887 **Wmk. 1**

142 A16 1r12c claret 37.50 32.50

For overprint see No. O18.

Issue of 1883-84 Surcharged

1888-90 **Wmk. 2**

143 A7 2c on 4c lilac rose 1.50 1.00
a. Inverted surcharge 25.00 24.00
b. Double surcharge, one invtd. 375.00
144 A7 2c on 4c rose 2.75 .50
a. Inverted surcharge 20.00 *21.00*
b. Double surcharge 400.00

Surcharged

145 A7 2c on 4c lilac rose 1.10 .30
a. Inverted surcharge 42.50 *42.50*
b. Double surcharge 125.00 130.00
c. Double surcharge, one invtd. 92.50 95.00
146 A7 2c on 4c rose 10.00 .25
a. Double surcharge, one invtd. 110.00 *135.00*
b. Double surcharge 110.00 *135.00*
c. Inverted surcharge 425.00

Surcharged

147 A7 2c on 4c lilac rose 80.00 45.00
a. Inverted surcharge 175.00 47.50
b. Double surcharge, one inverted 240.00
148 A7 2c on 4c rose 4.50 .80
a. Inverted surcharge 19.00 10.00
b. Double surcharge, one inverted 10.00 *15.00*
c. Double surcharge 210.00 160.00

Surcharged

149 A7 2c on 4c lilac rose 67.50 30.00
a. Inverted surcharge 200.00 32.50
150 A7 2c on 4c rose 3.00 1.25
a. Inverted surcharge 19.00 10.00
b. Double surcharge 160.00 150.00
c. Double surcharge, one inverted 20.00 12.50

Surcharged

151 A7 2c on 4c rose 15.00 1.10
a. Inverted surcharge 25.00 10.00
b. Double surcharge 145.00 150.00
c. Double surch., one invtd. 27.50 13.50
i. "S" of "Cents" inverted 650.00 350.00
151D A7 2c on 4c lilac rose 67.50 37.50
e. Inverted surcharge 100.00 45.00
f. Double surcharge 425.00
g. Double surch., one invtd. 150.00 150.00
h. "S" of "Cents" inverted 725.00

Counterfeit errors of surcharges of Nos. 143 to 151D are prevalent.

No. 136 Surcharged

1890

152 A24 5c on 15c ol green 4.00 2.75
a. "Flve" instead of "Five" 135.00 95.00
b. "REVENUE" omitted 210.00 190.00
c. Inverted surcharge 62.50 *75.00*
d. Double surcharge 125.00 *145.00*
e. As "a," inverted surcharge — 1,800.
f. Inverted "s" in "Cents" 130.00 *105.00*
g. As "f," inverted surcharge 2,200.
h. As "b," invtd. "s" in "Cents" 1,700.

Nos. 138-139 Surcharged

1891

153 A24 15c on 25c brown 19.00 20.00
154 A24 15c on 28c slate 20.00 10.00

Nos. 88, 89 and 139 Surcharged

1892

155 A7 3c on 4c lilac rose 2.00 *3.50*
156 A7 3c on 4c rose 9.50 *13.50*
a. Double surcharge, one invtd.
157 A24 3c on 28c slate 6.75 6.25
a. Double surcharge 180.00
Nos. 155-157 (3) 18.25 *23.25*

Type of 1879

1898

158 A16 2r50c violet, *red* 42.50 *65.00*

No. 136 Surcharged in Black

1899

159 A24 6c on 15c olive green 1.35 *.85*

Surcharged Type "g" in Black

1899 **Wmk. 1**

160 A16 1r50c on 2r50c gray 22.50 *52.50*
161 A16 2r25c on 2r50c yel 47.50 *85.00*

A35

1900 **Wmk. 1**

162 A35 1r50c car rose 35.00 *52.50*
163 A35 2r25c dull blue 37.50 *52.50*

Nos. 166-292 exist in many different shades, representing different printings for each stamp.

King Edward VII
A36 A37

A38

A39

A40

1903-05 Wmk. 2

166 A36 2c org brown 2.10 .25
167 A37 3c green 2.10 1.10
168 A37 4c yel & blue 2.10 *5.50*
169 A38 5c dull lilac 3.00 .65
170 A39 6c car rose 10.00 1.60
171 A37 12c ol grn & car 5.50 *11.50*
172 A40 15c ultra 6.75 3.50
173 A40 25c bister 6.00 *11.00*
174 A40 30c vio & green 3.50 *4.25*
175 A37 75c bl & org ('05) 4.00 *24.00*
176 A40 1r50c gray ('04) 67.50 67.50
177 A40 2r25c brn & grn ('04) 90.00 65.00
Nos. 166-177 (12) 202.55 195.85
Set, never hinged 400.00

For overprints see Nos. O19-O24.

1904-10 Wmk. 3

178 A36 2c orange brown 2.50 .25
a. 2c orange 1.60 .55
179 A37 3c green 1.75 .25
180 A37 4c yel & blue 3.00 1.60
181 A38 5c dull lilac 3.50 1.30
a. Booklet pane of 12
b. 5c dull lilac, "chalky paper" 7.00 .75
182 A39 6c car rose 5.25 .25
183 A40 10c ol grn & vio ('10) 2.60 3.50
184 A37 12c ol grn & car 1.75 *1.90*
185 A40 15c ultra 3.50 .65
186 A40 25c bister ('05) 6.25 4.00
187 A40 25c slate ('10) 2.75 3.00
188 A40 30c vio & grn ('05) 2.75 *3.25*
189 A40 50c brown ('10) 4.25 *7.75*
190 A37 75c bl & org ('05) 5.50 *8.25*
191 A40 1r vio, *yel* ('10) 8.50 *12.50*
192 A40 1r50c gray ('05) 45.00 20.00
193 A40 2r scar, *yel* ('10) 16.00 *30.00*
194 A40 2r25c brn & grn 24.00 *32.50*
195 A40 5r blk, *grn* ('10) 47.50 *115.00*
196 A40 10r blk, *red* ('10) 135.00 *290.00*
Nos. 178-196 (19) 321.35 *535.95*
Set, never hinged 600.00

A41

A42

1908

197 A41 5c deep red violet 7.50 .25
a. Booklet pane of 12
198 A42 6c carmine rose 3.50 .25

1911, July 5

199 A40 3c green 1.10 .85

A44

King George V — A45

Type I

Type II

3 AND 6 CENTS

Type I — Small "c" after value, 2¼mm wide and 2mm high.

Type II — Large "c" after value, 2½mm wide and 2¼mm high.

1, 5 AND 9 CENTS are Type II, other denominations Type I.

For description of dies I and II see "Dies of British Colonial Stamps" in the Table of Contents.

1912-25 Die I Wmk. 3

200 A44 1c dp brn (Die Ib) ('20) 1.20 .25
201 A44 2c brown org .45 .30
202 A44 3c dp grn (Die Ia, type II) 5.25 .50
a. 3c deep green, die I, type I 6.75 2.40
203 A44 5c red violet 1.20 .70
a. 5c purple 12.00 3.00
204 A44 6c car (Die Ib, type II) 1.50 1.60
a. 6c carmine, die I, type I 20.00 1.30
b. As "a," bklt. pane of 6
205 A44 10c olive green 3.50 2.00
206 A44 15c ultra 3.00 1.50

Chalky Paper

207 A44 25c yel & ultra 1.75 2.10
208 A44 30c green & vio 4.75 3.75
209 A44 50c black & scar 1.75 *2.10*
210 A44 1r violet, *yel* 6.00 4.25
211 A44 2r blk & red, *yel* 4.00 *15.00*
212 A44 5r blk, *green* 20.00 *47.50*
a. 5r black, *bl grn*, olive back 25.00 *50.00*
b. 5r blk, *emer* (Die II) ('20) 52.50 *120.00*
213 A44 10r vio & blk, *red* 85.00 *105.00*
a. Die II ('20) 95.00 *190.00*
214 A44 20r blk & red, *bl* 175.00 *170.00*
215 A45 50r dull violet 750.00 *1,500.*
216 A45 100r gray black 3,250.
217 A45 500r gray green *8,750.*
218 A45 1000r vio, *red* ('25) *37,500.*
Nos. 200-214 (15) 314.35 *356.55*
Set, never hinged 600.00

Although Nos. 217 and 218 were theoretically available for postage it is not probable that they were ever used for other than fiscal purposes.

The 1r through 100r with revenue cancellations sell for minimal prices.

For surcharge & overprints see Nos. 223, MR1-MR3.

Die I

1913-14 Surface-colored Paper

220 A44 1r violet, *yellow* 6.50 *5.75*
221 A44 2r black & red, *yel* 4.25 *17.50*
222 A44 5r black, *green* 26.00 *42.50*
Nos. 220-222 (3) 36.75 *65.75*

No. 203 Surcharged

1918

223 A44 1c on 5c red violet 3.50 *3.50*
a. 1c on 5c purple .25 .30

For overprint see No. MR4.

Die I

1921-33 Wmk. 4 Ordinary Paper

225 A44 1c dp brn (Die Ib) ('27) 1.20 .40
226 A44 2c brn org (Die II) .85 .30
227 A44 3c green (Die Ia, type II) 5.75 .90
228 A44 3c slate (Die Ia, type II) ('22) .90 .25
229 A44 5c red vio (Die I) .70 .25
230 A44 6c carmine (Die Ib, type II) 4.00 .90
231 A44 6c vio (Die Ib, type II) ('22) 3.00 .25
232 A44 9c red, *yel* (Die II) ('26) 3.25 .45
233 A44 10c olive green 1.60 .45
a. Die II 2.10 .70
234 A44 12c scarlet, Die II 1.20 *4.00*
a. Die I ('25) 10.00 *10.00*
235 A44 15c ultramarine 4.00 *22.50*
236 A44 15c green, *yel*, Die II 5.00 1.20
a. Die I ('22) 5.75 *3.00*
237 A44 20c ultra, Die II ('24) 4.25 .50
a. Die I ('22) 6.00 *7.25*
238 A44 25c yel & blue 3.25 2.25
a. Die II 5.75 1.50

For surcharges see Nos. 248-249.

Chalky Paper

239 A44 30c green & violet 1.90 *6.75*
a. Die II 6.25 1.50
240 A44 50c blk & scar (Die II) 2.25 .95
a. Die I 65.00 *100.00*
241 A44 1r vio, *yel*, Die II 26.00 *42.50*
a. Die I 16.00 *52.50*
242 A44 2r blk & red, *yel* (Die II) 8.50 *15.00*
243 A44 5r blk, *emer*, (Die II) 52.50 *97.50*
244 A44 20r blk & red, *bl*, (Die II) 325.00 *425.00*
245 A45 50r dull vio 825.00 *1,500.*
246 A45 100r gray black 3,250.
247 A45 100r ultra & dl vio ('27) 2,750.
Nos. 225-244 (20) 455.10 622.30
Set, never hinged 725.00

Nos. 228, 231 Surcharged

1926

248 A44 2c on 3c slate 3.50 1.20
a. Double surcharge 85.00
b. Bar omitted 90.00 *100.00*
249 A44 5c on 6c violet 1.25 .45
a. Double surcharge

A46

1927-29 Chalky Paper Wmk. 4

254 A46 1r red vio & dl vio ('28) 3.00 1.50
255 A46 2r car & green ('29) 4.50 3.25
256 A46 5r brn vio & grn ('28) 17.50 *30.00*
257 A46 10r org & green 75.00 *160.00*
258 A46 20r ultra & dl vio 325.00 *450.00*
Nos. 254-258 (5) 425.00 *644.75*
Set, never hinged 700.00

Nos. 256-258 are valued with postal cancellations. Revenue cancellations are more common.

Common Design Types pictured following the introduction.

Silver Jubilee Issue

Common Design Type

1935, May 6 Engr. *Perf. 13½x14*

260 CD301 6c gray blk & ultra .70 .35
261 CD301 9c indigo & green .70 2.50
262 CD301 20c blue & brown 4.00 2.75
263 CD301 50c brt vio & ind 5.00 16.00
Nos. 260-263 (4) 10.40 21.60
Set, never hinged 20.00

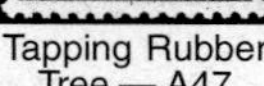
Tapping Rubber Tree — A47

Colombo Harbor — A49

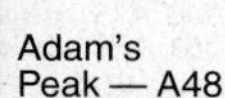
Adam's Peak — A48

Picking Tea — A50

Coconut Palms — A53

Rice Terraces A51

River Scene A52

Temple of the Tooth, Kandy A54

Ancient Reservoir A55

Wild Elephants A56

View of Trincomalee A57

Perf. 11x11½ (266, 267), 11½x11 (269, 269, 271, 272, 274), 11½x13 (264, 270), 13x11½ (265), 14 (273)

1935-36 Wmk. 4

264 A47 2c car rose & blk .45 *.55*
a. Perf. 14 12.00 .55
265 A48 3c olive & black 1.40 *.55*
a. Perf. 14 40.00 *.40*
266 A49 6c blue & black .45 .40
267 A50 9c org red & ol grn 1.50 .90
268 A51 10c dk vio & blk 1.75 *3.25*
269 A52 15c grn & org brn 2.25 .70
270 A53 20c ultra & black 2.75 *3.50*
271 A54 25c choc & dk ultra 2.00 1.75
272 A55 30c green & lake 3.00 *3.75*
273 A56 50c dk vio & blk 17.50 2.50
274 A57 1r brown & vio 40.00 29.00
Nos. 264-274 (11) 73.05 46.85
Set, never hinged 220.00

Issued: 2c, 15c, 25c, 5/1/35; 10c, 6/1/35; 1r, 7/1/35; 30c, 8/1/35; 3c, 10/1/35; 6c, 9c, 20c, 50c, 1/1/36.

Coronation Issue

Common Design Type

1937, May 12 *Perf. 11x11½*

275 CD302 6c dark carmine .75 1.10
a. Booklet pane of 10 25.00
276 CD302 9c deep green 3.00 *4.75*
a. Booklet pane of 10 300.00
277 CD302 20c deep ultra 4.50 *4.50*
Nos. 275-277 (3) 8.25 10.35
Set, never hinged 16.00

Types of 1935 with "Postage & Revenue Removed" and Picturing George VI and

Sigiriya (Lion Rock) — A61

Ancient Guard Stone — A68

George VI — A69

Perf. 11x11½, 11½x11; 12 (#286)

1938-52 Engr. Wmk. 4

278 A47 2c car rose & blk ('44) .45 *2.00*
- *a.* Perf. 13½x13 ('38) 100.00 2.00
- *b.* Perf. 13½ ('38) 2.00 .25
- *c.* Perf. 12 ('49) 1.25 *5.75*
- *d.* Perf. 11½x13 ('38) 10.00 3.75

279 A48 3c dk grn & blk ('42) .50 .25
- *a.* Perf. 13x13½ ('38) 225.00 17.50
- *b.* Perf. 14 ('41) 100.00 1.10
- *c.* Perf. 13½ ('38) 3.50 .25
- *d.* Perf. 12 ('46) .70 *.95*
- *e.* Perf. 13x11½ 8.00 3.75

280 A49 6c blue & black .25 .25
281 A61 10c blue & black 1.75 .25
282 A52 15c red brn & grn 1.25 .25
283 A50 20c dull bl & blk 2.25 .25
284 A54 25c choc & dk ultra 3.25 .30
285 A55 30c dk grn & rose car 8.00 3.75
286 A56 50c dk vio & blk ('46) 2.75 .25
- *a.* Perf. 14 ('42) 90.00 29.00
- *b.* Perf. 13x11½ ('38) 150.00 52.50
- *c.* Perf. 13x13½ ('38) 300.00 3.00
- *d.* Perf. 13½ ('38) 15.00 1.00
- *e.* Perf. 11½x11 ('42) 4.00 5.00

287 A57 1r dk brn & bl vio 10.50 2.00
288 A68 2r dark car & blk 9.25 5.00

Perf. 14

Typo.

289 A69 5r brn vio & grn 27.50 19.00
289A A69 10r yel org & dl grn ('52) 75.00 50.00
Nos. 278-289A (13) 142.70 83.55
Set, never hinged 265.00

No. 289A differs from type A69 in having "REVENUE" inscribed vertically at either side of the frame. This revenue 10r was valid for postage Dec. 1, 1952-Mar. 14, 1954.

Used examples of Nos. 278-289A are valued postally used.

See Nos. 292, 295. For surcharges see Nos. 290-291.

Catalogue values for unused stamps in this section, from this point to the end of the section, are for Never Hinged items.

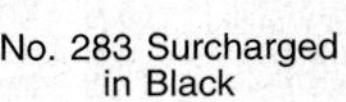
No. 283 Surcharged in Black

1940, Nov. 5 ***Perf. 11x11½***

290 A50 3c on 20c dull bl & blk *4.50* *4.50*

No. 280 Surcharged

1941, May 10

291 A49 3c on 6c blue & black .65 *1.00*

Coconut Palms — A70

1943-47 Wmk. 4 Engr. ***Perf. 12***

292 A70 5c red org & ol grn ('47) 2.10 .35
- *a.* Perf. 13½ ('43) .35 .25

Peace Issue

Common Design Type

1946, Dec. 10 ***Perf. 13½x14***

293 CD303 6c deep blue .30 *.35*
294 CD303 15c brown .30 *1.75*

Guard Stone Type of 1938

1947, Mar. 15 ***Perf. 11x11½***

295 A68 2r violet & black 2.75 *3.00*

Parliament Building, Colombo — A71

Adam's Peak A72

Dagoba at Anuradhapura A74

Temple of the Tooth, Kandy A73

1947, Nov. 25 ***Perf. 11x12, 12x11***

296 A71 6c deep ultra & black .25 .25
297 A72 10c car, orange & black .25 *.40*
298 A73 15c red vio & grnsh blk .25 *.80*
299 A74 25c brt green & bister .25 *1.75*
Nos. 296-299 (4) 1.00 3.20

New constitution of 1947.

National Flag A75

D. S. Senanayake A76

Engr., Flag Typo. (A75); Engr. (A76)

Perf. 12½x12, 12x12½, 13x12½

1949 Wmk. 4

300 A75 4c org brn, car & yel .25 .25
301 A76 5c dark green & brn .25 .25

Wmk. 290

302 A75 15c red org, car & yel 1.10 1.00
303 A76 25c dp blue & brown .25 1.00
Nos. 300-303 (4) 1.85 2.50

Size of No. 302: 28x22¼mm.

1st anniv. of Ceylon's independence.

Issued: Nos. 300-301, Feb. 4; Nos. 302-303, Apr. 5.

A77

A78

Design: 15c, Lion Rock and UPU symbols.

Wmk. 290

1949, Oct. 10 Engr. ***Perf. 12***

304 A77 5c dk green & brown .85 .25
305 A77 15c dark car & black 1.25 *2.75*
306 A78 25c ultra & black 1.25 1.25
Nos. 304-306 (3) 3.35 4.25

75th anniv. of the UPU.

Kandyan Dancer A79

Kiri Vehera, Polonnaruwa A80

Vesak Orchid — A81

Sigiriya — A82

Ratmalana, Plane — A83

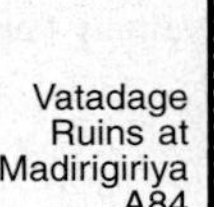

Vatadage Ruins at Madirigiriya A84

1950, Feb. 4 ***Perf. 12x12½***

307 A79 4c bright red & choc .25 .25
308 A80 5c green .25 .25
309 A81 15c pur & blue green 2.75 .50
310 A82 30c carmine & yel .40 *.70*

Perf. 11x11½, 11½x11

311 A83 75c red org & blue 8.75 .25
312 A84 1r red brn & dp blue 2.50 .45
Nos. 307-312 (6) 14.90 2.40

See Nos. 340-345.

Coconut Palms — A85

Star Orchid — A86

1951-52 Unwmk. Photo. ***Perf. 11½***

313 A85 10c gray & dark green 1.25 .75
314 A86 35c dk grn & rose brn ('52) 1.50 1.50
- *a.* Corrected inscription ('54) 6.50 .70

On No. 314a a dot has been added above the third character in the second line of the Tamil inscription.

Issue dates: 10c, Aug. 1; 35c, Feb. 1.

See No. 351.

Mace and Symbols of Industry A87

Perf. 12½x14

1952, Feb. 23 Wmk. 290

315 A87 5c green .25 .30
316 A87 15c brt ultramarine .40 .60

Colombo Plan Exhibition, February 1952.

Coronation Issue

Queen Elizabeth II — A88

1953, June 2 Engr. ***Perf. 12x12½***

317 A88 5c green 1.40 .25

Royal Procession A89

1954, Apr. 10 ***Perf. 13x12½***

318 A89 10c deep blue 1.00 .25

Visit of Queen Elizabeth II and the Duke of Edinburgh, 1954.

Sambar in Ruhuna National Park — A90

Rubber Trees — A91

Designs: 3c, Ancient guard stone. 6c and 10r, Harvesting rice. 25c, Sigiriya fresco. 50c, Outrigger fishing canoe. 85c, Tea Picker. 2r, Gal Oya dam. 5r, Bas-relief, "The Lovers."

1954 Unwmk. Photo. ***Perf. 11½***

Size: 21x25½mm

319 A90 2c green & brown .25 *1.25*
320 A90 3c violet & black .25 *1.00*
321 A90 6c yel grn & blk brn .25 *.30*
322 A90 25c vio bl, bl & brn orange .25 .25

Size: 25½x21mm

323 A91 40c black brown 5.50 1.25
324 A91 50c indigo .45 .25

Size: 23x32½mm, 32½x23mm

325 A90 85c dk grn & gray 1.50 .40
326 A91 2r blue & blk brn 9.25 1.40
327 A90 5r dp org & blk brn 8.00 1.50
328 A90 10r brown 52.50 20.00
Nos. 319-328 (10) 78.20 27.60

See Nos. 346-356.

Issued: 25c, 50c, 5r, 10r, 3/15; others, 5/15.

Nos. 327-328 with revenue cancellations sell for minimal prices.

King Coconuts — A92

1954, Dec. 1

329 A92 10c brown & orange .30 .25

See No. 349.

Symbols of Agriculture A93

Perf. 14x14½

1955, Dec. 10 — Wmk. 290

330 A93 10c orange & brown .30 .25

Royal Agricultural and Food Exhibition.

House of Representatives — A94

1956, Mar. 26 — Unwmk. — *Perf. 11½*

Granite Paper

331 A94 10c deep green .25 .25

25th anniv. of Prime Minister Sir John Kotelawala's entry into the Ceylon Legislature.

Arrival of Vijaya in Ceylon — A95

Dharmachakra Encircling Globe — A96

1956, May 23 — Granite Paper

332 A95 3c dull vio gray & saph .50 .25
333 A96 15c ultramarine .25 .25

Birth of Buddha, 2500th anniv. See Nos. B1-B2.

Methods of Transportation — A97

35c, 85c, Ceylon's 1st stamp & coat of arms.

1957, Apr. 1 — Photo. — *Perf. 12½x13*

334 A97 4c blue green & ver .70 .50
335 A97 10c blue & vermilion .70 .25

Perf. 11½

Granite Paper

336 A97 35c blue, yel & brown .40 *.40*
337 A97 85c dull grn, yel & brn .70 *1.25*
Nos. 334-337 (4) 2.50 2.40

Ceylon's 1st postage stamps, cent.

Nos. B1-B2 Overprinted with Black Bars and Squares

1958, Jan. 15 — Unwmk.

Granite Paper

338 SP1 4c dp blue & lt yel .25 .25
a. Inverted overprint 22.50 *37.50*
b. Double overprint 37.50 *50.00*
339 SP1 10c dk gray, yel & brt pink .25 .25
a. Inverted overprint 15.00 *20.00*

The overprint obliterates the surtax and inscription at right.

Types of 1950-54 Redrawn

Perf. 12x12½

1958-59 — Engr. — Wmk. 290

340 A79 4c brt red & chocolate .25 .25
341 A80 5c green .25 *1.60*
342 A81 15c purple & blue grn 3.50 1.10
343 A82 30c car & yel ('59) .25 *1.50*

Perf. 11½x11

344 A83 75c red org & bl ('59) 9.50 5.75

Perf. 11x11½

345 A84 1r red brn & dp blue .65 .25
Nos. 340-345 (6) 14.40 10.45

Issued: 4c, 5/14; 5c, 15c, 1r, 10/1; 30c, 75c, 5/1.

For surcharge see No. 368.

No. 328

No. 356

1958-59 — Unwmk. — Photo. — *Perf. 11½*

Granite Paper

346 A90 2c green & brown .25 .50
347 A90 3c violet & black .25 .70
348 A90 6c yel grn & blk brn .25 .65
349 A92 10c brown & orange .25 .25
350 A90 25c vio bl, bl & brn orange .25 .25
351 A86 35c dk grn & rose brn 7.75 .40
352 A91 50c indigo .25 .25
353 A90 85c dark green & gray 4.50 8.50
354 A91 2r blue & blk brn 2.00 .30
355 A90 5r dp org & blk brn 10.00 .40
356 A90 10r brown 12.00 1.40
Nos. 346-356 (11) 37.75 13.60

Designs and sizes of Nos. 340-356 remain as before, but wording has been changed to be predominantly Singhalese. "Ceylon" appears in small letters only in English and Tamil.

Nos. 355-356 with revenue cancellations sell for minimal prices.

Issue dates: 35c, 50c, July 15; 10c, Oct. 1; 85c, May 1, 1959; others, May 14, 1958.

For surcharges, see Sri Lanka Nos. 1572, 1577.

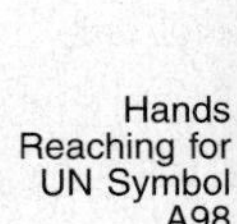

Hands Reaching for UN Symbol A98

Perf. 13x12½

1958, Dec. 10 — Photo. — Unwmk.

357 A98 10c red brown & red .25 .25
358 A98 85c Prus green & red .30 .30

10th anniv. of the signing of the Universal Declaration of Human Rights.

Pirivena Universities and Founders A99

1959, Dec. 31

359 A99 10c brt ultra & dp org .25 .25

Institution of Pirivena Universities; founders Hikkaduwe Sri Sumangala Nayaka Thero and Ratmalane Sri Dharmaloka Nayake Thero.

Uprooted Oak Emblem — A100

1960, Apr. 7 — Photo. — *Perf. 11½*

Granite Paper

360 A100 4c chocolate & gold .25 *.85*
361 A100 25c vio blue & gold .25 .25

World Refugee Year, 7/1/59-6/30/60.

Prime Minister Bandaranaike A101

Type I — Type II

Two types:
I — Gray hair at temple.
II — Dark hair at temple (redrawn).

1961, Jan. 8 — Granite Paper

362 A101 10c vio bl & gray bl (I) .30 .25
a. Type II .40 .25

Solomon West Ridgeway Dias Bandaranaike, assassinated Sept. 26, 1959.

Badge of Singhalese Scouts — A102

1962, Feb. 26 — Unwmk. — *Perf. 11½*

Granite Paper

363 A102 35c dark blue & ocher .35 .25

Boy Scouts of Ceylon, 50th anniv.

Malaria Eradication Emblem — A103

Perf. 14½x14

1962, Apr. 7 — Photo. — Wmk. 290

364 A103 25c lt sep, red org & brn .40 .40

WHO drive to eradicate malaria.

Monoplane 1938, and De Havilland Comet IV — A104

1963, Feb. 28 — Unwmk. — *Perf. 11½*

Granite Paper

365 A104 50c lt grnsh blue & blk .60 .60

25th anniv. of Ceylonese airmail service.

Stylized Vase and Wheat Emblem A105

1963, Mar. 21 — Granite Paper

366 A105 5c blue & orange ver 1.00 *2.50*
367 A105 25c olive & brown 3.00 .50

FAO "Freedom from Hunger" campaign.

No. 340 Surcharged

Perf. 12x12½

1963, June 1 — Engr. — Wmk. 290

368 A79 2c on 4c brt red & choc .40 .40
a. Inverted surcharge 20.00
b. Double surcharge 40.00

Rural Life — A106

1963, July 5 — Photo. — *Perf. 14x14½*

369 A106 60c dull red & black 2.00 .75

50th anniv. of the Cooperative Movement.

Landscape and Elephant A107

1963, Dec. 2 — Wmk. 290

370 A107 5c blue & black .65 .45

National Conservation Week.

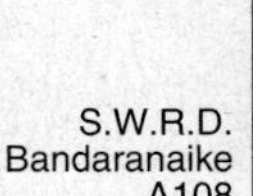

S.W.R.D. Bandaranaike A108

Perf. 11½

1963, Sept. 26 — Unwmk. — Engr.

Granite Paper

371 A108 10c blue .25 .25

Redrawn
Granite Paper

1964, July 1 Photo.
372 A108 10c grnsh gray & bl vio .25 .25

Frame redrawn on No. 372; inscription in bottom panel replaced by ornament.
For surcharge see No. 389.

Anagarika Dharmapala — A109

1964, Sept. 16 Unwmk. *Perf. 11½*
Granite Paper
373 A109 25c gray brn & dull yel .25 .25

Anagarika Dharmapala, Buddhist missionary, birth cent.

Ceylon Jungle Fowl — A110

Tea Picker — A112

Vatadage Ruins at Madirigiriya A111

Designs: 5c, Hill myna. 15c, Blue peafowl. 75c, Asiatic black-headed oriole. 5r, Girls, working in rice field. 10r, Map of Ceylon on scroll, showing agricultural development stations.

Wmk. 290, Unwmkd. (20c)
1964-69 Photo. *Perf. 14, 11½ (20c)*
374 A110 5c brt bl, blk, yel & grn 2.00 1.40
375 A110 15c yel, grn, blk, brt bl & rose 3.75 .30
376 A111 20c dk red brn, *buff* .25 .25
377 A110 60c yel & multi 4.50 1.10
a. Blue omitted 50.00
b. Red omitted 50.00
378 A110 75c ol, blk, org & brn 3.00 .75
a. Souvenir sheet of 4 10.00 14.00
b. As "a," overprinted 10.00
379 A112 1r brown & grn 1.00 .25
c. Brown omitted *1,500.*
379A A111 5r multicolored 9.50 9.50
379B A112 10r brown & multi 22.50 3.50
Nos. 374-379B (8) 46.50 17.05

No. 378a contains four imperf. stamps with simulated perforations similar to Nos. 374-375 and 377-378.
No. 378b is overprinted "First National Stamp Exhibition 1967" in two lines of black capitals.
No. 376 is on granite paper.
Issued: 20c, 1r, 10/1/; 5c, 15c, 60c, 75c, 2/5/66; 5r, 8/15/69; 10r, 10/1/69.
See No. 325.

Exhibition Buildings, Cogwheels — A113

"Industrial Exhibition" in Singhalese and English

1964, Dec. 1 Unwmk. *Perf. 11*
380 A113 5c multicolored .25 *.75*

"Industrial Exhibition" in Singhalese and Tamil

381 A113 5c multicolored .25 *.75*
a. Pair, #380-381 .35 *2.50*

1965 Industrial Exhibition.

Railroad Trains, 1864-1964 A114

"Railway Centenary" in Singhalese and English

Wmk. 290
1964, Dec. 21 Photo. *Perf. 14*
382 A114 60c lil rose, bl & yel grn 3.25 .55

"Railway Centenary" in Singhalese and Tamil

383 A114 60c lil rose, bl & yel grn 3.25 .55
a. Vertical pair, #382-383 7.75 7.75

Centenary of Ceylonese railroads.

ITU Emblem, Old and New Communication Equipment — A115

1965, May 17 *Perf. 14*
384 A115 2c ultra & red 1.60 1.40
385 A115 30c brown & red 4.50 .55

ITU, centenary.

ICY Emblem A116

1965, June 26 Unwmk. *Perf. 11½*
Granite Paper
386 A116 3c rose car & dk bl 1.50 1.25
387 A116 50c gold, rose car & blk 4.00 .60

International Cooperation Year.

Municipal Council Building A117

1965, Oct. 29 Photo. *Perf. 11½*
Granite Paper
388 A117 25c gray & green .30 .30

Centenary of Colombo Municipal Council.

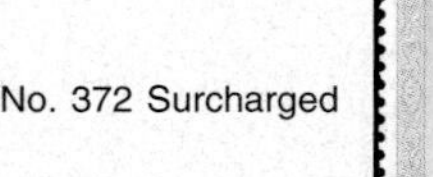
No. 372 Surcharged

1965, Dec. 18 Photo. *Perf. 11½*
389 A108 5c on 10c .25 1.25

D. S. Senanayake — A118

1966, Mar. 22 Unwmk. *Perf. 11½*
Granite Paper
390 A118 10c bright green .80 .25

D. S. Senanayake, first prime minister of Ceylon, 14th death anniv. See No. 418.

View and Arms of Kandy — A119

Perf. 14x13½
1966, June 15 Photo. Wmk. 290
391 A119 25c multicolored .25 .25

Centenary of Kandy Municipal Council.

Opening of WHO Headquarters, Geneva A120

Unwmk.
1966, Oct. 8 Litho. *Perf. 14*
392 A120 4c multicolored 2.50 3.00
393 A120 1r multicolored 8.00 1.60

Rice, Map of Ceylon, FAO Emblem — A121

Design: 30c, Rice and globe.

1966, Oct. 25 Photo. *Perf. 11½*
Granite Paper
394 A121 6c dk green, org & brn .25 *.75*
395 A121 30c brt blue, org & brn .50 .25

Intl. Rice Year under sponsorship of the FAO.

UNESCO Emblem A122

1966, Nov. 3 Litho. *Perf. 12*
396 A122 3c tan & multi 3.00 *3.50*
397 A122 50c brt green & multi 7.75 .75

20th anniv. of UNESCO.
For surcharge, see Sri Lanka No. 1578.

Map of Ceylon and UNESCO Emblem — A123

1966, Dec. 1 Unwmk. *Perf. 14*
398 A123 2c yel brn, yel & blue .35 *1.00*
399 A123 2r multicolored 1.50 *2.25*

Intl. Hydrological Decade (UNESCO), 1965-74.

Worshippers at Buddhist Shrine A124

Designs: 20c, Muhintale Rock. 35c, Sacred Bo Tree. 60c, Adam's Peak.

1967, Jan. 2 Photo. *Perf. 12*
400 A124 5c multicolored .25 .25
401 A124 20c multicolored .25 .25
402 A124 35c multicolored .25 .25
403 A124 60c multicolored .25 .25
Nos. 400-403 (4) 1.00 1.00

1st anniv. of the Poya Holiday System, Buddhist holiday replacing Sunday.
For surcharge, see Sri Lanka No. 1573.

Dutch Ramparts, Clock Tower and Arms of Galle A125

1967, Jan. 5 Litho. *Perf. 14x13½*
404 A125 25c dk green & multi .80 .25

Centenary of Galle Municipal Council.

Tea Research A126

40c, Tea tasting (cup & loose tea). 50c, Tea picking. 1r, Tea export (crate & freighter).

1967, Aug. 1 Unwmk. *Perf. 13½*
405 A126 4c multicolored .60 .60
406 A126 40c multicolored 1.75 1.60
407 A126 50c multicolored 1.75 .40
408 A126 1r multicolored 1.75 .25
Nos. 405-408 (4) 5.85 2.85

Centenary of the Ceylonese tea industry.

Elephant and ITY Emblem A127

1967, Aug. 15 Litho.
409 A127 45c multicolored 3.00 .85

Intl. Tourist Year.

Girl Guide, Jubilee Emblem and Flag — A128

1967, Sept. 19 *Perf. 12x12½*
410 A128 3c green & multi .60 .25
411 A128 25c org yel & multi .90 .25

Ceylon Girl Guide Assoc., 50th anniv.

Henry S. Olcott and Buddhist Flag A129

Perf. 13½

1967, Dec. 12 Unwmk. Litho.

412 A129 15c multicolored .40 .25

Colonel Henry S. Olcott (1832-1907), an American who reorganized the Buddhist hierarchy and school system in Ceylon and was the first president of the Theosophical Society.

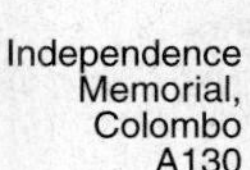

Independence Memorial, Colombo A130

Design: 1r, Flag of Ceylon and mace.

1968, Feb. 4 Wmk. 290 *Perf. 14*

413 A130 5c multicolored .25 .45
414 A130 1r multicolored .50 .25

20th anniversary of independence.

D. B. Jayatilaka — A131

1968, Feb. 14 Photo.

415 A131 25c brown .25 .25

Sir Don Baron Jayatilaka (1868-1944), Buddhist leader and scholar.

Hygiene Institute, Kalutara A132

Perf. 11½x12

1968, Apr. 4 Litho. Wmk. 290

416 A132 50c multicolored .25 .25

WHO, 20th anniversary.

Jet over Colombo Terminal A133

1968, Aug. 5 *Perf. 13½*

417 A133 60c org brn, dk bl & org .75 .25

Opening of Colombo Airport.

D. S. Senanayake — A134

1968, Sept. 23 Photo. *Perf. 14*

418 A134 10c deep green .25 .25

See No. 390.

Open Koran A135

1968, Oct. 14 Photo. *Perf. 14*

419 A135 25c org brn, blk, blue & emerald .25 .25

1,400th anniversary of the Koran.

Human Rights Flame A136

Perf. 12½x13½

1968, Dec. 10 Unwmk.

420 A136 2c multicolored .25 *.30*
421 A136 20c multicolored .25 .25
422 A136 40c multicolored .25 .25
423 A136 2r multicolored .90 *4.00*
Nos. 420-423 (4) 1.65 4.80

International Human Rights Year.

Ceylon Buddhist Headquarters, Colombo — A137

1968, Dec. 19 Litho. *Perf. 13½*

424 A137 5c multicolored .25 *.50*

All-Ceylon Buddhist Cong., 50th anniv.

A multicolored 50c showing the Sri Padmaya (Sacred Footprint) on Adam's Peak was prepared but the issuance order was countermanded on Dec. 18. Some were sold in ignorance of the withdrawal order. Value $65.

E. W. Perera — A138

Wmk. 290

1969, Feb. 17 Photo. *Perf. 14*

425 A138 60c brown .25 *.30*

E. W. Perera, member of Legislative Council.

"Strength in Saving" — A139

1969, Mar. 20

426 A139 3c blue, yel & black .25 *.30*

National Savings Movement, 25th anniv.

A140

4c, Seat of Enlightenment under Bodhi Tree. 6c, Buduresmala (disk symbolic of six-fold Buddha rays).

Wmk. 290

1969, Apr. 10 Litho. *Perf. 15*

427 A140 4c orange & multi .25 *.40*
428 A140 6c gold & multi .25 *.40*
429 A140 35c scarlet & multi .25 .25
Nos. 427-429 (3) .75 1.05

Vesak Day, which commemorates the birth, enlightenment and death of Buddha.

For surcharges see Nos. 463, 466.

A141

1969, Apr. 29 Photo. *Perf. 14x14½*

430 A141 15c org yel & multi .25 .25

Alexander Ekanayake Goonesingha (1891-1967), trade unionist, political leader and diplomat.

ILO, 50th Anniv. A142

1969, May 4 *Perf. 14½x14*

431 A142 5c grnsh bl & black .25 .25
432 A142 25c car rose & black .25 .25

Convocation Hall, University of Ceylon A143

Elephant Lamp (Ath Pana) — A144

35c, "Lamp of Education," globe & flags. 50c, Uranium atom diagram. 60c, Symbols of science education. 1r, Aerial view of Sigiriya rock fortress.

Inscribed: "SIYAWASA"

Unwmk.

1969, Aug. 1 Litho. *Perf. 14*

433 A143 4c yellow & multi .25 *.80*
434 A144 6c multicolored .30 *1.50*
435 A143 35c multicolored .25 .25
436 A144 50c red & multi .25 .25
437 A143 60c blue & multi .30 .25
438 A144 1r yel & multi .30 .25
Nos. 433-438 (6) 1.65 3.30

Centenary of public education and archaeological research.

For surcharges see Nos. 464-467.

Wild Water Buffalo A145

15c, Slender loris. 50c, Axis deer. 1r, Leopard.

Perf. 14x13½

1970, May 11 Litho. Unwmk.

439 A145 5c lt blue & multi 1.20 *1.25*
440 A145 15c buff & multi 2.00 1.00
441 A145 50c salmon & multi 1.40 1.25
442 A145 1r gray & multi 1.40 *1.75*
Nos. 439-442 (4) 6.00 5.25

Symbols of Agriculture and Industry A146

1970, June 17

443 A146 60c multicolored .25 .25

Asian Productivity Year.

Inauguration of UPU Headquarters, Bern — A147

1970, Aug. 14 Litho. Unwmk.

444 A147 50c org, black & blue .50 .25
445 A147 1.10r red, black & blue 4.25 .40

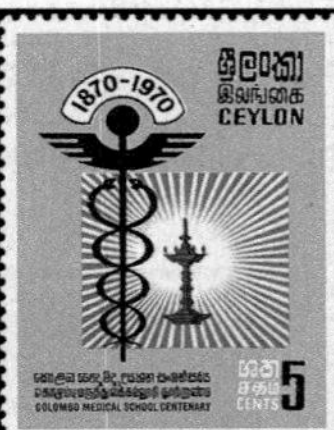

Caduceus and Oil Lamp — A148

1970, Sept. 1 *Perf. 13½x14*

446 A148 5c multicolored 1.00 *.75*
447 A148 45c gray & multi 1.00 *.60*

Centenary of the Ceylon Medical School.

Victory March and S.W.R.D. Bandaranaike A149

1970, Sept. 25 *Perf. 14*

448 A149 10c red & multi .25 .25

For surcharge see No. 465.

UN Emblem and Dove — A150

1970, Oct. 24 Photo. *Perf. 12½x14*

449 A150 2r dp orange & multi 2.75 *3.50*

25th anniversary of the United Nations.

Keppetipola Dissawe — A151

1970, Nov. 26 Litho. *Perf. 14x14½*

450 A151 25c multicolored .25 .25

The 152nd anniversary of the execution of Keppetipola Dissawe, leader of the Great Rebellion of 1817-18.

Ola Leaf Manuscript and Education Year Emblem — A152

1970, Dec. 21 Photo. *Perf. 13*
451 A152 15c brown & multi 2.75 1.50

International Education Year.

Charles Henry de Soysa — A153

1971, Mar. 3 Litho. *Perf. 14x13½*
452 A153 20c orange & multi .30 .30

de Soysa (1836-90), philanthropist who founded hospitals and schools.

Edward Henry Pedris — A154

1971, July 8 Litho. *Perf. 14x14½*
453 A154 25c blue & multi .30 .30

Edward Henry Pedris (1888-1925), patriot.

A 5c stamp for the 10th Conf. of World Fellowship of Buddhists, Ceylon, May 9-13, was supposedly not issued without "1972" overprint. See Sri Lanka No. 471.

Lenin (1870-1924) — A156

1971, Aug. 31 *Perf. 14½*
455 A156 40c dp car & multi .55 .55

Cumaratunga Munidasa — A157

Poets and Philosophers: No. 457, Ananda Coomaraswamy (1887-1947). No. 458, Rev. S. Mahinda Thero (1905-51). No. 459, Ananda Rajakaruna (1885-1957). No. 460, Arumuga Navalar (1822-78).

1971, Oct. 29 *Perf. 14*
456 A157 5c brown .25 .25
457 A157 5c slate .25 .25
458 A157 5c deep orange .25 .25
459 A157 5c dp vio blue .25 .25
460 A157 5c brown red .25 .25
Nos. 456-460 (5) 1.25 1.25

CARE Package A158

1971, Dec. 28 *Perf. 14x13*
461 A158 50c purple, blue & pink .55 .35

25th anniv. of CARE, a US-Canadian Co-operative for American Relief Everywhere.

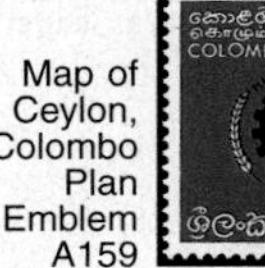

Map of Ceylon, Colombo Plan Emblem A159

1971, Dec. 28 Litho. *Perf. 14x14½*
462 A159 20c multicolored .30 .30

20th anniversary of the Colombo Plan.

Issues of 1969-70 Surcharged

a

b

c

d

e

Wmk. 290, Unwmkd.
1971, Dec. 5 *Perf. 15, 14*
463 A140 (a) 5c on 4c (#427) 6.00 2.50
464 A143 (b) 5c on 4c (#433) .25 1.90
465 A149 (c) 15c on 10c (#448) .25 .50
466 A140 (d) 25c on 6c (#428) .65 .95
467 A144 (e) 25c on 6c (#434) .65 *3.25*
Nos. 463-467 (5) 7.80 9.10

Nos. 463-466 exist with surcharge inverted.

WHO Emblem and Heart — A160

1972, May 2 Unwmk. *Perf. 13x13½*
468 A160 25c multicolored 2.75 .90

"Your heart is your health," World Health Day.

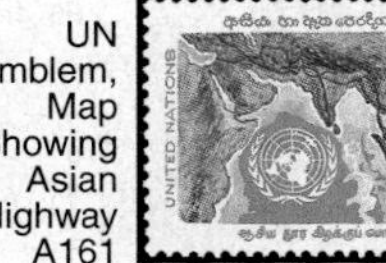

UN Emblem, Map Showing Asian Highway A161

1972, May 2 *Perf. 13x12½*
469 A161 85c lt blue & multi 5.25 3.25

Economic Commission for Asia and the Far East (ECAFE), 25th anniversary.

SEMI-POSTAL STAMPS

Catalogue values for unused stamps in this section are for Never Hinged items.

Lamp and Dharmachakra SP1

Design: 10c+5c, Hand of Peace.

Perf. 11½
1956, May 10 Unwmk. Photo.
Granite Paper
B1 SP1 4c + 2c dp bl & lt yel .35 *.75*
B2 SP1 10c + 5c dk gray, yel & brt pink .50 *1.00*

2500th anniv. of the birth of Buddha. The surtax went to the Buddha Jayanti Fund. For overprints, see Nos. 338-339.

WAR TAX STAMPS

Nos. 201, 202, 202a and 203 Overprinted

Die I
1918 Wmk. 3 *Perf. 14*
MR1 A44 2c brown orange .25 *.45*
a. Double overprint 35.00 47.50
b. Inverted overprint 75.00 *85.00*
MR2 A44 3c dp grn (Die Ia, type II) 4.00 .45
a. 3c dp green (Die I, type I) .25 *.60*
b. Double overprint (Die I) 110.00 *120.00*
c. 5c Double overprint (Die Ia, type II) 150.00
MR3 A44 5c red violet 4.75 3.50
a. Double overprint 75.00 *75.00*
b. Inverted overprint 75.00
c. 5c purple .60 .35

No. 223 Overprinted in Black

MR4 A44 1c on 5c red violet 3.50 *.45*
a. Double overprint 225.00
b. 1c on No. 223a .60 .45
Nos. MR1-MR4 (4) 12.50 4.85

OFFICIAL STAMPS

Regular Issues Overprinted

Black Overprint
1869 Wmk. 1 *Perf. 12½, 14*
O1 A4 1p blue 97.50
O2 A1 2p yellow 97.50
O3 A5 3p rose 190.00
O4 A2 8p red brown 97.50
O5 A1 1sh gray lilac 220.00

Red Overprint
O6 A1 6p brown 97.50
O7 A2 2sh blue 160.00
a. Imperf. *1,250.*
Nos. O1-O7 (7) 960.00

Nos. O1-O7 were never placed in use.
The overprint measures 15mm on Nos. O1, O3.

Regular Issues Overprinted in Black or Red

1895-1900 Wmk. 2 *Perf. 14*
O8 A6 2c green 17.00 .75
O9 A6 2c org brn ('00) 11.50 .65
O10 A24 3c org brn & grn 11.50 2.50
O11 A24 3c green ('00) 12.50 4.50
O12 A23 5c lilac 5.25 .35
O13 A24 15c olive green 24.00 .50
O14 A24 15c ultra ('00) 25.00 .60
O15 A24 25c brown 13.50 3.00
O16 A24 30c vio & org brn 13.50 .65
O17 A24 75c blk & org brn (R) ('99) 10.00 *8.50*

Wmk. 1
O18 A16 1r12c claret 100.00 62.50
Nos. O8-O18 (11) 243.75 84.50

1903-04 Wmk. 2
O19 A36 2c orange brown 24.00 1.75
O20 A37 3c green 17.50 2.10
O21 A38 5c dull lilac 32.50 1.60
O22 A40 15c ultramarine 40.00 3.25
O23 A40 25c bister 35.00 22.50
O24 A40 30c violet & green 20.00 1.50
Nos. O19-O24 (6) 169.00 32.70

CHAD

'chad

(Tchad)

LOCATION — Central Africa, south of Libya
GOVT. — Republic
AREA — 495,572 sq. mi.
POP. — 7,557,436 (1999 est.)
CAPITAL — N'Djamena

A former dependency of Ubangi-Shari, Chad became a separate French colony in 1920. In 1934, the colonies of Chad, Gabon, Middle Congo and Ubangi-Shari were grouped in a single administrative unit known as French Equatorial Africa, with the capital at Brazzaville. The Republic of Chad was proclaimed November 28, 1958.

100 Centimes = 1 Franc

Catalogue values for unused stamps in this country are for Never Hinged items, beginning with Scott 64 in the regular postage section, Scott B1 in the semi-postal section, Scott C1 in the air post section, Scott CB1 in the air post semi-postal section, Scott J23 in the postage due section, Scott M1 in the military stamp section, and Scott O1 in the officials section.

See French Equatorial Africa No. 190 for stamp inscribed "Tchad."

Types of Middle Congo, 1907-17, Overprinted

Perf. 14x13½, 13½x14

1922 **Unwmk.**

1 A1 1c red & violet .40 .55
a. Overprint omitted 225.00
2 A1 2c ol brn & salmon .40 .80
a. Overprint omitted 260.00
3 A1 4c ind & vio 1.20 1.60
4 A1 5c choc & grn 1.25 1.60
5 A1 10c dp grn & gray grn 2.40 2.75
6 A1 15c vio & red 2.50 2.75
7 A1 20c grn & vio 4.00 4.75
8 A2 25c ol brn & brn 12.00 12.00
9 A2 30c rose & pale rose 2.40 2.00
10 A2 35c dl bl & dl rose 3.25 3.25
11 A2 40c choc & grn 4.00 4.00
12 A2 45c vio & grn 3.25 3.25
13 A2 50c dk bl & pale bl 3.25 4.00
14 A2 60c on 75c vio, *pnksh* 4.00 4.75
a. "TCHAD" omitted 300.00
b. "60" omitted 300.00
15 A2 75c red & violet 4.00 4.00
16 A3 1fr indigo & salmon 12.00 16.00
17 A3 2fr indigo & violet 24.00 24.00
18 A3 5fr ind & olive brn 24.00 24.00
Nos. 1-18 (18) 108.30 116.05

See Nos. 26a, 32a, 38a, 55a.

Stamps of 1922 Overprinted in Various Colors

Nos. 19-28

Nos. 29-50

1924-33

19 A1 1c red & vio .40 .80
a. "TCHAD" omitted 225.00 *250.00*
b. Double overprint 300.00
c. Violet omitted 300.00
20 A1 2c ol brn & sal .40 *.50*
a. "TCHAD" omitted 225.00
b. Double overprint 240.00
21 A1 4c ind & vio .40 *.50*
a. "TCHAD" omitted 950.00
22 A1 5c choc & grn (Bl) 1.60 *2.00*
a. "TCHAD" omitted 200.00 225.00
23 A1 5c choc & grn .80 *.70*
a. "TCHAD" omitted 225.00
24 A1 10c dp grn & gray grn (Bl) 1.60 1.40
25 A1 10c dp grn & gray grn 1.60 1.40
26 A1 10c red org & blk ('25) .60 .80
a. "Afrique Equatoriale Française" omitted 225.00 250.00
b. "TCHAD" omitted 240.00 260.00
27 A1 15c vio & red .80 .85
28 A1 20c grn & vio .80 .80
a. "TCHAD" omitted 225.00
b. "Afrique Equatoriale Française" doubled 340.00
29 A2 25c ol brn & brn .80 .85
a. "Afrique Equatoriale Française" doubled 160.00
30 A2 30c rose & pale rose .80 1.10
31 A2 30c gray & bl (R) ('25) .40 .80
32 A2 30c dk grn & grn ('27) 1.20 1.60
a. "Afrique Equatoriale Française" omitted 340.00
33 A2 35c indigo & dl rose .80 .85
34 A2 40c choc & grn 1.25 1.60
a. Double overprint (R + Bk) 275.00
35 A2 45c vio & grn 1.20 1.40
a. Double overprint (R + Bk) 275.00
36 A2 50c dk bl & pale bl (R) 2.40 1.90
a. Inverted overprint 160.00
37 A2 50c grn & vio ('25) 2.40 2.00
38 A2 65c org brn & bl ('28) 2.40 2.40
a. "Afrique Equatoriale Française" omitted 260.00
39 A2 75c red & vio (Bl) 2.00 1.90
40 A2 75c dp bl & lt bl (R) ('25) .80 1.20
a. "TCHAD" omitted 260.00
41 A2 75c rose & dk brn ('28) 3.25 3.25
42 A2 90c brn red & pink ('30) 8.00 12.00
43 A3 1fr ind & salmon 2.40 2.50
44 A3 1.10fr dl grn & bl ('28) 4.00 4.00
45 A3 1.25fr org brn & lt bl ('33) 8.00 9.50
46 A3 1.50fr ultra & bl ('30) 8.00 12.00
47 A3 1.75fr ol brn & vio ('33) 40.00 45.00
48 A3 2fr ind & vio 3.25 3.50
a. Double impression of frame 550.00
49 A3 3fr red vio ('30) 12.00 16.00
50 A3 5fr ind & ol brn 4.00 4.75
Nos. 19-50 (32) 118.35 139.85

See No. 58a.

Types of 1922 Overprinted like Nos. 29-50 and Surcharged with New Values

1924-27

51 A2 60c on 75c dk vio, *pnksh* .80 1.20
a. "60" omitted 200.00
52 A3 65c on 1fr brn & ol grn ('25) 2.50 2.00
53 A3 85c on 1fr brn & ol grn ('25) 2.50 2.00
54 A2 90c on 75c brn red & rose red ('27) 2.50 2.00
55 A3 1.25fr on 1fr dk bl & ultra (R) ('26) 1.25 .80
a. "Afrique Equatoriale Française" omitted 175.00
56 A3 1.50fr on 1fr ultra & bl ('27) 2.50 2.00
57 A3 3fr on 5fr org brn & dl red ('27) 6.50 6.00
58 A3 10fr on 5fr ol grn & cer ('27) 16.00 14.50
a. "10fr" omitted 400.00 400.00
59 A3 20fr on 5fr vio & ver ('27) 20.00 21.00
Nos. 51-59 (9) 54.55 51.50

Common Design Types pictured following the introduction.

Colonial Exposition Issue
Common Design Types

1931 **Engr.** ***Perf. 12½***
Name of Country in Black

60 CD70 40c deep green 5.50 5.50
61 CD71 50c violet 5.50 5.50
62 CD72 90c red orange 5.50 5.50
63 CD73 1.50fr dull blue 5.50 5.50
Nos. 60-63 (4) 22.00 22.00

Catalogue values for unused stamps in this section, from this point to the end of the section, are for Never Hinged items.

Republic

"Birth of the Republic" A1

"Solidarity of the Community" A2

1959 **Unwmk.** **Engr.** ***Perf. 13***

64 A1 15fr ultra, grn & maroon .70 .25
65 A2 25fr dk grn & dp claret .90 .25

1st anniv. of the proclamation of the Republic.

Imperforates
Most Chad stamps from 1959 onward exist imperforate in issued and trial colors, and also in small presentation sheets in issued colors.

C.C.T.A. Issue
Common Design Type

1960

66 CD106 50fr rose lil & dk pur 1.75 .50

Flag and Map of Chad and UN Emblem — A3

Unwmk.

1961, Jan. 11 **Engr.** ***Perf. 13***
Flag in blue, yellow and carmine

67 A3 15fr brn & dk bl .60 .25
68 A3 25fr org brn & dk bl .90 .25
69 A3 85fr slate grn & dk bl 2.50 .40
Nos. 67-69 (3) 4.00 .90

Admission of Chad to United Nations.

Chari Bridge and Hippopotamus — A4

Abtouyoua Mountain and Ox — A5

Designs: 50c, Biltine and dorcas gazelle. 1fr, Logone and elephant. 2fr, Batha and lion. 3fr, Salamat and buffalo. 4fr, Ouaddai and Kudu. 15fr, Bessada and giant eland. 20fr, Tibesti mountains and mouflon. 25fr, Rocherg and antelope. 30fr, Kanem and cheetah. 60fr, Borkou and oryx. 85fr, Gorge of Archet and addax.

Perf. 13½x14, 14x13½

1961-62 **Typo.**

70 A5 50c yel grn & dk grn ('62) .25 .25
71 A5 1fr bl grn & dk bl grn ('62) .25 .25
72 A5 2fr dk red brn & blk ('62) .25 .25
73 A5 3fr ocher & dl grn ('62) .25 .25
74 A5 4fr dk crim & blk ('62) .25 .25
75 A4 5fr yellow & blk .25 .25
76 A5 10fr pink & blk .35 .25
77 A5 15fr lilac & blk ('62) .70 .25
78 A5 20fr red & blk .85 .25
79 A5 25fr blue & blk ('62) .90 .25
80 A5 30fr ultra & blk ('62) 1.00 .25
81 A5 60fr yel & ol grn ('62) 2.25 .25
82 A5 85fr org & blk 2.75 .25
Nos. 70-82 (13) 10.30 3.25

First anniversary of Independence.
For overprint see No. M1.

Abidjan Games Issue
Common Design Type

1962, July 21 **Photo.** ***Perf. 12½x12***

83 CD109 20fr Relay race .80 .25
84 CD109 50fr High jump 2.00 .30
Nos. 83-84,C8 (3) 5.80 1.55

African-Malgache Union Issue
Common Design Type

1962, Sept. 8 **Unwmk.**

85 CD110 30fr dk bl, bluish grn, red & gold 1.25 .25

Pres. Ngarta Tombalbaye — A7

1963, Apr. 22 ***Perf. 12x12½***

86 A7 20fr multi .50 .25
87 A7 85fr multi 1.40 .30

For surcharge, see No. 125.

Space Communciations Issue

Waves Around Globe — A8

Design: 100fr, Orbit patterns around globe.

Perf. 12½

1963, Sept. 19 **Unwmk.** **Photo.**

88 A8 25fr grn & pur .75 .25
89 A8 100fr pink & ultra 2.25 .60

Ancestral Mask — A9

Excavated Sao Art: 5fr, Clay weight in Pavia headform. 25fr, Ancestral clay statuette. 60fr, Gazelle, bronze. 80fr, Bronze pectoral.

1963, Dec. 2 **Engr.** ***Perf. 13***

90 A9 5fr brt grn & red brn .25 .25
91 A9 15fr gray, dl cl & red .25 .25
92 A9 25fr dk bl & org brn .90 .25

93 A9 60fr org brn & slate grn 2.25 .35
94 A9 80fr org red & olive 2.50 .40
Nos. 90-94 (5) 6.15 1.50

UNESCO Emblem, Scales and Tree — A10

1963, Dec. 10
95 A10 25fr green & maroon 1.00 .25

15th anniv. of the Universal Declaration of Human Rights.

Potter A11

Perf. 12½

1964, Feb. 5 Unwmk. Engr.
96 A11 10fr shown .30 .25
97 A11 30fr Boatmaker .80 .25
98 A11 50fr Weaver 1.35 .25
99 A11 85fr Smiths 2.00 .35
Nos. 96-99 (4) 4.45 1.10

Barograph and WMO Emblem A12

1964, Mar. 23 ***Perf. 13***
100 A12 50fr red lil, pur & ultra 1.40 .25

Fourth World Meteorological Day.

Cotton A13

1964, Apr. 6 Photo. ***Perf. 12½x13***
101 A13 20fr shown 1.40 .35
102 A13 25fr Royal poinciana 1.60 .40

Co-operation Issue
Common Design Type

1964, Nov. 7 Engr. ***Perf. 13***
103 CD119 25fr ver, dk bl & dk brn 1.00 .25

National Guard and Map of Chad A14

Design: 25fr, Infantry, flag and map, vert.

Perf. 12½x13, 13x12½

1964, Dec. 11 Photo.
104 A14 20fr multi .75 .25
105 A14 25fr lt bl & multi .90 .25

Issued to honor the army of Chad.

Aoudad or Barbary Sheep A15

10fr, Addax. 20fr, Oryx. 25fr, Derby's eland, vert. 30fr, Giraffe, buffalo & lion, Zakouma Park, vert. 85fr, Great kudu at water hole, vert.

Perf. 12½x12, 12x12½

1965, Jan. 11 Unwmk.
106 A15 5fr dk brn, ultra & yel .50 .25
107 A15 10fr ultra, org & blk .75 .25
108 A15 20fr multi 1.50 .25
109 A15 25fr multi 1.75 .25
110 A15 30fr multi 2.50 .40
111 A15 85fr multi 5.00 .75
Nos. 106-111 (6) 12.00 2.15

Olsen Perforator A16

Designs: 60fr, Mildé telephone, vert. 100fr, Distributor of Baudot telegraph.

1965, May 17 Engr. ***Perf. 13***
112 A16 30fr multi .65 .25
113 A16 60fr multi 1.10 .45
114 A16 100fr multi 1.80 .60
Nos. 112-114 (3) 3.55 1.30

Cent. of the ITU.

Motorized Police A17

Perf. 12½x12

1965, June 22 Photo. Unwmk.
115 A17 25fr ol, dk grn, gold & brn 1.00 .25

Issued to honor the national police.

Drum and stool — A18

Musical Instruments from National Museum: 2fr, Guitar. 3fr, Shoulder drums, vert. 15fr, Viol. 60fr, Harp, vert.

1965, Oct. 26 Engr. ***Perf. 13***
Size: 22x36mm, 36x22mm
116 A18 1fr car, emer & brn .25 .25
117 A18 2fr red, purple & brn .25 .25
118 A18 3fr red, brn lake & sepia .25 .25
119 A18 15fr red, ocher & sl grn .75 .25
120 A18 60fr maroon & slate grn 1.75 .60
Nos. 116-120,C23 (6) 5.25 2.60

See No. C23.

Head and Bowl — A19

Sao Art: 20fr, Head. 60fr, Head with crown. 80fr, Circlet with human head. From excavations at Bouta Kebira and Gawi.

1966, Apr. 1 Engr. ***Perf. 13***
121 A19 15fr ol, choc & ultra .40 .25
122 A19 20fr dk red, brn & bl grn .75 .25
123 A19 60fr brt bl, choc & ver 1.75 .50
124 A19 80fr brn org, grn & pur 2.50 .60
Nos. 121-124 (4) 5.40 1.60

Issued to publicize the International Negro Arts Festival, Dakar, Senegal, Apr. 1-24.

No. 86 Surcharged in Orange

1966, Apr. 15 Photo. ***Perf. 12x12½***
125 A7 25fr on 20fr multi 1.00 .30

WHO Headquarters, Geneva — A20

1966, May 3
126 A20 25fr car, lt ultra & yel .80 .25
127 A20 32fr emer, ultra & yel .90 .25

New WHO Headquarters, Geneva.

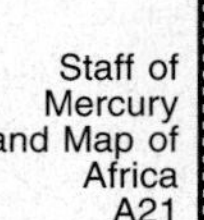

Staff of Mercury and Map of Africa A21

1966, May 24 ***Perf. 12½x12***
128 A21 30fr multi 1.00 .25

Central African Customs and Economic Union (Union Douaniere et Economique de l'Afrique Centrale, UDEAC).

Soccer Player — A22

Design: 60fr, Soccer player facing left.

1966, July 12 Engr. ***Perf. 13***
129 A22 30fr grn, bl grn & mar .80 .25
130 A22 60fr dk bl, gray & car 1.60 .40

8th World Cup Soccer Championship, Wembley, England, July 11-30.

Young Men, Flag and Emblem A23

1966, Aug. 11 Photo. ***Perf. 12½x13***
131 A23 25fr dk bl & multi 1.00 .25

Chad Youth Movement.

Greek Columns and UNESCO Emblem — A24

1966, Aug. 23 Engr. ***Perf. 13***
132 A24 32fr sl bl, vio & car rose 1.00 .25

20th anniv. of UNESCO.

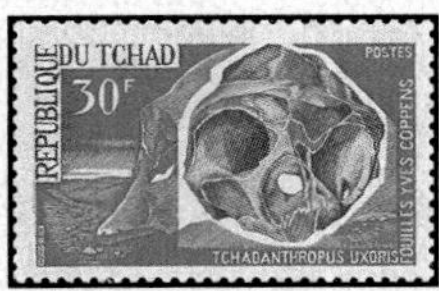

Reconstructed Skull of Chadanthropus — A25

1966, Sept. 20 Engr. ***Perf. 13***
133 A25 30fr gray, red & ocher 2.00 .50

Yves Coppens' discovery of Lake Chad man.

Stone Axe — A26

Prehistoric Tools: 30fr, Flint arrow head. 85fr, Bone harpoon. 100fr, Sandstone millstone with grinder.

1966, Dec. 11 Engr. ***Perf. 13***
134 A26 25fr dp bl, red & dk brn .70 .25
135 A26 30fr brn, dp bl & blk .80 .25
136 A26 85fr dk red, brt bl & brn 2.50 .50
137 A26 100fr Prus grn, dk brn & bis brn 2.75 .65
a. Miniature sheet of 4, #134-137 15.00 8.00
Nos. 134-137 (4) 6.75 1.65

Map of Chad and Various Sports — A27

1967, Apr. 10 Photo. ***Perf. 12x12½***
138 A27 25fr multi 1.00 .30

Issued for Sports Day, Apr. 10, 1967.

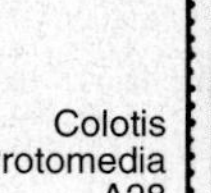

Colotis Protomedia A28

Various Butterflies.

1967, May 23 Photo. ***Perf. 12½x12***
139 A28 5fr blue & multi 2.00 .30
140 A28 10fr emerald & multi 4.25 .75
141 A28 20fr orange & multi 8.50 1.50
142 A28 130fr red & multi 17.50 2.50
Nos. 139-142 (4) 32.25 5.05

WHO Headquarters, Brazzaville — A29

1967, Sept. 23 Photo. ***Perf. 12½x13***
143 A29 30fr vio bl & multi 1.00 .25

Opening of the Regional Office of the WHO, Brazzaville.

Jamboree Emblem and Boy Scouts A30

32fr, Jamboree emblem and Boy Scout.

1967, Oct. 17 Photo. ***Perf. 12½x13***
144 A30 25fr multi .90 .25
145 A30 32fr multi 1.00 .25

12th Boy Scout World Jamboree, Farragut State Park, Idaho, Aug. 1-9.

Great Mills of Chad A31

30fr, Lake reclamation project, grain fields.

1967, Nov. 14 Engr. ***Perf. 13***
146 A31 25fr brt bl, ind & sep .90 .25
147 A31 30fr ultra, emer & ol brn 1.00 .25

Economic development of Chad.

Woman and Harp Player A32

Rock Paintings: 30fr, Giraffes. 50fr, Camel rider hunting ostrich.

1967, Dec. 19 Engr. ***Perf. 13***
Size: 36x22mm
148 A32 15fr bl, sal & mar 1.00 .25
149 A32 30fr grnsh bl, sal & mar 2.00 .40
150 A32 50fr emer, sal & mar 2.75 .55
Nos. 148-150,C38-C39 (5) 14.25 3.65

Balloud expedition in the Ennedi Mountains. See Nos. 163-166.

Rotary Emblem — A33

1968, Jan. 9 Photo. ***Perf. 13x12½***
151 A33 50fr multi 1.80 .50

Rotary Club of Chad, 10th anniversary.

Map of Chad, WHO Emblem, Well, Physicians, Mother and Child — A34

1968, Apr. 6 ***Perf. 13x12½***
152 A34 25fr multi .75 .25
153 A34 32fr multi .90 .25

20th anniv. of WHO.

"Water" Aiding Agriculture and Industry A35

1968, Apr. 23 Engr. ***Perf. 13***
154 A35 50fr grnsh bl, brn & brt grn 1.10 .25

Hydrological Decade (UNESCO), 1965-74.

National Administration School — A36

1968, Aug. 20 Engr. ***Perf. 13***
155 A36 25fr slate, brn red & rose vio 1.00 .25

Boy Learning to Write A37

1968, Sept. 10
156 A37 60fr dk bl, dk brn & blk 2.00 .50

Issued for National Literacy Day.

Cotton Harvest A38

Loom, Fort Archambault Factory — A39

1968, Sept. 24 Engr. ***Perf. 13***
157 A38 25fr Prus bl, choc & dk grn .90 .25
158 A39 30fr brt grn, ol & ultra 1.00 .25

Issued to publicize the cotton industry.

Tiger Moth — A40

Moths: 30fr, Owlet. 50fr, Saturnid (Gynanisa maja). 100fr, Saturnid (Epiphora bauhiniae).

1968, Oct. 1 **Photo.**
159 A40 25fr multi 5.25 .60
160 A40 30fr multi 6.25 .75
161 A40 50fr multi 9.50 .85
162 A40 100fr multi 11.00 1.50
Nos. 159-162 (4) 32.00 3.70

Rock Paintings Type of 1967

Rock Paintings: 2fr, Archers. 10fr, Costumes (4 women, 1 man). 20fr, Funeral vigil. 25fr, Dispute.

1968, Nov. 19 Engr. ***Perf. 13***
Size: 36x22mm
163 A32 2fr scar, salmon & brn .55 .25
164 A32 10fr pur, salmon & dk red 1.50 .25
165 A32 20fr grn, salmon & mar 1.90 .50
166 A32 25fr bl, salmon & maroon 3.25 .60
Nos. 163-166 (4) 7.20 1.60

Man and Human Rights Flame — A41

1968, Dec. 10 Engr. ***Perf. 13***
167 A41 32fr grn, brt bl & red 1.00 .25

International Human Rights Year.

St. Paul — A42

Apostles: 1fr, St. Peter. 2fr, St. Thomas. 5fr, St. John the Evangelist. 10fr, St. Bartholomew. 20fr, St. Matthew. 25fr, St. James the Less. 30fr, St. Andrew. 40fr, St. Jude. 50fr, St. James the Greater. 85fr, St. Philip. 100fr, St. Simon.

1969, May 6 Litho. ***Perf. 12½x13***
168 A42 50c multi .25 .25
169 A42 1fr multi .25 .25
170 A42 2fr multi .25 .25
171 A42 5fr multi .25 .25
172 A42 10fr multi .25 .25
173 A42 20fr multi .30 .25
174 A42 25fr multi .40 .25
175 A42 30fr multi .50 .25
176 A42 40fr multi .60 .25
177 A42 50fr multi .70 .25
178 A42 85fr multi 1.10 .40
179 A42 100fr multi 1.25 .40
a. Sheet of 12, #168-179 6.00 1.75

Jubilee Year of the Catholic Church in Chad.

Tractors and Trucks — A43

1969, June 19 Engr. ***Perf. 13***
180 A43 32fr grn, red brn & ind .75 .25

50th anniv. of the ILO.

Deborah Meyer, US, 200 Meter Freestyle A44

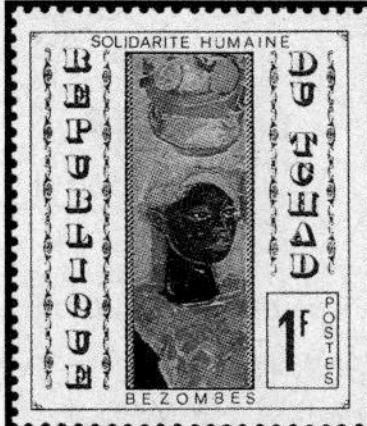

Woman with Flowers, by Veneto — A45

Portrait of an African Woman, by Bezombes — A45a

Winners of 1968 Olympic Games: No. 182, Roland Matthes, East Germany, 100m backstroke. No. 183, Klaus DiBiasi, Italy, springboard diving. No. 184, Bruno Cipolla, Primo Baran and Renzo Sambo, Italy, pair with coxswain. No. 185, Annemarie Zimmermann and Rosewitha Esser, West Germany, women's kayak tandem. No. 186, Sailing, G.B. No. 187, Pierre Trentin, France, 1000 meter bicycling. No. 188, Pier Franco Vianelli, Italy, 196k bicycle road race. No. 189, Daniel Morelon and Pierre Trentin, France, tandem.

No. 190, Daniel R. Rebillard, France, 4000m pursuit (bicycle). No. 191, Ingrid Becker, West Germany, pentathlon. No. 192, Jean J. Guyon, France, equestrian. No. 193, Olympic dressage team, West Germany. No. 194, Bernd Klinger, West Germany, small bore rifle. No. 195, Manfred Wolke, East Germany, welterweight. No. 196, Randy Matson, US, shot put. No. 197, Colette Besson, France, 400m run. No. 198, Mohammed Gammoudi, Tunisia, 5,000m run. No. 199, Tommie Smith, US, 200m run.

No. 200, David Hemery, G.B., 200m hurdles. No. 201, Willie Davenport, US, 110m hurdles. No. 202, Bob Beamon, US, long jump. No. 203, Sawao Kato, Japan, all around gymnastics. No. 204, Dick Fosbury, US, high jump.

Paintings: No. 206, Holy Family, by Murillo, horiz. No. 207, Adoration of the Magi, by Rubens. No. 209, Three Black Men, by Rubens. No. 210, Mother and Child, by Gauguin.

1969, June 30 Litho. ***Perf. 12½x13***
181-204 A44 1fr set of 24 8.00 8.00
Perf. 12½x13, 13x12½
205 A45 1fr shown .35 .35
206 A45 1fr multi .35 .35
207 A45 1fr multi .35 .35
208 A45a 1fr shown .35 .35
209 A45 1fr multi .35 .35
210 A45 1fr multi .35 .35

Issued to stress the brotherhood of mankind.

For overprints see Nos. 244A-244F, 245A-245X.

Cochlospermum Tinctorium — A46

Flowers: 4fr, Parkia biglobosa. 10fr, Pancratium trianthum. 15fr, Morning glory.

1969, July 8 Photo. ***Perf. 12½x13***
211 A46 1fr pink, yel & blk .60 .25
212 A46 4fr dk grn, yel & red .90 .25
213 A46 10fr dk grn, yel & gray 1.10 .25
214 A46 15fr vio bl & multi 1.90 .25
Nos. 211-214 (4) 4.50 1.00

Meat Freezer, Farcha A47

30fr, Cattle at Farcha slaughterhouse.

1969, Aug. 19 Engr. *Perf. 13*
215 A47 25fr sl grn, ocher & red brn .60 .25
216 A47 30fr red brn, sl grn & gray .75 .25

Economic development in Chad.

Development Bank Issue
Common Design Type

1969, Sept. 10
217 CD130 30fr dl red, grn & ocher .90 .25

Tilapia Nilotica A48

Fish: 3fr, Citharinus latus. 5fr, Tetraodon fahaka strigosus. 20fr, Hydrocyon forskali.

1969, Nov. 25 Engr. *Perf. 13*
218 A48 2fr choc, grn & gray .40 .25
219 A48 3fr gray, red & bl .90 .25
220 A48 5fr ocher, blk & yel 1.40 .25
221 A48 20fr blk, red & grn 3.75 .60
Nos. 218-221 (4) 6.45 1.35

ASECNA Issue
Common Design Type

1969, Dec. 12 Engr. *Perf. 13*
222 CD132 30fr orange 1.00 .25

Pres. François Tombalbaye A49

1970, Jan. 11 Litho. *Perf. 14*
223 A49 25fr multi 1.00 .25

Lenin — A50

1970, Apr. 22 Photo. *Perf. 11½*
224 A50 150fr gold, blk & buff 2.75 1.10

Lenin (1870-1924), Russian communist leader.

UPU Headquarters Issue
Common Design Type

1970, May 20 Engr. *Perf. 13*
225 CD133 30fr dk red, pur & brn 1.20 .25

During the 1970-73 period three different agents had entered into contracts to produce stamps with various officials of the Chad government, apparently including Pres. Tombalbaye.

In June 1973, Tombalbaye declared that some of the stamps produced by these agents were not recognized by the Chad government but might be put on sale at a later date, and that other stamps produced and shipped to Chad were refused by the government.

In July 1973, the Chad government announced that the stamps that were not recognized would be put on sale by the end of the year. We have no evidence that this actually happened.

Apollo Program A50a

Designs: 15fr, Apollo 11 in Lunar orbit. 25fr, Apollo 12 astronaut deploying lunar research equipment. 40fr, Astronaunt, lunar module on moon. 50fr, Astronauts Conrad and Bean in life raft after splashdown, horiz.

1970, June 12 Litho. *Perf. 12x12½*
225A A50a Strip of 3, #b-d 6.00 —

Souvenir Sheet
Perf. 13½x13
225E A50a 50fr multicolored 10.00 —

No. 225E contains one 66x44mm stamp. 15fr, 25fr are airmail.

Expo '70, Japan — A50b

Japanese prints of women: 50c, by Kiyonaga. 1fr, by Utamaro. 2fr, from Heian period.

1970, June 12 Litho. *Perf. 12x12½*
225F A50b Strip of 3, #a-c 13.50 —

For overprint see No. 239C.

Adult Education Class and UN Emblem — A52

1970, June 16 Litho. *Perf. 14*
226 A52 100fr blue & multi 1.75 .60

International Education Year.

Bull's Head, Symbols of Weather and Agriculture — A53

1970, July 22 Engr. *Perf. 13*
227 A53 50fr org, gray & grn .90 .25

Issued for World Meteorological Day.

1970 World Cup Soccer Championships, Mexico City — A53a

Designs: 1fr, Three players, Italian flag. 4fr, Franz Beckenbauer, German flag. Nos. 227C, 227E, English players receiving World Cup trophy, 1966. No. 227D, Three players, Brazilian flag. No. 227F, Four players, "1970."

1970-71 Litho. *Perf. 12*
227A A53a 1fr multicolored
227B A53a 4fr multicolored
227C A53a 5fr multicolored
227D A53a 5fr multicolored
Nos. 227A-227D 3.75 —

Embossed
Die Cut Perf 13
227E A53a 5fr gold 17.50 —

Souvenir Sheet
Litho.
Perf. 13½x13
227F A53a 15fr multicolored 6.25 —

No. 227F contains one 66x44mm stamp. Nos. 227D, 227F are airmail.

Issued: Nos. 227A-227D, 227F, 7/2; No. 227E, 11/1/71.

For overprints see Nos. 267A-267E.

Christmas A53b

Virgin and Child by: 3fr, Solario. 25fr, Durer. 32fr, Fouquet.

1970, Aug. 19 Litho. *Perf. 12x12½*
227G A53b 3fr multicolored
227H A53b 25fr multicolored
227I A53b 32fr multicolored
Nos. 227G-227I 14.00 —

No. 227I is airmail.

Ahmed Mangue, Minister of Education — A54

1970, Sept. 15 Litho. & Engr.
228 A54 100fr gold, car & blk 1.80 .50

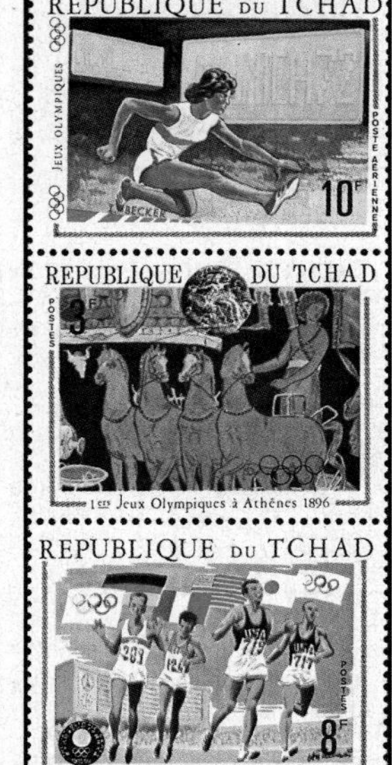

1972 Summer Olympics, Munich — A54a

Designs: No. 228A, 3fr, Horses pulling chariot. 8fr, Men running. 10fr, No. 228C, Woman hurdling. No. 228B, 20fr, Equestrian. 35fr, Woman diving. No. 228D, Woman diver in tuck position.

1970 Litho. *Perf. 12½x12*
228A A54a Strip of 3, #a-c 4.00 —

Perf. 12x12½
228B A54a Pair, #a-b + label 4.00 —

Embossed
Die Cut Perf 13
228C A54a 10fr gold 17.50 —

Souvenir Sheet
Litho.
Perf. 13½x13
228D A54a 40fr multicolored 10.00 —

10fr, 35fr, Nos. 228C-228D are airmail. No. 228D contains one 66x43mm stamp.

Issued: Nos. 228A-228B, 228D, Sept; No. 228C, 10/14.

For overprints see Nos. 239D-239F.

Tanner A55

Designs: 2fr, Cloth dyer, vert. 3fr, Camel turning oil press. 4fr, Water carrier, vert. 5fr, Copper worker.

1970, Oct. 10 Engr. *Perf. 13*
229 A55 1fr ol brn, bl & brn .25 .25
229A A55 2fr dk brn, ol & ind .25 .25
229B A55 3fr pur, ol brn & rose car .40 .25
229C A55 4fr choc, lem & bl grn .50 .25
229D A55 5fr red, choc & sl grn .50 .25
Nos. 229-229D (5) 1.90 1.25

UN Emblem, Grain and Dove — A56

1970, Oct. 24 Photo. *Perf. 12x12½*
230 A56 32fr dk bl & multi 1.00 .25

25th anniversary of United Nations.

OCAM Headquarters, Map of Africa, Stars — A57

1971, Jan. 23 Photo. *Perf. 12½x12*
231 A57 30fr dk grn & multi 1.00 .25

OCAM (Organisation Commune Africaine, Malgache et Mauricienne) Summit Conference, N'djamena, Jan. 22-30.

Space Exploration — A57a

10fr, Apollo 11. 35fr, Soviet space station. 40fr, John F. Kennedy, Apollo spacecraft, vert.

1971, Feb. 16 Litho. *Perf. 13x13½*
231A A57a 8fr shown .60 —
231B A57a 10fr multi .90 —
231C A57a 35fr multi 6.25 —
Nos. 231A-231C (3) 7.75

Embossed
Die Cut Perf 13
231D A57a 8fr gold, like #231A 8.25 —
f. Sheet of 1, Imperf.

Souvenir Sheet
Perf. 13½x13
231E A57a 40fr multi 10.00 —

Nos. 231C, 231E are airmail. No. 231Df contains one 73x45mm stamp with same size design as No. 231D. No. 231E contains one 33x50mm stamp.

Nos. 231D, 231Df probably were not available in Chad.

1972 Winter Olympics, Sapporo A57b

Paintings by Kiyonaga: 50c, Cherry Trees in Bloom, Tokyo. 1fr, Snowy Morning. 2fr, Sake Party.

1971 Litho. *Perf. 12x12½*
231G A57b 50c multicolored .80
231H A57b 1fr multicolored 1.40
231I A57b 2fr multicolored 2.25
Nos. 231G-231I (3) 4.45

Embossed
Die Cut Perf 13
231J A57b 2fr gold, like #231I 17.50
k. Sheet of 1, Imperf. 35.00

Issued: Nos. 231G-231I, 2/16; Nos. 231J-231Jk, 11/1. No. 231Jk contains one 43x54mm stamp with same size design as No. 231I.

For overprints see Nos. 246A-246C.

Nos. 231J-231Jk probably were not available in Chad.

Portraits of French Royalty — A57c

Designs: No. 232A, 25fr, The Dauphin (Louis XVII), by J.M. Vien the Younger. 32fr, Marie Antoinette, by E. Vigee-Lebrun. 60fr, Louis XVI, by J.S. Duplessis.

No. 232B, 25fr, Comtesse du Barry, by E. Vigee-Lebrun. 40fr, Louis XV, by M.Q. Delatour.

No. 232C, 40fr, Marie Antoinette, by Charpentier. 50fr, Louis XVI (Dauphin), by Michel Van Loo.

No. 232D, 35fr, Madame de Pompadour (detail), by Delatour. 70fr, Louis XV by Delatour.

No. 232E, 30fr, Madame de Pompadour (entire), by Delatour. 60fr, Marie Leszczynska, by Jean Marc Nattier. 80fr, Louis XV, by Van Loo.

No. 232F, 40fr, Duc D'Orleans as Regent, by 19th cent. French school. 200fr, Louis XIV, by H. Rigaud.

No. 232G, 100fr, Madame de Montespan, by Henry Gascard. 100fr, Madame de Maintenon, by Pierre Mignard.

No. 232H, 50fr, Colbert, by Claude Lefebvre. 200fr, Louis XIV, by J. Garnier.

No. 232J, 50fr, Marie Therese, by Mignard. 200fr, Louis XIV, by Marot.

No. 232K, 50fr, Marie de la Valliere, by English school. 200fr, Louis XIV, by French school.

No. 232L, 100fr, Giulio Cardinal Mazarin, by Mignard. 100fr, Anne of Austria, by Rubens.

No. 232M, 50fr, Vicomte de Turenne, by Champaigne. 200fr, Louis XIV as a Boy, by Mignard.

No. 232N, 100fr, Marquis de Cinq-Mars, by M. le Nain. 150fr, Cardinal Richelieu, by Champaigne.

No. 232P, 150fr, Anne of Austria, by Rubens. 250fr, Louis XIII (detail), by Simon Vouet.

No. 232Q, 150fr, Marriage of Marie de Medicis (looking right), by Rubens. 150fr, Mirror image.

No. 232R, 150fr, Duke of Sully, by Quesnel. 150fr, Mirror image.

No. 232S, 150fr, Henry IV, by Rubens. 150fr, Marie de Medicis, by Rubens.

No. 232T, 200fr, Gabrielle d'Estrees, by unknown artist. 250fr, Henry IV, by French school, c. 1595.

No. 232U, 150fr, Jeanne d'Albret, by Francois Clouet. 200fr, Marie de Medicis as a Girl, by Angelo Bronzino.

No. 232V, 200fr, Henry III, by Clouet. 250fr, Ambroise Pare, by 16th century French school.

No. 232W, 150fr, Catherine de Medicis, by Clouet. 250fr, Henry II, by Clouet.

No. 233A, 200fr, Elizabeth of Austria, by Clouet. 250fr, Charles IX, by Clouet.

No. 233B, 200fr, Mary Stuart, by 16th cent. Scottish school. 300fr, Diane of Poitiers, by Fontainbleu school.

No. 233C, 200fr, Elizabeth of Valois, by Alonso S. Coello. 250fr, Francis, Duke of Alencon, by Clouet.

No. 233D, 150fr, Marguerite d'Angouleme, by Clouet. 300fr, Francis I, by Clouet.

No. 233E, 200fr, Francis I, by Titian. 300fr, Francis I as Dauphin, by Corneille of Lyon.

No. 233F, 100fr, Anne of Austria, by Coello. 250fr, Louis XIII, by Champaigne.

No. 233G, 200fr, Marie de Medicis, by Rubens. 200fr, Marie de Medicis, Louis XIII, by Rubens.

No. 233H, 150fr, The Exchange of Princess Elizabeth of France and Princess Anne of Austria on the Andaye River, by Rubens. 250fr, Louis XIII of France and Navarre, by Vouet.

No. 233J, 250fr, Marie de Medicis, by Rubens. 250fr, Henry IV, by Rubens.

No. 233K, Louis XV and the Dauphin at Battle of Fontenoy. No. 233L, The Grand Dauphin and his Family, by Mignard. No. 233M, Madame de Montespan, horiz. No. 233N, Madame de la Valliere and her Children. No. 233P, The Birth of Louis XIII at Fontainebleau, by Rubens. No. 233Q, Reconciliation of the Queen and Louis XIII, by Rubens. No. 233R, Henry IV Entrusting Regency to Marie de Medici, by Rubens. No. 233S, The Majority of Louis XIII, by Rubens. No. 233T, The Apotheosis of Henry IV and the Proclamation of Regency, by Rubens. No. 233U, Felicity of the Regency, by Rubens.

Small numbers appear at the lower right on Nos. 232A-233J. To ease identication, these numbers are shown in parentheses after each listing.

1971-73 Litho. *Perf. 12½x13*
232A A57c Strip of 3, #aa-ac (58-60) *3.00*
232B A57c Pair, #aa-ab (53-54) *2.00*
232C A57c Pair, #aa-ab (56-57) *2.00*
232D A57c Pair, #aa-ab (51-52) *2.00*
232E A57c Strip of 3, #aa-ac (48-50) *4.00*
232F A57c Pair, #aa-ab (45, 47) *4.00*
232G A57c Pair, #aa-ab (44, 45B) *3.00*
232H A57c Pair, #aa-ab (42-43) *4.00*
232J A57c Pair, #aa-ab (40-41) *4.00*
232K A57c Pair, #aa-ab (38-39) *4.00*
232L A57c Pair, #aa-ab (36-37) *2.50*
232M A57c Pair, #aa-ab (34-35) *4.00*
232N A57c Pair, #aa-ab (32-33) *4.00*
232P A57c Pair, #aa-ab (30-31) *6.00*
232Q A57c Pair, #aa-ab (22-23) *4.00*
232R A57c Pair, #aa-ab (22A-22B) *4.50*
232S A57c Pair, #aa-ab (26, 27A) *4.50*
232T A57c Pair, #aa-ab (18-19) *7.50*
232U A57c Pair, #aa-ab (16-17) *5.50*
232V A57c Pair, #aa-ab (16-16A) *7.50*
232W A57c Pair, #aa-ab (14-15) *6.50*
233A A57c Pair, #aa-ab (13-13A) *7.50*
233B A57c Pair, #aa-ab (11-12) *8.00*
233C A57c Pair, #aa-ab (10, 11A) *6.50*
233D A57c Pair, #aa-ab (8-9) *7.50*
233E A57c Pair, #aa-ab (7, 8A) *8.00*
233F A57c Pair, #aa-ab (29, 32B) *6.00*
233G A57c Pair, #aa-ab (24-25) *6.00*
233H A57c Pair, #aa-ab (27-28) *6.00*
233J A57c Pair, #aa-ab (20-21) *7.50*
Nos. 232A-233J (30) *151.50*

Souvenir Sheets
Perf. 13x13½, 13½x13, 13½
233K A57c 75fr multi *6.50*
233L A57c 100fr multi *6.00*
233M A57c 200fr multi *6.00*
233N A57c 300fr multi *6.00*
233P A57c 350fr multi *12.00*
233Q A57c 400fr multi *16.00*
233R A57c 400fr multi *10.00*
233S A57c 400fr multi *10.00*
233T A57c 400fr multi *6.00*
233U A57c 500fr multi *13.50*
Nos. 233K-233U (10) *92.00*

Nos. 232A 60fr, 232B 40fr, 232C 50fr, 232D 70fr, 232E 80fr, 232F 200fr, 232G, 232H 200fr, 232J 200fr, 232K, 232L, 232M 200fr, 232N-233U are airmail.

Issued: 1971 — No. 232A, 2/24; No. 232B, 3/30; No. 232C, 3/4; Nos. 232D, 233K, 3/15; No. 232E, 4/12; Nos. 232F, 233L, 4/26; No. 232G, 8/10; No. 232H, 9/6; No. 232J, 9/23; No. 232K, 10/6; No. 232L, 10/26; No. 232M, 11/16; No. 232N, 11/20.

1972 — Nos. 232P, 233P, Jan.; Nos. 232Q, 233M-233N, Feb.; Nos. 233Q-233R, May; Nos. 232R, 233S, 6/15; Nos. 232S, 233T, 6/26; No. 232T, 8/8; No. 232U, 8/17; No. 232V, 8/30; Nos. 232W, 233U, 12/11; No. 233A, 12/18; No. 233B, 12/28.

1973 — Nos. 233C-233J.

Nos. 233K-233L, 233T-233U each contain one 37x62mm stamp. Nos. 233N, 233P each contain one 32x50mm stamp. No. 233M contains one 45x65mm stamp. Nos. 233Q-233R, 233U each contain one 65x45mm stamp.

Nos. 232Q-232V, 233G, 233J, 233R-233U and possibly 232P, 232W-233F, 233H probably were not available in Chad.

Symbolic Tree — A58

1971, Mar. 21 Engr. *Perf. 13*
236 A58 40fr bl grn, dk red & grn 1.00 .25

Intl. year against racial discrimination.

Paintings of Flowers A58a

Designs: 1fr, The Three Graces (detail), by Rubens. 4fr, Imperial Bouquet, by Van Os. 5fr, Bouquet, by Jan Brueghel.

1971, Apr. 28 Litho. *Perf. 12x12½*
236A A58a Strip of 3, #a-c 5.50 —

For overprint see No. 278A.

Summer Olympic Games — A58b

15fr, Swimming. 20fr, Women's relay races. 25fr, Swimming, medals. 50fr, Running.

Perf. 12x12½, 12½x12
1971, Apr. 28 Litho.
236B A58b 15fr multi, vert. 1.60 —
236C A58b 20fr multi, vert. 2.50 —
236D A58b 25fr multi 3.00 —
Nos. 236B-236D (3) 7.10

Embossed
Perf. 13
236E A58b 25fr gold, like No. 236D 17.50

Souvenir Sheet
Litho.
Die Cut Perf 13
236F A58b 50fr multicolored 10.00

Nos. 236D-236F are airmail. No. 236F contains one 62x36mm stamp.

Issued: Nos. 236B-236D, 236F, 4/28; No. 236E, 11/1.

For overprints see Nos. 251A-251D.

No. 236E probably was not available in Chad.

Map of Africa, Radar Antenna A59

Map of Africa and: 40fr, Communications tower. 50fr, Communications satellite.

1971, May 17 Engr. *Perf. 13*
237 A59 5fr ultra, org & dk red .25 .25
238 A59 40fr pur, emer & brn .75 .25
239 A59 50fr dk red, blk & brn 1.00 .25
Nos. 237-239 (3) 2.00 .75

3rd World Telecommunications Day.

Apollo 11 — A59a

1971, July 5 Embossed *Perf. 13*

239A A59a 10fr gold 22.50
b. Sheet of 1, Imperf. 40.00

No. 239Ab contains one 73x45mm stamp with same size design as No. 239A.

Nos. 239A-239Ab probably were not available in Chad.

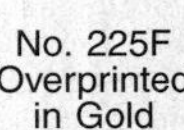

No. 225F Overprinted in Gold

1971, July 17 Litho. *Perf. 12x12½*

239C A50b Strip of 3, #a-c 4.75

1972 Winter Olympics, Sapporo.

Nos. 228A-228B, 228D Ovptd. with "MUNICH 72" and Olympic Rings in Gold

Perf. 12½x12, 12x12½

1971, Nov. 1 Litho.

239D A54a Strip of 3, #a-c 10.00
239E A54a Pair, #a-b + label 6.00

Souvenir Sheet

Perf. 13½x13

239F A54a 40fr on #228D 20.00

UNICEF Emblem and Children — A60

1971, Dec. 11 Engr. *Perf. 13*

240 A60 50fr Prus bl, emer & brt pink 2.00 .25

25th anniv. of UNICEF.

Gorane Nangara Dancers A61

Dancers: 15fr, Girls' initiation dance, Yondo. 30fr, Women of M'Boum, vert. 40fr, Men of Sara Kaba, vert.

1971, Dec. 18 Litho. *Perf. 13*

241 A61 10fr blk & multi .75 .25
242 A61 15fr brn org & multi 1.10 .25
243 A61 30fr bl & multi 1.50 .25
244 A61 40fr yel grn & multi 1.90 .25
Nos. 241-244 (4) 5.25 1.00

Nos. 205-210 Ovptd. in Gold

1971 Litho. *Perf. 12½x13, 13x12½*

244A-244F A45 1fr on #205-210 4.50

Nos. 244A-244F probably were not available in Chad.

Presidents Pompidou and Tombalbaye, Map with Paris and Fort Lamy — A62

1972, Jan. 25 Photo. *Perf. 13*

245 A62 40fr blue & multi 1.60 .25

Visit of Pres. Georges Pompidou of France, Jan. 1972.

Nos. 181-204 Ovptd. in Gold

1972, Feb. 7 Litho. *Perf. 12½x13*

245A-245X A44 1fr on #181-204 20.00

Nos. 245A-245X probably were not available in Chad.

Nos. 231G-231I Ovptd. in Gold

a

b

1972, Feb. Litho. *Perf. 12x12½*

246A A57b 50c Pair, #d.-e. 1.50
246B A57b 1fr Pair, #f.-g. 2.25
246C A57b 2fr Pair, #h.-i. 2.75

Nos. 246A-246C probably were not available in Chad.

President Tombalbaye — A63

1972, Apr. 13 Litho. *Perf. 13*

247 A63 30fr multi .40 .25
247A A63 40fr multi .60 .25
Nos. 247-247A,C112-C113 (4) 2.65 1.15

Downhill Skiing — A64

75fr, Women's figure skating. 150fr, Luge.

1972, Apr. 13 *Perf. 13½*

248 A64 25fr multi .30 .25
249 A64 75fr multi .75 .25
250 A64 150fr multi 1.50 .45
Nos. 248-250,C114-C115 (5) 6.45 2.00

11th Winter Olympic Games, Sapporo, Japan.

Heart — A65

1972, Apr. 25 Engr. *Perf. 13*

251 A65 100fr purple, bl & car 1.60 .25

"Your heart is your health," World Health Month.

Nos. 236B-236D, 236F Ovptd. in Gold

1972 Litho. *Perf. 12x12½, 12½x12*

251A A58b 15fr multicolored 3.25
251B A58b 20fr multicolored 5.00
251C A58b 25fr multicolored 7.75
Nos. 251A-251C (3) 16.00

Souvenir Sheet

Die Cut Perf 13

251D A58b 50fr multicolored 47.50

Nos. 251C-251D are airmail.

Gorrizia Dubiosa — A66

Insects and Spiders: 2fr, Spider (argiope sector). 3fr, Silk spider (nephila senegalense). 4fr, Beetle (oryctes boas). 5fr, Dragonfly (hemistigma albipunctata).

1972, May 6 Photo.

252 A66 1fr green & multi 1.25 .25
253 A66 2fr blue & multi 2.00 .25
254 A66 3fr car rose & multi 2.25 .30
255 A66 4fr yellow grn & multi 4.00 .40
256 A66 5fr dp green & multi 4.50 .60
Nos. 252-256 (5) 14.00 1.80

Trains — A66a

10fr, Orient Express. 40fr, Osaka Express. 50fr, St. Germain. 150fr, Blue train. 200fr, Trans-Europe Express.

300fr, Rogers "Madison," 1855.

1972 Litho. *Perf. 12*

256A A66a 10fr multi 1.00
256B A66a 40fr multi 2.25
256C A66a 50fr multi 2.50
256D A66a 150fr multi 5.00
256E A66a 200fr multi 9.25
Nos. 256A-256E (5) 20.00

Souvenir Sheet

256F A66a 300fr multi 14.00

No. 256F contains one 60x40mm stamp. See note before No. 225A.

Scout Greeting — A67

70fr, Mountain climbing. 80fr, Canoeing.

1972, May 15 Photo.

257 A67 30fr multi .75 .25
258 A67 70fr multi 1.40 .25
259 A67 80fr multi 1.75 .25
Nos. 257-259,C118-C119 (5) 8.55 1.65

Scout Jamboree.

Hurdles, Motion and Olympic Emblems A68

Motion and Olympic Emblems and: 130fr, Gymnast on rings. 150fr, Swimming. 300fr, Bicycling.

1972, June 9 Litho. *Perf. 13½*

260 A68 50fr blk & multi .75 .25
261 A68 130fr blk & multi 1.90 .25
262 A68 150fr blk & multi 2.25 .30
Nos. 260-262 (3) 4.90 .80

Souvenir Sheet

263 A68 300fr blk & multi 5.00 2.00

20th Olympic Games, Munich, Aug. 26-Sept. 10.

Ski Jump, Kasaya, Japan — A69

Designs: 75fr, Cross-country skiing, P. Tyldum, Sweden. 100fr, Figure-skating, pairs, L. Rodnina and A. Ulanov, USSR. 130fr, Men's speed skating, A. Schenk, Netherlands.

1972, June 15 *Perf. 14½*

264 A69 25fr gold & multi .40 .25
265 A69 75fr gold & multi 1.00 .25
266 A69 100fr gold & multi 1.50 .40
267 A69 130fr gold & multi 1.90 .50
Nos. 264-267,C130-C131 (6) 11.55 3.15

11th Winter Olympic Games, gold-medal winners. Nos. 264-267 exist se-tenant with label showing earth satellite.

Nos. 227A-227D, 227F Ovptd. in Gold

1972 Litho. *Perf. 12*

267A A53a 1fr multicolored .95
267B A53a 4fr multicolored 1.20
267C A53a 5fr multicolored 1.90
267D A53a 5fr multicolored 1.90
Nos. 267A-267D (4) 5.95

Souvenir Sheet

Perf. 13½x13

267E A53a 15fr multicolored 9.00

Nos. 267D-267E are airmail.
Nos. 267A-267E probably were not available in Chad.

TV Tower and Weight-lifting — A70

Designs (TV Tower, Munich and): 40fr, Woman sprinter. 60fr, Soccer goalkeeper.

1972, Aug. 15 Litho. *Perf. 14½*

268 A70 20fr gold & multi .65 .25
269 A70 40fr gold & multi .80 .25
270 A70 60fr gold & multi 1.40 .25
Nos. 268-270,C135-C137 (6) 10.70 2.65

20th Summer Olympic Games, Munich. Nos. 268-270 exist se-tenant with label showing arms of Munich.
Nos. 268-270, C135-C137 exist in souvenir sheets of one. Value, set, $130.

Domestic Animals A71

1972, Aug. 29 Engr. *Perf. 13*

271 A71 25fr Dromedary 1.40 .25
272 A71 30fr Horse 1.75 .25
273 A71 40fr Dog 2.75 .30
274 A71 45fr Goat 3.00 .40
Nos. 271-274 (4) 8.90 1.20

For surcharge see No. 293.

Tobacco Cultivation A72

1972, Oct. 24 Engr. *Perf. 13*

275 A72 40fr shown .75 .25
276 A72 50fr Plowing 1.25 .25

Massa Warrior — A73

Design: 20fr, Moundang warrior.

1972, Nov. 15 Photo. *Perf. 14x13*

277 A73 15fr orange & multi .70 .25
278 A73 20fr yellow & multi .90 .25

No. 236A Overprinted in Gold

1972 Litho. *Perf. 12x12½*

278A A58a Strip of 3, #a-c 5.50

No. 278A probably was not available in Chad.

King Faisal and Pres. Tombalbaye — A74

1972, Nov. 17 Litho. *Perf. 13*

279 A74 100fr gold & multi 2.50 .75

Visit of King Faisal of Saudi Arabia. See No. C143.

Gen. Gowon and Pres. Tombalbaye — A75

1972, Dec. 7

280 A75 70fr multi 1.00 .25

Visit of Gen. Yakubu Gowon of Nigeria.

Olympic Emblem and 100-meter Sprint, Valeri Borzov, USSR — A76

Designs (Olympic Emblem and): 20fr, Shotput, Komar, Poland. 40fr, Hammer throw, Bondartchuk, USSR. 60fr, Discus, Danek, Czechoslovakia.

1972, Dec. 22 *Perf. 11*

281 A76 10fr multi .55 .25
282 A76 20fr multi .55 .25
283 A76 40fr multi .70 .25
284 A76 60fr multi 1.10 .30
Nos. 281-284,C148-C149 (6) 10.15 2.40

20th Summer Olympic Games, winners.
Nos. 281-284, C148-C149 exist as souvenir sheets of one. Value, set, $150.

Olympic Emblem and Fencing, Woyda, Poland — A77

Olympic Emblem and: 30fr, 3-day equestrian event, Richard Meade, Gt. Britain. 50fr, Two-man sculls, Brietzke-Mager, East Germany.

1972, Dec. 22

285 A77 20fr gold & multi .65 .25
286 A77 30fr gold & multi .65 .25
287 A77 50fr gold & multi 1.00 .25
Nos. 285-287,C151-C152 (5) 10.55 2.50

20th Summer Olympic Games, winners.

1972 Summer Olympics Gold Medalists — A77a

20fr, Teofilo Stevenson, boxing, Cuba. 25fr, Yugoslavia, team handball. 30fr, M. Peters, pentathlon, Great Britain. 40fr, basketball, USSR. No. 287E, W. Ruska, judo, Netherlands. No. 287F, Women's gymnastics, Ludmila Tourischeva, USSR. 75fr, Men's volleyball, Japan. No. 287H, A. Scalzone, shooting, Italy. No. 287I, Soccer, Poland. 130fr, J. Williams, archery, US. No. 287K, A. Nakayama, men's rings, Japan. No. 287L, Field hockey, West Germany. 200fr, Vassily Alexeiev, weight lifting, USSR. 250fr, D. Morelon, cycling, France.

1972, Dec. 22 Litho. *Perf. 11½*

287A A77a 20fr multicolored
287B A77a 25fr multicolored
287C A77a 30fr multicolored
287D A77a 40fr multicolored
287E A77a 50fr multicolored
287F A77a 50fr multicolored
287G A77a 75fr multicolored
287H A77a 100fr multicolored
287I A77a 100fr multicolored
287J A77a 130fr multicolored
287K A77a 150fr multicolored
287L A77a 150fr multicolored
Nos. 287A-287L 18.00

Souvenir Sheets

Perf. 15

287M A77a 200fr multicolored 13.50
287N A77a 250fr multicolored 13.50

Nos. 287G-287N are airmail.

Soviet Flag and Shield — A78

1972, Dec. 30 Litho. *Perf. 12*

288 A78 150fr red & multi 1.90 .40

50th anniversary of the Soviet Union.

High Jump — A79

Designs (Games Emblem and): 125fr, Running. 200fr, Shot put. 250fr, Discus.

1973, Jan. 17 Litho. *Perf. 13½x13*

289 A79 50fr vio bl & multi .75 .25
290 A79 125fr olive & multi 1.60 .40
291 A79 200fr lilac & multi 3.00 .65
Nos. 289-291 (3) 5.35 1.30

Souvenir Sheet

292 A79 250fr brn & multi 3.75 2.25

2nd African Games, Lagos, Nigeria, 1/7-18.

Paintings with Musical Instruments — A79a

Details from Paintings: 30fr, Madeleine Playing her Lute, by unknown artist. 70fr, A Concert, by Lorenzo Costa. 100fr, Bass and Sheet Music, by Jean-Baptiste Oudry, horiz. 125fr, St. Cecilia and Angel, by Carlo Saraceni. 150fr, Woman Listening to Violinist, by Gabriel Metsu. 300fr, Still Life with Musical Instruments, by Pieter Claesz, horiz.

1973, Apr. Litho. *Perf. 11½*

292A A79a 30fr multicolored
292B A79a 70fr multicolored
292C A79a 100fr multicolored
292D A79a 125fr multicolored
292E A79a 150fr multicolored
Nos. 292A-292E 13.50

Souvenir Sheet

Perf. 15

292F A79a 300fr multicolored 13.50

Nos. 292D-292F are airmail.

No. 271 Srchd. and Ovptd. in Red

1973, Aug. 16 Engr. *Perf. 13*

293 A71 100fr on 25fr multi 2.25 .50

African solidarity in drought emergency.

African Postal Union Issue

Common Design Type

1973, Sept. 17 Engr. *Perf. 13*

294 CD137 100fr multicolored 1.75 .40

Easter A79b

Details from paintings: 40fr, Christ on the Cross, by Lucas Cranach. 60fr, Supper in Emmaus, by Titian, horiz. 120fr, The Crucifixion, by Durer. 150fr, The Tribute, by Titian. 250fr, The Pieta, by Botticelli. 400fr, Entombment of Christ, by Gaspard Isenmann, horiz.

1973 Litho. *Perf. 11½*

294A A79b 40fr multicolored
294B A79b 60fr multicolored
294C A79b 120fr multicolored
294D A79b 150fr multicolored
294E A79b 250fr multicolored
Nos. 294A-294E 13.50

Souvenir Sheet

Perf. 15

294F A79b 400fr multicolored 13.50

Nos. 294A, 294D-294F are airmail.

Animals A79c

1973 Litho. *Perf. 13½*

294G A79c 20fr Sheep
294H A79c 30fr Camels
294J A79c 100fr Cats
294K A79c 130fr Dogs
294L A79c 150fr Horses
Nos. 294G-294L 13.50

Nos. 294J-294L are airmail.
See note before No. 225A.

Christmas — A79d

30fr, The Virgin & Infant Surrounded by Saints, by Lorenzo Lotto. 40fr, Madonna and Child with St. Peter and a Martyred Saint, by Paolo Veronese (not Tintoretto), vert. 55fr, Nativity Scene, by Martin Schongauer, vert. 60fr, Nativity Scene, by Federico Barocci, vert. 250fr, Adoration of the Magi, by Stephan Lochner, vert. 400fr, Epiphany, by Hans Memling.

1973 Litho. *Perf. 11½*

294M A79d 30fr multicolored
294N A79d 40fr multicolored
294P A79d 55fr multicolored
294Q A79d 60fr multicolored
294R A79d 250fr multicolored
Nos. 294M-294R 13.50

Souvenir Sheet

Perf. 15

294S A79d 400fr multicolored 13.50

Nos. 294Q-294S are airmail.
See note before No. 225A.

Insects — A80

No. 295, Dinothrombium Tinctorium. No. 296, Bupreste sternocera. No. 297, Diptere hyperechia. No. 298, Chrysis. No. 299, Longicorn beetle. No. 300, Spider.

1974, Sept. 3 Photo. *Perf. 13*

295 A80 25fr multicolored 1.50 .25
296 A80 30fr multicolored 2.25 .25
297 A80 40fr multicolored 2.75 .25
298 A80 50fr multicolored 3.25 .35
299 A80 100fr multicolored 4.75 .65
300 A80 130fr multicolored 7.50 .95
Nos. 295-300 (6) 22.00 2.70

Rotary Emblem — A81

1975, Apr. 11 Typo. *Perf. 13*

301 A81 50fr multi 1.00 .25

Rotary International, 70th anniversary.

Craterostigma Plantagineum — A82

Flowers: 10fr, Tapinanthus globiferus. 15fr, Commelina forskalaei, vert. 20fr, Adenium obesum. 25fr, Yellow hibiscus. 30fr, Red hibiscus. 40fr, Kigelia africana.

1975, Sept. 25 Photo. *Perf. 13*

302 A82 5fr org & multi .40 .25
303 A82 10fr gray bl & multi .60 .25
304 A82 15fr yel grn & multi .75 .25
305 A82 20fr lt brn & multi 1.00 .25
306 A82 25fr lil & multi 1.75 .25
307 A82 30fr bis & multi 1.90 .35
308 A82 40fr ultra & multi 3.00 .50
Nos. 302-308 (7) 9.40 2.10

A. G. Bell, Satellite and Waves — A83

1976, June 10 Litho. *Perf. 12½*

309 A83 100fr bl, brn & ocher 1.40 .40
310 A83 125fr lt grn, brn & ocher 1.90 .60

Centenary of first telephone call by Alexander Graham Bell, Mar. 10, 1976.

Ice Hockey, USSR — A84

90fr, Ski jump, Karl Schnabl, Austria.

1976, June 21 *Perf. 14*

311 A84 60fr multi .75 .25
312 A84 90fr multi 1.25 .25
Nos. 311-312,C178-C179 (4) 8.25 2.10

12th Winter Olympic Games, winners. See No. C180.

High Hurdles A85

1976, July 12 Litho. *Perf. 13½*

313 A85 45fr multi .70 .25
Nos. 313,C187-C189 (4) 8.70 1.70

21st Summer Olympic Games, Montreal, Canada.
See No. C190.

Mars Landing and Viking Rocket A86

Mars Landing and: 90fr, Viking trajectory, Earth to Mars.

1976, July 23 *Perf. 14*

314 A86 45fr multi .50 .25
315 A86 90fr multi 1.00 .25
Nos. 314-315,C191-C193 (5) 7.35 2.10

Viking Mars project.

For overprints see Nos. 379-380.

Robert Koch, Medicine — A87

Design: 90fr, Anatole France, literature.

1976, Dec. 15

316 A87 45fr multi .75 .25
317 A87 90fr multi 1.50 .25
Nos. 316-317,C196-C198 (5) 9.75 2.05

Nobel Prize winners.

Map and Flag of Chad, Clasped Hands A88

120fr, Map of Chad, people & occupations.

1976, Sept. 15 Litho. *Perf. 12½x13*

318 A88 30fr multi .60 .25
319 A88 60fr orange & multi 1.10 .30
320 A88 120fr brown & multi 2.25 .50
Nos. 318-320 (3) 3.95 1.05

National reconciliation.

Freed Political Prisoners — A89

Designs: 60fr, Parade of cadets.

1976, Sept. 25 Litho. *Perf. 12½*

321 A89 30fr blue & multi .30 .25
322 A89 60fr black & multi .75 .25
323 A89 120fr red & multi 1.40 .25
Nos. 321-323 (3) 2.45 .75

Revolution of Apr. 13, 1975, 1st anniv.

Decorated Calabashes — A90

Designs: Various pyrographed calabashes.

1976, Nov. Litho. *Perf. 12½x13*

324 A90 30fr multi .40 .25
325 A90 60fr multi .90 .25
326 A90 120fr multi 1.75 .25
Nos. 324-326 (3) 3.05 .75

Germany No. C57 and Friedrichshafen, Germany — A91

1977, Mar. 30 *Perf. 14*
327 A91 100fr multi 1.40 .25
Nos. 327,C206-C209 (5) 11.55 2.10

75th anniversary of the Zeppelin.

Elizabeth II in Coronation Regalia and Clergy — A92

Design: 450fr, Elizabeth II and Prince Philip.

1977, June 15 Litho. *Perf. 14x13½*
328 A92 250fr multi 3.25 .75

Souvenir Sheet

329 A92 450fr multi 6.00 2.50

25th anniv. of the reign of Elizabeth II.
Nos. 328-329 exist imperf. For overprints see Nos. 347-348.

Simon Bolivar A93

Famous Personalities: 175fr, Joseph J. Roberts. No. 332, Queen Wilhelmina of Netherlands. No. 333, Charles de Gaulle. 325fr, King Baudouin and Queen Fabiola of Belgium.

1977, June 15 *Perf. 13½x14*
330 A93 150fr multi 1.50 .30
331 A93 175fr multi 2.25 .45
332 A93 200fr multi 3.00 .65
333 A93 200fr multi 3.00 .75
334 A93 325fr multi 4.00 1.00
Nos. 330-334 (5) 13.75 3.15

Post and Telecommunications Emblem — A94

Map of Chad and Waves — A95

Society Emblem — A96

1977, Aug. 15 Litho. *Perf. 13*
335 A94 30fr yel & blk .50 .25

Perf. 12½

336 A95 60fr multi .75 .25

Perf. 13½x13

337 A96 120fr multi 1.60 .50
Nos. 335-337 (3) 2.85 1.00

Telecommunications (30fr); Natl. Telecommunications School, 10th anniv. (60fr); Intl. Telecommunication Soc. of Chad (120fr).

WHO Emblem and Man (Back Pain) — A97

World Rheumatism Year (WHO Emblem and): 60fr, Woman's head (neck pain), horiz. 120fr, Leg (knee pain).

Perf. 12½x13, 13x12½

1977, Nov. 10 **Engr.**
338 A97 30fr multi .50 .25
339 A97 60fr multi 1.00 .25
340 A97 120fr multi 1.40 .40
Nos. 338-340 (3) 2.90 .90

World Cup Emblems and Saving a Goal — A98

Designs (Argentina '78, World Cup Emblems and): 60fr, Heading the ball. 100fr, Referee whistling a goal. 200fr, World Cup poster. 300fr, Pelé. 500fr, Helmut Schoen and Munich stadium.

1977, Nov. 25 Litho. *Perf. 13½*
341 A98 40fr multi .50 .25
342 A98 60fr multi .75 .25
343 A98 100fr multi 1.10 .25
344 A98 200fr multi 2.50 .50
345 A98 300fr multi 3.75 .75
Nos. 341-345 (5) 8.60 2.00

Souvenir Sheet

346 A98 500fr multi 5.75 3.00

World Cup Soccer Championship, Argentina '78.
For overprints see Nos. 359-364.

Nos. 328-329 Overprinted in Silver

1978, Sept. 13 *Perf. 14x13½*
347 A92 250fr multi 3.00 1.00

Souvenir Sheet

348 A92 450fr multi 5.50 4.50

25th anniv. of coronation of Elizabeth II.

Abraham and Melchisedek, by Rubens — A99

Rubens Paintings: 120fr, Helene Fourment, vert. 200fr, David and the Elders of Israel. 300fr, Anne of Austria, vert. 500fr, Marie de Medicis, vert.

1978, Nov. 23 Litho. *Perf. 13½*
349 A99 60fr multi .75 .25
350 A99 120fr multi 1.75 .35
351 A99 200fr multi 3.00 .75
352 A99 300fr multi 4.50 1.25
Nos. 349-352 (4) 10.00 2.60

Souvenir Sheet

353 A99 500fr multi 6.75 3.00

Peter Paul Rubens (1577-1640).

Dürer Portrait A100

Dürer Paintings: 150fr, Jacob Muffel. 250fr, Young Woman. 350fr, Oswolt Krel.

1978, Nov. 23
354 A100 60fr multi .60 .25
355 A100 150fr multi 1.75 .50
356 A100 250fr multi 3.00 .80
357 A100 350fr multi 4.50 1.25
Nos. 354-357 (4) 9.85 2.80

Head, Village and Fly — A101

1978, Nov. 28 *Perf. 13*
358 A101 60f multi .75 .25

National Health Day.

Nos. 341-346 Overprinted in Silver

a

b

c

d

e

f

1978, Dec. 30 Litho. *Perf. 13½*
359 A98(a) 40fr multi .50 .25
360 A98(b) 60fr multi .75 .25
361 A98(c) 100fr multi 1.40 .40
362 A98(d) 200fr multi 2.50 .75
363 A98(e) 300fr multi 3.50 1.25
Nos. 359-363 (5) 8.65 2.90

Souvenir Sheet

364 A98(f) 500fr multi 5.75 5.00

World Soccer Championship winners.

UPU Emblems, Camel Caravan, Satellites — A102

Design: 150fr, Obus woman and houses, Massa Territory, hibiscus.

1979, June 8 Litho. *Perf. 12x12½*
365 A102 60fr multi 3.00 .25
366 A102 150fr multi 5.00 .40

Philexafrique II, Libreville, Gabon, June 8-17. Nos. 365, 366 each printed in sheets of 10 with 5 labels showing exhibition emblem.

Wildlife Fund Emblem and Gazelle — A103

Protected Animals.

1979, Sept. 15 Litho. *Perf. 14½*

367	A103	40fr shown	1.75	.30
368	A103	50fr Addax	2.00	.50
369	A103	60fr Oryx antelope	2.50	.75
370	A103	100fr Cheetah	3.75	1.40
371	A103	150fr Wild Ass	5.25	1.90
372	A103	300fr Rhinoceros	10.00	3.00
		Nos. 367-372 (6)	25.25	7.85

Souvenir Sheet

Holy Family, by Dürer — A104

1979, Sept. 1 *Perf. 13½*

373	A104	500fr brown & dull red	6.75	2.50

Boy and Handpainted Doors — A105

IYC Emblem and: 75fr, Oriental girl. 100fr, Caucasian girl, doves. 150fr, African boys. 250fr, Pencil and outlines of child's hands.

1979, Sept. 19 Litho. *Perf. 13½*

374	A105	65fr multi	.60	.25
375	A105	75fr multi	.75	.25
376	A105	100fr multi	1.00	.25
377	A105	150fr multi	1.50	.40
		Nos. 374-377 (4)	3.85	1.15

Souvenir Sheet

378	A105	250fr multi	3.00	1.50

Nos. 314-315 Overprinted

1979, Nov. 26 Litho. *Perf. 13½x14*

379	A86	45fr multi	.60	.25
380	A86	90fr multi	1.00	.30
		Nos. 379-380,C240-C242 (5)	7.45	2.55

Apollo 11 moon landing, 10th anniversary.

Ski Jump, Lake Placid '80 Emblem — A106

Lake Placid '80 Emblem and: 20fr, Slalom, vert. 40fr, Biathlon, vert. 150fr, Women's slalom, vert. 350fr, Cross-country skiing. 500fr, Downhill skiing.

1979, Dec. 18 *Perf. 14½*

381	A106	20fr multi	.30	.25
382	A106	40fr multi	.65	.25
383	A106	60fr multi	.80	.25
384	A106	150fr multi	1.75	.50
385	A106	350fr multi	3.00	1.40
386	A106	500fr multi	4.50	1.90
		Nos. 381-386 (6)	11.00	4.55

13th Winter Olympic Games, Lake Placid, NY, Feb. 12-24, 1980.

Jet over Map of Africa A107

1980, Feb. 20 Litho. *Perf. 12½*

387	A107	15fr yellow & multi	.25	.25
388	A107	30fr blue & multi	.40	.25
389	A107	60fr red & multi	.60	.25
		Nos. 387-389 (3)	1.25	.75

ASECNA (Air Safety Board), 20th anniv.

A set of four stamps (50fr, 80fr, 100fr air post, 200fr air post) commemorating cooperation between Chad and Libya were prepared for use in 1981 but not issued. Value, $300.

1982 World Cup Soccer Championships, Spain — A108

1982 Litho. *Perf. 13½*

390	A108	30fr Hungary	.30	.25
391	A108	40fr Italy	.40	.25
392	A108	50fr Algeria	.50	.25
393	A108	60fr Argentina	.60	.25
		Nos. 390-393,C258-C259 (6)	5.80	1.75

21st Birthday of Princess Diana A109

1982, July 2 Litho. *Perf. 13½*

395	A109	30fr 1961	.30	.25
396	A109	40fr 1965	.40	.25
397	A109	50fr 1967	.50	.25
398	A109	60fr 1975	.60	.25
		Nos. 395-398,C260-C261 (6)	5.80	2.20

For overprints see Nos. 413-419B.

A110

1984 Summer Olympics, Los Angeles — A110a

No. 405A, Runner. No. 405B, Long jumper, vert.

1982, Aug. 2 Litho. *Perf. 13½*

399	A110	30fr Gymnast	.30	.25
400	A110	40fr Equestrian	.40	.25
401	A110	50fr Judo	.50	.25
402	A110	60fr High jump	.60	.25
403	A110	80fr Hurdles	1.00	.25
404	A110	300fr Woman gymnast	3.00	.95
		Nos. 399-404 (6)	5.80	2.20

Souvenir Sheet

405	A110	500fr Relay race	4.75	1.50

For surcharge see No. C302.

1982, July 31 Litho. & Embossed

405A	A110a	1500fr gold & multi	16.00

Souvenir Sheet

405B	A110a	1500fr gold & multi	10.00

No. 405 contains one 56x39mm stamp. Nos. 403-405B airmail.

No. 405A exists in a souvenir sheet of 1. Value $47.50.

Scouting Year — A111

Boy Scouts, 75th Anniv. A111a

Scouts from various countries. No. 412A, Lord Robert Baden-Powell. No. 412B, Scouts at campsite, Baden-Powell, horiz.

1982, July 15

406	A111	30fr West Germany	.30	.25
407	A111	40fr Upper Volta	.40	.25
408	A111	50fr Mali	.50	.25
409	A111	60fr Scotland	.60	.25
410	A111	80fr Kuwait	1.00	.25
411	A111	300fr Chad	3.00	.95
		Nos. 406-411 (6)	5.80	2.20

Souvenir Sheet

412	A111	500fr Chad, diff.	4.75	2.00

Litho. & Embossed

412A	A111a	1500fr gold & multi	14.00

Souvenir Sheet

412B	A111a	1500fr gold & multi	17.00

No. 412 contains one 53x35mm stamp. Nos. 410-412B airmail.

No. 412A exists in a souvenir sheet of 1. Value $40.

For overprints see Nos. 466-472B.

Nos. 395-398, C260-C262B Overprinted "21 JUIN 1982 / WILLIAM ARTHUR PHILIP LOUIS/ PRINCE DE GALLES"

1982, Oct. 4 Litho. *Perf. 13½*

413	A109	30fr multi	.30	.25
414	A109	40fr multi	.40	.25
415	A109	50fr multi	.50	.25
416	A109	60fr multi	.60	.25
417	A109	80fr multi	1.00	.25
418	A109	300fr multi	3.00	.95
		Nos. 413-418 (6)	5.80	2.20

Souvenir Sheet

419	A109	500fr multi	5.50	1.60

Litho. & Embossed

419A	AP71b	1500fr on #C262A	16.00

Souvenir Sheet

419B	AP71b	1500fr on #C262B	10.00

Birth of Prince William of Wales, June 21. Nos. 417-419B airmail.

No. 419A exists in a souvenir sheet of 1. Value $42.50.

A112

1982 World Cup Soccer Championships, Spain — A112a

Various players and flags. No. 426A, Dino Zoff, Italy, holding World Cup trophy. No. 426B, Paolo Rossi, Italy, two players, trophy, horiz.

1982, Nov. 30

420	A112	30fr multi	.30	.25
421	A112	40fr multi	.40	.25
422	A112	50fr multi	.50	.25
423	A112	60fr multi	.60	.25
424	A112	80fr multi	1.00	.25
425	A112	300fr multi	3.00	.95
		Nos. 420-425 (6)	5.80	2.20

Souvenir Sheet

426	A112	500fr multi	4.75	2.00

Litho. & Embossed

426A	A112a	1500fr gold & multi	16.00

Souvenir Sheet

426B	A112a	1500fr gold & multi	16.00

No. 426 contains one 56x32mm stamp. Nos. 424-426B airmail.

No. 426A exists in a souvenir sheet of 1. Value $42.50.

For surcharge see No. C306.

A113

Chess Champions — A113a

30fr, Philidor. 40fr, Paul Morphy. 50fr, Howard Staunton. 60fr, Capablanca. 80fr, Boris Spassky. 300fr, Anatoly Karpov.

500fr, Victor Korchnoi. No. 433A, Bobby Fischer. No. 433B, William Steinitz.

1982, Dec. 24

427 A113 30fr multi 1.00 .25
428 A113 40fr multi 1.10 .25
429 A113 50fr multi 1.25 .25
430 A113 60fr multi 1.40 .25
431 A113 80fr multi 2.10 .25
432 A113 300fr multi 3.75 .75
Nos. 427-432 (6) 10.60 2.00

Souvenir Sheet

433 A113 500fr multi 10.00 3.00

Litho. & Embossed

433A A113a 1500fr gold & multi 17.50

Souvenir Sheet

433B A113a 1500fr gold & multi 12.00

No. 433 contains one 53x35mm stamp. Nos. 431-433B airmail.

No. 433A exists in a souvenir sheet of 1. Value $50.

For overprints see Nos. 459-465.

2nd UN Conference on Peaceful Uses of Outer Space, Vienna, Aug. 9-21 — A114

A114a

Inventors and Satellites: 30fr, K.E. Tsiolkovsky, Soyuz. 40fr, R.H. Goddard, space telescope design. 50fr, Korolev, ultraviolet telescope. 60fr, von Braun, Columbia space shuttle. 80fr, Esnault Pelterie, Ariana rocket. 300fr, H. Oberth, orbital space station. 500fr, Pres. Kennedy, Apollo 11 badge, lunar rover. No. 440A, Sir Bernard Lovell, Viking I & II. No. 440B, Sir Isaac Newton, satellite TDF 1.

1983, Feb. 1 Litho. *Perf. 13½*

434 A114 30fr multi .30 .25
435 A114 40fr multi .40 .25
436 A114 50fr multi .50 .25
437 A114 60fr multi .60 .25
438 A114 80fr multi 1.00 .25
439 A114 300fr multi 3.00 .95
Nos. 434-439 (6) 5.80 2.20

Souvenir Sheet

440 A114 500fr multi 5.50 2.50

Litho. & Embossed

440A A114a 1500fr gold & multi 16.00

Souvenir Sheet

440B A114a 1500fr gold & multi 12.00

No. 440 contains one 42x50mm stamp. Nos. 438-440B airmail.

No. 440A exists in a souvenir sheet of 1. Value $50.

Bobsledding — A115

Woman Figure Skater A115a

40fr, Speed skating. 50fr, Cross-country skiing. 60fr, Hockey. 80fr, Ski jumping. 300fr, Downhill skiing.

500fr, Figure skating. No. 447B, Slalom skier, horiz.

1983, Apr. 25 Litho. *Perf. 13½*

441 A115 30fr shown .30 .25
442 A115 40fr multi .40 .25
443 A115 50fr multi .50 .25
444 A115 60fr multi .60 .25
445 A115 80fr multi 1.00 .30
446 A115 300fr multi 3.00 1.10
Nos. 441-446 (6) 5.80 2.40

Souvenir Sheet

447 A115 500fr multi 5.50 1.60

Litho. & Embossed

447A A115a 1500fr gold & multi 16.00

Souvenir Sheet

447B A115a 1500fr gold & multi 12.00

14th Winter Olympic Games, Sarajevo, Yugoslavia, Feb. 8-19, 1984.

Nos. 445-447B airmail.

No. 447A exists in a souvenir sheet of 1. Value $45.

For surcharge see No. C298.

First Manned Balloon Flight, 200th Anniv. A116

Designs: 25fr, Hot air balloon, Montgolfier Brothers. 45fr, Captive balloon, Pilatre De Rozier. 50fr, First parachute descent, Jacques Garnerin. 60fr, Chelsea balloon, J.P. Blanchard.

1983, May 30 Litho. *Perf. 13½*

448 A116 25fr multi .30 .25
449 A116 45fr multi .40 .25
450 A116 50fr multi .50 .25
451 A116 60fr multi .60 .25
Nos. 448-451,C268-C269 (6) 5.80 1.65

Automobiles — A116a

Automobiles and their builders: 25fr, 1927 Mercedes Type S, Gottlieb Daimler and Karl Benz. 45fr, 1913 Torpedo Martini Type GC 32-2, 6L, Friedrich Martini. 50fr, 1926 Chrysler "70," Walter P. Chrysler. 60fr, 1929 Alfa Romeo 6C 1750 Grand Sport, Nicola Romeo. 80fr, 1934 Phantom II Continental, Stewart Rolls and Henry Royce. 250fr, 1948 Talbot Lago, Lord Shrewsbury and Talbot.

1983, July 15 Litho. *Perf. 13½*

451A A116a 25fr multicolored
451B A116a 45fr multicolored
451C A116a 50fr multicolored
451D A116a 60fr multicolored
451E A116a 80fr multicolored
451F A116a 250fr multicolored
Nos. 451A-451F 6.75 1.60

Nos. 451E-451F are airmail.

1984 Summer Olympics, Los Angeles A117

A117a

1983, Nov. 15 Litho. *Perf. 13½*

452 A117 25fr Kayak .30 .25
453 A117 45fr Long jump .60 .25
454 A117 50fr Boxing .70 .25
455 A117 60fr Discus .75 .25
456 A117 80fr Running 1.00 .25
457 A117 350fr Equestrian 3.50 .75
Nos. 452-457 (6) 6.85 2.00

Souvenir Sheet

458 A117 500fr Gymnastics 5.50 2.50

Litho. & Embossed

458A A117a 1500fr Hurdles 16.00

Souvenir Sheet

458B A117a 1500fr Equestrian, vert. 13.00

Nos. 456-458B are airmail.

No. 458A exists in a souvenir sheet of 1. Value $47.50.

Pres. Hissein Habre — A117b

Designs: Nos. 458D, 458H, Sources of food. Nos. 458E, 458I, Dove of peace, different tribal groups, country map.

1983, Dec. 26 Litho. *Perf. 13½*

458C A117b 50fr multicolored .60 .25
458D A117b 50fr multicolored .60 .25
458E A117b 50fr multicolored .60 .25
458F A117b 60fr multicolored .70 .25
458G A117b 80fr multicolored .90 .25
458H A117b 80fr multicolored .90 .25
458I A117b 80fr multicolored .90 .25
458J A117b 100fr multicolored 1.10 .35

See Nos. C276-C279.

Nos. 427-433 Overprinted: "60e ANNIVERSAIRE FEDERATION / MONDIALE D'ECHECS 1924-1984"

1983, Dec. 27 Litho. *Perf. 13½*

459 A113 30fr multi .90 .25
460 A113 40fr multi 1.10 .25
461 A113 50fr multi 1.40 .25
462 A113 60fr multi 1.75 .25
463 A113 80fr multi 2.25 .30
464 A113 300fr multi 4.50 .75
Nos. 459-464 (6) 11.90 2.05

Souvenir Sheet

465 A113 500fr multi 4.50 2.50

World Chess Fedn., 60th anniv.

Nos. 406-412B Ovptd. with Emblem for the 15th World Scout Jamboree, Alberta, Canada, 1983

1983, Dec. 27 Litho. *Perf. 13½*

466 A111 30fr multi .30 .25
467 A111 40fr multi .40 .25
468 A111 50fr multi .50 .25
469 A111 60fr multi .60 .25
470 A111 80fr multi .70 .25
471 A111 300fr multi 3.00 .50
Nos. 466-471 (6) 5.50 1.75

Souvenir Sheet

472 A111 500fr multi 6.00 2.50

Litho. & Embossed

472A A111a 1500fr on #412A 16.00

Souvenir Sheet

472B A111a 1500fr on #412B 12.00

Locomotive "Lady," 1879 — A118

200fr, Sailboat, Lake Chad. 300fr, Graf Zeppelin. 350fr, Renault desert transport, 1930. 400fr, Bloch 120 monoplane. 500fr, Air Africa DC-8.

600fr, Intelsat V satellite.

1984, Mar. 15

473 A118 50fr shown .60 .25
474 A118 200fr multicolored 2.40 .60
475 A118 300fr multicolored 3.25 .90
476 A118 350fr multicolored 4.00 1.10
477 A118 400fr multicolored 4.25 1.25
478 A118 500fr multicolored 5.50 1.50
Nos. 473-478 (6) 20.00 5.60

Souvenir Sheet

479 A118 600fr multicolored 5.75 5.00

Nos. 477-479 airmail. For surcharge see No. 579.

Liberation, 2nd Anniv. — A119

1984, June 6 *Perf. 12½*

480 A119 50fr multi .60 .25

Pres. Hissein Habre — A120

1984, June 18 *Perf. 12½x13*
481 A120 125fr multi 1.50 .40

Anniversaries and Events — A121

Designs: 50fr, Pres. Habre, civil war martyrs. 200fr, Paul Harris, Rotary Intl. headquarters, Illinois. 300fr, Alfred Nobel, will establishing fund for Prizes. 350fr, Raphael, detail from Virgin with Child and St. John the Baptist. 400fr, Rembrandt, detail from The Holy Family. 500fr, J.W. Goethe, scene from Faust. 600fr, Rubens, detail from Helene Fourment and Her Two Children.

1984, Jan. 16 **Litho.** *Perf. 13½*
482 A121 50fr multi .50 .25
483 A121 200fr multi 1.90 .30
484 A121 300fr multi 3.00 .45
485 A121 350fr multi 3.75 .55
486 A121 400fr multi 4.50 .60
487 A121 500fr multi 5.75 .70
Nos. 482-487 (6) 19.40 2.85

Souvenir Sheet

488 A121 600fr multi 6.75 2.50

Nos. 486-488 are airmail.

Homage to Our Martyred Dead — A122

1984, Feb. 22 **Litho.** *Perf. 13½*
500 A122 50fr multi .50 .25
501 A122 80fr multi .75 .25
502 A122 120fr multi 1.10 .25
503 A122 200fr multi 1.90 .40
504 A122 250fr multi 2.50 .50
Nos. 500-504 (5) 6.75 1.65

Nos. 503-504 are airmail. For surcharge see C303.

World Communications Year — A123

1984, Feb. 29 **Litho.** *Perf. 13½*
505 A123 50fr sil & multi .50 .25
506 A123 60fr sil & multi .60 .25
507 A123 70fr sil & multi .75 .25
508 A123 125fr sil & multi 1.10 .25
509 A123 250fr sil & multi 2.50 .50
Nos. 505-509 (5) 5.45 1.50

Nos. 508-509 are airmail. For surcharge see C304.

Anniversaries and Events — A123a

50fr, Durer, detail from Madonna of the Rosary. 200fr, Henri Dunant, Red Cross founder, Battle of Solferino. 300fr, Early telephone, Goonhilly Downs Satellite Station, Britain. 350fr, J.F. Kennedy, Neil Armstrong's 1st step on Moon, 1969. 400fr, Europe-Africa Satellite infrared photograph. 500fr, Prince Charles & Lady Diana. 600fr, Wedding photograph of Prince Charles & Lady Diana.

1984
510 A123a 50fr multi .50 .25
511 A123a 200fr multi 2.10 .30
512 A123a 300fr multi 3.00 .45
513 A123a 350fr multi 3.50 .50
514 A123a 400fr multi 3.75 .55
515 A123a 500fr multi 5.00 .80
Nos. 510-515 (6) 17.85 2.85

Souvenir Sheet

516 A121 600fr multicolored 5.25

A souvenir sheet of 6 containing Nos. 510-515 exists. Nos. 514-516 are airmail.
For surcharge see No. 578.

Development of Communications — A123b

Ships and locomotives: 90fr, Indiaman, East India Co. 100fr, Nord 701, 1885. 125fr, Vera Cruz. 150fr, Columbia, 1888. 200fr, Carlisle Castle. 250fr, Rete Mediterranea, 1900. 300fr, Britannia. 350fr, Mav 114.

1984, Aug. 1 **Litho.** *Perf. 12½*
517 A123b 90fr multi 1.10 .25
518 A123b 100fr multi 1.10 .25
519 A123b 125fr multi 1.75 .25
520 A123b 150fr multi 1.75 .25
521 A123b 200fr multi 2.50 .25
522 A123b 250fr multi 3.00 .30
523 A123b 300fr multi 3.25 .35
524 A123b 350fr multi 3.75 .50
Nos. 517-524 (8) 18.20 2.40

Christmas — A124

1984, Dec. 28 **Litho.** *Perf. 13*
525 A124 50fr lt bl & org brn .50 .25
526 A124 60fr ver & org brn .60 .25
527 A124 80fr emer & org brn .75 .25
528 A124 85fr rose lil & org brn .75 .25
529 A124 100fr org yel & org brn 1.00 .30
530 A124 135fr dp bl vio & org brn 1.25 .40
Nos. 525-530 (6) 4.85 1.70

European Music Year — A125

Instruments.

1985, Apr. 30 **Litho.** *Perf. 12x12½*
531 A125 20fr Guitar .30 .25
532 A125 25fr Harp .35 .25
533 A125 30fr Xylophone .45 .25
534 A125 50fr Shoulder drum .55 .25
535 A125 70fr like #534 .80 .25
536 A125 80fr like #532 .85 .30
537 A125 100fr like #531 1.10 .40
538 A125 250fr like #533 2.75 .80
Nos. 531-538 (8) 7.15 2.75

Mushrooms A126

25fr, Chlorophyllum molybdites. 30fr, Tulostoma volvulatum. 50fr, Lentinus tuber-regium. 80fr, Podaxis pistillaris.

1985, May 15 **Litho.** *Perf. 12½*
539 A126 25fr multi .50 .25
540 A126 30fr multi .60 .25
541 A126 50fr multi .90 .25
542 A126 70fr like #541 1.25 .25
543 A126 80fr multi 1.40 .25
544 A126 100fr like #539 2.10 .35
Nos. 539-544 (6) 6.75 1.60

Anniversaries and Events — A127

25fr, Abraham Lincoln. 45fr, Henri Dunant, Geneva birthplace and red cross. 50fr, Gottlieb Daimler, 1887 Motor Carriage. 60fr, Louis Bleriot, Bleriot XI monoplane, 1909. 80fr, Paul Harris, Chicago site of Rotary Intl. founding. 350fr, Auguste Piccard, bathyscaphe Trieste, 1953.

600fr, Anatoly Karpov, 1981 world chess champion. 1500fr, Paul Harris on Medal.

1985, May 25 **Litho.** *Perf. 13½*
545 A127 25fr multi .30 .25
546 A127 45fr multi .60 .25
547 A127 50fr multi .75 .25
548 A127 60fr multi 1.00 .25
549 A127 80fr multi 1.10 .35
550 A127 350fr multi 4.00 1.25
Nos. 545-550 (6) 7.75 2.60

Souvenir Sheets

551 A127 600fr multi 6.75 5.00

Litho. & Embossed

551A A127 1500fr multi 14.50

No. 551A contains one 130x90mm stamp. Nos. 548-551A are airmail.
Souvenir sheets of 1 exist for Nos. 545-551.

Intl. Youth Year — A128

70fr, Development levels. 200fr, Globe, horiz.

1985, May 30 **Litho.** *Perf. 13*
552 A128 70fr multi .70 .25
553 A128 200fr multi 1.75 .50

A129

3rd Anniv. of the Republic A130

Perf. 13, 12½x13
1985, June 7 **Litho.**
554 A129 70fr Hand, claw .70 .25
555 A129 70fr Hands, map .70 .25
556 A130 70fr Pres. Hissein Habre .70 .25
557 A129 110fr like #554 1.10 .40
558 A129 110fr like #555 1.25 .40
559 A130 110fr like #556 1.25 .40
Nos. 554-559 (6) 5.70 1.95

Audubon Birth Bicent. — A131

1985, July 20 **Engr.** *Perf. 13*
560 A131 70fr Stork 1.10 .30
561 A131 110fr Ostrich 1.60 .40
562 A131 150fr Marabou 2.25 .65
563 A131 200fr Snake eagle 3.00 .90
Nos. 560-563 (4) 7.95 2.25

Souvenir Sheet

564 A131 500fr like 200fr 6.75 5.00

Mammals A132

1985, Aug. 25
565 A132 50fr Waterbuck .75 .25
566 A132 70fr Kudus, horiz. 1.00 .40
567 A132 250fr Shaggy mouflon 3.25 1.25
Nos. 565-567 (3) 5.00 1.90

Souvenir Sheet

568 A132 500fr White rhinoceros 5.75 5.00

UN, 40th Anniv. — A133

1985, Nov. 24
569 A133 200fr brt bl, red & brn 2.25 .75

Chad Admission to UN, 25th Anniv. — A134

1985, Nov. 24
570 A134 300fr red, brt bl & yel 3.25 1.00

President's Visit to the Nation's Interior A135

1986, June 7 Litho. *Perf. 12½x13*
571 A135 100fr multi 1.10 .25
572 A135 170fr multi 2.25 .35
573 A135 200fr multi 2.50 .45
Nos. 571-573 (3) 5.85 1.05

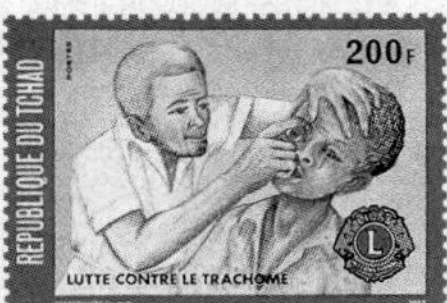

Lions Club Intl. — A135a

100fr, Sick child. 170fr, Three children, horiz. 200fr, Eye exam, horiz.

1987 Litho. *Perf. 14*
573A A135a 30fr Like #573C 50.00 —
573C A135a 100fr multi
573E A135a 170fr multi
573F A135a 200fr multi

There are two additional stamps in this set. The editors would like to examine them.

World Wildlife Fund — A136

Various mouflons, *Ammotragus lervia.*

1988, Nov. 10 Litho. *Perf. 13*
574 A136 25fr shown 2.00 .50
575 A136 45fr Adult, young 2.50 .75
576 A136 70fr Two adults, diff. 3.50 1.25
577 A136 100fr Adults, young 4.75 1.75
Nos. 574-577 (4) 12.75 4.25

Nos. 475, 512 and 570 Surcharged

Methods and Perfs. As Before
1987-89
578 A123a 170fr on 300fr #512
578A A134 230fr on 300fr #570
579 A118 240fr on 300fr #475

At least eleven additional stamps were issued in this set. The editors would like to examine any examples.

Liberation — A137

1989 *Perf. 11½x12*
580 A137 20fr multi .50 .30
581 A137 25fr multi .60 .30
582 A137 40fr multi 1.00 .50
583 A137 100fr multi 1.50 .75
584 A137 170fr multi 2.50 1.25
Nos. 580-584 (5) 6.10 3.10

World Post Day — A137a

1989, Oct. 9 Photo. *Perf. 12*
Granite Paper
584A A137a 100fr grn bl & multi
584B A137a 120fr red & multi
584C A137a 170fr pur & multi
584D A137a 250fr ol & multi
Nos. 584A-584D 160.00

Visit of Pope John Paul II — A138

Cathedral in Chad and: 20fr, 100fr, Pope holding crosier. 80fr, 170fr, Pope, diff.

1989, Dec. 20 Litho. *Perf. 13*
585 A138 20fr multicolored .25 .25
586 A138 80fr multicolored 1.00 .40
587 A138 100fr multicolored 1.25 .50
588 A138 170fr multicolored 2.10 1.10
Nos. 585-588 (4) 4.60 2.25

Traditional Hair Styles — A139

1989, Oct. 9 Photo. *Perf. 12*
Granite Paper
589 A139 100fr apple grn & multi
590 A139 120fr purple & multi
591 A139 170fr pink & multi
592 A139 250fr org yel & multi
Nos. 589-592 160.00

Vaccinations A140

1991, Dec. 1 Photo. *Perf. 11½*
Granite Paper
593 A140 30fr brown & multi .30 .25
594 A140 100fr green & multi 1.00 .45
595 A140 170fr vio & multi 1.60 .75
596 A140 180fr blue & multi 1.75 .80
597 A140 200fr red & multi 1.90 .90
Nos. 593-597 (5) 6.55 3.15

Liberty and Democracy Day — A141

1991, Dec. 1 Litho.
598 A141 10fr green & multi .25 .25
599 A141 20fr lilac & multi .25 .25
600 A141 40fr yellow & multi .40 .25
601 A141 70fr blue & multi .65 .30
602 A141 130fr tan & multi 1.25 .75
603 A141 200fr pink & multi 1.90 1.00
Nos. 598-603 (6) 4.70 2.80

Fight Against Insect Pests — A141a

1992, Sept. 1 Photo. *Perf. 12*
603A A141a 25fr multi 30.00 15.00
603B A141a 45fr multi 30.00 15.00
603C A141a 100fr multi 30.00 15.00
603D A141a 150fr multi 30.00 15.00
603E A141a 170fr multi 30.00 15.00
Nos. 603A-603E (5) 150.00 75.00

A142

1992, Nov. 15 Litho. *Perf. 11½*
604 A142 20fr bright yel & multi .25 .25
605 A142 45fr golden yel & multi .40 .25
606 A142 85fr pink & multi .75 .35
607 A142 170fr blue & multi 1.50 .70
608 A142 300fr gray & multi 3.00 1.40
Nos. 604-608 (5) 5.90 2.95

Doctors Without Borders, 20th anniv.

Campaign Against Illiteracy A143

1992, Nov. 30
609 A143 25fr yel grn & multi .25 .25
610 A143 40fr golden yel & multi .40 .25
611 A143 70fr pink & multi .60 .30
612 A143 100fr lilac & multi .75 .40
613 A143 180fr blue & multi 1.60 .60
614 A143 200fr gray & multi 1.75 .70
Nos. 609-614 (6) 5.35 2.50

Intl. Conference on Nutrition, Rome — A144

1992, Dec. 15
615 A144 10fr yellow & multi .25 .25
616 A144 60fr pink & multi 1.00 .25
617 A144 120fr yel grn & multi 1.75 .40
618 A144 500fr blue & multi 4.50 1.60
Nos. 615-618 (4) 7.50 2.50

Palace of the People A145

1993, Apr. 15 Litho. *Perf. 11½*
619 A145 80fr multi 40.00 5.00
620 A145 100fr multi 40.00 5.00
621 A145 130fr multi 40.00 5.00
622 A145 400fr multi 40.00 5.00
Nos. 619-622 (4) 160.00 20.00

Natl. Conference — A146

1993, Dec. 1 Litho. *Perf. 11¾*
Granite paper
623 A146 55fr multi .80 .35
624 A146 70fr multi 1.00 .45
625 A146 110fr multi 1.40 .80
626 A146 125fr multi 1.75 .90
Nos. 623-626 (4) 4.95 2.50

OAU, 30th Anniv. — A147

1993, Dec. 4 Litho. *Perf. 11½x11¾*
627 A147 15fr multi .25 .25
628 A147 30fr multi .30 .25
629 A147 110fr multi 1.10 .80
630 A147 190fr multi 2.00 1.50
Nos. 627-630 (4) 3.65 2.80

Victor Schoelcher (1804-93), Abolitionist A148

Perf. 11¾x11½
1993, Dec. 26 Litho.
631 A148 55fr multi .40 .40
632 A148 105fr multi 1.10 .75
633 A148 125fr multi 1.40 1.10
634 A148 300fr multi 2.75 2.00

Tourism A149

Perf. 11¾x11½

1993, Dec. 27 **Litho.**

635 A149 15fr multi *40.00 20.00*
636 A149 95fr multi *40.00 20.00*
637 A149 100fr multi *40.00 20.00*
638 A149 190fr multi — —

Bank of Central African States A150

1994 **Litho.** ***Perf. 11½***

639 A150 20fr multicolored .25 .25
640 A150 30fr pink & multi .40 .25
641 A150 105fr blue & multi .90 .30
642 A150 190fr lilac & multi 1.60 .90
Nos. 639-642 (4) 3.15 1.70

Huts for Storing Grain A151

Designs: 75fr, Arabe, kim. 150fr, Sara, moundang. 300fr, Boulala, kotoko. 450fr, Ouaddai, kenga.

1995, Oct. 15 **Litho.** ***Perf. 14***

643 A151 75fr multicolored .50 .25
644 A151 150fr multicolored .90 .30
645 A151 300fr multicolored 1.50 .75
646 A151 450fr multicolored 2.50 1.00
Nos. 643-646 (4) 5.40 2.30

Souvenir Sheet

Chinese Post, Cent. — A151a

1996 **Litho.** ***Perf. 13¼***

646A A151a 270fr multi 2.25 2.00

1996 Olympic Games, Atlanta A151b

No. 646B: e, Tennis. f, Equestrian. g, Soccer. h, Boxing.
No. 646C: i, Judo. j, Running. k, Cycling. l, Table tennis.
1500fr, Hurdler.

1996 **Litho.** ***Perf. 13¼***

646B A151b 250fr Sheet of 4, #e-h 3.00 4.00
646C A151b 300fr Sheet of 4, #i-l 4.00 5.00

Souvenir Sheet

646D A151b 1500fr multi 5.50 5.50

No. 646D contains one 39x57mm stamp.

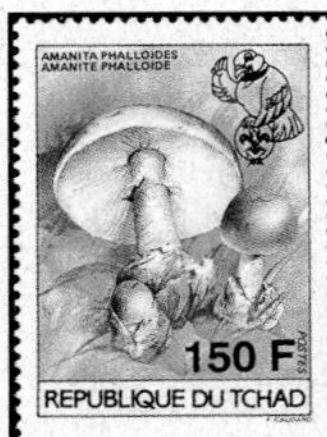

1995 Boy Scout Jamboree, Holland — A152

Mushrooms: 150fr, Amanita phalloides. 170fr, Phallus impudicus. 200fr, Lyloperdon perlatum. 350fr, Hydne commun. 450fr, Agaricus bisporus. 800fr, Cortinarius orellanus.
1500fr, Pleurotus ostreatus.

1996, Apr. 15 **Litho.** ***Perf. 13½***

647-652 A152 Set of 6 8.00 4.75
a. Souvenir sheet, #647-652 9.25 4.75

Souvenir Sheet

653 A152 1500fr multicolored 5.50 5.00

Nos. 647-652 exist in souvenir sheets of 1.

Butterflies, Mushrooms and Minerals A152a

No. 653A: g, Papilio zalmoxis. h, Anacridium melanorhodon. i, Otidea leporina. j, Haliaetus vocifer.
No. 653B: k, Amanita phalloides, Papilio dardanus. l, Papilio antimachus, Cortinarius praestans. m, Phallus impudicus, Chrysidia croesus. n, Papilio dardanus, Lycoperon perlatum.
No. 653C: o, Charaxes brutus. p, Epiphora albida. q, Euchloron megaera. r, Salamis duprei.
No. 653D: s, Disthene. t, Olivine. u, Sphene. v, Hemimorphite.
No. 653E, Argema mittrei. No. 653F, Zoisite.

1996 **Litho.** ***Perf. 13¼***

653A A152a 350fr Sheet of 4, #g-j 7.00 6.00
653B A152a 400fr Sheet of 4, #k-n 8.00 7.00
653C A152a 650fr Sheet of 4, #o-r 12.00 10.00
653D A152a 800fr Sheet of 4, #s-v 15.00 12.00
Nos. 653A-653D (4) 42.00 35.00

Souvenir Sheets

653E A152a 2000fr multi 7.50 7.50
653F A152a 2000fr multi 7.50 7.50

A number has been reserved for an additional sheet in this set. Nos. 653E-653F each contain one 42x36mm stamp.

Greenpeace, 25th Anniv. — A153

No. 654: a, 170fr, Green coral, school of small fish. b, 200fr, Yellow & orange coral. c, 300fr, Red orange coral. d, 350fr, White coral.
1500fr, Diver, coral, vert.

1996, July 16

654 A153 Block of 4, #a.-d. 5.00 5.00

Souvenir Sheet

655 A153 1500fr multicolored 9.50 9.50

Entertainers A154

Designs: No. 656, 170fr, Bob Marley. No. 657, 170fr, Marilyn Monroe. No. 658, 200fr, Elvis Presley. No. 659, 200fr, Monroe. No. 660, 300fr, Monroe. No. 661, 350fr, Stevie Wonder. No. 662, 350fr, Presley. No. 663, 400fr, John Lennon. No. 664, 500fr, Presley. No. 665, 600fr, Lennon. No. 666, 700fr, Madonna. No. 667, 800fr, Presley. No. 668, 1000fr, Monroe.
No. 669, 1500fr, Tina Turner. No. 670, 1500fr, Clint Eastwood. No. 670A, 1500fr, Presley.

1996, May 15

656-668 A154 Set of 13 29.00 22.50
665a Sheet of 2, #663, 665 4.50 2.25
667a Sheet of 4, #658, 662, 664, 667 8.00 3.75
668a Sheet of 4, #657, 659-660, 668 7.00 3.50

Souvenir Sheets

669-670A A154 Set of 3 18.00 10.00

Nos. 656-668 exist in souvenir sheets of 1. No. 670A contains one 51x90mm stamp.
See No. 674.

A155

No. 671: a, Pres. Bill Clinton. b, Elvis Presley in white jumpsuit.
No. 672: a, Pres. Richard Nixon. b, Presley in white shirt, black jacket.

1996, Dec. 17 **Litho.** ***Perf. 13½***

671 A155 1500fr Sheet of 2, #a.-b. 14.00 14.00
672 A155 1500fr Sheet of 2, #a.-b. 14.00 14.00

Giant Panda — A156

No. 673: a, Holding branch, left claw out. b, Holding branch. c, Lying on back. d, Holding branch in mouth.

1996, Oct. 15

673 A156 100fr Sheet of 4, #a.-d. 2.25 2.25

Entertainers Type of 1996

1996 **Litho.** ***Perf. 13½***

674 A154 500fr Jerry Garcia 2.50 1.75

No. 674 exists in a souvenir sheet of 1.

1998 World Cup Soccer Championships, France — A157

1998 World Cup Soccer Championships, France — A157a

Unidentified players, stadium: No. 675, 150fr, The Beaujoire, Nantes. No. 676, 200fr, Lescure Park, Bordeaux. No. 676A, 300fr, Municipal Stadium, Toulouse. No. 676B, 600fr, Felix Bollaert, Lens.
No. 677A: b, Player in white shirt. c, Player in red shirt.

1996, Dec. 17

675-676B A157 Set of 4 5.00 4.00

Souvenir Sheet

677 A157a 1500fr George Weah 7.50 5.00
677A A157a 3000fr Sheet of 2, #b-c 13.00 11.00

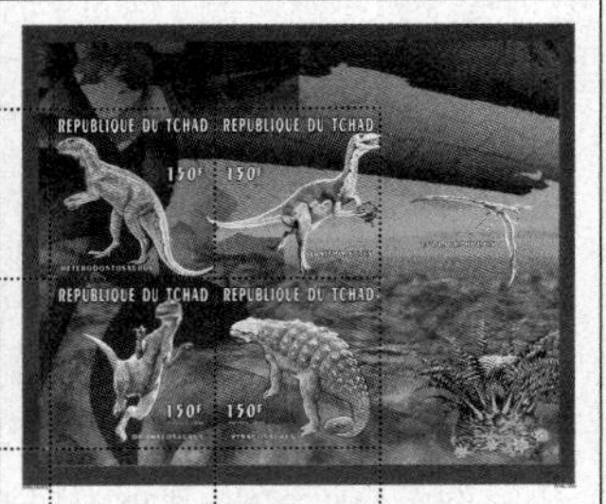

Dinosaurs, Dog & Cats, Butterflies & Insects — A158

No. 678 — Dinosaurs: a, Heterodontosaurus. b, Ornitholestes. c, Dromaeosaurus. d, Pinacosaurus.
No. 679 — Dinosaurs: a, Corythosaurus. b, Ankylosaurides. c, Ornithomimus. d, Styracosaurus.
No. 680 — Dogs & cats: a, Artois. b, Bengal. c, Persian. d, Vendeen.
No. 681 — Butterflies & insects: a, Euphaedra zaddachi. b, Pseudacraea dolomena. c, Cicindela barbara. d, Goliath.

1996, Oct. 15

678 A158 150fr Sheet of 4, #a.-d. 3.00 3.00
679 A158 200fr Sheet of 4, #a.-d. 3.75 3.75
680 A158 250fr Sheet of 4, #a.-d. 5.00 5.00
681 A158 300fr Sheet of 4, #a.-d. 6.00 4.00

Ovptd. in Gold in Sheet Margin

1997 **Litho.** ***Perf. 13½***

678e Sheet of 4 3.00 3.00
679e Sheet of 4 3.75 3.75
680e Sheet of 4 5.00 5.00

Gold overprints on Nos. 678e-680e contain two-line inscription in Chinese and Hong Kong '97 exhibition emblem.

UNICEF, UN, 50th Anniv., Lions Intl. — A159

No. 682 — UNICEF, 50th anniv.: a, 150fr, Girl, boy turtles. b, 400fr, Feeding small child.
No. 683 — UN, 50th anniv.: a, 170fr, Huygens probe, starving child. b, 500fr, Man with plant, Marsnet probe.
No. 684 — Lions Intl.: a, 200fr, Man carrying sack of grain. b, 800fr, Men examining plants, native man stirring kettle over fire.

1996, Oct. 15 Litho. *Perf. 13½*

682 A159 Pair, #a.-b. + label 3.00 2.00
683 A159 Pair, #a.-b. + label 3.50 2.50
684 A159 Pair, #a.-b. + label 5.50 3.50

Nos. 682-684 exist as souvenir sheets with colored margins. Value, each $13.

1996 European Soccer Championships — A160

No. 685: a, Oliver Bierhoff holding trophy. b, Two players. c, Two players, referee. d, Queen Elizabeth II, player holding trophy.

1996, Dec. 17

685 A160 350fr Sheet of 4, #a.-d. 6.00 4.75

Michael Schumacher, 1995 World Driving Champion — A161

No. 686: a, Ferrari Formula-1 race car. b, Schumacher close-up. c, Schumacher in Benetton uniform. d, Benetton Formula-1 race car.
No. 687, Schumacher with arms raised. No. 687A, Winner of 1996 Italian Grand Prix.

1997, June 16

686 A161 700fr Sheet of 4, #a.-d. 12.50 9.00

Souvenir Sheets

687 A161 2000fr multicolored 8.50 7.00
687A A161 2000fr multicolored 8.50 7.00

No. 687 contains one 36x51mm stamp.

1998 Winter Olympic Games, Nagano, Japan A162

Designs: 100fr, Women's figure skating. 170fr, Hockey. 350fr, Downhill skiing. 750fr, Speed skating.
1500fr, Slalom skiing.

1996, Dec. 17

688-691 A162 Set of 4 5.75 4.00

Souvenir Sheet

692 A162 1500fr multicolored 6.25 4.00

World Wildlife Fund — A163

No. 693 — Struthio camelus rothschildi: a, Female. b. Male. c, Chicks. d, Male, female up close.

1996, Dec. 17 Litho. *Perf. 13½*

693 A163 200fr Block of 4, #a.-d. 15.00 15.00

Jacqueline Kennedy Onassis (1929-94) — A164

Various portraits.

1996, Dec. 17

694 A164 200fr Sheet of 9, #a.-i. 8.00 6.00

Intl. Red Cross, Rotary Intl., Scouts — A165

No. 695 — Intl. Red Cross: a, 100fr, Woman, airplane. b, 350fr, Man, train.
No. 696 — Rotary Intl.: a, 300fr, Boy, water coming through pipes. b, 700fr, Native boy and man, volunteers.
No. 697 — Scouts: a, 250fr, Boy scout holding book, hyena. b, 1000fr, Garry Kasparov, chess player, scout.

1996, Oct. 15 Litho. *Perf. 13½*

695 A165 Pair, #a.-b. + label 2.50 1.75
696 A165 Pair, #a.-b. + label 5.50 3.50
697 A165 Pair, #a.-b. + label 6.50 4.50

Nos. 695-697 exist in souvenir sheets with colored margins. Value, each $13.

Japanese Sumo Wrestling — A166

Various wrestlers in ring.

1996, Dec. 17 Litho. *Perf. 13½*

698 A166 400fr Sheet of 4, #a.-d. 7.00 5.00

China '96 — A168

Various paintings showing mountains and trees.

1996

704 A168 100fr Sheet of 9, #a.-i. 4.50 3.50

Marilyn Monroe — A168a

Various portraits.

1997 Litho. *Perf. 13¼*

704J A168a 500fr Sheet of 9, #k-s 14.00 14.00

History of Space Travel — A169

No. 705: a, Lunar N1 rocket, USSR, Saturn 1, US, Apollo 1 crew, Grissom, White, Chaffee. b, Launch of Soyuz, USSR, V.M. Komarov. c, US Lunar Orbiter 4. d, Neil Armstrong, US, Molniya 1, USSR. e, Venera 4, USSR, Mariner, US. f, Surveyor 3, US.
No. 706: a, Ariane 1, Landsat 4, US. b, Spacelab & space shuttle, NASA, ESA, Thomas Mattingly, US. c, L-Sat Telecom Satelite, ESA. d, J.L. Chretien, Soviet Salyut 7, US Space Shuttle. e, Venera 13, USSR. f, Intelsat 6, US.
No. 707: a, John Glenn, Atlas rocket, Mercury capsule. b, Mariner 2, US. c, Scott Carpenter, US. d, Telstar, Tiros 6, US. e, Vostok capsule, USSR, Bell X15 airplane, US. f, Mars 1, USSR.
No. 708: a, "Sounds of Earth" record, Voyager 1 & 2, US. b, Himawari 1, MU-3H, Japan, Atlas Centaur, US. c, Soviet Salyut 6, Proton rocket, Galileo (1564-1642). d, Meteosat, SMS Geos, Atlas EF, US. e, Boeing 747, space shuttle, US. f, ISEE, US.
No. 709: a, Saturn 5, US, OAO 3 Copernicus. b, Pioneer 10, US. c, Luna 20, USSR, John F. Kennedy. d, Landsat 1, US. e, Apollo 16, US astronauts Mattingly, Duke, Young. f, Lunar Rover, US Apollo 17 astronauts Schmitt, Evans, Cernan.
No. 710: a, RD 107 rocket, USSR, Vanguard rocket, US, Vanguard I, US. b, Aerobee, Goddard rockets, Robert H. Goddard. c, Laika, 1st dog in space, USSR. d, Theodor von Karman, V2A, Gird 09 rockets, USSR. e, Sputnik 1, USSR, Korolev airplane. f, Sanger, Bell X1 airplanes, US, Eugene Sanger.
No. 711, US Astronauts, Neil Armstrong, Michael Collins, Edwin E. Aldrin, Jr., USSR animals in space, Laika, Felix the cat.
Illustration reduced.

1997 Litho. *Perf. 13½*

705 A169 150fr Sheet of 6, #a.-f. 3.25 3.25
706 A169 250fr Sheet of 6, #a.-f. 4.75 4.75
707 A169 300fr Sheet of 6, #a.-f. 6.00 6.00
708 A169 450fr Sheet of 6, #a.-f. 7.25 7.25
709 A169 475fr Sheet of 6, #a.-f. 9.25 9.25
710 A169 800fr Sheet of 6, #a.-f. 14.50 14.50

Souvenir Sheet

711 A169 2000fr multicolored 7.00 7.00

No. 711 contains one 80x85mm stamp.

Elvis Presley — A169a

Various portraits.

1997 Litho. *Perf. 13¼*

711A A169a 300fr Sheet of 9, #b-j 9.50 9.50

Jacqueline Kennedy Onassis (1929-94) — A170

Various portraits.

1997, July 15 Litho. *Perf. 13½*
712 A170 150fr Sheet of 9, #a.-i. 5.00 2.75

Pres. John F. Kennedy — A170a

No. 712J: k, Standing, looking right. l, With family. m, Looking left. n, With statue of George Washington. o, Seated, with Great Seal of the United States. p, Facing forward, with stars and arrows. q, In chair. r, With statue of Lincoln. s, Behind podium, with flag and Capitol.

1997 Litho. *Perf. 13¼*
712J A170a 250fr Sheet of 9, #k-s 7.00 7.00

Diana, Princess of Wales (1961-97) — A171

Various portraits.

1997
713 A171 300fr Sheet of 9, #a.-i. 9.00 9.00
714 A171 450fr Sheet of 9, #a.-i. 12.50 12.50

Souvenir Sheet

715 A171 2000fr multicolored 7.00 6.25

No. 715 contains one 42x60mm stamp.

Deng Xiaoping and Bruce Lee — A171a

No. 715A — Deng and: c, Child. d, Chinese flag. e, Dancer. f, Boats in water. g, Farmers. h, Cityscape.

No. 715B — Lee and movie titles: i, Operation Dragon. j, La Fureur du Dragon. k, La Fureur de Vaincre. l, La Flute Silencieuse. m, Le Jeu de la Mort. n, Le Retour du Dragon.

1000fr, Deng and stars.

1997 Litho. *Perf. 13¼*
715A A171a 75fr Sheet of 6, #c-h 1.75 1.75
715B A171a 125fr Sheet of 6, #i-n 3.00 3.00

Souvenir Sheet

715O A171a 1000fr multi — —

No. 715O contains one 36x41mm stamp.

Mahatma Gandhi (1869-1948), Mother Teresa (1910-97) — A172

No. 716: a, Gandhi seated, dendrobium speciosum. b, Mother Teresa with Indian people. c, Bulbophyllum umbellatum, Gandhi with 2 women.

1998, Feb. 5 Litho. *Perf. 13½*
716 A172 150fr Sheet of 3, #a.-c. 1.90 1.90

Famous Men — A173

Designs: 300fr, Nelson Mandela, Pres. of South Africa, diamond. 450fr, Albert Einstein (1879-1955), physicist, satellite. 800fr, Robert Barany (1876-1936), physician, Felix the space cat.

2000fr, Alfred Nobel (1833-96).

1998, Feb. 5
717-719 A173 Set of 3 7.00 5.50

Souvenir Sheet

720 A173 2000fr multicolored 8.25 7.50

Nos. 717-719 exist in souvenir sheets of 1. No. 720 contains one 41x60mm stamp.

See Nos. 729-734.

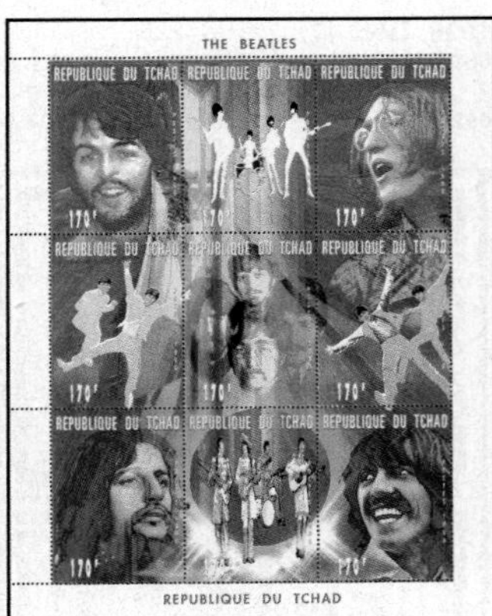

The Beatles — A174

No. 721: a-i, Various portraits of John Lennon.

No. 722 — The Beatles: a, Paul McCartney. b, Silhouettes. c, John Lennon. d, George Harrison, Lennon. e, Four faces. f, McCartney, Ringo Starr. g, Starr. h, Four in Sgt. Pepper's costumes. i, Harrison.

No. 723 — Life of John Lennon: a, Yoko Ono. b, With McCartney. c, In profile. d, Wearing suit. e, Wearing white shirt, tie. f, With mother. g, Wearing dark glasses. h, With guru. i, In white suit.

No. 724: Various portraits of Lennon, McCartney, Harrison, Starr.

No. 724J, Beatles in suits and ties. No. 724K, Beatles in Sgt. Pepper uniforms.

1996 Litho. *Perf. 13½*
721 A174 100fr Sheet of 9, #a-f 2.75 2.75
722 A174 170fr Sheet of 9, #a.-i. 5.50 5.50
723 A174 200fr Sheet of 9, #a.-i. 5.25 5.25
724 A174 300fr Sheet of 9, #a.-i. 12.00 12.00

Souvenir Sheets

724J A174 1500fr multi 7.50 6.00
724K A174 1500fr multi 7.50 6.00

Antelopes — A175

Designs: a, 170fr, Damaliscus dorcas. b, 350fr, Oryx gazella. c, 500fr, Addax nasomaculatus. d, 600fr, Aepyceros melampus.

1996, Dec. 17
725 A175 Block of 4, #a.-d. 6.00 6.00

Nos. 725a-725d exist in souvenir sheets of 1.

No. 725 Overprinted in Gold

1996
726 A175 Block of 4, #a.-d. 7.00 7.00

Nos. 726a-726d exist in souvenir sheets of 1.

Marilyn Monroe (1926-1962) — A176

Various portraits.

1996
727 A176 250fr Sheet of 9, #a.-i. 9.50 8.00

Souvenir Sheet

728 A176 1500fr multicolored 5.00 5.00

No. 728 contains one 51x90mm stamp.

Famous People Type of 1997

Nobel Prize winners: 100fr, Mother Teresa (1910-97), humanitarian. 150fr, Martin Luther King, Jr. (1929-68), civil rights leader. 475fr, Otto Hahn (1879-1968), chemist, nuclear powered ship. 500fr, Ivan Pavlov (1849-1936), physiologist, Russian space dog, Laika. 600fr, Johannes van der Waals (1837-1923), physicist. 1000fr, Sir Edward Appleton (1892-1965), physicist, Concorde jet.

1998, Feb. 5
729-734 A173 Set of 6 14.50 10.00

Nos. 729-734 exist in souvenir sheets of 1.

Scouting A177

Wild animals: No. 735: a, Hyena. b, Mongoose.

No. 736: a, Wildcat. b, Addax nasomaculatus.

No. 737: a, Fennec. b, Hyena, diff.

1998, Feb. 6
735 A177 150fr Pair, #a.-b. 1.75 1.75
736 A177 550fr Pair, #a.-b. 5.25 5.25
737 A177 600fr Pair, #a.-b. 6.25 6.25

Cats and Dogs — A178

No. 738: a, Maine coon. b, Singapore.

No. 739: a, Siberian husky. b, Malamute.

No. 740: a, Spitz. b, Eskimo.

No. 741: a, Siamese. b, Common cat.

No. 742, 1500fr, Abyssinian. No. 743, 1500fr, Samoyed.

1998, Feb. 6

738	A178	300fr Pair, #a.-b.	2.75	2.75
739	A178	450fr Pair, #a.-b.	3.00	3.00
740	A178	475fr Pair, #a.-b.	3.75	3.75
741	A178	500fr Pair, #a.-b.	4.00	4.00

Souvenir Sheets

742-743	A178	Set of 2	11.00	11.00

Nos. 742-743 each contain one 42x60mm stamp.

Airplanes, Ships, & Trains — A179

No. 743A — Early aircraft: b, Latecoere 28, France. c, D'Equeuilly, France. d, Liore et Olivier Leo-213, France. e, Louis Bleriot monoplane. f, Graf Zeppelin LZ 127. g, Caproni CA 133, Italy.

No. 744 — Airplanes: a, Sikorsky VS-44A. b, Short S25/V Sandringham 4. c, Bristol 167 Brabazon 1. d, Savoia S13 Bis. e, Curtiss CR-3. f, Curtiss R3C-2.

No. 745 — Ships: a, Normandy, 1935. b, Persia, 1856. c, Queen Elizabeth II, 1968. d, Christian Radich, 1937. e, Amerigo Vespucci, 1933. f, Tovarich, 1933.

No. 745G — Classic sports cars: h, 1963-65 Porsche 356 SC. i, 1961-66 AC Cobra. j, 1960-61 Maserati Tipo 63 Birdcage. k, 1962-63 Austin Healey 3000 MK11. l, 1959-62 Ferrari 250 GT Berlinetta SWB. m, 1958 Aston Martin DB4.

No. 746 — Trains: a, BRB cog steam train. b, AE 4/7 10969. c, Crocodile of Saint-Gothard BE 6/8 111. d, RAE 2/4 1001. e, Steam train, Spain. f, RE 6/6 11612 express.

No. 746G — High speed trains: h, ETR 470, Italy. i, TGV Metro, France. j, Hikari, Japan. k, TGV 001 turbotrain, France. l, Eurostar 3203/3204 Metro train, France, Germany, Great Britain. m, 990 ICE train, Germany.

1500fr, Steam locomotive, C5/6 2978. 2000fr, TGV, France.

1998, Feb. 4

743A	A179	150fr Sheet of 6, #b.-g.	3.50	3.50
744	A179	200fr Sheet of 6, #a.-f.	4.50	4.50
745	A179	250fr Sheet of 6, #a.-f.	5.50	5.50
745G	A179	300fr Sheet of 6, #h.-m.	6.75	6.75
746	A179	350fr Sheet of 6, #a.-f.	8.00	8.00
746G	A179	400fr Sheet of 6, #h.-m.	9.00	9.00

Souvenir Sheets

747	A179	1500fr multicolored	5.50	5.50
748	A179	2000fr multicolored	7.75	7.75

Nos. 747-748 contain one 36x42mm stamp.

Swiss rail service, 150th anniv. (Nos. 746-747).

Issued: No. 745G, 2/6.

See No. 758.

Diana, Princess of Wales (1961-97) A180

Various portraits.

2000fr, Portrait wearing high lace collar.

1997 **Litho.** ***Perf. 13½***

749	A180	250fr Sheet of 9, #a.-i.	8.00	8.00

Souvenir Sheet

749J	A180	2000fr multicolored	7.75	7.75

Literacy Campaign A181

1997, June 16

750	A181	150fr olive & multi	.80	.80
751	A181	300fr buff & multi	1.75	1.60
752	A181	475fr salmon & multi	2.50	2.50
		Nos. 750-752 (3)	5.05	4.90

Kellou Dahalob — A182

1998, Apr. 8

753	A182	50fr pink & multi	.30	.30
754	A182	100fr blue & multi	.40	.40
755	A182	150fr green & multi	.65	.65
756	A182	300fr lilac & multi	1.10	1.10
757	A182	400fr yellow & multi	1.50	1.50
		Nos. 753-757 (5)	3.95	3.95

Transportation Type of 1997

No. 758 — Modern aircraft: a, SAT, France, Germany. b, BAC/Aerospatiale Concorde. c, X001, Japan. d, Bell X-2, US. e, Douglas X-3, US. f, Aerospatiale STS 2000, France.

1998, Feb. 4 **Litho.** ***Perf. 13½***

758	A179	475fr Sheet of 6, #a.-f.	12.00	12.00

Women — A183

Women: 50fr, 100fr, 150fr, Using grindstone. 300fr, 450fr, 500fr, Kneeling.

1997, June 16

759	A183	50fr vio & multi, vert.	.30	.30
760	A183	100fr grn & multi, vert.	.40	.40
761	A183	150fr yel & multi, vert.	.55	.55
762	A183	300fr vio & multi	1.10	1.10
763	A183	450fr grn & multi	1.75	1.75
764	A183	500fr yel & multi	1.90	1.90
		Nos. 759-764 (6)	6.00	6.00

Protect the Ozone Layer — A184

1998 **Litho.** ***Perf. 13½***

765	A184	150fr blue & multi	.60	.60
766	A184	300fr green & multi	1.25	1.25
767	A184	475fr pink & multi	1.90	1.60
768	A184	500fr blue green & multi	1.90	1.90
		Nos. 765-768 (4)	5.65	5.35

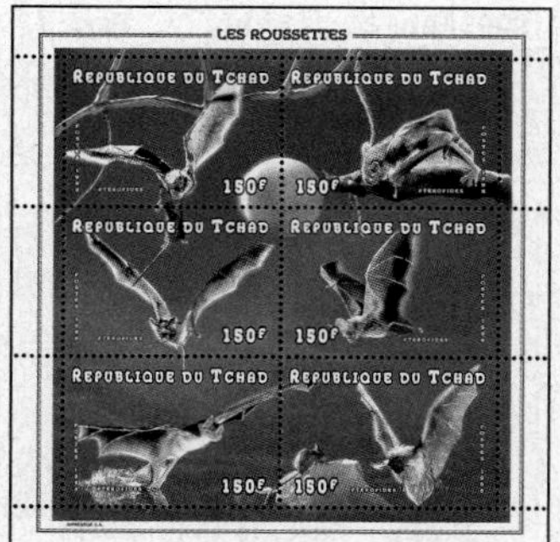

Fauna — A185

No. 769 — Bats: a, Holding mouse, tree branch. b, Drinking. c, One in flight, bottom of mouse. d, One flying left. e, One flying right. f, Mouse on rock, bat landing.

No. 769G — Horses: h, Gray Arabian. i, Brown Arabian. j, Przewalski's. k, Australian brumbies. l, Camargue. m, Zebras.

No. 769N — Sea mammals: o-t, Various portraits of Trichechus senegalensis.

No. 770 — Gorillas & chimpanzees: a, Chimpanzee scratching head. b, Gorilla walking on all fours. c, Gorilla seated. d, Chimpanzee swinging from branch. e, Chimpanzee using stick. f, Two gorillas.

No. 771 — Raptors: a, Terathopius ecaudatus. b, Buteo buteo. c, Sagittarius serpentarius. d, Polemaetus belligosus. e, Circaetus allicus. f, Aquila chrysaetos.

No. 771G — Reptiles: h, Crocodylus niloticus. i, Drendroaspis angusticeps. j, Bitis nasicornis. k, Chamaeleo johnstoni. l, Naja nigricolis. m, Meroles cuneirostris.

No. 771N — Mushrooms: o, Coprinus atramentarius. p, Romaria botrytis. q, Aleuria aurantia. r, Amanita muscaria. s, Macrolepiota rhacodes. t, Helvella crispa.

No. 771U — Mushrooms: v, Morchella vulgaris. w, Tuber aestiuum. x, Tuber melanosporum. y, Mitrophora hybrida. z, Morchella conica. aa, Choeromyces meandriformis.

No. 772 — Butterflies: a, Charaxes jasius. b, Hamanumidia daedalus. c, Charaxes bohemani. d, Hallimoides rumia, denomination LL. e, Hallimoides rumia, denomination LR. f, Pseudacraea boisduuali.

1500fr, Coelogyne ovalis, palla ussheri. 2000fr, Baleniceps, Neurophyllum clauatum.

1998, June 20

769	A185	150fr Sheet of 6, #a.-f.	5.00	5.00
769G	A185	250fr Sheet of 6, #h.-m.	5.50	5.50
769N	A185	300fr Sheet of 6, #o.-t.	6.50	6.50
770	A185	300fr Sheet of 6, #a.-f.	8.00	8.00
771	A185	350fr Sheet of 6, #a.-f.	10.00	10.00
771G	A185	450fr Sheet of 6, #h.-m.	12.00	12.00
771N	A185	475fr Sheet of 6, #o.-t.	10.50	10.50
771U	A185	500fr Sheet of 6, #v.-aa.	12.00	12.00
772	A185	600fr Sheet of 6, #a.-f.	16.00	8.00

Souvenir Sheets

773	A185	1500fr multicolored	6.50	6.50
773A	A185	2000fr multicolored	7.50	7.50

Nos. 773-773A contain one 51x42mm stamp.

Bela Lugosi as Dracula — A185a

Lugosi in various poses.

1998, Dec. 11 **Litho.** ***Perf. 13½***

773B	A185a	250fr Sheet of 9, #d.-l.	7.50	7.50

Souvenir Sheet

773C	A185a	1500fr multi, horiz.	5.00	5.00

Diana, Princess of Wales — A186

No. 774 — Various portraits: a, 200fr. b, 250fr. c, 300fr. d, 400fr. e, 475fr. f, 500fr. g, 800fr. h, 900fr. i, 1000fr.

1999, Jan. 10 **Litho.** ***Perf. 12½***

774	A186	Sheet of 9, #a.-i.	18.00	18.00

Birds — A187

Designs: 75fr, Ibis ibis. 150fr, Ephippiorhynchus senegalensis. 200fr, Phoenicopterus ruber. 300fr, Leptoptilus crumeniferus. 400fr, Scopus umbretta. 475fr, Platalea alba.

1000fr, Balaeniceps rex.

1999, Jan. 15 **Litho.** ***Perf. 12¾***

775-780	A187	Set of 6	5.75	5.75

Souvenir Sheet

781	A187	1000fr multicolored	3.50	3.50

No. 781 contains one 32x40mm stamp.

Fire Trucks A188

Designs: 50fr, 1840 model. 150fr, 1920 Fiat. 200fr, 1915 Mack. 300fr, 1930 Renault. 400fr, Pegaso M 1090. 500fr, 1960 Jet Fire Power.

700fr, 1720 King George III Fire Company.

1998, Dec. 30

782-787	A188	Set of 6	5.75	5.75

Souvenir Sheet

788	A188	700fr multicolored	2.50	2.50

No. 788 contains one 35x28mm stamp.

Minerals — A188a

No. 788A: a, Opal. b, Cyanite. c, Chalcopyrite. d, Apatite. e, Celestite. f, Scorodite.

No. 788B: a, Agate. b, Wulfenite. c, Barytine. d, Tanzanite. e, Amazonite. f, Malachite.

1998 Litho. *Perf. 13½*

788A A188a 475fr Sheet of 6, #a.-f. 10.00 10.00
788B A188a 500f Sheet of 6, #a.-f. 10.50 10.50

Dinosaurs — A188b

No. 788C: a, Dilophosaurus. b, Argentinosaurus. c, Kritosaurus. d, Scutellosaurus. e, Ornithomimosaurus. f, Bactrosaurus.

No. 788D: a, Coelophysis. b, Kannemeyeria. c, Apatosaurus. d, Scipionyx. e, Lystrosaurus. f, Kentrosaurus.

No. 788E, Giganotosaurus, vert.

1998, Nov. 12 Litho. *Perf. 13¼*

Sheets of 6

788C A188b 400fr #a.-f. 7.75 7.75
788D A188b 450fr #a.-f. 9.00 9.00

Souvenir Sheet

788E A188b 2000fr multi 6.50 6.50

US Pres. Ronald Reagan — A189

No. 789: a, Family portrait as young boy. b, In front of family home. c, In football uniform, as radio announcer. d, Riding horse. e, Up close portrait. f, With Nancy, greeting Pope John Paul II. g, Making speech at podium. h, Being sworn in as president. i, At desk in Oval Office.

2000fr, At desk, White House.

1999, Feb. 2 Litho. *Perf. 13½*

789 A189 450fr Sheet of 9, #a.-i. 14.00 14.00

Souvenir Sheet

790 A189 2000fr multicolored 6.50 6.50

American Railroads — A190

No. 791 — Train, railroad pioneer: a, "Alco" Santa Fe, 1945, Cyrus Holliday. b, Rio Grande, 1961, J.F. Stevens. c, Amtrak, 1976, Thomas Dehone Judah. d, 250 Gobernador, 1884, Mark Hopkins. e, Meeting of Central Pacific and Union Pacific at Promontory Point, 1869, Leland Stanford, Thomas Durant. f, Great Northern W1, 1947, Jim Hill. g, Union Pacific Railroad, 1951, G.M. Dodge. h, Pennsylvania GG1, 1934, S.M. Vauclain. i, 151 Santa Fe U.P, 1917, S. Barstow Strong.

1998, Dec. 11

791 A190 200fr Sheet of 9, #a.-i. 7.00 7.00

Fossils and Cave Paintings — A191

No. 792: a, Harlania enigmatica. b, Spirophyton. c, Fossils, dunes of Djourab. d, Chain of people, oxen, Bardai. e, Man of Gonoa. f, Oxen, Kozen, Borkou.

1998, Dec. 11

792 A191 150fr Sheet of 6, #a.-f. 4.00 4.00

Frank Sinatra — A191a

No. 792G — Sinatra with: h, Blonde actress. i, Green jacket. j, Ava Gardner. k, Striped suit. l, Actor. m, Gun. n, Dark green hat. o, Oscar statuette. p, Military cap.

1998, Dec. 30 Litho. *Perf. 13½*

792G A191a 300fr Sheet of 9, #h.-p. 9.50 9.50

James Dean (1931-55), Actor — A192

Various portraits.

1999, Feb. 2

793 A192 200fr Sheet of 9, #a.-i. 6.25 6.25

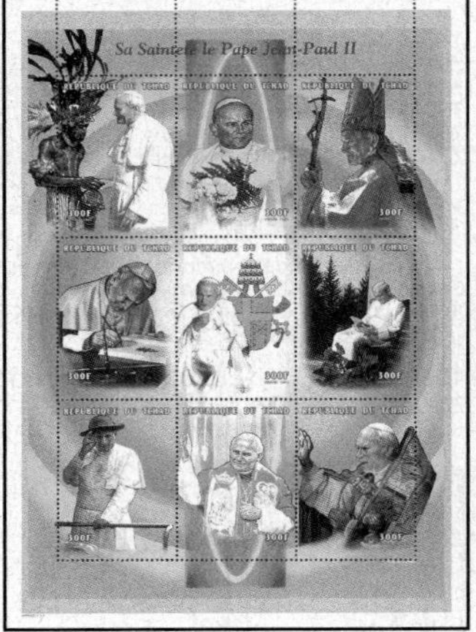

Pope John Paul II — A193

Various portraits.

1999, Feb. 2

794 A193 300fr Sheet of 9, #a.-i. 9.00 9.00

Souvenir Sheet

795 A193 1500fr multicolored 5.50 5.00

No. 795 contains one 58x51mm stamp.

John Glenn's Return to Space — A194

Various portraits.

1999, Feb. 11 Litho. *Perf. 13½*

796 A194 500fr Sheet of 9, #a.-i. 15.00 15.00

Souvenir Sheet

797 A194 2000fr multicolored 6.50 6.50

No. 797 contains one 57x51mm stamp.

Kofi Annan, UN Secretary-General — A195

Various portraits.

1998, Dec. 11

798 A195 150fr Sheet of 9, #a.-i. 4.75 4.75

Chess — A196

No. 798J: k, Paul Morphy. l, Chess board, Morphy-Anderssen, 1858. m, Adolf Anderssen. n, Emanuel Lasker. o, Chess board, Lasker-Capablanca, 1914. p, José Raul Capablanca. q, David Bronstein. r, Chess board, Bronstein-Botvinnik, 1951. s, Mikhail Botvinnik.

a, Bobby Fischer. b, Chess board, Fischer-Tal, 1961. c, Mikhail Tal. d, Boris Spassky. e, Chess board, Spassky-Petrosian, 1969. f, Tigran Petrosian. g, Garry Kasparov. h, Chess board, Kasparov-Karpov, 1960. i, Anatoly Karpov.

No. 800, Margrave Othon IV of Brandenburg.

No. 800A, King Louis XVI playing chess, horiz.

1999, Feb. 20

798J A196 375fr Sheet of 9, #k.-s. 11.00 11.00
799 A196 500fr Sheet of 9, #a.-i. 14.75 14.75

Souvenir Sheets

800 A196 2000fr multi 6.75 6.75
800A A196 2000fr multi 6.75 6.75

Dated 1998. No. 800 contains one 58x51mm stamp. No. 800A contains one 58x51mm stamp. Sheets of 3 stamps, containing Nos. 798Jk-798Jm, 798Jn-798Jp, 798Jq-798Js, 799a-799c, 799d-799f, or 799g-799i exist.

Souvenir Sheets

France, 1998 World Cup Champions — A197

No. 801: a, Bikente Lizarazu. b, Christian Karembeu. c, Frank Leboeuf. d, Emmanuel Petit.

No. 802: a, Fabien Barthez. b, Marcel Desailly. c, Didier Deschamps. d, Christophe Dugarry.

No. 803: Youri Djorkaeff. b, Aime Jacquet. c, Lilian Thuram. d, Zinedine Zidane.

2000fr, Deschamps holding World Cup.

1999, Feb. 20 Litho. ***Perf. 13½***

801 A197 300fr Sheet of 4, #a.-d. 4.00 4.00
802 A197 400fr Sheet of 4, #a.-d. 5.75 5.75
803 A197 500fr Sheet of 4, #a.-d. 7.25 7.25

Perf. 13¼

804 A197 2000fr multicolored 7.00 7.00

No. 804 contains one 57x51mm stamp.

Hokusai Paintings A198

Designs: a, Voyagers Crossing the Oi River. b, Bird. c, On Totomi Mountain. d, Evening at Ueno. e, Higashimachi-matsuri-yatai-tenjou. f, Evening shower at Yoshiwara. g. Woman with Umbrella. h, Cascade. i, Courtesan.

1999, Sept. 10 Litho. ***Perf. 13½***

805 A198 475fr Sheet of 9, #a.-i. 17.50 17.50

Japex '99.

Millennium — A199

No. 806 — Highlights of 1000-1899: a, Commercial routes in West Africa. b, Crusades. c, Notre Dame Cathedral. d, Ming dynasty tombs. e, Discovery of America. f, Albrecht Dürer. g, Sir Isaac Newton. h, American Independence. i, Napoleon.

No. 807 — 1900-24: a, Return of Halley's Comet. b, Lord Baden-Powell founds Scouting movement. c, Sinking of the Titanic. d, 1st film in Technicolor. e, Marconi sends 1st message across Atlantic, birth of radio. f, Harry Houdini. g, Capablanca-Lasker chess matches. h, Pierre & Marie Curie win Nobel Prize. i, Theft of the Mona Lisa.

No. 808 — 1925-49: a, Birth of Marilyn Monroe. b, Discovery of Pluto. c, Laurel and Hardy. d, Independence of India. e, Alexander Fleming discovers penicillin. f, Introduction of Volkswagen Beetle & Vespa motor scooter. g, Opening of film "Dracula." h, World War II. i, Discovery of Lascaux cave drawings.

No. 809 — 1950-74: a, 1st flight of the Concorde, 7 original astronauts. b, Death of Buddy Holly. c, 1st Super Bowl. d, Death of Eva Peron. e, Art by Andy Warhol. f, The Beatles. g, Cultural Revolution in China. h, Assassination of Pres. John F. Kennedy. i, Cuban Revolution.

No. 810 — 1975-99: a, Death of Princess Diana. b, Death of Enzo Ferrari. c, Akira. d, Argentina, 1986 World Cup Soccer champions. e, B. Lara breaks cricket records. f, France, 1998 World Cup Soccer champions. g, Explosion of the Space Shuttle Challenger. h, Pope John Paul II meets Lech Walesa. i, Deaths of Frank Sinatra, Freddie Mercury.

1999, Sept. 10

806 A199 150fr Sheet of 9, #a.-i. 5.25 5.25
807 A199 300fr Sheet of 9, #a.-i. 10.00 10.00
808 A199 450fr Sheet of 9, #a.-i. 15.00 15.00
809 A199 475fr Sheet of 9, #a.-i. 16.00 16.00
810 A199 500fr Sheet of 9, #a.-i. 16.00 16.00
Nos. 806-810 (5) 62.25 62.25

Souvenir Sheet

PhilexFrance '99 — A200

1999, Sept. 10

811 A200 1500fr multi 6.00 6.00

I Love Lucy — A201

No. 812: a, Lucy leaning against tree, Ricky. b, Lucy, Ricky kissing. c, Lucy pointing gun. d, Ricky falling to ground. e, Lucy in apartment. f, Ricky holding animal. g, Ricky drinking from canteen. h, Lucy, Ricky talking. i, Lucy behind bush.

No. 813, Lucy in grape vat. No. 814, Lucy, Ricky in bed.

1999, Feb. 20 Litho. ***Perf. 13¼***

812 A201 450fr Sheet of 9, #a.-i. 17.00 17.00

Souvenir Sheets

813 A201 1500fr multi 6.00 6.00
814 A201 2000fr multi 8.00 8.00

Dated 1998.

See Nos. 865-867.

Betty Boop — A202

No. 815: a, With cat and dog. b, In flowered dress. c, Looking back over shoulder. d, With hammer, dresser. e, As majorette. f, In red dress with fur collar. g, Holding paper. h, Holding blue dress. i, Holding telephone.

No. 816, With feathered hat. No. 817, In leopard-spotted blouse.

1999, Feb. 20 Litho. ***Perf. 13¼***

815 A202 450fr Sheet of 9, #a.-i. 16.00 16.00

Souvenir Sheets

816 A202 1500fr multi 5.00 5.00
817 A202 2000fr multi 7.00 7.00

Dated 1998.

See Nos. 856-858.

Antique Automobiles — A203

150fr, 1900 F.N. 300fr, 1906 Bianchi. 400fr, 1906 Renault. 500fr, 1919 Pierce-Arrow. 700fr, 1919 Citroen 5CV. 900fr, 1928 Ford. 1000fr, 1898 Renault.

1999 Litho. ***Perf. 13x12¾***

818-823 A203 Set of 6 11.00 11.00

Souvenir Sheet

Perf. 13x13¼

824 A203 1000fr multi 5.00 5.00

No. 824 contains one 40x31mm stamp.

Locomotives — A204

Designs: 150fr, 0-4-4-0. 300fr, Red 0-4-0. 400fr, Green 0-6-0. 500fr, Brown 0-4-0. 700fr, Blue 0-4-0. 900fr, Blue 0-6-0. 1000fr, Electric locomotive.

1999 ***Perf. 12¾***

825-830 A204 Set of 6 11.00 11.00

Souvenir Sheet

Perf. 13x13¼

831 A204 1000fr multi 5.00 5.00

No. 831 contains one 36x28mm stamp.

Wonders of Forgotten Cultures — A205

Designs: 50fr, Easter Island. 150fr, Stonehenge. 300fr, Jericho. 400fr, Machu Picchu. 500fr, Valley of Statues. 700fr, Chichén Itzá. 900fr, Persepolis.

1999 ***Perf. 12¾***

832-838 A205 Set of 7 15.00 15.00

Chad postal officials have declared the following items to be "not authorized:"

Set of six stamps of various denominations: New Year 2000 (Year of the Dragon)

Sheet of nine stamps of various denominations: Orchids

Sheet of nine 150fr stamps: Spanish Impressionist paintings

Sheet of nine 300fr stamps: Millennium (Composers), Van Gogh paintings

Sheet of nine 450fr stamps: Millennium (Marilyn Monroe), French Impressionist paintings

Sheet of nine 475fr stamps: Impressionist paintings

Sheet of nine 500fr stamps: Renoir nudes, Elvis Presley, Olympics

Souvenir sheets of one: Millennium (three 300fr, two 450fr, one 475fr, three 500fr, one 1500fr), New Year 2000 (1000fr), Palace of Versailles (1500fr, 2000fr), Hiroshige paintings (1500fr, 2000fr).

Minerals A206

Designs: 150fr, Wulfenite. 200fr, Argentite. 400fr, Siderite. 500fr, Dolomite and quartz. 700fr, Azurite. 900fr, Spinel and calcite. 1000fr, Cassiterite.

2000, Jan. 15 Litho. ***Perf. 12¾***

839-844 A206 Set of 6 14.00 14.00

Souvenir Sheet

845 A206 1000fr multi 5.00 5.00

Dated 1999.

Dogs — A206a

Designs: 150fr, Caucasian Mountain dog (Berger caucasique). 300fr, Belgian shepherd (Berger Belgue). 400fr, Spanish mastiff (Mâtin Espagne). 500fr, Kuvasz. 700fr, Beauceron. 900fr, Rough collie.

2000, Jan. 15 Litho. ***Perf. 13***

845A A206a 150fr multi —
845B A206a 300fr multi —
845C A206a 400fr multi —
845D A206a 500fr multi —
845E A206a 700fr multi —
845F A206a 900fr multi —

Dated 1999.

Elvis Presley — A207

No. 846: a, Playing guitar, wearing red jacket. b, Holding microphone and guitar, wearing red jacket. c, Holding guitar, wearing gold jacket. d, Playing guitar wearing black leather jacket. e, Playing guitar, wearing black jacket. f, Playing guitar, wearing blue jacket. g, Holding microphone, wearing blue shirt. h, Singing, wearing brown jacket. i, Holding microphone, wearing striped yellow jacket.

2000, Mar. 10 ***Perf. 13¼***

846 A207 300fr Sheet of 9, #a-i 10.00 10.00

Dated 1999.

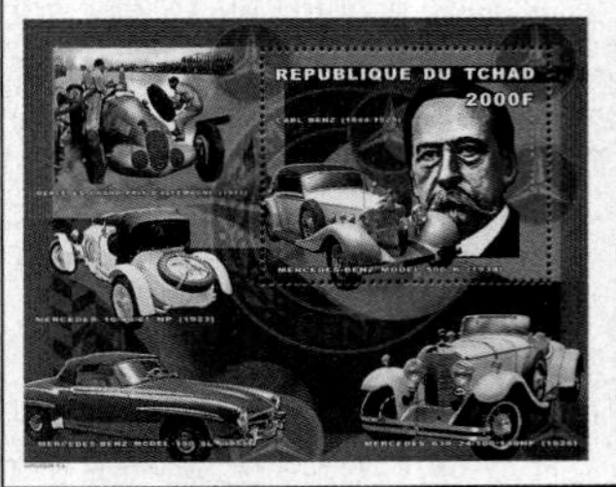

Carl Benz and Mercedes-Benz Automobiles — A208

No. 847: a, 1934 W-25. b, 1934 500 K. c, 1964 230 SL. d, 1935 150. e, 1954 300 SL. f, 1971 280 SE.

2000fr, 1934 500 K, diff.

2000, Mar. 10

847 A208 250fr Sheet of 6, #a-f 6.25 6.25

Souvenir Sheet

848 A208 2000fr multi 8.00 8.00

No. 847 contains six 30x30mm stamps. Dated 1999.

Trains — A209

No. 849: a, FES 3228, European Union flag. b, TGV Duplex, French flag. c, 500 Series Unit W1, Japanese flag. d, AVE Class 100, Spanish flag. e, ICE3, German flag. f, ETR 500, Italian flag.

2000fr, TGC 001 V56, TGV Duplex, Etienne Chambron.

2000, Mar. 10

849 A209 600fr Sheet of 6, #a-f 10.00 10.00

Souvenir Sheet

850 A209 2000fr multi 5.50 5.50

No. 849 contains six 30x30mm stamps. Dated 1999.

French Rulers — A210

No. 851, 150fr: a, Charlemagne. b, King Charles VIII. c, King Francis I. d, King Henry II. e, Catherine de Medici. f, King Henry III.

No. 852, 200fr: a, King Louis XII. b, King Louis XIII. c, King Louis XIV. d, King Louis XV. e, King Louis XVI. f, King Louis XVIII.

No. 853, 300fr — Napoleon Bonaparte: a, Standing, wearing red cape. b, On horseback, wearing red cape. c, On horseback, with soldier at right. d, On horseback, with crowd at right. e, Standing with other people. f, On white horse, leading battle.

2000, Mar. 10 **Sheets of 6, #a-f**

851-853 A210 Set of 3 17.50 17.50

Dated 1999.

Pope John Paul II — A211

No. 854 — Pope John Paul II and: a, Dalai Lama. b, Fidel Castro. c, King Hassan II of Morocco. d, Grand Rabbi Elio Toaff. e, Patriarch Bartholomew I. f, Mother Teresa.

2000, Mar. 10

854 A211 475fr Sheet of 6, #a-f 11.00 11.00

Dated 1999.

Space — A212

No. 855: a, Sputnik, dog Laika. b, Yuri Gagarin, Vostok 1. c, Konstantin Feoktistov, Vladimir Komarov, Boris Yegorov, Voskhod 1. d, Luna 1, chimpanzee Ham. e, Neil Armstrong, Michael Collins, Edwin Aldrin, Apollo 11. f, Aldrin, splashdown of capsule.

2000, Mar. 10

855 A212 500fr Sheet of 6, #a-f 11.00 11.00

Dated 1999.

Betty Boop Type of 1999

No. 856: a, Wearing red and violet striped leotard, kicking leg up. b, As cheerleader. c, At football field, holding pennant. d, At ice cream shop. e, Wearing yellow and green striped leotard. f, Wearing baseball cap and orange shorts. g, Wearing baseball cap and checked shirt. h, Seated, drinking beverage. i, Wearing cut-off shorts.

No. 857, 1500fr, Riding bicycle. No. 858, 2000fr, Wearing glasses, elbow and knee pads.

2000, Mar. 30

856 A202 250fr Sheet of 9, #a-i 8.50 8.50

Souvenir Sheets

857-858 A202 Set of 2 12.50 12.50

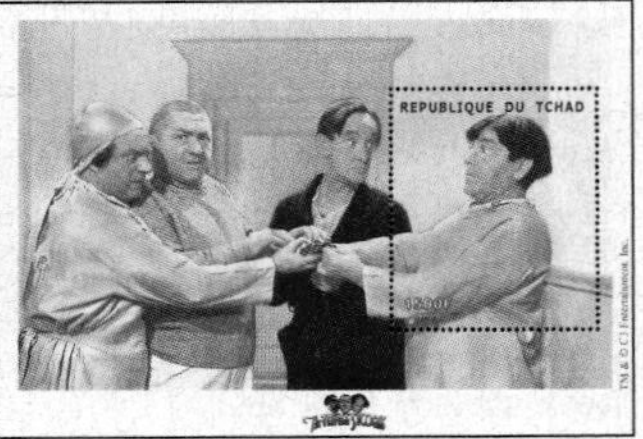

The Three Stooges — A213

No. 859, 250fr, horiz.: a, Larry, in surgeon's gown, and Curly. b, Curly, Moe, Larry around barrel. c, Moe, Larry and Curly on horse. d, Larry attacking man. e, Moe getting hair pulled. f, Moe with mallet. g, Curly, Moe and Larry in western outfits, outdoors. h, Larry, Curly and Moe in white doctor's jackets. i, Man looking at Moe.

No. 860, 300fr, horiz.: a, Larry grabbing Moe's chin. b, Moe and Larry holding scrolls. c, Moe, yellow background. d, Larry, blue background. e, Moe, Shemp and Larry. f, Shemp, blue background. g, Shemp, yellow background. h, Shemp pointing bellows at Larry. i, Moe and Larry in white.

No. 861, 1500fr, Moe in surgeon's gown. No. 862, 1500fr, Moe wearing hat. No. 863, 2000fr, Curly, Moe and Larry in western outfits, outdoors. No. 864, 2000fr, Larry with violin.

2000 **Sheets of 9, #a-i**

859-860 A213 Set of 2 20.00 20.00

Souvenir Sheets

861-864 A213 Set of 4 27.50 27.50

Issued: Nos. 859, 861, 863, 3/30; Nos. 860, 862, 864, 5/29.

I Love Lucy Type of 1999

No. 865: a, Lucy dancing, man in background. b, Lucy dancing, with knees bent and arms extended. c, Lucy in doorway. d, Lucy dancing behind sofa. e, Lucy kicking out leg. f, Lucy being caught by two men. g, Lucy with one arm extended. h, Lucy being sprayed with seltzer water. i, Lucy with leg on dance rail.

No. 866, 1500fr, Lucy looking at clock, horiz. No. 867, 2000fr, Lucy with clown costume and arms extended.

2000, May 29

865 A201 225fr Sheet of 9, #a-i 8.00 8.00

Souvenir Sheets

866-867 A201 Set of 2 14.50 14.50

N'Djamena, Cent. — A213a

Background colors: 150fr, Blue. 300fr, Red. 475fr, Green.

2000, May 29 **Litho.** ***Perf. 13¼***

867A-867C A213a Set of 3 — —

Chadian Political History — A214

No. 868, 150fr: a, Louis Léon César Faidherbe. b, François Joseph Lamy. c, Henri Eugène Gouraud. d, Gustav Nachtigal. e, Head of Rabah on spike. f, Fernand Foureau.

No. 869, 300fr: a, Pierre Savorgnan de Brazza. b, Philippe Marie de Hautecloque Leclerc. c, Emile Gentil. d, Gabriel Lisette. e, Charles de Gaulle. f, Felix Eboué.

2000, May 29 ***Perf. 13½***

Sheets of 6, #a-f

868-869 A214 Set of 2 16.00 16.00

Wildlife, Map of Chad, Scouting Emblem — A215

No. 870, 150fr — Giraffa camelopardalis: a, Pair, one with head lowered. b, Pair, both with heads extended. c, Pair near forest. d, Trio.

No. 871, 200fr: a, Pair of Gazella granti in field. b, Gazella cuiveri. c, Gazella dorcas. d, Pair of Gazella granti at waterhole.

No. 872, 250fr — Addax nasomaculatus: a, View of head. b, Lying in grass. c, Standing. d, Grazing.

No. 873, 300fr — Ammotragus lervia: a, Pair. b, View of head. c, Standing on mountain ledge. d, Standing, with purple mountain in background

No. 874, 375fr — Diceros bicornis: a, View of head. b, Facing right, line of dark green foliage in background. c, Facing left. d, Facing right, with trees in background.

No. 875, 400fr — Panthera pardus: a, On tree branch. b, Lying in grass. c, Standing. d, View of head.

No. 876, 450fr: a, Head of Theropithecus gelada. b, Cercopithecus aethiops. c, Papio anubis. d, Adult and juvenile Thereopithecus gelada.

No. 877, 450fr — Hippopotamus amphibius: a, Pair laying in mud. b, With open mouth. c, Standing. d, Herd.

No. 878, 475fr — Oryx dammah: a, Facing right, green foliage in background. b, View of head. c, Pair. d, Grazing, mountain in background.

No. 879, 500fr — Panthera leo: a, Male on female. b, Females at waterhole. c, Female and cub. d, Female and male.

No. 880, 600fr — Loxodonta africana: a, With tree at right. b, Facing right. c, View of head. d, With tree and mountain in background.

No. 881, 750fr — Syncerus caffer: a, Juvenile, adult grazing. b, Adult in field. c, Pair lying on ground. d, With grass in mouth.

No. 882, 1000fr, Pair of Diceros bicornis. No. 883, 1000fr, Pair of Hippopotamus amphibius fighting. No. 884, 1500fr, Panthera leo with kill.

Illustration reduced.

2000, Aug. 1 ***Perf. 13¼***

Horiz. Strips of 4, #a-d

870-881 A215 Set of 12 75.00 75.00

Souvenir Sheets

882-884 A215 Set of 3 14.00 14.00

Nos. 882-884 each contain one 36x51mm stamp.

Miniature Sheet

Baseball Player — A216

2000, Oct. 11 **Litho. & Embossed**
885 A216 3000fr gold & multi 10.00 10.00

Exists with silver background.

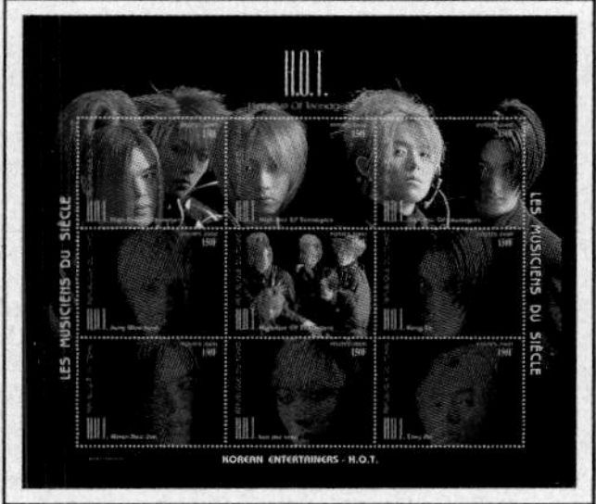

High-five of Teenagers — A217

No. 886: a, Moon Hee-jun and Lee Jae-won. b, Jang Woo-hyuk and ear of Tony An. c, Tony an and Kang Ta. d, Jang Woo-hyuk. e, Entire group. f, Kang Ta. g, Moon Hee-jun. h, Lee Jae-won. i, Tony An.

2000 **Litho.**
886 A217 150fr Sheet of 9, #a-i 4.50 4.50

Sports and Chess — A218

No. 887, 30fr — Dogs involved in sport activities: a, Sled dogs. b, Dog racing. c, Hunting dogs. d, Dogs and skier.

No. 888, 70fr — Various sports: a, Petanque. b, Rugby. c, Archery. d, Jai alai.

No. 889, 250fr — 2000 Summer Olympics, Sydney: a, Fencing. b, Judo. c, Tennis. d, Boxing.

No. 890, 300fr — 2000 Summer Olympics, Sydney: a, Cycling. b, Basketball. c, Beach volleyball. d, Baseball.

No. 891, 400fr — Soccer players: a, Zinedine Zidane. b, Lilian Thuram. c, Yuri Djorkaeff. d, Nicolas Anelka

No. 892, 475fr — 2000 Summer Olympics, Sydney: a, Table tennis. b, Equestrian. c, Swimming. d, Kayaking.

No. 893, 500fr — Golf: a, Man with white pants swinging club. b, Golfer analyzing putt. c, Man with black pants swinging club. d, Woman golfer.

No. 894, 750fr — Formula I race drivers: a, Michael Schumacher. b, Mikka Hakkinen. c, Ralf Schumacher. d, David Coulthard.

No. 895, 1000fr — Chess: a, Knight with shield. b, Knight on donkey. c, Knight with attendant. d, Horses and wheeled castle.

2000fr, Venus Williams.

2001, Jan. 31 ***Perf. 13¼***

Sheets of 4, #a-d

887-895 A218 Set of 9 75.00 75.00

Souvenir Sheet

896 A218 2000fr multi 9.00 9.00

2000 Summer Olympics, Sydney (No. 896). No. 896 contains one 36x51mm stamp.

Trains — A219

No. 897, 200fr: a, Mallard, 1935. b, P8 Prussian, 1908. c, F2A, 1936. b, 240 P, 1940.

No. 898, 300fr: a, NSB No. 3641. b, New Zealand Railways Sereis EW. c, Series 277, Renfe. d, Series DF4 Vent d'Est IV Co-Co.

No. 899, 400fr: a, SNCF Series 9100 2-D-2, 1950. b, SNCF Series 72000 C-C, 1967. c, CC 21000, 1969. d, VL-80, 1963.

No. 900, 475fr: a, GNER Eurostar. b, Electric EMU ETR 500. c, DER OBB 1016 001. d, GNER train.

No. 901, 500fr: a, OL-49, 1951. b, Pacific Series 16E, 1935. c, Andaluces 030, 1877. d, Franco-Crosti Gr. 743, 1937.

No. 902, 500fr: a, JR West 8-car unit E4. b, TGV KTX. c, 300 Series unit J3. d, E3 Series unit R6.

No. 903, 600fr: a, 2D2 PO, 1926. b, Metropolitan BB Vickers, 1920. c, DB ET 491, 1935. d, Series D, 1925.

No. 904, 600fr: a, Electric EMU 490. b, Acela, 2001. c, CFF-FFS Electric EMU RABe 500. d, ICE-T Bavereihe 41.

No. 905, 750fr: a, Single Driver, 1870. b, Great Western Railway Castle, 1923. c, Schools Class, 1930. d, 230 Besa, 1905.

No. 906, 750fr: a, TGV Thalys. b, TGV Duplex. c, TGV La Poste. d, TGV Atlantique.

1500fr, SAR Series 26 2-D-2. 2000fr, TGV Sud-est.

2001, June 22 **Litho.**

Sheets of 4, #a-d

897-906 A219 Set of 10 75.00 75.00

Souvenir Sheets

907-908 A219 Set of 2 13.50 13.50

Nos. 907-908 each contain one 51x36mm stamp.

British Royalty — A220

No. 909, 300fr — Queen Mother: a, With King George VI. b, With young daughter. c, With Prince Charles. d, Waving. e, Wearing tiara and yellow dress. f, Wearing pink dress and hat. g, Wearing green dress and hat. h, Holding flowers. i, With dogs.

No. 910, 300fr — Prince William wearing: a, Black suit with lapel handkerchief. b, Suit with red and blue vest. c, Suit with gold vest. d, Sweater, looking right. e, Black suit and dark blue tie. f, Sweater, facing forward. g, Blue shirt with button. h, Dark blue shirt without button. i, Light blue suit.

2001, July 22 ***Perf. 13¼***

Sheets of 9, #a-i

909-910 A220 Set of 2 20.00 20.00

No. 910 contains nine 36x51mm stamps.

French Rulers — A221

No. 911, 300fr: a, King Francis I. b, King Louis XIII. c, Elizabeth of Austria, consort of King Charles IX. d, King John II the Good.

No. 912, 375fr: a, King Louis XIV. b, King Francis I, diff. c, King Louis XVI. d, King Louis XVIII.

No. 913, 475fr: a, King Louis XV as child. b, King Louis XV as adult. c, Queen Marie Antoinette. d, King Charles VII.

No. 914, 500fr — Napoleon Bonaparte wearing: a, White tunic. b, Black jacket. c, Emperor's robes. d, Red tunic.

2001, July 22 **Sheets of 4, #a-d**

911-914 A221 Set of 4 25.00 25.00

Stamps of Nos. 911-913 exist in souvenir sheets of 1. Value, set $70.

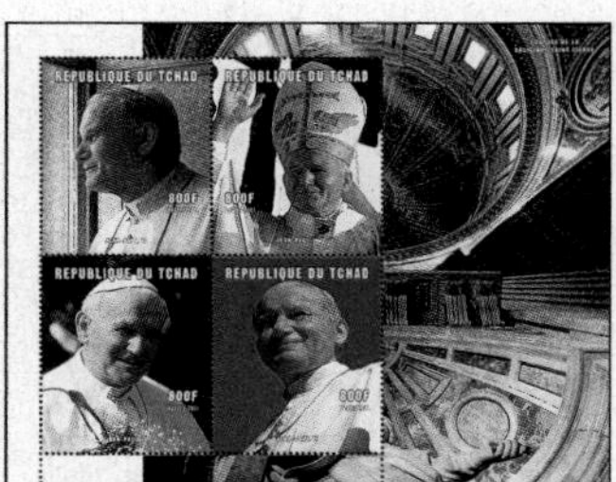

Pope John Paul II — A222

No. 915, 800fr: a, Standing in room, looking left. b, Waving, c, Holding flowers. d, With blue sky background.

No. 916, 1000fr: a, Wearing red hat. b, Wearing miter, waving. c, Bending to kiss ground. d, Wearing miter, holding crucifix.

4000fr, Wearing zucchetto.

2001 **Litho.** ***Perf. 13¼***

Sheets of 4, #a-d

915-916 A222 Set of 2 29.00 29.00

Miniature Sheet

Litho. & Embossed

917 A222 4000fr gold & multi 22.50 22.50

Issued: Nos. 915-916, 7/22; No. 917, 7/23. No. 917 contains one 60x90mm stamp and exists with a silver background. Stamps of Nos. 915-916 exist in souvenir sheets of 1. Value, set $60.

Famous Men — A223

Designs: 200fr, Charles Darwin (1809-82), naturalist. 250fr, Christopher Columbus (1451-1506), explorer. 300fr, Jacques-Yves Cousteau (1910-97), marine scientist. 350fr, Albert Schweitzer (1875-1965), missionary. 400fr, Juan Manuel Fangio (1911-95), race car driver. 450fr, Nicolaus Copernicus (1473-1543), astronomer. 500fr, Robert Stephenson (1803-59), engineer. 550fr, Etienne Chambron, high speed rail pioneer. 600fr, Garry Kasparov, chess player. 750fr, Lord Robert Baden-Powell (1857-1941), founder of scouting. 800fr, Neil Armstrong, astronaut. 1000fr, Sir Alexander Fleming (1881-1955), bacteriologist.

2001, Oct. 30 **Litho.**

918-929 A223 Set of 12 25.00 25.00

Nos. 918-929 exist in souvenir sheets of 1. Value, set $115.

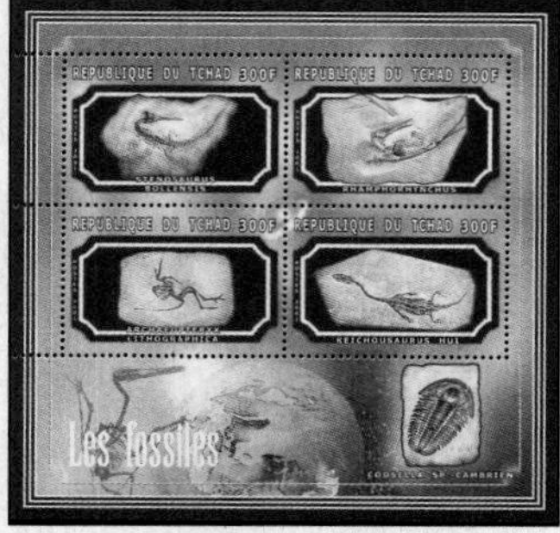

Fossils, Dinosaurs, Meteorites and Minerals — A224

No. 930, 300fr — Fossils: a, Stenosaurus bollensis. b, Rhamphorhynchus. c, Archaeopteryx lithographica. d, Keichousaurus hui.

No. 931, 375fr — Dinosaurs: a, Mesadactylus. b, Pteranodon. c, Tropeognathus. d, Quetzalcoatlus.

No. 932, 400fr — Meteorites found in: a, India. b, Nigeria. c, US. d, Australia.

No. 933, 500fr — Dinosaurs: a, Deinonychus. b, Seismosaurus. c, Pleurocoelus, Acrocanthosaur. d, Styracosaurus.

No. 934, 500fr — Minerals: a, Fluorite. b, Pyrite. c, Wulfenite. d, Merovingian scoria.

No. 935, 550fr — Meteorites found in: a, Antarctica. b, Libya. c, USSR. d, China.

No. 936, 600fr — Minerals: a, Magnetite. b, Kunzite. c, Apophyllite, Stilbite. d, Fluorite, diff.

No. 937, 750fr — Minerals: a, Quartz. b, Merovingian scoria, diff. c, Epidote. d, Amethyst, agate.

3000fr, Tyrannosaurus rex, vert.

2001, Dec. 27 **Litho.**

Sheets of 4, #a-d

930-937 A224 Set of 8 70.00 70.00

Miniature Sheet

Litho. & Embossed

938 A224 3000fr gold & multi 17.00 17.00

No. 938 contains one 60x90mm stamp and exists with silver background.

French Kings — A225

Designs: No. 939, 3000fr, Louis IX. No. 940, 3000fr, Francis I. No. 941, 3000fr, Henry IV. No. 942, 3000fr, Louis XIII. No. 943, 3000fr, Louis XV.

2002, Apr. 10 **Litho. & Embossed**

Gold & Multicolored

939-943 A225 Set of 5 50.00 50.00

Nos. 939-943 exist with silver background.

Egyptian Treasures A225a

Designs: No. 943A, 3000fr, Painted wooden box. No. 943B, 3000fr, Nekhbet vulture. No. 943C, 3000fr, Oushebti of Tutankhamen, vert. No. 943D, 3000fr, Pair of royal scepters, vert. No. 943E, 3000fr, Diadem, vert. No. 943F, 3000fr, Gold-plated throne, vert. No. 943G, 3000fr, Cynocephalic pectoral, vert. No. 943H, 3000fr, Coffin of Tutankhamen, vert. No. 943I, 3000fr, Statue of Ka, vert. No. 943J, 3000fr, Duck earring, vert. No. 943K, 3000fr, Lion-shaped vase, vert. No. 943L, 3000fr, Canopic dais and chapel, vert.

Embossed on Gold Paper

2002, Apr. 10 ***Perf. 13¼***

943A-943L A225a Set of 12 140.00 140.00

Artists and Their Paintings — A226

On Nos. 944-957, painting titles (in French) and artist's birth and death dates are in margins adjacent to each stamp. On Nos. 958-962 painting titles are not shown, but artist's name is in sheet margin

No. 944, 150fr: a, Berthe Morisot (1841-95). b, Cache-cache. c, Le Berceau. d, Au bal. e, Jeune femme se poudrant. f, Paule Gobillard peignant.

No. 945, 200fr: a, Marc Chagall (1887-1985). b, Nature morte. c, Le violoniste vert. d, La maison bleue. e, Mariage. f, Le soldat ivre.

No. 946, 250fr: a, Camille Pissarro (1830-1903). b, Les chataigniers a Osny. c, Le verger. d, Le repos des glaneuses. e, Jeune paysanne prenant son cafe. f, Le bergére.

No. 947, 300fr: a, Alfred Sisley (1839-99). b, Le pont de Villeneuve la Garenne. c, Allee de jardin a Louveciennes. d, Meule de foin bord du Loing. e, Moret sur Loing. f, Moulin a Moret.

No. 948, 325fr: a, Paul Delvaux (1897-1994). b, La voix publique. c, Nocturnes. d, Balgnade des Nymphes. e, Pygmalion. f, Jeunes femmes revant.

No. 949, 350fr: a, Edouard Manet (1832-83). b, Le Déjeuner sur l'herbe. c, Olympia. d, Le fifre. e, La serveuse de bocks. f, Le balcon.

No. 950, 375fr: a, Vincent van Gogh (1853-90). b, Champ de blé avec cypres. c, Rue a Auvers. d, La sieste. e, Chambre jaune a Arles. f, Rue de village.

No. 951, 400fr: a, Salvador Dali (1904-89). b, Cannibalisme en automne. c, Corpus Hypercubicus. d, Le sommeil. e, Le tentation de St. Antoine. f, Meditation sur harpe.

No. 952, 425fr: a, Paul Cézanne (1839-1906). b, Les baigneurs. c, Les grandes baigneuses (light blue background). d, Les grandes baigneuses, diff. (dark blue background). e, Les baigneueses. f, Les baigneurs au repos.

No. 953, 450fr: a, Pablo Picasso (1881-1973). b, Les demoiselles d'Avignon. c, Femme a l'eventail. d, La danse. e, La vie. f, La mere et son fils.

No. 954, 475fr: a, Amadeo Modigliani (1884-1920). b, Nu souche sur un divan. c, Nu debout. d, Cariatide debout. e, Nu allongé. f, Nu assis de dos.

No. 955, 500fr: a, Auguste Renoir (1841-1919). b, Diane chasseresse. c, Nu allongé. d, Baigneuses. e, Baigneuse assise. f, Nymphe au printemps.

No. 956, 550fr: a, Edgar Degas (1834-1917). b, Femme se coiffant. c, Aprés le bain (view of front of seated woman). d, Femme se peignant. e, Aprés le bain (view of back of woman). f, Aprés le bain (woman dressing).

No. 957, 600fr: a, Henri Matisse (1869-1954). b, Le nu bleu. c, Le genou levé. d, Nu assis sur un fauteuil. e, Odalisques. f, Nu allongé.

No. 958, 1500fr, Gustave Caillebotte. No. 959, 1500fr, Picasso, diff. No. 960, 1500fr, Auguste Renoir, diff. No. 961, 2000fr, Pablo Picasso, diff. No. 962, 2000fr, Van Gogh, diff.

2002, Apr. 10 ***Perf. 12¾x13¼***

Sheets of 6, #a-f

944-957 A226 Set of 14 110.00 110.00

Souvenir Sheets

Perf. 13¼x12¾

958-962 A226 Set of 5 27.50 27.50

Nos. 944a-955a and 957a exist in souvenir sheets of 1 that are perf. 13¼x12¾. Value, set $92.50.

Miniature Sheet

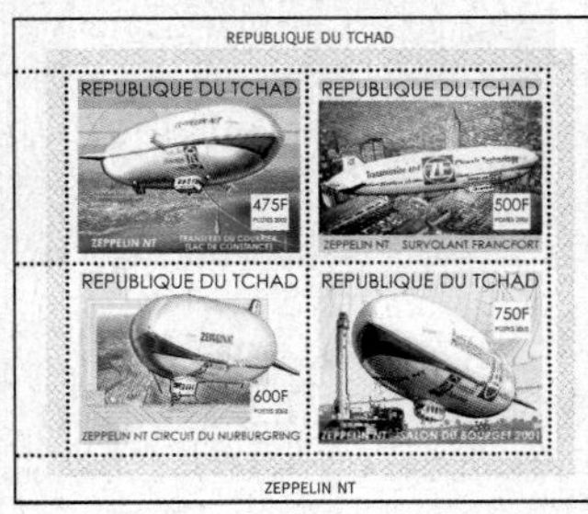

Zeppelin NT — A227

No. 963: a, 475fr, Over Lake Constance. b, 500fr, Over Frankfurt. c, 600fr, Over Nürburgring, Germany. d, 750fr, At 2001 Salon du Bourget.

2002, Oct. 30 ***Perf. 13¼***

963 A227 Sheet of 4, #a-d 10.00 10.00

Nos. 963a-963d exist in souvenir sheets of 1. Value, set $45.

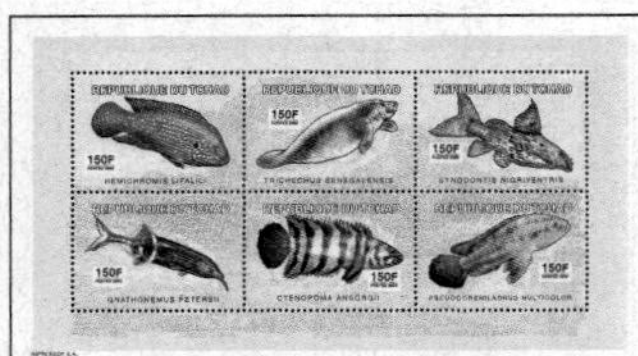

Fauna and Mushrooms — A228

No. 964, 150fr: a, Hemichromis lifalili. b, Trichechus senegalensis. c, Synodontis nigriventris. d, Gnathonemus petersii. e, Ctenopoma ansorgii. f, Pseudocrenilabrus multicolor.

No. 965, 300fr, vert.: a, Nectarina venusta. b, Lamprotornis splendidus. c, Poicephalus meyeri. d, Halcyon leucocephala. e, Quelea quelea. f, Merops pusillus.

No. 966, 350fr, vert.: a, Terathopius ecaudatus. b, Gymnogyps californianus. c, Buteo jamaicensis. d, Lophaetus occipitalis. e, Aquila rapax. f, Melierax metabates.

No. 967, 375fr, vert.: a, Elanus caeruleus. b, Harpia harpyja. c, Gyps rueppellii. d, Milvus migrans. e, Torgos tracheliotus. f, Aquila chrysaetos.

No. 968, 550fr: a, Kallimoides rumia. b, Zophopetes dysmephila. c, Megalopalpus zymna. d, Coeliades forestan. e, Catopsilia florella. f, Anaphaesis aurota.

No. 969, 600fr: a, Amanita muscaria. b, Amanita rubescens. c, Cortinarius orellanus. d, Hygrophorus hypothejus. e, Leccinum piceinum. f, Strobilomyces strobilaceus.

2003, June 2 **Litho.**

Sheets of 6, #a-f

964-969 A228 Set of 6 55.00 55.00

Stamps of Nos. 965-969 exist in a set of twelve souvenir sheets of two, with each souvenir sheet of two containing adjacent stamps found in the sheet of six. Value, set $160.

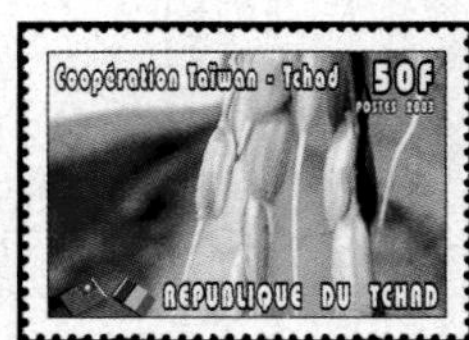

Chad — Taiwan Cooperation — A229

Flags and: 50fr, Grain. 100fr, Surgeon's hands, Red Cross. 150fr, Bridge. 300fr, Handshake, maps.

2003, Dec. 1

970-973	A229 Set of 4		2.50	2.50
973a	Booklet pane, 2 each #970-973		5.00	—
	Complete booklet, #973a		5.00	
973b	Souvenir sheet, #970-973		2.50	2.50

AIDS Prevention A230

Red ribbon and: 50fr, People under umbrella. 100fr, Man and woman. 150fr, Doctor. 300fr, "Prudence, Abstinence, Fidelité."

2004, July 7 **Litho.** ***Perf. 13x12¾***

974-977 A230 Set of 4 2.50 2.50

Opening of Petroleum Refinery, 1st Anniv. A231

Pres. Idriss Deby opening pipeline and: 150fr, Storage tank. 350fr, Storage tanks. 400fr, Refinery. 500fr, Tower, vert.

2004, Oct. 10 ***Perf. 12¾x13, 13x12¾***

978-981 A231 Set of 4 6.50 6.50

Women's Hairstyles A232

Designs: 150fr, Figuerier. 350fr, Sakkindjala. 550fr, Kileskou. 575fr, Dabbou.

2005, Mar. 8 ***Perf. 13***

982-985 A232 Set of 4 8.00 8.00

Toumai Skull A233

Color of skull: 25fr, Purple. 50fr, Green. 100fr, Gray. 150fr, Red. 1500fr, Gray.

2005, July 19 **Litho.** ***Perf. 12¾x13***

986-989 A233 Set of 4 1.40 1.40

Souvenir Sheet

990 A233 1500fr multi 5.75 5.75

Campaign Against Trypanosomiasis, 10th Anniv. — A234

Tsetse fly and: 150fr, Trypanosomiasis protozoa, eradication campaign emblem. 300fr, Eradication campaign emblem, map of Africa. 350fr, Pan-African Postal Union emblem, eradication campaign emblem, map of Africa. 550fr, Trypanosomiasis protozoa, maps of Chad and Africa.

2010 ***Perf. 12¾***

991-994 A234 Set of 4 5.50 5.50

Independence, 50th Anniv. — A235

Emblem with denomination color of: 150fr, Red. 300fr, White. 350fr, Yellow. 550fr, Blue.

2010

995-998 A235 Set of 4 5.50 5.50

A236

Designs: No. 999, 150fr, Cyphotilapia frontosa, Lysmata amboinensis. No. 1000, 150fr, Cyrtocara moorii, Potamonautes maculata. No. 1001, 150fr, Placidochromis milomo, Sesarma mederi. No. 1002, 150fr, Tropheus brichardi, Atyopsis gabonensis. No. 1003, 200fr, Phocidae, Swakopmund Lighthouse, Namibia. No. 1004, 200fr, Odobenus rosmarus, Nosy Iranja Lighthouse, Madagascar. No. 1005, 200fr, Lobodon carcinophaga, Pelican Point Lighthouse, Namibia. No. 1006, 200fr, Odobenus rosmarus, Katsepy Lighthouse, Madagascar. No. 1007, 300fr, Morus capensis, Pointe-Noire Lighthouse, Congo. No. 1008, 300fr, Phalacrocorax capensis, Slangkop Point Lighthouse, South Africa. No. 1009, 300fr, Fregata magnificens, Cap Agulhas Lighthouse, South Africa. No. 1010, 300fr, Phalacrocorax melanoleucos, Ngombe Lighthouse, Gabon. No. 1011, 300fr, Strombus gibberulus albus, Grand Bassam Lighthouse, Ivory Coast. No. 1012, 300fr, Argonauta cornuta, Cap Blanc Lighthouse, Mauritania. No. 1013, 300fr, Calpurnus verrucosus, Conakry Lighthouse, Guinea. No. 1014, 300fr, Haliotis quekettі, Cap Miné Lighthouse, Madagascar. No. 1015, 350fr, Galeocerdo cuvier, Cherchell Lighthouse, Algeria. No. 1016, 350fr, Isurus paucus, l'ilot d'Arzew Lighthouse, Algeria. No. 1017, 350fr, Sphyrna mokarran, Amirauté Lighthouse, Algeria. No. 1018, 350fr, Carcharodon carcharias, Cap Ivi Lighthouse, Algeria. No. 1019, 500fr, Amanita jacksonii, Eugaster spinulosa. No. 1020, 500fr, Amanita caesarea, Zographus regalis. No. 1021, 500fr, Armillaria gallica, Megaponera foetens. No. 1022, 500fr, Sarcoscypha coccinea, Mylabris sp. No. 1023, 600fr, Cystodermella cinnabarina, Schistocerca gregaria. No. 1024, 600fr, Marasmius rotula, Palpopleura lucia. No. 1025, 600fr, Periphragmoides lysurus, Myrmeleontidae. No. 1026, 600fr, Boletus edulis, Trithemis kirbyi. No. 1027, 750fr, Fluorine. No. 1028, 750fr, Malachite. No. 1029, 750fr, Pyrite. No. 1030, 750fr, Vanadinite.

2012, Sept. 4 **Litho.** ***Perf. 13¼***

999-1030 A236 Set of 32 50.00 50.00

Nos. 999-1030 each exist in souvenir sheets of 1.

SEMI-POSTAL STAMPS

Catalogue values for unused stamps in this section are for Never Hinged items.

Anti-Malaria Issue

Common Design Type

Perf. 12½x12

1962, Apr. 7 **Engr.** **Unwmk.**

B1 CD108 25fr + 5fr orange 1.00 .50

Freedom from Hunger Issue

Common Design Type

1963, Mar. 21 ***Perf. 13***

B2 CD112 25fr + 5fr dk grn, dk bl & brn 1.10 .50

Red Cross, Mother and Children — SP1

1974, Oct. 2 Photo. ***Perf. 12½x13***
B3 SP1 30fr + 10fr multi 1.25 .40

Red Cross of Chad, first anniversary.

AIR POST STAMPS

Catalogue values for unused stamps in this section are for Never Hinged items.

Olympic Games Issue

French Equatorial Africa No. C37 Surcharged in Red

Unwmk.
1960, Dec. 15 Engr. ***Perf. 13***
C1 AP8 250fr on 500fr grnsh blk, blk & slate 10.00 6.00

17th Olympic Games, Rome, Aug. 25-Sept. 11. Surcharge 46mm wide.

Red Bishops — AP1

Birds in pairs: 100fr, Scarlet-chested sunbird. 200fr, African paradise flycatcher. 250fr, Malachite kingfisher. 500fr, Nubian carmine bee-eater.

1961-63 Unwmk. Engr. ***Perf. 13***
C2 AP1 50fr dk grn, mag & blk 1.00 .35
C3 AP1 100fr multi 3.25 1.25
C4 AP1 200fr multi 5.75 1.90
C5 AP1 250fr dk bl, grn & dp org ('63) 7.50 3.00
C6 AP1 500fr multi 17.50 9.50
Nos. C2-C6 (5) 35.00 16.00

Air Afrique Issue

Common Design Type

1962, Feb. 17 Unwmk. ***Perf. 13***
C7 CD107 25fr lt bl, org brn & blk 1.00 .25

Abidjan Games Issue

Discus Thrower — AP2

1962, July 21 Photo. ***Perf. 12x12½***
C8 AP2 100fr brn, lt grn & blk 3.00 1.00

African Postal Union Issue

Common Design Type

1963, Sept. 8 Unwmk. ***Perf. 12½***
C9 CD114 85fr dk bl, ocher & red 1.80 .60

Air Afrique Issue, 1963

Common Design Type

1963, Nov. 19 ***Perf. 13x12***
C10 CD115 50fr multi 1.80 .60

Europafrica Issue

Common Design Type

1963, Nov. 30 Photo. ***Perf. 12x13***
C11 CD116 50fr dp grn, yel & dk brn 1.60 .50

Mail Truck and Broussard Plane — AP4

Unwmk.
1963, Dec. 16 Engr. ***Perf. 13***
C12 AP4 100fr sl grn, ultra & red brn 3.00 .90

Chiefs of State Issue

Map and Presidents of Chad, Congo, Gabon and Central African Republic AP4a

1964, June 23 Photo. ***Perf. 12½***
C13 AP4a 100fr multi 1.70 .60

See note after Central African Republic No. C19.

Europafrica Issue

Globe and Emblems of Industry and Agriculture — AP5

1964, July 20 ***Perf. 13x12***
C14 AP5 50fr brn, pur & dp org 1.60 .40

See note after Cameroun No. 402.

Soccer — AP6

Designs: 50fr, Javelin throw, vert. 100fr, High jump, vert. 200fr, Runners.

1964, Aug. 12 Engr. ***Perf. 13***
C15 AP6 25fr yel grn, sl grn & org brn .75 .30
C16 AP6 50fr org brn, ind & brt bl 1.50 .60
C17 AP6 100fr blk, red & brt grn 2.75 1.00
C18 AP6 200fr bis, blk & car 4.75 2.00
a. Min. sheet of 4, #C15-C18 14.00 6.50
Nos. C15-C18 (4) 9.75 3.90

18th Olympic Games, Tokyo, 10/10-25/64.

Communications Symbols — AP7

1964, Nov. 2 Litho. ***Perf. 12½x13***
C19 AP7 25fr lil, dk brn & lt red brn .80 .25

Pan-African and Malagasy Posts and Telecommunications Cong., Cairo, Oct. 24-Nov. 6.

President John F. Kennedy (1917-63) — AP8

1964, Nov. 3 Photo. ***Perf. 12½***
C20 AP8 100fr multi 1.90 .75
a. Souvenir sheet of 4 12.00 6.00

ICY Emblem — AP9

1965, July 5 Photo. ***Perf. 13***
C21 AP9 100fr multi 1.80 .60

International Cooperation Year, 1965.

Abraham Lincoln — AP10

1965, Sept. 7 Unwmk. ***Perf. 13***
C22 AP10 100fr multi 2.00 .75

Centenary of death of Abraham Lincoln.

Musical Instrument Type

Design: 100fr, Xylophone (marimba).

1965, Oct. 26 Engr. ***Perf. 13***
Size: 48x27mm
C23 A18 100fr ocher, brt bl & vio bl 2.00 1.00

Sir Winston Spencer Churchill (1874-1965) AP11

1965, Nov. 23 Engr. ***Perf. 13***
C24 AP11 50fr dk grn & blk 1.50 .50

Dr. Albert Schweitzer and Outstretched Hands — AP12

1966, Feb. 15 Photo. ***Perf. 12½***
C25 AP12 100fr multi 2.75 .80

Dr. Albert Schweitzer (1875-1965), medical missionary, theologian and musician.

Air Afrique Issue, 1966

Common Design Type

1966, Aug. 31 Photo. ***Perf. 13***
C26 CD123 30fr yel grn, blk & gray .85 .25

White-throated Bee-eater — AP13

Birds: 50fr, Blue-eared glossy starling. 200fr, African pygmy kingfisher. 250fr, Red-throated bee-eater. 500fr, Little green bee-eater.

1966-67 Photo. ***Perf. 13x12½***
C27 AP13 50fr gold & multi 1.20 .40
C28 AP13 100fr bluish gray & multi 2.75 1.00
C29 AP13 200fr grnsh gray & multi 5.25 1.75
C30 AP13 250fr pale bl & multi 6.00 1.75
C31 AP13 500fr pale sal & multi 11.00 3.25
Nos. C27-C31 (5) 26.20 8.15

Issued: 100fr, 200fr, 500fr, 8/18/66; others, 3/21/67.

For surcharges see Nos. C67-C69.

Congress Hall — AP14

1967, Jan. 5 Photo. ***Perf. 12½***
C32 AP14 25fr multi .70 .25

Opening of the new Congress Hall.

Breguet 19 Biplane — AP15

Planes: 30fr, Latécoère 631 hydroplane. 50fr, Douglas DC-3. 100fr, Piper Cherokee 6.

1967, Aug. 1 Engr. *Perf. 13*

C33	AP15	25fr sky bl, sl grn & lt brn	.75	.25
C34	AP15	30fr sky bl, indigo & grn	1.00	.30
C35	AP15	50fr sky bl, ol bis & sl grn	1.75	.60
C36	AP15	100fr dk bl, sl grn & dk red	3.50	.90
		Nos. C33-C36 (4)	7.00	2.05

First anniversary of Air Chad.

African Postal Union Issue, 1967
Common Design Type

1967, Sept. 9 Engr. *Perf. 13*

C37	CD124	100fr ol, brt pink & red brn	2.00	.60

Rock Painting Type of Regular Issue

1967, Dec. 19 Engr. *Perf. 13*
Size: 48x27mm

C38	A32	100fr Masked dancers	4.00	.95
C39	A32	125fr Rabbit hunt	4.50	1.50

Downhill Skiing — AP16

1968, Feb. 5 Engr. *Perf. 13*

C40	AP16	30fr shown	1.25	.30
C41	AP16	100fr Ski jump, vert.	3.25	.90

10th Winter Olympic Games, Grenoble, France, Feb. 6-18.

Konrad Adenauer (1876-1967), Chancellor of West Germany (1949-63) AP17

1968, Mar. 19 Photo. *Perf. 12½*

C42	AP17	52fr grn, dk brn & lt lil	1.30	.50
a.		Souvenir sheet of 4	5.00	4.50

The Snake Charmer, by Henri Rousseau — AP18

Design: 130fr, "War" by Henri Rousseau.

1968, May 14 Photo. *Perf. 13½*
Size: 41x41mm

C43	AP18	100fr ultra & multi	3.50	1.00

Size: 48x35mm
Perf. 12½

C44	AP18	130fr brn & multi	5.50	1.50

Hurdlers — AP19

1968, Oct. 16 Engr. *Perf. 13*

C45	AP19	32fr shown	1.00	.40
C46	AP19	80fr Relay race	2.25	.80

19th Olympic Games, Mexico City, 10/12-27.

PHILEXAFRIQUE Issue

The Actor Wolf (Bernard), by Jacques L. David AP20

1969, Jan. 15 Photo. *Perf. 12½*

C47	AP20	100fr multi	2.90	1.75

PHILEXAFRIQUE, Philatelic Exhib. in Abidjan, Feb. 14-23. Printed with alternating label. Value is for stamp with label attached.

2nd PHILEXAFRIQUE Issue
Common Design Type

50fr, Chad #J12 and Moundang Dancers.

1969, Feb. 14 Engr. *Perf. 13*

C48	CD128	50fr red, brt bl, brn & grn	2.40	1.00

Gustav Nachtigal and Tibesti Gorge, 1869 — AP21

No. C50, Heinrich Barth & Lake Chad, 1851.

1969, Feb. 17

C49	AP21	100fr vio bl, dk brn & brn	2.40	.60
C50	AP21	100fr grn, pur & bl	2.40	.60

German explorers Gustav Nachtigal (1834-85) and Heinrich Barth (1821-65), and state visit of the Pres. of West Germany Heinrich Lubke.

Apollo 8, Earth and Moon — AP22

1969, Apr. 10 Photo. *Perf. 13*

C51	AP22	100fr multi	2.50	.75

US Apollo 8 mission, the 1st men in orbit around the moon, Dec. 21-27, 1968.

Mahatma Gandhi — AP23

No. C53, John F. Kennedy. No. C54, Dr. Martin Luther King, Jr. No. C55, Robert F. Kennedy.

1969, May 20 Photo. *Perf. 12½*

C52	AP23	50fr blk & lt grn	1.25	.40
C53	AP23	50fr blk & tan	1.25	.40
C54	AP23	50fr blk & pink	1.25	.40
C55	AP23	50fr blk & lt vio bl	1.25	.40
a.		Souvenir sheet of 4, #C52-C55	6.00	6.00
		Nos. C52-C55 (4)	5.00	1.60

Issued to honor exponents of non-violence.

Presidents Tombalbaye and Mobutu, Map and Flags of Chad and Congo — AP24

Embossed on Gold Foil

1969 *Die-cut Perf. 13½*

C56	AP24	1000fr gold, dk bl & red	27.50	27.50

1st anniv. of the establishment of the Union of Central African States, comprising Chad, Congo Democratic Republic and Central African Republic.

Napoleon Visiting Hospital, by Alexandre Veron-Bellecourt — AP25

Paintings: 85fr, Battle of Wagram, by Horace Vernet. 130fr, Battle of Austerlitz, by Francois Pascal Gerard.

1969, July 23 Photo. *Perf. 12x12½*

C57	AP25	30fr multi	1.20	.40
C58	AP25	85fr multi	2.50	.75
C59	AP25	130fr multi	4.50	1.25
		Nos. C57-C59 (3)	8.20	2.40

Bicentenary of birth of Napoleon I.

Apollo 11 Issue

Astronaut on Moon — AP26

Embossed on Gold Foil

1969, Oct. 17 *Die-cut Perf. 13½*

C60	AP26	1000fr gold	27.50	27.50

See note after Algeria No. 427.

Village Life, by Goto Narcisse — AP27

No. 62, Women at the Market, by Iba N'Diaye. No. 63, Woman with Flowers, by Iba N'Diaye, vert.

1970 Photo. *Perf. 12x12½, 12½x12*

C61	AP27	100fr multi	3.25	.75
C62	AP27	250fr grn & multi	5.00	1.00
C63	AP27	250fr brn & multi	5.00	1.00
		Nos. C61-C63 (3)	13.25	2.75

Issued: 100fr, Mar. 17; Nos. C62-C63, Aug. 28.

Napoleon — AP27a

Designs: Nos. C63A, C63E, Napoleon II, Duke of Reichstadt, vert.

No. C63B: g, 10fr, Crossing the Grand St. Bernard, by David. h, 25fr, Emperor Napoleon, by Gerard. i, 32fr, Marriage of Napoleon and Marie Louise, by Rouget.

40fr, Napoleon after return from Elba, vert.

Perf. 12x12½, 12½x12

1970-71 Litho.

C63A	AP27a	10fr multicolored	4.00	—
C63B	AP27a	Strip of 3, #g.-i.	14.00	—

Embossed
Perf. 13

C63C	AP27a	10fr gold	20.00	—
f.		Sheet of 1, Imperf.	37.50	—

Souvenir Sheets
Litho.
Perf. 13x13½

C63D	AP27a	40fr multicolored	10.00	—

Embossed
Imperf

C63E	AP27a	10fr gold, like #C63A	37.50	—

No. C63A is printed se-tenant with label. No. C63D contains one 43x67mm stamp. No. C63Cf contains one 53x42mm stamp with same size design as No. C63Bg. No. C63E contains one 43x104mm stamp with same size design as No. C63A.

No. C63E probably was not available in Chad.

Issued: No. C63B, 6/12; Nos. C63A, C63D-C63E, 4/1971; No. C63C, 11/1/71.

EXPO Emblem and Osaka Print — AP28

EXPO Emblem and: 100fr, Tower of the Sun. 125fr, Osaka print, diff.

1970, June 30 Engr. *Perf. 13*

C64 AP28 50fr bl, red brn & sl grn .70 .25
C65 AP28 100fr red, yel grn & Prus bl 1.40 .40
C66 AP28 125fr blk, dk red & bis 1.90 .60
Nos. C64-C66 (3) 4.00 1.25

Issued to publicize EXPO '70 International Exhibition, Osaka, Japan, Mar. 15-Sept. 13.

1968 Summer Olympics, 1970 World Cup Soccer Championships, Mexico AP28a

5fr, Flags, soccer players. 15fr, Olympic torch, soccer player.

1970, July 1 Litho. *Perf. 12½x12*

C66A AP28a 5fr multicolored 1.50

Souvenir Sheet

Perf. 13½x13

C66C AP28a 15fr multicolored 6.50

No. C66A printed in sheets of 2 + 2 labels. No. C66C contains one 66x43mm stamp.

For overprints see Nos. C88A-C88B.

Nos. C28-C30 Surcharged and Overprinted in Carmine

a

b

c

1970, July 9 Photo. *Perf. 13x12½*

C67 AP13 (a) 50fr on 100fr 1.70 .25
C68 AP13 (b) 100fr on 200fr 2.75 .45
C69 AP13 (c) 125fr on 250fr 4.00 .55
Nos. C67-C69 (3) 8.45 1.25

Space missions of Apollo 11, 12 and 13.

DC-8 "Fort Lamy" over Airport — AP29

1970, Aug. 5 *Perf. 12½*

C70 AP29 30fr dk sl grn & multi 1.30 .30

Souvenir Sheet

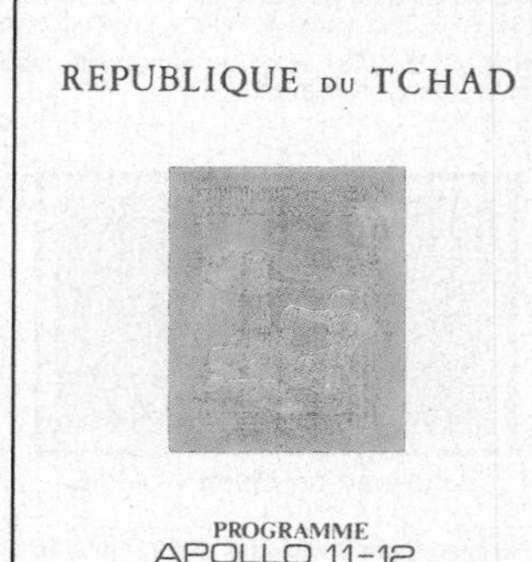

Apollo 12 — AP29a

1970, Sept. Embossed *Perf. 12¾*

C70A AP29a 25fr gold 18.00

No. C70A exists imperf. Value, $35.

No. C70A probably was not available in Chad.

The Visitation, Venetian School, 15th Century AP30

Paintings, Venetian School: 25fr, Nativity, 15th century. 30fr, Virgin and Child, c. 1350.

1970, Dec. 15 Photo. *Perf. 12½x12*

C71 AP30 20fr gold & multi .65 .25
C72 AP30 25fr gold & multi .90 .25
C73 AP30 30fr gold & multi 1.00 .25
Nos. C71-C73 (3) 2.55 .75

Christmas 1970. See Nos. C144-C147.

Post Office Mauritius and Emblem AP31

1971, Jan. 23 Engr. *Perf. 13*

C74 AP31 10fr shown .25 .25
C75 AP31 20fr Tuscany #23 .40 .25
C76 AP31 30fr France #8 .60 .25
C77 AP31 60fr US #2 1.10 .30
C78 AP31 80fr Japan #8 1.50 .60
C79 AP31 100fr Saxony #1 1.90 .75
a. Souvenir sheet of 6, #C74-C79 8.00 5.00
Nos. C74-C79 (6) 5.75 2.40

Publicity for PHILEXOCAM, philatelic exhibition, Fort Lamy, Jan. 23-30.

Gamal Abdel Nasser — AP32

1971, Feb. 16 Photo. *Perf. 12½*

C80 AP32 75fr multi 1.50 .50

In memory of Gamal Abdel Nasser (1918-1970), President of Egypt.

Presidents Mobutu, Bokassa and Tombalbaye — AP33

1971, Apr. 28 Photo. *Perf. 13*

C81 AP33 100fr multi 1.50 .60

Return of Central African Republic to the United States of Central Africa which also includes Congo Democratic Republic and Chad.

Map of Africa, Communications Network and Symbols — AP34

1971, May 17 Engr. *Perf. 13*

C82 AP34 125fr ultra, sl grn & brn red 3.00 .75

Pan-African telecommunications system.

Boys Around Campfire, Torii AP35

1971, Aug. 24 Photo. *Perf. 12½*

C83 AP35 250fr multi 1.50 .40

13th Boy Scout World Jamboree, Asagiri Plain, Japan, Aug. 2-10.

White Egret — AP36

1971, Sept. 28 Photo. *Perf. 13x12½*

C84 AP36 1000fr blk, dk bl & ocher 60.00 12.50

Greek Marathon Runners — AP37

45fr, Ancient Olympic Stadium. 75fr, Greek wrestlers. 130fr, Olympic Stadium, Athens, 1896.

1971, Oct. 5 *Perf. 12½*

C85 AP37 40fr multi .75 .25
C86 AP37 45fr multi 1.00 .25
C87 AP37 75fr multi 1.75 .40
C88 AP37 130fr multi 2.00 .75
Nos. C85-C88 (4) 5.50 1.65

75th anniv. of modern Olympic Games.

Nos. C66A, C66C Ovptd. in Gold

1971 Litho. *Perf. 12½x12*

C88A AP28a 5fr multi 2.50

Souvenir Sheet

Perf. 13½x13

C88B AP28a 15fr multi 5.50

Overprint on No. C88B is 36mm long.

Duke Ellington — AP38

50fr, Sidney Bechet. 100fr, Louis Armstrong.

1971, Oct. 20 Litho. *Perf. 13*

C89 AP38 50fr multi 2.00 .50
C90 AP38 75fr lt bl & multi 3.00 .70
C91 AP38 100fr multi 5.00 .85
Nos. C89-C91 (3) 10.00 2.05

Famous American jazz musicians.

Charles de Gaulle — AP39

Design: No. C93, Félix Eboué.

Lithographed and Embossed

1971, Nov. 9 *Perf. 12½*

C92 AP39 200fr grn, yel grn & gold 8.00 4.00
C93 AP39 200fr bl, lt bl & gold 8.00 4.00
a. Souv. sheet, #C92-C93 + label 15.00 15.00

Charles de Gaulle (1890-1970), pres. of France.

African Postal Union Issue, 1971

Common Design Type

Design: 100fr, Sao antelope head and UAMPT building, Brazzaville, Congo.

1971, Nov. 13 Photo. *Perf. 13x13½*

C94 CD135 100fr bl & multi 1.50 .50

Apollo 15 Rocket AP40

80fr, Apollo 15 capsule, horiz. 150fr, Lunar module on Moon, horiz. 250fr, Astronaut making tests. 300fr, Moon-buggy. No. C100, Successful splashdown, horiz. No. C101, Apollo 15 insignia.

1972, Jan. 5 Litho. *Perf. 13½*

C95 AP40 40fr multi .50 .25
C96 AP40 80fr multi .90 .25
C97 AP40 150fr multi 1.50 .30
C98 AP40 250fr multi 2.50 .45
C99 AP40 300fr multi 3.00 .60
C100 AP40 500fr multi 5.50 1.40
Nos. C95-C100 (6) 13.90 3.25

Souvenir Sheet

C101 AP40 500fr multi 8.00 2.50

Apollo 15 moon landing.

Soyuz 11 Link-up — AP41

Designs: 30fr, Soyuz 11 on launching pad, vert. 50fr, No. C108, Cosmonauts in uniform. 200fr, V. I. Patsayev. No. C106, V. N. Volkov. 400fr, G. L. Dobrovolsky. No. C109, Three cosmonauts.

1972, Jan. 5 *Perf. 13½x13*

C102 AP41 30fr multi .25 .25
C103 AP41 50fr multi .45 .25
C104 AP41 100fr multi .80 .25
C105 AP41 200fr multi 2.00 .50
C106 AP41 300fr multi 3.25 .75
C107 AP41 400fr multi 4.25 1.10
Nos. C102-C107 (6) 11.00 3.10

Souvenir Sheets

C108 AP41 300fr multi 3.50 1.25
C109 AP41 400fr multi 4.00 1.50

Soyuz 11 link-up project.

Bobsledding — AP42

Design: 100fr, Slalom.

1972, Feb. 24 Engr. *Perf. 13*

C110 AP42 50fr Prus bl & rose red .90 .30
C111 AP42 100fr red lil & slate grn 1.70 .50

11th Winter Olympic Games, Sapporo, Japan, Feb. 3-13.

Pres. Tombalbaye Type, 1972

1972, Apr. 13 Litho. *Perf. 13*

C112 A63 70fr multi .75 .30
C113 A63 80fr multi .90 .35

11th Winter Olympic Type, 1972

130fr, Speed skating. No. C115, Ice hockey. No. C116, Ski jumping. 250fr, 4-man bobsled.

1972, Apr. 13 *Perf. 13½*

C114 A64 130fr multi 1.40 .45
C115 A64 200fr multi 2.50 .60

Souvenir Sheets

C116 A64 200fr multi 3.50 1.25
C117 A64 250fr multi 4.50 1.50

Scout Jamboree Type, 1972

Designs: 100fr, Cooking preparation. 120fr, Lord Baden Powell. 250fr, Hiking.

1972, May 15

C118 A67 100fr multi 2.25 .40
C119 A67 120fr multi 2.40 .50

Souvenir Sheet

C120 A67 250fr multi 8.50 1.75

Zebras — AP43

African wild animals: 30fr, Mandrills. 100fr, African elephants. 130fr, Gazelles. 150fr, Hippopotamuses. 200fr, Lion cub.

1972, May 15 Litho. *Perf. 13*

C121 AP43 20fr multi .35 .25
C122 AP43 30fr multi .50 .25
C123 AP43 100fr multi 1.40 .35
C124 AP43 130fr multi 2.25 .50
C125 AP43 150fr multi 3.50 .75
Nos. C121-C125 (5) 8.00 2.10

Souvenir Sheet

C126 AP43 200fr multi 15.00 10.00

View of Venice, by Caffi — AP44

Paintings by Ippolito Caffi: 40fr, Sailing ship and Doge's Palace, vert. 140fr, Grand Canal, vert.

1972, May 23 Photo.

C127 AP44 40fr gold & multi 1.10 .25
C128 AP44 45fr gold & multi 1.90 .25
C129 AP44 140fr gold & multi 3.50 .60
Nos. C127-C129 (3) 6.50 1.10

UNESCO campaign to save Venice.

11th Winter Olympic Winners Type, 1972

Designs: 150fr, Slalom, B. Cochran, US. 200fr, Women's figure skating, B. Schuba, Austria. 250fr, Ice hockey, USSR. 300fr, 2-man bobsled. W. Zimmerer and P. Utzschneider, West Germany.

1972, June 15 *Perf. 14½*

C130 A69 150fr gold & multi 3.00 .75
C131 A69 200fr gold & multi 3.75 1.00

Souvenir Sheets

C132 A69 250fr gold & multi 3.25 2.75
C133 A69 300fr gold & multi 3.75 3.00

Nos. C130-C131 exist se-tenant with label showing earth satellite.

Daudet, "Tartarin de Tarascon," Book Year Emblem — AP45

1972, July 22 Engr. *Perf. 13*

C134 AP45 100fr dk red, lil & dk brn 1.70 .60

Intl. Book Year, 1972, and to honor Alphonse Daudet (1840-1897), French writer.

20th Summer Olympics Type, 1972

Designs (TV Tower, Munich and): 100fr, Gymnast. 120fr, Pole vault. 150fr, Fencing. 250fr, Hammer throw. 300fr, Boxing.

1972, Aug. 15 *Perf. 14½*

C135 A70 100fr gold & multi 2.10 .50
C136 A70 120fr gold & multi 2.50 .60
C137 A70 150fr gold & multi 3.25 .80
Nos. C135-C137 (3) 7.85 1.90

Souvenir Sheets

C138 A70 250fr gold & multi 3.50 2.75
C139 A70 300fr gold & multi 4.00 3.00

Nos. C135-C137 exist se-tenant with label showing arms of Munich.

Lunokhod on Moon — AP46

Russian moon missions: 100fr, Luna 16 on moon and rocket in flight, vert.

1972, Sept. 19 *Perf. 13*

C140 AP46 100fr dk bl, pur & bis 1.50 .50
C141 AP46 150fr slate, brn & lil 2.00 .75

Farcha Laboratory, Cattle, Scientist — AP47

1972, Nov. 11 Photo. *Perf. 13*

C142 AP47 75fr yellow & multi 1.40 .30

20th anniversary of the Farcha Laboratory for veterinary research.

King Faisal and Holy Kaaba, Mecca — AP48

1972, Nov. 17

C143 AP48 75fr multi 1.40 .40

Visit of King Faisal of Saudi Arabia.

Christmas Type of 1970

Christmas: 40fr, Virgin and Child, by Giovanni Bellini. 75fr, Virgin and Child, by Dall'Occhio. 80fr, Nativity, by Fra Angelico, horiz. 95fr, Adoration of the Kings, by Il Perugino.

1972, Dec. 15 Photo. *Perf. 13*

C144 AP30 40fr gold & multi .25 .25
C145 AP30 75fr gold & multi 1.75 .30
C146 AP30 80fr gold & multi 2.00 .40
C147 AP30 95fr gold & multi 2.00 .50
Nos. C144-C147 (4) 6.00 1.45

Summer Olympic Winners Type, 1972

Olympic Emblems and: 150fr, Pole vault, Nordwig, East Germany. 250fr, Hurdles, Milburn, US. 300fr, Javelin, Wolfermann, West Germany.

1972, Dec. 22 *Perf. 11*

C148 A76 150fr multi 3.00 .60
C149 A76 250fr multi 4.25 .75

Souvenir Sheet

C150 A76 300fr multi 12.00 3.00

Summer Olympic Winners Type, 1972

Olympic Emblem and: 150fr, Dressage, Mancinelli, Italy. No. C152, Finn class sailing, Serge Maury, France. No. C153, Swimming, Mark Spitz.

1972, Dec. 22 Litho. *Perf. 11*

C151 A77 150fr gold & multi 3.25 .75
C152 A77 250fr gold & multi 5.00 1.00

Souvenir Sheet

C153 A77 250fr multi 15.00 3.00

Copernicus and Solar System — AP49

1973, Mar. 31 Engr. *Perf. 13*

C154 AP49 250fr gray, mag & brn 5.25 1.25

500th anniversary of the birth of Nicolaus Copernicus (1473-1543), Polish astronomer.

Horses — AP49a

Details from paintings: 20fr, A Horse Frightened by Lightning, by Theordore Gericault. 60fr, The White Horse, by Paul Potter. 100fr, Mares and Foals, by George Stubbs. 150fr, Horse Head, by Theordore Gericault, vert. 500fr, The Carriage, by Vernet.

1973 Litho. *Perf. 11½*

C154A AP49a 20fr multi
C154B AP49a 60fr multi
C154C AP49a 100fr multi
C154D AP49a 150fr multi
Nos. C154A-C154D 14.00

Souvenir Sheet

Perf. 15

C154E AP49a 500fr multi 15.00

See note before No. 225A.

Airplanes — AP49b

5fr, Fokker F VII/3M. 25fr, DH 89A Rapide. 70fr, Viscount. 150fr, Boeing 747. 200fr, Concorde.
350fr, Concorde, diff.

1973 Litho. *Perf. 12*

C154F AP49b 5fr multi
C154G AP49b 25fr multi
C154H AP49b 70fr multi
C154J AP49b 150fr multi
C154K AP49b 200fr multi
Nos. C154F-C154K 14.00

Souvenir Sheet

Perf. 12

C154L AP49b 350fr multi 14.00

Nos. C154L contains one 60x40mm stamp.
See note before No. 225A.

Skylab over Africa — AP50

1974, Aug. 6 Engr. *Perf. 13*

C155 AP50 100fr shown 1.50 .25
C156 AP50 150fr Skylab 2.50 .60

Exploits of Skylab, US manned space station.

Soccer — AP51

125fr, 150fr, Soccer players; 125fr, vert.

1974, Oct. 22 Engr. *Perf. 13*

C157 AP51 50fr dl red & choc .75 .25
C158 AP51 125fr red & dp grn 1.75 .50
C159 AP51 150fr grn & rose red 2.50 .75
Nos. C157-C159 (3) 5.00 1.50

World Cup Soccer Championship, Munich, June 13-July 7.

Family and WPY Emblem — AP52

1974, Nov. 11

C160 AP52 250fr multi 4.00 1.25

World Population Year.

Mail Delivery by Canoe — AP53

UPU Cent.: 40fr, Diesel train. 100fr, Jet. 150fr, Spacecraft.

1974, Dec. 20 Engr. *Perf. 13*

C161 AP53 30fr car & multi .60 .25
C162 AP53 40fr ultra & blk 1.00 .25
C163 AP53 100fr brn, ultra & blk 1.90 .40
C164 AP53 150fr grn, lil & ol 2.40 .55
Nos. C161-C164 (4) 5.90 1.45

Women of Different Races, IWY Emblem — AP54

1975, June 25 Photo. *Perf. 13*

C165 AP54 250fr bl & multi 4.50 1.25

International Women's Year 1975.

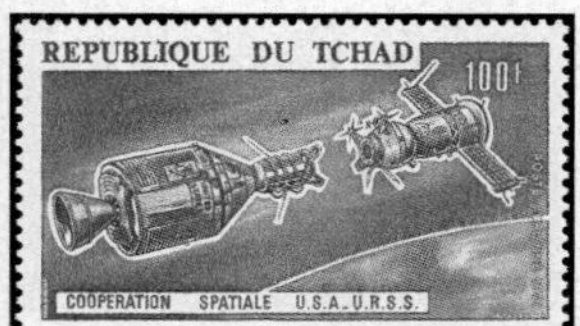

Apollo and Soyuz Before Link-up — AP55

130fr, Apollo and Soyuz after link-up.

1975, July 15 Engr. *Perf. 13*

C166 AP55 100fr ultra, choc & grn 1.50 .40
C167 AP55 130fr vio bl, brn & grn 2.00 .50

Apollo Soyuz space test project (Russo-American space cooperation), launching 7/15; link-up 7/17.

For overprints see Nos. C171-C172.

Soccer Player, View of Montreal — AP56

Olympic Rings, Montreal Skyline: 100fr, Discus thrower. 125fr, Runner.

1975, Oct. 14 Engr. *Perf. 13*

C168 AP56 75fr car & slate grn 1.00 .25
C169 AP56 100fr car, choc & bl grn 1.40 .40
C170 AP56 125fr brn, bl & car 1.90 .75
Nos. C168-C170 (3) 4.30 1.40

Pre-Olympic Year 1975.

Nos. C166-C167 Overprinted: "JONCTION / 17 JUILLET 1975"

1975, Nov. 4 Engr. *Perf. 13*

C171 AP55 100fr multi 1.75 .25
C172 AP55 130fr multi 2.10 .35

Apollo-Soyuz link-up in space, July 17.

Stylized British and American Flags, "200" — AP57

1975, Dec. 5 Engr. *Perf. 13*

C173 AP57 150fr vio bl, car & ol bis 2.25 .75

American Bicentennial.

Adoration of the Shepherds, by Murillo — AP58

Christmas (Paintings): 75fr, Adoration of the Shepherds, by Georges de La Tour. 80fr, Virgin and Child with Bible, by Rogier van der Weyden, vert. 100fr, Holy Family, by Raphael, vert.

1975, Dec. 15 Litho. *Perf. 13x12½*

C174 AP58 40fr yel & multi .75 .25
C175 AP58 75fr yel & multi 1.25 .35
C176 AP58 80fr yel & multi 1.75 .40
C177 AP58 100fr yel & multi 2.75 .75
Nos. C174-C177 (4) 6.50 1.75

12th Winter Olympic Winners Type, 1976

250fr, 4-man bobsled, West Germany. 300fr, Speed skating, J. E. Storholt, Norway. 500fr, Downhill skiing, F. Klammer, Austria.

1976, June 21 *Perf. 14*

C178 A84 250fr multi 2.75 .60
C179 A84 300fr multi 3.50 1.00

Souvenir Sheet

C180 A84 500fr multi 6.00 3.00

Paul Revere's Ride and Portrait by Copley — AP59

American Bicentennial: 125fr, Washington crossing Delaware. 150fr, Lafayette offering his services to America. 200fr, Rochambeau at Yorktown with Washington. 250fr, Franklin presenting Declaration of Independence. 400fr, Count de Grasse's victory at Cape Charles.

1976, July 4 Litho. *Perf. 14*

C181 AP59 100fr multi 1.10 .30
C182 AP59 125fr multi 1.25 .35
C183 AP59 150fr multi 1.90 .40
C184 AP59 200fr multi 2.25 .50
C185 AP59 250fr multi 3.00 .55
Nos. C181-C185 (5) 9.50 2.10

Souvenir Sheet

C186 AP59 400fr multi 6.00 3.00

Summer Olympics Type, 1976

1976, July 12 *Perf. 13½*

C187 A85 100fr Boxing 1.50 .30
C188 A85 200fr Pole vault 2.50 .50
C189 A85 300fr Shot put 4.00 .65
Nos. C187-C189 (3) 8.00 1.45

Souvenir Sheet

C190 A85 500fr Sprint 6.00 3.00

Viking Mars Project Type, 1976

Mars Lander and: 100fr, Viking landing on Mars. 200fr, Capsule over Mars. 250fr, Lander over Mars. 450fr, Lander and probe.

1976, July 23 Litho. *Perf. 14*

C191 A86 100fr multi 1.10 .30
C192 A86 200fr multi 2.25 .55
C193 A86 250fr multi 2.50 .75
Nos. C191-C193 (3) 5.85 1.60

Souvenir Sheet

C194 A86 450fr multi 7.50 3.00

For overprints see Nos. C240-C243.

Concorde — AP60

1976, Oct. 15 Litho. *Perf. 12½*

C195 AP60 250fr bl, blk & ver 6.00 1.75

First commercial flight of supersonic jet Concorde, Jan. 21.

Nobel Prize Type, 1976

100fr, Albert Einstein, physics. 200fr, Dag Hammarskjold, peace. 300fr, Shinichiro Tomanaga, physics. 500fr, Alexander Fleming, medicine.

1976, Dec. 15 *Perf. 14*

C196 A87 100fr multi 1.50 .30
C197 A87 200fr multi 2.50 .55
C198 A87 300fr multi 3.50 .70
Nos. C196-C198 (3) 7.50 1.55

Souvenir Sheet

C199 A87 500fr multi 8.00 3.50

Adoration of the Shepherds, by Gerard van Honthorst — AP61

Christmas (Paintings): 30fr, Nativity, by Albrecht Altdorfer, vert. 60fr, Nativity, by Hans Holbein, vert. 150fr, Adoration of the Kings, by Gerard David.

1976, Dec. 22 Litho. *Perf. 12½*

C200 AP61 30fr gold & multi .50 .25
C201 AP61 60fr gold & multi .75 .25
C202 AP61 120fr gold & blk 1.50 .50
C203 AP61 150fr gold & blk 2.25 .75
Nos. C200-C203 (4) 5.00 1.75

Lesdiguières Bridge, by Jongkind — AP62

Design: 120fr, Sailing Ship and Boats, by Johan Barthold Jongkind (1819-1891).

1976, Dec. 27 Photo. *Perf. 13*

C204 AP62 100fr multi 1.75 .55
C205 AP62 120fr multi 2.25 .60

Centenary of impressionism.

Zeppelin Type of 1977

125fr, Germany #C40, North Pole. 150fr, Germany #C45, Chicago department store. 175fr, Germany #C38 and scenes of NYC and London. 200fr, 500fr, US #C15, NYC.

1977, Mar. 30 *Perf. 11*

C206 A91 125fr multi 1.90 .35
C207 A91 150fr multi 2.25 .40
C208 A91 175fr multi 2.75 .50
C209 A91 200fr multi 3.25 .60
Nos. C206-C209 (4) 10.15 1.85

Souvenir Sheet

C210 A91 500fr multi 8.00 3.00

Sassenage Castle, Grenoble — AP63

1977, May 21 Litho. *Perf. 12½*

C211 AP63 100fr multi 1.00 .30

Intl. French Language Council, 10th Anniv.

Lafayette and Ships — AP64

American Bicentennial: 120fr, Abraham Lincoln, eagle and flags, vert. 150fr, James Madison and family.

1977, July 30 Engr. *Perf. 13*

C212 AP64 100fr multi 1.40 .35
C213 AP64 120fr multi 1.75 .40
C214 AP64 150fr multi 2.25 .50
Nos. C212-C214 (3) 5.40 1.25

Lindbergh and Spirit of St. Louis — AP65

100fr, Concorde. 150fr, 200fr, 300fr, Various Lindbergh portraits & Spirit of St. Louis.

1977, Sept. 27

C215	AP65	100fr multi	1.25	.30
C216	AP65	120fr multi	1.25	.40
C217	AP65	150fr multi	1.40	.55
C218	AP65	200fr multi	2.25	.65
C219	AP65	300fr multi	3.00	.90
		Nos. C215-C219 (5)	9.15	2.80

Charles A. Lindbergh's solo transatlantic flight from NY to Paris, 50th anniv., and 1st supersonic transatlantic flight of Concorde.

For overprint see No. C227.

Mariner 10 — AP66

Spacecraft: 200fr, Lunokhod on moon, Luna 21. 300fr, Viking on Mars.

1977, Oct. 10 Engr. *Perf. 13*

C220	AP66	100fr multi	1.25	.40
C221	AP66	200fr multi	2.00	.70
C222	AP66	300fr multi	2.75	.90
		Nos. C220-C222 (3)	6.00	2.00

Running — AP67

1977, Oct. 24 Engr. *Perf. 13*

C223	AP67	30fr shown	.40	.25
C224	AP67	60fr Volleyball	.85	.25
C225	AP67	120fr Soccer	1.50	.45
C226	AP67	125fr Basketball	1.25	.50
		Nos. C223-C226 (4)	4.00	1.45

No. C215 Overprinted: "PARIS NEW-YORK / 22.11.77"

1977, Nov. 22

C227	AP65	100fr multi	3.25	.25

Concorde, 1st commercial flight Paris-NYC.

Virgin and Child, by Rubens AP68

Rubens Paintings: 60fr, Virgin and Child and Two Donors. 100fr, Adoration of the Shepherds. 125fr, Adoration of the Kings.

1977, Dec. 20 Litho. *Perf. 12½x12*

C228	AP68	30fr multi	.75	.25
C229	AP68	60fr multi	1.10	.30
C230	AP68	100fr multi	1.50	.40
C231	AP68	125fr multi	1.90	.60
		Nos. C228-C231 (4)	5.25	1.55

Christmas 1977.

Antoine de Saint-Exupéry — AP69

50fr, Wilbur & Orville Wright & Flyer. 80fr, Hugo Junkers & his plane. 100fr, Gen. Italo Balbo & his plane. 120fr, Concorde. 500fr, Wilbur & Orville Wright & Flyer.

1978, Oct. 25 Litho. *Perf. 13½*

C232	AP69	40fr multi	.60	.25
C233	AP69	50fr multi	.75	.25
C234	AP69	80fr multi	1.10	.30
C235	AP69	100fr multi	1.50	.40
C236	AP69	120fr multi	1.75	.50
		Nos. C232-C236 (5)	5.70	1.70

Souvenir Sheet

C237	AP69	500fr multi	6.75	2.00

History of aviation and 75th anniversary of 1st powered flight.

Philexafrique II-Essen Issue

Common Design Types

No. C238, Rhinoceros & Chad #C6. No. C239, Kingfisher & Mecklenburg-Strelitz #1.

1978, Nov. 1 *Perf. 12½*

C238	CD138	100fr multi	3.00	1.00
C239	CD139	100fr multi	3.00	1.00
a.		Pair, #C238-C239 + label	7.50	4.00

Nos. C191-C194 Overprinted "ALUNISSAGE/APOLLO XI/ JUILLET 1969"

1979, Nov. 26 Litho. *Perf. 13½x14*

C240	A86	100fr multi	1.10	.35
C241	A86	200fr multi	2.25	.65
C242	A86	250fr multi	2.50	1.00
		Nos. C240-C242 (3)	5.85	2.00

Souvenir Sheet

C243	A86	450fr multi	5.50	4.50

Apollo 11 moon landing, 10th anniversary.

Hurdles, Moscow '80 Emblem — AP70

Emblem and: 30fr, Field hockey. 250fr, Swimming. 350fr, Running. 500fr, Yachting.

1979, Nov. 30 *Perf. 13½*

C244	AP70	15fr multi	.25	.25
C245	AP70	30fr multi	.30	.25
C246	AP70	250fr multi	1.90	.60
C247	AP70	350fr multi	3.00	1.10
		Nos. C244-C247 (4)	5.45	2.20

Souvenir Sheet

C248	AP70	500fr multi	5.75	3.00

Pre-Olympic Year.

For overprints see Nos. C254-C255.

Austria Jubilee Issue of 1910, Canoe, Hill — AP71

Hill, Stamps & Vessels: 100fr, US design A97, dhow. 200fr, France #21, Sidewheeler. 300fr, Holstein #16, ocean liner. 500fr, Chad #J13, ocean liner.

1979, Dec. 3 *Perf. 14x13½*

C249	AP71	65fr multi	.60	.25
C250	AP71	100fr multi	1.40	.25
C251	AP71	200fr multi	2.25	.45
C252	AP71	300fr multi	2.75	.70
		Nos. C249-C252 (4)	7.00	1.65

Souvenir Sheet

C253	AP71	500fr multi	5.75	3.00

Sir Rowland Hill (1795-1879), originator of penny postage.

For overprints see Nos. C256-C257.

Nos. C244-C245, C249-C250 Overprinted: "POSTES 1981" in Red or Overprinted and Surcharged Silver on Red

Perf. 13½, 14x13½

1981, Nov. 15 Litho.

C254	AP70	30fr on 15fr multi	1.25	.40
C255	AP70	30fr multi	1.25	.40
C256	AP71	60fr on 65fr multi	2.25	.70
C257	AP71	60fr on 100fr multi	2.25	.70
		Nos. C254-C257 (4)	7.00	2.20

Soccer Type of 1982 and

1982 World Cup Soccer Championships, Spain — AP71a

80fr, Brazil. 300fr, W. Germany.

No. C259C, Soccer players, ball, & trophy, vert.

1982 Litho. *Perf. 13½*

C258	A108	80fr multi	1.00	.25
C259	A108	300fr multi	3.00	.50

Souvenir Sheet

C259A	A108	500fr like 300fr	5.00	2.00

Litho. & Embossed

C259B	AP71a	1500fr shown	16.00	

Souvenir Sheet

C259C	AP71a	1500fr gold & multi	11.50	

No. C259A contains one 42x51mm stamp.

No. C259B exists in a souvenir sheet of 1. Value $42.50.

For surcharge see No. C305.

Diana Type of 1982 and

Princess Diana, 21st Birthday — AP71b

Design: No. C262A, Portrait, horiz.

1982, July 2 Litho. *Perf. 13½*

C260	A109	80fr 1977	1.00	.25
C261	A109	300fr 1980	3.00	.95

Souvenir Sheet

C262	A109	500fr 1981	4.50	2.00

Litho. & Embossed

C262A	AP71b	1500fr gold & multi	12.50	

Souvenir Sheet

C262B	AP71b	1500fr gold & multi	13.50	

No. C262A exists in a souvenir sheet of 1. Value $42.50.

For overprints see Nos. 419A-419B.

Manned Flight Bicentenary AP72

Balloons: 100fr, Charles' & Roberts', 1783. 200fr, J.P. Blanchard, Berlin, 1788. 300fr, Charles Green, London, 1837. 400fr, Modern blimp. 500fr, Montgolfiere, 1783.

1983, Apr. Litho. *Perf. 13*

C263	AP72	100fr multi, vert.	1.25	.25
C264	AP72	200fr multi, vert.	2.50	.40
C265	AP72	300fr multi	3.50	.60
C266	AP72	400fr multi	4.75	.75
		Nos. C263-C266 (4)	12.00	2.00

Souvenir Sheet

C267	AP72	500fr multi, vert.	5.75	2.50

Balloon Type and

First Balloon Ascension, Bicent. — AP72a

80fr, Steam Powered Airship, H. Giffard. 250fr, Graf Zeppelin; Airship L-1, 1st flight. 300fr, 1st Balloon Flight, Montgolfier & Rozier. No. C270A, Airship Hindenburg, Count Ferdinand von Zeppelin. No. C270B, Jean-Francois Pilatre de Rozier & Marquis d'Arlandes, 1st balloon ascension.

1983, May 30 Litho. *Perf. 13½*

C268	A116	80fr multi	1.00	.25
C269	A116	250fr multi	3.00	.40

Souvenir Sheet

C270	A116	300fr multi	3.75	2.50

Litho. & Embossed

Perf. 13½

C270A	AP72a	1500fr gold & multi	16.00	

Souvenir Sheet

C270B	AP72a	1500fr gold & multi	12.00	

No. C270A exists in a souvenir sheet of 1. Value $25.

For surcharge see No. C299.

1984 Summer Olympics — AP73

Various kayak scenes.

1984, Mar. 1 Litho. *Perf. 13*

No.	Type	Denomination	Color	Unused	Used
C271	AP73	100fr	multi	1.00	.25
C272	AP73	200fr	multi	2.00	.25
C273	AP73	300fr	multi	3.00	.50
C274	AP73	400fr	multi	4.00	.60
			Nos. C271-C274 (4)	10.00	1.60

Souvenir Sheet

No.	Type	Denomination	Color	Unused	Used
C275	AP73	500fr	multi	5.00	3.50

Natl. Goals AP73a

Nos. C276, C278, Peace & reconciliation. Nos. C277, C279, Self-sufficiency in food production.

1983, Dec. 26 Litho. *Perf. 13½*

No.	Type	Denomination	Color	Unused	Used
C276	AP73a	150fr	multi	1.50	.40
C277	AP73a	150fr	multi	1.50	.40
C278	AP73a	200fr	multi	2.25	.55
C279	AP73a	200fr	multi	2.25	.55
			Nos. C276-C279 (4)	7.50	1.90

For surcharges see Nos. C300-C301.

Souvenir Sheet

Paul P. Harris (1868-1947), Founder of Rotary Intl. — AP73b

Litho. & Embossed

1984, Jan. 16 *Perf. 13½*

No.	Type	Denomination	Color	Unused	Used
C279B	AP73b	1500fr	gold & multi	12.00	

IYY, PHILEXAFRICA '85 — AP74

No. C280, Boy scout, tree. No. C281, Air Chad Fokker 27.

1985, May 2 Litho. *Perf. 13*

No.	Type	Denomination	Color	Unused	Used
C280	AP74	200fr	multicolored	3.00	1.50
C281	AP74	200fr	multicolored	3.00	1.50
a.			Pair, #C280-C281 + label	6.75	5.00

IYY, PHILEXAFRICA Type of 1985

No. C283, Girl, Scout ceremony. No. C284, Communications and transportation.

1985, Nov. 1 Litho. *Perf. 13x12½*

No.	Type	Denomination	Color	Unused	Used
C283	AP74	250fr	multicolored	3.00	1.50
C284	AP74	250fr	multicolored	3.00	1.50
a.			Pair, #C283-C284 + label	6.75	5.00

ASCENA Airlines, 25th Anniv. — AP75

1985, Aug. 25 *Perf. 12½*

No.	Type	Denomination	Color	Unused	Used
C285	AP75	70fr	bl & multi	.60	.25
C286	AP75	110fr	org & multi	1.00	.25
C287	AP75	250fr	yel & multi	2.25	.80
			Nos. C285-C287 (3)	3.85	1.30

Victor Hugo (1802-1885), French Novelist — AP76

Scene from Les Miserables.

1985, Nov. 24 Engr. *Perf. 13*

No.	Type	Denomination	Color	Unused	Used
C288	AP76	70fr	org brn, chlky bl & dp brn	.75	.25
C289	AP76	110fr	lake, dk brn & dk grn	1.00	.30
C290	AP76	250fr	brt org, blk & dk red	2.50	.80
C291	AP76	300fr	dk red, cl & sl bl	2.75	.90
			Nos. C288-C291 (4)	7.00	2.25

Adoration of the Magi — AP77

1985, Dec. 22 Litho. *Perf. 13½*

No.	Denomination	Color	Unused	Used
C292	250fr	multicolored	2.25	.60

Christmas 1985.

1988 Summer Olympics, Seoul — AP78

100fr, 400-Meter hurdles, vert. 170fr, 5000-Meter race. 200fr, Long jump. 600fr, Triple jump, vert.

750fr, 10,000-Meter race, vert.

1988, June 1 Litho. *Perf. 13*

No.	Type	Denomination	Color	Unused	Used
C293	AP78	100fr	multi	1.10	.30
C294	AP78	170fr	multi	1.75	.55
C295	AP78	200fr	multi	2.25	.65
C296	AP78	600fr	multi	5.75	2.00
			Nos. C293-C296 (4)	10.85	3.50

Souvenir Sheet

No.	Type	Denomination	Color	Unused	Used
C297	AP78	750fr	multi	8.00	6.00

Stamps of 1982-84 Surcharged

1989 *Perfs. as Before*

No.	Type	Surcharge
C298	A115	100 on 300fr #446
C299	A116	100 on 250fr #C269
C300	AP73a	100 on 200fr #C278
C301	AP73a	100 on 200fr #C279
C302	A110	170 on 300fr #404
C303	A122	170 on 200fr #503
C304	A123	170 on 250fr #509
C305	A108	170 on 300fr #C259
C306	A112	240 on 300fr #425

AIR POST SEMI-POSTAL STAMPS

Catalogue values for unused stamps in this section are for Never Hinged items.

Ramses II Battling the Hittites (from Abu Simbel) — SPAP1

Unwmk.

1964, Mar. 9 Engr. *Perf. 13*

No.	Type	Denomination	Color	Unused	Used
CB1	SPAP1	10fr + 5fr	multi	.75	.25
CB2	SPAP1	25fr + 5fr	multi	1.40	.40
CB3	SPAP1	50fr + 5fr	multi	2.75	.75
			Nos. CB1-CB3 (3)	4.90	1.40

UNESCO world campaign to save historic monuments in Nubia.

Lions Emblem SPAP2

1967, July 5 Photo. *Perf. 13*

No.	Type	Denomination	Color	Unused	Used
CB4	SPAP2	50fr + 10fr	multi	2.00	.25

50th anniv. of Lions Intl. and to publicize the Lions work for the blind.

POSTAGE DUE STAMPS

Postage Due Stamps of France Overprinted

1928 Unwmk. *Perf. 14x13½*

No.	Type	Denomination	Color	Unused	Used
J1	D2	5c	light blue	.70	1.20
J2	D2	10c	gray brown	.70	1.20
J3	D2	20c	olive green	.70	1.20
J4	D2	25c	bright rose	1.10	1.60
J5	D2	30c	light red	1.10	1.60
J6	D2	45c	blue green	1.45	2.00
J7	D2	50c	brown violet	2.25	2.40
J8	D2	60c	yellow brown	2.25	2.40
J9	D2	1fr	red brown	2.25	2.75
J10	D2	2fr	orange red	5.00	6.00
J11	D2	3fr	bright violet	4.25	5.50
			Nos. J1-J11 (11)	21.75	27.85

Huts — D3

Canoe — D4

1930 Typo. *Perf. 14x13½, 13½x14*

No.	Type	Denomination	Color	Unused	Used
J12	D3	5c	dp bl & olive	.40	.80
J13	D3	10c	dk red & brn	.40	.80
J14	D3	20c	grn & brn	1.20	1.60
J15	D3	25c	lt bl & brn	1.20	2.40
J16	D3	30c	bis brn & Prus bl	1.60	2.00
J17	D3	45c	Prus bl & olive	2.40	2.75
J18	D3	50c	red vio & brn	2.40	4.00
J19	D3	60c	gray lil & bl blk	3.25	4.75
J20	D4	1fr	bis brn & bl blk	3.25	4.75
J21	D4	2fr	vio & brn	8.00	8.00
J22	D4	3fr	dp red & brn	35.00	40.00
			Nos. J12-J22 (11)	59.10	71.85

In 1934 stamps of Chad were superseded by those of French Equatorial Africa.

Catalogue values for unused stamps in this section, from this point to the end of the section, are for Never Hinged items.

Republic

Rhinoceros — D5

Tibesti Pictographs: #J24, Kudu. #J25, 2 antelopes. #J26, 3 antelopes. #J27, Ostrich. #J28, Horned bull. #J29, Bull. #J30, Wild swine. #J31, Elephant. #J32, Rhinoceros. #J33, Warrior with spear and shield. #J34, Masked archer.

Unwmk.

1962, Apr. 20 Engr. *Perf. 13*

No.	Type	Denomination	Color	Unused	Used
J23	D5	50c	olive bister	.30	.25
J24	D5	50c	brown red	.30	.25
a.			Pair, #J23-J24	.55	
J25	D5	1fr	blue	.40	.25
J26	D5	1fr	green	.40	.25
a.			Pair, #J25-J26	.75	
J27	D5	2fr	vermilion	.50	.25
J28	D5	2fr	maroon	.50	.25
a.			Pair, #J27-J28	1.00	
J29	D5	5fr	slate green	.75	.40
J30	D5	5fr	violet blue	.75	.40
a.			Pair, #J29-J30	1.50	
J31	D5	10fr	brown	1.40	.75
J32	D5	10fr	orange brown	1.40	.75
a.			Pair, #J31-J32	2.75	
J33	D5	25fr	carmine rose	3.25	1.75
J34	D5	25fr	violet	3.25	1.75
a.			Pair, #J33-J34	6.50	
			Nos. J23-J34 (12)	13.20	7.30

Dolls — D6

1969, Sept. 19 Engr. *Perf. 14x13*

No.	Type	Denomination	Color	Unused	Used
J35	D6	1fr	Kanem	.25	.25
J36	D6	2fr	Kotoko	.25	.25
J37	D6	5fr	Leather	.40	.25
J38	D6	10fr	Kotoko	.50	.25
J39	D6	25fr	Guera	.60	.25
			Nos. J35-J39 (5)	2.00	1.25

MILITARY STAMPS

Catalogue values for unused stamps in this section are for Never Hinged items.

No. 78 Overprinted "F.M."

1965 Typo. *Perf. 14x13½*

No.	Type	Denomination	Color	Unused	Used
M1	A5	20fr	red & black	300.00	300.00

Flag Bearer and Map of Chad — M1

1968 Unwmk. Litho. *Perf. 13x12½*

No.	Type	Color	Unused	Used
M2	M1	tan & multi	2.00	5.00

1st Regiment Emblem — M2

1972, Jan. 21 Photo. *Perf. 13*

M3	M2	blue & multi	1.00	2.00

OFFICIAL STAMPS

Catalogue values for unused stamps in this section are for Never Hinged items.

Flag and Map of Chad — O1

Perf. 13½x14

1966-71 Typo. Unwmk.

Flag in blue, yellow and carmine

O1	O1	1fr light blue	.25	.25
O2	O1	2fr gray	.25	.25
O3	O1	5fr black	.25	.25
O4	O1	10fr violet blue	.25	.25
O5	O1	25fr orange	.30	.25
O6	O1	30fr bright green	.50	.25
O7	O1	40fr carmine ('71)	.75	.25
O8	O1	50fr red lilac	.75	.25
O9	O1	85fr green	1.10	.30
O10	O1	100fr brown	1.75	.35
O11	O1	200fr red	3.00	.50
		Nos. O1-O11 (11)	9.15	3.15

Flag and Map Type of 1966-71 Redrawn with "N'Djamena" as Capital on Map

Perf. 13½x13¼, 11¾ (100fr)

1993-2000 ? Litho.

Center Flag Stripe in Yellow

Frame Color

O12	O1	30fr violet	—	—
O13	O1	100fr brown	—	—
O14	O1	200fr red	—	—

Nos. O13 and O14 have a large "F" in denomination, "POSTES" without serifs, and has printer's inscription of "COURVOISIER."

Center Flag Stripe in Orange

Frame Color

O17	O1	50fr green	—	—
O18	O1	85fr orange	—	—
O19	O1	100fr red orange	—	—
O20	O1	150fr blue green	—	—
O21	O1	200fr green	—	—
O22	O1	250fr lilac	—	—
O23	O1	300fr blue	—	—
O24	O1	500fr red	—	—
O25	O1	1000fr dark green	—	—

Additional stamps may have been issued in this set. The editors would like to examine any examples. Numbers may change.

CHILE

'chi-lē

LOCATION — Southwest corner of South America
GOVT. — Republic
AREA — 284,520 sq. mi.
POP. — 14,973,843 (1999 est.)
CAPITAL — Santiago

100 Centavos = 1 Peso
1000 Milésimos = 100 Centésimos = 1 Escudo (1960)
100 Centavos = 1 Peso (1975)

Catalogue values for unused stamps in this country are for Never Hinged items, beginning with Scott 257 in the regular postage section, Scott B3 in the semi-postal section, Scott C125 in the airpost section, Scott CB1 in the airpost semi-postal section, and Scott O60 in the officials section.

Issues of the Republic

Unused values for Nos. 1-14 are for stamps without gum. Examples with original gum are very scarce and are worth considerably more.

Pen cancellations are common on the 1862-67 issues. Such stamps sell for much less than the quoted values which are for those with handstamped postal cancellations.

Watermarks

1 5 5 5
a b c d

10 10 10 20
e f g

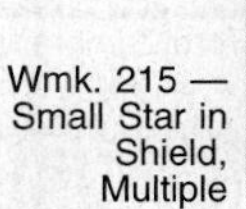

Wmk. 215 — Small Star in Shield, Multiple

Christopher Columbus — A1

London Prints

1853 Wmk. b Engr. *Imperf.*

Blued Paper

1 A1 5c brown red 650.00 125.00
a. White paper 250.00

Wmk. e

White Paper

2 A1 10c dp brt bl 1,000. 150.00
a. Blued paper 225.00
b. Diag. half used as 5c on cover 800.00
c. Horiz. half used as 5c on cover 800.00
d. Vert. half used as 5c on cover 800.00

Santiago Prints

Impressions Fine and Clear

1854 Wmk. b and e

White Paper

3 A1 5c pale red brn 600.00 75.00
a. 5c deep red brown 650.00 75.00
b. 5c chestnut 1,000. 200.00
e. Double impression 275.00
4 A1 5c burnt sienna 1,800. 300.00
a. 5c dull chocolate 3,500. 2,000.
5 A1 10c deep blue 1,200. 275.00
a. 10c slate blue 275.00
b. 10c greenish blue *475.00*
d. Diag. half used as 5c on cover 450.00
e. Horiz. half used as 5c on cover 450.00
f. Vert. half used as 5c on cover 450.00
6 A1 10c lt dl bl 800.00 150.00
a. 10c pale blue 190.00
b. Diag. half used as 5c on cover 425.00
c. Horiz. half used as 5c on cover 425.00
d. Vert. half used as 5c on cover 425.00

Litho.

7 A1 5c pale brown *1,200.* 300.00

London Print

1855 Blued Paper Wmk. c Engr.

8 A1 5c brown red 220.00 16.00
Fiscal cancellation 2.75

Santiago Prints

Impressions Worn and Blurred

1856-62 Wmk. b and e

White Paper

9 A1 5c rose red ('58) 60.00 8.00
Fiscal cancellation 1.40
a. 5c carmine red ('62) 90.00 20.00
b. 5c orange red ('61) *225.00* 100.00
c. 5c dull redsh brn ('57) *250.00* 27.50
f. Printed on both sides *450.00 250.00*
g. Double impression *450.00* 140.00
10 A1 10c sky blue ('57) 160.00 40.00
Fiscal cancellation 1.40
a. 10c deep blue *160.00* 40.00
b. 10c light blue ('59) *160.00* 40.00
c. 10c indigo blue ('60) *175.00* 50.00
k. Printed on both sides *350.00*
n. As "j," half used as 5c on cover 165.00
o. Any shade, horiz. half used as 5c on cover 200.00
p. Any shade, vert. half used as 5c on cover 200.00

London Prints

1862 Wmk. a, f and g

11 A1 1c lemon yellow 67.50 40.00
Fiscal cancellation 1.50
a. Double impression, one inverted *2,000. 200.00*
12 A1 10c bright blue 40.00 15.00
Fiscally used 1.50
a. 10c deep blue 32.50 21.00
b. Blued paper — 17.50
c. Wmkd. "20" (error) *5,000. 5,200.*
d. Diag. half used as 5c on cover 110.00
e. Horiz. half used as 5c on cover 125.00
f. Vert. half used as 5c on cover 125.00
13 A1 20c green 160.00 70.00
Fiscally used 6.75
Nos. 11-13 (3) 267.50 125.00

No. 11a is only known fiscally used.

Santiago Print

1865 Wmk. d

14 A1 5c rose red 80.00 20.00
Fiscally used 1.50
a. 5c carmine red 80.00 20.00
b. Printed on both sides *375.00 200.00*
c. Laid paper — *90.00*
d. Double impression, entire stamp *825.00 160.00*

The 5c rose red (shades) on unwatermaked paper, either wove or ribbed, and on paper watermarked Chilean arms in the sheet are reprints made about 1870.

No. 13 has been reprinted in the color of issue and in fancy colors, both from the original engraved plate and from lithographic transfers. The reprints are on paper without watermark or with watermark CHILE and Star.

A2

1867 Unwmk. *Perf. 12*

15 A2 1c orange 70.00 15.00
Pen cancellation 1.25
16 A2 2c black 80.00 30.00
Pen cancellation 2.00
17 A2 5c red 60.00 2.00
Pen cancellation .40
18 A2 10c blue 80.00 6.00
Pen cancellation 1.25
19 A2 20c green 80.00 8.00
Pen cancellation 1.60
Nos. 15-19 (5) 370.00 61.00

Unused values for Nos. 15-19 are for stamps with original gum.

A3

1877 *Rouletted*

20 A3 1c gray 10.00 3.00
Pen cancellation .60
21 A3 2c orange 30.00 3.00
Pen cancellation .60
22 A3 5c dull lake 24.00 2.00
Pen cancellation .40
23 A3 10c blue 18.00 2.75
a. Diagonal half used as 5c on cover —
24 A3 20c green 20.00 4.50
Nos. 20-24 (5) 102.00 15.25

The panel inscribed "CENTAVO" is straight on No. 22.

A4

A5

Columbus — A6

1878-99 *Rouletted*

25 A4 1c green ('81) 1.10 .30
26 A4 2c rose ('81) 1.10 .30
27 A5 5c dull lake ('78) 9.00 1.10
28 A5 5c ultra ('83) 2.40 .30
29 A5 10c orange ('85) 3.50 .40
a. 10c yellow 9.00 1.90
30 A5 15c dk grn ('92) 3.50 .70
31 A5 20c gray ('86) 3.50 .70
32 A5 25c org brn ('92) 3.50 .70
33 A5 30c rose car ('99) 9.00 4.75
34 A5 50c lilac ('78) 55.00 35.00
35 A5 50c violet ('85) 3.50 2.40
36 A6 1p dk brn & blk ('92) 26.00 3.50
a. Imperf. horiz. or vert., pair 75.00
Nos. 25-36 (12) 121.10 50.15

On Nos. 25-26 there is a small colorless ornament at each side of the base of the numeral, above the "E" and "V" of "CENTAVO."

For surcharge and overprint see Nos. 50, O16.

Columbus — A7

No. 25

No. 37

No. 26

No. 38

1894 Re-engraved

37 A7 1c blue green 1.10 .30
38 A7 2c carmine lake 1.10 .30

On Nos. 37-38 the ornaments on Nos. 25-26 are missing. On No. 37 the figure "1" is broader than on No. 25. On No. 38 the head of the figure "2" is formed by a curved line instead of a ball like on No. 26.

Columbus — A8

Type I

Type II

Type I — There is a heavy shadow, or shading, below "Chile" and the adjacent ornaments.

Type II — There is practically no shading below "Chile" and the ornaments.

Type I

1900-01

39 A8 1c yel grn .80 .25
40 A8 2c brn rose 1.25 .25
41 A8 5c dp bl 6.50 .35
42 A8 10c violet 6.50 .70
43 A8 20c gray 6.50 2.50
44 A8 30c dp org ('01) 6.50 2.50
45 A8 50c red brn 7.50 2.50
Nos. 39-45 (7) 35.55 9.05

Type II

No.	Type	Description	Unused	Used
46	A8	1c yel grn ('01)	.85	.25
47	A8	2c rose ('01)	.85	.30
48	A8	5c dull blue ('01)	5.00	.25
a.		Printed on both sides		—
49	A8	10c vio ('01)	6.00	.85
		Nos. 46-49 (4)	12.70	1.65

For surcharge see No. 57.

No. 33 Surcharged in Black

1900

No.	Type	Description	Unused	Used
50	A5	5c on 30c rose car	1.25	.75
a.		Inverted surcharge	32.50	24.00
b.		Double surcharge	90.00	60.00
c.		Double surcharge, both invtd.	90.00	60.00
d.		Double surcharge, one invtd.	90.00	60.00

Columbus — A10

1901-02 *Perf. 12*

No.	Type	Description	Unused	Used
51	A10	1c green	.50	.30
52	A10	2c carmine	.65	.25
53	A10	5c ultra	1.50	.25
54	A10	10c red & blk	2.25	.35
55	A10	30c vio & blk	6.75	.85
56	A10	50c red org & blk	7.25	2.25
		Nos. 51-56 (6)	18.90	4.25

No. 44 Surcharged in Dark Blue

1903 *Rouletted*

No.	Type	Description	Unused	Used
57	A8	10c on 30c orange	2.60	.50
a.		Inverted surcharge	18.00	12.00
b.		Double surcharge	25.00	15.00
c.		Double surch., one inverted	25.00	15.00
d.		Double surch., both invtd.	25.00	15.00
e.		Stamp design printed on both sides		

Telegraph Stamps Surcharged or Overprinted in Black

Pedro de Valdivia — A11

Coat of Arms — A12

A13

Type I

Type II

Type I — Animal at left has neither mane nor tail.

Type II — Animal at left has mane and tail.

1904 *Perf. 12*

No.	Type	Description	Unused	Used
58	A11	1c on 20c ultra	.50	.40
a.		Imperf. horiz., pair	40.00	40.00
b.		Inverted surcharge	50.00	50.00
59	A13	2c yel brn, I	.40	.30
a.		Inverted overprint	20.00	20.00
b.		Pair, one without overprint	50.00	50.00
60	A13	5c red, I	.60	.30
a.		Inverted overprint	20.00	20.00
c.		Pair, one without overprint	50.00	50.00
61	A13	10c ol grn, I	2.25	.60
a.		Inverted overprint	50.00	50.00
		Nos. 58-61 (4)	3.75	1.60

Perf. 12½ to 16

No.	Type	Description	Unused	Used
62	A13	2c yel, brn, II	7.00	*4.50*
63	A11	3c on 5c brn red	70.00	60.00
a.		Inverted surcharge		
64	A12	3c on 1p brn, II	.70	.40
a.		Double surcharge	50.00	50.00
65	A13	5c red, II	11.00	5.50
a.		Inverted overprint	30.00	20.00
66	A13	10c ol grn, II	25.00	10.00
67	A11	12c on 5c brn red	1.30	.70
a.		No star at left of "Centavos"	3.00	2.50
b.		Inverted surcharge	40.00	40.00
c.		Double surcharge	50.00	50.00
		Nos. 62-67 (6)	115.00	81.10

Counterfeits exist of the overprint and surcharge varieties of Nos. 57-67.

For overprint see No. O12.

A14

A15

Columbus — A16

1905-09 *Perf. 12*

No.	Type	Description	Unused	Used
68	A14	1c green	.25	.25
69	A14	2c carmine	.30	.25
70	A14	3c yel brn	.65	.30
71	A14	5c ultra	.70	.25
72	A15	10c gray & blk	1.10	.25
73	A15	12c lake & blk	5.50	2.25
74	A15	15c vio & blk	1.25	.25
75	A15	20c org brn & blk	2.25	.25
76	A15	30c bl grn & blk	3.50	.35
77	A15	50c ultra & blk	3.50	.40
78	A16	1p brnz, ol grn & gray ('08)	16.00	11.00
		Nos. 68-78 (11)	35.00	15.80

A 20c dull red and black, type A15, was prepared but not issued. Value $125. "Specimen" examples of Nos. 74, 76-78 exist, punched to prevent postal use.

For surcharges and overprints see Nos. 79-82, O9, O11-O15.

No. 78a lacks metallic gold sheen of No. 78.

Nos. 68-72 exist overprinted "Isla de Mas Afuera". Overprints were authorized for use only on Juan Fernandez Islands. Value, $125 each.

Nos. 73, 78 Surcharged in Blue or Red

a

b

1910

No.	Type	Description	Unused	Used
79	A15 (a)	5c on 12c (Bl)	.50	.25
80	A16 (b)	10c on 1p (R)	1.10	.30
81	A16 (b)	20c on 1p (R)	1.60	.60
82	A16 (b)	1p (R)	3.00	1.10
		Nos. 79-82 (4)	6.20	2.25

The 1p is overprinted "ISLAS DE JUAN FERNANDEZ" only. The use of these stamps throughout Chile was authorized.

Independence Centenary Issue

Oath of Independence — A17

Monument to O'Higgins — A26

Adm. Lord Thomas Cochrane — A29

Designs: 2c, Battle of Chacabuco. 3c, Battle of Roble. 5c, Battle of Maipu. 10c, Naval Engagement of "Lautaro" and "Esmeralda." 12c, Capturing the "Maria Isabel." 15c, First Sortie of Liberating Forces. 20c, Abdication of O'Higgins. 25c, Chile's First Congress. 50c, Monument to José M. Carrera. 1p, Monument to San Martin. 2p, Gen. Manuel Blanco Encalada. 5p, Gen. José Ignacio Zenteno.

1910 **Center in Black**

No.	Type	Description	Unused	Used
83	A17	1c dk green	.25	.25
a.		Center inverted	*50,000.*	*24,000.*
84	A17	2c lake	1.10	.75
85	A17	3c red brown	.80	.45
86	A17	5c dp blue	.45	.25
87	A17	10c gray brn	1.20	.30
88	A17	12c vermilion	2.50	1.00
89	A17	15c slate	1.90	.55
90	A17	20c red orange	2.50	.85
91	A17	25c ultra	3.25	2.00
92	A26	30c violet	3.25	1.40
93	A26	50c olive grn	6.75	2.25
94	A26	1p yel org	14.00	5.25
95	A29	2p red	14.00	5.25
96	A29	5p yel grn	37.50	17.50
97	A29	10p dk violet	35.00	16.00
		Nos. 83-97 (15)	124.45	54.05

Nos. 83-93 exist overprinted "Isla de Mas Afuera". Overprints were authorized for use only on Juan Fernandez Islands. Value, $200 each.

Columbus A32

Pedro de Valdivia A33

Mateo de Toro Zambrano A34

Bernardo O'Higgins A35

Ramón Freire — A36

F. A. Pinto — A37

Joaquín Prieto — A38

Manuel Bulnes — A39

Manuel Montt — A40

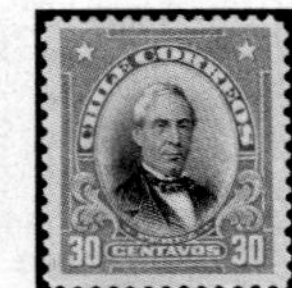
José Joaquín Pérez — A41

Federico Errázuriz Zanartu — A42

José de Balmaceda — A43

Designs: 1p, Anibal Pinto, 2p, Domingo Santa María. 10p, Federico Errázuriz Echaurren.

Outer backgrounds consist of horizontal and diagonal lines

1911 **Engr.** *Perf. 12*

No.	Type	Description	Unused	Used
98	A32	1c dp green	.25	.25
99	A33	2c scarlet	.25	.25
100	A34	3c sepia	.75	.25
101	A35	5c dk blue	.25	.25
102	A36	10c gray & blk	.75	.25
a.		Center inverted	1,800.	1,250.
103	A37	12c carmine & blk	1.00	.25
104	A38	15c reddsh pur & blk	.90	.25
a.		Center inverted	*2,000.*	25,000.
105	A39	20c org red & blk	1.75	.25
a.		Center inverted	125.00	125.00
106	A40	25c lt blue & blk	2.75	.60
107	A41	30c bis brn & blk	4.00	.30
108	A42	50c myr grn & blk	5.00	.30
109	A43	1p green & blk	11.00	.40
110	A43	2p ver & blk	22.00	2.00
111	A43	5p ol grn & blk	70.00	11.00
112	A43	10p org yel & blk	60.00	9.00
		Nos. 98-112 (15)	180.65	25.60

See Nos. 117, 121, 123, 127-128, 133-141, 143, 155A, 157-161, 165-169,171-172 and designs A47-A55, A57. For overprints see Nos. C6, C6B-C6D, C7-C8, C10-C11, C13-C21, O19-O22, O24-O27, O30-O34, O40.

Columbus A47

Toro Zambrano A48

Freire A49

O'Higgins A50

1912-13 **Engr.** *Perf. 12*

No.	Type	Description	Unused	Used
113	A47	2c scarlet	.25	.25
114	A48	4c black brn	.30	.25
115	A49	8c gray	1.00	.25
116	A50	10c blue & blk	1.00	.25
a.		Center inverted	625.00	500.00
b.		Imperf. horiz. or vert., pair	50.00	
117	A37	14c car & blk	1.50	.25
121	A38	40c violet & blk	5.75	.60
123	A40	60c lt blue & blk	14.00	1.75
		Nos. 113-123 (7)	23.80	3.60

See Nos. 125-126, 131, 164, 170, 173. For overprints see Nos. C6E, O18, O23, O28, O29.

Cochrane — A52

1915 Engr. *Perf. 13½x14*

124 A52 5c slate blue .60 .35
a. Imperf., pair 11.50

See Nos. 155, 162-163. For overprints see Nos. O17, O37.

1918

125 A49 8c slate 17.50 .80

No. 125 is from a plate made in Chile to resemble No. 115. The top of the head is further from the oval, the spots of color enclosed in the figures "8" are oval instead of round, and there are many small differences in the design.

1921 Worn Plate

126 A49 8c gray 20.00 5.00

No. 126 differs from No. 125 in not having diagonal lines in the frame and only a few diagonal lines above the shoulders (due to wear), while No. 125 has diagonal lines in the oval up to the level of the forehead.

Columbus — A53

1915-25 Typo. *Perf. 13½ to 14½*

127 A32 1c gray green .25 .25
128 A33 2c red .25 .25
129 A53 4c brown ('18) .25 .25

Frame Litho.; Head Engr.

131 A50 10c bl & blk 1.25 .25
a. 10c dark blue & black 1.25 .25
b. Imperf., pair 110.00
c. Center inverted 325.00
133 A38 15c vio & blk .90 .25
134 A39 20c org red & blk 1.40 .25
a. 20c brown orange & blk 1.75 .25
135 A40 25c dl bl & blk .55 .25
136 A41 30c bis brn & blk 1.75 .25
137 A42 50c dp grn & blk 1.75 .25

Perf. 14

138 A43 1p grn & blk 14.00 .50
139 A43 2p red & blk 17.00 .30
a. 2p vermilion & black 50.00 1.00
140 A43 5p ol grn & blk ('20) 40.00 1.00
141 A43 10p org & blk ('25) 40.00 2.50
Nos. 127-141 (13) 119.35 6.55

The frames have crosshatching on the 15c, 20c, 30c, 2p, 5p and 10p. They have no crosshatching on the 10c, 25c, 50c and 1p.

Nos. 131a and 134a are printed from new head plates which give blacker and heavier impressions. No. 131a exists with; (a) frame litho., head engr.; (b) frame typo., head engr.; (c) frame typo., head litho. No. 134a is with frame typo., head engr.

A 4c stamp with portrait of Balmaceda and a 14c with portrait of Manuel de Salas were prepared but not placed in use. Both stamps were sent to the paper mill at Puente Alto for destruction. They were not all destroyed as some were privately preserved and sold.

Columbus — A54

Types of 1915-20 Redrawn

1918-20 *Perf. 13½x14½*

143 A32 1c gray grn ('20) .30 .25
144 A54 4c brown .50 .25

No. 143 has all the lines much finer and clearer than No. 127. The white shirt front is also much less shaded.

Manuel Rengifo — A55

1921

145 A55 40c dk vio & blk 2.00 .40

For overprints see Nos. C6A, C9.

Pan-American Congress Building — A56

1923, Apr. 25 Typo. *Perf. 14½x14*

146 A56 2c red .25 .25
147 A56 4c brown .25 .25

Typo.; Center Engr.

148 A56 10c blue & blk .25 .25
149 A56 20c orange & blk .75 .25
150 A56 40c dl vio & blk 1.00 .30
151 A56 1p green & blk 1.25 .50
152 A56 2p red & blk 5.00 .60
153 A56 5p dk grn & blk 17.00 4.50
Nos. 146-153 (8) 25.75 6.90

Fifth Pan-American Congress.

Adm. Juan José Latorre — A57

Typographed; Head Engraved

1927 *Perf. 13½x14½*

154 A57 80c dk brn & blk 2.00 .60

Types of 1915-25 Issues Inscribed: "Chile Correos"

Perf. 13½x14½

1928-31 Engr. Wmk. 215

155 A52 5c slate blue 1.40 .25

Frame Typo.; Center Engr.

155A A38 15c violet & blk 2,200.
156 A55 40c dk vio & blk .60 .25
157 A42 50c dp grn & blk 2.50 .25

Perf. 14

158 A43 1p green & blk 1.00 .25
159 A43 2p red & blk 5.00 .25
160 A43 5p ol grn & blk 9.75 .45
161 A43 10p orange & blk 9.75 1.90
Nos. 155,156-161 (7) 30.00 3.60

Paper of Nos. 155-161 varies from thin to thick.

Types of 1915-25 Issues Inscribed: "Correos de Chile"

1928 Engr. *Perf. 13½x14½*

162 A52 5c deep blue .35 .25

1929 Litho.

163 A52 5c light green .50 .25

Frame Litho.; Center Engr.

164 A50 10c blue & blk 2.00 .25
165 A38 15c violet & blk 2.40 .25
166 A39 20c org red & blk 5.75 .25
167 A40 25c blue & blk .95 .25
168 A41 30c brown & blk .75 .25
169 A42 50c dp grn & blk .65 .25
Nos. 163-169 (7) 13.00 1.75

Redrawn

1929 Frame Typo.; Center Litho.

170 A50 10c blue & blk 3.00 .25
171 A38 15c violet & blk 2.75 .25
172 A39 20c org red & blk 4.25 .25
Nos. 170-172 (3) 10.00 .75

1931 Unwmk.

173 A50 10c blue & blk .70 .25

In the redrawn stamps the lines behind the portraits are heavier and completely fill the ovals. There are strong diagonal lines above the shoulders. On No. 170 the head is larger than on Nos. 164, 173.

A58

Prosperity of Saltpeter Trade
A59 A60

Perf. 13½x14

1930, July 21 Litho. Wmk. 215

Size: 20x25mm

175 A58 5c yellow grn .60 .40
176 A58 10c red brown .60 .30
177 A58 15c violet .60 .30
178 A59 25c deep gray 1.90 .60
179 A60 70c dark blue 4.50 1.50

Perf. 14

Size: 24½x30mm

180 A60 1p dk gray grn 3.75 .75
Nos. 175-180 (6) 11.95 3.85

Cent. of the 1st shipment of saltpeter from Chile, July 21, 1830.

Manuel Bulnes — A61

1931 *Perf. 13½, 14*

181 A61 20c brown 1.00 .30

For overprints see Nos. O35, O39.

Bernardo O'Higgins — A62

1932

182 A62 10c deep blue 1.50 .40

For overprints see Nos. O36, O38.

Mariano Egana — A63

Joaquin Tocornal — A64

1934 *Perf. 13½x14*

183 A63 30c magenta .65 .25

Perf. 14

184 A64 1.20p bright blue 1.10 .25

Centenary of the constitution.

José Joaquín Pérez — A65

1934 *Perf. 13½x14*

185 A65 30c bright pink 1.60 .35

Atacama Desert — A66

Designs: 10c, Fishing boats. 20c, Coquito palms. 25c, Sheep. 30c, Mining. 40c, Lonquimay forest. 50c, Colliery at Port Lota. 1p, Shipping at Valparaiso. 1.20p, Puntiagudo volcano. 2p, Diego de Almagro. 5p, Cattle. 10p, Mining saltpeter.

Wmk. 215

1936, Mar. 1 Litho. *Perf. 14*

186 A66 5c vermilion .60 .30
187 A66 10c violet .30 .25
188 A66 20c magenta .40 .25
189 A66 25c grnsh blue 3.00 .80
190 A66 30c lt green .40 .25
191 A66 40c blk, *cream* 3.25 .85
192 A66 50c bl, *bluish* 1.75 .30

Engr.

193 A66 1p dk green 1.75 .50
194 A66 1.20p dp blue 2.00 .70
195 A66 2p dk brown 2.50 .80
196 A66 5p copper red 5.75 2.25
197 A66 10p dk violet 14.00 8.00
Nos. 186-197 (12) 35.70 15.25

400th anniv. of the discovery of Chile by Diego de Almagro.

Laja Waterfall — A78

Fishing in Chiloé — A84

Designs: 10c, Agriculture. 15c, Boldo tree. 20c, Nitrate Industry. 30c, Mineral spas. 40c, Copper mine. 50c, Mining. 1.80p, Osorno Volcano. 2p, Mercantile marine. 5p, Lake Villarrica. 10p, State railways.

Perf. 13½x14

1938-40 Litho. Wmk. 215

198 A78 5c brn car ('39) .25 .25
199 A78 10c sal pink ('39) .25 .25
200 A78 15c brn org ('40) .25 .25
201 A78 20c light blue .25 .25
202 A78 30c brt pink .25 .25
203 A78 40c lt grn ('39) .25 .25
204 A78 50c violet .25 .25

Engr. *Perf. 14*

205 A84 1p orange brn .25 .25
206 A84 1.80p deep blue .45 .25
207 A84 2p car lake ('39) .25 .25
208 A84 5p dk slate grn ('39) .35 .25
209 A84 10p dp reddish lil ('40) .90 .25
Nos. 198-209 (12) 3.95 3.00

See Nos. 217-227. For surcharge and overprints see Nos. 253, O41-O66, O70-O71.

Map of the Americas — A89

Unwmk.

1940, Sept. 11 Litho. *Perf. 14*

210 A89 40c dl grn & yel grn .60 .25

Pan American Union, 50th anniversary.

Camilo Henríquez — A90

Founding of Santiago A93

Designs: 40c, Pedro de Valdivia. 1.10p, Benjamin Vicuna Mackenna. 3.60p, Diego Barros Arana.

Perf. 14½x14, 14½

1941, Jan. 23 Engr. Wmk. 215

211 A90 10c carmine lake .25 .25
212 A90 40c green .35 .25
213 A90 1.10p red 1.25 .70
214 A93 1.80p blue 1.25 .70
215 A90 3.60p indigo 3.75 2.75
Nos. 211-215 (5) 6.85 4.65

400th anniversary of Santiago.

Types of 1938

Perf. 13½x14

1942-46 Unwmk. Litho.

217 A78 10c sal pink ('43) .25 .25
218 A78 15c brown org ('43) .25 .25
219 A78 20c lt blue ('43) .25 .25
220 A78 30c brt pink ('43) .25 .25
221 A78 40c yellow grn .80 .25
222 A78 50c violet ('43) .25 .25

Engr. ***Perf. 14***

223 A84 1p brown orange 1.50 .25
225 A84 2p car lake ('43) .25 .25
226 A84 5p dk sl grn ('43) .50 .25
227 A84 10p rose violet ('46) .90 .25
Nos. 217-227 (10) 5.20 2.50

Valentin Letelier — A95

University of Chile — A98

Designs: 40c, Andrés Bello. 90c, Manuel Bulnes. 1.80p, Manuel Montt.

1942, Nov. 1 ***Perf. 14x14½, 14 (1p)***

228 A95 30c rose red .25 .25
229 A95 40c deep green .25 .25
230 A95 90c rose violet 1.90 1.50
231 A98 1p deep brown 1.10 .90
232 A95 1.80p dark blue 3.50 3.00
Nos. 228-232 (5) 7.00 5.90

University of Chile cent. See No. C89.

Manuel Bulnes — A100

Map Showing Strait of Magellan — A104

Designs: 30c, Juan Williams Wilson. 40c, Diego Duble Almeida. 1p, José Mardones.

1944, Mar. 2 Litho. ***Perf. 14***

233 A100 15c black .25 .25
234 A100 30c deep rose .25 .25
235 A100 40c yellow green .25 .25
236 A100 1p brown carmine .95 .25
237 A104 1.80p ultra 1.40 .95
Nos. 233-237 (5) 3.10 1.95

100th anniversary of the occupation of the Strait of Magellan.

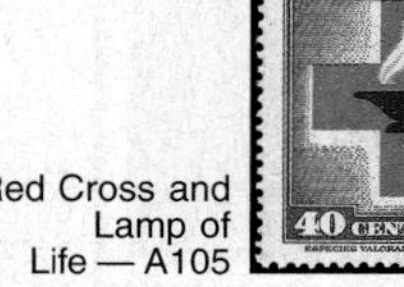
Red Cross and Lamp of Life — A105

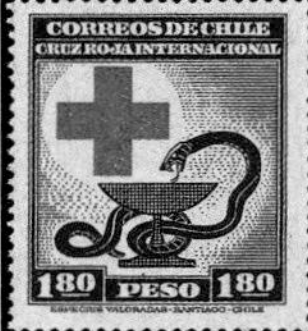

Serpent and Cup — A106

1944, Oct. 18 Unwmk.

238 A105 40c green, red & blk .30 .25
239 A106 1.80p ultra & red .90 .45

80th anniv. of the Intl. Red Cross Soc.

Bernardo O'Higgins — A107

"Embrace of Maipú" (O'Higgins Joining San Martin) — A108

Designs: 40c, Abdication of O'Higgins. 1.80p, Battle of Rancagua.

1945 Engr. ***Perf. 14 (15c), 14½***

Center in Black

240 A107 15c carmine .30 .25
241 A108 30c brown .30 .25
242 A108 40c deep green .40 .25
243 A108 1.80p dark blue 1.50 .90
Nos. 240-243 (4) 2.50 1.65

Death of Bernardo O'Higgins in 1842, cent.

A111

Proposed Columbus lighthouse.

Wmk. 215

1945, Sept. 10 Litho. ***Perf. 14***

244 A111 40c light green .50 .25

Issued in honor of the discovery of America by Columbus and the Memorial Lighthouse to be erected in his memory.

A112

1946 Engr.

245 A112 40c dark green .40 .25
246 A112 1.80p dark blue .40 .25

80th anniv. of the death of Andrés Bello, poet and educator.

Map Showing Chile's Claims of Antarctic Territory A113

1947, May 12 Litho. ***Perf. 14½***

247 A113 40c carmine 1.00 .30
248 A113 2.50p deep blue 2.00 .50

Eusebio Lillo and Ramon Carnicer A114

1947, Sept. 18 Engr.

249 A114 40c dark green .40 .25

Centenary of national anthem.

Miguel de Cervantes Saavedra A115

1947, Oct. 11 Wmk. 215

250 A115 40c dk carmine .40 .25

400th anniv. of the birth of Cervantes, novelist, playwright and poet.

Arturo Prat Chacón and Iquique Naval Battle A116

1948, Dec. 24 ***Perf. 14½***

251 A116 40c deep blue .40 .25

Centenary of the birth of Arturo Prat Chacon, Chilean naval hero.

Bernardo O'Higgins — A117

Perf. 13½x14

1948 Wmk. 215 Litho.

252 A117 60c black .30 .25

See No. 262. For surcharges see Nos. 266-267.

No. 203 Surcharged in Black

1948

253 A78 20c on 40c lt grn .25 .25

Chilean Pigeons — A118

FAUNA: a, Chilean Otter. b, tree. d, American skunk. f, Southern sea lions. g, Sugarcane borer moth. h, Emperor penguins. i, Bat. j, Chinchilla. k, Grant's stag beetle. l, Trevally (fish). m, Chilean slender lizard. o, Crested caracara. q, Red-gartered coot. r, Chilean guemal (deer). s, Spiny rock lobster. u, Tilefish. v, Praying mantis. x, Torrent duck. y, Red conger.

FLORA: b, Araucarian pine (monkey puzzle tree). e, Evening primrose. n, Chilean red bell flower. p, Loxodon (flower). t, Boldo tree. w, Coquito palm trees.

Wmk. 215

1948, Dec. 6 Litho. ***Perf. 14***

254 60c Block of 25 45.00 45.00
a.-y. A118 any single 1.00 .80
255 2.60p Block of 25 70.00 70.00
a.-y. A118 any single 1.75 1.25

Issued in panes of 100.

Cent. (in 1944) of the publication of the 1st volume of Claudio Gay's Natural History of Chile. See No. C124.

Catalogue values for unused stamps in this section, from this point to the end of the section, are for Never Hinged items.

Benjamin Vicuna Mackenna — A121

1949, Mar. 22 Engr. ***Perf. 13½x14***

257 A121 60c deep blue .30 .25

See No. C126.

Symbols of Arts and Crafts Education — A122

Design: 2.60p, Badge and book.

Unwmk.

1949, Nov. 11 Litho. ***Perf. 14***

258 A122 60c lilac rose .25 .25
259 A122 2.60p violet blue .40 .30
Nos. 258-259,C127-C128 (4) 2.90 1.55

Cent. of the foundation of Chile's School of Arts and Crafts.

Heinrich von Stephan — A123

1950, Jan. 6 Engr.

260 A123 60c deep carmine .25 .25
261 A123 2.50p deep blue .75 .50
Nos. 260-261,C129-C130 (4) 2.60 1.60

UPU, 75th anniv.

O'Higgins Type of 1948

1950 Litho. ***Perf. 13x14***

262 A117 60c black .40 .25

For surcharge see No. 266.

San Martín — A124

Wmk. 215

1951, Mar. 16 Engr. *Perf. 14*
263 A124 60c deep blue .40 .25

Cent. of the death of Gen. José de San Martin. See No. C165.

Isabella I — A125

1952, Mar. 20
264 A125 60c brt blue .35 .25

500th anniv. of the birth of Queen Isabella I of Spain. See No. C166.

Bernardo O'Higgins — A126

1952 Unwmk. Litho. *Perf. 13½x14*
265 A126 1p dk blue grn .30 .25

See No. 275. For overprints see Nos. O67-O69.

No. 262 Surcharged in Red, Numbers & Letters Thicker

No. 252 Surcharged in Red, Numbers & Letters Thinner

1952, Sept.
266 A117 40c on 60c black .35 .25

Wmk. 215
267 A117 40c on 60c black .35 .25

Mateo de Toro Zambrano — A127

1953, Mar. 13 Wmk. 215
268 A127 80c green .30 .25

See No. 285.

Valdivia Arms — A128

Old Fort — A129

3p, Modern Valdivia. 5p, Street in ancient Valdivia.

1953, May *Perf. 14*
269 A128 1p brt ultra .50 .25
270 A129 2p dull rose vio .50 .25
271 A129 3p blue green .75 .25
272 A129 5p deep brown .75 .25
Nos. 269-272,C167 (5) 4.75 1.45

4th centenary of the founding of Valdivia, capital of Valdivia province.

José Toribio Medina (1852-1930), Historian and Bibliographer A130

1953, June Engr. *Perf. 14½*
273 A130 1p brown .35 .25
274 A130 2.50p deep blue .45 .25

O'Higgins Type of 1952
Perf. 13½x14
1953, Oct. Wmk. 215 Litho.
275 A126 1p dk blue green .35 .25

For overprint see No. O69.

Stamp of 1853 — A131

1953, Oct. 15 Engr. *Perf. 14½*
276 A131 1p reddish brn .75 .25

Centenary of Chile's first postage stamps.
Souvenir sheet including No. 276 is noted below No. C168.

A132

Census chart and map.

1953, Nov. 5 Litho. *Perf. 13½x14*
277 A132 1p blue green .30 .25
278 A132 2.50p violet blue .30 .25
279 A132 3p chocolate .50 .25
280 A132 4p carmine .50 .25
Nos. 277-280 (4) 1.60 1.00

12th general census of population and housing.

Arms of Angol — A133

1954, May 28 Unwmk. *Perf. 14*
281 A133 2p deep carmine .40 .25

400th anniversary of the founding of Angol, capital of Malleco province.

Ignacio Domeyko — A134

1954, Aug. 16 Engr. *Perf. 13½x14*
282 A134 1p blue slate .35 .25

150th anniversary of the birth of Ignacio Domeyko (1802-89), mineralogist and educator. See No. C171.

Early Steam Locomotive — A135

1954, Sept. 10 Wmk. 215 *Perf. 14½*
283 A135 1p red .65 .30

Centenary (in 1951) of the first South American railroad. See No. C172.

Adm. Arturo Prat Chacón — A136

1954 Unwmk. Litho. *Perf. 14*
284 A136 2p dk violet blue .35 .25

75th anniv. of the naval Battle of Iquique.

Toro Zambrano Type of 1953
1954, Nov. 6 *Perf. 13½x14*
285 A127 80c green .30 .25

Arms of Viña del Mar — A137

Design: 2p, Arms of Valparaiso.

1955, Mar. 5 Wmk. 215 *Perf. 14*
286 A137 1p violet blue .35 .25
287 A137 2p carmine .35 .25

1st Intl. Phil. Exhib., Valparaiso, Mar. 1955.

Dr. Alejandro del Rio — A138

1955, May 24 *Perf. 13½x14*
288 A138 2p violet blue .40 .25

14th Pan-American Sanitary Conference.

Christ of the Andes, Emblems of Chile, Argentina A139

1955, Aug. 31 Unwmk. *Perf. 14½*
289 A139 1p violet blue .40 .25

Reciprocal visits of Presidents Juan D. Peron and Carlos Ibanez del Campo. See No. C173.

Manuel Rengifo — A140

5p, Mariano Egana. 50p, Diego Portales.

1955-56 Unwmk. *Perf. 14x14½*
290 A140 3p violet blue .35 .25
291 A140 5p dk car rose .35 .25
292 A140 50p rose lilac ('56) 1.90 .45
Nos. 290-292 (3) 2.60 .95

Joaquin Prieto (1786-1854), soldier and political leader; president, 1831-41. See No. QRA1.

Jose M. Carrera A141

Ramón Freire A142

Portraits: 5p, Manuel Bulnes. 10p, Pres. Francisco A. Pinto. 50p, Manuel Montt.

Perf. 14x14½
1956-58 Unwmk. Litho.
293 A141 2p purple .30 .25
293A A142 3p lt violet blue .25 .25
294 A141 5p redsh brn (19½x23mm) .30 .25
a. Size 19x22mm .30 .25
295 A142 10p vio (19x22¼mm) .30 .25
a. Perf. 13½x14 (19¼x22½mm) ('58) .55 .25
296 A141 50p rose red .50 .25
Nos. 293-296 (5) 1.65 1.25

Wmk. 215
297 A141 2p dull purple .30 .25
298 A142 3p violet blue .30 .25

No. 294 has yellow gum; No. 294a, white gum.

For overprints see Nos. O72-O76.

Federico Santa Maria — A143

Unwmk.

1957, Jan. 31 Engr. *Perf. 14*
299 A143 5p dk red brown .30 .25

25th anniv. of the Federico Santa Maria Technical University. See Nos. C190-C191.
Souvenir sheet including No. 299 is noted below No. C191.

Gabriela Mistral — A144

1958, Jan. 10
300 A144 10p red brown .50 .25

Issued in honor of Gabriela Mistral, poet and educator. See No. C192.

Arms of Osorno — A145

Design: 50p, Garcia Hdo. de Mendoza.

1958, Mar. 23 Litho. *Perf. 14*
301 A145 10p carmine .25 .25

Engr.
302 A145 50p green .40 .25

400th anniversary of the founding of the city of Osorno, capital of Osorno province.
Souvenir sheet including No. 302 in red brown is noted below No. C193.

Arms of Santiago — A146

1958, Oct. 18 Unwmk. *Perf. 14*
303 A146 10p dark violet .30 .25

Natl. Philatelic Exposition, Santiago, Oct. 18-26.
Souvenir sheet including No. 303 in deep red is noted below No. C194.

Symbolical Savings Bank — A147

1958, Dec. 18
304 A147 10p dark blue .40 .25

Savings Bank for Public Employees, cent.
Souvenir sheet including No. 304 in violet is noted below No. C195.

Modern Map of Antarctica — A148

1958, Aug. 28 Unwmk. *Perf. 14*
305 A148 40p rose carmine .60 .60

IGY, 1957-1958. See No. C214.

Antarctic Map and "La Araucana" A149

Map of Strait of Magellan, 1588 — A150

1958 Litho. *Perf. 14*
310 A149 10p violet blue 1.00 .25

Engr.
311 A150 200p dull purple 3.00 1.75
Nos. 310-311,C199-C200 (4) 10.00 4.00

For overprint see No. O77.

Valdivia River Bridge — A153

1959, Feb. 9 Engr. *Perf. 14*
319 A153 40p green .90 .25

Cent. of the German School in Valdivia and to publicize the Valdivia Phil. Exhib., 2/9-18.
Souvenir sheet including No. 319 is noted below No. C213.

Strait of Magellan, Map by Pedro Sarmiento de Gamboa, c. 1582 — A154

1959, Aug. 27 Litho.
320 A154 10p dull purple .45 .25

Juan Ladrillero expedition to explore the Strait of Magellan, 1557-58, 400th anniv. See No. C215.

Diego Barros Arana — A155

1959, Aug. 27
321 A155 40p ultra .45 .25

50th anniv. of the death of Diego Barros Arana (1830-1907), historian. See No. C216.

Henri Dunant — A156

1959, Oct. 6 Unwmk. *Perf. 14*
322 A156 20p red & red brn .45 .25

Cent. of the Red Cross idea. See No. C217.

Manuel Bulnes — A157

Francisco A. Pinto — A158

Choshuenco Volcano A159

No. 326, Choshuenco volcano, redrawn. 5c, Manuel Montt. 10c, Maule River Valley. 20c, 1e, Inca Lake.

1960-67 Litho. *Perf. 13x14*
323 A157 5m bluish grn .25 .25
324 A158 1c carmine .25 .25

Perf. 14
Size: 29x25mm
325 A159 2c ultra ('61) .25 .25

Perf. 14x13
Size: 23½x18mm
326 A159 2c ultra ('62) .25 .25

Perf. 13x14
327 A157 5c blue .25 .25

Perf. 14
Size: 29x25mm
328 A159 10c green ('62) .25 .25
329 A159 20c Prus blue ('62) .35 .25
329A A159 1e bluish grn ('67) .65 .25
Nos. 323-329A (8) 2.50 2.00

On No. 325 "Volcan Choshuenco" is at upper left, below "Correos." On No. 326, it is at bottom, above "Centesimos."
For overprint and surcharge see Nos. B7, O79, RA1.

Refugee Family A160

1960, Apr. 7 *Perf. 14½*
330 A160 1c green .30 .25

WRY, July 1, 1959-June 30, 1960. A souvenir sheet is noted below No. C218.

Type of Air Post Issue, 1962, and

Arms of Chile A161

José M. Carrera A162

No. 332, Palace of Justice. 5c, Natl. Memorial. 10c, Manuel de Toro y Zambrano and Martinez de Rozas. 20c, Manuel de Salas and Juan Egana. 50c, Manuel Rodriguez and Juan Mackenna.

Wmk. 215 (#331, 1e); Unwmk.

1960-65 Engr. *Perf. 14½*
331 A161 1c maroon & sepia .30 .25
332 A161 1c brn & claret ('62) .30 .25
333 A162 5c grn & Prus grn ('61) .30 .25
334 AP54 10c brn & vio brn ('64) .50 .25
334A AP54 20c ind & bl grn ('65) .50 .25
335 AP54 50c red brn & mar ('65) .80 .25
336 A162 1e gray ol & brn 1.50 .40
Nos. 331-336,C218A-C220D (14) 7.60 3.80

150th anniv. of the formation of the 1st Natl. Government. A souvenir sheet is noted below No. C220B. See No. C285.

Family — A163

Design: 10c, Various buildings.

Unwmk.

1960, Jan. 18 Litho. *Perf. 14*
337 A163 5c green .30 .25
338 A163 10c brt violet .30 .25

13th population census (No. 337) and 2nd housing census (No. 338).

Chamber of Deputies A164

1961, Aug. 14 Unwmk. *Perf. 14½*
339 A164 2c red brown .65 .25

150th anniv. of the 1st National Congress. See No. C245.

Soccer Players and Globe A165

Design: 5c, Goalkeeper and stadium, vert.

1962, May 30 Engr. *Perf. 14½*
340 A165 2c blue .45 .25
341 A165 5c green .60 .25

World Soccer Championship, Chile, May 30-June 17. Note on souvenir sheet follows No. C247.

Mother and Child — A166

1963, Mar. 21 Litho. *Perf. 14*
342 A166 3c maroon .35 .25

FAO "Freedom from Hunger" campaign. See No. C248.

Centenary Emblem — A167

1963, Aug. 23 Unwmk. *Perf. 14*
343 A167 3c red & gray .35 .25

Cent. of the Intl. Red Cross. See No. C249.

Fireman Carrying Woman — A168

1963, Dec. 20 Unwmk. *Perf. 14*
344 A168 3c violet .40 .25

Centenary of the Santiago Fire Brigade. See No. C250.

Enrique Molina — A169

Design: No. 346, Magr. Carlos Casanueva.

1964, Nov. 14 Litho. *Perf. 14*
345 A169 4c bister brown .30 .25
346 A169 4c rose claret .30 .25
Nos. 345-346,C257-C258 (4) 1.20 1.00

Enrique Molina, founder of the University of Concepcion, and Msgr. Carlos Casanueva, rector of the Catholic University, 1920-53.

Easter Island Statue — A170

Copihue, National Flower — A171

Design: 30c, Robinson Crusoe.

1965-69 Litho. *Perf. 14x14½*
347 A170 6c rose lilac 1.50 .25
347A A170 10c rose pink ('68) .50 .25

Perf. 14
348 A171 15c yel grn & rose red 1.00 .25
348A A171 20c yel grn & rose red ('69) .50 .25

Perf. 14x14½
349 A170 30c rose claret .75 .25
Nos. 347-349 (5) 4.25 1.25

For surcharge see No. RA2.

Skier — A172

1965, Aug. 30 *Perf. 14*
350 A172 4c blue green .40 .25

World Skiing Championships, Chile, 1966.

Lorenzo Sazie — A173

1966, Feb. 9 Litho. *Perf. 14x14½*
351 A173 1e green 1.50 .25

Cent. of the death of Dr. Lorenzo Sazie, dean of the Faculty of Medicine, University of Santiago.

German Riesco, President in 1901-1906 — A174

Portrait: 30c, Jorge Montt (1847-1922), president in 1891-1896.

1966 Unwmk. *Perf. 13x14*
354 A174 30c violet .30 .25
355 A174 50c dull brown .35 .25

For surcharge see No. 450.

William Wheelwright and S.S. Chile — A175

1966, Aug. 2 *Perf. 14½*
358 A175 10c ultra & lt bl .35 .25

125th anniv. (in 1965) of the arrival of the paddle steamers "Chile" and "Peru." See No. C268.

Learning to Read — A176

1966, Aug. 13 Litho. *Perf. 14*
359 A176 10c red brown .35 .25

Literacy campaign.

UN and ICY Emblems A177

1966, Oct. 28 Unwmk. *Perf. 14½*
360 A177 1e green & brown 1.40 .25

Intl. Cooperation Year, 1965. See No. C269.

Capt. Luis Pardo and Ship in Antarctica — A178

1967, Jan. Litho. *Perf. 14½*
361 A178 20c turquoise blue 1.50 .75

Rescue of the Shackleton South Pole expedition by Capt. Luis Pardo of Chile, 50th anniv. See No. C271.

Family — A179

1967, Apr. 13 Unwmk. *Perf. 14*
362 A179 10c magenta & blk .35 .25

8th Intl. Conf. for Family Planning, Santiago, Apr. 1967. See No. C272.

Trees and Mountains A180

1967, June 9 Litho. *Perf. 14½*
363 A180 10c blue grn & lt bl .60 .25

Reforestation Campaign. See No. C274.

Lions Emblem — A181

1967, July 12 Litho. *Perf. 14*
364 A181 20c Prus blue & yel .35 .25
Nos. 364,C275-C276 (3) 1.85 .80

50th anniv. of Lions Intl.

Chilean Flag A182

1967, Oct. 20 Unwmk. *Perf. 14½*
365 A182 80c crimson & ultra .60 .25

Natl, flag, 150th anniv. See No. C277.

José Maria Cardinal Caro — A183

1967, Dec. 4 Engr. *Perf. 14½*
366 A183 20c deep carmine .60 .35

Cent. of the birth of José Maria Cardinal Caro, the first Chilean cardinal. See No. C279.

San Martin and O'Higgins — A184

1968, Apr. 23 Litho. Unwmk.
367 A184 3e blue .65 .25

Sesquicentennial of the Battles of Chacabuco and Maipu. See No. C280.

Farm Couple — A185

1968, June 18 *Perf. 14½*
368 A185 20c black, org & grn .75 .25

Agrarian reforms. See No. C281.

Juan I. Molina A186

1968, Aug. 27 Litho. *Perf. 14½*
369 A186 2e red lilac .60 .25

Issued to honor Juan I. Molina, educator and scientist. See No. C282.

Hand Holding Cogwheel — A187

1968, Sept. *Perf. 14x14½*
370 A187 30c deep carmine .30 .25

Fourth census of manufacturers.

Map of Chiloé Province, Sailing Ship and Coastal Vessel A188

1968, Oct. 7 ***Perf. 14½***
371 A188 30c ultra .40 .25

Anniversaries of the founding of five towns in Chiloé Province. See No. C283.

Automobile Club Emblem A189

1968, Nov. 10 **Engr.** ***Perf. 14½x14***
372 A189 1e carmine rose .35 .25

40th anniversary of the Automobile Club of Chile. See No. C284.

Francisco Garcia Huidobro A190

Design: 5e, King Philip V of Spain.

1968, Dec. 31 **Litho.** ***Perf. 14½***
373 A190 2e pale rose & ultra .40 .25
374 A190 5e brown & yel grn .40 .25
Nos. 373-374,C288-C289 (4) 1.40 1.00

225th anniv. of the founding of the State Mint (Casa de Moneda de Chile).

Satellite and Radar Station A191

1969, May 20 **Litho.** ***Perf. 14½***
375 A191 30c blue .35 .30

Inauguration of ENTEL-Chile, the 1st commercial satellite communications ground station, Longovilo.

See No. C290. For surcharges see Nos. 397, C308.

Red Cross, Crescent and Lion and Sun Emblems A192

1969, Sept. **Litho.** ***Perf. 14½***
376 A192 2e violet blue & red .40 .25

50th anniversary of the League of Red Cross Societies. See No. C291.

Rapel Hydroelectric Plant — A193

1969, Nov. 18 **Litho.** ***Perf. 14½***
377 A193 40c green .30 .25

See No. C292. For surcharge see No. B8.

Col. Rodriguez Monument — A194

1969, Nov. 24
378 A194 2e rose claret .40 .25

150th anniversary of the death of Col. Manuel Rodriguez. See No. C293.

EXPO '70 Emblem — A195

1969, Dec. 2 **Litho.** ***Perf. 14***
379 A195 3e blue .55 .25

EXPO '70 Intl. Exhibition, Osaka, Japan, Mar. 15-Sept. 13, 1970. See No. C294.

Open Book A196

1969, Dec. 3 ***Perf. 14½***
380 A196 40c red brown .40 .25

Translation of the Bible into Spanish by Casiodoro de Reina, 400th anniv. See No. C295. For surcharge see No. B10.

Globes and ILO Emblem A197

1969, Dec. 17 ***Perf. 14½***
381 A197 1e green & blk .35 .25

ILO, 50th anniv. See No. C296.

Human Rights Flame A198

1969, Dec. 18
382 A198 4e blue & red .65 .25

Human Rights Year, 1968. See No. C297.

Policarpo Toro and Easter Island A199

1970, Jan. 26 ***Perf. 14½***
383 A199 5e lilac .90 .45

80th anniversary of the acquisition of Easter Island. See No. C298.

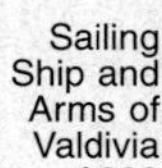

Sailing Ship and Arms of Valdivia A200

1970, Feb. 4 **Litho.** ***Perf. 14½***
384 A200 40c dk carmine .60 .25

150th anniv. of the capture of Valdivia during Chile's war of independence by Thomas Cochrane (1775-1860), naval commander. See No. C299.

Paul Harris and Rotary Emblem — A201

1970, Mar. 18 **Litho.** ***Perf. 14***
385 A201 10e violet blue .50 .25

Cent. of the birth of Paul Harris (1868-1947), founder of Rotary Intl. See No. C300.

Mahatma Gandhi — A202

1970, Apr. 1 **Litho.** ***Perf. 14½***
386 A202 40c blue green 3.50 .30

Mohandas K. Gandhi (1869-1948), leader in India's fight for independence, birth cent. See No. C301. For surcharge see No. 449.

Santo Domingo Church, Santiago, Chile — A203

Designs: 2e, Casa de Moneda de Chile, horiz. 3e, Pedro de Valdivia. 5e, Bridge, horiz. 10e, Ambrosio O'Higgins.

1970, Apr. 30 **Engr.**
387 A203 2e violet brown .40 .25
388 A203 3e dark red .40 .25
389 A203 4e dark blue .30 .25
390 A203 5e brown .30 .25
391 A203 10e green .30 .25
Nos. 387-391 (5) 1.70 1.25

Exploration and development of Chile by Spanish explorers.

A sheet containing imperf examples of Nos. 388, 390 and 391 exists. It was not valid for postage. Size:109x140mm, value $10.

Education Year Emblem — A204

1970, July 17 **Litho.** ***Perf. 14½***
392 A204 2e claret .35 .25

International Education Year. See No. C302.

Virgin and Child — A205

1970, July 28
393 A205 40c green .30 .25

O'Higgins National Shrine at Maipu. See No. C303. For surcharge see No. 454.

Torch and Snake — A206

1970, Aug. 11
394 A206 40c claret & light blue .60 .25

International Cancer Congress, Houston, Texas, May 22-29. See No. C304.

Copper Symbol, Chile Arms — A207

1970, Oct. 21 **Litho.** ***Perf. 14½***
395 A207 40c car & lt red brn .35 .25

Nationalization of the copper industry.

See No. C305. For surcharges see Nos. 459, B9.

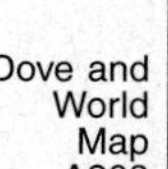

Dove and World Map A208

1970, Oct. 22
396 A208 3e rose magenta & pur .40 .25

25th anniv. of the UN. See No. C306.

No. 375 Surcharged in Red

1970, Dec. 24 Litho. *Perf. 14½*
397 A191 52c on 30c blue .45 .25

Freighter and Ship's Wheel — A209

1971, Jan. 18 Litho. *Perf. 14*
398 A209 52c deep carmine .35 .25

Natl. Maritime Commission. See No. C307.

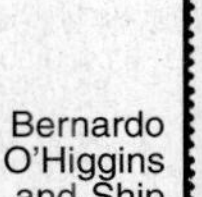

Bernardo O'Higgins and Ship A210

1971, Feb. 3 *Perf. 14½*
399 A210 5e pale blue and bluish grn .75 .25

150th anniv. of the expedition to liberate Peru from Spanish rule. See No. C309.

An imperforate souvenir sheet containing Nos. 399, C280, and C303 exists. Size: 120x150mm.

Youth, Girl and UN Emblem A211

1971, Feb. 11 Litho. *Perf. 14½*
400 A211 52c dk blue & brn .35 .25

1st meeting in Latin America of the Executive Council of UNICEF, Santiago, May 20-31, 1969. See No. C310.

Chilean Boy Scout Emblem — A212

1971, Feb. 10 *Perf. 14*
401 A212 1e green & brn .45 .25

Founding of Chilean Boy Scouts, 60th anniversary. See No. C311.

Satellite and Radar Station A213

1971, May 25 Litho. *Perf. 14½*
402 A213 40c dull green .50 .25

First commercial Chilean satellite communications ground station, Longovilo. See No. C312.

Diver with Harpoon Gun A214

1971, Sept. 1
403 A214 1.15e lt & dk green 1.10 .25
404 A214 2.35e vio bl & dp vio bl .40 .25

10th World Championship of Underwater Fishing.

Ferdinand Magellan and Sailing Ship — A215

1971, Nov. 3
405 A215 35c lt vio & brn vio .35 .25

450th anniv. of 1st trip through and discovery of the Strait of Magellan, Oct. 21-Nov. 28, 1520.

Dagoberto Godoy and Plane over Andes — A216

1971, Nov. 4
406 A216 1.15e blue & grn .40 .25

First trans-Andean flight, Dec. 12, 1918.

Virgin of San Cristobal — A217

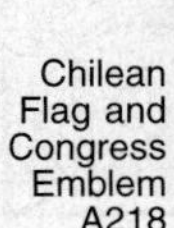

Chilean Flag and Congress Emblem A218

Congress Emblem and: 4.35e, Church of San Francisco. 9.35e, Central post office, horiz. 18.35e, La Posada (Inn) del Corregidor, horiz.

1971
407 A217 1.15e dk blue .60 .30
408 A218 2.35e ultra & car .60 .30
409 A217 4.35e brown red .60 .30
410 A217 9.35e violet .60 .30
411 A217 18.35e lilac rose 1.10 .30
Nos. 407-411 (5) 3.50 1.50

10th Cong. of the Postal Union of the Americas and Spain, Santiago.

An imperf souvenir sheet containing Nos. 407-411 was not valid for postage. Value $11.

Issued: 2.35e, 4.35e, Nov. 5; 1.15e, Nov. 11; 9.35e, Nov. 18; 18.35e, Nov. 19.

Observation Dome, Cerro el Tololo Observatory — A219

1971, Dec. 18
412 A219 1.95e lt & dk blue .35 .25

Boeing 707 over Easter Island A220

1971, Dec. 18
413 A220 2.35e vio brn and ocher .45 .25

Inauguration of regular flights: Santiago, Easter Island, Tahiti.

Alonso de Ercilla y Zuniga — A221

1972, Mar. 20 Engr. *Perf. 14*
414 A221 1e dark red .40 .25

4th centenary (in 1969) of "La Araucana," by Alonso de Ercilla y Zuniga (1533-1596), Spanish author. See No. C313.

Map of Antarctica and Dog Sled — A222

1972, Mar. 20 Litho. *Perf. 14½x15*
415 A222 1.15e vio bl & blk .70 .30
416 A222 3.50e blue grn & grn 1.10 .30

10th anniversary (in 1971) of the Antarctic Treaty pledging peaceful uses of and scientific cooperation in Antarctica.

For surcharge see No. 630.

"Your Heart is your Health" — A223

1972, Apr. 2 Litho. *Perf. 14½*
417 A223 1.15e black & car .40 .25

World Health Month.

For surcharge see No. 631.

People and Statement by Pres. Allende — A224

Conference Hall and UN Emblem — A225

1972, Apr. 13 Litho. *Perf. 14½*
418 A224 35c dl grn & buff .35 .25
419 A225 1.15e ultra & pur .40 .25
420 A224 4e dk pur & pale rose .60 .35
421 A225 6e orange & vio bl .50 .25
Nos. 418-421 (4) 1.85 1.10

3rd UN Conf. on Trade and Development (UNCTAD III), Santiago, Apr.-May 1972. Design A224 is perf. horiz. in the middle.

Soldier, 1822, Andes, Military College Emblem A226

1972, June 9
422 A226 1.15e blue & yel .40 .25

Sesquicentennial of Bernardo O'Higgins Military College.

Miner Holding Copper Ingot, Chilean Flag — A227

1972, July 11 Litho. *Perf. 15x14½*
423 A227 1.15e blue & rose red .35 .25
424 A227 5e blue, blk & rose red .45 .25

Nationalization of copper industry.

An imperforate souvenir sheet exists of Nos. 423-424. Size:110x140mm.

Sailing Ship — A228

1972, Aug. 4
425 A228 1.15e violet brown .55 .25

Arturo Pratt Naval Training School, sesqui.

Mt. Calan Observatory — A229

1972, Aug. 31 Litho. *Perf. 14½*

426 A229 50c ultra .40 .25

University of Chile Mt. Calan Observatory.

Carrier Pigeon — A230

1972, Oct. 9 Litho. *Perf. 14½*

427 A230 1.15e red lilac & vio .40 .25

Intl. Letter Writing Week, Oct. 9-15.

René Schneider and Army Flag — A231

1972, Oct. 25 *Perf. 14*

428 A231 2.30e multi .40 .30

2nd anniv. of the death of Gen. René Schneider. No. 428 is perforated vertically in the middle.

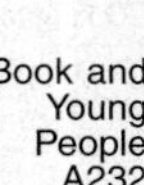

Book and Young People A232

1972, Oct. 31 *Perf. 14½*

429 A232 50c black & dp org .40 .25

International Book Year 1972.

Guitar and Earthen Jar A233

Designs: 2.65e, Fish and produce. 3.50e, Stove, pots and rug, vert.

1972, Nov. 20 Litho. *Perf. 14½*

430 A233 1.15e red & blk .50 .25
431 A233 2.65e ultra & rose lake .60 .25
432 A233 3.50e red & red brn .65 .25
Nos. 430-432 (3) 1.75 .75

Tourism Year of the Americas.

José M. Carrera Before Execution A234

1973, Feb. 1 Litho. *Perf. 14½*

433 A234 2.30e lt ultra .40 .25

Sesquicentennial of the death of José Miguel Carrera (1785-1821), Chilean revolutionist and dictator.

Map of Antarctica, Flag at Base — A235

1973, Feb. 8

434 A235 10e ultra & red 1.50 .25

Bernardo O'Higgins Antarctic Base, 25th anniv.

Naval Air Service Emblem, Destroyer A236

1973, Mar. 16 Litho. *Perf. 14½*

435 A236 20e brt bl & ocher .45 .25

Chilean Naval Aviation, 50th anniversary.

La Silla Observatory A237

1973, Apr. 25 Litho. *Perf. 14½*

436 A237 2.30e ultra & blk .40 .25

INTERPOL Emblem A238

Designs: 50e, Fingerprint over globe.

1973, Sept. 23 Litho. *Perf. 14½*

437 A238 30e bister & ultra 1.20 .75
438 A238 50e black & red 1.00 .50

50th anniversary of International Criminal Police Organization.

Grapes — A239

Chilean wine export: 100e, Globe inscribed "Chile Exporta Vino."

1973, Dec. 10 Litho. *Perf. 14½*

439 A239 20e buff & lilac .75 .25
440 A239 100e blue & claret 1.75 .25

UPU Headquarters, Bern — A240

1974, Apr. 4

441 A240 500e on 45c green .75 .25

UPU cent. No. 441 was not issued without dark green surcharge and overprint.

No. 441 exists on an imperforate souvenir sheet. Size: 115x140mm. Value, $20.

Bernardo O'Higgins, Armed Forces Emblems — A241

No. 443, Soldiers with mortar. No. 444, Navy anti-aircraft gunners. No. 445, Pilot in cockpit. No. 446, Mounted policeman.

1974, Apr. 11 Litho. *Perf. 14½*

442 A241 30e shown .30 .25
443 A241 30e multicolored .30 .25
444 A241 30e multicolored .30 .25
445 A241 30e multicolored .30 .25
446 A241 30e multicolored .30 .25
Nos. 442-446 (5) 1.50 1.25

Honoring the Armed Forces.

Soccer Ball and Globe — A242

1000e, Soccer ball and stadium, horiz.

1974 Litho. *Perf. 14*

447 A242 500e dk red & org .60 .25
448 A242 1000e bl & indigo 1.10 .30

World Cup Soccer Championship, Munich, June 13-July 7.

A souvenir sheet contains 2 imperf. stamps similar to Nos. 447-448, with blue marginal inscription. Printed on thin card. Size: 90x119mm. Value, $15.

Nos. 386, 355 Surcharged

1974, June Litho. *Perf. 14½*

449 A202 100e on 40c bl grn .30 .25

Perf. 13x14

450 A174 300e on 50c dl brn .35 .25

Traffic Police — A243

1974, June 20 *Perf. 14½*

451 A243 30e red brn & grn .40 .25

Traffic safety.

Santiago-Australia Air Service — A244

1974, Sept. 5 Litho. *Perf. 14½x14*

452 A244 Block of 4 6.00 3.00
a. 200e Easter Island turtle .90 .30
b. 200e Polynesian dancer .90 .30
c. 200e Map of Fiji Islands .90 .30
d. 200e Kangaroo .90 .30

Inauguration of air service by LAN (Chile's national airline) from Santiago to Easter Island, Tahiti, Fiji, Australia.

Globe Cut to Show Mantle and Core — A245

1974, Sept. 9 *Perf. 14x14½*

453 A245 500e red brn & org 1.50 1.50

International Volcanology Congress, Santiago, Sept. 9-14.

No. 393 Surcharged in Brown

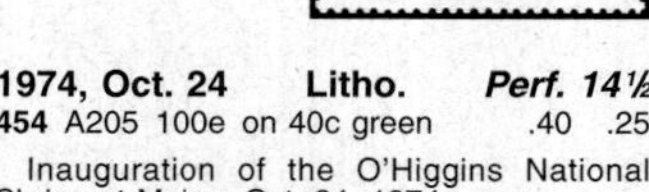

1974, Oct. 24 Litho. *Perf. 14½*

454 A205 100e on 40c green .40 .25

Inauguration of the O'Higgins National Shrine at Maipu, Oct. 24, 1974.

Juan Fernandez Archipelago — A246

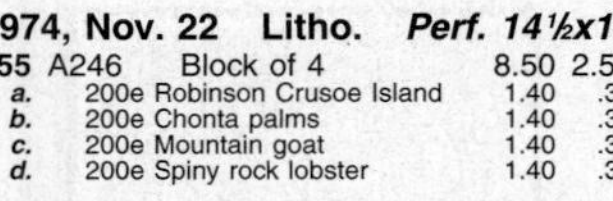

1974, Nov. 22 Litho. *Perf. 14½x14*

455	A246	Block of 4	8.50	2.50
a.		200e Robinson Crusoe Island	1.40	.35
b.		200e Chonta palms	1.40	.35
c.		200e Mountain goat	1.40	.35
d.		200e Spiny rock lobster	1.40	.35

400th anniversary of discovery of Juan Fernandez Archipelago.

O'Higgins and Bolivar A247

1974, Dec. 9 *Perf. 14½*

456	A247	100e red brn & buff	.30	.25

Sesquicentennial of the Battles of Junin and Ayacucho.

F. Vidal Gormaz and Institute Seal — A248

1975, Jan. 22 Litho. *Perf. 14½*

457	A248	100e rose claret & bl	.40	.25

Centenary of the Naval Hydrographic Institute; F. Vidal Gormaz was first commandant.

Albert Schweitzer — A249

1975, Apr. 7 Litho. *Perf. 14x14½*

458	A249	500e yel & red brn	.70	.25

Dr. Albert Schweitzer (1875-1965), medical missionary, birth centenary.

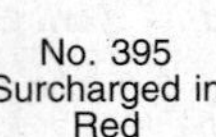
No. 395 Surcharged in Red

1975, Apr. 7 *Perf. 14½*

459	A207	70e on 40c car & lt red brn	.35	.25

Note: souvenir cards were issued by Chile starting in 1975 for various issues. They were printed on thin card. These are not souvenir sheets.

Volunteer Lifeboat Service — A250

1975, Apr. 15 Litho. *Perf. 14½x14*

460	A250	Block of 4	8.50	3.75
a.		150e Lighthouse	1.40	.30
b.		150e Shipwreck	1.40	.30
c.		150e Lifeboat	1.40	.30
d.		150e Sailor reaching for life preserver	1.40	.30

Valparaiso Volunteer Lifeboat service, 50th anniversary.

Frigate Lautaro A251

No. 462, Corvette Baquedano. No. 463, Cruiser Chacabuco. No. 464, Brigantine Goleta Esmeralda.

1975, May 21 Photo. & Engr.

461	A251	500e shown	.75	.30
462	A251	500e multi	.75	.30
463	A251	500e multi	.75	.30
464	A251	500e multi	.75	.30
a.		Block of 4, #461-464	7.50	7.50
465	A251	800e like #461	1.00	.35
466	A251	800e like #462	1.00	.35
467	A251	800e like #463	1.00	.35
468	A251	800e like #464	1.00	.35
a.		Block of 4, #465-468	10.00	10.00
469	A251	1000e like #461	1.50	.50
470	A251	1000e like #462	1.50	.50
471	A251	1000e like #463	1.50	.50
472	A251	1000e like #464	1.50	.50
a.		Block of 4, #469-472	12.50	12.50
		Nos. 461-472 (12)	13.00	4.60

Shipwreck of training frigate Lautaro, 30th anniversary. Se-tenant in sheets of 25 (5x5) with 7 Lautaro stamps and 6 each of the others.

Happy Mother, by Alfredo Valenzuela P. — A252

Paintings: No. 474, Young Girl, by Francisco Javier Mandiola. No. 475, Lucia Guzman, by Pedro Lira Rencoret. No. 476, Woman, by Magdalena Mira Mena.

1975, Oct. 13 Litho. *Perf. 14½*

473	A252	50c multicolored	.90	.25
474	A252	50c multicolored	.90	.25
475	A252	50c multicolored	.90	.25
476	A252	50c multicolored	.90	.25
		Nos. 473-476 (4)	3.60	1.00

International Women's Year 1975. Gray inscription on back, printed beneath gum, gives details about painting shown.

Diego Portales, Finance Minister — A253

Inscribed: D. Portales

1975-78 Litho. *Perf. 13½x14½*

477	A253	10c gray grn	.30	.25
478	A253	20c violet ('76)	.30	.25
479	A253	30c orange ('76)	.30	.25
480	A253	50c lt brown	.30	.25
481	A253	1p blue	.30	.25
482	A253	1.50p ocher ('76)	.30	.25
483	A253	2p gray ('77)	.30	.25
483A	A253	2.50p citron ('78)	.30	.25
483B	A253	3.50p pnksh rose ('78)	.35	.25
484	A253	5p rose claret	.35	.25
		Nos. 477-484 (10)	3.10	2.50

See Nos. 635-639. For surcharge see No. 533.

Cochrane and Liberating Squadron, 1820 — A254

No. 486, Capture of Valdivia, 1820. No. 487, Capture of Three-master Esmeralda, 1820. No. 488, Cruiser Cochrane, 1874. No. 489, Destroyer Cochrane, 1962.

1976, Jan. 6 *Perf. 14½*

485	A254	1p multicolored	.70	.25
486	A254	1p multicolored	.70	.25
487	A254	1p multicolored	.70	.25
488	A254	1p multicolored	.70	.25
489	A254	1p multicolored	.70	.25
a.		Strip of 5, #485-489	4.00	4.00

Lord Thomas Cochrane, first commander of Chilean Navy, birth bicentenary.

Flags of Chile and Bolivia A255

1976, May 25 Litho. *Perf. 14½*

490	A255	1.50p multicolored	1.60	.25

Sesquicentennial of Bolivia's independence.

Lake of the Inca, OAS Emblem A256

1976, June 11

491	A256	1.50p multicolored	1.40	.25

6th General Assembly of the Organization of American States.

George Washington A257

1976, July 3

492	A257	5p multicolored	1.25	.25

American Bicentennial.

Minerva and Academy Emblem A258

1976, July

493	A258	2.50p multicolored	.80	.25

Polytechnic Military Academy, 50th anniv.

Araucan Indian — A259

Designs: 2p, Condor with broken chain. 3p, Winged woman, symbolizing rebirth.

1976, Sept. 20 Litho. *Perf. 14½*

494	A259	1p blue & multi	.25	.25
495	A259	2p blue & multi	1.10	.75
496	A259	3p yellow & multi	.45	.25
a.		Strip of 3, #494-496	2.00	2.00

3rd anniversary of the Military Junta.

View, Antarctica — A260

1977, Feb. 10 Litho. *Perf. 14½*

497	A260	2p multicolored	6.00	1.20

Visit of President Augusto Pinochet to Antarctica.

School Emblem, Planted Field — A261

1977, Mar. 10 *Perf. 14½*

498	A261	2p multicolored	1.50	.30

Cent. of advanced agricultural education.

Justice — A262

1977, Mar. 30 Litho. *Perf. 14½*

499	A262	2p brown & slate	1.60	.35

Supreme Court of Justice, sesquicentennial.

Eye with Globe, Caduceus — A263

1977, Mar. 30 Litho. *Perf. 14½*

500	A263	2p multicolored	1.75	.55

11th Pan-American Ophthalmological Cong.

Mounted Policeman A264

Designs: No. 502, Policewoman with children. No. 503, Paine Peaks and Osorno Volcano, crossed rifle emblem. No. 504, Crossed rifle emblem, mounted and motorcycle policemen, helicopter and automobile, horiz.

1977, Apr. 27

501	A264	2p multicolored	.45	.25
502	A264	2p multicolored	.45	.25
503	A264	2p multicolored	.45	.25
504	A264	2p multicolored	.45	.25
		Nos. 501-504 (4)	1.80	1.00

Chilean police organization, 50th anniv.

Intelsat Satellite over Globe — A265

1977, May 17 Litho. *Perf. 14½*

505	A265	2p multi	1.50	.50

World Telecommunications Day.

El Mercurio's First Front Page, Press and Ship — A266

1977, July 5 Litho. *Perf. 14½*

506	A266	2p multi	.40	.25

El Mercurio de Valparaiso, first Chilean newspaper, 150th anniversary.

St. Francis, Birds and Cross — A267

1977, July 26 Litho. *Perf. 14½*

507	A267	5p multi	1.75	.30

St. Francis of Assisi, 750th death anniv.

Science and Technology A268

1977, Aug. 26 Litho. *Perf. 14½*

508	A268	4p multi	.55	.25

Young Mother Weaving — A269

No. 510, Handicapped boy in wheelchair & nurse. No. 511, Children dancing in circle. No. 512, Old man & home.

1977, Sept. 13 Litho. *Perf. 14½*

509	A269	5p multi	.60	.25
510	A269	5p multi	.60	.25
511	A269	10p multi, horiz.	1.25	.25
512	A269	10p multi, horiz.	1.25	.25
		Nos. 509-512 (4)	3.70	1.00

4th anniversary of Government Junta and social services of armed forces.

Diego de Almagro — A270

1977, Oct. 31 Engr. *Perf. 14½*

513	A270	5p rose & carmine	.40	.25

Diego de Almagro (1475-1538), leader of Spanish expedition to Chile.

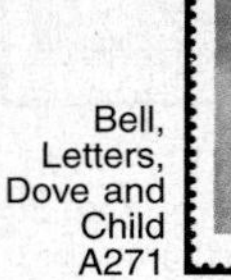

Bell, Letters, Dove and Child A271

1977, Dec. 12 Litho. *Perf. 14½*

514	A271	2.50p multi	.40	.25

Christmas 1977.

Loading Timber A272

1978 Litho. *Perf. 15*

515	A272	10p multi	1.25	.25
516	A272	20p multi	1.75	.35

No. 516 inscribed "CORREOS," ship is flying Chilean flag.

Papal Arms and Globe A273

University — A274

1978 Litho. *Perf. 14½*

521	A273	10p multi	1.25	.30
522	A274	25p multi	2.25	.75

World Peace Day (10p); Catholic University of Valparaiso, 50th anniversary (25p). Issue dates: 10p, July 28; 25p, July 31.

O'Higgins, by Gil de Castro — A275

1978, Aug. 20 Litho. *Perf. 15*

523	A275	10p multi	.90	.30

Bernardo O'Higgins (1778-1842), soldier and statesman.

Chacabuco Victory Monument A276

1978, Sept. 11

524	A276	10p multi	.90	.30

160th anniv. of O'Higgins victory at Chacabuco, and 5th anniv. of military government.

Teacher Writing on Blackboard — A277

1978, Sept. 21

525	A277	15p multi	1.10	.25

10th anniversary and 9th Reunion of Inter-american Council for Education, Science and Culture (C.I.E.C.C.), Sept. 21-29.

First National Fleet, by Thomas Somerscales — A278

Design: 30p, Last Moments of Rancagua Battle, by Pedro Subercaseaux.

1978 Litho. *Perf. 15*

526	A278	20p multi	3.00	.55
527	A278	30p multi	3.75	.90

Bernardo O'Higgins (1778-1842), soldier and statesman.
Issue dates: 20p, Oct. 9; 30p, Oct. 2.

San Martin-O'Higgins Medal, by Rene Thenot, 1942 — A279

1978, Oct. 20

528	A279	7p multi	.75	.25

José de San Martin and Bernardo O'Higgins, 200th birth anniversaries.

Council Emblem — A280

1978, Nov. 27 Litho. *Perf. 14½*

529	A280	50p multi	3.50	2.00

Intl. Council of Military Sports, 30th anniv.

Three Kings — A281

Virgin and Child — A282

1978, Dec. 14 Litho. *Perf. 14½*

530	A281	3p multi	.75	.25
531	A282	11p multi	1.40	.40

Christmas 1978.

Philippi Brothers A283

1978, Dec. 29 Litho. *Perf. 14½x15*

532	A283	3.50p multi	.70	.25

Bernardo E. Philippi (1811-1852) and Rodulfo A. Philippi (1808-1904), scientists and travelers.

No. 477 Surcharged in Bright Green

1979 Litho. *Perf. 13x14*

533	A253	3.50p on 10c gray grn	.30	.25

Flags of Chile and Salvation Army — A284

1979, Mar. 17 Litho. *Perf. 14½*
534 A284 10p multi 1.30 .65

Salvation Army in Chile, 70th anniversary.

Pope Paul VI (1897-1978) — A285

1979, Mar. 30
535 A285 11p multi 2.50 .90

Battle of Maipu Monument — A286

1979, Apr. 17 Litho. *Perf. 14½*
536 A286 8.50p multi 1.50 .50

Bernardo O'Higgins (1778-1842), Liberator of Chile.

Naval Battles A287

1979, May 21 Litho. *Perf. 14½*
537 A287 3.50p Angamos .80 .30
538 A287 3.50p Iquique .80 .30
539 A287 3.50p Punta Gruesa .80 .30
Nos. 537-539 (3) 2.40 .90

Centenary of victorious naval battles against Peru.

1903 Ambulance and Red Cross — A288

1979, June 29 Litho. *Perf. 14½*
540 A288 25p multi 3.50 1.10

75th anniversary of Chilean Red Cross.

Diego Portales — A289

1979-86 Litho. *Perf. 13½*
542 A289 1.50p ocher .25 .25
543 A289 2p gray ('81) .25 .25
544 A289 3.50p red .30 .25
545 A289 4.50p bl grn ('81) .40 .25
546 A289 5p rose claret .50 .25
547 A289 6p emerald .60 .30
548 A289 7p yellow ('82) .55 .30
549 A289 10p blue ('82) .80 .30
550 A289 12p orange ('86) .35 .25
Nos. 542-550 (9) 4.00 2.40

1.50p, 3.50p, 5p and 6p inscribed "D. Portales."

People and Flag — A290

1979, Aug. 28 Litho. *Perf. 14½*
551 A290 10p multi 1.00 .60

Yugoslavian immigration, centenary.

Coat of Arms and Mt. Castillo A290a

1979, Oct. 12 Litho. *Perf. 14½*
552 A290a 20p multi 1.90 .90

Coyhaique 50th anniv.

IYC Emblem, Playground — A291

IYC Emblem, Children's Drawings: 11p, Girl and shadow, vert. 12p, Dancing.

1979, Oct. 9 *Perf. 14½*
553 A291 9.50p multi .95 .60
554 A291 11p multi 1.00 .75
555 A291 12p multi 1.50 .85
Nos. 553-555 (3) 3.45 2.20

International Year of the Child.

Telecom 79 A292

1979, Oct. 26 Litho. *Perf. 14½*
556 A292 15p multi 1.50 .75

3rd World Telecommunications Exhibition, Geneva, Sept. 20-26.

Puerto Williams, 25th Anniversary — A293

1979, Nov. 21
557 A293 3.50p multi .60 .25

Adoration of the Kings A294

1979, Dec. 4 Litho. *Perf. 15*
558 A294 3.50p multi .60 .25

Christmas 1979.

Rafael Sotomayor, Minister of War — A295

Military heroes: No. 560, Erasmo Escala. No. 561, Emilio Sotomayor. No. 562, Eleuterio Ramirez.

1979, Dec. 29 *Perf. 13½*
559 A295 3.50p ocher & brn .50 .25
560 A295 3.50p multi .50 .25
561 A295 3.50p multi .50 .25
562 A295 3.50p multi .50 .25
a. Block of 4, #559-562 2.25 2.25

Bell UH-1 Rescue Helicopter at Tinguiririca Volcano, by S.O. Mococain — A296

Air Force, 50th Anniversary: No. 564, Flying boat Catalina Skua over Antarctic, by E.F. Alvarez. No. 565, F5-E Tiger II over Andes, by M.M. Barria.

1980, Mar. 21 Litho. *Perf. 13½*
563 A296 3.50p shown .55 .25
564 A296 3.50p Jet .55 .25
565 A296 3.50p Sea plane .55 .25
Nos. 563-565 (3) 1.65 .75

The Death of Bueras, by Pedro Leon Carmona — A297

1980, Apr. 14 Litho. *Perf. 13½*
566 A297 12p multi 1.40 .50

Charge of Bueras, Battle of Maipo, 1818.

Rotary International, 75th Anniversary — A298

1980, Apr. 15
567 A298 10p multi 1.25 .45

Gen. Manuel Baquedano, by Pedro Subercaseaux A299

Gen. Pedro Lagos, Battle Scene, by Subercaseaux — A300

Battle of Morro de Arica Centenary (Subercaseaux Paintings): No. 570, Commander Juan J. San Martin, battle scene.

1980, June 7 Litho. *Perf. 13½*
568 A299 3.50p multi .50 .25
569 A300 3.50p multi .50 .25
570 A300 3.50p multi .50 .25
Nos. 568-570 (3) 1.50 .75

Score and Perez's Silhouette — A301

1980, June 27 Litho. *Perf. 13½*
571 A301 6p multi .60 .30

Osman Perez Freire (1880-1930), composer, and fragment from his song "Ay, Ay, Ay."

Mt. Gasherbrum II, Chilean Flag, Ice Pick — A302

1980, July 9
572 A302 15p multi 1.40 .60

Chilean Himalayan expedition, June 1979.

"Charity," Stained-glass Window A303

1980, July 18
573 A303 10p multi 1.50 .35

Daughters of Charity, 125th anniv. in Chile.

Condor, Colors of Chile — A304

1980, Sept. 11 **Litho.** ***Perf. 13½***
574 A304 3.50p multi .60 .25

Plebiscite to vote on new constitution.

Inca Child Mummy — A305

1980, Sept. 14
575 A305 5p shown .75 .25
576 A305 5p Claudio Gay .75 .25
a. Pair, #575-576 + label 1.75 1.25

Natl. Museum of Natural History (founded by Claudio Gay, 1800-73) sesqui.

Pablo Burchard, by Pedro Lira — A306

1980, Sept. 27 **Litho.** ***Perf. 13½***
577 A306 3.50p multi .45 .25

Museum of Fine Art centenary (directed by Burchard, 1932).

Santiago International Fair — A307

1980, Oct. 30
578 A307 3.50p multi .50 .25

Nativity — A308

Christmas 1980: 3.50p, Family, vert.

1980, Nov. 25 **Litho.** ***Perf. 13½***
579 A308 3.50p multi .75 .30
580 A308 10.50p multi 1.50 .55

Infantryman 1879 — A309

Pacific War period uniforms, 1879.

1980, Nov. 27
581 A309 3.50p shown .75 .25
582 A309 3.50p Cavalry officer .75 .25
583 A309 3.50p Artillery officer .75 .25
584 A309 3.50p Engineer colonel .75 .25
a. Block of 4, #581-584 6.00 4.00

See Nos. 606-609.

Congress Emblem — A310

1980, Dec. 1
585 A310 11.50p multi 2.00 .60

23rd Intl. Cong. of Military Medicine & Pharmacy.

Eradication of Hoof and Mouth Disease A311

1981, Jan. 16 **Litho.** ***Perf. 13½***
586 A311 9.50p multi 1.20 .25

Moai Statues, Easter Island — A312

No. 588, Robinson Crusoe Island. No. 589, Penguins, Antarctic Territory.

1981, Jan. 28 **Litho.** ***Perf. 13½***
587 A312 3.50p shown 1.50 .40
588 A312 3.50p multi 2.50 .40
589 A312 10.50p multi 4.00 1.00
Nos. 587-589 (3) 8.00 1.80

National Heroine Javiera Carrera, by O.M. Pizarro, Birth Bicentenary — A313

1981, Mar. 20
590 A313 3.50p multi .40 .25

UPU Membership Centenary A314

1981, Apr. 1
591 A314 3.50p multi .40 .25

C130 Hercules Air Force Transport Plane Unloading Cargo — A315

1981, Apr. 21
592 A315 3.50p multi 1.25 .40

Lieutenant Marsh Air Force Base, 1st anniv.

13th World Telecommunications Day — A316

1981, May 17 **Litho.** ***Perf. 13½***
593 A316 3.50p multi .45 .25

Arturo Prat Naval Base A317

1981, June 23 **Litho.** ***Perf. 13½***
594 A317 3.50p multi 1.50 .25

Capt. Jose Luis Araneda A318

1981, June 26
595 A318 3.50p multi .45 .25

Battle of Sangrar centenary.

Philatelic Society of Chile, 90th Anniv. A319

1981, July 29 **Litho.** ***Perf. 13½***
596 A319 4.50p multi 1.25 .50

Minister Recabarren and Chief Conuepan Giving Speeches, by Hector Robles Acuna — A320

1981, Aug. 7
597 A320 4.50p multi 1.25 .25

Temuco city centenary.

Exports A321

1981, Aug. 31 **Litho.** ***Perf. 13½***
598 A321 14p multi 1.00 .35

Presidential Palace — A322

1981, Sept. 11
599 A322 4.50p multi 1.25 .40

Natl. liberation, 8th anniv.

St. Vincent de Paul, 400th Birth Anniv. A323

1981, Sept. 27 **Litho.** ***Perf. 13½***
600 A323 4.50p multi .60 .25

Andres Bello, Poet and Sholar, Birth Bicentenary A324

1981, Sept. 29
601 A324 4.50p Coin .45 .25
602 A324 9.50p Bust, books .75 .30
603 A324 11.50p Statue, arms 1.10 .40
Nos. 601-603 (3) 2.30 .95

2nd Congress of South American Uniformed Police A325

1981, Oct. 15
604 A325 4.50p multi .60 .25

World Food Day A326

1981, Oct. 16
605 A326 5.50p multi .55 .25

Uniform Type of 1980

1879 Parade Uniforms.

1981, Nov. 6 ***Perf. 13½***
606 A309 5.50p Infantry private .80 .25
607 A309 5.50p Cadet .80 .25
608 A309 5.50p Cavalryman .80 .25
609 A309 5.50p Artilleryman .80 .25
a. Block of 4, #606-609 6.00 3.00

Intl. Year of the Disabled A327

1981, Nov. 11
610 A327 5.50p multi 1.10 .30

Christmas 1981 — A328

1981, Nov. 25
611 A328 5.50p Nativity .50 .25
612 A328 11.50p Three Kings 1.00 .40

50th Anniv. of Federico Santa Maria Technical University — A329

1981, Dec 1 **Litho.** ***Perf. 13½***
613 A329 5.50p multi .50 .25

Dario Salas (1881-1941), Educator — A330

1981, Dec. 4
614 A330 5.50p multi .60 .25

FIDA '82, 2nd Natl. Air Force Fair — A331

1982, Mar. 6 **Litho.** ***Perf. 13½***
615 A331 4.50p multi .50 .25

1980 Constitution — A332

4.50p, Cardinal Caro, family. 11p, Diego Portales. 30p, Bernardo O'Higgins.

1982, Mar. 11
616 A332 4.50p multi .50 .25
617 A332 11p multi 1.25 .45
618 A332 30p multi 2.00 .90
Nos. 616-618 (3) 3.75 1.60

Panamerican Institute of Geography and History, 12th General Assembly A333

1982, Mar. 22 **Litho.** ***Perf. 13½***
619 A333 4.50p multi .50 .25

American Air Forces Cooperation System — A334

1982, Apr. 12
620 A334 4.50p multi .75 .25

Pedro Montt — A335

1982, Mar. 27
621 A335 4.50p light vio .50 .25

Fish Exports — A336

1982, May 3 **Litho.** ***Perf. 13½***
622 A336 20p multi 2.25 .75

Scouting Year — A337

No. 623b, Robert Baden-Powell.

1982, May 21 **Litho.** ***Perf. 13***
623 A337 Pair 40.00 25.00
a.-b. 4.50p, either single 12.50 6.00

Battle of Concepcion Centenary A338

Chacabuco Regiment officers killed in battle.

1982, June 18 **Litho.** ***Perf. 13½***
624 Block of 4 2.50 2.50
a. A338 4.50p I. Carrera Pinto .50 .25
b. A338 4.50p A. Perez Canto .50 .25
c. A338 4.50p J. Montt Salamanca .50 .25
d. A338 4.50p L. Cruz Martinez .50 .25

UN World Assembly on Aging, July 26-Aug. 6 — A339

1982, Aug. 5
625 A339 4.50p multi 1.00 .25

TB Bacillus Centenary A340

1982, Aug. 31
626 A340 4.50p multi .40 .25

9th Anniv. of National Liberation — A341

1982, Sept. 11 **Litho.** ***Perf. 13½***
627 A341 4.50p multi .40 .25

Christmas 1982 — A342

Children's drawings.

1982, Nov. 2
628 A342 10p multi 1.25 .25
629 A342 25p multi, vert. 1.50 .60

Nos. 416 Surcharged in Green

Nos. 417 Surcharged in Black

1982, Nov. ***Perf. 14½x15, 14½***
630 A222 1p on 3.50p bl grn & grn (G) 2.25 .50
631 A223 2p on 1.15p blk & car 3.50 .50

Marist Alumni, 9th World Congress A342a

Virgin Mary & Marcellus Champagnat (founder of Marist Brotherhood), stained glass window, Church of the Sacred Heart of Jesus, Barcelona.

1982, Nov. 11 Litho. *Perf. 13½*

631A A342a 7p multi 1.50 .40

El Sur Newspaper Centenary A342b

7p, Wooden handpress, masthead.

1982, Nov. 15

631B A342b 7p multi .50 .25

110th Anniv. of South American Steamship Co. — A342c

1982, Dec. 20

631C A342c 7p Steamer Copiapo 1.20 .35

60th Anniv. of Radio Club of Chile — A342d

1982, Dec. 29

631D A342d 7p multi 1.10 .25

First Anniv. of Postal Agreement with Order of Malta — A343

1983, Mar. 30 Litho. *Perf. 13½*

632 25p Arms of Order of Malta 2.50 .40
633 50p Chile 4.00 .80
a. Pair, #632-633 7.50 6.50

D.D. No. 20

This and similar inscriptions indicate that the stamps would be sold at a discount if purchased in large quantities.

D. Portales Type of 1975 Inscribed Diego Portales and

Ramon Barros Luco A344

Juan Luis Sanfuentes A344a

1983-88 Litho. *Perf. 13½*

634	A344	1p	grnsh bl	.25	.25
635	A253	1p	chalky bl	.25	.25
636	A253	1.50p	ocher	.25	.25
637	A344	2p	dl vio ('84)	.25	.25
638	A253	2p	ol gray	.25	.25
639	A253	2.50p	lemon	.25	.25
640	A253	5p	red lilac	.35	.25
641	A344	5p	crim rose	.25	.25
642	A344a	5p	red ('84)	.25	.25
643	A344	7p	ultra	.30	.25
644	A344a	9p	brn ('84)	.25	.25
645	A344a	9p	grn ('84)	.25	.25
646	A344	10p	black	.25	.25
646A	A344a	10p	gray ('84)	.25	.25
647	A344a	15p	ultra ('87)	.25	.25
a.			Booklet pane of 10	1.50	
648	A344a	20p	yel ('88)	.25	.25
b.			Booklet pane of 10	2.00	

Nos. 644, 647, 648 inscribed "D.S. No. 20."
Issued: No. 640, 8/85.
For surcharge see No. 779.

50th Anniv. of Bureau of Investigation A345

1983, June 19 Litho. *Perf. 13½*

649 A345 20p multi 1.25 .50

Antonio Cardinal Samore (1905-1983) — A346

1983, June 26

650 A346 30p multi 2.00 .60

Centenary of Cliff Elevators in Valparaiso A347

1983, Aug. 19 Litho. *Perf. 13½*

651 A347 40p multi 5.00 .45

Pucara de Quitor Settlement Ruins, San Pedro de Atacama — A348

No. 653, Llamas, rock painting, Rio Ibanez, Aisen. No. 654, Duck-shaped jug with human head, Diaguita cultures. No. 655, Puoko Tangata carved stone head, Easter Isld.

1983, Aug. 26

652 A348 7p multi 1.25 .40
653 A348 7p multi 1.25 .40
654 A348 7p multi 1.00 .40
655 A348 7p multi, vert. 1.00 .40
Nos. 652-655 (4) 4.50 1.60

10th Anniv. of National Liberation — A349

1983, Sept. 11 Litho. *Perf. 13½*

656 A349 7p Angel with broken chains .60 .25
657 A349 7p Couple, flag .60 .25
658 A349 10p Family, torch .60 .25
659 A349 40p Coat of arms, "10" 2.00 .75
a. Strip of 4, #656-659 5.00 3.50

For surcharges see Nos. 669-670.

Famous Hondurans A350

No. 660, Francisco Morazan (1792-1842), Advocate of United Central America. No. 661, Jose Cecilio Del Valle (1777-1834), Scholar and Leader of Pan Americanism.

1983, Oct. 3 Litho. *Perf. 13½*

660 A350 7p multi .40 .25
661 A350 7p multi .40 .25
a. Pair, #660-661 .80 .80

World Communications Year — A351

1983, Oct. 13 Litho. *Perf. 13½*

662 7p Central P.O. .85 .25
663 7p Challenger spaceship .85 .25
a. A351 Pair, #662-663 1.75 1.75

Christmas 1983 — A353

Childrens' Drawings: 10p Chilean Peasant, Hanny Chacon. 30p, Holy Family. Lucrecia Cardenas, vert.

1983, Nov. 14 Litho. *Perf. 13*

664 A353 10p multi .75 .25
665 A353 30p multi 1.50 .40

Design descriptions printed on back on top of gum.

State Railways Centenary — A354

Train Cars: a, Presidential coach, 1911. b, Service coach, 1910; tender, 1929. c, Locomotive Type 80, 1929.

1984, Jan. 4 Litho. *Perf. 13½*

666 A354 Strip of 3 10.00 8.75
a.-c. 9p, any single 2.40 .45

3rd Intl. Air Fair, Santiago, Mar. 3-11 — A355

1984, Jan. 31 Litho. *Perf. 13½*

667 A355 9p Flags, plane 1.10 .25

20th Anniv. of Nuclear Energy Commission — A356

1984, Apr. 16 Litho. *Perf. 13*

668 A356 9p multi .50 .25

Nos. 656-657 Surcharged in Purple

1984, June 11 Litho. *Perf. 13½*

669 A349 9p on 7p #656 .45 .25
670 A349 9p on 7p #657 .45 .25
a. Pair, #669-670 1.25 .95

Antarctic Colonization — A357

No. 671, Women's expedition. No. 672, Villa las Estrellas Station. No. 673, Scouts, flag, Air Force base.

1984, June 18

671 A357 15p multicolored 1.00 .35
672 A357 15p multicolored 1.00 .35
673 A357 15p multicolored 1.00 .35
a. Strip of 3, #671-673 6.50 4.50

10th Anniv. of Regionalization — A358

Designs: a, Parinacota Church, Tarapaca. b, El Tatio geyser, Antofagasta. c, Copper mining, Atacama. d, Tololo Observatory, Coquimbo. e, Valparaiso Harbor, Valparaiso. f, Ahu Akivi head sculptures, Easter Isld. g, St.

Francis Church, Santiago. h, El Hunique House, O'Higgins. i, Colburn Machicura Dam and Hydroelectric Power Station, Maule. j, Sta. Juana de Guadalcazar Fort, Bio-Bio. k, Indian woman, Araucania. l, Guar Isld. Church, Los Lagos. m, Main road, Gen. del Campo. n, Shepherds' Monument, Magellanes and Antarctic. o, Family, Villa las Estrellas Station, Antarctic.

1984, July 11

674 Sheet of 15 24.00 24.00
a.-o. A358 9p multi, any single 1.25 1.25

Capt. Pedro Sarmiento de Gamboa, Map, 1584 — A359

1984, July 31 Litho. *Perf. 13*

675 A359 100p multi 4.75 1.10

400th anniv. of Spanish presence in Straits of Magellan.

State Bank of Chile Centenary — A360

35p, Founder Antonio Varas de la Barra, coin.

1984, Sept. 6 Litho. *Perf. 13½*

676 A360 35p multi 1.25 .55

11th Anniv. of Liberation — A361

20p, Monument to O'Higgins.

1984, Sept. 11

677 A361 20p multi .90 .30

Circus Centenary — A362

1984, Sept. 28 Litho. *Perf. 13½*

678 A362 45p Clown 1.75 .70

Endangered Species, World Wildlife Emblem — A363

1985, July Litho. *Perf. 13½*

679 A363 9p Chinchilla *6.50* 2.50
680 A363 9p Blue whale *6.50* 2.50
681 A363 9p Sea lions *6.50* 2.50
682 A363 9p Chilean huemuls *6.50* 2.50
a. Block of 4, #679-682 *26.00* *15.00*

Christmas 1984 — A364

Children's drawings.

1984, Nov. 20 Litho. *Perf. 13½*

683 A364 9p Shepherds .40 .25
684 A364 40p Bethlehem 1.50 .40

Santiago University Planetarium Opening — A365

1984, Dec. 29

685 A365 10p multi 3.00 2.00

Flora and Fauna — A366

Wildlife: a, Conepatus chinga. b, Leucocoryne purpurea. c, Himantopus himantopus. d, Lutra felina. e, Balbisia peduncularis. f, Psittacus cyanalysias. g, Pudu pudu. h, Fuschia magellanica. i, Diuca diuca. j, Dusicyon griseus. k, Alstroemeria sierrae. l, Glaucidium nanum.

1985, Feb.

686 Block of 12 20.00 10.00
a.-l. A366 10p, Any single 1.50 .50

American Airforces Cooperation System, 25th Anniv. A367

1985, Mar. 26

687 A367 45p Emblem, flags 2.00 1.10

Chile-Argentina Peace Treaty — A368

1985, May 2 Litho. *Perf. 13½*

688 A368 20p Papal arms, flags 3.00 .60

Fr. Joseph Kentenich (1885-1968), Founder, Intl. Schonstatt Movement of Catholic Laymen A369

40p, Portrait, La Florida Sanctuary, Santiago.

1985, May 19 Litho. *Perf. 13½*

689 A369 40p multi .70 .40

Antarctic Treaty, 25th Anniv. — A370

Resources, research: 15p, Krill, pack ice, map. 20p, Seismological Station, O'Higgins' Base. 35p, Georeception Station, dish receiver.

1985, June 21

690 A370 15p multi .65 .35
691 A370 20p multi .85 .50
692 A370 35p multi 1.50 .75
Nos. 690-692 (3) 3.00 1.60

Canis Fulvipes — A371

Endangered wildlife: b, Phoenicoparrus jamesi. c, Fulica gigantea. d, Lutra provocax.

1985, Aug. 9 Litho. *Perf. 13½*

693 A371 Block of 4 12.00 4.50
a.-d. 20p, any single 1.75 .35

Intl. Youth Year A372

UN, 40th Anniv. A373

1985, Aug. 31

694 A372 15p multi .50 .25
695 A373 15p multi .50 .25
a. Pair, #694-695 1.50 1.50

Gen. Jose Miguel Carrera Verdugo (1785-1821) — A374

1985, Oct. 8 Litho. *Perf. 13½*

696 A374 40p multi 1.50 .55

Farmer and Ox-drawn Hay Cart — A375

Folklore: b, Street photographer, wet plate camera. c, One-man band. d, Basket maker.

1985, Oct.

697 A375 Block of 4 1.40 .90
a.-d. 10p, any single .30 .25

For surcharges see Nos. 770-771.

Christmas 1985 — A376

Winning children's drawings, 7th natl. design contest.

1985, Nov. 4

698 A376 15p Nativity .55 .25
699 A376 100p Father Christmas, vert. 3.75 1.00

Nos. 698-699 inscribed in black on gummed side with child's name, age, school and region.

Holy Family — A376a

1985 Litho. *Perf. 13½*

699A A376a 10p buff & brn .60 .25

For surcharge see No. 768.

16th Armed Forces Conference — A377

20p, Cavalryman, Directorial Escort, 1818. 35p, Officer, Grand Guard, 1813.

1985, Nov. 15 Litho. *Perf. 13½*

700 A377 20p multicolored .60 .25
701 A377 35p multicolored 1.00 .35

Halley's Comet — A378

1985, Nov. 29 Litho. *Perf. 13½*

702 A378 45p multicolored 1.00 .25
a. Souvenir sheet *40.00* 20.00

No. 702a exists imperf. Value $40.

Natl. Solidarity Campaign — A379

1985

703 A379 5p red & blue 2.25 .75

Campaign for Prevention of Forest Fires — A380

1985, Dec. 27

704 40p Forest .75 .40
705 40p Fire destruction .75 .40
a. A380 Pair, #704-705 2.75 1.50

No. 705a has continuous design.

Dungeness Point Lighthouse, Straits of Magellan — A381

1986, Jan. 26

706 A381 45p shown 1.50 .60
707 A381 45p Evangelistas Lighthouse 1.50 .60
a. Pair, #706-707 4.00 2.50

No. 707a continuous design.

View of Santiago, Mackenna — A382

1986, Jan. 28

708 A382 30p multi .45 .25

Benjamin Vicuna Mackenna (d. 1886), municipal superintendent of Santiago, 1872-1875.

Diego Portales, Natl. Crest, Text — A382a

1986, Feb. Litho. *Perf. 13½*

708A A382a 12p on 3.50p multi 2.75 1.25

No. 708A not issued without surcharge.

1986 World Cup Soccer Championships, Mexico — A383

Host stadiums: 15p, Natl. Stadium, Chile, 1962. 20p, Aztec Stadium, Mexico, 1970. 35p, Maracana Stadium, Brazil, 1950. 50p, Wembley Stadium, Great Britain, 1966.

1986, Feb. 18

709 A383 15p multi .40 .25
710 A383 20p multi .55 .25
711 A383 35p multi .80 .35
712 A383 50p multi 1.25 .50
Nos. 709-712 (4) 3.00 1.35

Environmental Conservation — A384

1986, Feb. 28

713 A384 20p Water .75 .25
714 A384 20p Air .75 .25
715 A384 20p Soil .75 .25
Nos. 713-715 (3) 2.25 .75

Sailing Ship Santiaguillo, Flags — A385

1986, Mar. 20

716 A385 40p multi 1.20 .55

Discovery of Valparaiso Bay, 450th anniv.

A386

1986, Apr. 9

717 A386 45p multi 1.20 .45

Interamerican Development Bank, 25th anniv.

A387

1986, Apr. 30 Litho. *Perf. 13½*

718 A387 15p multi .65 .25

St. Rosa de Lima (1586-1617), sanctuary at Pelequen.

Moai Statues, Easter Is. — A388

60p, Raraku Volcano. 100p, Tongariki Ruins.

1986, May 15

719 A388 60p multi 3.75 1.75
a. Souvenir sheet *12.50* *12.50*
720 A388 100p multi 6.75 3.25
a. Souvenir sheet *20.00* *20.00*

AMERIPEX '86 — A389

1986, May 23

721 A389 100p multi 2.50 1.10

Historic Naval Ships — A390

No. 722, Schooner Ancud, 1843. No. 723, Armed merchantman Aguilar, 1830. No. 724, Corvette Esmeralda, 1856. No. 725, Frigate O'Higgins, 1834.

1986, May 30

722 A390 35p multi 1.25 .60
723 A390 35p multi 1.25 .60
724 A390 35p multi 1.25 .60
725 A390 35p multi 1.25 .60
a. Block of 4, #722-725 7.00 6.50

See Nos. 752-753.

Paintings by Juan Francisco Gonzalez (1853-1933) A391

No. 726, Rush and Chrysanthemums. No. 727, Gate of La Serena.

1986, June 24

726 A391 30p multi 1.00 .35
727 A391 30p multi 1.00 .35
a. Pair, #726-727 2.50 1.75

Exports — A392

Designs: a, Saltpeter. b, Iron. c, Copper. d, Molybdenum.

1986 Litho. *Perf. 13½*

728 A392 Block of 4 1.60 1.25
a.-d. 12p, any single .30 .25

Antarctic Fauna — A393

a, Sterna vittata. b, Phalacrocorax atriceps. c, Aptenodytes forsteri. d, Catharacta lonnberg.

1986, July 16 Litho. *Perf. 13½*

729 Block of 4 8.00 5.00
a.-d. A393 40p, any single 1.75 .70

Writers — A394

No. 730, Pedro de Ona (1570-1643). No. 731, Vicente Huidobro (1893-1948).

1986, Aug. 19

730 A394 20p multi .65 .40
731 A394 20p multi .65 .40
a. Pair, #730-731 1.75 1.00

Has continuous design.

Military Academy, Cent. — A395

No. 732, Major-General, 1878. No. 733, Major, 1950.

1986, Sept. 8 Litho. *Perf. 13½*

732 A395 45p multi .90 .40
733 A395 45p multi .90 .40
a. Pair, #732-733 1.90 1.10

Art A396

No. 734, Diaguita urn, duck jug. No. 735, Mapuche silver ornament, embroidery.

1986, Oct. 17 *Perf. 13½*

734	A396 30p multi	.65	.40
735	A396 30p multi	.65	.40
a.	Pair, #734-735	2.50	1.60

Christmas — A397

8th Natl. design contest-winning children's drawings.

1986, Nov. 19 Litho. *Perf. 13½*

736	A397 15p multi	.65	.25
737	A397 105p multi	2.75	.70

Nos. 736-737 inscribed in black on gummed side with child's name, age, school and region.

Christmas A397a

Design: Shepherds see star, Bethlehem.

1986, Nov. Litho. *Perf. 13½*

737A	A397a 12p multi	.35	.25

Intl. Peace Year — A398

1986, Nov. 26

738	A398 85p multi	1.30	.60

Natl. Women Volunteers — A399

1986, Dec. 15 Litho. *Perf. 13½*

739	A399 15p multi	2.25	.25

Crowning of Our Lady of Mt. Carmel, Patron of Chile, by Pius XI, 60th Anniv. — A400

1986, Dec. 19

740	A400 25p multi	.75	.25

Andean Railways Kitson-Meyer No. 59, 1907, Designed by Robert Sterling — A401

1987, Jan. 27 Litho. *Perf. 13½*

741	A401 95p multi	2.90	1.25

Arturo Prat Naval Base, Greenwich Island, the Antarctic, 40th Anniv. — A402

No. 742, Storage and power supplies. No. 743, Working and living quarters.

1987, Feb. 6

742	100p multi	4.50	2.00
743	100p multi	4.50	2.00
a.	A402 Pair, #742-743	13.00	7.75

State Visit of Pope John Paul II, Apr. 1-6, 1987 — A403

Pope John Paul II and: 20p, Christ the Redeemer statue. 25p, Votive Church, Maipu. 90p, Cross of the Seas, Straits of Magellan. 115p, Virgin of the Hill.

1987 Litho. *Perf. 13½*

744	A403	20p multi	.30	.25
745	A403	25p multi	.40	.25
746	A403	90p multi	1.40	.60
747	A403	115p multi	1.90	.95
a.		Souv. sheet of one	6.50	5.25
747B	A403	115p multi	2.00	1.00
		Nos. 744-747B (5)	6.00	3.05

No. 747a sold for 250p.

No. 747B differs from No. 747 in that the Statue of the Virgin has a halo and Pope John Paul II is smiling.

Issue date: Nos. 744-747a, Apr. 6.

Los Carabineros (Natl. Guard), 60th Anniv. — A404

No. 748, Cavalry showmanship. No. 749, Air-sea rescue.

1987, Apr. 21

748	A404 50p multi	1.00	.40
749	A404 50p multi	1.00	.40
a.	Pair, #748-749	2.50	2.00

World Youth Soccer Championships — A405

b, Concepcion Stadium, kick play. c, Antofagasta Stadium, dribbling the ball. d, Valparaiso Stadium, heading the ball.

1987, May 28

750	A405	Block of 4	4.00	4.00
a.-d.		45p any single	1.00	.60

Souvenir Sheet

751	A405	45p Four players	4.00	4.00

No. 751 sold for 150p.

Naval Ships Type of 1986

No. 752, Battleship Almirante Latorre, 1913. No. 753, Cruiser O'Higgins, 1936.

1987, May 29

752	A390 60p multi	1.00	.60
753	A390 60p multi	1.00	.60
a.	Pair, #752-753	3.00	2.25

Diego Portales (1793-1837), Finance Minister — A406

1987, June 16

754	A406 30p multi	.50	.25

Public Works Ministry, Cent. — A407

1987, June 26

755	A407 25p multi	.85	.45

Infantry School, Cent. — A408

1987, July 9

756	A408 50p Entrance	.75	.25
757	A408 100p Soldiers, natl. flag	1.00	.50

Miniature Sheet

Flora and Fauna — A409

Designs: a, Chiasognathus granti. b, Calidris alba. c, Hippocamelus antisensis. d, Jubaea chilensis. e, Colias vauthieri. f, Pandion haliaetus. g, Cephalorhynchus commersonii. h, Austrocedrus chilensis. i, Jasus frontalis. j, Stephanoides fernandensis. k, Vicugna vicugna. l, Thyrsopteris elegans. m, Lithodes antarctica. n, Pterocnemia pennata. o, Lagidium viscacia. p, Cereus atacamensis.

1987, July 30

758		Sheet of 16	17.50	15.00
a.-p.	A409	25p any single	.75	.40

Intl. Year of Shelter for the Homeless A410

1987, Aug. 6

759	A410 40p multi	.90	.30

Legends and Folk Tales — A411

a, The Guitarist of Quinchamali. b, El Caleuche. c, El Pihuychen. d, La Lola.

1987, July Litho. *Perf. 13½*

760	A411	Block of 4	3.50	1.00
a.-d.		15p any single	.50	.25

Nos. 760a-760d exist ovptd. "D.S. No 20." in golden brown on back. Value $4.50.

For surcharges see Nos. 812, 1104.

FISA '87, Santiago — A412

1987, Oct. 16 Litho. *Perf. 13½*

761	A412 20p multi	.40	.25

25th Intl. agriculture and exports exhibition.

Rear Admiral Carlos Condell de la Haza (1843-1887), Naval Hero at the Battle of the Pacific — A413

1987, Nov. 7
762 A413 50p multi 1.00 .90

Christmas 1987 — A414

Children's drawings: 30p, Holy Family. 100p, Star Over Bethlehem, horiz.

1987, Nov. 13
763 A414 30p multi .75 .30
764 A414 100p multi 2.75 .95

COBRE '87, Intl. Conf. on Copper — A415

1987, Nov. 23
765 A415 40p Foundry 1.00 .60
a. Souv. sheet of one 2.60 2.60

No. 765 sold for 150p.

Natl. Antarctic Exploration Commission, 25th Anniv. — A415a

1987, Dec. 11 Litho. *Perf. 13½*
765B A415a 45p multi 1.25 .55

Ramon Freire Serrano (1787-1851), Chief of State — A416

1987, Dec. 29 *Perf. 13x13½*
766 A416 20p pale lil & rose clar .40 .30

To Smoke Is To Contaminate — A417

1987, Dec. Litho. *Perf. 13½*
767 A417 15p blue & ver .40 .25

Natl. Commission for the Control of Smoking.

No. 699A Surcharged in Green

1987 Litho. *Perf. 13½*
768 A376a 12p on 10p buff & brn .30 .25

Christmas 1987 — A418

1987, Dec.
769 A418 15p ultra, org yel & blk .30 .25
a. Bklt. pane of 10 4.75

No. 769a exists ovptd. "D.S. No 20." on back.

No. 697 Surcharged in Black and Rose Red

1987, Dec.
770 A375 Block of 4 (RR) 2.00 .80
a.-d. 12p on 10p, #697a-697d .40 .25
771 A375 Block of 4 (Blk) 2.00 .80
a.-d. 15p on 10p, #697a-697d .40 .25

St. John Bosco (1815-1888), Educator Canonized in 1934 — A419

1988, Jan. 29
772 A419 40p multi 2.50 .30

20th Music Week, Frutillar — A420

1988, Jan. 27
773 A420 30p multi .75 .25

FIDA '88, 5th Intl. Aviation Fair — A421

1988, Mar. 4 Litho. *Perf. 13½*
774 A421 60p dark blue & blue 1.20 .60

1988 Summer Olympics, Seoul — A422

Flags of Chile and Korea, events: 50p, Shot put, pole vault, javelin. 100p, Swimming, cycling, running.

1988, Mar. 18 *Perf. 13½*
775 A422 50p multi 1.25 .60
776 A422 100p multi 2.50 1.00
a. Souv. sheet of 2, #775-776 3.75 3.75

No. 776a sold for 250p.

Natl. Agricultural Soc., 150th Anniv. — A423

1988, Apr. 8
777 A423 45p multi 1.40 .35

Intl. Red Cross and Red Crescent Organizations, 125th Annivs. — A424

1988, May 10
778 A424 150p multi 1.75 .65

No. 645 Surcharged

1988 Litho. *Perf. 13½*
779 A344a 20p on 9p green .25 .25

Easter Island Folk Art — A425

Designs: Nos. 780, 782, Carved wooden head from Kava Kava. Nos. 781, 783, Bird man stone carving from Tangata Manu.

1988, Apr. 1 Litho. *Perf. 13½*
780 A425 20p brick red & blk .30 .25
781 A425 20p brick red & blk .30 .25
a. Bklt. pane, 6 #780, 4 #781 4.00
b. Pair, #780-781 2.40 2.40
782 A425 20p yel & blk .30 .25
783 A425 20p yel & blk .30 .25
a. Bklt. pane, 6 #782, 4 #783 4.00
b. Pair, #782-783 2.40 2.40
Nos. 780-783 (4) 1.20 1.00

Nos. 782-783 inscribed "D.S. No 20."
For surcharges see Nos. 813-816, 955-956.

Merino, Biplane, Jet Passenger Plane and Supersonic Fighter Plane — A426

1988, May 17 Litho. *Perf. 13½*
784 A426 35p multi 1.20 .25

Commodore Arturo Merino Benitez (b. 1888), aviation pioneer.

Naval Tradition — A427

Designs: No. 785, Training ship *Esmeralda*. No. 786, Capt. Arturo Pratt, a stained-glass window in the Naval Museum, Valparaiso.

1988, May 23
785 50p multi .90 .50
786 50p multi .90 .50
a. A427 Pair, #785-786 2.25 1.75

Pontifical Catholic University of Chile, Santiago, Cent. — A429

1988, June 21
787 A429 40p Papal & university arms 1.20 .25

Locomotives — A430

No. 788, Esslingen No. 3331. No. 789, North British No. 45.

1988, July 22 Litho. *Perf. 13½*
788 60p multi 1.00 .70
789 60p multi 1.00 .70
a. Souv. sheet, #788-789, imperf 7.00 7.00
b. A430 Pair, #788-789 2.40 2.40

Arica-La Paz Railway, 75th anniv. (No. 788); Antofagasta Bolivia Railway, cent. (No. 789).

Jose Miguel Carrera Natl. Institute, 175th Anniv. — A431

1988, Aug. 10 Litho. *Perf. 13½*
790 A431 45p multi 1.25 .35

Annexation of Easter Is., Cent. — A432

1988, Sept. 9
791 50p Ship, officer 2.00 .40
792 50p Map, globe 2.00 .40
a. A432 Pair, #791-792 4.50 1.50
793 100p Easter Is. folk dancers 3.00 .75
794 100p Stone ruins 3.00 .75
a. A432 Pair, #793-794 6.50 3.00
b. Souv. sheet of 4, #791-794, imperf. 12.50 6.50
Nos. 791-794 (4) 10.00 2.30

Miniature Sheet

Flowers — A433

Designs: a, Chloraea chrysantha. b, Lapageria rosea. c, Nolana paradoxa. d, Rhodophiala advena. e, Schizanthus hookeri. f, Acacia caven. g, Cordia decandra. h, Leontochir ovallei. i, Alstroemeria pelegrina. j, Copiapoa cinerea. k, Salpiglossis sinuata. l, Leucocoryne coquimbensis. m, Eucryphia glutinosa. n, Calandrinia longiscapa. o, Desfontainia spinosa. p, Sophora macrocarpa.

1988, Aug. 23 Litho. *Perf. 13½*
795 Sheet of 16 19.00 19.00
a.-p. A433 30p any single .85 .40

First Domestic Airmail Route, 1919 — A434

150p, Clodomiro Figueroa Ponce's aircraft.

1988, Oct. 11
796 A434 150p multi 2.00 1.10

Christmas 1988
A435 A436

Children's drawings: 35p, Nativity, by Paulette Thiers, age 8. 100p, Going to church, by Jose M. Lamas, age 9, horiz.

1988, Nov. 17
797 A435 20p rose lake & org yel .45 .25
a. Bklt. pane of 10 6.50
798 A435 20p rose lake & org yel .45 .25
a. Bklt. pane of 10 6.50
799 A436 35p multi .65 .25
800 A436 100p multi 1.10 .40
Nos. 797-800 (4) 2.65 1.15

No. 798 inscribed "D.S. No 20."

Artisans — A437

1988, Oct. 25 Litho. *Perf. 13½*
801 25p Potter .60 .25
802 25p Weaver .60 .25
a. A437 Pair, #801-802 1.50 1.25

No. 802a has continuous design.

Natl. Philatelic Soc., Cent. — A438

1988, Nov. 24
803 A438 40p No. 38, cancellation .60 .25

School Crossing Guards — A439

1988, Oct. 26
804 A439 45p multi .75 .25

A440

Battle scenes and: No. 805, Manuel Bulnes (1799-1866) Commander. No. 806, Cavalryman, Servicemen. No. 807, Roberto Simpson, Commander. No. 808, Seaman, Servicemen.

1989, Jan. 12 Litho. *Perf. 13½*
805 50p multi .85 .40
806 50p multi .85 .40
a. A440 Pair, #805-806 3.00 1.00
807 100p multi 1.60 .85
808 100p multi 1.60 .85
a. A440 Pair, #807-808 3.50 2.10
Nos. 805-808 (4) 4.90 2.50

Battles of 1839: Yungay (50p) and Casma (100p). Nos. 806a, 808a have continuous designs.

Municipal Annivs. A442

Municipal coats of arms and: 30p, San Ambrosio Church. 35p, Craftsman sculpting marble. 45p, Laja Spring and falls.

1989, Jan. 20
809 A442 30p multi .30 .25
810 A442 35p multi .45 .25
811 A442 45p multi .50 .25
Nos. 809-811 (3) 1.25 .75

Founding of Vallenar, 200th anniv. (30p); founding of Combarbala, 200th anniv. (35p); founding of Los Angeles, 250th anniv. (45p).

Nos. 760a-760d and 780-783 Surcharged

a b

1989, Mar. 20 Litho. *Perf. 13½*
812 Block of 4 1.75 .75
a.-d. A411(a) 25p on 15p #760a-760d, any single .25 .25
813 A425(b) 25p on 20p #780 .35 .25
814 A425(b) 25p on 20p #781 .35 .25
a. A425(b) Pair, #813-814 1.50 1.25
Complete booklet, 6 #813, 4 #814 5.00
815 A425(b) 25p on 20p #782 .35 .25
816 A425(b) 25p on 20p #783 .35 .25
a. A425(b) Pair, #815-816 1.50 1.25
Complete booklet, 6 #815, 4 #816 5.00
Nos. 812-816 (5) 3.15 1.75

Surcharge differs on Nos. 814, 816.
Issued: Nos. 812-814, 3/20. Nos. 815-816, 11/30.

Women Beatified — A443

No. 818, Sr. Teresa de Los Andes. No. 819, Laura Vicuna.

1989, Mar. 21 Litho. *Perf. 13½*
818 A443 40p multicolored .75 .35
819 A443 40p multicolored .75 .35
a. Pair, #818-819 2.00 1.10

No. 819a has continuous design.

EXFINA '89, Santiago — A444

No. 820, Christopher Columbus. No. 821, Galleons.

1989, Mar. 31
820 100p multi 1.75 .80
821 100p multi 1.75 .80
a. A444 Pair, #820-821 4.00 3.25
b. Souvenir sheet of 2, #820-821 9.00 5.25
c. Souvenir sheet of 2, #820-821 12.00 6.25

No. 821a has continuous design. No. 821b margin pictures Columbus's coat of arms and the Order of the Great Admiralty, No. 821c margin Nos. 55, 69, 18, 76, 37, 1, 20 and 98.

CORFO Development Corp., 50th Anniv. — A445

1989, Apr. 4
822 A445 60p Shipping .60 .30
823 A445 60p Lumber .60 .30
824 A445 60p Communication .60 .30
825 A445 60p Coal .60 .30
a. Block of 4, #822-825 3.00 2.50

Gabriela Mistral (1889-1957), Poet — A446

1989, Apr. 7 Litho. *Perf. 13½*
826 A446 30p Poet, steeple .60 .25
827 A446 30p Poet, children .60 .25
828 A446 30p Poet working .60 .25
829 A446 30p Receiving Nobel Prize, 1945 .60 .25
a. Block of 4, #826-829 3.00 2.00

Exports — A447

Nos. 830, 832, Grapes. Nos. 831, 833, Apple.

1989, Apr. 19
830 A447 25p indigo & brt yel grn .45 .25
831 A447 25p ver & brt yel grn .45 .25
a. Bklt. pane, 5 each #830-831 10.00
b. Pair, #830-831 2.00 1.00
832 A447 25p indigo & pale yel org .45 .25
833 A447 25p ver & pale yel org .45 .25
a. Bklt. pane, 5 each #832-833 10.00
b. Pair, #832-833 2.00 1.00
Nos. 830-833 (4) 1.80 1.00

Nos. 832-833 inscribed "D.S. No 20."
See Nos. 861-864, 943-946. For surcharges see Nos. 956B-956C, 1085-1088.

Military Justice Department, 150th Anniv. — A448

1989, Apr. 24 Litho. *Perf. 13½*
834 A448 50p multicolored .60 .25

Monument to the Martyrs of Carabineros de Chile — A449

1989, Apr. 26
835 A449 35p multicolored .50 .25

Surveyor and Penguins — A450

1989, May 29
836 A450 150p multicolored 4.75 1.00

Antarctic Research Institute expeditions, 25th anniv.

Naval Engineers, Cent. — A451

No. 837, Naval school. No. 838, Seamen in boiler room. No. 839, Ship, helicopter, submarine. No. 840, *Aquiles* launch, Asmar-Talcahuano.

1989, May 31

837 A451 45p multicolored .75 .25
838 A451 45p multicolored .75 .25
839 A451 45p multicolored .75 .25
840 A451 45p multicolored .75 .25
a. Block of 4, #837-840 3.50 3.50

Horse-drawn Carriage (Victoria), Vina del Mar — A452

Early transportation: 35p, Launch off Chiloe Is., vert. 40p, Cart, Cautin. 45p, Ferry, Rio Palena. 50p, Car transport, Lake Gral, Carretta. 60p, Incline railroad, Valparaiso. 100p, Cable car (funicular), Santiago.

1989-92 Litho. *Perf. 13½*

841 A452 30p black & orange .55 .25
842 A452 60p black & lemon .90 .45
843 A452 60p like No. 842 .85 .25
844 A452 100p black & brt yel grn 1.50 .75

1989-91

845 A452 35p black & brt blue .55 .25
846 A452 40p black & olive .65 .25
847 A452 45p blk & pale blue grn .65 .25
a. Inscribed "1991" .65 .25
848 A452 45p black & lt ol grn .35 .25
849 A452 50p black & scarlet .45 .25
a. Inscribed "1992" .45 .25
Nos. 841-849 (9) 6.45 2.95

Nos. 843, 848 inscribed DS No. 20.
Issued: Nos. 841-842, 844, 4/22/89; No. 848, 2/1/91; No. 843, 1992; others, 8/1989.
For surcharge see No. 1002.

Export Type of 1989

Nos. 861, 863, Grapes. Nos. 862, 864, Apple.

1989, May 22

861 A447 5p dark blue & gray .40 .40
862 A447 5p brt red, dark blue & gray .40 .40
a. Pair, #861-862 .90 .90
863 A447 10p dark blue & gray .40 .40
864 A447 10p brt red, dark blue & gray .40 .40
a. Pair, #863-864 .90 .90

World Stamp Expo '89 — A453

1989, Aug. 25 Litho. *Perf. 13½*

865 A453 250p multicolored 4.50 1.40
a. Souvenir sheet of 1 10.00 8.00

A454

UPAE emblem and pre-Columbian peoples: 30p, Atacamena potter. 150p, Selk'nam-onas bow hunter.

1989, Oct. 12

866 A454 30p multicolored 1.00 .25
867 A454 150p multicolored 3.75 .95

Drawing by Christina Lopez — A455

1989, Nov. 20 Litho. *Perf. 13½*

868 A455 100p multicolored 1.40 .45

Christmas.

Christmas Ornaments — A456

Nos. 869, 871, Balls. Nos. 870, 872, Bells.

1989

869 A456 25p dull green & org .45 .25
870 A456 25p dull green & org .45 .25
a. Bklt. pane, 5 each Nos. 869-870 4.50
b. Pair, #869-870 1.00 .70
871 A456 25p dull green & ver .45 .25
872 A456 25p dull green & ver .45 .25
a. Bklt. pane, 5 each Nos. 871-872 4.50
b. Pair, #871-872 1.00 .70
Nos. 869-872 (4) 1.80 1.00

Nos. 871-872 inscribed "D.S. No 20."

Miniature Sheet

16 SELLOS = $ 560.-

Wildlife, Natl. Parks — A457

Designs: a, Vicuna, Lauca Park. b, Chilean flamingos, Salar de Surire. c, Cactus, La Chimba Reserve. d, Guanaco, Pan de Azucar Park. e, Song bird, Father Jorge Park. f, Terns, Rapa Nui Park. g, Ferret, La Campana Park. h, Duck, Rio Clarillo Park. i, Cypress tree, Rio de Los Cipreses Reserve. j, Black-headed swan, Laguna de Torca Reserve. k, Puma, Laguna del Laja Park. l, Araucaria tree, Villarrica Park. m, Flower, Vicente Perez Rosales Park. n, Lenga tree, Dos Lagunas. o, Sea lion, Laguna San Rafael Park. p, Rhea, Torres del Paine Park.

1990, Jan. 25

873 A457 Sheet of 16 20.00 10.00
a.-p. 35p any single .80 .25

1990 World Cup Soccer Championships, Italy — A458

1990, Feb. 23

874 A458 50p Cleated shoe .80 .25
875 A458 50p Hand .80 .25
876 A458 50p Soccer ball .80 .25
877 A458 50p Athlete .80 .25
a. Block of 4, #874-877 4.50 2.40

Natl. Air Force A459

Various aircraft: No. 878, Vickers Wibault. No. 879, Curtiss O1E Falcon. No. 880, Pitts S2A. No. 881, Extra 300.

1990, Mar. 16 Litho. *Perf. 13½*

878 A459 40p multicolored .65 .25
879 A459 40p multicolored .65 .25
880 A459 40p multicolored .65 .25
881 A459 40p multicolored .65 .25
a. Souvenir sheet of 4, #878-881 2.75 2.75
Nos. 878-881 (4) 2.60 1.00

FIDAE '90.

Discovery of America 500th Anniv. (in 1992) — A460

Maps and 16th cent. men: No. 882, Incan. No. 883, Spanish infantryman.

1990, Apr. 20 Litho. *Perf. 13½*

882 60p multicolored 1.00 .25
883 60p multicolored 1.00 .25
a. A460 Pair, #882-883 4.00 3.00

Port Cities A462

1990, Apr. 27

884 A462 40p Valparaiso .50 .25
885 A462 40p San Vicente .50 .25
a. Pair, #884-885 1.25 1.25

Democracy — A463

1990, June 8 Litho. *Perf. 13½*

886 A463 20p Sunrise .25 .25
887 A463 30p Peace dove .50 .25
888 A463 60p Pleasure .80 .40
889 A463 100p Star 1.40 .60
a. Souvenir sheet of 4, #886-889 4.00 4.00
Nos. 886-889 (4) 2.95 1.50

Equality — A464

1990, June 8

890 A464 45p multicolored .60 .30
a. Souvenir sheet 1.40 1.40

No. 890a margin continues the design.

Naval Tradition — A465

No. 891, Transport ship Piloto Pardo. No. 892, Oceanographic research ship Yelcho.

1990, May 30 Litho. *Perf. 13½*

891 A465 50p multicolored .60 .25
892 A465 50p multicolored .60 .25
a. Pair, #891-892 1.50 1.00

A466

1990, June 12

893 A466 250p Sir Rowland Hill 3.50 1.25
a. Souvenir sheet of 1 6.00 4.50

Penny Black, 150th anniv.
No. 893a margin continues the design.

A467

1990, June 21

894 A467 150p multicolored 1.75 .75

Organization of American States, cent.

Marine Resources — A468

Designs: a, Scallop. b, Clam. c, Swordfish. d, Crab. e, Fish. f, Baiting, processing.

1990, July 27 Litho. *Perf. 13½*

895 A468 Block of 6 7.00 3.00
a.-f. 40p any single .70 .25

Curimon Convent A469

1990, Aug. 1
896 A469 50p multicolored .60 .25

250th anniversary of San Felipe.

Environmental Protection — A470

1990, Sept. 1 Litho. *Perf. 13½*

897	A470 35p Aerosol propellants	.35	.25
898	A470 35p Deforestation	.35	.25
899	A470 35p Smokestacks	.35	.25
900	A470 35p Oil slick, shore	.35	.25
901	A470 35p Forest fire	.35	.25
a.	Strip of 5, #897-901	2.00	2.00
b.	Bklt. pane, 2 each #897-901	5.50	

Inscribed "D.S. No 20"

902	A470 35p Aerosol propellants	.35	.25
903	A470 35p Deforestation	.35	.25
904	A470 35p Smokestacks	.35	.25
905	A470 35p Oil slick, shore	.35	.25
906	A470 35p Forest fire	.35	.25
a.	Strip of 5, #902-906	2.00	2.00
b.	Bklt. pane, 2 each #902-906	5.50	
	Nos. 897-906 (10)	3.50	2.50

See Nos. 988-997.

Presidents of Chile — A471

No. 912, Salvador Allende. No. 913, Eduardo Frei. No. 914, Jorge Alessandri. No. 915, Gabriel Gonzalez V. No. 916, Juan Antonio Rios. No. 917, Pedro Aguirre Cerda. No. 918, Juan E. Montero. No. 919, Carlos Ibanez. No. 920, Emiliano Figueroa. No. 921, Arturo Alessandri.

1990, Sept. 4

912	A471 35p multicolored	.35	.25
913	A471 35p multicolored	.35	.25
914	A471 40p multicolored	.50	.25
a.	Inscribed "1992"	.50	.25
915	A471 45p multicolored	.55	.25
916	A471 50p multicolored	.65	.35
917	A471 60p multicolored	.70	.40
918	A471 70p multicolored	.85	.40
a.	Inscribed "1992"	.85	.40
919	A471 80p multicolored	.90	.50
920	A471 90p multicolored	.95	.55
a.	Inscribed "1992"	1.00	.55
921	A471 100p multicolored	1.00	.65
a.	Inscribed "1992"	1.40	.75
	Nos. 912-921 (10)	6.80	3.85

Rodeos — A472

Designs: a, Rodeo ring. b, Men on horses. c, Man stopping horse. d, Men, horses, bull.

1990, Sept. 24

926	Block of 4	2.75	2.00
a.-d.	A472 45p any single	.45	.25

Discovery of America, 500th Anniv. (in 1992) — A473

30p, Phoenicopterus chilensis. 150p, Arctocephalus australis.

1990, Oct. 12 Litho. *Perf. 13½*

927	A473 30p multicolored	1.50	.25
928	A473 150p multicolored	5.00	.85

King and Queen of Spain's Visit — A474

No. 930, Arms of King Juan Carlos I, Chilean Arms.

1990, Oct. 18

929	A474 100p shown	1.25	.60
930	A474 100p Denomination at LR	1.25	.60
a.	Pair, #929-930	3.25	2.25

Malleco Bridge, Cent. — A475

Design: No. 932, Boy waving at train on bridge.

1990, Oct. 26 Litho. *Perf. 13½*

931	A475 60p multicolored	1.25	.55
932	A475 60p multicolored	1.25	.55
a.	Pair, #931-932	3.00	2.10

Chilean Antarctic Territorial Claims, 50th Anniv. — A476

Design: No. 934, Penguins, helicopter, camp.

1990, Nov. 6 *Perf. 13½*

933	250p multicolored	3.00	1.40
934	250p multicolored	3.00	1.40
a.	A476 Pair, #933-934	8.00	6.00
b.	Souvenir sheet of 2, #933-934	12.00	12.00

A477

Christmas — A478

150p, Underwater dwelling.

1990, Nov. 20 Litho. *Perf. 13½*

935	A477 35p lt green & bl grn	.45	.25
a.	Booklet pane of 10	4.00	
936	A477 35p dull org & bl grn	.30	.25
a.	Booklet pane of 10	4.00	
937	A478 35p shown	.65	.25
938	A478 150p multi	2.75	1.50
	Nos. 935-938 (4)	4.15	2.25

No. 936 inscribed "D.S. No.20."

National Congress — A479

No. 939, Congress chamber. No. 940, Early congressional session.

1990, Dec. 21 Litho. *Perf. 13½*

939	A479 100p multicolored	1.00	.55
940	A479 100p multicolored	1.00	.55
a.	Pair, #939-940	2.75	1.75

City of Santiago, 450th Anniv. — A480

1991, Feb. 7

941	A480 100p Colorado House	1.00	.55
942	A480 100p Skyline	1.00	.55
a.	Pair, #941-942	3.50	2.50
b.	Souvenir sheet of 2, #941-942	5.00	5.00

Exports Type of 1989

Nos. 943, 945, Grapes. Nos. 944, 946, Apple.

1991, Feb. 8 *Perf. 13½ on 3 Sides*

943	A447 45p indigo & brt pink	.50	.25
944	A447 45p ver & brt pink	.50	.25
a.	Bklt. pane, 5 each #943-944	5.00	
945	A447 45p indigo & yel	.50	.25
946	A447 45p ver & yel	.50	.25
a.	Bklt. pane, 5 each #945-946	5.00	
	Nos. 943-946 (4)	2.00	1.00

Nos. 945-946 inscribed "D.S. No.20."
For surcharges see Nos. 1085-1088.

Historical Aircraft — A481

Designs: a, Voisin. b, S.E. 5a. c, Morane Saulnier MS 35. d, Consolidated PBY-5A/OA-10 Catalina.

1991, Mar. 21 Litho. *Perf. 13½*

947	A481 150p Block of 4, #a.-d.	7.25	4.50

American Soccer Cup, Chile — A482

1991, Apr. 12 Litho. *Perf. 13½*

948	100p Player, map	1.10	.40
949	100p Ball, goalie	1.10	.40
a.	A482 Pair, #948-949	2.25	1.00

Coal Mining A483

Design: No. 951, Miners dumping cart of coal.

1991, Apr. 18

950	A483 200p shown	1.90	.95
951	A483 200p multicolored	1.90	.95
a.	Pair, #950-951	4.00	3.00

Cultural Art — A484

1991, Apr. 29

952	90p multicolored	1.00	.50
953	90p multicolored	1.00	.50
a.	A484 Pair, #952-953	2.25	1.40

Chilean Scientific Society, Cent. — A485

1991, Apr. 29

954	A485 45p blue grn & blk	.50	.25

Nos. 782-783 Surcharged

a

b

1991, Apr. 30

955	A425(a) 45p on 20p, #782	.50	.25
956	A425(b) 45p on 20p, #783	.50	.25
a.	Pair, #955-956	1.50	.75

Nos. 832-833 Surcharged

1991, May 6 Litho. *Perf. 13½*

956B	A447 45p on 25p, #832	.90	.25
956C	A447 45p on 25p, #833	.90	.25
d.	Pair, #956B-956C	2.00	1.10

Santiago Cathedral A486

1991, May 9 Litho & Engr.

957	A486 300p red brn, sal & blk	2.75	1.75

World Telecommunications Day — A487

1991, May 17 Litho.

958	A487 90p multicolored	1.25	.30

A488

1991, May 23
959 A488 100p Pope Leo XIII 1.00 .40

Rerum Novarum Encyclical, cent.

A489

Rescue of Shackleton Expedition, 75th anniv.: a, Lt. Luis Pardo, Sir Ernest Shackleton. b, Rescue ship, Yelcho. c, Sailor pointing to survivors. d, Shackleton's ship, Endurance.

1991, May 28 **Litho.** ***Perf. 13½***
960 A489 50p Block of 4, #a.-d. 3.50 1.50
e. Miniature sheet, #960 4.75 2.50

21st General Assembly of Organization of American States, Santiago — A490

1991, June 5
961 A490 70p multicolored 1.00 .25

New Carabinero School — A491

1991, June 12
962 A491 50p multicolored .60 .25

Natl. Merchant Marine Day — A492

1991, June 26
963 A492 45p black & red .60 .25

11th Pan American Games, Havana — A493

1991, July 23
964 A493 100p Runners, torch, flags 1.00 .50
965 A493 100p Cycling, running, basketball 1.00 .50
a. Pair, #964-965 2.50 1.75

Founding of the City of Los Andes, Bicent. — A494

1991, July 29
966 A494 100p multicolored 1.25 .40

Miniature Sheet

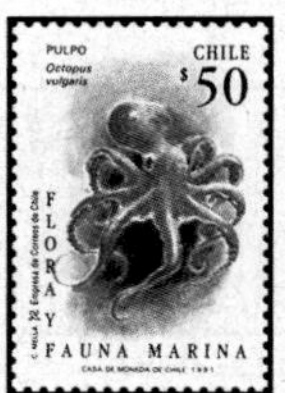

Marine Life — A495

Designs: No. 967a, Octopus vulgaris. b, Durvillaea antarctica. c, Paralichthys adspersus. d, Austromegabalanus psittacus. e, Concholepas concholepas. f, Cancer setosus. g, Lessonia nigrescens. h, Loxechinus albus. i, Homalaspis plana. j, Porphyra columbina. k, Oplegnathus insignis. l, Chorus giganteus. m, Rhynchocinetes typus. n, Engraulis ringens. o, Gracilaria spp. p, Pyura chilensis.

1991, Aug. 20 **Litho.** ***Perf. 13½***
967 Sheet of 16 20.00 7.50
a.-p. A495 50p any single .90 .25

1891 Revolution, Cent. — A496

Jose M. Balmaceda (1840-1891) and: No. 968, Machinery. No. 969, Teacher, students at Valentin Letelier School of Medicine.

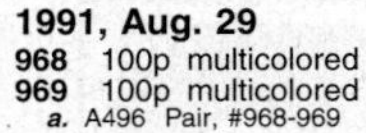
1991, Aug. 29
968 100p multicolored .90 .45
969 100p multicolored .90 .45
a. A496 Pair, #968-969 2.00 1.00

Chilean Art — A497

Paintings: 50p, Woman in Red, by Pedro Reszka. 70p, The Traveler, by Camilo Mori. 200p, Head of Child, by Benito Rebolledo. 300p, Boy Wearing a Fez, by A. Valenzuela Puelma.

1991, Sept. 26
970 A497 50p multicolored .50 .25
971 A497 70p multicolored .50 .30
972 A497 200p multicolored 2.25 .75
973 A497 300p multicolored 3.25 1.25
Nos. 970-973 (4) 6.50 2.55

Antarctic Treaty, 30th Anniv. — A498

1991, Oct. 7 **Litho.** ***Perf. 13½***
974 A498 80p shown 2.00 .70
975 A498 80p Birds, sea life 2.00 .70
a. Pair, #974-975 4.50 1.60

Intl. Letter Writing Week A499

1991, Oct. 9
976 A499 45p shown .45 .25
977 A499 70p Envelope filled with people .70 .30

America Issue — A500

UPAEP emblem, sailing ships and: 150p, Navigator.

1991, Oct. 14
978 A500 50p multicolored 1.50 .25
979 A500 150p multicolored 3.25 .75

A501

1991, Oct. 21
980 45p blue hat .75 .25
981 45p red hat .75 .25
a. A501 Pair, #980-981 2.00 .75
b. Souvenir sheet of 2, #980-981 4.00 2.75

Pablo Neruda, (1904-1973), Nobel Prize winner for literature, 1971.

A502

1991, Nov. 4
982 A502 45p Boy with stars .50 .25
983 A502 100p Girl with stars 1.00 .50

Christmas.

Christmas
A503 A504

1991, Nov. 18 **Litho.** ***Perf. 13½***
984 A503 45p violet & brt pink 1.10 .25
985 A504 45p violet & brt pink 1.10 .25
a. Pair, #984-985 2.50 .25
b. Bklt. pane of 5 #985a 7.00
986 A503 45p violet & brt pink 1.10 .25
987 A504 45p violet & brt pink 1.10 .25
a. Pair, #986-987 2.50 .25
b. Bklt. pane of 5 #987a 7.00
Nos. 984-987 (4) 4.40 1.00

Nos. 986-987 inscribed "D.S. No. 20."
For surcharges see Nos. 1016-1019.

Environmental Protection Type of 1990

1992, Jan. 28 **Litho.** ***Perf. 13½***

Lemon & Black

988 A470 60p like #897 .55 .25
989 A470 60p like #898 .55 .25
990 A470 60p like #899 .55 .25
991 A470 60p like #900 .55 .25
992 A470 60p like #901 .55 .25
a. Strip of 5, #988-992 3.50 2.50
b. Bklt. pane, 2 each #988-992 7.00

Inscribed "D.S. No. 20"

Orange & Dark Green

993 A470 60p like #902 .55 .25
994 A470 60p like #903 .55 .25
995 A470 60p like #904 .55 .25
996 A470 60p like #905 .55 .25
997 A470 60p like #906 .55 .25
a. Strip of 5, #993-997 3.50 2.50
b. Bklt. pane, 2 each #993-997 7.00
Nos. 988-997 (10) 5.50 2.50

Wolfgang Amadeus Mozart, Death Bicent. (in 1991) — A505

1992, Jan. 31
998 A505 60p shown .60 .25
999 A505 200p Hands at piano 1.90 .90
a. Sheet of 2, #998-999 4.00 4.00

FIDAE '92, Intl. Air and Space Fair — A506

1992, Mar. 5 Litho. *Perf. 13½*
1000 A506 60p multicolored .60 .25

16th Population and Housing Census A507

1992, Mar.
1001 A507 60p multicolored .60 .25

No. 847 Surcharged in Red Brown

1992, Mar.
1002 A452 60p on 45p .60 .25

Chilean Cities — A508

Cities' coat of arms and: 80p, Church of San Jose de Maipo. 90p, People making pottery. 100p, Lircunlauta House. 150p, Wine and lumber industries. 250p, Huilquilemu cultural center.

1992, Apr. 10 Litho. *Perf. 13½*
1003 A508 80p multicolored .65 .25
1004 A508 90p multicolored .75 .25
1005 A508 100p multicolored .90 .35
1006 A508 150p multicolored 1.40 .50
1007 A508 250p multicolored 2.10 .80
Nos. 1003-1007 (5) 5.80 2.15

80p, San Jose de Maipo, 200th anniv. 90p, Melipilla, 250th anniv. 100p, San Fernando, 250th anniv. 150p, Cauquenes, 250th anniv. 250p, Talca, 250th anniv.

Expo '92, Seville A509

1992, Apr. 23
1008 A509 150p Pavilion 1.40 .50
1009 A509 200p Iceberg 2.00 .65
a. Sheet of 2, #1008-1009 *4.50 4.50*

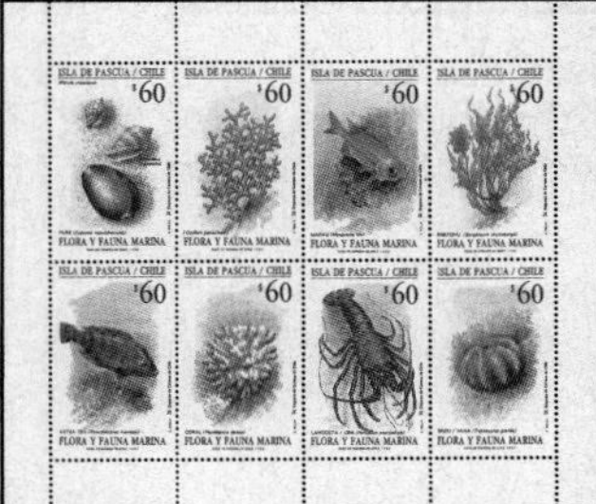

A510

Easter Island — A511

Marine life: No. 1010a, Morula praecipua, Strombus maculatus, Cypraea caputdraconis. b, Codium pocockiae. c, Myripristis tiki. d, Sargassum skottsbergii. e, Pseudolabrus fuentesi. f, Pocillopora danae. g, Panulirus pascuensis. h, Tripneustes gratilla.
No. 1011b, Natives, airplane, petroglyph.

1992, June 9 Litho. *Perf. 13½*
1010 A510 60p Sheet of 8, #a.-h. 10.00 2.75
1011 A511 200p Pair, #a.-b. 5.00 1.50

Natl. Council of the Disabled — A512

1992, June 23
1012 A512 60p multicolored .60 .25

Military Chiefs of Staff, 50th Anniv. — A513

1992, July 3
1013 A513 60p multicolored .60 .25

Submarine Forces, 75th Anniv. — A514

Coat of arms and: 250p, Officer using periscope, control room.

1992, July 4
1014 A514 150p multicolored 1.50 .50
1015 A514 250p multicolored 2.25 .90

Nos. 984-987 Surcharged

1992, Aug. 11 Litho. *Perf. 13½*
1016 A503 60p on 45p No. 984 .60 .25
1017 A504 60p on 45p No. 985 .60 .25
a. Pair, #1016-1017 2.50 .90
1018 A503 60p on 45p No. 986 .60 .25
1019 A504 60p on 45p No. 987 .60 .25
a. Pair, #1018-1019 2.50 .90
Nos. 1016-1019 (4) 2.40 1.00

Nos. 1018-1019 inscribed "D.S. No. 20."

Emperor Penguins — A515

1992, Sept. 28 Litho. *Perf. 13½*
1020 A515 200p shown 1.40 1.00
1021 A515 250p Adults with young 2.75 1.25
a. Souv. sheet of 2, #1020-1021 6.25 6.25

Central Post Office, Santiago, 1772 — A516

1992, Oct. 9
1022 A516 200p multicolored 1.75 .70

Discovery of America, 500th Anniv. — A517

UPAEP emblem and: 200p, Calendar stone, astrolabe, Columbus. 250p, Church, map of Central and South America, sailing ship.

1992, Oct. 20
1023 A517 200p multicolored 2.75 .65
1024 A517 250p multicolored 3.25 .75

Radio Chile, 75th Anniv. — A518

1992, Oct. 22
1025 A518 250p multicolored 2.00 .80

Bernardo O'Higgins (1778-1842) A519

1992, Oct. 23
1026 A519 60p multicolored .60 .25

Claudio Arrau, Pianist — A520

1992, Nov. 12 Litho. *Perf. 13½*
1027 A520 150p As child 1.25 .55
1028 A520 200p As adult 1.60 .75
a. Souv. sheet of 2, #1027-1028 3.50 3.50

Natl. Human Rights Day — A521

1992, Dec. 10
1029 A521 100p multicolored .80 .40
a. Souvenir sheet of 1 1.50 1.50

Christmas — A522

Designs: Nos. 1030, 1032, Denomination at LR. Nos. 1031, 1033, Denomination at LL.

1992, Dec. 12 Litho. *Perf. 13½*
1030 A522 60p buff & brown .60 .25
1031 A522 60p buff & brown .60 .25
a. Pair, #1030-1031 2.50 .45
b. Booklet pane of 5 #1031a 6.00 4.50
1032 A522 60p buff & red .60 .25
1033 A522 60p buff & red .60 .25
a. Pair, #1032-1033 2.50 .45
b. Booklet pane of 5 #1033a 6.00
Nos. 1030-1033 (4) 2.40 1.00

Nos. 1032-1033 inscribed "DS/20."

A523

University of Chile, 150th Anniv.: a, Statue. b, Coat of arms, facade of building.

1992, Nov. 19 Litho. *Perf. 13½*
1034 A523 200p Pair, #a.-b. 3.00 1.25
c. Souvenir sheet of 1, #1034 6.00 4.00

Nos. 1034a-1034b have a continuous design.

A524

1992, Dec. 12
1035 A524 70p black & yellow 1.00 .25

23rd meeting of Latin American Energy Ministers.

Churches of Chiloe — A525

Nos. 1036, 1038, Achao. Nos. 1037, 1039, Castro.

1993, Mar. 1 Litho. *Perf. 13½*

1036 A525 70p black & pink .70 .55
1037 A525 70p black & pink .70 .55
a. Pair #1036-1037 1.50 1.50
b. Booklet pane of 5 #1037a 7.50

Inscribed "DS/20"

1038 A525 70p black & yellow .70 .55
1039 A525 70p black & yellow .70 .55
a. Pair, #1038-1039 1.50 1.50
b. Booklet pane of 5 #1039a 7.50
Nos. 1036-1039 (4) 2.80 2.20

See Nos. 1053-1060, 1093-1098. For surcharges see Nos. 1129-1130.

Arrival of the Jesuits, 400th Anniv. — A526

Canonization of St. Teresa of the Andes, 1993 — A527

200p, St. Ignatius of Loyola. 300p, St. Teresa of the Andes.

1993 Litho. *Perf. 13½*

1040 A526 200p multicolored 2.10 1.00
a. Souvenir sheet of 1 3.00 3.00
1041 A527 300p multicolored 2.60 1.00

Issue dates: 200p, Mar. 15; 300p, Mar. 31. No. 1040a sold for 250p.

World Festival of Theatre of the Nations — A528

1993, Apr. 22

1042 A528 250p multicolored 1.75 .75

Second Space Conference of the Americas — A529

1993, Apr. 26

1043 A529 150p multicolored 1.30 .75
a. Souvenir sheet of 1 2.10 2.10

No. 1043a sold for 350p.

Clotario Blest (1899-1990), Syndicalist A530

1993, Apr. 30

1044 A530 70p multicolored .60 .25

Intl. Labor Day.

Vicente Huidobro, Poet (1893-1948) A531

1993, May 19 Litho. *Perf. 13½*

1045 A531 100p shown .90 .40
1046 A531 100p Portrait, seated .90 .40
a. Pair, #1045-1046 2.00 1.50

Antique Fire Engines — A532

Nos. 1047, 1902 Watterous Engineering Co. Ltd., Canada. Nos. 1048, 1872 Merryweather, England.

1993, June 30 Litho. *Perf. 13½*

1047 A532 100p multicolored 1.25 .50
1048 A532 100p multicolored 1.25 .50
a. Souv. sheet of 2, #1047-1048 3.00 3.00

No. 1048a sold for 400p.

Aircraft — A533

Designs: No. 1049, Douglas B-26 Invader. No. 1050, Mirage M50 Panther. No. 1051, Sanchez Besa. No. 1052, Bell 47D1 helicopter.

1993, July 13

1049 A533 100p multicolored .65 .35
1050 A533 100p multicolored .65 .35
1051 A533 100p multicolored .65 .35
1052 A533 100p multicolored .65 .35
a. Block of 4, #1049-1052 3.50 3.00

Church Type of 1993

Designs: 10p, Chonchi. 20p, Vilupulli. 30p, Llau-llao. 40p, Dalcahue. 50p, Tenaun. 80p, Quinchao. 90p, Quehui. 100p, Nercon.

1993, July Litho. *Perf. 13½*

1053 A525 10p green & black .25 .25
1054 A525 20p black & brown .25 .25
1055 A525 30p black & ver .25 .25
1056 A525 40p black & blue .30 .30
1057 A525 50p blk & grn blue .35 .35
1058 A525 80p black & buff .55 .55
a. Inscribed "1994" .60 .60
b. Booklet pane of 10 #1058a 8.25
Complete booklet, #1058b 8.25
1059 A525 90p olive & black .60 .60
a. Booklet pane of 10 8.25
Complete booklet, #1059a 8.25
1060 A525 100p gray vio & blk .65 .65
a. Booklet pane of 10 8.25
Complete booklet, #1060a 8.25
Nos. 1053-1060 (8) 3.20 3.20

Issued: No. 1058a, 1/1/94; No. 1059a, 1995; No. 1060a, 2/1/96.
See Nos. 1093-1097.

Natl. Dance, "La Cueca" — A534

1993, Sept. 15 Litho. *Perf. 13½*

1061 A534 70p Cueca chilota .65 .25
1062 A534 70p Cueca central .65 .25
1063 A534 70p Cueca nortina .65 .25
Nos. 1061-1063 (3) 1.95 .75

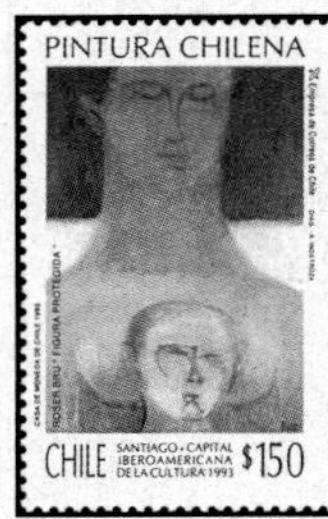

Paintings — A535

Designs: 80p, Tarde Amanecer, by Mario Carreno, horiz. 90p, Summer, by Gracia Barrios, horiz. 150p, Figura Protegida, by Roser Bru. 200p, Tangueria-Valparaiso, by Nemesio Antunez, horiz.

1993, Sept. 28

1064 A535 80p multicolored .70 .25
1065 A535 90p multicolored .80 .25
1066 A535 150p multicolored 1.50 .40
1067 A535 200p multicolored 2.00 .55
Nos. 1064-1067 (4) 5.00 1.45

Chilean Mint, 250th Anniv. A536

1993, Oct. 7 Litho. & Engr.

1068 A536 250p multicolored 2.40 .95
a. Souvenir sheet of 1 3.50 3.50

A537

1993, Oct. 19 Litho.

1069 A537 80p multicolored .70 .25

Urban transportation system, 25th anniv.

A538

150p, Cyanoliseus patagonus. 200p, Hippocamelus bisulcus.

1993, Oct. 12 Litho. *Perf. 13½*

1070 A538 150p multicolored 1.25 .55
1071 A538 200p multicolored 2.25 .75

America issue.

Chilean Possession of Straits of Magellan, 150th Anniv. — A539

1993, Oct. 21

1072 A539 100p multicolored 3.00 .35

Naval Anniversaries — A540

1993, Oct. 27

1073 A540 80p Sailing ships .60 .30
1074 A540 80p Schooner .60 .30
1075 A540 80p Assault ship .60 .30
1076 A540 80p Patrol boat .60 .30
Nos. 1073-1076 (4) 2.40 1.20

Sailing of first naval squadron (No. 1073), Arturo Prat Naval Academy (No. 1074), Marine Corps (No. 1075), 175th anniversaries. Alejandro Navarette School for Cadets (No. 1076), 125th anniv.

Intl. Year of Indigenous Peoples — A541

1993, Nov. 24

1077 A541 100p multicolored .90 .40

Christmas — A542

1993, Dec. 1 Litho. *Perf. 13½*

1078 A542 70p buff & brt lilac 1.10 .25
a. Booklet pane of 10 6.00
1079 A542 70p apple grn & brt blue 1.30 .25
a. Booklet pane of 10 7.00

No. 1079 inscribed "DS/20."
For surcharge see No. 1131.

Pygoscelis Adelie — A543

1993, Dec. 3
1080 A543 200p Nesting 2.40 .60
1081 A543 250p Adult, chicks 3.00 .80
a. Souv. sheet of 2, #1080-1081, imperf. 6.50 6.50

Chilean Antarctica.
No. 1081a has simulated perfs.

Chilean Cities — A544

1993, Dec. 15
1082 A544 80p Rancagua .50 .25
1083 A544 80p Curico .50 .25
1084 A544 80p Ancud .50 .25
Nos. 1082-1084 (3) 1.50 .75

Rancagua and Curico, 250th anniv. Ancud, 225th anniv.

Nos. 943-946 Surcharged

1993 Litho. *Perf. 13½ on 3 Sides*
1085 A447 60p on 45p, #943 .35 .25
1086 A447 60p on 45p, #944 .35 .25
a. Bklt. pane, 5 each #1085-1086 3.50
1087 A447 60p on 45p, #945 .35 .25
1088 A447 60p on 45p, #946 .35 .25
a. Bklt. pane, 5 each #1087-1088 3.50
Nos. 1085-1088 (4) 1.40 1.00

Nos. 1087-1088 inscribed "D.S. No. 20."

Intl. Year of the Family — A545

1994, Jan. 17 Litho. *Perf. 13½*
1089 A545 100p multicolored 1.00 .25

Musical Instruments — A546

Designs: a, Violin. b, Cello.

1994, Jan. 27 Litho. *Perf. 13½*
1091 A546 150p Pair, #a.-b. 3.25 3.25

No. 1091 has a continuous design.

Church Type of 1993

Designs: 80p, Quinchao. 90p, Quehui. Nos. 1097, 1098, Nercon.

1994-96 Litho. *Perf. 13½*
1093 A525 80p black & violet .50 .25
a. Booklet pane of 10 — —
Complete booklet, #1093a —
1095 A525 90p red & black .50 .25
a. Booklet pane of 10 4.75
Complete booklet, #1095a 4.75
1097 A525 100p yellow & black .55 .30
a. Booklet pane of 10 6.00
Complete booklet, #1097a 6.00
Nos. 1093-1097 (3) 1.55 .80

Issued: 80p, 1/13/94; 90p, 1995; 100p, 2/1/96.
Nos. 1093, 1095, 1097 inscribed "DS/20."

Souvenir Sheet

Natl. Aviation Museum, 50th Anniv. — A547

Aircraft: a, Sukhoi SU-30 Flanker. b, Vought-Sikorsky OS-2U3 Kingfisher. c, Lockheed F-117A Nighthawk. d, Northrop F-5E Tiger III.

1994, Mar. 17 Litho. *Perf. 13*
1102 A547 300p Sheet of 4, #a.-d. + 2 labels 10.00 5.50

Intl. Air and Space Fair, FIDAE '94.
See No. 1159.

College of Agronomy, 50th Anniv. — A548

1994, Apr. 28 Litho. *Perf. 13*
1103 A548 220p multicolored 1.50 .75

No. 760 Surcharged

1994, May 1 Litho. *Perf. 13½*
1104 Block of 4 2.50 1.50
a.-d. A411 80p on 15p any single .50 .25

Concepcion University, 75th Anniv. — A549

Sections of mural, by Jorge Gonzalez Camarena: No. 1105, Cactus plant, skeletons. No. 1106, Flags, pillars, nude woman, faces. No. 1107, Flags, bodies, woman, soldier in armor. No. 1108, Women's faces, pipelines.

1994, May 14 Litho. *Perf. 13*
1105 A549 250p multicolored 1.65 .75
1106 A549 250p multicolored 1.65 .75
1107 A549 250p multicolored 1.65 .75
1108 A549 250p multicolored 1.65 .75
a. Strip of 4, #1105-1108 + label 7.50 5.00

No. 1108a is a continuous design.

Chilean Antarctic Institute, 30th Anniv. — A550

Designs: No. 1109, Penguins, buildings. No. 1110, Buildings, coastal waters.

1994, May 31 *Perf. 13*
1109 300p multicolored 2.00 1.10
1110 300p multicolored 2.00 1.10
a. A550 Pair, #1109-1110 4.50 2.50

No. 1110a is a continuous design.

Antique Fire Engines — A551

No. 1111, Merryweather steam pumper, England, 1869. No. 1112, Western lever pumper, US, 1863. No. 1113, Mieusset steam pumper, France, 1905. No. 1114, Merryweather pumper, England, 1903.

1994, July 19 Litho. *Perf. 13*
1111 A551 150p multicolored .90 .50
1112 A551 150p multicolored .90 .50
1113 A551 150p multicolored .90 .50
1114 A551 150p multicolored .90 .50
a. Block of 4, #1111-1114 4.50 3.50

Javiera Carrera Girls' School, Cent. — A552

1994, Aug. 10
1115 A552 200p multicolored 1.50 .60

Arms, Sights from Chilean Cities — A553

Designs: 90p, Porvenir, cent. 100p, Villa Alemana, cent. 150p, Constitucion, bicent. 200p, Linares, bicent. 250p, Copiapo, 250th anniv. 300p, La Serena, 450th anniv.

1994, Aug. 26
1116 A553 90p multicolored .65 .25
1117 A553 100p multicolored .80 .30
1118 A553 150p multicolored 1.25 .40
1119 A553 200p multicolored 1.75 .55
1120 A553 250p multicolored 2.00 .65
1121 A553 300p multicolored 2.30 .85
Nos. 1116-1121 (6) 8.75 3.00

Butterflies — A554

Designs: a, Vanessa terpsichore. b, Hypsochila wagenknechti. c, Battus polydamas. d, Polythysana apollina. e, Satyridae. f, Tetraphloebia stellygera. g, Eroessa chilensis. h, Phoebis sennae.

1994, June 24 Litho. *Perf. 13*
1122 A554 100p Sheet of 8, #a.-h. 9.00 9.00

20th Intl. Conference on Data Bases — A555

1994, Sept. 21 Litho. *Perf. 13½*
1123 A555 100p multicolored .75 .30

America Issue — A556

Early postal transport vehicles: 80p, Van. 220p, DH-60-G, Gypsy Moth.

1994, Oct. 12
1124 A556 80p multicolored 1.25 .30
1125 A556 220p multicolored 2.25 .70

A557

1994, Oct. 31 Litho. & Engr.
1126 A557 300p multicolored 2.00 1.00

Beatification of Father Alberto Hurtado.

A558

1994 Litho. *Perf. 13½*
1127 A558 80p multicolored 1.00 .25
a. Booklet pane of 10 10.00

Complete booklet, #1127a 10.00

Inscribed "DS/20"

1128 A558 80p multicolored 1.00 .25
a. Booklet pane of 10 10.00
Complete booklet, #1128a 10.00

Christmas.

Nos. 1036-1037, 1079 Surcharged

Perf. 13½ on 3 Sides

1994, Nov. 4 **Litho.**

1129 A525 80p on 70p #1036 .90 .25
1130 A525 80p on 70p #1037 .90 .25
a. Pair, #1129-1130 1.80 .50
b. Booklet pane, 5 #1130a 4.50
Complete booklet, #1130b 4.50
1131 A542 80p on 70p #1079 .90 .25
a. Booklet pane, 10 #1131 9.00
Complete booklet, #1131a 9.00

Size and location of surcharge varies.

Miniature Sheet

Intl. Women's Day — A559

Designs: a, Star, "Women enriching the future." b, Moon, sun, "Women bringing harmony." c, Bird, "Women bringing peace." d, Earth, "Women changing the world."

1995, Mar. 8 **Litho.** ***Perf. 13½***
1132 A559 90p Sheet of 4, #a.-d. 6.00 2.50

Ancud Seminary of Conciliation, 150th Anniv. — A560

1995, Apr. 27
1133 A560 200p multicolored 1.60 .75

Destroyer Admiral Williams A561

1995, Apr. 21
1134 A561 100p multicolored 4.50 .30

World Conference on Social Development A562

1995, Apr. 25
1135 A562 150p multicolored 1.25 .45

Order of St. Augustine in Chile, 400th Anniv. — A563

Stained glass, Cathedral of Santiago.

1995, Apr. 28
1136 A563 250p multicolored 1.75 .75

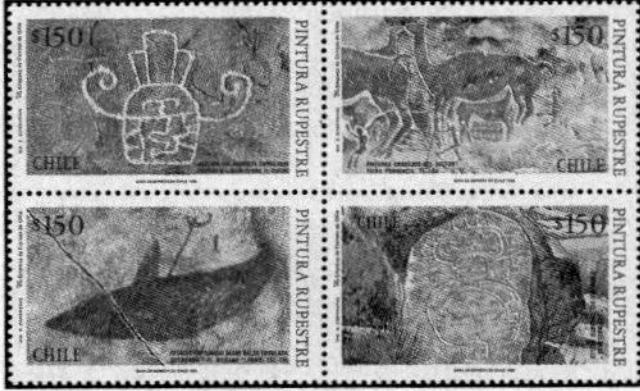

Petroglyphs — A564

Designs: a, Ceremonial mask, Buitre, Limari Province. b, Lamas, Taira Sector, El Loa Province. c, Harpooned whale, El Medano, Taltal Province. d, Two masks, Encanto, Ovalle.

1995, June 16 **Litho.** ***Perf. 13½***
1137 A564 150p Block of 4, #a.-d. 9.75 4.00

Miniature Sheet

Motion Pictures, Cent. — A565

Posters: a, Director's chair, camera. b, Charlie Chaplin in "The Kid." c, Lumiere brothers' 1895 Cinematographe. d, "Valparaiso, My Love", with Aldo Francia.

1995, June 21
1138 A565 100p Sheet of 4, #a.-d. 6.00 3.00

City of Parral, Bicent. A566

1995, June 30 **Litho.** ***Perf. 13½***
1139 A566 200p multicolored 1.60 .85

Miniature Sheet

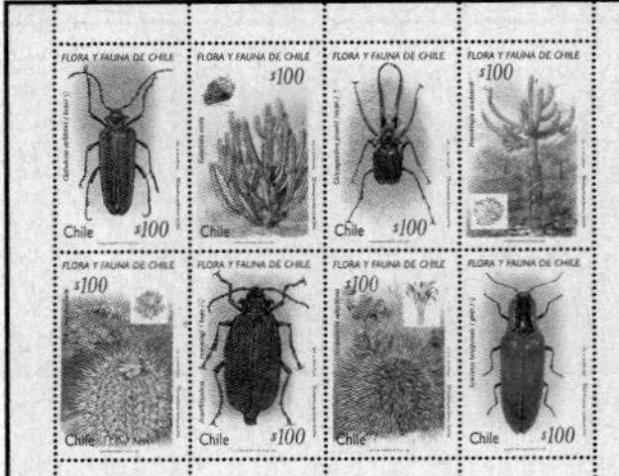

Insects and Cacti — A567

a, Cheloderus childreni. b, Eulychnia acida. c, Chiasognathus grantii. d, Browningia candelaris. e, Copiapoa dealbata. f, Acanthinodera cummingi. g, Neoporteria subgibbosa. h, Semiotus luteipennis.

1995, Aug. 10 **Litho.** ***Perf. 13½***
1140 A567 100p Sheet of 8, #a.-h. 11.50 7.50

2nd World Congress of Police, Santiago — A568

1995, Oct. 2
1141 A568 200p multicolored 1.60 .80

Ministry of Housing and Urban Development, 30th Anniv. — A569

Design: Tower of Babel V, by Mario Toral.

1995, Oct. 5 **Litho.** ***Perf. 13½***
1142 A569 200p multicolored 1.60 .85

Andres Bello (1781-1865), Scholar, Author A570

1995, Oct. 9 **Litho. & Engr.**
1143 A570 250p dk brn & blk 2.00 .85

Andres Bello Covenant, 25th anniv.

UNESCO, UN, FAO, 50th Anniv. — A571

Designs: a, Hands holding book, UNESCO emblem. b, Hands clasped between two globes, UN emblem. c, Hand holding seedling, FAO emblem.

1995, Oct. 10 **Litho.** ***Perf. 13½***
1144 A571 100p Strip of 3, #a.-c. 2.60 1.40

America Issue — A572

Children's drawings of environmental protection: 100p, Family in garden, trees, vert. 250p, Three people working with trees.

1995, Oct. 12 **Litho.** ***Perf. 13½***
1145 A572 100p multicolored 1.00 .45
1146 A572 250p multicolored 2.50 1.10

Chilean Soccer, Cent. — A573

Designs: a, Carlos Dittborn. b, Hugo Lepe. c, Eladio Rojas. d, Honorino Landa.

1995, Nov. 13 **Litho.** ***Perf. 13½***
1147 A573 100p Sheet of 4, #a.-d. 3.50 1.40

A574

1995, Oct. 24 **Litho.** ***Perf. 13½***
1148 A574 250p multicolored 2.25 .95

51st World Congress of Cape Horn captains.

Gabriela Mistral (1889-1957), 50th Anniv. of Receiving Nobel Prize for Literature A575

Litho. & Engr.

1995, Nov. 15 ***Perf. 13½***
1149 A575 300p blue black & blk 2.00 1.00

Eudyptes Chrysolophus A576

1995, Nov. 22 **Litho.** ***Perf. 13½***
1150 A576 100p shown 2.85 .60
1151 A576 250p Penguins, diff. 3.85 1.25
a. Souv. sheet, #1150-1151 11.00 6.00

No. 1151a sold for 600p.

Chilean Export Assoc., 60th Anniv. — A577

Cargo ship and: a, Kiwi fruit. b, Grapes. c, Peaches. d, Apples.
Jet plane and: e, Various berries.

1995, Dec. 1
1152 A577 100p Strip of 5, #a.-e. 8.50 3.50

Christmas
A578 A579

1995, Nov. 13 **Booklet Stamps**
1153 A578 90p brt blue & blue 1.00 .30
1154 A579 90p brt blue & blue 1.00 .30
a. Bklt. pane, 5 ea #1153-1154 10.00
Complete booklet, #1154a 10.25
1155 A578 90p brt grn & brown 1.00 .30
1156 A579 90p brt grn & brown 1.00 .30
a. Bklt. pane, 5 ea #1155-1156 10.00
Complete booklet, #1156a 10.25

Nos. 1155-1156 inscribed "DS/20."

End of World War II, 50th Anniv. A580

1995, Dec. 20 **Litho.** ***Perf. 13½***
1157 A580 200p multicolored 2.50 .75

Petroleum Production in Chile, 50th Anniv. — A581

Designs: a, Off-shore oil derrick, one main tower. b, Refinery, road trees, building. c, Refinery, up close. d, Off-shore oil derrick, four towers.

1995, Dec. 29
1158 A581 100p Block of 4, #a.-d. 5.00 4.00

Aviation Type of 1994

Designs: a, Embraer EMB-145. b, Mirage M5M Elkan. c, DHC-6 Twin Otter Series 300. d, SAAB JAS 39, Gripen.

1996, Mar. 9 **Litho.** ***Perf. 13½***
1159 A547 400p Sheet of 4, #a.-d. 13.00 8.50

Intl. Air and Space Fair, FIDAE '96.

Men's High School, La Serena, 175th Anniv. — A582

1996, Apr. 12
1160 A582 100p multicolored .70 .35

Espamer '96, World Philatelic Exhibition — A583

Designs: No. 1161, Old Train Station, Cordoba. No. 1162, Lope de Vega Theater.

1996, Apr. 25
1161 A583 200p multicolored 2.50 .70
1162 A583 200p multicolored 2.50 .70
a. Pair, #1161-1162 6.00 3.00

Accident Prevention A584

Traffic safety: No. 1163a, Cross street at crosswalk. b, Respect traffic police. c, Obey traffic signals. d, Wait for ride on sidewalk. e, Don't cross street between parked cars. f, Never ride on side of bus. g, Walk beside road facing oncoming traffic. h, Pay attention to where you are walking. i, Don't play on streets. j, Obey traffic rules while riding a bicycle.

Safety in the home: No. 1164a, Extinguish matches after using. b, Be careful with boiling water. c, Curb sharp objects. d, Protect electrical outlets. e, Don't improvise electrical connections. f, Don't play radio or TV too loudly. g, Check all gas connections. h, Don't overload electrical outlets. i, Keep flammable materials away from furnace. j, Keep toys off floor.

Recreational safety: No. 1165a, Swim only in designated areas. b, Keep hands, head inside the car. c, Don't get a sunburn. d, Don't contaminate water with detergents. e, Don't litter. f, Extinguish camp fires. g, Don't bother others when swimming. h, Check car safety features. i, Keep kites away from electrical wires. j, Don't run in swimming pool area.

Safety in the workplace: No. 1166a, Use protective gear. b, Use only safe tools. c, Keep you mind on your work. d, Use proper tools. e, Avoid work accidents. f, Keep stairs free of objects. g, Don't carry objects that obstruct your view. h, Check ladder before using. i, Keep area clean, organized. j, Be aware of protruding nails.

Proper use of drugs and alcohol: No. 1167a, Don't drink and drive. b, Don't drink if you are pregnant. c, Don't encourage friends to drink. d, Alcohol and work don't mix. e, Drinking could destroy your family. f, Drugs can't make you happy. g, Drugs don't make you successful. h, Be happy without drugs. i, For your family say "no" to drugs. j, Drug free, happy and confident.

Safety in schools: No. 1168a, Keep calm in case of fire. b, Don't run along sides of buildings. c, Don't play dangerous jokes. d, Don't sit or stand in high dangerous places. e, Don't run on stairs. f, Don't walk and drink at the same time. g, Don't rock on chairs. h, Don't play with sharp objects. i, Don't open doors abruptly. j, Don't talk to strangers outside the school.

1996, May 2
1163 A584 50p Block of 10, #a.-j. 8.50 2.60
1164 A584 50p Block of 10, #a.-j. 8.50 2.60
1165 A584 50p Block of 10, #a.-j. 8.50 2.60
1166 A584 50p Block of 10, #a.-j. 8.50 2.60
1167 A584 50p Block of 10, #a.-j. 8.50 2.60
1168 A584 50p Block of 10, #a.-j. 8.50 2.60

No. 1 Dry Dock, Talcahuano, Cent. — A585

1996, May 20
1169 A585 200p multicolored 1.40 .70

Sculptures — A586

No. 1170, Mariner's Compass, by Ricardo Mesa, vert. No. 1171, Friendship, by Francisca Cerda, vert. No. 1172, Andes Winds, by Benito Rojo. No. 1173, Memory, by Fernando Undurraga.

1996, June 20 **Litho.** ***Perf. 13½***
1170 A586 150p multicolored 1.75 .90
1171 A586 150p multicolored 1.75 .90
a. Pair, #1170-1171 4.75 4.75
1172 A586 200p multicolored 2.25 .90
1173 A586 200p multicolored 2.25 .90
a. Pair, #1172-1173 6.00 6.00
Nos. 1170-1173 (4) 8.00 3.60

Intl. Day Against Use of Illegal Drugs and Drug Trafficking — A587

1996, June 26
1174 A587 250p multicolored 3.50 1.25

1996 Summer Olympic Games, Atlanta — A588

Designs: a, Boxer's glove. b, Runner's shoe. c, Roller blade. d, Ball.

1996, July 3
1175 A588 450p Block of 4, #a.-d. 13.50 11.00

Order of Mother of God, 50th Anniv. of Presence in Chile — A589

1996, Aug. **Litho.** ***Perf. 13½***
1176 A589 200p multicolored 1.50 .75

Lyceum of San Fernando, 150th Anniv. — A590

1996, Aug. 2
1177 A590 200p multicolored 1.50 .75

4th Intl. Congress of Earth Sciences — A591

Globe showing portions of continents, and: a, Forest fire. b, Smoke stacks creating air pollution. c, Cutting down trees. d, Surveying equipment, desert.

1996, Aug. 5 Litho. *Perf. 13½*

1178 A591 200p Block of 4, #a.-d. 6.75 6.75

Minerals — A592

a, Kroehnkita. b, Lapis lazuli. c, Bornite. d, Azurite.

1996, Aug. 9

1179 A592 150p Block of 4, #a.-d. 5.00 4.25

German Immigration, 150th Anniv. — A593

Designs: 250p, House, lake, mountain. 300p, Monument showing arrival on boat.

1996, Aug. 22

1180 A593 250p multicolored 1.90 .90
1181 A593 300p multicolored 2.10 1.00

Aptenodytes Patagonica A594

1996, Sept. 9 Litho. *Perf. 13½*

1182 A594 250p shown 3.50 1.00
1183 A594 300p Molting 4.00 1.10
a. Souvenir sheet, #1182-1183 9.00 7.50

Castro Fire Dept., Cent. — A595

Designs: a, 1937 Italian pumper. b, 1940 Ford fire truck. c, Gorlitz G.A. Fischer manual 4-speed pumper. d, 1907 pumper.

1996, Sept. 14

1184 A595 200p Block of 4, #a.-d. 7.00 6.00

Ecotourism in National Parks — A596

Designs: a, River rafting. b, Horseback riding. c, Snow skiing. d, Hiking around cacti.

1996, Sept. 27

1185 A596 100p Sheet of 4, #a.-d. 3.25 3.25

Juan José Latorre Benavente (1846-1912), Admiral — A597

1996, Oct. 8

1186 A597 200p multicolored 1.50 .75

Historical Costumes — A598

America issue: No. 1187, Two women, child, dog, vert. No. 1188, Two men with horse, vert. 250p, Two men on horseback.

1996, Oct. 23

1187 A598 100p multicolored .95 .50
1188 A598 100p multicolored .95 .50
a. Pair, #1187-1188 2.00 2.00
1189 A598 250p multicolored 1.75 1.10

Church, City of Arica — A599

150p, Fauna, mountains, Parinacota Park.

1996, Nov. 18 Litho. *Perf. 13½*

1190 A599 100p multicolored .65 .35
1191 A599 150p multicolored .85 .45

Christmas — A600

1996, Nov. 25

1192 A600 100p black & multi .70 .30
a. Booklet pane of 10 7.50
Complete booklet, #1192a 8.00
1193 A600 100p orange & multi .70 .30
a. Booklet pane of 10 7.50
Complete booklet, #1193a 8.00

No. 1193 is inscribed DS/20.

Mythology

A601 A602

1997, Feb. 12 Litho. *Perf. 13½*

1194 A601 40p black & blue .25 .25
1195 A602 110p black & green .80 .40
a Booklet pane of 10 8.00
Complete booklet, #1195a 8.50
1196 A602 110p black & orange .80 .40
a. Booklet pane of 10 8.00
Complete booklet, #1196a 8.50

No. 1195 inscribed DS/20.

Sixth Summit of Spanish-Americana Heads of State and Government — A603

Mural, Visual Memory of the Nation, by Mario Toral: No. 1198, Left half. No. 1199, Right half.

1996, Nov. 6

1198 110p multicolored .90 .45
1199 110p multicolored .90 .45
a. A603 Pair, #1198-1199 2.00 .95

State Visit of King Carl XVI Gustaf, Queen Silvia of Sweden — A604

Design: Nobel Laureates Pablo Neruda, Gabriela Mistral, Nobel medal.

1996, Dec. 3

1200 A604 300p multicolored 2.25 1.10

UNICEF, 50th Anniv. — A605

1996, Dec. 11

1201 A605 200p multicolored 1.75 .90

Frontier Region, Cent. — A606

No. 1202, Christian Alliance & Missionary Church, cent. No. 1203, Lonquimay municipality, cent.

1997

1202 A606 110p multicolored .80 .40
1203 A606 110p multicolored .90 .45

Issued: No. 1202, 1/19; No. 1203, 1/25.

Arturo Prat Antarctic Naval Base, 50th Anniv. — A607

1997, Feb. 6 Litho. *Perf. 13½*

1204 A607 250p Aerial view, vert. 1.90 .95
1205 A607 300p shown 2.40 1.10

Controller General of the Republic, 70th Anniv. — A608

1997, Mar. 26

1206 A608 110p multicolored 2.00 .40

Opening of Metro Line 5 — A609

1997, Apr. 2

1207 A609 200p multicolored 1.50 .75

Interamerican Masonic Confederation, 50th Anniv. — A610

1200p, Emblems, compass, square, book.

1997, Apr. 8

1208 A610 250p shown 2.00 1.00

Souvenir Sheet

1209 A610 1200p multicolored 9.00 9.00

No. 1209 contains one 48x60mm stamp.

Heinrich von Stephan (1831-97) A611

1997, Apr. 15

1210 A611 250p multicolored 2.25 1.10

World Book and Copyright Day — A612

1997, Apr. 23
1211 A612 110p multicolored .80 .45

Details from "Death to the Invader," by David Alfaro Siqueiros (1896-1974), Muralist — A613

1997, June 26 Litho. *Perf. 13½*
1212 A613 150p shown 1.50 .40
1213 A613 200p Detail, diff. 1.75 .60

Souvenir Sheets
1214 A613 1000p like #1212 7.25 6.25
1215 A613 1000p like #1213 7.25 6.25

Nos. 1214-1215 each contain one 48x36mm stamp.

Providencia, Cent. — A614

1997, July 17
1216 A614 250p multicolored 1.60 1.60

A615

1997, Sept. 1
1217 A615 300p multicolored 2.00 2.00

Diplomatic relations between Chile and Japan, cent. See Japan No. 2578.

A616

1997, Oct. 1 Litho. *Perf. 13½*
1218 A616 110p Quality .80 .80

1st Radio Broadcast in Chile, 75th Anniv. — A617

1997 Litho. *Perf. 13½*
1219 A617 110p multicolored .80 .80

Chilean Opera Singers A618

Singer, opera: 120p, Carlo Morelli, "Rigoletto." 200p, Pedro Navia, "La Bohéme." 250p, Renato Zanelli, "Faust." 300p, Rayèn Quitral, "The Magic Flute." 500p, Ramón Vinay, "Othello."

1997, Oct. 15
1220 A618 120p multicolored 1.00 1.00
1221 A618 200p multicolored 1.75 1.75
1222 A618 250p multicolored 2.25 2.25
1223 A618 300p multicolored 2.50 2.50
1224 A618 500p multicolored 4.25 4.25
Nos. 1220-1224 (5) 11.75 11.75

America Issue — A619

Life of a postman: 110p, Delivering mail on bicycle. 250p, Delivering mail on horseback.

1997, Oct. 12 Litho. *Perf. 13½*
1225 A619 110p multicolored 1.00 1.00
1226 A619 250p multicolored 2.50 2.50

Christmas — A620

1997 Litho. *Perf. 13½*
1227 A620 110p multicolored 1.60 .80
a. Booklet pane of 10 16.00
Complete booklet, #1227a 16.00
1228 A620 110p multicolored 1.60 .80
a. Booklet pane of 10 16.00
Complete booklet, #1228a 16.00

No. 1228 is inscribed D/S20 and was only issued in booklets.

Chilean Post, 250th Anniv. A621

Designs: 120p, Postman canceling letters. 300p, Man depositing letter into postbox.

1997, Dec. 22
1229 A621 120p multicolored .75 .75
1230 A621 300p multicolored 1.90 .95

Dogs
A622 A623

1998 Litho. *Perf. 13½*
1231 A622 120p Great Dane .60 .25
1232 A623 120p Dalmatian .60 .25
a. Pair, #1231-1232 1.25 1.00
b. Booklet pane, 5 #1232a 7.00
Complete booklet, #1232b 7.00
1233 A622 120p Great Dane .60 .25
1234 A623 120p Dalmatian .60 .25
a. Pair, #1233-1234 1.25 1.00
b. Booklet pane, 5 #1234a 7.00
Complete booklet, #1234b 7.00

Nos. 1233-1234 are inscribed DS/20.

2nd Summit of the Americas, Santiago — A624

1998, Apr. 17 Litho. *Perf. 13½*
1235 A624 150p multicolored 1.20 1.20

Souvenir Sheet
1236 A624 1000p Logo, diff. 7.50 7.50

No. 1236 contains one 26x42mm stamp.

Paintings — A625

350p, "Los Zambos de Calama," by Mauricio Moran. 400p, "Sandia Calada," by Roser Bru.

1998, May 14 Litho. *Perf. 13½*
1237 A625 350p multicolored 2.10 2.10
1238 A625 400p multicolored 2.40 2.40

Capuchin Order in Chile, 150th Anniv. — A626

Designs: 150p, Native village, friar writing in book. 250p, Friar aiding injured man.

1998, May 18
1239 A626 150p multicolored .90 .90
1240 A626 250p multicolored 1.40 1.40

1998 World Cup Soccer Championships, France — A627

Players and: 250p, Crowd. 350p, World Cup Trophy. 500p, Map of France. 700p, Chilean flag.
1500p, Player, vert.

1998, May 23
1241 A627 250p multicolored 1.50 1.50
1242 A627 350p multicolored 2.50 2.00
1243 A627 500p multicolored 3.50 3.00
1244 A627 700p multicolored 4.50 4.25
Nos. 1241-1244 (4) 12.00 10.75

Souvenir Sheet
1245 A627 1500p multicolored 10.00 9.00

A628

Antarctic Research: 250p, Logo, penguin. 350p, Penguins, map, logo.

1998, July 22
1246 A628 250p multicolored 1.50 1.50
1247 A628 350p multicolored 2.25 2.25

No. 1246, Scientific Committee on Antarctic Research, 25th meeting. No. 1247, Natl. Administrators of Antarctic Programs, 10th meeting.

A629

1998, Apr. 3
1248 A629 120p multicolored .80 .80

Captain Arturo Prat Chacon, 150th birth anniv.

Army Veterinarian Service, Cent. — A630

350p, Veterinarian listening to horse's heartbeat.

1998, Apr. 20
1249 A630 250p multicolored 1.50 1.50
1250 A630 350p multicolored 2.25 2.25

Merchant Marine's Director General of Maritime Territory, 150th Anniv. — A631

1998, Aug. 31 **Litho.** ***Perf. 13½***
1251 A631 500p multicolored 3.00 3.00

Intl. Year of the Ocean.

Intl. Year of the Ocean A632

No. 1252, Nautical cartography. No. 1253, Iceberg. 500p, Silhouette of stone head, Easter Island.

1998, Sept. 10
1252 A632 400p multicolored 2.50 2.50
1253 A632 400p multicolored 2.50 2.50
1254 A632 500p multicolored 3.00 3.00
Nos. 1252-1254 (3) 8.00 8.00

Folk Singers and Composers — A633

Designs: 200p, Clara Solovera Cortes (1909-92). 250p, Francisco Flores del Campo (1908-93). 300p, Victor Jara Martinez (1932-73). 350p, Violeta Parra Sandoval (1917-67).

1998, Sept. 14
1255 A633 200p multicolored 1.00 1.00
1256 A633 250p multicolored 1.40 1.40
1257 A633 300p multicolored 1.50 1.50
1258 A633 350p multicolored 1.90 1.90
Nos. 1255-1258 (4) 5.80 5.80

World Stamp Day A634

1998, Oct. 9 **Litho.** ***Perf. 13½***
1259 A634 250p multicolored 1.50 1.50

Francisco Bilbao (1823-65), Writer A635

Litho. & Engr.

1998, Oct. 29 ***Perf. 13½***
1260 A635 250p multicolored 1.50 1.50

Chilean Painters — A636

Designs: 300p, Self-portrait, by Augusto Eguiluz (1894-1969), vert. 450p, Landscape, by Agustin Abarca (1882-1953).

1500p, "Two Nudes," by Henriette Petit (1894-1983).

1998, Nov. 3 **Litho.**
1261 A636 300p multi 2.25 1.50
1262 A636 450p multi 2.75 2.25

Souvenir Sheet

1262A A636 1500p multi 10.00 8.00

No. 1262A contains one 36x47mm stamp.

Catholic University of Valparaiso, 70th Anniv. — A637

1998, Nov. 18 **Litho.** ***Perf. 13½***
1263 A637 130p multicolored 1.20 1.20

Prominent Women from the University of Chile — A638

America Issue: 120p, Amanda Labarca, edcuator. 250p, Marta Brunet, writer.

1998, Nov. 19 **Litho.** ***Perf. 13½***
1264 A638 120p multicolored .85 .85
1265 A638 250p multicolored 1.60 1.60

1999 World Scout Jamboree, Chile — A639

Scouting emblems and: 120p, Children of two races, stylized tents. 200p, Robert Baden-Powell. 250p, Stylized doves. 300p, Scout, stylized tents. 1000p, Scouts, leaders seated in semi-circle, vert.

3000p, Jamboree emblem over drawing of Jamboree site at Picarquin, emblems of past jamborees, Intl. Scouting Emblem.

1998, Dec. 27
1266 A639 120p multicolored .75 .75
1267 A639 200p multicolored 1.10 1.10
1268 A639 250p multicolored 1.40 1.40
1269 A639 300p multicolored 1.50 1.50
1270 A639 1000p multicolored 5.25 5.25
Nos. 1266-1270 (5) 10.00 10.00

Imperf

Size: 126x104mm

1270A A639 3000p multi 16.00 16.00

Birds — A640

Designs: 10p, Zonotrichia capensis. 20p, Curaeus curaeus.

1998, Nov. 29
1271 A640 10p multicolored .80 .25
a. Inscribed "2000" .80 .25
1272 A640 20p multicolored .80 .25
a. Inscribed "2000" .80 .25

See Nos. 1313-1314, 1356, 1385-1386, 1418-1419.

World Equestrian High Jump Record, 50th Anniv. — A641

Captain Alberto Larraguibel and Huaso.

1999, Feb. 5 **Litho.** ***Perf. 13½***
1273 A641 200p multicolored 1.25 1.25

Temuco Fire Dept., Cent. — A642

Designs: 140p, 1900 pumper. 200p, 1929 Ford. 300p, 1955 Ford K tanker. 350p, 1967 Mercedes Benz hook and ladder truck.

1500p, Firefighter rescuing victim, vert.

1999, Feb. 18 **Litho.** ***Perf. 13½***
1274 A642 140p multicolored 1.25 .65
1275 A642 200p multicolored 1.50 .95
1276 A642 300p multicolored 2.25 1.50
1277 A642 350p multicolored 2.50 1.75
Nos. 1274-1277 (4) 7.50 4.85

Souvenir Sheet

1278 A642 1500p multicolored 12.00 8.50

Chilean Chamber of Deputies, 1000th Session — A643

1999, Mar. 3 ***Perf. 13½***
1279 A643 140p multicolored .70 .70

Sacred Heart College, 150th Anniv. — A644

1999, Mar. 15
1280 A644 250p multicolored 1.25 1.25

Economic Development Corporation (CORFO), 60th Anniv. — A645

Pedro Aguirre Cerda, former president of Chile.

1999, Apr. 29 ***Perf. 13½***
1281 A645 140p multicolored .90 .90

Chilean Insurance Assoc., Cent. — A646

1999, May 18 **Litho.** ***Perf. 13½***
1282 A646 140p multicolored .65 .65

Chilean Antarctica A647

Designs: 360p, Leptonychotes weddellii. 450p, Pygoscelis antarctica.

1500p, Arctocephalus gazella, penguins.

1999, June 15
1283 A647 360p multicolored 2.75 1.75
1284 A647 450p multicolored 4.75 3.25

Souvenir Sheet

1285 A647 1500p multicolored 13.50 8.50

No. 1285 contains one 35x48mm stamp.

Easter Island A648

1999, June 25
1286 A648 360p multicolored 5.00 2.10

Souvenir Sheet

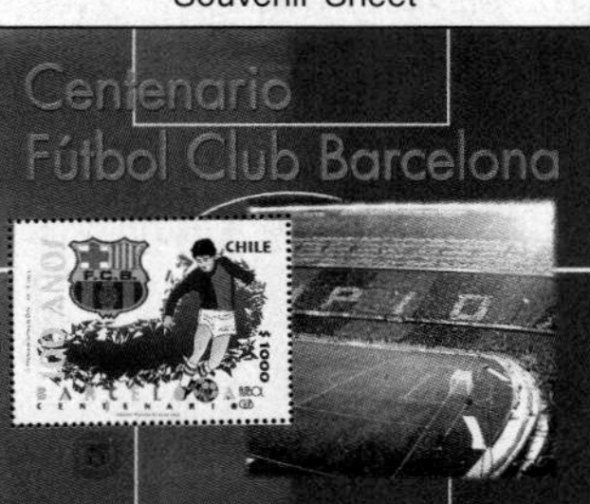

Barcelona Soccer Club, Cent. — A649

1999
1287 A649 1000p multicolored 10.00 5.00

University of Santiago, 150th Anniv. — A650

Designs: 140p, Monument, students in training room, School of Arts and Sciences, 1849. 250p, Technical equipment, building on campus, State Technical University, 1947. 300p, Student looking into microscope, computer, modern building, 1999.

1999, July 6 Litho. *Perf. 13½*
1288 A650 140p multicolored .75 .75
1289 A650 250p multicolored 1.25 1.25
1290 A650 300p multicolored 1.60 1.60
Nos. 1288-1290 (3) 3.60 3.60

Alexander von Humboldt (1769-1859), 200th Anniv. of Scientific Research in Latin America — A651

Face from monument and: 300p, Bust of Humboldt, wildlife, mountains. 360p, Portrait of Humboldt, penguins, sea.

1999, July 16
1291 A651 300p multicolored 2.25 1.75
1292 A651 360p multicolored 2.50 1.90

China '99, World Philatelic Exhibition, Beijing — A652

Chinese, Chilean flags and: 140p, Pagoda. 450p, Chinese junk.
1500p, Great Wall of China, Gate of Heavenly Peace.

1999, Aug. 10
1293 A652 140p multicolored .75 .75
1294 A652 450p multicolored 2.10 2.10

Souvenir Sheet

1295 A652 1500p multicolored 10.00 8.00

No. 1295 contains one 60x48mm stamp.

City of Quilpue, Cent. — A653

1999, Aug. 20
1296 A653 250p multicolored 1.60 1.60

Holy Year 2000 — A654

140p, Raúl Cardinal Silva Henriquez (1907-99). 200p, Walking in street clothes, administering sacrament, face of Christ.

1999, Aug. 9
1297 A654 140p shown .80 .80
1298 A654 200p multicolored 1.00 1.00

A655

1999, Sept. 23 Litho. *Perf. 13½*
1299 A655 140p multicolored .70 .70

Red Cross blood donation campaign.

2000 World Congress of Authors & Composers, Santiago — A656

1999, Oct. 5
1300 A656 170p multicolored 1.10 1.10

Intl. Year of Older Persons — A657

1999, Oct. 6
1301 A657 250p multicolored 1.35 1.35

UPU, 125th Anniv. — A658

1999, Oct. 9
1302 300p Red mailbox 2.75 2.75
1303 360p Gold mailbox 2.75 2.75
a. A658 Pair, #1302-1303 + label 6.75 6.75

Nos. 1302-1303 printed in sheets of 16 pairs, with label in central column.

America Issue, A New Millennium Without Arms — A659

1999, Oct. 12
1304 A659 140p shown 2.50 1.25
1305 A659 320p Broken bomb 3.50 1.75

Labor Management, 75th Anniv. — A660

1999, Aug. 23
1306 A660 320p multicolored 1.50 1.50

Interamerican Development Bank, 40th Anniv. — A661

1999, Oct. 29 Litho. *Perf. 13½*
1307 A661 360p multicolored 1.75 1.75

Holy Year 2000 — A662

1999, Dec. 1
1308 A662 450p multicolored 2.10 2.10

A663

1999, Dec. 1
1309 A663 170p multicolored 2.50 1.00

Inscribed "D.S. 20"

1310 A663 170p multicolored 2.50 1.00
a. Booklet pane of 10 25.00
Complete booklet, #1310a 26.00
b. Booklet pane of 5 12.50
Complete booklet, #1310b 13.00

Nos. 1309-1310 each were issued se-tenant with two labels that served as a lottery ticket and stub.

Union Leaders — A664

No. 1311, Luis Emilio Recabarren Serrano (1876-1924), Clotario Leopoldo Blest Riffo (1899-1990). No. 1312, Tucapel Jiménez Alfaro (1921-82), Manuel Bustos Huerta (1943-99).

1999, Dec. 29 Litho. *Perf. 13½*
1311 200p multi .90 .90
1312 200p multi .90 .90
a. A664 Pair, #1311-1312 + label 3.25 3.25

Bird Type of 1998

Designs: 50p, Campephilus magellanicus, vert. 100p, Falco peregrinus cassini, vert.

2000, Feb. *Perf. 13½*
1313 A640 50p multi .50 .25
1314 A640 100p multi 1.10 .25

Discovery of Juan Fernández, Archipelago, 425th Anniv. — A665

a, Más Afuera (Alejandro Selkirk) Island, Santa Clara Island, tip of Más a Tierra (Robinson Crusoe) Island. b, Más a Tierra Island. c, Dendroseris litoralis. d, Rhaphythamnus venustus. e, Lobster. f, Lobster's antenna, boat. g, Boat, Gavilea insularis. h, Gavilea insularis.

2000, Feb. 29 *Perf. 13¼*
1315 A665 360p Sheet of 8, #a.-h. 16.00 16.00

Condorito, Cartoon Character by Rene Rios Boettiger Pepo — A666

Condorito: 150p, Celebrating millennium. 260p, As soccer player. 480p, As fire fighter. 980p, On horse.
2000p, With people.

2000, Mar. 20 *Perf. 13½*
1316 A666 150p multi 1.25 1.25
1317 A666 260p multi 2.10 2.10
1318 A666 480p multi 4.00 4.00
1319 A666 980p multi 8.00 8.00
Nos. 1316-1319 (4) 15.35 15.35

Souvenir Sheet

1320 A666 2000p multi 15.00 15.00

Easter Island — A667

Designs: 200p, Dancer, stone weapon. 260p, Stone statue and carvings. 340p, Island native, stone statue. 480p, Female dancer, inscribed tablet, map of island.

2000, Apr. 27 Litho. *Perf. 13¼*
1321 A667 200p multi 1.75 1.75
1322 A667 260p multi 2.40 2.40
1323 A667 340p multi 3.25 3.25
1324 A667 480p multi 4.50 4.50
Nos. 1321-1324 (4) 11.90 11.90

Town of Carahue, Cent. (in 1998) — A668

Bridge and: No. 1325, Locomotive, pottery. No. 1326, Potatoes.

2000, May 5

1325	220p multi	1.10	1.10
1326	220p multi	1.10	1.10
a.	A668 Pair, #1325-1326	2.50	2.50

El Mercurio Newspaper, Cent. — A669

2000, June 1

1327 A669 370p multi 3.00 3.00

4th Natl. Masonic Convention — A670

2000, June 23

1328 A670 460p multi 4.00 4.00

Medicinal Plants — A671

Designs: 200p, Quillaja saponaria. 360p, Fabiana imbricata.

2000, July 3

1329	A671 200p multi	1.75	1.75
1330	A671 360p multi	3.25	3.25

Discovery of Brazil, 500th Anniv. — A672

Designs: 260p, Map of Brazil, butterfly, girl. 1500p, Monkey, parrots, boy.

2000, July 10

1331 A672 260p multi 2.00 2.00

Souvenir Sheet

1332 A672 1500p multi 10.00 10.00

No. 1332 contains one 48x36mm stamp.

Folklore A673

Religious festivals: 150p, Dancer in devil costume, La Tirana. 200p, Festival of San Pedro de Atacama. 370p, Candlemas Festival, Copiapo. 460p, Chinese dancers, Andacollo.

2000, July 13

1333	A673 150p multi	1.25	1.25
1334	A673 200p multi	1.60	1.60
1335	A673 370p multi	3.25	3.25
1336	A673 460p multi	3.70	3.70
	Nos. 1333-1336 (4)	9.80	9.80

Prehistoric Animals — A674

No. 1337: a, Milodon. b, Titanosaurus. c, Plesiosaurus. d, Iguanodon.

2000

1337 A674 150p Block of 4, #a-d 4.50 4.50

José de San Martín (1778-1850) — A675

2000, Aug. 25 Litho. *Perf. 13½*

1338 A675 320p multi 2.00 2.00

World Meteorological Organization, 50th Anniv. — A676

2000, Aug. 28

1339 A676 320p multi 2.00 2.00

Antarctic Fauna — A677

450p, Sphenis magellanicus, vert. 650p, Megaptera novaeangliae. 940p, Orcinus orca. 2000p, Mirounga leonina, vert.

2000, Sept. 15

1340-1342 A677 Set of 3 17.00 14.00

Souvenir Sheet

1343 A677 2000p multi 21.00 12.00

No. 1343 contains one 36x48mm stamp.

2000 Summer Olympics, Sydney — A678

Sydney Opera House, Olympic flag and: a, 290p, Chilean flag, tennis player, soccer player, sprinter. b, 290p, Australian flag, archer, high jumper, cyclist.

2000, Sept. 20

1344 A678 Pair, #a-b 5.00 5.00

City of Concepcion, 450th Anniv. — A679

Mural by Gregorio De la Fuente: a, Indian holding stick. b, Soldier on white horse. c, Finger pointing upward. d, Seated figure, arms, horse-drawn carriage. e, Horse, statue, train. f, People and rainbow.

2000, Oct. 2

1345	Horiz. strip of 6	15.00	15.00
a.-f.	A679 250p Any single	1.50	.75

America Issue, World AIDS Day — A680

Designs: 150p, Heart, clasped hands of adult and child. 220p, Clasped hands.

2000, Oct. 12

1346-1347 A680 Set of 2 3.00 3.00

Penal Reform — A681

Designs: 150p, Flag, court proceedings. 2000p, People, doors of Justice Ministry.

2000, Nov. 16

1348 A681 150p multi 1.25 1.25

Souvenir Sheet

1349 A681 2000p multi 14.00 14.00

Christmas — A682

Designs: a, Star of Bethlehem. b, Santa Claus flying over town. c, Three Magi on camels. d, Star on top of Christmas tree. e, Boy at mailbox. f, Sleeping child. g, Two Magi, cow. h, Baby Jesus, cow. i, Mary, Joseph. j, Girl putting ornaments on tree.

2000, Nov. 20 *Perf. 13½*

1350	Block of 10	10.00	10.00
a.-j.	A682 150p Any single	.75	.40

Inscribed "DS/20"

Perf. 13½ on 3 sides

1351	Booklet pane of 10	10.00	
a.-j.	A682 150p Any single	.90	.45
	Booklet, #1351	10.00	

National Zoo, 75th Anniv. — A683

Various animals and birds, denomination in: a, LL. b, LR. c, UL. d, UR.

2001, Jan. 13 Litho. *Perf. 13½*

1352 A683 160p Block of 4, #a-d 7.50 7.50

San Sebastian Festival, Yumbel — A684

2001, Jan. 18

1353 A684 210p multi 1.50 1.50

Father Alberto Hurtado (1901-52) A685

Hurtado and: 160p, Truck. 340p, Children.

2001, Jan. 20

1354-1355 A685 Set of 2 3.50 3.50

Bird Type of 1998

No. 1356, vert.: a, Sephanoides fernandensis. b, Mimus thenca. c, Pteroptochos megapodius. d, Enicognathus leptorhynchus. Size of Nos. 1356a-1356d: 24x29mm.

2001, Jan. 29

1356 A640 160p Block of 4, #a-d 4.75 4.75

Reunión Anual de las Asambleas de Gobernadores BID CII
Chile
$230

Assembly of Governors of Inter-American Development Bank and Investment Corporation — A686

2001, Mar. 16

1357 A686 230p multi 1.40 1.40

Souvenir Sheet

Air Force Anniversaries — A687

No. 1358: a, Lockheed C-130 Hercules, map of Antarctica. b, Flugzeugbau Extra-300, acrobatic squadron. c, North American AT-6 Texan. d, Consolidated PBY-5A/OA-10 Catalina, map of Easter Island.

2001, Mar. 29
1358 A687 260p Sheet of 4, #a-d 5.50 5.50

Air Force presence in Antarctica, 50th anniv. (No. 1358a); Halcones acrobatic squadron, 20th anniv. (No. 1358b); Aviation Group No. 1, 75th anniv. (No. 1358c); First flight of Easter Island, 50th anniv. (No. 1358d).

Nationalization of Copper Industry, 30th Anniv. — A688

Design: 2000p, Miner and equipment.

2001, Apr. 26 Litho. *Perf. 13¼*
1359 A688 400p multi 3.00 3.00

Souvenir Sheet

1359A A688 2000p multi 12.50 12.50

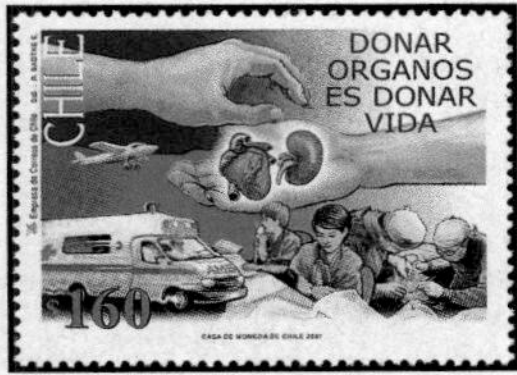

Organ Donation — A689

2001, May 3
1360 A689 160p multi 1.50 1.50

Easter Island — A690

Designs: No. 1361, Stone carvings, map of island and: a, Compass rose. b, Bird and native. No. 1361C, Artifact and map of island.

2001, June 25
1361 A690 260p Horiz. pair, #a-b 4.00 4.00

Souvenir Sheet

1361C A690 2000p multi 16.00 16.00

Lynchailurus Colocolo — A691

2001
1362 A691 100p multi 1.00 .30

Endangered species. See Nos. 1394-1395.

Valparaiso Firefighting Corps, 150th Anniv. — A692

Firefighters and: 160p, Manuel Blanco Encalada. 260p, Old pumper, building on fire, modern fire truck. 350p, Flags, building. 490p, Helicopter, rail tank car.
2000p, Helicopter, modern fire truck.

2001, June 28 Litho. *Perf. 13¼*
1363-1366 A692 Set of 4 7.00 7.00

Souvenir Sheet

1367 A692 2000p multi 11.50 11.50

Mushrooms A693

Designs: 300p, Macrolepiota rhacodes. 400p, Laccata ohiensis.

2001, July 25 Litho. *Perf. 13¼*
1368-1369 A693 Set of 2 4.50 4.50

24th Conference of American Armies, Santiago — A694

2001, Aug. 13
1370 A694 350p multi 2.00 2.00

Bernardo O'Higgins (1778-1842), Soldier and Statesman — A695

2001, Aug. 17
1371 A695 260p multi 1.90 1.90

Chilean Antarctic Research — A696

Designs: 350p, Researcher, Leptonychotes weddellii. 700p, Researchers, Macronectes giganteus. 2000p, Chionis alba.

2001, Aug. 29
1372-1373 A696 Set of 2 7.75 7.75

Souvenir Sheet

1374 A696 2000p multicolored 15.00 15.00

America Issue — UNESCO World Heritage — A697

World Heritage Sites and stamps: 160p, Quinchao Church, #1058. 230p, Tenaun Church, #1057.

2001, Oct. 9 Litho. *Perf. 13¼*
1375-1376 A697 Set of 2 9.00 9.00

Cape Horn A698

2001, Nov. 22
1377 A698 220p multi 1.75 1.75

El Indice del Indice, by Roberto Matta (1911-2002) — A699

2001, Nov. 5 Litho. *Perf. 13¼*
1378 A699 300p multi 2.50 2.50

Railroads in Chile, 150th Anniv. — A700

No. 1379 (50x29mm): a, Caldera Station, train cars. b, Locomotive and Copiapó Station.
220p, Train on bridge.

2001, Nov. 20
1379 A700 200p Horiz. pair, #a-b 3.50 3.50
1380 A700 220p multi 1.75 1.75

Christmas — A701

Designs: a, Heads of three shepherds. b, Shepherd and cow. c, Joseph and Mary. d, Donkey and Magus. e, Cow and two Magi. f, Head of shepherd. g, Two sheep. h, Infant Jesus. i, Shepherd with staff. j, One sheep.

2001, Nov.
1381 A701 160p Block of 10, #a-j 8.00 8.00

Inscribed "DS/20"

1382 A701 160p Block of 10, #a-j 9.00 9.00
k. Booklet pane, #1382 with straight edge at right 10.00 —
Complete booklet, #1382k 10.00

Rotary Intl. Emblem, Map of Chile, Globe, Tropic of Capricorn Monument — A702

2001, Dec. 21
1383 A702 240p multi 2.00 2.00

Antofagasta Rotary Club, 75th anniv.

Taxation Department, Cent. — A703

2002, Jan. 14
1384 A703 180p multi 1.10 1.10

Bird Type of 1998

Designs: 10p, Turdus falcklandii. 20p, Sturnella loyca.

2002, Jan. 25
1385 A640 10p multi .75 .25
1386 A640 20p multi .75 .25

City of Valdivia, 450th Anniv. — A704

2002, Feb. 9
1387 A704 260p multi 1.75 1.75

Carabinero Force, 75th Anniv. — A705

2002, Apr. 8
1388 A705 250p multi 1.75 1.75

Ignacy Domeyko (1802-89), Mineralogist — A706

2002, Apr. 11
1389 A706 290p multi *5.00 4.75*

See Poland No. 3645.

City of Villarrica, 450th Anniv. — A707

2002, Apr. 26
1390 A707 290p multi 2.00 2.00

Town of Calbuco, 400th Anniv. — A708

2002, May 2
1391 A708 230p multi 1.75 1.75

Barros Arana Natl. Boarding School — A709

2002, May 20
1392 A709 250p multi 1.75 1.75

Abolition of Death Penalty, 1st Anniv. — A710

2002, May 29
1393 A710 240p multi 1.75 1.75

Endangered Species Type of 2001

Designs: 10p, Oreailurus jacobita. 20p, Oncifelis geoffrovi.

2002, June 5
1394 A691 10p multi .55 .25
1395 A691 20p multi .65 .25

Easter Island A711

Map of Easter Island and: 250p, Toromiro sophora, moai. 450p, Bird, row of moai statues, native in traditional costume.
2000p, Toromiro sophora and bird.

2002, July 1
1396-1397 A711 Set of 2 6.50 5.75

Souvenir Sheet

1398 A711 2000p multi 13.00 13.00

No. 1398 contains one 47x47mm stamp.

World Heritage Sites — A712

Churches and stamps: 230p, Achao, #1036. 290p, Dalcahue, #1056.

2002, July 27
1399-1400 A712 Set of 2 3.00 3.00

America Issue — Youth, Education, and Literacy — A713

Designs: 230p, Adult students. 450p, Woman reading to child, teacher, boy at computer.

2002, Sept. 9
1401-1402 A713 Set of 2 3.75 3.75

Children's Toys — A714

Designs: 290p, Pinwheel. 380p, Kite, vert.

2002, Sept. 16
1403-1404 A714 Set of 2 3.00 3.00

Observatories — A715

Designs: 450p, Cerro-Tololo. 550p, Paranal. 2000p, Cerro-Tololo, diff.

2002, Sept. 27
1405-1406 A715 Set of 2 4.00 4.00

Souvenir Sheet

1407 A715 2000p multi 13.00 13.00

No. 1407 contains one 47x47mm stamp.

University of Chile Clinical Hospital, 50th Anniv. — A716

2002, Oct. 17
1408 A716 250p multi 1.50 1.50

Forestry Education, 50th Anniv. — A717

2002, Oct. 22
1409 A717 250p multi 1.50 1.50

12th Convention on International Trade in Endangered Species Conference — A718

Designs: 300p, Phoenicoparrus andinus. 450p, Vicugna vicugna.
2000p, Chinchilla lanigera.

2002, Oct. 29
1410-1411 A718 Set of 2 4.25 4.25

Souvenir Sheet

1412 A718 2000p multi 10.00 10.00

No. 1412 contains one 47x47mm stamp.

Protected Whales — A719

Designs: 250p, Eubalaena australis. 500p, Balaenoptera acutorostrata.
2000p, Physeter macrocephalus.

2002, Nov. 2
1413-1414 A719 Set of 2 3.25 3.25

Souvenir Sheet

1415 A719 2000p multi 11.00 11.00

Violence Against Women Prevention Day — A720

2002, Nov. 22
1416 A720 230p multi 1.00 1.00

Town of Puerto Varas, 150th Anniv. A721

2002, Nov. 29
1417 A721 190p multi 1.00 1.00

Bird Type of 1998

Designs: 500p, Campephilus magellanicus, vert. 1000p, Falco peregrinus cassini, vert.

2003, Jan. 15 Litho. *Perf. 13¼*
1418 A640 500p multi 2.50 1.25
1419 A640 1000p multi 5.00 2.50

Puerto Montt, 150th Anniv. A722

2003, Feb. 13
1420 A722 240p multi 1.40 1.40

Claudio Arrau (1903-91), Pianist — A723

2003, June 9 Litho. *Perf. 13¼*
1421 A723 200p multi 1.25 1.25

First Chilean Postage Stamps, 150th Anniv. — A724

No. 1422 — Mailbox, building and: a, #1. b, #2.
2000p, Building, #1 and various other stamps.

2003, July 1
1422 A724 300p Horiz. pair, #a-b 2.50 2.50

Souvenir Sheet

1423 A724 2000p multi 8.50 8.50

America Issue — Flora and Fauna — A725

Designs: 240p, Trees, flowers, cactus. 300p, Frog, fox, butterfly, pudu, parrot.

2003, Oct. 12 Litho. *Perf. 13¼*
1424-1425 A725 Set of 2 3.00 3.00

Supreme Court, 180th Anniv. — A726

2003, Nov. 5
1426 A726 200p multi 1.25 1.25

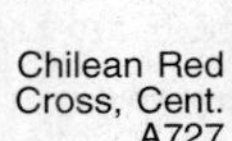

Chilean Red Cross, Cent. A727

2003, Nov. 18
1427 A727 200p black & red 1.35 1.35

Christmas — A728

2003, Nov. 28
1428 A728 190p multi 1.25 .60

Inscribed "DS-20"

1429 A728 190p multi 1.25 .60

Powered Flight, Cent. — A729

2003, Dec. 11
1430 A729 200p multi 1.50 1.50

Cristo Redentor Statue, Cent. A730

2004, Apr. 22 **Litho.**
1431 A730 200p multi 1.50 1.45

Seventh World Conference of Grand Masonic Lodges — A731

2004, May 5 ***Perf. 13¼***
1432 A731 190p multi 1.50 1.45

Pablo Neruda (1904-73), Poet — A732

2004, June 11
1433 A732 300p multi 1.40 1.40

Social Security, 80th Anniv. — A733

2004, Aug. 18
1434 A733 190p multi 1.25 1.25

America Issue — Environmental Protection — A734

Designs: 100p, Burnt forest, logs, field of flowers, puma, flower. 600p, Flower, wildlife, tanker truck, smokestacks.

2004, Sept. 27
1435-1436 A734 Set of 2 3.25 3.25

German Institute, Osorno, 150th Anniv. — A735

2004, Oct. 6
1437 A735 250p multi *70.00 70.00*

Tematica 2004 National Philatelic Exhibition A736

2004, Oct. 19
1438 A736 310p multi 1.90 1.90

Naval Telecommunications, Cent. — A737

2004, Nov. 5
1439 A737 400p multi 2.25 2.25

Electricity and Fuel Superintendency, Cent. — A738

2004, Dec. 7
1440 A738 240p multi 1.60 1.60

Chilean Air Force, 75th Anniv. — A739

2005, Mar. 15 **Litho.** ***Perf. 13¼***
1441 A739 230p multi 1.50 1.50

Law No. 20,000 — A740

2005, May 4
1442 A740 220p multi 1.25 1.25

Pope John Paul II (1920-2005) — A741

Pope John Paul II and: a, Child, condor, mountain. b, Crucifix, Chilean flag, mountain. c, Church, Chilean flag.

2005, May 13
1443 A741 Horiz. strip of 3 6.75 6.75
a.-c. 230p Any single 1.50 1.50

Rotary International, Cent. — A742

2005, June 30 **Litho.** ***Perf. 13¼***
1444 A742 230p multi 1.25 1.25

Treasury Building, Bicent. — A743

2005, June 30
1445 A743 230p multi 1.25 1.25

Publication of Don Quixote, 400th Anniv. A744

No. 1446: a, Don Quixote on horseback. b, Windmill. c, Windmills. d, Miguel de Cervantes, author.

2005, July 14
1446 Horiz. strip of 4 .50 .50
a.-b. A744 10p Either single .25 .25
c.-d. A744 20p Either single .25 .25

See No. 1462.

El Teniente Copper Mine, Cent. — A745

2005, Aug. 3
1447 A745 390p multi 2.40 2.40

Undersecretariat of Aviation, 75th Anniv. — A746

2005, Aug. 19
1448 A746 400p multi 2.00 2.00

Valparaiso Customs House, 150th Anniv. — A747

2005, Sept. 1
1449 A747 390p multi 2.00 2.00

Bicentennial Fountain, Santiago — A748

2005, Sept. 5

1450 A748 230p multi 1.50 1.50

America Issue — Fight Against Poverty — A749

No. 1451: a, Denomination at right. b, Denomination at left.

2005, Oct. 3 Litho. *Perf. 13¼*

1451 A749 250p Horiz. pair, #a-b 4.00 4.00

Canonization of Father Alberto Hurtado (1901-52) — A750

2005, Oct. 13 Litho. *Perf. 13¼*

1452 A750 390p multi 2.00 2.00

Expo Austral 2005 Philatelic Exhibition, Punta Arenas — A751

2005, Oct. 22

1453 A751 390p multi 3.00 3.00

New Civil Matrimony Law — A752

2005, Nov. 18 Litho. *Perf. 13¼*

1454 A752 260p multi 1.60 1.60

German Clinic, Cent. — A753

2005, Nov. 23

1455 A753 230p multi 1.50 1.50

Restoration of Central Post Office, Santiago A754

2005, Nov. 30

1456 A754 230p multi 1.25 1.25

Political Constitution A755

2005, Dec. 1

1457 A755 230p multi 1.25 1.25

An unissued version of this stamp, with a different design of a star over a black book, was leaked into the philatelic marketplace. The Chilean government considers these stolen property.

Department of Physical Education, Sports and Recreation, Cent. — A756

2006, Mar. 6 Litho. *Perf. 13¼*

1458 A756 230p multi 1.25 1.25

Intl. Women's Day — A757

2006, Mar. 7

1459 A757 390p multi 2.50 2.50

Wulff Castle, Cent. — A758

No. 1460 — Castle, arms of Vina del Mar and: a, Birds. b, Windmill.

2006, Mar. 21

1460 Horiz. pair 3.25 3.25
a. A758 230p multi 1.10 1.10
b. A758 390p multi 1.90 1.90

Tourism — A759

No. 1461: a, Morro de Arica. b, Moais, Easter Island. c, Palafittes, Castro. d, Torres del Paine. e, Penguins, Chilean Antarctic Territory.

2006, May 19

1461 Horiz. strip of 5 6.25 6.25
a.-e. A759 230p Any single 1.10 1.10

Don Quixote Type of 2005

No. 1462: a, Building. b, Windmills. c, Windmill, country name at LR. d, Don Quixote and Sancho Panza.

2006, May 31

1462 Horiz. strip of 4 1.00 1.00
a.-d. A744 10p Any single .25 .25

Catholic University of the North, 50th Anniv. — A760

No. 1463: a, Students using computers, denomination at UR. b, Students, denomination at LL.

2006, June 9

1463 Horiz. pair 2.50 2.50
a.-b. A760 230p Either single 1.10 1.10

Citizenship Plaza, Santiago — A761

2006, July 7

1464 A761 390p multi 1.90 1.90

World Quality Forum — A762

No. 1465: a, Building. b, Building and flags.

2006, Aug. 29 Litho. *Perf. 13¼*

1465 A762 230p Horiz. pair, #a-b 2.60 2.60

America Issue, Energy Conservation — A763

No. 1466: a, River and mountains. b, Clouds. c, Oil rigs in water. d, Windmill.

2006, Sept. 29

1466 A763 390p Block of 4, #a-d 7.50 7.50

Adventist University of Chile, Cent. — A764

No. 1467 — University emblem and: a, Building, 1906. b, Family and building, 1922. c, Building, 1960-70. d, Building, 2006.

2006, Oct. 20

1467 Horiz. strip of 4 + central label 4.50 4.50
a.-d. A764 250p Any single 1.10 1.10

Antarctic Wildlife — A765

No. 1468 — Chilean and Estonian flags and: a, Balaenoptera acutorostrata. b, Aptenodytes forsteri.

2006, Oct. 25 *Perf. 13½*

1468 A765 500p Horiz. pair, #a-b 4.50 4.50

See Estonia No. 555.

Anniversaries — A766

No. 1469: a, Colonization of the Straits of Magellan area, 160th anniv. b, Fort Bulnes, 160th anniv.

2006, Dec. 7 *Perf. 13¼*

1469 A766 250p Horiz. pair, #a-b 3.25 3.25

Gasco, 150th Anniv. — A767

No. 1470: a, San Borja facility. b, Gasco headquarters.

2006, Dec. 14

1470 A767 250p Horiz. pair, #a-b 3.25 3.25

Federico Santa Maria Technical University, 75th Anniv. — A768

2006, Dec. 20

1471 A768 250p multi 1.40 1.40

Carabineros, 80th Anniv. — A769

Expo Antarctica Chile 2009 Philatelic Exhibition, Pres. Eduardo Frei Montalva Antarctic Base — A807

Designs: 470p, Map of Antarctica, Pres. Eduardo Frei Montalva Antarctic Base. 3000p, Villa Las Estrellas, horiz.

2009, Mar. 12

1521 A807 470p multi 2.00 2.00

Souvenir Sheet

1522 A807 3000p multi 19.00 19.00

Antarctic Treaty, 50th anniv. No. 1522 contains one 48x30mm stamp.

Preservation of Polar Regions and Glaciers — A808

Nos. 1523, 1524 — Emblem and map of: a, Arctic area. b, Antarctic area. No. 1524 has vert. stamps.

Litho. with Foil Application

2009, Mar. 18 ***Perf. 13¼***

1523 A808 470p Vert. pair, #a-b 4.00 4.00

Souvenir Sheet

1524 A808 1500p Sheet of 2, #a-b 19.00 19.00

Miniature Sheets

Independence, Bicent. — A809

No. 1525: a, Chile #92. b, Chile #93. c, Chile #94. d, Chile #95. e, Chile #96. f, Chile #97.

No. 1526, horiz.: a, Chile #83. b, Chile #84. c, Chile #85. d, Chile #86. e, Chile #87. f, Chile #88. g, Chile #89. h, Chile #90. i, Chile #91. j, Bicentennial emblem.

2009, Apr. 20 **Litho.**

1525 A809 310p Sheet of 6, #a-f 6.50 6.50

1526 A809 310p Sheet of 10, #a-j 10.50 10.50

University of Concepción, 90th Anniv. — A810

No. 1527: a, Homage to the Founders, sculpture by Samuel Román. b, Campanile.

2009, May 14

1527 A810 310p Horiz. pair, #a-b 2.25 2.25

Santa María de Los Angeles Diocese, 50th Anniv. — A811

No. 1528: a, Virgin Mary, Jesus and angels. b, Los Angeles Cathedral.

2009, June 10

1528 A811 470p Horiz. pair, #a-b 3.50 3.50

Protected Birds — A812

Designs: 10p, Condor. 20p Tricahue parrot. 50p, Chilean flamingo. 100p, Humboldt penguin. 500p, Black-necked swan.

2009, July 15 **Litho.** ***Perf. 13¼***

1529 A812 10p black .25 .25

1530 A812 20p black .25 .25

1531 A812 50p black .25 .25

1532 A812 100p black .55 .55

1533 A812 500p black 2.25 2.25

Nos. 1529-1533 (5) 3.55 3.55

21st UPAEP Congress, Santiago — A813

2009, Aug. 17 **Litho.** ***Perf. 13¼***

1534 A813 500p multi 2.60 2.60

Mutual de Seguros Insurance Company, 90th Anniv. — A814

No. 1535: a, Old building, emblem with black gear. b, Modern building, emblem with blue gray gear.

Litho. With Foil Application

2009, Oct. 14 ***Perf. 13¼***

1535 A814 310p Horiz. pair, #a-b 2.75 2.75

A815

Winning Art in Bicentennial Stamp Design Contest — A816

No. 1536: a, Flag with mountains and city, by Andrea Barreda, elementary school competition. b, City, by Javiera Monreal Arcil, middle school competition.

No. 1537: a, People in various costumes, by Patricio Díaz Donay, visual arts competition. b, Pepper, by Joshua Arévalo Carreño, university and technical school competition.

2009, Oct. 15 **Litho.** ***Perf. 13¼***

1536 A815 310p Pair, #a-b 2.40 2.40

1537 A816 310p Horiz. pair, #a-b 2.40 2.40

America Issue, Traditional Games — A817

Designs: 310p, Spinning top. 470p, Girl flying kite.

2009, Oct. 30

1538-1539 A817 Set of 2 3.50 3.50

Christmas — A818

No. 1540 — Children: a, Painting nativity scene. b, Drawing pictures of Santa Claus. c, Opening presents under Christmas tree. d, Looking out of window.

2009, Nov. 26

1540 A818 310p Block of 4, #a-d 5.00 5.00

Gabriela Mistral (1889-1957), 1945 Nobel Laureate in Literature — A819

No. 1451: a, Mistral at left, mountain at right. b, Church at left, Mistral at right. c, Mistral at left, church at right. d, Mountain at left, Mistral at right.

2009, Dec. 18

1541 A819 500p Block of 4, #a-d 8.00 8.00

Chile Philatelic Society, 120th Anniv. — A820

2009, Dec. 30

1542 A820 500p multi 2.00 2.00

Bicentennial Art by National Art Prize Winners — A821

No. 1543 — Works of art by: a, José Balmes. b, Eugenio Dittborn. c, Guillermo Núñez.

2010, Mar. 3

1543 Horiz. strip of 3 6.75 6.75

a.-c. A821 290p Any single 2.25 2.25

Bicentenary Regatta — A822

No. 1544 — Flags and: a, Ships. b, Map of South America, ship.

2010, Apr. 15 Litho. *Perf. 13¼*
1544 A822 430p Horiz. pair, #a-b 3.75 3.75

Miniature Sheet

Pres. Eduardo Frei Montalva Antarctic Air Base, 40th Anniv. — A823

No. 1545: a, People near cargo airplane. b, Hangar. c, Airplane over base. d, Helicopter. e, Small airplane. f, Penguin, people, base.

2010, May 4
1545 A823 500p Sheet of 6, #a-f 11.50 11.50

Bauer Tower, Vicuña, 105th Anniv. — A824

Designs: 500p, Tower. 3000p, Tower, diff.

2010, May 7
1546 A824 500p multi 1.90 1.90

Souvenir Sheet

1547 A824 3000p multi 11.50 11.50

2010 World Cup Soccer Championships, South Africa — A825

No. 1548 — Flags of Chile and South Africa, emblem of Chile Soccer Federation and: a, Soccer ball and players. b, Map of Africa, leopard skin.

2010, June 25
1548 A825 500p Vert. pair, #a-b 5.00 5.00

Inauguration of Mini University of Tokyo Atacama Observatory Telescope, Mt. Chajnantor — A826

2010, July 7 Litho. *Perf. 13¼*
1549 A826 430p multi 1.60 1.60

Souvenir Sheet

1550 A826 3000p multi 11.00 11.00

Valparaiso, UNESCO World Heritage Site — A827

No. 1551: a, British Arch. b, Heroes of Iquique Monument.
No. 1552, horiz.: a, Palacio Polanco. b, Palacio Lyon.
No. 1553: a, Polanco Funicular. b, Artillería Funicular.
No. 1554, horiz.: a, Trolley bus with doors closed. b, Trolley bus with front doors open.

2010, July 12 Litho. *Perf. 13¼*
1551 A827 10p Horiz. pair, #a-b .25 .25
1552 A827 20p Horiz. pair, #a-b .25 .25
1553 A827 50p Horiz. pair, #a-b .40 .40
1554 A827 100p Horiz. pair, #a-b .75 .75
Nos. 1551-1554 (4) 1.65 1.65

Independence of Latin America, Bicent. — A828

2010, Sept. 10
1555 A828 430p multi 1.75 1.75

La Serena — A829

No. 1556: a, Monumental Lighthouse. b, Plaza de Armas Fountain.

2010, Sept. 15
1556 A829 420p Pair, #a-b 3.50 3.50

Bicentennial Naval Review — A830

No. 1557: a, Steamship from 1910 naval review. b, Ships and sailing vessel with flags hoisted from 1910 naval review. c, Ships from 2010, denomination at UR. d, Ships from 2010, denomination at UL.

2010, Sept. 20
1557 A830 430p Block of 4, #a-d 7.75 7.75

Miniature Sheet

Antofagasta — A831

No. 1558: a, La Portada. b, Fishing terminal. c, Costanera Avenue. d, Historic District. e, Huanchaca Ruins. f, Antofagasta at night.

2010, Sept. 24
1558 A831 500p Sheet of 6, #a-f 12.50 12.50

Arica — A832

No. 1559: a, Fountain, Morro de Arica. b, Fuerza del Sol Carnival.

2010, Sept. 30 Litho. *Perf. 13¼*
1559 A832 420p Horiz. pair, #a-b 3.50 3.50

America Issue, National Symbols — A833

2010, Oct. 12 Litho. *Perf. 13¼*
1560 A833 290p multi 2.60 2.60

Third International Culture Forum, Valparaíso A834

2010, Oct. 19
1561 A834 500p multi 2.10 2.10

Irishmen Involved With Chilean Independence — A835

No. 1562: a, Commander General John Mackenna (1771-1814). b, Supreme Director Bernardo O'Higgins (1778-1842).

2010, Oct. 28
1562 A835 500p Horiz. pair, #a-b 4.25 4.25

See Ireland Nos. 1902-1903.

Bicentennial Clock, La Serena University — A836

2010, Oct. 29 Litho. *Perf. 13¼*
1563 A836 420p multi 1.75 1.75

Souvenir Sheet

1564 A836 3000p Clock, vert. 12.50 12.50

Chile 2010 Bicentennial Philatelic Exhibition — A837

2010, Nov. 12 Litho. *Perf. 13¼*
1565 A837 290p multi 1.25 1.25

Christmas A838

2010, Nov. 26
1566 A838 290p multi 1.25 1.25

Miniature Sheet

Chilean Army, Bicent. — A839

No. 1567: a, Cavalry, back of army vehicle. b, Army vehicle, helicopter, tank, rocket launcher. c, Soldiers, flag, truck. d, Soldiers, people awaiting humanitarian aid. e, Soldiers at fort. f, Bulldozer and road grader. g, Soldiers working on railroad track and building. h, Soldiers on pontoon bridge beside damaged bridge.

2010, Dec. 2

1567 A839 500p Sheet of 8, #a-h 21.00 21.00

Purranque, Cent. — A840

2011, Apr. 8

1568 A840 290p multi 1.25 1.25

Pres. Eduardo Frei Montalva (1911-82) A841

2011, May 6

1569 A841 290p multi 1.25 1.25

Postal Union of the Americas, Spain and Portugal (UPAEP), Cent. — A842

2011, May 20

1570 A842 290p multi 1.25 1.25

National Congress, Bicent. — A843

2011, July 3

1571 A843 290p multi 1.25 1.25

First Competition of Urban Intervention Ideas — A844

2011, July 29 **Litho.** ***Perf. 13¼***

1572 A844 500p multi 2.25 2.25

Rapa Nui Face Decorations — A845

Various face decorations.

2011, Aug. 5

1573	A845	10p brown	.25	.25
1574	A845	20p lt brown	.25	.25
1575	A845	50p lt brown	.25	.25
1576	A845	100p brown	.45	.45
		Nos. 1573-1576 (4)	1.20	1.20

FAMAE (Weapons Manufacturer for Chilean Armed Forces), Bicent. — A846

2011, Sept. 30

1577 A846 290p multi 1.25 1.25

El Tabo, Cent. — A847

No. 1578 — Arms of El Tabo and: a, Nuestra Senora del Rosario Church, El Tabo. b, La Asuncion Church, Las Cruces.

2011, Oct. 7

1578 A847 290p Horiz. pair, #a-b 4.25 4.25

Talca University, 30th Anniv. — A848

No. 1579 — Sculpture and: a, Legal and Social Sciences Building. b, Kinetic Frieze, by Matilde Perez. c, Botanical Garden. d, Curicó Campus Engineering Building.

2011, Oct. 12

1579 A848 290p Block of 4, #a-d 4.75 4.75

Mailbox A849

2011, Oct. 21

1580 A849 290p multi 1.60 1.60

America issue.

Christmas — A850

2011, Nov. 28

1581 A850 310p multi 1.50 1.50

Carabineros, 85th Anniv. — A851

No. 1582 — Anniversary emblem and: a, Male and female carabineros. b, Flag and silhouettes of carabineros.

2012, Apr. 24

1582 A851 310p Horiz. pair, #a-b 2.60 2.60

Diplomatic Relations Between Chile and South Korea, 50th Anniv. — A852

2012, July 23 ***Perf. 13¼***

1583 A852 310p multi 1.40 1.40

University of Chile, 170th Anniv. — A853

No. 1584: a, University building. b, Statue of first University rector, Andrés Bello López (1781-1865). c, Valentín Letelier, (1852-1919) rector. d, Amanda Labarca (1886-1975), educator.

2012, Sept. 7

1584 A853 500p Block of 4, #a-d 8.50 8.50

Trauco (Mythological Forest Dweller) A854

2012, Oct. 22

1585 A854 310p multi 1.40 1.40

America issue.

Puente Alto, 120th Anniv. — A855

2012, Nov. 12

1586 A855 310p multi 1.40 1.40

Christmas — A856

No. 1587: a, Boy and open mail box. b, Children opening Christmas gifts.

2012, Nov. 30

1587 A856 310p Horiz. pair, #a-b 2.75 2.75

Diplomatic Relations Between Thailand and Chile, 50th Anniv. — A857

2012, Dec. 5

1588 A857 500p multi 2.25 2.25

Pontifical Catholic University of Chile, 125th Anniv. — A858

2013, May 15
1589 A858 500p multi 2.10 2.10

Arica-La Paz Railway, Cent. — A859

No. 1590: a, Steam locomotive. b, Diesel locomotive.

2013, May 29
1590 A859 310p Horiz. pair, #a-b 2.50 2.50

Salvador Allende School of Public Health at University of Chile, 70th Anniv. — A860

No. 1591: a, Dr. Benjamin Viel (1913-98), Dr. Abraham Horwitz (1910-2000), Dr. Hugo Behm (1913-2011). b, Building.

2013, June 7
1591 A860 500p Pair, #a-b 4.50 4.50

Historic Aricraft — A861

No. 1592: a, Voisin biplane, 1910 (airplane used in first flight in Chile). b, Batuco biplane, 1913 (first airplane made in Chile).

No. 1593: a, De Havilland DH-60G "Gipsy Moth," 1929 (airplane used on first airmail route in Chile). b, Junkers R42, 1930 (seaplane flown from Puerto Montt to Straits of Magellan).

No. 1594: a, Blériot XI, 1916 (airplane used in first military flight and first airmail flight in Chile). b, Bristol M1C, 1918 (first airplane to cross the Andes at highest point).

No. 1595: a, Let L-13 "Blanik," 1964 (first glider to cross Andes). b, Bell 47 D-1 "Sioux" helicopter, 1960 (helicopter used in airlift after Valdivia earthquake).

No. 1596: a, PBY-5A Catalina, 1951 (seaplane used in first flight to Easter Island). b, Vought Sikorsky OS2U-3 "Kingfisher," 1947 (seaplane used in first flight from Chile to Antarctica).

2013, Aug. 9 Litho. *Perf. 13¼*
1592 Horiz. pair .25 .25
a.-b. A861 10p Either single .25 .25
1593 Horiz. pair .25 .25
a.-b. A861 20p Either single .25 .25
1594 Horiz. pair .40 .40
a.-b. A861 50p Either single .25 .25
1595 Horiz. pair .60 .60
a.-b. A861 70p Either single .30 .30
1596 Horiz. pair .80 .80
a.-b. A861 100p Either single .40 .40
Nos. 1592-1596 (5) 2.30 2.30

Annexation of Easter Island, 125th Anniv. — A862

2013, Sept. 27 Litho. *Perf. 13¼*
1597 A862 500p multi 2.00 2.00

National Library, 200th Anniv. — A863

2013, Sept. 30 Litho. *Perf. 13¼*
1598 A863 310p multi 1.25 1.25

General José Miguel Carrera National Institute (School for Boys), 200th Anniv. — A864

2013, Sept. 30 Litho. *Perf. 13¼*
1599 A864 430p multi 1.75 1.75

Federation of Catholic University Students, 75th Anniv. — A865

2013, Oct. 8 Litho. *Perf. 13¼*
1600 A865 310p multi 1.25 1.25

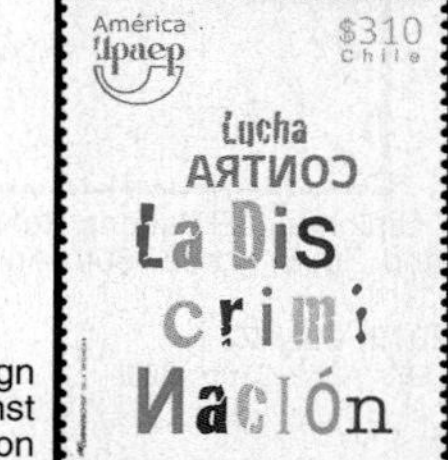

Campaign Against Discrimination A866

2013, Oct. 25 Litho. *Perf. 13¼*
1601 A866 310p multi 1.25 1.25

America Issue.

Miniature Sheet

San José Mine Rescue, 3rd Anniv. — A867

No. 1602: a, Fénix 2 rescue capsule. b, Names of 33 rescued miners. c, Note indicating condition and number of miners sent to surface on probe. d, Monument to the rescue of the miners. e, Drilling equipment at surface. f. 33 Chilean flags.

2013, Oct. 30 Litho. *Perf. 13¼*
1602 A867 500p Sheet of 6, #a-f 11.50 11.50

Christmas A868

2013, Nov. 27 Litho. *Perf. 13¼*
1603 A868 310p multi 1.25 1.25

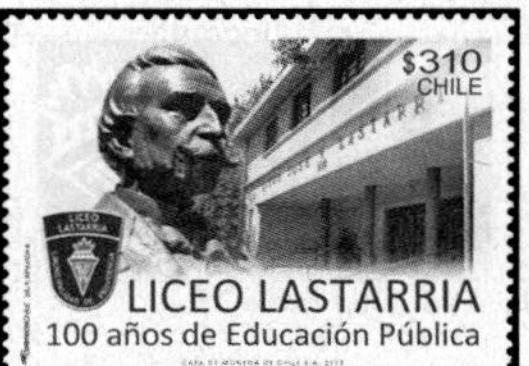

Public Education in Chile, Cent. — A869

2013, Dec. 30 Litho. *Perf. 13¼*
1604 A869 310p multi 1.25 1.25

Philatelic Society of Chile, 125th Anniv. — A870

2014, Mar. 18 Litho. *Perf. 13¼*
1605 A870 310p multi 5.25 5.25

Los Angeles, 275th Anniv. — A871

No. 1606: a, Statue of Bernardo O'Higgins. b, Liceo de Hombres. c, Laguna Esmeralda. d, Laja Waterfalls.

2014, May 26 Litho. *Perf. 13¼*
1606 A871 310p Block of 4, #a-d 5.50 5.50

Printed in sheets containing four blocks of 4 + 4 labels.

2014 World Cup Soccer Championships, Brazil — A872

2014, June 16 Litho. *Perf. 13¼*
1607 A872 500p multi 1.90 1.90

Battle of Rancagua, 200th Anniv. — A873

No. 1608 — Soldiers and: a, Angel holding shield. b, Swordsmen on horseback.

2014, Sept. 30 Litho. *Perf. 13¼*
1608 A873 Horiz pair 2.50 2.50
a.-b. 310p Either single 1.10 1.10

Printed in sheets containing 12 pairs and 6 labels.

Exfina 2014 Philatelic Exhibition, Santiago — A874

Designs: 470p, Chile #1. 500p, Chile #2. 1500p, Emblem of Philatelic Society of Chile.

2014, Oct. 14 Litho. *Perf. 13¼*
1609-1610 A874 Set of 2 3.50 3.50

Souvenir Sheet

1611 A874 1500p multi 5.75 5.75

Philatelic Society of Chile, 125th anniv.

America Issue — A875

No. 1612: a, Lautaro (c. 1534-1557), Mapuche leader of resistance to Spanish rule. b. Caupolicán (d. 1558), Mapuche military leader.

2014, Oct. 30 Litho. *Perf. 13¼*
1612 A875 310p Vert. pair, #a-b 2.10 2.10

Christmas
A876

2014, Nov. 10 Litho. *Perf. 13¼*
1613 A876 310p multi 1.00 1.00

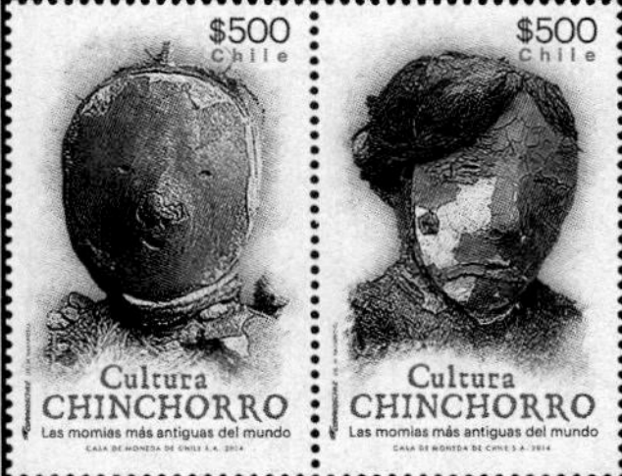

Chinchorro Mummies — A877

No. 1614: a, Mummy of a child with stake point at top of head. b, Mummy with outer coating missing under eye.

2014, Nov. 28 Litho. *Perf. 13¼*
1614 A877 500p Horiz. pair, #a-b 3.25 3.25

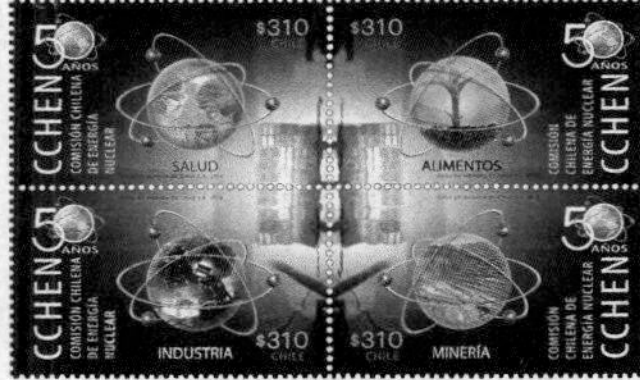

Chilean Nuclear Energy Commission, 50th Anniv. — A878

No. 1615 — Stylized atom with inscription: a, Salud (health). b, Alimentos (food). c, Industria (industry). d, Minería (mining).

2014, Dec. 10 Litho. *Perf. 13¼*
1615 A878 310p Block of 4, #a-d 4.25 4.25

Miniature Sheet

Talcahuano, 250th Anniv. — A879

No. 1616: a, Cacique Talcahueñu, painting by Héctor Robles Acuña. b, R.H. Huáscar. c, David Fuentes Sosa and his Blériot airplane "Talcahuano." d, Alcalde Luis Macera Dellarossa Coliseum. e, Boats in water near Caleta Tumbes. f, Sailboats off Talcahuano.

2014, Dec. 12 Litho. *Perf. 13¼*
1616 A879 500p Sheet of 6, #a-f 10.00 10.00

Hippocamelus Bisulcus — A880

No. 1617 — Huemul: a, Head, with foliage in background. b, Entire animal on hill, head at right. c, Entire animal with head at left. d, Head, Moon in clouds.

2015, Apr. 7 Litho. *Perf. 13¼*
1617 A880 600p Block of 4, #a-d 8.00 8.00

Protection of the huemul.

Miniature Sheet

Chuquicamata, Cent. — A881

No. 1618: a, Pres. Ramón Barros Luco. b, Steam shovel. c, Chuquicamata Mine. d, Chuquicamata Arch. e, Chile Theater. f, El Salvador Church.

2015, June 3 Litho. *Perf. 13¼*
1618 A881 500p Sheet of 6, #a-f 9.50 9.50

2015 Copa América Soccer Championships, Chile — A882

No. 1619 — Map of chile and; a, Soccer ball. b, Mascot and soccer ball.

2015, June 8 Litho. *Perf. 13¼*
1619 A882 500p Horiz. pair, #a-b 3.25 3.25

Josefina Martínez Children's Hospital, 75th Anniv. — A883

2015, July 28 Litho. *Perf. 13¼*
1620 A883 310p multi .95 .95

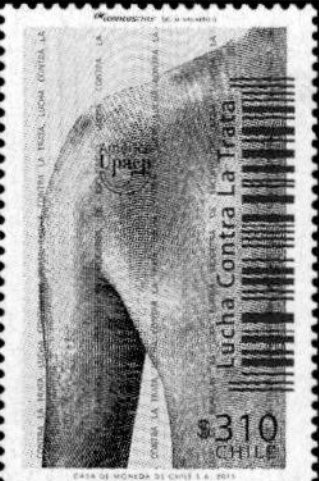

Campaign Against Human Trafficking A884

Designs: 310p, Man. 500p, Woman.

2015, Oct. 26 Litho. *Perf. 13¼*
1621-1622 A884 Set of 2 2.40 2.40

America Issue.

State Defence Council, 120th Anniv. — A885

2015, Oct. 29 Litho. *Perf. 13¼*
1623 A885 310p multi .90 .90

Maps — A886

Map of: 10p, Santiago, 1541. 50p, Antarctica, 1739. 60p, Antarctica, present day. 80p, Robinson Crusoe Island, 1753. 100p, Robinson Crusoe Island, 1744.

No. 1629 — Map of Easter Island from: a, 1770. b, 1777.

2015, Nov. 4 Litho. *Perf. 13¼*
1624 A886 10p multi .25 .25
1625 A886 50p multi .25 .25
1626 A886 60p multi .25 .25
1627 A886 80p multi .25 .25
1628 A886 100p multi .30 .30
1629 Horiz. pair 5.50 5.50
a.-b. A886 1000p Either single 2.75 2.75
Nos. 1624-1629 (6) 6.80 6.80

Christmas — A887

2015, Nov. 25 Litho. *Perf. 13¼*
1630 A887 310p multi .90 .90

Nacimiento — A888

No. 1631 — Arms of Nacimiento and: a, Nacimiento Fort. b, Potter and pottery.

2015, Dec. 21 Litho. *Perf. 13¼*
1631 Horiz. pair + flanking label 3.50 3.50
a.-b. A888 600p Either single 1.75 1.75

Pelluhue — A889

No. 1632 — Arms of Pelluhue and: a, Caleta Curanipe. b, Municipal Stadium. c, Pueño-La Sirena. d, Arcos de Calan, Tregualemu.

2015, Dec. 28 Litho. *Perf. 13¼*
1632 A889 310p Block of 4, #a-d 3.50 3.50

Miniature Sheet

Symbols of Chilean Justice — A890

No. 1633: a, Supreme Court Building. b, Statues at Supreme Court Building. c, Stained-glass window. d, Statue of Blind Justice. e, Court building and eagle sculpture. f, Court building and sculpture of Justice.

2015, Dec. 29 Litho. *Perf. 13¼*
1633 A890 500p Sheet of 6, #a-f 8.50 8.50

Naval Aviation — A891

No. 1634: a, Dornier Wal No. 16, 1928. b, Fairey III-F Mk 1, 1927.

2016, Mar. 16 Litho. *Perf. 13¼*
1634 A891 600p Horiz. pair, #a-b 3.75 3.75

A892

Design: Lieutenant Hernan Merino Correa (1936-65), Soldier Killed in Laguna del Desierto Incident.

2016, Apr. 25 Litho. *Perf. 13¼*
1635 A892 500p multi 1.50 1.50

2016 Summer Olympics, Rio de Janeiro — A893

2016, Oct. 21 Litho. *Perf. 13¼*
1636 A893 310p multi .95 .95

America issue.

National Monuments — A894

No. 1637: a, San Andrés Church, Pica. b, Matilla Church, Matilla.

2016, Oct. 27 Litho. *Perf. 13¼*
1637 A894 310p Horiz. pair, #a-b 1.90 1.90

Christmas A895

2016, Nov. 14 Litho. *Perf. 13¼*
1638 A895 310p multi .95 .95

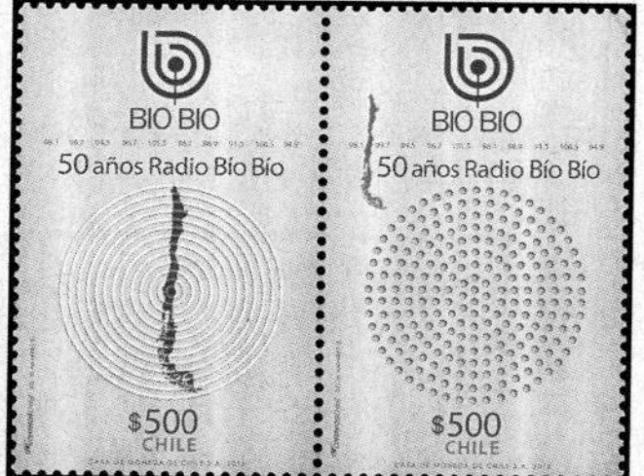

Radio Bío Bío, 50th Anniv. — A896

No. 1639 — Emblem and: a, Concentric circles, map of Chile in blue. b, Speaker holes, map of Chile in red.

2016, Dec. 7 Litho. *Perf. 13¼*
1639 A896 500p Horiz. pair, #a-b 3.00 3.00

Costumes of the Selk'nam People — A897

Inscriptions: 10p, Tanu. 20p, Halaháches. 30p, Matan. 50p, Shoort Jóichik. 100p, Kulan. 1000p, Ulen.

2016, Dec. 29 Litho. *Perf. 13¼*
1640-1645 A897 Set of 6 3.75 3.75

Pampilla Festival, Coquimbo — A898

2016, Dec. 30 Litho. *Perf. 13¼*
1646 A898 600p multi 1.90 1.90

Bernardo O'Higgins Military Academy, 200th Anniv. — A899

2017, Mar. 15 Litho. *Perf. 13¼*
1647 A899 600p multi 1.90 1.90

Independence, 200th Anniv. (in 2018) — A900

No. 1648: a, Fiscal Warehouse Buildings (Edificios Almacenes Fiscales). b, Juan O. Goñi (1854-1919), naval officer, and ship, Esmerelda, in Battle of Iquique. c, José Santiago Campino, first accountant of Chilean Navy. d, Naval Storehouse Building (Edificio de la Dirección de Abastecimiento de la Armada).

2017, June 15 Litho. *Perf. 13¼*
1648 Horiz. strip of 4 + label or block of 4 7.75 7.75
a.-d. A900 600p Any single 1.90 1.90

Battle of Chacabuco, 200th Anniv. — A901

2017, Aug. 20 Litho. *Perf. 13¼*
1649 A901 340p multi 1.10 1.10

Children's Rights — A902

No. 1650: a, Sun and heart with faces. b, Faces, crescent Moon and Sun.
1500p, Faces, crescent Moon and Sun, diff.

2017, Sept. 13 Litho. *Perf. 13¼*
1650 A902 500p Vert. pair, #a-b 3.25 3.25

Souvenir Sheet

1651 A902 1500p multi 4.75 4.75

Chilean ratification of United Nations Convention on the Rights of the Child, 25th anniv.

Murals by David Alfaro Sisqueiros and Xavier Guerrero at Mexico School, Chillán, 75th Anniv. — A903

2017, Sept. 14 Litho. *Perf. 13¼*
1652 A903 360p multi 1.25 1.25

Chilean Postal Service, 270th Anniv. — A904

2017, Oct. 25 Litho. *Perf. 13¼*
1653 A904 360p multi 1.25 1.25

Desert Flowers — A905

No. 1654: a, Leontochir ovallei. b, Leucocoryne vittata. c, Argylia radiata. d, Rhodophiala phycelloides.

2017, Oct. 25 Litho. *Perf. 13¼*
1654 A905 600p Block of 4, #a-d 7.75 7.75

Chilean Postal Service, 270th anniv.

Vicente Pérez Rosales National Park — A906

2017, Oct. 31 Litho. *Perf. 13¼*
1655 A906 360p multi 1.25 1.25

America issue.

Christmas A907

2017, Dec. 15 Litho. *Perf. 13¼*
1656 A907 360p multi 1.25 1.25

Violeta Parra (1917-67), Composer and Folklorist A908

2017, Dec. 28 Litho. *Perf. 13¼*
1657 A908 500p multi 1.75 1.75

Visit to Chile of Pope Francis A909

2018, Jan. 10 Litho. *Perf. 13¼*
1658 A909 600p multi 2.00 2.00

Battle of Maipú, 200th Anniv. A910

2018, Apr. 5 Litho. *Perf. 13¼*
1659 A910 360p multi 1.25 1.25

Chilean Navy, 200th Anniv. — A911

No. 1660 — Crest of Chilean Navy and: a, Capture of the Esmerelda, 1820. b, First national squadron, 1818. c, Ship and helicopters, 2018. d, Four sailors, 2018.

2018, Oct. 5 Litho. *Perf. 13¼*
1660 Horiz. strip of 5 + flanking label 7.00 3.50
a.-e. A911 600p Any single 1.75 .85

Vultur Gryphus — A912

2018, Oct. 13 Litho. *Perf. 13¼*
1661 A912 360p multi 1.10 .55

Souvenir Sheet

1662 A912 1500p multi 4.50 2.25

Exfil 2018 Philatelic Exhibition, Santiago. No. 1662 contains one 48x48mm stamp.

Canis Lupus Familiaris — A913

2018, Oct. 31 Litho. *Perf. 13¼*
1663 A913 360p multi 1.10 .55

America issue.

Christmas — A914

No. 1664 — Winning designs in children's art contest: a, Family and Christmas tree, by Fabián Manquepillán. b, Christmas tree, mailbox and children holding letters, by Emanuel Sepúlveda. c, Santa Claus and reindeer as penguins, by Bárbara Rivera. d, Pyramid of children, by Nicolette Sepúlveda. e, Children and snowman, by Nicolás Sandoval.

2018, Nov. 20 Litho. *Perf. 13¼*
1664 Horiz. strip of 5 7.50 3.75
a.-e. A914 500p Any single 1.50 .75

July 2, 2019, Total Solar Eclipse — A916

2019, July 2 Litho. *Perf. 13¼*
1666 A916 830p multi 2.40 1.25

Bass and Jorge Peña Hen (1928-73), Composer and Founder of Children's Symphony Orchestra A917

2019, July 12 Litho. *Perf. 13¼*
1667 A917 370p multi 1.10 .55

Youth and Children's Orchestras Foundation.

A918

A919

A920

University of Concepción, Cent. — A921

2019, Aug. 7 Litho. *Perf. 13¼*
1668 Horiz. strip of 4 + central label 4.00 2.00
a. A918 370p multi 1.00 .50
b. A919 370p multi 1.00 .50
c. A920 370p multi 1.00 .50
d. A921 370p multi 1.00 .50

Express Mail Service, 20th Anniv. — A922

2019, Oct. 9 Litho. *Perf. 13¼*
1669 A922 520p multi 1.40 .70

President Frei Antarctic Air Base, 50th Anniv. — A924

No. 1672 — Map and: a, Aerial view of base. b, Heliograph of the Meteorological Center. c, Teniente Marsh Aerodrome. d, Chilean Air Force Bell 412 helicopter and penguins.

2019, Oct. 29 Litho. *Perf. 13¼*
1672 A924 1000p Block of 4, #a-d 11.00 5.50

International Year of Indigenous Languages — A925

2019, Nov. 27 Litho. *Perf. 13¼*
1673 A925 480p multi 1.25 .60

Christmas A926

2019, Nov. 28 Litho. *Perf. 13¼*
1674 A926 370p multi .95 .45

POSTAL FISCAL STAMPS

Revenue stamps and telegraph stamp authorized for postal use until the end of 1914.

Arms — PF1

1880-91 Engr. Unwmk. *Perf. 12*
AR1 PF1 1c red 2.25 *6.75*
Revenue cancel .25
AR2 PF1 2c brown 2.25 *5.25*
Revenue cancel .25
AR3 PF1 5c blue 3.50 *4.50*
Revenue cancel .25
AR4 PF1 10c green ('91) 13.50 *13.50*
Revenue cancel .25
AR5 PF1 20c orange ('91) 13.50 *35.00*
Revenue cancel .25

Printed by the American Banknote Co. Issued: 1c, 2c, 11/27/80; 5c, 7/3/80; 10c, 20c, 4/1/91.
Counterfeit postal cancels exist.

Arms — PF2

1891, Apr. 21
AR6 PF2 2c yellow brown 2.00 *12.00*
Telegraph cancel .75
AR7 PF2 10c olive green 1.00 *12.00*
Telegraph cancel .75
AR8 PF2 20c blue 8.50 *6.00*
Telegraph cancel .75
AR9 PF2 1p brown 1.50 *20.00*
Revenue cancel .75

Printed by Bradbury, Wilkinson & Co. Nos. AR6-AR9 are telegraph stamps, authorized for postal use.
Counterfeit postal cancels exist.
Smaller format stamps of the same design as AR6-AR9 are 1894 telegraph stamps that were not authorized for postal use.

PF3

1900-13 *Perf. 14*
AR10 PF3 1c vermilion 2.25 3.00
Revenue cancel .25
AR11 PF3 2c brown ('13) 2.25 3.50
Revenue cancel .25
AR12 PF3 5c blue 3.00 4.50
Revenue cancel .25

Printed by Waterlow & Sons, London. Issued: 1c, 10/25/00; 2c, 1/21/13; 5c, 12/6/00.
Counterfeit postal cancels exist.

SEMI-POSTAL STAMPS

S. S. Abtao and Captain Policarpo Toro SP1

S. S. Abtao and Brother Eugenio Eyraud SP2

Perf. 14½x15

1940, Mar. 1 Engr. Unwmk.

B1	SP1	80c + 2.20p dk grn & lake	4.00	2.00
B2	SP2	3.60p + 6.40p lake & dk grn	4.00	2.00
a.		Pair, #B1-B2	10.00	8.00
		Set, never hinged	10.00	

50th anniv. of Chilean ownership of Easter Is. Surtax used for charitable institutions.

Sheets containing 15 of each value, with 9 se-tenant pairs.

Catalogue values for unused stamps in this section, from this point to the end of the section, are for Never Hinged items.

Pedro de Valdivia — SP3

Portraits: 10c+10c, Jose Toribio Medina.

1961, Apr. 29 Photo. *Perf. 13x12½*

B3	SP3	5c + 5c pale brn & sl grn	1.00	.35
B4	SP3	10c + 10c buff & vio blk	1.00	.30

Printed without charge by the Spanish Mint as a gift to Chile. The surtax was to aid the 1960 earthquake victims and to increase teachers' salaries. See Nos. CB1-CB2.

No. 402 Surcharged in Dark Green

1974, Mar. 25 Litho. *Perf. 14½*

B5	A213	27e + 3e on 40c dl grn	.60	.25

Cent. of intl. meteorological cooperation.

The 3e surtax of Nos. B5-B10 was for modernization of the postal system.

No. 412 Surcharged in Dark Blue

1974, Apr. 25 Litho. *Perf. 14½*

B6	A219	27e + 3e on 1.95e	.75	.30

500th anniversary of the birth of Nicolaus Copernicus (1473-1534), Polish astronomer.

No. 329A Surcharged

1974, May 2 Litho. *Perf. 14*

B7	A159	27e + 3e on 1e bluish grn	.40	.30

Centenary of the city of Vina del Mar.

No. 377 Surcharged in Blk, Nos. 395, 380 in Red

1974 Litho. *Perf. 14½*

B8	A193	47e + 3e on 40c grn	.25	.25
B9	A207	67e + 3e on 40c multi	.60	.40
B10	A196	97e + 3e on 40c red brn	.40	.35
		Nos. B8-B10 (3)	1.25	1.00

Issued: No. B8, 6/7; No. B9, 7/9; No. B10, 6/20.

AIR POST STAMPS

Surcharged in Black

Lithographed; Center Engraved

1927 Unwmk. *Perf. 13½x14*

Black Brown & Blue

C1	AP1	40c on 10c	350.00	50.00
C2	AP1	80c on 10c	350.00	65.00
C3	AP1	1.20p on 10c	350.00	75.00
C4	AP1	1.60p on 10c	350.00	75.00
C5	AP1	2p on 10c	350.00	75.00
		Nos. C1-C5 (5)	1,750.	340.00

Issued for air post service between Santiago and Valparaiso. The stamps picture Bernardo O'Higgins and are not known without surcharge.

Regular Issues of 1915-28 Overprinted or Surcharged in Black, Red or Blue

Inscribed: "Chile Correos"

1928-29 *Perf. 13½x14, 14*

C6	A39	20c brn org & blk (Bk)	.75	.35
C6A	A55	40c dk vio & blk (R)	1.00	.35
C6B	A43	1p grn & blk (Bl)	4.25	.80
C6C	A43	2p red & blk (Bl)	5.00	1.10
f.		2p ver & blk (Bl)	120.00	35.00
C6D	A43	5p ol grn & blk (Bl)	10.00	3.25
C6E	A50	6p on 10c dp bl & blk (R)	65.00	40.00
C7	A43	10p org & blk (Bk) ('29)	16.00	6.50
C8	A43	10p org & blk (Bl)	50.00	35.00
		Nos. C6-C8 (8)	152.00	87.35

On Nos. C6B to C6D, C7 and C8 the overprint is larger than on the other stamps of the issue.

Nos. 155, 156, 158-161 Ovptd. or Srchd. in Red, Blue or Black

Inscribed: "Chile Correos"

1928-32 Wmk. 215

C9	A55	40c vio & blk (R)	1.35	.25
C10	A43	1p gray grn & blk (Bl)	1.90	.25
C11	A43	2p red & blk (Bl)	11.00	2.25
C12	A52	3p on 5c sl bl (R)	65.00	42.50
C13	A43	5p ol grn & blk (Bl)	8.50	3.00
C14	A43	10p org & blk (Bk)	45.00	12.00
		Nos. C9-C14 (6)	132.75	60.25

Same Overprint on Nos. 166-169, 172 and 158 in Black or Red

Inscribed: "Correos de Chile"

1928-30

C15	A39	20c (#166) ('29)	1.25	.70
C16	A39	20c (#172) ('30)	.50	.25
C17	A40	25c bl & blk (R)	.60	.25
C18	A41	30c brn & blk	.40	.25
a.		Double ovpt., one inverted	250.00	250.00
C19	A42	50c dp grn & blk (R)	.50	.25
		Nos. C15-C19 (5)	3.25	1.70

No. 109 Overprinted in Black

Inscribed: "Chile Correos"

1932 *Perf. 13½x14, 14*

C21	A43	1p yel grn & blk (Bk)	6.00	1.75

Condor on Andes — AP1a

Airplane Crossing Andes — AP3

Los Cerrillos Airport — AP2

1931 Litho. *Perf. 13½x14, 14½x14*

C22	AP1a	5c yellow grn	.25	.25
C23	AP1a	10c yellow brn	.25	.25
C24	AP1a	20c rose	.25	.25
C25	AP2	50c dark blue	3.00	.75
C26	AP3	50c black brn	1.10	.50
C27	AP3	1p purple	1.75	.35
C28	AP3	2p blue blk	2.50	.50
a.		2p bluish slate	12.00	3.00
C29	AP2	5p lt red	4.25	.75
		Nos. C22-C29 (8)	13.35	3.60

For surcharges see Nos. C51-C53.

Airplane over City — AP4

Two Airplanes over Globe — AP9

Designs: 30c, 40c, 50c, Wings over Chile. 60c, Condor. 70c, Airplane and Star of Chile. 80c, Condor and Statue of Canpolican. 3p, 4p, 5p, Seaplane. 6p, 8p, 10p, Airplane. 20p, 30p, Airplane and Southern Cross. 40p, 50p, Airplane and symbols of space.

Perf. 13½x14

1934-39 Engr. Wmk. 215

C30	AP4	10c yel grn ('35)	.30	.25
C31	AP4	15c dk grn ('35)	.45	.25
C32	AP4	20c dp bl ('36)	.25	.25
C33	AP4	30c blk brn ('35)	.25	.25
C34	AP4	40c indigo ('38)	.25	.25
C35	AP4	50c dk brn ('36)	.25	.25
C36	AP4	60c vio blk ('35)	.25	.25
C37	AP4	70c blue ('35)	.45	.25
C38	AP4	80c ol blk ('35)	.25	.25

Perf. 14

C39	AP9	1p slate blk	.25	.25
C40	AP9	2p grnsh bl	.25	.25
C41	AP9	3p org brn ('35)	.30	.25
C42	AP9	4p brn ('35)	.30	.25
C43	AP9	5p org red	.30	.25
C44	AP9	6p yel brn ('35)	.45	.25
a.		6p brown ('39)	2.75	1.90
C45	AP9	8p grn ('35)	.40	.25
C46	AP9	10p brn lake	.45	.25
C47	AP9	20p olive	.45	.25
C48	AP9	30p gray blk	.50	.25
C49	AP9	40p gray vio	1.00	.70
C50	AP9	50p brn vio	2.50	.80
		Nos. C30-C50 (21)	9.85	6.25

Nos. C30-C50 have been re-issued in slightly different colors, with white gum. The first printings are considerably scarcer.

See Nos. C90-C107B, C148-C154.

Types of 1931 Surcharged in Black or Red

Perf. 13½x14, 14½x14

1940 Wmk. 215

C51	AP1a	80c on 20c lt rose	.40	.25
C52	AP2	1.60p on 5p lt red	4.25	1.50
C53	AP3	5.10p on 2p sl bl (R)	7.00	1.75
		Nos. C51-C53 (3)	11.65	3.50

The surcharge on No. C52 measures 21½mm.

Plane and Weather Vane — AP14

Plane and Caravel — AP23

Designs (Plane and): 20c, Globe. 30c, Chilean flag. 40c, Star of Chile and Southern Cross. 50c, Mountains. 60c, Tree. 70c, Lakes. 80c, Shore. 90c, Sunrise. 2p, Compass. 3p, Telegraph lines. 4p, Rainbow. 5p, Factory. 10p, Snow-capped mountain.

1941-42 Wmk. 215 Litho. *Perf. 14*

C54	AP14	10c ol gray	.25	.25
C55	AP14	20c dp rose	.25	.25
C56	AP14	30c blue vio	.25	.25
C57	AP14	40c dl red brn	.25	.25
C58	AP14	50c org red ('42)	.35	.25
C59	AP14	60c dp green	.25	.25
C60	AP14	70c rose	.30	.25
C61	AP14	80c ultra ('42)	1.50	.45
C62	AP14	90c dk brown	.45	.25
C63	AP23	1p brt blue	.30	.25
C64	AP23	2p rose lake	.80	.30
C65	AP23	3p dk bl grn & yel grn	1.20	.60
C66	AP23	4p bl vio & buff	1.75	1.00
C67	AP23	5p dk org red ('42)	17.00	6.00
C68	AP23	10p gray grn & bl grn	9.50	6.00
		Nos. C54-C68 (15)	34.40	16.60

The 1p, dated "1541-1941," commemorates the 400th anniversary of Santiago.

1942-46 Unwmk.

C69	AP14	10c ultra ('43)	.25	.25
C70	AP14	10c rose lil ('45)	.25	.25
C71	AP14	20c dull grn ('43)	.25	.25
C72	AP14	20c cop brn ('45)	.25	.25
C73	AP14	30c dull vio ('44)	.25	.25
C74	AP14	30c ol blk ('45)	.25	.25
C75	AP14	40c red brn ('44)	.30	.25
C76	AP14	40c ultra ('45)	.25	.25
C77	AP14	50c rose ('43)	.25	.25
C78	AP14	50c org red ('45)	.25	.25
C79	AP14	60c orange	.25	.25
C79B	AP14	60c dp grn ('46)	.25	.25
C80	AP14	70c rose ('45)	.45	.35
C81	AP14	80c slate grn	.25	.25
C82	AP14	90c brown ('45)	.45	.35
C83	AP23	1p gray grn & lt bl ('43)	.25	.25
C84	AP23	2p org red ('43)	.45	.25
C85	AP23	3p dk pur & pale org ('43)	.45	.25
C86	AP23	4p bl grn & yel grn	.45	.35
C87	AP23	5p dk rose car ('43)	.35	.25
a.		5p dk car rose ('44)	.25	.25
C88	AP23	10p sapphire ('43)	.45	.35
		Nos. C69-C88 (21)	6.60	5.65

No. C83 is without dates "1541-1941."

See Nos. C109-C123. For surcharges see Nos. C145-C147

Coat of Arms and Plane AP29

1942, Nov. 5 Engr. *Perf. 14½*

C89 AP29 100p car lake 40.00 35.00

University of Chile centenary.

Types of 1934-39

Perf. 13½x14

1944-55 Unwmk. Engr.

C90	AP4	10c yel grn ('55)	.25	.25
C92	AP4	20c deep blue	.25	.25
C93	AP4	30c black brn	.25	.25
C94	AP4	40c indigo	.25	.25
C95	AP4	50c dk brn ('47)	.25	.25
C96	AP4	60c slate vio	.25	.25
C97	AP4	70c blue ('48)	.25	.25
C98	AP4	80c olive blk	.25	.25

Perf. 14

C99	AP9	1p slate blk	.25	.25
C100	AP9	2p grnsh bl	.25	.25
C101	AP9	3p org brn ('45)	.25	.25
C102	AP9	4p brown	.25	.25
C103	AP9	5p org red	.35	.25
C104	AP9	6p yel brn ('46)	.40	.25
C105	AP9	8p green	.40	.25
C106	AP9	10p brn lake	1.10	.25
C107	AP9	20p ol gray ('45)	.75	.25
a.		Imperf., pair	70.00	
C107B	AP9	50p rose vio ('50)	17.50	2.50
		Nos. C90-C107B (18)	23.50	6.75

Plane and Radio Tower — AP30

1945 Unwmk. Litho. *Perf. 14*

C108 AP30 1.60p brt violet .55 .25

See Nos. C118-C119.

Types of 1941-45

1946-48 Wmk. 215

C109	AP14	10c rose lil ('47)	.25	.25
C110	AP14	20c dk red brn ('48)	.25	.25
C111	AP14	20c dull grn ('48)	1.50	.30
C112	AP14	30c black ('48)	.25	.25
C113	AP14	40c ultra ('48)	.25	.25
C114	AP14	60c ol grn ('48)	.25	.25
C115	AP14	80c ol blk ('48)	.25	.25
C116	AP14	90c choc ('48)	.25	.25
C117	AP23	1p gray grn & lt bl ('48)	.25	.25
C118	AP30	1.60p brt violet	.25	.25
C119	AP30	1.80p brt vio ('48)	.25	.25
C119A	AP23	2p org red	.40	.25
C120	AP23	3p dk pur & pale org ('47)	1.50	.30
C121	AP23	4p bl grn & yel grn ('48)	1.10	.45
C122	AP23	5p rose car ('47)	.80	.25
C123	AP23	10p sapphire ('47)	1.00	.25
		Nos. C109-C123 (16)	8.80	4.30

No. C117 is without dates "1541-1941."
For surcharges see Nos. C145, C147.

Flora and Fauna Type of 1948

1948

C124	A118	3p Block of 25	40.00	40.00
		Never hinged	75.00	
a.-y.		any single	1.10	1.00

Catalogue values for unused stamps in this section, from this point to the end of the section, are for Never Hinged items.

Air Line Emblem and Planes — AP32

1949 Wmk. 215 Litho. *Perf. 14*

C125 AP32 2p ultra .45 .25

20th anniversary of the establishment of Chile's National Air Line.

Benjamin Vicuna Mackenna — AP33

1949, Mar. 22 Engr. *Perf. 13½x14*

C126 AP33 3p dk car rose .30 .25

Factory, Badge and Book — AP34

Design: 10p, Column and cogwheel.

Unwmk.

1949, Nov. 11 Litho. *Perf. 14*

C127	AP34	5p green	.85	.45
C128	AP34	10p red brown	1.40	.55

Centenary of the founding of Chile's School of Arts and Crafts.

Plane and Globe — AP35

1950, Jan. Engr.

C129	AP35	5p green	.60	.25
C130	AP35	10p red brown	1.00	.60

75th anniv. of the UPU.

Plane over Snow-capped Mountain AP36

Araucarian Pine and Plane — AP38

Plane and: 40c, Coast and Sunrise. 60c, Over fishing boat. 2p, Chilean flag. 3p, Dock crane. 4p, Above river. 5p, Blast furnace. 10p, Mountain lake. 20p, Cable cars.

Imprint: "Especies Valoradas-Chile"

1950-54 Wmk. 215 Litho. *Perf. 14*

C135	AP36	20c yel brn ('54)	.35	.25
C136	AP36	40c purple ('52)	.35	.25
C137	AP36	60c lt bl ('53)	1.60	.90
C138	AP38	1p dull green	.35	.25
C139	AP38	2p brown red	.35	.25
C140	AP38	3p violet bl	.35	.25
C141	AP38	4p red org ('54)	.35	.25
C142	AP38	5p violet	.35	.25
C143	AP38	10p yel grn ('53)	.35	.25
C144	AP38	20p red brn ('54)	.60	.25
		Nos. C135-C144 (10)	5.00	3.15

See Nos. C155-C164, C207-C212.

Nos. C115, C81 and C116 Surcharged with New Value in Carmine or Black

1951-52 Wmk. 215

C145 AP14 40c on 80c ol blk (C) ('52) .25 .25

Unwmk.

C146 AP14 40c on 80c sl grn (C) ('52) 5.50 3.50

Wmk. 215

C147	AP14	1p on 90c choc	.25	.25
		Nos. C145-C147 (3)	6.00	4.00

Types of 1934-39

1951-53 Unwmk. Engr. *Perf. 14*

C148	AP9	1p deep blue	.25	.25
C149	AP9	2p blue	.35	.25
C150	AP9	6p bis brn ('52)	.45	.25
C151	AP9	30p dk gray ('53)	.60	.90
C152	AP9	40p dk pur brn	18.00	2.40
C153	AP9	50p dark purple	25.00	5.00
		Nos. C148-C153 (6)	44.65	9.05

Wmk. 215

C154 AP9 50p dk pur ('52) .80 .40

Types of 1950-54
Designs as Before
Imprint: "Especies Valoradas-Chile"

1951-55 Unwmk. Litho. *Perf. 14*

C155	AP36	20c yel brn ('54)	.25	.25
C156	AP36	40c purple	.25	.25
C157	AP36	60c lt blue ('53)	.25	.25
C158	AP38	1p dk bl grn ('55)	.25	.25
C159	AP38	2p brown red	.25	.25
C160	AP38	3p violet bl	.25	.25
C161	AP38	4p red org ('52)	.30	.25
C162	AP38	5p violet	.30	.25
C163	AP38	10p emerald	.30	.25
C164	AP38	20p brown	.40	.25
		Nos. C155-C164 (10)	2.80	2.50

San Martin Crossing Andes AP40

Wmk. 215

1951, Mar. 16 Engr. *Perf. 14½*

C165 AP40 5p red violet .90 .50

Gen. José de San Martín, death cent.

Isabella Type of Regular Issue, 1952

1952, Mar. 21 *Perf. 14*

C166 A125 10p carmine .70 .40

A souvenir card without franking value was issued for the Hispano-Chilean Philatelic Exhibition at Santiago, Oct. 12, 1969. It contains 2 imperf. stamps similar to Nos. 264 and C166-60c green and 10p rose red. Size: 115x137½mm.

Ancient Fortress AP42

1953, Apr. 28

C167 AP42 10p brown car 2.25 .45

4th centenary of the founding of Valdivia.

Stamp Centenary Type of 1953

1953, Oct. 15 Engr. *Perf. 14½*

C168 A131 100p grnsh blue 2.75 1.00

An imperf. souvenir sheet contains one each of Nos. 276 and C168, with inscriptions in black at top and bottom center. Sheet measures 178x229mm, value $375, or 172x226mm, value $130. It is stated that this sheet was not valid for postage.

Early Plane and Stylized Modern Version — AP44

Unwmk.

1954, May 26 Engr. *Perf. 14*

C170 AP44 3p deep blue .30 .25

25th anniversary of the founding of Chile's National Air Line.

Domeyko Type of Regular Issue, 1954

1954, Aug. 16 *Perf. 13½x14*

C171 A134 5p reddish brown .30 .25

Railroad Type of Regular Issue, 1954

1954, Sept. 10 Wmk. 215 *Perf. 14½*

C172 A135 10p dk purple 1.50 .25

An imperforate souvenir sheet contains one each of Nos. 283 and C172. Size: 195x235mm. Value $425.

Size: 174x232mm. Value, $110.

Presidential Visits Type of 1955

1955, May 24

C173 A139 100p red 1.50 1.25

Jet Plane in Clouds — AP48

Comet Air Liner — AP49

Designs: 2p, Helicopter over bridge. 10p, Oil derricks and plane. 50p, Control tower and plane. 200p, Beechcraft monoplane. 500p, Douglas DC-6.

Perf. 14½x14, 14x13½ (AP49)

1955-56 Engr. Wmk. 215

C174	AP48	1p dp red lil ('56)	.25	.25
C175	AP48	2p pale brn ('56)	.25	.25
C176	AP48	10p bluish grn ('56)	.25	.25
C177	AP48	50p rose ('56)	.60	.25
C178	AP49	100p green	1.00	.25
C179	AP49	200p dp ultra	6.50	.90
C180	AP49	500p dk carmine	7.50	.90
		Nos. C174-C180 (7)	16.35	3.05

Stamps similar to type AP49, but inscribed in escudo currency, are listed as type AP58.

1956-58 Unwmk.

Designs: 5p, Train and plane. 20p, Jet plane and Easter Island statue.

C183	AP48	5p violet	.25	.25
C184	AP48	10p grn ('57)	.25	.25
C185	AP48	20p ultra	.25	.25
C186	AP48	50p rose ('57)	.25	.25
C187	AP49	100p bl grn ('57)	.55	.25
a.		Lithographed ('60)	.55	.25
C188	AP49	200p dp ultra ('57)	.65	.25
C189	AP49	500p car ('58)	.85	.25
		Nos. C183-C189 (7)	3.05	1.75

Symbols of University Departments — AP50

Design: 100p, View of the University.

1956, Dec. 15 Unwmk. *Perf. 14½*

C190 AP50 20p green .35 .25
C191 AP50 100p dk vio bl 1.40 .80

25th anniversary of the Federico Santa Maria Technical University, Valparaiso.

A souvenir sheet contains one each of Nos. 299, C190-C191, imperf. It was not issued for postal use, though some served postally. Size: 185x251mm. Value, $75. Exists on sepia and white papers.

Mistral Type of Regular Issue, 1958

1958, Jan. 10 Engr. *Perf. 14*

C192 A144 100p green .25 .25

Ambrosio O'Higgins — AP51

1958, Mar. 23

C193 AP51 100p lt blue .40 .25

Founding of the city of Osorno, 500th anniv.

A souvenir sheet contains one each of Nos. 302 and C193, imperf. and printed in red brown. It was not issued for postal use, though some served postally. Size: 155x138mm. Value, $55.

Exhibition Type of Regular Issue

1958, Oct. 18 Unwmk.

C194 A146 50p dull green .45 .45

A souvenir sheet contains one each of Nos. 303 and C194, imperforate, printed in deep red or in purple and green. It was not issued for postal use, though some served postally. Size: 188x220mm. Value, $45.

Bank Type of Regular Issue, 1958

1958, Dec. 18 Engr. *Perf. 14*

C195 A147 50p redsh brown .25 .25

A souvenir sheet contains one each of Nos. 304 and C195, printed in dull violet, imperf. It was not issued for postal use, though some served postally. Size: 128x162mm. Value, $130.

Antarctic Types of Regular Issue

1958 Litho. *Perf. 14*

C199 A149 20p violet 1.00 .25

Engr.

C200 A150 500p dark blue 5.00 1.75

Symbols of Various Religions AP52

Perf. 14½

1959, Jan. 23 Unwmk. Engr.

C206 AP52 50p dk car rose .30 .25

10th anniversary of the Universal Declaration of Human Rights.

Types of 1950-54

Designs: 50p, Plane silhouette over shore. 100p, Plane over map of Antarctica. 200p, Plane over natural arch rock.

Imprint: "Casa de Moneda de Chile"

1959 Litho. *Perf. 14*

C207 AP38 1p dk blue grn .85 .50
a. Wmk. 215 30.00
C208 AP38 10p emerald .55 .25
C209 AP38 20p red brown .35 .25
C210 AP38 50p yellow grn .35 .25
C211 AP38 100p car rose .35 .25
C212 AP38 200p brt blue .55 .25
Nos. C207-C212 (6) 3.00 1.75

Carlos Anwandter AP53

1959, June 18 Engr. *Perf. 14*

C213 AP53 20p rose carmine .25 .25

Centenary of the German School in Valdivia, founded by Carlos Anwandter.

A souvenir sheet contains one each of Nos. 319 and C213, imperforate. It was not issued for postal use, though some served postally. Size: 144x213mm. Value, $50. Size: 190x273mm. Value, $70.

IGY Type of Regular Issue, 1958

1959, Aug. 28 Unwmk. *Perf. 14*

C214 A148 50p green .70 .25

Ladrillero Type of Regular Issue

1959, Aug. 28 Litho.

C215 A154 50p green .50 .25

Barros Arana Type of Regular Issue

1959, Aug. 28

C216 A155 100p purple .50 .25

Red Cross Type of Regular Issue

1959, Oct. 6

C217 A156 50p red & blk .60 .25

WRY Type of Regular Issue, 1960

1960, Apr. 7 Unwmk. *Perf. 14½*

C218 A160 10c violet .35 .25

A souvenir sheet contains two stamps similar to Nos. 330 and C218, the 1c printed in blue, the 10c airmail in maroon. The sheet is imperf., printed on thin cardboard. Size: 160x204mm. Value, $85.

Type of Regular Issue, 1960-62, and

José Agustin Eyzaguirre and José Miguel Infante — AP54

Designs: 2c, Palace of Justice. 5c, National memorial. No. C220, Arms of Chile. No. C220A, José Gaspar Marin and J. Gregorio Argomedo. 50c, Archbishop J. I. Cienfuegos and Brother Camilo Henriquez. 1e, Bernardo O'Higgins.

1960-65 Unwmk. Engr. *Perf. 14½*

C218A AP54 2c mar & gray vio ('62) .25 .25
C219 A162 5c vio bl & dl pur ('61) .25 .25

Wmk. 215

C220 A161 10c dk brn & red brn .25 .25

Unwmk.

C220A AP54 10c vio brn & brn ('64) .40 .25
C220B AP54 20c dk bl & dl pur ('64) .25 .25
C220C AP54 50c bl grn & ind ('65) 1.00 .25
C220D A162 1e dk red & red brn ('63) 1.00 .40
Nos. C218A-C220D (7) 3.40 1.90

150th anniv. of the formation of the 1st Natl. Government.

A souvenir sheet contains two airmail stamps: a 5c brown similar to No. C219 (National Memorial) and a 10c green, type A161. The sheet is imperf., printed on heavy paper with papermaker's watermark. Size: 120x168mm. Value, $75.

Map and Rotary Emblem — AP55

Unwmk.

1960, Dec. 1 Litho. *Perf. 14*

C221 AP55 10c blue .50 .25

South American Rotary Regional Conference, Santiago, 1960.

A souvenir sheet contains one 10c maroon, type AP55, with brown marginal inscription. Size: 118x158mm. Value, $15.

The souvenir sheet was overprinted in green "El Mundo Unida Contra la Malaria" and the outline of a mosquito, and released in October, 1962. Value, $110.

Araucan Pine and Plane — AP56

Designs: 2m, Chilean flag and plane. 3m, Plane and dock crane. 4m, Plane above river (vignette like AP39). 5m, Blast furnace. 1c, Plane over mountain lake. 2c, Plane over cable cars. 5c, Plane silhouette over shore. 10c, Plane over map of Antarctica. 20c, Plane over natural arch rock.

Imprint: "Casa de Moneda de Chile"

1960-62 Litho. *Perf. 14*

C222 AP56 1m orange .25 .25
C223 AP56 2m yellow grn .25 .25
C224 AP56 3m violet .25 .25
C225 AP56 4m gray olive .25 .25
C226 AP56 5m brt bl grn .25 .25
C227 AP56 1c ultra .25 .25
C228 AP56 2c red brn ('61) .35 .25
C229 AP56 5c yel grn ('61) 1.75 .25
C230 AP56 10c car rose ('62) .45 .25
C231 AP56 20c brt bl ('62) .50 .25
Nos. C222-C231 (10) 4.55 2.50

Oil Derricks and Douglas DC-6 — AP57

Beechcraft Monoplane AP58

5m, Train and plane. 2c, Jet plane & Easter Island statue. 5c, Control tower & plane. 10c, Comet airliner. 50c, Douglas DC-6.

Perf. 14x13½

1960-67 Unwmk. Litho.

C234 AP57 5m red brown .35 .35
C235 AP57 1c dull blue .35 .35
C236 AP57 2c ultra ('62) .35 .35
C237 AP57 5c rose red ('64) .35 .35
C238 AP58 10c ultra ('67) .35 .35
C239 AP58 20c car ('62) .35 .35
C240 AP58 50c green ('63) .35 .35
Nos. C234-C240 (7) 2.45 2.45

Stamps similar to type AP58, but inscribed in peso ($) currency, are listed as type AP49.

Congress Type of Regular Issue

1961, Oct. 5 *Perf. 14½*

C245 A164 10c gray green .95 .60

Soccer Type of Regular Issue, 1962

Designs: 5c, Goalkeeper and stadium, vert. 10c, Soccer players and globe.

1962, May 30 Unwmk. Engr.

C246 A165 5c rose lilac .25 .25
C247 A165 10c dk carmine .25 .25

A souvenir sheet of four contains one each of Nos. 340-341, C246-C247, imperf., with light brown marginal inscriptions. Size: 123x194mm. Sold for 7.50 escudos (face value, 22 centavos). Value $12.

It also exists with a different watermark in a smaller format, size: 122x162mm. Value is the same.

Hunger Type of Regular Issue

20c, Mother with empty bowl, horiz.

1963, Mar. 21 Litho. *Perf. 14*

C248 A166 20c green .25 .25

Red Cross Type of Regular Issue

Design: 20c, Centenary emblem and plane silhouette, horiz.

1963, Sept. 6 Unwmk. *Perf. 14*

C249 A167 20c gray & red .25 .25

Fire Engine of 1860's AP59

1963, Dec. 20 Litho. *Perf. 14½*

C250 AP59 30c red .50 .25

Centenary of the Santiago Fire Brigade.

Western Hemisphere AP60

1964, Apr. 9 Unwmk. *Perf. 14½*

C254 AP60 4c ultra .40 .25

Issued in memory of President John F. Kennedy and to honor the Alliance for Progress.

Battle of Rancagua — AP61

1965, May 7 Engr. *Perf. 14½*

C255 AP61 5c dull grn & sepia .40 .25

Battle of Rancagua, 10/7/14, 150th anniv.

ITU Emblem, Old and New Communication Equipment AP62

1965, May 7 Litho. *Perf. 14½x14*

C256 AP62 40c red & maroon .40 .25

ITU centenary.

Portrait Type of 1964

Portraits: No. C257, Enrique Molina. No. C258, Msgr. Carlos Casanueva.

1965, June Litho. *Perf. 14*

C257 A169 60c brt violet .30 .25
C258 A169 60c green .30 .25

See note after No. 346.

Skier Type of Regular Issue 1965

Design: 20c, Skier, horiz.

1965, Aug. 30 Unwmk. *Perf. 14*

C259 A172 20c ultra .30 .25

Fishing Boats, Angelmo Harbor AP63

Aviators' Monument AP64

1965
C260 AP63 40c brown .30 .25

Perf. 14x14½
C262 AP64 1e car rose .30 .25

Andrés Bello (1780?-1865), Venezuela-born Writer and Educator — AP65

1965, Nov. 29 Engr. Unwmk.
C263 AP65 10c dk car rose .35 .35

Skiers — AP66

1966, Apr. 6 Litho. *Perf. 14*
C264 AP66 4e dk bl & red brn 1.25 .25

World Skiing Championships, Partillo, Aug. 1966.

Basketball AP67

1966, Apr. 28
C265 AP67 13c rose carmine .40 .25

International Basketball Championships.

Slalom AP68

Perf. 14½x15
1966, July 20 Litho. Unwmk.
C266 AP68 75c rose car & lil .40 .25
C267 AP68 3e ultra & lt bl .40 .25

Intl. Skiing Championships, Partillo, August 1966. A souvenir sheet of 2 contains imperf. stamps similar to Nos. C266-C267. No gum. Size: 109x140mm. Value, $30.

Ship Type of Regular Issue

1966 Litho. *Perf. 14½*
C268 A175 70c Prus grn & yel grn .35 .25

See note below No. 358.

A souvenir sheet of design A177 was issued imperforate in deep red. Size: 140x119mm. Value $10.

ICY Type of Regular Issue

1966, Oct. 28 Unwmk. *Perf. 14½*
C269 A177 3e blue & carmine .50 .25

A souvenir sheet of 2 contains imperf. stamps similar to Nos. 360 and C269. No gum. Size: 111x140mm. Value $7.50.

Chilean Flag and Ships — AP69

1966, Nov. 21 Litho. *Perf. 14*
C270 AP69 13c dull red brn .40 .25

Centenary of the city of Antofagasta.

Pardo Type of Regular Issue

40c, Pardo & map of Chile's claim to Antarctica.

1967, Jan. 6 Unwmk. *Perf. 14½*
C271 A178 40c ultra .50 .25

See note below No. 361.

Family Type of Regular Issue

1967, Apr. 13 Litho. *Perf. 14*
C272 A179 80c brt bl & blk .35 .25

Ruben Dario and Title Page of "Azul" AP70

1967, May 15 Engr. *Perf. 14½*
C273 AP70 10c dark blue .30 .25

Ruben Dario (pen name of Felix Ruben Garcia Sarmiento, 1867-1916), Nicaraguan poet, newspaper correspondent and diplomat.

Tree Type of Regular Issue

1967, June 9 Litho.
C274 A180 75c grn & pale rose .35 .25

Lions Type of Regular Issue

1967 Litho. *Perf. 14*
C275 A181 1e purple & yel .40 .25
C276 A181 5e blue & yel 1.10 .30

A souvenir sheet without franking value contains 3 imperf. stamps, 20c, 1e and 5e, in violet blue and yellow. Size: 110x140mm. Value, $13.50. Also exists with the stamps in violet. Value, $18.

Issue dates: 1e, July 12; 5e, Aug. 11.

Flag Type of Regular Issue

1967, Oct. 20 Unwmk. *Perf. 14½*
C277 A182 50c ultra & crimson .35 .25

ITY Emblem AP71

1967, Nov. 22 Litho. *Perf. 14½*
C278 AP71 30c lt vio bl & blk .35 .25

Issued for International Tourist Year, 1967.

Caro Type of Regular Issue, 1967

1967, Dec. 4 Engr. *Perf. 14½*
C279 A183 40c violet .70 .35

Type of Regular Issue, 1968

1968, Apr. 23 Litho. *Perf. 14½*
C280 A184 2e brt violet .60 .25

Sesquicentennial of the Battles of Chacabuco and Maipu. A souvenir sheet of 2 contains imperf. stamps similar to Nos. 367 and C280. Value, $12. A second sheet exists with the 2e in green and the 3e in brown. Size: 139½x100mm. Value, $12.

Another imperforate souvenir sheet was issued in 1971 with Nos. 399, C280 and C303 in original colors. Size: 120x150mm.

Farm Type of Regular Issue

1968, June 18 Unwmk.
C281 A185 50c blk, org & grn .35 .25

Juan I. Molina, Educator and Scientist AP72

1968, Aug. 27 Litho. *Perf. 14½*
C282 AP72 1e bright green .30 .25

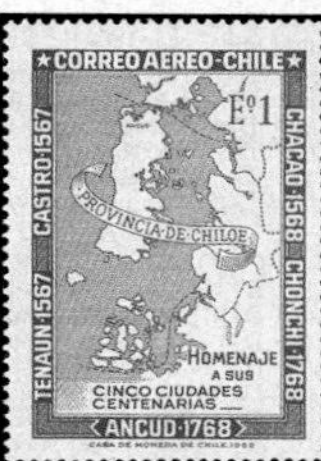

Map of Chiloé Province — AP73

Perf. 14½
1968, Oct. 7 Unwmk. Litho.
C283 AP73 1e rose claret .35 .35

Anniversaries of the founding of five towns in Chiloé Province.

Auto Club Type of Regular Issue

1968, Nov. 10 Engr. *Perf. 14½x14*
C284 A189 5e ultra .35 .25

British Crown and Map of Chile — AP74

50c, Chilean coat of arms (horiz.; similar to type A161). 3e, British coat of arms, horiz.

1968, Nov. 12 Litho. *Perf. 14½*
C285 AP74 50c green & brn .25 .25
C286 AP74 3e bl & org brn .40 .25

Engr.
C287 AP74 5e purple & mag .60 .25
Nos. C285-C287 (3) 1.25 .75

Visit of Queen Elizabeth II of Great Britain, Nov. 11-18. A souvenir sheet of 3 contains imperf., lithographed stamps similar to Nos. C285-C287. Size: 124½x190mm. The souvenir sheet also publicizes the British-Chilean Philatelic Exhibition. Value, $20.

First Coin Minted in Chile and Coin Press AP75

Design: 1e, Chile No. 128.

1968, Dec. 31 Litho. *Perf. 14½*
C288 AP75 50c ocher & vio brn .30 .25
C289 AP75 1e lt bl & dp org .30 .25

225th anniversary of the founding of the State Mint (Casa de Moneda de Chile).

A souvenir sheet of 4 contains imperf. stamps similar to Nos. 373-374, C288-C289. Size: 150x119mm. Value, $10.

Satellite Type of Regular Issue

1969, May 20 Litho. *Perf. 14½*
C290 A191 2e rose lilac .35 .30

Red Cross Type of Regular Issue

1969, Sept. Litho. *Perf. 14½*
C291 A192 5e black & red .50 .25

A souvenir card contains 2 imperf. stamps similar to Nos. 376 and C291, with red marginal inscription. Size: 109x140mm. Value $5.

Dam Type of Regular Issue

1969, Nov. 18 Litho. *Perf. 14½*
C292 A193 3e blue .50 .25

Rodriguez Type of Regular Issue

1969, Nov. 24
C293 A194 30c brown .35 .25

EXPO '70 Type of Regular Issue

1969, Dec. 1 Litho. *Perf. 14*
C294 A195 5e red .35 .25

Bible Type of 1969

1969, Dec. 2 *Perf. 14½*
C295 A196 1e green .30 .25

ILO Type of Regular Issue

1969, Dec. 17 *Perf. 14½*
C296 A197 2e rose lil & blk .35 .25

Human Rights Year Type of 1969

1969, Dec. 18
C297 A198 4e brown & red .35 .35

A souvenir sheet of 2 contains imperf. stamps similar to Nos. 382 and C297. Size: 110x140mm. Value, $9.

Easter Island Type of 1970

1970, Jan. 26
C298 A199 50c dull grnsh bl .70 .25

Ship Type of Regular Issue

1970, Feb. 4 Litho. *Perf. 14½*
C299 A200 2e deep ultra .40 .25

Rotary Type of Regular Issue

1970, Mar. 18 Litho. *Perf. 14*
C300 A201 1e rose claret .35 .25

Gandhi Type of Regular Issue

1970, Apr. 1 Litho. *Perf. 14½*
C301 A202 1e red brown .40 .25

Education Year Type of 1970

1970, July 17 Litho. *Perf. 14½*
C302 A204 4e red brown .30 .25

National Shrine Type of 1970

1970, July 28 Litho. *Perf. 14½*
C303 A205 1e ultra .35 .25

An imperforate souvenir sheet containing Nos. 399, C280, and C303 exists. Size: 120x150mm.

Cancer Type of Regular Issue

1970, Aug. 11
C304 A206 2e brn & lt olive .40 .25

A few stamps are known inscribed "Correos de Chile" instead of "Correos Aereo Chile." Value $350.

Copper Type of Regular Issue

1970, Oct. 21 Litho. *Perf. 14½*
C305 A207 3e grn & lt red brn .50 .25

United Nations Type of 1970

1970, Oct. 22
C306 A208 5e dk car & grn .50 .25

Freighter Type of Regular Issue

1971, Jan. 18 Litho. *Perf. 14*
C307 A209 5e lt red brown .50 .25

No. C290 Surcharged in Red

1971, Jan. 21 Litho. *Perf. 14½*
C308 A191 52c on 2e rose lil .40 .25

Liberation Type of Regular Issue

1971, Feb. 3 *Perf. 14½*
C309 A210 1e blue gray & vio brn .40 .25

UNICEF Type of Regular Issue

1971, Feb. 11 Litho. *Perf. 14½*

C310	A211	2e blue & grn	.30	.25

Boy Scout Type of Regular Issue

1971, Feb. 10 *Perf. 14*

C311	A212	5c dk car & ol	.40	.25

Satellite Type of Regular Issue

1971, May 25 Litho. *Perf. 14½*

C312	A213	2e brown	.40	.25

De Ercilla Type of Regular Issue

1972, Mar. 20 Engr. *Perf. 14*

C313	A221	2e Prussian blue	.30	.25

A souvenir card contains impressions of Nos. 414 and C313 with black marginal inscription commemorating España 75 Philatelic Exhibition. Size: 165x220mm. Value $19.

AIR POST SEMI-POSTAL STAMPS

Catalogue values for unused stamps in this section are for Never Hinged items.

Type of Semi-Postal Stamps, 1961

Portraits: 10c+10c, Alonso de Ercilla. 20c+20c, Gabriela Mistral.

Perf. 13x12½

1961, Apr. 29 Photo. Unwmk.

CB1	SP3	10c + 10c salmon & choc	1.00	.30
CB2	SP3	20c + 20c gray & dp cl	1.00	.30

Printed without charge by the Spanish Mint as a gift to Chile. The surtax was to aid the 1960 earthquake victims and to increase teachers' salaries.

ACKNOWLEDGMENT OF RECEIPT STAMPS

AR1

1894 Unwmk. *Perf. 11½*

H1	AR1	5c brown	3.00	*4.00*
a.		Imperf., pair	20.00	
b.		Pair, imperf. vert. or horiz.	20.00	

The black stamp of design similar to AR1 inscribed "Avis de Paiement" was prepared for use on notices of payment of funds but was not regularly issued. Value, $5.

A black stamp of design AR1 exists. Value $30.

POSTAGE DUE STAMPS

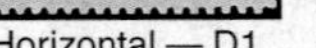
Horizontal — D1

Vertical — D2

Horizontal

Handstamped

1894 Unwmk. *Perf. 13*

J1	D1	2c black, *straw*	19.00	19.00
J2	D1	4c black, *straw*	19.00	19.00
J3	D1	6c black, *straw*	19.00	19.00
J4	D1	8c black, *straw*	19.00	19.00
J5	D2	10c black, *straw*	19.00	19.00
J6	D1	16c black, *straw*	19.00	19.00
J7	D1	20c black, *straw*	19.00	19.00
J8	D1	30c black, *straw*	19.00	19.00
J9	D1	40c black, *straw*	19.00	19.00
		Nos. J1-J9 (9)	171.00	171.00
J1a	D1	2c black, *yellow*	60.00	60.00
J2a	D1	4c black, *yellow*	40.00	40.00
J3a	D1	6c black, *yellow*	30.00	30.00
J4a	D1	8c black, *yellow*	19.00	19.00
J5a	D2	10c black, *yellow*	19.00	19.00
J6a	D1	16c black, *yellow*	19.00	19.00
J7a	D1	20c black, *yellow*	19.00	19.00
J8a	D1	30c black, *yellow*	19.00	19.00
J9a	D1	40c black, *yellow*	19.00	19.00
		Nos. J1a-J9a (9)	244.00	244.00

Vertical

J1b	D1	2c black, *straw*	27.50	27.50
J2b	D1	4c black, *straw*	27.50	27.50
J3b	D1	6c black, *straw*	27.50	27.50
J4b	D1	8c black, *straw*	27.50	27.50
J5b	D2	10c black, *straw*	27.50	27.50
J6b	D1	16c black, *straw*	27.50	27.50
J7b	D1	20c black, *straw*	27.50	27.50
J8b	D1	30c black, *straw*	27.50	27.50
J9b	D1	40c black, *straw*	27.50	27.50
		Nos. J1b-J9b (9)	247.50	247.50
J1c	D1	2c black, *yellow*	85.00	85.00
J2c	D1	4c black, *yellow*	57.50	57.50
J3c	D1	6c black, *yellow*	42.50	42.50
J4c	D1	8c black, *yellow*	27.50	27.50
J5c	D2	10c black, *yellow*	27.50	27.50
J6c	D1	16c black, *yellow*	27.50	27.50
J7c	D1	20c black, *yellow*	27.50	27.50
J8c	D1	30c black, *yellow*	27.50	27.50
J9c	D1	40c black, *yellow*	27.50	27.50
		Nos. J1c-J9c (9)	350.00	350.00

Counterfeits exist.

D3

1895 Litho. *Perf. 11*

J19	D3	1c red, *yellow*	7.50	5.50
J20	D3	2c red, *yellow*	7.50	5.50
J21	D3	4c red, *yellow*	7.50	5.50
J22	D3	6c red, *yellow*	7.50	5.50
J23	D3	8c red, *yellow*	7.50	5.50
J24	D3	10c red, *yellow*	7.50	5.50
J25	D3	20c red, *yellow*	7.50	5.50
J26	D3	40c red, *yellow*	7.50	5.50
J27	D3	50c red, *yellow*	7.50	5.50
J28	D3	60c red, *yellow*	7.50	5.50
J29	D3	80c red, *yellow*	7.50	5.50
J30	D3	1p red, *yellow*	13.00	13.00
		Nos. J19-J30 (12)	95.50	73.50

Nos. J19-J30 were printed in sheets of 100 (10x10) containing all 12 denominations.

Counterfeits of Nos. J19-J42 exist, but usually are perforated 11½ or 14.

No. J19 was surcharge '10c' in a circle. This surcharge was never issued. Value, $13.

1896 *Perf. 13½*

J31	D3	1c red, *straw*	1.50	.90
J32	D3	2c red, *straw*	1.50	.90
J33	D3	4c red, *straw*	1.50	.90
J34	D3	6c red, *straw*	1.50	.90
J35	D3	8c red, *straw*	1.50	.90
J36	D3	10c red, *straw*	1.50	.90
J37	D3	20c red, *straw*	1.50	.90
J38	D3	40c red, *straw*	13.50	7.50
J39	D3	50c red, *straw*	13.50	7.50
J40	D3	60c red, *straw*	13.50	7.50
J41	D3	80c red, *straw*	20.00	12.00
J42	D3	100c red, *straw*	20.00	12.00
		Nos. J31-J42 (12)	91.00	52.80

Counterfeits are perforated 11½ or 14.

D4

1898 *Perf. 13*

J43	D4	1c scarlet	.60	.50
J44	D4	2c scarlet	1.25	1.00
J45	D4	4c scarlet	.60	.50
J46	D4	10c scarlet	.60	.50
J47	D4	20c scarlet	.60	.50
		Nos. J43-J47 (5)	3.65	3.00

Counterfeits are perforated 11½ or 14.

D5

1924 *Perf. 12½*

J48	D5	2c blue & red	.60	1.75
J49	D5	4c blue & red	.60	1.75
J50	D5	8c blue & red	.60	1.75
J51	D5	10c blue & red	.60	1.75
J52	D5	20c blue & red	.60	1.75
J53	D5	40c blue & red	.60	1.75
J54	D5	60c blue & red	.60	1.75
J55	D5	80c blue & red	.60	1.75
J56	D5	1p blue & red	1.50	5.50
J57	D5	2p blue & red	2.75	7.50
J58	D5	5p blue & red	3.75	7.50
		Nos. J48-J58 (11)	12.80	34.50
		Set, never hinged	26.00	

Nos. J48-J58 were printed in sheets of 150 containing all 11 denominations, and a second printing was printed in sheets of 50 containing the five lower denominations, providing various se-tenants. Stamps from the second printing are of a slightly different shades, with the red appearing pinkish. Second printing stamps are worth 2.5x first printing stamps.

All values of this issue exist imperforate, also with center inverted, but are not believed to have been regularly issued. Those with inverted centers sell for about 10 times normal stamps.

Counterfeits are perforated 11½.

OFFICIAL STAMPS

Nos. O1A-O16 are departmental Official stamps for use by the Navy department.

Nos. 69-71, Handstamped

1906 Unwmk. *Perf. 12*

O1A	A14	2c carmine	175.00	—
O1B	A14	3c yel brn	175.00	—
O1C	A14	5c ultra	175.00	—

Nos. O1A-O1C exist with inverted or vertical overprints, and as pairs, one without overprint.

Counterfeits exist.

O1

Single-lined frame
Control number in violet

1907 *Imperf.*

O1	O1	dl bl, "CARTA" org	*175.00*	*175.00*
O2	O1	red, "OFICIO" bl	*350.00*	*250.00*
O3	O1	vio, "PAQUETE" red	*250.00*	*250.00*
O4	O1	org, *bl,* "EP" vio	*300.00*	*260.00*
		Nos. O1-O4 (4)	*1,075.*	*935.00*

The diagonal inscription in differing color indicates type of usage: CARTA for letters of ordinary weight; OFICIO, heavy letters to 100 grams; PAQUETE, parcels to 100 grams; E P (Encomienda Postal), heavier parcels; C (Certificado), as on No. O8, registration including postage.

Varieties include CARTA, PAQUETE and E P inverted, OFICIO omitted, etc.

Reprints lack control number.

Double-lined frame
Large control number in black

Perf. 11

O5	O1	bl, "CARTA" yel	90.00	60.00
O6	O1	red, "OFICIO" bl	160.00	80.00
O7	O1	brn, "PAQUETE" grn	160.00	80.00
O8	O1	grn, "C" red	*1,100.*	*600.00*
		Nos. O5-O8 (4)	1,510.	820.00

Nos. O5-O8 exist in tête bêche pairs; with CARTA, OFICIO or PAQUETE double or inverted, and other varieties.

Counterfeits of Nos. O1-O8 exist.

Reprints lack control number.

Regular Issues of 1892-1909 Overprinted in Red — a

On Stamps of 1904-09

1907 *Perf. 12*

O9	A14	1c green	50.00	*85.00*
a.		Inverted overprint	*75.00*	
O10	A12	3c on lp brn	80.00	*120.00*
a.		Inverted overprint	*150.00*	
O11	A14	5c ultra	60.00	*95.00*
a.		Inverted overprint	*120.00*	
O12	A15	10c gray & blk	65.00	*125.00*
O13	A15	15c vio & blk	65.00	*125.00*
O14	A15	20c org brn & blk	65.00	*125.00*
O15	A15	50c ultra & blk	125.00	*200.00*

On Stamp of 1892

Rouletted

O16	A6	1p dk brn & blk	375.00	*550.00*
		Nos. O9-O16 (8)	885.00	*1,425.*

Counterfeits of Nos. O9-O16 exist.

Regular Issues of 1915-25 Overprinted in Red or Blue

b

Nos. O21-O22

1926 *Perf. 13½x14, 14*

O17	A52	5c slate bl (R)	2.50	1.60
O18	A50	10c bl & blk (R)	4.25	2.00
O19	A39	20c org red & blk (Bl)	4.25	2.00
O20	A42	50c dp grn & blk (Bl)	2.10	1.50
O21	A43	1p grn & blk (R)	4.25	2.00
O22	A43	2p ver & blk (Bl)	6.25	3.00
		Nos. O17-O22 (6)	23.60	12.10
		Set, never hinged	42.50	

Nos. O21 and O22 are overprinted vertically at each side.

Nos. O17 to O22 were for the use of the Biblioteca Nacional.

1928 Wmk. 215

O22A	A42	50c dp grn & blk (Bl), #157	30.00	14.00

Regular Issue of 1915-25 Overprinted in Red — c

1928 Unwmk. *Perf. 13½x14, 14*

O23	A50	10c bl & blk	6.50	4.00
O24	A39	20c brn org & blk	6.25	4.00
O25	A40	25c dl bl & blk	10.00	6.00
O26	A42	50c dp grn & blk	10.00	6.00
O27	A43	1p grn & blk	10.00	6.00
		Nos. O23-O27 (5)	42.75	26.00
		Set, never hinged	120.00	

The overprint on Nos. O23 to O26 is 16½mm high; on No. O27 it is 20mm.

Regular Issues of 1928-30 Overprinted in Red — d

On Stamp Inscribed: "Correos de Chile"

1930-31

O28 A50 10c bl & blk, #173 2.50 1.25

On Stamp Inscribed: "Chile Correos"

O28A A42 50c dp grn & blk, #137 2.50 1.00

Wmk. 215

On Stamps Inscribed: "Correos de Chile"

O29 A50 10c bl & blk, #164 4.25 2.10
O29A A50 10c bl & blk, #170 4.25 2.00
O30 A39 20c org red & blk, #166 2.25 1.10
O31 A40 25c bl & blk, #167 2.25 1.10
O32 A42 50c dp grn & blk, #169 2.60 1.30

On Stamps Inscribed: "Chile Correos"

O33 A42 50c dp grn & blk, #157 2.60 1.30
O34 A43 1p grn & blk, #158 2.25 1.25
Nos. O28-O34 (7) 18.70 9.40
Set, never hinged 50.00

No. 181 Overprinted in Red

1933 ***Perf. 13½x14***
O35 A61 20c brown 2.50 1.25

No. 182 Overprinted in Red

1935 **Wmk. 215**
O36 A62 10c deep blue 4.25 2.25

No. 163 Overprinted in Red

Inscribed: "Correos de Chile"

1934
O37 A52 5c lt grn 1.75.75

No. 182 Overprinted in Red

1935
O38 A62 10c dp bl 1.75 .75

Same Overprint in Black on No. 181

1936 ***Perf. 13½x14***
O39 A61 20c dk brn 11.00 2.00

No. 158 Overprinted in Red

1938 ***Perf. 14***
O40 A43 1p grn & blk 4.25 2.10

Nos. 204 and 205 Overprinted Type "d" in Black

1939 ***Perf. 13½x14, 14***
O41 A78 50c violet 6.25 3.25
O42 A84 1p org brn 6.25 3.25

Stamps of 1938-40 Overprinted in Black, Red or Blue

1940-45 ***Perf. 13½x14, 14***
O43 A78 10c sal pink ('45) 2.50 1.25
O44 A78 15c brn org 1.25 .40
O45 A78 20c lt bl (R) ('42) 1.25 .60
O46 A78 30c brt pink (Bl) .90 .40
O47 A78 40c lt grn .90 .40
O48 A78 50c vio ('45) 2.50 1.00
O49 A84 1p org brn ('42) 3.75 1.75
O50 A84 1.80p dp bl (R) ('45) 10.00 7.50
O51 A84 2p car lake ('42) 2.50 1.25
Nos. O43-O51 (9) 25.55 14.55
Set, never hinged 50.00

Overprint "b" in Black on Nos. 223, 225

Unwmk.

O58 A84 1p brn org 5.00 2.00
O59 A84 2p car lake ('46) 5.00 2.00

Catalogue values for unused stamps in this section, from this point to the end of the section, are for Never Hinged items.

Regular Issues of 1938-43 Overprinted Diagonally in Carmine, Black or Blue — e

Wmk. 215, Unwmkd.

1948-54 ***Perf. 13½x14, 14***
O60 A78 20c lt bl, #219 (C) 1.25 .40
O61 A78 30c brt pink, #202 (Bl) ('54) 1.75 1.00
O62 A78 40c brt grn, #203 ('54) 6.75 2.50
O63 A78 50c vio #222 ('49) 1.60 .40
O64 A84 1p org brn, #205 4.25 1.10
O65 A84 2p car lake, #207 ('54) 5.00 1.10
O66 A84 5p dk sl grn, #208 (C) ('51) 5.00 1.10
Nos. O60-O66 (7) 25.60 7.60

Overprint "e" Diagonally on Nos. 265 and 275 in Red or Black

Wmk. 215, Unwmkd.

1953-55 ***Perf. 13½x14, 13x14***
O67 A126 1p dk bl grn, #265 (R) 1.25 .40
O68 A126 1p dk bl grn, #265 (Bk) ('55) 1.00 .40
O69 A126 1p dk bl grn, #275 (R) ('55) 1.00 .40
Nos. O67-O69 (3) 3.25 1.20

Overprint "e" Horizontally on Nos. 207, 209 in Black or Blue

1955-56 **Wmk. 215** ***Perf. 14***
O70 A84 2p car lake ('56) 4.25 1.25
O71 A84 10p rose vio (Bl) 6.75 1.75

Overprint "e" Horizontally on Nos. 293-295 and Types of 1956 Regular Issue in Black or Red

1956 **Unwmk.** ***Perf. 14x14½***
O72 A141 2p purple 2.50 .70
O73 A142 3p lt vio bl (R) 8.00 2.50
O74 A141 5p redsh brn 1.50 .35
O75 A142 10p vio (19x22¼mm) (R) 1.25 .40
a. Perf. 13½x14 (19½x22½mm) ('58) 8.00 1.75
O76 A141 50p rose red 5.00 1.75

No. 298 was overprinted, however it was never released.

No. 310 Overprinted in Red Vertically, Reading Down, Similar to Type "e"

Size of Overprint: 21x2½mm

1958 **Litho.** ***Perf. 14***
O77 A149 10p vio blue *125.00 42.50*

Overprint "e" Horizontally on No. 327 in Red

1960 **Unwmk.** ***Perf. 13x14***
O79 A157 5c blue 4.25 1.25

POSTAL TAX STAMPS

Catalogue values for unused stamps in this section are for Never Hinged items.

Talca Issue.

A 10c blue postal tax stamp, inscribed "Bicentenario de Talca" and picturing a coat of arms, was issued in 1942. It was sold only in Talca and was required for a time on all domestic letters sent from that city. The tax helped pay for Talca's bicentenary celebration. Value 20 cents.

Nos. 326 and 347 Surcharged

1970 **Unwmk.** **Litho.** ***Perf. 14x13***
RA1 A159 10c on 2c ultra .25 .25

Perf. 14x14½
RA2 A170 10c on 6c rose lil .25 .25

Chilean Arms — PT1

Perf. 14½x14
1970, Apr. 23 **Litho.** **Unwmk.**
RA3 PT1 10c blue .30 .25

See No. RA6.

No. RA3 Surcharged in Red

a b

1971-72
RA4 PT1 (a) 15c on 10c bl .75 .40
RA5 PT1 (b) 15c on 10c bl ('72) .30 .25

Type of 1970

1972, July **Litho.** ***Perf. 14½x14***
RA6 PT1 15c rose red .30 .25

No. RA6 Surcharged in Ultramarine

1972-73
RA7 PT1 20c on 15c rose red .30 .25
RA8 PT1 50c on 15c rose red ('73) .30 .25

No. RA8 has 9 bars instead of 8.

The surtax on Nos. RA1-RA8 was for modernization of postal system. Compulsory on all inland mail.

PARCEL POST POSTAL TAX STAMP

Catalogue values for unused stamps in this section are for Never Hinged items.

Pres. J. J. Prieto V. — PPT1

Unwmk.

1957, Apr. 8 **Litho.** ***Perf. 14***
QRA1 PPT1 15p green .35 .30

The surtax aided the Prieto Foundation. No. QRA1 was required on parcel post entering or leaving Chile.

CHINA

'chī-nə

LOCATION — Eastern Asia
GOVT. — Republic
AREA — 2,903,475 sq. mi.
POP. — 462,798,093 (1948)

10 Candareen = 1 Mace
10 Mace = 1 Tael
100 Cents = 1 Dollar (Yuan) (1897)

Watermarks

Wmk. 103 — Yin-Yang Symbol

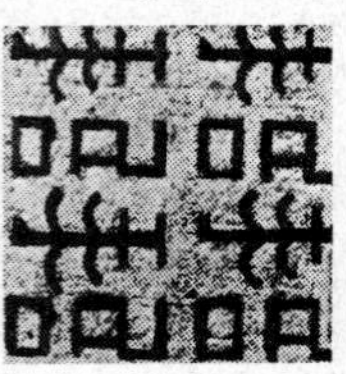

Wmk. 261 — Character Yu (Post) Multiple

Issues of the Imperial Maritime Customs Post

Imperial Dragon — A1

1878 Unwmk. Typo. *Perf. 12½*

Thin Paper

Stamps printed 2½-3¼mm apart

1	A1	1c green	725.00	400.00
b.		1c yellow green	750.00	425.00
2	A1	3c brown red	1,100.	400.00
3	A1	5c orange	1,450.	600.00

Imperforate essays of Nos. 1-3 have an extra circle near the dragon's lower left foot. Examples with the circle completely or mostly removed are proofs or unfinished stamps.

1882

Thin Paper

Stamps printed 4½mm apart

4	A1	1c green	600.00	400.00
5	A1	3c brown red	1,100.	400.00
6	A1	5c orange yellow	20,000.	1,500.

Nos. 4-5 exist on both thin paper and medium paper. Both are of equal value.

Nos. 4-5 sometimes show portions of papermaker's watermark "Monckton Kent."

1883 *Rough to smooth Perf. 12½*

Medium to Thick Opaque Paper

Stamps printed 2½ to 3¼mm apart

7	A1	1c green	675.00	475.00
c.		Vert. pair, imperf. between	*160,000.*	
8	A1	3c brown red	1,150.	400.00
b.		Vert. pair, imperf. between		*230,000.*
d.		3c dark vermilion	1,600.	400.00
9	A1	5c yellow	1,850.	650.00
b.		Horiz. pair, imperf. btwn. (rough)		*60,000.*
c.		Vert. pair, imperf. btwn. (smooth)		*60,000.*

Nos. 1-9 were printed from plates of 25, 20 or 15 individual copper dies, but only No. 5 exists in the 15-die setting. Many different printings and plate settings exist. All values occur in a wide variety of shades and papers. The effect of climate on certain papers has produced the varieties on so-called toned papers in Nos. 1-15.

Nos. 7-9 were printed with smooth perforations until mid-1885 when the pins became blunt. Stamps with rough perfs are worth approximately 30 percent more than stamps with smooth perfs.

Value for No. 8b is for a damaged example.

Counterfeits, frequently with forged cancellations, occur in all early Chinese issues.

Imperial Dragon — A2

1885 Wmk. 103 *Perf. 12½*

10	A2	1c green	175.00	110.00
a.		Vert. pair, imperf. btwn.	*20,000.*	*17,500.*
b.		Horiz. pair, imperf. btwn.		—
11	A2	3c lilac	400.00	140.00
a.		Horiz. pair, imperf. btwn.	*22,000.*	*17,500.*
b.		Vert. pair, imperf. btwn.		*24,000.*
12	A2	5c grnsh yellow	425.00	140.00
a.		5c bister brown	700.00	175.00
b.		Vert. pair, imperf. btwn.	*24,000.*	*24,000.*
c.		Horiz. pair, imperf. btwn.		*52,500.*
		Nos. 10-12 (3)	1,000.	390.00

Nos. 10-12 exist with rough and smooth perforations. Examples with smooth perfs are worth approximately 10 percent more than stamps with rough perfs.

1888 *Perf. 11½-12*

13	A2	1c green	85.00	60.00
14	A2	3c lilac	200.00	125.00
b.		Double impression		*1,100.*
15	A2	5c grnsh yellow	300.00	175.00
b.		Horiz. pair, imperf. vert.		*50,000.*
c.		Double impression	1,100.	1,100.
		Nos. 13-15 (3)	585.00	360.00

Nos. 10-15 were printed from plates made of 40 individual copper dies, arranged in two panes of 20 each. Several different settings exist of all values.

Nos. 10d and 13b have a smaller design, measuring 19mmx22mm. The regular design size is 19¼mmx22¼mm.

Imperforates of Nos. 13-15 are considered proofs by most authorities.

Stamps overprinted "Formosa" in English or Chinese are proofs.

For surcharges see Nos. 25-27, 75-77.

"Shou" and "Wu Fu" — A3

Dragon and Hydrangea Leaves — A4

"Pa Kua" Signs in Corners — A5

Dragon and Peony — A6

Carp, the Messenger Fish — A7

Dragon, "Pa Kua" and Immortelle A8

Dragons and "Shou" A9

Dragons and Giant Peony — A10

Junk on the Yangtse A11

1894 Lithographed in Shanghai

16	A3	1c orange red	60.00	*50.00*
a.		Vert. pair, imperf. btwn.	*4,500.*	*3,500.*
b.		Horiz. pair, imperf. btwn.	*17,500.*	*12,000.*
c.		Vert. pair, imperf. horiz.	*3,250.*	*3,250.*
17	A4	2c green	65.00	55.00
a.		Horiz. pair, imperf. btwn.	*3,750.*	*3,500.*
18	A5	3c orange	57.50	30.00
a.		Vert. pair, imperf. btwn.	*3,350.*	*3,500.*
b.		Horiz. pair, imperf. btwn.	*5,000.*	*13,340.*
19	A6	4c rose pink	225.00	*250.00*
a.		Horiz. pair, imperf. btwn.	*14,000.*	
20	A7	5c dull orange	350.00	*400.00*
a.		Horiz. pair, imperf. btwn.	*18,000.*	*18,000.*
21	A8	6c dark brown	175.00	70.00
a.		Vert. pair, imperf. btwn.	*26,500.*	
b.		Horiz. pair, imperf. btwn.	*15,000.*	
22	A9	9c dark green	200.00	135.00
a.		Imperf., pair	*2,250.*	
b.		Horiz. pair, imperf. vert.	*4,250.*	*3,750.*
c.		Vert. pair, imperf. horiz.	*5,000.*	
d.		Vert. pair, imperf. btwn.	*4,750.*	*4,250.*
e.		Tete beche pair, vert.	*2,000.*	*1,800.*
f.		Tete beche pair, imperf. horiz.	*5,500.*	
g.		Tete beche pair, imperf. vert.	*5,500.*	*4,750.*
h.		Vert. strip of 3, imperf. btwn.	*5,500.*	
i.		Tete beche pair, horiz.	*1,500.*	*1,300.*
23	A10	12c brown orange	700.00	300.00
b.		Vert. pair, imperf. btwn.	—	
24	A11	24c carmine	900.00	400.00
a.		Vert. pair, imperf. btwn.	*37,500.*	—
b.		Horiz. pair, imperf. btwn.		—
		Nos. 16-24 (9)	2,733.	1,690.

60th birthday of Tsz'e Hsi, the Empress Dowager. All values exist in several distinct shades.

On Mar. 20, 1896, the Customs Post was changed, by Imperial Edict, effective Jan. 1, 1897, to a National Post and the dollar was adopted as the unit of currency.

Time was required to work out details of the Imperial Post and design new stamps. As a provisional measure, stocks of Nos. 16-24 were ordered surcharged with new values in dollars and cents. It is believed that only the Shanghai office stock of Nos. 16-24 (plus any reserve stock at the printers) was surcharged with small figures of value. Other post offices throughout China were instructed to return all unoverprinted stocks on receipt of the new surcharges.

Early in the year it was apparent that all stamps would be exhausted before the new issues were ready (Nos. 86-97), and since the stones from which Nos. 16-24 had been printed no longer existed, new stones were made from the original transfers. A printing from the new stones was made early in 1897 and surcharged with large figures of value spaced 2½mm below the Chinese characters. During the surcharging, sheets from the 1894 (original) printing were received from outlying post offices and surcharged as they arrived. A small quantity of the 1897 printing reached the public without surcharge (Nos. 16n-24n).

Additional stamps were still required and another printing was made from the new stones and surcharged with large figures, but in a new setting with 1½mm between the Chinese characters and the value. Additional sheets of the 1894 printing were received from the most distant post offices and were also surcharged with the 1½mm setting. Thus there are four different sets of the large-figure surcharges. All these stamps were regularly issued but no attempt was made by the post office to separate printings. Some values are difficult to distinguish as to printing, particularly in used condition.

See No. 73. For surcharges see Nos. 28-72, 74.

1897 Lithographed in Shanghai

16n	A3	1c pink	*1,300.*
17n	A4	2c olive green	*1,300.*
18n	A5	3c chrome yellow	*1,000.*
p.		3c yellow buff	*1,100.*
19n	A6	4c pale rose	*1,000.*
20n	A7	5c yellow	*1,000.*
21n	A8	6c red brown	*1,100.*
22n	A9	9c yellowish green	*5,500.*
p.		9c emerald green	—
23n	A10	12c yellowish orange	*6,000.*
24n	A11	24c purplish red	*4,750.*

The colors of the 1897 printings are pale or dull; the gum is thin and white. The 1894 printing has a thicker, yellowish gum.

The set of 9 values on thick unwatermarked paper is a special printing of 5,000 sets ordered by P. G. von Mollendorf, a Customs official, for presentation purposes. Value, set $3,100.

For surcharges see Nos. 47-55, 65-72.

Issues of the Chinese Government Post

Preceding Issues Surcharged in Black

Small Numerals 2½mm Below Chinese Characters

Surcharged on Nos. 13-15

1897, Jan. 2 *Perf. 11½-12*

25	A2	1c on 1c	115.00	*85.00*
26	A2	2c on 3c	475.00	120.00
a.		Double surcharge	—	
27	A2	5c on 5c	150.00	57.50
		Nos. 25-27 (3)	740.00	262.50

Surcharged on Nos. 16-24

On No. 28 the "½" is 3mm high.

28	A5	½c on 3c	45.00	35.00
a.		"1" instead of "½"	750.00	375.00
b.		Horiz. pair, imperf. btwn.	*11,000.*	
c.		Vert. pair, imperf. horiz.	*11,000.*	—
d.		Double surcharge	*15,000.*	*17,000.*
e.		Vert. pair, imperf. btwn.	*11,000.*	
29	A3	1c on 1c	45.00	30.00
a.		Inverted surcharge	*50,000.*	*10,000.*
30	A4	2c on 2c	40.00	22.50
a.		Horiz. pair, imperf. vert.	*8,500.*	
b.		Vert. pair, imperf. btwn.	*8,750.*	*8,750.*
c.		Double surcharge	*20,000.*	11,500.
d.		Inverted surcharge	—	*15,000.*
e.		Horiz. pair, imperf. btwn.	*16,000.*	
31	A6	4c on 4c	45.00	27.50
a.		Double surcharge	*30,000.*	*20,000.*
b.		Vert. pair, imperf. btwn.	*27,500.*	—
c.		Horiz. pair, imperf. btwn.	*15,000.*	*15,000.*
32	A7	5c on 5c	50.00	22.50
a.		Vert. pair, imperf. btwn.	*20,000.*	*16,750.*
33	A8	8c on 6c	60.00	35.00
a.		Vert. pair, imperf. btwn.	*6,750.*	*6,750.*
b.		Vert. strip of 3, imperf. btwn.	*15,000.*	—
c.		Horiz. pair, imperf. btwn.	*7,000.*	*5,000.*
e.		Horiz. pair, imperf. vert.	*7,000.*	*7,000.*
34	A8	10c on 6c	140.00	90.00
b.		Vert. pair, imperf. btwn.	*11,750.*	*2,500.*
c.		Horiz. pair, imperf. vert.	*2,400.*	*2,400.*
d.		On #21c	150.00	100.00
35	A9	10c on 9c	475.00	200.00
a.		Double surcharge	*70,000.*	*40,000.*
b.		Inverted surcharge	*950,000.*	—
36	A10	10c on 12c	500.00	225.00
a.		Vert. pair, imperf. horiz.	*4,000.*	
b.		Vert. pair, imperf. btwn.	*4,500.*	*4,500.*
c.		Horiz. pair, imperf. btwn.	*6,000.*	
37	A11	30c on 24c	600.00	240.00
a.		Vert. pair, imperf. btwn.	*20,000.*	*20,000.*
		Nos. 28-37 (10)	2,000.	927.50

Small Numerals 4mm Below Chinese Characters

25a	A2	1c on 1c green	350.00	*100.00*
28f	A4	½c on 3c orange	400.00	400.00
i.		½c on 3c olive yellow	450.00	450.00
29b	A3	1c on 1c vermilion	500.00	400.00
30f	A4	2c on 2c dark green	600.00	500.00
31d	A6	4c on 4c dark pink	700.00	500.00
32b	A7	5c on 5c dull orange	800.00	600.00
33d	A8	8c on 6c brown	800.00	500.00
35c	A9	10c on 9c dark green	1,000.	700.00
37b	A11	30c on 24c dark red	1,200.	900.00

Preceding Issues Surcharged in Black

No. 38 the "½" is 4mm high.

Large Numerals 2½mm below Chinese characters

Surcharged on Nos. 16-24

1897, Mar.

38	A5	½c on 3c	2,500.	875.00
b.		Inverted surcharge		*13,500.*
39	A3	1c on 1c	700.00	300.00
40	A4	2c on 2c	375.00	350.00
41	A6	4c on 4c	475.00	375.00
b.		Horiz. pair, imperf. btwn.	*15,000.*	
42	A7	5c on 5c	250.00	210.00
43	A8	8c on 6c	2,400.	1,750.
44	A9	10c on 9c	800.00	375.00
45	A10	10c on 12c	*87,500.*	3,400.
46	A11	30c on 24c	1,750.	1,300.
b.		2mm spacing between "30" and "cents."	*15,000.*	*2,000.*

Same Surcharge on Nos. 16n-24n

47	A5	½c on 3c	37.50	*40.00*
a.		"cen" for "cent"	850.00	700.00
b.		Vert. pair, imperf. btwn.	*6,750.*	*6,000.*
c.		Vert. pair, imperf. horiz.	2,400.	1,600.
d.		As "a" and "c"	*4,500.*	*4,500.*
e.		As "a" and "b"	*7,500.*	*7,500.*
f.		Horiz. pair, imperf. btwn.	*3,000.*	*3,000.*

48	A3	1c on 1c	40.00	25.00
a.		Horiz. pair, imperf. btwn.		*4,000.*
49	A4	2c on 2c	32.50	19.00
50	A6	4c on 4c	40.00	19.00
a.		Horiz. pair, imperf. btwn.	*13,500.*	*13,500.*
b.		Vert. pair, imperf. btwn.		*5,000.*
51	A7	5c on 5c	50.00	30.00
52	A8	8c on 6c	600.00	300.00
53	A9	10c on 9c	300.00	125.00
a.		10c on 9c emerald	400.00	150.00
b.		Pair, one without surcharge	*3,000.*	*2,500.*
54	A10	10c on 12c	375.00	90.00
55	A11	30c on 24c	1,200.	400.00
a.		2mm spacing btwn "30" and "cents"	*1,700.*	750.00
b.		Vert. pair, imperf. btwn.	*17,500.*	*17,500.*

All recorded unused examples of No. 45 are flawed.

Numerals 1½mm below Chinese characters

1897, May

Surcharged on Nos. 16-24

56	A5	½c on 3c org yel	525.00	350.00
57	A3	1c on 1c	350.00	290.00
58	A4	2c on 2c	175,000.	*6,000.*
59	A6	4c on 4c	290.00	240.00
60	A7	5c on 5c	375.00	290.00
61	A8	8c on 6c	1,600.	1,300.
62	A9	10c on 9c	350.00	240.00
63	A10	10c on 12c	1,600.	1,000.
64	A11	30c on 24c	*80,000.*	—

Same Surcharge on Nos. 16n-24n

65	A5	½c on 3c	25.00	*30.00*
a.		Inverted surcharge	*4,500.*	*4,500.*
b.		½mm spacing	*8,000.*	*8,000.*
c.		"t." of "cent." missing	—	—
d.		Horiz. pair, imperf. between	*10,000.*	
66	A3	1c on 1c	40.00	25.00
67	A4	2c on 2c	35.00	17.50
a.		Inverted surcharge	*17,500.*	*8,750.*
b.		Vert. pair, imperf. btwn.		*20,000.*
68	A6	4c on 4c	300.00	225.00
a.		Inverted surcharge	3,000.	2,000.
69	A7	5c on 5c	300.00	225.00
70	A9	10c on 9c	225.00	110.00
a.		Inverted surcharge	3,000.	2,000.
71	A10	10c on 12c	400.00	225.00
72	A11	30c on 24c	*13,000.*	2,500.

Same Surcharge (1½mm Spacing) on Type A12, and

A12

A12a

Redrawn Designs Printed from New Stones

1897

73	A12	½c on 3c yel	250.00	190.00
a.		½mm spacing	*6,000.*	*4,000.*
74	A12a	2c on 2c yel grn	75.00	35.00
a.		Horiz. pair, imperf. btwn.	*10,000.*	*5,000.*

Nos. 73 and 74 were surcharged on stamps printed from new stones, which differ slightly from the originals. On No. 73 the numeral "3" and symbols in the four corner panels have been enlarged and strengthened. On No. 74, the numeral "2" has a thick, flat base.

Surcharged on Nos. 13-15

75	A2	1c on 1c green	500.00	*625.00*
a.		On #13b	550.00	*575.00*
76	A2	2c on 3c lilac	1,100.	*1,200.*
77	A2	5c on 5c grnsh yel	375.00	*525.00*

Revenue Stamps Surcharged in Black

A13

a

b

c

d

e

f

g

1897 Unwmk. *Perf. 12 to 15*

78	A13 (a)	1c on 3c red	525.00	350.00
a.		No period after "cent"	600.00	400.00
b.		Central character with large "box"	625.00	550.00
79	A13 (b)	2c on 3c red	850.00	450.00
a.		Inverted surcharge	*37,500.*	*27,500.*
b.		Inverted "S" in "CENTS"	*1,000.*	*600.00*
c.		No period after "CENTS"	*950.00*	*550.00*
d.		Comma after "CENTS"	*950.00*	*550.00*
e.		Double surcharge	*140,000.*	—
f.		Dbl. surch., both inverted	*150,000.*	
g.		Double surch. (blk & grn)	*220,000.*	
80	A13 (c)	2c on 3c red	500.00	400.00
81	A13 (d)	4c on 3c red	*75,000.*	*75,000.*
a.		Double surcharge (blk & vio)	*250,000.*	*250,000.*
82	A13 (e)	4c on 3c red	1,650.	800.00

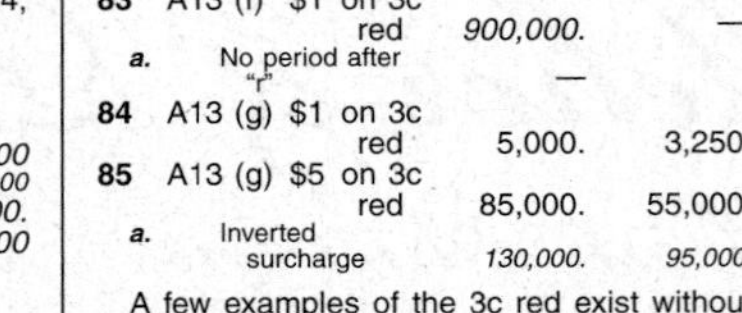

83	A13 (f)	$1 on 3c red	*900,000.*	—
a.		No period after "r"	—	
84	A13 (g)	$1 on 3c red	5,000.	3,250.
85	A13 (g)	$5 on 3c red	85,000.	55,000.
a.		Inverted surcharge	*130,000.*	*95,000.*

A few examples of the 3c red exist without surcharge; one canceled. Value, unused $85,000. No. 79 with green surcharge is a trial printing. Value, $220,000.

No. 79g is unique. The only canceled example of No. 83 is in a museum.

Normal spacing for No. 78 is 4mm between "one cent" and the Chinese character.

Dragon — A14

Carp — A15

Wild Goose — A16

"Imperial Chinese Post" Lithographed in Japan

Perf. 11, 11½, 12

1897, Aug. 16 Wmk. 103

86	A14	½c purple	7.00	4.50
a.		Horiz. pair, imperf. btwn.	*800.00*	
b.		Vert. pair, imperf. btwn.	*20,000.*	
87	A14	1c yellow	8.00	4.00
88	A14	2c orange	8.00	3.75
a.		Vert. pair, imperf. horiz.	—	
b.		Vert. pair, imperf. between	10.00	6.00
c.		2c orange red	10.00	5.00
89	A14	4c brown	11.00	3.75
a.		Horiz. pair, imperf. btwn.	*3,000.*	
b.		Horiz. pair, imperf. vert.	*3,000.*	
90	A14	5c rose red	14.00	5.00
91	A14	10c dk green	40.00	3.75
92	A15	20c maroon	85.00	19.00
93	A15	30c red	140.00	32.50
94	A15	50c yellow grn	100.00	45.00
a.		50c black green	1,750.	
b.		50c blue green	5,750.	
95	A16	$1 car & rose	325.00	200.00
a.		Horiz. pair, imperf. vert.	*8,000.*	
96	A16	$2 orange & yel	3,000.	1,600.
a.		Horiz. pair, imperf. vert.	*15,000.*	
97	A16	$5 yel grn & pink	1,800.	1,000.

The inner circular frames and outer frames of Nos. 86-91 differ for each denomination.

No. 97 imperforate and unwatermarked was not regularly issued. **Examples have been privately perforated and offered as No. 97.** Shades occur in most values of this issue.

A17

A18

A19

"Chinese Imperial Post" Engraved in London

1898 Wmk. 103 *Perf. 12 to 16*

98	A17	½c chocolate	6.00	4.00
a.		Vert. pair, imperf. btwn.	850.00	475.00
b.		Vert. pair, imperf. horiz.	850.00	475.00
99	A17	1c ocher	6.50	4.00
a.		Vert. pair, imperf. btwn.	300.00	250.00
b.		Horiz. pair, imperf. btwn.	400.00	350.00
100	A17	2c scarlet	8.00	4.00
a.		Vert. pair, imperf. btwn.	400.00	200.00
b.		Horiz. pair, imperf. vert.	400.00	200.00
101	A17	4c orange brn	7.50	4.00
a.		Vert. pair, imperf. btwn.	575.00	
b.		Horiz. pair, imperf. vert.	500.00	300.00
c.		Horiz. pair, imperf. btwn.	700.00	600.00
d.		Horiz. strip of 3, imperf. btwn.	2,250.	1,500.
102	A17	5c salmon	11.00	8.00
a.		Vert. pair, imperf. btwn.	400.00	300.00
b.		Horiz. pair, imperf. btwn.	775.00	500.00
c.		Vert. pair, imperf. horiz.	600.00	500.00
d.		5c pale reddish orange	16.00	5.50
e.		As "d," vert pair, imperf. btwn.	600.00	500.00
103	A17	10c dk blue grn	17.50	6.00
a.		Vert. or horiz, pair, imperf. btwn	—	—
104	A18	20c claret	70.00	9.00
a.		Horiz. pair, imperf. btwn.	850.00	750.00
b.		Vert. pair, imperf. horiz.	850.00	750.00
c.		Vert. pair, imperf. btwn.	900.00	800.00
105	A18	30c dull rose	60.00	15.00
a.		Horiz. pair, imperf. btwn.	*2,000.*	
b.		Vert. pair, imperf. horiz.	*1,750.*	
c.		Vert. pair, imperf. btwn.	*1,750.*	
106	A18	50c lt green	85.00	20.00
a.		Vert. pair, imperf. btwn.	*2,250.*	
107	A19	$1 red & pale rose	375.00	50.00
108	A19	$2 brn, red & yel	625.00	100.00
109	A19	$5 dp grn & sal	950.00	360.00
a.		Horiz. pair, imperf. btwn.	*77,500.*	
b.		Vert. pair, imperf. btwn.	*20,000.*	
		Nos. 98-109 (12)	2,222.	584.00

No. 98 surcharged "B. R. A.-5-Five Cents" in three lines in black or green, was surcharged by British military authorities shortly after the Boxer riots for use from military posts in an occupied area along the Peking-Mukden railway. Usually canceled in violet.

See note following No. 122.

1900(?)-06 Unwmk. *Perf. 12 to 16*

110	A17	½c brown	7.00	2.75
a.		Horiz. pair, imperf. btwn.	400.00	400.00
b.		Vert. pair, imperf. btwn.	400.00	400.00
111	A17	1c ocher	8.00	2.75
a.		Horiz. pair, imperf. btwn.	350.00	350.00
b.		Vert. pair, imperf. btwn.	350.00	350.00
c.		Vert. pair, imperf. horiz.	350.00	350.00
112	A17	2c scarlet	10.00	3.00
a.		Horiz. pair, imperf. btwn.	350.00	350.00
b.		Vert. pair, imperf. btwn.	350.00	350.00
c.		Vert. pair, imperf. horiz.	350.00	350.00
d.		Horiz. pair, imperf. vert.	350.00	350.00
e.		Vert. strip of 3, imperf. btwn.	1,000.	650.00
113	A17	4c orange brn	18.00	3.25
a.		Horiz. pair, imperf. btwn.	350.00	350.00
b.		Vert. pair, imperf. btwn.	350.00	350.00
114	A17	5c rose red	30.00	5.00
a.		Vert. pair, imperf. btwn.	350.00	350.00
b.		Vert. pair, imperf. horiz.	350.00	350.00
115	A17	5c orange	37.50	6.00
a.		5c yellow	450.00	100.00
b.		Vert. pair, imperf. btwn.	400.00	400.00
c.		Horiz. pair, imperf. btwn.	400.00	400.00
116	A17	10c green	40.00	2.75
a.		Vert. pair, imperf. btwn.	425.00	
b.		Horiz. pair, imperf. btwn.	725.00	
c.		Vert. pair, imperf. horiz.	425.00	
d.		Vert. strip of 3, imperf. btwn.	700.00	
117	A18	20c red brown	50.00	4.00
a.		Horiz. pair, imperf. btwn.	600.00	
b.		Vert. pair, imperf. btwn.	500.00	
c.		Vert. pair, imperf. horiz.	750.00	375.00
118	A18	30c dull red	50.00	4.00
a.		Vert. pair, imperf. btwn.	850.00	
119	A18	50c yellow grn	75.00	6.00
a.		Horiz. pair, imperf. btwn.	1,000.	
b.		Vert. pair, imperf. btwn.	*2,000.*	
120	A19	$1 red & pale rose ('06)	225.00	35.00
121	A19	$2 brn red & yel ('06)	450.00	75.00
122	A19	$5 dp grn & sal	875.00	250.00
		Nos. 110-122 (13)	1,876.	399.50

See No. 124-130. For surcharges and overprints see Nos. 123, 134-177, J1-J6, Offices in Tibet 1-11.

Diagonal Half of No. 112 Surcharged on Stamp and Envelope

1903

123	A17	1c on half of 2c scarlet, on cover		*1,500.*

Used Oct. 22 to Oct. 24. Value is for cover mailed to post office other than sending office (Foochow) and bearing backstamp showing arrival date. Locally addressed or unaddressed covers without backstamps properly used are worth approximately $900. Others are worth less.

Forgeries are plentiful, particularly on pieces of cover. Certificates of authenticity are mandatory.

1905-10

124	A17	2c green ('08)	3.25	3.25
a.		Horiz. pair, imperf. btwn.	350.00	350.00
b.		Vert. pair, imperf. btwn.	350.00	350.00
c.		Horiz. pair, imperf. vert.	350.00	350.00

d. Horiz. strip of 4, imperf. btwn. 800.00 *800.00*
125 A17 3c slate grn ('10) 8.00 2.50
a. Horiz. pair, imperf. btwn. 350.00
b. Vert. pair, imperf. btwn. 350.00
126 A17 4c vermilion ('09) 6.75 2.75
a. Vert. pair, imperf. btwn. 350.00 350.00
127 A17 5c violet 12.00 2.50
a. 5c lilac 10.00 2.75
b. Horiz. pair, imperf. btwn. 550.00
c. Vert. pair, imperf. btwn. 1,000.
d. Vert. pair, imperf. horiz. 600.00
128 A17 7c maroon ('10) 20.00 10.00
129 A17 10c ultra ('08) 25.00 2.75
a. Horiz. pair, imperf. btwn. 400.00 400.00
b. Vert. pair, imperf. btwn. 400.00
c. Vert. pair, imperf. horiz. 400.00 400.00
130 A18 16c olive grn ('07) 60.00 20.00
Nos. 124-130 (7) 135.00 43.75

Temple of Heaven, Peking — A20

1909 ***Perf. 14***

131 A20 2c orange & green 8.50 *10.00*
132 A20 3c orange & blue 10.00 *18.00*
133 A20 7c orange & brn vio 11.50 14.00
Nos. 131-133 (3) 30.00 *42.00*

1st year of the reign of Hsuan T'ung, who later became Henry Pu-yi and then Emperor Kang Teh of Manchukuo.

Stamps of 1902-10 Overprinted with Chinese Characters

Foochow Issue

Overprinted in Red or Black

1912 ***Perf. 12 to 16***

134 A17 3c slate grn (R) 300. 175.
135 A19 $1 red & pale rose 3,500. 2,500.
136 A19 $2 brn red & yel 6,000. 3,500.
137 A19 $5 dp grn & sal 7,250. 4,000.

The overprint "Ling Shih Chung Li" or "Provisional Neutrality," signified that the P.O. was conducted neutrally by agreement between the Manchu and opposing forces.

Nanking Issue

Overprinted in Red or Black

138 A17 1c ocher (R) 300. 190.
139 A17 3c slate grn (R) 300. 190.
140 A17 7c maroon 600. 400.
141 A18 16c olive grn (R) 3,500. 2,000.
142 A18 50c yellow grn (R) 3,750. 2,500.
143 A19 $1 red & pale rose 6,500. 2,250.
144 A19 $2 brn red & yel 7,500. 4,000.
145 A19 $5 dp green & sal 11,000. 9,000.

Vertical overprint reads: "Chung Hwa Min Kuo" (Republic of China).

Stamps of this issue were also used in Shanghai and Hankow.

Additional values were overprinted but not issued. Excellent forgeries of the overprints of Nos. 134-145 exist.

Issues of the Republic

Overprinted in Black or Red

Overprinted by the Maritime Customs Statistical Department, Shanghai

146 A17 ½c brown 1.50 1.25
a. Inverted overprint 60.00 50.00
b. Double overprint 100.00
147 A17 1c ocher (R) 2.25 1.25
a. Vert. pair, imperf. horiz. 200.00 200.00
b. Inverted overprint 225.00 150.00
c. Double overprint 225.00 200.00
d. Horiz. pair, imperf. btwn. 300.00 250.00
e. Horiz. pair, imperf. vert. 275.00
f. Pair, one without overprint 225.00
148 A17 2c green (R) 8.00 3.00
a. Vert. pair, imperf. btwn. 350.00 300.00
b. Horiz. pair, imperf. btwn. 350.00
149 A17 3c slate grn (R) 3.00 1.50
a. Inverted overprint 400.00 80.00
b. Horiz. pair, imperf. btwn. 500.00 500.00
c. Vert. pair, imperf btwn. 300.00 300.00
d. Horiz. pair, imperf. vert. 200.00
e. Horiz. strip of 3, imperf btwn. 450.00
f. Horiz. strip of 5, imperf btwn. 975.00
150 A17 4c vermilion 4.75 1.75
a. Vert. pair, imperf. btwn. 800.00
151 A17 5c violet (R) 6.25 1.75
a. Horiz. pair, imperf. btwn. —
b. Vert. pair, imperf btwn. — 1,000.
152 A17 7c maroon 8.25 3.50
153 A17 10c ultra (R) 8.50 1.75
a. Double overprint *300.00*
b. Pair, one without overprint *900.00*
c. Brownish red overprint 22.50 9.00
d. Inverted overprint *750.00* *750.00*
154 A18 16c olive grn (R) 22.50 8.50
155 A18 20c red brown 21.00 5.00
a. Vert. pair, imperf btwn. —
156 A18 30c rose red 26.00 6.00
157 A18 50c yel grn (R) 45.00 6.00
158 A19 $1 red & pale rose 450.00 35.00
a. Inverted overprint *27,500.*
159 A19 $2 brn red & yel 400.00 75.00
a. Inverted overprint 725.00 600.00
160 A19 $5 dp grn & sal 825.00 675.00
Nos. 146-160 (15) 1,832. 826.25

Stamps with blue overprint similar to the preceding were not an official issue but were privately made by a printer in Tientsin.

Overprinted in Red

Overprinted by the Commercial Press, Shanghai.

This type differs in that the top character is shifted slightly to right and the bottom character is larger and has small "legs".

161 A17 1c ocher 10.00 2.00
a. Inverted overprint 350.00 350.00
b. Vert. pair, imperf. btwn. 425.00
c. Double overprint 350.00
c. Double overprint 350.00
162 A17 2c green 37.50 3.50
a. Inverted overprint 1,100. 800.00
b. Vert. pair, imperf. btwn. 750.00
c. Horiz. pair, imperf. btwn. 650.00
d. Horiz. strip of 3, imperf. btwn. 850.00

Overprinted in Blue, Carmine or Black

Overprinted by Waterlow & Sons, London

163 A17 ½c brown (Bl) 3.00 2.00
a. Vert. pair, imperf. btwn. *1,350.* *1,250.*
164 A17 1c ocher (C) 3.00 2.00
a. Horiz. pair, imperf. btwn. *800.00*
165 A17 2c green (C) 3.75 2.00
166 A17 3c slate grn (C) 4.50 1.75
a. Inverted overprint *1,500.*
b. Vert. pair, imperf. btwn. 400.00
c. Horiz. pair, imperf. btwn. 400.00
167 A17 4c vermilion (Bk) 5.75 2.25
168 A17 5c violet (C) 12.50 2.25
169 A17 7c maroon (Bk) 40.00 *37.50*
170 A17 10c ultra (C) 19.50 2.75
a. Vert. pair, imperf. btwn. *1,500.* *2,600.*
171 A18 16c olive grn (R) 57.50 19.00
172 A18 20c red brn (Bk) 35.00 3.50
173 A18 30c dull red (Bk) 115.00 6.75
174 A18 50c yellow grn (R) 170.00 17.50
175 A19 $1 red & pale rose (Bk) 250.00 27.50
176 A19 $2 brn red & yel (Bk) 525.00 225.00
177 A19 $5 dp grn & sal (C) 850.00 525.00
Nos. 163-177 (15) 2,095. 876.75

Due to instructions issued to postmasters throughout China at the time of the Revolution, a number of them prepared unauthorized overprints using the same characters as the overprints prepared by the government. While many were made in good faith, some, like the blue overprints from Tientsin, were bogus, and the status of certain others is extremely dubious.

Dr. Sun Yat-sen — A21

1912, Dec. 14 ***Perf. 14½***

178 A21 1c orange 6.00 *3.25*
179 A21 2c yellow grn 6.00 *3.25*
180 A21 3c slate grn 6.00 *3.25*
181 A21 5c rose lilac 12.00 3.25
182 A21 8c dp brown 12.00 5.00
183 A21 10c dull blue 12.00 5.00
184 A21 16c olive grn 37.50 20.00
185 A21 20c maroon 47.50 15.00
186 A21 50c dk green 130.00 50.00
187 A21 $1 brown red 340.00 75.00
188 A21 $2 yellow brn 1,000. 675.00
189 A21 $5 gray 375.00 *250.00*
Nos. 178-189 (12) 1,984. 1,108.

Honoring the leader of the Revolution.

President Yuan Shih-kai — A22

1912, Dec. 14

190 A22 1c orange 4.00 3.00
191 A22 2c yellow green 4.00 3.00
192 A22 3c slate green 4.00 3.00
193 A22 5c rose lilac 4.00 *4.00*
194 A22 8c deep brown 11.50 4.00
195 A22 10c dull blue 10.00 2.50
196 A22 16c olive green 12.00 *12.00*
197 A22 20c maroon 9.00 *10.00*
198 A22 50c dark green 55.00 *35.00*
199 A22 $1 brown red 200.00 60.00
200 A22 $2 yellow brown 240.00 75.00
201 A22 $5 gray 725.00 325.00
Nos. 190-201 (12) 1,279. 536.50

Honoring the 1st pres. of the Republic.

Junk — A24

Reaping Rice — A25

Gateway, Hall of Classics, Peking — A26

DESIGN A24

London Printing: Vertical shading lines under top panel fine, junk with clear diagonal shading lines on sails, right pennant of junk usually long, lines in water weak except directly under junk.

Peking Printing: Vertical shading lines under top panel and inner vertical frame line much heavier, water and sails of junk more evenly and strongly colored, white wave over "H" of "CHINA" pointed upward, touching the junk.

DESIGN A25

London: Front hat brim thick and nearly straight, left foot touches shadow.

Peking: Front hat brim thin and strongly upturned, left foot and sickle clearly outlined in white, shadow of middle tree lighter than those of the right and left trees.

DESIGN A26

London: Light colored walk clearly defined almost to the doorway, figure in right doorway "T" shaped with strong horizontal cross-bar, white panel in base of central tower rectangular, vertical stroke in top left character uniformly thick at its base, tree to right of doorway ends in minute dots.

Peking: Walk more heavily shaded near doorway, especially at right; figure in right doorway more like a "Y", white panel at base of central tower is a long oval, right vertical stroke in top left character incurved near its base, tree at right has five prominent dots at top.

London Printing: By Waterlow & Sons, London, perf. 14 to 15.

Peking Printing: By the Chinese Bureau of Engraving and Printing, Peking, perf. 14.

London Printing

1913, May 5 ***Perf. 14-15***

202 A24 ½c black brn 1.00 .40
a. Horiz. or vert. pair, imperf. btwn. 300.00
203 A24 1c orange 1.00 .40
a. Horiz. pair, imperf. btwn. 300.00 *150.00*
b. Vert. pair, imperf. btwn. 300.00
c. Horiz. strip of 5, imperf. btwn 850.00
204 A24 2c yellow grn 3.00 .40
a. Horiz. pair, imperf. btwn. 375.00
205 A24 3c blue grn 7.00 .45
a. Horiz. pair, imperf. btwn. 290.00
b. Vert. pair, imperf. btwn. *400.00*
206 A24 4c scarlet 10.00 .70
207 A24 5c rose lilac 30.00 .60
208 A24 6c gray 6.00 .90
209 A24 7c violet 27.50 8.75
210 A24 8c brown org 50.00 2.50
211 A24 10c dk blue 40.00 1.10
a. Horiz. pair, imperf. btwn. — *2,000.*
b. Vert. pair, imperf. btwn. — 2,100.
212 A25 15c brown 40.00 5.75
213 A25 16c olive grn 27.50 2.25
214 A25 20c brown red 50.00 2.75
215 A25 30c brown vio 50.00 2.00
a. Horiz. pair, imperf. btwn. *5,000.* *5,000.*
216 A25 50c green 80.00 3.50
217 A26 $1 ocher & blk 260.00 3.00
218 A26 $2 blue & blk 425.00 25.00
219 A26 $5 scarlet & blk 825.00 125.00
220 A26 $10 yel grn & blk 2,350. 950.00
Nos. 202-220 (19) 4,283. 1,135.

First Peking Printing

1915 *Perf. 14*

221 A24 ½c black brn .80 .35
a. Vert. pair, imperf. btwn. 600.00
222 A24 1c orange .80 .35
223 A24 2c yellow grn 1.60 .35
224 A24 3c blue grn 1.75 .35
a. Horiz. pair, imperf. btwn. 175.00
225 A24 4c scarlet 20.00 .35
226 A24 5c rose lilac 8.50 .35
a. Booklet pane of 4 140.00
227 A24 6c gray 16.00 .35
228 A24 7c violet 25.00 4.50
229 A24 8c brown org 14.00 .40
230 A24 10c dk blue 15.00 .70
a. Booklet pane of 4 140.00
231 A25 15c brown 42.50 4.50
232 A25 16c olive grn 22.00 .70
233 A25 20c brown red 25.00 .70
234 A25 30c brown vio 17.50 .70
a. Hoirz. pair, imperf. btwn. 900.00
235 A25 50c green 42.50 .80
a. Vert. pair, imperf. btwn. 900.00
236 A26 $1 ocher & blk 140.00 .85
237 A26 $2 blue & blk 350.00 6.00
a. Center inverted 175,000. —
238 A26 $5 scarlet & blk 800.00 42.50
239 A26 $10 yel grn & blk 1,100. 300.00
Nos. 221-239 (19) 2,643. 364.80

1919

240 A24 1½c violet 3.75 .60
241 A25 13c brown 9.50 .70
242 A26 $20 yellow & blk 6,500. 3,900.

Nos. 226 and 230 overprinted in red with five characters in vertical column were for postal savings use.

The higher values of the 1913-19 issues are often overprinted with Chinese characters, which are the names of various postal districts. Stamps were frequently stolen while in transit to post offices. The overprints served to protect them, since the stamps could only be used in the districts for which they were overprinted.

Compare designs A24-A26 with designs A29-A31. For surcharges and overprints see Nos. 247, 288, B1-B3, Sinkiang 1-38.

Yeh Kung-cho, Hsu Shi-chang and Chin Yun-peng
A27

1921, Oct. 10

243 A27 1c orange 6.00 1.75
244 A27 3c blue green 6.50 1.50
245 A27 6c gray 7.50 5.00
246 A27 10c blue 8.50 4.00
Nos. 243-246 (4) 28.50 12.25

National Post Office, 25th anniversary.
For overprints see Sinkiang Nos. 39-42.

No. 224 Surcharged in Red

1922

247 A24 2c on 3c blue green 4.50 .70
a. Inverted surcharge 175,000. —

Second Peking Printing

A29

A30

A31

Types of 1913-19 Issues Re-engraved

Type A29: Most of the whitecaps in front of the junk have been removed and the water made darker. The shading lines have been removed from the arabesques and pearls above the top inscription. The inner shadings at the top and sides of the picture have been cut away.

Type A30: The heads of rice in the side panels have a background of crossed lines instead of horizontal lines. The Temple of Heaven is strongly shaded and has a door. There are rows of pearls below the Chinese characters in the upper corners. The arabesques above the top inscription have been altered and are without shading lines.

Type A31: The curved line under the inscription at top is single instead of double. There are four vertical lines, instead of eight, at each side of the picture. The trees at the sides of the temple had foliage in the 1913-19 issues, but now the branches are bare. There are numerous other alterations in the design.

1923 *Perf. 14*

248 A29 ½c black brown 1.40 .30
a. Horiz. pair, imperf. btwn. 290.00 275.00
b. Horiz. pair, imperf. vert. 290.00 275.00
c. Vert. pair, imperf. btwn. 250.00
249 A29 1c orange .80 .30
a. Imperf., pair 150.00
b. Horiz. pair, imperf. btwn. 150.00
c. Booklet pane of 6 90.00
d. Booklet pane of 4 45.00
e. Vert. pair, imperf. btwn. 150.00
f. Vert. pair, imperf. horiz. 150.00
250 A29 1½c violet 3.00 .90
251 A29 2c yellow grn 1.60 .30
252 A29 3c blue green 5.00 .30
a. Booklet pane of 6 80.00
253 A29 4c gray 22.00 .80
a. Horiz. pair, imperf. btwn. 300.00
254 A29 5c claret 3.25 .50
a. Booklet pane of 4 100.00
255 A29 6c scarlet 7.00 .50
256 A29 7c violet 7.00 .50
257 A29 8c orange 14.00 .50
258 A29 10c blue 12.00 .30
a. Booklet pane of 6 120.00
b. Booklet pane of 2 150.00
259 A30 13c brown 26.00 .60
260 A30 15c dp blue 8.00 .60
261 A30 16c olive grn 9.00 .60
262 A30 20c brown red 7.00 .40
263 A30 30c purple 26.00 .40
a. Horiz. pair, imperf. btwn. 650.00
264 A30 50c dp green 50.00 .55
265 A31 $1 org brn & sep 52.50 .65
266 A31 $2 blue & red brn 70.00 1.00
267 A31 $5 red & slate 115.00 4.25
268 A31 $10 green & claret 575.00 62.50
269 A31 $20 plum & blue 1,200. 175.00
Nos. 248-269 (22) 2,216. 251.75

Nos. 249 and 275 exist with webbing watermark from experimental printing. Value, $4,500 each.

To prevent speculation and theft, the dollar denominations were overprinted with single characters in red for use in Kwangsi ($1-$20) and Kweichow ($1-$5).

See Nos. 275, 324. For surcharges and overprints see Nos. 274, 289, 311, 325, 330, 339-340, Szechwan 1-3, Yunnan 1-20, Manchuria 1-20, Sinkiang 47-69, 114, C1-C4.

Temple of Heaven, Peking — A32

1923, Oct. 17 *Perf. 14*

270 A32 1c orange 5.00 1.00
271 A32 3c blue green 5.50 2.25
272 A32 4c red 10.50 2.50
273 A32 10c blue 16.50 5.00
Nos. 270-273 (4) 37.50 10.75

Adoption of Constitution, October, 1923.
For overprints see Sinkiang Nos. 43-46.

No. 253 Surcharged in Red

1925

274 A29 3c on 4c gray 3.50 .35
a. Inverted surcharge 300,000. 275,000.
b. Vert. pair, imperf. btwn.

Junk Type of 1923

1926

275 A29 4c olive green 1.60 .25
a. Horiz. pair, imperf. vert. 200.00 290.00
b. Horiz. pair, imperf. btwn. 200.00
c. Horiz. strip of 3, imperf. btwn. 350.00

Marshal Chang Tso-lin — A34

1928, Mar. 1 *Perf. 14*

276 A34 1c brown orange 1.50 1.50
277 A34 4c olive green 3.00 3.00
278 A34 10c dull blue 9.50 5.50
279 A34 $1 red 72.50 *80.00*
Nos. 276-279 (4) 86.50 90.00

Assumption of office by Marshal Chang Tso-lin. The stamps of this issue were only available for postage in the Provinces of Chihli and Shantung and at the Offices in Manchuria and Sinkiang.

For overprints see Manchuria Nos. 21-24, Sinkiang 70-73.

President Chiang Kai-shek — A35

1929, May

280 A35 1c brown orange 3.00 .40
281 A35 4c olive green 5.00 .75
282 A35 10c dark blue 23.00 3.50
283 A35 $1 dark red 90.00 70.00
Nos. 280-283 (4) 121.00 74.65

Unification of China.
For overprints see Yunnan Nos. 21-24, Manchuria 25-28, Sinkiang 74-77.

Sun Yat-sen Mausoleum, Nanking — A36

1929, May 30 *Perf. 14*

284 A36 1c brown orange 2.00 .75
285 A36 4c olive green 2.00 1.00
286 A36 10c dark blue 9.00 2.50
287 A36 $1 dark red 85.00 *90.00*
Nos. 284-287 (4) 98.00 94.25

The transfer of Dr. Sun Yat-sen's remains from Peiping to the mausoleum at Nanking.

For overprints see Yunnan Nos. 25-28, Manchuria 29-32, Sinkiang 78-81.

Nos. 224 and 252 Surcharged in Red

1930

288 A24 1c on 3c blue green 1.60 *2.75*
289 A29 1c on 3c blue green 1.20 .40
a. No period after "Ct" 25.00 25.00

See Nos. 311, 325, 330.

Dr. Sun Yat-sen — A37

Type I

Type II

Type I — Double-lined circle in the sun.
Type II — Heavy, single-lined circle in the sun.

Printed by De la Rue & Co., Ltd., London

Perf. 11½x12½ (Nos. 304-306), 12½

1931, Nov. 12 **Type I** **Engr.**

290 A37 1c orange .55 .30
291 A37 2c olive green .65 .40
292 A37 4c green 1.10 .30
293 A37 20c ultra 1.40 .30
294 A37 $1 org brn & dk brn 12.00 .50
295 A37 $2 blue & org brn 35.00 3.00
296 A37 $5 dull red & blk 50.00 5.00
Nos. 290-296 (7) 100.70 9.80

1931-37 **Type II**

Dry Printing

297 A37 2c olive grn .50 .25
298 A37 4c green 7.50 1.00
299 A37 5c green ('33) .40 .25
300 A37 15c dk green 4.25 1.25
301 A37 15c scarlet ('34) .50 .25
302 A37 20c ultra ('37) .90 .25
303 A37 25c ultra 3.00 1.00
304 A37 $1 org brn & dk brn 14.00 .50
305 A37 $2 blue & org brn 25.00 1.25
306 A37 $5 dull red & blk 50.00 6.00
Nos. 297-306 (10) 106.05 12.00

"Nomads in the Desert" — A38

1932 **Unwmk.** *Perf. 14*

307 A38 1c deep orange 45.00 90.00
308 A38 4c olive green 45.00 90.00
309 A38 5c claret 45.00 90.00
310 A38 10c deep blue 45.00 90.00
Nos. 307-310 (4) 180.00 360.00

Northwest Scientific Expedition of Sven Hedin. A small quantity of this issue was sold at face at Peking and several other cities. The bulk of the issue was furnished to Hedin and sold at $5 (Chinese) a set for funds to finance the expedition.

No. 252 Surcharged in Black Like 288

1932

311 A29 1c on 3c blue green 2.75 1.60

Martyrs Issue

Teng Keng
A39

Ch'en Ying-shih
A40

Chu Chih-hsin
A45

Sung Chiao-jen
A46

Huang Hsing
A47

Liao Chung-kai
A48

1932-34 *Perf. 14*

312 A39 ½c black brown .25 .25
313 A40 1c orange ('34) .25 .25
314 A39 2½c rose lilac ('33) .25 .25
315 A48 3c dp brown ('33) .25 .25
316 A45 8c brown orange .50 .30
317 A46 10c dull violet .60 .30
318 A45 13c blue green .65 .30
319 A46 17c brown olive .55 .30
320 A47 20c brown red 1.10 .30

321 A48 30c brown violet 1.50 .30
322 A47 40c orange 1.40 .35
323 A40 50c green ('34) 5.00 .50
Nos. 312-323 (12) 12.30 3.65

Perfs. 12 to 13 and compound and with secret marks are listed as Nos. 402-439. No. 316 re-drawn is No. 485.

For overprints and surcharge see Nos. 342, 472, 474, 478-479, 486-487, 490, 531-536, 539-541, 544-549, 616, 619, 622-624, 647-659, 662-663, 665, 669, 672, 698, 704, 711, 713-715, 720-721, 831, 846-847, 867, 870, 872, 881-882, J120-J121, 1N14-1N15, 1N59, 2N6-2N9, 2N32-2N56, 2N60, 2N76-2N82, 2N85, 2N87-2N90, 2N107-2N115, 2N118, 2N121-2N123, 3N6-3N10, 3N34-3N55, 3N59, 4N6-4N9, 4N39-4N64, 4N69, 5N5-5N8, 5N34-5N60, 5N65, 6N6-6N8, 6N35-6N61, 6N66, 7N5-7N7, 7N30-7N53, 7N55, 7N59, 8N1, 8N4, 8N28-8N42, 8N45, 8N47-8N50, 8N60-8N61, 8N68, 8N73, 8N76-8N79, 8N89, 8N97, 8N99-8N100, 8N103-8N104, 9N72-9N77, Taiwan 14-17, 20, 28A, 74, Northeastern Provinces 6-8, 11, Szechwan 12-23, Yunnan 49-60, Sinkiang 102-113, 140-161, 197.

Junk Type of 1923

1933 *Perf. 14*
324 A29 6c brown 25.00 3.00

No. 275 Surcharged in Red Like 288

1933
325 A29 1c on 4c olive green 3.00 .35
a. No period after "Ct" 30.00 25.00

Tan Yuan-chang — A49

1933, Jan. 9
326 A49 2c olive green 3.00 1.50
327 A49 5c green 6.50 .75
328 A49 25c ultra 10.00 1.75
329 A49 $1 red 75.00 35.00
Nos. 326-329 (4) 94.50 39.00

Tan Yuan-chang, more commonly known as Tan Yen-kai, a prominent statesman in China since the revolution of 1912 and Pres. of the Executive Dept. of the Natl. Government. Placed on sale Jan. 9, 1933, the date of the ceremony in celebration of the completion of the Tan Yuan-chang Memorial Hall and Tomb at Mukden.

For overprints see Yunnan Nos. 45-48, Sinkiang 98-101.

No. 251 Surcharged in Red Like 288

1935 *Perf. 14*
330 A29 1c on 2c yellow grn 2.50 .25
a. No peroid after "Ct" *30.00 25.00*

Emblem of New Life Movement A50

Four Virtues of New Life A51

Lighthouse — A52

1936, Jan. 1
331 A50 2c olive green 1.75 .75
332 A50 5c green 2.00 .25
333 A51 20c dark blue 6.00 .70
334 A52 $1 rose red 40.00 11.00
Nos. 331-334 (4) 49.75 12.70

"New Life" movement.

Methods of Mail Transportation A53

Maritime Scene — A54

Shanghai General Post Office — A55

Ministry of Communications, Nanking — A56

1936, Oct. 10
335 A53 2c orange 3.00 .70
336 A54 5c green 1.50 .25
337 A55 25c blue 5.00 .50
338 A56 $1 dk carmine 30.00 9.50
Nos. 335-338 (4) 39.50 10.95

Founding of the Chinese PO, 40th anniv.

Nos. 260 and 261 Surcharged in Red

1936, Oct. 11
339 A30 5c on 15c dp blue 2.75 .50
340 A30 5c on 16c olive grn 3.50 1.00

No. 298 Surcharged in Red

1937
341 A37 1c on 4c green (#298a) 1.25 .50
a. Upper left character missing
b. 1c on 4c green (#298) 750.00 40.00

Nos. 322 and 303 Surcharged in Black or Red

1938 *Perf. 12½, 14*
342 A47 8c on 40c orange (Bk) 2.00 .75
343 A37 10c on 25c ultra (R) 1.75 .30

Dr. Sun Yat-sen — A57

Type I

Type II

Type III

Type I — Coat button half circle. Six lines of shading above head. Top frame partially shaded with vertical lines.

Type II — Coat button complete circle. Nine lines of shading above head. Top frame partially shaded with vertical lines.

Type III — Coat button complete circle. Nine lines of shading above head. Top frame line fully shaded with vertical lines.

Printed by the Chung Hwa Book Co. Type I

1938 Unwmk. Engr. *Perf. 12½*
344 A57 $1 henna & dk brn 85.00 12.00
345 A57 $2 dp blue & org brn 17.50 4.25
346 A57 $5 red & grnsh blk 150.00 19.00
Nos. 344-346 (3) 252.50 35.25

1939 **Type II**
347 A57 $1 henna & dk brn 20.00 1.00
348 A57 $2 dp blue & org brn 20.00 4.00

1939-43 **Type III**
349 A57 2c olive green .25 .25
350 A57 3c dull claret .25 .25
351 A57 5c green .25 .25
352 A57 5c olive green .25 .25
353 A57 8c olive green .25 .25
a. Vert. pair, imperf. btwn. 250.00
b. Horiz. pair, imperf. btwn. 250.00
354 A57 10c green .25 .25
a. Horiz. pair, imperf. btwn. 250.00
355 A57 15c scarlet 1.25 *2.25*
356 A57 15c dk vio brn ('43) 17.50 *32.50*
357 A57 16c olive gray 1.75 .45
a. Vert. pair, imperf. btwn. 250.00
358 A57 25c dk blue .35 *2.00*
359 A57 $1 henna & dk brn 2.00 2.00
360 A57 $2 dp blue & org brn 4.50 1.00
a. Imperf., pair 300.00
361 A57 $5 red & grnsh blk 2.75 1.00
a. Vert. pair, imperf. btwn. 250.00
b. Horiz. pair, imperf. btwn. 250.00
362 A57 $10 dk green & dull pur 17.50 2.25
363 A57 $20 rose lake & dk blue 60.00 50.00
Nos. 349-363 (15) 109.10 *94.95*

Several values exist imperforate, but these were not regularly issued. No. 361 imperforate is printer's waste.

See Nos. 368-401, 506-524. For surcharges and overprints see Nos. 440-448, 473, 475-477, 480-481, 482-484, 489, 537-538, 615, 618, 620, 660-661, 664, 666-668, 673-676, 680-681, 686, 688, 699-703, 707-709, 717, 719, 830, J67-J68, M2, M11-M12, 1N2-1N13, 1N23-1N42, 1N57-1N58, 2N10-2N31, 2N61-2N75, 2N86, 2N91-2N93, 2N117, 2N119-2N120, 3N11-3N33, 3N56-3N58, 3N60-3N61, 4N10-4N38, 4N65-4N68, 4N70-4N71, 5N9-5N33, 5N61-5N64, 5N66-5N68, 6N9-6N34, 6N62-6N65, 6N67-6N69, 7N8-7N29, 7N56-7N58, 7N60-7N61, 8N5-8N27, 8N46, 8N51-8N53, 8N55-8N56, 8N58-8N59, 8N62-8N67, 8N72, 8N74-8N75, 8N80-8N84, 8N86-8N88, 8N90, 8N95-8N96, 8N98, 8N101-8N102, 8N105-8N106, 9N6-9N71, 9N97, 9N99, Taiwan 78, 84, Northeastern Provinces 9-10, Sinkiang 115-139, 174-188, 196, 198.

Chinese and American Flags and Map of China — A58

Printed by American Bank Note Co.

Frame Engr., Center Litho.

1939, July 4 Unwmk. *Perf. 12*

Flag in Deep Rose and Ultramarine

364 A58 5c dark green 1.75 .50
365 A58 25c deep blue 1.75 .90
366 A58 50c brown 4.00 1.10
367 A58 $1 rose carmine 6.50 2.25
Nos. 364-367 (4) 14.00 4.75

150th anniv. of the US Constitution.

Type of 1939-41 Re-engraved

2c, 1939-41

Re-engraved

8c, 1939-41

Re-engraved

1940 *Perf. 12½*
368 A57 2c olive green .25 .25
369 A57 8c olive green .25 .25

Type of 1938-41
Type III

1940 Unwmk. *Perf. 14*

No.	Type	Description	Unused	Used
370	A57	2c olive green	2.60	1.10
371	A57	5c green	5.25	2.25
372	A57	$1 henna & dk brn	115.00	24.00
373	A57	$2 dp blue & org brn	22.00	5.50
374	A57	$5 red & grnsh blk	27.00	18.00
a.		Vert. pair, imperf. btwn.	250.00	
b.		Horiz. pair, imperf. btwn.	250.00	
375	A57	$10 dk grn & dull pur	75.00	13.50
		Nos. 370-375 (6)	246.85	64.35

See surcharge note following No. 363.

Type of 1939-41

1940 Wmk. 261 *Perf. 12½*

Type III

No.	Type	Description	Unused	Used
376	A57	$1 henna & dk brn	7.00	*9.00*
377	A57	$2 dp blue & org brn	9.00	*9.00*
378	A57	$5 red & grnsh blk	10.00	*18.00*
379	A57	$10 dk green & dull pur	15.00	*30.00*
380	A57	$20 rose lake & dp blue	19.00	*30.00*
		Nos. 376-380 (5)	60.00	*96.00*

See surcharge note following No. 363.

Printed by the Dah Tung Book Co.

Five Cent

Type III - Characters joined | Secret Mark - Characters not joined

Eight Cent

Type III - Characters not joined | Secret Mark - Characters joined

Ten Cent

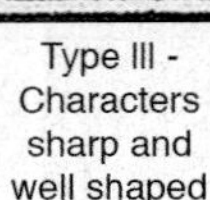

Type III - Characters sharp and well shaped | Secret Mark - Characters coarse and varying in thickness

Dollar Values

Type III | Secret Mark

1940 Unwmk. *Perf. 14*

Type III with Secret Marks

No.	Type	Description	Unused	Used
381	A57	5c green	.25	.25
382	A57	5c olive green	.25	.25
383	A57	8c olive green	.40	.25
a.		Without "star" in uniform button	1.50	*2.50*
384	A57	10c green	.25	.25
385	A57	30c scarlet	.35	.25
386	A57	50c dk blue	.45	.25
387	A57	$1 org brn & sepia	2.50	.25
388	A57	$2 dp blue & yel brn	1.00	.35
389	A57	$5 red & slate grn	1.00	.45
390	A57	$10 dk grn & dull pur	4.00	2.25
391	A57	$20 rose lake & dk blue	12.00	3.50
		Nos. 381-391 (11)	22.45	8.30

Type III with Secret Marks

1940 Wmk. 261 *Perf. 14*

No.	Type	Description	Unused	Used
392	A57	5c green	.25	.25
393	A57	5c olive green	.25	.25
394	A57	10c green	.35	.25
395	A57	30c scarlet	.25	.25
396	A57	50c dk blue	.55	.25
397	A57	$1 org brn & sepia	4.50	6.00
398	A57	$2 dp blue & yel brn	12.50	18.00
399	A57	$5 red & slate grn	11.50	*18.00*
400	A57	$10 dk grn & dull pur	16.00	*20.00*
401	A57	$20 rose lake & dk blue	25.00	37.00
		Nos. 392-401 (10)	71.15	100.25

Nos. 383, 384, 385, 397, 400 and 401 exist perf. 12½, but were not issued with this perforation.

See surcharge note following No. 363.

Types of 1932-34 Martyrs Issue with Secret Mark

1932-34 Issue. In the left Chinese character in bottom row, the two parts are not joined.

Secret Mark, 1940-41 Issue. The two parts are joined

Perf. 12½, 13 and Compound

1940-41 Wmk. 261

No.	Type	Description	Unused	Used
402	A39	½c olive blk	.25	.25
403	A40	1c orange	.25	.25
404	A46	2c dp blue ('41)	.25	*1.00*
405	A39	2½c rose lilac	.25	*1.00*
406	A48	3c dp yellow brn	.30	*1.00*
407	A39	4c pale vio ('41)	.30	*1.00*
408	A48	5c dull red org ('41)	.30	*1.00*
409	A45	8c dp orange	.25	*1.00*
410	A46	10c dull violet	.25	*1.00*
411	A45	13c dp yellow grn	.35	*1.00*
412	A48	15c brown car	.25	*1.00*
413	A46	17c brown olive	.25	.25
414	A47	20c lt blue	.25	.25
415	A45	21c olive brn ('41)	1.10	*1.25*
416	A40	25c red vio ('41)	.25	*1.00*
417	A46	28c olive ('41)	.30	*1.00*
418	A48	30c brown car	.45	.25
a.		Vert. pair, imperf. btwn.	140.00	
419	A47	40c orange	.30	.25
420	A40	50c green	.30	.25

Unwmk.

No.	Type	Description	Unused	Used
421	A39	½c olive black	.25	.25
422	A40	1c orange	.25	.25
a.		Without secret mark	2.75	2.75
b.		Horiz. pair, imperf. vert.	110.00	
423	A46	2c dp blue	.25	.25
a.		Vert. pair, imperf. horiz.	100.00	
b.		Horiz. pair, imperf. between	160.00	
424	A39	2½c rose lilac	.25	.25
425	A48	3c dp yellow brn	.25	.25
426	A39	4c pale violet	.25	.25
427	A48	5c dull red org	.25	.25
428	A45	8c dp orange	.25	.25
429	A46	10c dull violet	3.25	.40
430	A45	13c dp yel grn	.25	.65
431	A48	15c brown car	.35	*1.00*
432	A46	17c brn olive	.40	.25
433	A47	20c lt blue	.30	.25
a.		Vert. pair, imperf. horiz.	125.00	
b.		Horiz. pair, imperf. vert.	125.00	
434	A45	21c olive brn	.50	.35
435	A40	25c rose vio	.35	*.50*
436	A46	28c olive	.70	.50
437	A48	30c brown car	2.50	2.50
438	A47	40c orange	.35	.35
439	A40	50c green	3.50	.40
		Nos. 402-439 (38)	20.65	23.15

Several values exist imperforate, but they were not regularly issued.

Used values are for favor cancels. Postally used examples sell for more.

See surcharge note following No. 323.

Regional Surcharges.

The regional surcharges, Nos. 440-448, 482-484, 486-491, 525-549, have been listed according to the basic stamps, with black or red surcharges. The surcharges of the individual provinces, plus Hong Kong and Shanghai, are noted in small type. The numeral following each letter is the surcharge denomination. These surcharges are identified by the following letters:

a — Hong Kong	i — Kwangsi
b — Shanghai	j — Kwangtung
bx — Anhwei	k — Western Szechwan
c — Hunan	l — Yunnan
d — Kansu	m — Honan
e — Kiangsi	n — Shensi
f — Eastern Szechwan	o — Kweichow
g — Chekiang	p — Hupeh
h — Fukien	

Regional Surcharges on Stamps of 1939-40

Hong Kong — a4

Shanghai — b3

Hunan — c3

Kansu — d3

Kiangsi — e3

Eastern Szechwan — f3

Chekiang — g3

1940-41 Unwmk. *Perf. 12½, 14*

Carmine Surcharge

No.	Type	Description	Unused	Used
440	A57	4c on 5c ol grn (#382) (a4)	.60	.60
r.		Lower right character duplicated at left	30.00	32.50

Black Surcharge

No.	Type	Description	Unused	Used
441	A57	3c on 5c grn (#351) (b3)	1.25	*1.40*
442	A57	3c on 5c ol grn (#352) (c3, d3)	.65	*2.00*
443	A57	3c on 5c grn (#381) (b3)	.60	*1.25*
444	A57	3c on 5c ol grn (#382) (e3)	.70	*1.00*
r.		Lower left character duplicated at right (Kiangsi)	42.50	42.50
		(b3) Shanghai	.65	*1.40*
		(f3) Eastern Szechwan	.65	*1.60*

The Kansu surcharges of No. 442 are of 6 types. Differences include formation of top part of fen character (at left of "3"), fen with low right hook, height of "3" (5-4mm), space between upper and lower characters (6-9mm), etc.

1940-41 Wmk. 261 *Perf. 14*

No.	Type	Description	Unused	Used
445	A57	3c on 5c grn (#392) (e3)	.60	*1.40*
r.		Lower left character duplicated at right (Kiangsi)	35.00	35.00
		(b3, c3) Shanghai, Hunan	.60	*1.60*
446	A57	3c on 5c ol grn (#393) (f3)	.70	*1.75*
		(b3) Shanghai	.95	*1.75*
r.		Lower left character duplicated at right (f3)	60.00	65.00

Red Surcharge

No.	Type	Description	Unused	Used
447	A57	3c on 5c grn (#392) (g3)	1.25	3.25
448	A57	3c on 5c ol grn (#393) (g3)	6.00	6.00

Dr. Sun Yat-sen — A59

Printed by American Bank Note Co.

1941 Unwmk. Engr. *Perf. 12*

No.	Type	Description	Unused	Used
449	A59	½c sepia	.25	.30
450	A59	1c orange	.25	.25
451	A59	2c brt ultra	.25	.25
452	A59	5c green	.25	.25
453	A59	8c red orange	.60	.70
454	A59	8c turq green	.30	.25
455	A59	10c brt green	.25	.25
456	A59	17c olive	4.50	*12.00*
457	A59	25c rose violet	.30	1.00
458	A59	30c scarlet	.35	.25
459	A59	50c dk blue	.50	.25
460	A59	$1 brown & blk	.60	.25
461	A59	$2 blue & blk	.75	.25
a.		Center inverted	*180,000.*	
462	A59	$5 scarlet & blk	1.75	.65
463	A59	$10 green & blk	5.00	2.75
464	A59	$20 rose vio & blk	4.00	*6.00*
		Nos. 449-464 (16)	19.90	25.65

For surcharges see Nos. 488, 491, 542-543, 617, 621, 670, 677, 687, 705-706, 712, 716, 718, M1, M3-M4, 1N16-1N22, 1N43-1N56, 9N78-9N96, 9N98, 9N100.

Industry and Agriculture — A60

1941, June 21 *Perf. 12½*

No.	Type	Description	Unused	Used
465	A60	8c green	.50	.50
466	A60	21c red brown	.65	.65
467	A60	28c dk olive grn	.85	.85
468	A60	33c vermilion	1.10	*1.50*
469	A60	50c dp ultra	1.25	1.25
470	A60	$1 dk violet	1.75	1.75
		Nos. 465-470 (6)	6.10	6.50

Souvenir Sheet

Imperf

Typo.

No.	Type	Description	Unused	Used
471		Sheet of 6	70.00	*100.00*
a.		A60 8c dull green	8.00	*15.00*
b.		A60 21c dark orange brown	8.00	*15.00*
c.		A60 28c dull yellow green	8.00	*15.00*
d.		A60 33c red	8.00	*15.00*
e.		A60 50c dull blue	8.00	*15.00*
f.		A60 $1 dark violet	8.00	*15.00*

The Thrift Movement and its aim to "Save for Reconstruction."

Issued in sheets measuring 155x171mm, without gum.

This sheet exists with additional blue marginal overprints in Russian, French and Chinese reading "Souvenir of the Exhibition of the Russian Philatelic Society in China, Shanghai, China, Feb. 28, 1943." Value, $600 unused; $800 used.

The overprinting was applied by the society, and when so overprinted this sheet had no franking power.

Stamps of 1939-41 Overprinted in Carmine or Blue

1941, Oct. 10 *Perf. 12½, 14, 13*

No.	Type	Description	Unused	Used
472	A40	1c dull orange	.25	*4.00*
473	A57	2c olive grn (C)	.25	*4.00*
474	A39	4c pale violet (C)	.25	*4.00*
475	A57	8c ol grn (#369) (C)	.25	*4.00*
476	A57	10c green (#354) (C)	.25	*4.00*
477	A57	16c ol gray (#357) (C)	.25	*4.00*
478	A45	21c olive brn (C)	.25	*4.00*
479	A46	28c olive (C)	.60	*6.00*
480	A57	30c scarlet	1.00	*6.00*
481	A57	$1 hn & dk brn (#359)	4.00	*10.00*
		Nos. 472-481 (10)	7.35	*50.00*

Chinese Republic, 30th anniversary.

Kiangsi — e7

Eastern Szechwan — f7

Chekiang — g7

Fukien — h7

1941 Unwmk. *Perf. 12½, 14*

482 A57 7c on 8c (#353) (g7, h7) 1.00 1.10
483 A57 7c on 8c (#369) (f7) 1.00 .55
484 A57 7c on 8c (#383) (h7) 1.00 .90
(e7) Kiangsi 1.00 .90
(g7) Chekiang 1.00 1.10
r. Without "star" in uniform button 70.00

Type of 1932-34 Re-engraved

1941 Unwmk. *Perf. 14*

485 A45 8c deep orange 25.00 *60.00*

The original stamps are 19½mm wide, the re-engraved 21mm.

Eleven other values of the Martyrs Issue and types A37 and A57 exist re-engraved, but were not issued.

Hunan — c1

Kiangsi — e1

Fukien — h1

Kwangsi — i1

Kwangtung — j1

1942 Red Surcharge

486 A39 1c on ½c blk brn (#312) (i1) 1.00 *1.75*
(c1) Hunan 2.00 *2.75*
487 A39 1c on ½c ol blk (#421) (e1) .75 1.60
(c1) Hunan .85 *2.00*
(i1) Kwangsi 1.65 *2.50*
(h1) Fukien 6.00 *9.50*
488 A59 1c on ½c sepia (#449) (j1) 1.00 *1.60*
(c1) Hunan 1.25 *2.50*

Hunan — c40

Eastern Szechwan — f40

Western Szechwan — k40

Yunnan — l40

Red Surcharge

489 A57 40c on 50c dk bl (#386) (f40) .75 1.25
(k40) Western Szechwan 4.25 *6.00*
(l40) Yunnan 3.75 *5.50*
r. Inverted surcharge (Yunnan) 110.00

Wmk. 261

490 A40 40c on 50c grn (#420) (c40) 1.75 *6.50*

Unwmk.

491 A59 40c on 50c dk bl (#459) (c40) 3.25 *8.25*

Dr. Sun Yat-sen — A62

Central Trust Printing
Perf. 10½-11, 11½-12½, 13 and Compounds

1942-43 Without Gum Typo.

492 A62 10c dp green ('43) .25 *1.50*
493 A62 16c dull ol brn 13.50 *47.50*
a. Perf 10½ 550.00 *550.00*
494 A62 20c dk ol grn ('43) .25 *1.50*
a. Perf. 11 13.50 11.00
495 A62 25c brown vio .25 *1.00*
496 A62 30c dull ver .25 *1.00*
a. Perf. 11 3.00 5.00
497 A62 40c dk red brn ('43) .25 *1.00*
a. Perf. 11x13 85.00
b. Perf. 11 14.00 14.00
498 A62 50c sage green .25 .25
a. Perf. 11 7.00 *13.50*
499 A62 $1 rose lake .35 .25
a. Perf. 11 40.00 40.00
500 A62 $1 dull grn ('43) .35 .35
501 A62 $1.50 dp blue ('43) .35 *.45*
a. Perf. 11 290.00 290.00
502 A62 $2 dk blue grn .35 .35
503 A62 $3 dk yel ('43) .35 .35
504 A62 $4 red brown .40 .45
505 A62 $5 cerise ('43) .35 .35
Nos. 492-505 (14) 17.50 56.30

Many shades and part-perforate varieties exist.

See Nos. 550 to 563 for other stamps of type A62 with secret mark and new values and colors. For surcharges and overprints see Nos. 525-530, 671, 683, 692-694, 696, 771, 773, 807-809, 811-820, 824-827, 832, 834-834A, 836, 848-850, 852-854, 857, 860-863, 876, 879, M5-M10, Taiwan 55, 86, 99, Kwangsi 6-7, Sinkiang 162-173, 194-195.

Type of 1938
Thin Paper Without Gum

1942-44 Unwmk. Engr. *Imperf.*

506 A57 $10 red brown 1.75 1.25
507 A57 $20 blue grn 1.75 1.00
508 A57 $20 rose red ('44) 17.00 11.00
509 A57 $30 dull vio ('43) 1.25 1.00
510 A57 $40 rose red ('43) 1.40 1.00
511 A57 $50 blue 2.00 1.25
512 A57 $100 org brn ('43) 8.00 5.00

Rouletted

513 A57 $5 lilac gray ('44) 14.00 *14.00*
a. Rouletted x perf. 12½ 25.00 30.00
514 A57 $10 red brown 6.75 5.00
515 A57 $50 blue 7.25 6.00
a. Rouletted x imperf. 6.50 —
Nos. 506-515 (10) 61.15 46.50

1942-45 *Perf. 12½ to 15*

516 A57 $4 dp blue ('43) .80 1.25
517 A57 $5 lil gray ('43) 1.75 1.25
518 A57 $10 red brown 1.75 1.25
519 A57 $20 blue grn ('43) 1.75 1.00
520 A57 $20 rose red ('45) 125.00 *175.00*
521 A57 $30 dull vio ('43) 1.25 1.00
522 A57 $40 rose ('43) 1.25 1.00
523 A57 $50 blue 5.50 2.50
524 A57 $100 org brn ('45) 120.00 *125.00*
Nos. 516-524 (9) 259.05 309.25

Beware of Nos. 508 and 512 with faked perforations that are offered as Nos. 520 and 524.

See surcharge note following No. 363.

No. 493 Overprinted in Black or Red

1942

525 A62 (i) 16c (Bk) 85.00 100.00
(c) Hunan 500.00
(k) Western Szechwan 190.00 190.00
(m) Honan 850.00 850.00
(n) Shensi 250.00 260.00
r. Perf. 10½ (Kwangsi) 550.00
s. Inverted ovpt. (Shensi) 300.00
526 A62 (d) 16c (R) 60.00 50.00
(bx) Anhwei 550.00 550.00
(e) Kiangsi 77.50 60.00
(f) Eastern Szechwan 120.00 75.00
(h) Fukien 300.00 225.00
(j) Kwangtung 675.00 675.00
(l) Yunnan 60.00 50.00
(o) Kweichow 275.00 200.00
(p) Hupeh, perf. 10½ 925.00 850.00
r. Perf. 10½ (E. Szechwan) 500.00
s. Horiz. pair, imperf. btwn (Yunnan) 650.00
t. Perf. 13 (Hupeh) — —

This overprint means "Domestic Ordinary Letter Surcharge Paid." It was applied in various sizes and types by 14 districts, 9 using red ink, 5 using black. (The Anhwei overprint comes in two types.) These overprinted stamps were briefly sold for $1.16 before the government ordered their sale suspended. The vertical bars and 50c surcharge of Nos. 527-528 were then applied.

Nos. 525-526 Surcharged "50 cents" and 2 Vertical Bars in Black or Red

Anhwei — bx

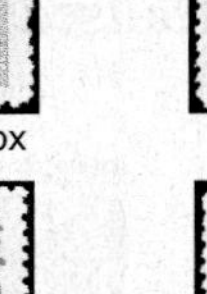
Hunan — c

Kansu — d

Kiangsi — e

Eastern Szechwan — f

Fukien — h

Kwangsi — i

Kwangtung — j

Western Szechwan — k

Yunnan — l

Honan — m

Shensi — n

Kweichow — o

Hupeh — p

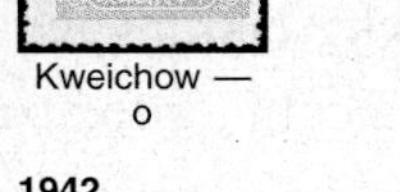

1942 Unwmk.

527 A62 50c on 16c (Bk) (c,f) 3.25 3.00
(i) Kwangsi 6.00 6.00
(k) Western Szechwan 11.00 8.50
(m) Honan 11.50 10.00
(n) Shensi 4.25 *5.00*
r. Inverted surch. (W. Szech.) 250.00
s. "k" surcharge on #493 350.00
528 A62 50c on 16c (R) (p) 5.00 5.00
(bx) Anhwei 95.00 *300.00*
(d) Kansu 3.25 *5.00*
(e) Kiangsi 5.50 *10.00*
(h) Fukien 6.50 *8.50*
(j) Kwangtung 6.50 6.00
(l) Yunnan 6.50 8.00
(o) Kweichow 4.00 7.00
r. "o" surcharge inverted 300.00
s. "p" surch. on #526(f) 100.00 *47.50*

Many varieties of Nos. 527-528 exist, including narrow or wide spacing between the two top characters, or between the vertical bars, or both.

Surcharges on stamps perf. 10½ (basic No. 493a) usually sell at much higher prices.

No. 493 Surcharged in Black, Red or Carmine

General Issue

Hunan — c50

Eastern Szechwan — f50

Chekiang — g50

Kwangsi — i50

Kwangtung — j50

Western Szechwan — k50

Honan — m50

Shensi — n50

Kweichow — o50

1943 Unwmk.

529 A62 50c on 16c (Bk) (m50) 11.00 11.00
(n50) Shensi 11.00 11.00
r. Perf. 11x13 (Shensi) 95.00
530 A62 50c on 16c (C) 1.00 *2.00*
(c50) Hunan 3.00 6.00
(f50) Eastern Szechwan 3.75 2.75
(g50) Chekiang 42.50 *50.00*
(i50) Kwangsi 6.50 *7.50*
(j50) Kwangtung 5.00 *7.00*
(k50) Western Szechwan 5.00 *6.50*
(m50) Honan 8.50 *9.50*
(o50) Kweichow 11.00 13.00
r. Inverted surch. (Hunan) 65.00
s. "05" instead of "50" (Kweichow) 450.00

Many varieties of Nos. 529-530 exist, such as narrow or wide spacing horizontally or vertically between the overprinted Chinese characters.

Surcharges on No. 493a (perf. 10½) usually sell at much higher pricess.

The General Issue type, No. 530, was distributed to all head offices, which in turn supplied the post offices under their direction. It is surcharged in carmine; the other stamps listed under No. 530 are surcharged in red or carmine.

Hunan — c20

Kansu — d20

Kiangsi — e20

Eastern Szechwan — f20

Fukien — h20

Kwangsi — i20

Kwangtung — j20

Western Szechwan — k20

Yunnan — l20

Honan — m20

Shensi — n20

Kweichow — o20

Hupeh — p20

On No. 318

1943 Wmk. 261, Unwmkd.

531 A45 20c on 13c (k20) 2.25 *5.00*
(d20) Kansu 2.25 *6.00*
(n20) Shensi 3.50 *5.50*
532 A45 20c on 13c (i20;R) 1.00 *2.75*
(c20) Hunan 1,100.
(e20) Kiangsi 275.00
(j20) Kwangtung 85.00 95.00
(p20) Hupeh 2.00 *4.00*

On No. 411

533 A45 20c on 13c (n20) 2.25 *4.25*
(d20) Kansu 2.75 *7.50*
(k20) Western Szechwan 2.00 *7.50*
(l20) Yunnan 21.00 *35.00*
(m20) Honan 350.00
534 A45 20c on 13c (p20;R) 1.75 *5.25*
(c20) Hunan 2.50 1.75
(e20) Kiangsi 9.00 2.10
(f20) Eastern Szechwan 2.50 *2.75*
(h20) Fukien 9.50 *11.00*
(i20) Kwangsi 2.00 *2.75*
(j20) Kwangtung 22.00 22.00
(o20) Kweichow 3.75 *3.25*

On No. 430

535 A45 20c on 13c (l20) 2.25 *4.75*
(d20) Kansu 2.25 *2.75*
(k20) Western Szechwan 35.00 *42.50*
(m20) Honan 9.50 *9.25*
(n20) Shensi 3.50 *5.50*
536 A45 20c on 13c (f20;i20;R) 2.25 *3.50*
(c20) Hunan 11.00 *9.75*
(e20) Kiangsi 4.50 *4.00*
(j20) Kwangtung 2.25 *2.75*
(o20) Kweichow 2.25 *10.00*
(p20) Hupeh 2.25 *4.00*

On No. 357

537 A57 20c on 16c (k20) 2.25 *2.75*
(c20) Hunan 3.50 *13.50*
(d20) Kansu 3.50 *13.50*
(m20) Honan 11.00 *17.50*
(n20) Shensi 3.50 *13.50*
538 A57 20c on 16c (e20, o20; R) 2.25 *13.50*
(c20) Hunan 11.00 *17.50*
(i20) Kwangsi 11.00 *13.50*
(j20) Kwangtung 52.50 *55.00*

On No. 413

539 A46 20c on 17c (c20;R) 2.75 *4.25*
(i20) Kwangsi 2.25 *2.75*
(j20) Kwangtung 30.00 *42.50*

On No. 432

540 A46 20c on 17c (k20) 3.50 *5.50*
(d20) Kansu 3.50 *6.50*
(m20) Honan 40.00 *47.50*
541 A46 20c on 17c (e20;R) 2.25 *5.50*
(j20) Kwangtung 3.75 *15.00*
(o20) Kweichow 2.50 *6.75*

On No. 456

542 A59 20c on 17c (m20) 210.00 *275.00*
543 A59 20c on 17c (c20;R) 18.00 30.00

On No. 415

544 A45 20c on 21c (e20;R) 11.00 *12.00*

On No. 434

545 A45 20c on 21c (c20, k20) 2.25 *4.00*
(d20) Kansu 2.50 *6.75*
(l20) Yunnan 2.50 *4.00*
(m20) Honan 2.50 *9.25*
546 A45 20c on 21c (f20;R) 1.75 *4.25*
(e20) Kiangsi 1.75 *5.50*
(h20) Fukien 2.50 *4.75*
(i20) Kwangsi 2.75 *4.00*
(j20) Kwangtung 3.75 *5.00*
(o20) Kweichow 2.50 *2.75*
(p20) Hupeh 2.50 *5.50*

On No. 417

547 A46 20c on 28c (e20;R) 775.00 *725.00*

On No. 436

548 A46 20c on 28c (l20) 3.50 *6.25*
(d20) Kansu 17.50 *24.00*
(k20) Western Szechwan 25.00 *65.00*
(m20) Honan 40.00 *47.50*
549 A46 20c on 28c (e20;R) 1.75 *3.25*
(c20) Hunan 1.90 *4.75*
(h20) Fukien 3.50 *4.75*
(i20) Kwangsi 4.75 *4.75*
(j20) Kwangtung 4.25 *6.25*
(o20) Kweichow 4.75 *4.75*

Many varieties of Nos. 531-549 exist, such as narrow or wide spacing between the overprinted Chinese characters, and "20" higher or lower than illustrated.

Type of 1942-43
Pacheng Printing

1944-46 Unwmk. *Perf. 12*
Without Gum

550 A62 30c chocolate .40 *13.00*
551 A62 $1 green 4.00 *5.00*
552 A62 $2 dk vio brn .25 .25
a. Imperf., pair 30.00 25.00
553 A62 $2 dk bl grn .25 *2.00*
a. Perf. 10½ 47.50 35.00
554 A62 $2 deep blue 1.75 *6.00*
555 A62 $3 lt yellow 1.60 *2.00*
556 A62 $4 violet brn .25 *2.00*
a. Imperf., pair 60.00
557 A62 $5 car ('46) .25 *1.00*
a. Perf. 10½ 75.00 75.00
558 A62 $6 gray vio ('45) .25 *.40*
559 A62 $10 red brn ('45) .25 .25
a. Imperf., pair 60.00
560 A62 $20 dp ultra ('46) .25 .25
561 A62 $50 dk green ('46) 4.00 .25
562 A62 $70 lilac ('46) 5.00 .25
563 A62 $100 lt brown ('46) .30 .25
Nos. 550-563 (14) 18.80 *32.90*

In the Pacheng printing of the Central Trust type stamps, the secret mark "C" has been added below the lower left foliate ornament beneath the sun emblem. On the $3, it is below the right ornament. New values also include a "P" at right of sun emblem on the $6 and $10, and at right of necktie on the $20.

Seven different varieties of paper were used in the printing of Nos. 550-563. Some values exist on laid paper with elephant watermark in sheet.

See surcharge note following No. 505.

Dr. Sun Yat-sen — A63

1944-46 Unwmk. Typo. *Perf. 12½*
Without Gum

565 A63 40c brown red .35 .35
566 A63 $2 gray brown .35 .35
567 A63 $3 red .35 .35
a. $3 orange red 4.00 4.00
568 A63 $3 lt red brn ('45) .95 .75
569 A63 $6 pale lilac gray ('45) .35 .45
570 A63 $10 dull lake ('45) .35 .35
571 A63 $20 rose ('45) .35 .35
a. Perf. 16 400.00 400.00
572 A63 $50 lt brown ('46) .45 .55
573 A63 $70 rose vio ('46) .55 .55
Nos. 565-573 (9) 4.05 4.05

For surcharges see Nos. 772, 774, 828, 833, 835, 836A, 839, 842, 851, 864, 868, 873-875, 877, 880. Taiwan 81, 98, Sinkiang 200-201.

Allegory of Savings — A64

1944-45 Engr. *Perf. 13*
Without Gum

574 A64 $40 indigo ('45) .35 *.90*
575 A64 $50 yellow grn ('45) .35 .35
576 A64 $100 yellow brn .35 .35
577 A64 $200 dk green ('45) .35 .35
Nos. 574-577 (4) 1.40 1.95

All four values were printed on thick paper; the first three were also printed on thin paper.

For surcharges see Szechwan Nos. F1, F3.

A65

1944, Dec. 25 Litho.
Without Gum

578 A65 $2 deep green .70 *2.00*
579 A65 $5 fawn .70 *2.00*
580 A65 $6 dull rose vio 1.40 *3.50*
581 A65 $10 violet blue 2.75 *7.00*
582 A65 $20 carmine 5.25 *9.00*
Nos. 578-582 (5) 10.80 23.50

50th anniversary of the Kuomintang.

Dr. Sun Yat-sen — A66

1945, Mar. 12 Without Gum

583 A66 $2 gray green .45 *1.75*
584 A66 $5 red brown .55 *1.75*
585 A66 $6 dk vio blue .65 *2.25*
586 A66 $10 lt blue 1.00 *1.75*
587 A66 $20 rose 1.25 *4.00*
588 A66 $30 buff 2.00 *6.00*
Nos. 583-588 (6) 5.90 17.50

Death of Dr. Sun Yat-sen, 20th anniv.

Dr. Sun Yat-sen — A67

1945-46 Without Gum *Perf. 12½*

589 A67 $2 green .25 .35
590 A67 $5 dull green .25 .35
591 A67 $10 dk blue .25 .35
a. Imperf., pair 120.00
592 A67 $20 carmine ('46) .25 .35
a. Imperf., pair 120.00
Nos. 589-592 (4) 1.00 1.40

For surcharges see Nos. 695, 697, 837, 855, Taiwan 58, 82, 87-88.

Statue of Liberty, Map of China, Flags of Great Britain, China and United States, and Chiang Kai-shek
A68

Unwmk.
1945, July 7 Engr. *Perf. 12*
Flags in Dark Blue and Red

593 A68 $1 deep blue .50 *1.00*
594 A68 $2 dull green .50 *1.00*
595 A68 $5 olive gray .50 *1.00*
596 A68 $6 brown 1.00 *2.00*
597 A68 $10 rose lilac 5.00 *7.00*
598 A68 $20 carmine rose 5.00 *9.50*
Nos. 593-598 (6) 12.50 *21.50*

Signing of a Treaty in 1943 between Great Britain, the US and China.

Pres. Lin Sen (1864-1943) — A69

1945, Aug. Unwmk. *Perf. 12*

599 A69 $1 dp ultra & blk .65 *4.00*
600 A69 $2 myrtle grn & blk .65 *4.00*
601 A69 $5 red & blk .65 *4.00*
602 A69 $6 purple & blk .90 *4.00*
603 A69 $10 choc & blk 4.00 *12.00*
604 A69 $20 olive grn & blk 4.25 *12.00*
Nos. 599-604 (6) 11.10 *40.00*

Pres. Chiang Kai-shek — A70

1945, Oct. 10
Flag in Rose Red and Violet Blue

605 A70 $2 green .45 *2.00*
606 A70 $4 dark blue .50 *2.00*
607 A70 $5 olive gray .50 *3.00*
608 A70 $6 bister brown 1.50 *4.00*
609 A70 $10 gray 4.00 *8.00*
610 A70 $20 red violet 5.00 *8.00*
Nos. 605-610 (6) 11.95 27.00

Inauguration of Chiang Kai-shek as president, Oct. 10, 1943.

President Chiang Kai-shek — A71

1945, Oct. 10 Typo. *Perf. 13*
Without Gum
Flag in Carmine and Blue

611 A71 $20 green & blue .25 .25
612 A71 $50 bister brn & bl .50 .50
613 A71 $100 blue .50 .40
614 A71 $300 rose red & blue .50 .40
Nos. 611-614 (4) 1.75 1.55

Victory of the Allied Nations over Japan.

C. N. C. Surcharges

The green surcharges on Nos. 615 to 621, and the surcharges on Nos. 647 to 721, and 768 to 774 represent Chinese National Currency and were applied at Shanghai.

Stamps of 1938-41 Srchd. in Black with Chinese Characters and New Value in Checkered Rectangle at Bottom, Resrchd. in Green

1945 *Perf. 12, 12½*

615 A57 10c on $20 on 3c (#350) .25 *5.00*
616 A46 15c on $30 on 2c (#423) .25 *5.00*
a. Horiz. pair, imperf. between 90.00
b. Vert. pair, imperf. between 85.00
617 A59 25c on $50 on 1c (#450) .25 *5.00*
618 A57 50c on $100 on 3c (#350) .25 *5.00*
619 A40 $1 on $200 on 1c (#422) .25 *5.00*
a. Horiz. pair, imperf. between 90.00
620 A57 $2 on $400 on 3c (#350) .25 *5.00*
621 A59 $5 on $1000 on 1c (#450) .25 *5.00*
Nos. 615-621 (7) 1.75 *35.00*

The black (first) surcharges on Nos. 615 to 621 represent Nanking puppet government currency.

In the green surcharge, the characters at the left express the new value and are either two or four in number.

Types of 1932-34, Re-engraved, and Srchd. in Green with Horiz. Bar and Four or Five Chinese Characters and Ovptd. in Black

Perf. 14

622 A47 $10 on 20c brown red 10.00 *12.00*
623 A47 $20 on 40c orange 25.00 *29.00*
a. Green surcharge inverted 150.00 85.00
624 A48 $50 on 30c violet brn 18.50 *22.00*
Nos. 622-624 (3) 53.50 *63.00*

These provisional surcharges were applied in Honan in National currency to stamps of the Hwa Pei (North China) government. The black overprint reads: "Hwa Pei."

The two-character "Hwa Pei" overprint was applied to various stamps in 1941-43 by the North China puppet government. See Nos. 8N1-8N53, 8N60-8N84.

Dr. Sun Yat-sen — A72

1945, Dec. **Typo.** *Perf. 12*
Without Gum

625 A72 $20 dp carmine .25 .25
626 A72 $30 dp blue .25 .25
627 A72 $40 orange .60 1.25
628 A72 $50 green 1.00 .35
629 A72 $100 dk brown .25 .25
630 A72 $200 brown violet .25 .25
Nos. 625-630 (6) 2.60 2.60

For surcharges see Nos. 810, 829, 838, 865, J110-J119, Taiwan 75, Kwangsi F2, Szechwan F2, F4, Yunnan 66-67, 71.

Type of 1931-37
Perf. 12½, 13x12½, 13½

1946 **Unwmk.**

631 A37 $1 dk violet .30 *1.50*
632 A37 $2 olive green .30 *3.00*
633 A37 $20 brt yellow grn .30 *.55*
634 A37 $30 chocolate .30 *.50*
635 A37 $50 red orange .30 *.50*
Nos. 631-635 (5) 1.50 6.05

$4 blue and $5 red values were prepared but not issued. Value $400.

For surcharges see Nos. 678, 684, 689-690, 768, 843.

Dr. Sun Yat-sen — A73

1946-47 **Engr.** *Perf. 14*
Without Gum

636 A73 $20 carmine 6.25 .25
637 A73 $30 dk blue ('47) .35 .25
638 A73 $50 purple .25 .25
639 A73 $70 red org ('47) 18.50 3.00
640 A73 $100 dk carmine .25 .25
641 A73 $200 olive grn ('47) .25 .25
642 A73 $500 brt bl grn ('47) .35 .25
643 A73 $700 red brown ('47) .25 .25
644 A73 $1000 rose lake .35 .35
645 A73 $3000 blue 1.00 .40
646 A73 $5000 dp green & ver 1.00 .40
Nos. 636-646 (11) 28.80 5.90

For surcharges see Nos. 679, 769, 775, 823, 837A, 844-845, 856, 866, 875A, 878, Taiwan 18, 23-28, 54, 76-77, 100, Northeastern Provinces 41-43, Fukien 5-6, Hunan 1, E1, Kwangsi 11, F2, Szechwan F5-F8, Sinkiang 202-204, People's Republic of China 3L53, 3L67-3L68, 6L28.

Stamps of 1932-41 Surcharged in Black

Perf. 12½, 13, 13x12, 14
Wmk. 261

647 A45 $20 on 8c (#409) .25 *2.00*
648 A39 $30 on ½c (#402) 4,000.
649 A45 $50 on 21c (#415) .25 *.25*
650 A45 $70 on 13c (#411) .25 .25
651 A46 $100 on 28c (#417) 1.00 *.65*

Unwmk.

652 A39 $3 on 2½c (#424) 7.50 *8.00*
653 A48 $10 on 15c (#431) .25 .25
654 A45 $20 on 8c (#428) .25 .25
655 A47 $20 on 20c (#433) .35 .35
656 A39 $30 on ½c (#421) .25 .25
657 A45 $50 on 21c (#434) .40 *.55*
657A A45 $70 on 13c (#318) 210.00 *250.00*
658 A45 $70 on 13c (#430) .40 *.55*
659 A46 $100 on 28c (#436) .40 .40

Forgeries of No. 648 exist.

Stamps and Types of 1931-1946 Surcharged in Black or Carmine

Perf. 12½, 13, 14

1946-47 **Wmk. 261**

660 A57 $50 on 5c green (#392) .35 .85
661 A57 $50 on 5c ol grn (#393) 25.00 20.00
662 A48 $50 on 5c dl red org (#408) .25 *1.25*
663 A40 $100 on 1c org (#403) .25 *1.10*

Perf. 12, 12½, 12½x13, 13, 14

1946-47 **Unwmk.**

664 A57 $20 on 3c (#350) .25 *.35*
665 A45 $20 on 8c (#428) .25 .25
666 A57 $50 on 3c (#350) .25 .25
667 A57 $50 on 5c (#352) .25 .25
668 A57 $50 on 5c (#382) .95 *1.75*
669 A48 $50 on 5c (#427) .25 .25
670 A59 $50 on 5c (#452) .25 .25
671 A62 $50 on $1 (#500) .25 .25
672 A40 $100 on 1c (#422) .25 .25
a. Without secret mark (#422a) 67.50 67.50
673 A57 $100 on 3c (#350) .25 .25
674 A57 $100 on 8c (#353) 14.00 14.00
675 A57 $100 on 8c (#369) 2.00 .35
676 A57 $100 on 8c (#383) .35 .35
a. Without "star" in uniform button (No. 383a) 25.00 16.00
677 A59 $100 on 8c (#454) .25 .25
678 A37 $100 on $1 (#631) .25 .25
679 A73 $100 on $20 (#636) .35 .35
680 A57 $200 on 10c (#354) .75 .25
681 A57 $200 on 10c (#384) .40 1.10
682 A37 $200 on $4 dl bl .50 .25
a. Double surcharge 16.00
683 A62 $250 on $1.50 (#501) .30 *2.50*
a. Perf. 11 250.00 250.00
684 A37 $250 on $2 (#632) .50 .25
685 A37 $250 on $5 car .50 .25
686 A57 $300 on 10c (#354) .25 .25
687 A59 $300 on 10c (#455) .25 .25
688 A57 $500 on 3c (#350) .50 .25
689 A37 $500 on $20 (#633) .25 .25
690 A37 $800 on $30 (#634) .30 .25
691 A37 $1000 on 2c (#297) .65 .35
692 A62 $1000 on $2 (#552) .30 .25
a. Imperf., pair 30.00 20.00
693 A62 $1000 on $2 (#553) .25 .25
694 A62 $1000 on $2 (#554) .25 *.55*
695 A67 $1000 on $2 (#589) .25 .25
696 A62 $2000 on $5 (#557) .30 .25
697 A67 $2000 on $5 dl grn (C) (#590) .25 .25
Nos. 664-697 (34) 27.15 27.65

Nos. 660-697 have a double row of dots in the surcharge box frame.

Nos. 682 and 685 were not issued without surcharge. No. 682 is perf. 13x13½; No. 685, perf. 12x12½.

The characters at the left express the new value and vary in number.

Stamps of 1938-41 Surcharged in Black

Perf. 12, 12½, 13, 14

1946 **Wmk. 261**

698 A45 $20 on 8c (#409) 250.00 190.00
699 A57 $50 on 5c (#392) 3.00 *3.00*
700 A57 $50 on 5c (#393) 5.00 *8.00*

1946-48 **Unwmk.**

700A A57 $20 on 5c (#381) 900.00
701 A57 $20 on 8c (#353) .25 .35
702 A57 $20 on 8c (#369) .35 .35
703 A57 $20 on 8c (#383) .25 .50
a. Without "star" in uniform button (No. 383a) 4.50 4.50
b. Inverted surcharge 20.00
c. Dbl. surch., one on back 32.50 32.50
d. Double surcharge 32.50
704 A45 $20 on 8c (#428) .25 .25
a. Double surcharge 22.50
705 A59 $20 on 8c (#453) .25 .25
706 A59 $20 on 8c (#454) .25 .25
a. Inverted surcharge 13.00
b. Double surcharge 13.00
707 A57 $50 on 5c (#351) 7.25 6.75
708 A57 $50 on 5c (#352) .25 .25
a. Inverted surcharge 27.50
709 A57 $50 on 5c (#381) .70 .70
710 A57 $50 on 5c (#382) .50 .35
711 A48 $50 on 5c (#427) .25 .25
a. Inverted surcharge 27.50
712 A59 $50 on 5c (#452) .50 .25
a. Double surcharge 16.00

Stamps of 1939-41 Surcharged in Blue or Red

1946 **Wmk. 261** *Perf. 12½*

713 A40 $10 on 1c org (#403) .25 .25
a. Inverted surcharge 40.00
714 A48 $20 on 3c dp yel brn (#406) 800.00 800.00

Forgeries of No. 714 exist. Expertizing is recommended.

1946 **Unwmk.** *Perf. 12, 12½, 13*

715 A40 $10 on 1c org (#422) .25 .25
a. Without secret mark (#422a) 10.00 12.00
b. Inverted surcharge 8.00 10.00
716 A59 $10 on 1c org (#450) .25 .25
a. Double surcharge 27.50
717 A57 $20 on 2c ol grn (R) (#368) .25 .25
718 A59 $20 on 2c brt ultra (R) (#451) .25 .25
a. Inverted surcharge 20.00
b. Double surcharge 16.00
719 A57 $20 on 3c dl cl (#350) .25 .25
a. Double surcharge 22.50
720 A48 $20 on 3c dp yel brn (#425) .25 .35
721 A39 $30 on 4c pale vio (R) (#426) .25 .25
a. Inverted surcharge 9.00
Nos. 715-721 (7) 1.75 1.85

President Chiang Kai-shek — A74

Perf. 10½-11½

1946, Oct. 31 **Engr.** **Unwmk.**

722 A74 $20 carmine 3.00 3.00
723 A74 $30 green 3.00 3.00
724 A74 $50 vermilion 3.00 3.00
725 A74 $100 yellow grn 5.00 5.00
726 A74 $200 yellow org 5.00 5.00
727 A74 $300 magenta 5.00 5.00
Nos. 722-727 (6) 24.00 24.00

60th birthday of Chiang Kai-shek.

Printed by Dah Yeh Printing Co.; the earlier ones are gumless, the later ones gummed.

For stamps of Type A74 with additional characters on either side of the portrait see Taiwan Nos. 29-34, Northeastern Provinces 30-35.

Printed by Dah Tung Book Co.
Without Gum
Perf. 14

722a A74 $20 carmine 1.10 1.50
723a A74 $30 green 1.10 1.50
724a A74 $50 vermilion 1.10 1.50
725a A74 $100 yellow green 3.00 3.00
726a A74 $200 yellow orange 2.00 2.00
727a A74 $300 magenta 2.50 2.50
Nos. 722a-727a (6) 10.80 12.00

Assembly House, Nanking A75

1946, Nov. 15 **Litho.** *Perf. 14*
Without Gum

728 A75 $20 green .75 .40
729 A75 $30 blue .75 .40
730 A75 $50 dk brown .75 .40
a. Horiz. pair, imperf. between 95.00 95.00
731 A75 $100 carmine .75 .40
Nos. 728-731 (4) 3.00 1.60

Convening of National Assembly.

For surcharges see Taiwan Nos. 10-13, Northeastern Provinces 26-29.

Entrance to Dr. Sun Yat-sen Mausoleum A76

1947, May 5 **Engr.**

732 A76 $100 dp green .35 .35
733 A76 $200 deep blue .35 .35
734 A76 $250 carmine .35 .35
735 A76 $350 lt brown .35 .35
736 A76 $400 dp claret .35 .35
Nos. 732-736 (5) 1.75 1.75

First anniversary of return of Chinese National Government to Nanking.

See Taiwan Nos. 35-39, Northeastern Provinces 36-40.

Dr. Sun Yat-sen — A77

1947 *Perf. 12½, 11½x12½*

737 A77 $500 olive green .25 .25
738 A77 $1000 green & car .25 .25
739 A77 $2000 dp blue & red brn .30 .25
740 A77 $5000 org red & blk .30 .25
Nos. 737-740 (4) 1.10 1.00

For surcharge see Szechwan No. 50.

Confucius A78

Confucius' Lecturing School A79

Tomb of Confucius A80

Temple of Confucius A81

1947, Aug. 27 **Litho.** *Perf. 14*
Without Gum

741 A78 $500 carmine rose .60 *.65*

Engr.

742 A79 $800 yellow brown .50 *.80*
743 A80 $1250 blue green .50 *1.25*
744 A81 $1800 blue .50 *1.90*
Nos. 741-744 (4) 2.10 4.60

Sun Yat-sen and Plum Blossoms — A82

1947-48 **Engr.** *Perf. 14*
Without Gum

745 A82 $150 dk blue .25 *.25*
746 A82 $250 dp lilac .35 .25
747 A82 $500 blue grn .25 .25
748 A82 $1000 red .25 .25
749 A82 $2000 vermilion .25 .25
750 A82 $3000 blue .25 .25
751 A82 $4000 gray ('48) .25 .25
752 A82 $5000 dk brown .25 .25
753 A82 $6000 rose lil ('48) .25 .25
754 A82 $7000 lt red brn ('48) .25 .25
755 A82 $10,000 dp blue & car 1.10 .25
756 A82 $20,000 car & yel grn .35 .25
757 A82 $50,000 grn & dk bl 1.25 .25
758 A82 $100,000 dl yel & ol grn ('48) 1.80 2.00
759 A82 $200,000 vio brn & dp bl ('48) 2.25 .45
760 A82 $300,000 sep & org brn ('48) 2.25 .55
761 A82 $500,000 dk Prus grn & sep ('48) 3.00 .55
Nos. 745-761 (17) 14.60 6.80

See Nos. 788-799. For similar type see Formosa A1. For surcharges see Nos. 770, 804-806, 821-822, 840-841, 858-859, 869, 871, 880A-880B, 885A-885E, 1025-1036, Taiwan 56-57, 59, 89, Fukien 1-4, 7-12, 19-23, Hunan 2-5, C1, F1, Kiangsi 1-3, C1, E1, F1-F2, Kwangsi 8-10, 12-17, Shensi 1-2, C1, E1, Szechwan 24-49, Yunnan 61-62, 69, 205-207, People's Republic of China 3L69-3L70, 3L76, 4L63-4L64, 6L22, 6L27, 6L29, 6L32.

Chinese Flag and Map of Taiwan — A83

1947, Oct. 25 **With Gum**

762 A83 $500 carmine .35 *1.00*
763 A83 $1250 deep green .35 *1.00*

Restoration of Taiwan to China, 2nd anniv.

Mobile Post Office — A84

Street-Corner Branch Post Office — A85

1947, Nov. 5

764 A84 $500 carmine .25 *.50*
765 A85 $1000 lilac .25 *1.00*
766 A85 $1250 green .25 *.85*
767 A84 $1800 deep blue .25 *1.10*
Nos. 764-767 (4) 1.00 3.45

Stamps and Type of 1943-47 Surcharged in Black or Green

1947-48 **Unwmk.** *Perf. 12½, 13, 14*

768 A37 $500 on $20 brt yel grn (#633) .25 .25
769 A73 $1250 on $70 red org (#639) .25 .25
770 A82 $1800 on $350 yel org .25 .25
771 A62 $2000 on $3 dk yel ('48) (#503) .50 .25
772 A63 $2000 on $3 red (#567) .25 .25
a. On #567a 6.50 2.25
773 A62 $3000 on $3 lt yel ('48) (#555) .25 .25
774 A63 $3000 on $3 lt red brn (G) ('48) (#568) .25 .25
Nos. 768-774 (7) 2.00 1.75

Nos. 768-774 have a single row of dots in the surcharge box frame.

The characters at the left express the new value and vary in number.

No. 640 Surcharged

1948, Aug. *Perf. 14*

775 A73 $5000 on $100 dk car 7.00 *80.00*

No. 775 received its surcharge in Kwangsi for use in that province.

Map of China and Mail-carrying Vehicles A86

Rural Mail Delivery — A87

Early and Modern Mail Transportation A88

1947, Dec. 16 **Engr.** *Perf. 12*

776 A86 $100 violet .25 *1.00*
777 A87 $200 brt green .25 *1.00*
778 A87 $300 red brown .25 *1.00*
779 A88 $400 scarlet .25 *1.00*
780 A88 $500 brt vio blue .25 *1.00*
Nos. 776-780 (5) 1.25 5.00

Chinese Postal Administration, 50th anniv.

National Assembly Building and New Constitution A89

1947, Dec. 25 *Perf. 14*
Without Gum

781 A89 $2000 brt red .50 .60
782 A89 $3000 blue .50 .60
783 A89 $5000 deep green .50 .60
Nos. 781-783 (3) 1.50 1.80

1st anniv. of the adoption of China's new constitution, Dec. 25, 1946.

Chinese Stamps of 1947 and 1912 — A90

Perf. 14, Imperf.

1948, Mar. 20 **Litho.**
Without Gum

784 A90 $5000 dk car rose 1.00 *4.00*
a. Vert. pair, imperf. btwn 40.00
785 A90 $5000 dk green 1.00 *4.00*
a. Vert. pair, imperf. btwn 40.00

Stamp exhibitions at Nanking, Mar. 20 (No. 784), and at Shanghai, May 19 (No. 785).

Sun Yat-sen Memorial Hall, Taipei — A91

1948, Apr. 28 **Engr.** *Perf. 14*

786 A91 $5000 violet .30 *1.25*
787 A91 $10000 red .30 *2.00*

Restoration of Formosa to China, 3rd anniv.

Sun Yat-sen Type of 1947-48

1948 **Without Gum**

788 A82 $20000 rose pink .50 .35
789 A82 $30000 chocolate .25 .25
790 A82 $40000 green .25 .25
791 A82 $50000 dp blue .25 .25
792 A82 $100000 dull grn .25 .25
793 A82 $200000 brn vio .75 .25
794 A82 $300000 yel grn 2.75 1.00
795 A82 $500000 lil rose 1.25 .25
796 A82 $1000000 claret .75 .25
797 A82 $2000000 vermilion 1.50 .25
798 A82 $3000000 ol bis 3.00 .55
799 A82 $5000000 ultra 6.00 .90
Nos. 788-799 (12) 17.50 4.80

Zeros for "cents" omitted.

For surcharges see Nos. 841, 871, 880A-880B, 885A-885E, 1025-1028, 1031-1036.

Early Ship and Modern Hai Tien — A92

Passenger Ship Kiang Ya — A93

1948, Aug. 16 **Without Gum**

800 A92 $20000 blue .60 *1.75*
801 A92 $30000 rose lilac .60 *2.00*
802 A93 $40000 yel brown .60 *2.75*
803 A93 $60000 vermilion .60 *2.75*
Nos. 800-803 (4) 2.40 9.25

75th anniversary of the China Merchants' Steam Navigation Company.

Type of 1947-48 Surcharged in Black

1948 **Unwmk.** *Perf. 14*

804 A82 $4000 on $100 car .25 *25.00*
805 A82 $5000 on $100 car .25 .25
806 A82 $8000 on $700 red brn .35 *.90*
Nos. 804-806 (3) .85 26.15

Stamps of 1942-46 Surcharged in Black or Red

1948 *Perf. 12½, 13*

807 A62 $5000 on $1 (#500) .25 .25
808 A62 $5000 on $1 (#551) 20.00 *20.00*
809 A62 $5000 on $2 (#502) .25 .25
810 A72 $10000 on $20 (#625) .25 .25
811 A62 $20000 on 10c (#492) .25 .25
812 A62 $20000 on 50c (#498;R) .25 *.50*
813 A62 $30000 on 30c (#496) .25 *.50*
a. Perf. 10½ 22.00 22.00
Nos. 807-813 (7) 21.50 22.00

Nos. 492, 556 and 558 Surcharged in Black or Carmine

1948

814 A62 $15,000 on 10c dp grn .25 .25
815 A62 $15,000 on $4 vio brn .25 .25
816 A62 $15,000 on $6 gray vio (C) .25 .25
Nos. 814-816 (3) .75 .75

No. 498, 494 and 504 Surcharged in Black

1948 **Unwmk.** *Perf. 11½, 13*

817 A62 $15,000 on 50c, perf. 13 .25 *.50*
a. Perf. 11½ 10.00 *15.00*
818 A62 $40,000 on 20c dk ol grn .25 .90
a. Perf. 11 10.00 7.50
819 A62 $60,000 on $4 red brn .45 *.50*
Nos. 817-819 (3) .95 1.90

Gold Yuan Surcharges
(Nos. 820-885E)

Stamps of 1942-47 Surcharged in Black, Carmine or Red

1948 *Perf. 14, 13, 11*

820 A62 ½c on 30c (#496) .25 *5.00*
821 A82 ½c on $500 (Bk) (#747) .25 .25
822 A82 ½c on $500 (C) (#747) .25 *.90*
823 A73 1c on $20 (#636) .25 *2.25*
824 A62 2c on $1.50 (R) (#501) .25 *3.25*
825 A62 3c on $5 (#505) .25 *3.25*
826 A62 4c on $1 (#499) .25 *3.25*

827 A62 5c on 50c (#498) .25 *1.00*
a. Perf. 11 6.50 *8.00*
Nos. 820-827 (8) 2.00 *19.15*

On No. 820-827, the position of the surcharged denomination and "Gold Yuan" characters varies, the aim being to obliterate the original denomination.

Stamps of 1940-48 Surcharged in Black, Violet, Carmine, Blue or Green

Perf. 12, 12½, 13, 14, 12½x13

1948-49

828 A63 5c on $20 (#571) .25 *1.10*
829 A72 5c on $30 (C) (#626) .25 *2.00*
a. Double surcharge 17.50
830 A57 10c on 2c (#368) .25 *1.75*
831 A39 10c on 2½c (#424) .25 *1.10*
832 A62 10c on 25c (V) (#495) .25 *1.25*
833 A63 10c on 40c (#565) .25 *1.40*
834 A62 10c on $1 (#500) .25 *.35*
834A A62 10c on $1 (#551) 275.00 *250.00*
835 A63 10c on $2 (#566) .25 .25
836 A62 10c on $20 (C) (#560) .25 .25
836A A63 10c on $20 (#571) 300.00 *300.00*
837 A67 10c on $20 (#592) .25 .25
837A A73 10c on $20 (#636) 1.00 *3.50*
838 A72 10c on $30 (C) (#626) .25 *1.50*
839 A63 10c on $70 (#573) .25 .50
a. Double surcharge 15.00
840 A82 10c on $7000 (#754) 1.00 1.00
841 A82 10c on $20,000 (#788) .25 *4.75*
842 A63 20c on $6 (#569) .25 *.35*
843 A37 20c on $30 (#634) .45 *4.75*
844 A73 20c on $30 (C) (#637) .65 *3.75*
845 A73 20c on $100 (#640) .25 *3.00*
a. Inverted surcharge 22.00
b. Double surcharge 16.00
846 A39 50c on ½c (#312) 75.00 75.00
847 A39 50c on ½c (#421) .25 *.65*
a. Inverted surcharge 30.00
848 A62 50c on 20c (#494) .25 *2.00*
849 A62 50c on 30c (Bl) (#496) .25 *3.00*
850 A62 50c on 40c (V) (#497) .25 *2.00*
a. Perf. 11 9.00 *10.00*
851 A63 50c on 40c (V) (#565) .25 *1.00*
852 A62 50c on $4 (#556) 1.00 *3.50*
853 A62 50c on $4 (Bl) (#556) .25 *2.00*
854 A62 50c on $20 (C) (#560) .25 *2.00*
855 A67 50c on $20 (V) (#592) .50 *1.50*
856 A73 50c on $20 (#636) .25 *1.25*
857 A62 50c on $70 (C) (#562) .30 .30
858 A82 50c on $6000 (#753) 2.00 *3.50*
859 A82 50c on $6000 (Bl) (#753) .25 *1.50*
860 A62 $1 on 30c (#550) .25 .25
a. Perf. 11 22.00 22.00
861 A62 $1 on 40c (#497) .25 .25
a. Perf. 11 4.00 4.00
862 A62 $1 on $1 (#499) .55 *2.00*
863 A62 $1 on $5 (#557) .70 .40
864 A63 $2 on $2 (R) (#566) .25 *1.00*
865 A72 $2 on $20 (#625) .25 .25
866 A73 $2 on $100 (#640) .25 .25
867 A46 $5 on 17c (#432) .90 .90
868 A63 $5 on $2 (#566) .25 .25
869 A82 $5 on $3000 (C) (#750) .25 *1.50*
870 A47 $8 on 20c (#433) .50 .50
871 A82 $8 on $30,000 (C) (#789) .25 *2.50*
872 A47 $10 on 40c (#438) 1.25 1.00
873 A63 $10 on $2 (G) (#566) .25 .35
874 A63 $10 on $2 (C) (#566) .25 .25
875 A63 $20 on $2 (C) (#566) .25 .25
875A A73 $20 on $20 (#636) 4.75 3.00
876 A62 $50 on 30c (#496) .25 *.30*
877 A63 $50 on $2 (Bl) (#566) .30 .25
878 A73 $80 on $20 (#636) .25 *1.00*
879 A62 $100 on $1 (#551) .25 *1.00*
a. Perf. 11 100.00 *100.00*
880 A63 $100 on $2 (C) (#566) .35 .35
880A A82 $50,000 on $20,000 (#788) 1.40 .40
880B A82 $100,000 on $30,000 (V) (#789) 2.75 .90

Wmk. 261

881 A39 10c on 2½c (#405) .40 *4.00*
882 A39 50c on ½c (#402) .25 *2.00*
Nos. 828-882 (61) 680.50 *707.10*

Characters at left express the new value. Style of characters and numerals varies.

Nos. Q7 to Q9 Surcharged in Black or Carmine

1948 Unwmk. *Perf. 12½*

883 PP2 $200 on $3000 red org .70 .50
884 PP2 $500 on $5000 dk bl (C) .70 .45
885 PP2 $1000 on $10,000 vio .70 .50
Nos. 883-885 (3) 2.10 1.45

Nos. 788-791 Surcharged in Gold Yuan in Red (Nos. 885A, 885D-885E) or Black (Nos. 885B-885C) at Foochow

1949, Apr. 30 Unwmk. *Perf. 14*

885A $20,000 on $40,000 16.00 *21.00*
885B $50,000 on $30,000 16.00 *21.00*
885C $100,000 on $20,000 16.00 *21.00*
885D $200,000 on $40,000 16.00 *21.00*
885E $200,000 on $50,000 16.00 *21.00*
Nos. 885A-885E (5) 80.00 *105.00*

Issued in Fukien Postal District.

Dr. Sun Yat-sen — A94

1949 Unwmk. Engr. *Perf. 14*
Without Gum

886 A94 $1 orange .45 *1.00*
887 A94 $10 green .50 *.65*
888 A94 $20 vio brown .45 *.65*
889 A94 $50 dk Prus grn .45 *.65*
890 A94 $100 org brn .45 *.65*
891 A94 $200 red org .45 *.65*
892 A94 $500 rose lilac .45 *.65*
893 A94 $800 car rose .45 *2.50*
894 A94 $1000 blue .45 .65

Redrawn
Engr.
Perf. 12½

895 A94 $10 green .45 *5.00*
a. Perf. 14 4.00 *8.00*
b. Perf. 13 .45 *5.50*
896 A94 $20 violet brn .45 *.55*
a. Perf. 14 1.10 *4.50*
b. Perf. 13 .45 *.90*
Nos. 886-896 (11) 5.00 *13.60*

Small "T" at left of necktie on Nos. 895-896a.

Redrawn

1949 Litho. *Perf. 12½*
Without Gum

897 A94 $50 grnsh gray .30 *2.75*
898 A94 $100 dk org brn .30 *.50*
899 A94 $200 orange red .60 *3.00*
900 A94 $500 rose lilac .30 *.50*
901 A94 $1000 deep blue .30 *.50*
902 A94 $2000 violet .30 *1.50*
903 A94 $5000 light blue .30 *.45*
904 A94 $10,000 sepia .30 *.45*
905 A94 $20,000 apple grn .30 *1.50*
906 A94 $50,000 rose pink .30 *1.00*
907 A94 $80,000 brn red .70 *4.50*
908 A94 $100,000 bl grn .45 *1.00*
Nos. 897-908 (12) 4.45 *17.65*

Diagonal lines have been added to the background of the redrawn design.

Zeros for "cents" omitted on No. 908.

See Nos. 973-981. For surcharges see Nos. 991-1006, 1057-1060, Fukien 13-17, Szechwan 51, Tsingtau 1-4, Yunnan 63-65, 68, 70, People's Republic of China 4L34-4L44, 4L48-4L60, 5L43-5L50, 5L54-5L59, 5L91-5L95, 6L1-6L16, 6L23-6L26, 6L30-6L31, 7L6-7L8, 7L13-7L16, 8L12-8L13, 8L48-8L51.

Plane, Train and Ship — A95

Gold Yuan Surcharge in Black or Other Colors on Revenue Stamps

Two types, 50c on $20:
I — Thick numerals in "20." Vertical stroke in lower right corner of vignette. (Dah Tung Book Co.)
II — Thin "20." No vertical stroke in corner. (Central Trust.)

Two types, $2 on $50, $10 on $30, $100 on $50 and $300 on $50:
III — "Y" in lower right corner of vignette. (Dah Yeh Printing Co.)
IV — No "Y" in corner. (Dah Tung, Central Trust or Chung Ming.)

Two types, $50 on $300 and $1000 on $100:
V — Projection on left frame column below foliate ornament. (Dah Yeh Printing Co.)
VI — No projection. (Dah Tung Book Co.)

Litho.; Nos. 923, 933, 935-936 Engr.

1949 *Perf. 12½, 13, 14*
Without Gum

913 A95 50c on $20 red brn, I .25 *.50*
a. 50c on $20 brown, II .25 *.50*
914 A95 $1 on $15 red org .25 *9.00*
915 A95 $2 on $50 dk bl, IV (C) .25 *1.00*
a. Type III .40 *1.25*
916 A95 $3 on $50 dk bl (Bl) .25 *1.00*
917 A95 $3 on $50 dk bl .25 *1.00*
918 A95 $5 on $500 brn .25 *.90*
919 A95 $10 on $30 dk vio, III (Bl) .25 *.45*
a. Type IV .70 *1.75*
b. Double surcharge, IV
920 A95 $15 on $20 org brn (Bl) .25 *.45*
921 A95 $25 on $20 org brn (G) .25 *1.00*
922 A95 $50 on $50 dk bl (R O) .25 *.45*
923 A95 $50 on $300 grn, VI (C) .25 *.60*
a. $50 on $300 yel grn, V (C) .25 *.50*
924 A95 $80 on $50 dk bl (Dk Br) .25 *1.25*
925 A95 $100 on $50 dk bl, IV 1.00 .60
a. Type III 8.00 *17.50*
926 A95 $200 on $50 dk bl .90 .90
927 A95 $200 on $500 brn (Bl) .60 *1.00*
928 A95 $300 on $50 dk bl, III (C) 1.25 1.25
a. Type IV 1.75 *2.00*
929 A95 $300 on $50 dk bl (Br) 2.00 2.00
930 A95 $500 on $15 red org (Bl) 1.50 *4.25*
931 A95 $500 on $30 dk vio .75 *3.00*
932 A95 $1000 on $50 dk bl (C) 12.00 9.00
933 A95 $1000 on $100 ol grn, V 3.00 *4.50*
a. Type VI 14.00 *15.00*
934 A95 $1500 on $50 dk bl (Bl) 2.50 *3.00*
935 A95 $2000 on $300 grn (Bl) .45 .65
a. Horiz. pair, imperf. between
936 A95 $5000 on $100 ol grn (C) 350.00
Nos. 913-936 (24) 378.95
Nos. 913-935 (23) 28.95 47.75

No. 936 was officially authorized, but never issued.

Key pattern of overprinted border inverted and in 2 or 3 detached sections at top and bottom in Blue, Black or Green
Without Gum
Type A95

1949 Hankow Prints Litho.

937 A95 $50 on $10 (Bk) 9.50 *11.00*
938 A95 $100 on $10 11.00 *14.00*
939 A95 $500 on $10 (Bk) 9.00 *6.50*
940 A95 $1000 on $10 7.00 *9.00*
941 A95 $5000 on $20 29.00 25.00
942 A95 $10,000 on $20 (Bk) 17.50 14.00
943 A95 $50,000 on $20 20.00 *25.00*
944 A95 $100,000 on $20 (Bk) 25.00 25.00
945 A95 $500,000 on $20 350.00 300.00
946 A95 $2,000,000 on $20 (G) 900.00 375.00
947 A95 $5,000,000 on $20 1,600. 950.00
Nos. 937-944 (8) 128.00 129.50

The $10 stamp is slate green, the $20 red brown.

The basic revenue stamps of Nos. 915-947 were the work of several printers. There are three main types, differing in the bottom label. Nos. 922 and 925 are in a second type; Nos. 923 and 930 in a third. Varieties of paper, color and overprint exist.

Counterfeits exist of Nos. 945-947.

For surcharges and overprints see Nos. 960-970, C63, E13, F3, J122-J126, Hupeh 1-2, People's Republic of China 5L51-5L53, 6L17-6L21.

Redrawn Coarse Impression

1949 Litho. Without Gum
Size: 18¼x20¾mm

951 A94 $50 green .40 *30.00*
952 A94 $1000 dp blue .50 *4.00*
953 A94 $5000 carmine .65 *4.00*
954 A94 $10,000 brown 4.00 *10.00*
955 A94 $20,000 orange 1.25 *4.00*
956 A94 $50,000 blue 3.00 8.00
957 A94 $200,000 violet 5.00 8.00
958 A94 $500,000 vio brn 6.00 10.00
Nos. 951-958 (8) 20.80 *78.00*

Zeros for "cents" omitted on Nos. 957-958.
See surcharge note following No. 900.

Locomotive and Ship — A96

1949, May 1 Litho. *Perf. 12½*
Without Gum

959 A96 orange 5.00 2.50
a. Rouletted 13.50 10.00

Nos. 959, C62, E12 and F2 were printed without denomination and sold at the daily rate of the yuan. This was necessitated by the gold yuan inflation.

For surcharges and overprints see Nos. 1130, 1213, Taiwan 97, Fukien 18, Kansu 1, People's Republic of China 24-29, 101-104, 4L31-4L33, 4L45-4L47, 4L61-4L62, 7L9-7L12, 8L52-8L54.

Revenue Stamps Overprinted in Black

1949, May *Perf. 12½, 13, 14*

Without Gum

960 A95 $30 dark violet 125.00 120.00

Engr.

961 A95 $200 violet brown 15.00 12.00
962 A95 $500 dark green 25.00 20.00
Nos. 960-962 (3) 165.00 152.00

A similar overprint appears on Nos. C63, E13, F3, differing in 2nd and 3rd characters of bottom row.

Silver Yuan Surcharge in Black or Other Colors

1949 **Litho.**

963 A95 1c on $5000 brn (G) 8.50 7.00
964 A95 4c on $100 ol grn (Bl) 6.00 3.75
965 A95 4c on $3000 org) 6.00 2.00
966 A95 10c on $50 dk bl (RV) 8.50 2.75
967 A95 10c on $1000 car 8.50 8.50
a. Inverted surcharge 60.00
968 A95 20c on $1000 red (V) 8.50 8.50
b. Inverted surcharge
968A A95 50c on $30 dk vio (C) 47.50 10.00
969 A95 50c on $50 dk bl (C) 21.00 10.00
970 A95 $1 on $50 dk bl 25.00 *35.00*
Nos. 963-970 (9) 139.50 87.50

Nos. 963-965 and 967 are engraved.

Sun Type of 1949 Redrawn
Coarse Impression

1949 *Perf. 12½, 13 or Compound*

973 A94 1c apple green 29.00 *11.00*
974 A94 2c orange 9.00 *17.50*
975 A94 4c blue green .35 *2.00*
976 A94 10c deep lilac .35 *2.00*
977 A94 16c orange red .75 *17.50*
978 A94 20c blue .45 *5.50*
979 A94 50c dk brown 2.40 *48.00*
980 A94 100c deep blue 475.00 475.00
981 A94 500c scarlet 525.00 525.00
Nos. 973-981 (9) 1,042. 1,104.

For surcharges see Nos. 1057-1060.

Flying Geese Over Globe — A97

1949, May **Litho.** *Perf. 12½*

Without Gum

984 A97 $1 brown org 15.00 *20.00*
985 A97 $2 blue 75.00 *90.00*
986 A97 $5 car rose 75.00 *90.00*
987 A97 $10 blue grn 75.00 *90.00*
Nos. 984-987 (4) 240.00 *290.00*

Five other denominations — 10c, 16c, 50c, $20 and $50 — were also printed at Shanghai, but were not issued.

For surcharges see Nos. 1007-1011, 1042-1045, 1061-1063, People's Republic of China 49-56, 5LQ17-5LQ26, 7L17-7L18, 8L14-8L16.

Pigeons, Globe and Wreath A98

Engraved and Typographed

1949, Aug. 1 **Without Gum** *Imperf.*

988 A98 $1 org red & blk 12.00 *17.50*

75th anniv. of the UPU.
Exists with black denomination omitted.

Summer Palace, Peiping — A99

Bronze Bull and Kunming Lake — A100

Engraved and Typographed

1949, Aug. *Rouletted*

Without Gum

989 A99 15c org brn & grn 8.00 *12.00*
990 A100 40c dl grn & car 9.25 *12.00*
a. 2nd and 3rd characters at top transposed 160.00 200.00

Silver Yuan Surcharge in Black on 1949 Sun Yat-sen Issues

1949 *Perf. 12½, 14*

991 A94 1c on $100 org brn 15.00 10.00
992 A94 1c on $100 dk org brn 15.00 10.00
993 A94 2½c on $500 rose lil 19.00 11.00
a. Inverted surcharge 60.00
994 A94 2½c on $500 rose lil 21.00 12.00
995 A94 15c on $10 grn 30.00 40.00
a. Inverted surcharge 67.50
996 A94 15c on $20 vio brn 42.50 *65.00*
Nos. 991-996 (6) 142.50 148.00

Silver Yuan Surcharge in Black or Carmine

997 A94 2½c on $50 grn 2.75 *3.75*
998 A94 2½c on $50,000 bl 7.50 3.75
999 A94 5c on $1000 dp bl (C) 6.00 *8.00*
1000 A94 5c on $20,000 org 4.00 *7.00*
1001 A94 5c on $200,000 vio (C) 5.50 3.25
1002 A94 5c on $500,000 vio brn 5.50 3.25
1003 A94 10c on $5000 car 11.00 *12.00*
1004 A94 10c on $10,000 brn 11.00 *12.00*
1005 A94 15c on $200 red org 13.50 *14.00*
1006 A94 25c on $100 dk org brn 27.50 *40.00*
Nos. 997-1006 (10) 94.25 *107.00*

REPUBLIC OF CHINA

ri-'pə-blik of 'chī-nə

(Taiwan)

LOCATION — Taiwan (since 1949) (Formosa)
GOVT. — Republic
AREA — 13,970 sq. mi.
POP. — 22,113,250 (1999 est.)
CAPITAL — Taipei

Stamps issued and used in Taiwan after Communist forces occupied the Chinese mainland include Taiwan Nos. 91-96, 101-103, J10-J17.

Catalogue values for unused stamps in this country are for Never Hinged items, beginning with Scott 1124 in the regular postage section, Scott B17 in the semi-postal section, Scott C69 in the airpost section, and Scott J142 in the postage due section.

Watermarks

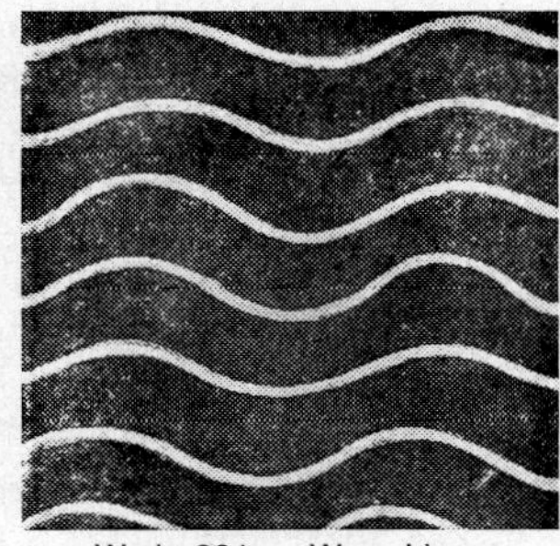

Wmk. 281 — Wavy Lines

Wmk. 323 — Seal Character (found with "Yu" in various arrangements)

Wmk. 368 — JEZ Multiple

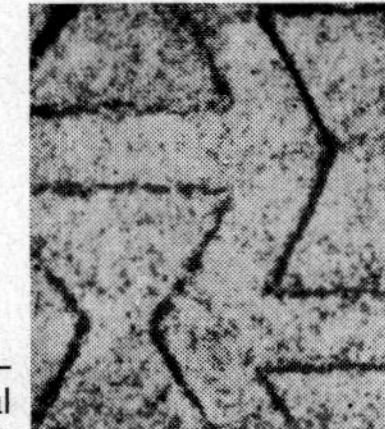

Wmk. 370 — Geometrical Design

Type of 1949 with Value Omitted Surcharged in Various Colors

1950, Jan. 1 **Unwmk.** *Perf. 12½*

Without Gum

1007 A97 $1 green (Bk) 150.00 11.00
1008 A97 $2 green (C) 200.00 20.00
1009 A97 $5 green (V) 2,000. 110.00
1010 A97 $10 green (Br) 2,750. 275.00
1011 A97 $20 green (Dk Bl) 4,500. 900.00
Nos. 1007-1011 (5) 9,600. 1,316.

Two printings of the $1 and $2 show minor differences.

Cheng Ch'eng-kung (Koxinga) — A101

1950, June 26 **Typo.** *Rouletted*

Without Gum

1012 A101 3c dk gray grn 4.50 5.00
1013 A101 10c orange brn 3.25 .30
1014 A101 15c orange yel 14.50 10.00
1015 A101 20c emerald 4.00 .25
1016 A101 30c claret 60.00 16.00
1017 A101 40c red orange 4.50 .30
1018 A101 50c chocolate 7.25 1.00
1019 A101 80c carmine 21.50 3.50
1020 A101 $1 ultra 18.00 1.00
1021 A101 $1.50 green 67.50 13.00
1022 A101 $1.60 blue 60.00 1.60
1023 A101 $2 red violet 24.50 1.25
1024 A101 $5 aqua 170.00 20.00
Nos. 1012-1024 (13) 459.50 73.20

Part perf pairs exist of the 10c, 20c, 80c.

The 10c and 20c were reprinted from new plates. There are slight differences.

For surcharges see Nos. 1070-1072, 1105-1108, 1118-1119. See No. C64.

Nos. 751, 753, 788-791, 793, 795-799 Surcharged in Carmine or Black

1950 **Engr.** *Perf. 14*

Without Gum

1025 A82 3c on $30,000 3.75 5.00
1026 A82 3c on $40,000 (C) 3.25 5.00
1027 A82 3c on $50,000 (C) 3.25 5.00
1028 A82 5c on $200,000 3.75 5.00
1029 A82 10c on $4000 32.00 35.00
1030 A82 10c on $6000 23.00 26.00
1031 A82 10c on $20,000 23.00 26.00
1032 A82 10c on $2,000,000 23.00 15.00
1033 A82 20c on $500,000 35.00 20.00
1034 A82 20c on $1,000,000 60.00 20.00
1035 A82 30c on $3,000,000 90.00 30.00
1036 A82 50c on $5,000,000 (C) 150.00 45.00
Nos. 1025-1036 (12) 450.00 237.00

Issued: Nos. 1025-1027, 3/6; No. 1028, 3/25; No. 1031, 6/10: Nos. 1029-1030, 1032, 1035-1036, 8/1; No. 1033-1034, 8/25.

Forgeries exist.

Inverted Surcharge

1029a A82 10c on $4000 175.00
1030a A82 10c on $6000 375.00
1031a A82 10c on $20,000 210.00
1032a A82 10c on $2,000,000 225.00
1033a A82 20c on $500,000 300.00
1034a A82 20c on $1,000,000 300.00

Allegory of Election A102

Perf. 12x12½, Imperf.

1951, Mar. 20 **Engr.** **Unwmk.**

Without Gum

1037 A102 40c carmine 15.00 2.00
1038 A102 $1 dp blue 35.00 4.00
1039 A102 $1.60 purple 62.50 5.00
1040 A102 $2 brown 85.00 5.00
Nos. 1037-1040 (4) 197.50 16.00

Value, imperf. set, $250.

Souvenir Sheet

Imperf

1041 A102 $2 dp blue grn *400.00 400.00*

Adoption of local self-government in Taiwan.

Design A97 Surcharged — A103

Surcharge in Various Colors

1951, July 19 ***Perf. 12½***

Without Gum

1042 A103 $5 grn (R Br)	90.00	15.00
1043 A103 $10 green (Bk)	180.00	16.50
1044 A103 $20 green (R)	775.00	47.50
1045 A103 $50 green (P)	1,300.	120.00
Nos. 1042-1045 (4)	2,345.	199.00

Farmer and Scroll Announcing Tax Reduction — A104

1952, Jan. 1 **Without Gum** ***Perf. 14***

1046 A104 20c red orange	11.00	1.20
1047 A104 40c dk green	15.00	2.25
1048 A104 $1 brown	26.00	5.25
1049 A104 $1.40 dp blue	42.50	3.75
1050 A104 $2 dk gray	120.00	40.00
1051 A104 $5 brown car	160.00	14.00
Nos. 1046-1051 (6)	374.50	66.45

Land tax reduction of 37.5% in Taiwan.
Value, imperf. set, $1,000.

Pres. Chiang Kai-shek, Flag and Followers A105

Flag in Violet Blue and Carmine

1952, Mar. 1 **Unwmk.** ***Perf. 14***

Without Gum

1052 A105 40c rose car	16.00	.50
1053 A105 $1 dp green	30.00	2.25
1054 A105 $1.60 brown org	62.50	1.10
1055 A105 $2 brt blue	125.00	19.00
1056 A105 $5 violet brn	145.00	5.00
Nos. 1052-1056 (5)	378.50	27.85

2nd anniv. of Chiang Kai-shek's return to the presidency.
Value, imperf. set, $500.
See Nos. 1064-1069.

Nos. 975-976, 978-979 Surcharged in Black

1952, Aug. 1 ***Perf. 12½***

Without Gum

1057 A94 3c on 4c bl grn	5.50	5.25
1058 A94 3c on 10c dp lil	5.50	5.25
1059 A94 3c on 20c blue	7.75	7.50
1060 A94 3c on 50c dk brn	8.75	8.75
Nos. 1057-1060 (4)	27.50	26.75

Forgeries exist.

Geese Type of 1949 with Value Omitted Surcharged

1952, Dec. 8

Without Gum

1061 A97 $10 green (P)	80.00	16.00
1062 A97 $20 green (R)	250.00	27.50
1063 A97 $50 green (Bk)	2,000.	750.00
Nos. 1061-1063 (3)	2,330.	793.50

Chiang Type of 1952 Redrawn

Perf. 12½

1953, Mar. 1 **Engr.** **Unwmk.**

Without Gum

Flag in Dark Blue & Carmine

1064 A105 10c red orange	6.00	1.60
1065 A105 20c green	1.25	1.60
1066 A105 40c rose pink	17.50	2.25
1067 A105 $1.40 blue	55.00	3.50
1068 A105 $2 brown	135.00	7.00
1069 A105 $5 rose violet	200.00	19.00
Nos. 1064-1069 (6)	414.75	34.95

Chiang Kai-shek's return to presidency, 3rd anniv.
Many differences in redrawn design. Value, imperf. set, $650.

Nos. 1020, 1014, 1016 and 1022 Surcharged in Various Colors

1953 ***Rouletted***

Without Gum

1070 A101 3c on $1 ultra (C)	3.25	1.00
1070A A101 10c on 15c org yel (G) ('54)	12.00	3.00
1071 A101 10c on 30c cl (Bl)	12.00	6.00
1072 A101 20c on $1.60 bl (Bk)	7.00	3.00
Nos. 1070-1072 (4)	34.25	13.00

Chinese characters and ornamental device at bottom differ on each value.
Issued: No. 1071, 2/1; No. 1070, 5/25; No. 1072, 6/13; No. 1070A, 7/16.

Nurse & Patients — A106

Cross in Red, Burelage Color in Italics

1953, July 1 **Litho.** ***Perf. 12½***

Without Gum

1073 A106 40c brown, *buff*	15.00	2.00
1074 A106 $1.60 blue, *bl*	35.00	2.00
1075 A106 $2 green, *yel*	55.00	2.25
1076 A106 $5 red org, *org*	95.00	10.00
Nos. 1073-1076 (4)	200.00	16.25

Chinese Anti-Tuberculosis Association.

Chiang Kai-shek — A107

1953, Oct. 31 **Engr.** **Without Gum**

1077 A107 10c dk brown	4.50	.25
1078 A107 20c lilac	4.50	.25
1079 A107 40c dp green	4.50	.25
1080 A107 50c dp pink	6.75	.45
1081 A107 80c brown bis	20.00	2.40
1082 A107 $1 dp olive grn	9.00	.25
1083 A107 $1.40 dp blue	9.00	.25
1084 A107 $1.60 dp carmine	9.00	.25
1085 A107 $1.70 apple grn	9.50	1.35
1086 A107 $2 brown	9.50	.25
1087 A107 $3 dark blue	170.00	11.00
1088 A107 $4 aqua	11.50	.70
1089 A107 $5 red orange	14.50	.70
1090 A107 $10 dk green	57.50	3.50
1091 A107 $20 dk brn lake	72.50	10.00
a. Souvenir folder	*500.00*	
Nos. 1077-1091 (15)	412.25	31.85

67th birthday of Pres. Chiang Kai-shek.
No. 1091a contains Nos. 1077-1091 imperf, arranged in 3 sheets of 5 stamps each.

Silo Highway Bridge — A108

$1.60 and $5, Silo bridge, side view.

Without Gum

Various Frames

1954, Jan. 28 **Unwmk.** ***Perf. 12½***

1092 A108 40c vermilion	16.00	2.00
1093 A108 $1.60 blue violet	80.00	4.00
1094 A108 $3.60 sepia	60.00	11.00
1095 A108 $5 magenta	140.00	19.50
a. Souvenir folder	*1,100.*	*750.00*
Nos. 1092-1095 (4)	296.00	36.50

Opening of Silo bridge, 1st anniversary.
No. 1095a contains one sheet of 4 containing Nos. 1092-1095 imperforate. Beware of stapled folders.

Forest of Evergreens — A109

1954, Mar. 12 ***Perf. 12x12½***

Without Gum

1096 A109 40c shown	22.50	1.00
1097 A109 $10 Nursery	160.00	10.00

Issued to publicize forest conservation.

Runner — A110

1954, Mar. 29 **Without Gum**

1098 A110 40c dp ultra	13.50	.75
1099 A110 $5 carmine	77.50	10.00

11th Youth Day, Mar. 29, 1954.

Globe, Bridge and Ship — A111

1954, Oct. 21 ***Perf. 12***

Without Gum

1100 A111 40c red orange	16.50	.90
1101 A111 $5 deep blue	19.00	4.00

2nd Overseas Chinese Day, Oct. 21, 1954.

Ex-Prisoner with Broken Chains — A112

Designs: $1, Ex-prisoner with torch and flag, UN emblem. $1.60, Torch and date.

1955, Jan. 23

Without Gum

1102 A112 40c blue green	3.50	.65
1103 A112 $1 sepia	25.00	6.00
1104 A112 $1.60 lake	25.00	4.25
Nos. 1102-1104 (3)	53.50	10.90

Honoring Chinese who fought on the side of the North Korean army, who, when released January 23, 1954, chose to return to the Republic of China.

Nos. 1019-1021, 1017 Surcharged in Brown, Blue or Green

a

b

c

1955 ***Rouletted***

Without Gum

1105 A101(a) 3c on $1 (Br)	5.50	.60
1106 A101(b) 10c on 80c (Bl)	10.75	1.00
1107 A101(b) 10c on $1.50 (Bl)	10.75	1.50
1108 A101(c) 20c on 40c (G)	3.50	.85
Nos. 1105-1108 (4)	30.50	3.95

Issued: No. 1105, 1108, 2/18; Nos. 1106-1107, 8/1.

Hand Planting Evergreen Tree — A113

Design: $50, Seedling and map of Taiwan.

1955, Apr. 1 ***Perf. 12***

Without Gum

1109 A113 $20 dp carmine	35.00	1.50
1110 A113 $50 blue	87.50	7.00

Issued to publicize forest conservation.

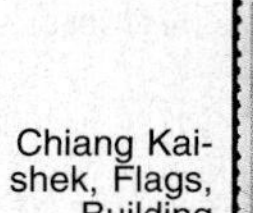

Chiang Kai-shek, Flags, Building A114

1955, May 20 **Engr.** ***Perf. 12***

Without Gum

1111 A114 20c olive	6.50	.40
1112 A114 40c blue green	5.50	.25
1113 A114 $2 car rose	16.00	1.50
1114 A114 $7 dp ultra	25.00	2.50
a. Souv. sheet of 4, #1111-1114, imperf.	*300.00*	*200.00*
Nos. 1111-1114 (4)	53.00	4.65

First anniversary of Pres. Chiang Kai-shek's re-election.
No. 1114a is perf. 12 at right edge of sheet. Value is for sheet with right selvage.

Armed Forces Emblem — A115

1955, Sept. 3 **Without Gum**

1115 A115 40c dk blue	2.00	.40
1116 A115 $2 org ver	20.00	1.75
1117 A115 $7 bl grn	24.00	1.75
a. Sheet of 3, #1115-1117, imperf.	*450.00*	*350.00*
Nos. 1115-1117 (3)	46.00	3.90

Armed Forces Day, Sept. 3.
No. 1117a is perf. 12 at right edge of sheet. Value is for sheet with right selvage.

Nos. 1017, 1018 and C64 Surcharged in Magenta

1955, Sept. 16 Typo. *Rouletted*
Without Gum

1118 A101 20c on 40c org 4.50 .40
1119 A101 20c on 50c choc 5.25 1.00
1120 AP6 20c on 60c dp blue 22.50 3.50
Nos. 1118-1120 (3) 32.25 4.90

Flags of UN and China A116

1955, Oct. 24 Engr. *Perf. 11½*
Without Gum

1121 A116 40c dk blue 1.75 .40
1122 A116 $2 dk car rose 8.50 1.25
1123 A116 $7 slate green 11.75 2.00
Nos. 1121-1123 (3) 22.00 3.65

10th anniv. of the UN, Oct. 24, 1955.

Catalogue values for unused stamps in this section, from this point to the end of the section, are for Never Hinged items.

Pres. Chiang Kai-shek — A117

1955, Oct. 31 Photo. *Perf. 13½*

1124 A117 40c dk bl, red & brn 6.50 .60
1125 A117 $2 grn, red & dk bl 18.00 2.00
1126 A117 $7 brn, red & grn 23.50 3.25
a. Souv. sheet of 3, #1124-1126, imperf. *175.00 175.00*
Nos. 1124-1126 (3) 48.00 5.85

69th birthday of Pres. Chiang Kai-shek.
No. 1126a is perf. 12 at right edge of sheet. Value is for sheet with right selvage. Issued without gum.

Birthplace of Sun Yat-sen — A118

1955, Nov. 12 Engr. *Perf. 12*
Without Gum

1127 A118 40c blue 3.25 .40
1128 A118 $2 red brown 14.50 1.25
1129 A118 $7 rose lake 18.00 2.00
Nos. 1127-1129 (3) 35.75 3.65

90th anniversary, birth of Sun Yat-sen.

No. 959a Surcharged in Bright Green

1956, Feb. 10 Litho. *Rouletted*
Without Gum

1130 A96 20c on orange .75 .25

See No. 1213.

China Map and Transportation Methods — A119

Wmk. 281
1956, Mar. 20 Engr. *Perf. 12*
Without Gum

1131 A119 40c dk carmine 3.00 .40
1132 A119 $1 intense blk 9.00 .80
1133 A119 $1.60 chocolate 10.00 .80
1134 A119 $2 dk green 14.50 1.20
Nos. 1131-1134 (4) 36.50 3.20

60th anniv. of the founding of the modern Chinese postal system.

Souvenir Sheets
Imperf
Without Gum

1135 A119 $2 magenta *72.50 35.00*
1136 A119 $2 red *72.50 35.00*

Exhib. for the 60th anniv. of the modern Chinese postal system, Mar. 20, 1956.

Children at Play — A120

1956, Apr. 4 Unwmk. *Perf. 12*
Without Gum

1137 A120 40c emerald 2.10 .30
1138 A120 $1.60 dk blue 5.25 .60
1139 A120 $2 dk carmine 8.75 1.20
Nos. 1137-1139 (3) 16.10 2.10

Children's Day, Apr. 4, 1956.

Early and Modern Locomotives A121

1956, June 9 Wmk. 281 Vert.
Without Gum

1140 A121 40c rose car 5.00 .30
1141 A121 $2 blue 7.25 .75
1142 A121 $8 green 12.00 2.10
Nos. 1140-1142 (3) 24.25 3.15

75th anniversary of Chinese Railroads.

Pres. Chiang Kai-shek
A122 A123

A124

Various Portraits of Chiang
Perf. 14½x13½, 14½ (A123), 13½x14½
1956, Oct. 31 Photo. Unwmk.

1143 A122 20c red orange 2.50 .25
1144 A122 40c carmine rose 12.00 .25
1145 A123 $1 brt ultra 16.00 .30
1146 A123 $1.60 red lilac 20.00 .25
1147 A124 $2 red brown 28.00 .60
1148 A124 $8 brt grnsh blue 62.50 1.90
Nos. 1143-1148 (6) 141.00 3.55

70th birthday of Pres. Chiang Kai-shek.

Types of Special Delivery, Air Post and Registration Stamps of 1949 Surcharged in Black or Maroon

a

b

c

1956 Unwmk. Litho. *Rouletted*
Without Gum

1150 SD2(a) 3c red violet 6.00 .60
a. Perf. 12½ 2.25 .30
1151 AP5(b) 3c blue green (M) 1.50 .25
1152 R2(c) 10c bright red 1.75 .25
Nos. 1150-1152 (3) 9.25 1.10

Issued: No. 1150, 4/25; No. 1151, 11/11; No. 1152, 12/25.

Telecommunications Emblem and Radio Tower — A125

Wmk. 281
1956, Dec. 28 Engr. *Perf. 12*
Without Gum

1153 A125 40c deep ultra 2.75 .25
1154 A125 $1.40 carmine 4.75 .40
1155 A125 $1.60 dark green 7.25 .60
1156 A125 $2 chocolate 9.00 1.00
Nos. 1153-1156 (4) 23.75 2.25

Chinese telegraph service, 75th anniv.

Map of China — A126

Pin Perf., Perf. 12x12½
1957 Litho. Wmk. 281
Without Gum

1157 A126 3c brt blue .40 .25
1158 A126 10c violet 6.25 .60
1159 A126 20c red orange .75 .25
1160 A126 40c rose red 1.00 .25

Unwmk.

1161 A126 $1 orange brown 3.75 .50
1162 A126 $1.60 green 6.25 .50
Nos. 1157-1162 (6) 18.40 2.35

Map inscription reads: "Recovery of Mainland."
See Nos. 1177-1182.

Mother Instructing Mencius — A127

Design: $3, Mother tattooing Yueh Fei.

Without Gum
Unwmk.
1957, May 12 Engr. *Perf. 12*

1163 A127 40c green 1.75 .25
1164 A127 $3 redsh brown 7.25 .60

Issued to honor Mother's Day, 1957.

Badge of Chinese Boy Scouts — A128

1957, Aug. 11 Without Gum

1165 A128 40c lilac .50 .25
1166 A128 $1 green 2.75 .40
1167 A128 $1.60 dk blue 3.50 .50
Nos. 1165-1167 (3) 6.75 1.15

Cent. of the birth of Lord Baden-Powell and to publicize the World Scout Jubilee Jamboree, England, Aug. 1-12.

Globe, Radio Tower and Microphone A129

1957, Sept. 16 Without Gum

1168 A129 40c vermilion 1.00 .25
1169 A129 50c brt rose lilac 2.00 .30
1170 A129 $3.50 dark blue 3.25 .85
Nos. 1168-1170 (3) 6.25 1.40

30th anniv. of Chinese broadcasting.

Map of Taiwan — A130

1957, Oct. 26 Without Gum

1171 A130 40c blue green 3.50 .40
1172 A130 $1.40 lt ultra 8.75 2.25
1173 A130 $2 gray 12.00 2.25
Nos. 1171-1173 (3) 24.25 4.90

Start of construction on the Cross Island Highway, Taiwan.

Freighter "Hai Min" and River Boat "Kiang Foo" — A131

1957, Dec. 16 Engr. *Perf. 12*
Without Gum

1174 A131 40c deep ultra 1.35 .25
1175 A131 80c rose lake 2.75 .95
1176 A131 $2.80 vermilion 4.75 1.40
Nos. 1174-1176 (3) 8.85 2.60

85th anniv. of the establishment of the China Merchants Steam Navigation Co.

Type of 1957
Pin Perf., Perf. 12x12½
1957, Dec. 25 Typo. Unwmk.
Without Gum
Dark Blue Frames

1177 A126 3c brt blue 1.35 .25
1178 A126 10c violet 2.75 .50
1179 A126 20c brick red .90 .25
1180 A126 40c rose red 1.10 .25
1181 A126 $1 dp org brn 6.75 .70
1182 A126 $1.60 dp green 7.25 .80
Nos. 1177-1182 (6) 20.10 2.75

On Feb. 20, 1958, two booklets were issued. One contained 6 #1179 and 22 #1180. The other contained 10 #1179, 30 #1180, and 6 #1181.

Stamps with bars obliterating the face value are specimens.

Butterfly — A132

Various Insects in Natural Colors

Perf. 13½

1958, Mar. 20 Unwmk. Photo.

1183 A132 10c pale grn, grn & blk 1.50 .40
1184 A132 40c lem, pink, grn & blk .50 .25
1185 A132 $1 yel grn & mar 4.00 .60
1186 A132 $1.40 yel, org & blk 4.75 .75
1187 A132 $1.60 pale brn & dk pur 5.25 1.00
1188 A132 $2 brt yel, org & blk 6.00 1.25
Nos. 1183-1188 (6) 22.00 4.25

Mme. Chiang Kai-shek Orchid — A133

Orchids: 20c, Formosan Wilson, horiz. $1.40, Klotzsch. $3, Fitzgerald, horiz.

Orchids in Natural Colors

1958, Mar. 20

1189 A133 20c chocolate 1.50 .25
1190 A133 40c purple 1.50 .25
1191 A133 $1.40 dk vio brn 6.25 .60
1192 A133 $3 dark blue 7.00 2.00
Nos. 1189-1192 (4) 16.25 3.10

World Health Organization Emblem — A134

1958, May 28 Engr. *Perf. 12*

Without Gum

1193 A134 40c dark blue .60 .25
1194 A134 $1.60 brick red 1.50 .30
1195 A134 $2 deep red lilac 1.90 .50
Nos. 1193-1195 (3) 4.00 1.05

10th anniv. of the WHO.

President's Mansion, Taipei — A135

Wmk. 323

1958, Sept. 20 Engr. *Perf. 12*

Without Gum

1196 A135 $10 blue green 7.50 .35
a. Granite paper 17.00 .50
1197 A135 $20 car rose 19.00 .60
a. Granite paper 42.50 1.50
1198 A135 $50 red brown 67.50 2.40
1199 A135 $100 dk blue 170.00 8.00
Nos. 1196-1199 (4) 264.00 11.35

Issued: Nos. 1196a, 1197a, 5/24/63.

See Nos. 1349-1351. For surcharge see No. J131.

Taiwan Farm Scene A136

1958, Oct. 1 Unwmk.

Without Gum

1200 A136 20c emerald 1.25 .25
1201 A136 40c black 1.25 .25
1202 A136 $1.40 brt magenta 3.00 .30
1203 A136 $3 ultra 4.50 .75
Nos. 1200-1203 (4) 10.00 1.55

10th anniversary of the Joint Commission on Rural Reconstruction.

Pres. Chiang Kai-shek A137

1958, Oct. 31 Photo. *Perf. 13½*

1204 A137 40c multicolored 1.50 .40

Pres. Chiang Kai-shek on his 72nd birthday.

UNESCO Building, Paris A138

1958, Nov. 3 Engr. *Perf. 12*

Without Gum

1205 A138 20c dark blue .50 .25
1206 A138 40c green .50 .25
1207 A138 $1.40 orange ver 1.25 .40
1208 A138 $3 red lilac 2.00 .60
Nos. 1205-1208 (4) 4.25 1.50

UNESCO Headquarters in Paris opening, Nov. 3.

Flame from Liberty Torch Encircling Globe — A139

1958, Dec. 10 Unwmk.

Without Gum

1209 A139 40c green .35 .25
1210 A139 60c gray brown 1.05 .25
1211 A139 $1 carmine 1.05 .25
1212 A139 $3 ultra 1.75 .60
Nos. 1209-1212 (4) 4.20 1.35

10th anniversary of the signing of the Universal Declaration of Human Rights.

No. 959a Surcharged in Bright Green

Rouletted

1958, Dec. 11 Litho. Unwmk.

Without Gum

1213 A96 20c on orange .75 .25

Ballot Box, Scales and Constitution — A140

1958, Dec. 25 Engr. *Perf. 12*

Without Gum

1214 A140 40c green 1.00 .25
1215 A140 50c dull purple 1.60 .25
1216 A140 $1.40 car rose 3.75 .40
1217 A140 $3.50 dk blue 9.50 1.75
Nos. 1214-1217 (4) 15.85 2.65

Adoption of the constitution, 10th anniv.

Chu Kwang Tower, Quemoy — A141

1959-60 Wmk. 323 Litho. *Perf. 12*

Without Gum

1218 A141 3c orange .25 .25
1218A A141 5c lt yel grn ('60) 4.75 .30
1219 A141 10c lilac .45 .25
1220 A141 20c ultra .55 .25
1221 A141 40c brown .25 .25
1222 A141 50c bluish grn 1.60 .25
1223 A141 $1 rose red 1.10 .25
1224 A141 $1.40 yel grn 2.10 .25
1225 A141 $2 gray grn 2.75 .30
1226 A141 $2.80 rose pink 9.50 .75
1227 A141 $3 slate blue 8.25 .35
Nos. 1218-1227 (11) 31.55 3.45

See Nos. 1270-1283.

ILO Emblem and Headquarters, Geneva — A142

1959, June 15 Engr. *Perf. 12*

Without Gum

1228 A142 40c blue .40 .25
1229 A142 $1.60 dk brown 1.00 .25
1230 A142 $3 brt blue grn 1.40 .30
1231 A142 $5 orange ver 2.50 .60
Nos. 1228-1231 (4) 5.30 1.40

40th anniversary of the ILO.

Bugler and Tents A143

1959, July 8 Unwmk.

Without Gum

1232 A143 40c carmine 1.00 .25
1233 A143 50c dark blue 1.75 .30
1234 A143 $5 green 4.50 .70
Nos. 1232-1234 (3) 7.25 1.25

10th World Boy Scout Jamboree, Makiling National Park, Philippines, July 17-26.

Inscribed Stone, Mt. Tai-wu, Quemoy — A144

Map of Taiwan Straits A145

1959, Sept. 3 Engr. *Perf. 12*

Without Gum

1235 A144 40c brown 2.00 .25
1236 A145 $1.40 ultra 2.10 .25
1237 A145 $2 green 4.00 .50
1238 A144 $3 dark blue 4.75 .75
Nos. 1235-1238 (4) 12.85 1.75

Defense of Quemoy and Matsu islands. For overprints see Nos. 1258-1259.

Pigeons Circling Globe A146

1959, Oct. 4 Without Gum

1239 A146 40c blue .70 .25
1240 A146 $1 rose carmine 1.20 .30
1241 A146 $2 gray brown 1.60 .25
1242 A146 $3.50 red orange 2.10 .60
Nos. 1239-1242 (4) 5.60 1.40

Intl. Letter Writing Week, Oct. 4-10.

National Taiwan Science Hall, Taipei — A147

1959, Nov. 12 Photo. *Perf. 13x13½*

1243 A147 40c shown .35 .25
1244 A147 $3 Front view 1.25 .90

Emblem A148

1959, Dec. 7 Engr. *Perf. 12*

Without Gum

1245 A148 40c blue green .60 .25
1246 A148 $1.60 red lilac 1.60 .30
1247 A148 $3 orange 2.40 .75
Nos. 1245-1247 (3) 4.60 1.30

Intl. Confederation of Free Trade Unions, 10th anniv.

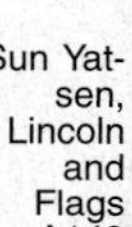

Sun Yat-sen, Lincoln and Flags A149

Perf. 13½, 12

1959, Dec. 25 Photo. Unwmk.

1248 A149 40c multicolored .65 .30
1249 A149 $3 multicolored 2.00 .60

Issued to honor Sun Yat-sen and Abraham Lincoln as "Leaders of Democracy."

Mailman on Motorcycle Delivering Night Mail — A150

Postal Launch A151

1960, Mar. 20 Engr. *Perf. 11½*
Without Gum

1250 A150 $1.40 dk violet brn 2.40 .40
1251 A151 $1.60 ultra 2.75 .50

Issued to publicize the Prompt Delivery Service.

WRY Uprooted Oak Emblem — A152

1960, Apr. 7 Photo. *Perf. 13*

1252 A152 40c blk, red brn & emer .75 .25
1253 A152 $3 blk, red org & grn 1.75 .30

World Refugee Year, 7/1/59-6/30/60.

Cross Island Highway, Taiwan — A153

Design: $1, $2, Road through tunnel, vert.

Perf. 11½

1960, May 9 Engr. Unwmk.
Without Gum

1254 A153 40c green 1.60 .25
1255 A153 $1 dk blue 3.25 .50
1256 A153 $2 brown vio 3.00 .40
1257 A153 $3 brown 5.00 1.00
a. Souv. sheet of 2, #1255, 1257, wmk. 323, imperf. 300.00 140.00
Nos. 1254-1257 (4) 12.85 2.15

Opening of the Cross Island Highway, Taiwan.

Red Overprint on Nos. 1237-1238 Chinese and English: "Welcome U.S. President Dwight D. Eisenhower 1960"

1960, June 18 Unwmk. *Perf. 12*

1258 A145 $2 green 2.25 .40
1259 A144 $3 dk blue 3.00 .90

Eisenhower's visit to China, June 18, 1960.

Phonopost — A154

1960, June 27 Without Gum

1260 A154 $2 red orange 2.50 .50

Phonopost Service of the Chinese armed forces.

Two Horses and Groom, by Han Kan — A155

Paintings from Palace Museum, Taichung: $1, Two Riders, by Wei Yen. $1.60, Flowers and Birds by Hsiao Yung, vert. $2, Pair of Mandarin Ducks by Monk Hui Ch'ung.

1960, Aug. 4 Photo. *Perf. 13*

1261 A155 $1 ol gray, blk & brn 6.00 .70
1262 A155 $1.40 bis brn, blk & fawn 8.00 1.20
1263 A155 $1.60 multicolored 14.00 2.10
1264 A155 $2 beige, blk & gray grn 20.00 4.00
Nos. 1261-1264 (4) 48.00 8.00

Chinese paintings, 7th-11th centuries.

For other painting types with large straight numerals in the upper corners and large Chinese characters on the side see A186, A241 and A285.

Youth Corps Flag and Summer Activities — A156

Design: $3, similar to 50c, horiz.

1960, Aug. 20 Engr. *Perf. 12*
Without Gum

1265 A156 50c slate green .60 .25
1266 A156 $3 copper brown 2.40 .60

Summer activities of China Youth Corps.

Reforestation A157

$2, Protection of forest. $3, Timber industry.

1960, Aug. 29 Photo. *Perf. 13½x13*

1267 A157 $1 multicolored 1.90 .25
1268 A157 $2 multicolored 4.00 .70
1269 A157 $3 multicolored 5.75 1.25
a. Souvenir sheet of 3 26.00 22.50
Nos. 1267-1269 (3) 11.65 2.20

Fifth World Forestry Congress, Seattle, Washington, Aug. 29-Sept. 10.

No. 1269a contains Nos. 1267-1269 assembled as a triptych, 65½x40mm and imperf., but with simulated black perforations.

Chu Kwang Tower, Quemoy — A158

1960-61 Wmk. 323 Litho. *Perf. 12*
Without Gum

1270 A158 3c lt red brown .25 .25
1271 A158 40c pale violet .25 .25
1272 A158 50c orange ('61) 1.00 .25
1273 A158 60c rose lilac .75 .25
1274 A158 80c pale green .25 .25
1275 A158 $1 gray grn ('61) .80 .25
1276 A158 $1.20 gray olive 1.50 .25
1277 A158 $1.50 ultra 1.75 .25
1278 A158 $2 car rose ('61) 1.25 .25
1279 A158 $2.50 pale blue 2.50 .25
1280 A158 $3 bluish green 3.75 .25
1281 A158 $3.20 lt red brown 1.90 .25
1282 A158 $3.60 vio blue ('61) 7.50 .25
1283 A158 $4.50 vermilion 14.00 .60
Nos. 1270-1283 (14) 37.45 3.85

Issue dates: Nos. 1272, 1275, 1278 and 1282, Jan. 28, 1961; all others Oct. 5, 1960.

For surcharges see Nos. J132-J134.

Without Gum

1962-64 Granite Paper

1270a A158 3c light red brown .25 .25
1270B A158 10c emer ('63) 1.50 .25
1271a A158 40c pale violet .25 .25
1274a A158 80c pale green .25 .25
1275a A158 $1 gray grn ('63) 12.00 .25
1278a A158 $2 carmine rose 9.00 .25
1281a A158 $3.20 red brn ('64) 40.00 .50
1282A A158 $4 brt blue grn 15.00 .25
1283a A158 $4.50 vermilion 45.00 1.00
Nos. 1270a-1283a (9) 123.25 3.25

Two types of No. 1271a: I. Seven lines in "0" of "40." II. Eight lines in "0."

Issue dates: Nos. 1270a, 1271a, Feb. 20, 1962; No. 1274a, March 20, 1962; No. 1282A, June 30, 1962; Nos. 1278a, 1283a, Dec. 1, 1962; No. 1270B, Dec. 15, 1963; No. 1281a, Jan. 25, 1964.

Sports — A159

Perf. 12½

1960, Oct. 25 Photo. Unwmk.

1284 A159 50c Diving 1.25 .25
1285 A159 80c Discus thrower 1.00 .25
1286 A159 $2 Basketball 1.75 .30
1287 A159 $2.50 Soccer 3.50 .55
1288 A159 $3 Hurdling 4.00 .75
1289 A159 $3.20 Runner 5.25 1.00
Nos. 1284-1289 (6) 16.75 3.10

Bronze Wine Container, 1751-1111 B.C. — A160

Ancient Chinese Art Treasures: $1, Cauldron, 1111-771 B.C. $1.20, Porcelain vase, 960-1126 A.D. $1.50, Perforated tube, 1111-771 B.C. $2, Jug in shape of monk's cap, 1368-1661 A.D. $2.50, Jade flower vase, 1368-1661, A.D.

1961 Photo. *Perf. 13*

1290 A160 80c lt ol, blk & dk vio .60 .30
1291 A160 $1 sal, bl & blk 1.20 .45
1292 A160 $1.20 yel, brn & ultra 2.00 .60
1293 A160 $1.50 lil, bl & sep 3.00 .80
1294 A160 $2 pale grn, dk grn & red brn 5.00 .85
1295 A160 $2.50 grnsh bl & dk vio 8.25 1.00
Nos. 1290-1295 (6) 20.05 4.00

Issue dates: Nos. 1290, 1292, 1295, Feb. 1. Nos. 1291, 1293-1294, May 1.

Flat Bowl, 1111-771 B.C. — A161

80c, Palace perfumer, 1662-1911. $1, Corn vase, 770-221 B.C. $2, Jade tankard, 960-1126 A.D. $4, Glazed washer, 1127-1279 A.D. $4.50, Jade chimera, 8 B.C.-206 A.D.

1961

1296 A160 80c pink, brn, bl & yel .60 .30
1297 A160 $1 cit, blk & brn 4.00 1.00
1298 A161 $1.50 sal & ind 4.50 1.25
1299 A160 $2 bl, blk & rose 23.00 2.25
1300 A161 $4 red, blk & bluish gray 8.00 1.00
1301 A161 $4.50 grnsh bl, blk & brn 60.00 4.25
Nos. 1296-1301 (6) 100.10 10.05

Issued: Nos. 1296-1298, 8/15; Nos. 1299-1301, 9/15.

1962

Designs: 80c, Topaz twin wine vessels, 1662-1911 A.D. $1, Squat pouring vase, 1751-1111 B.C. $2.40, Vase, 1368-1661 A.D. $3, Wine vase, 1751-1111 B.C. $3.20, Covered porcelain jar, 1662-1911 A.D. $3.60, Perforated disc, 206 B.C.-8 A.D.

1302 A160 80c crim, blk & ocher .75 .30
1303 A160 $1 blue & vio blk 3.25 1.00
1304 A160 $2.40 hn brn, blk & bl 13.50 2.00
1305 A160 $3 blue, blk & pink 95.00 6.00
1306 A160 $3.20 ultra, lt grn & red 28.00 3.00
1307 A160 $3.60 yel, blk & brn 34.00 3.25
Nos. 1302-1307 (6) 174.50 15.55

Issue dates: Nos. 1303-1304, 1307, Jan. 15. Nos. 1302, 1305-1306, Feb. 15.

Farmer with Mechanized Plow — A162

1961, Feb. 4 Engr. *Perf. 12*
Without Gum

1308 A162 80c rose violet 1.50 .25
1309 A162 $2 green 3.50 .50
1310 A162 $3.20 vermilion 5.50 .35
Nos. 1308-1310 (3) 10.50 1.10

1961 agricultural census.

Madame Chiang Kai-shek and League Emblem — A163

Unwmk.

1961, Mar. 8 Photo. *Perf. 13*
Portrait in Black

1311 A163 80c lt grn & car rose 3.50 .25
1312 A163 $1 yel grn & car rose 7.25 .50

1313 A163 $2 org brn & car rose 7.25 .75
1314 A163 $3.20 lil & car rose 11.25 2.00
Nos. 1311-1314 (4) 29.25 3.50

10th anniversary of the Chinese Women's Anti-Aggression League.

Spiny Lobster and Mail Order Service Emblem — A164

1961, Mar. 20 Engr. *Perf. 11½*
Without Gum

1315 A164 $3 slate green 6.75 .75

Issued to publicize the mail order service for consumer goods.

Jeme Tien-yow and Pataling Tunnel — A165

$2, Jeme Tien-yow & 1909 locomotive.

1961, Apr. 26 *Perf. 11½*
Without Gum

1316 A165 80c lilac 1.75 .25
1317 A165 $2 black, horiz. 5.50 .75

Centenary of the birth of Jeme Tien-yow, builder of the Peking-Kalgan railroad.

Map of China inscribed: "Recovery of the Mainland" — A166

Pres. Chiang Kai-shek — A167

1961, May 20 Photo. *Perf. 13½*

1318 A166 80c multicolored 3.00 .25
1319 A167 $2 multicolored 11.00 1.50
a. Souvenir sheet of 2 32.50 30.00

1st anniversary of Pres. Chiang Kai-shek's 3rd term inauguration.

No. 1319a contains one each of Nos. 1318-1319, imperf. with simulated perforations. Without gum.

Convair 880-M, Biplane of 1921 and Flag — A168

1961, July 1 *Perf. 13x12½*

1320 A168 $10 multicolored 7.25 1.20

40th anniversary of civil air service.

Sun Yat-sen and Chiang Kai-shek — A169

Flag and Map of China — A170

Perf. 13½

1961, Oct. 10 Unwmk. Photo.

1321 A169 80c gray, lt brn & sl 1.50 .25
1322 A170 $5 gray, ultra, red & beige 9.50 1.75
a. Souvenir sheet of 2 20.00 20.00

50th anniv. of the Republic of China. No. 1322a contains one each of Nos. 1321-1322, imperf. with simulated perforations. No gum.

Green Lake — A171

Lotus Pond A172

Taiwan Scenery: $2, Sun-Moon Lake. $3.20, Wulai waterfalls.

Perf. 13½x14, 14x13½

1961, Oct. 31 Unwmk.

1323 A171 80c multicolored 2.50 .25
1324 A172 $1 multicolored 8.75 1.00
1325 A172 $2 multicolored 13.50 1.40
1326 A171 $3.20 multicolored 28.00 2.25
Nos. 1323-1326 (4) 52.75 4.90

Oil Refinery — A173

Designs: $1.50, Steel works. $2.50, Aluminum plant. $3.20, Fertilizer plant, horiz.

1961, Nov. 14 *Perf. 11½*

1327 A173 80c multicolored .85 .25
1328 A173 $1.50 multicolored 5.75 .80
1329 A173 $2.50 multicolored 8.00 1.00
1330 A173 $3.20 multicolored 9.25 1.75
Nos. 1327-1330 (4) 23.85 3.80

Chinese industrial development and the Golden Jubilee Convention of the Chinese Institute of Engineers, Nov. 13-16.

Atomic Reactor, Tsing-Hwa University A174

Atomic Reactor in Operation A175

Design: $3.20, Atomic symbol and laboratory, Tsing-Hwa, horiz.

1961-62 Photo. *Perf. 12½*

1331 A174 80c multicolored 3.00 .25
1332 A175 $2 multicolored 6.75 2.00
1333 A175 $3.20 multicolored 7.25 1.00
Nos. 1331-1333 (3) 17.00 3.25

Inauguration on Apr. 13, 1961, of the 1st Chinese atomic reactor at the National Tsing-Hwa University Institute of Nuclear Science.
Issued: 80c, 12/2; $2, $3.20, 3/20/62.

Microwave Reflector and Telegraph Wires — A176

Design: $3.20, Microwave parabolic antenna and mountains, horiz.

1961, Dec. 28 *Perf. 12½*

1334 A176 80c multicolored 1.75 .25
1335 A176 $3.20 multicolored 3.75 1.00

80th anniv. of Chinese telecommunications.

Mechanical Postal Equipment and Twine Tying Machine — A176a

Wmk. 323
1962, Mar. 20 Engr. *Perf. 11½*
Without Gum

1336 A176a 80c chocolate 2.50 .50

Yu Shan Observatory — A177

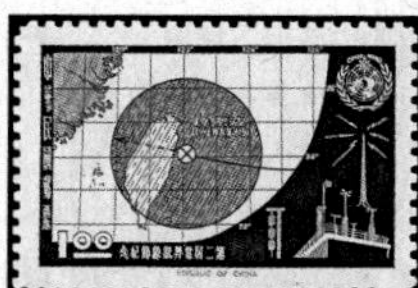

Map Showing Route of Typhoon Pamela, Sept. 1961 — A177a

Observation Balloon, Earth and Cumulus Clouds — A178

1962 Without Gum

1337 A177 80c brown .75 .25
1338 A177a $1 bluish black 2.25 .45
1339 A178 $2 green 4.00 .70
Nos. 1337-1339 (3) 7.00 1.40

Issue dates: 80c, $2, Mar. 23; $1, May 7.
World Meteorological Day, Mar. 23.

Child Receiving Milk, UN Emblem A179

1962, Apr. 4 Without Gum

1340 A179 80c rose red .85 .25
1341 A179 $3.20 green 4.00 .60
a. Souvenir sheet of 2 17.50 5.50

15th anniv. of UNICEF. No. 1341a contains one each of Nos. 1340-1341 imperf. with simulated perforations.

Malaria Eradication Emblem — A180

Unwmk.
1962, Apr. 7 Photo. *Perf. 13*

1342 A180 80c dk bl, red & lt grn .65 .25
1343 A180 $3.60 brn, pink & grn 2.75 .90

WHO drive to eradicate malaria.

Yu Yu-jen — A181

1962, Apr. 24 *Perf. 13*

1344 A181 80c gray, blk & pink 3.00 .40

Issued to honor Yu Yu-jen, newspaper reporter, revolutionary leader and co-worker of Sun Yat-sen, on his 84th birthday.

Cheng Ch'eng-kung (Koxinga) — A182

1962, Apr. 29

1345 A182 80c deep claret 2.40 .25
1346 A182 $2 dark green 11.00 1.25

300th anniversary (in 1961) of the recovery of Taiwan from the Dutch by Koxinga.

Emblem of Intl. Cooperative Alliance — A183

Clasped Hands Across Globe — A184

Wmk. 323

1962, July 7 Engr. *Perf. 12*

Without Gum

1347	A183	80c brown	.50	.25
1348	A184	$2 violet	3.75	.75

Intl. Cooperative Movement and 40th Intl. Cooperative Day, July 7, 1962.

Mansion Type of 1958

1962, July 20 Without Gum

1349	A135	$5 gray green	7.50	.25
1350	A135	$5.60 violet	10.50	.35
1351	A135	$6 orange	9.25	.30
		Nos. 1349-1351 (3)	27.25	.90

1963 Granite Paper

1349a	A135	$5 gray green	6.00	.25
1350a	A135	$5.60 violet	6.00	.25
1351a	A135	$6 orange	15.00	.40
		Nos. 1349a-1351a (3)	27.00	.90

"Art and Science" — A185

$2, "Education," book and UNESCO emblem, horiz. $3.20, "Communications," globes, horiz.

1962, Aug. 28 Wmk. 323 *Perf. 12*

Without Gum

1352	A185	80c lilac rose	.40	.25
1353	A185	$2 rose claret	3.00	.50
1354	A185	$3.20 yellow green	3.00	.40
		Nos. 1352-1354 (3)	6.40	1.15

UNESCO activities in China.

Emperor T'ai Tsung, T'ang Dynasty, 627-649 A186

Emperors: $2, T'ai Tsu, Sung dynasty, 960-975. $3.20, T'ai Tsu, Yuan dynasty (Genghis Khan), 1206-27. $4, T'ai Tsu, Ming dynasty, 1368-98.

1962, Sept. 20 Photo. Unwmk.

1355	A186	80c multicolored	20.00	1.00
1356	A186	$2 multicolored	75.00	8.00
1357	A186	$3.20 multicolored	125.00	6.00
1358	A186	$4 multicolored	150.00	14.00
		Nos. 1355-1358 (4)	370.00	29.00

Lions International Emblem A187

1962, Oct. 8 *Perf. 13½*

1359	A187	80c multicolored	1.10	.25
1360	A187	$3.60 multicolored	3.25	1.00
a.		Souvenir sheet of 2	35.00	17.00

45th anniv. of Lions Intl. No. 1360a contains one each of Nos. 1359-1360, imperf. with simulated perforations.

Pole Vaulting — A188

Shooting A189

1962, Oct. 25 Unwmk. *Perf. 13*

1361	A188	80c multicolored	1.00	.25
1362	A189	$3.20 multicolored	3.75	.60

Sports meet.

Young Farmers and 4-H Emblem — A190

Design: $3.20, 4-H emblem and rice.

Wmk. 323

1962, Dec. 7 Engr. *Perf. 12*

Without Gum

1363	A190	80c carmine	.75	.25
1364	A190	$3.20 green	3.75	.80
a.		Souvenir sheet of 2	24.00	12.00

10th anniv. of the 4-H Club in China. No. 1364a contains one each of Nos. 1363-1364, imperf. with simulated perforations.

Flag, Liner of China Merchants' Steam Navigation Co. — A191

Design: $3.60, Company's Pacific navigation chart and freighter, horiz.

Perf. 13½

1962, Dec. 16 Unwmk. Photo.

1365	A191	80c multicolored	1.25	.25
1366	A191	$3.60 multicolored	6.50	1.60

90th anniversary of the China Merchants' Steam Navigation Co., Ltd.

Farm Woman, Tractor and Plane Dropping Food over Mainland — A192

Perf. 12½

1963, Mar. 21 Unwmk. Photo.

1367	A192	$10 multicolored	7.25	1.20

FAO "Freedom from Hunger" campaign.

Torch, Young Couple and Martyrs' Monument, Canton A193

Wmk. 323

1963, Mar. 29 Engr. *Perf. 11½*

Without Gum

1368	A193	80c purple	.50	.25
1369	A193	$3.20 green	3.00	.60

Issued for the 20th Youth Day.

Swallows, Pagoda and AOPU Emblem — A194

Designs: $2, Northern gannet, horiz. $6, Japanese crane and pine.

Unwmk.

1963, Apr. 1 Photo. *Perf. 13*

1370	A194	80c multicolored	2.00	.25
1371	A194	$2 multicolored	4.00	.65
1372	A194	$6 multicolored	16.50	3.25
		Nos. 1370-1372 (3)	22.50	4.15

1st anniversary of the formation of the Asian-Oceanic Postal Union, AOPU.

Refugee Girl (Li Ying) and Map of China — A195

Refugees Fleeing Mainland A196

Wmk. 323

1963, June 27 Engr. *Perf. 11½*

Without Gum

1373	A195	80c bluish black	2.40	.25
1374	A196	$3.20 dp claret	7.25	.60

1st anniv. of the evacuation of Chinese mainland refugees from Hong Kong to Taiwan. Designs from photographs of refugees.

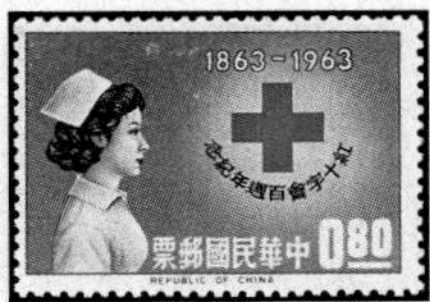

Nurse and Red Cross A197

Design: $10, Globe and Red Cross.

Perf. 12½

1963, Sept. 1 Unwmk. Photo.

1375	A197	80c black & carmine	3.00	.25
1376	A197	$10 slate, gray & car	12.00	4.25

Centenary of International Red Cross.

Basketball Player, Stadium and Asian Cup — A198

$2, Hands reaching for ball and Asian cup.

Wmk. 323

1963, Nov. 20 Engr. *Perf. 12*

Without Gum

1377	A198	80c lilac rose	1.00	.25
1378	A198	$2 violet	2.75	.80

The 2nd Asian Basketball Championship, Taipei, Nov. 20.

UN Emblem, Torch and Men — A199

Scales and Men of Various Races A200

1963, Dec. 10 Wmk. 323 *Perf. 11½*

Without Gum

1379	A199	80c brt green	.50	.25
1380	A200	$3.20 maroon	2.25	.65

Universal Declaration of Human Rights, 15th anniversary.

Village and Orchids A201

"Kindle the Fire of Conscience" A202

Perf. 13½x13

1963, Dec. 17 Photo. Unwmk.

1381	A201	40c multicolored	2.75	.30
1382	A202	$4.50 multicolored	11.00	2.50

Contribution of the Good-People-Good-Deeds campaign to improve ethical standards.

Sun Yat-sen and Book, "Three Principles of the People" A203

1963, Dec. 25 *Perf. 13*

1383	A203	$5 blue & multi	14.00	2.00

"Land-to-the-Tillers" program, 10th anniv. An 80c was prepared but not issued.

Torch — A204

Hands Unchained — A205

Wmk. 323

1964, Jan. 23 Engr. *Perf. 11½*

Without Gum

1384	A204	80c red orange	.85	.25
1385	A205	$3.20 indigo	3.75	.60

Liberty Day, 10th anniversary.

Broadleaf Cactus — A206

Designs: $1, Crab cactus. $3.20, Nopalxochia. $5, Grizzly bear cactus.

Perf. 12½

1964, Feb. 27 Unwmk. Photo.
Plants in Original Colors

1386	A206	80c dp plum & fawn	4.50	.25
1387	A206	$1 dk blue & car	9.50	1.20
1388	A206	$3.20 green	9.50	.60
1389	A206	$5 lilac & yellow	12.50	2.40
		Nos. 1386-1389 (4)	36.00	4.45

Wu Chih-hwei — A207

Wmk. 323
1964, Mar. 25 Engr. *Perf. 11½*
Without Gum

1390	A207	80c black brown	2.25	.40

Centenary of the birth of Wu Chih-hwei (1865-1953), politician and leader of the Kuomintang.

Chu Kwang Tower, Quemoy — A208

Perf. 13x12½

1964-66 Wmk. 323 Litho.
Granite Paper; Without Gum

1391	A208	3c sepia	.25	.25
1392	A208	5c brt yel grn ('65)	.25	.25
1393	A208	10c yellow grn	.25	.25
1394	A208	20c slate grn ('65)	.25	.25
1395	A208	40c rose red	.25	.25
1396	A208	50c brown	.45	.25
1397	A208	80c orange ('65)	.90	.25
1398	A208	$1 violet ('65)	.45	.25
1399	A208	$1.50 brt lilac ('66)	9.00	1.20
1400	A208	$2 lilac rose	1.15	.25
1401	A208	$2.50 ultra ('65)	3.50	.25
1402	A208	$3 slate	5.25	.40
1403	A208	$3.20 brt blue	5.75	.30
1404	A208	$4 brt green	4.50	.25
		Nos. 1391-1404 (14)	32.20	4.65

Nurses Holding Candles A209

Florence Nightingale and Student Nurse — A210

1964, May 12 Engr. *Perf. 11½*
Without Gum

1406	A209	80c violet blue	1.50	.25
1407	A210	$4 red	6.25	1.40

Issued for Nurses Day.

Shihmen Reservoir A211

Designs: $1, Irrigation system. $3.20, Main dam and power plant. $5, Spillway.

Perf. 12½

1964, June 14 Unwmk. Photo.

1408	A211	80c multicolored	3.00	.30
1409	A211	$1 multicolored	3.25	.80
1410	A211	$3.20 multicolored	6.00	.70
1411	A211	$5 multicolored	19.00	3.25
		Nos. 1408-1411 (4)	31.25	5.05

Completion of Shihmen Reservoir.

15th Century Ship, Modern Liner — A212

Wmk. 323
1964, July 11 Engr. *Perf. 11½*
Without Gum

1412	A212	$2 orange	1.00	.25
1413	A212	$3.60 brt green	4.00	.80

China's 10th Navigation Day.

Bananas A213

Unwmk.
1964, July 25 Photo. *Perf. 14*

1414	A213	80c shown	*7.00*	.50
1415	A213	$1 Oranges	*20.00*	2.00
1416	A213	$3.20 Pineapple	*23.50*	2.00
1417	A213	$4 Watermelon	*37.50*	5.00
		Nos. 1414-1417 (4)	*88.00*	9.50

Artillery, Warships, Jet Fighters A214

Wmk. 323
1964, Sept. 3 Engr. *Perf. 11½*
Without Gum

1418	A214	80c dk blue	1.60	.35
1419	A214	$6 violet brown	6.75	1.75

Issued for the 10th Armed Forces Day.

Unisphere, Flags of China and U.S. — A215

Chinese Pavilion, NY World's Fair — A216

1964, Sept. 10 Photo. Unwmk.

1420	A215	80c violet & multi	1.60	.25
1421	A216	$5 blue & multi	12.50	2.25

NY World's Fair, 1964-65. See Nos. 1450-1451.

Cowboy Carrying Calf, and Ranch — A217

Wmk. 323
1964, Sept. 24 Engr. *Perf. 11½*
Without Gum

1422	A217	$2 brown lake	1.60	.30
1423	A217	$4 dark violet blue	6.50	1.60

Animal Protection Week, Sept. 24-30.

Bicycling — A218

Sports: $1, Runner. $3.20, Gymnast on rings. $10, High jump.

1964, Oct. 10 Without Gum

1424	A218	80c violet blue	.40	.25
1425	A218	$1 rose red	.60	.40
1426	A218	$3.20 dull blue grn	3.00	.60
1427	A218	$10 lilac	9.00	2.40
		Nos. 1424-1427 (4)	13.00	3.65

18th Olympic Games, Tokyo, Oct. 10-25.

Xu Guangqi — A219

1964, Nov. 8 Engr. *Perf. 11½*
Without Gum

1428	A219	80c indigo	3.25	.50

Issued to honor Xu Guangqi (1562-1633), scholar and statesman.

Pharmaceutical Industry — A220

Textile Industry A221

$2, Chemical industry. $3.60, Cement industry.

1964, Nov. 11 Photo. Unwmk.

1429	A220	40c multi	1.00	.25
1430	A221	$1.50 multi	8.00	1.75
1431	A220	$2 multi	4.50	.75
1432	A221	$3.60 multi	12.00	1.90
		Nos. 1429-1432 (4)	25.50	4.65

Dr. Sun Yat-sen — A222

1964, Nov. 24 Engr. Wmk. 323
Without Gum

1433	A222	80c green	2.50	.25
1434	A222	$3.60 purple	9.75	1.75

Founding of the Kuomintang by Sun Yat-sen, 70th anniversary.

Eleanor Roosevelt and Scales of Justice — A223

Unwmk.
1964, Dec. 10 Photo. *Perf. 13*

1435	A223	$10 violet & brown	3.25	.80

Issued to honor Eleanor Roosevelt (1884-1962) on the 16th anniversary of the Universal Declaration of Human Rights.

Scales, Code Book and Plum Blossom — A224

Wmk. 323
1965, Jan. 11 Engr. *Perf. 11½*
Without Gum

1436	A224	80c carmine rose	.60	.25
1437	A224	$3.20 dull slate grn	4.00	.80

The 20th Judicial Day.

Rotary Emblem and Mainspring — A225

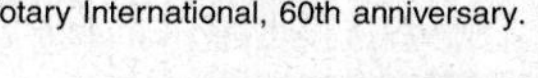
1965, Feb. 23 Wmk. 323 *Perf. 11½*
Without Gum

1438	A225	$1.50 vermilion	1.00	.25
1439	A225	$2 emerald	2.00	.40
1440	A225	$2.50 blue	2.75	.60
		Nos. 1438-1440 (3)	5.75	1.25

Rotary International, 60th anniversary.

Double Carp Design — A226

Wmk. 323
1965, Mar. 29 Engr. *Perf. 11½*
Granite Paper; Without Gum

1441	A226	$5 purple	12.00	.40
1442	A226	$5.60 dp blue	10.00	5.00
1443	A226	$6 brown	10.50	.60
1444	A226	$10 lilac rose	12.00	.40
1445	A226	$20 rose car	23.00	1.00

1446 A226 $50 green 40.00 4.00
1447 A226 $100 crim rose 160.00 12.00
Nos. 1441-1447 (7) 267.50 23.40

New dies used to reprint Nos. 1444-1447, 8/20/67. Remainders of Nos. 1441-1447 issued with gum, 11/1/71.

Madame Chiang Kai-shek — A227

1965, Apr. 17 Photo. Unwmk.
1448 A227 $2 multicolored 10.00 1.00
1449 A227 $6 salmon & multi 65.00 9.00

Chinese Women's Anti-Aggression League, 15th anniversary.

Unisphere and Chinese Pavilion — A228

"100 Birds Paying Homage to Queen Phoenix" and Unisphere — A229

1965, May 8
1450 A228 $2 blue & multi 22.00 .60
1451 A229 $10 red, ocher & bis 33.00 4.00

New York World's Fair, 1964-65.

ITU Emblem, Old and New Communication Equipment A230

Design: $5, similar to 80c, vert.

Perf. 13½x13, 13x13½
1965, May 17 Photo. Unwmk.
1452 A230 80c multicolored 1.25 .25
1453 A230 $5 multicolored 5.00 1.00

Centenary of the ITU.

Red Sea Bream A231

Fish: 80c, White pomfret. $2, Skipjack, vert. $4, Moonfish.

1965, July 1 ***Perf. 13***
1454 A231 40c multicolored 2.00 .25
1455 A231 80c multicolored 4.00 .40
1456 A231 $2 multicolored 9.00 1.20
1457 A231 $4 multicolored 20.00 2.25
Nos. 1454-1457 (4) 35.00 4.10

Issued for Fishermen's Day.

Confucius — A232

Portraits: $2.50, Yueh Fei. $3.50, Wen Tien-hsiang. $3.60, Mencius.

Wmk. 323
1965-66 Engr. ***Perf. 11½***
Without Gum
1458 A232 $1 deep carmine 2.25 .40
1459 A232 $2.50 black brown 2.00 .40
1460 A232 $3.50 dark red 10.00 2.00
1461 A232 $3.60 dark blue 11.00 2.25
Nos. 1458-1461 (4) 25.25 5.05

The $2.50 and $3.50 have colored background.
Forgeries of No. 1461 exist.
Issued: Nos. 1458, 1461, 9/28/65; Nos. 1459-1460, 9/3/66.
See Nos. 1507-1508, design A251.

ICY Emblem — A233

Design: $6, ICY emblem, horiz.

Unwmk.
1965, Oct. 24 Photo. ***Perf. 13***
1462 A233 $2 brn, blk & gold 1.25 .30
1463 A233 $6 brt grn, red & gold 8.50 1.75

International Cooperation Year, 1965.

Street Crossing, Traffic Light — A234

Wmk. 323
1965, Nov. 1 Engr. ***Perf. 11½***
Without Gum
1464 A234 $1 brown violet 1.10 .25
1465 A234 $4 crimson rose 5.50 1.00

Issued to publicize traffic safety.

Sun Yat-sen — A235

Designs: $4, Dr. Sun Yat-sen, portrait at right. $5, Sun Yat-sen and flags, horiz.

Perf. 13½
1965, Nov. 12 Unwmk. Photo.
1466 A235 $1 multicolored 3.00 .40
1467 A235 $4 multicolored 6.00 1.00
1468 A235 $5 multicolored 17.50 4.75
Nos. 1466-1468 (3) 26.50 6.15

Children with New Year's Firecrackers A236

Dragon Dance, "Dragon Playing Ball" A237

1965, Dec. 1 Photo. ***Perf. 13***
1469 A236 $1 multi 4.00 .40
1470 A237 $4.50 multi 18.50 2.50

Lien Po from "Marshal and Prime Minister Reconciled" — A238

Facial Paintings for Chinese Operas: $3, Kuan Yü from "Reunion at Ku City." $4, Gen. Chang Fei from "The Battle of Chang Pan Hill." $6, Buddha from "The Flower-Scattering Angel."

1966, Feb. 15 Unwmk. ***Perf. 11½***
1471 A238 $1 olive & multi 8.00 1.00
1472 A238 $3 multicolored 17.50 2.00
1473 A238 $4 multicolored 38.00 4.00
1474 A238 $6 ver & multi 42.50 6.00
Nos. 1471-1474 (4) 106.00 13.00

Labels with a similar appearance to these stamps exist. These labels have the numbers 1 to 20 in the upper right corner, but lack the "00."

Postal Service Emblem Held by Carrier Pigeon — A239

Stone, Mt. Tai-wu, Quemoy, and Mailman A240

postal service emblem and: $3, Postal Museum. $4, Mailman climbing symbolic slope.

1966, Mar. 20 Photo. ***Perf. 12½***
1475 A239 $1 green & multi 1.60 .25
1476 A240 $2 multicolored 5.50 .60
1477 A240 $3 multicolored 7.25 .75
1478 A239 $4 multicolored 12.00 2.25
Nos. 1475-1478 (4) 26.35 3.85

China postal service, 70th anniversary.

Fishing on a Snowy Day, "Five Dynasties" (907-960) A241

Paintings from Palace Museum: $3.50, Calves on the Plain, Sung artist (960-1126). $4.50, Winter landscape, Sung artist (960-1126). $5, Magpies, by Lin Ch'un, Southern Sung dynasty (1127-1279).

1966, May 20 Photo. ***Perf. 13***
1479 A241 $2.50 blk, brn & red 11.50 .60
1480 A241 $3.50 bis brn, blk & gray 30.00 .75
1481 A241 $4.50 blk, buff & sl 42.50 2.25
1482 A241 $5 multicolored 55.00 4.50
Nos. 1479-1482 (4) 139.00 8.10

Inauguration of Pres. Chiang Kai-shek for a 4th term.

Dragon Boat Race A242

Lion Dance — A243

$4, Lady Chang O flying to the Moon.

1966 Unwmk.
1483 A242 $2.50 multi 5.50 .60
1484 A242 $4 multi 10.00 .80
1485 A243 $6 multi 20.00 1.75
Nos. 1483-1485 (3) 35.50 3.15

Dragon Boat, Mid-Autumn and Lunar New Year Festivals. Issued: $2.50, 6/23; $4, 9/29; $6, 11/26.

Flags of China and Argentina A244

1966, July 9 Photo. ***Perf. 13***
1486 A244 $10 multicolored 6.00 .75

Argentina's Independence. 150th anniv.

Lin Sen — A245

Wmk. 323
1966, Aug. 1 Engr. ***Perf. 11½***
Without Gum
1487 A245 $1 dk brown 3.00 .40

Centenary of the birth of Lin Sen (1867-1943), Chairman of the Nationalist Government of China (1931-43).

Flying Geese — A246

1966-67 ***Perf. 11½ Rough***
Granite Paper; Without Gum
1496 A246 $3.50 brown 1.50 .25
1497 A246 $4 vermilion 1.00 .25
1498 A246 $4.50 brt green 1.25 .25
1499 A246 $5 rose lilac 1.25 .25
1500 A246 $5.50 yel grn ('67) 1.25 .25
1501 A246 $6 brt blue 7.50 .90
1502 A246 $6.50 violet 1.50 .50
1503 A246 $7 black 3.00 .25
1504 A246 $8 car rose ('67) 1.50 .25
Nos. 1496-1504 (9) 19.75 3.15

The $4.50, $5, $6, $7 and $8 were reissued with gum in 1970-71.

For similar design, see Nos. 1566-1567.

Pres. Chiang Kai-shek in Chung San Robe — A247

$5, Chiang Kai-shek in marshal's uniform.

Unwmk.

1966, Oct. 31 Photo. *Perf. 13*

1505	A247	$1	multicolored	2.50	.25
1506	A247	$5	multicolored	10.75	2.10

Chiang Kai-shek's inauguration for a fourth term as president, May 20, 1966.

Famous Men Type of 1965-66 with Frame Line

Portraits: No. 1507, Tsai Yuan-pei (1868-1940), educator. No. 1508, Chiu Ching (1875-1907), woman educator and revolutionist.

1967 Wmk. 323 Engr. *Perf. 11½*
Without Gum

1507	A232	$1	violet blue	2.50	.50
1508	A232	$1	black	5.00	.60

Issue dates: No. 1507, Jan. 11. No. 1508, July 15.

No. 1507 is on granite paper.

Motorized Mailman and Microwave Station — A248

"Transportation" and Radar Weather Station — A249

Unwmk.

1967, Mar. 15 Photo. *Perf. 13*

1511	A248	$1	multicolored	1.90	.25
1512	A249	$5	multicolored	4.25	.80

Issued to publicize the progress in communication and transportation services.

Pres. Chiang Kai-shek and Chinese Flag — A250

Design: $4, Different frame.

1967, May 20 Litho. *Perf. 13*

1513	A250	$1	multicolored	2.25	.25
1514	A250	$4	multicolored	6.50	1.25

First anniversary of President Chiang Kai-shek's 4th-term inauguration.

Chu Yuan, 332-295 B.C. — A251

Portraits: $2, Li Po (705-760). $2.50, Tu Fu (712-770). $3, Po Chu-i (772-846).

Granite Paper; Without Gum
Wmk. 323

1967, June 12 Engr. *Perf. 11½*

1515	A251	$1	black	1.10	.25
1516	A251	$2	brown	5.50	.50
1517	A251	$2.50	brown blk	7.00	1.20
1518	A251	$3	grnsh black	8.25	1.40
			Nos. 1515-1518 (4)	21.85	3.35

Issued for Poets' Day.

See design A232.

Hotei, Wood Carving — A252

Handicrafts: $2.50, Vase and plate. $3, Dolls. $5, Palace lanterns.

Perf. 11½

1967, Aug. 12 Unwmk. Photo.

1519	A252	$1	gray & multi	1.90	.25
1520	A252	$2.50	multi	3.75	.60
1521	A252	$3	multi	5.75	1.00
1522	A252	$5	multi	11.50	3.25
			Nos. 1519-1522 (4)	22.90	5.10

Taiwan handicraft industry.

World Map — A253

Granite Paper; Without Gum
Wmk. 323

1967, Sept. 25 Engr. *Perf. 11½*

1523	A253	$1	vermilion	.35	.25
1524	A253	$5	blue	2.75	.50

1st Conference of the World Anti-Communist League, WACL, Taipei, Sept. 25-29.

Players on Stilts: "The Fisherman and the Woodcutter" A254

Unwmk.

1967, Oct. 10 Photo. *Perf. 13*

1525	A254	$4.50	multi	2.60	.60

Issued for the 56th National Day.

Maroon Oriole — A255

Formosan Birds: $1, Formosan barbet, vert. $2.50, Formosan green pigeon. $3, Formosan blue magpie. $5, Crested serpent eagle, vert. $8, Mikado pheasants.

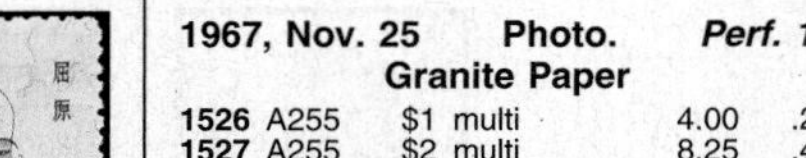

1967, Nov. 25 Photo. *Perf. 11*
Granite Paper

1526	A255	$1	multi	4.00	.25
1527	A255	$2	multi	8.25	.40
1528	A255	$2.50	multi	9.25	.60
1529	A255	$3	multi	10.00	.75
1530	A255	$5	multi	11.00	1.25
1531	A255	$8	multi	12.50	2.50
			Nos. 1526-1531 (6)	55.00	5.75

Chung Hsing Pagoda — A256

Buddha, Changhua A257

Designs: $2.50, Seashore, Yeh Liu Park. $5, National Palace Museum, Taipei.

Unwmk.

1967, Dec. 10 Photo. *Perf. 13*

1532	A256	$1	multi	2.25	.25
1533	A257	$2.50	multi	6.00	.50
1534	A257	$4	multi	7.50	1.00
1535	A257	$5	multi	8.50	2.50
			Nos. 1532-1535 (4)	24.25	4.25

Issued for International Tourist Year 1967.

China Park, Manila, and Flags — A258

1967, Dec. 30 *Perf. 13½*

1536	A258	$1	multicolored	.50	.25
1537	A258	$5	multicolored	3.50	.70

Sino-Philippine Friendship Year 1966-67.

Sun Yat-sen Building, Yangmingshan

A259 A259a

Perf. 13x12½

1968-75 Litho. Wmk. 323
Granite Paper

1538	A259	5c	lt brown	.65	.25
1539	A259	10c	grnsh black	.65	.25
1540	A259	50c	brt rose lilac	.30	.25
1541	A259	$1	vermilion	.40	.25
1542	A259	$1.50	emerald	2.25	.70
1543	A259	$2	plum	1.90	.25
1544	A259	$2.50	blue	1.40	.25
1545	A259	$3	grnsh blue	2.25	.35
			Nos. 1538-1545 (8)	9.80	2.55

See Nos. 1702-1709. For overprints see Nos. 1723-1725.

Issued: 50c, $1, $2.50, 1/23/1968; others 7/11/68.

All reprinting of this issue after Sept. 1969 are on a whiter paper with fewer colored fibers.

On Dec. 10, 1969, a booklet containing 12 #1540, 24 #1541, and 8 #1544 was issued.

Coil Stamps

Perf. 13 Horiz.

Photo. Unwmk.

1546	A259a	$1	carmine rose	1.20	.30
1547	A259a	$1	vermilion	.55	.25

Issued: No. 1546, 3/20/70; No. 1547, 1/28/75.

Inscription on No. 1546 is in color with white background. On No. 1547 it is white with colored background.

Harvesting Sugar Cane — A260

Unwmk.

1968, Mar. 1 Photo. *Perf. 13*

1548	A260	$1	olive & multi	1.25	.25
1549	A260	$4	multicolored	4.00	.70

Jade Cabbage, 1662-1911 — A261

Ancient Art Treasures: $1.50, Jade battle axe. $2, Porcelain flower bowl, 960-1126 A.D., horiz. $2.50, Cloisonné enamel vase, 1723-1736 A.D. $4, Agate flower holder in shape of finger citrus, 1662-1911 A.D., horiz. $5, Sacrificial kettle, 1111-771 B.C.

1968, Mar. 29 Unwmk. *Perf. 13*

1550	A261	$1	rose & multi	1.75	.25
1551	A261	$1.50	blue & multi	5.75	.50
1552	A261	$2	blue & multi	6.25	.70
1553	A261	$2.50	dull rose & multi	7.50	1.00
1554	A261	$4	pink & multi	10.50	1.20
1555	A261	$5	blue & multi	11.75	2.00
			Nos. 1550-1555 (6)	43.50	5.65

For similar artifact designs inscribed "Republic of China," with single-color denominations in slanted numerals and the cents underlined, see types A276, A291, A323, A336, A384, A395, A411.

Artifact designs with denominations in outlined numerals begin with type A439.

View of City in Cathay (1) — A262

Views: No. 1557, City and wall of Forbidden City (2). No. 1558, Wall at right, bridge at left (3). No. 1559, Queen's ship landing at left (4). No. 1560, Palace (5). $5, City wall and gate. $8, Suburb around Great Bridge. Design from scroll "A City in Cathay," painted 1736.

1968, June 18 Photo. *Perf. 13½*
Size: 50x29mm

1556	A262	$1	multicolored	4.00	.40
1557	A262	$1	multicolored	4.00	.40
1558	A262	$1	multicolored	4.00	.40
1559	A262	$1	multicolored	4.00	.40
1560	A262	$1	multicolored	4.00	.40
a.			Strip of 5, #1556-1560	20.00	20.00

Size: 60x31mm

Perf. 13x13½

1561	A262	$5	multicolored	20.00	4.25
1562	A262	$8	multicolored	35.00	6.00
			Nos. 1556-1562 (7)	75.00	12.25

See Nos. 1610-1614. For similar designs see types A281, A299, A326, A343.

Entrance Gate, Taroko Gorge A263

$8, Sun Yat-sen Building, Yangmingshan.

1968, Feb. 12 Photo. *Perf. 13*

1563	A263	$5 multicolored	4.25	.60
1564	A263	$8 multicolored	4.25	1.00

The 17th Annual Conference of the Pacific Area Travel Association.

Vice President Chen Cheng — A264

1968, Mar. 5

1565	A264	$1 brown & multi	2.75	.25

Vice President Chen Cheng (1898-1965).

Flying Geese — A265

Wmk. 323

1968, Mar. 20 Litho. *Perf. 12*

Granite Paper

1566	A265	$1 vermilion	9.00	.25

Souvenir Sheet

Imperf

1567	A265	$3 green	16.50	3.50

90th anniv. of Chinese postage stamps. No. 1567 contains one stamp with simulated perforations.

See Nos. 1496-1504.

WHO Emblem and "20" — A266

1968, Apr. 7 Engr. *Perf. 12*

Granite Paper

1568	A266	$1 green	.45	.25
1569	A266	$5 scarlet	1.60	.50

20th anniv. of WHO.

Symbolic Water Cycle — A267

Wmk. 323

1968, June 6 Litho. *Perf. 11½*

Granite Paper

1570	A267	$1 green & org	.60	.25
1571	A267	$4 brt blue & org	1.40	.30

Hydrological Decade (UNESCO) 1965-74.

Broadcasting to Mainland China — A268

Dual Carriers for FM Broadcasting A269

Wmk. 323

1968, Aug. 1 Litho. *Perf. 12*

Granite Paper

1572	A268	$1 bl, vio bl & gray	.70	.25
1573	A269	$4 lt ultra & ver	1.35	.30

40th anniv. of the Broadcasting Corp. of China, and the inauguration of frequency modulation broadcasting.

Human Rights Flame — A270

1968, Sept. 3 Granite Paper

1574	A270	$1 multicolored	.60	.25
1575	A270	$5 multicolored	1.40	.30

International Human Rights Year 1968.

Crop Improvement and Extension Work — A271

Wmk. 323

1968, Sept. 30 Litho. *Perf. 12*

Granite Paper

1576	A271	$1 yel, bister & dk brn	.45	.25
1577	A271	$5 yel, emer & dk grn	1.90	.50

Joint Commission on Rural Reconstruction, 20th anniversary.

Javelin — A272

Designs: $2.50, Weight lifting. $5, Pole vault, horiz. $8, Woman hurdling, horiz.

Unwmk.

1968, Oct. 12 Photo. *Perf. 13*

1578	A272	$1 multi	.60	.25
1579	A272	$2.50 multi	1.60	.30
1580	A272	$5 multi	1.60	.60
1581	A272	$8 pink & multi	1.60	.40
		Nos. 1578-1581 (4)	5.40	1.55

19th Olympic Games, Mexico City, 10/12-27.

Pres. Chiang Kai-shek and Whampoa Military Academy — A273

Designs: $2, Pres. Chiang Kai-shek reviewing forces of the Northern Expedition. $2.50, Suppression of bandits, reconstruction work and New Life Movement emblem. $3.50, Marco Polo Bridge near Peking and victory parade, Nanking. $4, Original copy of Constitution of Republic of China. $5, Nationalist Chinese flag flying over mainland China.

1968, Oct. 31 *Perf. 11½x12*

1582	A273	$1 multi	.60	.25
1583	A273	$2 multi	1.75	.30
1584	A273	$2.50 multi	2.10	.40
1585	A273	$3.50 multi	3.25	.50
1586	A273	$4 multi	3.50	.80
1587	A273	$5 multi	4.00	.90
		Nos. 1582-1587 (6)	15.20	3.15

Chiang Kai-shek's achievements for China.

Cock — A274

1968, Nov. 12 Litho. *Perf. 12*

Granite Paper

1588	A274	$1 pink & multi	11.00	.75
1589	A274	$4.50 lilac & multi	62.50	13.00

Issued for use on New Year's greetings.

Flag — A275

1968, Dec. 25 Wmk. 323 *Perf. 12½*

Granite Paper

1590	A275	$1 multicolored	.70	.25
1591	A275	$5 lt blue & multi	2.75	.60

Constitution of the Republic of China, 20th anniversary.

Jade Belt Buckle, 1662-1911 A276

Ancient Art Treasures: $1.50, Yellow jade vase, 960-1126 A.D., vert. $2, Cloisonne enamel square teapot, 1662-1911 A.D. $2.50, Kuei, sacrificial bronze vessel, 722-481 B.C. $4, Heavenly ball vase, 1368-1661 A.D., vert. $5, Gourd-shaped vase, 1662-1911 A.D., vert.

Unwmk.

1969, Jan. 15 Photo. *Perf. 13*

1592	A276	$1 dl rose & multi	.75	.25
1593	A276	$1.50 rose & multi	2.75	.30
1594	A276	$2 brt rose & multi	3.50	.40
1595	A276	$2.50 lt blue & multi	3.75	.60
1596	A276	$4 tan & multi	4.00	.80
1597	A276	$5 pale blue & multi	4.25	1.00
		Nos. 1592-1597 (6)	19.00	3.35

Servicemen and Savings Emblem A277

Wmk. 323

1969, Feb. 1 Engr. *Perf. 12*

Granite Paper

1598	A277	$1 dull red brown	.40	.25
1599	A277	$4 deep blue	1.75	.55

Military Savings Program, 10th anniv.

Ti (Flute) A278

Musical Instruments: $2.50, Sheng (13 bamboo pipes connected at the base). $4, P'i p'a (lute). $5, Cheng (zither).

Unwmk.

1969, Mar. 16 Photo. *Perf. 13*

1600	A278	$1 buff & multi	.70	.25
1601	A278	$2.50 lt ap grn & multi	1.60	.50
1602	A278	$4 pink & multi	3.50	.75
1603	A278	$5 lt grnsh bl & multi	2.50	.60
		Nos. 1600-1603 (4)	8.30	2.10

Sun Yat-sen Building and Kuomintang Emblem A279

1969, Mar. 29 Litho. *Perf. 13½*

1604	A279	$1 multicolored	1.25	.25

10th Natl. Cong. of the Chinese Nationalist Party (Kuomintang), Mar. 29. A $2.50 stamp portraying Sun Yat-sen and Chiang Kai-shek was prepared but not issued.

Double Carp Design — A280

Perf. 13½x12½

1974, Aug. 2 Engr. Wmk. 323

Granite Paper

1606	A280	$10 dark blue	3.50	.40
1607	A280	$20 dark brown	8.50	.40
1608	A280	$50 green	9.00	.75
1609	A280	$100 bright red	16.00	1.40
		Nos. 1606-1609 (4)	37.00	2.95

1969, Apr. 21 *Perf. 11½*

1606a	A280	$10	4.00	.25
1607a	A280	$20	6.00	.25
1608a	A280	$50	7.00	.45
1609a	A280	$100	13.00	.90
		Nos. 1606a-1609a (4)	30.00	1.85

1976, Dec. 15 *Perf. 11½*

White Paper

1606b	A280	$10	3.00	.25
1607b	A280	$20	5.00	.25
1608b	A280	$50	7.00	.50
1609b	A280	$100	10.00	1.00
		Nos. 1606b-1609b (4)	25.00	2.00

The 1969 issue is 27mm high; 1974 and 1976, 28mm.

See No. 1980.

Bridal Procession — A281

Designs: No. 1610, Musicians and standard bearer from bridal procession. $2.50, Emigrant farm family in oxcart. $5, Art gallery. $8, Roadside food stands. Designs from scroll "A City in Cathay," painted in 1736.

Perf. 13½

1969, May 20 Unwmk. Photo.

1610	A281	$1 multi	1.75	.25
1611	A281	$1 multi	1.75	.25
a.		Pair, #1610-1611	3.75	3.75
1612	A281	$2.50 multi	5.75	.60
1613	A281	$5 multi	7.00	1.50
1614	A281	$8 multi	8.00	2.10
		Nos. 1610-1614 (5)	24.25	4.70

ILO Emblem A282

Wmk. 323

1969, June 15 Engr. *Perf. 11½*

Granite Paper

1615 A282 $1 dark blue .50 .25
1616 A282 $8 dark carmine 1.50 .50

ILO, 50th anniversary.

Family at Dinner Table and Dressing A283

Designs: $2.50, Housecleaning and obeying traffic rules. $4, Recreation (music, fishing, basketball) and education.

Wmk. 323

1969, July 15 Engr. *Perf. 11½*

1617 A283 $1 brick red .45 .25
1618 A283 $2.50 blue 1.40 .35
1619 A283 $4 green 1.15 .30
Nos. 1617-1619 (3) 3.00 .90

Model Citizen's Life Movement.

Pupils in Laboratory and Playing — A284

Design: $1, $5, Pupils with book and various school activities, horiz.

Granite Paper

1969, Sept. 1 Wmk. 323 *Perf. 11½*

1620 A284 $1 brt red .25 .25
1621 A284 $2.50 brt green .60 .25
1622 A284 $4 dk blue 1.50 .30
1623 A284 $5 brown 1.60 .55
Nos. 1620-1623 (4) 3.95 1.35

Free 9-year education system, 1st anniv.

Wild Flowers and Pheasants, by Lu Chih (Ming) A285

Paintings: $2.50, Bamboo and birds, Sung dynasty. $5, Flowers and Birds, Sung dynasty. $8, Cranes and Flowers, by G. Castiglione, S.J. (1688-1766).

1969, Oct. 9 Photo. *Perf. 13½*

1624 A285 $1 multi 2.25 .25
1625 A285 $2.50 multi 6.75 .80
1626 A285 $5 multi 13.50 1.75
1627 A285 $8 multi 19.00 3.00
Nos. 1624-1627 (4) 41.50 5.80

Golden Scepter Rose — A286

Roses: $1, "Charles Mollerin," called black rose. $5, Peace. $8, Josephine Bruce.

1969, Oct. 31 Litho. *Perf. 14*

1628 A286 $1 lt vio & multi 1.00 .25
1629 A286 $2.50 lt bl & multi 5.00 .40
1630 A286 $5 dl org & multi 6.25 .90
1631 A286 $8 ap grn & multi 5.75 .70
Nos. 1628-1631 (4) 18.00 2.25

Rocket and Radar Station — A287

Wmk. 323

1969, Nov. 21 Engr. *Perf. 11½*

1632 A287 $1 rose claret 1.75 .25

The 30th Air Defense Day.

Symbol of International Cooperation A288

1969, Nov. 25

1633 A288 $1 rose claret .50 .25
1634 A288 $5 green 1.40 .40

5th General Assembly of the Asian Parliamentary Union, Taipei, Nov. 24-28.

Pekingese — A289

1969, Dec. 1 Litho. *Perf. 12*

Granite Paper

1635 A289 50c red & multi 2.40 .50
1636 A289 $4.50 green & multi 12.00 2.00

Issued for use on New Year's greetings.

Satellite, Earth Station and Map of Taiwan A290

Unwmk.

1969, Dec. 28 Photo. *Perf. 13*

1637 A290 $1 brown & multi .45 .25
1638 A290 $5 vio blue & multi 1.60 .35
1639 A290 $8 purple & multi 2.25 .65
Nos. 1637-1639 (3) 4.30 1.25

Inauguration of the Communication Satellite Earth Station at Chin-Shan-Li, Dec. 28.

Agate Grinding Stone, 1662-1911 A291

Ancient Art Treasures: $1, Carved lacquer ware vase, 1662-1911, vert. $2, White jade Chin-li-chih melons, 1662-1911. $2.50, Black jade shepherd and ram, 206 B.C.-220 A.D. $4, Chien-lung twin porcelain vase, 1736-1796, vert. $5, Ju porcelain vase with 3 bulls, 960-1126, vert.

1970, Jan. 23

1640 A291 $1 lt grnsh bl & multi .40 .25
1641 A291 $1.50 pale bl & multi 1.90 .25
1642 A291 $2 green & multi 2.50 .30
1643 A291 $2.50 pink & multi 3.00 .50
1644 A291 $4 ol bis & multi 5.00 .75
1645 A291 $5 ultra & multi 6.25 .80
Nos. 1640-1645 (6) 19.05 2.85

Hsuan Chuang — A292

Chu Hsi — A293

Design: $2.50, Hua To.

1970 Wmk. 323 Engr. *Perf. 11½*

Granite Paper

1646 A292 $1 car rose .75 .25
1647 A293 $2.50 blue grn 2.10 .40
1648 A293 $4 blue 2.50 .50
Nos. 1646-1648 (3) 5.35 1.15

Issued in memory of Hsuan Chuang (602-664), who propagated Buddhism in China; Chu Hsi (1130-1200), who developed Neo-Confucianism, and Hua To (3rd century A.D.) physician and surgeon.

Issued: $2.50, 3/17; others, 2/20.

EXPO '70 Pavilion, Emblem and Flags of Participants A294

Design: $5, Chinese pavilion, EXPO '70 emblem, exhibition and Chinese flags.

Unwmk.

1970, Mar. 13 Photo. *Perf. 13*

1649 A294 $5 org red & multi 1.25 .25
1650 A294 $8 lt blue & multi 1.75 .60

EXPO '70 International Exhibition, Osaka, Japan, Mar. 15-Sept. 13.

Nimbus III and WMO Emblem A295

Design: $1, Agricultural meteorological station and tropical landscape, vert.

Perf. 14x13½, 13½x14

1970, Mar. 23 Litho. Wmk. 323

Granite Paper

1651 A295 $1 green & multi .35 .25
1652 A295 $8 blue & multi 2.25 .65

10th Annual World Meteorological Day.

Martyrs' Shrine, Taipei A296

Shrine's Gate A297

Unwmk.

1970, Mar. 29 Photo. *Perf. 13*

1653 A296 $1 multicolored .65 .25
1654 A297 $8 multicolored 2.40 .65

Completion of the Martyrs' Shrine in Northern Taipei, dedicated to the memory of 72 young revolutionaries who died Mar. 29, 1911.

Yueh Fei Fighting for Lost Territories A298

Characters from Chinese Operas: $2.50, Emperor Shun and stepmother. $5, The Lady Warrior Chin Liang-yu. $8, Kuan Yu and groom.

1970, May 4 Unwmk. *Perf. 13½*

1655 A298 $1 multi .40 .25
1656 A298 $2.50 multi 3.50 .30
1657 A298 $5 multi 5.50 .75
1658 A298 $8 multi 7.50 1.20
Nos. 1655-1658 (4) 16.90 2.50

A299

Three Horses Playing — A300

Horses: No. 1659, Barren tree at right. No. 1660, Horse standing in river. No. 1661, Tree trunk in lower left corner. No. 1662, Trees in left background. No. 1663, shown. $8, Groom roping horses. Designs from scroll "One Hundred Horses" by Lang Shih-ning (Giuseppe Castiglione, 1688-1766).

Perf. 13½

1970, June 18 Unwmk. Photo.

1659 A299 $1 multi 1.40 .25
1660 A299 $1 multi 1.40 .25
1661 A299 $1 multi 1.40 .25
1662 A299 $1 multi 1.40 .25
1663 A299 $1 multi 1.40 .25
a. Strip of 5, #1659-1663 8.00 8.00
1664 A300 $5 bister & multi 14.00 2.00
1665 A300 $8 dl yel & multi 16.50 3.00
Nos. 1659-1665 (7) 37.50 6.25

Lai-tsu Amusing his Old Parents — A301

Chinese Fairy Tales: No. 1667, Man disguised as deer, and hunters. No. 1668, Boy cooling his father's bed. No. 1669, Boy fishing through ice. No. 1670, Son reunited with old mother. No. 1671, Emperor tasting mother's medicine. No. 1672, Boy saving oranges for mother. No. 1673, Boy saving father from tiger.

Wmk. 323

1970, July 10 Litho. *Perf. 13½*

Granite Paper

1666 A301 10c red & multi .25 .25
1667 A301 10c car rose & multi .25 .25
1668 A301 10c lt vio & multi .25 .25
1669 A301 10c gray & multi .25 .25
1670 A301 10c emerald & multi .25 .25
1671 A301 50c bister & multi .40 .25

1672 A301 $1 sky blue & multi .60 .25
1673 A301 $1 dp blue & multi .60 .25
Nos. 1666-1673 (8) 2.85 2.00

See Nos. 1726-1733.

Man's First Step onto Moon — A302

$1, Pres. Chiang Kai-shek's message brought to the moon. $5, Neil A. Armstrong, Michael Collins, Edwin E. Aldrin, Jr., and moon, horiz.

Perf. 13½x13, 13x13½

1970, July 21 Photo. Unwmk.

1674 A302 $1 yellow & multi .50 .25
1675 A302 $5 lt yel grn & multi 2.75 .40
1676 A302 $8 blue & multi 3.25 .50
Nos. 1674-1676 (3) 6.50 1.15

1st anniv. of man's 1st landing on the moon.

Asian Productivity Year Symbol A303

Wmk. 323

1970, Aug. 18 Litho. *Perf. 13½*

Granite Paper

1677 A303 $1 emerald & multi .55 .25
1678 A303 $5 blue & multi 1.25 .40

Issued to publicize Asian Productivity Year.

Flags of China and UN — A304

1970, Sept. 19 Wmk. 323 *Perf. 12*

Granite Paper

1679 A304 $5 blue, car & blk 2.75 .65

25th anniversary of the United Nations.

Postal Zone Map — A305

Postal Code Emblem A306

1970, Oct. 8 Litho.

1680 A305 $1 lt blue & multi .70 .25
1681 A306 $2.50 green & multi 1.10 .40

Issued to publicize the postal code system.

Eleventh Month Scroll — A307

Designs: A scroll series, "Activities of the 12 Months," painted on silk by a group of painters of the Ch'ien Lung court (1736-1796). Chinese number in parenthesis at right of denomination tells month.

Jan., Feb., Mar.
(一) (二) (三)

Perf. 13½x13

1970-71 Photo. Unwmk.

1682 A307 $1 multi 1.60 .40
1683 A307 $2.50 multi 14.00 3.00
1684 A307 $5 multi 20.00 4.00

Apr., May, June
(四) (五) (六)

1685 A307 $1 multi 1.60 .40
1686 A307 $2.50 multi 5.00 1.00
1687 A307 $5 multi 8.00 1.40

July, Aug., Sept.
(七) (八) (九)

1688 A307 $1 multi 1.60 .40
1689 A307 $2.50 multi 5.00 1.00
1690 A307 $5 multi 8.00 1.40

Oct., Nov., Dec.
(十) (一十) (二十)

1691 A307 $1 multi 1.60 .40
1692 A307 $2.50 multi 5.00 1.00
1693 A307 $5 multi 8.00 1.40
Nos. 1682-1693 (12) 79.40 15.80

Issued: Nos. 1691-1693, 10/21/70; Nos. 1682-1684, 1/14/71; Nos. 1685-1687, 4/26/71; Nos. 1688-1690, 8/27/71.

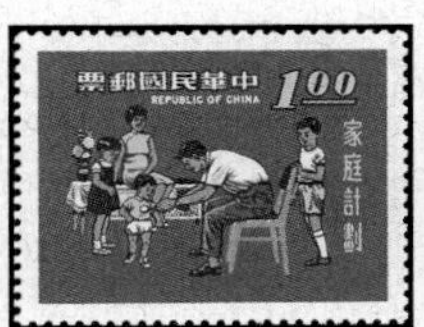

Family at Home A308

$4, Family of 5 going on an excursion, vert.

Perf. 13½x14, 14x13½

1970, Nov. 11 Litho. Wmk. 323

Granite Paper

1694 A308 $1 multicolored .50 .25
1695 A308 $4 yel grn & multi 2.50 .40

Issued to publicize family planning.

Piggy Bank — A309

1970, Dec. 1 *Perf. 12½x12*

Granite Paper

1696 A309 50c multi 1.50 .25
1697 A309 $4.50 blue & multi 9.50 1.50

Issued for use on New Year's greetings.

Tibia Fusus Shells A310

Rare Taiwan Shells: $2.50, Harpeola kurodai. $5, Conus stupa kuroda. $8, Entemnotrochus rumphii.

1971, Feb. 25 *Perf. 13x13½*

1698 A310 $1 vio & multi .85 .25
1699 A310 $2.50 multi 2.60 .25
1700 A310 $5 org & multi 3.50 .40
1701 A310 $8 grn & multi 4.50 .70
Nos. 1698-1701 (4) 11.45 1.60

Sun Yat-sen Building, Yangmingshan A311

Perf. 13½x12½

1971 Litho. Wmk. 323

Granite Paper

1702 A311 5c brown .25 .25
1703 A311 10c dk gray .25 .25
1704 A311 50c brt rose lilac .25 .25
1705 A311 $1 vermilion .25 .25
1706 A311 $1.50 ultra 2.75 .50
1707 A311 $2 plum 5.75 .50
1708 A311 $2.50 emerald 1.90 .25
1709 A311 $3 aqua 6.50 .75
Nos. 1702-1709 (8) 17.90 3.00

Passbook and Postal Savings Certificate A312

$4, People and hand dropping coin into bank.

Perf. 13½x14

1971, Mar. 20 Litho. Wmk. 323

1712 A312 $1 yel grn & multi .80 .25
1713 A312 $4 ver & multi 2.40 .45

Publicizing Chinese Postal Savings Service.

Cooperation Emblem, Farmers — A313

Design: $8, Chinese teaching rice farming to Africans, horiz.

Unwmk.

1971, May 20 Photo. *Perf. 13*

1714 A313 $1 multicolored .75 .25
1715 A313 $8 multicolored 2.25 .50

Sino-African Technical Cooperation Committee, 10th anniversary.

Rock Monkey — A314

Taiwan Animals: $2, White-face flying squirrel. $3, Chinese pangolin. $5, Formosan sika deer. $2, $3, $5 are horiz.

1971, June 25 *Perf. 11½*

1716 A314 $1 gold & multi .40 .25
1717 A314 $2 gold & multi 1.25 .25
1718 A314 $3 gold & multi 1.75 .45
1719 A314 $5 gold & multi 2.50 .75
Nos. 1716-1719 (4) 5.90 1.70

Pitcher — A315

Designs: $2.50, Players at base, horiz. $4, Batter and catcher.

1971, July 29 Photo. *Perf. 13*

1720 A315 $1 multi .30 .25
1721 A315 $2.50 multi .70 .25
1722 A315 $4 multi 1.40 .35
Nos. 1720-1722 (3) 2.40 .85

Pacific Regional competition for the 1971 Little League World Series.

Nos. 1541, 1544-1545 Overprinted in Magenta or Red

Perf. 13x12½

1971, Sept. 9 Litho. Wmk. 323

Granite Paper

1723 A259 $1 vermilion (M) .45 .25
1724 A259 $2.50 blue (R) .80 .25
1725 A259 $3 grnsh blue (R) .80 .35
Nos. 1723-1725 (3) 2.05 .85

Chinese victory in 1971 Little League World Series, Williamsport, Pa., Aug. 24.

Fairy Tale Type of 1970

Chinese Fairy Tales (Filial Piety): No. 1726, Birds and elephant helping in rice field. No. 1727, Son gathering mulberries for mother. No. 1728, Son gathering firewood. No. 1729, Son, mother and bandits. No. 1730, Son carrying heavy burden. 50c, Son digging for bamboo shoots in winter. No. 1732, Man and wife working as slaves. No. 1733, Father, son and carriage.

1971, Sept. 22 *Perf. 13½*

Granite Paper

1726 A301 10c dp org & multi .25 .25
1727 A301 10c lilac & multi .25 .25
1728 A301 10c ocher & multi .25 .25
1729 A301 10c dp car & multi .25 .25
1730 A301 10c lt ultra & multi .25 .25
1731 A301 50c multicolored .50 .25
1732 A301 $1 emerald & multi 1.20 .25
1733 A301 $1 lt red brn & multi 1.20 .25
Nos. 1726-1733 (8) 4.15 2.00

Flag of China, "Double Ten" and Anniversary Emblems A316

Designs (Flag of China and): $2.50, National anthem. $5, Gen. Chiang Kai-shek. $8, Sun Yat-sen.

1971, Oct. 10 Photo. *Perf. 13*

1734 A316 $1 orange & multi .35 .25
1735 A316 $2.50 multi .90 .25
1736 A316 $5 green & multi 2.75 .50
1737 A316 $8 olive & multi 1.75 .50
Nos. 1734-1737 (4) 5.75 1.50

60th National Day.

Bird in Flight (AOPU Emblem) A317

Perf. 13½x14

1971, Nov. 8 Litho. Wmk. 323

1738 A317 $2.50 yellow & multi .85 .25
1739 A317 $5 orange & multi 1.10 .25

Asian-Oceanic Postal Union Executive Committee Session, Taipei, Nov. 8-15.

"White Frost Hawk," by Lang Shih-ning A318

Dog Series I

Designs: $2, "Star-Glancing Wolf." $2.50, "Golden-Winged Face." $5, "Young Black Dragon." $8, "Young Gray Dragon."

Designs from painting series "Ten Prized Dogs," by Lang Shih-ning (Giuseppe Castiglione, 1688-1766).

Perf. 13½x13

1971, Nov. 16 Litho. Unwmk.

1740 A318 $1 Facing left 1.00 .25
1741 A318 $2 Lying down 2.00 .40
1742 A318 $2.50 Scratching 3.00 .50
1743 A318 $5 Facing right 5.25 .75
1744 A318 $8 Looking back 14.50 2.25
Nos. 1740-1744 (5) 25.75 4.15

Dog Series II

Designs: $1, "Black with Snow-white Paws." $2, "Yellow Leopard." $2.50, "Flying Magpie." $5, "Heavenly Lion." $8, "Mottled Tiger."

1972, Jan. 12

1745 A318 $1 Facing right 1.10 .25
1746 A318 $2 Walking 8.50 .80
1747 A318 $2.50 Sleeping 3.50 .60
1748 A318 $5 Facing left 12.50 1.40
1749 A318 $8 Sitting 34.00 7.00
Nos. 1745-1749 (5) 59.60 10.05

Squirrels — A319

Perf. 13½x12½

1971, Dec. 1 Wmk. 323

1750 A319 Block of 4 7.00 2.50
a. 50c in UL corner 1.40 .25
b. 50c in UR corner 1.40 .25
c. 50c in LL corner 1.40 .25
d. 50c in LR corner 1.40 .25
1751 A319 Block of 4 28.00 7.00
a. $4.50 in UL corner 6.00 1.25
b. $4.50 in UR corner 6.00 1.25
c. $4.50 in LL corner 6.00 1.25
d. $4.50 in LR corner 6.00 1.25

New Year 1972.

Flags of China and Jordan A320

1971, Dec. 16 *Perf. 13½*

Granite Paper

1752 A320 $5 multicolored 1.90 .25

50th anniversary of the founding of the Hashemite Kingdom of Jordan.

Cargo Ship "Hai King" — A321

$7, Ocean liner & map of Pacific Ocean, vert.

1971, Dec. 16 *Perf. 12½*

1753 A321 $4 grn, dk bl & red 1.45 .25
1754 A321 $7 ocher & multi 1.45 .30

China Merchants Steam Navigation Co., cent.

Downhill Skiing, Olympic Rings A322

$5, Cross-country skiing. $8, Giant slalom.

1972, Feb. 3 *Perf. 13½*

1755 A322 $1 org, blk & bl .50 .25
1756 A322 $5 yel grn, dp org & blk 1.10 .25
1757 A322 $8 red, gray & blk 1.25 .25
Nos. 1755-1757 (3) 2.85 .75

11th Winter Olympic Games, Sapporo, Japan, Feb. 3-13.

Vase, 18th Century — A323

Porcelain Series I

Porcelain Masterworks of Ching Dynasty: $2, Covered jar. $2.50, Pitcher. $5, Vase with 5 openings and dragon design. $8, Covered jar with children design.

Perf. 11½

1972, Mar. 20 Photo. Unwmk.

1758 A323 $1 violet & multi .50 .25
1759 A323 $2 plum & blue 2.00 .30
1760 A323 $2.50 org ver & bl 2.25 .40
1761 A323 $5 bis brn & bl 3.00 .06
1762 A323 $8 sl grn & multi 3.50 1.00
Nos. 1758-1762 (5) 11.25 2.55

See Nos. 1812-1821, 1864-1868.

Nine Flying Doves A324

Perf. 13½x14

1972, Apr. 1 Litho. Wmk. 323

1763 A324 $1 lt blue & blk .75 .25
1764 A324 $5 lt violet & blk 2.10 .35

Asian-Oceanic Postal Union, 10th anniv.

"Dignity with Self-reliance" — A325

Perf. 13½x12½

1972-75 Litho. Wmk. 323

1765 A325 5c brown & yel .25 .25
1766 A325 10c blue & org .25 .25
1767 A325 20c cl & yel grn ('75) .25 .25
1768 A325 50c lil & lil rose .25 .25
1769 A325 $1 red & brt bl .25 .25
1770 A325 $1.50 yel & dk bl .60 .25
1771 A325 $2 maroon & org .45 .25
1772 A325 $2.50 emer & ver .50 .25
1773 A325 $3 red & lt grn .90 .25
Nos. 1765-1773 (9) 3.70 2.25

Souvenir Sheet

Imperf

1775 A325 Sheet of 2 6.00 3.75

No. 1775 commemorates ROCPEX '72 Philatelic Exhibition, Taipei, Oct. 24-Nov. 2. It contains 2 stamps similar to Nos. 1771 and 1773 with simulated perforations.

Issued: $1, $1.50, $2, $3, 5/20/72; 5c, 10c, 50c, $2.50, No. 1775, 10/24/72; 20c, 1975.

For overprints see Nos. 1787-1790.

Emperor Shih-tsung's Procession — A326

Messengers on Horseback — A327

Designs from scrolls depicting Emperor Shih-tsung's (reigned 1522-1566) journey to and from tombs at Cheng-tien. No. 1776 shows land journey departure and is designed from right to left. No. 1779 shows return trip by boat and is designed from left to right. The 5 stamps of Nos. 1776 and 1780 are numbered 1 to 5 in Chinese (see illustrations with Nos. 1682-1686 for numerals).

1972 Photo. Unwmk. *Perf. 13½*

1776 Strip of 5 3.00 6.00
a. A326 $1 shown .45 .35
b. A326 $1 Seven carriages .45 .35
c. A326 $1 Carriage drawn by 23 horses .45 .35
d. A326 $1 Procession .45 .35
e. A326 $1 Emperor under 2 canopies .45 .35
1777 A327 $2.50 shown 1.50 .50
1778 A327 $5 Guards with flags, fans & spears 4.50 2.00
1779 A327 $8 Sedan chair carried by 28 men 3.50 1.40
1780 Strip of 5 3.00 6.00
a. A326 $1 Three barges .45 .35
b. A326 $1 Procession, sedan chairs .45 .35
c. A326 $1 Two barges with trunks .45 .35
d. A326 $1 Procession on land .45 .35
e. A326 $1 Procession, 2 sedan chairs .45 .35
1781 A326 $2.50 Courtiers at city welcoming Emperor 1.50 .40
1782 A327 $5 Orchestra on horseback 4.50 2.00
1783 A326 $8 Barges 3.50 1.40
Nos. 1776-1783 (8) 25.00 19.70

Issue dates: No. 1776-1779, June 14; Nos. 1780-1783, July 12.

First Day Covers — A328

Magnifying Glass, Tongs, Gauge — A329

Design: $2.50, Sun Yat-sen stamp of 1971 (type A311) under magnifying glass.

Wmk. 323

1972, Aug. 9 Engr. *Perf. 12*

1784 A328 $1 dk vio blue .40 .25
1785 A328 $2.50 brt green .80 .25
1786 A329 $8 scarlet 1.20 .50
Nos. 1784-1786 (3) 2.40 1.00

Promotion of philately. Printed in sheets of 40. Each sheet contains 4 blocks of 10 stamps surrounded by margins with inscriptions.

Nos. 1768-1770, 1772 Overprinted in Dark Blue or Red

Perf. 13½x12½

1972, Sept. 9 Litho. Wmk. 323

1787 A325 $1 red & brt bl (DB) .40 .25
1788 A325 $1.50 yel & dk bl (R) .65 .25
1789 A325 $2 mar & org (R) .75 .25
1790 A325 $3 red & lt grn (DB) .80 .35
Nos. 1787-1790 (4) 2.60 1.10

China's championship victories in the Little League World Series, Gary, Ind., and in the Senior League World Series, Williamsport, Pa., Aug. 1972.

Emperor Yao (2357-2258 B.C.) — A330

Rulers: $4, Emperor Shun (ruled 2255-2208 B.C.). $4.50, Yu, the Great (ruled 2205-2198 B.C.). $5, King T'ang (ruled 1783-1754 B.C.). $5.50, King Wen (ruled 1171-1122 B.C.). $6, King Wu (ruled 1121-1114 B.C.). $7, Chou Kung (died 1105 B.C.). $8, Confucius (551-479 B.C.).

1972-76 Engr. *Perf. 12*

Granite Paper

1791 A330 $3.50 dk blue 1.50 .25
1792 A330 $4 rose red .50 .25
1793 A330 $4.50 bluish lil 1.60 .25
1794 A330 $5 brt green .50 .25
1795 A330 $5.50 dp claret 2.00 .60
1796 A330 $6 dp org 2.10 .25
a. Perf. 13½x12½ ('76) .80 .25
1797 A330 $7 sepia .95 .25
a. Perf. 13½x12½ ('76) .95 .25
1798 A330 $8 indigo 1.20 .25
a. gray, perf. 13½x12½ ('76) .60 .25
Nos. 1791-1798 (8) 10.35 2.35

In the first printing, Nos. 1791-1794, 1796-1798 measure 32mm high. In a 1974 reissue they are 33mm.

1974, July 25 *Perf. 12*

Large Wmk. 323

1791a A330 $3.50 .90 .25
1792a A330 $4 .60 .25
1793a A330 $4.50 1.50 .25
1794a A330 $5 .70 .25
1796b A330 $6 2.10 .45
1797b A330 $7 1.20 .25
1798b A330 $8 1.20 .25
Nos. 1791a-1798b (7) 8.20 1.95

Issued: Nos. 1791-1794, 9/20/1972; Nos. 1795-1798, 4/2/1973; Nos. 1791a-1794a, 1796b-1798b, 7/25/1974; Nos. 1796a-1798a, 1/26/1976.

The 1972 issue was printed using a wet copper plate and the designs are 32mm high. The 1973 printings were done on dry copper plates resulting in a taller design of 33mm. The 1974 printing was printed on a locally made paper with a larger version of the "post" watermark No. 323, using dry copper plates resulting in the design being 33mm high.

Mountain Climbing — A331

Designs (China Youth Corps emblem and): $2.50, Skiing (skiers forming circle). $4, Diving. $8, Parachute jumping.

Unwmk.

1972, Oct. 31 Photo. *Perf. 12*

1800	A331	$1 green & multi	.25	.25
1801	A331	$2.50 blue & multi	.65	.25
1802	A331	$4 orange & multi	1.00	.25
1803	A331	$8 multicolored	1.30	.40
		Nos. 1800-1803 (4)	3.20	1.15

China Youth Corps, 20th anniversary.

JCI Emblem A332

1972, Nov. 12 Litho. Wmk. 323

1804	A332 $1 multicolored	.25	.25
1805	A332 $5 orange & multi	.45	.25
1806	A332 $8 multicolored	.85	.40
	Nos. 1804-1806 (3)	1.55	.90

27th Junior Chamber International (JCI) World Congress, Taipei, Nov. 12-19.

Electronic Mail Sorter — A333

Plane, Ship and Pier — A334

Progress of Communications System on Taiwan: $5, Highway overpass over railroad.

Wmk. 323

1972, Nov. 12 Engr. *Perf. 11½*

1807	A333 $1 red	.35	.25
1808	A334 $2.50 blue	.80	.25
1809	A334 $5 dk violet brn	1.25	.40
	Nos. 1807-1809 (3)	2.40	.90

Cow and Calf (Parental Love) — A335

1972, Dec. 1 Litho. *Perf. 12*

1810	A335 50c red & blk	2.50	.25
1811	A335 $4.50 yel, red & brn	4.50	.90

New Year 1973. Printed in sheets of 80, divided into 4 panes of 20, separated by vertical and horizontal gutters 2 rows wide. 20 red chops meaning "Happy New Year" are printed in the gutters.

Porcelain Type of 1972 and

Stem Bowl with Dragons A336

Porcelain Series II

Porcelain Masterworks of Ming Dynasty: $1, Covered vase with fruits and flowers. $2, Vase with ornamental and floral design. $2.50, Vase imitating ancient bronze. $5, Flask with flowers of 4 seasons. $8, Garlic head vase.

1973 Photo. *Perf. 11½*

1812	A323 $1 gray & multi	1.90	.25
1813	A323 $2 lt brn & multi	2.75	.25
1814	A323 $2.50 brt grn & multi	3.75	.25
1815	A323 $5 ultra & multi	4.00	.35
1816	A323 $8 olive & multi	6.00	.60
	Nos. 1812-1816 (5)	18.40	1.70

Porcelain Series III

Ming Porcelain: $2, Refuse container with dragons. $2.50, Covered jar with lotus. $5, Covered jar with horses. $8, Bowl with figures of immortals.

1817	A336 $1 gray & multi	1.60	.25
1818	A336 $2 lt vio & multi	2.40	.25
1819	A336 $2.50 dk red & multi	3.50	.25
1820	A336 $5 blue & multi	3.75	.35
1821	A336 $8 dp org & multi	5.25	.60
	Nos. 1817-1821 (5)	16.50	1.70

Issued: Nos. 1812-1816, 1/10; Nos. 1817-1821, 3/24.

See Nos. 1864-1868.

Oyster Fairy and Fisherman's Dance — A337

$1, Kicking shuttlecock, vert. $5, Rowing boat over land. $8, Old man carrying young lady, vert.

1973, Feb. 7 Photo. *Perf. 11½*

Granite Paper

1822	A337 $1 multicolored	.65	.25
1823	A337 $4 Shown	1.05	.25
1824	A337 $5 multicolored	1.90	.25
1825	A337 $8 multicolored	2.10	.40
	Nos. 1822-1825 (4)	5.70	1.15

Chinese folklore popular entertainment.

Bamboo Boat A338

Taiwanese Handicrafts: $2.50, Painted marble vase, vert. $5, Painted glass plate. $8, Doll, bridegroom carrying bride on back, vert.

Perf. 13½x14½, 14½x13½

1973, Mar. 9 Photo.

1826	A338 $1 multi	.25	.25
1827	A338 $2.50 multi	1.10	.25
1828	A338 $5 multi	1.75	.25
1829	A338 $8 multi	2.40	.30
	Nos. 1826-1829 (4)	5.50	1.05

Federation Emblem, Cargo Hook, Crane — A339

Emblem, Tractor, New Buildings A340

Wmk. 323

1973, Apr. 2 Litho. *Perf. 12½*

1830	A339 $1 salmon & multi	.40	.25
1831	A340 $5 blue & blk	1.25	.25

12th convention of International Federation of Asian and Western Pacific Contractors Association, Taipei, Apr. 2-10.

Pres. Chiang Kai-shek, Flag of China — A341

Design: $4, like $1 with different border.

Unwmk.

1973, May 20 Photo. *Perf. 12*

1832	A341 $1 yellow & multi	.65	.25
1833	A341 $4 dk grn & multi	2.00	.50

First anniversary of Pres. Chiang Kai-shek's inauguration for a fifth term.

Lin Tse-hsü — A342

Wmk. 323

1973, June 3 Engr. *Perf. 12*

1834	A342 $1 sepia	1.10	.25

Lin Tse-hsü (1785-1850), Governor of Hunan and Kwantung, who destroyed large quantity of opium at Humen, Kwantung, June 3, 1839.

Willows and Palace Gate in the Morning — A343

Lady Watering Peonies, Stone Ornament A344

Design from scroll "Spring Morning in the Han Palace," by Chiu Ying. The five stamps of No. 1835 are numbered 1 to 5 and the five stamps of No. 1838 are numbered 6-10 in Chinese (see illustrations with Nos. 1682-1691 for numerals). The stamps are numbered and listed from right to left.

1973 Photo. Unwmk. *Perf. 11½*

Granite Paper

1835		Strip of 5	3.50	3.50
	a.	A343 $1 shown	.45	.25
	b.	A343 $1 Ladies feeding peacocks	.45	.25
	c.	A343 $1 Lady watering peonies	.45	.25
	d.	A343 $1 Pear tree in bloom	.45	.25
	e.	A343 $1 Lady musicians	.45	.25
1836		A344 $5 shown	2.75	.80
1837		A344 $8 Lady musicians	4.00	2.40
1838		Strip of 5	3.50	3.00
	a.	A343 $1 Ladies playing go	.45	.25
	b.	A343 $1 Various games	.45	.25
	c.	A343 $1 Talking and playing music	.45	.25
	d.	A343 $1 Artist painting portrait	.45	.25
	e.	A343 $1 Sentries guarding wall	.45	.25
1839		A344 $5 Ladies playing go	2.75	.80
1840		A344 $8 Girl chasing butterfly	4.00	2.40
		Nos. 1835-1840 (6)	20.50	12.90

Issued: Nos. 1835-1837, 6/20; Nos. 1838-1840, 7/18.

Fan, Bamboo Design, by Hsiang Te-hsin — A345

Designs: Painted fans, Ming dynasty.

Perf. 12½x13

1973, Aug. 15 Photo. Wmk. 368

1841	A345 $1 bister & multi	.50	.25
1842	A345 $2.50 bister & multi	1.25	.25
1843	A345 $5 bister & multi	2.25	.50
1844	A345 $8 bister & multi	3.50	.60
	Nos. 1841-1844 (4)	7.50	1.60

See Nos. 1934-1937.

Little League Emblem — A346

Wmk. 370

1973, Sept. 9 Litho. *Perf. 13½*

1845	A346 $1 yel, car & dk bl	1.00	.25
1846	A346 $4 yel, grn & dk bl	2.00	.30

Chinese victory in Little League Twin Championships, Gary, Ind., and Williamsport, Pa.

INTERPOL Emblem — A347

Wmk. 370

1973, Sept. 11 Litho. *Perf. 12*

1847	A347 $1 blue & org	.95	.25
1848	A347 $5 green & org	1.40	.25
1849	A347 $8 magenta & org	2.60	.40
	Nos. 1847-1849 (3)	4.95	.90

Intl. Criminal Police Organization, 50th anniv.

Ch'iu Feng-chia — A348

Wmk. 323

1973, Oct. 5 Engr. *Perf. 11½*

1850	A348 $1 violet black	.70	.25

2nd meeting of overseas Hakkas, Taipei, Oct. 5-7, and to honor Ch'iu Feng-chia (1864-1912), Hakka scholar, poet and revolutionist.

Tsengwen Reservoir A349

Tsengwen Dam — A350

Perf. 13½

1973, Oct. 31 Photo. Unwmk.

1851 Strip of 3 1.00 .70
a. A349 $1 Upper shore .25 .25
b. A349 $1 shown .25 .25
c. A349 $1 Lower shore .25 .25

Perf. 12x11½

1852 A350 $5 shown 1.40 .30
1853 A350 $8 Spillway 2.00 .60
Nos. 1851-1853 (3) 4.40 1.60

Inauguration of Tsengwen Reservoir. No. 1851 printed in sheets of 15.

Tiger — A351

Wmk. 370

1973, Dec. 1 Litho. *Perf. 12½*

1854 A351 50c multi 1.40 .25
1855 A351 $4.50 multi 2.75 .40

New Year 1974.

"Snow-dotted Eagle," by Lang Shih-ning — A352

No. 1857, "Comfortable Ride." No. 1858, "Red Flower Eagle." No. 1859, "Cloud-running Steed." No. 1860, "Sky-running steed." $2.50, "Red Jade Seat." $5, "Thunderclap Steed." $8, "Arabian Champion." Designs from painting series "Ten Prized Horses," by Lang Shih-ning (Giuseppe Castiglione, 1688-1766).

1973 Litho. Unwmk. *Perf. 13*

1856 A352 50c shown 1.10 .25
1857 A352 $1 Pinto, blk tail 1.25 .35
1858 A352 $1 Facing left 1.25 .35
1859 A352 $1 Facing right 1.25 .35
1860 A352 $1 Pinto, white tail 1.25 .35
a. Horiz. or vert. strip of 4, #1857-1860 6.00 5.00
1861 A352 $2.50 Palomino 3.25 .60
1862 A352 $5 Grazing 5.50 2.40
a. Souvenir sheet of 4 60.00 35.00
1863 A352 $8 Brown stallion 8.75 1.25
Nos. 1856-1863 (8) 23.60 5.90

No. 1862a contains 4 stamps with simulated perforations similar to Nos. 1856-1857, 1861-1862.

Issued: 50c, $2.50, $5, 11/21; others 12/21.

Porcelain Types of 1972-73
Porcelain Series IV

Porcelain Masterworks of Sung Dynasty: $1, Vase. $2, Three-tiered vase. $2.50, Lotus-shaped bowl. $5, Incense burner. $8, Incense burner on stand.

1974, Jan. 16 Photo. *Perf. 11½*

1864 A323 $1 ultra & multi .55 .25
1865 A336 $2 multicolored 1.75 .25
1866 A336 $2.50 red & multi 2.10 .30
1867 A336 $5 lilac & multi 2.25 .40
1868 A336 $8 green & multi 2.25 .50
Nos. 1864-1868 (5) 8.90 1.70

Juggler — A353

Design: $8, Magician producing dishes from his robe, horiz.

1974, Feb. 6 Photo. *Perf. 11½*

1869 A353 $1 yellow & multi .60 .25
1870 A353 $8 yellow & multi 1.80 .25

Taroko Gorge, Hualien — A354

Designs: $2.50, Luce Chapel, Tunghai University. $5, Tzu En Pagoda, Sun Moon Lake. $8, Goddess of Mercy, Keelung.

1974, Mar. 22 Photo. *Perf. 12*

1871 A354 $1 multi .50 .25
1872 A354 $2.50 multi 1.10 .25
1873 A354 $5 multi 1.30 .30
1874 A354 $8 multi 2.00 .50
Nos. 1871-1874 (4) 4.90 1.30

Taiwan landmarks.

Fighting Cocks (Brass) A355

Designs: $2.50, Grapes and bowl with fruit (imitation jade). $5, Fisherman (wood carving), vert. $8, Basket with plastic roses, vert.

Perf. 13½x14½, 14½x13½

1974, Apr. 10

1875 A355 $1 bl grn & multi .40 .25
1876 A355 $2.50 brown & multi .85 .25
1877 A355 $5 crimson & multi 1.00 .30
1878 A355 $8 multicolored 1.50 .50
Nos. 1875-1878 (4) 3.75 1.30

Taiwanese handicraft products.

Sun Yat-sen Memorial Hall — A356

Taiwan landmarks: $2.50, Reaching-moon Tower, Cheng Ching Lake. $5, Orchid Island (boats). $8, Penghu Interisland Bridge.

1974, May 15 Photo. *Perf. 11½*

Granite Paper

1879 A356 $1 blue & multi .25 .25
1880 A356 $2.50 blue & multi .60 .25
1881 A356 $5 blue & multi .75 .25
1882 A356 $8 blue & multi 1.00 .30
Nos. 1879-1882 (4) 2.60 1.05

Pres. Chiang and Gate of Whampoa Military Academy A357

Marching Cadets and Entrance Gate — A358

Wmk. 323

1974, June 16 Engr. *Perf. 11½*

1883 A357 $1 carmine rose .75 .25
1884 A358 $14 violet blue 1.00 .25

50th anniversary of the founding of the Whampoa Military Academy.

Long-distance Runner and Olympic Rings — A359

$8, Women's relay race, Olympic rings.

1974, June 23 Litho. *Perf. 12½*

1885 A359 $1 blue, blk & red .50 .25
1886 A359 $8 pink, blk & red 1.25 .30

80th anniv. of Intl. Olympic Committee.

The Boy Wang Ch'i Fighting Invaders — A360

Folk Tales: No. 1888, T'i Ying pleading for her father before the Emperor. No. 1889, Wen Yen-po flushing out ball caught in tree. No. 1890, Boy Wang Hua returning gold piece he found. No. 1891, Pu Shih, a rich sheep raiser and benefactor. No. 1892, K'ung Yung as a child choosing smallest pear. No. 1893, Tung Yu studying. No. 1894, Szu Ma-kuang saving playmate from drowning in water jar.

1974, July 15 Wmk. 370 *Perf. 13½*

1887 A360 50c olive & multi .30 .25
1888 A360 50c ultra & multi .30 .25
1889 A360 50c ocher & multi .30 .25
1890 A360 50c red brn & multi .30 .25
a. Block of 4, #1887-1890 1.50 1.20
1891 A360 $1 green & multi .50 .25
1892 A360 $1 lilac & multi .50 .25
1893 A360 $1 blue & multi .50 .25
1894 A360 $1 car & multi .50 .25
a. Block of 4, #1891-1894 2.50 2.00
Nos. 1887-1894 (8) 3.20 2.00

For similar designs see A380, A427, A456, A495.

Myrtle, by Wei Sheng — A361

Silk Fan Paintings, Sung Dynasty (960-1279 A.D.): $2.50, Cabbage and Insects, by Hsu Ti. $5, Hibiscus, Cat and Dog, by Li Ti. $8, Pomegranate and Birds, by Wu Ping. Fans from National Palace Museum.

Perf. 13x12½

1974, Aug. 14 Photo. Wmk. 368

1895 A361 $1 multi .25 .25
1896 A361 $2.50 multi 1.00 .25
1897 A361 $5 multi 1.75 .40
1898 A361 $8 multi 2.50 .50
Nos. 1895-1898 (4) 5.50 1.40

See Nos. 1950-1953.

Battle at Marco Polo Bridge, July 7, 1937 A362

Wmk. 370

1974, Sept. 3 Litho. *Perf. 13½*

1899 A362 $1 multicolored 1.25 .25

Souvenir Sheet

Wmk. 323

Without Gum; Granite Paper

1900 Sheet of 8 7.00 7.00
a. A362 $1, single stamp .55 .55

20th Armed Forces Day. No. 1900 commemorates Armed Forces Stamp Exhibition, Sun Yat-sen Memorial Hall, Sept. 3-9.

Chrysanthemum A363

Designs: Various chrysanthemums.

Unwmk.

1974, Sept. 30 Photo. *Perf. 12*

Granite Paper

1901 A363 $1 lilac & multi .25 .25
1902 A363 $2.50 multi .70 .25
1903 A363 $5 orange & multi 1.00 .25
1904 A363 $8 multi 1.60 .35
Nos. 1901-1904 (4) 3.55 1.10

Rep. of China Pavilion, EXPO Emblem A364

Map of Fair Grounds, Chinese Flag A364a

Wmk. 370

1974, Oct. 10 Litho. *Perf. 13*

1905 A364 $1 multi .50 .25
1906 A364a $8 multi 1.00 .25

EXPO '74, Spokane, Wash., May 4-Nov. 4. Theme, "Preserve the Environment."

Steel Mill, Kaohsiung A365

Taichung Harbor A366

Designs: $1, Taiwan North Link Railroad and map. $2, Oil refinery. $2.50, Electric train. $3.50, Taoyuan International Airport. $4, Taiwan North-South Highway and map. $4.50, Kaohsiung shipyard. $5, Su-ao Port.

Perf. 13x12½, 12½x13

1974, Oct. 31 Wmk. 323

1907 A365 50c lilac, yel & brn .25 .25
1908 A365 $1 green & org .25 .25
1909 A365 $2 blue & yel .25 .25
1910 A365 $2.50 emer & org .35 .25
1911 A366 $3 ocher & ultra .25 .25
1912 A366 $3.50 sl grn & yel .30 .25
1913 A366 $4 brown & yel .30 .25

1914	A366	$4.50 ver & bl	.35	.25
1915	A366	$5 sepia & dk bl	.30	.25
		Nos. 1907-1915 (9)	2.60	2.25

Major construction projects.

See Nos. 2009-2017, 2068-2076. For overprints see Nos. 2064-2065, 2112-2113.

Agaricus Bisporus A367

Edible Mushrooms: $2.50, Pleurotus ostreatus. $5, Dictyophora indusiata. $8, Flammulina velutipes.

Perf. 11½

1974, Nov. 15 Unwmk. Photo.

1916	A367	$1 multi	.25	.25
1917	A367	$2.50 multi	.40	.25
1918	A367	$5 multi	.75	.25
1919	A367	$8 multi	.85	.35
		Nos. 1916-1919 (4)	2.25	1.10

9th Intl. Scientific Congress on the Cultivation of Edible Fungi, Taipei, Nov. 1974.

Batters and World Map — A368

Pitcher and Championship Banners — A369

Wmk. 323

1974, Nov. 24 Litho. *Perf. 13½*

1920	A368	$1 multicolored	.60	.25
1921	A369	$8 multicolored	.90	.25

China's victory in 1974 Little League Baseball World Series Triple Championships.

Rabbit — A370

Wmk. 323

1974, Dec. 10 Photo. *Perf. 12½*

1922	A370	50c orange & multi	.25	.25
1923	A370	$4.50 brown & multi	1.25	.25

New Year 1975.

Acrobat with Iron Rod — A371

$5, Two acrobats spinning tops, horiz.

Granite Paper

1975, Jan. 15 Unwmk. *Perf. 11½*

1924	A371	$4 yellow & multi	.50	.25
1925	A371	$5 yellow & multi	1.00	.30

Children Watching Puppet Show — A372

Ceremonial New Year Greetings — A373

Designs from scroll "Festivals for the New Year," by Ting Kuan-p'eng. Nos. 1926a-1926e are numbered 1-5 in Chinese.

$5, Children buying firecrackers. $8, Children and man with trained monkey.

1975, Feb. 25 Photo. *Perf. 11½*

Granite Paper

1926		Strip of 5	4.25	3.50
a.		A372 $1 Ceremonial New Year Greetings	.65	.25
b.		A372 $1 Man with trained monkey	.65	.25
c.		A372 $1 Crowd and musicians	.65	.25
d.		A372 $1 Picnic under a tree	.65	.25
e.		A372 $1 shown	.65	.25
1927	A373	$2.50 shown	3.00	.30
1928	A373	$5 multi	3.50	.75
1929	A373	$8 multi	6.00	1.00
		Nos. 1926-1929 (4)	16.75	5.55

Sun Yat-sen Memorial Hall, Taipei A374

Sun Yat-sen's Handwriting — A375

Sun Yat-sen, Bronze Statue in Memorial Hall — A376

Sun Yat-sen Memorial Hall, St. John's University, NY A377

Perf. 13½x14, 14x13½

1975, Mar. 12 Litho.

1930	A374	$1 green & multi	.50	.25
1931	A375	$4 yel grn & multi	1.10	.25
1932	A376	$5 yellow & multi	1.25	.25
1933	A377	$8 gray & multi	1.40	.30
		Nos. 1930-1933 (4)	4.25	1.05

Dr. Sun Yat-sen (1866-1925), statesman and revolutionary leader.

Fan Type of 1973 Inscribed "Landscape" (1st Character, 2nd Row)

Painted fans, Ming Dynasty. Second row of inscription gives design description.

Perf. 12½x13

1975, Apr. 16 Photo. Wmk. 368

1934	A345	$1 bister & multi	.30	.25
1935	A345	$2.50 bister & multi	.95	.25
1936	A345	$5 bister & multi	2.00	.40
1937	A345	$8 bister & multi	2.25	1.20
		Nos. 1934-1937 (4)	5.50	2.10

Yuan-chin coin, 1122-221 B.C. — A378

Ancient Chinese Coins: $4, Pan-liang, 221-207 B.C. $5, Five chu, 206 B.C.-220 A.D. $8, Five chu, 502-557 A.D.

Wmk. 323

1975, May 20 Litho. *Perf. 13*

1938	A378	$1 salmon & multi	.25	.25
1939	A378	$4 yellow & multi	1.20	.25
1940	A378	$5 dl yel & multi	1.35	.25
1941	A378	$8 lt vio & multi	2.00	.25
		Nos. 1938-1941 (4)	4.80	1.00

The Cloth-bag Monk, by Chang Hung (1577-1668) A379

Chinese Paintings: $4, Lao-tzu Riding Buffalo, by Chao Pu-chih (1053-1110). $5, Portrait of Shih-te, by Wang Wen (1497-1576). $8, Splashed-ink Immortal, by Liang K'ai (early 13th century).

Perf. 11½

1975, June 18 Photo. Unwmk.

Granite Paper

1942	A379	$2 blk, buff & ver	.50	.25
1943	A379	$4 blk, gray & red	1.90	.25
1944	A379	$5 blk, yel & ver	2.50	.40
1945	A379	$8 tan, red & blk	3.75	.60
		Nos. 1942-1945 (4)	8.65	1.50

Chu Yin Reading by the Light of Fireflies — A380

Folk Tales: No. 1947, Hua Mu-lan going to war for her father. No. 1948, King Kou Chien tasting gall. $5, Chou Ch'u killing tiger.

Perf. 14x13½

1975, July 16 Litho. Wmk. 368

1946	A380	$1 olive & multi	.25	.25
1947	A380	$2 bis brn & multi	.40	.25
1948	A380	$2 lt grn & multi	.60	.25
1949	A380	$5 blue & multi	1.20	.25
		Nos. 1946-1949 (4)	2.45	1.00

See Nos. 2108-2111.

Cherry-Apple Blossoms, by Lin Ch'un — A381

Silk Fan Paintings, Sung Dynasty: $2, Spring Blossoms and Butterfly, by Ma K'uei. $5, Monkeys and Deer, by I Yüan-chih. $8, Tame Sparrow among Bamboo.

Perf. 13x12½

1975, Aug. 15 Litho. Wmk. 323

1950	A381	$1 multicolored	.30	.25
1951	A381	$2 multicolored	1.10	.25
1952	A381	$5 multicolored	1.75	.30
1953	A381	$8 multicolored	2.75	.50
		Nos. 1950-1953 (4)	5.90	1.30

See Nos. 2001-2004.

Gen. Chang Tzu-chung (1891-1940) A382

No. 1955, Maj. Gen. Kao Chih-hong (1908-37). No. 1956, Capt. Sha Shih-chiun (1896-1938). No. 1957, Maj. Gen. Hsieh Chin-yuan (1905-41). No. 1958, Lt. Yen Hai-wen (1916-37). No. 1959, Lt. Gen. Tai An-lan (1905-42).

Wmk. 323

1975, Sept. 3 Engr. *Perf. 12*

1954	A382	$2 carmine	.25	.25
1955	A382	$2 sepia	.25	.25
1956	A382	$2 dull green	.25	.25
1957	A382	$5 violet black	.55	.25
1958	A382	$5 violet blue	.55	.25
1959	A382	$5 dark blue	.55	.25
		Nos. 1954-1959 (6)	2.40	1.50

Martyrs of the resistance fight against Japan.

Lotus Pond with Willows, by Madame Chiang — A383

Paintings by Madame Chiang Kai-shek: $5, Sun Breaks through Mountain Clouds. $8, A Pair of Pine Trees. $10, Fishing and Farming.

Perf. 13½

1975, Oct. 31 Litho. Unwmk.

1960	A383	$2 multicolored	1.20	.25
1961	A383	$5 multicolored	4.75	.30
1962	A383	$8 multicolored	4.75	.40
1963	A383	$10 multicolored	6.00	.75
		Nos. 1960-1963 (4)	16.70	1.70

For similar design see type A404.

Cauldron with Phoenix Handles, 481-221 B.C. A384

Ancient Bronzes: $2, Rectangular cauldron, 1122-722 B.C., vert. $8, Flat jar, 481-221 B.C. $10, 3-legged wine vessel, 1766-1122 B.C., vert.

1975, Nov. 12 Photo. *Perf. 12*
1964 A384 $2 pink & multi .25 .25
1965 A384 $5 lt blue & multi .75 .25
1966 A384 $8 yellow & multi .90 .25
1967 A384 $10 lilac & multi 1.00 .25
Nos. 1964-1967 (4) 2.90 1.00

For similar design see type A395. No. 1964 has 7 Chinese characters at left, No. 2005 has 4. No. 1967 has 4 characters at left, No. 2008 has 5.

Dragon, Nine-Dragon Wall, Peihai — A385

Wmk. 323
1975, Dec. 1 Litho. *Perf. 12½*
1968 A385 $1 orange & multi .50 .25
1969 A385 $5 green & multi 2.00 .75

New Year 1976.

Techi Dam — A386

Design: $10, Panoramic view of Techi Dam.

1975, Dec. 17 Unwmk. *Perf. 13½*
1970 A386 $2 green & multi .30 .25
1971 A386 $10 blue & multi 1.00 .35

Completion of Techi Dam, Tachia River.

Biathlon and Olympic Rings — A387

Olympic Rings and: $5, Luge. $8, Skiing.

1976, Jan. 15 Litho. *Perf. 13½*
1972 A387 $2 blue & multi .25 .25
1973 A387 $5 blue & multi .50 .25
1974 A387 $8 blue & multi .80 .30
Nos. 1972-1974 (3) 1.55 .80

12th Winter Olympic Games, Innsbruck, Austria, Feb. 4-15.

Chin, Oldest Chinese Instrument A388

Musical Instruments: $5, Se, c. 2900 B.C. $8, Standing kong-ho (harp). $10, Sleeping kong-ho.

1976, Feb. 11 Unwmk. *Perf. 14*
1975 A388 $2 yellow & multi .50 .25
1976 A388 $5 orange & multi .60 .25
1977 A388 $8 grnsh bl & multi .75 .25
1978 A388 $10 multicolored .85 .30
Nos. 1975-1978 (4) 2.70 1.05

For similar design see Type A407.

Double Carp Type of 1969
Perf. 13½x12½
1976, Dec. 15 Engr. Unwmk.
1980 A280 $14 carmine rose 2.25 .25

Mail Collecting A389

Mail Sorting — A390

Postal Service, 80th Anniv.: $8, Mail transport. $10, Mail delivery.

Wmk. 323
1976, Mar. 20 Litho. *Perf. 13½*
1984 A389 $2 yellow & multi .40 .25
1985 A390 $5 green & multi .70 .30
1986 A390 $8 blue & multi 1.05 .30
1987 A389 $10 orange & multi 1.25 .40
a. Souv. sheet of 4, #1984-1987 11.00 9.00
Nos. 1984-1987 (4) 3.40 1.25

Pres. Chiang Kai-shek A391

People Paying Homage — A392

No. 1990, Pres. Chiang lying in state. No. 1991, Hearse leaving funeral chapel. $5, People along funeral route. $8, Spirit tablet in Tzuhu Guest House. $10, Tzuhu Guest House, Pres. Chiang's burial place.

1976, Apr. 4
1988 A391 $2 gray & multi .40 .25
1989 A392 $2 gray & multi .40 .25
1990 A392 $2 gray & multi .40 .25
1991 A392 $2 gray & multi .40 .25
1992 A392 $5 gray & multi .50 .25
1993 A392 $8 gray & multi .50 .25
1994 A392 $10 gray & multi .60 .35
Nos. 1988-1994 (7) 3.20 1.85

Pres. Chiang Kai-shek (1887-1975), first death anniversary.

Flags of China and US — A393

Wmk. 323
1976, May 29 Litho. *Perf. 13½*
1995 A393 $2 multicolored .30 .25
1996 A393 $10 yellow & multi 1.30 .40

American Bicentennial.

Coin, 12th Century B.C. — A394

Bronze Shovel Coins (pu): $5, Pointed-feet coin, 481-221 B.C. $8, Round-feet coin, 722-481 B.C. $10, Square-feet coin, 3rd-2nd centuries B.C.

1976, June 16
1997 A394 $2 salmon & multi .30 .25
1998 A394 $5 lt blue & multi .80 .30
1999 A394 $8 gray & multi 1.00 .30
2000 A394 $10 multicolored 1.00 .30
Nos. 1997-2000 (4) 3.10 1.15

Fan Painting Type of 1975

Silk Fan Paintings, Sung Dynasty: $2, Hibiscus, by Li Tung. $5, Lilies, by Lin Ch'un. $8, Deer and Pine, by Mou Chung-fu. $10, Quail and Wild Flowers, by Li An-chung.

Perf. 13x12½
1976, July 14 Litho. Wmk. 323
2001 A381 $2 multicolored .85 .25
2002 A381 $5 multicolored 2.00 .30
2003 A381 $8 multicolored 2.10 .35
2004 A381 $10 multicolored 2.10 .30
Nos. 2001-2004 (4) 7.05 1.20

Cauldron, Shang Dynasty — A395

Ancient Bronzes: $5, 3-legged cauldron, Chou Dynasty (1122-722 B.C.). $8, Wine container, Chou Dynasty. $10, Wine vessel with spout, Shang Dynasty (1766-1122 B.C.).

1976, Aug. 25 Photo. *Perf. 11½*
Granite Paper
2005 A395 $2 rose & multi .25 .25
2006 A395 $5 lt blue & multi .90 .25
2007 A395 $8 yellow & multi 1.00 .25
2008 A395 $10 lilac & multi 1.10 .25
Nos. 2005-2008 (4) 3.25 1.00

Construction Types of 1974

Designs: $1, Taiwan North Link railroad and map. $2, Railroad electrification. $3, Taichung Harbor. $4, Taiwan North-South Highway and map. $5, Steel Mill, Kaohsiung. $6, Taoyuan International Airport. $7, Kao-hsiung shipyard. $8, Oil refinery. $9, Su-ao Port.

Perf. 13½x12½, 12½x13½
1976 Litho. Wmk. 323
2009 A365 $1 carmine & grn .25 .25
2010 A365 $2 orange & multi .25 .25
2011 A366 $3 violet & multi .25 .25
2012 A366 $4 carmine & multi .25 .25
2013 A365 $5 green & brn .25 .25
2014 A366 $6 brown & multi .50 .25
2015 A366 $7 brown & multi .40 .25
2016 A365 $8 carmine & grn .55 .25
2017 A366 $9 olive & blue .75 .40
Nos. 2009-2017 (9) 3.45 2.40

Chiang Kai-shek and Mother A396

Sun Yat-sen and Chiang Kai-shek at Canton Station — A397

Design: $5, Chiang Kai-shek, portrait.

1976, Oct. 31 Litho. *Perf. 13½*
2023 A396 $2 multicolored .40 .25
2024 A396 $5 multicolored 1.20 .50
2025 A397 $10 multicolored 1.20 .40
Nos. 2023-2025 (3) 2.80 1.15

Pres. Chiang Kai-shek, 90th anniv. of birth.

Flags of Kuomintang and China A398

Sun Yat-sen and Chiang Kai-shek A399

1976, Nov. 12 *Perf. 13½x14*
2026 A398 $2 multicolored .35 .25
2027 A399 $10 multicolored 1.10 .45
a. Souv. sheet of 2, #2026-2027 6.00 6.00

11th National Kuomintang Cong., Taipei.

Brazen Serpent — A400

1976, Dec. 15 Wmk. 323 *Perf. 12½*
2028 A400 $1 red, lilac & gold .60 .25
2029 A400 $5 plum, yel & gold 1.75 .25

New Year 1977.

Bird and Plum Blossoms, by Ch'en Hung-shou A401

Chinese Paintings: $8, "Wintry Days" (pine), by Yang Wei-chen. $10, Rock and Bamboo, by Hsia Ch'ang.

Perf. 11½
1977, Jan. 12 Photo. Unwmk.
Granite Paper
2030 A401 $2 multicolored .90 .25
2031 A401 $8 multicolored 2.75 .30
2032 A401 $10 multicolored 3.75 .75
Nos. 2030-2032 (3) 7.40 1.30

Black-naped Orioles — A402

Birds of Taiwan: $8, Common Kingfisher. $10, Chinese pheasant-tailed jacana.

1977, Feb. 16 **Litho.**

2033	A402	$2 multicolored	.50	.25
2034	A402	$8 multicolored	1.60	.25
2035	A402	$10 multicolored	1.75	.30
		Nos. 2033-2035 (3)	3.85	.80

See Nos. 2163-2165.

Census Emblem, Industry and Commerce A403

Perf. 13½

1977, Mar. 16 **Litho.** **Unwmk.**

2036	A403	$2 red & multi	.25	.25
2037	A403	$10 purple & multi	.90	.25

Industry and Commerce Census.

Green Mountains Rising into Clouds, by Madame Chiang — A404

Landscapes, by Madame Chiang Kai-shek: $5, Boat in the Beauty of Spring. $8, Scholar beside Waterfall. $10, Water Rises to Meet the Bridge.

Perf. 11½

1977, Mar. 31 **Unwmk.** **Photo.**

Granite Paper

2038	A404	$2 multi	.65	.25
2039	A404	$5 multi	2.60	.40
2040	A404	$8 multi	3.25	.50
2041	A404	$10 multi	3.50	.60
		Nos. 2038-2041 (4)	10.00	1.75

League Emblem — A405

1977, Apr. 18 **Litho.** ***Perf. 12½***

2042	A405	$2 carmine & multi	.25	.25
2043	A405	$10 green & multi	1.00	.65

10th World Anti-Communist League Conference.

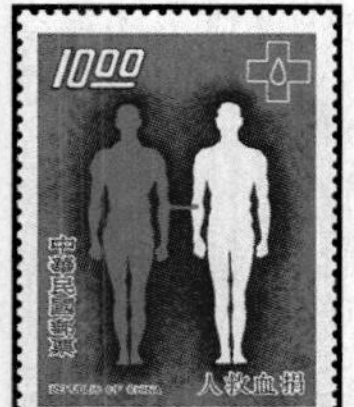

Blood Donation — A406

Design: $2, Donating blood, horiz.

1977, May 5 **Wmk. 323** ***Perf. 13½***

2044	A406	$2 red & black	.25	.25
2045	A406	$10 red & black	.90	.65

Blood donation movement.

San-hsien A407

Musical Instruments: $5, Tung-hsiao (bamboo flute). $8, Yang-chin (butterfly harpsichord). $10, Pai-hsiao (pipes). Background shows musician playing instrument.

Unwmk.

1977, June 21 **Photo.** ***Perf. 14***

2046	A407	$2 multicolored	.35	.25
2047	A407	$5 multicolored	.60	.25
2048	A407	$8 multicolored	.80	.25
2049	A407	$10 multicolored	1.00	.30
		Nos. 2046-2049 (4)	2.75	1.05

Idea Leuconoe — A408

Protected Butterflies: $4, Hebomoia glaucippe formosana. $6, Stichophthalma howqua formosana. $10, Atrophaneura horishana.

1977, July 20 **Litho.** ***Perf. 13½***

2050	A408	$2 ver & multi	.40	.25
2051	A408	$4 lt grn & multi	1.15	.25
2052	A408	$6 lt bl & multi	1.40	.40
2053	A408	$10 yellow & multi	1.75	.40
		Nos. 2050-2053 (4)	4.70	1.30

National Palace Museum A409

Temple — A410

Children's Drawings: $2, Sea Goddess Festival. $4, Boats on Shore of Lan-yu.

Wmk. 323

1977, Aug. 27 **Litho.** ***Perf. 13½***

2054	A409	$1 multicolored	.25	.25
2055	A409	$2 multicolored	.25	.25
2056	A409	$4 multicolored	.40	.25
2057	A410	$5 multicolored	.50	.25
		Nos. 2054-2057 (4)	1.40	1.00

8th Exhib. of World School Children's Art.

Carved Lacquer Plate, Wan-li Ware A411

Ancient Carved Lacquer Ware: $5, Bowl, Ching dynasty. $8, Round box, Ming dynasty. $10, Four-tiered box, Ching dynasty.

Perf. 13x14

1977, Sept. 28 **Photo.** **Wmk. 368**

2058	A411	$2 multicolored	.30	.25
2059	A411	$5 multicolored	.90	.30
2060	A411	$8 multicolored	1.10	.25
2061	A411	$10 multicolored	1.35	.30
		Nos. 2058-2061 (4)	3.65	1.10

Lions International, Emblem and Activities — A412

Unwmk.

1977, Oct. 8 **Litho.** ***Perf. 13***

2062	A412	$2 multicolored	.25	.25
2063	A412	$10 multicolored	.85	.25

Intl. Association of Lions Clubs, 60th anniv.

Nos. 2069 and 2075 Overprinted in Claret

Perf. 13½x12½

1977, Sept. 9 **Litho.** **Unwmk.**

2064	A365	$2 orange & multi	.35	.25
2065	A365	$8 carmine & grn	1.00	.25

Little League baseball championship.

Chinese Quality Mark — A413

Perf. 13x12½

1977, Oct. 14 **Litho.** **Unwmk.**

2066	A413	$2 red & multi	.50	.25
2067	A413	$10 blue & multi	1.75	.25

International Standardization Day.

Construction Types of 1974 Redrawn: Numerals Outlined

Designs as 1976 Issue.

Perf. 13½x12½, 12½x13½

1977 **Litho.** **Unwmk.**

Granite Paper

2068	A365	$1 car & dp grn	.25	.25
2069	A365	$2 ver & multi	.25	.25
2070	A366	$3 violet & multi	.55	.25
2071	A366	$4 carmine & multi	.30	.25
2072	A365	$5 green & multi	.25	.25
2073	A366	$6 sepia & multi	.30	.25
2074	A366	$7 sepia & multi	.70	.25
2075	A365	$8 red lil & multi	.65	.25
2076	A366	$9 olive & multi	.80	.25
		Nos. 2068-2076 (9)	4.05	2.25

Numerals are in solid color on Nos. 1907-1915, 2009-2017; in outline on Nos. 2068-2076.

For overprints see Nos. 2064-2065, 2112-2113.

Man and Heart — A414

Perf. 13½x12½

1977, Nov. 12 **Litho.** **Wmk. 323**

2077	A414	$2 multicolored	.35	.25
2078	A414	$10 multicolored	.95	.25

Physical health, cardiac care.

White Stallion — A415

New Year 1978: $5, Two horses, horiz. Designs from painting "100 Horses," by Lang Shih-ning.

Perf. 12½

1977, Dec. 1 **Unwmk.** **Litho.**

2079	A415	$1 red & multi	.50	.25
2080	A415	$5 emerald & multi	1.60	.30

First Page of Constitution A416

Pres. Chiang Accepting Constitution, 1946 — A417

1977, Dec. 25 **Litho.** ***Perf. 13½***

2081	A416	$2 multicolored	.25	.25
2082	A417	$10 multicolored	1.10	.30

30th anniversary of the Constitution.

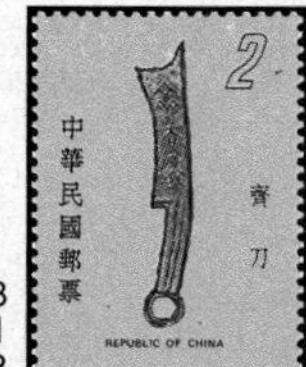

Knife Coin with 3 Characters, 403-221 B.C. — A418

Designs: Ancient knife coins.

1978, Jan. 18 **Wmk. 323** ***Perf. 13½***

2083	A418	$2 salmon & multi	.25	.25
2084	A418	$5 lt blue & blk	1.40	.25
2085	A418	$8 lt gray & multi	1.50	.25
2086	A418	$10 tan & multi	1.90	.30
		Nos. 2083-2086 (4)	5.05	1.05

China No. 1 and Flag of China — A419

Designs: $5, No. 464 (Sun Yat-sen). $10, No. 1204 (Chiang Kai-shek).

1978, Feb. 21 **Litho.** ***Perf. 13½***

2087	A419	$2 brown & multi	.40	.25
2088	A419	$5 blue & multi	.90	.25
2089	A419	$10 orange & multi	1.75	.40
a.		Souv. sheet of 3, #2087-2089	13.50	7.00
		Nos. 2087-2089 (3)	3.05	.90

Centenary of Chinese postage stamps.

Sun Yat-Sen Memorial Hall A420

China Nos. 2079 and 2 — A421

Perf. 14x12½, 12½x14

1978, Mar. 20 **Wmk. 323**

No.	Type	Value	Description	Unused	Used
2090	A420	$2	multicolored	.35	.25
2091	A421	$10	multicolored	1.00	.25

ROCPEX '78 Phil. Exhib., Taipei, Mar. 20-29.

Chiang Kai-shek with Revolutionary Army — A422

Pres. Chiang Kai-shek (1887-1975); $2, as young man, 1912, vert. $8, Making speech at Mt. Lu, July 17, 1937. $10, Reviewing Armed Forces on National Day, 1956, and Chinese flags, vert.

1978, Apr. 5 **Wmk. 323** ***Perf. 13½***

No.	Type	Value	Description	Unused	Used
2092	A422	$2	violet & multi	.25	.25
2093	A422	$5	green & multi	.90	.30
2094	A422	$8	blue & multi	1.15	.30
2095	A422	$10	vio blue & multi	1.25	.40
			Nos. 2092-2095 (4)	3.55	1.25

Nuclear Reactor and Plant — A423

Perf. 13½x12½

1978, Apr. 26 **Unwmk.**

No.	Type	Value	Description	Unused	Used
2096	A423	$10	multicolored	1.00	.25

First nuclear power plant on Taiwan.

Poem by Wen Cheng-ming (1470-1559) A424

Chinese Calligraphy: $2, Letter by Wang Hsi-chih (307-365). $4, Eulogy by Chu Sui-liang (596-658). $8, From Autobiography of Huai-su, Tang Dynasty. $10, Poem by Ch'ang Piao, Sung Dynasty.

1978, May 20 **Wmk. 323** ***Perf. 13½***

No.	Type	Value	Description	Unused	Used
2097	A424	$2	multicolored	*.85*	.25
2098	A424	$4	multicolored	*3.00*	.40
2099	A424	$6	multicolored	*3.00*	.60
2100	A424	$8	multicolored	*3.50*	.40
2101	A424	$10	multicolored	*4.50*	.60
			Nos. 2097-2101 (5)	*14.85*	2.25

Head and Dao Cancer Fund Emblem — A425

1978, June 15 **Litho.** ***Perf. 13½***

No.	Type	Value	Description	Unused	Used
2102	A425	$2	red, org & ol	.35	.25
2103	A425	$10	dk & lt bl & grn	1.00	.25

Cancer prevention.

Carved Lacquer Vase, Ming Dynasty — A426

Ancient Carved Lacquer Ware: $2, Box with dragon and cloud design, Ch'ing dynasty, horiz. $5, Double box on legs, Ch'ing dynasty, horiz. $8, Round box with peonies, Ming dynasty, horiz.

1978, July 12

No.	Type	Value	Description	Unused	Used
2104	A426	$2	gray olive & multi	.25	.25
2105	A426	$5	gray olive & multi	.75	.30
2106	A426	$8	gray olive & multi	.90	.25
2107	A426	$10	gray olive & multi	1.00	.30
			Nos. 2104-2107 (4)	2.90	1.10

Tsu Ti Practicing with his Sword — A427

Folk Tales: No. 2109, Pan Ch'ao, diplomat and governor. No. 2110, Tien Tan's "Fire Bull Battle." $5, Liang Hung-yu, a general's wife, who served as drummer in battle.

Wmk. 323

1978, Aug. 16 **Litho.** ***Perf. 13½***

No.	Type	Value	Description	Unused	Used
2108	A427	$1	multicolored	.25	.25
2109	A427	$2	bister & multi	.95	.25
2110	A427	$2	gray & multi	.95	.25
2111	A427	$5	multicolored	1.25	.25
			Nos. 2108-2111 (4)	3.40	1.00

For similar designs see types A456, A495.

Nos. 2071 & 2073 Overprinted in Red

1978, Sept. 9 ***Perf. 12½x13***

No.	Type	Value	Description	Unused	Used
2112	A366	$4	multicolored	.30	.25
2113	A366	$6	multicolored	.85	.30

Triple championships won by Chinese teams in Little League World Series. "1978" overprint on $4 at left, on $6 at right.

Ixias Pyrene A428

Protected Butterflies: $4, Euploea sylvestor swinhoei. $6, Cyrestis thyodamas formosana. $10, Byasa polyeuctes termessus.

1978, Sept. 20

No.	Type	Value	Description	Unused	Used
2114	A428	$2	multicolored	.50	.25
2115	A428	$4	multicolored	1.50	.25
2116	A428	$6	multicolored	1.75	.30
2117	A428	$10	multicolored	2.40	.30
			Nos. 2114-2117 (4)	6.15	1.10

Scout Symbols — A429

1978, Oct. 5 **Litho.** ***Perf. 13½***

No.	Type	Value	Description	Unused	Used
2118	A429	$2	multicolored	.50	.25
2119	A429	$10	multicolored	.75	.25

5th Chinese Boy Scout Jamboree, Cheng Ching Lake, Oct. 5-12.

Tropical Tomatoes — A430

Design: $10, Tropical tomatoes, horiz.

1978, Oct. 23 **Wmk. 323**

No.	Type	Value	Description	Unused	Used
2120	A430	$2	multicolored	.45	.25
2121	A430	$10	multicolored	1.50	.30

International Symposium on Tropical Tomatoes, Taiwan, Oct. 23-28.

Sino-Saudi Bridge A431

Design: $6, Buttresses of bridge, flags of Taiwan and Saudi Arabia, horiz.

1978, Oct. 31

No.	Type	Value	Description	Unused	Used
2122	A431	$2	multicolored	.50	.25
2123	A431	$6	multicolored	1.40	.25

Completion of Sino-Saudi Bridge over Cho-Shui River.

National Flag — A432

1978-80 ***Perf. 13½***

No.	Type	Value	Description	Unused	Used
2124	A432	$1	red & dk bl, I	.25	.25
a.			Bklt. pane of 16 ($5, $6, $8, $10, 3 $1, 9 $2)	7.75	
b.			Type II	1.50	.25
2125	A432	$2	red & dk bl, I	.25	.25
a.			Bklt. pane of 15 + label	11.00	
b.			Type II	.25	.25
2126	A432	$3	yel grn & multi	.30	.25
2127	A432	$4	bis & multi	.25	.25
2128	A432	$5	dk grn & multi, I	.30	.25
a.			Type II	.30	.25
2129	A432	$6	brn org & multi	1.00	.25
2130	A432	$7	dk brn & multi	1.00	.25
2131	A432	$8	dk grn & multi, I	1.00	.25
a.			Type II	1.00	.25
2132	A432	$10	brt bl & multi	.80	.25
2133	A432	$12	brt rose lil & multi	.80	.25
			Nos. 2124-2133 (10)	5.95	2.50

Two types exist: I. Second line (red) below flag is same width as blue line. II. Second line is a hairline, notably thinner. The $3, $4, $7 and $12 were issued only in type II; $6, $10, No. 2124a, only in type I.

Nos. 2129-2133 have colorless inscriptions and denomination in a panel of solid color.

Issued: Nos. 2124, 2125, 2128, 2129, 2121, 11/12/1978; No. 2132, 1/23/1979; No. 2124a, selvage inscription in blue, 10/10/1979, selvage inscription in green or red, 1/23/1980; No. 2125a, selvage inscription in blue, 10/25/1979, selvage inscription in green or red 4/24/1980; Nos. 2125b, 2128a, 2130, 2131a, 2133, 5/31/1980; Nos. 2124b, 2126, 2127, 7/31/1980.

1980 booklets are worth approximately 50 percent more than 1979 booklets.

A432a

Coil Stamp

1980, Jan. 15 ***Perf. 12 Horiz.***

No.	Type	Value	Description	Unused	Used
2134	A432a	$2	multicolored	.50	.25

See Nos. 2288-2300. For overprints see Nos. 2540-2541.

Three Rams, by Emperor Hsuan-tsung A433

Wmk. 323

1978, Dec. 1 **Litho.** ***Perf. 12½***

No.	Type	Value	Description	Unused	Used
2135	A433	$1	multicolored	.30	.25
2136	A433	$5	multicolored	1.40	.30

New Year 1979.

Taoyuan International Airport — A434

$10, Passenger terminal, control tower.

1978, Dec. 31 ***Perf. 13½***

No.	Type	Value	Description	Unused	Used
2137	A434	$2	multi	.40	.25
2138	A434	$10	multi, horiz.	.70	.25

Completion of Taoyuan Intl. Airport.

Oracle Bones and Inscription, 1766-1123 B.C. — A435

Antiquities and Inscriptions: $5, Lehchi cauldron, 722-481 B.C. $8, Small seal (turtle), 206 B.C.-8 A.D. $10, Inscribed stone tablet, 175-183 A.D.

1979, Jan. 17

No.	Type	Value	Description	Unused	Used
2139	A435	$2	multicolored	.65	.25
2140	A435	$5	multicolored	1.60	.40
2141	A435	$8	multicolored	1.90	.30
2142	A435	$10	multicolored	2.25	.40
			Nos. 2139-2142 (4)	6.40	1.35

Origin and development of Chinese characters.

Chihkan Tower, 1653 A436

Taiwan Scenery: $5, Shrine of Confucius, 1665. $8, Shrine of Koxinga, 1661. $10, Eternal Castle and moat.

1979, Feb. 11 **Litho.** ***Perf. 13½***

No.	Type	Value	Description	Unused	Used
2143	A436	$2	multicolored	.45	.25
2144	A436	$5	multicolored	1.10	.30
2145	A436	$8	multicolored	1.30	.25
2146	A436	$10	multicolored	1.60	.30
			Nos. 2143-2146 (4)	4.45	1.10

Children Playing on Winter Day, Sung Dynasty — A437

1979, Mar. 8

2147	A437	Block of 4	15.00	15.00
a.		$5 in UL corner	3.75	.50
b.		$5 in UR corner	3.75	.50
c.		$5 in LL corner	3.75	.50
d.		$5 in LR corner	3.75	.50
e.		Souvenir sheet of 4, #2147, imperf.	*32.00*	16.00

No. 2147e has simulated perforations.

Lu Hao-tung — A438

Perf. 13x12½

1979, Mar. 29 Engr. Wmk. 323

2148	A438	$2 blue	1.00	.25

Lu Hao-tung (1868-1895), revolutionist.

Yellow Jade Brush Holder — A439

Ancient Brush Washers: $5, White jade, Ming Dynasty. $8, Dark green jade, Ch'ing Dynasty. $10, Bluish jade, Ch'ing Dynasty. All horiz.

Granite Paper

Unwmk.

1979, Apr. 12 Photo. *Perf. 12*

2149	A439	$2 multicolored	.50	.25
2150	A439	$5 multicolored	1.25	.30
2151	A439	$8 multicolored	1.35	.30
2152	A439	$10 multicolored	1.60	.30
		Nos. 2149-2152 (4)	4.70	1.15

For similar artifacts designs with single-color background and denominations in outlined numerals with the cents, see types A453, A469, A489, A523, A547, A582.

A440

A440a

Designs: National flower plum blossoms.

Perf. 13½x12½

1979-92 Engr. Wmk. 323

Granite Paper

2153	A440	$10 dk blue	1.50	.25
a.		Plain paper	1.00	.25
2154	A440	$20 brown	1.00	.25
b.		Plain paper	1.10	.25
2154A	A440	$40 brt car	2.10	.25
c.		Plain paper	2.00	.25
2155	A440	$50 dull green	3.50	.75
a.		Plain paper	2.50	.30
2156	A440	$100 vermilion	7.00	1.00
e.		Plain paper	3.50	.60

Perf. 14x13½

2156A	A440a	$300 pur & red org	28.00	7.00
c.		Plain paper	15.00	1.80
2156B	A440a	$500 ver & brn	32.00	6.00
d.		Plain paper	25.00	3.00
		Nos. 2153-2156B (7)	75.10	15.50

Issued: Nos. 2153, 2154, 5/20/1979; No. 2155, 6/5/1979; No. 2156, 8/8/1979; No. 2156B, 11/15/1982; No. 2156A, 6/6/1983; No. 2154A, 4/15/1985; Nos. 2154b, 2155a, 1/5/1987; No. 2153a, 5/10/1988; No. 2156e, 3/20/1989; No. 2154Ac, 2/2/1990; Nos. 2156Ac, 2156Bd, 5/1/1991.

City Houses and Garden — A441

Design: $10, Rural landscape, horiz.

Perf. 13x12½, 12½x13

1979, June 5 Litho.

2157	A441	$2 multicolored	.45	.25
2158	A441	$10 multicolored	.95	.25

Protection of the Environment.

Bankbook and Computer Department A442

Designs: $2, Children at counter, vert. $5, People standing in line, vert. $10, Hand putting coin in savings bank, symbolic tree.

1979, July 1 Wmk. 323 *Perf. 13½*

2159	A442	$2 multicolored	.25	.25
2160	A442	$5 multicolored	.80	.25
2161	A442	$8 multicolored	1.10	.25
2162	A442	$10 multicolored	1.30	.30
		Nos. 2159-2162 (4)	3.45	1.05

Postal savings, 60th anniversary.

Bird Type of 1977

Birds of Taiwan: $2, Swinoe's pheasant. $8, Steere's babbler. $10, Formosan yuhina.

1979, Aug. 8 *Perf. 11½*

2163	A402	$2 multicolored	.45	.25
2164	A402	$8 multicolored	1.50	.25
2165	A402	$10 multicolored	1.75	.40
		Nos. 2163-2165 (3)	3.70	.90

Rowland Hill, Penny Black A443

Perf. 13½x13

1979, Aug. 27 Litho. Wmk. 323

2166	A443	$10 multicolored	1.25	.30

Sir Rowland Hill (1795-1879), originator of penny postage.

Jar with Rope Design, Shang Dynasty — A444

Ancient Chinese Pottery: $5, Two-handled jar, Shang dynasty. $8, Red jar with "ears," Han dynasty. $10, Green glazed jar, Han dynasty.

1979, Sept. 12 *Perf. 13½*

2167	A444	$2 multicolored	.40	.25
2168	A444	$5 multicolored	1.50	.25
2169	A444	$8 multicolored	1.75	.25
2170	A444	$10 multicolored	2.00	.35
		Nos. 2167-2170 (4)	5.65	1.10

Children and IYC Emblem — A445

1979, Sept. 28 Litho. *Perf. 13½*

2171	A445	$2 multicolored	.40	.25
2172	A445	$10 multicolored	.80	.30

International Year of the Child.

Trade Symbols, Competition Emblem A446

1979, Dec. 9 Litho. *Perf. 13½*

2173	A446	$2 blue & multi	.40	.25
2174	A446	$10 green & multi	.80	.25

10th National Vocational Training Competition, Taichung, Dec. 9.

Trees on a Winter Plain, by Li Ch'eng A447

Paintings: $5, Bamboo, Wen T'ung. $8, Old tree, bamboo and rock, by Chao Meng-fu. $10, Twin Pines, by Li K'an.

1979, Nov. 21

2175	A447	$2 multicolored	.65	.25
2176	A447	$5 multicolored	1.90	.40
2177	A447	$8 multicolored	2.50	.40
2178	A447	$10 multicolored	3.25	.50
		Nos. 2175-2178 (4)	8.30	1.55

Monkey — A448

1979, Dec. 1 *Perf. 12½*

2179	A448	$1 yellow & multi	.75	.25
2180	A448	$6 tan & multi	2.60	.35

New Year 1980.

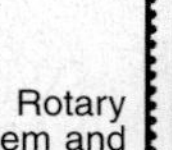

Rotary Emblem and "75" — A449

Rotary Intl., 75th Anniv.: $12, Anniv. emblem.

1980, Feb. 23 Litho. *Perf. 13½*

2181	A449	$2 multicolored	.40	.25
2182	A449	$12 multi, vert.	.90	.25

Mt. Hohuan A450

Taiwan Landscapes (East-West Cross-Island Highway): $2, Tunnel of Nine Turns, vert. $12, Bridge, Tien Hsiang, vert.

1980, Mar. 1 Wmk. 323

2183	A450	$2 multicolored	.35	.25
2184	A450	$8 multicolored	1.20	.25
2185	A450	$12 multicolored	1.90	.45
		Nos. 2183-2185 (3)	3.45	.95

A451

1980, Mar. 29 Engr. *Perf. 13½x12½*

Granite Paper

2186	A451	$2 red brown	.80	.25

Shih Chien-Ju (1879-1900), revolutionist.

A452

$2, Chung-cheng Memorial Hall. $8, Quotation. $12, Bronze statue.

1980, Apr. 4 Litho. *Perf. 13½*

2187	A452	$2 multicolored	.35	.25
2188	A452	$8 multicolored	.60	.25
2189	A452	$12 multicolored	1.15	.50
		Nos. 2187-2189 (3)	2.10	1.00

Chiang Kai-shek (1887-1975).

Melon-shaped Jade Brush Washer, Ming Dynasty — A453

Jade Pottery: $2, Jar with dragons, Sung dynasty, vert. $8, Monk's alms bowl, Ch'ing dynasty. $10, Yellow jade brush washer, Ch'ing dynasty.

1980, May 20 Photo. *Perf. 12*
Granite Paper

No.	Type	Value	Color	Mint	Used
2190	A453	$2	multicolored	.50	.25
2191	A453	$5	multicolored	1.60	.30
2192	A453	$8	multicolored	1.15	.25
2193	A453	$10	multicolored	1.75	.40
			Nos. 2190-2193 (4)	5.00	1.20

Energy Conservation A454

1980, July 15 Litho. *Perf. 13½*

No.	Type	Value	Color	Mint	Used
2194	A454	$2	multicolored	.45	.25
2195	A454	$12	multicolored	.90	.30

A455

T'ang Dynasty pottery.

1980, Aug. 18 Litho. *Perf. 13½*

No.	Type	Value	Description	Mint	Used
2196	A455	$2	Soldier	.50	.25
2197	A455	$5	Roosters	1.50	.30
2198	A455	$8	Horse	1.90	.25
2199	A455	$10	Camel	2.25	.35
			Nos. 2196-2199 (4)	6.15	1.15

A456

Folk Tales: $1, Grinding mortar into a needle. No. 2201, Confucius Returning Lost Article (shown). No. 2202, Wen Tien-hsiang in jail. $5, Sending coal in snow.

Perf. 14x13½
1980, Sept. 23 Litho. Wmk. 323

No.	Type	Value	Color	Mint	Used
2200	A456	$1	multicolored	.25	.25
2201	A456	$2	multicolored	.70	.25
2202	A456	$2	multicolored	.70	.25
2203	A456	$5	multicolored	1.20	.25
			Nos. 2200-2203 (4)	2.85	1.00

Railroad Electrification A457

No. 2205, Taichung Harbor. No. 2206, Chiang Kai-shek Airport. No. 2207, Steel Mill. No. 2208, Sun Yat-sen Freeway. No. 2209, Nuclear power plant. No. 2210, Petrochemical plants. No. 2211, Su-ao Harbor. No. 2212, Kaohsiung shipyard. No. 2213, North link railroad.

1980, Oct. 10 *Perf. 13½x14*

No.	Type	Value	Color	Mint	Used
2204	A457	$2	shown	.35	.25
2205	A457	$2	multicolored	.35	.25
2206	A457	$2	multicolored	.35	.25
2207	A457	$2	multicolored	.35	.25
2208	A457	$2	multicolored	.50	.25
2209	A457	$2	multicolored	.35	.25
2210	A457	$2	multicolored	.35	.25
2211	A457	$2	multicolored	.35	.25
2212	A457	$2	multicolored	.35	.25
2213	A457	$2	multicolored	.50	.25
a.			Souv. sheet of 10, #2204-2213	12.50	7.50
b.			Block of 10, #2204-2213	7.50	3.75
			Nos. 2204-2213 (10)	3.80	2.50

Completion of major construction projects.

10th National Savings Day — A458

$2, Ancient coin and coin banks.

Wmk. 323
1980, Oct. 25 Litho. *Perf. 13½*

No.	Type	Value	Color	Mint	Used
2214	A458	$2	multicolored	.65	.25
2215	A458	$12	shown	1.00	.30

Landscape, by Ch'iu Ying, Ming Dynasty — A459

1980, Nov. 12 Litho. *Perf. 13½*

No.	Type	Description	Mint	Used
2216	A459	Block of 4	12.50	5.00
a.		$5 in UL corner	2.50	.40
b.		$5 in UR corner	2.50	.40
c.		$5 in LL corner	2.50	.40
d.		$5 in LR corner	2.50	.40
e.		Souvenir sheet, imperf.	30.00	30.00

No. 2216e has simulated perforations.

Cock — A460

1980, Dec. 1 *Perf. 12½*

No.	Type	Value	Color	Mint	Used
2217	A460	$1	multicolored	.70	.25
2218	A460	$6	multicolored	3.50	.25
a.			Souv. sheet, 2 each #2217-2218	12.50	12.50

New Year 1981.

Faces, Flag, Census Form — A461

1980, Dec. 13 *Perf. 13½*

No.	Type	Value	Description	Mint	Used
2219	A461	$2	shown	.30	.25
2220	A461	$12	Buildings, horiz.	1.20	.30

1980 population and housing census.

TIROS-N Satellite — A462

Design: $10, Central weather bureau, horiz.

1981, Jan. 28 Litho. *Perf. 13½*

No.	Type	Value	Color	Mint	Used
2221	A462	$2	multicolored	.40	.25
2222	A462	$10	multicolored	1.00	.25

Completion of meteorological satellite ground station, Taipei.

"Happiness" A463

New Year 1981 (Calligraphy): No. 2224, Wealth. No. 2225, Longevity. No. 2226, Joy.

1981, Feb. 3 *Perf. 13½x12½*

No.	Type	Value	Description	Mint	Used
2223	A463	$5	multi, 5 at B	.80	.25
2224	A463	$5	multi, 5 at R	.80	.25
2225	A463	$5	multi, 5 at L	.80	.25
2226	A463	$5	multi, 5 at T	.80	.25
a.			Block of 4, #2223-2226	6.00	1.40

International Year of the Disabled — A464

1981, Feb. 19 Litho. *Perf. 13½*

No.	Type	Value	Color	Mint	Used
2227	A464	$2	multicolored	.35	.25
2228	A464	$12	multicolored	1.00	.25

Mt. Ali — A465

1981, Mar. 1

No.	Type	Value	Description	Mint	Used
2229	A465	$2	shown	.35	.25
2230	A465	$7	Oluanpi Beach	1.00	.25
2231	A465	$12	Sun Moon Lake	1.40	.40
			Nos. 2229-2231 (3)	2.75	.90

A $2 multicolored stamp for the 12th National Kuomintang Congress at Taipei was prepared for release Mar. 29, 1981, but not issued. It showed Sun Yat-sen, Chiang Kai-shek, flags of China and the Kuomintang and a map of China.

Children in Forest A467

Children's Day: Drawings.

1981, Apr. 4

No.	Type	Value	Color	Mint	Used
2233	A467	$1	multicolored	.25	.25
2234	A467	$2	multicolored	.25	.25
2235	A467	$5	multicolored	.35	.25
2236	A467	$7	multicolored	.40	.25
			Nos. 2233-2236 (4)	1.25	1.00

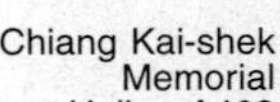

Chiang Kai-shek Memorial Hall — A468

1981, Apr. 5 *Perf. 12½x13½*

No.	Type	Value	Color	Mint	Used
2237	A468	20c	bluish lilac	.30	.25
a.			Photo. ('87)	.25	.25
2238	A468	40c	crim rose	.30	.25
a.			Photo. ('87)	.25	.25
2239	A468	50c	dull red brn	.30	.25
a.			Photo. ('88)	.25	.25
			Nos. 2237-2239 (3)	.90	.75

Chiang Kai-shek (1887-1975).

See Nos. 2601-2603.

Issued: Nos. 2237a-2238a, 1/16/1987; No. 2239, 8/15/1987.

Cloisonne Enamel Brush Washer, 15th Cent. A469

Cloisonne Enamel: $5, Ritual vessel, 15th cent., vert. $8, Plate, 17th cent. $10, Vase, Ming Dynasty, vert.

1981, May 20 Photo. *Perf. 12*
Granite Paper

No.	Type	Value	Color	Mint	Used
2240	A469	$2	multicolored	.35	.25
2241	A469	$5	multicolored	1.15	.30
2242	A469	$8	multicolored	1.30	.25
2243	A469	$10	multicolored	1.45	.30
			Nos. 2240-2243 (4)	4.25	1.10

For similar enamelware stamps see Nos. 2318-2321, 2348-2351, 2410-2413.

Early & Modern Locomotives A470

Wmk. 323
1981, June 9 Litho. *Perf. 12½*

No.	Type	Value	Description	Mint	Used
2244	A470	$2	shown	.60	.25
2245	A470	$14	Trains, horiz.	1.75	.40

Railroad service centenary.

Linnaeus Crab — A471

1981, June 14 *Perf. 13½*

No.	Type	Value	Description	Mint	Used
2246	A471	$2	De Haan crab, horiz.	.30	.25
2247	A471	$5	shown	.60	.25
2248	A471	$8	Miers crab, horiz.	.90	.25
2249	A471	$14	Rathbun crab	1.75	.40
			Nos. 2246-2249 (4)	3.55	1.15

Central Weather Bureau, 40th Anniv. — A472

1981, July 1 Litho. *Perf. 13½*

No.	Type	Value	Color	Mint	Used
2250	A472	$2	multicolored	.40	.25
2251	A472	$14	multicolored	1.60	.30

Scene from The Cowherd and the Weaving Maid — A473

Designs: Scenes from the Cowherd and the Weaving Maid.

1981, Aug. 6 Litho. ***Perf. 13½x14***

2252 A473 $2 multicolored .60 .25
2253 A473 $4 multicolored 1.00 .25
2254 A473 $8 multicolored 1.75 .25
2255 A473 $14 multicolored 2.75 .50
Nos. 2252-2255 (4) 6.10 1.25

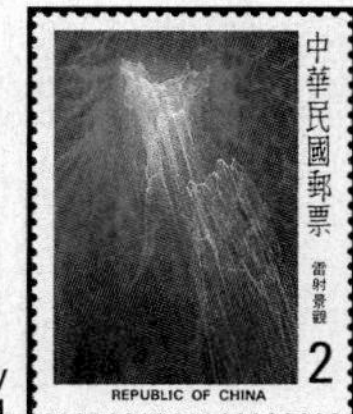

First Lasography Exhibition — A474

Lasography Designs.

1981, Aug. 15 ***Perf. 13½***

2256 A474 $2 multicolored .25 .25
2257 A474 $5 multicolored .30 .25
2258 A474 $8 multicolored .65 .25
2259 A474 $14 multicolored 1.10 .50
Nos. 2256-2259 (4) 2.30 1.25

Soccer Players — A475

1981, Sept. 9 Litho. ***Perf. 13½***

2260 $5 multicolored .60 .25
2261 $5 multicolored .60 .25
a. A475 Pair, #2260-2261 1.40 .65

Sports Day.

A477

70th Anniv. of Republic: No. 2263, Eastward Expedition (soldiers on Hill). No. 2264, Northward Expedition (Chiang on horse). No. 2265, Resistance War with Japan (Chiang, fist raised). No. 2266, Suppression of Communist Rebels (Battle scene). No. 2267, Counter-offensive and unification. $8, Chiang Kai-shek. $14, Sun Yat-sen.

1981, Oct. 10 ***Perf. 13½***

2262 A477 $2 multicolored .40 .25
2263 A477 $2 multicolored .40 .25
2264 A477 $2 multicolored .40 .25
2265 A477 $2 multicolored .40 .25
2266 A477 $3 multicolored .40 .25
2267 A477 $3 multicolored .40 .25
2268 A477 $8 multicolored .70 .25
2269 A477 $14 multicolored 1.60 .45
a. Souv. sheet of 8, #2262-2269 11.50 6.50
Nos. 2262-2269 (8) 4.70 2.20

No. 2269a issued Oct. 25.

ROCPEX TAIPEI '81 Intl. Philatelic Exhibition, Taipei, Oct. 25-Nov. 2 A478

1981, Oct. 25

2270 A478 $2 multicolored .25 .25
2271 A478 $14 multicolored 1.15 .25

Nos. 2269a, 2270-2271 overprinted with four characters meaning "Best of Show" were not valid for postage. They were inserted in a special "ROCPEX" book, edition of 10,000. Value $25.

Boys Playing Games (#2272a) — A479

Designs: a.-j. "One Hundred Boys," Sung Dynasty scroll (each stamp is numbered from 1 to 10 in Chinese. See illustrations with Nos. 1682-1691 for numerals.) Two strips of 5 each in continuous design.

1981, Nov. 12

2272 Block of 10 22.50 22.50
a.-e. A479 $2 single (top row) 2.00 .25
f.-j. A479 $2 single (bottom row) 2.00 .25

New Year 1982 (Year of the Dog) — A480

Wmk. 323

1981, Dec. 1 Litho. ***Perf. 12½***

2273 A480 $1 multicolored .70 .25
2274 A480 $10 multicolored 2.25 .30
a. Souv. sheet, 2 ea #2273-2274 12.50 5.00

Information Week, Dec. 6-12 — A481

1981, Dec. 7 ***Perf. 14x13½***

2275 A481 $2 multicolored .95 .25

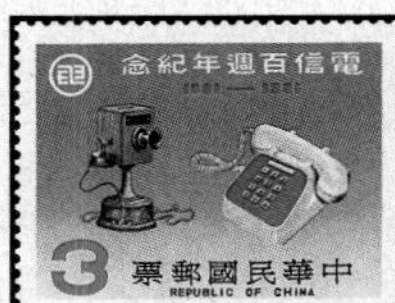

Telecommunications Centenary — A482

1981, Dec. 28 ***Perf. 14x13½, 13½x14***

2276 A482 $2 Telephone, vert. .35 .25
2277 A482 $3 Old, new phones .70 .25
2278 A482 $8 Submarine cable 1.00 .25
2279 A482 $18 Computers, vert. 1.45 .40
Nos. 2276-2279 (4) 3.50 1.15

Floral Arrangement A483

Various floral arrangements in Ming vases.

Wmk. 323

1982, Jan. 23 Litho. ***Perf. 13½***

2280 A483 $2 multicolored .30 .25
2281 A483 $3 multicolored .60 .25
2282 A483 $8 multicolored .95 .25
2283 A483 $18 multicolored 1.25 .50
Nos. 2280-2283 (4) 3.10 1.25

Compare with designs A559, A584.

The Ku Cheng Reunion — A484

Designs: Opera scenes.

Wmk. 323

1982, Feb. 15 Litho. ***Perf. 13½***

2284 A484 $2 multicolored .60 .25
2285 A484 $3 multicolored 1.15 .25
2286 A484 $4 multicolored 1.70 .25
2287 A484 $18 multicolored 2.25 .50
Nos. 2284-2287 (4) 5.70 1.25

Flag Type of 1978
Value Colorless in Colored Panel

1981 Litho. ***Perf. 13½***

Panel Color

2288 A432 $1 dk blue .25 .25
2289 A432 $1.50 lt olive .25 .25
2290 A432 $2 dk olive bis .25 .25
2291 A432 $3 red .25 .25
2292 A432 $4 blue .50 .25
2293 A432 $5 sepia .60 .25
2294 A432 $6 orange .70 .25
2295 A432 $7 green .85 .25
2296 A432 $8 magenta .95 .25
2297 A432 $9 olive grn 1.00 .25
2298 A432 $10 dk purple 1.20 .25
2299 A432 $12 lilac 1.40 .25
2300 A432 $14 dk green 1.75 .40
Nos. 2288-2300 (13) 9.95 3.40

Second line (red) below flag is a hairline, notably thinner.

For overprints see Nos. 2540-2541.

Robert Koch — A485

Wmk. 323

1982, Mar. 24 Litho. ***Perf. 13½***

2309 A485 $2 multicolored .95 .25

Tubercle Bacillus centenary.

Cheng Shih-liang, Revolutionary A486

1982, Mar. 29 Engr. ***Perf. 13½x12½***

Granite Paper

2310 A486 $2 carmine rose .70 .25

Children's Day A487

Designs: Various children's drawings.

1982, Apr. 4 Litho.

2311 A487 $2 multi, vert. .30 .25
2312 A487 $3 multicolored .30 .25
2313 A487 $5 multicolored .80 .25
2314 A487 $8 multicolored .90 .25
Nos. 2311-2314 (4) 2.30 1.00

Dentists' Day A488

$2, Tooth, boy. $3, Flossing, brushing. $10, Examination.

1982, May 4 Litho. ***Perf. 13½***

2315 A488 $2 multicolored .25 .25
2316 A488 $3 multicolored .60 .25
2317 A488 $10 multicolored 1.00 .25
Nos. 2315-2317 (3) 1.85 .75

Champleve Enamel Cup and Saucer, 18th Cent. A489

Painted Enamelware: $5, Cloisonne gold-plated duck Ch'ien-lung period (1736-1795), vert. $8, Incense burner, K'ang-hsi period (1662-1722). $12, Cloisonne pitcher, Ch'ien-lung period, vert.

1982, May 20 Photo. ***Perf. 12***

Granite Paper

2318 A489 $2 multicolored .55 .25
2319 A489 $5 multicolored 1.35 .25
2320 A489 $8 multicolored 1.90 .25
2321 A489 $12 multicolored 2.60 .40
Nos. 2318-2321 (4) 6.40 1.15

See Nos. 2348-2351.

Poets' Day — A490

Tang Dynasty Poetry Illustrations (618-906): $2, Spring Dawn, by Meng Hao-Jan. $3, On Looking for a Hermit and Not Finding Him, by Chia Tao. $5, Summer Dying, by Liu Yu-Hsi. $18, Looking at the Snow Drifts on South Mountain, by Tsu Yung. Chinese characters are to the left of the denominations on Nos. 2322-2325, Nos. 2396-2399 have no characters to the left of the denominations.

Wmk. 323

1982, June 25 Litho. ***Perf. 13½***

2322 A490 $2 multicolored *1.15* .25
2323 A490 $3 multicolored *3.75* .25
2324 A490 $5 multicolored *5.75* .35
2325 A490 $18 multicolored *20.00* 1.90
Nos. 2322-2325 (4) *30.65* 2.75

See Nos. 2352-2355.

5th World Women's Softball Championship, Taipei, July 1-12 — A491

1982, July 2
2326 A491 $2 lt grn & multi .85 .25
2327 A491 $18 tan & multi 1.75 .40

Scouting Year A492

$2, Crossing bridge, Baden-Powell. $18, Emblem, camp.

1982, July 18
2328 A492 $2 multicolored .65 .25
2329 A492 $18 multicolored 1.00 .40

Stamp in Tongs A493

$18, Album stamps magnified.

1982, Aug. 9
2330 A493 $2 shown .65 .25
2331 A493 $18 multicolored 1.40 .40

Carved Lion, Tsu Shih Temple — A494

Tsu Shih Temple of Sanhsia Architecture: $3, Lion brackets, horiz. $5, Sub-lintels. $18, Tiled roof, horiz.

1982, Sept. 1 Litho. ***Perf. 13½***
2332 A494 $2 multicolored .25 .25
2333 A494 $3 multicolored .65 .25
2334 A494 $5 multicolored 1.90 .25
2335 A494 $18 multicolored 2.60 .50
Nos. 2332-2335 (4) 5.40 1.25

Hsun Kuan Saving Hsiang-cheng City — A495

Designs: Scenes from The Thirty-Six Examples of Filial Piety, Folk Tale collection by Wu Yen-huan.

1982, Oct. 15 ***Perf. 14x13½***
2336 A495 $1 multicolored .25 .25
2337 A495 $2 multicolored .80 .25
2338 A495 $3 multicolored 1.00 .25
2339 A495 $5 multicolored 1.20 .25
Nos. 2336-2339 (4) 3.25 1.00

30th Anniv. of China Youth Corps A496

$2, Riding. $3, Raising flag, vert. $18, Mountain climbing.

1982, Oct. 31
2340 A496 $2 multicolored .25 .25
2341 A496 $3 multicolored .25 .25
2342 A496 $18 multicolored 1.25 .50
Nos. 2340-2342 (3) 1.75 1.00

Seated Lohan (Buddhist Saint) — A497

Paintings of Lohan, Hanging Scrolls by Liu Sung-nien, 13th cent.

Perf. 13x12½
1982, Nov. 12 Litho. Wmk. 323
2343 A497 $2 multicolored .75 .25
2344 A497 $3 multicolored 2.00 .25
2345 A497 $18 multicolored 7.25 .90
a. Souv. sheet, #2343-2345 *27.50* 13.00
Nos. 2343-2345 (3) 10.00 1.40

No. 2345a comes overprinted in red in the sheet margins. Value, unused $45, Used $20.

New Year 1983 (Year of the Boar) — A498

1982, Dec. 1 ***Perf. 12½***
2346 A498 $1 multicolored 1.40 .25
2347 A498 $10 multicolored 3.00 .25
a. Souv. sheet, 2 ea #2346-2347 *17.50* 5.50

Enamelware Type of 1982

Designs: $2, Square basin, Ch'ing Dynasty (1644-1911). $3, Vase, Ch'ien-lung period (1736-1795). $4, Tea pot, Ch'ien-lung period. $18, Elephant vase, Ch'ing Dynasty.

1983, Jan. 5 Photo. ***Perf. 12***
Granite Paper
2348 A489 $2 multi .65 .25
2349 A489 $3 multi, vert. .85 .25
2350 A489 $4 multi 1.40 .25
2351 A489 $18 multi, vert. 2.25 .50
Nos. 2348-2351 (4) 5.15 1.25

Poetry Illustration Type of 1982

Sung Dynasty Poetry: $2, Seeing the Flowers Fade Away. $3, River. $5, Freckled with Clouds is the Azure Sky. $11, Yielding Fine Fragrance in the Snow. Nos. 2352-2355 vert.

Wmk. 323
1983, Feb. 10 Litho. ***Perf. 13½***
2352 A490 $2 multicolored *1.25* .25
2353 A490 $3 multicolored *2.50* .30
2354 A490 $5 multicolored *8.75* 1.20
2355 A490 $11 multicolored *7.50* .80
Nos. 2352-2355 (4) *20.00* 2.55

Mt. Jade, Taiwan — A499

$2, Wawa Valley, vert. $3, University Pond, vert.

1983, Mar. 1
2356 A499 $2 multicolored .25 .25
2357 A499 $3 multicolored .60 .25
2358 A499 $18 shown 2.75 .50
Nos. 2356-2358 (3) 3.60 1.00

400th Anniv. of Arrival of Matteo Ricci (1552-1610), Italian Missionary A500

Perf. 14x13½
1983, Apr. 3 Litho. Wmk. 323
2359 A500 $2 Astrolabe .25 .25
2360 A500 $18 Great Wall 1.25 .35

Mandarin Phonetic Symbols, 70th Anniv. — A501

$2, Wu Ching-heng, inventor. $18, Children writing.

Wmk. 323
1983, May 22 Litho. ***Perf. 13½***
2361 A501 $2 multicolored .35 .25
2362 A501 $18 multicolored 1.75 .35

Scenes from Lady White Snake Fairytale — A502

1983, June 15 ***Perf. 14x13½***
2363 A502 $2 multicolored .25 .25
2364 A502 $3 lt blue & multi .25 .25
2365 A502 $3 orange & multi .25 .25
2366 A502 $18 multicolored 4.00 .60
Nos. 2363-2366 (4) 4.75 1.35

A503

Various bamboo carved objects: $2, Bamboo jug. $3, Tao-t'ieh motif vase. $4, Landscape sculpture. $18, Brush holder, Ming dynasty.
Nos. 2367-2369 Ch'ing dynasty.

Wmk. 323
1983, July 14 Litho. ***Perf. 13½***
2367 A503 $2 multicolored .30 .25
2368 A503 $3 multicolored .80 .25
2369 A503 $4 multicolored 1.00 .25
2370 A503 $18 multicolored 2.00 .50
Nos. 2367-2370 (4) 4.10 1.25

A504

Wmk. 323
1983, Aug. 5 Litho. ***Perf. 13½***
2371 A504 $2 Globe .55 .25
2372 A504 $18 Emblem .95 .35

World Communications Year.

Fishing Industry (Local Fish) A505

$2, Epinephelus tauvina. $18, Saurida undosquamis.

1983, Aug. 20
2373 A505 $2 multicolored 1.00 .25
2374 A505 $18 multicolored 1.75 .35

40th Journalists' Day — A506

1983, Sept. 1
2375 A506 $2 multicolored .75 .25

Views of Mongolia and Tibet — A507

1983, Sept. 15
2376 A507 $2 Village .45 .25
2377 A507 $3 Potala Palace .65 .25
2378 A507 $5 Sheep grazing 1.20 .25
2379 A507 $11 Camel caravan 2.40 .30
Nos. 2376-2379 (4) 4.70 1.05

2nd East Asian Bird Protection Conference, Oct. — A508

$2, Lanius cristatus, vert. $18, Butastur indicus.

1983, Oct. 8 Litho. ***Perf. 13½***
2380 A508 $2 multicolored .50 .25
2381 A508 $18 multicolored 2.75 .40

A509

Plum Blossoms, photography by Hu Ch'ung-hsien.

1983, Oct. 31 Litho. ***Perf. 14x13½***
2382 A509 $2 multicolored .75 .25
2383 A509 $3 multi, diff. .25 .25
2384 A509 $5 multi, diff. 1.25 .30
2385 A509 $11 multi, diff. .75 .25
Nos. 2382-2385 (4) 3.00 1.05

A510

$2, JCI and Congress emblems. $18, Globe and emblems, horiz.

1983, Nov. 6 ***Perf. 13x13½, 13½x13***
2386 A510 $2 multicolored .25 .25
2387 A510 $18 multicolored 1.35 .40

Jaycees Intl., 38th World Congress, Taipei.

8th Asian-Pacific Cardiology Congress — A511

$18, Electrocardiogram.

1983, Nov. 27 **Litho.** ***Perf. 13½***
2388 A511 $2 shown .30 .25
2389 A511 $18 multicolored 1.40 .40

New Year 1984 (Year of the Rat) — A512

1983, Dec. 1 **Litho.** ***Perf. 12½***
2390 A512 $1 multicolored 1.50 .70
2391 A512 $10 multicolored 4.75 .30
a. Souv. sheet, 2 each #2390-2391 *30.00* 9.00

Literacy Week A513

$18, Modern family, vert.

1983, Dec. 17 **Litho.** ***Perf. 13½***
2392 A513 $2 shown .25 .25
2393 A513 $18 multicolored 1.50 .40

World Freedom Day A514

$2, Korean War Patriots. $18, Intl. support.

1984, Jan. 23 **Litho.** ***Perf. 13½***
2394 A514 $2 multicolored .35 .25
2395 A514 $18 multicolored 2.10 .35

Drama Day — A515

Yuan Dynasty Poetry Illustrations by Tien-shih Lin (Poems by): $2, Kuan Yun-shih. $3, Po Pu. $5, Chang Ko-chiu. $18, Shang Cheng-shu. (See note with Nos. 2322-2325.)

1984, Feb. 15 **Litho.** ***Perf. 13½***
2396 A515 $2 multicolored *.85* .25
2397 A515 $3 multicolored *3.50* .30
2398 A515 $5 multicolored *4.50* .60
2399 A515 $18 multicolored *9.00* 2.40
Nos. 2396-2399 (4) *17.85* 3.55

A516

A517

A518

Arbor Day — A519

1984, Mar. 12 **Litho.** ***Perf. 13½x14***
2400 A516 $2 multicolored 1.00 .25
2401 A517 $2 multicolored 1.00 .25
2402 A518 $2 multicolored 1.00 .25
2403 A519 $2 multicolored 1.00 .25
a. Block of 4, #2400-2403 5.75 3.00

Lin Chueh-min — A520

1984, Mar. 29 **Engr.** ***Perf. 13x12½***
Granite Paper
2404 A520 $2 dark green .75 .25

Central News Agency, 60th Anniv. — A521

$2, Emblem. $10, Emblem, satellite, dish antenna.

Perf. 14x13½
1984, Apr. 1 **Litho.** **Wmk.**
2405 A521 $2 multicolored .25 .25
2406 A521 $10 multicolored 1.00 .25

God of Longevity — A522

Paintings by Chang Ta-chien (1899-1983): $2, Five Auspicious Tokens. $18, Lotus Blossoms in Ink Splash.

Wmk. 323
1984, Apr. 20 **Litho.** ***Perf. 11½***
2407 A522 $2 multicolored 1.25 .25
2408 A522 $5 multicolored 2.25 .30
2409 A522 $18 multicolored 6.75 1.25
Nos. 2407-2409 (3) 10.25 1.80

Ch'ing Dynasty Enamelware A523

$2, Cup, pot, plate, horiz. $3, Wine jug. $4, Teapot. $18, Candle holder.

1984, May 20 **Photo.** ***Perf. 12***
Granite Paper
2410 A523 $2 multicolored .50 .25
2411 A523 $3 multicolored .50 .25
2412 A523 $4 multicolored .75 .25
2413 A523 $18 multicolored 2.25 .50
Nos. 2410-2413 (4) 4.00 1.25

China Airlines World-wide Service Inauguration A524

1984, May 31 **Litho.** ***Perf. 13½x14***
2414 A524 $2 Jet circling globe .25 .25
2415 A524 $7 Globe, jet .75 .25
2416 A524 $11 New York City .85 .30
2417 A524 $18 Amsterdam 1.10 .50
Nos. 2414-2417 (4) 2.95 1.30

30th Navigation Day A525

Perf. 13½x13
1984, July 11 **Litho.** **Wmk. 323**
2418 A525 $2 Container ship .85 .25
2419 A525 $18 Oil tanker 2.10 .45

1984 Summer Olympics — A526

Perf. 13½x14, 14x13½
1984, June 23
2420 A526 $2 Judo, horiz. .30 .25
2421 A526 $5 Archery .60 .30
2422 A526 $18 Swimming, horiz. 1.40 .50
Nos. 2420-2422 (3) 2.30 1.05

Alpine Plants — A527

$2, Gentiana arisanensis. $3, Epilobium nankotaizanense. $5, Adenophora uehatae. $18, Aconitum fukutomei.

1984, Aug. 8 ***Perf. 13***
2423 A527 $2 multi .25 .25
2424 A527 $3 multi .70 .25
2425 A527 $5 multi 1.10 .25
2426 A527 $18 multi 2.00 .50
Nos. 2423-2426 (4) 4.05 1.25

The Eighteen Scholars, Sung Dynasty Hanging Scroll — A528

$2, Playing instruments. $3, Playing chess. $5, Practicing calligraphy. $18, Painting.

Wmk. 323
1984, Aug. 20 **Litho.** ***Perf. 13***
2427 A528 $2 multicolored *1.00* .25
2428 A528 $3 multicolored *3.00* .25
2429 A528 $5 multicolored *5.00* .50
2430 A528 $18 multicolored *15.00* 1.00
Nos. 2427-2430 (4) *24.00* 2.00

Athletics Day — A529

1984, Sept. 9
2431 $5 Two players .75 .25
2432 $5 One player .75 .25
a. A529 Pair, #2431-2432 1.50 .75

A531

1984, Sept. 9
2433 A531 $10 "20," map of Asia 1.00 .25

Asian-Pacific Parliamentarians' Union, 20th anniv.

A532

1984, Oct. 10 Litho. *Perf. 12½*

2434 A532 $2 No. 1458 .25 .25
2435 A532 $5 No. 296 .60 .25
2436 A532 $18 Museum 1.75 .50
a. Souv. sheet of 3, #2434-2436 9.50 4.00
Nos. 2434-2436 (3) 2.60 1.00

Postal Museum opening.

Flag, Alliance Emblem — A533

1984, Oct. 16 *Perf. 13½*

2437 A533 $2 multicolored 1.00 .25

Grand Alliance for China's Reunification Under the Three Principles of the People Convention, Taipei, Oct. 16-17.

Veteran's Assistance A534

1984, Nov. 1 Litho. *Perf. 13½*

2438 A534 $2 Vignettes .80 .25

Pine Tree A535

Bamboo A535a

Plum Tree — A535b

1984-88

2439 A535 $2 multicolored .30 .25
2440 A535a $8 multicolored .80 .25
2441 A535b $10 pale yellow bister background .85 .25
a. Grayish tan background .65 .25
Nos. 2439-2441 (3) 1.95 .75

Issued: Nos. 2439-2440, 2441a, 11/12; No. 2441,1/12/88.

See Nos. 2495-2503, 3303.

A536

1984, Dec. 1 *Perf. 12x12½*

2442 A536 $1 multicolored .75 .25
2443 A536 $10 multicolored 2.40 .30
a. Min. sheet, 2 ea #2442-2443 *5.25* 2.75

New Year 1985 (Year of the Ox).

Scales, Legal Codes — A537

1985, Jan. 11 Litho. *Perf. 13½*

2444 A537 $5 multicolored .90 .25

Judicial Day 1985.

Quemoy and Matsu Scenes A538

$2, Ku-kang Lake, Quemoy. $5, Kuang-hai Stone, Quemoy. $8, Sheng-li Reservoir, Matsu. $10, Tung-chu Lighthouse, Matsu.

1985, Jan. 23 Litho. *Perf. 13½x14*

2445 A538 $2 multicolored .30 .25
2446 A538 $5 multicolored .80 .25
2447 A538 $8 multicolored 1.00 .25
2448 A538 $10 multicolored 1.25 .25
Nos. 2445-2448 (4) 3.35 1.00

Sir Robert Hart (1835-1911) A539

1985, Feb. 15 Litho. *Perf. 14x13½*

2449 A539 $2 No. 1 .80 .25

Inspector General of Chinese Customs, 1863-1908, and founder of the Chinese Postal Service.

Lo Fu-hsing (1886-1914) A540

1985, Feb. 24 *Perf. 13x13½*

2450 A540 $2 multicolored .80 .25

Tsou Jung (1882-1905) A541

1985, Mar. 29 Engr. *Perf. 13½x12½*
Granite Paper

2451 A541 $3 green .80 .25

Chung-cheng Memorial Hall Main Gate — A542

$8, Tzuhu Memorial. $10, Chiang Kai-shek, vert.

1985, Apr. 5 Litho. *Perf. 13*

2452 A542 $2 shown .40 .25
2453 A542 $8 multicolored 1.50 .25
2454 A542 $10 multicolored 1.60 .35
Nos. 2452-2454 (3) 3.50 .85

Tenth death anniv. of Chiang Kai-shek.

A543

1985, May 8 Litho. *Perf. 13½*

2455 A543 $2 Carnation .75 .25
2456 A543 $2 Day lily .75 .25
a. Pair, #2455-2456 2.00 .75

Mother's Day.

Tunnel to Chi-chin Island — A544

1985, May 18

2457 A544 $5 multicolored .60 .25

Kaohsiung Cross-Harbor Tunnel, 1st anniv.

Girl Scouts, 75th Anniv. — A545

Wmk. 323
1985, June 1 Litho. *Perf. 13½*

2458 A545 $2 multicolored .40 .25
2459 A545 $18 multicolored 2.20 .30

The Book of Odes, Confucius A545a

1985, June 22 Litho. Wmk. 323

2460 A545a $2 Spring 1.00 .25
2461 A545a $5 Summer 3.50 .25
2462 A545a $8 Fall 5.25 .25
2463 A545a $10 Winter 6.00 .30
Nos. 2460-2463 (4) *15.75* 1.05

Fruit — A546

Perf. 13½x14
1985, July 5 Litho. Wmk. 323

2464 A546 $2 Wax Jambo .55 .25
2465 A546 $3 Guava 1.25 .25
2466 A546 $5 Carambola 1.50 .25
2467 A546 $8 Litchi nut 1.60 .30
Nos. 2464-2467 (4) 4.90 1.05

Ch'ing Dynasty (1644-1911) Ivory Carvings — A547

$2, Dragon Boat. $3, Landscape. $5, Melon, water container. $18, Brush holder, vert.

1985, July 18 Wmk. 323 *Perf. 13½*

2468 A547 $2 multicolored .35 .25
2469 A547 $3 multicolored .30 .25
2470 A547 $5 multicolored .50 .25
2471 A547 $18 multicolored 1.90 .50
Nos. 2468-2471 (4) 3.05 1.25

T'ang Dynasty (618-907) Aristocrat — A548

Designs: $5, Sung Dynasty (960-1280) palace woman. $8, Yuan Dynasty (1280-1368) aristocrat. $11, Ming Dynasty (1368-1644) aristocrat.

1985, Aug. 1 Wmk. 323 *Perf. 13½*

2472 A548 $2 multicolored .50 .25
2473 A548 $5 multicolored 2.40 .25
2474 A548 $8 multicolored 2.75 .30
2475 A548 $11 multicolored 3.00 .40
Nos. 2472-2475 (4) 8.65 1.20

4th Asian Conf. on Costume, Aug. 3.

In the 2 rows of Chinese characters above the denomination, the right row has 3 characters and a dot on Nos. 2472-2475, 4 characters and a dot on Nos. 2549-2552. Nos. 2605-2608, 2660-2663 have solid black numerals.

See Nos. 2549-2552, 2605-2608, 2660-2663, 2721-2724, 2794-2797.

Social Welfare Program A549

Perf. 13½x14
1985, Aug. 15 Wmk. 323

2476 A549 $2 Heart, bird feeding young .80 .25

Historic Sites A550

$2, Taipei North Gate. $5, San Domingo Fort, Tamsui. $8, Lung Shun Temple, Lukang. $10, Confucius Temple, Changhua.

Wmk. 323

1985, Sept. 3 Litho. ***Perf. 13½***

2477 A550	$2 multicolored	.25	.25
2478 A550	$5 multicolored	.90	.25
2479 A550	$8 multicolored	1.20	.25
2480 A550	$10 multicolored	1.40	.35
	Nos. 2477-2480 (4)	3.75	1.10

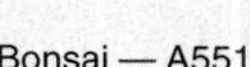

Bonsai — A551

Perf. 13½x14

1985, Sept. 22 Wmk. 323

2481 A551	$2 Oak	.25	.25
2482 A551	$5 Five-leaf pine	.60	.25
2483 A551	$8 Lohan pine	.75	.25
2484 A551	$18 Banyan	1.50	.50
	Nos. 2481-2484 (4)	3.10	1.25

Trade Shows — A552

Taipei World Trade Center and show emblems: a, Sporting goods. b, Toys and gifts. c, Electronics. d, Machinery. Se-tenant in continuous design.

1985, Oct. 5 ***Perf. 13½***

2485 A552	Strip of 4	3.75	1.00
a.-d.	$2 any single	.50	.25

Scenes of Modern Taiwan, Map, Flag A553

$18, Chiang Kai-shek, Triumphal Arch.

1985, Oct. 25

2486 A553	$2 shown	.50	.25
2487 A553	$18 multicolored	4.25	.50

Defeat of Japanese army, end of World War II, and return of Taiwan to control of the Republic, 40th anniv.

7th Asian Conference on Mental Retardation A554

1985, Nov. 8 ***Perf. 14x13½***

2488 A554	$2 multicolored	.75	.25
2489 A554	$11 multicolored	1.75	.25

Sun Yat-sen and Birthplace A555

1985, Nov. 12 ***Perf. 13½***

2490 A555	$2 multicolored	.50	.25
2491 A555	$18 multicolored	1.90	.40

Postal Life Insurance, 50th Anniv. — A556

1985, Dec. 1

2492 A556	$2 multicolored	.80	.25

New Year 1986 (Year of the Tiger) — A557

1985, Dec. 1 ***Perf. 12½***

2493 A557	$1 multicolored	.60	.25
2494 A557	$10 multicolored	2.25	.25
a.	Min. sheet, 2 ea #2493-2494	*12.50*	3.25

Flora Types of 1984

1986, Jan. 10 Litho. ***Perf. 13½***

2495 A535	$1 multicolored	.30	.25
2496 A535a	$11 multicolored	.70	.25
2497 A535b	$18 multicolored	1.00	.25

1988, Feb. 12

2498 A535	$1.50 multicolored	.25	.25
2499 A535a	$7.50 multicolored	.65	.25
2500 A535b	$16 multicolored	1.25	.30

No. 2500 has value expressed in dollars and cents. For surcharge, see No. 3303.

1989, Feb. 24

2501 A535	$3 multicolored	.25	.25
2502 A535a	$16.50 multicolored	1.25	.30
2503 A535b	$21 multicolored	1.60	.35
	Nos. 2495-2503 (9)	7.25	2.45

Cultural Renaissance Movement — A558

Painting: Hermit Anglers on a Mountain Stream, Ming Dynasty, 1386-1644. Continuous design. (Each stamp is numbered from 1 to 5 in Chinese. See illustrations with Nos. 1682-1691 for numerals.)

1986, Jan. 28 Litho. ***Perf. 13½***

2507	Strip of 5	9.00	7.00
a.-e.	A558 $2 any single	*1.50*	.25

See No. 2604.

Floral Arrangements A559

Wmk. 323

1986, Feb. 20 Litho. ***Perf. 13½***

2517 A559	$2 denom. UL	.35	.25
2518 A559	$5 denom. UR	.75	.25
2519 A559	$8 shown	.85	.25
2520 A559	$10 denom. UL	1.25	.30
	Nos. 2517-2520 (4)	3.20	1.05

Compare with designs A483, A584.

Natl. Postal Service, 90th Anniv. A560

$2, Unloading express mail at airport. $5, Motorcycle delivery. $8, Technological innovations. $10, Electronic sorting machine.

1986, Mar. 20

2521 A560	$2 multi	.25	.25
2522 A560	$5 multi, vert.	.50	.25
2523 A560	$8 multi, vert.	.75	.25
2524 A560	$10 multi	1.10	.30
a.	Souv. sheet of 4, #2521-2524	5.75	2.55
	Nos. 2521-2524 (4)	2.60	1.05

Chen Tien-hua (1875-1905), Revolutionary A561

1986, Mar. 29 Engr. ***Perf. 13½x12½***

Granite Paper

2525 A561	$2 violet	.80	.25

Yushan Natl. Park A562

1986, Apr. 10 Litho. ***Perf. 13½***

2526 A562	$2 multicolored	.40	.25
2527 A562	$5 multi, diff.	1.00	.25
2528 A562	$8 multi, diff.	1.30	.25
2529 A562	$10 multi, diff.	1.60	.30
	Nos. 2526-2529 (4)	4.30	1.05

Power Plants A563

1986, Apr. 29

2530 A563	$2 Hydro-electric	.25	.25
2531 A563	$8 Thermo-electric	.65	.25
2532 A563	$10 Nuclear	.90	.25
	Nos. 2530-2532 (3)	1.80	.75

Economic prosperity through energy development.

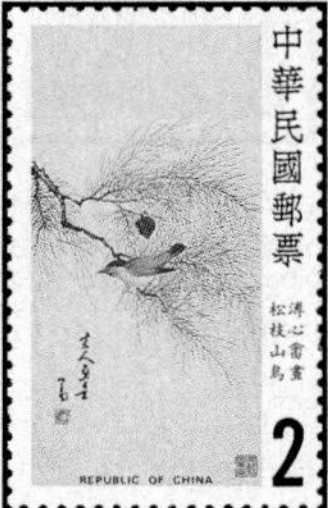

Paintings by P'u Hsin-yu (1896-1963) A564

1986, May 22 ***Perf. 11½***

2533 A564	$2 Bird	.90	.25
2534 A564	$8 Landscape	3.50	.40
2535 A564	$10 Woman in forest	4.50	.50
	Nos. 2533-2535 (3)	8.90	1.15

Asian Productivity Org., 25th Anniv. — A565

1986, June 3 ***Perf. 13x13½***

2536 A565	$2 multicolored	.25	.25
2537 A565	$11 multicolored	.90	.25

Natl. Productivity Center, 30th anniv.

Coral-reef Fish A566

Designs: a, Chrysiptera starcki. b, Chelmon rostratus. c, Chaetodon xanthurus. d, Chaetodon quadrimaculatus. e, Chaetodon meyeri. f, Genicanthus semifasciatus. g, Genicanthus semifasciatus. h, Pomacanthus annularis. i, Lienardella fasciata. j, Balistapus undulatus.

1986, June 27 ***Perf. 13½***

2538	Block of 10	5.25	4.25
a.-j.	A566 $2 any single	.50	.25

Protection of Intellectual Property Rights — A567

1986, June 12

2539 A567	$2 Macaw	1.10	.25

Nos. 2294, 2297 Surcharged

1986, July 9 Litho. ***Perf. 13½***

2540 A432	$2 on $6 multi	.25	.25
2541 A432	$8 on $9 multi	1.00	.25

60th Anniv. of northward expedition by the national revolutionary army.

Bridges A568

$2, Tzu Mu, 1965. $5, Chang Hung, 1968. $8, Kuan Fu, 1977. $10, Kuan Tu, 1983.

1986, July 30

2542 A568	$2 multicolored	.45	.25
2543 A568	$5 multicolored	1.10	.25
2544 A568	$8 multicolored	1.60	.25
2545 A568	$10 multicolored	2.00	.30
	Nos. 2542-2545 (4)	5.15	1.05

Love between Liang Shanpo and Chu Yingtai, Folk Tale — A569

Cartoons by Huang Mu-ts'un: a, Yingtai disguised to go to school. b, Yingtai and Shanpo meet in class. c, The friends at pond. d,

Yingtai summoned home for arranged marriage. e, Yingtai and Shanpo ascend to heaven as butterflies (each stamp is numbered from 1 to 5 in Chinese. See illustrations with Nos. 1682-1691 for numerals.)

1986, Aug. 12 *Perf. 12½*

2546	Strip of 5	4.00	1.60
a.-e.	A569 $5 any single	.50	.25

Social Awareness Campaign A570

1986, Sept. 12 **Litho.** *Perf. 13½*

2547	A570	$2 Rainbow, children	.40	.25
2548	A570	$8 Children, adults	.90	.25

Folk Costumes — A571

Designs: $2, Shang Dynasty (1766-1122 B.C.) aristocrat. $5, Warring States (403-221 B.C.) aristocrat. $8, Later Han Dynasty (A.D. 25-221) empress. $10, Flying ribbons gown, Wei and Tsin Dynasties (A.D. 221-420) aristocrat.

1986, Sept. 23 **Litho.** *Perf. 13½*

2549	A571	$2 multicolored	.60	.25
2550	A571	$5 multicolored	1.40	.25
2551	A571	$8 multicolored	1.75	.25
2552	A571	$10 multicolored	2.75	.35
		Nos. 2549-2552 (4)	6.50	1.10

Ch'ing Dynasty Ju-i Scepters A572

$2, White jade. $3, Red coral. $4, Redwood and gems. $18, Gilded wood.

1986, Oct. 10 **Photo.** *Perf. 14x14½*

2553	A572	$2 multicolored	.25	.25
2554	A572	$3 multicolored	.35	.25
2555	A572	$4 multicolored	.45	.25
2556	A572	$18 multicolored	2.00	.40
		Nos. 2553-2556 (4)	3.05	1.15

See Nos. 2582-2585.

Chiang Kai-shek A573

Portrait and: $5, Map and flag. $8, Emblem. $10, Flags on globe.

1986, Oct. 31 **Litho.** *Perf. 13½*

2557	A573	$2 multicolored	.30	.25
2558	A573	$5 multicolored	1.15	.25
2559	A573	$8 multicolored	1.50	.25
2560	A573	$10 multicolored	1.90	.30
a.		Souv. sheet of 4, #2557-2560	12.00	6.00
		Nos. 2557-2560 (4)	4.85	1.05

Cultural Heritage A574

Architecture: $2, Chin-Kuang Fu land development and defense fund building, 1826. $5, Erh-sha-wan Gun Emplacement, Keelung, 1841, restored 1979. $8, Fort Hsi T'ai, 1886. $10, Matsu Temple, Peng-hu, renovated 1563-1624.

1986, Nov. 14 **Litho.** *Perf. 13½*

2561	A574	$2 multicolored	.25	.25
2562	A574	$5 multicolored	.85	.25
2563	A574	$8 multicolored	1.00	.25
2564	A574	$10 multicolored	1.20	.30
		Nos. 2561-2564 (4)	3.30	1.05

New Year 1987 (Year of the Hare) — A575

1986, Dec. 1 *Perf. 12½*

2565	A575	$1 dl pink & multi	.50	.25
2566	A575	$10 pale grn & multi	2.50	.25
a.		Souv. sheet, 2 each #2565-2566	*11.50*	3.50

Kenting, 1st Natl. Park A576

1987, Jan. 8 **Litho.** *Perf. 13½*

2567	A576	$2 Garden	.50	.25
2568	A576	$5 Shore rocks	1.45	.25
2569	A576	$8 Shore and hill	1.75	.25
2570	A576	$10 Shore and rocks, diff.	2.00	.30
		Nos. 2567-2570 (4)	5.70	1.05

Folk Art — A577

Puppets: $2, Hand puppet. $5, Marionette. $18, Shadow puppet.

1987, Feb. 12 **Litho.** *Perf. 14x13½*

2571	A577	$2 multicolored	.40	.25
2572	A577	$5 multicolored	1.00	.25
2573	A577	$18 multicolored	1.75	.40
		Nos. 2571-2573 (3)	3.15	.90

Speedpost A578

1987, Mar. 20 **Litho.** *Perf. 14x13½*

2574	A578	$2 multicolored	.35	.25
2575	A578	$18 multicolored	1.25	.30

Stamp Day.

Wu Yueh (1878-1905), Revolutionary A579

1987, Mar. 29 **Engr.** *Perf. 13½x12½*

2576	A579	$2 orange	1.25	.25

Landscapes Painted by Madame Chiang Kai-shek — A580

$2, Singing Creek with Bamboo Orchestra. $5, Mountains Draped in Clouds. $8, Vista of Tranquility. $10, Mountains after a Snowfall.

1987, Apr. 10 **Litho.** *Perf. 13½*

2577	A580	$2 blk, buff & ver	.80	.25
2578	A580	$5 blk, buff & ver	2.60	.30
2579	A580	$8 blk, buff & ver	3.50	.30
2580	A580	$10 blk, buff & ver	4.25	.50
		Nos. 2577-2580 (4)	11.15	1.35

Stone Sculptures — A581

Designs: a, Head of a Bodhisattva, sandstone, Northern Wei Dynasty (386-534). b, Standing Buddha, limestone, Northern Ch'i Dynasty (550-577). c, Head of a Bodhisattva, sandstone, T'ang Dynasty (618-907). d, Seated Buddha, alabaster, T'ang Dynasty.

1987, Apr. 23

2581	Strip of 4	3.00	1.75
a.-d.	A581 $5 any single	.60	.25

No. 2581a shows seven Chinese characters at left; No. 2581c shows five.

Ju-i Scepters, Ch'ing Dynasty A582

$2, Silver and gems. $3, Gold and gems. $4, Gilded, jade and inlaid gems. $18, Gilded, inlaid malachite.

1987, May 7 **Photo.** *Perf. 14x14½*

2582	A582	$2 multicolored	.60	.25
2583	A582	$3 multicolored	1.45	.25
2584	A582	$4 multicolored	2.25	.25
2585	A582	$18 multicolored	3.00	.45
		Nos. 2582-2585 (4)	7.30	1.20

Feitsui Reservoir Inauguration A583

$2, Reservoir. $18, Hsintien Stream, reservoir.

1987, June 6 **Litho.** *Perf. 13½x14*

2586	A583	$2 multicolored	.50	.25
2587	A583	$18 multicolored	2.10	.30

Flower Arrangements by Huang Yung-ch'uan A584

$8, Flowers in brown vase.

1987, June 19 *Perf. 13½*

2588	A584	$2 denom. LL	.25	.25
2589	A584	$5 denom. LL	.80	.25
2590	A584	$8 denom. UR	1.00	.25
2591	A584	$10 denom. UR	1.10	.25
		Nos. 2588-2591 (4)	3.15	1.00

Compare with designs A483, A559.

Lions Club Intl. 70th Annual Convention, Taipei — A585

1987, July 1

2592	A585	$2 multicolored	.35	.25
2593	A585	$18 multicolored	1.75	.30

Sino-Japanese War, 50th Anniv. — A586

$1, Battle front. $2, Chiang Kai-shek giving speech. $5, Public donating funds. $6, Troops marching. $8, Signing of peace treaty. $18, Parade.

1987, July 7 *Perf. 14x13½*

2594	A586	$1 multicolored	.35	.25
2595	A586	$2 multicolored	.55	.25
2596	A586	$5 multicolored	.65	.25
2597	A586	$6 multicolored	.85	.25
2598	A586	$8 multicolored	1.20	.25
2599	A586	$18 multicolored	1.35	.45
		Nos. 2594-2599 (6)	4.95	1.70

Wang Yun-wu (1888-1979), Lexicographer A587

1987, Aug. 14 *Perf. 13½*

2600	A587	$2 gray black	.80	.25

Memorial Hall Type of 1981

Perf. 12½x13½

1987, Sept. 24 **Photo.**

2601	A468	10c lake	.25	.25
2602	A468	30c brt green	.25	.25
2603	A468	60c brt blue	.25	.25
		Nos. 2601-2603 (3)	.75	.75

A588

Cultural Renaissance Movement — A589

Scroll, 1543, by Weng Chen-ming (1470-1559), a copy of Chao Po-su's *Red Cliff*. Nos.

2604a-2604e and 2604f-2604j are printed in continuous designs. (Each stamp is numbered from 1 to 10 in Chinese. See illustrations with Nos. 1682-1691 for numerals.)

1987, Sept. 22 Engr. *Perf. 13½*

2604 Block of 10 11.00 11.00
a.-e. A588 $3 any single .80 .25
f.-j. A589 $3 any single .80 .25

Folk Costumes — A590

$1.50, Han woman, early Ch'ing Dynasty (1644-1911). $3, Wife of a Ch'ing Dynasty Manchu Bannerman. $7.50, Urban woman wearing Manchu ch'i-p'ao dress, c. 1912. $18, Short jacket over long skirt, c. 1920.

1987, Oct. 2 Litho.

2605 A590 $1.50 multicolored *1.00* .25
2606 A590 $3 multicolored *1.20* .25
2607 A590 $7.50 multicolored *1.40* .25
2608 A590 $18 multicolored *1.75* .60
Nos. 2605-2608 (4) *5.35* 1.35

Nos. 2605-2608 have 3 groups of 2 smaller Chinese characters above denomination. Nos. 2660-2663 have 2 groups of 2 and 4 characters.

A591

$3, Ta Chen Tian temple, Taichung. $18, Confucius.

1987, Nov. 12 *Perf. 13½x14*

2609 A591 $3 multicolored .45 .25
2610 A591 $18 multicolored 1.90 .80

Intl. Symposium on Confucianism, Taipei, Nov. 12-17.

A592

1987, Dec. 1 *Perf. 12½*

2611 A592 $1.50 multicolored .50 .25
2612 A592 $12 multicolored 2.00 .40
a. Souv. sheet, 2 ea #2611-2612 9.00 2.50

New Year 1988 (Year of the Dragon).

Constitution, 40th Anniv. — A593

1987, Dec. 25 Litho. *Perf. 13½*

2613 A593 $3 multicolored .45 .25
2614 A593 $16 multi, diff. 1.30 .30

Prevent Hypertension Campaign A594

1988, Jan. 8 *Perf. 12½x13½*

2615 A594 $3 multicolored .45 .25

Fruit Tree Blossoms — A595

No. 2616, Prunus mume. No. 2617, Prunus armeniaca. No. 2618, Prunus persica.

No. 2619, Paeonia suffruticosa. No. 2620, Punica granatum. No. 2621, Nelumbo nucifera.

No. 2622, Impatiens balsamina. No. 2623, Osmanthus fragrans. No. 2624, Chrysanthemum morifolium.

No. 2625, Hibiscus mutabilis. No. 2626, Camellia japonica. No. 2627, Narcissus tazetta.

Wmk. 323

1988, Feb. 4 Litho. *Perf. 13½*

2616 A595 $3 multi .65 .25
2617 A595 $7.50 multi 1.90 .25
2618 A595 $12 multi 2.90 .30
a. Min. sheet of 3, #2616-2618 *25.00* *25.00*

Wmk. 323

1988, May 5 Litho. *Perf. 13½*

2619 A595 $3 multi .60 .25
2620 A595 $7.50 multi 1.75 .25
2621 A595 $12 multi 2.60 .30
a. Min. sheet of 3, #2619-2621 *15.00* *15.00*

Wmk. 323

1988, Aug. 9 Litho. *Perf. 13½*

2622 A595 $3 multi .60 .25
2623 A595 $7.50 multi 1.75 .25
2624 A595 $12 multi 2.60 .30
a. Min. sheet of 3, #2622-2624 *12.50* *12.50*

Wmk. 323

1988, Nov. 7 Litho. *Perf. 13½*

2625 A595 $3 multi .60 .25
2626 A595 $7.50 multi 1.75 .25
2627 A595 $12 multi 2.60 .30
a. Min. sheet of 3, #2625-2627 *12.50* *12.50*
Nos. 2616-2627 (12) 20.30 3.20

Tourism Day — A596

Folk art: $3, Modeled dough figurines. $7.50, Blown sweet-malt sugar candy. $16, Sugar paintings.

Perf. 13½x14

1988, Mar. 2 Litho. Wmk. 323

2628 A596 $3 multicolored .60 .20
2629 A596 $7.50 multicolored 1.20 .30
2630 A596 $16 multicolored 2.20 .50
Nos. 2628-2630 (3) 4.00 1.00

A597

Perf. 13½x12½

1988, Mar. 29 Engr. Wmk. 323

2631 A597 $3 brown .80 .25

Hsu Hsi-lin (1873-1907), hero of the revolution.

A598

$1.50, Biotechnology. $3, Energy resources. $7, Immunization. $7.50, Automation. $10, Telecommunications. $12, Laser technology. $16, Micro-optics. $16.50, Agricultural research.

1988 Litho. *Perf. 13½*

2632 A598 $1.50 multicolored .25 .25
2633 A598 $3 multicolored .25 .25
2634 A598 $7 multicolored .35 .25
2635 A598 $7.50 multicolored .35 .25
2636 A598 $10 multicolored .50 .30
2637 A598 $12 multicolored .55 .30
2638 A598 $16 multicolored .75 .60
2639 A598 $16.50 multicolored 1.00 .60
Nos. 2632-2639 (8) 4.00 2.80

Industrialization by technological development. Issued: $3, $7.50, $10, $16, Apr. 22; others, May 9.

Police Day A599

Wmk. 323

1988, June 15 Litho. *Perf. 13½*

2640 A599 $3 Traffic control .30 .25
2641 A599 $12 Rescue operations 1.20 .30

Amphibians A600

$1.50, Microhyla butleri. $3, Rana taipehensis. $7.50, Microhyla inornata. $16, Rhacophorus smaragdinus.

1988, July 8 *Perf. 13½x14*

2642 A600 $1.50 multicolored *1.30* .25
2643 A600 $3 multicolored *2.00* .25
2644 A600 $7.50 multicolored *2.50* .30
2645 A600 $16 multicolored *3.50* .60
Nos. 2642-2645 (4) *9.30* 1.40

China Broadcasting Corp. (BBC), 60th Anniv. — A601

Wmk. 323

1988, Aug. 1 Litho. *Perf. 13½*

2646 A601 $3 multicolored .80 .25

Victory at the Battle of Kinmen, 30th Anniv. A602

Designs: $1.50, Chiang Kai-shek and artillery commander. $3, With troops. $7.50, Cannon. $12, Tanks.

1988, Aug. 23

2647 A602 $1.50 multicolored .40 .25
2648 A602 $3 multicolored .60 .25
2649 A602 $7.50 multicolored .90 .25
2650 A602 $12 multicolored 1.10 .40
Nos. 2647-2650 (4) 3.00 1.15

Sports Promotion — A603

Nos. 2651-2652, Basketball. Nos. 2653-2654, Baseball.

1988, Sept. 9

2651 $5 Players .90 .25
2652 $5 Players .90 .25
a. A603 Pair, #2651-2652 2.25 1.10
2653 $5 Batter .90 .25
2654 $5 Catcher .90 .25
a. A603 Pair, #2653-2654 2.25 1.10
Nos. 2651-2654 (4) 3.60 1.00

Nos. 2652a, 2654a have continuous designs.

Yangmingshan Natl. Park — A604

$1.50, Volcanic crater. $3, Lake. $7.50, Tatun Volcanic Range. $16, Dormant volcano.

1988, Sept. 16

2655 A604 $1.50 multicolored *.25* .25
2656 A604 $3 multicolored *.55* .25
2657 A604 $7.50 multicolored *1.00* .25
2658 A604 $16 multicolored *2.25* .50
Nos. 2655-2658 (4) *4.05* 1.25

Lofty Mount Lu, a Hanging Scroll, 1467, By Shen Chou (1427-1509) — A605

Painting details: a, UL. b, UR. c, LL. d, LR.

Wmk. 323

1988, Oct. 19 Litho. *Perf. 11½*

2659 A605 Block of 4 *7.00* 5.00
a.-d. $5 any single *1.50* .35

Folk Costumes — A606

Designs: $2, Shang Dynasty (1766-1122 B.C.) nobleman. $3, Warring States (403-221) B.C.) ruler. $7.50, Wei-Chin Period (221-420) official. $12, Northern Dynasties (502-581) official.

Perf. 13½x14

1988, Nov. 23 Litho. Wmk. 323

2660 A606	$2 multicolored	*.60*	.25
2661 A606	$3 multicolored	*1.00*	.25
2662 A606	$7.50 multicolored	*2.00*	.30
2663 A606	$12 multicolored	*2.75*	.50
	Nos. 2660-2663 (4)	6.35	1.30

Nos. 2721-2724 have groups of 2 and 6 Chinese characters above denomination; Nos. 2660-2663 groups of 2 and 4; Nos. 2794-2797 groups of 1 and 5.

A607

1988, Dec. 1 ***Perf. 12½***

2664 A607 $2 multicolored	*.65*	.25
2665 A607 $13 multicolored	*5.00*	.50
a. Souv. sheet, 2 each #2664-2665	*16.50*	11.50

New Year 1989 (Year of the Snake).

A608

Wmk. 323

1989, Jan. 4 Litho. *Perf. 13½*

2666 A608 $3 black	.70	.25

Tai Ch'uan-hsien (1890-1949), party leader.

Pres. Chiang Ching-kuo (1910-88) A609

1989, Jan. 13

2667 A609	$3 shown	.25	.25
2668 A609	$6 Suffrage	.40	.25
2669 A609	$7.50 Industry	.80	.30
2670 A609	$16 Children	1.40	.50
	Nos. 2667-2670 (4)	2.85	1.30

Ni Ying-tien (1884-1910), Revolution Leader — A610

Perf. 13½x12½

1989, Mar. 28 Engr. Wmk. 323

2671 A610 $3 black	.80	.25

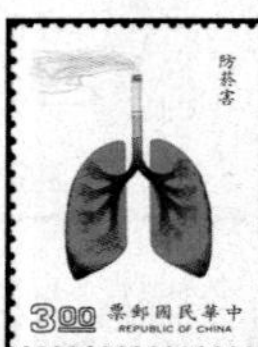

Stop Smoking — A611

Perf. 13½x12½

1989, Apr. 7 Litho. Wmk. 323

2672 A611 $3 multicolored	.80	.25

Lighthouses — A612

75c, Mu Tou Yu. $2, Lu Tao. $2.25, Pen Chia Yu. $3, Pitou Chiao. $4.50, Tungyin Tao. $6, Chilai Pi. $7, Fukwei Chiao. $7.50, Hua Yu. $9, Oluan Pi. $10, Kaohsiung. $10.50, Yuweng Tao. $12, Tungchu Tao. $13, Yeh Liu. $15, Tungchi Yu. $16.50, Chimei Yu.

1989-91 ***Perf. 13½***

2673	A612	75c multi	.25	.25
2674	A612	$2 multi	.60	.25
2675	A612	$2.25 multi	.25	.25
2676	A612	$3 multi	.65	.25
2677	A612	$4.50 multi	.50	.25
2678	A612	$6 multi	.65	.25
2679	A612	$7 multi	.80	.25
2680	A612	$7.50 multi	1.60	.35
2681	A612	$9 multi	1.00	.25
2682	A612	$10 multi	2.10	.45
2683	A612	$10.50 multi	1.20	.25
2683A	A612	$12 multi	1.35	.25
2683B	A612	$13 multi	1.45	.25
2683C	A612	$15 multi	1.60	.25
2684	A612	$16.50 multi	3.50	.75
		Nos. 2673-2684 (15)	17.50	4.55

Issued: 75c, $2.25, 4/21/1989; $4.50, 8/6/1989; $9, $10.50, $13, 8/16/1989; $7, $15, 5/19/90; $6, $12, 1/9/91; $2, $3, $7.50, $10, $16.50, 5/20/91.

See Nos. 2811-2823.

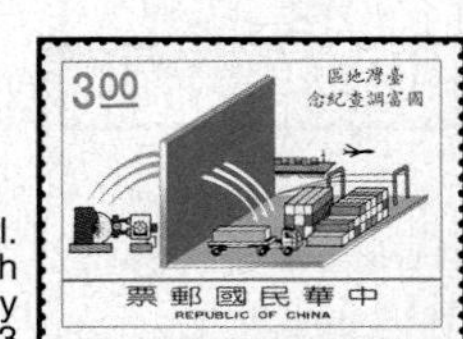

1st Natl. Wealth Survey A613

1989, May 18 Litho. *Perf. 13½*

2685 A613 $3 multicolored	.50	.25

Ch'u Ts'u Collection of Poems, 722-481 B.C. — A614

Designs: $3, Man overlooking fields. $7.50, Man, woman on path. $12, Man holding staff. $16, Man, stallion, stone gate. Excerpts: $3, "I once tended nine fields of orchids; Also I had planted a hundred rods of melilotus" (Li Sao). $7.50, "No grief is greater than parting of the living; No joy is more than making new friends" (Chiu Ko, shao ssu ming). $12, "Since my heart is straight and good, Why should I be chagrined at living remote and neglected?" (Chiu Chang, she chiang). $16, "The steed will not gallop itself into servitude; The phoenix has no appetite for slave food." (Chiu Pien).

1989, June 7 Photo. *Perf. 11½x12*

Granite Paper

2686 A614	$3 multicolored	.35	.25
2687 A614	$7.50 multicolored	.90	.35
2688 A614	$12 multicolored	1.75	.55
2689 A614	$16 multicolored	2.00	.75
	Nos. 2686-2689 (4)	5.00	1.90

Compare with types A629, A663. Nos. 2686-2689 have two Chinese characters near denomination. Nos. 2725-2728 have groups of 3 and 4 characters.

Taipei Subway Inauguration — A615

$3, Subway tunnel. $16, Entering underground.

1989, June 27 Litho. *Perf. 13½*

2690 A615 $3 multicolored	.35	.25
2691 A615 $16 multicolored	1.40	.60

A616

A616a

A616b

Butterflies A616c

$2, Graphium sarpedon connectens. $3, Papilo memnon heronus. $7.50, Princeps demoleus libanius. $9, Pachliopa aristolochiae interpositas.

Wmk. 323

1989, July 14 Litho. *Perf. 13½*

2692 A616	$2 multicolored	.75	.25
2693 A616a	$3 multicolored	.75	.25
2694 A616b	$7.50 multicolored	3.00	.40
2695 A616c	$9 multicolored	2.40	.30
	Nos. 2692-2695 (4)	6.90	1.20

Compare with design A627.

Ch'ing Dynasty Teapots from I-Hsing of Kiangsu, 1644-1911 A617

1989, July 28 ***Perf. 13½x14***

2696 A617	$2 multicolored	.65	.25
2697 A617	$3 multi, diff.	.65	.25
2698 A617	$12 multi, diff.	2.25	.45
2699 A617	$16 multi, diff.	2.40	.60
	Nos. 2696-2699 (4)	5.95	1.55

For stamps with teapot designs and solid black denominations see Nos. 2760-2764.

Intl. Seminar on Fan Chung-yen (989-1052), Military Leader and Civil Service Reformer — A618

Perf. 14x13½

1989, Sept. 1 Litho. Wmk. 323

2700 A618 $12 multicolored	1.25	.55

Autumn Colors on the Ch'iao and Hua Mountains, 14th Cent., by Ch'iao Meng-fu A619

a, Right side of mountain, trees. b, Trees, left side of mountain. c, House, trees. d, shown.

Wmk. 323

1989, Oct. 5 Litho. *Perf. 13½*

2701 Strip of 4	10.00	4.00
a.-d. A619 $7.50 any single	2.25	.50

Social Welfare A619a

1989, Nov. 3 Litho. *Perf. 13½*

2701E A619a $3 multicolored	.80	.25

Taroko Natl. Park — A620

Designs: $2, Marble gorge, Liwu River. $3, Hohuan Mountain. $12, Waterfall, Cirque of Nanhu. $16, Chingshui Cliff.

Wmk. 323

1989, Nov. 28 Litho. *Perf. 13½*

2702 A620	$2 multicolored	.35	.25
2703 A620	$3 multicolored	.35	.25
2704 A620	$12 multicolored	1.00	.45
2705 A620	$16 multicolored	1.25	.50
	Nos. 2702-2705 (4)	2.95	1.45

New Year 1990 (Year of the Horse) — A621

1989, Dec. 1 ***Perf. 12½***

2706 A621 $2 multicolored	.35	.25
2707 A621 $13 multicolored	1.40	.50
a. Souv. sheet, 2 ea #2706-2707	6.40	3.00

Yu Lu — A622

Men Shen, "guardian spirits" (likenesses of legendary beings placed on residence doors at the new year): No. 2708, Yu Lu. No. 2709, Shen Shu. No. 2710, Wei-ch'ih Ching-te. No. 2711, Ch'in Shu-pao.

Wmk. 323

1990, Jan. 19 Litho. *Perf. 13½*

2708 A622	$3 shown	1.00	.25
2709 A622	$3 "$3" at LR	1.00	.25
a.	Pair, #2708-2709	2.00	1.75

2710 A622 $7.50 "$7.50" at LL 2.40 .40
2711 A622 $7.50 "$7.50" at LR 2.40 .40
a. Pair, #2710-2711 5.00 4.25
Nos. 2708-2711 (4) 6.80 1.30

Nos. 2709a, 2711a have continuous designs.

A623

Scenery — A624

Designs: $2, Lishan House, Pear Mountain. $18, Tayu Pass, Tayuling, vert.

Wmk. 323

1990, Feb. 10 Litho. *Perf. 13½*
2712 A623 $2 multicolored .50 .25
2713 A624 $18 multicolored 1.75 .80

Labor Insurance System, 40th Anniv. — A625

1990, Mar. 1
2714 A625 $3 multicolored .80 .25

Liquefied Natural Gas A626

$3, Terminal, Yung-an Hsiang of Kaohsiung. $16, Container ship, map, refinery.

1990, Mar. 31 Litho. *Perf. 13½*
2715 A626 $3 multi .40 .25
2716 A626 $16 multi, vert. 1.20 .50

A627

A627a

A627b

Butterflies A627c

$2, Salatura genutia. $3, Hypolimnas misippus. $7.50, Pieris canidia. $9, Precis almana.

1990, Apr. 20
2717 A627 $2 multicolored .35 .25
2718 A627a $3 multicolored .35 .25
2719 A627b $7.50 multicolored 1.00 .25
2720 A627c $9 multicolored 1.40 .35
Nos. 2717-2720 (4) 3.10 1.10

Compare with design A616.

Folk Costumes — A628

$2, Official, Sui & T'ang Dynasties (589-907). $3, Official, T'ang & Sung Dynasties (618-1280). $7.50, Royal guardsman, Chin & Yuan Dynasties (1115-1368). $12, Highest ranking civil official, Ming Dynasty (1368-1644).

1990, May 10 Litho. *Perf. 13½*
2721 A628 $2 multicolored .50 .25
2722 A628 $3 multicolored .60 .25
2723 A628 $7.50 multicolored 1.35 .25
2724 A628 $12 multicolored 1.40 .45
Nos. 2721-2724 (4) 3.85 1.20

See note after No. 2663.

Yueh Fu Classical Poetry A629

Lyrics from Tzu-yeh folk songs, Six Dynasties (222-589): $3, Spring Song at Midnight. $7.50, Summer Song at Midnight. $12, Autumn Song at Midnight. $16, Winter Song at Midnight.

Wmk. 323

1990, June 27 Litho. *Perf. 11½*
Granite Paper
2725 A629 $3 shown .25 .25
2726 A629 $7.50 Couple, river 1.10 .25
2727 A629 $12 Washing clothes, river 2.40 .45
2728 A629 $16 River in winter 3.25 .65
Nos. 2725-2728 (4) 7.00 1.60

Compare with designs A614 and A663.

Bonsai A630

Designs: $3, Pinus thunbergii parl. $6.50, Ehretia microphylla lamk. $12, Buxus harlandii hance. $16, Celtis sinensis pers.

1990, July 20 Litho. *Perf. 13½*
2729 A630 $3 multicolored .25 .25
2730 A630 $6.50 multicolored .75 .25
2731 A630 $12 multicolored 1.15 .45
2732 A630 $16 multicolored 1.75 .65
Nos. 2729-2732 (4) 3.90 1.60

Snuff Bottles — A631

$3, Bamboo stem shaped. $6, Peony motif. $9, Amber. $16, White jade.

1990, Aug. 9
2733 A631 $3 multicolored .35 .25
2734 A631 $6 multicolored .50 .25
2735 A631 $9 multicolored .95 .35
2736 A631 $16 multicolored 1.50 .60
Nos. 2733-2736 (4) 3.30 1.45

Formosan Firecrest A632

$3, Laughing thrush. $7.50, White-eared sibia. $16, Yellow tit.

1990, Aug. 20 Litho. *Perf. 13½*
2737 A632 $2 shown .50 .25
2738 A632 $3 multicolored .50 .25
2739 A632 $7.50 multicolored 1.15 .25
2740 A632 $16 multicolored 2.50 .50
Nos. 2737-2740 (4) 4.65 1.25

Sports — A633

1990, Sept. 8 Litho. *Perf. 13½*
2741 A633 $2 Sprint .25 .25
2742 A633 $3 Long jump .25 .25
2743 A633 $7 Pole vault .90 .30
2744 A633 $16 High hurdle 1.20 .60
Nos. 2741-2744 (4) 2.60 1.40

Flying Tigers, 50th Anniv. A634

1990, Sept. 26 Litho. *Perf. 13½*
2745 A634 $3 multicolored 1.00 .25

Children's Drawings A635

1990, Oct. 9
2746 A635 $2 Cat .25 .25
2747 A635 $3 Peacocks .25 .25
2748 A635 $7.50 Chickens .75 .25
2749 A635 $12 Cattle 1.10 .40
Nos. 2746-2749 (4) 2.35 1.15

National Theater A636

Photo. & Engr.

1990, Oct. 30 *Perf. 13½*
2750 A636 $3 shown .45 .25
2751 A636 $12 Natl. concert hall 1.50 .60

A637

Ancient money.

1990, Nov. 5 Litho. *Perf. 13x13½*
2752 A637 $2 Shell .35 .25
2753 A637 $3 Oyster .35 .25
2754 A637 $6.50 Bone .50 .25
2755 A637 $7.50 Jade .65 .35
2756 A637 $9 Bronze .75 .40
Nos. 2752-2756 (5) 2.60 1.50

A638

1990, Dec. 1 *Perf. 12½*
2757 A638 $2 multicolored .60 .25
2758 A638 $13 multicolored 2.50 .60
a. Souv. sheet, 2 ea #2757-2758 *10.00* 2.50

New Year 1991 (Year of the Sheep).

Hu Shih (1891-1962), Educator — A639

Wmk. 323

1990, Dec. 17 Engr. *Perf. 13½*
2759 A639 $3 purple .80 .25

Teapots, Natl. Palace Museum A640

Teapots: $2, Blue phoenix, Ming Dynasty. $3, Dragon handle and spout, Ming Dynasty. $9, Blue landscape, flowered top, Ch'ing Dynasty. $12, Rectangular, passion flower motif, Ch'ing Dynasty. $16, Rectangular, flower motif, Ch'ing Dynasty.

1991, Jan. 18 Photo. *Perf. 12*
Granite Paper
2760 A640 $2 yel, blk & blue .40 .25
2761 A640 $3 brt yel grn & blk .55 .25
2762 A640 $9 pink & multi .85 .30
2763 A640 $12 violet & multi 1.15 .40
2764 A640 $16 lt blue & multi 1.30 .60
Nos. 2760-2764 (5) 4.25 1.80

God of Happiness A641

God of Joy — A642

No. 2766, God of Wealth. No. 2768, God of Longevity.

1991, Feb. 7 Litho. *Perf. 13½*

2765	A641	$3 shown		.50	.25
2766	A641	$3 multi		.50	.25
2767	A642	$7.50 shown		1.10	.25
2768	A642	$7.50 multi		1.10	.25
		Nos. 2765-2768 (4)		3.20	1.00

Perf. 13½ Vert.

2765a	A641	$3		*1.20*	.25
2766a	A641	$3		*1.20*	.25
2767a	A642	$7.50		*1.20*	.25
2768a	A642	$7.50		*1.20*	.25
b.		Bklt. pane of 8, 2 each #2765a-2768a + label		*11.50*	

Native Plants A643

Designs: $2, Petasites formosanus. $3, Heloniopsis acutifolia. $7.50, Disporum shimadai. $9, Viola nagasawai.

1991, Mar. 12 Litho. *Perf. 13½*

2769	A643	$2	multicolored	.50	.25
2770	A643	$3	multicolored	.55	.25
2771	A643	$7.50	multicolored	.90	.30
2772	A643	$9	multicolored	1.10	.35

1991, June 12

Designs: $2, Gaultheria itoana. $3, Lysionotus montanus. $7.50, Leontopodium microphyllum. $9, Gentiana flavo-maculata.

2773	A643	$2	multicolored	.30	.25
2774	A643	$3	multicolored	.45	.25
2775	A643	$7.50	multicolored	1.10	.30
2776	A643	$9	multicolored	1.30	.35

1991, Sept. 12

Designs: $3.50, Rosa transmorrisonensis. $5, Impatiens devolii. $9, Impatiens uniflora. $12, Impatiens tayemonii.

2777	A643	$3.50	multicolored	.40	.25
2778	A643	$5	multicolored	.55	.25
2779	A643	$9	multicolored	1.00	.30
2780	A643	$12	multicolored	1.20	.35

1991, Dec. 12

Designs: $3.50, Kalanchoe garambiensis. $5, Pieris taiwanensis. $9, Pleione formosana. $12, Elaeagnus oldhamii.

2781	A643	$3.50	multicolored	.40	.25
2782	A643	$5	multicolored	.55	.25
2783	A643	$9	multicolored	.75	.45
2784	A643	$12	multicolored	1.00	.55
		Nos. 2769-2784 (16)		12.05	4.95

Hsiung Cheng-Chi (1887-1910), Revolutionary A644

1991, Mar. 28 Engr. *Perf. 13½x12½*

2785	A644	$3	blue	.80	.25

Republic of China, 80th Anniv. A645

$3, Agriculture. $7.50, Science & technology. $12, Cultural activities. $16, Transportation.

1991, Mar. 28 Litho. *Perf. 13½*

2786	A645	$3	multicolored	.35	.25
2787	A645	$7.50	multicolored	.65	.30
2788	A645	$12	multicolored	1.10	.50
2789	A645	$16	multicolored	1.25	.75
		Nos. 2786-2789 (4)		3.35	1.80

Children's Toys — A646

No. 2790, Bamboo pony. No. 2791, Woven-grass grasshopper. No. 2792, Top. No. 2793, Pinwheels.

1991, Apr. 20 Litho. *Perf. 13½*

2790	A646	$3	multicolored	.50	.25
2791	A646	$3	multicolored	.50	.25
2792	A646	$3	multicolored	.50	.25
2793	A646	$3	multicolored	.50	.25
a.		Souv. sheet of 4, #2790-2793		*6.50*	3.50
		Nos. 2790-2793 (4)		2.00	1.00

See Nos. 2840-2843. Compare with designs A676, A696.

No. 2793a exists with a red overprint in Chinese characters in the selvage. The overprinted sheet was sold at an exhibition in Singapore. Value, $23.

Perf. 13½ Vert.

2790a	A646	$3		*1.00*	.25
2791a	A646	$3		*1.00*	.25
2792a	A646	$3		*1.00*	.25
2793b	A646	$3		*1.00*	.25
c.		Bklt. pane, 2 each #2790a-2793b + label		*8.00*	
		Nos. 2790a-2793b (4)		4.00	1.00

Folk Costumes — A647

Ch'ing Dynasty (1644-1911): $2, Winter court hat, Mang robe. $3, Summer court hat, surcoat. $7.50, Winter overcoat. $12, Common hat, traveling robe.

1991, June 29 Litho. *Perf. 13½*

2794	A647	$2	multicolored	.60	.25
2795	A647	$3	multicolored	.75	.25
2796	A647	$7.50	multicolored	1.90	.25
2797	A647	$12	multicolored	2.50	.35
		Nos. 2794-2797 (4)		5.75	1.10

See note after No. 2663.

Nos. 2794-2797 have groups of one and five Chinese characters.

Traffic Safety Year A648

$7.50, Don't drink & drive.

1991, July 17 Litho. *Perf. 13½*

2798	A648	$3	shown	.40	.25
2799	A648	$7.50	multicolored	1.40	.30

Cloisonne Enamel Lions, Ch'ing Dynasty (1644-1911)
A649 A649a

1991, July 20 Litho. *Perf. 12½*

2800	A649	yel grn & multi		.55	.25
2801	A649a	violet & multi		2.25	.60
		Nos. 2800-2801 (2)		2.80	.85

No. 2800 paid basic domestic rate, No. 2801 paid basic express mail rate on date of issue.

Fruits — A650

1991, Aug. 10 Litho. *Perf. 14x13½*

2802	A650	$3	Strawberry	.30	.25
2803	A650	$7.50	Grapes	.55	.40
2804	A650	$9	Mango	.75	.50
2805	A650	$16	Sugar apple	1.25	.75
		Nos. 2802-2805 (4)		2.85	1.90

Birds — A651

Designs: a, Myiophoneus insularis. b, Cinclus pallasii. c, Aix galericulata. d, Nycticorax nycticorax. e, Egretta garzetta. f, Rhyacornis fuliginosus. g, Enicurus scouleri. h, Motacilla cinerea. i, Alcedo atthis. j, Motacilla alba.

1991, Aug. 24 *Perf. 13½*

2806		Block of 10		5.75	3.25
a.-j.		A651 $5 any single		.40	.25

Outdoor Activities A652

Wmk. 323

1991, Sept. 27 Litho. *Perf. 13½*

2807	A652	$2	Rock climbing	.25	.25
2808	A652	$3	Fishing	.35	.25
2809	A652	$7.50	Bird watching	.70	.30
2810	A652	$10	Playing in water	1.00	.40
		Nos. 2807-2810 (4)		2.30	1.20

Intl. Federation of Camping and Caravaning, 1991 Rally.

Lighthouse Type of 1989
Inscription Panel in Blue

1991-92 *Perf. 13½*

2811	A612	50c	like #2683C	.25	.25
2812	A612	$1	like #2674	.35	.25
2813	A612	$3.50	like #2678	.25	.25
2814	A612	$5	like #2679	.45	.25
a.		Booklet pane of 10		4.00	
2815	A612	$7	like #2676	.50	.25
2816	A612	$9	like #2681	.75	.25
2817	A612	$10	like #2682	.90	.35
2818	A612	$12	like #2683A	1.00	.40
a.		$12 Bklt. pane of 5 + label		5.00	
2819	A612	$13	like #2675	1.00	.40
2820	A612	$19	like #2680	1.50	.65
2821	A612	$20	like #2683B	1.60	.65
2822	A612	$26	like #2683	1.75	.90
2823	A612	$28	like #2684	1.75	.90
		Nos. 2811-2823 (13)		12.05	5.75

Issued: 50c, $3.50, $5, $12, 10/2; No. 2818a, 9/26/92; $1, $19, $20, 3/2/92; $26, $28, 5/20/92; $7, $9, $10, $13, 8/21/92.

Peacocks by Lan Shih-ning (Giuseppe Castiglione, 1688-1768) A653

$20, Peacock spreading tail feathers.

Perf. 12x11½

1991, Oct. 30 Photo. Unwmk.

Granite Paper

2826	A653	$5	multicolored	.90	.30
2827	A653	$20	multicolored	3.25	.80
a.		Souvenir sheet of 1		5.00	4.25

New Year 1992 (Year of the Monkey) — A654

Wmk. 323

1991, Nov. 30 Litho. *Perf. 12½*

2828	A654	$3.50	orange & multi	.50	.25
2829	A654	$13	tan & multi	1.75	.50
a.		Souv. sheet, 2 ea #2828-2829		5.50	2.00

Chinese Books A655

$3.50, Scroll. $5, Fold bindings. $9, Butterfly bindings. $15, String bindings.

Wmk. 323

1992, Jan. 17 Litho. *Perf. 13½*

2830	A655	$3.50	multicolored	.25	.25
2831	A655	$5	multicolored	.65	.25
2832	A655	$9	multicolored	1.25	.25
2833	A655	$15	multicolored	1.90	.50
		Nos. 2830-2833 (4)		4.05	1.25

Good Fortune and Satisfaction A656

Five Blessings Upon the House — A657

Nienhwa paintings: No. 2835, Peace in the Wake of Firecrackers. No. 2837, An Abundance for Every Year.

1992, Jan. 27 Litho. *Perf. 13½*

2834	A656	$5	multicolored	.55	.25
2835	A656	$5	multicolored	.55	.25
2836	A657	$12	multicolored	1.45	.50
2837	A657	$12	multicolored	1.45	.50
a.		Bklt. pane, 2 each #2834-2837 + label		*4.00*	
		Nos. 2834-2837 (4)		4.00	1.50

Lunar New Year.

A658

Lunar New Year: a, like #2664. b, like #2611. c, like #2565. d, like #2493. e, like #2442. f, like #2390. g, like #2346. h, like #2273. i, like #2217. j, like #2828. k, like #2757. l, like #2706.

Wmk. 323

1992, Feb. 18 Litho. *Perf. 12½*

2838 A658 $5 Block of 12, #a.-l., ver & multi 7.50 2.75
m. Sheet of 12, #2838a-2838 l 8.00 3.00

A659

Trees: a, Chamaecyparis formosensis. b, Chamaecyparis taiwanensis. c, Calocedrus formosana. d, Cunninghamia konishii. e. Taiwania crypto- merioides.

1992, Mar. 12 *Perf. 13½*

2839 A659 $5 Strip of 5, #a.-e. 3.00 1.50

Children's Toys Type of 1991

1992, Apr. 29 Litho. *Perf. 13½*

2840 A646 $5 Walking on iron pots .75 .25
a. Perf. 13½ vert. .55 .25
2841 A646 $5 Chopstick gun .75 .25
a. Perf. 13½ vert. .55 .25
2842 A646 $5 Hoop rolling .75 .25
a. Perf. 13½ vert. .55 .25
2843 A646 $5 Grass fighting .75 .25
a. Sheet of 4, #2840-2843 *4.75 4.75*
b. As "a," imperf. (simulated perfs), red inscription in sheet margin *13.00 13.00*
c. Perf. 13½ vert. .55 .25
d. Bklt. pane, 2 each #2840a-2842a, 2843c + label 4.75
Nos. 2840-2843 (4) 3.00 1.00

Issue date: No. 2843b, May 15.

A660

Mother and son in: $3.50, Spring. $5, Summer. $9, Autumn. $10, Winter.

Wmk. 323

1992, May 9 Litho. *Perf. 13½*

2844 A660 $3.50 multicolored .25 .25
2845 A660 $5 multicolored .55 .25
2846 A660 $9 multicolored 1.00 .30
2847 A660 $10 multicolored 1.10 .35
Nos. 2844-2847 (4) 2.90 1.15

Parent-child relationships.

A661

Glassware Decorated with Enamel — Vases: $3.50, Faceted, decorated with bats and longevity characters. $5, Double-lobed, with children at play. $7, Flowered. $17, Tutoring scene.

Wmk. 323

1992, June 25 Litho. *Perf. 13½*

Background colors

2848 A661 $3.50 pink .25 .25
2849 A661 $5 green .50 .25
2850 A661 $7 bister .75 .25
2851 A661 $17 blue 2.25 .55
Nos. 2848-2851 (4) 3.75 1.30

Stone Lion of Lugouqiao A662

Various stone lions.

Wmk. 323

1992, July 7 Engr. *Perf. 13½*

2852 A662 $5 olive grn & pur .50 .25
2853 A662 $5 blue & brown .50 .25
2854 A662 $12 org & olive grn 1.10 .40
2855 A662 $12 purple & black 1.10 .40
Nos. 2852-2855 (4) 3.20 1.30

Compare with designs A614, A629, A663.

Ku Shih Classical Poetry — A663

Excerpts: $3.50, "Flesh and body are as closely linked as leaves to a tree." $5, "Once a man and woman get married, conjugal love will last forever without doubt." $9, "Man takes pains to uphold virtue." $15, "Tartar horses lean toward the northern wind."

1992, Aug. 8 Litho.

2856 A663 $3.50 Children playing near tree .25 .25
2857 A663 $5 Man & woman .65 .25
2858 A663 $9 Couple near stream 1.15 .30
2859 A663 $15 Horse, tree 1.60 .50
Nos. 2856-2859 (4) 3.65 1.30

Life in the Countryside A664

Scenes of temple fair: a, Two women, man beating drum, crowd. b, Vendor with basket. c, People playing musical instruments. d, Man with food cart. e, Women with umbrella, basket.

Wmk. 323

1992, Sept. 22 Litho. *Perf. 11½*

2860 A664 $5 Strip of 5, #a.-e. 4.00 2.75

Silk Tapestries A665

Ming Dynasty Silk Tapestry Drawing on Life: $5, Two Birds Perched on a Red Camellia Branch. $12, Two Birds Playing on a Peach Branch.

1992, Oct. 9 Litho. *Perf. 11½*

Granite Paper

2861 A665 $5 multicolored .65 .25
2862 A665 $12 multicolored 1.75 .50
a. Sheet of 2, #2861-2862 2.75 .75

Chinese Opera A666

Actors, props: $3.50, Nin Hsiang-ju's carting to a party from "The General and Premier." $5, Hsao En rowing a boat from "The Lucky Pearl." $9, Wang Chao-chun making peace with the frontier from "Chao-chun Serves as an Envoy." $12, Scene with red sedan chair from "Escort to the Wedding."

Wmk. 323

1992, Oct. 21 Litho. *Perf. 13½*

2863 A666 $3.50 multicolored .25 .25
2864 A666 $5 multicolored .60 .25
2865 A666 $9 multicolored 1.05 .30
2866 A666 $12 multicolored 1.00 .45
Nos. 2863-2866 (4) 2.90 1.25

Alishan Forest Railway — A667

1992, Nov. 5 *Perf. 11½*

2867 A667 $5 Steam engine .55 .25
2868 A667 $15 Diesel engine 1.20 .50

Endangered Mammals of Taiwan A668

Designs: a, Lutra lutra chinensis. b, Pteropus dasymallus formosus. c, Neofelis nebulosa brachyurus. d, Selenarctos thibetanus formosanus.

Perf. 11½x12

1992, Nov. 25 Photo. Unwmk.

Granite Paper

2869 A668 $5 Block of 4, #a.-d. 3.00 1.25

New Year 1993 (Year of the Rooster) — A669

Design: $13, Rooster facing left.

Wmk. 323

1992, Dec. 1 Litho. *Perf. 12½*

2870 A669 $3.50 red & multi .55 .25
a. Perf. 13½ vert. .40 .25
2871 A669 $13 pur & multi 1.35 .35
a. Souv. sheet, 2 ea #2870-2871 4.75 4.75
b. As "a" with added inscription in border 4.75 4.75
c. Bklt. pane, 5 ea #2870-2871 8.00
d. Perf. 13½ vert. 1.00 .40
e. Booklet pane, 6 each #2870a, 2871d + label 8.75

Inscription on No. 2871b reads "Philippine Stamp Exhibition 1992-Taipei" in English and Chinese.

Johann Adam Schall von Bell (1592-1666), Astronomer and Missionary — A670

1992 Dec. 10 *Perf. 11½*

2872 A670 $5 multicolored .75 .25

Traditional Nienhwas of Window Frames — A671

Wmk. 323

1993, Jan. 7 Litho. *Perf. 11½*

Background Color

2873 A671 $5 brt green .25 .25
2874 A671 $5 pink .25 .25
2875 A671 $12 yellow 1.05 .40
2876 A671 $12 red 1.05 .40
Nos. 2873-2876 (4) 2.60 1.30

Lunar New Year.

Perf. 13½ Vert.

2873a A671 $5 *1.00* .45
2874a A671 $5 *1.00* .45
2875a A671 $12 *1.00* .45
2876a A671 $12 *1.00* .45
b. Booklet pane, 2 each #2873a-2876a + label *9.00*

Nos. 2873a-2876a are 29x43mm.

Traditional Crafts A672

$3.50, Clip & paste moldings. $5, Lanterns. $9, Pottery jars. $15, Oil paper umbrella.

1993, Jan. 16

2877 A672 $3.50 multi .25 .25
2878 A672 $5 multi .40 .25
2879 A672 $9 multi .90 .30
2880 A672 $15 multi 1.35 .50
Nos. 2877-2880 (4) 2.90 1.30

Chinese Creation Story — A673

Designs: $3.50, Pan Gu's creation of the universe, vert. $5, Pan Gu transmitted himself into all creatures. $9, Nu Wa created human beings with pestled earth. $19, Nu Wa mended sky with smelted stone, vert.

1993, Feb. 6 *Perf. 12x11½, 11½x12*

2881 A673 $3.50 multicolored .25 .25
2882 A673 $5 multicolored .55 .25
2883 A673 $9 multicolored 1.05 .50
2884 A673 $19 multicolored 2.00 1.10
Nos. 2881-2884 (4) 3.85 2.10

Lucky Animals — A674

$3.50, Mandarin duck. $5, Chinese unicorn. $10, Deer. $15, Crane.

Wmk. 323

1993, Mar. 2 Litho. *Perf. 13½*

2885	A674	$3.50 multi	.25	.25
2886	A674	$5 multi	.40	.25
2887	A674	$10 multi	.90	.40
2888	A674	$15 multi	1.35	1.00
		Nos. 2885-2888 (4)	2.90	1.90

See Nos. 2920-2923.

Water Plants — A675

$5, Nymphaea x hybrida. $9, Nuphar shimadai. $12, Eichhornia crassipes.

1993, Mar. 12 *Perf. 11½*

2889	A675	$5 multicolored	.50	.25
2890	A675	$9 multicolored	.75	.30
2891	A675	$12 multicolored	1.00	.40
		Nos. 2889-2891 (3)	2.25	.95

A676

No. 2892, Sandbag tossing. No. 2893, Bamboo dragonfly twisting. No. 2894, Rubber band skipping. No. 2895, Waist-strength dueling.

1993 Litho. Wmk. 323 *Perf. 11½*

2892	A676	$5 multicolored	.50	.30
2893	A676	$5 multicolored	.50	.30
2894	A676	$5 multicolored	.50	.30
2895	A676	$5 multicolored	.50	.30
a.		Souv. sheet, #2892-2895	3.00	3.00
b.		As "a," with green & black inscriptions in border	3.25	3.25
c.		As "a," with red inscription in border	3.00	3.00
		Nos. 2892-2895 (4)	2.00	1.20

Inscriptions on No. 2895b read "AUSTRALIAN STAMP EXHIBITION 1993-TAIPEI" in Chinese and English.

Inscription on No. 2895c reads "Chinese Stamp Exhibition-Thailand" in Chinese.

Nos. 2895b-2895c each have perforations extending into the margin at top (No. 2895c) or bottom (No. 2895b).

Issue dates: Nos. 2892-2895, 2895a, Apr. 20; No. 2895b, Apr. 23; No. 2895c, Apr. 30.

Perf. 13½ Vert.

2892a	A676	$5	.90	.30
2893a	A676	$5	.90	.30
2894a	A676	$5	.90	.30
2895d	A676	$5	.90	.30
e.		Bklt. pane, 2 each #2892a-2894a, 2895d + label	7.50	

A677

Yangtze River A678

Designs: No. 2896, Source on Ching-Kang-Chang Plateau. No. 2897, Abrupt bend, Chinsha River. No. 2898, Narrow waterway, Roaring Tiger Gorge, Chinsha River. No. 2899, Sheer cliffs, Chuntang Gorge. $9, Three Small Gorges (Dragon Gate, Pawu, and Titsui).

Perf. 13x13½

1993, May 15 Litho. Wmk. 323

2896	A677	$3.50 shown	.25	.25
2897	A677	$3.50 multicolored	.25	.25
2898	A678	$5 shown	.60	.25
2899	A677	$5 multicolored	.60	.25
2900	A677	$9 multicolored	1.10	.30
		Nos. 2896-2900 (5)	2.80	1.30

Environmental Protection
A679 A680

Children's paintings: $5, No More Noise Pollution, by Yen Chao-min. $17, Clothing My Hometown with Green, by Hu Hui-chun.

Perf. 12½x13½, 13½x12½

1993, June 5

2901	A679	$5 multicolored	.55	.25
2902	A680	$17 multicolored	1.60	1.00

Ch'eng-hua Porcelain, Natl. Palace Museum A681

Cups decorated in tou-ts'ai: $3.50, Human figures. $5, Chickens. $7, Flowers and fruits. $9, Dragon.

1993, June 30 *Perf. 12*

2903	A681	$3.50 multicolored	.25	.25
2904	A681	$5 multicolored	.65	.25
2905	A681	$7 multicolored	.90	.40
2906	A681	$9 multicolored	1.10	.65
		Nos. 2903-2906 (4)	2.90	1.55

Vocational Training A682

$3.50, Graphic artist. $5, Computer operator. $9, Carpenter. $12, Welder.

Wmk. 323

1993, July 24 Litho. *Perf. 12½*

2907	A682	$3.50 multicolored	.25	.25
2908	A682	$5 multicolored	.45	.25
2909	A682	$9 multicolored	.90	.50
2910	A682	$12 multicolored	1.25	.75
		Nos. 2907-2910 (4)	2.85	1.75

Parent-Child Relationship A683

Silhouettes: $3.50, Adult carrying child on shoulders. $5, Father playing flute for daughter. $9, Father teaching daughter. $10, Father, adult son enjoying wildlife.

Wmk. 323

1993, Aug. 4 Litho. *Perf. 11½*

Background Color

2911	A683	$3.50 tan	.25	.25
2912	A683	$5 green	.40	.25
2913	A683	$9 lilac	.85	.55
2914	A683	$10 red brown	1.00	.65
		Nos. 2911-2914 (4)	2.50	1.70

Souvenir Sheet

Taipei '93, Asian Intl. Philatelic Exhibition — A684

Enjoying Antiques, by Tu Chin, 15th cent: a, Man carrying stick. b, Man selecting antiques from table. c, Man seated in chair. d, Two people at table.

Perf. 12x11½

1993, Aug. 14 Photo. Unwmk.

Granite Paper

2915	A684	$5 Sheet of 4, #a.-d.	3.25	2.40

Persimmon A685 Loquat A686

1993, Sept. 10 Litho. *Perf. 12½*

2916	A685	$5 shown	.60	.25
2917	A685	$5 Peach	.60	.25
2918	A686	$12 shown	1.50	.75
2919	A686	$12 Papaya	1.50	.75
		Nos. 2916-2919 (4)	4.20	2.00

Lucky Animals Type of 1993

Wmk. 323

1993, Sept. 29 Litho. *Perf. 13½*

2920	A674	$1 Blue dragon	.25	.25
2921	A674	$2.50 White tiger	.25	.25
2922	A674	$9 Linnet	.80	.40
2923	A674	$19 Black tortoise	1.50	.90
		Nos. 2920-2923 (4)	2.80	1.80

Taiwan Area Games, Taoyuan — A687

Designs: a, Taekwondo. b, Pommel horse.

Wmk. 323

1993, Oct. 20 Litho. *Perf. 12½*

2924	A687	$5 Pair, #a.-b.	1.00	.65

Stone Lions — A688

Stone lions from: $3.50, Taipei New Park. $5, Hsinchu City Council. $9, Hsinchu City God Temple. $12, Fort Providentia, Tainan.

1993, Oct. 30

2925	A688	$3.50 multicolored	.25	.25
2926	A688	$5 multicolored	.35	.25
2927	A688	$9 multicolored	.75	.45
2928	A688	$12 multicolored	1.00	.60
		Nos. 2925-2928 (4)	2.35	1.55

Syrmaticus Mikado A689

Designs: a, Hatchling. b, Mother with chicks. c, Immature female, male. d, Adult female, male (profile, showing plumage).

Perf. 11½

1993, Nov. 17 Photo. Unwmk.

Granite Paper

2929	A689	$5 Strip of 4, #a.-d.	2.25	1.60

New Year 1994 (Year of the Dog) — A690

Design: $13, Dog facing left.

Wmk. 323

1993, Dec. 1 Litho. *Perf. 12½*

2930	A690	$3.50 red & multi	.25	.25
a.		Perf. 13½ vert.	.50	.25
b.		As "a," bklt. pane of 12 + label	3.00	
2931	A690	$13 green & multi	1.10	.55
a.		Souv. sheet, 2 ea #2930-2931	2.75	1.60
b.		As "a," overprinted in red	3.00	1.60

No. 2931b is inscribed in Chinese for Kaohsiung Kuo-kuang Stamp Exhibition-1993, and has additional perforations extending into top and bottom margins.

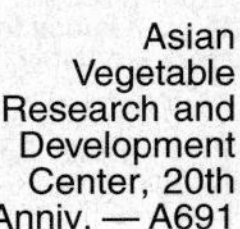

Asian Vegetable Research and Development Center, 20th Anniv. — A691

$13, Researchers in field.

1993, Dec. 7

2932	A691	$5 shown	.30	.25
2933	A691	$13 multicolored	1.00	.75

Formation of Constitutional Court — A692

Wmk. 323

1994, Jan. 11 Litho. *Perf. 12½*

2934	A692	$5 multicolored	.75	.30

Paper Making — A693

Designs: No. 2935, Cutting bamboo. No. 2936, Cooking bamboo. No. 2937, Pouring syrup into wooden panel. No. 2938, Stacking panel. No. 2939, Drying paper.

1994, Jan. 24 *Perf. 12x12½*

2935	A693	$3.50 multicolored	.25	.25
2936	A693	$3.50 multicolored	.25	.25
2937	A693	$5 multicolored	.50	.25
2938	A693	$5 multicolored	.50	.25
2939	A693	$12 multicolored	1.00	.65
		Nos. 2935-2939 (5)	2.50	1.65

See Nos. 2993-2997, 3071-3075, 3098-3102, 3174-3177.

Flowers — A694

$5, Clivia miniata. $12, Cymbidium sinense. $19, Primula malacoides.

1994, Feb. 17 *Perf. 12½*

2940	A694	$5 multicolored	.30	.25
2941	A694	$12 multicolored	.90	.60
2942	A694	$19 multicolored	1.35	1.00
		Nos. 2940-2942 (3)	2.55	1.85

Kinmen Wind Lion Lords — A695

Various Wind Lion Lords.

1994, Mar. 18 Litho. *Perf. 12½*

2943	A695	$5 green & multi	.40	.25
2944	A695	$9 yellow & multi	.60	.40
2945	A695	$12 org yel & multi	.95	.50
2946	A695	$17 blue & multi	1.15	.75
		Nos. 2943-2946 (4)	3.10	1.90

Children at Play — A696

No. 2947, Playing with paper boat. No. 2948, Fighting with water gun. No. 2949, Throwing paper airplane. No. 2950, Playing "train" with rope.

Wmk. 323

1994, Apr. 2 Litho. *Perf. 12½*

2947	A696	$5 multicolored	.40	.25
2948	A696	$5 multicolored	.40	.25
2949	A696	$5 multicolored	.40	.25
2950	A696	$5 multicolored	.40	.25
a.		Souv. sheet, #2947-2950	2.00	1.25
		Nos. 2947-2950 (4)	1.60	1.00

Perf. 13½ Vert.

2947a	A696	$5	.45	.25
2948a	A696	$5	.45	.25
2949a	A696	$5	.45	.25
2950b	A696	$5	.45	.25
c.		Bklt. pane, 2 ea #2947a-2949a, 2950b + label	3.50	1.50
		Nos. 2947a-2950b (4)	1.80	1.00

A697

Life in the countryside: $5, Playing chess. $10, Playing musical instruments. $12, Telling stories. $19, Drinking tea.

Wmk. 323

1994, Apr. 25 Litho. *Perf. 12½*

2951	A697	$5 multicolored	.25	.25
2952	A697	$10 multicolored	.60	.50
2953	A697	$12 multicolored	.80	.70
2954	A697	$19 multicolored	1.15	1.00
		Nos. 2951-2954 (4)	2.80	2.45

A698

Mother, baby birds: $5, Malay bittern. $7, Little tern, horiz. $10, Common noddy, horiz. $12, Muller's barbet.

1994, May 7

2955	A698	$5 multicolored	.35	.30
2956	A698	$7 multicolored	.55	.35
2957	A698	$10 multicolored	.90	.50
2958	A698	$12 multicolored	1.00	.60
		Nos. 2955-2958 (4)	2.80	1.75

A699

Protection of Intellectual Property Rights: $5, Palm-shaped book. $15, Human head, computer disk.

Wmk. 323

1994, May 28 Litho. *Perf. 12½*

2959	A699	$5 multicolored	.50	.25
2960	A699	$15 multicolored	1.25	.75

A700

Designs: $5, Care for Lost Children. $17, Care for the aged.

1994, June 11

2961	A700	$5 multicolored	.25	.25
2962	A700	$17 multicolored	.90	.60

Intl. Olympic Committee, Cent. — A701

1994, June 23

2963	A701	$5 shown	.40	.25
2964	A701	$15 Sporting events	1.20	.75

A702

Shei-pa Natl. Park: $5, Tapachienshan. $7, Shei-san Landslide Scar. $10, Holy Ridge. $17, Shiah-tsuei Lake.

Wmk. 323

1994, July 1 Litho. *Perf. 12½*

2965	A702	$5 multicolored	.45	.25
2966	A702	$7 multicolored	.55	.35
2967	A702	$10 multicolored	.90	.50
2968	A702	$17 multicolored	1.40	.90
		Nos. 2965-2968 (4)	3.30	2.00

A703

$5, Portrait of Chien Mu (b. 1895), educator.

1994, July 30 *Perf. 11½x12*

2969	A703	$5 multicolored	.75	.25

Intl. Year of the Family A704

$5, Rainbow, window. $15, Globe, house.

1994, Aug. 25 *Perf. 11½*

2970	A704	$5 multicolored	.40	.25
2971	A704	$15 yel & multi	1.20	.75

Invention Myths — A705

Designs: $5, Sueirenjy digging wood to obtain fire. $10, Fushijy drawing Pa-Kua. $12, Shennungjy making agricultural tools. $15, Tsang-jier creating written characters.

1994, Sept. 17 Photo. *Perf. 11½*

Granite Paper

2972	A705	$5 multicolored	.40	.25
2973	A705	$10 multicolored	.85	.50
2974	A705	$12 multicolored	1.00	.75
2975	A705	$15 multicolored	1.25	.85
		Nos. 2972-2975 (4)	3.50	2.35

A706

Design: $5, Dr. Lin Yutang, linguist, writer, 100th birthday.

Wmk. 323

1994, Oct. 8 Litho. *Perf. 12½*

2976	A706	$5 multicolored	.45	.30

A707

$5, Cheng Ho's ship. $17, Chart, ship, Cheng Ho.

1994, Oct. 17

2977	A707	$5 multicolored	.40	.25
2978	A707	$17 multicolored	1.20	.75

World Trade Week.

Sun Yat-sen, Founding of Kuomintang, Cent. — A708

Design: $19, Democratic elections, factories, economic development.

Wmk. 323

1994, Nov. 24 Litho. *Perf. 12½*

2979	A708	$5 multicolored	.50	.25
2980	A708	$19 multicolored	1.75	.90

A709

1994, Nov. 29

2981	A709	$3.50 Facing right	.35	.25
a.		Perf. 13½ vert.	.35	.25
b.		As "a," booklet pane of 6	2.00	
		Complete booklet, 2 #2981b + label	4.00	
2982	A709	$13 Facing left	1.10	.75
a.		Souv. sheet, 2 ea #2981-2982	2.90	2.00

New Year 1995 (Year of the Boar).

A710

$5, Portrait. $15, Greeting farm family.

1994, Dec. 24 Litho. *Perf. 12½*

2983	A710	$5 multicolored	.40	.25
2984	A710	$15 multicolored	1.20	.75

Pres. Yen Chia-kan, 1st death anniv.

Horse's Back Roofline A711

Swallow's Tail Roofline — A711a

Talisman (Stove & Bowl) Roofline — A711b

Cylinder-Shaped Brick Roofline — A711c

Traditional Architecture: Roof lines.

Perf. 12½x12

1995, Jan. 10 Litho. Wmk. 323

2985	A711	$5 multicolored	.35	.25
2986	A711a	$5 multicolored	.35	.25
2987	A711b	$12 multicolored	1.00	.60
2988	A711c	$19 multicolored	1.50	1.00
		Nos. 2985-2988 (4)	3.20	2.10

See Nos. 3079-3082, 3113-3116, 3187-3190, 3235-3238.

Ancient Chinese Engravings — A712

Various floral designs.

1995, Jan. 24 *Perf. 13½*

Denomination in Black

2989	A712	$3.50 multicolored	.25	.25
2990	A712	$5 multicolored	.50	.25
2991	A712	$19 multicolored	1.40	1.00
2992	A712	$26 multicolored	2.25	1.40
		Nos. 2989-2992 (4)	4.40	2.90

See Nos. 3018-3021, 3044-3047, 3076-3078, 3178-3181, 3221-3226, 3254-3256, 3299-3300.

Ancient Skills Type of 1994

Methods of irrigation: No. 2993, Water wheel. No. 2994, Gear-driven bucket lift. $5, Pedal-powered hoist. $12, Hand-cranked hoist. $13, Using pole with counter-weight to raise bucket.

Perf. 12x11½

1994, Feb. 14 Litho. Wmk. 323

2993	A693	$3.50	multicolored	.25	.25
2994	A693	$3.50	multicolored	.25	.25
2995	A693	$5	multicolored	4.00	.25
2996	A693	$12	multicolored	1.00	.70
2997	A693	$13	multicolored	1.10	.75
	Nos. 2993-2997 (5)			6.60	2.20

Beauties on an Outing, by Lee Gong-lin — A713

a, Two riders. b, Rider on black horse, woman with child on horse. c, Three riders. d, One rider.

Unwmk.

1995, Mar. 3 Photo. *Perf. 12*

Granite Paper

2998	A713 $9 Strip of 4, #a.-d.		3.25	2.00
e.	Souv. sheet, #2998b-2998c		1.75	1.00

No. 2998 is a continuous design.

Natl. Health Insurance Plan — A714

Perf. 11½x12½

1995, Mar. 1 Litho. Wmk. 323

2999	A714	$12	multicolored	1.75	.80

Flowers — A715

$5, Lilium speciosum. $12, Haemanthus multiflorus. $19, Hyacinthus orientalis.

1995, Mar. 20 Litho. *Perf. 12½*

3000	A715	$5	multicolored	.30	.25
3001	A715	$12	multicolored	.75	.60
3002	A715	$19	multicolored	1.50	1.00
	Nos. 3000-3002 (3)			2.55	1.85

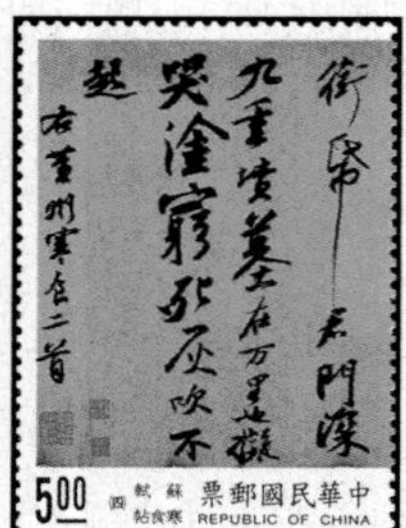

Chinese Calligraphy A716

Cold Food Observance, poem by Su Shih, red inscriptions at: a, Lower left. b, Middle. c, Upper right. d, Right half of design.

1995, Apr. 6 *Perf. 13½*

3003	Strip of 4	3.50	2.25
a.-d.	A716 $5 any single	.40	.25

Paintings by Tsou I Kuei's — A717

1995, May 5 Photo. *Die Cut*

Self-Adhesive

3004	A717	$5	Red peony	.60	.25
3005	A717	$5	Pink peony	.60	.25
a.	Bklt. pane, 9 ea #3004-3005			12.50	

By its nature, No. 3005a is a complete booklet. The peelable backing serves as a booklet cover.

Campaign Against Illegal Drugs — A718

$15, Arm, hypodermic needle.

Wmk. 323

1995, June 1 Litho. *Perf. 12½*

3006	A718	$5	shown	.40	.25
3007	A718	$15	multicolored	1.10	.75

Natl. Taiwan University Hospital, Cent. — A719

Designs: $5, Medical treatment, old hospital. $19, Medical research, new hospital.

1995, June 20

3008	A719	$5	multicolored	.50	.25
3009	A719	$19	multicolored	1.40	1.00

East Coast Scenes A720

Designs: No. 3010, Green hills above Chichi Bay. No. 3011, Rocky promontory, Shihyuesan. $12, Hsiaoyehlieu. $15, Changhong Bridge.

Wmk. 323

1995, July 1 Litho. *Perf. 12½*

3010	A720	$5	multicolored	.40	.25
3011	A720	$5	multicolored	.40	.25
3012	A720	$12	multicolored	1.00	.65
3013	A720	$15	multicolored	1.40	.90
	Nos. 3010-3013 (4)			3.20	2.05

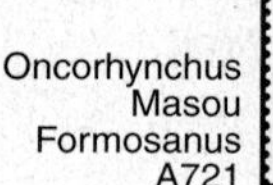

Oncorhynchus Masou Formosanus A721

Designs: $5, Mating. $7, Female digging a spot to lay eggs. $10, Hatching of fry. $17, Fry swimming in river.

Perf. 14x14½

1995, July 27 Litho. Unwmk.

3014	A721	$5	multicolored	.40	.25
3015	A721	$7	multicolored	.60	.40
3016	A721	$10	multicolored	.75	.60
3017	A721	$17	multicolored	1.40	1.00
	Nos. 3014-3017 (4)			3.15	2.25

Ancient Chinese Engraving Type

Various pictures of birds on tree branches.

Wmk. 323

1995, Aug. 18 Litho. *Perf. 13½*

Denomination in Black

3018	A712	$2.50	multicolored	.25	.25
3019	A712	$7	multicolored	.60	.35
3020	A712	$13	multicolored	1.10	.80
3021	A712	$28	multicolored	2.75	1.60
	Nos. 3018-3021 (4)			4.70	3.00

Marine Life — A722

No. 3022, Tubastraea aurea. No. 3023, Chromodoris elizabethina. $5, Spirobranchus gigateus. $17, Himerometra magnipinna.

Wmk. 323

1995, Sept. 7 Litho. *Perf. 12½*

3022	A722	$3.50	multicolored	.25	.25
3023	A722	$3.50	multicolored	.25	.25
3024	A722	$5	multicolored	.50	.30
3025	A722	$17	multicolored	1.50	.80
	Nos. 3022-3025 (4)			2.50	1.60

Louis Pasteur (1822-95) — A723

1995, Sept. 20

3026	A723	$17	multicolored	1.40	.80

Natl. Palace Museum, 70th Anniv. A724

Designs: No. 3027, Painting, "Strange Peaks and Myriad Trees." No. 3028, Greenish blue porcelain vase, vert. $5, Bronze X Fu-K'uei Ting vessel, vert. $26, Calligraphy of quatrain in seven-character verse, "The Fragrance of Flowers."

Perf. 12x11½, 11½x12

1995, Oct. 9 Photo. Unwmk.

3027	A724	$3.50	multicolored	.30	.25
3028	A724	$3.50	multicolored	.30	.25
3029	A724	$5	multicolored	.50	.25
3030	A724	$26	multicolored	2.40	1.50
	Nos. 3027-3030 (4)			3.50	2.25

A725

End of World War II, 50th Anniv.: $5, Chinese soldiers in battle. $19, Flag, outline map of Taiwan, presidential mansion.

Perf. 11½x12

1995, Oct. 24 Litho. Wmk. 323

3031	A725	$5	multicolored	.60	.25
3032	A725	$19	multicolored	2.10	.65
a.	Souvenir sheet, #3031-3032			3.25	2.50

A726

Sea Turtles: No. 3033, Chelonia mydas. No. 3034, Caretta caretta. No. 3035, Lepidochelys olivacea. No. 3036, Eretmochelys imbricata.

Wmk. 323

1995, Nov. 10 Litho. *Perf. 12½*

3033	A726	$5	multicolored	.65	.25
3034	A726	$5	multicolored	.65	.25
3035	A726	$5	multicolored	.65	.25
3036	A726	$5	multicolored	.65	.25
	Nos. 3033-3036 (4)			2.60	1.00

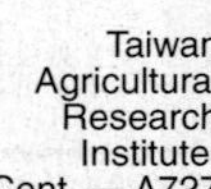

Taiwan Agricultural Research Institute, Cent. — A727

Perf. 12x11½

1995, Nov. 22 Litho. Wmk. 323

3037	A727	$5	In rice field	.60	.25
3038	A727	$28	In anthurium field	2.00	.75

New Year 1996 (Year of the Rat) — A728

Designs: $3.50, $13, Different stylized rats.

Wmk. 323

1995, Dec. 1 Litho. *Perf. 12½*

3039	A728	$3.50 pink & multi	.35	.25
a.	Perf. 13½ vert.		.60	.25
b.	As "a," booklet pane of 6		2.10	
	Complete booklet, 2 #3039b + gutter		4.25	
3040	A728	$13 olive & multi	.95	.45
a.	Souv. sheet, 2 ea #3039-3040		3.00	1.50

Traditional Wedding Ceremony A729

Designs: $5, Escorting bride. $12, Kowtowing Heaven, Earth, and ancestors. $19, Seated in bridal chamber.

1996, Jan. 10

3041	A729	$5	multicolored	.30	.25
3042	A729	$12	multicolored	1.00	.40
3043	A729	$19	multicolored	1.75	.60
	Nos. 3041-3043 (3)			3.05	1.25

Ancient Chinese Engraving Type

Various pictures of fruit.

Wmk. 323

1996, Jan. 25 Litho. *Perf. 13½*

Denomination in Black

3044	A712	$9	multicolored	.75	.30
3045	A712	$12	multicolored	1.00	.50
3046	A712	$15	multicolored	1.20	.60
3047	A712	$17	multicolored	1.40	.70
	Nos. 3044-3047 (4)			4.35	2.10

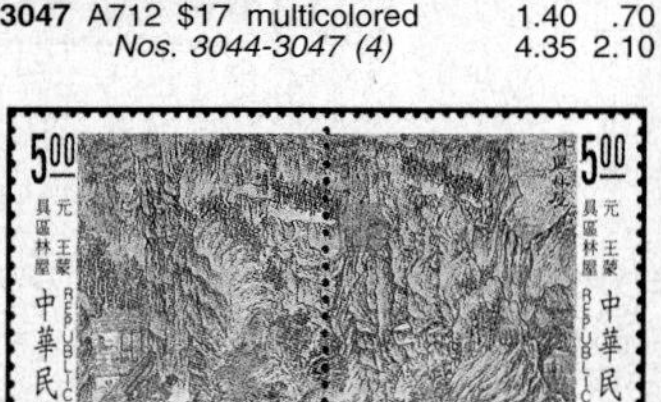

Scenic Dwelling at Chü-Ch'ü, by Wang Meng, Yüan Dynasty — A730

Denominations: a, UL. b, UR. c, LL. d, LR.

Perf. 12½x12

1996, Feb. 15 Litho. Unwmk.

3048	A730 Block of 4, #a.-d.	2.50	2.25
a.-d.	$5 any single	.65	.50

Herbaceous Flowers: $5, Gaillardia pulchella. $12, Kalanchoe blossfeldiana. $19, Portulaca oleracea.

Wmk. 323

1998, Mar. 1 **Litho.** ***Perf. 12½***

3161 A764 $5 multicolored .35 .25
3162 A764 $12 multicolored .80 .40
3163 A764 $19 multicolored 1.75 .65
Nos. 3161-3163 (3) 2.90 1.30

Emperor Shih-tzu, on Hunting Expedition, by Liu Kuan-tao
A765

$5, Horseman drawing bow. $19, Emperor Shih-tzu leading hunting party on horseback.

1998, Mar. 20 **Photo.** ***Perf. 12***

Granite Paper

3164 A765 $5 multicolored .75 .25

Size: 64x40mm

3165 A765 $19 multicolored 1.50 .50

Souvenir Sheet

3165A A765 Sheet of 2, b.-c. 2.50 1.00
b. A765 $5 multi 1.20 .25
c. A765 $19 multi 1.20 .75

No. 3165A is a continuous design.

Children's Folk Rhymes
A766

No. 3166, "A Frog Has One Mouth." No. 3167, "A Little Mouse Climbs an Oil Lamp." $12, "Fireflies." $19, "Egrets."

Wmk. 323

1998, Apr. 4 **Litho.** ***Perf. 11½***

3166 A766 $5 multicolored .40 .25
3167 A766 $5 multicolored .40 .25
3168 A766 $12 multicolored .60 .50
3169 A766 $19 multicolored 1.40 .65
Nos. 3166-3169 (4) 2.80 1.65

Copyright Law in Taiwan, 70th Anniv.
A767

1998, Apr. 30

3170 A767 $19 multicolored 1.40 .65

A768

Portraits of Mythological Character, Chung K'uei: $5, Making ghosts work for him, from Kung Kai's "Chung K'uei Moving," Song Dynasty. $20, Dancing beside small ghost, from "An Auspicious Occasion," Ming Dynasty.

1998, May 15 **Photo.** ***Perf. 11½***

Granite Paper

3171 A768 $5 multicolored 1.00 .25
3172 A768 $20 multicolored 1.75 .75

A769

Wmk. 323

1998, May 25 **Litho.** ***Perf. 11½***

3173 A769 $15 multicolored 1.25 .60

Intl. Law Assoc., 125th anniv.

Ancient Skills Type of 1994

Ships and methods of transport, horiz.: $5, Grain barge. $7, Six-oared boat. $10, One-wheeled carriage. $13, Southern Chinese one-man push cart.

1998, June 10 ***Perf. 12x11½***

3174 A693 $5 multicolored .45 .25
3175 A693 $7 multicolored .55 .25
3176 A693 $10 multicolored .75 .30
3177 A693 $13 multicolored .90 .40
Nos. 3174-3177 (4) 2.65 1.20

Ancient Chinese Engravings Type of 1995 Redrawn with Chinese Inscription Reading Left to Right

Various floral designs. Denominations do not include two zeros.

Wmk. 323

1998, July 8 **Litho.** ***Perf. 13½***

Denomination in Red

3178 A712 $7 like #2989 .45 .25
3179 A712 $19 like #2990 1.25 .60
3180 A712 $20 like #2991 1.40 .70
3181 A712 $26 like #2992 1.75 .85
Nos. 3178-3181 (4) 4.85 2.40

Novel, "Red Chamber Dream," by Tsao Hsueh-chin
A770

Scenes from love story: No. 3182, Chia Pao-yu visits the garden (with group of women). No. 3183, Lin Tai-yu buries flowers (with hoe). $5, Hsueh Pao-chai plays with butterflies. $20, Shih Hsiang-yun in a drunken sleep (on bench).

1998, July 16 ***Perf. 11x11½***

3182 A770 $3.50 multicolored .30 .25
3183 A770 $3.50 multicolored .30 .25
3184 A770 $5 multicolored .40 .25
3185 A770 $20 multicolored 1.60 1.00
Nos. 3182-3185 (4) 2.60 1.75

20th Asia Pacific Jamboree, 8th Taiwan Jamboree — A771

1998, Aug. 5 **Litho.** ***Perf. 11***

3186 A771 $5 Emblem .30 .25
3186A A771 $5 Tents .30 .25
b. Pair, #3186-3186A 1.00 .50

Traditional Architecture Type of 1995

Terraces set on raised platforms: No. 3187, Spirit way (carved stone ramp between two staircases). No. 3188, Octagonal base of a column. $10, Carved cornerstone. $19, Carved stone drainage spout.

Perf. 11½x12

1998, Aug. 26 **Litho.** **Wmk. 323**

3187 A711 $5 multi, vert. .50 .25
3188 A711 $5 multi, vert. .50 .25
3189 A711 $10 multi, vert. .75 .30
3190 A711 $19 multi, vert. 1.25 .55
Nos. 3187-3190 (4) 3.00 1.35

Sports Stamps — A772

Table tennis: No. 3191, Player awaiting serve. No. 3192, Player serving.
Rugby: No. 3193, Two players. No. 3194, Three players.

Wmk. 323

1998, Sept. 9 **Litho.** ***Perf. 11½***

Denomination Color

3191 $5 green .40 .25
3192 $5 red .40 .25
a. A772 Pair, #3191-3192 .80 .30
3193 $7 red .50 .25
3194 $7 blue .50 .25
a. A772 Pair, #3193-3194 1.00 .40
Nos. 3191-3194 (4) 1.80 1.00

Chinese Fables
A773

Designs: No. 3195, "A Frog in a Well." No. 3196, "The Fox Borrows the Tiger's Ferocity." $12, "Adding Legs to a Drawing of a Snake." $19, "The Snipe and the Clam are at a Deadlock."

Wmk. 323

1998, Sept. 25 **Litho.** ***Perf. 11½***

3195 A773 $5 multicolored .40 .25
3196 A773 $5 multicolored .40 .25
3197 A773 $12 multicolored .80 .40
3198 A773 $19 multicolored 1.20 .55
Nos. 3195-3198 (4) 2.80 1.45

Kinmen National Park
A774

No. 3199, Taiwushan mountain area. No. 3200, Kunningtou Cliff, beach. $12, Teyueh Tower, Huang Hui-huang's house, Shuitou village. $19, Putou Beach, Liehyu Coast.

1998, Oct. 16

3199 A774 $5 multicolored .40 .25
3200 A774 $5 multicolored .40 .25
3201 A774 $12 multicolored .90 .40
3202 A774 $19 multicolored 1.40 .55
Nos. 3199-3202 (4) 3.10 1.45

Birds — A775

Spizaetus nipalensis: No. 3203, On tree branch. No. 3204, In flight.
Spilornis cheela: No. 3205, On tree branch. No. 3206, In flight.
Ictinaetus malayensis: No. 3207, On tree branch. No. 3208, In flight.
Milvus migrans: No. 3209, Perched on rock. No. 3210, In flight.

1998, Oct. 30 **Litho.** ***Perf. 11½***

3203 $5 multicolored .35 .25
3204 $5 multicolored .35 .25
a. A775 Pair, #3203-3204 .70 .25
3205 $5 multicolored .35 .25
3206 $5 multicolored .35 .25
a. A775 Pair, #3205-3206 .70 .25
3207 $10 multicolored .65 .25
3208 $10 multicolored .65 .25
a. A775 Pair, #3207-3208 1.30 .50
3209 $10 multicolored .65 .25
3210 $10 multicolored .65 .25
a. A775 Pair, #3209-3210 1.30 .50
Nos. 3203-3210 (8) 4.00 2.00

Ancient Jade Carvings
A776

No. 3211, 2 men mining jade on a mountain. No. 3212, Mountain with 2 pavilions, stream. $7, Figures washing an elephant. $26, Mountain, trees, men.

Perf. 11½x12, 12x11½

1998, Nov. 13 **Photo.**

Granite Paper

3211 A776 $5 multi .35 .25
3212 A776 $5 multi, vert. .35 .25
3213 A776 $7 multi .50 .25
3214 A776 $26 multi, vert. 1.60 .80
a. Souvenir sheet, #3211-3214 3.50 1.60

New Year 1999 (Year of the Rabbit)
A777 A778

Wmk. 323

1998, Dec. 2 **Litho.** ***Perf. 12½***

3215 A777 $3.50 multicolored .35 .25
a. Perf. 14 vert. .50 .25
b. As "a," booklet pane of 6 2.50
Complete bklt., 2 #3215b + gutter 5.00
3216 A778 $13 multicolored 1.25 .35
a. Souv. sheet, 2 ea #3215-3216 3.25 2.00
b. As "a," ovptd. in margin, perf. 12½x11¾ 3.25 2.00

No. 3216b was issued 1/30/99 and is inscribed in sheet margin, "ALLIANCE '99 INT'L. FAIR OF PRODUCTS & TRAVEL / Jan. 30-Feb. 1, 1999" and four lines of Chinese text.

Common Expressions of Good Fortune — A779

Expressions, designs: No. 3217, "To have prosperous descendants," gourd on a vine. No. 3218, "A good marriage that soon brings sons," pair of Mandarin ducks, lotus flowers, seeds. No. 3219, "Prosperity from start to finish," egret, flowers. No. 3220, "Reunion and abundance," fish surrounded by flowers.

Perf. 11½x12

1999, Jan. 6 **Litho.** **Wmk. 323**

3217 A779 $5 multicolored .55 .25
3218 A779 $5 multicolored .55 .25
3219 A779 $12 multicolored 1.10 .40
3220 A779 $12 multicolored 1.10 .40
Nos. 3217-3220 (4) 3.30 1.30

Ancient Chinese Engravings Type of 1995 Redrawn with Chinese Inscription Reading Left to Right; No Zeros

Various pictures of birds on tree branches, bamboo and orchid.

1999, Jan. 20 ***Perf. 13½***

Denomination in Red

3221 A712 $1 like #3018 .25 .25
3222 A712 $3.50 like #3019 .30 .25
3223 A712 $5 like #3020 .35 .25
3224 A712 $10 like #3021 .60 .30
3225 A712 $12 like #3076 .80 .35
3226 A712 $28 like #3077 1.90 .90
Nos. 3221-3226 (6) 4.20 2.30

Indoor Potted Plants — A781

$5, Sinningia speciosa. $12, Saintpaulia x hybrida. $19, Anthurium scherzerianum.

Perf. 12½

1999, Feb. 10 Litho. Unwmk.

3228 A781 $5 multicolored .50 .25
3229 A781 $12 multicolored 1.10 .35
3230 A781 $19 multicolored 1.90 .65
Nos. 3228-3230 (3) 3.50 1.25

Ancient Chinese Painting, "Joy in Peacetime" A782

No. 3231, Woman holding child, boy with small elephant. No. 3232, Boy carrying lantern, crane on leash, people under tree. $7, Family, children playing with toy animals on wheels. $26, Women in front of steps, children playing with toys, boy on edge of balcony.

1999, Mar. 2 Photo. *Perf. 12*
Granite Paper

3231 A782 $5 multicolored .50 .25
3232 A782 $5 multicolored .50 .25
3233 A782 $7 multicolored .65 .25
3234 A782 $26 multicolored 2.00 .65
a. Souvenir sheet, #3231-3234 3.50 1.75
Nos. 3231-3234 (4) 3.65 1.40

A782a

A782b

A782c

Traditional Architecture — A782d

Decorative features: No. 3235, Hanging cylinder with carving of woman and deer. No. 3236, Taishi screen. $10, Xuanyu (decorative element on gable). $19, Wood carving.

1999, Mar. 20 Litho. Wmk. 323

3235 A782a $5 multicolored .45 .25
3236 A782b $5 multicolored .45 .25
3237 A782c $10 multicolored .90 .30
3238 A782d $19 multicolored 1.75 .50
Nos. 3235-3238 (4) 3.55 1.30

Children's Folk Rhymes A783

Titles: No. 3239, "Baby Sleep." No. 3240, "Be Brave." $12, "Rock, Rock, Rock." $19, "Buggie Flies."

Perf. 11½x11

1999, Apr. 2 Litho. Unwmk.

3239 A783 $5 multicolored .55 .25
3240 A783 $5 multicolored .55 .25
3241 A783 $12 multicolored 1.00 .30
3242 A783 $19 multicolored 1.60 .45
Nos. 3239-3242 (4) 3.70 1.25

Taiwan's Aboriginal Culture A784

Celebrations wearing traditional costumes: a, Dancing in row, mountain in background, Atayal Ancestor Festival. b, People wearing hip bells, Saisiat Festival of the Dwarfs. c, Standing arm in arm in circle, Bunun eight-part contrapuntal vocals. d, Row of people standing inside building, Tsou Victory Festival. e, Group outside before large display board, Rukai Harvest Festival. f, Holding bamboo poles in air, Paiwan "Maleveq" Bamboo Festival. g, Men walking while holding millet leaves in air, Puyuma Harvest Ceremony. h, Women dancing in row, tree in background, Ami Harvest Ceremony. i, Holding boat in air, Yami Boat Ceremony.

Block of 9

1999, Apr. 22 *Perf. 13*

3243 A784 $5 #a.-i. + label 4.75 4.50

No. 3243 was issued in sheets of 2 blocks + 2 labels. The labels contain the upper and lower halves of Taiwan. The lower block of 9 is in reverse order.

Intl. Council of Nurses, Cent. A785

1999, May 12 Litho. *Perf. 11½*

3244 A785 $5 shown .50 .25
3245 A785 $17 Nurse, world map 1.40 .50

Chinese Classical Opera — A786

Legends of the Ming Dynasty: No. 3246, Fan Li watching Hsi-shih wash yarn, "Wuan Sha Chi.". No. 3247, Tsai Pochieh, Niu looking at moon, Chao Waniang with pipa (stringed instrument) on her back, "The Story of a Pipa." $12, Hung Funu surprising Li Ching, "The Story of Hung Fu." $15, Jueilan setting up incense table, "Paiyueh Pavilion."

1999, May 27 *Perf. 13*

3246 A786 $5 multicolored .40 .25
3247 A786 $5 multicolored .50 .25
3248 A786 $12 multicolored 1.10 .30
3249 A786 $15 multicolored 1.30 .35
a. Souvenir sheet, #3246-3249 3.50 1.40
b. As "a," imperf., with added inscription 3.50 1.40
Nos. 3246-3249 (4) 3.30 1.15

No. 3249b was issued 7/23 and is inscribed in sheet margin with exhibition emblem, two lines of Chinese text and "TAIPEI INTERNATIONAL STAMP EXHIBITION 1999 (INVITATIONAL)."

New Taiwan Dollar, 50th Anniv. A787

1999, June 15 *Perf. 11½*

3250 A787 $5 Coins .40 .25
3251 A787 $25 Currency 1.60 .60

Carp Type of 1997 Redrawn With Denominations at Right

1999, July 1 Engr. *Perf. 13½x12½*

3252 A745 $50 green 3.25 2.40
3253 A745 $100 brown 7.25 3.25

Ancient Chinese Engravings Type of 1995 Redrawn with Chinese Inscription Reading Left to Right

Perf. 13½

1999, July 15 Litho. Unwmk.
Denomination in Red

3254 A712 50c like #3044 .25 .25
3255 A712 $6 like #3045 .60 .25
3256 A712 $25 like #3046 2.10 .75
Nos. 3254-3256 (3) 2.95 1.25

Father's Day A788

Designs: $5, Children with large present, silhouette of their father. $25, Father teaching son how to ride bicycle, girl.

1999, Aug. 8 *Perf. 11½*

3257 A788 $5 multicolored .50 .25
3258 A788 $25 multicolored 2.00 1.00

Chinese Gourmet Food A789

Dish, region: a, Peony lobster, Taiwan. b, "Buddha Jumps the Wall" steamed seafood (with blue & white teapot, bowl), Fukien. c, Hors d'oeuvres shaped as star, Canton. d, "Dongpo Pork" (on yellow plate, bowl), Kiangsu and Chekiang. e, "Stewed Fish Jaws" (surrounded by strawberries, pineapple), Shanghai. f, "Beggar's Chicken" (with napkin), Hunan. g, "Carp Jumping over Dragon's Gate," Szechwan. h, "Peking Duck" (in footed dish), Beijing.

Perf. 11½x11¼

1999, Aug 20 Litho. Unwmk.

3259 A789 $5 Block of 8, #a.-h. 3.25 1.60

Outdoor Activities — A790

1999, Sept. 9 *Perf. 11¼x11½*

3260 A790 $5 Diving .40 .25
3261 A790 $6 Rafting .45 .35
3262 A790 $10 Surfing .90 .40
3263 A790 $25 Windsurfing 2.25 .40
Nos. 3260-3263 (4) 4.00 1.40

Taiwanese Opera A791

$5, Stage, audience. $6, Dressing room. $10, Actress, tents. $25, Actress as clown.

1999, Oct. 15 Litho. *Perf. 11½x11¼*

3264 A791 $5 multicolored .35 .25
3265 A791 $6 multicolored .40 .35
3266 A791 $10 multicolored .75 .40
3267 A791 $25 multicolored 1.90 .65
Nos. 3264-3267 (4) 3.40 1.65

Illustrations from Ching Dynasty Bird Manual A792

No. 3268, Yellow-headed parrot. No. 3269, Blue-winged parrotlet (4 characters at LL). $12, African gray parrot (5 characters at UL). $25, King parrot (5 characters at UL).

1999, Nov. 11 Litho. *Perf. 11½*

3268 A792 $5 multicolored .75 .30
3269 A792 $5 multicolored .75 .30
3270 A792 $12 multicolored 1.50 .50
3271 A792 $25 multicolored 3.25 1.10
Nos. 3268-3271 (4) 6.25 2.20

Compare with No. 3152.

See Nos. 3316-3319, 3379-3381, 3509-3512.

New Year 2000 (Year of the Dragon)
A793 A794

1999, Dec. 1 Litho. *Perf. 12½*

3272 A793 $3.50 multicolored .30 .25
a. Perf. 13¼ vert. .30 .25
b. As "a," booklet pane of 6 1.60
Complete booklet, 2 #3272b + gutter 3.50
3273 A794 $13 multicolored 1.00 .40
a. Souv. sheet, 2 ea #3272-3273 2.50 1.50

Millennium A795

No. 3274, ROCSAT-1. No. 3275, Deer. $12, Train. $15, Dove, St. Peter's Basilica.

1999, Dec. 31 Litho. *Perf. 11½*

3274 A795 $5 multicolored .40 .25
3275 A795 $5 multicolored .40 .25
3276 A795 $12 multicolored .90 .40
3277 A795 $15 multicolored 1.10 .55
a. Souvenir sheet of 4, #3274-3277, perf. 12 2.75 1.50
b. Souvenir sheet of 4, #3274-3277, imperf. 3.00 1.60
Nos. 3274-3277 (4) 2.80 1.45

Taipei 2000 Stamp Exhibition (No. 3277b). No. 3277b has simulated perforations.

Calligraphy Tools A796

Designs: No. 3278, "Colored Cloud Dragon" writing brushes of Ming Emperor Chia-Ching. No. 3279, "Imperial Dragon Fragrance" ink stick of Ming Emperor Lung-Ching, vert. $7, "Clear Heart House" calligraphic work by Tsai Hsiang, Sung Dynasty, vert. $26, Celadon toad inkstone, Sung Dynasty.

2000, Jan. 12 Photo. *Perf. 11¾*
Granite Paper

3278 A796 $5 multicolored .50 .30
3279 A796 $5 multicolored .60 .30
3280 A796 $7 multicolored .70 .40
3281 A796 $26 multicolored 2.75 1.00
Nos. 3278-3281 (4) 4.55 2.00

Opening of Second Southern Freeway A797

Designs: $5, $25, Kaoping River bridge. $12, Interchange.

2000, Feb. 2 Litho. *Perf. 13x13¼*

3282 A797 $5 multi .50 .25
3283 A797 $12 multi .95 .40

Souvenir Sheet

Perf. 12

3284 A797 $25 multi 2.00 1.00

No. 3284 contains one 80x30mm stamp.

Seasons A798

Spring — No. 3285: a, Buds on tree. b, Farmer plowing. c, Cranes. d, Farmers planting. e, Basket of offerings to dead ancestors. f, Farmer's clothing.

Summer — No. 3286: a, Rice seedlings. b, Water wheel. c, Ripened rice. d, Cicada on tree. e, Palm leaf fan. f, Watermelons.

Autumn — No. 3287: a, Farmers in field. b, Granary. c, Dew on grass. d, Reddened maple leaves. e, Leafless tree. f, Hoarfrost on leaves.

Winter — No. 3288: a, Jar on table. b, Snow-covered pine trees. c, Snow-covered mountains. d, Bowl of rice balls. e, Snow-covered plum blossoms. f, House and village.

2000, Feb. 3 *Perf. 11¾*

3285 Strip of 6 4.50 3.25
a.-f. A798 $5 multicolored .60 .25
3286 Strip of 6 4.50 3.25
a.-f. A798 $5 multicolored .60 .25
3287 Strip of 6 4.50 3.25
a.-f. A798 $5 multicolored .60 .25
3288 Strip of 6 4.50 3.25
a.-f. A798 $5 multicolored .60 .25
Nos. 3285-3288 (4) 18.00 13.00

Issued: No. 3285, 2/3; No. 3286, 5/5; No. 3287, 8/4; No. 3288, 11/3.

Soochow University, Cent. A799

Designs: $5 School gate. $25, Justice statue at Law School.

2000, Mar. 16 *Perf. 13x13¼*

3289 A799 $5 multi .40 .25
3290 A799 $25 multi 1.90 1.00

Novel "The Romance of the Three Kingdoms" A800

No. 3291, Gathering of Liu Bei, Guan Yu and Chang Fei. No. 3292, Guan Yu reading. $5, Three visits to the thatched cottage. $20, Filling boats with straw for making arrows.

2000, Apr. 12 Litho. *Perf. 11½*

3291 A800 $3.50 multi .50 .25
3292 A800 $3.50 multi .50 .25
3293 A800 $5 multi .65 .35
3294 A800 $20 multi 1.40 .55
a. Souv. sheet, #3291-3294, perf. 12 3.00 2.60
Nos. 3291-3294 (4) 3.05 1.40

Inauguration of New President and Vice-president — A801

a, Pres. Chen Shui-bian, Vice-pres. Lu Hsiu-lien. b, Presidential Office Building.

2000, May 20 Litho. *Perf. 11¾*

3295 A801 $5 Pair, #a-b .90 .30
c. Souvenir sheet, 2 #3295 2.25 1.00

Tropic of Cancer Monuments A802

2000, June 21 *Perf. 13*

3296 A802 $5 Hsialiao .40 .25
3297 A802 $12 Wuho 1.25 .50
3298 A802 $25 Chingpu 2.25 .90
Nos. 3296-3298 (3) 3.90 1.65

Ancient Chinese Engravings Type of 1995 Redrawn with Chinese Inscription Reading Left to Right

2000, July 5 Litho. *Perf. 13½*

Denomination in Red

3299 A712 $32 like #3046 2.25 1.40
3300 A712 $34 like #3078 2.60 1.40

Sacred Trees — A803

Designs: $5, Taiwan Giant, Miaoli County. $39, Sleeping Moon, Chiayi County.

2000, July 20 Litho. *Perf. 11¼x11½*

3301 A803 $5 multi .30 .25
3302 A803 $39 multi 2.60 1.25

No. 2499 Surcharged in Red

2000, Aug. 24 Litho. *Perf. 13½*

3303 A535a $3.50 on $7.50 multi .60 .25

Poisonous Plants — A804

Designs: No. 3304, $5, Lycoris radiata. No. 3305, $5, Cerbera manghas. $12, Abrus precatorius. $20, Nerium indicum.

2000, Sept. 8 Litho. *Perf. 13*

3304-3307 A804 Set of 4 3.50 1.60

Sept. 21, 1999 Earthquake, 1st Anniv. — A805

Designs: $5, Map, seismograph reading. $12, Rescue workers. $25, Earthquake preparedness.

2000, Sept. 21 *Perf. 11¼x11½*

3308-3310 A805 Set of 3 3.50 1.60

Dragonflies A806

Designs: Nos. 3311, 3315a, $5, Lamelligomphus formosanus. Nos. 3312, 3315b, $5, Anotogaster sieboldii, vert. Nos. 3313, 3315c, $12, Trithemis festiva, vert. Nos. 3314, 3315d, $12, Neurothemis ramburii.

2000, Oct. 11 *Perf. 13*

3311-3314 A806 Set of 4 2.75 1.25

Souvenir Sheet

Stamps Without White Margins

Perf. 11¾

3315 A806 Sheet of 4, #a-d 2.75 1.25

Bird Manual Type of 1999

No. 3316, $5, Corn bunting (2 characters at UR). No. 3317, $5, Brambling (3 characters at UL). $12, Bali mynah (3 characters at LR). $25, Indian grackle (2 characters at LR).

2000, Oct. 26 *Perf. 11½*

3316-3319 A792 Set of 4 5.50 2.50

Compare No. 3317 with No. 3378.

Tamkang University, 50th Anniv. A807

$5, Palace Lamp Boulevard, classroom buildings. $25, Maritime Museum, Scroll Plaza.

2000, Nov. 8 *Perf. 13*

3320-3321 A807 Set of 2 2.40 1.25

A808

New Year 2001 (Year of the Snake) — A809

2000, Dec. 1 *Perf. 12½*

3322 A808 $3.50 multi .40 .25
a. Perf. 13¼ vert. .40 .25
b. As "a," booklet pane of 6 2.40
Booklet, 2 #3322b + gutter 4.80
3323 A809 $13 multi 1.00 .35
a. Souv. sheet, 2 ea #3322-3323 2.75 1.25
b. As "a," with added marginal inscription in red 2.75 1.25

Added marginal inscription of No. 3323b reads in Chinese "Turn-of-the-Century Intl. Stamp Exhibition, Kaohsiung / Dec. 25, 2000-Jan. 3, 2001" in red

Issued: No. 3323b, 12/25/00.

Establishment of Trade Links with People's Republic of China — A810

Ships in Taiwan Strait and: $9, Building. $25, Obelisk.

2001, Jan. 1 Litho. *Perf. 11½*

3324-3325 A810 Set of 2 2.50 2.00

A811

Common Chinese expressions of good fortune: No. 3326, $5, "Marital bliss," twin lotus blossoms on one stalk (pink background). No. 3327, $5, "Success in one's career," longan, lichee and walnuts (light green background). No. 3328, $12, "Producing many offspring," split pomegranates (buff background). No. 3329, $12, "Growing old together with wealth and high position," bulbuls flying around peonies (light orange background).

2001, Jan. 2 *Perf. 11¾x12¼*

3326-3329 A811 Set of 4 3.75 2.00

See Nos. 3404-3407.

Zodiac Signs A812

Designs: No. 3330, $5, Aquarius. No. 3331, $12, Gemini. No. 3332, $25, Libra. No. 3333, $5, Capricorn. No. 3334, $12, Taurus. No. 3335, $25, Virgo. No. 3336, $5, Aries. No. 3337, $12, Leo. No. 3338, $25, Sagittarius. No. 3339, $5, Pisces. No. 3340, $12, Cancer. No. 3341, $25, Scorpio.

2001 *Perf. 12*

3330-3341 A812 Set of 12 15.00 10.00

Values are for stamps with surrounding selvage.

Issued: Nos. 3330-3332, 2/14. Nos. 3333-3335, 4/20. Nos. 3336-3338, 7/25. Nos. 3339-3341, 11/8.

Fruit — A813

$1, Plums. $3.50, Tangerines. $5, Apples. $7, Pears. $12, Guavas. $20, Longans. $25, Cantaloupes. $40, Grapefruit.

2001-05 Litho. *Perf. 12½x13¼*

3342 A813 $1 multi .25 .25
3343 A813 $3.50 multi .30 .25
a. "Republic of China" 12½mm long ('05) .30 .25
3344 A813 $5 multi .35 .25
3345 A813 $7 multi .50 .25
3346 A813 $12 multi .85 .50
3347 A813 $20 multi 1.25 .80
a. "Republic of China" 12½mm long ('05) 1.25 .70
3348 A813 $25 multi 1.60 .85
3349 A813 $40 multi 3.00 2.60
Nos. 3342-3349 (8) 8.10 5.75

Issued: $5, $7, $12, $25, 2/23. $1, $3.50, $20, $40, 8/23. Nos. 3343a, 3347a, 5/16/05.

"Republic of China" on Nos. 3343 and 3347 is 12mm long and is in taller letters.

See Nos. 3408-3411, 3472-3475.

Mount Jade A814

Designs: No. 3350, $5, Main peak (shown). No. 3351, $5, Western peak, flowers in foreground. $12, Northern peak. $25, Eastern peak.

2001, Mar. 8 Litho. *Perf. 11½x11¼*

3350-3353 A814 Set of 4 3.75 3.00

Compare Type A814 with Types A834-A837, A855-A858.

Children's Rhymes A815

Designs: No. 3354, $5, Little Ball (blue background). No. 3355, $5, Point to the Water Vat (pink background). $12, Pangolin. $25, Shake and Stamp.

2001, Apr. 4
3354-3357 A815 Set of 4 4.50 3.00

Buddhist Statues — A816

Designs: $5, Sakyamuni Buddha, Northern Wei Dynasty. $9, Seated Buddha, Tang Dynasty. $12, Mahavairocana Buddha, Sung Dynasty.

2001, May 11 ***Perf. 11¼x11½***
3358-3360 A816 Set of 3 2.00 1.60
3360a Souvenir sheet, #3358-3360, perf. 12 2.00 2.00

Agricultural Implements — A817

Designs: $5, Rice wind drum. $7, Plow. $10, Bamboo rice baskets. $25, Coir rainwear.

2001, May 25 ***Perf. 11½x11¼***
3361-3364 A817 Set of 4 3.75 3.00

Dr. George Leslie Mackay (1844-1901) A818

2001, June 1 ***Perf. 11¼x11½***
3365 A818 $25 multi 1.90 1.60

2001 Kiwanis International Convention A819

Designs: $5, Girl, Earth. $25, Mother and child, map.

2001, June 22 ***Perf. 13***
3366-3367 A819 Set of 2 2.00 1.60

Kites — A820

No. 3368: a, Dragon. b, Phoenix. c, Tiger. d, Fish.

2001, July 13 ***Perf. 11¼x11½***
3368 Horiz. strip of 4 1.90 1.50
a.-d. A820 $5 Any single .40 .35

Carp Encircled by Dragons Type of 1997 With Denominations at Right

2001, Aug. 3 Engr. *Perf. 13*
Size: 25x33mm
3369 A745 $300 red vio & dk bl 16.00 8.00
3370 A745 $500 red & brown 36.00 16.00

Rapid Transit A821

Designs: $5, Train, transit system emblem. $12, Passengers in station, fare card. $25, Chientan Station.

2001, Aug. 14 Litho. *Perf. 13*
3371-3372 A821 Set of 2 1.50 .80

Souvenir Sheet

Perf. 11¾
3373 A821 $25 multi 2.25 1.25

No. 3373 contains one 85x42mm stamp.

Fables — A822

Designs: No. 3374, $5, Now Three, Now Four (man and monkeys). No. 3375, $5, Selling the All-Penetrating Sword and Unyielding Shield (men watching man with sword and shield). $12, Waiting by the Tree for the Rabbit. $25, An Old Fool Moves Mountains.

2001, Sept. 6 Litho. *Perf. 11½*
3374-3377 A822 Set of 4 3.00 2.50

Bird Manual Type of 1999 and

Siberian Rubythroat A823

Designs: No. 3379, Waxwing (3 characters at UR). $12, White-rumped munia (2 characters at R). $25, Great barbet (3 characters at LL).

2001, Sept. 28 Litho. *Perf. 11½*
3378 A823 $5 shown 2.00 1.00
3379 A792 $5 multi 2.00 1.00
3380 A792 $12 multi 3.75 1.90
3381 A792 $25 multi 6.75 3.25
Nos. 3378-3381 (4) 14.50 7.15

Republic of China, 90th Anniv. A824

Designs: No. 3382, $5, Terminal, Chiang Kai-shek Intl. Airport. No. 3383, $5, Electronic products made in Republic of China. $12, Dancers at National Theater. $15, Dolphins.

2001, Oct. 9 Litho. *Perf. 11½*
3382-3385 A824 Set of 4 3.00 2.25

2001 National Games — A825

Athletes and: $5, Torch. $25, Map.

2001, Oct. 18 Litho. *Perf. 12½*
3386-3387 A825 Set of 2 2.50 2.00

34th Baseball World Cup A826

Emblem, map and: No. 3388, $5, Pitcher. No. 3389, $5, Batter. $12, Catcher. $20, Runner sliding.

2001, Oct. 30 ***Perf. 11½***
3388-3391 A826 Set of 4 3.00 2.40
3391a Souvenir sheet, #3388-3391, perf. 12 3.75 3.00

Puppet Theater A827

Designs: $5, Mozhaonu, from "Thunder Storm." $6, Taiyangnu, from "Rising Winds, Surging Clouds." $10, Kuangdao, from "Thunder Crazy Sword." $25, Chin Chia-chien, from "Thunder Golden Light."

2001, Nov. 16 Litho. *Perf. 11½*
3392-3395 A827 Set of 4 3.50 2.40

National Defense Medical Center, Cent. A828

Designs: $5, Medical students, old medical school building. $25, Doctors, new medical school building.

2001, Nov. 23 ***Perf. 13***
3396-3397 A828 Set of 2 2.60 2.10

New Year 2002 (Year of the Horse) — A829

Horse and: $3.50, Clouds. $13, Flowers.

2001, Dec. 3 Litho. *Perf. 12½*
3398 A829 $3.50 multi .40 .25
a. Perf. 13¾ vert. .40 .25
b. Booklet pane, 12 #3398a 4.50 —
Booklet, #3398b 5.00

3399 A829 $13 multi 1.20 .80
a. Souvenir sheet, 2 each #3398-3399 3.25 2.00

Paul Cardinal Yu Pin (1901-78) — A830

2001, Dec. 7 ***Perf. 11½***
3400 A830 $25 multi 2.40 .75
a. Souvenir sheet of 1, perf. 12 1.90 1.50

Greetings A831

No. 3401: a, Pink chrysanthemums, red background. b, White lilies, red background. c, Pink flowers, yellow background. d, Red orange flowers, yellow background. e, Pink flowers, green background. f, Coral roses, blue green background. g, Star and wreath, blue background. h, Poinsettias, blue background. i, Red violet flowers, purple background. j, Yellow flowers, purple background.

2001, Dec. 12 ***Perf. 12½***
3401 Sheet of 10 + 10 labels 6.00 4.00
a.-j. A831 $5 Any single .60 .40

Labels could be personalized for an additional fee.

Sheets with blank (unprinted) labels were not released.

Fu Hsing Kang College, 50th Anniv. A832

Designs: $5, Students with flags. $25, Tower, administration building, statue of students.

2002, Jan. 4 ***Perf. 11½***
3402-3403 A832 Set of 2 2.75 2.10

Expressions of Good Fortune Type of 2001

Designs: No. 3404, $5, "Continuously produce good offspring," lotus and sweet osmanthus flowers in a vase (gradiated pink background). No. 3405, $5, "A high, moral gentleman," orchid and sweet osmanthus in containers (gradiated green background). No. 3406, $12, "A hall full of the rich and famous," flowering crabapple in a vase (gradiated orange background). No. 3407, $12, "Safe and peaceful in all seasons," roses in vase (gradiated purple background).

2002, Jan. 16 ***Perf. 11¾x12¼***
3404-3407 A811 Set of 4 2.75 1.60

Fruit Type of 2001

2002-05 Litho. *Perf. 12½x13¼*
3408 A813 $6 Avocados .35 .25
3409 A813 $10 Lichees .75 .30
a. "Republic of China" 12½mm long ('05) .60 .30
3410 A813 $17 Dates 1.20 .50
a. "Republic of China" 12½mm long ('05) 1.00 .55
3411 A813 $32 Passion fruit 2.20 .85
a. "Republic of China" 12½mm long ('05) 2.00 1.00
Nos. 3408-3411 (4) 4.50 1.90

Issued: Nos. 3408-3411, 2/8/02; 3409a, 3410a, 3411a, 5/16/05.

"Republic of China" on Nos. 3409-3411 is 12mm long and is in taller letters.

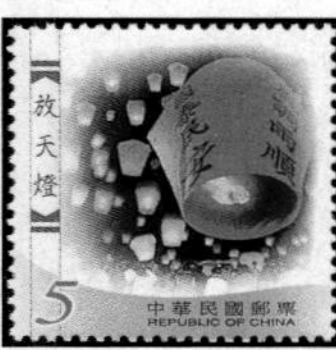

Folk Traditions A833

Designs: No. 3412, $5, Release of sky lanterns (orange background). No. 3413, $5, Fireworks display (blue background). $10, Matsu procession (lilac background). $20, Dragon boat race (pink background).

2002, Feb. 26 Litho. *Perf. 12½*
3412-3415 A833 Set of 4 3.25 2.40

See Nos. 3440-3443.

Winter, Mount Hsueh A834

North Ridge, Mount Hsueh A835

Autumn, Mount Hsueh A836

Glacial Cirques, Mount Hsueh A837

2002, Mar. 20 *Perf. 11½*
3416 A834 $5 multi .35 .35
3417 A835 $5 multi .35 .35
3418 A836 $12 multi .80 .70
3419 A837 $25 multi 1.60 1.40
Nos. 3416-3419 (4) 3.10 2.80

Compare with Types A814, A855-A858.

Novel "The Romance of the Three Kingdoms" A838

Designs: No. 3420, $3.50, Three heroes battling Lu Bu (warriors on horseback). No. 3421, $3.50, To the rescue of his master's family (one warrior on horseback). $5, Scraping away the poison from the bone (medicinal bleeding). $20, Playing a lute to make the enemy retreat (horseman and gate).

2002, Apr. 4
3420-3423 A838 Set of 4 4.00 1.75
a. Souvenir sheet, #3420-3423, perf. 12 4.00 4.00

Endangered Bird Thalasseus Bernsteini — A839

No. 3424: a, Two birds in flight. b, Bird in flight heading left. c, Bird landing on rock carrying fish. d, Bird on rock with beak open. e, Adult feeding chick. f, Bird diving. g, Bird landing with bill open. h, Bird standing on rock, looking left. i, Adult with chick. j, Adult on nest. $25, Bird in flight.

2002, May 15 Litho. *Perf. 11½*
3424 A839 $5 Sheet of 10, #a-j 4.00 3.25

Souvenir Sheet

Perf. 12

3425 A839 $25 multi 2.40 1.60

No. 3424 contains ten 40x30mm stamps.

Dragon & Carp Type of 1997 Redrawn With Denomination at Right

2002, June 5 Engr. *Perf. 13¼x12½*
3426 A745 $80 brown 5.00 3.00

Porcelain Bowls A840

Ching Dynasty bowls depicting: No. 3427, $5, Peacock (salmon background). No. 3428, $5, Lotus flowers (blue green background). $7, Peonies. $32, Sparrows and bamboo.

2002, June 21 Litho. *Perf. 11½*
3427-3430 A840 Set of 4 6.00 4.50

Flowers — A841

Designs: $5, Matthiola incana. $12, Gardenia jasminoides. $25, Michelia figo.

2002, July 5 *Perf. 13*
3431-3433 A841 Set of 3 3.50 1.60

Cetaceans A842

Designs: No. 3434, $5, Megaptera novaeangliae, whaling ship. No. 3435, $5, Tursiops truncatus, people on shore attracting cetacean. $10, Orcinus orca, boat following cetaceans. $25, Grampus griseus, people rescuing beached dolphin.

2002, July 25 Litho. *Perf. 11½x11¼*
3434-3437 A842 Set of 4 3.50 1.40
a. Souvenir sheet, #3434-3437, perf. 12 4.00 2.60

Intl. Paralympic Committee World Table Tennis Championships — A843

Player: No. 3438, $5, On crutches. No. 3439, $5, In wheelchair.

2002, Aug. 13 *Perf. 11½x11¼*
3438-3439 A843 Set of 2 1.00 .65

Folk Traditions Type of 2002

Designs: No. 3440, $5, Launching of water lanterns (green background). No. 3441, $5, Snatching flags for good luck (yellow background). $10, Worship of the just (blue background). $20, Burning the Prince's boat (red orange background).

2002, Aug. 22 *Perf. 12½*
3440-3443 A833 Set of 4 3.00 2.25

Republic of China — Vatican City Diplomatic Relations, 60th Anniv. A844

Designs: $5, Chinese and Vatican flags, Chinese Presidential building, St. Peter's Basilica. $17, Flags, doves, Celso Cardinal Costantini.

2002, Sept. 20 *Perf. 11½x11¼*
3444-3445 A844 Set of 2 2.00 1.25

Bird Manual Type of 1999 and

White-rumped Munia — A845

Designs: No. 3446, $5, Vernal hanging parrot (3 characters at LL). $12, White-headed greenfinch (4 characters at LL). $25, Yunnan greenfinch (2 characters at UL).

2002, Oct. 9
3446 A792 $5 multi .85 .75
3447 A845 $5 multi .85 .75
3448 A792 $12 multi 1.60 1.50
3449 A792 $25 multi 3.25 2.75
Nos. 3446-3449 (4) 6.55 5.75

Taiwanese Opera A846

Designs: $5, Liang Shan-po and Chu Ying-tai. $6, Hsueh Ting-shan and Fan Li-hua. $10, Hsueh Ping-kuei and Wang Pao-chuan. $25, The Living Buddha Chikung.

2002, Oct. 25
3450-3453 A846 Set of 4 3.00 1.50

Koalas — A847

Designs: No. 3454, $5, Adult with cub. No. 3455, $5, Adult on branch. $9, Adult with head on branch. $21, Adult with cub, diff.

2002, Nov. 15 *Perf. 11¼x11½*
3454-3457 A847 Set of 4 2.75 1.40
a. Souvenir sheet, #3454-3457, perf. 12 2.75 2.25

Knots A848

Nos. 3458-3459 — Various knots (Denomination location, denomination color and background color): a, UL, orange, light orange. b, UL, purple, yellow. c, UL, green, light green. d, UL, yellow, light blue. e, UL, blue, pink. f, UR, orange, light orange. g, UR, red violet, yellow. h, UR, blue, light green. i, UR, yellow, light blue. j, UR, red violet, pink.

No. 3460 (yellow denominations, olive green background): a, Like #3458a. b, Like #3458b. c, Like #3458c, d, #3458d, e, Like #3458e. f, Like #3458f. g, Like #3458g. h, Like #3458h. i, Like #3458i. j, Like #3458j.

2002, Nov. 22 Litho. *Perf. 12½*
3458 Block of 10 3.00 3.00
a.-j. A848 $3.50 Any single .30 .25
k. Sheet of 10 #3458f + 10 attached labels 15.00 15.00
l. Sheet of 10 #3458g + 10 attached labels 15.00 15.00
m. Sheet of 10 #3458h + 10 attached labels 15.00 15.00
n. Sheet of 10 #3458i + 10 attached labels 15.00 15.00
o. Sheet of 10 #3458j + 10 attached labels 15.00 15.00
p. Sheet , #3458a-3458j + 10 attached labels 15.00 15.00
q. Sheet, #3458a, 3458b, 3458d, 3458f, 3458g, 3458i + 6 attached labels ('04) 10.50 10.50
3459 Block of 10 4.50 4.50
a.-j. A848 $5 Any single .45 .25
k. Sheet of 10 #3459a + 10 attached labels 15.50 15.50
l. Sheet of 10 #3459b + 10 attached labels 15.50 15.50
m. Sheet of 10 #3459c + 10 attached labels 15.50 15.50
n. Sheet of 10 #3459d + 10 attached labels 15.50 15.50
o. Sheet of 10 #3459e + 10 attached labels 15.50 15.50
p. Sheet of 10 #3459f + 10 attached labels 15.50 15.50
q. Sheet of 10 #3459g + 10 attached labels 15.50 15.50
r. Sheet of 10 #3459h + 10 attached labels 15.50 15.50
s. Sheet of 10 #3459i + 10 attached labels 15.50 15.50
t. Sheet of 10 #3459j + 10 attached labels 15.50 15.50
3460 Block of 10 22.00 22.00
a.-j. A848 $25 Any single 2.10 1.10
k. Sheet of 10 #3460a + 10 attached labels 30.00 30.00
l. Sheet of 10 #3460b + 10 attached labels 30.00 30.00
m. Sheet of 10 #3460c + 10 attached labels 30.00 30.00
n. Sheet of 10 #3460d + 10 attached labels 30.00 30.00
o. Sheet of 10 #3460e + 10 attached labels 30.00 30.00
p. Sheet, #3460a-3460j + 10 attached labels 30.00 30.00
Nos. 3458-3460 (3) 29.50 29.50

Nos. 3458k-3458p sold for $185 each; Nos. 3459k-3459u for $200 each; Nos. 3460k-3460p for $400 each. Labels, which were personalized, were separated from stamps on Nos. 3458k-3458p, 3459k-3459u, 3460k-3460p by vertical rows of simulated perforations.

No. 3458q sold for $141 and has labels, which could be personalized, that are separated from the stamps by simulated perforations. Issued 9/30/04.

New Year 2003 (Year of the Ram) — A849

Designs: $3.50, Yellow ram. $13, Red ram.

2002, Dec. 2 Litho. *Perf. 12¼*
3461 A849 $3.50 multi .40 .25
a. Perf. 12¼ Vert. .40 .25
b. As "a," booklet pane of 6 2.25 —
Booklet, 2 #3461b 5.25
3462 A849 $13 multi 1.00 .40
a. Souvenir sheet, 2 each #3461-3462 2.75 1.50
b. As "a," with Chinese text in red in L & R sheet margins 2.40 1.25

Issued: No. 3462b, 1/1/03. Chinese text in left and right sheet margins on No. 3462b commemorates the establishment of Chunghwa Post Co., Ltd.

Street Scene on a Summer Day, by Chen Cheng-po A850

Girl in the White Dress, by Li Mei-shu — A851

Courtyard with Banana Trees, by Liao Chi-chun — A852

Sunrise, by Kuo Po-chuan A853

Perf. 11½x11¼, 11¼x11½

2002, Dec. 6

3463	A850 $5 multi		.40	.25
3464	A851 $5 multi		.40	.25
3465	A852 $10 multi		.70	.30
3466	A853 $20 multi		1.50	.50
	Nos. 3463-3466 (4)		3.00	1.30

Admission to World Trade Organization, 1st Anniv. — A854

2003, Jan. 1 Litho. ***Perf. 11½x11¼***

3467	A854 $17 multi	2.25	.90

Spring on Wuyen Peak A855

Glacial Cirques, Mt. Nanhu A856

Mt. Nanhu A857

Snow on Mt. Chungyang Chien A858

2003, Jan. 23

3468	A855 $5 multi	.35	.25
3469	A856 $5 multi	.35	.25
3470	A857 $12 multi	.75	.30
3471	A858 $25 multi	1.25	.55
	Nos. 3468-3471 (4)	2.70	1.35

Compare with Types A814, A834-A837.

Fruit Type of 2001

2003-05 Litho. ***Perf. 12½x13¼***

3472	A813 $9 Rose apples	.60	.25
a.	"Republic of China" 12½mm long ('05)	.60	.30
3473	A813 $13 Kumquats	.90	.40
3474	A813 $15 Lemons	1.10	.45
a.	"Republic of China" 12½mm long ('05)	.95	.50
3475	A813 $34 Coconuts	2.00	1.00
	Nos. 3472-3475 (4)	4.60	2.10

Issued: Nos. 3472-3475, 2/14/03; 3472a, 3474a, 5/16/05.

"Republic of China" on Nos. 3472 and 3474 is 12mm long and is in taller letters.

Love — A859

Hearts and: No. 3476, $5, Woman tending to man in wheelchair. No. 3477, $5, Family. $10, Landscape. $25, Girl and dogs.

2003, Mar. 20 ***Perf. 11¼x11½***

3476-3479	A859 Set of 4	3.00	2.25

Puppet Theater A860

Designs: No. 3480, $5, *Journey to the West* performed on outdoor stage. No. 3481, $5, Puppets on television. $10, *Mysteries of the Wolf Castle* performed at the National Opera House. $25, Screening of movie, *Legend of the Sacred Stone.*

2003, Apr. 3 ***Perf. 11½x11¼***

3480-3483	A860 Set of 4	3.00	2.25

Merops Philippinus A861

Designs: Nos. 3484, 3488a, $5, Foraging. Nos. 3485, 3488b, $5, Roosting. Nos. 3486, 3488c, $10, Bathing. Nos. 3487, 3488d, $20, Feeding chick.

2003, May 8 ***Perf. 12½***

With White Frame

3484-3487	A861 Set of 4	3.00	2.25

Souvenir Sheet

Without White Frame

3488	A861 Sheet of 4, #a-d	3.50	3.00

No. 3488 contains four 33x25mm stamps.

Furniture — A862

Designs: No. 3489, $5, Wash basin stand. No. 3490, $5, Canopy bed. $12, Taishi chair. $20, Pahsien table.

2003, May 22 ***Perf. 11¼x11½***

3489-3492	A862 Set of 4	3.00	1.50

Folktale "Eight Immortals Cross the Sea" — A863

Immortal: No. 3493, $5, Riding catfish. No. 3494, $5, On donkey. $10, Holding fan. $25, In brown robe.

2003, June 12

3493-3496	A863 Set of 4	6.75	3.50

See Nos. 3535-3538.

Moths A864

Designs: No. 3497, $5, Antitrygodes divisaria perturbata. No. 3498, $5, Vamuna virilis. $12, Sinna extrema. $20, Thyas juno.

2003, June 26 ***Perf. 11½x11¼***

3497-3500	A864 Set of 4	3.00	1.50

Dragonflies A865

Designs: Nos. 3501, 3505a, $5, Acisoma panorpoides panorpoides. Nos. 3502, 3505b, $5, Sympetrum eroticu ardens, vert. Nos. 3503, 3505c, $10, Anax parthenope julius. Nos. 3504, 3505d, $17, Rhyothemis variegata arria, vert.

2003, July 25 ***Perf. 12½***

With White Frames

3501-3504	A865 Set of 4	2.60	1.50

Souvenir Sheet

Without White Frames

Perf. 11¾

3505	A865 Sheet of 4, #a-d	3.00	2.60

Stamp size: Nos. 3505a, 3505c, 33x25mm; Nos. 3505b, 3505d, 25x33mm.

Greetings A866

No. 3506: a, Cranes. b, Wood carving and red plate. c, Fish and coin. d, Bamboo. e, Wood carving of bird.

No. 3507: a, Vase with tasseled rope. b, Like #3506a. c, Like #3506b. d, Three brown containers. e, Like #3508. f, Dragon. g, Like #3506c. h, Like #3506d. i, Horse and rider. j, Like #3506e.

No. 3508, Vase with flowers.

2003, Aug. 9 ***Perf. 12½***

3506	Horiz. strip of 5	1.90	1.90
a.-e.	A866 $3.50 Any single	.35	.25
f.	Sheet of 10 #3506a+ 10 attached labels	18.00	18.00
g.	Sheet of 10 #3506b+ 10 attached labels	18.00	18.00
h.	Sheet of 10 #3506c + 10 attached labels	18.00	18.00
i.	Sheet of 10 #3506d + 10 attached labels	18.00	18.00
j.	Sheet of 10 #3506e + 10 attached labels	18.00	18.00
k.	Sheet , 2 each #3506a-3506e + 10 attached labels	18.00	18.00
3507	Block of 10	5.00	5.00
a.-j.	A866 $5 Any single	.50	.25
k.	Sheet of 10 #3507a + 10 attached labels	19.00	19.00
l.	Sheet of 10 #3507b + 10 attached labels	19.00	19.00
m.	Sheet of 10 #3507c + 10 attached labels	19.00	19.00
n.	Sheet of 10 #3507d + 10 attached labels	19.00	19.00
o	Sheet of 10 #3507e + 10 attached labels	19.00	19.00
p.	Sheet of 10 #3507f + 10 attached labels	19.00	19.00
q.	Sheet of 10 #3507g + 10 attached labels	19.00	19.00
r.	Sheet of 10 #3507h + 10 attached labels	19.00	19.00
s.	Sheet of 10 #3507i + 10 attached labels	19.00	19.00
t.	Sheet of 10 #3507j + 10 attached labels	19.00	19.00
u.	Sheet, #3507a-3507j + 10 attached labels	19.00	19.00
v.	Sheet, #3507d, 3507e, 3507f, 3507g, 3507h, 3507j + 6 attached labels ('04)	13.50	13.50
3508	A866 $12 multi	1.25	.65
a.	Sheet of 10 #3508 + 10 attached labels	25.00	25.00
	Nos. 3506-3508 (3)	8.15	7.55

Nos. 3506f-3506k sold for $185 each; Nos. 3507k-3507u for $200 each; No. 3508a for $270 each. Labels, which were personalized, were separated from stamps on Nos. 3506f-3506k, 3507k-3507u, 3508a by vertical rows of simulated perforations.

No. 3507v sold for $150 and has labels, which could be personalized, that are separated from the stamps by simulated perforations. Issued 5/30/04.

Bird Manual Type of 1999 and

White-throated Laughing Thrush — A867

Designs: No. 3510, Great mynah (2 characters at LR). $12, Yellow-legged buttonquail (3 characters at UL). $25, Crested lark (4 characters at L).

Perf. 11½x11¼

2003, Sept. 10 Litho.

3509	A867 $5 multi	.75	.40
3510	A792 $5 multi	.75	.40
3511	A792 $12 multi	1.60	.85
3512	A792 $25 multi	3.25	1.60
	Nos. 3509-3512 (4)	6.35	3.25

Chungshan Park, Taichung A868

Tourist attractions: No. 3514, $5, Dongshan River Bridge, Ilan. $11, Badlands, Tianliao. $20, Sansiantai, Chenggong.

2003, Oct. 28 Litho. ***Perf. 11½***

3513-3516	A868 Set of 4	2.75	1.25

Chungshan Park, cent. (No. 3513).

Veterans Day, 25th Anniv. A869

Veterans Affairs Commission insignia and: $5, Veterans building Central Cross-Island Highway. $25, Veterans, homes and hospital for veterans.

2003, Oct. 31

3517-3518	A869 Set of 2	1.90	.90

The Back Yard, by Lu Tie-jhou — A870

A Gold Mine Tower: Jioufen, by Lin Ke-gong — A871

Leisurely, by Chen Jin — A872

East Gate, by Li Ze-fan A873

2003, Nov. 20

3519 A870 $5 multi .40 .25
3520 A871 $5 multi .40 .25
3521 A872 $10 multi .70 .30
3522 A873 $20 multi 1.40 .60
Nos. 3519-3522 (4) 2.90 1.40

New Year 2004 (Year of the Monkey) — A874

Monkey holding fruit: $3.50, With tail. $13, In hand.

2003, Dec. 1 ***Perf. 12¼***

3523-3524 A874 Set of 2 2.60 1.40
3523a Perf. 12¼ vert. .70 .35
3524a Sheet, 2 each #3523-3524 7.00 3.50
3523b Booklet pane, 12 #3523a 8.50 —
Complete booklet, #3523b 9.00

Springs A875

Designs: No. 3525, $5, Yangmingshan Hot Springs, fumaroles (light orange background). No. 3526, $5, Suao Cold Springs, Nanfangao Bridge (light blue background). $10, Guanziling Murky Hot Spring, Shuei Huo Tong Yuan. $25, Green Island Seabed Hot Springs, Green Island Lighthouse.

2003, Dec. 14 ***Perf. 13***

3525-3528 A875 Set of 4 3.50 1.50
3528a Souvenir sheet, #3525-3528 3.50 2.00

Completion of Highway 3 — A876

Designs: $5, Jhonggang Interchange. $25, Cingshuei Service Area.
$20, Cingshuei Service Area, diff.

2004, Jan. 8 **Litho.** ***Perf. 12½***

3529-3530 A876 Set of 2 2.00 .90

Souvenir Sheet

Perf. 11½x11¼

3531 A876 $20 multi 1.60 1.25

No. 3531 contains one 80x30mm stamp.

Flowers — A877

Designs: No. 3532, $5, Lilium formosanum. No. 3533, $5, Hippeastrum x hybridum. $12, Fressia x hybrida.

2004, Jan. 17 ***Perf. 12¼***

3532-3534 A877 Set of 3 1.75 .70
3534a Souvenir sheet, #3532-3534, perf. 13 1.75 1.25
3534b As "a," with Taiwan Flower Expo emblem and text added in margin 1.90 1.25

Eight Immortals Cross the Sea Type of 2003

Immortal: No. 3535, $5, With crane and flute. No. 3536, $5, With lotus flower. $10, Holding stick, wearing red robe. $25, Carrying flower basket.

2004, Feb. 25 ***Perf. 11¼x11½***

3535-3538 A863 Set of 4 3.25 1.50

Red Cross Society, Cent. — A878

No. 3539: a, Heart, stylized people with arms raised. b, Heart, stylized people doing Red Cross activities.

2004, Mar. 9 ***Perf. 11¼x11½***

3539 A878 $5 Horiz. pair, #a-b 1.10 .55

A Young Girl From Lu Kai, by Yan Shui-long A879

Old Street in Taipei, by Yang San-lang A880

Happy Farmers, by Lee Shih-chiao A881

Fish Shop, by Liu Chi-hsiang A882

Perf. 11¼x11½, 11½x11¼

2004, Mar. 25

3540 A879 $5 multi .40 .25
3541 A880 $5 multi .40 .25
3542 A881 $10 multi .80 .30
3543 A882 $20 multi 1.40 .60
Nos. 3540-3543 (4) 3.00 1.40

Butterflies A883

Designs: No. 3544, $5, Parantica sita niphonica. No. 3545, $5, Choaspes benjaminii formosanus. $17, Junonia almana. $20, Artipe eryx horiella.

2004, Apr. 21 ***Perf. 11½x11¼***

3544-3547 A883 Set of 4 3.00 1.50

Yijhen Folk Art Performers A884

Designs: No. 3548, $5, Eight Generals (buff background). No. 3549, $5, Song Jiang Battle Array (grayish blue background). $11, Drum Dance. $25, Stilt walkers.

2004, May 11

3548-3551 A884 Set of 4 3.00 1.50

Inauguration of Pres. Chen Shiu-bian and Vice-President Hsiu-lien Annette Lu — A885

No. 3552 — President, Vice-President and: a, Map of Taiwan, flag, crowd. b, Map of People's Republic of China and Taiwan, handshake, flowers. c, Buildings, crowd. d, Train, highway, buildings.

$12, President, Vice-President, buildings, train, highway.

2004, May 20 ***Perf. 12½***

3552 Horiz. strip of 4 1.75 .70
a.-d. A885 $5 Any single .40 .25

Souvenir Sheet

Perf. 12

3553 A885 $12 multi 1.50 1.25

No. 3553 contains one 80x30mm stamp.

Opening of Movie, *Harry Potter and the Prisoner of Azkaban* — A886

No. 3554: a, $5, Harry, messenger owl, Hedwig, with letter. b, $5, Hedwig, rose background. c, $5, Harry riding Hippogriff. d, $5, Hippogriff, green background. e, $5, Harry, Monster Book of Monsters. f, $25, Crookshanks the Cat.

No. 3555: a, $5, Harry playing quidditch. b, $5, Harry playing quidditch, Dementors. c, $5, Harry and Hermoine riding Hippogriff. d, $5, Harry holding wand, Hogwarts. e, $5, Harry practicing Patronus Charm to repel Dementors. f, $25, Harry thrusting wand.

2004, June 4 ***Perf. 12***

Sheets of 6, #a-f

3554-3555 A886 Set of 2 10.00 6.00

Postal administrators said that Nos. 3554-3555 would not be not sold directly to customers at foreign addresses. The sheets were made available abroad through Canada Post's philatelic agency, and also were sent to foreign standing order customers.

Old Train Stations A887

Designs: No. 3556, $5, Keelung Station, rickshaws. No. 3557, $5, Taipei Station, automobile. $15, Hsinchu Station, ox and cart. $25, Taichung Station, wagons.

2004, June 9 ***Perf. 13½x13¾***

3556-3559 A887 Set of 4 3.75 1.50

Compare Type A887 with Types A926-A929.

Iron Fort, Nangan Island A888

Cinbi, Beigan Island A889

Fujheng, Tungchu Island A890

Lienyuyikeng, Tungyin Island — A891

2004, July 1 **Litho.** ***Perf. 11½x11¼***

3560 A888 $5 multi .40 .25
3561 A889 $5 multi .40 .25
3562 A890 $9 multi .60 .25
3563 A891 $25 multi 1.60 .75
Nos. 3560-3563 (4) 3.00 1.50

Matsu National Scenic Area.

Crabs A892

Designs: No. 3564, $3.50, Uca formosensis. No. 3565, $3.50, Uca borealis. $5, Uca arcuata. $25, Uca lactea.

2004, July 21
3564-3567 A892 Set of 4 2.50 1.10

Souvenir Sheet

Listening to the Lute, Attributed to Li Sung — A893

No. 3568: a, $5, Lute player. b, $25, Scholar and woman.

2004, Aug. 6 ***Perf. 12***
3568 A893 Sheet of 2, #a-b 3.00 3.00

Souvenir Sheet

Taipei 2005 Intl. Stamp Exhibition — A894

No. 3569: a, $5, Sun Moon Lake. b, $25, Mt. Ali.

2004, Aug. 27 ***Perf. 11½x11¼***
3569 A894 Sheet of 2, #a-b 3.25 3.25

Intl. Day of Peace A895

2004, Sept. 21 ***Perf. 12¼x11¾***
3570 A895 $15 multi 1.10 .55

Souvenir Sheets

Hello Kitty — A896

No. 3571, oval stamps: a, $5, Dear Daniel, donuts. b, $15, Hello Kitty, Taipei 101 Building. No. 3572, rectangular stamps: a, $5, Hello Kitty, bird, horiz. b, $15, Dear Daniel, Fisherman's Wharf, Danshuei.

2004, Sept. 24 ***Perf.***
3571 A896 Sheet of 2, #a-b 2.00 1.50

Perf. 12
3572 A896 Sheet of 2, #a-b 2.00 1.50

Sayings With Numbers Greeting Stamps

One Sea of Smooth Sailing A897

Two Lions Bring Good Fortune A898

Three Goats of Auspiciousness — A899

Safety in All Four Seasons A900

Five Blessings at the Door A901

Six is Silky Smooth A902

Married for Seven Lives A903

Eight Immortals Wish for Your Perfection A904

Nine Means Success A905

Ten is All Around Perfection A906

2004, Oct. 10 ***Perf. 12½***

3573	Block of 10	3.25	1.10
a.	A897 $3.50 multi	.30	.25
b.	A898 $3.50 multi	.30	.25
c.	A899 $3.50 multi	.30	.25
d.	A900 $3.50 multi	.30	.25
e.	A901 $3.50 multi	.30	.25
f.	A902 $3.50 multi	.30	.25
g.	A903 $3.50 multi	.30	.25
h.	A904 $3.50 multi	.30	.25
i.	A905 $3.50 multi	.30	.25
j.	A906 $3.50 multi	.30	.25

Changed Colors

3574	Block of 10	4.25	1.50
a.	A897 $5 multi	.40	.25
b.	A898 $5 multi	.40	.25
c.	A899 $5 multi	.40	.25
d.	A900 $5 multi	.40	.25
e.	A901 $5 multi	.40	.25
f.	A902 $5 multi	.40	.25
g.	A903 $5 multi	.40	.25
h.	A904 $5 multi	.40	.25
i.	A905 $5 multi	.40	.25
j.	A906 $5 multi	.40	.25
k.	Sheet, #3574a-3574j + 10 attached labels ('04)	11.00	11.00

No. 3574k sold for $170 and has labels, which could be personalized, that are separated from the stamps by simulated perforations. Issued 10/10/04.

Kaohsiung Medical University. 50th Anniv. A907

Designs: No. 3575, $5, University gate and buildings. No. 3576, $5, Building, researcher, beaker, mosquito and snake.

2004, Oct. 16 ***Perf. 12½***
3575-3576 A907 Set of 2 1.15 .65

Main Peak, Mt. Cilai A908

North Peak, Mt. Cilai A909

South Peak, Mt. Cilai A910

Grasslands, Mt. Cilai — A911

2004, Oct. 16 ***Perf. 11½x11¼***

3577	A908 $5 multi		.30	.25
3578	A909 $5 multi		.30	.25
3579	A910 $12 multi		.80	.40
3580	A911 $25 multi		1.60	.75
	Nos. 3577-3580 (4)		3.00	1.65

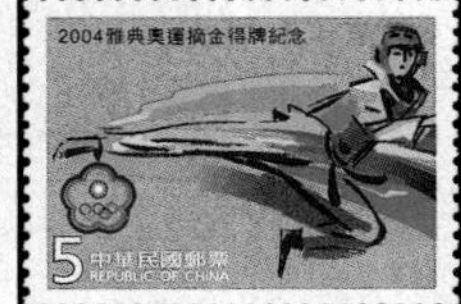

Taiwanese Mealist at 2004 Summer Olympics A912

Designs: No. 3581, $5, Women's Taekwondo. No. 3582, $5, Men's Taekwondo, vert. $9, Archery. $12, Athletes on winner's platform, vert.

Perf. 11¼x11½, 11½x11¼
2004, Oct. 22
3581-3584 A912 Set of 4 2.50 1.25

Platalea Minor A913

Designs: No. 3585, $2.50, Pair in flight. No. 3586, $2.50, Pair standing on one leg. $15, With wings spread. $25, Foraging for food. $20, Birds in water.

2004, Oct. 30 ***Perf. 13½x13¼***
3585-3588 A913 Set of 4 3.00 1.65

Souvenir Sheet

3589 A913 $20 multi 2.25 1.75

No. 3589 contains one 80x30mm stamp.

Pres. Yen Chia-kan (1905-93) A914

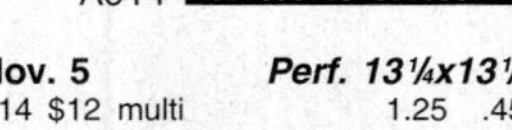

2004, Nov. 5 ***Perf. 13¼x13½***
3590 A914 $12 multi 1.25 .45

New Year 2005 (Year of the Cock) — A915

Designs: $3.50, Cock on lantern. $13, Lanterns, cock
$5, Cock, hen and chick, horiz.

2004, Nov. 10 ***Perf. 12¼x11¾***

3591-3592 A915 Set of 2 2.40 1.25

Souvenir Sheet

Perf. 11¾x11¼

3593 A915 $5 multi .95 .75

No. 3593 contains one 46x26mm stamp.

Prefectural Hall, Chiayi A916

East Gate, Chiayi A917

2004, Nov. 20 ***Perf. 13½x13¼***

3594 A916 $5 multi .80 .50
3595 A917 $5 multi .80 .50

Chiayi, 300th anniv.

Embroidered Squares for Ching Dynasty Civil Official Court Dresses — A918

Designs: No. 3596, $3.50, Manchurian crane (orange background). No. 3597, $3.50, Golden pheasant (green background). $5, Peacock. $25, Goose.

2005, Jan. 20 Litho. ***Perf. 11½x11¼***

3596-3599 A918 Set of 4 2.60 1.40

See Nos. 3727-3730.

Greetings A919

No. 3600 — Cartoon balloon with various keyboard characters creating faces and backgrounds with: a, Hands. b, Envelopes. c, Hearts. d, Flowers.

2005, Jan. 31 ***Perf. 12½***

3600 Horiz. strip of 4 1.60 .85
a.-d. A919 $5 Any single .40 .25
e. Sheet, #3600a-3600d + 4 attached labels 11.50 11.50

No. 3600e sold for $140 and has labels, which could be personalized, that are separated from the stamps by simulated perforations. Sheets exist with various arrangements of stamps and positions of labels respective to the stamps (at left, above or below).

Rotary International, Cent. — A920

Rotary emblem and: $5, Map of Taiwan. $12, Dove.

2005, Feb. 23 ***Perf. 13½x13¼***

3601-3602 A920 Set of 2 1.30 1.00

Mangroves A921

Designs: No. 3603, $3.50, Kandelia obovata. No. 3604, $3.50, Rhizophora stylosa. No. 3605, $5, Avicennia marina. No. 3606, $5, Lumnitzera racemosa.

2005, Mar. 10 ***Perf. 11½x11¼***

3603-3606 A921 Set of 4 1.25 1.00

Longshan Temple, Mengjia A922

Lin Ben Yuan Garden, Banciao A923

Designs: $13, Chaotain Temple, Beigang. $15, Fort Anping, Tainan.

2005, Mar. 18

3607 A922 $5 multi .35 .25
3608 A923 $5 multi .35 .25
3609 A923 $13 multi .85 .40
3610 A923 $15 multi .95 .45
Nos. 3607-3610 (4) 2.50 1.35

Souvenir Sheet

Taipei 2005 Intl. Stamp Exhibition — A924

No. 3611: a, $5, Wood carving, Mandarin Ducks Playing in a Lotus Pond. b, $25, Hand puppets, horiz.

2005, Apr. 19 ***Perf. 12***

3611 A924 Sheet of 2, #a-b 2.40 2.40

Coral Reef Fish A925

Designs: No. 3612, $5, Rhinomuraena quaesita. No. 3613, $5, Pomacanthus semicirculatus. $12, Forcipiger flavissimus. $25, Pterois volitans.

2005, May 16 ***Perf. 11½x12***

3612-3615 A925 Set of 4 3.50 1.75
a. Sheet, 2 each #3612-3615 7.00 7.00

Changhua Train Station, 1918 A926

Chiayi Train Station, 1933 A927

Tainan Train Station, 1936 A928

Kaohsiung Train Station, 1941 A929

2005, June 9 ***Perf. 13½x13¾***

3616 A926 $5 multi .35 .25
3617 A927 $5 multi .35 .25
3618 A928 $15 multi .90 .50
3619 A929 $25 multi 1.40 .80
Nos. 3616-3619 (4) 3.00 1.80

Compare with type A887.

Novel "The Romance of the Three Kingdoms" A930

Designs: No. 3620, $3.50, Mayhem in the Fengyi Pavilion (man and woman near pavilion railing). No. 3621, $3.50, Deterring the Enemy in Changban (horse and rider on bridge). $5, Releasing Tsao Tsao (rider on horse near flag). $20, A Trick in the Bag (man in bed holding bag).

Perf. 11½x11¼

2005, June 23 **Litho.**

3620-3623 A930 Set of 4 3.25 3.00
3623a Souvenir sheet, #3620-3623 3.25 3.25

Lifeline Suicide Prevention Hotline — A931

2005, July 1 ***Perf. 12x11½***

3624 A931 $12 multi 1.25 .75

Albert Einstein's Theory of Relativity, Cent. — A932

2005, July 1

3625 A932 $15 multi 1.10 .55

Souvenir Sheets

Mickey Mouse — A933

No. 3626: a, $5, At ship's wheel, in *Steamboat Willie*. b, $25. As wizard, in *Fantasia*.

No. 3627: a, $5, Holding sword, in *The Prince and the Pauper*. b, $25. With Pluto, in *Mickey's Twice Upon a Christmas*.

2005, Aug. 3 ***Perf. 12***

Sheets of 2, #a-b

3626-3627 A933 Set of 2 3.50 2.00

Rooster-shaped Wine Vessel — A934

2005, Aug. 19 ***Perf. 11¼x11½***

3628 A934 $15 multi .95 .45
a. Sheet of 6, perf. 12 5.75 3.00

Taipei 2005 Intl. Stamp Exhibition.

Souvenir Sheets

A935

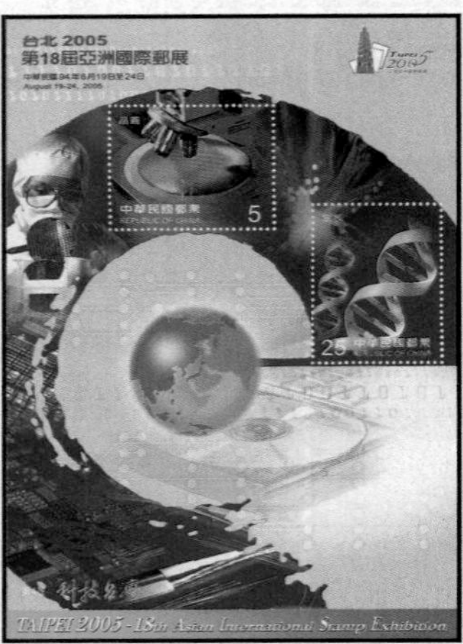

A936

A937

A938

A939

Taipei 2005 Intl. Stamp Exhibition — A940

No. 3629: a, $5, Green Island and shoreline. b, $25, Formosan rock monkey.

No. 3630: a, $5, Microscope. b, $25, DNA double helices, vert.

No. 3631: a, $5, Flowers. $25, Fruit.

No. 3632: a, $5, Ear Shooting Ceremony, vert. b, $25, Dragon boat in race.

No. 3633: a, $5, Bowl of food and ladle. b, $25, Rice cakes.

No. 3634: a, $5, Royal empress angelfish. b, $25, Red horny coral.

2005 ***Perf.***

3629 A935 Sheet of 2, #a-b 2.25 .95

Perf. 13½x13, 13x13½

3630 A936 Sheet of 2, #a-b 2.25 .95

Perf. 13½

3631 A937 Sheet of 2, #a-b 2.25 .95

Perf. 13¼x13½, 13½x13¼

3632 A938 Sheet of 2, #a-b 2.25 .95

Perf. 12

3633 A939 Sheet of 2, #a-b 2.25 .95

Perf.

3634 A940 Sheet of 2, #a-b 2.25 .95

Nos. 3629-3634 (6) 13.50 5.70

Issued: No. 3629, 8/19; No. 3630, 8/20; No. 3631, 8/21; No. 3632, 8/22; No. 3633, 8/23; No. 3634, 8/24. No. 3629 contains two 38mm diameter stamps. No. 3634 contains two 43x33mm oval stamps.

Novel, "Journey to the West" — A941

Designs: No. 3635, $3.50, Stone Monkey (monkeys at waterfall). No. 3636, $3.50, Buddhist Baby in the River. $5, Making a Pass at Chang E. $20, Taming the Monster of the River of Flowing Sands.

2005, Sept. 15 ***Perf. 11¼x11½***

3635-3638 A941 Set of 4 9.00 7.00

Souvenir Sheet

Kaohsiung 2005 Intl. Stamp Exhibition — A942

No. 3639: a, $5, Loyalty and Filial Piety, by Cian Syuan, vert. b, Gilt scepter.

Perf. 13¼x13½, 13½x13¼

2005, Oct. 7

3639 A942 Sheet of 2, #a-b 2.00 2.00

Souvenir Sheets

A943

Opening of Movie, *Harry Potter and the Goblet of Fire* — A944

No. 3640: a, $5, Triwizard Cup. b, $5, Harry and Hungarian Horntail. c, $5, Golden Egg. d, $5, Harry swimming. e, $5, Harry summoning Firebolt with wand. f, $25, Harry and Triwizard Cup.

No. 3641: a, $5, Hungarian Horntail. b, $5, Harry on Firebolt. c, $5, Voldemort's snake, Nagini. d, $5, Grindylows. e, $5, Dumbledore's phoenix, Fawkes. f, $25, Merchieftainess.

2005, Nov. 18 ***Perf. 12***

3640 A943 Sheet of 6, #a-f 5.00 2.50

3641 A944 Sheet of 6, #a-f 5.00 2.50

New Year 2006 (Year of the Dog) — A945

Designs: $3.50, Dog at left. $13, Dog at lower right.

$12, Three dogs, horiz.

2005, Dec. 1 ***Perf. 12¼x11¾***

3642-3643 A945 Set of 2 2.50 2.00

Souvenir Sheet

Perf. 11¾x11¼

3644 A945 $12 multi 1.50 1.00

No. 3644 contains one 46x26mm stamp.

Pets — A946

Designs: $3.50, Siberian husky. $5, Golden retriever. $12, Himalayan cat. $25, Scottish fold cat.

Perf. 13½x12½

2005, Dec. 22 **Litho.**

Country Name in Green

3645 A946 $3.50 multi .30 .25

3646 A946 $5 multi .35 .25

3647 A946 $12 multi .75 .35

3648 A946 $25 multi 1.40 .75

Nos. 3645-3648 (4) 2.80 1.60

See Nos. 3652-3655, 3685-3688 3712-3715.

Tea Ceremony — A947

No. 3649: a, Preparation of tea set (dull orange panel). b, Placing of tea leaves in pot (lemon panel). c, Pouring hot water over pots and cups (light green panel). d, Drying of pot and pouring of tea (blue geen panel). e, Smelling and drinking of tea (gray blue panel).

2006, Jan. 26 ***Perf. 13½***

3649 A947 Horiz. strip of 5 1.90 1.00

a.-e. $5 Any single .35 .25

Taipei 101 Building — A948

Designs: $5, In day. $12, At night.

2006, Feb. 23 ***Perf. 12***

3650-3651 A948 Set of 2 3.50 2.25

Pets Type of 2005

Designs: $2.50, Labrador retriever. $7, St. Bernard. $10, Siamese cat. $32, Persian cat.

2006, Mar. 8 *Perf. 13½x12½*

Country Name in Blue

3652	A946	$2.50 multi	.25	.25
3653	A946	$7 multi	.45	.25
3654	A946	$10 multi	.60	.30
3655	A946	$32 multi	2.00	1.00
		Nos. 3652-3655 (4)	3.30	1.80

See Nos. 3712-3715.

King Penguins A949

Aptenodytes patagonicus: No. 3656, $5, Adult and juvenile. No. 3657, $5, Courtship. $9, Swimming and diving, horiz. $12, Gliding and preening, horiz.
$15, Colony, horiz.

Perf. 11¼x11½, 11½x11¼

2006, Mar. 26

3656-3659 A949 Set of 4 2.00 1.60

Souvenir Sheet

Perf. 12

3660 A949 $15 multi 1.25 1.00

No. 3660 contains one 80x30mm stamp.

Miniature Sheet

Children's Art — A950

No. 3661 — Winning drawings in children's stamp design competition: a, Birds with black bills. b, People with red faces. c, Pheasants. d, Chinese celebration. e, Fishing boats and catch. f, People with large flowers and fruit. g, Man painting Chinese lantern. h, Bridge and ducks. i, Train. j, Bees and flowers. k, People with black faces. l, Boy on ladder. m, People and chickens. n, Ring of people around dancers and musicians. o, People and large lions. p, Two cats. q, People and cow. r, Whale and fish. s, People with white faces bending backwards. t, Bus.

2006, Apr. 4 *Perf. 11½*

3661 A950 $5 Sheet of 20, #a-t 6.00 3.50

Fireflies A951

Designs: No. 3662, $5, Pyrocoelia analis. No. 3663, $5, Diaphanes citrinus. No. 3664, $5, Diaphanes niveus. No. 3665, $5, Diaphanes formosus.

2006, May 25 *Perf. 13½x13¼*

3662-3665 A951 Set of 4 1.75 1.00

Souvenir Sheet

Completion of Nangang to Suao Section of National Expressway 5 — A952

2006, June 16 **Litho.** *Perf. 11½*

3666 A952 $12 multi 1.50 .80

Souvenir Sheets

Winnie the Pooh — A953

No. 3667: a, $5, Winnie the Pooh pushing Piglet in wheelbarrow. b, $25, Winnie the Pooh, Piglet and Tigger floating in inner tube.
No. 3668: a, $5, Winnie the Pooh and Piglet running in autumn. b, $25, Winnie the Pooh and Tigger ice fishing.

2006, June 21 *Perf. 12*

Sheets of 2, #a-b

3667-3668 A953 Set of 2 4.00 2.00

Tourism Greeting Stamps A954

Designs: Nos. 3669a, 3670a, Satchel and cliff. Nos. 3669b, 3670b, Camera and boat. Nos. 3669c, 3670c, Notebook, pen and bridge. No. 3669d, 3670d, Sailboat and rock. No. 3669e, 3670e, Heart and train.

2006, June 30 *Perf. 12½*

3669	Horiz. strip of 5	1.50	.55
a.-e.	A954 $3.50 Any single	.30	.25
f.	Sheet, 2 each #3669a-3669e, + 5 labels	7.00	—
3670	Horiz. strip of 5	2.00	.80
a.-e.	A954 $5 Any single	.40	.25
f.	Sheet, 2 each #3670a-3670e, + 5 labels	7.00	—

Nos. 3669f and 3670f each sold for $100. Labels could be personalized.

Fish A955

Designs: No. 3671, $5, Amphiprion ocellaris. No. 3672, $5, Zanclus cornutus. No. 3673, $12, Coris gaimard. No. 3674, $12, Oxycirrhites typus.

2006, July 14 *Perf. 11½*

3671-3674	A955 Set of 4	2.75	2.25
3674a	Miniature sheet, 2 each #3671-3674, perf. 11½x12	5.75	5.75

A956

Sung Dynasty Calligraphy and Painting — A957

Designs: $5, Poem by Huang T'ing-chien. $9, Calligraphy on silk, by Mi Fu. Nos. 3677, 3679a, $12, Detail of magpie in flight, from Magpies and Hare, by Ts'ui Po. Nos. 3678, 3679b, $15, Detail of magpie on branch, from Magpies and Hare.

2006, Aug. 4 *Perf. 11½*

Denominations in Black

3675-3678 A956 Set of 4 9.00 7.00

Souvenir Sheet

Denominations in Black and Orange

Perf. 12½

3679 A957 Sheet of 2, #a-b 4.00 3.00

Dragonflies A958

Designs: Nos. 3680, 3684a, $5, Crocothemis servilia servilia. Nos. 3681, 3684b, $5, Orthetrum, pruinosum neglectum, vert. Nos. 3682, 3684c, $12, Diplacodes trivialis, vert. No. 3683, 3684d, $12, Orthetrum sabina sabina.

Perf. 13x13¼, 13¼x13

2006, Aug. 16 **With White Frames**

3680-3683 A958 Set of 4 2.00 1.75

Souvenir Sheet

Without White Frames

Perf. 11¾

3684 A958 Sheet of 4, #a-d 2.40 2.00

Pets Type of 2005

Designs: $1, Yorkshire terrier. $9, Pomeranian. $15, Abyssinian cat. $20, Norwegian Forest cat.

2006, Aug. 30 *Perf. 13½x12½*

Country Name in Blue

3685	A946	$1 multi	.25	.25
3686	A946	$9 multi	.55	.25
3687	A946	$15 multi	.90	.45
3688	A946	$20 multi	1.25	.60
		Nos. 3685-3688 (4)	2.95	1.55

Aerial Activities — A959

Designs: No. 3689, $3.50, Paragliding. No. 3690, $3.50, Hang gliding, horiz. $12, Ultralight aircraft, horiz. $15, Parasailing.

2006, Sept. 15 *Perf. 13½*

3689-3692 A959 Set of 4 2.50 1.50

Pitta Nympha — A960

Designs: Nos. 3693, 3697a, $5, On branch. Nos. 3694, 3697b, $5, In flight, horiz. Nos. 3695, 3697c, $10, With young at nest, horiz. Nos. 3696, 3697d, $10, With insect in beak.

Perf. 13¼x13, 13x13¼

2006, Sept. 30 **With White Frames**

3693-3696 A960 Set of 4 2.25 1.10

Souvenir Sheet

Without White Frames

Perf. 11¾

3697 A960 Sheet of 4, #a-d 2.25 1.10

Cetaceans A961

Designs: No. 3698, $5, Stenella attenuata. No. 3699, $5, Stenella longirostris. $10, Feresa attenuata. $15, Physeter macrocephalus.

Perf. 13x12 Syncopated

2006, Oct. 18 **Litho.**

3698-3701	A961 Set of 4	2.50	1.50
3701a	Souvenir sheet, #3698-3701	2.50	1.50

Flowers A962

Designs: No. 3702, $5, Ludwigia octovalvis. No. 3703, $5, Hygrophila pogonocalyx, vert. $12, Titanotrichum oldhamii, vert.

2006, Nov. 8 *Perf. 11½*

3702-3704 A962 Set of 3 1.75 .90

Scenic Areas A963

Designs: No. 3705, $5, Jhongshan Building, Yangmingshan National Park. No. 3706, $5, Taroko Gorge, vert. $9, Queen's Head Rock, vert. $12, Sun Moon Lake.

2006, Nov. 11 *Perf. 12½*

3705-3708 A963 Set of 4 2.75 1.50

A964

New Year 2007 (Year of the Pig) — A965

Designs: $3.50, Pig on drum. $13, Pig and drums.

2006, Dec. 1 ***Perf. 12¼x11¾***

3709-3710	A964	Set of 2	1.50	.75

Souvenir Sheet

Perf. 11½x11¼

3711	A965	$12 multi	2.40	1.25

Pets Type of 2005

Designs: 50c, Border collie. $13, Beagle. $17, American Shorthair cat. $34, Maine Coon cat.

2006, Dec. 18 ***Perf. 13½x12½***

Country Name in Green

3712	A946	50c multi	.25	.25
3713	A946	$13 multi	.75	.40
3714	A946	$17 multi	1.00	.55
3715	A946	$34 multi	2.00	1.10
		Nos. 3712-3715 (4)	4.00	2.30

Inauguration of High Speed Rail Line — A966

No. 3716: a, 700T Series train. b, Hsinchu Station.

2006, Dec. 25 ***Perf. 11½***

3716	A966	$12 Horiz. pair, #a-b	1.60	.80

Orchids — A967

Designs: $3.50, Phaius tankervilleae. $5, Spiranthes sinensis. $12, Vanda x hybrida. $25, Cattleya sp.

2007, Jan. 10 **Litho.** ***Perf. 13½x12½***

3717	A967	$3.50 multi	.25	.25
3718	A967	$5 multi	.35	.25
3719	A967	$12 multi	.80	.40
3720	A967	$25 multi	1.60	.80
		Nos. 3717-3720 (4)	3.00	1.70

See Nos. 3751-3754, 3768-3771.

Ching Dynasty Jewelry A968

Designs: No. 3721, $5, Earrings. No. 3722, $5, Hairpin. $12, Fingernail guard. $25, Ring.

2007, Jan. 17 ***Perf. 11½***

3721-3724	A968	Set of 4	2.75	1.50

Valentine's Day — A969

Heart and faces in: $5, White. $20, Red.

2007, Feb. 6

3725-3726	A969	Set of 2	1.50	.75

Embroidered Squares Type of 2005

Embroidered squares for Ching Dynasty military officials: No. 3727, $3.50, Cilin (light green background). No. 3728, $3.50, Lion (light orange background). $5, Leopard (bright orange background). $25, Tiger (light blue background).

2007, Feb. 16 ***Perf. 11½x11¼***

3727-3730	A918	Set of 4	2.25	1.10

Feb. 28, 1947 Massacre Memorial Museum A970

2007, Feb. 28

3731	A970	$5 multi	6.00	3.00

Bridges A971

Designs: No. 3732, $5, Kanjin Bridge, Taoyuan (green panel). No. 3733, $5, Fusing Bridge, Luofu (purple panel). $12, MacArthur Second Bridge, Taipei. $15, Dajhih Bridge, Taipei.

2007, Apr. 12 **Litho.** ***Perf. 11½x12***

3732-3735	A971	Set of 4	2.40	1.20

See Nos. 3808-3811.

Lesser Panda A972

Panda: No. 3736, $5, Eating bamboo. No. 3737, $5, Resting on rock. No. 3738, $10, Walking near tree, vert. No. 3739, $10, Scratching on rock, vert.

$12, Two pandas, vert.

Perf. 11½x11¼, 11¼x11½

2007, Apr. 25

3736-3739	A972	Set of 4	2.00	1.00

Souvenir Sheet

Perf. 12

3740	A972	$12 multi	1.00	1.00

No. 3740 contains one 40x50mm stamp.

Dharma Drum Mountain Intl. Buddhist Educational Complex — A973

Chung Tai Chan Monastery A974

Fo Guang Shan Monastery A975

Tzu Chi Foundation Building — A976

2007, May 24 ***Perf. 13¼x13***

3741	A973	$5 multi	.45	.25
3742	A974	$5 multi	.45	.25
3743	A975	$5 multi	.45	.25
3744	A976	$5 multi	.45	.25
		Nos. 3741-3744 (4)	1.80	1.00

Dahlia and Butterflies A977

Iris and Butterfly A978

Clematis and Ladybugs A979

Tung Blossom and Butterflies A980

Rose and Butterfly A981

Sunflower and Insects — A982

Bird-of-Paradise Flower and Butterfly A983

Lotus and Butterflies A984

English Daisies and Dragonfly A985

Balloon Flower and Dragonfly A986

2007, May 28 ***Perf. 12½***

3745		Block of 10	2.10	1.10
a.	A977	$3.50 multi	.25	.25
b.	A978	$3.50 multi	.25	.25
c.	A979	$3.50 multi	.25	.25
d.	A980	$3.50 multi	.25	.25
e.	A981	$3.50 multi	.25	.25
f.	A982	$3.50 multi	.25	.25
g.	A983	$3.50 multi	.25	.25
h.	A984	$3.50 multi	.25	.25
i.	A985	$3.50 multi	.25	.25
j.	A986	$3.50 multi	.25	.25

Changed Colors

3746		Block of 10	3.00	1.50
a.	A977	$5 multi	.30	.25
b.	A978	$5 multi	.30	.25
c.	A979	$5 multi	.30	.25
d.	A980	$5 multi	.30	.25
e.	A981	$5 multi	.30	.25
f.	A982	$5 multi	.30	.25
g.	A983	$5 multi	.30	.25
h.	A984	$5 multi	.30	.25
i.	A985	$5 multi	.30	.25
j.	A986	$5 multi	.30	.25

Food Preparation Implements — A987

Designs: No. 3747, $5, Rice bucket and shelf (light blue background). No. 3748, $5, Steamer (green background). No. 3749, $12, Rice baskets (tan background). No. 3750, $12, Dinnerware (lilac background).

2007, June 28 ***Perf. 11½x11¼***

3747-3750	A987	Set of 4	2.25	1.10

Orchids Type of 2007 Inscribed "Taiwan" Instead of "Republic of China"

Designs: $1, Paphiopedilum sp. $2.50, Phalaenopsis aphrodite. $10, Dendrobium sp. $32, Oncidium x hybridum.

2007, July 12 *Perf. 13½x12½*

3751 A967	$1 multi		.25	.25
3752 A967	$2.50 multi		.25	.25
3753 A967	$10 multi		.60	.30
3754 A967	$32 multi		2.10	1.00
Nos. 3751-3754 (4)			3.20	1.80

End of Martial Law, 20th Anniv. — A988

2007, July 15 *Perf. 11¼x11½*

3755 A988 $12 multi .85 .40

Fish A989

Designs: No. 3756, $5, Nemateleotris magnifica. No. 3757, $5, Balistoides conspicillum. $12, Paracanthurus hepatus. $25, Cetoscarus bicolor.

2007, July 27 *Perf. 11½x11¼*

3756-3759 A989 Set of 4 6.00 3.00

Chiang Wei-shui (1890-1931), Political and Social Leader — A990

2007, Aug. 6 **Engr.** *Perf. 11¼x11½*

3760 A990 $25 brown 1.60 .80

Taiwan - African Heads of State Summit, Taipei A991

2007, Sept. 9 **Litho.** *Perf. 11½x11¼*

3761 A991 $12 multi 1.20 .60

Miniature Sheet

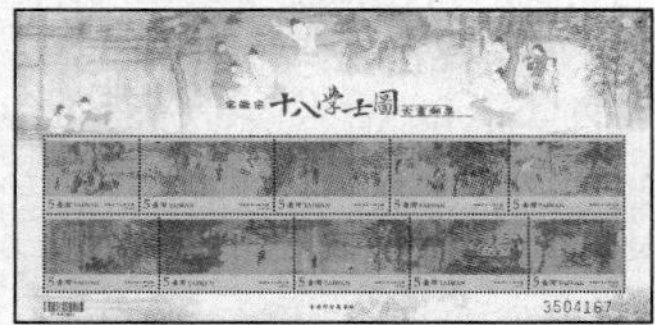

Eighteen Scholars of T'ang, by Emperor Hui-tsung. — A992

No. 3762 — Various portions of painting numbered: a, (10-5), 36x30mm. b, (10-4), 51x30mm. c, (10-3), 43x30mm. d, (10-2), 45x30mm. e, (10-1), 43x30mm. f, (10-10), 43x30mm. g, (10-9), 51x30mm. h, (10-8), 43x30mm. i, (10-7), 45x30mm. j, (10-6), 36x30mm.

2007, Sept. 21 *Perf. 13¼*

3762 A992 Sheet of 10 3.00 1.50
a.-j. $5 Any single .30 .25

Doves — A993

2007, Sept. 28 *Perf. 11¼x11½*

3763 A993 $5 multi .60 .30

Portions of the design were applied by a thermographic process producing a shiny, raised effect.

Shells A994

Designs: No. 3764, $5, Marchia loebbeckei. No. 3765, $5, Harpa major. No. 3766, $12, Epitonium scalare. No. 3767, $12, Cypraea aurantium.

2007, Oct. 11 **Litho.** *Perf. 11½x11¼*

3764-3767 A994 Set of 4 2.40 1.20

Orchids Type of 2007 Inscribed "Taiwan" Instead of "Republic of China"

Designs: $7, Ascocentrum sp. $9, Arundina graminifolia. $15, Vanda teres. $20, Epidendrum sp.

2007, Oct. 24 *Perf. 13½x12½*

3768 A967	$7 multi	.45	.25
3769 A967	$9 multi	.55	.30
3770 A967	$15 multi	.95	.45
3771 A967	$20 multi	1.25	.60
Nos. 3768-3771 (4)		3.20	1.60

Birds — A995

Designs: $3.50, Pericrocotus solaris. $5, Parus varius. $12, Luscinia calliope. $25, Phoenicurus auroreus.

2007, Nov. 3

3772 A995	$3.50 multi	.25	.25
3773 A995	$5 multi	.30	.25
3774 A995	$12 multi	.75	.35
3775 A995	$25 multi	1.60	.80
Nos. 3772-3775 (4)		2.90	1.65

See Nos. 3792-3795, 3819-3822, 3845-3848.

Outdoor Activities — A996

Designs: No. 3776, $5, Speed walking. No. 3777, $5, Cycling. $12, Skateboarding. $25, Rollerblading.

2007, Nov. 9 *Perf. 11½*

3776-3779 A996 Set of 4 3.00 1.50

Scouting, Cent. — A997

2007, Nov. 28 *Perf. 12½*

3780 A997 $12 multi .80 .40

A998

New Year 2008 (Year of the Rat) — A999

2007, Dec. 3 *Perf. 12½x11¾*

3781 A998 $3.50 Rat at left .45 .25
3782 A998 $13 Rat at right 1.45 .70

Souvenir Sheet

Perf. 12½

3783 A999 $12 multi 1.75 .85

Democracy Movement Leaders A1000

Designs: No. 3784, Lei Chen (1897-1979), publisher. No. 3785, Fu Jheng (1927-91), editor. No. 3786, Kuo Yu Shing (1908-85), politician. No. 3787, Huang Hsin Chieh (1928-99), politician.

2007, Dec. 10 **Engr.** *Perf. 11½*

3784 A1000	$5 brown	.35	.25
3785 A1000	$5 green	.35	.25
3786 A1000	$5 claret	.35	.25
3787 A1000	$5 brown black	.35	.25
Nos. 3784-3787 (4)		1.40	1.00

Liou Family Compound, Shangfangliao — A1001

Lin Family Mansion, Banciao — A1002

Li Teng-fang Compound, Dasi — A1003

Siao Family Compound, Jiadong — A1004

2008, Jan. 23 **Litho.** *Perf. 12*

3788 A1001	$5 multi	.35	.25
3789 A1002	$5 multi	.35	.25
3790 A1003	$5 multi	.35	.25
3791 A1004	$12 multi	.95	.45
Nos. 3788-3791 (4)		2.00	1.20

Birds Type of 2007

Designs: $1, Dicrurus aeneus. $2.50, Lanius schach. $10, Dendrocitta formosae. $32, Pycnonotus sinensis.

2008, Jan. 30 *Perf. 13½x12½*

3792 A995	$1 multi	.25	.25
3793 A995	$2.50 multi	.25	.25
3794 A995	$10 multi	.65	.30
3795 A995	$32 multi	2.00	1.00
Nos. 3792-3795 (4)		3.15	1.80

A1005

Puppet Theater — A1006

No. 3796: a, Mirror Man, denomination at UL. b, Old Oddball, denomination at UR.
No. 3797: a, Shih Yan-wun, denomination at UL. b, Dragon Lady of the Bitter Sea, denomination at UR.

2008, Feb. 4 *Perf. 11½*

3796 A1005 $5 Horiz. pair, #a-b .80 .40
3797 A1006 $5 Horiz. pair, #a-b .80 .40
c. Souvenir sheet, #3796-3797, perf. 11½x11 1.75 .80

Syrmaticus Mikado — A1007

Litho. & Engr.

2008, Mar. 7 *Perf. 12*
3798 A1007 $25 multi 1.75 .85

Taipei 2008 Intl. Stamp Exhibition A1008

Paintings: $5, Plum Blossoms and Solitary Bird, by Pien Wen-chin. $9, Apricot Blossoms and Peacocks, by Lü Chi. $13, Wild Duck by a Brook, by Ch'en Lin. $15, Bamboo and Shrike, by Li An-chung.

2008, Mar. 7 **Litho.** *Perf. 12½*
3799-3802 A1008 Set of 4 2.75 1.40
3802a Souvenir sheet, #3799-3802, perf. 12½ syncopated 2.75 2.50

Miniature Sheets

A1009

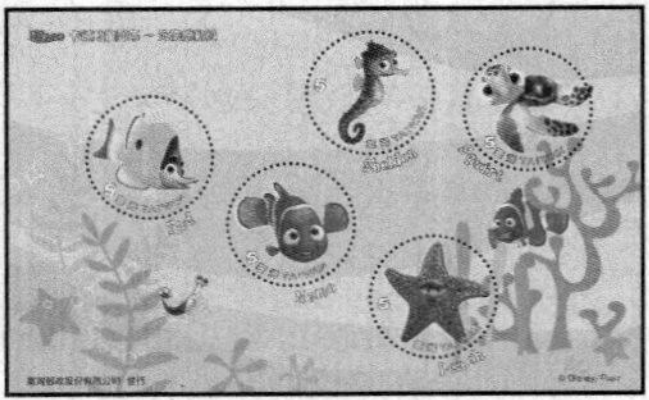

Characters From Animated Film, "Finding Nemo" — A1010

No. 3803: a, Turtles (32mm diameter). b, Dory (26x34mm). c, Bubbles (32mm diameter). d, Nemo (34x26mm). e, Pearl (32mm diameter).

No. 3804 (all stamps 32mm diameter): a, Sheldon. b, Squirt. c, Tad. d, Nemo. e, Peach.

Perf. 13x13½ (#3803b), 13½x13 (#3803d)

2008, Apr. 3
3803 A1009 $5 Sheet of 5, #a-e 1.75 .85
3804 A1010 $5 Sheet of 5, #a-e 1.75 .85

Cactus Flowers — A1011

Designs: No. 3805, $5, Hylocerus undatus. No. 3806, $5, Thelocactus bicolor. $12, Rhipsalidopsis gaertneri.

2008, Apr. 30 **Litho.** *Perf. 11¼x11½*
3805-3807 A1011 Set of 3 1.50 .75

Bridges Type of 2007 Inscribed "Taiwan"

Designs: No. 3808, $5, Wurih Bridge, Taichung. No. 3809, $5, Jilu Bridge, Nantou, at night. $12, Shueiyun Bridge, Shueili. $15, Sindong Bridge, Miaoli.

2008, May 12 *Perf. 11½x11¼*
3808-3811 A971 Set of 4 2.50 1.25

A1012

A1013

A1014

Inauguration of President Ma Ying-jeou and Vice-president Vincent C. Siew — A1015

2008, May 20 *Perf. 13½x13¼*
3812 A1012 $5 multi .35 .25
3813 A1013 $5 multi .35 .25
3814 A1014 $13 multi .85 .45
3815 A1015 $15 multi 1.00 .50
a. Miniature sheet, #3812-3815, perf. 12 2.60 1.40
Nos. 3812-3815 (4) 2.55 1.45

Yellow Tiger Flag A1016

Portrait of Jheng Cheng-gong A1017

2008, May 29 *Perf. 12½*
Stamps With White Frames
3816 A1016 $5 multi .35 .25
3817 A1017 $25 multi 1.90 .95

Souvenir Sheet
Perf. 13½
Stamps Without White Frames
3818 Sheet of 2 2.75 1.40
a. A1016 $5 multi .45 .25
b. A1017 $25 multi 2.25 1.10

National Taiwan Museum, cent.

Birds Type of 2007

Designs: $7, Streptopelia orientalis. $15, Passer montanus. $20, Pica pica. $34, Zosterops japonicus.

2008, June 5 *Perf. 13½x12½*
3819 A995 $7 multi .50 .25
3820 A995 $15 multi 1.00 .50
3821 A995 $20 multi 1.40 .70
3822 A995 $34 multi 2.25 1.10
Nos. 3819-3822 (4) 5.15 2.55

Stag Beetles — A1018

Designs: No. 3823, $5, Neolucanus swinhoei. No. 3824, $5, Dorcus schenklingi. $10, Lucanus datunensis. $12, Cyclommatus asahinai.

2008, June 5 *Perf. 12¼*
3823-3826 A1018 Set of 4 2.10 1.10

Shells A1019

Designs: No. 3827, $5, Murex troscheli. No. 3828, $5, Lambis chiragra. No. 3829, $12, Spondylus regius. No. 3830, $12, Cymatium pyrum.

2008, July 9 **Litho.** *Perf. 13½*
3827-3830 A1019 Set of 4 2.25 1.10

Urocissa Caerulea A1020

Designs: Nos. 3831, 3835a, $5, Adults feeding hatchlings in nest. Nos. 3832, 3835b, $5, Bird holding snake in beak. Nos. 3833, 3835c, $12, Bird in flight. Nos. 3834, 3835d, $12, Bird on branch with spread wings.

2008, July 9 *Perf. 13x13¼*
Stamps With White Frames
3831-3834 A1020 Set of 4 2.25 1.10

Souvenir Sheet
Stamps Without White Frames
Perf. 11¾
3835 A1020 Sheet of 4, #a-d 2.25 1.10

No. 3835 contains four 34x25mm stamps.

Miniature Sheet

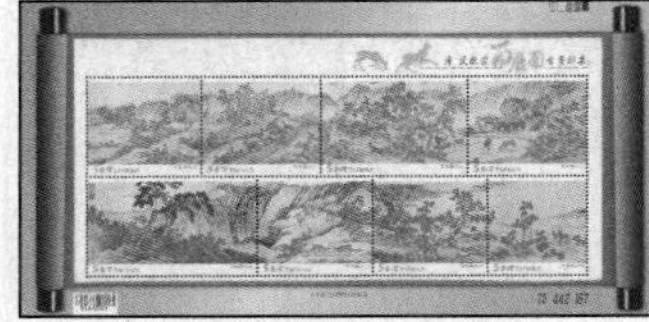

A Hundred Deers, by Ignace Sichelbart — A1021

No. 3836 — Parts of painting numbered: a, 8-1 (45x38mm). b, 8-2 (55x38mm). c, 8-3 (45x38mm). d, 8-4 (43x38mm). e, 8-5 (37x38mm). f, 8-6 (43x38mm). g, 8-7 (43x38mm). h, 8-8 (65x38mm).

2008, July 16 *Perf. 13¼*
3836 A1021 Sheet of 8, #a-h 2.75 1.40
a.-h. $5 Any single .30 .25

Items From Aboriginal Culture — A1022

Designs: $5, Paiwan earthenware pot. No. 3838, $12, Ami lover's bag (orange background). No. 3839, $12, Rukai men's headdress (lt. green background). $25, Bunun men's neck ornament.

2008, Aug. 1 *Perf. 11¼x11½*
3837-3840 A1022 Set of 4 3.50 1.75

Miniature Sheet

Yimin Festival — A1023

No. 3841: a, Erection of lantern poles. b, Bowl of congee, spoon, flowers. c, Sinpu Yimin Temple, horiz. d, Pig competition, horiz.

2008, Aug. 20 **Litho.** *Perf. 12½*
3841 A1023 $5 Sheet of 4, #a-d 1.25 .65

New Year 2009 (Year of the Ox) — A1024

Designs: $3.50, Head of ox. $13, Ox. $12, Ox in water, horiz.

2008, Dec. 1 *Perf. 12¼x11¾*
3842-3843 A1024 Set of 2 1.75 .85

Souvenir Sheet
Perf. 11¾x11¼
3844 A1024 $12 multi 1.10 1.10

No. 3844 contains one 50x30mm stamp.

Birds Type of 2007 Inscribed "Republic of China (Taiwan)"

Designs: 50c, Rostratula benghalensis. $9, Turdus poliocephalus. $13, Amaurornis phoenicurus. $17, Cettia acanthizoides.

2009, Jan. 15 *Perf. 13½x12½*
3845 A995 50c multi .25 .25
3846 A995 $9 multi .55 .25
3847 A995 $13 multi .80 .40
3848 A995 $17 multi 1.00 .50
Nos. 3845-3848 (4) 2.60 1.40

Giant Pandas in Taipei Zoo A1025

Designs: $5, Tuan Tuan on log bridge. $9, Yuan Yuan eating.
$25, Tuan Tuan and Yuan Yuan.

2009, Jan. 20 *Perf. 11½x11¼*
3849-3850 A1025 Set of 2 1.25 .60

Souvenir Sheet

Perf. 12

3851 A1025 $25 multi 1.50 1.50

No. 3851 contains one 50x40mm stamp.

Ceremonial Objects A1026

Designs: No. 3852, $5, Gift basket with handle, two women in background. No. 3853, $5, Wooden carrying box, men carrying box in background. No. 3854, $12, Bridal sedan chair, wedding procession in background. No. 3855, $12, Candlesticks, bride and groom holding incense sticks in background.

2009, Feb. 10 *Perf. 11½x11¼*
3852-3855 A1026 Set of 4 2.50 1.25

Shells A1027

Designs: No. 3856, $5, Strombus sinuatus. No. 3857, $5, Hydatina amplustre. No. 3858, $12, Cymatium hepaticum. No. 3859, $12, Mitra mitra.

2009, Feb. 26 *Perf. 13½*
3856-3859 A1027 Set of 4 2.25 1.10

Flowers — A1028

Designs: $3.50, Lantana camara. $5, Murraya paniculata. $12, Tabebuia chrysantha. $25, Hibiscus sabdariffa.

2009, Mar. 12 *Perf. 13½x12½*
3860 A1028 $3.50 multi .25 .25
3861 A1028 $5 multi .30 .25
3862 A1028 $12 multi .75 .35
3863 A1028 $25 multi 1.50 .75
Nos. 3860-3863 (4) 2.80 1.60

See Nos. 3890-3893, 3905-3908, 3934-3937.

Opening of Red and Orange Lines of Kaohsiung Mass Rapid Transit System A1029

Train and: $5, Central Park Station. $25, World Games Station.

2009, Apr. 7 *Perf. 11½x11¼*
3864-3865 A1029 Set of 2 2.00 1.00

A1030

Pres. Chiang Ching-kuo (1910-88) — A1031

Pres. Chiang: No. 3866, $5, Wearing hat (gray panel). No. 3877, $5, Wearing suit and tie (dull purple panel). $10, Holding cane (blue panel), horiz. $12, Holding baby (brown panel), horiz.

Perf. 11¼x11½, 11½x11¼

2009, Apr. 13
3866-3869 A1030 Set of 4 2.25 1.10

Souvenir Sheet

3870 A1031 $25 shown 2.00 1.00

Dragons Circling Two Carps By Type of 1997 With Denominations at Lower Right and Inscribed "Republic of China (Taiwan)"

2009, May 20 Engr. *Perf. 13¼x12½*
3871 A745 $50 cobalt blue 3.25 1.60

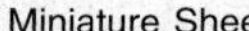

Miniature Sheet

Butterflies — A1032

No. 3872: a, $5, Papilio xuthus (butterfly cutout at LL). b, $5, Troides aeacus formosanus (butterfly cutout at LR). c, $12, Graphium agamemnon (butterfly cutout at UL). d, Papilio paris nakaharai (butterfly cutout at UR).

2009, June 25 Litho. *Perf. 11½x12*
3872 A1032 Sheet of 4, #a-d 2.10 1.10

2009 World Games, Kaohsiung — A1033

Designs: $5, Kaohsiung Arena and World Games mascots Kao Mei and Syong Ge. $12, Main Stadium and World Games emblem.

2009, July 16 *Perf. 12*
3873-3874 A1033 Set of 2 1.10 .55
3874a Souvenir sheet, #3873-3874 1.10 .55

Ancient Art Treasures — A1034

Designs: No. 3875, $5, Two Qing Dynasty gold gourds. No. 3876, $5, Gold bowl used by Emperor Qianlong. No. 3877, $12, Mughal Empire inlaid round urn. No. 3878, $12, Qing Dynasty gilt ewer.

2009, July 20 *Perf. 12¼*
3875-3878 A1034 Set of 4 2.10 1.10
3878a Souvenir sheet, #3875-3878, perf. 12¼x11¾ 2.25 1.10

Sites in Kinmen — A1035

Designs: $5, Guningtou. $9, Zhaishan Tunnel. No. 3881, $10, Interior of Qingtian Hall. No. 3882, $10, Lake Taihu.

2009, July 29 *Perf. 12½*
3879-3882 A1035 Set of 4 2.10 1.10

Paintings by Lin Yu-shan (1907-2004) — A1036

No. 3883: a, $5, On the Way Home. b, $25, Two Heads of Cattle.

2009, Aug. 7 Litho. *Perf. 12½x12*
3883 A1036 Horiz. pair, #a-b, + central label 2.50 1.25

Nursery Rhymes — A1037

Designs: No. 3884, $5, Little Girl and Her Doll (blue denomination). No. 3885, $5, Kingdom of Dolls (king and soldier on horses, yellow denomination). No. 3886, $5, Train, horiz. (red denomination). No. 3887, $5, Thunder Shower, horiz. (fish, fireflies, lotus flower, denomination in orange).

2009, Aug. 26 *Perf. 12¼*
3884-3887 A1037 Set of 4 1.25 .60

21st Summer Deaflympics, Taipei — A1038

Designs: $5, Badminton, running. $25, Taekwondo, tennis.

2009, Sept. 5 *Perf. 11½*
3888-3889 A1038 Set of 2 1.90 .95

Flowers Type of 2009

Designs: $1, Calliandra emarginata. $2.50, Bombax ceiba. $10, Delonix regia. $32, Spathodea campanulata.

2009, Oct. 14 Litho. *Perf. 13½x12½*
3890 A1028 $1 multi .25 .25
3891 A1028 $2.50 multi .25 .25
3892 A1028 $10 multi .65 .30
3893 A1028 $32 multi 2.00 1.00
Nos. 3890-3893 (4) 3.15 1.80

Greetings A1039

No. 3894: a, Necklace (orange background). b, Gift boxes (pink background). c, Bouquet of roses (yellow background). d, Lollipop and candy (light blue background). e, Balloons (orange red background). f, Champagne flutes (blue violet background). g, Hearts (yellow green background). h, Cake and strawberry (rose background). i, Sparklers (red violet background). j, Four-leaf clover (light green background).

No. 3895: a, Necklace (orange red background). b, Gift boxes (yellow green background). c, Bouquet of roses (pink background). d, Lollipop and candy (yellow background). e, Balloons (red background). f, Champagne flutes (red violet background). g, Hearts (orange background). h, Cake and strawberry (green background). i, Sparklers (blue background). j, Four-leaf clover (yellow background).

2009, Nov. 12 *Perf. 12½*
3894 Block of 10 2.50 1.25
a.-j. A1039 $3.50 Any single .25 .25
3895 Block of 10 3.00 1.50
a.-j. A1039 $5 Any single .30 .25

Nos. 3894 and 3895 were each printed in sheets containing two blocks + 5 labels.

Ferns — A1040

Designs: $5, Asplenium nidus. $9, Cyathea spinulosa. $12, Cyathea lepifera. $25, Cibotium taiwanense.

2009, Nov. 26 *Perf. 11¼x11½*
3896-3899 A1040 Set of 4 3.25 1.60
3899a Souvenir sheet, #3896-3899 3.25 1.60

See Nos. 4060-4063.

A1041

New Year 2010 (Year of the Tiger) — A1042

Tiger at: $3.50, Left. $13, Right.

2009, Dec. 1 *Perf. 12¼x12½*
3900-3901 A1041 Set of 2 1.50 .75

Souvenir Sheet

Perf. 12½

3902 A1042 $12 multi 1.10 1.10

Anti-Corruption Day — A1043

Background color: $5, Light blue. $25, Mauve.

2009, Dec. 9 Litho. *Perf. 11½*
3903-3904 A1043 Set of 2 1.90 .95

Flowers Type of 2009

Designs: $7, Michelia champaca. $15, Duranta repens. $20, Ixora chinensis. $34, Lagerstroemia speciosa.

2010, Jan. 20 *Perf. 13½x12½*

3905	A1028	$7 multi	.45	.25
3906	A1028	$15 multi	.95	.45
3907	A1028	$20 multi	1.25	.65
3908	A1028	$34 multi	2.25	1.10
		Nos. 3905-3908 (4)	4.90	2.45

Lin An-tai Historical Home, Taipei — A1044

Li Family Compound, Luzhou — A1045

Lin Family Compound, Wufeng — A1046

Xiaoyun Villa, Shengang — A1047

2010, Feb. 9 *Perf. 13½x13¼*

3909	A1044	$5 multi	.35	.25
3910	A1045	$5 multi	.35	.25
3911	A1046	$5 multi	.35	.25
3912	A1047	$12 multi	.75	.35
		Nos. 3909-3912 (4)	1.80	1.10

Little Taiwan, Qimei Islet A1048

Whale Arch, Xiaomen Islet A1049

Scenery of Penghu Islands: No. 3914, Basalt rocks, Xiaomen Islet. No. 3916, Twin heart-shaped stone weir, Qimei Islet.

2010, Feb. 24 *Perf. 13½*

3913	A1048	$5 shown	.35	.25
3914	A1048	$5 multi	.35	.25
3915	A1049	$10 shown	.65	.30
3916	A1049	$10 multi	.65	.30
		Nos. 3913-3916 (4)	2.00	1.10

Bridges A1050

Designs: No. 3917, $5, Jinde Bridge, Donggang (shown). No. 3918, $5, Qigu River Bridge, Tainan. No. 3919, $12, Anyi Bridge, Tainan. No. 3920, $12, Wangyue Bridge, Tainan (blue bridge at night).

2010, Mar. 10 *Perf. 11½*

3917-3920 A1050 Set of 4 2.25 1.10

Mushrooms A1051

Designs: Nos. 3921, 3925a, $5, Dictyphora multicolor. Nos. 3922, 3925b, $5, Pleurotus salmoneostramineus. Nos. 3923, 3925c, $12, Pseudocolus fusiformis. Nos. 3924, 3925d, $12, Coprinus disseminatus.

2010, Mar. 25 *Perf. 13*

Stamps With White Frames

3921-3924 A1051 Set of 4 2.25 1.10

Miniature Sheet

Stamps Without White Frames

Perf. 11¾

3925 A1051 Sheet of 4, #a-d 2.25 1.10

Crabs A1052

Designs: No. 3926, $5, Cardisoma carnifex. No. 3927, $5, Scandarma lintou. $10, Sesarmops intermedius. $25, Gecarcoidea lalandii.

2010, Apr. 15 *Perf. 11½*

3926-3929 A1052 Set of 4 3.00 1.50

Scenes From *The Romance of the Three Kingdoms* A1053

Designs: No. 3930, $3.50, Shooting an Arrow at the Halberd Beside the Gate of the Camp (shown). No. 3931, $3.50, Commenting on Heroes Over Wine. $5, Zhou Yu's Anger at Being Tricked by Zhuge Liang Three Times. $20, Holding Meng Huo Captive Seven Times.

2010, Apr. 29 *Perf. 11½*

3930-3933	A1053	Set of 4	2.10	1.10
3933a		Sheet of 4, #3930-3933, perf. 12	2.10	1.10

Flowers Type of 2009

Designs: 50c, Bauhinia variegata. $9, Euphorbia milii. $13, Brunfelsia hopeana. $17, Plumeria rubra.

2010, May 12 Litho. *Perf. 13½x12½*

3934	A1028	50c multi	.25	.25
3935	A1028	$9 multi	.55	.30
3936	A1028	$13 multi	.80	.40
3937	A1028	$17 multi	1.10	.55
		Nos. 3934-3937 (4)	2.70	1.50

Long-horned Beetles A1054

Designs: 75c, Erythrus formosanus. $2.50, Rosalia formosa conviva. $5, Aphrodisium faldermannii yuagii. $25, Anoplophora horsfieldi tonkinensis.

2010, May 21 *Perf. 12½x13½*

3938	A1054	75c multi	.25	.25
3939	A1054	$2.50 multi	.25	.25
3940	A1054	$5 multi	.30	.25
3941	A1054	$25 multi	1.60	.80
		Nos. 3938-3941 (4)	2.40	1.55

See Nos. 3976-3979, 4027-4030, 4134-4137.

Girl Scouts, Cent. — A1055

Emblems and: $5, Two doves, stylized globe. $25, Dove, ribbon hearts.

2010, June 1 *Perf. 12½*

3942-3943 A1055 Set of 2 1.90 .95

Souvenir Sheet

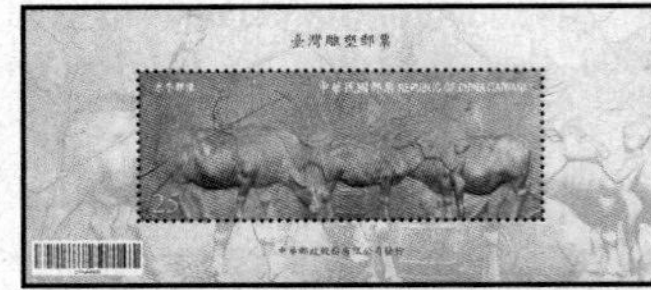

Water Buffaloes, Sculpture by Huang Tu-shui (1895-1930) — A1056

Litho. & Embossed

2010, June 22 *Perf. 11½x11¼*

3944 A1056 $25 multi 1.60 .80

A1057

Scenes From Novel "Journey to the West" — A1058

Designs: No. 3945, Complete Enlightenment. No. 3946, Sun Wukong Wreaks Havoc in Heaven. $12, Dreaming of Beheading the Jing River Dragon King. $25, Stealing the Ginseng Fruits.

2010, July 7 Litho. *Perf. 11¼x11½*

3945	A1057	$5 multi	.35	.25
3946	A1058	$5 multi	.35	.25
3947	A1058	$12 multi	.75	.35
3948	A1058	$25 multi	1.60	.80
		Nos. 3945-3948 (4)	3.05	1.65

Compare with Nos. 4003-4006.

Lighthouses A1059

Designs: No. 3949, $5, Chilung Tao Lighthouse (denomination in yellow). No. 3950, $5, Wenkan Tui Lighthouse (denomination in blue). $10, Paisha Chia Lighthouse (denomination in lilac), horiz. $25, Liuchiu Yu Lighthouse (denomination in light green), horiz.

Perf. 11¼x11½, 11½x11¼

2010, July 28

3949-3952 A1059 Set of 4 3.00 1.50

See Nos. 4160-4163.

Modern Taiwanese Paintings — A1060

No. 3953: a, $5, Bamboo Grove in Early Summer, by Tsai Yun-yan. b, $25, Pear Espalier, by Lu Yun-sheng.

2010, Aug. 9 *Perf. 12x12½*

3953 A1060 Horiz. pair, #a-b, + central label 1.90 .95

Souvenir Sheet

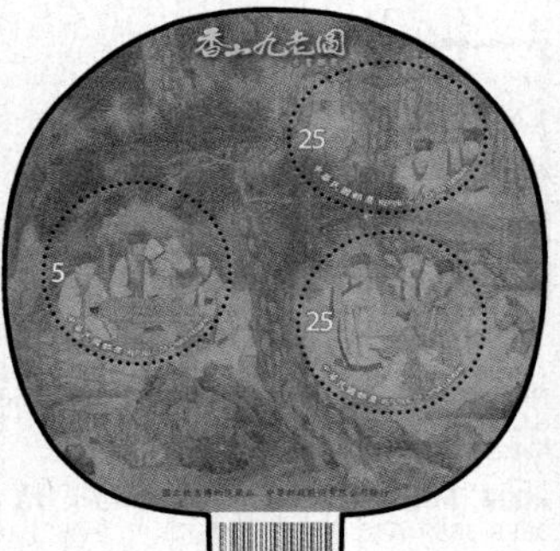

Nine Elders of Mt. Hsiang, by Unknown Painter — A1061

No. 3954: a, $5, Servant and elders playing game (35mm diameter). b, $25, Three elders and dancer (35mm diameter). c, $25, Elders in bamboo grove (37x29mm oval stamp).

2010, Sept. 9 *Perf.*

3954 A1061 Sheet of 3, #a-c 3.50 1.75

Stamps Depicting Educators A1062

Designs: $5, Republic of China No. 1648 (Chu Hsi). $25, Republic of China No. 1798 (Confucius).

Perf. 11¼x11½

2010, Sept. 28 **Litho.**

3955-3956 A1062 Set of 2 1.90 .95

Shells A1063

Designs: No. 3957, $5, Thatcheria mirabilis. No. 3958, $5, Tibia martinii. No. 3959, $12, Stellaria solaris. No. 3960, $12, Rapa rapa.

2010, Oct. 4 *Perf. 11½x11¼*

3957-3960 A1063 Set of 4 2.25 1.10

Bridges A1064

Designs: No. 3961, $5, Lizejian Bridge, Yilan (shown). No. 3962, $5, Taroko Bridge, Hualien. $12, Hongye Bridge, Taitung. $15, Pudu Bridge, Hualien.

2010, Oct. 20
3961-3964 A1064 Set of 4 2.50 1.25

National Taipei University of Technology, Cent. — A1065

No. 3965: a, $5, Building, old gate. b, $25, Sixth Instructional Building, Technology Building, new gate.

2010, Nov. 1 ***Perf. 12½***
3965 A1065 Horiz. pair, #a-b 2.00 1.00

A1066

A1067

A1068

A1069

A1070

A1071

A1072

A1073

A1074

A1075

A1076

A1077

A1078

A1079

A1080

A1081

A1082

A1083

A1084

2010, Nov. 6 Litho. ***Perf. 13½x13¼***

3966	Sheet of 9	3.25	1.60
a.	A1066 $5 multi	.35	.25
b.	A1067 $5 multi	.35	.25
c.	A1068 $5 multi	.35	.25
d.	A1069 $5 multi	.35	.25
e.	A1070 $5 multi	.35	.25
f.	A1071 $5 multi	.35	.25
g.	A1072 $5 multi	.35	.25
h.	A1073 $5 multi	.35	.25
i.	A1074 $5 multi	.35	.25

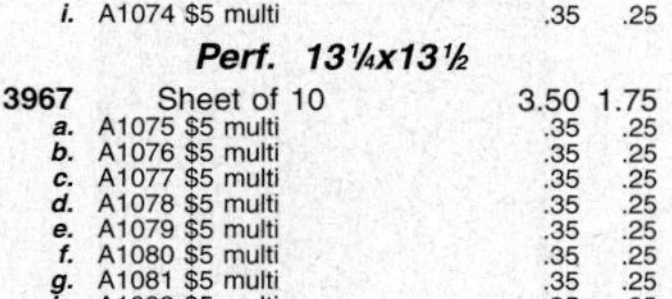

Perf. 13¼x13½

3967	Sheet of 10	3.50	1.75
a.	A1075 $5 multi	.35	.25
b.	A1076 $5 multi	.35	.25
c.	A1077 $5 multi	.35	.25
d.	A1078 $5 multi	.35	.25
e.	A1079 $5 multi	.35	.25
f.	A1080 $5 multi	.35	.25
g.	A1081 $5 multi	.35	.25
h.	A1082 $5 multi	.35	.25
i.	A1083 $5 multi	.35	.25
j.	A1084 $5 multi	.35	.25

Taipei International Flora Expo.

Qing Dynasty Gilt Copper Censers A1085

Censer with: No. 3968, $5, Turquoise inlays (shown). No. 3969, $5, Lotus flower designs. $10, Glass and enamel inlays. $25, White jade, turquoise and glass inlays.

2010, Nov. 18 ***Perf. 11½***
3968-3971 A1085 Set of 4 3.00 1.50
3971a Souvenir sheet of 4, #3968-3971, perf. 12 3.00 1.50

New Year 2011 (Year of the Rabbit) A1086

Designs: $3.50, Two rabbits. $13, One rabbit.
$12, One rabbit, diff.

2010, Dec. 1 ***Perf. 12¼***
3972-3973 A1086 Set of 2 1.10 .55

Souvenir Sheet

Perf. 12½

3974 A1086 $12 multi .80 .40

No. 3974 contains one 61x37mm stamp.

Miniature Sheet

Fireworks Displays — A1087

No. 3975: a, $5, Double Tenth Day display, Taipei (30x30mm). b, $5, New Year's display at Taipei 101 Building (24x48mm). c, $25, Lantern Festival display, Kaohsiung (30x30mm). d, $25, Dragon Boat Festival display, Longtan (24x48mm).

Litho. With Hologram

2011, Jan. 1 ***Perf. 13¼***
3975 A1087 Sheet of 4, #a-d 4.25 2.10

Long-horned Beetles Type of 2010

Designs: $1, Aeolesthes oenochrous. $3.50, Doliops similis. $10, Thermistis taiwanensis. $32, Dorysthenes pici.

2011, Jan. 26 Litho. ***Perf. 12½x13½***

3976	A1054	$1 multi	.25	.25
3977	A1054	$3.50 multi	.25	.25
3978	A1054	$10 multi	.70	.35
3979	A1054	$32 multi	2.25	1.10
	Nos. 3976-3979 (4)		3.45	1.95

Valentine's Day — A1088

Quick response code and: $5, Outline of heart. $25, Heart.

2011, Feb. 14 ***Perf. 12½***
3980-3981 A1088 Set of 2 2.10 1.10

Values are for stamps with surrounding selvage.

Fish A1089

Designs: No. 3982, $5, Candidia barbatus. No. 3983, $5, Opsariichthys pachycephalus. $12, Spinibarbus hollandi. $25, Squalidus banarescui.

2011, Mar. 18 ***Perf. 13½x13¼***
3982-3985 A1089 Set of 4 4.00 1.60

Miniature Sheet

Butterflies — A1090

No. 3986: a, $5, Euploea eunice hobsoni (butterfly cutout at LL). b, $5, Euploea sylvester swinhoei (butterfly cutout at LR). c, $12, Euploea tulliolus koxinga (denomination at LL). d, $12, Euploea mulciber barsine (denomination at LR).

2011, Apr. 8 ***Perf. 12½x12***
3986 A1090 Sheet of 4, #a-d 2.40 1.25

National Tsing Hua University, Cent. A1091

Designs: $5, Second campus gate, old library building. $25, Current campus gate, Humanities and Social Sciences Building.

2011, Apr. 20 ***Perf. 12½***
3987-3988 A1091 Set of 2 2.10 1.10

Alpine Flowers — A1092

Designs: No. 3989, $5, Gentiana scabrida var. punctulata. No. 3990, $5, Euphrasia transmorrisonensis. No. 3991, $10, Clematis montana, horiz. No. 3992, $10, Cypripedium formosanum, horiz.

2011, May 16		*Perf. 12*	
3989-3992 A1092	Set of 4	2.10	1.10

A Singularly Harmonious Vibration — A1093

Double Happiness A1094

Blessings From the Three Stars A1095

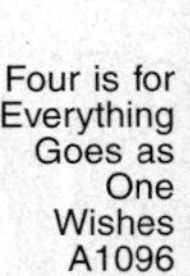

Four is for Everything Goes as One Wishes A1096

Bumper Crops of All Five Grains A1097

Spring in All Six Directions A1098

Seven is for a Match Made in Heaven A1099

The Eight Immortals Wish for Your Longevity A1100

Nine Similes and Three Abundances — A1101

Ten Complete A1102

No. 3993 — Color of denomination: a, Blue green. b, Pink. c, Gray. d, Orange red. e, Red violet. f, Red. g, Blue gray. h, Purple. i, Green. j, Olive green.

No. 3994 — Color of denomination: a, Olive green. b, Gray. c, Pink. d, Purple. e, Red. f, Blue gray. g, Orange red. h, Green. i, Red violet. j, Blue green.

2011, May 27		*Perf. 12½*	
3993	Block of 10	2.50	1.25
a.	A1093 $3.50 multi	.25	.25
b.	A1094 $3.50 multi	.25	.25
c.	A1095 $3.50 multi	.25	.25
d.	A1096 $3.50 multi	.25	.25
e.	A1097 $3.50 multi	.25	.25
f.	A1098 $3.50 multi	.25	.25
g.	A1099 $3.50 multi	.25	.25
h.	A1100 $3.50 multi	.25	.25
i.	A1101 $3.50 multi	.25	.25
j.	A1102 $3.50 multi	.25	.25
3994	Block of 10	3.50	1.75
a.	A1093 $5 multi	.35	.25
b.	A1094 $5 multi	.35	.25
c.	A1095 $5 multi	.35	.25
d.	A1096 $5 multi	.35	.25
e.	A1097 $5 multi	.35	.25
f.	A1098 $5 multi	.35	.25
g.	A1099 $5 multi	.35	.25
h.	A1100 $5 multi	.35	.25
i.	A1101 $5 multi	.35	.25
j.	A1102 $5 multi	.35	.25

Sea Slugs A1103

Designs: No. 3995, $5, Mexichromis multituberculata. No. 3996, $5, Chromodoris willani. $12, Gymnodoris ceylonica. $25, Glossodoris averni.

2011, June 8		*Perf. 12½*	
3995-3998 A1103	Set of 4	3.25	1.60

Owls — A1104

Designs: No. 3999, $5, Asio otus. No. 4000, $5, Otus sunia. $10, Strix aluco. $25, Glaucidium brodiei.

2011, July 7	**Engr.**	*Perf. 12¾x12½*	
3999-4002 A1104	Set of 4	3.25	1.60

See Nos. 4051-4054, 4122-4125.

Swindling Treasures A1105

Red Boy — A1106

Crossing the River on a Turtle's Back — A1107

Achieving Nirvana — A1108

2011, July 21		**Litho.**	
4003 A1105	$5 multi	.35	.25
4004 A1106	$5 multi	.35	.25
4005 A1107	$12 multi	.85	.40
4006 A1108	$25 multi	1.75	.85
	Nos. 4003-4006 (4)	3.30	1.75

Scenes from Novel "Journey to the West." Compare with Nos. 3945-3948.

Atayal Facial Tattoos A1109

2011, Aug. 1		*Perf. 12½*	
4007 A1109	$25 multi	1.75	.85

Souvenir Sheet

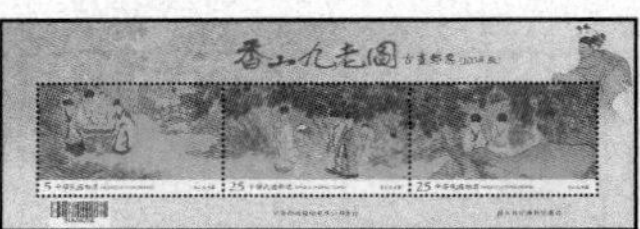

Scroll Painting, "Nine Elders of Mt. Hsiang" — A1110

No. 4008: a, $5, Three elders and attendant at game table. b, $25, Three elders and three attendants dancing. c, $25, Two elders reading, attendant, tree in foreground.

2011, Sept. 9		*Perf. 13½x13¼*	
4008 A1110	Sheet of 3, #a-c	3.75	1.90

National Palace Museum A1111

Taipei 101 Building A1112

Sun Moon Lake A1113

Yushan (Jade Mountain) A1114

Alishan A1115

Love River, Kaohsiung A1116

Beach, Kenting A1117

Day Lilies in Liushidan Mountains A1118

Taroko National Park A1119

Jiufen A1120

2011, Sept. 27		*Perf. 12½*	
4009	Block of 10	2.50	1.25
a.	A1111 $3.50 multi	.25	.25
b.	A1112 $3.50 multi	.25	.25
c.	A1113 $3.50 multi	.25	.25
d.	A1114 $3.50 multi	.25	.25
e.	A1115 $3.50 multi	.25	.25
f.	A1116 $3.50 multi	.25	.25
g.	A1117 $3.50 multi	.25	.25
h.	A1118 $3.50 multi	.25	.25
i.	A1119 $3.50 multi	.25	.25
j.	A1120 $3.50 multi	.25	.25
4010	Block of 10	3.50	1.75
a.	A1111 $5 multi	.35	.25
b.	A1112 $5 multi	.35	.25
c.	A1113 $5 multi	.35	.25
d.	A1114 $5 multi	.35	.25
e.	A1115 $5 multi	.35	.25
f.	A1116 $5 multi	.35	.25
g.	A1117 $5 multi	.35	.25

h.	A1118 $5 multi	.35	.25
i.	A1119 $5 multi	.35	.25
j.	A1120 $5 multi	.35	.25

Travel destinations. Nos. 4009 and 4010 were each printed in sheets containing two blocks + 5 labels.

A1121

Republic of China, Cent. — A1122

No. 4011: a, Flag of Republic of China, Sun Yat-sen, doves over buildings. b, Presidential Office Building, bananas, pineapple, sugar cane. c, Building, highway bridge, airplane, ship. d, Train, silicon wafers, satellite dish. No. 4012, Flag of Republic of China, Presidential Office Building, Sun Yat-sen.

Perf. 12½x13¼ Syncopated

2011, Oct. 10 Litho.

4011	Horiz. strip of 4	3.25	1.60
a.-b.	A1121 $5 Either single	.35	.25
c.	A1121 $10 multi	.65	.35
d.	A1121 $25 multi	1.75	.85

Souvenir Sheet

Litho. With Foil Application

Perf. 13¼

4012	A1122 $25 multi	1.75	.85

The syncopation between Nos. 4011a and 4011b is a rectangle, and oval between Nos. 4011b and 4011c and 4011c and 4011d.

Plum Blossoms A1123

Perf. 13¼x13½

2011, Oct. 10 Litho. & Engr.

4013	A1123 $100 multi	6.75	3.25

No. 4013 was printed in sheets of 10 + 8 labels.

Scouting in China, Cent. — A1124

Scout and: $5, City. $12, Mountain, horiz.

Perf. 12¾x12½, 12½x12¾

2011, Nov. 1 Litho.

4014-4015	A1124 Set of 2	1.25	.60

Railway Branch Lines — A1125

No. 4016: a, $5, Shalun Branch Line (denomination in pink). b, $5, Jiji Branch Line (denomination in orange). c, $12, Neiwan Branch Line (denomination in blue). d, $12, Liujia Branch Line (denomination in pink). e, $15, Pingxi Branch Line.

2011, Nov. 12 ***Perf. 12½***

4016	Vert. strip of 5	3.50	1.75
a.-b.	A1125 $5 Either single	.35	.25
c.-d.	A1125 $12 Either single	.80	.40
e.	A1125 $15 multi	1.00	.50

New Year 2012 (Year of the Dragon) A1126

Designs: $3.50, Two dragons. $13, Dragon facing left.

$12, Dragon facing right.

2011, Dec. 1 ***Perf. 13***

4017-4018	A1126 Set of 2	1.10	.55

Souvenir Sheet

Perf. 12½

4019	A1126 $12 multi	.80	.40

No. 4019 contains one 64x40mm stamp.

Souvenir Sheet

Alishan Forest Railway, Cent. — A1127

No. 4020: a, $5, Diesel engine, tunnel. b, $25, Steam engine.

2011, Dec. 25 ***Perf. 12½x12¾***

4020	A1127 Sheet of 2, #a-b	2.00	1.00

Berries — A1128

Designs: $3.50, Actinidia callosa. $5, Sypsepalum dulcificum. $12, Solanum americanum. $25, Solanum verbascifolium.

2012, Jan. 12 ***Perf. 13¼x12½***

4021	A1128 $3.50 multi	.25	.25
4022	A1128 $5 multi	.35	.25
4023	A1128 $12 multi	.85	.40
4024	A1128 $25 multi	1.75	.85
	Nos. 4021-4024 (4)	3.20	1.75

See Nos. 4084-4087, 4106-4109, 4164-4167..

A1129

Roses — A1130

No. 4025: a, Rose. b, Rose, stem and leaves.

$32, Two roses.

Litho. & Embossed

2012, Feb. 10 ***Perf. 14½***

4025	A1129 Horiz. pair + central label	2.60	1.25
a.	$12 multi	.85	.40
b.	$25 multi	1.75	.85

Souvenir Sheet

Litho.

Perf.

4026	A1130 $32 multi	2.25	1.10

No. 4026 is impregnated with a rose scent.

Long-horned Beetles Type of 2010

Designs: $7, Leptura formosomontana formosomontana. $12, Pyrestes curticornis. $15, Anaglyptus meridionalis. $20, Anoplophora albopicta.

2012, Mar. 9 Litho. ***Perf. 12½x13½***

4027	A1054 $7 multi	.50	.25
4028	A1054 $12 multi	.85	.40
4029	A1054 $15 multi	1.00	.50
4030	A1054 $20 multi	1.40	.70
	Nos. 4027-4030 (4)	3.75	1.85

Mushrooms A1131

Designs: Nos. 4031, 4035a, $5, Amanita rubrovolvata. Nos. 4032, 4035b, $5, Entoloma murraii. Nos. 4033, 4035c, $12, Geastrum sessile. Nos. 4034, 4035d, $12, Clavulinopsis miyabeana.

2012, Mar. 23 ***Perf. 13¼x13***

Stamps With White Frames

4031-4034	A1131 Set of 4	2.40	1.25

Souvenir Sheet

Stamps Without White Frames

Perf. 12¾x13

4035	A1131 Sheet of 4, #a-d	2.40	1.25

No. 4035 contains four 26x34mm stamps.

Fish A1132

Designs: No. 4036, $5, Formosania lacustre. No. 4037, $5, Tanakia himantegus. $12, Channa asiatica. $25, Sinogastromyzon puliensis.

2012, Apr. 11 ***Perf. 12½x13¼***

4036-4039	A1132 Set of 4	3.25	1.60

Scenes From Novel "Outlaws of the Marsh" A1133

Designs: No. 4040, $5, Demons Released (denomination at LL). No. 4041, $5, Slaying the Tiger on Jingyang Ridge (denomination at LR). $10, Mountain God Temple on a Stormy Night. $25, Knocking the Lord of the West Dead.

2012, Apr. 25 ***Perf. 12½x12¾***

4040-4043	A1133 Set of 4	3.25	1.60

See Nos. 4110-4113.

"A Match Made in Heaven" A1134

"One Child After Another" A1135

Congratulatory greetings: $5, "The Hall is Packed with Wealth and Riches." $12, "A Family Experinces Two Joys."

2012, May 4 ***Perf. 13***

4044	A1134 $3.50 multi	.25	.25
4045	A1135 $3.50 multi	.25	.25
4046	A1135 $5 multi	.35	.25
4047	A1135 $12 multi	.80	.40
	Nos. 4044-4047 (4)	1.65	1.15

Booklet Stamp

Perf. 13½ Vert.

4048	A1135 $5 multi	.35	.25
a.	Booklet pane of 12	4.25	—
	Complete booklet, #4048a	4.25	

Inauguration of President Ma Ying-jeou and Vice President Wu Den-yih — A1136

No. 4049 — President, Vice president and: a, Flag and Presidental Palace. b, Taipei 101 building, train, ship and airplane. c, Children, dancers, National Theater. d, Map of Taiwan, stylized globe. $32, President, Vice President, flag, Presidential Palace, plum blossoms, horiz.

2012, May 20 ***Perf. 13¼x13½***

4049	Horiz. strip of 4	2.40	1.25
a.-b.	A1136 $5 Either single	.35	.25
c.-d.	A1136 $12 Either single	.80	.40

Souvenir Sheet

Perf. 13½x13¼

4050	A1136 $32 multi	2.25	1.10

No. 4050 contains one 80x30mm stamp.

Owls Type of 2011

Designs: No. 4051, $5, Asio flammeus. No. 4052, $5, Otus spilocephalus. $10, Strix leptogrammica. $25, Ninox scutulata.

2012, June 6 Engr. ***Perf. 12¾x12½***

4051-4054	A1104 Set of 4	3.00	1.50

Festivals A1137

Designs: No. 4055, $5, Chinese New Year (fireworks and calligraphic couplets). No.

4056, $5, Lantern Festival (lanterns and sandals). $10, Dragon Boat Festival (herb sachets and covered wine containers). $25, Mid-autumn Festival (Jade Hare, Lady Chang'e, moon cakes).

2012, June 20 Litho. *Perf. 12½*
4055-4058 A1137 Set of 4 3.00 1.50

Miniature Sheet

Bees and Wasps — A1138

No. 4059: a, $5, Phimenes flavopictus. b, $5, Xanthopimpla pedator. c, $5, Vespa ducalis. d, $10, Apis mellifera. e, $10, Xylocopa tranquebarorum. f, $10, Apis cerana.

2012, July 12 *Perf. 13*
4059 A1138 Sheet of 6, #a-f 3.00 1.50

Ferns Type of 2009

Designs: No. 4060, $5, Polystichum lepidocaulon. No. 4061, $5, Bolbitis heteroclita. $10, Adiantum malesianum, horiz. $25, Asplenium prolongatum, horiz.

Perf. 12¾x12½, 12½x12¾
2012, July 25
4060-4063 A1040 Set of 4 3.00 1.50
4063a Sheet of 4, #4060-4063, perf. 12, + label 3.00 1.50

Familial Bonds A1139

Silhouettes of: $5, Father and daughter. $7, Mother and son. $10, Mother, father and child. $12, Grandparents and child.

2012, Aug. 24 *Perf. 12½x13¼*
4064-4067 A1139 Set of 4 2.40 1.25

Miniature Sheet

Teas and Tourist Attractions — A1140

No. 4068: a, Baozhong tea, Pinglin Tea Museum (bright yellow frame). b, Tieguanyin tea, Maokong Funicular (yellow orange frame). c, Black tea, Sun Moon Lake Wharf (orange frame). d, Oolong tea, Alishan Forest train (bister frame). e, Oriental Beauty tea, Emei Lake Suspension Bridge (red brown frame).

2012, Sept. 12 *Perf. 12½*
4068 A1140 $10 Sheet of 5, #a-e 3.50 1.75

Nos. 4068a-4068e each have a cut-out of a teapot under the denomination.

Cotton Rose — A1141

Bird-of-Paradise Flower — A1142

Clary Sage — A1143

Dancing Lady Orchid — A1144

Zinnia — A1145

Marigold A1146

Chinese Hibiscus — A1147

Fragrant Olive — A1148

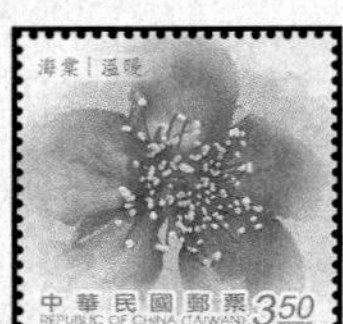

Flowering Crab Apple — A1149

Hydrangea A1150

2012, Sept. 28 *Perf. 13¼*

4069	Block of 10	2.50	1.25
a.	A1141 $3.50 multi	.25	.25
b.	A1142 $3.50 multi	.25	.25
c.	A1143 $3.50 multi	.25	.25
d.	A1144 $3.50 multi	.25	.25
e.	A1145 $3.50 multi	.25	.25
f.	A1146 $3.50 multi	.25	.25
g.	A1147 $3.50 multi	.25	.25
h.	A1148 $3.50 multi	.25	.25
i.	A1149 $3.50 multi	.25	.25
j.	A1150 $3.50 multi	.25	.25
4070	Block of 10	3.50	1.75
a.	A1141 $5 multi	.35	.25
b.	A1142 $5 multi	.35	.25
c.	A1143 $5 multi	.35	.25
d.	A1144 $5 multi	.35	.25
e.	A1145 $5 multi	.35	.25
f.	A1146 $5 multi	.35	.25
g.	A1147 $5 multi	.35	.25
h.	A1148 $5 multi	.35	.25
i.	A1149 $5 multi	.35	.25
j.	A1150 $5 multi	.35	.25

Miniature Sheets

A1151

Characters From *Toy Story* — A1152

No. 4071: a, $5, Mr. Pricklepants, Peas-in-a-Pod (40x30mm). b, $5, Aliens (35mm diameter). c, $5, Trixie, Buttercup (40x30mm). d, $12, Lotso-Huggin Bear (30x40mm). e, $12, Woody (35mm diameter).
No. 4072: a, $5, Woody on Bullseye (35mm diameter). b, $5, Rex (35mm diameter). c, $5, Hamm (35mm diameter). d, $12, Buzz Lightyear (35mm diameter). e, $12, Jessie (30x40mm).

Serpentine Die Cut (round stamps), Serpentine Die Cut 14x13½ (horiz. stamps), Serpentine Die Cut 13½x14 (vert. stamps)
2012, Oct. 23 Self-Adhesive
4071 A1151 Sheet of 5, #a-e 2.75 1.40
4072 A1152 Sheet of 5, #a-e 2.75 1.40

Protected Mammals A1153

Designs: No. 4073, $5, Paguma larvata taivana. No. 4074, $5, Mustela nivalis formosana. $10, Martes flavigula chrysopila. $25, Viverricula indica pallida.

2012, Nov. 7 Litho. *Perf. 12½x13¼*
4073-4076 A1153 Set of 4 3.25 1.60

A1154

Three Friends and a Hundred Birds, by Pien Wen-chin (c. 1356-c. 1428) — A1155

No. 4077 — Details from painting of various birds in tree: a, $5. b, $10. c, $12.
$70, Entire painting.

2012, Nov. 22 *Perf. 13¼x13*
4077 A1154 Sheet of 3, #a-c 1.90 .95

Souvenir Sheet
Silk-Faced Paper
Perf. 14x14¼
4078 A1155 $70 multi 5.00 2.50

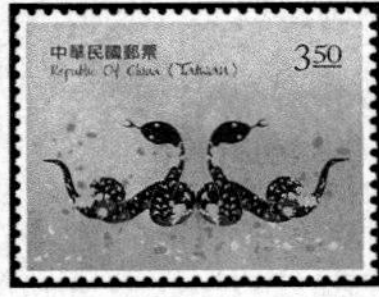

New Year 2013 (Year of the Snake) A1156

Designs: $3.50, Two snakes. $13, Snake, head at left.
$12, Snake, head at right.

2012, Dec. 3 *Perf. 13*
4079-4080 A1156 Set of 2 1.25 .60

Souvenir Sheet
Perf. 12½
4081 A1156 $12 multi .85 .45

No. 4081 contains one 64x40mm stamp.

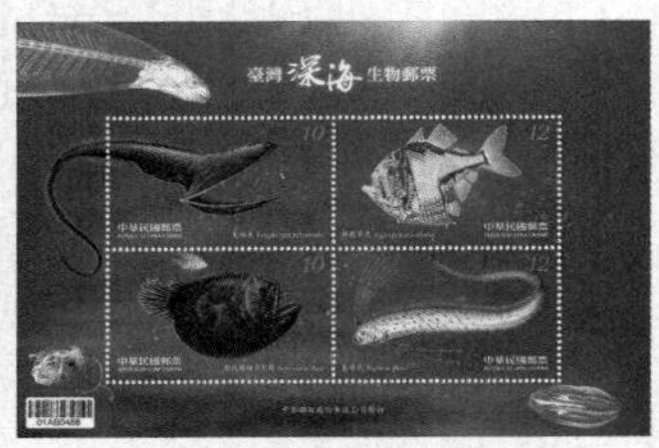

Marine Life — A1157

No. 4082: a, $10, Eurypharynx pelecanoides. b, $10, Bufoceratias shaoi. c, $12, Argyropelecus aculeatus. d, $12, Regalecus glesne.
$25, Histioteuthis celetaria pacifica, vert.

Litho., Litho. With Foil Application (#4082c)
2012, Dec. 12 *Perf. 14x13¼*
4082 A1157 Sheet of 4, #a-d 3.00 1.50

Souvenir Sheet
Perf. 13¼x14
4083 A1157 $25 multi 1.75 .85

Berries Type of 2012

Designs: $2.50, Rhodomyrtus tomentosa. $7, Ardisia squamulosa. $10, Hylocereus undatus. $32, Mahonia japonica.

2013, Jan. 17 Litho. *Perf. 13¼x12½*

4084 A1128	$2.50 multi	.25	.25
4085 A1128	$7 multi	.50	.25
4086 A1128	$10 multi	.70	.35
4087 A1128	$32 multi	2.25	1.10
	Nos. 4084-4087 (4)	3.70	1.95

Chinese Dishes — A1158

No. 4088 — Chopsticks and: a, Kung Pao Chicken, bowl of rice, spoon. b, Mud Crab with Glutinous Rice Cake, cup of green tea, salt shaker. c, Three-cup Chicken, bowl of sauce, salt shaker. d, Hakka Stir-fry, bowl of rice, salt shaker.

2013, Jan. 31 ***Perf. 13¼x13***

4088 A1158 $5 Horiz. strip of 4, #a-d 1.40 .70

Compare with Type A1176.

St. Valentine's Day — A1159

Designs: $12, Colored roses. $25, White roses.

Litho. & Embossed

2013, Feb. 4 ***Perf. 13¼x13½***

4089-4090 A1159 Set of 2 2.50 1.25

4090a Souvneir sheet of 2, #4089-4090 2.50 1.25

Grain Farming — A1160

Designs: $5, Oryza sativa. $7, Setaria italica. $10, Zea mays. $25, Triticum aestivum.

2013, Mar. 5 **Litho.** ***Perf. 12½***

4091-4094 A1160 Set of 4 3.25 1.60

A1161

A1162

A1163

A1164

A1165

Qing Dynasty Embroidery — A1166

2013, Mar. 20 **Litho.** ***Perf. 14***

4095	A1161 $10 multi	.70	.35
4096	A1162 $10 multi	.70	.35
4097	A1163 $10 multi	.70	.35
4098	A1164 $10 multi	.70	.35
4099	A1165 $10 multi	.70	.35
	Nos. 4095-4099 (5)	3.50	1.75

Litho. & Embossed With Foil Application

Souvenir Sheet

Silk-Faced Paper

Perf. 13x13¼

4100 A1166 $100 multi 6.75 3.50

Children at Play — A1167

Children: No. 4101, $5, Carrying lantern. No. 4102, $5, Flying paper airplanes. No. 4103, $5, With pinwheels. No. 4104, $5, With spinning top. No. 4105, $5, With hand puppets.

2013, Apr. 2 **Litho.** ***Perf. 12½***

4101-4105 A1167 Set of 5 1.75 .85

4105a Booklet pane of 10, 2 each #4101-4105, perf. 12½ on 3 sides 3.50 —

Complete booklet, #4105a 3.50

See Nos. 4168-4172.

Berries Type of 2012

Designs: $1, Ribes formosanum. $15, Garcinia subelliptica. $17, Coffea arabica. $20, Smilax ocreata.

2013, Apr. 17 ***Perf. 13¼x12½***

4106	A1128 $1 multi	.25	.25
4107	A1128 $15 multi	1.00	.50
4108	A1128 $17 multi	1.25	.60
4109	A1128 $20 multi	1.40	.70
	Nos. 4106-4109 (4)	3.90	2.05

Capturing Daming Prefecture by Ruse A1168

Heavenly Inscriptions on Stele A1169

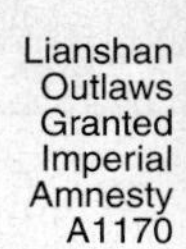

Lianshan Outlaws Granted Imperial Amnesty A1170

Successful Expedition Against Liao Empire A1171

2013, May 10 ***Perf. 12½x12¾***

4110	A1168 $5 multi	.35	.25
4111	A1169 $5 multi	.35	.25
4112	A1170 $10 multi	.70	.35
4113	A1171 $25 multi	1.75	.85
	Nos. 4110-4113 (4)	3.15	1.70

Scenes from novel "Outlaws of the Marsh." Compare with Nos. 4040-4043.

Congratulations — A1172

Designs: No. 4114, $3.50, Tropical fish. No. 4115, $3.50, Swans. No. 4116, $5, Penguins. No. 4117, $5, Mandarin ducks.

2013, May 22 ***Perf. 12½***

4114-4117 A1172 Set of 4 1.25 .60

Values are for stamps with surrounding selvage.

Herbs — A1173

Designs: No. 4118, $5, Mentha x piperita. No. 4119, $5, Rosmarinus officinalis. $12, Salvia elegans. $15, Artemisia indica.

2013, June 11

4118-4121 A1173 Set of 4 2.50 1.25

See Nos. 4179-4182, 4244-4247.

Owls Type of 2011

Designs: No. 4122, $5, Otus lettia. No. 4123, $5, Tyto longimembris. $10, Ketupa flavipes. $25, Otus elegans botelensis.

Perf. 12¾x12½

2013, June 26 **Engr.**

4122-4125 A1104 Set of 4 3.00 1.50

Vases — A1174

Designs: $12, Ming Dynasty vase with "One Hundred Deer" design. $25, Qing Dynasty vase with "One Hundred Boys" design.

2013, July 10 **Litho.**

4126-4127 A1174 Set of 2 2.50 1.25

4127a Souvenir sheet of 2, #4126-4127 2.50 1.25

Mushrooms A1175

Designs: Nos. 4128, 4132a, $5, Ramaria botrytis. Nos. 4129, 4132b, $5, Morchella elata. Nos. 4130, 4132c, $12, Gomphus floccosus. Nos. 4131, 4132d, $12, Aleuria aurantia.

2013, July 24 ***Perf. 12½***

Stamps With White Frames

4128-4131 A1175 Set of 4 2.25 1.10

Souvenir Sheet

Stamps Without White Frames

Perf. 12½x13

4132 A1175 Sheet of 4, #a-d 2.25 1.10

No. 4132 contains four 26x34mm stamps.

Chinese Dishes — A1176

No. 4133 — Chopsticks and: a, Stinky tofu, condiment bowl at UL. b, Taiwanese meatball, two sauce bottles at UL. c, Oyster omelet, teapot and condiment bowl at UL. d, Braised pork rice, salt and pepper shakers at UL.

2013, Aug. 16 ***Perf. 13¼x13***

4133 A1176 $5 Horiz. strip of 4, #a-d 1.40 .70

Compare with Type A1158.

Long-horned Beetles Type of 2010

Designs: No. 4134, Parandra lanyuana. No. 4135, Bunothorax takasagoensis. $10, Oplatocera mandibulata. $25, Cyrtoclytus kusumai.

2013, Aug. 28 ***Perf. 12½x13½***

4134	A1054 $5 multi	.35	.25
4135	A1054 $5 multi	.35	.25
4136	A1054 $10 multi	.70	.35
4137	A1054 $25 multi	1.75	.85
	Nos. 4134-4137 (4)	3.15	1.70

Soong May-ling (Madame Chiang) (1898-2003), First Lady — A1177

2013, Sept. 12 ***Perf. 12¾x12½***
4138 A1177 $12 multi .80 .40

A1178

Emperor Gaozong Era Artifacts — A1179

No. 4139: a, Qing Dynasty gourd-shaped vase. b, Qing Dynasty carved red lacquer bowl, horiz. c, Northern Song Dyanasty plate with celadon glaze, horiz. d, Qing Dynasty jade bear-shaped vessel.
$25, Qing Dynasty New Year's silk tapestry scroll.

2013, Oct. 8 **Litho.** ***Perf. 12***
4139 A1178 Sheet of 4 + label 2.50 1.25
a. $5 multi .35 .25
b.-c. $10 Either single .65 .30
d. $12 multi .85 .40

Souvenir Sheet
Perf. 12¾x12½
4140 A1179 $25 multi 1.75 .85

Presidential Office Building, Taipei — A1180

Sun Yat-sen Memorial Hall, Taipei — A1181

National Palace Museum, Taipei — A1182

Taipei 101 Building — A1183

Chiang Kai-shek Memorial Hall, Taipei — A1184

Jiufen — A1185

Alishan — A1186

Qingshui Cliff — A1187

Queen's Head Rock Formation A1188

Sun Moon Lake — A1189

2013, Oct. 22 **Litho.** ***Perf. 13¼***
4141 Block of 6 2.10 1.10
a. A1180 $5 multi .35 .25
b. A1181 $5 multi .35 .25
c. A1182 $5 multi .35 .25
d. A1183 $5 multi .35 .25
e. A1184 $5 multi .35 .25
f. A1185 $5 multi .35 .25
4142 Block of 4 3.50 1.60
a. A1186 $12 multi .85 .40
b. A1187 $12 multi .85 .40
c. A1188 $12 multi .85 .40
d. A1189 $12 multi .85 .40

Bicycle Paths — A1190

Bicyclist on: No. 4143, $5, Yangguang Bridge on Xindian River Bicycle Path, New Taipei City (pale orange panel). No. 4144, $5, Bali Zuoan Bicycle Path, New Taipei City (pink panel). No. 4145, $10, Sankeng Bicycle Path, Taoyuan (green panel). No. 4146, $10, Hsinchu Coast Bicycle Path (yellow panel).

2013, Nov. 8 **Litho.** ***Perf. 13¼x13***
Stamp + Label
4143-4146 A1190 Set of 4 2.10 1.10

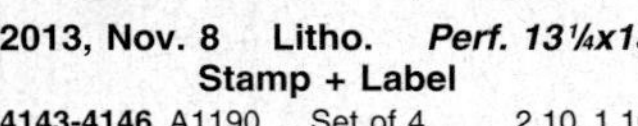

Dragon and Phoenix — A1191

2013, Nov. 15 **Engr.** ***Perf. 13¼x12½***
4147 A1191 $50 car & rose 3.50 1.75

Qing Dynasty Bowl, 1723-35 A1192

Wash Bowl, Southern Song to Yuan Dynasties, 13th-14th Cent. A1193

Ming Dynasty Jar With Lid, 1465-87 A1194

12th Cent. Ding Ware Pillow A1195

Ming Dynasty Flower Holder A1196

Qing Dynasty Covered Box, 1874-1908 A1197

Qing Dynasty Jadeite Cabbage and Insects Figurine A1198

Ru Ware Warming Bowl, 11th-12th Cent. A1199

Qing Dynasty Stone With Meat Design A1200

Western Zhoud Dynasty Mao-gong Ding (Ritual Vessel) A1201

2013, Nov. 22 **Litho.** ***Perf. 12½***
4148 Block of 6 2.10 1.10
a. A1192 $5 multi .35 .25
b. A1193 $5 multi .35 .25
c. A1194 $5 multi .35 .25
d. A1195 $5 multi .35 .25
e. A1196 $5 multi .35 .25
f. A1197 $5 multi .35 .25
4149 Block of 4 3.50 1.60
a. A1198 $12 multi .85 .40
b. A1199 $12 multi .85 .40
c. A1200 $12 multi .85 .40
d. A1201 $12 multi .85 .40

Items in National Palace Museum.

New Year 2014 (Year of the Horse) A1202

Designs: $3.50, Horse with leg lifted. $13, Horse leaping.
$12, Two leaping horses.

2013, Dec. 2 **Litho.** ***Perf. 13***
4150-4151 A1202 Set of 2 1.10 .55

Souvenir Sheet
Perf. 12½
4152 A1202 $12 multi .85 .40

No. 4152 contains one 64x40mm stamp.

Corals A1203

Designs: $3.50, Dendronephthya gigantea. $5, Pavona cactus. $10, Acropora granulosa. $15, Melithaea ochracea.

2014, Jan. 8 **Litho.** ***Perf. 12½x13¼***
4153-4156 A1203 Set of 4 2.25 1.10

See Nos. 4257-4260, 4308-4311, 4425-4428.

Chinese Desserts — A1204

No. 4157: a, Pineapple-filled shortcrust pastries, orange shopping bag and box. b, Mochi, green shopping bag and box. c, Sun cakes, red shopping bag and box. d, Egg yolk pastries, rose lilac shopping bag and box.

2014, Jan. 22 **Litho.** ***Perf. 13¼x13***
4157 A1204 $5 Horiz. strip of 4, #a-d 1.40 .70

Lophura Swinhoii — A1205

No. 4158: a, Immature male. b, Head of mature male. c, Chicks. d, Hen and chick. $25, Male and female.

Perf. 12½x13¼

2014, Feb. 20 **Litho.**

4158 A1205 Block of 4 2.25 1.25
a.-b. $5 Either single .35 .25
c. $10 multi .65 .35
d. $12 multi .80 .40

Souvenir Sheet

Perf. 13½

4159 A1205 $25 multi 1.75 .85

No. 4159 contains one 80x50mm stamp.

Lighthouses Type of 2010

Designs: No. 4160, $5, Fangyuan Lighthouse (denomination in rose), horiz. No. 4161, $5, Chamu Yu Lighthouse (denomination in blue), horiz. $10, Lanyu Lighthouse (denomination in purple), horiz. $25, Sandiaojiao Lighthouse (denomination in yellow), horiz.

2014, Mar. 6 **Litho.** ***Perf. 12½x12¾***

4160-4163 A1059 Set of 4 3.00 1.50

Berries Type of 2012

Designs: No. 4164, Lycium chinense. No. 4165, Dianella ensifolia. $15, Ampelopsis brevipedunculata var. hancei. $34, Diplocylos palmatus.

Perf. 13¼x12½

2014, Mar. 27 **Litho.**

4164 A1128 $5 multi .35 .25
4165 A1128 $5 multi .35 .25
4166 A1128 $15 multi 1.00 .50
4167 A1128 $34 multi 2.25 1.10
Nos. 4164-4167 (4) 3.95 2.10

Children at Play Type of 2013

Designs: No. 4168, $5, Boy on hobby horse. No. 4169, $5, Children playing with bamboo helicopters. No. 4170, $5, Child flying kite. No. 4171, $5, Children playing marbles. No. 4172, $5, Children with Lion Dance costumes.

2014, Apr. 2 **Litho.** ***Perf. 12½***

4168-4172 A1167 Set of 5 1.75 .85
4172a Booklet pane of 10, 2 each #4168-4172, perf. 12½ on 3 sides 3.50 —
Complete booklet, #4172a 3.50

Children at Play Bathing a Buddha, Scroll Painting by Su Hanchen A1206

Children Playing in an Autumn Garden, Scroll Painting by Su Hanchen A1207

Children Playing in Summer, Scroll Painting by Unknown Artist — A1208

Children Playing in Autumn, Scroll Painting by Unknown Artist — A1209

Children Painting in Winter, Scroll Painting by Unknown Artist — A1210

2014, Apr. 30 **Litho.** ***Perf. 13¼x12½***

4173 A1206 $5 multi .35 .25
4174 A1207 $5 multi .35 .25
4175 A1208 $10 multi .70 .35
4176 A1209 $10 multi .70 .35
4177 A1210 $12 multi .80 .40
Nos. 4173-4177 (5) 2.90 1.60

"The Swan Goose Carries a Message" — A1211

Perf. 13½x13¼

2014, May 9 **Litho. & Engr.**

4178 A1211 $9 multi .60 .30

See People's Republic of China No. 4189.

Herbs Type of 2013

Designs: $3.50, Foeniculum vulgare. $5, Perilla frutescens. $12, Lavandula angustifolia. $25, Ocimum basilicum.

2014, June 11 **Litho.** ***Perf. 12½***

4179-4182 A1173 Set of 4 3.00 1.50

Souvenir Sheet

Electrification of the Hua-tung Railway — A1212

No. 4183: a, $5, Trains in Hualien Station. b, $12, Train and Kecheng bridge. c, $25, Train exiting Shanli Tunnel.

Perf. 12½x12¾

2014, June 28 **Litho.**

4183 A1212 Sheet of 3, #a-c 3.00 1.50

Cuichi Pond A1213

Tunlu Pond A1214

Designs: $10, Qicai Lake. $12, Jiaming Lake.

2014, July 17 **Litho.** ***Perf. 13¼***

4184 A1213 $5 multi .35 .25
4185 A1214 $5 multi .35 .25
4186 A1214 $10 multi .70 .35
4187 A1214 $12 multi .80 .40
Nos. 4184-4187 (4) 2.20 1.25

Compare with Nos. 4340-4343.

National Taiwan Library, Cent. — A1215

2014, Aug. 9 **Litho.** ***Perf. 12½***

4188 A1215 $12 multi .80 .40

Jugang Tower and Residential Buildings, Kinmen — A1216

Wentai Pagoda and Buildings, Kinmen — A1217

2014, Aug. 28 **Litho.** ***Perf. 12½***

4189 Horiz. pair 1.10 .65
a. A1216 $5 multi .35 .25
b. A1217 $12 multi .80 .40

Kinmen County, cent.

Miniature Sheet

Museums — A1218

No. 4190: a, $5, National Taiwan Museum of Fine Arts (modern building with lawn), Taichung. b, $5, National Taiwan Museum, Taipei (building with 6 pillars). c, $5, National Museum of Taiwan Literature (building with domes at sides). d, $5, National Museum of Taiwan History (building with solar panels). e, $12, National Palace Museum, vert.

2014, Sept. 10 **Litho.** ***Perf. 12½***

4190 A1218 Sheet of 5, #a-e, + 4 labels 2.10 1.10

Blue and White Porcelain A1219

Designs: $5, Qing Dynasty dish with floral design. $10, Ming Dynasty jar with peony design. $12, Ming Dynasty jar with dragon design. $20, Qing Dynasty vase depicting women.

$25, Qing Dynasty plate with bird and flowers design, horiz.

Litho. & Embossed

2014, Sept. 19 ***Perf. 13¾x13½***

4191-4194 A1219 Set of 4 3.25 1.60

Souvenir Sheet

Perf. 13½x13¾

4195 A1219 $25 multi 1.75 .85

Miniature Sheet

Taipei 2015 Asian International Stamp Exhibition — A1220

No. 4196: a, $5, Pink azalea blossoms in spring, Mt. Hehuan. b, $5, Tung trees in summer, Pingxi Railway. c, $10, Maple trees in autumn, Wuling Farm. d, $25, Cherry blossoms in winter, Mt. Xue.

2014, Oct. 3 **Litho.** ***Perf. 12½***

4196 A1220 Sheet of 4, #a-d, + 4 labels 3.00 1.50

Miniature Sheet

Taipei Zoo, Cent. — A1221

No. 4197: a, $5, Formosan serow (30x40mm). b, $5, Formosan pangolin (40x30mm). c, $10, Asian elephant (55x38mm). d, $10, Formosan black bear (30x40mm). e, $12, Bengal tiger (55x38mm). f, $12, Giant pandas (38x55mm).

Perf. 13¼x12½, 12½x13¼

2014, Oct. 16 Litho.
4197 A1221 Sheet of 6, #a-f 3.50 1.75

A1222

Scenes From Novel "The Dream of Red Mansions," by Cao Xueqin: No. 4198, $5, Women standing around seated man. No. 4199, $5, Woman and five men looking at garden. $10, Visit of Yuanchun at Lantern Festival. $25, Baochai chasing butterflies.

2014, Oct. 27 Litho. *Perf. 13x13½*
4198-4201 A1222 Set of 4 3.00 1.50

See Nos. 4228-4231, 4304-4307, 4361-4364.

Flowers in Koji Pottery Vases — A1223

Large vases with: No. 4202, $5, Peonies (yellow green panel). No. 4203, $5, Lotuses (blue panel). $10, Chrysanthemums (orange panel). $25, Camellias (pink lilac panel).

2014, Nov. 14 Litho. *Perf. 13½*
4202-4205 A1223 Set of 4 3.00 1.50

Bride and Groom In Chinese Attire A1224

Bride and Groom in Western Attire A1225

Bride and groom with: No. 4206, Red ribbon. No. 4207, Angels and flowers. No. 4208, Red streamer and bow. No. 4209, Hearts and horses.

2014, Nov. 21 Litho. *Perf. 12½*

4206	A1224 $3.50 multi		.25	.25
4207	A1225 $3.50 multi		.25	.25
4208	A1224 $5 multi		.35	.25
4209	A1225 $5 multi		.35	.25
	Nos. 4206-4209 (4)		1.20	1.00

New Year 2015 (Year of the Ram) — A1226

Designs: $3.50, Bright pink ram. $13, Purple ram.
$12, Two rams.

2014, Dec. 1 Litho. *Perf. 13*
4210-4211 A1226 Set of 2 1.10 .55

Souvenir Sheet

Perf. 12½

4212 A1226 $12 multi .80 .40

No. 4212 contains one 64x40mm stamp.

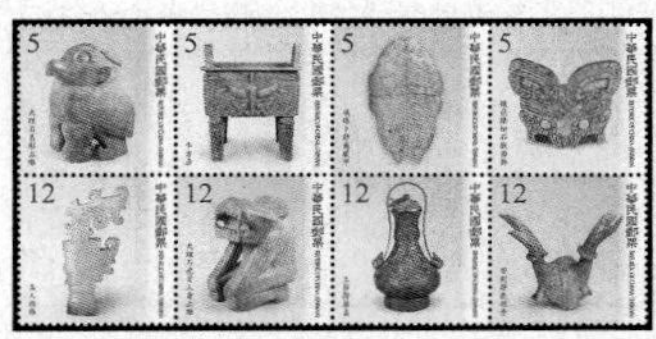

Archaeological Treasures From Yin Ruins — A1227

No. 4213: a, Marble figurine depicting owl, rose brown background. b, Cauldron with handles, light blue background. c, Oracle bone, rose brown background. d, Mask for horse with turquoise inlays, gray blue background. e, Figurine of human head with crest, light blue background. f, Anthropomorphic figurine with tiger's head, rose brown background. g, Wine container with detachable cap, gray blue background. h, Deer skull with inscriptions, rose brown background.

2014, Dec. 10 Litho. *Perf. 12½*

4213	A1227 Block of 8	4.25	2.10
a.-d.	$5 Any single	.25	.25
e.-h.	$12 Any single	.80	.40
i.	Souvenir sheet of 8, #4213a-4213h + 4 labels	4.25	2.10

Jellyfish — A1228

Designs: $5, Pelagia noctiluca. $7, Physophora hydrostatica. $10, Mastigias papua. $12, Cyanea capillata.

2015, Jan. 8 Litho. *Perf. 13¼x13*
4214-4217 A1228 Set of 4 2.25 1.10

Legumes A1229

Designs: $5, Arachis hypogaea. $7, Vigna angularis. $10, Glycine max. $25, Vigna radiata.

2015, Jan. 28 Litho. *Perf. 13¼x12½*
4218-4221 A1229 Set of 4 3.00 1.50

Animals — A1230

Nos. 4222 and 4223: a, Rabbits. b, Squirrels. c, Dogs. d, Bears. e, Elephants. f, Cats. g, Deer. h, Sheep. i, Zebras. j, Giraffes.

2015, Feb. 12 Litho. *Perf. 13¼*

4222	Block of 10	2.50	1.25
a.-j.	A1230 $3.50 Any single	.25	.25
4223	Block of 10	3.50	1.75
a.-j.	A1230 $5 Any single	.35	.25

Bo Le Appraises the Horse A1231

The Ambition of a Swan A1232

Adept With Both the Pen and the Sword A1233

Tiny Blade of Grass and Spring Sun A1234

Perf. 12½x12¾

2015, Mar. 20 Litho.

4224	A1231 $5 multi	.35	.25
4225	A1232 $5 multi	.35	.25
4226	A1233 $5 multi	.35	.25
4227	A1234 $5 multi	.35	.25
	Nos. 4224-4227 (4)	1.40	1.00

Chinese idioms.

Daiyu Burying the Flowers A1235

Tanchun Starting a Poetry Club A1236

Grandmother Liu Touring Daguanyuan — A1237

Miaoyu Tasting Tea A1238

2015, Mar. 30 Litho. *Perf. 13x13¼*

4228	A1235 $5 multi	.35	.25
4229	A1236 $5 multi	.35	.25
4230	A1237 $10 multi	.65	.30
4231	A1238 $25 multi	1.60	.80
	Nos. 4228-4231 (4)	2.95	1.60

Scenes from "The Dream of Red Mansions," by Cao Xueqin. Compare with Nos. 4198-4201, 4304-4307, 4361-4364.

Teresa Teng (1953-95), Singer — A1239

Various photographs of Teng with panel color of: $5, Pink. $9, Orange. $13, Dull rose. $15, Lilac.

2015, Apr. 15 Litho. *Perf. 12½*
4232-4235 A1239 Set of 4 2.75 1.40

Control Yuan Building, Cent. — A1240

2015, Apr. 24 Litho. *Perf. 13¼*
4236 A1240 $25 multi 1.75 .85

Taipei 2015 Intl. Stamp Exhibition — A1241

No. 4237: a, Dragon. b, Geese.

2015, Apr. 24 Litho. *Perf. 14*

4237	A1241 Horiz. pair + central label	2.10	1.10
a.	$5 multi	.35	.25
b.	$25 multi	1.75	.85
c.	Souvenir sheet of 4, 2 each #4237a-4237b, perf. 13¼x13½ syncopated	4.25	2.25

Black-faced Spoonbills on Zengwen River — A1242

Black-winged Stilt, Sicao Wetlands A1243

2015, Apr. 25 Litho. *Perf. 14*

4238 A1242 $10 multi		.65	.30
4239 A1243 $25 multi		1.75	.85
a.	Horiz. pair, #4238-4239, + central label	2.40	1.25
b.	Vert. pair, #4238-4239, no label	2.40	1.25

Taipei 2015 Intl. Stamp Exhibition. Nos 4238-4239 were printed in sheets of 16 (8 of each stamp) + 9 labels.

A1244

Taipei 2015 Intl. Stamp Exhibition — A1245

No. 4240: a, Family, child playing with blocks. b, Family on bicycle.

No. 4241: a, Family, child playing with blocks at left, on bicycle at right. b, Family, child playing with blocks at right, on bicycle at left.

2015, Apr. 26 Litho. *Perf. 12¾x12½*

4240 A1244	Horiz. pair + central label	2.10	1.10
a.	$5 multi	.35	.25
b.	$25 multi	1.75	.85

Souvenir Sheet

4241 A1245	Sheet of 2	3.50	1.75
a.-b.	$25 Either single	1.75	.85

Taipei 2015 Intl. Stamp Exhibition — A1246

No. 4242: a, Sky Lantern Festival, Pingxi. b, Xiao Liuqiu coral island.

2015, Apr. 27 Litho. *Perf. 14*

4242 A1246	Horiz. pair + central label	2.60	1.25
a.	$12 multi	.80	.40
b.	$25 multi	1.75	.85

Taipei 2015 Intl. Stamp Exhibition — A1247

No. 4243 — Scroll paintings: a, Literary Gathering, by Emperor Huizong. b, Elegant Gathering in the Western Garden, by Zhao Mengfu.

2015, Apr. 28 Litho. *Perf. 13¼x12½*

4243 A1247	Horiz. pair + central label	2.40	1.25
a.	$9 multi	.60	.30
b.	$25 multi	1.75	.85
c.	Souvenir sheet of 2, #4243a-4243b, + label	2.40	1.25

Herbs Type of 2013

Designs: $3.50, Allium schoenoprasum. $5, Borago officinalis. $12, Tropaeolum majus. $25, Chamaemelum nobile.

2015, June 11 Litho. *Perf. 12½*

4244-4247 A1173 Set of 4 3.00 1.50

Liberation of Taiwan in World War II, 70th Anniv. — A1248

Designs: No. 4248, $3.50, Soldiers carrying flags. No. 4249, $3.50, Farm woman holding sheaf of rice, Shimen Reservoir. No. 4250, $5, People cheering Chiang Kai-shek, horiz. No. 4251, $5, Crowd in plaza celebrating Taiwan Retrocession Day, 1963, horiz.

2015, July 7 Litho. *Perf. 12½*

4248-4251 A1248 Set of 4 1.10 .55

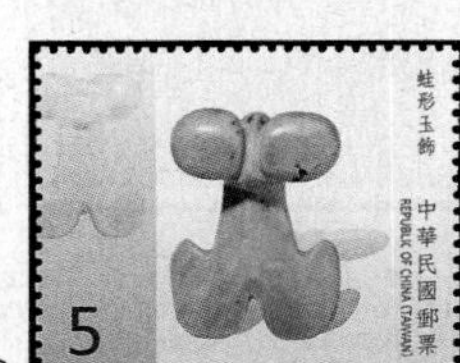
A1249

Prehistoric Artifacts — A1250

Designs: $5, Frog-shaped jade ornament. $7, Jade tubes. $9, Circular jade bangle. $12, String of jade beads.
$20, Jade earring.

2015, Aug. 21 Litho. *Perf. 12½*

4252-4255 A1249 Set of 4 2.10 1.10

Souvenir Sheet

4256 A1250 $20 multi 1.25 .60

Corals Type of 2014

Designs: $3.50, Montipora foliosa. $5, Sarcophyton ehrenbergi. $10, Ellisella robusta. $15, Stylaster gracilis.

2015, Sept. 10 Litho. *Perf. 12½*

4257-4260 A1203 Set of 4 2.10 1.10

A1251

Paintings by Giuseppe Castiglione (Lang Shining) — A1252

Designs: No. 4261, $5, Gathering of Auspicious Signs (flowers in vase). No. 4262, $5, Long-haired Dog Beneath Blossoms. No. 4263, $9, Ayusi Sweeping Bandits with a Lance, horiz. No. 4264, $9, Cochin Lemur, horiz.

No. 4265 — Golden Pheasant in Spring: a, $12. b, $70.

2015, Oct. 8 Litho. *Perf. 13¼*

4261-4264 A1251 Set of 4 1.75 .85

Souvenir Sheet
Silk-Faced Paper

4265 A1252 Sheet of 2, #a-b 5.00 2.50

Sun Yat-sen (1866-1925), First President of Republic of China — A1253

Various depictions of Sun Yat-sen: $5, $12, horiz.

2015, Nov. 12 Litho. *Perf. 12½*

4266-4267 A1253 Set of 2 1.10 .55

Rail Tourism — A1254

Designs: $5, Yuli-Taitung Summer Formosa train, railroad bridge. $10, South Link Line train, bridge near coast. $15, Jiji Line Evolution No. 1001 train, bicyclists.

2015, Nov. 25 Litho. *Perf. 13x13¼*

4268-4270 A1254 Set of 3 1.90 .95

New Year 2016 (Year of the Monkey) A1255

Designs: $3.50, Monkey facing right. $13, Monkey facing left.
$12, Two monkeys.

2015, Dec. 1 Litho. *Perf. 13*

4271-4272 A1255 Set of 2 1.00 .50

Souvenir Sheet
Perf. 12½

4273 A1255 $12 multi .75 .35

No. 4273 contains one 64x40mm stamp.

A1256

Opening of National Palace Museum Southern Branch — A1257

Designs: $5, Right-spiraling conch, Qing dynasty. $10, Jade bowl with handles and lid. $12, Hanging scroll with deities Good Fortune, Wealth and Long Life.

No. 4277: a, Board from Tibetan Kangyar with text and two deities. b, Board from Tibetan Kangyar with five deities.

Perf. 14¼x14½

2015, Dec. 10 Litho.

4274-4276 A1256 Set of 3 1.75 .85

Souvenir Sheet
Perf. 14¾

4277 A1257 $25 Sheet of 2, #a-b 3.00 1.50

Souvenir Sheets

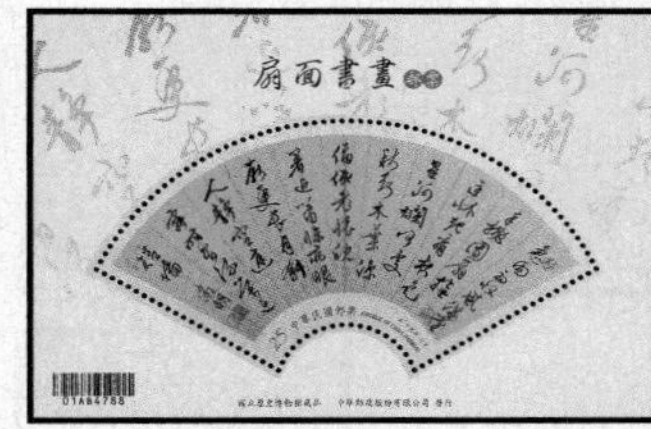
Fan With Verse in Calligraphy by Wen Zhengming (1470-1559) — A1258

2016, Jan. 13 Litho. *Perf. 13½*

4278 A1258 $25 multi 1.50 .75

Litho. With Bamboo Veneer Affixed

4279 A1258 $80 multi 4.75 2.40

Fruit — A1259

Designs: $1, Atemoyas. $2.50, Papayas. $5, Lychees. $15, Dates.

2016, Jan. 28 Litho. *Perf. 12½x13½*

4280 A1259	$1 multi	.25	.25
4281 A1259	$2.50 multi	.25	.25
4282 A1259	$5 multi	.30	.25
4283 A1259	$15 multi	.90	.45
	Nos. 4280-4283 (4)	1.70	1.20

See Nos. 4365-4368, 4383-4386.

Churches — A1260

Designs: No. 4284, $5, Church of St. Joseph, Jinlun (with "Kiokai ni Santo Yosef" sign). No. 4285, $5, Holy Family Church, Taipei. No. 4286, $12, Minor Basilica of the Immaculate Conception, Wanjin. No. 4287, $12, Cathedral of the Holy Rosary, Kaohsiung, vert.

2016, Feb. 4 Litho. *Perf. 13¼*
4284-4287 A1260 Set of 4 2.10 1.10

Souvenir Sheet

Chinese Postal Service, 120th Anniv. — A1261

No. 4288 — Mailbox and: a, $5, Bicycle. b, $12, Motorcycle.

2016, Mar. 18 Litho. *Perf. 13*
4288 A1261 Sheet of 2, #a-b 1.10 .55

Tree Peonies — A1262

Peach Blossoms A1263

Herbaceous Peonies — A1264

Flowering Crab Apple and Magnolia Blossoms A1265

Corn Poppies and Fringed Iris — A1266

Yellow Prickly Roses and Peonies — A1267

Carnations A1268

Cherries and Grosbeaks A1269

Perf. 13¼x12½
2016, Mar. 29 Litho.

4289	A1262	$5 multi	.30	.25
4290	A1263	$5 multi	.30	.25
4291	A1264	$7 multi	.45	.25
4292	A1265	$9 multi	.55	.30
4293	A1266	$10 multi	.65	.30
4294	A1267	$10 multi	.65	.30
4295	A1268	$12 multi	.75	.35
4296	A1269	$12 multi	.75	.35
	Nos. 4289-4296 (8)		4.40	2.35

Paintings by Giuseppe Castiglione (1688-1766).

Miniature Sheet

Taitung County — A1270

No. 4297: a, $5, Footbridge, Sanxiantai. b, $5 People watching hot air balloons over Luye Highlands. c, $10, Fishing boat, Lanyu Island. d, $12, National Museum of Prehistory, Taitung.

2016, Apr. 20 Litho. *Perf. 12½x12¾*
4297 A1270 Sheet of 4, #a-d 2.00 1.00

Tea Grinding, by Liu Songnian (1174-1224) A1271

Lu Tong Brewing Tea, by Qian Xuan (1235-1305) A1272

Tasting Tea, by Wen Zhengming (1470-1559) A1273

2016, May 5 Litho. *Perf. 12¾*

4298	A1271	$5 multi	.30	.25
4299	A1272	$15 multi	.95	.45
4300	A1273	$25 multi	1.60	.80
	Nos. 4298-4300 (3)		2.85	1.50

South China Sea Peace Initiative A1274

No. 4301: a, Map of South China Sea, memorial plaque, Taiping Island. b, Taiping Lighthouse. c, Solar panels, Taiping Island National Monument and flags. d, Trail, goat and chickens.

2016, May 5 Litho. *Perf. 12½x12¾*

4301	Horiz. strip of 4	2.60	1.40
a.	A1274 $5 multi	.30	.25
b.	A1274 $9 multi	.55	.30
c.	A1274 $13 multi	.80	.40
d.	A1274 $15 multi	.95	.45

Pixelated Faces — A1275

Line-Drawn Faces — A1276

No. 4302 — Images of newly-elected Pres. Tsai Ing-wen and Vice-president Chen Chien-jen with background colors of: a, Light gray brown. b, Orange. c, Brownish gray. d, Turquoise.

$32, 20 pixelated faces.

2016, May 20 Litho. *Perf. 12½*

4302	Strip of 4	2.10	1.10
a.	A1275 $5 multi	.30	.25
b.	A1276 $5 multi	.30	.25
c.	A1275 $12 multi	.75	.35
d.	A1276 $12 multi	.75	.35

Souvenir Sheet

Perf. 12½x12¾

4303 A1275 $32 multi 2.00 1.00

No. 4303 contains one 80x30mm stamp.

Xiangling Studies Poetry A1277

White Snow and Pink Plum Blossoms A1278

Qingwen Repairs a Coat A1279

Lantern Festival Feast A1280

2016, June 29 Litho. *Perf. 14*

4304	A1277	$5 multi	.30	.25
4305	A1278	$5 multi	.30	.25
4306	A1279	$10 multi	.65	.30
4307	A1280	$25 multi	1.60	.80
	Nos. 4304-4307 (4)		2.85	1.60

Scenes from "The Dream of Red Mansions," by Cao Xueqin. Compare with Nos. 4198-4201, 4228-4231, 4361-4364.

Corals Type of 2014

Designs: $3.50, Euphyllia ancora. $5, Fungia (Pleuractis) taiwanensis. $10, Scleronephthya gracillimum. $15, Anella mollis.

2016, July 14 Litho. *Perf. 12½x13¼*
4308-4311 A1203 Set of 4 2.10 1.10

Carp Encircled by Dragons Type of 1997 With Denomination at Right and Inscribed "Republic of China (Taiwan)"

2016, Aug. 3 Engr. *Perf. 13¼x12½*
4312 A745 $100 dk purple 6.25 3.25

Fruit Type of 2016

Designs: $7, Tomatoes. $17, Guavas. $25, Persimmons. $34, Pineapple.

Perf. 12½x13½
2016, Aug. 17 Litho.

4313	A1259	$7 multi	.45	.25
4314	A1259	$17 multi	1.10	.55
4315	A1259	$25 multi	1.60	.80
4316	A1259	$34 multi	2.25	1.10
	Nos. 4313-4316 (4)		5.40	2.70

A1281

A1282

A1283

A1284

A1285

A1286

A1287

A1288

A1289

Seals — A1290

Perf. 13½x12½

2016, Sept. 14 **Litho.**

4317	Block of 10	2.50	1.25
a.	A1281 $3.50 multi	.25	.25
b.	A1282 $3.50 multi	.25	.25
c.	A1283 $3.50 multi	.25	.25
d.	A1284 $3.50 multi	.25	.25
e.	A1285 $3.50 multi	.25	.25
f.	A1286 $3.50 multi	.25	.25
g.	A1287 $3.50 multi	.25	.25
h.	A1288 $3.50 multi	.25	.25
i.	A1289 $3.50 multi	.25	.25
j.	A1290 $3.50 multi	.25	.25
4318	Block of 10	3.00	1.50
a.	A1281 $5 multi	.30	.25
b.	A1282 $5 multi	.30	.25
c.	A1283 $5 multi	.30	.25
d.	A1284 $5 multi	.30	.25
e.	A1285 $5 multi	.30	.25
f.	A1286 $5 multi	.30	.25
g.	A1287 $5 multi	.30	.25
h.	A1288 $5 multi	.30	.25
i.	A1289 $5 multi	.30	.25
j.	A1290 $5 multi	.30	.25

Hu Shih (1891-1962), Writer and Diplomat A1291

Chien Shih-Liang (1908-83), Chemist — A1292

Wu Ta-You (1907-2000), Physicist A1293

2016, Sept. 28 **Engr.** ***Perf. 12½***

4319	A1291 $5 slate blue	.30	.25
4320	A1292 $5 red violet	.30	.25
4321	A1293 $5 brown	.30	.25
	Nos. 4319-4321 (3)	.90	.75

Past presidents of Academia Sinica.

Balloon and Bicyclist — A1294

Bird and Open Box — A1295

2016, Oct. 21 **Litho.** ***Perf. 14***

4322	A1294 $5 multi	.35	.25
4323	A1295 $25 multi	1.60	.80

Souvenir Sheet

Litho. & Embossed With Foil Application

4324	Sheet of 2	4.00	2.00
a.	A1294 $32 multi	2.00	1.00
b.	A1295 $32 multi	2.00	1.00

PhilaTaipei 2016 World Stamp Exhibition, Taipei.

PhilaTaipei 2016 World Stamp Exhibition, Taipei — A1296

No. 4325: a, Yushan, Sun Moon Lake, butterfly, dragon boat. b, Map of Taiwan, birds, Taipei 101 Building, 85 Sky Tower, Kaohsiung.

Perf. 14 Syncopated

2016, Oct. 21 **Litho.**

4325	A1296 Horiz. pair	3.00	1.40
a.	$13 gold & multi	.85	.40
b.	$32 gold & multi	2.00	1.00
c.	Souvenir sheet of 4, 2 each #4325a-4325b	6.00	3.00

A1297

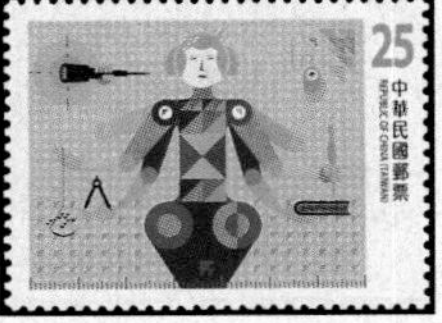
PhilaTaipei 2016 World Stamp Exhibition, Taipei A1298

2016, Oct. 22 **Litho.** ***Perf. 13½***

4326	A1297 $9 multi	.60	.30
4327	A1298 $25 multi	1.60	.80
a.	Souvenir sheet of 6, 3 each #4326-4327	6.75	3.50

Souvenir Sheet

PhilaTaipei 2016 World Stamp Exhibition, Taipei — A1299

No. 4328: a, Animals and birds in tree (64x40mm). b, Fish and marine life in ocean (50x30mm).

2016, Oct. 22 **Litho.** ***Perf. 14***

4328	A1299 Sheet of 2	3.00	1.50
a.	$15 multi	.95	.50
b.	$32 multi	2.00	1.00

PhilaTaipei 2016 World Stamp Exhibition, Taipei — A1300

No. 4329 — Little Yam: a, Mailing letter. b, Holding opened envelope.

2016, Oct. 22 **Litho.** ***Perf. 13¼x12¾***

4329	A1300 Horiz. pair + central label	2.00	1.00
a.	$5 multi	.35	.25
b.	$25 multi	1.60	.80
c.	Souvenir sheet of 4, 2 each #4329a-4329b, + 2 labels	4.00	2.00

Souvenir Sheet

PhilaTaipei 2016 World Stamp Exhibition, Taipei — A1301

No. 4330: a, Bird carrying flower (39x30mm heart-shaped). b, Person, flowers, hearts (30x40mm).

Perf. ($17), Perf. 12¾x12½ ($25)

2016, Oct. 22 **Litho.**

4330	A1301 Sheet of 2	2.75	1.40
a.	$17 multi	1.10	.55
b.	$25 multi	1.60	.80

Souvenir Sheet

Traveler at Shanyin County, Fan Painting by Lan Ying (c. 1585-1664) — A1302

2016, Oct. 24 **Litho.** ***Perf. 14***

4331	A1302 $25 multi	1.60	.80

New Year 2017 (Year of the Rooster) — A1303

Rooster and: $3.50, Chinese character in black. $13, Fish.
$12, Two roosters, horiz.

2016, Dec. 1 **Litho.** ***Perf. 13***

4332-4333	A1303 Set of 2	1.10	.55

Souvenir Sheet

Perf. 12½

4334	A1303 $12 multi	.75	.40

No. 4334 contains one 64x40mm stamp.

Starfish A1304

Designs: No. 4335, $5, Fromia monilis. No. 4336, $5, Culcita novaeguineae. No. 4337, $5, Acanthaster planci. No. 4338, $5, Linckia laevigata.

2017, Jan. 5 **Litho.** ***Perf. 12½x12¾***

4335-4338	A1304 Set of 4	1.40	1.40

Lions Clubs International, Cent. — A1305

Lions Clubs International emblem, "100," club members and inscription: a, "We Serve." b, "100th Anniversary."

2017, Jan. 20 **Litho.** ***Perf. 13¼x12½***

4339	A1305 Horiz. pair	1.40	1.40
a.	$5 multi	.30	.30
b.	$15 multi	1.10	1.10

Wanli Pond A1306

Baishi Pond A1307

Jialuo Lake A1308

Dagui Lake A1309

2017, Feb. 23 Litho. *Perf. 14*

4340	A1306	$5	multi	.35	.25
4341	A1307	$5	multi	.35	.25
4342	A1308	$10	multi	.65	.30
4343	A1309	$12	multi	.80	.40
	Nos. 4340-4343 (4)			2.15	1.20

Compare with Nos. 4184-4187.

Miniature Sheet

Tainan City — A1310

No. 4344: a, $5, Jingzaijiao Tile-paved Salt Fields. b, $9, Tainan Confucian Temple. c, $12, Chikan Lou. d, $12, Anping Sword Lion architectural decoration.

2017, Mar. 28 Litho. *Perf. 14*

4344	A1310	Sheet of 4, #a-d	2.50	1.25

Poppies A1311

White and Purple Lilacs — A1312

Tiger Lilies and Winding Peonies — A1313

Emerald Bamboo and Morning Glories — A1314

Lotuses and Arrowhead A1315

Pea Blossoms and Millet Stalks — A1316

Cockscomb A1317

Chrysanthemums A1318

2017, Apr. 26 Litho. *Perf. 13¼x12½*

4345	A1311	$5	multi	.35	.25
4346	A1312	$5	multi	.35	.25
4347	A1313	$7	multi	.50	.25
4348	A1314	$9	multi	.60	.30
4349	A1315	$10	multi	.70	.35
4350	A1316	$10	multi	.70	.35
4351	A1317	$12	multi	.80	.40
4352	A1318	$12	multi	.80	.40
	Nos. 4345-4352 (8)			4.80	2.55

Paintings by Giuseppe Castiglione (1688-1766).

This Infant Can Be Taught A1319

To Hold Bamboo in Your Breast A1320

To Rub Your Eyes and See Anew A1321

To Add Eyes to the Dragon A1322

2017, May 10 Litho. *Perf. 12½x13¼*

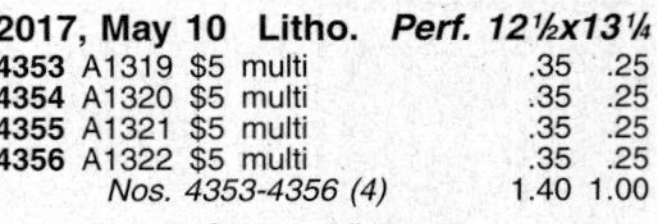

4353	A1319	$5	multi	.35	.25
4354	A1320	$5	multi	.35	.25
4355	A1321	$5	multi	.35	.25
4356	A1322	$5	multi	.35	.25
	Nos. 4353-4356 (4)			1.40	1.00

Chinese idioms.

Train and Dongshan River Bridge — A1323

Train and Youkeng Bridge — A1324

Train and Carp Pond Bridge — A1325

Train and Da-an River Bridge — A1326

2017, June 9 Litho. *Perf. 12½x13¼*

4357	A1323	$5	multi	.35	.25
4358	A1324	$5	multi	.35	.25
4359	A1325	$12	multi	.80	.40
4360	A1326	$12	multi	.80	.40
	Nos. 4357-4360 (4)			2.30	1.30

Xiangyun Sleeps in Inebriation A1327

Daiyu Burns Manuscripts — A1328

Jia Mansion Ransacked A1329

Baoyu Becomes a Monk A1330

2017, June 29 Litho. *Perf. 13x13½*

4361	A1327	$5	multi	.35	.25
4362	A1328	$5	multi	.35	.25
4363	A1329	$10	multi	.65	.35
4364	A1330	$25	multi	1.75	.85
	Nos. 4361-4364 (4)			3.10	1.70

Scenes from "The Dream of Red Mansions," by Cao Xueqin. Compare with Nos. 4198-4201, 4228-4231, 4304-4307.

Fruit Type of 2016

Designs: $3.50, Mangos. $5, Oranges. $12, Watermelon. $32, Grapes.

2017, July 20 Litho. *Perf. 12½x13½*

4365	A1259	$3.50	multi	.25	.25
4366	A1259	$5	multi	.35	.25
4367	A1259	$12	multi	.80	.40
4368	A1259	$32	multi	2.10	1.10
	Nos. 4365-4368 (4)			3.50	2.00

Carrier Dove

A1331 A1332

2017, Aug. 1 Litho. *Perf. 12½*

4369	A1331	($6)	orange & multi	.40	.25
4370	A1332	($8)	blue & multi	.55	.25

Tungyin Tao Lighthouse — A1333

Qinbi Village — A1334

Chinese Crested Terns — A1335

Dinoflagellates Glowing Blue in Sea Water — A1336

2017, Aug. 9 Litho. *Perf. 14½x14*

4371	A1333	$5	multi	.35	.25
4372	A1334	$9	multi	.60	.30
4373	A1335	$10	multi	.65	.35
4374	A1336	$20	multi	1.40	.70
	Nos. 4371-4374 (4)			3.00	1.60

Matsu Islands tourist attractions.

2017 Summer Universiade, Taipei — A1337

No. 4375 — Universiade mascot Bravo Bear participating in: a, Weight lifting. b, Archery. c,

Track. d, Taekwondo. e, Baseball. f, Basketball. g, Volleyball. h, Table tennis.
$25, Stylized figures participating in weight lifting, archery, track, volleyball, taekwondo, table tennis, basketball, and baseball.

Perf. 13¼x13½ Syncopated

2017, Aug. 16 Litho.

4375	Block of 8	5.50	3.00
a.-d.	A1337 $5 Any single	.35	.25
e.-h.	A1337 $15 Any single	1.00	.50

Souvenir Sheet

Litho. & Embossed

Perf. 13x12¾ Syncopated

4376	A1337 $25 multi	1.75	.85

No. 4376 contains one 100x30mm rectangular stamp.

Magpie, by Xu Beihong — A1338

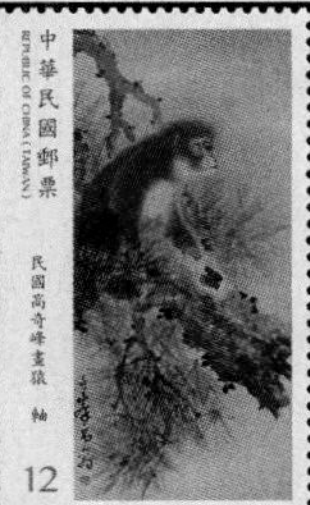

Macaque, by Gao Xifeng — A1339

A Secluded Scene of Remote Mountains, by Huang Chun-pi — A1340

Pumpkin Vines of Abundant Growth, by Qi Baishi — A1341

2017, Sept. 6 Litho. *Perf. 13¼x12¼*

4377	A1338 $5 multi	.35	.25
4378	A1339 $12 multi	.80	.40
4379	A1340 $15 multi	1.00	.50
4380	A1341 $25 multi	1.75	.85
	Nos. 4377-4380 (4)	3.90	2.00

A1342

Cross-Strait Exchanges, 30th Anniv. — A1343

2017, Sept. 20 Litho. *Perf. 13x12¾*

4381	A1342 $9 multi	.60	.30
4382	A1343 $28 multi	1.90	.95

Fruit Type of 2016

Designs: $3, Asian pears. $6, Rose apples. $8, Bananas. $28, Pomelos.

Perf. 12¼x13½

2017, Sept. 20 Litho.

4383	A1259 $3 multi	.25	.25
4384	A1259 $6 multi	.40	.25
4385	A1259 $8 multi	.55	.25
4386	A1259 $28 multi	1.90	.95
	Nos. 4383-4386 (4)	3.10	1.70

Hydrophasianus Chirurgus — A1344

No. 4387: a, $5, Bird and eggs in nest (denomination in yellow). b, $5, Bird in flight, horiz. (denomination in light blue). c, $10, Juvenile bird walking on water plants, horiz. (denomination in orange). d, $10, Adult and chick walking on water plants (denomination in pink).
$32, Bird grabbing tail feather in beak, horiz.

2017, Oct. 11 Litho. *Perf. 13*

4387	A1344 Sheet of 4, #a-d	2.00	1.00

Souvenir Sheet

Perf. 12¾x12½

4388	A1344 $32 multi	2.10	1.10

No. 4388 contains one 60x40mm stamp.

National Taipei University of Business, Cent. A1345

Designs: $8, Japanese era building. $28, Current school building.

Perf. 12½x13¼

2017, Nov. 16 Litho.

4389-4390	A1345 Set of 2	2.40	1.25

Cheirostylis Octodactyla A1346

2017, Nov. 16 Litho. *Perf. 12½*

4391	A1346 $35 multi	2.40	1.25

New Year 2018 (Year of the Dog)
A1347 A1348

Design: $15, Dog and fan, horiz.

2017, Dec. 1 Litho. *Perf. 13*

4392	A1347 $6 gold & multi	.40	.25
4393	A1348 $13 gold & multi	.90	.45

Souvenir Sheet

4394	A1348 $15 gold & multi	1.00	.50

No. 4394 contains one 64x40mm stamp.

Wild Orchids — A1349

Designs: $8, Calanthe puberula. $15, Calanthe sieboldii. $16, Habenaria dentata. $22, Neottia meifongensis. $23, Dendrobium chryseum, horiz. $28, Bulbophyllum pectinatum, horiz. $43, Dendrobium linawianum, horiz.

2018 Litho. *Perf. 13½x13*

4395	A1349 $8 multi	.55	.25
4396	A1349 $15 multi	1.00	.50

Perf. 12½

4397	A1349 $16 multi	1.10	.55
4398	A1349 $22 multi	1.50	.75
4399	A1349 $23 multi	1.60	.80

Perf. 13x13½

4400	A1349 $28 multi	1.90	.95

Perf. 12½

4401	A1349 $43 multi	3.00	1.50
	Nos. 4395-4401 (7)	10.65	5.30

Self-Adhesive

Die Cut Perf. 13½x13

4402	A1349 $8 multi	.55	.25

Die Cut Perf. 13x13½

4403	A1349 $28 multi	1.90	.95

Issued: $8, $15, $28, 1/26; $16, $22, $23, $43, 2/27. See Nos. 4433-4436.

Souvenir Sheet

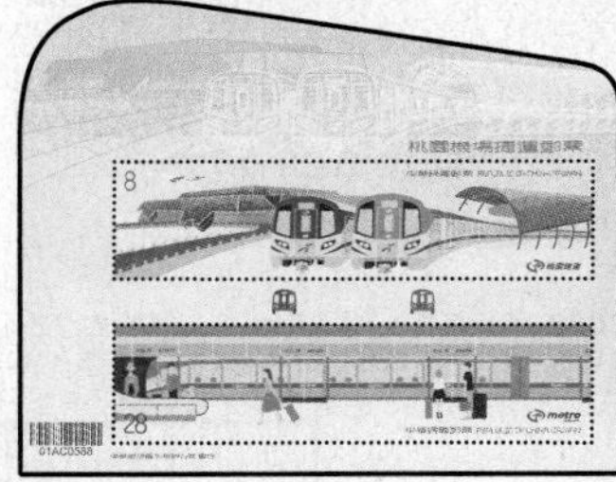

Taoyuan Airport Mass Transit Rail Line, 1st Anniv. — A1350

No. 4404: a, $8, Airport, commuter and express trains at station. b, $28, Escalator, passengers on platform, train at station.

2018, Mar. 2 Litho. *Perf. 13*

4404	A1350 Sheet of 2, #a-b	2.50	1.25

Jiemei Lakes A1351

Cueifong Lake — A1352

Yuanyang Lake — A1353

Songluo Lake — A1354

Perf. 13½x13¼

2018, Mar. 21 Litho.

4405	A1351 $6 multi	.40	.25
4406	A1352 $6 multi	.40	.25
4407	A1353 $8 multi	.55	.25
4408	A1354 $8 multi	.55	.25
	Nos. 4405-4408 (4)	1.90	1.00

A1355

A1356

A1357

A1358

A1359

A1360

A1361

A1362

A1363

Best Wishes — A1364

2018, Apr. 12 Litho. *Perf. 13¼x12½*

4409	Block of 10	4.00	2.50
a.	A1355 $6 multi	.40	.25
b.	A1356 $6 multi	.40	.25
c.	A1357 $6 multi	.40	.25
d.	A1358 $6 multi	.40	.25
e.	A1359 $6 multi	.40	.25
f.	A1360 $6 multi	.40	.25
g.	A1361 $6 multi	.40	.25
h.	A1362 $6 multi	.40	.25
i.	A1363 $6 multi	.40	.25
j.	A1364 $6 multi	.40	.25
4410	Block of 10	5.50	2.50
a.	A1355 $8 multi	.55	.25
b.	A1356 $8 multi	.55	.25
c.	A1357 $8 multi	.55	.25
d.	A1358 $8 multi	.55	.25
e.	A1359 $8 multi	.55	.25
f.	A1360 $8 multi	.55	.25
g.	A1361 $8 multi	.55	.25
h.	A1362 $8 multi	.55	.25
i.	A1363 $8 multi	.55	.25
j.	A1364 $8 multi	.55	.25

Taichung Park — A1365

National Taichung Theater — A1366

Wuling Farm — A1367

Gaomei Wetlands — A1368

2018, May 3 **Litho.** ***Perf. 12¾***

4411	A1365	$8 multi	.55	.25
4412	A1366	$9 multi	.60	.30
4413	A1367	$12 multi	.80	.40
4414	A1368	$15 multi	1.00	.50
	Nos. 4411-4414 (4)		2.95	1.45

Taichung City tourist attractions.

Kaomei Lighthouse A1369

Wuchiu Yu Lighthouse A1370

Suao Lighthouse A1371

Anping Lighthouse A1372

2018, May 23 **Litho.** ***Perf. 12½***

4415	A1369	$8 multi	.55	.25
4416	A1370	$8 multi	.55	.25
4417	A1371	$12 multi	.80	.40
4418	A1372	$15 multi	1.00	.50
	Nos. 4415-4418 (4)		2.90	1.40

Miniature Sheet

Aerial Views — A1373

No. 4419: a, $8, Cattle on Mount Daijan. b, $9, Choir on Mount Jade. c, $13, Sunset over fish farms, Yongan. d, $15, Giant footprints in paddies, Yuli.

2018, June 8 **Litho.** ***Perf. 13¼***

4419 A1373 Sheet of 4, #a-d 3.00 1.50

Souvenir Sheet

Marine Life — A1374

No. 4420: a, $13, Carcharhinus melanopterus. b, $28, Chelonia mydas.

2018, June 26 **Litho.** ***Perf. 12¾***

4420 A1374 Sheet of 2, #a-b 2.75 1.40

Chinese Poetry — A1375

Scenes depicting poem: $6, Climbing White Stork Tower, by Wang Zhihuan (temple and tree). $8, River Snow, by Liu Zhongyuan (fishing boat in river). $9, Longing, by Wang Wei (woman holding bean and fan). $15, Quiet Night Thoughts, by Li Bai (Moon over shelter with sleeping man).

2018, July 6 **Litho.** ***Perf. 12¾***

4421-4424 A1375 Set of 4 2.50 1.25

Compare with Nos. 4470-4473, 4556-4559.

Corals Type of 2014

Designs: No. 4425, $6, Leptoseris yabei. No. 4426, $6, Clavularia viridis. No. 4427, $15, Lobophytum crassum. No. 4428, $15, Melithaea formosa.

2018, July 19 **Litho.** ***Perf. 12½x13¼***

4425-4428 A1203 Set of 4 2.75 1.40

Ocean Fireworks Festival, Magong City — A1376

Erkan Village, Xiyu Island — A1377

Low Tide Path, Kueibishan — A1378

Daguoye Columnar Basalt — A1379

2018, Aug. 2 **Litho.** ***Perf. 12½x13¼***

4429	A1376	$6 multi	.40	.25
4430	A1377	$8 multi	.55	.25
4431	A1378	$12 multi	.80	.40
4432	A1379	$15 multi	1.00	.50
	Nos. 4429-4432 (4)		2.75	1.40

Penghu County tourist attractions.

Wild Orchids Type of 2018

Designs: $7, Phalaenopsis equestris. $9, Odontochilus nanlingensis. $10, Bulbophyllum retusiusculum, horiz. $20, Bulbophyllum griffithii, horiz.

Perf. 13¼x12½

2018, Aug. 22 **Litho.**

4433	A1349	$7 multi	.45	.25
4434	A1349	$9 multi	.60	.30

Perf. 12½x13¼

4435	A1349	$10 multi	.65	.35
4436	A1349	$20 multi	1.40	.70
	Nos. 4433-4436 (4)		3.10	1.60

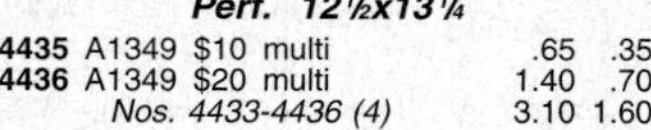

Red Sunset, by Lin Chih-chu (1917-2008) A1380

By the Window, by Liao Te-cheng (1920-2015) A1381

Day and Night, by Chen Ting-shih (1916-2002) A1382

Work No. 057, by Lee Chun-shan (1912-84) A1383

Perf. 12½x12¾, 12¾x12½

2018, Sept. 12 **Litho.**

4437	A1380	$8 multi	.55	.30
4438	A1381	$8 multi	.55	.30
4439	A1382	$10 multi	.65	.35
4440	A1383	$10 multi	.65	.35
	Nos. 4437-4440 (4)		2.40	1.30

Miniature Sheet

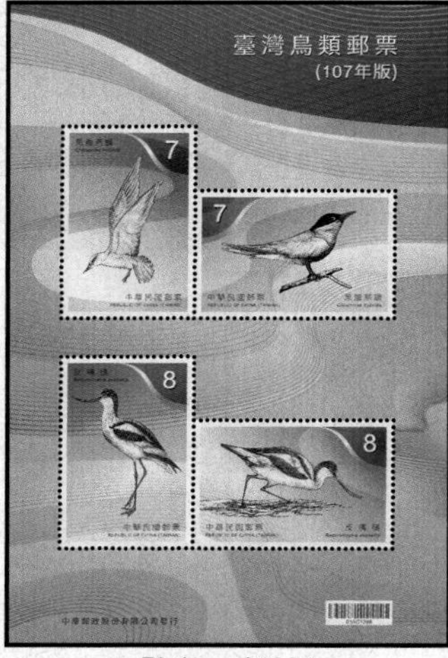

Birds — A1384

No. 4441: a, Chlidonias hybrida in flight. b, Chlidonias hybrid on branch, horiz. c, Recurvirostra avosetta. d, Recurvirostra avosetta, horiz.

2018, Oct. 3 **Litho.** ***Perf. 13¼***

4441	A1384	Sheet of 4	2.00	1.00
a.-b.		$7 Either single	.45	.25
c.-d.		$8 Either single	.55	.25

A1385

Taichung World Flora Exposition — A1386

Designs: $6, Lily. $8, Oncidium orchid. $9, Gladioli. $28, Flamingo flower.

No. 4446: a, $13, Leopard cat mascot holding potted lilies. b, $15, Leopard kitten mascot on pot holding hygrophila. c, $17, Leopard cat mascot holding potted butterfly orchid.

2018, Oct. 31 **Litho.** ***Perf. 14x13¾***

Stamps + Label

4442-4445 A1385 Set of 4 3.50 1.75

Souvenir Sheet

Perf. 13¼ on Top and Bottom

4446 A1386 Sheet of 3, #a-c 3.00 1.50

Blue and White Porcelain A1387

Designs: $6, Ming Dynasty water container with fish design. $9, Ming Dynasty bowl with phoenix and flower design. $15, Qing Dynasty ewer with fruits and flowers design. $16, Qing Dynasty vase with flower design.

$28, Ming Dynasty vase with dragon and lotus blossom designs.

Perf. 13¾x13½

2018, Nov. 15 **Litho.**

4447-4450 A1387 Set of 4 3.00 1.50

Souvenir Sheet

4451 A1387 $28 multi 1.90 .95

Compare with types A1424-A1428.

New Year 2019 (Year of the Pig) — A1388

Designs: $6, Red pig and gold piglet. $13, Pig with plum blossoms and red piglet. $15, Two pigs with plum blossoms.

2018, Dec. 3 **Litho.** ***Perf. 13***

4452-4453 A1388 Set of 2 1.25 .60

Souvenir Sheet

4454 A1388 $15 multi 1.00 .50

No. 4454 contains one 64x40mm stamp.

Goldfish A1389

Goldfish varieties: No. 4455, $6, Red Swallowtail facing right. No. 4456, $6, Ryukin facing left. $12, Dragon Eye. $28, Goose Head Pearl Scale.

2019, Jan. 24 **Litho.** ***Perf. 12½***

4455-4458 A1389 Set of 4 3.50 1.75

Compare with types A1450-A1453.

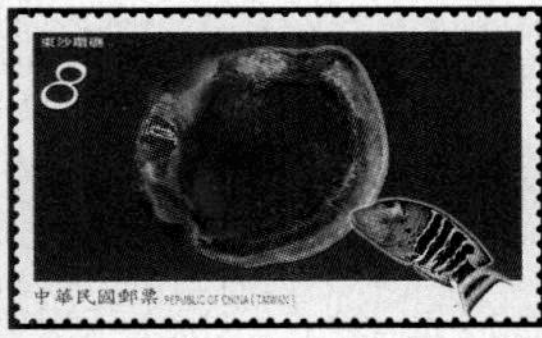

Dongsha Atoll National Park — A1390

Designs: $8, Aerial view of Dongsha Atoll and red-breasted wrasse. $13, Dongsha Coral Reef and yellowhead demoiselle. $15, Dongsha Seagrass Bed and spotted eagle ray. $28, Aerial view of Dongsha Island and white-breasted waterhen.

Perf. 12½x13½

2019, Feb. 21 **Litho.**

4459-4462 A1390 Set of 4 4.25 2.10

Education Benefits Both Students and Teachers A1391

Offering Bricks to Elicit Jade A1392

Love House and Crow A1393

True to Life A1394

Perf. 12½x12¾

2019, Mar. 20 **Litho.**

4463 A1391 $8 multi .55 .25
4464 A1392 $8 multi .55 .25
4465 A1393 $8 multi .55 .25
4466 A1394 $8 multi .55 .25
Nos. 4463-4466 (4) 2.20 1.00

Chinese idioms.

A1395

A1396

A1397

Presidential Office Building, Cent. — A1398

2019, Apr. 2 **Litho.** ***Perf. 12¾x12½***

4467 Horiz. strip of 3 2.40 1.25
a. A1395 $8 multi .55 .25
b. A1396 $13 multi .85 .40
c. A1397 $15 multi 1.00 .50

Souvenir Sheet

4468 A1398 $28 multi 1.90 .95

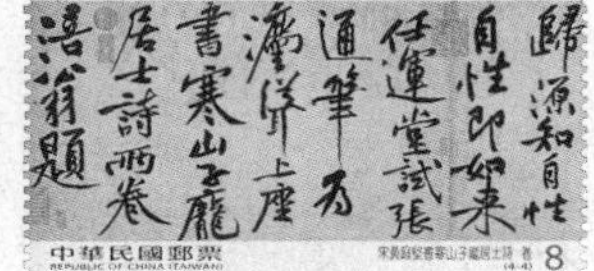

A1399

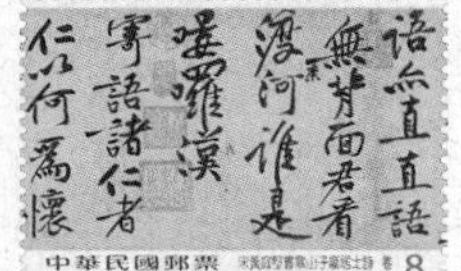

A1400

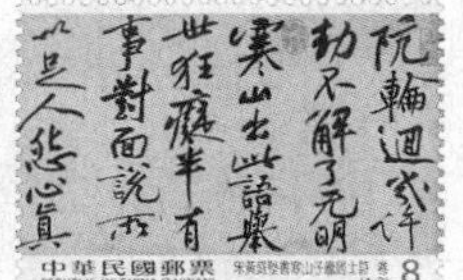

A1401

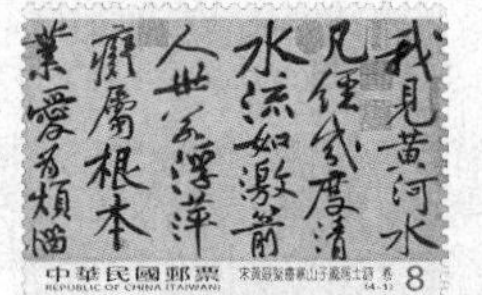

Poetry of Hanshan and Recluse Pang, by Huang Ting-chien (1045-1105) A1402

2019, May 29 **Litho.** ***Perf. 12½x13¼***

4469 Horiz. strip of 4 2.00 1.00
a. A1399 $8 multi .50 .25
b. A1400 $8 multi .50 .25
c. A1401 $8 multi .50 .25
d. A1402 $8 multi .50 .25

Exists in a sheet containing 4 no. 4469.

"Spring Wind," by Bai Juyi — A1403

"Summer Fun on the Farm," by Fan Chengdai A1404

"An Autumn Evening," by Du Mu — A1405

"After Snowfall in the Mountains," by Zheng Banqiao — A1406

2019, June 12 **Litho.** ***Perf. 12¾***

4470 A1403 $6 multi .40 .25
4471 A1404 $8 multi .55 .25
4472 A1405 $9 multi .60 .30
4473 A1406 $15 multi 1.00 .50
Nos. 4470-4473 (4) 2.55 1.30

Chinese poetry. Compare with Nos. 4421-4424, 4556-4559.

Festival on South Street, by Kuo Hsueh-hu (1908-2012) A1407

Ferry of the Egret, by Chen Yung-sen (1913-97) A1408

Guitar, by Chang Yi-hsiung (1914-2016) A1409

Studio, by Hsiao Ju-sung (1922-92) A1410

Perf. 12¾x12½

2019, June 21 **Litho.**

4474 A1407 $8 multi .55 .25
4475 A1408 $8 multi .55 .25
4476 A1409 $15 multi 1.00 .50

Perf. 12½x12¾

4477 A1410 $15 multi 1.00 .50
Nos. 4474-4477 (4) 3.10 1.50

Han Dynasty Jade Items From National Palace Museum — A1411

Designs: $6, Jade beast. $8, Jade seal. $13, Jade camel, horiz. $15, Jade bixie beast, horiz.

2019, July 5 **Litho.** ***Perf. 13¼x13***

4478-4481 A1411 Set of 4 3.50 1.75

Compare with Types A1440-A1443.

Lanyang Museum, Toucheng Township, Yilan County — A1412

Surfer at Wai'ao, Toucheng Township, Yilan County — A1413

Chiang Ku Ceremony, Toucheng Township, Yilan County — A1414

Lizejian Bridge Over Dongshan River, Yilan County — A1415

2019, July 16 Litho. *Perf. 13¼*

4482	A1412	$6 multi	.40	.25
4483	A1413	$8 multi	.50	.25
4484	A1414	$12 multi	.80	.40
4485	A1415	$13 multi	.85	.40
	Nos. 4482-4485 (4)		2.55	1.30

Yilan County tourist attractions.

Tamsui Church, Tamsui — A1416

Thài-Pêng-Kéng Maxwell Memorial Church, Tainan — A1417

Grace Baptist Church, Taipei — A1418

Tainan Holiness Church, Tainan — A1419

2019, Aug. 7 Litho. *Perf. 12¾*

4486	A1416	$8 multi	.50	.25
4487	A1417	$8 multi	.50	.25
4488	A1418	$12 multi	.80	.40
4489	A1419	$12 multi	.80	.40
	Nos. 4486-4489 (4)		2.60	1.30

Famous church architecture.

Field of Rapeseed Flowers, East Rift Valley — A1420

Qixingtan Bay — A1421

Rafters on Xiuguluan River — A1422

Swallow Grotto, Taroko National Park — A1423

2019, Aug. 28 Litho. *Perf. 12¾*

4490	A1420	$6 multi	.40	.25
4491	A1421	$6 multi	.40	.25
4492	A1422	$12 multi	.80	.40
4493	A1423	$12 multi	.80	.40
	Nos. 4490-4493 (4)		2.40	1.30

Tourist attractions of Hualien County.

Ming Dynasty Teapot — A1424

Qing Dynasty Tea Bowl — A1425

Qing Dynasty Teapot — A1426

Ming Dynasty Teacup A1427

Ming Dynasty Pilgrim Bottle — A1428

Litho. & Embossed

2019, Sept. 9 *Perf. 13¾x13½*

4494	A1424	$8 multi	.55	.25
4495	A1425	$12 multi	.80	.40
4496	A1426	$13 multi	.85	.25
4497	A1427	$18 multi	1.25	.60
	Nos. 4494-4497 (4)		3.45	1.50

Souvenir Sheet

4498	A1428	$28 multi	1.90	.95

Blue and white porcelain. Compare with type A1387.

Little Green Man Pedestrian Signal — A1429

Electronic Toll Collection A1430

Multipurpose Smartcard for Fare Collection A1431

Transportation Information and Management A1432

2019, Sept. 25 Litho. *Perf. 13½x13*

4499	A1429	$8 multi	.55	.25
4500	A1430	$8 multi	.55	.25
4501	A1431	$8 multi	.55	.25
4502	A1432	$8 multi	.55	.25
a.	Souvenir sheet of 4, #4499-4502, perf.12¾x12½		2.25	1.00
	Nos. 4499-4502 (4)		2.20	1.00

National Chung Hsing University, Taichung City, Cent. A1433

Designs: $8, Main entrance. $28, Auditorium.

2019, Oct. 9 Litho. *Perf. 12½x13¼*

4503-4504	A1433	Set of 2	2.40	1.25

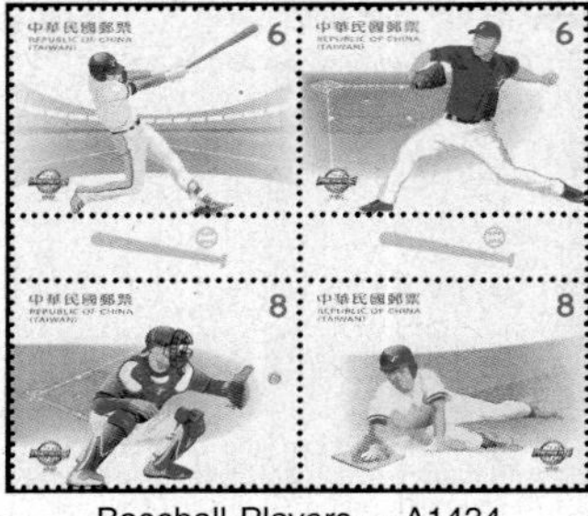
Baseball Players — A1434

No. 4505: a, Batter. b, Pitcher. c, Catcher. d, Runner.

2019, Nov. 1 Litho. *Perf. 12½*

4505	A1434	Block of 4, #a-d, + 2 central labels	1.90	1.00
a.-b.		$6 Either single	.40	.25
c.-d.		$8 Either single	.55	.25

Group B Games of World Baseball Softball Confederation Premier 12 Competition, Republic of China.

Keelung Lighthouse A1435

Tungting Tao Lighthouse A1436

Taichung Port Lighthouse A1437

Tamsui Harbor Lighthouse A1438

2019, Nov. 20 Litho. *Perf. 12½*

4506	A1435	$8 multi	.55	.25
4507	A1436	$8 multi	.55	.25
4508	A1437	$12 multi	.80	.40
4509	A1438	$15 multi	1.00	.50
	Nos. 4506-4509 (4)		2.90	1.40

New Year 2020 (Year of the Rat) — A1439

Designs: $6, Blue green rat. $13, Magenta rat.
$15, Magenta and purple rats, horiz.

2019, Dec. 3 Litho. *Perf. 13*

4510-4511	A1439	Set of 2	1.25	.65

Souvenir Sheet

Perf. 12½

4512	A1439	$15 multi	1.00	.50

No. 4512 contains one 64x40mm stamp.

Jade Hornless Dragons Cup A1440

Jade Bottle With Phoenixes A1441

Jade Goblet A1442

Jade Four-legged Cauldron A1443

Perf. 13¼x12½

2019, Dec. 10 Litho.

4513	A1440	$7 multi	.50	.25
4514	A1441	$12 multi	.80	.40
4515	A1442	$15 multi	1.00	.50
4516	A1443	$35 multi	2.40	1.25
	Nos. 4513-4516 (4)		4.70	2.40

Jade items from National Palace Museum. Compare with Nos. 4478-4481.

Baimi Viaduct — A1444

Nan'ao Beixi Bridge — A1445

2020, Jan. 3 Litho. *Perf. 13¼x13*

4517	A1444	$28 multi	1.90	.95
4518	A1445	$35 multi	2.40	1.25

Completion of Suhua Highway Improvement Project.

Dapeng Bay Bridge — A1446

Kenting National Park — A1447

Little Liuqiu Flower Vase Rock — A1448

Hengchun Old Town — A1449

2020, Jan. 10 Litho. *Perf. 12¾*

4519	A1446	$6 muti	.40	.25
4520	A1447	$6 multi	.40	.25
4521	A1448	$8 multi	.55	.25
4522	A1449	$15 multi	1.00	.50
	Nos. 4519-4522 (4)		2.35	1.25

Tourist attractions in Pingtung County.

Red Crane Crest Oranda A1450

Ranchu A1451

Broadtail Ryukin A1452

Pompons A1453

Perf. 12½x13¼

2020, Feb. 26 Litho.

4523	A1450	$6 multi	.40	.25
4524	A1451	$9 multi	.60	.30
4525	A1452	$15 multi	1.00	.50
4526	A1453	$17 multi	1.25	.60
	Nos. 4523-4526 (4)		3.25	1.65

Compare with Type A1389.

Dalongdong Basin Temple, Taipei A1454

Taiwan Tainan District Court Building, Tainan A1455

Railway Division of Taiwan Governor General's Bureau of Transportation, Taipei — A1456

Gongziliao Fort, Keelung A1457

2020, Mar. 20 Litho. *Perf. 12½*

4527	A1454	$8 multi	.55	.25
4528	A1455	$8 multi	.55	.25
4529	A1456	$8 multi	.55	.25
4530	A1457	$8 multi	.55	.25
	Nos. 4527-4530 (4)		2.20	1.00

Taijiang National Park — A1458

Designs: $6, Oysters and Cigu Lagoon. $8, Black-faced Spoonbill Reserve. $15, Beach morning glories and Wangzailiao Sand Bar. $28, Mangrove blossom and Sicao Mangrove Green Tunnel.

2020, Apr. 24 Litho. *Perf. 12¾*

4531-4534	A1458	Set of 4	4.00	2.00

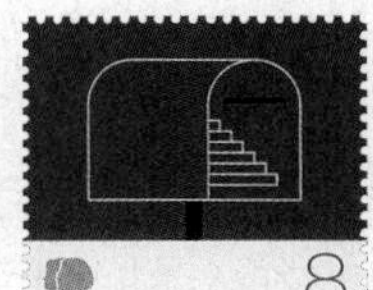
A1459

A1460

A1461

A1462

Inauguration of President Tsai Ing-wen and Vice President Lai Ching-te — A1463

2020, May 20 Litho. *Perf. 12½*

4535		Horiz. strip or block of 4	3.25	1.50
a.	A1459	$8 multi	.55	.25
b.	A1460	$8 multi	.55	.25
c.	A1461	$15 multi	1.00	.50
d.	A1462	$15 multi	1.00	.50

Souvenir Sheet

4536	A1463	$35 multi	2.40	1.25

Annular Solar Eclipse — A1464

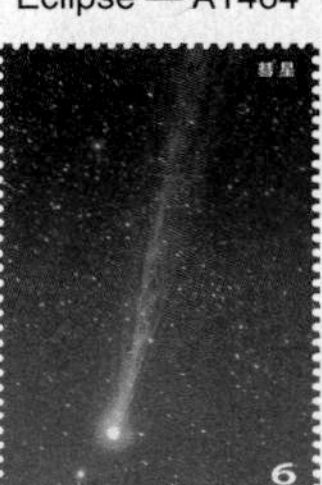
Comet — A1465

Total Solar Eclipse — A1466

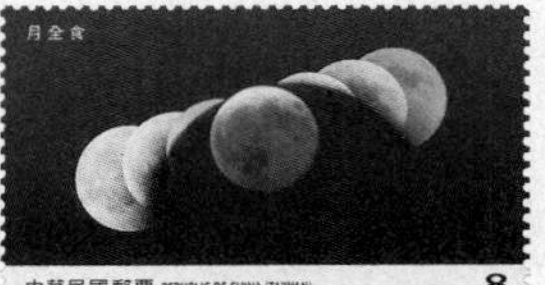
Total Lunar Eclipse — A1467

Perf. 13¼x13½

2020, June 20 Litho.

4537	A1464	$6 multi	.40	.25
4538	A1465	$6 multi	.40	.25

Perf. 13½x13¼

4539	A1466	$8 multi	.55	.25
4540	A1467	$8 multi	.55	.25
a.		Souvenir sheet of 4, #4537-4540, perf. 13¼	1.90	1.00

Sports A1468

Designs: No. 4541, $6, Badminton. No. 4542, $6, Archery. $8, Weight lifting. $12, Men's pommel horse gymnastics.

2020, July 10 Litho. *Perf. 12½x12¾*

4541-4544	A1468	Set of 4	2.25	1.10

COVID-19 Prevention — A1469

No. 4545: a, Five people wearing masks. b, Manufacturing inspection, bus, train, ambulance, commuter wearing mask, handwashing and medical research.

2020, July 21 Litho. ***Perf. 12¾x12½***

4545	A1469	Horiz. pair + central label	1.90	.95
a.		$13 multi	.90	.45
b.		$15 multi	1.00	.50

Sun Moon Lake — A1470

Jiji Green Tunnel — A1471

Qingjing Farm — A1472

Hehuan Mountain Dark Sky Park — A1473

Perf. 12½x13¼

2020, Aug. 12 Litho.

4546	A1470	$8 multi	.55	.25
4547	A1471	$8 multi	.55	.25
4548	A1472	$13 multi	.90	.45
4549	A1473	$15 multi	1.10	.55
		Nos. 4546-4549 (4)	3.10	1.50

Nantou County tourist attractions.

Hanshan Culture Jade Bird — A1474

Liangzhu Culture Jade Ornament — A1475

Longshan-Qijia Culture Jade Cong Tube — A1476

Shang Dynasty Jade Disc — A1477

Perf. 13¼x12½, 12½x13¼

2020, Aug. 26 Litho.

4550	A1474	$8 multi	.55	.25
4551	A1475	$9 multi	.65	.30
4552	A1476	$17 multi	1.25	.60
4553	A1477	$22 multi	1.50	.75
		Nos. 4550-4553 (4)	3.95	1.90

Taipei Grand Mosque — A1478

Taichung Mosque — A1479

Perf. 12½x13¼

2020, Sept. 29 Litho.

4554	A1478	$15 multi	1.10	.55
4555	A1479	$28 multi	2.00	1.00

Plum Blossoms, Poem by Wang Anshi (1021-86) A1480

Orchid River, Poem by Du Mu (803-52) — A1481

New Bamboo, Poem by Zheng Banqiao (1693-1765) A1482

Chrysanthemums, Poem by Yuan Zhen (779-831) A1483

2020, Oct. 14 Litho. ***Perf. 12¾***

4556	A1480	$8 multi	.55	.30
4557	A1481	$8 multi	.55	.30
4558	A1482	$12 multi	.85	.40
4559	A1483	$15 multi	1.10	.55
		Nos. 4556-4559 (4)	3.05	1.55

Chinese poetry. Compare with Nos. 4421-4424, 4470-4473.

SEMI-POSTAL STAMPS

China 1913-1919 Issues Surcharge in Red or Blue

1920, Dec. 1 Unwmk. ***Perf. 14, 15***

B1	A24	1c on 2c green	7.00	3.00
B2	A24	3c on 4c scar (Bl)	8.00	4.00
B3	A24	5c on 6c gray	13.00	6.00
		Nos. B1-B3 (3)	28.00	13.00

The surcharge represents the actual franking value. The extra cent helped victims of the 1919 Yellow River flood.

War Refugees SP2

Black Surcharge

1944, Oct. 10 Engr. ***Perf. 12***

B4	SP2	$2 +$2 on 50c + 50c	3.00	*4.00*
B5	SP2	$4 +$4 on 8c + 8c	3.00	*6.00*
B6	SP2	$5 +$5 on 21c + 21c	3.00	*4.00*
B7	SP2	$6 +$6 on 28c + 28c	5.00	*5.00*
B8	SP2	$10 +$10 on 33c + 33c	5.50	*7.00*
B9	SP2	$20 +$20 on $1 + $1	8.00	*10.00*
a.		Sheet of 6, #B4-B9	200.00	350.00
		Nos. B4-B9 (6)	27.50	*36.00*

The borders of each stamp differ slightly in design. The surtax was for war refugees.

Nos. B4-B8 exist without surcharge, but were not regularly issued.

Great Wall of China — SP4

1948, July 5 Litho. ***Perf. 14, Imperf.***

Without Gum

Cross in Carmine

B11	SP4	$5000 + $2000 vio	.75	*3.00*
B12	SP4	$10,000 + $2000 brn	.75	*3.00*
B13	SP4	$15,000 + $2000 gray	.75	*3.00*
		Nos. B11-B13 (3)	2.25	*9.00*

The surtax was for anti-tuberculosis work. Value, imperf. set, $3.

Republic of China (Taiwan)

Chinese Refugee Family — SP5

1954, Oct. 1 Engr. ***Perf. 12***

Without Gum

B14	SP5	40c + 10c dp bl	20.00	4.00
B15	SP5	$1.60 + 40c lil rose	55.00	21.00
B16	SP5	$5 + $1 red	100.00	87.50
		Nos. B14-B16 (3)	175.00	112.50

The surtax was used to aid in the evacuation of Chinese from North Viet Nam.

Catalogue values for unused stamps in this section, from this point to the end of the section, are for Never Hinged items.

Sept. 21, 1999 Earthquake Relief — SP6

a, Damaged buildings, map, rescue workers. b, Hands, heart, earthquake fault.

1999, Nov. 1 Litho. ***Imperf.***

Sheet of 2

B17	SP6	$25 +$25, #a.-b.	7.25	7.25

No. B17 has simulated perforations.

Souvenir Sheet

Typhoon Morakot Relief — SP7

No. B18: a, Map of Taiwan surrounded by clouds, rescuers and rafts. b, House, construction equipment and workers.

2009, Oct. 9 Litho. ***Imperf.***

B18	SP7	$25 +$25 Sheet of 2, #a-b	19.50	19.50

No. B18 has simulated perforations.

AIR POST STAMPS

Curtiss "Jenny" over Great Wall (Bars of Republic flag on tail) — AP1

Unwmk.

1921, July 1 Engr. ***Perf. 14***

C1	AP1	15c bl grn & blk	40.00	*70.00*
C2	AP1	30c scar & blk	40.00	*70.00*
C3	AP1	45c dull vio & blk	40.00	*70.00*
C4	AP1	60c dk blue & blk	52.50	*85.00*
C5	AP1	90c ol grn & blk	57.50	*90.00*
		Nos. C1-C5 (5)	230.00	*385.00*

(Nationalist sun emblem on tail) — AP2

1929, July 5

C6 AP2 15c blue grn & blk 10.00 3.00
C7 AP2 30c dk red & blk 15.00 5.00
C8 AP2 45c dk vio & blk 24.00 10.00
C9 AP2 60c dk blue & blk 27.50 12.00
C10 AP2 90c ol grn & blk 27.50 18.00
Nos. C6-C10 (5) 104.00 48.00

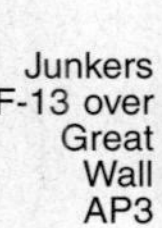

Junkers F-13 over Great Wall AP3

1932-37

C11 AP3 15c gray grn .70 .45
C12 AP3 25c orange ('33) 5.00 3.00
C13 AP3 30c red 10.00 2.50
C14 AP3 45c brown vio 1.00 .45
C15 AP3 50c dk brown ('33) 1.00 .45
C16 AP3 60c dk blue 1.00 .45
C17 AP3 90c olive grn 1.00 1.00
C18 AP3 $1 yellow grn ('33) 1.50 1.00
C19 AP3 $2 brown ('37) 1.50 *2.00*
C20 AP3 $5 brown car ('37) 4.00 *5.00*
Nos. C11-C20 (10) 26.70 *16.30*

See #C21-C40. For surcharges and overprints see #C41-C52, C54-C60, 9N111-9N114, 9NC1-9NC7, Szechwan C1, C3-C6, Sinkiang C5-C19.

Type of 1932-37, with secret mark

1932-37 Issue, Lower part of left character joined

Secret Mark, 1940-41 Issue, Separated

Perf. 12, 12½, 12½x13, 13

1940-41 **Wmk. 261**

C21 AP3 15c gray green 1.00 1.00
C22 AP3 25c yellow org 1.25 1.25
C23 AP3 30c red 1.00 1.00
a. Vert. pair, imperf. between *500.00*
C24 AP3 45c dull rose vio ('41) 1.00 1.00
C25 AP3 50c brown 1.00 1.00
C26 AP3 60c dp blue ('41) 1.00 1.00
C27 AP3 90c olive ('41) 1.00 1.00
C28 AP3 $1 apple grn ('41) 1.00 1.00
C29 AP3 $2 lt brown ('41) 1.00 1.00
C30 AP3 $5 lake 2.50 *3.00*
Nos. C21-C30 (10) 11.75 12.25

Unwmk.

Perf. 12½, 13, 13½

C31 AP3 15c gray green ('41) .70 *1.00*
C32 AP3 25c lt orange ('41) .70 *1.00*
C33 AP3 30c lt red ('41) .70 *1.00*
C34 AP3 45c dl rose vio ('41) .70 *1.00*
C35 AP3 50c brown .70 *1.00*
C36 AP3 60c blue ('41) .70 *1.00*
C37 AP3 90c lt olive ('41) .70 *1.00*
C38 AP3 $1 apple grn ('41) .70 *1.00*
a. Horiz. pair, imperf. between *500.00*
C39 AP3 $2 lt brown ('41) 3.00 2.00
C40 AP3 $5 lake ('41) 2.00 2.00
Nos. C31-C40 (10) 10.60 *12.00*

For surcharges see note following No. C20.

Nos. C11 and C12 Surcharged

1946, May 2 **Unwmk.** ***Perf. 14***

C41 AP3 $53 on 15c 1.50 *1.50*
C42 AP3 $73 on 25c 1,750. *1,750.*

Forgeries of No. C42 exist.

On Nos. C23, C21, C22, C29 and C30

Perf. 13, 13x12, 12½

Wmk. 261

C43 AP3 $23 on 30c red .75 *.75*
C44 AP3 $53 on 15c gray grn 25.00 *30.00*
C45 AP3 $73 on 25c yel org 1.00 *1.00*
C46 AP3 $100 on $2 lt brown 1.50 *2.00*
C47 AP3 $200 on $5 lake 1.00 *1.00*
Nos. C43-C47 (5) 29.25 34.75

On Nos. C33, C31, C32, C39 and C40

Perf. 13, 13x12, 13x12½, 12½

Unwmk.

C48 AP3 $23 on 30c lt red .75 *1.00*
a. Inverted surcharge *400.00*
b. "2300" omitted *50.00*
c. Last character (kuo) of surch. omitted *120.00*
C49 AP3 $53 on 15c gray grn .75 *1.00*
a. Horiz. pair, imperf. btwn. *1,500.* *675.00*
C50 AP3 $73 on 25c lt org .75 *1.50*
a. Inverted surcharge *1,100.* *350.00*
C51 AP3 $100 on $2 lt brn .75 *1.00*
C52 AP3 $200 on $5 lake .75 *1.00*
a. Inverted surcharge *400.00*
Nos. C48-C52 (5) 3.75 *5.50*

The surcharges on Nos. C41-C52 represent Chinese natl. currency and were applied at Shanghai.

Douglas DC-4 over Sun Yat-sen Mausoleum, Nanking — AP4

1946, Sept. 10 **Litho.** ***Perf. 14***

Without Gum

C53 AP4 $27 blue .65 *1.00*

For surcharges see Nos. C61, Szechwan C2.

No. C23 Surcharged in Black

Perf. 13x12

1948, May 18 **Wmk. 261**

C54 AP3 $10,000 on 30c red .60 *1.25*

Same, in Black or Carmine, on Nos. C33, C32, C37, C36, C18 and C38

Unwmk.

Perf. 12½, 13x12½, 14

C55 AP3 $10,000 on 30c lt red .60 *1.00*
C56 AP3 $20,000 on 25c lt org .60 *1.00*
C57 AP3 $30,000 on 90c lt ol (C) .60 *1.25*
C58 AP3 $50,000 on 60c blue (C) .60 *1.25*
C59 AP3 $50,000 on $1 yel grn (C) (#C18) 160.00 150.00
C60 AP3 $50,000 on $1 ap grn (C) (#C38) .60 *1.10*

No. C53 Surcharged in Black

Perf. 14

C61 AP4 $10,000 on $27 bl .75 *3.00*
a. Inverted surcharge *175.00*
Nos. C54-C61 (8) 164.35 159.85

Douglas DC-4 and Arrow — AP5

Perf. 12½

1949, May 2 **Unwmk.** **Litho.**

Without Gum

C62 AP5 blue green 7.50 *8.00*
a. Rouletted 12.00 *17.50*

See note after No. 959.
For surcharge see No. 1151.
For overprints see Taiwan No. C1, Fukien No. C1, Kansu No. C1, PRC Nos. 26, 102.

Revenue Stamp Overprinted in Blue

1949, May **Engr.** ***Perf. 14***

C63 A95 $100 olive green 125.00 125.00

See note after No. 962.

Republic of China (Taiwan)

Cheng Ch'eng-kung (Koxinga) — AP6

Rouletted

1950, Sept. 26 **Unwmk.** **Typo.**

Without Gum

C64 AP6 60c deep blue 14.00 14.00

For surcharge see No. 1120.

Plane over City Gate, Taipei — AP7

Jet Planes above Chung Shan Bridge — AP8

Two Doves Near Koxinga Shrine — AP9

1954 **Engr.** ***Perf. 11½***

Without Gum

C65 AP7 $1 dk brown 18.00 2.40
a. Vert. pair, imperf. btwn. 200.00
C66 AP8 $1.60 olive blk 23.00 1.60
a. Vert. pair, imperf. btwn. 140.00
b. Horiz. pair, imperf. btwn. 100.00 110.00
C67 AP9 $5 grnsh blue 33.00 2.00
Nos. C65-C67 (3) 74.00 6.00

Issued: No. C66, 8/14; Nos. C65, C67, 9/1.

No. C67 Surcharged in Red

1958, Dec. 11 **Without Gum**

C68 AP9 $3.50 on $5 grnsh bl 11.00 1.25

Catalogue values for unused stamps in this section, from this point to the end of the section, are for Never Hinged items.

Sea Gull — AP10

1959, Mar. 20 **Photo.** ***Perf. 13***

C69 AP10 $8 blue, gray & blk 8.25 .80

Sabre Jets in Bomb Burst Formation — AP11

Plane Formations: $2, Loop, horiz. $5, Diamond formation passing over grounded plane, horiz.

1960, Feb. 29 **Unwmk.** ***Perf. 13***

C70 AP11 $1 multicolored 6.50 .50
C71 AP11 $2 multicolored 6.00 .50
C72 AP11 $5 multicolored 10.00 .60
Nos. C70-C72 (3) 22.50 1.60

Issued to honor the Chinese Air Force and the "Thunder Tiger" aerobatic team.

Jet Airliner over Pitan Bridge AP12

Designs: $6, Jet over Tropic of Cancer monument, Kiai, vert. $10, Jet over Lion Head mountain, Sinchu, vert.

1963, Aug. 14 **Photo.** ***Perf. 13***

C73 AP12 $2.50 multi 7.25 .25
C74 AP12 $6 multi 12.50 .40
C75 AP12 $10 multi 16.00 .65
Nos. C73-C75 (3) 35.75 1.30

Boeing 727 over Chilin Pavilion, Grand Hotel — AP13

Design: $8, Boeing 727 over National Palace Museum, Taipei.

1967, Apr. 1 **Unwmk.** ***Perf. 13***

C76 AP13 $5 multicolored 3.75 .25
C77 AP13 $8 multicolored 5.50 .50

Wild Geese Flying over Mountains — AP14

Wild Geese flying over: $5, The sea. $8, The land, horiz.

1969, Aug. 14 **Photo.** ***Perf. 13***

C78 AP14 $2.50 multicolored 3.00 .25
C79 AP14 $5 multicolored 4.75 .45
C80 AP14 $8 multicolored 5.75 .60
Nos. C78-C80 (3) 13.50 1.30

Presidential Palace and Tzu-Ch'iang Squadron AP15

$7, China Airlines jet. $12, China flag, jet.

1980, June 18 Litho. *Perf. 13½*

C81	AP15	$5 shown	.45	.30
C82	AP15	$7 multicolored	1.25	.30
C83	AP15	$12 multicolored	1.75	.50
		Nos. C81-C83 (3)	3.45	1.10

Civil Aeronautics Administration, 37th Anniv. — AP16

Jet Airliners over: $7, Chiang Kai-shek Intl. Airport, vert. $11, Chung Cheng Memorial Hall. $18, Sun Yat-sen Memorial Hall.

Perf. 14x13½, 13½x14

1984, Jan. 20 Litho.

C84	AP16	$7 multicolored	.90	.30
C85	AP16	$11 multicolored	.90	.40
C86	AP16	$18 multicolored	1.00	.40
		Nos. C84-C86 (3)	2.80	1.10

Airplane AP17

1987, Aug. 4 Litho. *Perf. 13½*

C87	AP17	$9 multicolored	.70	.40
C88	AP17	$14 multicolored	.95	.55
C89	AP17	$18 multicolored	1.25	.65
		Nos. C87-C89 (3)	2.90	1.60

SPECIAL DELIVERY STAMPS

Used values of Nos. E1-E8 are for mailer's receipts. Complete unused strips of four are exceptionally scarce because the first section (#1) was to remain in the P.O. booklet.

The mailer received the righthand section (#4), usually canceled, as a receipt. The middle two sections were canceled and attached to the letter. Upon arrival at the destination P.O. they were canceled again, usually on the back, with the righthand copy (#3) retained by that P.O. The lefthand copy (#2) was signed by the recipient and returned to the original P.O. as evidence of delivery. Sections 2 and 3 usually are thin or badly damaged.

Unused strips of three (#2-4) can be found of Nos. E3-E8.

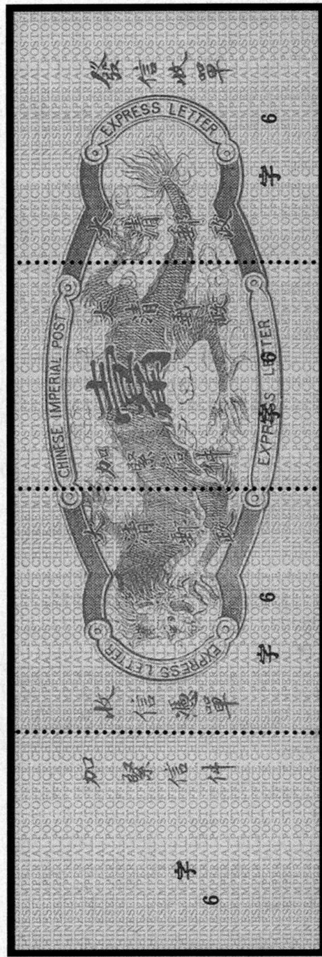

Type E1-E2

Design: Dragon in irregular oval, dragon's head facing downward, with no date, and background with period after "POSTOFFICE."

"Chinese Imperial Post Office" in lines, repeated to form the background which is usually lighter in color than the rest of the design.

Stamp 8x2½ inches, divided into four parts by perforation or serrate rouletting.

1905 Unwmk. *Perf. 11*

E1	10c grass green	*12,000.*	550.00

Serrate Roulette in Black

E2	10c deep green	*15,000.*	500.00

Type, E3-E8

Designs: Dragon's head facing forward. Background with no period after "POSTOFFICE".

1907-10 No Date

E3	10c light bluish green	*4,000.*	250.00

Background with date at bottom

1909-11

E4	10c grn (Feb. 1909)	*2,000.*	400.00
E5	10c bl grn (Jan. 1911)	4,000.	500.00

"IMPERIAL POST OFFICE" in serifed letters repeated to form the background.

No Date, No Border

Background of 30 or 28 lines

1912

E6	10c green (30 lines)	2,000.	300.00
a.	28 lines	*2,250.*	*1,500.*

Background of 35 lines of sans-serif letters

Colored Border

E8	10c green	1,600.	190.00

On No. E8 the medallion in the third section has Chinese characters in the background instead of the usual English inscriptions. E6 and E8 occur with many types of four-character overprints reading "Republic of China," applied locally but unofficially at various post offices.

Type, E9, E10

Design: Wild Goose. Stamp 7½x2¾ inches, divided into five parts.

"CHINESE POST OFFICE" in sans-serif letters, repeated to form the background of 28 lines, with border.

1913 Serrate Roulette in Black

E9	10c green	900.00	110.00

Unused values for Nos. E9-E10 are for complete strips of five parts. Used values are for single parts.

"CHINESE POST OFFICE" in antique letters, forming a background of 29, 30 or 31 lines. No border.

1914 Serrate Roulette in Green

E10	10c green	350.00	50.00

On No. E9 the background is in sans-serif capitals, the Chinese and English inscriptions are on white tablets and the serial numbers are in black.

On No. E10 the background is in antique capitals and extends under the inscriptions. The serial numbers are in green.

Black overprint on No. E10

1916
E10A 10c green 300.00

Yuan Si-Kai proclaimed himself Emperor of China, Dec. 15, 1915, naming his reign "Hung Hsien." No E10A is overprinted "Hung Hsien" in Chinese characters.

NOTE: In February 1916, the Special Delivery Stamps were demonetized and became merely receipts without franking value. To mark this, four of the five sections of the stamp had the letters A, B, C, D either handstamped or printed on them.

SD1

1941 Unwmk. Typo. *Rouletted*
Without Gum
E11 SD1 ($2) car & yel 40.00 32.50

Motorcycle Messenger — SD2

1949, July Litho. *Perf. 12½*
Without Gum
E12 SD2 red violet 9.00 *22.50*
a. Rouletted 13.00 *25.00*

See note after No. 959.
For surcharge and overprints see Nos. 1150, Taiwan E1, Fukien E1.

Revenue Stamp Overprinted in Purple Brown

1949 Without Gum
E13 A95 $10 grnsh gray 55.00 55.00

See note after No. 962.

REGISTRATION STAMPS

R1

1941 Unwmk. Typo. *Rouletted*
Without Gum
F1 R1 ($1.50) green & buff 30.00 21.00

Mountain Scene — R2

1949, July Litho. *Perf. 12½*
Without Gum
F2 R2 carmine 10.50 *19.00*
a. Rouletted 14.00 *24.00*

See note after No. 959.
For surcharge and overprints see Nos. 1152, Taiwan F1, Fukien F1, PRC 103.

Revenue Stamp Overprinted in Carmine

1949
F3 A95 $50 dark blue 35.00 35.00

See note after No. 962.

POSTAGE DUE STAMPS

Regular Issue of 1902-03 Overprinted in Black

1904 Unwmk. *Perf. 14 to 15*
J1 A17 ½c chocolate 16.00 16.00
J2 A17 1c ocher 16.00 16.00
J3 A17 2c scarlet 19.50 16.00
a. red *20.00* *10.00*
J4 A17 4c red brn 20.50 20.00
J5 A17 5c salmon 23.00 23.00
J6 A17 10c dk blue grn 40.00 35.00
a. Vert. pair, imperf. btwn. *2,000.* *2,000.*
Nos. J1-J6 (6) 135.00 126.00

D1

1904 Engr.
J7 D1 ½c blue 7.00 4.00
a. Horiz. pair, imperf. btwn. *3,000.* *2,000.*
J8 D1 1c blue 12.00 4.00
J9 D1 2c blue 12.00 4.00
a. Horiz. pair, imperf. btwn. *2,000.* *1,800.*
J10 D1 4c blue 15.00 6.00
J11 D1 5c blue 18.00 7.00
J12 D1 10c blue 20.00 9.00
J13 D1 20c blue 50.00 12.00
J14 D1 30c blue 70.00 40.00
Nos. J7-J14 (8) 204.00 86.00

Arabic numeral of value at left on Nos. J12-J14.

1911
J15 D1 1c brown 22.50 *25.00*
J16 D1 2c brown 37.50 *40.00*

The ½c, 4c, 5c and 20c in brown exist but were not issued as they arrived in China after the downfall of the Ching dynasty.

Issues of 1904 Overprinted in Red

1912
J19 D1 ½c blue 625. *825.*
J20 D1 4c blue 800. *900.*
J21 D1 5c blue 900. 900.
J22 D1 10c blue 1,400. 900.
J23 D1 20c blue 2,750. 2,600.
J24 D1 30c blue 2,750. 2,600.

Nos. J15-J16 exist with this overprint, but were not regularly issued. Value, $9,500, each.

Nos. J1-J14 Overprinted in Red

1912
J25 D1 ½c blue 4.00 2.50
J26 D1 1c brown 5.00 2.50
a. Horiz. pair, imperf. btwn. *3,000.* *3,000.*
b. Inverted overprint 550.00 550.00
J27 D1 2c brown 6.50 3.25
J28 D1 4c blue 12.00 5.00
J29 D1 5c blue 220.00 *240.00*
J30 D1 5c brown 16.00 *8.00*
a. Inverted overprint 550.00 *340.00*
J31 D1 10c blue 20.00 *10.50*
J32 D1 20c blue 22.00 14.00
J33 D1 30c blue 28.00 24.00
Nos. J25-J33 (9) 333.50 309.75

Nos. J19-J24 and the two unissued stamps from that set exist additionally overprinted 'Republic of China' in Chinese characters. The same overprint as J25-J33 value for set of 8, $65,000.

Issues of 1904 Overprinted in Black

1912
J34 D1 ½c blue 12.50 9.25
J35 D1 ½c brown 6.50 2.75
J36 D1 1c brown 6.50 2.75
a. Inverted overprint 350.00 350.00
b. Horiz. pair, imperf. btwn. 1,800
J37 D1 2c brown 8.25 *4.75*
J38 D1 4c blue 16.50 *8.75*
J39 D1 5c brown 22.00 *13.00*
a. Horiz. pair, imperf. btwn. *3,000.* *3,000.*
J40 D1 10c blue 35.00 *25.00*
J41 D1 20c brown 52.50 *92.50*
J42 D1 30c blue 90.00 60.00
Nos. J34-J42 (9) 249.75 218.75

D4

Printed by Waterlow & Sons

1913, May *Perf. 14, 15*
J43 D4 ½c blue 3.00 1.50
a. Horiz. pair, imperf. btwn. *3,500.* *2,600.*
J44 D4 1c blue 3.50 1.50
a. Vert. pair, imperf. btwn. 2,500
J45 D4 2c blue 5.00 3.00
J46 D4 4c blue 8.00 3.00
J47 D4 5c blue 12.00 6.00
J48 D4 10c blue 17.50 8.00
J49 D4 20c blue 27.50 13.00
J50 D4 30c blue 35.00 15.00
Nos. J43-J50 (8) 111.50 51.00

Printed by the Chinese Bureau of Engraving & Printing

1915 Re-engraved *Perf. 14*
J51 D4 ½c blue 2.50 *1.00*
J52 D4 1c blue 3.00 .65
J53 D4 2c blue 3.25 .65
J54 D4 4c blue 4.00 .75
J55 D4 5c blue 5.75 1.50
J56 D4 10c blue 8.75 2.50
J57 D4 20c blue 14.00 8.00
J58 D4 30c blue 40.00 20.00
Nos. J51-J58 (8) 81.25 35.05

In the upper part of the stamps of type D4 there is an ornament of five marks like the letter "V". Below this is a curved label with an inscription in Chinese characters. On the 1913 stamps there are two complete background lines between the ornament and the label. The 1915 stamps show only one unbroken line at this place. There are other minute differences in the engraving of the stamps of the two issues.

D5

1932 *Perf. 14*
J59 D5 ½c orange .50 *.30*
J60 D5 1c orange .50 *.30*
J61 D5 2c orange .50 *.30*
J62 D5 4c orange .50 *.30*
J63 D5 5c orange 1.25 *1.50*
J64 D5 10c orange 1.60 2.00
J65 D5 20c orange 2.25 3.00
J66 D5 30c orange 3.25 *4.00*
Nos. J59-J66 (8) 10.35 11.70

See Nos. J69-J79. For surcharges see Nos. 1NJ1, 9NJ1-9NJ4.

Nos. 387-388 Overprinted in Black or Red

1940
J67 A57 $1 henna & dk brn (Bk) 10.00 *25.00*
J68 A57 $2 dl bl & org brn (R) 10.00 *20.00*

Type of 1932
Printed by The Commercial Press, Ltd.
Perf. 12½, 12½x13, 13

1940-41 Engr.
J69 D5 ½c yellow orange .80 *1.25*
J70 D5 1c yellow orange .80 *1.25*
J71 D5 2c yel org ('41) .80 *1.25*
J72 D5 4c yellow orange .80 *1.25*
J73 D5 5c yel org ('41) 1.20 *1.25*
J74 D5 10c yel org ('41) .80 *1.25*
J75 D5 20c yel org ('41) .80 *1.25*
J76 D5 30c yellow orange .80 *2.00*
J77 D5 50c yellow orange 1.00 *2.00*
J78 D5 $1 yellow orange 1.20 *2.00*
J79 D5 $2 yellow orange 1.50 *3.00*
Nos. J69-J79 (11) 10.50 *17.75*

For surcharge see No. 1NJ1.

D6

Thin Paper Without Gum

1944 Typo. *Perf. 13*
J80 D6 10c bluish green .80 *3.00*
J81 D6 20c light chalky blue .80 *3.00*
J82 D6 40c dull rose .80 *3.00*
J83 D6 50c bluish green .80 *3.00*
J84 D6 60c dull blue .80 *3.00*
J85 D6 $1 dull rose .80 *2.00*
J86 D6 $2 lilac brown .80 *2.00*
Nos. J80-J86 (7) 5.60 *19.00*

D7

1945 Without Gum Unwmk.
J87 D7 $2 rose carmine .80 *2.00*
J88 D7 $6 rose carmine .80 *2.00*
J89 D7 $8 rose carmine .80 *2.00*
J90 D7 $10 rose carmine .80 *2.00*
J91 D7 $20 rose carmine .80 *2.00*
J92 D7 $30 rose carmine 1.00 *2.00*
Nos. J87-J92 (6) 5.00 *12.00*

For surcharges see Nos. J102-J109.

D8

Thin Paper Without Gum

1947 Litho. *Perf. 14*
J93 D8 $50 plum .80 *2.00*
J94 D8 $80 plum .80 *2.00*
J95 D8 $100 plum .80 *2.00*
J96 D8 $160 plum .80 *2.00*
J97 D8 $200 plum .80 *2.00*
J98 D8 $400 violet brown .80 *2.00*
J99 D8 $500 violet brown .80 *2.00*
a. Vert. pair, imperf. between 80.00
J100 D8 $800 violet brown .80 *2.00*
J101 D8 $2000 violet brown .80 *2.00*
Nos. J93-J101 (9) 7.20 *18.00*

Type of 1945, Redrawn Surcharged in Black

Without Gum
Deep claret

1948 **Engr.** ***Perf. 13½x14***
J102 D7 $1000 on $20 .70 *3.00*
J103 D7 $2000 on $30 .70 *3.00*
J104 D7 $3000 on $50 .70 *3.00*
J105 D7 $4000 on $100 .70 *3.00*
J106 D7 $5000 on $200 .70 *3.00*
J107 D7 $10,000 on $300 .70 *3.00*
J108 D7 $20,000 on $500 .70 *3.00*
J109 D7 $30,000 on $1000 .70 *3.00*
Nos. J102-J109 (8) 5.60 *24.00*

There are many differences in the redrawn design.

No. 627 Surcharged in Black

1949 ***Perf. 12***
J110 A72 1 (c) on $40 org .70 *10.00*
J111 A72 2 (c) on $40 org .70 *10.00*
J112 A72 5 (c) on $40 org .70 *10.00*
J113 A72 10 (c) on $40 org .70 *10.00*
J114 A72 20 (c) on $40 org .70 *10.00*
J115 A72 50 (c) on $40 org .70 *10.00*
J116 A72 $1 on $40 org .70 *10.00*
J117 A72 $2 on $40 org .70 *10.00*
J118 A72 $5 on $40 org 1.00 *10.00*
J119 A72 $10 on $40 org 1.00 *10.00*
Nos. J110-J119 (10) 7.60 *100.00*

Republic of China (Taiwan)

No. 438 Surcharged in Green or Black

1951 **Unwmk.** ***Perf. 12½***
J120 A47 40c on 40c org (G) 47.50 *47.50*
J121 A47 80c on 40c org (Bk) 47.50 *47.50*

Revenue Stamps Surcharged in Various Colors

1953 **Unwmk.** ***Perf. 12½, 14***
Without Gum
J122 A95 10c on $50 dk bl (O) 30.00 4.50
J123 A95 20c on $100 ol grn (Dk Br) 30.00 4.50
J124 A95 40c on $20 org brn 34.00 6.00
J125 A95 80c on $500 sl grn (Dk Bl) 52.50 9.00
J126 A95 $1 on $30 dk vio (G) 52.50 15.00
Nos. J122-J126 (5) 199.00 39.00

D9

1956 **Unwmk.** **Litho.** ***Perf. 12½***
Without Gum
J127 D9 20c rose car, & lt bl 3.25 .40
J128 D9 40c green & buff 4.50 .60
J129 D9 80c brown & gray 8.75 1.00
J130 D9 $1 ultra & pink 10.00 2.00
Nos. J127-J130 (4) 26.50 4.00

No. 1197 Surcharged in Dark Violet

Wmk. 323
1961, Dec. 28 **Engr.** ***Perf. 12***
Without Gum
J131 A135 $5 on $20 car rose 12.00 2.40

Nos. 1274, 1282-1283 Surcharged in Black, Carmine Rose or Blue

1964-65 **Litho.**
J132 A158 10c on 80c pale grn .55 .25
J133 A158 20c on $3.60 vio bl (CR) ('65) .65 .25
J134 A158 40c on $4.50 ver (B) ('65) 1.40 .30
Nos. J132-J134 (3) 2.60 .80

D10

1966-76 **Wmk. 323** ***Perf. 12½***
Granite Paper; Without Gum
J135 D10 10c dk brn & lil .25 .25
J136 D10 20c blue & yel .40 .25
J137 D10 50c vio bl & lt bl ('70) .65 .25
J138 D10 $1 purple & sal .50 .25
J139 D10 $2 grn & lt bl .65 .25
J140 D10 $5 red & sal 1.25 .60
a. $5 org red & pale yel 1.25 .60
J141 D10 $10 lil rose & pink ('76) *22.50* 1.00
Nos. J135-J141 (7) 26.20 2.85

The 50c, $10 and No. J140a are gummed. The $1 and $2 were reissued with gum in 1968 and 1973 respectively. No. J140a and the $10 are on ordinary paper.

Catalogue values for unused stamps in this section, from this point to the end of the section, are for Never Hinged items.

D11

1984-88 **Litho.** ***Perf. 12½***
J142 D11 $1 rose & violet .25 .25
J143 D11 $2 yellow & blue .25 .25
J144 D11 $3 pale grn & brt rose lil .25 .25
J145 D11 $5 blue & yellow .25 .25
J146 D11 $5.50 rose lil & brt blue .40 .35
J147 D11 $7.50 bis yel & dp vio .60 .45
J148 D11 $10 yel & lil rose .50 .30
J149 D11 $20 sky blue & citron 1.60 1.25
Nos. J142-J149 (8) 4.10 3.35

Issued: $3, $5.50, $7.50, $20, Apr. 1, 1988; others, Mar. 15, 1984.

D12

1998, Sept. 30 **Litho.** ***Perf. 12½***
Background Color
J150 D12 50c orange yellow .25 .25
J151 D12 $1 pink .30 .25
J152 D12 $2 deep pink .30 .25
J153 D12 $5 yellow green .50 .25
J154 D12 $10 blue .90 .30
J155 D12 $20 green 1.75 .60
Nos. J150-J155 (6) 4.00 1.90

Lotus Flower, Peach, Bats, Coins and Chinese Characters — D13

Perf. 12½x12¼
2008, Nov. 12 **Litho.**
Denomination Color
J156 D13 $1 dark red .25 .25
J157 D13 $3 green .30 .25
J158 D13 $5 olive green .40 .25
J159 D13 $10 purple .75 .35
J160 D13 $20 bister 1.50 .75
Nos. J156-J160 (5) 3.20 1.85

Type of 2008
Die Cut Perf. 22
2015, Oct. 28 **Litho.**
Self-Adhesive
Denomination Color
J161 D13 50c red brown .25 .25
J162 D13 $2 dark blue .25 .25

PARCEL POST STAMPS

PP1

PP2

PP3

1945-48 **Unwmk.** **Engr.** ***Perf. 13***
Without Gum
Q1 PP1 $500 green 12.00 1.00
Q2 PP1 $1000 blue 12.00 1.00
Q3 PP1 $3000 rose red 22.50 1.60
Q4 PP1 $5000 brown 140.00 30.00
Q5 PP1 $10,000 lil gray 250.00 50.00
Q6 PP1 $20,000 red org *4,500.*
Nos. Q1-Q5 (5) 436.50 83.60

No. Q6 was sold through the philatelic counter in Shanghai.

For surcharges see People's Republic of China Nos. 5LQ1-5LQ2, 5LQ27-5LQ28.

Perf. 12½
Q7 PP2 $3000 red org 30.00 2.00
Q8 PP2 $5000 dk blue 40.00 2.00
Q9 PP2 $10,000 violet 45.00 5.00
Q10 PP2 $20,000 dk red 50.00 8.00
Nos. Q7-Q10 (4) 165.00 17.00

Perf. 13½
Q11 PP3 $1000 org yel 9.00 1.50
Q12 PP3 $3000 bl grn 9.00 1.50
Q13 PP3 $5000 org red 9.00 1.50
Q14 PP3 $7000 dl blue 9.00 1.50
Q15 PP3 $10,000 car rose 10.00 2.00
Q16 PP3 $30,000 olive 10.00 2.00
Q17 PP3 $50,000 indigo 10.00 2.00
Q18 PP3 $70,000 org brn 14.00 4.00
Q19 PP3 $100,000 dp plum 14.00 4.00

Denomination Tablet Without Inner Frame
Q20 PP3 $200,000 dk grn 18.50 6.00
Q21 PP3 $300,000 pink 18.50 4.00
Q22 PP3 $500,000 vio brn 18.50 4.00
Q23 PP3 $3,000,000 sl bl 20.00 10.00
Q24 PP3 $5,000,000 lilac 20.00 10.00
Q25 PP3 $6,000,000 ol gray 22.00 10.00
Q26 PP3 $8,000,000 scar 22.00 11.00
Q27 PP3 $10,000,000 sage grn 25.00 14.00
Nos. Q11-Q27 (17) 258.50 89.00

Zeros for "cents" omitted on Nos. Q23-Q27.

See Taiwan Nos. Q1-Q5. For surcharges see Nos. 883-885, Northeastern Provinces Q1, Szechwan Q1, People's Republic of China 3LQ1-3LQ9, 5LQ3-5LQ16, 5LQ29-5LQ30.

#Q11-Q15, Q23-Q24 Surcharged in Black or Carmine (#Q35)

1949 **Unwmk.** ***Perf. 13½***
Q32 PP3 $10 on $3000 5.00 1.00
Q33 PP3 $20 on $5000 5.00 1.00
Q34 PP3 $50 on $10,000 5.00 1.00
Q35 PP3 $100 on $3,000,000 8.00 2.00
Q36 PP3 $200 on $5,000,000 12.00 2.00
Q37 PP3 $500 on $1000 22.50 .25
Q38 PP3 $1000 on $7000 22.50 .30
Nos. Q32-Q38 (7) 80.00 7.55

5 characters in each line on Nos. Q33-Q38.

MILITARY STAMPS

No. 454 Overprinted in Dull Red

1943-44 **Unwmk.** ***Perf. 12***
M1 A59 8c turquoise green 6.00 *9.00*

Nos. 383, 453-454 Overprinted in Red or Black

6mm between characters
Perf. 14, 12½
M2 A57 8c olive green 6.00 *9.00*
a. 8mm between characters 6.00 *9.00*
M3 A59 8c red orange (B) 600.00
M4 A59 8c turquoise green 12.00 10.00

Forgeries of No. M3 abound.

No. 493 Overprinted in Red

Perf. 13
M5 A62 16c dull olive brn 11.00 *15.00*
a. Perf. 10½-11 350.00

No. M5 overprinted in black is a proof.

Stamps of 1942-44 Overprinted in Carmine or Black

M6 A62 50c sage grn (C) 6.00 *7.00*
M7 A62 $1 rose lake 8.00 *9.00*
M8 A62 $1 dull green 8.00 *9.00*
M9 A62 $2 dk bl grn (C) 10.00 *14.00*
M10 A62 $2 dk vio brn ('44) 200.00 150.00
Nos. M6-M10 (5) 232.00 189.00

Nos. 383 and 357 Overprinted in Red

1944 *Perf. 12, 14*

No.	Type	Description	Unused	Used
M11	A57	8c olive green	6.00	*10.00*
a.		Right character inverted	1,000.	
M12	A57	16c olive gray	90.00	*100.00*

Anti-Aircraft Guns — M1

1945, Jan. 1 Typo. *Perf. 12½*

Thin Paper Without Gum

No.	Type	Description	Unused	Used
M13	M1	rose	3.00	*10.00*

For overprints see Northeastern Provinces Nos. M2-M3.

TAIWAN

(Formosa)

100 Sen = 1 Yen

100 Cents = 1 Dollar

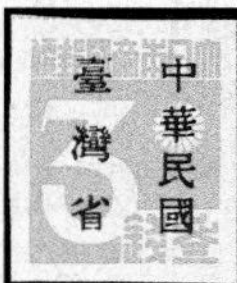

Stamps and Types of Japan (Taiwan) Overprinted in Black

Stamps Divided by Lines of Colored Dashes

Values in Sen and Yen

1945 Unwmk. Litho. *Imperf.*

Without Gum

No.	Type	Description	Unused	Used
1	A1	3s carmine	2.50	10.00
2	A1	5s blue grn	2.50	2.00
3	A1	10s pale blue	2.50	.55
a.		Inverted overprint	375.00	
b.		Double overprint	375.00	
4	A1	30s dk blue	14.00	10.00
5	A1	40s violet	14.00	7.00
6	A1	50s gray brn	10.00	5.00
7	A1	1y olive grn	12.00	10.00

Same Overprint on Types of Japan

No.	Type	Description	Unused	Used
8	A99	5y gray grn	24.00	18.00
9	A100	10y brown vio	45.00	45.00
a.		Inverted overprint	375.00	
		Nos. 1-9 (9)	126.50	107.55

The basic stamps of this issue were prepared by Japanese authorities for Taiwan use before the end of World War II when the island reverted to Chinese control. They are printed on crude buff or white wove paper. The overprint translates: "For Use in Taiwan, Chinese Republic."

A second overprinting of Nos. 2-3 was made with a different font.

China, Nos. 728-731, Srchd. in Black

1946 Without Gum *Perf. 14*

No.	Type	Description	Unused	Used
10	A75	70s on $20 green	3.50	*5.50*
a.		Inverted surcharge	*1,200.*	
11	A75	1y on $30 blue	3.50	*5.50*
12	A75	2y on $50 dk brn	3.50	*5.75*
13	A75	3y on $100 car	3.75	*5.75*
		Nos. 10-13 (4)	14.25	*22.50*

Convening of the Chinese Natl. Assembly.

China Issues and Types of 1940-1946 Srchd. in Black — a

Perf. 12½, 12½x13, 13, 13x12½, 14

1946-47

Nos. 18, 23-28 Without Gum

No.	Type	Description	Unused	Used
14	A46	2s on 2c dp bl	.80	*1.50*
15	A48	5s on 5c dl red org	.80	*1.00*
16	A39	10s on 4c pale vio	.80	*1.50*
17	A48	30s on 15c brn car	.80	*1.00*
18	A73	50s on $20 car	.80	*1.00*
19	A37	65s on $20 brt yel grn	1.00	*2.00*
20	A47	1y on 20c lt bl	.80	*2.00*
a.		Inverted surcharge	*950.00*	
21	A37	1y on $30 choc	1.00	*1.75*
22	A37	2y on $50 red org	1.50	2.00
23	A73	3y on $100 dk car	.80	*2.00*
24	A73	5y on $200 ol grn	.80	*2.00*
25	A73	10y on $500 brt bl grn	.80	*1.50*
26	A73	20y on $700 red brn	1.00	1.00
27	A73	50y on $1000 rose lake	2.00	1.50
28	A73	100y on $3000 blue	2.75	1.60
		Nos. 14-28 (15)	16.45	*23.35*

The bottom line of the surcharge expresses the new value and consists of 2, 3 or 4 characters.

Nos. 14, 18-19, 21-28 issued in 1947.

Same Surcharge on China No. 412

1947 Wmk. 261 *Perf. 13*

No.	Type	Description	Unused	Used
28A	A48	30s on 15c brn car	135.00	150.00

Type of China, 1946, with additional inscription on both sides of head

1947 Unwmk. Engr. *Perf. 11, 11½*

No.	Type	Description	Unused	Used
29	A74	70c carmine	3.50	*4.75*
30	A74	$1 green	3.50	*4.75*
31	A74	$2 vermilion	3.50	*4.75*
32	A74	$3 yel grn	3.50	*4.75*
33	A74	$7 yel org	3.50	*4.75*
34	A74	$10 magenta	3.50	*4.75*
		Nos. 29-34 (6)	21.00	*28.50*

60th birthday of Chiang Kai-shek.

Type of China, 1947, with additional inscription above value

1947 *Perf. 14*

No.	Type	Description	Unused	Used
35	A76	50c deep green	3.50	*5.50*
36	A76	$3 deep blue	3.50	*5.50*
37	A76	$7.50 carmine	3.50	*5.50*
38	A76	$10 light brown	3.50	*5.50*
39	A76	$20 deep claret	3.50	*5.50*
		Nos. 35-39 (5)	17.50	*27.50*

First anniversary of return of Chinese National Government to Nanking.

Dr. Sun Yat-sen — A3

1947, July 10 Without Gum

No.	Type	Description	Unused	Used
40	A3	$1 dk brown	1.00	2.50
41	A3	$2 org brn	1.20	2.00
42	A3	$3 blue grn	1.20	2.00
43	A3	$5 vermilion	2.50	*2.75*
44	A3	$9 deep blue	1.00	1.20
45	A3	$10 brt rose car	1.00	.80
46	A3	$20 deep green	.85	.70
47	A3	$50 rose lilac	.85	.60
48	A3	$100 blue	.85	.60
49	A3	$200 dark red	.85	.60
		Nos. 40-49 (10)	11.30	13.75

The 30c gray and $7.50 orange were not regularly issued without surcharge. Value for the two stamps, $450.

See Nos. 63-68. For overprint and surcharges see Nos. 51-53, 69-73, 102, J10-J17.

Type of 1947 Surcharged in Black — b

1948 Unwmk. *Perf. 14*

No.	Type	Description	Unused	Used
51	A3	$25 on $100 blue	2.50	*3.00*
52	A3	$500 on $7.50 org	6.75	3.50
53	A3	$1000 on 30c gray	14.00	9.00
		Nos. 51-53 (3)	23.25	15.50

Stamps of China, 1943-48, Surcharged Type "a" in Black or Carmine

1948-49 *Perf. 12½, 14*

Without Gum

No.	Type	Description	Unused	Used
54	A73	$5 on $70 red org (#639)	1.00	*2.50*
55	A62	$10 on $3 dk yel (#555)	4.50	*3.50*
56	A82	$10 on $150 dk bl (C) (#745)	1.20	*1.75*
57	A82	$20 on $250 dp lil (C) (#746)	1.10	*1.20*
58	A67	$100 on $20 car (#592)	1,600.	—
59	A82	$1000 on $20,000 rose pink ('49) (#788)	6.50	3.50
		Nos. 54-59 (6)	1,614.	12.45

The bottom line of the surcharge expresses the new value and consists of 2 or 3 characters.

Forgeries of No. 58 abound.

Type of 1947

1949 Engr. *Perf. 14*

No.	Type	Description	Unused	Used
63	A3	$25 olive grn	1.20	1.00
64	A3	$5000 ocher	10.00	2.00
65	A3	$10,000 apple grn	10.00	5.00
66	A3	$20,000 ol bister	10.00	5.00
67	A3	$30,000 indigo	10.00	2.00
68	A3	$40,000 violet brn	9.00	2.00
		Nos. 63-68 (6)	50.20	17.00

For overprint and surcharges see Nos. 101, 103, J12.

No. 42 and type of 1947 Surcharged Type "b" in Black, Carmine Violet or Red Violet

1949

No.	Type	Description	Unused	Used
69	A3	$300 on $3 bl grn	1.75	1.00
70	A3	$1000 on $3 bl grn (C)	3.00	1.00
71	A3	$2000 on $3 bl grn (V)	2.50	1.00
72	A3	$3000 on $3 bl grn (RV)	12.00	4.25
73	A3	$3000 on $7.50 org	120.00	5.50
		Nos. 69-73 (5)	139.25	12.75

For overprints see Nos. J10-J11.

Stamps of China, 1940-47, Surcharged Type "a" in Black or Carmine

Perf. 12½, 13x13½, 14

No.	Type	Description	Unused	Used
74	A39	$2 on 2½c rose lil (#424)	.80	.80
75	A72	$5 on $40 org (#627)	1.00	*2.00*
76	A73	$5 on $50 pur (C) (#638)	1.00	1.50
77	A73	$5 on $100 dk car (#640)	1.25	.80
78	A57	$20 on 2c ol grn (#368)	1.00	1.75
81	A63	$100 on $20 rose (#571)	1.10	.50
82	A67	$200 on $10 dk bl (C) (#591)	8.00	1.75
84	A57	$500 on $30 dl vio (#521)	18.00	5.00
86	A62	$800 on $4 red brn (#504)	15.00	10.00
87	A67	$5000 on $10 dk bl (#591)	18.00	5.00
88	A67	$10,000 on $20 car (#592)	18.00	4.00
89	A82	$200,000 on $3000 bl (C) (#750)	900.00	50.00
		Nos. 74-89 (12)	983.15	83.10

Northeastern Provinces No. 47, Surcharged in Green, Red Violet, Black or Blue

1949-50

No.	Type	Description	Unused	Used
91	A2	2c on $44 (G)	62.50	10.00
92	A2	5c on $44 (RV) ('50)	57.50	20.00
a.		Violet surcharge	85.00	11.50
93	A2	10c on $44 (RV) ('50)	75.00	6.00
94	A2	20c on $44 (Bk) ('50)	100.00	7.00
a.		Double surcharge	200.00	
95	A2	30c on $44 (Bl) ('50)	110.00	14.00
96	A2	50c on $44 (Bl) ('50)	130.00	17.00
		Nos. 91-96 (6)	535.00	74.00

There were two printings of Nos. 91-93, with minor differences.

China 959a, Overprinted in Black

Overprint 15mm Wide

1949 Unwmk. *Rouletted 9½*

No.	Type	Description	Unused	Used
97	A96	orange	5.50	1.75

China Nos. 567, 498 and 640 Surcharged Type "a" in Black

1948-49 Unwmk. *Perf. 12½, 13, 14*

No.	Type	Description	Unused	Used
98	A63	$20 on $3 red	3.50	2.50
99	A62	$50 on 50c sage grn	3.75	5.00
a.		Perf. 11	50.00	75.00
100	A73	$600 on $100 dk car	6.50	9.00
		Nos. 98-100 (3)	13.75	16.50

Botton line of surcharge consists of 3 characters.

No. 99 has two settings of surcharge: I. Spacing 10mm between rows of characters. II. Spacing 12mm.

#67, 47 and 68 Surcharged in Violet (#101) or Black

1949 *Perf. 14*

No.	Type	Description	Unused	Used
101	A3	2c on $30,000 ind	52.50	30.00
102	A3	10c on $50 rose lil	52.50	15.00
103	A3	10c on $40,000 vio brn	125.00	45.00
		Nos. 101-103 (3)	230.00	90.00

Numerals slightly larger on Nos. 101-103.

For similar surcharges on China type A82 see China Nos. 1025-1036.

AIR POST STAMP

China No. C62a, Overprinted in Black

Overprint 15mm Wide

1949 Unwmk. *Rouletted 9½*

No.	Type	Description	Unused	Used
C1	AP5	blue green	2.50	2.50

SPECIAL DELIVERY STAMP

China No. E12a, Overprinted in Black

Overprint 12½mm Wide

1950 Unwmk. *Rouletted 9½*

No.	Type	Description	Unused	Used
E1	SD2	red violet	10.00	4.50

REGISTRATION STAMP

China No. F2a Overprinted in Black

Overprint 12mm Wide

1950 Unwmk. *Rouletted 9½*

No.	Type	Description	Unused	Used
F1	R2	carmine	10.00	4.50

POSTAGE DUE STAMPS

D1

Unwmk.

1948, Feb. 10 Litho. *Perf. 14*

Without Gum

No.	Description	Unused	Used
J1	D1 $1 blue	2.50	*5.00*
J2	D1 $3 blue	2.50	*5.75*
J3	D1 $5 blue	2.50	*5.75*
J4	D1 $10 blue	2.50	*7.75*
J5	D1 $20 blue	2.50	*4.75*
	Nos. J1-J5 (5)	12.50	*29.00*

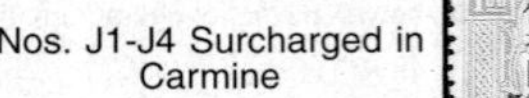
Nos. J1-J4 Surcharged in Carmine

1948, Dec. 4

No.	Description	Unused	Used
J6	D1 $50 on $1 blue	24.00	*13.00*
J7	D1 $100 on $3 blue	24.00	*13.00*
J8	D1 $300 on $5 blue	24.00	*13.00*
J9	D1 $500 on $10 blue	24.00	*13.00*
	Nos. J6-J9 (4)	96.00	*52.00*

Nos. 70, 72 and 64 Handstamped in Violet

1949, Aug. 5

No.	Description	Unused	Used
J10	A3 $1000 on $3 bl grn	35.00	22.00
J11	A3 $3000 on $3 bl grn	54.00	29.00
J12	A3 $5000 ocher	120.00	70.00
	Nos. J10-J12 (3)	209.00	121.00

No. 48 Surcharged in Various Colors

1950

No.	Description	Unused	Used
J13	A3 4c on $100 bl (Br)	12.00	10.00
J14	A3 10c on $100 bl (RV)	22.50	*26.00*
J15	A3 20c on $100 bl (Bk)	10.00	*22.50*
J16	A3 40c on $100 bl (C)	47.50	*90.00*
J17	A3 $1 on $100 bl (Bl)	35.00	*47.50*
	Nos. J13-J17 (5)	127.00	*196.00*

PARCEL POST STAMPS

Type of China, Parcel Post Stamps of 1945-48 With Added Inscription

1949 Unwmk. Engr. *Perf. 14*

No.	Description	Unused	Used
Q1	PP3 $100 bluish grn	*265.00*	1.00
Q2	PP3 $300 rose car	*265.00*	1.00
Q3	PP3 $500 olive green	*265.00*	1.00
Q4	PP3 $1000 slate	*265.00*	1.00
Q5	PP3 $3000 deep plum	*265.00*	1.00
	Nos. Q1-Q5 (5)	*1,325.*	5.00

Chinese characters in lower corners have colorless background; denomination tablet in color.

OCCUPATION STAMPS

Issued Under Japanese Occupation

Unused values for Japanese occupation issues are for never hinged examples.

Canceled Stamps
Postally used stamps of the Japanese occupation generally have heavy, smudgy cancels.

Kwangtung

China No. 297 Overprinted in Black

1942 Unwmk. *Perf. 12½*

No.	Description	Unused	Used
1N1	A37 2c olive green	8.00	8.00
a.	Inverted overprint	120.00	165.00

Same Overprint in Red or Black on Stamps of China, 1939-41

Perf. 12½, 14

No.	Description	Unused	Used
1N2	A57 3c dl cl (#350)	2.75	2.75
1N3	A57 8c ol grn (#383)	2.75	2.75
1N4	A57 10c grn (#354) (R)	2.50	2.75
1N5	A57 10c grn (#384) (R)	3.50	3.50
1N6	A57 16c ol gray (#357)	7.50	*7.25*
1N7	A57 30c scar (#385)	4.00	3.00
1N8	A57 50c dk bl (#386) (R)	5.00	*9.00*
1N9	A57 $1 org brn & sep (#387)	10.00	*10.00*
1N10	A57 $2 dp bl & yel brn (#388)	12.00	*9.50*
1N11	A57 $5 red & sl grn (#389)	15.00	*10.00*
1N12	A57 $10 dk grn & dl pur (#390)	30.00	*20.00*
1N13	A57 $20 rose lake & dk bl (#391)	13.00	*13.00*

Same Overprint on China Nos. 422 and 433

Perf. 12½

No.	Description	Unused	Used
1N14	A40 1c orange	3.00	*2.40*
a.	Inverted overprint	87.50	80.00
1N15	A47 20c lt blue	6.00	*5.00*

Same Overprint on Stamps of China, 1941

Perf. 12

No.	Description	Unused	Used
1N16	A59 1c orange	4.50	*4.50*
1N17	A59 5c green	2.50	*4.50*
1N18	A59 8c turq green	2.75	*3.75*
1N19	A59 10c brt green	3.25	*3.75*
1N20	A59 17c olive	4.00	*6.00*
1N21	A59 30c scarlet	6.00	*7.00*
1N22	A59 50c dark blue	4.00	*4.00*
	Nos. 1N1-1N22 (22)	152.00	*142.40*

Stamps of China, 1939-41 Overprinted in Black

1942 *Perf. 12½, 14*

No.	Description	Unused	Used
1N23	A57 2c olive grn (#368)	1.50	*2.00*
1N24	A57 3c dl claret (#350)	1.50	*2.00*
1N25	A57 5c olive grn (#352)	1.50	*1.25*
1N26	A57 8c olive grn (#353)	300.00	—
1N27	A57 8c olive grn (#369)	1.00	*1.00*
1N28	A57 10c green (#354)	1.50	*2.00*
1N29	A57 16c ol gray (#357)	1.50	*3.00*
1N30	A57 25c dk bl (#358)	2.00	*4.00*
1N31	A57 30c scarlet (#385)	2.50	*3.00*
1N32	A57 50c dk blue (#386)	2.25	*2.75*
1N33	A57 $1 org brn & sep (#387)	13.00	*17.00*
1N34	A57 $2 dp bl & yel brn (#388)	13.00	*14.00*
1N35	A57 $5 red & sl grn (#389)	14.00	*17.00*
1N36	A57 $10 dk grn & dl pur (#390)	20.00	*20.00*
1N37	A57 $20 rose lake & dk bl (#391)	14.00	*27.50*
	Nos. 1N23-1N25,1N27-1N37 (14)	89.25	*116.50*

No. 1N26 is valued in fine condition.

Same Overprint on China Nos. 397-401

1942 Wmk. 261 *Perf. 14*

No.	Description	Unused	Used
1N38	A57 $1 org brn & sep	10.00	*9.00*
1N39	A57 $2 dp bl & yel brn	9.00	13.00
1N40	A57 $5 red & sl grn	11.00	*14.00*
1N41	A57 $10 dk grn & dl pur	22.50	26.50
1N42	A57 $20 rose lake & dk bl	22.50	24.00
	Nos. 1N38-1N42 (5)	75.00	86.50

Same Overprint on Stamps of China, 1941

1942 Unwmk. *Perf. 12*

No.	Description	Unused	Used
1N43	A59 2c brt ultra	1.00	*2.00*
1N44	A59 5c green	1.00	*2.00*
1N45	A59 8c red org	2.00	*3.00*
1N46	A59 8c turq grn	2.00	*3.00*
1N47	A59 10c brt green	2.00	*5.00*
1N48	A59 17c olive	2.00	*5.00*
1N49	A59 25c rose vio	2.00	*4.00*
1N50	A59 30c scarlet	2.00	*3.00*
1N51	A59 50c dk blue	3.00	*3.00*
1N52	A59 $1 brn & blk	7.00	*8.00*
1N53	A59 $2 bl & blk	7.00	*8.75*
1N54	A59 $5 scar & blk	13.00	13.00
1N55	A59 $10 grn & blk	17.00	*17.00*
1N56	A59 $20 rose vio & blk	11.00	*20.00*
	Nos. 1N43-1N56 (14)	72.00	*96.75*

China Nos. 354 and 369 Surcharged in Black

1945 Unwmk. *Perf. 12½*

No.	Description	Unused	Used
1N57	A57 $200 on 10c grn	200.00	110.00
1N58	A57 $400 on 8c ol grn	200.00	110.00

China No. 422 Surcharged in Black

1945

No.	Description	Unused	Used
1N59	A40 $400 on 1c org	750.00	600.00

Forgeries exist.

OCCUPATION POSTAGE DUE STAMPS

China, No. J79 Surcharged Diagonally with New Value Between Parallel Lines in Black

1945 Unwmk. *Perf. 12½*

No.	Description	Unused	Used
1NJ1	D5 $100 on $2 yel org	825.00	*900.00*
a.	Inverted surcharge	1,100.	1,100.

MENG CHIANG (Inner Mongolia)

Nos. 297-298, 301-303 Overprinted

Characters 4mm High — I

Characters 5mm High — II

1941 Engr. Unwmk.

No.	Description	Unused	Used
2N1	A37 2c #297, I	3.00	*2.00*
a.	Type II	2.00	*2.00*
2N2	A37 4c #298, II	55.00	—
a.	Type I	60.00	55.00
2N3	A37 15c #301, I	6.00	*5.50*
a.	Type II	45.00	6.00
2N4	A37 20c #302, II	11.00	8.75
a.	Type I	12.00	*16.00*
2N5	A37 25c #303, II	12.00	*14.00*
a.	Type I	92.50	92.50
	Nos. 2N1-2N5 (5)	87.00	*30.25*

For surcharge see No. 2N116.

On Nos. 312, 314, 318, 321

1941 *Perf. 14*

No.	Description	Unused	Used
2N6	A39 ½c #312, I	14.00	*17.50*
a.	Type II	47.50	—
2N7	A39 2½c #314, II	5.00	*6.00*
a.	Type I	8.75	*8.75*
2N8	A45 13c #318, II	7.50	7.50
a.	Type I	120.00	110.00
2N9	A48 30c #321, II	87.50	92.50
	Nos. 2N6-2N9 (4)	114.00	123.50

On Stamps of 1939-41

1941 *Perf. 12½*

No.	Description	Unused	Used
2N10	A57 2c #368, II	2.40	*3.00*
2N11	A57 3c #350, II	1.00	1.00
a.	Type I	2.00	2.00
2N12	A57 5c #352, II	2.10	*2.50*
a.	Type I	2.75	*6.00*
2N13	A57 8c #353, I	2.50	2.00
a.	Type II	2.00	2.00
2N14	A57 8c #369, II	20.00	11.00
2N15	A57 10c #354, II	3.00	3.00
2N16	A57 16c #357, II	6.00	6.00
2N17	A57 $1 #359, II	30.00	30.00
a.	Type I	440.00	440.00
b.	#347, I	87.50	80.00
2N18	A57 $5 #361, II	100.00	100.00
	Nos. 2N10-2N18 (9)	167.00	158.50

For surcharges see Nos. 2N117, 2N119.

On Stamps of 1940 with Secret Marks

1941 Unwmk. *Perf. 14*

No.	Description	Unused	Used
2N19	A57 5c #382, II	2.50	*2.00*
2N20	A57 8c #383, I	4.00	3.25
a.	Type II	55.00	—
2N21	A57 10c #384, II	2.25	2.00
a.	Type I	4.00	4.00
2N22	A57 30c #385, II	3.00	4.00
a.	Type I	5.00	5.00
2N23	A57 50c #386, I	9.00	9.00
a.	Type II	7.25	7.25
2N24	A57 $1 #387, I	22.50	*17.50*
a.	Type II	30.00	29.00
2N25	A57 $2 #388, I	30.00	22.50
a.	Type II	35.00	32.50
2N26	A57 $5 #389, I	42.50	45.00
a.	Type II	87.50	
2N27	A57 $10 #390, II	87.50	87.50
a.	Type I	87.50	87.50
2N28	A57 $20 #391, II	120.00	*120.00*
a.	Type I	120.00	*110.00*
	Nos. 2N19-2N28 (10)	323.25	*312.75*

For surcharge see No. 2N120.

On Stamps of 1940 with Secret Marks

1941 Wmk. 261 *Perf. 14*

No.	Description	Unused	Used
2N29	A57 10c #394, II	4.50	4.50
2N30	A57 30c #395, II	6.00	*6.00*
a.	Type I	120.00	110.00
2N31	A57 50c #396, II	8.00	*9.00*
	Nos. 2N29-2N31 (3)	18.50	*19.50*

On Stamps of 1940-41 (Martyrs) with Secret Marks

Perf. 12½, 13 & Compound

1941 Wmk. 261

No.	Description	Unused	Used
2N32	A39 ½c #402, II	12.00	*14.00*
2N33	A40 1c #403, II	3.00	2.00
a.	Type I	5.00	3.50
2N34	A39 2½c #405, I	80.00	72.50
a.	Type II	80.00	80.00
2N35	A48 3c #406, II	6.00	4.00
2N36	A46 10c #410, I	12.50	12.50
a.	Type II	21.00	—
2N37	A46 17c #413, II	62.50	—
a.	Type I	80.00	80.00
2N38	A40 25c #416, II	8.00	10.00
2N39	A48 30c #418, II	72.50	77.50
a.	Type I	77.50	87.50
2N40	A47 40c #419, II	8.50	7.00
a.	Type I	14.50	13.00
2N41	A40 50c #420, I	13.00	14.00
a.	Type II	60.00	—

Unwmk.

No.	Description	Unused	Used
2N42	A39 ½c #421, II	2.00	*3.00*
a.	Type I	5.00	5.00
2N43	A40 1c #422, I	2.00	2.00
a.	Type II	4.25	3.50
2N44	A46 2c #423, I	8.50	9.00
2N45	A48 3c #425, II	4.00	3.50
a.	Type I	5.00	4.00
2N46	A39 4c #426, II	2.00	2.00
2N47	A45 8c #428, II	19.00	—
a.	Type I	100.00	—
2N48	A46 10c #429, I	24.00	24.00
a.	Type II	72.50	
2N49	A45 13c #430, I	8.00	*7.25*
a.	Type II	24.00	—
2N50	A48 15c #431, II	5.00	5.00
2N51	A46 17c #432, II	5.00	*5.00*
a.	Type I	7.25	6.00

2N52 A47 20c #433, II 5.00 5.00
a. Type I 6.00 7.00
2N53 A45 21c #434, II 5.00 5.00
2N54 A40 25c #435, I 6.00 8.00
2N55 A46 28c #436, II 5.00 7.00
2N56 A40 50c #439, I 21.50 18.00
a. Type II 18.00 9.00
Nos. 2N42-2N56 (15) 122.00 103.75

For surcharges see Nos. 2N114-2N115, 2N118, 2N121-2N122.

China Nos. 297-298, 302 Surcharged in Black

1942 Unwmk. *Perf. 12½, 13*
2N57 A37 1c on 2c ol grn 55.00 55.00
2N58 A37 2c on 4c grn 14.00 14.00
2N59 A37 10c on 20c ultra 85.00 42.50
Nos. 2N57-2N59 (3) 154.00 111.50

Same, on China No. 313

Perf. 14
2N60 A40 ½c on 1c org 62.50 62.50

Same, on Stamps of China, 1938-41

Perf. 12½
2N61 A57 1c on 2c (#368) 2.00 1.25
2N62 A57 4c on 8c (#353) 14.00 13.00
a. Inverted surcharge 47.50 —
2N63 A57 4c on 8c (#369) 6.00 7.00
2N64 A57 5c on 10c (#354) 3.00 3.00
2N65 A57 8c on 16c (#357) 11.00 7.00
2N66 A57 50c on $1 (#359) 15.00 17.50
a. On No. 347 220.00 220.00
b. On No. 344 660.00 —
2N67 A57 $1 on $2 (#360) 87.50 72.50
Nos. 2N61-2N67 (7) 138.50 121.25

No. 2N66b was issued without gum.

Same, on Stamps of China, 1940

Perf. 14
2N68 A57 4c on 8c (#383) 3.00 1.50
2N69 A57 15c on 30c (#385) 10.00 10.00
a. Inverted surcharge 55.00 55.00
2N70 A57 25c on 50c (#386) 10.00 10.00
2N71 A57 50c on $1 (#387) 30.00 18.00
2N72 A57 $1 on $2 (#388) 30.00 18.00
2N73 A57 $5 on $10 (#390) 75.00 62.50
2N74 A57 $10 on $20 (#391) 140.00 110.00
Nos. 2N68-2N74 (7) 298.00 230.00

Same, on China No. 395

1942 Wmk. 261 *Perf. 14*
2N75 A57 15c on 30c scar 140.00 100.00

Same, on China Nos. 418 and 419

Perf. 12½, 13
2N76 A48 15c on 30c brn car 47.50 47.50
2N77 A47 20c on 40c org 20.00 13.50
Nos. 2N75-2N77 (3) 207.50 161.00

Same, on Stamps of China, 1940-41

1942 Unwmk.
2N78 A40 ½c on 1c org 3.00 3.00
2N79 A39 2c on 4c pale vio 6.00 6.00
2N80 A47 10c on 20c lt bl 6.00 6.00
2N81 A47 20c on 40c org 17.50 14.50
2N82 A40 25c on 50c grn 24.00 24.00
Nos. 2N78-2N82 (5) 56.50 53.50

Same Surcharge on "New Peking" Prints

Perf. 14
2N83 A37 1c on 2c ol grn 14.50 25.00
2N84 A37 2c on 4c dl grn 1.40 1.00
2N85 A46 5c on 10c dl vio 5.00 9.00
2N86 A57 8c on 16c ol gray 2.00 2.75
2N87 A47 10c on 20c red brn 5.00 7.25
2N88 A48 15c on 30c brn car 4.00 4.00
2N89 A47 20c on 40c org 9.00 10.00
2N90 A40 25c on 50c grn 6.00 6.00
2N91 A57 50c on $1 org brn & sep 8.50 14.50
2N92 A57 $1 on $2 dp bl & org brn 40.00 45.00
2N93 A57 $5 on $10 dk grn & dl pur 60.00 80.00
Nos. 2N83-2N93 (11) 155.40 204.50

The "New Peking" printings were made by the Chinese Bureau of Engraving and Printing for use in Japanese controlled areas of North China. They are on thin, poor quality paper, with dull gum or without gum and there are slight alterations in the designs.

Dragon-Carved Pillar and Doves — A1

Wmk. Characters in Circle in Sheet

1943 Engr. *Perf. 12xPin-perf. 12*
2N94 A1 4f deep orange 4.00 10.00
2N95 A1 8f dark blue 5.00 10.00

5th anniv. of the Inner Mongolia post and telegraph service.

The watermark, which is 40mm in diameter and covers four stamps, occurs three times in the sheet.

Mining Coal — A2

1943 Unwmk. Photo. *Perf. 12*
2N96 A2 4f Prus green 4.00 10.00
2N97 A2 8f brown red 4.00 10.00

2nd anniv. of the "Greater East Asia War."

Flying Horse — A3

Yun Wang — A4

1944 *Perf. 12½x12, 12x12½*
2N98 A3 4f rose 3.00 10.00
2N99 A4 8f dull blue 3.00 10.00

5th anniv. of the founding of the Federal Autonomous Government of Mongolia, Sept. 1, 1939.

Industrial Plant — A5

1944, Dec. 8 Photo. *Perf. 12x12½*
2N100 A5 8f red brown 4.00 12.00

3rd anniv. of the "Greater East Asia War" and to encourage production increase.

New Peking Printings of 1942 Overprinted in Black

1945 Unwmk. Engr. *Perf. 14*

Without Gum
2N101 A37 2c olive grn 12.00 —
2N102 A37 4c dull grn 20.00 —
2N103 A37 5c green 21.00 27.50
2N104 A57 $1 org brn & sep 6.00 8.00
2N105 A57 $2 dp bl & org brn 15.00 19.00
2N106 A57 $5 red & grnsh blk 50.00 50.00

Same Overprint on New Peking Printings of Martyrs Issue
2N107 A40 1c orange 2.00 2.50
2N108 A45 8c dp orange 3.00 4.00
2N109 A46 10c dl violet 3.00 4.00
2N110 A47 20c red brown 3.00 4.00
2N111 A48 30c brown car 3.00 4.00
2N112 A47 40c orange 2.00 3.00
2N113 A40 50c green 8.00 10.00

For surcharges see Nos. 2N123-2N127.

Stamps of Meng Chiang, 1941, Surcharged in Red or Black

50c

10c

$1

1945
2N114 A39 10c on ½c ol blk (#2N42, II, R) 4.00 5.00
a. On #2N42a, I 7.25 8.00
2N115 A40 10c on 1c org (#2N43a, II, R) 2.00 3.00
a. Without secret mark (China #422a) 40.00 40.00
b. On #2N43, I 3.00 3.50
2N116 A37 50c on 2c ol grn (#2N1a, II, B) 18.00 35.00
b. On #2N1, I 18.00 35.00
2N117 A57 50c on 2c ol grn (#2N10, II, B)) 1.40 2.50
2N118 A39 50c on 4c pale vio (#2N46, II, R) 2.00 3.00
2N119 A57 50c on 5c ol grn (#2N12, II, R) 1.00 1.90
a. On #2N12a, I 12.50 12.50
2N120 A57 50c on 5c ol grn (#2N19, II, R) 1.50 2.75
Nos. 2N114-2N120 (7) 29.90 53.15

Same Surcharge on #2N32, 2N33

1945 Wmk. 261
2N121 A39 10c on ½c ol blk, II (R) 29.00 35.00
2N122 A40 10c on 1c orange, II (R) 6.00 7.00
a. On #2N33a, I 35.00 —

Same Surcharge on Nos. 2N107, 2N101-2N103 and 2N108

1945 Unwmk.
2N123 A40 10c on 1c org (R) 2.00 3.00
2N124 A37 50c on 2c ol grn (Bk) 5.00 6.00
2N125 A37 50c on 4c dl grn (R) 10.00 12.00
2N126 A37 50c on 5c green 1.00 3.00
2N127 A45 $1 on 8c dp org (R) 4.00 6.00
Nos. 2N123-2N127 (5) 22.00 30.00

NORTH CHINA

Honan

Nos. 297-298, 301-303 Overprinted

I

II

1941 Engr. Unwmk.
3N1 A37 2c #297, II 18.00 18.00
a. Type I 30.00 30.00
3N2 A37 4c #298, I 12.00 7.25
a. Type II 32.50 32.50
3N3 A37 15c #301, I 3.00 3.00
a. Type II 40.00 3.00
3N4 A37 20c #302, I 11.00 8.00
3N5 A37 25c #303, II 24.00 24.00
Nos. 3N1-3N5 (5) 68.00 60.25

1941 *Perf. 14*
3N6 A39 ½c #312, I 3.00 4.00
a. Type II 40.00 —
3N7 A39 2½c #314, I 4.00 5.00
a. Type II 4.00 3.00
3N8 A45 13c #318, II 4.00 5.00
a. Type I 100.00 100.00
3N9 A48 30c #321, II 18.00 22.00
3N10 A47 40c #322, II 100.00 115.00
Nos. 3N6-3N10 (5) 129.00 151.00

On Stamps of 1939-41

1941 *Perf. 12½*
3N11 A57 2c #368, II 4.00 2.50
3N12 A57 3c #350, I 2.00 2.50
a. Type II 3.00 2.50
3N13 A57 5c #352, II 4.00 2.50
a. Type I 2.40 2.40
3N14 A57 8c #353, II 4.00 2.50
a. Type I 3.00 2.00
3N15 A57 10c #354, II 8.00 7.00
3N16 A57 16c #357, II 3.00 5.00
3N17 A57 $1 #359, II 20.00 25.00
a. Type I 325.00 325.00
b. On #347, I 80.00 75.00
3N18 A57 $5 #361, II 80.00 80.00
Nos. 3N11-3N18 (8) 125.00 127.00

For overprints see Nos. 3N56, 3N58, 3N61.

On Stamps of 1940 with Secret Marks

1941 Unwmk. *Perf. 14*
3N20 A57 5c #382, II 5.00 4.00
3N21 A57 8c #383, II 4.00 1.00
3N22 A57 10c #384, II 6.00 5.00
3N23 A57 30c #385, I 9.00 12.00
a. Type II 15.00 11.00
3N24 A57 50c #386, I 8.00 8.00
a. Type II 18.00 17.00
3N25 A57 $1 #387, I 12.00 15.00
a. Type II 80.00 80.00
3N26 A57 $2 #388, I 18.00 18.00
a. Type II 24.00 24.00
3N27 A57 $5 #389, I 40.00 35.00
a. Type II 62.50 57.50
3N28 A57 $10 #390, II 65.00 62.50
a. Type I 195.00 195.00
3N29 A57 $20 #391, II 125.00 140.00
a. Type I 125.00 140.00
Nos. 3N20-3N29 (10) 292.00 300.50

On Stamps of 1940 with Secret Marks

1941 Wmk. 261 *Perf. 14*
3N30 A57 5c #392, II 24.00 20.00
3N31 A57 5c #393, II 15.00 15.00
3N32 A57 30c #395, I 32.50 31.00
a. Type II 40.00 40.00
3N33 A57 50c #396, II 75.00 75.00
Nos. 3N30-3N33 (4) 146.50 141.00

On Stamps of 1940-41 (Martyrs) with Secret Marks

Perf. 12½, 13 & Compound

1941 Wmk. 261
3N34 A39 ½c #402, II 3.00 3.50
3N35 A40 1c #403, II 3.00 2.00
a. Type I 5.00 3.00
3N36 A39 2½c #405, II 18.00 17.00
3N37 A46 10c #410, II 20.00 18.50
a. Type I 35.00 35.00
3N38 A45 13c #411, II 5.00 5.00
3N39 A46 17c #413, II 6.00 5.00
a. Type I 13.00 9.00
3N40 A40 25c #416, II 7.50 8.00
3N41 A47 40c #419, II 9.00 6.00
a. Type I 20.00 20.00
Nos. 3N34-3N41 (8) 71.50 65.00

Unwmk.
3N42 A39 ½c #421, II 4.00 6.00
a. Type I 6.00 8.00
3N43 A40 1c #422, I 3.00 5.00
a. Type II 6.00 8.00
3N44 A46 2c #423, I 15.00 16.00
3N45 A48 3c #425, I 4.00 6.00
3N46 A39 4c #426, II 6.00 7.00
3N47 A46 10c #429, I 50.00 60.00
3N48 A45 13c #430, II 5.50 7.00
a. Type I 30.00 30.00
3N49 A48 15c #431, II 6.00 7.00
3N50 A46 17c #432, II 6.00 7.00
a. Type I 20.00 20.00
3N51 A47 20c #433, II 6.00 8.00
a. Type I 62.50 62.50
3N52 A45 21c #434, II 7.50 9.00
3N53 A40 25c #435, I 8.00 10.00
3N54 A46 28c #436, II 5.00 8.00
Nos. 3N42-3N54 (13) 126.00 156.00

For overprints see Nos. 3N55, 3N59.

Overprinted in Red

1942
3N55 A39 4c #3N46 6.00 10.00
3N56 A57 8c #3N14 50.00 60.00
3N57 A57 8c #369, II 25.00 30.00
Nos. 3N55-3N57 (3) 81.00 100.00

The fall of Singapore.

Overprinted in Red

1942
3N58 A57 2c #3N11 15.00 15.00
3N59 A39 4c #3N46 20.00 25.00
3N60 A57 8c #369, II 72.50 72.50
3N61 A57 8c #3N14 65.00 72.50
Nos. 3N58-3N61 (4) 172.50 185.00

Formation of Manchukuo, 10th anniv.

Hopei

On Stamps of 1940-41 (Martyrs) with Secret Marks

I

II

1941 Engr. Unwmk.
4N1 A37 2c #297, II 4.00 6.00
a. Type I 11.00 15.00
4N2 A37 4c #298, I 4.50 8.00
a. Type II 85.00 —
4N3 A37 15c #301, II 5.00 5.00
a. Type I 4.25 8.00
4N4 A37 20c #302, II 37.50 35.00
4N5 A37 25c #303, II 35.00 12.00
a. Type I 95.00 110.00
Nos. 4N1-4N5 (5) 86.00 66.00

On Nos. 312, 314, 318, 321

1941 Perf. 14
4N6 A39 ½c #312, II 3.00 6.00
a. Type I 10.00 12.00
4N7 A39 2½c #314, II 4.00 6.00
a. Type I 4.00 6.00
4N8 A45 13c #318, II 5.00 8.00
a. Type I 5.00 8.00
4N9 A48 30c #321, II 7.00 10.00
Nos. 4N6-4N9 (4) 19.00 30.00

On Stamps of 1939-41

1941 Perf. 12½
4N10 A57 2c #368, II 5.00 3.00
4N11 A57 2c #349, II 4.00 2.00
4N12 A57 3c #350, II 6.00 2.00
a. Type I 3.00 2.00
4N13 A57 5c #352, II 3.00 2.00
a. Type I 4.00 2.00
4N14 A57 8c #353, II 2.00 1.00
a. Type I 2.00 1.60
4N15 A57 8c #369, II 6.00 6.00
4N16 A57 10c #354, II 3.00 1.00
4N17 A57 16c #357, II 4.00 4.00
4N18 A57 $1 #359, II 175.00 165.00
a. On #347, I 250.00 —
4N19 A57 $2 #360, II 62.50 55.00
a. Type I 65.00 65.00
4N20 A57 $5 #361, I 65.00 65.00
a. Type II 65.00 75.00
4N21 A57 $10 #362, II 200.00 200.00
4N22 A57 $20 #363, II 450.00 450.00
Nos. 4N10-4N22 (13) 985.50 956.00

For overprints see Nos. 4N66-4N68, 4N70.

On Stamps of 1940 with Secret Marks

1941 Unwmk. Perf. 14

Type II
4N24 A57 5c #382 4.00 1.00
4N25 A57 8c #383 4.00 1.00
4N26 A57 10c #384 8.00 3.00
4N27 A57 30c #385 8.00 3.00
4N28 A57 50c #386 8.00 3.00
4N29 A57 $1 #387 12.00 6.00
4N30 A57 $2 #388 45.00 20.00
4N31 A57 $5 #389 55.00 50.00
4N32 A57 $10 #390 65.00 55.00
4N33 A57 $20 #391 75.00 72.50
Nos. 4N24-4N33 (10) 284.00 214.50

For overprints see Nos. 4N65, 4N71.

Type I
4N24a A57 5c 3.00 1.50
4N25a A57 8c 80.00 70.00
4N26a A57 10c 4.00 2.40
4N28a A57 50c 8.00 3.00
4N29a A57 $1 11.00 6.00
4N30a A57 $2 45.00 32.50
4N31a A57 $5 55.00 55.00
4N32a A57 $10 45.00 65.00
4N33a A57 $20 110.00 110.00
Nos. 4N24a-4N33a (9) 361.00 345.40

On Stamps of 1940 with Secret Marks

1941 Wmk. 261 Perf. 14
4N34 A57 5c #392, II 5.00 3.00
4N35 A57 5c #393, II 5.00 3.00
4N36 A57 10c #394, II 4.00 2.00
4N37 A57 30c #395, II 10.00 10.00
a. Type I 15.00 16.00
4N38 A57 50c #396, II 5.00 5.00
Nos. 4N34-4N38 (5) 29.00 23.00

On Stamps of 1940-41 (Martyrs) with Secret Marks

Perf. 12½, 13 & Compound

1941 Wmk. 261
4N39 A39 ½c #402, II 3.00 3.00
4N40 A40 1c #403, I 2.50 3.00
a. Type II 3.00 3.00
4N41 A46 2c #404, II 4.00 4.00
4N42 A39 2½c #405, II 5.00 5.00
4N43 A48 3c #406, II 4.00 4.00
4N44 A46 10c #410, II 5.00 5.00
a. Type I 6.00 6.00
4N45 A45 13c #411, II 4.00 4.00
4N46 A46 17c #413, II 5.00 3.50
a. Type I 4.25 4.25
4N47 A40 25c #416, II 7.50 5.00
4N48 A48 30c #418, II 30.00 30.00
a. Type I 50.00 50.00
4N49 A47 40c #419, II 6.00 6.00
a. Type I 6.00 6.00
Nos. 4N39-4N49 (11) 76.00 72.50

Unwmk.
4N50 A39 ½c #421, II 3.00 2.00
a. Type I 4.00 2.25
4N51 A40 1c #422, II 4.00 2.00
a. Type I 5.00 2.00
4N52 A46 2c #423 4.00 2.00
4N53 A48 3c #425, I 4.00 4.00
a. Type II 5.50 4.25
4N54 A39 4c #426, II 4.50 2.50
4N55 A45 8c #428, II 4.00 2.50
a. Type I 5.00 5.00
4N56 A46 10c #429, II 5.00 3.00
4N57 A45 13c #430, I 5.00 4.00
a. Type II 4.50 4.50
4N58 A48 15c #431, II 9.00 8.00
4N59 A46 17c #432, II 8.00 10.00
a. Type I 8.00 6.00
4N60 A47 20c #433, II 6.00 6.00
a. Type I 6.00 6.00
4N61 A45 21c #434, II 6.00 8.00
4N62 A40 25c #435, I 6.00 8.00
a. Type II 5.00 5.00
4N63 A46 28c #436, II 5.00 8.00
Nos. 4N50-4N63 (14) 73.50 70.00

For overprints see Nos. 4N64, 4N69.

Honan Singapore Overprint in Red

1942
4N64 A39 4c #4N54 5.00 6.00
4N65 A57 8c #4N25 8.00 10.00
4N66 A57 8c #4N14 12.00 14.00
4N67 A57 8c #4N15 12.00 15.00
Nos. 4N64-4N67 (4) 37.00 45.00

Honan Anniv. of Manchukuo Overprint in Red

1942
4N68 A57 2c #4N10 16.00 20.00
4N69 A39 4c #4N54 7.00 10.00
4N70 A57 8c #4N14 90.00 105.00
4N71 A57 8c #4N25 15.00 20.00
Nos. 4N68-4N71 (4) 128.00 155.00

Shansi

Nos. 297-298, 301, 303 Overprinted

I

II

1941 Engr. Unwmk.
5N1 A37 2c #297, II 65.00 75.00
a. Type I 87.50 80.00
5N2 A37 4c #298, I 50.00 62.50
a. Type II 125.00 165.00
5N3 A37 15c #301, II 8.00 10.00
a. Type I 9.00 11.00
5N4 A37 25c #303, II 9.00 13.50
a. Type I 62.50 67.50
Nos. 5N1-5N4 (4) 132.00 161.00

On Nos. 312, 314, 318, 321

1941 Perf. 14
5N5 A39 ½c #312, II 55.00 55.00
a. Type I 4.00 4.00
5N6 A39 2½c #314, II 3.00 3.00
a. Type I 4.00 4.00
5N7 A45 13c #318, II 6.00 4.00
a. Type I 240.00 240.00
5N8 A48 30c #321, II 15.00 12.00
Nos. 5N5-5N8 (4) 79.00 74.00

On Stamps of 1939-41

1941 Perf. 12½
5N9 A57 2c #368, II 2.40 2.00
5N10 A57 3c #350, II 2.00 2.00
a. Type I 15.00 15.00
5N11 A57 5c #352, II 7.00 3.50
a. Type I 7.50 5.00
5N12 A57 8c #353, II 1.50 1.50
a. Type I 4.00 3.50
5N13 A57 8c #369, II 42.50 25.00
5N14 A57 10c #354, II 17.00 8.00
5N15 A57 16c #357, II 7.50 5.00
5N16 A57 $1 #359, II 20.00 17.00
5N17 A57 $2 #360, II 50.00 50.00
5N18 A57 $5 #361, II 40.00 57.50
Nos. 5N9-5N18 (10) 189.90 171.50

For overprints see Nos. 5N62-5N64, 5N66-5N67.

On Stamps of 1940 with Secret Marks

1941 Unwmk. Perf. 14
5N19 A57 5c #382, II 3.00 2.00
5N20 A57 8c #383, II 3.00 2.00
5N21 A57 10c #384, I 6.00 2.00
a. Type II 32.50 5.00
5N22 A57 30c #385, II 9.00 4.00
a. Type I 7.50 3.00
5N23 A57 50c #386, I 7.50 5.00
a. Type II 5.75 5.75
5N24 A57 $1 #387, I 18.00 14.00
a. Type II 45.00 37.50
5N25 A57 $2 #388, II 40.00 25.00
a. Type I 25.00 25.00
5N26 A57 $5 #389, II 32.50 32.50
a. Type I 97.50 97.50
5N27 A57 $10 #390, II 70.00 70.00
a. Type I 75.00 75.00
5N28 A57 $20 #391, II 70.00 70.00
a. Type I 125.00 135.00
Nos. 5N19-5N28 (10) 259.00 226.50

For overprints see Nos. 5N61, 5N68.

On Stamps of 1940 with Secret Marks

1941 Wmk. 261 Perf. 14
5N29 A57 5c #392, II 6.00 3.00
5N30 A57 5c #393, II 3.00 2.00
5N31 A57 10c #394, II 6.00 3.00
5N32 A57 30c #395, I 37.50 80.00
5N33 A57 50c #396, I 15.00 11.00
Nos. 5N29-5N33 (5) 67.50 99.00

On Stamps of 1940-41 (Martyrs) with Secret Marks

Perf. 12½, 13 & Compound

1941 Wmk. 261
5N34 A39 ½c #402, II 3.00 3.00
5N35 A40 1c #403, II 3.00 2.00
a. Type I 3.00 2.00
5N36 A46 2c #404, II 7.50 5.00
5N37 A39 2½c #405, II 9.00 10.50
5N38 A46 10c #410, I 9.75 9.75
5N39 A45 13c #411, II 6.00 5.00
5N40 A46 17c #413, I 47.50 32.50
5N41 A40 25c #416, II 5.00 5.00
5N42 A48 30c #418, I 150.00 150.00
a. Type II 150.00 150.00
5N43 A47 40c #419, II 6.00 6.00
a. Type I 37.50 37.50
5N44 A40 50c #420, II 7.50 7.50
a. Type I 42.50 42.50
Nos. 5N34-5N44 (11) 254.25 236.25

Unwmk.
5N45 A39 ½c #421, II 3.00 3.75
a. Type I 5.25 5.75
5N46 A40 1c #422, I 4.50 3.00
a. Type II 3.00 3.00
5N47 A46 2c #423, II 4.00 4.00
5N48 A48 3c #425, I 11.00 9.00
5N49 A39 4c #426, II 5.00 5.00
5N50 A45 8c #428, I 17.00 15.00
a. Type II 35.00 21.00
5N51 A46 10c #429, I 50.00 50.00
a. Type II 57.50 57.50
5N52 A45 13c #430, I 30.00 20.00
a. Type II 22.50 22.50
5N53 A48 15c #431, II 6.75 6.75
5N54 A46 17c #432, II 6.00 6.00
a. Type I 6.00 5.50
5N55 A47 20c #433, II 7.50 6.00
a. Type I 7.50 4.00
5N56 A45 21c #434, II 6.00 6.00
5N57 A40 25c #435, I 9.00 5.00
5N58 A46 28c #436, II 7.50 6.00
5N59 A40 50c #439, II 17.00 15.00
Nos. 5N45-5N59 (15) 184.25 160.50

For overprints see Nos. 5N60, 5N65.

Honan Singapore Overprint in Red

1942
5N60 A39 4c #5N49 6.00 7.00
5N61 A57 8c #5N20 18.00 22.50
5N62 A57 8c #5N12 18.00 18.00
5N63 A57 8c #5N13 50.00 55.00
Nos. 5N60-5N63 (4) 92.00 102.50

Honan Anniv. of Manchukuo Overprint in Red

1942
5N64 A57 2c #5N9 18.00 17.00
5N65 A39 4c #5N49 13.50 17.00
5N66 A57 8c #5N12 50.00 62.50
5N67 A57 8c #5N13 72.50 85.00
5N68 A57 8c #5N20 55.00 55.00
Nos. 5N64-5N68 (5) 209.00 236.50

Shantung

Nos. 297-298, 301-303 Overprinted

I

II

1941 Engr. Unwmk.
6N1 A37 2c #297, II 2.50 2.00
a. Type I 5.00 5.00
6N2 A37 4c #298, II 8.00 7.25
a. Type I 9.25 8.00
6N3 A37 15c #301, II 3.00 2.50
a. Type I 4.00 3.50
6N4 A37 20c #302, II 6.00 5.00
6N5 A37 25c #303, II 12.00 7.25
a. Type I 265.00 225.00
Nos. 6N1-6N5 (5) 31.50 24.00

On Nos. 312, 314, 318

1941 Perf. 14
6N6 A39 ½c #312, II 3.00 2.00
a. Type I 3.00 2.00
6N7 A39 2½c #314, II 3.00 2.10
a. Type I 4.50 2.00
6N8 A45 13c #318, II 6.00 3.00
a. Type I 40.00 25.00
Nos. 6N6-6N8 (3) 12.00 7.10

On Stamps of 1939-41

1941 Perf. 12½
6N9 A57 2c #349, II 3.00 2.00
6N10 A57 2c #368, II 2.00 2.00
6N11 A57 3c #350, II 2.00 2.00
a. Type I 3.00 1.50
6N12 A57 5c #352, II 3.50 2.00
a. Type I 3.00 1.50
6N13 A57 8c #353, II 3.00 2.00
a. Type I 2.00 1.00
6N14 A57 8c #369, II 2.00 2.00
6N15 A57 10c #354, II 3.50 2.00
6N16 A57 16c #357, II 5.50 7.50
6N17 A57 $1 #359, II 27.00 13.00
a. Type I 425.00 425.00
b. On No. 347, I 62.50 57.50
6N18 A57 $5 #361, II 60.00 55.00
Nos. 6N9-6N18 (10) 111.50 89.50

For overprints see Nos. 6N62, 6N64-6N65, 6N67-6N68.

On Stamps of 1940 with Secret Marks

1941 Unwmk. Perf. 14
6N20 A57 5c #382, II 2.00 1.25
6N21 A57 8c #383, II 3.00 1.00
a. Type I 3.00 1.50
6N22 A57 10c #384, II 3.00 2.00
6N23 A57 30c #385, II 4.00 2.00
a. Type I 7.00 7.50
6N24 A57 50c #386, I 8.00 6.75
a. Type II 9.00 8.00
6N25 A57 $1 #387, II 9.00 5.00
a. Type I 24.00 22.50
6N26 A57 $2 #388, II 18.00 15.00
a. Type I 24.50 27.50
6N27 A57 $5 #389, II 30.00 30.00
a. Type I 42.50 40.00
6N28 A57 $10 #390, II 67.50 67.50
a. Type I 72.50 72.50
6N29 A57 $20 #391, II 97.50 97.50
a. Type I 100.00 125.00
Nos. 6N20-6N29 (10) 242.00 228.00

For overprints see Nos. 6N63, 6N69.

On Stamps of 1940 with Secret Marks

1941 Wmk. 261 Perf. 14
6N30 A57 5c #392, II 3.00 2.00
6N31 A57 5c #393, II 3.00 2.00
6N32 A57 10c #394, II 10.00 8.00
6N33 A57 30c #395, II 7.50 7.00
a. Type I 25.00 25.00
6N34 A57 50c #396, II 10.00 4.25
a. Type I 12.00 11.50
Nos. 6N30-6N34 (5) 33.50 23.25

On Stamps of 1940-41 (Martyrs) with Secret Marks

Perf. 12½, 13 & Compound

1941 **Wmk. 261**

6N35 A39 ½c #402, II 4.50 3.00
6N36 A40 1c #403, II 4.50 2.00
a. Type I 3.00 2.00
6N37 A39 2½c #405, II 25.00 *17.00*
6N38 A46 10c #410, I 11.00 4.00
6N39 A45 13c #411, II 10.00 5.00
6N40 A46 17c #413, II 5.00 5.00
a. Type I 11.00 *11.00*
6N41 A40 25c #416, II 7.50 5.00
6N42 A48 30c #418, I 60.00 37.50
6N43 A47 40c #419, II 6.00 6.00
a. Type I 37.50 37.50
6N44 A40 50c #420, II 12.00 9.00
Nos. 6N35-6N44 (10) 145.50 93.50

Unwmk.

6N45 A39 ½c #421, II 4.00 2.00
a. Type I 7.50 4.25
6N46 A40 1c #422, II 3.00 2.00
a. Type I 3.25 3.25
b. On No. 422a, II 97.50 97.50
6N48 A46 2c #423, II 5.00 2.50
6N49 A48 3c #425, I 6.00 *5.00*
a. Type II 5.00 *6.75*
6N50 A39 4c #426, II 5.00 3.00
6N51 A45 8c #428, II 4.00 3.50
a. Type I 40.00 40.00
6N52 A46 10c #429, I 15.00 15.00
6N53 A45 13c #430, I 6.00 4.50
a. Type II 4.50 4.50
6N54 A48 15c #431, II 5.00 5.00
6N55 A46 17c #432, II 5.00 4.00
a. Type I 5.00 5.00
6N56 A47 20c #433, II 6.00 4.50
a. Type I 6.75 6.75
6N57 A45 21c #434, II 9.00 5.00
6N58 A40 25c #435, I 7.00 5.75
6N59 A46 28c #436, II 5.00 4.00
6N60 A40 50c #439, II 55.00 55.00
Nos. 6N45-6N60 (15) 140.00 120.75

For overprints see Nos. 6N61, 6N66.

Honan Singapore Overprint in Red

1942

6N61 A39 4c #6N50 5.00 *5.00*
6N62 A57 8c #6N13 24.50 *30.00*
6N63 A57 8c #6N21 30.00 24.50
6N64 A57 8c #6N14 40.00 *40.00*
Nos. 6N61-6N64 (4) 99.50 *99.50*

Honan Anniv. of Manchukuo Overprint in Red

1942

6N65 A57 2c #6N10 9.00 *9.00*
6N66 A39 4c #6N50 11.00 *11.00*
6N67 A57 8c #6N13 40.00 *30.00*
6N68 A57 8c #6N14 65.00 *72.50*
6N69 A57 8c #6N21 32.50 *37.50*
Nos. 6N65-6N69 (5) 157.50 *160.00*

Supeh

Nos. 297-298, 301-302 Overprinted

I

II

1941 **Engr.** **Unwmk.**

7N1 A37 2c #297, I 24.00 13.00
a. Type II 27.50 15.00
7N2 A37 4c #298, I 100.00 57.50
a. Type II 110.00
7N3 A37 15c #301, II 8.00 6.00
a. Type I 6.00 6.00
7N4 A37 20c #302, II 15.00 6.00
Nos. 7N1-7N4 (4) 147.00 82.50

On Nos. 312, 314, 318

1941 ***Perf. 14***

7N5 A39 ½c #312, I 4.50 4.25
7N6 A39 2½c #314, II 6.00 4.00
a. Type I 5.50 4.00
7N7 A45 13c #318, II 6.00 5.00
a. Type I 160.00 160.00
Nos. 7N5-7N7 (3) 16.50 13.25

On Stamps of 1939-41

1941 ***Perf. 12½***

7N8 A57 2c #368, II 5.50 *5.00*
7N9 A57 3c #350, II 5.50 5.00
a. Type I 24.50 24.50
7N10 A57 5c #352, II 6.00 6.00
a. Type I 7.50 8.00
7N11 A57 8c #353, I 6.00 6.00
a. Type II 8.00 5.00
7N12 A57 8c #369, II 50.00 50.00
7N13 A57 10c #354, II 9.00 *8.00*
7N14 A57 16c #357, II 9.00 *9.00*
7N15 A57 $1 #359, II 18.00 *19.00*
a. On No. 347, I 210.00 210.00
Nos. 7N8-7N15 (8) 109.00 *108.00*

For overprints see Nos. 7N56-7N58, 7N60-7N61.

On Stamps of 1940 with Secret Marks

1941 **Unwmk.** ***Perf. 14***

7N17 A57 5c #382, II 7.50 4.00
7N18 A57 8c #383, II 6.00 2.00
7N19 A57 10c #384, I 7.50 4.25
a. Type II 4.25 4.25
7N20 A57 30c #385, I 8.00 *5.00*
a. Type II 12.00 *9.00*
7N21 A57 50c #386, II 8.00 *5.50*
a. Type I 12.00 7.00
7N22 A57 $1 #387, I 45.00 *30.00*
a. Type II 40.00 *50.00*
7N23 A57 $2 #388, II 29.00 29.00
a. Type I 32.50 *40.00*
7N24 A57 $5 #389, I 50.00 50.00
a. Type II 100.00 100.00
7N25 A57 $10 #390, I 80.00 80.00
a. Type II 90.00 90.00
7N26 A57 $20 #391, II 100.00 *100.00*
a. Type I 100.00 *110.00*
Nos. 7N17-7N26 (10) 341.00 309.75

On Stamps of 1940 with Secret Marks

1941 **Wmk. 261** ***Perf. 14***

7N27 A57 10c #394, II 9.00 8.00
7N28 A57 30c #395, I 25.00 *25.00*
7N29 A57 50c #396, I 18.00 *18.50*
Nos. 7N27-7N29 (3) 52.00 *51.50*

On Stamps of 1940-41 (Martyrs) with Secret Marks

Perf. 12½, 13 & Compound

1941 **Wmk. 261**

7N30 A39 ½c #402, II 5.75 *6.50*
7N31 A40 1c #403, I 7.00 7.00
a. Type II 6.00 6.00
7N32 A46 2c #404, II 6.00 *6.50*
7N33 A39 2½c #405, I 40.00 40.00
7N34 A46 10c #410, I 32.50 32.50
7N35 A45 13c #411, II 12.00 9.00
7N36 A46 17c #413, II 9.00 9.00
a. Type I 100.00 100.00
7N37 A40 25c #416, II 10.00 10.00
7N38 A48 30c #418, I 25.00 15.00
7N39 A47 40c #419, II 10.00 10.00
a. Type I 15.00 15.00
7N40 A40 50c #420, I 100.00 100.00
Nos. 7N30-7N40 (11) 257.25 245.50

Unwmk.

7N41 A39 ½c #421, II 6.00 *7.00*
a. Type I 9.00 8.50
7N42 A40 1c #422, II 4.50 *5.00*
7N43 A46 2c #423, I 14.50 *15.00*
7N44 A48 3c #425, I 9.00 *10.00*
7N45 A39 4c #426, II 11.00 *12.00*
7N46 A46 10c #429, I 50.00 *55.00*
7N47 A45 13c #430, I 9.00 *10.00*
7N48 A48 15c #431, II 7.50 *8.00*
7N49 A46 17c #432, II 8.00 *9.00*
a. Type I 12.00 12.00
7N50 A47 20c #433, II 12.00 12.00
a. Type I 12.00 11.00
7N51 A45 21c #434, II 12.00 12.00
7N52 A40 25c #435, I 12.00 12.00
a. Type II 18.00 18.00
7N53 A46 28c #436, II 6.75 *7.50*
Nos. 7N41-7N53 (13) 162.25 *174.50*

For overprints see Nos. 7N55, 7N59.

Honan Singapore Overprint in Red

1942

7N54 A37 4c #298, II 95.00 *110.00*
7N55 A39 4c #7N45 7.50 *13.00*
7N56 A57 8c #7N11a 40.00 *40.00*
7N57 A57 8c #7N12 24.00 *20.00*
Nos. 7N54-7N57 (4) 166.50 *183.00*

Honan Anniv. of Manchukuo Overprint in Red

1942

7N58 A57 2c #7N8 17.00 *24.50*
7N59 A39 4c #7N45 30.00 *17.00*
7N60 A57 8c #7N11a 115.00 *130.00*
7N61 A57 8c #7N12 100.00 *97.50*
Nos. 7N58-7N61 (4) 262.00 *269.00*

North China

For use in Honan, Hopei, Shansi, Shantung and Supeh (Northern Kiangsu)

Stamps of China, 1931-37 Surcharged North China (Hwa Pei) and Half of Original Value

1942 **Unwmk.** ***Perf. 14, 12½***

8N1 A40 ½c on 1c (#313) 2.00 *2.50*
8N2 A37 1c on 2c (#297) .75 1.10
8N3 A37 2c on 4c (#298) 1.50 1.25
8N4 A45 4c on 8c (#316) 150.00

Same Surcharge on Stamps of 1938-41

Perf. 12½

8N5 A57 1c on 2c (#349) 5.00 *8.50*
8N6 A57 1c on 2c (#368) .50 .30
8N7 A57 4c on 8c (#353) 2.10 1.25
8N8 A57 4c on 8c (#369) .60 .35
8N9 A57 5c on 10c grn .65 .50
8N10 A57 8c on 16c ol gray 2.00 .80
8N11 A57 50c on $1 (#359) 8.00 8.00
8N12 A57 50c on $1 (#344) 575.00 575.00
8N13 A57 50c on $1 (#347) 110.00 110.00
8N14 A57 $1 on $2 (#360) 12.50 12.50
8N15 A57 $1 on $2 (#345) 40.00 32.50
8N16 A57 $1 on $2 (#348) 155.00 155.00

No. 8N12 was issued without gum.
For overprint see No. 8N58.

Same Surcharge on China Nos. 383-388, 390-391

Perf. 14

8N17 A57 4c on 8c ol grn .80 .65
8N18 A57 5c on 10c grn 1.25 2.00
8N19 A57 15c on 30c scar 1.50 1.25
a. Inverted surcharge 80.00 80.00
8N20 A57 25c on 50c dk bl 2.00 1.75
8N21 A57 50c on $1 org brn & sep 4.50 4.50
8N22 A57 $1 on $2 dp bl & yel brn 5.75 5.75
8N23 A57 $5 on $10 dk grn & dl pur 50.00 50.00
8N24 A57 $10 on $20 rose lake & dk bl 50.00 60.00
Nos. 8N17-8N24 (8) 115.80 125.90

For overprint see No. 8N55.

Same Surcharge on China Nos. 394-396

Wmk. 261

8N25 A57 5c on 10c grn 1.00 *1.50*
8N26 A57 15c on 30c scar 3.50 *5.00*
8N27 A57 25c on 50c dk bl 1.50 1.50
Nos. 8N25-8N27 (3) 6.00 *8.00*

Same Surcharge on Stamps of 1940-41

1942 **Wmk. 261** ***Perf. 12½, 13***

8N28 A40 ½c on 1c org .30 *1.00*
8N29 A46 1c on 2c dp bl 2.50 2.50
8N30 A45 4c on 8c dp org 20.00 *24.50*
8N31 A46 5c on 10c dl vio 3.00 *3.00*
8N32 A48 15c on 30c brn car 9.75 9.75
8N33 A47 20c on 40c org 5.75 2.50
8N34 A40 25c on 50c grn 5.75 5.00
Nos. 8N28-8N34 (7) 47.05 48.25

Unwmk.

8N35 A40 ½c on 1c org (#422) .30 .25
a. ½c on 1c org (#422a) 37.00 37.00
8N36 A46 1c on 2c dp bl 1.40 1.40
8N37 A39 2c on 4c pale vio 1.00 .85
8N38 A45 4c on 8c dp org 1.25 2.00
8N39 A46 5c on 10c dl vio 3.00 3.00
8N40 A47 10c on 20c lt bl 3.75 .75
8N41 A47 20c on 40c org 4.00 1.00
8N42 A40 25c on 50c grn 32.50 32.50
Nos. 8N35-8N42 (8) 47.20 41.75

Same Surcharge on "New Peking" Prints

Perf. 14

8N43 A37 1c on 2c ol grn .35 .25
8N44 A37 2c on 4c dl grn .90 .25
a. Inverted surcharge 42.50
8N45 A45 4c on 8c dp org .65 .25
8N46 A57 8c on 16c ol gray .35 .25
8N47 A47 10c on 20c red brn 1.75 1.50
8N48 A48 15c on 30c brn car .85 .85
8N49 A47 20c on 40c org 2.10 .50
a. Inverted surcharge 55.00
8N50 A40 25c on 50c grn 1.75 1.50
8N51 A57 50c on $1 org brn & sep 3.50 3.50
8N52 A57 $1 on $2 dp bl & org brn 5.75 3.50
8N53 A57 $5 on $10 dk grn & dl pur 30.00 24.50
Nos. 8N43-8N53 (11) 47.95 *36.85*

See note after No. 2N93. For overprints see #8N54, 8N56-8N57, 8N59.

Nos. 8N44, 8N17 and 8N46 with Additional Overprint in Red

1943 **Unwmk.** ***Perf. 14***

8N54 A37 2c on 4c dl grn .30 *3.00*
8N55 A57 4c on 8c ol grn 1.50 *5.00*
8N56 A57 8c on 16c ol gray 1.50 *8.00*
Nos. 8N54-8N56 (3) 3.30 *16.00*

Return of the Foreign Concessions to China.

Nos. 8N44, 8N8 and 8N46 with Additional Overprint in Red

1943, Aug. 15 ***Perf. 14, 12½***

8N57 A37 2c on 4c dl grn .55 *3.00*
8N58 A57 4c on 8c ol grn 1.00 *5.00*
8N59 A57 8c on 16c ol gray 2.00 *3.00*
Nos. 8N57-8N59 (3) 3.55 *11.00*

North China Postal Service, 5th anniv.

Stamps of China, 1934-41, Overprinted in Black

1943, Nov. 1

8N60 A40 1c org (#313) .85 1.00
8N61 A40 1c org (#422) .85 1.00
8N62 A57 10c grn (#354) .50 1.00
8N63 A57 $2 dp bl & yel brn (#388) 30.00 30.00
8N64 A57 $5 red & grnsh blk (#361) 24.00 24.00
8N65 A57 $5 red & sl grn (#389) 9.75 9.75
8N66 A57 $10 dk grn & dl pur (#390) 14.50 14.50
8N67 A57 $20 rose lake & dk bl (#391) 90.00 *110.00*
Nos. 8N60-8N67 (8) 170.45 *191.25*

Same Overprint on "New Peking" Prints

8N68 A40 1c orange .30 .25
8N69 A37 2c olive grn .30 *.75*
8N70 A37 4c dull green .30 *1.50*
8N71 A37 5c green .60 *.75*
8N72 A57 9c olive grn .35 *.60*
8N73 A46 10c dl violet .35 *.75*
8N74 A57 16c olive gray .30 *.45*
8N75 A57 18c olive gray .30 *.45*
8N76 A47 20c henna .50 *.60*
8N77 A48 30c brown car .45 .45
8N78 A47 40c brt orange .45 *.75*
a. Inverted overprint 42.50 42.50
8N79 A40 50c green 2.50 2.50
8N80 A57 $1 org brn & sep 4.25 1.25
8N81 A57 $2 bl & org brn 2.50 2.20
8N82 A57 $5 red & sl grn 5.00 *7.50*
8N83 A57 $10 dk grn & dl pur 9.00 9.00
8N84 A57 $20 rose lake & dk bl 10.00 *12.50*
Nos. 8N68-8N84 (17) 37.45 *42.25*

See note after No. 2N93. For overprints see Nos. 8N85-8N90, 8N95-8N106.

Nos. 8N70 and 8N62 with Additional Overprint in Red

1944, Jan. 9

8N85 A37 4c dull green .35 *2.00*
8N86 A57 10c green .35 *.75*

1st anniv. of the declaration of war against the Allies by North China.

Nos. 8N72, 8N75, 8N79 and 8N80 with Additional Overprint in Red

1944, Mar. 30

8N87 A57 9c olive green 1.00 *2.00*
8N88 A57 18c olive gray 3.50 *4.00*
8N89 A40 50c green 5.75 *7.50*
8N90 A57 $1 org brn & sepia 2.10 *3.00*
a. Red overprint inverted 37.00 37.00
Nos. 8N87-8N90 (4) 12.35 *16.50*

North China Political Council, 4th anniv.

Shanghai-Nanking Nos. 9N101-9N104 Surcharged North China (Hwa Pei) and New Value in Red or Black

a

b

c

d

1944 *Perf. 12½x12, 12x12½*

8N91 OS1 (a) 9c on 50c org 2.00 8.00
8N92 OS1 (b) 18c on $1 grn (R) 2.00 10.00
a. Double surcharge 37.00 37.00
8N93 OS2 (c) 36c on $2 dp bl (R) 3.00 12.00
8N94 OS2 (d) 90c on $5 car rose 4.00 12.00
Nos. 8N91-8N94 (4) 11.00 42.00

Nos. 8N72, 8N75, 8N79 and 8N80 Overprinted in Red or Blue

1944, Aug. 15

8N95 A57 9c olive grn 4.00 *4.00*
8N96 A57 18c olive gray 3.00 *4.00*
8N97 A40 50c green 4.00 *5.00*
8N98 A57 $1 org brn & sep (Bl) 5.00 *8.00*
Nos. 8N95-8N98 (4) 16.00 *21.00*

6th anniv. of the General P.O. Dept. of North China.

North China Nos. 8N76, 8N79-8N81 Overprinted in Blue or Black

1944, Dec. 5

8N99 A47 20c henna (Bl) 3.00 *4.00*
8N100 A40 50c green (Bl) 3.00 *4.00*
8N101 A57 $1 org brn & sep (Bl) 5.75 *8.00*
8N102 A57 $2 bl & org brn 1.75 *3.00*
Nos. 8N99-8N102 (4) 13.50 *19.00*

Death of Wang Ching-wei, puppet ruler of China.

North China Nos. 8N76, 8N79-8N81 Overprinted in Red or Black

1945

8N103 A47 20c henna 3.00 *5.00*
8N104 A40 50c green (R) 9.00 *10.00*
8N105 A57 $1 org brn & sep 3.25 *4.00*
8N106 A57 $2 bl & org brn 5.75 *6.00*
Nos. 8N103-8N106 (4) 21.00 *25.00*

2nd anniv. of the declaration of war.

Shanghai-Nanking Nos. 9N105-9N106 Surcharged in Red

1945 *Perf. 12x12½*

8N107 OS3 50c on $3 lt org .65 *8.00*
8N108 OS3 $1 on $6 blue .65 *8.00*

Return of the foreign concessions in Shanghai.

Dragon Pillar — OS1

Designs: $2, Long Bridge and White Pagoda. $5, Tower in Imperial City. $10, Marble Boat, Summer Palace.

1945 **Unwmk.** **Litho.** *Perf. 14*

Various Papers

8N109 OS1 $1 dull yellow 1.50 *6.00*
8N110 OS1 $2 deep blue .30 *6.00*
8N111 OS1 $5 carmine 3.00 *6.00*
8N112 OS1 $10 dull green .50 *6.00*
Nos. 8N109-8N112 (4) 5.30 *24.00*

North China Political Council, 5th anniv.

Dr. Sun Yat-sen — OS2

Various Papers

1945 **Without Gum**

8N113 OS2 $1 bister .30 .25
8N114 OS2 $2 dark blue 1.10 .35
8N115 OS2 $5 fawn 2.50 2.50
8N116 OS2 $10 sage green 2.50 *3.00*
8N117 OS2 $20 dull violet 2.50 *3.00*
8N118 OS2 $50 brown 50.00 *60.00*
Nos. 8N113-8N118 (6) 58.90 *69.10*

Nos. 8N113-8N118 without "Hwa Pei" overprint are proofs.

Wutai Mountain, Shansi — OS3

Designs: $10, Kaifeng Iron Pagoda. $20, International Bridge, Tientsin. $30, Taishan Mountain, Shantung. $50, General Post Office, Peking.

Various Papers

1945, Aug. 15 **Without Gum**

8N119 OS3 $5 gray green .30 *6.00*
8N120 OS3 $10 dull brown .75 *6.00*
8N121 OS3 $20 dull purple .55 *6.00*
8N122 OS3 $30 slate blue 1.10 *6.00*
8N123 OS3 $50 carmine 3.25 10.00
Nos. 8N119-8N123 (5) 5.95 *34.00*

North China Postal Directorate, 7th anniv.

SHANGHAI AND NANKING

China Nos. 299-303 Surcharged

a

b

Surcharged Type "b"

1942-45 **Unwmk.** *Perf. 12½, 13½*

9N1 A37 $6 on 5c green .90 *1.25*
9N2 A37 $20 on 15c scar .45 *.90*
9N3 A37 $500 on 15c dk grn .30 *1.25*
9N4 A37 $1000 on 20c ultra 3.50 3.50
9N5 A37 $1000 on 25c ultra 3.50 3.50
Nos. 9N1-9N5 (5) 8.65 *10.40*

A $1000 on 20c ultramarine, No. 293, exists.

Surcharged Type "a" (Nos. 9N6-9N10) or Type "b" (Nos. 9N11-9N40) on Type A57 Stamps of 1939-41

Perf. 12½

9N6 25c on 5c (#352) 2.50 *4.00*
9N7 30c on 2c (#368) .25 *.30*
9N8 50c on 3c (#350) .30 *1.00*
9N9 50c on 5c (#352) .30 .30
9N10 50c on 8c (#353) 2.00 *1.00*
9N11 $1 on 8c (#353) .30 .25
9N12 $1 on 8c (#369) 14.50 14.50
9N13 $1 on 15c (#356) 1.00 .25
9N14 $1.30 on 16c (#357) .30 *1.00*
9N15 $1.50 on 3c (#350) .30 *1.00*
9N16 $2 on 5c (#352) 1.40 1.40
9N17 $2 on 10c (#354) .30 *.35*
9N18 $3 on 15c (#356) 1.00 *.35*
9N19 $4 on 16c (#357) .50 1.00
9N20 $5 on 15c (#356) .30 .30
9N21 $6 on 5c (#351) .75 *1.75*
a. Perf. 14 (#371) 62.50 62.50
9N22 $6 on 5c (#352) .30 *.45*
9N23 $6 on 8c (#353) .50 *1.25*
9N24 $6 on 8c (#369) *990.00* *990.00*
9N25 $6 on 10c (#354) .30 .30
9N26 $10 on 10c (#354) .30 .35
9N27 $10 on 16c (#357) .60 .30
9N28 $20 on 3c (#350) .30 *1.00*
9N29 $20 on 15c (#355) 1.40 *3.00*
9N30 $20 on 15c (#356) .50 .50
9N31 $20 on $2 (#360) 3.00 *5.00*
9N32 $100 on 3c (#350) 1.00 .50
9N33 $500 on 8c (#353) 3.00 *5.50*
9N34 $500 on 8c (#369) 42.50 *57.50*
9N35 $500 on 10c (#354) 3.00 *4.25*
9N36 $500 on 15c (#355) 1.50 *3.00*
9N37 $500 on 15c (#356) 1.25 *2.50*
9N38 $500 on 16c (#357) 1.50 *5.00*
9N39 $1000 on 25c (#358) 1.50 *3.00*
9N40 $2000 on $5 (#361) 1.75 *3.00*
Nos. 9N1-9N23,9N25-9N40 (39) 98.85 *135.55*

Nos. 381-391 (Type A57) Surcharged with Type "b"

Perf. 14

9N41 $1 on 8c ol grn .30 *1.00*
9N42 $1.70 on 30c scar .35 *2.00*
a. Perf. 12½ 4.00 6.00
9N43 $2 on 5c ol grn .50 *2.00*
9N44 $2 on $1 org brn & sep 1.25 *3.00*
9N45 $3 on 8c ol grn .75 *.75*
a. $3 on 8c olive green (#383a) 42.50 42.50
b. "3" with flat top .50 .50
9N46 $6 on 5c grn .50 *.60*
9N47 $6 on 5c ol grn 1.00 *2.00*
9N48 $6 on 8c ol grn .45 *1.00*
9N49 $10 on 10c grn .50 *2.50*
a. Perf. 12½ 2.50 *7.50*
9N50 $20 on $2 dp bl & yel brn 2.00 *3.00*
9N51 $50 on 30c scar 2.00 *3.00*
9N52 $50 on 50c dk bl 1.00 *2.00*
9N53 $50 on $5 red & sl grn 2.00 3.00
9N54 $50 on $20 rose lake & dk bl 4.00 *6.00*
9N55 $100 on $10 dk grn & dl pur 4.00 *5.00*
9N56 $200 on $20 rose lake & dk bl 1.00 *2.00*
9N57 $500 on 8c ol grn 13.50 *16.00*
a. $500 on 8c ol grn (#383a) 30.50 30.00
9N58 $500 on 10c grn 3.00 *4.25*
9N59 $1000 on 30c scar 3.00 *4.00*
9N60 $1000 on 50c dk bl 3.00 *4.00*
9N61 $1000 on $2 dp bl & yel brn 5.00 *10.00*
9N62 $2000 on $5 red & sl grn 5.00 *5.00*

China Nos. 392-395 and 399-401 (Type A57) Surcharged with Type "b"

1942-45 **Wmk. 261** *Perf. 14*

9N63 $2 on $1 org brn & sep, perf. 12½ 1.00 *1.75*
9N64 $6 on 5c grn .50 *1.05*
9N65 $6 on 5c ol grn 1.40 *2.00*
9N66 $50 on $5 red & sl grn .85 *1.25*
a. Numeral tablet violet 1.00 *1.25*
9N67 $100 on $10 dk grn & dl pur .50 *.75*
9N68 $200 on $20 rose lake & dk bl .60 *.75*
9N69 $500 on 10c grn 2.50 *3.00*
9N70 $1000 on 30c scar 3.50 *4.00*
9N71 $5000 on $10 dk grn & dl pur, perf. 12½ 8.00 *9.75*
a. Perf. 14 125.00 125.00
Nos. 9N41-9N71 (31) 72.95 *106.40*

Nos. 9N63 and 9N71 were not issued without surcharge. A $50 on 30c scarlet exists.

Same Surch. on Stamps of 1940-41

Perf. 12½, 13

Wmk. 261

9N72 A46 $30 on 2c dp bl 150.00 150.00

A $7.50 on ½c and a $15 on 1c are known.

Unwmk.

9N73 A39 $7.50 on ½c ol blk 2.50 *3.00*
9N74 A40 $15 on 1c org .35 *1.50*
a. Without secret mark 62.50 62.50
9N75 A46 $30 on 2c dp bl 1.40 *2.00*
9N76 A40 $200 on 1c org .30 *.35*
9N77 A45 $200 on 8c dp org .85 *1.25*
Nos. 9N73-9N77 (5) 5.40 *8.10*

Surcharged Type "a" (Nos. 9N78-9N81) or Type "b" (Nos. 9N82-9N96) on Type A59 Stamps of 1941

Perf. 12

9N78 5c on ½c sepia .25 *.35*
9N79 10c on 1c orange .25 *.35*
9N80 20c on 1c orange .25 *.50*
9N81 40c on 5c green .25 *.50*
9N82 $5 on 5c green .25 *.35*
9N83 $10 on 10c brt grn .25 *.35*
9N84 $50 on ½c sepia .25 *.35*
9N85 $50 on 1c orange .45 *.50*
9N86 $50 on 17c olive .45 *.60*
9N87 $200 on 5c green .45 *.50*
9N88 $200 on 8c turq grn .25 *.30*
9N89 $200 on 8c red org .45 *.75*
9N90 $500 on $5 scar & blk .50 *.50*
9N91 $1000 on 1c orange .45 *.65*
9N92 $1000 on 25c rose vio .50 *.65*
9N93 $1000 on 30c scarlet 1.25 .65
9N94 $1000 on $2 bl & blk 1.25 *1.25*
9N95 $1000 on $10 grn & blk .50 *.65*
9N96 $2000 on $5 scar & blk 1.25 *1.25*
Nos. 9N78-9N96 (19) 9.50 *11.00*

Stamps of China 1939-41 Surcharged in Red or Blue

1943 **Unwmk.** *Perf. 12, 12½*

9N97 A57 25c on 5c grn .25 *1.50*
9N98 A59 50c on 8c red org (Bl) .25 *.90*
9N99 A57 $1 on 16c ol gray .25 *1.75*
9N100 A59 $2 on 50c dk bl .25 *.90*
Nos. 9N97-9N100 (4) 1.00 *5.05*

Return of the foreign concessions in Shanghai.

Wheat and Cotton — OS1

Purple Mountain, Nanking
OS2

Perf. 12½x12, 12x12½

1944 Engr. Unwmk.

9N101 OS1 50c orange .90 *6.00*
9N102 OS1 $1 green .90 *6.00*
9N103 OS2 $2 deep blue .90 *6.00*
9N104 OS2 $5 carmine rose .90 *6.00*
Nos. 9N101-9N104 (4) 3.60 *24.00*

Puppet government at Nanking, 4th anniv.
For surcharges see Nos. 8N91-8N94, 9N107-9N110.

Map of Foreign Concessions in Shanghai — OS3

1944 ***Perf. 12x12½***

9N105 OS3 $3 lt orange .90 *1.10*
9N106 OS3 $6 blue .90 *1.10*

1st anniversary of the return of the foreign concessions in Shanghai.
For surcharges see Nos. 8N107-8N108.

Nos. 9N101-9N104 Surcharged in Black with Type "b"

1945, Mar. 30

9N107 OS1 $15 on 50c orange .90 *1.10*
9N108 OS1 $30 on $1 green .90 *1.10*
9N109 OS2 $60 on $2 dp blue .90 *1.10*
9N110 OS2 $200 on $5 car rose .90 *1.10*
Nos. 9N107-9N110 (4) 3.60 *4.40*

China Nos. C31, C32, C36 and C38 Srchd. in Red, Green, Orange or Carmine

1945 ***Perf. 12½, 13***

9N111 AP3 $150 on 15c (R) .45 *3.00*
9N112 AP3 $250 on 25c (G) .45 *3.00*
9N113 AP3 $600 on 60c (O) .45 *3.00*
9N114 AP3 $1,000 on $1 (C) .45 *3.00*
Nos. 9N111-9N114 (4) 1.80 *12.00*

Issue as air raid precaution propaganda.

AIR POST STAMPS

China Nos. C35 and C38 Surcharged in Black

The surcharges on Nos. 9NC1-9NC7 were in Japanese currency because all air mail then was carried by Japanese planes.

The surcharges translate: (10c) "Airmail fee for postcard within the nation has been paid." (20c) "Airmail fee for letter within the nation has been paid."

1941 Unwmk. ***Perf. 12½***

9NC1 AP3 10(s) on 50c brown .55 *1.00*
9NC2 AP3 20(s) on $1 apple grn .90 *.90*

Two types of surcharge exist on No. 9NC1.

Similar Surcharge on No. C28

1941 Wmk. 261 ***Perf. 13***

9NC3 AP3 20(s) on $1 ap grn 18.00 18.00

Nos. C37 and C39 Surcharged

The surcharges translate: (18c and 25c) "Airmail fee for postcard to Japan has been paid." (35c) "Airmail fee for letter to Japan has been paid."

1941 Unwmk. ***Perf. 12½, 13***

9NC4 AP3 18(s) on 90c lt olive .55 *6.00*
9NC5 AP3 25(s) on 90c lt olive .45 *6.00*
9NC6 AP3 35(s) on $2 lt brown .45 *6.00*
Nos. 9NC4-9NC6 (3) 1.45 *18.00*

No. 9NC6 with Additional Surcharge in Red

Perf. 12½

9NC7 AP3 60(s) on 35(s) on $2 .45 *6.00*

POSTAGE DUE STAMPS

Postage Due Stamps of China 1932 Surcharged in Black

1945 Unwmk. ***Perf. 14***

9NJ1 D5 $1 on 2c org .90 *10.00*
9NJ2 D5 $2 on 5c org .90 *10.00*
9NJ3 D5 $5 on 10c org .90 *10.00*
9NJ4 D5 $10 on 20c org .90 *15.00*
Nos. 9NJ1-9NJ4 (4) 3.60 *45.00*

Northeastern Provinces

With the end of World War II and the collapse of Manchukuo, the Northeastern Provinces reverted to China. In many Manchurian towns and cities, the Manchukuo stamps were locally handstamped in ideograms: "Republic of China," "China Postal Service" or "Temporary Use for China." A typical example is shown above.

Dr. Sun Yat-sen — A1

Black Surcharge

1946, Feb. Unwmk. Typo. ***Perf. 14***

1 A1 50c on $5 red .35 *2.00*
2 A1 50c on $10 green .90 *3.00*
3 A1 $1 on $10 green .35 *2.00*
4 A1 $2 on $20 brown vio .35 *2.00*
5 A1 $4 on $50 brown .35 *2.00*
Nos. 1-5 (5) 2.30 *11.00*

The two characters at left express the new value.

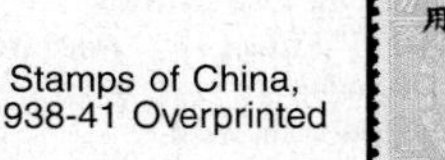

Stamps of China, 1938-41 Overprinted

1946, Apr. ***Perf. 12½, 13, 13½, 14***

6 A40 1c org (#422) .35 *3.75*
7 A48 3c dp yel brn (#425) .35 *4.75*
8 A48 5c dl red org (#427) .35 *4.75*
9 A57 10c grn (#354) .35 *3.75*
10 A57 10c grn (#384) .35 *3.75*
11 A47 20c lt bl (#433) .35 *3.75*
a. Horiz. pair, imperf. btwn 100.00
Nos. 6-11 (6) 2.10 *24.50*

Dr. Sun Yat-sen — A2

1946, July Engr. ***Perf. 14***
Without Gum

12 A2 5c lake .35 *3.50*
13 A2 10c orange .35 *3.50*
14 A2 20c yel grn .35 *4.00*
15 A2 25c blk brn .35 *3.50*
16 A2 50c red org .35 *2.75*
17 A2 $1 blue .35 *2.25*
18 A2 $2 dk vio .35 *2.75*
19 A2 $2.50 indigo .35 *3.50*
20 A2 $3 brown .35 *2.75*
21 A2 $4 org brn .35 *3.50*
22 A2 $5 dk grn .35 *2.75*
23 A2 $10 crimson .35 *1.75*
24 A2 $20 olive .35 *1.40*
25 A2 $50 blue vio .40 *1.00*
Nos. 12-25 (14) 4.95 *38.90*

Two types of $4, $10, $20 and $50: I- Character *kuo* directly left of sun emblem is open at upper and lower left corners of "box." Diagonal stroke from top center to lower right has no hook at bottom. II- Character is closed at left corners. Diagonal stroke has hook at bottom.
See Nos. 47-52, 61-63. For surcharges see Nos. M1, Taiwan 91-96, People's Republic of China 35-48, 3L37-3L52, 3L55-3L66, 3L71-3L75.

China Nos. 728-731 Surcharged in Black

1946

26 A75 $2 on $20 green .35 *3.25*
27 A75 $3 on $30 blue .35 *3.25*
28 A75 $5 on $50 dark brown .35 *3.25*
29 A75 $10 on $100 carmine .35 *3.25*
Nos. 26-29 (4) 1.40 *13.00*

Convening of Chinese National Assembly.

Type of China, 1946, with added inscriptions on both sides of head

1947 Engr. ***Perf. 11, 11½***

30 A74 $2 carmine .65 *4.00*
31 A74 $3 green 1.10 *4.00*
32 A74 $5 vermilion 1.10 *4.00*
33 A74 $10 yel grn 1.10 *4.00*
34 A74 $20 yel org 1.40 *4.00*
35 A74 $30 magenta 1.40 *4.00*
Nos. 30-35 (6) 6.75 *24.00*

60th birthday of Chiang Kai-shek.

Type of China, 1947, with additional inscription above value

1947 Unwmk. Engr. ***Perf. 14***

36 A76 $2 deep green .65 *2.00*
37 A76 $4 deep blue .65 *2.00*
38 A76 $6 carmine .65 *2.00*
39 A76 $10 lt brown .65 *2.00*
40 A76 $20 deep claret .65 *2.00*
Nos. 36-40 (5) 3.25 *10.00*

First anniversary of return of Chinese National Government to Nanking.

China Nos. 644 to 646 and 634 Surcharged in Black

1947 ***Perf. 12½, 14***

41 A73 $100 on $1000 rose lake 1.10 *4.25*
42 A73 $300 on $3000 bl 1.10 *4.25*
43 A73 $500 on $5000 dp grn & ver .55 *5.00*
44 A37 $500 on $30 choc 1.00 *4.25*
Nos. 41-44 (4) 3.75 *17.75*

Type of 1946

1947 Engr. ***Perf. 14***
Without Gum

47 A2 $44 dk car rose *40.00* *85.00*
48 A2 $100 dp grn .35 *.70*
49 A2 $200 rose brn .35 *1.40*
50 A2 $300 bluish grn .35 *2.75*
51 A2 $500 rose car .35 *.70*
52 A2 $1000 dp orange .35 *.60*
Nos. 47-52 (6) *41.75* *91.15*

For surcharges see note following No. 25.

Stamps and Types of 1946-47 Surcharged in Black or Red

1948 Unwmk. ***Perf. 14***

53 A2 $1500 on 20c yel grn .90 *4.50*
54 A2 $3000 on $1 blue .45 *5.00*
55 A2 $4000 on 25c blk brn (R) .45 *4.00*
56 A2 $8000 on 50c red org .45 *3.25*
57 A2 $10,000 on 10c org .55 *3.25*
58 A2 $50,000 on $109 dk grn (R) 1.00 *6.25*
59 A2 $100,000 on $65 dl grn .90 *6.25*
60 A2 $500,000 on $22 gray (R) 1.50 *6.25*
Nos. 53-60 (8) 6.20 *38.75*

Type of 1946

1947, Nov. 5 Without Gum

61 A2 $22 gray 80.00 85.00
62 A2 $65 dull green 80.00 100.00
63 A2 $109 dark green 85.00 100.00
Nos. 61-63 (3) 245.00 285.00

For surcharges see note following No. 25.

POSTAGE DUE STAMPS

D1

1947 Unwmk. Engr. ***Perf. 14***
Without Gum

J1 D1 10c dark blue .55 *7.75*
J2 D1 20c dark blue .55 *7.75*
J3 D1 50c dark blue .55 *5.75*
J4 D1 $1 dark blue .25 *4.25*
J5 D1 $2 dark blue .25 *5.50*
J6 D1 $5 dark blue .25 *5.50*
Nos. J1-J6 (6) 2.40 *36.50*

Nos. J4-J6 are known on paper with the papermaker's watermark, "COSMOS BOND."

Nos. J1 to J3 Surcharged in Red

1948

J7 D1 $10 on 10c dark blue .35 *9.00*
J8 D1 $20 on 20c dark blue .35 *9.00*
J9 D1 $50 on 50c dark blue .35 *9.00*
Nos. J7-J9 (3) 1.05 *27.00*

The surcharge reads "Changed to . . . dollars." Characters at the left express the new value and vary on each denomination.

MILITARY STAMPS

No. 16 Surcharged in Black

1947 Unwmk. *Perf. 14*

M1 A2 $44 on 50c red org 11.00 *40.00*

The surcharge reads: "Army Post. Temporarily for 44 dollars."

China No. M13 Overprinted in Black

Thin Paper Without Gum
Perf. 12½

M2 M1 rose 2.75 *18.00*

China No. M13 Overprinted in Black

M3 M1 rose 62.50 *80.00*

PARCEL POST STAMP

China No. Q25 Surcharged in Black

1948 Unwmk. Engr. *Perf. 13½*
Without Gum

Q1 PP3 $500,000 on $5,000,000 lil 180.00

Used value is for CTO.

The use of this handstamp from Anhwei has not been verified.

FUKIEN PROVINCE

Stamps of China, 1945-49, Surcharged

1949 Engr. *Perf. 14*
Without Gum

1 A82 1c on $500 bl grn 10.00 *6.25*
2 A82 1c on $7000 lt red brn 15.00 *22.50*
3 A82 2c on $2,000,000 ver 5.00 *6.75*
4 A82 2½c on $50,000 dp bl 35.00 35.00
5 A73 4c on $100 dk car 4.50 4.50
6 A73 10c on $200 ol grn 7.25 9.00
7 A82 10c on $3000 bl 5.50 *4.50*
8 A82 10c on $4000 gray 7.25 *10.75*
9 A82 10c on $6000 rose lil 4.50 *6.25*
10 A82 10c on $100,000 dl grn 5.75 *6.75*
11 A82 10c on $1,000,000 cl 5.75 *6.25*
12 A82 40c on $200,000 brn vio 9.00 *10.00*
Nos. 1-12 (12) 114.50 128.50

The surcharge on No. 2 is handstamped and in slightly larger characters.
Issue dates: No. 2, May 10; others, June.

China Nos. 973, 975-978 Overprinted

1949, June Litho. *Perf. 12½, 13*

13 A94 1c apple grn 18.00 5.50
14 A94 4c blue green 5.50 2.00
15 A94 10c deep lilac 55.00 27.50
16 A94 16c orange red 11.00 *27.50*
17 A94 20c blue 55.00 27.50
Nos. 13-17 (5) 144.50 90.00

Same Overprint on China No. 959

1949, July Litho. *Perf. 12½*

18 A96 orange 72.50 72.50

Same Overprint on Fukien Nos. 1, 3-4, 8, 11 in Black or Red

1949, June Engr. *Perf. 14*

19 A82 1c on $500 bl grn 150.00 150.00
20 A82 2c on $2,000,000 ver 55.00 55.00
21 A82 2½c on $50,000 dp bl 90.00 90.00
22 A82 10c on $4000 gray 37.50 37.50
23 A82 10c on $1,000,000 cl 145.00 145.00
Nos. 19-23 (5) 477.50 477.50

AIR POST STAMP

China #C62 Overprinted as #13-17

1949, July Litho. *Perf. 12½*

C1 AP5 blue green 72.50 37.50

SPECIAL DELIVERY STAMP

China #E12 Overprinted as #13-17

1949, July Litho. *Perf. 12½*

E1 SD2 red violet 50.00 35.00

REGISTRATION STAMP

China #F2 Overprinted as #13-17

1949, July Litho. *Perf. 12½*

F1 R2 carmine 50.00 35.00

HUNAN PROVINCE

China No. 640 Surcharged

1949, May Engr. *Perf. 14*

1 A73 on $100 dk car 14.50 8.50

The first printing of surcharge on No. 1 is in smaller characters.

China Nos. 797, 788, 750, 747 Surcharged

1949, May Engr. *Perf. 14*

2 A82 1c on $2,000,000 ver 27.50 27.50
3 A82 2c on $20,000 rose pink 27.50 27.50
4 A82 5c on $3000 blue 35.00 *40.00*
5 A82 10c on $500 blue grn 30.00 27.50
Nos. 2-5 (4) 120.00 122.50

AIR POST STAMP

China No. 790 Surcharged

1949, May Engr. *Perf. 14*

C1 A82 On $40,000 green 22.50 *24.00*

SPECIAL DELIVERY STAMP

China No. 637 Surcharged as No. F1 in Red

1949, May Engr. *Perf. 14*

E1 A73 On $30 dark blue 27.50 27.50

REGISTRATION STAMP

China No. 754 Surcharged

1949, May Engr. *Perf. 14*

F1 A82 On $7000 lt red brn 27.50 27.50

HUPEH PROVINCE

China Type A95 Surcharged

1949, May Litho.

1 A95 1c on $20 red brn 67.50 67.50
2 A95 10c on $20 red brn 67.50 67.50

KANSU PROVINCE

China No. 959 Handstamped in Purple

1949, Aug. Litho. *Perf. 12½*

1 A96 orange *1,100.*

AIR POST STAMP

Same Handstamp Overprinted on China No. C62 in Red

1949, Aug. Litho. *Perf. 12½*

C1 AP5 blue green *1,100.*

Counterfeits exist.

KIANGSI PROVINCE

China Nos. 789-791 Surcharged

1949 Engr. *Perf. 14*

1 A82 On $30,000 choc 57.50 55.00
2 A82 On $40,000 green 57.50 55.00
3 A82 On $50,000 dp bl 57.50 55.00
Nos. 1-3 (3) 172.50 165.00

AIR POST STAMP

Similar Surcharge on China No. 754

1949 Engr. *Perf. 14*

C1 A82 On $7000 lt red brn 62.50 62.50

Third and fourth characters in right column of surcharge read "Air Mail" in Chinese on No. C1, "Registered" on Nos. F1-F2.

SPECIAL DELIVERY STAMP

Similar Surcharge on China No. 750

1949 Engr. *Perf. 14*

E1 A82 On $3000 blue 67.50 45.00

See note below No. C1.

REGISTRATION STAMPS

Similar Surcharge on China Nos. 747 and 754

1949 Engr. *Perf. 14*

F1 A82 On $500 bl grn 67.50 45.00
F2 A82 On $7000 lt red brn 67.50 55.00

KWANGSI PROVINCE

China Nos. 811 and 818 Also Surcharged in Red

1949, May 21 Typo.

6 A62 5c on $20,000 on 10c dp grn 30.00 30.00
7 A62 5c on $40,000 on 20c dk ol grn 67.50 67.50

China Stamps of 1946-48 Surcharged in Black or Red

a

b

1949 Engr. *Perf. 14*
Type "a" Surcharge

8 A82 ½c on $500,000 lil rose 40.00 27.50
9 A82 1c on $200,000 brn vio 35.00 12.00
10 A82 2c on $300,000 yel grn 120.00 72.50
11 A73 5c on $3000 blue 35.00 20.00
12 A82 5c on $3000 blue 18.00 11.00
13 A82 5c on $40,000 grn 35.00 20.00

Type "b" Surcharge

14	A82	13c on $50,000 dp bl (R)	25.00	16.00
15	A82	13c on $50,000 dp bl	100.00	25.00
16	A82	17c on $7000 lt red brn	27.50	27.50
17	A82	21c on $100,000 dl grn	32.50	29.00
		Nos. 8-17 (10)	468.00	260.50

SHENSI PROVINCE

China Nos. 747, 750 Surcharged

1949, May — Engr. — *Perf. 14*

1	A82	On $500 bl grn	45.00	45.00
2	A82	On $3000 blue	45.00	45.00

AIR POST STAMP

Similar Surcharge on China No. 754

1949, May — Engr. — *Perf. 14*

C1	A82	On $7000 lt red brn	55.00	55.00

SPECIAL DELIVERY STAMP

Similar Surcharge on China No. 746 in Red

1949, May — Engr. — *Perf. 14*

E1	A82	On $250 dp lil	62.50	62.50

REGISTRATION STAMPS

Similar Surcharge on China Nos. 626, 637 in Red

1949, May — Typo. — *Perf. 12*

F1	A72	on $30 dp bl	62.50	62.50
F2	A73	on $30 dk bl	55.00	55.00

SZECHWAN PROVINCE

Re-engraved Issue of China, 1923, Overprinted

1933 — Unwmk. — *Perf. 14*

1	A29	1c orange	11.00	1.00
2	A29	5c claret	11.00	1.40
3	A30	50c deep green	32.50	6.75
		Nos. 1-3 (3)	54.50	9.15

The overprint reads "For use in Szechwan Province exclusively."

Same on Sun Yat-sen Issue of 1931-37
Type II

1933-34 — *Perf. 12½*

4	A37	2c olive grn	2.00	1.00
5	A37	5c green	22.50	2.40
6	A37	15c dk green	7.75	3.50
7	A37	15c scar ('34)	9.00	12.00
8	A37	25c ultra	7.50	1.75
9	A37	$1 org brn & dk brn	22.50	4.00
10	A37	$2 bl & org brn	55.00	6.75
11	A37	$5 dl red & blk	125.00	37.50
		Nos. 4-11 (8)	251.25	68.90

Same on Martyrs Issue of 1932-34

1933 — *Perf. 14*

12	A39	½c black brn	.80	.80
13	A40	1c orange	1.25	.55
14	A39	2½c rose lilac	3.50	3.75
15	A48	3c deep brown	3.00	3.00
16	A45	8c brown org	1.75	1.50
17	A46	10c dull violet	4.50	.55
18	A45	13c blue green	5.00	1.00
19	A46	17c brown olive	5.50	1.40
20	A47	20c brown red	8.50	1.00
21	A48	30c brown violet	6.75	1.00
22	A47	40c orange	18.00	1.40
23	A40	50c green	37.50	2.10
		Nos. 12-23 (12)	96.05	18.05

Stamps of China, 1947-48, Surcharged

1949 — Engr. — *Perf. 14*

24	A82	on $150 dk bl	72.50	55.00
25	A82	on $250 dp lil	72.50	55.00
26	A82	on $500 bl grn	21.00	12.50
27	A82	on $1000 red	55.00	42.50
28	A82	on $2000 ver	21.00	9.50
29	A82	on $3000 blue	21.00	9.50
30	A82	on $4000 gray	21.00	9.50
31	A82	on $5000 dk brn	62.50	62.50
32	A82	on $6000 rose lil	21.00	21.00
33	A82	on $7000 lt red brn	55.00	45.00
34	A82	on $10,000 dk bl & car	30.50	16.00
35	A82	on $20,000 rose pink	22.50	16.00
36	A82	on $30,000 choc	29.00	22.50
37	A82	on $50,000 grn & dk bl	29.00	25.00
38	A82	on $50,000 dp bl	29.00	22.50
39	A82	on $100,000 dl yel & ol	29.00	22.50
40	A82	on $100,000 dl grn	29.00	25.00
41	A82	on $200,000 vio brn & dp bl	29.00	22.50
42	A82	on $200,000 brn vio	29.00	22.50
43	A82	on $300,000 sep & org brn	40.00	27.50
44	A82	on $300,000 yel grn	55.00	40.00
45	A82	on $500,000 dk Prus grn & sep	29.00	22.50
46	A82	on $1,000,000 claret	55.00	40.00
47	A82	on $2,000,000 ver	29.00	27.50
48	A82	on $3,000,000 ol bis	29.00	27.50
49	A82	on $5,000,000 ultra	110.00	67.50
		Nos. 24-49 (26)	1,026.	769.00

Several of Nos. 24-49 exist with inverted surcharge and a few with bottom character of left row repeated in right row, same position.
Counterfeits exist.

China No. 737 Surcharged in Black

1949 — *Perf. 12½*

50	A77	2c on $500 ol grn	40.00	55.00

China No. 975 Handstamp Surcharged in Purple

1949 — Litho.

51	A94	2½c on 4c bl grn	55.00	40.00

AIR POST STAMPS

China Nos. C55-C58, C60-C61 Surcharged

Perf. 12½, 13x12½, 14

1949, July — Unwmk.

C1	AP3	On $10,000 on 30c	9.00	15.00
a.		On #C54		500.00
C2	AP4	On $10,000 on $27	14.50	20.00
a.		Second surcharge inverted	250.00	
b.		On #C53	125.00	
C3	AP3	On $20,000 on 25c	14.50	20.00
C4	AP3	On $30,000 on 90c	16.00	27.50
C5	AP3	On $50,000 on 60c	125.00	155.00
C6	AP3	On $50,000 on $1	17.00	30.00
		Nos. C1-C6 (6)	196.00	267.50

REGISTRATION STAMPS

Stamps of China, 1944-47, Surcharged

Engraved; Typographed (A72)

1949 — *Perf. 12, 13, 14*

F1	A64	On $100 yel brn	77.50
F2	A72	On $100 dk brn	77.50
F3	A64	On $200 dk grn	155.00
F4	A72	On $200 brn vio	72.50
F5	A73	On $200 ol grn	77.50
F6	A73	On $500 brt bl grn	155.00
F7	A73	On $700 red brn	275.00
F8	A73	On $5000 dp grn & ver	120.00
		Nos. F1-F8 (8)	1,010.

PARCEL POST STAMP

China No. Q10 Surcharged

1949 — Engr. — *Perf. 12½*

Q1	PP2	1c on $20,000 dk red	—	—

TSINGTAU PROVINCE

China Nos. 890, 903, 900, 894 Handstamp Surcharged in Purple (#1-2), Blue (#3) or Red (#4)

Engraved; Lithographed

1949, May — *Perf. 14, 12½*

1	A94	1c on $100 org brn	100.00	90.00
2	A94	4c on $5000 lt bl	100.00	90.00
3	A94	6c on $500 rose lil	100.00	90.00
4	A94	10c on $1000 bl	100.00	90.00
		Nos. 1-4 (4)	400.00	360.00

YUNNAN PROVINCE

Stamps of China, 1923-26, Overprinted

The overprint reads "For exclusive use in the Province of Yunnan." It was applied to prevent stamps being purchased in the depreciated currency of Yunnan and used elsewhere.

1926 — Unwmk. — *Perf. 14*

1	A29	½c blk brn	1.10	.35
2	A29	1c orange	1.75	.35
3	A29	1½c violet	3.75	4.25
4	A29	2c yellow grn	2.75	.50
5	A29	3c blue green	2.75	.35
6	A29	4c olive grn	3.50	.50
7	A29	5c claret	3.50	.50
8	A29	6c red	5.25	1.25
9	A29	7c violet	5.50	1.90
10	A29	8c brown org	4.75	1.40
11	A29	10c dark blue	3.00	.30
12	A30	13c brown	3.00	1.90
13	A30	15c dark blue	3.00	1.90
14	A30	16c olive grn	3.50	1.90
15	A30	20c brown red	8.50	3.25
16	A30	30c brown vio	8.00	5.75
17	A30	50c deep green	8.00	5.75
18	A31	$1 org brn & sep	20.50	14.00
19	A31	$2 blue & red brn	35.00	14.00
20	A31	$5 red & slate	240.00	260.00
		Nos. 1-20 (20)	367.10	320.10

Unification Issue of China, 1929, Overprinted in Red

1929 — *Perf. 14*

21	A35	1c brown org	2.25	2.25
22	A35	4c olive grn	3.75	5.75
23	A35	10c dark blue	12.00	15.00
24	A35	$1 dark red	120.00	130.00
		Nos. 21-24 (4)	138.00	153.00

Similar Overprint in Black on Sun Yat-sen Mausoleum Issue
Characters 15½-16mm apart

25	A36	1c brown orange	2.25	2.00
26	A36	4c olive green	2.25	3.75
27	A36	10c dark blue	9.00	8.50
28	A36	$1 dark red	77.50	67.50
		Nos. 25-28 (4)	91.00	81.75

London Print Issue of China, 1931-37, Overprinted

1932-34 — Unwmk. — *Perf. 12½*

Type I (double circle)

29	A37	1c orange	4.00	2.75
30	A37	2c olive grn	5.00	5.50
31	A37	4c green	3.25	5.50
32	A37	20c ultra	3.25	3.00
33	A37	$1 org brn & dk brn	50.00	55.00
34	A37	$2 bl & org brn	82.50	85.00
35	A37	$5 dl red & blk	250.00	295.00
		Nos. 29-35 (7)	398.00	451.75

Type II (single circle)

36	A37	2c olive grn	26.00	26.00
37	A37	4c green	17.00	10.75
38	A37	5c green	15.00	10.00
39	A37	15c dk green	8.00	8.75
40	A37	15c scar ('34)	8.00	10.00
41	A37	25c ultra	11.00	11.50
42	A37	$1 org brn & dk brn	67.50	67.50
43	A37	$2 bl & org brn	125.00	125.00
44	A37	$5 dl red & blk	260.00	260.00
		Nos. 36-44 (9)	537.50	529.50

Nos. 36-39, 41-44 were overprinted in London as well as in Peking. The London overprints are 11mm in length; the Peking overprints are 12mm in length. There are other minor differences. Value of London overprints is significantly more than the Peking overprints, which are valued above.

Tan Yuan-chang Issue of China, 1933, Overprinted

1933 *Perf. 14*

No.	Type	Description	Unused	Used
45	A49	2c olive green	1.75	1.75
46	A49	5c green	3.00	2.40
47	A49	25c ultra	5.25	*7.00*
48	A49	$1 red	80.00	*105.00*
		Nos. 45-48 (4)	90.00	*116.15*

Martyrs Issue of China, 1932-34, Overprinted

1933

No.	Type	Description	Unused	Used
49	A39	½c blk brown	1.75	1.60
50	A40	1c orange	3.50	2.75
51	A39	2½c rose lilac	4.00	4.50
52	A48	3c deep brown	6.25	2.25
53	A45	8c brown org	2.75	2.75
54	A46	10c dull vio	4.00	4.50
55	A45	13c blue grn	2.50	1.10
56	A46	17c brn olive	12.50	12.50
57	A47	20c brown red	3.25	3.25
58	A48	30c brown vio	10.00	10.00
59	A47	40c orange	47.50	47.50
60	A40	50c green	47.50	47.50
		Nos. 49-60 (12)	145.50	140.20

China No. 324 was overprinted with characters arranged vertically, like Sinkiang No. 114, but was not issued.

China Stamps of 1945-49 Surcharged in Black or Blue

Engraved; Lithographed; Typographed

1949 *Perf. 12, 12½, 14*

No.	Type	Description	Unused	Used
61	A82	1c on $200,000 brn vio	19.00	19.00
62	A82	1.2c on $40,000 grn	19.00	*21.00*
63	A94	6c on $200 red org	19.00	19.00
64	A94	10c on $20,000 org	19.00	*21.00*
65	A94	12c on $50 dk Prus grn (Bl)	19.00	19.00
66	A72	12c on $50 grnsh gray (Bl)	19.00	19.00
67	A72	12c on $200 brn vio (Bl)	19.00	*21.00*
68	A94	30c on $20 vio brn	19.00	19.00
69	A82	$1.20 on $100,000 dl grn	30.00	*35.00*
		Nos. 61-69 (9)	182.00	193.00

China No. 888 and 630 Surcharged

1949 **Engr.** *Perf. 14*

No.	Type	Description	Unused	Used
70	A94	4c on $20 vio brn	360.00	225.00

Typo. *Perf. 12*

No.	Type	Description	Unused	Used
71	A72	12c on $200 brn vio	310.00	200.00

MANCHURIA

Kirin and Heilungkiang Issue

Stamps of China, 1923-26, Overprinted

The overprint reads: "For use in Ki-Hei District" the two names being abbreviated.

The intention of the overprint was to prevent the purchase of stamps in Manchuria, where the currency was depreciated, and their resale elsewhere.

1927 **Unwmk.** *Perf. 14*

No.	Type	Description	Unused	Used
1	A29	½c black brn	1.90	.35
2	A29	1c orange	1.90	.35
3	A29	1½c violet	2.50	1.90
4	A29	2c yellow grn	2.50	1.90
5	A29	3c blue grn	1.75	.75
6	A29	4c olive grn	.85	.35
7	A29	5c claret	1.75	.35
8	A29	6c red	2.50	1.90
9	A29	7c violet	5.25	1.90
10	A29	8c brown org	3.50	1.90
11	A29	10c dk blue	1.90	.50
12	A30	13c brown	4.00	3.00
13	A30	15c dk blue	4.00	3.00
14	A30	16c olive grn	4.00	2.75
15	A30	20c brown red	6.00	3.50
16	A30	30c brown vio	8.75	3.50
17	A30	50c dp green	12.00	4.25
18	A31	$1 org brn & sep	26.00	8.75
19	A31	$2 bl & red brn	70.00	19.00
20	A31	$5 red & slate	325.00	325.00
		Nos. 1-20 (20)	486.05	384.90

Several values of this issue exist with inverted overprint, double overprint and in pairs with one overprint omitted. These "errors" were not regularly issued. Forgeries also exist.

Chang Tso-lin Stamps of 1928 Overprinted in Red or Blue

1928 *Perf. 14*

No.	Type	Description	Unused	Used
21	A34	1c brown org (R)	2.75	1.75
22	A34	4c olive grn (R)	1.75	1.75
23	A34	10c dull blue (R)	5.00	3.75
24	A34	$1 red (Bl)	50.00	45.00
		Nos. 21-24 (4)	59.50	52.25

Unification Issue of China, 1929, Overprinted in Red as in 1928

1929

No.	Type	Description	Unused	Used
25	A35	1c brown orange	2.00	2.00
26	A35	4c olive green	3.75	3.25
27	A35	10c dark blue	13.00	12.50
28	A35	$1 dark red	110.00	*100.00*
		Nos. 25-28 (4)	128.75	*117.75*

Similar Overprint in Black on Sun Yat-sen Mausoleum Issue of China Characters 15-16mm apart

1929 *Perf. 14*

No.	Type	Description	Unused	Used
29	A36	1c brown orange	2.25	*2.50*
30	A36	4c olive green	2.75	*3.00*
31	A36	10c dark blue	8.50	10.00
32	A36	$1 dark red	85.00	85.00
		Nos. 29-32 (4)	98.50	100.50

SINKIANG

Stamps of China, 1913-19, Overprinted in Black or Red

The first character of overprint is ½mm out of alignment, to the left, and the overprint measures 16mm.

1915 **Unwmk.** *Perf. 14*

No.	Type	Description	Unused	Used
1	A24	½c black brn	1.75	.95
2	A24	1c orange	1.75	.70
3	A24	2c yellow grn	2.40	1.25
4	A24	3c slate grn	2.40	.65
5	A24	4c scarlet	4.75	1.10
6	A24	5c rose lilac	3.50	.95
7	A24	6c gray	6.50	2.75
8	A24	7c violet	12.00	*8.50*
9	A24	8c brown orange	8.00	5.50
10	A24	10c dark blue	5.50	2.75
11	A25	15c brown	6.50	3.50
12	A25	16c olive grn	13.00	9.25
13	A25	20c brown red	13.00	7.25
14	A25	30c brown violet	14.50	11.00
15	A25	50c deep green	40.00	18.50
16	A26	$1 ocher & blk (R)	145.00	62.50
a.		Second & third characters of overprint transposed	*70,000.*	
		Nos. 1-16 (16)	280.55	137.10

Stamps of China, 1913-19, Overprinted in Black or Red

The five characters of overprint are correctly aligned and measure 15½mm.

1916-19

No.	Type	Description	Unused	Used
17	A24	½c black brn	2.00	2.40
18	A24	1c orange	3.25	1.75
19	A24	1½c violet	4.50	4.00
20	A24	2c yellow grn	3.25	1.75
21	A24	3c slate grn	5.50	.70
22	A24	4c scarlet	5.50	1.25
23	A24	5c rose lilac	5.50	.90
24	A24	6c gray	8.00	1.25
25	A24	7c violet	8.00	*11.00*
26	A24	8c brown org	8.75	8.50
27	A24	10c dark blue	8.75	1.25
28	A25	13c brown	4.75	*8.00*
29	A25	15c brown	6.00	*8.50*
30	A25	16c olive grn	5.50	4.00
31	A25	20c brown red	4.50	3.00
32	A25	30c brown vio	6.75	6.00
33	A25	50c deep green	9.25	5.50
34	A26	$1 ocher & blk (R)	29.00	11.00
35	A26	$2 dk bl & blk (R)	27.50	12.00
36	A26	$5 scar & blk (R)	110.00	37.50
37	A26	$10 yel grn & blk (R)	275.00	175.00
38	A26	$20 yel & blk (R)	1,435.	875.00
		Nos. 17-38 (22)	1,976.	1,180.

For overprint see No. C4.

China Nos. 243-246 Overprinted

1921 *Perf. 14*

No.	Type	Description	Unused	Used
39	A27	1c orange	1.75	1.75
40	A27	3c blue green	3.50	3.50
41	A27	6c gray	13.50	13.50
42	A27	10c blue	80.00	80.00
		Nos. 39-42 (4)	98.75	98.75

Constitution Issue of China, 1923, Overprinted

1923

No.	Type	Description	Unused	Used
43	A32	1c orange	1.55	1.55
44	A32	3c blue green	6.50	6.50
45	A32	4c red	9.75	9.75
46	A32	10c blue	27.50	27.50
		Nos. 43-46 (4)	45.30	45.30

Stamps of China, 1923-26, Overprinted as in 1916-19, in Black or Red

1924

Re-engraved

No.	Type	Description	Unused	Used
47	A29	½c black brn	1.50	*3.00*
48	A29	1c orange	1.50	1.25
49	A29	1½c violet	2.75	*5.00*
50	A29	2c yellow grn	4.25	1.40
51	A29	3c blue grn	4.25	1.25
52	A29	4c gray	4.25	*6.75*
53	A29	5c claret	1.40	3.00
54	A29	6c red	7.50	10.00
55	A29	7c violet	8.50	7.50
56	A29	8c org brn	17.00	*15.00*
57	A29	10c dark blue	6.75	1.90
58	A30	13c red brown	6.00	*8.50*
59	A30	15c deep blue	8.75	6.75
60	A30	16c olive grn	10.00	9.75
61	A30	20c brown red	8.50	6.25
62	A30	30c brown vio	9.75	6.75
63	A30	50c deep green	10.00	6.75
64	A31	$1 org brn & sep (R)	18.00	8.50
65	A31	$2 bl & red brn (R)	40.00	12.00
66	A31	$5 red & slate (R)	95.00	19.00
67	A31	$10 grn & claret (R)	300.00	170.00
68	A31	$20 plum & bl (R)	425.00	325.00
		Nos. 47-68 (22)	990.65	635.30

See #69, 114. For overprints see #C1-C3.

Same Overprint on China No. 275

1926

No.	Type	Description	Unused	Used
69	A29	4c olive green	8.00	5.50

Chang Tso-lin Stamps of China, 1928, Overprinted in Red or Blue

1928 *Perf. 14*

No.	Type	Description	Unused	Used
70	A34	1c brn org (R)	1.75	1.75
71	A34	4c ol grn (R)	2.75	2.75
72	A34	10c dull bl (R)	6.50	6.50
73	A34	$1 red (Bl)	55.00	55.00
		Nos. 70-73 (4)	66.00	66.00

Unification Issue of China, 1929, Overprinted in Red as in 1928

1929

No.	Type	Description	Unused	Used
74	A35	1c brown org	2.75	2.75
75	A35	4c olive grn	4.75	4.75
76	A35	10c dk blue	11.50	11.50
77	A35	$1 dk red	90.00	90.00
		Nos. 74-77 (4)	109.00	109.00

Similar Overprint in Black on Sun Yat-sen Mausoleum Issue of China Characters 15mm apart

1929 *Perf. 14*

No.	Type	Description	Unused	Used
78	A36	1c brown org	2.25	2.25
79	A36	4c olive grn	3.50	*3.50*
80	A36	10c dark blue	8.00	*8.00*
81	A36	$1 dark red	95.00	95.00
		Nos. 78-81 (4)	108.75	108.75

Stamps of Sun Yat-sen Issue of 1931-37 Overprinted

1932 **Type I** *Perf. 12½*

No.	Type	Description	Unused	Used
82	A37	1c orange	1.75	*4.00*
83	A37	2c olive grn	4.25	*5.75*
84	A37	4c green	2.50	*6.50*
85	A37	20c ultra	4.00	*8.25*
86	A37	$1 org brn & dk brn	12.00	*20.00*
87	A37	$2 bl & org brn	35.00	*42.50*
88	A37	$5 dl red & blk	40.00	*60.00*
		Nos. 82-88 (7)	99.50	*147.00*

No. 83 was overprinted in Shanghai in 1938. The overprint differs in minor details.

1932-38 **Type II**

No.	Type	Description	Unused	Used
89	A37	2c olive grn	.45	*2.00*
90	A37	4c green	1.25	*4.00*
91	A37	5c green	.80	*4.00*
92	A37	15c dk green	1.10	*4.00*
93	A37	15c scar ('34)	1.10	*4.00*
93A	A37	20c ultra ('38)	.80	*2.75*
94	A37	25c ultra	1.25	*4.00*
95	A37	$1 org brn & dk brn	9.50	*11.00*
96	A37	$2 bl & org brn	20.00	*32.50*
97	A37	$5 dl red & blk	40.00	*65.00*
		Nos. 89-97 (10)	76.25	*133.25*

Nos. 89, 90 and 94 were overprinted in London, Peking and Shanghai. Nos. 92, 95-97 exist with London and Peking overprints. Nos. 91 and 93 exist with Peking and Shanghai overprints. No. 93A is a Shanghai overprint. The overprints differ in minor details.

Tan Yuan-chang Issue of China, 1933, Overprinted as in 1928

1933 *Perf. 14*

98	A49	2c olive grn	3.75	3.75
99	A49	5c green	4.75	4.75
100	A49	25c ultra	15.00	15.00
101	A49	$1 red	75.00	95.00
		Nos. 98-101 (4)	98.50	118.50

Stamps of China Martyrs Issue of 1932-34 Overprinted

1933-34

102	A39	½c black brown	.25	*3.50*
103	A40	1c orange	1.10	*4.25*
104	A39	2½c rose lilac	.25	*3.25*
105	A48	3c deep brown	.25	*3.25*
106	A45	8c brown orange	.75	*3.50*
107	A46	10c dull violet	.25	*3.25*
108	A45	13c blue green	.25	*4.50*
109	A46	17c brown olive	.25	*2.50*
110	A47	20c brown red	1.10	*6.50*
111	A48	30c brown violet	.40	*4.50*
112	A47	40c orange	.60	*3.25*
113	A40	50c green	.70	*2.50*
		Nos. 102-113 (12)	6.15	*44.75*

Nos. 102-113 were originally overprinted in Peking. In 1938, Nos. 103-105, 108-112 were overprinted in Shanghai. The two overprints differ in minor details. No. 105, Shanghai overprint, is scarce. Value $35.

China No. 324 Overprinted as in 1916-19

1936 *Perf. 14*

114	A29	6c brown	20.00	*25.00*

Stamps of China, 1939-40 Overprinted in Black Type III

1940-45 **Unwmk.** *Perf. 12½*

115	A57	2c olive green	.85	*3.00*
116	A57	3c dull claret ('41)	.25	*3.00*
117	A57	5c green	.25	*3.00*
118	A57	5c olive green	.25	*3.00*
119	A57	8c olive green ('41)	.25	*3.00*
120	A57	10c green ('41)	.25	*3.00*
121	A57	15c scarlet	.55	*4.00*
122	A57	16c olive gray ('41)	.40	*3.00*
123	A57	25c dark blue	.55	*5.00*
124	A57	$1 hn & dk brn (type II)	6.25	*11.00*
125	A57	$2 dp bl & org brn (type I)	4.50	*11.00*
126	A57	$5 red & grnsh blk	26.00	*32.50*
		Nos. 115-126 (12)	40.35	*84.50*

Perf. 14

With Secret Marks

127	A57	8c ol grn (#383a)	1.10	*3.00*
a.		On #383	19.00	*22.50*
128	A57	10c green ('41)	10.00	*15.00*
129	A57	30c scarlet ('45)	.30	*3.00*
130	A57	50c dk blue ('45)	.55	*3.50*
131	A57	$1 org brn & sep	.55	*4.00*
132	A57	$2 dp bl & org brn	.55	*4.00*
133	A57	$5 red & sl grn	.65	*6.00*
134	A57	$10 dk grn & dl pur	1.90	*5.00*
135	A57	$20 rose lake & dk bl	3.50	*8.00*
		Nos. 127-135 (9)	19.10	*51.50*

Wmk. Character Yu (Post) (261)

Perf. 14

136	A57	5c olive green	.30	*2.50*
137	A57	10c green	.35	*3.75*
138	A57	30c scarlet	.35	*5.00*
139	A57	50c dark blue	.45	*2.50*
		Nos. 136-139 (4)	1.45	*13.75*

Martyrs Issue, 1940-41, Overprinted in Black

Perf. 12, 12½, 13, 13x12, 13½x13

1941-45 **Wmk. 261**

140	A40	1c orange	.35	*2.40*
141	A39	2½c rose lilac	.35	*4.50*
142	A45	8c dp org ('45)	5.75	12.00
143	A46	10c dull vio	.45	*3.00*
144	A45	13c dp yel grn	1.00	*5.50*
145	A46	17c brown olive	1.00	*5.25*
146	A40	25c red vio ('45)	2.00	*7.25*
147	A47	40c orange ('45)	3.50	*9.25*
		Nos. 140-147 (8)	14.40	*49.15*

Unwmk.

148	A39	½c olive blk	.35	*3.25*
149	A40	1c orange ('45)	.35	*2.40*
150	A46	2c dp blue ('45)	3.25	*3.75*
151	A48	3c dp yel brn	.35	*4.50*
152	A39	4c pale vio ('45)	.35	*4.50*
153	A45	8c dp orange	.35	*5.50*
154	A45	13c dp yel grn ('45)	.65	*4.00*
155	A48	15c brn car ('45)	.35	*4.00*
156	A46	17c brn ol ('45)	1.00	*4.50*
157	A47	20c lt blue ('45)	.35	*3.25*
158	A45	21c ol brn ('45)	1.25	*4.50*
159	A46	28c olive ('45)	1.45	*5.50*
160	A47	40c orange ('45)	3.00	*14.00*
161	A40	50c green ('45)	2.00	*7.00*
		Nos. 148-161 (14)	15.05	*70.65*

Stamps of China, 1942-43 Overprinted in Carmine, Black or Red

1944 **Without Gum** *Perf. 12½, 13*

162	A62	10c dp grn (C)	1.75	*7.75*
163	A62	20c dk ol grn (C)	2.00	*7.75*
164	A62	25c violet brn	.30	*8.50*
165	A62	30c dk orange	.95	*9.00*
166	A62	40c red brown	.30	*8.50*
167	A62	50c sage green	.30	*5.00*
a.		Perf. 11	16.00	24.00
168	A62	$1 rose lake	3.75	5.00
169	A62	$1 dull green	.30	*8.50*
170	A62	$1.50 dp bl (C)	.30	*9.50*
171	A62	$2 dk bl grn (R)	2.40	*7.00*
172	A62	$3 yellow	.30	*12.00*
173	A62	$5 cerise	2.40	*11.00*
		Nos. 162-173 (12)	15.05	*99.50*

For surcharges see Nos. 194-195.

Same Overprint on Stamps of China, 1942-43, in Black

1944-46 ***Imperf.***

174	A57	$10 red brown	140.00	125.00
175	A57	$20 rose red	6.75	*17.00*
176	A57	$30 dull vio	5.00	*17.00*
177	A57	$40 rose red	5.00	*17.00*
178	A57	$50 blue ('46)	1,080.	*1,170.*
179	A57	$100 orange brn	14.50	*22.50*

Perf. 13½

180	A57	$4 dp blue	2.00	*13.50*
181	A57	$5 lilac gray	3.50	*13.50*
182	A57	$10 red brn	3.50	*13.50*
183	A57	$20 blue grn	2.00	*15.00*
184	A57	$20 rose red	140.00	140.00
185	A57	$30 dull vio	4.00	*17.00*
186	A57	$40 rose	4.00	*16.00*
187	A57	$50 blue	4.50	*17.00*
188	A57	$100 orange brn	160.00	140.00
		Nos. 174-177,179-188 (14)	494.75	584.00

Beware of trimmed examples of Nos. 182 and 187 offered as Nos. 174 and 178.

Nos. 162 and 164 Surcharged in Black

1944, Aug. 1

194	A62	12c on 10c dp grn	9.00	*27.50*
195	A62	24c on 25c brn vio	9.00	*27.50*

Stamps of China, 1940-41, Overprinted in Black at Chengtu, Szechwan

1943

196	A57	10c green (#354)	25.00	*45.00*
197	A47	20c lt blue (#433)	25.00	*45.00*

Wmk. 261 *Perf. 14*

198	A57	50c dk blue (#396)	25.00	*30.00*

China Nos. 565 and 567 Overprinted in Black

1945 **Unwmk.** *Perf. 12½*

200	A63	40c brown red	.45	20.00
201	A63	$3 red	.45	18.00

China Nos. 640-642, 788, 751, 753 Surcharged in Black or Red

1949 **Engr.** *Perf. 14*

202	A73	1c on $100 dk car	29.00	*35.00*
203	A73	3c on $200 ol grn (R)	29.00	*35.00*
204	A73	5c on $500 brt bl grn (R)	29.00	*35.00*
205	A82	10c on $20,000 rose pink	25.00	*30.00*
206	A82	50c on $4000 gray (R)	100.00	100.00
207	A82	$1 on $6000 rose lil	110.00	110.00
		Nos. 202-207 (6)	322.00	*345.00*

AIR POST STAMPS

Sinkiang Nos. 53, 57, 59, 32 Overprinted in Red

1932-33 **Unwmk.** *Perf. 14*

C1	A29	5c claret ('33)	400.00	290.00
C2	A29	10c dark blue ('33)	400.00	225.00
C3	A30	15c deep blue	2,700.	775.00
C4	A25	30c brown violet	1,170.	990.00

Counterfeits exist of Nos. C1-C4.

Air Post Stamps of China, 1932-37 Handstamped in Dull Red

1942

C5	AP3	15c gray green	7.25	*9.00*
C6	AP3	25c orange	425.00	375.00
C7	AP3	30c red	15.50	*27.50*
C8	AP3	45c brown vio	11.00	*18.00*
C9	AP3	50c dk brown	45.00	*50.00*
C10	AP3	60c dk blue	11.00	*21.00*
C11	AP3	90c olive grn	57.50	*80.00*
C12	AP3	$1 yellow grn	12.00	*20.00*
		Nos. C5-C12 (8)	584.25	*600.50*

Same Handstamped Overprint on Air Post Stamps of China, 1940-41 in Dull Red

1942 **Wmk. 261** *Perf. 12½, 13, 13½*

C13	AP3	15c gray green	6.75	*15.00*
C14	AP3	25c yellow orange	6.75	*17.00*

1942 **Unwmk.**

C15	AP3	25c light orange	6.75	13.50
C16	AP3	30c light red	6.75	13.50
C17	AP3	50c brown	9.00	15.00
C18	AP3	$2 light brown	42.50	42.50
C19	AP3	$5 lake	42.50	42.50
		Nos. C15-C19 (5)	107.50	127.00

Twelve values exist with this overprint in black. Their status has not been determined. Inverted overprints exist in both red and black.

Official Perforated Characters

For use on official mail, various Sinkiang stamps were perforated with an arrangement of four Chinese characters ("For Official Business Only"). These include Nos. 1-38, 47-69, 114.

OFFICES IN TIBET

12 Pies = 1 Anna
16 Annas = 1 Rupee

Stamps of China, Issues of 1902-10, Surcharged

1911 **Unwmk.** *Perf. 12 to 16*

1	A17	3p on 1c ocher	27.50	*45.00*
a.		Inverted surcharge	*3,500.*	
2	A17	½a on 2c grn	27.50	*45.00*
3	A17	1a on 4c ver	27.50	*45.00*
4	A17	2a on 7c mar	27.50	*45.00*
5	A17	2½a on 10c ultra	35.00	*55.00*
6	A18	3a on 16c ol grn	70.00	*80.00*
a.		Large "S" in "Annas"	*1,250.*	
7	A18	4a on 20c red brn	70.00	*80.00*
8	A18	6a on 30c rose red	125.00	*140.00*
9	A18	12a on 50c yel grn	325.00	*400.00*
10	A19	1r on $1 red & pale rose	900.00	*900.00*
11	A19	2r on $2 red & yel	1,620.	*1,800.*
		Nos. 1-11 (11)	3,255.	3,635.

Beware of fake overprints.

PEOPLE'S REPUBLIC OF CHINA

ˈpē-pəls ri-ˈpə-blik of ˈchī-nə

LOCATION — Eastern Asia
GOVT. — Communist Republic
POP. — 1,339,724,852 (2010 est.)
CAPITAL — Beijing (Peking)

The communists completed their conquest of all mainland China in 1949. They established the Central Government and General Postal Administration in Peking. They ordered all but two regions to stop selling regional issues by June 30, 1950, extending validity one year from that date. The Northeast and Port Arthur-Dairen regions were exempted because their currency had a different value. These two regions stopped using separate issues at the end of 1950. Thereafter unified issues were used throughout mainland China.

On July 1, 1997 Hong Kong returned to Chinese control as an administrative district. Hong Kong stamps issued under Chinese rule will continue to be listed under "Hong Kong."

Reprints

After currency revaluation Mar. 1, 1955, reprints were prepared and put on sale by the Philatelic Agency in order to supply stocks of exhausted issues for collectors. Minor differences in design or paper distinguish the reprints. They are of commemorative and special issues up to the gymnastics set of 1952. Reprints are less expensive. Values are for original issues. Reprint distinctions are footnoted.

Used Stamps

Most used stamps before 1970 exist primarily canceled to order. Postally used stamps generally sell for ½ the unused value.

Beginning in 1987 the PRC stopped furnishing quantities of used stamps to the philatelic market. When available, used stamps of these issues sell for the same or more than unused stamps.

China Post Issue Numbers

Commemorative issues, beginning in 1949, and special issues, beginning in 1951, bear 4 numbers in lower margin: 1. Issue number. 2. Total of stamps in set. 3. Position of stamp in set. 4. Cumulative number of stamp (usually in parenthesis). A fifth number, the year of issue, was added in 1952.

The numbering system varies at times, and changed in 1992 to listing the year of issue followed by the set number on the right hand lower margin. Stamps with the "R" prefix do not have serial numbers on them.

We have listed the China Post issue number on all sets to 1992. In certain sets listings include parenthetically the position-in-set number. During some periods these parentheses in listings hold the stamp's cumulative number.

Gum

All stamps to the beginning of 1960 were issued without gum, except as noted. After that date, most stamps have gum, which is translucent and almost invisible. Catalogue values are for stamps with fresh, untoned paper and gum. Stamps with toned paper or gum sell for approximately 20% to 50% less. All issues are unwatermarked, unless otherwise noted.

100 fen = 1 yuan ($)

Catalogue values for unused stamps in this country are for Never Hinged items, beginning with Scott 487 in the regular postage section, Scott B1 in the semi-postal section.

Lantern and Gate of Heavenly Peace — A1

Original Reprint

Reprints have altered ornament on lantern base. On originals, it is a full oval; on reprints, only a partial circle. Value, set: unused $11; used $3.

China Post No. C1

1949, Oct. 8 Litho. *Perf. 12½*

No.	Type	Description	Unused	Used
1	A1	$30 blue	7.25	5.50
2	A1	$50 rose red	8.25	5.50
3	A1	$100 green	12.00	6.00
4	A1	$200 maroon	12.00	6.00
		Nos. 1-4 (4)	39.50	23.00

1st session of Chinese People's Consultative Political Conference. See Nos. 1L121-1L124.

Globe and Hand Holding Hammer — A2

Original Reprint

Reprints show heavier shading on index finger and thumb. Value, set $6.50 unused or $3.50 used.

China Post No. C3

1949, Nov. 16

No.	Type	Description	Unused	Used
5	A2	$100 carmine	14.50	10.00
6	A2	$300 slate green	14.50	10.00
7	A2	$500 dark blue	42.50	10.00
		Nos. 5-7 (3)	71.50	30.00

Asiatic and Australasian Congress of the World Federation of Trade Unions, Peking.
The $100, imperf., is of dubious status.
See Nos. 1L133-1L135.

Conference Hall, Peking — A3

Mao Tse-tung on Rostrum A4

Original Reprint

Nos. 8-9: First character in top inscription shows a square, reprints an oblong.

Nos. 10-11: Originals have heavy cross-hatching and lines which touch back of head and top of rostrum. Reprints have lighter lines which do not touch head or top of rostrum. Reprints, value set $19 unused, $8 used.

China Post No. C2

1950, Feb. 1 Engr. *Perf. 14*

No.	Type	Description	Unused	Used
8	A3	$50 red	12.50	8.00
9	A3	$100 blue	12.50	8.00
10	A4	$300 red brown	13.50	9.50
11	A4	$500 green	21.00	16.00
		Nos. 8-11 (4)	59.50	41.50

Chinese People's Consultative Political Conference. See Nos. 1L136-1L139.

Gate of Heavenly Peace (actual size) — A5

China Post No. R1

First Issue: Top line of shading broken at right.

1950, Feb. 10 Litho. *Perf. 12½*

No.	Type	Description	Unused	Used
12	A5	$200 green	13.00	6.50
13	A5	$300 brown red	1.00	*1.00*
14	A5	$500 red	1.00	1.00
15	A5	$800 orange	12.00	1.00
16	A5	$1000 dull violet	5.00	1.00
17	A5	$2000 olive	18.00	3.00
18	A5	$5000 brt pink	2.00	*2.75*
19	A5	$8000 blue	1.00	*9.00*
20	A5	$10,000 brown	1.25	*9.00*
		Nos. 12-20 (9)	54.25	*34.25*

China Post No. R2

1950, June 9 Typo.

Second Issue: Top line of shading extends to frame line at right.

No.	Type	Description	Unused	Used
21	A5	$1000 dull violet	2.25	2.10
22	A5	$3000 red brown	1.75	1.75
23	A5	$10,000 brown	1.00	*2.50*
		Nos. 21-23 (3)	5.00	*6.35*

Other Gate of Heavenly Peace issues are illustrated where they are listed. See A10, A13, A14 and A42 for similar designs.

For similar types with Chinese characters in upper right corner see Northeast China A28, A29, Port Arthur & Darien A11, North China A8.

As part of the second issue, a $4,000 value in deep blue was prepared by not issued. Value, $8,250.

China Nos. 959, C62, E12, F2 Surcharged in Blue, Black, Green or Red

China Post Nos. SC1 and SC4

Rouletted, Perf. 12½ (#27, 29)

1950, Mar. Litho.

No.	Type	Description	Unused	Used
24	SD2	$100 on red vio (Bl)	1.50	*8.50*
a.		Perf. 12½	12.50	6.50
25	R2	$200 on red (Bk)	7.50	8.00
a.		Perf. 12½	60.00	3.25
26	AP5	$300 on bl grn (Bk)	1.40	*3.25*
a.		Perf. 12½	1.60	1.10
27	A96	$500 on org (Gr)	1.00	.60
a.		Perf. 14	80.00	67.50
28	A96	$800 on org (R)	8.50	1.00
a.		Perf. 12½	30.00	5.50
b.		Perf. 14	*850.00*	90.00
29	A96	$1000 on org (Bk)	1.00	.70
a.		Perf. 14	27.50	3.00
		Nos. 24-29 (6)	20.90	22.05

In Nos. 24-29 the rouletted stamps are China Post No. SC4, the perforated stamps are China Post No. SC1.

Harvesters with Ox — A6

China Post No. SC2

1950, May

No.	Type	Description	Unused	Used
30	A6	$20,000 on $10,000 red	*790.00*	130.00

No. 30 is surcharged on an unissued stamp of East China. Value, without surcharge (unissued) *$1,500.*

Flag, Mao Tse-tung, Gate of Heavenly Peace — A7

Original Reprint

Originals have a single curved line in jacket button, reprints have an extra dot in button. Value, set unused $32.50 used $11.50.

China Post No. C4

1950, July 1 *Perf. 14*

Yellow Stars

No.	Type	Description	Unused	Used
31	A7	$800 green & red	55.00	17.50
32	A7	$1000 brn & red	80.00	22.50
33	A7	$2000 dk brn & red	95.00	24.00
34	A7	$3000 dk blue & red	140.00	35.00
		Nos. 31-34 (4)	370.00	99.00

Inauguration of the People's Republic, Oct. 1, 1949. See Nos. 1L150-1L153.

Sun Yat-sen Stamps of Northeastern Provinces Surcharged in Red, Black or Blue

China Post No. SC3

1950, July 1 Engr.

No.	Type	Description	Unused	Used
35	A2	$50 on 20c yel grn	8.00	*8.00*
36	A2	$50 on 25c blk brn	5.00	5.50
37	A2	$50 on 50c red org (Bk)	1.75	*2.25*
38	A2	$100 on $2.50 ind	1.40	*2.00*
39	A2	$100 on $3 brn (Bk)	2.25	*4.25*
40	A2	$100 on $4 org brn, Type II (Bl)	4.75	*7.00*
a.		Type I	*450.00*	*225.00*
41	A2	$100 on $5 dk grn (Bk)	7.00	6.00
42	A2	$100 on $10 crim, Type II (Bl)	23.00	12.00
a.		Type I	*2,250.*	—
43	A2	$400 on $20 ol, Type II (Bl)	87.50	87.50
a.		Type I	*800.00*	*275.00*
44	A2	$400 on $44 dk car rose (Bl)	2.75	*5.50*
45	A2	$400 on $65 dl grn	140.00	100.00
46	A2	$400 on $100 dp grn	22.00	15.00
47	A2	$400 on $200 rose brn (Bk)	47.50	22.00
48	A2	$400 on $300 bluish grn	60.00	26.00
		Nos. 35-48 (14)	412.90	303.00

Flying Geese Type of China Surcharged in Red, Blue, Green, Brown or Black

China Post No. SC5

1950, Aug. 1 *Perf. 12½, Imperf.*

No.	Type	Description	Unused	Used
49	A97	$50 on 10c dk bl (R)	.40	1.00
50	A97	$100 on 16c ol, imperf. (Bl)	.45	1.00
51	A97	$100 on 50c dl grn, imperf. (Bl)	.45	1.00
52	A97	$200 on $1 org (G)	.60	1.00
53	A97	$200 on $2 bl (Br)	5.00	4.00
54	A97	$400 on $5 car rose (Bk)	1.00	2.00
55	A97	$400 on $10 bl grn (Bk)	2.50	*5.00*
56	A97	$400 on $20 pur (Bk)	3.00	*6.50*
		Nos. 49-56 (8)	13.40	21.50

Dove of Peace, by Picasso — A8

China Post No. C5

1950, Aug. 1 **Engr.** ***Perf. 14***

57	A8	$400	brown	30.00	8.50
58	A8	$800	green	32.50	10.00
59	A8	$2000	blue	50.00	15.00
		Nos. 57-59 (3)		112.50	33.50

World Peace Campaign. See Nos. 1L154-1L156.

Paper of originals appears bright under ultraviolet lamp. That of reprints looks dull. Value, set unused $7.50 used $3.25.

Chinese Flag and "1" — A9

$800

Original Reprint

Reprints are a brighter red, leaves beside "1" are gray brown instead of reddish brown. On the large format stamp, the arrangement of dots in background differs in relationship to large star: in the originals the dots run about parellel to the bottom edge of the upper right point of the large star, in the reprints the dots run in lines almost parellel to the left edge of the top point of the large star. Value, set unused $20 used $9.

China Post No. C6

1950 **Engr. & Litho.**

Flag in Red & Yellow

60	A9	$100	purple	35.00	18.00
61	A9	$400	red brown	37.50	20.00
62	A9	$800	green	55.00	17.50
63	A9	$1000	lt olive	80.00	30.00
64	A9	$2000	blue	120.00	45.00
		Nos. 60-64 (5)		327.50	130.50

1st anniv. of the Chinese People's Republic. Size of $800: 38x46mm; others 26x32mm.

Issue dates: No. 62, Oct. 1; others Oct. 31. See Nos. 1L157-1L161.

Gate of Heavenly Peace (actual size) — A10

China Post No. R3

Third Issue: Cloud almost touches character at upper left. Cloud breaks inner frame line at top.

1950 **Litho.**

65	A10	$100	lt grnsh bl	45.00	22.00
66	A10	$200	green	325.00	16.00
67	A10	$300	dk carmine	2.25	*4.25*
68	A10	$400	grnsh gray	8.25	*4.50*
69	A10	$500	carmine	2.00	*2.75*
70	A10	$800	orange	8.25	1.90
71	A10	$2000	gray olive	3.25	3.25
		Nos. 65-71 (7)		394.00	*54.65*

Issued: $800, 10/8; $500, $2000, 12/1; others, 10/6.

"Communication" and Map of China — A11

Original

Reprint

Originals have 3 lines below horizontal bar (2nd character); reprints have four. Value, set unused $3.50, used $1.50.

China Post No. C7

1950, Nov. 1 **Litho.**

72	A11	$400	green & brn	37.50	15.00
73	A11	$800	carmine & grn	40.00	13.00

First All-China Postal Conference, Peking. See Nos. 1L162-1L163.

Stalin and Mao Tse-tung — A12

China Post No. C8

1950, Dec. 1 **Engr.** ***Perf. 14***

74	A12	$400	red	22.50	15.00
75	A12	$800	dp green	22.50	16.00
76	A12	$2000	dk blue	37.50	22.50
		Nos. 74-76 (3)		82.50	53.50

Signing of Sino-Soviet Treaty of Friendship, Alliance and Mutual Assistance. See Nos. 1L176-1L178.

Paper of originals appears bright under ultraviolet lamp. That of reprints looks dull. Value, set unused $18.50, used $7.

East China Issue of 1949 Surcharged in Red, Black, Brown or Blue

Train and Postal Runner — A12a

China Post No. SC7

1950, Dec. **Litho.** ***Perf. 12½***

77	A12a	$50 on $10 dp ultra (R)		.65	1.10
78	A12a	$100 on $15 org ver (Bk)		.65	1.10
a.		$100 on $15 red (Bk), perf. 14		3.00	3.00
79	A12a	$300 on $50 car (Bk)		.70	3.00
80	A12a	$400 on $1600 vio bl (Br)		2.00	2.25
81	A12a	$400 on $2000 brn vio (Bl)		1.00	1.25
		Nos. 77-81 (5)		5.00	8.70

East China Issue of 1949 Surcharged in Red or Black

Chairman Mao — A12b

China Post No. SC6

1950, Dec.

82	A12b	$50 on $10 ultra (R)	.90	.70
83	A12b	$400 on $15 ver (Bk)	1.00	.90
84	A12b	$400 on $2000 grn (Bk)	3.00	3.00
		Nos. 82-84 (3)	4.90	4.60

(actual size) — A13

China Post No. R4

Fourth Issue: Similar to 3rd issue, but large cloud does not break inner frame line at top.

1950-51 **Litho.**

85	A13	$100	lt blue	1.00	*2.00*
86	A13	$200	dull green	14.00	4.50
87	A13	$300	dull lilac	.75	*5.00*
88	A13	$400	gray grn	8.50	1.75
89	A13	$500	carmine	.85	1.75
90	A13	$800	orange	80.00	3.00
a.		Imperf., pair		*725.00*	
91	A13	$1000	violet	1.50	*2.75*
92	A13	$2000	olive	300.00	7.50
93	A13	$3000	brown	1.00	*3.50*
94	A13	$5000	pink	1.00	*5.50*
		Nos. 85-94 (10)		408.60	*37.25*

Issued: $200, $300, $500, $800, $2000, $5000, 12/22/50; others 6/8/51.

(actual size) — A14

China Post No. R5

Fifth Issue: Colored network on surface in salmon.

1951, Jan. 18 **Engr.** ***Perf. 14***

95	A14	$10,000	brown	2.50	*35.00*
96	A14	$20,000	olive	4.00	*15.00*
97	A14	$30,000	green	175.00	*110.00*
98	A14	$50,000	violet	275.00	80.00
99	A14	$100,000	scar	3,000.	425.00
100	A14	$200,000	blue	3,500.	800.00
		Nos. 95-100 (6)		6,957.	1,465.

Unit Issue of China Surcharged

China Post No. SC8

1951, May 2 **Litho.** ***Perf. 12½***

101	SD2	$5	on rose lilac	3.00	*3.25*
102	AP5	$10	on brt grn	2.00	*2.25*
103	R2	$15	on red	1.00	*1.00*
104	A96	$25	on orange	1.00	*1.00*
		Nos. 101-104 (4)		7.00	7.50

Issued for use in Northeast China, but available for use throughout China. Nos. 101-104 rouletted (China Post No. SC9) were sold for philatelic purposes only. Value, set unused $8, used $7.

Chairman Mao Tse-tung — A15

China Post No. C9

1951, July 1 **Engr.** ***Perf. 14***

105	A15	$400	chestnut	11.00	7.50
106	A15	$500	deep green	14.00	7.00
107	A15	$800	crimson	16.00	6.00
		Nos. 105-107 (3)		41.00	20.50

Chinese Communist Party, 30th anniv.

Reprints are on whiter, thinner and harder paper. Value, set unused $20, used $8.

Picasso Dove — A16

China Post No. C10

1951, Aug. 15 ***Perf. 12½***

108	A16	$400	orange brn	24.00	19.00
109	A16	$800	blue grn	22.50	12.00
110	A16	$1000	dull vio	31.00	19.00
		Nos. 108-110 (3)		77.50	50.00

Reprints are perf 14. Value, set unused $32.50, used $11.

Remittance Stamp of China Surcharged in Carmine or Black

(same size) — A17

China Post No. SC10

Engraved, Commercial Press

1951, Sept. ***Perf. 12, 12½, 13***

111 A17 $50 on $2 bl grn (C) 1.00 *2.00*

Rouletted 9½

Typo., Kang Hwa Printing Co.

112 A17 $50 on $2 gray bl (C) 3.75 *4.50*
113 A17 $50 on $5 red org (Bk) 1.00 *2.50*
114 A17 $50 on $50 gray (C) 6.00 *7.50*

Perf. 13

Lithographed, Central Trust Co.

115 A17 $50 on $50 gray blk (C) .75 *1.00*

Perf. 10x11½, 11½x9½, 11½x10

Lithographed, Chung Hwa Book Co.

116 A17 $50 on $50 gray (C) 3.50 6.00
a. Perf. 11½ 2.50 2.50
Nos. 111-116 (6) 16.00 *23.50*

National Emblem — A18

China Post No. S1

Engraved; Background Network Lithographed in Yellow

1951, Oct. 1 ***Perf. 14***

117 A18 $100 Prus blue 19.00 6.50
118 A18 $200 brown 13.00 6.00
119 A18 $400 orange 12.00 6.00
120 A18 $500 green 14.00 8.00
121 A18 $800 carmine 16.00 6.50
Nos. 117-121 (5) 74.00 33.00

Reprints exist but are difficult to distinguish; paper whiter, and colors slightly brighter. Value, set unused $18 or used $5.

Rough Perfs

Rough perforations are normal on many early issues. These include Nos. 122-123, 136-140, 155-176, 239-240, 299-300, 453-456, 467-482, 629-634, 684-707, 737-745 and probably others.

Lu Hsun and Quotation A19

Original

Reprint

Reprints have dot in triangle at lower right; no dot in original. Value, set unused $5, used $2.25.

China Post No. C11

1951, Oct. 19 **Litho.** ***Perf. 12½***

122 A19 $400 lilac 11.00 6.50
123 A19 $800 green 20.00 10.00

15th anniversary of the death of Lu Hsun (1881-1936), writer.

Peasant Uprising, Chintien — A20

Design: Nos. 126-127, Coin of Taiping Regime and decrees of peasant government.

Original

Reprint

Reprints of Nos. 124-125 have additional short stroke at upper left.

Original

Reprint

Reprints of Nos. 126-127 have two short strokes on scale near tail of right dragon on coin. Value, Nos. 124-127 unused $8.50, used $3.75.

China Post No. C12

1951, Dec. 15 **Engr.** ***Perf. 14***

124 A20 $400 green 19.00 12.00
125 A20 $800 scarlet 13.00 10.00
126 A20 $800 orange 13.00 10.00
127 A20 $1000 deep blue 22.00 10.50
Nos. 124-127 (4) 67.00 42.50

Centenary of Taiping Peasant Rebellion.

Old and New Methods of Agriculture — A21

Original

Reprint

One short horizontal line between legs of plower; 2 lines in reprints. Value, set unused $8.50, used $3.50.

China Post No. S2

1952, Jan. 1

128 A21 $100 scarlet 11.00 7.00
129 A21 $200 bright blue 11.00 7.00
130 A21 $400 deep brown 12.00 8.00
131 A21 $800 green 14.00 8.00
Nos. 128-131 (4) 48.00 30.00

Agrarian reform.

Potala Monastery, Lhasa — A22

China Post No. C13

Nos. 134-135, Farmer plowing with yaks.

1952, Mar. 15 ***Perf. 12½***

132 A22 $400 vermilion 17.50 10.00
133 A22 $800 claret 15.00 7.50
134 A22 $800 blue grn 15.00 7.50
135 A22 $1000 dull vio 17.50 10.00
Nos. 132-135 (4) 65.00 35.00

Liberation of Tibet.

Reprints, perf 14, have a small Chinese character at lower left of the vignette which is missing in the original. Value, set unused $16, used $7.

Some reprints of No. 132 are perf 14x14½. Value, $200.

Children of Four Races — A23

China Post No. C14

1952, Apr. 12 **Litho.**

136 A23 $400 dull grn 1.50 .40
137 A23 $800 vio blue 1.75 .55

Intl. Child Protection Conf., Vienna.

Hammer and Sickle on Numeral 1 — A24

China Post No. C15

Labor Day: No. 139, Dove rising from worker's hand. No. 140, Dove, hammer, wheat & chimneys.

1952, May 1

138 A24 $800 scarlet 2.00 .45
139 A24 $800 blue grn 2.00 .45
140 A24 $800 orange brn 2.00 .45
Nos. 138-140 (3) 6.00 1.35

Physical Exercises — A25

China Post No. S4

Stamps printed in blocks of four for each color, each block representing a specific setting-up exercise; exercises coincided with a national radio program. Where exercise positions are identical within the block, the serial number in the LL margin of each stamp (and in parenthesis in the listings below) is the only means of differentiation.

1952, June 20

141 A25 Block of 4 140.00 100.00
a. $400 vermilion 8.50 6.00
b. $400 vermilion 8.50 6.00
c. $400 vermilion 8.50 6.00
d. $400 vermilion 8.50 6.00
142 A25 Block of 4 140.00 100.00
a. $400 blue 8.50 6.00
b. $400 blue 8.50 6.00
c. $400 blue 8.50 6.00
d. $400 blue 8.50 6.00
143 A25 Block of 4 140.00 100.00
a. $400 brown red 8.50 6.00
b. $400 brown red 8.50 6.00
c. $400 brown red 8.50 6.00
d. $400 brown red 8.50 6.00
144 A25 Block of 4 140.00 100.00
a. $400 yellow green 8.50 6.00
b. $400 yellow green 8.50 6.00
c. $400 yellow green 8.50 6.00
d. $400 yellow green 8.50 6.00
145 A25 Block of 4 140.00 100.00
a. $400 red orange 8.50 6.00
b. $400 red orange 8.50 6.00
c. $400 red orange 8.50 6.00
d. $400 red orange 8.50 6.00
146 A25 Block of 4 140.00 100.00
a. $400 dull blue 8.50 6.00
b. $400 dull blue 8.50 6.00
c. $400 dull blue 8.50 6.00
d. $400 dull blue 8.50 6.00
147 A25 Block of 4 140.00 100.00
a. $400 orange 8.50 6.00
b. $400 orange 8.50 6.00
c. $400 orange 8.50 6.00
d. $400 orange 8.50 6.00
148 A25 Block of 4 140.00 100.00
a. $400 dull purple 8.50 6.00
b. $400 dull purple 8.50 6.00
c. $400 dull purple 8.50 6.00
d. $400 dull purple 8.50 6.00
149 A25 Block of 4 140.00 100.00
a. $400 yellow bister 8.50 6.00
b. $400 yellow bister 8.50 6.00
c. $400 yellow bister 8.50 6.00
d. $400 yellow bister 8.50 6.00
150 A25 Block of 4 140.00 100.00
a. $400 sky blue 8.50 6.00
b. $400 sky blue 8.50 6.00
c. $400 sky blue 8.50 6.00
d. $400 sky blue 8.50 6.00
Nos. 141-150 (10) 1,400. 1,000.

Originals are on thin gray paper, colors darker. Reprints on thicker white paper, colors brighter. Value, set of blocks unused $55, used $37.50.

Hunting, Wei Dynasty, A.D. 386-580 A26

China Post No. S3

Designs from Murals in Cave Temples at Tunhuang, Kansu Province: No. 152, Lady attendants, Sui Dynasty, 581-617 A.D. No. 153, Gandharvas (mythology), Tang Dynasty, 618-906. No. 154, Dragon, Tang Dynasty.

1952, July 1 **Engr.**

151 A26 $800 slate green 2.00 .65
152 A26 $800 chocolate 2.00 .65
a. Vert. pair, imperf. between 500.00
153 A26 $800 indigo 2.00 .65
154 A26 $800 dk vio 2.00 .65
Nos. 151-154 (4) 8.00 2.60

"Glorious Mother Country," 1st series.

Marco Polo Bridge, near Peking A27

China Post No. C16

Designs: No. 156, Cavalry passing through Great Wall. No. 157, Departure of New Fourth Army. No. 158, Mao Tse-tung and Gen. Chu Teh planning counter-attack.

1952, July 7 **Litho.** ***Perf. 14***

155 A27 $800 brt blue 2.50 .75
156 A27 $800 blue grn 2.50 .75
157 A27 $800 plum 2.50 .75
158 A27 $800 scarlet 2.50 .75
Nos. 155-158 (4) 10.00 3.00

15th anniversary of war against Japan.

Soldier, Sailor & Airman — A28

Soldier & Tanks — A28a

China Post No. C17

No. 161, Sailor & warships, horiz. No. 162, Airman & planes, horiz.

1952, Aug. 1 **Engr.** ***Perf. 12½***

159 A28 $800 carmine 2.50 .65
160 A28a $800 deep green 2.50 .65
161 A28a $800 purple 2.50 .65
162 A28a $800 orange brown 2.50 .65
Nos. 159-162 (4) 10.00 2.60

25th anniv. of People's Liberation Army.

Huai River Sluice Dam — A29

China Post No. S5

No. 164, Train on the Chengtu-Chungking Railway. No. 165, Oil refinery and derricks in the Northwest. No. 166, Mechanized state farm.

1952, Oct. 1 ***Perf. 14***

163	A29	$800 dk violet	2.50	.75
164	A29	$800 red	2.50	.75
165	A29	$800 dk vio brn	2.50	.75
166	A29	$800 dp green	2.50	.75
		Nos. 163-166 (4)	10.00	3.00

"Glorious Mother Country," 2nd series.

Doves and Globe A30

China Post No. C18

Designs: Nos. 167-168, Picasso dove over Pacific, vert. $2500, as No. 169.

1952, Oct. 2 ***Perf. 14***

167	A30	$400 maroon	1.75	.50
168	A30	$800 red	1.00	.40
169	A30	$800 brown orange	1.00	.40
170	A30	$2500 deep green	3.00	.70
		Nos. 167-170 (4)	6.75	2.00

Peace Conf. of the Asian and Pacific Regions.

Volunteers on the March — A31

China Post No. C19

No. 172, Chinese peasants loading supplies. No. 173, Volunteers attacking across river. No. 174, Meeting of Chinese & Korean troops.

1952, Oct. 25

171	A31	$800 blue green	2.25	.50
172	A31	$800 vermilion	2.75	.60
173	A31	$800 violet	2.75	.60
174	A31	$800 lake brown	2.75	.60
		Nos. 171-174 (4)	10.50	2.30

2nd anniv. of Chinese Volunteers in Korea.

Woman Textile Worker A32

China Post No. C21

Design: No. 176, Farm woman with sickle.

1953, Mar. 10

175	A32	$800 carmine	1.75	.50
176	A32	$800 emerald	1.75	.50

International Women's Day.

Textile Worker — A33

China Post No. R6

$200, Shepherdess. $250, Stone lion. $800, Lathe operator. $1600, Coal miners. $2000, Corner tower of Forbidden City, Peking.

1953 Litho. ***Perf. 14, 12½ ($250)***

177	A33	$50 magenta	.75	.30
178	A33	$200 emerald	1.50	.50
179	A33	$250 ultra	4.50	2.00
180	A33	$800 blue grn	.85	.35
181	A33	$1600 gray	1.25	1.00
182	A33	$2000 red org	2.25	.45
		Nos. 177-182 (6)	11.10	4.60

Issued: Nos. 177-181, Mar. 25; No. 182, May 23.

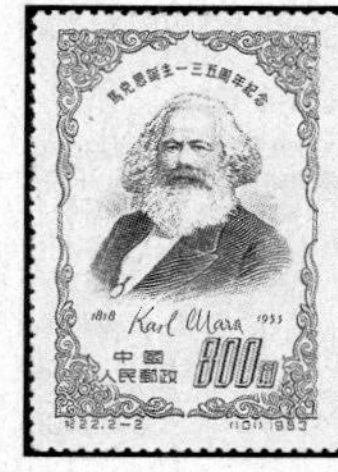

Karl Marx — A34

China Post No. C22

1953, May 20 Engr. ***Perf. 14***

183	A34	$400 dk brown	2.50	.75
184	A34	$800 slate grn	2.25	.75

135th anniv. of the birth of Karl Marx.

Workers and Banners — A35

China Post No. C23

1953, June 25

185	A35	$400 Prus blue	2.25	.65
186	A35	$800 carmine	2.25	.65

7th All-China Trade Union Congress.

Picasso Dove — A36

China Post No. C24

1953, July 25

187	A36	$250 blue grn	3.00	.90
188	A36	$400 orange brn	2.00	.70
189	A36	$800 purple	2.00	.60
		Nos. 187-189 (3)	7.00	2.20

World Peace.

Groom, Wei Dynasty, 386-580 A37

China Post No. S6

Scenes from Tunhuang Murals: No. 191, Court Players, Wei Dynasty. No. 192, Battle Scene, Sui Dynasty, 581-617. No. 193, Ox-drawn palanquin, Tang Dynasty, 618-906.

1953, Sept. 1

190	A37	$800 dp green	2.00	.75
191	A37	$800 red org	2.00	.75
192	A37	$800 Prus blue	2.00	.75
193	A37	$800 carmine	2.00	.75
		Nos. 190-193 (4)	8.00	3.00

"Glorious Mother Country," 3rd series.

Stalin and Mao on Kremlin Terrace A38

Statue of Stalin at Volga-Don Canal — A39

China Post No. C20

Designs: No. 195, Lenin proclaiming Soviet power. No. 197, Stalin as orator.

1953, Oct. 5

194	A38	$800 green	2.75	1.25
195	A38	$800 carmine	2.75	1.25
196	A39	$800 brt blue	3.75	2.00
197	A39	$800 org brn	4.00	1.50
		Nos. 194-197 (4)	13.25	6.00

Russian October Revolution, 35th anniv.

Stamps in same designs with two additional characters meaning "Soviet" in the single-line Chinese inscription, and in different colors, were unofficially released at several small post offices in Hunan, Fukien and Canton areas in February, 1953, but were withdrawn after only a small number had been sold. Value, set $30,000. unused, $12,000 canceled.

Compass, 3rd Century B.C. A40

China Post No. S7

No. 199, Seismoscope, later Han Dynasty. No. 200, Drum cart to measure distance, Chin Dynasty. No. 201, Armillary sphere, Ming Dynasty.

1953, Dec. 1

198	A40	$800 indigo	2.00	.90
199	A40	$800 dk green	2.00	.90
200	A40	$800 dk blue	2.00	.90
201	A40	$800 choc	2.00	.90
		Nos. 198-201 (4)	8.00	3.60

Major inventions by ancient and medieval Chinese scientists.

"Glorious Mother Country," 4th series.

Francois Rabelais — A41

China Post No. C25

Designs: $400, Jose Marti, Cuban revolutionary. $800, Chu Yuan (350-275 B.C.), philosopher. $2200, Nicolaus Copernicus, astronomer.

1953, Dec. 30

202	A41	$250 slate grn	1.50	.50
203	A41	$400 brown blk	1.50	.50
204	A41	$800 indigo	1.50	.50
205	A41	$2200 choc	2.50	.85
		Nos. 202-205 (4)	7.00	2.35

(same size) Gate of Heavenly Peace — A42

China Post No. R7

Sixth Issue: Inscription at upper right.

1954, Apr. 16 **Litho.**

206	A42	$50 carmine	.55	.35
207	A42	$100 lt blue	.55	.35
208	A42	$200 green	.55	.35
209	A42	$250 ultra	3.75	.95
210	A42	$400 gray grn	1.10	.25
211	A42	$800 orange	.65	.25

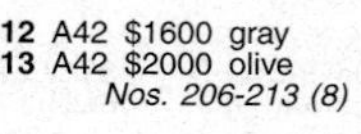

212	A42	$1600 gray	.90	*.75*
213	A42	$2000 olive	1.40	.60
		Nos. 206-213 (8)	9.45	3.85

Textile Plant, Harbin — A43

China Post No. S8

Designs: $200, Tangku Harbor. $250, Tienshui-Lanchow railroad bridge, Kansu Province. $400, Heavy machine-building plant, Taiyuan, Shansi. No. 218, Automatic blast, furnace, Anshan, Manchuria. No. 219, Fushun open-cut coal mine. $2000, Automatic power plant, Northeast. $3200, Prospecting in Tayeh district, Hupeh.

1954, May 1 **Engr.**

214	A43	$100 brown olive	1.60	1.00
215	A43	$200 blue green	2.10	1.00
216	A43	$250 violet	1.90	.75
217	A43	$400 black	1.90	1.00
218	A43	$800 claret	1.90	.75
219	A43	$800 indigo	1.90	.75
220	A43	$2000 red	2.10	1.00
221	A43	$3200 dark brown	2.10	1.00
		Nos. 214-221 (8)	15.50	7.25

Economic progress.

Lenin — A44

China Post No. C26

$400, Lenin and Stalin Monument, Gorki, horiz. $2000, Lenin proclaiming Soviet power.

1954, June 30 **Engr.**

222	A44	$400 deep green	2.50	1.25
223	A44	$800 dark brown	3.50	1.50
224	A44	$2000 deep carmine	4.00	2.00
		Nos. 222-224 (3)	10.00	4.75

30th anniversary of the death of Lenin.

Pottery Vessels, Neolithic Period, 2000 B. C. — A45

China Post No. S9

Archeological Treasures: No. 226, Stone clime, Shang Dynasty, c. 1200 B.C. No. 227, Kuo Chi Tsu-pai bronze basin, Middle Chou Dynasty, 816 B.C. No. 228, Lacquered box and wine cup, Warring States Period, 403-221 B.C.

1954, Aug. 25

225	A45	$800 brown	2.00	.60
226	A45	$800 indigo	2.00	.60
227	A45	$800 Prus bl	2.00	.60
228	A45	$800 dk car	2.00	.60
		Nos. 225-228 (4)	8.00	2.40

"Glorious Mother Country," 5th series.

Pipe Production, Anshan Steel Mill — A46

China Post No. S10

Design: $800, Rolling mill, Anshan.

1954, Oct. 1

229 A46 $400 Prus green 3.25 .75
230 A46 $800 vio brown 3.25 .75

Stalin Statue, by Tomsky — A47

China Post No. C27

Designs: $800, Stalin portrait. $2000, Stalin viewing hydroelectric plant.

1954, Oct. 15 **Size: 21x45mm**

231 A47 $400 black 5.00 .90

Size: 26x37mm

232 A47 $800 black brown 2.25 .80

Size: 42x26mm

233 A47 $2000 deep red 3.00 .80
Nos. 231-233 (3) 10.25 2.50

First anniversary of the death of Stalin.

Exhibition Building, Peking — A48

China Post No. C28

1954, Nov. 7

234 A48 $800 brown, *cream* 57.50 12.00
a. Size: 53½x24mm 72.50 20.00

Russian Economic and Cultural Exhibition, Peking. No. 234 measures 52½x24½mm.

Apprentices and Lathe — A49

China Post No. S11

Progress in Technology: $800, Heavy machinery and workers.

1954, Dec. 15

235 A49 $400 dk olive grn 2.40 .70
236 A49 $800 bright red 3.60 .80

Woman Worker Voting — A50

People Celebrating Opening of Congress — A51

China Post No. C29

1954, Dec. 30

237 A50 $400 deep claret 3.50 2.00
238 A51 $800 bright red 4.25 2.25

First National Congress.

Flags, Worker and Woman Holding Constitution — A52

China Post No. C30

1954, Dec. 30

239 A52 $400 brown, *buff* 3.50 .75
240 A52 $800 brt red, *yel* 4.25 1.50

Adoption of Constitution.

High-tension Pylon — A53

China Post No. S12

1955, Feb. 25

241 A53 $800 dk Prus bl 6.75 1.50

Development of electric power.

Factory Health Workers and Red Cross A54

China Post No. C31

1955, June 25 **Engr.; Cross Typo.**

242 A54 8f dp grn & red 20.00 3.00

50th anniversary of Chinese Red Cross.

Stalin and Mao in Kremlin A55

Soviet Specialist and Chinese Worker — A56

China Post No. C32

1955, July 25 **Engr.**

243 A55 8f brown red 20.00 1.50
244 A56 20f olive blk 27.50 3.25

5th anniv. of Sino-Soviet Friendship Treaty.

Chang Heng (78-139), Astronomer — A57

China Post No. C33

Portraits of Scientists: No. 246, Tsu Chung-chih (429-500), mathematician. No. 247, Chang Sui (683-727), astronomer. No. 248, Li Shih-chen (1518-1593), physician and pharmacologist.

1955, Aug. 25 ***Perf. 14***

245 A57 8f sepia, *buff* 6.00 1.25
a. Min. sheet, sepia, *white* 65.00 20.00
246 A57 8f dp grn, *buff* 6.00 1.25
a. Min. sheet, deep green, *white* 65.00 20.00
247 A57 8f black, *buff* 6.00 1.25
a. Min. sheet, blk, *white* 65.00 20.00
248 A57 8f claret, *buff* 6.00 1.25
a. Min. sheet, claret, *white* 65.00 20.00
Nos. 245-248 (4) 24.00 5.00

Miniature sheets contain one imperf. stamp.

Steel Pouring Ladle A58

China Post No. S13

No. 250, High tension line (2). No. 251, Mechanized coal mining (3). No. 252, Tank cars and derricks (4). No. 253, Heavy machine shop (5). No. 254, Soldier on guard (6). No. 255, Spinning machine (7). No. 256, Workers discussing 5-year plan (8). No. 257, Combine harvester (9). No. 258, Milk production (10). No. 259, Dam (11). No. 260, Pottery industry (12). No. 261, Truck (13). No. 262, Ship at dock (14). No. 263, Geological survey (15). No. 264, Higher education (16). No. 265, Family (17). No. 266, Workers' rest home (18).

1955-56 **Litho.**

249 A58 8f shown 4.25 .90
250 A58 8f multicolored 4.25 .90
251 A58 8f multicolored 4.25 .90
252 A58 8f multicolored 4.25 .90
253 A58 8f multicolored 4.25 .90
254 A58 8f multicolored 4.25 .90
255 A58 8f multicolored 4.25 .90
256 A58 8f multicolored 4.25 .90
257 A58 8f multicolored 4.25 .90
258 A58 8f multicolored 4.25 .90
259 A58 8f multicolored 4.25 .90
260 A58 8f multi ('56) 4.25 .90
261 A58 8f multicolored 4.25 .90
262 A58 8f multicolored 4.25 .90
263 A58 8f multicolored 4.25 .90
264 A58 8f multicolored 4.25 .90
265 A58 8f multicolored 4.25 .90
266 A58 8f multi ('56) 4.25 .90
Nos. 249-266 (18) 76.50 16.20

1st 5 Year Plan. Issued: Nos. 249-257, 10/1; Nos. 258-259, 261-265, 12/15; Nos. 260, 266, 2/24/56.

Lenin — A59

China Post No. C34

1955, Dec. 15 **Engr.** ***Perf. 14***

267 A59 8f dk blue grn 22.50 1.75
268 A59 20f dk rose car 27.50 2.75

85th anniversary of the birth of Lenin.

Engels — A60

China Post No. C35

1955, Dec. 15

269 A60 8f deep orange 20.00 1.75
270 A60 20f brown 30.00 2.75

135th anniversary of the birth of Friedrich Engels (1820-1895), German socialist.

Storming Lu Ting Bridge — A61

Crossing Great Snow Mountains A62

China Post No. C36

1955, Dec. 30

271 A61 8f dark red 20.00 1.25
272 A62 8f dark blue 28.00 3.50

Long March of Chinese Communist army, 20th anniversary.

Miner — A63

Gate of Heavenly Peace — A64

China Post No. R8

Designs: 1f, Machinist. 2f, Airman. 2½f, Nurse. 4f, Soldier. 8f, Steel worker. 10f, Scientist. 20f, Farm woman. 50f, Sailor.

1955-56 **Litho.** ***Perf. 14***

273 A63 ½f orange brn 1.75 .70
274 A63 1f purple 1.75 .35
275 A63 2f green 3.50 .80
276 A63 2½f blue ('56) 3.00 .40
277 A63 4f gray olive 2.25 .50
278 A63 8f red org (Peking printing) 15.00 .75
a. Perf. 12½ (Shanghai printing) 400.00 40.00
279 A63 10f claret ('56) 7.00 .70
280 A63 20f dp blue 12.00 .80
281 A63 50f gray 3.75 .95
Nos. 273-281 (9) 50.00 5.95

China Post No. R9

Engr.

282 A64 $1 claret ('56) 5.00 .60
283 A64 $2 sepia ('55) 4.00 .60
284 A64 $5 indigo ('56) 8.50 1.00
285 A64 $10 dp org ('56) 15.00 8.00
286 A64 $20 gray vio ('56) 23.50 *17.50*
Nos. 282-286 (5) 56.00 27.70

Nos. 282-286 are the 7th Gate Issue. Used values for Nos. 282-286 are for postally used examples.

Trucks, Mountains, Highway Map — A65

Suspension Bridge over Tatu River — A66

China Post No. S14

No. 289, 1st truck arriving in Lhasa, & the Potala.

1956, Mar. 10 **Engr.**

287	A65	4f dp blue	4.25	.95
288	A66	8f dk brown	2.40	.65
289	A65	8f carmine	2.40	.65
		Nos. 287-289 (3)	9.05	2.25

Completion of Sikang-Tibet and Chinghai-Tibet Highways.

Summer Palace and Marble Boat A67

China Post No. S15

Famous Views of Imperial Peking: No. 291, Peihai Park with Jade Belt Marble Bridge. No. 292, Gate of Heavenly Peace. No. 293, Temple of Heaven. No. 294, Great Throne Hall, Forbidden City.

1956-57

290	A67	4f car rose	6.00	1.00
291	A67	4f blue grn	6.00	1.00
292	A67	8f red org ('57)	9.00	1.00
293	A67	8f Prus blue	9.00	1.00
294	A67	8f yellow brn	9.00	1.00
		Nos. 290-294 (5)	39.00	5.00

Issued: No. 292, 2/20/57; others, 6/15/56.
No. 292 exists with sun rays in background. Values: unused, $250,000; used, $80,000.

Salt Making A68

China Post No. S16

Designs: No. 296, Dwelling of the Eastern Han period. No. 297, Duck hunting and harvesting. No. 298, Carriage crossing bridge.

1956, Oct. 1

295	A68	4f gray olive	2.00	.40
296	A68	4f slate blue	2.00	.40
297	A68	8f gray brown	2.00	.40
298	A68	8f sepia	2.00	.40
		Nos. 295-298 (4)	8.00	1.60

Murals, Tung Han Dynasty, 250 B.C.-220 A.D., found near Chengtu.

Ancient Coins and "Save" A69

China Post No. S17

1956, Oct. 1

299	A69	4f yellow brown	10.00	1.25
300	A69	8f rose red	14.00	2.00

Promotion of saving.

Gate of Heavenly Peace — A70

China Post No. C37

1956, Nov. 10

301	A70	4f dk green	14.00	.90
302	A70	8f brt red	17.50	.90
303	A70	16f dk carmine	27.50	1.50
		Nos. 301-303 (3)	59.00	3.30

8th National Congress of the Communist Party of China.

Sun Yat-sen — A71

China Post No. C38

1956, Nov. 12

304	A71	4f brown, *cream*	22.50	2.00
305	A71	8f dp blue, *cream*	32.50	3.25

90th anniversary of birth of Sun Yat-sen.

Weight Lifting — A72

China Post No. C39

1957, Mar. 20 **Litho.** ***Perf. 12½***

Hibiscus red and green; inscription brown

306	A72	4f Shot put	3.00	.50
307	A72	4f shown	3.00	.50
308	A72	8f Track	3.00	.50
309	A72	8f Soccer	3.00	.50
310	A72	8f Bicycling	3.00	.50
		Nos. 306-310 (5)	15.00	2.50

First National Workers' Sports Meeting.

Truck Factory No. 1, Changchun — A73

China Post No. C40

China's truck industry: 8f, Trucks rolling off assembly line.

1957, May 1 **Engr.** ***Perf. 14***

311	A73	4f light brown	3.00	.75
312	A73	8f slate green	4.00	.75

Nanchang Uprising — A74

China Post No. C41

No. 314, Mao and Chu Teh at Chingkanshan. No. 315, Crossing Yellow River. No. 316, Liberation of Nanking, 4/23/49.

1957

313	A74	4f blk vio	31.00	3.25
314	A74	4f slate grn	31.00	2.75
315	A74	8f red brn	31.00	2.75
316	A74	8f dp blue	31.00	2.75
		Nos. 313-316 (4)	124.00	11.50

People's Liberation Army, 30th anniv. Issued: Nos. 313, 315, 8/10; No. 314, 8/30; No. 316, 12/30.

Congress Emblem — A75

China Post No. C42

1957, Sept. 30

317	A75	8f chocolate	9.00	1.50
318	A75	22f indigo	12.00	1.10

4th Intl. Trade Union Cong., Leipzig, 10/4-15.

Yangtze River Bridge A76

China Post No. C43

20f, Road leading to and over bridge.

1957, Oct. 1

319	A76	8f scarlet	3.00	.60
320	A76	20f slate blue	5.25	1.20

Completion of Yangtze River Bridge at Wuhan.

Fireworks over Kremlin — A77

China Post No. C44

Designs: 8f, Hammer and sickle over globe and broken chain. 20f, Stylized dove and olive branch. 22f, Hands of three races holding book with Marx and Lenin. 32f, Star and pylon.

1957, Nov. 7

321	A77	4f brt red	5.00	.95
322	A77	8f chocolate	6.00	.95
323	A77	20f dp green	11.00	.95
324	A77	22f red brown	13.50	2.50
325	A77	32f dp blue	27.50	3.00
		Nos. 321-325 (5)	63.00	8.35

40th anniv. of Russian October Revolution.

Map of Yellow River Basin A78

China Post No. S19

No. 327, Sanmen Gorge dam & powerhouse. No. 328, Ocean liner on Yellow River. No. 329, Dam, irrigation canals & tree-bordered fields.

1957, Dec. 30

326	A78	4f deep orange	19.00	2.25
327	A78	4f deep blue	19.00	2.25
328	A78	8f deep lake	31.00	2.00
329	A78	8f blue green	31.00	2.00
		Nos. 326-329 (4)	100.00	8.50

Yellow River control plan.

Old Man and Young Drummer — A79

China Post No. S20

1957, Dec. 30 **Litho.**

330	A79	8f shown	2.60	.70
331	A79	8f Plowman	2.60	.70
332	A79	8f Woman planting tree	2.60	.70
333	A79	8f Harvest	2.60	.70
		Nos. 330-333 (4)	10.40	2.80

Agricultural cooperation.

Train on Bridge, Ship and Train — A80

China Post No. C45

Designs (Congratulatory Banner and): 4f, Crane, dove and flowers. 8f, Crane with hot ingots, cotton bolls and wheat.

1958, Jan. 30 **Engr.**

334	A80	4f emer, *cream*	2.50	1.50
335	A80	8f red, *cream*	2.50	1.50
336	A80	16f ultra, *cream*	2.50	1.50
		Nos. 334-336 (3)	7.50	4.50

Fulfillment of First Five-Year Plan.

Sungyu Pagoda, Honan — A81

China Post No. S21

Ancient Pagodas: No. 338, Chienhsun Pagoda, Yunnan. No. 339, Sakyamuni Pagoda, Shansi. No. 340, Flying Rainbow Pagoda, Shansi.

1958, Mar. 15 **Engr.**

337	A81	8f sepia	4.75	1.10
338	A81	8f Prus blue	4.75	1.10
339	A81	8f maroon	4.75	1.10
340	A81	8f dp green	4.75	1.10
		Nos. 337-340 (4)	19.00	4.40

Trilobite, Kaoli — A82

China Post No. S22

Designs: 8f, Lufeng dinosaur. 16f, Choukoutien sino-megaceros.

1958, Apr. 15

341	A82	4f blue	2.50	.80
342	A82	8f sepia	3.50	.50
343	A82	16f slate green	3.75	.50
		Nos. 341-343 (3)	9.75	1.80

Prehistoric animals of China.

Heroes Monument A83

China Post No. C47

1958, May 1

344 A83 8f scarlet 42.50 4.25
a. Souvenir sheet, imperf. *275.00* 110.00

Unveiling of People's Heroes Monument, Peking. No. 344a issued May 30.

Karl Marx — A84

China Post No. C46

Design: 22f, Marx Speaking to German Workers' Educational Association, London, painting by Zhukow.

1958, May 5

345 A84 8f chocolate 22.00 1.75
346 A84 22f dk green 28.00 4.00

Karl Marx (1818-83), 140th birth anniv.

Cogwheels and Factories — A85

China Post No. C48

1958, May 25

347 A85 4f brt grnsh bl 22.50 2.25
348 A85 8f red lilac 35.00 3.50

8th All-China Trade Union Cong., Peking.

Dove over Globe — A86

China Post No. C49

1958, June 1

349 A86 8f violet blue 10.00 1.75
350 A86 20f blue green 17.50 3.25

4th Congress of the Intl. Democratic Women's Federation, Vienna, June 1958.

Mother and Child — A87

China Post No. S18

Children's Day: No. 352, Watering sunflowers. No. 353, Playing hide-and-seek. No. 354, Sailing toy boat.

1958, June 1 **Litho.**

351 A87 8f green & multi 25.00 2.40
352 A87 8f green & multi 25.00 2.40
353 A87 8f green & multi 25.00 2.40
354 A87 8f green & multi 25.00 2.40
Nos. 351-354 (4) 100.00 9.60

Kuan Han-ching A88

China Post No. C50

Designs (Operas): 4f, "Dream of Butterflies." 20f, "The Riverside Pavilion."

1958, June 20 **Engr.**

355 A88 4f indigo, *cr* 32.50 3.00
356 A88 8f brown, *cr* 35.00 2.50
357 A88 20f black, *cr* 50.00 4.50
a. Souvenir sheet of 3, *ivory* 475.00 100.00
Nos. 355-357 (3) 117.50 10.00

700th anniversary of publication of works of Kuan Han-ching (1210-1280), dramatist. No. 357a contains 3 imperf. stamps similar to Nos. 355-357. Size: 130x100mm. Issued June 28.

Planetarium A89

China Post No. S23

20f, Telescope and stars over Peking.

1958, June 25

358 A89 8f dk green 9.00 2.00
359 A89 20fr indigo 13.50 2.50

First Chinese planetarium, Peking.

Marx and Engels — A90

China Post No. C51

8f, Cover of 1st edition of the Communist Manifesto.

1958, July 1

360 A90 4f dk red vio 29.00 3.50
361 A90 8f Prus blue 34.00 2.00

110th anniversary of publication of the Communist Manifesto.

Wild Goose and Broadcasting Tower — A91

China Post No. C52

1958, July 10

362 A91 4f ultra 20.00 3.75
363 A91 8f deep green 25.00 2.00

1st Conference of the Ministers of Posts and Telecommunications of Socialist Countries, Moscow, Dec. 3-17, 1957.

Peony and Doves — A92

China Post No. C53

8f, Olive branch with ribbon & clouds. 22f, Atomic energy symbol over factories.

1958, July 20

364 A92 4f red 20.00 3.25
365 A92 8f green 16.00 2.75
366 A92 22f red brown 27.50 5.00
Nos. 364-366 (3) 63.50 11.00

Congress for Disarmament and International Cooperation, Stockholm, July 17-22.

Bronze Weather Vane — A93

China Post No. S24

Designs: No. 368, Weather balloon. No. 369, Typhoon tower and weather map of Asia.

1958, Aug. 25

367 A93 8f yel bis & blk 2.25 .65
368 A93 8f blue & blk 2.25 .65
369 A93 8f brt grn & blk 2.25 .65
Nos. 367-369 (3) 6.75 1.95

Meteorological services in ancient and modern China.

"5" Encircling IUS Emblem — A94

China Post No. C54

1958, Sept. 4

370 A94 8f rose lilac 25.00 2.25
371 A94 22f dp blue grn 42.50 3.75

Intl. Union of Students, 5th Cong., Peking, 9/4-13.

Nos. 370-371 exist with incorrect inscription. Values: No. 370, unused $15,000; used $6,000; No. 371, unused $160,000; used $120,000.

Telegraph Building, Peking A95

China Post No. C56

1958, Sept. 29

372 A95 4f greenish black 6.00 1.00
373 A95 8f rose red 6.00 1.00

Opening of Telegraph Building, Peking.

Exhibition Emblem and Exhortation A96

China Post No. C55

Designs: No. 375, Dragon over clouds signifying "aiming high." No. 376, Flying horses, signifying "great leap forward" in production.

1958, Oct. 1

374 A96 8f slate grn 20.00 1.50
375 A96 8f rose car 20.00 1.50
376 A96 8f red brown 20.00 1.75
Nos. 374-376 (3) 60.00 4.75

National Exhibition of Industry and Communications, Peking.

Worker and Excavator A97

China Post No. S26

Design: 8f, Completed dam and pylon.

1958, Oct. 25

377 A97 4f dark brown 3.50 .75
378 A97 8f deep Prussian blue 5.50 .60

13 Ming Tombs Reservoir completion.

Sputnik 3 in Orbit — A98

China Post No. S25

Designs: 4f, Sputnik over armillary sphere. 10f, Trajectories of 3 Sputniks over earth.

1958, Oct. 30

379 A98 4f scarlet 8.00 1.25
380 A98 8f dp violet bl 6.00 1.10
381 A98 10f dp green 9.00 1.90
Nos. 379-381 (3) 23.00 4.25

Anniversary of first earth satellite launched by the USSR.

Chinese and North Korean Soldiers A99

China Post No. C57

Designs: No. 383, Chinese soldier embracing Korean woman. No. 384, Chinese girl presenting flowers to returning soldier.

1958, Nov. 20

382 A99 8f brt purple 7.50 .90
383 A99 8f chestnut 7.50 1.25
384 A99 8f rose car 7.50 1.25
Nos. 382-384 (3) 22.50 3.40

Return of the Chinese Volunteers from Korea.

Forest and Mountains A100

China Post No. S27

Afforestation: No. 386, Mounted forest patrol. No. 387, Mechanized lumbering, horiz. No. 388, Tree-planting: "Turning the Country Green," horiz.

1958, Dec. 15

385 A100 8f dp blue grn 5.50 1.00
386 A100 8f slate grn 5.50 1.00
387 A100 8f dk purple 5.50 1.00
388 A100 8f indigo 5.50 1.00
Nos. 385-388 (4) 22.00 4.00

Peony — A101

China Post No. R10

Designs: 3f, Lotus. 5f, Chrysanthemums.

1958, Sept. 25 **Litho.**
389 A101 1½f lilac rose 3.75 1.00
390 A101 3f blue grn 15.00 2.40
391 A101 5f dp orange 2.00 .55
Nos. 389-391 (3) 20.75 3.95

Atomic Reactor A102

China Post No. S28

1958, Dec. 30 **Engr.**
392 A102 8f shown 18.00 2.50
393 A102 20f Cyclotron 25.00 3.00

Inauguration of China's first atomic reactor and cyclotron, Peking.

Children Launching Model Planes — A103

China Post No. S29

8f, Gliders over trees. 10f, Parachutists descending. 20f, Small monoplanes in mid-air.

1958, Dec. 30
394 A103 4f carmine 2.25 .50
395 A103 8f dp slate grn 2.25 .50
396 A103 10f dk brown 3.00 .65
397 A103 20f Prus blue 4.00 .85
Nos. 394-397 (4) 11.50 2.50

Sports-aviation publicity.

Camel Carrying Load — A104

China Post No. S30

Designs: No. 399, Pomegranates. No. 400, Rooster. No. 401, Theatrical figure.

1959, Jan. 1
398 A104 8f vio & blk 17.50 1.10
399 A104 8f dp bl grn & blk 17.50 1.10
400 A104 8f red & blk 17.50 1.10
401 A104 8f dp bl & blk 17.50 1.10
Nos. 398-401 (4) 70.00 4.40

Paper cut-outs (folk art).

Red Flag, Mao and Workers — A105

China Post No. C58

Designs: 8f, Traditional and modern blast furnaces. 10f, Steel works and workers.

1959
402 A105 4f brt red 30.00 1.75
403 A105 8f lake 30.00 1.75
404 A105 10f deep red 35.00 2.25
Nos. 402-404 (3) 95.00 5.75

"Great Leap Forward" in steel production. Issue dates: 4f, 8f, Feb. 19; 10f, May 25.

Women Workers and Atomic Model — A106

China Post No. C59

Design: 22f, Chinese and Soviet women holding banners dated "3.8."

1959, Mar. 8
405 A106 8f emerald, *cr* 3.00 .60
406 A106 22f magenta, *cr* 4.50 1.25

International Women's Day.

Natural History Museum A107

China Post No. S31

1959, Apr. 1
407 A107 4f greenish blue 3.25 1.00
408 A107 8f olive brown 3.25 .75

Opening of Museum of Natural History, Peking.

Wheat — A108

China Post No. C60

Designs on Chinese Flag: No. 410, Rice. No. 411, Cotton bolls. No. 412, Soybeans, rapeseed and peanuts.

1959, Apr. 25
409 A108 8f red 5.00 .70
410 A108 8f red 5.00 .70
411 A108 8f red 5.00 .70
412 A108 8f red 5.00 .70
a. Block of 4, #409-412 47.50 12.00

Successful harvest, 1958.

A109

China Post No. C61

Designs: 4f, Marx, Lenin and workers. 8f, Black, yellow and white fists holding banner. 22f, Steel workers parading with banners dated "5.1."

1959, May 1
413 A109 4f ultra 7.50 1.60
414 A109 8f red 10.00 1.25
415 A109 22f emerald 20.00 2.25
Nos. 413-415 (3) 37.50 5.10

International Labor Day.

A110

China Post No. S34

8f, Peking airport. 10f, Plane loading on runway.

1959, June 20
416 A110 8f lilac & blk 24.00 2.00
417 A110 10f ol gray & blk 32.50 2.50

Opening of new Peking Airport.

Students with Marx-Lenin Banners A111

China Post No. C62

Design: 8f, Workers with banners of Mao.

1959, July 1 **Photo.** ***Perf. 11x11½***
418 A111 4f gray, red & dk brn 32.50 12.00
419 A111 8f bis, red & dk brn 60.00 8.00

40th anniv. of the May 4th students' uprising.

Frederick Joliot-Curie — A112

China Post No. C63

22f, Three races, dove and olive branch.

1959, July 25 **Engr.** ***Perf. 11½***
420 A112 8f violet brn 10.00 2.75
421 A112 22f dk violet 20.00 3.25

10th anniv. of the World Peace Movement.

Stamp Printing Plant, Peking A113

China Post No. C65

1959, Aug. 15 ***Perf. 11x11½***
422 A113 8f dp blue grn 15.00 2.00

Sino-Czechoslovak cooperation in stamp production.

Table Tennis — A114

China Post No. C66

1959, Aug. 30 **Litho.** ***Perf. 14***
423 A114 4f black & blue 8.50 1.25
424 A114 8f black & red 7.50 .90

25th World Table Tennis Championships, Dortmund, German Democratic Republic.

Soviet Space Rocket — A115

China Post No. S33

1959, Sept. 10 **Photo.** ***Perf. 11½***
425 A115 8f Prus bl, red & blk 25.00 3.25

Launching of first Russian space rocket, Jan. 2, 1959.

Backyard Steel Production — A116

China Post No. S35

Designs: No. 426, Sun rising over "industry and agriculture." No. 428, Farming. No. 429, Trade. No. 430, Education. No. 431, Militia. No. 432, Communal dining. No. 433, Nursery. No. 434, Care for the aged. No. 435, Health services. No. 436, Flutist; culture and sports. No. 437, Flower symbolizing unity of industry, agriculture, trade, education and armed forces.

Position-in-set number in ( ).

1959, Sept. 25 **Engr.**
426 A116 8f rose 5.00 .80
427 A116 8f violet brn 5.00 .80
428 A116 8f dp orange 5.00 .80
429 A116 8f slate grn 5.00 .80
430 A116 8f dp blue 5.00 .80
431 A116 8f olive 5.00 .80
432 A116 8f indigo 5.00 .80
433 A116 8f lilac rose 5.00 .80
434 A116 8f gray blk 5.00 .80
435 A116 8f emerald 5.00 .80
436 A116 8f dk violet 5.00 .80
437 A116 8f red 5.00 .80
Nos. 426-437 (12) 60.00 9.60

First anniversary of Peoples' Communes.

Mao and Gate of Heavenly Peace — A117

China Post No. C67

Designs: No. 439, Marx, Lenin and Kremlin. 22f, Dove over globe.

Perf. 11½ x 11

1959, Sept. 28 **Photo.**

With Gum

438 A117 8f lt brown & red 55.00 3.75
439 A117 8f dull blue & red 25.00 2.25
440 A117 22f blue grn & red 27.50 8.50
Nos. 438-440 (3) 107.50 14.50
Set, never hinged 170.00

National Emblem A118

China Post No. C68

1959, Oct. 1 **Litho.** ***Perf. 14***
441 A118 4f pale grn, red & gold 12.00 2.10
442 A118 8f gray, red & gold 14.00 2.10
443 A118 10f lt blue, red & gold 22.50 3.75
444 A118 20f pale brn, red & gold 32.50 4.75
Nos. 441-444 (4) 81.00 12.70

Blast Furnaces — A119

China Post No. C69

No. 446, Large coal mine. No. 447, Planer, Wuhan heavy machinery plant. No. 448, Wuhan Yangtze River Bridge. No. 449, Combine harvester. No. 450, Hsinankiang hydroelectric station. No. 451, Spinning machine. No. 452, Kirin chemical fertilizer plant.

Engraved and Photogravure

1959, Oct. 1 ***Perf. 11½ x 11***

With Gum

No.	Type	Description	Unused	Used
445	A119	8f brown & rose red	4.50	1.50
446	A119	8f brown & gray	4.50	1.50
447	A119	8f brown & yel brn	4.50	1.50
448	A119	8f brown & stl bl	4.50	1.50
449	A119	8f brown & org	4.50	1.50
450	A119	8f brown & ol	4.50	1.50
451	A119	8f brown & bl grn	4.50	1.50
452	A119	8f brown & vio	4.50	1.50
		Nos. 445-452 (8)	36.00	12.00
		Set, never hinged	62.50	

Celebration at Gate of Heavenly Peace — A120

China Post No. C70

Designs: 10f, Workers and factory, vert. 20f, People rejoicing, vert.

1959, Oct. 1 **Litho.** ***Perf. 14***

No.	Type	Description	Unused	Used
453	A120	8f cream & multi	9.50	3.25
454	A120	10f cream & multi	17.50	3.75
455	A120	20f cream & multi	22.50	5.50
		Nos. 453-455 (3)	49.50	12.50

Mao Proclaiming Republic — A121

China Post No. C71

1959, Oct. 1 **Engr.**

No.	Type	Description	Unused	Used
456	A121	20f deep carmine	280.00	75.00

Nos. 438-456 commemorate 10th anniversary of the Proclamation of the People's Republic of China.

A122

China Post No. C64

Designs: No. 457, Pioneers' emblem. No. 458, Pioneer Bugler. No. 459, Schoolgirl. No. 460, Girl using rain gauge. No. 461, Boy planting tree. No. 462, Girl figure skater.

1959, Nov. 10 **Photo.** ***Perf. 11½***

No.	Type	Description	Unused	Used
457	A122	4f red yel & blk	13.00	1.00
458	A122	4f Prus bl & red	13.00	1.00
459	A122	8f brn & red	12.00	1.00
460	A122	8f dk bl & red	12.00	1.00
461	A122	8f red & grn	12.00	1.00
462	A122	8f mag & red	12.00	1.00
		Nos. 457-462 (6)	74.00	6.00

10th anniversary of the Young Pioneers. Black inscription on No. 457 engraved.

A123

China Post No. C73

4f, Exhibition emblem, communications symbols. 8f, Exhibition emblem & chimneys.

1959, Dec. 1 **Engr.**

No.	Type	Description	Unused	Used
463	A123	4f dark blue	2.75	.80
464	A123	8f red	3.25	.80

Exhibition of Industry and Communications, Peking.

Palace of Nationalities A124

China Post No. S36

Engraved, Frame Lithographed

1959, Dec. 10 ***Perf. 14***

No.	Type	Description	Unused	Used
465	A124	4f red & blk	13.00	1.75
466	A124	8f brt grn & blk	14.00	1.50

Inauguration of the Cultural Palace of Nationalities, Peking.

Athletes' Monument and Track — A125

China Post No. C72

Sports: No. 468, Parachuting. No. 469, Marksmanship. No. 470, Diving. No. 471, Table tennis. No. 472, Weight lifting. No. 473, High jump. No. 474, Rowing. No. 475, Track. No. 476, Basketball. No. 477, Traditional Chinese fencing. No. 478, Motorcycling. No. 479, Gymnastics. No. 480, Bicycling. No. 481, Horsemanship. No. 482, Soccer.

1959, Dec. 28 **Litho.**

No.	Type	Description	Unused	Used
467	A125	8f bis, blk & gray	7.50	1.00
468	A125	8f dl bl, blk & gray	7.50	1.00
469	A125	8f red brn & blk	7.50	1.00
470	A125	8f grn, blk & brn	7.50	1.00
471	A125	8f brt grn, blk, brn & gray	7.50	1.00
472	A125	8f gray, blk & brn	7.50	1.00
473	A125	8f dl bl, blk & brn	7.50	1.00
474	A125	8f Prus grn, blk & brn	7.50	1.00
475	A125	8f org, blk & brn	7.50	1.00
476	A125	8f dl vio, blk & brn	7.50	1.00
477	A125	8f lt ol, blk & brn	7.50	1.00
478	A125	8f bl, blk & gray	7.50	1.00
479	A125	8f gray bl, blk, grn, & bl	7.50	1.00
480	A125	8f gray, blk, brn, & vio	7.50	1.00
481	A125	8f red org, blk, brn, & gray	7.50	1.00
482	A125	8f lt gray, blk, brn, & red	7.50	1.00
		Nos. 467-482 (16)	120.00	16.00

First National Sports Meeting, Peking.

Wheat and Main Pavilion A126

China Post No. S37

Designs (Pavilion and): 8f, Meteorological symbols. 10f, Domestic animals. 20f, Fish.

1960, Jan. 20 **Engr. & Litho.**

Cream Background

No.	Type	Description	Unused	Used
483	A126	4f black & org	2.00	.85
484	A126	8f black & dull bl	2.00	.85
485	A126	10f black & org brn	2.00	.85
486	A126	20f black & grnsh bl	2.25	1.00
		Nos. 483-486 (4)	8.25	3.55

Opening of the National Agricultural Exhibition Halls, Peking.

With Gum

From No. 487 onward all stamps were issued with gum except as noted.

Catalogue values for unused stamps in this section, from this point to the end of the section, are for Never Hinged items without gum toning.

Conference Hall, Tsunyi A127

China Post No. C74

Designs: 8f, Mao addressing conference. 10f, Crossing Chinsha River.

Engraved (4f, 10f); Photogravure (8f)

1960, Jan. 25 ***Perf. 11x11½***

No.	Type	Description	Unused	Used
487	A127	4f violet & blue	60.00	9.50
488	A127	8f red & multi	77.50	7.75
489	A127	10f slate green	140.00	11.00
		Nos. 487-489 (3)	277.50	28.25

25th anniversary of the Communist Party Conference at Tsunyl.

Clara Zetkin (1857-1933) A128

China Post No. C76

8f, Mother, child and dove. 10f, Woman tractor driver. 22f, Women of three races.

1960, Mar. 8 **Photo.** ***Perf. 11½x11***

No.	Type	Description	Unused	Used
490	A128	4f black & multi	6.50	1.00
491	A128	8f black & multi	11.00	1.00
492	A128	10f black & multi	15.00	1.50
493	A128	22f black & multi	17.50	2.25
		Nos. 490-493 (4)	50.00	5.75

50th anniv. of International Women's Day.

Chinese and Russian Workers — A129

China Post No. C75

Designs: 8f, Chinese and Russian flags. 10f, Chinese and Russian soldiers.

1960, Mar. 10

No.	Type	Description	Unused	Used
494	A129	4f dk brown	26.00	5.00
495	A129	8f red, yel & blk	34.00	3.00
496	A129	10f dp blue	47.50	9.00
		Nos. 494-496 (3)	107.50	17.00

10th anniv. of Sino-Soviet Treaty of Friendship. Black inscription engraved on No. 495.

Flags of Hungary and China A130

China Post No. C78

Design: 8f, Parliament Building, Budapest.

1960, Apr. 4 ***Perf. 11 x 11½***

No.	Type	Description	Unused	Used
497	A130	8f yel, blk, red & grn	52.50	7.25
498	A130	8f blue, red & blk	52.50	7.25

15th anniv. of the liberation of Hungary.

Lenin Speaking — A131

China Post No. C77

Designs: 8f, Portrait of Lenin. 20f, Lenin talking with Smolny Palace guard.

Engraved (4f, 20f); Engraved and Photogravure (8f)

1960, Apr. 22 ***Perf. 11½ x 11***

No.	Type	Description	Unused	Used
499	A131	4f violet brn	27.50	1.90
500	A131	8f org red & blk	30.00	2.75
501	A131	20f dk brown	50.00	4.50
		Nos. 499-501 (3)	107.50	9.15

90th anniversary of the birth of Lenin.

Lunik 2, Moon and Russian Arms — A132

China Post No. S39

Design: 10f, Lunik 3 over moon.

1960, Apr. 30 **Engr.** ***Perf. 11½***

No.	Type	Description	Unused	Used
502	A132	8f red	11.00	1.90
503	A132	10f green	17.50	2.50

Russian space flights.

Pioneers and Flags of Czechoslovakia and China — A133

View of Prague with Charles Bridge A134

China Post No. C79

Perf. 11½x11; 11x11½

1960, May 9 **Photo.**

No.	Type	Description	Unused	Used
504	A133	8f yellow & multi	50.00	6.50
505	A134	8f deep green	50.00	6.50

Liberation of Czechoslovakia, 15th anniv.

Nostril Bouquet A135

China Post No. S38

Various goldfish: No. 507, Black-back dragon eye (2). No. 508, Bubble eye (3). No. 509, Red tiger head (4). No. 510, Pearl scale (5). No. 511, Blue dragon eye (6). No. 512, Skyward eye (7). No. 513, Red cap (8). No. 514, Purple cap (9). No. 515, Red head (10). No. 516, Red and white dragon eye (11). No. 517, Red dragon eye (12).

1960, June 1 ***Perf. 11x11½***

506 A135 4f shown 72.50 7.00
507 A135 4f multi 72.50 7.00
508 A135 4f multi 85.00 7.00
509 A135 4f multi 72.50 7.00
510 A135 8f multi 200.00 7.00
511 A135 8f multi 85.00 7.00
512 A135 8f multi 160.00 7.00
513 A135 8f multi 52.50 10.50
514 A135 8f multi 52.50 10.50
515 A135 8f multi 52.50 10.50
516 A135 8f multi 225.00 10.50
517 A135 8f multi 58.00 20.00
Nos. 506-517 (12) 1,188. 111.00

Unused values for Nos. 506-517 are for examples with untoned gum.

Sow with Litter A136

China Post No. S40

No. 519, Pig being inoculated. No. 520, Pigs. No. 521, Pig and mechanized feeding. No. 522, Pig and bales.

1960, June 15

518 A136 8f red & blk 60.00 9.25
519 A136 8f dp grn & blk 60.00 9.25
520 A136 8f lil rose & blk 60.00 9.25
521 A136 8f lt yel grn & blk 60.00 9.25
522 A136 8f org & blk 60.00 9.25
Nos. 518-522 (5) 300.00 46.25

Flag Inscribed "Serving the Workers" — A137

China Post No. C81

Design: 8f, Inscribed stone seal.

1960, July 30 Photo. ***Perf. 11½x11***

523 A137 4f lt grn, red, pink & brn 47.50 7.00

Photogravure & Engraved

524 A137 8f pale bl, red & bis 60.00 5.50

3rd Natl. Cong. for Literature and Arts, Peking.

Flowers, Flags of North Korea and China — A138

China Post No. C82

Design: 8f, Flying horse of Korea.

1960, Aug. 15 **Photo.**

525 A138 8f red & multi 57.50 10.00
526 A138 8f ultra, red & indigo 72.50 10.00

15th anniversary of the liberation of Korea.

Railroad Station, Peking — A139

China Post No. S42

Design: 10f, Train arriving at station.

1960, Aug. 30 ***Perf. 11½***

527 A139 8f blue, cream & brn 47.50 15.00
528 A139 10f bluish grn, cr & ind 67.50 16.00

Opening of new Peking Railroad Station.

Girls and Flags of North Viet Nam and China A140

Lake of the Returning Sword, Hanoi — A141

China Post No. C83

1960, Sept. 2 ***Perf. 11x11½, 11½x11***

529 A140 8f red & multi 20.00 5.50
530 A141 8f red, gray grn & gray 27.50 3.50

15th anniversary of the Democratic Republic of North Viet Nam.

Worker and Fresh-air Installation — A142

China Post No. S43

Designs: No. 532, Exterminator. No. 533, Window cleaning. No. 534, Medical examination of child. No. 535, Physical exercise.

1960, Sept. 10 ***Perf. 11½***

531 A142 8f black & orange 13.50 1.25
532 A142 8f indigo & slate 13.50 1.25
533 A142 8f brown & blue 13.50 1.25
534 A142 8f maroon & ocher 13.50 1.25
535 A142 8f indigo & brt grn 13.50 1.25
Nos. 531-535 (5) 67.50 6.25

National health campaign.

Great Hall of the People — A143

China Post No. S41

Design: 10f, Inside view.

1960, Oct. 1

536 A143 8f yellow & multi 47.50 15.00
537 A143 10f brown & multi 67.50 17.00

Completion of the Great Hall of the People, Peking.

Dr. Norman Bethune — A144

China Post No. C84

No. 539, Dr. Bethune operating on a soldier.

Photo. (No. 538); Engr. (No. 539)

1960, Nov. 20 ***Perf. 11½x11***

538 A144 8f red & multi 24.00 3.00
539 A144 8f sepia 24.00 3.00

Dr. Norman Bethune (1890-1939), Canadian surgeon with 8th Route Army.

Engels Addressing Congress at The Hague — A145

China Post No. C80

1960, Nov. 28 **Engr.**

540 A145 8f shown 50.00 3.25

Photo.

541 A145 10f Portrait of Engels 55.00 8.00

140th anniversary of the birth of Friedrich Engels (1820-1895), German Socialist.

"Hwang Shi Ba" — A146

China Post No. S44

1960-61 **Photo.**

Various Chrysanthemums in Natural Colors

542 A146 4f bl gray 19.00 3.25
543 A146 4f pink 19.00 3.25
544 A146 8f dk gray 21.00 3.25
545 A146 8f dp blue 21.00 3.25
546 A146 8f green 21.00 3.25
547 A146 8f magenta 21.00 3.25
548 A146 8f olive 20.00 3.25
549 A146 8f grnsh bl 21.00 3.25
550 A146 10f gray 25.00 4.75
551 A146 10f choc 26.00 4.75
552 A146 20f dp blue 47.50 5.50
553 A146 20f brt red 47.50 6.50
554 A146 22f olive bis 110.00 9.25
555 A146 22f carmine 175.00 12.00
556 A146 30f grnsh gray 250.00 13.00
557 A146 30f brt pink 160.00 8.25
558 A146 35f dp green 110.00 10.00
559 A146 52f brt lilac rose 110.00 20.50
Nos. 542-559 (18) 1,224. 120.50

Issued: Nos. 548-550, 557-559, 12/10/60; Nos. 545-547, 554-556, 1/18/61; Nos. 542-544, 2/24/61.

Freighter — A147

China Post No. S32

1960, Dec. 15 ***Perf. 11½***

Without Gum

560 A147 8f deep blue 14.00 2.25

1st 10,000-ton Chinese-built freighter, launching.

Pantheon, Paris — A148

China Post No. C85

Design: 8f, Proclamation of the Commune.

Engraved and Photogravure

1961, Mar. 18 ***Perf. 11½x11***

561 A148 8f gray blk & red 37.50 5.75
562 A148 8f brown & red 37.50 6.75

90th anniversary of the Paris Commune.

Championship Symbol and Jasmine — A149

China Post No. C86

Designs: 10f, Table tennis racket and ball; Temple of Heaven. 20f, Table tennis match. 22f, Peking workers' gymnasium.

1961, Apr. 5 **Photo.** ***Perf. 11***

563 A149 8f multicolored 7.50 .75
564 A149 10f multicolored 8.50 1.00
565 A149 20f multicolored 9.50 1.50
566 A149 22f multicolored 11.00 2.00
a. Souv. sheet, #563-566 *900.00 700.00*
Nos. 563-566 (4) 36.50 5.25

26th World Table Tennis Championships, Peking.

Jeme Tien-yow — A150

China Post No. C87

Design: 10f, Train and tunnel, Peking-Changchow Railroad.

1961, June 20 ***Perf. 11½x11***

567 A150 8f ol grn & blk 11.00 1.25
568 A150 10f org brn & brn 26.50 3.75

Centenary of the birth of Jeme Tien-yow, railroad construction engineer.

Congress Building, Shanghai — A151

China Post No. C88

Designs: 8f, August 1st Building, Nanchang. 10f, Provisional Central Government Office, Juikin. 20f, Pagoda Hill, Yenan. 30f, Gate of Heavenly Peace, Peking.

1961, July 1 ***Perf. 11½***

569 A151 4f gold, red & cl 105.00 11.50
570 A151 8f gold, red & bl grn 105.00 11.50
571 A151 10f gold, red & yel brn 92.50 7.00

No.	Type	Denom.	Color	Unused	Used
572	A151	20f	gold, red & ultra	180.00	14.00
573	A151	30f	gold, red & org red	210.00	26.00
			Nos. 569-573 (5)	692.50	70.00

40th anniv. of the Chinese Communist Party.

August 1 Building, Nanchang — A152

China Post No. R11

3f, 4f, 5f, Trees & Sha Cho Pa Building, Juikin. 8f, 10f, 20f, Pagoda Hill, Yenan. 22f, 30f, 50f, Gate of Heavenly Peace, Peking.

1961-62 Engr. *Perf. 11*

Without Gum

Size: 24x16mm

No.	Type	Denom.	Color	Unused	Used
574	A152	1f	vio blue	15.00	.70
575	A152	1½f	maroon	45.00	2.50
576	A152	2f	indigo	18.00	1.10
577	A152	3f	dull vio	67.50	3.25
578	A152	4f	green	4.00	.75
579	A152	5f	gray	4.00	.60
580	A152	8f	dark olive	4.00	.50
581	A152	10f	brt lil rose	10.00	.50
582	A152	20f	grnsh bl	3.00	.50
583	A152	22f	brown	1.75	.50
584	A152	30f	blue	3.00	.50
585	A152	50f	vermilion	3.00	.50
			Nos. 574-585 (12)	178.25	11.90

Issued: 1f, 1½f, 5f, 7/20/62; others 7/20/61.

See Nos. 647-654, 1059-1064.

Flowers, Flags of Mongolia and China A153

China Post No. C89

Design: 10f, Parliament, Ulan Bator, and statue of Sukhe Bator.

1961, July 11 Photo. *Perf. 11x11½*

No.	Type	Denom.	Color	Unused	Used
586	A153	8f	crim, ultra & yel	120.00	20.00
587	A153	10f	orange, blk & yel	175.00	27.50

40th anniv. of the Mongolian People's Republic.

Military Museum — A154

China Post No. S45

Photo. & Engr.

1961, Aug. 1 *Perf. 11½*

No.	Type	Denom.	Color	Unused	Used
588	A154	8f	gray bl, brn & grn	82.50	3.25
a.			Inscribed series "" (error)	*200.00*	*17.50*
589	A154	10f	gray, blk & grn	87.50	3.75

Opening of the People's Revolutionary Military Museum.

Uprising at Wuchang A155

Sun Yat-sen — A156

China Post No. C90

Perf. 11x11½, 11½x11

1961, Oct. 10 Photo.

No.	Type	Denom.	Color	Unused	Used
590	A155	8f	gray & blk	62.50	5.00
591	A156	10f	tan & black	77.50	5.50

50th anniversary of the 1911 Revolution.

Donkey — A157

China Post No. S46

Designs: 8f, 10f, 20f, 22f, Horses; 30f, 50f, Camels. Ceramic statuettes from Tang Dynasty (618-906) graves.

1961, Nov. 10 *Perf. 11½x11*

Statuettes in Original Colors

No.	Type	Denom.	Color	Unused	Used
592	A157	4f	dull blue	21.00	2.10
593	A157	8f	gray green	21.00	2.10
594	A157	8f	dp purple	21.00	2.10
595	A157	10f	dp blue	21.00	2.10
596	A157	20f	olive	24.00	2.60
597	A157	22f	blue grn	44.00	3.75
598	A157	30f	red brown	90.00	9.50
599	A157	50f	slate	55.00	5.75
			Nos. 592-599 (8)	297.00	30.00

Rejoicing Tibetans — A158

China Post No. S47

Designs: 8f, Woman sower. 10f, Celebration of bumper crop. 20f, People's representatives. 30f, Tibetan children.

1961, Nov. 25

No.	Type	Denom.	Color	Unused	Used
600	A158	4f	brn & ocher	52.50	4.00
601	A158	8f	brn & lt bl grn	45.00	3.50
602	A158	10f	brn & yel	62.50	4.00
603	A158	20f	brn & rose	135.00	9.00
604	A158	30f	brn & bluish gray	150.00	10.00
			Nos. 600-604 (5)	445.00	30.50

Rebirth of the Tibetan people.

Lu Hsun — A159

China Post No. C91

1962, Feb. 26

No.	Type	Denom.	Color	Unused	Used
605	A159	8f	red brown & blk	7.25	1.75

80th anniv. of the birth of Lu Hsun, writer.

An Chi Bridge, Chao Hsien — A160

China Post No. S50

Bridges of Ancient China: 8f, Pao Tai, Soochow. 10f, Chu Pu, Kwan Hsien. 20f, Chen Yang, San Kiang.

1962, May 15 *Perf. 11*

No.	Type	Denom.	Color	Unused	Used
606	A160	4f	dk gray blue	5.75	1.00
607	A160	8f	dp green	5.75	1.00
608	A160	10f	brown	33.00	3.75
609	A160	20f	grnsh blue	24.00	2.50
			Nos. 606-609 (4)	68.50	8.25

Tu Fu — A161

China Post No. C93

4f, Tu Fu memorial pavilion, Chengtu.

1962, May 25 *Perf. 11½x11*

No.	Type	Denom.	Color	Unused	Used
610	A161	4f	ol bis & blk	65.00	3.00
611	A161	8f	grnsh bl & blk	75.00	4.00

Poet Tu Fu, 1,250th anniversary of birth.

Cranes and Bamboo — A162

China Post No. S48

10f, Two cranes in flight. 20f, Crane on rock.

1962, June 10

No.	Type	Denom.	Color	Unused	Used
612	A162	8f	tan & multi	25.00	2.50
613	A162	10f	blue & multi	50.00	4.75
614	A162	20f	bister & multi	67.50	8.00
			Nos. 612-614 (3)	142.50	15.25

"The Sacred Crane," from paintings by Chen Chi-fo.

Cuban Soldier and Flag A163

China Post No. S51

Designs: 10f, Sugar cane worker. 22f, Militiaman and woman.

1962, July 10 *Perf. 11x11½*

No.	Type	Denom.	Color	Unused	Used
615	A163	8f	car, rose & blk	45.00	6.50
616	A163	10f	green & blk	90.00	11.00
617	A163	22f	ultra & blk	200.00	47.50
			Nos. 615-617 (3)	335.00	65.00

Support of Cuba.

Torch and Map of Algeria — A164

China Post No. S52

Design: 22f, Algerian soldiers and flag.

1962, July 10 *Perf. 11½x11*

No.	Type	Denom.	Color	Unused	Used
618	A164	8f	dp brown & red org	2.75	1.20
619	A164	22f	ocher & dp brn	8.25	1.90

Support of Algeria.

Mei Lan-fang — A165

China Post No. C94

Designs (Mei Lan-fang in Women's Roles): No. 621, Beating drum. No. 622, With fan. 10f, Lady Yu with swords. 20f, With bag. 22f, Heavenly Maiden, horiz. 30f, With spinning wheel, horiz. 50f, Kneeling, horiz. $3, Scene from opera "Drunken Beauty."

1962 *Perf. 11½x11, 11x11½*

No.	Type	Denom.	Color	Unused	Used
620	A165	4f	tan & multi	220.00	35.00
621	A165	8f	tan & multi	120.00	15.00
622	A165	8f	gray & multi	120.00	15.00
623	A165	10f	gray & multi	220.00	20.00
624	A165	20f	lt grn & multi	220.00	30.00
625	A165	22f	cream & multi	375.00	65.00
626	A165	30f	lt blue & multi	475.00	80.00
627	A165	50f	buff & multi	475.00	80.00
			Nos. 620-627 (8)	2,225.	340.00

Souvenir Sheet

Perf. 11

No.	Type	Denom.	Color	Unused	Used
628	A165	$3	brown & multi	*18,500.*	*6,250.*

Stage art of Mei Lan-fang, actor.

Issued: 4f, 8f, 10f, 8/8; $3, 9/15; others 9/1.

Nos. 620-627 exist imperf. Value, set unused $6,750, used $2,350.

No. 628 contains one 48x58mm stamp and almost always has some faults. Values above are for fault-free examples. Value for No. 628 with small faults, unused $10,000. Excellent forgeries exist.

Flower Drum Dance, Han — A166

China Post No. S49

Folk Dances: 8f, Ordos, Mongolia. 10f, Catching shrimp, Chuang. 20f, Friend, Yi. 30f, Fiddle dance, Tibet. 50f, Tambourine dance, Uighur.

Cumulative numbers 246-251 at lower right.

1962, Oct. 15 Litho. *Perf. 12½*

Without Gum

No.	Type	Denom.	Color	Unused	Used
629	A166	4f	cream & multi	3.00	.80
630	A166	8f	cream & multi	3.00	.80
631	A166	10f	cream & multi	3.75	1.00
632	A166	20f	cream & multi	5.00	1.50
633	A166	30f	cream & multi	6.00	1.75
634	A166	50f	cream & multi	7.00	2.25
			Nos. 629-634 (6)	27.75	8.10

See Nos. 696-707.

Lenin Leading Soldiers — A167

Soldiers Storming Winter Palace — A167a

China Post No. C95

1962, Nov. 7 Photo. *Perf. 11½*

635	A167	8f black & red	90.00	6.00
636	A167a	20f slate grn & red	175.00	13.00

45th anniversary of the Russian Revolution.

Monument and Map of Albania — A168

China Post No. C96

Design: 10f, Albanian flag and Girl Pioneer.

1962, Nov. 28 *Perf. 11½x11*

637	A168	8f Prus blue & sepia	4.50	1.50
638	A168	10f red, yel, & blk	6.75	1.75

50th anniversary of Albanian independence.

Tsai Lun, Inventor of Papermaking A169

China Post No. C92

Designs: No. 640, Paper making. No. 641, Sun Szu-miao, physician. No. 642, Writing medical treatise. No. 643, Shen Ko, geologist. No. 644, Making field notes. No. 645, Kuo Shou-chin, astronomer. No. 646, Astronomical instrument.

Cumulative numbers 297-304 at lower right.

1962, Dec. 1 *Perf. 11½x11*

639	A169	4f multicolored	10.50	1.20
640	A169	4f multicolored	13.50	1.20
641	A169	8f multicolored	15.00	1.60
642	A169	8f multicolored	15.00	3.00
643	A169	10f multicolored	15.00	4.75
644	A169	10f multicolored	15.00	4.75
645	A169	20f multicolored	24.00	8.00
646	A169	20f multicolored	29.00	8.00
		Nos. 639-646 (8)	137.00	32.50

Scientists of ancient China.

No. 639 exists with an extra character in the inscription. Value, unused *$12,500*, used *$2,500*.

Building Type of 1961
China Post No. R12

Designs: 1f, 2f, Building, Nanchang. 3f, 4f, Trees and Sha Cho Pa Building. 8f, 10f, 20f, Pagoda Hill, Yenan. 30f, Gate of Heavenly Peace, Peking.

1962, Jan. Litho. *Rough Perf. 12½*
Size: 21x16mm
Without Gum

647	A152	1f ultra	*1.50*	*.50*
648	A152	2f greenish gray	*2.60*	*.50*
649	A152	3f violet gray	*1.50*	*.50*
650	A152	4f green	*1.50*	*.50*
651	A152	8f dk olive, perf. 14	*10.00*	*.50*
b.		Perf. 11x11½	*20.00*	
652	A152	10f brt rose lilac	*6.75*	*.50*
653	A152	20f slate blue	*11.00*	*1.00*
654	A152	30f dull blue	*8.00*	*1.00*
		Nos. 647-654 (8)	*42.85*	*5.00*

Tank Monument, Havana A170

Crowd in Peking — A171

China Post No. C97

Designs: No. 656, Cuban revolutionaries. No. 658, Crowd in Havana. No. 659, Cuban soldier. No. 660, Castro and Cuban flag.

Perf. 11½, 11x11½

1963, Jan. 1 Photo.

655	A170	4f red & blk brn	75.00	5.00
656	A170	4f green & blk	75.00	5.00
657	A171	8f dull red & brn	110.00	12.50
658	A171	8f dull red & brn	110.00	20.00
659	A170	10f ocher & blk	160.00	22.50
660	A170	10f red, blue & blk	190.00	*50.00*
		Nos. 655-660 (6)	720.00	*115.00*

4th anniversary of the Cuban revolution.

Green Dragontail — A172

China Post No. S56

No. 661, Tibetan clouded yellow (1). No. 662, Tritailed glory (2). No. 663, Neumogeni jungle queen (3). No. 664, Washan swordtail (4). No. 665, Striped ringlet (5). No. 667, Dilunulated peacock (7). No. 668, Yamfly (8). No. 669, Golden kaiser-i-hind (9). No. 670, Mushaell hairstreak (10). No. 671, Yellow orange-tip (11). No. 672, Great jay (12). No. 673, Striped punch (13). No. 674, Hainan violet-beak (14). No. 675, Omeiskipper (15). No. 676, Philippines birdwing (16). No. 677, Richtofenis red apollo (17). No. 678, Blue-banded king crow (18). No. 679, Solskyi copper (19). No. 680, Yunnan clipper (20).

1963 Without Gum *Perf. 11*

661	A172	4f multi	15.00	2.00
662	A172	4f multi	15.00	2.00
663	A172	4f multi	15.00	2.00
664	A172	4f multi	15.00	2.00
665	A172	4f multi	15.00	2.00
666	A172	8f shown	19.00	2.50
667	A172	8f multi	19.00	2.50
668	A172	8f multi	19.00	2.50
669	A172	8f multi	19.00	2.50
670	A172	8f multi	19.00	2.50
671	A172	10f multi	25.00	3.00
672	A172	10f multi	25.00	3.00
673	A172	10f multi	25.00	3.00
674	A172	10f multi	25.00	*3.00*
675	A172	10f multi	25.00	3.00
676	A172	20f multi	37.50	8.00
677	A172	20f multi	37.50	8.00
678	A172	22f multi	45.00	12.50
679	A172	30f multi	60.00	20.00
680	A172	50f multi	70.00	22.50
		Nos. 661-680 (20)	545.00	108.50

Issued: Nos. 666-675, July 15; others Apr. 5.

Karl Marx — A173

China Post No. C98

Designs: No. 682, "Workers of the World, Unite" on cover of first edition of Communist Manifesto. No. 683, Marx and Engels.

1963, May 5 *Perf. 11½*
Without Gum

681	A173	8f black, gold & sal	30.00	3.50
682	A173	8f gold & red	30.00	4.00
683	A173	8f gold & choc	25.00	4.00
		Nos. 681-683 (3)	85.00	11.50

145th anniversary of birth of Karl Marx (1818-1883), German political philosopher.

Child with Top — A174

China Post No. S54

Child: No. 685, eating berries. No. 686, as traffic policeman. No. 687, with windmill. No. 688, listening to caged cricket. No. 689, with sword. No. 690, embroidering. No. 691, with umbrella. No. 692, playing with sand. No. 693, playing table tennis. No. 694, learning to add. No. 695, with kite.

1963, June 1 Litho. *Perf. 12½*
Without Gum
Multicolored Designs

684	A174	4f grnsh gray	5.25	.80
685	A174	4f tan	5.25	.80
686	A174	8f gray	5.25	.60
687	A174	8f blue	5.25	.80
688	A174	8f tan	5.25	.80
689	A174	8f dp gray	5.25	.80
690	A174	8f citron	5.25	1.20
691	A174	8f gray	5.25	1.20
692	A174	10f green	7.75	1.90
693	A174	10f violet	7.75	1.90
694	A174	20f bister	17.00	4.75
695	A174	20f green	17.00	4.75
		Nos. 684-695 (12)	91.50	20.30

Children's Day. Value, imperf set unused $450, used $200.

Dance Type of 1962
China Post No. S53

Folk Dances: 4f, Weavers' dance, Puyi. 8f, Kazakh. 10f, Olunchun. 20f, Labor dance, Kaochan. 30f, Reed pipe dance, Miao. 50f, Fan dance, Korea.

Cumulative numbers 261-266 at lower right.

1963, June 15 *Perf. 12½*
Without Gum

696	A166	4f cream & multi	3.00	.40
697	A166	8f cream & multi	3.00	.50
698	A166	10f cream & multi	4.00	.60
699	A166	20f cream & multi	5.00	1.75
700	A166	30f cream & multi	5.00	1.75
701	A166	50f cream & multi	8.00	3.25
		Nos. 696-701 (6)	28.00	8.25

China Post No. S55

1963, June 30 Without Gum

Folk Dances: 4f, "Wedding Ceremony," Yu. 8f, "Encircling Mountain Forest," Pai. 10f, Long drum dance, Yao. 20f, Third day of the third month dance, Li. 30f, Knife dance, Kawa. 50f, Peacock dance, Thai.

Cumulative numbers 279-284 at lower right.

702	A166	4f cream & multi	3.00	.40
703	A166	8f cream & multi	3.00	.50
704	A166	10f cream & multi	3.00	.60
705	A166	20f cream & multi	6.00	1.25
706	A166	30f cream & multi	6.00	1.25
707	A166	50f cream & multi	6.00	1.25
		Nos. 702-707 (6)	27.00	5.25

Giant Panda Eating Apples — A175

China Post No. S59

Designs: No. 709, Giant panda eating bamboo shoots. 10f, Two pandas, horiz.

1963, Aug. 5 Photo. *Perf. 11½x11*
Size: 28x38mm

708	A175	8f pale blue & blk	45.00	3.50
709	A175	8f pale blue & blk	45.00	6.00

Size: 50x29mm
Perf. 11½

710	A175	10f olive & blk	60.00	4.00
		Nos. 708-710 (3)	150.00	13.50

Value, imperf set unused $330, used $150.

Table Tennis Player — A176

China Post No. C99

No. 712, Trophies won by Chinese team.

1963, Sept. 10 Engr. *Perf. 11½*

711	A176	8f dk olive grn	28.00	2.75
712	A176	8f brown	28.00	2.75

27th World Table Tennis Championships.

Snub-nosed Langur — A177

China Post No. S60

Designs: 10f, Two monkeys playing. 22f, Two monkeys grooming.

1963, Sept. 23 Photo. *Perf. 11½x11*

713	A177	8f gray & multi	20.00	2.25
714	A177	10f gray & multi	20.00	2.25
715	A177	22f gray & multi	35.00	7.75
		Nos. 713-715 (3)	75.00	12.25

Value, imperf set unused $300, used $130.

Jade-green Screen Mountain — A178

China Post No. S57

Hwang Shan Landscapes (Yellow Mountains), Anhwei Province: No. 717, "Guests Welcoming Pines" (2). No. 718, Pines and Rock Behind the Sea (3). No. 719, Terrace of Keeping Cool (4). No. 720, Mount of Heavenly Capital (5). No. 721, Mount of Scissors (6). No. 722, Forest of Ten Thousand Pines (7). No. 723, "Brush Blooming in Dream" (8). No. 724, Mount of Lotus Flower (9). No. 725, Cumulus Cloud over West Sea (10). No. 726, Old Pines of Hwang Shan (11). No. 727, "Watching the Clouds over West Sea" (12). No. 728, Mount of Stalagmites (13). No. 729, "Stone Monkey Watching the Sea" (14). No. 730, Forest of Lions (15). No. 731, Three Fairy Tales of Pen Lai (16).

Nos. 724-731 horiz.

Engraved and Photogravure

1963, Oct. 15 *Perf. 11½*

No.	Type	Denom.	Color	Unused	Used
716	A178	4f	shown	42.50	5.50
717	A178	4f	multi	42.50	5.50
718	A178	4f	multi	42.50	5.50
719	A178	4f	multi	42.50	5.50
720	A178	8f	multi	32.50	5.00
721	A178	8f	multi	32.50	5.00
722	A178	8f	multi	32.50	6.00
723	A178	8f	multi	32.50	5.00
724	A178	10f	multi	67.50	9.00
725	A178	10f	multi	67.50	9.00
726	A178	10f	multi	67.50	9.00
727	A178	10f	multi	67.50	9.00
728	A178	20f	multi	87.50	14.00
729	A178	22f	multi	85.00	13.00
730	A178	30f	multi	190.00	40.00
731	A178	50f	multi	190.00	60.00
	Nos. 716-731 (16)			1,123.	206.00

Soccer Player — A179

Athletes and Banners — A180

China Post No. C100

No. 733, Discus, women's. No. 734, Diving, men's. No. 735, Gymnastics, women's.

Engraved and Photogravure

1963, Nov. 17 *Perf. 11*

No.	Type	Denom.	Color	Unused	Used
732	A179	8f	gray, red & blk	19.00	2.00
733	A179	8f	gray, ultra & blk	19.00	2.00
734	A179	8f	lt grn, brn & blk	19.00	2.00
735	A179	8f	gray, lil rose & blk	19.00	2.00

Photo.

Perf. 11½

No.	Type	Denom.	Color	Unused	Used
736	A180	10f	red & multi	65.00	6.00
	Nos. 732-736 (5)			141.00	14.00

Games of the Newly Emerging Forces, Djakarta.

Clay Rooster and Goat — A181

China Post No. S58

Chinese Folk Toys: No. 738, Cloth camel. No. 739, Cloth tigers. No. 740, Clay ox and rider. No. 741, Cloth rabbit, wooden doll, clay roosters. No. 742, Straw rooster. No. 743, Cloth donkey and bird. No. 744, Clay lion. No. 745, Cloth tiger and tumbler doll.

1963, Dec. 10 Litho. *Perf. 11½*

Toys Multicolored; Without Gum

No.	Type	Denom.	Color	Unused	Used
737	A181	4f	bister	2.25	1.00
738	A181	4f	gray	2.25	1.00
739	A181	4f	lt blue	2.25	1.00
740	A181	8f	bister	2.25	1.00
741	A181	8f	gray	2.25	1.00
742	A181	8f	lt blue	2.25	1.00
743	A181	10f	bister	4.50	1.00
744	A181	10f	gray	4.50	1.00
745	A181	10f	lt blue	4.50	1.00
	Nos. 737-745 (9)			27.00	9.00

Armed Vietnamese Family — A182

China Post No. C101

Liberation of South Viet Nam: No. 747, Militia with Vietnamese flag.

1963, Dec. 20 Photo. *Perf. 11½x11*

No.	Type	Denom.	Color	Unused	Used
746	A182	8f	tan, blk & red	11.00	2.00
747	A182	8f	red & multi	11.00	2.00

Flags of Cuba and China — A183

China Post No. C102

Design: No. 749, Boy waving Cuban flag.

1964, Jan. 1

No.	Type	Denom.	Color	Unused	Used
748	A183	8f	red, yel, bl & ind	65.00	7.00
749	A183	8f	multicolored	65.00	7.00

5th anniversary of the liberation of Cuba.

Woman Driving Tractor — A184

China Post No. S64

Woman of the People's Commune: No. 751, harvesting. No. 752, picking cotton. No. 753, picking fruit. No. 754, reading book. No. 755, on guard duty.

1964, Mar. 8

No.	Type	Denom.	Color	Unused	Used
750	A184	8f	ol, pink & brn	5.50	1.00
751	A184	8f	brn yel & org	5.50	1.00
752	A184	8f	gray & multi	5.50	1.00
753	A184	8f	black, org & bl	5.50	1.00
754	A184	8f	green & multi	5.50	2.00
755	A184	8f	lilac & multi	5.50	2.00
	Nos. 750-755 (6)			33.00	8.00

Chinese and African Men A185

China Post No. C103

Design: No. 757, African drummer.

1964, Apr. 12 Photo. *Perf. 11*

No.	Type	Denom.	Color	Unused	Used
756	A185	8f	red & multi	5.00	.95
757	A185	8f	black & dk brn	5.00	.95

African Freedom Day.

Marx, Engels, Lenin and Stalin — A186

China Post No. C104

Design: No. 759, Banners and workers.

1964, May 1 *Perf. 11½*

No.	Type	Denom.	Color	Unused	Used
758	A186	8f	gold, red & blk	*55.00*	*7.50*
759	A186	8f	gold, red & blk	*55.00*	*7.50*

Labor Day.

Orchard, Yenan A187

China Post No. S65

Yenan, Shrine of the Chinese Revolution: No. 761, Central Auditorium, Yang Chia Ling. No. 762, Mao's office and residence. No. 763, Auditorium, Wang Chia Ping. No. 764, Border Region Assembly Hall. No. 765, Pagoda Hill and Bridge.

1964, July 1 Photo. *Perf. 11x11½*

No.	Type	Denom.	Color	Unused	Used
760	A187	8f	multicolored	14.00	3.00
761	A187	8f	multicolored	14.00	3.00
762	A187	8f	multicolored	14.00	3.00
763	A187	8f	multicolored	14.00	3.00
764	A187	8f	multicolored	14.00	3.00
765	A187	52f	multicolored	90.00	19.50
	Nos. 760-765 (6)			160.00	34.50

Map and Flag of Viet Nam — A188

China Post No. C105

1964, July 20 *Perf. 11½*

No.	Type	Denom.	Color	Unused	Used
766	A188	8f	multicolored	60.00	6.00

Victory in South Viet Nam.

Alchemist's Glowing Crucible — A189

China Post No. S61

No. 768, Night-shining jade (2). No. 769, Purple Kuo's cap (3). No. 770, Chao pink (4). No. 771, Yao yellow (5). No. 772, Twin beauty (6). No. 773, Ice-veiled ruby (7). No. 774, Gold-sprinkled Chinese ink (8). No. 775, Cinnabar jar (9). No. 776, Lan Tien jade (10). No. 777, Imperial robe yellow (11). No. 778, Hu red (12). No. 779, Pea green (13). No. 780, Wei purple (14). No. 781, Intoxicated celestial peach (15).

No. 782, Glorious crimson & great gold pink.

1964, Aug. 5 *Perf. 11½x11*

No.	Type	Denom.	Color	Unused	Used
767	A189	4f	shown	18.50	2.10
768	A189	4f	multi	18.50	2.10
769	A189	8f	multi	12.00	2.10
770	A189	8f	multi	12.00	2.10
771	A189	8f	multi	12.00	2.10
772	A189	8f	multi	12.00	2.10
773	A189	8f	multi	12.00	2.10
774	A189	10f	multi	20.50	2.10
775	A189	10f	multi	20.50	2.10
776	A189	10f	multi	20.50	2.10
777	A189	10f	multi	20.50	2.10
778	A189	10f	multi	20.50	2.10
779	A189	20f	multi	75.00	*18.50*
780	A189	43f	multi	120.00	*23.00*
781	A189	52f	multi	190.00	*34.00*
	Nos. 767-781 (15)			584.50	*100.70*

Souvenir Sheet

Perf. 11½

Without Gum

No.	Type	Denom.	Color	Unused	Used
782	A189	$2	multi	*2,500.*	*925.00*

No. 782 contains one 48x59mm stamp.

Eight values depicting theatrical masks of the Peking Opera were prepared in 1964 but not issued. The designs are as design type A398: 4f, Meng Lang. 4f, Li Kui. 8f, Huang Gai. 8f, Monkey King. 10f, Lu Zhishen. 10f, Lian Po. 20f, Zhang Fei. 20f, Dou Erdun. The unissued stamps are numbered 352-359 and dated "1964." Sound examples are rare and sell for between $125,000 and $275,000. See Nos. 1574-1581.

Wine Cup — A190

China Post No. S63

Sacrificial bronze vessels of Yin dynasty, prior to 1050 B.C.: No. 784, Ku beaker (2). No. 785, Kuang wine urn (3). No. 786, Chia wine cup (4). No. 787, Tsun wine vessel (5). No. 788, Yu wine urn (6). No. 789, Tsun wine vessel (7). No. 790, Ceremonial cauldron (8).

Engraved and Photogravure

1964, Aug. 25 *Perf. 11½x11*

No.	Type	Denom.	Color	Unused	Used
783	A190	4f	shown	11.50	1.75
784	A190	4f	multi	11.50	1.75
785	A190	8f	multi	10.50	1.75
786	A190	8f	multi	10.50	1.75
787	A190	10f	multi	24.00	2.00
788	A190	10f	multi	24.00	2.00
789	A190	20f	multi	42.50	4.75
790	A190	20f	multi	42.50	4.75
	Nos. 783-790 (8)			177.00	20.50

Grain Harvest — A191

China Post No. S66

Designs: No. 792, Students planting trees. No. 793, Study period. No. 794, Scientific experimentation.

1964, Sept. 26 **Photo.**

No.	Type	Denom.	Color	Unused	Used
791	A191	8f	multicolored	7.25	1.25
792	A191	8f	multicolored	7.25	1.25
793	A191	8f	multicolored	7.25	1.25
794	A191	8f	multicolored	7.25	1.25
	Nos. 791-794 (4)			29.00	5.00

Youth helping in agriculture.

Marx, Engels, Trafalgar Square, London — A192

China Post No. C107

1964, Sept. 28 ***Perf. 11½***

795 A192 8f red, gold & red brn 130.00 25.00

Centenary of the First International.

Gold Ink

Stamps with gold ink often show some tarnishing. Values are for untarnished gold color. Tarnished stamps will sell for less.

People with Banners — A193

China Post No. C106

No. 797, Gate of Heavenly Peace and Chinese flag. No. 798, People with banners, facing left.

1964, Oct. 1

796	A193 8f cream & multi	50.00	7.50
797	A193 8f cream & multi	50.00	7.50
798	A193 8f cream & multi	50.00	7.50
a.	Souvenir sheet of 3	*4,250.*	*1,350.*
b.	Strip of 3, #796-798	300.00	80.00
	Nos. 796-798 (3)	150.00	22.50

15th anniv. of the People's Republic.

No. 798a contains No. 798b in continuous design without separating perfs. No. 798a almost always has disturbed gum, with interleaving paper sticking to it, or tarnished gilt. Such examples sell for considerably less than the very fine example valued above.

Values for No. 798b are for an unfolded strip.

Oil Derricks — A194

China Post No. S67

Oil industry: 4f, Geological surveyors and truck, horiz. 8f, "Christmas tree" and extraction accessories. 10f, Oil refinery. 20f, Tank cars, horiz.

1964, Oct. 1

799	A194 4f lt blue & multi	75.00	11.00
800	A194 8f shown	125.00	15.00
801	A194 8f lilac & multi	70.00	8.00
802	A194 10f slate & multi	70.00	8.00
803	A194 20f brown & multi	240.00	30.00
	Nos. 799-803 (5)	580.00	72.00

Albanian and Chinese Flags A195

China Post No. C108

10f, Enver Hoxha and Albanian coat of arms.

1964, Nov. 29 ***Perf. 11x11½***

804	A195 8f red & multi	40.00	13.50
805	A195 10f red, yel & blk	62.50	22.00

20th anniv. of the liberation of Albania.

Power Dam Construction A196

China Post No. S68

No. 807, Installation of turbogenerator rotor. No. 808, Main dam. 20f, Pylon.

1964, Dec. 15 ***Perf. 11½***

806	A196 4f multicolored	75.00	10.00
807	A196 8f multicolored	70.00	5.00
808	A196 8f multicolored	92.50	5.00
809	A196 20f multicolored	220.00	27.50
	Nos. 806-809 (4)	457.50	47.50

Hsin An Kiang Dam and hydroelectric power station.

Fertilizer Industry — A197

China Post No. S69

Chemical Industry: No. 811, Plastics. No. 812, Medicines. No. 813, Rubber. No. 814, Insecticides. No. 815, Industrial acids. No. 816, Industrial alkaloids. No. 817, Synthetic fibers.

1964, Dec. 30 **Photo. & Engr.**

810	A197 8f red & blk	10.00	1.50
811	A197 8f yel grn & blk	10.00	1.50
812	A197 8f brown & blk	10.00	1.50
813	A197 8f lilac rose & blk	10.00	1.50
814	A197 8f blue & blk	10.00	1.50
815	A197 8f orange & blk	10.00	1.50
816	A197 8f violet & blk	10.00	1.50
817	A197 8f brt green & blk	10.00	1.50
	Nos. 810-817 (8)	80.00	12.00

Mao Studying Map — A198

Mao Tse-tung — A199

China Post No. C109

Design: No. 819, Victory at Lushan Pass.

1965, Jan. 31 **Photo.** ***Perf. 11***

818	A198 8f red & multi	75.00	22.50
819	A198 8f red & multi	75.00	22.50

Perf. 11½x11

820	A199 8f gold & multi	125.00	30.00
	Nos. 818-820 (3)	275.00	75.00

Tsunyi Conference, 30th anniversary.

Conference Hall, Bandung — A200

China Post No. C110

No. 822, Asians and Africans applauding.

1965, Apr. 18 ***Perf. 11½x11***

821	A200 8f cream & multi	4.00	.90
822	A200 8f cream & multi	4.00	.90

10th anniversary of the Bandung, Indonesia, Conference, Apr. 1955.

Lenin — A201

China Post No. C111

1965, Apr. 25 ***Perf. 11½***

823 A201 8f red, choc & salmon 30.00 5.00

95th anniversary of the birth of Lenin.

Chinese Player — A202

China Post No. C112

No. 825, European woman (2). No. 826, Chinese woman (3). No. 827, European man (4).

1965, Apr. 25 ***Perf. 11½***

824	A202 8f shown	.90	.45
825	A202 8f multi	.90	.45
826	A202 8f multi	.90	.45
827	A202 8f multi	.90	.45
a.	Block of 4, #824-827	10.00	5.00

28th World Table Tennis Championships, Ljubljana, Yugoslavia, Apr. 15-25.

Climbers on Mt. Minya Konka — A203

China Post No. S70

Mountain Climbers: No. 829, on Muztagh Ata. No. 830, on Mt. Jolmo Lungma (Mt. Everest). No. 831, Women camping on Kongur Tiubie Tagh. No. 832, on Shisha Pangma.

1965, May 25 **Photo. & Engr.**

828	A203 8f blue, blk & ol	17.00	2.10
829	A203 8f blue, blk & ol	17.00	2.10
830	A203 8f ultra, blk & gray	17.00	2.10
831	A203 8f lt bl, blk & yel gray	17.00	2.10
832	A203 8f ultra, blk & gray	17.00	2.10
	Nos. 828-832 (5)	85.00	10.50

Chinese mountaineering achievements, 1957-64.

Marx and Lenin — A204

China Post No. C113

1965, June 21 **Photo.** ***Perf. 11½x11***

833 A204 8f red, yel & blk 27.50 4.50

Postal Ministers' Congress, Peking.

Tseping Valley A205

China Post No. S73

Chingkang Mountains, Cradle of the Chinese Revolution: No. 835, San Wan Tsun (2). No. 836, Octagon Bldg., Mao Ping (3). No. 837, River and Bridge at Lung Shih (4). No. 838, Ta Ching Tsun (5). No. 839, Bridge across the Lung Yuan (6). No. 840, Hwang Yang Mountain (7). No. 841, Chingkang peaks (8).

1965, July 1 ***Perf. 11x11½***

834	A205 4f shown	32.50	8.50
835	A205 8f multi	32.50	3.00
836	A205 8f multi	32.50	3.00
837	A205 8f multi	35.00	3.00
838	A205 8f multi	35.00	3.00
839	A205 10f multi	55.00	3.00
840	A205 10f multi	55.00	10.00
841	A205 52f multi	35.00	19.00
	Nos. 834-841 (8)	312.50	52.50

Soldiers with Books — A206

China Post No. S74

No. 843, Soldiers reading Little Red Books (2). No. 844, With shell and artillery (3). No. 845, Rifle instruction (4). No. 846, Sewing jacket (5). No. 847, Bayonet charge (6). No. 848, With Banner (7). No. 849, Military band (8).

1965, Aug. 1 ***Perf. 11½***

Without Gum

842	A206 8f shown	45.00	6.50
843	A206 8f multi	45.00	6.50
844	A206 8f multi	45.00	6.50
845	A206 8f multi	45.00	6.50
846	A206 8f multi	45.00	6.50
847	A206 8f multi	45.00	11.00
848	A206 8f multi	45.00	11.00
849	A206 8f multi	45.00	11.00
	Nos. 842-849 (8)	360.00	65.50

People's Liberation Army. Nos. 846-849 vertical.

"Welcome to Peking" — A207

China Post No. C114

No. 851, Chinese and Japanese young men. No. 852, Chinese and Japanese girls. No. 853, Musical entertainment. No. 854, Emblem of meeting.

1965, Aug. 25 ***Perf. 11½x11***

No.	Type	Description	Unused	Used
850	A207	4f yellow & multi	2.00	1.00
851	A207	8f pink & multi	2.00	1.00
852	A207	8f multicolored	3.75	1.00
853	A207	10f multicolored	4.50	2.00
854	A207	22f lt blue & multi	9.25	3.00
		Nos. 850-854 (5)	21.50	8.00

Chinese-Japanese Youth Meeting, Peking.

North Vietnamese Soldier — A208

Peoples of the World — A209

China Post No. C117

Designs: No. 856, Soldier with guns. No. 857, Soldier giving victory salute.

1965, Sept. 2 ***Perf. 11½x11***

No.	Type	Description	Unused	Used
855	A208	8f red & red brn	4.50	1.25
856	A208	8f red & blk	4.50	1.25
857	A208	8f red & vio brn	4.50	1.25

Perf. 11½

No.	Type	Description	Unused	Used
858	A209	8f black & red	7.00	1.75
		Nos. 855-858 (4)	20.50	5.50

Struggle of the people of Viet Nam.

Mao Tse-tung at His Desk — A210

Crossing Yellow River A211

Victory Monument A212

China Post No. C115

Design: No. 862, Recruits in cart.

1965, Sept. 3 ***Perf. 11***

No.	Type	Description	Unused	Used
859	A210	8f red & multi	57.50	15.00

Perf. 11x11½, 11½x11

No.	Type	Description	Unused	Used
860	A211	8f red & dk grn	40.00	3.75
861	A212	8f red & dk brn	40.00	3.75
862	A211	8f red & dk grn	40.00	3.75
		Nos. 859-862 (4)	177.50	26.25

20th anniversary of victory over Japan.

2nd National Games — A213

National Games Opening Ceremonies — A214

China Post No. C116

Perf. 11½x11, 11 (A214)

1965, Sept. 28

No.	Type	Description	Unused	Used
863	A213	4f Soccer	19.50	1.75
864	A213	4f Archery	19.50	1.75
865	A213	8f Javelin	19.50	1.75
866	A213	8f Gymnastics	19.50	1.75
867	A213	8f Volleyball	19.50	1.75
868	A214	10f shown	52.50	4.00
869	A213	10f Bicyling	57.50	4.00
870	A213	20f Diving	62.50	7.50
871	A213	22f Hurdles	62.50	7.50
872	A213	30f Weight lifting	72.50	20.00
873	A213	43f Basketball	72.50	25.00
		Nos. 863-873 (11)	477.50	76.75

Government Building — A215

China Post No. R13

1½f, 5f, 22f, Gate of Heavenly Peace. 2f, 8f, 30f, People's Hall. 3f, 10f, 50f, Military Museum.

1964-66 ***Perf. 11½x11***

Without Gum

No.	Type	Description	Unused	Used
874	A215	1f brown	.60	.35
875	A215	1½f red lilac	.60	*.35*
876	A215	2f green	.60	.35
877	A215	3f blue grn	.60	.35
878	A215	4f brt blue	.70	.35
879	A215	5f vio brn ('66)	2.25	.35
880	A215	8f rose red	.80	.35
881	A215	10f gray olive	2.25	.35
882	A215	20f violet	2.25	.35
883	A215	22f orange	2.25	.35
884	A215	30f yellow grn	3.50	.50
885	A215	50f dp blue ('66)	16.00	4.00
		Nos. 874-885 (12)	32.40	*8.00*

No. 878 exists as perf. 12. No 880 exists with other perforation varieties. Nos. 879 and 885 were issued March 10, 1966; all others issued June 17, 1964.

Textile Workers — A216

China Post No. S71

No. 887, Machine shop (2). No. 888, Welder (3). No. 889, Students (4). No. 890, Militia (5).

1965, Nov. 30

No.	Type	Description	Unused	Used
886	A216	8f shown	35.00	3.25
887	A216	8f multicolored	35.00	3.25
888	A216	8f multicolored	35.00	3.25
889	A216	8f multicolored	35.00	3.25
890	A216	8f multicolored	35.00	3.25
		Nos. 886-890 (5)	175.00	16.25

Women workers.

Soccer — A217

China Post No. S72

Children's Sports: No. 892, Racing. No. 893, Tobogganing and skating. No. 894, Gymnastics. No. 895, Swimming. No. 896, Rifle practice. No. 897, Jumping rope. No. 898, Table tennis.

1966, Feb. 25 ***Perf. 11***

No.	Type	Description	Unused	Used
891	A217	4f emer & multi	1.60	.55
892	A217	4f yel brn & multi	1.60	.55
893	A217	8f blue & multi	1.60	.55
894	A217	8f yellow & multi	1.60	.70
895	A217	8f grnsh bl & multi	1.60	.70
896	A217	8f green & multi	1.60	.70
897	A217	10f org & multi	5.00	1.50
898	A217	52f grnsh gray & multi	15.00	7.00
		Nos. 891-898 (8)	29.60	12.25

Mobile Transformer A218

China Post No. S62

New Industrial Machinery: No. 900, Electron microscope, vert. No. 901, Lathe. No. 902, Vertical boring and turning machine, vert. No. 903, Gear-grinding machine. No. 904, Hydraulic press. No. 905, Milling machine. No. 906, Electron accelerator, vert.

Perf. 11x11½, 11½x11

1966, Mar. 30 **Photo. & Engr.**

No.	Type	Description	Unused	Used
899	A218	4f yellow & blk	35.00	3.00
900	A218	8f blk & lt ultra	35.00	2.00
901	A218	8f sal pink & blk	35.00	2.00
902	A218	8f olive & blk	35.00	2.00
903	A218	8f rose lil & blk	35.00	2.00
904	A218	10f gray & blk	45.00	8.50
905	A218	10f bl grn & blk	45.00	11.00
906	A218	22f lilac & blk	50.00	9.00
		Nos. 899-906 (8)	315.00	39.50

Military and Civilian Workers A219

China Post No. S75

Women in Various Occupations: No. 908, Train conductor. No. 909, Red Cross worker. No. 910, Kindergarten teacher. No. 911, Road sweeper. No. 912, Hairdresser. No. 913, Bus conductor. No. 914, Traveling saleswoman. No. 915, Canteen worker. No. 916, Rural mail carrier.

1966, May 10 ***Perf. 11x11½***

No.	Type	Description	Unused	Used
907	A219	8f red & multi	2.75	1.10
908	A219	8f pale grn & multi	2.75	1.10
909	A219	8f yellow & multi	2.75	1.10
910	A219	8f green & multi	2.75	1.10
911	A219	8f salmon & multi	2.75	1.10
912	A219	8f pale bl & bl	2.75	1.10
913	A219	8f yellow & multi	2.75	1.10
914	A219	8f tan & multi	2.75	1.10
915	A219	8f yel grn & multi	2.75	1.10
916	A219	8f green & multi	2.75	1.10
		Nos. 907-916 (10)	27.50	11.00

Statue "Thunderstorm" — A220

China Post No. C119

22f, Open book and association emblem.

1966, June 27 ***Perf. 11***

No.	Type	Description	Unused	Used
917	A220	8f red & black	12.50	3.00
918	A220	22f red, gold & yel	24.00	4.50

Afro-Asian Writers' Assoc. Conf., Peking.

Sun Yat-sen — A221

China Post No. C120

1966, Nov. 12 ***Perf. 11½x11***

No.	Type	Description	Unused	Used
919	A221	8f sepia & lt buff	105.00	27.50

Birth centenary of Sun Yat-sen.

Athletes Holding Portrait of Mao — A222

Two Women Athletes with Little Red Book A223

China Post No. C121

No. 921, Athletes holding Little Red Books. No. 923, Athletes reading Mao texts.

1966, Dec. 31 ***Perf. 11***

No.	Type	Description	Unused	Used
920	A222	8f red & multi	90.00	16.50
921	A222	8f red & multi	90.00	16.50

Perf. 11x11½

No.	Type	Description	Unused	Used
922	A223	8f blue & multi	70.00	17.00
923	A223	8f blue & multi	70.00	17.00
		Nos. 920-923 (4)	320.00	67.00

1st Athletic Games of the New Emerging Nations.

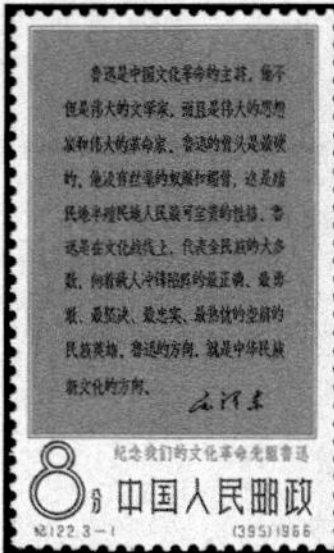

Appreciation of Lu Hsun by Mao — A224

China Post No. C122

Designs: No. 925, Portrait of Lu Hsun. No. 926, Lu Hsun's handwriting (3 vert. rows).

Engr. & Photo.; Photo. (#925)

1966, Dec. 31 ***Perf. 11½***

No.	Type	Description	Unused	Used
924	A224	8f red & black	60.00	25.00
925	A224	8f red & multi	120.00	25.00
926	A224	8f red & black	60.00	25.00
		Nos. 924-926 (3)	240.00	75.00

Lu Hsun, Revolutionary writer (1881-1936).

"Be Resolute ...," by Mao Tse-tung — A225

China Post No. C124

Designs: No. 928, Drilling crew fighting natural gas fire, horiz. No. 929, Attempt to close fire-engulfed valve.

Sizes: Nos. 927, 929, 26x38mm; No. 928, 49x29mm

Perf. 11½x11, 11½ (No. 928)

1967, Mar. 10 **Photo.**

927 A225 8f red, gold & blk 65.00 17.50
928 A225 8f brick red & blk 65.00 17.50
929 A225 8f brick red & blk 65.00 17.50
Nos. 927-929 (3) 195.00 52.50

Heroic oil well firefighters.

Liu Ying-chun A226

China Post No. C123

No. 931, With book by Mao (2). No. 932, Holding bridle of horse (3). No. 933, With film slide (4). No. 934, Lecturing (5). No. 935, Fatal attempt to stop runaway horse (6).

1967, Mar. 25 ***Perf. 11½x11***

930 A226 8f shown 65.00 17.50
931 A226 8f multi 65.00 17.50
932 A226 8f multi 65.00 17.50
933 A226 8f multi 65.00 17.50
934 A226 8f multi 65.00 17.50
935 A226 8f multi 65.00 17.50
Nos. 930-935 (6) 390.00 105.00

In memory of soldier Liu Ying-chun, hero.

Third 5-Year Plan — A227

China Post No. C118

Design: No. 936, Banners, 3 workers and male soldier facing right (industrial growth). No. 937, Banners, 3 workers and female militia member facing left (agricultural growth).

1967, Apr. 15 ***Perf. 11***

936 A227 8f red & multi 90.00 19.00
937 A227 8f red & multi 90.00 19.00

Third Five-Year Plan.

Mao Tse-tung — A228

Thoughts of Mao — A229

China Post No. W1

1967, Apr. 20 ***Perf. 11½***

938 A228 8f red & multi 110.00 45.00

Red & Gold

939 A229 8f 39 characters 110.00 55.00
940 A229 8f 50 characters 110.00 55.00
941 A229 8f 39 characters in 6 lines 110.00 55.00
942 A229 8f 53 characters 110.00 55.00
943 A229 8f 46 characters 110.00 55.00
a. Strip of 5, #939-943 1,600. 525.00

Gold & Red

944 A229 8f 41 characters 160.00 90.00
945 A229 8f 49 characters 160.00 90.00
946 A229 8f 35 characters 160.00 90.00
947 A229 8f 22 characters 160.00 90.00
948 A229 8f 29 characters 160.00 90.00
a. Strip of 5, #944-948 2,600. 725.00
Nos. 938-948 (11) 1,460. 770.00

Thoughts of Mao Tse-tung.

Values for Nos. 943a and 948a are for unfolded strips without tarnishing. Strips with folds and/or tarnishing sell for much less.

For Nos. 938-1046, beware of forgeries, removed cancels and repairs. No numbers appear below design on Nos. 938-1046.

Gate of Heavenly Peace and Text from C. C. P. Communique Praising Mao — A230

Mao and Lin Piao A231

China Post No. W2

No. 950, Mao and poem. No. 951, Mao among people of various races. No. 952, Mao facing left and Red Guards with books. No. 953, Mao with upraised right hand. No. 954, Mao leaning on rail, horiz. 10f, Mao and Lin Piao in discussion, horiz.

Engraved and Photogravure

1967 ***Perf. 11x11½***

Size: 36x56mm

949 A230 4f yel, red & mar 140.00 47.50

Photo.

950 A230 8f yel, brn, & red 140.00 47.50
951 A230 8f yel, red & multi 140.00 47.50
952 A230 8f yel, red & multi 140.00 47.50

Size: 36x50mm, 50x36mm

Perf. 11

953 A231 8f black & multi 175.00 42.50
954 A231 8f lt blue & multi 400.00 160.00
955 A231 8f black & multi 135.00 42.50
956 A231 10f black & multi 400.00 160.00
Nos. 949-956 (8) 1,670. 595.00

"Mao Tse-tung Our Great Teacher."

Issued: Nos. 949-953, 5/1; Nos. 954-956, 9/20.

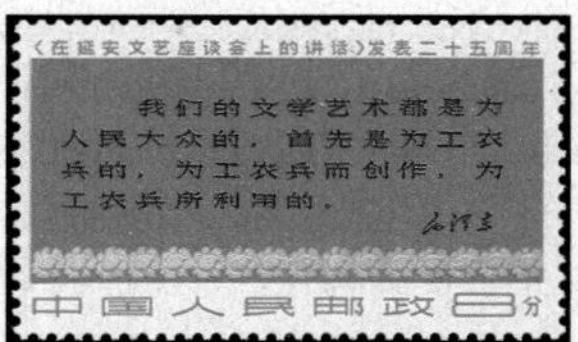

Mao Text (4 lines) — A232

Parade of Supporters — A233

China Post No. W3

Design: No. 958, Mao text (5 lines).

Engraved and Photogravure

1967, May 23 ***Perf. 11½***

957 A232 8f black, red & yel 325.00 135.00
958 A232 8f black, red & yel 325.00 160.00

Photo.

Perf. 11

959 A233 8f multicolored 325.00 160.00
Nos. 957-959 (3) 975.00 455.00

25th anniversary of Mao Tse-tung's "Talks on Literature and Art" in Yenan.

A stamp was prepared in August 1967 for the 40th anniversary of the Autumn Harvest March. It was not issued, but a few examples have entered the marketplace. It depicts Mao Tse-tung on the left and Lin Piao on the right at podium, against a blue sky. A cut example comprising the right half of the stamp was sold in a Jan. 2010 Hong Kong auction for the equivalent of U.S. $285,000. Presumably, an intact example would sell for far more.

Mao Tse-tung — A234

China Post No. W4

1967 **Engr.** ***Perf. 11***

960 A234 4f brown 100.00 *30.00*
961 A234 8f carmine 200.00 *50.00*
962 A234 35f dk brown 40.00 *12.50*
963 A234 43f vermilion 45.00 *12.50*
964 A234 52f carmine 50.00 *17.50*
Nos. 960-964 (5) 435.00 *122.50*

46th anniv. of Chinese Communist Party. Issue dates: 8f, July 1; others Sept. 18.

Mao, "Sun of the Revolution" — A235

China Post No. W6

No. 966, Mao and people of various races.

1967, Oct. 1 ***Perf. 11½x11***

965 A235 8f multicolored *75.00* *40.00*
966 A235 8f multicolored *170.00* *47.50*

People's Republic of China, 18th anniv.

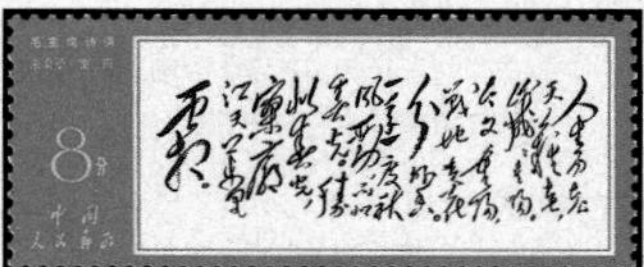

"September 9" — A236

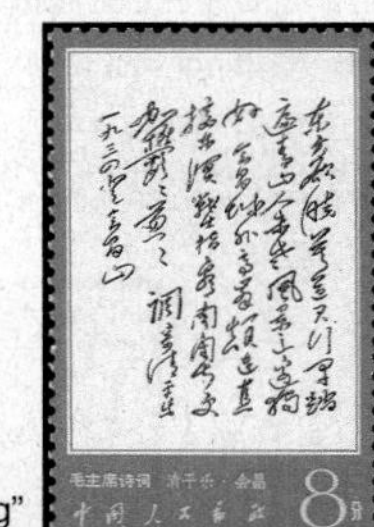

"Huichang" A237

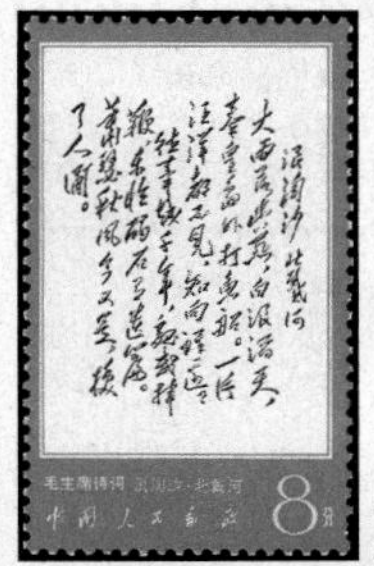

"Peitaiho" A238

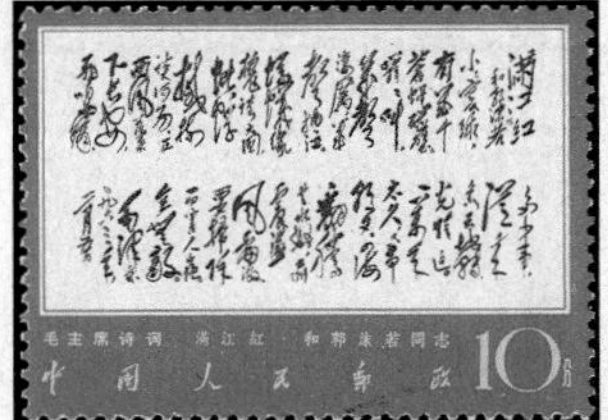

Reply to Comrade Kuo Mo-jo — A239

Mao Tse-tung Writing Poems — A240

China Post No. W7

Poems by Mao: No. 967, "The Long March." No. 968, "Liupanshan." No. 969, shown. No. 970, "The Cave of the Fairies." No. 971, "Snow." No. 972, "Lushan Pass." No. 975, "Conquest of Nanking." No. 976, "The Yellow Crane Pavilion." No. 977, "Swimming." No. 979, "Changsha."

1967-68 Photo. *Perf. 11*

Size: 79x18½mm

No.	Type	Description	Unused	Used
967	A236	4f 9 characters, UL panel	140.00	100.00
968	A236	4f 11 characters, UL panel	140.00	33.00

Size: 60x24mm

Perf. 11½

No.	Type	Description	Unused	Used
969	A236	8f shown, 10 characters in UL panel	100.00	50.00
970	A236	8f 21 characters in UL panel	130.00	50.00
971	A236	8f 11 characters in UL panel	115.00	67.50
972	A236	8f 9 characters in UL panel	115.00	67.50

Size: 29x50mm

No.	Type	Description	Unused	Used
973	A237	8f shown	675.00	155.00
974	A238	8f shown	875.00	250.00
975	A238	8f 3 rows in bottom panel	600.00	160.00
976	A238	8f 2 rows in bottom panel	310.00	155.00

Size: 52x38mm

Perf. 11

No.	Type	Description	Unused	Used
977	A239	8f 3 short vert. rows, at left of poem	450.00	160.00
978	A239	10f shown	67.50	33.00
979	A239	10f undivided text	145.00	33.00
980	A240	10f red, yel & multi	145.00	50.00
		Nos. 967-980 (14)	4,008.	1,364.

Issued: Nos. 969-970, 980, 10/1; Nos. 973-974, 977, 5/20/68; others 7/20/68.

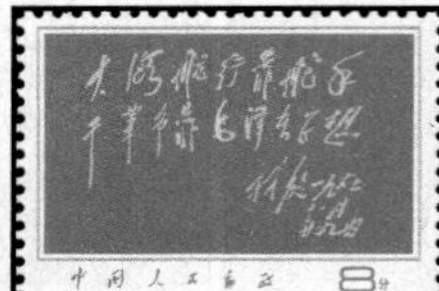

Lin Piao's Epigram on Mao Tse-tung A241

China Post No. W8

1967, Dec. 26 Photo. *Perf. 11x11½*

No.	Type	Description	Unused	Used
981	A241	8f red & gold	42.50	15.00

Mao and Parade of Artists — A242

"Raid on White Tiger Regiment" — A243

"Red Detachment of Women" — A244

China Post No. W5

No. 983, "The Red Lantern," vert. No. 985, "Shachiapang" (women & soldier). No. 986, "On the Dock". No. 987, "Taking Bandits' Fort". No. 989, "The White-haired Girl". No. 990, Mao with Orchestra & Chorus (50x36mm).

1968 *Perf. 11½x11; 11 (983, 990)*

No.	Type	Description	Unused	Used
982	A242	8f shown (56x36mm)	160.00	40.00
983	A242	8f multi	160.00	40.00
984	A243	8f shown	160.00	40.00
985	A243	8f multi	160.00	40.00
986	A243	8f multi	160.00	40.00
987	A243	8f multi	160.00	40.00
988	A244	8f shown	160.00	40.00
989	A244	8f multi	160.00	40.00
990	A242	8f multi	160.00	40.00
		Nos. 982-990 (9)	1,440.	360.00

Mao's direction for revolutionary literature and art. Issued: Nos. 982-987, Jan. 30; Nos. 988-990, May 1.

"Unite still more closely . . ." — A245

China Post No. W9

1968, May 31 Photo. *Perf. 11*

No.	Type	Description	Unused	Used
991	A245	8f red, gold & red brn	400.00	100.00

Mao Tse-tung's statement of support of Afro-Americans.

Statement about Cultural Revolution A246

China Post No. W10

Directives of Chairman Mao: No. 993, Experiences of Revolutionary Committee. No. 994, Leadership role of Revolutionary Committee. No. 995, Basic principle of reform. No. 996, Purpose of Cultural Revolution.

1968, July 20 Photo. *Perf. 11½*

No. of Lines Over Signature

No.	Type	Description	Unused	Used
992	A246	8f 6	475.00	250.00
993	A246	8f 5	475.00	250.00
994	A246	8f 4½	475.00	250.00
995	A246	8f 4	475.00	250.00
996	A246	8f 8	475.00	250.00
a.		Strip of 5, #992-996	*7,000.*	2,350.
		Nos. 992-996 (5)	2,375.	1,250.

Value for No. 996a is for an unfolded strip.

Lin Piao's Statement, July 26, 1965 — A247

China Post No. W11

1968, Aug. 1 Engr. & Photo.

No.	Type	Description	Unused	Used
997	A247	8f red, gold & blk	37.50	11.00

Chinese People's Liberation Army, 41st anniv.

Mao Tse-tung Going to An Yuan, 1921 A248

China Post No. W12

1968, Aug. 1 *Perf. 11x11½*

No.	Type	Description	Unused	Used
998	A248	8f multicolored	210.00	50.00

Shade varieties include varying amount of red in clouds.

An 8f stamp was prepared in Sept. 1968, showing black writing on a red background, regarding Chairman Mao's inscriptions to Japanese Labor Friends. It was not issued, but a few examples have reached the marketplace. Value, *$175,000.*

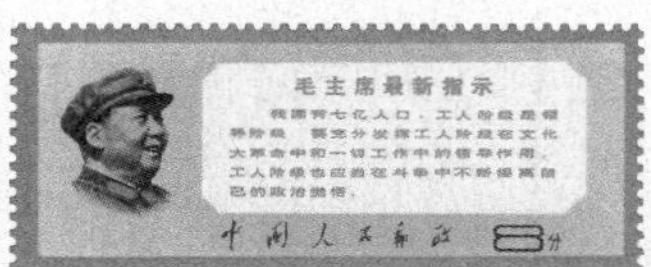

Directive of Chairman Mao — A249

China Post No. W13

1968, Nov. 30 *Perf. 11½*

No.	Type	Description	Unused	Used
999	A249	8f red & blk brn	*240.00*	50.00

China Map, Worker, Farmer and Soldier — A249a

China Post No. W14

1968, Nov. 25 Photo. *Perf. 11½x11*

No.	Type	Description	Unused	Used
999A	A249a	8f red, bl & bis	*135,000.*	*80,000.*

Map inscribed: "The entire nation is red." Although officially issued in Canton Nov. 25, some post offices began selling the stamp Nov. 24. Because of inaccuracies in the map (the archipelagos of Xisha and Nanshi were omitted), the stamp was withdrawn from sale Nov. 26.

No. 999A most often is found repaired. Values are for sound, unrepaired examples.

Counterfeits exist.

Two values were prepared to celebrate the Great Victory of the Cultural Revolution but were not issued, although a few examples were sold through the post office at Hebei prior to the recall and issue date. Values for sound stamps: 8f, Mao Tse-tung and Lin Piao, $300,000; 8f, map and workers, $1,150,000.

Woman, Miner and Soldier Holding Little Red Book A250

China Post No. W16

1968, Dec. 26 *Perf. 11x11½*

No.	Type	Description	Unused	Used
1000	A250	8f multicolored	65.00	15.00

Canceled-to-order

From about this point on stamps are valued postally used.

Yangtze Bridge, Nanking A251

Road across Bridge — A252

China Post No. W15

No. 1003, Side view. 10f, Aerial view.

Lithographed, *Perf. 11½x11 (A251);* Photogravure, *Perf. 11½ (A252)*

1969, May 1 Without Gum

No.	Type	Description	Unused	Used
1001	A251	4f multicolored	8.75	3.00
1002	A252	8f multicolored	72.50	11.00
1003	A252	8f multicolored	22.50	6.00
1004	A251	10f multicolored	6.75	3.00
		Nos. 1001-1004 (4)	110.50	23.00

Inauguration of Yangtze Bridge at Nanking on Dec. 29, 1968.

Singer and Pianist A253

China Post No. W17

(Piano Music from the Opera, "The Red Lantern"): No. 1006, Woman singer and pianist.

1969, Aug. 1 Photo. *Perf. 11x11½*
Without Gum

1005	A253	8f multicolored	40.00	12.50
1006	A253	8f multicolored	110.00	18.50

Harvest A254

China Post No. W18

No. 1008, Two harvesters. No. 1009, Harvesters with Little Red Books. No. 1010, Red Cross Worker examining baby.

1969, Oct. 1 Without Gum

1007	A254	4f shown	13.50	3.50
1008	A254	8f multi	62.50	8.50
1009	A254	8f multi	82.50	19.00
1010	A254	10f multi	9.00	3.75
		Nos. 1007-1010 (4)	167.50	34.75

Agriculture students.

Armed Forces and Slogan — A255

Guarding the Coast — A256

China Post No. W19

Designs: No. 1013, 43f, Snow patrol, vert.

1969, Oct. 1 *Perf. 11½*
Without Gum

1011	A255	8f red & multi	72.50	*15.00*
1012	A256	8f blue & multi	15.50	*4.50*
1013	A256	8f blue & multi	15.50	*4.50*
1014	A256	35f black & multi	12.00	*6.00*
1015	A256	43f black & multi	15.50	*8.00*
		Nos. 1011-1015 (5)	131.00	*38.00*

Defense of Chen Pao-tao (Damansky Islands) in Ussuri River.

Farm Woman A257

China Post No. RW2

Designs: 8f, Foundry worker. 10f, Soldier.

1969, Oct. 1 *Perf. 10; 11½*
Without Gum

1016	A257	4f ver & dk pur	2.75	*.80*
a.		Perf 11½	8.25	1.60
1017	A257	8f ver & dk brn	3.25	*.80*
a.		Perf 11½	5.00	1.60
1018	A257	10f ver & blk	5.50	*1.75*
a.		Perf 11½	—	*900.00*
		Nos. 1016-1018 (3)	11.50	*3.35*

Perforation

Nos. 1016-1018 and some succeeding issues bear two kinds of perforation: clean (Peking) and rough (Shanghai).

Building — A258

Communist Party Building, Shanghai A259

Agriculture Building, Canton — A260

Foundry Worker — A261

Type I

China Post Nos. RW1 and R14

Two types of 8f Gate of Heavenly Peace:
I — Strong, definite halo around sun.
II — Halo missing, white shades gradually into red.

No. 1022, 1929 Party Day House, Pu Tien. No. 1023, Mao's Home and Office, Yunnan. No. 1024, Woman Tractor Driver. No. 1025, Gate of Heavenly Peace. No. 1026, Heroes Monument. No. 1027, Pagoda Hill, Yenan. No. 1028, Gate of Heavenly Peace (no sun). No. 1029, Monument, Tsu Ping. No. 1030, Conference Hall, Tsunyi. No. 1031, Highway ('72). No. 1032, Shao Shan Village, Birthplace of Mao. No. 1033, Conference Hall. No. 1034, Chingkang Peaks. No. 1035, as 4f, different view. No. 1036, People's Hall, Peking.

1969-72 Photo. *Perf. 10*
Without Gum

1019	A258	1f shown	.50	.50
1020	A259	1½f shown	1.30	.95
a.		Perf. 11½	8.75	4.50
1021	A260	2f shown	.50	.40
1022	A260	3f multi	.75	.40
1023	A260	4f multi	.95	.30
1024	A261	5f multi	1.90	.75
1025	A260	8f multi, type II	4.25	1.30
a.		Type I	8.50	1.60
1026	A259	8f multi	2.40	2.10
a.		Perf. 11½	8.50	4.00
1027	A260	8f multi	20.00	*3.25*
1028	A260	8f multi	1.00	.40
1029	A260	10f multi	1.00	.40
1030	A259	20f multi	3.50	1.90
a.		Perf. 11½	25.00	6.00
1031	A260	20f multi	3.00	.50
1032	A260	22f multi	1.60	.75
1033	A260	35f multi	1.25	.65
1034	A260	43f multi	3.00	.65
1035	A259	50f multi	2.50	.75
1036	A260	52f multi	5.25	.85
1037	A261	$1 shown	6.00	2.25
		Nos. 1019-1037 (19)	60.65	19.05

China Post No. RW1 includes Nos. 1019, 1024-1027, 1030, 1035, and 1037. The rest are China Post No. R14.

Issue dates: Nos. 1025 and 1027, Oct. 1, 1969; Nos. 1030 and 1035, Jan. 1, 1970; Nos. 1020, 1024 and 1026, April 1, 1970; No. 1037, April 20, 1970; Nos. 1019 and 1031, Dec. 20, 1971; Nos. 1023 and 1028, March 25, 1972; others, Sept. 25, 1971.

Kin Hsün-hua A262

China Post No. W21

1970, Jan. Without Gum *Perf. 11½*

1045	A262	8f red & black	37.50	*17.50*
a.		8f red & gray brown	45.00	15.00

Death of Kin Hsün-hua in Kirin border flood.

Mounted Patrol — A263

China Post No. 1046

1970, Aug. 1 Without Gum

1046	A263	8f yel grn & multi	25.00	9.25

People's Liberation Army, 43rd anniv.

Commemorative stamps from Nos. 1047 to 1142 and 1211-1214, carry a cumulative number in parentheses at lower left and the year at lower right. Where such numbers help to identify, they are quoted in parentheses.

Cpl. Yang Tse-jung — A264

Ensemble A265

China Post No. N1

No. 1048, Armed guards (2) horiz. No. 1049, Yang leaping through forest (3). No. 1051, Yang in folk costume (5). No. 1052, Four actors (6) horiz.

Perf. 11½x11 (1047, 1049), 11x11½ (1048,1052), 11½ (1050-1051)

1970-1971
Without Gum

1047	A264	8f shown	55.00	14.00
1048	A264	8f multi	18.50	2.75
1049	A264	8f multi	23.00	4.75
1050	A265	8f shown	87.50	14.00
1051	A265	8f multi	14.00	3.75
1052	A264	8f multi	32.00	8.25
		Nos. 1047-1052 (6)	230.00	47.50

Scenes from opera "Taking Tiger Mountain by Strategy."

Frontier Guard A266

China Post No. N2

1971, Jan. Litho. *Perf. 10*
Without Gum

1053	A266	4f multicolored	6.50	1.90
a.		Perf. 11½	7.00	1.90
b.		Perf. 11½x10	8.00	3.00
c.		Perf. 10x11½	8.00	3.50

Banner of the Commune A267

Street Battle, Paris, 1871 A268

China Post No. N3

10f, Proclamation of the Commune. 22f, Rally.

Perf. 11½x11, 11x11½
1971, Mar. 18 Litho. & Engr.
Without Gum

1054	A267	4f sal & multi	40.00	18.00
1055	A268	8f ver, pink & brn	230.00	50.00
1056	A267	10f ver, pink & dk brn	15.00	11.00
1057	A268	22f ver, pink & dk brn	11.00	10.00
		Nos. 1054-1057 (4)	296.00	89.00

Centenary of the Paris Commune.

Redrawn Building Type of 1961
China Post No. R12

Designs: 2f, 3f, August 1 building, Nanchang. 4f, 52f, Gate of Heavenly Peace, Peking. 10f, 20f, Pagoda Hill, Yenan.

1971, July 1 Litho. *Perf. 11x11½*
Size: 21x16mm
Without Gum

1059	A152	2f slate green	2.00	.75
1060	A152	3f sepia	3.00	1.25
1061	A152	4f brt pink	5.00	2.00
1062	A152	10f brt rose lil	1.50	1.25
1063	A152	20f dk blue grn	3.75	1.25
1064	A152	52f orange	2.50	3.00
		Nos. 1059-1064 (6)	17.75	9.50

Paper of Nos. 1059-1064 is white. That of Nos. 647-654 is toned.

Communist Party Building, Shanghai — A269

People and Factories — A270

China Post No. N4

Designs: No. 1068, Peasant Movement Training Institute. No. 1069, Ching Kang Peaks. No. 1070, Conference Building, Tsunyi. No. 1071, Pagoda Hill, Yenan. No. 1073, People and People's Hall, Peking. No. 1074, People and Pagoda Hill, Yenan. 22f, Gate of Heavenly Peace, Peking.

1971, July 1 Photo. *Perf. 11½*
Red and Gold Frame
Without Gum

No.	Type	Description	Unused	Used
1067	A269	4f vermilion	23.00	4.00
1068	A269	4f brt grn	23.00	4.00
1069	A269	8f grnsh bl & red	29.00	4.00
1070	A269	8f ol blk	35.00	4.00
1071	A269	8f bis, grn & red	35.00	4.00
1072	A270	8f yel, red & multi	35.00	6.50
1073	A270	8f yel, red & multi	35.00	6.50
1074	A270	8f yel, red & multi	35.00	6.50
a.		Strip of 3, #1072-1074	180.00	60.00
1075	A269	22f red, gold & brn	18.00	7.25
		Nos. 1067-1075 (9)	268.00	46.75

50th anniv. of the Chinese Communist Party. No. 1073 has date of 1921-1971 at top. No. 1074a has a continuous design and is valued as an unfolded strip.

Chinese Welcome A271

China Post No. N5

No. 1077, Chinese & African players. No. 1078, Chinese & African girl players. 43f, Games' emblem.

1971, Nov. 3 Litho. *Perf. 11½*
Without Gum

No.	Type	Description	Unused	Used
1076	A271	8f lil rose & multi	21.00	5.75
1077	A271	8f lt yellow & multi	21.00	5.75
1078	A271	8f dk grn & multi	21.00	5.75
1079	A271	43f grn, gold & org	85.00	16.00
		Nos. 1076-1079 (4)	148.00	33.25

Afro-Asian Table Tennis Games, Peking.

Enver Hoxha — A272

China Post No. N6

No. 1081, Party's birthplace. No. 1082, Albanian flag. 52f, Albanian partisans, horiz.

1971, Nov. 3 Photo. *Perf. 11*
Without Gum

No.	Type	Description	Unused	Used
1080	A272	8f Prus blue & multi	32.50	8.00
1081	A272	8f buff & multi	20.00	7.00
1082	A272	8f red, yel & multi	20.00	7.00
1083	A272	52f lt blue & multi	35.00	10.00
		Nos. 1080-1083 (4)	107.50	32.00

30th anniversary of the founding of Albanian Communist Party.

Yenan Pagoda and 1942 Meeting House A273

China Post No. N8

No. 1085, Uniformed choir (34). No. 1086, "Brother & Sister" (35). No. 1087, Outdoor performance (36). No. 1088, "The Red Signal Lantern" (37). No. 1089, Dancer from "The Red Company of Women" (38).

1972, May 23 Photo. *Perf. 11*
Without Gum

No.	Type	Description	Unused	Used
1084	A273	8f shown	25.00	7.50
1085	A273	8f multi	25.00	7.50
1086	A273	8f multi	25.00	7.50
1087	A273	8f multi	25.00	7.50
1088	A273	8f multi	25.00	7.50
1089	A273	8f multi	25.00	7.50
		Nos. 1084-1089 (6)	150.00	45.00

30th anniversary of the publication of the Discussions on Literature and Art at the Yenan Forum.

Various Ball Games — A274

Workers' Gymnastics A275

China Post No. N9

No. 1092, Tug of war (41). No. 1093, Mountain climbers and tents (42). No. 1094, Children diving & swimming (43).

1972, June 10

No.	Type	Description	Unused	Used
1090	A274	8f shown	*47.50*	5.00
1091	A275	8f shown	*24.00*	5.00
1092	A275	8f multi	*24.00*	5.00
1093	A275	8f multi	*21.50*	5.00
1094	A275	8f multi	*24.00*	5.00
		Nos. 1090-1094 (5)	141.00	25.00

10th anniversary of Mao Tse-tung's edict on physical culture.

Ocean Freighter Fenglei — A276

China Post No. N7

No. 1096, Tanker Taching No. 30 (30). No. 1097, Cargo-passenger ship Changzeng (31). No. 1098, Dredger Xienfeng (32).

1972, July 10 Photo. *Perf. 11½*
Without Gum

No.	Type	Description	Unused	Used
1095	A276	8f shown	77.50	12.50
1096	A276	8f multi	40.00	11.00
1097	A276	8f multi	40.00	11.00
1098	A276	8f multi	62.50	12.50
		Nos. 1095-1098 (4)	220.00	47.00

Table Tennis Players' Welcome A277

China Post No. N11

No. 1099, Championship emblem, vert. (45). No. 1101, Table tennis (47). No. 1102, Women from different countries, vert. (48).

1972, Sept. 2 *Perf. 11½x11, 11x11½*
Without Gum

No.	Type	Description	Unused	Used
1099	A277	8f multi	13.50	5.00
1100	A277	8f shown	37.50	5.00
1101	A277	8f multi	25.00	5.00
1102	A277	22f multi	22.00	6.00
		Nos. 1099-1102 (4)	98.00	21.00

First Asian table tennis championships.

Wang Chin-hsi — A278

China Post No. N10

Engraved and Photogravure
1972, Dec. 25 *Perf. 11½x11*

No.	Type	Description	Unused	Used
1103	A278	8f multicolored	65.00	20.00

Wang Chin-hsi, the Iron Man, fighter for the working class.

Workers on Cliffs along Canal — A279

China Post No. N12

No. 1105, Canal flowing through tunnel (50). No. 1106, Bridge (51). No. 1107, Canal along cliffs (52).

1972, Dec. 30

No.	Type	Description	Unused	Used
1104	A279	8f multi	30.00	7.00
1105	A279	8f multicolored	30.00	7.00
1106	A279	8f multicolored	40.00	10.00
1107	A279	8f multicolored	40.00	10.00
		Nos. 1104-1107 (4)	140.00	34.00

Construction of Red Flag Canal, Linhsien county, Honan.

Giant Panda — A280

China Post No. N14

Designs: Pandas in various positions. The 8f stamps are horizontal.

Perf. 11½x11, 11x11½
1973, Jan. 15 Photo.
Designs in Black and Red

No.	Type	Description	Unused	Used
1108	A280	4f lt yel grn	10.00	8.00
1109	A280	8f buff	10.00	6.00
1110	A280	8f lt tan	10.00	6.00
1111	A280	10f pale grn	115.00	18.00
1112	A280	20f pale bl gray	57.50	10.00
1113	A280	43f pale lil	17.00	14.00
		Nos. 1108-1113 (6)	219.50	62.00

Woman Coal Miner — A281

China Post No. N15

No. 1115, Committee member (64). No. 1116, Telephone line worker (65).

1973, Mar. 8 Photo. *Perf. 11½x11*

No.	Type	Description	Unused	Used
1114	A281	8f shown	24.00	5.00
1115	A281	8f multi	17.50	6.00
1116	A281	8f multi	17.50	5.00
		Nos. 1114-1116 (3)	59.00	16.00

Intl. Working Women's Day. Designs are after paintings from an exhib. for 30th anniv. of the Yenan Forum on Literature and Art.

Dancing Girl — A282

China Post No. N19

No. 1118, Musician, boy (87). No. 1119, Girl with scarf (88). No. 1120, Boy with tambourine (89). No. 1121, Girl with drum (90).

1973, June 1 Photo. *Perf. 11*

No.	Type	Description	Unused	Used
1117	A282	8f shown	3.00	1.75
1118	A282	8f multi	3.00	1.75
1119	A282	8f multi	3.00	1.75
1120	A282	8f multi	3.00	1.75
1121	A282	8f multi	3.00	1.75
a.		Strip of 5, #1117-1121	65.00	20.00
		Nos. 1117-1121 (5)	15.00	8.75

Values for No. 1121a are for an unfolded strip.

Tournament Emblem — A283

China Post No. N20

No. 1123, Visitors from Asia, Africa and Latin America arriving by plane (92). No. 1124, Woman player (93). No. 1125, African, Asian & Latin American women (94).

1973, Aug. 25 Photo. *Perf. 11½*

No.	Type	Description	Unused	Used
1122	A283	8f multi	16.00	2.75
1123	A283	8f multicolored	13.00	2.75
1124	A283	8f multicolored	13.00	2.75
1125	A283	22f multicolored	13.00	2.75
		Nos. 1122-1125 (4)	55.00	11.00

Asian, African and Latin American Table Tennis Friendship Invitational Tournament.

The White-haired Girl — A284

China Post No. N13

Designs: Scenes from the ballet "The White-haired Girl." Nos. 1126, 1129 vert.

1973, Sept. 25 Photo. *Perf. 11½*

No.	Type	Description	Unused	Used
1126	A284	8f multi	40.00	11.00
1127	A284	8f multi	50.00	11.00
1128	A284	8f multi	40.00	11.00
1129	A284	8f multi	45.00	11.00
		Nos. 1126-1129 (4)	175.00	44.00

Fair Building, Canton — A285

China Post No. N21

1973, Oct. 15 Photo. *Perf. 11*

1130	A285	8f multicolored	30.00	3.00

Export Commodities Fall Fair, Canton.

Teapot with Blue Phoenix Design — A286

China Post No. N16

Excavated Works of Art: No. 1132, Silver pot with horse design. No. 1133, Black pottery horse. No. 1134, Woman, clay figurine. No. 1135, Carved stone pillar base. No. 1136, Galloping bronze horse. No. 1137, Bronze inkwell (toad). No. 1138, Bronze lamp, Chang Hsin Palace. No. 1139, Bronze tripod. No. 1140, Square bronze pot. 20f, Bronze wine vessel. 52f, Painted red clay tripod.

1973, Nov. 20 *Perf. 11½*

1131	A286	4f	ol bis & multi	5.50	.75
1132	A286	4f	ver & multi	5.50	.75
1133	A286	8f	yel grn & multi	4.50	.75
1134	A286	8f	brt rose & multi	4.50	.75
1135	A286	8f	lt vio & multi	4.50	.75
1136	A286	8f	yel bis & multi	4.50	.75
1137	A286	8f	lt bl & multi	4.50	.75
1138	A286	8f	gray & multi	4.50	.75
1139	A286	10f	yel bis & multi	4.50	.75
1140	A286	10f	dp org & multi	9.00	.75
1141	A286	20f	lil & multi	9.00	2.00
1142	A286	52f	grn & multi	14.50	4.00
	Nos. 1131-1142 (12)			70.50	13.50

Marginal Markings

Marginal inscriptions on stamps of 1974-91 start at lower left with "J" for commemoratives and "T" for "special issues," followed by three numbers indicating (a) set sequence for the year, (b) total of stamps in set, and (c) number of stamp within set. At right appears the year date. Listings include the "c" number parenthetically. The "a" number is included only when it will help identify stamps not illustrated.

Example: T26 (6-3), the 3rd stamp of 6 from the 26th special set. Set numbers and or positions will be shown only when they help identify a stamp. An illustrated single stamp set will not have these numbers in the listings.

Woman Gymnast — A287

China Post No. T.1.

Designs: No. 1144, Gymnast on rings. No. 1145, Aerial split over balance beam, woman. No. 1146, Gymnast on parallel bars. No. 1147, Uneven bars, woman. No. 1148, Gymnast on horse.

1974, Jan. 1 Photo. *Perf. 11½x11*

1143	A287	8f lt grn & multi	10.00	3.50
1144	A287	8f lt vio & multi	10.00	3.50
1145	A287	8f lt blue & multi	10.00	3.50
1146	A287	8f sal & multi	12.50	4.50
1147	A287	8f yel & multi	10.00	4.50
1148	A287	8f lil rose & multi	12.50	4.50
	Nos. 1143-1148 (6)		65.00	24.00

Girls Twirling Bamboo Diabolos — A288

China Post No. T.2.

Designs: No. 1149, Lion Dance, vert. No. 1150, Handstand on chairs, vert. No. 1152, Men balancing jar. No. 1153, Plate spinning, vert. No. 1154, Twirling umbrella, vert.

1974, Jan. 21 *Perf. 11*

1149	A288	8f brn & multi	7.00	2.75
1150	A288	8f Prus bl & multi	7.00	2.75
1151	A288	8f lilac & multi	10.00	2.75
1152	A288	8f dull bl & multi	7.00	2.75
1153	A288	8f ol grn & multi	7.00	2.75
1154	A288	8f gray & multi	10.00	2.75
	Nos. 1149-1154 (6)		48.00	16.50

Traditional acrobatics.

Shao Shan — A289

Site of 1st National Communist Party Congress — A289a

Peasant Movement Institute, Kwangchow — A289b

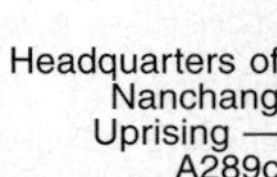

Headquarters of Nanchang Uprising — A289c

Great Hall of the People, Beijing — A289d

View of Wen Chia Shih — A289e

Tien An Men, Beijing — A289f

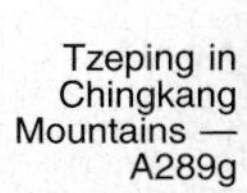

Tzeping in Chingkang Mountains — A289g

Site of Kutien Meeting — A289h

Tsunyi Conference Site — A289i

Yenan (bridge) — A289j

Hsi Pai Ho, Communist Party Meeting Site — A289k

Fairy Cave, Lushan — A289l

Monument to People's Heroes — A289m

Transportation by Railroad — A289n

Trucks on Mountain Road — A289o

China Post No. R15

1973-74 Litho. *Perf. 11*
Without Gum

1163	A289	1f	sl grn & pale grn	.65	.35
1164	A289a	1½f	car & buff	.65	.35
1165	A289b	2f	dk blue & pale grn	.70	.35
1166	A289c	3f	dk ol & yel	.70	.35
1167	A289d	4f	red & yel	1.50	.35
1168	A289e	5f	brn & lt yel	.80	.35
1169	A289f	8f	dull mag & buff	1.00	.35
a.			Perf. 11½x12	17.50	9.75
1170	A289g	10f	blue & buff	.80	.40
1171	A289h	20f	dk red & buff	2.40	.40
1172	A289i	22f	vio & lt yel	5.00	1.60
1173	A289j	35f	mar & lt yel	4.25	1.75
1174	A289k	43f	red brn & buff	5.00	2.00
1175	A289l	50f	dk blue & pink	4.00	.50
1176	A289m	52f	sepia & buff	3.00	.50

China Post No. R16
Photogravure & Engraved

1177	A289n	$1	multicolored	5.00	1.00
1178	A289o	$2	multicolored	6.50	1.10
	Nos. 1163-1178 (16)			41.95	11.70

Issue dates: No. 1177, Oct. 20, 1973; No. 1178, Feb. 20, 1974; all others April 1, 1974.

Capital Stadium — A290

China Post No. R17

Design: 8f, Hotel Peking.

1974, Dec. 1 Photo. *Perf. 11*
Without Gum

1179	A290	4f black & yel grn	.85	.25

Nos 1179 and 1180 also exist with gum.

1180	A290	8f black & ultra	.50	.25

"Veteran Secretary" — A291

Well Diggers — A292

China Post No. T.3.

Designs: Nos. 1183-1186 horizontal.

1974, Apr. 20 Photo. *Perf. 11*

1181	A291	8f shown	4.50	2.25
1182	A292	8f shown	4.50	2.25
1183	A291	8f Spring hoeing	5.50	2.25
1184	A291	8f Farmers	5.50	2.25
1185	A292	8f Farm	5.50	2.25
1186	A291	8f Bumper crops	5.50	2.50
	Nos. 1181-1186 (6)		31.00	13.75

Paintings by farmers of Huhsien County, shown at exhibition in Peking.

Mailman on Motorcycle — A293

China Post No. J.1.

1974, May 15 Photo. *Perf. 11*

1187	A293	8f shown	10.00	4.50
1188	A293	8f People of the world	10.00	3.50
1189	A293	8f Great Wall	15.00	3.50
	Nos. 1187-1189 (3)		35.00	11.50

Centenary of the UPU.

Barefoot Doctor Inoculating Children A294

China Post No. N18

Designs (Barefoot Doctors): No. 1191, Crossing stream at night to reach patient, vert. No. 1192, Gathering herbs, vert. No. 1193, Acupuncture treatment for farmer in the field.

Perf. 11x11½, 11½x11
1974, June 26 Photo.

1190	A294	8f multicolored	14.00	2.00
1191	A294	8f multicolored	19.00	3.00
1192	A294	8f multicolored	16.50	2.00
1193	A294	8f multicolored	14.00	2.00
	Nos. 1190-1193 (4)		63.50	9.00

Steel Worker Wang Chin-hsi — A295

China Post No. T.4.

No. 1195, Workers studying Mao's writings around campfire. No. 1196, Drilling for oil in winter. No. 1197, Scientific industrial management. No. 1198, Oil derricks and farms.

1974, Sept. 30 Photo. *Perf. 11*

1194 A295 8f multi (5-1) 6.50 3.00
1195 A295 8f multi (5-2) 6.00 2.75
1196 A295 8f multi (5-3) 6.00 2.75
1197 A295 8f multi (5-4) 6.00 2.75
1198 A295 8f multi (5-5) 6.50 3.00
Nos. 1194-1198 (5) 31.00 14.25

Workers of Taching as examples of achievement.

Members of Tachai Commune — A296

China Post No. T.5.

No. 1200, Farmers leveling mountains and fields in winter. No. 1201, Scientific farming. No. 1202, Trucks carrying surplus harvest. No. 1203, Young workers with banner.

1974, Sept. 30

1199 A296 8f multi (5-1) 5.50 1.50
1200 A296 8f multi (5-2) 5.50 1.50
1201 A296 8f multi (5-3) 5.50 1.50
1202 A296 8f multi (5-4) 6.50 1.50
1203 A296 8f multi (5-5) 6.50 1.50
Nos. 1199-1203 (5) 29.50 7.50

Farmers of Tachai as examples of achievement.

Arms of Republic and Members of Ethnic Groups — A297

China Post No. J.2.

1974, Oct. 1

1204 A297 8f multi (1-1) 40.00 8.50

Taching Steel Worker — A298

China Post No. J.3.

Designs: No. 1206, Tachai farm woman. No. 1207, Soldier, planes and ships.

1974, Oct. 1

1205 A298 8f multi (3-1) 4.50 2.00
1206 A298 8f multi (3-2) 4.50 2.00
1207 A298 8f multi (3-3) 4.50 2.00
a. Strip of 3, #1205-1207 25.00 12.00

People's Republic of China, 25th anniv.
Values for No. 1207a are for an unfolded strip.

Export Commodities Fair Building, Canton — A299

China Post No. T.6.

1974, Oct. 15

1208 A299 8f multicolored 12.50 2.00

Chinese Export Commodities Fair, Canton.

Guerrillas' Monument, Permet, Albania — A300

Albanian Patriots and Coat of Arms — A301

China Post No. J.4.

1974, Nov. 29 Photo. *Perf. 11½x11*

1209 A300 8f multicolored 8.50 2.75
1210 A301 8f multicolored 8.50 2.75

Albania's liberation, 30th anniversary.

Water-cooled Generator — A302

China Post No. N17

Industrial Products: No. 1212, Motorized rice sprouts transplanter. No. 1213, Universal cylindrical grinding machine. No. 1214, Open-air rock drill, vert. All dated 1973.

Photogravure and Engraved

1974, Dec. 23 *Perf. 11*

1211 A302 8f vio & multi 67.50 10.50
1212 A302 8f yel grn & multi 90.00 22.50
1213 A302 8f ver & multi 67.50 10.50
1214 A302 8f blue & multi 135.00 22.50
Nos. 1211-1214 (4) 360.00 66.00

Congress Delegates — A303

China Post No. J.5.

Designs: No. 1216, Red flags, constitution and flowers. No. 1217, Worker, farmer and soldier, agriculture and industry.

1975, Jan. 25 Photo. *Perf. 11½*

1215 A303 8f gold & multi (3-1) 16.00 4.00
1216 A303 8f gold & multi (3-2) 20.00 4.00
1217 A303 8f gold & multi (3-3) 25.00 10.00
Nos. 1215-1217 (3) 61.00 18.00

Fourth National People's Congress, Peking.

Teacher Studying Revolutionary Works — A304

China Post No. T.9.

No. 1219, Teacher, children and horse. No. 1220, Outdoors class. No. 1221, Class held in boat.

1975, Mar. 8 Photo. *Perf. 11*

1218 A304 8f multi (4-1) 18.00 5.25
1219 A304 8f multi (4-2) 29.00 6.25
1220 A304 8f multi (4-3) 21.00 5.25
1221 A304 8f multi (4-4) 18.00 4.25
Nos. 1218-1221 (4) 86.00 21.00

Rural women teachers and for International Working Women's Day.

"Broadsword," Encounter Position — A305

China Post No. T.7.

No. 1223, Exercise with 2 swords (woman). No. 1224, Graceful boxing (woman). No. 1225, Man leaping with spear. No. 1226, Woman holding fighting staff. 43f, 2 women with spears against man with 3-section staff.

1975, June 10 Photo. *Perf. 11x11½*

Size: 39x29mm

1222 A305 8f (6-1) 6.00 2.10
1223 A305 8f (6-2) 7.00 2.10
1224 A305 8f (6-3) 5.00 2.10
1225 A305 8f (6-4) 5.00 2.10
1226 A305 8f (6-5) 6.00 2.10

Size: 59x29mm

1227 A305 43f red & multi (6-6) 12.00 7.75
Nos. 1222-1227 (6) 41.00 18.25

Wushu ("Kung Fu"), self-defense exercises. Tête bêche in sheets of 50 (5x10). Value, set of pairs $120.

Mass Judgment and Criticisms — A306

China Post No. T.8.

No. 1229, Brigade leader writing wall newspaper. No. 1230, Study and criticism on battlefield, horiz. No. 1231, Former "slave" led into battle by criticism of Lin Piao and Confucius, horiz.

Perf. 11½x11, 11x11½

1975, Aug. 20 Photo.

1228 A306 8f red & multi (4-1) 20.00 4.25
1229 A306 8f red & multi (4-2) 20.00 4.25
1230 A306 8f red & multi (4-3) 18.50 4.25
1231 A306 8f red & multi (4-4) 20.00 4.25
Nos. 1228-1231 (4) 78.50 17.00

Campaign to encourage criticism of Lin Piao and Confucius.

Athletes Studying Theory of Dictatorship of Proletariat — A307

China Post No. J.6.

3rd National Sports Meet: No. 1232, Women athletes leading parade, vert. No. 1234, Women volleyball players. No. 1235, Runner, soldier, farmer and worker, vert. No. 1236, Young athlete and various sports. No. 1237, Athletes of various races and horse race. 35f, Children and diving tower, vert.

1975, Sept. 12 Photo. *Perf. 11½*

1232 A307 8f multi (7-1) 4.00 1.00
1233 A307 8f multi (7-2) 8.50 1.00
1234 A307 8f multi (7-3) 14.00 1.50
1235 A307 8f multi (7-4) 4.00 1.00
1236 A307 8f multi (7-5) 4.00 1.00
1237 A307 8f multi (7-6) 4.00 1.00
1238 A307 35f multi (7-7) 4.00 2.00
Nos. 1232-1238 (7) 42.50 8.50

Mountaineers A308

Mt. Everest A309

China Post No. T.15.

Design: No. 1240, Mountaineers raising Chinese flag on summit, horiz.

1975 Photo. *Perf. 11½x11, 11x11½*

1239 A308 8f multi (3-2) 2.75 1.00
1240 A308 8f multi (3-3) 2.75 1.00
1241 A309 43f multi (3-1) 4.00 1.25
Nos. 1239-1241 (3) 9.50 3.25

Chinese Mt. Everest expedition.

Agricultural Workers with Book — A310

China Post No. J.7.

No. 1243, Workers carrying load. No. 1244, Woman driving harvester combine.

1975, Oct. 1 *Perf. 11½*

1242 A310 8f multi (3-1) 9.00 1.90
1243 A310 8f multi (3-2) 9.00 1.90
1244 A310 8f multi (3-3) 13.00 1.90
Nos. 1242-1244 (3) 31.00 5.70

National Conference to promote learning from Tachai's achievements in agriculture.

Girl Giving Boy Red Scarf — A311

China Post No. T.14.

Designs (Children): No. 1246, Putting up wall posters criticizing Lin Piao and Confucius. No. 1247, Studying. No. 1248, Harvesting. 52f, Physical training.

1975, Dec. 1 Photo. *Perf. 11½*

1245 A311 8f multi (5-1) 4.50 1.25
1246 A311 8f multi (5-2) 4.50 1.25
1247 A311 8f multi (5-3) 4.50 1.25
1248 A311 8f multi (5-4) 4.50 1.25
1249 A311 52f multi (5-5) 9.00 2.50
Nos. 1245-1249 (5) 27.00 7.50

Moral, intellectual and physical progress of Chinese children.

Woman Plowing Rice Field A312

China Post No. T.13.

No. 1251, Mechanized rice planting. No. 1252, Drainage and irrigation. No. 1253, Woman spraying insecticide over cotton field. No. 1254, Combine.

1975, Dec. 15 *Perf. 11*

1250	A312	8f multi (5-1)	7.50	1.75
1251	A312	8f multi (5-2)	7.50	1.75
1252	A312	8f multi (5-3)	5.25	1.75
1253	A312	8f multi (5-4)	5.25	1.75
1254	A312	8f multi (5-5)	5.25	1.75
		Nos. 1250-1254 (5)	30.75	8.75

Priority program of farm mechanization.

Farmland and Irrigation Canal — A313

China Post No. J.8.

Designs: No. 1256, Irrigation canal (16-2). No. 1257, Fertilizer plant (16-3). No. 1258, Textile plant (16-4). No. 1259, Anshan Iron and Steel Co. (16-5). No. 1260, Coal freight trains (16-6). No. 1261, Hydroelectric station (16-7). No. 1262, Ship building (16-8). No. 1263, Oil industry (16-9). No. 1264, Pipe line and port (16-10). No. 1265, Train on viaduct (16-11). No. 1266, Scientific research (16-12). No. 1267, Classroom (16-13). No. 1268, Health Center (16-14). No. 1269, Apartment houses (16-15). No. 1270, Department store (16-16).

1976 **Photo.** *Perf. 11½*

1255	A313	8f shown (16-1)	10.00	2.25
1256	A313	8f multi	9.00	2.25
1257	A313	8f multi	20.00	2.25
1258	A313	8f multi	9.50	2.25
1259	A313	8f multi	9.50	2.25
1260	A313	8f multi	11.50	2.25
1261	A313	8f multi	11.50	2.25
1262	A313	8f multi	11.50	2.25
1263	A313	8f multi	11.50	2.25
1264	A313	8f multi	11.50	2.25
1265	A313	8f multi	11.50	2.25
1266	A313	8f multi	8.00	2.25
1267	A313	8f multi	30.00	5.50
1268	A313	8f multi	8.00	2.25
1269	A313	8f multi	15.00	2.25
1270	A313	8f multi	37.50	5.50
		Nos. 1255-1270 (16)	225.50	42.50

Nos. 1255-1270 commemorate fulfillment of 4th Five-year Plan.

Issued: Nos. 1255-1259, 2/20; Nos. 1260-1264, 4/9; Nos. 1265-1270, 6/12.

Heart Surgery with Acupuncture Anesthesia — A314

China Post No. T.12.

Operating Room and: No. 1272, Man driving tractor with severed arm restored. No. 1273, Man exercising broken arm in cast. No. 1274, Patient threading needle after cataract operation.

1976, Apr. 9 **Photo.** *Perf. 11½*

1271	A314	8f brn & multi (4-1)	8.25	2.00
1272	A314	8f yel grn & multi (4-2)	21.50	3.00
1273	A314	8f bl grn & multi (4-3)	8.00	1.75
1274	A314	8f vio bl & multi (4-4)	8.00	1.75
		Nos. 1271-1274 (4)	45.75	8.50

Achievements in medical and health services.

Students in May 7 School — A315

China Post No. J.9.

Designs: No. 1276, Students as farm workers. No. 1277, Production brigade.

1976, May 7 **Photo.** *Perf. 11½*

1275	A315	8f multi (3-1)	11.00	2.00
1276	A315	8f multi (3-2)	4.50	2.00
1277	A315	8f multi (3-3)	11.00	2.00
		Nos. 1275-1277 (3)	26.50	6.00

Chairman Mao's May 7 Directive, 10th anniv.

Mass Training in Swimming — A316

China Post No. J.10.

No. 1279, Swimmers crossing Yangtze River. No. 1280, Swimmers walking into the surf.

1976, July 16 **Photo.** *Perf. 11½*

Size: 47x27mm

1278	A316	8f multi (3-1)	8.50	2.00

Size: 35x27mm

1279	A316	8f multi (3-2)	8.50	2.00
1280	A316	8f multi (3-3)	8.50	2.00
		Nos. 1278-1280 (3)	25.50	6.00

Chairman Mao's swim in Yangtze River, 10th anniversary.

Workers, Peasants and Soldiers Going to College — A317

China Post No. T.18.

No. 1282, Classroom. No. 1283, Instruction on construction site. No. 1284, Computer room. No. 1285, Graduates returning home.

1976, Sept. 6 **Photo.** *Perf. 11½*

1281	A317	8f multi (5-1)	11.00	2.75
1282	A317	8f multi (5-2)	11.00	2.75
1283	A317	8f multi (5-3)	13.00	3.50
1284	A317	8f multi (5-4)	17.00	3.50
1285	A317	8f multi (5-5)	11.00	3.25
		Nos. 1281-1285 (5)	63.00	15.75

Success of proletarian education system.

Power Line Repair by Woman — A318

China Post No. T.16.

No. 1287, Insulator repair. No. 1288, Cherry picker. No. 1289, Transformer repair.

1976, Sept. 15

1286	A318	8f multi (4-1)	9.00	1.75
1287	A318	8f multi (4-2)	9.00	1.75
1288	A318	8f multi (4-3)	6.00	1.75
1289	A318	8f multi (4-4)	6.00	1.75
		Nos. 1286-1289 (4)	30.00	7.00

Maintenance of high power lines.

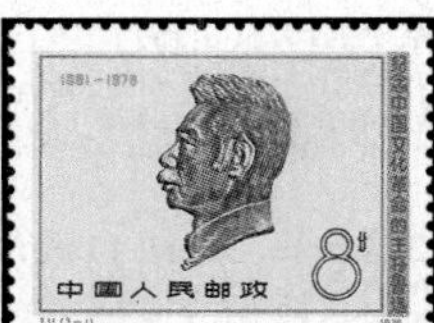

Lu Hsun A319

China Post No. J.11.

No. 1291, Lu Hsun sick, writing in bed. No. 1292, Lu Hsun with worker, soldier and peasant.

Photo. & Engr.

1976, Oct. 19 *Perf. 11x11½*

1290	A319	8f multi (3-1)	6.00	2.00

Photo.

1291	A319	8f multi (3-2)	15.00	4.00
1292	A319	8f multi (3-3)	9.00	2.00
		Nos. 1290-1292 (3)	30.00	8.00

Lu Hsun (1881-1936), writer and revolutionary leader.

Old Farmer Tying Towel on Student's Head — A320

China Post No. T.17.

Designs: No. 1294, Student teaching farm woman, horiz. No. 1295, Students climbing mountain for new water resources. No. 1296, Student testing wheat, horiz. 10f, Student feeding lamb. 20f, Frontier guards, horiz.

1976, Dec. 22 **Photo.** *Perf. 11½*

1293	A320	4f multi (6-1)	4.50	.85
1294	A320	8f multi (6-2)	4.50	.90
1295	A320	8f multi (6-3)	4.50	.90
1296	A320	8f multi (6-4)	10.00	3.25
1297	A320	10f multi (6-5)	7.00	.90
1298	A320	20f multi (6-6)	8.00	2.60
		Nos. 1293-1298 (6)	38.50	9.40

Students' efforts to help poor country people.

Mao's Home, Shaoshan — A321

China Post No. T.11.

Shaoshan, Mao's birthplace: No. 1300, School building. No. 1301, Farmers' Association building. 10f, Railroad station.

1976, Dec. 26 *Perf. 11*

1299	A321	4f multi (4-1)	3.75	1.50
1300	A321	8f multi (4-2)	3.75	1.50
1301	A321	8f multi (4-3)	7.00	1.50
1302	A321	10f multi (4-4)	3.75	1.50
		Nos. 1299-1302 (4)	18.25	6.00

Chou En-lai — A322

China Post No. J.13.

No. 1304, Chou giving report at 10th Party Congress. No. 1305, Chou with Wang Chin-hsi, famous oil worker, horiz. No. 1306, Chou with people of Tachai, 1973, horiz.

1977, Jan. 8 **Photo.** *Perf. 11½*

1303	A322	8f multi (4-1)	3.75	1.60
1304	A322	8f multi (4-2)	7.50	1.60
1305	A322	8f multi (4-3)	3.75	1.60
1306	A322	8f multi (4-4)	12.50	1.60
		Nos. 1303-1306 (4)	27.50	6.40

Premier Chou En-lai (1898-1976), a founder of Chinese Communist Party, 1st death anniversary.

Liu Hu-lan, an Inspiration A323

China Post No. J.12.

Liu Hu-lan, Chinese heroine: No. 1307, Liu Hu-lan monument. No. 1308, Mao Tse-tung quotation: "A great life-a glorious death."

1977, Jan. 31

1307	A323	8f multi (3-1)	18.00	4.00
1308	A323	8f multi (3-2)	5.00	2.00
1309	A323	8f multi (3-3)	5.00	2.00
		Nos. 1307-1309 (3)	28.00	8.00

Uprising in Taiwan A324

China Post No. J.14.

Design: 10f, Gate of Heavenly Peace, Peking; Sun Moon Lake, Taiwan, Taiwanese people holding PRC flag.

1977, Feb. 28 **Photo.** *Perf. 11*

1310	A324	8f multi (2-1)	9.00	1.25
1311	A324	10f multi (2-2)	11.00	1.75

Uprising of the people of Taiwan, 2/28/47.

Sharpshooters — A325

China Post No. T.10.

Militia Women: No. 1313, Women horseback riders. No. 1314, Underground defense tunnel.

1977, Mar. 8 *Perf. 11½*

1312	A325	8f multi (3-1)	7.50	3.00
1313	A325	8f multi (3-2)	7.50	3.00
1314	A325	8f multi (3-3)	11.00	3.00
		Nos. 1312-1314 (3)	26.00	9.00

Coal Mining — A326

Sheepherding — A326a

Export (Loading Railroad Car onto Ship) — A326b

Forestry — A326c

Hydroelectric Station — A326d

Fishery — A326e

Combine in Field — A326f

Radio Tower, Mail Truck — A326g

Steel Production — A326h

Trucks on Mountain Road — A326i

Textiles — A326j

Tractor Assembly Line — A326k

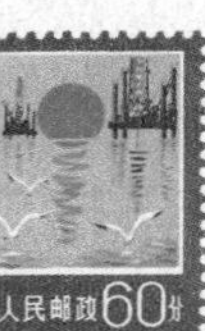

Offshore Oil Rigs, Birds, Setting Sun — A326l

Railroad Bridge, Yangtze Gorge — A326m

China Post No. R18

1977		Photo.		*Perf. 11½*
1315	A326	1f yel grn, red & blk	.45	.30
1316	A326a	1½f bl grn, yel grn & brn	.50	.30
1317	A326b	2f org, bl & blk	.50	.30
1318	A326c	3f ol & dk grn	.60	.30
1319	A326d	4f lil, org & blk	.85	.30
1320	A326e	5f lt ol & ultra	.85	.30
1321	A326f	8f red & yel	.85	.30
1322	A326g	10f lt grn, org & bl	.85	.30
1323	A326h	20f org, yel & brn	.95	.30
1324	A326i	30f bl, gray grn & blk	1.25	.35
1325	A326j	40f multicolored	1.40	.35
1326	A326k	50f cit, red & blk	1.25	.35
1327	A326l	60f pur, lt & dk org	1.25	.50
1328	A326m	70f blue & multi	2.00	.75
		Nos. 1315-1328 (14)	13.55	5.00

Nos. 1316, 1317 and 1325 exist imperf. Value, pair each $1,000.

Issue dates: Nos. 1318, 1322-1323, 1325-1328, March 18; all others Aug. 11.

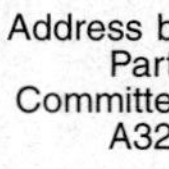

Address by Party Committee A327

China Post No. T.22.

Designs: No. 1330, Planting new rice fields. No. 1331, Farmers reading wall newspaper. No. 1332, Land reclamation.

1977, Apr. 9			*Perf. 11x11½*	
1329	A327	8f multi (4-1)	4.50	1.00
1330	A327	8f multi (4-2)	4.50	1.00
1331	A327	8f multi (4-3)	4.50	1.00
1332	A327	8f multi (4-4)	4.50	1.00
		Nos. 1329-1332 (4)	18.00	4.00

Building Tachai-type communities throughout China.

Worker at Microphone — A328

China Post No. J.15.

Designs: No. 1334, Drilling for oil during snowstorm. No. 1335, Crowd advancing under Red banner. No. 1336, Workers, industrial complex, rocket blast-off.

1977, Apr. 25			*Perf. 11*	
1333	A328	8f multi (4-1)	7.00	1.25
1334	A328	8f multi (4-2)	7.00	1.25
1335	A328	8f multi (4-3)	7.00	1.25
1336	A328	8f multi (4-4)	7.00	1.25
		Nos. 1333-1336 (4)	28.00	5.00

Conference on learning from Taching workers in industry.

Mongolians Hailing Anniversary A329

China Post No. J.16.

10f, Iron and steel complex, iron ore train. 20f, Cattle grazing in improved pasture.

1977, May 1			*Perf. 11x11½*	
1337	A329	8f multi (3-1)	5.00	.85
1338	A329	10f multi (3-2)	1.50	.75
1339	A329	20f multi (3-3)	3.00	1.10
		Nos. 1337-1339 (3)	9.50	2.70

30th anniversary of Inner Mongolian Autonomous Region.

1877 Flag of Romania and Oak Leaves — A330

Mihai Viteazu Memorial (16th Century Hero) — A331

China Post No. J.17.

10f, Battle of Smirdan, by N. Grigorescu.

1977, May 9		Photo.	*Perf. 11*	
1340	A330	8f multi (3-1)	5.25	1.25
1341	A331	10f multi (3-2)	1.10	1.00
1342	A331	20f multi (3-3)	1.10	1.00
		Nos. 1340-1342 (3)	7.45	3.25

Centenary of Romanian independence.

Yenan "Let 100 Flowers Bloom" A332

China Post No. J.18.

No. 1344, Hammer, sickle, gun & flowers; "Proletarian revolutionary literature will prosper."

1977, May, 23				
1343	A332	8f grn, red & gold	1.90	.75
1344	A332	8f lt brn, red & gold	1.90	.75

Yenan Forum on Literature & Art, 35th anniv.

Zhu De — A333

China Post No. J.19.

Designs: No. 1346, Zhu De, last address to Congress. No. 1347, Zhu De at his desk, horiz. No. 1348, Zhu De on horseback as commander of Red Army.

1977, July 6		Photo.	*Perf. 11½*	
1345	A333	8f multi (4-1)	1.75	.70
1346	A333	8f multi (4-2)	1.75	.70
1347	A333	8f multi (4-3)	2.10	.80
1348	A333	8f multi (4-4)	2.10	.80
		Nos. 1345-1348 (4)	7.70	3.00

Zhu De (1886-1976), Commander of Red Army, Chairman of National People's Congress.

Military under Mao's Banner — A334

China Post No. J.20.

No. 1350, Red Flag, Soldiers, Chingkang Mountains. No. 1351, Guerrilla fighters returning to base. No. 1352, Guerrillas crossing Yangtze. No. 1353, National defense.

1977, Aug. 1				
1349	A334	8f multi (5-1)	7.00	1.50
1350	A334	8f multi (5-2)	4.00	1.50
1351	A334	8f multi (5-3)	6.00	1.50
1352	A334	8f multi (5-4)	6.00	1.50
1353	A334	8f multi (5-5)	4.75	1.50
		Nos. 1349-1353 (5)	27.75	7.50

Liberation Army Day, 50th anniversary of People's Army.

Gate of Heavenly Peace, People and Red Flags — A335

China Post No. J.23.

Designs: No. 1355, People marching under Red Flag with Mao's portrait. No. 1356, People marching under Red Flag with hammer and sickle.

1977, Aug. 22		Photo.	*Perf. 11½x11*	
1354	A335	8f multi (3-1)	16.00	3.75
1355	A335	8f multi (3-2)	16.00	3.75
1356	A335	8f multi (3-3)	16.00	3.75
		Nos. 1354-1356 (3)	48.00	11.25

11th National Congress of the Communist Party of China.

Chairman Mao — A336

China Post No. J.21.

Designs (Mao Portraits): No. 1358, as young man in Shansi. No. 1359, addressing Communist Party in Plenary Session. No. 1360, Proclaiming People's Republic at Gate of Heavenly Peace. No. 1361, at airport with Chou En-lai and Zhu De, horiz. No. 1362, Reviewing Army as old man.

1977, Sept. 9		Photo.	*Perf. 11½*	
1357	A336	8f multi (6-1)	4.00	1.10
1358	A336	8f multi (6-2)	4.00	1.10
1359	A336	8f multi (6-3)	4.00	1.10
1360	A336	8f multi (6-4)	4.00	1.10
1361	A336	8f multi (6-5)	6.00	1.10
1362	A336	8f multi (6-6)	4.00	1.10
		Nos. 1357-1362 (6)	26.00	6.60

Mao-Tse-tung (1893-1976), first death anniversary.

Mao Memorial Hall — A337

China Post No. J.22.

Completion of Mao Memorial Hall: No. 1364, Chairman Hua's inscription.

1977, Sept. 9				
1363	A337	8f lt ultra & multi	5.00	1.50
1364	A337	8f lt grn, tan & gold	7.50	2.25

Tractors Moving Drilling Tower — A338

China Post No. T.19.

No. 1366, Shui Pow Tsi oil well and women workers. No. 1367, Construction of oil pipe line, Taching, and silos. No. 1368, Tung Fang Hung oil refinery, Peking. No. 1369, Taching oil loaded into tanker in harbor. 20f, Off-shore drilling platform "Pohai No. 1."

1978, Jan. 31		Photo.	*Perf. 11*	
1365	A338	8f multi (6-1)	2.00	1.00
1366	A338	8f multi (6-2)	2.00	1.00
1367	A338	8f multi (6-3)	2.00	1.00
1368	A338	8f multi (6-4)	5.00	1.00
1369	A338	8f multi (6-5)	5.00	1.00
1370	A338	20f multi (6-6)	4.00	2.00
		Nos. 1365-1370 (6)	20.00	7.00

Development of Chinese oil industry.

"Army Teaching Militia" — A339

China Post No. T.23.

No. 1372, "Army helping with rice planting."

1978, Feb. 5		Photo.	*Perf. 11*	
1371	A339	8f multi (2-1)	4.75	1.25
1372	A339	8f multi (2-2)	4.75	1.25

Army and people working as a family.

Red Flags, Mao Tse-tung — A340

Constitution and Red Flags — A341

China Post No. J.24.

No. 1375, Atom symbol over symbols of agriculture & industry. All designs include Great Hall of the People, Peking, & flowers.

1978, Feb. 26

1373 A340 8f multi (3-1)	4.00	.85
1374 A341 8f multi (3-2)	4.00	.85
1375 A340 8f multi (3-3)	4.00	.85
Nos. 1373-1375 (3)	12.00	2.55

5th National People's Congress.

Mao's Eulogy for Lei Feng — A342

Lei Feng, Studying Mao's Works — A343

China Post No. J.26.

No. 1377, Chairman Hua's thoughts (5 lines).

1978, Mar. 5

1376 A342 8f gold & red (3-1)	8.00	2.00
1377 A342 8f gold & red (3-2)	8.00	2.00
1378 A343 8f multicolored (3-3)	8.00	2.00
Nos. 1376-1378 (3)	24.00	6.00

Lei Feng (1940-1962), communist fighter; 15th anniversary of Chairman Mao's eulogy "Learn from Comrade Lei Feng."

Hsiang Ching-yu — A344

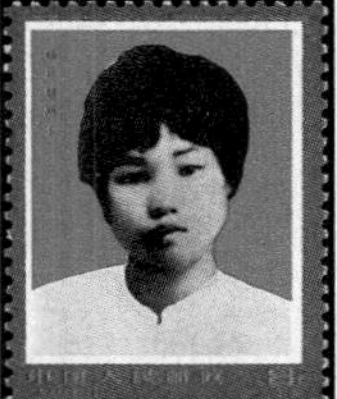
Yang Kai-hui — A345

China Post No. J.27.

1978, Mar. 8

1379 A344 8f multi (2-1)	4.00	1.00
1380 A345 8f multi (2-2)	4.00	1.00

Hsiang Ching-yu, pioneer of Women's Movement, executed 1928; Yang Kai-hui, communist fighter, executed 1930.

A346

A346a

A346b

China Post No. J.25.

No. 1381, Conference emblem. No. 1382, Banners symbolizing industry, agriculture, defense & science. No. 1383, Red flag, atom symbol & globe.

1978, Mar. 18 Litho. *Perf. 11½x11*

1381 A346 8f gold & red (3-1)	3.00	.90
1382 A346a 8f multi (3-2)	3.00	.90
1383 A346b 8f multi (3-3)	3.00	.90
a. Souvenir sheet of 3	*500.00*	*250.00*
Nos. 1381-1383 (3)	9.00	2.70

Natl. Science Conf. No. 1383a contains Nos. 1381-1383 with simulated perforations. Sold for 50f.

Release of Weather Balloon A347

China Post No. T.24.

Weather Observations: No. 1385, Radar station, typhoon watch. No. 1386, Computer, weather maps. No. 1387, Local weather observers. No. 1388, Rockets intercepting hail clouds.

1978, Apr. 25 Photo. *Perf. 11x11½*

1384 A347 8f multi (5-1)	1.50	.70
1385 A347 8f multi (5-2)	1.50	.70
1386 A347 8f multi (5-3)	1.50	.70
1387 A347 8f multi (5-4)	1.50	.70
1388 A347 8f multi (5-5)	1.50	.70
Nos. 1384-1388 (5)	7.50	3.50

Galloping Horse — A348

China Post No. T.28.

Designs: Galloping Horses, by Hsu Peihung (1895-1953). 40f, 50f, 60f, 70f, $5, horiz.

1978, May 5 *Perf. 11½x11, 11x11½*

1389 A348 4f multi (10-1)	3.00	1.00
1390 A348 8f multi (10-2)	3.00	1.00
1391 A348 8f multi (10-3)	3.00	1.00
1392 A348 10f multi (10-4)	4.00	1.00
1393 A348 20f multi (10-5)	4.00	1.00
1394 A348 30f multi (10-6)	8.50	2.00
1395 A348 40f multi (10-7)	6.50	1.75
1396 A348 50f multi (10-8)	25.00	3.00
1397 A348 60f multi (10-9)	8.00	2.00
1398 A348 70f multi (10-10)	7.00	2.00
Nos. 1389-1398 (10)	72.00	15.75

Souvenir Sheet

1399 A348 $5 multicolored	*550.00*	250.00

No. 1399 contains one stamp showing 4 horses, size: 89x39mm.

Children Playing Soccer — A349

China Post No. T.21.

Designs: No. 1401, Children on the beach. No. 1402, Little girls dancing. No. 1403, Children taking long walks. 20f, Children exercising for good health.

Size: 22x27mm

1978, June 1 *Perf. 11½*

1400 A349 8f multi (5-2)	1.00	.60
1401 A349 8f multi (5-3)	1.00	.60
1402 A349 8f multi (5-4)	1.00	.60
1403 A349 8f multi (5-5)	1.00	.60

Size: 48x28mm

1404 A349 20f multi (5-1)	1.25	.95
Nos. 1400-1404 (5)	5.25	3.35

Build up your health while young.

Synthetic Fiber Feeder A350

China Post No. T.25.

Designs: No. 1406, Drawing out threads. No. 1407, Weaving. No. 1408, Dyeing and printing. No. 1409, Finished products.

1978, June 15 Photo. *Perf. 11½*

1405 A350 8f multi (5-1)	1.00	.60
1406 A350 8f multi (5-2)	1.00	.60
1407 A350 8f multi (5-3)	1.00	.60
1408 A350 8f multi (5-4)	1.00	.60
1409 A350 8f multi (5-5)	1.00	.60
a. Strip of 5, #1405-1409	12.00	11.00
Nos. 1405-1409 (5)	5.00	3.00

Chemical fiber industry. No. 1409a has continuous design. No. 1409a is valued as an unfolded strip. Folded strips sell for less.

Conference Emblem A351

"Develop Economy and Ensure Supplies" A352

China Post No. J.28.

1978, June 20 *Perf. 13*

1410 A351 8f multi (2-1)	2.25	.75
1411 A352 8f multi (2-2)	2.25	.75

Natl. Conf. on Learning from Taching and Tachai in Finance and Trade.

New Pastures, Mongolia — A353

China Post No. T.27.

Designs: No. 1413, Kazakh shepherds selecting sheep for breeding. No. 1414, Mechanized shearing of sheep, Tibet.

1978, June 30 Photo. *Perf. 11½*

1412 A353 8f multi (3-1)	3.00	.80
1413 A353 8f multi (3-2)	3.00	.80
1414 A353 8f multi (3-3)	3.00	.80
Nos. 1412-1414 (3)	9.00	2.40

Learning from Tachai in developing animal husbandry and new pastoral areas.

Coke Oven — A354

China Post No. T.26.

Iron and Steel Industry: No. 1416, Iron furnace. No. 1417, Pouring steel. No. 1418, Steel rolling. No. 1419, Finished iron and steel products.

1978, July 22

1415 A354 8f multi (5-1)	2.25	.50
1416 A354 8f multi (5-2)	2.25	.50
1417 A354 8f multi (5-3)	2.25	.50
1418 A354 8f multi (5-4)	2.25	.50
1419 A354 8f multi (5-5)	2.25	.50
Nos. 1415-1419 (5)	11.25	2.50

Iron Fist to Prevent Revisionism A355

China Post No. T.32.

No. 1421, "Carrying forward revolutionary tradition." No. 1422, "Strenuous training in military skills to wipe out enemy."

1978, Aug. 1 Photo. *Perf. 11½*

1420 A355 8f multi (3-1)	3.50	.70
1421 A355 8f multi (3-2)	3.50	.70
1422 A355 8f multi (3-3)	3.50	.70
Nos. 1420-1422 (3)	10.50	2.10

"Learn from Hard-boned 6th Company." (A military unit since 1939).

Jug in Shape of Sheep — A356

China Post No. T.29.

Arts and Crafts: 4f, Giant lion (toy; horiz.). No. 1425, Rhinoceros (lacquer ware; horiz). 10f, Cat (embroidery). 20f, Bag (weaving; horiz.). 30f, Teapot in shape of peacock (cloisonné). 40f, Plate with lotus, and swan-shaped box (lacquer ware; horiz.). 50f, Dragon flying in sky (ivory). 60f, Sun rising (jade; horiz.). 70f, Flight to human world (ivory). $3, Flying fairies (arts and crafts; horiz.).

1978, Aug. 26

1423	A356	4f multi (10-1)	.95	.45
1424	A356	8f multi (10-2)	.95	.45
1425	A356	8f multi (10-3)	.95	.45
1426	A356	10f multi (10-4)	.95	.55
1427	A356	20f multi (10-5)	.95	.55
1428	A356	30f multi (10-6)	2.00	.80
1429	A356	40f multi (10-7)	2.50	1.10
1430	A356	50f multi (10-8)	6.00	2.75
1431	A356	60f multi (10-9)	3.50	2.75
1432	A356	70f multi (10-10)	3.50	1.60
		Nos. 1423-1432 (10)	22.25	11.45

Souvenir Sheet

1433	A356	$3 multi	*300.00*	190.00

No. 1433 contains one 85x36mm stamp.

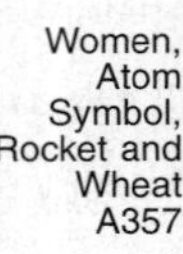

Women, Atom Symbol, Rocket and Wheat A357

China Post No. J.30.

1978, Sept. 8 Photo. *Perf. 11*

1434	A357	8f multicolored	2.50	1.00

4th National Women's Congress.

Ginseng — A358

China Post No. T.30.

Medicinal Plants: No. 1436, Horn of plenty. No. 1437, Blackberry lily. No. 1438, Balloon-flower. 55f, Rhododendron dauricum.

1978, Sept. 15

1435	A358	8f multi (5-1)	1.00	.35
1436	A358	8f multi (5-2)	1.00	.35
1437	A358	8f multi (5-3)	1.00	.35
1438	A358	8f multi (5-4)	1.00	.35
1439	A358	55f multi (5-5)	4.00	1.25
		Nos. 1435-1439 (5)	8.00	2.65

Flag, Wheat, Cogwheel, Plane, Atom Symbols — A359

China Post No. J.31.

1978, Oct. 11 Photo. *Perf. 11*

1440	A359	8f multicolored	4.00	1.00

9th National Trade Union Congress.

Youth League Emblem A360

China Post No. J.32.

1978, Oct. 16

1441	A360	8f multicolored	4.25	1.00

10th Natl. Communist Youth League Cong.

Chinese and Japanese Girls Exchanging Gifts A361

Great Wall and Mt. Fuji A362

China Post No. J.34.

1978, Oct. 22

1442	A361	8f multicolored	1.60	.75
1443	A362	55f multicolored	2.60	1.50

Signing of Sino-Japanese Peace and Friendship Treaty.

Moslem, Chinese and Mongolian People — A363

China Post No. J.29.

No. 1445, Loading coal at Holan Mountain. 10f, Irrigated rice fields & boxthorn.

1978, Oct. 25

1444	A363	8f multi (3-1)	2.75	1.00
1445	A363	8f multi (3-2)	2.75	1.00
1446	A363	10f multi (3-3)	3.25	1.00
		Nos. 1444-1446 (3)	8.75	3.00

20th anniversary of founding of Ningsia Moslem Autonomous Region.

Chinsha River Bridge, West Szechuan A364

China Post No. T.31.

Highway Bridges: No. 1448, Hsinhong bridge, Wuhsi. No. 1449, Chiuhsikou bridge, Fengdu. No. 1450, Chinsha River bridge, West Szechuan. 60f, Shangyeh bridge, Sanmen. $2, Hsiang-kiang River bridge.

1978, Nov. 1 Photo. *Perf. 11½x11*

1447	A364	8f multi (5-1)	2.00	.40
1448	A364	8f multi (5-2)	1.60	.40
1449	A364	8f multi (5-3)	1.60	.40
1450	A364	8f multi (5-4)	1.60	.40
1451	A364	60f multi (5-5)	3.50	1.25
		Nos. 1447-1451 (5)	10.30	2.85

Souvenir Sheet

1452	A364	$2 multi	*300.00*	180.00

No. 1452 contains one 86x37mm stamp.

Mechanical Transplanting of Rice Seedlings A365

China Post No. T.34.

Paintings: No. 1454, Spraying fields. No. 1455, Seed selection. No. 1456, Trade. No. 1457, Delivery of public grain in city.

1978, Nov. 30 *Perf. 11½*

1453	A365	8f multi (5-1)	3.25	1.50
1454	A365	8f multi (5-2)	3.25	1.50
1455	A365	8f multi (5-3)	3.25	1.50
1456	A365	8f multi (5-4)	3.25	1.50
1457	A365	8f multi (5-5)	3.25	1.50
a.		Strip of 5, #1453-1457	25.00	16.50

Agricultural progress. No. 1457a has a continuous design. Value is for unfolded strip. Folded strips are worth less.

Dancers and Fireworks — A366

China Post No. J.33.

Designs: No. 1459, Industry, vert. 10f, Agriculture, vert.

1978, Dec. 11 Photo. *Perf. 11*

1458	A366	8f multi (3-1)	4.50	1.00
1459	A366	8f multi (3-2)	3.00	1.00
1460	A366	10f multi (3-3)	1.50	1.00
		Nos. 1458-1460 (3)	9.00	3.00

20th anniversary of Kwangsi Chuang Autonomous Region.

Miners with Pneumatic Drill A367

China Post No. T.20.

Mine Development: 4f, Old Tibetan peasant reporting to surveyor. 10f, Open-cut mining with power shovel. 20f, Loaded electric train in pit.

1978, Dec. 29 Photo. & Engr.

1461	A367	4f multi (4-1)	2.50	1.00
1462	A367	8f multi (4-2)	3.50	1.75
1463	A367	10f multi (4-3)	2.50	1.00
1464	A367	20f multi (4-4)	2.50	1.00
		Nos. 1461-1464 (4)	11.00	4.75

A368

China Post No. T.35.

Golden Pheasants: 4f, Roosting on rock. 8f, In flight. 45f, Seeking food.

1979, Jan. 25 Photo. *Perf. 11½*

1465	A368	4f multi (3-1)	2.00	1.00
1466	A368	8f multi (3-2)	2.50	2.00
1467	A368	45f multi (3-3)	4.00	3.00
		Nos. 1465-1467 (3)	8.50	6.00

Albert Einstein, Equation — A369

China Post No. J.36.

1979, Mar. 14 Photo. *Perf. 11½x11*

1468	A369	8f multi	2.50	1.25

Phoenix Battling Monster, Praying Woman A370

China Post No. T.33.

60f, Man riding dragon to heaven. Designs from silk paintings found in Changsha tomb, Warring States Period (475-221 B.C.).

1979, Mar. 29 *Perf. 11*

1469	A370	8f multi (2-1)	2.50	1.50
1470	A370	60f multi (2-2)	3.50	1.50

Summer Palace — A371

China Post No. R20

Photo., Photo. & Engr. ($5)

1979-80 *Perf. 13*

1471	A371	$1 Pagoda ('80)	2.00	.70
1472	A371	$2 Shown	1.75	.80
1473	A371	$5 Temple, Beihai Park	5.75	1.50
		Nos. 1471-1473 (3)	9.50	3.00

Issued: $1, Nov. 24, 1980; $2, June 16, 1979; $5, June 20, 1980.

Hammer and Sickle "51" and Bars from "International" — A372

China Post No. J.35.

1979, May 1 Photo. *Perf. 11*

1474	A372	8f multicolored	2.50	1.00

International Labor Day, 90th anniv.

"Tradition of May 4th Movement" A373

Young Woman, Rocket, Antenna, Nuclear Reactor A374

China Post No. J.37.

1979, May 4

1475	A373	8f multicolored	1.25	.65
1476	A374	8f multicolored	1.25	.65

60th anniversary of May 4th Movement.

IYC Emblem, Children Holding Balloons — A375

Children of Three Races, IYC Emblem — A376

China Post No. J.38.

1979, May 25 ***Perf. 11½***
1477 A375 8f multicolored 2.00 1.00
1478 A376 60f multicolored 12.00 4.50

International Year of the Child.

Great Wall in Spring A377

China Post No. T.38.

Designs (The Great Wall): No. 1480, in summer. No. 1481, in autumn. 60f, in winter. $2, Guard tower.

1979, June 25 Photo. ***Perf. 11***
1479 A377 8f multi (4-1) 2.00 .95
1480 A377 8f multi (4-2) 2.00 .95
1481 A377 8f multi (4-3) 2.00 1.00
1482 A377 60f multi (4-4) 10.00 4.50
Nos. 1479-1482 (4) 16.00 7.40

Souvenir Sheet

1483 A377 $2 multi *125.00* 60.00

For overprint see No. 1492.

Roaring Tiger — A379

China Post No. T.40.

Manchurian Tiger: 8f, Two young tigers. 60f, Tiger at rest.

1979, July 20 ***Perf. 11½x11***
1484 A379 4f multi (3-1) 4.25 1.00
1485 A379 8f multi (3-2) 2.50 1.00
1486 A379 60f multi (3-3) 3.00 1.75
Nos. 1484-1486 (3) 9.75 3.75

Mechanical Harvesting — A380

China Post No. T.39.

Work of the Communes: No. 1488, Forestry. No. 1489, Raising ducks. No. 1490, Women weaving baskets. 10f, Fishing.

1979, Aug. 10 ***Perf. 11½***
1487 A380 4f multi (5-1) 6.00 2.00
1488 A380 8f multi (5-2) 3.25 1.00
1489 A380 8f multi (5-3) 3.25 1.00
1490 A380 8f multi (5-4) 3.25 1.00
1491 A380 10f multi (5-5) 4.00 1.75
Nos. 1487-1491 (5) 19.75 6.75

No. 1483 Overprinted with Gold Inscription and "1979"
China Post No. J.41.
Souvenir Sheet

1979, Aug. 25 Photo. ***Perf. 11***
1492 A377 $2 multi (1-1) *575.00 200.00*

31st International Stamp Exhibition, Riccione, Italy.
Forged overprints exist.

Games Emblem, Sports — A381

China Post No. J.43.

No. 1494, Soccer, badminton, high jump, speed skating. No. 1495, Fencing, skiing, gymnastics, diving. No. 1496, Motorcycling, table tennis, basketball, archery. No. 1497, Emblem only.

1979, Sept. 15 ***Perf. 11½x11***
1493 A381 8f multi (4-1) 1.25 .80
1494 A381 8f multi (4-2) 1.25 .80
1495 A381 8f multi (4-3) 1.25 .80
1496 A381 8f multi (4-4) 1.25 .80
a. Block of 4, #1493-1496 7.50 5.00

Souvenir Sheet
Perf. 11½

1497 A381 $2 multi, vert. *90.00 45.00*

4th National Games. Size of stamp in No. 1497: 22x26mm.

Flag and Rainbow — A382

China Post No. J.44.

Design: No. 1499, Flag and mountains.

1979, Oct. 1 Photo. ***Perf. 11½***
1498 A382 8f multicolored 2.40 1.00
1499 A382 8f multicolored 5.25 1.50

National Emblem — A383

China Post No. J.45.

1979, Oct. 1 Photo. ***Perf. 11½***
1500 A383 8f multicolored 5.75 1.50

Souvenir Sheet

1501 A383 $1 multicolored *85.00* 35.00

Dancers — A384

China Post No. J.47.

Designs: Nos. 1503-1505, various dances.

1979, Oct. 1 Photo. ***Perf. 11½***
1502 A384 8f multi (4-1) .85 .40
1503 A384 8f multi (4-2) .85 .40
1504 A384 8f multi (4-3) .85 .40
1505 A384 8f multi (4-4) .85 .40
a. Block of 4, #1502-1505 7.00 5.00

Tractor, Aerial Crop Spraying, Irrigation — A385

China Post No. J.48.

No. 1507, Gear, computers. No. 1508, Rocket, submarine, jets. No. 1509, Atom symbol.

1979, Oct. 1 Photo. ***Perf. 11½***
1506 A385 8f multi (4-1) 2.75 1.00
1507 A385 8f multi (4-2) 2.75 1.00
1508 A385 8f multi (4-3) 1.60 .90
1509 A385 8f multi (4-4) 2.25 .90
Nos. 1506-1509 (4) 9.35 3.80

National Anthem A386

China Post No. J.46.

1979, Oct. 1 Engr. ***Perf. 11***
1510 A386 8f multicolored 12.50 2.00

Exhibition Emblem — A387

China Post No. J.40.

1979, Oct. 3
1511 A387 8f multicolored 1.25 1.00

Junior National Scientific and Technological Exhibition.

Children Flying Model Planes — A388

China Post No. T.41.

No. 1513, Girls and microscope. No. 1514, Children and telescope. No. 1515, Boy catching butterflies. No. 1516, Girl taking meteorological readings. No. 1517, Boys sailing model boat. No. 1518, Girl with book.

1979, Oct. 3
1512 A388 8f multi (6-1) 1.50 .70
1513 A388 8f multi (6-2) 1.50 .70
1514 A388 8f multi (6-3) 1.50 .70
1515 A388 8f multi (6-4) 1.50 .70
1516 A388 8f multi (6-5) 1.50 .70
1517 A388 60f multi (6-6) 7.00 3.00
Nos. 1512-1517 (6) 14.50 6.50

Souvenir Sheet
Perf. 11

1518 A388 $2 multi *1,500.* 850.00

Study Science from Childhood. No. 1518 contains one stamp, size: 90x40mm.

Yu Shan Mountain A389

China Post No. T.42.

Taiwan Landscapes: No. 1520, Sun and Moon Lake. No. 1521, Chihkan Tower. No. 1522, Suao-Hualien Highway. 55f, Tian Xiang Falls. 60f, Banping Mountain.

1979, Oct. 20 Photo. ***Perf. 11x11½***
1519 A389 8f multi (6-1) 1.50 .85
1520 A389 8f multi (6-2) 1.50 .85
1521 A389 8f multi (6-3) 1.50 .85
1522 A389 8f multi (6-4) 1.50 .85
1523 A389 55f multi (6-5) 4.00 1.50
1524 A389 60f multi (6-6) 11.00 3.00
Nos. 1519-1524 (6) 21.00 7.90

Arts Symbols A390

China Post No. J.39.

8f, Seals and modernization symbols.

1979, Oct. 30
1525 A390 4f multicolored 1.25 .65
1526 A390 8f multicolored 2.00 .85

4th Natl. Cong. of Literary and Art Workers.

Train in Tunnel A391

China Post No. T.36.

Railroads: No. 1528, Mountain bridge. No. 1529, Freight train.

1979, Oct. 30 **Photo. & Engr.**
1527 A391 8f multi (3-1) 3.00 1.00
1528 A391 8f multi (3-2) 3.00 1.25
1529 A391 8f multi (3-3) 3.00 1.50
Nos. 1527-1529 (3) 9.00 3.75

Chrysanthemum Petal — A392

China Post No. T.37.

Camellias: No. 1531, Lion head. No. 1532, Camellia chryantha. 10f, Small osmanthus leaf. 20f, Baby face. 30f, Cornelian. 40f, Peony camellia. 50f, Purple gown. 60f, Dwarf rose. 70f, Willow leaf spinel pink. $2, Red jewelry.

1979, Nov. 10 Photo. ***Perf. 11x11½***
1530 A392 4f multi (10-1) 5.25 1.00
1531 A392 8f multi (10-2) 1.75 .65
1532 A392 8f multi (10-3) 1.75 .65
1533 A392 10f multi (10-4) 1.75 .65
1534 A392 20f multi (10-5) 1.75 1.00
1535 A392 30f multi (10-6) 14.00 3.00
1536 A392 40f multi (10-7) 2.75 1.25
1537 A392 50f multi (10-8) 1.50 1.00
1538 A392 60f multi (10-9) 3.25 1.00
1539 A392 70f multi (10-10) 3.50 1.00
Nos. 1530-1539 (10) 37.25 11.20

Souvenir Sheet
Perf. 11½x11

1540 A392 $2 multi *260.00 130.00*

No. 1540 contains one 86x36mm stamp.

No. 1540 Overprinted and Numbered in Gold in Margin
China Post No. J.42.
Souvenir Sheet

Souvenir Sheet

1979, Nov. 10

1541 A392 $2 multi (1-1) *400.00 150.00*

People's Republic of China Phil. Exhib., Hong Kong, 1979.

Forged overprints exist.

Norman Bethune Treating Soldier — A393

China Post No. J.50.

Design: 70f, Bethune statue.

1979, Nov. 12

1542 A393 8f multi (2-2) 1.50 .45
1543 A393 70f multi (2-1) 4.50 2.00

Dr. Norman Bethune, 40th death anniv.

Central Archives Hall A394

China Post No. J.51.

Intl. Archives Weeks: No. 1545, Gold archive cabinet, vert. 60f, Pavilion.

Perf. 11x11½, 11½x11

1979, Nov. 26 **Photo.**

1544 A394 8f multi (3-1) 2.00 1.00
1545 A394 8f multi (3-2) 2.00 1.00
1546 A394 60f multi (3-3) 11.00 2.25
Nos. 1544-1546 (3) 15.00 4.25

Monkey King in Waterfall Cave — A395

China Post No. T.43.

Monkey King, Scenes from Pilgrimage to the West (Novel): No. 1548, Fighting Necha, son of Prince Li. No. 1549, In Mother Queen's peach orchard. No. 1550, In the alchemy furnace. 10f, Subduing the white bone demon. 20f, With palm leaf fan. 60f, In cobweb cave. 70f, Walking on scripture-seeking route.

1979, Dec. 1 ***Perf. 11½x11***

1547 A395 8f multi (8-1) 5.25 1.75
1548 A395 8f multi (8-2) 5.25 1.75
1549 A395 8f multi (8-3) 5.25 1.75
1550 A395 8f multi (8-4) 5.25 1.75
1551 A395 10f multi (8-5) 7.25 1.75
1552 A395 20f multi (8-6) 7.25 1.75
1553 A395 60f multi (8-7) 32.50 10.00
1554 A395 70f multi (8-8) 19.50 6.00
Nos. 1547-1554 (8) 87.50 26.50

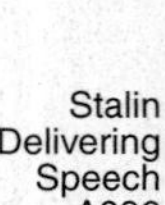

Stalin Delivering Speech A396

China Post No. J.49.

Joseph Stalin (1879-1953): No. 1555, Portrait of Stalin, vert.

Perf. 11x11½, 11½x11

1979, Dec. 21 **Engr.**

1555 A396 8f brown (2-1) 1.50 1.00
1556 A396 8f black (2-2) 2.00 1.60

A397

China Post No. T.44.

No. 1557, Peony (16-1). No. 1558, Squirrels and grapes (16-2). No. 1559, Crabs candle and wine (16-3). No. 1560, Tadpoles in mountain spring (16-4). No. 1561, Chicks (16-5). No. 1562, Lotus (16-6). No. 1563, Red plum (16-7). No. 1564, Kingfisher (16-8). No. 1565, Bottle gourd (16-9). No. 1566, Voice of autumn (16-10). No. 1567, Wisteria (16-11). No. 1568, Chrysanthemums (16-12). No. 1569, Shrimp (16-13). No. 1570, Litchi (16-14). No. 1571, Cabbages, mushrooms (16-15). No. 1572, Peaches (16-16).

No. 1573, Hyacynth.

1980 **Photo.** ***Perf. 11½***

1557 A397 4f multi 2.50 1.00
1558 A397 4f multi 2.50 1.00
1559 A397 8f multi 2.00 .75
1560 A397 8f multi 2.00 .75
1561 A397 8f multi 2.00 .75
1562 A397 8f multi 2.00 .75
1563 A397 8f multi 2.00 .75
1564 A397 8f multi 2.00 .75
1565 A397 10f multi 5.00 1.75
1566 A397 20f multi 5.00 1.75
1567 A397 30f multi 6.00 2.00
1568 A397 40f multi 30.00 8.00
1569 A397 50f multi 7.50 2.00
1570 A397 55f multi 7.50 3.00
1571 A397 60f multi 37.50 8.00
1572 A397 70f multi 15.00 5.00
Nos. 1557-1572 (16) 130.50 38.00

Souvenir Sheet

1573 A397 $2 multi *240.00 125.00*

Qi Baishi paintings. Issued: Nos. 1557-1560, 1569-1572, 1/15; others, 5/20. No. 1573 contains one 37½x61mm stamp.

A398

China Post No. T.45.

Opera Masks: No. 1574, Meng Liang Mask from Hongyang Cave Opera. No. 1575, Li Kui, from Black Whirlwind. No. 1576, Huang Gai, from Meeting of Heroes. No. 1577, Monkey King. 10f, Lu Zhishen, from Wild Boar Forest. 20f, Lian Po, from Reconciliation between the General and Minister. 60f, Zhang Fei, from Reed Marsh. 70f, Dou Erdun, from Stealing the Emperor's Horse.

1980, Jan. 25 ***Perf. 11½x11***

1574 A398 4f multi (8-1) 4.25 1.25
1575 A398 4f multi (8-2) 28.00 5.50
1576 A398 8f multi (8-3) 4.00 1.25
1577 A398 8f multi (8-4) 3.50 1.75
1578 A398 10f multi (8-5) 4.00 1.75
1579 A398 20f multi (8-6) 4.00 1.75
1580 A398 60f multi (8-7) 7.00 3.00
1581 A398 70f multi (8-8) 8.00 4.00
Nos. 1574-1581 (8) 62.75 20.25

A set of eight similar to Nos. 1574-1581 was prepared but not issued in 1964. See note below No. 782.

Speed Skating, Olympic Rings — A399

China Post No. J.54.

Olympic Rings and: No. 1582, Chinese flag. No. 1584, Figure skating. 60f, Downhill skiing.

1980, Feb. 13

1582 A399 8f multi (4-1) 2.50 .75
1583 A399 8f multi (4-2) 2.50 .75
1584 A399 8f multi (4-3) 2.50 .75
1585 A399 60f multi (4-4) 9.00 3.00
Nos. 1582-1585 (4) 16.50 5.25

13th Winter Olympic Games, Lake Placid, NY, Feb. 12-24.

Monkey, New Year — A400

China Post No. T.46.
Engraved and Photogravure

1980, Feb. 15 ***Perf. 11½***

1586 A400 8f multicolored *1,900. 675.00*

Excellent forgeries of No. 1586 exist.

Clara Zetkin — A401

China Post No. J.53.
Photogravure & Engraved

1980, Mar. 8 ***Perf. 11½x11***

1587 A401 8f black & yellow 2.50 1.10

International Working Women's Day, 70th anniv., founded by Clara Zetkin (1857-1933).

Orchard A402

China Post No. T.48.

Afforestation: 8f, Trees lining highway. 10f, Aerial seeding. 20f, Trees surrounding factory.

1980, Mar. 12 ***Perf. 11x11½***

1588 A402 4f multi (4-1) 3.25 .95
1589 A402 8f multi (4-2) 3.25 .95
1590 A402 10f multi (4-3) 1.50 .75
1591 A402 20f multi (4-4) 1.50 .75
Nos. 1588-1591 (4) 9.50 3.40

Apsaras, Symbols of Modernization — A403

China Post No. J.52.

1980, Mar. 15 **Photo.** ***Perf. 11½***

1592 A403 8f multicolored 3.00 1.40

2nd National Conference of the Scientific and Technical Association of China.

Mail Transport — A404

China Post No. T.49.

1980, Mar. 20 ***Perf. 11x11½***

1593 A404 2f Ship (4-1) 1.75 1.50
1594 A404 4f Bus (4-2) 5.50 2.00
1595 A404 8f Train (4-3) 4.75 2.00
1596 A404 10f Jet (4-4) 3.75 2.25
Nos. 1593-1596 (4) 15.75 7.75

Forgeries exist.

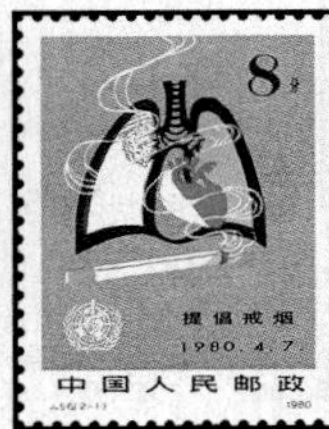

Lungs, Heart, Cigarette, WHO Emblem — A405

China Post No. J.56.

1980, Apr. 7 ***Perf. 11½x11***

1597 A405 8f shown (2-1) 2.00 .60
1598 A405 60f Faces (2-2) 14.00 3.50

Fight against cigarette smoking.

Statue of Chien Chen (688-763) — A406

China Post No. J.55.

Loan to China by Japan of statue of Chien Chen (Jian Zhen), Buddhist missionary to Japan (754-763): No. 1600, Chien Chen Memorial Hall, Yangchou, horiz. 60f, Chien Chen's ship, horiz. His name in Japan is Ganjin.

1980, Apr. 13 ***Perf. 11x11½, 11½x11***

1599 A406 8f multi (3-1) 4.00 1.10
1600 A406 8f multi (3-2) 4.00 1.10
1601 A406 60f multi (3-3) 35.00 7.75
Nos. 1599-1601 (3) 43.00 9.95

Lenin's 110th Birthday — A407

China Post No. J.57.
Photogravure and Engraved

1980, Apr. 22 ***Perf. 11½x11***

1602 A407 8f multicolored 4.00 1.10

Swallow Chick Kite — A408

China Post No. T.50.

Kites: No. 1604, Slender-swallow (4-2). No. 1605, Semi-slender swallow (4-3). No. 1606, Dual swallows (4-4).

1980, May 10 Photo. *Perf. 11½*
1603 A408 8f shown (4-1) 5.50 1.75
1604 A408 8f multi 5.50 1.75
1605 A408 8f multi 5.50 1.75
1606 A408 70f multi 30.00 6.25
Nos. 1603-1606 (4) 46.50 11.50

Hare Running from Fallen Papaya A409

China Post No. T.51.

1980, June 1 Photo. *Perf. 11x11½*
1607 Strip of 4 + label 20.00 20.00
a. A409 8f shown (4-1) 2.00 1.60
b. A409 8f Hare fox, monkey running away (4-2) 2.00 1.60
c. A409 8f Lion instructing animals (4-3) 2.00 1.60
d. A409 8f Discovery of fallen papaya (4-4) 2.00 1.60
e. Bklt. pane, 2 #1607 *500.00*
Complete booklet *900.00*

Gu Dong fairy tale.

Beware of complete booklets of No. 1607e with forged booklet covers.

Terminal Building, Jets — A410

China Post No. T.47.

1980, June 20 *Perf. 11½*
1608 A410 8f Shown (2-1) 4.00 1.40
1609 A410 10f Runways, jets (2-2) 4.00 1.40

Peking Intl. Airport opening.

Sika Stag — A411

China Post No. T.52.

8f, Doe and fawn (3-2). 60f, Herd (3-3).

1980, July 18 Photo. *Perf. 11½*
1610 A411 4f Shown (3-1) 2.25 1.40
1611 A411 8f multi 2.25 1.40
1612 A411 60f multi 11.00 5.25
Nos. 1610-1612 (3) 15.50 8.05

White Lotus — A412

China Post No. T.54.

No. 1614, Rose-tipped snow (4-2). No. 1615, Buddha's seat (4-3). No. 1616, Variable charming face (4-4).

No. 1617, Fresh lotus on rippling water.

1980, Aug. 4
1613 A412 8f Shown (4-1) 6.00 2.00
1614 A412 8f multi 6.00 2.00
1615 A412 8f multi 6.00 2.00
1616 A412 70f multi 60.00 8.00
Nos. 1613-1616 (4) 78.00 14.00

Souvenir Sheet

1617 A412 $1 multi *250.00 120.00*

No. 1617 contains one 48x88mm stamp.

Pearl Cave, Sword-cut Stone Sculptures — A413

China Post No. T.53.

Guilin Landscapes: No. 1619, Three mountains, distant views. No. 1620, Nine-horse fresco hill. No. 1621, Egrets around aged banyan. No. 1622, Western hills at sunset, vert. No. 1623, Moonlight on Lijiang River, vert. 60f, Springhead, ancient ferry, vert. 70f, Scenic path, Yangshue, vert.

1980, Aug. 30 Photo. *Perf. 11½*
1618 A413 8f multi (8-1) 2.00 1.00
1619 A413 8f multi (8-2) 2.00 1.00
1620 A413 8f multi (8-3) 2.00 1.00
1621 A413 8f multi (8-4) 2.00 1.00
1622 A413 8f multi (8-5) 2.00 1.00
1623 A413 8f multi (8-6) 2.00 1.00
1624 A413 60f multi (8-7) 20.00 4.00
1625 A413 70f multi (8-8) 25.00 5.00
Nos. 1618-1625 (8) 57.00 15.00

Entrance Gate and Good Fairies A414

Great Wall, Symbols of Chicago, San Francisco and New York A415

China Post No. J.59.

1980, Sept. 13 Photo. *Perf. 11x11½*
1626 A414 8f multicolored 2.00 .90
1627 A415 70f multicolored 14.00 3.75

Exhibitions of the People's Republic of China in San Francisco, Chicago and New York, Sept.-Dec. Sheets of 12 were sold only at the US exhibitions at increasing prices. Value, set of two sheets of 12, $1,500.

Romanian Flag, Warrior and Scroll — A416

China Post No. J.61.

1980, Sept. 20 Photo. *Perf. 11½x11*
1628 A416 8f multicolored 2.50 1.40

2050th anniv. of Dacia, 1st independent Romanian state.

UNESCO Exhibition of Drawings and Paintings — A417

China Post No. J.60.

No. 1629, Sea of Clouds, by Liu Haisu (3-1). No. 1630, Oriole and Magnolia, by Yu Feian, vert., (3-2). No. 1631, Camels, by Wu Zuoren (3-3).

1980, Oct. 8 *Perf. 11½*
1629 A417 8f multi 2.00 .85
1630 A417 8f multi 2.00 .85
1631 A417 8f multi 2.00 .85
Nos. 1629-1631 (3) 6.00 2.55

Scenes from Tarrying Garden — A418

China Post No. T.56.

No. 1632, Quxi Tower (4-1). No. 1633, Yuancui Pavilion (4-2). No. 1634, Hanbi Shanfang (4-3). No. 1635, Guanyun Peak (4-4).

1980, Oct. 25 Photo. *Perf. 11½*
1632 A418 8f multi *7.25* 4.00
1633 A418 8f multi *7.25* 4.00
1634 A418 10f multi *12.00* 4.00
1635 A418 60f multi *62.50* 22.50
Nos. 1632-1635 (4) *89.00* 34.50

Xu Guangqi (1562-1633), Agronomist A419

China Post No. J.58.

Scientists of Ancient China: No. 1637, Li Bing, hydraulic engineer, 3rd century B.C. No. 1638, Jia Sixie, agronomist, 5th century. 60f, Huang Daopo, textile expert, 13th century.

Photogravure and Engraved

1980, Nov. 20 *Perf. 11½x11*
1636 A419 8f multi (4-1) 7.00 2.00
1637 A419 8f multi (4-2) 7.00 2.00
1638 A419 8f multi (4-3) 7.00 2.00
1639 A419 60f multi (4-4) 42.50 11.00
Nos. 1636-1639 (4) 63.50 17.00

Shooting, Olympic Rings — A420

China Post No. J.62.

1980, Nov. 26 Photo.
1640 A420 4f shown (5-1) 2.25 .45
1641 A420 8f Gymnastics (5-2) 2.25 .45
1642 A420 8f Diving (5-3) 2.25 .45
1643 A420 10f Volleyball (5-4) 2.25 .75
1644 A420 60f Archery (5-5) 14.00 2.75
Nos. 1640-1644 (5) 23.00 4.85

Return to International Olympic Committee, 1st anniversary.

Chinese River Dolphin A421

China Post No. T.57.

Photogravure & Engraved

1980, Dec. 25 *Perf. 11x11½*
1645 A421 8f shown (2-1) 3.50 .75
a. Booklet pane of 6 50.00
1646 A421 60f Dolphins (2-2) 8.00 1.90
a. Booklet pane of 1 50.00

Stamps from No. 1645a have straight edges on top or bottom.

Cock — A422

China Post No. T.58.

Photogravure & Engraved

1981, Jan. 5 *Perf. 11½*
1647 A422 8f multicolored 35.00 6.00
a. Booklet pane of 12 275.00
Complete booklet 300.00

New Year 1981.

Stamps from booklet pane have straight edges on top or bottom.

Early Morning in Xishuang Bana A423

China Post No. T.55.

No. 1649, Dai mountain village (6-2). No. 1650, Rainbow over Lanchang River (6-3). No. 1651, Ancient temple vert. (6-4). No. 1652, Moonlit night, vert. (6-5). No. 1653, Phoenix tree, vert. (6-6).

Perf. 11x11½, 11½x11

1981, Jan. 20 Photo.
1648 A423 4f shown (6-1) 7.00 1.50
1649 A423 4f multi 2.60 .75
1650 A423 8f multi 2.60 .75
1651 A423 8f multi 2.60 .75
1652 A423 8f multi 2.60 .75
1653 A423 60f multi 13.00 3.50
Nos. 1648-1653 (6) 30.40 8.00

Flower Basket Palace Lantern — A424

China Post No. T.60.

Designs: Palace lanterns.

1981, Feb. 19 Photo. *Perf. 11½*
1654 A424 4f multi (6-1) 2.00 1.00
1655 A424 8f multi (6-2) 2.00 1.00
1656 A424 8f multi (6-3) 2.00 1.00
1657 A424 8f multi (6-4) 2.00 1.00
1658 A424 20f multi (6-5) 4.50 3.50
1659 A424 60f multi (6-6) 25.00 7.50
Nos. 1654-1659 (6) 37.50 15.00

Crossing River, Scene from Marking the Gunwale A425

China Post No. T.59.

Scenes from Marking the Gunwale fable: No. 1660, Text (5-1). No. 1662, Dropping sword in water (5-3). No. 1663, Marking gunwale (5-4). No. 1664, Searching for sword (5-5).

1981, Mar. 10 Photo. ***Perf. 11x11½***

1660 A425 8f multi 2.00 1.25
1661 A425 8f shown (5-2) 2.00 1.25
1662 A425 8f multi 2.00 1.25
1663 A425 8f multi 2.00 1.25
1664 A425 8f multi 2.00 1.25
a. Bklt. pane, 2 each #1660-1664 50.00
Complete booklet, #1664a 55.00
b. Strip of 5, #1660-1664 16.00 10.00

Chinese Juniper A426

China Post No. T.61.

Designs: Miniature landscapes: No. 1665, Chinese elm, vert. (6-1). No. 1666, Juniper, vert. (6-2). No. 1667, Maidenhair tree, vert. (6-3). No. 1669, Persimmon (6-5). No. 1670, Juniper (6-6).

1981, Mar. 31 ***Perf. 11½***

1665 A426 4f multi 3.00 1.40
1666 A426 8f multi 2.00 1.10
1667 A426 8f multi 2.00 1.10
1668 A426 10f shown (6-4) 2.00 1.10
1669 A426 20f multi 2.00 1.25
1670 A426 60f multi 12.50 4.25
Nos. 1665-1670 (6) 23.50 10.20

Vase with Tiger-shaped Handles — A427

China Post No. T.62.

Cizhou Kiln Ceramic Pottery: 4f, Vase with 2 tigers, Song Dynasty. No. 1672, Black glazed jar, Jin Dynasty. No. 1673, Amphora. No. 1674, Jar with 2 phoenixes (Yuan Dynasty). 10f, Flat flask, Yuan Dynasty.

1981, Apr. 15 Photo. ***Perf. 11½x11***

1671 A427 4f multi, vert. (6-1) 1.50 .90
1672 A427 8f multi (6-2) 1.50 .90
1673 A427 8f multi, vert. (6-3) 1.50 .90
1674 A427 8f multi (6-4) 1.50 .90
1675 A427 10f multi (6-5) 1.50 .90
1676 A427 60f multi (6-6) 7.50 3.75
Nos. 1671-1676 (6) 15.00 8.25

Panda and Colored Stamps — A428

China Post No. J.63.

1981, Apr. 29 Photo. ***Perf. 11½x11***

1677 A428 8f shown (2-1) .90 .50
1678 A428 60f Boat, bird (2-2) 3.25 1.60
a. Booklet pane (8 #1677, souv. sheet with 1677-1678) 20.00
Complete booklet, #1678a 23.00

Qinchuan Steer A429

China Post No. T.63.

Cattle Breeds: No. 1680, Binhu buffalo. No. 1681, Yak. No. 1682, Black and white dairy cows. 10f, Pasture red cow. 55f, Simmental cross-breed.

1981, May 5 ***Perf. 11x11½***

1679 A429 4f multi (6-1) 2.00 1.00
1680 A429 8f multi (6-2) 3.00 1.25
1681 A429 8f multi (6-3) 2.75 1.25
1682 A429 8f multi (6-4) 2.25 1.00
1683 A429 10f multi (6-5) 2.25 1.00
1684 A429 55f multi (6-6) 3.50 1.00
Nos. 1679-1684 (6) 15.75 6.50

Mail Delivery Slogan — A430

China Post No. J.70.

1981, May 9 ***Perf. 11***

1685 A430 8f multicolored 1.25 .35

13th World Telecommunications Day — A431

China Post No. J.69.

1981, May 17 ***Perf. 11½x11***

1686 A431 8f multicolored 1.00 .35

Construction Worker — A432

China Post No. J.65.

No. 1688, Miner (4-2). No. 1689, Children crossing street (4-3). No. 1690, Farm worker (4-4).

1981, May 20 ***Perf. 11½***

1687 A432 8f shown (4-1) 1.75 .60
1688 A432 8f multi 1.75 .60
1689 A432 8f multi 1.75 .60
1690 A432 8f multi 1.75 .60
Nos. 1687-1690 (4) 7.00 2.40

National Safety Month.

Telephone Building, Peking — A433

China Post No. R19

1981, June 5 Engr. ***Perf. 11½x11***

1691 A433 8f violet brown 1.40 .65

Swaythling Cup, Men's Team Table Tennis — A434

China Post No. J.71.

36th World Table Tennis Championships Victory — No. 1692: a, St. Bride Vase, men's singles (7-3). b, Iran Cup, men's doubles (7-4). c, G. Geist Prize, women's singles (7-5). d, W.J. Pope Trophy, women's doubles (7-6). e, Heydusek Prize, mixed doubles (7-7). No. 1694, Marcel Corbillon Cup, women's team. Nos. 1693-1694 printed in sheets of 16 (8 each) + 2 labels.

1981, June 30 Photo. ***Perf. 11½x11***

1692 Strip of 5 6.50 3.75
a.-e. A434 8f multi .45 .25
1693 A434 20f multi (7-1) 1.75 .85
1694 A434 20f multi (7-2) 1.75 .85

Chinese Communist Party, 60th Anniv. A435

China Post No. J.64.

1981, July 1 Photo. ***Perf. 11x11½***

1695 A435 8f multicolored 1.50 .60

Hanpo Pass, Lushan Mountains A436

China Post No. T.67.

No. 1696, Five-veteran Peak, vert. (7-1). No. 1698, Yellow Dragon Pool, vert. (7-3). No. 1699, Sunlit Peak (7-4). No. 1700, Three-layer Spring, vert. (7-5). No. 1701, Stone and pines (7-6). No. 1702, Dragon-head Cliff, vert. (7-7).

Photogravure & Engraved

1981, July 20 ***Perf. 12½x12***

1696 8f multi 2.40 .70
1697 8f shown (7-2) 2.40 .70
1698 8f multi 2.40 .70
1699 8f multi 2.40 .70
1700 8f multi 2.40 .70
1701 8f multi 2.40 .70
1702 60f multi 23.00 4.75
Nos. 1696-1702 (7) 37.40 8.95

Tremella Fuciformis A437

China Post No. T.66.

Edible mushrooms: No. 1704, Dictyophora indusiata (6-2). No. 1705, Hericium erinaceus (6-3). No. 1706, Russula rubra (6-4). No. 1707, Lentinus edodes (6-5). No. 1708, Agaricus bisporus (6-6).

1981, Aug. 6 Photo. ***Perf. 11½***

1703 A437 4f shown (6-1) 1.00 .55
1704 A437 8f multi 1.00 .55
1705 A437 8f multi 1.00 .55
1706 A437 8f multi 1.00 .55
1707 A437 10f multi 1.00 .55
1708 A437 70f multi 8.25 2.50
Nos. 1703-1708 (6) 13.25 5.25

Quality Month — A438

China Post No. J.66.

1981, Sept. 1 Photo. ***Perf. 11½x11***

1709 A438 8f Silver medal (2-1) 2.50 .75
1710 A438 8f Gold medal (2-2) 2.50 .75

Lunan Stone Forest, Yunn — A439

China Post No. T.64.

Designs: Views of limestone formations, Lunan Stone Forest. Nos. 1711-1713 horiz.

1981, Sept. 18 ***Perf. 11½***

1711 A439 8f multi (5-1) 1.40 .60
1712 A439 8f multi (5-2) 1.40 .60
1713 A439 8f multi (5-3) 1.40 .60
1714 A439 10f multi (5-4) 1.40 .60
1715 A439 70f multi (5-5) 13.00 4.75
Nos. 1711-1715 (5) 18.60 7.15

Lu Xun, Writer, Birth Centenary A440

China Post No. J.67.

1981, Sept. 25

1716 A440 8f shown (2-1) 2.25 .50
1717 A440 20f Portrait (diff.) (2-2) 3.50 1.50

Sun Yat-sen and Text A441

China Post No. J.68.

70th Anniv. of 1911 Revolution: No. 1719, 72 Martyrs Grave, Huang Hua Gang. No. 1720, Hubei Provincial Government Headquarters, 1911.

1981, Oct. 10 Photo. ***Perf. 11x11½***

1718 A441 8f multi (3-1) 1.90 .60
1719 A441 8f multi (3-2) 1.90 .60
1720 A441 8f multi (3-3) 1.90 .60
Nos. 1718-1720 (3) 5.70 1.80

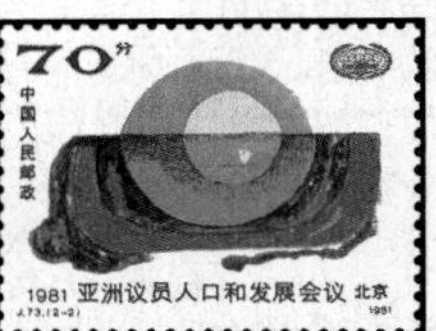

Asian Conference of Parliamentarians on Population and Development, Peking, Oct. 27 — A442

China Post No. J.73.

1981, Oct. 27 ***Perf. 11½x11, 11x11½***

1721 A442 8f Tree, vert. (2-1) .75 .40
1722 A442 70f shown (2-2) 1.50 1.10

Xishuang Banna — A443

Mt. Hua — A443a

Mt. Tai — A443b

Huang Guo Shu Falls — A443c

Hainan Island — A443d

Tiger Hill, Suzhou — A443e

Great Wall — A443f

Immense Forest — A443g

Mt. Tian — A443h

Grassland, Inner Mongolia — A443i

Stone Forest — A443j

Banping Mountain — A443k

Mt. Qomolangma — A443l

Seven-Star Crag — A443m

Three Gorges, Changjiang River — A443n

Guilin landscape — A443o

Mt. Huangshan — A443p

China Post No. R21

Nos. 1731-1739 are horizontal.

Perf. 11¼, 13x13¼ (#1726, 1729), 13¼x13 (#1731)

1981-83 **Engr.**

1723 A443 1f blue green .35 .25
1724 A443a 1½f red orange .35 .25
1725 A443b 2f gray green .35 .25
1726 A443c 3f red brown .40 .25
1727 A443d 4f purple .50 .25
1728 A443e 5f brown .45 .25
1729 A443f 8f blue .45 .25
1730 A443g 10f purplish brn .50 .25
1731 A443h 20f blue green .50 .25
1732 A443i 30f light brown .50 .25
1733 A443j 40f blue black .60 .25
1734 A443k 50f violet .80 .25
1735 A443l 70f greenish blk 1.00 .50
1736 A443m 80f rose lake 1.15 .70
1737 A443n $1 violet black 1.25 .75
1738 A443o $2 green 2.00 1.40
1739 A443p $5 Prussian blue 5.00 2.75
Nos. 1723-1739 (17) 16.15 9.10

Issued: Nos. 1737-1739, 10/9/82; Nos. 1732, 1734-1736 4/1/83.

China Post No. R22
Photo.

Perf. 11½

1726a A443 3f tan & brown .25 .25
1727a A443 4f pink & purple .25 .25
1727b Perf. 11½x11 7.50 7.50
1729a A443 8f blue .35 .25
1730a A443 10f dark brown .60 .50
1731a A443 20f blue green 1.40 .80
Nos. 1726a-1731a (5) 2.85 2.05

Nos. 1727a, 1729a, 1730a exist tagged. Values 10-15% higher.

Cowrie Shell and Shell-shaped Coin — A444

China Post No. T.65.

Ancient Coins. T.65.

Photogravure and Engraved

1981, Oct. 29 ***Perf. 11½x11***

1740 A444 4f shown (8-1) 1.35 .50
1741 A444 4f Shovel (8-2) 1.35 .50
1742 A444 8f Shovel, diff. (8-3) 1.35 .50
1743 A444 8f Shovel, diff. (8-4) 1.75 .50
1744 A444 8f Knife (8-5) 1.75 .50
1745 A444 8f Knife (8-6) 1.75 .50
1746 A444 60f Knife, diff. (8-7) 8.00 2.50
1747 A444 70f Gong (8-8) 10.50 3.00
Nos. 1740-1747 (8) 27.80 8.50

See Nos. 1765-1772.

A445

China Post No. J.72.

1981, Nov. 10 Photo. ***Perf. 11½x11***

1748 A445 8f multicolored 1.00 .40

Intl. Year of the Disabled.

A446

China Post No. T.69.

Twelve Beauties, from The Dream of Red Mansions, by Cao Xueqin: No. 1749, Daiyu (12-1). No. 1750, Baochai (12-2). No. 1751, Yuanchun (12-3). No. 1752, Yingchun (12-4). No. 1753, Tanchun (12-5). No. 1754, Xichun (12-6). No. 1755, Xiangyuh (12-7). No. 1756, Liwan (12-8). No. 1757, Xifeng (12-9). No. 1758, Sister Qiao (12-10). No. 1759, Keqing (12-11). No. 1760, Miaoyu (12-12).

No. 1761, Baoyu, Daiyu.

1981-82 Photo. ***Perf. 11***

1749 A446 4f multi 5.00 .95
1750 A446 4f multi 3.00 .95
1751 A446 8f multi 4.00 1.50
1752 A446 8f multi 3.00 1.00
1753 A446 8f multi 3.00 1.00
1754 A446 8f multi 3.00 1.00
1755 A446 8f multi 3.00 1.25
1756 A446 10f multi 3.00 1.25
1757 A446 20f multi 3.00 1.25
1758 A446 30f multi 5.00 1.75
1759 A446 40f multi 22.50 6.00
1760 A446 80f multi 8.00 2.75
Nos. 1749-1760 (12) 65.50 20.65

Souvenir Sheet

1761 A446 $2 multi *210.00 95.00*

No. 1761 contains one 59x39mm stamp. Issued: Nos. 1749, 1751, 1753, 1755, 1757, 1759, 1761, 11/20/81; others, 4/24/82.

A447

China Post No. J.76.

8f, Girl playing (2-1). 20f, Girl holding trophy (2-2).

1981, Dec. 21 **Photo.**

1762 A447 8f multi .60 .30
1763 A447 20f multi 1.10 .60

Women's team victory in 3rd World Cup Volleyball Championship.

A448

China Post No. T.70.

Photogravure & Engraved

1982, Jan. 5 ***Perf. 11½***

1764 A448 8f multicolored 7.75 3.00
a. Booklet pane of 10 + label 77.50
Complete booklet, #1764a 85.00 *85.00*

New Year 1982 (Year of the Dog). Stamps from No. 1764a have straight edges at top or bottom.

Coin Type of 1981
China Post No. T.71.

No. 1765, Guilian mask (8-1). No. 1766, Shu shovel (8-2). No. 1767, Xia zhuan shovel (8-3). No. 1768, Han Dan shovel (8-4). No. 1769, Knife (8-5). No. 1770, Ming knife (8-6). No. 1771, Jin hua knife (8-7). No. 1772, Yi Liu Hua coin (8-8).

1982, Feb. 12

1765 A444 4f multi 1.20 .65
1766 A444 4f multi 1.20 .65
1767 A444 8f multi 1.20 .65
1768 A444 8f multi 1.20 .65
1769 A444 8f multi 1.20 .65
1770 A444 8f multi 1.20 .80

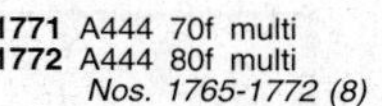

1771 A444 70f multi 4.25 2.25
1772 A444 80f multi 5.50 3.00
Nos. 1765-1772 (8) 16.95 9.30

Nie Er (1912-1935), Natl. Anthem Composer — A449

China Post No. J.75.

1982, Feb. 15 ***Perf. 11x11½***

1773 A449 8f multicolored 2.25 .55

Intl. Drinking Water and Sanitation Decade, 1981-1990
A450

China Post No. J.77.

1982, Mar. 1 ***Perf. 11½x11***

1774 A450 8f multicolored 1.20 .50

TB Bacillus Centenary
A451

China Post No. J.74.

1982, Mar. 24 ***Perf. 11x11½***

1775 A451 8f multicolored 1.50 .50

Fire Control — A452

China Post No. T.76.

No. 1776, Water hoses (2-1). No. 1777, Chemical extinguisher (2-2).

1982, May 8 Photo. ***Perf. 11½x11***

1776 A452 8f multicolored 1.50 .50
1777 A452 8f multicolored 1.50 .50

Syzygy of the Nine Planets, Mar. 10 and May 16 — A453

China Post No. T.78.

1982, May 16 ***Perf. 11½***

1778 A453 8f multicolored 2.25 .60

Medicinal Herbs — A454

China Post No. T.72.

No. 1779, Hemerocallis flava (6-1). No. 1780, Fritillaria unibracteata (6-2). No. 1781, Aconitum carmichaeli (6-3). No. 1782, Lilium brownii (6-4). No. 1783, Arisaema (6-5). No. 1784, Paeonia lactiflora (6-6).
No. 1785, Iris tectorum maxim.

1982, May 20 ***Perf. 11½x11***

1779	A454	4f multi	.65	.45
1780	A454	8f multi	.65	.45
1781	A454	8f multi	.65	.45
1782	A454	10f multi	1.40	.65
1783	A454	20f multi	1.75	.75
1784	A454	70f multi	5.25	1.50
		Nos. 1779-1784 (6)	10.35	4.25

Souvenir Sheet

1785	A454	$2 multi	30.00	19.50

No. 1785 contains one 89x39mm stamp.

Soong Ching Ling (1893-1981), Sun Yat-sen's Widow — A455

China Post No. J.82.

8f, Addressing Consultative Conf. (2-1). 20f, Portrait (2-2).

1982, May 29 ***Perf. 11½***

1786	A455	8f multi	1.00	.45
1787	A455	20f multi	4.00	1.40

Sable A456

China Post No. T.68.

1982, June 20 Photo. ***Perf. 11½***

1788	A456	8f shown (2-1)	1.50	.60
1789	A456	80f Sable, diff. (2-2)	5.00	3.75
a.		Bklt. pane of 8, 6 8f plus sheetlet of 2 (8f, 80f)	37.50	
		Complete booklet, #1789a	45.00	

A457

China Post No. J.78.

1982, June 30 ***Perf. 11½x11***

1790	A457	8f multicolored	1.75	.40

Natl. census, July 1.

A458

China Post No. J.81.

1982, July 25 Photo. ***Perf. 11½x11***

1791	A458	8f multicolored	1.40	.40

2nd UN Conference on Peaceful Uses of Outer Space, Vienna, Aug. 9-21.

Strolling in Autumn Woods, by Shen Zhou, Ming Dynasty — A459

China Post No. T.77.

Fan Paintings (Ming or Qing Dynasty): No. 1793, Jackdaw on Withered Tree, by Tang Yin. No. 1794 Bamboo and Sparrows, by Zhou Zhimian. 10f, Writing Poem under Pine, by Chen Hongshou and Bai Han. 20f, Chrysanthemums, by Yun Shouping, Qing. 70f, Birds, Crape Myrtle and Chinese Parasol, by Wang Wu, Qing.

1982, July 31 ***Perf. 11½***

1792	A459	4f multi (6-1)	3.00	.80
1793	A459	8f multi (6-2)	1.30	.70
1794	A459	8f multi (6-3)	1.30	.70
1795	A459	10f multi (6-4)	2.10	.75
1796	A459	20f multi (6-5)	2.10	.80
1797	A459	70f multi (6-6)	6.00	2.25
		Nos. 1792-1797 (6)	15.80	6.00

A460

China Post No. J.79.

1982, Aug. 25 ***Perf. 11½x11***

1798	A460	8f multicolored	1.00	.35

60th anniv. of Chinese Geological Society.

A461

China Post No. T.73.

1982, Aug. 25 Photo. ***Perf. 11½x11***

1799	A461	4f Orpiment (4-1)	.75	.30
1800	A461	8f Stibnite (4-2)	.75	.30
1801	A461	10f Cinnabar (4-3)	1.50	.30
1802	A461	20f Wolframite (4-4)	1.50	.55
		Nos. 1799-1802 (4)	4.50	1.45

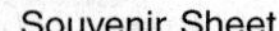

Souvenir Sheet

Messenger, Tomb Mural, Jiayu Pass, Wei-Jin Period — A462

China Post No. J.85.

1982, Aug. 25

1803	A462	$1 multicolored	29.00	12.50

All-China Philatelic Federation, 1st Cong.

12th Natl. Communist Party Congress A463

China Post No. J.86.

1982, Sept. 1 ***Perf. 11½***

1804	A463	8f multicolored	1.75	.45

Hoopoe — A464

China Post No. T.79.

No. 1806, Swallows (5-2). No. 1807, Oriole (5-3). No. 1808, Chickadees (5-4). No. 1809, Woodpecker (5-5).
No. 1810, Cuckoos.

1982, Sept. 10 ***Perf. 11½x11***

1805	A464	8f shown (5-1)	1.25	.40
1806	A464	8f multi	1.25	.40
1807	A464	8f multi	1.25	.40
1808	A464	20f multi	3.25	.80
1809	A464	70f multi	9.00	3.25
		Nos. 1805-1809 (5)	16.00	5.25

Souvenir Sheet

1810	A464	$2 multi	55.00	20.00

No. 1810 contains one 56x36mm stamp.

Japan-China Relations Normalization, 10th Anniv. — A465

China Post No. J.84.

Flower Paintings: 8f, Plum blossoms, by Guan Shanyue. 70f, Hibiscus, by Xiao Shufang.

1982, Sept. 29 ***Perf. 11***

1811	A465	8f multi (2-1)	1.40	.40
1812	A465	70f multi (2-2)	2.50	1.00

World Food Day — A466

China Post No. J.80.

1982, Oct. 16 ***Perf. 11½***

1813	A466	8f multicolored	1.25	.40

Guo Morou (1892-1978), Acad. of Sciences Pres. — A467

China Post No. J.87.

Designs: Portraits.

1982, Nov. 16 Photo. ***Perf. 11½x11***

1814	A467	8f multi (2-1)	.75	.50
1815	A467	20f multi (2-2)	1.75	.60

Bodhisattva, 11th Cent. Sculpture — A468

China Post No. T.74.

Liao Dynasty Buddha Sculptures, Lower Huayan Monastery.

1982, Nov. 19 ***Perf. 11***

1816	A468	8f multi (4-1)	1.40	.40
1817	A468	8f multi (4-2)	1.40	.40
1818	A468	8f multi (4-3)	1.90	.40
1819	A468	70f multi (4-4)	5.25	3.00
		Nos. 1816-1819 (4)	9.95	4.20

Souvenir Sheet

Perf. 11x11½

1820	A468	$2 multicolored	57.50	22.00

No. 1820 contains one 36x55mm stamp.

Dr. D.S. Kotnis, Indian Physician in 8th Army A469

China Post No. J.83.

Perf. 11½x11, 11x11½

1982, Dec. 9 **Photo.**

1821	A469	8f Portrait, vert. (2-1)	.60	.30
1822	A469	70f Riding horse (2-2)	2.50	1.60

11th Communist Youth League Natl. Congress A470

China Post No. J.88.

1982, Dec. 20 ***Perf. 11x11½***

1823	A470	8f multicolored	1.50	.50

Bronze Wine Container — A471

China Post No. T.75.

Western Zhou Dynasty Bronze (1200-771 B.C.): No. 1825, Three-legged cooking pot. No. 1826, Food bowl. No. 1827, Three-legged cooking pot (diff.). No. 1828, Animal-shaped wine container. 10f, Wine container with lid. 20f, Round food bowl. 70f, Square wine container.

Photogravure & Engraved

1982, Dec. 25 *Perf. 11*

1824	A471	4f multi (8-1)	1.75	.90
1825	A471	4f multi (8-2)	1.75	.90
1826	A471	8f multi (8-3)	1.75	.90
1827	A471	8f multi (8-4)	3.00	1.40
1828	A471	8f multi (8-5)	1.75	.90
1829	A471	10f multi (8-6)	2.75	.90
1830	A471	20f multi (8-7)	3.50	1.60
1831	A471	70f multi (8-8)	17.50	5.00
		Nos. 1824-1831 (8)	33.75	12.50

A472

China Post No. T.80.

1983, Jan. 5 *Perf. 11½*

1832	A472	8f multicolored	14.00	3.75
a.		Booklet pane of 12	150.00	*77.50*
		Complete booklet, #1832a	150.00	

New Year 1983 (Year of the Pig).

Stamps from No. 1832a have straight edges at top or bottom and sell for less as singles than No. 1832.

A473

China Post No. T.81.

Stringed Instruments.

1983, Jan. 20 *Perf. 11½x11, 11x11½*

1833	A473	4f Konghou (5-1)	3.75	.80
1834	A473	8f Ruan (5-2)	3.75	.80
1835	A473	8f Qin, horiz. (5-3)	3.75	.80
1836	A473	10f Piba (5-4)	3.75	.80
1837	A473	70f Sanxian (5-5)	29.00	5.25
		Nos. 1833-1837 (5)	44.00	8.45

A474

China Post No. J.89.

No. 1838, Monument, Jiangan (2-1). No. 1839, Erqi Memorial Tower, Zhengzhou (2-2).

1983, Feb. 7 Photo. *Perf. 11½x11*

1838	A474	8f multi	1.00	.50
1839	A474	8f multi	1.25	.50

60th Anniv. of Peking-Hankow Railroad Workers' Strike.

The Western Chamber, Traditional Opera, by Wang Shifu (1271-1368) A475

China Post No. T.82.

Scenes from the opera.

1983, Feb. 21 Photo. *Perf. 11x11½*

1840	A475	8f multi (4-1)	3.50	1.30
1841	A475	8f multi (4-2)	3.50	1.30
1842	A475	10f multi (4-3)	6.00	1.60
1843	A475	80f multi (4-4)	27.50	5.00
		Nos. 1840-1843 (4)	40.50	9.20

Souvenir Sheet

Photogravure and Engraved

Perf. 12

1844	A475	$2 multicolored	155.00	50.00

No. 1844 contains one 27x48mm stamp.

Karl Marx (1818-1883) A476

China Post No. J.90.

8f, Portrait (2-1). 20f, Making speech (2-2).

Photogravure & Engraved

1983, Mar. 14 *Perf. 11½x11*

1845	A476	8f multicolored	.90	.50
1846	A476	20f multicolored	1.40	.60

Tomb of the Yellow Emperor A477

China Post No. T.84.

8f, Tomb, vert. (3-1). 10f, Hall of Founder of Chinese Culture (3-2). 20f, Cypress tree, vert. (3-3).

Photogravure & Engraved

1983, Apr. 5 *Perf. 11½*

1847	A477	8f multi	1.50	.60
1848	A477	10f multi	2.00	.60
1849	A477	20f multi	3.25	.90
		Nos. 1847-1849 (3)	6.75	2.10

World Communications Year — A478

China Post No. J.91.

1983, Apr. 28 Photo. *Perf. 11½*

1850	A478	8f multicolored	1.00	.50

Male Chinese Alligator — A479

China Post No. T.85.

20f, Female, hatching eggs (2-2).

Photogravure & Engraved

1983, May 24 *Perf. 11*

1851	A479	8f shown (2-1)	1.10	.50
1852	A479	20f multicolored	1.90	.75

Kitten, by Tan Arxi — A480

China Post No. T.86.

Various children's drawings.

1983, June 1 *Perf. 11½x11*

1853	A480	8f multi (4-1)	.45	.30
1854	A480	8f multi (4-2)	.45	.30
1855	A480	8f multi (4-3)	.45	.30
1856	A480	8f multi (4-4)	.45	.30
		Nos. 1853-1856 (4)	1.80	1.20

6th Natl. People's Congress A481

China Post No. J.94.

8f, Hall (2-1). 20f, Natl. anthem score (2-2).

1983, June 6 *Perf. 11x11½*

1857	A481	8f multicolored	1.50	.50
1858	A481	20f multicolored	3.75	.90

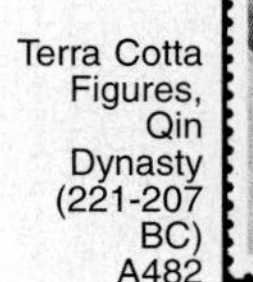

Terra Cotta Figures, Qin Dynasty (221-207 BC) A482

China Post No. T.88.

No. 1859, Soldiers (4-1). No. 1860, Heads (4-2). No. 1861, Soldiers, horses (4-3). No. 1862, Excavation site (4-4).

No. 1863, Soldier leading horse.

1983, June 30

1859	A482	8f multi	1.25	.55
1860	A482	8f multi	1.25	.55
1861	A482	10f multi	2.00	.65
1862	A482	70f multi	5.75	2.40
a.		Bklt. pane of 8 (#1859, 3 #1860, 3 #1861, #1862)	*97.50*	*75.00*
		Nos. 1859-1862 (4)	10.25	4.15

Souvenir Sheet

1863	A482	$2 multi	*80.00*	*25.00*
a.		Booklet pane of 1	*70.00*	
		Complete booklet, #1862a, #1863a	100.00	*65.00*

No. 1863 contains one 59x39mm stamp.

A483

China Post No. T.87.

Female roles in Peking opera: 4f, Sun Yujiao (8-1). No. 1865, 8f, Chen Miaochang (8-2). No. 1866, 8f, Bai Suzhen (8-3). No. 1867, 8f, Sister Thirteen (8-4). 10f, Qin Xianglian (8-5). 20f, Yang Yuhuan (8-6). 50f, Cui Yingying (8-7). 80f, Mu Guiying (8-8).

1983, July 20 Photo. *Perf. 11*

1864	A483	4f multi	2.40	.65
1865	A483	8f multi	2.40	.65
1866	A483	8f multi	2.40	.65
1867	A483	8f multi	2.40	.65
1868	A483	10f multi	2.40	.65
1869	A483	20f multi	2.40	.65
1870	A483	50f multi	13.50	3.00
1871	A483	80f multi	17.50	4.25
		Nos. 1864-1871 (8)	45.40	11.15

A484

China Post No. J.92.

Paintings by Liu Lingcang: No. 1872, Li Bai (4-1). No. 1873, Du Fu (4-2). No. 1874, Han Yu (4-3). No. 1875, Liu Zongyuan (4-4).

1983, Aug. 10 Photo. *Perf. 11½*

1872	A484	8f multi	2.25	.40
1873	A484	8f multi	2.25	.40
1874	A484	8f multi	2.25	.40
1875	A484	70f multi	13.00	3.25
		Nos. 1872-1875 (4)	19.75	4.45

Poets and philosophers of ancient China.

5th Natl. Women's Congress — A485

China Post No. J.95.

1983, Sept. 1 Photo. *Perf. 11½*

1876	A485	8f multicolored	1.00	.40

5th National Games — A486

China Post No. J.93.

No. 1877, Emblem (6-1). No. 1878, Gymnast (6-2). No. 1879, Badminton (6-3). No. 1880, Diving (6-4). No. 1881, High jump (6-5). No. 1882, Wind surfing (6-6).

1983, Sept. 16 Photo. *Perf. 11½*

1877	A486	4f multi	.85	.35
1878	A486	8f multi	.85	.35
1879	A486	8f multi	.85	.35
1880	A486	8f multi	.85	.35

1881 A486 20f multi 1.50 .40
1882 A486 70f multi 5.50 2.25
Nos. 1877-1882 (6) 10.40 4.05

Family Planning A487

China Post No. T.91.

No. 1883, One child (2-1). No. 1884, Cultivated land (2-2).

1983, Sept. 19 ***Perf. 11x11½***
1883 A487 8f multicolored .50 .30
1884 A487 8f multicolored .50 .30

10th Intl. Trade Union Congress — A488

China Post No. J.98.

1983, Oct. 18 Litho. ***Perf. 11½***
1885 A488 8f multicolored 1.00 .40

Mute Swans A489

China Post No. T.83.

Cygnus Olor: No. 1886, One swan (4-1). No. 1887, Two swans (4-2). No. 1888, Four swans (4-3). No. 1889, Six swans (4-4).

Perf. 11x11½ on 3 sides
1983, Nov. 18 **Photo.**
1886 A489 8f multi .40 .30
1887 A489 8f multi 1.45 .50
1888 A489 10f multi 1.45 .50
1889 A489 80f multi 3.25 1.75
a. Booklet pane, 7 #1886, 1 each #1887-1889 35.00 *20.00*
Complete booklet, #1889a 55.00 *27.50*
Nos. 1886-1889 (4) 6.55 3.05

A490

China Post No. J.96.

Various photos.

1983, Nov. 24 Photo. ***Perf. 11½***
1890 A490 8f multi (4-1) 1.40 .50
1891 A490 8f multi (4-2) 1.40 .50
1892 A490 8f multi (4-3) 1.40 .50
1893 A490 8f multi (4-4) 1.40 .50
Nos. 1890-1893 (4) 5.60 2.00

85th birth anniv. of Liu Shaoqi, political leader.

A491

China Post No. J.99.

1983, Nov. 29 Photo. ***Perf. 11½***
1894 A491 8f No. 117 (2-1) .60 .35
1895 A491 20f No. 4L1 (2-2) .90 .45

CHINAPEX '83 Natl. Philatelic Exhibition.

A492

China Post No. J.97.

Various portraits.

1983, Dec. 26 Photo. ***Perf. 11½***
1896 A492 8f 1925 (4-1) 1.25 .35
1897 A492 8f 1945 (4-2) 1.25 .35
1898 A492 10f 1952 (4-3) 6.00 1.00
1899 A492 20f 1961 (4-4) 3.50 .60
Nos. 1896-1899 (4) 12.00 2.30

90th birth anniv. of Mao Tse-tung.

A493

China Post No. T.90.

Photogravure and Engraved

1984, Jan. 5 ***Perf. 11½***
1900 A493 8f multicolored 7.00 2.50
a. Booklet pane of 12 *85.00 30.00*
Complete booklet, #1900a 100.00 *60.00*

New Year 1984 (Year of the Rat).
Stamps from No. 1900a have straight edge at top or bottom.

Beauties Wearing Flowers — A494

China Post No. T.89.

Portions of painting by Zhou Fang (Tang Dynasty).

1984, Mar. 24 Photo. ***Perf. 11***
1901 A494 8f multi (3-1) 2.50 .40
1902 A494 10f multi (3-2) 4.00 .60
1903 A494 70f multi (3-3) 12.50 3.00
Nos. 1901-1903 (3) 19.00 4.00

Souvenir Sheet

1904 A494 $2 Entire painting *210.00* 55.00

No. 1904 contains one 162x40mm stamp.

Chinese Roses — A495

China Post No. T.93.

No. 1905, Spring of Shanghai (6-1). No. 1906, Rosy Dawn of Pujiang River (6-2). No. 1907, Pearl (6-3). No. 1908, Black whirlwind (6-4). No. 1909, Yellow flower in battlefield (6-5). No. 1910, Blue Phoenix (6-6).

1984, Apr. 20 Photo. ***Perf. 11½***
1905 A495 4f multi .80 .30
1906 A495 8f multi .80 .30
1907 A495 8f multi .80 .30
1908 A495 10f multi .80 .35
1909 A495 20f multi 1.75 .45
1910 A495 70f multi 4.00 1.40
Nos. 1905-1910 (6) 8.95 3.10

Ren Bishi (1904-50), Statesman A496

China Post No. J.100.

1984, Apr. 30 ***Perf. 11½x11***
1911 A496 8f multicolored 1.10 .50

Crested Ibis A497

China Post No. T.94.

1984, May 15 Photo. ***Perf. 11x11½***
1912 A497 8f Flying (3-1) .70 .25
1913 A497 8f Wading (3-2) .70 .25
1914 A497 80f Perching (3-3) 2.10 1.40
Nos. 1912-1914 (3) 3.50 1.90

Chinese Red Cross Society, 80th Anniv. — A498

China Post No. J.102.

1984, May 29 ***Perf. 11½***
1915 A498 8f multicolored .90 .40

Gezhou Dam, Yangtze River — A499

China Post No. T.95.

8f, Dam (3-1). 10f, Bridge, vert. (3-2). 20f, Lock Gate #2 (3-3).

1984, June 15 **Photo.**
1916 A499 8f multi .50 .35
1917 A499 10f multi .75 .40
1918 A499 20f multi 1.60 .75
Nos. 1916-1918 (3) 2.85 1.50

Zhuo Zheng Garden, Suzhou — A500

China Post No. T.96.

No. 1919, Inverted Image Tower (4-1). No. 1920, Loquat Garden (4-2). No. 1921, Water Court, Xiao Cang Lang (4-3). No. 1922, Yuanxiang Hall, Yiyu Study (4-4).

Photogravure & Engraved

1984, June 30 ***Perf. 11½x11***
1919 A500 8f multi .75 .45
1920 A500 8f multi .75 .45
1921 A500 10f multi .85 .45
1922 A500 70f multi 2.25 1.50
Nos. 1919-1922 (4) 4.60 2.85

1984 Summer Olympics A501

China Post No. J.103.

No. 1923, Shooting (6-1). No. 1924, High jump (6-2). No. 1925, Weight lifting (6-3). No. 1926, Gymnastics (6-4). No. 1927, Volleyball (6-5). No. 1928, Diving (6-6).
No. 1929, Athletes, rings.

1984, July 28 Photo. ***Perf. 11½***
1923 A501 4f multi .35 .35
1924 A501 8f multi .40 .40
1925 A501 8f multi .40 .40
1926 A501 10f multi .45 .45
1927 A501 20f multi .50 .50
1928 A501 80f multi 1.25 1.25
Nos. 1923-1928 (6) 3.35 3.35

Souvenir Sheet

1929 A501 $2 multi 14.00 6.00

No. 1929 contains one 61x38mm stamp.

Calligraphy — A502

China Post No. T.98.

Artworks by Wu Changshuo: No. 1931, A Pair of Peaches (8-2). No. 1932, Lotus (8-3). No. 1933, Wisteria (8-4). No. 1934, Peony (8-5). No. 1935, Chrysanthemum (8-6). No. 1936, Plum Blossom (8-7). No. 1937, Seal Cutting (8-8).

1984, Aug. 27 Photo. ***Perf. 11½***
1930 A502 4f shown (8-1) .85 .30
1931 A502 4f multi .85 .30
1932 A502 8f multi 1.75 .30
1933 A502 8f multi .75 .30
1934 A502 8f multi 7.25 1.60
1935 A502 10f multi 1.60 .50
1936 A502 20f multi 1.75 .50
1937 A502 70f multi 4.50 1.60
Nos. 1930-1937 (8) 19.30 5.40

Luanhe River Water Diversion Project — A503

China Post No. T.97.

Perf. 11½x11, 11 (#1939)

1984, Sept. 11		**Photo.**	
1938 A503	8f multi (3-1)	.45	.40
1939 A503	10f multi, horiz. (3-2)	.45	.40
1940 A503	20f multi (3-3)	.65	.50
	Nos. 1938-1940 (3)	1.55	1.30

Chinese-Japanese Youth — A504

China Post No. J.104.

1984, Sept. 24	**Photo.**	***Perf. 11½***	
1941 A504	8f Neighbors (3-1)	.35	.30
1942 A504	20f Planting tree (3-2)	.55	.40
1943 A504	80f Dancing (3-3)	1.10	.90
	Nos. 1941-1943 (3)	2.00	1.60

People's Republic, 35th Anniv. — A505

China Post No. J.105.

No. 1944, Engineer (5-1). No. 1945, Farm woman (5-2). No. 1946, Scientist (5-4). No. 1947, Soldier (5-5). No. 1948, Cranes (5-3).

1984, Oct. 1 Photo. *Perf. 11½x11*

Size: 26x35mm

1944 A505	8f multi	.40	.30
1945 A505	8f multi	.40	.30
1946 A505	8f multi	.40	.30
1947 A505	8f multi	.40	.30

Size: 36x48mm

Perf. 11

1948 A505	20f multi	1.50	1.00
	Nos. 1944-1948 (5)	3.10	2.20

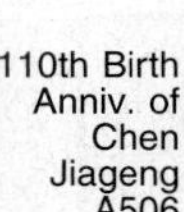

110th Birth Anniv. of Chen Jiageng A506

China Post No. J.106.

8f, Chen Jiageng (2-1). 80f, Jimei School (2-2).

1984, Oct. 21	**Photo.**	***Perf. 12½x12***	
1949 A506	8f multi	.65	.25
1950 A506	80f multi	2.10	.75

The Maiden's Study A507

China Post No. T.99.

Scenes from The Peony Pavilion, by Tang Xianzu: No. 1952, In the dreamland (4-2). No. 1953, Du Liniang drawing self-portrait (4-3). No. 1954, Married to Liu Mengmai (4-4).

No. 1955, Playing in the garden.

Photogravure & Engraved

1984, Oct. 30		***Perf. 11***	
1951 A507	8f shown (4-1)	.75	.40
1952 A507	8f multi	.75	.40
1953 A507	20f multi	1.60	.80
1954 A507	70f multi	3.25	1.75
	Nos. 1951-1954 (4)	6.35	3.35

Souvenir Sheet

Perf. 11½

1955 A507	$2 multi	*40.00*	*20.00*

No. 1955 contains one 90x60mm stamp.

Emei Shan Mountain Scenery — A508

China Post No. T.100.

No. 1956, Baoguo Temple (6-1). No. 1957, Leiyin Temple (6-2). No. 1958, Hongchun Lawn (6-3). No. 1959, Elephant bath (6-4). No. 1960, Woyun Temple (6-5). No. 1961, Shining Cloud Sea at Jinding (6-6).

1984, Nov. 16		***Perf. 11***	
1956 A508	4f multi	1.00	.50
1957 A508	8f multi	.70	.35
1958 A508	8f multi	.40	.40
1959 A508	10f multi	.90	.45
1960 A508	20f multi	1.75	.90
1961 A508	80f multi	5.50	2.25
	Nos. 1956-1961 (6)	10.25	4.85

A509

China Post No. J.101.

Portraits: 8f, During the Long March (3-1). 10f, At 7th Natl. Party Congress (3-2). 20f, In motorcade (3-3).

1984, Dec. 15	**Photo.**	***Perf. 11½x11***	
1962 A509	8f multi	.45	.45
1963 A509	10f multi	.55	.50
1964 A509	20f multi	.80	.50
	Nos. 1962-1964 (3)	1.80	1.45

Former party secretary Ren Bishi (1904-50).

Flower Arrangement A510

China Post No. T.101.

1984, Dec. 25		***Perf. 11***	
1965 A510	8f multi	.75	.40

Chinese insurance industry.

New Year 1985 (Year of the Ox) — A511

China Post No. T.102.

Photogravure & Engraved

1985, Jan. 5		***Perf. 11½***	
1966 A511	8f multi	2.00	.50
a.	Bklt. pane of 4 + 8 plus label	20.00	10.00
	Complete booklet, #1966a	30.00	

Stamps from No. 1966a have straight edge at top or bottom.

Zunyi Meeting, 50th Anniv. — A512

China Post No. J.107.

Paintings: 8f, The Zunyi Meeting, by Liu Xiangping. 20f, The Red Army Successfully Arrived in Northern Shaanxi, by Zhao Yu.

1985, Jan. 15	**Photo.**	***Perf. 11x11½***	
1967 A512	8f multi (2-1)	1.10	.30
1968 A512	20f multi (2-2)	1.90	.70

A513

China Post No. T.104.

Lantern Folk Festival: No. 1969, Lotus of Good Luck. No. 1970, Auspicious dragon and phoenix. No. 1971, A hundred flowers blossoming. 70f, Prosperity and affluence.

1985, Feb. 28		***Perf. 11½***	
1969 A513	8f multi (4-1)	1.05	.40
1970 A513	8f multi (4-2)	1.05	.40
1971 A513	8f multi (4-3)	1.05	.40
1972 A513	70f multi (4-4)	3.25	1.05
	Nos. 1969-1972 (4)	6.40	2.25

A514

China Post No. J.108.

1985, Mar. 8			
1973 A514	20f multicolored	.80	.35

UN Decade for Women (1976-85).

Mei (Prunus mume) — A515

China Post No. T.103.

No. 1974, Green calyx (6-1). No. 1975, Pendant mei (6-2). No. 1976, Contorted dragon (6-3). No. 1977, Cinnabar (6-4). No. 1978, Versicolor mei (6-5). No. 1979, Apricot mei (6-6).

No. 1980, Duplicate and condensed fragrance mei.

1985, Apr. 5		***Perf. 11***	
1974 A515	8f multi	.90	.35
1975 A515	8f multi	.90	.35
1976 A515	8f multi	.90	.35
1977 A515	10f multi	1.60	.35
1978 A515	20f multi	2.50	.75
1979 A515	80f multi	6.50	2.25
	Nos. 1974-1979 (6)	13.30	4.40

Souvenir Sheet

Perf. 11½

1980 A515	$2 multi	*47.50*	*20.00*

No. 1980 contains one 93x52mm stamp.

Huizo Guild Hall, Guangzhou — A516

China Post No. J.109.

1985, May 1	**Photo.**	***Perf. 11***	
1981 A516	8f multi	.80	.30

All-China Fed. of Trade Unions.

Intl. Youth Year A517

China Post No. J.110.

1985, May 4		**Photo.**	
1982 A517	20f multicolored	1.00	.30

A518

China Post No. T.106.

Paintings of giant pandas: 8f, 20f, 50f, 80f, by Han Meilin; $3, by Wu Zuoren. T.106.

1985, May 24		***Perf. 11½***	
1983 A518	8f multi (4-1), vert.	1.15	.35
1984 A518	20f multi (4-2)	1.40	.40
1985 A518	50f multi (4-3), vert.	1.40	.50
1986 A518	80f multi (4-4)	3.75	.70
	Nos. 1983-1986 (4)	7.70	1.95

Souvenir Sheet

Perf. 11x11½

1987 A518	$3 multi, vert.	7.50	3.00
a.	Ovptd. in sheet margin	6.25	

No. 1987 contains one 39x59mm stamp.

No. 1987a ovptd. in sheet margin with panda hologram, PJZ-4 and horizontal Chinese inscription in gold. Issued 10/9/96.

No. 1987a was sold in a mount affixed to a small card.

Xian Xinghai (1905-1945), Composer A519

China Post No. J.111.

Design: Bust, by Cao Chongen and music from The Yellow River Cantata.

1985, June 13	**Photo.**	***Perf. 11½x11***	
1988 A519	8f multicolored	1.00	.35

Agnes Smedley, 1892-1950 (3-1) — A520

China Post No. J.112.

American journalists: 20f, Anna Louise Strong, 1885-1970 (3-2). 80f, Edgar Snow, 1905-1972 (3-3).

1985, June 25

1989	A520	8f multicolored	.30	.30
1990	A520	20f multicolored	.40	.30
1991	A520	80f multicolored	.80	.60
		Nos. 1989-1991 (3)	1.50	1.20

Zheng He's West Seas Expedition, 580th Anniv. — A521

China Post No. J.113.

No. 1992, Portrait of the navigator. No. 1993, Peace envoy. 20f, Trade, cultural exchange. 80f, Honored for navigational feats.

1985, July 11 ***Perf. 11½***

1992	A521	8f multi (4-1)	.40	.30
1993	A521	8f multi (4-2)	.40	.30
1994	A521	20f multi (4-3)	.75	.45
1995	A521	80f multi (4-4)	1.75	.90
		Nos. 1992-1995 (4)	3.30	1.95

Self-portrait A522

Xu Beihong, 1895-1953, Painter — A522a

China Post No. J.114.

1985, July 19 ***Perf. 11½x11, 11x11½***

1996	A522	8f multi (2-1)	.40	.25
1997	A522a	20f multi (2-2)	.90	.40

A523

China Post No. J.115.

Designs: 8f, Lin Zexu, 1785-1850, statesman, patriot. 80f, Burning opium at Humen, bas-relief.

1985, Aug. 30 ***Perf. 11***

1998	A523	8f multi (2-1)	.40	.35

Size: 51x22mm

1999	A523	80f multi (2-2)	1.15	.50

Lin Zexu's ban of the opium trade catalyzed the Anglo-Chinese Opium Wars.

A524

China Post No. J.116.

8f, Prosperity (3-1). 10f, Celebration (3-2). 20f, Abundant Harvest (3-3).

1985, Sept. 1 ***Perf. 11½x11***

2000	A524	8f multi	.45	.30
2001	A524	10f multi	.60	.35
2002	A524	20f multi	1.15	.40
		Nos. 2000-2002 (3)	2.20	1.05

Tibet Autonomous Region, 20th anniv.

End of World War II, 40th Anniv. A525

China Post No. J.117.

Woodcuts by Wu Biduan: 8f, The Chinese Army Rose Against the Japanese Agressors at Logouqiao (2-1). 80f, The Eighth Route Army and Militia Fought Around the Great Wall (2-2).

1985, Sept. 3 ***Perf. 11***

2003	A525	8f multi	.50	.30
2004	A525	80f multi	.95	.55

2nd Natl. Worker's Games, Sept. 8-15, Beijing A526

China Post No. J.118.

Competitors from various events and: 8f, Men's bicycling (2-1). 20f, Women hurdlers (2-2).

1985, Sept. 8 ***Perf. 11x11½***

2005	A526	8f multi	.50	.45
2006	A526	20f multi	.75	.60

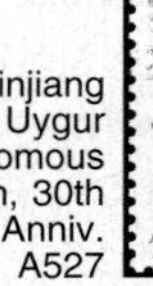

Xinjiang Uygur Autonomous Region, 30th Anniv. A527

China Post No. J.119.

8f, Oasis in the Gobi, woman (3-1). 10f, Oil field, Lake Tianchi (3-2). 20f, Tianshan pasture, woman (3-3).

1985, Oct. 1 **Photo.** ***Perf. 11½***

2007	A527	8f multi	.35	.30
2008	A527	10f multi	.40	.30
2009	A527	20f multi	.65	.35
		Nos. 2007-2009 (3)	1.40	.95

Size of No. 2008, 60x30mm.

1st Natl. Youth Games, Oct. 6-15, Zhengzhou A528

China Post No. J.121.

8f, Girls' track & field (2-1). 20f, Boys' basketball (2-2).

1985, Oct. 6 ***Perf. 11½x11***

2010	A528	8f multi	.40	.30
2011	A528	20f multi	.65	.40

Forbidden City Main Buildings — A529

China Post No. J.120.

1985, Oct. 10 ***Perf. 11½***

2012	A529	8f multi (4-1)	.35	.30
2013	A529	8f multi (4-2)	.35	.30
2014	A529	20f multi (4-3)	.35	.30
2015	A529	80f multi (4-4)	.70	.70
a.		Vert. strip of 4, #2012-2015	2.75	2.75

Palace Museum, 60th anniv.

Zou Taofen (1895-1935), Journalist — A530

China Post No. J.122.

1985, Nov. 5 ***Perf. 11½x11***

2016	A530	8f Portrait (2-1)	.35	.35
2017	A530	20f Epitaph by Zhou Enlai (2-2)	.35	.35
a.		Pair, #2016-2017	1.00	.90

December 9th Revolution, 50th Anniv. — A531

China Post No. J.125.

1985, Dec. 9 ***Perf. 11½***

2018	A531	8f Memorial Pavilion	1.10	.30

New Year 1986 — A532

China Post No. T.107.

Photogravure & Engraved

1986, Jan. 5 ***Perf. 11½***

2019	A532	8f multicolored	1.50	.50
a.		Bklt. pane of 4 + 8 with label btwn	*8.00*	
		Complete booklet, #2019a	20.00	

Natl. Space Industry — A533

China Post No. T.108.

4f, 1st experimental satellite. No. 2021, Recoverable satellite. No. 2022, Underwater rocket launch. 10f, Rocket launch. 20f, Earth satellite receiver. 70f, Satellite trajectory diagram.

1986, Feb. 1 **Photo.**

2020	A533	4f multi (6-1)	.65	.35
2021	A533	8f multi (6-2)	.65	.35
2022	A533	8f multi (6-3)	.65	.35
2023	A533	10f multi (6-4)	.65	.40
2024	A533	20f multi (6-5)	1.50	.40
2025	A533	70f multi (6-6)	3.25	.80
		Nos. 2020-2025 (6)	7.35	2.65

Dong Biwu (1886-1975), Party Founder — A534

China Post No. J.123.

Photogravure and Engraved

1986, Mar. 5 ***Perf. 11½x11***

2026	A534	8f 1975 (2-1)	.90	.30
2027	A534	20f 1945 (2-2)	1.10	.65

Lin Boqu (1886-1960), Party Leader — A535

China Post No. J.124.

1986, Mar. 20

2028	A535	8f shown (2-1)	.75	.30
2029	A535	20f Lin standing (2-2)	1.00	.50

Marshal He Long (1896-1969), Revolution Leader — A536

China Post No. J.126.

20f, On horseback (2-2).

1986, Mar. 22 ***Perf. 11x11½***

2030	A536	8f shown (2-1)	1.10	.30
2031	A536	20f multicolored	1.25	.45

Halley's Comet — A537

China Post No. T.109.

1986, Apr. 11 **Photo.** ***Perf. 11½***

2032	A537	20f dk bl & gray	1.00	.30

White Crane A538

China Post No. T.110.

8f, Two cranes (3-1). 10f, One flying (3-2), vert. 70f, Four cranes (3-3), vert. $2, Flock.

1986, May 22 ***Perf. 11x11½, 11½x11***

2033	A538	8f multi	.60	.30
2034	A538	10f multi	.60	.30
2035	A538	70f multi	1.60	.75
		Nos. 2033-2035 (3)	2.80	1.35

Souvenir Sheet

2036 A538 $2 multi *12.50 4.50*

No. 2036 contains one 116x25mm stamp.

Li Weihan (1896-1984), Party Leader — A539

China Post No. J.127.

1986, June 2 ***Perf. 11x11½***

2037	A539	8f Portrait (2-1)	.50	.30
2038	A539	20f Writing (2-2)	.65	.50

Intl. Peace Year A540

China Post No. J.128.

1986, June 16 ***Perf. 11***

2039 A540 8f multi 1.00 .30

Mao Dun (1896-1981), Writer — A541

China Post No. J.129.

1986, July 4 ***Perf. 11x11½***

2040	A541	8f Portrait (2-1)	.50	.30
2041	A541	20f Portrait, diff. (2-2)	.65	.50

Wang Jiaxiang (1906-1974), Party Leader — A542

China Post No. J.130.

1986, Aug. 15

2042	A542	8f Portrait (2-1)	.50	.30
2043	A542	20f Portrait, diff. (2-2)	.65	.50

Teacher's Day A543

China Post No. J.131.

1986, Sept. 10 ***Perf. 11***

2044 A543 8f multi 1.00 .30

Magnolia Liliflora A544

China Post No. T.111.

No. 2045, Blossom (3-1). No. 2046, Two blossoms (3-2). No. 2047, Blossom, diff. (3-3). No. 2048, Three blossoms.

1986, Sept. 23 ***Perf. 11x11½***

2045	A544	8f multi	.45	.30
2046	A544	8f multi	.45	.30
2047	A544	70f multi	2.60	1.60
		Nos. 2045-2047 (3)	3.50	2.20

Souvenir Sheet

2048 A544 $2 multi *13.50 8.00*

No. 2048 contains one 132x70mm stamp.

Inner Mongolia — A545

Tibet — A545a

Northeastern China — A545b

Hunan — A545c

So. Yangtze River — A545d

Beijing — A545e

Yunnan — A545f

Shanghai — A545g

Anhui — A545h

No. Shaanxi — A545i

Sichuan — A545j

Taiwan — A545k

Fujian — A545l

Zhejiang — A545m

China Post No. R23

Folk Houses.

Perf. 13x13½, 11x11½, (1½f, 3f, #2057-2062)

1986, Apr. 1 **Photo.**

2049	A545	1f multi	.25	.25
2050	A545a	1½f multi	.25	.25
2051	A545b	2f multi	.25	.25
2052	A545c	3f multi	.25	.25
2053	A545d	4f multi	.25	.25
2054	A545e	8f multi	.25	.25
2055	A545f	10f multi	.25	.25
2056	A545g	20f multi	.25	.25
2057	A545h	30f multi	.30	.25
2058	A545i	40f multi	.40	.30
2059	A545j	50f multi	.60	.40
2060	A545k	90f multi	.80	.55
2061	A545l	$1 multi	.85	.65
2062	A545m	$1.10 multi	.90	.75
		Nos. 2049-2062 (14)	5.85	4.90

Issue dates: 3f, Dec. 25; 4f, $1, Oct. 15; 20f, 50f, Sept. 10; 40f, Nov. 15; others, Apr. 1.
Postal forgeries of No. 2056 exist.
See Nos. 2198-2204.

1989-90 **Photo.**

2055a	Perf. 11x11½ ('89)	1.00	.65
2056a	Perf. 11x11½ ('89)	1.00	.65
2057a	Perf. 13x13½ ('90)	.50	.35
2058a	Perf. 13x13½	6.00	*3.00*
2059a	Perf. 13x13½ ('89)	1.00	.60
2061a	Perf. 13x13½ ('90)	1.90	1.00
	Nos. 2055a-2061a (6)	11.40	6.25

Souvenir Sheet

All-China Philatelic Federation, 2nd Congress — A546

China Post No. J.135.

1986, Oct. 17 **Litho.** ***Perf. 11½***

2063 A546 $2 Jade lion *8.50 3.50*

Leaders of the 1911 Revolution A547

China Post No. J.132.

1986, Oct. 10 **Photo.** ***Perf. 11x11½***

2064	A547	8f Sun Yat-sen (3-1)	1.00	.40
2065	A547	10f Huang Xing (3-2)	1.40	.70
2066	A547	40f Zhang Taiyan (3-3)	3.00	1.50
		Nos. 2064-2066 (3)	5.40	2.60

Souvenir Sheet

Sun Yat-sen (1866-1925) — A548

China Post No. J.133.

1986, Nov. 12 ***Perf. 11½***

2067 A548 $2 multicolored *14.00 6.00*

Marshal Zhu De (1886-1976) A549

China Post No. J.134.

Designs: 20f, Orating.

1986, Dec. 1 **Engr.** ***Perf. 11½x11***

2068	A549	8f sepia (2-1)	2.25	.35
2069	A549	20f myrtle grn (2-2)	4.25	.50

Sports of Ancient China A550

China Post No. T.113.

Stone carvings: No. 2070, Archery (4-1), vert. No. 2071, Weiqi (4-2). No. 2072, Golf (4-3). No. 2073, Soccer (4-4), vert..

Perf. 11½x11, 11x11½

1986, Dec. 20 **Photo.**

2070	A550	8f multi	.60	.30
2071	A550	8f multicolored	.60	.30
2072	A550	10f multicolored	.90	.40
2073	A550	50f multicolored	3.75	1.75
		Nos. 2070-2073 (4)	5.85	2.75

A551

China Post No. T.112.

Photogravure & Engraved

1987, Jan. 5 ***Perf. 11½***

2074	A551	8f blk, dk pink & yel grn	1.20	.40
a.		Bklt. pane of 4 + 8 + label	*10.50*	—
		Complete booklet, #2074a	19.50	

New Year 1987 (Year of the Hare).

A552

China Post No. J.136.

8f, Traveling (3-1). 20f, Cave writing (3-2). 40f, Mountain climbing (3-3).

1987, Feb. 20 **Photo.** ***Perf. 11½***

2075	A552	8f multi	.80	.30
2076	A552	20f multi	2.60	1.25
2077	A552	40f multi	4.75	2.25
		Nos. 2075-2077 (3)	8.15	3.80

Xu Xiake (1587-1621), Ming Dynasty geographer.

Birds of Prey — A553

China Post No. T.114.

No. 2078, Kite (4-1). No. 2079, Sea eagle (4-2), vert. No. 2080, Vulture (4-3), vert. No. 2081, Buzzard (4-4).

1987, Mar. 20

2078	A553	8f multi	.60	.30
2079	A553	8f multi	.60	.30
2080	A553	10f multi	.95	.30
2081	A553	90f multi	5.75	1.25
		Nos. 2078-2081 (4)	7.90	2.15

Liao Zhongkai (1877-1925), National Party Leader — A554

China Post No. J.137.

20f, Liao, He Xiangning (2-2).

1987, Apr. 23 ***Perf. 11½x11***

2082	A554	8f shown (2-1)	.75	.30
2083	A554	20f multi	1.30	.35

Kites — A555

China Post No. T.115.

No. 2084, Hawk (4-1). No. 2085, Dragon (4-2). No. 2086, Symbolic octagon (4-3). No. 2087, Phoenix (4-4).

1987, Apr. 1

2084	A555	8f multi	.75	.35
2085	A555	8f multi	.75	.35
a.		Pair, #2084-2085	2.75	2.25
2086	A555	30f multi	2.00	.95
2087	A555	30f multi	2.00	.95
a.		Pair, #2086-2087	5.25	4.00
		Nos. 2084-2087 (4)	5.50	2.60

Nos. 2085a, 2087a have continuous designs.

A556

China Post No. J.138.

Portraits of Ye Jianying (1897-1986), central committee vice chairman.

1987, Apr. 28

2088	A556	8f multi (3-3)	.85	.30
2089	A556	10f multi (3-2)	1.25	.40
2090	A556	30f multi (3-1)	4.50	1.50
		Nos. 2088-2090 (3)	6.60	2.20

Caves of the Thousand Buddhas, Dunhuang, Gansu Province — A557

China Post No. T.116.

Wall Paintings: 8f, Worshipping Bodhisattvas, Northern Liang Dynasty. 10f, Deer King Jatka, Northern Wei Dynasty. 20f, Heavenly Musicians, Northern Wei Dynasty. 40f, Flying Devata, Northern Wei Dynasty. $2, Mahasattva Jataka.

1987, May 20 ***Perf. 11½***

2091	A557	8f multi (4-1)	.60	.30
2092	A557	10f multi (4-2)	.75	.30
2093	A557	20f multi (4-3)	1.90	.75
2094	A557	40f multi (4-4)	3.25	1.25
		Nos. 2091-2094 (4)	6.50	2.60

Souvenir Sheet

2095	A557	$2 multi	*27.50*	*15.00*

No. 2095 contains one 92x73mm stamp.

See Nos. 2149-2152, 2283-2286, 2407-2411, 2505-2508, 2704-2707.

Children's Day Festival A558

China Post No. T.117.

Children's drawings: No. 2096, Happy Holiday, by Yan Qinghui, age 7. No. 2097, Peace and Happiness, by Liu Yuan, age 7.

1987, June 1 ***Perf. 12½x12***

2096	A558	8f shown (2-1)	.80	.25
2097	A558	8f multi, vert. (2-2)	1.05	.45

Rural Development A559

China Post No. T.118.

No. 2098, Village, southeast China (4-1). No. 2099, Market, horiz. (4-2). No. 2100, Dairy industry, horiz. (4-3). No. 2101, Theater, horiz. (4-4).

1987, June 25 ***Perf. 11½***

2098	A559	8f multi	.55	.45
2099	A559	8f multi	.55	.45
2100	A559	10f multi	.75	.60
2101	A559	20f multi	1.50	1.25
		Nos. 2098-2101 (4)	3.35	2.75

Postal Savings Bank Inauguration A560

China Post No. T.119.

1987, July 1

2102	A560	8f multicolored	1.30	.30

Esperanto Language Movement, Cent. — A561

China Post No. J.139.

1987, July 26

2103	A561	8f lt olive grn, blk & brt blue	1.15	.30

People's Liberation Army, 60th Anniv. A562

China Post No. J.140.

No. 2104, Flag, Great Wall (4-1). No. 2105, Rocket launch, soldier, village (4-2). No. 2106, Submarine, sailor (4-3). No. 2107, Aircraft, pilot (4-4).

1987, Aug. 1 ***Perf. 11***

2104	A562	8f multi	.55	.30
2105	A562	8f multi	.55	.30
2106	A562	10f multi	1.30	.35
2107	A562	30f multi	1.80	.60
		Nos. 2104-2107 (4)	4.20	1.55

Intl. Year of Shelter for the Homeless A563

China Post No. J.141.

1987, Aug. 20 ***Perf. 11***

2108	A563	8f gray, dk car rose & blk	1.00	.30

Chinese Art Festival, Sept. 5-25, Beijing — A564

China Post No. J.142.

1987, Sept. 5 ***Perf. 11***

2109	A564	8f brt red, gold & blk	1.90	.40

Fairy Tales — A565

China Post No. T.120.

4f, Pan Gu inventing the universe. No. 2111, Nu Wa creating man. No. 2112, Yi shooting nine suns. 10f, Chang'e flying to the moon. 20f, Kua Fu pursuing the sun. 90f, Jing Wei filling the sea.

1987, Sept. 25 ***Perf. 11½***

2110	A565	4f multi (6-1)	.55	.30
2111	A565	8f multi (6-2)	.65	.30
2112	A565	8f multi (6-3)	.65	.30
2113	A565	10f multi (6-4)	.80	.30
2114	A565	20f multi (6-5)	1.10	.50
2115	A565	90f multi (6-6)	2.50	1.50
		Nos. 2110-2115 (6)	6.25	3.20

Communist Party of China, 13th Natl. Congress A566

China Post No. J.143.

1987, Oct. 25 ***Perf. 11***

2116	A566	8f multicolored	1.00	.40

Yellow Crane Tower A567

China Post No. T.121.

No. 2118, Yue Yang Tower (4-2). No. 2119, Teng Wang Pavilion (4-3). No. 2120, Peng Lai Pavilion (4-4).

1987, Oct. 30

2117	A567	8f shown (4-1)	.45	.25
2118	A567	8f multi	.45	.25
2119	A567	10f multi	.60	.35
2120	A567	90f multi	3.50	2.40
a.		Min. sheet of 4, #2117-2120	*17.00*	*9.00*
		Nos. 2117-2120 (4)	5.00	3.25

No. 2120a sold for $1.50.

6th Natl. Games — A568

China Post No. J.144.

No. 2121, Pole vault (4-1). No. 2122, Softball (4-2). No. 2123, Weight lifting (4-3). No. 2124, Diving (4-4).

1987, Nov. 20 ***Perf. 11½x11***

2121	A568	8f multi	.35	.25
2122	A568	8f multi	.35	.25
2123	A568	30f multi	.60	.35
2124	A568	50f multi	1.00	.55
		Nos. 2121-2124 (4)	2.30	1.40

Souvenir Sheet

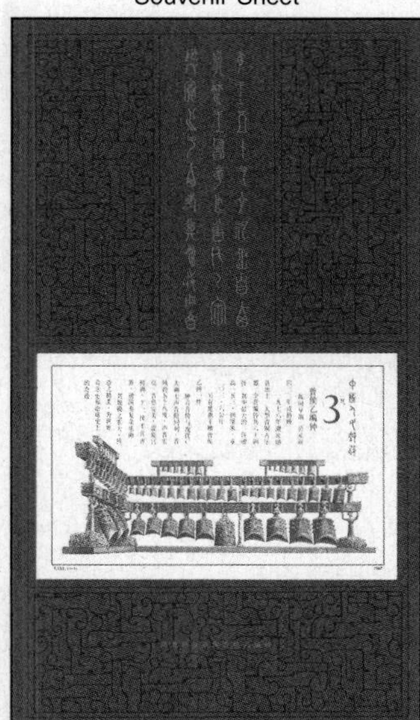

Bronze Bells from the Tomb of Marquis Yi of the Zeng State (c. 433 B.C.), Hubei Province — A569

China Post No. T.122.

1987, Dec. 10 Litho. *Imperf.*
2125 A569 $3 multicolored *9.50 4.50*

Classic Literature — A570

China Post No. T.123.

Outlaws of the Marsh: 8f, Shi Jin practicing martial arts. 10f, Sagacious Lu, the "Tattooed Monk," uprooting a willow tree. 30f, Lin Chong seeking shelter from snow storm at the Mountain Spirit Temple. 50f, Song Jiang helps Ward Chief Chao Gai flee. $2, Outlaws of the Marsh capture treasures.

1987, Dec. 20 Photo. *Perf. 11*
2126 A570 8f multi (4-1) .50 .25
2127 A570 10f multi (4-2) .65 .25
2128 A570 30f multi (4-3) 2.00 .60
2129 A570 50f multi (4-4) 3.00 1.25
Nos. 2126-2129 (4) 6.15 2.35

Souvenir Sheet
Perf. 11½x11

2130 A570 $2 multi *32.00 16.00*

No. 2130 contains one 90x60mm stamp.
See Nos. 2216-2219, 2373-2377, 2449-2452, 2822-2826, 2889-2893.

New Year 1988 (Year of the Dragon) — A571

China Post No. T.124.
Photo. & Engr.

1988, Jan. 5 *Perf. 11½*
2131 A571 8f multicolored *3.00* .45
a. Bklt. pane of 4 + 8 with label between *24.00* —
Complete booklet, #2131a *40.00*

Cai Yuanpei (1868-1940), Education Reformer — A572

China Post No. J.145.

1988, Jan. 11 Photo. *Perf. 11½x11*
2132 A572 8f shown (2-1) .80 .25
2133 A572 20f Seated (2-2) 1.20 .50

Tao Zhu (1908-1969), Party Leader — A573

China Post No. J.146.

1988, Jan. 16 *Perf. 11x11½*
2134 A573 8f shown (2-1) .80 .30
2135 A573 20f Tao, diff. (2-2) 1.05 .50

Folklore A574

China Post No. T.125.

1988, Feb. 10
2136 A574 8f shown (4-1) .45 .25
2137 A574 10f multi, diff. (4-2) .60 .25
2138 A574 20f multi, diff. (4-3) .75 .40
2139 A574 30f multi, diff. (4-4) 1.50 .70
Nos. 2136-2139 (4) 3.30 1.60

A575

China Post No. J.147.

1988, Mar. 25 Photo. *Perf. 11½*
2140 A575 8f multicolored 1.00 .30

7th Natl. People's Congress.

A576

China Post No. J.148.

8f, Wuzhi Mountain (4-1). 10f, Wanquan River (4-2). 30f, "End of the Earth" (4-3). $1.10, "Deer Turning Its Head" (4-4).

1988, Apr. 20 Photo. *Perf. 11½*
2141 A576 8f multi .35 .25
2142 A576 10f multi .45 .25
2143 A576 30f multi .65 .30
2144 A576 $1.10 multi .85 .50
Nos. 2141-2144 (4) 2.30 1.30

Establishment of Hainan Province.

Modern Scientists A577

China Post No. J.149.

Designs: 8f, Li Siguang, geologist. 10f, Zhu Kezhen, meteorologist and geographer. 20f, Wu Youxun, physicist. 30f, Hua Luogeng, mathematician.

1988, Apr. 28 *Perf. 11x11½*
2145 A577 8f multi (4-1) .45 .25
2146 A577 10f multi (4-2) .55 .25
2147 A577 20f multi (4-3) .70 .30
2148 A577 30f multi (4-4) 1.20 .60
Nos. 2145-2148 (4) 2.90 1.40

Wall Paintings Type of 1987
China Post No. T.126.

Caves of the Thousand Buddhas, Dunhuang, Gansu Province: No. 2149, Hunting, Western Wei Dynasty. No. 2150, Fishing, Western Wei Dynasty. 10f, Farming, Northern Zhou Dynasty. 90f, Building a Pagoda, Northern Zhou Dynasty.

1988, May 25 *Perf. 11½x11*
2149 A557 8f multi (4-1) .50 .25
2150 A557 8f multi (4-2) .50 .25
2151 A557 10f multi (4-3) .65 .30
2152 A557 90f multi (4-4) 2.10 .75
Nos. 2149-2152 (4) 3.75 1.55

Environmental Protection — A578

China Post No. T.127.

No. 2153, Soil (4-1). No. 2154, Air (4-2). No. 2155, Water (4-3). No. 2156, Prevent noise pollution (4-4).

1988, June 5 Photo. *Perf. 11*
2153 8f multi .40 .30
2154 8f multi .40 .30
2155 8f multi .40 .30
2156 8f multi .40 .30
a. A578 Block of 4, #2153-2156 3.25 1.75

Souvenir Sheet

China Nos. 1-3 — A579

China Post No. J.150.
Photo. & Engr.

1988, July 2 *Perf. 13*
2157 A579 $3 multicolored *11.00 6.00*

Postage stamps of China, 110th anniv.

11th Asian Games (in 1990), Beijing A580

China Post No. J.151.

8f, Emblem (2-1). 30f, Character trademark (2-2).

1988, July 20 Photo. *Perf. 11x11½*
2158 A580 8f multi .30 .25
2159 A580 30f multi .70 .45

See No. 2300a.

Signing of the Sino-Japanese Peace Treaty, 10th Anniv. — A581

China Post No. J.152.

1988, Aug. 12 Photo. *Perf. 11*
2160 A581 8f Peony (2-1) .30 .25
2161 A581 $1.60 Sakura (2-2) .85 .50
a. Pair, #2160-2161 2.75 1.50

Achievements in Construction — A582

China Post No. T.128.

Designs: 8f, Coal-loading wharf, Ch'in-huang-tao Port. 10f, Ethylene refinery, Qilu. 20f, Pao-shan steel plant, Shanghai. 30f, Central Television Broadcasting Station.

1988, Sept. 2 Photo. *Perf. 11*
2162 A582 8f multi (4-1) .50 .25
2163 A582 10f multi (4-2) .70 .30
2164 A582 20f multi (4-3) .85 .30
2165 A582 30f multi (4-4) .95 .40
Nos. 2162-2165 (4) 3.00 1.25

See Nos. 2221-2224, 2279-2282, 2354-2357.

Mt. T'ai Shan, Shantung Province — A583

China Post No. T.130.

8f, T'ai Shan Temple (4-1). 10f, Ladder to Heaven (4-2). 20f, Daguang peak (4-3). 90f, Sun-watching peak (4-4).

1988, Sept. 14 Photo. & Engr.
2166 A583 8f multi .35 .25
2167 A583 10f multi .40 .35
2168 A583 20f multi .75 .40
2169 A583 90f multi 3.00 1.25
Nos. 2166-2169 (4) 4.50 2.25

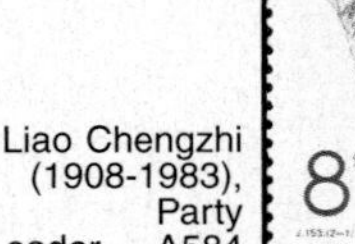

Liao Chengzhi (1908-1983), Party Leader — A584

China Post No. J.153.

1988, Sept. 25 Photo. ***Perf. 11½x11***

2170 A584 8f shown (2-1) .40 .25
2171 A584 20f Writing (2-2) .75 .45

Marshal Peng Dehuai (1898-1974), Party Leader — A585

China Post No. J.155.

20f, Peng in uniform (2-2).

1988, Oct. 24 Photo. ***Perf. 11x11½***

2172 A585 8f shown (2-1) .50 .25
2173 A585 20f multi 1.35 .60

1st Natl. Farmers' Games A586

China Post No. J.154.

1988, Oct. 9 Photo. ***Perf. 11½***

2174 A586 8f Cycling (2-1) .35 .25
2175 A586 20f Javelin (2-2) .65 .40

Literary Masterpieces — A587

China Post No. T.131.

The Romance of the Three Kingdoms, by Luo Guanzhong, 14th cent.: No. 2176, Three heroes' sworn brotherhood (4-1). No. 2177, Battle between Lu Bu and the heroes, vert. (4-2). No. 2178, Struggle between man and woman at Fengyi Pavilion (4-3). No. 2179, Two noblemen, vert. (4-4). No. 2180, Guan Yu's battle through five passes.

Perf. 11½x11, 11x11½

1988, Nov. 25 Photo.

2176 A587 8f multicolored .50 .25
2177 A587 8f multicolored .50 .35
2178 A587 30f multicolored 1.25 .70
2179 A587 50f multicolored 1.60 1.20
Nos. 2176-2179 (4) 3.85 2.50

Souvenir Sheet

Perf. 11

2180 A587 $3 multicolored *32.50 16.00*

See Nos. 2310-2313, 2403-2406, 2539-2543.

Intl Volunteers' Day — A588

China Post No. J.156.

1988, Dec. 5 Photo. ***Perf. 11***

2181 A588 20f multicolored 1.00 .30

A589

China Post No. T.132.

Milu, *Elaphurus davidianus*

1988, Dec. 20 Photo. ***Perf. 11½x11***

2182 A589 8f Buck (2-1) .85 .25
2183 A589 40f Herd (2-2) 2.25 1.50

Exist imperf. Value, pairs each $6.50.

Orchids — A590

China Post No. T.129.

8f, Da yi pin (4-1). 10f, Dragon (4-2). 20f, Large phoenix tail (4-3). 50f, Silver-edged black (4-4).
Red lotus petal.

1988, Dec. 25 ***Perf. 12***

2184 A590 8f multi .70 .30
2185 A590 10f multi .85 .35
2186 A590 20f multi 1.10 .45
2187 A590 50f multi 1.40 .75
a. Strip of 4, #2184-2187 6.25 3.75
Nos. 2184-2187 (4) 4.05 1.85

Souvenir Sheet

Perf. 11½x11

2188 A590 $2 multi *16.00 8.00*

No. 2188 contains one 55x37mm stamp.

A591

China Post No. R24

Grotto Statuary: $2, Buddha. $5, Warrior, Longmen Grotto, Henan. $10, Goddess. $20, Woman and birds.

Photo & Engr.

1988-89 ***Perf. 11½x11***

2189 A591 $2 buff & reddish blk 1.35 .30
2190 A591 $5 buff & grnh blk 1.60 .65
2191 A591 $10 buff & brn blk 2.60 1.25
a. Souv. sheet of 1, buff & sep *22.00* 20.00
2192 A591 $20 buff & indigo 6.50 2.50
Nos. 2189-2192 (4) 12.05 4.70

Issued: $2, 11/30; $5, 8/10; $10, 10/15; $20, 10/20.

No. 2191a released on Oct. 12, 1989, for the China Natl. Philatelic Exhibition and the 40th anniv. of the People's Republic.

Nos. 2189-2192, 2191a are almost always found with small ink spots on the stamps. Values are for stamps in this condition.

A592

China Post No. T.133.

Photo. & Engr.

1989, Jan. 5 ***Perf. 11½***

2193 A592 8f multicolored 2.10 .30
a. Bklt. pane of 4+8 with label between *12.00* —
Complete booklet, #2193a *18.00*

New Year 1989 (Year of the Snake).

Stamps from No. 2193a have one or two straight edges and sell for less as singles than No. 2193.

Qu Qiubai (1899-1935), Party Leader (J.157) — A593

China Post No. J.157.

1989, Jan. 29 Photo. ***Perf. 11x11½***

2194 A593 8f multi (2-1) .55 .30
2195 A593 20f multi, diff. (2-2) .90 .45

Brown-eared Pheasant, *Crossoptilon mantchuricum* (T.134) — A594

China Post No. T.134.

1989, Feb. 21 ***Perf. 11½***

2196 A594 8f multi (2-1) .55 .25
2197 A594 50f multi, diff. (2-2) .95 .40

Shandong — A594a

Guangxi — A594b

Ningxia — A594c

Shanxi — A594d

Qinghai — A594e

Guizhou — A594f

Jiangxi — A594g

China Post Nos. R25-R27

1989-91 Photo. ***Perf. 13x13½***

2198 A594a 5f multicolored .25 .25
2199 A594b 15f blk, gray & brt grn .25 .25
2200 A594c 25f blk, gray & rose .30 .25
2201 A594d 80f blk, gray & pale bl .60 .25
2202 A594e $1.30 blk, gray & brn red .60 .35
2203 A594f $1.60 blk, gray & pale ultra .75 .35
2204 A594g $2 multicolored 1.00 .35
Nos. 2198-2204 (7) 3.75 2.05

Issued: 5f, 6/10/91; 15f, 11/25/90; 25f, 11/10/90; 80f, 9/20/90; $1.30, $1.60, 3/10/89; $2, 4/25/91.

China Post Nos.: R25, $1.30, and $1.60; R26, 15f, 25f, and 80f; R27, 5f, and $2.00.

Silk Painting Excavated from Han Tomb No. 1 at Mawangdui, Changsha A595

China Post No. T.135.

8f, In the Heavens (3-1). 20f, On the Earth, vert. (3-2). 30f, In the Netherworld, vert. (3-3). $5, Entire painting.

1989, Mar. 25 Photo. ***Perf. 11x11½***

2208 A595 8f multi .50 .25
a. Perf. 11½ 5.50 5.50

Perf. 11½x11

2209 A595 20f multi .50 .25
a. Perf. 11½ 5.50 5.50
2210 A595 30f multi .50 .25
a. Perf. 11½ 5.50 5.50
Nos. 2208-2210 (3) 1.50 .75

Textured Paper, Without Gum

Size: 90x165mm

Imperf

2211 A595 $5 multi *4.50 3.00*

Prevention and Resistance of Cancer — A596

China Post No. T.136.

20f, Woman's thermogram (2-2).

1989, Apr. 7 Litho. ***Perf. 12***

2212 A596 8f shown (2-1) .35 .25
2213 A596 20f multicolored .65 .30

May Fourth Movement, 70th Anniv. A597

China Post No. J.158.

1989, May 4 Photo. ***Perf. 11***

2214 A597 8f Bas-relief .60 .30

Interparliamentary Union, Cent. — A598

China Post No. J.159.

1989, June 29 Photo. ***Perf. 11x11½***

2215 A598 20f multi .70 .30

Literature Type of 1987
China Post No. T.138.

Outlaws of the Marsh: 8f, Wu Song slaying a tiger on Jingyang Ridge. 10f, Qin Ming dodging arrows. 20f, Hua Rong shooting a wild goose on Mt. Liangshan. $1.30, Li Kui fighting Zhang Shun from a junk.

1989, July 25 Photo. *Perf. 11*

2216 A570 8f multi (4-1) .30 .25
2217 A570 10f multi (4-2) .30 .25
2218 A570 20f multi (4-3) .40 .35
2219 A570 $1.30 multi (4-4) .75 .50
Nos. 2216-2219 (4) 1.75 1.35

Asia-Pacific Telecommunity, 10th Anniv. — A599

China Post No. J.160.

1989, Aug. 4 Litho. *Perf. 12*

2220 A599 8f multi .55 .25

Type of 1988
China Post No. T.139.

Achievements in Engineering and Construction: 8f, Beijing Intl. Telecommunications Building, vert. 10f, Xi Qu Coal Mine, Gu Jiao, Shanxi Province. 20f, Long Yang Gorge Hydroelectric Power Station, Qinghai Province. 30f, Da Yao Shan Tunnel of the Guangzhou-Heng Yang Railway.

1989, Aug. 10 Photo. *Perf. 11*

2221 A582 8f multi (4-1) .30 .25
2222 A582 10f multi (4-2) .30 .25
2223 A582 20f multi (4-3) .30 .30
2224 A582 30f multi (4-4) .35 .30
Nos. 2221-2224 (4) 1.25 1.10

Mt. Huashan — A601

China Post No. T.140.

Designs: 8f, Five prominent peaks. 10f, View from atop Huashan. 20f, 1000-foot precipice. 90f, Blue Dragon Ridge.

1989, Aug. 25 Photo. & Engr.

2225 A601 8f multi (4-1) .35 .25
2226 A601 10f multi (4-2) .45 .25
2227 A601 20f multi (4-3) .50 .35
2228 A601 90f multi (4-4) 1.10 .55
Nos. 2225-2228 (4) 2.40 1.40

Modern Art — A602

China Post No. T.141.

Paintings: 8f, *The Fable of the White Snake*, by Ye Qianyu. 20f, *Li River in Fine Rain*, by Li Keran. 50f, *Marching Together*, by Wu Zuoren.

1989, Sept. 1 Photo.

2229 A602 8f multi (3-1) .40 .25
2230 A602 20f multi (3-2) .50 .25
2231 A602 50f multi (3-3) .90 .40
Nos. 2229-2231 (3) 1.80 .90

People's Political Conference A603

China Post No. J.161.

1989, Sept. 21 *Perf. 12*

2232 A603 8f No. 2 .80 .30

A604

Confucius (551-479 B.C.) — A605

China Post No. J.162.

Designs: 8f, The lecture in the Apricot Temple, Qufu. $1.60, Confucius riding in an ox cart.

1989, Sept. 28 Photo. *Perf. 11*

2233 A604 8f shown (2-1) .65 .30
2234 A604 $1.60 multi (2-2) 1.90 .90

Souvenir Sheet
Without Gum

Litho. *Imperf.*

2235 A605 $3 multicolored *5.75 3.25*

A606

Gate of Heavenly Peace — A607

China Post No. J.163.

1989, Oct. 1 Photo. *Perf. 11x11½*

2236 A606 8f shown (4-1) .25 .25
2237 A606 10f Flowers (4-2) .25 .25
2238 A606 20f Five stars (4-3) .35 .25
2239 A606 40f Construction (4-4) .55 .25
Nos. 2236-2239 (4) 1.40 1.00

Souvenir Sheet
Without Gum

Litho. *Imperf.*

2240 A607 $3 shown 4.50 3.00

PRC, 40th anniv.

Photography, Sesquicentennial — A608

China Post No. T.142.

1989, Oct. 15 Photo. *Perf. 11*

2241 A608 8f multicolored .75 .30

Li Dazhao (1889-1927), Party Leader — A609

China Post No. J.164.

1989, Oct. 29 Photo. *Perf. 11x11¼*

2242 A609 8f Li, soldiers (2-1) .75 .30
 a. Perf. 11½x11¼ 6.00 6.00
2243 A609 20f Li, text (2-2) 1.25 .30
 a. Perf. 11½x11¼ 6.00 6.00

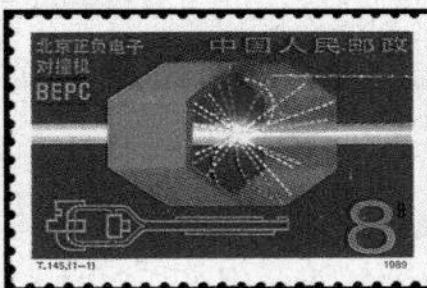

Positron Collider Produced in Beijing A610

China Post No. T.145.

1989, Nov. 1 *Perf. 11*

2244 A610 8f multicolored .90 .60

Rocket Defense A611

China Post No. T.143.

Designs: 4f, Transporting 3 rockets. 8f, Disassembled rocket on transport. 10f, Launch, vert. 20f, Stage separation in space.

1989, Nov. 15 Litho. *Perf. 12*

2245 A611 4f multicolored (4-1) .25 .25
2246 A611 8f multicolored (4-2) .35 .25
2247 A611 10f multicolored (4-3) .45 .30
2248 A611 20f multicolored (4-4) .60 .40
Nos. 2245-2248 (4) 1.65 1.20

A612

Views of West Lake — A613

China Post No. T.144.

1989, Nov. 25 Photo. *Perf. 11x11½*

2249 A612 8f multi (4-1) .45 .25
2250 A612 10f multi, diff. (4-2) .60 .30
2251 A612 30f multi, diff. (4-3) .75 .35
2252 A612 40f multi, diff. (4-4) .95 .40
Nos. 2249-2252 (4) 2.75 1.30

Souvenir Sheet
Perf. 11½x11

2253 A613 $5 multicolored 7.50 3.50

11th Asian Games A614

China Post No. J.165.

Various stadiums.

1989, Dec. 15 *Perf. 11x11½*

2254 A614 8f multi (4-1) .30 .25
2255 A614 10f multi (4-2) .30 .25
2256 A614 30f multi (4-3) .30 .25
2257 A614 $1.60 multi (4-4) .55 .40
Nos. 2254-2257 (4) 1.45 1.15

See Nos. 2295-2300.

A615

China Post No. T.146.
Photo & Engr.

1990, Jan. 5 *Perf. 11½*

2258 A615 8f multicolored 1.50 .30
 a. Bklt. pane of 12 + 4 labels *18.00* —
 Complete booklet, #2258a 21.00
 b. As. No. 2258, perf. 11½x11 16.00 16.00

New Year 1990 (Year of the Horse).
Stamps from No. 2258a have straight edges at top or bottom and sell for less as singles than No. 2258.

Narcissus A616

China Post No. T.147.

1990, Feb. 10 Photo. *Perf. 11x11½*

2259 A616 8f multi (4-1) .25 .25
2260 A616 20f multi, diff. (4-2) .30 .30
2261 A616 30f multi, diff. (4-3) .45 .30
2262 A616 $1.60 multi, diff. (4-4) .55 .40
Nos. 2259-2262 (4) 1.55 1.25

Norman Bethune (1890-1939), Surgeon — A617

China Post No. J.166.
Litho. & Engr.

1990, Mar. 3 *Perf. 11x11½*

2263 A617 8f In Canada (2-2) .30 .25
2264 A617 $1.60 In China (2-1) .60 .50
 a. Pair, #2263-2264 1.60 1.25

See Canada Nos. 1264-1265.

Intl. Women's Day — A618

China Post No. J.167.

1990, Mar. 8 Photo. *Perf. 11½x11*

2265 A618 20f multicolored .60 .30

Afforestation — A619

China Post No. T.148.

8f, Bird, flora (4-1). 10f, Buildings (4-2). 20f, Great Wall, forest, (4-3). 30f, Bushes, evergreens (4-4).

1990, Mar. 12 ***Perf. 11***
2266 A619 8f multi .30 .25
2267 A619 10f multi .30 .25
2268 A619 20f multi .40 .25
2269 A619 30f multi .50 .25
Nos. 2266-2269 (4) 1.50 1.00

Pottery — A620

China Post No. T.149.

1990, Apr. 10 **Litho.** ***Perf. 12***
2270 A620 8f multi (4-1) .25 .25
2271 A620 20f multi (4-2) .30 .25
2272 A620 30f multi (4-3) .50 .30
2273 A620 50f multi (4-4) .65 .30
Nos. 2270-2273 (4) 1.70 1.10

Li Fuchun (1900-1975), Party Leader — A621

China Post No. J.168.

1990, May 22 **Photo.** ***Perf. 11x11½***
2274 A621 8f shown .40 .30
2275 A621 20f In uniform (2-2) .60 .35

Bronze Head — A622

China Post No. T.151.

Bronze treasures from Emperor Qin Shi Huang Mausoleum: 50f, Horse head. $5, Chariots.

1990, June 20 **Photo.** ***Perf. 11½x11***
2276 A622 8f shown (2-1) .45 .25
2277 A622 50f multicolored (2-2) .75 .35

Miniature Sheet

Size: 141x79mm

2278 A622 $5 multicolored *7.50 4.25*

Achievements Type of 1988

China Post No. T.152.

Designs: 8f, 2nd automobile factory. 10f, Yizheng Joint Corporation of Chemical Fiber Industry. 20f, Shengli Oil Field. 30f, Qinshan Nuclear Power Station.

1990, June 30 **Litho.** ***Perf. 12***
2279 A582 8f shown (4-1) .30 .25
2280 A582 10f multicolored (4-2) .30 .25
2281 A582 20f multicolored (4-3) .40 .25
2282 A582 30f multicolored (4-4) .55 .30
Nos. 2279-2282 (4) 1.55 1.05

Wall Paintings Type of 1987

China Post No. T.150.

8f, Flying Devatas. 10f, Worshipping Bodhisatva. 30f, Savior Avolokitesvara. 50f, Indra.

1990, July 10 ***Perf. 11½x11***
2283 A557 8f multi (4-1) .35 .25
2284 A557 10f multi, vert. (4-2) .35 .25
2285 A557 30f multi, vert. (4-3) .45 .30
2286 A557 50f multi (4-4) .85 .40
Nos. 2283-2286 (4) 2.00 1.20

Snow Leopard (Uncia Uncia) A624

China Post No. T.153.

1990, July 20 **Photo.** ***Perf. 11½***
2287 A624 8f multicolored (2-1) .40 .25
2288 A624 50f multicolored (2-2) .75 .30

Chinese Soviet Post Stamp of 1931 A625

China Post No. J.169.

Design: 20f, Chinese Red Post issue of West Fukien, 1929.

1990, Aug. 1 **Litho.** ***Perf. 12***
2289 A625 8f multi (2-1) .40 .25
2290 A625 20f multi, diff. (2-2) .75 .25

Zhang Wentian (1900-1990) — A626

China Post No. J.170.

1990, Aug. 30 ***Perf. 11x11½***
2291 A626 8f shown (2-1) .35 .25
2292 A626 20f multi, diff. (2-2) .75 .25

Intl. Literacy Year — A627

China Post No. J.171.

1990, Sept. 8 ***Perf. 11½x11***
2293 A627 20f multicolored .75 .30

Chinese Films — A628

China Post No. T.154.

1990, Sept. 21 **Litho.** ***Perf. 11***
2294 A628 20f multicolored .90 .25

11th Asian Games, Beijing A629

China Post No. J.172.

4f, Running (6-1). 8f, Gymnastics (6-2). 10f, Karate (6-3). 20f, Volleyball (6-4). 30f, Swimming (6-5). $1.60, Shooting (6-6).

1990, Sept. 22 ***Perf. 11x11½***
2295 A629 4f multi .25 .25
2296 A629 8f multi .25 .25
2297 A629 10f multi .30 .25
2298 A629 20f multi .30 .25
2299 A629 30f multi .40 .30
2300 A629 $1.60 multi .90 .65
a. Souv. sheet of 12, #2158-2159, 2254-2257, 2295-2300 *9.50 6.00*
Nos. 2295-2300 (6) 2.40 1.95

Souvenir Sheet

Sportphilex '90, Beijing — A629a

1990, Sept. 21 **Litho.** ***Perf. 11½***
2300B A629a $10 multi *20.00 15.00*

No. 2300B exists imperf. Value, *$700.*

Modern Scientists A630

China Post No. J.173.

Designs: 8f, Lin Qiaozhi, obstetrician. 10f, Zhang Yuzhe, astronomer. 20f, Hou Debang, chemist. 30f, Ding Ying, agronomist.

1990, Oct. 10 **Litho.** ***Perf. 12***
2301 A630 8f multicolored (4-1) .45 .25
2302 A630 10f multicolored (4-2) .45 .25
2303 A630 20f multicolored (4-3) .75 .25
2304 A630 30f multicolored (4-4) .80 .25
Nos. 2301-2304 (4) 2.45 1.00

Mt. Hengshan — A631

China Post No. T.155.

Designs: 8f, Towering Temple. 10f, South Sacred Mountain. 20f, Forested mountainside. 50f, Imposing Zhurong Peak.

Photo. & Engr.

1990, Nov. 5 ***Perf. 11***
2305 A631 8f multicolored (4-1) .35 .30
2306 A631 10f multicolored (4-2) .50 .30
2307 A631 20f multicolored (4-3) .65 .35
2308 A631 50f multicolored (4-4) 1.05 .45
Nos. 2305-2308 (4) 2.55 1.40

See Nos. 2342-2345. 2628-2631.

Souvenir Sheet

China Philatelic Federation, 3rd Congress — A632

China Post No. J.174.

1990, Nov. 28 ***Perf. 11½x11***
2309 A632 $2 multicolored 5.50 4.00

Two types of No. 2309 exist. Either two or three of the horizontal bars in seventh character from top right are connected at left side. Value for No. 2309 is for the first type. Examples with three bars connected, value $7.50.

Literature Type of 1988

China Post No. T.157.

Romance of the Three Kingdoms by Luo Guanzhong: No. 2310, Night Attack on Wuchao. No. 2311, Making Three Calls at the Thatched Cottage. 30f, Rescuing the Master Single-handedly. 50f, Turning the Changban Bridge Upside Down.

1990, Dec. 10 **Photo.** ***Perf. 11½x11***
2310 A587 20f multicolored (4-1) .35 .25
2311 A587 20f multi, vert. (4-2) .35 .25
2312 A587 30f multicolored (4-3) .40 .30
2313 A587 50f multi, vert. (4-4) .60 .35
Nos. 2310-2313 (4) 1.70 1.15

Han Xizai's Night Revels by Gu Hongzhong — A633

China Post No. T.158.

Designs: a, Guests enjoying food, music (5-1). b, Music and dance (5-2). c, Hand washing (5-3). d, Musicians (5-4). e, Guests departing (5-5).

1990, Dec. 20 **Litho.** ***Perf. 12***
2314 Strip of 5 5.00 3.25
a.-e. A633 50f any single .70 .40

New Year 1991 (Year of the Sheep) — A634

China Post No. T.159.

Photo. & Engr.

1991, Jan. 5 ***Perf. 11½***
2315 A634 20f multicolored 1.75 .40
a. Bklt. pane of 12 + label 15.00 —
Complete booklet, #2315a 15.00

Stamps from No. 2315a have straight edges at top or bottom and sell for less as singles than No. 2315.

Dujiangyan Irrigation Project — A635

China Post No. T.156.

Designs: 20f, Yuzui, flood control. 50f, Feishayan, drainage. 80f, Baopingkou, water volume control.

1991, Feb. 20 Photo. *Perf. 11½x11*
2316 A635 20f multicolored .40 .25
2317 A635 50f multicolored .80 .45
2318 A635 80f multicolored 1.40 .80
Nos. 2316-2318 (3) 2.60 1.50

A636

China Post No. J.175.

1991, Mar. 18
2319 A636 20f multicolored .80 .40

Paris Commune, 120th anniv.

A637

China Post No. T.160.

1991, Apr. 20 Photo. *Perf. 10*
2320 A637 20f multi (2-1) .45 .30
a. Perf. 11½x11 1.50 .90

Perf. 11½x11
2321 A637 50f Child & adult hands (2-2) .55 .30

Family planning.

Horned Animals A638

China Post No. T.161.

No. 2322, Saiga tatarica (4-1). No. 2323, Budorcas taxicolor (4-2). No. 2324, Ovis ammon (4-3). No. 2325, Capra ibex (4-4).

1991, May 10 *Perf. 11x11½*
2322 A638 20f multi .30 .25
2323 A638 20f multi .30 .25
a. Perf. 11 7.00 7.00
2324 A638 50f multi .50 .30
a. Perf. 11 17.50 17.50
2325 A638 $2 multi .75 .35
Nos. 2322-2325 (4) 1.85 1.15

No. 2322 exists imperf. Value, pair *$140.*

A639

China Post No. J.176.

25f, Song and dance (2-1). 50f, Golden bridge (2-2).
$2, PRC No. 132, cranes.

1991, May 23 Photo. *Perf. 11*
2326 A639 25f multi .45 .30
2327 A639 50f multi .75 .40

Souvenir Sheet
2328 A639 $2 multi *10.00 4.50*

Occupation of Tibet, 40th anniv.

A640

China Post No. J.177.

1991, June 22 *Perf. 11½x11*
2329 A640 20f multicolored 1.00 .35

Antarctic Treaty, 30th anniv.

Rhododendrons — A641

China Post No. T.162.

Varieties of rhododendrons: No. 2330, Delavayi (8-1). No. 2331, Molle (8-2). No. 2332, Simsii (8-3). No. 2333, Fictolacteum (8-4). No. 2334, Agglutinatum, vert. (8-5). No. 2335, Fortunei, vert. (8-6). No. 2336, Giganteum, vert. (8-7). No. 2337, Rex, vert. (8-8).
$5, Wardii.

1991, June 25 Litho. *Perf. 12*
2330 A641 10f multi .30 .25
2331 A641 15f multi .30 .25
2332 A641 20f multi .30 .25
2333 A641 20f multi .30 .25
2334 A641 50f multi .55 .25
2335 A641 80f multi .80 .35
2336 A641 90f multi .95 .50
2337 A641 $1.60 multi 1.60 .75
Nos. 2330-2337 (8) 5.10 2.85

Souvenir Sheet
Perf. 11½
2338 A641 $5 multi *11.50 8.50*

No. 2338 contains one 80x40mm stamp.

Chinese Communist Party, 70th Anniv. A642

China Post No. J.178.

50f, Hammer and sickle (2-2).

1991, July 1 Photo. *Perf. 11x11½*
2339 A642 20f shown (2-1) .80 .30
2340 A642 50f multicolored 1.20 .50

Peasant Uprising, 209B.C. A643

China Post No. J.179.

1991, July 7
2341 A643 20f brown .60 .25

Mt. Hengshan Type of 1990
China Post No. T.163.

Designs: No. 2342, Monastery on mountainside. No. 2343, Snow-covered mountain top. 55f, Inscription carved into mountainside. 80f, Hidden monastery.

Photo. & Engr.
1991, July 20 *Perf. 11*
2342 A631 20f multi (4-1) .30 .25
2343 A631 20f multi (4-2) .30 .25
2344 A631 55f multi (4-3) .65 .30
2345 A631 80f multi (4-4) .90 .45
Nos. 2342-2345 (4) 2.15 1.25

Intl. Union for Quaternary Research, 13th Conf. A644

China Post No. J.180.

1991, Aug. 2 Photo. *Perf. 11x11½*
2346 A644 20f multicolored .70 .30
a. Perf. 11½ *13.00 13.00*

Chengde Mountain Resort — A645

China Post No. T.164.

Ch'ing Dynasty Royal Gardens: 15f, Pine valleys. 20f, Mid-lake pavilion. 90f, Islet, maple trees. $2, Chengde Royal Summer Resort.

1991 *Perf. 11½x11*
2347 A645 15f multi (3-1) .30 .25
2348 A645 20f multi (3-2) .40 .30
2349 A645 90f multi (3-3) .90 .60
Nos. 2347-2349 (3) 1.60 1.15

Souvenir Sheet
2350 A645 $2 multicolored *9.00 3.75*

No. 2350 contains one 90x40mm stamp. Issue dates: $2, Aug. 19; others, Aug. 10.

A646

China Post No. J.181.

Chen Yi, (b. 1901), party leader.

1991, Aug. 26 Photo. *Perf. 11½x11*
2351 A646 20f shown (2-1) .50 .25
2352 A646 50f Verse (2-2) .90 .40

A647

China Post No. T.168.

1991, Sept. 14
2353 A647 80f Disaster relief .65 .40

Achievements Type of 1988
China Post No. T.165.

20f, Luoyang glassworks. 25f, Urumchi chemical fertilizer project. 55f, Dalian expressway, Shenyang. 80f, Xichang satellite launching center.

1991, Sept. 20 Litho. *Perf. 12*
2354 A582 20f multi (4-1) .30 .25
2355 A582 25f multi (4-2) .30 .30
2356 A582 55f multi (4-3) .55 .35
2357 A582 80f multi (4-4) .65 .45
Nos. 2354-2357 (4) 1.80 1.35

Revolutionary Heroes — A648

China Post No. J.182.

Designs: No. 2358, Xu Xilin (1873-1907). No. 2359, Qiu Jin (1879-1907). No. 2360, Song Jiaoren (1882-1913).

Perf. 10 (#2358), 11x11½
1991, Oct. 10 Photo.
2358 A648 20f multi (3-1) .75 .35
a. Perf. 11x11½ 6.00 1.60
2359 A648 20f multi (3-2) .55 .30
2360 A648 20f multi (3-3) .55 .30
Nos. 2358-2360 (3) 1.85 .95

Jingdezhen Chinaware A649

China Post No. T.166.

Designs: 15f, Glazed wine pot and warming bowl, Song Dynasty, vert. No. 2362, Porcelain vase, Yuan Dynasty, vert. No. 2363, Jar, Ming Dynasty. 25f, Porcelain vase, Ch'ing Dynasty, vert. 50f, Modern underglazed plate, vert. $2, Modern octagonal eggshell bowl.

Perf. 11¼x11½, 11½x11¼ (#2363, 2366)
1991, Oct. 11 Photo.
2361 A649 15f multi (6-1) .45 .25
2362 A649 20f multi (6-2) .45 .25
2363 A649 20f multi (6-3) .45 .25
2364 A649 25f multi (6-4) .45 .25
2365 A649 50f multi (6-5) .45 .30
2366 A649 $2 multi (6-6) 1.10 .50
Nos. 2361-2366 (6) 3.35 1.80

Perf. 11¼x11, 11x11¼ (#2363a, 2366a)
1991
2361a A649 15f multi .55 .25
2362a A649 20f multi .55 .25
2363a A649 20f multi .55 .25
2364a A649 25f multi .55 .30
2365a A649 50f multi .55 .30
2366a A649 $2 multi 1.00 .55
Nos. 2361a-2366a (6) 3.75 1.90

Tao Xingzhi, Educator, Birth Cent. — A650

China Post No. J.183.

50f, Wearing robe (2-2).

1991, Oct. 18 Litho. *Perf. 12*
2367 A650 20f shown (2-1) .40 .25
2368 A650 50f multicolored .60 .35

Xu Xiangqian, Revolutionary Leader, 90th Birth Anniv. — A651

China Post No. J.184.

1991, Nov. 8 ***Perf. 11x11½***

2369 A651 20f shown (2-1) .45 .30
2370 A651 50f In uniform (2-2) .65 .40

1st Women's Soccer World Championships, Guangdong Province — A652

China Post No. J.185.

Designs: 50f, Woman kicking soccer ball.

1991, Nov. 16 ***Perf. 11½x11***

2371 A652 20f red & multi (2-1) .40 .30
2372 A652 50f grn & multi (2-2) .50 .35

Literature Type of 1987

China Post No. T.167.

Outlaws of the Marsh: 20f, Dai Zong sends a false letter from Liangshan Marsh. No. 2374, Ten feet of steel alone captures Stumpy Tiger Wang. No. 2375, Mistress Gu breaks open the jail in Dengzhou to rescue the Xie Brothers. 90f, Sun Li offers a plan to attack Zhu Family manor. $3, Mount Liangshan gallants raid the execution grounds.

1991, Nov. 19 ***Perf. 11***

2373 A570 20f multi (4-1) .25 .25
2374 A570 25f multi (4-2) .30 .30
2375 A570 25f multi (4-3) .35 .35
2376 A570 90f multi (4-4) 1.20 .55
Nos. 2373-2376 (4) 2.10 1.45

Souvenir Sheet

Perf. 11x11½

2377 A570 $3 multicolored *9.00 5.00*

No. 2377 contains one 60x90mm stamp.

Beginning with No. 2378 stamps are inscribed "CHINA" and are numbered chronologically with the year followed by the number of the set. Additional numbers in parentheses indicate the number and position of each stamp in a set. A typical inscription looks like this: 1992-2 (2-2)T. We will note these only when helpful in identifying stamps.

New Year 1992, Year of the Monkey

A653 A654

20f, Monkey, peach. 50f, Magpies, plum branches.

Photo. & Engr.

1992, Jan. 25 ***Perf. 11½***

2378 A653 20f multicolored .40 .30
2379 A654 50f multicolored .70 .35

Storks — A655

1992, Feb. 20 Photo. ***Perf. 11x11½***

2380 A655 20f Ciconia nigra .30 .25
2381 A655 $1.60 Ciconia ciconia .80 .45

Conifers — A656

Designs: 20f, Metasequoia glyptostroboides. 30f, Cathaya argyrophylla. 50f, Taiwania flousiana. 80f, Abies beshanzuensis.

1992, Mar. 10 Litho. ***Perf. 12½***

2382 A656 20f multicolored .30 .25
2383 A656 30f multicolored .30 .25
2384 A656 50f multicolored .35 .30
2385 A656 80f multicolored .55 .35
Nos. 2382-2385 (4) 1.50 1.15

Marine Life A660

20f, Pagrosomus major. 25f, Penaeus chinesis. 50f, Chlamys farreri. 80f, Laminaria japonica.

1992, Apr. 15 Photo. ***Perf. 11***

2386 A660 20f multi .25 .25
2387 A660 25f multi .25 .25
2388 A660 50f multi .35 .25
2389 A660 80f multi .40 .30
Nos. 2386-2389 (4) 1.25 1.05

Publication of "Discussions on Literature and Art at the Yenan Forum," 50th Anniv. — A661

1992, May 23 Photo. ***Perf. 11½x11***

2390 A661 20f org, blk & red .90 .30

A662

1992, June 5 Litho. ***Perf. 12***

2392 A662 20f multicolored .75 .30

UN Conf. on Human Development, 20th anniv.

A663

Insects: 20f, Coccinella septempunctata. 30f, Sympetrum croceolum. 50f, Chrysopa septempunctata. $2, Tenodera aridifolia sinensis.

1992, June 28

2393 A663 20f multicolored .30 .25
2394 A663 30f multicolored .30 .25
2395 A663 50f multicolored .35 .30
2396 A663 $2 multicolored .95 .45
Nos. 2393-2396 (4) 1.90 1.25

1992 Summer Olympics, Barcelona A664

20f, Basketball, vert. 25f, Women's gymnastics. 50f, Women's diving. 80f, Weight lifting, vert.

$5, Runners.

1992, July 25 Photo. ***Perf. 11***

2397 A664 20f multi .30 .25
2398 A664 25f multi .35 .25
2399 A664 50f multi .35 .30
2400 A664 80f multi .45 .35
Nos. 2397-2400 (4) 1.45 1.15

Souvenir Sheet

2401 A664 $5 multi 2.50 1.75

No. 2401 contains one 54x40mm stamp.

Intl. Space Year — A665

1992, Aug. 18 Litho. ***Perf. 12***

2402 A665 20f multicolored .80 .30

Literature Type of 1988

Romance of the Three Kingdoms by Luo Guanzhong: 20f, Verbal battle with scholars. 30f, Goading Sun Quan with sarcasm, vert. 50f, Jiang Gan stealing the letter. $1.60, Gathering arrows with straw-covered boats, vert.

Perf. 11½x11, 11x11½

1992, Aug. 25 **Photo.**

2403 A587 20f multi .30 .25
2404 A587 30f multi .35 .30
2405 A587 50f multi .35 .30
2406 A587 $1.60 multi .75 .45
Nos. 2403-2406 (4) 1.75 1.30

Wall Paintings Type of 1987

20f, Bodhisattva, vert. 25f, Musical performance, vert. 55f, Flight of a dragon. 80f, Envoy to the western regions. $5, Avalokitesvara-Bodhisattva, vert.

1992, Sept. 15 ***Perf. 11***

2407 A557 20f multicolored .30 .25
2408 A557 25f multicolored .35 .30
2409 A557 55f multicolored .35 .30
2410 A557 80f multicolored .60 .40
Nos. 2407-2410 (4) 1.60 1.25

Souvenir Sheet

Perf. 11½

2411 A557 $5 multicolored *3.00 2.00*

No. 2411 contains one 52x70mm stamp.

Normalization of Diplomatic Relations Between China and Japan, 20th Anniv. — A666

20f, Cranes, Great Wall of China, Mt. Fuji. $2, Japanese, Chinese children, dove.

1992, Sept. 29 Photo. ***Perf. 11x11½***

2412 A666 20f multicolored .25 .25
2413 A666 $2 multicolored .95 .55

A667

Statue of Mazu, Chinese Goddess of the Sea.

1992, Oct. 4 Litho. ***Perf. 12***

2414 A667 20f multicolored .60 .30

A667a

1992, Oct. 12 Photo. ***Perf. 11½x11***

2414A A667a 20f multicolored 1.25 .30

14th Chinese Communist Party Congress.

Jiao Yulu (1922-1964), Communist Party Leader — A668

1992, Oct. 28 Litho. ***Perf. 12***

2415 A668 20f multicolored .60 .30

Famous Men A669

Designs: 20f, Xiong Qinglai, mathematician. 30f, Tang Feifan, microbiologist. 50f, Zhang Xiaoqian, physician. $1, Liang Sicheng, architect.

1992, Nov. 20

2416 A669 20f multicolored .25 .25
2417 A669 30f multicolored .30 .25
2418 A669 50f multicolored .40 .25
2419 A669 $1 multicolored .65 .30
Nos. 2416-2419 (4) 1.60 1.05

Luo Ronghuan, Leader of People's Army, 90th Anniv. of Birth A670

1992, Nov. 26 Photo. ***Perf. 11x11½***

2420 A670 20f In dress uniform .35 .25
2421 A670 50f In field uniform .60 .35

Constitution of the People's Republic of China, 10th Anniv. — A671

1992, Dec. 4 ***Perf. 11½x11***
2422 A671 20f multicolored .70 .40

Liu Bocheng, Leader of People's Army, Birth Cent. A672

Designs: 20f, In dress uniform. 50f, During period of Long March, vert.

1992, Dec. 4 ***Perf. 11x11½, 11½x11***
2423 A672 20f multicolored .35 .25
2424 A672 50f multicolored .60 .30

Quingtian Stone Carvings — A673

10f, Spring. 20f, Chinese sorghum. 40f, Harvest. $2, Blooming flowers, full moon.

1992, Dec. 15 **Litho.** ***Perf. 12***
2425 A673 10f multicolored .25 .25
2426 A673 20f multicolored .25 .25
2427 A673 40f multicolored .30 .25
2428 A673 $2 multicolored .50 .30
Nos. 2425-2428 (4) 1.30 1.05

New Year 1993 (Year of the Rooster)
A674 A675

Photo. & Engr.

1993, Jan. 5 ***Perf. 11½***
2429 A674 20f red & black .50 .25
2430 A675 50f red, white & blk .70 .30

Madam Song Quingling, Chinese Communist Leader, Birth Cent. A676

1993, Jan. 20 **Photo.** ***Perf. 11x11½***
2431 A676 20f Portrait .35 .30
a. Perf. 11 5.00 5.00
2432 A676 $1 With children .65 .45
a. Perf. 11 5.00 5.00

No. 2431 exists imperf. Value, pair $140.

Camelus Bactrianus Ferus A677

1993, Feb. 20 **Litho.** ***Perf. 12***
2433 A677 20f shown .30 .25
2434 A677 $1.60 Adult, young .70 .35

8th Natl. People's Congress A678

1993, Mar. 15 **Litho.** ***Perf. 12***
2435 A678 20f multicolored .60 .25

A679

Game of Weiqi (Go): 20f, Painting of players of ancient times. $1.60, Game board showing Chinese-style position.

1993, Apr. 30 **Litho.** ***Perf. 12***
2436 A679 20f multi .30 .25
2437 A679 $1.60 multi .60 .40

A680

20th Cent. Revolutionaries: 20f, Li Jishen (1885-1959), horiz. 30f, Zhang Lan (1872-1955). 50f, Shen Junru (1875-1963). $1, Huang Yanpei (1878-1965), horiz.

1993, May 15 **Litho.** ***Perf. 12***
2438 A680 20f multi .30 .25
2439 A680 30f multi .30 .25
2440 A680 50f multi .35 .30
2441 A680 $1 multi .50 .35
Nos. 2438-2441 (4) 1.45 1.15

See Nos. 2483-2486.

A681

1993, May 9 **Photo.** ***Perf. 12***
2442 A681 50f Runner (2-1) .35 .25
2443 A681 50f Mascot (2-2) .35 .25
a. Pair, #2442-2443 .85 .75

First East Asian Games. No. 2443a printed in continuous design.

A682

Bamboo: 20f, Phyllostachys nigra. 30f, Phyllostachys aureosulcata spectabilis. 40f, Bambusa ventricosa. $1, Pseudosasa amabilis. $5, Phyllostachys heterocycla pubescens, horiz.

1993, June 15 **Litho.** ***Perf. 12½***
2444 A682 20f multi .30 .25
2445 A682 30f multi .40 .25
2446 A682 40f multi .50 .30
2447 A682 $1 multi .65 .35
Nos. 2444-2447 (4) 1.85 1.15

Souvenir Sheet

Photo.

Perf. 11

2448 A682 $5 multicolored 2.75 2.25
a. As #2448, added inscription 7.50 7.50

No. 2448 contains one 54x40mm stamp.

No. 2448a is inscribed in sheet margin with hologram of panda at left, Chinese inscription for CHINA '96 and PJZ-3 at bottom, and flag and tagged security emblem at right. Soaking in water may affect the hologram. Issued: May 10, 1996.

Literature Type of 1987

Outlaws of the Marsh: 20f, Chai Jin is trapped in Gaotang. 30f, Shi Qian steals armor. 50f, Xu Ning teaches how to use barbed lance. $2, Shi Xiu leaps from building to rescue condemned man from execution.

1993, Aug. 20 **Photo.** ***Perf. 11***
2449 A570 20f multi .35 .25
2450 A570 30f multi .40 .25
2451 A570 50f multi .50 .30
2452 A570 $2 multi .90 .40
Nos. 2449-2452 (4) 2.15 1.20

Changbai Mountains — A683

1993, Sept. 3 ***Perf. 11½x11***
2453 A683 20f Tianchi .25 .25
2454 A683 30f Alpine tundra .30 .25
2455 A683 50f Waterfall .35 .30
2456 A683 $1 Mixed forest .45 .35
Nos. 2453-2456 (4) 1.35 1.15

Seventh Natl. Games — A684

1993, Sept. 4
2457 A684 20f multicolored .75 .30

Longmen Grottoes — A685

Designs: 20f, Rocana, Ancestor Worshipping Temple. 30f, Sakyamuni, Middle Binyang Cave, Northern Wei. 50f, Maharaja, devas treading on Yaksha. $1, Bodhisattva at the left side of Rocana, Guyang Cave, Northern Wei. $5, Ancestor Worshipping Temple.

1993, Sept. 5 **Litho.** ***Perf. 12***
2458 A685 20f multi .30 .25
2459 A685 30f multi .45 .25
2460 A685 50f multi .65 .30
2461 A685 $1 multi 1.20 .45
Nos. 2458-2461 (4) 2.60 1.25

Souvenir Sheets

2462 A685 $5 multicolored *3.00* *2.25*
a. Overprinted in gold *7.50* *4.50*
b. Overprinted in silver *5.00* *3.50*

No. 2462 contains one 120x40mm stamp.

Overprint in margin of No. 2462a includes Chinese characters and "PJZ-1." Bangkok '95 (No. 2462a). No. 2462a sold for $6.

No. 2462a exists with serial number inscribed in sheet margin. The same number is inscribed on Thailand No. 1615b. These were sold as a set. Value for the two sheets with matching numbers, $26.50.

Sheet margin of No. 2462b contains silver lettering in Chinese for Thailand stamp exhibition and "PJZ-7." No. 2462b exists with serial number inscribed in sheet margin. Value: *$11.50.*

Issued: No. 2462a, 8/95; No. 2462b, 12/5/97.

Honey Bees A686

10f, Queen and two bees. 15f, Extracting nectar. 20f, Two Zhonghua bees. $2, Two bees in flight.

1993, Sept. 21 **Photo.** ***Perf. 11½***
2463 A686 10f multi .30 .25
a. Perf. 11x11½ 5.00 5.00
2464 A686 15f multi .30 .25
a. Perf. 11x11½ 5.00 5.00
2465 A686 20f multi .30 .25
2466 A686 $2 multi .70 .50
Nos. 2463-2466 (4) 1.60 1.25

Lacquerware — A687

1993, Oct. 20 **Photo.** ***Perf. 12***
2467 A687 20f Bowl .25 .25
2468 A687 30f Duck .30 .25
2469 A687 50f Round tray .35 .25
2470 A687 $1 Lidded box .40 .30
Nos. 2467-2470 (4) 1.30 1.05

Paintings, by Zheng Banqiao — A688

Designs: 10f, Bamboo, rock on fan. No. 2472, Orchard. No. 2473, Orchard, bamboo, rock on scroll, vert. 30f, Bamboo, rock on scroll, vert. 50f, Vase and chrysanthemums. $1.60, Chinese calligraphy on fan.

1993, Nov. 22 **Litho.** ***Perf. 12½***
2471 A688 10f multi (6-1) .25 .25
2472 A688 20f multi (6-2) .25 .25
2473 A688 20f multi (6-3) .25 .25
2474 A688 30f multi (6-4) .35 .30
2475 A688 50f multi (6-5) .35 .30
2476 A688 $1.60 multi (6-6) .55 .35
Nos. 2471-2476 (6) 2.00 1.70

No. 2476 exists imperf. Value, pair *$240.*

A689

1993, Nov. 26 ***Perf. 12***
2477 A689 20f multicolored .60 .30

Yang Hucheng, birth cent.

Mao Tse-tung (1893-1976) A690

$1, Portrait, seated.
$5, Standing by Great Wall.

1993 Photo. *Perf. 11½*
2478 A690 20f shown *1.15* .35
2479 A690 $1 multicolored *3.25* .55

Souvenir Sheet

2480 A690 $5 multicolored *4.00 3.00*
a. Overprinted in gold in margin *4.00 5.50*

No. 2480 contains one 48x58mm stamp. No. 2480a sold for $8.

No. 2478 exists imperf. Value, pair *$350.*

Issued: $5, 11/16; 20f, $1, 12/26; No. 2480a, 4/9/99.

New Year 1994 (Year of the Dog)
A691 A692

1994, Jan. 5 Photo. *Perf. 11½*
2481 A691 20f multi .50 .25
2482 A692 50f yel, red & blk .70 .30

20th Cent. Revolutionaries Type

Designs: No. 2483, Chen Qiyou, horiz. No. 2484, Chen Shutong. No. 2485, Ma Xulun. No. 2486, Xu Deheng, horiz.

1994, Feb. 25 Litho. *Perf. 12*
2483 A680 20f blk & brn (4-1) .30 .30
2484 A680 20f blk & brn (4-2) .30 .30
2485 A680 50f blk & brn (4-3) .35 .30
2486 A680 50f blk & brn (4-4) .35 .30
Nos. 2483-2486 (4) 1.30 1.20

Sturgeon — A693

20f, Huso dauricus. 40f, Acipenser sinensis. 50f, Psephurus gladius. $1, Acipenser dabryanus.

1994, Mar. 18 Litho. *Perf. 12½*
2487 A693 20f multi .30 .25
2488 A693 40f multi .35 .25
2489 A693 50f multi .40 .30
2490 A693 $1 multi .50 .40
Nos. 2487-2490 (4) 1.55 1.20

Afforestation Campaign — A694

Designs: 15f, Sand dunes. 20f, Flowers on sand dune. 40f, Forest of poplars. 50f, Oasis.

1994, Apr. 21 Litho. *Perf. 12*
2491 A694 15f multi .25 .25
2492 A694 20f multi .30 .25
2493 A694 40f multi .35 .25
2494 A694 50f multi .40 .30
Nos. 2491-2494 (4) 1.30 1.05

Teapots — A695

Style of teapot: 20f, Round, three-legged. 30f, Square, four-legged. 50f, Eight diagrams. $1, Round-eared.

1994, May 5 Litho. *Perf. 12*
2495 A695 20f multi .30 .25
2496 A695 30f multi .35 .25
2497 A695 50f multi .40 .30
2498 A695 $1 multi .75 .35
Nos. 2495-2498 (4) 1.80 1.15

Huangpu Military School, 70th Anniv. A696

1994, June 16 Litho. *Perf. 12*
2499 A696 20f multicolored .65 .25

Intl. Olympic Committee, Cent. A697

1994, June 23
2500 A697 20f multicolored .65 .25

Ancient Chinese Writers — A698

Designs: 20f, Tao Yuanming holding basket of flowers. 30f, Cao Zhi holding sword at side. 50f, Si Maqian writing on scroll. $1, Qu Yuan walking away with sword under arm.

1994, June 25
2501 A698 20f multi .25 .25
2502 A698 30f multi .30 .25
2503 A698 50f multi .35 .30
2504 A698 $1 multi .50 .35
Nos. 2501-2504 (4) 1.40 1.15

Wall paintings Type of 1987

10f, Flying Devata. 20f, Vimalakirti. 50f, Z. Yichao on the march. $1.60, Sorceresses.

1994, July 16 Photo. *Perf. 11*
2505 A557 10f multi .25 .25
2506 A557 20f multi .30 .25
2507 A557 50f multi .35 .30
2508 A557 $1.60 multi .55 .35
Nos. 2505-2508 (4) 1.45 1.15

Zhaojun's Marriage to Xiongnu — A699

1994, Aug. 25 Photo. *Perf. 11½x11*
2509 A699 20f Zhaojun .30 .25
2510 A699 50f Leaving home .60 .30

Souvenir Sheet

Perf. 11½

2511 A699 $3 Wedding 3.25 2.10

No. 2511 contains one 85x46mm stamp.

Sixth Far East and South Pacific Games for the Disabled, Beijing — A700

1994, Sept. 4 Litho. *Perf. 12*
2512 A700 20f multicolored .75 .25

Wulingyuan State Forest Park — A701

20f, South Gate to Heaven. 30f, Shentangwan. 50f, No. One Bridge. $1, Writing-brush Peak. $3, Picturesque corridor.

1994, Sept. 25 Litho. *Perf. 12*
2513 A701 20f multi, vert. .25 .25
2514 A701 30f multi, vert. .35 .25
2515 A701 50f multi .40 .35
2516 A701 $1 multi .60 .40
Nos. 2513-2516 (4) 1.60 1.25

Souvenir Sheet

Perf. 11½x12

2517 A701 $3 multicolored *3.25 1.75*

No. 2517 contains one 50x36mm stamp.

Wuyi Mountains — A702

Designs: a, Jade-girl Peak (4-1). b, Nine-bend Brook (4-2). c, Guadun Village (4-3). d, Alpine Grassland (4-4).

1994, Sept. 30 *Perf. 12*
2518 Strip of 4 1.90 1.50
a.-d. A702 50f any single .35 .25

No. 2518 exists imperf. Value, *$225.*

Listening to the Rapids, by Fu Baoshi (1904-65) A703

Paintings: No. 2520, Appreciating a Painting. No. 2521, Dadi's Thatched Hut. 40f, Playing the Ruan. 50f, At Hupao. $1, The Road to Shanyin.

1994, Oct. 5
2519 A703 10f multi (6-1) .25 .25
2520 A703 20f multi (6-2) .25 .25
2521 A703 20f multi (6-3) .25 .25
2522 A703 40f multi (6-4) .35 .30
2523 A703 50f multi (6-5) .45 .35
2524 A703 $1 multi (6-6) .80 .40
Nos. 2519-2524 (6) 2.35 1.80

Cranes — A704

20f, Whooping crane. $2, Black-necked crane.

Photo. & Engr.

1994, Oct. 9 *Perf. 11x11½*
2528 A704 20f multi .50 .25
2529 A704 $2 multi .85 .55

See US Nos. 2867-2868.

Souvenir Sheet

UPU, 120th Anniv. — A705

1994, Oct. 9 Litho. *Perf. 12*
2530 A705 $3 multicolored 2.50 1.30
a. Ovptd. in sheet margin 3.50 2.00

No. 2530a ovptd. in sheet margin with UPU hologram, vertical Chinese inscription in gold. Issued: July 18, 1996.

Gorges of Yangtze River — A706

Designs: 10f, Baidicheng. No. 2532, Qutang Gorge. No. 2533, Wuxia Gorge. 30f, Goddess Peak. 50f, Xiling Gorge. $1, Qu Yuan Memorial Temple.

$5, The Three Gorges.

1994, Nov. 4 Photo. *Perf. 12*
2531 A706 10f multi (6-1) .30 .25
2532 A706 20f multi (6-2) .30 .25
2533 A706 20f multi (6-3) .30 .25
2534 A706 30f multi (6-4) .30 .25
2535 A706 50f multi (6-5) .35 .30
2536 A706 $1 multi (6-6) .40 .35
Nos. 2531-2536 (6) 1.95 1.65

Souvenir Sheet

Perf. 11½x11

2537 A706 $5 multicolored 3.00 2.00

No. 2537 contains one 116x35mm stamp.

Souvenir Sheet

All-China Philatelic Federation, 4th Congress — A707

1994, Nov. 17 Litho. *Perf. 11*
2538 A707 $3 multicolored 2.00 1.30

Literature Type of 1988

Romance of the Three Kingdoms by Luo Guanzhong: 20f, Composing a poem with a lance in hands. 30f, Liu Bei's marriage, vert. 50f, Overwhelming Xiaoyaojin with prowess. $1, Campsites burned, vert.
$5, Fierce battle at Chibi.

Perf. 11½x11, 11x11½
1994, Nov. 24 Photo.
2539 A587 20f multicolored .25 .25
2540 A587 30f multicolored .30 .25
2541 A587 50f multicolored .35 .30
2542 A587 $1 multicolored .40 .35
Nos. 2539-2542 (4) 1.30 1.15

Souvenir Sheet
Perf. 11
2543 A587 $5 multicolored 4.50 2.60

No. 2543 contains one 158x36mm stamp.

Special Economic Zones A708

Designs: a, Shenzhen (5-1). b, Zhuhai (5-2). c, Shantou (5-3). d, Xiamen (5-4). e, Hainan (5-4).

1994, Dec. 10 Litho. *Perf. 12*
2544 A708 50f Strip of 5, #a.-e. 2.40 *1.90*

Pagodas of Ancient China — A709

Designs: No. 2545, Dayan Pagoda, Cien Temple. No. 2546, Zhenguo Pagoda, Kaiyuan Temple. 50f, Liuhe Pagoda, Kaihua Temple. $2, Youguo Temple.

Photo. & Engr.
1994, Dec. 15 *Perf. 11½x11*
2545 20f tan, brn & blk (4-1) .30 .25
2546 20f tan, brn & blk (4-2) .35 .25
2547 50f tan, brn & blk (4-3) .40 .25
2548 $2 tan, brn & blk (4-4) .75 .30
a. Souvenir sheet of 4, #2545-2548 *4.50 3.00*
Nos. 2545-2548 (4) 1.80 1.05

No. 2548a sold for $5.

New Year 1995 (Year of the Boar)
A711 A712

Photo. & Engr.
1995, Jan. 5 *Perf. 11½*
2550 A711 20f multicolored .70 .25
2551 A712 50f multicolored .80 .30

Winter Scenes A713

Designs: 20f, Snow willows, Cold River. 50f, Ice & snow on jade trees, vert.

1995, Jan. 12 Litho. *Perf. 12*
2552 A713 20f multicolored .35 .25
2553 A713 50f multicolored .65 .30

Mt. Dinghushan — A714

Designs: 15f, Topographical map. No. 2555, Stream flowing down from mountain. No. 2556, Buildings on mountain side. $2.30, Silver pheasants.

1995, Feb. 15 Litho. *Perf. 12½*
2554 A714 15f multi (4-1) .25 .25
2555 A714 20f multi (4-2) .35 .30
2556 A714 20f multi (4-3) .35 .30
2557 A714 $2.30 multi (4-4) 1.00 .35
Nos. 2554-2557 (4) 1.95 1.20

World Summit for Social Development, Copenhagen — A715

1995, Mar. 6 Photo. *Perf. 11x11½*
2558 A715 20f multicolored 2.50 .40

Owls — A716

1995, Mar. 22 Photo. *Perf. 11½*
2559 A716 10f Eagle owl .25 .25
2560 A716 20f Long-eared owl .30 .25
2561 A716 50f Snowy owl .40 .35
2562 A716 $1 Grass owl .75 .40
Nos. 2559-2562 (4) 1.70 1.25

Sweet Osmanthus A717

No. 2563, Thunbergii (4-1). No. 2564, Latifolius (4-2). No. 2565, Aurantiacus (4-3). No. 2566, Semperflorens (4-4).

1995, Apr. 14 Litho. *Perf. 12*
2563 A717 20f multicolored .25 .25
2564 A717 20f multicolored .25 .25
2565 A717 50f multicolored .35 .30
2566 A717 $1 multicolored .60 .40
Nos. 2563-2566 (4) 1.45 1.20

A souvenir sheet of 4, Nos. 2563-2566, exists, both perf and imperf. Value, perf $4.25, imperf $85.

43rd World Table Tennis Championships, Tianjin — A718

1995, May 1 Litho. *Perf. 12*
2567 A718 20f Athlete .35 .25
2568 A718 50f Arena .55 .30
a. Souv. sheet of 2, #2567-2568 *19.00 9.25*

No. 2568a sold for $7. Issued 8/14/95.

Spring Outing — A719

Designs: No. 2569, Group riding horses. No. 2570, Three riding horses.

1995, May 23 Litho. *Perf. 12*
2569 A719 50f multi (2-1) .30 .30
2570 A719 50f multi (2-2) .70 .30
a. Pair, #2569-2570 2.50 1.00

No. 2570a is a continuous design.

Shadow Play — A720

Various costumed characters.

1995, June 8 Photo. *Perf. 12x12½*
2571 A720 20f multi (4-1) .25 .25
2572 A720 40f multi (4-2) .25 .25
2573 A720 50f multi (4-3) .35 .30
2574 A720 50f multi (4-4) .35 .30
Nos. 2571-2574 (4) 1.20 1.10

Highway Interchanges, Beijing — A721

1995, June 20 Photo. *Perf. 11½x11*
2575 A721 20f Siyuan .25 .25
2576 A721 30f Tianningsi .30 .25
2577 A721 50f Yuting .35 .25
2578 A721 $1 Anhui .50 .30
Nos. 2575-2578 (4) 1.40 1.05

Diplomatic Relations Between China & Thailand, 20th Anniv. — A722

No. 2579, Elephants walking right into water. No. 2580, Elephants walking left into water.

1995, July 1
2579 $1 multi (2-1) .45 .30
2580 $1 multi (2-2) .45 .30
a. A722 Pair, #2579-2580 1.25 .85

Taihu Lake A723

Lake scenes: No. 2581, Yellow trees. No. 2582, Structures on bank, boats, hills. No. 2583, Structures across inlet. No. 2584, Red trees, home. 230f, Winter scene. 500f, Houses on cliff, lighthouse.

1995, July 20 Photo. *Perf. 11½*
2581 A723 20f multi (5-1) .25 .25
2582 A723 20f multi (5-2) .25 .25
2583 A723 50f multi (5-3) .35 .30
2584 A723 50f multi (5-4) .35 .30
2585 A723 230f multi (5-5) .85 .70
Nos. 2581-2585 (5) 2.05 1.80

Souvenir Sheet
Perf. 11
2586 A723 500f multicolored 3.00 1.90
a. Ovptd. in sheet margin 7.00 4.75

No. 2586 contains one 90x60mm stamp with continuing design.

No. 2586a issued 3/24/97. Gold overprint in sheet margin contains an emblem, Chinese inscription saying "Hong Kong Returns to China" and "PJZ-5."

Posts of Ancient China A724

1995, Aug. 17 Photo. *Perf. 12*
2587 A724 20f Yucheng .30 .25
2588 A724 50f Jimingshan .50 .30

Shaolin Temple, 1500th Anniv. A725

No. 2589, Entrance (4-1). No. 2590, Pagoda Forest (4-2). No. 2591, Martial arts (4-3). No. 2592, Historical rescue (4-4).

1995, Aug. 30
2589 A725 20f multicolored .40 .25
2590 A725 20f multicolored .40 .25
2591 A725 50f multicolored .50 .25
2592 A725 100f multicolored 1.00 .45
Nos. 2589-2592 (4) 2.30 1.20

Cultural Relics of Tibet — A726

20f, Jar. 30f, Casque. 50f, Celestial motion chart. 100f, Pearl mandala.

1995, Sept. 1
2593 A726 20f multicolored .25 .25
2594 A726 30f multicolored .30 .25
2595 A726 50f multicolored .35 .25
2596 A726 100f multicolored .40 .30
Nos. 2593-2596 (4) 1.30 1.05

Wildlife A727

1995, Sept. 1 *Perf. 11x11½*
2597 A727 20f Koalas .30 .25
2598 A727 $2.90 Pandas 1.10 .75

See Australia No. 1459.

End of World War II, 50th Anniv. A728

10f, July 7th event. No. 2600, Victory at Taier village. No. 2601, Soldier, hundred-regiment battle. No. 2602, Guerrilla war. No. 2603, Troops on parade, joining forces at Mangyo. 60f, Aircraft donated by Chinese living abroad. No. 2605, Taiwan recovered. No. 2606, Japanese surrender aboard USS Missouri.

1995, Sept. 3
2599 A728 10f multi (8-1) .25 .25
2600 A728 20f multi (8-2) .25 .25
2601 A728 20f multi (8-3) .25 .25
2602 A728 50f multi (8-4) .30 .25
2603 A728 50f multi (8-5) .30 .25
2604 A728 60f multi (8-6) .35 .30
2605 A728 100f multi (8-7) .50 .40
2606 A728 100f multi (8-8) .50 .40
Nos. 2599-2606 (8) 2.70 2.35

4th World Conference on Women, Beijing A729

Symbols of: 15f, Equality. 20f, Development. 50f, Peace. 60f, Friendship.

1995, Sept. 4 *Perf. 12*
2607 A729 15f multi .25 .25
2608 A729 20f multi .30 .25
2609 A729 50f multi .35 .25
2610 A729 60f multi .40 .30
Nos. 2607-2610 (4) 1.30 1.05

The Great Wall — A730

China Post No. R28

230f, Shanhaiguan Pass. 290f, Jinshanling.

1995, Oct. 5 **Photo.** *Perf. 12½*
2611 A730 60f shown .30 .25
2612 A730 230f multicolored .85 .30
2613 A730 290f multicolored 1.05 .35
Nos. 2611-2613 (3) 2.20 .90

See Nos. 2755, 2792-2795, 2907-2910, 2934-2941, 2952-2955.

Jiuhua Mountains A731

10f, Sunrise at Peak Terrace, horiz. No. 2615, Hall of Meditation. No. 2616, Temple of Bodhisattva, horiz. No. 2617, Sunset at Zhiyuan, horiz. No. 2618, Great Rock. No. 2619, Phoenix Pine, horiz.

1995, Oct. 9 *Perf. 12*
2614 A731 10f multi (6-1) .25 .25
2615 A731 20f multi (6-2) .25 .25
2616 A731 20f multi (6-3) .25 .25
2617 A731 50f multi (6-4) .35 .30
2618 A731 50f multi (6-5) .35 .30
2619 A731 290f multi (6-6) 1.00 .45
Nos. 2614-2619 (6) 2.45 1.80

Motion Pictures, Cent. A732

Projector and: 20f, Black and white film. 50f, Color film.

1995, Oct. 13
2620 A732 20f blue & black .35 .25
2621 A732 50f multicolored .65 .30

A733

UN, 50th Anniv. — A733a

Designs: 20f, UN flag, Headquarters. 50f, Stylized flags, UN emblem, "50."

1995, Oct. 24 **Litho.**
2622 A733 20f multi .35 .25
2623 A733a 50f multi .90 .30

Sanqing Mountains — A734

No. 2624, Good Fortune Land. No. 2625, Sichun Goddess. 50f, Bodhisattva Enjoys Music. 100f, Huge Boa out of Mountain.

1995, Nov. 1 **Photo.** *Perf. 12*
2624 A734 20f multi (4-1) .25 .25
2625 A734 20f multi (4-2) .25 .25
2626 A734 50f multi, vert. (4-3) .30 .25
2627 A734 100f multi, vert. (4-4) .45 .40
Nos. 2624-2627 (4) 1.25 1.15

Mt. Hengshan Type of 1990

Songshan Mountains: 20f, Ancient Temple of Mount Song. 50f, Moon waiting at Songmen Gate. 60f, Shaolin Temple. $1, Panorama view of Mt. Song.

Photo. & Engr.

1995, Nov. 10 *Perf. 11*
2628 A631 20f multi .25 .25
2629 A631 50f multi .25 .25
2630 A631 60f multi .30 .30
2631 A631 $1 multi .70 .40
Nos. 2628-2631 (4) 1.50 1.20

Scenic Views of Hong Kong — A735

Designs: 20f, Victoria Harbor. 50f, Central Plaza at night. 60f, Hong Kong Cultural Center. 290f, Repulse Bay.

1995, Nov. 28 **Photo.** *Perf. 12*
2632 A735 20f multi .25 .25
2633 A735 50f multi .25 .25
2634 A735 60f multi .30 .30
2635 A735 290f multi .95 .40
Nos. 2632-2635 (4) 1.75 1.20

No. 2635 exists imperf. Value, pair *$140.*

Sun Zi's Art of War — A736

Drawings depicting: No. 2637, Discussing strategy. 30f, Capturing Ying. 50f, Battle at Ailing. 100f, Meeting of sovereigns, Huangchi.

1995, Dec. 4 *Perf. 11x11½*
2636 A736 20f multi (5-1) .25 .25
2637 A736 20f multi (5-2) .25 .25
2638 A736 30f multi (5-3) .30 .25
2639 A736 50f multi (5-4) .35 .30
2640 A736 100f multi (5-5) .70 .45
Nos. 2636-2640 (5) 1.85 1.50

New Year 1996 (Year of the Rat)
A737 A738

Photo. & Engr.

1996, Jan. 5 *Perf. 11½*
2641 A737 20f multi .60 .25
2642 A738 50f multi 1.40 .35

3rd Asian Winter Games A739

No. 2643, Speed skating. No. 2644, Ice hockey. No. 2645, Figure skating. No. 2646, Skiing.

1996, Feb. 4 **Litho.** *Perf. 12*
2643 A739 50f multi (4-1) .25 .25
2644 A739 50f multi (4-2) .25 .25
2645 A739 50f multi (4-3) .25 .25
2646 A739 50f multi (4-4) .25 .25
a. Block of 4, #2643-2646 1.40 1.00

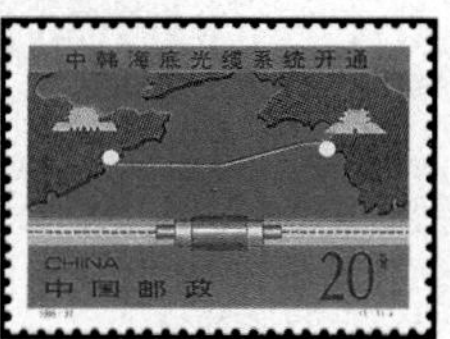

China/Korea Submarine Fiber Optic Cable System — A740

1996, Feb. 8 **Litho.** *Perf. 12*
2647 A740 20f multicolored .60 .25

First day covers are dated 12/15/95.
See Korea No. 1863.

Shenyang Imperial Palace — A741

Designs: No. 2648, Buildings, denomination UL. No. 2649, Buildings, denomination LR.

1996, Mar. 18 **Photo.** *Perf. 12*
2648 A741 50f multi (2-1) .35 .25
2649 A741 50f multi (2-2) .35 .25
a. Pair, Nos. 2648-2649 1.00 .75

China Post, Cent. A742

Post Office buildings: 10f, Tianjin Posts Bureau. 20f, Beijing Postal Administration. 50f, Directorate of Posts of China. 100f, Beijing postal hub.
500f, China #78-85.

1996, Mar. 20 *Perf. 11½*
2650 A742 10f multi .25 .25
2651 A742 20f multi .35 .25
2652 A742 50f multi .35 .30
2653 A742 100f multi .45 .40
Nos. 2650-2653 (4) 1.40 1.20

Souvenir Sheet

Perf. 11

2654 A742 500f multicolored *5.00* 3.25

No. 2654 contains one 89x59mm stamp.
No. 2654 exists with a red overprint in the bottom margin. Value, $15.

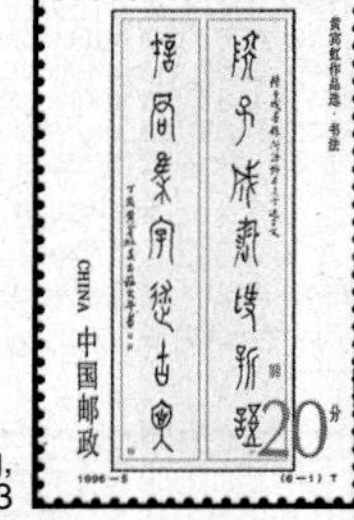

Huang Binhong, Artist — A743

No. 2655, Calligraphy. No. 2656, Landscape. 40f, Qingcheng Mts. No. 2658, View from Xiing. No. 2659, Colored landscape. 230f, Flowers.

1996, Apr. 5 *Perf. 11½*
2655 A743 20f multi (6-1) .25 .25
2656 A743 20f multi (6-2) .25 .25
2657 A743 40f multi (6-3) .40 .30
2658 A743 50f multi (6-4) .45 .30
2659 A743 50f multi (6-5) .45 .35
2660 A743 230f multi (6-6) 1.75 .50
Nos. 2655-2660 (6) 3.55 1.95

Aircraft — A744

1996, Apr. 17 *Perf. 12*
2661 A744 20f F-8 (4-1) .35 .25
2662 A744 50f A-5 (4-2) .55 .30
2663 A744 50f Yun-7 (4-3) .55 .30
2664 A744 100f Yun-12 (4-4) .90 .40
Nos. 2661-2664 (4) 2.35 1.25

Potted Landscapes — A745

Nos. 2665-2666, Lijing & Divine Peak. Nos. 2667-2668, Melting Snow & Eagle Rock. Nos. 2668-2669, Manch & Rosy Clouds.

1996, Apr. 18
2665 A745 20f multi (6-1) .25 .25
2666 A745 20f multi (6-2) .25 .25
a. Pair, #2665-2666 .60 .50
2667 A745 50f multi (6-3) .25 .25
2668 A745 50f multi (6-4) .25 .25
a. Pair, #2667-2668 .80 .60
2669 A745 100f multi (6-5) .35 .30
2670 A745 100f multi (6-6) .35 .30
a. Pair, #2669-2670 1.25 1.00
Nos. 2665-2670 (6) 1.70 1.60

Iron Trees — A746

No. 2671, Cycas revoluta. No. 2672, Cycas panzhihuaensis. 50f, Cycas pectinata. 230f, Cycas multipinnata.

1996, May 2 Litho. *Perf. 12*

2671 A746 20f multi (4-1) .30 .25
2672 A746 20f multi (4-2) .30 .25
2673 A746 50f multi (4-3) .30 .25
2674 A746 230f multi (4-4) .70 .30
Nos. 2671-2674 (4) 1.60 1.05

Nos. 2671-2674 exist imperf. Value, set of pairs *$325.*

China-San Marino Relations, 25th Anniv. A747

No. 2675, Great Wall of China (2-1). No. 2676, Mt. Titano (2-2).

1996, May 6 Photo. *Perf. 12*

2675 A747 100f multi .40 .30
2676 A747 100f multi .40 .30
a. Pair, #2675-2676 1.20 .80

See San Marino Nos. 1356-1357.

Artifacts from Hemudu Ruins — A748

Designs: 20f, Agricultural tool. 50f, Pile to support building. 100f, Paddles for boats. 230f, Bird and sun carved in wood.

1996, May 12 Litho. *Perf. 12*

2677 A748 20f multi .25 .25
2678 A748 50f multi .30 .25
2679 A748 100f multi .35 .30
2680 A748 230f multi .70 .40
Nos. 2677-2680 (4) 1.60 1.20

Souvenir Sheet

CHINA '96, 9th Asian Intl. Philatelic Exhibition — A749

1996, May 18 *Perf. 11½x12*

2681 A749 500f multicolored 8.00 3.00
a. Overprinted in gold 7.00 5.00

No. 2681 exists imperf. Value, $20.

Overprint in margin of No. 2681a includes Chinese characters, Shanghai '97 exhibition emblem, and "PJZ-6." Issued in 1998.

Children's Activities A750

Designs: 20f, Singing, playing musical instruments. 30f, Pushing child in wheelchair, holding umbrella. 50f, Placing flag on South Pole, penguins. 100f, Planting tree.

1996, June 1 *Perf. 12*

2682 A750 20f multi .25 .25
2683 A750 30f multi .30 .25
2684 A750 50f multi .35 .25
2685 A750 100f multi .45 .30
Nos. 2682-2685 (4) 1.35 1.05

Modern Olympic Games, Cent. — A751

1996, June 23 Photo. *Perf. 12*

2686 A751 20f multicolored 1.00 .25

Protection of Land A752

Stylized designs representing: 20f, Making use of land. 50f, Protection of farmland.

1996, June 25 *Perf. 11x11½*

2687 A752 20f multi .40 .25
2688 A752 50f multi .60 .30

A753

Military Terraces — A754

1996, July 9 Litho. *Perf. 12*

2689 A753 20f multi .35 .25
2690 A754 50f multi .50 .30

Vehicles — A755

No. 2691, Red Flag, 4-door limousine. No. 2692, Dongfeng, stake truck. 50f, Jiefang, 4-door truck. 100f, Beijing, canvas-topped jeep.

1996, July 15 Photo. *Perf. 12*

2691 A755 20f multi (4-1) .25 .25
2692 A755 20f multi (4-2) .25 .25
2693 A755 50f multi (4-3) .35 .25
2694 A755 100f multi (4-4) .50 .35
Nos. 2691-2694 (4) 1.35 1.10

New Tangshan Built Following 1976 Earthquake — A756

No. 2695, Farm cottages (4-1). No. 2696, Factory (4-2). No. 2697, Street (4-3). No. 2698, Port (4-4).

1996, July 28 *Perf. 11½*

2695 A756 20f multi .25 .25
2696 A756 50f multi .30 .25
2697 A756 50f multi .30 .25
2698 A756 100f multi .40 .30
Nos. 2695-2698 (4) 1.25 1.05

30th Intl. Geological Conference — A757

1996, Aug. 4 Litho. *Perf. 12*

2699 A757 20f multicolored .70 .30

Tianchi Lake, Tianshan Mountains — A758

20f, High mountain lake. No. 2701, Splendid Waterfalls. No. 2702, Snow-capped peaks. 100f, Lakeside scenery.

1996, Aug. 8

2700 A758 20f multi (4-1) .25 .25
2701 A758 50f multi, vert. (4-2) .35 .25
2702 A758 50f multi, vert. (4-3) .35 .25
2703 A758 100f multi (4-4) .45 .30
Nos. 2700-2703 (4) 1.40 1.05

Wall Paintings Type of 1987

10f, Illustration of Mount Wutai. 20f, King of Khotan, vert. 50f, Savior Avalokitesvara. 100f, Worshipping Bodhisattvas.
$5, Thousand Arm Avalokitesvara.

1996, Aug. 15 Photo. *Perf. 11*

2704 A557 10f multi, vert. .30 .25
2705 A557 20f multi .30 .25
2706 A557 50f multi .35 .30
2707 A557 100f multi .55 .40
Nos. 2704-2707 (4) 1.50 1.20

Souvenir Sheet

2708 A557 500f multicolored 5.50 2.60

No. 2708 contains one 46x102mm stamp.

Mausoleums of Western Xia — A759

Designs: No. 2709: Mausoleum terrace. No. 2710, Ornament on Divine Gate. 50f, Stele. 100f, Stele remnant, Shouling.

1996, Aug. 22 Photo. *Perf. 11½*

2709 A759 20f multi (4-1) .25 .25
2710 A759 20f multi (4-2) .25 .25
2711 A759 50f multi (4-3) .30 .25
2712 A759 100f multi (4-4) .45 .30
Nos. 2709-2712 (4) 1.25 1.05

Railways in China — A760

Designs: 15f, Datong-Quinhuangdao Railway. 20f, Lanzhou-Xinjiang Two-Track Railway. 50f, Beijing-Kowloon Railway. 100f, Beijing Western Railway Station

1996, Sept. 1

2713 A760 15f multi .35 .25
2714 A760 20f multi .50 .25
2715 A760 50f multi .50 .30
2716 A760 100f multi 1.05 .55
Nos. 2713-2716 (4) 2.40 1.35

A761

Chinese Archives: No. 2717, Archives on tortoise shells, Shang Dynasty. No. 2718, Archives on wood slips, Han Dynasty. 50f, Iron scrolls, Ming Dynasty. 100f, Books of Ch'ing Dynasty.

1996, Sept. 2 Litho. *Perf. 12*

2717 A761 20f multi (4-1) .40 .25
2718 A761 20f multi (4-2) .40 .25
2719 A761 50f multi (4-3) .55 .30
2720 A761 100f multi (4-4) 1.15 .45
Nos. 2717-2720 (4) 2.50 1.25

A762

1996, Sept. 10 *Perf. 12*

2721 A762 20f Portrait .45 .25
2722 A762 50f In uniform .75 .35

Ye Ting (1896-1946), co-founder of Chinese People's Liberation Army.

96th Conference of Inter-Parliamentary Union — A763

1996, Sept. 16 *Perf. 11½*

2723 A763 20f multi .75 .25

Shanghai — A764

No. 2724, Communication (6-1). No. 2725, Lujiazui (6-2). No. 2726, Jinqiao (6-3). No. 2727, Zhanghiang (6-4). No. 2728, Waigaoqiao (6-5). No. 2729, Residential (6-6). No. 2730, Panoramic view.

Photo. & Engr.

1996, Sept. 21 *Perf. 11½*

2724 A764 10f multicolored .25 .25
2725 A764 20f multicolored .35 .25
2726 A764 20f multicolored .40 .25
2727 A764 50f multicolored .45 .30
2728 A764 60f multicolored .50 .30
2729 A764 100f multicolored .90 .35
Nos. 2724-2729 (6) 2.85 1.70

Souvenir Sheet

Perf. 11

2730 A764 500f multicolored 7.50 4.25
a. Margin ovptd. 12.00 6.50

No. 2730 contains one 90x45mm stamp.
No. 2730a issued 10/20/01. It is inscribed in margin with multicolored emblems and gold "PJZ-14," "APEC CHINA 2001," and Chinese characters.

Space Navigation — A765

1996, Oct. 7 **Litho.** *Perf. 12*

2731 A765 20f Rocket lift-off .45 .25
2732 A765 100f Satellite in orbit .65 .35

Singapore Waterfront — A766

Design: 290f, Panmen, Suzhou, China.

1996, Oct. 9 **Photo.** *Perf. 11½*

2733 A766 20f multi .30 .25
2734 A766 290f multi 1.00 .40

See Singapore Nos. 768-769.

Victory of Long March, 60th Anniv. — A767

Designs: 20f, Red Army through Marshland. 50f, Reunion of Three Armies.

1996, Oct. 22 **Litho.** *Perf. 12*

2735 A767 20f multi .50 .30
2736 A767 50f multi 1.00 .50

Colored Sculpture of Tianjin A768

Designs: 20f, The Two Immortals. No. 2738, Making Candy. No. 2739, Returning from Fishing. 100f, Xi Chun in Painting.

1996, Nov. 5 **Photo.** *Perf. 11½*

2737 A768 20f multi (4-1) .25 .25
2738 A768 50f multi (4-2) .30 .25
2739 A768 50f multi (4-3) .30 .25
2740 A768 100f multi (4-4) .35 .30
Nos. 2737-2740 (4) 1.20 1.05

Hong Kong A769

20f, Bank of China. 40f, Container Terminal. 60f, Kai Tak Airport. 290f, Stock Exchange.

1996, Dec. 19 **Litho.** *Perf. 12*

2741 A769 20f multi (4-1) .25 .25
2742 A769 40f multi (4-2) .25 .25
2743 A769 60f multi (4-3) .35 .25
2744 A769 290f multi (4-4) 1.00 .35
Nos. 2741-2744 (4) 1.85 1.10

Nos. 2741-2744 exist imperf. Value, set of pairs *$700.*

Visit China — A770

1997, Jan. 1

2745 A770 50f multi 1.00 .25

A771

1997, Jan. 1

2746 A771 50f multicolored .90 .25

First natl. agricultural census.

New Year 1997 (Year of the Ox)
A772 A773

Photo. & Engr.

1997, Jan. 5 *Perf. 11½*

2747 A772 50f multi (2-2) .60 .25
2748 A773 150f multi (2-1) 1.40 .50

Paintings by Pan Tianshou (1897-1971) A774

No. 2749, Pines on the Yellow Mountain. No. 2750, Rosy Clouds of Dawn. No. 2751, Clearing Up after Mould Rains. No. 2752, Chrysanthemum and Bamboo. No. 2753, Sleeping Cat. No. 2754, A Corner of Lingyan Brook.

1997, Mar. 14 **Photo.** *Perf. 11½*

2749 A774 50f multi (6-1) .25 .25
2750 A774 50f multi (6-2) .25 .25
2751 A774 100f multi (6-3) .50 .35
2752 A774 100f multi (6-4) .50 .35
2753 A774 150f multi (6-5) .95 .40
2754 A774 150f multi (6-6) .95 .40
Nos. 2749-2754 (6) 3.40 2.00

Great Wall Type of 1995
China Post No. R29

1997, Apr. 1 **Photo.** *Perf. 13x12*

2755 A730 50f multicolored .25 .25

A776

Tea: No. 2756, People forming circle beside tea tree. No. 2757, Statue of tea sage. No. 2758, Tea utensils, horiz. No. 2759, Painting of tea party, horiz.

1997, Apr. 8 **Litho.** *Perf. 12*

2756 A776 50f multi (4-1) .50 .25
2757 A776 50f multi (4-2) .50 .25
2758 A776 150f multi (4-3) .90 .40
2759 A776 150f multi (4-4) .90 .40
Nos. 2756-2759 (4) 2.80 1.30

A777

Stylized designs depicting: No. 2760, Celebration. No. 2761, Unity (group of people), horiz. 200f, Advance (horses running), horiz.

1997, May 1 **Photo.** *Perf. 11½*

2760 A777 50f multi (3-1) .30 .25
2761 A777 50f multi (3-2) .30 .25
2762 A777 200f multi (3-3) .85 .35
Nos. 2760-2762 (3) 1.45 .85

Inner Mongolia Autonomous Region, 50th anniv.

Pheasants A778

Designs: 50f, Chinese copper pheasant. 540f, Common pheasant.

Litho. & Engr.

1997, May 9 *Perf. 11½x11*

2763 A778 50f multi (2-1) .25 .25
2764 A778 540f multi (2-2) 1.40 1.00

See Sweden Nos. 2225-2226.

Dong Architecture A779

No. 2765, Zengchong Drum Tower. No. 2766, Bai'er Drum Tower. No. 2767, Wind and Rain Bridge over the River, horiz. No. 2768, Wind and Rain Bridge in the Field, horiz.

1997, June 2 **Litho.** *Perf. 12*

2765 A779 50f multi (4-1) .25 .25
2766 A779 50f multi (4-2) .25 .25
a. Pair, #2765-2766 .70 .60
2767 A779 150f multi (4-3) .40 .25
2768 A779 150f multi (4-4) .40 .25
a. Pair, #2767-2768 1.15 1.10
Nos. 2765-2768 (4) 1.30 1.00

Maiji Grottoes — A780

Statues: No. 2769, Buddha and Xieshi Bodhisattva. No. 2770, Xieshi Bodhisattva and his disciple. 100f, Maid. No. 2772, Buddha. No. 2773, Xieshi Bodhisattva. 200f, Provider.

1997, June 13

2769 A780 50f multi (6-1) .25 .25
2770 A780 50f multi (6-2) .25 .25
2771 A780 100f multi (6-3) .35 .25
2772 A780 150f multi (6-4) .45 .30
2773 A780 150f multi (6-5) .45 .30
2774 A780 200f multi (6-6) .60 .35
Nos. 2769-2774 (6) 2.35 1.70

A780a

A781

Texts surrounded by flowers: 50f, Sino-British Joint Declaration. 150f, Basic Law of the Hong Kong Special Adminstrative Region. 800f, Deng Xiaoping.

1997, July 1 **Litho.** *Perf. 12*

2774A A780a 50f multi (2-1) .30 .25
2774B A780a 150f multi (2-2) .80 .50

Souvenir Sheets

2774C A781 800f multi 3.50 2.40
d. Overprinted in sheet margin 5.00 3.25

Litho. (stamp) & Embossed (margin)

Perf. 13½

2775 A781 $50 gold & multi *30.00 30.00*
a. Overprinted in margin *37.50 37.50*

Deng Xiaoping (1904-97), return of Hong Kong to China.
No. 2775 was released in special souvenir folder.
No. 2744C exists imperf. Value, *$500.*
No. 2774Cd contains gold Chinese inscription for Hong Kong's Return Exhibition Tour, emblem, and "PJZ-8" in sheet margin. Issued: 6/19/98.
Overprint in margin on No. 2775a is Chinese inscription, "2000-1" and "(2-1)J." Issued: 1/1/00.

Ancient Temples of Wutai Mountain — A782

Designs: 40f, Taihuai Township. No. 2777, Nanchan Temple. No. 2778, Foguang Temple.

No. 2779, Xiantong Temple. No. 2780, Bodhisattva Summit. 200f, Zhenhai Temple.

1997, July 26 Litho. *Perf. 12*

2776	A782	40f multi (6-1)	.25	.25
2777	A782	50f multi (6-2)	.30	.25
2778	A782	50f multi (6-3)	.30	.25
2779	A782	150f multi (6-4)	.50	.30
2780	A782	150f multi (6-5)	.50	.30
2781	A782	200f multi (6-6)	.60	.35
		Nos. 2776-2781 (6)	2.45	1.70

Chinese People's Liberation Army, 70th Anniv. — A783

No. 2782, Land Force. No. 2783, Naval Force. No. 2784, Air Force. No. 2785, Strategic Missile Troops. 200f, Joint military maneuvers.

1997, Aug. 1

2782	A783	50f multi (5-1)	.45	.25
2783	A783	50f multi (5-2)	.45	.25
2784	A783	50f multi (5-3)	.45	.25
2785	A783	50f multi (5-4)	.45	.25
2786	A783	200f multi (5-5)	1.90	.75
		Nos. 2782-2786 (5)	3.70	1.75

Shoushan Stone Carvings A784

Designs: No. 2787, "Rhythm of Autumn," vert. No. 2788, "Rhinoceros under Sunshine,", vert. No. 2789, "Jade's Fragrance," (basket of fruit). No. 2790, "Drunken Joy."
800f, Qianlong's Chain Seals.

1997, Aug. 17 Litho. *Perf. 12*

2787	A784	50f multi (4-1)	.30	.25
2788	A784	50f multi (4-2)	.30	.25
2789	A784	150f multi (4-3)	.50	.30
2790	A784	150f multi (4-4)	.50	.30
		Nos. 2787-2790 (4)	1.60	1.10

Souvenir Sheet

2791	A784	800f multi	4.00	3.00

No. 2791 contains one 60x60mm stamp.

Great Wall Type of 1995
China Post No. R29

Gates: 30f, Huangyaguan. 100f, Badaling. 150f, Joyongguan. 200f, Zijingguan.

1997, Sept. 1 Photo. *Perf. 13x12*

2792	A730	30f yellow & black	.30	.45
2793	A730	100f vermilion & black	.50	.45
2794	A730	150f green & black	.70	.45
2795	A730	200f red & black	.85	.50
		Nos. 2792-2795 (4)	2.35	1.85

Communist Party of China, 15th Natl. Congress A785

1997, Sept. 12 Litho. *Perf. 12*

2796	A785	50f multicolored	1.00	.30

A786

No. 2797, China Rose. No. 2798, New Zealand Monthly Rose.

1997, Oct. 9 Photo. *Perf. 11½*

2797	150f multi (2-1)	.50	.30
2798	150f multi (2-2)	.50	.30
a.	A786 Pair, #2797-2798	1.50	1.40

See New Zealand Nos. 1469-1470.

Eighth Natl. Games A788

1997, Oct. 12 Litho. *Perf. 12*

2799	A788	50f Athletes (2-1)	.30	.25
2800	A788	150f Stadium)2-2)	.60	.30
a.		Souv. sheet, #2799-2800	4.00	2.60

No. 2800a sold for 300f.

Temple of Heaven, Beijing — A789

No. 2801, Hall of Prayers for Bumper Harvests. No. 2802, Imperial Vault of Heaven. No. 2803, Circular Mound Altar. No. 2804, Fasting Palace.

1997, Oct. 16 Litho. *Perf. 12*

2801	A789	50f multi (4-1)	.30	.25
2802	A789	50f multi (4-2)	.30	.25
a.		Pair, #2801-2802	.80	.70
2803	A789	150f multi (4-3)	.45	.25
2804	A789	150f multi (4-4)	.45	.25
a.		Pair, #2803-2804	1.40	1.10
		Nos. 2801-2804 (4)	1.50	1.00

Mt. Huangshan — A790

a, Mt. Huangshan at sunrise (8-1). b, Xihai Peaks (8-2). c, Flying Rock in surging clouds (8-3). d, Beihai in drifting clouds (8-4). e, Yuping Peak (8-5). f, Mystical stone (8-6). g, Tiandu Peak over clouds (8-7). h, Fabled Abode of Immortals (8-8).

1997, Oct. 20 Photo. *Perf. 11½*
Sheet of 8 + Label

2805	A790	200f #a.-h.	9.00	6.50

Nos. 2805d, 2805e are each 36x46mm.
22nd UPU Congress, Beijing, 1999.

City Wall of Xi'an A791

Designs: No. 2806, Surrounding tower. No. 2807, Arrow Tower. No. 2808, Watch Tower. No. 2809, Corner Tower.

1997, Oct. 24 Litho. *Perf. 12*

2806	A791	50f multi (4-1)	.30	.25
2807	A791	50f multi (4-2)	.30	.25
2808	A791	150f multi (4-3)	.50	.25
2809	A791	150f multi (4-4)	.50	.25
		Nos. 2806-2809 (4)	1.60	1.00

Three Gorges Dam Project on Yangtze River — A792

No. 2810, New channel being opened to navigation. No. 2811, Damming Yangtze River.

1997, Nov. 8 Photo. *Perf. 11½*

2810	A792	50f multi (2-1)	.35	.25
2811	A792	50f multi (2-2)	.35	.25
a.		Pair, #2810-2811	1.00	.75

Macao Landmarks — A793

50f, Ma Kok Temple. 100f, Lin Fong Temple. 150f, St. Paul's Ruins. 200f, Guia Lighthouse.

1997, Nov. 11 Litho. *Perf. 12*

2812	A793	50f multi (4-1)	.25	.25
2813	A793	100f multi (4-2)	.40	.25
2814	A793	150f multi (4-3)	.45	.35
2815	A793	200f multi (4-4)	.60	.40
		Nos. 2812-2815 (4)	1.70	1.25

Steel Production Exceeds 100 Million Tons in 1996 A794

50f, Ancient method of producing steel. 150f, Modern mill, pouring steel from smelter.

1997, Nov. 25

2816	A794	50f multi (2-1)	.30	.25
2817	A794	150f multi (2-2)	.70	.40

Telecommunications — A795

Stylized designs: No. 2818, Digital transmissions. No. 2819, Computer, "X-changing" data. No. 2820, Computer receiving signals, Chinese landmarks. No. 2821, Cellular phone transmission, man's head.

1997, Dec. 10

2818	A795	50f multi (4-1)	.30	.25
2819	A795	50f multi (4-2)	.30	.25
2820	A795	150f multi (4-3)	.50	.25
2821	A795	150f multi (4-4)	.50	.25
		Nos. 2818-2821 (4)	1.60	1.00

Literature Type of 1987

Outlaws of the Marsh: 40f, Huyan Zhuo coaxes Guan Sheng in a moonlit night. No. 2823, Lu Junyi captures Shi Wengong. No. 2824, Yan Qing defeats sky supporting pillar. 150f, Thunderbolt defeats Imperial Army.
800f, Heroes of Mount Liangshan take seats in order of rank.

1997, Dec. 22 Photo. *Perf. 11*

2822	A570	40f multi (4-1)	.25	.25
2823	A570	50f multi (4-2)	.35	.25
2824	A570	50f multi (4-3)	.35	.25
2825	A570	150f multi (4-4)	.70	.40
		Nos. 2822-2825 (4)	1.65	1.15

Souvenir Sheet

2826	A570	800f multicolored	4.00	2.75

No. 2826 contains one 60x90mm stamp.

New Year 1998 (Year of the Tiger)
A796 A797

Photo. & Engr.

1998, Jan. 5 *Perf. 11½*

2827	A796	50f multi (2-1)	.55	.25
2828	A797	150f multi (2-2)	1.25	.40

Gardens of Lingnan — A798

1998, Jan. 18 Litho. *Perf. 12*

2829	A798	50f Keyaun (4-1)	.30	.25
2830	A798	50f Liangyuan (4-2)	.30	.25
2831	A798	100f Qinghui (4-3)	.40	.30
2832	A798	200f Yuyin Villa (4-4)	.70	.35
		Nos. 2829-2832 (4)	1.70	1.15

Deng Xiaoping (1904-97) — A799

No. 2833, At middle age. No. 2834, During Liberation War. No. 2835, With Mao Tse-tung. 100f, As Chairman of Central Military Commission. 150f, Making speech on 35th anniversary of People's Republic. 200f, Making speech, hand raised, 1992.

1998, Feb. 19 Photo. *Perf. 11½*

2833	A799	50f multi (6-1)	.35	.25
2834	A799	50f multi (6-2)	.35	.25
2835	A799	50f multi (6-3)	.35	.25
2836	A799	100f multi (6-4)	.50	.30
2837	A799	150f multi (6-5)	.70	.40
2838	A799	200f multi (6-6)	.85	.55
		Nos. 2833-2838 (6)	3.10	2.00

Chinese People's Police — A800

Designs: 40f, Golden shield. No. 2840, Blitz operation. No. 2841, Cooperation between police and people. 100f, Traffic control. 150f, Fire police. 200f, Border guards.

1998, Feb. 28 Litho. *Perf. 12*

2839	A800	40f multi (6-1)	.25	.25
2840	A800	50f multi (6-2)	.30	.25
2841	A800	50f multi (6-3)	.30	.25
2842	A800	100f multi (6-4)	.40	.30
2843	A800	150f multi (6-5)	.55	.30
2844	A800	200f multi (6-6)	.70	.35
		Nos. 2839-2844 (6)	2.50	1.70

A801

1998, Mar. 5
2845 A801 50f multi (1-1) 1.00 .25

Ninth Natl. People's Congress, Beijing.

A802

Chou En-lai (1898-1976), Communist Party leader: No. 2846, In military uniform on horse. No. 2847, As First Premier, walking. No. 2848, As diplomat wearing lei. No. 2849, Standing and applauding.

1998, Mar. 5 Photo. *Perf. 11½*
2846 A802 50f multi (4-1) .80 .25
2847 A802 50f multi (4-2) .80 .25
2848 A802 150f multi (4-3) 1.10 .50
2849 A802 150f multi (4-4) 1.10 .50
Nos. 2846-2849 (4) 3.80 1.50

Nine-Village Valley — A803

Designs: No. 2850, Fangcao Lake. No. 2851, Wuhua Lake. No. 2852, Shuzheng Waterfalls. No. 2853, Nuorilang Waterfalls.
No. 2854, Long Lake.

1998, Mar. 26 Litho. *Perf. 12*
2850 A803 50f multi (4-1) .30 .25
2851 A803 50f multi (4-2) .30 .25
2852 A803 150f multi (4-3) .50 .35
2853 A803 150f multi (4-4) .50 .35
Nos. 2850-2853 (4) 1.60 1.20

Souvenir Sheet
2854 A803 800f multicolored 3.50 2.75

No. 2854 contains one 93x52mm stamp.

Dai Architecture — A804

No. 2855, Building on stilts. No. 2856, Well. No. 2857, Pavilion. No. 2858, Pagoda.

1998, Apr. 12 Photo. *Perf. 11½*
2855 A804 50f multi (4-1) .30 .25
2856 A804 50f multi (4-2) .30 .25
2857 A804 150f multi (4-3) .55 .35
2858 A804 150f multi (4-4) .55 .35
Nos. 2855-2858 (4) 1.70 1.20

Construction, Hainan Special Economic Zone — A805

No. 2859, Urban construction, Haikou. No. 2860, Economic development zone, Yangpu. No. 2861, Phoenix Intl. Airport, Sanya. No. 2862, Natl. tourism and resort zone, Yalongwan.

1998, Apr. 13 Litho. *Perf. 12*
2859 A805 50f multi (4-1) .25 .25
2860 A805 50f multi (4-2) .25 .25
a. Pair, #2859-2860 .75 .65
2861 A805 150f multi (4-3) .55 .30
2862 A805 150f multi (4-4) .55 .30
a. Pair, #2861-2862 1.25 1.00
Nos. 2859-2862 (4) 1.60 1.10

Ancient Academies — A806

Designs: No. 2863, Yingtian. No. 2864, Songyang. No. 2865, Yuelu. No. 2866, Bailu.

1998, Apr. 29
2863 A806 50f multi (4-1) .35 .25
2864 A806 50f multi (4-2) .35 .25
2865 A806 150f multi (4-3) .65 .35
2866 A806 150f multi (4-4) .65 .35
Nos. 2863-2866 (4) 2.00 1.20

Beijing University, Cent. A807

1998, May 4 Litho. *Perf. 12*
2867 A807 50f multicolored 1.00 .25

22nd UPU Congress, Beijing A808

50f, Emblem (2-1). 540f, Emblem, vert. (2-2).

1998, May 15 Litho. *Perf. 12*
2868 A808 50f multicolored .25 .25
2869 A808 540f multicolored 1.75 .85

Shennongjia Nature Reserve — A809

No. 2870, Mountain peaks. No. 2871, River, gorge. No. 2872, Primitive forest. No. 2873, Grasslands.

1998, June 6
2870 A809 50f multi (4-1) .30 .25
2871 A809 50f multi (4-2) .30 .25
2872 A809 150f multi (4-3) .55 .35
2873 A809 150f multi (4-4) .55 .35
Nos. 2870-2873 (4) 1.70 1.20

Chongqing — A810

1998, June 18 Litho. *Perf. 12*
2874 A810 50f Great Hall (2-1) .45 .25
2875 A810 150f Port (2-2) .75 .45

Xilinguole Grassland — A811

Designs: No. 2876, Sheep grazing, sheep herders. No. 2877, Cattle grazing, flowers. 150f, Poplar and birch forest, deer.
800f, Horses at Xilinguole River Bend.

1998, June 24
2876 A811 50f multi (3-1) .30 .25
2877 A811 50f multi (3-2) .30 .25
2878 A811 150f multi (3-3) .60 .40
Nos. 2876-2878 (3) 1.20 .90

Souvenir Sheet
2879 A811 800f multicolored 3.00 2.75

No. 2879 contains one 56x36mm stamp.

Paintings, by He Xiangning (1878-1972) — A812

50f, Tiger (3-1). 100f, Lion, vert. (3-2). 150f, Plum blossom, vert. (3-3).

Perf. 12½ Syncopated
1998, June 27 Photo.
2880 A812 50f multi .40 .25
2881 A812 100f multi .65 .35
2882 A812 150f multi .80 .50
Nos. 2880-2882 (3) 1.85 1.10

Jingpo Lake — A813

Views of lake: No. 2883, Bridge, houses on cliff, boat. No. 2884, Islands, boats at shore. No. 2885, Boat, island. No. 2886, Waterfalls.

1998, Aug. 15 Litho. *Perf. 12*
2883 A813 50f multi (4-1) .30 .25
2884 A813 50f multi (4-2) .30 .25
2885 A813 50f multi (4-3) .30 .25
2886 A813 50f multi (4-4) .30 .25
a. Strip of 4, #2883-2886 1.50 1.25

Würzburg Palace — A814

Puning Temple, Chengde — A815

1998, Aug. 20 Litho. *Perf. 12*
2887 A814 50f multi (2-1) .35 .25
2888 A815 540f multi (2-2) 1.90 1.40

See Germany Nos. 2012-2013.

Literature Type of 1987

Romance of the Three Kingdoms: No. 2889, Liu Bei finds a guardian for his heir at Baidi City. No. 2890, Zhuge Liang leads his army home, vert. 100f, Death of Zhuge Liang. 150f, Three Kingdoms united under the reign of Jin, vert.
800f, The Stratagem of Empty City.

1998, Aug. 26 Photo. *Perf. 11½*
2889 A570 50f multi (4-1) .25 .25
2890 A570 50f multi (4-2) .25 .25
2891 A570 100f multi (4-3) .50 .35
2892 A570 150f multi (4-4) .75 .55
Nos. 2889-2892 (4) 1.75 1.40

Souvenir Sheet
2893 A570 800f multicolored 5.00 3.00

No. 2893 contains one 158x37mm stamp.

The Louvre, France A817

Design: 200f, Hall of Heavenly Peace, Imperial Palace, China.

1998, Sept. 12 Photo. *Perf. 13x13½*
2895 A817 50f multi (2-1) .75 .25
2896 A817 200f multi (2-2) .85 .55

See France Nos. 2669-2670.

Cliff Paintings of Helan Mountains — A818

50f, Human face (3-1). 100f, Hunting (3-2). 150f, Ox (3-3).

1998, Sept. 23 Litho. *Perf. 12*
2897 A818 50f multi .30 .25
2898 A818 100f multi .40 .35
2899 A818 150f multi .55 .45
Nos. 2897-2899 (3) 1.25 1.05

Longquan Pottery and Porcelain — A819

Designs: No. 2900, Vase with five spouts. No. 2901, Vase with phoenix ears. No. 2902, Double gourd vase. 150f, Ewer.

1998, Oct. 13
2900 A819 50f multi (4-1) .30 .25
2901 A819 50f multi (4-2) .30 .25
2902 A819 50f multi (4-3) .30 .25
2903 A819 150f multi (4-4) .65 .50
Nos. 2900-2903 (4) 1.55 1.25

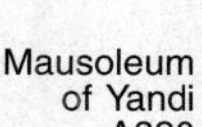

Mausoleum of Yandi A820

Designs: 50f, Meridian Gate. 100f, Saluting Pavilion. 150f, Tomb.

1998, Oct. 28 Litho. *Perf. 12*

2904	A820	50f multi (3-1)	.25	.25
2905	A820	100f multi (3-2)	.40	.30
2906	A820	150f multi (3-3)	.60	.45
a.		Souvenir sheet, #2904-2906	2.50	1.75
		Nos. 2904-2906 (3)	1.25	1.00

Great Wall Type of 1995
China Post No. R29

10f, Jiumenko Pass. 300f, Niagziguan Pass. 420f, Pianguan Pass. 500f, Bianjing Tower.

1998, Nov. 1 Photo. *Perf. 13x12*

2907	A730	10f apple grn & blk	.25	.25
2908	A730	300f olive & black	1.30	1.25
2909	A730	420f brn org & blk	1.70	1.60
2910	A730	500f blue, blk & brn	2.00	1.75
		Nos. 2907-2910 (4)	5.25	4.85

Major Campaigns in Liberation War — A821

No. 2911, Making plans. No. 2912, Conquering Jinzhou. No. 2913, Battle in Huaihai. No. 2914, Liberating Beijing. 150f, People moving supplies.

1998, Nov. 14 Litho. *Perf. 12*

2911	A821	50f red & multi (5-1)	.45	.25
2912	A821	50f gray & multi (5-2)	.45	.25
2913	A821	50f org yel & multi (5-3)	.45	.25
2914	A821	50f org & multi (5-4)	.45	.25
2915	A821	150f brn org & multi (5-5)	1.00	.75
		Nos. 2911-2915 (5)	2.80	1.75

Liu Shaoqi (1898-1969), Communist Party Leader — A822

Various portraits.

1998, Nov. 24 Photo. *Perf. 11½*

2916	A822	50f multi (4-1), vert.	.35	.25
2917	A822	50f multi (4-2), vert.	.35	.25
2918	A822	50f shown (4-3)	.35	.25
2919	A822	150f multi (4-4)	1.00	.50
		Nos. 2916-2919 (4)	2.05	1.25

Chillon Castle, Lake Geneva A823

Bridge 24, Slender West Lake, Yangzhou A824

1998, Nov. 25 *Perf. 11x11½*

2920	A823	50f multi (2-1)	.35	.25
2921	A824	540f multi (2-2)	1.75	1.00

See Switzerland Nos. 1037-1039.

Lingqu Canal — A825

No. 2922, Dam. No. 2923, Bridge over canal, vert. 150f, Boat approaching lock, vert.

1998, Dec. 1 Litho. *Perf. 12*

2922	A825	50f multi (3-1)	.30	.25
2923	A825	50f multi (3-2)	.30	.25
2924	A825	150f multi (3-3)	.60	.45
		Nos. 2922-2924 (3)	1.20	.95

Buildings in Macao — A826

Designs: 50f, Building complex, Nanwan. 100f, Friendship Bridge. 150f, Macao Stadium. 200f, Macao Intl. Airport.

1998, Dec. 12 Litho. *Perf. 12*

2925	A826	50f multi (4-1)	.25	.25
2926	A826	100f multi (4-2)	.40	.30
2927	A826	150f multi (4-3)	.55	.40
2928	A826	200f multi (4-4)	.70	.60
		Nos. 2925-2928 (4)	1.90	1.55

11th Communist Party Congress, 20th Anniv. — A827

50f, Deng Xiaoping (2-1). 150f, Handbill, buildings (2-2).

1998, Dec. 18

2929	A827	50f multicolored	.90	.25
2930	A827	150f multicolored	1.60	.45

Fish of the Coral Reef — A828

a, Pomacanthus imperator (8-1). b, Plectropomus maculatus (8-2). c, Chaetodon plebeius (8-3). d, Chaetodon chrysurus (8-4), vert. e, Heniochus acuminatus (8-5), vert. f, Lutjanus sebae (8-6). g, Balistoides conspicillum (8-7). h, Pygoplites diancanthus (8-8).

1998, Dec. 22 Photo. *Perf. 11½*
Sheet of 8

2931	A828	200f #a.-h. + label	6.75	6.00
i.		As No. 2931, with margin ovptd. in gold	*8.00*	*8.00*

UPU, 22nd Congress, Beijing '99 World Philatelic Exhibition.

Nos. 2931d-2931e are each 40x49mm.

No. 2931i issued 7/15/00. No. 2931i inscribed in margin in gold "PJZ-12," "1997-1999" and Chinese characters. Inscription for best philatelic item from 1997-99.

New Year 1999 (Year of the Rabbit)
A829 A830

50f, Stylized rabbit (2-1). 150f, Symbol for rabbit (2-2).

Photo. & Engr.

1999, Jan. 5 *Perf. 11½*

2932	A829	50f multicolored	1.10	.25
2933	A830	150f multi	1.60	.50

Great Wall Type of 1995
China Post No. R29

5f, Hushan Section. 20f, Shanhaiguan Pass. 40f, Jinshanling Section. 80f, Mutianyu Section. 270f, Pingxingguan Pass. 320f, Desheng Pass. 440f, Yanmen Pass. 540f, Zhenbei Tower.

1999, Mar. 1 Photo. *Perf. 13x12*

2934	A730	5f bl, blk & bl grn	.25	.25
2935	A730	20f vio & blk	.35	.25
2936	A730	40f pink & blk	.40	.30
2937	A730	80f grn, blk & ol	.50	.40
2938	A730	270f grn, blk & brn	1.30	.65
2939	A730	320f vio, blk & bwn	1.75	1.10
2940	A730	440f red brn, blk & bwn	3.25	2.00
2941	A730	540f blue & black	3.00	1.50
		Nos. 2934-2941 (8)	10.80	6.45

Stone Carvings of the Han Dynasty A831

No. 2942, Plowing fields with oxen. No. 2943, Group weaving. No. 2944, Three figures dancing in front of fire. No. 2945, Horses, carriage. No. 2946, Group in assassination attempt. No. 2947, Goddess Chang'e.

1999, Mar. 16 *Perf. 12*

2942	A831	50f dark green & blk	.25	.25
2943	A831	50f brown & blk	.25	.25
2944	A831	50f dark blue & blk	.25	.25
2945	A831	150f dark brown & blk	.55	.45
2946	A831	150f brown olive & blk	.55	.45
2947	A831	150f dark purple & blk	.55	.45
		Nos. 2942-2947 (6)	2.40	2.10

A832

Chinese Ceramics (Porcelain from the Jun Kiln): 80f, Halberd-shaped cup. 100f, Cup. 150f, Dual-handled stove. 200f, Dual-handled vase with base.

1999, Apr. 8 Photo. *Perf. 11½*

2948	A832	80f multi (4-1)	.35	.25
2949	A832	100f multi (4-2)	.45	.30
2950	A832	150f multi (4-3)	.65	.45
2951	A832	200f multi (4-4)	.90	.60
		Nos. 2948-2951 (4)	2.35	1.60

Great Wall Type of 1995
China Post No. R29

Designs: 60f, Huanghua Tower. $10, Huama section. $20, Sanguankou Pass. $50 Jiayuguan Pass.

1999, May 1 Photo. *Perf. 13x12*

2952	A730	60f multicolored	.30	.30

Size: 28x22mm
Perf. 11½
Photo. & Engr.

2953	A730	$10 multicolored	4.00	3.00
2954	A730	$20 multicolored	8.00	5.75
2955	A730	$50 multicolored	20.00	14.50
		Nos. 2952-2955 (4)	32.30	23.55

A833

1999, May 1 Litho. *Perf. 12*

2956	A833	80f shown (2-1)	.40	.25
2957	A833	200f Tree (2-2)	.80	.55

Kunming World Horticultural Fair.

Red Deer A834

1999, May 18 Litho. *Perf. 11x11½*

2958	A834	80f Bucks	.35	.25
2959	A834	80f Does	.35	.25
a.		Pair, #2958-2959	1.00	.70

See Russia No. 6514.

Beauty of Putuo Mountain — A835

No. 2960, Puji Temple (6-1). No. 2961, Nantian Gate, vert. (6-2). No. 2962, 100-step Sand (6-3). No. 2963, Pantuo Rock (6-4). No. 2964, Fanyin Cave, vert. (6-5). No. 2965, Fayu Temple (6-6).

1999, June 3 Litho. *Perf. 12*

2960	A835	30f multicolored	.25	.25
2961	A835	60f multicolored	.30	.25
2962	A835	60f multicolored	.30	.25
2963	A835	80f multicolored	.35	.30
2964	A835	80f multicolored	.35	.30
2965	A835	280f multicolored	.85	.75
		Nos. 2960-2965 (6)	2.40	2.10

Fang Zhimin (1899-1935), Revolutionary A836

1999, Aug. 21 Photo. *Perf. 11¼*

2966	A836	80f Close-up (2-1)	.45	.35
2967	A836	80f Standing (2-2)	.45	.35

Souvenir Sheet

China 1999 World Philatelic Exhibition — A837

1999, Aug. 21 *Perf. 11½x11¼*

2968	A837	800f multicolored	5.00	3.75

Exists overprinted in upper corners in gold. Value, $7.50.

A838

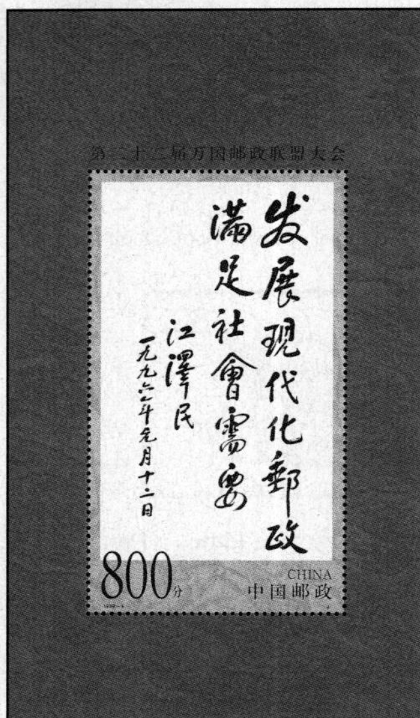

22nd UPU Congress — A839

Congress sites: 80f, 1st, Bern. 540f, 22nd, Beijing.
800f, Inscription by Pres. Jiang Zemin.

1999, Aug. 23 Litho. *Perf. 12*

2969 A838 80f multi (2-1) .35 .25
2970 A838 540f multi (2-2) 1.90 1.25

Souvenir Sheet

Perf. 12¼

2971 A839 800f multicolored 5.00 3.25

UPU, 125th Anniv. — A840

1999, Sept. 7 Litho. *Perf. 12*

2972 A840 80f multicolored .65 .35

Intl. Year of the Elderly — A841

1999, Sept. 9

2973 A841 80f multicolored .65 .25

Chinese People's Political Consultative Conference, 50th Anniv. — A842

60f, Building (2-1). 80f, Mao Zedong, vert. (2-2).

1999, Sept. 21

2974 A842 60f multi .40 .25
2975 A842 80f multi 1.20 .35

Ethnic Groups in China — A843

Designs (stamp number following "56-" at LR): a, Han (1). b, Mongols (2). c, Hui (3). d, Tibetans (4). e, Uygurs (5) f, Miao (6). g, Yi (7). h, Zhuang (8). i, Bouyei (9). j, Koreans (10). k, Manchu (11). l, Dongs (12). m, Yao (13). n, Bai (14). o, Tujia (15). p, Hani (16). q, Kazak (17). r, Dai (18). s, Li (19). t, Lisu (20). u, Va (21). v, She (22). w, Gaoshan (23). x, Lahu (24). y, Shui (25). z, Dongxiang (26). aa, Naxi (27). ab, Jingpo (28). ac, Kirgiz (29). ad, Tu (30). ae, Daur (31). af, Mulam (32). ag, Qiang (33). ah, Blang (34). ai, Salas (35). aj, Maonan (36). ak, Gelao (37). al, Xibe (38). am, Achang (39). an, Pumi (40). ao, Tajiks (41). ap, Nu (42). aq, Uzbeks (43). ar, Russians (44). as, Ewenki (45). at, De'ang (46). au, Bonan (47). av, Yugur (48). aw, Jing (49). ax, Tartars (50). ay, Drung (51). az, Oroqen (52). ba, Hezhe (53). bb, Moiba (54). bc, Lhoba (55). bd, Jino (56).

1999, Oct. 7 Photo. *Perf. 13¼*

2976 A843 80f Sheet of 56, #a.-bd. 20.00 17.00
be. As #2976, overprinted in margin *45.00 45.00*

No. 2976be includes the inscription "PJZ-17" in the selvage at the bottom right of the sheet.

Mountains — A844

1999, Oct. 5 *Perf. 11½x11¼*

2977 A844 80f Lushan (2-1) .50 .30
2978 A844 80f Kuryongyon (2-2) .50 .30

Project Hope, 10th Anniv. — A845

1999, Oct. 30 Photo. *Perf. 11½*

2979 A845 80f multi .75 .30

Scientific and Technological Achievements — A846

Designs: No. 2980, Cambrian era fossil. No. 2981, Underwater robot. No. 2982, Best result of Goldbach conjecture, vert. No. 2983, 2.16m telescope, vert.

1999, Nov. 1 Litho. *Perf. 12*

2980 A846 80f multi (4-1) .50 .25
2981 A846 80f multi (4-2) .50 .25
a. Pair, #2980-2981 2.00 1.75
2982 A846 80f multi (4-3) .50 .25
2983 A846 80f multi (4-4) .50 .25
a. Pair, #2982-2983 2.00 1.75
Nos. 2980-2983 (4) 2.00 1.00

Li Lisan (1899-1967), Minister of Labor — A847

No. 2984, As young man (2-1). No. 2985, Wearing glasses (2-2).

1999, Nov. 19 Photo. *Perf. 11½*

2984 A847 80f multi .45 .30
2985 A847 80f multi .45 .30

Return of Macao to China — A848

Designs: 80f, Sino-Portuguese declaration, flower. 150f, Basic Law of Macao Special Administrative Region, Great Wall.
800f, $50, Deng Xiaoping.

1999-2000 Photo. *Perf. 11¾x11½*

2986 A848 80f multi (2-1) .55 .25
2987 A848 150f multi (2-2) .75 .50

Souvenir Sheets

Perf. 13

2988 A848 800f multi 4.00 2.40

Litho. (stamp) & Embossed (margin)

Perf. 12

2989 A848 $50 multi *20.00 15.00*
a. Overprinted in margin *40.00 40.00*

No. 2988 contains one 60x50mm stamp with star-shaped perforations in the corners.
Overprint in margin on No. 2989a is Chinese inscription, "2000-1" and "(2-2)J."
Issued: No. 2989a, 1/1/00; others, 12/20/99.

Nie Rongzhen (1899-1992), Military Leader — A849

1999, Dec. 29 Litho. *Perf. 12*

2990 A849 80f In uniform (2-1) .50 .30
2991 A849 80f Seated (2-2) .50 .30

Millennium — A850

No. 2992, Sun Yat-sen, #590. No. 2993, #2214. No. 2994, #2339. No. 2995, #2601. No. 2996, Mao Zedong, #456. 200f, #2248. 260f, #2730. 280f, Deng Xiaoping, #2774C.

1999, Dec. 31 Litho. *Perf. 12*

2992 A850 60f multi (8-1) .30 .25
2993 A850 60f multi (8-2) .30 .25
2994 A850 80f multi (8-3) .40 .30
2995 A850 80f multi (8-4) .40 .30
2996 A850 80f multi (8-5) .40 .30
2997 A850 200f multi (8-6) .80 .65
2998 A850 260f multi (8-7) .90 .75
2999 A850 280f multi (8-8) 1.05 .85
Nos. 2992-2999 (8) 4.55 3.65

New Year 2000 (Year of the Dragon) — A851

80f, Dragon (2-1). $2.80, Rising sun (2-2).

Photo. & Engr.

2000, Jan. 5 *Perf. 11½x11¾*

3000 A851 80f copper & multi *8.75 .85*
3001 A851 $2.80 copper & multi *13.25 1.25*

A852

Spring Festival: No. 3002, Welcoming the Spring Festival. No. 3003, Bidding farewell to outgoing year. $2.80, Offering sacrifices to god of land.
$8, Family reunion, horiz.

2000, Jan. 29 Photo. *Perf. 11¼*

3002 A852 80f multi (3-1) .50 .25
3003 A852 80f multi (3-2) .50 .25
3004 A852 $2.80 multi (3-3) 1.60 .80
Nos. 3002-3004 (3) 2.60 1.30

Souvenir Sheet

Perf. 11¼x11

3005 A852 $8 multi *4.50 3.50*
a. Ovptd. in sheet margin *9.00 5.75*

Nos. 3002-3004 were issued in miniature sheets of 9. Value, $8, each.
No. 3005 contains one 90x60mm stamp.
No. 3005a contains gold Chinese inscription for New Century Philatelic Exhibition, "2000," and "PJZ-11" in sheet margin. Issued: 4/28.

A853

Wildlife.

2000, Feb. 25 Photo. *Perf. 13¼x13*

3006 A853 Sheet of 10 + 2 labels 7.50 7.50
a. 30f Nipponia nippon .25 .25
b. 60f Teinopalpus aureus .25 .25
c. 80f Ailuropoda melanoleuca .30 .25
d. $1 Crossoptilon manichuricum .35 .25
e. $1.50 Acipenser sinensis .50 .25
f. $2 Rhinopithecus roxellanae .65 .35
g. $2.60 Lipotes vexillifer .80 .40
h. $2.80 Grus japonensis .85 .45
i. $3.70 Panthera tigris 1.20 .60
j. $5.40 Alligator sinensis 1.75 .95

Cultural Relics — A854

Designs; 60f, Neolithic Age jade dragon. No. 3008, Dragon-shaped ornament. No. 3009, Carved tile with dragon. No. 3010, Copper mirror with dragon. No. 3011, Bronze dragon. $2.80, Dragon on sandalwood throne.

2000, Mar. 7 Litho. *Perf. 12*

3007 A854	60f multi (6-1)	.85	.25
3008 A854	80f multi (6-2)	1.25	.30
3009 A854	80f multi (6-3)	1.25	.30
3010 A854	80f multi (6-4)	1.25	.30
3011 A854	80f multi (6-5)	1.25	.30
3012 A854	$2.80 multi (6-6)	4.25	1.75
Nos. 3007-3012 (6)		10.10	3.20

Yangtze River Highway Bridges — A855

2000, Mar. 26 Litho. *Perf. 12*

3013 A855	80f Wanxian (4-1)	.35	.30
3014 A855	80f Huangshi (4-2)	.35	.30
3015 A855	80f Tongling (4-3)	.35	.30
3016 A855	$2.80 Jiangyin (4-4)	1.30	.75
Nos. 3013-3016 (4)		2.35	1.65

Landscapes in Dali — A856

Designs: No. 3017, Cangshan Mountain and Erhai Lake. No. 3018, Pagodas at Chongsheng Temple. No. 3019, Jizu Mountain. $2.80, Shibao Mountain.

Perf. 11¾x11½

2000, Apr. 19 Photo.

3017 A856	80f multi (4-1)	.30	.25
3018 A856	80f multi (4-2)	.30	.25
3019 A856	80f multi (4-3)	.30	.25
3020 A856	$2.80 multi (4-4)	1.00	.70
Nos. 3017-3020 (4)		1.90	1.45

Legend of Mulan — A857

Mulan: No. 3021, Weaving cloth. No. 3022, Joining army. No. 3023, On expedition. No. 3024, Returning home.

2000, Apr. 30 Litho. *Perf. 12*

3021 A857	80f multi (4-1)	.30	.30
3022 A857	80f multi (4-2)	.30	.30
3023 A857	80f multi (4-3)	.30	.30
3024 A857	80f multi (4-4)	.30	.30
a.	Strip, #3021-3024	*2.00*	*1.60*

Taer Lamasery A858

No. 3025, Good Luck Treasure Pagoda. No. 3026, Big Golden Tile Palace. No. 3027, Big Scripture Hall. $2.80, Banqen residence.

2000, May 5

3025 A858	80f multi (4-1)	.35	.30
3026 A858	80f multi (4-2)	.35	.30
3027 A858	80f multi (4-3)	.35	.30
3028 A858	$2.80 multi (4-4)	1.00	.75
Nos. 3025-3028 (4)		2.05	1.65

Cai Chang and Li Fuchun A859

2000, May 22

3029 A859 80f multi .80 .30

Stampin' the Future Children's Stamp Design Contest Winners — A860

Various children's drawings: No. 3030, 30f, (8-1). No. 3031, 60f, (8-2). No. 3032, 60f, (8-3). No. 3033, 80f, (8-4). No. 3034, 80f, (8-5). No. 3035, 80f, (8-6). $2.60, (8-7). $2.80, (8-8).

Perf. 11½x11¼

2000, June 1 Photo.

3030-3037 A860 Set of 8 3.50 2.50

Chen Yun (1905-95), Statesman A861

No. 3038, 80f, As a young man (4-1). No. 3039, 80f, In uniform, vert. (4-2). No. 3040, 80f, In black jacket, vert. (4-3). $2.80, As old man (4-4).

Perf. 13x13¼, 13¼x13

2000, June 13

3038-3041 A861 Set of 4 2.25 1.50

Pots A862

Designs: No. 3042, 80f, Wine vessel (2-1). No. 3043, 80f, Horse milk pot (2-2).

2000, June 28 Litho. *Perf. 12*

3042-3043 A862 Set of 2 1.00 .50

See Kazakhstan No. 305.

Laoshan Mountain — A863

No. 3044, 80f, Huge Peak (4-1). No. 3045, 80f, Yangkou Bay (4-2). No. 3046, 80f, Beijiu Lake (4-3). $2.80, Taiqing Palace (4-4).

Perf. 11½x11¼

2000, July 15 Photo.

3044-3047 A863	Set of 4	2.00	1.75
3047a	Souvenir sheet, #3044-3047	*5.00*	*4.00*

Souvenir Sheet

All-China Philatelic Federation, Fifth Congress — A864

2000, July 18 Litho. *Perf. 12*

3048 A864	$8 multi	4.75	3.75
a.	Margin ovptd. in gold	5.75	5.00

No. 3048a issued 9/21/01. It is inscribed in margin in gold "PJZ-13," "2001," with Chinese characters and Nanjing 2001 Philatelic Exhibition mascot.

Small Carp Leap Through Dragon Gate Legend — A865

No. 3049: a, Grandma Carp tells a story (5-1). b, Small Carp look for Dragon Gate (5-2). c, Help from Uncle Crab (5-3). d, Small Carp leap through Dragon Gate (5-4). e, Aunt Swallow passes on a letter (5-5).

2000, Aug. 8 Photo. *Perf. 11½*

3049 A865	80f Horiz. strip of 5, #a-e	2.50	2.00
f.	Booklet pane, #3049 + 2 labels, perf. 12	9.00	
	Booklet, #3049f	10.00	

Shenzhen Special Economic Zone — A866

No. 3050: a, 80f, Financial Center district (5-1). b, 80f, China Intl. Exhibition Center (5-2). c, 80f, Yantian Harbor area (5-3). d, 80f, Shenzhen Bay tourist area (5-4). e, $2.80, Shekou industrial district (5-5).

2000, Aug. 26 Litho. *Perf. 12*

3050 A866 Horiz. strip of 5, #a-e 2.75 2.00

2000 Summer Olympics, Sydney — A867

2000, Sept. 15 Photo. *Perf. 13¼x13*

3051 A867	$8 multi	*4.00*	*3.00*
a.	Sheet of 2	*32.00*	*32.00*

No. 3051a issued 10/31/00.

Beaches — A868

a, Coconuts Bay, PRC (2-1). b, Varadero Beach, Cuba (2-2).

2000, Sept. 26 Litho. *Perf. 12*

3052 A868	Pair	1.00	.75
a.-b.	80f Any single	.85	.25

See Cuba Nos. 4108-4109.

Masks and Puppets A869

No. 3053, Tan background (2-1). No. 3054, Violet blue background (2-2).

2000, Oct. 9 Photo. *Perf. 13x13½*

3053-3054 A869 80f Set of 2 1.25 .60

See Brazil Nos. 2767-2768.

Relics from the Tomb of Prince Jing of Zhongshan — A870

No. 3055, 80f, Eternal Fidelity palace lamp (4-1). No. 3056, 80f, Bronze pot (4-2). No. 3057, 80f, Boshan incense burner (4-3). $2.80, Cup (4-4).

2000, Oct. 20 *Perf. 13½x13¼*

3055-3058 A870 Set of 4 2.25 1.75

Ancient Thinkers — A871

No. 3059, 60f, Confucius (6-1). No. 3060, 80f, Mencius (6-2). No. 3061, 80f, Lao Zi (6-3). No. 3062, 80f, Zhuang Zi (6-4). No. 3063, 80f, Mo Zi (6-5). $2.80, Xun Zi (6-6).

Photo. & Engr.

2000, Nov. 11 *Perf. 11¼x11*

3059-3064 A871 Set of 6 6.25 2.50

Test of Shenzhou Spacecraft, 1st Anniv. — A872

No. 3065: a, Launch (2-1). b, In orbit (2-2).

2000, Nov. 20 Photo. *Perf. 11½*

3065 A872	Pair	*4.50*	*3.00*
a.-b.	80f Any single	.80	.35
c.	Sheet, 6 #3065	*40.00*	*40.00*

World Meteorological Organization, 50th Anniv. — A873

Designs: No. 3066, 80f, Weather satellite (4-1). No. 3067, 80f, Weather measuring equipment on Qinghai-Tibetan Plateau (4-2). No. 3068, 80f, Weather-predicting computer (4-3). $2.80, Airplane for cloud seeding (4-4).

2000, Nov. 22 Litho. *Perf. 12*

3066-3069 A873 Set of 4 1.90 1.50

Flowers — A874

No. 3070, 80f, Scarlet kaffir lily (4-1). No. 3071, 80f, Noble clivia (4-2). No. 3072, 80f, Golden striated lily (4-3). $2.80, White kaffir lily (4-4).

Perf. 11¼x11½

2000, Dec. 12 Photo.

3070-3073 A874 Set of 4 3.00 1.75
3073a Souv. sheet, #3070-3073 5.00 4.00

Ancient Bells — A875

No. 3074, 80f, Jingshu bell (4-1). No. 3075, 80f, Su chime bell (4-2). No. 3076, 80f, Jingyun bell (4-3). $2.80, Qianlong bell (4-4).

2000, Dec. 31 *Perf. 11¼x11½*

3074-3077 A875 Set of 4 2.25 1.60

Advent of New Millennium A876

Designs: 60f, Sun, moon, date, time, building (5-1). No. 3079, 80f, Dove, Earth (5-2). No. 3080, 80f, Map, leaf, infant's hands (5-3). No. 3081, 80f, Circuitboard, head, Earth, horiz. (5-4). $2.80, Moon, stars, sundial (5-5).

2001, Jan. 1 Litho. *Perf. 12*

3078-3082 A876 Set of 5 5.00 2.00

New Year 2001 (Year of the Snake) — A877

Snake and: 80f, Flower (2-1). $2.80, Chinese character for snake (2-2).

Photo. & Engr.

2001, Jan. 5 *Perf. 11½x11¾*

3083 A877 80f multi 3.25 .75
a. Sheet of 6 *17.00 17.00*
3084 A877 $2.80 multi 3.75 1.25
a. Sheet of 6 *23.00 23.00*

Clown Roles in Peking Opera — A878

Designs: No. 3085, 80f, Tang Qin (6-1). No. 3086, 80f, Lin Lihua (6-2). No. 3087, 80f, Gao Lishi (6-3). No. 3088, 80f, Jiang Gan (6-4). No. 3089, 80f, Yang Xiangwu (6-5). $2.80, Shi Qian (6-6).

2001, Feb. 15 Photo. *Perf. 11½x11*

3085-3090 A878 Set of 6 2.75 2.25

Wildlife — A879

2001, Mar. 16 *Perf. 13¼x13*

3091 Sheet of 10 + 2 labels *6.50 6.50*
a. A879 30f Budorcas taxicolor .25 .25
b. A879 60f Psephurus gladius .30 .30
c. A879 60f Elaphurus davidianus .30 .30
d. A879 80f Acipenser dabryanus .35 .35
e. A879 80f Capra ibex .35 .35
f. A879 80f Haliaeetus pelagicus .35 .35
g. A879 80f Camelus bactrianus .35 .35
h. A879 $1 Uncia uncia .45 .45
i. A879 $2.60 Martes zibellina 1.15 1.15
j. A879 $5.40 Saiga tatarica 2.40 2.40

Ancient Towns — A880

Designs: No. 3092, 80f, Zhouzhuang, Kunshan (6-1). No. 3093, 80f, Tongli, Wujiang (6-2). No. 3094, 80f, Wuzhen, Tongxiang (6-3). No. 3095, 80f, Nanxun, Huzhou (6-4). No. 3096, 80f, Luzhi, Wuxian (6-5). $2.80, Xitang, Jiashan (6-6).

2001, Apr. 7 Photo. *Perf. 11½x11¼*

3092-3097 A880 Set of 6 2.25 2.10
3097a Booklet pane, #3092-3097 + 6 labels *9.00*
Booklet, #3097a *11.50*

Strange Stories From a Chinese Studio, by Pu Songling A881

Designs: 60f, Ying Ning (4-1). No. 3099, 80f, A Bao (4-2). No. 3100, 80f, Mask of Evildoer (4-3). $2.80, Stealing Peach (4-4).
$8, Taoist Priest from Laoshan.

2001, Apr. 21 *Perf. 11½*

3098-3101 A881 Set of 4 2.25 2.00

Souvenir Sheet

Perf. 13½x13

3102 A881 $8 multi *6.50 6.50*

No. 3102 contains one 90x60mm stamp.

Yongle Temple Murals A882

No. 3103: a, Lady Queen Mother (4-1). b, Jade Lady Presenting Treasure (4-2). c, Celestial Worthy of the East (4-3). d, Venus and Mercury (4-4).

2001, May 5 Litho. *Perf. 12*

3103 Horiz. strip of 4 3.00 2.50
a. A882 60f multi .30 .25
b.-c. A882 80f Any single .40 .35
d. A882 $2.80 multi 1.10 .95

Mount Wudang — A883

Designs: 60f, Nanyan Hall (3-1). No. 3105, 80f, Zixiao Temple (3-2). No. 3106, 80f, Taizi Slope (3-3).
$8, Golden Crown in spring.

Perf. 11¼x11½

2001, May 26 Photo.

3104-3106 A883 Set of 3 2.10 1.00

Souvenir Sheet

Perf. 12¼x12½

3107 A883 $8 multi + label *6.00 4.75*

No. 3107 contains one 47x71mm stamp.

Ancient Chinese Receptacles A884

Designs: No. 3108, 80f, Earthenware vase. No. 3109, 80f, Porcelain coffee pot.

2001, June 12 *Perf. 11¼x11½*

3108-3109 A884 Set of 2 1.25 .60

See Belgium Nos. 1858-1859.

Dragon Boat Festival A885

Designs: No. 3110, Dragon boat race (3-1). No. 3111, Making Zongzi (3-2). $2.80, Expelling five poisons (3-3).

2001, June 25 Photo. *Perf. 13x13½*

3110 A885 80f multi .40 .25
a. Sheet of 9 *8.00* —
3111 A885 80f multi .40 .25
a. Sheet of 9 *8.00* —
3112 A885 $2.80 multi 1.00 .90
a. Sheet of 9 *27.50* —
Nos. 3110-3112 (3) 1.80 1.40

Nos. 3110-3112 each issued in sheets of 40.

Early Leaders of the Communist Party — A886

Designs: No. 3113, 80f, Wang Jinmei (5-1). No. 3114, 80f, Zhao Shiyan (5-2). No. 3115, 80f, Deng Enming (5-3). No. 3116, 80f, Cai Hesen (5-4). No. 3117, 80f, He Shuheng (5-5).

2001, June 28 *Perf. 11¼x11*

3113-3117 A886 Set of 5 3.50 2.00

Communist Party, 80th Anniv. A887

2001, July 1 Photo. *Perf. 13x13¼*

3118 A887 80f multi 1.75 .40
a. Sheet of 8 *26.00* —

No. 3118 issued in sheets of 40.

Emblem of 2008 Summer Olympics, Beijing — A888

2001, July 14 *Perf. 13x13¼*

3119 A888 80f multi + label .95 .75
a. Sheet of 36 + 39 labels *35.00* —

No. 3119 printed in sheets of 12 stamp + label pairs with one large central label. See Hong Kong No. 940, Macao No. 1067.
No. 3119a contains 12 each of No. 3119, Hong Kong No. 940 (with different adjacent label), and Macao No. 1067 (with different adjacent label).

Waterfalls A889

Designs: No. 3120, 80f, Yinlianzhuitan (3-1). No. 3121, 80f, Doupotang, horiz. (3-2). No. 3122, 80f, Dishuitan (3-3).
$8, Huangguoshu.

Perf. 12¼x12, 12x12¼

2001, July 22 Litho.

3120-3122 A889 Set of 3 1.60 .95

Souvenir Sheet

Perf. 12

3123 A889 $8 multi *4.75 4.75*

No. 3123 contains one 40x60mm stamp.

Beidaihe Beach — A890

Designs: 60f, Pigeon Nest (4-1). No. 3125, 80f, Zhonghai Beach (4-2). No. 3126, 80f, Lianfeng Hill (4-3). $2.80, Tiger Stone (4-4).

2001, Aug. 5 Litho. *Perf. 12*

3124-3127 A890 Set of 4 1.90 1.75

21st Universiade A891

Emblem, "2001" and: 60f, Concentric circles (3-1). 80f, Runners (3-2). $2.80, Hemispheres of globe (3-3).

2001, Aug. 22 **Litho.**

3128-3130	A891	Set of 3	1.75	1.40
3129a		Sheet of 20 +20 labels	*18.00*	

No. 3129a exists with different margin designs.

Sheets of four No. 3129 plus four labels were not placed on sale but were included with 2001 year sets. Uncut sheets containing two of these sheets also exist.

Datong River Diversion Project — A892

Designs: No. 3131, 80f, Sluice gates (4-1). No. 3132, 80f, Xianming Gorge water pipeline (4-2). No. 3133, 80f, Tunnel (4-3). $2.80, Zhuanglang River Aqueduct (4-4).

2001, Aug. 26

3131-3134	A892	Set of 4	2.00	1.75

Wuhu Bridge — A893

View from: 80f, Shore (2-1). $2.80, Roadway (2-2).

Photo. & Engr.

2001, Sept. 20 ***Perf. 11½x11¼***

3135-3136	A893	Set of 2	1.50	1.20

Orchids A894

Designs: No. 3137, 80f, Paphiopedilum malipoense (4-1). No. 3138, 80f, Paphiopedilum dianthum (4-2). No. 3139, 80f, Paphiopedilum markianum (4-3). $2.80, Paphiopedilum appletonianum (4-4).

2001, Sept. 28 **Photo.** ***Perf. 12½***

3137-3140	A894	Set of 4	2.50	2.00
3140a		Souvenir sheet, #3137-3140	*6.50*	3.00

Ancient Gold Masks — A895

Designs: No. 3141, 80f, Mask of San Xing Dui (2-1). No. 3142, 80f, Funerary mask of King Tutankhamun, Egypt (2-2).

2001, Oct. 12 ***Perf. 11¾x11½***

3141-3142	A895	Set of 2	2.50	.80

See Egypt Nos. 1807-1808.

People's Republic of China as 2001 Asia-Pacific Economic Cooperation Head — A896

2001, Oct. 20 **Litho.** ***Perf. 12***

3143	A896	80f multi	.90	.35

Souvenir Sheet

Ertan Hydroelectric Plant — A897

2001, Oct. 20 **Litho.** ***Perf. 12¼***

3144	A897	$8 multi	*4.00*	*3.00*

Horses, Zhaoling Mausoleum A898

Horse: a, Facing right, galloping (6-1). b, Facing right, galloping, diff. (6-2). c, Facing right, walking (6-3). d, With attendant (6-4). e, Facing left, walking (6-5). f, Facing left, galloping (6-6).

2001, Oct. 28 **Photo.** ***Perf. 12***

Fawn Background

3145	Horiz. strip of 6	3.50	2.40
a.	A898 60f multi	.30	.25
b.-e.	A898 80f multi	.40	.30
f.	A898 $2.80 multi	1.00	.90
g.	Sheet, 2 each #3145a-3145c, white background, photo. & embossed	*16.00*	—
h.	Sheet, 2 each #3145d-3145f, white background, photo. & embossed	*16.00*	—

Sailing Ships — A899

No. 3146: a, Chinese junk, 13th cent. (2-1). b, Portuguese caravel, 15th cent. (2-2).

2001, Nov. 8 ***Perf. 13x13¼***

3146	A899	80f Horiz. pair, #a-b	2.00	1.00

See Portugal No. 2454.

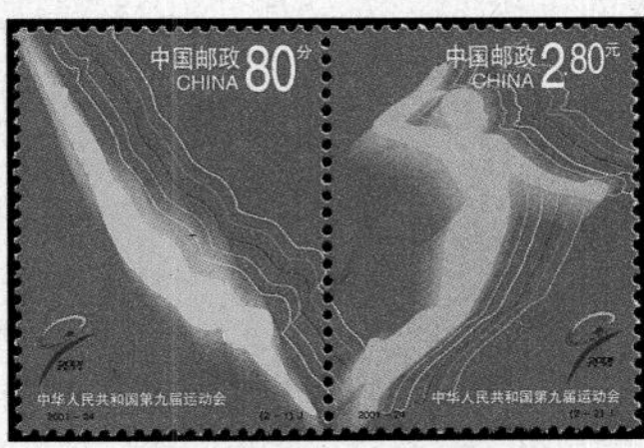

9th Natl. Games — A900

No. 3147: a, 80f, Diving (2-1). b, $2.80, Volleyball (2-2).

2001, Nov. 11 **Litho.** ***Perf. 12***

3147	A900	Horiz. pair, #a-b	1.50	1.50
c.		Souvenir sheet, #3147	*2.75*	*2.40*

Liupan Shan Mountains — A901

Various landscapes: No. 3148, 80f (4-1). No. 3149, 80f (4-2). No. 3150, 80f (4-3). $2.80, (4-4).

Photo. & Engr.

2001, Nov. 24 ***Perf. 11¼x11½***

3148-3151	A901	Set of 4	2.25	2.00

Xiu Xian and the White Snake — A902

Designs: No. 3152, Women, umbrella (4-1). No. 3153, Three men (4-2). No. 3154, Man with sword, man with bowl (4-3). $2.80, Women on bridge (4-4).

Perf. 11½, 11½x11 (#3153-3154)

2001, Dec. 5 **Photo.**

3152	A902	80f multi	.40	.30
a.		Booklet pane of 1	*1.10*	—
3153	A902	80f multi	.40	.30
a.		Booklet pane of 1	*1.10*	—
3154	A902	80f multi	.40	.30
a.		Booklet pane of 1	*1.10*	—
3155	A902	$2.80 multi	1.25	.90
a.		Booklet pane of 1	*4.00*	—
		Booklet, #3152a-3155a	*8.00*	
		Nos. 3152-3155 (4)	2.45	1.80

Admission to World Trade Organization A903

2001, Dec. 11 **Photo.** ***Perf. 13¼x13***

3156	A903	80f multi	1.00	.80

Koxinga's Recovery of Taiwan from the Dutch, 340th Anniv. — A904

Koxinga and: No. 3157, 80f, Warriors, ships (3-1). No. 3158, 80f, Warriors, horse (3-2). $2.80, People, trees (3-3).

Perf. 11½x11¼

2001, Dec. 13 **Photo.**

3157-3159	A904	Set of 3	1.90	1.50

Souvenir Sheet

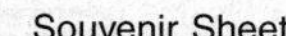

Qinhai - Tibet Railway — A905

2001, Dec. 29 ***Perf. 13¼***

3160	A905	$8 multi	4.50	3.25

New Year 2002 (Year of the Horse) — A906

Designs: 80f, Ceramic horse (2-1). $2.80, Flowers, Chinese symbol for horse (2-2).

Photo. & Engr.

2002, Jan. 5 ***Perf. 11½***

3161-3162	A906	Set of 2	4.50	2.00

Nos. 3161-3162 each exist in a miniature sheet of six. Value, each $18.50.

Art of Badashanren (1626-1705) A907

Designs: 60f, Two Eagles (6-1). No. 3164, 80f, Pine Tree (6-2). No. 3165, 80f, Lotus Flowers (6-3). No. 3166, 80f, Chysanthemum in Vase (6-4). $2.60, Two Magpies on a Rock (6-5). $2.80, Landscape After Dong Yuan (6-6).

Perf. 11¼x11½

2002, Jan. 20 **Photo.**

3163-3168	A907	Set of 6	3.75	3.00

Environmental Protection — A908

China Post No. R30

Designs: 5f, Keeping birth rate low. 10f, Forest conservation. 30f, Conservation of mineral resources. 60f, Preventing air pollution. 80f, Conservation of water. $1.50, Conservation of ocean resources.

Perf. 12¾x13¼ Syncopated

2002 **Photo.**

3169	A908	5f multi	.25	.25
3170	A908	10f multi	.30	.25
3171	A908	30f multi	.30	.25
3172	A908	60f multi	.35	.25
3173	A908	80f multi	.40	.25
3174	A908	$1.50 multi	.75	.40
		Nos. 3169-3174 (6)	2.35	1.65

Issued: 10f, 60f, 2/1; others, 4/1. See Nos. 3334-3335.

Birds — A909

China Post No. R31

Designs: 80f, Yellow-bellied tragopan. $1, Biddulph's ground jay. $2, Taiwan blue magpies. $4.20, Alashan redstart. $5.40, Kozlov's bunting.

2002 *Perf. 13¼*
3175 A909 80f multi .40 .30
a. Booklet pane of 10 +2 labels 5.00
Booklet, #3175a 5.00
3176 A909 $1 multi .50 .35
3177 A909 $2 multi .90 .65
3178 A909 $4.20 multi 1.60 1.25
3179 A909 $5.40 multi 2.00 1.50
Nos. 3175-3179 (5) 5.40 4.05

Issued: 80f, $1, $2, 2/1; Nos. 3178, 3179, 4/1. No. 3175a, 12/7.

See Nos. 3336-3337, 3547-3548.

Flowers — A910

No. 3180: a, Camellia nitidissima (2-1). b, Couroupita guianensis (2-2).

2002, Feb. 5 *Perf. 13¼x13*
3180 A910 80f Horiz. pair, #a-b 1.50 .80

See Malaysia Nos. 861-864.

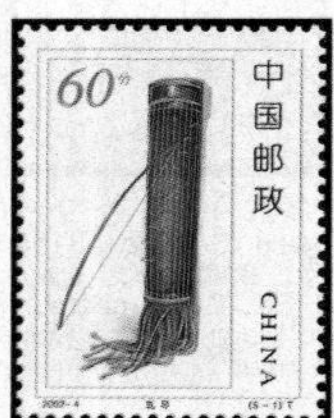

Musical Instruments A911

Designs: 60f, Yaqin (5-1). No. 3182, 80f, Erhu (5-2). No. 3183, 80f, Banhu (5-3). No. 3184, 80f, Satar (5-4). $2.80, Matouqin (5-5).

2002, Feb. 23 **Litho.** *Perf. 12*
3181-3185 A911 Set of 5 2.50 2.00

Souvenir Sheet

The Royal Carriage, by Yan Liben — A912

2002, Mar. 16 **Photo.**
3186 A912 $8 multi 9.00 6.00

Song Dynasty Pottery and Porcelain from Ruyao Kilns A913

Designs: 60f, Wine vessel (4-1). No. 3188, 80f, Three-legged basin (4-2). No. 3189, 80f, Bowl (4-3). $2.80, Dish (4-4).

2002, Mar. 30 **Litho.**
3187-3190 A913 Set of 4 2.50 2.00

Strange Stories from a Chinese Studio, by Pu Songling A914

No. 3191: a, 60f, Xi Fangping (4-1). b, 80f, Pianpian (4-2).

No. 3192: a, 80f, Tian Qilang (4-3). b, $2.80, Bai Qiulian (4-4).

2002, Apr. 21 **Photo.** *Perf. 11½*
3191 A914 Vert. pair, #a-b .85 .75
3192 A914 Horiz. pair, #a-b 1.30 1.00

Qianshan Mountain — A915

No. 3193: a, Wuliang Taoist Temple (4-1). b, Maitreya Peak (4-2). c, Longquan Temple (4-3). d, Terrace of Immortals (4-4).

2002, Apr. 26 *Perf. 12*
3193 A915 Horiz. strip of 4 2.10 1.90
a.-c. 80f Any single .30 .25
d. $2.80 multi .90 .70

Ancient City of Lijiang — A916

Designs: No. 3194, 80f, Sifang Street (3-1). No. 3195, 80f, Stream, vert. (3-2). $2.80, House of Naxi people (3-3).

2002, May 1 *Perf. 11½*
3194-3196 A916 Set of 3 2.50 1.50
a. Souvenir sheet, #3194-3196 4.25 3.25

No. 3196a sold for $6.60.

Ruyi (Good Luck Symbol) — A917

2002, May 10 **Litho.** *Perf. 12*
3197 A917 80f multi + label .90 .50

Exists in miniature sheet of 4 + 4 vert. labels (value $6) and in sheet of 16 + 16 horiz. labels (value $20).

Stamps with Attached Labels

Starting with No. 3197, stamps listed as having attached labels are known to have been issued in dozens of different sheets having various margin and label designs, various numbers of stamps and labels in the sheets, and different stamp and label combinations. Little information has been made available about these sheets, and all seem to have been sold for prices significantly above face value. Labels on these sheets do not seem to have been personalizable with personal photos but have illustrations with approved designs.

2002 World Cup Soccer Championships, Japan and Korea — A918

No. 3198: a, 80f, Player (2-1). b, $2.80, Players (2-2).

2002, May 16 **Photo.** *Perf. 12¼*
3198 A918 Horiz. pair, #a-b 1.40 1.25

A souvenir sheet containing People's Republic of China No. 3198, Hong Kong Nos. 978a-978b and Macao 1091a-1091b exists, and sold for premium over face value. Value $17.50.

Lighthouses A919

Nautical charts and: No. 3199, 80f, Maota Pagoda Lighthouse (5-1). No. 3200, 80f, Jiangxin Pagoda Lighthouses (5-2). No. 3201, 80f, Huaniaoshan Lighthouse (5-3). No. 3202, 80f, Laotieshan Lighthouse (5-4). No. 3203, 80f, Lin'gao Lighthouse (5-5).

Photo. & Engr.

2002, May 18 *Perf. 11½x11*
3199-3203 A919 Set of 5 2.00 1.50

Yellow River Dams A920

Designs: No. 3204, 80f, Lijia Gorge (4-1). No. 3205, 80f, Liujia Gorge (4-2). No. 3206, 80f, Qingtong Gorge (4-3). No. 3207, 80f, Sanmen Gorge (4-4).

$8, Xiaolangdi, vert.

2002, June 8 **Photo.** *Perf. 12*
3204-3207 A920 Set of 4 1.60 1.25

Souvenir Sheet

Perf. 13x13¼

3208 A920 $8 multi 3.50 3.00

No. 3208 contains one 40x60mm stamp.

Dazu Stone Carvings — A921

Designs: No. 3209, 80f, Avalokitesvara of the Sun and Moon, North Mountain (4-1). No. 3210, 80f, Samantabhadra, North Mountain (4-2). No. 3211, 80f, Three Avatamasaka Sages, Holy Summit Mountain (4-3). No. 3212, 80f, Statue in Cave of the Three Emperors, Stone Gate Mountain (4-4).

$8, Avalokitesvara of a Thousand Hands, Holy Summit Mountain.

2002, June 18 **Litho.** *Perf. 12*
3209-3212 A921 Set of 4 1.40 1.00

Souvenir Sheet

Photo.

Perf. 13x13¼

3213 A921 $8 multi 3.50 2.75

No. 3213 contains one 40x60mm stamp.

Desert Flowers A922

No. 3214: a, Ammopiptanthus mongolicus (4-1). b, Calligonum rubicandum (4-2). c, Hedysarum scoparium (4-3). d, Tamarix leptostachys (4-4).

2002, June 29 **Photo.** *Perf. 13x13¼*
3214 Vert. strip of 4 1.75 1.50
a.-c. A922 80f Any single .35 .25
d. A922 $2 multi .70 .60

Antarctic Scenes A923

Designs: No. 3215, 80f, Penguins (3-1). No. 3216, 80f, Aurora Australis (3-2). $2, Bird, Grove Mountains (3-3).

2002, July 15 **Litho.** *Perf. 12*
3215-3217 A923 Set of 3 2.25 1.25

Qinghai Lake — A924

Designs: No. 3218, 80f, Lake shore (3-1). No. 3219, 80f, Birds on rock (3-2). $2.80, View of lake and birds (3-3).

2002, July 20
3218-3220 A924 Set of 3 1.60 1.40

Early Communist Party Leaders — A925

Designs: No. 3221, 80f, Huang Gonglue (1898-1931) (5-1). No. 3222, 80f, Xu Jishen (1901-31) (5-2). No. 3223, 80f, Cai Shengxi (1906-32) (5-3). No. 3224, 80f, Wei Baqun (1894-1932) (5-4). No. 3225, 80f, Liu Zhidan (1903-36) (5-5).

2002, Aug. 1 **Photo.**
3221-3225 A925 Set of 5 2.75 1.50

Scientists of Ancient China — A926

Designs: No. 3226, 80f, Bian Que (4-1). No. 3227, 80f, Liu Hui (4-2). No. 3228, 80f, Su Song (4-3). No. 3229, 80f, Song Yingxing (4-4).

Photo. & Engr.

2002, Aug. 20 ***Perf. 11¼x11***
3226-3229 A926 Set of 4 1.60 1.25

Yandangshan Mountain — A927

Designs: No. 3230, 80f, Xianshengmen Gate (4-1). No. 3231, 80f, Dalongqui Pond (4-2). No. 3232, 80f, Beidou Cave, horiz. (4-3). No. 3233, 80f, Guanyin Peak, horiz. (4-4).

2002, Sept. 7 **Litho.** ***Perf. 12¾***
3230-3233 A927 Set of 4 1.50 1.25

Mid-Autumn Festival — A928

Designs: No. 3234, 80f, Family reunion (3-1). No. 3235, 80f, People looking at Moon (3-2). $2, The Moon as a matchmaker (3-3).

2002, Sept. 21 ***Perf. 12***
3234-3236 A928 Set of 3 1.75 1.40

Each printed in sheets of 20. Sheets of nine containing three of each stamp exist with a decorative border (value $25) and a border with Chinese text for the Beijing 2002 Stamp Exhibition (value $55).

Peng Zhen (1902-97) — A929

Designs: No. 3237, 80f, Head of Peng Zhen (2-1). No. 3238, 80f, Peng Zhen standing (2-2).

2002, Oct. 12 ***Perf. 11¾x12***
3237-3238 A929 Set of 2 1.00 .60

Architecture in Slovakia and China — A930

No. 3239: a, Bojnice Castle, Slovakia (2-1). b, Handan Congtai Pavilion, China (2-2).

Photo. & Engr.

2002, Oct. 12 ***Perf. 11¼x11***
3239 A930 80f Horiz. pair, #a-b 1.25 .60

See Slovakia No. 410.

Dong Yong and Lady — A931

No. 3240: a, Dong Yong's filial love moves immortals (5-1). b, Dong Yong marries seventh immortal maiden (5-2). c, Immortal maiden weaving brocade (5-3). d, Dong Yong returns home (5-4). e, Everlasting love (5-5).

2002, Oct. 26 **Litho.** ***Perf. 13¼x13***
3240 Horiz. strip of 5 2.25 2.00
a.-d. A931 80f Any single .35 .25
e. A931 $2 multi .70 .50

Nos. 3240a-3240e exist in booklet panes of one that made up a booklet that had limited distribution to people with standing order accounts. Value, $8, for complete booklet.

Flower — A932

2002, Nov. 8 **Litho.** ***Perf. 12***
3241 A932 80f multi + label .75 .50

Exists in a miniature sheet of 4 + 4 labels. Value, $4.

Souvenir Sheet

Hukou Waterfall — A933

Photo. (Margin Photo. & Embossed)

2002, Nov. 8 ***Perf. 13¼x13***
3242 A933 $8 multi *17.50 6.50*

Museums — A934

Designs: No. 3243, 80f, Shanxi History Museum (5-1). No. 3244, 80f, Shanghai Museum (5-2). No. 3245, 80f, Henan Museum (5-3). No. 3246, 80f, Tibet Museum (5-4). No. 3247, 80f, Tianjin Natural Museum.

2002, Nov. 9 **Photo.** ***Perf. 12¾***
3243-3247 A934 Set of 5 2.00 1.50

Martial Arts A935

No. 3248: a, Kung Fu (2-1). b, Taekwondo (2-2)

2002, Nov. 20 **Photo.** ***Perf. 12***
3248 A935 80f Vert. pair, #a-b 1.10 .80

No. 3248 is a joint issue with South Korea No. 2109.

Gibbons — A936

Designs: No. 3249, 80f, Hylobates lar (4-1). No. 3250, 80f, Hylobates leucogenys (4-2). No. 3251, 80f, Hylobates concolor (4-3). $2, Hylobates hoolock (4-4).

Photo. & Engr.

2002, Dec. 7 ***Perf. 11¼x11***
3249-3252 A936 Set of 4 1.75 1.40

New Year 2003 (Year of the Ram) — A937

Designs: 80f, Ram (2-1). $2, Chinese symbol (2-2).

Photo. & Engr.

2003, Jan. 5 ***Perf. 11½***
3253-3254 A937 Set of 2 5.75 3.50

Sheets of 8 + central label of Nos. 3253-3254 exist. Value, each $37.50. Sheets of 6 of Nos. 3253-3254 also exist. Value, each $30.

Yangliuqing New Year Woodprints A938

Designs: No. 3255, 80f, Five boys wrestling for a lotus (4-1). No. 3256, 80f, Zhong Kui, vert. (4-2). No. 3257, 80f, Steaing the herb of immortality (4-3). $2, Wealth in a jade hall (4-4).

2003, Jan. 25 **Photo.** ***Perf. 12***
3255-3258 A938 Set of 4 3.75 1.90

A sheet containing two each Nos. 3255-3258 exists. Value $22.50.

Seal Characters A939

Designs: No. 3259, 80f, 24 characters (2-1). No. 3260, 80f, 12 characters (2-2).

2003, Feb. 22 **Litho.**
3259-3260 A939 Set of 2 4.50 1.25

A sheet exists containg four each Nos. 3259-3260. Value $55.

Knot A940

2003, Feb. 3
3261 A940 80f multi + label 1.00 .60

Exists in sheets of 4 stamps + 4 labels. Value $13.

Perf 12¾ examples come from a sheetlet containing four examples with labels below the stamps that also contain four No. 3375. The sheetlet sold for $15.

Lilies A941

Designs: 60f, Lilium taliense (4-1). No. 3263, 80f, Lilium lankongense (4-2). No. 3264, 80f, Lilium distichum (4-3). $2, Lilium lophophorum (4-4).

$8, Lilium leucanthum.

2003, Mar. 5 **Photo.** ***Perf. 13x13¼***
3262-3265 A941 Set of 4 4.25 2.25

Souvenir Sheet

Perf. 13¼

3266 A941 $8 multi 5.00 2.50

Nos. 3262-3265 each exist in sheets of 10. Value, set of 4, $35.

No. 3266 contains one 75x53mm stamp.

Arch Bridges — A942

Designs: No. 3267, 80f, Maple Bridge (4-1). No. 3268, 80f, Xiaoshang Bridge (4-2). No. 3269, 80f, Lugouqiao Bridge (4-3). No. 3270, 80f, Double Dragon Bridge (4-4).

Photo. & Engr.

2003, Mar. 29 ***Perf. 11½***
3267-3270 A942 Set of 4 2.00 1.25

A sheet of 8 exists for each of Nos. 3267-3270. Value, set of 2, $72.50.

Chinese and Iranian Buildings A943

Designs: No. 3271, 80f, Bell Tower, Xian, China (2-1). No. 3272, 80f, Mosque, Isfahan, Iran (2-2).

2003, Apr. 15 **Photo.** ***Perf. 13x13¼***
3271-3272 A943 Set of 2 2.25 1.50

See Iran No. 2856.

A sheet exists containing 4 each Nos. 3271-3272. Value $25.

Souvenir Sheet

Leshan Giant Buddha — A944

Photo. & Engr.

2003, Apr. 28 ***Perf. 12***
3273 A944 $8 multi 5.00 3.50

Gulangyu Island — A945

No. 3274: a, Eight Diagram Building (3-1). b, Sunlight Rock (3-2). c, Shuzhuang Park (3-3)

2003, May 2 **Photo.** ***Perf. 12***
3274 Horiz. strip of 3 1.80 1.50
a.-b. A945 80f Either single .35 .25
c. A945 $2 multi .75 .60
d. Souvenir sheet, #3274 4.50 3.00

A souvenir sheet exists containing 3 No. 3274. Value $50.

Campaign to Combat Epidemic of Severe Acute Respiratory Syndrome — A946

2003, May 19 ***Perf. 13¼x13***
3275 A946 80f multi *35.00 11.00*

Beware of counterfeits of No. 3275.

Strange Stories from a Chinese Studio, by Pu Songling A947

Designs: 10f, Xiang Yu (6-1). 30f, Tiger of Zhaocheng (6-2). 60f, Huanniang (6-3). 80f, Ah Xiu (6-4). $1.50, Wang Gui'an (6-5). $2, Goddess (6-6).
$8, Princess of Dongting Lake, horiz.

2003, May 16 ***Perf. 12***
3276-3281 A947 Set of 6 2.50 2.50

Souvenir Sheet

Perf. 13¼x13

3282 A947 $8 multi 5.50 3.75

No. 3282 contains one 90x60mm stamp.
Sheets exist containing 4 each of Nos. 3276-3277, 3278-3279 and 3280-3281. Value, set $42.50

1976 Meteorite Shower Over Jilin — A948

Designs: No. 3283, 80f, Meteorites falling (3-1). No. 3284, 80f, Dispersal of meteorites (3-2). $2, Meteorite (3-3).

2003, June 21 **Litho.**
3283-3285 A948 Set of 3 2.25 1.75

A sheet exists containing 3 each of Nos. 3283-3285. Value $45.

Master-of-Nets Garden, Suzhou — A949

No. 3286: a, 80f, Late Spring Cottage (4-1). b, 80f, Pavilion Greeting the Moon and Breeze (4-2). c, 80f, Veranda of Bamboo (4-3). d, $2, Hall of Ten Thousand Volumes (4-4).

2003, June 29 **Photo.** ***Perf. 12¾***
3286 A949 Horiz. strip of 4, #a-d 2.60 2.00

A sheet exists containing 2 No. 3286. Value $17.50.

Tibetan Antelopes A950

Designs: 80f, Antelopes and mountain (2-1). $2, Antelope's head, adult with young (2-2).

Photo. & Engr.

2003, July 20 ***Perf. 11x11¼***
3287-3288 A950 Set of 2 1.50 1.50

Sheets exist containing 3 each of Nos. 3287-3288. Value, set $25.

Kongtong Mountain — A951

No. 3289: a, 80f, Town of Huangcheng (4-1). b, 80f, Gorge of Playing the Zither (4-2). c, 80f, Pagoda Courtyard (4-3). d, $2, Peak of Thunder (4-4).

2003, July 26 **Litho.** ***Perf. 12***
3289 A951 Block of 4, #a-d 2.25 2.00

A sheet exists containing 2 No. 3289. Value, $65.

Sailing Ship — A952

2003, Aug. 5
3290 A952 80f multi + label 1.00 1.00

No. 3290 exists in sheets of 4 stamps + 4 labels. Value $5.

Powered Flight, Cent. — A953

Designs: 80f, Foreign airplanes (2-1). $2, Chinese airplanes (2-2).

2003, Aug. 9 **Photo.** ***Perf. 12¾***
3291-3292 A953 Set of 2 1.90 1.25

A sheet exists containing 6 each of Nos. 3291-3292. Value, $22.

Jinci Temple Painted Statues — A954

Designs: No. 3293, 80f, Ruyi maid (4-1). No. 3294, 80f, Maid holding a towel (4-2). No. 3295, 80f, Maid carrying a royal seal (4-3). $2, Maid singing and dancing (4-4).

2003, Aug. 16 ***Perf. 11¾x12***
3293-3296 A954 Set of 4 3.00 1.50

Sheets exist containing four each of Nos. 3293-3294 and 3295-3296. Value, set of 2 sheets $40. Value, set of 2 sheets with gold overprint $45.

Three Gorges Project — A955

Designs: No. 3297, 80f, Dam and reservoir (3-1). No. 3298, 80f, Ship locks (3-2). $2, Power plant and high tension wire towers (3-3).

2003, Aug. 20 **Litho.** ***Perf. 12***
3297-3299 A955 Set of 3 1.90 1.40

A sheet exists containing 3 each of Nos. 3297-3299. Value, $22.

Traditional Sports of Ethnic Minorities A956

Designs: No. 3300, 80f, Wrestling (4-1). b, No. 3301, 80f, Archery (4-2). No. 3302, 80f, Horse racing (4-3). No. 3303, 80f, Swinging (4-4).

2003, Sept. 5 **Photo.** ***Perf. 13x13½***
3300-3303 A956 Set of 4 1.50 1.10
3303a Souvenir sheet, #3300-3303 3.00 2.00

No. 3303a sold for $5. Sheets exist containing four each of No. 3300-3301 and 3302-3303. Value, set $19.
The sheets exist with overprint in selvage. Value, set $30.

Tiananmen Gate, Beijing — A957

2003, Sept. 10 **Litho.** ***Perf. 12***
3304 A957 80f multi + label 1.00 .50

Two different sheets each containing four examples of No. 3304 were included in a souvenir folder sold only at the International Stamp and Coin Expo in Beijing in 2004. Value, set of 2 $8. Two additional sheets of four stamps + four labels, perf. 12½, exist. Value, set of 2 $30.

General Yue Fei (1103-42) — A958

Designs: No. 3305, 80f, Mother tattooing "Loyalty to the Country" on Yue Fei's back (3-1). No. 3306, 80f, Yue Fei standing with sword (3-2). $2, Yue Fei seated (3-3).

2003, Sept. 25
3305-3307 A958 Set of 3 1.75 1.25

A sheet exists containing 3 each of Nos. 3305-3307. Value, $30.

Souvenir Sheet

Water Diversion Projects — A959

2003, Sept. 26 **Photo.** ***Perf. 12¾***
3308 A959 $8 multi 3.75 2.50

Book Printing — A960

Designs: No. 3309, 80f, Ritual of Zhou, China (2-1). No. 3310, 80f, Hungarian Illuminated Chronicle, 1473 (2-2).

2003, Sept. 30 **Litho.** ***Perf. 12***
3309-3310 A960 Set of 2 1.25 .80

Nos. 3309-3310 have large perforation holes at the stamp corners. A sheet exists containing 4 each of Nos. 3309-3310 in se-tenant pairs. Value, $27.50.
See Hungary Nos. 3863-3864.

Double Ninth Festival — A961

Designs: No. 3311, 80f, Climbing mountain (3-1). No. 3312, 80f, Enjoying the beauty of chrysanthemums (3-2). $2, Playing chess and drinking wine (3-3).

2003, Oct. 4 **Photo.** ***Perf. 11½***
3311-3313 A961 Set of 3 1.75 1.25

A sheet exists containing 3 each of Nos. 3311-3313 in strips of 3. Value, $15.

Launch of First Manned Chinese Spacecraft A962

No. 3314: a, 80f, Astronaut, Shenzhou spacecraft (2-1). b, $2, Yang Liwei, flag (2-2).

2003, Oct. 16 ***Perf. 13x13¼***
3314 A962 Pair, #a-b 10.00 6.00

A booklet containing No. 3314, Hong Kong No. 1062 and Macao No. 1128 exists. The booklet sold for a premium over face value. Value, $20.

Folktale of Liang Shanbo and Zhu Yingtai — A963

Designs: No. 3315, 80f, Zhu Yingtai, disguised as a man, and Liang Shanbo become sworn brothers at Caoqiao (5-1). No. 3316, 80f, Classmates for three years (5-2). No. 3317, 80f, Bidding farewell (5-3). No. 3318, 80f, Sad parting on the terrace (5-4). $2, Turning into butterflies (5-5).

2003, Oct. 18 ***Perf. 12***
3315-3319 A963 Set of 5 3.00 1.75

A booklet containing booklet panes of 1 of each of Nos. 3315-3319 exists. Value, $7.50. A sheet exists containing 2 each of Nos. 3315-3319. Value, $18. The sheet exists overprinted in the selvage. Value, $30.

China 2003 Intl. Stamp Exhibition, Mianyang A964

2003, Nov. 20 **Photo.** ***Perf. 13¼***
3320 A964 80f multi 1.00 .60

No. 3320 exists as a minature sheet of 8. Value, $10. The sheet exists overprinted in the selvage. Value, $10.

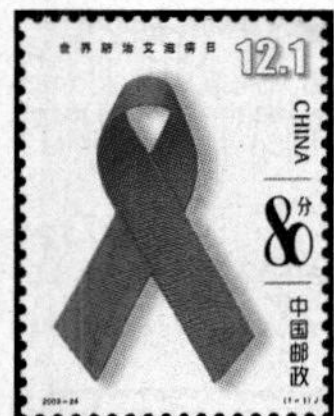

World AIDS Day — A965

2003, Dec. 1 ***Perf. 11¼x11***
3321 A965 80f multi 2.00 1.00

No. 3321 exists as a miniature sheet of 8. Value, $27.50.

Mao Zedong (1893-1976) — A966

Mao: No. 3322, 80f, Seated in folding chair (4-1). No. 3323, 80f, Standing (4-2). No. 3324, 80f, Seated on bench (4-3). No. 3325, 80f, Seated at desk (4-4).

Litho. & Engr.

2003, Dec. 6 ***Perf. 12***
3322-3325 A966 Set of 4 15.00 6.75

A sheet exists containing 2 each of Nos. 3322-3325 in se-tenant strips of 4. Value, $100.

Bronze Objects of Eastern Zhou Dyansty — A967

Designs: No. 3326, 60f, Square plate with turtle and fish patterns (8-1). No. 3327, 60f, Gui of the Duke of Qin (handled bowl with lid) (8-2). No. 3328, 80f, Iron-footed tripod of the King of Zhongshan (8-3). No. 3329, 80f, Gourd-shaped ladle of Yi, the Marquis of Zeng (8-4). No. 3330, 80f, Divine animal wine vessel, vert. (8-5). No. 3331, 80f, Wine vessel with phoenix pattern, vert. (8-6). $1, Square pot with lotus and cranes design, vert. (8-7). $2, Tripod with a dragon-shaped handle, vert. (8-8).

Perf. 11½x11¼, 11¼x11½

2003, Dec. 13 **Photo. & Engr.**
3326-3333 A967 Set of 8 5.50 2.75

A sheet of 8 No. 3328 exists. Value, $40.

Environmental Protection Type of 2002
China Post No. R30

Designs: 50f, Prevention and control of desertification. $4.50, Protection of biodiversity.

Perf. 12¾x13¼ Syncopated

2004, Jan. 1 **Photo.**
3334 A908 50f multi .35 .35
3335 A908 $4.50 multi 1.75 .90

Bird Type of 2002
China Post No. R31

Designs: $5, Yellow-bellied tit. $6, Yunnan nuthatch.

2004, Jan. 1 ***Perf. 13¼***
3336 A909 $5 multi 1.75 1.60
3337 A909 $6 multi 2.00 1.90

New Year 2004 (Year of the Monkey) A968

2004, Jan. 5 ***Perf. 13 Syncopated***
3338 A968 80f multi 2.10 1.25
 a. Booklet pane of 10 25.00 —
 Complete booklet, #3338a 27.00

Sheets of 4 and sheets of 6 exist. Value, set $65.

Taohuawu New Year Pictures — A969

Designs: No. 3339, 80f, Feelings of Pipa (4-1). No. 3340, 80f, Kylin Bringing a Son (4-2). No. 3341, 80f, Liu Hai Playing with the Golden Toad (4-3). $2, Ten Beauties Playing Football (4-4).

2004, Jan. 14 **Litho.** ***Perf. 12***
3339-3342 A969 Set of 4 1.50 1.25
3342a Souvenir sheet, #3339-3342 5.50 3.75

A sheet of 2 each of Nos. 3339-3342 in se-tenant blocks of 4 exists. Value, $7. Sheet exists with overprint in selvage. Value, $21.

Deng Yingchao (1904-92), Communist Party Leader — A970

No. 3343: a, Holding book. b, Portrait.

2004, Feb. 4 **Litho. & Engr.**
3343 A970 80f Vert. pair, #a-b 1.10 1.00

No. 3343 exists in miniature sheets of 10. Value, $11.

Suzhou Industrial Park, 10th Anniv. A971

2004, Mar. 1 **Photo.** ***Perf. 13x13¼***
3344 A971 80f multi 1.00 .50

No. 3344 exists in miniature sheets of 12. Value, $27.50.

See Singapore No. 1084.

Red Cross Society, Cent. — A972

2004, Mar. 10 ***Perf. 11¼x11***
3345 A972 80f multi .90 .35

Stories Explaining Chinese Idioms A973

Idioms: No. 3346, 80f, Trying to learn the Handan walk (4-1). No. 3347, 80f, Lord Ye's love for dragon (4-2). No. 3348, 80f, Filling a position in a Yu band (4-3). No. 3349, 80f, When the snipe and the clam grapple (4-4).

Perf. 12½x13¼ Syncopated

2004, Apr. 2
3346-3349 A973 Set of 4 1.60 1.25

A sheet of 2 each of Nos. 3346-3349 in se-tenant strips of 4 exists. Value, $12.

Peacocks — A974

Designs: No. 3350, 80f, Blue peacock (2-1). No. 3351, 80f, Albino peacock, vert. (2-2). $6, Green peacocks.

2004, Apr. 13 ***Perf. 12¾***
3350-3351 A974 Set of 2 1.00 .60

Souvenir Sheet
Perf. 13¼x13

3352 A974 $6 multi 4.50 3.25

No. 3352 contains one 60x40mm stamp

Nanxi River — A975

No. 3353: a, River and mountain (4-1). b, Tree and boat in foreground, mountains in background (4-2). c, Rocks, boat in river (4-3). d, Boat, spit of land with trees (4-4).

2004, Apr. 24 **Photo.** ***Perf. 12¾***
3353 Horiz. strip of 4 2.00 1.60
 a. A975 60f multi .30 .25
 b.-c. A975 80f Either single .40 .30
 d. A975 $2 multi .75 .55

Danxia Mountain — A976

Designs: 60f, Sengmao Peak (4-1). No. 3355, 80f, Xianlong Lake (4-2). No. 3356, 80f, Chahu Peak (4-3). $2, Jinjiang River (4-4).

2004, May 1 **Litho. & Engr.** ***Perf. 12***
3354-3357 A976 Set of 4 1.75 1.40

Economic and Technological Development Zones, 20th Anniv. — A977

2004, May 4 **Litho.**
3358 A977 80f multi 1.00 .40

Exists in a sheet of 8 stamps + 8 labels. Value, $7.50.

Hometowns of Returned Chinese — A978

Designs: No. 3359, 80f, Xinglong Overseas Chinese Farm (4-1). No. 3360, 80f, Jinan University (4-2). No. 3361, 80f, Fuqing Rongqiao Development Zone (4-3). No. 3362, 80f, Kaiping (4-4).

2004, May 15 Photo. ***Perf. 11x11¼***
3359-3362 A978 Set of 4 1.50 1.10

Sima Guang Breaking the Vat — A979

Designs: No. 3363, 80f, Sima Guang falling into water (3-1). No. 3362, 80f, Breaking vat (3-2). No. 3363, $2, Rescued (3-3).

2004, June 1 ***Perf. 12***
3363-3365 A979 Set of 3 1.50 1.25

A sheet of 2 each of Nos. 3363-3365 exists. Value, $17.50.

Scenes of Villages of Southern Anhui Province A980

Designs: No. 3366, 80f, Archway (4-1). No. 3367, 80f, Old buildings (4-2). No. 3368, 80f, Buildings on South Lake (4-3). No. 3369, 80f, Moon Pond (4-4).

Photo. & Engr.

2004, June 25 ***Perf. 11x11¼***
3366-3369 A980 Set of 4 1.60 1.25

Liu Yi Delivering a Letter — A981

Designs: No. 3370, 80f, Dragon Princess asking Liu Yi to deliver a letter (4-1). No. 3371, 80f, Delivering letter to Dongting Lake (4-2). No. 3372, 80f, Family reunion (4-3). $2, Couple embracing (4-4).

2004, July 17 Photo. ***Perf. 13¼x13***

3370	A981 80f multi	.35	.30
a.	Booklet pane of 1	.90	—
3371	A981 80f multi	.35	.30
a.	Booklet pane of 1	.90	—
3372	A981 80f multi	.35	.30
a.	Booklet pane of 1	.90	—
3373	A981 $2 multi	.75	.30
a.	Booklet pane of 1	2.50	—
	Complete booklet, #3370a-3373a	6.75	
	Nos. 3370-3373 (4)	1.80	1.20

Complete booklet sold for $6.

Nos. 3370a-3373a exist with additional overprint in the margin. Value for complete booklet, $9.

Souvenir Sheet

Eight Immortals Crossing the Sea — A982

2004, July 30 ***Perf. 12 Syncopated***
3374 A982 $6 multi 5.00 5.00

Peony — A983

2004, July 31 Litho. ***Perf. 12¾***
3375 A983 80f multi + label .75 .50

Perf 12¾ examples come from a sheet containing four examples with labels below the stamps that also contain four No. 3261. The sheetlet sold for $15. Value, $14.

2004 Summer Olympics, Athens — A984

Olympic rings and: No. 3376, 80f, Parthenon, Athens (2-1). No. 3377, 80f, Hall of Good Harvest, Temple of Heaven, Beijing.

2004, Aug. 13 Photo. ***Perf. 12¾***
3376-3377 A984 Set of 2 1.00 1.00

Perf. 12¾ examples come from a sheet containing four examples with labels below the stamps that also contain four No. 3261. The sheetlet sold for $15. Value, $14.

See Greece Nos. 2124-2125.

A985

Deng Xiaoping (1904-97), Chinese Leader

Designs: No. 3378, 80f, Walking (2-1). No. 3379, 80f, Saluting, horiz. (2-2). $6, Seated.

2004, Aug. 22 ***Perf. 12 Syncopated***
3378-3379 A985 Set of 2 1.90 1.00

Souvenir Sheet

Perf. 13 Syncopated

3380 A985a $6 brnz & multi 5.00 2.25

No. 3380 contains one 47x57mm stamp.

South China Tiger A986

Designs: 80f, Head (2-1). $2, Adult and young (2-2).

2004, Aug. 23 Litho. ***Perf. 12***
3381-3382 A986 Set of 2 1.25 .90

A sheet of 4 each of Nos. 3381-3382 in se-tenant pairs exists. Value, $17.50.

People's Congress, 50th Anniv. — A987

Designs: No. 3383, 80f, Congress members arriving at Huairentang Hall of Zhongnanhai (2-1). No. 3384, 80f, Interior of Great Hall of the People (2-2).

2004, Sept. 15 ***Perf. 13¼***
3383-3384 A987 Set of 2 1.00 .80

A sheet containing 3 pairs of Nos. 3383-3384 exists. Value, $11.

Bloodstone Seals A988

No. 3385: a, 80f, Seal of Emperor Qianlong (2-1). b, $2, Seal of Emperor Jiaqing (2-2).

Litho. & Embossed

2004, Sept. 17 ***Perf. 13x13¼***
3385 A988 Pair, #a-b 1.75 1.10

A sheet coitaining four pairs of No. 3385 exists. Value, $10.

Celery Wormwood A989

Designs: No. 3386, 80f, Purple flowers (4-1). No. 3387, 80f, Blue flowers (4-2). No. 3388, 80f, Red flowers (4-3). $2, Yellow flowers (4-4).

2004, Sept. 19 Photo. ***Perf. 13¼x13***
3386-3389 A989 Set of 4 1.75 1.50

A sheet containing 2 strips of 3386-3389 exists. Value, $11.

Chinese and Romanian Handicrafts A990

Designs: No. 3390, 80f, Drum with tigers and birds, China (2-1). No. 3391, 80f, Cucuteni pottery jar, Romania (2-2).

2004, Sept. 22 ***Perf. 13 Syncopated***
3390-3391 A990 Set of 2 1.10 1.00

A sheet containing 4 pairs of Nos. 3390-3391 exists. Value, $13.

See Romania No. 4668.

Sheet exists with additional overprint in selvage. Value, $16.

National Symbols A991

Designs: No. 3392, 80f, Flag (2-1). No. 3393, 80f, Arms, vert. (2-2).

Perf. 13¼x13 Syncopated, 13x13¼ Syncopated

2004, Sept. 30
3392-3393 A991 Set of 2 2.50 2.50

A sheet of 4 self-adhesive examples of both Nos. 3392 and 3393 was included in a souvenir folder sold only at the International Stamp and Coin Expo in Beijing in 2004. Value, $25.

Landscapes of Chinese Borderlands — A992

Designs: No. 3394, 80f, Forest, Xing'an Mountains (12-1). No. 3395, 80f, Lake in Yalu River Basin (12-2). No. 3396, 80f, Reefs in Yellow Sea (12-3). No. 3397, 80f, Zhoushan Archipelago (12-4). No. 3398, 80f, Coast of Taiwan (12-5). No. 3399, 80f, Xisha Islands (12-6). No. 3400, 80f, Karst landscape, Southern Guangxi (12-7). No. 3401, 80f, Rain forest, Southern Yunnan (12-8). No. 3402, 80f, Mt. Qomolangma (12-9). No. 3403, 80f, Pamirs (12-10). No. 3404, 80f, Badain Jaran Desert (12-11). No. 3405, 80f, Hulun Buir Steppe (12-12).

2004, Oct. 1 ***Perf. 12¾***
3394-3405 A992 Set of 12 3.75 3.50
3405a Sheet of 12, #3394-3405 + central label 10.00 7.50

Buildings in China and Spain — A993

Designs: No. 3406, 80f, Jinmao Tower, China (2-1). No. 3407, 80f, Park Guell, Spain.

2004, Oct. 8 ***Perf. 13¼x13***
3406-3407 A993 Set of 2 1.40 .90

See Spain Nos. 3319-3320.

Miniature Sheet

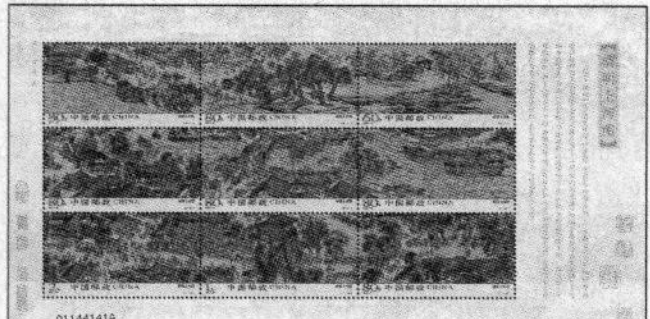

The Festival of Pure Brightness on the River, by Zhang Zeduan — A994

No. 3408 — Various details from painting: a, 60f, Trees (9-1). b, 80f, Trees, people on horseback (9-2). c, 80f, Buildings, boats on river (9-3). d, 80f, Buildings, boats on river, diff. (9-4). e, 80f, Bridge (9-5). f, 80f, Buildings, boats on river (9-6). g, 80f, Buildings (9-7). h, $1, Tower (9-8). i, $2, Intersection (9-9).

Litho. & Engr.

2004, Oct. 18 ***Perf. 12***
3408 A994 Sheet of 9, #a-i 15.00 9.75

Phoenix — A995

2004, Nov. 1 **Litho.** ***Perf. 12¾***
3409 A995 80f multi + label .80 .30

A sheet of 4 No. 3409 + label exists. Value, $6.

A sheet of 10 serpentine die cut 12¼ self-adhesive stamps like No. 3409 + 10 labels depicting Snoopy for 25 yuan. Value, $15.

Pavilions — A996

Designs: No. 3410, 80f, Aiwan (4-1). No. 3411, 80f, Pipa (4-2). No. 3412, 80f, Lan (4-3). No. 3413, 80f, Zuiweng (4-4).

2004, Nov. 6 **Photo.** ***Perf. 13¼x13***
3410-3413 A996 Set of 4 1.60 1.00

A sheet of 2 each of Nos. 3410-3413 exists. Value, $14.

Ancient Calligraphy A997

Designs: No. 3414, 80f, Yiying stele (4-1). No. 3415, 80f, Zhangqian stele (4-2). No. 3416, 80f, Caoquan stele (4-3). No. 3417, 80f, Shimen song (4-4).

Photo. & Engr.

2004, Dec. 5 ***Perf. 11¼x11***
3414-3417 A997 Set of 4 2.25 .90

A sheet of 2 each of Nos. 3414-3417 exists. Value, $16.

New Year 2005 (Year of the Rooster) A998

Perf. 13 Syncopated

2005, Jan. 5 **Photo.**
3418 A998 80f multi 1.75 .40
a. Booklet pane of 10 16.00 —
Complete booklet, #3418a 17.00

No. 3418 exists in sheets of 4 and 6. Value, $11 and 15, respectively.

The sheet of 6 exists with an additional overprint "PJZ-18." Value, $60. Some also exist overprinted "PJZ-17." Value, $200.

Tarim-Baihe Gas Pipeline — A999

No. 3419: a, 80f, Derrick (2-1). b, $3, Pipes (2-2).

2005, Jan. 8 **Litho.** ***Perf. 12***
3419 A999 Horiz. pair, #a-b 2.25 1.25

Historic Structures in Taiwan A1000

No. 3420: a, North Gate, Taipei City Wall (5-1). b, Confucian Temple (5-2). c, Longshan Temple, Lugang (5-3). d, Erkunshen Cannon Fort, Tainan (5-4). e, Matsu Temple, Penghu (5-5).

Perf. 13 Syncopated

2005, Jan. 30 **Litho. & Engr.**
3420 Vert. strip of 5 2.75 1.75
a.-d. A1000 80f Any single .30 .25
e. A1000 $1.50 multi .60 .45

Exists in a sheet with 2 No. 3420. Value, $6.

Yangjiabu New Year Woodprints A1001

Designs: No. 3421, 80f, Door God (4-1). No. 3422, 80f, Abundance for year (4-2). No. 3423, 80f, Good news on New Year's Day (4-3). No. 3424, 80f, Goddess strewing flowers from heaven (4-4).

2005, Feb. 1 **Litho.** ***Perf. 13¼x13***
3421-3424 A1001 Set of 4 1.75 1.10
3424a Souvenir sheet, #3421-3424 7.50 2.50

No. 3424a sold for $4.80. A miniature sheet containing 2 of each stamp exists. Value, $8.

Magnolias A1002

Designs: No. 3425, 80f, Magnolia denudata (4-1). No. 3426, 80f, Magnolia delavayi (4-2). No. 3427, 80f, Magnolia grandiflora (4-3). No. 3428, 80f, Magnolia liliflora (4-4).

2005, Mar. 5 **Photo.** ***Perf. 13x13¼***
3425-3428 A1002 Set of 4 2.50 1.10

Great Wall of China — A1003

2005, Apr. 1 **Litho.** ***Perf. 12¾***
3429 A1003 80f multi + label .60 .30

See note following No. 3462. See No. 3846A.

Earth Day — A1004

2005, Apr. 22 **Photo.** ***Perf. 13¼***
3430 A1004 80f multi 1.00 .30

A ring of syncopated perforations surrounds the vignette.

Jigong Mountains A1005

No. 3431: a, Mountain at daybreak (4-1). b, Garden in clouds (4-2). c, Moon Pond (4-3). d, Black Dragon Waterfall (4-4).

Perf. 12½ Syncopated

2005, Apr. 28 **Litho.**
3431 Horiz. strip of 4 2.00 1.25
a.-d. A1005 80f Any single .35 .25

No. 3431 exists in a sheet comprised of two strips of 4. Value, $6.

All-China Federation of Trade Unions, 80th Anniv. — A1006

2005, May 1 ***Perf. 12***
3432 A1006 80f multi 2.40 .40

Paintings of Flower Arrangements A1007

Designs: No. 3433, 80f, Magnolia Flowers, by Chen Hongshou (2-1). No. 3434, 80f, Flower Vase in a Window Niche, by Ambrosius Bosschaert the Elder (2-2).

Perf. 12½ Syncopated

2005, May 18 **Photo.**
3433-3434 A1007 Set of 2 1.50 .50

See Liechtenstein Nos. 1315-1316.

Dalian Bay Area Views — A1008

No. 3435: a, Tiger Beach (4-1). b, Bangchui Island (4-2). c, Golden Pebble Beach (4-3). d, Lushunkou (4-4).

2005, May 21 ***Perf. 12¾ Syncopated***
3435 Horiz. strip of 4 2.50 1.25
a.-d. A1008 80f Any single .40 .25

Exists in a sheet with 2 No. 3435. Value, $7.

Fudan University, Cent. A1009

Litho., Engr. & Embossed

2005, May 27 ***Perf. 12***
3436 A1009 80f multi .85 .25

Hans Christian Andersen (1805-75), Author A1010

No. 3437 — Fairy tales by Andersen: a, The Emperor's New Clothes (5-1). b, The Little Mermaid (5-2). c, Thumbelina (5-3). d, The Little Match Girl (5-4). e, The Ugly Duckling (5-5).

Perf. 13¼ Syncopated

2005, June 1 **Photo.**
3437 Horiz. strip of 5 3.00 1.40
a.-e. A1010 60f Any single .30 .25
f. Booklet pane of 1, #3437a .50 —
g. Booklet pane of 1, #3437b .50 —
h. Booklet pane of 1, #3437c .50 —
i. Booklet pane of 1, #3437d .50 —
j. Booklet pane of 1, #3437e .50 —
Complete booklet, #3437f-3437j 6.00

The complete booklet sold for $6.

A sheet of ten serpentine die cut 10 self-adhesive stamps containing two of each of the designs of Nos. 3437a-3437e and ten labels exists. Value, $10.

Voyages of Admiral Zheng He, 600th Anniv. — A1011

No. 3438: a, Admiral Zheng He (3-1). b, Building, map of voyages (3-2). c, Compass, drawing of ship (3-3)

$6, Ship, horiz.

2005, June 28 **Litho.**
3438 Horiz. strip of 3 3.00 1.00
a.-c. A1011 80f Any single .30 .25

Souvenir Sheet

3439 A1011 $6 multi 4.00 2.50

No. 3439 contains one 70x50mm stamp.

Nantong Museum — A1012

No. 3440: a, Southern Hall (2-1). b, Central Hall (2-2).

Photo. & Engr.

2005, July 16 ***Perf. 12½x12¾***
3440 A1012 80f Horiz. pair, #a-b 1.20 .75

Xianghai National Nature Reserve — A1013

Designs: No. 3441, 80f, Red-crowned cranes in nest (4-1). No. 3442, 80f, Three birds in flight, trees (4-2). No. 3443, 80f, Birds at lake (4-3). No. 3444, 80f, Eagles flying above steppe (4-4).

2005, July 30 **Photo.** ***Perf. 12¾***
3441-3444 A1013 Set of 4 2.50 1.00

Miniature Sheet

People's Army Generals — A1014

No. 3445: a, Yang Jingyu (5-1). b, Zuo Quan (5-2). c, Peng Xuefeng (5-3). d, Luo Binghui (5-4). e, Guan Xiangying (5-5).

2005, Aug. 1 ***Perf. 12***
3445 A1014 80f Sheet of 10, 2 each #a-e 7.00 4.00

End of World War II, 60th Anniv. — A1015

No. 3446: a, Soldiers with machine guns (4-1). b, Bugler (4-2). c, Soldier holding gun, troops landing in Normandy (4-3). d, Conquering Berlin (4-4).
$6, Dove, vert.

Perf. 12¾ Syncopated

2005, Aug. 15 **Litho.**
3446 A1015 80f Block of 4, #a-d 3.00 1.25

Souvenir Sheet

Photo.

Perf. 12¾

3447 A1015 $6 multi 4.50 2.00

Tibet Autonomous Region, 40th Anniv. — A1016

2005, Aug. 26 **Photo.** ***Perf. 13¼***
3448 A1016 80f multi 1.25 .30

Chinese Motion Pictures, Cent. — A1017

2005, Aug. 28 **Litho.** ***Perf. 12¾x13***
3449 A1017 80f multi .85 .25

Exists in a sheet of 8 stamps + 8 labels.

"Five Happinesses Arrive" — A1018

2005, Sept. 16 ***Perf. 12¾***
3450 A1018 80f multi + label 1.00 .35

See note following No. 3462.

Fanjing Mountain Nature Reserve A1019

No. 3451: a, Golden Summit (4-1). b, Mushroom Rock (4-2). c, Forest (4-3). d, Heiwan River (4-4).

2005, Sept. 18 **Photo.** ***Perf. 13x13¼***
3451 Horiz. strip of 4 1.60 1.25
a.-d. A1019 80f Any single .30 .25

Exists in a sheet with 2 No. 3451. Value, $7.50.

Farm Technology A1020

Sheep and: No. 3452, 80f, Chinese water wheel (2-1). No. 3453, 80f, Dutch windmill (2-2).

2005, Sept. 22 ***Perf. 12***
3452-3453 A1020 Set of 2 2.00 .50

See Netherlands Nos. 1203-1204.
Exists in a sheet with 4 No. 3453 and 8 No. 3452. Value, $27.50.

Miniature Sheet

People's Liberation Army Generals — A1021

No. 1021: a, Su Yu (10-1). b, Xu Haidong (10-2). c, Huang Kecheng (10-3). d, Chen Geng (10-4). e, Tan Zheng (10-5). f, Xiao Jinguang (10-6). g, Zhang Yunyi (10-7). h, Luo Ruiqing (10-8). i, Wang Shusheng (10-9). j, Xu Guangda (10-10).

Litho. & Engr.

2005, Sept. 27 ***Perf. 13¼x13***
3454 A1021 80f Sheet of 10, #a-j 8.00 3.25

Miniature Sheet

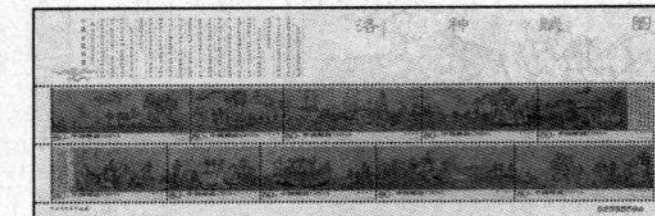

Goddess of the River Luo, by Gu Kaizhi — A1022

Various painting details with width of: a, 50mm (10-1). b, 50mm (10-2). c, 60mm (10-3). d, 40mm (10-4). e, 60mm (10-5). f, 60mm (10-6). g, 60mm (10-7). h, 50mm (10-8). i, 40mm (10-9). j, 50mm (10-10).

2005, Sept. 28 ***Perf. 12***
3455 A1022 80f Sheet of 10, #a-j 15.00 7.50

Xinjiang Uygur Autonomous Region, 50th Anniv. — A1023

No. 3456: a, Male dancers and musicians (3-1). b, Male and female dancers (3-2). c, Women carrying plates of food (3-3).

Perf. 12x12½ Syncopated

2005, Oct. 1 **Litho.**
3456 A1023 Horiz. strip of 3 1.25 1.00
a.-c. 80f Any single .30 .25

Souvenir Sheet

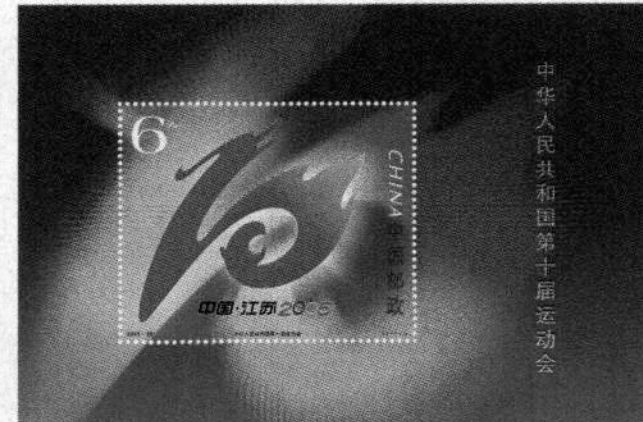

10th National Games, Jiangsu Province — A1024

2005, Oct. 12 **Photo.** ***Perf. 12¾***
3457 A1024 $6 multi 3.00 2.00

Wild Cats A1025

Designs: No. 3458, 80f, Panthera pardus orientalis (2-1). No. 3459, 80f, Puma concolor (2-2).

2005, Oct. 13 **Photo.** ***Perf. 13x13¼***
3458-3459 A1025 Set of 2 1.75 .50

See Canada Nos. 2122-2123.

"Be Safe Every Year" — A1026

2005, Nov. 6 **Litho.** ***Perf. 13¼***
3460 A1026 80f red & blk + label 3.50 1.00

A serpentine die cut 10 self-adhesive stamp of type A1026 exists. Value, $22.50.

Relics From Chengtoushan Archaeological Site — A1027

2005, Nov. 6 **Photo.** ***Perf. 12½***
3461 A1027 80f multi 1.00 .25

"Beam With Delight" — A1028

2005, Nov. 11 **Litho.** ***Perf. 12¾***
3462 A1028 80f multi + label 1.10 .25

A sheet of 2 each of Nos. 3429, 3450 and 3462 exists. Value, $6.

2008 Summer Olympics, Beijing — A1029

Designs: No. 3463, Beijing Olympics emblem, Olympic rings (6-1).
No. 3464 — Beijing Olympic mascots with emblem on chest: a, Beibei (6-2). b, Jingjing (6-3). c, Huanhuan (6-4). d, Yingying (6-5). e, Nini (6-6).
No. 3465: a, Like #3463. b, Like #3464a. c, Like #3464b. d, Like #3464c. e, Like #3464d. f, Like #3464e.

2005, Nov. 12 **Photo.** ***Perf. 13¼x13***
3463 A1029 80f multi .65 .25
3464 A1029 80f Horiz. strip of 5, #a-e 10.00 7.50

Self-Adhesive

Serpentine Die Cut 11¾

3465 A1029 80f Sheet, 2 each #a-f *26.00 26.00*

A sheet of 5 30x30mm stamps with the Beijing Olympics emblem and Olympic rings was issued in 2008. Value, $15.

New Year 2006 (Year of the Dog) A1030

Perf. 13 Syncopated

2006, Jan. 5 **Photo.**

3466 A1030 80f multi 1.00 .25
a. Sheet of 6 *9.00 7.25*
b. Booklet pane of 10 10.00 —
Complete booklet, #3466b 10.00

A sheet of 4 exists that was a giveaway for standing-order customers. Value, $15.

Wuqiang New Year Woodprints A1031

Designs: No. 3467, 80f, Being Safe All Year Round (4-1). No. 3468, 80f, Five Blessings Approach Your Door (4-2). No. 3469, 80f, Flower of Prosperity Blossoms (4-3). No. 3470, 80f, Lion Rolling the Embroidered Ball (4-4).

Litho. & Engr.

2006, Jan. 22 ***Perf. 12***

3467-3470 A1031 Set of 4 2.75 1.25
3470a Souvenir sheet, #3467-3470 6.00 2.50
3470b Souvenir sheet, 2 each #3467-3470 *9.00 6.00*

Lanterns A1032

Designs: No. 3471, 80f, Fish lantern (5-1). No. 3472, 80f, Chinese white cabbage lantern (5-2). No. 3473, 80f, Lotus lantern (5-3). No. 3474, 80f, Dragon and phoenix lantern (5-4). $1.50, Butterfly lantern (5-5).

2006, Feb. 12 **Photo.** ***Perf. 13¼x13***

3471-3475 A1032 Set of 5 5.00 2.00
3475a Sheet, 2 each #3471-3475 *14.00 8.00*

Abolition of Agricultural Tax — A1033

Perf. 13½ Syncopated

2006, Feb. 22

3476 A1033 80f multi 7.00 2.00

Lijiang River — A1034

No. 3477: a, Yangdi (4-1). b, Langshi (4-2). c, Huangbu (4-3). d, Xingping (4-4).

2006, Feb. 25 ***Perf. 12¾***

3477 A1034 Horiz. strip of 4 4.00 2.00
a.-d. 80f Any single .60 .25

Relic Plants — A1035

Designs: No. 3478, 80f, Ginkgo biloba (4-1). No. 3479, 80f, Glyptostrobus pensilis (4-2). No. 3480, 80f, Davidia involucrata (4-3). No. 3481, 80f, Liriodendron chinense (4-4).

Perf. 12x12¼ Syncopated

2006, Mar. 12 **Litho.**

3478-3481 A1035 Set of 4 4.75 1.50

Dogs A1036

Designs: Nos. 3482, 3486a, 80f, Pekingese (4-1). Nos. 3483, 3486b, 80f, Pug, vert. (4-2). Nos. 3484, 3486c, 80f, Chow chow (4-3). Nos. 3485, 3486d, 80f, Tibetan mastiff, vert. (4-4).

Perf. 13¼ Syncopated

2006, Mar. 19 **Litho. & Engr.**

3482-3485 A1036 Set of 4 2.00 1.40

Self-Adhesive

Serpentine Die Cut 11¾ on 2 Sides

3486 A1036 80f Sheet, 2 each #3486a-3486d 10.00 *7.00*

Qingcheng Mountain A1037

Designs: 60f, Remote mountain gate (4-1). No. 3488, 80f, Winding path (4-2). No. 3489, 80f, Ancient temple (4-3). No. 3490, 80f, Spring (4-4).

2006, Apr. 12 ***Perf. 13¼ Syncopated***

3487-3490 A1037 Set of 4 3.50 1.50

Statues in Yungang Grottoes — A1038

Designs: No. 3491, 80f, Sakyamuni (4-1). No. 3492, 80f, Bodhisattva (4-2). No. 3493, 80f, Head of Bodhisattva (4-3). No. 3494, 80f, Xieshi Bodhisattva (4-4).
$6, Sakyamuni, diff.

Perf. 13¼x13½ Syncopated

2006, Apr. 13 **Photo.**

3491-3494 A1038 Set of 4 5.00 1.00

Souvenir Sheet

Perf. 13 Syncopated

3495 A1038 $6 multi 3.25 3.00

No. 3495 contains one 40x60mm stamp.

Tianzhu Mountain — A1039

Designs: 60f, Green Dragon Mountain Stream (4-1). No. 3497, 80f, Taoist Practice Terrace (4-2). No. 3498, 80f, Sanzu Temple (4-3). No. 3499, 80f, Qingtian Peak (4-4).

2006, Apr. 22 ***Perf. 11½x11¼***

3496-3499 A1039 Set of 4 2.40 1.00

Scientists A1040

Designs: No. 3500, 80f, Liang Xi (1883-1958), forester (4-1). No. 3501, 80f, Mao Yisheng (1896-1989), civil engineer (4-2). No. 3502, 80f, Yan Jici (1900-96), physicist (4-3). No. 3503, 80f, Zhou Peiyuan (1902-93), physicist (4-4).

Litho. & Engr.

2006, May 13 ***Perf. 12***

3500-3503 A1040 Set of 4 5.50 2.00

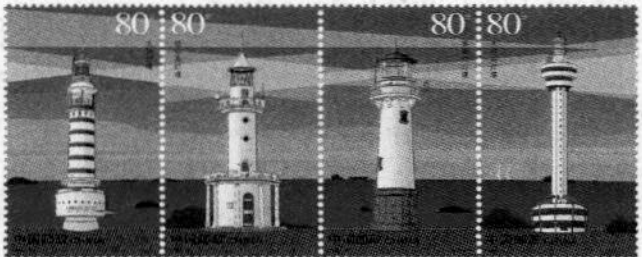

Lighthouses — A1041

No. 3504: a, Dagu Lighthouse (4-1). b, Guishan Island Lighthouse (4-2). c, Wusongkou Lighthouse (4-3). d, Mulantou Lighthouse (4-4).

2006, May 22 **Photo.** ***Perf. 12¾***

3504 A1041 Horiz. strip of 4 2.50 1.50
a.-d. 80f Any single .40 .25

Chinese Space Program, 50th Anniv. — A1042

No. 3505: a, Geospace Double Star Exploration (2-1). b, Shenzhou 6 (2-2).

Perf. 12x11¼ Syncopated

2006, June 8 **Litho.**

3505 A1042 80f Horiz. pair, #a-b 2.25 1.00

Silver and Gold Objects — A1043

Designs: No. 3506, 80f, Jeeweled Qing Dynasty cup, China (2-1). No. 3507, 80f, Tankard with Biblical designs, by Peter Rohde, Poland.

2006, June 20 **Photo.** ***Perf. 13¼x13***

3506-3507 A1043 Set of 2 1.50 .65

See Poland No. 3829.

Olympic Rings and Emblem of 2008 Summer Olympics, Beijing — A1043a

2006, June 23 **Litho.** ***Perf. 12***

3507A A1043a 80f multi + label 1.25 .45

Printed in sheets of 15 stamps + 15 labels, sheets of 5 stamps + 5 labels, sheets of 4 stamps + 4 labels to right of stamps, sheets of 4 stamps + 4 labels below stamps, and sheets of 8 stamps + 8 labels. Value, set of 5 sheets $50.

Early Communist Leaders A1044

Designs: No. 3508, 80f, Gao Junyu (1896-1925) (5-1). No. 3509, 80f, Wang Hebo (1882-1927) (5-2). No. 3510, 80f, Su Zhaozheng (1885-1929) (5-3). No. 3511, 80f, Peng Pai (1896-1929) (5-4). No. 3512, 80f, Deng Xhongxia (1894-1933) (5-5).

2006, June 30 **Litho. & Engr.**

3508-3512 A1044 Set of 5 *35.00 12.50*

Opening of Qinghai-Tibet Railway — A1045

Designs: No. 3513, 80f, Bridge across Kekexili, antelopes (3-1). No. 3514, 80f, Train crossing Danggula Mountains, cattle (3-2). No. 3515, 80f, Lhasa Railway Station, birds (3-3).

Perf. 12½x12 Syncopated

2006, July 1 **Litho.**

3513-3515 A1045 Set of 3 6.75 2.00

Kanasi Nature Reserve — A1046

Designs: No. 3516, 80f, Kanasi Lake (4-1). No. 3517, 80f, Crouching Dragon Bend (4-2). No. 3518, 80f, Celestial Bend (4-3). No. 3519, 80f, Moon Bend (4-4).

2006, July 8 **Photo.** ***Perf. 12¾***

3516-3519 A1046 Set of 4 6.00 1.75

Earthquake Protection and Damage Mitigation A1047

2006, July 26 ***Perf. 13½x13***

3520 A1047 80f multi 4.00 .65

2008 Summer Olympics, Beijing — A1048

Designs: Nos. 3521, 3525a, 60f, Basketball (4-1). Nos. 3522, 3525b, 80f, Fencing (4-2). Nos. 3523, 3525c, Sailing (4-3). Nos. 3524, 3525d, $3, Gymnastics (4-4).

2006, Aug. 8 Photo. *Perf. 13¼x13*
3521-3524 A1048 Set of 4 3.25 2.00

Self-Adhesive

Serpentine Die Cut 11¾

3525 A1048 Sheet of 8, 2 each #a-d 20.00 *10.00*

Portions of the designs of Nos. 3525a-3525d were applied by a thermographic process, producing a shiny, raised effect.

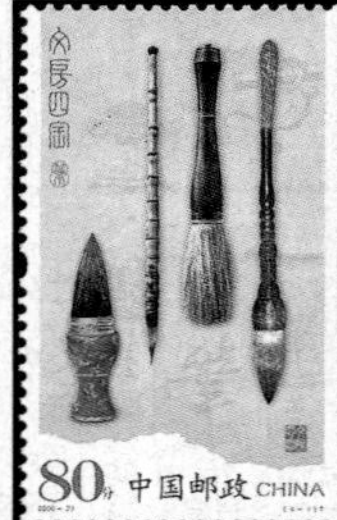

Treasures of the Study — A1049

Designs: No. 3526, 80f, Brushes (4-1). No. 3527, 80f, Ink (4-2). No. 3528, 80f, Paper (4-3). No. 3529, 80f, Ink stone (4-4).

Perf. 12x12½ Syncopated

2006, Sept. 10 Litho.
3526-3529 A1049 Set of 4 5.25 1.90

A sheet of 2 each of Nos. 3526-3529 exists. Value, $60.

All-China Federation of Returned Overseas Chinese, 50th Anniv. A1050

Perf. 12½x12 Syncopated

2006, Sept. 25
3530 A1050 80f multi 1.00 .30

Musical Instruments — A1051

Designs: No. 3531, 80f, Seven-stringed qin, China (2-1). No. 3532, 80f, Bösendorfer piano, Austria (2-2).

Perf. 13x12½ Syncopated

2006, Sept. 26 Litho.
3531-3532 A1051 Set of 2 2.00 .60

See Austria Nos. 2066-2067.

Chinese Export Commodities Fair — A1052

Perf. 13½x13¼ Syncopated

2006, Oct. 15 Photo.
3533 A1052 80f multi 1.00 .25

Long March, 70th Anniv. — A1053

Designs: No. 3534, 80f, Setting Out (4-1). No. 3535, 80f, Zunyi Conference (4-2). No. 3536, 80f, Speedily Occupy the Luding Bridge (4-3). No. 3537, 80f, The Red Army Through the Marshland (4-4).
$6, Reunion.

2006, Oct. 22 *Perf. 13x13¼*
3534-3537 A1053 Set of 4 3.50 1.60

Souvenir Sheet

3538 A1053 $6 multi 4.00 2.50

No. 3538 contains one 80x50mm stamp. A souvenir sheet of one of No. 3535 exists.
No. 3538 exists imperf.

Dialogue With ASEAN, 15th Anniv. A1054

Perf. 12½x12 Syncopated

2006, Oct. 30 Litho.
3539 A1054 80f multi 1.50 .30

"Enjoying Prosperity Year After Year" A1055

"Happy New Year" — A1055a

Perf. 12¾ Syncopated

2006, Nov. 1 Photo.
3540 A1055 80f multi .30 .25
3541 A1055a $3 multi 1.10 .85

A souvenir sheet containing Nos. 3540-3541 exists. Value, $19.
See note following No. 3628. See Nos. 3708a, 3869b, 3978a, 4048a, 4158a, 4238a, 4326a, 4409a, 4488a, 4582a, 4683a.

Beijing Summit of Forum on China-Africa Cooperation — A1056

2006, Nov. 3 Litho. *Perf. 13¼*
3542 A1056 80f multi 1.25 .25

Buildings Associated With Dr. Sun Yat-sen (1826-1925) A1057

Designs: No. 3543, 80f, Sun Yat-sen Villa (4-1). No. 3544, 80f, Mausoleum (4-2). No. 3545, 80f, Sun Yat-sen Memorial Hall (4-3). No. 3546, 80f, Sun Yat-sen University (4-4).

Perf. 13¼ Syncopated

2006, Nov. 12 Litho. & Engr.
3543-3546 A1057 Set of 4 4.00 1.75

Birds Type of 2002

China Post No. R31

Designs: 40f, Chinese monal pheasant. $1.20, Taiwan yuhinas.

Perf. 13½ Syncopated

2006, Nov. 15 Photo.
3547 A909 40f multi .30 .25
3548 A909 $1.20 multi .45 .35

Heavenly Steed, Silk Roll Painting — A1058

No. 3549: a, Horse and rider. b, People looking at horse.

2006, Dec. 3 Photo. *Perf. 12¾*
3549 A1058 $1.20 Horiz. pair, #a-b 1.50 1.00

Wu Lanfu (1906-88), Politician A1059

2006, Dec. 23 *Perf. 13¼x13*
3550 A1059 $1.20 multi *11.00 4.00*

Trains — A1060

Designs: No. 3551, $1.20, Locomotive, blue background (4-1). No. 3552, $1.20, Locomotive, red brown background (4-2). No. 3553, $1.20, Box car (4-3). No. 3554, $1.20, Log cars and gateway (4-4).
$6, Locomotive and city skyline.

2006, Dec. 28 *Perf. 13x13¼*
3551-3554 A1060 Set of 4 *20.00 10.00*

Souvenir Sheet

Perf. 13¼x13

3555 A1060 $6 multi *10.50 8.00*

No. 3555 contains one 90x40mm stamp.

China Post, 110th Anniv. — A1061

Perf. 12x11½ Syncopated

2006, Dec. 30 Litho.
3556 A1061 $1.20 multi 1.50 .60

A sheet containing 6 No. 3556 exists. Value, $8.50.

New Year 2007 (Year of the Pig) — A1062

Perf. 13 Syncopated

2007, Jan. 5 Photo.
3557 A1062 $1.20 multi 1.00 .35
a. Souvenir sheet of 6 11.00 *6.00*
b. Booklet pane of 10 10.00 —
Complete booklet, #3557b 10.00

A sheet containing 4 No. 3557 exists. Value, $12.50.

6th Asian Winter Games — A1063

Perf. 12x12½ Syncopated

2007, Jan. 28 Litho.
3558 A1063 $1.20 multi 1.30 .35

Shiwan Pottery Figurines A1064

Designs: No. 3559, $1.20, Ta Xue Xun Mei (2-1). No. 3560, $1.20, Wang Zhaojun Chu Sai (2-2).

2007, Feb. 3 Photo. *Perf. 13¼x13*
3559-3560 A1064 Set of 2 1.25 .65
3560a Miniature sheet, 4 each #3559-3560 7.00 3.50

"Divine Birds of the Sun" — A1065

2007, Feb. 9 Litho. *Perf. 12*

3561 A1065 $1.20 multi + label .65 .35

Printed in sheets of 6 + 6 labels (value, $11), 8 + 8 labels and 15 + 15 labels (value, $20).

Mianzhu New Year Woodcuts A1066

Designs: No. 3562, $1.20, Zuo Zuo Ti Dao (4-1). No. 3563, $1.20, Mu Guiying (4-2). No. 3564, $1.20, Shuang Xi Tong Zi (4-3). No. 3565, $1.20, Zhang Xian She Gou (4-4).

Perf. 12x11½ Syncopated

2007, Feb. 10 Litho. & Engr.

3562-3565 A1066 Set of 4 3.00 1.50
3565a Souvenir sheet of 4, #3562-3565 4.50 2.50
3565b Miniature sheet of 8, 2 each #3562-3565 8.00 5.25

A lithographed sheet similar to No. 3565b on a textured silk-faced paper exists. Value, $16.

Beijing Opera — A1067

Designs: 80f, Lin Xiangru (6-1). No. 3567, $1.20, Song Shijie (6-2). No. 3568, $1.20, Zhou Yu (6-3). No. 3569, $1.20, Xu Xian (6-4). No. 3570, $1.20, Gao Chong (6-5). No. 3571, $1.20, Ren Tanghui (6-6).

2007, Mar. 10 Photo. *Perf. 13¼x13*

3566-3571 A1067 Set of 6 2.75 1.90

Postal Savings Bank — A1068

2007, Mar. 20 *Perf. 12¾*

3572 A1068 $1.20 multi 1.00 .35
a. Miniature sheet of 8 *9.00 4.50*

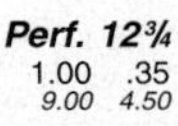

Writings of Li Keran A1069

Designs: No. 3573, $1.20, Man viewing waterfall (6-1). No. 3574, $1.20, Mountains with red-leaved trees (6-2). No. 3575, $1.20, People looking at scroll (6-3). No. 3576, $1.20, Crane flying above man under tent (6-4). No. 3577, $1.20, Cattle and driver in pond (6-5). No. 3578, $1.20, Raining in Jiangnan (6-6).

Perf. 13x13¼ Syncopated

2007, Mar. 26

3573-3578 A1069 Set of 6 3.50 2.25

Modern Chinese Drama, Cent. A1070

Perf. 13 Syncopated

2007, Apr. 6 Litho.

3579 A1070 $1.20 multi .80 .35

Yangzhou Garden — A1071

No. 3580: a, He Garden (3-1). b, Ge Garden (3-2). c, Xu Garden (3-3).

Perf. 12x11½ Syncopated

2007, Apr. 8

3580 A1071 Horiz. strip of 3 1.75 1.40
a.-c. $1.20 Any single .50 .35

Dances — A1072

Designs: No. 3581, $1.20, Dragon dance (2-1). No. 3582, $1.20, Lion dance (2-2).

2007, Apr. 13 Litho. *Perf. 12¾x13*

3581-3582 A1072 Set of 2 2.25 .75

See Indonesia No. 2100.

Torch Relay for 2008 Summer Olympics, Beijing — A1073

2007, Apr. 27 *Perf. 12*

3583 A1073 $1.20 multi + label 1.75 .60
a. Sheet of 4 + 4 labels 3.00 2.50

Inner Mongolia Autonomous Region, 60th Anniv. — A1074

Designs: No. 3584, $1.20, Horsemen, wrestlers, archer (2-1). No. 3585, $1.20, Seven women (2-2).

Perf. 12½x12 Syncopated

2007, May 1

3584-3585 A1074 Set of 2 1.00 .70
3585a Souvenir sheet, #3584-3585 2.00 1.50

Mausoleums of Qing Emperors A1075

Designs: No. 3586, $1.20, Zhaoling Mausoleum (3-1). No. 3587, $1.20, Xiaoling Mausoleum (3-2). No. 3588, Tailing Mausoleum (3-3).

2007, May 12 Photo. *Perf. 12¾*

3586-3588 A1075 Set of 3 1.50 1.00

Tongji University, Cent. A1076

2007, May 20 *Perf. 12½ Syncopated*

3589 A1076 $1.20 multi .85 .50

Kong Rong and Pears — A1077

Nos. 3590 and 3591: a, Denomination at LL (2-1). b, Denomination at LR (2-2).

2007, June 1 *Perf. 13¼x13*

3590 A1077 $1.20 Horiz. pair, #a-b 1.45 .85

Self-Adhesive

Booklet Stamps

Serpentine Die Cut 11¾

3591 A1077 $1.20 Horiz. pair, #a-b .85 .85
c. Booklet pane, 4 #3591 5.00

Chongqing — A1078

No. 3592: a, City skyline (2-1). b, City and highway interchange (2-2).

Perf. 12x11½ Syncopated

2007, June 8 Litho.

3592 A1078 $1.20 Horiz. pair, #a-b 1.10 .90

Wudalianchi Natl. Park — A1079

No. 3593: a, Heilong Mountain (3-1). b, Sanchi Pool (3-2). c, Sea of Rock (3-3).

2007, June 19 Photo. *Perf. 12¾*

3593 A1079 Horiz. strip of 3 1.95 1.25
a.-c. $1.20 Any single .45 .35

Return of Hong Kong, 10th Anniv. A1080

Designs: No. 3594, $1.20, Flags of People's Republic of China and Hong Kong, doves, monument (3-1). No. 3595, $1.20, "CEPA" and stylized buildings (3-2). No. 3596, $1.20, Hong Kong buildings, bridge (3-3).

Perf. 13¼x12¾ Syncopated

2007, July 1

3594-3596 A1080 Set of 3 2.00 1.50

A souvenir sheet containing Nos. 3594-3596 and Hong Kong No. 1275 sold for $12.95 in Hong Kong currency. Value, $27.50.

Pres. Yang Shangkun (1907-98) A1081

Designs: No. 3597, $1.20, Standing in uniform (2-1). No. 3598, $1.20, Seated at desk, horiz. (2-2).

Perf. 11½x11, 11x11½

2007, July 5 Photo. & Engr.

3597-3598 A1081 Set of 2 3.25 .85

Nanji Islands Marine Reserve — A1082

Shells and: No. 3599, $1.20, Sanpanwei (3-1). No. 3600, $1.20, Longchuanjiao (3-2). No. 3601, $1.20, Dashaao (3-3).

Perf. 12¾x12½ Syncopated

2007, July 10 Photo.

3599-3601 A1082 Set of 3 1.95 1.00

Emblem of People's Liberation Army — A1083

2007, July 15 Litho. *Perf. 12*

3602 A1083 $1.20 multi + label 1.25 .45

Souvenir Sheet

All-China Philatelic Federation, 6th Congress — A1084

Perf. 12½ Syncopated

2007, July 28 **Litho. & Engr.**

3603 A1084 $6 multi 3.75 2.25

A sheet of 2 No. 3603 exists. Value, $9.

People's Liberation Army, 80th Anniv. — A1085

Designs: No. 3604, $1.20, Soldiers saluting (4-1). No. 3605, $1.20, Soldier carrying sack (4-2). No. 3606, $1.20, Soldier with rifle (4-3). No. 3607, $1.20, Soldiers wearing UN Peacekeeper berets (4-4).

Perf. 13¼x12½ Syncopated

2007, Aug. 1 **Photo.**

3604-3607 A1085 Set of 4 3.50 2.00

A sheet of eight (two each Nos. 3604-3607) exists. Value, $10.

Olympic Sports — A1086

Designs: Nos. 3608, 3614a, $1.20, Diving (6-1). Nos. 3609, 3614b, $1.20, Shooting (6-2). Nos. 3610, 3614c, $1.20, Athletics (6-3). Nos. 3611, 3614d, $1.20, Volleyball (6-4). Nos. 3612, 3614e, $1.20, BMX bicycling (6-5). Nos. 3613, 3614f, $1.20, Weight lifting (6-6).

2007, Aug. 8 **Photo.** ***Perf. 13¼x13***

3608-3613 A1086 Set of 6 4.00 2.25

3613a Sheet of 10, #3521-3524, 3608-3613, + label 21.00 18.00

Self-Adhesive

Serpentine Die Cut 11¾

3614 Miniature sheet of 12, 2 each #a-f *23.00*

a.-f. A1086 $1.20 Any single .40 .30

No. 3613a sold for $18.60.

Tengchong Volcano Area — A1087

Designs: No. 3615, $1.20, Rehai (3-1). No. 3616, $1.20, Volcanoes, vert. (3-2). No. 3617, $1.20, Shenzhu Valley, vert. (3-3).

Perf. 12x12½ Syncopated, 12½x12 Syncopated

2007, Aug. 18

3615-3617 A1087 Set of 3 1.50 1.00

Nos. 3615-3617 were printed together in a sheet of 15 stamps + a horizontal label. The first row consists of the label and 2 No. 3615; the second row, 3 No. 3615; the third row, 5 No. 3616; and the fourth row, 5 No. 3617.

Jin Hu — A1088

No. 3618: a, Da Chibi (2-1). b, Maoer Mountain (2-2).

Perf. 12¾ Syncopated

2007, Sept. 2 **Litho.**

3618 A1088 $1.20 Horiz. pair, #a-b 1.45 .95

2007 Women's Soccer World Cup, People's Republic of China A1089

2007, Sept. 10 **Photo.** ***Perf. 13¼***

3619 A1089 $1.20 multi 1.75 .75

Values are for stamps with surrounding selvage.

2007 World Summer Special Olympics, Shanghai — A1090

2007, Oct. 2 ***Perf. 13¼***

3620 A1090 $1.20 multi 1.00 .40

Historic Sites in Three Gorges Reservoir Area — A1091

Designs: No. 3621, $1.20, Zhang Fei Temple (4-1). No. 3622, $1.20, Shibaozhai Village, vert. (4-2). No. 3623, $1.20, Ancient Dachang, vert. (4-3). No. 3624, $1.20, Quyuan's Grave (4-4).

Perf. 13¼ Syncopated

2007, Oct. 13 **Litho. & Engr.**

3621-3624 A1091 Set of 4 2.00 1.50

17th Natl. Communist Party Congress — A1092

Designs: No. 3625, $1.20, Memorial for First Natl. Communist Party Congress (2-1). No. 3626, $1.20, Site of Second Plenary Session of the Seventh Central Committee.

$6, Dove and monument.

Perf. 13¼x13 Syncopated

2007, Oct. 15 **Photo.**

3625-3626 A1092 Set of 2 2.75 1.00

Souvenir Sheet

Perf. 13¼x13

3627 A1092 $6 multi 4.75 2.75

No. 3627 contains one 60x40mm stamp.

A souvenir sheet of 2 of Nos. 3625-3626 exists. Value, $65.

"Happiness" A1093

Perf. 12¾ Syncopated

2007, Nov. 1 **Photo.**

3628 A1093 $1.20 multi .45 .40

A sheet containing Nos. 3628, 3541 and four labels exists. Value, $10.

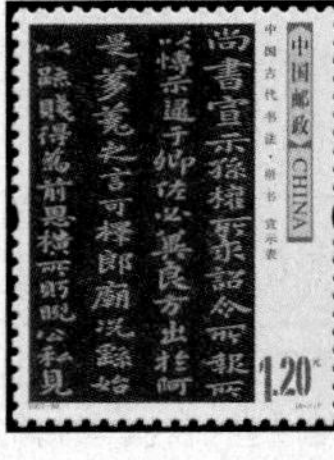

Ancient Calligraphy A1094

Designs: No. 3629, $1.20, Proclamation (6-1). No. 3630, $1.20, Zhang Menglong Stele (6-2). No. 3631, $1.20, Inscription for Sweet Spring at Jiucheng Palace (6-3). No. 3632, $1.20, Preface for Sacred Religion at Wild Goose Pagoda (6-4). No. 3633, $1.20, Yan Qinli Stele (6-5). No. 3634, $1.20, Mysterious Pagoda Stele (6-6).

Perf. 12x11½ Syncopated

2007, Nov. 5 **Litho.**

3629-3634 A1094 Set of 6 3.25 2.25

A sheet containing 2 each of lithographed and embossed examples of Nos. 3629-3634 exists. Value, $10.

Mountains — A1095

Designs: No. 3635, $1.20, Mount Gongga, People's Republic of China (2-1). No. 3636, $1.20, Popocatepetl, Mexico (2-2).

Perf. 12¾ Syncopated

2007, Nov. 22

3635-3636 A1095 Set of 2 2.00 .75

See Mexico Nos. 2561-2562.

Launch of China's First Lunar Probe A1096

2007, Nov. 26 **Litho. & Embossed**

3637 A1096 $1.20 multi 4.00 1.75

Emblem of Expo 2010, Shanghai A1097

Mascot of Expo 2010 — A1098

Perf. 11½ Syncopated

2007, Dec. 19 **Litho.**

3638 A1097 $1.20 multi .60 .45

a. Booklet pane of 1 .70 —

3639 A1098 $1.20 multi .60 .45

a. Booklet pane of 1 .70 —

b. Booklet pane of 10, 5 each #3638-3639 7.00 —

Complete booklet, #3638a, 3639a, 3639b 7.00

Compare with Type A1131.

Venues at 2008 Summer Olympics, Beijing — A1099

Designs: 80f, China Agricultural University Gymnasium (6-1). No. 3641, $1.20, Laoshan Mountain Bike Course (6-2). No. 3642, $1.20, National Indoor Stadium (6-3). No. 3643, $1.20, Beijing University Gymnasium (6-4). No. 3644, $1.20, National Aquatics Center (6-5). No. 3645, $3, Qingdao Olympic Sailing Center (6-6).

$6, National Stadium.

2007, Dec. 20 **Photo.** ***Perf. 13x13¼***

3640-3645 A1099 Set of 6 3.75 2.75

Souvenir Sheet

Perf. 13

3646 A1099 $6 multi 4.00 2.75

No. 3646 contains one pentagonal 65x62mm stamp.

A self-adhesive sheet of 2 each of Nos. 3640-3645 exists. Value, $12.

New Year 2008 (Year of the Rat) A1100

Perf. 12¾ Syncopated

2008, Jan. 5 **Photo.**

3647 A1100 $1.20 multi .80 .40

a. Booklet pane of 10 8.00 —

Complete booklet, #3647a 17.50

Miniature sheets containing 4 and 6 stamps exist. Value, $11 and $12, respectively.

Zhuxian New Year Woodprints A1101

Designs: No. 3648, $1.20, Gate guardian (4-1). No. 3649, $1.20, Woman lecturing son (4-2). No. 3650, $1.20, Come back with fruitful result (4-3). No. 3651, $1.20, Chivalrous women (4-4).

2008, Jan. 15 **Photo.** ***Perf. 13¼x13***

3648-3651 A1101 Set of 4 2.75 1.75

3651a Souvenir sheet of 4, #3648-3651 4.00 2.25

No. 3651a sold for $7.20. A miniature sheet containing two each of Nos. 3648-3651 exists. Value, $7.50.

Beijing Opera Characters A1102

Designs: 80f, Zhang Fei (6-1). No. 3653, $1.20, Cao Cao (6-2). No. 3654, $1.20, Bao Zheng (6-3). No. 3655, $1.20, Lian Po (6-4). No. 3656, $1.20, Xu Yanzhao (6-5). No. 3657, $1.20, Yang Yansi (6-6).

Perf. 12x11½ Syncopated

2008, Feb. 23 **Litho.**
3652-3657 A1102 Set of 6 3.00 2.25

Miniature Sheet

Birds — A1103

No. 3658: a, Urocissa caerulea (6-1). b, Emberiza koslowi (6-2). c, Tragopan caboti (6-3). d, Garrulax sukatschewi (6-4). e, Chrysolophus pictus (6-5). f, Podoces biddulphi (6-6).

2008, Feb. 28 Photo. *Perf. 13¼x13*
3658 A1103 $1.20 Sheet of 6, #a-f 3.25 2.50

11th National People's Congress — A1104

2008, Mar. 5
3659 A1104 $1.20 multi .80 .40

Olympic Torch Relay — A1105

Designs: $1.20, Lighting of torch in Greece, mascot holding torch (2-1). $3, Torch, torch bearer, vert. (2-2).

2008, Mar. 5 Photo. *Perf. 13¼*
3660-3661 A1105 Set of 2 2.00 1.25
3661a Souvenir sheet, #3660-3661 *6.00 3.00*

No. 3661a sold for $6.30. A sheet containing 4 self-adhesive examples each of Nos. 3660-3661 exists. Value, $15.

Suzhou-Nantong Yangtze River Bridge — A1106

No. 3662 — Denomination at: a, Left (2-1). b, Right (2-2).

2008, Apr. 12 ***Perf. 13¼***
3662 A1106 $1.20 Horiz. pair, #a-b 1.60 .90

Boao Forum For Asia — A1107

No. 3663: a, Dongyu Island (2-1). b, Forum venue (2-2).

Perf. 12x11½ Syncopated

2008, Apr. 13 **Litho.**
3663 A1107 $1.20 Horiz. pair, #a-b 1.45 .90

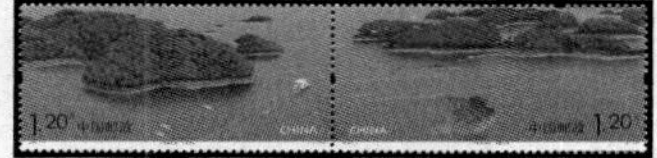

Qiandao Lake — A1108

No. 3664 — Islands with denomination at: a, Left (2-1). b, Right (2-2).

2008, Apr. 16 *Perf. 12¾ Syncopated*
3664 A1108 $1.20 Horiz. pair, #a-b 1.75 .90
c. Souvenir sheet, #3664 3.75 2.00

No. 3664c sold for $3.60.

A1109

Olympic Expo, Beijing — A1110

2008, Apr. 30 Photo. *Perf. 11¼x11*
3665 A1109 $1.20 multi .60 .40

Litho.

Perf. 12½

3666 A1110 $1.20 multi .60 .40

A circle of perforations surrounds the circular design on No. 3665.

Summer Palace — A1111

Designs: No. 3667, $1.20, Shiqikong Bridge (6-1). No. 3668, $1.20, Corridor (6-2). No. 3669, $1.20, Boat (6-3). No. 3670, $1.20, Garden of Harmonious Pleasures (6-4). No. 3671, $1.20, Yudai Bridge (6-5). No. 3672, $1.20, Houhu Lake (6-6).

$6, Tower of the Fragrance of Buddha, vert.

Litho. & Engr.

2008, May 10 ***Perf. 12***
3667-3672 A1111 Set of 6 3.00 2.00

Souvenir Sheet

Perf. 12x11¾

3673 A1111 $6 multi 2.75 2.00

No. 3673 contains one 50x62mm stamp.

Cao Chong Weighs the Elephant A1112

Cao Chong: Nos. 3674, 3676, $1.20, Marking water level on boat carrying elephant (2-1). Nos. 3675, 3677, $1.20, Replacing elephant with weighable objects (2-2).

2008, June 1 Photo. *Perf. 13x13¼*
3674-3675 A1112 Set of 2 1.00 1.00

Booklet Stamps

Self-Adhesive

Serpentine Die Cut 11¾

3676-3677 A1112 Set of 2 .85 —
3677a Booklet pane of 8, 4 each #3676-3677 3.50 —
Complete booklet, #3677a 4.00

Temples A1113

Designs: No. 3678, $1.20, White Horse Temple, China (2-1). No. 3679, $1.20, Mahabodhi Temple, India (2-2).

2008, June 6 ***Perf. 13¼x13***
3678-3679 A1113 Set of 2 1.25 .75

See India No. 2246.

Development on the Taiwan Strait — A1114

Designs: No. 3680, $1.20, Minjiang River development (4-1). No. 3681, $1.20, Port of Xiamen (4-2). No. 3682, $1.20, Exhibition Hall (4-3). No. 3683, $1.20, Fujian-Taiwan Kinship Museum (4-4).

2008, June 18 ***Perf. 12¾***
3680-3683 A1114 Set of 4 1.90 1.50

A sheet containing 2 each of Nos. 3680-3683 + 1 label exists. Value, $7.

Second Land Survey — A1115

Designs: No. 3684, $1.20, Satellite, rural land survey (2-1). No. 3685, $1.20, Theodolite, urban land survey (2-2).

Perf. 12¾x12½

2008, June 25 **Litho.**
3684-3685 A1115 Set of 2 1.20 .75

Qiuci Grotto Murals A1116

Designs: No. 3686, $1.20 Heavenly Kings (4-1). No. 3687, $1.20, Bodhisattva (4-2). No. 3688, $1.20, Flying Apsaras, horiz. (4-3). No. 3689, $1.20, Maitreya Preaching, horiz. (4-4).

2008, July 6 Photo. *Perf. 13¼*
3686-3689 A1116 Set of 4 2.00 1.50

General Qi Jiguang (1528-88) A1117

Qi Jiguang: No. 3690, $1.20, Standing (2-1). No. 3691, $1.20, On horse (2-2).

Perf. 12x12½ Syncopated

2008, July 19 **Litho.**
3690-3691 A1117 Set of 2 1.25 .90

Opening of 2008 Summer Olympics, Beijing — A1118

2008, Aug. 8 Photo. *Perf. 13¼*
3692 A1118 $1.20 multi 2.25 .50

A sheet of 8 self-adhesive stamps similar to No. 3692 exists. Value, $11. A sheet of 8 stamps with a holographic background exists. Value, $35.

Olympex 2008 Philatelic Exhibition, Beijing — A1119

Designs: No. 3693, $1.20, Greece #127 (2-1). No. 3694, $1.20, Portugal #RA14 (2-2).

$6, Greece #127, gold medal and mascots of 2004 Summer Olympics.

2008, Aug. 8 Photo. *Perf. 13¼x13*
3693-3694 A1119 Set of 2 1.25 .85

Souvenir Sheet

Litho.

Perf.

3695 A1119 $6 multi 4.50 3.50

No. 3695 contains one 56mm diameter stamp. No. 3695 exists on silk paper. Value, $20.

2008 Summer Olympics Gold Medal
A1119a

2008, Aug. 9 **Litho.** ***Perf. 12***
3695A A1119a $1.20 multi + label 4.00 4.00

Labels could be personalized. No. 3695A was printed in sheets of various sizes, with many sheets having pre-printed labels depicting Olympic athletes.

Closing of 2008 Summer Olympics
A1120

Designs: No. 3696, $1.20, National Stadium, Beijing (4-1). No. 3697, $1.20, Tower, Forbidden City, Beijing (4-2). No. 3698, $1.20, Millennium Wheel, London (4-3). No. 3699, $1.20, Tower of London (4-4).

2008, Aug. 24 **Photo.** ***Perf. 13¼***
3696-3699 A1120 Set of 4 3.00 2.25

A sheet containing 3 self-adhesive examples each of Nos. 3696-3699 exists. Value, $11.

China Central Television, 50th Anniv.
A1121

Perf. 13½x13 Syncopated
2008, Sept. 2
3700 A1121 $1.20 multi .85 .40

Emblem of 2008 Paralympic Games, Beijing — A1122

Paralympic Games Mascot — A1123

2008, Sept. 6 ***Perf. 13¼x13***
3701 A1122 $1.20 multi .65 .40
3702 A1123 $1.20 multi .65 .40

University of Science and Technology, 50th Anniv. — A1124

Perf. 12x11¼ Syncopated
2008, Sept. 20 **Litho.**
3703 A1124 $1.20 multi 1.25 .40

Ningxia Hui Autonomous Region, 50th Anniv. — A1125

No. 3704: a, Windmills (3-1). b, Trees and wildlife in desert (3-2). c, People holding flower bouquets (3-3).

Perf. 13¼x12¾ Syncopated
2008, Sept. 23 **Photo.**
3704 A1125 Horiz. strip of 3 1.40 1.25
a. 80f multi .25 .25
b.-c. $1.20 Either single .45 .35

Airports — A1126

No. 3705: a, Beijing Capital International Airport (3-1). b, Shanghai Pudong International Airport (3-2). c, Guangzhou Baiyun International Airport (3-3).

2008, Sept. 28 ***Perf. 12¾***
3705 Vert. strip of 3 1.75 1.50
a.-c. A1126 $1.20 Any single .45 .35

Guangxi Zhuang Autonomous Region, 50th Anniv. — A1127

No. 3706: a, Dancers (3-1). b, Building (3-2). c, Port (3-3).

Perf. 12¾ Syncopated
2008, Oct. 18 **Litho.**
3706 A1127 Horiz. strip of 3 1.25 1.25
a. 80f multi .25 .25
b.-c. $1.20 Either single .45 .35

Happy New Year Type of 2006 and

"Blossom of Fortune"
A1128

Perf. 11¾ Syncopated
2008, Oct. 9 **Litho.**
3707 A1128 $1.20 multi .50 .35

Souvenir Sheet

3708 Sheet of 2, #3707, 3708a 12.00 8.00
a. A1055a $3 gold & multi 6.25 6.25

Seventh Asia-Europe Meeting, Beijing — A1129

Perf. 12x11¼ Syncopated
2008, Oct. 24
3709 A1129 $1.20 multi 1.00 .40
a. Miniature sheet of 12 8.50 8.50

"Harmony" — A1130

2008, Dec. 3 ***Perf. 12***
3710 A1130 $1.20 multi + label .50 .40

Expo 2010, Shanghai — A1131

2008, Dec. 13 ***Perf. 12***
3711 A1131 $1.20 multi + label .60 .45

Compare with Type A1097.

A1132

Reform in China, 30th Anniv. — A1133

Perf. 12x11¼ Syncopated
2008, Dec. 18 **Litho.**
3712 A1132 $1.20 multi 1.00 .60
a. Miniature sheet of 8 6.50 6.50

Souvenir Sheet
Photo.
Perf.

3713 A1133 $6 multi + label 3.00 3.00

A sheet containing 2 examples of No. 3713 exists. Value, $12.

New Year 2009 (Year of the Ox) — A1134

Perf. 13 Syncopated
2009, Jan. 5 **Photo.**
3714 A1134 $1.20 multi .85 .45
a. Miniature sheet of 6 17.00 5.00
b. Booklet pane of 10 8.50 —
Complete booklet, #3714b 11.00

A sheet of 4 No. 3714 exists. Value, $7.

Bo Yibo (1908-2007), Politician
A1135

Bo Yibo: No. 3715, $1.20, Standing (2-1). No. 3716, $1.20, Seated, horiz. (2-2).

2009, Jan. 15 ***Perf. 13¼x13, 13x13¼***
3715-3716 A1135 Set of 2 1.25 .90

Zhangzhou New Year Woodprints
A1136

Designs: No. 3717, $1.20, Lion holding a sword in mouth (4-1). No. 3718, $1.20, The coming flood of wealth, vert. (4-2). No. 3719, $1.20, Goddess sending children, vert. (4-3). No. 3720, $1.20, Rat marrying off its daughter (4-4).

2009, Jan. 18 ***Perf. 12***
3717-3720 A1136 Set of 4 2.00 1.50
3720a Souvenir sheet, #3717-3720 + label 2.50 2.50
3720b Miniature sheet of 8, 2 each #3717-3720 4.50 4.50

No. 3720b exists on silk paper. Value, $5.50.

A1137

24th Winter Universiade, Harbin — A1138

2009, Feb. 18 **Litho.** ***Perf. 12¾***
3721 A1137 $1.20 multi .40 .40
3722 A1138 $1.20 multi .40 .40

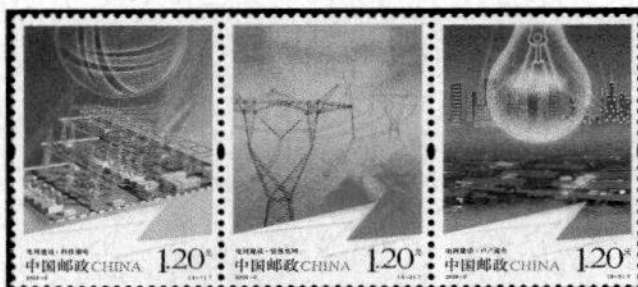

Electric Power Grid Construction — A1139

No. 3723: a, Power station (3-1). b, Transmission towers and power lines (3-2). c, Light bulb, city skyline (3-3).

Perf. 12x12½ Syncopated
2009, Feb. 24
3723 A1139 $1.20 Horiz. strip of 3, #a-c 2.00 1.50

Paintings by Shi Tao (1642-1707) A1140

No. 3724: a, Chaohu Lake (30x55mm) (6-1). b, Enjoying Fountain Sound (25x55mm) (6-2). c, Double Chrysanthemums (30x55mm) (6-3). d, Plum Blossoms and Bamboo (25x55mm) (6-4). e, Horse and its Owner (30x55mm) (6-5). f, Lotus (25x55mm) (6-6).

2009, Mar. 22 Litho. *Perf. 12½x13*

3724 Horiz. strip of 6 4.25 3.00
a. A1140 80f multi .35 .25
b.-f. A1140 $1.20 Any single .65 .45

A1141

China 2009 World Stamp Exhibition, Luoyang — A1142

Designs: No. 3725, $1.20, Vase (2-1). No. 3726, $1.20, Jar with stopper (2-2).
$6, National Beauty and Heavenly Fragrance.

Perf. 12¾ Syncopated

2009, Apr. 10 Litho. & Embossed

3725-3726 A1141 Set of 2 1.10 .85

Souvenir Sheet

Litho.

Perf. 13 Syncopated

3727 A1142 $6 multi 3.50 3.00

Nos. 3725 and 3726 both exist in sheets of 4. Value, set $7.50.
No. 3727 exists in a sheet of 2. Value, $10. No. 3727 exists in a sheet of 2 on silk paper. Value, $19.

China at World Expos A1143

Scenes from Expos from: No. 3728, $1.20, 1904, 1915, 1926, 1933 (red panel) (4-1). No. 3729, $1.20, 1982, 1982 (brown panel) (4-2). No. 3730, $1.20, 1999 (green panel) (4-3). No. 3731, $1.20, 2010 (blue panel) (4-4).

Perf. 13¼x12¾ Syncopated

2009, May 1 Photo.

3728-3731 A1143 Set of 4 3.00 2.00
3731a Miniature sheet of 8, 2 each #3728-3731 7.00 7.00

Fenghuang — A1144

No. 3732: a, North Gate (3-1). b, Rainbow Bridge (3-2). c, Street (3-3).

Perf. 12¾ Syncopated

2009, May 23 Litho.

3732 A1144 Horiz. strip of 3 1.25 1.25
a.-c. $1.20 Any single .40 .35

Children's Art — A1145

Designs: Nos. 3733, 3737, 80f, Love for the Motherland (yellow orange panel) (4-1). Nos. 3734, 3738, $1.20, Happy Life, horiz. (red panel) (4-2). Nos. 3735, 3739, $1.20, Peace Lovers (blue panel) (4-3). Nos. 3736, 3740, $1.20, Enthusiasm for Science, horiz. (green panel) (4-4).

Perf. 13¼x13, 13x13¼

2009, June 1 Photo.

3733-3736 A1145 Set of 4 2.00 1.40

Booklet Stamps

Self-Adhesive

Serpentine Die Cut 12

3737-3740 A1145 Set of 4 1.40 1.40
3740a Booklet pane of 8, 2 each #3737-3740 3.00

Hangzhou Bay Bridge — A1146

No. 3741: a, Bridge. b, Marine platform.

2009, June 18 Litho. *Perf. 12*

3741 A1146 $1.20 Horiz. pair, #a-b 1.00 .80

Li Xiannian (1909-92), People's Republic of China President A1147

Designs: No. 3742, $1.20, Wearing army uniform and cap (3-1). No. 3743, $1.20, Wearing gray suit with collar buttoned (3-2). No. 3744, $1.20, Wearing gray suit and eyeglasses (3-3).

2009, June 23 Photo. *Perf. 13¼x13*

3742-3744 A1147 Set of 3 1.50 1.25

A1148

16th Asian Games, Guangzhou — A1149

2009, June 30 Photo. *Perf. 13¼*

3745 A1148 $1.20 multi .60 .50
3746 A1149 $1.20 multi .60 .50

A sheet containing four each of Nos. 3745-3746 exists. Value, $8.

Great Hall of the People — A1150

Designs: No. 3747, East Gate (2-1). No. 3748, Great Auditorium (2-2).

2009, July 18 Litho. *Perf. 13¼x12½*

3747 A1150 $1.20 multi .55 .45
3748 A1150 $1.20 multi .55 .45
a. Booklet pane of 2, #3747-3748 1.10 —
b. Booklet pane of 8, 4 each #3747-3748 4.50 —
Complete booklet, #3748a, 3748b 7.50

Sanjiangyuan Nature Reserve — A1151

No. 3749: a, Geladandong (3-1). b, Eling Lake (3-2). c, Dza Chu (3-3).

Perf. 13¼x12½ Syncopated

2009, July 25 Photo.

3749 A1151 Horiz. strip of 3 1.40 1.25
a.-c. $1.20 Any single .40 .35

Flag, 60th Anniv. — A1152

2009, Aug. 2 Litho. *Perf. 13¼*

3750 A1152 $1.20 multi + label .80 .60

A souvenir sheet of 4 No. 3750 + one label exists.

Labrang Lamasery A1153

No. 3751: a, Grand Sutra Hall (2-1). b, Gongtang Pagoda (2-2).

Perf. 13x12¾ Syncopated

2009, Aug. 2

3751 A1153 $1.20 Vert. pair, #a-b .90 .80

Stork Tower A1154

Golden Gate A1155

2009, Aug. 14 Photo.

3752 A1154 $1.20 multi .55 .40
3753 A1155 $1.20 multi .55 .40

A1156

Huang Long Scenic Area — A1157

Designs: No. 3754, $1.20, Guest Welcome Ponds (3-1). No. 3755, $1.20, Waterfall (3-2). No. 3756, $1.20, Erdao Lake (3-3).
$6, Five-color Ponds.

2009, Aug. 27 *Perf. 12¾*

3754-3756 A1156 Set of 3 1.25 1.10

Souvenir Sheet

Perf. 13¼x12¾ Syncopated

3757 A1157 $6 multi 2.50 2.50

A miniature sheet containing 2 each of Nos. 3754-3756 exists. Value, $6.

National Library of China — A1158

Books and: No. 3758, $1.20, Old building (2-1). No. 3759, $1.20, Modern building (2-2).

2009, Sept. 9 *Perf. 13¼ Syncopated*

3758-3759 A1158 Set of 2 1.10 1.10

Miniature Sheet

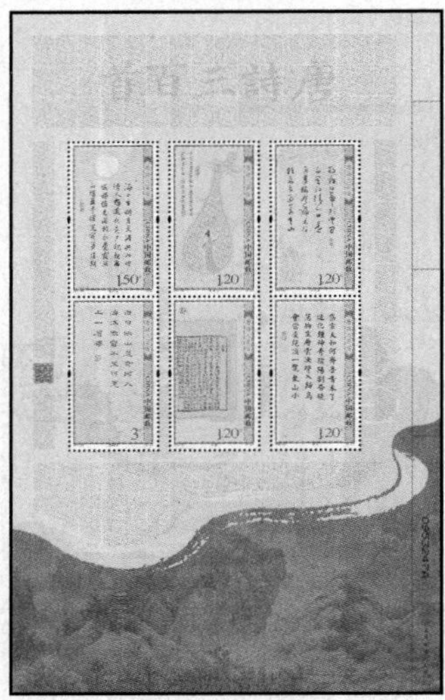

Tang Poems — A1159

No. 3760: a, $1.20, Downstream to Jiangling, by Il Bai (boat near rocks) (6-1). b, $1.20, A View of Taishan Mountain, by Du Fu (mountains) (6-2). c, $1.20, The Song of Pipa, by Bai Juyi (musician) (6-3). d, $1.20, To One Unnamed, by Li Shangyin (book) (6-4). e, $1.50, Looking at the Moon and Thinking of One Far Away, by Zhang Jiulin (Moon) (6-5). f, $3, On the Stork Tower, by Wang Zhihuan (Stork Tower) (6-6).

Litho., Engr. & Silk-screened
Perf. 12¾x13¼ Syncopated

2009, Sept. 13
3760 A1159 Sheet of 6, #a-f 9.00 6.50

Lanzhoui University, Cent. A1160

Perf. 13x12½ Syncopated

2009, Sept. 17 **Litho.**
3761 A1160 $1.20 multi .65 .50

Chinese People's Political Consultative Conference, 60th Anniv. — A1161

Flowers and: No. 3762, $1.20, Conference emblem (2-1). No. 3763, $1.20, Conference venue, horiz. (2-2).

Perf. 13¼ Syncopated

2009, Sept. 17
3762-3763 A1161 Set of 2 1.50 1.10

A1162

Beijing-Hangzhou Grand Canal — A1163

Designs: No. 3764, $1.20, Lantern Lighting Pagoda (6-1). No. 3765, $1.20, Boats and Tianhou Temple (6-2). No. 3766, $1.20, Shanshan Guild Hall (6-3). No. 3767, $1.20, Qingjiang Water Gate (6-4). No. 3768, $1.20, Boats and Wenfeng Pagoda (6-5). No. 3769, $1.20, Gongchen Bridge (6-6).
$6, Canal.

Perf. 13x13¼ Syncopated

2009, Sept. 26 **Photo.**
3764-3769 A1162 Set of 6 3.25 2.10

Souvenir Sheet
Perf. 13¼ Syncopated

3770 A1163 $6 multi 3.00 3.00

A1164

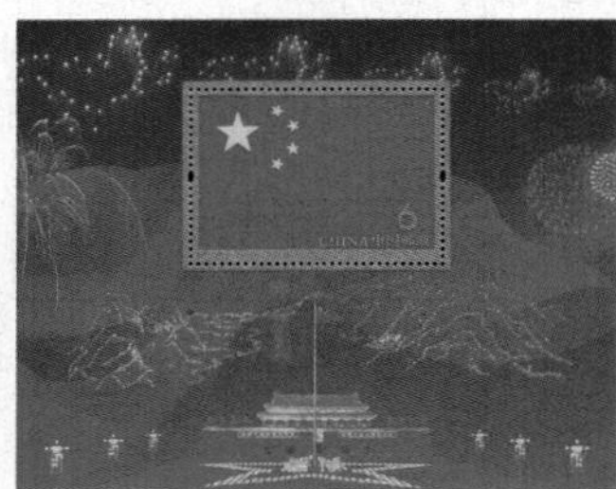

People's Republic of China, 60th Anniv. — A1165

Designs: No. 3771, $1.20, Marchers (4-1). No. 3772, $1.20, Tractors pulling floats bearing Chinese symbols (4-2). No. 3773, $1.20, Flag, emblems of Macao and Hong Kong (4-3). No. 3774, $1.20, Olympic rings and torch (4-4).
$6, Flag.

Perf. 13x12½ Syncopated

2009, Oct. 1
3771-3774 A1164 Set of 4 1.80 1.50

Souvenir Sheet
Perf. 13¼x13½ Syncopated

3775 A1165 $6 multi 3.00 3.00

A miniature sheet containing two each of Nos. 3771-3774 exists. Value, $6.

National Day Parade — A1166

Designs: No. 3776, $1.20, Infantry Group (red background) (4-1). No. 3777, $1.20, Army and 2nd Artillery Group (green background) (4-2). No. 3778, $1.20, Navy Equipment Group (blue background) (4-3). No. 3779, $1.20, Air Group (orange background) (4-4).

Perf. 13¼x12½ Syncopated

2009, Oct. 1
3776-3779 A1166 Set of 4 2.25 2.00

A miniature sheet containing two each of Nos. 3776-3779 exists. Value, $9.

"Music" — A1167

2009, Sept. 29 **Litho.** ***Perf. 12***
3780 A1167 $1.20 multi + label .75 .35

See Stamps With Attached Labels note after No. 3197.

"Happiness With the Spring" — A1168

2009, Oct. 9 ***Perf. 13 Syncopated***
3781 A1168 $1.20 multi .75 .35

A souvenir sheet containing Nos. 3781 and 3708a exists. Value, $13.

A1169

11th National Games, Shandong A1170

Perf. 13¼x13 Syncopated

2009, Oct. 16
3782 A1169 $1.20 multi .50 .45
3783 A1170 $1.20 multi .50 .45
a. Souvenir sheet, #3782-3783 1.75 1.75

No. 3783a sold for $3.60.

Ancient Academies A1171

Designs: No. 3784, $1.20, Stone Drum Academy (4-1). No. 3785, $1.20, Anding Academy (4-2). No. 3786, $1.20, Ehu Academy (4-3). No. 3787, $1.20, Dongpo Academy (4-4).

Perf. 13¼ Syncopated

2009, Nov. 15 **Photo.**
3784-3787 A1171 Set of 4 1.75 1.50

A souvenir sheet containing two each of Nos. 3784-3787 exists. Value, $6.

Guangji Bridge — A1172

No. 3788: a, Building at left on shore, bridge, ships (3-1). b, Ships, central part of bridge (3-2). c, Bridge, building at right on shore (3-3).

Perf. 12¾ Syncopated

2009, Nov. 16 **Litho.**
3788 A1172 Horiz. strip of 3 1.10 1.10
a.-c. $1.20 Any single .35 .35

Ma Lianliang (1901-66), Opera Performer, in Kong Ming Borrows the East Wing — A1173

Ma Lianliang in Zhao the Orphan — A1174

Perf. 13¼x13½ Syncopated

2009, Nov. 28 **Photo.**
3789 A1173 $1.20 multi .60 .35
3790 A1174 $1.20 multi .60 .35

Return of Macao to China, 10th Anniv. A1175

Doves and: No. 3791, $1.20, Golden Lotus sculpture, flags of People's Republic of China and Macao (3-1). No. 3792, $1.20, "CEPA," buildings (3-2). $1.50, Bridge, buildings (3-3).

Perf. 13¼x13 Syncopated

2009, Dec. 20
3791-3793 A1175 Set of 3 1.25 1.25
3793a Souvenir sheet, #3791-3793, Macao #1302a-1302c 2.40 2.40

See Macao Nos. 1302-1303. No. 3793a was not offered for sale in Macao.

16th Asian Games, Guangzhou — A1176

2009, Dec. 25 **Litho.** ***Perf. 12***
3794 A1176 $1.20 multi + label 1.00 .40

Compare with Type A1148. See Stamps With Attached Labels note after No. 3197.

Gutian Conference, 80th Anniv. — A1177

Perf. 13¼x13 Syncopated

2009, Dec. 28
3795 A1177 $1.20 multi .80 .35

Ballet Dancers in Red Detachment of Women — A1178

Designs: No. 3796, $1.20, Dancer in red (2-1). No. 3797, $1.20, Dancers in blue (2-2).

2010, Jan. 1 Photo. *Perf. 13¼*
3796-3797 A1178 Set of 2 2.00 1.00

New Year 2010 (Year of the Tiger) A1179

2010, Jan. 5 *Perf. 12¾ Syncopated*
3798 A1179 $1.20 multi 1.00 .40
a. Booklet pane of 10 4.00 —
Complete booklet, #3798a 7.50

No. 3798 exists in sheets of 4 and 6. Value, $10 each.

Gen. Song Renqiong (1909-2005) — A1180

Designs: No. 3799, $1.20, Wearing cap (2-1). No. 3800, $1.20, Reading book (2-2).

Perf. 13 Syncopated
2010, Jan. 8 Litho.
3799-3800 A1180 Set of 2 1.00 .70

Expo 2010, Shanghai — A1181

Designs: 80f, Expo Center (4-1). No. 3802, $1.20, China Pavilion (4-2). No. 3803, $1.20, Expo Performance Center (4-3). $3, Theme Pavilion (4-4).
$6, Shanghai Expo Park, vert.

Perf. 13¼x13 Syncopated
2010, Jan. 21 Photo.
3801-3804 A1181 Set of 4 2.00 2.00

Souvenir Sheet
Perf. 13x12¾ Syncopated
3805 A1181 $6 multi 6.00 4.50

No. 3805 contains one 30x75mm stamp. A sheet containing two each of Nos. 3801-3804 exists. A sheet containing two examples of No. 3805 exists.

Liangping New Year Woodprints A1182

Designs: No. 3806, $1.20, Gate god (4-1). No. 3807, $1.20, Stealing the immortal grass (4-2). No. 3808, $1.20, Peace leads to happiness (4-3). No. 3809, $1.20, Exiting the pass with a stolen token (4-4).

2010, Feb. 6 *Perf. 13¼x13*
3806-3809 A1182 Set of 4 1.40 1.40
3809a Souvenir sheet, #3806-3809 + label 2.50 2.50
3809b Souvenir sheet of 8, 2 each #3806-3809 on fabric-faced paper *10.00 8.00*
3809c As "b," plain paper *6.25 6.25*

No. 3809a sold for $7.20.

Intl. Women's Day, Cent. — A1183

Perf. 13¼x13 Syncopated
2010, Mar. 8
3810 A1183 $1.20 multi .85 .40

Dwelling in Fuchun Mountains, Painting by Huang Gongwang — A1184

No. 3811 — Various parts of painting with inscription: a, (6-1). b, (6-2). c, (6-3). d, (6-4). e, (6-5). f, (6-6).

2010, Mar. 20 *Perf. 13¼*
3811 A1184 Block of 6 12.50 10.00
a.-d. $1.20 Any single .60 .35
e. $1.50 multi .75 .50
f. $3 multi 1.25 .95

Tomb Sweeping Festival — A1185

Designs: No. 3812, $1.20, Ancestor worship (3-1). No. 3813, $1.20, Spring outing (3-2). No. 3814, $1.20, Planting willows (3-3).

Perf. 13¼x13½ Syncopated
2010, Apr. 5 Litho.
3812-3814 A1185 Set of 3 1.50 1.10

A sheet containing three each of Nos. 3812-3814 exists.

Idioms — A1186

Designs: No. 3815, $1.20, The foolish old man removes the mountains (4-1). No. 3816, $1.20, Sleeping on brushwood and tasting gall (4-2). No. 3817, $1.20, Mao Sui recommending himself (4-3). No. 3818, $1.20, Rising to practice swordplay upon hearing the rooster crow (4-4).

Perf. 13¼x13½ Syncopated
2010, Apr. 18 Photo.
3815-3818 A1186 Set of 4 1.40 1.40

Opening of Expo 2010, Shanghai A1187

2010, May 1 *Perf. 13¼ Syncopated*
3819 A1187 $1.20 multi 1.00 .40

A sheet of six exists.

A1188

A1189

Ancient Calligraphy — A1190

No. 3820 — Preface to the Orchid Pavilion: a, Denomination at right (6-1). b, Denomination at left (6-2).
No. 3821 — Poems Composed During the Cold Food Festival in Huangzhou: a, Denomination at right (6-3). b, Denomination at left (6-4).
No. 3822 — Elegiac Lament for My Nephew: a, Denomination at right (6-5). b, Denomination at left (6-6).

2010, May 15 *Perf. 13x13¼*
3820 A1188 $1.20 Horiz. pair, #a-b .70 .70
3821 A1189 $1.20 Horiz. pair, #a-b .70 .70
3822 A1190 $1.20 Horiz. pair, #a-b .70 .70
Nos. 3820-3822 (3) 2.10 2.10

A sheet containing two each Nos. 3820-3822 exists.

Tenth Global Travel and Tourism Summit, Beijing — A1191

2010, May 25 *Perf. 13¼ Syncopated*
3823 A1191 $1.20 multi 3.50 .50

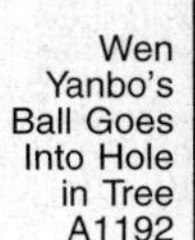

Wen Yanbo's Ball Goes Into Hole in Tree A1192

Wen Yanbo Retrieves Ball With Water A1193

2010, June 1 *Perf. 13 Syncopated*
3824 A1192 $1.20 multi .35 .35
3825 A1193 $1.20 multi .35 .35
a. Booklet pane of 2, #3824-3825 .70 —
b. Booklet pane of 8, 4 each #3824-3825 3.00 —
Complete booklet, #3825a, 3825b 4.00

A1194

Environmental Protection A1195

Perf. 13¼x13½ Syncopated
2010, June 5
3826 A1194 $1.20 multi 1.25 .40
3827 A1195 $1.20 multi 1.25 .40

Kunqu Opera — A1196

Designs: No. 3828, $1.20, Washing the Silken Gauze (3-1). No. 3829, $1.20, The Peony Pavilion (3-2). No. 3830, $1.20, The Palace of Long Life (3-3).

Perf. 13¼ Syncopated
2010, June 12 Photo.
3828-3830 A1196 Set of 3 1.10 1.10

A miniature sheet containing 3 each of Nos. 3828-3830 exists.

Pearl River Scenes — A1197

Designs: No. 3831, $1.20, Five Goats Statue, Guangzhou (4-1). No. 3832, $1.20, Guangzhou Center for the Performing Arts (4-2). No. 3833, $1.20, Guangzhou skyline (4-3). No. 3834, $1.20, Guangzhou Intl. Convention and Exhibition Center (4-4).

Perf. 13¼x13 Syncopated
2010, June 28
3831-3834 A1197 Set of 4 1.40 1.40
3834a Souvenir sheet of 8, 2 each #3831-3834 *9.50 4.75*

Loulan — A1198

Designs: No. 3835, $1.20, Ruins of Buddhist stupa (2-1). No. 3836, $1.20, Ruins of building (2-2).

2010, July 3 **Litho.**

3835-3836 A1198 Set of 2 .70 .70

Maritime Day — A1199

Perf. 13½x13 Syncopated

2010, July 11 **Photo.**

3837 A1199 $1.20 multi .80 .35

Composers — A1200

Designs: No. 3838, $1.20, Johann Sebastian Bach (1685-1750) (4-1). No. 3839, $1.20, Joseph Haydn (1732-1809) (4-2). No. 3840, $1.20, Wolfgang Amadeus Mozart (1756-91) (4-3). $4.50, Ludwig van Beethoven (1770-1827) (4-4).

Perf. 13¼x12¾ Syncopated

2010, July 25 **Litho. & Engr.**

3838-3841 A1200 Set of 4 2.40 2.40

Legend of the Cowherd and the Weaving Maid — A1201

Designs: No. 3842, Dress-linked affection (4-1). No. 3843, Happy lovers (4-2). No. 3844, Carrying children to chase wife (4-3). No. 3845, Heavenly reunion (4-4).

Perf. 13¼x13¾ Syncopated

2010, Aug. 16 **Photo.**

3842 A1201 $1.20 multi .40 .35
 a. Booklet pane of 1 + 5 labels .60 —
3843 A1201 $1.20 multi .40 .35
 a. Booklet pane of 1 + 5 labels .60 —
3844 A1201 $1.20 multi .40 .35
 a. Booklet pane of 1 + 5 labels .60 —
3845 A1201 $1.20 multi .40 .35
 a. Booklet pane of 1 + 5 labels .60 —
 Complete booklet, #3842a-3845a 3.00
 Nos. 3842-3845 (4) 1.60 1.40

Complete booklet sold for $8.

2010 Asian Para Games, Guangzhou — A1202

2010, Sept. 3 ***Perf. 13***

3846 A1202 $1.20 multi .80 .35

Values are for stamp with adjacent selvage.

Great Wall Type of 2005

2010, Sept. 3 **Litho.** ***Perf. 12***

3846A A1003 $1.20 multi + label *5.00 5.00*

See note following No. 3462.

A1203

Shangri-La (Zhongdian) — A1204

Designs: No. 3847, $1.20, Songzanlin Lamasery (4-1). No. 3848, $1.20, Napa Lake and grassland (4-2). No. 3849, $1.20, Pudacuo National Park (4-3). No. 3850, $1.20, Dukezong (4-4).

$6, Meili Snow Mountain.

Perf. 13¼x13 Syncopated

2010, Sept. 13

3847-3850 A1203 Set of 4 1.50 1.50

Souvenir Sheet

Perf. 13¼x13¾ Syncopated

3851 A1204 $6 multi 2.50 1.90

Confucius and Buildings — A1205

No. 3852: a, $1.20, Confucius and temple (3-1). b, $1.20, Family home of Confucius (3-2). c, $3, Cemetery of Confucius (3-3).

Perf. 13¼ Syncopated

2010, Sept. 28 **Litho.**

3852 A1205 Horiz. strip of 3, #a-c 2.00 1.60
 d. Souvenir sheet, #3852a-3852c 3.00 3.00

Huai River Water Control Project — A1206

Designs: No. 3853, $1.20, Nanwan Reservoir (4-1). No. 3854, $1.20, Linhuaigang Water Control Project (4-2). No. 3855, $1.20, Huai River Outflow Project (4-3). No. 3856, $1.20, Nansi Lake Water Control Project (4-4).

Perf. 12¾x13 Syncopated

2010, Oct. 14

3853-3856 A1206 Set of 4 1.50 1.50

Flora — A1207

Drawings of: No. 3857, $1.20, Plum blossom (4-1). No. 3858, $1.20, Orchid (4-2). No. 3859, $1.20, Bamboo (4-3). No. 3860, $1.20, Chrysanthemums (4-4).

2010, Oct. 18 ***Perf. 13¼ Syncopated***

3857-3860 A1207 Set of 4 2.50 1.50
 3860a Souvenir sheet of 8, 2 each #3857-3860 *20.00 15.00*

No. 3860a exists imperf.

Zhu Xi (Chu Hsi) (1130-1200), Philosopher A1208

Designs: No. 3861, $1.20, Portrait of Zhu Xi (2-1). No. 3862, $1.20, Zhu Xi, student and horse (2-2).

Perf. 13¼x13½ Syncopated

2010, Oct. 22 **Litho. & Engr.**

3861-3862 A1208 Set of 2 1.00 .75

A souvenir sheet of two exists.

2010 Asian Games, Guangzhou A1209

Designs: 80f, Badminton (6-1). No. 3864, $1.20, Wushu (6-2). No. 3865, $1.20, Hurdles (6-3). No. 3866, $1.20, Equestrian (6-4). No. 3867, $1.20, Dragon boat racing (6-5). $3, Weiqi (6-6).

Perf. 13¼ Syncopated

2010, Nov. 12 **Photo.**

3863-3868 A1209 Set of 6 2.60 2.60
 3868a Sheet of 12, 2 each #3863-3868 *8.00 8.00*

Souvenir Sheet

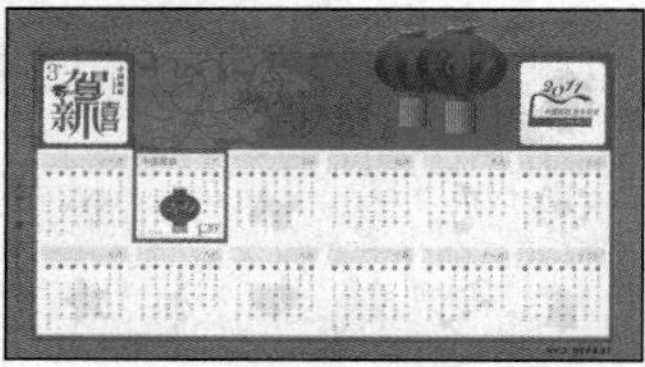

New Year 2011 — A1210

No. 3869: a, $1.20, Chinese lantern, calendar for February 2011. b, $3, Like #3541, with copper frame.

Serpentine Die Cut 12¼

2010, Oct. 9 **Self-Adhesive** **Litho.**

3869 A1210 Sheet of 2, #a-b, + 13 labels *4.75 4.75*

Traditional Chinese Medicine Stores — A1211

Designs: No. 3870, $1.20, Tongren Tang (4-1). No. 3871, $1.20, Huqing Yu Tang (4-2). No. 3872, $1.20, Lei Yongshang (4-3). No. 3873, $1.20, Chen Liji (4-4).

Perf. 13¼ Syncopated

2010, Nov. 20 **Photo.**

3870-3873 A1211 Set of 4 1.50 1.50

High-speed Train — A1212

Perf. 13¼x12¾ Syncopated

2010, Dec. 7 **Photo.**

3874 A1212 $1.20 multi 1.50 .80

Chinese Capital Markets A1213

Bar graph and: No. 3875, $1.20, Bull, computers at capital market (2-1). No. 3876, $1.20, City, satellite dish, train (2-2).

Perf. 13¼ Syncopated

2010, Dec. 12 **Litho.**

3875-3876 A1213 Set of 2 1.75 1.25
 3876a Souvenir sheet of 8, 4 each #3875-3876 *30.00 20.00*

New Year 2011 (Year of the Rabbit) A1214

Perf. 13 Syncopated

2011, Jan. 5 **Photo.**

3877 A1214 $1.20 multi .80 .60
 a. Booklet pane of 10 8.00 —
 Complete booklet, #3877a 8.00
 b. Souvenir sheet of 6 *12.50 10.00*

A souvenir sheet containing 4 No. 3877 exists. Value, $12.50.

Fengxiang New Year Woodprints A1215

Designs: No. 3878, $1.20, General Yuchi Jingde (4-1). No. 3879, $1.20, Fortune boy (4-2). No. 3880, $1.20, Beauties (4-3). No. 3881, $1.20, Fortune flower vase (4-4).

Perf. 13¼x13¾ Syncopated

2011, Jan. 10 **Litho.**

3878-3881 A1215 Set of 4 2.00 1.50

Sheet of eight containing two each Nos. 3878-3881 on plain and fabric-faced paper exist.

Early Leaders of the Communist Party of China — A1216

Designs: No. 3882, $1.20, Chen Yannian (1898-1927) (5-1). No. 3883, $1.20, Zhang Tailei (1898-1927) (5-2). No. 3884, $1.20, Luo Yinong (1902-28) (5-3). No. 3885, $1.20, Yun Daiying (1895-1931) (5-4). No. 3886, $1.20, Xiang Ying (1898-1941) (5-5).

2011, Feb. 21

3882-3886 A1216 Set of 5 3.00 1.90

Liangzhu Jade — A1217

Designs: No. 3887, $1.20, Cong (carved block of jade) (2-1). No. 3888, $1.20, Bi (ring of jade) (2-2).

2011, Mar. 8 **Photo.**

3887-3888 A1217 Set of 2 1.50 .75

Scenes From "The Scholars," Novel by Wu Jingzi — A1218

Designs: 80f, Lotus painter Wang Mian (6-1). No. 3890, $1.20, Fanjin passing the Imperial exam (6-2). No. 3891, $1.20, Two lamp wicks (6-3). No. 3892, $1.20, Ma Er tours West Lake (6-4). No. 3893, $1.20, Mr. and Mrs. Du Shaoqing (6-5). No. 3894, $1.20, Shen Qunzhi selling writings by Sheli Bridge (6-6).

2011, Mar. 21

3889-3894 A1218 Set of 6 2.10 2.10

A sheet of 12 containing two each of Nos. 3889-3894 exists.

Chinese Calligraphy A1219

Designs: No. 3895, $1.20, Pingfu Tie, by Lu Ji (4-1). No. 3896, $1.20, Chuyue Tie, by Wang Xizhi (4-2). No. 3897, $1.20, Gushi Si Tie, by Zhangxu (4-3). No. 3898, $1.20, Zixu Tie, by Huaisu (4-4).

2011, Apr. 15 ***Perf. 13¼ Syncopated***

3895-3898 A1219 Set of 4 2.25 1.50

A sheet of eight containing two each Nos. 3895-3896, printed on rice paper exists.

Military Aircraft — A1220

Designs: No. 3899, $1.20, J-10 fighter (3-1). No. 3900, $1.20, JH-7 fighter (3-2). No. 3901, $1.20, AC313 helicopter (3-3).

Perf. 13¼x12¾ Syncopated

2011, Apr. 17 **Litho.**

3899-3901 A1220 Set of 3 1.50 1.25

World Reading Day A1221

2011, Apr. 23 ***Perf. 13 Syncopated***

3902 A1221 $1.20 multi .60 .50

Tsinghua University, Cent. A1222

2011, Apr. 24 **Litho. & Embossed**

3903 A1222 $1.20 multi .80 .50

Expo 2011, Xi'an — A1223

Designs: $1.20, Emblem (2-1). $3, Mascot (2-2).

Perf. 13¼x13¾ Syncopated

2011, Apr. 28 **Photo.**

3904-3905 A1223 Set of 2 2.00 1.40

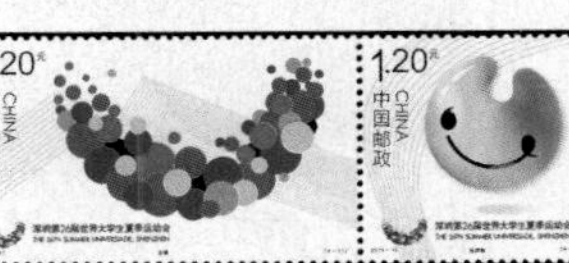

26th Summer Universiade, Shenzhen — A1224

No. 3906: a, $1.20, Emblem (50x30mm, 4-1). b, $1.20, Mascot (30x30mm, 4-2).

No. 3907: a, $1.20, Shenzhen Universiade Sports Center (50x30mm, 4-3). b, $3, Torch, Chinese and English text (30x30mm, 4-4).

2011, May 4 **Litho.** ***Perf. 13¼***

Horiz. Pairs, #a-b

3906-3907 A1224 Set of 2 2.10 2.10

3907a Sheet of 8 2 each #3906a-3906b, 3907a-3907b *6.50 5.50*

Cloud Brocade A1225

Designs: No. 3908, $1.20, Dragon (3-1). No. 3909, $1.20, Crane insignia of first-rank civil official (3-2). No. 3910, $1.20, Fish (Double happiness, 3-3).

Perf. 13¼x12¾

2011, May 10 **Photo.**

3908-3910 A1225 Set of 3 1.50 1.25

3910a Souvenir sheet of 3, #3908-3910, + 3 labels *5.50 3.50*

Emblem of Communist Party of China — A1226

2011, May 21 **Litho.** ***Perf. 13¼***

3911 A1226 $1.20 multi + label 1.00 .75

See Stamps With Attached Labels note after No. 3187.

Liberation of Tibet, 60th Anniv. — A1227

Designs: No. 3912, $1.20, Potala Palace, Chinese soldiers, Tibetans and livestock (3-1). No. 3913, $1.20, Airplane over building, dancers (3-2). No. 3914, $1.20, Building, dancers (3-3).

Perf. 13¼x13¾ Syncopated

2011, May 23 **Photo.**

3912-3914 A1227 Set of 3 1.50 1.25

Scientists A1228

Designs: No. 3915, $1.20, Bei Shizhang (1903-2009), biologist (4-1). No. 3916, $1.20, Qian Xuesen (1911-2009), rocket scientist (4-2). No. 3917, $1.20, Hou Xianglin (1912-2008), chemical engineer (4-3). No. 3918, $1.20, Qian Sanqiang (1913-92), nuclear physicist (4-4).

Perf. 13x12¾ Syncopated

2011, May 25

3915-3918 A1228 Set of 4 2.25 1.50

Ming and Qing Dynasty Furniture — A1230

No. 3919: a, 80f, Qing Dynasty rosewood-embedded copper dragon throne (6-1). b, $1.20, Ming Dynasy pearwood folding chair (6-2).

No. 3920: a, $1.20, Ming Dynasty pearwood official's armchair with carved Chinese characters (6-3). b, $1.20, Ming Dynasty pearwood armchair with carved dragons (6-4).

No. 3921: a, $1.20, Qing Dynasty rosewood-embedded marble armchair (6-5). b, $1.20, Ming Dynasty marble-embedded rosewood drum stool (6-6).

Perf. 13¼x13¾ Syncopated

2011, June 20 **Litho.**

3919 A1230 Horiz. pair, #a-b .65 .65

c. Booklet pane, #3919a-3919b + 2 labels *.90* —

3920 A1230 $1.20 Horiz. pair, #a-b .75 .75

c. Booklet pane, #3920a-3920b + 2 labels *1.10* —

3921 A1230 $1.20 Horiz. pair, #a-b .75 .75

c. Booklet pane, #3921a-3921b + 2 labels *1.10* —

d. Booklet pane, #3919a-3919b, 3920a-3920b, 3921a-3921b *3.25* —

Complete booklet, #3919c, 3920c, 3921c, 3921d *6.50*

Nos. 3919-3921 (3) 2.15 2.15

A1231

Communist Party of China, 90th Anniv. — A1232

Flag of the Communist Party of China and: No. 3922, $1.20, People and building (6-1). No. 3923, $1.20, Soldiers and monument (6-2). No. 3924, $1.20, Sculpture and building (6-3). No. 3925, $1.20, City skyline, sculpture of bull (6-4). No. 3926, $1.20, City skyline and modern building (6-5). No. 3927, $1.20, Beijing National Stdium, Chinese Pavilion, Shanghai (6-6).

$6, Flag of the Communist Party of China.

2011, June 22 **Photo.** ***Perf. 13¼***

3922-3927 A1231 Set of 6 3.25 2.50

3924a Sheet of 6, 2 each #3922-3924 *8.75 8.75*

3927a Sheet of 6, 2 each #3925-3927 *8.75 8.75*

Souvenir Sheet

Perf. 13¼x13

3928 A1232 $6 multi 3.50 2.75

Opening of Beijing-Shanghai High Speed Railway — A1233

Perf. 13¼x12¾ Syncopated

2011, June 30

3929 A1233 $1.20 multi 1.75 .90

Cycling — A1234

Designs: No. 3930, $1.20, Cyclists on bike path (2-1). No. 3931, $1.20, Cyclists racing (2-2).

2011, July 2 **Litho.**

3930-3931 A1234 Set of 2 1.00 .80

Folk Vocal Arts — A1235

Designs: No. 3932, $1.20, Xiangsheng (4-1). No. 3933, $1.20, Singer with drum (4-2). No. 3934, $1.20, Pingtan (4-3). No. 3935, $1.20, Performer in black robe (4-4).

2011, July 8 ***Perf. 13¼ Syncopated***

3932-3935 A1235 Set of 4 1.50 1.50
3935a Sheet of 8, 4 each #3932-3935 *9.50 9.50*

Chinese Culture Abroad — A1236

No. 3936: a, Chinese Festival, London Eye (4-1). b, Chinese Benevolent Association sculpture and building, Buddhist temple, modern building (4-2). c, Chinatown, Transamerica Pyramid, San Francisco (4-3). d, Chinese school building, mountain (4-4).

Perf. 13¼x13¾ Syncopated

2011, July 10

3936 Horiz. strip of 4 3.00 2.60
a.-c. A1236 $1.20 Any single .40 .40
d. A1236 $4.50 multi 1.40 1.40

Cargo Ships — A1237

No. 3937: a, Cosco Asia container ship (4-1). b, Xinsheng Hai bulk transport ship (4-2).

Perf. 13¼x12¾ Syncopated

2011, Aug. 8 **Photo.**

3937 A1237 $1.20 Horiz. pair, #a-b 1.00 .85

Peonies — A1238

Lilies — A1239

Sunflowers — A1240

Chinese Rose — A1241

Carnations — A1242

Camellias — A1243

Azalea Flowers — A1244

Lotus Flowers — A1245

Plum Blossoms — A1246

Magnolia Blossoms — A1247

2011, Sept. 1 **Litho.** ***Perf. 12***

3938 A1238 $1.20 multi + label .65 .50
3939 A1239 $1.20 multi + label .65 .50
3940 A1240 $1.20 multi + label .65 .50
3941 A1241 $1.20 multi + label .65 .50
3942 A1242 $1.20 multi + label .65 .50
3943 A1243 $1.20 multi + label .65 .50
3944 A1244 $1.20 multi + label .65 .50
3945 A1245 $1.20 multi + label .65 .50
3946 A1246 $1.20 multi + label .65 .50
3947 A1247 $1.20 multi + label .65 .50
Nos. 3938-3947 (10) 6.50 5.00

See Stamps With Attached Labels note after No. 3197.

Traditional Games of Ethnic Minorities A1248

No. 3948, $1.20: a, Men in board shoe race (4-1). b, Women with bamboo poles (4-2).
No. 3949, $1.20: a, Top spinning (4-3). b, Stilt racing (4-4).

Perf. 13x12¾ Syncopated

2011, Sept. 10 **Photo.**

Vert. Pairs, #a-b

3948-3949 A1248 Set of 2 1.50 1.50

A1249

Lord Guan Yu (?-219) — A1250

Lord Guan Yu: No. 3950, $1.20, On horse (2-1). No. 3951, $1.20, Seated, reading annals (2-2).

Perf. 13x13¼ Syncopated

2011, Sept. 12

3950-3951 A1249 Set of 2 2.75 1.00

Souvenir Sheet

Perf. 13¼x13 Syncopated

3952 A1250 $6 multi 6.50 6.00

A limited edition souvenir sheet of 6 containing three each Nos. 3950-3951 exists.

Details From the Scroll of the 87 Immortals A1251

Various details with stamps numbered: No. 3953, $1.20, (6-1). No. 3954, $1.20, (6-2). No. 3955, $1.20, (6-3). No. 3956, $1.20, (6-4). $1.50, (6-5). $3, (6-6).

Perf. 13¼ Syncopated

2011, Sept. 26 **Litho.**

3953-3958 A1251 Set of 6 3.00 3.00
3958a Booklet pane of 6, #3953-3958 *4.00* —
Complete booklet, #3958a *8.50*

A1252

Chinese Revolution, Cent. — A1253

Designs: No. 3959, $1.20, Wuchang Uprising (2-1). No. 3960, $1.20, Revolution leaders (2-2).
$6, Dr. Sun Yat-sen (1866-1925), leader of revolution.

Perf. 13¼x13 Syncopated

2011, Oct. 10 **Photo.**

3959-3960 A1252 Set of 2 1.00 .85
3960a Sheet of 8, 4 each #3959-3960 *8.00 7.00*

Souvenir Sheet

Perf. 13¼x12¾ Syncopated

3961 A1253 $6 multi 2.00 2.00

A1254

Rebuilding Efforts After May 12, 2008 Sichuan Earthquake — A1255

Designs: No. 3962, $1.20, Clock, rebuilt town (4-1). No. 3963, $1.20, Sculpture, rebuilt sections of ancient town (4-2). No. 3964, $1.20, Sculpture, buildings (4-3). No. 3965, $1.20, Flag, sculpture, rebuilt village (4-4).
$6, Rebuilt town, sculpture, wind generators.

Perf. 13¼ Syncopated

2011, Oct. 13 **Litho.**
3962-3965 A1254 Set of 4 2.25 1.50

Souvenir Sheet

Perf. 13 Syncopated

3966 A1255 $6 multi 2.00 2.00

A1256

Tianjin Binhai New Area — A1257

Building and: No. 3967, $1.20, New downtown (3-1). No. 3968, $1.20, Yujiabao Financial District (3-2). No. 3969, $1.20, Map of National Animation Industry Park (3-3).
$6, Port, crane, container ship.

Perf. 13¼x12¾ Syncopated

2011, Oct. 21 **Photo.**
3967-3969 A1256 Set of 3 1.25 1.25

Souvenir Sheet

Perf. 13x13¾ Syncopated

3970 A1257 $6 multi 1.90 1.90

A1258

China 2011 Intl. Philatelic Exhibition, Wuxi — A1259

Designs: No. 3971, $1.20, Flat-sided container with spout and handle (2-1). No. 3972, $1.20, A-fu (2-2).
$6, Yu Zhuang Qiu, by Ni Zan.

Perf. 13¼x13¾ Syncopated

2011, Oct. 10
3971-3972 A1258 Set of 2 .75 .75
3972a Sheet of 8, 4 each #3971-3972 + label *6.50 6.50*

Souvenir Sheet

Perf. 13¼x13 Syncopated

3973 A1259 $6 multi 1.90 1.90

No. 3973 exists imperf.

Xinhua News Agency, 80th Anniv. A1260

Various buildings: No. 3974, $1.20, Red electric wave (4-1). No. 3975, $1.20, Anti-Japanese War (4-2). No. 3976, $1.20, War of Liberation (4-3). No. 3977, $1.20, Going global (4-4).

Perf. 13¼ Syncopated

2011, Nov. 7 **Litho.**
3974-3977 A1260 Set of 4 1.50 1.50

Bird on Branch A1261

2011, Oct. 9 ***Perf. 11¾ Syncopated***
3978 A1261 $1.20 multi .40 .40
a. Souvenir sheet of 2, #3708a, 3978 *3.75 3.75*

Armillary Spheres A1262

Designs: No. 3980, $1.20, Simplified armillary sphere built by Guo Shoujing, 1276 (2-1). No. 3981, $1.20, Equatorial armillary sphere built by Tycho Brahe, 1595 (2-2).

Perf. 13¼x12¾ Syncopated

2011, Dec. 10 **Litho. & Engr.**
3980-3981 A1262 Set of 2 1.00 .90

See Denmark Nos. 1576-1577.

New Year 2012 (Year of the Dragon) A1263

Perf. 12¾ Syncopated

2012, Jan. 5 **Photo.**
3982 A1263 $1.20 multi 1.50 1.00
a. Booklet pane of 10 15.00 —
Complete booklet, #3982a 16.00

Limited edition sheets of 4 and 6 stamps exist.

Bank of China, Cent. — A1264

Designs: $1.20, Old bank building (2-1). $1.50, Modern bank building (2-2).

2012, Feb. 5 ***Perf. 13 Syncopated***
3983-3984 A1264 Set of 2 3.50 2.00

Emblem and Building of Zhonghua Book Company A1265

Perf. 13¼x13¾ Syncopated

2012, Feb. 23 **Litho.**
3985 A1265 $1.20 multi 1.00 .50

Diplomatic Relations Between People's Republic of China and Israel, 20th Anniv. — A1266

Designs: No. 3986, $1.20, Waxwing, five-pointed star (2-1). No. 3987, $1.20, White dove, Star of David (2-2).

2012, Mar. 20 **Litho. & Embossed**
3986-3987 A1266 Set of 2 1.50 1.50

See Israel Nos. 1923-1924.

Asian-Pacific Postal Union, 50th Anniv. — A1267

2012, Apr. 1 **Photo.** ***Perf. 13x13¼***
3988 A1267 $1.20 multi .80 .80

Musicians A1268

Designs: No. 3989, $1.20, Xiao Youmei (1884-1940) (4-1). No. 3990, $1.20, Liu Tianhua (1895-1932) (4-2). No. 3991, $1.20, He Lvting (1903-99) (4-3). No. 3992, $1.20, Ma Sicong (1912-87) (4-4).

2012, Apr. 15 ***Perf. 13 Syncopated***
3989-3992 A1268 Set of 4 1.60 1.60

Chinese Characters A1269

Embellished character for: No. 3993, $1.20, Good luck (fu) (4-1). No. 3994, $1.20, Richness (lu) (4-2). No. 3995, $1.20, Longevity (shou) (4-3). No. 3996, $1.20, Happiness (xi) (4-4).

Litho With Foil Application

2012, Apr. 27
3993-3996 A1269 Set of 4 4.50 2.50
3996a Souvenir sheet of 8, 2 each #3993-3996 *16.00 13.00*

Communist Youth League, 90th Anniv. A1270

Designs: 80f, Building, flag of Youth League (2-1). $1.20, Emblem, Great Wall of China, boy and girl (2-2).

Perf. 13x12¾ Syncopated

2012, May 4 **Photo.**
3997-3998 A1270 Set of 2 .65 .65
3998a Souvenir sheet of 8, 4 each #3997-3998 *6.00 4.50*

International Nurses Day — A1271

2012, May 12
3999 A1271 $1.20 multi .40 .40

Nanjing University, 110th Anniv. — A1272

Perf. 13¼x13¾ Syncopated

2012, May 20 **Litho.**
4000 A1272 $1.20 multi .40 .40

Publication of *Talks at Yan'an Forum on Literature and Art*, 70th Anniv. — A1273

Flowers and: No. 4001, $1.20, Former building of Chinese Communist Party Central Committee (2-1). No. 4002, $1.20, National Performing Arts Center, Beijing (2-2).

2012, May 23 **Photo.**
4001-4002 A1273 Set of 2 1.25 .80

Tables — A1274

No. 4003: a, Ming Dynasty pear wood drawing table (50x30mm) (4-1). b, Qing Dynasty square pear wood table (40x30mm) (4-2).
No. 4004: a, Ming Dynasty pear wood incense stand with base (40x30mm) (4-3). b, Ming Dynasty rock wood table (50x30mm) (4-4).

Perf. 13¼x13 Syncopated

2012, June 9 Litho. & Embossed

4003 A1274 $1.20 Horiz. pair, #a-b 1.00 .75
c. Booklet pane of 1 #4003a + 2 labels .40 —
d. Booklet pane of 1 #4003b + 2 labels .40 —
4004 A1274 $1.20 Horiz. pair, #a-b 1.00 .75
c. Booklet pane of 1 #4004a + 2 labels .40 —
d. Booklet pane of 1 #4004b + 2 labels .40 —
e. Booklet pane of 4, #4003a-4003b, 4004a-4004b 1.50 —
Complete booklet, #4003c, 4003d, 4004c, 4004d, 4004e 3.25

Third Asian Beach Games, Haiyang
A1275

Designs: No. 4005, $1.20, Beach volleyball (3-1). No. 4006, $1.20, Inline skating (3-2). No. 4007, $1.20, Waterskiing (3-3).

Perf. 13¼ Syncopated

2012, June 16 Photo.

4005-4007 A1275 Set of 3 1.25 1.25

Rocket Launch and Spacecraft — A1276

2012, June 25 Litho. *Perf. 12*

4008 A1276 $1.20 multi + label .40 .40

See Stamps With Attached Labels note after No. 3197.

Places in People's Republic of China — A1277

Designs: No. 4009, $1.20, Jingangshan Mountain (6-1). No. 4010, $1.20, Ruijin (6-2). No. 4011, $1.20, Zunyi (6-3). No. 4012, $1.20, Huining (6-4). No. 4013, $1.20, Yan An (6-5). No. 4014, $1.20, Xibaipo (6-6).

Perf. 13¼x12¾ Syncopated

2012, June 30 Litho. & Engr.

4009-4014 A1277 Set of 6 2.25 2.25
4014a Sheet of 12, 2 each #4009-4014 5.75 5.75

Full Coverage in Insurance Systems
A1278

Perf. 13¼x13¾ Syncopated

2012, July 1 Photo.

4015 A1278 $1.20 gold & red 1.50 .75

Emblem of Chinese Olympic Committee — A1279

2012, July 17 Litho. *Perf. 12*

4016 A1279 $1.20 multi + label 1.00 .70

See Stamps With Attached Labels note after No. 3197.

National Museum and Stamps — A1280

No. 4017 — Museum and: a, $1.20, People's Republic of China #787. b, $3, People's Republic of China #790.

Perf. 13¼ Syncopated

2012, July 8 Litho. & Engr.

4017 A1280 Horiz. pair, #a-b 1.40 1.40

2012 Summer Olympics, London
A1281

Designs: No. 4018, $1.20, Soccer (4-1). No. 4019, $1.20, Tennis (4-2). No. 4020, $1.20, Equestrian (4-3). No. 4021, $1.20, Hurdles (4-4).

Perf. 13¼x13 Syncopated

2012, July 27 Photo.

4018-4021 A1281 Set of 4 1.50 1.50
4021a Sheet of 8, 2 each #4018-4021 *6.25 6.25*

Generals
A1282

Designs: No. 4022, $1.20, Zhao Bosheng (1897-1933) (5-1). No. 4023, $1.20, Duan Dechang (1904-33) (5-2). No. 4024, $1.20, Xie Zichang (1897-1935) (5-3). No. 4025, $1.20, Zeng Zhongsheng (1900-35) (5-4). No. 4026, $1.20, Dong Zhentang (1895-1937) (5-5).

Perf. 13¼x13¾ Syncopated

2012, Aug. 1

4022-4026 A1282 Set of 5 2.00 1.90

A1283

Silk Road — A1284

Designs: No. 4027, $1.20, Buildings, figurines of camel and man (4-1). No. 4028, $1.20, Building, horse figurine (4-2). No. 4029, $1.20, Mountains, pitcher (4-3). No. 4030, $1.20, Cliff buildings, horse and rider figurine (4-4).

Perf. 13¼x12¾ Syncopated

2012, Aug. 1

4027-4030 A1283 Set of 4 1.50 1.50
4030a Sheet of 8, 2 each #4027-4030 *7.25 7.25*

Souvenir Sheet

Perf. 13¼ Syncopated

4031 A1284 $6 shown 1.90 1.90

Liu Sanjie — A1285

Designs: No. 4032, $1.20, Song fairy (4-1). No. 4033, $1.20, Singing, horiz. (4-2). No. 4034, $1.20, Couple with embroidered ball, horiz. (4-3). No. 4035, $1.20, Riding a carp to heaven (4-4).

Perf. 13¼x13½ Syncopated, 13 Syncopated

2012, Aug. 23

4032-4035 A1285 Set of 4 1.90 1.50
4032a Booklet pane of 1 .65 —
4033a Booklet pane of 1 .65 —
4034a Booklet pane of 1 .65 —
4035a Booklet pane of 1 .65 —
Complete booklet, #4032-4035a 2.60

Complete booklet sold for $8.

Hetian Jade
A1286

Designs: No. 4036, $1.20, Figurine of dragon (4-1). No. 4037, $1.20, Bi with grain design, vert. (4-2). No. 4038, $1.20, Cup on plate (4-3). No. 4039, $1.20, Figurine of children washing elephant, vert. (4-4).

Litho. & Embossed

2012, Aug. 28 *Perf. 12*

4036-4039 A1286 Set of 4 1.50 1.50
4039a Souvenir sheet of 4, #4036-4039 + label 2.40 2.40

A1287

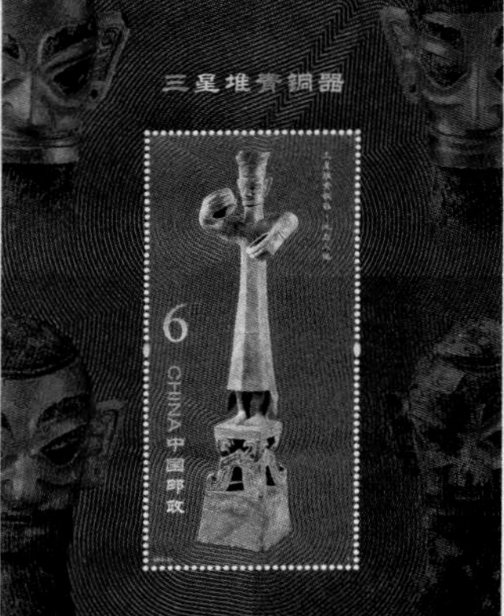
Sanxingdui Bronze Relics — A1288

Designs: No. 4040, $1.20, Mask (2-1). No. 4041, $1.20, Statue of person kneeling (2-2). $6, Statue of person standing.

Perf. 13¼x13½ Syncopated

2012, Sept. 26 Litho.

4040-4041 A1287 Set of 2 .80 .80

Souvenir Sheet

Perf. 13x13¼

4042 A1288 $6 multi 1.90 1.90

Miniature Sheet

Song Poetry — A1289

No. 4043: a, 80f, Sand of Silk Washing, by Yan Shu (6-1). b, $1.20, Meditating on the Past at Chibi, by Su Shi (6-2). c, $1.20, Fairy of the Magpie Bridge, by Qin Guan (6-3). d, $1.20, A Twig of Plum Blossoms (6-4). e, $1.20, Ode to the Plum Blossom, by Lu You (6-5). f, $3, This Unconstrained Poem to Chen Tongfu, by Xin Qiji (6-6).

Perf. 13x13¼ Syncopated

2012, Aug. 31

4043 A1289 Sheet of 6, #a-f 3.75 3.75

Yanbian Culture — A1290

Designs: No. 4044, $1.20, Harvest Dance (3-1). No. 4045, $1.20, Dancers (3-2). No. 4046, $1.20, Hymn for harmony (3-3).

Perf. 13¼x13 Syncopated

2012, Sept. 3 **Photo.**

4044-4046 A1290 Set of 3 2.00 1.25
4046a Sheet of 9, 3 each #4044-4046 7.50 3.75

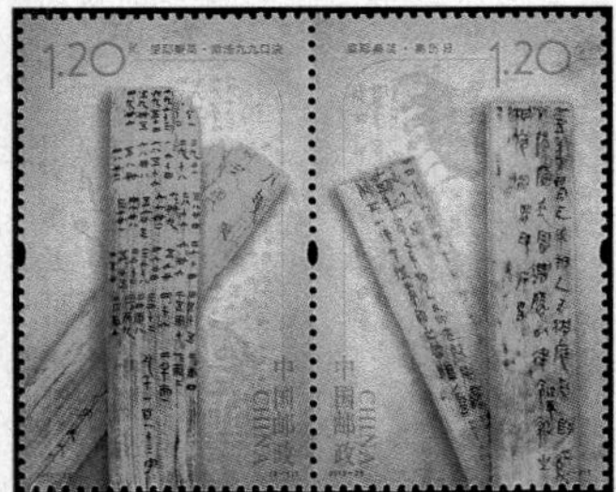

Qin Dynasty Liye Bamboo Slips — A1291

No. 4047: a, Multiplication table, denomination at UL (2-1). b, Calendar, denomination at UR (2-2).

Perf. 13¼ Syncopated

2012, Sept. 13

4047 A1291 $1.20 Horiz. pair, #a-b .80 .80

"Good Fortune" A1292

Perf. 11¾ Syncopated

2012, Oct. 9 **Litho.**

4048 A1292 $1.20 multi .40 .40
a. Souvenir sheet of 2, #3708a, 4048 *1.90 1.90*

Porcelain Objects From Dehua Kiln — A1293

No. 4049, $1.20: a, Three-legged pot with dragon decoration (4-1). b, Vase with handles (4-2).
No. 4050, $1.20: a, Seated Guanyin figurine (4-3). b, Bodhidharma figurine (4-4).

Perf. 13¼ Syncopated

2012, Oct. 20 **Photo.**

Horiz. Pairs, #a-b

4049-4050 A1293 Set of 2 2.00 1.60

History of Merchants — A1294

Designs: No. 4051, $1.20, Steamship, 1872 (3-1). No. 4052, $1.20, Shekou skyline (3-2). $1.50, Hong Kong skyline (3-3)

Perf. 13¼x13 Syncopated

2012, Oct. 26 **Litho.**

4051-4053 A1294 Set of 3 1.75 1.25
4053a Souvenir sheet of 6, 2 each #4051-4053 *4.75 4.75*

A1295

18th National Congress of Chinese Communist Party — A1296

No. 4054: a, Rocket launch (2-1). b, Great Wall of China (2-2).

Perf. 13¼ Syncopated

2012, Nov. 8 **Photo.**

4054 A1295 $1.20 Horiz. pair, #a-b .80 .80

Souvenir Sheet

Perf. 13 Syncopated

4055 A1296 $6 multi 2.00 2.00

A sheet containing four No. 4054 exists.

Bridges — A1297

Designs: No. 4056, $1.20, Taizhou Yangtze River Bridge (2-1). No. 4057, $1.20, Bosporus Bridge, Istanbul, Turkey (2-2).

Perf. 13¼x13 Syncopated

2012, Nov. 26 **Litho.**

4056-4057 A1297 Set of 2 .80 .80

See Turkey No. 3319.

Auditing — A1298

No. 4058: a, Three-legged pot, bas-relief (4-1). b, Imperial Chinese chop (4-2). c, Auditing document of Communist era with red circular seal, building, star, hammer and sickle (4-3). d, Modern auditing documents, building (4-4).

Perf. 13 Syncopated

2012, Nov. 30 **Photo.**

4058 A1298 Horiz. strip of 4 1.60 1.60
a.-d. $1.20 Any single .40 .40

Confucius Institute — A1299

No. 4059: a, $1.20, Stylized dove and globe (2-1). b, $3, Panda (2-2).

2012, Dec. 1

4059 A1299 Horiz. pair, #a-b 1.40 1.40

Constitution of People's Republic of China, 30th Anniv. — A1300

Perf. 13½x13¼ Syncopated

2012, Dec. 4 **Litho.**

4060 A1300 $1.20 multi 1.00 .40

New Year 2013 (Year of the Snake) A1301

Perf. 12¾ Syncopated

2013, Jan. 5 **Photo.**

4061 A1301 $1.20 multi *.40 .40*
a. Booklet pane of 10 *8.75* —
Complete booklet, #4061a 8.75

A limited edition sheet of 6 stamps exists.

Offshore Oil Exploration — A1302

Designs: No. 4062, $1.20, Exploration ship (3-1). No. 4063, $1.20, Offshore drilling rig (3-2). $3, Production ship (3-3).

Perf. 13¼x13 Syncopated

2013, Jan. 18

4062-4064 A1302 Set of 3 1.75 1.75

Heart and Flowers — A1303

2013, Feb. 28 **Litho.** ***Perf. 12***

4065 A1303 $1.20 multi + label .40 .40

See Stamps With Attached Labels note after No. 3197.

Lanterns — A1304

2013, Mar. 3

4066 A1304 $1.20 multi + label .40 .40

See Stamps With Attached Labels note after No. 3197.

12th National People's Congress A1305

Perf. 13¼x13½ Syncopated

2013, Mar. 5 **Photo.**

4067 A1305 $1.20 multi .40 .40
a. Souvenir sheet of 6 4.50 4.50

Mao Zedong's Instruction to Follow Examples of Comrade Lei Feng, 50th Anniv. — A1306

Lei Feng (1940-62), model soldier: 80f, Holding gun (4-1). No. 4069, $1.20, Studying book (4-2). No. 4070, $1.20, Polishing object (4-3). No. 4071, $1.20, Holding baby (4-4).

Perf. 13¼ Syncopated

2013, Mar. 5 **Litho. & Engr.**

4068-4071 A1306 Set of 4 1.40 1.40
4071a Sheet of 8, 2 each #4068-4071 *5.50 5.50*

Party School of the Central Committee, 80th Anniv. A1307

Perf. 13 Syncopated

2013, Mar. 13 **Litho.**

4072 A1307 $1.20 multi .40 .40

Peach Blossoms A1308

Various peach blossoms in decorative frames: No. 4073, 80f, (12-1). No. 4074, 80f, (12-2). No. 4075, $1.20. (12-3). No. 4076, $1.20, (12-4). No. 4077, $1.20, (12-5). No. 4078, $1.20 (12-6). No. 4079, $1.20, (12-7). No. 4080, $1.20, (12-8). No. 4081, $1.20, (12-9). No. 4082, $1.20 (12-10). No. 4083, $1.20, (12-11). $1.50, (12-12).

Perf. 13¼x13 Syncopated

2013, Mar. 16 **Photo.**

4073-4084 A1308 Set of 12 6.50 4.50
4078a Sheet of 12, 2 each #4073-4078 *5.50 5.50*
4084a Sheet of 12, 2 each #4079-4084 *6.50 6.50*

World Water Day — A1309

2013, Mar. 22

4085 A1309 $1.20 multi .40 .40

Painting of Women Producing Silk — A1310

Details from painting: No. 4086, $1.20, Women beating silk in basin (3-1). No. 4087, $1.20, Women working silk thread (3-2). No. 4088, $1.20, Women pulling silk cloth (3-3). $6, Entire painting.

Perf. 13 Syncopated

2013, Apr. 13 **Litho.**
4086-4088 A1310 Set of 3 1.25 1.25

Souvenir Sheet

Perf. 13½ Syncopated

4089 A1310 $6 multi 2.00 2.00

No. 4089 contains one 59x37mm stamp.

Cloisonné Ware — A1311

Designs: 80f, Yuan Dynasty three-legged pot (6-1). No. 4091, $1.20, Ming Dynasty container (6-2). No. 4092, $1.20, Qing Dynasty Zun vessel (6-3). No. 4093, $1.20, Qing Dynasty pot with spout and handle (6-4). No. 4094, $1.20, Hanging vase with handle (6-5). $3, Ming Dynasty bottle vase (6-6).

Perf. 13¼x13½ Syncopated

2013, Apr. 21
4090-4095 A1311 Set of 6 3.00 3.00
4095a Sheet of 12, 2 each #4090-4095 *7.75 7.75*

Souvenir Sheet

7th Congress of All-China Philatelic Federation — A1312

2013, Apr. 25 **Litho. & Embossed**
4096 A1312 $6 multi 2.00 2.00

Earthquake Relief A1313

Perf. 13x12½ Syncopated

2013, May 3 **Photo.**
4097 A1313 $1.20 multi *7.50 7.50*

Mother's Day — A1314

Litho. With Foil Application

Perf. 13x12¾ Syncopated

2013, May 11
4098 A1314 $1.20 multi .40 .40

Exists in a sheet of 8.

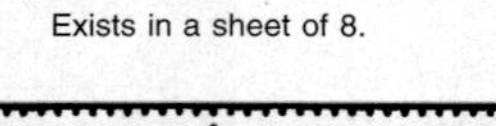

Galloping Horse — A1315

2013, May 19 **Litho.** ***Perf. 12***
4099 A1315 $1.20 multi + label .40 .40

See Stamps With Attached Labels note after No. 3197.

Town Scenes A1316

Designs: No. 4100, $1.20, Qiantong (8-1). No. 4101, $1.20, Laitan (8-2). No. 4102, $1.20, Heping (8-3). No. 4103, $1.20, Jingziuan (8-4). No. 4104, $1.20, Heshun (8-5). No. 4105, $1.20, Tangjiawan (8-6). No. 4106, $1.20, Lizhuang (8-7). No. 4107, $1.20, Jingsheng (8-8).

Perf. 13¼x12¾ Syncopated

2013, May 19 **Litho. & Engr.**
4100-4107 A1316 Set of 8 3.25 3.25

Zhangjiajie Tianzi Mountain A1317

Xiapu Beaches A1318

Qilian Yu Island Group, Paracel Islands A1319

Panjin Red Beach A1320

Longsheng Terraced Fields A1321

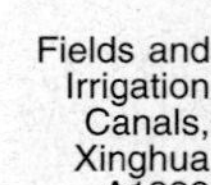

Fields and Irrigation Canals, Xinghua A1322

Perf. 13x12¾ Syncopated

2013, May 19 **Photo.**

4108	A1317	80f multi	.25	.25
4109	A1318	80f multi	.25	.25
4110	A1319	$1.20 multi	.40	.40
4111	A1320	$1.20 multi	.40	.40
4112	A1321	$1.50 multi	.50	.50
4113	A1322	$3 multi	1.00	1.00
		Nos. 4108-4113 (6)	2.80	2.80

Tadpoles and Pond Life A1323

No. 4114 — Tadpoles and: a, Shrimp. b, Goldfish. c, Crab. d, Turtles. e, Frog.

Perf. 13x12½ Syncopated

2013, June 1 **Photo.**

4114	Horiz. strip of 5	1.90	1.90
a.	A1323 80f multi	.25	.25
b.-e.	A1323 $1.20 Any single	.40	.40
f.	Booklet pane of 5, #4114a-4114e	1.90	—
	Complete booklet, #4114f	1.90	

Gold and Bronze Statues of Buddha — A1324

Buddha statue from: 80f, Five Dynasties period (6-1). No. 4116, $1.20, Song Dynasty (6-2). No. 4117, $1.20, Ming Dynasty (6-3). No. 4118, $1.20, Ming Dynasty, diff. (6-4). No. 4119, $1.20, Ming Dynasty, diff. (6-5). No. 4120, $1.20, Ming Dynasty, diff. (6-6). $6, Five Buddha statues.

Perf. 13¼ Syncopated

2013, June 16 **Litho.**
4115-4120 A1324 Set of 6 2.25 2.25

Souvenir Sheet

Perf. 13 Syncopated

4121 A1324 $6 multi 2.00 2.00

No. 4121 contains one 74x83mm stamp.
No. 4115-4120 exist in a sheet of 12 (2 of each value).

Four Arts of Chinese Scholars A1325

Designs: No. 4122, $1.20, Scholar playing a qin (4-1). No. 4123, $1.20, Scholars playing game of Go (4-2). No. 4124, $1.20, Scholars learning calligraphy (4-3). No. 4125, $1.20, Scholar and wall painting (4-4).

Perf. 13¼ Syncopated

2013, July 13 **Litho.**
4122-4125 A1325 Set of 4 1.60 1.60

A sheet containing two No. 4122-4125 exists. The stamps exist printed on silk paper.

Longhu Mountain — A1326

No. 4126: a, Elephant Trunk Hill (3-1). b, Rocks of Immortals (3-2). c, Zhengyi Taoist Abbey (3-3).
$6, Longhu Mountain and lake, horiz.

Perf. 13¼ Syncopated

2013, July 27 **Photo.**
4126 A1326 $1.20 Horiz. strip of 3, #a-c 1.25 1.25

Souvenir Sheet

Perf. 13x13½ Syncopated

4127 A1326 $6 multi 2.00 2.00

Ship — A1327 Stars — A1328

Knot — A1329

Painting of Bamboo — A1330

Die Cut Perf. 12¾ Syncopated

2013, Aug. 8 **Photo.**

Self-Adhesive

4128 A1327 80f multi .25 .25

Die Cut Perf. 13¼x13 Syncopated

4129	A1328	$1.20 multi	.40	.40
4130	A1329	$2.40 multi	.80	.80
4131	A1330	$3 multi	1.00	1.00
		Nos. 4128-4131 (4)	2.45	2.45

Mascot of 2014 Youth Olympic Games, Nanjing — A1331

2013, Aug. 15 **Litho.** ***Perf. 12***
4132 A1331 $1.20 multi + label .40 .40

See Stamps With Attached Labels note after No. 3197.

China-ASEAN Expo, 10th Anniv. — A1332

Perf. 13¼x12¾ Syncopated

2013, Aug. 15 **Photo.**
4133 A1332 $1.20 multi .40 .40

Cats A1333

Cat breed: No. 4134, $1.20, Chinese Li Hua (4-1). No. 4135, $1.20, Maine Coon (4-2). No. 4136, $1.20, Abyssinian, vert. (4-3). No. 4137, $1.20, Exotic shorthair, vert. (4-4).

Perf. 13 Syncopated, 13¼x13¾ Syncopated (#4136-4137)

2013, Aug. 18 Litho. & Engr.

4134-4137 A1333 Set of 4 1.60 1.60

Sun and Peonies — A1334

2013, Aug. 26 Litho. *Perf. 12*

4138 A1334 $1.20 multi + label .40 .40

See Stamps with Attached Labels note after No. 3197.

12th National Games, Liaoning — A1335

Designs: No. 4139, $1.20, Rhythmic gymnastics (2-1). No. 4140, $1.20, Fencing (2-2).

Perf. 13¼x13 Syncopated

2013, Aug. 31 Litho.

4139-4140 A1335 Set of 2 .80 .80

4140a Souvenir sheet of 2, #4139-4140 *1.40 1.40*

Wei Guoqing (1913-89), Political and Military Leader — A1336

Wei Guoqing: No. 4141, $1.20, Wearing army cap (2-1). No. 4142, $1.20, Without cap (2-2).

Perf. 13¼x13¾ Syncopated

2013, Sept. 2 Litho.

4141-4142 A1336 Set of 2 .80 .80

Yu Yuan Garden, Shanghai — A1337

Designs: 80f, Zigzag Bridge and Mid-lake Pavilion (4-1). No. 4144, $1.20, Grand Rockery (4-2). No. 4145, $1.20, Yuan-yu Building (4-3). No. 4146, $1.20, Exquisite Jade Rock (4-4).

Perf. 13¼x12¾ Syncopated

2013, Sept. 7 Litho. & Engr.

4143-4146 A1337 Set of 4 1.50 1.50

Nanhua Temple — A1338

No. 4147: a, Cao Xi Gate (4-1). b, Mahavira Hall (4-2). c, Ling Zhao Pagoda (4-3). d, Liu Zu Hall (4-4).

Perf. 13¼x13 Syncopated

2013, Sept. 7 Photo.

4147 Horiz. strip of 4 1.60 1.60

a.-d. A1338 $1.20 Any single .40 .40

Poets — A1339

Designs: No. 4148, $1.20, Jia Yi (200 B.C.-168 B.C.) (4-1). No. 4149, $1.20, Sima Xiangru (179 B.C.-118 B.C.) (4-2). No. 4150, $1.20, Yang Xiong (53 B.C.-18 A.D.) (4-3). No. 4151, $1.20, Ban Gu (32-92) (4-4).

Perf. 13¼ Syncopated

2013, Sept. 15 Photo.

4148-4151 A1339 Set of 4 1.60 1.60

Table Tennis — A1340

Players: No. 4152, $1.20, Woman (2-1). No. 4153, $1.20, Man (2-2).

Perf. 13½x13 Syncopated

2013, Sept. 27 Photo.

4152-4153 A1340 Set of 2 .80 .80

See Sweden No. 2715.

Chinese Technical Achievements — A1341

Designs: 80f, Rendezvous of Shenzhou and Tiangong spacecraft (4-1). No. 4155, $1.20, Beidou Navigation Satellite System (4-2). No. 4156, $1.20, Liaoning Aircraft Carrier (4-3). No. 4157, $1.20, Jiaolong Manned Submersible (4-4).

Perf. 13x12¾ Syncopated

2013, Sept. 29 Photo.

4154-4157 A1341 Set of 4 2.75 1.50

4157a Souvenir sheet of 4, #4154-4157 1.50 1.50

Fish and Flowers A1342

Perf. 12¾x12 Syncopated

2013, Oct. 9 Litho.

4158 A1342 $1.20 multi .40 .40

a. Souvenir sheet of 2, #3708a, 4158, perf. 11¾ syncopated 2.50 2.50

Tenth China Art Festival A1343

Perf. 13¼x13 Syncopated

2013, Oct. 11 Litho.

4159 A1343 $1.20 multi .40 .40

Xi Zhongxun (1913-2002), Communist Party Official — A1344

Xi Zhnongxun: No. 4160, $1.20, As young man in military uniform (2-1). No. 4161, $1.20, As older man (2-2).

Perf. 13¼x13½ Syncopated

2013, Oct. 15 Litho. & Engr.

4160-4161 A1344 Set of 2 .80 .80

21st Intl. Congress of Supreme Audit Institutions, Beijing — A1345

No. 4162: a, Congress emblem, Gate of Heavenly Peace (2-1). b, Emblem of Intl. Organization of Supreme Audit Institutions, Great Wall of China (2-2)

Perf. 13¼ Syncopated

2013, Oct. 22 Litho.

4162 A1345 $1.20 Horiz. pair, #a-b .80 .80

Hybrid Rice — A1346

No. 4163: a, Seed production (2-1). b, Stalk of rice, rice bowl (2-2).

2013, Oct. 25 Litho. *Perf. 13¼x13¾*

4163 A1346 $1.20 Horiz. pair, #a-b .80 .80

Mao Zedong (1893-1976), Chairman of People's Republic of China — A1347

Various paintings of Mao Zedong: No. 4164, $1.20, With boats in background (4-1). No. 4165, $1.20, With opened overcoat (4-2). No. 4166, $1.20, With arm extended, vert. (4-3). No. 4167, $1.20, Watching waves come ashore (4-4).

Perf. 13¼ Syncopated

2013, Nov. 16 Litho.

4164-4167 A1347 Set of 4 1.60 1.60

Wuhan University, 120th Anniv. A1348

Perf. 13 Syncopated

2013, Nov. 29 Litho.

4168 A1348 $1.20 multi .40 .40

Chinese Junk — A1349

2013, Nov. 22 Litho. *Perf. 12*

4169 A1349 $1.20 multi + label .40 .40

See Stamps With Attached Labels note under No. 3197.

First Moon Landing by Chinese Space Vehicles — A1350

No. 4170: a, $1.20, Chang'e 3 Lander (2-1). b, $1.50, Yutu Moon Rover (2-2).

Perf. 13¼x13 Syncopated

2014, Jan. 1 Photo.

4170 A1350 Horiz. pair, #a-b .90 .90

New Year 2014 (Year of the Horse) A1351

Perf. 12¾ Syncopated

2014, Jan. 5 Photo.

4171 A1351 $1.20 multi .40 .40

a. Booklet pane of 10 4.00 —

Complete booklet, #4171a 4.00

Diplomatic Relations Between France and People's Republic of China, 50th Anniv. — A1352

Desings: No. 4172, $1.20, Qinhuai River, Nanjing (2-1). No. 4173, $1.20, Seine River, Paris (2-2).

Perf. 13x12½ Syncopated

2014, Jan. 27 Litho. & Engr.

4172-4173 A1352 Set of 2 .80 .80

See France Nos. 4587-4588.

Birds of Prey — A1353

Designs: No. 4174, $1.20, Aquila heliaca (4-1). No. 4175, $1.20, Circus cyaneus, horiz. (4-2). No. 4176, $1.50, Accipiter gentilis, horiz. (4-3). No. 4177, $1.50, Falco tinnunculus (4-4).

Perf. 12¾ Syncopated (vert. stamps), 13x12½ Syncopated

2014, Feb. 23 **Litho. & Engr.**

4174-4177 A1353 Set of 4 1.75 1.75

Bathing Horses, by Zhao Mengfu (1254-1322) — A1354

No. 4179: a, 7 horses and rider. (50x38mm) (3-1). b, 5 horses, 3 riders, 3 grooms, Chinese text (57x38mm) (3-2). c, 2 horses, 2 men (50x38mm) (3-3).

$6, Entire painting.

Perf. 13¼ Syncopated

2014, Mar. 1 **Litho.**

4178	Horiz. strip of 3	1.40	1.40
a.-b.	A1354 $1.20 Either single	.40	.40
c.	A1354 $1.50 multi	.50	.50

Souvenir Sheet

Perf. 13½x14 Syncopated

4179 A1354 $6 multi 2.00 2.00

No. 4179 contains one 153x31mm stamp.

Strengthening of Consumer Rights in China — A1355

Designs: No. 4180, $1.20, Scales, book and Consumer Rights Day emblem (2-1). No. 4181, $1.20, Hands, bowl, shirt, house, steering wheel. (2-2).

Perf. 13¼x13¾ Syncopated

2014, Mar. 15 **Litho.**

4180-4181 A1355 Set of 2 .80 .80

Internet Life — A1356

Designs: No. 4182, $1.20, Internet icons, man and woman touching hands (4-1). No. 4183, $1.20, Computer screen, mouse, man pushing shopping cart with Internet icons (4-2). No. 4184, $1.20, Hand holding smart phone showing picture of man on laptop computer (4-3). $1.50, Clouds with Internet icons, people on hills (4-4).

Perf. 13¼x13½ Syncopated

2014, Apr. 20 **Photo.**

4182-4185 A1356 Set of 4 1.75 1.75

Exists in a sheet of 2 each, No. 4182-4185.

Theme Pavilion and Emblem A1357

Botanical Pavilion and Mascot A1358

Perf. 13 Syncopated

2014, Apr. 25 **Photo.**

4186	A1357 $1.20 multi (2-1)	.40	.40
4187	A1358 $1.20 multi (2-2)	.40	.40

Intl. Horticultural Exposition, Qingdao.

Chinese People's Association for Friendship With Foreign Countries, 60th Anniv. — A1359

Perf. 13¼ Syncopated

2014, May 3 **Litho.**

4188 A1359 $1.20 multi .40 .40

Wild Goose Delivering Letters — A1360

Perf. 13¼x13 Syncopated

2014, May 10 **Litho. & Engr.**

4189 A1360 $1.20 multi .40 .40

See Republic of China No. 4178.

Buddhist Art — A1361

Designs: No. 4190, $1.20, Sakyamuni Buddha (4-1). No. 4191, $1.20, Amitayus Buddha (4-2). No. 4192, $1.20, Green Tara (4-3). No. 4193, $1.20, White Tara (4-4).

$6, Sahasra-bhuja Sahasra-netra Avalokitesvara.

Perf. 13¼x13 Syncopated

2014, May 18 **Litho.**

4190-4193 A1361 Set of 4 1.60 1.60

Souvenir Sheet

Perf. 13x13¼ Syncopated

4194 A1361 $6 multi 1.90 1.90

No. 4194 contains one 66x108mm stamp.

A sheet containing 2 each No. 4190-4193 exists.

Birds in Bamboo Forest — A1362

2014, May 28 **Litho.** ***Perf. 12***

4195 A1362 $1.20 multi + label .40 .40

See Stamps With Attached Labels note after No. 3197.

Premiere of Animated Movie *The Monkey King* — A1363

Designs: No. 4196, 80f, Monkey King seeking weapon in Dragon King's palace (6-1). No. 4197, 80f, Horses in water and in flight (6-2). No. 4198, $1.20, Monkey King, other monkeys, banner (6-3). No. 4199, $1.20, Monkey King in peach tree (6-4). No. 4200, $1.20, Monkey King in battle (6-5). No. 4201, $1.20, Monkey King breaking picture frame (6-6).

Perf. 13¼x12¾ Syncopated

2014, June 1 **Photo.**

4196-4201	A1363 Set of 6	2.10	2.10
4201a	Booklet pane of 6, #4196-4201	2.10	—
	Complete booklet, #4201a	2.10	

Huangpu Military Academy, 90th Anniv. — A1364

Perf. 13¼x12¾ Syncopated

2014, June 16 **Litho. & Engr.**

4202 A1364 $1.20 multi .40 .40

The Dream of Red Mansions, Novel by Cao Xueqin A1365

Scenes from novel: No. 4203, $1.20, Lady Dowager sends for her motherless granddaughter (4-1). No. 4204 $1.20, Confounded monk ends a confounding case (4-2). No. 4205, $1.20, Grandmother Liu saw Madam Phoenix first (4-3). $1.50, Baoyu recognizes the gold locket (4-4).

$6, Spirit of Baoyu.

Perf. 13 Syncopated

2014, June 21 **Photo.**

4203-4206 A1365 Set of 4 1.75 1.75

Souvenir Sheet

4207 A1365 $6 multi 2.00 2.00

No. 4207 contains one 45x70mm stamp. Compare with Nos. 4375-4379.

Huangmei Opera — A1366

Designs: 80f, A Happy Marriage with a Fairy (3-1). No. 4209, $1.20, Royal Son-in-law (3-2). No. 4210, $1.20, Collecting Grass for Pig (3-3).

Perf. 13¼ Syncopated

2014, July 6 **Litho.**

4208-4210 A1366 Set of 3 1.10 1.10

Fruit — A1367

Designs: No. 4211, $1.20, Apples (4-1). No. 4212, $1.20, Peaches (4-2). No. 4213, $1.50, Pomegranates (4-3). No. 4214, $1.50, Kumquats (4-4).

Perf. 13¼x13 Syncopated

2014, July 15 **Litho.**

4211-4214 A1367 Set of 4 1.75 .75

Exists in a sheet of 2 each, No. 4211-4214.

2014 Youth Olympic Games, Nanjing — A1368

Perf. 13¼x13½ Syncopated

2014, Aug. 16 **Litho.**

4215 A1368 $1.20 multi .40 .40

Basin — A1369

2014, Aug. 20 **Litho.** ***Perf. 12***

4216 A1369 $1.20 multi + label .40 .40

See Stamps With Attached Labels note after No. 3197.

Deng Xiaoping (1904-97), Leader of People's Republic of China A1370

Deng Xiaoping: No. 4217, $1.20, In military uniform, Red Army flag (4-1). No. 4218, $1.20, At lectern, United Nations Building and flag (4-

2). No. 4219, $1.50, Reading speech, microphones, teapot, flag of Chinese Communist Party (4-3). No. 4220, $1.50, With extended arm, flag of People's Republic of China (4-4)

Perf. 13 Syncopated

2014, Aug. 22 **Litho.**
4217-4220 A1370 Set of 4 1.75 1.75

Exists in a sheet of 2 each, No. 4217-4220.

Zhuge Liang (181-234), Chancellor of Shu Han — A1371

Designs: No. 4221, $1.20, Zhuge Liang standing (2-1). No. 4222, $1.20, Zhuge Liang writing (2-2).
$6, Zhuge Liang standing, diff.

Perf. 13¼ Syncopated

2014, Aug. 28 **Litho.**
4221-4222 A1371 Set of 2 .80 .80

Souvenir Sheet

4223 A1371 $6 multi 2.00 2.00

No. 4223 contains one 38x62mm stamp.
A sheet containing 4 each No. 4221-4222 exists.

Teacher's Day — A1372

Designs: $1.20, Candles in hot-air balloon basket, eyeglasses and book on desk (2-1). $1.50, Tree with symbols of education, stylized faces (2-2).

Perf. 13¼x13¾ Syncopated

2014, Sept. 10 **Photo.**
4224-4225 A1372 Set of 2 .90 .90

Exists in a sheet of 4 each, No. 4224-4225.

Miniature Sheet

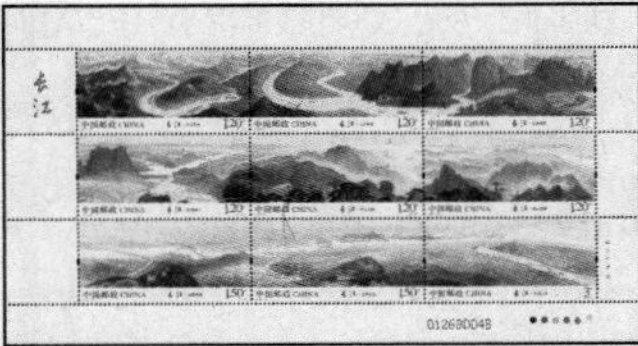

Yangtze River — A1373

No. 4226: a, $1.20, River running through mountains (9-1). b, $1.20, River passing Chongqing (9-2). c, $1.20, Three Gorges (9-3). d, $1.20, Hubei and Hunan (9-4). e, $1.20, Mount Lu and Jiujang River (9-5). f, $1.20, Yellow Mountain (9-6). g, $1.50, Bridges over river (9-7). h, $1.50, River passing towns (9-8). i, $3, River running into sea (9-9).

Perf. 13¼x12¾ Syncopated

2014, Sept. 13 **Photo.**
4226 A1373 Sheet of 9, #a-i 4.50 4.50

People's Congress, 60th Anniv. — A1374

60th anniv. emblem and: No. 4227, $1.20, Building and people (2-1). No. 4228, $1.20, Great Hall of the People and flags (2-2).

Perf. 12¾x12½ Syncopated

2014, Sept. 15 **Litho.**
4227-4228 A1374 Set of 2 1.25 .80

National Rejuvenation — A1375

Ribbons and: 80f, Buildings, flags and ship (4-1). No. 4230, $1.20, Buildings, construction cranes, harvesters (4-2). No. 4231, $1.20, China Central Television Building, Ferris wheel, buildings, dancers (4-3). No. 4232, $1.20, Ethnic dancers and musicians, buildings (4-4).

Perf. 13 Syncopated

2014, Sept. 20 **Photo.**
4229-4232 A1375 Set of 4 1.50 1.50
4232a Souvenir sheet of 4, #4229-4232 1.50 1.50

Filial Piety — A1376

Designs: No. 4233, $1.20, Yu Shun, elephants and birds (4-1). No. 4234, $1.20, Wife of Jiang Shi holding tray with bowl and plate, carp jumping from spring (4-2). No. 4235, $1.50, Hua Mulan with spear on horseback (4-3). No. 4236, $1.50, Sun Simao studying medicine (4-4).

Perf. 13¼ Syncopated

2014, Sept. 30 **Litho. & Engr.**
4233-4236 A1376 Set of 4 1.75 1.75

Exists in a sheet of 2 each, No. 4233-4236.

A1377

A1378

Xinjiang Production and Construction Corps, 60th Anniv. — A1379

Perf. 13 Syncopated

2014, Oct. 7 **Litho.**
4237 Horiz. strip of 3 1.25 1.25
a. A1377 $1.20 multi .40 .40
b. A1378 $1.20 multi .40 .40
c. A1379 $1.20 multi .40 .40

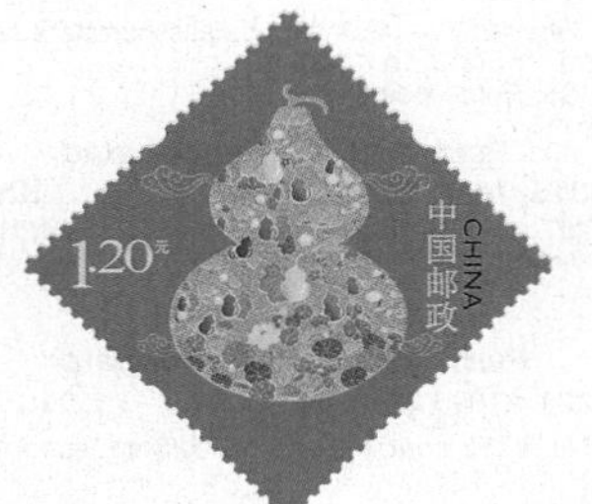

Calabash — A1380

Perf. 12¾ Syncopated

2014, Oct. 9 **Litho.**
4238 A1380 $1.20 multi .40 .40
a. Souvenr sheet of 2, #3708a (perf. 12 syncopated), #4238 1.40 1.40

Scientists A1381

Designs: No. 4239, $1.20, Wang Ganchang (1907-98), nuclear physicist (6-1). No. 4240, $1.20, Zhou Jiuzhang (1907-68), spacecraft engineer (6-2). No. 4241, $1.20, Guo Yonghuai (1909-68), physicist (6-3). No. 4242, $1.20, Deng Jiaxian (1924-86), nuclear physicist (6-4). No. 4243, $1.20, Zhu Guangya (1924-2011), nuclear physicist (6-5). No. 4244, $1.20, Wang Xuan (1937-2006), computer scientist (6-6).

Perf. 13¼ Syncopated

2014, Oct. 16 **Photo.**
4239-4244 A1381 Set of 6 2.40 2.40

Sail Your Dreams — A1382

2014, Oct. 31 **Litho.** ***Perf. 13¼***
4245 A1382 $1.20 multi + label .40 .40

See Stamps With Attached Labels note after No. 3197.

Meeting of Leaders of Asia-Pacific Economic Cooperation, Beijing — A1383

2014, Nov. 10 **Litho.** ***Perf. 13¼x13***
4246 A1383 $1.20 multi .40 .40

10th China Intl. Aviation and Aerospace Exhibition — A1384

No. 4247: a, Helicopter, airplanes, city skyline (2-1). b, Space Station, rockets, astronaut (2-2).

2014, Nov. 11 **Litho.** ***Perf. 13¼x13***
4247 A1384 $1.20 Horiz. pair, #a-b .80 .80

Chinese Character for "Congratulations" — A1385

2014, Nov. 12 **Litho.** ***Perf. 12***
4248 A1385 $1.20 multi + label .40 .40

See Stamps With Attached Labels note after No. 3197.

Chinese Arctic and Antarctic Research Expeditions, 30th Anniv. — A1386

No. 4249: a, $1.20, Map of Antarctica, research expedition station, buildings, penguins (2-1). b, $1.50, Map of Arctic region, ship, buildings and polar bears (2-2).

Perf. 13x12¾ Syncopated

2014, Nov. 20 **Litho.**
4249 A1386 Vert. pair, #a-b .90 .90

Double Happiness — A1387

2014, Dec. 1 **Litho.** ***Perf. 13¼x13***
4250 A1387 $3 multi 1.00 1.00

Values are for stamp with surrounding selvage.

Miniature Sheet

Yuan Dramatic Works — A1388

No. 4251: a, 80f, Sand and Sky — Autumn Thoughts, by Ma Zhiyuan (6-1). b, $1.20, Sheep on the Slope — Meditation on the Past at Tong Pass, by Zhang Yanghao (6-2). c, $1.20, Dou E Yuan, by Guan Hanqing (6-3). d, $1.20, Over the Wall, by Bai Pu (6-4). e, $1.50,

The Orphan of Zhao, by Ji Junxiang (6-5). f, $3, Premature Death of a Beautiful Young Girl, by Zheng Guangzu (6-6).

Litho. & Engr.

2014, Dec. 1 *Perf. 13¼*

4251 A1388 Sheet of 6, #a-f 3.00 3.00

New Year 2015 (Year of the Ram) A1389

Perf. 13 Syncopated

2015, Jan. 5 **Photo.**

4252 A1389 $1.20 multi .40 .40
a. Booklet pane of 10 4.00 —
Complete booklet, #4252a 4.00

Exists in a sheet of 4.

Greeting Chinese New Year A1390

Perf. 13 Syncopated

2015, Jan. 10 **Litho.**

4253 A1390 $1.20 multi .40 .40

Exists in a sheet of 8.

Zunyi Conference, 80th Anniv. — A1391

Designs: No. 4254. $1.20, Conference site (2-1). No. 4255, $1.20, Conference participants (2-2).

Perf. 13¼x13 Syncopated

2015, Jan. 15 **Litho.**

4254-4255 A1391 Set of 2 .80 .80

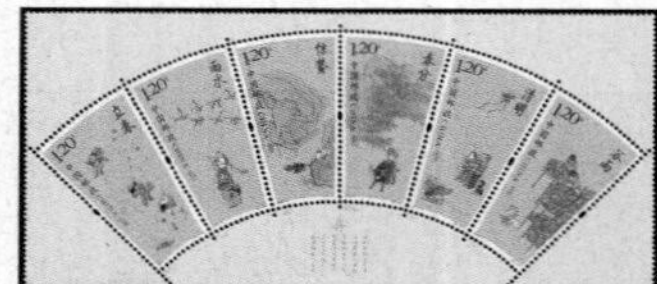

24 Solar Terms — A1392

No. 4256: a, Beginning of Spring (children and flowers) (6-1). b, Rain water (fisherman and birds). (6-2). c, Waking of insects (cowherd and bulls) (6-3). d, Spring equinox (boy on bull) (6-4). e, Pure brightness (kite flying) (6-5). f, Grain rain (women tending to vegetables on racks, rabbits) (6-6).

Perf. 13 Syncopated

2015, Feb. 4 **Photo.**

4256 A1392 $1.20 Block of 6, #a-f 2.40 2.40

Values are for stamps with surrounding selvage.

Court Ladies Swinging Fans, by Zhou Fang — A1393

No. 4257 — Painting details numbered: a, (3-1). b, (3-2). c, (3-3).
$6, Entire painting.

Perf. 13¼x13 Syncopated

2015, Mar. 22 **Litho.**

4257 Horiz. strip of 3 1.40 1.40
a.-b. A1393 $1.20 Either single .40 .40
c. A1393 $1.50 multi .50 .50

Souvenir Sheet

Perf. 12¾x12½ Syncopated

4258 A1393 $6 multi 2.00 2.00

No. 4258 contains one 157x28mm stamp.

Writers — A1394

Designs: No. 4259, $1.20, Tang Xianzu (1550-1616) (6-1). No. 4260, $1.20, Feng Menglong (1574-1645) (6-2). No. 4261, $1.20, Pu Songling (1640-1715) (6-3). No. 4262, $1.20, Hong Sheng (1645-1704) (6-4). No. 4263, $1.20, Kong Shangren (1648-1718) (6-5). No. 4264, $1.20, Cao Xueqin (c.1715-c.1763) (6-6).

Perf. 13 Syncopated

2015, Apr. 4 **Litho. & Engr.**

4259-4264 A1394 Set of 6 2.40 2.40

Slender West Lake — A1395

Designs: No. 4265, $1.20, Lotus Bridge (3-1). No. 4266, $1.20, Twenty-four Bridge (3-2). $1.50, White Pagoda (3-3).

Perf. 13¼x13 Syncopated

2015, Apr. 18 **Litho. & Engr.**

4265-4267 A1395 Set of 3 1.25 1.25

Exists in a sheet containing 3, No. 4265-4267.

Scenes from *Journey to the West,* by Wu Cheng'en A1396

Designs: No. 4268, $1.20, Great sage equalling heaven (4-1). No. 4269, $1.20, Sun Wukong surrendered to Buddha (4-2). No. 4270, $1.50, Tang monk makes vows to go to the West (4-3). No. 4271, $1.50, Tang monk disciples Monkey King (4-4).
$6, Making havoc in heaven.

Perf. 13¼ Syncopated

2015, May 3 **Litho.**

4268-4271 A1396 Set of 4 1.75 1.75

Souvenir Sheet

Photo.

Perf. 13¼x13 Syncopated

4272 A1396 $6 multi 2.00 2.00

Vacation Activities A1397

Designs: 80f, Man taking photograph. $1.20, Family in automobile on bridge. $3, Backpacking.

Die Cut Perf. 12½ Syncopated

2015, May 19 **Photo.**

Self-Adhesive

4273 A1397 80f multi .25 .25
4274 A1397 $1.20 multi .40 .40
4275 A1397 $3 multi 1.00 1.00
Nos. 4273-4275 (3) 1.65 1.65

World Metrology Day — A1398

Perf. 13¼x12¾ Syncopated

2015, May 20 **Litho.**

4276 A1398 $1.20 multi .40 .40

Ships — A1399

Designs: No. 4277, $1.20, Space tracking ship (4-1). No. 4278, $1.20, Liquified natural gas tanker (4-2). No. 4279, $1.20, Floating Production Storage and Offloading ship (4-3). $1.50, Guided missile destroyer (4-4).

Perf. 13¼x12¾ Syncopated

2015, June 3 **Litho.**

4277-4280 A1399 Set of 4 1.75 1.75

World Environment Day — A1400

Perf. 13¼x12¾ Syncopated

2015, June 5 **Photo.**

4281 A1400 $1.20 multi .40 .40

Exists in a sheet of 6.

Father's Day — A1401

Litho. With Foil Application

Perf. 13¼x13 Syncopated

2015, June 13

4282 A1401 $1.20 multi .40 .40

Rainbows, Hearts and Gift Box — A1402

2015, June 18 **Litho.** *Perf. 13¼*

4283 A1402 $1.20 multi + label .40 .40

See Stamps With Attached Labels note after No. 3197.

Mickey Mouse — A1403

2015, June 20 **Litho.** *Perf. 12*

4284 A1403 $1.20 multi .40 .40

See Stamps With Attached Labels note after No. 3197.

Qiantang River Tidal Bores — A1404

No. 4285: a, Crossing bores (3-1). b, Spectators watching wave (3-2). c, Spectators watching reverse bore (3-3).

Perf. 13¼x12¾ Syncopated

2015, July 1 **Litho. & Engr.**

4285 Horiz. strip of 3 1.40 1.40
a.-b. A1404 $1.20 Either single .40 .40
c. A1404 $1.50 multi .50 .50

Peace Dove — A1405

2015, July 3 **Litho.** *Perf. 13¼*

4286 A1405 $1.20 multi + label .40 .40

See Stamps With Attached Labels note after No. 3197.

Qingyuan Mountain — A1406

Designs: 80f, Sky Lake (3-1). No. 4288, $1.20, Rock carvings (3-2). No. 4289, $1.20, Statue of Lao Zi (3-3).

Perf. 13¼x12¾ Syncopated

2015, July 18 **Litho. & Engr.**

4287-4289 A1406 Set of 3 1.10 1.10

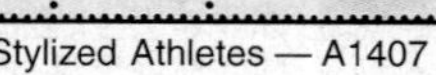

Stylized Athletes — A1407

2015, July 20 **Litho.** *Perf. 13¼*

4290 A1407 $1.20 multi + label .40 .40

See Stamps With Attached Labels note after No. 3197.

Happiness of the People A1408

Buildings and: 80f, Fruit sellers, machine (4-1). No. 4292, $1.20, Bus, medical care (4-2). No. 4293, $1.20, Automobile, person in wheelchair, voters (4-3). No. 4294, $1.20, Ferris wheel, tai chi, woman pushing baby carriage (4-4).

Perf. 13x12¾ Syncopated

2015, July 25 **Photo.**

4291-4294	A1408 Set of 4	1.40	1.40
4294a	Souvenir sheet of 4, #4291-4294	1.40	1.40

Awarding of 2022 Winter Olympics to Beijing — A1409

Perf. 13¼x13½ Syncopated

2015, July 31 **Photo.**

4295	A1409 $1.20 multi	.40	.40

Lord Bao (999-1062), Government Official A1410

Designs: No. 4296, $1.20, Lord Bao throwing inkstone into water (2-1). No. 4297, $1.20, Case of Chen Shimei (2-2).

$6, Lord Bao seated.

Perf. 13¼ Syncopated

2015, Aug. 8 **Photo.**

4296-4297	A1410 Set of 2	.75	.75

Souvenir Sheet

Perf. 13¼x13½ Syncopated

4298	A1410 $6 multi	1.90	1.90

No. 4298 contains one 60x67mm stamp.

A sheet of 6 exists comprised of 3 each, No. 4296-4297.

Mandarin Ducks A1411

Perf. 13x12¾ Syncopated

2015, Aug. 20 **Litho. & Engr.**

4299	A1411 $1.20 multi	.40	.40

Exists in a sheet of 8.

Lunar Exploration by China — A1412

2015, Aug. 20 **Litho.** ***Perf. 13¼***

4300	A1412 $1.20 multi + label	.40	.40

See Stamps With Attached Labels note after No. 3197.

Miniature Sheet

Yellow River — A1413

No. 4301: a, $1.20, Beginning of river (9-1). b, $1.20, Nine Bays (9-2). c, $1.20, River bend in Hinterland (9-3). d, $1.20, Great bend (9-4). e, $1.20, River approaching Hukou Waterfalls (9-5). f, $1.20, Hukou Waterfalls and Sanjing (9-6). g, $1.50, Helou area (9-7). h, $1.50, Zhongshou Plain (9-8). i, $3, Mountains and buildings in foreground (9-9).

Perf. 13¼x12¾ Syncopated

2015, Aug. 23 **Photo.**

4301	A1413 Sheet of 9, #a-i	4.25	4.25

Tibet Autonomous Region, 50th Anniv. — A1414

No. 4302: a, Tibetans, symbols of Tibet, cranes and mountains (3-1). b, Tibetans, doves, buildings (3-2). c, Tibetan family, house, symbols of Tibet (3-3).

Perf. 13¼x12¾ Syncopated

2015, Sept. 1 **Photo.**

4302	Horiz. strip of 3	1.25	1.25
a.-c.	A1414 $1.20 Any single	.40	.40

Victory in World War II, 70th Anniv. — A1415

Soldiers and: No. 4303, 80f, September 18 Memorial Museum (13-1). No. 4304, 80f, Northeast China Revolutionary Martyrs Memorial Hall (13-2). No. 4305, $1.20, Museum of the War of Chinese People's Resistance Against Japanese Aggression (13-3). No. 4306, $1.20, Shanghai Songhu Anti-Japanese War Memorial Hall (13-4). No. 4307, $1.20, Museum of Victims in the Nanjing Massacre by Japanese Invaders (13-5). No. 4308, $1.20, Taierzhuang Campaign Memorial Hall (13-6). No. 4309, $1.20, Yan'an Revolutionary Memorial Hall (13-7). No. 4310, $1.20, Memorial Hall of Former Site of the Eighth Route Army Headquarters (13-8). No. 4311, $1.20, Hundred Regiments Offensive Memorial Hall (13-9). No. 4312, $1.20, Pingxingguan Victory Memorial Hall (13-10). No. 4313, $1.20, Museum of Tunnel Warfare at Ranzhuang (13-11). No. 4314, $1.20, New Fourth Army Memorial Hall (13-12). No. 4315, $1.20, Memorial Hall of Anti-Japanese War in Western Yunnan (13-13).

$6, Statue of soldier with sword, vert.

Perf. 13¼x13 Syncopated

2015, Sept. 3 **Photo.**

4303-4315	A1415 Set of 13	4.75	4.75

Souvenir Sheet

4316	A1415 $6 multi	1.90	1.90

No. 4316 contains one 50x60mm stamp.

Flying Fairies — A1416

2015, Sept. 9 **Litho.** ***Perf. 13¼***

4317	A1416 $1.20 multi	.40	.40

See Stamps With Attached Labels note after No. 3197.

Birthday Cake — A1417

2015, Sept. 10 **Litho.** ***Perf. 12***

4318	A1417 $1.20 multi	.40	.40

See Stamps With Attached Labels note after No. 3197.

Synthetic Crystalline Bovine Insulin, 50th Anniv. A1418

Perf. 13x12¾ Syncopated

2015, Sept. 17 **Photo.**

4319	A1418 $1.20 multi	.40	.40

10th International Garden Expo, Wuhan — A1419

Designs: $1.20, Buildings (2-1). $1.50, Buildings, diff. (2-2).

Perf. 13x12¾ Syncopated

2015, Sept. 25 **Photo.**

4320-4321	A1419 Set of 2	.85	.85

United Nations, 70th Anniv. — A1420

Designs: $1.20, United Nations emblem, stylized dove (2-1). $1.50, United Nations Headquarters, arrows (2-2).

Perf. 13¼x13 Syncopated

2015, Sept. 26 **Litho.**

4322-4323	A1420 Set of 2	.85	.85

Xianjiang Production and Construction Corps, 60th Anniv. — A1421

No. 4324: a, Building, wind generators, airplane, train, bridge (3-1). b, Agricultural products, city skyline, airplane, bridge over river, doves, farm community (3-2). c, Dancers (3-3).

Perf. 13¼x13 Syncopated

2015, Oct. 1 **Photo.**

4324	Horiz. strip of 3	1.25	1.25
a.-c.	A1421 $1.20 Any single	.40	.40

Tianjin University, 120th Anniv. A1422

Perf. 13x12¾ Syncopated

2015, Oct. 2 **Photo.**

4325	A1422 $1.20 multi	.40	.40

Good Fortune and Longevity A1423

Perf. 12¾ Syncopated

2015, Oct. 9 **Litho.**

4326	A1423 $1.20 multi	.40	.40
a.	Souvenir sheet of 2, #3708a (perf. 12¾), 4326	1.40	1.40

Palace Museum — A1424

Designs: No. 4327, $1.20, Meridian Gate (4-1). No. 4328, $1.20, Hall of Supreme Harmony (4-2). No. 4329, $1.50, Corner Tower (4-3). No. 4330, $1.50, Gate of Heavenly Purity (4-4).

Perf. 13¼x12 Syncopated

2015, Oct. 10 **Litho.**

Stamp + Label

4327-4330	A1424 Set of 4	1.75	1.75

Poets — A1425

Designs: No. 4331, $1.20, Du Fu (712-70) (4-1). No. 4332, $1.20, Su Dongpo (1037-1101) (4-2). No. 4333, $1.20, Bai Juyi (772-846) (4-3). No. 4334, $1.20, Cao Zhi (192-232) (4-4).

Perf. 13¼ Syncopated

2015, Nov. 12 **Litho. & Engr.**

4331-4334	A1425 Set of 4	1.50	1.50

Delivery of First ARJ21 Airplane to Chengdu Airlines — A1426

Perf. 13¼x13 Syncopated

2015, Nov. 28 **Photo.**

4335	A1426 $1.20 multi	.40	.40

Chinese Values A1427

Designs: No. 4336, $1.20, Bird's nest (importance of family) (3-1). No. 4337, $1.20, Ox (dreams and spirit, 47x28mm) (3-2). $1.50, Child daydreaming (unity of personal and national dreams) (3-3).

Perf. 13 Syncopated, 13¼x13 Syncopated (#4337)

2015, Nov. 29 Photo.

4336-4338 A1427 Set of 3 1.25 1.25

Exists in a sheet containing 3, No. 4336-4338.

New Year 2016 (Year of the Monkey) A1428

Designs: No. 4339, $1.20, Monkey with peach (2-1). No. 4340, $1.20, Three monkeys (2-2).

Perf. 13 Syncopated

2016, Jan. 5 Litho. & Engr.

4339-4340	A1428	Set of 2	.75	.75
4340a		Booklet pane of 10, 5 each #4339-4340	7.50	—
		Complete booklet, #4340a	7.50	
4340b		Souvenir sheet of 4, 2 each #4339-4340	4.50	4.50

Children Celebrating Chinese New Year A1429

Perf. 13 Syncopated

2016, Jan. 10 Litho.

4341 A1429 $1.20 multi .40 .40

Paintings by Liu Haisu (1896-1994) — A1430

Designs: No. 4342, $1.20, Land So Rich in Beauty (3-1). No. 4343, $1.20, Ink Lotus (3-2). $1.50, Yellow Mountain Renzi Waterfall (3-3).

Litho. (#4342), Photo. (#4343), Litho. & Engr. (#4344)

2016, Mar. 16 ***Perf. 13 Syncopated***

4342-4344 A1430 Set of 3 1.25 1.25

China Post, 120th Anniv. — A1431

Designs: No. 4345, $1.20, Mailbox, post office, statue of postman on horse, bicycle (4-1). No. 4346, $1.20, All-day automated kiosk, modern post office interior (4-2). No. 4347, $1.20, Airplane, parcel sorting conveyors, mail van (4-3). No. 4348, $1.20, Automated savings bank kiosks, credit cards (4-4).

Perf. 13¼x13 Syncopated

2016, Mar. 20 Litho.

4345-4348 A1431 Set of 4 1.50 1.50

Painting of Gaoyi Tu, by Sun Wei — A1432

No. 4349: a, Right side of painting (47x35mm) (3-1). b, Center of painting (62x35mm) (3-2). c, Left side of painting (47x35mm) (3-3).

$6, Entire painting.

Perf. 13¼ Syncopated

2016, Apr. 2 Photo.

4349		Horiz. strip of 3	1.25	1.25
a.-b.		A1432 $1.20 Either single	.40	.40
c.		A1432 $1.50 multi	.45	.45

Souvenir Sheet

Perf. 13½x13¾ Syncopated

4350 A1432 $6 multi 1.90 1.90

No. 4350 contains one 134x35mm stamp.

Jiaotong University, 120th Anniv. — A1433

Perf. 13½ Syncopated

2016, Apr. 8 Photo.

4351 A1433 $1.20 multi .40 .40

Song Ci (1186-1249), Forensic Medicine Expert — A1434

Song Ci, Scribe and Child — A1435

Perf. 13½ Syncopated

2016, Apr. 13 Litho. & Engr.

4352 A1434 $1.20 multi .40 .40

4353 A1435 $1.50 multi .45 .45

Nationwide Reading A1436

Perf. 13¼x13½ Syncopated

2016, Apr. 23 Litho.

4354 A1436 $1.20 multi .40 .40

A1437

Tangshan International Horticulture Exposition — A1438

Perf. 13 Syncopated

2016, Apr. 29 Litho.

4355 A1437 $1.20 multi .40 .40

4356 A1438 $1.50 multi .45 .45

24 Solar Terms — A1439

No. 4357: a, Beginning of summer (woman, butterflies and flowers) (6-1). b, Lesser fullness of grain (woman at loom) (6-2). c, Grain in beard (man in rice paddy) (6-3). d, Summer solstice (crouching children and flowers) (6-4). e, Lesser heat (man and goat near water wheel) (6-5). f, Greater heat (children looking at scroll under vines) (6-6).

Perf. 13 Syncopated

2016, May 5 Photo.

4357 A1439 $1.20 Block of 6, #a-f 2.25 2.25

Values are for stamps with surrounding selvage.

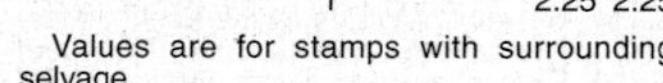

Scientists A1440

Designs: No. 4358, $1.20, Ding Wenjiang (1887-1936), geologist (4-1). No. 4359, $1.20, Jin Shanbao (1895-1997), agronomist (4-2). No. 4360, $1.20, Ye Qisun (1898-1977), physicist (4-3). No. 4361, $1.20, Ye Duzheng (1916-2013), meteorologist (4-4).

Perf. 13¼ Syncopated

2016, May 8 Litho. & Engr.

4358-4361 A1440 Set of 4 1.50 1.50

Snow-covered Landscape — A1441

Wanfeng Peaks Forest A1442

Sand Lake A1443

Xixi National Wetland Park A1444

Perf. 13x12¾ Syncopated

2016, May 12 Photo.

4362	A1441	40f multi	.25	.25
4363	A1442	$1 multi	.30	.30
4364	A1443	$2 multi	.60	.60
4365	A1444	$4.20 multi	1.25	1.25
		Nos. 4362-4365 (4)	2.40	2.40

Ancient Chinese Towns — A1445

Designs: No. 4366, $1.20, Zhentong (6-1). No. 4367, $1.20, Qiliping (6-2). No. 4368, $1.20, Qingyan (6-3), No. 4369, $1.20, Zhujiajiao (6-4). No. 4370, $1.20, Sanhe (6-5). No. 4371, $1.20, Huangyao (6-6).

Perf. 13¼x12¾ Syncopated

2016, May 19 Litho. & Engr.

4366-4371 A1445 Set of 6 2.25 2.25

Cultural Heritage Day — A1446

No. 4372 — Inscription on emblem: a, $1.20, China Intangible Cultural Heritage (2-1). b, $1.50, China Cultural Heritage (2-2).

Perf. 13¼x13½ Syncopated

2016, June 11 Litho.

4372 A1446 Horiz. pair, #a-b .85 .85

Opening of Shanghai Disney Resort — A1447

Designs: $1.20, Mickey and Minnie Mouse (2-1). $1.50, Tinker Bell, Enchanted Storybook Castle (2-2).

Perf. 13¼x13 Syncopated

2016, June 16 **Photo.**

4373-4374 A1447 Set of 2 .85 .85
4374a Souvenir sheet of 2, #4373-4374 1.25 1.25

No. 4374a sold for $4.

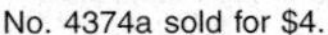

A1448

The Dream of Red Mansions, Novel by Cao Xueqin — A1449

Scenes from novel: No. 4375, $1.20, Xifeng abuses her power (4-1). No. 4376, $1.20, Lingguan writes on the ground (4-2). No. 4377, $1.20, Qingwen, the maid, tearing the fan (4-3). $1.50, Baoyu receives a flogging (4-4).

$6, Rong-guo House makes itself ready for an important visitor.

Perf. 13 Syncopated

2016, June 18 **Photo.**

4375-4378 A1448 Set of 4 1.60 1.60

Souvenir Sheet

4379 A1449 $6 multi 1.90 1.90

Compare with Nos. 4203-4207.

Longxing Temple, Zhengding — A1450

Designs: $1.20, Moni Hall (2-1). $1.50, Dabei Pavilion (2-2).

Perf. 13¼x13 Syncopated

2016, June 26 **Litho.**

4380-4381 A1450 Set of 2 .85 .85

Pass the Flame — A1451

2016, July 8 **Litho.** ***Perf. 13¼***

4382 A1451 $1.20 multi + label .40 .40

See Stamps With Attached Labels note after No. 3197.

Artifacts From Ruins of Yin — A1452

No. 4383: a, 80f, Oracle bone with inscription (3-1). b, $1.20, Bronze ware (3-2). c, $1.50, Jadeware (3-3)

Perf. 11¾ Syncopated

2016, July 13 **Litho. & Engr.**

4383 A1452 Horiz. strip of 3, #a-c 1.10 1.10

Fruit — A1453

Designs: No. 4384, $1.20, Apricots (4-1). No. 4385, $1.20, Grapes (4-2). No. 4386, $1.50, Watermelons (4-3). No. 4387, $1.50, Litchis (4-4).

Perf. 13¼x13 Syncopated

2016, July 23 **Litho. & Embossed**

4384-4387 A1453 Set of 4 1.75 1.75

Exists in a sheet containing 2 each of Nos. 4384-4387.

2016 Summer Olympics, Rio de Janeiro A1454

Designs: $1.20, Women's volleyball (2-1). $1.50, Men's relay race (2-2).

Perf. 13 Syncopated

2016, Aug. 5 **Photo.**

4388-4389 A1454 Set of 2 .80 .80

Red-billed Leiothrix A1455

Perf. 13x12¾ Syncopated

2016, Aug. 9 **Litho. & Engr.**

4390 A1455 $1.20 multi .40 .40

Miniature Sheet

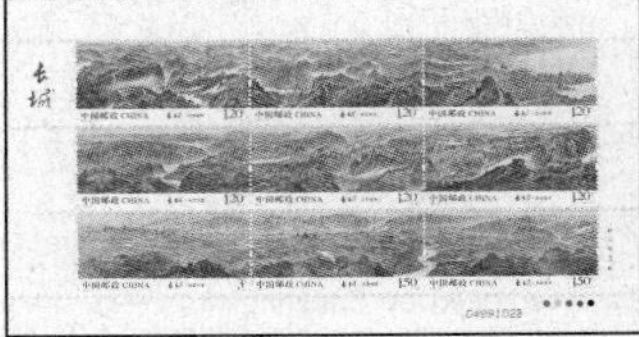

Great Wall of China — A1456

No. 4391: a, $1.20, Shanhai Pass and Old Dragon Head (9-1). b, $1.20, Hushan Great Wall (9-2). c, $1.20, Jinshanling, Jiumenkou and Huangyaguan (9-3). d, $1.20, Gubeikou, Huanghuacheng, Mutianyu, Badaling and Juyongguan (9-4). e, $1.20, Zijingguan, Pingxingguan, Niangziguan, Yanmenguan, Deshengkou and Bianjinlou (9-5). f, $1.20, Pianguan (9-6). g, $1.50, Zhenbeitai and Huamachi (9-7). h, $1.50, Sanguankou (9-8). i, $3, Yumenguan and Jiayuguan (9-9).

Perf. 13¼x12¾ Syncopated

2016, Aug. 20 **Litho. & Engr.**

4391 A1456 Sheet of 9, #a-i 4.00 4.00

G20 Summit, Hangzhou — A1457

Perf. 13¼x13 Syncopated

2016, Aug. 27 **Photo.**

4392 A1457 $1.20 multi .40 .40

Silk-Faced Paper

4392A A1457 $1.20 multi .40 .40

No. 4392 exists in a sheet of 8 on regular and silk papers.

Full Moon on Mid-Autumn Night — A1458

Perf. 13¼ Syncopated

2016, Aug. 28 **Litho.**

4393 A1458 $1.20 multi .40 .40

Microperforations surround the Moon in the vignette.

Exists in a sheet of 6.

A1459

Xuan Zang, Character From *Journey to the West* — A1460

Xuan Zang: No. 4394, $1.20, Walking with items on back (2-1). No. 4395, $1.20, Translating Buddhist scriptures (2-2).

Perf. 13¼ Syncopated

2016, Sept. 4 **Photo.**

4394-4395 A1459 Set of 2 .75 .75

Souvenir Sheet

Perf. 13¼x13 Syncopated

4396 A1460 $6 multi 1.90 1.90

Foreign Trade — A1461

Buildings, ships and: No. 4397, $1.20, Doves, lectern and microphones (6-1). No. 4398, $1.20, Train, offshore platform (6-2). No. 4399, $1.20, Truck at airport (6-3). No. 4400, $1.20, Arrow charts, stacks of coins (6-4). No. 4401, $1.50, Sculpture, dancers and fireworks (6-5). No. 4402, $1.50, Crane and shipping containers (6-6).

Perf. 13¼x13½ Syncopated

2016, Sept. 10 **Photo.**

4397-4402 A1461 Set of 6 2.40 2.40
4402a Souvenir sheet of 6, #4397-4402 3.50 3.50

No. 4402a sold for $11.

39th International Organization for Standardization General Assembly, Beijing — A1462

Perf. 13¼x13½ Syncopated

2016, Sept. 11 **Litho.**

4403 A1462 $1.20 multi .35 .35

Sichuan University, 120th Anniv. A1463

Perf. 13 Syncopated

2016, Sept. 28 **Litho.**

4404 A1463 $1.20 multi .35 .35

Filial Piety — A1464

Designs: No. 4405, $1.20, Carrying rice for more than 1,000 li (4-1). No. 4406, $1.20, Personally checking his mother's prescriptions (4-2). No. 4407, $1.50, Wenji returning to Han (4-3). No. 4408, $1.50, Gu Kaizhi painting his mother (4-4).

Perf. 13¼ Syncopated

2016, Oct. 7 **Litho. & Engr.**

4405-4408 A1464 Set of 4 1.60 1.60

New Year 2017 (Year of the Rooster) A1465

Perf. 12¾ Syncopated

2016, Oct. 9 **Litho.**

4409 A1465 $1.20 multi .35 .35
a. Souvenir sheet of 2, #3708a (perf. 12¾ syncopated), 4409 1.25 1.25

Poverty Alleviation Day — A1466

Perf. 13¼ Syncopated

2016, Oct. 14 **Litho.**

4410 A1466 $1.20 multi .35 .35

Red Army — A1467

Designs: No. 4411, $1.20, Start of the Long March (6-1). No. 4412, $1.20, Zunyi Conference (6-2). No. 4413, $1.20, Army crossing the Chishui River four times (6-3). No. 4414, $1.20, Army crossing the Snow Mountain and grasslands (6-4). No. 4415, $1.50, Union of the three Red Armies (6-5). No. 4416, $1.50, Soldiers and flags (6-6).

Perf. 13¼x13 Syncopated

2016, Oct. 22 **Litho.**

4411-4416 A1467 Set of 6 2.40 2.40

End of Long March, 80th anniv.

Lighthouses A1468

No. 4417: a, Huayang Lighthouse (5-1). b, Chigua Lighthouse (5-2). c, Zhubi Lighthouse (5-3). d, Yongshu Lighthouse (5-4). e, Meiji Lighthouse (5-5).

Perf. 13¼ Syncopated

2016, Oct. 28 **Photo.**

4417 Horiz. strip of 5 2.00 2.00
a.-c. A1468 $1.20 Any single .35 .35
d.-e. A1468 $1.50 Either single .45 .45

Sun Yat-sen (1866-1925), First President of Republic of China — A1469

Designs: No. 4418, $1.20, Museum of Dr. Sun Yat-sen (4-1). No. 4419, $1.20, Statue of Sun Yat-sen, vert. (4-2). No. 4420, $1.50, Sun Yat-sen Memorial Hall (4-3). No. 4421, $1.50, Sun Yat-sen Memorial Secondary School, vert. (4-4).

Perf. 13 Syncopated, 13¼ Syncopated (vert. stamps)

2016, Nov. 12 **Photo.**

4418-4421 A1469 Set of 4 1.60 1.60

A1470

China 2016 International Stamp Exhibition, Nanning — A1471

Designs: No. 4422, $1.20, Zhuang brocade (2-1). No. 4423, $1.20, Silk ball and tassels (2-2).

Perf. 13¼ Syncopated

2016, Dec. 2 **Litho.**

4422-4423 A1470 Set of 2 .70 .70

Souvenir Sheet

Perf. 13¼x13½ Syncopated

4424 A1471 $6 multi 1.75 1.75

New Year 2017 (Year of the Rooster) A1472

Designs: No. 4425, $1.20, Rooster running (2-1). No. 4426, $1.20, Rooster and chicks (2-2).

Perf. 13 Syncopated

2017, Jan. 5 **Litho. & Engr.**

4425-4426 A1472 Set of 2 .70 .70
4426a Booklet pane of 10, 5 each #4425-4426 3.50 —
Complete booklet, #4426a 3.50
4426b Souvenir sheet of 4, 2 each #4425-4426 1.40 1.40

New Year's Greetings A1473

Perf. 13 Syncopated

2017, Jan. 10 **Litho.**

4427 A1473 $1.20 multi .35 .35

Miniature Sheet

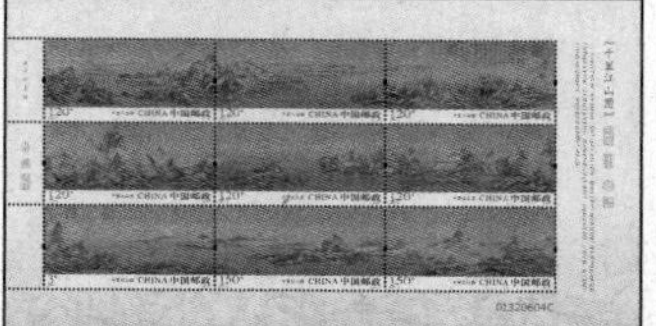
One Thousand Li of Rivers and Mountains, Painting by Wang Ximeng (1096-1119) — A1474

No. 4428 — Various parts of painting numbered: a, $1.20, (9-1). b, $1.20, (9-2). c, $1.20, (9-3). d, $1.20, (9-4). e, $1.20, (9-5). f, $1.20, (9-6). g, $1.50, (9-7). h, $1.50, (9-8). i, $3 (9-9).

Perf. 13¼x13 Syncopated

2017, Feb. 25 **Photo.**

4428 A1474 Sheet of 9, #a-i 4.00 4.00

Commercial Press, 120th Anniv. A1475

Perf. 13 Syncopated

2017, Feb. 27 **Litho.**

4429 A1475 $1.20 multi .35 .35

Development of Beijing, Tianjin and Hebei Province A1476

Designs: No. 4430, $1.20, City, train, airplane, ship, highways. (3-1). No. 4431, $1.20, Buildings, wind generators, cars at charging stations, cyclists on road (3-2). No. 4432, $1.50, Manufacturing, agriculture, trucks at warehouse, airplane (3-3).

Perf. 13 Syncopated

2017, Mar. 9 **Litho.**

4430-4432 A1476 Set of 3 1.25 1.25
4432a Souvenir sheet of 3, #4430-4432 1.75 1.75

No. 4432a sold for $5.80.

Four Seasons A1477

Designs: No. 4433, $1.20, Spring Swallows Flying Through Willows (4-1). No. 4434, $1.20, Paddling in a Summer Lotus Pond (4-2). No. 4435, $1.50, Rooster Crowing at Autumn Harvest (4-3). No. 4436, $1.50, Plum Blossoms in Winter (4-4).

Perf. 13¼ Syncopated

2017, Mar. 20 **Photo.**

4433-4436 A1477 Set of 4 1.60 1.60

Scenes From *Journey to the West*, by Wu Cheng'en A1478

Designs: No. 4437, $1.20, White dragon horse is reined in (4-1). No. 4438, $1.20, Zhu Bajie recruited by Sanzang (4-2). No. 4439, $1.50, Friar Sand joins the pilgrims (4-3). No. 4440, $1.50, Wuzhuang Temple Monkey (4-4).

Perf. 13x13¼ Syncopated

2017, Mar. 30 **Photo.**

4437-4440 A1478 Set of 4 1.60 1.60

Jade Figurines of Hongshan Culture — A1479

No. 4441: a, Dragon (3-1). b, Phoenix (3-2). c, Man (3-3).

Perf. 13¼ Syncopated

2017, Apr. 9 **Litho. & Embossed**

4441 A1479 $1.20 Horiz. strip of 3, #a-c 1.10 1.10

A1480

A1481

Inner Mongolian Autonomous Region, 70th Anniv. — A1482

Perf. 13 Syncopated

2017, May 1 **Photo.**

4442 Horiz. strip of 3 1.10 1.10
a. A1480 $1.20 multi .35 .35
b. A1481 $1.20 multi .35 .35
c. A1482 $1.20 multi .35 .35

Belt and Road Forum for International Cooperarion, Beijing — A1483

Perf. 13 Syncopated

2017, May 14 **Photo.**

4443 A1483 $1.20 multi .35 .35

No. 4443 exists in sheets of 8 on silk paper.

Dinosaurs — A1484

No. 4444: a, $1.20, Tsintaosaurus (6-1). b, $1.20, Yangchuanosaurus (6-2). c, $1.20, Huayangosaurus (6-3). d, $1.20, Sinosauropteryx (6-4). e, $1.50, Gigantoraptor (6-5). f, $3, Microraptor (6-6).
$6, Mamenchisaurus.

Perf. 13 Syncopated

2017, May 19 **Litho. & Engr.**

4444	A1484	Sheet of 6, #a-f	2.75	.75

Souvenir Sheet

Perf. 12½x12¾ Syncopated

4445	A1484	$6 multi	1.75	1.75

No. 4445 contains one 49x68mm stamp.

Zhejiang University, 120th Anniv. — A1485

Perf. 13 Syncopated

2017, May 21 **Litho. & Embossed**

4446	A1485	$1.20 multi	.35	.35

Children at Play — A1486

Children: No. 4447, 80f, Rolling iron rings (6-1). No. 4448, 80f, Playing leapfrog (6-2). No. 4449, $1.20, Tossing beanbag (6-3). No. 4450, $1.20, On swings (6-4). No. 4451, $1.20, Kicking shuttlecock (6-5). No. 4452, $1.20, Playing hopscotch (6-6).

Perf. 13¼x13½ Syncopated

2017, May 31 **Litho. & Engr.**

4447-4452	A1486	Set of 6	1.90	1.90

One Belt and One Road — A1487

2017, June 11 **Litho.** ***Perf. 13¼***

4453	A1487	$1.20 multi + label	.35	.35

See Stamps With Attached Labels note after No. 3197.

International Day Against Drug Abuse and Illicit Trafficking — A1488

Perf. 13 Syncopated

2017, June 26 **Photo.**

4454	A1488	$1.20 multi	.35	.35

Return of Hong Kong, 20th Anniv. A1489

Buildings and: No. 4455, $1.10, Flags of Hong Kong and People's Republic of China, people waving flags, people in dragon and lion costumes (3-1). No. 4456, $1.20, Doves (3-2). No. 4457, $1.50, Airplane, train, bridge (3-3).

Perf. 13¼x13 Syncopated

2017, July 1 **Photo.**

4455-4457	A1489	Set of 3	1.25	1.25

See Hong Kong No. 1855.

Emblem of Chinese Soccer Super League — A1490

2017, July 24 **Litho.** ***Perf. 13¼***

4458	A1490	$1.20 multi + label	.35	.35

See Stamps With Attached Labels note after No. 3197.

Neolithic Age Jade Phoenix — A1491

Western Zhou Dynasty Phoenix Wine Container A1492

Tang Dynasty Celadon Pot With Phoenix-head Cover — A1493

Tang Dynasty Golden Phoenix — A1494

Ming Dynasty Phoenix and Peonies Silk Tapestry — A1495

Qing Dynasty Phoenix and Peonies Porcelain Jar — A1496

Perf. 13¼x13½ Syncopated

2017, July 29 **Litho. & Embossed**

4459	A1491	$1.20 multi	.35	.35

Litho. & Engr.

4460	A1492	$1.20 multi	.35	.35

Litho. & Embossed

4461	A1493	$1.20 multi	.35	.35

Litho. & Embossed With Foil Application

4462	A1494	$1.20 multi	.35	.35

Litho.

4463	A1495	$1.50 multi	.45	.45
4464	A1496	$1.50 multi	.45	.45
	Nos. 4459-4464 (6)		2.30	2.30

A1497

Chinese People's Liberation Army, 90th Anniv. — A1498

Designs: No. 4465, $1.20, Soldier, tanks and helicopters (6-1). No. 4466, $1.20, Sailor, ship and airplane (6-2). No. 4467, $1.20, Air Force pilot and airplane (6-3). No. 4468, $1.20, Rocket Force member, trucks and rocket launch (6-4). No. 4469, $1.20, Strategic Support Force member at computer, digital code (6-5). No. 4470, $1.20, Armed Police Force member, ship and helicopter (6-6).
$6, Soldiers, sailor and flag.

Perf. 13¼x13½ Syncopated

2017, Aug. 1 **Photo.**

4465-4470	A1497	Set of 6	2.25	2.25

Souvenir Sheet

4471	A1498	$6 multi	1.90	1.90

2017 BRICS (Brazil, Russia, India, China and South Africa) Summit, Xiamen — A1499

Perf. 13¼x13½ Syncopated

2017, Aug. 19 **Photo.**

4472	A1499	$1.20 multi	.40	.40

Litho.

Perf. 13¼x13½ Syncopated

On Silk-Faced Paper

4472A	A1499	$1.20 multi	.40	.40

No. 4472A exists in sheets of 8.

13th National Games, Tianjin and Luoyang — A1500

Mascots playing: No. 4473, $1.20, Volleyball and tennis (2-1). No. 4474, $1.20, Table tennis and gymnastics (2-2)

Perf. 13¼ Syncopated

2017, Aug. 27 **Litho.**

4473-4474	A1500	Set of 2	.75	.75
4474a		Souvenir sheet of 2, #4473-4474	.75	.75

Magpies A1501

Perf. 13x13¼ Syncopated

2017, Aug. 28 **Litho. & Engr.**

4475	A1501	$1.20 multi	.40	.40

No. 4475 comes printed in sheets of 8.

Composers — A1502

Designs: No. 4476, $1.20, Franz Schubert (1797-1828) (4-1). No. 4477, $1.20, Frédéric Chopin (1810-49) (4-2). No. 4478, $1.50, Franz Liszt (1811-86) (4-3). No. 4479, $1.50, Gustav Mahler (1860-1911) (4-4).

Perf. 13 Syncopated

2017, Sept. 9 **Litho. & Engr.**

4476-4479	A1502	Set of 4	1.75	1.75

Scientific and Technological Innovations — A1503

Designs: No. 4480, $1.20, Radio telescope (5-1). No. 4481, $1.20, Mozi Quantum Science Experiment Satellite (5-2). No. 4482,

$1.20, Discovery 1 research ship (5-3). No. 4483, $1.50, Bohai Rim agricultural project (5-4). No. 4484, $1.50, Sunway TaihuLight supercomputer (5-5).

Perf. 13x12¾ Syncopated

2017, Sept. 17 Litho.

4480-4484 A1503 Set of 5 2.00 2.00

Zhang Qian (d. 113 B.C.), Diplomat and Developer of Silk Road Trade Routes A1504

Designs: No. 4485, $1.20, Zhang Qian facing left (2-1). No. 4486, $1.20, Zhang Qian giving rolled-up scroll to another man (2-2).

$6, Zhang Qian holding open scroll.

Perf. 13x13¼ Syncopated

2017, Sept. 20 Photo.

4485-4486 A1504 Set of 2 .75 .75

Souvenir Sheet

Perf. 13x12¾ Syncopated

4487 A1504 $6 silver & multi 1.90 1.90

No. 4487 contains one 60x90mm stamp.

New Year 2018 (Year of the Dog) A1505

Perf. 12½ Syncopated

2017, Oct. 9 Litho.

4488 A1505 $1.20 gold & multi .40 .40

a. Souvenir sheet of 2, #3708a, perf. 12½ syncopated, 4488 1.40 1.40

Cantonese Opera — A1506

Designs: No. 4489, $1.20, Fragrant Mountain Birthday Celebration (3-1). No. 4490, $1.20, Six States Installation of Minister (3-2). $1.50, The Imperial Emperor of Heaven Holds Court (3-3).

Perf. 13¼x13½ Syncopated

2017, Oct. 15 Photo.

4489-4491 A1506 Set of 3 1.25 1.25

A1507

Designs: No. 4492, $1.20, Monument, building, boat and bridge (2-1). No. 4493, $1.20, Wind turbines, solar panels, airplane, road, rocket, ship and high-speed train (2-2).

$6, Hammer and sickle, Gate of Heavenly Peace.

Perf. 13x12¾ Syncopated

2017, Oct. 18 Photo.

4492-4493 A1507 Set of 2 .75 .75

Souvenir Sheet

Perf.

4494 A1507 $6 gold & multi 1.90 1.90

19th National Congress of the Communist Party of People's Republic of China.

No. 4494 contains one 56mm diameter stamp.

Journalist's Day — A1508

Perf. 13¼x13½ Syncopated

2017, Nov. 8 Photo.

4495 A1508 $1.20 sil & multi .40 .40

Statues Depicting Lions A1509

Designs: No. 4496, $1.20, Iron Lion of Cangzhou (2-1). No. 4497, $1.20, Stone Lion, Temple Phnom Bakheng, vert. (2-2).

Perf. 13x13¼ Syncopated, 13¼x13½ Syncopated

2017, Nov. 16 Litho. & Engr.

4496-4497 A1509 Set of 2 .75 .75

See Cambodia Nos. 2458-2459.

Development of High-Speed Rail Transportation — A1510

Designs: No. 4498, $1.20, Construction of elevated high-speed rail line, high-speed train and tunnels (4-1). No. 4499, $1.20, High-speed trains at servicing depot (4-2). No. 4500, $1.20, Completed high-speed rail bridges (4-3). No. 4501, $1.20, High-speed railway stations (4-4).

$6, High-speed trains and city skylines.

Perf. 13¼x13 Syncopated

2017, Nov. 25 Photo.

4498-4501 A1510 Set of 4 1.50 1.50

Souvenir Sheet

Perf. 12¾ Syncopated

4502 A1510 $6 gold & multi 1.90 1.90

No. 4502 contains one 78x46mm stamp.

Disney Princesses and Castle — A1511

2017, Dec. 2 Litho. *Perf. 13¼*

4503 A1511 $1.20 multi + label .40 .40

See Stamps with Attached Labels note after No. 3197.

Xiongan New Area — A1512

No. 4504: a, Sculpture, gate, front page of *Renmin Ribao* newspaper (2-1). b, Gate of Heavenly Peace, buildings, lion statue (2-2).

Perf. 13x12¾ Syncopated

2017, Dec. 22 Litho.

4504 A1512 $1.20 Horiz. pair, #a-b .75 .75

Emblem of 2022 Winter Olympics, Beijing — A1513

Emblem of 2022 Winter Paralympics, Beijing — A1514

Perf. 13¼x13½ Syncopated

2017, Dec. 31 Photo.

4505 A1513 $1.20 multi .40 .40

4506 A1514 $1.20 multi .40 .40

New Year 2018 (Year of the Dog) — A1515

Designs: No. 4507, $1.20, Dog facing right (2-1). No. 4508, $1.20, Dog and puppy (2-2).

Perf. 13 Syncopated

2018, Jan. 5 Litho. & Engr.

4507-4508 A1515 Set of 2 .80 .80

a. Booklet pane of 10, 5 each #4507-4508 4.00 —

Complete booklet, #4508a 4.00

b. Souvenir sheet of 4, 2 each #4507-4508 1.60 1.60

New Year's Greetings A1516

Perf. 13x12¾ Syncopated

2018, Jan. 10 Photo.

4509 A1516 $1.20 multi .40 .40

Paper Cuttings — A1517

Designs: No. 4510, $1.20, Luhua Dang, character from Beijing Opera (4-1). No. 4511, $1.20, Shepherd and sheep (4-2). No. 4512, $1.20, Jiangwa leading Meixiang on horse (4-3). No. 4513, $1.20, The son's farewell to his mother (4-4).

Perf. 13¼ Syncopated

2018, Jan. 24 Litho.

4510-4513 A1517 Set of 4 1.60 1.60

Lantern Festival — A1518

Designs: No. 4514, $1.20, Family eating rice dumpling balls (3-1). No. 4515, $1.20, People looking at large lanterns (3-2). $1.50, Dragon and lion dance (3-3).

Perf. 13¼x13½ Syncopated

2018, Mar. 2 Photo.

4514-4516 A1518 Set of 3 1.25 1.25

Exists in a sheet containing 3 sets, No. 4514-4516.

13th National People's Congress — A1519

Perf. 13x12¾ Syncopated

2018, Mar. 5 Litho.

4517 A1519 $1.20 multi .40 .40

Crabapple Blossoms A1520

Designs: No. 4518, $1.20, Malus prunifolia (4-1). No. 4519, $1.20, Malus micromalus (4-2). No. 4520, $1.20, Malus honanensis (4-3). No. 4521, $1.20, Malus sieboldii (4-4).

Perf. 13x12¾ Syncopated

2018, Mar. 25 Litho. & Engr.

4518-4521 A1520 Set of 4 1.60 1.60

Central Academy of Fine Arts, Cent. — A1521

Perf. 13x12¾ Syncopated

2018, Apr. 1 Litho. & Engr.

4522 A1521 $1.20 gold & multi .40 .40

A1522

The Dream of Red Mansions, Novel by Cao Xueqin — A1523

Designs: No. 4523, $1.20, Miao Yu makes tea (4-1). No. 4524, $1.20, Xi Chun painting (4-2). No. 4525, $1.20, Pinger and her attendants at dressing table (4-3). $1.50, Baoyu visits Bamboo Lodge at night (4-4).
$6, Tanchun and the Crab Flower Club.

Perf. 13 Syncopated

2018, Apr. 22 Litho.

4523-4526 A1522 Set of 4 1.60 1.60

Souvenir Sheet

Perf. 12¾ Syncopated

4527 A1523 $6 multi 1.90 1.90

Karl Marx (1818-83), Political Theorist — A1524

Designs: No. 4528, $1.20, Statue of Marx (2-1). No. 4529, $1.20, Statues of Marx and Friedrich Engels, book covers (2-2).

Perf. 13¼ Syncopated

2018, May 5 Photo.

4528-4529 A1524 Set of 2 .75 .75

I Looked Up to Them and They Seemed to Become More High, by Feng Zikai (1898-1975) A1525

Autumn Mountain Stream, by Guan Shanyue (1912-2000) A1526

Two Eagles, by Li Kuchan (1898-1983) A1527

Perf. 13¼ Syncopated

2018, May 11 Litho. & Engr.

4530 A1525 $1.20 multi .40 .40

Litho.

4531 A1526 $1.20 multi .40 .40

Photo.

4532 A1527 $1.50 multi .45 .45
Nos. 4530-4532 (3) 1.25 1.25

Buffalo — A1528

2018, May 19 Litho. *Perf. 13¼*

4533 A1528 $1.20 multi + label .40 .40

See Stamps With Attached Labels note after No. 3197.

Relics of the Silk Road A1529

Designs: No. 4534, $1.20, Gilt bronze figurine of silkworm (4-1). No. 4535, $1.20, Gold horse figurine (4-2). No. 4536, $1.20, Agate wine cup with head of animal (4-3). No. 4537, $1.20, Gold-painted blue glass plate (4-4).

Perf. 13 Syncopated

2018, May 19 Litho. & Embossed

4534-4537 A1529 Set of 4 1.50 1.50

National Day of the Disabled — A1530

Perf. 13¼x13½ Syncopated

2018, May 20 Litho.

4538 A1530 $1.20 multi .40 .40

Scientists and Scientific Works — A1531

Designs: No. 4539, $1.20, Li Shizhen (1518-93), compiler of medical knowledge (4-1). No. 4540, $1.20, *Compendium of Materia Medica,* by Li Shizhen (4-2). No. 4541, $1.20, Song Yingxing (1587-1666), scientist and encyclopedia writer (4-3). No. 4542, $1.20, *Exploitation of the Works of Nature,* by Song Yingxing (4-4).

Perf. 13¼x13½ Syncopated

2018, May 26 Litho.

4539-4542 A1531 Set of 4 1.50 1.50

Sites in Kashgar Prefecture — A1532

Designs: 80f, Ancient town of Kashgar (4-1). No. 4544, $1.20, Ruins of Stone City, Tashkurgan (4-2). No. 4545, $1.20, Zepu Jinhu Yang National Forest Park (4-3). No. 4546, $1.20, Khunjerab Pass border gate (4-4).

Perf. 13 Syncopated

2018, June 9 Photo.

4543-4546 A1532 Set of 4 1.40 1.40

Shanghai Cooperation Organization Summit, Qingdao — A1533

Perf. 13 Syncopated

2018, June 9 Litho.

4547 A1533 $1.20 multi .40 .40

On Silk-Faced Paper

Perf. 13¼x13 Syncopated

4547A A1533 $1.20 multi .40 .40

A1534

Qu Yuan (c. 340-278 B.C.), Poet — A1535

Qu Yuan: No. 4548, $1.20, Seated behind table (The Lament) (2-1). No. 4549, $1.20, Pointing to sky (Asking the Heaven) (2-2).
$6, Qu Yuan holding scroll.

Perf. 13x13¼ Syncopated

2018, June 18 Photo.

4548-4549 A1534 Set of 2 .75 .75

Souvenir Sheet

Perf. 13 Syncopated

4550 A1535 $6 multi 1.90 1.90

Uprightness and Incorruptibility A1536

Designs: No. 4551, $1.20, Han treasuring incorruptibility (4-1). No. 4552, $1.20, Yang Xu hung fish to refuse gifts (4-2). No. 4553, $1.20, Yu Qian's sleeves swaying in the breeze (4-3). No. 4554, $1.20, Yu Chenglong making public declaration to refuse gifts (4-4).

Perf. 13¼ Syncopated

2018, June 24 Litho.

4551-4554 A1536 Set of 4 1.50 1.50

Buildings and Doves — A1537

2018, July 1 Litho. *Perf. 13¼*

4555 A1537 $1.20 multi + label .35 .35

See Stamps With Attached Labels note after No. 3197.

Fruits — A1538

Designs: No. 4556, $1.20, Pineapples (4-1). No. 4557, $1.20, Cherries (4-2). No. 4558, $1.20, Mangos (4-3). $1.50, Oranges (4-4).

Perf. 13¼x13 Syncopated

2018, July 14 Litho.

4556-4559 A1538 Set of 4 1.60 1.60

National Heroes — A1539

Designs: No. 4560, $1.20, Guan Tianpei (1781-1841), admiral (5-1). No. 4561, $1.20, Lin Zexu (1785-1850), viceroy (5-2). No. 4562, $1.20, Feng Zicai (1818-1903), general (5-3). No. 4563, $1.20, Liu Yongfu (1837-1917), President of Republic of Formosa (5-4). No. 4564, $1.20, Deng Shichang (1849-94), naval officer (5-5).

Perf. 13¼x13½ Syncopated

2018, July 29 Photo.

4560-4564 A1539 Set of 5 1.75 1.75

Landscapes of the Four Seasons, by Liu Songnian (c. 1155-1224) — A1540

Various sections of the painting numbered: No. 4565, 80f, (4-1). No. 4566, 80f, (4-2). No. 4567, $1.20, (4-3). No. 4568, $1.20, (4-4).

Perf. 13¼x13 Syncopated

2018, Aug. 4 Litho. & Engr.

4565-4568 A1540 Set of 4 1.25 1.25
4568a Souvenir sheet of 4, #4565-4568 1.25 1.25

24 Solar Terms — A1541

No. 4569: a, Autumn begins (family at table) (6-1). b, Stopping the heat (people winnowing rice) (6-2). c, White dews (people in tai chi poses) (6-3). d, Autumn equinox (man and boy picking fruit) (6-4). e, Cold dews (woman and tailor) (6-5). f, Hoarfrost falls (man with camera, two women in coats near tree with changing leaves) (6-6).

Perf. 13 Syncopated

2018, Aug. 7 **Photo.**

4569 A1541 $1.20 Block of 6, #a-f 2.10 2.10

Values are for stamps with surrounding selvage.

Geese in Flight A1542

Perf. 13 Syncopated

2018, Aug. 17 **Litho. & Engr.**

4570 A1542 $1.20 multi .35 .35

Yangtze River Economic Belt — A1543

Designs: No. 4571, $1.20, Ecology protection plan (6-1). No. 4572, $1.20, Multimoda transport corridor (6-2). No. 4573, $1.20, Transformation and upgrading of industry (6-3). No. 4574, $1.20, New urbanization (6-4). No. 4575, $1.50, Airplane, train and ships at port (6-5). No. 4576, $1.50, Regional coordinated development (6-6).

Perf. 13¼x13 Syncopated

2018, Aug. 26 **Litho.**

4571-4576 A1543 Set of 6 2.25 2.25

4576a Souvenir sheet of 6, #4571-4576 2.25 2.25

Miniature Sheet

Book of Songs — A1544

No. 4577: a, 80f, The Songs of Zhou and the South (woman, birds and flowers) (6-1). b, $1.20, The Songs of Qin (man in robe) (6-2). c, $1.20, The Songs of Qin (two men and wheel) (6-3). d, $1.20, Minor Songs of the Kingdom (four men) (6-4). e, $1.50, Minor Songs of the Kingdom (three cranes and six fish) (6-5). f, $3, Songs of Lu (horses) (6-6).

Perf. 13 Syncopated

2018, Sept. 8 **Litho. & Engr.**

4577 A1544 Sheet of 6, #a-f 2.60 2.60

Round Moon Over Mid-Autumn Festival — A1545

Perf. 13¼x13 Syncopated

2018, Sept. 15 **Litho.**

4578 A1545 $1.20 multi .35 .35

Perforations encircle most of the moon.

Windmills, Solar Panels, Factory, Airships, Computer and Head — A1546

Houses and People of Ningxia Hui Autonomous Region — A1547

City — A1548

Designs: a, Innovation driven. b, Poverty alleviation. c, Establishing autonomous region by ecological way.

Perf. 13 Syncopated

2018, Sept. 19 **Litho.**

4579 Horiz. strip of 3 1.10 1.10

a. A1546 $1.20 multi .35 .35

b. A1547 $1.20 multi .35 .35

c. A1548 $1.20 multi .35 .35

Ningxia Hui Autonomous Region, 60th anniv.

Farmers' Harvest Festival A1549

Perf. 13 Syncopated

2018, Sept. 23 **Photo.**

4580 A1549 $1.20 multi .35 .35

International Day of Older Persons A1550

Perf. 13¼ Syncopated

2018, Oct. 1 **Litho.**

4581 A1550 $1.20 gold & multi .35 .35

Happiness and Longevity A1551

Perf. 12½ Syncopated

2018, Oct. 9 **Litho.**

4582 A1551 $1.20 gold & multi .35 .35

a. Souvenir sheet of 2, #3708a (perf. 12½ syncopated), 4582 1.25 1.25

Dancers and Buildings — A1552

Ships, Trains and City Skyline — A1553

Waterfront Houses Near Mountains — A1554

Designs: a, Harmonious homeland. b, Openning-up door. c, Eco-friendly land.

Perf. 13 Syncopated

2018, Oct. 18 **Photo.**

4583 Horiz. strip of 3 1.10 1.10

a. A1552 $1.20 multi .35 .35

b. A1553 $1.20 multi .35 .35

c. A1554 $1.20 multi .35 .35

Guangxi Zhuang Autonomous Region, 60th anniv.

Qingzhou Navigational Channel Bridge — A1555

East Artificial Island — A1556

Tunnel — A1557

Perf. 13¼ Syncopated

2018, Oct. 30 **Photo.**

4584 A1555 $1.20 multi .35 .35

4585 A1556 $1.20 multi .35 .35

4586 A1557 $1.20 multi .35 .35

Nos. 4584-4586 (3) 1.05 1.05

Opening of Hong Kong-Zhuhai-Macao Bridge. See Hong Kong No. 1970.

China International Import Expo Emblem — A1558

China International Import Expo Mascot — A1559

Perf. 13¼ Syncopated

2018, Nov. 5 **Photo.**

4587 A1558 $1.20 multi .35 .35

4588 A1559 $1.20 multi .35 .35

2022 Winter Olympics, Beijing A1560

Designs: No. 4589, $1.20, Cross-country skiing (4-1). No. 4590, $1.20, Alpine skiing (4-2). No. 4591, $1.20, Biathlon (4-3). No. 4592, $1.20, Freestyle skiing (4-4).

Perf. 13 Syncopated

2018, Nov. 16 **Photo.**

4589-4592 A1560 Set of 4 1.40 1.40

Direct Postal, Transportation and Trade Links Across the Taiwan Straits, 10th Anniv. — A1561

Perf. 13¼ Syncopated

2018, Dec. 15 **Photo.**

4593 A1561 $1.20 multi .35 .35

A1562

Governmental Reform, 40th Anniv. — A1563

Designs: No. 4594, $1.20, Leaders at table, statue of bull, tractor in field (2-1). No. 4595, $1.20, Dancers, buildings, airplane and train (2-2).

$6, People raising hands in Tiananmen Square.

Perf. 13x12¾ Syncopated

2018, Dec. 18 **Photo.**

4594-4595 A1562 Set of 2 .70 .70

Souvenir Sheet

Perf. 13¼ Syncopated

4596 A1563 $6 multi 1.75 1.75

New Year 2019 (Year of the Pig) — A1564

Designs: No. 4597, $1.20, Pig (2-1). No. 4598, $1.20, Two pigs and three piglets (2-2).

Perf. 13 Syncopated

2019, Jan. 5 **Litho. & Engr.**

4597-4598	A1564	Set of 2	.70	.70
4597a		Souvenir sheet of 6	3.25	3.25
4598a		Booklet pane of 10, 5 each #4597-4598	3.50	—
		Complete booklet, #4598a	3.50	
4598b		Souvenir sheet of 4, 2 each #4597-4598	1.40	1.40
4598c		Souvenir sheet of 6 #4598	3.25	3.25

New Year Greetings A1565

Perf. 13 Syncopated

2019, Jan. 10 **Litho.**

4599 A1565 $1.20 multi .35 .35
a. Souvenir sheet of 8 3.00 3.00

Knot — A1566

2019, Jan. 26 **Litho.** ***Perf. 13¼***

4600 A1566 $1.20 multi + label .35 .35

See Stamps With Attached Labels note after No. 3197.

A1567

Designs: No. 4601, $1.20, Purple Sand tea pot and cup (2-1). No. 4602, $1.20, Silver tea pot (2-2).

Perf. 13 Syncopated

2019, Feb. 8 **Photo.**

4601-4602 A1567 Set of 2 .75 .75

Diplomatic relations between People's Republic of China and Portugal, 40th anniv. See Portugal Nos. 4091-4092.

Arbor Day — A1568

Perf. 13¼ Syncopated

2019, Mar. 12 **Photo.**

4603 A1568 $1.20 multi .35 .35

Marathon Runners — A1569

Various marathon runners with denomination at: No. 4604, $1.20, UL (2-1). No. 4605, $1.20, UR (2-2).

Perf. 13¼ Syncopated

2019, Mar. 31 **Photo.**

4604-4605 A1569 Set of 2 .70 .70

A1570

Journey to the West, Novel by Wu Cheng'en (c. 1500-c.1580) — A1571

Designs: No. 4606, $1.20, Monkey subdues the white-boned demon (4-1). No. 4607, $1.20, Battles with the Red Boy (4-2). No. 4608, $1.50, In the Kingdom of Chechi, the Monkey King shows his powers (4-3). No. 4609, $1.50, Escape from the Kingdom of Women (4-4).

$6, Immortals subdue the water buffalo.

Perf. 13¼x13 Syncopated

2019, Apr. 20 **Photo.**

4606-4609 A1570 Set of 4 1.60 1.60

Souvenir Sheet

Perf. 13x13¼ Syncopated

4610 A1571 $6 multi 1.90 1.90

No. 4606-4609 exists in a sheet of 8 with 2 sets of each.

2019 International Horiticultural Exhibition, Beijing — A1572

Designs: 80f, Emblem, roses, Great Wall of China (2-1). $1.20, Mascots and exhibition buildings (2-2).

Perf. 13¼x13 Syncopated

2019, Apr. 29 **Photo.**

4611-4612 A1572 Set of 2 .60 .60

May Fourth Movement, Cent. — A1573

"100" and: No. 4613, $1.20, Sculptures, May 4th movement spirit (2-1). No. 4614, $1.20, Doves and people with raised hands, new era of endeavor (2-2).

Perf. 11¾x12¼ Syncopated

2019, May 4 **Litho.**

4613-4614 A1573 Set of 2 .70 .70

2022 Asian Games, Hangzhou — A1574

2019, May 11 **Litho.** ***Perf. 13¼***

4615 A1574 $1.20 multi + label .35 .35

See Stamps With Attached Labels note after No. 3197.

Peonies A1575

Designs: No. 4616, $1.20, Paeonia lactiflora (4-1). No. 4617, $1.20, Paeonia veitchii (4-2). No. 4618, $1.20, Paeonia obovata (4-3). No. 4619, $1.20, Paeonia mairei (4-4).

Perf. 13 Syncopated

2019, May 11 **Litho. & Engr.**

4616-4619 A1575 Set of 4 1.40 1.40

Exists in sheet of 8 with 2 sets, No. 4616-4619.

Ancient Cities — A1576

Designs: No. 4620, 80f, Yangliuqing (4-1). No. 4621, 80f, Guangfu (4-2). No. 4622, $1.20, Nianbadu (4-3). No. 4623, $1.20, Furong (4-4).

Perf. 13¼x13 Syncopated

2019, May 19 **Litho. & Engr.**

4620-4623 A1576 Set of 4 1.25 1.25

Exists in sheet of 8 with 2 sets, No. 4620-4623.

Children at Play — A1577

Children: No. 4624, 80f, Completing jigsaw puzzle (4-1). No. 4625, 80f, Building sand castle (4-2). No. 4626, $1.20, Roller skating (4-3). No. 4627, $1.20, Playing with building blocks (4-4).

Perf. 13¼ Syncopated

2019, June 1 **Photo.**

4624-4627 A1577 Set of 4 1.25 1.25
4627a Souvenir sheet of 8, 2 each #4624-4627 3.00 3.00

A1578

China 2019 World Stamp Exhibition, Wuhan — A1579

Various details of *The Three Towns of Wuhan*: No. 4628, $1.20, (2-1). No. 4629, $1.20 (2-2).

$6, Bronze Zun-pan from tomb of Zenghouyi.

Perf. 13¼ Syncopated

2019, June 11 **Litho.**

4628-4629 A1578 Set of 2 .70 .70
4629a Souvenir sheet of 8, 4 each #4628-4629 3.75 3.75

Souvenir Sheet

Litho. & Engr.

Perf.

4630 A1579 $6 multi 1.75 1.75

Yiwu Train — A1580

Madrid Train — A1581

Perf. 13½ Syncopated

2019, June 15 **Litho. & Engr.**

4631 Horiz. pair .70 .70
a. A1580 $1.20 multi .35 .35
b. A1581 $1.20 multi .35 .35

Chine-Europe Railway Express.

Seventh World Military Games, Wuhan — A1582

Designs: No. 4632, 80f, Javelin (4-1). No. 4633, 80f, Obstacle course (4-2). No. 4634, $1.20, Naval pentathlon (4-3). No. 4625, $1.20, Four-person formation skydiving (4-4).

Perf. 13¼x13 Syncopated

2019, July 10 **Photo.**

4632-4635 A1582 Set of 4 1.25 1.25

4635a Souvenir sheet of 8, 2 each #4632-4635 3.00 3.00

Poyang Lake — A1583

Designs: 80f, Stone Bell Mountain (3-1). No. 4637, $1.20, Shoe-shape Island (3-2). No. 4638, $1.20, Birds over Poyang Lake National Wetland Park (3-3).

Perf. 13½x13 Syncopated

2019, July 20 **Photo.**

4636-4638 A1583 Set of 3 .95 .95

Five Sacred Mountains — A1584

Designs: No. 4639, $1.20, Sunrise on Mount Tai (5-1). No. 4640, $1.20, Mount Hua in Late Autumn (5-2). No. 4641, $1.20, Mount Zhurong in Rain (5-3). No. 4642, $1.20, Mount Heng in Snow (5-4). No. 4643, $1.20, Mounts Taishi and Shaoshi (5-5).

Perf. 13 Syncopated

2019, Aug. 3 **Litho. & Engr.**

4639-4643 A1584 Set of 5 1.75 1.75

4643a Souvenir sheet of 5, #4639-4643 1.75 1.75

Ancient Mythology A1585

Designs: No. 4644, 80f, Suiren producing fire by drilling in wood (6-1). No. 4645, 80f, Fuxi drawing trigrams (6-2). No. 4646, $1.20, Shennong tasting herbs (6-3). No. 4647, $1.20, Leizu and the origins of Chinese silk (6-4). No. 4648, $1.20, Cangjie creating Chinese characters (6-5). No. 4649, $1.20, Yu the Great taming waters (6-6).

2019, Aug. 6 **Photo.** ***Perf. 13¼***

4644-4649 A1585 Set of 6 1.90 1.90

Highways to Tibet — A1586

Designs: 80f, Sichuan-Tibet Highway (2-1). $1.20, Qinghai-Tibet Highway (2-2).

Perf. 13¼x13 Syncopated

2019, Aug. 10 **Litho. & Embossed**

4650-4651 A1586 Set of 2 .55 .55

A1587

Lu Ban (c. 507-444 B.C.), God of Carpenters and Masons — A1588

Lu Ban holding: No. 4652, $1.20, Model of building (2-1). No. 4653, $1.20, Hammer and chisel (2-2).

$6, Lu Ban holding invention.

Perf. 13x13¼ Syncopated

2019, Aug. 24 **Photo.**

4652-4653 A1587 Set of 2 .70 .70

4653a Souvenir sheet of 6, 3 each #4652-4653 2.75 2.75

Souvenir Sheet

Perf. 13 Syncopated

4654 A1588 $6 multi 1.75 1.75

Chinese People's Political Consultative Conference, 70th Anniv. — A1589

National Political Consultative Conference Auditorium, Beijing — A1590

Perf. 13¼x13½ Syncopated

2019, Sept. 21 **Photo.**

4655 A1589 $1.20 gold & multi .35 .35

Perf. 13 Syncopated

4656 A1590 $1.20 gold & multi .35 .35

Guangdong-Hong Kong-Macao Greater Bay Area — A1591

Designs: No. 4657, $1.20, Drone, Pearl River and buildings (3-1). No. 4658, $1.20, Bridge, airplane over runway, ship near port (3-2). No. 4659, $1.20, Dragon boats, buildings, bicyclist, woman in traditional costume, runners, Tsai chi practitioner (3-3).

Perf. 13¼x13 Syncopated

2019, Sept. 26 **Photo.**

4657-4659 A1591 Set of 3 1.00 1.00

4659a Souvenir sheet of 3, #4657-4659 1.00 1.00

Opening of Beijing Daxing International Airport — A1592

Perf. 13¼x13 Syncopated

2019, Sept. 26 **Photo.**

4660 A1592 $1.20 multi + label .35 .35

A1593

People's Republic of China, 70th Anniv. — A1594

Designs: No. 4661, $1.20, Drone, airplane, satellite, robotic arm, woman and man with computer, buildings and train (5-1). No. 4662, $1.20, People at governmental meeting (5-2). No. 4663, $1.20, Athletes and entertainers, China Central Television Building (5-3). No. 4664, $1.20, Buildings, school children, farmer, doctor, nurse and patient (5-4). No. 4665, $1.20, Wind generators, solar panels, woman and chld watering tree (5-5).

$6, Ship, doves, 70th anniv. emblem.

Perf. 13 Syncopated

2019, Oct. 1 **Photo.**

4661-4665 A1593 Set of 5 1.75 1.75

4665a Souvenir sheet of 10, 2 each #4661-4665 4.50 4.50

Souvenir Sheet

4666 A1594 $6 multi 1.75 1.75

Chaotianmen Bridge, Chongqing — A1595

Saratov Bridge, Saratov, Russia — A1596

Perf. 12x12¼ Syncopated

2019, Oct. 2 **Litho.**

4667 A1595 $1.20 multi .35 .35

4668 A1596 $1.20 multi .35 .35

Diplomatic relations between People's Republic of China and Russia, 70th anniv.

Chinese Incense Burner on Hook, c. 880 — A1597

Slovakian Bronze Horse Harness Fitting, c. 795 — A1598

Perf. 13¼x13 Syncopated

2019, Oct. 6 **Litho. & Embossed**

4669 A1597 $1.20 multi .35 .35

4670 A1598 $1.20 multi .35 .35

Diplomatic relations between People's Republic of China and Slovakia, 70th anniv. See Slovakia No. 828.

Famous Men — A1599

Designs: No. 4671, 80f, Wang Shouren (1472-1529), philosopher (6-1). No. 4672, 80f, Huang Zongxi (1610-95), philosopher (6-2). No. 4673, 80f, Gu Yanwu (1613-82), philologist (6-3). No. 4674, $1.20, Wang Fuzhi (1619-92), historian (6-4). No. 4675, $1.20, Dai Zhen (1724-77), philosopher (6-5). No. 4676, $1.20, Zhang Xuecheng (1738-1801), historian (6-6).

Perf. 13¼ Syncopated

2019, Oct. 7 **Litho. & Engr.**

4671-4676 A1599 Set of 6 1.75 1.75

Nankai University, Tianjin, Cent. — A1600

Perf. 13x13¼ Syncopated

2019, Oct. 17 **Litho.**

4677 A1600 $1.20 multi .35 .35

Chang'e 4 Probe A1601

Cloned Monkeys A1602

Experimental Discovery of Quantum Anomalous Hall Effect — A1603

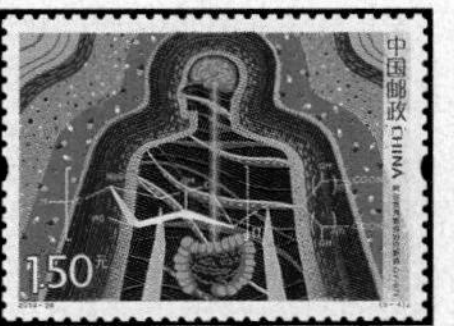

Human Body and Chemical Diagram for New Drug to Treat Alzheimer's Disease A1604

China Spallation Neutron Source A1605

Litho. With Foil Application

2019, Nov. 1 *Perf. 13 Syncopated*

4678 A1601 $1.20 gold & multi .35 .35
4679 A1602 $1.20 gold & multi .35 .35
4680 A1603 $1.20 gold & multi .35 .35
4681 A1604 $1.50 gold & multi .45 .45
4682 A1605 $1.50 gold & multi .45 .45
Nos. 4678-4682 (5) 1.95 1.95

Golden Rat — A1606

Perf. 12¾ Syncopated

2019, Nov. 1 **Photo.**

4683 A1606 $1.20 gold & multi .35 .35
a. Souvenir sheet of 2, #3708a (perf. 12¾ syncopated), 4683 1.25 1.25

24 Solar Terms — A1607

No. 4684: a, Beginning of winter (pigs, woman and bok choy) (6-1). b, Slight snow (man pruning tree) (6-2). c, Great snow (children making snowman) (6-3). d, The winter solstice (woman knitting and child painting) (6-4). e, Slight cold (children on chairs with ice skate blades) (6-5). f, Great cold (man and child looking at tree in snow) (6-6).

Perf. 13 Syncopated

2019, Nov. 8 **Photo.**

4684 A1607 $1.20 Block of 6, #a-f 2.10 2.10

Values are for stamps with surrounding selvage.

Poverty Alleviation — A1608

Designs: No. 4685, $1.20, Flag of People's Republic of China, family, medical clinic, school (6-1). No. 4686, $1.20, Boat on river, Chixi Village (6-2). No. 4687, $1.20, Tree, buildings in Shibadong Village (6-3). No. 4688, $1.20, Raspberries, women, motorized cart, Minning Village (6-4). No. 4689, $1.20, Statue of man, buildings in Lankao County (6-5). No. 4690, $1.20, Peaches, sculpture, truck, buildings in Jinggangshan City (6-6).

Perf. 13 Syncopated

2019, Nov. 29 **Photo.**

4685-4690 A1608 Set of 6 2.10 2.10

Emblems of 2022 Winter Olympics and Paralympics, Beijing — A1609

No. 4691 — Emblem of: a, Winter Olympics. b, Winter Paralympics.

2019, Dec. 7 **Litho.** *Perf. 12*

4691 A1609 $1.20 Vert. pair, #a-b, + 2 labels .70 .70

Return of Macao to People's Republic of China, 20th Anniv. A1610

Designs: No. 4692, $1.20, Flags of People's Republic of China and Macao, people, Lotus Flower sculpture (3-1). No. 4693, $1.20, Dragon, dancers, buildings of Macao (3-2). $1.50, Buildings and bridges of Macao (3-3).

Perf. 13¼x13 Syncopated

2019, Dec.20 **Photo.**

4692-4694 A1610 Set of 3 1.10 1.10

New Year 2020 (Year of the Rat) — A1611

Designs: No. 4695, $1.20, Rat (2-1). No. 4696, $1.20, Three rats (2-2).

Perf. 13 Syncopated

2020, Jan. 5 **Litho. & Engr.**

4695-4696 A1611 Set of 2 .70 .70
4696a Booklet pane of 10, 5 each #4695-4696 3.50 —
Complete booklet, #4696a 3.50

Mascot of 2022 Winter Olympics, Beijing — A1612

Mascot of 2022 Winter Paralympics, Beijing — A1613

Perf. 13x13¼ Syncopated

2020, Jan. 16 **Photo.**

4697 A1612 $1.20 multi .35 .35
4698 A1613 $1.20 multi .35 .35

Paper Cutting Art — A1614

Designs: No. 4699, $1.20, Sanniang Teaches Her Son (4-1). No. 4700, $1.20, Celebrating Spring Festival With Waist Drums (4-2). No. 4701, $1.20, Wang Xiao Serves With a Donkey (4-3). No. 4702, $1.20, Auspicious Road for Ginseng Digging (4-4).

Perf. 13¼x12¾ Syncopated

2020, Feb. 8 **Litho.**

4699-4702 A1614 Set of 4 1.40 1.40

Paintings by Wu Guanzhong (1919-2010) A1615

Designs: No. 4703, $1.20, Sorghum and Cotton (6-1). No. 4704, $1.20, Melon Vines (6-2). No. 4705, $1.20, Water Lane (6-3). No. 4706, $1.50, Spring Snow in Daba Mountains (50x30mm) (6-4). No. 4707, $1.50, Double Swallows (50x30mm) (6-5). $3, Dancing Cranes (50x30mm) (6-6).

Perf. 13¼ Syncopated (vert. stamps), 13¼x13 Syncopated (horiz. stamps)

2020, Mar. 20 **Litho.**

4703-4708 A1615 Set of 6 2.75 2.75

Launch of First Chinese Satellite, Dong Fang Hong I, 50th Anniv. A1616

Perf. 13 Syncopated

2020, Apr. 24 **Litho.**

4709 A1616 $1.20 multi .35 .35

Ancient Asian Civilizations — A1618

Designs: No. 4711, $1.20, Ziggurat of Ur (6-1). No. 4712, $1.20, Akkadian-language tablet with Gilgamesh Flood Myth, vert. (6-2). No. 4713, $1.20, Harappan seal, vert. (6-3). No. 4714, $1.20, Mohenjo-daro ruins (6-4). No. 4715, $1.20, Liangzhu jade cong, vert. (6-5). No. 4716, $1.20, Ruins at Shimao archaeological site (6-6).

Perf. 13¼x13 Syncopated (horiz. stamps), 13¼ Syncopated (vert. stamps)

2020, May 15 **Litho. & Engr.**

4711-4716 A1618 Set of 6 2.10 2.10

A1619

The Dream of Red Mansions, Novel by Cao Xueqin — A1620

Designs: No. 4717, $1.20, Yuanyang vows never to marry (4-1). No. 4718, $1.20, Baoqin stands in snow (4-2). No. 4719, $1.20, You Sanjie returns the love token sword (4-3). $1.50, Malicious talk makes Lady Wang have a search made of the garden (4-4).

$6, Xiangyun sleeps among the peonies.

Perf. 13 Syncopated

2020, May 17 **Photo.**

4717-4720 A1619 Set of 4 1.50 1.50

Souvenir Sheet

Perf. 13¼x13

4721 A1620 $6 multi 1.75 1.75

Roses A1621

Designs: No. 4722, $1.20, Red rose and swallows in flight (4-1). No. 4723, $1.20, Pink roses and ducks (4-2). No. 4724, $1.50, White roses and birds in flight (4-3). No. 4725, $1.50, Purple roses and swans (4-4).

Litho. & Embossed With Holographic Foil Affixed

2020, May 20 ***Perf. 13¼ Syncopated***

4722-4725 A1621 Set of 4 1.50 1.50

Ascent of Mount Everest by Chinese Mountaineering Team, 60th Anniv. — A1622

Perf. 13 Syncopated

2020, May 25 **Photo.**

4726 A1622 $1.20 multi .35 .35

Harbin Institute of Technology, Cent. — A1624

Perf. 13¼x13½ Syncopated

2020, June 6 **Litho. & Engr.**

4733 A1624 $1.20 multi .35 .35

Publication of Chinese Edition of *The Communist Manifesto*, Cent. — A1632

Perf. 13¼x12¾ Syncopated

2020, Aug. 22 **Litho.**

4749 A1632 $1.20 multi .35 .35

Scientists — A1633

Designs: No. 4750, $1.20, Wang Daheng (1915-2011), optical engineer (4-1). No. 4751, $1.20, Huang Kun (1919-2005), physicist (4-2). No. 4752, $1.20, Yu Min (1926-2019), nuclear physicist (4-3). No. 4753, $1.20, Chen Jingrun (1933-96), mathematician (4-4).

Perf. 13¼x12¾ Syncopated

2020, Sept. 19 **Litho. & Engr.**

4750-4753 A1633 Set of 4 1.40 1.40

SEMI-POSTAL STAMPS

Catalogue values for unused stamps in this section are for Never Hinged items.

Girl Holding Ball — SP1

China Post No. T.92

1984, Feb. 16 **Photo.** ***Perf. 11½***

B1 SP1 8f + 2f shown (2-1)	1.25	.30
B2 SP1 8f + 2f Boy, panda (2-2)	1.25	.30

Surtax for China Children's Fund.

Hands Reading Braille — SP2

China Post No. T.105

No. B4, Sign language, lip reading. No. B5, Artificial limb. No. B6, Handicapped person in wheelchair.

1985, Mar. 15 **Photo.** ***Perf. 11½***

B3 SP2 8f + 2f shown (4-1)	.60	.35
B4 SP2 8f + 2f multi (4-2)	.60	.35
B5 SP2 8f + 2f multi (4-3)	.60	.35
B6 SP2 8f + 2f multi (4-4)	.60	.35
Nos. B3-B6 (4)	2.40	1.40

Surtax for China Welfare Fund.

Children SP3

China Post No. T.137

No. B7, Friends. No. B8, Penguins. No. B9, Bird, Moon, Sun. No. B10, Girl, boy playing ball.

1989, June 1 **Litho.** ***Perf. 12***

B7 SP3 8f +4f multi (4-1)	.25	.25
B8 SP3 8f +4f multi (4-2)	.25	.25
B9 SP3 8f +4f multi (4-3)	.25	.25
B10 SP3 8f +4f multi (4-4)	.25	.25
a. Strip of 4, #B7-B10	1.50	1.50

Intl Children's Day, 40th anniv., and 10th Intl. Year of the Child. Surtax for China Children's Fund.

Flood Victims Relief — SP4

1998, Sept. 10 **Photo.** ***Perf. 13x13½***

B10B SP4 50f + 50f label .75 .40

Sichuan Earthquake Relief — SP5

2008, May 20 **Photo.** ***Perf. 13x13¼***

B11 SP5 $1.20 + $1 multi + label *14.00 8.00*

AIR POST STAMPS

Mail Plane and Temple of Heaven — AP1

China Post No. A1

1951, May 1 **Engr.** ***Perf. 12½***

Without Gum

C1 AP1 $1000 carmine	1.00	.40
C2 AP1 $3000 green	1.00	.40
C3 AP1 $5000 orange	1.00	.40
a. Pair, imperf. between	600.00	—
C4 AP1 $10,000 vio brn & grn	3.00	1.00
C5 AP1 $30,000 dk bl & brn	24.00	4.25
Nos. C1-C5 (5)	30.00	6.45

Planes at Airport — AP2

China Post No. A2

Designs: 28f, Plane over winding mountain highway. 35f, Plane over railroad yard. 52f, Plane over ship.

1957-58 **Without Gum** ***Perf. 14***

C6 AP2 16f indigo	16.00	1.00
C7 AP2 28f olive black	16.00	1.00
C8 AP2 35f slate	16.00	5.00
C9 AP2 52f Prus blue ('58)	16.00	2.00
Nos. C6-C9 (4)	64.00	9.00

POSTAGE DUE STAMPS

Grain and Cogwheel — D1

China Post No. D1

1950, Sept. 1 **Typo.** ***Perf. 12½***

Without Gum

J1 D1 $100 steel blue	.25	1.00
J2 D1 $200 steel blue	.25	1.00
J3 D1 $500 steel blue	.25	1.00
J4 D1 $800 steel blue	30.00	6.00
J5 D1 $1000 steel blue	.45	1.00
J6 D1 $2000 steel blue	.70	1.00
J7 D1 $5000 steel blue	.70	1.00
J8 D1 $8000 steel blue	.70	5.00
J9 D1 $10,000 steel blue	2.00	15.00
Nos. J1-J9 (9)	35.30	32.00

D2

China Post No. D2

1954, Aug. 18 **Litho.** ***Perf. 14***

Without Gum

J10 D2 $100 red	1.50	1.25
J11 D2 $200 red	1.00	1.25
J12 D2 $500 red	1.50	1.25
J13 D2 $800 red	1.00	1.25
J14 D2 $1600 red	1.00	1.25
Nos. J10-J14 (5)	6.00	6.25

MILITARY STAMP

Red Star, 8-1 in Center — M1

China Post No. M1

1953, Aug. **Litho.** ***Perf. 14***

Without Gum

M1 M1 $800 yel, org & red *300.00 125.00*

This stamp also was printed in deep purple, orange & red (value, *$3,500.*), and blue, orange & red (value, *$315,000*). These were not issued.

While it has been assumed for many years that each color was for a separate branch of the armed forces (army, air force and navy), there is no documentation to support that theory. Quantities printed also do not correspond to the number of servicemen in each branch.

M2

China Post No. M2

1995 **Litho.** ***Perf. 12***

M4 M2 20f multicolored 13.00 *4.00*

NORTHEAST CHINA

The Northeast Liberation Area included the provinces of Liaoning, Kirin, Jehol and Heilungkiang, the area generally known as Manchuria under the Japanese. The first post war issues were local overprints on stamps of Manchukuo. In early 1946, a Ministry of Posts and Telegraphs served the areas already liberated, and in August, 1946, a Communications Committee of the Political Council was established. In June, 1947, these postal services were subordinated to the Harbin General Post Office, and this was extended to Changchun on Oct. 22, 1948, and to Mukden on Nov. 4, 1948. It was rapidly extended to cover all Manchuria.

Rough Perfs

Rough perforations are normal on most regional issues.

All Stamps Issued without Gum

Mao Tse-tung

A1 A2

1946, Feb. **Unwmk.** **Litho.**

1L1 A1 $1 violet	22.50	25.00
1L2 A2 $2 vermilion	2.50	5.00
1L3 A2 $5 orange	2.75	5.00
a. Booklet pane of 6	250.00	
1L4 A2 $10 blue	3.00	4.00
a. Booklet pane of 6	250.00	
Nos. 1L1-1L4 (4)	30.75	39.00

Value, imperf set $125.

For surcharges see Nos. 1L20-1L23, 1L49-1L50, 1L89, 1L91, 1L93.

Map of China, Lion, Hyena and Chiang Kai-shek — A3

1946, Dec. 12 *Perf. 10½*

1L5 A3 $1 violet 2.25 4.00
1L6 A3 $2 orange 2.25 4.00
1L7 A3 $5 org brn 7.50 *12.00*
1L8 A3 $10 lt grn 12.00 20.00
a. Imperf., pair 60.00
Nos. 1L5-1L8 (4) 24.00 40.00

10th anniversary of the capture of Chiang Kai-shek at Sian.

Railroad Workers, Chengchow A4

1947, Feb. 7 *Perf. 10½*

1L9 A4 $1 pink 3.00 *4.00*
1L10 A4 $2 dull grn 3.00 *4.00*
1L11 A4 $5 pink 4.00 *5.00*
1L12 A4 $10 dull grn 8.00 *9.00*
Nos. 1L9-1L12 (4) 18.00 *22.00*

24th anniversary of the Chengchow railroad workers' strike and massacre.

Women (Worker, Soldier and Farmer) — A5

Wmk. Chinese Characters in Sheet

1947, Mar. 8 *Perf. 10½x11*

1L13 A5 $5 brick red 5.00 8.00
1L14 A5 $10 brown 5.00 8.00

International Women's Day, March 8. Exists imperf.

Same Overprinted in Green ("Northeast Postal Service")

1947, Mar. 18

1L15 A5 $5 brick red 9.50 12.00
1L16 A5 $10 brown 9.50 12.00

Exists imperf.

Children Carrying Banner — A6

1947, Apr. 4 *Perf. 11x10½*

Granite Paper

1L17 A6 $5 rose red 7.00 10.00
1L18 A6 $10 lt green 12.00 15.00
1L19 A6 $30 orange 17.50 20.00
Nos. 1L17-1L19 (3) 36.50 45.00

Children's Day.

Nos. 1L1-1L2 Surcharged in Red, Brown, Black, Blue or Green

1947, Apr. **Unwmk.** *Perf. 11*

1L20 A1 $50 on $1 vio (R) 30.00 *32.50*
a. Brown surcharge 30.00 *32.50*
1L21 A2 $50 on $2 ver 30.00 *32.50*
a. Brown surcharge 30.00 *32.50*
1L22 A1 $100 on $1 vio 30.00 *32.50*
a. Green surcharge 30.00 *32.50*
1L23 A2 $100 on $2 ver (Bl) 30.00 *32.50*
a. Green surcharge 30.00 *32.50*
Nos. 1L20-1L23 (4) 120.00 *130.00*

Farmer and Worker — A7

Wmk. Chinese Characters in Sheet

1947, May 1 *Perf. 10½x11*

Granite Paper

1L24 A7 $10 orange red 6.00 *8.00*
1L25 A7 $30 ultra 10.00 *15.00*
1L26 A7 $50 gray green 6.50 *8.00*
Nos. 1L24-1L26 (3) 22.50 *31.00*

Labor Day. Value, imperf. pairs, set $425.

Ax Severing Chain — A8

1947, May 4 *Perf. 11*

1L27 A8 $10 brt green 8.00 *10.00*
1L28 A8 $30 brown 8.00 *10.00*
1L29 A8 $50 violet 10.00 *15.00*
Nos. 1L27-1L29 (3) 26.00 *35.00*

28th anniversary of the students' revolt at Peking University against the 1918 peace treaty. Value, imperf. pairs, set $525.

Workers with Banner: "Oppose Imperialist Aggression" — A9

1947, May 30 *Perf. 10½x11*

Banner in Red

1L30 A9 $2 brt lilac 7.50 *10.00*
1L31 A9 $5 brt green 7.50 *10.00*
1L32 A9 $10 yellow 9.50 *10.00*
1L33 A9 $20 violet 9.00 *10.00*
1L34 A9 $30 red brown 9.00 *12.00*
1L35 A9 $50 dk blue 12.00 *15.00*
1L36 A9 $100 brown 15.00 *20.00*
a. Souvenir sheet of 7 375.00
Nos. 1L30-1L36 (7) 69.50 *87.00*

22nd anniversary of the Shanghai-Nanking Road incident. No. 1L36a is on granite paper and contains 7 imperf. stamps similar to Nos. 1L30-1L36. Size: 215x158mm. Value, imperf. pairs, ordinary paper, set $1,300.

Mao and Communist Flag — A10

1947, July 1 *Perf. 10½x11*

1L37 A10 $10 red 20.00 *24.00*
1L38 A10 $30 brt lilac 20.00 *24.00*
1L39 A10 $50 rose brn 60.00 *65.00*
1L40 A10 $100 vermilion 70.00 *80.00*
Nos. 1L37-1L40 (4) 170.00 *193.00*

26th anniversary of the founding of the Chinese Communist Party.

Hand Holding Rifle — A11

1947, July 7 *Perf. 10½*

1L41 A11 $10 orange 10.00 *12.00*
1L42 A11 $30 green 10.00 *12.00*
1L43 A11 $50 dull blue 15.00 14.00
1L44 A11 $100 brown 20.00 18.00
a. Souvenir sheet of 4 475.00 *600.00*
Nos. 1L41-1L44 (4) 55.00 56.00

10th anniversary of the start of Sino-Japanese War. No. 1L44a contains 4 imperf. stamps similar to Nos. 1L41-1L44. Size: 149x107mm.

Exist imperf. Value, set of pairs $1,100.

White Mountain and Black Water, Northeast China — A12

Wmk. Zigzag Lines (141)

1947, Aug. 15 *Perf. 10½*

1L45 A12 $10 brown org 5.50 *8.50*
1L46 A12 $30 lt ol grn 5.50 *8.50*
1L47 A12 $50 blue grn 17.50 *16.00*
1L48 A12 $100 sepia 27.50 *22.50*
Nos. 1L45-1L48 (4) 56.00 *55.50*

2nd anniversary of the reoccupation of Northeast China and the surrender of Japan.

Exist imperf. Value, set of pairs $700.

Nos. 1L1-1L2 Surcharged in Black, Red, Green or Blue

1947, Aug. 29 **Unwmk.** *Perf. 11*

1L49 A1 $5 on $1 vio 40.00 40.00
a. Red surcharge 40.00 40.00
b. Green surcharge 40.00 40.00
1L50 A2 $10 on $2 ver 40.00 40.00
a. Blue surcharge 40.00 40.00
b. Green surcharge 40.00 40.00

Map of Manchuria — A13

1947, Sept. 18 **Unwmk.**

White Paper

1L51 A13 $10 gray green 7.00 10.00
1L52 A13 $20 rose lilac 7.00 10.00
1L53 A13 $30 black brown 13.00 10.00
1L54 A13 $50 carmine 13.00 10.00
Nos. 1L51-1L54 (4) 40.00 40.00

16th anniversary of Japanese attack on Mukden, Sept. 18, 1931.

Northeast Political Council Offices — A14

1947, Oct. 10 *Perf. 10½*

1L55 A14 $10 yel orange 50.00 *75.00*
1L56 A14 $20 rose red 50.00 *75.00*
1L57 A14 $100 brown 110.00 *120.00*
Nos. 1L55-1L57 (3) 210.00 *270.00*

35th anniversary of the founding of the Chinese Republic.

Mao Tse-tung (Value figures repeated) — A15

1947, Oct. 10 **White Paper** *Perf. 11*

1L58 A15 $1 brown 3.50 *6.00*
1L59 A15 $5 gray green 2.50 *6.00*
1L60 A15 $10 brt green 18.00 *25.00*
1L61 A15 $15 bluish lilac 18.00 *25.00*
1L62 A15 $20 brt rose 1.00 *6.00*
1L63 A15 $30 green 1.00 *8.00*
1L64 A15 $50 black brown 25.00 *30.00*
1L65 A15 $90 blue 6.50 *10.00*
Nos. 1L58-1L65 (8) 75.50 *116.00*

Newsprint

1L66 A15 $100 red .80
a. White paper 8.00 5.00
1L67 A15 $500 red orange 40.00 40.00
a. White paper 32.50 30.00

Type A22 resembles A15, but has "YUAN" at upper right.

The $1, $90 were also printed on newsprint. See footnote following No. 1L72.

See Nos. 1L68-1L72. For surcharges see Nos. 1L84-1L88, 1L90, 1L92, 1L94.

White Paper

1947, Nov. **Redrawn**

1L68 A15 $50 lt grn 1.00 *3.00*
1L69 A15 $150 red org, wmkd. Chinese characters 2.25 4.00
a. Unwatermarked 2.75
1L70 A15 $250 bluish lil .90 *1.50*
a. Wmkd. Chinese characters 1.25 *1.50*

Nos. 1L69 and 1L69a exist in same sheet.

1947, Dec. **Unwmk.** **Newsprint**

1L71 A15 $300 green 55.00 30.00
1L72 A15 $1000 yellow 1.50 *2.00*
a. White paper 1.50 *2.00*
Nos. 1L68-1L72 (5) 60.65 40.50

Panel below portrait 8½x3mm on Nos. 1L68-1L70; 7x3mm on No. 1L58-1L67. Nos. 1L68-1L70 have different ornamental border. Nos. 1L71-1L72 without zeros for cents.

For surcharges see Nos. 1L90, 1L92, 1L94.

Hand Holding Torch — A16

1947, Dec. 12 **Unwmk.** *Perf. 11*

White Paper

1L73 A16 $30 rose red 17.50 *22.50*
1L74 A16 $90 dk bl 19.00 *22.50*
1L75 A16 $150 green 21.00 *27.50*
Nos. 1L73-1L75 (3) 57.50 *72.50*

11th anniversary of the capture of Chiang Kai-shek at Sian.

Tomb of Gen. Li Chao-lin — A17

1948, Mar. 9 **Unwmk.** *Perf. 10½x11*

1L76 A17 $30 green 24.00 *26.00*
a. Granite paper, wmkd. 24.00 *26.00*
1L77 A17 $150 vio gray 24.00 *26.00*
a. Granite paper, wmkd. 24.00 26.00

2nd anniversary of the assassination of Gen. Li Chao-lin, Commander of 3rd Army.

Globe and Banner — A18

Wmk. Chinese Characters in Sheet

1948, May 1 *Perf. 11x10½*

1L78	A18	$50	red	17.00	*20.00*
1L79	A18	$150	green	9.50	*20.00*
1L80	A18	$250	lilac	9.50	*40.00*
	Nos. 1L78-1L80 (3)			36.00	*80.00*

Labor Day.

Student, Torch and Banner — A19

1948, May 4 Unwmk. *Perf. 10½x11*

Granite paper

1L81	A19	$50	green	21.00	25.00
1L82	A19	$150	brown	21.00	*25.00*
1L83	A19	$250	red	25.00	*30.00*
	Nos. 1L81-1L83 (3)			67.00	80.00

Youth Day, May 4.

Nos. 1L58, 1L61, 1L59, 1L63, 1L65, 1L2-1L4, 1L68-1L69, 1L71 Srchd. in Black, Blue, Red or Green

1948-49 *Perf. 11*

1L84	A15	$100 on $1		75.00	90.00
a.		Blue surcharge		50.00	50.00
1L85	A15	$100 on $15		28.00	28.00
a.		Blue surcharge		50.00	50.00
1L86	A15	$300 on $5 (R)		55.00	42.50
1L87	A15	$300 on $30 (R)		20.00	20.00
1L88	A15	$300 on $90 (R)		15.00	15.00
1L89	A2	$500 on $2		12.00	12.00
1L90	A15	$500 on $50 (R, '49)		30.00	25.00
1L91	A2	$1500 on $5 (Bl)		12.00	10.00
1L92	A15	$1500 on $150 (G; '49)		25.00	25.00
a.		Blue surcharge		50.00	50.00
1L93	A2	$2500 on $10 (R)		15.00	15.00
1L94	A15	$2500 on $300 ('49)		20.00	20.00
	Nos. 1L84-1L94 (11)			307.00	302.50

Crane Operator — A20

Wmk. Chinese Characters in Sheet

1948, May *Perf. 11*

1L95	A20	$100	red & pink	4.50	6.00
1L96	A20	$300	vio brn & yel	7.50	10.00
1L97	A20	$500	bl & grn	11.00	15.00
	Nos. 1L95-1L97 (3)			23.00	31.00

6th All-China Labor Conference, Harbin.

Farmer, Worker and Soldier Saluting — A21

1948, Dec. 3 Unwmk. *Perf. 11x10½*

White paper

1L98	A21	$500	vermilion	17.50	*20.00*
1L99	A21	$1500	brt grn	20.00	*24.00*
1L100	A21	$2500	brown	32.50	*37.50*
	Nos. 1L98-1L100 (3)			70.00	*81.50*

Liberation of Northeast China.

Values for Nos. 1L98-1L100 are for fine stamps.

Mao Tse-tung ("YUAN" at upper right) — A22

1949, Feb. *Perf. 11*

1L101	A22	$300	olive	.90	*1.75*
1L102	A22	$500	orange	8.50	*10.00*
1L103	A22	$1500	bl grn	.90	*1.75*
1L104	A22	$4500	brown	.90	*1.75*
1L105	A22	$6500	dk bl	.90	*1.75*
	Nos. 1L101-1L105 (5)			12.10	*17.00*

See type A15. For surcharges see Nos. 1L126-1L129, 1L131-1L132.

Workers, Globe and Flag — A23

1949, May 1 *Perf. 11½*

1L106	A23	$1000	red & dl bl	.65	*1.75*
1L107	A23	$1500	red & pale bl	.65	*1.75*
1L108	A23	$4500	rose & ol brn	.85	*1.75*
1L109	A23	$6500	dl org & grn	.85	*1.75*
1L110	A23	$10,000	mar & ultra	4.00	*5.00*
	Nos. 1L106-1L110 (5)			7.00	*12.00*

Labor Day.

Fields and Factories — A24

1949 *Perf. 10, 11*

1L111	A24	$5000	Prus bl	7.75	*7.75*
1L112	A24	$10,000	org brn	.60	*2.00*
1L113	A24	$50,000	green	.90	*3.25*
1L114	A24	$100,000	violet	1.25	*13.00*
	Nos. 1L111-1L114 (4)			10.50	*26.00*

Production in agriculture and industry.

Workers with Flags — A25

1949, July 1 *Perf. 11*

1L115	A25	$1500	vio, lt bl & red	1.50	*2.00*
1L116	A25	$4500	dk brn, lt bl & ver	1.50	*2.25*
1L117	A25	$6500	gray, lt bl & rose red	3.25	*5.50*
	Nos. 1L115-1L117 (3)			6.25	*9.75*

28th anniversary of the founding of the Chinese Communist Party.

Heroes' Monument, Harbin — A26

1949, Aug. 15 *Perf. 11½x11*

1L118	A26	$1500	brick red	1.50	*4.00*
1L119	A26	$4500	yel grn	2.00	*4.00*
1L120	A26	$6500	lt blue	4.00	*6.00*
	Nos. 1L118-1L120 (3)			7.50	*14.00*

4th anniversary of the Reoccupation, and the surrender of Japan.

東北貼用

"Northeast Postal Service"

The following commemorative issues are similar to those of the People's Republic of China, 1949-1950, with the 4 characters shown added in different sizes and various arrangements.

Reprints were also issued similar to those of the PRC.

Chinese Lantern Type of PRC, 1949
China Post No. C1NE

1949, Sept. 12 Litho. *Perf. 12½*

1L121	A1	$1000	dp blue	35.00	11.00
1L122	A1	$1500	scarlet	35.00	13.00
1L123	A1	$3000	green	65.00	*17.50*
1L124	A1	$4500	maroon	65.00	*17.50*
	Nos. 1L121-1L124 (4)			200.00	*59.00*

Reprints exist. Value, set $14.

Factory — A27

1949, Oct. *Perf. 11x10½*

1L125	A27	$1500	orange	1.50	*3.00*

For surcharge see No. 1L130.

Nos. 1L101, 1L103-1L105, 1L125 Surcharged in Black or Green

1949, Nov. 20

1L126	A22	$2000 on $300		37.50	*40.00*
1L127	A22	$2000 on $4500 (G)		50.00	*50.00*
1L128	A22	$2500 on $1500		.70	*25.00*
1L129	A22	$2500 on $6500		37.50	*40.00*
1L130	A27	$5000 on $1500		.60	*2.00*
1L131	A22	$20,000 on $4500		.40	*7.00*
1L132	A22	$35,000 on $300		.50	*11.00*
	Nos. 1L126-1L132 (7)			127.20	*175.00*

Globe and Hammer Type of PRC
China Post No. C3NE

1949, Nov. 15 *Perf. 12½*

1L133	A2	$5000	crimson	650.00	250.00
1L134	A2	$20,000	dp green	950.00	275.00
1L135	A2	$35,000	vio blue	1,250.	325.00
	Nos. 1L133-1L135 (3)			2,850.	850.00

Reprints, value; Nos. 1L133-1L134, each $2; No. 1L135, $575.

Mao and Conference Hall Types of PRC
China Post No. C2NE

1950, Feb. 1 *Perf. 14*

1L136	A3	$1000	vermilion	35.00	29.00
1L137	A3	$1500	dp blue	35.00	29.00
1L138	A4	$5000	dk vio brn	60.00	45.00
1L139	A4	$20,000	green	60.00	*55.00*
	Nos. 1L136-1L139 (4)			190.00	158.00

Reprints exist. Value, set $13.

Gate of Heavenly Peace — A28

1950 *Perf. 10, 10½, 11*

Narrow horizontal shading

1L140	A28	$500	olive	2.00	2.00
1L141	A28	$1000	orange	2.25	4.00
1L142	A28	$1000	lil rose	4.00	4.00
1L143	A28	$2000	gray grn	1.75	*2.50*
1L144	A28	$2500	yellow	4.50	4.50
1L145	A28	$5000	dp org	35.00	2.00
1L146	A28	$10,000	brn org	2.50	2.50
1L147	A28	$20,000	vio brn	1.50	*3.00*
1L148	A28	$35,000	dp blue	1.50	*4.00*
1L149	A28	$50,000	brt grn	22.50	20.00
	Nos. 1L140-1L149 (10)			77.50	48.50

See A29.

Flag and Mao Type of PRC
China Post No. C4NE

1950, July 1 *Perf. 14*

Yellow Stars

1L150	A7	$5000	grn & red	200.00	115.00
1L151	A7	$10,000	brn & red	225.00	115.00
1L152	A7	$20,000	dk brn & red	225.00	115.00
1L153	A7	$30,000	dk vio bl & red	375.00	150.00
	Nos. 1L150-1L153 (4)			1,025.	495.00

Reprints exist. Value, set $55.

Picasso Dove Type of PRC
China Post No. C5NE

1950, Aug. 1 Engr. *Perf. 14*

1L154	A8	$2500	brown	16.00	*20.00*
1L155	A8	$5000	green	21.00	20.00
1L156	A8	$20,000	blue	28.00	20.00
	Nos. 1L154-1L156 (3)			65.00	60.00

Reprints exist. Value, set $6.

Flag Type of PRC
China Post No. C6NE

1950, Oct. 1 Engr. & Litho.

Flag in Red & Yellow

1L157	A9	$1000	purple	160.00	32.50
1L158	A9	$2500	org brn	175.00	32.50
1L159	A9	$5000	dp grn	190.00	40.00
1L160	A9	$10,000	olive	200.00	45.00
1L161	A9	$20,000	blue	225.00	100.00
	Nos. 1L157-1L161 (5)			950.00	250.00

Size of No. 1L159: 38x47mm, others 26x33mm.

Reprints exist. Value, set $30.

Postal Conference Type of PRC
China Post No. C7NE

1950, Nov. 1 Litho.

1L162	A11	$2500	grn & dp org	45.00	20.00
1L163	A11	$5000	car & grn	45.00	20.00

Reprints exist. Value, set, $5.

Gate of Heavenly Peace — A29

China Post No. RN1-RN2

1950-51 *Perf. 10½*

Wide horizontal shading

1L164	A29	$5000	orange	15.00	*15.00*
1L165	A29	$30,000	scarlet	9.00	*20.00*
1L166	A29	$100,000	violet	16.00	*24.00*

Wmk. Zigzag Lines (141)

1L167	A29	$250	brown	1.75	*2.50*
1L168	A29	$500	olive	1.75	*2.50*
1L169	A29	$1000	lil rose	2.00	*4.00*
1L170	A29	$2000	dl grn ('51)	3.00	*4.00*
1L171	A29	$2500	yellow	1.75	*4.00*
1L172	A29	$5000	orange	3.75	*4.00*
1L173	A29	$10,000	brn org ('51)	2.50	*4.00*
1L174	A29	$12,500	maroon	1.75	*4.00*
1L175	A29	$20,000	dp brn ('51)	2.75	*7.50*
	Nos. 1L164-1L175 (12)			61.00	*95.50*

A $50,000 green was prepared, but not issued. Value $200.

Nos. 1L167, 1L168, 1L172 and 1L174 exist on grayish paper.

Stalin and Mao Tse-tung Type of PRC

Unwmk.

1950, Dec. 1 Engr. *Perf. 14*

1L176	A12	$2500	red	24.00	17.50
1L177	A12	$5000	dp green	29.00	17.50
1L178	A12	$20,000	dk blue	29.00	17.50
	Nos. 1L176-1L178 (3)			82.00	52.50

Reprints exist. Value, set $16.

NORTHEAST CHINA PARCEL POST STAMPS

Locomotive — PP1

1951 **Litho.** ***Perf. 10½***
1LQ1 $100,000 purple *500.00*

Imperf

1LQ2 $300,000 brown *1,600.*
1LQ3 $500,000 grnsh bl *2,400.*
1LQ4 $1,000,000 ver *4,750.*

Value, Nos. 1LQ2-1LQ4 perf. 10½, $2,650.
For similar type see North China PP1.

PORT ARTHUR AND DAIREN

The Liaoning Postal Administration was established on April 1, 1946, in accordance with the Sino-Soviet Treaty, but was renamed one week later the Port Arthur and Dairen Postal Administration. On Apr. 3, 1947, it was combined with telecommunications and renamed the Kwantung Post and Telegraph General Administration.

On May 1, 1949, the name was again changed to Port Arthur and Dairen Post and Telegraph Administration. Postal tariffs were based on local currency and both Manchukuo and Japanese stamps were overprinted for use.

Gum

Nos. 2L1-2L35, 2L37-2L55 and 2L62-2L66 were issued with gum.

Manchukuo Nos. 162 and 94 Handstamp Surcharged in Violet ("Liaoning Post")

1946, Mar. 15
2L1 A19 20f on 30f buff 72.50 72.50
2L2 A18 1y on 12f org 37.50 37.50

Same Surcharge on Japan Nos. 260, 337, 195, 244, 263, 342 in Violet, Red or Black

1946, Apr. 1
2L3 A85 20f on 3s grn (V) 19.50 *21.00*
2L4 A151 1y on 17s gray vio (R) 16.00 *18.00*
2L5 A57 5y on 6s car 30.00 30.00
2L6 A57 5y on 6s crim 30.00 20.00
2L7 A88 5y on 6s org 22.00 22.00
2L8 A154 15y on 40s dk vio 110.00 *125.00*
Nos. 2L1-2L8 (8) 337.50 346.00

Surcharge sideways on Nos. 2L5-2L6.

Japan Nos. 260 and 263 Surcharged

1946, Apr.
2L9 A85 1y on 3s grn —
2L10 A88 5y on 6s org —

Sha Ho Kow (suburb of Dairen) issue. The status of this issue is in question.

Manchukuo Nos. 84, 88 and 98 Handstamp Surcharged in Green, Red or Black

1946, May 1
2L11 A16 1y on 1f red brn (G) 18.00 *24.00*
2L12 A18 5y on 4f lt ol grn (R) 24.00 *32.50*
2L13 A19 15y on 30f chnt brn 52.50 *62.50*
Nos. 2L11-2L13 (3) 94.50 *119.00*

Transfer of postal administration and Labor Day.

Manchukuo Nos. 159, 86 and 94 Surcharged in Green, Red or Black

1946, July 7
2L14 A17 1y on 6f crim rose (G) 11.50 *20.00*
2L15 A17 5y on 2f lt grn (R) 52.50 *85.00*
2L16 A18 15y on 12f dp org 110.00 110.00
Nos. 2L14-2L16 (3) 174.00 215.00

Outbreak of war with Japan, 9th anniv.

Manchukuo Nos. 94, 84 and 158 Surcharged in Black, Green or Red

1946, Aug. 15
2L17 A18 1y on 12f dp org 22.50 *27.50*
2L18 A16 5y on 1f red brn (G) 52.50 50.00
2L19 A10 15y on 5f gray blk (R) 110.00 100.00
Nos. 2L17-2L19 (3) 185.00 177.50

Surrender of Japan, first anniversary.

Manchukuo Nos. 159, 94 and 86 Surcharged in Green, Black or Red

1946, Oct. 10
2L20 A17 1y on 6f crim rose (G) 32.50 30.00
2L21 A18 5y on 12f dp org 57.50 55.00
2L22 A17 15y on 2f lt grn (R) 110.00 100.00
Nos. 2L20-2L22 (3) 200.00 185.00

35th anniversary of Chinese revolution.

Manchukuo Nos. 84, 159 and 94 Surcharged in Black, Green or Blue

1946, Oct. 19
2L23 A16 1y on 1f red brn 50.00 50.00
2L24 A17 5y on 6f crim rose (G) 100.00 100.00
2L25 A18 15y on 12f dp org (Bl) 135.00 135.00
Nos. 2L23-2L25 (3) 285.00 285.00

10th anniversary of the death of Lu Hsun (1881-1936), writer.

Manchukuo Nos. 86, 159 and 95 Surcharged in Red, Green or Black

1947, Feb. 20
2L26 A17 1y on 2f lt grn (R) 85.00 85.00
2L27 A17 5y on 6f crim rose (G) 175.00 175.00
2L28 A18 15y on 13f dk red brn 325.00 325.00
Nos. 2L26-2L28 (3) 585.00 585.00

29th anniversary of the Red (USSR) Army.

Manchukuo Nos. 86, 159 and 162 Surcharged in Red, Green or Black

1947, May 1
2L29 A17 1y on 2f lt grn (R) 24.00 24.00
2L30 A17 5y on 6f crim rose (G) 67.50 65.00
2L31 A19 15y on 30f buff 110.00 100.00
Nos. 2L29-2L31 (3) 201.50 189.00

Labor Day.

Manchukuo Nos. 86, 88, 98 and 162 Surcharged ("Kwantung Postal Service, China")

1947, Sept. 15
2L32 A17 5y on 2f lt grn 40.00 40.00
2L33 A18 15y on 4f lt ol grn 65.00 62.50
2L34 A19 20y on 30f red brn 100.00 95.00
2L35 A19 20y on 30f buff 110.00 100.00
Nos. 2L32-2L35 (4) 315.00 297.50

Manchukuo Nos. 86 and 159 Surcharged in Red and Green

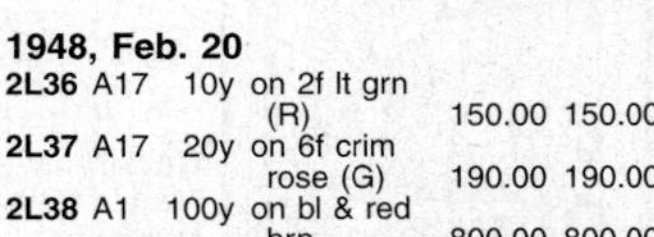

Sacred Golden Kite (same size) — A1

1948, Feb. 20
2L36 A17 10y on 2f lt grn (R) 150.00 150.00
2L37 A17 20y on 6f crim rose (G) 190.00 190.00
2L38 A1 100y on bl & red brn 800.00 800.00

30th anniversary of the Red (USSR) Army. No. 2L38 is on an ungummed label for the 2600th anniv. of the Japanese Empire.

Japan No. 260 and Manchukuo Nos. 84, 86 and 88 Surcharged in Red, Blue or Black

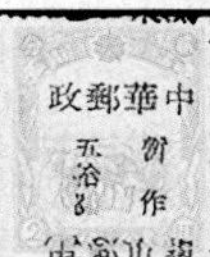

1948, July
2L39 A85 5y on 3s grn (R) 125.00 125.00
2L40 A16 10y on 1f red brn (Bl) 250.00 250.00
2L41 A17 50y on 2f lt grn 500.00 500.00
2L42 A18 100y on 4f lt ol grn (R) 900.00 900.00

Smaller Characters on Bottom Line

2L43 A17 10y on 2f lt grn (R) 300.00 250.00
2L44 A16 50y on 1f red brn 350.00 300.00

政 郵 東 關
年週一卅念紀
壹 暫
仟
圓 作
節命革月十

Stamps of Manchukuo Nos. 84, 86 and 88 Surcharged in Blue, Red or Black

1948, Nov. 1
2L45 A16 10y on 1f red brn (Bl) 275.00 600.00
2L46 A17 50y on 2f lt grn (R) 450.00 600.00
2L47 A18 100y on 4f lt ol grn 1,100. 600.00

31st anniversary of the Russian Revolution.

年八四祝慶
揍勞業農東關
念紀會大覽展
拾 暫
圓 作
電郵東關

Manchukuo Nos. 86 and 161 Surcharged in Red or Green

1948, Nov. 15
2L48 A17 10y on 2f lt grn 1,050. 1,050.
2L49 A17 50y on 20f brn (G) 1,200. 1,200.

Kwantung Agricultural and Industrial Exhibition.

Manchukuo Nos. 86, 88 and 161 Surcharged in Red, Black or Green

1949, Jan.
2L50 A17 20y on 2f lt grn (R) 500.00
2L51 A18 50y on 4f lt ol grn 700.00
2L52 A17 100y on 20f brn (G) 700.00

Without Gum

From No. 2L56 onward all stamps were issued without gum except as noted.

Farmer and Worker — A2

Train and Ship — A3

Ship at Dock (No. 2L55) — A4

(No. 2L56)

1949 **Litho.** ***Perf. 11, 11½***
2L53 A2 5y pale grn 3.00 *5.00*
2L54 A3 10y orange 20.00 25.00
2L55 A4 50y vermilion 22.50 30.00
2L56 A4 50y red (redrawn) 24.00 30.00
Nos. 2L53-2L56 (4) 69.50 90.00

Issue dates: No. 2L56, July 7; others Apr. 1.
For surcharges see Nos. 2L62-2L66.

Worker, Flag and Means of Transport A5

1949, May 1 ***Perf. 11***

2L57 A5 10y rose pink 55.00 *55.00*
 a. 10y vermilion 75.00 75.00

Labor Day. No. 2L57a is from a worn plate.

Mao Tse-tung and Red Flag — A6

1949, July 1

2L59 A6 50y red 45.00 45.00

28th anniversary of the founding of the Chinese Communist Party.

Heroes Monument, Dairen — A7

1949, Sept.

2L60 A7 10y red, bl & olive 45.00 45.00
 a. 10y red, blue & pale blue 100.00 85.00

4th anniversary of victory over Japan and opening of the Dairen Industrial Fair.

Nos. 2L53-2L54 Surcharged in Red or Black

a

b

c

1949, Sept. **With Gum**

2L62 A2(a) 7y on 5y (R) 40.00 40.00
2L63 A2(a) 7y on 5y 40.00 40.00
2L64 A2(b) 50y on 5y (R) 95.00 95.00
2L65 A3(b) 100y on 10y 500.00 400.00
2L66 A3(c) 500y on 10y (R) 650.00 475.00
 Nos. 2L62-2L66 (5) 1,325. 1,050.

Size of surcharge on No. 2L63: 16x19mm.
A 500y on 5y, red surcharge "c," and a 500y on 10y orange, surcharge "b" were prepared but not issued.

Stalin and Lenin — A8

1949, Nov. 7 ***Perf. 11x11½***

2L68 A8 10y dl bl grn (shades) 100.00 *65.00*

32nd anniversary of the Russian Revolution.

Workers Saluting Mao, Star and Flag — A9

1949, Nov. 16 ***Perf. 11***

2L69 A9 35y dk bl, red, & yel *175.00 110.00*

Founding of the People's Republic of China.

Stalin — A10

1949, Dec. 20 ***Perf. 11½***

2L70 A10 20y dull magenta *90.00 110.00*
2L71 A10 35y rose red *90.00 110.00*

70th birthday of Stalin.

Gate of Heavenly Peace — A11

China Post No. RL1

1950, Mar. 10 **Typo.** ***Perf. 10½***

2L72 A11 10y Prus blue *425.00 400.00*
2L73 A11 20y dull grn *225.00 150.00*
2L74 A11 35y red *15.00 20.00*
2L75 A11 50y deep pur *15.00 25.00*
2L76 A11 100y lilac rose *55.00 55.00*
 Nos. 2L72-2L76 (5) 735.00 650.00

NORTH CHINA

The North China Liberation Area included the provinces of Hopeh, Chahar, Shansi and Suiyuan. The original postal service, begun in the Shansi-Hopeh-Chahar Border Area in December, 1937, became the North China Postal and Telegraph Administration in May, 1949.

All Stamps Issued without Gum Except as Noted
Large Victory Issue

Cavalry Man Holding Nationalist Flag — A1

Wmk. Wavy Lines

1946, Mar. ***Perf. 10½***

Granite Paper
Size: 34½x42mm

3L1 A1 $1 red brown 4.50 4.50
 a. Newsprint 10.00 12.00
3L2 A1 $2 gray grn 4.50 4.50
3L3 A1 $4 vermilion 5.00 5.00
3L4 A1 $5 vio brn 16.00 16.00
3L5 A1 $8 vio bl 16.00 16.00
3L6 A1 $10 dp car 5.00 5.00
3L7 A1 $12 yellow 15.00 15.00
3L8 A1 $20 lt green 34.00 34.00
 Nos. 3L1-3L8 (8) 100.00 100.00

Defeat of Japan.

Small Victory Issue
Perf. 10½x10, 9½ rough

1946, May **Unwmk.**

Granite paper
Size: 20x21mm

3L9 A1 $1 red org 1.60 *2.25*
3L10 A1 $2 green 2.50 2.25
3L11 A1 $3 lt lilac 4.75 *8.50*
3L12 A1 $5 dull pur 6.25 .40
3L13 A1 $8 dk blue 13.50 *17.50*
3L14 A1 $10 rose red 2.50 *4.50*
3L15 A1 $15 purple *77.50 67.50*
3L16 A1 $20 green 4.75 *6.25*
3L17 A1 $30 brt grnsh bl 4.00 *7.25*
3L18 A1 $40 brt rose lilac 4.75 3.25
3L19 A1 $50 brown *36.00* .75
3L20 A1 $60 myrtle green *67.50* 1.60

Wmk. Wavy Lines

3L21 A1 $100 orange 9.00 *4.50*
3L22 A1 $200 dull blue 12.00 *4.50*
3L23 A1 $500 rose 57.50 *70.00*
 Nos. 3L9-3L23 (15) 304.10 201.00

North China Postal and Telegraph Administration

Charging Infantrymen A2

Agriculture and Industry A3

1949, Jan. **Unwmk.** ***Imperf.***

White Paper

3L24 A2 50c brown lake 3.50 *4.00*
3L25 A2 $1 Prussian blue 3.50 *4.00*

Newsprint

3L26 A2 $2 apple green 3.50 *4.00*
3L27 A3 $3 dull violet 3.50 *4.00*
3L28 A2 $5 brown 3.50 *4.00*
3L29 A3 $6 deep rose 3.50 3.00
 a. White paper 3.50 3.50
3L30 A2 $10 blue grn 1.25 *3.00*
3L31 A2 $12 dp car 3.75 *5.00*
 Nos. 3L24-3L31 (8) 26.00 *31.00*

No. 3L29 issued in Peking, others in Tientsin.

Remittance Stamps of China Surcharged

A4

壹
$1

叁
$3

1949, Jan. **Engr.** ***Perf. 13***

Small Central Characters

3L32 A4 50c on $50 brn blk 3.25 *3.50*
3L33 A4 $1 on $50 gray blk 5.50 *2.75*
3L34 A4 $3 on $50 gray 5.50 2.50

Large Central Characters

3L35 A4 50c on $50 blk 2.50 1.60
3L36 A4 $6 on $20 dk vio brn 7.50 1.60
 Nos. 3L32-3L36 (5) 24.25 11.95

Issued in Tientsin.
For surcharges see Nos. 3LQ10-3LQ21.

Sun Yat-sen Type A2 of Northeastern Provinces and China No. 640 Srchd. in Black, Red, Green or Blue

#3L37-3L45, 3L47-3L50, 3L52

#3L46, 3L51, 3L53

c

Type "b," bottom character of left vertical row (yuan) differs. Type "c," top character of right vertical row differs.

1949, Mar. 7 ***Perf. 14***

3L37 A2 50c on 5c lake .85 *2.75*
3L38 A2 $1 on 10c org .85 *2.25*
3L39 A2 $2 on 20c yel grn 80.00 25.00
3L40 A2 $3 on 50c red org .85 *1.75*
3L41 A2 $4 on $5 dk grn 9.50 2.25
3L42 A2 $6 on $10 crim 2.75 *2.25*
3L43 A2 $10 on $300 bluish grn 6.00 *3.25*
3L44 A2 $12 on $1 bl 4.00 *3.25*
3L45 A2 $18 on $3 brn 7.00 *1.75*
3L46 A2 $20 on 50c red org (Bl) 2.75 1.50
3L47 A2 $20 on $20 ol, II 5.50 *4.50*
 a. Type I 20.00 *13.50*
3L48 A2 $30 on $2.50 ind (R) 7.00 *4.00*
3L49 A2 $40 on 25c blk brn (R) 9.00 *6.25*
3L50 A2 $50 on $109 dk grn (R) 17.50 9.00
3L51 A2 $80 on $1 bl (R) 22.50 4.50
3L52 A2 $100 on $65 dl grn (R) 30.00 9.00
3L53 A73 $100 on $100 dk car, surch. 16mm wide (Bl) 30.00 3.25
 a. Surcharge 14mm wide 30.00 10.00

1949, Apr.

3L55 A2 (c) $2 on 20c yel grn 1.75 *3.25*
3L56 A2 (c) $3 on 50c red org .85 *2.25*
3L57 A2 (c) $4 on $5 dk grn 7.00 4.25
3L58 A2 (c) $6 on $10 crim, I 4.50 4.25
 a. Type II 15.00 10.00
3L59 A2 (c) $12 on $1 blue 1.75 *1.75*

d

e

1949, Apr. **Type "d"**

3L60 A2 $1 on 25c blk grn (G) .50 *1.25*
3L61 A2 $10 on $300 bluish grn (R) 13.00 5.75
3L62 A2 $20 on 50c red org (G) 26.00 *25.00*
3L63 A2 $20 on $20 ol (R) 11.00 4.25
3L64 A2 $40 on 25c blk brn (R) 11.00 5.00
3L65 A2 $50 on $109 dk grn, surch. 15mm wide (R) 13.00 *13.00*
 a. Surcharge 13mm wide 30.00 *30.00*
3L66 A2 $80 on $1 bl (R) 8.00 6.50

Type "d" On Stamps on China

3L67 A73 $100 on $100 dk car (G) 65.00 35.00
3L68 A73 $300 on $700 red brn (Bl) 20.00 12.50
3L69 A82 $500 on $500 bl grn (R) 20.00 4.50
3L70 A82 $3000 on $3000 bl (R) 20.00 8.25

Type "e" On Stamps of Northeastern Provinces

1949, Aug.

3L71 A2 $10 on $10 crim, II (Bl) 8.00 3.50
 a. Type I 12.50 12.00
3L72 A2 $30 on 20c yel grn (R) 8.00 2.25
3L73 A2 $50 on $44 dk car rose (Bl) 8.00 1.25
3L74 A2 $100 on $3 brn (Bl) 14.00 6.50
3L75 A2 $200 on $4 org brn, II (Bl) 40.00 24.00
 a. Type I 1,100. 450.00

On China No. 754 in Blue

3L76 A82 $10 on $7000 lt red brn 12.50 8.50
 Nos. 3L37-3L76 (39) 549.90 *269.25*

Overprints on Nos. 3L71 and 3L76 have 2 characters in center row.

Farmer and Worker on Globe — A5

1949, May 1 **Engr.** ***Perf. 14***

3L77	A5	$20 crimson	9.50	9.50
3L78	A5	$40 dark blue	9.50	9.50
3L79	A5	$60 brown org	9.50	9.50
3L80	A5	$80 dk green	9.50	9.50
3L81	A5	$100 purple	9.50	9.50
		Nos. 3L77-3L81 (5)	47.50	47.50

Labor day. Exists imperf. Value, set $50. Also issued in blocks of 4, imperf between. Value, unused or used, $17.50.

Mao Tse-tung (Chinese Numeral) — A6

Mao Tse-tung (Arabic Numeral) — A7

1949, July 1 ***Perf. 14***

3L82	A6	$10 red	8.00	*8.00*
3L83	A7	$20 dk blue	2.00	*7.00*
3L84	A6	$50 orange	13.00	8.00
3L85	A7	$80 dk green	5.50	*8.00*
3L86	A6	$100 purple	10.00	10.00
3L87	A7	$120 olive	2.00	*7.00*
3L88	A6	$140 vio brn	10.00	*12.00*
		Nos. 3L82-3L88 (7)	50.50	*60.00*

28th anniv. of the founding of the Chinese Communist Party. Value, imperf, set $150.

Gate of Heavenly Peace — A8

1949, Nov. 26 **Litho.** ***Perf. 12½***

3L89	A8	$50 orange	*1.00*	*7.00*
3L90	A8	$100 crimson	.50	*2.00*
3L91	A8	$200 green	2.00	*2.00*
3L92	A8	$300 rose brn	15.00	4.50
3L93	A8	$400 blue	15.00	4.50
3L94	A8	$500 brown	15.00	2.50
3L95	A8	$700 violet	8.00	7.00
		Nos. 3L89-3L95 (7)	56.50	29.50

Farmers and Factory — A9

1949, Dec. **Engr.** ***Perf. 14***

3L96	A9	$1000 orange	19.00	6.00
3L97	A9	$3000 dark blue	1.00	*1.50*
3L98	A9	$5000 crimson	1.00	*2.75*
3L99	A9	$10,000 red brown	1.00	*5.75*
		Nos. 3L96-3L99 (4)	22.00	*16.00*

NORTH CHINA PARCEL POST STAMPS

Parcel Post Stamps of China Nos. Q23-Q27 (Type PP3) Srchd. in Red, Black (#3LQ6-3LQ9) or Blue (#3LQ2)

政郵民人

元百捌

北 華

a

b

c

1949, June

Surcharged Type "a"

3LQ1	$300 on $6,000,000		55.00
3LQ2	$400 on $8,000,000		55.00
3LQ3	$500 on $10,000,000		55.00
3LQ4	$800 on $5,000,000		55.00
3LQ5	$1000 on $3,000,000		75.00

Surcharged Type "b"

3LQ6	$500 on $3,000,000		75.00
3LQ7	$1000 on $5,000,000		90.00

Surcharged Type "c"

3LQ8	$3000 on $8,000,000		225.00
3LQ9	$5000 on $10,000,000		300.00
	Nos. 3LQ1-3LQ9 (9)		985.00

Nos. 3LQ8-3LQ9 have large numerals unboxed.

Remittance Stamps of China (like North China Type A4) Surcharged in Black or Red

政郵民人

紙印褰包

元 六

北 華

a

b

Peking Surcharge "a"

1949, June **Litho.** ***Perf. 13***

3LQ10	$6 on $5 ver	11.00	3.50
3LQ11	$20 on $50 gray	11.00	3.50
3LQ12	$50 on $20 dk vio brn	11.00	3.50
3LQ13	$100 on $10 ol grn	11.00	7.00

Tientsin Surcharge "b"

Engr. ***Perf. 14***

3LQ14	$20 on $1 brn org	14.00	15.00
a.	Perf. 12½	22.50	7.50
3LQ15	$30 on $2 dk grn	14.00	20.00
a.	Red surcharge	22.50	11.00
3LQ16	$30 on $10 ol grn	*125.00*	*15.00*
3LQ17	$100 on $10 gray grn (R)	14.50	25.00

Litho.

Perf. 13

3LQ18	$50 on $5 red	14.00	125.00

Engr.

Perf. 14

3LQ19	$20 on $1 org brn	40.00	17.00

Perf. 12½

3LQ20	$100 on $10 yel grn (R)	65.00	30.00

Typo.

Roulette 9½

3LQ21	$30 on $2 bl grn (R)	50.00	20.00

The surcharge on No. 3LQ19 is without first and last lines.

Nos. 3LQ14, 3LQ14a, 3LQ15, 3LQ15a, 3LQ16-3LQ17, 3LQ19-3LQ20 issued with gum.

Locomotive — PP1

1949, Nov. **Engr.** ***Perf. 14***

3LQ22	PP1	$500 crim	17.50	*17.50*
3LQ23	PP1	$1000 dp bl	*175.00*	50.00
3LQ24	PP1	$2000 green	*250.00*	75.00
3LQ25	PP1	$5000 dp ol	*350.00*	125.00
3LQ26	PP1	$10,000 org	*650.00*	250.00
3LQ27	PP1	$20,000 red brn	*1,400.*	750.00
3LQ28	PP1	$50,000 brn pur	*3,000.*	1,200.
		Nos. 3LQ22-3LQ28 (7)	5,843.	2,468.

NORTHWEST CHINA

The Northwest China Liberation Area consisted of the provinces of Sinkiang, Tsinghai, Ningsia and the western part of Shensi. The area was first established as the Shensi-Kansu-Ningsia Border Area in October, 1936, after the Long March to Yenan. Remote Sinkiang was not included until late 1949.

All Stamps Issued without Gum

Pagoda on Yenan Hill — A1

1945, Mar. **Litho.** ***Imperf.***

4L1	A1	$1 green	26.00
4L2	A1	$5 dk blue	150.00
4L3	A1	$10 rose red	25.00
4L4	A1	$50 dull pur	30.00
4L5	A1	$100 yel org	55.00
		Nos. 4L1-4L5 (5)	286.00

Rouletted 9

4L1a	A1	$1	95.00
4L2a	A1	$5	160.00
4L3a	A1	$10	100.00

First issue; denomination in Chinese and Arabic. Heavy shading at top of vignette. Columns at sides.

See types A2, A3 and A4. For surcharges see Nos. 4L6-4L10, 4L23.

Nos. 4L1-4L2 Surcharged in Red

三暫

十

圓作

a b

九暫

十

元作

c d

1946, Nov.

4L6	A1 (a)	$30 on $1 grn	35.00
4L7	A1 (b)	$30 on $1 grn	*160.00*
a.		Rectangular lower left character	*1,000.*
4L8	A1 (c)	$30 on $1 grn	20.00
4L9	A1 (b)	$60 on $1 grn	2,500.
4L10	A1 (d)	$90 on $5 dk bl	37.50

Surcharge on Nos. 4L7a is type "b" as illustrated. Surcharge on No. 4L7 differs from "b," having lower left character as in type "a."

Surcharge on No. 4L9 the upper left surcharge character differs from that shown in "b."

Pagoda on Yenan Hill — A2

1948, June

4L11	A2	$100 buff	175.00
4L12	A2	$300 rose pink	8.00
4L13	A2	$500 red	8.50
4L14	A2	$1000 blue	8.00
4L15	A2	$2000 yel grn	24.00
4L16	A2	$5000 dull pur	22.50
		Nos. 4L11-4L16 (6)	246.00

Second issue; denominations in Chinese only. Many shades and proofs exist.

For surcharge see No. 4L24.

Pagoda on Yenan Hill (same size) — A3

1948, Dec.

4L17	A3	10c yel org	2.00
4L18	A3	20c lemon	2.00
4L19	A3	$1 dk blue	2.00
4L20	A3	$2 vermilion	2.00
4L21	A3	$5 pale bl grn	11.00
4L22	A3	$10 violet	18.00
		Nos. 4L17-4L22 (6)	37.00

Third issue; ornamental border at sides. Many shades exist.

Nos. 4L2 and 4L13 Surcharged in Red or Black

1949, Jan.

4L23	A1	$1 on $5 dk bl	80.00	80.00
4L24	A2	$2 on $500 red	40.00	40.00

Pagoda on Yenan Hill — A4

1949, May 1

4L25	A4	50c yel to olive	.85	*2.00*
4L26	A4	$1 dl bl to indigo	.85	*2.00*
4L27	A4	$3 ol yel to org yel	.85	*2.00*
4L28	A4	$5 blue green	2.25	*3.00*
a.		Upper left character as on #4L25		
4L29	A4	$10 vio to dp vio	7.50	*9.00*
4L30	A4	$20 pink to rose red	13.50	*20.00*
		Nos. 4L25-4L30 (6)	25.80	*38.00*

Fourth issue; light shading at top of vignette, columns without ornaments at sides. Many shades exist.

China Nos. 959, F2 and E12 Overprinted ("People's Post, Shensi")

1949, June 13 **Engr.** ***Perf. 12½***

4L31	A96	orange	25.00	16.00
4L32	R2	carmine	35.00	35.00
4L33	SD2	red vio	35.00	35.00
		Nos. 4L31-4L33 (3)	95.00	86.00

Stamps of China, Sun Yat-sen Type A94 of 1949, Overprinted in Black or Red ("People's Post, Shensi")

Lithographed; Engraved

1949, July 1 ***Perf. 14, 12½***

4L34	$10 green	1.25	3.00
4L35	$20 vio brn	1.25	*3.00*
4L36	$20 vio brn	1.25	4.00
4L37	$50 dk Prus grn (889; R)	6.00	8.00
4L38	$50 grn	6.00	8.00
4L39	$100 org brn	14.50	15.00
4L40	$500 ros lil	20.00	25.00
4L41	$1000 dp bl (952; R)	27.50	30.00
4L42	$2000 vio (902;R)	30.00	35.00
4L43	$5000 car	45.00	30.00
4L44	$10,000 brn	80.00	90.00
	Nos. 4L34-4L44 (11)	232.75	251.00

Kansu-Ningsia-Tsinghai Area, Lanchow Overprints

China Nos. 959a, F2 and E12 Overprinted ("People's Post, Kansu")

1949, Oct. Engr. *Rouletted*

4L45 A96 orange 22.50 22.50

Perf. 12½

4L46 R2 carmine 32.50 32.50
4L47 SD2 red vio 32.50 32.50
Nos. 4L45-4L47 (3) 87.50 87.50

Stamps of China, Sun Yat-sen Type A94 of 1949, Overprinted ("People's Post, Kansu")

Engraved; Lithographed

1949, Oct. *Perf. 14, 12½*

4L48 $10 grn 2.25 2.25
4L49 $20 vio brn 2.25 3.25
4L50 $50 dk Prus grn 5.25 *8.25*
4L51 $100 org brn 3.50 3.25
4L52 $100 dk org brn 5.25 *6.00*
4L53 $200 red org 6.50 5.25
4L54 $500 rose lil 6.50 5.25
4L55 $1000 blue 3.50 3.25
4L56 $1000 dp bl 6.50 *7.50*
4L57 $2000 vio 11.00 *15.00*
4L58 $5000 lt bl 22.00 *27.50*
4L59 $10,000 sepia 30.00 *37.50*
4L60 $20,000 ap grn 60.00 *72.50*
Nos. 4L48-4L60 (13) 164.50 196.75

No. 4L54-4L60 exist with wider spaced overprints.

China Nos. 959, F2 and 791-792 Surcharged in Black or Red ("People's Post, Sinkiang")

1949, Oct.

4L61 A96 $1 on org 12.00 *13.50*
4L62 R2 $3 on car 18.00 *20.00*
4L63 A82 10c on $50,000 dp bl (R) 40.00 40.00
4L64 A82 $1.50 on $100,000 dl grn (R) 80.00 80.00
Nos. 4L61-4L64 (4) 150.00 153.50

Northwest People's Post

Mao Tse-tung — A5

Great Wall — A6

1949, Oct. 15 Litho. *Imperf.*

4L65 A5 $50 rose 7.00 *3.75*
a. $200 cliche in $50 plate *225.00*
4L66 A6 $100 dark blue 1.75 *2.00*
4L67 A5 $200 dark orange 6.50 *6.00*
4L68 A6 $400 sepia 12.00 *7.50*
Nos. 4L65-4L68 (4) 27.25 *19.25*

EAST CHINA

The East China Liberation Area included the provinces of Shantung, Kiangsu, Chekiang, Anhwei and Fukien. The original postal service established in Shantung in 1941, became the East China Posts and Telegraph General Office in July, 1948.

All Stamps Issued without Gum

Mao Tse-tung — A1

1948, Mar. Litho. *Perf. 10½*

5L1 A1 $50 yel org 2.00 *3.00*
5L2 A1 $100 dp rose 6.00 *8.00*
5L3 A1 $200 dk vio bl 6.00 *8.00*
5L4 A1 $300 brt grn 7.50 *8.00*
5L5 A1 $500 dp blue 2.50 *8.00*
5L6 A1 $800 vermilion 7.50 *8.00*
5L7 A1 $1000 dk blue 12.00 *15.00*
5L8 A1 $5000 rose 30.00 30.00
5L9 A1 $10,000 dp car 75.00 75.00
Nos. 5L1-5L9 (9) 148.50 *163.00*

Many varieties, including unissued imperforates exist.

Transportation and Tower — A2

Perf. 9 to 11 and compound

1949, Apr. Litho.

5L10 A2 $1 yel grn .95 *1.00*
5L11 A2 $2 blue grn .60 *1.00*
5L12 A2 $3 dull red .60 *1.00*
5L13 A2 $5 pale brn (ovpt. 4x4mm) .60 *1.00*
a. Without overprint 65.00 65.00
b. Overprint 3x3mm 1.25 *3.00*
c. As "b," purple overprint 65.00
5L14 A2 $10 ultra .90 *1.00*
5L15 A2 $13 brt vio .60 *1.00*
5L16 A2 $18 brt blue .60 *1.00*
5L17 A2 $21 vermilion .90 *1.00*
5L18 A2 $30 gray .60 *3.00*
5L19 A2 $50 crimson 2.25 *4.00*
5L20 A2 $100 olive 27.50 27.50
Nos. 5L10-5L20 (11) 36.10 *42.50*

Seventh anniv. of Shantung Communist Postal Administration. The overprint on the $5, character "yu" meaning "Posts," obliterates Japanese flag on tower, erroneously included in design. Value, imperfs. of Nos. 5L10-5L12, 5L13c, 5L14-5L20 on different paper, set $150.

Train and Postal Runner (1949.2.7) — A3

1949, Apr. Litho. *Perf. 8 to 11*

5L21 A3 $1 brt emer .25 *1.50*
5L22 A3 $2 blue grn .25 *1.50*
5L23 A3 $3 dk red .25 *1.50*
5L24 A3 $5 brown .35 *2.00*
5L25 A3 $10 ultra .60 *2.25*
5L26 A3 $13 brt vio .35 *1.75*
5L27 A3 $18 brt blue .35 *1.75*
5L28 A3 $21 vermilion 3.50 *4.00*
5L29 A3 $30 slate .35 *2.25*
5L30 A3 $50 crimson .45 *2.25*
5L31 A3 $100 olive 2.00 *3.50*
Nos. 5L21-5L31 (11) 8.70 24.25

7th anniv. of Shantung P. O., Feb. 7. Imperf. sets were sold by the Philatelic Dept., Tientsin P.O. Value $40. See Nos. 5L69-5L76. For surcharges see People's Republic of China Nos. 77-81.

Mao, Soldiers, Map — A4

Perf. 9½ to 11 and comp.

1949, Apr.

5L32 A4 $1 brt emer .40 *1.00*
5L33 A4 $2 blue grn .40 *1.00*
5L34 A4 $3 dull red .40 *1.00*
5L35 A4 $5 brown .40 *1.00*
5L36 A4 $10 ultra .60 *1.00*
5L37 A4 $13 brt vio .60 *1.50*
5L38 A4 $18 brt blue .60 *1.50*
5L39 A4 $21 vermilion .60 *1.50*
5L40 A4 $30 gray .60 *1.50*
5L41 A4 $50 crimson .60 *1.50*
5L42 A4 $100 olive 6.75 *8.00*
Nos. 5L32-5L42 (11) 11.95 *20.50*

Victory of Hwai-Hai (Hwaiying and Haichow). Imperf. sets were sold by the Philatelic Dept., Tientsin P.O. Value, set $100.

Stamps of China, Sun Yat-sen Type of 1949, Surcharged in Red or Black

(Nanking) — a

(Wuhu) — b

1949, May 4 Engr. *Perf. 12½*

5L43 A94 (a) $1 on $10 grn (895, R) 1.00 2.00
a. Perf. 13 3.25 3.00
5L44 A94 (a) $3 on $20 vio brn 3.00 4.00
a. Perf. 13 3.00 4.50
b. Perf. 14 5.75 5.50
c. Surcharge inverted 200.00

Sun Yat-sen Type A94 Surcharged Type "b"

Lithographed, Engraved

1949, May *Perf. 12½, 14*

5L45 $30 on $1000 dp bl 10.00 7.50
5L46 $30 on $1000 bl 10.00 7.50
5L47 $50 on $200 org red 10.00 7.50
5L48 $100 on $5000 lt bl (903, R) 22.50 20.00
5L49 $300 on $10,000 sep (904, R) 67.50 60.00
5L50 $500 on $200 org red 100.00 85.00
Nos. 5L45-5L50 (6) 220.00 187.50

Many varieties exist.

China Nos. 913a and 913 Srchd. in Blue, Green, Black or Red, (East China)

1949, May Litho. *Perf. 12½*

5L51 A95 $5 on 50c on $20 brn, II (B) 17.50 16.00
a. Green surcharge 100.00 *100.00*
5L52 A95 $10 on 50c on $20 brn, II 17.50 16.00
5L53 A95 $20 on 50c on $20 red brn, II (R) 17.50 16.00
a. Type I (R) 21.00 21.00
Nos. 5L51-5L53 (3) 52.50 48.00

Stamps of China, Sun Yat-sen Type of 1949, Srchd. in Black or Red, (Hangchow)

Engr., Litho. (No. 5L57)

1949, June 25 *Perf. 14, 12½*

5L54 A94 $1 on $1 org 4.00 4.00
5L55 A94 $3 on $20 vio brn (896, R) 2.00 2.00
5L56 A94 $5 on $100 org brn 7.50 7.50
5L57 A94 $5 on $100 dk org brn 5.00 5.00
5L58 A94 $10 on $50 dk Prus grn (889, R) 24.00 24.00
5L59 A94 $13 on $10 grn 2.75 *2.75*
Nos. 5L54-5L59 (6) 45.25 45.25

East China Liberation Area

Maps of Shanghai and Nanking — A5

1949, May 30 Litho. *Perf. 8½ to 11*

5L60 A5 $1 orange ver .30 *3.50*
5L61 A5 $2 blue green .30 *3.50*
5L62 A5 $3 brt violet .40 *3.50*
5L63 A5 $5 violet brn .40 *.50*
5L64 A5 $10 ultra .40 *1.00*
5L65 A5 $30 slate .40 *3.00*
5L66 A5 $50 carmine .40 *3.00*
5L67 A5 $100 olive .40 *1.00*
5L68 A5 $500 orange 15.00 8.00
Nos. 5L60-5L68 (9) 18.00 *27.00*

Liberation of Shanghai and Nanking. Many shades, paper and perforation varieties and imperfs. exist.

Train and Postal Runner Type Dated "1949"

1949, July-1950, Feb. *Perf. 12½, 14*

5L69 A3 $10 dp ultra .25 *.25*
a. $15 red, perf. 14 .50 .30
5L70 A3 $15 orange ver .25 *.45*
5L71 A3 $30 slate green .25 .25
a. Perf. 12½ .50 .30
5L72 A3 $50 carmine .25 *.50*
5L73 A3 $60 bl grn, perf. 14 .25 *1.50*
5L74 A3 $100 ol, perf. 14 8.00 2.00
5L75 A3 $1600 vio bl ('50) .90 *4.00*
5L76 A3 $2000 brn vio ('50) 1.00 *4.00*
Nos. 5L69-5L76 (8) 11.15 *12.95*

Chu Teh, Mao, Troops with Flags — A7

1949, Aug. 17 *Perf. 12½*

5L77 A7 $70 orange .40 *.35*
5L78 A7 $270 crimson .50 *.35*
5L79 A7 $370 emerald .60 .50
5L80 A7 $470 vio brn 1.00 .60
5L81 A7 $570 blue .50 *.50*
Nos. 5L77-5L81 (5) 3.00 2.30

22nd anniv. of the People's Liberation Army. For similar type see Southwest China A1.

Mao Tse-tung — A8

1949, Oct.

5L82 A8 $10 dk blue 8.00 *15.00*
5L83 A8 $15 vermilion 10.00 *15.00*
5L84 A8 $70 brown .50 .50
5L85 A8 $100 vio brn .50 .50
5L86 A8 $150 orange .50 .50
5L87 A8 $200 grnsh gray .50 .50
5L88 A8 $500 gray bl .50 .50
5L89 A8 $1000 rose .50 .50
5L90 A8 $2000 emerald .50 .50
Nos. 5L82-5L90 (9) 21.50 *33.50*

For surcharges see People's Republic of China Nos. 82-84.

Stamps of China, Sun Yat-sen Type of 1949 Surcharged in Black or Red

1949, Nov. Litho. *Perf. 12½*

5L91 A94 $400 on $200 org red 22.50 1.50
5L92 A94 $1000 on $50 grnsh gray (897, R) 2.25 .70
5L93 A94 $1200 on $100 dk org brn .30 *1.50*
5L94 A94 $1600 on $20,000 ap grn .30 *3.00*
5L95 A94 $2000 on $1000 dp bl (952,R) .30 *.75*
a. Perf. 14 45.00 25.00
Nos. 5L91-5L95 (5) 25.65 *7.45*

EAST CHINA PARCEL POST STAMPS

Parcel Post Stamps of China 1945-48 Surcharged, (Shantung)

1949, Aug. 1 Engr. *Perf. 13*

5LQ1	PP1 $200 on $500 grn	*10.00*	8.00
5LQ2	PP1 $500 on $1000 bl	30.00	18.00

Type PP3 *Perf. 13½*

5LQ3	$200 on $200,000 dk grn	32.50	32.00
5LQ4	$200 on $10,000,000 sage grn	32.50	32.00
5LQ5	$500 on $7000 dl bl	65.00	65.00
5LQ6	$500 on $50,000 indigo	12.00	12.00
5LQ7	$1000 on $10,000 car rose	12.00	12.00
5LQ8	$1000 on $100,000 dk rose brn	37.50	12.00
5LQ9	$1000 on $300,000 pink	12.00	37.00
5LQ10	$1000 on $500,000 vio brn	90.00	12.00
5LQ11	$1000 on $8,000,000 org ver	15.00	90.00
5LQ12	$2000 on $5,000,000 dl vio	30.00	30.00
5LQ13	$2000 on $6,000,000 brn blk	55.00	55.00
5LQ14	$3000 on $30,000 ol	60.00	60.00
5LQ15	$3000 on $70,000 org brn	30.00	30.00
5LQ16	$5000 on $3,000,000 dl bl	90.00	90.00
	Nos. 5LQ1-5LQ16 (16)	613.50	595.00

China Type A97, No. 987 Surcharged

包裹印紙 圓萬壹 — $200 — $500
華東郵政 — $1000 — $2000
$5000 — $10,000

1949, Sept. 7 Litho. *Perf. 12½*

5LQ17	$200 on $10	35.00	15.00
5LQ18	$500 on $10	35.00	15.00
5LQ19	$1000 on $10	35.00	15.00
5LQ20	$2000 on $10	50.00	32.50
5LQ21	$5000 on $10	75.00	50.00
5LQ22	$10,000 on $10	150.00	75.00
	Nos. 5LQ17-5LQ22 (6)	380.00	202.50

Flying Geese Type of China, 1949, and China Nos. 984-986 Surcharged in Red or Black

1950, Jan. 28

5LQ23	A97 $5000 on 10c bl vio (R)	30.00	25.00
5LQ24	A97 $10,000 on $1 brn org	45.00	40.00
5LQ25	A97 $20,000 on $2 bl	75.00	70.00
5LQ26	A97 $50,000 on $5 car rose	130.00	130.00
	Nos. 5LQ23-5LQ26 (4)	280.00	265.00

Parcel Post Stamps of China Type PP3, Nos. Q1-Q2, Q12-Q13 Surcharged in Red or Black

1950, Jan. 28 Engr. *Perf. 13, 13½*

5LQ27	$5000 on $500 grn (R)	.75	*15.00*
5LQ28	$10,000 on $1000 bl (R)	80.00	65.00
5LQ29	$20,000 on $3000 bl grn	140.00	110.00
5LQ30	$50,000 on $5000 org red	7.50	*75.00*
	Nos. 5LQ27-5LQ30 (4)	228.25	265.00

CENTRAL CHINA

The Central Chinese Liberation Area included the provinces of Honan, Hupeh, Hunan and Kiangsi. The area was established between August and September, 1949, following the occupation of Hankow by Red Army forces.

All Stamps Issued without Gum

Hupeh Postal and Telegraph Administration

Stamps of China, Sun Yat-sen Type A94 of 1949, Surcharged ("Chinese P.O., Temporary Use")

Engraved; Lithographed

1949, June 4 *Perf. 14, 12½*

Thin parallel lines

6L1	$1 on $200 red org	4.00	*4.50*
6L2	$6 on $10,000 sep	4.00	*4.50*
6L3	$15 on $1 org	4.00	*4.50*
6L4	$30 on $100 org brn	7.50	6.00
6L5	$30 on $100 dk org brn	4.00	*4.50*
6L6	$50 on $20 vio brn	25.00	14.00
6L7	$80 on $1000 dp bl	5.50	5.00

Thick parallel lines

6L8	$1 on $200 red org	7.00	7.00
6L9	$3 on $5000 lt bl	3.50	*4.00*
6L10	$10 on $500 rose lil	3.50	*4.00*
6L11	$10 on $500 rose lil	5.25	*5.75*
6L12	$50 on $20 vio brn	7.00	*7.50*
6L13	$50 on $20 vio brn	4.00	*5.00*
6L14	$80 on $1000 bl	6.50	5.00
6L15	$80 on $1000 dp bl	27.00	16.00
6L16	$100 on $50 dk Prus grn	5.00	*6.00*
	Nos. 6L1-6L16 (16)	122.75	103.25

Kiangsi Postal and Telegraph Administration.

Central Trust Revenue Stamps of China Surcharged ("People's Post, Kiangsi")

(same size) — A1

$30

$60

1949, June 20 Engr. *Perf. 12½*

6L17	A1 $3 on $30 pur	2.50	3.00
6L18	A1 $15 on $15 red org	7.00	3.00
6L19	A1 $30 on $50 dk bl	7.00	3.00
6L20	A1 $60 on $50 dk bl	7.00	3.00
6L21	A1 $130 on $15 red org	4.00	3.00

The $15 surcharge has 3 characters in left vertical row, the $130 surcharge has 5.

Same Surcharge on Sun Yat-sen Issues of China, 1945-49

Engraved, Lithographed

Perf. 14, 12½

6L22	A82 $1 on $250 dp lil	6.50	10.00
6L23	A94 $5 on $1000 dp bl	6.50	10.00
6L24	A94 $5 on $2000 vio	6.50	10.00
6L25	A94 $5 on $5000 lt bl	3.50	8.00
6L26	A94 $10 on $1000 bl	6.50	10.00
6L27	A82 $20 on $4000 gray	4.50	9.00
6L28	A73 $30 on $100 dk car	6.50	10.00
6L29	A82 $30 on $20,000 rose pink	4.50	8.00
6L30	A94 $80 on $500 rose lil	4.00	8.00
6L31	A94 $100 on $1000 dp bl	3.50	8.00
6L32	A82 $200 on $250 dp lil	4.50	8.00
	Nos. 6L17-6L32 (16)	84.50	114.00

Central China Posts and Telegraph Administration

Farmer, Soldier and Worker
A2 A3

I — Top white line of square character (yuan) at upper left does not touch left vertical stroke. No gap in shading between soldier's feet.

II — Top line connects with left vertical stroke. Gap in shading between feet.

Perf. 10 to 11½ & Comp.

1949 Litho.

6L33	A2 $1 orange	10.00	12.00
6L34	A2 $3 brn org	6.00	8.00
6L35	A2 $6 emerald	7.50	10.00
6L36	A3 $7 yel brn	1.00	*4.00*
6L37	A2 $10 bl grn	.25	*3.00*
6L38	A3 $14 org brn	35.00	35.00
6L39	A2 $15 ultra	2.00	*5.00*
6L40	A2 $30 grn, type I	.25	*3.00*
a.	Type II	.80	.70
6L41	A3 $35 gray bl	25.00	*30.00*
6L42	A2 $50 rose vio	12.00	14.00
6L43	A3 $70 dp grn	.70	3.00
6L44	A2 $80 pink	.90	*10.00*
6L45	A3 $100 bl grn	.80	*8.00*
6L46	A3 $220 rose red	4.00	*6.00*
	Nos. 6L33-6L46 (14)	105.40	151.00

Nos. 6L33 and 6L34 exist imperf. Value, each $13.50.

For surcharges & overprints see Nos. 6L63-6L65, 6L66-6L73, 6L75, 6L90-6L98, 6L100-6L108.

Star Enclosing Map of Hankow Area — A4

Two types of $500:
I — Thick numerals of "500." No period after "500."
II — Thin numerals and period.

Two types of $1000:
I — No period after "1000."
II — Period after "1000."

1949, July

6L48	A4 $110 org brn	1.00	*1.25*
6L49	A4 $130 violet	5.00	3.00
6L50	A4 $200 dp org	.50	*.50*
6L51	A4 $290 brown	1.75	1.25
6L52	A4 $370 dk bl	1.75	1.25
6L53	A4 $500 lt bl, I	7.50	1.50
a.	$500 blue, II	20.00	7.00
6L54	A4 $1000 dull red, II	20.00	2.00
a.	$1000 dark red, I	27.50	8.00
6L55	A4 $5000 brown	5.00	5.00
6L56	A4 $10,000 brt pink	6.00	6.00
	Nos. 6L48-6L56 (9)	48.50	21.75

For surcharges and overprints see Nos. 6L74, 6L76-6L81, 6L99, 6L109.

Hankow River Customs Building A5

River Wall, Wuchang — A6

Design: $290, $370, River scene, Hanyang.

1949, Aug. 16 *Perf. 11*

6L57	A5 $70 green	3.00	3.00
6L58	A5 $220 crimson	3.00	3.00
6L59	A5 $290 brown	3.00	3.00
6L60	A5 $370 brt blue	3.00	3.00
6L61	A6 $500 purple	7.00	7.00
6L62	A6 $1000 vermilion	7.00	7.00
	Nos. 6L57-6L62 (6)	26.00	26.00

Liberation of Hankow, Wuchang and Hanyang.
Exist imperf. Twice the value of used.
For overprints see Nos. 6L82-6L87.

Nos. 6L35, 6L39 and 6L40 Surcharged in Red ("Honan Renminbi Currency")

1949, July

6L63	A2 $7 on $6 emer	7.00	7.00
6L64	A2 $14 on $15 ultra	7.50	*7.50*
6L65	A2 $70 on $30 grn	9.00	*10.00*
	Nos. 6L63-6L65 (3)	23.50	24.50

Surcharge shown is for $70. The $7 has 5 characters in left column and no bottom line.

Issues of 1949 Overprinted ("Honan Renminbi Currency")

1949, Aug.

6L66	A2 $3 brn org	.95	*2.00*
6L67	A3 $7 yel brn	.95	*2.00*
6L68	A2 $10 bl grn	1.90	*4.00*
6L69	A3 $14 org brn	1.90	*5.00*
6L70	A2 $30 yel grn (6L40a)	2.00	*5.00*
6L71	A3 $35 gray bl	.95	*5.00*
6L72	A2 $50 rose vio	7.00	*8.00*
6L73	A3 $70 dp grn	2.00	*5.00*
6L74	A4 $110 org brn	7.00	*8.00*
6L75	A3 $220 rose red	6.00	6.00
6L76	A4 $290 brown	6.00	*8.00*
6L77	A4 $370 blue	10.00	*12.00*
6L78	A4 $500 bl, II	12.00	*15.00*
6L79	A4 $1000 dk red, I	25.00	*30.00*
6L80	A4 $5000 brown	100.00	*125.00*
6L81	A4 $10,000 brt pink	200.00	*225.00*
	Nos. 6L66-6L81 (16)	383.65	*465.00*

Width of the overprint varies slightly.

Nos. 6L57-6L62 Overprinted ("Honan Renminbi Currency")

1949, Aug. *Perf. 11*

6L82	A5 $70 green	2.50	*5.00*
6L83	A5 $220 crimson	4.00	*7.00*
6L84	A5 $290 brown	4.00	*8.00*
6L85	A5 $370 brt bl	6.00	*8.00*
6L86	A6 $500 purple	6.00	*10.00*
6L87	A6 $1000 vermilion	8.00	*14.00*
	Nos. 6L82-6L87 (6)	30.50	*52.00*

Width of overprint on Nos. 6L82-6L85, 7mm; on Nos. 6L86-6L87, 12mm.
Exist imperf. About the same value.

Changchow Issue Surcharged in Red ("Honan Renminbi Currency")

(same size) Mao Tse-tung — A7

1949, Sept. *Perf. 10*

6L88	A7 $290 on $30 yel grn	30.00	*32.50*
6L89	A7 $370 on $30 yel grn	37.50	*50.00*

Issues of 1949 Surcharged

1950, Jan.

6L90	A2	$200 on $1	.55	*1.75*
6L91	A2	$200 on $3	3.00	1.60
6L92	A2	$200 on $6	.55	*1.75*
6L93	A3	$200 on $7	3.00	1.60
6L94	A3	$200 on $14	3.00	1.60
6L95	A3	$200 on $35	3.25	2.40
6L96	A3	$200 on $70	3.00	1.60
6L97	A2	$200 on $80	3.00	1.60
6L98	A3	$200 on $220	3.00	1.60
6L99	A4	$200 on $370	.50	*1.75*
6L100	A3	$300 on $70	.50	*2.50*
6L101	A2	$300 on $80	.50	*1.75*
6L102	A3	$300 on $220	.25	*1.75*
6L103	A2	$1200 on $3	27.50	27.50
6L104	A3	$1200 on $7	5.25	5.00
6L105	A3	$1500 on $14	7.00	6.75
6L106	A2	$2100 on $1	35.00	35.00
6L107	A2	$2100 on $6	35.00	35.00
6L108	A3	$2100 on $35	10.00	9.00
6L109	A4	$5000 on $370	4.50	4.50
		Nos. 6L90-6L109 (20)	148.35	146.00

Two types of surcharge exist, differing in spacing of characters in top row.

CENTRAL CHINA PARCEL POST STAMPS

Star and Map of Hankow — PP1

1949, Nov. Litho. *Perf. 11, 11½*

6LQ1	PP1	$5000 brown	4.50	*5.75*
6LQ2	PP1	$10,000 scarlet	19.00	17.00
6LQ3	PP1	$20,000 dk sl grn	9.50	*18.00*
6LQ4	PP1	$50,000 vermilion	5.00	*35.00*
		Nos. 6LQ1-6LQ4 (4)	38.00	*75.75*

SOUTH CHINA

The South China Liberation Area included the provinces of Kwangtung and Kwangsi and Hainan Island. The South China Postal and Telegraph Administration was organized on or about Nov. 4, 1949.

All Stamps Issued without Gum

Pearl River Bridge, Canton — A1

1949, Nov. 4 Litho. *Imperf.*

7L1	A1	$10 green	.85	*4.00*
7L2	A1	$20 sepia	.85	*4.00*
7L3	A1	$30 violet	.85	*4.00*
7L4	A1	$50 carmine	.85	*4.00*
7L5	A1	$100 ultramarine	1.50	*4.00*
		Nos. 7L1-7L5 (5)	4.90	*20.00*

For surcharges see Nos. 7L19-7L23.

China Nos. 993-995 With Additional Overprint in Red ("Liberation of Swatow")

1949, Nov. 9

7L6	A94	2½c on $500 rose lil	35.00	35.00
a.		Handstamped	80.00	80.00
7L7	A94	2½c on $500 rose lil	40.00	40.00
a.		Handstamped	95.00	95.00
7L8	A94	15c on $10 grn	50.00	50.00
a.		Handstamped	175.00	175.00

On Unit Issues of China, 1949

7L9	A96	org	19.00	12.50
7L10	AP5	bl grn (C62)	24.00	*27.50*
7L11	SD2	red vio (E12)	24.00	*27.50*
7L12	R2	car (F2)	20.00	*27.50*

On Sun Yat-sen and Flying Geese Issues of China

7L13	A94	2c org	150.00	*200.00*
7L14	A94	4c bl grn	300.00	*400.00*
7L15	A94	10c dp lil	20.00	*20.00*
7L16	A94	20c bl	40.00	*32.50*
7L17	A97	$1 brn org	45.00	30.00
7L18	A97	$10 bl grn	450.00	400.00
		Nos. 7L6-7L18 (13)	1,217.	1,303.

Forgeries exist of Nos. 7L13-7L14, 7L18.

Nos. 7L1-7L3 Surcharged in Red or Green

1950, Jan.

7L19	A1	$300 on $30 vio (R)	4.00	6.00
7L20	A1	$500 on $20 brn (R)	4.00	6.00
7L21	A1	$800 on $30 vio (G)	5.00	8.00
7L22	A1	$1000 on $10 gray grn (R)	5.00	8.00
7L23	A1	$1000 on $20 brn (R)	5.00	8.00
		Nos. 7L19-7L23 (5)	23.00	36.00

SOUTHWEST CHINA

The Southwest China Liberation Area included the provinces of Kweichow, Szechwan, Yunnan, Sikang and Tibet. The Southwest Postal and Telegraph Administration was organized on or about Nov. 15, 1949 after the liberation of Kweiyang, capital of Kweichow Province.

All Stamps Issued without Gum

Chu Teh, Mao and Troops — A1

1949, Dec. Litho. *Perf. 12½*

8L1	A1	$10 deep blue	4.00	*4.25*
8L2	A1	$20 rose claret	.45	*2.00*
8L3	A1	$30 dp org	.60	*2.00*
8L4	A1	$50 gray grn	1.00	*2.00*
8L5	A1	$100 carmine	.90	*1.50*
8L6	A1	$200 blue	1.25	*1.50*
8L7	A1	$300 bl vio	1.50	*2.00*
8L8	A1	$500 dk gray	3.00	*4.00*
8L9	A1	$1000 pale pur	11.00	*12.00*
8L10	A1	$2000 green	20.00	*20.00*
8L11	A1	$5000 orange	57.50	*60.00*
		Nos. 8L1-8L11 (11)	101.20	*111.25*

For surcharges and overprints see Nos. 8L21-8L29, 8L40-8L47, 8L55.

China Nos. 974-975, 984, 986-987 Surcharged ("Kweichow People's Post")

1949, Dec. 1 *Perf. 12½*

8L12	A94	$20 on 2c org	12.00	*15.00*
8L13	A94	$50 on 4c bl grn	18.00	18.00
8L14	A97	$100 on $1 brn org	30.00	21.00
8L15	A97	$400 on $5 car rose	60.00	*65.00*
8L16	A97	$2000 on $10 bl grn	210.00	130.00
		Nos. 8L12-8L16 (5)	330.00	249.00

Map of China, Flag Planted in Southwest — A2

1950, Jan. Litho. *Perf. 9 to 11½*

8L17	A2	$20 dark blue	1.25	*2.50*
8L18	A2	$30 green	2.75	*3.00*
8L19	A2	$50 red	1.75	*3.50*
8L20	A2	$100 brown	2.75	*3.50*
		Nos. 8L17-8L20 (4)	8.50	*12.50*

Liberation of the Southwest.

For surcharges see Nos. 8L30-8L39, 8L56-8L59.

Nos. 8L5-8L6 Surcharged

No. 8L22

$300

$1200

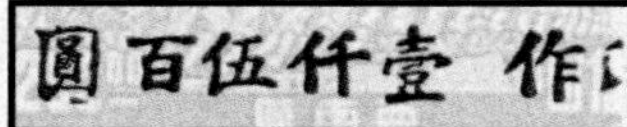

$1500

$2000

Perf. 12½

8L21	A1	$300 on $100 car	3.50	4.00
8L22	A1	$500 on $100 car	3.50	4.00
8L23	A1	$1200 on $100 car	7.00	7.00
8L24	A1	$1500 on $200 bl	7.00	7.00
8L25	A1	$2000 on $200 bl	11.00	10.00
		Nos. 8L21-8L25 (5)	32.00	32.00

Nos. 8L5-8L6 Overprinted ("East Szechwan")

1950, Jan.

8L26	A1	$100 carmine	9.00	9.00
8L27	A1	$200 blue	9.00	9.00

Nos. 8L5-8L6 Handstamp Surcharged

1950, Jan.

8L28	A1	$1200 on $100 car	15.00	*27.50*
8L29	A1	$1500 on $200 bl	40.00	*27.50*

Many varieties, including wide and narrow settings, exist.

Nos. 8L17-8L20 Surcharged in Black or Red

$60

$150

$300

$1500

$3000

$5000

$10,000

$20,000

$50,000

1950 *Perf. 9 to 11½*

8L30	A2	$60 on $30	12.00	9.00
8L31	A2	$150 on $30	12.00	9.00
8L32	A2	$300 on $20 (R)	2.00	*4.00*
8L33	A2	$300 on $100	12.00	9.00
8L34	A2	$1500 on $100	72.50	22.50
8L35	A2	$3000 on $50	7.75	*22.50*
8L36	A2	$5000 on $50	3.50	*22.50*
8L37	A2	$10,000 on $50	120.00	42.50
8L38	A2	$20,000 on $50	4.00	*42.50*
8L39	A2	$50,000 on $50	5.75	*60.00*
		Nos. 8L30-8L39 (10)	251.50	243.50

Nos. 8L5-8L7 Overprinted ("West Szechwan")

1950, Jan. ***Perf. 12½***

8L40	A1	$100 carmine	22.50	*24.00*
8L41	A1	$200 pale blue	30.00	*32.50*
8L42	A1	$300 blue violet	40.00	*42.50*
		Nos. 8L40-8L42 (3)	92.50	99.00

Nos. 8L4-8L7 Surcharged

No. 8L43

No. 8L44

No. 8L45

No. 8L46

No. 8L47

1950, Jan.

8L43	A1	$500 on $100	8.75	8.75
a.		Narrow spacing	70.00	60.00
8L44	A1	$800 on $100	8.75	8.75
8L45	A1	$1000 on $50	11.00	11.00
8L46	A1	$2000 on $200	22.50	27.50
8L47	A1	$3000 on $300	35.00	45.00
		Nos. 8L43-8L47 (5)	86.00	101.00

Two lines of surcharge 7mm apart on No. 8L43, 4mm on No. 8L43a.

China Nos. 975 and 977 Surcharged

No. 8L48 No. 8L50

Perf. 12½, 13 or Compound

1950, Jan.

8L48	A94	$100 on 4c	7.50	*13.50*
8L49	A94	$200 on 4c	12.00	*22.50*
8L50	A94	$800 on 16c	67.50	67.50
8L51	A94	$1000 on 16c	300.00	*375.00*
		Nos. 8L48-8L51 (4)	387.00	478.50

Unit Issue of China Overprinted ("Southwest People's Post")

1950, Jan. **Engr.** ***Rouletted***

8L52	A96	orange	150.00	175.00
a.		Perf. 12½	225.00	250.00

Perf. 12½

8L53	SD2	red violet	225.00	250.00
8L54	R2	carmine	225.00	250.00
		Nos. 8L52-8L54 (3)	600.00	675.00

On No. 8L54, space between overprint columns is 3mm and right column is raised to height of left.

Nos. 8L3, 8L17-8L20 Surcharged in Black or Red

1950, Mar. ***Perf. 12½, 9 to 11½***

8L55	A1	$800 on $30	45.00	45.00
8L56	A2	$1000 on $50	9.00	*12.00*
8L57	A2	$2000 on $100	13.50	*18.00*
8L58	A2	$4000 on $20 (R)	35.00	*40.00*
8L59	A2	$5000 on $30	55.00	55.00
		Nos. 8L55-8L59 (5)	157.50	*170.00*

CHRISTMAS ISLAND

'kris-məs 'ī-lənd

LOCATION — In the Indian Ocean, 230 miles south of Java
GOVT. — A territory of Australia
AREA — 52 sq. mi.
POP. — 2,373 (1999 est.)

Australia took over Christmas Island from Singapore in 1958.

Catalogue values for all unused stamps in this country are for Never Hinged items.

Queen Elizabeth II — A1

Engr.; Name and Value Typo. in Black

1958, Oct. 15 **Unwmk.** ***Perf. 14½***

1	A1	2c yellow orange	.45	.80
2	A1	4c brown	.55	.35
3	A1	5c lilac	.55	.50
4	A1	6c dull blue	1.60	.35
5	A1	8c gray brown	3.00	.50
6	A1	10c violet	2.25	.35
7	A1	12c carmine rose	3.25	2.00
8	A1	20c ultramarine	2.25	2.00
9	A1	50c yellow green	3.25	2.00
10	A1	$1 greenish blue	3.50	2.00
		Nos. 1-10 (10)	20.65	10.85
		Set, hinged	11.00	

Map of Island — A2

Island Scene — A3

4c, Moonflower. 5c, Robber crab. 8c, Phosphate train. 10c, Crane loading phosphate. 12c, Flying fish cove. 20c, Loading ship. 50c, Frigate bird. $1, Yellow-billed tropic bird.

Perf. 14x14½, 14½x14

1963, Aug. 28 **Engr.**

11	A2	2c orange	1.00	.55
12	A2	4c red brown	.40	.25
13	A2	5c rose lilac	.40	.35
14	A3	6c slate	.35	*.45*
15	A2	8c black	2.00	.45
16	A2	10c violet	.35	.25
17	A3	12c dull red	.30	.40
18	A3	20c dark blue	1.00	.35
19	A3	50c green	1.25	.35

Size: 35x21mm

20	A3	$1 orange yellow	1.75	.45
		Nos. 11-20 (10)	8.80	3.85
		Set, hinged	6.50	

"Simpson and His Donkey" by Wallace Anderson — A3a

1965, Apr. 14 **Photo.** ***Perf. 13½x13***

21	A3a	10c brt grn, sepia & blk	.55	*1.25*

ANZAC issue. See note after Australia No. 387.

Moorish Goddess A4

Fish: 1c, Golden striped grouper. 3c, Forceps fish. 4c, Queen triggerfish. 5c, Regal angelfish. 9c, Surgeonfish. 10c, Turkeyfish. 15c, Saddleback butterflyfish. 20c, Clown butterflyfish. 30c, Ghost pipefish. 50c, Lined surgeonfish. $1, Meyer's butterflyfish.

1968-70 **Photo.** ***Perf. 13½***

22	A4	1c multicolored	.55	.55
23	A4	2c multicolored	.75	.25
24	A4	3c multicolored	.75	.35
25	A4	4c multicolored	.75	.25
a.		Dark blue ("4c") omitted	3,000.	
26	A4	5c multicolored	.75	.30
27	A4	9c multicolored	.75	.60
28	A4	10c multicolored	.75	.30
29	A4	15c multicolored	6.00	3.00
30	A4	20c multicolored	1.75	.90
31	A4	30c multicolored	6.00	3.00
32	A4	50c multicolored	2.25	*2.50*
33	A4	$1 multicolored	2.25	*2.50*
		Nos. 22-33 (12)	23.30	14.50
		Set, hinged	15.00	

Issued: 15c, 30c, 12/14/70; others, 5/6/68.

Christmas Issues

"Hark the Herald Angels Sing" — A5

1969, Nov. 10 **Photo.** ***Perf. 13½***

34	A5	5c dk blue, gold, buff & red	.35	.35

A6

3c, The Ansidei Madonna, by Raphael. 5c, Virgin and Child, by Morando.

1970, Oct. 26 **Photo.** ***Perf. 14x14½***

35	A6	3c gold & multi	.25	.25
36	A6	5c silver & multi	.25	.25

A7

5c, Adoration of the Shepherds, Seville School. 20c, Adoration of the Shepherds, by Guido Reni.

1971, Oct. 4

37	A7	6c black & multi	.50	.50
38	A7	20c dark blue & multi	1.15	1.15

"Flying Fish," 1887 — A8

Ships and Map of Christmas Island: 1c, "Eagle," 1714. 2c, "Redpole," 1890. 3c, "Hoi Houw," 1959. 4c, "Pigot," 1771. 5c, "Valetta," 1968. 7c, "Asia," 1805. 8c, "Islander," 1929-60. 9c, "Imperieuse," 1888 (incorrectly inscribed "Imperious"). 10c, "Egeria," 1887. 20c, "Thomas," 1615. 25c, "Gordon," 1864. 30c, "Cygnet," 1688. 35c, "Triadic," 1958. 50c, "Amethyst," 1857. $1, "Royal Mary," 1643.

1972-73 **Photo.** ***Perf. 14½x13½***

39	A8	1c yel green & multi	.30	*.55*
40	A8	2c lt red brn & multi	.35	*.65*
41	A8	3c dp rose & multi	.35	*.70*
42	A8	4c multicolored	.45	*.70*
43	A8	5c multicolored	.45	*.70*
44	A8	6c lilac & multi	.45	*.70*
45	A8	7c lt green & multi	.45	*.70*
46	A8	8c blue & multi	.50	*.70*
47	A8	9c org & multi	.75	*.65*
48	A8	10c lem & multi	.45	*.50*
49	A8	20c tan & multi	.50	*.80*
50	A8	25c multicolored	.60	*1.60*
51	A8	30c multicolored	.75	*1.00*
52	A8	35c tan & multi	.80	*1.00*
53	A8	50c ultra & multi	.90	*1.60*
54	A8	$1 yellow & multi	1.25	*1.90*
		Nos. 39-54 (16)	9.30	*14.45*

Issued: 6c, 7c, 8c, 20c, 2/5/72; 1c, 2c, 3c, $1, 6/5/72; 4c, 5c, 9c, 50c, 2/6/73; 10c, 25c, 30c, 35c, 6/4/73.

A9 "Peace" A9a "Joy"

1972, Oct. 2 **Litho.** ***Perf. 14½***

55	A9	3c black & multi	.50	.50
56	A9a	3c black & multi	.50	.50
a.		Pair, #55-56	1.25	1.25
57	A9	7c black & multi	.65	.65
58	A9a	7c black & multi	.65	.65
a.		Pair, #57-58	1.50	1.50
		Nos. 55-58 (4)	2.30	2.30

Mother and Child, Christmas Island Map — A10

1973, Oct. 2 **Photo.** ***Perf. 14½x13½***

59	A10	7c blue & multi	.60	.60
60	A10	25c brt green & multi	1.75	1.75

Christmas.

Mother and Child with Star and Cross — A11

1974, Oct. 2 Photo. *Perf. 13½x14½*

61	A11	7c black & lilac rose	.55	.55
62	A11	30c black & yellow	1.60	*2.00*

Christmas.

Flight into Egypt — A12

1975, Oct. 2 Photo. *Perf. 14½x13½*

63	A12	10c gold, black & yel	.40	.40
64	A12	35c gold, vio blk & rose	.90	*1.25*

Christmas.

Star of Bethlehem and Dove
A13 A14

1976, Oct. 2 Photo. *Perf. 13½*

65	A13	10c red & multi	.25	.35
66	A14	10c red & multi	.25	.35
a.		Pair, #65-66	.90	*1.50*
67	A13	35c blue & multi	.40	.55
68	A14	35c blue & multi	.40	.55
a.		Pair, #67-68	1.10	*1.75*
		Nos. 65-68 (4)	1.30	1.80

Christmas.

Andrew Clunies-Ross (first settler) A15

Famous Visitors: 1c, William Dampier, explorer, buccaneer. 2c, Capt. Willem de Vlamingh, Dutch explorer. 3c, Vice Adm. John F. L. P. Maclear, Royal Navy. 4c, John Murray, oceanographer, scientist. 5c, Adm. Pelham Aldrich and crew collecting specimen. 7c, Joseph Jackson Lister, naturalist, and arenga listeri plant. 8c, Adm. William Henry May. 9c, Henry Nicholas Ridley, botanist. 10c, George Clunies-Ross, pioneer phosphate miner. 20c, Capt. Joshua Slocum. 45c, Charles William Andrews, zoologist, and frigate birds. 50c, Karl Richard Hanitsch, zoologist, and fruit pigeon. 75c, Victor W. W. Saunders Purcell, Sinologist. $1, Fam Choo Beng, educator. $2, Harold Spencer-Jones, astronomer.

1977-78 Photo. *Perf. 14x13½*

69	A15	1c multicolored	.25	*.80*
70	A15	2c multicolored	.25	*.90*
71	A15	3c multicolored	.25	*.90*
72	A15	4c multicolored	.25	*.90*
73	A15	5c multicolored	.30	*.40*
74	A15	6c multicolored	.30	*.70*
75	A15	7c multicolored	.30	*.45*
76	A15	8c multicolored	.30	*.75*
77	A15	9c multicolored	.35	*1.75*
78	A15	10c multicolored	.30	*.55*
79	A15	20c multicolored	.35	*.70*
80	A15	45c multicolored	.65	.45
81	A15	50c multicolored	.90	*2.00*
82	A15	75c multicolored	.70	*1.25*
83	A15	$1 multicolored	.80	*1.25*
84	A15	$2 multicolored	1.30	*2.00*
		Nos. 69-84 (16)	7.55	*15.75*

Issued: 1c, 6c, 9c, $1, 4/30/77; 2c, 3c, 4c, $2, 2/22/78; 5c, 7c, 45c, 50c, 5/31/78; 8c, 10c, 20c, 75c, 9/1/78.

Australian Arms, Map of Christmas Island — A16

1977, June 2 Litho. *Perf. 14½x13½*

85	A16	45c multicolored	.50	.50

25th anniv. of reign of Elizabeth II.

Souvenir Sheet

The Twelve Days of Christmas — A17

Twelve Days of Christmas: a, Partridge in a pear tree. b, 2 turtle doves. c, 3 French hens. d, 4 calling birds. e, 5 gold rings. f, 6 geese. g, 7 swans. h, 8 maids a-milking. i, 9 ladies dancing. j, 10 lords a-leaping. k, 11 pipers piping. l, 12 drummers drumming.

Unwmk.

1977, Oct. 20 Litho. *Perf. 14*

86	A17	Sheet of 12	1.50	*2.00*
a.-l.		10c, any single	.25	.25
m.		Wmk. 373 ('78)	2.75	*3.75*

Christmas.

Common Design Types pictured following the introduction.

Elizabeth II Coronation Anniversary

Common Design Types

Souvenir Sheet

1978, Apr. 21 Litho. *Perf. 15*

87	Sheet of 6	3.50	*4.00*
a.	CD326 45c White swan of Bohun	.55	*.60*
b.	CD327 45c Elizabeth II	.55	*.60*
c.	CD328 45c Abbott's booby	.55	*.60*

No. 87 contains 2 se-tenant strips of Nos. 87a-87c, separated by horizontal gutter with commemorative and descriptive inscriptions.

Souvenir Sheet

The Song of Christmas — A18

Song of Christmas: a, Christ Child. b, Herald angels. c, Redeemer. d, Israel. e, Star. f, Three Wise Men. g, Manger. h. "All He stands for." i, "Shepherds came."

1978, Oct. 2 Litho. *Perf. 14*

88	A18	Sheet of 9	1.50	*1.75*
a.-i.		10c single stamp	.25	.25

Christmas. Each stamp design incorporates one letter of "Christmas."

IYC Emblem, Oriental Children — A19

Design: IYC emblem and children of different races holding hands, continuous design.

1979, Apr. 20 Litho. *Perf. 14*

89		Strip of 5	1.50	2.25
a.-e.		A19 20c single stamp	.25	.45

International Year of the Child.

Rowland Hill and No. 25 A20

Sir Rowland Hill (1795-1879), originator of penny postage, and Christmas Island stamps: a, #1. b, #11. c, #21. d, #25. e, #34.

1979, Aug. 27 Litho. *Perf. 13x13½*

90		Strip of 5	1.10	1.75
a.-e.		A20 20c any single	.25	.40

Three Kings Bearing Gifts — A21

Christmas: 55c, Virgin and Child, globe.

1979, Oct. 22 Litho. *Perf. 14x14½*

91	A21	20c multicolored	.25	*.30*
92	A21	55c multicolored	.45	*.70*

25 Years of Golf — A22

1980, Feb. 12 Litho. *Perf. 14½x14*

93	A22	20c shown	.35	.55
94	A22	55c Clubhouse	.95	1.40

Surveyor, Phosphate Industry A23

No. 96, Drilling for samples. No. 97, Sample analysis. No. 98, Mine planning. No. 99, Jungle clearing. No. 100, Overburden removal. No. 101, Open cut mining. No. 102, Restoration. No. 103, Screening and stockpiling. No. 104, Loading train. No. 105, Rail transport. No. 106, Drying. No. 107, Crushing. No. 108, Pipeline. No. 109, Bulk storage. No. 110, Loading ship.

1980-81 Litho. *Perf. 14x14½*

95	A23	15c shown	.25	.25
96	A23	22c multicolored	.25	.25
97	A23	40c multicolored	.30	.30
98	A23	55c multicolored	.45	.45
99	A23	15c multicolored	.25	.25
100	A23	22c multicolored	.25	.25
101	A23	40c multicolored	.30	.30
102	A23	55c multicolored	.45	.45
103	A23	22c multicolored	.30	.30
104	A23	28c multicolored	.35	.35
105	A23	40c multicolored	.45	.45
106	A23	60c multicolored	.55	.55
107	A23	22c multicolored	.30	.30
108	A23	28c multicolored	.35	.35
109	A23	40c multicolored	.45	.45
110	A23	60c multicolored	.55	.55
		Nos. 95-110 (16)	5.80	5.80

Issued: Nos. 96-98, 5/5/80; Nos. 99-102, 7/14/80; Nos. 103-106, 2/9/81; NOs. 107-110, 5/4/81.

Souvenir Sheet

Christmas — A24

1980, Oct. 6 Litho. *Perf. 13½x13*

111	A24	Sheet of 6	1.60	*2.25*
a.		15c Angel	.25	.25
b.		22c Virgin and child	.25	.35
c.		60c Angel	.30	.35
d.		15c Angel holding soldier	.25	.35
e.		22c Kneeling woman and man	.25	.35
f.		60c Chinese, Indian, European children	.30	.35

Christmas. No. 111 contains 2 strips of 3 (Nos. 111a-111c and 111d-111f) with gutter between.

Cryptoblepharus Egeriae — A25

Reptiles: 30c, Emoia nativitata. 40c, Lepidodactylus listeri. 60c, Cyrtodactylus nov.

1981, Aug. 10 Litho. *Perf. 13x13½*

112	A25	24c shown	.25	.25
113	A25	30c multicolored	.30	.30
114	A25	40c multicolored	.45	.45
115	A25	60c multicolored	.55	.55
		Nos. 112-115 (4)	1.55	1.55

Souvenir Sheet

Christmas — A26

1981, Oct. 19 Litho. *Perf. 14½x14*

116	A26	Sheet of 4	1.60	*2.00*
a.		18c Angels, star	.25	*.30*
b.		24c Nativity	.25	*.35*
c.		40c Children praying to Jesus	.50	*.60*
d.		60c Children praying	.55	*.75*

Reef Heron A27

2c, Noddies. 3c, Glossy swiftlet. 4c, Imperial pigeon. 5c, Christmas Isld. silvereyes. 10c, Thrush. 25c, Silver bosunbird. 30c, Christmas Isld. emerald doves. 40c, Brown boobies. 50c,

Red-footed boobies. 65c, Christmas Isld. frigatebird. 75c, Golden bosunbirds. 80c, Nankeen kestrel, vert. $1, Christmas Isld. hawk owl, vert. $2, Goshawk, vert. $4, Abbott's boobies, vert.

1982-83 Litho. *Perf. 14*

117 A27	1c shown	.65	.25
118 A27	2c multicolored	.65	.25
119 A27	3c multicolored	.65	.75
120 A27	4c multicolored	.65	.75
121 A27	5c multicolored	.80	.95
122 A27	10c multicolored	.65	.75
123 A27	25c multicolored	1.00	.75
124 A27	30c multicolored	.70	.75
125 A27	40c multicolored	.70	.60
126 A27	50c multicolored	.70	.60
127 A27	65c multicolored	.70	.60
128 A27	75c multicolored	.85	.75
129 A27	80c multicolored	1.00	*2.00*
130 A27	$1 multicolored	2.00	2.25
131 A27	$2 multicolored	1.75	*4.00*
132 A27	$4 multicolored	2.75	3.00
	Nos. 117-132 (16)	16.20	19.00

Issued: 1c, 2c, 25c $4, 3/8; 3c, 4c, 10c, $2, 6/14; 40c, 50c, 65c, 75c, 8/23; 5c, 30c, 80c, $1, 2/21/83.

Christmas — A28

Paper sculptures.

1982, Oct. 18 Litho. & Embossed

135 A28	27c Joseph	.30	.30
136 A28	50c Angel	.40	.40
137 A28	75c Mary, Baby Jesus	.50	.65
a.	Strip of 3, #135-137	1.30	1.60

25th Anniv. of Boat Club — A29

Designs: Various boating activities.

Perf. 14x14½, 14½x14

1983, May 2 Litho.

138 A29	27c multicolored	.30	.30
139 A29	35c multicolored	.30	.30
140 A29	50c multi, horiz.	.45	.45
141 A29	75c multi, horiz.	.45	.45
	Nos. 138-141 (4)	1.50	1.50

25th Anniv. of Australian Territory A30

24c, Maps. golden bosun bird, kangaroo. 30c, Map, flag. 85c, Boeing 727, maps.

1983, Oct. 1 Litho. *Perf. 14*

142 A30	24c multicolored	.70	.45
143 A30	30c multicolored	.80	.80
144 A30	85c multicolored	1.60	2.00
	Nos. 142-144 (3)	3.10	3.25

Christmas — A31

Designs: Christmas candles.

1983, Oct. 31 Litho. *Perf. 13½x13*

145 A31	24c multicolored	.25	.30
146 A31	30c multicolored	.35	.50
147 A31	85c multicolored	.75	1.50
	Nos. 145-147 (3)	1.35	2.30

Red Land Crab — A32

30c, Feeding. 40c, Migration. 55c, Developmental stages. 85c, Adult female, young.

1984, Feb. 20 Litho. *Perf. 14x14½*

148 A32	30c multicolored	.30	.30
149 A32	40c multicolored	.40	.40
150 A32	55c multicolored	.40	.40
151 A32	85c multicolored	.80	.80
	Nos. 148-151 (4)	1.90	1.90

Local Fungi — A33

30c, Leucocoprinus fragilissimus. 40c, Microporus xanthopus. 45c, Trogia anthidepas. 55c, Haddowia longipes. 85c, Phillipsia domingensis.

1984, Apr. 30 *Perf. 13½x14½*

152 A33	30c multicolored	.45	.45
153 A33	40c multicolored	.50	.50
154 A33	45c multicolored	.65	.65
155 A33	55c multicolored	.75	.75
156 A33	85c multicolored	.95	.95
	Nos. 152-156 (5)	3.30	3.30

Cricket on Christmas Isld., 25th Anniv. A34

1984, July 23 Litho. *Perf. 14*

157 A34	30c Runout	.50	*.75*
158 A34	40c Catch at point	.55	*1.00*
159 A34	55c Batsman	.65	*1.25*
160 A34	85c Batsman hitting	.75	*1.50*
	Nos. 157-160 (4)	2.45	*4.50*

Souvenir Sheet

Christmas; Ausipex '84 A35

1984, Sept. 21 Litho. *Perf. 13½*

161	Sheet of 3 + 3 labels	2.60	2.60
a.	A35 30c Father Christmas arriving	.45	.45
b.	A35 55c Distributing gifts	.75	.75
c.	A35 85c Waving good-bye	1.25	1.25

Crabs A36

No. 162, Birgus latro. No. 163, Cardiosoma hirtipes. No. 164, Gecarcoidea natalis. No. 165, Ocypode ceratophthalma. No. 166, Coenobita rugosa. No. 167, Metasesarma rousseauxi. No. 168, Coenobita brevimana. No. 169, Geograpsus stormi. No. 170, Grapsus tenuicrustatus. No. 171, Geograpsus grayi. No. 172, Ocypode cordimana. No. 173, Geograpsus crinipes.

1985 Litho. *Perf. 13x13½*

162 A36	30c multicolored	1.00	.90
163 A36	33c multicolored	1.00	.90
164 A36	33c multicolored	1.10	1.00
165 A36	40c multicolored	1.10	1.00
166 A36	45c multicolored	1.10	1.25
167 A36	45c multicolored	1.25	1.50
168 A36	55c multicolored	1.25	1.50
169 A36	60c multicolored	1.75	1.75
170 A36	60c multicolored	2.25	2.50
171 A36	85c multicolored	2.50	2.50
172 A36	90c multicolored	2.50	*3.25*
173 A36	90c multicolored	3.00	*4.00*
	Nos. 162-173 (12)	19.80	22.05

Issued: 30c, 40c, 55c, 85c, 1/30; Nos. 163, 166, 169, 172, 4/29; Nos. 164, 167, 170, 173, 7/22.

Once in Royal David's City — A37

Songs: 33c, While Shepherds Watched Their Flocks by Night. 45c, Away in a Manger. 60c, We Three Kings of Orient Are. 90c, Hark! The Herald Angels Sing.

1985, Oct. 28 Litho. *Perf. 14x14½*

174 A37	27c multicolored	.80	*1.25*
175 A37	33c multicolored	.90	*1.40*
176 A37	45c multicolored	1.10	*1.50*
177 A37	60c multicolored	1.20	*1.60*
178 A37	90c multicolored	1.30	*1.75*
a.	Strip of 5, #174-178	6.75	*9.00*
	Nos. 174-178 (5)	5.30	*7.50*

Christmas.

Halley's Comet A38

33c, Over island. 45c, Edmond Halley. 60c, Over phosphate shipping. 90c, Over Flying Fish Cove.

1986, Apr. 30 Litho. *Perf. 14*

179 A38	33c multicolored	.40	*.70*
180 A38	45c multicolored	.50	*1.10*
181 A38	60c multicolored	.75	*2.10*
182 A38	90c multicolored	1.10	*2.50*
	Nos. 179-182 (4)	2.75	*6.40*

Indigenous Flowers — A39

1986, June 30 Litho. *Perf. 14*

183 A39	33c Ridley's orchid	.85	.55
184 A39	45c Hanging flower	.60	*.85*
185 A39	60c Hoya	.60	*1.50*
186 A39	90c Sea hibiscus	.70	*2.00*
	Nos. 183-186 (4)	2.75	*4.90*

Royal Wedding Issue, 1986

Common Design Type

Designs: 33c, Couple in Buckingham Palace garden. 90c, Andrew operating helicopter.

1986, July 23 Litho. *Perf. 14½x14*

187 CD338	33c multicolored	.45	*.45*
188 CD338	90c multicolored	1.00	*1.75*

Christmas A40

Santa Claus at Christmas Island: 30c, Speedboating. 36c, At the beach. 55c, Fishing. 70c, Golfing. $1, Sleeping in hammock.

1986, Sept. 30 Litho. *Perf. 13x13½*

189 A40	30c multicolored	.80	.60
190 A40	36c multicolored	.95	.60
191 A40	55c multicolored	1.40	1.50
192 A40	70c multicolored	2.50	*3.50*
193 A40	$1 multicolored	2.50	*4.00*
	Nos. 189-193 (5)	8.15	10.20

Visiting Ships, Cent. A41

1987, Jan. 21 *Perf. 14½*

194 A41	36c Flying Fish	1.00	.80
195 A41	90c Egeria	1.90	2.50

Wildlife A42

1c, Blind snake. 2c, Blue-tailed skink. 3c, Insectivorous bat. 5c, Green cricket. 10c, Christmas Is. fruit bat. 25c, Gecko. 30c, Praying mantis. 36c, Hawk owl. 40c, Bull-mouth helmet shell. 41c, Nudibranch. 50c, Textile cone shell. 65c, Brittle-stars. 75c, Royal angelfish. 90c, Christmas Is. white butterfly. $1, Mimic butterfly. $2, Shrew. $5, Green turtle.

1987-89 Litho. *Perf. 14*

196 A42	1c multicolored	.40	.90
197 A42	2c multicolored	.40	.90
198 A42	3c multicolored	.75	.90
199 A42	5c multicolored	1.10	.90
200 A42	10c multicolored	.90	.90
201 A42	25c multicolored	.90	1.00
202 A42	30c multicolored	1.00	1.25
203 A42	36c multicolored	2.25	1.75
204 A42	40c multicolored	1.50	2.75
204A A42	41c multi ('89)	3.25	1.00
205 A42	50c multicolored	1.60	2.75
206 A42	65c multicolored	1.00	*1.25*
207 A42	75c multicolored	1.00	*1.75*
208 A42	90c multicolored	3.25	3.00
209 A42	$1 multicolored	3.25	3.00
210 A42	$2 multicolored	3.25	*6.50*
211 A42	$5 multicolored	4.00	*6.50*
a.	Sheet of 16, #196-204, 205-211	*47.50*	*47.50*
	Nos. 196-211 (17)	29.80	37.00

Issued: 1c, 2c, 25c, $5, 3/25; 3c, 10c, 36c, $2, 6/24; 40c, 50c, 65c, 75c, 8/26; 5c, 30c, 90c, $1, 3/1/88; 41c, 9/1/89.

Stamps contained in No. 211a inscribed "1988" at bottom.

For overprint see Nos. 246-247.

Souvenir Sheet

Santa Claus Delivering Presents — A43

1987, Oct. 7 Litho. *Perf. 13½*

212 A43	Sheet of 4	5.50	5.50
a.	30c multicolored	.60	.60
b.	37c multicolored	.65	.65
c.	90c multicolored	1.75	1.75
d.	$1 multicolored	1.90	1.90

Christmas. Nos. 212a-212d printed in a continuous design.

Australia Bicentennial A44

Designs: a, First Fleet sighted by 5 Aborginals on land. b, Four Aboriginals on land, one in canoe. c, Ships entering bay, kangaroos. d, Europeans land. e, Flag raising.

1988, Jan. 26 Litho. *Perf. 13*

213		Strip of 5	10.00	10.00
a.-e.	A44	37c any single	1.75	1.75

Nos. 213a-213e printed in a continuous design. See Cocos Islands No. 172.

Annexation of the Island, Cent. — A45

37c, Capt William Henry May. 53c, Annexation ceremony. 95c, HMS Imperieuse. $1.50, Building cairn of stones.

1988, June 8 Litho. *Perf. 14½*

214	A45	37c multicolored	.65	.65
215	A45	53c multicolored	.90	.90
216	A45	95c multicolored	1.50	1.50
217	A45	$1.50 multicolored	2.00	2.00
		Nos. 214-217 (4)	5.05	5.05

Settlement of Christmas Is., Cent. — A46

Transportation: 37c, Horse and cart, 1910. 55c, Phosphate mining, 1910. 70c, Steam locomotive, 1914. $1, Arrival of first aircraft, 1957.

1988, Aug. 24 Litho. *Perf. 14½*

218	A46	37c multicolored	.95	.55
219	A46	55c multicolored	1.40	.75
220	A46	70c multicolored	1.40	1.00
221	A46	$1 multicolored	2.25	1.60
		Nos. 218-221 (4)	6.00	3.90

Christmas Presents — A47

32c, Bucket, shovel, boat. 39c, Snorkeling equipment. 90c, Toy soldier, doll, stuffed animals. $1, Race car, truck, plane.

1988, Nov. 15 *Perf. 14x14½*

222	A47	32c multicolored	.50	.50
223	A47	39c multicolored	.60	.60
224	A47	90c multicolored	1.25	1.25
225	A47	$1 multicolored	1.50	1.00
		Nos. 222-225 (4)	3.85	3.35

Chinese New Year — A48

1989, Jan. 31 *Perf. 14½*

226	A48	39c Good harvest	.70	.70
227	A48	70c Prosperity	1.00	1.00
228	A48	90c Good fortune	1.25	1.25
229	A48	$1 Progress	1.50	1.50
		Nos. 226-229 (4)	4.45	4.45

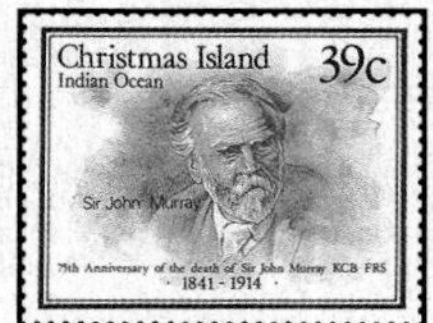

Sir John Murray (1841-1914), Oceanographer — A49

39c, Portrait. 80c, Murray Hill (map). $1, Murray's equipment. $1.10, HMS Challenger.

1989, Mar. 16 *Perf. 14½x14*

230	A49	39c multicolored	.70	.70
231	A49	80c multicolored	1.25	1.25
232	A49	$1 multicolored	1.60	1.60
233	A49	$1.10 multicolored	1.90	1.90
		Nos. 230-233 (4)	5.45	5.45

Malay-Hari Raya Folk Celebration — A50

39c, Children. 55c, Tambourine player. 80c, Girl. $1.10, Minaret.

1989, May 31 *Perf. 14*

234	A50	39c multicolored	.50	.50
235	A50	55c multicolored	.85	.85
236	A50	80c multicolored	1.10	1.10
237	A50	$1.10 multicolored	1.75	1.75
		Nos. 234-237 (4)	4.20	4.20

Ferns — A51

41c, Huperzia phlegmaria. 65c, Asplenium polydon. 80c, Davallia denticulata. $1.10, Asplenium nidus.

1989, Aug. 16

238	A51	41c multicolored	.90	.90
239	A51	65c multicolored	1.25	1.25
240	A51	80c multicolored	1.40	1.25
241	A51	$1.10 multicolored	2.10	2.10
		Nos. 238-241 (4)	5.65	5.50

Christmas — A52

Biblical scenes: 36c, Joseph. 41c, Manger. 80c, Shepherds see star. $1.10, Magi riding camels.

1989, Oct. 4 Litho. *Perf. 14½x15*

242	A52	36c multicolored	.65	.55
243	A52	41c multicolored	.70	.60
244	A52	80c multicolored	1.75	.90
245	A52	$1.10 multicolored	1.90	1.25
		Nos. 242-245 (4)	5.00	3.30

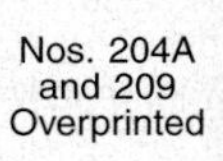

Nos. 204A and 209 Overprinted

1989, Oct. 18 Litho. *Perf. 14*

246	A42	41c multicolored	*1.40*	.60
247	A42	$1 multicolored	*4.75*	1.40

STAMPSHOW '89, Melbourne.
No. 247 is dated "1989."

1st Sighting of Christmas Is., 375th Anniv. — A53

Sightings of the island: 41c, John Milward, master of the British East India ship *Thomas,* 1615. $1.10, William Mynors, captain of *Royal Mary,* 1643.

1990, Jan. 31 Litho. *Perf. 14x15*

248	A53	41c multicolored	2.00	.50
249	A53	$1.10 multicolored	2.40	1.50

Transport Through the Ages — A55

1c, Phosphate transport. 2c, Phosphate train. 3c, Rail car, vert. 5c, Road train. 10c, Trishaw, vert. 15c, Terex. 25c, Long bus. 30c, Passenger rake, vert. 40c, Passenger barge, vert. 50c, Kolek canoe. 65c, Flying doctor, ambulance. 75c, Tradestore van. 90c, Vintage truck. $1, Water tanker. $2, Traction engine. $5, Steam locomotive, flat car.

Perf. 14x13½, 13½x14

1990 Litho. Unwmk.

254	A55	1c multicolored	.25	.25
255	A55	2c multicolored	.45	.45
256	A55	3c multicolored	.30	.30
257	A55	5c multicolored	.50	.50
258	A55	10c multicolored	.45	.45
259	A55	15c multicolored	.75	.75
260	A55	25c multicolored	.40	.40
261	A55	30c multicolored	.40	.40
262	A55	40c multicolored	.45	.45
263	A55	50c multicolored	.65	.65
264	A55	65c multicolored	3.75	1.75
265	A55	75c multicolored	1.75	1.75
266	A55	90c multicolored	1.75	1.75
267	A55	$1 multicolored	1.90	1.90
268	A55	$2 multicolored	2.50	2.50
269	A55	$5 multicolored	3.50	*3.75*
		Nos. 254-269 (16)	19.75	18.00

Issued: 1c, 3c, 10c, 25c, 30c, 40c, 50c, $5, Apr. 18; others, Aug. 22.

World Wildlife Fund — A56

No. 274e

Abbott's boobies *(Sula abbotti):* 20c, Adult (facing left). 29c, Adult (facing right). No. 273, Adults, nest, hatchling. No. 274a, Adult landing on tree branch. No. 274b, Adult resting on branch. No. 274c, Adult, young in nest.

Perf. 14x14½

1990, June 6 Litho. Unwmk.

270	A56	10c shown	1.25	1.25
271	A56	20c multicolored	1.75	1.75
272	A56	29c multicolored	2.00	2.00
273	A56	41c multicolored	3.25	3.25
		Nos. 270-273 (4)	8.25	8.25

Souvenir Sheet

Perf. 14½

274		Sheet of 3	8.25	8.25
a.-c.		A56 41c any single	2.50	2.50
d.		Overprinted in purple	*13.50*	*13.50*
e.		Overprinted in green	*17.50*	*17.50*

No. 274d overprint reads "WORLD STAMP EXHIBITION / AUCKLAND, NEW ZEALAND, 24 AUGUST-2 SEPTEMBER 1990."

Issued: No. 274d, Aug. 24; No. 274e, Dec. 6.

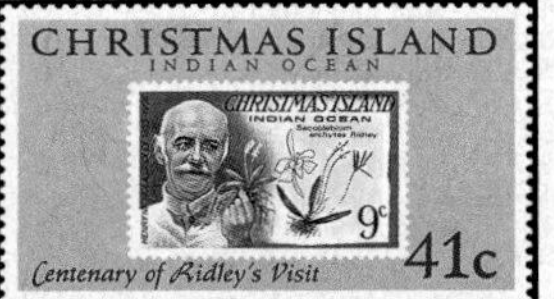

Centenary of Visit by Botanist Henry Ridley — A57

1990, July 11 Litho. *Perf. 14½*

275	A57	41c No. 77	.85	*.90*
276	A57	75c Ridley, vert.	1.30	*2.00*

Christmas A58

Flowers: 38c, Corymborkus veratrifolia. 43c, Hoya aldrichii. 80c, Quisqualis indica. $1.20, Barringtonia racemosa.

1990, Oct. 3 Litho. *Perf. 14½*

294	A58	38c multicolored	1.00	1.00
295	A58	43c multicolored	1.30	1.10
296	A58	80c multicolored	2.10	2.25
297	A58	$1.20 multicolored	3.00	*3.75*
		Nos. 294-297 (4)	7.40	8.10

1st Phosphate Mining Lease, Cent. — A59

1991, Feb. 13 Litho. *Perf. 14½*

298	A59	43c Freighter	1.15	1.15
299	A59	43c Loading rail cars	1.15	1.15
300	A59	85c Shay locomotive	1.30	1.30
301	A59	$1.20 Bucket shovel	1.90	1.90
302	A59	$1.70 Reforestation	2.25	2.25
a.		Strip of 5, #298-302	8.00	8.00
		Nos. 298-302 (5)	7.75	7.75

Island Police Force — A60

No. 303, Community relations. No. 304, Traffic control. 90c, Customs and quarantine. $1.20, Search and rescue.

1991, Apr. 17 Litho. *Perf. 14½*

303	A60	43c multicolored	1.75	1.75
304	A60	43c multicolored	1.75	1.75
305	A60	90c multicolored	2.50	2.50
306	A60	$1.20 multicolored	3.25	3.25
a.		Souvenir sheet of 4, #303-306	9.25	9.25
		Nos. 303-306 (4)	9.25	9.25

Maps — A61

75c, Goos Atlas, 1666. $1.10, Apres De Manevillette, 1745. $1.20, Comberford, 1667.

1991, June 19 Litho. *Perf. 14*

307 A61 43c shown, 1991 1.10 1.10
308 A61 75c multicolored 2.10 2.10
309 A61 $1.10 multicolored 2.75 2.75
310 A61 $1.20 multicolored 3.00 3.00
Nos. 307-310 (4) 8.95 8.95

Trees A62

43c, Bruguiera gymnorrhiza. 70c, Syzygium operculatum. 85c, Ficus microcarpa. $1.20, Arenga listeri.

1991, Aug. 21 Litho. *Perf. 14*

311 A62 43c multicolored 1.25 1.25
312 A62 70c multicolored 1.75 1.75
313 A62 85c multicolored 2.00 2.00
314 A62 $1.20 multicolored 2.25 2.25
Nos. 311-314 (4) 7.25 7.25

Christmas A63

Drawings of "What Christmas Means to Me" by: No. 315a, S'ng Yen Luiw. b, Liew Ann Nee. c, Foo Pang Chuan. d, Too Lai Peng. e, Jesamine Wheeler. 43c, Ho Puay Ha. $1, Ng Hooi Hua. $1.20, Yani Kawi.

1991, Oct. 2 Litho. *Perf. 14½*

315 Strip of 5 4.25 4.25
a.-e. A63 38c any single .75 .75
316 A63 43c multicolored .85 .70
317 A63 $1 multicolored 1.90 1.90
318 A63 $1.20 multicolored 2.10 2.10
Nos. 315-318 (4) 9.10 8.95

A64

War Time Evacuation, 50th Anniv.: No. 319, Conference to decide upon evacuation. No. 320, Europeans awaiting barge. $1.05, Barge approaching waiting ship. $1.20, Remaining population waving to TSS Islander.

1992, Feb. 19 Litho. *Perf. 14½*

319 A64 45c multicolored 1.25 1.25
320 A64 45c multicolored 1.25 1.25
321 A64 $1.05 multicolored 2.60 2.60
322 A64 $1.20 multicolored 2.75 2.75
Nos. 319-322 (4) 7.85 7.85

Shells — A65

5c, Cypraea tigris. 10c, Cypraea caputserpentis. 15c, Lambis scorpius. 20c, Chlamys pallium. 25c, Engina mendicaria. 30c, Drupa ricinus. 40c, Distorsio reticulata. 45c, Turbo petholatus. 50c, Cantharus pulcher. 60c, Conus capitaneus. 70c, Turbo lajonkairii. 80c, Lambis chiragra. 90c, Angaria delphinus. $1, Vasum ceramicum. $2, Tonna perdix. $5, Drupa rubusidaea.

1992 Litho. *Perf. 15x14½*

326 A65 5c multicolored .60 *.90*
327 A65 10c multicolored .90 .80
328 A65 15c multicolored 1.40 .80
329 A65 20c multicolored 1.40 .80
330 A65 25c multicolored 1.40 .80
331 A65 30c multicolored 1.40 .80
332 A65 40c multicolored 1.40 .80
333 A65 45c multicolored 1.75 .90
334 A65 50c multicolored 1.75 .90
335 A65 60c multicolored 2.25 1.00
336 A65 70c multicolored 2.75 1.25
337 A65 80c multicolored 2.75 1.75
338 A65 90c multicolored 2.75 2.00
339 A65 $1 multicolored 2.75 2.10
340 A65 $2 multicolored 2.00 *3.50*
341 A65 $5 multicolored 5.00 *5.50*
Nos. 326-341 (16) 32.25 24.60

Issued: 10c, 20c, 30c, 45c, 60c, 80c, $1, $2, 4/15; 5c, 15c, 25c, 40c, 50c, 70c, 90c, $5, 8/19.

For overprint see No. 348.

Sinking of Eidsvold and Nissa Maru, 50th Anniv. A66

Designs: 45c, Eidsvold hit by torpedo. 80c, Eidsvold sinking. $1.05, Nissa Maru hit by torpedo. $1.20, Nissa Maru sinking.

1992, June 17 Litho. *Perf. 14x13½*

343 A66 45c multicolored 2.25 2.25
344 A66 80c multicolored 3.00 3.00
345 A66 $1.05 multicolored 3.50 3.50
346 A66 $1.20 multicolored 3.75 3.75
Nos. 343-346 (4) 12.50 12.50

Christmas — A67

Coastline, booby birds: a, 40c, Plants on shore, birds. b, 40c, Birds, rocks offshore. c, 45c, Birds on shore. d, $1.05, Birds in flight, coastline. e, $1.20, Forest, rocky coastline.

1992, Oct. 7 Litho. *Perf. 14½*

347 A67 Strip of 5, #a.-e. 7.00 *9.00*

No. 341 Ovptd. in Red Violet

1992, Sept. 1 Litho. *Perf. 15x14½*

348 A65 $5 on #342 11.00 8.75

Kuala Lumpur Philatelic Exhibition.

Starting with No. 349, Christmas Island stamps are valid for postage on items mailed in Australia and Australian stamps are valid on items posted on Christmas Island.

Seabirds — A68

Designs: a, Abbott's booby. b, Christmas Island frigatebird. c, Common noddy. d, Golden bosunbird. e, Brown booby.

1993, Mar. 4 Litho. *Perf. 14½x14*

349 A68 45c Strip of 5, #a.-e. 3.75 *4.25*
f. Souvenir sheet of 5, #a.-e. 4.00 *4.50*
g. As "f," overprinted 9.00 *9.00*
h. As "f," overprinted 7.00 *7.00*

No. 349g Ovptd. in Gold in sheet margin with Taipei '93 emblem and: "ASIAN INTERNATIONAL INVITATION STAMP EXHIBITION / TAIPEI '93" in Chinese and English.

No. 349h Ovptd. in Gold in Sheet Margin with "INDOPEX '93 / 6TH ASIAN INTERNATIONAL PHILATELIC EXHIBITION 1993 / PAMERAN INTERNASIONAL PENGUMPULAN / KEENAM DI ASIA TAHUN 1993" and show emblem.

Issued: No. 349g, 4/93; No. 349h, 5/29/93.

Scenic Views — A69

1993, June 1 *Perf. 14x14½*

350 A69 85c Dolly Beach 1.75 1.75
351 A69 95c Blow holes 2.10 2.10
352 A69 $1.05 Merrial Beach 2.25 2.25
353 A69 $1.20 Rain forest 2.50 2.50
Nos. 350-353 (4) 8.60 8.60

Christmas — A70

40c, Turtle on beach. 45c, Crabs, wave. $1, Frigatebird, rainforest.

1993, Sept. 2 Litho. *Perf. 14½x14*

354 A70 40c multicolored 1.25 1.25
355 A70 45c multicolored 1.25 1.25
356 A70 $1 multicolored 2.50 2.50
Nos. 354-356 (3) 5.00 5.00

Naming of Christmas Island, 350th Anniv. — A71

1993, Dec. 1 Litho. *Perf. 14x14½*

357 A71 $2 multicolored 3.75 3.75

New Year 1994 (Year of the Dog) — A72

1994, Jan. 20 Litho. *Perf. 14x14½*

358 A72 45c shown 1.25 *1.50*
359 A72 45c Pekingese 1.25 *1.50*
a. Pair, #358-359 3.00 *4.00*
b. Souvenir sheet of 1, #359a 4.00 *4.00*
c. As "b," overprinted 4.75 *4.75*
d. As "b," overprinted 7.75 *7.75*
e. As "b," overprinted 8.00 *8.00*
f. As "b," overprinted 15.50 *15.50*

No. 359c Ovptd. in gold in sheet margin with dog and "Melbourne / STAMP & COIN SHOW / 11-13 February 1994;" No. 359d with "HONG KONG '94 STAMP EXHIBITION" and show emblem; No. 359e with "Canberra /Stamp Show '94 / 19-21 March / 1994" and show emblem; No. 359f with "QUEENSLAND STAMP & COIN SHOW 1994 / JUNE 11, 12, 13."

Issued: No. 359c, 2/11/94; No. 359d, 2/18/94; No. 359e, 3/19/94; No. 359f, 1995.

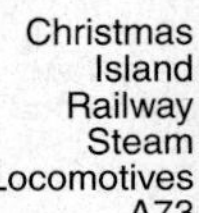

Christmas Island Railway Steam Locomotives A73

85c, Locomotive No. 4. 95c, Locomotive No. 9. $1.20, Locomotive No. 1.

1994, May 19 Litho. *Perf. 14x14½*

360 A73 85c multicolored 2.00 2.00
361 A73 95c multicolored 2.25 2.25
362 A73 $1.20 multicolored 2.60 2.60
Nos. 360-362 (3) 6.85 6.85

Orchids — A74

a, Brachypeza archytas. b, Thelasis capitata. c, Corymborkis veratrifolia. d, Flickingeria nativitatis. e, Dendrobium crumenatum.

1994, Aug. 16 Litho. *Perf. 14½x14*

363 A74 45c Strip of 5, #a.-e. 7.00 7.00

Christmas A75

1994, Sept. 8 Litho. *Perf. 14x14½*

364 A75 40c Angel .70 .60
365 A75 45c Wise man .90 .60
366 A75 80c Bethlehem 1.50 1.50
Nos. 364-366 (3) 3.10 2.70

New Year 1995 (Year of the Boar) — A76

Design: 85c, Stylized boar, diff.

1995, Jan. 12 Litho. *Perf. 14x14½*

367 A76 45c shown .80 .80
368 A76 85c multicolored 1.40 1.40
a. Souvenir sheet, #367-368 3.00 3.00
b. As "a," overprinted *7.00 7.00*
c. As "a," overprinted *15.00 15.00*

No. 368b ovptd. in gold in sheet margin with outline of boar and: "STAMP & COIN FAIR / ROYAL EXHIBITION BUILDING / MELBOURNE VIC. 3000 . 10-12 FEB 1995."

No. 368c ovptd. in sheet margin with Taiwan flag and map of Australia with flag, and also Chinese characters, dates and "STAMP TAIWAN, SYDNEY, / AUSTRALIA MAY 20-28 1995."

Christmas Island Golf Course, 40th Anniv. — A77

1995, May 11 Litho. *Perf. 14*

369 A77 $2.50 multicolored 6.00 6.00

Christmas A78

Santa Claus riding great frigatebird: 40c, Reading map. 45c, Dropping presents. 80c, Waving.

1995, Sept. 14 Litho. *Perf. 14x14½*

370 A78 40c multicolored .90 .75
371 A78 45c multicolored 1.00 .75
372 A78 80c multicolored 1.50 1.50
Nos. 370-372 (3) 3.40 3.00

End of World War II, 50th Anniv. — A79

No. 373a, RAAF reconnaissance flight, 1945. No. 373b, Arrival of HMS Rother, 1945.

Litho. & Engr.

1995, Oct. 12 *Perf. 14x14½*

373 Pair 2.75 2.75
a.-b. A79 45c any single 1.00 1.00

Angelfish A80

1995, Oct. 12 **Litho.**

374 A80 75c Lemonpeel 1.25 *1.75*
375 A80 $1 Emperor 1.90 *2.50*

See also Nos. 381-387.

New Year 1996 (Year of the Rat) A81

Litho. with Foil Application

1996, Jan. 9 *Perf. 14x14½*

376 A81 45c Facing right 1.25 1.25
377 A81 45c Facing left 1.25 1.25
a. Pair, #376-377 3.00 3.00
b. Souvenir sheet, #377a 3.75 3.75
c. As "b," overprinted *10.00 10.00*

No. 377c overprinted in gold in sheet margin "STAMP AND COIN FAIR / MELBOURNE / 23-25 February 1996."

Fish — A82

20c, Pinktail triggerfish. 30c, Longnose filefish. 45c, Princess anthias. 85c, Green moon wrasse. 90c, Spotted boxfish. 95c, Moorish idol. $1.20, Glass bigeye.

1996-97 **Litho.** *Perf. 14x14½*

381 A82 20c multicolored .40 .40
382 A82 30c multicolored .60 .50
383 A82 45c multicolored .90 .50
384 A82 85c multicolored 1.75 *2.00*
385 A82 90c multicolored 1.00 1.00
386 A82 95c multicolored 1.75 1.75
387 A82 $1.20 multicolored 2.25 *3.25*
Nos. 381-387 (7) 8.65 9.40

Issued: 20c, 30c, 45c, 90c, 4/18/96; 85c, 95c, $1.20, 7/17/97.

Birds — A83

1996, July 11 **Litho.** *Perf. 14½x14*

399 A83 45c White-eye 1.25 1.25
400 A83 85c Hawk-owl 2.00 2.00

Christmas A84

Sailing ships, words from Christmas carol: 40c, "I Saw Three Ships." 45c, "Come sailing in." 80c, "On Christmas day in the morning."

1996, Sept. 12 **Litho.** *Perf. 14*

401 A84 40c multicolored 1.00 .75
402 A84 45c multicolored 1.10 .90
403 A84 80c multicolored 1.60 1.60
Nos. 401-403 (3) 3.70 3.25

Exploration of Australian Coast & Christmas Island by Willem de Vlamingh, 300th Anniv. — A85

"Portrait of a Dutch Navigator," by Jan Verkolje.

1996, Oct. 27 **Litho.** *Perf. 14*

404 A85 45c multicolored 1.25 1.25

No. 404 was issued se-tenant with Australia No. 1571 (No. 1571a). Value, pair $4.

New Year 1997 (Year of the Ox) — A86

Constellation and: No. 405, Ox facing right. No. 406, Ox facing left.

Litho. with Foil Application

1997, Jan. 6 *Perf. 14x14½*

405 A86 45c multicolored 1.00 1.00
406 A86 45c multicolored 1.00 1.00
a. Pair, #405-406 2.75 2.75
b. Souvenir sheet, #405-406 3.00 3.00

Christmas A87

Santa on Christmas Island: 40c, Reading letters. 45c, Making toys. 80c, In sleigh.

1997, Sept. 11 **Litho.** *Perf. 14x14½*

407 A87 40c multicolored .65 .65
408 A87 45c multicolored .75 .75
409 A87 80c multicolored 1.75 1.75
Nos. 407-409 (3) 3.15 3.15

New Year 1998 (Year of the Tiger) — A88

Litho. with Foil Application

1998, Jan. 5 *Perf. 14x14½*

410 A88 45c shown 1.25 1.25
411 A88 45c Looking backward 1.25 1.25
a. Pair, #410-411 3.00 3.00
b. Souvenir sheet of 2, #410-411 3.50 3.50

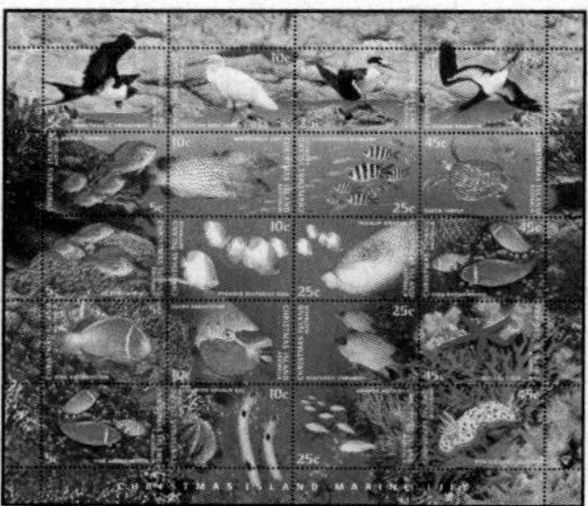
Marine Life — A89

Designs: a, 5c, Frigatebird. b, 5c, Ambon chromis, denomination LR. c, 5c, Ambon chromis, denomination LL. d, 5c, Pink anemonefish, denomination, UR. e, 5c, Pink anemonefish, denomination LL. f, 10c, Eastern reef egret. g, 10c, Whitelined cod. h, 10c, Pyramid butterfly fish. i, 10c, Dusky parrotfish. j, 10c, Spotted garden eel. k, 25c, Sooty tern. l, 25c, Scissortail sergeant. m, 25c, Thicklip wrasse. n, 25c, Blackaxil chromis. o, 25c, Orange anthias. p, 45c, Brown booby. q, 45c, Green turtle. r, 45c, Pink anemonefish. s, 45c, Blue sea star. t, 45c, Kunie's chromodoris.

1998, Mar. 12 **Litho.** *Perf. 14*

412 A89 Sheet of 20, #a.-t. 10.00 10.00

Tree Flowers of Christmas — A90

1998, Sept. 3 **Litho.** *Perf. 14½x14*

413 A90 40c Orchid tree .80 .80
414 A90 80c Flame tree 1.60 1.60
415 A90 95c Sea hibiscus 1.60 1.60
Nos. 413-415 (3) 4.00 4.00

New Year 1999 (Year of the Rabbit) A91

Litho. with Foil Application

1999, Jan. 14 *Perf. 14x14½*

416 A91 45c shown 1.00 1.00
417 A91 45c Rabbit looking left 1.00 1.00
a. Pair, #416-417 2.75 2.75
b. Souvenir sheet, #417a 3.25 3.25

Festivals on Christmas Island — A92

Children's drawings: No. 418, Carrying balloons in parade, by Fong Jason. No. 419, Giant crab, by Siti Zanariah Zainal. 85c, Children at night, by Tan Diana, vert. $1.20, Green mosque, tree, by Anwar Ramian, vert.

1999, July 15 **Litho.** *Perf. 14x14½*

418 A92 45c multicolored .75 .75
419 A92 45c multicolored .75 .75
a. Pair, #418-419 1.75 1.75

Perf. 14½x14

420 A92 85c multicolored 1.00 1.00
421 A92 $1.20 multicolored 1.75 1.75
Nos. 418-421 (4) 4.25 4.25

Christmas A93

Designs: 40c, Santa Claus in hammock. 45c, Santa, birds, crab, lizard, cake. 95c, Santa, booby-drawn sleigh.

1999, Sept. 9 **Litho.** *Perf. 14x14½*

422 A93 40c multicolored .95 .80
423 A93 45c multicolored 1.10 .95
424 A93 95c multicolored 1.75 1.75
Nos. 422-424 (3) 3.80 3.50

New Year 2000 (Year of the Dragon) A94

Litho. with Foil Application

2000, Jan. 13 *Perf. 14x14½*

425 A94 45c shown 1.10 1.10
426 A94 45c Dragon facing left 1.10 1.10
a. Pair, #425-426 3.00 3.00
b. Souvenir sheet, #426a 3.50 3.50

Faces of Christmas Island — A95

Ordinary people: a, Yeow Jian Min, without shirt. b, Ida Chin, with blue shirt. c, Ho Tak Wah, old man. d, Thomas Faul and James Neill. e, Siti Sanniah Kawi, with striped blouse.

2000, Apr. 13 **Litho.** *Perf. 14½x14*

427 A95 45c Strip of 5, #a.-e. 4.75 4.75

Christmas — A96

No. 428: a, We three kings of Orient are. b, Bearing gifts we traverse afar. 45c, Star of wonder, star of night.

2000, Sept. 5 **Litho.** *Perf. 14½x14*

428 Pair 1.90 1.90
a.-b. A96 40c Any single .60 .60
429 A96 45c multi .60 .60

New Year 2001 (Year of the Snake) A97

Snake color: 45c, Green. $1.35, Silver.

Litho. with Foil Application

2001, Jan. 8 *Perf. 14x14½*

430-431 A97 Set of 2 3.00 3.00
a. Souvenir sheet, #430-431 4.00 *4.00*

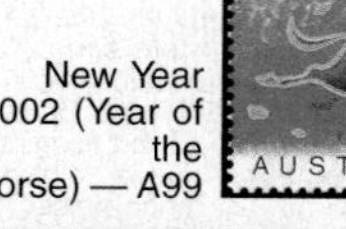
Fungi — A98

Designs: $1, Chaetocalathus semisupinus. $1.50, Pycnoporus sanguineus.

2001, Oct. 25 **Litho.** *Perf. 14x14½*

432-433 A98 Set of 2 4.00 *4.00*

New Year 2002 (Year of the Horse) — A99

Zodiac Animals and Their Chinese Characters A100

Designs: 45c, Purple horse. $1.35, Gold horse.

No. 436: a, Rat. b, Ox. c, Tiger. d, Rabbit. e, Dragon. f, Snake. g, Horse. h, Sheep. i, Monkey. j, Cock. k, Dog. l, Boar.

Litho. With Gold Foil Application

2002, Jan. 8 *Perf. 14x14½*

434-435 A99 Set of 2 3.00 3.00
a. Souvenir sheet, #434-435 4.00 4.00
436 Sheet of 14, #a-l, #435a 12.00 12.00
a.-d. A100 5c Any single .55 .55
e.-h. A100 15c Any single, orange background .60 .60
i.-l. A100 25c Any single, orange background .65 .65

See Nos. 442, 447, 451, 456, 462-463.

Worldwide Fund for Nature (WWF) — A101

Christmas Island birds — No. 437: a, Imperial pigeon. b, Hawk owl.
$1, Goshawk. $1.50, Thrush.

2002, May 1 Litho. *Perf. 14½x14*

437 A101 45c Horiz. pair, #a-b 1.60 1.60
438 A101 $1 multi 1.60 1.60
439 A101 $1.50 multi 2.75 2.75
Nos. 437-439 (3) 5.95 5.95

Zodiac Animals Type of 2002 and

New Year 2003 (Year of the Ram) A102

Designs: 50c, Yellow and orange ram. $1.50, Blue ram.

No. 442: a, Rat. b, Ox. c, Tiger. d, Rabbit. e, Dragon. f, Snake. g, Horse. h, Sheep. i, Monkey. j, Cock. k, Dog. l, Boar.

Litho. With Gold Foil Application

2003, Jan. 7 *Perf. 14x14½*

440-441 A102 Set of 2 3.50 3.50
a. Souvenir sheet, #440-441 4.00 4.00
442 Sheet of 14, #a-l, #441a 12.00 12.00
a.-d. A100 10c Any single, red violet background .50 .50
e.-h. A100 15c Any single, red violet background .60 .60
i.-l. A100 25c Any single, red violet background .70 .70

See No. 463.

Christmas — A103

Designs: 45c, Arrival of Santa Claus on whale shark. 50c, Santa giving gifts to red crabs.

2003, Oct. 31 Litho. *Perf. 14½x14*

443-444 A103 Set of 2 3.00 3.00

Zodiac Animals Type of 2002 and

New Year 2004 (Year of the Monkey) A104

Designs: 50c, Yellow and orange monkey. $1.45, Red orange monkey, lotus flower.

No. 447: a, Rat. b, Ox. c, Tiger. d, Rabbit. e, Dragon. f, Snake. g, Horse. h, Sheep. i, Monkey. j, Cock. k, Dog. l, Boar.

Litho. With Gold Foil Application

2004, Jan. 6 *Perf. 14x14½*

445-446 A104 Set of 2 4.50 4.50
446a Souvenir sheet, #445-446 5.50 5.50
447 Sheet of 14, #a-l, #446a 12.00 12.00
a.-d. A100 10c Any single, light and dark blue background .50 .50
e.-h. A100 15c Any single, light and dark blue background .60 .60
i.-l. A100 25c Any single, light and dark blue background .70 .70

No. 446a exists with a 2004 Hong Kong Stamp Expo overprint in sheet margin in red. This sheet was sold at the show and was sold at some post offices in Australia, but not on Christmas Island. Value: *$15.*

See No. 463.

Marine Life — A105

No. 448: a, Two butterflyfish, rear of whale shark. b, Three striped fish, front of whale shark. c, Four fish. d, Two fish. e, Two green turtles. f, Two triggerfish (polka dots), red coral at LL. g, Two fish with thin horizontal stripes with yellow tails. h, Two fish with thick vertical stripes. i, Black and white fish. j, Three fish. k, Yellow fish with black spot, blue fish, red coral, yellow coral. l, Striped fish, clam. m, Black fish, small red fish. n Red fish, divers. o, Two striped fish, red coral under denomination. p, Blue and yellow fish, red and white spotted fish, yellow coral. q, Blue and yellow fish, yellow coral, sea anemones. r, Three blue fish with orange spots. s, Sea anemone and two anemonefish. t, Nudibranch, red coral and starfish.

2004, July 13 Litho. *Perf. 14½x14*

448 A105 Sheet of 20 11.00 11.00
a.-e. 10c Any single .25 .25
f.-o. 25c Any single .45 .45
p.-t. 50c Any single .95 .95

Zodiac Animals Type of 2002 and

New Year 2005 (Year of the Cock) A106

Designs: 50c, Cock, spirals at right. $1.45, Cock, spirals at right.

No. 451: a, Rat. b, Ox. c, Tiger. d, Rabbit. e, Dragon. f, Snake. g, Horse. h, Sheep. i, Monkey. j, Cock. k, Dog. l, Boar.

Litho. With Gold Foil Application

2005, Jan. 4 *Perf. 14x14½*

449-450 A106 Set of 2 4.50 4.50
450a Souvenir sheet, #449-450 4.50 4.50
450b As "a," with Taipei 2005 emblem overprinted in margin 5.00 5.00
451 Sheet of 14, #a-l, #450a 14.00 14.00
a.-d. A100 10c Any single, red and yellow background .45 .45
e.-h. A100 15c Any single, red and yellow background .45 .45
i.-l. A100 25c Any single, red and yellow background .65 .65

See No. 463.

Christmas A107

Santa Claus, birds and: 45c, Palm tree, presents. 90c, Sleigh, crabs.

2005, Nov. 1 Litho. *Perf. 14¼x14*

452 A107 45c multi 1.25 1.25
a. Booklet pane of 4 5.00 —
453 A107 90c multi 2.25 2.25

No. 452a exists with two different margins. These two panes were issued in a booklet that also contained three examples of Australia No. 2423a. The entire booklet sold for $9.95.

Zodiac Animals Type of 2002 and

New Year 2006 (Year of the Dog) A108

Designs: 50c, Purple dog. $1.45, Copper dog.

No. 456: a, Rat. b, Ox. c, Tiger. d, Rabbit. e, Dragon. f, Snake. g, Horse. h, Sheep. i, Monkey. j, Cock. k, Dog. l, Boar.

Litho. With Copper Foil Application

2006, Jan. 5 *Perf. 14x14½*

454-455 A108 Set of 2 3.25 3.25
455a Souvenir sheet, #454-455 3.25 3.25
456 Sheet of 14, #a-l, #455a 9.00 9.00
a.-d. A100 10c Any single, brown and yellow background .30 .30
e.-h. A100 15c Any single, brown and yellow background .35 .35
i.-l. A100 25c Any single, brown and yellow background .50 .50

See No. 463.

Buildings — A109

Designs: 50c, Mosque. $1.45, Tai Jin House.

No. 458: a, Tai Pak Kong Temple. b, Soon Tian Temple.

2006, June 13 Litho. *Perf. 14½x14*

457 A109 50c multi 1.25 1.25
458 A109 $1 Horiz. pair, #a-b 4.50 4.50
459 A109 $1.45 multi 3.25 3.25
Nos. 457-459 (3) 9.00 9.00

Zodiac Animals Types of 1996-2006 and

New Year 2007 (Year of the Boar) A110

Zodiac Animals A111

Designs: Nos. 460, 463l, 50c, Boar facing right. $1.45, Boar facing left.

No. 462: a, Rat. b, Ox. c, Tiger. d, Rabbit. e, Dragon. f, Snake. g, Horse. h, Sheep. i, Monkey. j, Cock. k, Dog. l, Boar.

Litho. With Copper Foil Application

2007, Jan. 9 *Perf. 14x14½*

460-461 A110 Set of 2 4.25 4.25
461a Souvenir sheet, #460-461 4.25 4.25
462 Sheet of 14, #a-l, #461a 10.00 10.00
a.-d. A100 10c Any single, multicolored background .25 .25
e.-h. A100 15c Any single, multicolored background .30 .25
i.-l. A100 25c Any single, multicolored background .50 .50

Self-Adhesive

Serpentine Die Cut 12¼ Syncopated (#463a-463l), Serpentine Die Cut (#463m)

463 Sheet of 13 19.00
a. A81 50c Like #376 1.10 1.10
b. A86 50c Like #405 1.10 1.10
c. A88 50c Like #410 1.10 1.10
d. A91 50c Like #416 1.10 1.10
e. A94 50c Like #425 1.10 1.10
f. A97 50c Like #430 1.10 1.10
g. A99 50c Like #434 1.10 1.10
h. A102 50c Like #440 1.10 1.10
i. A104 50c Like #445 1.10 1.10
j. A106 50c Like #449 1.10 1.10
k. A108 50c Like #454 1.10 1.10
l. A110 50c Like #460 1.10 1.10
m. A111 $1 multi 3.00 3.00
n. Booklet pane, 2 each #463a-463b 4.00
o. Booklet pane, 2 each #463c-463d 4.00
p. Booklet pane, 2 each #463e-463f 4.00
q. Booklet pane, 2 each #463g-463h 4.00
r. Booklet pane, 2 each #463i-463j 4.00
s. Booklet pane, 2 each #463k-463l 4.00
Complete booklet, #463n-463s 25.00

Complete booklet sold for $12.95.

Christmas A112

Santa Claus: 45c, In boat. 50c, Hoisted by crane. $1.10, On beach.

2007, Nov. 1 Litho. *Perf. 14x14½*

464-466 A112 Set of 3 4.00 4.00

New Year 2008 (Year of the Rat) — A113

Designs: 50c, Rat. $1.45, Chinese character for "rat."

No. 469: a, Rat, diff. b, Ox. c, Dragon. d, Snake. e, Tiger. f, Rabbit. g, Horse. h, Pig. i, Goat. j, Monkey. k, Rooster. l, Dog.

Litho. With Foil Application

2008, Jan. 8 *Perf. 14*

467 A113 50c multi 1.00 1.00
a. Perf. 14¾x14 7.00 7.00

Perf. 14¾x14

468 A113 $1.45 multi 2.75 2.75
a. Souvenir sheet, #467a, 468 3.75 3.75
b. As "a," with Olympex emblem in margin 3.75 3.75
469 Sheet of 14, #467a, 468, 469a-469l 11.00 11.00
a.-d. A113 10c Any single .25 .25
e.-h. A113 15c Any single .35 .35
i.-l. A113 25c Any single .50 .50
m. Booklet pane of 4, #469a, 469b, 2 #468 6.75 —
n. Booklet pane of 4, #469e, 469f, 2 #467a 2.75 —
o. Booklet pane of 4, #469c, 469d, 2 #467a 2.75 —
p. Booklet pane of 4, #469g, 469i, 2 #467a 3.00 —
q. Booklet pane of 4, #469j, 469k, 2 #467a 3.25 —
r. Booklet pane of 4, #469h, 469l, 2 #467a 3.00 —
Complete booklet, #469m-469r 22.00

Complete booklet sold for $10.95. Issued: No. 468b, 8/8. See Nos. 512g, 546d.

Territorial Status of Christmas Island, 50th Anniv. A114

No. 470: a, Gecarcoidea natalis. b, Papasula abbotti. c, Asplenium listeri.

$1.45, Seal of Union of Christmas Island Workers. $2.45, Christmas Island flag.

2008, June 10 Litho. *Perf. 14¼*

470 Horiz. strip of 3 3.75 3.75
a.-c. A114 50c Any single 1.00 1.00
471 A114 $1.45 multi 3.50 3.50
472 A114 $2.45 multi 5.50 5.50
Nos. 470-472 (3) 12.75 12.75

Christmas — A115

Designs: Nos. 473, 475, 50c, Christmas tree, bird, crabs and shells. Nos. 474, 476, $1.20, Crabs with gifts and Christmas lights.

2008, Oct. 31 Litho. *Perf. 14½x14*

473-474 A115 Set of 2 3.00 3.00

Serpentine Die Cut 11¼ Syncopated

Self-Adhesive

475 A115 50c multi 1.00 1.00
a. Booklet pane of 10 10.00

Booklet Stamp

476 A115 $1.20 multi 2.00 2.00
a. Booklet pane of 5 10.00

No. 475 was also printed in sheets of 10.

Christmas With Personalized Picture — A116

Designs as before.

Serpentine Die Cut 11½x11¼ Syncopated

2008, Oct. 31 Litho.

Self-Adhesive

477 A116 50c multi *4.00 4.00*
478 A116 $1.20 multi *7.00 7.00*

Nos. 477-478 each were sold in sheets of 20 and have personalized pictures and a straight edge at right, and lack separations between the stamp and the personalized photo. Sheets of 20 of No. 477 sold for $23, and No. 478 sold for $37.

New Year 2009 (Year of the Ox) — A117

Designs: 55c, Rat. $1.65, Chinese character for "ox."

No. 481: a, Rat. b, Ox, diff. c, Dragon. d, Snake. e, Tiger. f, Rabbit. g, Horse. h, Pig. i, Goat. j, Monkey. k, Rooster. l, Dog.

Litho. With Foil Application

2009, Jan. 8 *Perf. 14¾x14*

479 A117 55c multi .90 .90
480 A117 $1.65 multi 2.75 2.75
a. Souvenir sheet, #479-480 4.00 4.00
481 Sheet of 14, #479-480, 481a-481l 13.00 13.00
a.-d. A117 10c Any single .30 .30
e.-h. A117 20c Any single .35 .35
i.-l. A117 25c Any single .50 .50
m. Booklet pane of 4, #481b, 481e, 2 #480 6.50 —
n. Booklet pane of 4, #481c, 481f, 2 #479 2.75 —
o. Booklet pane of 4, #481d, 481g, 2 #479 2.75 —
p. Booklet pane of 4, #481i, 481j, 2 #479 3.00 —
q. Booklet pane of 4, #481k, 481l, 2 #479 3.00 —
r. Booklet pane of 4, #481a, 481h, 2 #479 2.75 —
Complete booklet, #481m-481r 21.00

No. 479 was issued in a sheet of 9 + 9 labels that could be personalized and removed. The sheet sold for $15.95. Gutter strips of 10 of No. 484 exist with five labels forming a picture featuring the 12 Zodiac animals.

Complete booklet sold for $12.95. See Nos. 512h, 546e.

Christmas — A118

2009, Nov. 2 Litho. *Perf. 14¾x14*

482 A118 $1.25 multi 3.25 3.25

Booklet Stamp

Self-Adhesive

Serpentine Die Cut 11¼ Syncopated

483 A118 $1.25 multi 3.25 3.25
a. Booklet pane of 5 16.50

New Year 2010 (Year of the Tiger) — A119

Designs: 55c, Tiger. $1.65, Chinese character for "tiger."

No. 486: a, Rat. b, Ox. c, Dragon. d, Snake. e, Tiger, diff. f, Rabbit. g, Horse. h, Pigs. i, Goat. j, Monkey. k, Rooster. l, Dog.

Litho. With Foil Application

2010, Jan. 12 *Perf. 14¾x14*

484 A119 55c multi 1.25 1.25
485 A119 $1.65 multi 3.25 3.25
a. Souvenir sheet, #484-485 5.50 5.50
486 Sheet of 14, #484-485, 486a-486l 14.50 14.50
a.-d. A119 10c Any single .30 .30
e.-h. A119 20c Any single .40 .40
i.-l. A119 25c Any single .55 .55
m. Booklet pane of 4, #486e, 486f, 2 #485 8.00 —
n. Booklet pane of 4, #486c, 486d, 2 #484 3.25 —
o. Booklet pane of 4, #486g, 486i, 2 #484 4.00 —
p. Booklet pane of 4, #486j, 486k, 2 #484 4.00 —
q. Booklet pane of 4, #486h, 486l, 2 #484 4.00 —
r. Booklet pane of 4, #486a, 486b, 2 #484 3.25 —
Complete booklet, #486m-486r 23.00

Complete booklet sold for $12.95. A sheet of 13 self-adhesive stamps containing a round $1 stamp depicting a flower and stamps similar to Nos. 467, 479, 484, 486c, 486d, 486f, 486g, 486h, 486i, 486j, 486k, 486l, sold for $9.95.

No. 484 was issued in a sheet of 9 + 9 labels that could be personalized and removed. The sheet sold for $15.95. Gutter strips of 10 of No. 484 exist with five labels forming a picture featuring the 12 Zodiac animals.

A sheet containing lithographed versions of Nos. 486a-486l and 12 labels that could not be personalized sold for $10.

See Nos. 512i, 546f.

Worldwide Fund for Nature (WWF) A120

No. 487 — Christmas Island frigatebird: a, Adult on nest. b, Adults and chick at nest.

No. 488 — Christmas Island frigatebird: a, Chick and adult at nest. b, Adult in flight.

2010, Aug. 17 Litho. *Perf. 14¼*

487 Horiz. pair 4.25 4.25
a.-b. A120 60c Either single 1.60 1.25
488 Horiz. pair 9.75 9.75
a.-b. A120 $1.80 Either single 4.25 2.75
c. Souvenir sheet, #487a-487b, 488a-488b 14.00 14.00

Christmas — A121

Golden bosunbird: 60c, Carrying gift. $1.30, Flying away from gift on beach.

2010, Nov. 1 Litho. *Perf. 14¾x14*

489 A121 60c multi 2.25 2.25
490 A121 $1.30 multi 4.50 4.50

Booklet Stamp

Self-Adhesive

Serpentine Die Cut 11¼ Syncopated

491 A121 60c multi 2.25 2.25
a. Booklet pane of 10 22.50
491B A121 $1.30 multi 4.50 4.25
c. Booklet pane of 5 22.50

New Year 2011 (Year of the Rabbit) — A122

Designs: 60c, Rabbit. $1.80, Chinese character for "rabbit."

No. 494: a, Rat. b, Ox. c, Dragon. d, Snake. e, Tiger. f, Rabbit, diff. g, Horse. h, Pig. i, Goat. j, Monkey. k, Rooster. l, Dog.

Litho. With Foil Application

2011, Jan. 11 *Perf. 14¾x14*

492 A122 60c multi 1.25 1.25
493 A122 $1.80 multi 3.75 3.75
a. Souvenir sheetof 2, #492-493 5.50 5.50
494 Sheet of 14, #492-493, 494a-494l 13.00 13.00
a.-d. A122 15c Any single .30 .30
e.-h. A122 20c Any single .40 .40
i.-l. A122 25c Any single .50 .50
m. Booklet pane of 4, #494a, 494b, 2 #492 3.75 —
n. Booklet pane of 4, #494e, 494f, 2 #492 4.00 —
o. Booklet pane of 4, #494g, 494i, 2 #492 4.25 —
p. Booklet pane of 4, #494h, 494l, 2 #492 4.25 —
q. Booklet pane of 4, #494j, 494k, 2 #492 4.25 —
r. Booklet pane of 4, #494c, 494d, 2 #493 9.75 —
Complete booklet, #494m-494r 31.00

Complete booklet sold for $14.95. A sheet of 12 containing Nos. 494a-494l + 12 labels that could not be personalized sold for $15.95.

See Nos. 512j, 546g.

Crabs — A123

No. 495: a, Red crab. b, Robber crab.
No. 496: a, Jackson's crab. b, Blue crab.

2011, June 7 Litho. *Perf. 14¾x14*

495 A123 60c Horiz. pair, #a-b 4.00 4.00
496 A123 $1.20 Horiz. pair, #a-b 7.50 7.50

Christmas A124

Santa Claus: 55c, Giving cracker to crab. $1.50, In water holding flippers.

2011, Oct. 31 *Perf. 14x14¾*

497 A124 55c multi 1.75 1.75
498 A124 $1.50 multi 4.00 4.00

Booklet Stamps

Self-Adhesive

Serpentine Die Cut 11¼ Syncopated

499 A124 55c multi 1.75 1.75
a. Booklet pane of 10 17.50
500 A124 $1.50 multi 4.00 4.00
a. Booklet pane of 5 20.00

New Year 2012 (Year of the Dragon) — A125

Designs: 60c, Dragon. $1.80, Chinese character for "dragon."

No. 503: a, Rat. b, Ox. c, "Dragon" in circle. d, Snake. e, Tiger. f, Rabbit. g, Horse. h, Pig. i, Goat. j, Monkey. k, Rooster. l, Dog.

Litho. with Foil Application

2012, Jan. 10 *Perf. 14¾x14*

501 A125 60c multi 1.40 1.40
502 A125 $1.80 multi 4.00 4.00
a. Souvenir sheet of 2, #501-502 5.50 5.50
b. As "a," with 2012 Beijing Intl. Stamp & Coin Expo overprint in sheet margin in gold 5.00 5.00
503 Sheet of 14, #501-502, 503a-503l 11.00 11.00
a.-d. A125 15c Any single .35 .35
e.-h. A125 20c Any single .45 .45
i.-l. A125 25c Any single .55 .55
m. Booklet pane of 4, #503c, 503d, 2 #502 8.75 —
n. Booklet pane of 4, #503g, 503i, 2 #501 4.00 —
o. Booklet pane of 4, #503j, 503k, 2 #501 4.00 —
p. Booklet pane of 4, #503h, 503l, 2 #501 4.00 —
q. Booklet pane of 4, #503a, 503b, 2 #501 3.50 —
r. Booklet pane of 4, #503e, 503f, 2 #501 3.75 —
Complete booklet, #503m-503r 28.00

Complete booklet sold for $12.95.
Issued: No. 502b, 11/2.
See Nos. 512k, 546h.

Ferns A126

No. 504: a, Tectaria devexa. b, Asplenium listeri.

No. 505: a, Bolbitis heteroclita. b, Pteris tripartita.

2012, May 1 Litho. *Perf. 14x14¾*

504 Horiz. pair 3.00 3.00
a.-b. A126 60c Either single 1.25 1.25
505 Horiz. pair 6.00 6.00
a.-b. A126 $1.20 Either single 2.50 2.50

Christmas — A127

Designs: 55c, Sand sculpture of Santa Claus, frigatebirds, turtle and crabs. $1.60,

Santa Claus decorating sand sculpture of Christmas tree, starfish, crabs, bird.

2012, Nov. 1 *Perf. 14¾x14*

506 A127 55c multi 1.50 1.50
507 A127 $1.60 multi 3.75 3.75
a. Souvenir sheet of 2, #506-507 5.25 5.25

Booklet Stamp
Self-Adhesive
Serpentine Die Cut 11¼ Syncopated

508 A127 $1.60 multi 3.75 3.75
a. Booklet pane of 5 19.00

New Year Types of 2008-12 and

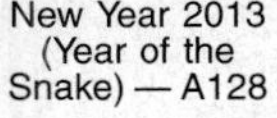

New Year 2013 (Year of the Snake) — A128

Rat and Apples — A129

Flower A130

Designs: No. 509, 60c, Snake. $1.80, Chinese character for "snake."

No. 511: a, Rat and apples. b, Ox and cherries. c, Dragon and tomatoes. d, Snake amd eggs. e, Tiger and fish. f, Rabbit and oranges. g, Horse and bananas. h, Boar and spinach. i, Goat and onions. j, Monkey and grapes. k, Rooster and pumpkins. l, Dog and milk bottles.

No. 512: a, Like No 511g. b, Like No. 511h. c, Like No. 511i. d, Like No. 511j. e, Like No. 511k. f, Like No. 511l. g, Rat with purple foil. h, Ox with purple foil. i, Tiger with purple foil. j, Rabbit with purple foil. k, Dragon with purple foil. l, Like No. 509.

Litho. With Foil Application

2013, Jan. 13 *Perf. 14¾x14*

509 A128 60c multi 1.25 1.25
510 A128 $1.80 multi 3.75 3.75
a. Souvenir sheet of 2, #509-510 5.25 5.25
b. As "a," with emblem overprinted in gold in sheet margin 4.75 4.75
511 Sheet of 14, #509-510, 511a-511l 10.00 10.00
a.-d. A129 15c Any single .30 .30
e.-h. A129 20c Any single .40 .40
i.-l. A129 25c multi .55 .55
m. Booklet pane of 4, #511d, 511g, 2 #510 9.00 —
n. Booklet pane of 4, #511i, 511j, 2 #509 4.00 —
o. Booklet pane of 4, #511k, 511l, 2 #509 4.00 —
p. Booklet pane of 4, #511a, 511h, 2 #509 3.50 —
q. Booklet pane of 4, #511b, 511e, 2 #509 3.50 —
r. Booklet pane of 4, #511c, 511f, 2 #509 3.50 —
Complete booklet, #511m-511r 27.50

Issued: No. 510b, 9/26. China International Collection Expo (No. 510b).

Self-Adhesive
Serpentine Die Cut 12¼, Serpentine Die Cut (#512m)

512 Sheet of 13 25.00
a.-b. A129 20c Either single .70 .70
c.-f. A129 25c Any single .90 .90
g. A113 50c pur & multi 1.75 1.75
h. A117 55c pur & multi 2.00 2.00
i. A119 55c pur & multi 2.00 2.00
j. A122 60c pur & multi 2.10 2.10
k. A125 60c pur & multi 2.10 2.10
l. A128 60c pur & multi 2.10 2.10
m. A130 $1 pur & multi 3.75 3.75

Complete booklet sold for $12.95. No. 512 sold for $9.95.

See Nos. 546i.

Fish — A131

No. 513: a, Cocos angelfish. b, Ladder wrasse.

$1.20, Redtooth triggerfish. $1.80, Red-striped pigfish.

2013, May 21 **Litho.** *Perf. 14x14¾*

513 Horiz. pair 2.50 2.50
a.-b. A131 60c Either single 1.25 1.25
514 A131 $1.20 multi 2.50 2.50
515 A131 $1.80 multi 3.50 3.50
Nos. 513-515 (3) 8.50 8.50

Flowering Shrubs — A132

No. 516: a, Colubrina pedunculata. b, Abutilon listeri.

No. 517: a, Urena lobata var. sinuata. b, Indigofera hirsuta.

No. 518, Like No. 516a. No. 519, Like No. 516b.

2013, June 18 *Perf. 14¾x14*

516 A132 60c Horiz. pair, #a-b 2.40 2.40
517 A132 $1.20 Horiz. pair, #a-b 4.50 4.50

Booklet Stamps
Self-Adhesive
Serpentine Die Cut 11¼ Syncopated

518 A132 60c multi 1.25 1.25
519 A132 60c multi 1.25 1.25
a. Booklet pane of 10, 5 each #518-519 16.00

Christmas A133

Designs: 55c, Santa Claus riding on frigatebird. $1.80, Frigatebird and crab in balloon gondola.

2013, Nov. 1 **Litho.** *Perf. 14x14¾*

520 A133 55c multi 1.10 1.10
521 A133 $1.80 multi 3.50 3.50
a. Souvenir sheet of 2, #520-521 5.00 5.00

Booklet Stamps
Self-Adhesive
Serpentine Die Cut 11¼ Syncopated

522 A133 $1.80 multi 3.50 3.50
a. Booklet pane of 5 20.00

Litho. With Foil Application

523 A133 $1.80 multi 3.50 3.50
a. Booklet pane of 10 40.00

New Year 2014 (Year of the Horse) — A134

Designs: 60c, Horse. $1.80, Chinese character for "horse."

No. 526: a, Rat. b, Ox. c, Dragon. d, Snake. e, Tiger. f, Rabbit. g, Horse, diff. h, Pig. i, Goat. j, Monkey. k, Rooster. l, Dog.

Litho. With Foil Application

2014, Jan. 7 *Perf. 14¾x14*

524 A134 60c multi 1.10 1.10
525 A134 $1.80 multi 3.25 3.25
a. Souvenir sheet of 2, #524-525 4.50 4.50
526 Sheet of 14, #524-525, 526a-526l 8.75 8.75
a.-d. A134 15c Any single .25 .25
e.-h. A134 20c Any single .35 .35
i.-l. A134 25c Any single .45 .45
m. Booklet pane of 4, #526g, 526i, 2 #525 7.75 —
n. Booklet pane of 4, #526j, 526k, 2 #524 3.25 —
o. Booklet pane of 4, #526h, 526l, 2 #524 3.25 —
p. Booklet pane of 4, #526a, 526b, 2 #524 3.00 —
q. Booklet pane of 4, #526e, 526f, 2 #524 3.25
r. Booklet pane of 4, #526c, 526d, 2 #524 3.00 —
Complete booklet, #526m-526r 23.50

Complete booklet sold for $12.95. See No. 546j.

Christmas Island National Park — A135

Designs: No. 527a, Forest. No. 527b, Beach. $1.40, Sea cliffs. $2.10, Wetlands.

2014, June 17 **Litho.** *Perf. 14x14¾*

527 Horiz. pair 3.00 3.00
a.-b. A135 70c Either single 1.40 1.40
528 A135 $1.40 multi 2.75 2.75
529 A135 $2.10 multi 4.00 4.00
Nos. 527-529 (3) 9.75 9.75

Red Crab Migration A136

Designs: 70c, Red crab. $2.10, Red crabs migrating.

2014, Aug. 12 **Litho.** *Perf. 14x14¾*

530-531 A136 Set of 2 5.25 5.25

Christmas — A137

Designs: 65c, Crab offering gift to Santa Claus. $1.80, Crab holding gift-wrapped coconut.

2014, Oct. 31 **Litho.** *Perf. 14¾x14*

532 A137 65c multi 1.25 1.25
533 A137 $1.80 multi 3.25 3.25
a. Souvenir sheet of 2, #532-533 4.50 4.50

Booklet Stamps
Self-Adhesive
Serpentine Die Cut 11¼ Syncopated

534 A137 65c multi 1.25 1.25
a. Booklet pane of 10 + 10 etiquettes 12.50
535 A137 $1.80 multi 3.25 3.25
a. Booklet pane of 5 16.50

New Year 2015 (Year of the Goat) — A138

Designs: 70c, Goat. $2.10, Chinese character for "goat."

No. 538: a, Rat. b, Ox. c, Dragon. d, Snake. e, Goat, diff. f, Monkey. g, Rooster. h, Dog. i, Tiger. j, Rabbit. k, Horse. l, Pig.

Litho. With Foil Application

2015, Jan. 8 *Perf. 14¾x14*

536 A138 70c multi 1.10 1.10
537 A138 $2.10 multi 3.25 3.25
a. Souvenir sheet of 2, #536-537 4.50 4.50
538 Sheet of 14, #536-537, 538a-538l 9.00 9.00
a.-d. A138 15c Any single .25 .25
e.-h. A138 25c Any single .40 .40
i.-l. A138 30c Any single .50 .50
m. Booklet pane of 4, #538e, 538f, 2 #537 8.00 —
n. Booklet pane of 4, #538g, 538h, 2 #536 3.25 —
o. Booklet pane of 4, #538a, 538l, 2 #536 3.25 —
p. Booklet pane of 4, #538b, 538i, 2 #536 3.25 —
q. Booklet pane of 4, #538c, 538j, 2 #536 3.25
r. Booklet pane of 4, #538d, 538k, 2 #536 3.25 —
Complete booklet, #538m-538r 24.50

Complete booklet sold for $14.95. See No. 546k.

Christmas — A139

Designs: 65c, Waterfall, Christmas tree made of red crabs. $1.80, Red crabs, snowman made of turtle and coconut.

2015, Oct. 30 **Litho.** *Perf. 14¾x14*

539 A139 65c multi .95 .95
540 A139 $1.80 multi 2.60 2.60
a. Souvenir sheet of 2, #539-540 3.75 3.75

Booklet Stamps
Self-Adhesive
Serpentine Die Cut 11¼ Syncopated

541 A139 $1.80 multi 2.60 2.60
a. Booklet pane of 5 13.00

Litho. With Foil Application

542 A139 65c multi .95 .95
a. Booklet pane of 10 9.50

New Year Types of 2008-15 and

New Year 2016 (Year of the Monkey) — A140

Peach A141

Designs: $1, Monkey. $3, Chinese character for "monkey."

No. 545: a, Rat. b, Rabbit. c, Goat. d, Dog. e, Ox. f, Dragon. g, Monkey, diff. h, Pig. i, Tiger. j, Snake. k, Horse. l, Rooster.

Litho. With Foil Application

2016, Feb. 3 *Perf. 14¾x14*

543 A140 $1 multi 1.50 1.50
544 A140 $3 multi 4.50 4.50
a. Souvenir sheet of 2, #543-544 6.00 6.00
545 Sheet of 14, #543-544, 545a-545l 12.00 12.00
a.-d. A140 20c Any single .30 .30
e.-h. A140 30c Any single .45 .45
i.-l. A140 50c Any single .75 .75
m. Booklet pane of 4, #543, 544, 545a, 545e 6.75 —
n. Booklet pane of 4, #545b, 545i, 2 #543 4.25 —
o. Booklet pane of 4, #545f, 545j, 2 #543 4.25 —
p. Booklet pane of 4, #543, 544, 545c, 545k 7.25 —
q. Booklet pane of 4, #545g, 545l, 2 543 4.25 —
r. Booklet pane of 4, #545d, 545h, 2 #543 3.75 —
Complete booklet, #545m-545r 30.50

Self-Adhesive
Serpentine Die Cut 12¼ Syncopated, Serpentine Die Cut (#546m)

546 Sheet of 13 14.50
a. A140 20c Like #545d .35 .35
b. A140 30c Like #545h .50 .50
c. A140 50c Like #545l .85 .85
d. A113 50c Rat .85 .85
e. A117 55c Ox .90 .90
f. A119 55c Tiger .90 .90
g. A122 60c Rabbit 1.00 1.00
h. A125 60c Dragon 1.00 1.00
i. A128 60c Snake 1.00 1.00
j. A134 60c Horse 1.00 1.00
k. A136 70c Goat 1.10 1.10
l. A140 $1 Like #543 1.60 1.60
m. A141 $2 multi 3.25 3.25

Complete booklet sold for $20.95. No. 546 sold for $9.95.

With Personalized Photo at Right Like Type A116 Litho.

Serpentine Die Cut 11½x11¼ Syncopated

Self-Adhesive

547 A140 $1 gold & multi 2.40 2.40

No. 547 was printed in a sheet of 20 and has personalized pictures and a straight edge at right and lack separations between the stamp and the personalized photo. Sheets of 20 sold for $33 each.

Robber Crab — A142

Various depictions of crab with denomination in: No. 548a, Greenish yellow. No. 548b, Turquoise green. $2, Red.

2016, Apr. 26 Litho. ***Perf. 14x14¾***

548 Horiz. pair 3.00 3.00
a.-b. A142 $1 Either single 1.50 1.50
549 A142 $2 multi 3.00 3.00

Shells A143

No. 550: a, Lambis scorpius. b, Tectus niloticus.
No. 551: a, Conus canonicus. b, Tridacna squamosa.

2016, Aug. 23 Litho. ***Perf. 14x14¾***

550 Horiz. pair 3.00 3.00
a.-b. A143 $1 Either single 1.50 1.50
551 Horiz. pair 6.00 6.00
a.-b. A143 $2 Either single 3.00 3.00

Christmas — A144

Birds and: 65c, Santa Claus in sleigh. $1.80, Rudolph, the red-nosed reindeer.

2016, Oct. 31 Litho. ***Perf. 14¾x14***

552 A144 65c multi 1.00 1.00
553 A144 $1.80 multi 2.75 2.75
a. Souvenir sheet of 2, #552-553 3.75 3.75

Booklet Stamps Self-Adhesive

Serpentine Die Cut 11¼ Syncopated

554 A144 $1.80 multi 2.75 2.75
a. Booklet pane of 5 14.00

Litho. With Foil Application

555 A144 65c multi 1.00 1.00
a. Booklet pane of 10 + 10 etiquettes 10.00

New Year 2017 (Year of the Rooster) — A145

Designs: $1, Rooster. $3, Chinese character for "rooster."
No. 558: a, Rat. b, Rabbit. c, Goat. d, Dog. e, Ox. f, Dragon. g, Monkey. h, Pig. i, Tiger. j, Snake. k, Horse. l, Chicks.

Litho. With Foil Application

2017, Jan. 10 ***Perf. 14¾x14***

556 A145 $1 multi 1.50 1.50
557 A145 $3 multi 4.50 4.50
a. Souvenir sheet of 2, #556-557 6.00 6.00

558 Sheet of 14, #556-557, 558a-558l 12.00 12.00
a.-d. A145 20c Any single .30 .30
e.-h. A145 30c Any single .45 .45
i.-l. A145 50c Any single .75 .75
m. Booklet pane of 4, #556, 557, 558d, 558l 7.50 —
n. Booklet pane of 4, #558a, 558h, 2 #556 4.00 —
o. Booklet pane of 4, #558e, 558i, 2 #556 4.50 —
p. Booklet pane of 4, #558b, 558f, 2 #556 4.00 —
q. Booklet pane of 4, #558j, 558k, 2 #556 4.75 —
r. Booklet pane of 4, #556, 557, 558c, 558g 7.25 —
Complete booklet, #558m, 558n, 558o, 558p, 558q, 558r 32.00

With Personalized Photo at Right Like Type A116 Self-Adhesive

Litho.

Serpentine Die Cut 11½x11¼ Syncopated

559 A145 $1 multi 2.50 2.50

Complete booklet sold for $20.95.
No. 559 was printed in a sheet of 20 and has personalized pictures and a straight edge at right and lack separations between the stamp and the personalized photo. Sheets of 20 sold for $33 each.

Early Voyages to Christmas Island A146

Quotation, map of Christmas Island and: $1, Mary, ship of island's discoverer William Mynors. $2, William Dampier and crab.

2017, Aug. 15 Litho. ***Perf. 14x14¾***

560 A146 $1 multi 1.60 1.60
561 A146 $2 multi 3.25 3.25
a. Souvenir sheet of 2, #560-561 5.00 5.00

Christmas — A147

Designs: 65c, Reindeer and elf on golf course. $2, Santa Claus swinging golf club.

2017, Nov. 1 Litho. ***Perf. 14¾x14***

562 A147 65c multi 1.00 1.00
563 A147 $2 multi 3.25 3.25
a. Souvenir sheet of 2, #562-563 4.25 4.25

Booklet Stamps Self-Adhesive

Serpentine Die Cut 11¼ Syncopated

564 A147 $2 multi 3.25 3.25
a. Booklet pane of 5 16.50

Litho. & Silk-Screened

565 A147 65c multi 1.00 1.00
a. Booklet pane of 10 + 10 etiquettes 10.00

New Year 2018 (Year of the Dog) — A148

Designs: $1, Dog. $3, Chinese character for "dog."
No. 568: a, Rat and Narcissus. b, Rabbit and Jonquil. c, Goat and Larkspur. d, Dog and Marigold. e, Ox and Carnation. f, Dragon and Sweet pea. g, Monkey and Gladiolus. h, Pig and Chrysanthemum. i, Tiger and Violet. j, Snake and Passion flower. k, Horse and Rose. l, Rooster and Aster.

Litho. With Foil Application

2018, Jan. 8 ***Perf. 14¾x14***

566 A148 $1 gold & multi 1.60 1.60
567 A148 $3 gold & multi 5.00 5.00
a. Souvenir sheet of 2, #566-567 6.75 6.75

568 Sheet of 14, #566-567, 568a-568l 13.50 13.50
a.-d. A148 20c Any single .35 .35
e.-h. A148 30c Any single .50 .50
i.-l. A148 50c Any single .80 .80
m. Booklet pane of 4, #566-567, 568d, 568h 7.50 —
n. Booklet pane of 4, #568a, 568e, 2 #566 4.25 —
o. Booklet pane of 4, #568b, 568i, 2 #566 4.50 —
p. Booklet pane of 4, #568f, 568j, 2 #566 4.75 —
q. Booklet pane of 4, #568c, 568k, 2 #566 4.50 —
r. Booklet pane of 4, #566-567, 568g, 568l 9.00 —
Complete booklet, #568m, 568n, 568o, 568p, 568q, 568r 35.00

With Personalized Photo at Right Like Type A116 Self-Adhesive

Litho.

Serpentine Die Cut 11½x11¼ Syncopated

569 A148 $1 multi 2.75 2.75

Complete booklet sold for $20.95.
No. 569 was printed in a sheet of 20 and has personalized pictures and a straight edge at right and lack separations between the stamp and the personalized photo. Sheets of 20 sold for $33 each.

Illustrations of Birds by John Gerrard Keulemans (1842-1912) — A149

Designs: No. 570, Christmas boobook. No. 571, White-tailed tropicbird. No. 572, Brown goshawk. No. 573, Christmas white-eye.

2018, Aug. 28 Litho. ***Perf. 14¾x14***

570 A149 $1 multi 1.50 1.50
571 A149 $1 multi 1.50 1.50
572 A149 $2 multi 3.00 3.00
573 A149 $2 multi 3.00 3.00
a. Souvenir sheet of 4, #570-573 9.00 9.00
Nos. 570-573 (4) 9.00 9.00

Christmas — A150

Designs: 65c, Santa Claus and Golden bosunbird on surfboard. $2, Red-footed booby with Christmas tree on surfboard.

2018, Nov. 1 Litho. ***Perf. 14¾x14***

574 A150 65c multi .95 .95
575 A150 $2 multi 3.00 3.00
a. Souvenir sheet of 2, #574-575 4.00 4.00

Booklet Stamps Self-Adhesive

Serpentine Die Cut 11¼ Syncopated

576 A150 $2 multi 3.00 3.00
a. Booklet pane of 5 15.00

Litho. & Silk-Screened

577 A150 65c multi .95 .95
a. Booklet pane of 10 + 10 etiquettes 9.50

New Year 2019 (Year of the Pig) — A151

Designs: $1, Pig. $3, Chinese character for "pig."
No. 568: a, Rat and kangaroo. b, Rabbit and platypus. c, Goat and echidna. d, Dog and dingo. e, Ox and wombat. f, Dragon and frilled lizard. g, Monkey and ringtail possum. h, Pig and koala. i, Tiger and Tasmanian Tiger. j, Snake and goanna. k, Horse and kookaburra. l, Rooster and emu.

Litho. With Foil Application

2019, Jan. 8 ***Perf. 14¾x14***

578 A151 $1 multi 1.50 1.60
579 A151 $3 multi 4.50 4.50
a. Souvenir sheet of 2, #578-579 6.00 6.00

580 Sheet of 14, #578-579, 580a-580l 12.00 12.00
a.-d. A151 20c Any single .30 .30
e.-h. A151 30c Any single .45 .45
i.-l. A151 50c Any single .75 .75
m. Booklet pane of 4, #578, 579, 580a, 580h 7.00 —
n. Booklet pane of 4, #580e, 580i, 2 #578 4.25 —
o. Booklet pane of 4, #580b, 580f, 2 #578 3.75 —
p. Booklet pane of 4, #580j, 580k, 2 #578 4.75 —
q. Booklet pane of 4, #578, 579, 580c, 580g 7.00 —
r. Booklet pane of 4, #580d, 580l, 2 #578 4.25 —
Complete booklet, #580m, 580n, 580o, 580p, 580q, 580r 31.00

With Personalized Photo at Right Like Type A116 Litho.

Serpentine Die Cut 11½x11¼ Syncopated

Self-Adhesive

581 A151 $1 multi — —

No. 581 was printed in a sheet of 20 and has personalized pictures, a straight edge at right and lacks separation between the stamp and the personalized photo. Sheets of 20 sold for $33 each.
Complete booklet sold for $20.95.

Explorers A152

Designs: $1, Captain John Fiot Lee Pearse Maclear (1838-1907), discoverer of Flying Fish Cove. $2, Captain Pelham Aldrich (1844-1930), explorer of Christmas Island jungle and discoverer of phosphates.

2019, Aug. 27 Litho. ***Perf. 14x14¾***

582-583 A152 Set of 2 4.00 4.00
583a Souvenir sheet of 2, #582-583 4.00 4.00

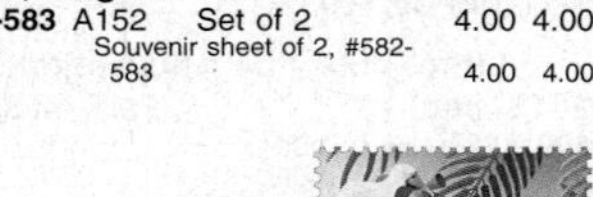

Christmas — A153

Designs: 65c, Santa Claus, crab and bird at dinner table. $2.20, Reindeer, crab and bird at dinner table.

2019, Nov. 1 Litho. ***Perf. 14¾x14***

584 A153 65c multi .90 .90
585 A153 $2.20 multi 3.00 3.00
a. Souvenir sheet of 2, #584-585 4.00 4.00

Booklet Stamps Self-Adhesive

Serpentine Die Cut 11¼ Syncopated

586 A153 $2.20 multi 3.00 3.00
a. Booklet pane of 5 15.00

Litho. & Silk-Screened

587 A153 65c multi .90 .90
a. Booklet pane of 20 + 20 etiquettes 18.00
Complete booklet, #587a 18.00

New Year 2020 (Year of the Rat) — A154

Designs: Nos. 588, 591a, Rat with fan. Nos. 589, 591b, Rat with red robe. Nos. 590, 591c, Rat with bowl.

No. 592: a, Ox. b, Goat. c, Dog. d, Rabbit. e, Horse. f, Monkey. g, Tiger. h, Dragon. i, Rooster. j, Rat. k, Snake. l, Pig.

Litho. & Embossed

2020, Jan. 8 ***Perf. 14¼***

588 A154 $1.10 multi 1.50 1.50
a. Booklet pane of 4 6.00 —
589 A154 $2.50 multi 3.50 3.50
a. Booklet pane of 4, 2 each #588, 589 10.00 —
590 A154 $3.30 multi 4.50 4.50
a. Booklet pane of 4, 2 each #588, 590 12.00 —
Complete booklet, #589a, 590a, 3 #588a 40.00
Nos. 588-590 (3) 9.50 9.50

Souvenir Sheet

591 Sheet of 3 9.50 9.50
a. A154 $1.10 multi (50x50mm diamond-shaped) 1.50 1.50
b. A154 $2.50 multi (50x50mm diamond-shaped) 3.50 3.50
c. A154 $3.30 multi (50x50mm diamond-shaped) 4.50 4.50

Miniature Sheet

592 Sheet of 15, #591a-591c, 592a-592l 19.00 19.00
a.-c. A154 10c Any single (30x30mm) .25 .25
d.-f. A154 50c Any single (30x30mm) .70 .70
g.-i. A154 70c Any single (30x30mm) .95 .95
j.-l. A154 $1 Any single (30x30mm) 1.25 1.25

Booklet Stamp Self-Adhesive

Litho.

Serpentine Die Cut 11½ Syncopated

593 A154 $2.50 multi 3.50 3.50
a. Booklet pane of 5 17.50

Complete booklet sold for $29.95. The three examples of No. 588a in the complete booklet have different pane margins. A sheet containing self-adhesive stamps like Nos. 592a-592l sold for $15.50.

Crabs A155

Designs: No. 594, $1.10, Bright-eyed crab. No. 595, $1.10, Kuhl's ghost crab. No. 596, $2.20, Red nipper. No. 597, $2.20, White-stripe crab.

2020, Aug. 17 Litho. ***Perf. 14x14¾***

594-597 A155 Set of 4 9.75 9.75
597a Souvenir sheet of 4, #594-597 9.75 9.75

Christmas A156

Designs: 65c, Santa Claus conducting choir of birds. $2.20, Reindeer, red crabs and giant geckos playing percussion instruments.

2020, Oct. 30 Litho. ***Perf. 14x14¾***

598 A156 65c multi .95 .95
599 A156 $2.20 multi 3.25 3.25
a. Souvenir sheet of 2, #598-599 4.25 4.25

Booklet Stamps Self-Adhesive

Serpentine Die Cut 11¼ Syncopated

600 A156 $2.20 multi 3.25 3.25
a. Booklet pane of 5 16.50

Litho. With Foil Application

601 A156 65c multi .95 .95
a. Booklet pane of 10 + 10 etiquettes 9.50

CILICIA

sə-ˈli-shē-ə

LOCATION — A territory of Turkey, in Southeastern Asia Minor
GOVT. — Former French occupation
AREA — 6,238 sq. mi.
POP. — 383,645
CAPITAL — Adana

British and French forces occupied Cilicia in 1918 and in 1919 its control was transferred to the French. Eventually part of Cilicia was assigned to the French Mandated Territory of Syria but by the Lausanne Treaty of 1923 which fixed the boundary between Syria and Turkey, Cilicia reverted to Turkey.

40 Paras = 1 Piaster

Issued under French Occupation

Numbers in parentheses are those of basic Turkish or French stamps.

Turkish Stamps of 1913-19 Handstamped

Perf. 11½, 12, 12½, 13½

1919 **Unwmk.**

On Pictorial Issue of 1913

2 A24 2pa red lilac 9.00 9.00
a. Inverted overprint 20.00 20.00
b. Double overprint 30.00 30.00
3 A25 4pa dk brn 7.25 7.25
a. Inverted overprint 20.00 20.00
b. Double overprint 22.50 22.50
4 A27 6pa dk blue 27.50 20.00
a. Inverted overprint 32.50 32.50
b. Double overprint 50.00 50.00
5 A32 1¾pi slate & red brn 8.75 8.75
a. Inverted overprint 20.00 20.00
b. Double overprint 22.50 22.50

On Issue of 1915

6 A17 1pi blue 4.00 4.00
a. Inverted overprint 10.00 10.00
b. Double overprint 10.00 10.00
c. In pair with unovptd. stamp 20.00 20.00
7 A21 20pa car rose 13.50 12.00
a. Inverted overprint 20.00 20.00
b. Double overprint 35.00 35.00
9 A22 20pa car rose 35.00 32.50
a. Inverted overprint 45.00 45.00
b. Double overprint 45.00 45.00

On Commemorative Issue of 1916

9A A41 5pa grn 130.00 92.50
10 A41 20pa ultra 7.25 7.25
a. Double overprint 15.00 15.00
11 A41 1pi vio & blk 9.50 9.50
a. Double overprint 27.50 27.50
b. Perf 12½ 9.50 9.50
c. In pair with unovptd. stamp 19.00 19.00
12 A41 5pi yel brn & blk 4.00 4.00
a. Double overprint 7.50 7.50

On Issue of 1916-18

13 A44 10pa grn 8.75 8.75
a. Perf 11½ (424a) 8.75 8.75
b. Double overprint 24.00 24.00
14 A47 50pa ultra 45.00 35.00
a. Perf 11½ (428a) 45.00 35.00
b. Double overprint 90.00 90.00
15 A51 25pi car, *straw* 8.75 8.75
16 A52 50pi car 8.75 8.75
17 A52 50pi ind 32.50 32.50

On Issue of 1917

18 A53 5pi on 2pa Prus blue 15.00 15.00
a. Perf 11½ (547c) 15.00 15.00

On Issue of 1919

19 A47 50pa ultra 40.00 32.50
a. Perf 11½ (555a) 40.00 32.50
b. Double overprint 80.00 80.00
20 A48 2pi org brn & indigo 40.00 32.50
21 A49 5pi pale bl & blk (557a) 40.00 32.50
a. Perf 11½ 40.00 32.50
b. Perf 11½x12½ (557b) 40.00 32.50
c. Double overprint 95.00 95.00

On Newspaper Stamp of 1916

22 A10 5pa on 10pa gray grn (P137) 4.75 4.75
d. Inverted overprint 11.00 11.00
e. Double overprint 14.00 14.00

On Semi-Postal Stamps of 1915

22A A21 20pa car rose (B8) 92.50 80.00
22B A21 1pi ultra (B9) 2,250. 1,700.
22C A21 1pi ultra (B13) 1,900. 1,200.

On Semi-Postal Stamps of 1916

23 A17 1pi bl (B19) 10.50 10.50
a. Inverted overprint 16.00 16.00
b. Double overprint 16.00 16.00
c. Perf 13¼ 25.00 25.00
24 A21 20pa car rose (B28) 4.00 4.00
a. Inverted overprint 7.50 7.50
b. Double overprint 10.00 10.00
25 A21 1pi ultra (B29) 8.75 8.75
a. Inverted overprint 15.00 15.00
b. Double overprint 25.00 25.00

Turkish Stamps of 1913-18 Handstamped

1919 **On Pictorial Issue of 1913**

31 A24 2pa red lil 5.00 5.00
a. Inverted overprint 8.00 8.00
b. Double overprint 12.00 12.00
c. In pair with unovptd. stamp 16.00 16.00
32 A25 4pa dk brn 15.00 15.00
a. Inverted overprint 25.00 25.00
b. Double overprint 45.00 45.00

On Issue of 1915

33 A17 1pi blue 13.50 13.50
a. Inverted overprint 22.50 22.50
b. Double overprint 40.00 40.00
34 A22 20pa car rose 5.00 5.00
a. Inverted overprint 11.00 11.00
b. Double overprint 17.50 17.50
c. In pair with unovptd. stamp 22.50 22.50

On Commemorative Issue of 1916

35 A41 20pa ultra 15.00 15.00
a. Inverted overprint 32.50 32.50
b. Perf 12½ (347a) 17.50 17.50
36 A41 1pi vio & blk 3.60 3.60
a. Inverted overprint 7.50 7.50
b. Perf 12½ (348a) 3.75 3.75

On Issue of 1917

40 A53 5pi on 2pa Prus bl 13.50 13.50
a. Perf 11½ (547c) 13.50 13.50

On Newspaper Stamp of 1916

41 A10 5pa on 10pa gray grn (P137) 27.50 27.50
a. Inverted overprint 50.00 50.00
b. In pair with unovptd. stamp 60.00 60.00

On Semi-Postal Stamp of 1915

41A A21 20pa car rose (B8) 225.00 150.00

On Semi-Postal Stamps of 1916

42 A17 1pi blue (B19) 6.50 6.50
a. Inverted overprint 14.00 14.00
b. Double overprint 15.00 15.00
c. Perf 12 (B19a) 8.00 8.00
d. Perf 12x13¼ (B19b) 8.00 8.00
43 A21 20pa car rose (B28) 4.25 4.25
a. Inverted overprint 10.00 *10.00*
b. Double overprint 11.00 *11.00*
Nos. 31-43 (11) 333.85 258.85

Turkish Stamps of 1913-19 Handstamped

1919 **On Pictorial Issue of 1913**

51 A24 2pa red lil 11.00 11.00
a. Inverted overprint 18.00 18.00
b. Double overprint 27.50 27.50
c. In pair with unovptd. stamp 45.00 45.00
52 A25 4pa dk brn 4.50 4.50
a. Inverted overprint 9.00 9.00
b. Double overprint 12.00 12.00

On Issue of 1915

53 A17 1pi blue 5.50 5.50
a. Inverted overprint 13.00 13.00
b. Double overprint 17.00 17.00
55 A22 5pa ocher 40.00 35.00
a. Double overprint 80.00 80.00
56 A22 20pa car rose 4.00 4.00
a. Inverted overprint 10.00 10.00
b. Double overprint 14.00 14.00
c. In pair with unovptd. stamp 25.00 25.00

On Commemorative Issue of 1916

57 A41 20pa ultra 4.00 4.00
a. Inverted overprint 8.00 8.00
b. Double overprint 12.00 12.00
c. Double overprint, one inverted 9.50 9.50
d. In pair with unovptd. stamp 17.50 17.50
58 A41 1pi vio & blk 4.50 4.50
a. Inverted overprint 7.50 7.50
b. Double overprint 10.00 10.00
59 A41 5pi yel brn & blk 12.00 12.00
a. Inverted overprint 18.00 18.00
b. Double overprint 24.00 24.00

On Issue of 1916

59A A17 1pi blue — —

On Issue of 1916-18

60 A43 5pa org 45.00 40.00
a. Inverted overprint 70.00 70.00
b. Perf 11½ (421a) 45.00 40.00
61 A46 1pi dl vio 13.50 13.50
a. Inverted overprint 21.00 21.00
b. Double overprint 35.00 35.00
63 A52 50pi green, *straw* 35.00 27.50

On Issue of 1917

64 A53 5pi on 2pa Prus bl 32.50 27.50
a. Double overprint 75.00 75.00
b. Perf 11½ (421a) 32.50 27.50

On Newspaper Stamp of 1916

65 A10 5pa on 10pa gray grn (P137) 8.75 8.75
a. Inverted overprint 13.50 13.50
b. Double overprint 24.00 24.00

On Semi-Postal Stamp of 1915

65A A21 20pa car rose (B8) 1,200. 850.00

On Semi-Postal Stamps of 1916

66 A17 1pi blue (B19) 30.00 30.00
a. Inverted overprint 55.00 55.00
67 A19 20pa car (B26) 13.50 13.50
a. Inverted overprint 17.50 17.50
b. Double overprint 17.50 17.50
68 A21 20pa car rose (B28) 180.00 92.50
69 A21 20pa car rose (B31) 8.00 8.00
a. Inverted overprint 15.00 15.00
b. Double overprint 22.50 22.50
69C A21 1pi ultra 110.00 80.00
Nos. 51-69C (20) 1,762. 1,272.

Turkey No. 424 Handstamped

1919

71 A44 10pa green 9.50 9.50
a. Inverted overprint 17.50 17.50
b. Double overprint 25.00 25.00
c. Perf 11½ (420a) 11.00 11.00

"T.E.O." stands for "Territoires Ennemis Occupés."

Turkish Stamps of 1913-19 Overprinted in Black, Red or Blue

In this setting there are various broken and wrong font letters and the letter "i" is sometimes replaced by a "t."

1919 **On Pictorial Issue of 1913**

75 A30 1pi blue (R) (260) 4.75 4.75
a. Inverted overprint 11.00 11.00
b. Double overprint 11.00 11.00
c. Double overprint, one inverted 20.00 20.00

On Issue of 1915

76 A21 20pa car rose 8.75 8.75

On Commemorative Issue of 1916

76A A41 5pa grn 200.00 110.00
77 A41 20pa ultra 13.50 13.50
a. Inverted overprint 20.00 20.00
b. Double overprint 30.00 30.00
c. Perf 12½ (347a) 13.50 13.50
78 A41 1pi vio & blk 24.00 24.00
a. Inverted overprint 35.00 35.00
b. Double overprint 60.00 60.00
c. Double overprint, one inverted 65.00 65.00

On Issue of 1916-18

79 A43 5pa org (Bl) (421) 4.75 4.75
a. Inverted overprint 9.50 9.50
b. Double overprint 13.00 13.00
c. Double overprint, one inverted 11.00 11.00
d. Perf 11½ (421a) 4.75 4.75
80 A44 10pa grn 8.75 8.75
a. Inverted overprint 16.00 16.00
b. Double overprint 22.50 22.50
c. Double overprint, one inverted 20.00 20.00
d. Perf 11½ (424a) 8.75 8.75
81 A45 20pa dp rose (Bk) (425) 27.50 27.50
a. Double overprint 60.00 60.00
82 A45 20pa dp rose (Bl) (425) 2.00 2.00
a. Inverted overprint 5.50 5.50
b. Double overprint 8.00 8.00
c. Double overprint, one inverted 10.00 10.00
83 A48 2pi org brn & indigo 1.60 1.60
a. Double overprint 5.50 5.50
b. Perf 11½ (429a) 1.60 1.60
83C A49 5pi pale blue & black (R) (430) 1.60 1.60
a. Inverted overprint 10.00 10.00
b. Double overprint 10.00 10.00
c. Double overprint, one inverted 13.00 13.00
d. Perf 11½ (430a) 1.75 1.75

84 A51 25pi car, *straw* 6.50 6.50
a. Inverted overprint 15.00 15.00
b. Double overprint 20.00 20.00
c. Double overprint, one inverted 13.50 13.50
85 A52 50pi grn, *straw* 92.50 87.50
a. Inverted overprint 150.00 150.00
b. Double overprint 150.00 150.00
c. Double overprint, one inverted 160.00 160.00

On Issue of 1917

85A A53 5pi on 2pa Prus bl —
86 A53 5pi on 2pa Prus bl 13.50 13.50
a. Perf 11½ (548c) 13.50 13.50

On Newspaper Stamps of 1916-19

87 A10 5pa on 10p gray grn (P137) 3.00 3.00
a. Inverted overprint 5.50 5.50
b. Double overprint 7.00 7.00
c. Double overprint, one inverted 13.50 13.50
88 A21 5pa on 2pa ol grn (P173) 1.50 1.50
a. Inverted overprint 5.50 5.50
b. Double overprint 7.00 7.00
c. Double overprint, one inverted 6.50 6.50

On Semi-Postal Stamps of 1915-17

90 A21 20pa car rose (B28) 8.75 8.75
a. Double overprint 16.00 16.00
91 A41 10pa car (B42) 4.50 4.50
a. Inverted overprint 7.75 7.75
b. Double overprint 9.50 9.50
c. Double overprint, one inverted 12.50 12.50
d. Perf 12½ (B42b) 3.25 3.25
92 A11 10pa on 20pa vio brn (B38) 3.25 3.25
a. Inverted overprint 10.00 10.00
b. Double overprint 12.50 12.50
c. Double overprint, one inverted 14.50 14.50
93 SP1 10pa red vio (B46) 3.25 3.25
a. Overprint sideways 8.50 8.50

It is understood that the newspaper and semi-postal stamps overprinted "Cilicie" were used as ordinary postage stamps.

A1

1920 Blue Surcharge ***Perf. 11½***

98 A1 70pa on 5pa red 2.40 2.40
a. Double surcharge 40.00 40.00
b. Triple surcharge 250.00
c. Inverted surcharge 35.00 35.00
d. Double overprint, one inverted 47.50 47.50
e. In pair with unovptd. stamp 120.00
99 A1 3½pi on 5pa red 3.00 2.75
a. Se-tenant with No. 98, horiz. pair 120.00 120.00
b. As "a," inverted surcharge 240.00 240.00
c. Double surcharge 40.00 40.00
d. Inverted surcharge 35.00 35.00
e. Double surcharge, one inverted 45.00 45.00

Nos. 98-99 exist with a variety of surcharge misspellings. For detailed listings, see the *Scott Classic Specialized Catalogue.*

French Offices in Turkey No. 26 Surcharged

1920 ***Perf. 14x13½***

100 A3 20pa on 10c rose red (I) 2.00 2.00
a. "PARAS" omitted 72.50 72.50

Three types of "20" exist on No. 100: I, "2" bold; II "2" faint; III, "0" distinctly taller than "2." See the *Scott Classic Specialized Catalogue of Stamps and Covers* for detailed listings.

Stamps of France, 1900-17, Surcharged

1920

101 A16 5pa on 2c vio brn 1.60 1.60
102 A22 10pa on 5c green 2.00 2.00
103 A22 20pa on 10c red 4.00 4.00
104 A22 1pi on 25c blue 2.75 2.25
105 A20 2pi on 15c gray green 12.00 12.00
106 A18 5pi on 40c red & gray bl 26.00 26.00
107 A18 10pi on 50c bis brn & lav 32.50 32.50
108 A18 50pi on 1fr claret & ol grn 180.00 180.00
109 A18 100pi on 5fr dk bl & buff 900.00 900.00
Nos. 101-109 (9) 1,161. 1,160.

Nos. 106 to 109 surcharged in four lines. "O.M.F." stands for "Occupation Militaire Francaise."

1917 Stamps of France Surcharged

No. 110

No. 115

1920

110 A16 5pa on 2c vio brn (109b) 13.00
111 A22 10pa on 5c grn (110b) 13.00
b. Double surcharge 75.00
c. On ordinary paper 19.00
112 A22 20pa on 10c red 9.75
a. Inverted surcharge 75.00
b. Double surcharge 67.50
113 A22 1pi on 25c bl (168d) 6.00
114 A20 2pi on 15c gray grn (139c) 27.00
115 A18 5pi on 40c red & gray bl 50.00
116 A18 20pi on 1fr claret & ol grn 190.00
a. "O.M.F. Cilicie" omitted 625.00
b. Double surcharge 625.00
Nos. 110-116 (7) 308.75

On Nos. 115 and 116 "SAND. EST" is placed vertically. "Sand. Est" is an abbreviation of Sandjak de l'Est (Eastern County).

Nos. 110-116 were prepared for use, but never issued.

Stamps of France, 1900-17, Surcharged

First Setting: 1.75-2mm spacing between "Cilicie" and figures of value

1920

117 A16 5pa on 2c vio brn 1.50 1.50
a. Inverted surcharge 32.50 27.50
b. "Cililie" 35.00 35.00
c. Surcharge 5pi (error) 60.00 60.00
h. Double surcharge 35.00 35.00
119 A22 10pa on 5c grn 1.50 1.50
a. Inverted surcharge 30.00 26.00
b. Surch. 5pa (error), upright 55.00 55.00
c. Surch. 5pa (error), invtd. 75.00 67.50
121 A22 20pa on 10c red 1.75 1.75
a. Inverted surcharge 32.50 27.50
b. Surch. 10pa (error), upright 60.00 60.00
c. Surch. 10pa (error), invtd. 80.00 72.50
f. Double surcharge 35.00 35.00
g. Double surcharge, one inverted 47.50 47.50
122 A22 1pi on 25c blue 2.00 2.00
a. Double surcharge 72.50 72.50
b. Inverted surcharge 55.00 52.50
123 A20 2pi on 15c gray green 2.25 2.25
a. Double surcharge 45.00 45.00
b. Inverted surcharge 35.00 32.50
c. Double surcharge, one inverted 55.00 55.00
124 A18 5pi on 40c red & gray blue 4.00 4.00
a. Double surcharge 65.00 65.00
b. Inverted surcharge 40.00 40.00
e. "PIASRTES" 72.50 72.50
125 A18 10pi on 50c bis brn & lav 12.50 12.50
a. Double surcharge 60.00 60.00
b. Inverted surcharge 55.00 47.50
c. First "S" in "PIASTRES" inverted 110.00 110.00
e. "PIASRTES" 72.50 72.50
126 A18 50pi on 1fr clar & ol grn 17.50 17.50
a. Inverted surcharge 130.00
b. Double surcharge 180.00
e. "PIASRTES" 87.50
127 A18 100pi on 5fr dk bl & buff 45.00 45.00
a. Inverted surcharge 180.00
d. "PIASRTES" *925.00*
Nos. 117-127 (9) 88.00 88.00

This surcharge has "O.M.F." in thicker letters than the preceding issues.

There were two printings of this surcharge, which may be distinguished by the spacing between "Cilicie" and figures of value. See the *Scott Classic Specialized Catalogue of Stamps and Covers* for detailed listings.

For overprints see Nos. C1-C2.

AIR POST STAMPS

Nos. 123 and 124 Handstamped

Perf. 14x13½

1920, July 15 **Unwmk.**

C1 A20 2pi on 15c gray grn *9,250.* 9,250.
C2 A18 5pi on 40c red & gray blue 9,500. 9,500.
a. "PIASRTES"

A very limited number of Nos. C1 and C2 were used on two air mail flights between Adana and Aleppo. At a later date impressions from a new handstamp were struck "to oblige" on stamps of the regular issue of 1920 (Nos. 123, 124, 125 and 126) that were in stock at the Adana Post Office.

Counterfeits exist.

POSTAGE DUE STAMPS

Turkish Postage Due Stamps of 1914 Handstamped

Handstamped

1919 **Unwmk.** ***Perf. 12***

J1 D1 5pa claret 22.00 22.00
a. Inverted overprint 35.00 35.00
b. Double overprint 50.00 50.00
J2 D2 20pa red 22.50 22.50
a. Inverted overprint 35.00 35.00
b. Double overprint 50.00 50.00
J3 D3 1pi dark blue 35.00 35.00
a. Inverted overprint 50.00 50.00
J4 D4 2pi slate 45.00 45.00
a. Inverted overprint 65.00 65.00
Nos. J1-J4 (4) 124.50 124.50

Handstamped

J5 D1 5pa claret 26.00 26.00
a. Inverted overprint 40.00 40.00
b. Double overprint 55.00 55.00
J6 D2 20pa red 30.00 30.00
a. Inverted overprint 45.00 45.00
b. Double overprint 60.00 60.00
J7 D3 1pi dark blue 35.00 35.00
a. Inverted overprint 47.50 47.50
J8 D4 2pi slate 35.00 35.00
a. Inverted overprint 47.50 47.50
Nos. J5-J8 (4) 126.00 126.00

Handstamped

J9 D1 5pa claret 22.00 22.00
a. Inverted overprint 32.50 32.50
b. Double overprint 32.50 32.50
J10 D2 20pa red 22.50 22.50
a. Inverted overprint 32.50 32.50
b. Double overprint 35.00 35.00
J11 D3 1pi dark blue 35.00 35.00
a. Inverted overprint 47.50 47.50
J12 D4 2pi slate 22.00 22.00
a. Inverted overprint 32.50 32.50
Nos. J9-J12 (4) 101.50 101.50

Postage Due Stamps of France Surcharged

1921

J13 D2 1pi on 10c choc 15.00 15.00
a. Inverted overprint 130.00
J14 D2 2pi on 20c olive grn 15.00 15.00
a. Inverted overprint 130.00
J15 D2 3pi on 30c red 15.00 15.00
a. Inverted overprint 92.50
J16 D2 4pi on 50c vio brn 14.00 14.00
a. Inverted overprint 92.50
Nos. J13-J16 (4) 59.00 59.00

COCHIN CHINA

'kō-chən 'chī-nə

LOCATION — The southernmost state of French Indo-China in the Cambodian Peninsula.
GOVT. — French Colony
AREA — 26,476 sq. mi.
POP. — 4,615,968
CAPITAL — Saigon

100 Centimes = 1 Franc

Surcharged in Black on Stamps of French Colonies

a

b

c

1886-87 Unwmk. *Perf. 14x13½*

1	A9(a) 5c on 25c yel, *straw*	225.00	120.00
2	A9(b) 5c on 2c brn, *buff*	40.00	*32.50*
3	A9(b) 5c on 25c yel, *straw*	32.50	27.50
a.	Inverted surcharge	*275.00*	*275.00*
4	A9(c) 5c on 25c blk, *rose* ('87)	60.00	47.50
a.	Double surch., one of type b	*3,750.*	*2,750.*
b.	Triple surch., two of type b	—	—
c.	Inverted surcharge	375.00	375.00
d.	Double surch., both type "c"	*2,750.*	*3,250.*
e.	Triple surch., types "a," "b" and "c"		*8,750.*
	Nos. 1-4 (4)	357.50	227.50

1888

5 A9 15c on half of 30c brn, *bis* 125.00

No. 5 was prepared but not issued.

The so-called Postage Due stamps were never issued.

Stamps of Cochin China were superseded by those of Indo-China in 1892.

COCOS ISLANDS

'kō-kəs 'ī-ləndz

(Keeling Islands)

LOCATION — Indian Ocean, 1,330 miles northwest of Australia, 580 miles southwest of Java
GOVT. — A territory of Australia
AREA — 6 sq. mi.
POP. — 670 (1994)

Of 27 small coral islands making up two atolls, two islands are inhabited. Cocos Islands stamps are also valid within Australia.

12 Pence = 1 Shilling
100 Cents = 1 Dollar (1969)

Catalogue values for all unused stamps in this country are for Never Hinged items.

Copra Industry — A1

Super Constellation A2

Map of Islands — A3

Designs: 1sh, Coco palms. 2sh, Sailboat (dukong). 2sh3p, Fairy tern.

Perf. 14½

1963, June 11 Unwmk. Engr.

No.	Type	Value	Description	Unused	Used
1	A1	3p	dk red brown	1.25	1.25
2	A2	5p	vio blue	1.50	.85
3	A3	8p	red	1.75	1.25
4	A1	1sh	green	1.75	.85
5	A3	2sh	dull purple	7.00	2.50
6	A2	2sh3p	green	13.00	4.00
			Nos. 1-6 (6)	26.25	10.70
			Set, hinged	13.00	

"Simpson and His Donkey" by Wallace Anderson — A3a

1965, Apr. 14 Photo. *Perf. 13½x13*

No.	Type	Value	Description	Unused	Used
7	A3a	5p	brt grn, sepia & blk	.85	.85

ANZAC issue. See note after Australia No. 387.

Nos. 8-31 are valid for postage in Australia.

Turbo Lajonkairii — A4

Blenny — A5

Designs: 2c, Tridacna crocea (shell). 3c, Tridacna derasa (shell). 5c, Porites cocosensis (coral). 6c, Flyingfish. 10c, Banded rail (bird). 15c, Java sparrow. 20c, Red-tailed tropic bird. 30c, Sooty tern. 50c, Eastern reef heron. $1, Great frigate bird.

Perf. 13½

1969, July 9 Unwmk. Photo.

Size: 21½x27mm, 26½x22mm

No.	Type	Value	Description	Unused	Used
8	A4	1c	multicolored	.30	.55
9	A4	2c	multicolored	1.00	.70
10	A5	3c	multicolored	.40	.25
11	A5	4c	multicolored	.30	.45
a.			Salmon omitted	2,000.	
12	A5	5c	multicolored	.35	.30
13	A5	6c	multicolored	.60	.65
14	A5	10c	multicolored	.75	.75
15	A5	15c	multicolored	.90	.30
16	A5	20c	multicolored	.75	.30
17	A5	30c	multicolored	.75	.30
18	A4	50c	multicolored	.90	.50

Size: 21½x34mm

No.	Type	Value	Description	Unused	Used
19	A4	$1	multicolored	2.00	1.25
			Nos. 8-19 (12)	9.00	6.30

"Dragon" — A6

"Juno" — A7

Perf. 13½x13, 13x13½

1976, Mar. 29 Photo.

No.	Type	Value	Description	Unused	Used
20	A6	1c	shown	.30	.30
21	A7	2c	shown	.30	.30
22	A7	5c	"Beagle"	.30	.30
23	A7	10c	"Sydney"	.35	.35
24	A7	15c	"Emden"	.55	.55
25	A7	20c	"Ayesha"	.55	.55
26	A6	25c	"Islander"	.55	.55
27	A6	30c	"Cheshire"	.55	.55
28	A7	35c	"Jukung"	.55	.55
29	A7	40c	"Scotia"	.55	.55
30	A6	50c	"Orontes"	.70	.70
31	A6	$1	Royal Yacht "Gothic"	.90	.90
			Nos. 20-31 (12)	6.15	6.15

Historic ships.

Flag, Southern Cross, Islands' Map — A8

Council Emblem, Sailboat A9

1979, Sept. 3 Litho. *Perf. 15½*

No.	Type	Value	Description	Unused	Used
32	A8	20c	multicolored	.35	.35
33	A9	50c	multicolored	.55	.75

Inauguration of Cocos Islands' postal service (20c), and establishment of Cocos Islands Council (50c).

Forcipiger Flavissimus A10

Fish: 2c, Chaetodon ornatissimus. 5c, Anthias. 10c, Meyer's coralfish. 15c, Halichoeres. 20c, Amphiprion clarkii. 22c, Balistapus undulatus. 25c, Maori wrasse. 28c, Macropharyngodon meleagris. 30c, Chaetodon madagascariensis. 35c, Centropyge colini. 40c, Bodianus axillaris. 50c, Coris gaimardi. 55c, Spotted wrasse. 60c, Epinephelus tauvina. $1, Paracanthurus hepatus. $2, Striped butterflyfish.

1979-80 Litho. *Perf. 15½*

No.	Type	Value	Description	Unused	Used
34	A10	1c	multicolored	.25	1.00
35	A10	2c	multicolored	.25	.35
36	A10	5c	multicolored	.35	1.10
37	A10	10c	multi ('80)	.25	1.00
38	A10	15c	multicolored	.30	.35
39	A10	20c	multicolored	.40	.35
40	A10	22c	multi ('80)	.35	.35
41	A10	25c	multi ('80)	.40	1.00
42	A10	28c	multi ('80)	.35	.35
43	A10	30c	multicolored	.50	.45
44	A10	35c	multicolored	.55	1.25
45	A10	40c	multicolored	.65	.55
46	A10	50c	multicolored	.85	.75
47	A10	55c	multi ('80)	.60	1.10
48	A10	60c	multi ('80)	.70	.75
49	A10	$1	multicolored	1.15	2.25
50	A10	$2	multi ('80)	2.25	2.75
			Nos. 34-50 (17)	10.15	15.70

Sailboats in Lagoon A11

Christmas: 25c, Yachts and seagulls, vert.

1979, Oct. 22 Litho. *Perf. 15½*

No.	Type	Value	Description	Unused	Used
51	A11	25c	multicolored	.40	.30
52	A11	55c	multicolored	.60	.70

Star of Bethlehem, Map of Cocos Islands A12

Christmas (Map of Cocos Islands and): 28c, Three kings. 60c, Nativity.

1980, Oct. 22 Litho. *Perf. 13½x13*

No.	Type	Value	Description	Unused	Used
53	A12	15c	multicolored	.25	.25
54	A12	28c	multicolored	.30	.30
55	A12	60c	multicolored	.70	.70
			Nos. 53-55 (3)	1.25	1.25

Flag and Arms of Great Britain — A13

Australian Territory Status, 25th Anniv. (British Flag and Arms of Past Administrators): No. 57, Ceylon, 1878, 1942-1946. No. 58, Straits Settlements, 1886. No. 59, Singapore, 1946. No. 60, Australia (flag), 1955.

1980, Nov. 24 Litho. *Perf. 13½x13*

No.	Type	Value	Description	Unused	Used
56	A13	22c	multicolored	.25	.25
57	A13	22c	multicolored	.25	.25
58	A13	22c	multicolored	.25	.25
59	A13	22c	multicolored	.25	.25
60	A13	22c	multicolored	.25	.25
a.			Strip of 5, Nos. 56-60	1.75	1.75

Eye of the Wind, Map of Cocos Islands — A14

28c, Expedition routes, horiz. 35c, Francis Drake, Golden Hinde. 60c, Prince Charles, Eye of the Wind.

1980, Dec. 18 *Perf. 13x13½, 13½x13*

No.	Type	Value	Description	Unused	Used
61	A14	22c	shown	.35	.35
62	A14	28c	multicolored	.35	.35
63	A14	35c	multicolored	.35	.35
64	A14	60c	multicolored	.60	.60
			Nos. 61-64 (4)	1.65	1.65

Operation Drake circumnavigation.

Livestock in Quarantine A15

22c, Aerial view of station. 60c, Livestock, diff.

1981, May 12 Litho. *Perf. 13½x13*

No.	Type	Value	Description	Unused	Used
65	A15	22c	multicolored	.30	.30
66	A15	45c	shown	.40	.40
67	A15	60c	multicolored	.70	.70
			Nos. 65-67 (3)	1.40	1.40

West Island Quarantine Station opening.

Catalina Guba II A16

Inauguration of Air Service to Indian Ocean: No. 69, Avro Lancastrian. No. 70, Douglas DC4 Skymaster, Lockheed Constellation. No. 71, Lockheed Electra. No. 72, Boeing 727.

1981, June 23 Litho. *Perf. 13½x13*

No.	Type	Value	Description	Unused	Used
68	A16	22c	multicolored	.30	.30
69	A16	22c	multicolored	.30	.30
70	A16	22c	multicolored	.30	.30
71	A16	22c	multicolored	.30	.30
72	A16	22c	multicolored	.30	.30
a.			Strip of 5, #68-72	1.75	1.75

Prince Charles and Lady Diana — A17

1981, July 29 Litho. *Perf. 13½x13*

No.	Type	Value	Description	Unused	Used
73	A17	24c	multicolored	.25	.25
74	A17	60c	multicolored	.70	.70

Royal Wedding.

Angels We Have Heard on High — A18

Christmas: Carols: 30c, Shepherds Why this Jubilee. 60c,

1981, Oct. 22 Photo. *Perf. 13½x13*

No.	Type	Value	Description	Unused	Used
75	A18	18c	shown	.30	.30
76	A18	30c	multicolored	.35	.35
77	A18	60c	multicolored	.45	.45
			Nos. 75-77 (3)	1.10	1.10

Sesquicentennial of Charles Darwin's Visit — A19

1981, Dec. 28 Litho. *Perf. 13½x13*

No.	Type	Value	Description	Unused	Used
78	A19	24c	Coral	.30	.30
79	A19	45c	Darwin, coral	.40	.40
80	A19	60c	Beagle, coral	.55	.55
			Nos. 78-80 (3)	1.25	1.25

Souvenir Sheet

No.	Type	Value	Description	Unused	Used
81			Sheet of 2	1.00	1.00
a.	A19	24c	Atoll	.45	.45
b.	A19	24c	Atoll, diff.	.45	.45

125th Anniv. of Annexation to the British Dominions A20

1982, Mar. 31 Litho. *Perf. 13½x14*

No.	Type	Description	Unused	Used
82	A20	24c Queen Victoria	.30	.30
83	A20	45c British flag	.50	.50
84	A20	60c Capt. Fremantle	.60	.60
		Nos. 82-84 (3)	1.40	1.40

Scouting Year — A21

Perf. 13½x14, 14x13½

1982, July 21 Litho.

No.	Type	Description	Unused	Used
85	A21	27c Baden-Powell	.40	.40
86	A21	75c Emblem, map, vert.	.90	.90

Macroglossum Corythus — A22

1c, Presic villida, vert. 2c, Cephonodes picus. 10c, Chasmina candida, vert. 20c, Nagia linteola. 25c, Eublemma rivula, vert. 30c, Eurrhyparodes tricoloralis, vert. 35c, Hippotion boerhaviae. 40c, Euploea core corinna, vert. 45c, Psara hipponalis. 50c, Danaus chrysippus. 55c, Hypolimas misippus, vert. 60c, Spodoptera litura, vert. $1, Achaea janata, vert. $2, Hippotion velox. $3, Utetheisa pulchelloides.

1982, Sept. 6

No.	Type	Description	Unused	Used
87	A22	1c multicolored	1.00	.65
88	A22	2c multicolored	.40	*.50*
89	A22	5c shown	1.50	.80
90	A22	10c multicolored	.40	*.50*
91	A22	20c multicolored	.40	*.60*
92	A22	25c multicolored	.40	*.70*
93	A22	30c multicolored	.40	*.60*
94	A22	35c multicolored	1.75	.80
95	A22	40c multicolored	.40	*.75*
96	A22	45c multicolored	.50	*.75*
97	A22	50c multicolored	.60	*1.40*
98	A22	55c multicolored	.55	*.90*
99	A22	60c multicolored	.60	*1.75*
100	A22	$1 multicolored	2.25	2.75
101	A22	$2 multicolored	1.50	*2.75*
102	A22	$3 multicolored	2.00	*2.50*
		Nos. 87-102 (16)	14.65	*18.70*

Christmas A23

1982, Oct. 25 *Perf. 13x13½*

No.	Type	Description	Unused	Used
104	A23	21c Holy Family	.25	.25
105	A23	35c Angel	.30	.30
106	A23	75c Flight into Egypt	.90	.90
		Nos. 104-106 (3)	1.45	1.45

Christmas — A24

The Birth of Christ: a, God Will Look After Us; b, Our Baby King Jesus; c, Your Saviour is Born; d, Wise Men Followed the Star; e, And Worship the Lord.

1983, Oct. 31 Litho. *Perf. 14x13½*

No.	Type	Description	Unused	Used
107	A24	Strip of 5	1.50	1.50
a.-e.		24c any single	.25	.25

Cocos-Malay Culture — A25

Festive Occasions: 45c, Hari Raya. 75c, Melenggok dance. 85c, Wedding.

1984, Jan. 27 Litho. *Perf. 14x13½*

No.	Type	Description	Unused	Used
108	A25	45c multicolored	.50	.40
109	A25	75c multicolored	.75	.65
110	A25	85c multicolored	.90	.75
		Nos. 108-110 (3)	2.15	1.80

75th Anniv. of Barrel Mail (1909-1955) A26

Designs: 35c, Mail distribution, Direction Isld. 55c, Jukongs retrieving barrels from ocean liner. 70c, Morea receiving outgoing barrel mail, 1909. $1, Barrel mail recovery.

1984, Apr. 20 Litho. *Perf. 13½x14*

No.	Type	Description	Unused	Used
111	A26	35c multicolored	.55	.55
112	A26	55c multicolored	.95	.95
113	A26	70c multicolored	1.10	1.10
		Nos. 111-113 (3)	2.60	2.60

Souvenir Sheet

No.	Type	Description	Unused	Used
114	A26	$1 multicolored	2.25	*2.25*

375th Anniv. of Islands' Discovery — A27

30c, Capt. William Keeling. 65c, The Hector. 95c, Astrolabe. $1.10, Map, 1666.

1984, July 10 Litho. *Perf. 14x13½*

No.	Type	Description	Unused	Used
115	A27	30c multicolored	.60	.50
116	A27	65c multicolored	1.20	1.15
117	A27	95c multicolored	1.50	1.40
118	A27	$1.10 multicolored	1.75	1.75
		Nos. 115-118 (4)	5.05	4.80

AUSIPEX '84 — A28

45c, Malay Settlement, Home Island. 55c, West Island Air Strip, settlement. $2, Jukong ships racing, Melbourne Exhibition Center.

1984, Sept. 21 Litho. *Perf. 13½*

No.	Type	Description	Unused	Used
119	A28	45c multicolored	.65	.55
120	A28	55c multicolored	.70	.70

Souvenir Sheet

No.	Type	Description	Unused	Used
121	A28	$2 multicolored	2.75	2.75

Christmas A29

1984, Oct. 31 Litho. *Perf. 13½*

No.	Type	Description	Unused	Used
122	A29	24c Fish	.40	.40
123	A29	35c Butterfly	.60	*1.10*
124	A29	55c Bird	1.00	*1.50*
		Nos. 122-124 (3)	2.00	*3.00*

Souvenir Sheet

Act of Self-Determination — A30

Integration with Australia: a, Australians welcoming Cocos islanders. b, Australian flag over the islands.

1984, Nov. 30 Litho. *Perf. 13½x14*

No.	Type	Description	Unused	Used
125	A30	Sheet of 2	2.50	2.50
a.-b.		30c any single	1.10	1.10

Crafts — A31

1985, Jan. 30 *Perf. 14x13½*

No.	Type	Description	Unused	Used
126	A31	30c Boat building	.55	.35
127	A31	45c Blacksmith	.80	.50
128	A31	55c Woodcarving	1.15	.80
		Nos. 126-128 (3)	2.50	1.65

Cable-laying Ships — A32

1985, Apr. 24 *Perf. 13½x14*

No.	Type	Description	Unused	Used
129	A32	33c Scotia	1.45	1.00
130	A32	65c Anglia	2.10	1.60
131	A32	80c Patrol	2.10	*2.10*
		Nos. 129-131 (3)	5.65	4.70

Birds A33

33c, Redfooted booby, vert. 60c, Nankeen night heron. $1, Buff-banded rail.

1985, July 17 *Perf. 13½*

No.	Type	Description	Unused	Used
132	A33	33c multicolored	2.50	2.50
133	A33	60c multicolored	2.75	2.75
134	A33	$1 multicolored	3.00	3.00
a.		"Block" of 3, #132-134	9.00	9.00

Nos. 132-134 printed in a continuous design.

Seashells A34

1c, Trochus maculatus. 2c, Smaragdia rangiana. 3c, Chama. 4c, Cypraea moneta. 5c, Drupa morum. 10c, Conus miles. 15c, Terebra maculata. 20c, Fragum fragum. 30c, Turbo lajonkairii. 33c, Mitra fissurata. 40c, Lambis lambis. 50c, Tridacna squamosa. 60c, Cypraea histrio. $1, Phillidia varicosa. $2, Halgerda tessellata. $3, Harminoea cymbalum.

1985-86 Litho. *Perf. 13½x14*

No.	Type	Description	Unused	Used
135	A34	1c multicolored	.65	*1.25*
136	A34	2c multicolored	.65	*1.25*
137	A34	3c multicolored	.65	*1.25*
138	A34	4c multicolored	1.10	*1.25*
139	A34	5c multicolored	.65	*1.25*
140	A34	10c multicolored	.75	*1.75*
141	A34	15c multicolored	2.25	1.50
142	A34	20c multicolored	2.25	1.75
143	A34	30c multicolored	2.25	1.75
144	A34	33c multicolored	2.25	1.75
145	A34	40c multicolored	2.25	1.75
146	A34	50c multicolored	2.25	*2.25*
147	A34	60c multicolored	2.25	*2.75*
148	A34	$1 multicolored	3.25	*3.25*
149	A34	$2 multicolored	3.25	*4.00*
150	A34	$3 multicolored	3.75	*4.50*
		Nos. 135-150 (16)	30.45	33.25

Issue dates: 1c, 5c, 33c, $1, Sept. 18. 2c, 3c, 10c, $3, Jan. 29, 1986. 15c-30c, 40c, Apr. 30, 1986. 4c, 50c, 60c, $2, July 30, 1986.

For surcharges see Nos. 225, 228-229, 231-233.

Souvenir Sheet

Christmas — A35

a, Star LR. b, Star LL. c, Star UR. d, Star UL.

1985, Oct. 30 *Perf. 13½x14*

No.	Type	Description	Unused	Used
151	A35	Sheet of 4	2.50	2.50
a.-d.		27c any single	.60	.60

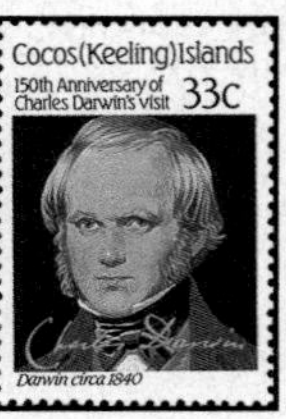

Darwin's Visit to the Islands — A36

33c, Charles Darwin. 60c, Map of voyage. $1, HMS Beagle.

1986, Apr. 1 Litho. *Perf. 14x13½*

No.	Type	Description	Unused	Used
152	A36	33c multicolored	.75	.75
153	A36	60c multicolored	1.50	*2.25*
154	A36	$1 multicolored	2.25	*2.75*
		Nos. 152-154 (3)	4.50	*5.75*

Christmas A37

30c, Coconut palm, holly. 90c, Shell, ornament. $1, Tropical fish, bell.

1986, Oct. 20 Litho. *Perf. 13½x14*

No.	Type	Description	Unused	Used
155	A37	30c multicolored	.70	.70
156	A37	90c multicolored	2.50	*3.00*
157	A37	$1 multicolored	2.50	*3.00*
		Nos. 155-157 (3)	5.70	*6.70*

Sailboats A38

a, Jukong. b, Ocean racers. c, Sarimanok. d, Ayesha. No. 158 has a continuous design.

1987, Jan. 28

No.	Type	Description	Unused	Used
158		Strip of 4	5.00	*6.00*
a.-d.		A38 36c any single	.95	*1.25*

Island Views — A39

70c, Direction Island. 90c, West Island. $1, Golf course, Cocos.

1987, Apr. 8

No.	Type	Description	Unused	Used
159	A39	70c multicolored	1.60	1.60
160	A39	90c multicolored	2.25	*2.50*
161	A39	$1 multicolored	2.60	*3.25*
		Nos. 159-161 (3)	6.45	*7.35*

Communications — A40

1987, July 29 Litho. *Perf. 13½x14*

162	A40	70c Radio	1.25	*1.50*
163	A40	75c Air service	1.25	*1.75*
164	A40	90c Satellite	1.50	*2.25*
165	A40	$1 Airmail	1.75	*2.25*
		Nos. 162-165 (4)	5.75	*7.75*

Industries A41

1987, Sept. 16

166	A41	45c Batik printing	1.10	*1.50*
167	A41	65c Boat building	1.50	*2.00*
168	A41	75c Copra production	1.75	*2.25*
		Nos. 166-168 (3)	4.35	*5.75*

Industrial activities of the Cocos Malay people.

Christmas — A42

30c, Peace on Earth. 90c, Unity. $1, Goodwill Towards All.

1987, Oct. 28 *Perf. 14x13½*

169	A42	30c multicolored	.45	.45
170	A42	90c multicolored	1.25	*1.90*
171	A42	$1 multicolored	1.60	*1.90*
		Nos. 169-171 (3)	3.30	*4.25*

Australia Bicentennial A43

Arrival of the First Fleet, Sydney Cove, Jan. 1788: a, Five aboriginals on shore. b, Four aboriginals on shore, one in canoe. c, Ships entering bay, kangaroos. d, Europeans land, white cranes. e, Flag raising.

1988, Jan. 26 Litho. *Perf. 13*

172		Strip of 5	8.50	8.50
a.-e.		A43 37c any single	1.05	1.05

No. 172 has a continuous design. See Christmas Is. No. 213.

Life Cycle of the Coconut — A44

1988, Apr. 13 Litho. *Perf. 14x13½*

173	A44	37c Flower	.60	.60
174	A44	65c Small nut stage	1.10	1.10
175	A44	90c Mature nuts	1.30	1.30
176	A44	$1 Seedlings	1.75	1.75
a.		Souvenir sheet of 4, #173-176	6.75	6.75
		Nos. 173-176 (4)	4.75	4.75

For surcharge see No. O1.

Cocos Postage Stamps, 25th Anniv. A45

Litho. & Engr.

1988, June 15 *Perf. 15x14*

177	A45	37c No. 1	1.00	1.00
178	A45	55c No. 4	1.35	*1.50*
179	A45	65c No. 2	1.50	*2.25*
180	A45	70c No. 3	1.75	*2.25*
181	A45	90c No. 5	2.00	*2.50*
182	A45	$1 No. 6	2.25	*2.50*
		Nos. 177-182 (6)	9.85	*12.00*

For overprint and surcharge see Nos. 216, 236.

Flowering Plants — A46

1c, Pisonia grandis. 2c, Cocos nucifera. 5c, Morinda citrifolia. 10c, Cordia subcordata. 30c, Argusia argentea. 37c, Calophyllum inophyllum. 40c, Barringtonia asiatica. 50c, Caesalpinia bonduc. 90c, Terminalia catappa. $1, Pemphis acidula. $2, Scaevola sericea. $3, Hibiscus tiliaceus.

1988-89 Litho. *Perf. 14x13½*

183	A46	1c multicolored	.55	*.90*
184	A46	2c multicolored	.55	*.90*
185	A46	5c multicolored	1.10	1.00
186	A46	10c multicolored	.75	*1.00*
189	A46	30c multicolored	1.10	*1.40*
190	A46	37c multicolored	1.60	1.25
191	A46	40c multicolored	1.10	*1.40*
192	A46	50c multicolored	1.40	*3.00*
194	A46	90c multicolored	2.00	*4.25*
195	A46	$1 multicolored	2.00	*2.50*
197	A46	$2 multicolored	2.50	*2.75*
198	A46	$3 multicolored	3.75	*4.00*
		Nos. 183-198 (12)	18.40	*24.35*

Issued: 1c, 5c, 37c, $3, 7/29; 2c, 10c, 30c, $2, 1/18/89; 40c, 50c, 90c, $1, 4/19/89.

For self-adhesive sheet of 3 see No. 217.

Souvenir Sheet

1988, July 30

199	A46	$3 like No. 198	*7.50*	*7.50*

SYDPEX '88.

Christmas A47

1988, Oct. 12 Litho. *Perf. 13½x14*

200	A47	32c multicolored	.85	.85
201	A47	90c multicolored	1.90	1.90
202	A47	$1 multicolored	2.25	2.25
		Nos. 200-202 (3)	5.00	5.00

1st Aerial Survey of the Indian Ocean Air Route, 50th Anniv. — A48

40c, P.G. Taylor, pilot. 70c, *Guba II* seaplane and crew. $1, *Guba II* landing off Direction Island. $1.10, Unissued 5sh stamp of Australia, 1939.

1989, July 19 Litho. *Perf. 14x13½*

203	A48	40c multicolored	.90	.90
204	A48	70c multicolored	1.40	1.40
205	A48	$1 multicolored	2.00	2.00
206	A48	$1.10 multicolored	2.25	2.25
		Nos. 203-206 (4)	6.55	6.55

Jukong, Traditional Sailing Vessel of the Cocos Malay People — A49

1989, Oct. 18 Litho. *Perf. 14x13½*

207	A49	35c multicolored	.85	.85
208	A49	80c multicolored	1.90	1.90
209	A49	$1.10 multicolored	2.75	2.75
		Nos. 207-209 (3)	5.50	5.50

Christmas.

A50

Designs: 40c, HMAS *Sydney.* 70c, SMS *Emden.* $1, Steam launch belonging to the *Emden.* $1.10, HMAS *Sydney* and naval crest.

1989, Nov. 9 Litho. *Perf. 13½x14*

210		Strip of 4 + label	6.75	6.75
a.		A50 40c multicolored	.60	.60
b.		A50 70c multicolored	1.15	1.15
c.		A50 $1 multicolored	1.60	1.60
d.		A50 $1.10 multicolored	1.75	1.75
e.		Souvenir sheet of 4, #210a-210d	8.25	8.25

Naval Engagement of the HMAS *Sydney* and the German Raider SMS *Emden,* 75th Anniv.

Crabs — A52

45c, Xanthid. 75c, Ghost. $1, Red-backed mud crab. $1.30, Coconut, vert.

1990, May 31 Litho. *Perf. 14½*

212	A52	45c multicolored	1.20	1.20
213	A52	75c multicolored	2.10	2.10
214	A52	$1 multicolored	2.40	2.40
215	A52	$1.30 multicolored	3.00	3.00
		Nos. 212-215 (4)	8.70	8.70

No. 180 Ovptd. in Red

Litho. & Engr.

1990, Aug. 24 *Perf. 15x14*

216	A45	70c gray, black & red	*9.50*	*9.50*

Flowering Plants Type of 1988

1990, Aug. 24 Photo. *Rouletted 9½*

Self-Adhesive

217		Sheet of 3	8.75	8.75
a.		A46 10c like No. 186	.30	.30
b.		A46 90c like No. 194	2.00	2.00
c.		A46 $2 like No. 197	4.50	4.50

World Stamp Exhibition, New Zealand 1990. Nos. 217a-217c inscribed 1990.

Explorers and Their Ships A54

45c, Capt. Keeling, Hector, 1609. 75c, Capt. Fitzroy, Beagle, 1836. $1, Capt. Belcher, Samarang, 1846. $1.30, Capt. Fremantle, Juno, 1857.

1990, Aug. 24 Litho. *Perf. 14½*

218	A54	45c violet brown	1.60	1.50
219	A54	75c pale bl & vio brn	2.75	*3.50*
220	A54	$1 pale yel & vio brn	3.25	*4.25*
221	A54	$1.30 buff & vio brn	5.25	*6.50*
a.		Souv. sheet of 4, #218-221, imperf.	11.00	11.00
		Nos. 218-221 (4)	12.85	15.75

Christmas — A55

1990, Dec. 12 Litho. *Rouletted 5*

222	A55	40c Star at left	1.00	1.00
a.		Bklt. pane of 10 + 2 labels	20.00	
223	A55	70c Star in center	1.75	1.75
a.		Bklt. pane, 4 #222, 2 #223 + 6 labels	25.00	
224	A55	$1.30 Star at right	3.50	3.50
		Nos. 222-224 (3)	6.25	6.25

Nos. 140, 141, 143, 146-147, 179 Surcharged in Blue or Black

No. 225

No. 228

No. 229

No. 231

No. 232

No. 233

No. 236

Litho., Litho. & Engr.

1990-91				***Perf. 13½x14, 15x14***	
225	A34	(1c)	on 30c #143	*6.50*	*6.50*
228	A34	(43c)	on 10c #140	*47.50*	*47.50*
229	A34	(43c)	on 10c #140	*19.00*	*19.00*
231	A34	70c	on 60c #147 (bk)	*10.00*	*10.00*
232	A34	80c	on 50c #146 (bk)	*10.00*	*10.00*
233	A34	$1.20	on 15c #141 (bk)	*10.00*	*10.00*
236	A45	$5	on 65c #179	*45.00*	*45.00*
			Nos. 225-236 (7)	*148.00*	*148.00*

Issued: No. 236, 11/11; No. 228, 12/18; Nos. 225, 229, 231-233, 1/1991.

Beaded Sea Star — A56

75c, Feather star. $1, Slate pencil urchin. $1.30, Globose sea urchin.

1991, Feb. 28		**Litho.**	***Perf. 14½***	
237	A56	45c shown	1.05	1.05
238	A56	75c multicolored	1.50	1.50
239	A56	$1 multicolored	2.10	2.10
240	A56	$1.30 multicolored	2.50	2.50
		Nos. 237-240 (4)	7.15	7.15

Hari Raya — A57

1991, Mar.		**Litho.**	***Perf. 14½***	
241	A57	45c multicolored	1.10	1.10
242	A57	75c multi, diff.	1.60	1.60
243	A57	$1.30 multi, diff.	3.00	3.00
		Nos. 241-243 (3)	5.70	5.70

Christmas — A58

1991, Nov. 6		**Litho.**	***Perf. 15½***	
244	A58	38c Child praying	.85	.85
245	A58	43c Child sleeping	1.05	1.05
246	A58	$1 Child singing	2.10	2.10
247	A58	$1.20 Child in wonder	2.75	2.75
		Nos. 244-247 (4)	6.75	6.75

Souvenir Sheet

248		Sheet of 4	7.00	7.00
a.		A58 38c Two children	.75	.75
b.		A58 43c Three girls	.85	.85
c.		A58 $1 Boy, two girls	2.00	2.00
d.		A58 $1.20 Boy, girl	2.25	2.25

Nos. 248a-248d are in a continuous design depicting a children's choir.

Crustaceans A59

Designs: 5c, Lybia tessellata. 10c, Pilodius areolatus. 20c, Trizopagurus strigatus. 30c, Lophozozymus pulchellus. 40c, Thalamitoides quadridens. 45c, Calcinus elegans, vert. 50c, Clibarius humilis. 60c, Trapezia rufopunctata, vert. 80c, Pylopaguropsis magnimanus, vert. $1, Trapezia ferruginea, vert. $2, Trapezia guttata, vert. $3, Trapezia cymodoce, vert.

1992		**Litho.**	***Perf. 14½***	
249	A59	5c multicolored	1.20	*1.60*
250	A59	10c multicolored	1.20	*1.75*
251	A59	20c multicolored	1.20	*1.75*
252	A59	30c multicolored	1.25	*2.50*
253	A59	40c multicolored	1.40	*2.50*
254	A59	45c multicolored	1.50	*2.50*
255	A59	50c multicolored	1.50	*4.00*
256	A59	60c multicolored	1.75	*4.00*
257	A59	80c multicolored	2.10	*4.00*
258	A59	$1 multicolored	2.75	*4.00*
259	A59	$2 multicolored	5.50	5.50
260	A59	$3 multicolored	8.50	7.00
		Nos. 249-260 (12)	29.85	*41.10*

Issued: 10c, 30c, 50c, 80c, $1, $2, 8/11; others, 2/28.

Discovery of America, 500th Anniv. — A60

1992, May 22		**Litho.**	***Perf. 14½***	
261	A60	$1.05 multicolored	3.75	*4.25*

Buff-banded Rail — A61

No. 262: a, 10c, Bird looking for food. b, 15c, Adult with chick. c, 30c, Two adults eating. d, 45c, Adult with eggs, hatchling.

No. 263: a, 45c, Two birds, one in water. b, 85c, Chick in nest. c, $1.20, Bird's head.

1992, June 18		**Litho.**	***Perf. 14***	
262	A61	Strip of 4, #a.-d.	5.25	5.25

Souvenir Sheet

263	A61	Sheet of 3, #a.-c.	8.00	8.00

World Wildlife Fund (No. 262).

World War II, 50th Anniv. — A62

45c, Royal Air Force Spitfire fighters. 85c, Japanese bombing of Kampong. $1.20, Sunderland reconnaissance flying boat.

1992, Oct. 13		**Litho.**	***Perf. 14½***	
264	A62	45c multicolored	1.75	1.75
265	A62	85c multicolored	3.00	3.00
266	A62	$1.20 multicolored	4.25	4.25
		Nos. 264-266 (3)	9.00	9.00

Festive Season — A63

40c, Storm waves on reef edge. 80c, Direction Island. $1, Moorish idols among coral.

1992, Nov. 10		**Litho.**	***Perf. 15x14½***	
267	A63	40c multicolored	1.40	1.40
268	A63	80c multicolored	2.50	2.50
269	A63	$1 multicolored	3.25	3.25
		Nos. 267-269 (3)	7.15	7.15

Corals — A64

45c, Lobophyllia hemprichii. 85c, Pocillopora eydouxi. $1.05, Fungia scutaria. $1.20, Sarcophyton sp.

1993, Jan. 28		**Litho.**	***Perf. 14½***	
270	A64	45c multicolored	.80	.80
271	A64	85c multicolored	1.45	1.45
272	A64	$1.05 multicolored	2.00	2.00
273	A64	$1.20 multicolored	2.50	2.50
		Nos. 270-273 (4)	6.75	6.75

A65

Island Currency Tokens: 45c, 5r token, 1968. 85c, Island scene token, 1968. $1.05, 150r token, 1977. $1.20, Token, 1910.

1993, Mar. 30		**Litho.**	***Perf. 15x14½***	
274	A65	45c multicolored	1.20	1.20
275	A65	85c multicolored	2.00	2.00
276	A65	$1.05 multicolored	2.60	2.60
277	A65	$1.20 multicolored	3.25	3.25
		Nos. 274-277 (4)	9.05	9.05

A66

Education: 5c, Primary classroom activities. 45c, Secondary studies. 85c, Crafts, traditional basket weaving. $1.05, Office staff, higher education. $1.20, Marine officers, coxswain's training.

1993, June 1		**Litho.**	***Perf. 14½***	
278	A66	5c multicolored	.80	.80
279	A66	45c multicolored	1.25	1.25
280	A66	85c multicolored	2.10	2.10
281	A66	$1.05 multicolored	2.40	2.40
282	A66	$1.20 multicolored	2.75	2.75
		Nos. 278-282 (5)	9.30	9.30

Air-Sea Rescue Service A67

45c, Men in lifeboat. 85c, Westwind Seascan. $1.05, R.J. Hawke inter-island ferry.

1993, Aug. 17		**Litho.**	***Perf. 14½***	
283	A67	45c multicolored	2.00	2.00
284	A67	85c multicolored	3.00	3.00
285	A67	$1.05 multicolored	4.00	4.00
a.		Souvenir sheet of 3, #283-285	11.00	11.00
		Nos. 283-285 (3)	9.00	9.00

A limited printing exists of No. 285a overprinted *Taipei '95* for the 1995 show. Value, $110.

Festive Season — A68

1993, Oct. 24		**Litho.**	***Perf. 14½***	
286	A68	40c pink & multi	1.25	1.25
287	A68	80c blue & multi	2.50	2.50
288	A68	$1 yellow & multi	3.50	3.50
		Nos. 286-288 (3)	7.25	7.25

From No. 289 on, Cocos Island stamps are valid for postage in Australia.

Map and Reef Life — A69

Reef triggerfish — No. 289: a, Two fish, purple coral (b). b, Three fish. c, Two fish. d, Two fish, red coral (e). e, One fish.

Green turtles — No. 290: a, Eggs, turtles. b, Two turtles (c). c, Group of baby turtles. d, Baby turtle. e, Fish, large turtle.

Pyramid butterflyfish — No. 291: a, Three fish. b, Two small, one large fish, coral (c). c, One small, one large fish, coral (d). d, Three fish, coral (e). e, Coral, one fish.

Junkongs sailing craft — No. 292: a, One boat, red sail. b, Two boats, one blue & white sail, one red sail. c, One boat, yellow sail. d, Two boats sailing away. e, Two boats, one red sail, one white & blue sail.

1994, Feb. 17		**Litho.**	***Perf. 14½x14***	
289	A69	5c Strip of 5, #a.-e.	1.25	*1.60*
290	A69	10c Strip of 5, #a.-e.	1.60	*2.00*
291	A69	20c Strip of 5, #a.-e.	2.00	*2.75*
292	A69	45c Strip of 5, #a.-e.	4.75	*5.25*
f.		Sheet of 20, #289-292	10.00	*13.00*
		Nos. 289-292 (4)	9.60	11.60

No. 292 also produced in sheets of 20.

Puppets — A70

1994, June 16		**Litho.**	***Perf. 14½x14***	
293	A70	45c Prabu Abjasa	.80	.80
294	A70	90c Prabu Pandu	1.50	1.50
295	A70	$1 Judistra	1.60	1.60
296	A70	$1.35 Abimanju	2.10	2.10
		Nos. 293-296 (4)	6.00	6.00

Christmas A71

1994, Oct. 31		**Litho.**	***Perf. 14x14½***	
297	A71	40c Angel	.70	.70
298	A71	45c Wise man	.90	.90
299	A71	80c Bethlehem	1.40	1.40
		Nos. 297-299 (3)	3.00	3.00

Seabirds A72

45c, White-tailed tropicbird, masked booby. 85c, Great frigatebird, white tern.

1995, Mar. 16 Litho. *Perf. 14x14½*

300	A72 45c multicolored		.80	.80
301	A72 85c multicolored		1.60	1.60
a.	Souvenir sheet of 2, #300-301		3.00	3.00
b.	As "a," overprinted		*15.00*	*15.00*

No. 301b ovptd. in gold in sheet margin with Jakarta '95 exhibition emblem and: "8th Asian International Philatelic Exhibition / PAMERAN FILATELI INTERNASIONAL ASIA VIII."

No. 301b issued 8/19/95.

Insects — A73

No. 302: a, Yellow crazy ant. b, Aedes mosquito. c, Hawk moth. d, Scarab beetle. e, Lauxaniid fly.

$1.20, Common eggfly butterfly.

1995, July 13 Litho. *Perf. 14½x14*

302	A73 45c Strip of 5, #a.-e.	5.25	5.25
303	A73 $1.20 multicolored	2.50	2.50

Fish — A74

Designs: 5c, Redspot wrasse. 30c, Gilded triggerfish. 40c, Saddled butterflyfish. 45c, Ringeyed hawkfish. 75c, Orangespine unicornfish. 80c, Blue tang. 85c, Humpback wrasse. 90c, Threadfin butterflyfish. $1, Bluestripe snapper. $1.05, Longnosed butterflyfish. $1.20, Freckled hawkfish. $2, Powder blue surgeonfish.

1995-97 Litho. *Perf. 14x14½*

304	A74	5c multicolored	.40	.40
305	A74	30c multicolored	.60	.60
306	A74	40c multicolored	.95	.95
307	A74	45c multicolored	1.10	1.10
308	A74	75c multicolored	1.60	1.60
309	A74	80c multicolored	1.75	1.75
310	A74	85c multicolored	1.75	1.75
311	A74	90c multicolored	2.00	2.00
312	A74	$1 multicolored	2.25	2.25
313	A74	$1.05 multicolored	2.25	2.25
314	A74	$1.20 multicolored	3.00	3.00
315	A74	$2 multicolored	5.25	5.25
	Nos. 304-315 (12)		22.90	22.90

Issued: 40c, 80c, $1.05, 11/1/95; 30c, 45c, 85c, $2, 8/8/96; 5c, 75c, 90c, $1, $1.20, 8/14/97.

See Nos. 327-329, 335.

Festive Season — A75

Designs: 45c, Greeting others, asking forgiveness. 75c, Drum beaters celebrate Hari Raya Puasa. 85c, Sharing food with friends.

1996, Feb. 19 Litho. *Perf. 14*

316	A75 45c multicolored	.65	.65
317	A75 75c multicolored	1.60	1.60
318	A75 85c multicolored	1.75	1.75
	Nos. 316-318 (3)	4.00	4.00

Animals Imported Into Australia Through Cocos Islands Quarantine Station — A76

45c, Black rhinoceros. 50c, Alpacas. $1.05, Boran cattle. $1.20, Ostrich.

1996, June 13 Litho. *Perf. 14½x14*

319	A76 45c multicolored	1.20	1.20
320	A76 50c multicolored	1.35	1.35
321	A76 $1.05 multicolored	2.40	2.40
322	A76 $1.20 multicolored	3.25	3.25
	Nos. 319-322 (4)	8.20	8.20

A77

Festive Season: 45c, Tambourine, dancing on shore, bird. 75c, Woman clapping, sailboats racing. 85c, Fish, night scene on beach.

1997, Jan. 6 Litho. *Perf. 14x14½*

323	A77 45c multicolored	.95	.95
324	A77 75c multicolored	1.50	1.50
325	A77 85c multicolored	1.90	1.90
	Nos. 323-325 (3)	4.35	4.35

A78

Children's drawings: a, Gift package. b, Mosque. c, Cocos Malay woman. d, Island scene. e, Two dancers.

1998, Jan. 22 Litho. *Perf. 14*

326	A78 45c Strip of 5, #a.-e.	4.00	4.00

Festive Season.

Fish Type of 1995

Designs: 70c, Crowned squirrelfish. 95c, Sixstripe wrasse. $5, Goldback anthias.

1998, Aug. 13 Litho. *Perf. 14x14½*

327	A74	70c multicolored	1.15	1.15
328	A74	95c multicolored	1.35	1.35
329	A74	$5 multicolored	7.50	7.50
	Nos. 327-329 (3)		10.00	10.00

Jukong Boats, Hari Raya Festival — A79

a, Women placing items in leaves, people along beach. b, Two women, boats along beach. c, Flowers, man in boat. d, Palm trees, two men, man in boat. e, Two people in boat.

1999, Feb. 11 Litho. *Perf. 14½x14*

330	A79 45c Strip of 5, #a.-e.	4.25	4.25

Flora and Fauna — A80

a, 45c, Two birds on tree branch. b, 25c, Bird in flight. c, 10c, Sailboat with sail down. d, 5c, Sailboat with red sails. e, 45c, Two birds in flight. f, 25c, Butterflies. g, 10c, School of fish. h, 5c, School of fish swimming left, coral. i, 45c, Red hibiscus flower. j, 25c, Three birds in flight. k, 10c, Two moorish idols. l, 5c, Turtles. m, 45c, Butterfly, flowers. n, 25c, Moth with wings folded, flowers. o, 10c, Two gold fish. p, 5c, Various fish swimming right. q, 45c, Yellow hibiscus. r, 25c, Butterfly on flowers. s, 10c, Two birds in flight. t, 5c, Large fish, coral.

1999, June 17 Litho. *Perf. 14x14½*

331	A80 Sheet of 20, #a.-t.	16.00	16.00

Faces of Cocos Islands A81

Ordinary people: a, Ratma Anthoney, with white shirt. b, Nakia Haji Dolman, with multicolored head covering. c, Muller Eymin, with white head covering. d, Courtney Press, with flowered outfit. e, Mhd Abu-Yazid, with blue shirt with stripes.

2000, Apr. 13 Litho. *Perf. 14x14½*

332	A81 45c Strip of 5, #a.-e.	4.50	4.50

Worldwide Fund for Nature — A82

No. 333: a, Purple crab. b, Little nipper crab.
No. 334: a, Horn-eyed ghost crab. b, Smooth-banded ghost crab.

2000, June 20 Litho. *Perf. 14x14¾*

333	A82 5c Pair, #a-b	1.00	1.00
334	A82 45c Pair, #a-b	2.00	2.00

Fish Type of 1995

No. 335: a, Wideband fusilier. b, Striped surgeonfish. c, Orangeband surgeonfish. d, Indo-Pacific sergeant.

2001, Feb. 8 Litho. *Perf. 14x14½*

335	Block of 4	5.00	5.00
a.-d.	A74 45c Any single	.90	.90

Turtles — A83

No. 336: a, Loggerhead. b, Hawksbill. c, Leatherback. d, Green.

2002, Oct. 1 Litho. *Perf. 14x14½*

336	A83 Block of 4	6.00	6.00
a.-d.	45c Any single	1.10	1.10

Shore Birds — A84

No. 337: a, Eastern reef egret. b, Sooty tern. c, Ruddy turnstone. d, Whimbrel.

2003, June 17

337	Horiz. strip of 4	7.50	7.50
a.-d.	A84 50c Any single	1.45	1.45

Royal Visit, 50th Anniv. — A85

Queen Elizabeth II and: No. 338a, Cocos Malay musicians. No. 338b, Royal Yacht Gothic. $1, Clunies Ross (Oceania) House. $1.45, Dignitary presenting model of Malay jukong.

2004, Mar. 16

338	A85 50c Horiz. pair, #a-b	2.75	2.75
339	A85 $1 multi	2.75	2.75
340	A85 $1.45 multi	3.50	3.50
a.	Souvenir sheet, #338a, 338b, 339, 340	10.00	10.00
b.	As "a," with 2004 World Stamp Championship emblem ovptd. in gold in margin	*15.00*	*15.00*
	Nos. 338-340 (3)	9.00	9.00

No. 340b issued 8/28.

Worldwide Fund for Nature (WWF) — A86

Designs: No. 341a, Blacktip reef shark. No. 341b, Gray reef sharks. $1, Blacktip reef sharks. $1.45, Gray reef shark.

2005, Jun 21 *Perf. 14½x14*

341	A86 50c Horiz. pair, #a-b	3.50	3.50
342	A86 $1 multi	3.50	3.50
343	A86 $1.45 multi	5.00	5.00
	Nos. 341-343 (3)	12.00	12.00

Wildlife — A87

No. 344: a-e, Various birds. f-t, Various fish and marine life.

2006, June 13 *Perf. 14¾x14*

344	A87 Sheet of 20	21.00	21.00
a.-e.	10c Any single	.50	.50
f.-o.	25c Any single	.80	.80
p.-t.	50c Any single	1.75	1.75

Mollusks — A88

Designs: No. 345a, Oriental moonsnail. No. 345b, Perly nautilus. $1, Partridge tun. $1.45, Giant clam.

2007, Mar. 20 *Perf. 14x14½*

345	A88 50c Horiz. pair, #a-b	4.50	4.50
346	A88 $1 multi	4.50	4.50
347	A88 $1.45 multi	4.50	4.50
	Nos. 345-347 (3)	13.50	13.50

Birds — A89

No. 345, a, Black-winged stilt. b, Chinese pond heron.

$1, White-breasted waterhen, horiz. $1.45, Saunders' tern, horiz.

2008, Feb. 26 *Perf. 14*

348	A89 50c Horiz. pair, #a-b	4.50	4.50
349	A89 $1 multi	4.50	4.50
350	A89 $1.45 multi	7.00	7.00
	Nos. 348-350 (3)	16.00	16.00

History of Cocos Islands — A90

No. 351: a, Sighting of islands by Captain William Keeling, 1609. b, Visit of Charles Darwin, 1836.

$1.10, Control of islands by Clunies Ross family, 1827-1978. $1.65, Australian territory, 1955.

2009, Apr. 21 ***Perf. 14¼***

351	A90	55c Horiz. pair, #a-b	4.50	4.50
352	A90	$1.10 multi	4.50	4.50
353	A90	$1.65 multi	7.00	7.00
		Nos. 351-353 (3)	16.00	16.00

Flowers — A91

No. 354: a, Ipomoea pes-caprae. b, Hibiscus tiliaceus.

No. 355: a, Suriana maritima. b, Morinda citrifolia.

2010, Sept. 15 Litho. ***Perf. 14¾x14***

354	A91	60c Horiz. pair, #a-b	4.75	4.75
355	A91	$1.20 Horiz. pair, #a-b	9.50	9.50

Boats — A92

Designs: 60c, Jukongs. $1.20, Small boat. $1.80, Glass-bottom boat, horiz. $3, Yacht, horiz.

Perf. 14¾x14, 14x14¾

2011, Jan. 18 **Litho.**

356	A92	60c multi	1.25	1.25
357	A92	$1.20 multi	2.40	2.40
358	A92	$1.80 multi	3.75	3.75
359	A92	$3 multi	6.00	6.00
		Nos. 356-359 (4)	13.40	13.40

Miniature Sheet

Marine Life — A93

No. 360: a, Sea cucumbers with red coloring. b, Fan coral with breaks at right. c, Sea cucumbers with purple coloring. d, Pink anemonefish in sea anemone. e, Christmas tree worm, tip at upper left. f, Mushroom coral. g, Giant clam. h, Fin of Spotted lionfish. i, Eye of Scribbled filefish (brown and blue fish). j, School of Neon fusiliers. k, Fan coral (intact). l, Nudibranch. m, Pink anemonefish in sea anemone, close-up. n, Christmas tree worms. o, Eye of Foster's hawkfish (pink and red fish). p, Foliaceous coral. q, Durban dancing shrimp. r, Magnificent sea anemone. s, Brain coral. t, Crown of thorns sea star.

2011, Sept. 6 ***Perf. 14¼***

360	A93	Sheet of 20	25.00	25.00
a.-t.		60c Any single	1.25	1.25

A sheet of 9 stamps containing stamps similar to Nos. 360a, 360b, 360d, 360e, 360j, 360l, 360m, 360n, and 360t but with glossy varnish was sold only with a set of nine gift cards for $9.99.

Colorful Skies Over Cocos Islands A94

Skies over: 60c, Pier. $1.20, Rocks in water. $1.80, Beach. $3, Palm trees.

2012, May 22 ***Perf. 14x14¾***

361-364	A94	Set of 4	13.00	13.00

Butterflies — A95

No. 365: a, Meadow argus. b, Common crow.

No. 366: a, Australian painted lady. b, Varied eggfly.

2012, Aug. 2

365	A95	Horiz. pair	3.00	3.00
a.-b.		60c Either single	1.50	1.50
366	A95	Horiz. pair	6.00	6.00
a.-b.		$1.20 Either single	3.00	3.00

Cocos Islands Postage Stamps, 50th Anniv. — A96

Designs: 5c, Sea turtle and underwater photographer. 60c, Man in outrigger canoe. $1, Sailboarder. $1.20, Coconut. $2, Egret.

2013, June 4 ***Perf. 14¾x14***

367-371	A96	Set of 5	11.00	11.00
371a		Souvenir sheet of 5, #367-371	11.00	11.00

A booklet containing five of No. 368 was produced locally and in very limited quantities. Value $110.

Barrel Mail — A97

Designs: 60c, Men and barrels in ocean, cover franked with Australia #213. $3, Men on shore signaling ship, cover franked with Australia #166 and 236.

2013, Aug. 6 Litho. ***Perf. 14¼***

372-373	A97	Set of 2	7.75	7.75

Historical Cocos Islands Maps — A98

Designs: No. 374a, 17th cent. map with natives at right. No. 374b, Map from 18th cent. with French inscriptions. $1.40, Map from 19th cent. $2.10, Map from 20th cent.

2014, June 24 Litho. ***Perf. 14¼***

374		Horiz. pair	2.80	2.80
a.-b.		A98 70c Either single	1.40	1.40
375	A98	$1.40 multi	2.75	2.75
376	A98	$2.10 multi	4.00	4.00
		Nos. 374-376 (3)	9.55	9.55

Battle of the Cocos Islands, Cent. — A99

Warships: 70c, HMAS Sydney. $3.50, SMS Emden.

2014, Oct. 14 Litho. ***Perf. 14¼***

377-378	A99	Set of 2	7.25	7.25

Worldwide Fund for Nature (WWF) A100

Birds: No. 379, 70c, Herald petrels. No. 380, 70c, Oriental pratincoles. No. 381, 70c, Little curlews. No. 382, 70c, Indian yellow-nosed albatrosses.

2015, Apr. 22 Litho. ***Perf. 14¼***

379-382	A100	Set of 4	4.50	4.50

A101

Uninhabited Islands — A102

No. 383: a, Pulu Klapa Satu (green water in foreground). b, Pulu Maraya (white beach in foreground).

No. 384: a, Pulu Blan Madar (at twilight). b, Pulu Beras (at midday).

2015, Aug. 25 Litho. ***Perf. 14¾x14***

383	A101	Horiz. pair	2.00	2.00
a.-b.		70c Either single	1.00	1.00
384	A102	Horiz. pair	4.00	4.00
a.-b.		$1.40 Either single	2.00	2.00

Dolphins A103

Designs: No. 385, $1, Common dolphin. No. 386, $1, Indo-Pacific bottlenose dolphin. No. 387, $1, Spinner dolphin.

2016, May 17 Litho. ***Perf. 14x14¾***

385-387	A103	Set of 3	4.50	4.50

A104

Art — A105

Nos. 388 and 389 — Various works with denomination at: a, UL. b, UR.

2016, Oct. 18 Litho. ***Perf. 14x14¾***

388	A104	Horiz. pair	3.25	3.25
a.-b.		$1 Either single	1.60	1.60
389	A105	Horiz. pair	6.50	6.50
a.-b.		$2 Either single	3.25	3.25
c.		Souvenir sheet of 4, #388a, 388b, 389a, 389b	9.75	9.75

Fruit — A106

No. 390: a, West Indian limes. b, Rose apples.

No. 391: a, Sapodillas. b, Breadfruit.

2017, May 30 Litho. ***Perf. 14x14¾***

390	A106	Horiz. pair	3.00	3.00
a.-b.		$1 Either single	1.50	1.50
391	A106	Horiz. pair	6.00	6.00
a.-b.		$2 Either single	3.00	3.00
c.		Souvenir sheet of 4, #390a, 390b, 391a, 391b	9.00	9.00

Airplanes A107

Designs: No. 392, $1, Consolidated Model 28-3. No. 393, $1, Avro Lancastrian. No. 394, $1, Lockheed Electra. No. 395, $1, Boeing 727.

2017, Oct. 31 Litho. ***Perf. 14x14¾***

392-395	A107	Set of 4	6.25	6.25
395a		Souvenir sheet of 4, #392-395	6.25	6.25

Basket Weaving A108

Hands of weaver making: No. 396, $1, Rice parcels. No. 397, $1, Basket with handle. $2, Round basket.

2018, June 26 Litho. ***Perf. 14x14¾***

396-398	A108	Set of 3	6.00	6.00
398a		Souvenir sheet of 3, #396-398	6.00	6.00

Shadow Puppets — A109

Puppet facing: No. 399, $1, Right. No. 400, $1, Left, diff. No. 401, $2, Right, diff. No. 402, $2, Left, diff.

2018, Oct. 16 Litho. ***Perf. 14¾x14***

399-402	A109	Set of 4	8.75	8.75
402a		Souvenir sheet of 4, #399-402	8.75	8.75

Water Sports A110

Designs: No. 403, $1, Windsurfing. No. 404. $1, Surfing. No. 405, $2, Snorkeling. No. 406, $2, Kitesurfing.

2019, May 28 Litho. *Perf. 14x14¾*

403-406	A110	Set of 4	8.50	8.50
406a		Souvenir sheet of 4, #403-406	8.50	8.50

Boobies — A111

Designs: No. 407, $1.10, Brown boobies. No. 408, $1.10, Red-footed booby. $2.20, Masked boobies.

2020, May 12 Litho. *Perf. 14¾x14*

407-409	A111	Set of 3	6.00	6.00
409a		Souvenir sheet of 3, #407-409	6.00	6.00

1902 Scrip — A112

1910 Ivorine Tokens A113

1968 Plastic Tokens A114

1977 Metal Coins A115

2020, Oct. 20 Litho. *Perf. 14x14¾*

410	A112	$1.10 multi	1.60	1.60
411	A113	$1.10 multi	1.60	1.60
412	A114	$2.20 multi	3.25	3.25
413	A115	$2.20 multi	3.25	3.25
a.		Souvenir sheet of 4, #410-413	9.75	9.75
		Nos. 410-413 (4)	9.70	9.70

Currencies used in Cocos Islands under rule by Clunies-Ross family.

OFFICIAL STAMP

No. 175 Ovptd. and Srchd. in Dark Blue

1991, Jan. 25 Litho. *Perf. 14x13½*

O1	A44 (43c) on 90c multi		*115.00*

No. O1 was not sold to the public unused. Used value is for a canceled-to-order example.

Mint examples exist in the marketplace. Value, $250.

COLOMBIA

kə-ˈləm-bē-ə

LOCATION — On the northwest coast of South America, bordering on the Caribbean Sea and the Pacific Ocean
GOVT. — Republic
AREA — 456,535 sq. mi.
POP. — 39,309,422 (1999 est.)
CAPITAL — Bogota

In 1810 the Spanish Viceroyalty of New Granada gained its independence and with Venezuela and Ecuador formed the State of Greater Colombia. In 1832 this state split into three independent units as Venezuela, Ecuador and the Republic of New Granada. The name of the country has been, successively, Granadine Confederation (1858-61), United States of New Granada (1861), United States of Colombia (1861-65), and the Republic of Colombia (1885 to date).

100 Centavos = 1 Peso

Catalogue values for unused stamps in this country are for Never Hinged items, beginning with Scott 594 in the regular postage section, Scott B1 in the semi-postal section, Scott C200 in the airpost section, Scott CE1 in the airpost special delivery section, Scott E2 in the special delivery section, and Scott RA33 in the postal tax section.

In the earlier days many towns did not have handstamps for canceling and stamps were canceled with pen and ink. Pen cancellations, therefore, do not indicate fiscal use. (Postage stamps were not used for revenue purposes.) Used values for Nos. 1-128 are for stamps with illegible manuscript cancels or handstamp cancels of Bogota or Medellin. Stamps with legible manuscript or other handstamped town-name cancels sell for more.

Fractions of many Colombian stamps of both early and late issues are found canceled, their use to pay postage having been tolerated even though forbidden by the postal laws and regulations. Many are known to have been made for philatelic purposes.

Watermarks

Wmk. 116 — Crosses and Circles

Wmk. 127 — Quatrefoils

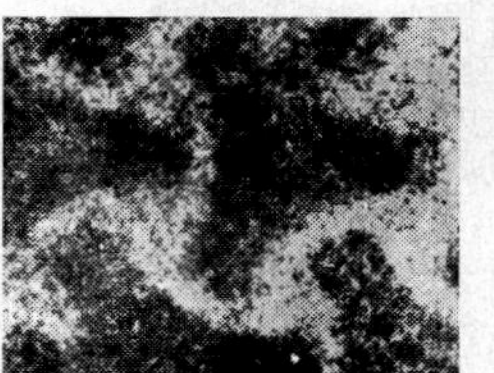
Wmk. 194 — Multiple Curvilinear Triangles

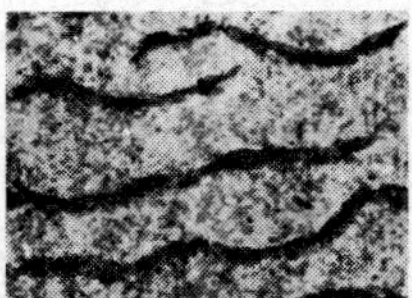
Wmk. 229 — Wavy Lines

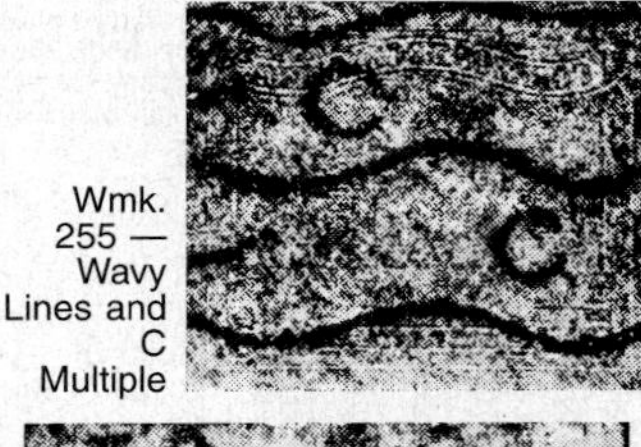
Wmk. 255 — Wavy Lines and C Multiple

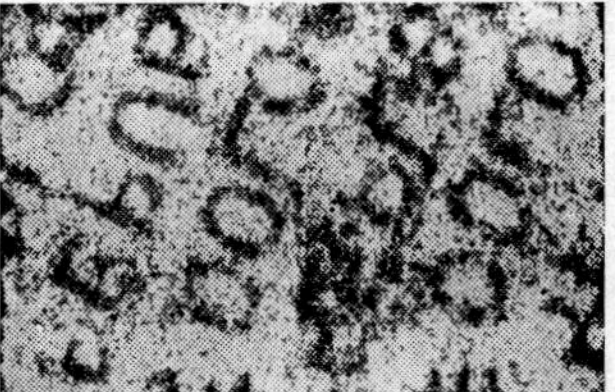
Wmk. 331 — REPUBLICA DE COLOMBIA

Wmk. 334 — Rectangles

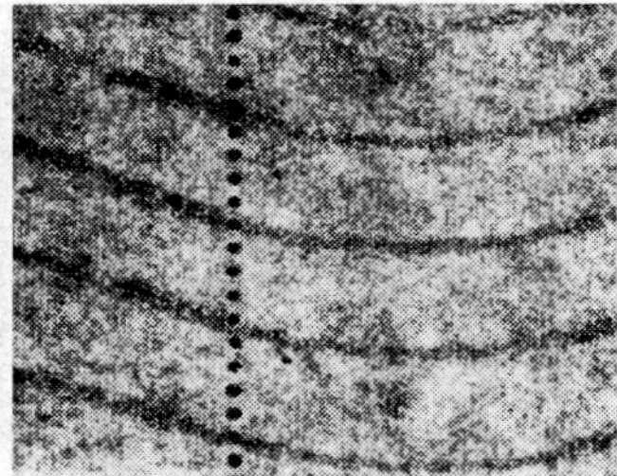
Wmk. 346 — Parallel Curved Lines

Stamps inscribed "Colombia" that show the Panama Canal area were used in Panama and can be found in Vol. 5.

Granadine Confederation

Coat of Arms — A1

Type A1 — Asterisks in frame. Wavy lines in background.

Type A2 — Diamond-shaped ornaments in frame. Straight lines in background. Numerals larger.

1859 Unwmk. Litho. *Imperf.*

Wove Paper

1	A1	2½c green	120.00	120.00
a.		2½c yellow green	120.00	120.00
2	A1	5c blue	140.00	87.50
a.		Tête bêche pair	*4,500.*	*10,000.*
b.		"50" instead of "5"		*7,500.*
3	A1	5c violet	375.00	120.00
a.		Tête bêche pair	*6,250.*	*6,000.*
b.		"50" instead of "5"		*15,000.*
4	A1	10c red brown	140.00	80.00
a.		10c buff	140.00	80.00
6	A1	20c blue	120.00	90.00
a.		20c gray blue	120.00	90.00
b.		Se-tenant with 5c	—	
c.		Tête bêche pair	*40,000.*	*32,500.*

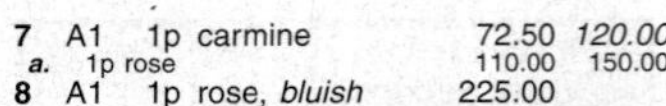

7	A1	1p carmine	72.50	*120.00*
a.		1p rose	110.00	150.00
8	A1	1p rose, *bluish*	225.00	

The 10c green is an essay.

Reprints of No. 7 are in brown rose or brown red. Wavy lines of background are much broken; no dividing lines between stamps.

Coat of Arms — A2

1860 Laid Paper

9	A2	5c lilac	325.00	200.00

Wove Paper

10	A2	5c gray lilac	90.00	90.00
a.		5c lilac	90.00	90.00
11	A2	10c yellow buff	90.00	90.00
a.		Tête bêche pair	*5,000.*	*5,000.*
12	A2	20c blue	260.00	175.00

United States of New Granada

Arms of New Granada — A3

1861

13	A3	2½c black	1,050.	400.00
14	A3	5c yellow	375.00	150.00
a.		5c buff	375.00	150.00
16	A3	10c blue	1,250.	175.00
17	A3	20c red	400.00	400.00
18	A3	1p pink	1,000.	400.00

There are 54 varieties of the 5c, 20c, and 1 peso.

Forgeries exist of Nos. 13-18.

United States of Colombia

Coat of Arms — A4

1862

19	A4	10c blue	250.00	125.00
20	A4	20c red	*11,000.*	725.00
21	A4	50c green	250.00	160.00
22	A4	1p red lilac	550.00	160.00
23	A4	1p red lil, *bluish*	*4,500.*	*1,000.*

No. 23 is on a thinner, coarser wove paper than Nos. 19-22.

Coat of Arms — A5

1863

24	A5	5c orange	100.00	65.00
a.		Star after "Cent"	110.00	72.50
25	A5	10c blue	175.00	50.00
a.		Period after "10"	200.00	50.00
26	A5	20c red	225.00	75.00
a.		Star after "Cent"	250.00	82.50
b.		Transfer of 50c in stone of 20c	*10,000.*	*2,500.*

Bluish Paper

28	A5	10c blue	175.00	32.50
a.		Period after "10"	190.00	35.00
29	A5	50c green	210.00	75.00
a.		Star after "Cent"	210.00	77.50

Ten varieties of each.

Coat of Arms — A6

1864 Wove Paper

30	A6	5c orange	60.00	37.50
a.		Tête bêche pair	475.00	400.00
31	A6	10c blue	55.00	15.00
a.		Period after 10	55.00	15.00

No.	Type	Description	Unused	Used
32	A6	20c scarlet	100.00	55.00
33	A6	50c green	85.00	65.00
34	A6	1p red violet	400.00	150.00

Two varieties of each.

Arms of Colombia
A7 A9

A8

1865

No.	Type	Description	Unused	Used
35	A7	1c rose	12.00	12.00
a.		bluish pelure paper	30.00	21.00
36	A8	2½c black, *lilac*	21.00	14.00
37	A9	5c yellow	47.50	20.00
a.		5c orange	47.50	20.00
38	A9	10c violet	67.50	4.50
39	A9	20c blue	67.50	20.00
40	A9	50c green	120.00	52.50
41	A9	50c grn (small figures)	120.00	52.50
42	A9	1p vermilion	125.00	18.00
a.		1p rose red	125.00	18.00
b.		Period after "PESO"	150.00	20.00

Ten varieties of each of the 5c, 10c, 20c, and 50c, and six varieties of the 1 peso. No. 36 was used as a carrier stamp.

A10 A11 A12

A13 A14

A15 A16

1866 **White Wove Paper**

No.	Type	Description	Unused	Used
45	A10	5c orange	72.50	27.50
46	A11	10c lilac	17.00	5.25
a.		Pelure paper	21.00	11.50
47	A12	20c light blue	42.50	21.00
a.		Pelure paper	67.50	52.50
48	A13	50c green	17.00	13.00
49	A14	1p rose red, *bluish*	92.50	32.50
a.		1p vermilion	92.50	32.50
51	A15	5p blk, *green*	500.00	190.00
52	A16	10p blk, *vermilion*	350.00	190.00

There are several varieties of the 1 peso having the letters "U," "N," "S" and "O" smaller.

A17 A18

A19 A20

A21

TEN CENTAVOS:

Type I — "B" of "COLOMBIA" over "V" of "CENTAVOS".

Type II — "B" of "COLOMBIA" over "VO" of "CENTAVOS."

ONE PESO:

Type I — Long thin spear heads. Diagonal lines in lower part of shield.

Type II — Short thick spear heads. Horizontal and a few diagonal lines in lower part of shield.

Type III — Short thick spear heads. Crossed lines in lower part of shield. Ornaments at each side of circle are broken. (See No. 97.)

1868

No.	Type	Description	Unused	Used
53	A17	5c orange	67.50	52.50
54	A18	10c lilac (I)	4.25	1.10
a.		10c red violet (I)	4.25	1.10
b.		10c lilac (II)	4.25	1.10
c.		10c red violet (II)	4.25	1.10
d.		Printed on both sides	7.50	2.50
55	A19	20c blue	3.00	1.25
56	A20	50c yellow green	3.50	2.40
57	A21	1p ver (II)	4.25	2.10
a.		Tête bêche pair	140.00	100.00
b.		1p rose red (I)	60.00	27.50
c.		1p rose red (II)	4.00	2.10
		Nos. 53-57 (5)	82.50	59.35

See Nos. 83-84, 96-97.

Counterfeits or reprints.

10c — There is a large white dot at the upper left between the circle enclosing the "X" and the ornament below.

50c — There is a shading of dots instead of dashes below the ribbon with motto. There are crossed lines in the lowest section of the shield instead of diagonal or horizontal ones.

1p — The ornaments in the lettered circle are broken. There are crossed lines in the lowest section of the shield. These counterfeits, or reprints, are on white paper, wove and laid, on colored wove paper and in fancy colors.

A22

Two varieties

1869-70 **Wove Paper**

No.	Type	Description	Unused	Used
59	A22	2½c black, *lilac*	4.75	2.50
a.		Laid paper ('70)	325.00	250.00
b.		Laid batonné paper ('70)	30.00	24.00

Nos. 59, 59a, 59b were used as carrier stamps.

Counterfeits, or reprints, are on magenta paper wove or ribbed.

A23 A24

1870 **Wove Paper**

No.	Type	Description	Unused	Used
62	A23	5c orange	2.00	1.25
a.		5c yellow	2.00	1.25
63	A24	25c black, *blue*	16.00	13.00

See No. 89.

In the counterfeits, or reprints, of No. 63, the top of the "2" of "25" does not touch the down stroke. The counterfeits are on paper of various colors.

A25 A26

5 pesos — The ornament at the left of the "C" of "Cinco" cuts into the "C," and the shading of the flag is formed of diagonal lines.

10 pesos — The stars have extra rays between the points, and the central part of the shield has some horizontal lines of shading at each end.

Surface Colored, Chalky Paper

1870

No.	Type	Description	Unused	Used
64	A25	5p blk, *green*	100.00	67.50
65	A26	10p blk, *vermilion*	120.00	67.50

See Nos. 77-79, 125-126.

A27 A28

A29

TEN CENTAVOS:

Type I — "S" of "CORREOS" 2½mm high. First "N" of "NACIONALES" small.

Type II — "S" of "CORREOS" 2mm high. First "N" of "NACIONALES" wide.

1871-74 **Thin Porous Paper**

No.	Type	Description	Unused	Used
66	A27	1c green ('72)	3.50	3.50
67	A27	1c rose ('73)	3.50	3.50
a.		1c carmine ('73)	3.50	3.50
68	A28	2c brown	1.60	1.60
a.		2c red brown	1.60	1.60
69	A29	10c vio (I) ('74)	2.50	2.50
a.		10c lilac (I) ('74)	2.50	2.50
b.		10c violet (II) ('74)	2.50	2.50
c.		10c lilac (II) ('74)	2.50	2.50
d.		As #69, laid paper ('72)	140.00	140.00
e.		As "b," laid paper ('72)	140.00	140.00
		Nos. 66-69 (4)	11.10	11.10

Counterfeits or reprints.

1c — The outer frame of the shield is broken near the upper left corner and the "A" of "Colombia" has no cross-bar.

2c — There are scratches across "DOS" and many white marks around the letters on the large "2." The counterfeits, or reprints, are on white wove and bluish white laid paper.

Condor — A30

Liberty Head
A31 A32

5 pesos, redrawn — The ornament at the left of the "C" only touches the "C," and the shading of the flag is formed of vertical and diagonal lines.

10 pesos, redrawn — The stars are distinctly five pointed, and there is no shading in the central part of the shield.

1877 **Wove Paper**

No.	Type	Description	Unused	Used
73	A30	5c purple	7.25	2.10
a.		5c lilac	7.25	2.10
74	A31	10c bister brown	3.50	.90
a.		10c red brown	3.50	.90
b.		10c violet brown	3.50	.90
75	A32	20c blue	4.25	1.40
a.		20c violet blue	25.00	3.50
77	A26	10p blk, *rose*	120.00	67.50
78	A25	5p blk, *lt grn*, redrawn	42.50	32.50
79	A26	10p blk, *rose*, redrawn	17.00	2.75
a.		10p blk, *dark rose*, redrawn	17.00	2.75
		Nos. 73-79 (6)	194.50	107.15

Stamps of the issues of 1871-77 are known with private perforations of various gauges, also with sewing machine perforation.

In the counterfeits, or reprints, of the 5 pesos the ornament at the left of the "C" of "Cinco" is separated from the "C" by a black line.

In the counterfeits, or reprints, of the 10 pesos the outer line of the double circle containing "10" is broken at the top, below "OS" of "Unidos," and the vertical lines of shading contained in the double circle are very indistinct.

There is a colorless dash below the loop of the "P" of "Pesos."

1876-79 **Laid Paper**

No.	Type	Description	Unused	Used
80	A30	5c lilac	85.00	65.00
81	A31	10c brown	47.50	2.75
82	A32	20c blue	100.00	67.50
83	A20	50c green ('79)	97.50	65.00
84	A21	1p pale red (II) ('79)	62.50	15.00
		Nos. 80-84 (5)	392.50	215.25

1879 **Wove Paper**

No.	Type	Description	Unused	Used
89	A24	25c green	32.50	32.50

1881 **Blue Wove Paper**

No.	Type	Description	Unused	Used
93	A30	5c violet	20.00	13.00
a.		5c lilac	20.00	13.00
94	A31	10c brown	12.00	2.50
95	A32	20c blue	12.00	3.75
96	A20	50c yellow green	12.50	7.50
97	A21	1p ver (III)	17.00	7.50
		Nos. 93-97 (5)	73.50	34.25

For types of 1p, see note over No. 53.

Reprints of the 10c and 20c are much worn. On the 10c the letters "TAVOS" of "CENTAVOS" often touch. On the 20c the letters "NT" of "VEINTE" touch and the left arm of the "T" is too long. Reprints of the 25c, 50c and 1p have the characteristics previously described. The reprints are on white wove or laid paper, on colored papers, and in fancy colors. Stamps on green paper exist only as reprints.

A34 A35

A36

1 centavo — The period before "UNION" is round and there are rays between the stars and the condors.

2 centavos — The "2's" and "C's" in the corners are placed upright.

5 centavos — The last star at the right almost touches the frame.

10 centavos — The letters of the inscription are thin; there are rays between the stars and the condor.

1881 **White Wove Paper** ***Imperf.***

No.	Type	Description	Unused	Used
103	A34	1c green	5.00	4.00
104	A35	2c vermilion	2.10	1.60
a.		2c rose	2.50	1.60
106	A34	5c blue	5.00	1.60
a.		Printed on both sides		
107	A36	10c violet	4.25	1.25
108	A34	20c black	4.75	2.00
		Nos. 103-108 (5)	21.10	10.45

The stamps of this issue are found with perforations of various gauges, also sewing machine perforation, all of which are unofficial.

See Nos. 112, 114-115.

Liberty Head — A37

1881 ***Imperf.***

No.	Type	Description	Unused	Used
109	A37	1c blk, *green*	3.50	*5.00*
110	A37	2c blk, *lilac rose*	3.50	*5.00*
111	A37	5c blk, *lilac*	8.50	1.75
		Nos. 109-111 (3)	15.50	*11.75*

Nos. 109 to 111 are found with regular or sewing machine perforation, unofficial.

Reprints:

1c — The top line of the stamp and the top frame extend to the left. 2c — There is a curved line over the scroll below the "AV" of "CENTAVOS."

5c — There are scratches across the "5" in the upper left corner. All three values were reprinted on the three colors of paper of the originals.

A37a

Redrawn

1 centavo — The period before "UNION" is square and the rays between the stars and the condor have been wholly or partly erased.

2 centavos — The "2's" and "C's" in the corners are placed diagonally.

5 centavos — The last star at the right touches the wing of the condor.

10 centavos — The letters of the inscription are thick; there are no rays under the stars; the last star at the right touches the wing of the condor and this wing touches the frame.

1883 ***Imperf.***

No.	Type	Description	Unused	Used
112	A34	1c green	4.75	4.25
113	A37a	2c rose	2.10	1.75
114	A34	5c blue	4.00	1.00
a.		5c ultramarine	4.00	1.00
b.		Printed on both sides, reverse ultra	25.00	20.00
115	A36	10c violet	5.00	1.40
		Nos. 112-115 (4)	15.85	8.40

The stamps of this issue are found with regular or sewing machine perforation, privately applied.

A38

A39

1883 ***Perf. 10½, 12, 13½***

No.	Type	Description	Unused	Used
116	A38	1c gray grn, *grn*	1.00	1.00
a.		Imperf., pair	5.00	5.00
117	A39	2c red, *rose*	1.00	*1.25*
a.		2c org red, *rose*	1.00	*1.25*
b.		2c red, *buff*	12.00	12.00
c.		Imperf., pair (#117 or 117a)	7.75	7.75
d.		"DE LOS" in very small caps	15.00	15.00
118	A38	5c blue, *bluish*	2.50	1.50
a.		5c dk bl, *bluish*	2.50	1.00
b.		5c blue	3.25	2.50
c.		Imperf., pair (#118 or 118a)	7.75	7.75
d.		As "b," imperf., pair	12.00	12.00
119	A39	10c org, *yel*	1.25	*1.40*
a.		"DE LOS" in large caps	60.00	26.00
b.		Imperf., pair	16.00	16.00
120	A39	20c vio, *lilac*	1.40	1.40
a.		Imperf., pair	16.00	16.00
122	A38	50c brn, *buff*	3.00	3.25
a.		Perf. 12	3.00	3.25
123	A38	1p claret, *bluish*	5.50	1.90
a.		Imperf., pair	16.00	16.00
		Nos. 116-123 (7)	15.65	11.70

Redrawn Types of 1877

1883 (?) ***Perf. 10½, 12***

No.	Type	Description	Unused	Used
125	A25	5p orange brown	10.00	6.00
126	A26	10p black, *gray*	10.00	7.25

1886 ***Perf. 10½, 11½, 12***

No.	Type	Description	Unused	Used
127	A38	5p brown, *straw*	10.00	5.50
a.		Imperf., pair	32.50	32.50
128	A38	10p black, *rose*	10.00	5.50
a.		Imperf., pair	32.50	32.50

Republic of Colombia

A40

Simón Bolívar — A41

Pres. Rafael Núñez — A42

1886 ***Perf. 10½ and 13½***

No.	Type	Description	Unused	Used
129	A40	1c grn, *grn*	1.75	.70
a.		Imperf., pair	6.75	6.75
130	A41	5c blue, *bl*	1.75	.40
a.		5c ultra, *blue*	1.75	.40
b.		Imperf., pair (#130)	6.75	6.75
131	A42	10c orange	3.50	.70
a.		Imperf., pair	9.25	9.25
b.		Pelure paper	4.50	1.00
		Nos. 129-131 (3)	7.00	1.80

Gen. Antonio Jose de Sucre y Alcala — A43

Gen. Antonio Nariño — A44

1887

No.	Type	Description	Unused	Used
133	A43	2c org red, *rose*	2.25	1.00
a.		2c orange red, *yellowish*	6.00	6.00
b.		2c orange red	7.25	7.25
c.		Imperf., pair (#133)	10.00	10.00
134	A44	20c pur, *grysh*	3.00	1.10
a.		Imperf., pair	8.50	8.50
b.		Pelure paper	3.50	2.25

Impressions of No. 134 on white, blue or greenish blue paper were not regularly issued.

Arms — A45

1888

No.	Type	Description	Unused	Used
135	A45	50c brn, *buff*	1.75	*1.90*
a.		Imperf., pair	6.00	6.00
136	A45	1p claret, *bluish*	8.00	2.10
137	A45	1p claret	3.50	1.60
138	A45	5p org brn	8.50	6.50
139	A45	5p black	14.50	9.50
140	A45	10p black, *rose*	21.00	6.75
		Nos. 135-140 (6)	57.25	28.35

See Nos. 155, 158-159.

Nariño — A46

1889

No.	Type	Description	Unused	Used
141	A46	20c pur, *grayish*	1.90	1.25
a.		Imperf., pair	9.25	9.25

Impressions on white, blue or greenish blue paper were not regularly issued.

A47

A48

A49

A50

A51

1890-91 ***Perf. 10½, 13½, 11***

No.	Type	Description	Unused	Used
142	A47	1c grn, *grn*	1.90	1.60
143	A48	2c org red, *rose*	.95	.95
144	A49	5c bl, *grnsh bl*	1.40	.40
a.		5c deep blue, *blue*	1.40	.40
b.		Imperf., pair	5.50	5.50
146	A50	10c brn, *yel*	1.00	.40
a.		10c brown, *buff*	1.00	.40
147	A51	20c vio, pelure paper	3.50	*3.50*
		Nos. 142-147 (5)	8.75	*6.85*

A52

A52a

A53

A53a

A54

Perf. 10½, 12, 13½, 14 to 15½

1892-99 **Ordinary Paper**

No.	Type	Description	Unused	Used
148	A47	1c red, *yel*	.85	.40
149	A52	2c red, *rose*	42.50	42.50
150	A52	2c green	.50	.30
a.		2c yellow green	.50	.30
151	A49	5c blk, *buff*	13.00	.35
152	A52a	5c org brn, *pale buff*	1.00	.30
a.		5c red brown, *salmon* ('97)	1.00	.30
153	A50	10c bis brn, *rose*	.75	.40
a.		10c brown, *brownish*	2.00	1.60
154	A53	20c brn, *bl*	.75	.40
a.		20c red brown, *blue*	.75	.40
b.		20c yel brn, *grnsh bl* ('97)	5.50	*13.00*
c.		20c brown, *buff* ('97)	19.00	13.00
155	A45	50c vio, *vio*	1.25	.75
156	A53a	50c red vio, *vio* ('99)	1.75	
157	A54	1p bl, *grnsh*	2.10	.90
a.		1p blue, *buff*	2.10	.90
158	A45	5p red, *pale rose*	8.50	3.25
159	A45	10p blue	16.00	3.25
a.		Thin, pale rose paper	27.50	7.25
		Nos. 148-159 (12)	88.95	
		Nos. 148-155,157-159 (11)		52.80

Type A53a is a redrawing of type A45. The letters of the inscriptions are slightly larger and the numerals "50" slightly smaller than in type A45.

The 20c brown on white paper is believed to be a chemical changeling.

Nos. 148, 150-152a, 153-155, 157, 159 exist imperf. Value per pair, $6-9.

A56

1899

No.	Type	Description	Unused	Used
162	A56	1c red, *yellow*	.70	.35
163	A56	5c red brn, *sal*	.70	.35
164	A56	10c brn, *lil rose*	2.00	.95
165	A56	50c blue, *lilac*	1.40	1.25
		Nos. 162-165 (4)	4.80	2.90

Cartagena Issues

A57

1899 **Blue Overprint** ***Imperf.***

No.	Type	Description	Unused	Used
167	A57	5c red, *buff*	30.00	30.00
a.		Sewing machine perf.	30.00	30.00
168	A57	10c ultra, *buff*	30.00	30.00
a.		Sewing machine perf.	30.00	30.00

Nos. 167 and 167a differ slightly from the illustration.

Bolivar No. 55 Overprinted with 7 Parallel Wavy Lines and

A58

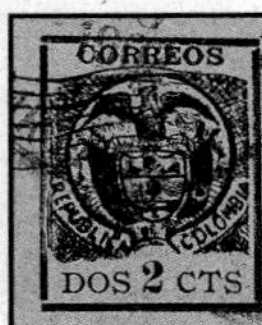

A59

A60

A61

Perf. 14 (#169), Sewing Machine Perf.

1899 **Purple Overprint**

No.	Type	Description	Unused	Used
169	A18	1c black	60.00	60.00
170	A58	1c brn, *buff*	20.00	20.00
a.		Altered from 10c	30.00	30.00
171	A59	2c blk, *buff*	20.00	20.00
a.		Altered from 10c	30.00	30.00
172	A60	5c mar, *grnsh bl*	18.00	18.00
a.		Perf. 12	18.00	18.00
b.		Without overprint	10.50	10.50
173	A61	10c red, *sal*	18.00	18.00
a.		Perf. 12	18.00	18.00
		Nos. 169-173 (5)	136.00	136.00

Types A58 and A59 illustrate Nos. 170a and 171a, which were made from altered plates of the 10c (No. 168). Nos. 170 and 171 were made from altered plate of the 5c denomination (No. 167), show part of the top flag of the "5" and differ slightly from the illustrations.

Nos. 170-173 exist imperf. Values about same as perf.

A62

1900 **Purple Overprint** ***Imperf.***

No.	Type	Description	Unused	Used
174	A62	5c red	25.00	25.00
a.		Perf. 12	35.00	35.00

A63

A64

"Gobierno Provisorio" at Top

1900 **Litho.** ***Perf. 12 Vertically***

No.	Type	Description	Unused	Used
175	A63	1c (ctvo) blk, *bl grn*	47.50	8.00
a.		"cvo."	120.00	14.50
b.		"cvos."	47.50	8.00
c.		"centavo"	55.00	47.50
176	A63	2c black	26.00	6.00
177	A63	5c blk, *pink*	26.00	6.00
a.		Name at side (V)	62.50	9.00
178	A63	10c blk, *pink*	26.00	6.00
a.		Name at side (V)	62.50	9.00
179	A63	20c blk, *yellow*	47.50	8.00
a.		Name at side (G)	92.50	12.00
		Nos. 175-179 (5)	173.00	34.00

"Gobierno Provisional" at Top

Name at Side in Black or Green

No.	Type	Description	Unused	Used
180	A64	1c (ctvo.) blk, *bl grn*	47.50	8.00
a.		"centavo"	125.00	47.50
181	A64	2c blk, *bl grn*	30.00	5.00
182	A64	5c blk (G)	30.00	5.00
a.		"ctvos." smaller	47.50	9.00
183	A64	10c blk, *pink*	30.00	5.00
184	A64	20c blk, *yel* (G)	47.50	8.00
		Nos. 180-184 (5)	185.00	31.00

Issues of the rebel provisional government in Cucuta.

A65

A66

Purple Overprint

1901 ***Sewing Machine Perf.***

185 A65 1c black 1.00 1.00
a. Without overprint 2.25 2.25
b. Double overprint 2.50 2.50
c. Imperf., pair 2.50 2.50
d. Inverted overprint 1.25 1.25
186 A66 2c blk, *rose* 1.00 1.00
a. Imperf., pair 2.50 2.50
b. Without overprint 2.25 2.25
c. Double overprint 2.50 2.50

A67

A68

1901 **Rose Overprint**

187 A67 1c blue 1.00 1.00
a. Imperf., pair 4.00 4.00
188 A68 2c brown 1.00 1.00
a. Imperf., pair 4.00 4.00
b. Without overprint 1.00 1.00

A69

A70

Sewing Machine or Regular Perf. 12, 12½

1902 **Magenta Overprint**

189 A69 5c violet 2.25 2.25
a. Without overprint 2.25 2.25
b. Double overprint 2.25 2.25
c. Imperf., pair 4.75 4.75
190 A70 10c yel brn 2.25 2.25
a. Double overprint 2.25 2.25
b. Imperf., pair 4.75 4.75
c. Without overprint 2.25 2.25
d. Printed on both sides 3.25 3.25

A71

A72

1902 **Magenta Overprint**

191 A71 5c yel brn 2.25 2.25
a. Without overprint 2.10 2.10
b. Imperf., pair 6.00 6.00
192 A71 10c black 1.75 1.75
a. Without overprint 1.50 1.50
b. Imperf., pair 9.00 9.00
193 A72 20c maroon 5.50 4.50
b. Imperf., pair 15.00 15.00
Nos. 191-193 (3) 9.50 8.50

Nos. 191-193 exist tête bêche. Value of 10c and 20c, each $15.

Washed examples of Nos. 167-174, 185-193 are offered as "without overprint."

Barranquilla Issues

Magdalena River — A75

Iron Quay at Sabanilla — A76

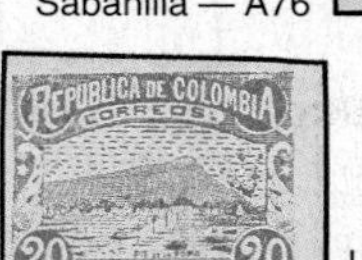
La Popa Hill — A77

1902-03 ***Imperf.***

194 A75 2c green 1.60 1.60
195 A75 2c dk bl 1.60 1.60
196 A75 2c rose 22.50 22.50
197 A76 10c scarlet 1.10 1.10
198 A76 10c orange 13.00 13.00
199 A76 10c rose 1.75 1.75
200 A76 10c maroon 1.90 1.90
201 A76 10c claret 1.90 1.90
202 A77 20c violet 3.50 3.50
a. Laid paper 9.50
203 A77 20c dl bl 9.50 9.50
204 A77 20c dl bl, *pink* *125.00 125.00*
205 A77 20c car rose 20.00 20.00
Nos. 194-205 (12) *203.35 203.35*

Sewing Machine Perf. and Perf. 12

194a A75 2c green 9.50 9.50
195a A75 2c dark blue 9.50 9.50
196a A75 2c carmine *47.50 47.50*
197a A76 10c scarlet 4.75 4.75
198a A76 10c orange *35.00 35.00*
199a A76 10c rose 6.50 6.50
200a A76 10c maroon 6.50 6.50
201a A76 10c claret 6.00 6.00
202b A77 20c purple .70 .70
c. 20c lilac .70 .70
203a A77 20c dull blue 9.50 9.50
204a A77 20c dull blue, *rose* *150.00 150.00*
205b A77 20c carmine rose *72.50 72.50*
Nos. 194a-205b (12) *357.95 357.95*

See Nos. 240-245.

Cruiser "Cartagena" — A78

Bolívar — A79

General Próspero Pinzón — A80

A81

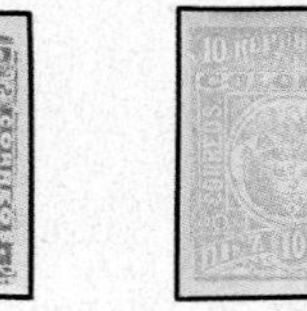
A82

1903-04 ***Imperf.***

209 A78 5c blue 2.75 2.75
210 A78 5c bister 4.50 4.50
211 A79 50c yellow 3.75 3.75
212 A79 50c green 4.50 4.50
213 A79 50c scarlet 4.50 4.50
214 A79 50c carmine 4.50 4.50
a. 50c rose 4.50 4.50
215 A79 50c pale brown 4.50 4.50
216 A80 1p yellow brn 1.60 1.60
217 A80 1p rose 2.50 2.50
218 A80 1p blue 2.50 2.50
219 A80 1p violet 25.00 25.00
220 A81 5p claret 5.50 5.50
221 A81 5p pale brown 8.00 8.00
222 A81 5p blue green 7.50 7.50
223 A82 10p pale green 7.75 7.75
224 A82 10p claret 25.00 25.00
Nos. 209-224 (16) 114.35 114.35

Nos. 216 and 217 measure 20½x26½mm and No. 218, 18x24mm. Stamps of this issue exist with forged perforations.

Perf. 12

209a A78 5c blue 9.50 9.50
210a A78 5c bister 9.50 9.50
211a A79 50c yellow 9.50 9.50
b. 50c orange 25.00 25.00
212a A79 50c green 25.00 25.00
213a A79 50c scarlet 11.50 11.50
214b A79 50c rose 11.50 11.50
215a A79 50c pale brown 11.50 11.50
216a A80 1p yellow brown 5.25 5.25
217a A80 1p rose 7.50 7.50
218a A80 1p blue 9.50 7.50
219a A80 1p violet 62.50 62.50
220a A81 5p claret 20.00 20.00
221a A81 5p pale brown 22.50 22.50
222a A81 5p blue green 22.50 22.50
223a A82 10p pale green 30.00 30.00
224a A82 10p claret 77.50 77.50
Nos. 209a-224a (16) 345.25 343.25

Laid Paper ***Imperf.***

240 A76 10c dk bl, *lil* 6.25 6.25
241 A76 10c dk bl, *bluish* 3.75 3.75
242 A76 10c dk bl, *brn* 3.75 3.75
243 A76 10c dk bl, *sal* 9.25 9.25
244 A76 10c dk bl, *grnsh bl* 5.00 5.00
245 A76 10c dk bl, *dp rose* 3.75 3.75
Nos. 240-245 (6) 31.75 31.75

Perf. 12

240a A76 10c dk bl, *lilac* 13.50 13.50
241a A76 10c dk bl, *bluish* 9.25 9.25
242a A76 10c dk bl, *brn* 9.25 9.25
243a A76 10c dk bl, *salmon* 72.50 72.50
244a A76 10c dk bl, *grnsh bl* 20.00 20.00
245a A76 10c dk bl, *deep rose* 9.25 9.25
Nos. 240a-245a (6) 133.75 133.75

A82a

Imperf., Sewing Machine Perf.

1902 **Typeset**

255 A82a 10c black, *rose* 3.50 3.50
256 A82a 20c blk, *orange* 2.50 2.50

This issue was printed in either Cali or Popayan.

Medellin Issue

A83

1902

257 A83 1c grn, *straw* .35 *.50*
258 A83 2c salmon, *rose* .35 *.50*
259 A83 5c dp bl, *grnsh* .35 *.50*
260 A83 10c pale brn, *straw* .35 *.50*
261 A83 20c pur, *rose* .45 *.50*
262 A83 50c dl rose, *grnsh* 2.25 *3.00*
263 A83 1p blk, *yellow* 4.50 *6.75*
264 A83 5p slate, *blue* 35.00 35.00
265 A83 10p dk brn, *rose* 22.50 22.50
Nos. 257-265 (9) 66.10 69.75

For overprint see No. L8.

Imperf., Pairs

257a A83 1c 11.00 11.00
258a A83 2c 11.00 11.00
259a A83 5c 11.00 11.00
260a A83 10c 11.00 11.00
261a A83 20c 11.00 11.00
262a A83 50c 11.00 11.00
263a A83 1p 27.50 27.50
264a A83 5p 80.00 80.00
265a A83 10p 50.00 50.00

Regular Issue

A84

A85

A86 A87

A88

A89

A90

A91

A92

1902 ***Imperf.***

266 A84 2c blk, *rose* .25 .25
267 A85 4c red, *grn* .25 .25
268 A86 5c grn, *grn* .25 .25
269 A87 10c blk, *pink* .25 .25
c. 10c blk, *rose* 1.10 1.10
270 A88 20c brn, *buff* .25 .25
271 A89 50c dk grn, *rose* 1.40 1.40
272 A90 1p pur, *buff* .60 .60
273 A91 5p grn, *bl* 4.25 4.25
274 A92 10p grn, *pale grn* 13.00 6.50
Nos. 266-274 (9) 20.50 14.00

For overprint see No. H4.

Sewing Machine Perf.

266a A84 2c blk, *rose* 1.90 1.90
267a A85 4c red, *grn* 1.60 1.60
268a A86 5c grn, *blue* 1.90 1.90
269a A87 10c blk, *pink* 1.90 1.90
270a A88 20c brn, *buff* 3.25 2.50
271a A89 50c dk grn, *rose* 6.50 5.25
272a A90 1p pur, *buff* 7.75 6.50
273a A91 5p grn, *blue* 35.00 35.00
274a A92 10p grn, *pale grn* 65.00 65.00
Nos. 266a-274a (9) 124.80 121.55

1903 ***Perf. 12***

266b A84 2c blk, *rose* 1.40 1.40
269b A87 10c blk, *pink* 1.60 1.60
270b A88 20c brn, *buff* 1.60 1.60
272b A90 1p pur, *buff* 3.25 3.25
273b A91 5p grn, *blue* 27.50 27.50
274b A92 10p grn, *pale grn* 52.50 45.00
Nos. 266b-274b (6) 87.85 80.35

1903 ***Imperf.***

284 A85 4c blue, *grn* .35 .35
285 A86 5c blue, *blue* .35 .35
286 A88 20c blue,*buff* .35 .35
288 A89 50c blue, *rose* 1.75 1.75
Nos. 284-288 (4) 2.80 2.80

Sewing Machine Perf.

284a A85 4c blue, *grn* 2.25 1.75
285a A86 5c blue, *blue* 2.25 1.75
286a A88 20c blue, *buff* 3.25 2.50
288a A89 50c blue, *rose* 6.50 5.75
Nos. 284a-288a (4) 14.25 11.75

Perf. 12

284b A85 4c blue, *grn* 2.50 2.50
285b A86 5c blue, *blue* 2.50 2.50
286b A88 20c blue, *buff* 3.50 3.50
288b A89 50c blue, *rose* 9.75 9.75
Nos. 284b-288b (4) 18.25 18.25

A93

1904 **Pelure Paper** ***Imperf.***

303 A93 ½c yellow brn 1.10 1.10
304 A90 1c blue green 1.10 1.10
a. 1c yellow green 1.10 1.10
306 A84 2c blue .90 .65
307 A86 5c carmine 1.00 1.00
308 A87 10c violet 1.10 .90
Nos. 303-308 (5) 5.20 4.75

For overprint see No. H13.

1904 ***Perf. 13***

303a A93 ½c yellow brown 4.25 4.25
304b A90 1c blue green 5.50 5.00
c. 1c yellow green 7.50 7.00
306a A84 2c blue 2.50 2.50

Perf. 12

307a A86 5c carmine 2.25 2.25
308a A87 10c violet 2.25 2.25
Nos. 303a-308a (5) 16.75 16.25

A94

A95

Pres. José Manuel Marroquín — A96

Imprint: "Lit. J.L.Arango Medellin. Col."

1904 **Wove Paper** ***Perf. 12***

314 A94 ½c yellow .85 .25
315 A94 1c green .85 .25
316 A94 2c rose .85 .25
317 A94 5c blue 1.40 .25
318 A94 10c violet 1.75 .25
319 A94 20c black 1.75 .25
320 A95 1p brown 19.00 3.00
321 A96 5p red & blk, *yel* 60.00 60.00
322 A96 10p bl & blk, *grnsh* 60.00 60.00
Nos. 314-322 (9) 146.45 124.50

Redrawn

314a A94 ½c .85 .25
315a A94 1c .85 .25
316a A94 2c .85 .25
317a A94 5c 1.40 .25
319a A94 20c 1.75 .25
Nos. 314a-319a (5) 5.70 1.25

Imperf., Pairs

314b A94 ½c 3.25 3.25
315b A94 1c 2.50 2.50
316b A94 2c 3.25 3.25
317b A94 5c 3.25 3.25
318a A94 10c 4.25 4.25
319b A94 20c 7.75 7.75
320a A95 1p 65.00 65.00
Nos. 314b-320a (7) 89.25 89.25

On the redrawn types, the imprint is close to the base of the design instead of being spaced from it. On the redrawn 2c and 5c, the lower end of the vertical white line below "OR" of "CORREOS" forms a hook which turns to the right instead of to the left as in the originals.

See Nos. 325-330. For surcharges see Nos. 351-354, L1-L7, L9-L13, L15-L25.

A97

100p has different frame.

1903 ***Imperf.***

323 A97 50p org yel, *pale pink* 92.50 92.50
324 A97 100p dk bl, *dk rose* 77.50 77.50

Imprint: "Lit. Nacional"

Perf. 10, 13, 13½ and Compound

1908

325 A94 ½c orange .85 .25
a. ½c yellow .85 .25
b. Imperf., pair 2.50 1.90
c. Without imprint 5.25 5.25
326 A94 1c yel grn .75 .25
a. Without imprint .75 .25
d. Imperf., pair 4.00 3.25
327 A94 2c red .75 .25
a. 2c carmine .75 .25
b. Imperf., pair 4.00 3.25
328 A94 5c blue .60 .25
a. Imperf., pair 4.25 5.25
329 A94 10c violet *50.00* 1.00
330 A94 20c gray blk *50.00* 1.00
Nos. 325-330 (6) *102.95* 3.00

The above stamps may be easily distinguished from those of 1904 by the perforation, by the height of the design, 24mm instead of 23mm, and by the "Lit. Nacional" imprint.

Camilo Torres A99

Policarpa Salavarrieta A100

Bolívar Demanding Liberation of Slaves — A105

Designs: 2c, Nariño. 5c, Bolívar. 10c, Francisco José de Caldas. 20c, Francisco de Paula Santander. 10p, Bolívar Resigning.

1910, Aug. **Engr.** ***Perf. 12***

331 A99 ½c violet & blk .50 .30
a. Center inverted 390.00 390.00
332 A100 1c deep green .40 .25
333 A100 2c scarlet .40 .25
334 A100 5c deep blue 1.25 .45
335 A100 10c plum 10.00 5.00
336 A100 20c black brn 15.00 5.50
337 A105 1p dk violet 85.00 25.00
338 A105 10p claret 325.00 250.00
Nos. 331-338 (8) 437.55 286.75

Colombian independence centenary.

Caldas A107

Monument to Battle of Boyacá A113

View of Cartagena A114

Coat of Arms A118

Designs: 1c, Torres. 2c, Narino. 4c, Santander. 5c, Bolivar. 10c, Jose Maria Cordoba. 1p, Sucre. 2p, Rufino Cuervo. 5p, Antonio Ricaurte y Lozano.

1917 **Engr.** ***Perf. 14***

339 A107 ½c bister .35 .25
340 A107 1c green .30 .25
341 A107 2c car rose .30 .25
342 A107 4c violet .90 .30
343 A107 5c dull blue 3.00 .25
344 A107 10c gray 3.00 .25
345 A113 20c red 1.50 .25
346 A114 50c carmine 1.75 .25
347 A107 1p brt blue 12.00 .40
348 A107 2p orange 13.50 .45
349 A107 5p gray 40.00 11.00
350 A118 10p dk brown 47.50 11.50
Nos. 339-350 (12) 124.10 25.40

The 1c, 5c, 10c, 50c, 2p, 5p and 10p also exist perf. 11½ and 11½ compounded with 14.

Litho. varieties of Nos. 343, 345 and 346 are counterfeits made to defraud the government.

Imperforate examples of Nos. 339-350 are not known to have been regularly issued.

See Nos. 373-374, 400-405. For overprints and surcharges see Nos. 369-370, 377, 409-410, 440, C1, O3, O5-O9.

Nos. 318-319, 329-330 Surcharged in Red

1918 **On Issue of 1904**

351 A94 ½c on 20c black 1.25 .35
352 A94 3c on 10c violet 3.00 .60

On Issue of 1908

353 A94 ½c on 20c gray blk 10.00 6.25
354 A94 3c on 10c violet 15.00 5.00
Nos. 351-354 (4) 29.25 12.20

Nos. 351-354 inclusive exist with surcharge reading up or down. On one stamp in each sheet the letter "S" in "Especie" is omitted. All denominations exist with a small zero before the decimal in the surcharge.

A119

1918 **Litho.** ***Perf. 13½***

358 A119 3c red .95 .25
a. Imperf., pair 5.00 5.00

A120

1920 **Engr.** ***Perf. 14***

359 A120 3c red, *org* .40 .25
a. Imperf., pair 3.75 3.75

See No. 371-372. For surcharge see No. 453.

A121

A122

A123

Perf. 10, 13½ and Compound

1920-21 **Litho.**

360 A121 ½c yellow 1.40 .50
361 A121 1c green .85 .25
362 A121 2c red .65 .25
363 A122 3c green .65 .25
a. 3c yellow green .65 .25
364 A121 5c blue 1.25 .25
365 A121 10c violet 6.00 1.50
366 A121 20c deep green 6.75 4.00
367 A123 50c dark red 8.50 4.00
Nos. 360-367 (8) 26.05 11.00

The tablet with "PROVISIONAL" was added separately to each design on the various lithographic stones and its position varies slightly on different stamps in the sheet. For some values there were two or more stones, on which the tablet was placed at various angles.

Nos. 360-366 exist imperf.

See No. 375.

No. 342 Surcharged in Red

a

(15mm wide) — b

1921

369 A107 (a) 3c on 4c violet .95 .25
a. Double surcharge 22.50
370 A107 (b) 3c on 4c violet 3.75 2.00

See No. 377.

Types of 1917-21

1923-24 **Engr.** ***Perf. 13½***

371 A120 1½c chocolate 1.25 .60
372 A120 3c blue .50 .25
373 A107 5c claret ('24) 3.00 .25
374 A107 10c blue 9.25 .50

Litho.

375 A121 10c dark blue 12.50 7.25
Nos. 371-375 (5) 26.50 8.85

No. 342 Surcharged in Red

(18mm wide)

1924

377 A107 3c on 4c vio 3.75 1.50
a. Double surcharge 22.50
b. Double surch., one invtd. 22.50
c. With added surch. "3cs." in red

A124

1924-25 **Litho.** ***Perf. 10, 10x13½***

379 A124 1c red .85 .25
380 A124 3c dp blue ('25) .85 .25

Exist imperf. Value, each pair $6.25.

A125

A126

Black, Red or Green Srch. & Ovpt.

Imprint of Waterlow & Sons

1925 ***Perf. 14, 14½***

382 A125 1c on 3c bis brn .70 .25
383 A126 4c violet (R) .50 .25
a. Inverted surcharge 12.50 8.75

Imprint of American Bank Note Co.

Perf. 12

384 A125 1c on 3c bis brn 7.50 6.25
a. Inverted surcharge 19.00 19.00
385 A126 4c violet (G) .50 .30
a. Inverted overprint 12.50 9.50
Nos. 382-385 (4) 9.20 7.05

Correos
Provisional

Revenue stamps of basic types A125 and A126 were handstamped as above in violet or blue by the Cali post office in 1925, but were not authorized by the government. Denominations so overprinted are 1c, 2c, 3c, 4c and 5c.

A127 A128

Perf. 10, 13½x10

1926 Litho. Wmk. 194
395 A127 1c yellow green .50 .25
396 A128 4c blue .55 .25

Exist imperf. Value, each pair $5.

Types of 1917 and

Sabana Station — A129

1926-29 Unwmk. Engr. *Perf. 14*
400 A107 4c deep blue .50 .25
401 A118 8c dark blue .60 .25
402 A107 30c olive bister 6.00 .70
403 A129 40c brn & yel brn 9.25 1.25
404 A107 5p violet 9.25 .90
a. Perf. 11 ('29) 12.00 1.00
405 A118 10p green 15.00 2.50
a. Perf. 11 ('29) 30.00 4.75
Nos. 400-405 (6) 40.60 5.85

For surcharges & overprint see Nos. 409-410, 453, O4.

Death of Bolívar A130

1930, Dec. 17 *Perf. 12½*
408 A130 4c dk blue & blk .80 .35

Cent. of the death of Simón Bolívar. See Nos. C80-C82.

Nos. 400 and 402 Surcharged in Red or Dark Blue

1932, Jan. 20 *Perf. 14*
409 A107 1c on 4c dp bl (R) .30 .25
a. Inverted surcharge 5.25 5.25
410 A107 20c on 30c ol bis 10.00 .70
a. Inverted surcharge 21.00
b. Double surcharge 21.00

Emerald Mine — A131

Oil Wells — A132

Coffee Cultivation A133

Platinum Mine — A134

Gold Mining — A135

Christopher Columbus — A136

Imprint: "Waterlow & Sons Ltd. Londres"

1932 Wmk. 229 *Perf. 12½*
411 A131 1c green .60 .25
412 A132 2c red .60 .25
413 A133 5c brown .70 .25
414 A134 8c blue blk 4.75 .60
415 A135 10c yellow 3.50 .25
416 A136 20c dk blue 10.00 .40
Nos. 411-416 (6) 20.15 2.00

See Nos. 441-442, 464-466a, 517. For surcharges see Nos. 455, 527, O1, O10-O11, O13, RA30.

Pedro de Heredia — A137

Perf. 11½

1934, Jan. 10 Unwmk. Litho.
417 A137 1c dark green 3.00 .80
418 A137 5c chocolate 3.75 .65
419 A137 8c dark blue 3.00 .80
Nos. 417-419 (3) 9.75 2.25

Cartagena, 400th anniv. See Nos. C111-C114.

Coffee Picking — A138

1934, Dec. Engr. *Perf. 12*
420 A138 5c brown 3.00 .25

Soccer — A139

Condor — A145

Allegory of Olympic Games at Barranquilla — A140

Foot Race A141

Tennis A142

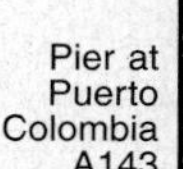

Pier at Puerto Colombia A143

View of the Bay A144

Designs: 4c, Discus Thrower. 10c, Hurdling. 15c, Athlete in stadium. 18c, Baseball. 24c, Swimming. 50c, View of Barranquilla. 1p, Post and Telegraph Building. 2p, Monument to Flag. 5p, Coat of Arms.

1935, Jan. 26 Litho. *Perf. 11½*
421 A139 2c bluish grn & buff 1.60 .50
422 A139 4c deep green 1.60 .50
423 A140 5c dk brn & yel 1.60 .50
a. Horiz. pair, imperf. btwn. 240.00
424 A141 7c dk carmine 3.00 1.75
425 A142 8c blk & pink 2.50 2.50
426 A141 10c brown & bl 3.50 1.75
427 A143 12c indigo 4.25 3.00
428 A141 15c bl & red brn 7.25 5.50
429 A141 18c dk vio & buff 10.00 8.25
430 A144 20c purple & grn 8.50 7.00
431 A144 24c bluish grn & ultra 8.50 6.75
432 A144 50c ultra & buff 13.00 10.00
433 A145 1p drab & blue 110.00 60.00
434 A145 2p dull grn & gray 125.00 100.00
435 A145 5p pur blk & bl 425.00 450.00
436 A145 10p black & gray 500.00 525.00
Nos. 421-436 (16) 1,225. 1,183.

3rd Natl. Olympic Games, Barranquilla. Counterfeits of 10p exist.

Oil Wells — A155

Gold Mining — A157

Imprint: "American Bank Note Co."

1935, Mar. Unwmk. Engr. *Perf. 12*
437 A155 2c carmine rose .45 .25
439 A157 10c deep orange 25.00 .25

See Nos. 468, 470, 498, 516. For surcharge and overprints see Nos. 496, 596, O2.

No. 347 Surcharged in Black

1935, Aug. *Perf. 14*
440 A107 12c on 1p brt bl 4.75 1.50

Types of 1932
Imprint: "Lit. Nacional Bogotá"

1935-36 Litho. *Perf. 11, 11½, 12½*
441 A131 1c lt green .25 .25
a. Imperf., pair 6.00
442 A133 5c brown ('36) .70 .25
a. Imperf., pair 6.00 4.00

For overprints and surcharges, see Nos. 527, O1.

Bolívar A159

Tequendama Falls A160

Wmk. Wavy Lines. (229)

1937 Engr. *Perf. 12½*
443 A159 1c deep green .25 .25
a. Perf. 14 .25 .25
444 A160 12c deep blue 5.00 1.50

See No. 570. For surcharges and overprints see Nos. 454, 456, C231, C326, O12.

Soccer Player A161

Discus Thrower A162

Runner — A163

1937, Jan. 4 Photo. Unwmk.
445 A161 3c lt green 1.40 .85
446 A162 10c carmine rose 3.75 1.75
447 A163 1p black 32.50 26.00
Nos. 445-447 (3) 37.65 28.60

National Olympic Games, Manizales. For surcharge see No. 452.

Exposition Palace — A164

Stadium at Barranquilla A165

Monument to the Colors A166

1937, Jan. 4
448 A164 5c violet brown 2.50 .40
449 A165 15c blue 7.00 5.00
450 A166 50c orange brn 20.00 9.00
Nos. 448-450 (3) 29.50 14.40

Barranquilla National Exposition.

Stamps of 1926-37 Surcharged in Black

Perf. 12½, 14 (#453)

1937-38 Unwmk.
452 A161 1c on 3c lt grn 1.00 1.00
a. Inverted surcharge 5.00 2.25
453 A118 5c on 8c dk bl .55 .45
a. Inverted surcharge 5.00 2.25

Wmk. 229
454 A160 2c on 12c dp bl .55 .45
455 A134 5c on 8c bl blk .65 .65
a. Invtd. surcharge 5.00 2.00
456 A160 10c on 12c dp bl ('38) 5.50 1.00
a. Dbl. surcharge 11.00 11.00
Nos. 452-456 (5) 8.25 3.55

Calle del Arco — A168

Entrance to Church of the Rosary — A169

Arms of Bogotá A170

Gonzálo Jiménez de Quesada A171

Bochica A172

Santo Domingo Convent A173

Mass of the Conquistadors — A174

1938, July 27 Unwmk. *Perf. 12½*

457	A168	1c yellow green	.25	.25
458	A169	2c scarlet	.25	.25
459	A170	5c brown blk	.40	.25
460	A171	10c brown	.75	.50
461	A172	15c brt blue	3.75	1.60
462	A173	20c brt red vio	3.75	1.75
463	A174	1p red brown	50.00	29.00
		Nos. 457-463 (7)	59.15	33.60

Bogotá, 400th anniversary.

Types of 1932
Imprint: "Litografia Nacional Bogotá"

1938, Dec. 5 Litho. *Perf. 10½, 11*

464	A132	2c rose	1.00	.35
465	A135	10c yellow	2.50	.35
466	A136	20c dull blue	10.00	1.25
a.		20c dark blue, perf. 12½ ('44)	62.50	6.25
		Nos. 464-466 (3)	13.50	1.95

Types of 1935 and

Bolívar A175

Coffee Picking A176

Arms of Colombia A177

Christopher Columbus A178

Caldas A179

Sabana Station A180

Imprint: "American Bank Note Co."

Wmk. 255

1939, Mar. 3 Engr. *Perf. 12*

467	A175	1c green	.25	.25
468	A155	2c car rose	.25	.25
469	A176	5c dull brown	.25	.25
470	A157	10c deep orange	.50	.25
471	A177	15c dull blue	1.75	.25
472	A178	20c violet blk	19.00	.25
473	A179	30c olive bister	5.50	.35
474	A180	40c bister brn	17.00	3.75
		Nos. 467-474 (8)	44.50	5.60

See Nos. 497-499, 515, 518, 574. For surcharges and overprints see Nos. 506-507, 520-522, 596, RA26, RA47.

Gen. Santander A181

Allegory A182

Gen. Santander A183

Statue at Cúcuta A184

Birthplace of Santander A185

Church at Rosario A186

Paya — A187

Bridge at Boyacá — A188

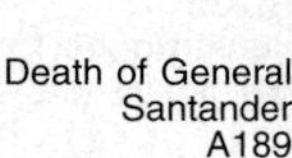

Death of General Santander A189

Invasion of the Liberators A190

Perf. 13x13½, 13½x13

1940, May 6 Engr. Wmk. 229

475	A181	1c olive green	.25	.25
476	A182	2c dk carmine	.50	.35
477	A183	5c sepia	.25	.25
478	A184	8c carmine	1.75	1.50
479	A185	10c orange yel	.80	.60
480	A186	15c dark blue	2.00	1.40
481	A187	20c green	2.75	2.00
482	A188	50c violet	6.00	5.00
483	A189	1p deep rose	20.00	17.50
484	A190	2p orange	62.50	60.00
		Nos. 475-484 (10)	96.80	88.85

Death of General Francisco Santander, cent.

Tobacco Plant A194

Gen. Santander A195

Garcia Rovira — A196

R. Galan — A197

Antonio Sucre — A198

1940-43 Engr. Wmk. 255 *Perf. 12*

488	A194	8c rose car & grn	1.25	.65
489	A195	15c dp blue ('43)	1.25	.25
490	A196	20c slate ('41)	4.75	.50
491	A197	40c brown bis ('41)	2.75	.50
492	A198	1p black	5.00	1.25
		Nos. 488-492 (5)	15.00	3.15

See Nos. 500, 554. For overprint see No. RA28.

Arms of Palmira — A199

Unwmk.

1942, July 4 Litho. *Perf. 11*

493	A199	30c claret	5.50	.75

8th Natl. Agricultural Exposition, held at Palmira.

Paradise of Isaacs, Palmira — A200

1942, July 4

494	A200	50c lt blue grn	5.50	.85

Issued in honor of the writer, Jorge Isaacs.

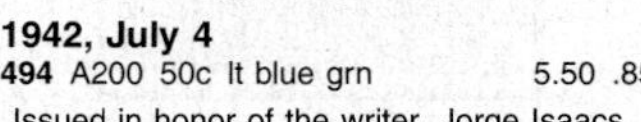

Signing Treaty of the Wisconsin A201

1942, Nov. 21 *Perf. 10½*

495	A201	10c dull orange	3.75	.50
a.		"2. XI.1902" instead of "21. XI. 1902"	22.50	22.50
b.		Perf. 12	6.00	6.00

40th anniv. of the signing of the Treaty of the Wisconsin, Nov. 21, 1902.

No. 470 Surcharged in Black

1944 Wmk. 255 *Perf. 12*

496	A157	5c on 10c dp org	.25	.25

Counterfeits exist of No. 496 with inverted or double surcharge.

Types of 1935-41 and

National Shrine — A202

San Pedro Alejandrino A203

Imprint: "Columbian Bank Note Co."

1944-45 Unwmk. Engr. *Perf. 11*

497	A175	1c green	.25	.25
498	A155	2c rose	.25	.25
499	A176	5c dull brown	.25	.25
500	A196	20c gray black	3.75	.75
501	A202	30c dl ol grn ('45)	2.25	1.25
502	A203	50c rose	2.25	1.25
		Nos. 497-502 (6)	9.00	4.00

No. 499 Surcharged in Black

1944, Oct.

506	A176	1c on 5c dull brn	.25	.25
507	A176	2c on 5c dull brn	.25	.25

Nos. 506 and 507 exist with inverted or double surcharge, created by favor.

Flag — A204

Arms — A205

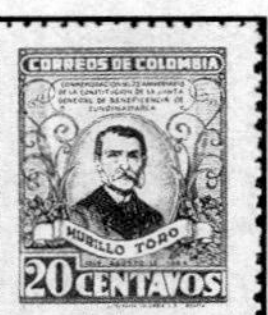
Murillo Toro — A206

Hospital of St. John of God A207

Virrey Solis A208

1944, Oct. 10 **Litho.**

508 A204 2c ultra & bis .30 .25
a. Sheet of 18 15.00
b. Imperf., pair 15.00
509 A205 5c ultra & bis .30 .25
a. Sheet of 22 18.00
b. Imperf., pair 15.00
510 A206 20c blk & bluish grn 1.00 .80
a. Sheet of 8 16.00
b. Imperf., pair 22.50
511 A207 40c blk & red 4.00 3.50
a. Sheet of 4 27.50
512 A208 1p blk & red 11.00 10.00
a. Sheet of 2 32.50
Nos. 508-512 (5) 16.60 14.80

Souvenir Sheet

Perf. 11x11½ All Around, Stamps Imperf.

513 Sheet of 5, #508-512 25.00 *40.00*
Never hinged 40.00

75th anniv. of Gen. Benevolent Assoc. of Cundinamarca.

Nos. 508-513 were printed in composite sheets containing one each of Nos. 508a, 509a, 510a, 511a and 512a, and two of 513. Fifty of these were presented to government officials.

Murillo Toro — A210

1944, Nov. 10 ***Perf. 11***

514 A210 5c lt brown .40 .25

Types of 1932-39 and

San Pedro Alejandrino A211

Imprint: "Litografia Nacional Bogota"

1944 **Litho.** ***Perf. 12½***

515 A175 1c dp green .25 .25
a. 1c olive green .35 .25
b. Imperf., pair 1.75 1.75
516 A155 2c dk carmine .25 .25
a. Imperf., pair 1.75 1.75
517 A135 10c yellow org 3.50 .45
518 A179 30c gray olive 12.00 1.75
a. Imperf., pair 35.00
519 A211 50c rose 12.00 5.25
Nos. 515-519 (5) 28.00 7.95

No. 469 Overprinted in Green, Blue or Red

Wmk. 255

1945, July 19 **Engr.** ***Perf. 12***

520 A176 5c dull brn (G) .40 .25
521 A176 5c dull brn (R) .40 .25
522 A176 5c dull brn (Bl) .40 .25
Nos. 520-522 (3) 1.20 .75

Portraits are Joseph Stalin, Franklin D. Roosevelt and Winston Churchill.

Nos. 520-522 exist with overprint inverted. Value, $20 each.

Clock Tower, Cartagena — A212

1945, Nov. 15

523 A212 50c olive black 4.25 1.60

For overprints see Nos. 543-544.

Sierra Nevada of Santa Marta A213

Designs: 30c, Seaplane Tolima. 50c, San Sebastian Fort, Cartagena.

Unwmk.

1945, Dec. 14 **Litho.** ***Perf. 11***

524 A213 20c light green 2.50 1.40
525 A213 30c pale blue 2.50 1.40
526 A213 50c salmon pink 2.50 1.40
Nos. 524-526 (3) 7.50 4.20

25th anniv. of the 1st airmail service in America, according to the inscription, but earlier services are known to have existed.

No. 442 Surcharged in Black

1946, Mar. 8 ***Perf. 12½***

527 A133 1c on 5c brown .25 .25
a. Inverted surcharge 5.00
b. Perf. 11x11½ 6.00 6.00

Gen. Antonio Jose de Sucre — A216

Wmk. 255

1946, Apr. 16 **Engr.** ***Perf. 12***

Size: 19x26½mm

528 A216 1c brn & turq grn .25 .25
529 A216 2c vio & rose car .25 .25

Size: 23x31mm

530 A216 5c sepia & blue .25 .25
531 A216 9c dk grn & red .80 *1.25*
532 A216 10c ultra & org .65 .50
533 A216 20c blk & dp org .65 .50
534 A216 30c brn red & grn .90 .40
535 A216 40c ol blk & red vio .90 .40
536 A216 50c dp brn & vio .90 .40
Nos. 528-536 (9) 5.55 4.20

Map of South America — A217

Unwmk.

1946, June 7 **Litho.** ***Perf. 11***

537 A217 15c ultra .65 .50
a. Imperf., pair 5.00

National Observatory — A218

1946, Aug.

538 A218 5c fawn .30 .25
a. Imperf., pair 6.00

See No. 565.

Andrés Bello — A219

Wmk. 255

1946, Sept. 3 **Engr.** ***Perf. 12***

539 A219 3c sepia .25 .25
540 A219 10c orange .60 .35
541 A219 15c slate black .70 .35
Nos. 539-541,C145 (4) 1.80 1.20

Bello (1781-1865), poet and educator.

Joaquín de Cayzedo y Cuero — A220

1946, Sept. 20 **Wmk. 229** ***Perf. 12½***

542 A220 2p bluish green 4.50 1.25

See No. 568. For surcharge see No. 613.

Type of 1945, Overprinted in Black or Green

1946, Dec. 6 **Wmk. 255** ***Perf. 12***

543 A212 50c red (Bk) 4.00 2.75
a. Double overprint 25.00
544 A212 50c red (G) 4.00 2.75
a. Double overprint 25.00

5th Central American and Caribbean Championship Games.

Coffee — A221

Engraved and Lithographed

1947, Jan. 10 **Wmk. 229** ***Perf. 12½***

545 A221 5c multicolored .40 .25

Colombian Orchid: Masdevallia Nycterina A222

Designs (Orchids): 2c, Miltonia vexillaria. No. 548, Cattleya chocoensis. No. 549, Odontoglossum crispum. No. 550, Cattleya dowiana aurea. 10c, Cattleya labiata trianae.

1947, Feb. 7 **Wmk. 255** ***Perf. 12***

546 A222 1c multicolored 1.25 .25
547 A222 2c multicolored 1.25 .25
548 A222 5c multicolored 1.25 .25
549 A222 5c multicolored 1.25 .25
550 A222 5c multicolored 1.25 .25
551 A222 10c multicolored 2.25 .35
Nos. 546-551 (6) 8.50 1.60

Antonio Nariño — A228

Alberto Urdaneta y Urdaneta — A229

Perf. 12½

1947, May 9 **Litho.** **Unwmk.**

552 A228 5c blue, *grnsh* .40 .25
553 A229 10c red brn, *grnsh* .40 .25
Nos. 552-553,C146-C147 (4) 2.10 1.30

4th Pan-American Press Congress, 1946.

Sucre Type of 1940

1947 **Wmk. 255** **Engr.** ***Perf. 12***

554 A198 1p violet 2.75 1.25

José Celestino Mutis and José Jerónimo Triana A230

Miguel A. Caro and Rufino J. Cuervo — A231

1947 **Wmk. 229** ***Perf. 12½***

555 A230 25c olive green .50 .40
556 A231 3p dark purple 4.00 3.75

See Nos. 567, 569. For surcharge see No. 610.

Metropolitan Cathedral, Plaza Bolívar, Bogotá — A232

National Capitol A233

Ministry of Foreign Affairs A234

A235

1948, Apr. 2

557 A232 5c black brown .25 .25
558 A233 10c orange .60 .55
559 A234 15c dark blue .60 .55
Nos. 557-559,C148-C149 (5) 2.70 2.60

Miniature Sheet

Imperf

560 A235 50c slate 2.00 1.60

9th Pan-American Conf., Bogotá.

No. RA5A Overprinted in Black

1948 Unwmk. *Perf. 12½*
Without Gum

561 PT3 1c yellow orange .25 .25

The letter "C" is the initial of "CORREOS." Exists with inverted overprint. Value $5.

Nos. RA33, RA24 and RA25 Overprinted in Black

1948 Wmk. 255 *Perf. 12.*

562 PT6 1c olive .25 .25
563 PT6 2c green .25 .25
564 PT6 20c brown .25 .25
Nos. 562-564 (3) .75 .75

Nos. 561-564 exist with inverted and double overprints.

Observatory Type of 1946
Unwmk.

1948, June 30 Litho. *Perf. 11*

565 A218 5c blue .25 .25

Simón Bolívar — A236

Wmk. 255

1948, May 29 Engr. *Perf. 12*

566 A236 15c green .40 .25

Types of 1946-47

1948 Unwmk. *Perf. 12½*

567 A230 25c green .25 .25
568 A220 2p dp green .55 .25
569 A231 3p dp red violet .55 .35
Nos. 567-569 (3) 1.35 .85

Falls Type of 1937

1948 Wmk. 229

570 A160 10c red .25 .25

For overprints see Nos. C231, C326.

Carlos Martinez Silva — A237

Perf. 13½

1948, Dec. 21 Unwmk. Litho.

571 A237 40c carmine .40 .25

Juan de Dios Carrasquilla A238

1949, May 20 Wmk. 229 *Perf. 12½*

572 A238 5c bister .35 .25

75th anniv. of the foundation of the Colombian Soc. of Agriculture.

Julio Garavito Armero — A239

Wmk. 229

1949, Apr. 24 Engr. *Perf. 12*

573 A239 4c green .35 .25

Issued to honor Julio Garavito Armero (1865-1920), mathematician.

Coffee Type of 1939
Imprint: "American Bank Note Co."

1949, Aug. 4 Wmk. 255

574 A176 5c blue .25 .25

Arms of Colombia — A240

1949, Oct. 7 Unwmk. *Perf. 13*

575 A240 15c blue .25 .25

Issued to honor the new Constitution. See Nos. C164-C165.

Shield and Tree — A241

1949, Oct. 13 Wmk. 229 *Perf. 12½*

576 A241 5c olive .25 .25

4th anniv. of Colombia's 1st Forestry Cong. and propaganda for the government's reforestation program.

Francisco Javier Cisneros — A242

1949, Dec. 15 Photo. Unwmk.

577 A242 50c red vio & yel 1.10 .60
578 A242 50c green & vio 1.10 .60
579 A242 50c brown & lt bl 1.10 .60
Nos. 577-579 (3) 3.30 1.80

50th anniv. (in 1948) of the death of Francisco Javier Cisneros.

Masdevallia Chimaera A243

Odontoglossum Crispum — A244

Eastern Hemisphere — A245

Designs: 3c, Cattleya labiata trianae. 4c, Masdevallia nycterina. 5c, Cattleya dowiana aurea. 11c, Miltonia vexillaria. 18c, Santo Domingo post office.

1950, Aug. 22 Photo. *Perf. 13*

580 A243 1c brown .25 .25
581 A244 2c violet .25 .25
582 A243 3c rose lilac .30 .25
583 A243 4c emerald .40 .25
584 A243 5c red orange .60 .25
585 A244 11c red 1.75 1.25
586 A244 18c ultra 2.75 .50
Nos. 580-586 (7) 6.30 3.00

Miniature Sheet

Imperf

587 A245 50c orange yel 2.00 2.00

75th anniv. (in 1949) of the UPU. See No. C199. For surcharge see No. C232.

Antonio Baraya — A246

Perf. 12½

1950, Nov. 27 Unwmk. Engr.

588 A246 2c red .25 .25

Colombian Farm A247

1950, Dec. 28 Photo. *Perf. 11½*

589 A247 5c dp car & buff .25 .25
590 A247 5c bl grn & gray .25 .25
591 A247 5c vio bl & gray .25 .25
Nos. 589-591 (3) .75 .75

Issued to publicize rural life.

Arms of Bogotá A248

Arms of Colombia A249

Perf. 12x12½

1950, Dec. 28 Engr. Wmk. 255

592 A248 5p deep green 2.75 1.50
593 A249 10p red orange 6.75 2.00

Catalogue values for unused stamps in this section, from this point to the end of the section, are for Never Hinged items.

Map and Badge — A250

Perf. 12½x13

1951, Jan. 30 Photo. Unwmk.

594 A250 20c red, yel & bl .55 .25

60th anniversary (in 1947) of the formation of the Colombian Society of Engineers.

Guillermo Valencia — A251

1951, Oct. 20 Engr. *Perf. 13x13½*

595 A251 25c black 1.10 .25

Issued to honor Guillermo Valencia (1873-1943), newspaper founder, governor of Cauca, presidential candidate, author.

No. 468 Overprinted in Black

1951, Dec. 11 Wmk. 255 *Perf. 12*

596 A155 2c carmine rose .30 .25

Issued to publicize the reversion of the Mares oil concession to Colombia.

Nicolas Osorio — A252

No. 598, Pompilio Martinez. No. 599, Ezequiel Uricoechea. No. 600, Jose M. Lombana.

Perf. 11½

1952, Aug. 6 Unwmk. Engr.
Various Frames

597 A252 1c deep blue .25 .25
598 A252 1c deep blue .25 .25
599 A252 1c deep blue .25 .25
600 A252 1c deep blue .25 .25
Nos. 597-600 (4) 1.00 1.00

Nos. 597-600 were printed in a single sheet containing four panes of twenty-five each, separated by double rows of ornamental tabs. Although inscribed "sobretasa," the stamps were for ordinary postage.

Types of Postal Tax Stamps of 1945-50 and

Communications Building
A253 A253a

1952 *Perf. 12*
601 A253 5c ultra .35 .25

Wmk. 255

602 PT10 20c brown 10.00 4.50
603 PT6 25c dk gray *42.50 42.50*
604 PT10 25c blue green 1.00 .25
605 A253a 50c orange yel 25.00 13.00
606 A253a 1p rose carmine 2.25 .30
607 A253a 2p lilac rose 25.00 9.75
608 A253a 2p violet 3.00 .65
Nos. 601-608 (8) 109.10 71.20

Although inscribed "sobretasa," Nos. 601-608 were issued for ordinary postage.
For surcharges see Nos. 612, RA48.

Cathedral of Manizales — A254

Perf. 11½
1952, Oct. 10 Photo. Unwmk.
609 A254 23c blue & gray blk .50 .25

Centenary of city of Manizales.
For surcharge see No. 619.

No. 555 Surcharged in Blue

1952, Oct. 30 Wmk. 229 *Perf. 12½*
610 A230 15c on 25c olive green .45 .25

Latin American Siderurgical Conf., 1952.
See No. C226.

Queen Isabella I and Monument A255

Perf. 12½
1953, Mar. 10 Unwmk. Engr.
611 A255 23c blue & black .95 .70

5th cent. of the birth of Queen Isabella I of Spain.
For surcharge see No. 693.

Nos. 606 and 568 Surcharged with New Values in Dark Blue

1953, Oct. 19 Wmk. 255
612 A253a 40c on 1p rose car 1.50 .25
613 A220 50c on 2p dp green 1.50 .25

Manuel Ancizar A256

Portraits: 23c, José Jeronimo Triana. 30c, Manuel Ponce de Leon. 1p, Agustin Codazzi.

Perf. 12½x13
1953, Nov. Engr. Unwmk.
Frames in Black

614 A256 14c rose red .65 .65
615 A256 23c ultra .55 .25
616 A256 30c chocolate .45 .25
617 A256 1p emerald .45 .25
Nos. 614-617 (4) 2.10 1.40

Cent. (in 1950) of the establishment of the Chorographic Commission. For surcharges and overprint see Nos. 620, 687, 690, 692, C284.

Murillo Toro and Map — A257

Black Surcharge
Engraved and Lithographed

1953, Dec. 12 Wmk. 255 *Perf. 12*
618 A257 5c on 5p multi .40 .25

2nd Natl. Phil. Exhib., Bogotá, Dec. 1953. See No. C237.

Nos. 609 and 614 Surcharged with New Value or New Value and Ornaments

1953 Unwmk. *Perf. 11½, 12½x13*
619 A254 5c on 23c (C) .45 .25
620 A256 5c on 14c (Bk) .45 .25

No. 614 surcharged "CINCO" in blue is listed as No. 687.

Symbolical of St. Francis Receiving Christ's Wounds — A258

1954, Apr. 23 Photo. *Perf. 11½*
621 A258 5c sepia & green .40 .25

400th anniversary of the establishment of Colombia's first Franciscan community.

Soldier, Map and Arms A259

1954, June 13 Engr. *Perf. 13*
622 A259 5c dull blue .25 .25

1st anniv. of the assumption of the presidency by Gen. Gustavo Rojas Pinilla. See Nos. C255, 637a.

Sports Emblem — A260

Design: 10c, Stadium and athlete holding arms of Colombia.

1954, July 18 Unwmk.
623 A260 5c deep blue .60 .25
624 A260 10c red .90 .25
Nos. 623-624,C256-C257 (4) 3.60 1.10

7th Natl. Athletic Games, Cali, July 1954.

History Academy Seal — A261

1954, July 24
625 A261 5c ultra & green .30 .25

50th anniversary (in 1952) of the Colombian Academy of History.

Convent and Cell of St. Peter Claver — A262

1954, Sept. 9
627 A262 5c dark green .25 .25
a. Souvenir sheet 8.00 *12.00*

300th anniv. of the death of St. Peter Claver.
No. 627a contains one stamp similar to No. 627, but printed in greenish black. Sheet size: 121x129½mm. See Nos. C258-C258a.

Mercury — A263

1954, Oct. 29
628 A263 5c orange .55 .25
Nos. 628,C259-C260 (3) 1.65 .75

1st Intl. Fair and Exhibition, Bogota, 1954.

Tapestry Madonna A264

College Cloister A265

Designs: 10c, Brother Cristobal de Torres. 20c, College chapel and arms.

Perf. 12½x11½, 11½x12½
1954, Dec. 6
629 A264 5c orange & blk .40 .25
630 A264 10c blue .40 .25
631 A265 15c violet brn .40 .25
632 A265 20c black & brn 1.00 .35
a. Souvenir sheet 6.50 *10.50*
Nos. 629-632,C263-C266 (8) 6.65 2.55

Founding of the Senior College of Our Lady of the Rosary, Bogota, 300th anniv. (in 1953).
No. 632a contains four stamps similar to Nos. 629-632, but printed in different colors: 5c yellow and black, 10c green, 15c dull violet, 20c black and light-blue.

Steel Mill — A266

1954, Dec. 12 *Perf. 12½x13*
633 A266 5c ultra & blk .50 .25

Issued to mark the opening of the Paz del Rio steel mill, October 1954. See No. C267.

José Marti — A267

1955, Jan. 28 *Perf. 13½x13*
634 A267 5c deep carmine .25 .25

Centenary of the birth of José Marti (1853-1895), Cuban patriot. See No. C268.

Arms, Flags and Soldiers Building Bridge A268

1955, Mar. 23 *Perf. 12½*
635 A268 10c claret .30 .25

Issued to honor Colombian soldiers who served in Korea, 1951-53. See Nos. 637a, C269.

Fleet Emblem — A269

M. S. City of Manizales and New York Skyline A270

1955, Apr. 12 Unwmk.
636 A269 15c deep green .25 .25
637 A270 20c violet .45 .25
a. Souvenir sheet *7.50 10.00*
Nos. 636-637,C270-C271 (4) 1.95 1.15

Grand-Colombian Merchant Fleet.
No. 637a contains four stamps similar to Nos. 622, 635-637, but printed in different colors: 5c blue, 10c dark carmine, 15c green, 20c purple.

Hotel Tequendama and Church of San Diego — A271

1955, May 16 Photo. ***Perf. 11½x12***
638 A271 5c blue .25 .25

See No. C273.

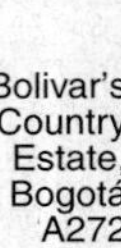

Bolivar's Country Estate, Bogotá A272

1955, Sept. 28 Engr. ***Perf. 12½***
639 A272 5c deep ultra .25 .25

50th anniv. of Rotary Intl. See No. C274.

Belalcazar, Jiménez de Quesada and Balboa A273

Caravels and Columbus A274

5c, San Martin, Bolivar and Washington.

Engraved and Photogravure

1955, Oct. 29 ***Perf. 13x12½***
640 A273 2c yel grn & brn .50 .25
641 A273 5c brt bl & brn .50 .25
642 A274 23c lt ultra & blk .55 .25
a. Souvenir sheet 24.00 24.00
Nos. 640-642,C275-C280 (9) 29.85 15.00

7th Cong. of the Postal Union of the Americas and Spain, Bogota, Oct. 12-Nov. 9, 1955.
No. 642a contains one each of Nos. 640-642, printed in slightly different shades.

José Eusebio Caro — A275

1955, Nov. 29 Engr. ***Perf. 13½x13***
643 A275 5c brown .35 .25

José Eusebio Caro (1817-53), poet. See No. C281.

Departmental Issue

Map — A276

View of San Andres Harbor — A277

Cattle at Waterhole A278

Designs: 2c, Docks, Atlantico. 3c, "Industry," Antioquia. 4c, Cartagena Harbor, Bolivar. No. 647, Steel Mill, Boyaca. No. 648, Cattle, Cordoba. No. 649, Map. No. 650, San Andres Harbor. No. 651, Cacao picker, Cauca. 10c, Coffee picker, Caldas. 15c, Salt Mine Chapel, Zipaquira, Cundinamarca. 20c, Tropical plants and map, Choco. 23c, Harvester, Huila. 25c, Banana plantation, Magdalena. 30c, Gold mining, Nariño. 40c, Tobacco plantation, Santander. 50c, Oil wells, North Santander. 60c, Cotton plantation, Tolima. 1p, Sugar industry, Cauca. 3p, Amazon river at Leticia, Amazonas. 5p, Windmills and panoramic view, La Guajira. 10p, Rubber plantation, Vaupes.

Perf. 13½x13, 13x13½, 13
Engr.; Engr. & Litho.

1956 Unwmk.

Various Frames

No.	Type	Value	Color	Unused	Used
644	A277	2c	car & grn	.25	.25
645	A276	3c	brn vio & blk	.25	.25
646	A277	4c	grn & blk	.25	.25
647	A276	5c	dk brn & bl	.25	.25
648	A277	5c	ol & dk vio brn	.30	.25
649	A276	5c	bl & blk	.25	.25
650	A277	5c	car & grnsh bl	.25	.25
651	A277	5c	ol grn & red brn	.25	.25
652	A276	10c	org & blk	.40	.25
653	A276	15c	ultra & blk	.25	.25
654	A276	20c	dk brn & bl	.25	.25
655	A277	23c	ultra & ver	.30	.25
656	A277	25c	ol grn & blk	.30	.25
657	A277	30c	ultra & brn	.25	.25
658	A277	40c	dl pur & red brn	.25	.25
659	A277	50c	dk grn & blk	.25	.25
660	A277	60c	pale brn & grn	.25	.25
661	A278	1p	mag & grnsh bl	1.90	.25
662	A278	2p	grn & red brn	2.75	.25
663	A278	3p	car & blk	4.25	.50
664	A278	5p	brn & lt ultra	7.50	1.00
665	A276	10p	red brn & grn	20.00	6.00
			Nos. 644-665 (22)	40.95	12.25

Nos. 645, 647, 649, 652-654 measure 27x32mm, No. 665 27x37mm. See Nos. 681-684, 685, 688-689. For surcharges and overprints see Nos. 685, 688-689, C289, C312.

Columbus and Proposed Lighthouse A279

1956, Oct. 12 Photo. ***Perf. 12***
666 A279 3c gray black .50 .25

Issued in honor of Christopher Columbus. See Nos. C285, C306.

Altar of St. Elizabeth and Tomb of Jimenez de Quesada A280

1956, Nov. 19 Unwmk.
667 A280 5c red lilac .25 .25

7th cent. of St. Elizabeth of Hungary, patron saint of Sante Fé de Bogotá. See No. C286.

St. Ignatius of Loyola — A281

1956, Nov. 26 Engr. ***Perf. 12½x13***
668 A281 5c blue .25 .25

400th anniv. of the death of St. Ignatius of Loyola. See No. C287. For overprint see No. C324.

Javier Pereira — A282

1956, Dec. 28 Unwmk. ***Perf. 12***
669 A282 5c blue .25 .25

Issued to honor 167-year-old Javier Pereira. See No. C288.

Emblem and Dairy Farm A283

Designs: 2c, Emblem and tractor. 5c, Emblem, coffee and corn.

1957, Mar. 5 Photo. ***Perf. 14x13½***
670 A283 1c lt ol grn .25 .25
671 A283 2c lt brn .25 .25
672 A283 5c lt bl .25 .25
Nos. 670-672,C292-C296 (8) 3.00 2.05

Agrarian Savings Bank of Colombia, 25th anniv.
For overprint see No. C322.

Arms of Military Academy and Gen. Rafael Reyes A284

Design: 10c, Arms and Academy.

1957, July 20 Engr. ***Perf. 12½***
673 A284 5c blue .25 .25
674 A284 10c orange .40 .25
a. Souv. sheet of 2 20.00 20.00
Nos. 673-674,C299-C300 (4) 1.40 1.00

50th anniv. of the Colombian Military Academy.
No. 674a contains one each of Nos. 673-674 in slightly different shades.
For overprints see Nos. C328, C312.

Statue of José Matias Delgado — A285

1957, Sept. 16 Photo. ***Perf. 12***
675 A285 2c rose brn .25 .25

Issued in honor of Jose Matias Delgado, liberator of El Salvador. See No. C301.

Santo Michelena, Marcos y Crespo, P. Alcantara Herran and UPU Monument A286

1957, Oct. 10 Unwmk.
676 A286 5c green .30 .25
677 A286 10c gray .30 .25
Nos. 676-677,C302-C303 (4) 1.30 1.00

Intl. Letter Writing Week and 14th UPU Cong.

St. Vincent de Paul and Children — A287

1957, Oct. 18
678 A287 1c dark olive green .25 .25

Colombian Society of St. Vincent de Paul, cent. See No. C304. For overprint see No. C323.

Fencer A288

1957, Nov. 22 Photo. ***Perf. 12***
679 A288 4c lilac .25 .25

3rd South American Fencing Championship. See No. C305. For overprint see No. C332.

Francisco José de Caldas and Hypsometer — A289

1958, May 12 Unwmk. ***Perf. 12***
680 A289 10c black .50 .25
Nos. 680,C309-C310 (3) 1.65 .75

International Geophysical Year, 1957-58.

Departmental Issue
Type of 1956

Designs as before.

1958 Engr. ***Perf. 13***
681 A276 3c ultra & brn .25 .25
682 A276 3c ol grn & pur .25 .25
683 A276 10c grn & brn .25 .25
684 A276 10c dk bl & brn .25 .25
Nos. 681-684 (4) 1.00 1.00

Nos. 646, C291, 614, 653, 655, 616, C308, 615 and 611 Surcharged or Overprinted in Dark Blue or Green

Perf. 12½, 12½x13, 13

1958-59			**Unwmk.**	
685	A277	2c on 4c grn & blk	.25	.25
686	AP48	5c dp plum & multi ('59)	.25	.25
687	A256	5c on 14c blk & rose red ("CINCO") ('59)	.30	.30
688	A276	5c on 15c ultra & blk	.25	.25
689	A277	5c on 23c ultra & ver (G)	.25	.25
690	A256	5c on 30c blk & choc ("CINCO")	.25	.25
691	AP40	10c on 25c rose vio	.25	.25
692	A256	20c on 23c blk & ultra (G) ("VEINTE") ('59)	.30	.25
693	A255	20c on 23c lt bl & blk ('59)	.30	.25
		Nos. 685-693 (9)	2.40	2.30

On No. 686 the words "Correo Extra Rapido" are obliterated in dark blue.

Father Rafael Almanza and Church of San Diego, Bogota
A290

1958, Oct. 23		**Photo.**	***Perf. 14x13***	
695	A290	10c purple	.30	.25
		Nos. 695,C313-C314 (3)	1.00	.75

For overprint see No. C336.

Msgr. R. M. Carrasquilla and Church
A291

1959, Jan. 22			***Perf. 14x13***	
696	A291	10c dk red brn	.25	.25
		Nos. 696,C315-C316 (3)	1.30	.75

Cent. of the birth of Msgr. R. M. Carrasquilla (1857-1930), rector of Our Lady of the Rosary Seminary, Bogotá. For overprints see Nos. C335, C341.

Miss Universe 1959 — A292

1959, June 26		**Photo.**	***Perf. 11½***	
697	A292	10c multi	.80	.25
		Nos. 697,C317-C318 (3)	47.55	46.65

Luz Marina Zuluaga, Miss Universe, 1959.
For overprint see No. C342.

Jorge Eliecer Gaitan — A293

1959, July 28		**Engr.**	***Perf. 12x13½***	
698	A293	10c on 3c gray bl (Bl)	.25	.25
699	A293	30c rose vio	.45	.25
		Nos. 698-699,C319-C320 (4)	4.70	3.30

Issued in honor of Jorge Eliecer Gaitan (1898-1948), lawyer and politician.
No. 698 exists without blue surcharge.

Gen. Francisco de Paula Santander — A294

Designs: Nos. 701, 703, Simon Bolivar.

1959	**Litho.**	**Wmk. 331**	***Perf. 12½***	
700	A294	5c brown & yel	.25	.25
701	A294	5c ultra & bl	.25	.25
702	A294	10c gray & grn	.30	.25
703	A294	10c gray & red	.30	.25
		Nos. 700-703,C389 (5)	4.60	1.45

Capitol, Bogota
A295

1959				
704	A295	2c dk bl & red brn	.25	.25
705	A295	3c blk brn & lilac	.25	.25

Stamp of 1859 and Mail Transport by Mule — A296

Designs (various stamps of 1859 and): 10c, Mail boat on the Magdalena river. 15c, as 5c. 25c, Train.

Unwmk.

1959, Dec. 1		**Photo.**	***Perf. 12***	
709	A296	5c org & grn	.25	.25
710	A296	10c rose cl & bl	.25	.25
711	A296	15c car rose & grn	.40	.40
712	A296	25c bl & red brn	.50	.50
		Nos. 709-712,C351-C354 (8)	6.00	4.25

Centenary of Colombian postage stamps.

Two-Toed Sloth — A297

Designs: 10c, Alexander von Humboldt. 20c, Spider monkey.

1960, Feb. 12			***Perf. 12***	
713	A297	5c grnsh bl & brn	.25	.25
714	A297	10c blk & dp car	.25	.25
715	A297	20c cit & gray brn	.45	.25
		Nos. 713-715,C357-C359 (6)	8.30	5.40

Cent. of the death of Alexander von Humboldt (1769-1859), German naturalist and geographer.
For overprint and surcharge see Nos. C411, C413.

Anthurium Andreanum A298

Flower: 20c, Espeletia grandiflora.

1960, May 10				
716	A298	5c multi	.85	.25
717	A298	20c brn, yel & gray ol	.85	.25
		Nos. 716-717,C360-C370 (13)	17.85	18.30

See Nos. C420-C425. For overprint see No. C412.

Lincoln Statue, Washington
A299

Wmk. 331

1960, June 10		**Litho.**	***Perf. 10½***	
718	A299	20c rose lil & blk	.35	.25
		Nos. 718,C375-C376 (3)	2.25	1.50

Florero House, Cradle of the Republic
A300

Arms of Santa Cruz de Mompox — A301

Design: 5c, First coins of Republic.

Unwmk.

1960, July 19		**Photo.**	***Perf. 12***	
719	A301	5c grn & ocher	.25	.25
720	A300	20c ol bis & mar	.25	.25
721	A301	20c multi	.25	.25
		Nos. 719-721,C377-C385 (12)	7.90	6.05

Colombia's independence, 150th anniv.

St. Isidore and Farm Animals — A302

Design: 20c, Nativity by Gregorio de Arce Vasquez y Ceballos.

1960, Sept. 26			***Perf. 12***	
722	A302	10c multi	.25	.25
723	A302	20c multi	.25	.25
		Nos. 722-723,C387 (3)	.75	.75

St. Isidore the Farmer, patron saint of the rural people.
See Nos. 747, C388, C439-C440.

UN Headquarters and Emblem
A303

Wmk. 331

1960, Oct. 24		**Litho.**	***Perf. 11***	
724	A303	20c blk & pink	.25	.25

Souvenir Sheet

Imperf

725	A303	50c dk brn, brt grn & blk	3.75	3.75

15th anniversary of the United Nations.

Pan-American Highway through Colombia — A304

1961, Mar. 7	**Unwmk.**		***Perf. 10½x11***	
726	A304	20c brn & grnsh bl	1.00	.70
		Nos. 726,C390-C393 (5)	3.40	2.90

8th Pan-American Highway Congress, Bogota, May 20-29, 1960.

Alfonso Lopez — A305

1961, Mar. 22		**Photo.**	***Perf. 12½***	
727	A305	10c brt rose & brn	.25	.25
728	A305	20c vio & brn	.25	.25
		Nos. 727-728,C394-C395 (4)	1.25	1.00

Alfonso Lopez (1886-1959), President of Colombia. See No. C396.

Cauca River Bridge, Cali
A306

Page from Resolutions of Confederated Cities — A307

1961-62			***Perf. 12½x13, 13½x13***	
729	A306	10c red brn, bl, grn & red ('62)	.50	.25
730	A307	20c pale brn & blk	.50	.25
		Nos. 729-730,C397-C401 (7)	4.05	2.45

50th anniversary (in 1960) of the Department of Valle del Cauca.

View of Cucuta and Arms
A308

No. 732, Arms of Ocana and Pamplona.

1961, Aug. 29			***Perf. 13x13½***	
731	A308	20c bl, blk, yel & red	.30	.25
732	A308	20c ocher, ultra & red	.30	.25
		Nos. 731-732,C402-C403 (4)	1.50	1.00

50th anniv. (in 1960) of the Department of North Santander.

Arms of Popayan — A309

Designs: No. 734, Arms of Barranquilla. No. 735, Arms of Bucaramanga.

Perf. 12½x13

1961, Oct. 10 **Unwmk.**

Arms in Multicolor

733	A309	10c blue & silver	.25	.25
734	A309	20c blue & yellow	.25	.25
735	A309	20c blue & gold	.25	.25
		Nos. 733-735,C404-C408 (8)	2.80	2.00

Issued to honor Atlantico Department.

Basketball A310

1961, Dec. 16 **Litho.** ***Perf. 13½x14***

736	A310	20c shown	.30	.25
737	A310	20c Runners	.30	.25
738	A310	20c Boxers	.50	.25
739	A310	25c Soccer	.30	.25
		Nos. 736-739,C414-C418 (9)	4.50	2.65

4th Bolivarian Games, Barranquilla, 1961.

Colombian Anti-Malaria Emblem — A311

Design: 50c, Malaria eradication emblem and mosquito in swamp.

1962, Apr. 12 **Unwmk.** ***Perf. 12***

740	A311	20c lt bis & red	.25	.25
741	A311	50c bis & ultra	.30	.25
		Nos. 740-741,C426-C428 (5)	5.45	5.15

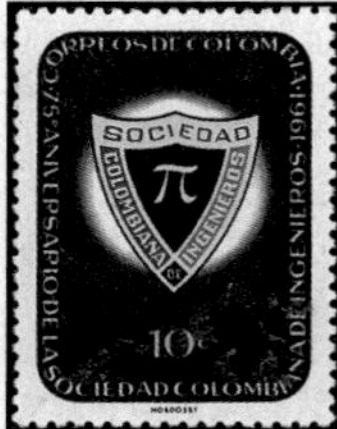

Engineers Society Emblem — A312

1962, June 12 **Photo.** ***Perf. 11½x12***

742	A312	10c multi	.25	.25
		Nos. 742,C429-C432 (5)	3.40	3.30

Colombian Society of Engineers, 75th anniv.

Flags of American Nations — A313

1962, June 28 ***Perf. 13***

Flags in National Colors

743	A313	25c blk & org ver	.25	.25

Souvenir Sheet

744	A313	2.50p blk & yel	5.50	5.50

70th anniv. of the founding of the Organization of American States.

See No. C433.

Woman Casting Ballot and Statue of Policarpa Salavarrieta — A314

Perf. 12x12½

1962, July 20 **Litho.** **Wmk. 229**

745	A314	10c lt bl, gray & blk	.25	.25

Issued to publicize women's political rights. See Nos. 752, C434, C448-C450.

Scouts at Campfire and Tents — A315

Perf. 11½x12

1962, July 28 **Photo.** **Unwmk.**

746	A315	10c brt grnsh bl & brn	.35	.30
		Nos. 746,C435-C438 (5)	6.75	5.40

Colombian Boy Scouts, 30th anniv.

St. Isidore Type of 1960 Redrawn

1962, Aug. 28 ***Perf. 12***

747	A302	10c pink & multi	.50	.25
		Nos. 747,C439-C440 (3)	5.25	5.00

The frame on No. 747 is solid color with white inscription similar to type AP82.

Railroad Map of Colombia — A316

1962, Sept. 28 ***Perf. 12½***

748	A316	10c blk, gray, grn & red	.25	.25
		Nos. 748,C441-C444 (5)	7.75	5.50

Progress of Colombian railroads and the completion of the Atlantic Line from Santa Marta to Bogota.

Post Horn — A317

Perf. 13½x14

1962, Oct. 18 **Litho.** **Wmk. 346**

749	A317	20c gold, dl gray vio & blk	.25	.25
		Nos. 749,C445-C446 (3)	.90	.75

50th anniv. of the founding of the Postal Union of the Americas and Spain, UPAE.

"Virgin of the Rock" — A318

1963, Mar. 11 **Wmk. 346**

750	A318	60c multi	.25	.25

Vatican II, the 21st Ecumenical Council of the Roman Catholic Church. See No. C447.

Red Cross Centenary Emblem — A319

1963, May 1 ***Perf. 12x12½***

751	A319	5c olive bister & red	.30	.25

Centenary of International Red Cross.

Women's Rights Type of 1962

1963, July 11 **Wmk. 346**

752	A314	5c org, gray & blk	.25	.25
		Nos. 752,C448-C450 (4)	1.30	1.00

Manuel Mejia J. and Flag of National Coffee Growers Assn. A320

Perf. 12½x13

1965, Feb. 10 **Engr.** **Unwmk.**

753	A320	25c rose & blk	.25	.25
		Nos. 753,C464-C466 (4)	6.50	1.15

Manuel Mejia J. (1887-1958), banker and manager of the National Coffee Growers Association.

Julio Arboleda (1817-62), Writer, Soldier and Statesman A321

1966, Mar. 9 **Litho.** ***Perf. 14x13½***

754	A321	5c lt brn, lt yel grn & blk	.30	.25

Spanish Galleon, 16th Century A322

History of Maritime Mail: 15c, Rio Hacha brigantine, 1850. 20c, Uraba canoe. 40c, Magdalena River steamship and barge, 1900. 50c, Modern motor ship and sea gull.

1966, June 16 **Photo.** **Unwmk.**

755	A322	5c org & multi	.40	.25
756	A322	15c car rose, blk & brn	.40	.25
757	A322	20c brt grn, org & blk	.40	.25
758	A322	40c dp bl & multi	.50	.25
759	A322	50c pale bl & multi	1.25	.60
		Nos. 755-759 (5)	2.95	1.60

Plumed Hogfish A323

Design: 10p, Bat ray and brittle starfish.

1966, Aug. 25 **Photo.** ***Perf. 12½x13***

760	A323	80c multi	.25	.25
761	A323	10p multi	8.50	5.50
		Nos. 760-761,C481-C483 (5)	27.25	19.90

Arms of Venezuela, Colombia and Chile A324

1966, Oct. 11 **Litho.** ***Perf. 14x13½***

762	A324	40c yel & multi	.25	.25
		Nos. 762,C484-C485 (3)	.95	.75

Visits of Eduardo Frei and Raul Leoni, presidents of Chile and Venezuela.

Camilo Torres, 1766-1816, Lawyer — A325

Portraits: 60c, Jorge Tadeo Lozano (1771-1816), naturalist. 1p, Francisco Antonio Zea (1776-1822), naturalist and politician.

Perf. 13½x14

1967, Jan. 18 **Litho.** **Unwmk.**

763	A325	25c vio & bis	.25	.25
764	A325	60c dk red brn & bis	.25	.25
765	A325	1p grn & bis	.40	.25
		Nos. 763-765,C486-C487 (5)	1.70	1.25

Issued to honor famous men of Colombia.

Map of South America and Arms A326

1967, Feb. 2 **Litho.** ***Perf. 14x13½***

766	A326	40c multi	.30	.25
767	A326	60c multi	.30	.25
		Nos. 766-767,C488 (3)	1.10	.75

Declaration of Bogota for cooperation and world peace, signed by Colombia, Chile, Ecuador, Peru and Venezuela.

Monochaetum Orchid and Bee — A327

Orchid: 2p, Passiflora vitifolia and butterfly.

1967, May 23 **Litho.** ***Perf. 14***

768	A327	25c multi	.35	.25
769	A327	2p multi	2.50	1.50
		Nos. 768-769,C489-C491 (5)	8.70	3.15

1st Natl. Orchid Exhib. and the Topical Phil. Flora and Fauna Exhib., Medellin, Apr. 1967.

Lions Emblem — A328

1967, July 12 Litho. *Perf. 13½x14*
770 A328 10p multi 3.50 2.00

50th anniv. of Lions Intl. See No. C492.

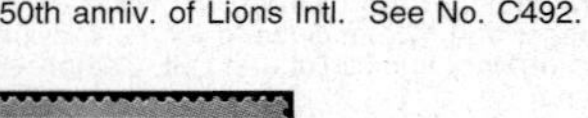

SENA Emblem — A329

Lithographed and Embossed

1967, Sept. 20 Unwmk.
771 A329 5p gold, brt grn & blk 1.50 .25

10th anniv. of Natl. Apprenticeship Service, SENA. See No. C494.

Gold Diadem in Calima Style — A330

Pre-Columbian Art: 3p, Gold statuette, ornamental globe and bird, horiz.

Perf. 13½x14, 14x13½

1967, Oct. 13 Photo.
772 A330 1.60p brt rose lil, gold & brn .95 .25
773 A330 3p dk bl, gold & brn 1.25 .40
Nos. 772-773,C495-C497 (5) 20.85 11.40

Meeting of the UPU Committee of Postal Studies, Bogota, Oct., 1967.

Radar Installation A331

1p, Map of communications network.

1968, May 14 Litho. *Perf. 13½x14*
774 A331 50c brt yel grn, blk & org brn .25 .25
775 A331 1p multi .35 .25
Nos. 774-775,C498-C499 (4) 1.15 1.00

20th anniv. of the National Telecommunications Service (TELECOM).

The Eucharist — A332

1968, June 6 Litho. *Perf. 13½x14*
776 A332 60c multi .25 .25
Nos. 776,C500-C501 (3) .80 .75

39th Eucharistic Cong., Bogotá, 8/18-25.

St. Augustin, by Gregorio Vasquez — A333

Designs: 60c, The Gathering of Manna, by Gregorio Vasquez. 1p, The Marriage of the Virgin, by Baltazar de Figueroa. 5p, Jeweled monstrance, c. 1700. 10p, Pope Paul VI, painting by Roman Franciscan nuns.

1968, Aug. 13 Photo. *Perf. 13*
777 A333 25c multicolored .25 .25
778 A333 60c multicolored .25 .25
779 A333 1p multicolored .25 .25
780 A333 5p multicolored .65 .25
781 A333 10p multicolored 1.25 .45
a. Souvenir sheet of 2 3.75 3.75
Nos. 777-781,C502-C506 (10) 9.55 4.95

39th Eucharistic Congress. Bogotá, Aug. 18-25. No. 781a contains two imperf. stamps similar to Nos. 780-781.

Pope Paul VI — A334

1968, Aug. 22 Litho. *Perf. 13½x14*
782 A334 25c multi .30 .25
Nos. 782,C507-C509 (4) 1.30 1.00

Visit of Pope Paul VI to Colombia, 8/22-24.

Arms of National University — A335

1968, Oct. 29 Litho. *Perf. 13½x14*
783 A335 80c multi .35 .25

Centenary of the founding of the National University. See No. C510.

Stamp of Antioquia, 1868 — A336

1968, Nov. 20 Litho. *Perf. 12x12½*
784 A336 30c emer & bl .30 .25

Souvenir Sheet

785 A336 5p lt olive & blue 5.00 5.00

Cent. of the 1st postage stamps of Antioquia and the 7th Natl. Phil. Exhib., Medellin, Nov. 20-29.

Institute Emblem — A337

1969, Mar. 5 Litho. *Perf. 13½x14*
786 A337 20c multi .35 .25

25th anniv. (in 1967) of the Inter-American Agricultural Sciences Institute. See No. C511.

Battle of Boyaca (Detail), by José Maria Espinosa — A338

Design: 30c, Army of liberation crossing Pisba Pass, by Francisco Antonio Caro.

1969, July 24 Litho. *Perf. 13½x14*
787 A338 20c gold & multi .35 .25
788 A338 30c gold & multi .35 .25
Nos. 787-788,C517 (3) 1.70 .85

Fight for independence, sesquicentennial.

"Poverty" A339

1970, Mar. 1 Litho. *Perf. 14*
789 A339 30c bl & multi .75 .25

Colombian Institute for Family Welfare and 10th anniv. of the Children's Rights Law.

Greek Mask and Pre-Columbian Symbol of Literary Contest — A340

1970, Sept. 12 Litho. *Perf. 14x13½*
790 A340 30c dk brn, red org & ocher 1.00 .25

3rd Latin American Theatrical Festival of the Universities, Manizales, Sept. 12-20.

Colombian Stamps, Envelope and Emblem A341

1970, Sept. 24 Litho. *Perf. 14x13½*
791 A341 2p brt bl & multi .75 .25

Issued to publicize Philatelic Week.

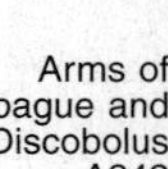

Arms of Ibague and Discobolus A342

1970, Oct. 13
792 A342 80c buff, emer & sepia .40 .25

9th National Games in Ibague.

St. Theresa, by Baltazar de Figueroa — A343

1970, Oct. 28 Litho. *Perf. 13½x14*
793 A343 2p multi .75 .25

Elevation of St. Theresa (1515-1582), to Doctor of the Church. See No. C568. For overprint see No. C568.

Casa Cural A344

1971, May 20 Litho. *Perf. 14x13½*
794 A344 1.10p multi .80 .25

Fourth centenary (in 1970) of the founding of Guacari, Valle. See No. 809.

Dancers and Music, Currulao — A345

1p, Chicha Maya dancers and music.

1971 Litho. *Perf. 13½x14*
795 A345 1p pink & multi 1.00 .25
796 A345 1.10p lt bl & multi 1.00 .25

Souvenir Sheets

Imperf

797 Sheet of 3 8.00 6.00
a. A345 2.50p Napanga 1.50 .65
b. A345 2.50p Joropo 1.50 .65
c. A345 5p Guabina 3.35 1.25
798 Sheet of 3 8.00 6.00
a. A345 4p Bambuco 1.50 1.00
b. A345 4p Cumbia 1.50 1.00
c. A345 4p Currulao 3.35 1.00

Issued: No. 795, 12/20; No. 796, 8/5; Nos. 797-798, 8/10.

Constitutional Assembly, by Delgado A346

1971, Oct. 2 *Perf. 14*
801 A346 80c multi 1.00 .25

Sequicentennial of Gran Colombian Constitutional Assembly in Rosario del Cucuta.

See No. C589. For overprint see No. C589.

Arrows Emblem — A347

1972, Feb. 24 ***Perf. 13½x14***

802 A347 60c blk & gray .30 .25

Inter-Governmental Committee on European Migration, 20th anniversary.

Student and World Map A348

1972, Mar. 15 ***Perf. 14x13½***

803 A348 1.10p lt grn & brn 1.00 .25

20th anniv. of ICETEX, an organization which furnishes financial help for educational purposes and for technical studies abroad.

UN Emblem, Soldier and Frigate A349

1972, Apr. 7

804 A349 1.20p lt bl & multi 1.00 .25

Colombian Battalion in Korea, 20th anniv.

Mother Francisca Josefa del Castillo — A350

1972, Apr. 6 ***Perf. 13½x14***

805 A350 1.20p brn & multi 1.00 .25

Tercentenary (in 1971) of the birth of Mother Francisca Josefa del Castillo, Poor Clare abbess and writer.

Handicraft A351

1972, Apr. 11

806 A351 1.10p multi .60 .25

Nos. 806,C569-C571 (4) 1.80 1.00

Colombian artisans.

Maxillaria Triloris — A352

1972, Apr. 20

807 A352 20p green & multi 9.75 .75

10th Natl. Phil. Exhib., Medellin.

Emeralds — A353

1972, June 16 Litho. ***Perf. 13½x14***

808 A353 1.10p multi 2.00 .25

Type of 1971

Design: Antonio Nariño House.

1972, June 17 ***Perf. 14x13½***

809 A344 1.10p multi 1.00 .25

4th centenary, town of Leyva.

San Andres and Providencia Islands — A354

1972, June 24 ***Perf. 13½x14***

810 A354 60c bl & multi 1.00 .25

Sesquicentennial of annexation by Colombia of San Andres and Providencia Islands.

Postal Service Emblem A355

1972, Nov. 15 Litho. ***Perf. 12½x12***

811 A355 1.10p emerald .30 .25

Family A356

1972, Nov. 23

812 A356 60c orange .30 .25

Social progress.

Radio League Emblem — A357

1973, Apr. 6 Litho. ***Perf. 12x12½***

813 A357 60c lt bl, ultra & red .30 .25

40th anniversary of the Colombian Radio Amateurs' League.

Human Figure, Tamalameque A358

Excavated Ceramic Artifacts: 1p, Winged urn, Tairona. 1.10p, Jug, Muisca.

1973, June 15 Litho. ***Perf. 13½x14***

814 A358 60c lt bl & multi .40 .25

815 A358 1p org & multi .80 .25

816 A358 1.10p vio bl & multi .80 .25

Nos. 814-816,C583-C586 (7) 8.00 2.75

Antonio Nariño, by José M. Espinosa — A359

1973, Dec. 13 Litho. ***Perf. 13½x14***

817 A359 60c multi .25 .25

Sesquicentennial of the death of General Antonio Nariño (1765-1823).

Child — A360

1973, Dec. 17

818 A360 1.10p multi .25 .25

National Campaign for Children's Welfare.

Symbols of Financial Controls A361

1973, Dec. 20 Litho. ***Perf. 14x13½***

819 A361 80c ultra, ocher & blk .25 .25

50th anniv. of Comptroller-general's Office.

Mother Laura Montoya — A362

1974, June 18 Litho. ***Perf. 13½x14***

820 A362 1p multi .25 .25

Mother Laura Montoya (1874-1949), founder and Mother Superior of the Missionaries of Mary Immaculata and St. Catherine of Siena.

Runner and Games' Emblem A363

1974, July 18 Litho. ***Perf. 14x13½***

821 A363 2p ver, yel & brn .35 .25

10th National Games, Pereira.

José Rivera A364

1974, Aug. 3 Litho. ***Perf. 14x13½***

822 A364 10p grn & multi 1.30 .25

50th anniv. of the publication of "La Voragine" (The Whirlpool) by José Eustasio Rivera.

Abstract Pattern — A365

1974, Oct. 24 Litho. ***Perf. 13½x14***

823 A365 1.10p multi .90 .25

Cent. of Natl. Insurance Co. See No. C610.

Train Emerging from Tunnel — A366

1974, Nov. 27 Litho. ***Perf. 13½x14***

824 A366 1.10p multi .90 .25

Centenary of the Antioquia railroad.

Boy, Puppy and Soccer Ball — A367

Christmas: 1p, Girl with racket and kitten.

1974, Dec. 9

825 A367 80c multi .50 .25
826 A367 1p multi .50 .25

A368

1975, Apr. 11 Litho. *Perf. 14x13½*

827 A368 80c Gold Animal .45 .25
828 A368 1.10p Gold necklace .45 .25
Nos. 827-828,C621-C622 (4) 6.65 1.35

Pre-Columbian Sinu culture artifacts.
For surcharge see No. 840.

Guglielmo Marconi — A369

1975, June 2 Litho. *Perf. 13½x14*

829 A369 3p multi .75 .25

Birth centenary of Guglielmo Marconi (1874-1937), Italian electrical engineer and inventor.

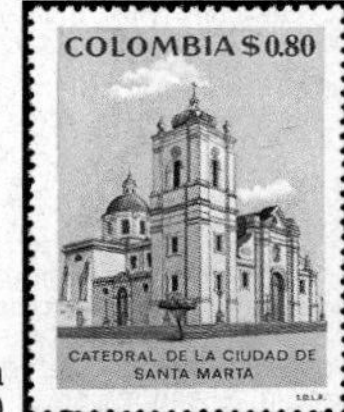
Santa Marta Cathedral — A370

1975, July 26

830 A370 80c multi .30 .25

400th anniv. of Santa Marta City. See No. C623.

Rafael Nuñez — A371

1975, Sept. 28 Litho. *Perf. 13½x14*

831 A371 1.10p multi .30 .25

Rafael Nunez (1825-1894), philosopher, poet, political leader, birth sesquicentenary.
For surcharge see No. 848.

A372

A372a

Arms of Medellin — A372b

1975-79 *Perf. 13½x14, 12 (1.20p)*

832	A372	1p	shown	.40	.25
833	A372b	1.20p	Ibagué	.35	.25
834	A372b	1.20p	Tunja	.25	.25
835	A372a	1.50p	Cucuta	.55	.25
836	A372b	1.50p	Cartagena	.25	.25
836A	A372b	4p	Sogamoso	1.00	.25
837	A372	5p	Popayan	.50	.25
838	A372b	5p	Barranquilla	.55	.25
839	A372a	10p	San Gil	1.00	.25
839A	A372a	10p	Socorro	1.00	.25
	Nos. 832-839A (10)			5.85	2.50

1p for the tercentenary of Medellin; No. 835, the cent. of Cucuta's reconstruction.

Issued: 1p, 11/4; No. 835, 11/29; No. 836, 2/10/76; No. 833, 7/30/76; No. 834, 12/20/76; No. 837, 8/30/77; No. 838, 9/20/77; 10p, 8/9/79; 4p, 9/14/79.

See Nos. 905-913, C818. For surcharge see No. 849.

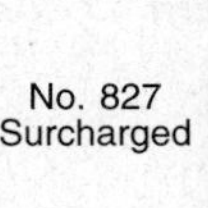
No. 827 Surcharged

1975 *Perf. 14x13½*

840 A368 1.20p on 80c multi .35 .25

Purace Indians, Cauca — A373

1976, Nov. 10 Litho. *Perf. 13½x14*

841 A373 1.50p multi .25 .25

Callicore A374

5p, Morpho (butterfly). 20p, Anthurium.

1976, Nov. 17 *Perf. 12*

842 A374 3p multicolored .90 .25
843 A374 5p multicolored 1.50 .25
844 A374 20p multicolored 4.25 1.00
Nos. 842-844 (3) 6.65 1.50

Rotary Emblem — A375

1976, Dec. 3 Litho. *Perf. 12*

845 A375 1p multicolored .25 .25

Rotary Club of Colombia, 50th anniversary.

Declaration of Independence, by John Trumbull — A376

1976, Dec. 21 Litho. *Perf. 12*

846 A376 Strip of 3 10.00 *11.50*
a.-c. 30p any single 2.75 2.00

American Bicentennial. No. 846 printed in sheets of 4 triptychs.

Policeman with Dog — A377

1976, Dec. 29 *Perf. 13½x14*

847 A377 1.50p multicolored .25 .25

Honoring the National Police.
For surcharge see No. 850.

Nos. 831, 834, 847 Surcharged in Light Brown

1977, June Litho. *Perf. 13½x14, 12*

848 A371 2p on 1.10p multi .65 .25
849 A372b 2p on 1.20p multi .50 .25
850 A377 2p on 1.50p multi .50 .25
Nos. 848-850 (3) 1.65 .75

Souvenir Sheet

Postal Museum, Bogota — A378

1977, July 27 Litho. *Perf. 14*

855 A378 25p multi 3.50 3.50

Postal Museum, Bogota.

Mother and Child — A379

1977-78 Litho. *Perf. 12*

856 A379 2p multi .50 .25
857 A379 2.50p multi ('78) 2.25 .25

National good nutrition plan.
Issue dates: 2p, Aug. 30; 2.50p, Jan. 26.

Jacana and Eichhornia A380

20p, Mayan cotinga and pyrostegia venusta.

1977, Sept. 6 Litho. *Perf. 14*

858 A380 10p multicolored 2.50 .25
859 A380 20p multicolored 4.00 .50
Nos. 858-859,C644-C647 (6) 10.20 1.75

Fidel Cano, by Francisco Cano — A381

1977, Sept. 16 *Perf. 14*

860 A381 4p multicolored .25 .25

90th anniversary of El Espectador, newspaper founded by Fidel Cano.

Abacus and Alphabet — A382

1977, Sept. 16 *Perf. 13½x14*

861 A382 3p multicolored .25 .25

Popular education.

Cattleya Triannae — A383

1978-79 Litho. *Perf. 12*

862 A383 2.50p multi .75 .25
863 A383 3p multi ('79) .75 .25

Issue dates: 2.50p, Apr. 18. 3p, May 10.

Sprinting and Games Emblem A384

Sports: a, sprinting. b, basketball. c, baseball. d, boxing. e. bicycling. f, fencing. g, soccer. h, gymnastics. i, judo. j, weight lifting. k, wrestling. l, swimming. m, tennis. n, target shooting. o, volleyball. p, water polo.

1978, June 27 Litho. *Perf. 14*

868 Sheet of 16 29.00 29.00
a.-p. A384 10p, any single 1.25 .25

13th Central American and Caribbean Games, Medellin.

"Sigma 2" by Alvaro Herrán A385

1978, June 30

869 A385 8p multicolored .55 .25

Chamber of Commerce, Bogota, centenary.

Gen. Tomás Cipriano de Mosquera (1778-1878), Statesman A386

1978, Oct. 6 Litho. *Perf. 12*

870 A386 6p multicolored .45 .25

Anthurium Narinenses — A387

1979, July 23 *Perf. 12*

871 A387 3p red & multi .30 .25
872 A387 3p purple & multi .30 .25
873 A387 3p rose & purple .30 .25
874 A387 3p white & multi .30 .25
a. Block of 4, #871-874 2.50 2.50

Gen. Rafael Uribe, by Acevedo Bernal — A388

1979, Oct. 31 Litho. *Perf. 12*

875 A388 8p multicolored .50 .25

Gen. Uribe, statesman, 60th death anniv.

Village, by Leonor Alarcon — A389

1979, Nov. 22 *Perf. 14*

876 A389 15p multicolored 1.50 .60

Community Work Boards, 20th anniversary.

Introduction of Color Television A390

1980, Mar. 4 Litho. *Perf. 14*

877 A390 5p multicolored .60 .25

Bullfight, Arms of Cali A391

1980, Mar. 25

878 A391 5p multicolored .70 .25

Cali Tourist Festival, 12/25/79-1/2/80.

"Learn to Write" — A392

a, shown. b, "a." c, "b." d, "c." e, "ch." f, "d." g, "e." h, "f." i, "g." j, "h." k, "i." l, "j." m, "k." n, "l." o, "ll." p, "m." q, "n." r, "ñ." s, "o." t, "p." u, "q." v, "r." w, "s." x, "t." y, "u." z, "v." aa, "w." ab, "x." ac, "y." ad, "z."

1980, Apr. 25 Litho. *Perf. 12½*

879 Block of 30 27.50 27.50
a.-ad. A392 4p any single .75 .25

Each stamp shows letter of alphabet and corresponding animal or subject. Issued in sheets of 90 (10x9).

Villavicencio Festival — A393

Design: 9p, Vallenato festival.

1980 Litho. *Perf. 14*

880 A393 5p multicolored .55 .25
881 A393 9p multicolored .55 .25

Issue dates: 5p, July 15; 9p, June 17.

Gustavo Uribe Ramirez and Tree A394

1980, Aug. 5 Litho. *Perf. 12*

882 A394 10p multicolored 1.20 .25

Gustavo Uribe Ramirez (1893-1968), ecologist.

Narino Palace (Former Presidential Residence) — A395

1980, Sept. 19 Litho. *Perf. 14*

883 A395 5p multicolored .70 .25

Monument to First Pioneers of 1819, Armenia A396

1980, Oct. 14

884 A396 5p multicolored .60 .25

11th National Games, Neiva — A397

1980, Nov. 28 *Perf. 13½x14*

885 A397 5p multicolored .60 .25

Fight against Cancer — A398

1980, Dec. 9

886 A398 10p multicolored .50 .25

Xavier University Law Faculty, 50th Anniversary A399

1980, Dec. 16 Litho. *Perf. 14½*

887 A399 20p multicolored .85 .30

Death of Bolivar — A400

1980, Dec. 17 *Perf. 12*

888 A400 25p multicolored 1.25 .60

Simon Bolivar, death sesquicentennial. See No. C696.

José Maria Obando, President of Colombia A401

115th Anniv. of Constitution (Former Presidents): b, Jose Hilario Lopez. c, Manuel Murillo Toro. d, Santiago Perez. e, Rafael Reyes. f, Carlos E. Restrepo. g, Jose Vicente Concha. h, Miguel Abadia Mendez. i, Eduardo Santos. j, Mariano Ospina Perez.

1981, June 9 Litho. *Perf. 12*

889 Strip of 10 *9.00*
a.-j. A401 5p multicolored .90 .25

1981, Sept. 23 Litho. *Perf. 12*

Designs: a, Rafael Nunez (1825-94). b, Marco Fidel Suarez (1855-1927). c, Pedro Nel Ospina (1858-1927). d, Enrique Olaya Herrera (1880-1937). e, Alfonso Lopez Pumarejo (1886-1959). f, Aquileo Parra (1825-1900). g, Santos Gutierrez (1820-72). h, Tomas Cipriano de Mosquera (1789-1878). i, Mariano Ospina Rodriguez. j, Pedro Alcantara Herran (1800-72).

890 Strip of 10 *65.00*
a.-j. A401 7p multicolored 6.50 .50

1981, Aug. 11 Litho. *Perf. 12*

Designs like No. 889.

891 Strip of 10 *75.00*
a.-j. A401 7p multicolored 7.50 1.00

1981, Nov. 11 Litho. *Perf. 12*

Designs: a, Manuel Maria Mallarino. b, Santos Acosta. c, Eustorgio Salgar. d, Julian Trujillo. e, Francisco Javier Zaldua. f, Guillermo Leon Valencia. g, Laureano Gomez. h, Manuel A. Sanclemente. i, Miguel Antonio Caro. j, Jose Eusebio Otalora.

892 Strip of 10 *45.00*
a.-j. A401 7p multicolored 4.50 .40

1981, Dec. 15 Litho. *Perf. 12*

Designs: a, Ruben Piedrahita Arango. b, Jorge Holguin. c, Ramon Gonzalez Valencia. d, Jose Manuel Marroquin. e, Carlos Holguin. f, Bartolome Calvo. g, Sergio Camargo. h, Jose Maria Rojas Garrido. i, J.M. Campo Serrano. j, Eliseo Payan.

893 Strip of 10 *30.00*
a.-j. A401 7p multicolored 3.00 .30

1982, May 3 *Perf. 12*

Designs: a, Simon Bolivar. b, Francisco de Paula Santander. c, Joaquin Mosquera. d, Domingo Caicedo. e, Jose Ignacio de Marquez. f, Roberto Urdaneta Arbelaez. g, Carlos Lozano y Lozano. h, Guillermo Quintero Calderon. i, Jose de Obaldia. j, Juan de Dios Aranzazu.

894 Strip of 10 12.50
a.-j. A401 7p multicolored 1.20 .25

See No. 1110, 1329.

Jose Maria Villa and West Bridge over Cauca River A404

1981, Nov. 25 Litho. *Perf. 14x13½*

895 A404 60p multicolored 1.50 .30

Agrarian, Mineral and Industrial Credit Bank, 50th Anniv. — A405

1981, Dec. 9 Litho. *Perf. 14*

896 A405 15p multicolored 1.00 .25

Los Nevados Park — A406

1981, Dec. 10 Litho. *Perf. 13½x14*
897 A406 20p multicolored 1.00 .25

Girl Sitting on Fence — A407

1982, Feb. 22 Litho. *Perf. 12½x12*
898 Strip of 3 5.00 5.00
a. A407 30p shown 1.10 .40
b. A407 30p Girl, basket 1.10 .40
c. A407 30p Boy, wheelbarrow 1.10 .40

Floral Bouquet — A408

Various floral arrangements (background): a, Flowers in vase (gray). b, Roses (red). c, Daisies (green). d, Roses (blue). e, Assorted (red). f, Yellow & orange flowers (green). g, Assorted (lilac). h, Roses (gray). i, Pink flowers (green). j, Flowers in basket (gray).

1982, July 28
900 Strip or block of 10 16.00 16.00
a.-j. A408 7p, any single 1.50 .30

Hipotecario Bank, 50th Anniv. — A409

1982, July 29 *Perf. 14*
901 A409 9p black & green .50 .25

St. Thomas Aquinas (1225-1274) A410

Paintings by Zurbaran.

1982 Litho. *Perf. 12*
902 A410 5p multicolored .60 .25
903 A410 5p St. Teresa of Avila .60 .25
904 A410 5p St. Francis of Assisi .60 .25
Nos. 902-904 (3) 1.80 .75

Issued: No. 902, 8/6; No. 903, 9/28; No. 904, 10/4.

Arms Type of 1975

No. 905, Buga. No. 906, San Juan de Pasto. No. 907, Rionegro. No. 908, Santa Fe de Bogota. No. 909, Santiago de Cali. No. 910, Honda. No. 911, Cartago. No. 912, Antioquia ('86).

1982-90 Litho. *Perf. 14, 12 (50p)*
905 A372 10p .40 .25
906 A372 10p multicolored 1.25 .25
907 A372 16p multicolored .70 .25
908 A372 20p multicolored 1.00 .25
909 A372 20p multicolored .30 .25
910 A372 23p multicolored .75 .25
911 A372 50p multicolored .70 .25
912 A372 55p multicolored 1.00 .25
Nos. 905-912 (8) 6.10 2.00

Issued: 16p, 23p, No. 905, 12/7; No. 908, 3/1/83; No. 906, 4/12/83; No. 909, 7/25/86; 55p, 8/5/86; 50p, 5/30/90.

See No. C818.

Gabriel Marquez, 1982 Nobel Prize, Literature — A412

1982, Dec. 10 *Perf. 13½x14*
917 A412 7p gray & green .25 .25

See Nos. C731-C732.

Public Education Bicentenary (Society of Mary for Education) A413

1983, May 6
918 A413 9p gold & blk .35 .25

José Maria Espinosa Prieto, Painter — A414

1983, June 3 *Perf. 12*
919 A414 9p Self-portrait, 1860 .40 .25

250th Anniv. of City of Cucuta — A415

1983, June 23 Litho. *Perf. 12*
920 A415 9p multicolored .35 .25

Porfirio Barba-Jacob (1883-1942), Poet — A416

1983, July 29 Litho. *Perf. 13½x14*
921 A416 9p Portrait .35 .25

Simon Bolivar, 200th Birth Anniv. A417

1983, July 24 *Perf. 12*
922 A417 9p multicolored .30 .25

See Nos. C736-C737.

Royal Spanish Botanical Expedition, 200th Anniv. — A418

No. 923, Cinchona lancefolia. No. 924, Passiflora laurifolia. No. 925, Cinchona cordiflora.

1983, Aug. 18 *Perf. 14*
923 A418 9p multicolored .25 .25
924 A418 9p multicolored .25 .25
925 A418 60p multicolored 1.75 .40
Nos. 923-925,C738-C740 (6) 5.05 2.80

Dawn in the Andes, by Alejandro Obregon A420

1983, Oct. 5 Litho. *Perf. 12*
928 A420 20p multicolored .40 .25

See No. C741.

Francisco de Paula Santander (1792-1840), General — A421

1984, Mar. 6 Litho. *Perf. 14½x14*
929 A421 12p light olive green .30 .25
930 A421 12p pale carmine .30 .25
931 A421 12p light ultra .30 .25
Nos. 929-931 (3) .90 .75

Admiral Jose Prudencio Padilla (1784-1831) — A423

1984, May 17 Litho. *Perf. 12*
933 A423 10p multicolored .40 .25

Luis Antonio Calvo (1882-1945) Composer — A424

1984, July 26
934 A424 18p multicolored .40 .25

Diego Fallon (1834-1905), Educator, Musician, Poet — A425

1984, Aug. 31 *Perf. 12*
935 A425 20p multicolored .45 .25

Candelario Obeso (1849-1884), Writer — A426

1984, Sept. 4 *Perf. 14x13½*
936 A426 20p multicolored .45 .25

Site of Marandua, Future City A427

1984, Sept. 28 *Perf. 12*
937 A427 15p multicolored .35 .25

See No. C744.

Christmas 1984 A428

Nativity and Children Playing, by Jose Uriel Sierra, Age 7.

1984, Dec. 14
938 A428 12p multicolored .35 .25

See No. C746.

Dr. Luis Eduardo Lopez, Education Minister A429

1984, Dec. 21
939 A429 22p multicolored .45 .25

Maria Concepcion Loperena de Fernandez de Castro, Independence War Heroine — A430

1985, Jan. 6
940 A430 12p multicolored .35 .25

Gonzalo Mejia (1885-1956) — A431

12p, Portrait, biplane, camera.

1985, Feb. 25
941 A431 12p multicolored .45 .25

Aviation, motion picture and meat exporting industrialist.

Self-portrait with Wife — A432

1985, Feb. 25
942 A432 37p multicolored .80 .30

Pedro Nel Gomez (1899-1984), painter. See No. C748.

Fauna A433

No. 943, Hydrochaeris hydrochaeris. No. 944, Felis pardalis. No. 945, Tremarctos ornatus, vert. No. 946, Tapirus pinchaque.

1985 ***Perf. 14***
943 A433 12p multicolored .50 .30

Perf. 13
944 A433 15p multicolored .50 .25
945 A433 15p multicolored .50 .25
946 A433 20p multicolored .85 .30
Nos. 943-946,C758 (5) 3.85 1.35

Carlos Gardel (1890-1935), Entertainer A434

15p, Portrait, Fokker F-31 Trimotor.

1985, June 23 ***Perf. 14***
947 A434 15p multicolored .30 .25

Camina Literacy Program — A435

1985, Nov. 25 ***Perf. 13½x14***
948 A435 15p Tree, alphabet .30 .25

Christmas 1985 A436

1985, Dec. 4 **Litho.** ***Perf. 13***
949 A436 15p multicolored .40 .25

Rafael Pombo Children's Foundation. See No. C755.

Eduardo Carranza (b. 1913), Poet — A437

1986, Feb. 13
950 A437 18p multicolored .30 .25

Colombian Free University, Cent. — A438

1986, Feb. 14
951 A438 18p multicolored .30 .25

Gen. Antonio Ricaurte (b. 1786), Liberator A439

1986, May 7 **Litho.** ***Perf. 13***
952 A439 18p Leiva birthplace .30 .25

Jose Asuncion Silva (1865-1896), Poet, and Scene from Nocturno — A440

1986, May 30 **Litho.** ***Perf. 12***
953 A440 18p multicolored .30 .25

Fernando Gomez Martinez (1897-1985), Journalist — A441

1986, June 19
954 A441 24p multicolored .30 .25

Santiago de Cali, 450th Anniv. A442

1986, July 25 **Litho.** ***Perf. 13***
955 A442 25p La Merced .30 .25

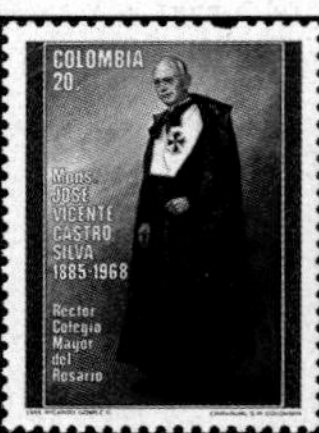

A443

Monsignor Jose Vicente Castro Silva (1885-1968), rector of the Mayor del Rosario School: portrait by Ricardo Gomez.

1986, Aug. 4 **Litho.** ***Perf. 12***
956 A443 20p multicolored .35 .25

Natl. University — A444

1986, Oct. 14 **Litho.** ***Perf. 12***
957 A444 40p multicolored .60 .40

Faculties: Fine Arts, cent., and Architecture, 50th anniv.

Rafael Maya (1897-1980), Poet, and Salamanca University Entrance — A445

1986, Oct. 15
958 A445 25p multicolored .35 .25

See No. C772.

Condor in Flight — A446

30
correos de colombia

Inia goefrenis A446a

No. 962, Inia goeffrensis. No. 963, Procyon cancrivorus. No. 964, Monachus tropicalis. No. 965, Pteronura brasiliensis. No. 966, Trichechus manatus. No. 967, Odocoileus virginianus. No. 968, Trogon personatus personatus. Nos. 962-968 horiz.

1986-89 **Litho.** ***Perf. 12***
959 A446 20p ultra .35 .25
960 A446 25p ultra ('87) .50 .25

Perf. 14½x14, 14x14½
961 A446a 30p grn ('87) .50 .25
962 A446a 30p dull vio ('87) .50 .25

Engr.
Wmk. 334
963 A446a 35p chest brn ('88) .75 .25
964 A446a 35p dark grn ('88) .75 .25
965 A446a 40p deep org ('88) .75 .25
966 A446a 40p gray ('88) .85 .25
967 A446a 40p tan ('89) .85 .25
968 A446a 45p dark vio ('88) .85 .25
Nos. 959-968 (10) 6.65 2.50

Issued: 20p, 11/6; 25p, 5/25; No. 961, 6/8; No. 962, 12/24; No. 963, 8/6; No. 964, 9/20; No. 965, 9/20; No. 966, 11/29; No. 967, 4/29; No. 968, 12/16.

See Nos. 996-1001, C778-C781.

A447

1987, Jan. 29 **Unwmk.** ***Perf. 12***
969 A447 25p multicolored .50 .25

Pedro Uribe Mejia (1886-1972), pioneer of Colombian coffee industry.

Santa Barbara Church — A448

1987, May 3 ***Perf. 13½x13***
970 A448 500p multicolored 5.00 1.75

Mompox, 450th anniv.

Writers A449

Portraits and scenes from works: 70p, Jorge Isaacs (1837-1895), novelist, and scene from *Maria.* 90p, Aurelio Martinez Mutis (1884-1954), poet, and scene from *La Epopeya del Condor.*

1987 ***Perf. 12***
971 A449 70p multicolored .90 .25
972 A449 90p multicolored 1.25 .40

Issue dates: 70p, July 28. 90p, Sept. 2.

A450

Social Security & Communications.

1987 **Litho.** ***Perf. 13½x13***
973 A450 35p multicolored .40 .25

A451

Natl. Anthem, Cent.: Score, lyricist Rafael Nunez and composer Oreste Sindici. Dated 1987.

1988, May 25 Litho. *Perf. 12*
974 A451 70p multicolored .90 .25

Human Rights — A452

Perf. 14½x14, 14x14½

1988-89 Engr.
975 A452 30p Life .35 .25
976 A452 35p Suffrage .35 .25
977 A452 40p Association, horiz. .45 .25
978 A452 45p Culture, horiz. .35 .25
Nos. 975-978 (4) 1.50 1.00

Issued: 30p, 35p, 5/12; 40p, 7/1; 45p, 10/27/89.

See Nos. C797, C807.

Pasto, 450th Anniv. A453

1988, May 20 Litho. *Perf. 12*
979 A453 60p Cathedral, Pasto .70 .35

Dated 1987.

Bogota Aqueduct and Sewage System, Cent. — A454

1988, May 20
980 A454 100p Waterfall 1.25 .35

Maria Currea de Aya (1888-1985), Women's Rights Activist — A455

1988, May 27
981 A455 80p multicolored .95 .25

A456

Sailfish, Istiaophorus Americanus.

Perf. 14x13½

1988, July 19 Engr. Wmk. 334
982 A456 (A) dark blue 4.00 2.25
983 A456 (B) Prus blue 1.00 .40

At the time of issue, No. 982 was sold for 400p and No. 983 for 100p. See type A486.

A457

Unwmk.

1988, Aug. 10 Litho. *Perf. 12*
984 A457 120p multicolored 1.25 .35

San Bartolome College, founded in 1604.

Jorge Alvarez Lleras (1885-1952), Engineer and Director of the Natl. Astronomical Observatory — A458

1988, Aug. 17
985 A458 90p multicolored 1.00 .45

Pres. Eduardo Santos (1888-1974) A459

1988, Aug. 30
986 A459 80p multicolored .85 .25

Andres Bello Seminary A460

Unwmk.

1988, Dec. 27 Litho. *Perf. 12*
987 A460 115p multicolored 1.25 .25

Adpostal, 25th Anniv. A461

1989, May 3
988 A461 45p multicolored .40 .25

Military Leaders — A462

Bolivar and Santander at the Los Llanos Campaign — A463

1989 Litho. *Perf. 12*
989 A462 40p Santander .60 .25
990 A462 40p Bolivar .60 .25
991 A463 45p multicolored .60 .25
Nos. 989-991 (3) 1.80 .75

Liberation campaign, 170th anniv.

Issued: No. 989, 8/25; No. 990, 7/25; 45p, 8/7.

From Boyaca to Santa Fe — A464

1989, Aug. 7 Litho. *Perf. 12*
992 45p multicolored 1.50 .45
993 45p multicolored 1.50 .45
a. A464 Pair, #992-993 4.00 2.00

Liberation campaign, 170th anniv.

Liberation Campaign Triptych — A466

Designs: a, Gen. Santander, liberation force. b, Simon Bolivar riding mount. c, Insurgent cavalry.

Unwmk.

1989, Aug. 7 Litho. *Perf. 13*
994 A466 Strip of 3 4.50 1.75
a.-c. 45p any single 1.25 .55

Liberation Campaign, 170th anniv.

Tunja, 450th Anniv. A467

1989, Aug. 8 *Perf. 12*
995 A467 45p multicolored .40 .25

Fauna Type of 1988

Designs: No. 996, Harpia harpyja, horiz. No. 997, Urocyon cinereoargenteus. No. 998, Dendrobates histrionicus. No. 999, Phenacosaurus indenenae. No. 1000, Cebuella pygmaea. No. 1001, Eurypyga helias, horiz.

Perf. 14½x14, 14x14½

1989-90 Engr. Wmk. 334
996 A446a 45p black 1.00 .25
997 A446a 50p blue gray .60 .25
998 A446a 50p deep claret .40 .25
999 A446a 55p red brown .85 .25
1000 A446a 60p brown .60 .25
1001 A446a 60p org brown .60 .25
Nos. 996-1001 (6) 4.05 1.50

Issued: 45p, 9/7; Nos. 997, 1000, 3/1/90; No. 998, 4/25; 55p, 8/18; No. 1001, 8/6.

City of Armenia, Cent. — A468

1989, Aug. 30 Unwmk. *Perf. 12*
1011 A468 135p multicolored 1.25 .80

Espeletia Hartwegiana A469

1990, Mar. 28 Litho. *Perf. 12*
1012 A469 60p multicolored .35 .25

Gen. Francisco De Paula Santander (1792-1840) — A470

1990, May 6 *Perf. 14x13½*
1013 A470 50p multicolored .35 .25
Nos. 1013,C823-C827 (6) 3.30 2.75

See Nos. 1046-1047.

General Santander Police Academy, 50th Anniv. — A471

1990, May 16 *Perf. 12*
1014 A471 60p multicolored .40 .25

Department of La Guajira A473

1990, July 1 *Perf. 12*
1016 A473 60p multicolored .60 .25

Ceiba Pentandra A474

1990, July 15 Litho. *Perf. 12*
1017 A474 60p multicolored .50 .25

Tibouchina lepidota — A475

1990, Aug. 8 Litho. *Perf. 12*
1018 A475 70p multicolored .90 .25

Ceroxylon quindiuense A476

Unwmk.

1990, Aug. 28 Litho. *Perf. 14*
1019 A476 70p multicolored .50 .25

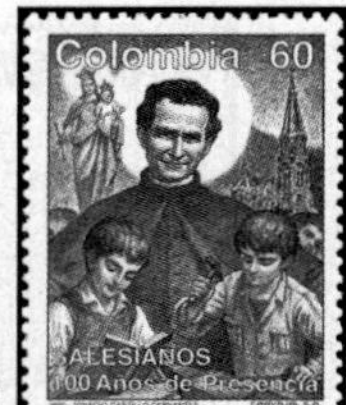

St. John Bosco — A477

1990, Sept. 28 *Perf. 12*
1020 A477 60p multicolored .60 .25

Salesian Order in Colombia, cent.

A478

1991, Mar. 28 Litho. *Perf. 12*
1021 A478 70p multicolored .40 .25

Miraculous Christ, Pilgrimage Church of Buga.

Moths and Butterflies A479

No. 1022, Callithea philotima. No. 1023, Anaea syene, vert. No. 1024, Thecla coronata, vert. No. 1025, Agrias amydon. No. 1026, Morpho rhetenor. No. 1027, Heliconius longarenus.

1991, Apr. 18 Litho. *Perf. 14*
1022 A479 70p multicolored .90 .25
1023 A479 70p multicolored .90 .25
1024 A479 80p multicolored 1.10 .25
1025 A479 80p multicolored 1.20 .25
1026 A479 170p multicolored 2.50 .35
1027 A479 190p multicolored 2.50 .35
Nos. 1022-1027 (6) 9.10 1.70

Nos. 1025-1027 are airmail.

New Constitution A480

1991, July 4 Litho. *Perf. 14*
1028 A480 70p multicolored .40 .25

A481

1991, July 19 *Perf. 12*
1029 A481 80p multicolored .40 .30

Pres. Dario Echandia Olaya (1897-1989). See No. 1042.

A482

1991, Aug. 7
1030 A482 70p multicolored .35 .25

Col. Antanasio Girardot (1791-1813).

A483

1991, Aug. 15 Litho. *Perf. 14*
1031 A483 80p multicolored .50 .25

Luis Carlos Galan Sarmiento (1943-1989), political reformer.

A484

Pre-Columbian Artifacts: 80p, Statue of cat god. No. 1033, Pitcher from tomb of high official. No. 1034, Statue with two heads. 210p, Flying fish, horiz.

1991, Aug. 24 *Perf. 12*
1032 A484 80p multicolored .75 .25
1033 A484 90p multicolored .90 .25
1034 A484 90p multicolored .90 .25
1035 A484 210p multicolored 2.00 .30
Nos. 1032-1035 (4) 4.55 1.05

Nos. 1034-1035 are airmail.

Colonial Architecture A485

80p, Cloister of St. Augustine, Tunja. No. 1037, Community Bridge, Chia. No. 1038, Roadside Chapel, Pamplona. 190p, Church of Immaculate Conception, Bogota.

1991 Litho. *Perf. 12*
1036 A485 80p multi .75 .25
1037 A485 90p multi 1.25 .25
1038 A485 90p multi, vert. 1.00 .30
1039 A485 190p multi, vert. 2.00 .35
Nos. 1036-1039 (4) 5.00 1.15

Issue dates: No. 1037, Sept. 9; others, Sept. 27. Nos. 1038-1039 are airmail.

Istiaphorus Americanus A486

1991, Sept. 3 *Perf. 14*
1040 A486 830p multicolored 5.75 1.50

Colombian Police Force, Cent. A487

1991, Oct. 12 *Perf. 12*
1041 A487 80p multicolored .60 .25

President Type of 1991

Pres. Alberto Lleras Camargo (1906-1990)

1991, Nov. 5
1042 A481 80p multicolored .45 .25

Sogamoso City Hall — A489

1991, Dec. 17 Litho. *Perf. 12*
1043 A489 80p multicolored .50 .25

A490

Designs: No. 1044, Diana Turbay Quintero (1950-91), journalist. No. 1045, Indalecio Lievano Aguirre (1917-82), diplomat.

1992 Litho. *Perf. 14*
1044 A490 80p multicolored .45 .25
1045 A490 80p multicolored .45 .25

Issued: No. 1044, Jan. 24; No. 1045, Apr. 21.

Santander Type of 1990 and

Battle of Boyaca — A491a

1992, Apr. 2 *Perf. 14*
Size: 26x37mm
1046 A470 80p Monument .50 .30
1047 A470 190p Portrait 1.20 .70

Souvenir Sheet
Perf. 13½x14
1047A A491a 950p multicolored 5.25 5.25

Nos. 1047-1047A are airmail. Gen. Francisco de Paula Santander, bicent. of birth.

A492

Ministers of Justice: 100p, Enrique Low Murtra (1939-91). 110p, Rodrigo Lara Bonilla (1946-84).

1992, Apr. 30 Litho. *Perf. 12*
1048 A492 100p multicolored .60 .30
1049 A492 110p multicolored .70 .30

A493

1992, May 18 *Perf. 14*
1050 A493 110p multicolored .50 .40

15th natl. games, Barranquilla.

Wildlife — A494

No. 1051, Oroaetus icidori. No. 1052, Tremarctos ornatus.

1992, Apr. 14 Litho. *Perf. 12*
1051 A494 (B) multicolored 1.60 .80
1052 A494 (A) multicolored 8.50 3.50

Nos. 1051-1052 had face values of 200p and 950p respectively on date of issue.

Endangered Species A495

No. 1053, Crocodylus acutus. No. 1054, Vultur gryphus, vert.

1992, Aug. 4

1053 A495 100p multicolored 1.25 .40
1054 A495 100p multicolored 1.25 .40

On No. 1053 acutus is misspelled.

A496

1992, Aug. 24 Litho. *Perf. 14*

1055 A496 100p multicolored .60 .30
1056 A496 110p multicolored .60 .30

Maria Lopez de Escobar, founder of the House of the Mother and Child. No. 1056 is airmail.

A497

1992, Sept. 23 Litho. *Perf. 12*

1057 A497 100p multicolored .50 .30

Conference of First Ladies of the Americas and Caribbean, Cartagena.

Recycling — A498

1992, Oct. 9 Litho. *Perf. 12*

1058 A498 100p multicolored .50 .30

Discovery of America, 500th Anniv. — A499

Paintings: 100p, Zenaida, by Ana Mercedes Hoyos. No. 1060, Estudio Para 1/500, by Beatriz Gonzalez. No. 1061, Blue Eagle, by Alejandro Obregon. 230p, Cantileo, by Luis Luna. 260p, Corn, by Antonio Caro. 400p, Grand Curtain, by Luis Caballero. 440p, Homage to Guatavita, by Alejandro Obregon.

1992, Oct. 5 Litho. *Perf. 13½x14*

1059 A499 100p multicolored .50 .30
1060 A499 110p multicolored .50 .30
1061 A499 110p multicolored .50 .30
1062 A499 230p multicolored 1.25 .70
1063 A499 260p multicolored 1.50 .80
Nos. 1059-1063 (5) 4.25 2.40

Souvenir Sheets

Perf. 12

1064 A499 400p multicolored 3.50 3.50
1065 A499 440p multicolored 3.50 3.50

Nos. 1061-1063 are airmail.

World Post Day — A500

1992, Oct. 19 Litho. *Perf. 12*

1066 A500 (B) multicolored 1.20 .65

No. 1066 had face value of 200p on day of issue.

Christmas — A501

Children's paintings of: 100p, Nativity scene. 110p, Adoration of the Magi.

1992, Nov. 20 Litho. *Perf. 12*

1067 A501 100p multicolored .60 .30
1068 A501 110p multicolored .60 .30

No. 1068 is airmail.

Three Musicians, by Fernando Botero
A502

1993, Feb. 5 Litho. *Perf. 12*

1069 A502 (B) multicolored 1.25 .80

No. 1069 had a face value of 250p on day of issue.

Lions Intl. Campaign Against Amblyopia
A503

1993, Mar. 26 *Perf. 14*

1070 A503 100p multicolored .40 .30

Holy Week in Popayan
A504

1993, Apr. 5 *Perf. 14x13½*

1071 A504 (B) multicolored 1.25 .80

No. 1071 had a face value of 250p on day of issue.

A505

1993, Apr. 7 *Perf. 12*

1072 A505 (B) multicolored 1.25 .80

Pan American Health Org., 90th anniv.
No. 1072 had a face value of 250p on day of issue.

A506

1993, Apr. 14

1073 A506 (B) multicolored 1.25 .80

Franciscans of Mary Immaculate, cent. No. 1073 had a face value of 250p on day of issue.

A507

1993, Apr. 22 Litho. *Perf. 14*

1074 A507 (B) multicolored .90 .80

EXFILBO '93, 18th Natl. Philatelic Exhibition. No. 1074 had a face value of 250p on day issue.

Guillermo Cano, writer — A508

1993, July 2 Litho. *Perf. 12*

1075 A508 250p multicolored 1.25 .75

Human Rights
A509

Rights: a, 150p, Of prisoners. b, 150p, Of the elderly. c, 200p, Of the infirm. d, 200p, Of children. e, 220p, Of women. f, 220p, Of the poor. g, 460p, To clean environment. h, 520p, Of indigenous people.

Painting: 800p, Peace, Rights, and Freedom, by Alfredo Vivero, vert.

1993, June 10 *Perf. 14*

1076 A509 Block of 8, #a.-h. 12.00 7.50

Souvenir Sheet

1077 A509 800p multicolored 5.50 5.50

Nos. 1076e-1076h are airmail.

Amazon Region of Colombia — A510

No. 1078a, Parrot. No. 1078b, Anaconda. No. 1079a, Victoria regia. No. 1079b, Flor ipecacuana. 880p, Map, native, horiz.

1993 Litho. *Perf. 12*

1078 A510 150p Pair, #a.-b. 1.50 1.25
1079 A510 220p Pair, #a.-b. 2.00 1.50

Souvenir Sheet

1080 A510 880p multicolored 5.00 5.00

Nos. 1079-1080 are airmail.

Famous People — A511

Designs: a, 150p, Alberto Pumarejo (1893-1970). b, 150p, Lorencita Villegas de Santos (1892-1960). c, 200p, Meliton Rodriguez (1875-1942). d, 200p, Tomas Carrasquilla (1858-1940).

1993 Litho. *Perf. 14x13½*

1081 A511 Block of 4, #a.-d. 4.00 2.75

Christmas — A512

1993, Nov. 30 *Perf. 12*

1082 A512 200p Holy Family .95 .60
1083 A512 220p Shepherd 1.60 1.10

No. 1083 is airmail.

Tourism
A513

Designs: No. 1084a, San Andres Providence. b, Cocuy Natl. Park. c, Lake Cocha. d, Waterfalls, Serrania de la Macarena. 250p, Lake Otun. No. 1086a, Chicamocha River. b, Sierra Nevada de Santa Marta mountains. 520p, Penol Reservoir.

1993, Dec. 1 Litho. *Perf. 12*

1084 A513 220p Block of 4, #a.-d. 4.50 3.00
1085 A513 250p multicolored 1.25 .75

1086 A513 460p Pair, #a.-b. 4.75 3.00
1087 A513 520p multicolored 2.75 1.50
Nos. 1084-1087 (4) 13.25 8.25

Nos. 1084, 1086-87 are airmail.

A514

1993, Dec. 21 Litho. *Perf. 14*
1088 A514 150p multicolored .75 .40

Natl. Museum, 170th anniv.

Marie Poussepin A515

1994, Jan. 25 Litho. *Perf. 14*
1089 A515 300p multicolored 1.40 .80

A516

Birds: 180p, Ognorhynchus icterotis. 240p, Rallus semiplumbeus. 270p, Semnornis ramphastinus. 560p, Anas cyanoptera.

1994, Mar. 4
1090 A516 180p multi 1.40 .40
1091 A516 240p multi 1.60 .55
1092 A516 270p multi, horiz. 2.00 .70
1093 A516 560p multi, horiz. 4.00 1.40
Nos. 1090-1093 (4) 9.00 3.05

Nos. 1092-1093 are airmail.

A517

1994, Apr. 11 Litho. *Perf. 14*
1094 A517 300p multicolored 1.40 .80

Air Force, 75th anniv.

Latin American Presidential Summit, Cartagena A518

1994, June 14 Litho. *Perf. 14*
1095 A518 300p shown 1.00 .65
1096 A518 630p Flags 2.10 1.60

No. 1096 is airmail.

1994 World Cup Soccer Championships, US — A519

World Cup Trophy and: 180p, Soccer player, Colombian flag. 270p, Two players with ball. 560p, Soccer ball, Colombian flag, vert.
1110p, Soccer player offering hand to another.

1994, May 26 *Perf. 12*
1097 A519 180p multicolored .60 .40
1098 A519 270p multicolored 1.00 .55
1099 A519 560p multicolored 2.00 1.40
Nos. 1097-1099 (3) 3.60 2.35

Souvenir Sheet

1100 A519 1110p multicolored 5.50 5.50

Nos. 1098-1099 are airmail.

Ricardo Rendon (1894-1931), Artist — A520

1994, June 30 Litho. *Perf. 12*
1101 A520 240p black 1.25 .65

1993 Census — A521

1994, Aug. 12 *Perf. 14*
1102 A521 240p multicolored 1.00 .40

Ministry of Communications Inravision, 30th Anniv. — A522

1994, Aug. 3
1103 A522 180p multicolored .80 .40

Intl. Year of the Family A523

1994, Sept. 1 Litho. *Perf. 14*
1104 A523 300p multicolored 1.25 .65

America Issue — A524

Methods of mail delivery: 270p, Horse, bicycle. 300p, Men holding stamps showing truck, ship, plane.

1994, Oct. 18 Litho. *Perf. 13*
1105 A524 270p multicolored 1.60 .65
1106 A524 300p multicolored 2.40 .70

No. 1105 is airmail.

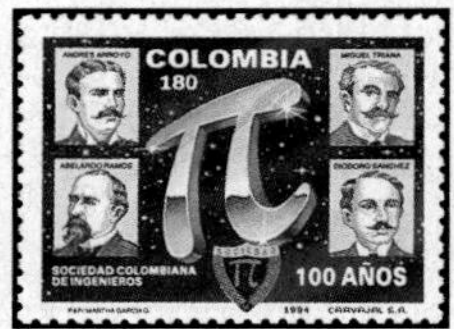

Colombian Society of Engineers, Cent. A525

1994, Oct. 20 Litho. *Perf. 12*
1107 A525 180p multicolored .75 .40

Christmas A526

1994, Nov. 22 Litho. *Perf. 13½x13*
1108 A526 270p Magi .95 .65
1109 A526 300p Holy family 1.10 .70

No. 1108 is airmail.

Former President Type of 1981

Miniature Sheet of 20

Designs: a, Jose Miguel Pey. b, Jorge Tadeo Lozano. c, Antonio Narino. d, Camilo Torres. e, Jose Fernandez Madrid. f, Jose Maria del Castillo y Rada. g, Custodio Garcia Rovira. h, Antonio Villavicencio. i, Liborio Mejia. j, Rafael Urdaneta. k, Juan Garcia del Rio. l, Jose Maria Melo. m, Tomas Herrera. n, Froilan Largacha. o, Salvador Camacho Roldan. p, Ezequiel Hurtado. q, Dario Echandia Olaya. r, Alberto Lleras Camargo. s, Gustavo Rojas Pinilla. t, Carlos Lleras Restrepo.

1995, Apr. 4 Litho. *Perf. 12*
1110 A401 270p #a.-t. 35.00 35.00

World Offroad Bicycle Championships, Melgar — A527

1995, Mar. 30 *Perf. 14*
1111 A527 400p multicolored 1.50 .90

A528

1995, Oct. 12 Litho. *Perf. 12*
1112 A528 220p multicolored 1.00 .45

Gen. Jose Maria Obando (1795-1861), President.

A529

1995, Nov. 28 *Perf. 14*
1113 A529 400p Clean air 1.50 .75
1114 A529 400p Clean water 1.50 .75

Preserve the environment. America issue.

Christmas A530

Stained glass windows: 220p, Flight into Egypt. 330p, Nativity.

1995, Dec. 18 *Perf. 12*
1115 A530 220p multicolored .75 .40
1116 A530 330p multicolored 1.10 .65

No. 1116 is airmail.

Bogotá to Boyacá World Cycling Championship — A531

1995, Oct. 4 Litho. *Perf. 12*
1117 A531 400p multicolored 1.75 .75

León De Greiff (1895-1976), Poet — A532

1996, May 2 Litho. *Perf. 12*
1118 A532 400p black 1.40 .60

Mosquera Courtyard, Natl. Capitol A533

1996, July 18 **Litho.** ***Perf. 14***
1119 A533 400p multicolored 1.25 .60

Medellin Rapid Transit System A534

1996, July 2 ***Perf. 12***
1120 A534 500p multicolored 2.00 .90

A535

1996, June 20
1121 A535 500p multicolored 1.50 .75

Community of St. John of God in Colombia, 400th anniv.

A536

Arms: a, Santa Maria la Antigua del Darien. b, San Sebastian de Mariquita. c, Villa de la Marinilla. d, Villa of Santa Cruz of Mompox.

1996, June 25
1122 A536 400p Block of 4, #a.-d. 4.75 4.75
e. As "d," inscribed AEREO 15.00 15.00
f. Block of 4, #1122a-1122c, 1122e 20.00 20.00

Issued in sheets of 16 stamps.

1996 Summer Olympic Games, Atlanta — A537

1996, July 16
1123 A537 500p multicolored 1.60 .75

SAYCO (Colombian Authors and Composers Society), 50th Anniv. — A538

1996, Aug. 17 **Litho.** ***Perf. 12***
1124 A538 400p multicolored 1.40 .60

Exfilbo '96, 20th Natl. Philatelic Exhibition A539

Jewelry from Gold Museum, Bogotá.

1996, Oct. 19 **Litho.** ***Perf. 12***
1125 A539 400p multicolored 1.40 .60

Souvenir Sheet

Founders Theater, Manizales, 30th Anniv. — A540

Drop curtain: a, Eagle, people watching man drawing on ground, vert. b, People, animals on hillside.

1996, Oct. 28 ***Perf. 14***
1126 A540 4000p #a.-b. 25.00 25.00

Christmas A541

No. 1127, Mailman handing woman letter. No. 1128, Woman reading letter, mailman holding bundle of mail.

1996, Nov. 22
1127 A541 400p multicolored 1.75 .40
1128 A541 400p multicolored 1.75 .40

No. 1128 is airmail.

America Issue — A542

No. 1129, Men's costume. No. 1130, Women's costume.

1996, Nov. 29 ***Perf. 12***
1129 A542 500p multicolored 1.50 .60
1130 A542 500p multicolored 1.50 .60

Historical Landmarks — A543

a, Cemetery, Santa Cruz of Mompox. b, Carved face, San Agustin Archaelogical Park. c, Entrance, Palace of the Inquisition, Cartagena de Indias. d, Inside ruins, Tierradentro Archaelogical Park.

1996, Dec. 6 ***Perf. 14***
1131 A543 400p Block of 4, #a.-d. 10.00 10.00

Alvaro Gomez Hurtado (1919-95), Politician, Writer — A544

1997, Mar. 18 **Litho.** ***Perf. 12***
1132 A544 400p multicolored 1.50 .75

Bogotá Journalists Assoc., 50th Anniv. A545

1997, July 10 **Litho.** ***Perf. 12***
1133 A545 400p multicolored 1.00 .40

Natl. Festival of Porro — A546

1997, June 26 ***Perf. 13½x14***
1134 A546 400p multicolored 1.00 .40

Pres. Virgilio Barco (1921-97) — A547

1997, Nov. 27 **Litho.** ***Perf. 14***
1135 A547 500p multicolored 1.15 .40

Colombia in Peace A548

500p, Children playing. 1100p, Children dancing.

1997, Dec. 30 **Litho.** ***Perf. 12***
1136 A548 500p multicolored 1.25 .40
1137 A548 1100p multicolored 2.50 .90

No. 1137 is airmail.

America Issue A549

500p, Postman by day. 1100p, Postman by night.

1997, Dec. 30
1138 A549 500p multicolored 1.75 .50
1139 A549 1100p multicolored 3.75 1.25

No. 1139 is airmail.

Jorge Eliecer Gaitan (1903-48), Politician — A550

1998, Apr. 24 **Litho.** ***Perf. 14***
1140 A550 500p multicolored 1.75 .80

Free University, 75th Anniv. A551

1998, July 1 **Litho.** ***Perf. 14***
1141 A551 500p black & red 2.50 .75

Santander Industrial University, 50th Anniv. — A552

1998, May 14 ***Perf. 12***
1142 A552 500p multicolored 1.75 .80

City of Manizales, 150th Anniv. — A553

1998, July 24 Litho. *Perf. 12*
1143 A553 500p multicolored 2.50 .75

A554

Pre-Columbian art, agency: a, Tairona, Bank of the Republic. b, Malagana, Controller General. c, Quimbaya, Bank Superintendent.

1998, July 24
1144 A554 500p Strip of 3, #a.-c. 7.25 7.25

Natl. financial agencies, 70th anniv.

A555

1998, Aug. 21 *Perf. 14*
1145 A555 500p multicolored 2.50 .80

Pres. Misael Pastrana Borrero (1923-97).

University of the Andes, 50th Anniv. A556

1998, Sept. 28
1146 A556 500p multicolored 2.10 .80

Christmas A557

Designs: 500p, Woman kneeling down to get water with bowl, cherubs in sky. No. 1148a, Magi. No. 1148b, Nativity scene.

1998, Nov. 19 Litho. *Perf. 14*
1147 A557 500p multicolored 1.25 .75
1148 A557 1000p Pair, #a.-b. 4.75 3.25

No. 1148 is airmail.

A558

Emblems of Colombian Academies: a, Language. b, Medicine. c, Law. d, History. e, Science. f, Ecomonics. g, Religion.

1998, Dec. 15 *Perf. 12*
Sheet of 7 + Label
1149 A558 500p #a.-g. 15.00 13.50

A559

1999, Apr. 16 *Perf. 14*
1150 A559 1000p multicolored 2.10 1.00

Gen. José Hilario López.

Famous Women — A559a

America Issue: 600p, Soledad Román de Nuñez. 1200p, Bertha Herández de Ospina.

1999, Mar. 25 Litho. *Perf. 12*
1151 A559a 600p multicolored 1.50 1.50
1152 A559a 1200p multicolored 2.75 2.75

No. 1152 is airmail.

Turtles — A560

a, Chelonia mydas. b, Dermochelys coriacea. c, Eretmochelys imbricata.

1999, Apr. 16 *Perf. 14*
1153 A560 1300p Strip of 3, #a.-c. 12.50 12.50

Dr. Eduardo Zuleta Angel, Diplomat (b. 1899) — A561

1999, Sept. 9 Litho. *Perf. 12*
1154 A561 600p multicolored 1.35 1.35

Pamplona, 450th Anniv. A562

1999 Litho. *Perf. 12*
1155 A562 1000p multicolored 2.50 2.50

Sovereign Military Order of Malta, 900th Anniv. — A563

1999, June 24 *Perf. 14*
1156 A563 1200p multicolored 4.75 4.00

Japanese Immigration to Colombia — A564

Designs: a, Red at right. b, Red at left.

1999, May 12 *Perf. 13½x14*
1157 A564 1300p Pair, #a.-b. 5.50 5.50

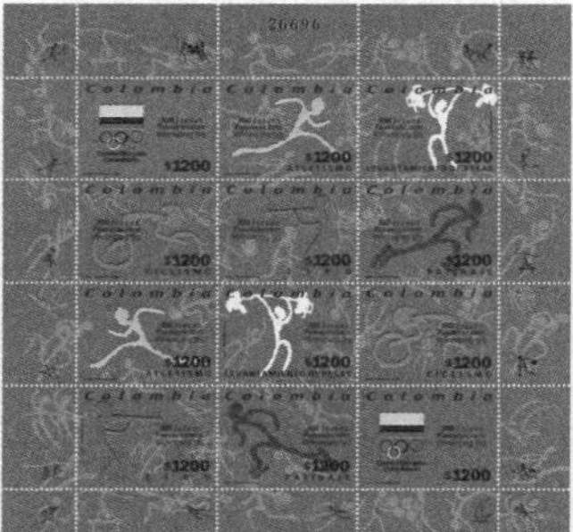

Pan American Games, Winnipeg, Manitoba — A565

Designs: a, Flag, Olympic rings. b, Runner facing right. c, Weight lifter facing left. d, Cyclist facing right. e, Shooter facing left. f, Roller skater facing right. g, Runner facing left. h, Weight lifter facing right. i, Cyclist facing left. j, Shooter facing right. k, Roller skater facing left. l, Like "a," with lilac vertical line under "12."

1999, July 23 Litho. *Perf. 14*
1158 A565 1200p Sheet of 12, #a.-l. 30.00 30.00

Luis A. Robles (b. 1849) — A566

1999, Oct. 27
1159 A566 600p multi 1.10 1.10

Manufacture of Aspirin, Cent. A567

1999, Dec. 1 *Perf. 12¾*
1160 A567 600p multi 1.10 1.10

Value is for stamp with surrounding selvage.

UPU, 125th Anniv. A568

1999, Oct. 29 *Perf. 14¼*
1161 A568 1000p "125" 1.75 1.75
1162 A568 1300p "1874-1999" 2.75 2.75

Inter-American Development Bank, 40th Anniv. — A569

Abstract art: a, "Colombia" in yellow. b, "Colombia" in red.

1999, Nov. 19 *Perf. 14x14¼*
1163 A569 1000p Pair, #a.-b. 3.50 3.50

America Issue, A New Millennium Without Arms — A570

a, Stylized hands. b, Large flower at LR.

1999, Nov. 9 *Perf. 14*
1164 A570 1200p Pair, #a.-b. 4.50 4.50

Christmas — A571

a, Holy Family, animals. b, Angel, Magi.

1999, Nov. 29 *Perf. 13½x14*
1165 A571 600p Pair, #a.-b. 2.40 2.40

Millennium — A572

Designs: a, Nude man, flag, dove. b, Globe, rainbow, "2000."

2000, Jan. 3 ***Perf. 14***
1166 A572 1000p Pair, #a.-b. 4.00 4.00

University of Medellin, 50th Anniv. A573

2000, Feb. 1 **Litho.** ***Perf. 14***
1167 A573 1000p multi 2.00 2.00

Father José Rafael Faría Bermúdez (1896-1979) A574

2000, Mar. 6 **Litho.** ***Perf. 14***
1168 A574 1300p multi 2.60 2.60

2000 Summer Olympics, Sydney A575

2000, Apr. 21
1169 A575 1000p multi 2.00 2.00

Popayán Religious Music Festival A576

2000, July 7
1170 A576 1000p multi 2.25 2.25

America Issue, Campaign Against AIDS A577

2000, Sept. 19 **Litho.** ***Perf. 14x13½***
1171 A577 1000p multi 4.00 4.00

Radio Station HJCK, 50th Anniv. — A578

2000, Sept. 28 **Litho.** ***Perf. 14***
1172 A578 1000p multi 2.00 2.00

Birth Registration A579

2000, Nov. 14 **Litho.** ***Perf. 14¼***
1173 A579 1000p multi 2.00 2.00

Paintings A580

No. 1174: a, Archangel, by Fernando Botero. b, Gypsy Woman With Tamourine, by Jean-Baptiste-Camille Corot. c, Vera Sergine Renoir, by Renoir. d, Man on Horse, by Botero. e, Mother Superior, by Botero. f, A Town, by Botero. g, Flowers, by Botero. h, Cézanne, by Botero. i, Patio, by Botero. j, Absinthe Drinker in Grenelle, by Toulouse-Lautrec. k, A Little Valley, by Corot. l, The Studio, by Botero.

2001, Jan. 31 ***Perf. 12***
1174 Sheet of 12 32.50 32.50
a.-l. A580 650p Any single 2.00 2.00

Children's Day — A581

2001, Mar. 15 **Litho.** ***Perf. 14***
1175 A581 1100p multi 3.75 3.50

Abolition of Slavery, 150th Anniv. — A582

2001, May 21 **Litho.** ***Perf. 14¼x14***
1176 A582 1100p multi 4.00 3.50

Discovery of Magdalena River, 500th Anniv. — A583

2001, June 13 **Litho.** ***Perf. 14***
1177 A583 1100p multi 4.00 3.50

Copa America Soccer Tournament A584

2001, July 18 **Litho.** ***Perf. 12¾***
1178 A584 1900p multi 5.25 5.00

Values are for examples with surrounding selvage.

America Issue — Los Katios Natl. Park, UNESCO World Heritage Site — A585

2001, Aug. 17 ***Perf. 13¾x14***
1179 A585 2100p multi 8.00 7.00

Year of Dialogue Among Civilizations A586

2001, Oct. 9 ***Perf. 14***
1180 A586 650p multi 2.75 2.25

Reclining Woman, by Fernando Botero — A587

2001, Oct. 23 ***Perf. 14¼***
1181 A587 1100p multi 4.50 4.00

Christmas A588

2001, Nov. 19 ***Perf. 14***
1182 A588 1100p multi 4.50 4.00

National Beauty Pageant — A589

Flag, Miss Colombia Vanesa A. Mendoza Bustos and: a, Cartagena de Indias. b, St. Francis of Assisi Cathedral, Quibdo.

2002, Jan. 22 ***Perf. 14x14¼***
1183 A589 800p Horiz. pair, #a-b 3.75 2.75

Natural Riches of Colombia — A590

Parts of map of Colombia, various wildlife and/or natives and: a, Bird and clouds at left. b, Turtle at upper left. c, Fish and whales at left. d, Man on horse at center. e, Volcano at upper left. f, Red and blue parrots at right. g, Flamingos at left. h, Snake at upper left.

2002, Feb. 1 ***Perf. 14¼x14***
1184 A590 2300p Sheet of 8, #a-h 50.00 45.00

Children's Day — A591

2002, Feb. 18 ***Perf. 12***
1185 A591 1400p multi 2.75 2.75

New Emblem of Adpostal — A592

2002, Mar. 7 ***Perf. 14***
1186 A592 800p multi 1.75 1.75

7th South American Games A593

2002, Jan. 7
1187 A593 2100p multi 4.00 4.00

Oxyura Jamaicensis A594

2002, Apr. 30 Litho. *Perf. 12*
1188 A594 3900p multi 7.25 7.25

Souvenir Sheet

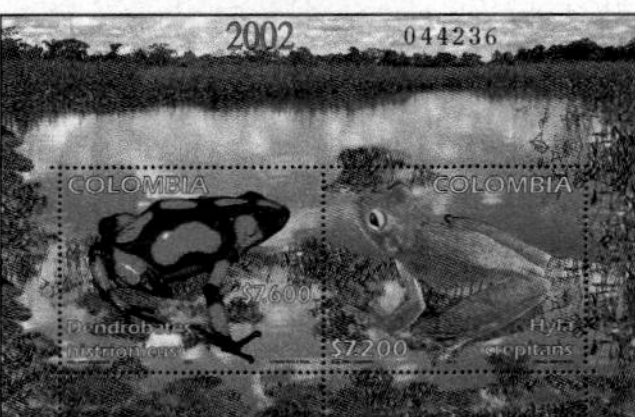

Frogs — A595

No. 1189: a, 7200p, Hyla crepitans. b, 7600p, Dendrobates histrionicus.

2002, Apr. 30 *Perf. 13¾x14*
1189 A595 Sheet of 2, #a-b 27.50 27.50

Souvenir Sheet

Butterflies — A596

No. 1190: a, Dryas iulia. b, Dryadula phaetusa, vert.

2002, Apr. 30 *Perf. 12*
1190 A596 13,700p Sheet of 2, #a-b *50.00 50.00*

Foundation for Reconstructive Surgery, 25th Anniv. — A597

2002, May 24 *Perf. 14*
1191 A597 1000p multi 2.00 2.00

Pre-Columbian Art — A598

No. 1192, 800p: a, Nariño pectoral. b, Nariño disc.
No. 1193, 1400p: a, Calima diadem. b, Calima pectoral.
No. 1194, 2100p: a, Anthropomorphic Tairona pectoral. b, Round Tairona pectoral.

2002, June 7 *Perf. 13½x14*
Horiz. Pairs, #a-b
1192-1194 A598 Set of 3 *40.00 40.00*

Surgical Society of Bogota San José Hospital, Cent. — A599

No. 1195: a, Early doctors and nurse. b, Hospital.

2002, July 22 *Perf. 14*
1195 A599 800p Horiz. pair, #a-b 3.00 3.00

Consuelo Araújo Noguera (1940-2001), Assassinated Former Minister of Culture — A600

2002, Aug. 1
1196 A600 1400p multi 2.75 2.75

Union Network International A601

2002, Aug. 12
1197 A601 1000p multi 1.90 1.90

America Issue — Youth, Education and Literacy — A602

No. 1198: a, Person reading book. b, Letters amd words.

2002, Oct. 9
1198 A602 2500p Horiz. pair, #a-b 7.25 7.25

Christmas A603

2002, Nov. 6 Litho. *Perf. 14x13¾*
1199 A603 800p multi 2.75 2.00

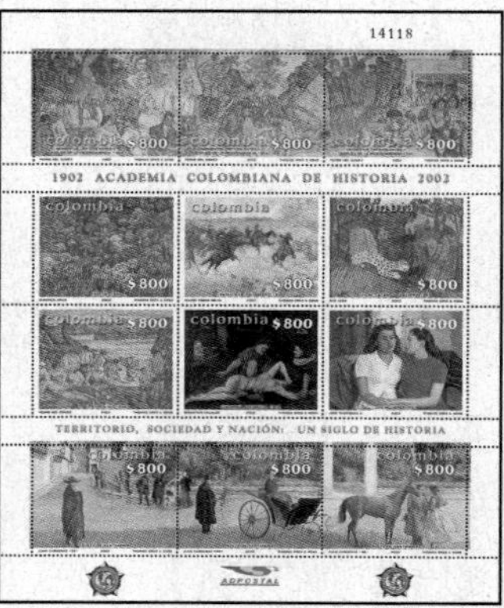

Colombian History Academy, Cent. — A604

No. 1200: a, Mural scene with Simon Bolivar at UR. b, Mural scene with horsemen at top. c, Mural scene with man with outstretched arms at UL. d, Cafetal, 1956. e, Batalla de Palonegro, 1905. f, Tigre Cazando Sabanera, 1963. g, El Barqueo, 1936. h, Colombia Asesinada, 1902. i, Dos Mujeres, 1951. j, Bearded man at left, Plaza de Santander. k, Carriage, Plaza de Santander. l, Horse, man and woman, Plaza de Santander.

2002, Nov. 19 *Perf. 13¾x14*
1200 A604 800p Sheet of 12, #a-l *45.00 45.00*

Peace Treaty Ending War of 1,000 Days, Cent. A605

2002, Nov. 21 *Perf. 14x13¾*
1201 A605 1600p multi 4.50 4.50

Carnival A606

No. 1202: a, shown. b, Participants holding masks on sticks. c, Participants on float.

2003, Jan. 4 *Perf. 14*
1202 Horiz. strip of 3 6.50 6.50
a.-b. A606 1000p Either single 1.25 1.25
c. A606 1200p multi 1.60 1.60

Printed in sheets of 3 horizontal strips and 2 horiz. strips of 3 labels.

Articulated Bus, Bogota A607

2003, Mar. 13 *Perf. 12*
1203 A607 1000p multi 2.00 2.00

Departments — A608

No. 1204 — Caldas Department: a, 1200p, Arms. b, 1200p, Government office building, Manizales, horiz. c, 1200p, Campesinos, 1957. d, 2400p, Church, Salamina. e, 2400p, Neira, 1997, horiz. f, 2400p, Enea Chapel, Manizales. g, 2800p, Laguna Verde, Villamaria. h, 2800p, Aguadas, horiz. i, 2800p, Devil's carnival, Riosucio. j, 4100p, Miner, Marmato. k, 4100p, Mariposas del Eje Cafetero, 2001, horiz. l, 4100p, Pacora.

No. 1205, 1000p — Huila Department: a, Arms. b, Government office building, Neiva, horiz. c, La Gaitana. d, Bordones Waterfall, Isnos. e, San Agustín World Heritage Archaeological Park, horiz. f, Lavapatas Spring, San Agustín. g, La Tatacoa Desert, Villavieja. h, Liberty tree, Gigante, horiz. i, Sombrero maker, Suaza. j, Nuestra Señora de los Dolores Church, Aipe. k, Paisaje, horiz. l, Dancers.

No. 1206 — 2400p: a, Historic center of Barichara. b, Ophthalmologic Foundation of Santander, Bucaramanga, horiz. c, Girón. d, Santander Industrial University Intl. Piano Festival, 20th anniv. emblem. e, Petroleum Christ Statue, refinery, Barrancabermeja, horiz. f, Church, San Andrés. g, Gustavo Cote Uribe (1918-94), writer. h, Chamber of Commerce, Bucaramanga, horiz. i, Carnival of Eastern Colombia, Bucaramanga. j, Historic center of Albania. k, Chicamocha River Canyon, Cepitá, horiz. l, Entreguerras.

Sheets of 12, #a-l, + 8 labels

2003 *Perf. 12*
1204 A608 Caldas *45.00 45.00*
1205 A608 Huila *19.00 19.00*
1206 A608 Santander *40.00 40.00*

Issued: No. 1204, Apr. 11. No. 1205, June 29. No. 1206, July 22. Size of horiz. stamps: 46x37mm.

See Nos. 1224-1226, 1246, 1265-1267, 1273, 1288-1289, 1316, 1335-1336, 1359, 1377, 1393, 1430, 1454, 1476, 1532-1533.

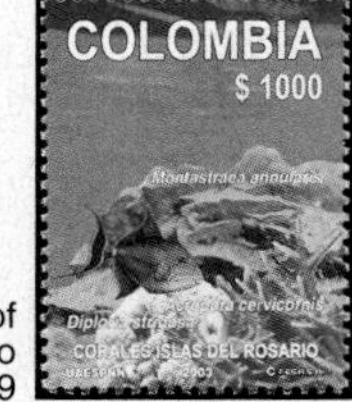

Fish and Coral of the Rosario Islands — A609

2003, Jan. 16 Litho. *Perf. 12*
1207 A609 1000p multi 3.50 3.00

Hapalopsittaca Fuertesi — A610

2003, June 13
1208 A610 1000p multi 3.50 3.00

Souvenir Sheets

Orchids — A611

No. 1209 — 2400p: a, Masdevallia ignea. b, Miltoniopsis vexillaria.
No. 1210 — 2800p: a, Odontoglossum crispum, horiz. b, Masdevallia macrura.
No. 1211, vert. — 5000p: a, Cimbidium. b, Oncidium obryzatum.
No. 1212 — 7000p: a, Cattleya dowiana. b, Cattleya trianaei (49x49mm).

Sheets of 2, #a-b

Perf. 14¼, 13¾x14 (#1212b)

2003, June 13
1209-1212 A611 Set of 4 57.50 57.50

Tejo, National Sport A612

No. 1213: a, Players, tree in foreground (49x39mm). b, Players, light poles (49x39mm). c, Cacique Turmeque.

2003, July 25 *Perf. 12*
1213 Horiz. strip of 3 11.00 11.00
a.-c. A612 2400p Any single 2.25 2.25

America Issue — A613

Flora and fauna: a, Denomination at UR. b, Denomination at LR.

2003, Oct. 9 **Litho.** *Perf. 12*
1214 A613 1600p Vert. pair, #a-b 6.25 6.25

Printed in sheets of four pairs and four labels.

Souvenir Sheet

Colombia Libraries National Reading Plan — A614

No. 1215: a, 1200p, Building. b, 4100p, Building, diff.

2003, Oct. 30 **Litho.** *Perf. 12*
1215 A614 Sheet of 2, #a-b 9.00 9.00

General Ramón Arturo Rincón Quiñones (1922-75) — A615

2003, Oct. 31
1216 A615 1000p multi 1.90 1.90

Souvenir Sheet

Administrative Security Deparment, 50th Anniv. — A616

2003, Oct. 31
1217 A616 4100p multi 6.50 6.50

Armed Forces A617

No. 1218 — Arms and mottos: a, General Command of Military Forces. b, National Army. c, National Navy. d, Air Force. e, Colombian Forces in Korea, 50th anniv.

2003, Nov. 7
1218 Vert. strip of 5 8.50 8.50
a.-e. A617 1200p Any single 1.10 .60

Christmas — A618

No. 1219: a, Good Shepherd, sheep. b, Tree, comet, airplane, rabbit. c, Rabbits, dog. d, Automobile, angel, reindeer, horse. e, Sheep, woman with basket, swan, house. f, Branch with leaves, horse and rider, duck, Indian with bow and arrow.

2003, Dec. 2 **Litho.** *Perf. 12*
1219 Block of 6 12.00 12.00
a.-f. A618 1000p Any single 1.40 1.40

Colombia and the Eldorado Legend — A619

No. 1220: a, Print of Eldorado ceremony, by Teodoro De Bry, 1595. b, Watercolor painting of Lake Guatavita, by M. María Paz, 1855. c, Watercolor painting of Lake Guatavita, by Gonzalo Ariza, 1984. d, Print of Lake Guatavita, by A. Humboldt Thibault and F. Schoell, 1813. e, Photo of Lake Guatavita, by Fernando Urbina Rangel, 1983. f, Print of Lake Guatavita, by Eustacio Barreto, 1883.

No. 1221 — Muisca raft: a, 1700p, Front. b, 2000p, Back, vert.

2004, Mar. 10
1220 A619 2800p Sheet of 6, #a-f, + 3 labels 32.00 32.00

Souvenir Sheet

1221 A619 Sheet of 2, #a-b 7.00 7.00

Locomotives — A620

No. 1222, 1100p: a, 2-8-2. b, 4-8-0.
No. 1223, 1300p: a, 2-6-2. b, 4-6-2.

2004, Mar. 19 **Horiz. Pairs, #a-b**
1222-1223 A620 Set of 2 8.00 8.00

Nos. 1222-1223 each printed in sheets of four pairs and two pairs of labels.

Departments Type of 2003

No. 1224, 1100p — Nariño Department: a, Galeras Volcano, San Juan de Pasto, horiz. b, Statue of Gen. Antonio Nariño. c, Nariño Government Building, San Juan de Pasto, horiz. d, Farm, Catambuco, horiz. e, Nuestra Señora de las Lajas Sanctuary, Ipiales. f, Sandoná city center, horiz. g, Gallery of Mirrors, horiz. h, Barnizadores de Pasto Chorography Commission. i, Golden palms, horiz. j, El Morro, Tumaco, horiz. k, Virgen de la Playa Sanctuary, San Pablo. l, Festival of Whites and Blacks, horiz.

No. 1225, 2000p — Tolima Department: a, Nevado del Tolima, horiz. b, Tolima arms. c, Ambalema, horiz. d, Bowls, La Chamba, horiz. e, Natural Bridge, Icononzo. f, Hermitage, Mariquita, horiz. g, Matachos, horiz. h, Prison, Ibagué. i, Alberto Castilla Conservatory Room, horiz. j, Fishermen, Magdalena River, horiz. k, Cacique Calarcá. l, Tolima Art Museum, Ibagué.

No. 1226, 3000p — Chocó Department: a, Coat of Arms. b, Quibdó skyline, horiz. c, Indian girls. d, San Pacho Fiesta. e, Carrasquilla College, Quibdó, horiz. f, Houses, Nóvita. g, Canoe on San Juan River. h, Women grinding corn meal, horiz. i, Nuestra Senora del Rosario Church, Condoto. j, Utría Bay. k, Bellavista Church, Bojayá, horiz. l, Goldsmith, Acandi.

Horiz. stamps are 46x37mm.

Sheets of 12, #a-l, +8 labels

2004 **Litho.** *Perf. 13¾x14*
1224 A608 Nariño 20.00 20.00
1225 A608 Tolima 35.00 35.00
1226 A608 Chocó 50.00 50.00
Nos. 1224-1226 (3) 105.00 105.00

Issued: No. 1224, 8/5; No. 1225, 4/16. No. 1226, 11/17

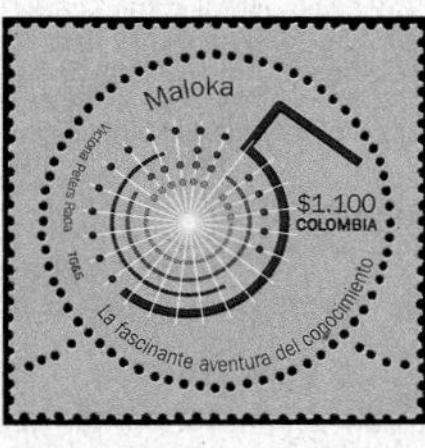

Maloka Science and Technology Center A621

2004, July 6 **Litho.** *Perf. 12¾*
1227 A621 1100p multi 1.75 1.75

Values are for stamps with surrounding selvage.

2004 Summer Olympics, Athens — A622

2004, Aug. 5 *Perf. 13¾x14*
1228 A622 4400p multi 9.00 9.00

Natl. Association of Contractors, 60th Anniv. A623

No. 1229: a, Denomination in white. b, Denomination in black.

2004, Aug. 5 *Perf. 14x13¾*
1229 Pair 5.00 5.00
a.-b. A623 2800p Either single 2.25 2.25

Printed in sheets containing 6 pairs and one large central label.

FIFA (Fédération Internationale de Football Association), Cent. — A624

2004, Aug. 25 *Perf. 13¼x14*
1230 A624 3500p multi 4.75 4.75

Women's Citizenship, 50th Anniv. — A625

2004, Sept. 24 *Perf. 14*
1231 A625 15,000p multi 12.50 12.50

Fair and Expositions Corporation, 50th Anniv. — A626

2004, Oct. 14 *Perf. 13½x13*
1232 A626 1300p multi 1.60 1.60

Colombian Radio Announcers Association, 50th Anniv. — A627

2004, Oct. 21 *Perf. 14*
1233 A627 1700p multi 3.25 3.25

17th National Games — A628

2004, Dec. 10 **Litho.** *Perf. 12¾*
1234 A628 7000p multi + label 12.50 12.50

Printed in sheets of 4 + 5 labels.

America Issue — Environmental Conservation — A629

Designs: No. 1235, 5000p, Whale, Gorgona National Nature Park. No. 1236, 5000p, Hammerhead sharks, Malpelo Flora and Fauna Sanctuary.

2004, Dec. 14 ***Perf. 14***
1235-1236 A629 Set of 2 9.00 9.00

Miniature Sheet

Christmas — A630

No. 1237 — Inscriptions: a, Jesús en la mansion de su padre. b, Eterna sumision a Dios. c, Jesús desciende al seno de su madre. d, Aceptacion de milagro divino. e, La ilusion de Maria. f, Voluntad divina en manos del emperador. g, Paciencia, expectativa y anhelo. h, Belén: Humilde hospedaje. i, Nacimiento, la faz de Dios encarnado.

2004, Dec. 15
1237 A630 2800p Sheet of 9, #a-i 28.50 28.50

Pre-Columbian Gold Artifacts From Gold Museum — A631

No. 1238, 1200p: a, Tumaco ear covering. b, Zenú nose ring.
No. 1239, 1800p: a, Cauma nose ring. b, Tierradentro bracelet.

Pairs, #a-b

2005, Jan. 21 ***Perf. 12x12½***
1238-1239 A631 Set of 2 6.50 6.50

Issued: No. 1238, 1/21; No. 1239, 3/28.

Rotary International, Cent. — A632

2005, Feb. 23 ***Perf. 13½x14***
1240 A632 3100p multi 3.00 3.00

Souvenir Sheet

Butterflies — A633

No. 1241: a, Protographium tyastes panamensis. b, Dismorphia zaela laura. c, Actinote ozomene.

2005, June 7 **Litho.** ***Perf. 14¼***
1241 A633 4600p Sheet of 3, #a-c 20.00 20.00

FENALCO (Natl. Federation of Retailers), 60th Anniv. A634

2005, June 10 ***Perf. 14***
1242 A634 1200p multi 1.75 1.75

Souvenir Sheets

Department Centenaries — A635

No. 1243, 3100p: a, Map of Caldas Department. b, Map of Colombia highlighting Caldas.
No. 1244, 3700p: a, Map of Huila Department. b, Map of Colombia highlighting Huila.
No. 1245, 4200p: a, Map of Atlantico Department. b, Map of Colombia highlighting Atlantico.

Sheets of 2, #a-b

2005, June ***Perf. 14x13½***
1243-1245 A635 Set of 3 35.00 35.00

Departments Type of 2003

No. 1246 — San Andrés y Providencia Department: a, Aerial view of San Andrés, horiz. b, Arms. c, Aerial view of Johnny Cay, horiz. d, Cayo Cangrejo, horiz. e, Artisan. f, Culture House, San Andrés, horiz. g, Morgan Head, Santa Catalina Island, horiz. h, Island view. i, Ensenada, San Andrés, horiz. j, Island architecture, horiz. k, Baptist Church, San Andrés. l, Aerial view of Providencia and Santa Catalina Islands.
Horiz. stamps are 46x37mm.

2005, July 20 ***Perf. 13¾x14***
1246 A608 1200p Sheet of 12, #a-l 30.00 30.00

Bogota Botanical Gardens — A636

2005, Aug. 5 ***Perf. 14***
1247 A636 1400p multi 1.75 1.75

15th Bolivarian Games — A637

2005, Aug. 11 ***Perf. 13¾x14***
1248 A637 3500p multi 3.75 3.75

Association of Graduates of the University of the Andes, 50th Anniv. A638

2005, Sept. 14 ***Perf. 14***
1249 A638 2000p multi 3.00 3.00

Intl. Day of Ozone Layer Protection A639

2005, Sept. 16
1250 A639 2000p multi 3.00 3.00

Souvenir Sheet

Publication of Don Quixote, 400th Anniv. — A640

No. 1251 — Paintings of Miguel de Cervantes by: a, Ricardo Rendón Bravo. b, Eduardo Ramírez Villamizar, vert. c, Santiago Martínez Delgado, vert.

Perf. 13½x14 (#1251a), 14x13½
2005, Oct. 25
1251 A640 1300p Sheet of 3, #a-c 6.50 6.50

Colpatria Bank, 50th Anniv. A641

2005, Nov. 2 ***Perf. 14x13½***
1252 A641 1200p multi 1.40 1.40

Arms of City of Facatativá A642

2005, Oct. 30 **Litho.** ***Perf. 14***
1253 A642 1800p multi 1.75 1.75

Latin Union, 50th Anniv. — A643

2005, Dec. 1 ***Perf. 13½x14***
1254 A643 5000p multi 6.00 6.00

Printed in sheets of 4.

Souvenir Sheet

America Issue, Fight Against Poverty — A644

2005, Nov. 30 ***Perf. 14x13½***
1255 A644 Sheet of 2 #1255a 13.00 13.00
a. 5000p Single stamp 6.25 6.25

Souvenir Sheet

Escuela de Lanceros (Military School), 50th Anniv. — A645

2005, Nov. 30 ***Perf. 14***
1256 A645 Sheet of 2 #1256a 31.00 31.00
a. 10,000p Single stamp 9.50 9.50

Christmas A646

2005, Dec. 9 *Perf. 14*
1257 A646 3100p multi 5.75 5.75

Printed in sheets of 7.

Colombian Journalism A647

2006, Feb. 9 **Litho.**
1258 A647 2000p multi 3.00 3.00

St. Francis Xavier (1506-52) A648

2006, Apr. 7
1259 A648 4500p multi 4.25 4.25

Pope John Paul II (1920-2005) A649

2006, Apr. 4
1260 A649 4800p multi 4.25 4.25

Frederic Chopin (1810-49), Composer — A650

2006, May 25 *Perf. 13½x13*
1261 A650 5300p multi 5.00 5.00

Printed in sheets of 4.

Gold Artifacts Type of 2005

No. 1262: a, Quimbaya striated lime receptacle with handles. b, Quimbaya thin lime receptacle.

2006, Jan. 26 *Perf. 12x12½*
1262 A631 1500p Pair, #a-b 3.75 3.75

Italian Cultural Institute of Bogota, 50th Anniv. — A651

No. 1263: a, Lute at lower left. b, Violin at lower right.

2006, Feb. 23 *Perf. 14*
1263 A651 1300p Horiz. pair, #a-b 3.50 3.50

Souvenir Sheet

Rayo Museum, 25th Anniv. — A652

No. 1264: a, Artwork in blue, white, red, yellow and black. b, Artwork in white, blue, tan and black.

2006, Jan. 21 *Perf. 13½x13*
1264 A652 Sheet, 2 each #a-b 7.00 7.00
a.-b. 1300p Either single 1.50 1.50

Departments Type of 2003

No. 1265 — Valle del Cauca Department: a, Mapping Commission drawing of Cali, horiz. b, Arms of Valle del Cauca. c, Arms and panoramic view of Sevilla, horiz. d, Calima Lake, El Darién, horiz. e, La Ermita, Santiago de Cali. f, Port of Buenaventura, horiz. g, Railroad station, Palmira, horiz. h, Sugar cane. i, Salsa dancers, Cali, horiz. j, El Paraiso Museum, El Cerrito, horiz. k, Basilica, Buga. l, Aerial view of Valle del Cauca, horiz.

No. 1266 — Boyacá Department: a, Plaza de Bolivar, Tunja, horiz. b, Arms of Boyacá. c, Mapping Commission drawing of Campo de Boyacá, horiz. d, Bolivar Monument, Campo de Boyacá, horiz. e, Altar of the Virgin of Chiquinquirá. f, Panoramic view of Garagoa, horiz. g, Plaza de los Libertadores, Duitama, horiz. h, Emeralds. i, Plaza Mayor, Villa de Leyva, horiz. j, Sierra Nevada del Cocuy, horiz. k, Temple of the Sun, Sogamoso. l, El Salitre Farm, Paipa, horiz.

No. 1267 — Quindío Department: a, Quindío Pass, 1836, horiz. b, Quimbaya culture sculpture. c, Coffee plantation house, Quimbaya, horiz. d, Coffee bean picker, Pijao, horiz. e, Valle de Cocora, Salento. f, Botanical Gardens, Calarca, horiz. g, La Estación Metropolitan Cultural Center, Armenia, horiz. h, Monument and government building, Armenia. i, Free Cemetery, Circasia, horiz. j, Aerial view of Buenavista, horiz. k, San José Temple, Génova. l, Founding of Armenia, horiz.

Horizontal stamps are 46x37mm.

Sheets of 12, #a-l, + 8 labels

2006 *Perf. 13½x14*
1265 A608 1300p Valle del Cauca 20.00 20.00
1266 A608 2000p Boyacá 30.00 30.00
1267 A608 3300p Quindío 45.00 45.00
Nos. 1265-1267 (3) 95.00 95.00

20th Central American and Caribbean Games A653

2006, July 15 **Litho.** *Perf. 14*
1268 A653 2000p multi 2.50 2.50

Pres. Alberto Lleras Camargo (1906-90) — A654

Denominations: a, 1300p. b, 3300p.

2006, Dec. 6 **Litho.** *Perf. 14x13¾*
1269 A654 Horiz. pair, #a-b + alternating labels 7.00 7.00

Souvenir Sheet

America Issue, Energy Conservation — A655

No. 1270: a, Left hand. b, Right hand.

2006, Dec. 28 *Perf. 12*
1270 A655 5000p Sheet of 2, #a-b 12.00 12.00

Christmas — A656

Denominations: a, 1300p. b, 3300p.

2006, Dec. 13 *Perf. 13¾x14*
1271 A656 Vert. pair, #a-b 5.75 5.75

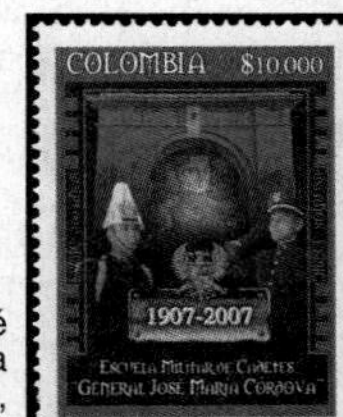

General José Maria Cordova Military School, Cent. — A657

2007, May 30 *Perf. 14*
1272 A657 10,000p multi 11.00 11.00

Departments Type of 2003

No. 1273 — Sucre Department: a, Coat of arms. b, St. Francis of Assisi Cathedral, Sincelejo, horiz. c, Palm trees, Tolú. d, Cattle, Sucre. e, Bull ring, Sincelejo, horiz. f, Church, Corozal. g, Musical score of "Fiesta en Corraleja." h, Painting of fandango dancers, horiz. i, Fisherman, Caimito. j, Palm trees, Sincelejo. k, Cane weaver, Sampués, horiz. l, Hammocks, Morroa.

Horizontal stamps are 46x37mm.

Sheet of 12, #a-l, + 8 Labels

2007, May 30 *Perf. 12*
1273 A608 3300p Sucre 50.00 50.00

Miniature Sheet

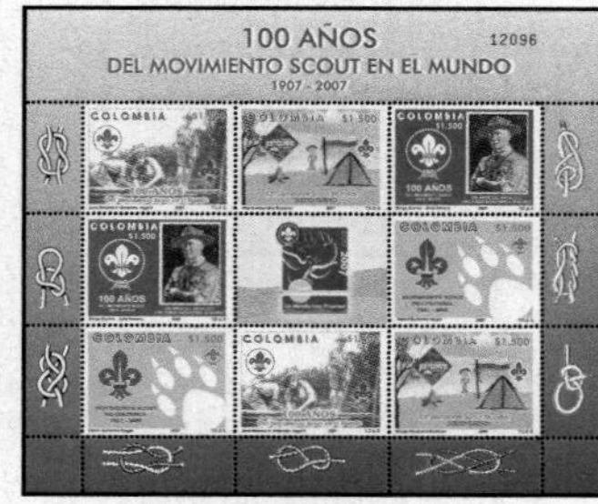

Scouting, Cent. — A658

No. 1274: a, International and Colombian Scouting emblems, Scouts with Lord Robert Baden-Powell. b, Emblem of 21st World Scout Jamboree, Colombian Scouting emblem, children's drawing of Colombian scout. c, Scouting emblem, Lord Robert Baden-Powell. d, International and Colombian Scouting emblems, animal track.

2007, June 26 *Perf. 14*
1274 A658 1500p Sheet of 8, 2 each #a-d, + central label 13.00 13.00

Souvenir Sheet

El Espectador Newspaper, 120th Anniv. — A659

No. 1275: a, Newspaper from 1887. b, Paperboy, horiz.

2007, June 28 *Perf. 12*
1275 A659 4500p Sheet of 2, #a-b 17.50 17.50

Pan American Games, Rio de Janeiro — A660

2007, July 9 *Perf. 14*
1276 A660 3700p multi 3.75 3.75

Fourth Spanish Language Intl. Congress — A661

2007, June 25
1277 A661 5300p multi + label 7.25 7.25

Caja de Compensación Familiar, 50th Anniv. — A662

2007, Oct. 10 Litho. *Perf. 14*
1278 A662 3500p multi 4.75 4.75

Colombian Association of Engineers, 50th Anniv. A663

2007, Oct. 17
1279 A663 1400p multi 1.50 1.50

Bogota Honors and Awards — A664

No. 1280: a, 2007 UNESCO World Book Capital. b, Venice Biennale Golden Lion Award for Architecture. c, 2007 Latin American Cultural Capital.

2007, Oct. 23
1280 A664 3700p Horiz. strip of 3, #a-c 20.00 20.00

Minuto de Dios, 50th Anniv. A665

2007, Nov. 22
1281 A665 1600p multi 2.00 2.00

Christmas A666

2007, Nov. 27
1282 A666 3300p multi 3.75 3.75

America Issue, Education For All — A667

2007, Dec. 13
1283 A667 3500p multi 4.25 4.25

Pres. Carlos Lleras Restrepo (1908-94) A668

2008, Apr. 8 Litho. *Perf. 12*
1284 A668 1400p multi 1.75 1.75

Colombian Friendship With Japan, Cent. A669

2008, May 22 *Perf. 14*
1285 A669 5200p multi 6.25 6.25

New Emblem of Postal Network of Colombia A670

2008, May 28
1286 A670 2100p multi 2.50 2.50

Compare with Type A685.

National Institute for the Blind, 50th Anniv. A671

Litho. & Embossed

2008, June 10
1287 A671 1400p multi 1.75 1.75

Departments Type of 2003

No. 1288 — Antioquia Department: a, Medellín skyline, horiz. b, Arms of Antioquia. c, Necoclí, horiz. d, Silleteros Parade, horiz. e, Purse. f, Rafael Uribe Uribe Palace of Culture, horiz. g, Molas, horiz. h, Lipaugus weberi. i, Waterfall, Támesis, horiz. j, Coffee cups, horiz. k, Santa Fé de Antioquia Church. l, Orquideorama, Medellín Botanical Gardens, horiz.

No. 1289 — Amazonas Department: a, Departmental emblem. b, Monkey, Isla de los Micos, horiz. c, Victoria Regia water lily. d, Butterfly, Puerto Nariño. e, Indigenous child, horiz. f, Caiman. g, Beaded mask. h, Dolphin, horiz. i, Amazonas landscape. j, Flower. k, Fisherman casting net, horiz. l, Fruits at Plaza de Mercado, Puerto Leticia.

Horizontal stamps are 50x40mm.

Sheets of 12, #a-l, + 8 labels

2008 Litho. *Perf. 13¾x14*
1288 A608 1500p Antioquia 17.50 17.50

Perf. 12
1289 A608 1600p Amazonas 24.00 24.00

Issued: No. 1288, 10/22; No. 1289, 7/18.

Battle of Maracaibo Lake, 185th Anniv. — A672

2008, July 30 *Perf. 12*
1290 A672 3900p multi 5.00 5.00

Treaty of Amity and Commerce Between Colombia and Switzerland, Cent. — A673

2008, July 31 *Perf. 14*
1291 A673 5200p multi 6.00 6.00

2008 Summer Olympics, Beijing — A674

2008, Aug. 1
1292 A674 5000p multi 5.75 5.75

Souvenir Sheet

1293 A674 10,000p multi 11.50 11.50

Aguadas, Bicent. — A675

2008, Aug. 15
1294 A675 3500p multi 4.00 4.00

Accordion Festival, Villanueva A676

2008, Sept. 25
1295 A676 5600p multi 6.00 6.00

Pres. Alfonso López Michelsen (1913-2007) A677

2008, Oct. 8
1296 A677 5100p multi 4.50 4.50

Miniature Sheet

Ministry of Communications, 85th Anniv. — A678

No. 1297 — Arms of Colombia and: a, Stylized person, emblem for Government Online program. b, Children, emblem for Computers for Education progam, vert. c, Girl with "@" balloon, campaign for clean Internet. d, Emblem for Compartel, vert.

2008, Oct. 29
1297 A678 1500p Sheet of 4, #a-d 5.50 5.50

Episcopal Conference of Colombia, Cent. — A679

2008, Nov. 6
1298 A679 1500p multi 1.40 1.40

18th Carlos Lleras Restrepo National Games A680

2008, Nov. 21
1299 A680 1500p multi 1.40 1.40

Natl. Department of Planning, 50th Anniv. A681

2008, Dec. 9
1300 A681 1500p multi 1.40 1.40

Christmas A682

Adoration of the Shepherds, by Gregorio Vásquez de Arce y Ceballos: a, 1400p. b, 3500p.

2008, Dec. 12
1301 A682 Vert. pair, #a-b 6.00 6.00

Miniature Sheet

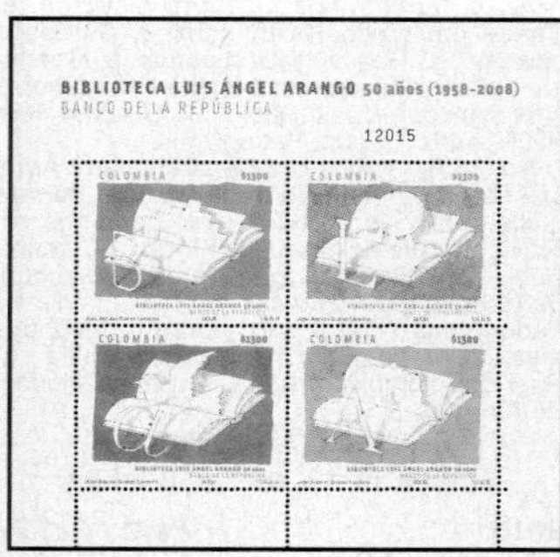

Luis Angel Arango Library, 50th Anniv. — A683

No. 1302 — Open book with: a, Ship page and "B." b, Sun page and "L." c, Dove page and "a." d, Face page and "A."

2008, Dec. 16 ***Perf. 13¾x14***
1302 A683 1300p Sheet of 4, #a-d 5.75 5.75

America Issue, National Festivals — A684

Paintings: No. 1303, 1400p, November 11, 1811, Absolute Independence of Cartagena, by Cecilia Porras. No. 1304, 1400p, Liberty Indian, by unknown artist, vert.

2008, Dec. 29 ***Perf. 13¾x14, 14x13¾***
1303-1304 A684 Set of 2 3.25 3.25

4-72 Colombia Postal Network Emblem — A685

Designs: 200p, Emblem on blue background with red frame. 400p, Emblem against blue background, and three arrows against red, blue and yellow backgrounds. 500p, Emblem against white background with blue frame. 600p, Emblem and map of Colombia.

2009, Mar. 1 **Litho.** ***Perf. 14***
1305-1308 A685 Set of 4 1.40 1.40

Souvenir Sheet

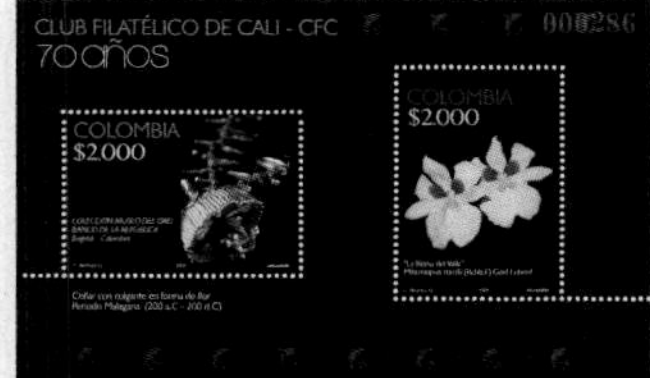

Cali Philatelic Club, 70th Anniv. — A686

No. 1309: a, Necklace with flower-shaped pendant. b, Miltoniopsis roezlii, vert.

2009, Mar. 12 ***Perf. 12***
1309 A686 2000p Sheet of 2, #a-b 7.25 7.25

Inter-America Development Bank, 50th Anniv. — A687

2009, Mar. 27
1310 A687 3700p multi 3.25 3.25

President Julio César Turbay (1916-2005) — A688

2009, Apr. 1 ***Perf. 14x13½***
1311 A688 1700p multi 1.60 1.60

Printed in sheets of 9 + 6 labels.

Naval School for Non-Commissioned Officers, Barranquilla, 75th Anniv. — A689

2009, Apr. 17 ***Perf. 14***
1312 A689 4000p multi 4.25 4.25

Colombian War School, Cent. A690

2009, May 8 ***Perf. 12***
1313 A690 5500p multi 5.50 5.50

President Guillermo León Valencia (1909-71) A691

2009, May 27
1314 A691 4200p multi 5.00 5.00

Fight of July 20, 1810, by Julián Rubiano Chávez A692

2009, June 25 ***Perf. 12***
1315 A692 1700p multi 1.75 1.75

Departments Type of 2003

Miniature Sheet

No. 1316 — La Guajira Department: a, Arms of La Guajira. b, Francisco el Hombre, mural in La Guajira Cultural Center, horiz. c, Waterfall, Montes de Oca. d, Phoenicopterus ruber. e, Domingueka, Kogui village, horiz. f, Cape of La Vela. g, Majayuts (Wayuu women). h, Riohacha Cathedral, horiz. i, Cardinalis phoeniceus. j, Aloe vulgaris. k, Caesalpinia coriaria, horiz. l, Wayuu mochilas (bags).

Horizontal stamps are 50x40mm.

Sheet of 12, #a-l, + 8 Labels

2009, July 24 **Litho.** ***Perf. 12***
1316 A608 1700p La Guajira 24.00 24.00

Miniature Sheet

Heliconia Varieties — A693

No. 1317: a, Heliconia stricta. b, Heliconia rostrata. c, Heliconia wagneriana. d, Heliconia orthotricha. e, Heliconia psittacorum.

2009, Aug. 14 **Litho.** ***Perf. 12***
1317 A693 2000p Sheet of 5, #a-e, + 5 labels 11.00 11.00

Miniature Sheet

First Colombian Postage Stamps, 150th Anniv. — A694

No. 1318: a, Colombia #1. b, Colombia #6. c, Colombia #4. d, Colombia #3. e, Colombia #7. f, Map of Colombia and text on gray background.

10,000p, Like No. 1318f with blue background.

2009, Aug. 25 ***Perf. 12***
1318 A694 4000p Sheet of 6, #a-f 28.00 28.00

Souvenir Sheet

1319 A694 10,000p multi 11.50 11.50

America Issue, Traditional Games — A695

No. 1320 — Chaza player: a, Bare-handed. b, Holding racquet.

2009, Oct. 13 **Litho.** ***Perf. 14***
1320 A695 5000p Horiz. pair, #a-b 12.00 12.00

Rafael Uribe Uribe (1859-1914), General — A696

2009, Oct. 20
1321 A696 1500p multi 1.75 1.75

Madrid Town Hall A697

2009, Nov. 13
1322 A697 10,000p multi 12.00 12.00

Madrid, Cundinamarca Department, 450th anniv.

Miniature Sheet

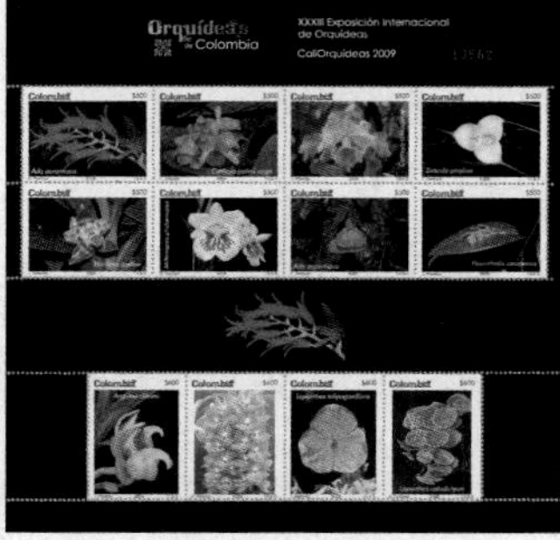

Orchids — A698

No. 1323: a, 500p, Ada aurantiaca (many flowers). b, 500p, Cattleya patinii cogn. c, 500p, Cattleya schroderae. d, 500p, Dracula amaliae. e, 500p, Huntleya gustavi. f, 500p, Miltoniopsis phalaenopsis. g, 500p, Ada aurantiaca (one flower). h, 500p, Pleurothallis casapensis. i, 600p, Anguloa cliftonii, vert. j, 600p, Cycnoche barthriorum, vert. k, 600p, Lepanthes telipogoniflora, vert. l, 600p, Lepanthes calodictyon, vert.

2009, Nov. 20
1323 A698 Sheet of 12, #a-l 11.00 11.00

33rd Intl. Orchid Exposition, Cali.

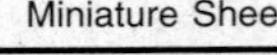

Miniature Sheet

Independence, Bicent. — A699

No. 1324: a, Bishop Andrés Rosillo y Meruelo (1758-1835). b, Josè Félix de Restrepo (1760-1832), statesman. c, Camilo Torres Tenorio (1766-1816), President of the Congress. d, Bishop Juan Fernández de Sotomayor (1777-1849). e, Antonio Villavicencio y Berástegui (1775-1816), President of the United Provinces of New Granada. f, Juan de Dios Morales (1767-1810), governmental minister and revolutionary. g, José María Carbonel (1778-1816), revolutionary agitator. h, Antonio Morales Galavís (1784-1852), military commander. i, José Ramón de Leyva (1747-1816), military commander. j, Nicolás Mauricio de Omaña, priest, lawyer.

2009, Nov. 24
1324 A699 6000p Sheet of 10, #a-j 70.00 70.00

Christmas A700

2009, Nov. 27 ***Perf. 12***
1325 A700 5000p multi 7.75 7.75

Souvenir Sheet

Campaign for a Mine-free World — A701

2009, Dec. 3 ***Perf. 14***
1326 A701 20,000p multi 25.00 20.00

Winning Designs in Stamp Design Contest — A702

No. 1327: a, Abstract face, by Vito. b, Collage, by Caracha. c, People holding hands, by D. Bueno.

2009, Dec. 15
1327 A702 1800p Horiz. strip of 3, #a-c 7.50 7.50

Miniature Sheet

Famous People — A703

No. 1328: a, Mercedes Abrego (1770-1813), spy. b, Gerardo Molina R. (1906-91), politician. c, Virginia Gutiérrez (1922-99), social anthropologist. d, María Mercedes Carranza (1945-2003), poet. e, Gonzalo Arango (1931-76), poet. f, Adolfo Mejía (1905-76), composer. g, General Benjamin Herrera (1853-1924). h, César Uribe Piedrahita (1896-1951), medical writer. i, Emilio Robledo (1875-1962), medical educator. j, Luis Duque Gómez (1916-2000), archaeologist. k, Enrique A. Becerra (1883-1954), jurist. l, Hugo Escobar Sierra (1927-2003), politician.

2010, Jan. 28 ***Perf. 13½x14***
1328 A703 4000p Sheet of 12, #a-l 60.00 60.00

Presidents Type of 1981

Miniature Sheet

No. 1329 — Presidents, coup leaders and other leaders of Colombia: a, Virgilio Barco Vargas. b, Julio César Turbay Ayala. c, Alfonso López Michelsen. d, Misael Pastrana Borrero. e, Carlos Lemos Simmonds. f, Victor Mosquera Chaux. g, Indalecio Liévano Aguirre. h, Rafael Azuero Manchola. i, Gabriel París Gordillo. j, Deogracias Fonseca. k, Rafael Navas Pardo. l, Luis Ernesto Ordóñez. m, Diego Euclides de Angulo. n, Clímaco Calderón Reyes. o, Andrés Cerón Serrano. p, Ignacio Gutiérrez Vergara. q, Juan José Nieto Gil. r, Rufino Cuervo. s, Manuel Rodríguez Torices. t, José Joaquín Camacho.

2010, Jan. 28 ***Perf. 14***
1329 Sheet of 20 47.50 47.50
a.-t. A401 1900p Any single 2.00 2.00

Ninth South American Games, Medellin — A704

2010, Feb. 18
1330 A704 5800p multi 8.00 8.00

Pope John Paul II (1920-2005) — A705

2010, Feb. 19 ***Perf. 13x13¼***
1331 A705 4400p multi 5.50 5.50

Miniature Sheet

Endangered Birds — A706

No. 1332: a, Crax alberti. b, Ognorhynchus icterotis. c, Hapalopsittaca fuertesi. d, Amazilia castaneiventris. e, Rallus semiplumbeus. f, Coeligena prunellei. g, Grallaria gigantea. h, Bangsia aureocincta. i, Hypopyrrhus pyrohypogaster.

2010, Apr. 6 ***Perf. 13¼x13***
1332 A706 1900p Sheet of 9, #a-i 22.50 22.50

Souvenir Sheet

Expo 2010, Shanghai — A707

2010, May 7 ***Perf. 13¾x14***
1333 A707 5000p multi 6.00 6.00

Miniature Sheet

Discovery of San Andrés, Providencia and Santa Catalina Archipelago, 500th Anniv. — A708

No. 1334: a, San Andrés Island. b, Providencia and Santa Catalina Islands. c, Quitasueño Keys. d, Bolivar Key. e, Roncador Keys. f, Bajo Nuevo Keys. g, Serranilla Keys. h, Serrana Keys. i, Alburquerque Keys.

2010, June 12 **Litho.** ***Perf. 14***
1334 A708 5900p Sheet of 9, #a-i, + 3 labels 85.00 85.00

Departments Type of 2003

No. 1335 — Guainía Department: a, Arms of Guainía. b, Princess Inírida Monument, horiz. c, Egretta alba. d, Cerro Mavicure. e, Canoe on Inírida River, horiz. f, Curripaco baskets. g, Guacamaya superba. h, Confluence of the Guaviare and Inírida Rivers, horiz. i, Remanso. j, Cualé Rapids. k, Children from Paujil, horiz. l, Coco Petroglyphs.

No. 1336 — Atlántico Department: a, Arms of Atlántico. b, Palacio de la Cultura, Barranquilla, horiz. c, Tubará rock paintings. d, Fluvicola pica. e, Julio Flórez Museum, Usiacurí, horiz. f, Tocagua Marsh, Luruaco. g, Bull's head carnival mask. h, San Antonio de Padua Church, Soledad, horiz. i, Tabebuya rosea. j, Iraca Palm handicrafts. k, Pier at Puerto Colombia, horiz. l, Customs House, Barranquilla.

Horiz. stamps are 50x40mm.

Sheets of 12, #a-l, + 8 labels

2010 ***Perf. 12x12½***
1335 A608 600p Guainía 15.00 15.00
1336 A608 2000p Atlántico 35.00 35.00

Issued: No. 1335, 7/24; No. 1336, 6/15.

Gonzalo Jiménez de Quesada Police Academy A709

2010, June 24 ***Perf. 14***
1337 A709 2000p multi 2.50 2.50

Bambuco National Pageant and Folklore Festival, Neiva, 50th Anniv. — A710

2010, June 22 ***Perf. 13¼x13***
1338 A710 4200p multi 5.50 5.50

Admiral Padilla Naval Academy A711

2010, July 3 ***Perf. 14***
1339 A711 500p multi 4.00 4.00

Miniature Sheet

Norte de Santander Department, Cent. — A712

No. 1340: a, Map of Norte de Santander Department. b, Government building. c, Estoraques Nature Area. d, Catatumbo River. e, Santa Ana de Ocaña Cathedral. f, Santa Clara de Pamplona Cathedral.

2010, July 14 **Litho.**
1340 A712 6000p Sheet of 6, #a-f 47.50 47.50

Teresa Pizarro de Angulo (c. 1930-2000), National Beauty Pageant Director — A713

2010, Aug. 3
1341 A713 5900p multi 8.00 8.00

Pinillos National College, Bicent. (in 2009) A714

2010, Aug. 27 **Litho.** ***Perf. 14***
1342 A714 4000p multi 5.25 5.25

America Issue, National Symbols — A715

No. 1343: a, Colombian flag. b, Colombian coat of arms.

2010, Oct. 12 ***Perf. 13½x14***
1343 A715 2100p Horiz. pair, #a-b 6.50 6.50

Medellin Institute of Fine Arts, Cent. A716

2010, Oct. 19 ***Perf. 14x13¾***
1344 A716 4400p multi 5.50 5.50

Miniature Sheet

Valle del Cauca Department, Cent. — A717

No. 1345: a, Map of Valle del Cauca Department. b, Sula granti. c, Overo Chapel. d, Pance River, Farallones Park. e, Ilama Culture vessel. f, Sonso Lake, Buga.

2010, Nov. 18 ***Perf. 14***
1345 A717 4000p Sheet of 6, #a-f 32.50 32.50

Colombia National Ballet, 50th Anniv. — A718

2010, Nov. 22
1346 A718 1200p multi 6.00 6.00

Christmas A719

2010, Nov. 23 ***Perf. 13x13¼***
1347 A719 5000p multi 6.50 6.50

Eduardo Caballero Calderón (1910-93), Writer A720

2010, Dec. 1 ***Perf. 14***
1348 A720 3000p multi 4.00 4.00

Miniature Sheet

Independence, Bicent. — A721

No. 1349 — Various paintings depicting scenes from towns declaring independence in 1810: a, Caratgena. b, Mompox. c, Pamplona. d, Socorro. e, Santa Marta. f, Chocó. g, Popayán. h, Cali. i, Tunja. j, Santa Fé de Bogotá. k, Santa Fé de Antioquia. l, Pore.

2010, Oct. 22 ***Perf. 13½x14***
1349 A721 2000p Sheet of 12, #a-l 32.50 32.50

Radio Station HJCK, Bogota A722

2011, Feb. 10 ***Perf. 14***
1350 A722 600p multi 1.50 1.50

4-72 Colombia Postal Network Emblem and "Es Tu Correo!" — A723

Frame Color

Serpentine Die Cut 12½

2011, Mar. 22 **Self-Adhesive**
1351 A723 10,000p blue 13.50 13.50
1352 A723 20,000p red 27.50 27.50

El Catolicismo Newspaper, 162nd Anniv. — A724

2011, Mar. 30 ***Perf. 13x13¼***
1353 A724 1700p multi 2.75 2.75

Souvenir Sheet

Biological Diversity — A725

2011, Apr. 11 ***Perf. 13***
1354 A725 6100p multi 10.00 10.00

Office of the Attorney General — A726

2011, May 10 ***Perf. 14***
1355 A726 1600p multi 3.00 3.00

Under-20 World Cup Soccer Championships, Colombia A727

2011, July 21 **Litho.** ***Perf. 13¼x13***
1356 A727 2000p multi 3.25 3.25

Rufino José Cuervo (1844-1911), Writer — A728

2011, July 27 ***Perf. 14***
1357 A728 5000p multi 8.00 8.00

Alfonso López Pumarejo National Carabiniers School, 50th Anniv. — A729

2011, Aug. 9 ***Perf. 14***
1358 A729 2100p multi 3.25 3.25

Departments Type of 2003

Miniature Sheet

No. 1359 — Norte de Santander Department: a, Arms of Norte de Santander. b, Virgin of Torcoroma and church, horiz. c, Locomotive. d, Sculpture of Barí Indian. e, Laguna Brava and Sisavita Complex, horiz. f, Southern tamandua, El Bojoso Reserve. g, Clock Tower, Cucuta. h, Street in La Play de Belén, horiz. i, Historic church, Rosario. j, Piedras Negras National Park. k, Pamplona University, horiz. l, Páramo de Guerrero.

Horiz. stamps are 46x37mm.

Sheet of 12, #a-l, + 8 labels

2011, Aug. 25 ***Perf. 13¼x13***
1359 A608 3000p Norte de Santander *55.00 55.00*

Souvenir Sheet

Intl. Year of Forests — A730

2011, Aug. 30 ***Perf. 14***
1360 A730 6200p multi 10.00 10.00

Miniature Sheet

Heroines of Independence — A731

No. 1361: a, Manuela Beltrán Archila. b, Manuela Cañizares. c, Manuela Sanz de Santamaría. d, Policarpa Salvarrieta. e, Matilde Anaray. f, Juana Velasco de Gallo. g, Simona Amaya. h, Antonia Santos. i, Simona Duque de Alzate. j, Manuela Sáenz de Thorne.

2011, Sept. 12 ***Perf. 13x13¼***
1361 A731 1500p Sheet of 10, #a-j 24.00 24.00

Intl. Year of People of African Descent — A732

2011, Oct. 12 *Perf. 13¼x13*
1362 A732 5000p multi 8.00 8.00

2011 Pan American Games, Guadalajara, Mexico — A733

2011, Oct. 19 *Perf. 14*
1363 A733 600p multi 1.00 1.00

Souvenir Sheet

Postal Union of the Americas, Spain and Portugal (UPAEP), Cent. — A734

2011, Nov. 11
1364 A734 1800p multi 3.00 3.00

Bolívar House, Bucaramanga — A735

2011, Nov. 15 *Perf. 13x13¼*
1365 A735 1200p multi 2.00 2.00

Declaration of Independence of Cartagena, 200th Anniv. — A736

2011, Nov. 26 *Perf. 14*
1366 A736 6000p multi 9.00 9.00

Emblem of United Nations AIDS Program A737

2011, Dec. 1
1367 A737 1900p multi 3.25 3.25

Mailbox — A738

2011, Dec. 2 **Litho.**
1368 A738 500p multi 1.25 1.25

America issue.

Christmas A739

2011, Dec. 2
1369 A739 1600p multi 2.75 2.75

Souvenir Sheet

El Tiempo Newspaper, Cent. — A740

2011, Dec. 13 *Perf. 13x13¼*
1370 A740 4000p multi 6.50 6.50

2012 Summer Olympics, London — A741

No. 1371: a, Swimming, fencing, wrestling. b, Equestrian, running, cycling. c, Judo, boxing, weight lifting. d, Shot put, soccer, tennis.

2012, Mar. 6 *Perf. 14x14¼*
1371 Horiz. strip of 4 20.00 20.00
a.-d. A741 3000p Any single 4.00 4.00

Nos. 1371a-1371d were printed in sheets of 8 containing two of each stamp.

National Police Magazine, Cent. — A742

2012, Mar. 23 *Perf. 14*
1372 A742 2000p multi 3.50 3.50

National Police Symphony, Cent. — A743

2012, Mar. 23
1373 A743 6400p multi 11.00 11.00

Diplomatic Relations Between Colombia and South Korea, 50th Anniv. — A744

No. 1374: a, Ginseng flowers and root. b, Coffee bush and beans.

2012, May 1 *Perf. 13x13¼*
1374 A744 600p Horiz. pair, #a-b 2.50 2.50

See South Korea No. 2379.

Souvenir Sheet

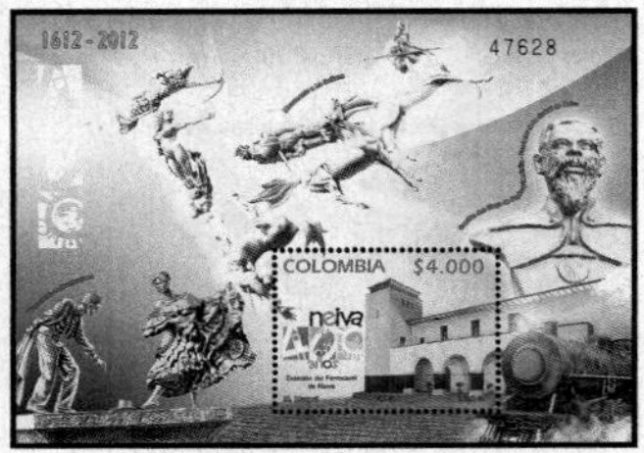
Neiva, 400th Anniv. — A745

2012, May 4 *Perf. 14*
1375 A745 4000p multi 6.50 6.50

Souvenir Sheet

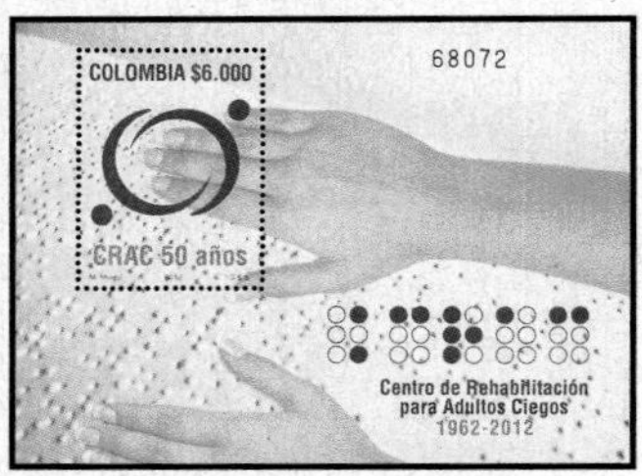
Rehabilitation Center for Blind Adults, 50th Anniv. — A746

2012, June 3 **Litho. & Embossed**
1376 A746 6000p multi 10.00 10.00

Departments Type of 2003
Miniature Sheet

No. 1377 — Cauca Department: a, Arms of Cauca. b, Puracé National Park, horiz. c, Gorgona National Park. d, Samanea saman. e, Laguna Grande de la Magdalena, horiz. f, Niña Maria de Caloto icon. g, Street in San Sebastian. h, Nuestra Senñora de la Asuncion Cathedral, Popayán, horiz. i, Battle of Bajo Palacé. j, Tierradentro National Archaeological Park. k, San Andrés Church, Pisimbalá, horiz. l, Megaptera novaeangliae.
Horiz. stamps are 46x37mm.

Sheet of 12, #a-l, + 8 labels

2012, July 24 **Litho.** *Perf. 12x12½*
1377 A608 1200p Cauca 24.00 24.00

Miniature Sheet

Famous Men — A747

No. 1378: a, Diego de Torres y Moyachoque (1549-90), Turmequé cacique. b, Pantaléon Germán Ribón (1774-1816), military leader. c, Cayetano Betancur (1910-82), philosopher. d, Luis Bermúdez (1912-94), composer.

2012, Aug. 16 *Perf. 13¼*
1378 A747 4600p Sheet of 4, #a-d 30.00 30.00

Rafael Pombo (1833-1912), Writer of Children's Literature — A748

2012, Aug. 23 *Perf. 13x13¼*
1379 A748 2100p multi + label 3.50 3.50

Voceadores de Prensa, Painting by Débora Arango Pérez (1907-2005) A749

2012, Aug. 28 *Perf. 14*
1380 A749 2400p multi 4.00 4.00

19th National Games and 3rd Paranational Games — A750

2012, Sept. 5
1381 A750 1500p multi 2.75 2.75

Art by Omar Rayo A751

No. 1382 — Art with stripes of: a, White, black and red. b, White, black and yellow. c, White, green, yellow, red and blue.

2012, Sept. 20 *Perf. 13x13¼*
1382 Horiz. strip of 3 5.00 5.00
a.-c. A751 1000p Any single 1.50 1.50

Jorge Palacios Preciado (1940-2003), Historian — A752

2012, Sept. 29
1383 A752 500p multi .85 .85

Plaza Mayor, Leyva
A753

2012, Oct. 4
1384 A753 4500p multi 8.50 8.50

First Congress of the United Provinces of New Granada, Bicent.

Souvenir Sheet

America Issue, Myths and Legends — A754

No. 1385: a, El Hojarasquin. b, El Ribiel and El Tesoro de Morgan.

2012, Oct. 9
1385 A754 4000p Sheet of 2, #a-b 13.00 13.00

Fedepalma (National Federation of Oil Palm Growers), 50th Anniv. — A755

2012, Oct. 24 *Perf. 14*
1386 A755 6000p multi 9.50 9.50

Gen. Francisco de Paula Santander (1792-1840) — A756

2012, Nov. 16 *Perf. 13¼*
1387 A756 1000p multi 1.75 1.75

Christmas
A757

2012, Dec. 14 *Perf. 14*
1388 A757 2500p multi 4.25 4.25

Medals Won at 2012 Summer Olympics, London
A758

2012, Dec. 18 *Perf. 13*
1389 A758 1800p multi 4.00 4.00

A souvenir sheet containing one 30,000p stamp depicting medals won at the 2012 Summer Olympics was produced in limited quantities.

Miniature Sheet

Proclamation of State Constitutions, 200th Anniv. — A759

No. 1391 — Seals of state of: a, Socorro. b, Cundinamarca. c, Tunja. d, Antioquia. e, Cartagena de Indias. f, Neiva.

Litho. & Embossed
2012, Dec. 19 *Perf. 13¼x13*
1391 A759 500p Sheet of 6, #a-f 5.00 5.00

Renaming of Las Hermosas National Natural Park After Gloria Valencia de Castaño (1927-2011), Television Personality — A760

2013, Apr. 29 **Litho.**
1392 A760 1800p multi + label 2.00 2.00

Departments Type of 2003
Miniature Sheet

No. 1393 — Cundinamarca Department: a, Arms of Cundinamarca. b, Tequendama Falls, Soacha, horiz. c, Poster commemorating bicentennial of Cundinamarca's independence. d, Basilica del Santo Cristo, Ubaté. e, Salt Cathedral, Zipaquirá, horiz. f, Ironworks, Pacho. g, Lagunas del Cerro, Machetá. h, Cliffs, Suesca, horiz. i, St. John the Baptist Parish Church, San Juan de Rioseco. j, Chapel, Siecha. k, Bridge of the Commoners, Chía, horiz. l, Versalles Falls, Guaduas.
Horiz. stamps are 46x37mm.

2013, July 16 *Perf. 13¼x13*
Sheet of 12, #a-l, + 8 labels
1393 A608 2100p Cundinamarca 27.00 27.00

2013 World Games, Cali — A761

2013, July 26 **Litho.** *Perf. 14*
1394 A761 2200p multi + label 2.40 2.40

Deportivo Independiente Medellín Soccer Team, Cent. — A762

2013, July 28 *Perf. 14x13½*
1395 A762 4500p multi 4.75 4.75

Town of Río de Oro, 355th Anniv. — A763

2013, Aug. 1 *Perf. 13½x14*
1396 A763 800p multi .85 .85

Alfonso Palacio Rudas (1912-96), Politician — A764

2013, Aug. 9 **Litho.**
1397 A764 7000p multi 7.50 7.50

Soledad Acosta de Samper (1833-1913), Writer — A765

2013, Sept. 3 *Perf. 13¼x13*
1398 A765 2500p multi 2.60 2.60

Campaign Against Crime
A766

2013, July 19 **Litho.** *Perf. 14x13½*
1399 A766 2000p multi 2.25 2.25

Aspects of Life of Coffee Pickers — A767

2013, July 30 **Litho.** *Perf. 14½x14¼*
1400 A767 2000p multi 2.25 2.25

Discovery of the Pacific Ocean by Vasco Núñez de Balboa, 500th Anniv. — A768

2013, Sept. 9 **Litho.** *Perf. 13½x14*
1401 A768 1400p multi 1.50 1.50

Pres. Alfonso López Michelsen (1913-2007)
A769

2013, Sept. 9 **Litho.** *Perf. 13½x14*
1402 A769 2500p multi 2.60 2.60

Christmas
A770

2013, Nov. 26 **Litho.** *Perf. 14x13½*
1403 A770 3500p multi 3.75 3.75

Pereira, 150th Anniv. (in 2013)
A771

2014, Mar. 13 **Litho.** *Perf. 13x13¼*
1404 A771 2500p multi 2.60 2.60

Gimnasio Moderno, Bogota, Cent.
A772

2014, Mar. 18 **Litho.** *Perf. 13x13¼*
1405 A772 800p multi .85 .85

Jaguar Mask — A773

2014, May 13 Litho. *Perf. 13½*
1406 A773 7200p multi + label 7.75 7.75

Artisans of Colombia, 50th anniv. No. 1406 was printed in sheets of 4 + 4 labels.

Souvenir Sheet

2014 World Cup Soccer Championships, Brazil — A774

No. 1407: a, Soccer ball. b, Emblem of the Colombian Soccer Federation, vert.

2014, May 23 Litho. *Perf. 13¾*
1407 A774 2600p Sheet of 2, #a-b 5.50 5.50
c. Booklet pane of 2, #1407a-1407b *10.00* —
Complete booklet, 5 #1407c *50.00*

Issued: No. 1407c, 7/8. Each example of No. 1407c in the complete booklet has a different pane margin. These pane margins differ from the sheet margin on No. 1407.

Official Journal, 150th Anniv. A775

2014, Oct. 9 Litho. *Perf. 13x13¼*
1408 A775 1300p multi 1.25 1.25

4-72 Colombia Postal Network Emblem and Text — A776

Serpentine Die Cut 12¼x12¾
2014, Aug. 25 Litho.
Self-Adhesive
Frame Color
1409 A776 10,000p blue 10.50 10.50
1410 A776 20,000p red 21.00 21.00

Scouting in Colombia, Cent. (in 2013) — A777

2014, Nov. 22 Litho. *Perf. 13¼x13*
1411 A777 3000p multi 2.60 2.60

Fanny Mikey (c. 1930-2008), Founder of Bogota Ibero-American Theater Festival — A778

2014, Dec. 2 Litho. *Perf. 13¼x13*
1412 A778 500p multi .45 .45

Christmas — A779

Perf. 13½x13¼
2014, Dec. 10 Litho.
1413 A779 100p multi .25 .25

Augusto Ramirez Ocampo (c. 1934-2011), Politician — A780

2014, Dec. 23 Litho. *Perf. 13¼x13*
1414 A780 1000p multi .85 .85

Gabriel García Márquez (1927-2014), 1982 Nobel Literature Laureate — A781

2015, July 14 Litho. *Perf. 13¼x13*
1415 A781 200p multi .25 .25

Souvenir Sheet
Imperf
1416 A781 10,000p multi 7.00 7.00

No. 1416 contains one 45x56mm stamp.

Fauna — A782

Designs: 200p, Allobates juanii. 500p, Eriocnemis mirabilis. 1000p, Diglossa gloriosissima. 2000p, Crocodylus intermedius. 5000p, Ateles hybridus. 10,000p, Phyllobates terribilis. 20,000p, Batrachemys dahli.

Serpentine Die Cut 12¾
2015, July 14 Litho.
Self-Adhesive

1417	A782	200p multi	.25	.25
1418	A782	500p multi	.35	.35
1419	A782	1000p multi	.70	.70
1420	A782	2000p multi	1.40	1.40
1421	A782	5000p multi	3.50	3.50
1422	A782	10,000p multi	7.00	7.00
1423	A782	20,000p multi	14.00	14.00
	Nos. 1417-1423 (7)		27.20	27.20

20th National and 4th Paranational Games, Chocó and Tolima — A783

2015, Nov. 7 Litho. *Perf. 13¼x13*
1424 A783 5000p multi + label 3.25 3.25

Souvenir Sheet
Litho. & Embossed With Foil Application
Perf. 13
1425 A783 12,000p gold & multi 7.75 7.75

No. 1425 contains one 40x52mm stamp.

Manuel Mejía Vallejo (1923-89), Writer — A784

Serpentine Die Cut 12¾
2015, Nov. 12 Litho.
Self-Adhesive
1426 A784 20,000p multi 13.00 13.00

Paulina Vega Dieppa, 2014 Miss Universe — A785

2015, Nov. 14 Litho. *Perf. 13¼x13*
1427 A785 20,000p multi 13.00 13.00

National Police School of Criminal Investigation, Cent. (in 2014) — A786

2015, Dec. 10 Litho. *Perf. 13¼x13*
1428 A786 1000p multi .65 .65

Christmas A787

2015, Dec. 11 Litho. *Perf. 13¼x13*
1429 A787 10,000p multi 6.25 6.25

Departments Type of 2003
Miniature Sheet

No. 1430 — Risaralda Department: a, Arms of Risaralda. b, Cathedral of Our Lady of Poverty, Pereira, horiz. c, Pseudoscada lavinia. d, Santa Rosa de Cabal Thermal Springs. e, House of Culture, Marsella, horiz. f, Immaculate Mary Church, Marsella. g, Magnolia wolfi. h, Emberá-Chamí women, horiz. i, Dosquebradas Viaduct. j, Alouatta seniculus. k, Oxypogon stubelii, horiz. l, Old Railway Station, Pereira.

Horiz. stamps are 46x37mm.

2015, Dec. 14 Litho. *Perf. 13¼x13*
Sheet of 12, #a-l, + 8 labels
1430 A608 100p Risaralda .75 .75

Aerial Mapping — A788

2016, Apr. 19 Litho. *Perf. 13¼x13*
1431 A788 5000p multi 3.50 3.50

Agustín Codazzi Geographical Institute.

José Francisco Socarrás Colina (1906-95), Physician and Educator — A789

2016, May 18 Litho. *Perf. 13½*
1432 A789 10,000p multi 6.50 6.50

Values are for stamps with surrounding selvage.

Rafael Escalona (1926-2009), Composer A790

2016, May 26 Litho. *Perf. 13¼x13*
1433 A790 5000p multi 3.25 3.25

ARC Gloria and Humpback Whales A791

2016, June 8 Litho. *Perf. 13x13¼*
1434 A791 2000p multi 1.40 1.40

Colombian Ocean Commission.

2016 Summer Olympics, Rio de Janeiro — A792

Designs: 500p, Dove and olive branch. 25,000p, Dove and olive branch, diff.

2016, July 7 Litho. *Perf. 13¼x13*
1435 A792 500p multi + label .35 .35

Souvenir Sheet
Silk-Faced Paper
Perf. 13¼

1436 A792 25,000p multi 16.50 16.50

No. 1436 contains one 30x60mm stamp.

A793

Quindío Department, 50th Anniv. — A794

No. 1437 — Arms of Quindío Department and: a, Spizaetus isidori. b, Horse and Ceroxylon quindiuense spp.

No. 1438: a, Spizaetus isidori. b, Horse and Ceroxylon quindiuense spp., vert.

2016, July 29 Litho. *Perf. 13x13¼*

1437 A793 200p Pair, #a-b .30 .30

Perf. 13¼

1438 A794 10,000p Sheet of 2, #a-b 13.00 13.00

No. 1437 was printed in sheets of 16, containing 8 each Nos. 1437a-1437b + 4 labels.

Malpelo Fauna and Flora Sanctuary UNESCO World Heritage Site A795

2016, Aug. 11 Litho. *Perf. 13x13¼*

1439 A795 2000p multi + label 1.40 1.40

Souvenir Sheet

Peace Dove Watering Plant — A796

Perf. 13¼x13½

2016, Sept. 13 Litho.

Flocked Paper

1440 A796 10,000p multi 7.00 7.00

No. 1440 is impregnated with a floral scent.

Ismael Enrique Arciniegas (1865-1938), Poet — A797

2016, Nov. 4 Litho. *Perf. 13½*

1441 A797 20,000p multi 13.00 13.00

Values are for stamps with surrounding selvage.

Colombian Geological Service, Cent. A798

2016, Nov. 10 Litho. *Perf. 13½*

1442 A798 20,000p multi 13.00 13.00

Miniature Sheet

Tourist Network of Heritage Towns — A799

No. 1443: a, Monument, Ciénaga, Magdalena Department. b, Santa Barbara Church, Santa Cruz de Mompox, Bolívar Department. c, Public Market, Santa Cruz de Lorica, Córdoba Department. d, Church, Aguadas, Caldas Department. e, Fountain and staute, Salamina, Caldas Department. f, Basilica of Our Lady of Monguí, Monguí, Boyacá Department. g, Central plaza and fountain, Villa de Leyva, Boyacá Department, h, Santa Barbara Church, Santa Fe de Antioquia, Antioquia Department. i, Church and building, Jericó, Antioquia Department. j, Building, Jardín, Antioquia Department. k, Lord of the Miracles Basilica, Guadelajara de Buga, Valle del Cauca Department. l, Navarro Bridge, Honda, Tolima Department. m. St. Michael Archangel Cathedral, Villa de Guaduas, Cundinamarca Department. n, Cathedral, Barichara, Santander Department. o, Building, San Juan Girón, Santander Department. p, St. Joseph's Church, La Playa de Belén, Norte de Santander Department. q, Cathedral, El Soccoro, Santander Department.

2016, Nov. 15 Litho. *Perf. 13½*

1443 A799 100p Sheet of 17, #a-q, + 3 labels *34.00 34.00*

Hands and Relay Network A800

2016, Dec. 3 Litho. *Perf. 13x13¼*

1444 A800 5000p multi 3.50 3.50

Souvenir Sheet
Self-Adhesive
Serpentine Die Cut

1445 A800 20,000p multi 13.50 13.50

No. 1445 contains one 28x36mm oval stamp on a 150mm diameter backing paper that is covered by a spinnable paper wheel that is attached by a metal grommet at the center.

Miniature Sheets

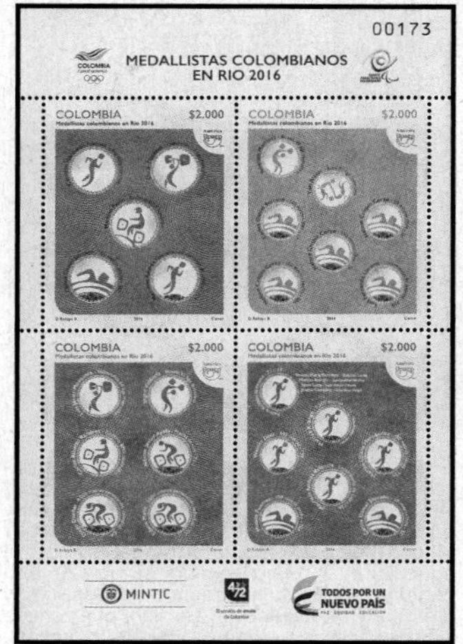

Medalists at 2016 Summer Olympics — A801

Nos. 1446 and 1447 — Emblem of sporting event and names of: a, Five gold medalists. b, Seven silver medalists. c, Six bronze medalists. d, Seven bronze medalists.

2016, Dec. 12 Litho. *Perf. 14*

1446 A801 2000p Sheet of 4, #a-d 5.50 5.50

1447 A801 10,000p Sheet of 4, #a-d 27.00 27.00

America Issue.

Colombian Antarctic Program — A802

2016, Dec. 13 Litho. *Perf. 13¼x13*

1448 A802 10,000p multi 6.75 6.75

Christmas — A803

2016, Dec. 14 Litho. *Perf. 14*

1449 A803 500p multi .35 .35

Sucre Department, 50th Anniv. — A804

No. 1450 — Arms of Sucre Department and: a, Dancers. b, Church.

2017, Mar. 1 Litho. *Perf. 13x13¼*

1450 A804 2000p Pair, #a-b 2.75 2.75

Printed in sheets of 16, containing 8 each Nos. 1450a-1450b + 4 labels.

Souvenir Sheet

Telegraph Key and Map of Colombia — A805

2017, Mar. 24 Litho. *Perf. 13¼x13*

1451 A805 2000p multi 1.40 1.40

Pres. Manuel Murillo Toro (1816-80).

Risaralda Department, 50th Anniv. — A806

No. 1452 — Arms of Risaralda Department and: a, Clouds covering Tatamá and Los Nevados National Parks. b, Bangsia aureocincta.

2017, Apr. 7 Litho. *Perf. 13x13¼*

1452 A806 500p Pair, #a-b .70 .70

Printed in sheets of 16, containing 8 each Nos. 1452a-1452b + 4 labels.

Enrique Santos Castillo (1917-2001), Lawyer and Journalist — A807

2017, Apr. 17 Litho. *Perf. 13¼x13*

1453 A807 5000p multi 3.50 3.50

Departments Type of 2003

Miniature Sheet

No. 1454 — Cesar Department: a, Arms of Cesar. b, 50th anniversary emblem of Cesar Department, horiz. c, 50th anniversary emblem of Vallenato Legend Festival. d, Ardea alba. e, Fisherman fishing Zapatosa Marsh, horiz. f, Vallenato musician playing accordion. g, Train hauling coal. h, Río Guatapurí, horiz. i, Cañaguate tree in bloom, Valledupar. j, Almojábana Monument, La Paz. k, Tamalameque folk dancers, horiz. l, Kankuama bags.

Horiz. stamps are 46x37mm.

2017, Apr. 27 Litho. *Perf. 13¼x13*
Sheet of 12, #a-l, + 8 labels

1454 A608 100p Cesar .85 .85

Julio Flórez (1867-1923), Poet — A808

2017, May 26 Litho. *Perf. 13¼*

1455 A808 1000p multi .70 .70

First Grand Masonic Lodge, 300th Anniv. — A809

2017, July 6 Litho. *Perf. 13¼x13*
1456 A809 500p multi .35 .35

Souvenir Sheet
Perf. 13½x13
1457 A809 10,000p multi 6.75 6.75

National Federation of Coffee Growers, 90th Anniv. — A810

2017, July 10 Litho. *Perf. 13¼*
1458 A810 50p multi .25 .25

Matamoros Corporation, 30th Anniv. (in 2016) — A811

2017, Aug. 14 Litho. *Perf. 13½*
1459 A811 20,000p multi 13.50 13.50

No. 1459 was printed in sheets of 2.

Caro y Cuervo Institute, 75th Anniv. — A812

No. 1460: a, Neon pink "I." b, Neon orange "C." c, Neon green "C."

2017, Aug. 24 Litho. *Perf. 13¼*
1460 A812 500p Horiz. strip of 3, #a-c 1.00 1.00

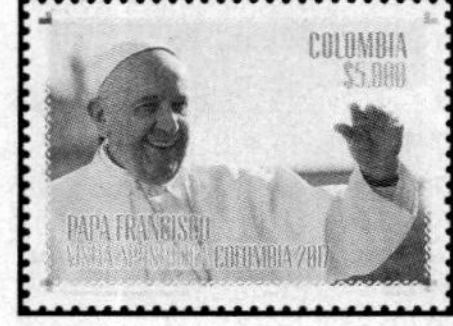

Visit of Pope Francis to Colombia A813

Design: 10,000p, Pope Francis, vert.

2017, Aug. 30 Litho. *Perf. 13x13¼*
1461 A813 5000p gold & sil 3.50 3.50

Souvenir Sheet
Perf. 13¼x13
1462 A813 10,000p gold & sil 6.75 6.75

Miniature Sheet

National University of Colombia, 150th Anniv. — A814

No. 1463: a, Balance (symbol of social sciences and humanities. b, Sesquicentenario symbols in deep turquoise-blue circle. c, Sesquicentenario symbols surrounding University crest, white background. d, Wheat (symbol of agriculture). e, Harp (symbol of arts). f, 19th century University monogram. g, University crest. h, Greek letter "pi" (symbol of science). i, Bowl of Hygieia (symbol of health sciences). j, Sesquicentenario symbols surrounding University crest, blue violet bacground. k, Sesquicentenario symbols in white circle. l, Greek letter "phi" (symbol of engineering).

2017, Aug. 31 Litho. *Perf. 13¼*
1463 A814 2000p Sheet of 12, #a-l, + 8 labels 16.50 16.50

Policarpa Salvarrieta (1795-1817), Executed Spy for Revolutionary Forces — A815

2017, Sept. 14 Litho. *Perf. 13½*
1464 A815 100p multi .25 .25

Ara Ararauna A816

2017, Sept. 22 Litho. *Perf. 13¼*
1465 A816 1000p multi .70 .70

Bio Program.

America Issue — A817

No. 1466 — Tourist attractions: a, Caño Cristales River. b, Serranía de la Lindosa.

2017, Oct. 9 Litho. *Perf. 13x13¼*
1466 A817 1000p Pair, #a-b 1.40 1.40

New Future of Colombia Association, 25th Anniv. (in 1998) — A818

2017, Oct. 18 Litho. *Perf. 13¼x13*
1467 A818 2000p multi 1.40 1.40

Lions Clubs International, Cent. — A819

2017, Oct. 30 Litho. *Perf. 13¼x13*
1468 A819 5000p blue & yel 3.25 3.25

18th Bolivarian Games, Santa Marta — A820

No. 1469: a, Emblem. b, Mascot Ajaytuké.

2017, Nov. 10 Litho. *Perf. 13¼*
1469 A820 3000p Pair, #a-b 4.00 4.00

Colombian Marine Corps, 80th Anniv. A821

2017, Nov. 30 Litho. *Perf. 13x13¼*
1470 A821 10,000p multi 6.75 6.75

Christmas — A822

Serpentine Die Cut 12¾x12½
2017, Dec. 1 Litho.
Self-Adhesive
1471 A822 4000p gold & multi 2.75 2.75

National Police, 126th Anniv. A823

2017, Dec. 7 Litho. *Perf. 13x13¼*
1472 A823 1000p multi .70 .70

Publication of *María,* Novel by Jorge Isaacs (1837-95), 150th Anniv. — A824

Perf. 13½x13¼
2017, Dec. 15 Litho.
1473 A824 4000p multi 2.75 2.75

Improvement and Decoration Society of Bogota, Cent. — A825

2017, Dec. 20 Litho. *Perf. 13*
1474 A825 200p multi .25 .25

Miniature Sheet

Endemic Birds — A826

No. 1475: a, Capito hypoleucus. b, Pyrrhura calliptera. c, Vireo caribaeus. d, Pyrrhura viridicata. e, Anisognathus melanogenys. f, Bangsia melanochlamys. g, Metallura iracunda. h, Cercomacra parkeri. i, Ramphomicron dorsale. j, Bucco noanamae. k, Atlapetes flaviceps. l, Coeligena orina. m, Hummingbird and "CO Colombia."

2018, Jan. 23 Litho. *Perf. 14¼*
1475 A826 1000p Sheet of 13, #a-m 9.25 9.25

Departments Type of 2003
Miniature Sheet

No. 1476 — Meta Department: a, Arms of Meta. b, Aerial view of Villavicencio, horiz. c, Joropo Music International Tournament, 50th anniv. d, Laguna de Lomalinda Natural Regional Park. e, Cuadrillas de San Martín Festival, horiz. f, Maloca Museum of Pope Francis, Villavicencio. g, Llano cowboys moving herd of cattle. h, Laguna del Amor, Puerto Rico, horiz. i, Dancers at Joropódromo. j, Monument at geographical center of Colombia, Puerto López. k, Sikuani canoe, horiz. l, Hato Santa Helena.

Horiz. stamps are 46x37mm.

2018, Jan. 26 Litho. *Perf. 13¼x13*
Sheet of 12, #a-l, + 8 labels
1476 A608 500p Meta 4.25 4.25

Miniature Sheet

Barranquilla Carnival, Cent. — A827

No. 1477: a, Carnival emblem. b, Alicia Lafaurie Roncallo, first Carnival Queen. c, Carnival reveler wearing tiger head covering and makeup. d, Torito Ribeño dancers. e, Cumbia singer. f, Fire-breathing clown.

2018, Feb. 9 Litho. *Perf. 13x13¼*
1477 A827 3000p Sheet of 6, #a-f 12.50 12.50

Corn Dishes A828

No. 1478 — Ear of corn and: a, Mazamorra and arepas. b, Empanadas and tamales. c, Envueltos. d, Tortas, chicha and buñuelas.

2018, Mar. 15 Litho. *Perf. 13x13¼*
1478 Block or horiz. strip of 4 15.00 15.00
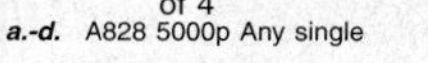
a.-d. A828 5000p Any single 3.75 3.75

National Institute of Health, Cent. — A829

2018, Mar. 20 Litho. *Perf. 13½*
1479 A829 2000p multi 1.50 1.50

General Rafael Reyes Prieto Military School, 109th Anniv. A830

2018, May 5 Litho. *Perf. 13x13¼*
1480 A830 20,000p multi 14.00 14.00

Butterflies — A831

No. 1481 — Flowers and: a, Danaus plexippus. b, Morpho peleides.

2018, May 9 Litho. *Perf. 13x13¼*
1481 A831 10,000p Pair, #a-b 14.00 14.00

See Mexico Nos. 3104-3105.

Miniature Sheet

Barranquilla Attractions — A832

No. 1482: a, Plaza de Intendencia Fluvial. b, Gran Malecón del Río. c, Yellow Butterflies Monument. d, Port of Barranquilla. e, Metropolitan Cathedral. f, Barranquilla sign.

2018, May 18 Litho. *Perf. 13¼*
1482 A832 5000p Sheet of 6, #a-f 21.00 21.00

Directorate of National Taxes and Customs, 25th Anniv. A833

2018, June 1 Litho. *Perf. 13x13¼*
1483 A833 10,000p multi 7.00 7.00

International History Festival, Villa de Leyva — A834

2018, June 15 Litho. *Perf. 13¼*
1484 A834 1000p multi .70 .70

Miniature Sheet

Ceramic Art of Cecilia Vargas Muñoz — A835

No. 1485: a, Chiva Expreso del Café . b, Sculpture of mammal without tail. c, Sculpture of mammal with tail. d, Chiva Expreso Macondo.

2018, July 13 Litho. *Perf. 13x13¼*
1485 A835 5000p Sheet of 4, #a-d 14.00 14.00

Awarding of 2016 Nobel Peace Prize to Pres. Juan Manuel Santos Calderón — A836

2018, July 18 Litho. *Perf. 13¼x13*
1486 A836 2000p multi 1.40 1.40

23rd Central American and Caribbean Sports Games, Barranquilla — A837

No. 1487: a, Mascot. b, Emblem.

2018, July 19 Litho. *Perf. 13½*
1487 A837 2000p Pair, #a-b 2.75 2.75

Miniature Sheet

Commissioning of ARC Gloria as Training Ship, 50th Anniv. — A838

No. 1482: a, Ship with flag at right, builidngs at LR. b, Ship and bridge. c, Stylized ship with flag at right. d, Aerial view of ship. e, View of ship's stern, large flag. f, 50th anniversary emblem.

2018, July 24 Litho. *Perf. 13¼x13*
1488 A838 5000p Sheet of 6, #a-f 21.00 21.00

Miniature Sheet

Orchids — A839

No. 1489: a, Acineta antioquiae. b, Anguloa uniflora. c, Coryanthes mastersiana. d, Coryanthes misasii. e, Epidendrum ciliare. f, Epidendrum fimbriatum. g, Epidendrum sp. h, Erycina glossomystax. i, Gongora gratulabunda (multiple orchids). j, Gongora gratulabunda (single orchid). k, Gongora sp. l, Lepanthes sp. m, Odontoglossum gloriosum. n, Pescatorea pulvinaris. o, Platistele sp. p, Pleurothallis gracilicolumna. q, Pleurothallis jaramilloi. r, Psychopsis krameriana. s, Stelis nanegalensis. t, Telipogon pulcher.

2018, Aug. 9 Litho. *Perf. 13½*
1489 A839 500p Sheet of 20, #a-t 6.50 6.50

Presidential Guard Batallion, 90th Anniv. — A840

2018, Aug. 13 Litho. *Perf. 13½x13*
1490 A840 200p multi .25 .25

Miniature Sheet

Catatumbo Region and Ocaña Province of Norte de Santander Department — A841

No. 1491: a, Catatumbo River, El Tarra. b, Pineapple cultivation, Teorama. c, Pink bean cultivation, Abrego. d, Páramo de Guerrero, Cáchira and Villa Caro. e, Site of the Convention of Ocaña, Ocaña. f, Cliffs, La Playa de Belén.

2018, Aug. 17 Litho. *Perf. 13x13½*
1491 A841 1000p Sheet of 6, #a-f 4.00 4.00

Miniature Sheet

Risaralda Bird Festival — A842

No. 1492 — Birds and butterflies: a, Dacnis hartlaubi. b, Penelope perspicax. c, Pipreola jucunda. d, Boissonneaua jardini. e, Myiarchus apicalis. f, Eueides isabella arquata. g, Eueides procula edias. h, Heliconius cydno cydnides. i, Heliconius erato chestertoni. j, Heliconius doris obscurus. k, Calliphlox mitchelli. l, Picumnus granadensis. m, Tangara ruficervix. n, Bangsia melanochlamys. o, Chlorochrysa nitidissima.

2018, Aug. 24 Litho. *Perf. 13*
1492 A842 1000p Sheet of 15, #a-o 9.75 9.75

Military Communications, 74th Anniv. — A843

2018, Aug. 31 Litho. *Perf. 13½x13*
1493 A843 20,000p multi 13.00 13.00

Souvenir Sheet

Domesticated Animals — A844

No. 1494: a, Horses, rabbit, cow, cat. dog, geese. b, Cow, donkey, sheep, dogs, goats, chickens, pigs.

2018, Oct. 9 Litho. *Perf. 13x13½*
1494 A844 4000p Sheet of 2, #a-b 5.00 5.00

America issue.

University of Caldas, 75th Anniv.
A845

2018, Oct. 23 **Litho.** ***Perf. 13***
1495 A845 10,000p multi 6.25 6.25

Restoration of Polish Independence, Cent. — A846

2018, Nov. 9 **Litho.** ***Perf. 13x13½***
1496 A846 5000p multi 3.25 3.25

National Civil Registry, 70th Anniv.
A847

2018, Dec. 5 **Litho.** ***Perf. 13***
1497 A847 2000p multi 1.25 1.25

Christmas
A848

Serpentine Die Cut
2018, Dec. 11 **Litho.**
On Plastic Film
Self-Adhesive
1498 A848 10,000p multi 6.25 6.25

A849

A850

A851

A852

A853

A854

A855

Details of Mural, "History of the Lord of the Miracles of Buga," by Gustavo Rojas
A856

2018, Dec. 13 **Litho.** ***Perf. 13x13½***

1499	Sheet of 8	20.00	20.00
a.	A849 4000p multi	2.50	2.50
b.	A850 4000p multi	2.50	2.50
c.	A851 4000p multi	2.50	2.50
d.	A852 4000p multi	2.50	2.50
e.	A853 4000p multi	2.50	2.50
f.	A854 4000p multi	2.50	2.50
g.	A855 4000p multi	2.50	2.50
h.	A856 4000p multi	2.50	2.50

Carlos Gaviria Díaz (1937-2015), Politician — A857

No. 1500: a, Gaviria Díaz facing right. b, Gaviria Díaz seated with legs crossed. c, Gaviria Díaz facing forward. d, Books authored by Gaviria Díaz.

2018, Dec. 17 **Litho.** ***Perf. 13¼***
1500 A857 500p Block of 4, #a-d 1.25 1.25

Diplomatic Relations Between Colombia and India, 60th Anniv. — A858

2019, Jan. 28 **Litho.** ***Perf. 13¼***
1501 A858 4000p multi 2.60 2.60

No. 1501 was printed in sheets of 8 + 4 flanking labels.

Miniature Sheet

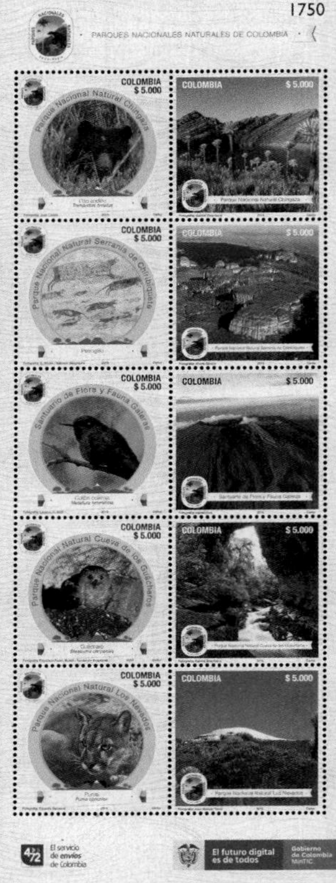

Colombian Parks — A859

No. 1502: a, Tremarctos ornatus, Chingaza National Natural Park. b, Lake and hills, Chingaza National Natural Park. c, Rock painting, Serranía de Chiribiquete National Natural Park. d, Aerial view of Chiribiquete National Natural Park. e, Metallura tyrianthina, Galeras Flora and Fauna Sanctuary. f, Volcano, Galeras Flora and Fauna Sanctuary. g, Steatornis caripensis, Cueva de los Guácharos National Park. h, Cave, Cueva de los Guácharos National Natural Park. i, Puma concolor, Los Nevados National Natural Park. j, Mountain, Los Nevados National Natural Park.

2019, Apr. 5 **Litho.** ***Perf. 14¼***
1502 A859 5000p Sheet of 10, #a-j 31.00 31.00

Latin American Integration Association — A860

2019, Apr. 12 **Litho.** ***Perf. 13½***
1503 A860 20,000p multi 12.50 12.50

Values are for stamps with surrounding selvage.

Gilberto Alejandro Durán Díaz (1919-89), Composer and Accordion Player
A861

2019, Apr. 21 **Litho.** ***Perf. 13***
1504 A861 500p multi .30 .30

Mohandas K. Gandhi (1869-1948), Indian Nationalist Leader — A862

2019, May 5 **Litho.** ***Perf. 13¼x13***
1505 A862 10,000p multi 6.00 6.00

Miniature Sheet

19th Century Colombian Watercolor Landscapes — A863

No. 1506: a, Market of Plaza Mayor, Santa Fé de Bogotá, by José Santiago del Castillo, 1837 (80x30mm). b, Los Llanos, Casanare Province, by Manuel María Paz, 1856 (40x30mm). c, Main House, Cachirí, Soto Province, by Carmelo Fernández, 1850 (40x30mm). d, Scene of the Battle of Boyaca, Tunja Province, by Fernández, 1850 (40x30mm). e, Bridge over Funza River, Bogotá, Cundinamarca Province, by María Paz, 1858 (40x30mm). f, Ambalema, Magdalena River, Tolima, by Edward Mark, 1846 (40x30mm). g, San Felipe Castle and La Popa Hill, Cartagena de Indias, by Mark, 1845 (40x30mm). h, Santa Marta, by Mark, 1844 (40x30mm). i, View of the Farallones de Cali from a Street in Cali, Buenaventura Province, by María Paz, 1853 (40x30mm). j, View of Village of Puracé from Alto de los Pesares, Popayán Province, by María Paz, 1855 (40x30mm). k, View of Cumbal and Chiles Volcanos, Túquerres Province, by María Paz, 1853 (40x30mm). l, Cabin, Chocó Province, by Mark, 1843 (40x30mm). m, City of Antioquia, by Henry Price, 1852 (80x30mm).

2019, May 13 **Litho.** ***Perf. 13x13¼***
1506 A863 2000p Sheet of 13, #a-m 15.50 15.50

Colombian independence, 200th anniv.

Diplomatic Relations Between Colombia and Russia, 160th Anniv. — A864

No. 1507: a, Russian Tsar Alexnder II (1818-81) and balalaika. b, Colombian President Mariano Ospina Rodríguez (1805-85) and tiple.

2019, May 24 **Litho.** ***Perf. 13x13¼***
1507 A864 20,000p Horiz. pair, #a-b 24.00 24.00

Riosucio Carnival A865

2019, May 28 Litho. *Perf. 13x13¼*
1508 A865 10,000p multi 6.00 6.00

Colombian Air Force, Cent. A866

2019, June 13 Litho. *Perf. 13x13¼*
1509 A866 10,000p multi 6.25 6.25

Diplomatic Relations Between Colombia and Morocco, 40th Anniv. — A867

No. 1510: a, Hassan tower, Rabat, Morocco. b, Monserrate Monastery, Bogota, Colombia.

2019, June 19 Litho. *Perf. 13x13¼*
1510 A867 10,000p Pair, #a-b 12.50 12.50

51st International Joropo Tournament, Villavicencio A868

2019, June 28 Litho. *Perf. 13¼x13*
1511 A868 2000p multi 1.25 1.25

Colombian National Army, 200th Anniv. — A869

2019, July 29 Litho. *Perf. 13¼x13*
1512 A869 5000p multi 3.00 3.00

Miniature Sheet

19th Century Watercolors of Colombians — A870

No. 1513: a, A Llapanga and Mestizo of Cauca, by Manuel María Paz, 1855. b, Customs, Plaza Mayor, Bogota, by François Désiré Roulin, 1824. c, Exterior of Houses of Nóvita, Chocó Province, by Marí Paz, 1853. d, Habitants of the Shores of the Magdalena, by Ramón Torres Méndez, c. 1850. e, Beggar of Sogamoso, by Edward Mark, 1845. f, Peasant of Ibagué, by Mark, 1847. g, Dinner at Santa Marta, by Roulin, 1823. h, Prortait of Three Young Boys of Túquerres, by María Paz, 1853. i, Notables of the Capital, by Carmelo Fernández, 1851. j, Family of Churruyes Indians on a Trip, by José María Gutiérrez de Alba, 1871. k, Peasant of Guaduas, by Mark, 1846. l, Antioquia, by Henry Price, 1852.

2019, Aug. 15 Litho. *Perf. 14*
1513 A870 5000p Sheet of 12, #a-l 35.00 35.00

Colombian independence, 200th anniv.

Solidarity Foundation for Colombia, 44th Anniv. — A871

2019, Aug. 25 Litho. *Perf. 13¼x13*
1514 A871 500p multi .30 .30

Souvenir Sheet

Marly Clinic, Bogota, 115th Anniv. — A872

2019, Aug. 28 Litho. *Perf. 13x13¼*
1515 A872 20,000p multi 12.00 12.00

Miniature Sheet

Traditional Dishes — A873

No. 1516: a, Sugar cane and panela (unrefined sugar). b, Panela. c, Plantain chips and dip. d, Green plantains, caramelized plantains.

2019, Oct. 9 Litho. *Perf. 13x13¼*
1516 A873 2000p Sheet of 4, #a-d 4.75 4.75

America issue.

Jorge Barón Television Production Company, 50th Anniv. — A874

2019, Oct. 15 Litho. *Perf. 13¼x13*
1517 A874 5000p multi 3.00 3.00

Radio Broadcasting in Colombia, 90th Anniv. — A875

2019, Oct. 30 Litho. *Perf. 13x13¼*
1518 A875 500p multi .30 .30

Miniature Sheet

Art Depicting Colombian Women of the 19th Century — A876

No. 1519 — Inscriptions: a, Frutera de la Mesa (Fruit Seller), attributed to Ramón Torres Méndez, 19th cent. b, Mujeres Blancas (White Women), Ocaña Province, by Carmelo Fernández, 1851. c, Sombrerera de Guaduas (Sombrero Maker of Guaduas), by Edward Mark, 1846. d, Plaza de Quibdó, Chocó Province, by Manuel María Paz, 1853. e, Campesinas Conduciendo Naranjas al Mercado de Bogotá (Peasants Bringing Oranges to Market in Bogotá), by Torres Méndez, 19th cent. f, Hilanderas de Lana (Wool Spinners), Pasto Province, by María Paz, 1853. g, Lavadoras de Oro Río Guadalupe (Gold Washers), Río Guadalupe, Medellin Province, by Henry Price, 1852. h, Bogotá, Mujeres del Pueblo (Bogotá, Village Women), attributed to Torres Méndez, 1872. i, Mujer de Vélez (Vélez Woman), attributed to Torres Méndez, 19th cent. j, Beata Carmelita (Blessed Carmelite), attributed to Torres Méndez, 19th cent. k, Llapangas de Popayán (Llapangas of Popayán), Popayán Province, by María Paz, 1855. l, India de Funza (Indian of Funza), attributed to Torres Méndez, 19th cent.

2019, Nov. 14 Litho. *Perf. 13½*
1519 A876 2000p Sheet of 12, #a-l 14.00 14.00

Colombian Independence, 200th anniv.

Lawyers' Club, Cent. — A877

2019, Nov. 14 Litho. *Perf. 13¼x13*
1520 A877 5000p multi 3.00 3.00

Andean Community, 50th Anniv. — A878

2019, Nov. 21 Litho. *Perf. 13¼x13*
1521 A878 2000p multi 1.25 1.25

Colombian Chamber of Informatics and Telecommunications, 25th Anniv. — A879

2019, Nov. 28 Litho. *Perf. 13¼x13*
1522 A879 5000p multi 3.00 3.00

21st National Games and 5th Paranational Games, Bolívar Deparatment — A880

2019, Nov. 29 Litho. *Perf. 13½*
1523 A880 5000p multi 3.00 3.00

Values are for stamps with surrounding selvage.

Bogota District Printing Office, Cent. — A881

2019, Dec. 2 Litho. *Perf. 13¼x13*
1524 A881 5000p multi 3.00 3.00

Avianca Airlines, Cent. — A882

No. 1525: a, SCADTA emblem, map of Colombia, crowd of people near seaplane. b, Seaplane with pilot and ground crew.

2019, Dec. 2 Litho. *Perf. 13¼x13*
1525 A882 2000p Pair, #a-b 2.25 2.25

Superintendent of Public Home Services, 25th Anniv. — A883

2019, Dec. 3 Litho. *Perf. 13¼x13*
1526 A883 5000p multi 3.25 3.25

Souvenir Sheet

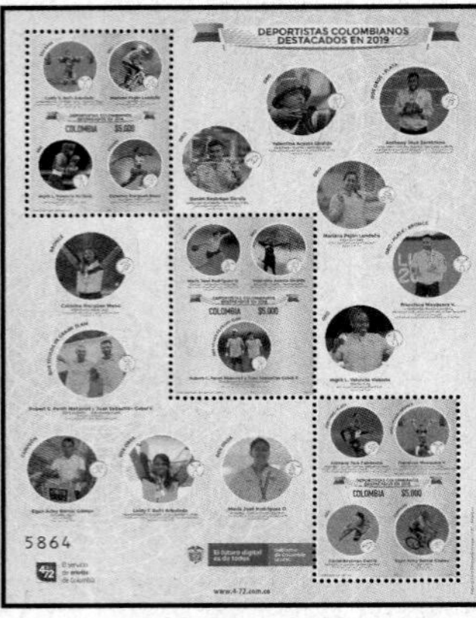

Athletes — A884

No. 1527: a, Weight lifter Leidy Y. Solís Arboleta, BMX bicyclist Mariana Pajón Londoño, boxer Ingrit L. Valencia Victoria, Triple jumper Caterine Ibargüen Mena. b, Bowler María José Rodríguez, archer Valentina Acosta Giraldo, tennis players Robert C. Farah Maksoud and Juan Sebastián Cabal Valdés. c, Runner Anthony José Zambrano, weight lifter Francisco Mosquera Valencia, diver Daniel Restrepo García, cyclist Egan Arley Bernal Gómez.

2019, Dec. 3 Litho. *Perf. 13¼x13*
1527 A884 5000p Sheet of 3, #a-c 9.25 9.25

Pereira Campus of Free University of Colombia, 50th Anniv. A885

2019, Dec. 9 Litho. *Perf. 13x13¼*
1528 A885 2000p multi 1.25 1.25

Rotary International Projects in Colombia A886

2019, Dec. 10 Litho. *Perf. 13*
1529 A886 500p multi .30 .30

Promotion of Tourism in Santander Department A887

2019, Dec. 12 Litho. *Perf. 13¼x13*
1530 A887 5000p multi 3.25 3.25

Christmas — A888

2019, Dec. 12 Litho. *Perf. 13¼x13*
1531 A888 5000p multi 3.25 3.25

Departments Type of 2003
Miniature Sheets

No. 1532 — Caquetá Department: a, Arms of Caquetá. b, Thraupis episcopus, horiz. c, El Paujil. d, Araracuara Canyon and Caquetá River. e, Sanjuanero dancers, horiz. f, Maloca of an indigenous community. g, Las Dalias Nature Reserve, La Montañita. h, Our Lady of Lourdes Cathedral, Florencia, horiz. i, St. John the Baptist Parish Church, El Doncello. j, Milán. k, Prafa Museum, Belén de los Andaquíes, horiz. l, Chairá Lake.

No. 1533 — Putumayo Department: a, Arms of Putumayo. b, Sunset on Putumayo River, Puerto Asís, horiz. c, Woman weaving. d, Betsknaté y Kalusturinda Carnival of Forgiveness, Sibundoy Valley. e, Ara ararauna, horiz. f, Putumayo Governmental Building, Mocoa. g, End of the World Waterfall, Mocoa. h, Indigenous mask makers, horiz. i, Pirarucu ceviche. j, Plukenetia volubilis fruits. k, St. Michael Archangel Cathedral, Mocoa, horiz. l, Piedra del Pijili, Orito.

Horiz. stamps are 46x37mm.

2019 Litho. *Perf. 13¼x13*
Sheets of 12, #a-l, + 8 labels
1532 A608 2000p Caquetá 15.00 15.00
1533 A608 2000p Putumayo 15.00 15.00

Issued: No. 1532, 12/20; No. 1533, 12/27.

A889

A890

Artillery Batallion No. 3, Cent. A891

2020, Jan. 17 Litho. *Perf. 13x13¼*
1534 Horiz. strip of 3 9.00 9.00
a. A889 5000p multi 3.00 3.00
b. A890 5000p multi 3.00 3.00
c. A891 5000p multi 3.00 3.00

Miniature Sheet

Diplomatic Relations Between Colombia and People's Republic of China, 40th Anniv. — A892

No. 1535 — UNESCO World Heritage Sites: a, Terracotta Army of Emperor Qin Shi Huang, People's Republic of China. b, Walls of Cartagena, Colombia. c, Great Wall of China. d, Stone sculptures, San Agustín Archaeological Park, Colombia.

2020, Feb. 7 Litho. *Perf. 13*
1535 A892 5000p Sheet of 4, #a-d 11.50 11.50

Miniature Sheet

Guadalajara de Buga, 450th Anniv. — A893

No. 1536: a, 1844 map of Guadalajara de Buga, Puente de la Libertad over Río Guadalajara. b, Sculpture of Rodrigo Díez de Fuenmayor, old train station. c, Bowls of Manjar blanco and Guiso Bugueño. d, Chloroceryle amazona, fishermen in Laguna de Sonso Nature Reserve.

2020, Mar. 4 Litho. *Perf. 13x13¼*
1536 A893 2000p Sheet of 4, #a-d 4.00 4.00

Miniature Sheet

2020 Risaralda Bird Festival — A894

No. 1537: a, Spizaetus isidori. b, Pseudocolopteryx acutipennis. c, Rupicola peruvianus. d, Machaeropterus striolatus. e, Ceratopipra erythrocephala. f, Atlapetes flaviceps. g, Penelope perspicax. h, Bangsia melanochlamys. i, Hapalopsittaca fuertesi. j, Megoleria susiana susanna.

2020, Mar. 20 Litho. *Perf. 13*
1537 A894 5000p Sheet of 10, #a-j 25.00 25.00

Leonardo da Vinci (1452-1519), Sculptor and Painter — A895

2020, May 29 Litho. *Perf. 13¼*
On Paper Faced With Synthetic Fabric
1538 A895 5000p multi 2.75 2.75

Miniature Sheet

Colombian Parks — A896

No. 1539: a, Podocnemis expansa, El Tuparro National Natural Park (35x35mm). b, Maipures Rapids, El Tuparro National Natural Park (35x35mm). c, Coeligena helianthea, Sumapaz National Natural Park (35x35mm). d, Laguna Larga, Sumapaz National Natural Park (35x35mm). e, Cardinalis phoeniceus, Macuira National Natural Park (35x35mm). f, Aleewolu Dunes, Macuira National Natural Park (35x35mm). g, Sphyrna lewini, Malpelo Flora and Fauna Sanctuary (35x35mm). h, Malpelo Island, Malpelo Flora and Fauna Sanctuary (35x35mm). i, "60 años" and National Natural Parks of Colombia emblem (70x35mm).

2020, June 6 Litho. *Perf. 14¼x14½*
1539 A896 500p Sheet of 9, #a-i 2.40 2.40

Mono Núñez Andean Music Festival — A897

2020, June 28 Litho. *Perf. 13¼*
1540 A897 200p multi .25 .25

RegioTram de Occidente Tramway Project A899

2020, July 16 Litho. ***Perf. 13x13¼***
1542 A899 5000p multi 2.75 2.75

No. 1542 was printed in sheets of 9 + 6 labels.

Miniature Sheet

Colombian Parks — A900

No. 1543: a, Anas georgica, Isla de la Corota Flora and Fauna Sanctuary. b, Aerial view of Isla de la Corota Flora and Fauna Sanctuary. c, Leptosciurus pucheranil, Las Hermosas Gloria Valencia de Castaño National Natural Park. d, Flora near Laguna las Mellizas, Las Hermosas Gloria Valencia de Castaño National Natural Park. e, Merganetta armetta, Nevado del Huila National Natural Park. f, Mountain, Nevado del Huila National Natural Park. g, Eriocnemis vestita, Doña Juana Cascabel Volcanic Complex National Natural Park. h, Laguna del Silencio, Doña Juana Cascabel Volcanic Complex National Natural Park. i, Lepanthes sp., Puracé National Natural Park. j, San Juan Hot Springs, Puracé National Natural Park.

2020, Aug. 14 Litho. ***Perf. 14½***
1543 A900 2000p Sheet of 10, #a-j 11.00 11.00

Julio Garavito Armero (1865-1920), Astronomer — A901

2020, Aug. 14 Litho. ***Perf. 13x13¼***
1544 A901 5000p multi 2.75 2.75

Campaign Against COVID-19 in Colombia — A902

2020, Aug. 26 Litho. ***Perf. 13¼x13***
1545 A902 10,000p multi 5.50 5.50

Miniature Sheet

Diplomatic Relations Between Colombia and Indonesia, 40th Anniv. — A903

No. 1546 — 40th anniv. emblem and: a, Chlorochrysa nitidissima, flag of Colombia. b, Artisan making batik, flag of Indonesia. c, Artisan making mola, flag of Colombia. d, Paradisaea minor, flag of Indonesia.

2020, Sept. 16 Litho. ***Perf. 13½***
1546 A903 500p Sheet of 4, #a-d 1.10 1.10

Reactivation of Aviation in Colombian Army, 25th Anniv. — A904

2020, Sept. 25 Litho. ***Perf. 13¼x13***
1547 A904 100p multi .25 .25

Miniature Sheet

Colombian Parks — A905

No. 1548: a, Bangsia aureocincta, Tatamá National Natural Park. b, Valle de las Lagunas, Tatamá National Natural Park. c, Otoglossum scansor, Las Orquidéas National Natural Park. d, Páramo Morro Pelao, Las Orquidéas National Natural Park. e, Alouatta seniculus, Otún Quimbaya Flora and Fauna Sanctuary. f, Hills, Otún Quimbaya Flora and Fauna Sanctuary. g, Andinobates opisthomelas, Selva de Florencia National Natural Park. h, El Escondido Volcano, Selva de Florencia National Natural Park.

2020, Sept. 29 Litho. ***Perf. 14½***
1548 A905 2000p Sheet of 8, #a-h 8.50 8.50

SEMI-POSTAL STAMP

Catalogue values for unused stamps in this section are for Never Hinged items.

Girl Giving First Aid — SP1

Perf. 13½x14
1966, Apr. 26 Litho. Unwmk.
B1 SP1 5c + 5c multicolored .25 .25

Issued for the Red Cross.

AIR POST STAMPS

No. 341 Overprinted

1919 Unwmk. ***Perf. 14***
C1 A107 2c car rose 3,500. 1,200.
a. Numerals "1" with serifs *6,000.* *2,000.*

Used for the first experimental flight from Barranquilla to Puerto Colombia, 6/18/19.

Issued by Compania Colombiana de Navegacion Aerea

From 1920 to 1932 the internal airmail service of Colombia was handled by the Compania Colombiana de Navegacion Aerea (1920) and the Sociedad Colombo-Alemana de Transportes Aéreos, known familiarly as "SCADTA" (1920-1932).

These organizations, under government contracts, operated and maintained their own post offices and issued stamps which were the only legal franking for airmail service during this period, both in the internal and international mails. All letters had to bear government stamps as well.

Woman and Boy Watching Plane — AP1

Designs: No. C3, Clouds and small biplane at top. No. C4, Tilted plane viewed close-up from above. No. C5, Flier in plane watching biplane. No. C6, Lighthouse. No. C7, Fuselage and tail of biplane. No. C8, Condor on cliff. No. C9, Plane at rest; pilot foreground. No. C10, Ocean liner.

1920, Feb. Unwmk. Litho. ***Imperf.***
Without Gum

C2	AP1	10c	multi	4,500.	1,750.
C3	AP1	10c	multi	4,500.	1,750.
C4	AP1	10c	multi	4,500.	1,750.
C5	AP1	10c	multi	4,500.	1,750.
C6	AP1	10c	multi	4,500.	1,750.
C7	AP1	10c	multi	12,500.	2,500.
C8	AP1	10c	multi	8,000.	3,000.
C9	AP1	10c	multi	4,500.	1,750.
C10	AP1	10c	multi	6,000.	1,500.

Nos. C2-C10 were overprinted on the nine lighter-colored varieties of a set of 18 publicity labels produced by the Curtiss Co. for inclusion with packs of cigarettes. These labels were printed setenant, in panes of 18 (3x6). Value for the set of 18 values without overprint: $4,750.

No. C8 exists uniquely on cover with the overprint omitted.

Flier Watching Plane — AP2

AP2a

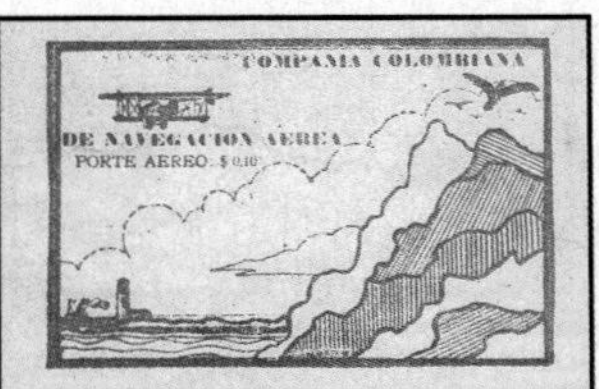

AP2b

1920, Mar.

No.	Type	Description	Unused	Used
C11	AP2	10c green	60.00	*92.50*
C11A	AP2a	10c green	65.00	*750.00*
C11B	AP2b	10c green	65.00	*750.00*
C11C	AP2a	10c red brown	65.00	—
C11D	AP2b	10c red brown	65.00	—

No. C11 Handstamp Surcharged

1920, Mar.

No.	Type	Description	Unused	Used
C11E	AP2	30c on 10c	250.00	—

Nos. C11C-C11D Handstamp Surcharged

1920, Dec.

No.	Type	Description	Unused	Used
C11F	AP2a	20c on 10c	250.00	—
C11G	AP2b	20c on 10c	250.00	—
C11H	AP2b	30c on 10c	250.00	—
i.		"0.30."		

No. C11C exists with "0-30." surcharge, however there is no evidence of postal usage.

Issued by Sociedad Colombo-Alemana de Transportes Aereos (SCADTA)

Seaplane over Magdalena River — AP3

1920-21 Litho. *Perf. 12*

No.	Type	Description	Unused	Used
C12	AP3	10c yellow ('21)	60.00	47.50
C13	AP3	15c blue ('21)	65.00	52.50
C14	AP3	30c blk, *rose*	30.00	16.00
a.		Horiz. pair, imperf. btwn.	600.00	
C15	AP3	30c rose ('21)	60.00	45.00
C16	AP3	50c pale green	60.00	*125.00*
a.		Horiz. pair, imperf. btwn.	600.00	
		Nos. C12-C16 (5)	275.00	286.00

For surcharges see Nos. C17-C24, C36-C37.

No. C16 Handstamp Surcharged in Violet, Black, Gray, or Blue Green

a

b

c

d

e

f

g

1921-23

No.	Type	Description	Unused	Used
C17	AP3 (a)	10c on 50c (V or B) ('23)	1,500.	825.
C18	AP3 (b)	10c on 50c (G or bl grn)	1,900.	825.
C19	AP3 (c)	10c on 50c (B)	1,500.	825.
a.		Imperf.		—
C20	AP3 (b)	30c on 50c (V or B)	925.	575.
C21	AP3 (d)	30c on 50c (V or B)	925.	575.
C22	AP3 (e)	30c on 50c (V)	4,500.	950.
C23	AP3 (f)	30c on 50c (V or G)	3,250.	950.
C24	AP3 (g)	30c on 50c (V)	3,250.	950.
C24A	AP3 (g)	20c on 50c (V)		—
C24B	AP3	30c on 50c "c 30" (V), on cover		—

No. C16 with Typewritten Surcharge in Red or Violet

1921

No.	Type	Description	Unused	Used
C24C	AP3	10c on 50c (R or V)	—	600.
C24D	AP3	30c on 50c (V)		*3,000.*

Plane over Magdalena River — AP4

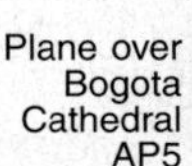

Plane over Bogota Cathedral AP5

1921 *Perf. 11½*

No.	Type	Description	Unused	Used
C25	AP4	5c orange yellow	4.50	4.00
C26	AP4	10c slate green	2.10	1.50
C27	AP4	15c orange brown	2.10	1.60
C28	AP4	20c red brown	4.50	2.10
a.		Horiz. pair, imperf. vert.	*225.00*	
C29	AP4	30c green	2.10	1.10
C30	AP4	50c blue	3.25	1.25
C31	AP4	60c vermilion	85.00	32.50
C32	AP5	1p gray black	22.50	5.00
C33	AP5	2p rose	40.00	20.00
C34	AP5	3p violet	110.00	72.50
C35	AP5	5p olive green	325.00	300.00
		Nos. C25-C35 (11)	601.05	441.55

Exist imperf.

For surcharge see No. C52.

Nos. C16 and C12 Handstamp Surcharged in Black or Violet

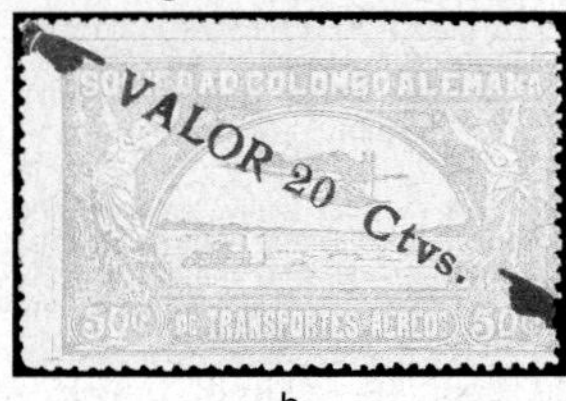

h

i

1921-22 *Perf. 12*

No.	Type	Description	Unused	Used
C36	AP3 (h)	20c on 50c (B or V)	3,500.	1,500.
C37	AP3 (i)	30c on 10c (V)	1,500.	575.

Seaplane over Magdalena River — AP6

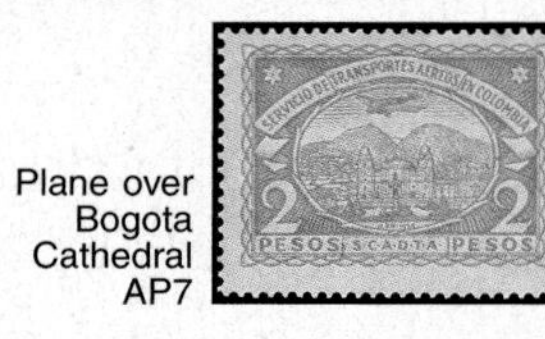

Plane over Bogota Cathedral AP7

1923-28 Wmk. 116 *Perf. 14x14½*

No.	Type	Description	Unused	Used
C38	AP6	5c orange yellow	1.75	.25
C39	AP6	10c green	1.75	.25
C40	AP6	15c carmine	1.75	.25
C41	AP6	20c gray	1.75	.25
C42	AP6	30c blue	1.75	.25
C43	AP6	40c purple ('28)	12.50	8.00
C44	AP6	50c green	2.10	.25
C45	AP6	60c brown	3.25	.25
C46	AP6	80c olive grn ('28)	32.50	30.00
C47	AP7	1p black	14.50	3.25
C48	AP7	2p red orange	21.00	6.00
C49	AP7	3p violet	37.50	25.00
C50	AP7	5p olive green	67.50	32.50
		Nos. C38-C50 (13)	199.60	106.50

For surcharges and overprints see Nos. C51, C53-C54, CF1.

Nos. C41 and C31 Surcharged in Carmine and Dark Blue

No. C51

No. C52

1923

No.	Type	Description	Unused	Used
C51	AP6	30c on 20c gray (C)	92.50	57.50
C52	AP4	30c on 60c ver	85.00	37.50

Nos. C41-C42 Overprinted in Black

1928 Wmk. 116 *Perf. 14x14½*

No.	Type	Description	Unused	Used
C53	AP6	20c gray	80.00	62.50
C54	AP6	30c blue	80.00	62.50

Goodwill flight of Lt. Benjamin Mendez from New York to Bogota.

Magdalena River and Tolíma Volcano AP8

Columbus' Ship and Plane AP9

1929, June 1 Wmk. 127 *Perf. 14*

No.	Type	Description	Unused	Used
C55	AP8	5c yellow org	1.25	.25
C56	AP8	10c red brown	1.25	.25
C57	AP8	15c deep green	1.25	.25
C58	AP8	20c carmine	1.25	.25
C59	AP8	30c gray blue	1.25	.25
C60	AP8	40c dull violet	1.25	.25
C61	AP8	50c dk olive grn	2.50	.25
C62	AP8	60c orange brown	3.75	.25
C63	AP8	80c green	11.00	3.25
C64	AP9	1p blue	12.00	2.50
C65	AP9	2p brown orange	18.00	5.75
C66	AP9	3p pale rose vio	42.50	18.00
C67	AP9	5p olive green	100.00	37.50
		Nos. C55-C67 (13)	197.25	69.00

For surcharges and overprints see Nos. C80-C95, CF2, CF4.

For International Airmail

AP10

AP11

1929, June 1 Wmk. 127 *Perf. 14*

No.	Type	Description	Unused	Used
C68	AP10	5c yellow org	6.25	*7.25*
C69	AP10	10c red brown	1.25	*3.00*
C70	AP10	15c deep green	1.25	*3.00*
C71	AP10	20c carmine	1.25	*3.75*
C72	AP10	25c violet blue	1.25	.85
C73	AP10	30c gray blue	1.25	.95
C74	AP10	50c dk olive grn	1.25	*1.90*
C75	AP10	60c brown	2.50	*3.00*
C76	AP11	1p blue	5.50	*7.25*
C77	AP11	2p red orange	8.50	*10.00*
C78	AP11	3p violet	100.00	100.00
C79	AP11	5p olive green	125.00	*140.00*
		Nos. C68-C79 (12)	255.25	*280.95*

This issue was sold abroad for use on correspondence to be flown from coastal to interior points of Colombia. Cancellations are those of the country of origin rather than Colombia.

For overprint see No. CF3.

Nos. C63, C66 and C64 Surcharged in Black

m

n

1930, Dec. 15

C80 AP8(m) 10c on 80c 7.00 7.00
C81 AP9(n) 20c on 3p 12.50 12.50
C82 AP9(n) 30c on 1p 15.00 12.50
Nos. C80-C82 (3) 34.50 32.00

Simon Bolivar (1783-1830).

Colombian Government Issues
Nos. C55-C67 Overprinted in Black

o

CORREO AEREO

p

Wmk. 127

1932, Jan. 1 Typo. *Perf. 14*

C83 AP8(o) 5c yellow org 10.00 10.00
C84 AP8(o) 10c red brown 2.25 .60
C85 AP8(o) 15c deep green 3.75 3.75
C86 AP8(o) 20c carmine 1.90 .35
a. Double overprint —
C87 AP8(o) 30c gray blue 1.90 .60
C88 AP8(o) 40c dull violet 2.50 1.25
C89 AP8(o) 50c dk ol grn 5.00 3.75
C90 AP8(o) 60c orange brn 4.25 3.75
C91 AP8(o) 80c green 17.00 17.00
C92 AP9(p) 1p blue 14.50 12.00
C93 AP9(p) 2p brown org 37.50 35.00
C94 AP9(p) 3p pale rose vio 77.50 65.00
C95 AP9(p) 5p olive green 125.00 *140.00*
Nos. C83-C95 (13) 303.05 293.05

Coffee
AP12

Gold
AP16

Designs: 10c, 50c, Cattle. 15c, 60c, Petroleum. 20c, 40c, Bananas. 3p, 5p, Emerald.

1932-39 Wmk. 127 Photo. *Perf. 14*

C96 AP12 5c org & blk brn .90 .25
C97 AP12 10c lake & blk 1.00 .25
C98 AP12 15c bl grn & vio blk .50 .25
C99 AP12 15c ver & vio blk ('39) 4.00 .25
C100 AP12 20c car & ol blk .85 .25
C101 AP12 20c turq grn & ol blk ('39) 4.25 .35
C102 AP12 30c dk bl & blk brn 2.40 .25
C103 AP12 40c dk vio & ol bis 1.10 .25
C104 AP12 50c dk grn & brnsh blk 6.75 1.50
C105 AP12 60c dk brn & blk vio 1.40 .25
C106 AP12 80c grn & blk brn 9.50 2.00
C107 AP16 1p dk bl & ol bis 10.00 1.25
C108 AP16 2p org brn & ol bis 16.00 2.75
C109 AP16 3p dk vio & emer 26.00 7.25
C110 AP16 5p gray blk & emer 57.50 21.00
Nos. C96-C110 (15) 142.15 38.10

For overprint see No. CF5.

Nos. C104, C106-C108 Surcharged

a

b

1934, Jan. 5

C111 AP12(a) 10c on 50c 4.50 4.50
C112 AP12(a) 15c on 80c 6.25 6.25
C113 AP16(b) 20c on 1p 6.50 6.50
C114 AP16(b) 30c on 2p 7.25 7.25
Nos. C111-C114 (4) 24.50 24.50

400th anniversary of Cartagena.

Nos. C100 and C103 Surcharged in Black or Carmine

1939, Jan. 15

C115 AP12 5c on 20c (Bk) .35 .35
C116 AP12 5c on 40c (C) .40 .25
C117 AP12 15c on 20c (Bk) 1.50 .50
a. Double surcharge 50.00
b. Pair, one with dbl. surch. 60.00
c. Inverted surcharge 50.00 50.00

No. CF5 Surcharged in Black

C118 AP12 5c on 20c .70 .70
Nos. C115-C118 (4) 2.95 1.80

Nos. C102-C103 Surcharged in Black or Red

1940, Oct. 20

C119 AP12 15c on 30c 1.75 .55
a. Inverted surcharge 50.00
C120 AP12 15c on 40c (R) 2.75 .80
a. Double surcharge 50.00

Pre-Columbian Monument — AP18

Proclamation of Independence — AP22

Designs: 10c, 40c, Symbol of Legend of El Dorado. 15c, 50c, Spanish Fortifications, Cartagena. 20c, 60c, Colonial Bogotá. 2p, 5p, National Library, Bogota.

Unwmk.

1941, Jan. 28 Engr. *Perf. 12*

C121 AP18 5c gray black .25 .25
C122 AP18 10c yellow org .25 .25
C123 AP18 15c carmine rose .25 .25
C124 AP18 20c yellow grn .35 .25
a. Horiz. pair, imperf. vert. 87.50
C125 AP18 30c deep blue .35 .25
C126 AP18 40c rose lake 1.40 .25
C127 AP18 50c turq green 1.40 .25
C128 AP18 60c sepia 1.40 .25
C129 AP18 80c olive blk 3.25 .40
C130 AP22 1p blue & blk 4.00 .50
C131 AP22 2p red org & blk 8.00 2.00
C132 AP22 3p violet & blk 16.00 6.50
C133 AP22 5p lt green & blk 40.00 20.00
Nos. C121-C133 (13) 76.90 31.40

See Nos. C151-C163, C217-C225. For overprints see Nos. C175-C198, C200-C216, C226, C290.

San Sebastian Fort, Cartagena — AP24

National Capitol, Bogotá AP27

Designs: 5c, 20c, 50c, San Sebastian Fort, Cartagena. 10c, 30c, 60c, Tequendama Waterfall. 15c, 40c, 80c, Bay of Santa Maria.

Unwmk.

1945, Nov. 3 Litho. *Perf. 11*

C134 AP24 5c blue gray .25 .25
C135 AP24 10c yellow org .25 .25
C136 AP24 15c rose .25 .25
C137 AP24 20c lt yel grn .30 .25
C138 AP24 30c ultra .30 .25
C139 AP24 40c claret .50 .25
C140 AP24 50c bluish grn .55 .25
C141 AP24 60c lt vio brn 2.25 .80
C142 AP24 80c dk slate grn 3.50 .80
C143 AP27 1p dk blue 5.00 .75
C144 AP27 2p red orange 7.00 2.50
Nos. C134-C144 (11) 20.15 6.60

Part-perforate varieties exist for all denominations except 80c.

Imperf., Pairs

C134a AP24 5c 8.50
C135a AP24 10c 8.50
C136a AP24 15c 8.50
C137a AP24 20c 8.50
C138a AP24 30c 8.50
C139a AP24 40c 8.50
C140a AP24 50c 8.50
C141a AP24 60c 8.50
C142a AP24 80c 10.50
C143a AP27 1p 17.50
C144a AP27 2p 60.00
Nos. C134a-C144a (11) 156.00

Bello Type of Regular Issue, 1946

Wmk. 255

1946, Sept. 3 Engr. *Perf. 12*

C145 A219 5c deep blue .25 .25

Francisco José de Caldas AP29

COLOMBIA

10 CENTAVOS 10

Manuel del Socorro Rodriguez AP30

Perf. 12½

1947, May 9 Litho. Unwmk.

C146 AP29 5c dp bl, *grnsh* .50 .35
C147 AP30 10c red org, *grnsh* .80 .45

4th Pan-American Press Congress (1946).

Chancellery Patio — AP31

Capitol, Patio Rafael Nunez AP32

AP33

1948, Apr. 2 Engr. Wmk. 229

C148 AP31 5c dark brown .25 .25
C149 AP32 15c deep blue 1.00 1.00

Miniature Sheet

Imperf

C150 AP33 50c brown 1.90 1.90

9th Pan-American Conference, Bogotá.

Types of 1941

1948, July 21 Unwmk. *Perf. 12*

C151 AP18 5c orange yel .25 .25
C152 AP18 10c scarlet .25 .25
C153 AP18 15c deep blue .25 .25
C154 AP18 20c violet .25 .25
C155 AP18 30c yellow grn .35 .25
C156 AP18 40c gray .40 .25
C157 AP18 50c rose lake .40 .25
C158 AP18 60c olive gray .70 .25
C159 AP18 80c red brn .85 .25
C160 AP22 1p ol grn & vio brn 1.50 .30
C161 AP22 2p dp grn & brt bl 2.50 .65
C162 AP22 3p rose car & blk 5.50 3.75
C163 AP22 5p lt brn & turq grn 14.00 7.00
Nos. C151-C163 (13) 27.20 13.95

"Air Week" 5c Blue

The War and Air Department issued a 5c blue stamp in May, 1949, to publicize Air Week (Semana de Aviacion). This stamp had no franking value and its use was optional during May 16-23.

Justice and Liberty — AP34

Design: 10c, Liberty holding tablet of laws.

1949, Oct. 7 Unwmk. *Perf. 13*

C164 AP34 5c blue green .25 .25
C165 AP34 10c orange .25 .25

Issued to honor the new Constitution.

Wing — AP35

For Domestic Postage

1950, June 22 Litho. *Perf. 12*

C166 AP35 5c org yel .25 .30
C167 AP35 10c brown red .35 .30
C168 AP35 15c lt blue .40 .40
C169 AP35 20c lt green .60 *.95*
C170 AP35 30c lilac gray 1.50 *2.40*
C171 AP35 60c chocolate 1.90 *3.50*

With Network

With Network as in Parenthesis

C172 AP35 1p dk gray (yel) 14.00 *16.00*
C173 AP35 2p bl (pale grn) 14.00 *20.00*
C174 AP35 5p claret (claret) 40.00 *60.00*
Nos. C166-C174 (9) 73.00 *103.85*

No. C172 was issued both with and without network.

Nos. C151-C157 and C160-C163 Overprinted in Black

1950, July 18

C175 AP18 5c orange yel .25 .25
C176 AP18 10c scarlet .25 .25
C177 AP18 15c deep blue .25 .25
C178 AP18 20c violet .25 .25
C179 AP18 30c yellow green .30 .25
C180 AP18 40c gray 2.50 .80
C181 AP18 50c rose lake .75 .40
C182 AP22 1p ol grn & vio brn 4.00 4.50
C183 AP22 2p dp grn & brt bl 7.50 6.00
C184 AP22 3p rose car & blk 10.00 16.00
C185 AP22 5p lt brn & turq grn 35.00 52.50
Nos. C175-C185 (11) 61.05 81.45

Nos. C151-C163 Overprinted in Black

1950, July 12

C186 AP18 5c orange yel .25 .25
C187 AP18 10c scarlet .25 .25
C188 AP18 15c deep blue .25 .25
C189 AP18 20c violet .25 .25
C190 AP18 30c yellow green .25 .25
C191 AP18 40c gray .55 .25
C192 AP18 50c rose lake .55 .25
C193 AP18 60c olive gray .85 .25
C194 AP18 80c red brown 1.25 .50
C195 AP22 1p ol grn & vio brn 1.50 .70
C196 AP22 2p dp grn & brt bl 4.50 2.40
C197 AP22 3p rose car & blk 10.00 12.00
C198 AP22 5p lt brn & turq grn 30.00 35.00
Nos. C186-C198 (13) 50.45 52.60

On Nos. C175-C198, "L" stands for LANSA, "A" for AVIANCA.

UPU Type
Miniature Sheet

Unwmk.

1950, Aug. 22 Photo. *Imperf.*

C199 A245 50c gray 2.25 2.25

75th anniv. (in 1949) of the UPU.

Catalogue values for unused stamps in this section, from this point to the end of the section, are for Never Hinged items.

Types of 1941 Overprinted at Lower Right in Black

Unwmk.

1951, Sept. 15 Engr. *Perf. 12*

C200 AP18 40c orange yel 1.60 1.00
C201 AP18 50c ultra 2.10 1.40
C202 AP18 60c gray 1.60 1.00
C203 AP18 80c car rose 1.50 1.00
C204 AP22 1p red org & red brn 6.00 6.00
C205 AP22 2p rose car & bl 7.25 7.25
C206 AP22 3p choc & emer 18.00 20.00
C207 AP22 5p org & gray 47.50 52.50
Nos. C200-C207 (8) 85.55 90.15

Types of 1941 Overprinted at Lower Right in Black

1951-54

C208 AP18 40c orange yel 5.50 .55
C209 AP18 50c ultra 16.00 .65
C210 AP18 60c gray 4.50 .55
a. Overprint centered 5.00 .55
C211 AP18 80c car rose 1.00 .35
C212 AP22 1p red org & red brn 4.75 .50
C213 AP22 1p ol grn & vio brn ('54) 7.00 .95
C214 AP22 2p rose car & bl 4.75 .70
C215 AP22 3p choc & emer 8.75 2.10
C216 AP22 5p org & gray 16.00 2.25
Nos. C208-C216 (9) 68.25 8.60

All values except the 2p and 3p exist without overprint.

Types of 1941

1952, May 10 Engr.

C217 AP18 5c ultra .50 .25
C218 AP18 10c ultra .50 .25
C219 AP18 15c ultra .50 .25
C220 AP18 20c ultra .90 .40
C221 AP18 30c ultra 2.50 .95

Color Change

C222 AP18 5c car rose .50 .25
C223 AP18 10c car rose .50 .25
C224 AP18 20c car rose .95 .25
C225 AP18 30c car rose 2.00 .55
Nos. C217-C225 (9) 8.85 3.40

Type of 1941 Surcharged in Blue

1952, Oct. 30

C226 AP18 70c on 80c car rose 2.00 .80

Latin American Siderurgical Conf., 1952.

Type of Postal Tax Stamps, 1948-50, Nos. 602 and 604 Surcharged or Overprinted in Black

1953 Wmk. 255 *Perf. 12*

C227 PT10 5c on 8c blue .25 .25
C228 PT10 15c on 20c brown .30 .25
C229 PT10 15c on 25c bl grn 1.50 .25
C230 PT10 25c blue green .80 .25
Nos. C227-C230 (4) 2.85 1.00

Many varieties of overprint or surcharge exist on Nos. C227-C231.

No. 570 Overprinted in Blue

1953, Aug. Wmk. 229 *Perf. 12½*

C231 A160 10c red .25 .25

"Extra Rapido"

Stamps inscribed "Extra Rapido" are for use on domestic airmail carried by airlines other than AVIANCA.

No. 585 Surcharged and Overprinted in Dark Blue

1953 Unwmk. *Perf. 13*

C232 A244 5c on 11c red .50 .35

Capitol and Arms — AP37

Revenue Stamps Overprinted "Correo Extra-Rapido"
Gray Security Paper

1953 Wmk. 255 Engr. *Perf. 12*

C233 AP37 1c on 2c green .25 .25
C234 AP37 50c red orange .25 .25

AP38

Real Estate Tax Stamps Ovptd. "Correo Extra-Rapido" in Black or Carmine

1953

C235 AP38 5c red orange .25 .25
C236 AP38 20c brown (C) .30 .25

On 20c, overprint is at bottom of stamp and two lines of ornaments cover real estate tax inscription at top.

Castillo y Rada and Map — AP39

Real Estate Tax Stamp Surcharged "Correo Aereo, II Exposicion Filatelica Nacional, Bogota Dicbre 1953, 15 Centavos"

1953, Dec. 12 Engr. & Litho.

C237 AP39 15c on 10p multi .50 .35

2nd Natl. Philatelic Exhib., Bogota, Dec. 1953.

No. RA45 Overprinted in Black

1953

C238 PT10 10c purple .25 .25

Galeras Volcano — AP40

Retreat of San Diego — AP41

Designs: No. C241, Las Lajas Shrine, Narino. No. C242, 50c, Bolivar monument. 20c, 80c, Ruiz mountain, Manizales. 40c, George Isaacs monument, Cali. 60c, Mono Fountain, Tunja. 1p, Stadium, Medellin. 2p, Pastelillo Fort, Cartagena. 3p, Santo Domingo University gate. 5p, Las Lajas Shrine. 10p, Map of Colombia.

Perf. 13½x13, 13

1954, Jan. 15 Engr. Unwmk.

C239 AP40 5c dp red vio .25 .25
C240 AP41 10c black .25 .25
C241 AP40 15c red orange .25 .25
C242 AP40 15c car rose .25 .25
C243 AP40 20c brown .25 .25
C244 AP40 30c brown org .25 .25
C245 AP40 40c blue .35 .25
C246 AP40 50c dk violet brn .40 .25
C247 AP40 60c dk brown .50 .25
C248 AP40 80c red brown .75 .25

Size: 37x27mm

Center in Black

C249 AP41 1p deep blue 3.75 .25
C250 AP41 2p dark green 5.00 .40
C251 AP41 3p carmine rose 12.00 1.40

Size: 38x32mm, 32x38mm

C252 AP41 5p dk grn & red brn 15.00 3.50
C253 AP40 10p gray grn & red org 22.00 7.50
Nos. C239-C253 (15) 61.25 15.55

See Nos. C307-C308. For surcharges and overprints see Nos. 691, C321, C325, C330, C333-C334, C343-C346.

Condor Carrying Shield AP42

Inscribed: "Correo Extra-Rapido"

1954, Apr. 23 Litho. *Perf. 12½*
C254 AP42 5c reddish lilac .95 .30

For overprint see No. RA53.

Soldier-Map-Arms Type

1954, June 13 Engr. *Perf. 13*
C255 A259 15c carmine .40 .25

See No. C271a.

Games Type

Design: 20c, Stadium and Athlete holding arms of Colombia.

1954, July 18
C256 A260 15c chocolate .70 .25
C257 A260 20c deep blue green 1.40 .35

Church of St. Peter Claver, Cartagena AP45

1954, Sept. 9
C258 AP45 15c brown 1.25 .35
a. Souvenir sheet 8.00 12.00

St. Peter Claver, 300th death anniv.
No. C258a contains one stamp similar to No. C258, but printed in red brown.

Mercury Type

1954, Oct. 29
C259 A263 15c deep blue .55 .25

Inscribed "Extra Rapido"

C260 A263 50c scarlet .55 .25

Archbishop Manuel José Mosquera, Death Cent. — AP47

Inscribed: "Correo Extra Rapido"

1954, Nov. 17
C261 AP47 2c yellow green .25 .25

Virgin of Chiquinquira — AP48

Inscribed: "Correo Extra Rapido"

1954, Dec. 4 Engr. & Litho.
C262 AP48 5c org brn & multi .25 .25

See No. C291. For overprint see No. 686.

College Types

Designs: 20c, Brother Cristobal de Torres. 50c, College chapel and arms.

Perf. 12½x11½, 11½x12½

1954, Dec. 6 Engr. Unwmk.
C263 A264 15c orange & blk .50 .25
C264 A264 20c ultra .85 .25
C265 A265 25c dark brown .85 .25
C266 A265 50c black & car 2.25 .70
a. Souvenir sheet 12.00 16.00
Nos. C263-C266 (4) 4.45 1.45

No. C266a contains four stamps similar to Nos. C263-C266, but printed in different colors: 15c red and black, 20c pale purple, 25c brown, 50c black and olive green.

Steel Mill Type

1954, Dec. 12 *Perf. 12½x13*
C267 A266 20c green & blk 1.75 .60

Marti Type

1955, Jan. 28 *Perf. 13½x13*
C268 A267 15c deep green .30 .25

Korean Veterans Type

1955, Mar. 23 *Perf. 12½*
C269 A268 20c dark green .55 .25

Merchant Fleet Types

1955, Apr. 12 *Perf. 12½*
C270 A269 25c black .40 .25
C271 A270 50c dark green .85 .40
a. Souvenir sheet 9.50 12.00

No. C271a contains 4 stamps similar to Nos. C255, C269-C271, but printed in different colors; 15c lilac red, 20c olive, 25c bluish black, 50c bluish green.

Marco Fidel Suarez (1855-1927), Pres. 1918-21 — AP56

Inscribed: "Correo Extra Rapido"

1955, April 23 *Perf. 13*
C272 AP56 10c deep blue .25 .25

Hotel-Church Type

1955, May 16 Photo. *Perf. 11½x12*
C273 A271 15c rose brown .40 .25

Rotary Type

Unwmk.

1955, Oct. 17 Engr. *Perf. 13*
C274 A272 15c dk carmine rose .40 .25

Atahualpa, Tisquesuza and Montezuma AP59

Ferdinand the Catholic and Queen Isabella I AP60

Designs: 15c, O'Higgins, Santander and Sucre. 20c, Marti, Hidalgo and Petion. 1p, Artigas, Solano Lopez and Murillo. 2p, Abdon Calderon, Baron de Rio Branco and José de La Mar.

1955, Oct. 12 Engr. & Photo.

Inscribed: "Extra Rapido"

C275 AP59 2c dull brn & blk .45 .25
C276 AP60 5c dk brn & yel .45 .25

Regular Air Post

C277 AP59 15c rose car & blk .55 .25
C278 AP59 20c pale brn & blk .85 .25
a. Souvenir sheet of 2 30.00 30.00

Inscribed: "Extra Rapido"

C279 AP60 1p ol gray & brn 15.00 7.50
C280 AP60 2p violet & blk 11.00 5.75
Nos. C275-C280 (6) 28.30 14.25

7th Cong. of the Postal Union of the Americas and Spain, Bogota, Oct. 12-Nov. 9, 1955.
No. C278a contains one each of Nos. C277-C278 printed in different shades.

Caro Type

1955, Nov. 29 Engr. *Perf. 13½x13*
C281 A275 15c gray green .40 .25

University of Salamanca AP62

Inscribed: "Extra Rapido"

1955, Nov. 29 Unwmk. *Perf. 13*
C282 AP62 20c dark brown .25 .25

University of Salamanca, 7th centenary.

Type of Postal Tax Stamp of 1948-50 Surcharged

1956 Wmk. 255 Engr. *Perf. 12*
C283 PT10 2c on 8c blue .25 .25

No. 617 Overprinted in Black

1956 Unwmk. *Perf. 12½x13*
C284 A256 1p black & emerald .40 .25

Columbus Type

1956, Oct. 11 Photo. *Perf. 12*
C285 A279 15c intense blue .65 .25

See No. C306.

St. Elizabeth Type

1956, Nov. 19
C286 A280 15c red brown .50 .25

St. Ignatius Type

1956, Nov. 26 Engr. *Perf. 12½x13*
C287 A281 5c brown .25 .25

Javier Pereira — AP63

1956, Dec. 28 Unwmk. *Perf. 12*
C288 AP63 20c rose carmine .25 .25

Issued to honor 167-year-old Javier Pereira.

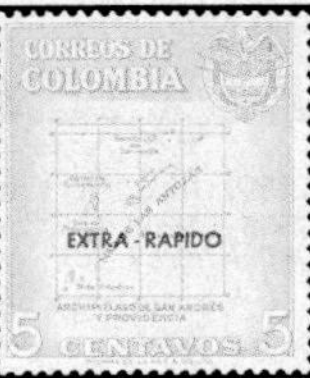

No. 649 and Type of 1941 Overprinted in Red

1957 *Perf. 13½x13*
C289 A276 5c blue & black 7.50 3.25

Perf. 12

C290 AP22 5p orange & gray 11.00 7.50

The overprint measures 14mm.

Virgin Type of 1954

Engraved and Lithographed

1957, May 23 Unwmk. *Perf. 13*
C291 AP48 5c dp plum & multi .25 .25

Bank Type

No. C292, 20c, Emblem, cow, horse & herd. 10c, Emblem & tractor. 15c, Emblem, coffee & corn. No. C293, Emblem & dairy farm.

1957 Photo. *Perf. 14x13½*
C292 A283 5c chocolate .25 .25
C293 A283 5c orange .25 .25
C294 A283 10c green .55 .25
C295 A283 15c black .35 .25
C296 A283 20c dull red .85 .30
Nos. C292-C296 (5) 2.25 1.30

No. C292 is inscribed "Extra Rapido."
Issued: No. C292, 3/5; others 5/23.

Cyclist AP64

1957, July 6 Unwmk. *Perf. 12*
C297 AP64 2c brown .25 .25
C298 AP64 5c ultra .25 .25

Seventh Bicycle Tour of Colombia.

Academy Type

Designs: 15c, Coat of arms and Gen. Rafael Reyes. 20c, Coat of arms and Academy.

1957, July 20 Engr. *Perf. 12½*
C299 A284 15c rose carmine .30 .25
C300 A284 20c brown .45 .25

Delgado Type

1957, Sept. 15 Photo. *Perf. 12*
C301 A285 10c slate blue .25 .25

UPU Type

1957, Oct. 10
C302 A286 15c dark red brown .30 .25
C303 A286 25c dark blue .40 .25

St. Vincent de Paul Type

1957, Oct. 18
C304 A287 5c rose brown .25 .25

Fencing Type

1957, Nov. 23 *Perf. 12*
C305 A288 20c dark red brown .50 .30

Columbus Type Inscribed "Extra Rapido"

1958, Jan. 8 Unwmk. *Perf. 12*
C306 A279 3c dark green .25 .25

Scenic Type

Design: 25c, Las Lajas Shrine.

1958, June 20 Engr. *Perf. 13*
C307 AP40 25c dark blue .30 .25
C308 AP40 25c rose violet .30 .25

IGY Type

1958, May 12 Photo. *Perf. 12*
C309 A289 25c green .50 .25

Inscribed "Extra Rapido"

C310 A289 1p purple .65 .25

No. 659 Ovptd. in Carmine

1958, Oct. 16 Engr. *Perf. 13*
C312 A277 50c dk green & blk .50 .25

Almanza Type

1958, Oct. 23 Photo. *Perf. 14x13*
C313 A290 25c dark gray .40 .25

Inscribed "Extra Rapido"

C314 A290 10c olive green .30 .25

Carrasquilla Type

1959, Jan. 22 Photo. *Perf. 14x13*
C315 A291 25c carmine rose .25 .25
C316 A291 1p dark blue .80 .25

Miss Universe Type

1959, June 26 Unwmk. *Perf. 11½*
C317 A292 1.20p multicolored 1.75 1.40
C318 A292 5p multicolored 45.00 45.00

Gaitan Type Inscribed and Surcharged in Black or Blue

1959, July 28 Engr. *Perf. 12x13½*
C319 A293 2p on 1p black 2.00 1.40
C320 A293 2p on 1p black (Bl) 2.00 1.40

The 1p black, type A293, exists without surcharge. Value $10.

No. C247 Surcharged in Dark Blue

1959, Aug. 24 Unwmk. *Perf. 13*
C321 AP40 50c on 60c dk brown 2.25 .40

Regular and Air Post Issues of 1948-59 Ovptd. in Black or Red

1959-60
C322 A283 5c orange .50 .50
C323 A287 5c rose brn ('60) .50 .35
C324 A281 5c brown (R) .45 .40
C325 AP41 10c black .35 .25
a. Double overprint 2.50 2.50
C326 A160 10c red, #C231 .35 .25
a. Double overprint 1.40 1.40
C328 A284 15c rose car .35 .25
a. Inverted overprint 3.00 3.00
C330 AP40 20c brown .35 .25
a. Double overprint 1.40 1.40
C331 A284 20c brown .35 .25
C332 A288 20c dk red brn ('60) .40 .25
C333 AP40 25c rose vio ('60) .35 .25
C334 AP40 25c dark blue .35 .25
C335 A291 25c car rose .35 .25
C336 A290 25c dark gray .35 .25
C338 AP40 30c brown org .35 .25
C340 AP40 50c on 60c dk brn .50 .25
C341 A291 1p dark blue 1.15 .25
a. Double overprint 2.50 2.50
C342 A292 1.20p brn, ultra, car & ol 1.40 1.15
C343 AP41 2p dk grn & blk 2.75 .25
C344 AP41 3p car rose & blk 6.75 .85
a. Double overprint 10.00 10.00
C345 AP41 5p dk grn & red brn 9.00 1.15
a. Double overprint 10.00 10.00
b. Inverted overprint 10.00 10.00
C346 AP40 10p gray grn & red org 12.00 3.25
Nos. C322-C346 (21) 38.90 11.15

Issued following agreement between the Colombian government and AVIANCA to unify the air postage used on all mail carried by AVIANCA.

Vertical overprint on Nos. C342 and C346.

Airmail Stamp of 1919 and Planes AP66

60c, Nos. C349a, C350a, Planes of 1919 and 1959. Nos. C349b, C350b, Stamp of 1919 and Planes.

Unwmk.
1959, Dec. 5 Photo. *Perf. 12*
C347 AP66 35c lt bl, blk & red .65 .25
C348 AP66 60c yel grn & gray 1.10 .75

Souvenir Sheets
C349 Sheet of 2 11.50 11.50
a. AP66 1p orange & gray 2.00 1.50
b. AP66 1p lilac, gray & red 2.00 1.50

Inscribed "Extra Rapido"
1960, May 17
C350 Sheet of 2 11.00 11.00
a. AP66 1.50p red orange & gray 2.00 1.50
b. AP66 1.50p olive, gray & rose 2.00 1.50

Nos. C347-C350 for the 40th anniv. of air post service and of the AVIANCA company.

Type of Regular Issue and

1859 Stamp and Seaplane AP67

Designs (various stamps of 1859 and): 10c, Map of Colombia. 25c, Pres. Mariano Ospina. 1.20p, Plane over mountains.

1959, Dec. 1 Photo. *Perf. 12*
C351 A296 25c choc & red .50 .35
C352 AP67 50c ver & ultra 1.25 .65
C353 AP67 1.20p yel grn & car 2.60 1.60

Inscribed "Extra Rapido"
C354 A296 10c lemon & vio .25 .25
Nos. C351-C354 (4) 4.60 2.85

Souvenir Sheet

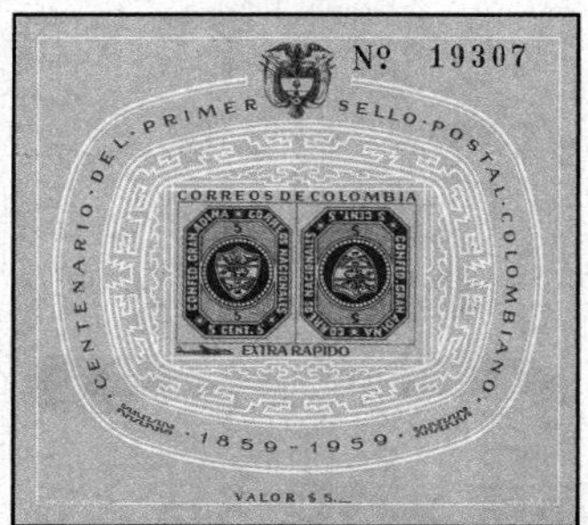

Tête Bêche 5c Stamps of 1859 — AP68

Wmk. 331
1959, Dec. 23 Litho. *Imperf.*
C355 AP68 5p blue, *pink* 19.00 19.00

Cent. of Colombian postage stamps.

No. C355 exists with inscription "VALOR $5.10" instead of "VALOR $5."

Eldorado Airport, Bogota AP69

1960, Jan. 5 Wmk. 331 *Perf. 12½*
C356 AP69 35c black & ocher .65 .25
C356A AP69 60c ver & gray .75 .45

Inscribed "Extra Rapido"
C356B AP69 1p Prus bl & gray 1.25 .70
Nos. C356-C356B (3) 2.65 1.40

Ant Bear AP70

1.30p, Armadillo. 1.45p, Parrot fish.

Unwmk.
1960, Feb. 12 Photo. *Perf. 12*
C357 AP70 35c sepia 1.60 .25
C358 AP70 1.30p rose car & dk brn 3.00 2.40
C359 AP70 1.45p lt bl, bl & yel 2.75 2.00
Nos. C357-C359 (3) 7.35 4.65

Alexander von Humboldt, German naturalist and geographer (1769-1859).

Flower Type

Nos. C360, C362, C366, Passiflora mollissima. Nos. C361, C364, C367, Odontoglossum luteo purpureum. Nos. C363, C369, Anthurium andreanum. Nos. C365, C370, Stanhopea tigrina. No. C368, Espeletia grandiflora.

1960, May 10 Photo. *Perf. 12*
Flowers in Natural Colors
C360 A298 5c dark blue .25 .25
C361 A298 35c maroon .55 .25
C362 A298 60c dark blue 1.10 .70
C363 A298 1.45p dark brown 1.25 1.10

Inscribed "Extra Rapido"
C364 A298 5c maroon .25 .25
C365 A298 10c brown .25 .25
C366 A298 1p dark blue 2.50 *3.00*
C367 A298 1p maroon 2.50 *3.00*
C368 A298 1p brown 2.50 *3.00*
C369 A298 1p brown 2.50 *3.00*
C370 A298 1p brown 2.50 *3.00*
Nos. C360-C370 (11) 16.15 *17.80*

See Nos. C420-C425.

Fleeing Family and Uprooted Oak Emblem AP71

Perf. 10, 11
1960, May 24 Litho. Wmk. 331
C371 AP71 60c bl grn & gray .40 .25

World Refugee Year, 7/1/59-6/30/60.

Souvenir Sheet

Pan-American Highway Through Colombia — AP72

1960, May 28 Litho. *Imperf.*
C372 AP72 2.50p brn & aqua 7.50 7.25

8th Pan-American Highway Congress, Bogota, May 20-29.

Lincoln Type
1960, June 6 *Perf. 10½*
C375 A299 40c dl red brn & blk 1.50 1.00
C376 A299 60c rose red & blk .40 .25

No. C376 exists imperforate. Value $25.

Type of Regular Issue and

Joaquin Camacho, Jorge Tadeo Lozano and Jose Miguel Pey AP73

Flag, Coins and Arms of Mompox and Cartagena — AP74

No. C378, Arms of Cartagena. 35c, 1.45p, Colombian flag. 60c, Andres Rosillo, Antonio Villavicencio and Joaquin Caicedo. 1p, Manuel de Bernardo Alvarez and Joaquin Gutierrez. 1.20p, Jose Antonio Galan statue. 1.30p, Front page of newspaper La Bagatela, 1811. 1.65p, Antonia Santos, Jose Acevedo y Gomez and Liborio Mejia.

Unwmk.
1960, July 20 Photo. *Perf. 12*
C377 AP73 5c lilac & brn .25 .25
C378 A301 5c dp bl grn & multi .25 .25
C379 AP73 35c multicolored .25 .25
C380 AP73 60c red brn & grn .45 .25
C381 AP73 1p ver & sl grn 1.10 .70
C382 A301 1.20p ultra & ind 1.10 .70
C383 AP73 1.30p orange & blk 1.10 .70
C384 AP73 1.45p multicolored 1.40 1.10
C385 AP73 1.65p green & brn 1.25 1.10
Nos. C377-C385 (9) 7.15 5.30

Souvenir Sheet
Stamps Inscribed "Extra Rapido"
C386 AP74 Sheet of 4 7.25 7.25
a. 50c deep claret & multi 1.00 1.00
b. 50c green & multi 1.00 1.00
c. 1p brown olive, yel, blue & car 1.00 1.00
d. 1p lilac & gray 1.00 1.00

150th anniv. of Colombia's independence.

St. Isidore Type

Designs: 35c, No. C388a, St. Isidore and farm animals. No. C388b, Nativity.

Unwmk.
1960, Sept. 26 Photo. *Perf. 12*
C387 A302 35c multicolored .25 .25

Souvenir Sheet
Stamps Inscribed "Extra Rapido"
C388 A302 Sheet of 2 9.75 9.75
a. 1.50p multicolored 3.00 3.00
b. 1.50p multicolored 3.00 3.00

See Nos. C439-C440.

Type of Regular Issue, 1959
Wmk. 331
1960, Nov. 23 Litho. *Perf. 12½*
C389 A294 35c Bolivar 3.50 .45

Pan-American Highway Type
1961, Mar. 7 Unwmk. *Perf. 10½x11*
C390 A304 10c rose lil & emer .60 .55
C391 A304 20c ver & lt bl .60 .55
C392 A304 30c black & emer .60 .55

Inscribed "Extra Rapido"
C393 A304 10c dk blue & emer .60 .55
Nos. C390-C393 (4) 2.40 2.20

8th Pan-American Highway Congress, Bogota, May 20-29, 1960.

Lopez Type
1961, Mar. 22 Photo. *Perf. 12½*
C394 A305 35c blue & brown .50 .25

Inscribed "Extra Rapido"
C395 A305 10c emerald & brn .25 .25

Souvenir Sheet
C396 A305 1p lilac & brn 5.75 5.75

Brother Damian and San Francisco Church, Cali AP75

Designs: 10c, View of Cali, vert. No. 398, Emblem of University del Valle, vert. 1.30p, Fine Arts School, Cali. 1.45p, Agricultural College, Palmira.

Perf. 13x13½, 13½x13
1961, Aug. 17 Photo. Unwmk.
C397 AP75 35c vio brn & ol .40 .25
C398 AP75 35c olive & grn .40 .25
C399 AP75 1.30p sepia & pink 1.00 .50
C400 AP75 1.45p multicolored 1.00 .70

Inscribed: "Extra Rapido"
C401 AP75 10c brn & yel grn .25 .25
Nos. C397-C401 (5) 3.05 1.95

50th anniv. (in 1960) of the department of Valle del Cauca.

View of Cucuta AP76

10c, Church of the Rosary, Cucuta, vert.

1961, Aug. 29

C402 AP76 35c brn ol & grn .65 .25

Inscribed: "Extra Rapido"

C403 AP76 10c dk brn & gray grn .25 .25

50th anniv. (in 1960) of the department of North Santander.

Old and New Ships of Barranquilla AP77

Arms and View of San Gil — AP78

Hotel, Popayan AP79

Statue of Christ in Procession AP80

Design: 1.45p, View of Velez.

Perf. 12½x13, 13x12½

1961, Oct. 10 Photo. Unwmk.

C404 AP77 35c gold & bl .45 .25
C405 AP78 35c bl grn, yel & red .45 .25
C406 AP79 35c car & brn .45 .25
C407 AP78 1.45p brown & grn .45 .25

Inscribed: "Extra Rapido"

C408 AP80 10c brown & yel .25 .25
Nos. C404-C408 (5) 2.05 1.25

Types of Regular and Air Post
Souvenir Sheets

Designs, No. C409: 35c, Barranquilla arms. 40c, Popayan arms. c, Arms and view of San Gil. d, Holy Week in Popayan.

No. C410: a, Old and new ships at Barranquilla. b, Hotel, Popayan. c, Bucaramanga arms. d, Holy Week in Popayan.

C409 Sheet of 4 11.50 11.50
a. A309 35c gold & multi 1.00 1.00
b. A309 40c gold & multi 1.00 1.00
c. AP78 1p blue, yellow & red 2.00 2.00
d. AP80 1p car rose & yellow 2.00 2.00

Stamps Inscribed: "Extra Rapido"

C410 Sheet of 4 11.50 11.50
a. AP77 50c gold & car rose 1.50 1.50
b. AP79 50c gold & blue 1.50 1.50
c. A309 50c pink & multi 1.50 1.50
d. AP80 50c blue & yellow 1.50 1.50

Nos. C404-C408 are in honor of the Atlantico Department. Nos. C409-C410 are in honor of the Departments of Atlantico, Cauca and Santander.

Nos. 713, 716 and 715 Overprinted and Surcharged

1961, Sept. *Perf. 12*

C411 A297 5c grnsh bl & brn .35 .25
C412 A298 5c multicolored .35 .25
C413 A297 10c on 20c cit & gray brn .35 .25
Nos. C411-C413 (3) 1.05 .75

"Aereo" in script on No. C412.
See Nos. C420-C425.

Sports Type

Designs: No. C414, Women divers. No. C415, Tennis, mixed doubles. 1.45p, No. C419b, Baseball. No. C417, Torch bearer. Nos. C418, C419a, Bolivar statue and flags of six participating nations. No. C419c, Soccer. No. C419d, Basketball.

1961, Dec. 16 Litho. *Perf. 13½x14*

C414 A310 35c ultra, yel & brn .75 .25
C415 A310 35c car, yel & brn .75 .25
C416 A310 1.45p Prus grn, yel & brn 1.10 .65

Inscribed: "Extra Rapido"

C417 A310 10c car lake, yel & brn .25 .25
C418 A310 10c ol, yel, bl & red .25 .25
Nos. C414-C418 (5) 3.10 1.65

Souvenir Sheet
Stamps Inscribed: "Extra Rapido"
Imperf

C419 Sheet of 4 7.25 7.25
a. A310 50c multi .60 .60
b. A310 50c multi .60 .60
c. A310 1p multi 1.25 1.25
d. A310 1p multi 1.25 1.25

Flower Type of 1960

5c, Passiflora mollissima. 10c, Espeletia grandiflora. 20c, 2p, Odontoglossum luteo purpureum. 25c, Stanhopea tigrina. 60c, Anthurium Andreanum.

Unwmk.
1962, Jan. 30 Photo. *Perf. 12*
Flowers in Natural Colors

C420 A298 5c gray .25 .25
C421 A298 10c gray blue .25 .25
C422 A298 20c rose lilac .25 .25
C423 A298 25c citron .40 .25
C424 A298 60c light brown .40 .25

Inscribed "Extra Rapido"

C425 A298 2p salmon pink 3.75 1.25
Nos. C420-C425 (6) 5.30 2.50

Anti-Malaria Type

Designs: 40c, Colombian anti-malaria emblem. 1p, 1.45p, Malaria eradication emblem and mosquito in swamp.

1962, Apr. 12 Litho. *Perf. 12*

C426 A311 40c yellow & red .25 .25
C427 A311 1.45p gray & ultra .65 .40

Inscribed "Extra Rapido"

C428 A311 1p yel grn & ultra 4.00 4.00
Nos. C426-C428 (3) 4.90 4.65

WHO drive to eradicate malaria.

Type of Regular Issue, 1962 and

Abelardo Ramos and Engineering School, Cauca — AP81

Designs: 10c, Miguel Triana, Andres A. Arroyo and Monserrate shrine with cable cars. 15c, Diodoro Sanchez and first meeting place of Engineers Society. 2p, Engineers Society emblem.

1962, June 12 Photo. *Perf. 11½x12*

C429 AP81 5c blue & dp rose .25 .25
C430 AP81 10c green & sepia .25 .25
C431 AP81 15c lilac & sepia .40 .30

Inscribed: "Extra Rapido"

C432 A312 2p blk, yel, red & bl 2.25 2.25
Nos. C429-C432 (4) 3.15 3.05

75th anniv. of the founding of the Colombian Soc. of Engineers and 6th Natl. Cong. of Engineers.

American States Type

1962, June 28 Photo. *Perf. 13*
Flags in National Colors

C433 A313 35c black & blue .35 .25

Women's Rights Type
Perf. 12x12½

1962, July 20 Litho. Wmk. 229

C434 A314 35c buff, gray & blk .25 .25

See Nos. C448-C450.

Scout Type

Designs: 15c, No. C438, Scouts at campfire and tents. 40c and No. C437, Girl Scouts.

Perf. 11½x12

1962, July 26 Photo. Unwmk.

C435 A315 15c brown & rose .30 .25
C436 A315 40c dp cl & pink .40 .30
C437 A315 1p blue & buff .70 .55

Inscribed "Extra Rapido"

C438 A315 1p purple & yel 5.00 4.00
Nos. C435-C438 (4) 6.40 5.10

Nos. C435 and C438 for 30th anniv. of the Colombian Boy Scouts. Nos. C436 and C437 for the 25th anniv. of the Girl Scouts.

Nativity by Gregorio Vasquez AP82

Design: 2p, St. Isidore, similar to type A302.

Inscribed "Extra Rapido"
Unwmk.

1962, Aug. 28 Photo. *Perf. 12*

C439 AP82 10c gray & multi .25 .25
C440 AP82 2p gray & multi 4.50 4.50

See Nos. C387-C388.

Type of Regular Issue, 1962 and

Locomotives of 1854 and 1961 — AP82a

Pres. Aquileo Parra and Magdalena River Bridge AP83

Design: 10c, Railroad map of Colombia.

1962, Sept. 28 Photo. *Perf. 12½*

C441 AP82a 5c sep & slate grn .25 .25
C442 A316 10c multicolored .25 .25

Engr.

C443 AP83 1p dull pur & brn 2.00 .25

Inscribed: "Extra Rapido."

C444 AP83 5p bl, brn & dl grn 5.00 4.50
Nos. C441-C444 (4) 7.50 5.25

Progress of Colombian railroads and completion of the Atlantic Line from Santa Maria to Bogota.
No. C444 inscribed "EXTRA RAPIDO."

UPAE Type

Designs: 50c, Map of Americas and carrier pigeon. 60c, Post horn.

Perf. 13½x14

1962, Oct. 18 Litho. Wmk. 346

C445 A317 50c slate grn & gold .40 .25
C446 A317 60c gold & plum .25 .25

Pope John XXIII AP84

1963, Mar. 11

C447 AP84 60c gold, red brn, buff & red .40 .25

Vatican II, the 21st Ecumenical Council of the Roman Catholic Church.

Women's Rights Type of 1962

1963-64 *Perf. 12x12½*

C448 A314 5c sal, gray & blk ('64) .25 .25
C449 A314 45c pale grn, gray & blk .40 .25
C450 A314 45c brt pink, gray & blk .40 .25
Nos. C448-C450 (3) 1.05 .75

Games Emblem — AP85

1963, Aug. 12 *Perf. 13x14*

C451 AP85 20c gray & multi .35 .25
C452 AP85 80c buff & multi .35 .25

South American Athletic Championships (22nd for men, 12th for women), Cali, June 30-July 7.

Bolivar Statue by Arenas-Betancourt — AP86

Perf. 14x13½

1963, Aug. 30 Unwmk.

C453 AP86 1.90p olive bis & blue .25 .25

Centenary of the city of Pereira.
For surcharge see No. C574.

Tennis Player — AP87

1963, Oct. 11 *Perf. 13½x14*

C454 AP87 55c multicolored .25 .25

30th South American Tennis Championships, Medellin, Oct. 3-13.

Pres. John F. Kennedy and Alliance for Progress Emblem AP88

1963, Dec. 17 Litho. *Perf. 14x13½*

C455 AP88 10c multicolored .25 .25

President John F. Kennedy (1917-1963).

Church of the True Cross, National Pantheon, Bogota — AP89

2p, Christ of the Martyrs, bell and tomb.

Perf. 13½x14

1964, Mar. 10 Photo. Unwmk.

C459	AP89	1p multicolored	.25	.25
C460	AP89	2p multicolored	.35	.25

View of Cartagena AP90

1964, Mar. 18 Litho. *Perf. 14x13½*

C461	AP90	3p vio, bl, ocher & brn	1.50	.60

Cartagena's independence in 1811, Simon Bolivar's visit in 1812 and the siege of 1815.

Eleanor Roosevelt AP91

1964, Nov. 10 Photo. *Perf. 12*

C462	AP91	20c ol & dl red brn	.25	.25

Eleanor Roosevelt (1884-1962).

Alberto Castilla and Score of "El Bunde" AP92

1964, Nov. 10 Unwmk.

C463	AP92	30c ol bis & Prus grn	.25	.25

Department of Tolima and Maestro Alberto Castilla (1878-1937) who in 1906 founded the Tolima Conservatory of Music in Ibague.

Mejia Type

Mejia portrait and: 45c, Women picking coffee. 5p, Mules carrying coffee bags. 10p, Loading coffee on freighter "Manuel Mejia."

1965, Feb. 10 Engr. *Perf. 12½x13*

C464	A320	45c brown & blk	.25	.25
C465	A320	5p gray grn & blk	2.50	.25
C466	A320	10p ultra & blk	3.50	.40
		Nos. C464-C466 (3)	6.25	.90

ITU Emblem AP93

1965, Oct. 25 Photo. *Perf. 12*

C467	AP93	80c Prus bl, lt bl & red	.25	.25

Cent. of the ITU.

Cattleya Truanae — AP94

1965, Oct. 3 Litho. *Perf. 13½x14*

C468	AP94	20c yellow & multi	1.00	.40

Fifth Philatelic Exhibition.

Cent. of the Telegraph in Colombia — AP95

No. C469, Pres. Manuel Murillo Toro statue, telegraph and orbits. No. C470, Telegraph and satellites over South America, horiz.

1965, Nov. 1 *Perf. 13½x14, 14x13½*

C469	AP95	60c multicolored	.25	.25
C470	AP95	60c multicolored	.25	.25

Junkers F-13 Seaplane, 1920 AP96

History of Colombian Aviation: 10c, Dornier Wal, 1924. 20c, Dornier Mercur, 1926. 50c, Trimotor Ford, 1932. 60c, De Havilland biplane, 1930. 1p, Douglas DC-4, 1947. 1.40p, Douglas DC-3, 1944. 2.80p, Superconstellation 1049, 1951. 3p, Boeing 720B jet, 1961.

Perf. 14x13½

1965-66 Photo. Unwmk.

C471	AP96	5c multicolored	.25	.25
C472	AP96	10c multicolored	.25	.25
C473	AP96	20c multicolored	.25	.25
C474	AP96	50c multicolored	.25	.25
C475	AP96	60c multicolored	.40	.25
C476	AP96	1p multicolored	.75	.25
C477	AP96	1.40p multicolored	1.00	.25
C478	AP96	2.80p multicolored	2.60	.60
C479	AP96	3p multicolored	3.40	.85
		Nos. C471-C479 (9)	9.15	3.20
		Nos. C471-C479,CE4 (10)	9.70	3.45

Issued: 5c, 60c, 3p, 12/13/65; 10c, 1p, 1.40p, 7/15/66; 20c, 50c, 2.80p, 12/14/66.

Automobile Club Emblem and Car on Road AP97

1966, Feb. 16 Litho. *Perf. 14x13½*

C480	AP97	20c multicolored	.60	.25

25th anniv. (in 1965) of the Automobile Club of Colombia.

Fish Type

Fish: 2p, Flying fish. 2.80p, Queen angelfish. 20p, King mackerel.

1966, Aug. 25 Photo. *Perf. 12½x13*

C481	A323	2p multicolored	.50	.25
C482	A323	2.80p multicolored	1.00	.90
C483	A323	20p multicolored	17.00	13.00
		Nos. C481-C483 (3)	18.50	14.15

Coat of Arms Type

1966, Oct. 11 Litho. *Perf. 14x13½*

C484	A324	1p ultra & multi	.40	.25
C485	A324	1.40p red & multi	.30	.25

Portrait Type

80c, Father Felix Restrepo Mejia, S.J. (1887-1965), theologian, scholar. 1.70p, José Joaquin Casas (1866-1951), educator, diplomat.

Perf. 13½x14

1967, Jan. 18 Litho. Unwmk.

C486	A325	80c dk bl & bis	.30	.25
C487	A325	1.70p blk & bis	.50	.25

Declaration of Bogota Type

1967, Feb. 2 Litho. *Perf. 14x13½*

C488	A326	3p multicolored	.50	.25

See note after No. 767.

Orchid Type

Orchids: 1p, Cattleya dowiana aurea, vert. 1.20p, Masdevallia coccinea, vert. 5p, Catasetum macrocarpum and bee.

1967, May 23 Litho. *Perf. 14*

C489	A327	1p multicolored	.90	.25
C490	A327	1.20p multicolored	.70	.25
C491	A327	5p multicolored	4.25	.90
a.		Souv. sheet of 3, #C489-C491	26.00	25.00
		Nos. C489-C491 (3)	5.85	1.40

Lions Type

1967, July 12 Litho. *Perf. 13½x14*

C492	A328	25c multicolored	.25	.25

"First Caesarean Section" by Grau AP98

Perf. 14x13½

1967, Sept. 7 Litho. Unwmk.

C493	AP98	80c multicolored	.25	.25

Issued to publicize the 6th Congress of Colombian Surgeons, Bogota, Sept. 25.

SENA Type

Lithographed and Embossed

1967, Sept. 20 *Perf. 13½x14*

C494	A329	2p gold, ver & blk	.50	.25

Pre-Columbian Art Type

Designs: 30c, Bird pectoral. 5p Ornamental pectoral. 20p, Pitcher.

1967, Oct. 13 Photo. *Perf. 13½x14*

C495	A330	30c ver, gold & brn	.40	.25
C496	A330	5p red, gold & brn	3.25	.50
a.		Souvenir sheet of 2	12.00	12.00
C497	A330	20p vio, gold & brn	15.00	10.00
		Nos. C495-C497 (3)	18.65	10.75

No. C496a also commemorates the 6th Natl. Phil. Exhib. No. C496a contains 2 imperf. stamps in changed colors similar to Nos. C495-C496 (30c has green background and 5p maroon background).

Telecommunications Type

Designs: 50c, Signal lights. 1p, Early Bird satellite, Southern Cross and radar.

Perf. 13½x14

1968, May 14 Litho. Unwmk.

C498	A331	50c blk, ver & emer	.25	.25
C499	A331	1p ultra, yel & gray	.30	.25

Eucharist Type

1968, June 6 Litho. *Perf. 13½x14*

C500	A332	80c rose lil, red, yel & blk	.25	.25
C501	A332	3p bl, red, yel & blk	.30	.25

Eucharistic Congress Type

Designs: 80c, The Last Supper, by Gregorio Vasquez, horiz. 1p, St. Francis Xavier Preaching, by Gregorio Vasquez. 2p, The Dream of the Prophet Elias, by Gregorio Vasquez. 3p, Monstrance, c. 1700. 20p, Pope Paul VI, painting by Roman Franciscan nuns.

1968, Aug. 13 Photo. *Perf. 13*

C502	A333	80c multicolored	.25	.25
C503	A333	1p multicolored	.40	.25
C504	A333	2p multicolored	.45	.25
C505	A333	3p lil & multi	.80	.25
C506	A333	20p gold & multi	5.00	2.50
		Nos. C502-C506 (5)	6.90	3.50

Shrine of the Eucharist, Bogotá AP99

1.20p, Pope Paul VI giving blessing and Papal arms. 1.80p, Cathedral of Bogotá.

Perf. 14x13½, 13½x14

1968, Aug. 22 Litho.

C507	AP99	80c multi	.30	.25
C508	AP99	1.20p multi, vert.	.30	.25
C509	AP99	1.80p multi, vert.	.40	.25
		Nos. C507-C509 (3)	1.00	.75

Visit of Pope Paul VI to Colombia.

Computer Symbols — AP100

1968, Oct. 29 Litho. *Perf. 13½x14*

C510	AP100	20c buff, car & grn	.25	.25

Cent. of the Natl. University and the 1st Data Processing Cong. in 1967 at the University.

Agriculture Institute Type

1968, Mar. 5 Litho. *Perf. 13½x14*

C511	A337	1p gray & multi	.25	.25

Microscope and Pen — AP101

1969, Mar. 24 Litho. *Perf. 14*

C512	AP101	5p blk, yel, ver & pur	2.00	.35

20th anniv. (in 1968) of the University of the Andes.

Alexander von Humboldt and Andes AP102

1969, May 3 Litho. *Perf. 14x13½*

C513	AP102	1p grn & brn	.65	.35

Alexander von Humboldt (1769-1859), German naturalist and traveler.

Map of Colombia, Amphibian Plane and Letter AP103

Design: 1.50p, No. C516b, Globe, letter, and jet of Avianca airlines.

1969, June 18 Litho. *Perf. 14x13½*

C514	AP103	1p multi	.45	.25
C515	AP103	1.50p multi	.65	.25

Souvenir Sheet

Imperf

C516		Sheet of 2	7.25	7.25
a.		AP103 5p green & multi	1.00	1.00
b.		AP103 5p violet & multi	1.00	1.00

50th anniv. of the 1st air post flight in Colombia. No. C516 also for 8th Natl. Philatelic Exhibition, EXFILBA 69, Barranquilla, June 18-22. No. C516 contains 2 stamps in the designs of the 1p and 1.50p.

Independence Type

2.30p, Simon Bolivar, José Antonio Anzoategui, Francisco de Paula Santander and victorious army entering Bogotá, 9/18/1819; painting by Ignacio Castillo Cervantes.

1969, July 24 Litho. *Perf. 13½x14*

C517	A338	2.30p gold & multi	1.00	.35

Social Security Emblem — AP104

1969, Oct. 29 Litho. *Perf. 13½x14*
C518 AP104 20c emer & blk .25 .25

20th anniv. of the Colombian Institute of Social Security.

Neurosurgeons' Congress Emblem — AP105

1969, Oct. 29
C519 AP105 70c vio, red & yel .50 .30

Issued to publicize the 13th Congress of Latin-American Neurosurgeons, Bogotá.

Junkers F-13 AP106

Nos. C521, C522b, Globe with airlines from Bogota & Boeing jet. No. C522a, like No. C520.

1969, Nov. 28 Litho. *Perf. 14x13½*
C520 AP106 2p grn & multi .60 .25
C521 AP106 3.50p ultra & multi 1.00 .50

Souvenir Sheet

Imperf

C522 Sheet of 2 6.50 6.50
a. AP106 3.50p lt grn & multi .75 .75
b. AP106 5p ultra & multi 1.00 1.00

50th anniv. of AVIANCA; No. C522 also publicizes the 1st Interamerican Phil. Exhib., Bogota, Nov. 28-Dec. 7.
No. C522 contains 2 imperf. stamps.

Child Mailing Letter — AP107

Christmas: 1.50p, Praying child and gifts.

1969, Dec. 16 Litho. *Perf. 13½x14*
C523 AP107 60c ocher & multi .60 .25
C524 AP107 1p multicolored .65 .25
C525 AP107 1.50p multicolored .75 .25
Nos. C523-C525 (3) 2.00 .75

Radar Station and Pre-Columbian Head — AP108

1970, Mar. 25 Litho. *Perf. 14x13½*
C526 AP108 1p dl grn, blk & brick red .95 .25

Issued to publicize the opening of the communications satellite earth station at Chocontá in Cundinamarca Province.

Emblem of Colombian Youth Sports Institute — AP109

2.30p, Games' emblem (dove and 3 rings).

1970, Apr. 6 Litho. *Perf. 13½x14*
C527 AP109 1.50p dk ol grn, yel & blk .30 .25
C528 AP109 2.30p red & multi .40 .25

9th Natl. Youth Games, Ibague, July 10-20.

Art Exhibition Emblem — AP110

1970, Apr. 30 Litho. *Perf. 13½x14*
C529 AP110 30c multicolored .25 .25

2nd Biennial Art Exhib., Medellin, 6/1-7/14.

Eduardo Santos, Rural and Urban Buildings AP111

1970, June 18 Litho. *Perf. 14x13½*
C530 AP111 1p grn, yel & blk .25 .25

Issued to commemorate the founding (in 1939) of the Territorial Credit Institute.

UN Emblem, Scales and Dove — AP112

1970, June 26 *Perf. 13½x14*
C531 AP112 1.50p dk bl, lt bl & yel .25 .25

25th anniversary of United Nations.

EXFILCA Emblem — AP113

1970, Nov. Litho. *Perf. 13½x14*
C532 AP113 10p bl, gold & blk 4.50 .25

EXFILCA 70, 2nd Interamerican Philatelic Exhib., Caracas, Venezuela, Nov. 27-Dec. 6.

Mother Juana Ruperta in Napanga Costume and Music by Efrain Orozco — AP114

Designs: 1p, Dancers from Eastern Plains and music by Alejandro Wills. No. C535, Guabina man, woman and folk song. No. C536, Bambuco man and woman, and music. No. C537, Man and woman dancing the Cumbia, and music.

1970-71 Litho. *Perf. 13½x14*
C533 AP114 60c dp lil rose & multi .80 .25
C534 AP114 1p ultra & multi .75 .25
C535 AP114 1.30p bl & multi .85 .25
C536 AP114 1.30p emer & multi ('71) 1.00 .25
C537 AP114 1.30p lil & multi ('71) .70 .25
Nos. C533-C537 (5) 4.10 1.25

Athlete and Games Emblem — AP115

Design: 2p, Games emblem.

1971, Mar. 11
C542 AP115 1.50p multicolored 1.10 1.00
C543 AP115 2p blk, org & grn 1.00 .75

6th Pan-American Games, Cali, 7/30-8/13.

Gilberto Alzate Avendano AP116

1971, Apr. 29 Litho. *Perf. 14x13½*
C544 AP116 1p bl & multi .85 .25

Avendano (1910-60), journalist, popular leader.

Commemorative Medal — AP117

Lithographed and Embossed

1971, June 21 *Perf. 14x13½*
C545 AP117 1p slate grn & gold .60 .30

Centenary (in 1970) of the Bank of Bogota.

Olympic Center — AP118

Soccer — AP119

Designs (Games Emblem and): Nos. C546-C546C, Olympic Center. No. 547, Soccer. No. C548, Wrestling. No. C549, Bicycling. No. C550, Volleyball. No. C551, Diving (women). No. C552, Fencing. No. C553, Sailing. No. C554, Equestrian. No. C555, Jumping. No. C556, Rowing. No. C557, Cali emblem. No. C558, Basketball (women). No. C559, Stadium. No. C560, Baseball. No. C561, Hockey. No. C562, Weight lifting. No. C563, Medals. No. C564, Boxing. No. C565, Gymnastics (women). No. C566, Sharpshooting.

1971, July 16 Litho. *Perf. 13½x14*

Multicolored and Emblem Color:

C546	AP118	1.30p	yellow	2.60	.30
C546A	AP118	1.30p	green	2.60	.30
C546B	AP118	1.30p	blue	2.60	.30
C546C	AP118	1.30p	carmine	2.60	.30
C547	AP119	1.30p	emerald	2.60	.30
C548	AP119	1.30p	lilac	2.60	.30
C549	AP119	1.30p	blue	2.60	.30
C550	AP119	1.30p	carmine	2.60	.30
C551	AP119	1.30p	blue	2.60	.30
C552	AP119	1.30p	carmine	2.60	.30
C553	AP119	1.30p	blue	2.60	.30
C554	AP119	1.30p	gray	2.60	.30
C555	AP119	1.30p	green	2.60	.30
C556	AP119	1.30p	blue	2.60	.30
C557	AP118	1.30p	orange	2.60	.30
C558	AP119	1.30p	carmine	2.60	.30
C559	AP118	1.30p	light blue	2.60	.30
C560	AP119	1.30p	plum	2.60	.30
C561	AP119	1.30p	yel grn	2.60	.30
C562	AP119	1.30p	pink	2.60	.30
C563	AP118	1.30p	deep org	2.60	.30
C564	AP119	1.30p	plum	2.60	.30
C565	AP119	1.30p	lilac rose	2.60	.30
C566	AP119	1.30p	green	2.60	.30
a.	Sheet of 25, #C546-C566			65.00	60.00

6th Pan American Athletic Games, Cali. No. C546B appears twice in sheet.

Battle of Carabobo, by Martin Tovar y Tovar — AP120

1971, Nov. 25 Litho. *Perf. 13½x14*
C567 AP120 1.50p multicolored 1.20 .25

Sesquicentennial of the Battle of Carabobo.

St. Theresa Type Overprinted

1972 Litho. *Perf. 13½x14*
C568 A343 2p multicolored .60 .25

See note after No. 793.

Vendor — AP121

Designs: 50c, Woman wearing shawl, and woven shawl. 3p, Fruit vendor (puppet).

1972, Apr. 11 Litho. *Perf. 13½x14*

C569 AP121	50c	multicolored	.35	.25
C570 AP121	1p	multicolored	.35	.25
C571 AP121	3p	multicolored	.50	.25
	Nos. C569-C571 (3)		1.20	.75

Colombian artisans.

Mormodes Rolfeanum AP122

1972, Apr. 20 *Perf. 14x13½*
C572 AP122 1.30p multicolored 1.15 .25

7th World Orchidology Congress, Medellin.

Congo Grande Dancer — AP123

1972, June 21 Litho. *Perf. 13½x14*
C573 AP123 1.30p multicolored .60 .25

International Carnival of Barranquilla.

No. C453 Surcharged in Brown

1972, Oct. 5 Litho. *Perf. 14x13½*
C574 AP86 1.30p on 1.90p .85 .25

Laureano Gomez, by Ridriguez Cubillos — AP124

No. C576, Guillermo Leòn Valencia Muñoz.

1972 *Perf. 13½x14*

C575 AP124	1.30p	multicolored	.25	.25
C576 AP124	1.30p	multicolored	.25	.25

Laureano Gomez (1898-1966), Guillermo Leon Valencia Munoz (1909-71), Presidents of Colombia.

Issued: No. C575, 10/17; No. C576, 11/28.

Benito Juarez — AP125

1972, Dec. 12 *Perf. 13½x14*
C577 AP125 1.50p multicolored .25 .25

Benito Juarez (1806-1872), revolutionary leader and president of Mexico.

Rebecca Fountain AP126

1972, Dec. 19 Litho.

C578 AP126	80c	multicolored	.70	.45
C579 AP126	1p	multicolored	.65	.25

"Bucaramanga" — AP127

1972, Dec. 22 *Perf. 14x13½*
C580 AP127 5p multicolored 1.00 .25

Founding of Bucaramanga, 350th anniv.

Xavier University AP128

1973, May 8 Litho. *Perf. 14x13½*

C581 AP128	1.30p	lt grn & sep	.30	.25
C582 AP128	1.50p	lt bl & sep	.30	.25

350th anniversary of the founding of Xavier University in Bogotá.

Ceramic Type

Excavated Ceramic Artifacts: 1p, Winged urn, Tairona. 1.30p, Woman and child, Sinu. 1.70p, Two-headed figure, Quimbaya. 3.50p, Man, Tumaco.

1973 Litho. *Perf. 13½x14*

C583 A358	1p	multicolored	1.75	1.20
C584 A358	1.30p	multicolored	1.00	.25
C585 A358	1.70p	multicolored	1.25	.25
C586 A358	3.50p	multicolored	2.00	.30
	Nos. C583-C586 (4)		6.00	2.00

Issue dates: 1p, Oct. 11; others, June 15.

Battle of Maracaibo, by Manuel F. Rincon AP129

1973, July 24 Litho. *Perf. 14x13½*
C587 AP129 10p bl & multi 2.50 .25

Battle of Maracaibo, sesquicentennial.

Bank Emblem AP130

1973, Oct. 1 Litho. *Perf. 14x13½*
C588 AP130 2p multicolored .30 .25

50th anniv. of the Bank of the Republic.

No. 801 Overprinted "AEREO"

1973, Oct. 11 *Perf. 14*
C589 A346 80c multicolored .30 .25

Pres. Pedro Nel Ospina, by Coroleano Leudo — AP131

1973, Nov. 9 *Perf. 13½x14*
C590 AP131 1.50p multicolored .25 .25

50th anniversary of the Ministry of Communications founded under Pres. Ospina.

Arms of Toro — AP132

1973, Dec. 1
C591 AP132 1p multicolored .25 .25

Founding of Toro, Valle del Cauca, 4th cent.

Bolivar, Battle of Bombona AP133

1973, Dec. 7 Litho. *Perf. 14x13½*
C592 AP133 1.30p multicolored .25 .25

Sesquicentennial (in 1972) of the Battle of Bombona.

Nicolaus Copernicus AP134

1974, Feb. 19 Litho. *Perf. 13½x14*
C593 AP134 2.50p multicolored .70 .25

500th anniversary of the birth of Nicolaus Copernicus (1473-1543), Polish astronomer.

Andes, Map of South America AP135

1974, May 11 Litho. *Perf. 14*
C594 AP135 2p multicolored .50 .25

Meeting of Communications Ministers of Members of the Andean Group, Cali, May 7-11, 1974.

Television Set AP136

1974, July 16 Litho. *Perf. 14x13½*
C595 AP136 1.30p org, blk & brn .40 .25

20th anniversary of Colombian television and 10th anniversary of INRAVISION, the National Institute of Radio and Television.

Championship Emblem — AP137

1974, Aug. 5 Litho. *Perf. 14x13½*
C596 AP137 4.50p multicolored .40 .25

2nd World Swimming Championships, Cali.

Condor — AP138

1974, Aug. 28 *Perf. 14*
C597 AP138 1.50p multicolored .65 .25

Bank of Colombia centenary.

UPU Envelope AP139

1974, Sept. 9 Litho. *Perf. 14*
C598 AP139 20p multicolored 2.75 2.60

Centenary of Universal Postal Union.

Symbol of Flight — AP140

1974, Sept. *Perf. 12x12½*
C599 AP140 20c olive .60 .25

Gen. José Maria Cordoba — AP141

1974, Oct. 14 Litho. *Perf. 13½x14*
C609 AP141 1.30p multicolored .25 .25

Sesquicentennial of the Battles of Junin and Ayacucho.

Insurance Type

Design: 3p, Abstract pattern.

1974, Oct. 24 Litho. *Perf. 13½x14*
C610 A365 3p multicolored .30 .25

White-tailed Trogon, Letter — AP142

Designs (UPU Letter and): 1.30p, Keelbilled Toucan, horiz. 2p, Peruvian cock-of-the-rock, horiz. 2.50p, Scarlet macaw.

Perf. 13½x14, 14x13½

1974, Nov. 14

C611	AP142	1p	multicolored	1.25	.25
C612	AP142	1.30p	multicolored	1.25	.25
C613	AP142	2p	multicolored	1.90	.25
C614	AP142	2.50p	multicolored	1.90	.25
			Nos. C611-C614 (4)	6.30	1.00

Centenary of Universal Postal Union.
For surcharge see No. C656.

Forest No. 1, by Roman Roncancio — AP143

Boy with Thorn in Finger, by Gregorio Vazquez AP144

Paintings: 3p, Women Fruit Vendors, by Miguel Diaz Vargas (1886-1956). 5p, Annunciation, Santafereña School, 17th-18th cent.

Perf. 13½x14, 14x13½

1975, Mar. 12 **Litho.**

C615	AP143	2p	multicolored	.75	.25
C616	AP144	3p	multicolored	.50	.25
C617	AP144	4p	multicolored	.65	.25
C618	AP144	5p	multicolored	1.10	.25
			Nos. C615-C618 (4)	3.00	1.00

Modern and Colonial Colombian paintings.

Trees and Lake AP145

Design: 6p, Victoria regia, Amazon River.

1975, Mar. 12 ***Perf. 14x13½***

C619	AP145	1p	yellow & multi	.25	.25
C620	AP145	6p	yellow & multi	.75	.25

Nature conservation of trees and Amazon Region.

Gold Treasure Type

Designs: 2p, Nose pendant. 10p, Alligator-shaped staff ornament.

1975, Apr. 11 **Litho.** ***Perf. 14x13½***

C621	A368	2p	grn, gold & brn	1.00	.25
C622	A368	10p	multicolored	4.75	.60

El Rodadero, Santa Maria AP146

1975, July 26 **Litho.** ***Perf. 14x13½***

C623	AP146	2p	multicolored	.25	.25

400th anniversary of Santa Marta City.

AP147

1975, Aug. 31 **Litho.** ***Perf. 13½x14***

C624	AP147	4p	multicolored	.25	.25

Intl. Women's Year 1975. Maria de Jesus Paramo de Collazos founded 1st normal school for women in Bucaramanga in 1875.

"Sugar Cane" — AP148

1976, Mar. 12 **Litho.** ***Perf. 13½x14***

C625	AP148	5p	blk & grn	1.25	.25

4th Congress of Latin-American and Caribbean sugar-exporting countries, Cali, 3/8-12.

View of Bogota — AP149

1976, July 2 **Litho.** ***Perf. 12***

C626	AP149	10p	shown	1.40	.90
C627	AP149	10p	Barranquilla	1.40	.90
C628	AP149	10p	Cali	1.40	.90
C629	AP149	10p	Medellin	1.40	.90
a.			Block of 4, #C626-C629	6.25	6.25

Habitat, UN Conf. on Human Settlements, Vancouver, Canada, May 31-June 11.

University Emblem and "90" — AP150

1976, Aug. 6 **Litho.** ***Perf. 13½x14***

C630	AP150	5p	lt blue & multi	.50	.25

Univ. of Colombia day school, 90th anniv.

Miguel Samper — AP151

1976, Oct. 29 **Litho.** ***Perf. 13½x14***

C631	AP151	2p	multicolored	.25	.25

Samper (1825-99), economist and writer.

Telephone, 1895 — AP152

1976, Nov. 2

C632	AP152	3p	multicolored	.25	.25

Centenary of first telephone call by Alexander Graham Bell, Mar. 10, 1876.

747 Jumbo Jet AP153

1976, Dec. 3 **Litho.** ***Perf. 12***

C633	AP153	2p	multicolored	.25	.25

Inauguration of 747 jumbo jet service by Avianca.
For surcharge see No. C636.

Convent, Church and Plaza de San Francisco — AP154

1976, Dec. 29 **Litho.** ***Perf. 14***

C634	AP154	6p	multicolored	.50	.25

150th anniv. of the Congress of Panama.

Souvenir Sheet

Bank of the Republic Emblem — AP155

1977, June 6 **Litho.** ***Perf. 14***

C635	AP155	25p	multicolored	12.00	12.00

Opening of Philatelic Museum of Medellin under auspices of Banco de la Republica.

No. C633 Surcharged in Light Brown

1977, June **Litho.** ***Perf. 12***

C636	AP153	3p on 2p	multi	.25	.25

Coffee — AP156

1977-78 **Litho.** ***Perf. 12½***

C640	AP156	3p	multi	.50	.25
C641	AP156	3.50p	multi ('78)	.50	.25

Colombian coffee.

Coffee Grower, Pack Mule — AP157

1977, Aug. 9 **Litho.** ***Perf. 13½x14***

C642	AP157	10p	multicolored	.50	.25

National Federation of Coffee Growers, 50th anniversary.

Beethoven and 9th Symphony AP158

1977, Aug. 17

C643	AP158	8p	multicolored	1.25	.25

Sesquicentennial of the death of Ludwig van Beethoven (1770-1827).

Bird Type

Tropical Birds and Plants: No. C644, Woodpecker and Meriania. C645, Purple gallinule and water lilies. No. C646, Xipholaena punicea and Cochlospermum orinocense. No. C647, Crowned flycatcher and Jacaranda copaia.

1977, Sept. 6 **Litho.** ***Perf. 14***

C644	A380	5p	multicolored	.75	.25
C645	A380	5p	multicolored	.75	.25
C646	A380	10p	multicolored	1.10	.25
C647	A380	10p	multicolored	1.10	.25
			Nos. C644-C647 (4)	3.70	1.00

Games' Emblem — AP159

1977, Sept. 9 ***Perf. 12x12½***

C648	AP159	6p	multicolored	.25	.25

13th Central American and Caribbean Games, Medellin, 1978.

La Cayetana, by Enrique Grau AP160

No. C650, Water Nymphs, by Beatriz Gonzalez.

1977, Sept. 13 *Perf. 14x13½*

C649 AP160 8p multicolored 1.25 .25
C650 AP160 8p multicolored 1.25 .25

Women's suffrage, 20th anniversary.

Judge Francisco Antonio Moreno, by Joaquin Gutierrez AP161

Design: 25p, Viceroy Manuel de Guirior.

1977, Sept. 13 *Perf. 12*

C651 AP161 20p multicolored 1.60 .75
C652 AP161 25p multicolored 2.40 1.10

Bicentenary of National Library.

Federico Lleras Acosta — AP162

1977, Sept. 27 **Litho.** *Perf. 14*

C653 AP162 5p multicolored .30 .25

Dr. Federico Lleras Acosta, veterinarian and bacteriologist; birth centenary.

Cauca University Arms — AP163

1977, Oct. 14

C654 AP163 5p multicolored .30 .25

Sesquicentennial of the University of Cauca.

CUDECOM Building, Bogota AP164

1977, Oct. 14

C655 AP164 1.50p multicolored .25 .25

Colombian Society of Engineers, 90th anniv.

No. C612 Surcharged with New Value and Bars in Brown

1977, Dec. 3 **Litho.** *Perf. 14x13½*

C656 AP142 2p on 1.30p multi .30 .25

Lost City, Tayrona Culture — AP165

1978, Apr. 18 **Litho.** *Perf. 12½*

C657 AP165 3.50p multicolored .25 .25

Creator of Energy, by Arenas Betancourt AP166

1978, Apr. 25 *Perf. 12*

C658 AP166 4p blue & multi .35 .25

Sesquicentennial of Antioquia University Law School.

Column of the Slaves — AP167

1978, May 9

C659 AP167 2.50p multicolored .25 .25

Sesquicentennial of Ocana Convention (meeting of various political groups).

Statue of Catalina, Cartagena AP168

1978, May 30 **Litho.** *Perf. 12*

C660 AP168 4p blk & lt bl .25 .25

Sesquicentennial of University of Cartagena.

Gold Pendant, Tolima — AP169

1978, July 11 **Litho.** *Perf. 12x12½*

C661 AP169 3.50p multicolored .25 .25

Apotheosis of Spanish Language, by Luis Alberto Acuña — AP170

1978, Aug. 9 *Perf. 14*

C662 AP170 Strip of 3 5.75 5.00
a.-c. 11p, any single 1.40 1.25

Millennium of Spanish language.

Presidential Guard — AP171

1978, Aug. 16 *Perf. 13½x14*

C663 AP171 9p multicolored .45 .45

Presidential Guard Battalion, 50th anniv.

Figure, Muisca Culture — AP172

1978, Sept. 12 **Litho.** *Perf. 12½*

C664 AP172 3.50p multicolored .30 .25

Apse of Carmelite Church — AP173

1978, Oct. 12 *Perf. 13*

C665 AP173 30p multicolored 2.60 .40

Souvenir Sheet

Perf. 13½x14

C666 AP173 50p multicolored 4.50 3.75

ESPAMER '78 Philatelic Exhibition, Bogota, Oct. 12-21.

Owl, Gold Ornament, Calima — AP174

No. C669, Gold frog, Quimbaya culture. No. C670, Gold nose pendant, Tairona, horiz.

1978-80 **Litho.** *Perf. 12½*

C667 AP174 3.50p multi .50 .25
C668 AP174 4p multi ('79) .30 .25
C669 AP174 4p multi ('79) .50 .25
C670 AP174 5p multi ('80) .80 .25
Nos. C667-C670 (4) 2.10 1.00

Virgin and Child, by Gregorio Vasquez — AP175

1978, Nov. 28 *Perf. 13½x14*

C671 AP175 2.50p multicolored .25 .25

Christmas 1978.

Bull Ring, Cathedral, Manizales AP176

1979, Jan. 6 **Litho.** *Perf. 14*

C672 AP176 7p multicolored .80 .25

Manizales Fair.

Children Playing Hopscotch, and IYC Emblem — AP177

No. C674, Child at blackboard and UNESCO emblem. No. C675, The Paper Collector, by Omar Gordillo, and UN emblem.

1979, July 19 *Perf. 13½x14, 14x13½*

C673 AP177 8p multi .40 .30
C674 AP177 12p multi, horiz. .55 .45
C675 AP177 12p multi .55 .45
Nos. C673-C675 (3) 1.50 1.20

International Year of the Child.

Rio Prado Hydroelectric Station — AP178

1979, Aug. 24 *Perf. 13½x14*

C676 AP178 5p multicolored .80 .25

Tomb, 6th Century — AP179

1979, Sept. 25 **Litho.** *Perf. 14*

C677 AP179 8p multicolored .80 .35

San Augustin Archaeological Park.

Gonzalo Jimenez de Quesada, by C. Leudo AP180

1979, Oct. 11 *Perf. 12*

C678 AP180 20p multicolored 3.25 1.00

Gonzalo Jimenez de Quesada (1500-1579), Spanish conquistador.

Hill, Penny Black, Colombia No. 1 — AP181

1979, Oct. 23 ***Perf. 13½x14***
C679 AP181 15p multicolored .90 .25

Sir Rowland Hill (1795-1879), originator of penny postage.

Amazon Region — AP182

Tourism: 14p, San Fernando Fortress.

1979 **Litho.** ***Perf. 13½x14***
C680 AP182 7p multicolored .60 .25
C681 AP182 14p multicolored 1.60 .75

Issue dates: 7p, Nov. 16; 14p, Nov. 9.
See Nos. C717-C719.

AP183

Creche Sculptures: No. C682, Three Kings and soldiers. No. C683, Nativity. No. C684, Shepherds.

1979, Nov. 30 ***Perf. 12***
C682 AP183 3p multicolored 1.25 1.10
C683 AP183 3p multicolored 1.25 1.10
C684 AP183 3p multicolored 1.25 1.10
a. Strip of 3, #C682-C684 4.50 3.50

Christmas 1979.

AP184

Magdalena Bridge, Avianca emblem.

1979, Dec. 5 ***Perf. 14***
C685 AP184 15p multicolored .70 .25

Barranquilla, 350th anniversary; Avianca National Airline, 60th anniversary.

AP185

Boy Playing Flute, by Judith Leyster.

1980, Feb. 15 ***Perf. 13½x14***
C686 AP185 6p multicolored .60 .25

2nd Intl. Music Competition, Ibague, Dec. 1979.

Gen. Antonio José de Sucre, 150th Death Anniversary AP186

1980, Feb. 15 **Litho.** ***Perf. 12½x12***
C687 AP186 12p multicolored .60 .25

The Watchman, by Edgar Negret AP187

1980, Feb. 26 ***Perf. 12x12½***
C688 AP187 25p multicolored 2.50 1.40

Virgin Mary, by Real del Sarte, 1929 AP188

1980, May 23 **Litho.** ***Perf. 14x13½***
C689 AP188 12p multicolored .60 .25

Apparition of the Virgin Mary to Sister Catalina Labouri Gontard, 150th anniv.

San Gil Produce Market, by Luis Roncancio — AP189

1980, May 27 ***Perf. 13½x14***
C690 AP189 12p multicolored .70 .25

Pres. Enrique Olaya Herrera, by Miguel Diaz Vargas — AP190

1980, Oct. 28 **Litho.** ***Perf. 12***
C691 AP190 20p multicolored 1.40 .40

Enrique Olaya Herrera (1880-1936), president, 1930-1934.

The Boy Fishing in a Bucket AP191

Christmas (Christmas Stories by Rafael Pombo): No. C693, The Frog and the Mouse. No. C694, The Seven Lives of the Cat.

1980, Nov. 21 **Litho.** ***Perf. 14½***
C692 AP191 4p multicolored .60 .25
C693 AP191 4p multicolored .60 .25
C694 AP191 4p multicolored .60 .25
Nos. C692-C694 (3) 1.80 .75

28th World Golf Cup, Cajica — AP192

1980, Dec. 9 **Litho.** ***Perf. 13½x14***
C695 AP192 30p multicolored 5.50 3.00

Bolivar Type

Simon Bolivar Death Sesquicentennial: 6p, Portrait, last words to Colombia, vert.

1980, Dec. 17 ***Perf. 12***
C696 A400 6p multicolored .80 .45

St. Peter Claver Holding Cross AP193

1981, Jan. 13 ***Perf. 14½***
C697 AP193 15p multicolored .80 .30

St. Peter Claver (1580-1654), helped American Indians.

Sculptured Bird, San Augustin AP194

Archaeological Finds: No. C699, Funeral chamber, Tierradentro. No. C700, Chamber hallway, Tierradentro. No. C701, Statue of man, San Augustin.

1981, May 12 **Litho.** ***Perf. 14***
C698 AP194 7p multicolored 1.25 .25
C699 AP194 7p multicolored 1.25 .25
C700 AP194 7p multicolored 1.25 .25
C701 AP194 7p multicolored 1.25 .25
a. Block of 4, #C698-C701 6.00 5.00

See Nos. C707-C710D.

Child with Hobby Horse, by Fernando Botero — AP195

4th Biennial Arts show, Medellin: 20p, Square Abstract, by Omar Rayo. 25p, Flowers, by Alejandro Obregon.

1981, May 15 ***Perf. 12***
C702 AP195 20p multicolored 1.35 .25
C703 AP195 25p multicolored 1.50 .40
C704 AP195 50p multicolored 2.75 .75
Nos. C702-C704 (3) 5.60 1.40

8th South American Swimming Championships, Medellin — AP196

1981, June 5
C705 AP196 15p multicolored .60 .25

Santamaria Bull Ring, 50th Anniv. — AP197

1981, June 9 **Litho.** ***Perf. 12***
C706 AP197 30p multicolored 3.25 1.75

Quimbaya Culture — AP197a

1981, Sept. 23 **Litho.** ***Perf. 14***

Yellow Background

C707 9p Man 1.25 .25
C708 9p Seated man 1.25 .25
C709 9p Seal, print 1.25 .25
C710 9p Jug 1.25 .25
e. AP197a Block of 4, #C707-C710 6.00 3.50

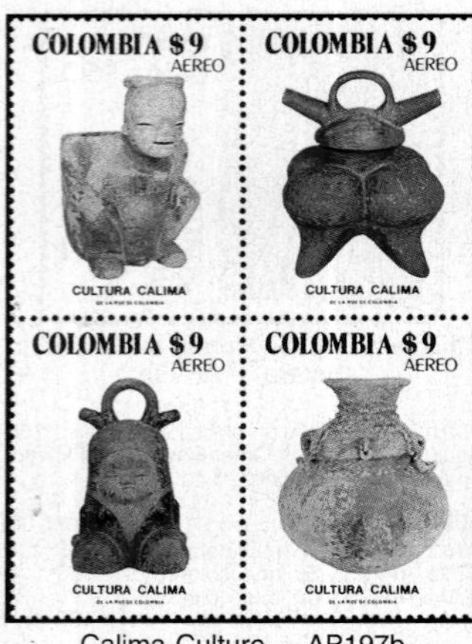

Calima Culture — AP197b

No. C710A, Anthropomorphic container. No. C710B, Jar. No. C710C, Anthropomorphic jar. No. C710D, Urn.

1981, Dec. 17 **White Background**

C710A	9p multicolored	1.75	.25
C710B	9p multicolored	1.75	.25
C710C	9p multicolored	1.75	.25
C710D	9p multicolored	1.75	.25
f.	AP197b Block of 4, #C710A-C710D	9.00	9.00

Fruit AP198

1981, Nov. 3 **Litho.** ***Perf. 14***

C711	Block of 6	25.00	20.00
a.-f.	AP198 25p, any single	4.00	1.50

Revolt of the Comuneros, 200th Anniv. — AP199

1981, Nov. 21 **Litho.** ***Perf. 12***

C712 AP199 20p multicolored .90 .40

Jose Manuel Restrepo, Historian, 1775?-1860? AP200

1981, Dec. 1 **Litho.** ***Perf. 12***

C713 AP200 35p multicolored 1.25 .75

Andres Bello, 1780?-1865 AP201

1981, Dec. 11 **Litho.** ***Perf. 12***

C714 AP201 18p multicolored .70 .25

Colombia's Admission to UPU, 100th Anniv. AP202

30p, No. 103. 50p, Hemispheres, Nos. 104-108.

1981 **Litho.** ***Perf. 12***

C715 AP202 30p multicolored 1.25 .35

Size: 100x70mm

Imperf

C716 AP202 50p multicolored 4.50 4.50

Issued: No. C715, Dec. 18. No. C716, Dec. 28.

Tourism Type of 1979

No. C717, Solano Bay. No. C718, Tota Lake, Boyaca. No. C719, Corrales, Boyaca.

1982 **Litho.** ***Perf. 12***

C717	AP182 20p multicolored	.60	.25
C718	AP182 20p multicolored	.60	.25
C719	AP182 20p multicolored	.60	.25
	Nos. C717-C719 (3)	1.80	.75

Issued: No. C717, 6/2; others, 6/16.

1982 World Cup — AP202a

Players and team emblems: a, "America." b, "A. B." c, "Cali." d, "C." e, "C/D." f, "Junior F.B.C." g, "D/M." h, Stadium. i, "M." j, "Club Atletico Nacional." k, "D/P." l, "Quindio." m, "Santa Fe." n, "T." o, "Santa Marta."

1982, June 21 ***Perf. 14***

C720	Sheet of 15	10.00	6.75
a.-o.	AP202a 9p, any single	.80	.30

Bogota Gun Club Centenary AP202b

1982, July 16 ***Perf. 12***

C721 AP202b 20p multicolored .70 .25

Gold Crocodile Figure, Tairona Culture AP202c

Tairona Culture Exhibit, Gold Museum: Various figures. Nos. C723-C727 vert.

1982, July 28

Gold, Black and

C722	AP202c 25p light brown	2.50	.95
C723	AP202c 25p bright pink	2.50	.95
C724	AP202c 25p green	2.50	.95
C725	AP202c 25p dark blue	2.50	.95
C726	AP202c 25p violet	2.50	.95
C727	AP202c 25p red	2.50	.95
	Nos. C722-C727 (6)	15.00	5.70

Government Buildings, Pereira — AP203

1982, Aug. 4 **Litho.** ***Perf. 12***

C728 AP203 35p multicolored 1.25 .40

Biplane in Flight, by Edgar Antonio Bustos AP204

1982, Aug. 5 ***Perf. 14***

C729 AP204 18p multicolored 1.20 .25

American Air Forces Cooperation System.

Magdalena River AP205

1982, Oct. 21 **Litho.** ***Perf. 12***

C730 AP205 30p multicolored 1.40 .35

Marquez Type

1982, Dec. 10 ***Perf. 13½x14***

C731	A412 25p gray & blue	.70	.25
C732	A412 30p gray & brown	1.00	.25

San Andres Archipelago — AP206

1983, Apr. 9 **Litho.** ***Perf. 12***

C733 AP206 25p Liberty Fort .60 .25

Opening of Las Gaviotas (The Seagulls) Ecological Center, Bogota — AP207

1983, June 1 **Litho.**

C734 AP207 12p multicolored .40 .25

50th Anniv. of Radio Amateurs League AP208

1983, June 11 ***Perf. 14x13½***

C735 AP208 12p multicolored .30 .25

Bolivar Type

1983, July 24 ***Perf. 12***

C736	A417 30p multicolored	.80	.25
C737	A417 100p multicolored	2.50	1.75

Botanical Exhibition Type

No. C738, Begonia guaduensis. No. C739, Chinchona ovaliflora. No. C740, Begonia urticae.

1983, Aug. 18 ***Perf. 14***

C738	A418 12p multicolored	.40	.25
C739	A418 12p multicolored	.40	.25
C740	A418 40p multicolored	2.00	1.40
	Nos. C738-C740 (3)	2.80	1.90

Cartagena, 450th Anniv. — AP208a

12p, Customs Square. 35p, Historic sites, Cartagena.

1983, Sept. 9 **Litho.** ***Perf. 12***

C740A	AP208a 12p multi	.50	.25
C740B	AP208a 35p multi	1.25	.30

Painting Type

1983, Oct. 5 **Litho.** ***Perf. 12***

C741 A420 30p multicolored 1.50 .50

Scouting Year — AP209

1983, Oct. 24

C742 AP209 12p multicolored .25 .25

Coffee Beans — AP210

1984, Mar. 28 **Litho.** ***Perf. 14½x14***

C743 AP210 14p multicolored .25 .25

Marandua City Type

1984, Sept. 28 ***Perf. 12***

C744 A427 30p multicolored .75 .25

AP211

1984, Nov. 2

C745 AP211 45p multicolored 1.50 .80

45th Cong. of Americanists, Bogota, 1985.

Christmas Type

1984, Dec. 14

C746 A428 14p multicolored .35 .25

AP212

Design: Dove, map and flags of Colombia, Mexico, Costa Rica and Venezuela.

1985, Feb. 15
C747 AP212 40p multicolored 1.50 .30

Contadora Group of Latin American countries.

Gomez Type

1985, Feb. 25
C748 A432 40p multicolored 1.00 .30

Birds — AP213

14p, Dryocopus lineatus nuperus. 20p, Xiphorhynchus picus. 50p, Eriocnemis cupreoventris. 55p, Momotus momota.

1985
C749 AP213 14p multicolored .80 .30
C750 AP213 20p multicolored 1.50 .30
C751 AP213 50p multicolored 3.50 1.00
C752 AP213 55p multicolored 4.50 1.25
Nos. C749-C752 (4) 10.30 2.85

Issued: 14p, 4/12; 20p, 50p, 8/6; 55p, 8/29.

AP214

1985, July 15
C753 AP214 20p multicolored .30 .25

Admiral Padilla Naval School, 50th anniv.

1985 Census AP215

1985, Oct. 15 *Perf. 12*
C754 AP215 20p multicolored .45 .25

Christmas Type

1985, Dec. 4 **Litho.** *Perf. 13*
C755 A436 20p Girl, Christmas tree .40 .25

Alfonso Lopez Pumarejo (1886-1959), President, 1934-38, 1942-45 — AP216

1986, Jan. 31
C756 AP216 24p multicolored .35 .25

Coffee Berries, Natl. Cycling Team AP217

1986, Feb. 4
C757 AP217 60p multicolored 1.25 .75

Natl. Coffee Producers Assoc. sponsorship of natl. cycling team, 25th anniv.

Fauna Type of 1985

1986, Feb. 18
C758 A433 50p Pudu mephistophiles 1.50 .25

World Communications Day — AP218

1986, May 17 **Litho.** *Perf. 13*
C759 AP218 50p multicolored .65 .25

Intl. Peace Year — AP219

1986, June 13 **Litho.** *Perf. 13*
C760 AP219 55p multicolored 1.00 .45

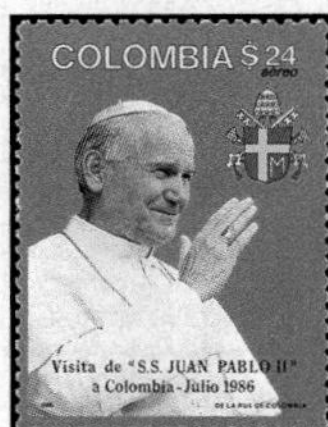

AP220

24p, Portrait, papal arms. 55p, Portrait, Medellin cathedral, horiz. 60p, Blessing crowd, horiz.

200p, Praying, Madonna of Bogota.

1986, July 1 **Litho.** *Perf. 13*
C761 AP220 24p multicolored 1.50 .25
C762 AP220 55p multicolored 1.50 .25
C763 AP220 60p multicolored 1.50 .25
Nos. C761-C763 (3) 4.50 .75

Souvenir Sheet

C764 AP220 200p multicolored 4.50 3.50

Visit of Pope John Paul II.

Nos. C762-C763 each printed in sheets of 20 with se-tenant labels picturing religious symbols.

AP221

1986, July 15 *Perf. 12*
C765 AP221 25p multicolored .30 .25

Enrique Santos Montejo (1886-1971), journalist.

Bach, Handel and Schutz, Composers AP222

1986, July 17 *Perf. 13*
C766 AP222 70p Bach 1.60 .40
C767 AP222 100p Text, music 2.10 .55

Salesian Order Education in Colombia, Cent. AP223

1986, July 23 *Perf. 12*
C768 AP223 25p De La Salle, founder .35 .25

Completion of Coal Mining Complex, El Cerrejon AP224

1986, July 29 **Litho.** *Perf. 12*
C769 AP224 55p multi 1.25 .75

AP225

Natl. Constitution, Cent. — AP226

25p, The Five Signators, by R. Vasquez, detail, & Bogota Cathedral. 200p, Pres. Nunez & Miguel Antonio Caro, Natl. Council of Delegates chairman, & Presidential Palace, constitution.

1986, Aug. 5 **Litho.** *Perf. 14*
C770 AP225 25p multi .35 .25

Souvenir Sheet

Perf. 12

C771 AP226 200p multi 3.00 3.00

Poet Type

Federico Garcia Lorca (1898-1936), poet, and birthplace, Fuentevaqueros, Granada, Spain.

1986, Sept. 26 **Litho.** *Perf. 12*
C772 A445 60p multi 1.00 .50

Gratitude for Intl. Aid after the Armero Mudslide Disaster AP227

1986, Nov. 13
C773 AP227 50p multi 1.00 .75

Christmas AP228

Wood sculpture: Virgin Mestiza, Nerina.

1986, Dec. 19 **Litho.** *Perf. 12*
C774 AP228 25p multi .35 .25

The Apotheosis of Popayan, by Ephrain Martinez Zambrano (1898-1956) — AP229

1987, Jan. 13
C775 100p Popayan riding horse 2.50 1.25
C776 100p Onlookers 2.50 1.25
a. AP229 Pair, #C775-C776 5.00 3.50

AP230

1987, Mar. 16 **Litho.** *Perf. 12*
C777 AP230 30p multi .50 .25

The Conversion of St. Augustine of Hippo, 1600th anniv.

Type of 1987

30p, Phoenicopterus ruber. 35p, Pseudemys scripta, horiz. No. C780, Crax alberti. No. C781, Symphysodon aequifasciatum, horiz.

Perf. 14½x14, 14x14½

1987-89 **Wmk. 334**
C778 A446a 30p lake .35 .25
C779 A446a 35p dark red brn .40 .25
C780 A446a 45p dark blue gray .30 .25
C781 A446a 45p blue .30 .25
Nos. C778-C781 (4) 1.35 1.00

Issue dates: 30p, June 8. 35p, Dec. 24. No. C780, Dec. 6, 1988. No. C781, June 23, 1989.

AP231

Perf. 13½x13

1987, Apr. 10 **Unwmk.**
C783 AP231 25p multi .30 .25

Natl. University School of Mining, Medellin, cent.

Purebred Horses AP232

1987, June 17 ***Perf. 12***
C784 AP232 60p White horse 1.25 .30
C785 AP232 70p Black horse 1.25 .30

El Espectador Newspaper, Cent. AP233

Design: Frontispieces from 1887, 1915, 1948, 1974 and portraits of founder Don Fidel Cano, editors Don Luis Cano, Luis Gabriel Cano Isaza and Alfonso Cano Isaza.

1987, July 24 ***Perf. 12½x12***
C786 AP233 60p multi .85 .25

Intl. Year of Shelter for the Homeless AP234

1987, Sept. 21 ***Perf. 14***
C787 AP234 60p multi 1.00 .25

Flags AP235

1987, Nov. 27 **Litho.** ***Perf. 13x13½***
C788 AP235 80p multi 1.00 .30

Ist Meeting of the eight Latin-American Presidents, Acapulco, Nov.

Christmas AP236

1987, Dec. 8 **Litho.** ***Perf. 14***
C789 AP236 30p multi .45 .25

Rural Telephone System AP237

1988, Feb. 4 **Litho.** ***Perf. 14***
C790 AP237 70p multi .80 .30

Founding of Bogota, 450th Anniv. — AP238

1988, Apr. 11 **Litho.** ***Perf. 12***
C791 AP238 70p multi .80 .25

Bogota, 450th Anniv. AP238a

80p, Modern district, vert. 90p, Colonial district.

Unwmk.

1988, July 1 **Litho.** ***Perf. 12***
C792 AP238a 80p multi .75 .25
C793 AP238a 90p multi .85 .30

Gold Artifacts AP239

Artifacts in the Gold Museum: 70p, Mask. 80p, Two-headed human figure inside a circle, Muisca tribe. 90p, Ritual figure of the Quimbaya.

1988 ***Perf. 12***
C794 AP239 70p multi 1.10 .50
C795 AP239 80p multi 1.50 .60
C796 AP239 90p multi 2.00 .75
Nos. C794-C796 (3) 4.60 1.85

Issue dates: 70p, May 13; 80p, 90p, Oct. 7.

Human Rights Type

Perf. 14x14½

1988, July 1 **Engr.** **Wmk. 334**
C797 A452 40p Communication, horiz. .40 .25

AP240

1988, Sept. 28 **Litho.** ***Perf. 12***
C798 AP240 80p multi .90 .25

Zipa Tisquesusa (d. 1538), Chibcha Indian leader during revolt against Spanish Conquistadors.

Christmas AP241

1988, Nov. 23 **Litho.** ***Perf. 12***
C799 AP241 40p multi .60 .25

Agustin Nieto Caballero (1889-1975), Educator — AP242

Unwmk.

1989, Mar. 18 **Litho.** ***Perf. 12***
C800 AP242 100p multi 1.00 .50

Pres. Laureano Gomez (1889-1965) AP243

1989, Mar. 29
C801 AP243 45p multi .45 .25

Intl. Coffee Organization — AP244

1989, Apr. 3
C802 AP244 110p multi 1.00 .50

12th Session of the UN Commission on Human Rights — AP245

1989, Apr. 28
C803 AP245 100p multi 1.00 .40

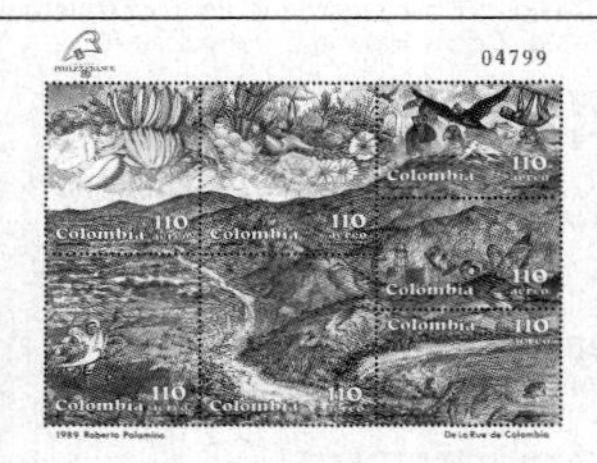
French Revolution, Bicent. AP246

1989, June 29 **Litho.** ***Perf. 12***
C804 AP246 100p multi .90 .40

PHILEXFRANCE '89 — AP247

a, Bananas, tropical fruits. b, Fruits, flowers. c, Birds, animals. d, Precious gems, metals and mineral resources. e, View of fields, Colombian carrying produce basket. f, Waterfall. g, Fish, coast.

1989 **Litho.** ***Perf. 14***
C805 AP247 Pane of 7 17.50 17.50
a.-g. 110p any single 1.75 .40

No. C805 printed in sheets containing panes of 7, rouletted between.

Souvenir Sheet

Los Lanceros, by R. Arenas Betancur — AP248

1989 **Litho.** ***Perf. 12***
C806 AP248 250p multicolored 2.25 1.25

Human Rights Type

Perf. 14½x14

1989, Aug. 18 **Engr.** **Wmk. 334**
C807 A452 55p Family .40 .25

Natl. Anti-Drugs Campaign AP249

Unwmk.

1989, Aug. 23 **Litho.** ***Perf. 12***
C808 AP249 115p multicolored 1.00 .25

America Issue AP250

UPAE emblem and artifacts or customs of pre-Columbian peoples: 115p, Quimbaya, Calima or Tolima gold smiths. 130p, Potter and Sinu ceramic figurine.

1989 ***Perf. 12***
C809 AP250 115p multicolored 1.25 .40
C810 AP250 130p multicolored 1.25 .60

Issue dates: 115p, Oct. 12; 130p, Aug. 23.

Joaquin Quijano Mantilla (1878-1944), Journalist — AP251

1989, Sept. 29 ***Perf. 12***
C811 AP251 170p multicolored 1.50 .50

Arts and Crafts in Barro-Raquira AP252

1989 **Litho.** ***Perf. 12***
C812 AP252 55p multicolored .40 .25

Christmas.

Boeing 767 AP253

1989, Dec. 5 **Litho.** ***Perf. 12***
C813 AP253 130p multicolored 1.25 .30

Bolivar Installed at the Congress of Angostura, by Tito Salas — AP254

1989, Dec. 12
C814 AP254 130p multicolored 1.10 .50

Creation of the Republic, 1819.

Fathers of the Nation Leaving the Constitutional Convention AP255

1989, Dec. 12
C815 AP255 130p shown 1.00 .50
C816 AP255 130p Arms 1.00 .50
C817 AP255 130p Temple of the Rosary 1.00 .50
Nos. C815-C817 (3) 3.00 1.50

Constitution of the Republic, 1821.

Arms Type of Regular Issue, 1982

1990, Mar. 1 **Litho.** ***Perf. 12***
C818 A372 60p Velez .30 .25

Presidential Summit, Cartagena AP256

130p, Plaza de la Aduana.

1990, Feb. 15 **Litho.** ***Perf. 12***
C819 AP256 130p multi .55 .25

Colombian National Radio, 50th Anniv. — AP257

1990, Feb. 16 **Litho.** ***Perf. 12***
C820 AP257 150p multicolored 1.00 .25

Teresa Cuervo Borda (1889-1976), Art Historian — AP258

1990, Mar. 28 **Litho.** ***Perf. 12***
C821 AP258 60p multicolored .35 .25

Second Latin American Theater Festival, Bogota — AP259

1990, Apr. 10
C822 AP259 150p buff, tan & gold 1.00 .25

Santander Type

No. C823, Santander holding the Constitution. No. C824, Central Cemetery, Bogota and National Pantheon. No. C825, Santander, as organizer of public education. No. C826, "Postman of New Granada" (Man and burro) by Joseph Brown and Jose Maria del Castillo, horiz. 500p, Santander on death bed.

1990, May 6 ***Perf. 14x13½***
C823 A470 60p multicolored .25 .25
C824 A470 60p multicolored .25 .25
C825 A470 70p multicolored .35 .25
C826 A470 70p multicolored .35 .25
Nos. C823-C826 (4) 1.20 1.00

Souvenir Sheet

Perf. 12

C827 A470 500p multi 1.75 1.50

No. C827 contains one 54x40mm stamp.

First Postage Stamp, 150th Anniv. AP260

1990, May 6 ***Perf. 14***
C828 AP260 150p multicolored .80 .40

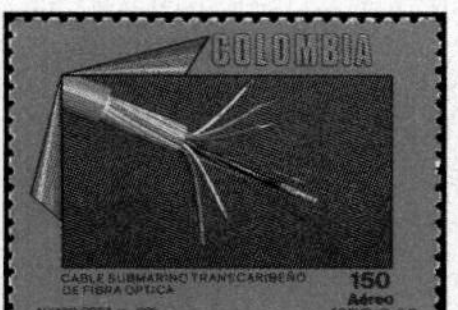

Trans-Caribbean Fiber Optic Cable — AP261

1990, May 19 ***Perf. 12***
C829 AP261 150p multicolored 1.00 .40

Institute of Industrial Development, 25th Anniv. — AP262

1990, May 22
C830 AP262 60p multicolored .40 .25

Souvenir Sheet

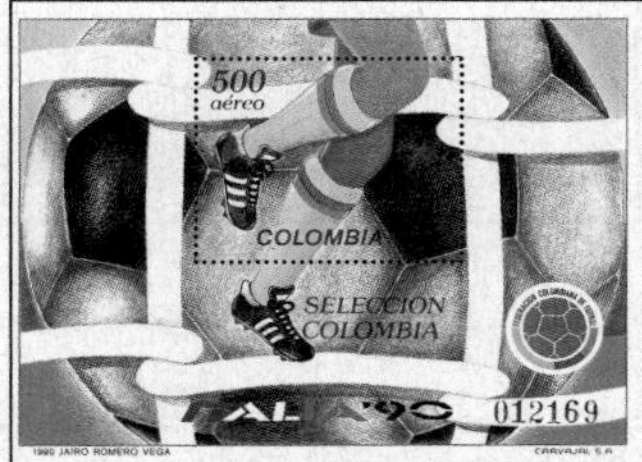

World Cup Soccer Championships, Italy — AP263

1990, June 8
C831 AP263 500p multicolored 4.50 3.50

AP264

1990, June 27
C832 AP264 130p multicolored .80 .25

Organization of American States, cent.

AP265

1990, July 26
C833 AP265 170p multicolored 1.25 .50

Museum of Gold, 50th Anniv.

Dolphins, Marine Birds AP266

170p, Jungle fauna, vert.

1990, Oct. 12 **Litho.** ***Perf. 12***
C834 AP266 150p shown 2.50 .25
C835 AP266 170p multi 2.50 .25

AP267

1990, Nov. 16 **Litho.** ***Perf. 12***
C836 AP267 70p multicolored .50 .25

Monastery of Our Lady of Las Lajas.

AP268

1991, Feb. 8 **Litho.** ***Perf. 12***
C837 AP268 170p multicolored 1.25 .50

Newspaper Publishing, 200th Anniv.

Christmas AP269

1990, Nov. 1 **Litho.** ***Perf. 12***
C838 AP269 70p multicolored .60 .25

AP270

Whales and Dolphins: 80p, Megaptera novaeangliae, breaching. 170p, Megaptera novaeangliae, diving. 190p, Inia geoffrensis, Sotalia fluviatilis, horiz.

1991, May 31 **Litho.** ***Perf. 14***
C839 AP270 80p multicolored 1.25 .25
C840 AP270 170p multicolored 2.50 .30
C841 AP270 190p multicoloed 3.25 .30
Nos. C839-C841 (3) 7.00 .85

America Issue AP271

190p, Ship arriving in New World.

1991, Oct. 11 **Litho.** ***Perf. 14***
C842 AP271 90p shown .60 .30
C843 AP271 190p multi 1.25 .50

Adoration of the Magi — AP272

1991, Dec. 20 Litho. *Perf. 14*
C844 AP272 90p multicolored .60 .30

Christmas.

Country Flags — AP273

1991, Dec. 2
C845 AP273 190p multi 1.00 .50

Fifth summit of Latin American presidents.

AP274

1992, Feb. 8 Litho. *Perf. 12*
C846 AP274 210p multicolored 1.25 .60

8th UNCTAD Conference, Cartagena.

Proclamation of New Constitution, July 4, 1991 — AP275

1991, Nov. 27 Litho. *Perf. 14*
C847 AP275 90p multicolored .40 .25

Export Products AP276

90p, Flowers. 210p, Fruits, vegetables, horiz.

1992, Mar. 11 *Perf. 12*
C848 AP276 90p multi .60 .30
C849 AP276 210p multi 1.40 .65

Copyright Protection AP277

1992, Apr. 13 Litho. *Perf. 12*
C850 AP277 190p multicolored 1.40 .60

1992 Summer Olympics AP278

1992, June 4 Litho. *Perf. 14*
C851 AP278 110p multicolored 1.25 .30

Earth Summit '92 — AP279

a, Tree, mountain landscape. b, Birds in tree.

1992, June 2 Litho. *Perf. 14*
C852 A279 230p Pair, #a.-b. 2.50 2.00

America Issue AP280

Paintings: 230p, Discovery of America by Christopher Columbus, by Salvador Dali. 260p, Magical America, Myth and Legend, by Alfredo Vivero.

1992, July 22 *Perf. 14x13½*
C853 AP280 230p multicolored 1.75 .70
C854 AP280 260p multicolored 2.00 .75

McDonnell Douglas MD83 AP281

1992, Sept. 22 Litho. *Perf. 12*
C855 AP281 110p multicolored .75 .30

Curtain of Colon Theatre AP282

1992, Oct. 12 Litho. *Perf. 12*
C856 AP282 230p multicolored 1.25 .65

Gloria Lara, 1938-82 — AP283

1992, Nov. 27 Litho. *Perf. 12*
C857 AP283 230p multicolored 2.00 .65

AP284

1993, June 7 Litho. *Perf. 12*
C858 AP284 220p multicolored 1.25 .60

1993 American Soccer Cup, Ecuador.

Intl. Year of Indigenous People — AP285

1993, July 1 *Perf. 14*
C859 AP285 460p multicolored 2.50 1.25

South American Eliminations for 1994 World Cup Soccer Championships, US — AP286

1993, July 31 Litho. *Perf. 12*
C860 AP286 220p multicolored 1.60 .60

AP287

America Issue (Endangered species): a, 220p, Saguinus oedipus. b, 220p, Porphyrula martinica. c, 460p, Rupicola peruviana. d, 520p, Trichecus manatus.

1993, Oct. 19 Litho. *Perf. 12*
C861 AP287 Block of 4, #a.-d. 7.50 7.50

AP288

1994, Mar. 21 Litho. *Perf. 12*
C862 AP288 630p multicolored 3.00 1.50

Intl. Decade for Natural Disaster Reduction.

Beatification of Josemaria Escriva de Balaguer — AP289

1994, May 17 Litho. *Perf. 13½x14*
C863 AP289 560p multicolored 2.25 1.40

First Airmail Delivery, 75th Anniv. AP290

Design: 270p, William Knox Martin, airplane over Port Colombia, 1919.

1994, July 29 Litho. *Perf. 14*
C864 AP290 270p multicolored 1.25 .55

Natl. Institute of Medical Law & Forensic Sciences, 80th Anniv. AP291

1994, Oct. 27 Litho. *Perf. 12*
C865 AP291 560p multicolored 2.25 1.25

Sociedad Colombo-Alemana de Transportes Aereos (SCADTA), 75th Anniv. — AP292

1995, Jan. 2 Litho. *Perf. 12*
C866 AP292 330p No. C15 1.10 .50

Flora and Fauna — AP293

Iguana iguana: No. C867a, Facing right. b, Facing left.

Rain forest: No. C868a, Nuts on branch, flowers. b, Waterfall, hanging red flower.

1995, Jan. 17
C867 AP293 650p Pair, #a.-b. 5.00 5.00
C868 AP293 750p Pair, #a.-b. 5.00 5.00

Nos. C867-C868 are continuous designs.

SCADTA, 75th Anniv. AP294

1995, Mar. 30 Litho. *Perf. 14*
C869 AP294 330p No. C9 1.50 .75

FAO, 50th Anniv. AP295

1995, Apr. 25 Litho. *Perf. 13x13½*
C870 AP295 750p multicolored 2.50 1.50

Andres Bello Organization, 25th Anniv. — AP296

1995, Apr. 27 *Perf. 13½x13*
C871 AP296 650p multicolored 2.50 1.25

Colombian Firefighters, Cent. — AP297

1995, May 5 *Perf. 12*
C872 AP297 330p multicolored 1.50 .75

Fenalco, 50th Anniv. — AP298

1995, May 25 *Perf. 13½*
C873 AP298 330p multicolored 1.25 .65

UN, 50th Anniv. — AP299

1995, June 21 *Perf. 12*
C874 AP299 750p multicolored 2.75 1.50

First Pacific Ocean Games — AP300

1995, June 23
C875 AP300 750p multicolored 2.75 1.50

11th Summit of Non-Aligned Countries, Cartagena — AP302

1995, Oct. 13 Litho. *Perf. 12*
C877 AP302 650p multicolored 2.75 1.25

Motion Pictures, Cent. AP303

Design: 330p, Charlie Chaplin and Jackie Coogan in "The Kid," Estela López Pomareda in "Maria," first Colombian feature length film.

1995, Oct. 19 *Perf. 14*
C878 AP303 330p black & sepia 1.50 .75

AP304

1995, Nov. 23 *Perf. 12*
C879 AP304 650p multicolored 2.10 1.00

Andes Development Corporation (CAF), 25th Anniv.

AP305

Fight against illegal drug trafficking: No. C880, Locating illegally grown plants. No. C881, Hands in handcuffs, horiz.

1995, Nov. 21 *Perf. 14*
C880 AP305 330p multicolored .70 .45
C881 AP305 330p multicolored .70 .45

Miniature Sheet of 16

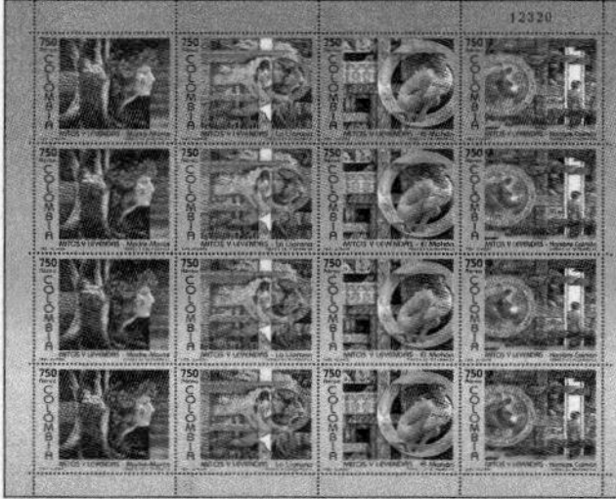

Myths and Legends — AP306

Madre-Monte: a.-d.
La Llorona: e.-h.
El Mohán: i.-l.
Hombre Caimán: m.-p.

Background color changes from top to bottom rows. Top row is blue. Row 2 is blue green. Row 3 is green. Row 4 is lilac. Each design comes in all four colors.

1995, Dec. 6
C882 AP306 750p #a.-p. 40.00 40.00

See No. C886.

José Asunción Silva (1865-96), Poet AP307

1996, Apr. 23 Litho. *Perf. 12*
C883 AP307 400p multicolored 1.25 .75

Isla de Providencia AP308

1996, Apr. 25 *Perf. 14*
C884 AP308 800p multicolored 2.75 1.40

Policarpa Salavarrieta (1796-1817), Patriot — AP309

1996, Apr. 26
C885 AP309 900p multicolored 3.00 1.50

Myths and Legends Type

Designs: a, Kogui Creation. b, Yonna Wayu. c, Jaguar Man. d, Master of the Animals.

1996, Aug. 12 Litho. *Perf. 13½x14*
C886 AP306 900p Block of 4, #a.-d. 13.00 13.00

Metropolitan Basilica, Medellin AP310

1996, July 12
C887 AP310 400p multicolored 1.05 .55

National Archives Building AP311

1996, July 30 Litho. *Perf. 14*
C888 AP311 400p multicolored 1.05 .55

CERLALC, 25th Anniv. AP312

1996, Aug. 16 Litho. *Perf. 12*
C889 AP312 800p multicolored 2.75 1.25

UNESCO.

Pioneers in Petroleum Industry — AP313

a, Jorge Isaacs, pumping oil. b, Francisco Burgos Rubio, refinery at night. c, Diego Martínez Camargo, derrick. d, Prisciliano Cabrales Lora, off-shore drilling. e, Manuel María Palacio, oil tanker loading offshore. f, Roberto De Mares, refinery, lake. g, General Virgilio Barco Maldonado, men positioning equipment. h, Roustabout, "ECOPETROL" emblem.

1996, Sept. 5 Litho. *Perf. 13½x14*
C890 AP313 800p Block of 8, #a.-h. 20.00 20.00

Colombian Golf Federation, 50th Anniv. AP314

1996, Sept. 19 Litho. *Perf. 12*
C891 AP314 400p multicolored 2.25 .60

Covenant for the Children AP315

1997, Feb. 28 Litho. *Perf. 14*
C892 AP315 400p multicolored 1.80 .75

AP316

1997, Apr. 25 ***Perf. 12***
C893 AP316 800p multicolored 3.75 1.75

Motion pictures in Colombia, cent.

AP317

1997, May 13 Litho. ***Perf. 12***
C894 AP317 400p multicolored 1.90 .75

Social Security Institute, 50th anniv.

Ericsson in Colombia, Cent. — AP318

1997, May 22 ***Perf. 13½x14***
C895 AP318 900p multicolored 4.50 2.00

Bogotá Colonial Bldg., Home of Natl. Mint and Numismatic Museum — AP319

1997, July 10 ***Perf. 12***
C896 AP319 800p multicolored 3.00 1.40

Phytelephas Seemannii — AP320

1997, July 23 ***Perf. 13½x14***
C897 AP320 900p multicolored 3.00 .90

Cordoba Cattle Fair AP321

1997, June 21 ***Perf. 14***
C898 AP321 400p multicolored 1.50 .45

Personalities — AP322

No. C899: a, Cacique Gaitana, 16th cent., Indian resistance leader. b, Josefa Acevedo de Gómez (1803-61), writer. c, Domingo Bioho (d. 1621), black leader. d, Soledad Acosta de Samper (1831-1913), historian. e, Maria Cano Márquez (1897-1967), popular leader. f, Manuel Quintín Lame (1880-1967), native leader. g, Ezequiel Uricoechea (1834-80), linguist, naturalist. h, Juan Rodríguez Freyle (1566-1642), colonial reporter. i, Gerardo Reichel-Dolmatoff (1912-94), archaeologist. j, Ramón de Zubiría (1922-95), writer, educator. k, Esteban Jaramillo (1874-1947), economist. l, Pedro Fermín de Vargas (1762-c. 1810), economist.

No. C900: a, Luis Carlos "el tuerto" López (1879-1950), poet. b, Aurelio Arturo (1906-74), poet. c, Enrique Pérez Arbeláez (1896-1972), botanist. d, José Maria González Benito (1843-1903), mathematician, astronomer. e, José Manuel Rivas Sacconi (1917-91), diplomat. f, Eduardo Lemaitre Román (1914-94), historian. g, Diójenes Arrieta (1848-93), politician. h, Gabriel Turbay Abunader (1901-47), politician, diplomat. i, Guillermo Echavarría Misas (1888-1985), aviation pioneer. j, Juan Friede Alter (1901-90), historian. k, Fabio Lozano Torrijos (1865-1947), diplomat. l, Lino de Pombo (1797-1862), engineer, diplomat.

Sheets of 12

1997, Dec. 19 Litho. ***Perf. 13½x14***
C899 AP322 500p #a.-l. 25.00 25.00
C900 AP322 500p #a.-l. 25.00 25.00

Colombian Society of Orthopedic Surgery and Traumatology, 50th Anniv. — AP323

1997 ***Perf. 12***
C901 AP323 1000p multicolored 3.00 1.00

AP324

1998, Apr. 30 Litho. ***Perf. 14***
C902 AP324 1000p multicolored 3.00 .80

Organization of American States, 50th anniv.

AP325

1998, May 22
C903 AP325 1000p bl & org 3.00 .80

4th Bolivar Philatelic Exhibition, Santa Fe de Bogota.

World Health Organization, 50th Anniv. — AP326

1998, Apr. 7 ***Perf. 12***
C904 AP326 1100p multicolored 3.00 1.00

1998 World Cup Soccer Championships, France — AP327

Stylized designs: a, Foot. b. Soccer ball. c, Hand.

1998, June 9 Litho. ***Perf. 14***
C905 AP327 1100p Strip of 3, #a.-c. 12.00 12.00

Intl. Year of the Ocean — AP328

1998, May 22 ***Perf. 12***
C906 AP328 1100p ARC Gloria 3.75 .95

Myths and Legends — AP329

Designs: a, Bochica. b, Chimingagua. c, Bachue and Huitica.

Perf. 13¼x12¾

1998, Nov. 27 Litho.
C907 AP329 1000p Strip of 3, #a.-c. 17.00 15.00

AIR POST SPECIAL DELIVERY STAMPS

Catalogue values for unused stamps in this section are for Never Hinged items.

Post Horn and Wings APSD1

Unwmk.

1958, May 19 Litho. ***Perf. 12***
CE1 APSD1 25c dk bl & red .55 .25

No. CE1 Ovptd. in Red

1959
CE2 APSD1 25c dk bl & red .50 .25

Jet Plane and Envelope — APSD2

1963, Oct. 4 ***Perf. 14***
CE3 APSD2 50c red & blk .25 .25

Aviation Type

80c, Boeing 727 jet, 1966.

Perf. 14x13½

1966, Dec. 14 Photo. Unwmk.
CE4 AP96 80c crim & multi .55 .25

AIR POST REGISTRATION STAMPS

Issued by Sociedad Colombo-Alemana de Transportes Aereos (SCADTA)

No. C41 Overprinted in Red

1923 Wmk. 116 ***Perf. 14x14½***
CF1 AP6 20c gray 4.75 1.10

Nos. C58 and C71 Overprinted in Black

1929 Wmk. 127 ***Perf. 14***
CF2 AP8 20c carmine 8.00 7.00
CF3 AP10 20c carmine 6.50 6.00

Colombian Government Issues

No. C86 Overprinted in Black

1932
CF4 AP8 20c carmine 6.50 6.00

No. C100 Overprinted

CF5 AP12 20c car & ol blk 6.00 1.25

For surcharge see No. C118.

SPECIAL DELIVERY STAMPS

Special Delivery Messenger — SD1

1917 Unwmk. Engr. *Perf. 14*
E1 SD1 5c dark green *60.00 150.00*

Catalogue values for unused stamps in this section, from this point to the end of the section, are for Never Hinged items.

SD2

1987, July 31 Litho. *Perf. 14*
E2 SD2 25p emerald & ver .30 .30
E3 SD2 30p emerald & ver .35 .35

REGISTRATION STAMPS

R1

R2

1865 Unwmk. Litho. *Imperf.*
F1 R1 5c black 87.50 47.50
F2 R2 5c black 110.00 50.00

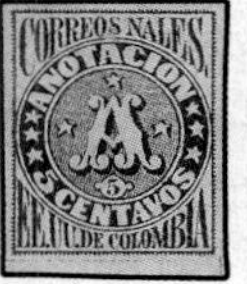

R3

R4

Vertical Lines in Background

1870 White Paper
F3 R3 5c black 3.00 2.50
F4 R4 5c black 3.00 2.50

Horizontal Lines in Background
F5 R3 5c black 10.00 8.50
F6 R4 5c black 3.00 2.50
Nos. F3-F6 (4) 19.00 16.00

Reprints of Nos. F3 to F6 show either crossed lines or traces of lines in background.

R5

1881 *Imperf.*
F7 R5 10c violet 60.00 52.50
a. Sewing machine perf. 67.50 60.00
b. Perf. 11 75.00 62.50

R6

1883 *Perf. 12, 13½*
F8 R6 10c red, *orange* 2.00 *2.50*

R7

1889-95 *Perf. 12, 13½*
F9 R7 10c red, *grysh* 9.50 4.50
F10 R7 10c red, *yelsh* 9.50 4.50
F11 R7 10c dp brn, *rose buff* ('95) 2.00 1.60
F12 R7 10c yel brn, *lt buff* ('92) 2.00 1.60
Nos. F9-F12 (4) 23.00 12.20

Nos. F9-F12 exist imperf.

R9

1902 *Imperf.*
F13 R9 20c red brown, *blue* 1.60 1.60
a. Sewing machine perf. 4.75 4.75
b. Perf. 12 4.75 4.75

Medellin Issue

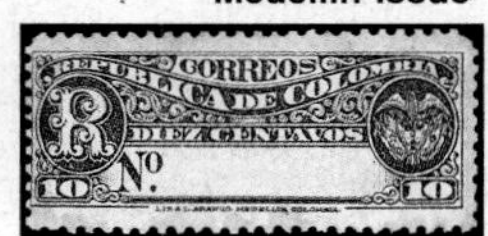

R10

1902 Laid Paper *Perf. 12*
F16 R10 10c blk vio 15.00 15.00
a. Wove paper 21.00 21.00

Regular Issue
Imperf

1903
F17 R9 20c blue, *blue* 1.60 1.60
a. Sewing machine perf. 4.75 4.75
b. Perf. 12 4.75 4.75

R11

1904 Pelure Paper *Imperf.*
F19 R11 10c purple 3.75 3.75
a. Sewing machine perf. 5.00 3.75
b. Perf. 12 6.25 5.00

R12

Imprint: "J. L. Arango"

1904 Wove Paper *Perf. 12*
F20 R12 10c purple 2.50 .60
a. Imperf., pair 7.75 7.75

Imprint: "Lit. Nacional"

1909 *Perf. 10, 14, 10x14, 14x10*
F21 R12 10c purple 2.75 .85
a. Imperf., pair 6.25 6.25

For overprints see Nos. LF1-LF4.

Execution at Cartagena in 1816 — R13

1910, July 20 Engr. *Perf. 12*
F22 R13 10c red & black 21.00 *90.00*

Centenary of National Independence.

Pier at Puerto Colombia — R14

Tequendama Falls — R15

Perf. 11, 11½, 14, 11½x14
1917, Aug. 25
F23 R14 4c green & ultra .55 *3.50*
a. Center inverted 575.00 575.00
F24 R15 10c deep blue 8.00 .60

R16

1925 Litho. *Perf. 10x13½*
F25 R16 (10c) blue 4.25 1.90
a. Imperf., pair 15.00 12.50
b. Perf. 13½x10 7.50 5.00

ACKNOWLEDGMENT OF RECEIPT STAMPS

AR1

1893 Unwmk. Litho. *Perf. 13½*
H1 AR1 5c ver, *blue* 4.75 4.75

1894 *Perf. 12*
H2 AR1 5c vermilion 4.50 *5.00*

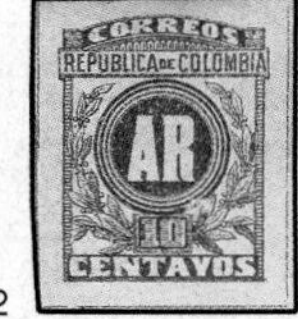

AR2

1902-03 *Imperf.*
H3 AR2 10c blue, *blue* 3.50 5.00
a. 10c, blue, *greenish blue* 3.50 5.00
b. Sewing machine perf. 3.50 5.00
c. Perf. 12 3.50 5.00

The handstamp "AR" in circle is believed to be a postmark.

AR2a

Purple Handstamp

1903 *Imperf.*
H4 AR2a 10c black, *pink* 25.00 25.00

AR3

1904 Pelure Paper *Imperf.*
H12 AR3 5c pale blue 10.50 10.50
a. Perf. 12 10.50 10.50

No. 307 Overprinted in Black, Green or Violet

H13 A86 5c carmine 17.50 17.50

AR4

1904 *Perf. 12*
H16 AR4 5c blue 3.25 2.75
a. Imperf., pair 8.75 8.75

For overprints see Nos. LH1-LH2.

General José Acevedo y Gómez — AR5

1910, July 20 Engr.
H17 AR5 5c orange & green 7.00 *17.50*

Centenary of National Independence.

Sabana Station AR6

Map of Colombia AR7

1917 *Perf. 14*
H18 AR6 4c bister brown 5.50 *6.00*
H19 AR7 5c orange brown 5.50 *4.50*
a. Imperf., pair 14.00

LATE FEE STAMPS

LF1

1886 Unwmk. Litho. *Perf. 10½*

I1	LF1	2½c blk, *lilac*	4.00	3.25
a.		Imperf., pair	15.00	15.00

LF2

1892 *Perf. 12, 13½*

I2	LF2	2½c dk bl, *rose*	3.50	2.50
a.		Imperf., pair	15.00	
I3	LF2	2½c ultra, *pink*	3.50	2.50

LF3

1902 *Imperf.*

I4	LF3	5c purple, *rose*	1.00	1.00
a.		Perf. 12	2.10	2.10

LF4

1914 *Perf. 10, 13½*

I6	LF4	2c vio brown	5.00	5.00
I7	LF4	5c blue green	5.00	4.25

Overprints illustrated above are unauthorized and of private origin.

POSTAGE DUE STAMPS

These are not, strictly speaking, postage due stamps but were issued to cover an additional fee, "Sobreporte," charged on mail to foreign countries with which Colombia had no postal conventions.

D1

D2

D3

1866 Unwmk. Litho. *Imperf.*

J1	D1	25c black, *blue*	80.00	55.00
J2	D2	50c black, *yellow*	55.00	*80.00*
J3	D3	1p black, *rose*	160.00	*125.00*
		Nos. J1-J3 (3)	295.00	260.00

DEPARTMENT STAMPS

These stamps are said to be for interior postage, to supersede the separate issues for the various departments.

Regular Issues Handstamped in Black, Violet, Blue or Green — a

On Stamps of 1904

1909 Unwmk. *Perf. 12*

L1	A94	½c yellow	2.50	2.50
a.		Imperf., pair	7.50	7.50
L2	A94	1c yel grn	3.75	2.50
L3	A94	2c red	5.50	3.75
a.		Imperf., pair	15.00	15.00
L4	A94	5c blue	6.25	4.00
L5	A94	10c violet	8.75	8.75
L6	A94	20c black	14.00	14.00
L7	A95	1p brown	22.50	21.00

On Stamp of 1902

L8	A83	10p dk brn, *rose*	25.00	25.00
		Nos. L1-L8 (8)	88.25	81.50

On Stamps of 1908

Perf. 10, 13, 13½ and Compound

L9	A94	½c orange	2.90	2.90
a.		Imperf., pair	7.50	7.50
L10	A94	1c green	5.00	5.00
a.		Without imprint	6.25	6.25
L11	A94	2c red	5.50	5.50
a.		Imperf., pair		
L12	A94	5c blue	5.50	5.50
a.		Imperf., pair	15.00	15.00
L13	A94	10c violet	8.75	8.75

On Tolima Stamp of 1888

Perf. 10½

L14	A23	1p red brn	27.50	27.50
		Nos. L9-L14 (6)	55.15	55.15

Regular Issues Handstamped — b

On Stamps of 1904

Perf. 12

L15	A94	½c yellow	2.50	2.50
L16	A94	1c yellow grn	4.25	4.25
L17	A94	2c red	7.50	7.50
L18	A94	5c blue	7.50	7.50
L19	A94	10c violet	10.00	10.00
L20	A94	20c black	14.00	14.00
L21	A94	1p brown	25.00	25.00
		Nos. L15-L21 (7)	70.75	70.75

On Stamps of 1908

Perf. 10, 13, 13½

L22	A94	½c orange	2.75	2.75
L23	A94	1c yellow grn	7.75	7.75
L24	A94	2c red	6.25	6.25
a.		Imperf., pair	15.00	15.00
L25	A94	5c light blue	7.50	7.50
		Nos. L22-L25 (4)	24.25	24.25

The handstamps on Nos. L1-L25 are, as usual, found inverted and double.

DEPARTMENT REGISTRATION STAMPS

Registration Stamps of 1904 Handstamped like Nos. L1-L25

1909 Unwmk. *Perf. 12*

LF1	R12 (a)	10c purple	30.00	30.00
LF2	R12 (b)	10c purple	30.00	30.00

On Registration Stamp of 1909

Perf. 10, 13

LF3	R12 (a)	10c purple	30.00	30.00
LF4	R12 (b)	10c purple	30.00	30.00
		Nos. LF1-LF4 (4)	120.00	120.00

Nos. LF1-LF4 exist imperf. Value per pair, $125.

DEPARTMENT ACKNOWLEDGMENT OF RECEIPT STAMPS

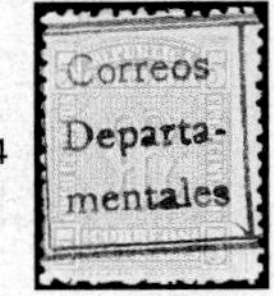

Acknowledgment of Receipt Stamp of 1904 Hstmpd.

1909 Unwmk. *Perf. 12*

LH1	AR4 (a)	5c blue	30.00	30.00
a.		Imperf., pair	125.00	
LH2	AR4 (b)	5c blue	30.00	30.00
a.		Imperf., pair	125.00	

LOCAL STAMPS FOR THE CITY OF BOGOTA

A1

Pelure Paper

1889 Unwmk. Litho. *Perf. 12*

LX1	A1	½c black	1.10	1.10
a.		Imperf., pair	7.25	7.25

Impressions on bright blue and blue-gray paper were not regularly issued.

A2

White Wove Paper

1896 *Perf. 12, 13½*

LX2	A2	½c black	1.10	1.10

A3

1903 *Imperf.*

LX3	A3	10c black, *pink*	7.25	1.40
a.		Perf. 12	7.25	1.40

OFFICIAL STAMPS

Stamps of 1917-1937 Overprinted in Black or Red

a

b

1937 Unwmk. *Perf. 11, 12, 13½*

O1	A131 (a)	1c green	.25	.25
O2	A157 (a)	10c dp org	.25	.25
O3	A107 (b)	30c olive bis	2.10	1.00
O4	A129 (b)	40c brn & yel brn	1.60	.80
O5	A114 (b)	50c car	1.60	.80
O6	A107 (b)	1p lt bl	13.00	5.50
O7	A107 (b)	2p org	15.00	6.50
O8	A107 (b)	5p gray	47.50	*52.50*
O9	A118 (b)	10p dk brn	110.00	*125.00*

Wmk. 229

Perf. 12½

O10	A132 (a)	2c red	.25	.25
O11	A133 (a)	5c brn	.25	.25
O12	A160 (a)	12c dp bl (R)	1.00	.50
O13	A136 (b)	20c dk bl (R)	1.60	.80
		Nos. O1-O13 (13)	194.40	194.40

Tall, wrong font "I's" in OFICIAL exist on all stamps with "a" overprint.

POSTAL TAX STAMPS

"Greatest Mother" PT1

Perf. 11½

1935, May 27 Unwmk. Litho.

RA1	PT1	5c olive blk & scar	4.00	1.25

Required on all mail during Red Cross Week in 1935 (May 27-June 3) and in 1936.

Mother and Child — PT2

Perf. 10½, 10½x11

1937, May 24 Unwmk.

RA2	PT2	5c red	2.75	.90

Required on all mail during Red Cross Week. The tax was for the Red Cross.

Ministry of Posts and Telegraphs Building — PT3

1939-45 Litho. *Perf. 10½, 12½*

RA3	PT3	¼c dp bl	.25	.25
RA3A	PT3	¼c dk vio brn ('45)	.25	.25
RA4	PT3	½c pink	.25	.25
RA5	PT3	1c violet	.30	.25
RA5A	PT3	1c yel org ('45)	1.75	.70
RA6	PT3	2c pck grn	.55	.25
RA7	PT3	20c lt brn	4.50	1.50
		Nos. RA3-RA7 (7)	7.85	3.45

Obligatory on all mail. The tax was for the construction of the new Communications Building.

The 25c of type PT3 and PT4 were not usable on postal matter.

For overprint see No. 561.

Ministry of Posts and Telegraphs Building — PT4

Perf. 12½x13

1940, Jan. 20 Engr. Wmk. 229

RA8 PT4 ¼c ultra .25 .25
RA9 PT4 ½c carmine .25 .25
RA10 PT4 1c violet .25 .25
RA11 PT4 2c bl grn .30 .25
RA12 PT4 20c brown 1.25 .25
Nos. RA8-RA12 (5) 2.30 1.25

See note after No. RA7. See No. RA18.

"Protection" — PT5

1940, Apr. 25 Wmk. 255 *Perf. 12*

RA13 PT5 5c rose carmine .30 .25

See No. RA17.

Postal Tax Stamps of 1939 Surcharged in Black

1943 Unwmk. *Perf. 10½*

RA14 PT3 ½c on 1c violet .25 .25
a. Inverted surcharge 2.00
RA15 PT3 ½c on 2c pck grn .25 .25
RA16 PT3 ½c on 20c lt brn .25 .25
Nos. RA14-RA16 (3) .75 .75

Types of 1940

Imprint: "Litografia Colombia Bogota S.A."

1944 Litho. *Perf. 11*

RA17 PT5 5c dark rose .40 .25

Imprint: "Lito-Colombia Bogota-Colombia"

RA18 PT4 ¼c ultra .25 .25

Ministry of Posts and Telegraphs Building — PT6

1945-48 Wmk. 255 Engr. *Perf. 12*

RA19 PT6 ¼c ultra .25 .25
RA20 PT6 ¼c sepia ('46) .25 .25
RA21 PT6 ½c car rose .25 .25
RA22 PT6 ½c dp mag ('46) .25 .25
RA23 PT6 1c vio ('46) .25 .25
RA23A PT6 1c red org ('46) .25 .25
RA24 PT6 2c grn ('46) .25 .25
RA25 PT6 20c brn ('47) 7.50 .30
a. 20c red brown ('48) .70 .25
Nos. RA19-RA25 (8) 9.25 2.05

These stamps were obligatory on all mail. The surtax was for the construction of the new Communications Building. See Nos. 603, RA33. For overprints see Nos. 562-564.

No. 469 Overprinted in Carmine

1946, May 25

RA26 A176 5c dull brown .40 .25

The surtax was for the Red Cross.

Ministry of Posts and Telegraphs Building — PT7

1946 Unwmk. Litho. *Perf. 11*

RA27 PT7 3c blue .25 .25

No. 490 Overprinted in Carmine

1947 Wmk. 255 *Perf. 12*

RA28 A196 20c gray black 5.25 2.90

Arms of Colombia and Red Cross — PT8

Perf. 12½

1947, Sept. Unwmk. Engr.

RA29 PT8 5c car lake .25 .25

The surtax of Nos. RA29 and RA40 was for the Red Cross. See No. RA40.

No. 466 Overprinted in Carmine

RA30 A136 20c dark blue 32.50 20.00

Catalogue values for unused stamps in this section, from this point to the end of the section, are for Never Hinged items.

Type of 1945

1947 Wmk. 255 Engr. *Perf. 12*

RA33 PT6 1c olive bister .30 .25

Black Surcharge — PT9

1948 Unwmk. Litho. *Perf. 11*

RA36 PT9 1c on 5c lt brn .30 .25
RA37 PT9 1c on 10c lt vio .30 .25
RA38 PT9 1c on 25c red .30 .25
RA39 PT9 1c on 50c ultra .30 .25
Nos. RA36-RA39 (4) 1.20 1.00

Type of 1947

1948 *Perf. 10½*

RA40 PT8 5c vermilion .25 .25

Ministry of Posts and Telegraphs Building — PT10

1948-50 Wmk. 255 Engr. *Perf. 12*

RA41 PT10 1c rose car ('49) .30 .25
RA42 PT10 2c green ('50) .30 .25
RA43 PT10 3c blue .30 .25
RA44 PT10 5c gray .30 .25
RA45 PT10 10c purple .30 .25
Nos. RA41-RA45 (5) 1.50 1.25

A 25c stamp of type PT10 was for use on telegrams, later for regular postage. See Nos. 602, 604. For overprints and surcharge see Nos. C227-C230, C238, C283, RA51.

Mother and Child — PT11

Dark Blue Surcharge

Unwmk.

1950, May 25 Litho. *Perf. 11*

RA46 PT11 5c on 2c gray, red, blk & yel 1.25 .90
a. "195" instead of "1950" 2.50 2.50
b. Top bar and "19" of "1950" omitted 2.50 2.50

Marginal perforations omitted, creating 26 straight-edged stamps in each sheet of 44. Surtax for Red Cross.

No. 574 Overprinted in Black

1950, May 26 Wmk. 255 *Perf. 12*

RA47 A176 5c blue .25 .25
a. Inverted overprint 8.00

Telegraph Stamp Surcharged in Black

RA48 A253a 8c on 50c org yel .25 .25

Fiscal stamps of type A253a were available for postal use after May 9, 1952. See Nos. 605-608.

Arms and Cross — PT12

Bartolome de Las Casas Aiding Youth — PT13

Perf. 12½

1951, May Unwmk. Engr.

RA49 PT12 5c red .25 .25
RA50 PT13 5c carmine .25 .25

The surtax was for the Red Cross.

No. RA43 Surcharged in Black

1951 Wmk. 255 *Perf. 12*

RA51 PT10 1c on 3c blue .25 .25

Type of 1951

Engraved; Cross Lithographed

1953 Unwmk. *Perf. 12½*

RA52 PT13 5c grn & car .35 .25

Surtax of Nos. RA52-RA60 for the Red Cross.

No. C254 Overprinted in Carmine

1954

RA53 AP42 5c lilac rose 2.00 .90

St. Peter Claver Offering Gifts to Slaves — PT14

Engraved; Cross Typographed

1955, May 2 Unwmk. *Perf. 13*

RA54 PT14 5c dp plum & red .30 .25

Death of St. Peter Claver, 300th anniv.

Jean Henri Dunant and Santiago Samper Brush PT15

Photo.; Red Cross & "Cruz Roja" Engr.

1956, June 1 Unwmk. *Perf. 13*

RA55 PT15 5c brown & red .45 .25

Nurses and Ambulances PT16

1958, June 2 Photo. *Perf. 12*

RA56 PT16 5c gray & red .25 .25

St. Louisa de Marillac and Church PT17

No. RA58, Henri Dunant and battle scene.

1960, Sept. 1 Litho. *Perf. 11*

RA57 PT17 5c brown & rose .30 .25
RA58 PT17 5c vio blue & rose .30 .25

No. RA57 for 3rd cent. of the Sisters of Charity. No. RA58 for cent. (in 1959) of the Red Cross idea.

Manuelita de la Cruz — PT18

1961, Nov. 2 Engr. *Perf. 13*

RA59 PT18 5c dull pur & red .25 .25
RA60 PT18 5c brown & red .25 .25

Issued in memory of Red Cross Nurse Manuelita de la Cruz, who died in the line of duty during the floods of 1955. Obligatory on domestic mail for a month.

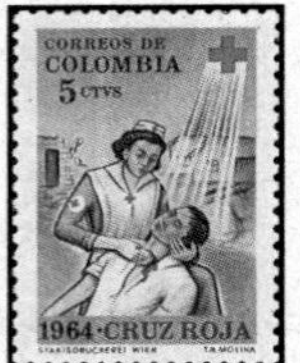

Red Cross Worker, Patient — PT19

1965, Apr. 30 Photo. *Perf. 12*

RA61 PT19 5c blue gray & red	.25	.25

Obligatory on domestic mail during May.

Nurse's Cap — PT20

1967, June 1 Litho. *Perf. 12*

RA62 PT20 5c brt bl & red	.25	.25

Red Cross — PT21

1969, July 1 Litho. *Perf. 12x12½*

RA63 PT21 5c vio bl & red	.25	.25

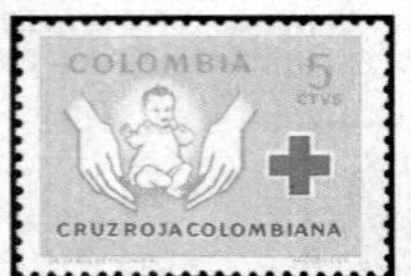

Child Care — PT22

1970, July 1 Litho. *Perf. 12½x12*

RA64 PT22 5c light bl & red	.25	.25

ANTIOQUIA

ant-ē-'ō-kē-ə

Originally a State, now a Department of the Republic of Colombia. Until the revolution of 1885, the separate states making up the United States of Colombia were sovereign governments in their own right. On August 4, 1886, the National Council of Bogotá, composed of two delegates from each state, adopted a new constitution which abolished the sovereign rights of states, which then became departments with governors appointed by the President of the Republic. The nine original states represented at the Bogotá Convention retained some of their previous rights, as management of their own finances, and all issued postage stamps until as late as 1904. For Panama's issues, see Panama Nos. 1-30.

Coat of Arms
A1 A2

A3 A4

Wove Paper

1868 Unwmk. Litho. *Imperf.*

1	A1	2½c blue	*1,000.*	*750.*
2	A2	5c green	*750.*	*575.*
3	A3	10c lilac	*3,000.*	*1,000.*
4	A4	1p red	*675.*	*750.*

Reprints of Nos. 1, 3 and 4 are on a bluish white paper and all but No. 3 have scratches across the design.

A5 A6

A7 A8

A9 A10

1869

5	A5	2½c blue	7.50	6.50
6	A6	5c green	11.00	10.00
7	A7	5c green	11.00	10.00
8	A8	10c lilac	14.50	7.00
9	A9	20c brown	14.50	7.00
10	A10	1p rose red	29.00	26.00
a.		1p vermilion	55.00	50.00
		Nos. 5-10 (6)	87.50	66.50

Reprints of Nos. 7, 8 and 10 are on a bluish white paper; reprints of Nos. 5 and 10a on white paper. The 10c blue is believed to be a reprint.

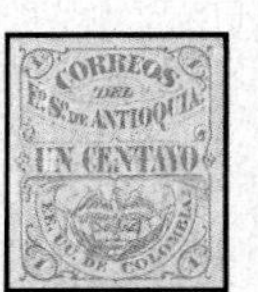

A11 A12

A13 A14

A15 A16

A17 A18

1873

12	A11	1c yellow grn	10.50	8.00
a.		1c green	10.50	8.00
13	A12	5c green	17.50	13.00
14	A13	10c lilac	50.00	42.50
15	A14	20c yellow brn	17.50	15.00
a.		20c dark brown	17.50	15.00

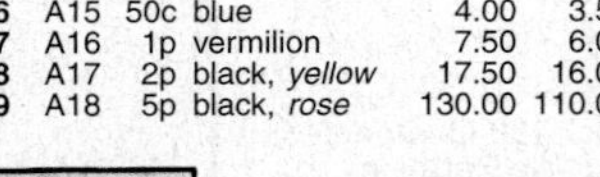

16	A15	50c blue	4.00	3.50
17	A16	1p vermilion	7.50	6.00
18	A17	2p black, *yellow*	17.50	16.00
19	A18	5p black, *rose*	130.00	110.00

A19 A20

Liberty Head
A21 A22

Pedro Justo Berrio — A23

1875-85

20	A19	1c blk, *grn*, unglazed ('76)	3.20	4.75
a.		Glazed paper	5.25	6.50
b.		1c blk, *lt grn*, laid paper ('85)	7.50	7.00
21	A19	1c black ('76)	2.25	2.00
a.		Laid paper	325.00	225.00
22	A19	1c bl grn ('85)	5.00	8.00
23	A19	1c red lil, laid paper ('85)	5.00	8.00
24	A20	2½c blue	5.00	3.75
a.		Pelure paper ('78)	*1,500.*	*1,100.*
25	A21	5c green	32.50	29.00
a.		Laid paper	325.00	175.00
26	A22	5c green	32.50	29.00
a.		Laid paper	325.00	175.00
27	A23	10c lilac	50.00	42.50
a.		Laid paper	325.00	250.00
28	A20	10c vio, pelure paper ('78)	*900.00*	*675.00*

Arms — A24 Liberty — A25

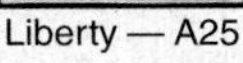

A26 A27

1878-85

29	A24	2½c blue, pelure paper	5.50	5.00
30	A24	2½c green ('83)	5.00	4.25
a.		Laid paper ('83)	160.00	110.00
31	A24	2½c blk, *buff* ('85)	14.50	13.00
32	A25	5c green ('83)	9.00	8.00
a.		Pelure paper	65.00	55.00
b.		Laid paper ('82)	80.00	*13.00*
33	A25	5c violet ('83)	19.00	15.00
a.		5c blue violet ('83)	19.00	15.00
34	A26	10c vio, laid paper ('82)	375.00	125.00
35	A26	10c scar ('83)	5.00	4.25
a.		Tete beche pair	225.00	225.00
36	A27	20c brown ('83)	9.00	8.00
a.		Laid paper ('82)	12.00	11.00

A28 A29

Liberty — A30

1883-85

37	A28	5c brown	10.50	7.00
a.		Laid paper	450.00	175.00
38	A28	5c green ('85)	275.00	90.00
a.		Laid paper ('85)	325.00	150.00
39	A28	5c yel, laid paper ('85)	11.00	9.00
40	A29	10c bl grn, laid paper	11.00	9.50
41	A29	10c bl, *bl* ('85)	11.00	9.00
42	A29	10c lil, laid paper ('85)	24.00	15.00
a.		Wove paper ('85)	3,360.	1,680.
43	A30	20c bl, laid paper ('85)	9.00	8.00

Coat of Arms — A31

1886 Wove Paper

55	A31	1c grn, *pink*	1.25	1.10
56	A31	2½c blk, *orange*	1.25	1.10
57	A31	5c ultra, *buff*	5.00	4.00
a.		5c blue, *buff*	7.50	6.50
58	A31	10c rose, *buff*	3.50	3.25
a.		Transfer of 50c in stone of 10c	275.00	275.00
59	A31	20c dk vio, *buff*	3.50	3.25
61	A31	50c yel brn, *buff*	6.50	5.50
62	A31	1p yel, *grn*	10.50	9.00
63	A31	2p green, *vio*	10.50	9.00
		Nos. 55-63 (8)	42.00	36.20

1887-88

64	A31	1c red, *vio*	1.00	.90
65	A31	2½c lil, *pale lil*	1.00	1.00
66	A31	5c car, *buff*	1.25	1.25
67	A31	5c red, *grn*	7.50	3.50
68	A31	10c brn, *grn*	1.50	*2.00*
		Nos. 64-68 (5)	12.25	8.65

Medellin Issue

A32 A33

A34

1888 Typeset

69	A32	2½c blk, *yellow*	32.50	29.00
70	A33	5c blk, *yellow*	17.50	15.00
71	A34	5c red, *yellow*	10.50	9.00
		Nos. 69-71 (3)	60.50	53.00

Two varieties of No. 69, six of No. 70 and ten of No. 71.

A35

1889

72	A35	2½c red	16.00	13.00

Ten varieties including "eentavos."

Regular Issue

Coat of Arms — A36

1889 Litho. *Perf. 13½*

No.	Type	Description	Unused	Used
73	A36	1c blk, *rose*	.50	.50
74	A36	2½c blk, *blue*	.50	.50
75	A36	5c blk, *yellow*	.60	.60
76	A36	10c blk, *green*	.60	.60
		Nos. 73-76 (4)	2.20	2.20

A37

A38

A39

A40

Coat of Arms — A41

1890

No.	Type	Description	Unused	Used
78	A37	20c blue	2.75	2.75
79	A38	50c vio brn	5.00	5.00
a.		Transfer of 20c in stone of 50c	200.00	200.00
80	A38	50c green	4.50	4.50
81	A39	1p red	4.00	4.00
82	A40	2p blk, *mag*	29.00	29.00
83	A41	5p blk, *org red*	45.00	45.00
		Nos. 78-83 (6)	90.25	90.25

Nos. 73-76, 82-83 exist imperf.

The so-called "errors" of Nos. 73 to 76, printed on paper of wrong colors, are essays or, possibly, reprints. They exist perforated and imperforate.

See No. 96.

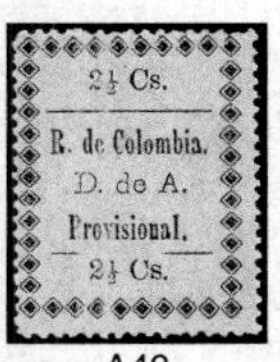
A42

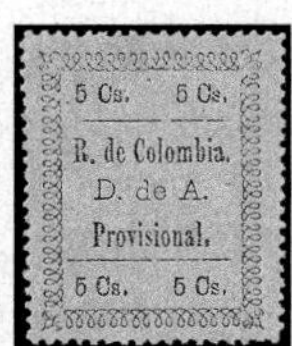
A43

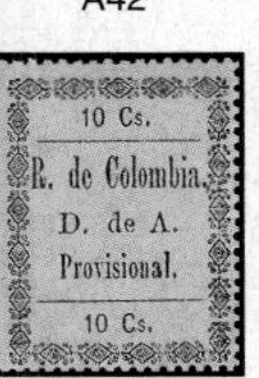
A44

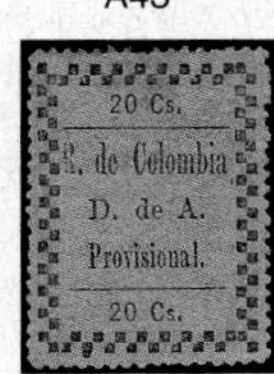
A45

1890 Typeset *Perf. 14*

No.	Type	Description	Unused	Used
84	A42	2½c blk, *buff*	4.50	4.50
85	A43	5c blk, *orange*	4.50	4.50
86	A44	10c blk, *buff*	14.00	14.00
87	A44	10c blk, *rose*	18.00	18.00
88	A45	20c blk, *orange*	18.00	18.00
		Nos. 84-88 (5)	59.00	59.00

20 varieties of the 5c, 10 each of the other values.

A46

1892 Litho. *Perf. 13½*

No.	Type	Description	Unused	Used
89	A46	1c brn, *brnsh*	.80	.80
90	A46	2½c pur, *lil*	.80	.80
92	A46	5c blk, *gray*	4.50	2.25
a.		Transfer of 2½c in stone of 5c	400.00	
		Nos. 89-92 (3)	6.10	3.85

1893

No.	Type	Description	Unused	Used
93	A46	1c blue	.50	.50
94	A46	2½c green	.80	.80
95	A46	5c vermilion	.50	.50
96	A36	10c pale brown	.50	.50
		Nos. 93-96 (4)	2.30	2.30

A47

1896 *Perf. 14*

No.	Type	Description	Unused	Used
97	A47	2c gray	.50	.50
98	A47	2c lilac rose	.50	.50
99	A47	2½c brown	.50	.50
100	A47	2½c steel blue	.50	.50
101	A47	3c orange	.50	.50
102	A47	3c olive grn	.50	.50
103	A47	5c green	.50	.50
104	A47	5c yellow buff	.60	.60
105	A47	10c brown vio	1.10	1.10
106	A47	10c violet	1.10	1.10
107	A47	20c brown org	2.75	2.75
108	A47	20c blue	2.75	2.75
109	A47	50c gray brn	2.75	2.75
110	A47	50c rose	2.75	2.75
111	A47	1p blue & blk	35.00	35.00
112	A47	1p rose red & blk	35.00	35.00
113	A47	2p orange & blk	110.00	110.00
114	A47	2p dk grn & blk	110.00	110.00
115	A47	5p red vio & blk	200.00	200.00
116	A47	5p purple & blk	200.00	200.00
		Nos. 97-116 (20)	707.30	707.30

#115-116 with centers omitted are proofs.

General José María Córdoba — A48

1899 *Perf. 11*

No.	Type	Description	Unused	Used
117	A48	½c grnsh bl	.50	.50
118	A48	1c slate blue	.50	.50
119	A48	2c slate brown	.50	.50
120	A48	3c red	.50	.50
121	A48	4c bister brown	.50	.50
122	A48	5c green	.50	.50
123	A48	10c scarlet	.50	.50
124	A48	20c gray violet	.50	.50
125	A48	50c olive bister	.50	.50
126	A48	1p greenish blk	.50	.50
127	A48	2p olive gray	.50	.50
		Nos. 117-127 (11)	5.50	5.50

Numerous part-perf. and imperf. varieties of Nos. 117-127 exist.

Used values for Nos. 117-127 are for favor-canceled stamps with oval cancels in violet. Postally used examples are valued at $3.50 each.

A49

A50

A50a

1901 Typeset *Perf. 12*

No.	Type	Description	Unused	Used
128	A49	1c red	.50	.50
129	A50	1c ultra	1.25	1.25
130	A50	1c bister	1.25	1.25
130A	A50a	1c dull red	1.25	1.25
130B	A50a	1c ultra	9.00	9.00
		Nos. 128-130B (5)	13.25	13.25

Eight varieties of No. 128, four varieties of Nos. 129-130B.

A51

A52

Atanasio Girardot
A53

Dr. José Félix Restrepo
A54

1902 Litho. Wove Paper

No.	Type	Description	Unused	Used
131	A51	1c brt rose	.50	.50
a.		Laid paper	1.25	1.25
b.		Imperf., pair	5.50	
132	A51	2c blue	.50	.50
a.		Transfer of 3c in stone of 2c	12.00	12.00
133	A51	3c green	.50	.50
a.		Imperf., pair	10.00	
134	A51	4c dull violet	.50	.50
135	A52	5c rose red	.50	.50
136	A53	10c rose lilac	.50	.50
a.		Small head	11.00	11.00
b.		10c rose	.50	.50
137	A53	20c gray green	.50	.50
138	A53	30c brt rose	.50	.50
139	A53	40c blue	.50	.50
140	A53	50c brn, *yel*	.50	.50

Laid Paper

No.	Type	Description	Unused	Used
141	A54	1p purple & blk	1.60	1.60
142	A54	2p rose & blk	1.60	1.60
143	A54	5p sl bl & blk	3.00	3.00
		Nos. 131-143 (13)	11.20	11.20

1903 Wove Paper

No.	Type	Description	Unused	Used
143A	A51	1c blue	.50	.50
144	A51	2c violet	.50	.50
a.		Imperf.	6.00	

A55

A56

A57

Designs: 1p, Francisco Antonio Zea. 2p, Custodio Garcia Rovira. 3p, La Pola (Policarpa Salavarrieta). 4p, J. M. Restrepo. 5p, José Fernández Madrid. 10p, Juan del Corral.

1903-04

No.	Type	Description	Unused	Used
145	A55	4c yellow brn	.70	.60
146	A55	5c blue	.70	.60
147	A56	10c yellow	.70	.60
148	A56	20c purple	.70	.60
149	A56	30c brown	1.75	1.75
150	A56	40c green	1.75	1.75
151	A56	50c rose	.70	.60
152	A57	1p olive gray	1.75	1.75
153	A57	2p purple	1.75	1.75
154	A57	3p dark blue	1.75	1.75
155	A57	4p dull red	3.00	3.00
156	A57	5p red brown	9.00	4.25
157	A57	10p scarlet	19.00	11.00
		Nos. 145-157 (13)	43.25	30.00

Nos. 145-146, 151, 153-157 exist imperf. Value of pairs, $8 to $10.

Manizales Issue

Stamps of these designs are local private post issues.

OFFICIAL STAMPS Stamps of 1903-04 with overprint "OFICIAL" were never issued.

REGISTRATION STAMPS

R1

1896 Unwmk. Litho. *Perf. 14*

No.	Type	Description	Unused	Used
F1	R1	2½c rose	2.50	2.50
F2	R1	2½c dull blue	2.50	2.50

Córdoba
R2

R3

1899 *Perf. 11*

No.	Type	Description	Unused	Used
F3	R2	2½c dull blue	.50	.50
F4	R3	10c red lilac	.50	.50

R4

1902 *Perf. 12*

No.	Type	Description	Unused	Used
F5	R4	10c purple, *blue*	.60	.60
a.		Imperf.	—	

ACKNOWLEDGMENT OF RECEIPT STAMPS

AR1

1902-03 Unwmk. Litho. *Perf. 12*

No.	Type	Description	Unused	Used
H1	AR1	5c black, *rose*	2.25	2.25
H2	AR1	5c slate ('03)	.75	.75

LATE FEE STAMPS

Córdoba — LF1

1899 Unwmk. Litho. *Perf. 11*

No.	Type	Description	Unused	Used
I1	LF1	2½c dark green	.70	.70
a.		Imperf., pair	6.00	

LF2

1901 **Typeset** ***Perf. 12***
I2 LF2 2½c red violet 2.00 2.00
a. 2½c purple 2.00 2.00

LF3

1902 **Litho.**
I3 LF3 2½c violet .50 .50

City of Medellin

Stamps of the designs shown were not issued by any governmental agency but by the Sociedad de Mejoras Publicas.

BOLIVAR

bə-ˈlē-ˌvär

Originally a State, now a Department of the Republic of Colombia. (See Antioquia.)

A1

1863-66 **Unwmk.** **Litho.** ***Imperf.***
1 A1 10c green *1,200. 600.00*
a. Five stars below shield *2,500. 2,400.*
2 A1 10c red ('66) 55.00 *60.00*
a. Diagonal half used as 5c on cover 240.00
b. Five stars below shield 175.00 145.00
3 A1 1p red 13.50 *15.50*

Fourteen varieties of each. Counterfeits of Nos. 1 and 1a exist.

Coat of Arms
A2 A3

A4

A5

1873
4 A2 5c blue 14.50 14.50
5 A3 10c violet 14.50 14.50
6 A4 20c yellow green 65.00 65.00
7 A5 80c vermilion 130.00 130.00
Nos. 4-7 (4) 224.00 224.00

A6

A7

A8

1874-78
8 A6 5c blue 55.00 28.00
9 A7 5c blue ('78) 16.00 14.50
10 A8 10c violet ('77) 8.00 7.50
Nos. 8-10 (3) 79.00 50.00

Bolívar — A9

Dated "1879"

1879 **White Wove Paper** ***Perf. 12½***
11 A9 5c blue .60 .60
a. Imperf., pair 4.00
12 A9 10c violet .50 .50
13 A9 20c red .60 .60
a. 20c green (error) 22.50 22.50

Bluish Laid Paper

15 A9 5c blue .60 .60
a. Imperf., pair 10.00
16 A9 10c violet 3.25 3.25
a. Imperf., pair 17.50
17 A9 20c red .80 .80
a. Imperf., pair 8.00
Nos. 11-17 (6) 6.35 6.35

Stamps of 80c and 1p on white wove paper and 1p on bluish laid paper were prepared but not placed in use.

Dated "1880"

1880 **White Wove Paper** ***Perf. 12½***
19 A9 5c blue .60 .60
a. Imperf., pair 4.00
20 A9 10c violet .80 .80
a. Imperf., pair 4.00
21 A9 20c red .80 .80
a. 20c green (error) 28.00 28.00
23 A9 80c green 5.00 5.00
24 A9 1p orange 5.50 5.50
a. Imperf., pair 22.00
Nos. 19-24 (5) 12.70 12.70

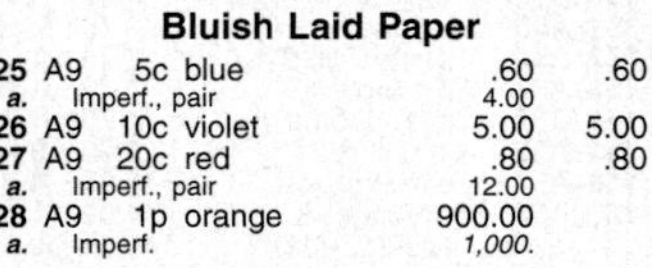

Bluish Laid Paper

25 A9 5c blue .60 .60
a. Imperf., pair 4.00
26 A9 10c violet 5.00 5.00
27 A9 20c red .80 .80
a. Imperf., pair 12.00
28 A9 1p orange 900.00
a. Imperf. *1,000.*

A11

A12

A13

A15

A16

Dated "1882"
White Wove Paper

1882 ***Perf. 12, 16x12***
29 A11 5c blue .70 .70
30 A12 10c lilac .70 .70
31 A13 20c red .70 .70
33 A15 80c green 1.25 1.25
34 A16 1p orange 1.25 1.25
Nos. 29-34 (5) 4.60 4.60

Nos. 29, 30 and 34 are known imperforate. They are printer's waste and were not issued through post offices.

A17

1882 **Engr.** ***Perf. 12***
35 A17 5p blue & rose red 1.25 1.25
a. Imperf., pair 11.00
b. Perf. 16 16.00 13.50
c. Perf. 14 13.50 13.50
36 A17 10p brown & blue 3.50 3.50
a. Imperf., pair 18.00
b. Perf. 16 14.50 12.00
c. Rouletted 17.00 17.00

Dated "1883"

1883 **Litho.** ***Perf. 12, 16x12***
37 A11 5c blue .50 .50
a. Imperf., pair 2.00
b. Perf. 12 25.00 5.00
38 A12 10c lilac .60 .60
39 A13 20c red .60 .60
41 A15 80c green .60 .60
42 A16 1p orange 3.25 3.25
a. Perf. 16x12 5.00 5.00
Nos. 37-42 (5) 5.55 5.55

1884 **Dated "1884"**
43 A11 5c blue .75 .75
a. Perf. 12 32.50 32.50
44 A12 10c lilac .60 .60
45 A13 20c red .60 .60
a. Perf. 12 16.00 16.00
47 A15 80c green .75 .75
a. Perf. 12 8.00 8.00
48 A16 1p orange .60 .60
Nos. 43-48 (5) 3.30 3.30

1885 **Dated "1885"**
49 A11 5c blue .50 .50
50 A12 10c lilac .50 .50
51 A13 20c red .50 .50
53 A15 80c green .50 .50
54 A16 1p orange .60 .60
Nos. 49-54 (5) 2.60 2.60

The note after No. 34 will also apply to imperforate stamps of the 1884-85 issues.

A18

1891 ***Perf. 14***
55 A18 1c black .60 .60
56 A18 5c orange .60 .60
a. Imperf., pair 1.75
57 A18 10c carmine .60 .60
58 A18 20c blue 1.25 1.25
59 A18 50c green 2.00 2.00
60 A18 1p purple 2.00 2.00
Nos. 55-60 (6) 7.05 7.05

For overprint see Colombia No. 169.

Bolívar
A19

José Fernández Madrid
A20

Manuel Rodriguez Torices
A21

José María García de Toledo
A22

1903 **Laid Paper** ***Imperf.***
62 A19 50c dk bl, *pink* 1.25 1.25
a. Bluish paper 1.25 1.25
63 A19 50c sl grn, *pink* 1.25 1.25
a. Rose paper 4.50 4.50
b. Greenish blue paper 6.50 6.50
c. Yellow paper 9.00 9.00
d. Brown paper 9.00 9.00
e. Salmon paper 16.00 16.00
64 A19 50c pur, *pink* 4.50 4.50
a. White paper 9.00 9.00
b. Brown paper 9.00 9.00
c. Greenish blue paper 9.00 9.00
d. Lilac paper 9.00 9.00
e. Rose paper 8.00 8.00
f. Yellow paper 9.00 9.00
g. Salmon paper 13.00 13.00
h. As "a," wove paper 20.00 20.00
65 A20 1p org, *sal* 1.25 1.25
a. Yellow paper 10.00 10.00
b. Greenish blue paper 32.50 32.50
66 A20 1p gray grn, *lil* 3.25 3.25
a. Yellow paper 14.00 14.00
b. Salmon paper 16.00 16.00
c. Green paper 16.00 16.00
d. White wove paper 24.00
67 A21 5p car rose, *lil* 1.25 1.25
a. Brown paper 2.50 2.50
b. Yellow paper 2.50 2.50
c. Greenish blue paper 10.00 10.00
d. Bluish paper 12.50 12.50
e. Salmon paper 16.00 16.00
f. Rose paper 20.00 20.00
68 A22 10p dk bl, *bluish* 2.75 2.75
a. Greenish blue paper 2.75 2.75
b. Rose paper 16.00 16.00
c. Salmon paper 16.00 16.00
d. Yellow paper 16.00 16.00
e. Brown paper 18.00 18.00
f. Lilac paper 24.00 24.00
g. White paper 20.00 20.00
69 A22 10p pur, *grnsh bl* 7.50 7.50
a. Bluish paper 16.00 16.00
b. Rose paper 15.00 15.00
c. Yellow paper 16.00 16.00
d. Brown paper 16.00 16.00
Nos. 62-69 (8) 23.00 23.00

Sewing Machine Perf.
Laid Paper

70 A19 50c dk bl, *pink* 2.25 2.25
a. Bluish paper 2.25 2.25
71 A19 50c sl grn, *pink* 4.50 4.50
72 A19 50c pur, *grnsh bl* 9.00 9.00
a. White paper 9.00 9.00
b. White wove paper 16.00
73 A20 1p org, *sal* 4.50 4.50
74 A20 1p gray grn, *lil* 20.00 20.00
a. Yellow paper 20.00 20.00
75 A21 5p car rose, *yel* 3.50 3.50
a. Lilac paper 9.00 9.00
b. Brown paper 9.00 9.00
c. Bluish paper 12.00 12.00
d. White wove paper 20.00
76 A22 10p dk bl, *grnsh bl* 10.00 10.00
a. Bluish paper 14.00 14.00
b. Yellow paper 20.00 20.00
c. As "b," wove paper 24.00
77 A22 10p pur, *grnsh bl* 15.00 15.00
a. Bluish paper 26.00 26.00
b. Rose paper 17.00 17.00
c. Yellow paper 26.00 26.00
Nos. 70-77 (8) 68.75 68.75

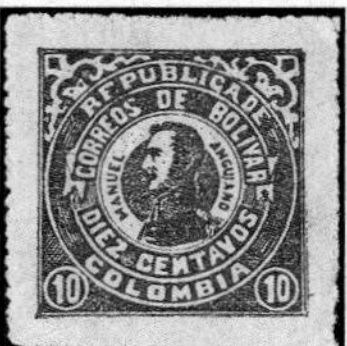

José María del Castillo y Rada — A23

Manuel Anguiano — A24

Pantaleón C. Ribón — A25

1904 ***Sewing Machine Perf.***

89 A23 5c black .50 .50
90 A24 10c brown .50 .50
91 A25 20c red .60 .60
92 A25 20c red brown 1.25 1.25
Nos. 89-92 (4) 2.85 2.85

Imperf., pairs

89a A23 5c black 8.00 8.00
90a A24 10c brown 6.00 6.00
91a A25 20c red 15.00 15.00
92a A25 20c red brown 15.00 15.00

A26

A27

A28

1904 ***Imperf.***

93 A26 ½c black 1.25 1.25
a. Tête bêche pair 7.50 7.50
94 A27 1c blue 2.50 2.50
95 A28 2c purple 2.75 2.75
Nos. 93-95 (3) 6.50 6.50

REGISTRATION STAMPS

Simón Bolívar — R1

White Wove Paper

Perf. 12½, 16x12

1879 **Unwmk.** **Litho.**

F1 R1 40c brown 1.50 1.50

Bluish Laid Paper

F2 R1 40c brown 1.50 1.50
a. Imperf., pair 7.00

Dated "1880"

1880 **White Wove Paper**

F3 R1 40c brown .70 .70

Bluish Laid Paper

F4 R1 40c brown 1.50 1.50
a. Imperf., pair 7.00

Simón Bolívar — R2

Dated "1882" to "1885"
White Wove Paper

1882-85 ***Perf. 16x12***

F5 R2 40c brown .70 .70
F6 R2 40c brown .60 .60
F7 R2 40c brown .60 .60
F8 R2 40c brown .60 .60
Nos. F5-F8 (4) 2.50 2.50

Perf. 12

F5a R2 40c 40.00
F6a R2 40c 32.50
F7a R2 40c 32.50
F8a R2 40c 32.50
Nos. F5a-F8a (4) 137.50

R3

1903 **Laid Paper** ***Imperf.***

F9 R3 20c orange, *rose* 1.25 1.25
a. Salmon paper 2.50 2.50
b. Greenish blue paper 13.00 13.00

Sewing Machine Perf.

F10 R3 20c orange, *rose* 5.50 5.50
a. Salmon paper 5.50 5.50
b. Greenish blue paper 13.00 13.00

R4

1904 **Wove Paper**

F11 R4 5c black 6.50 6.50

ACKNOWLEDGMENT OF RECEIPT STAMPS

AR1

1903 **Unwmk.** **Litho.** ***Imperf.***

Laid Paper

H1 AR1 20c org, *rose* 5.50 5.50
a. Yellow paper 2.75 2.75
b. Greenish blue paper 11.00 11.00
H2 AR1 20c dk bl, *yel* 4.50 4.50
a. Brown paper 7.50 7.50
b. Rose paper 5.50 5.50
c. Salmon paper 15.00 15.00
d. Greenish blue paper 15.00 15.00

Sewing Machine Perf.

H3 AR1 20c org, *grnsh bl* 13.50 13.50
a. Yellow paper 15.00 15.00
H4 AR1 20c dk bl, *yel* 15.00 15.00
a. Lilac paper 15.00 15.00
Nos. H1-H4 (4) 38.50 38.50

AR2

1904 **Wove Paper**

H5 AR2 2c red 2.50 2.50

LATE FEE STAMPS

LF1

1903 **Unwmk.** **Litho.** ***Imperf.***

Laid Paper

I1 LF1 20c car rose, *bluish* 1.25 1.25
I2 LF1 20c pur, *bluish* 1.25 1.25
a. Rose paper 4.50 4.50
b. Brown paper 4.50 4.50
c. Lilac paper 4.50 4.50
d. Yellow paper 14.00 14.00

Sewing Machine Perf.

I3 LF1 20c car rose, *bluish* 7.50 7.50
I4 LF1 20c pur, *bluish* 7.50 7.50
a. Rose paper 13.00 13.00
b. Lilac paper 13.00 13.00
c. Yellow paper 24.00 24.00
Nos. I1-I4 (4) 17.50 17.50

BOYACA

bō-yä-cä

Originally a State, now a Department of the Republic of Colombia. (See Antioquia.)

Diego Mendoza Pérez — A1

1902 **Unwmk.** **Litho.** ***Perf. 13½***

Wove Paper

1 A1 5c blue green 1.60 1.60
a. Bluish paper 190.00 190.00
b. Imperf., pair 32.50 32.50

Laid Paper

Perf. 12

2 A1 5c green 225.00 225.00

Coat of Arms

A2 A3

Gen. Próspero Pinzón — A4

A5

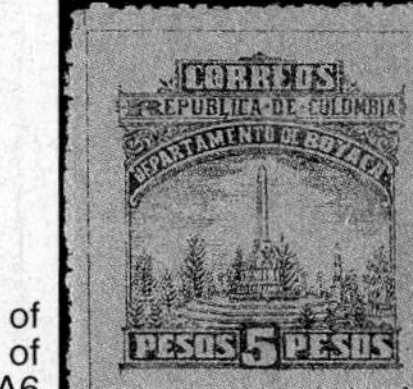

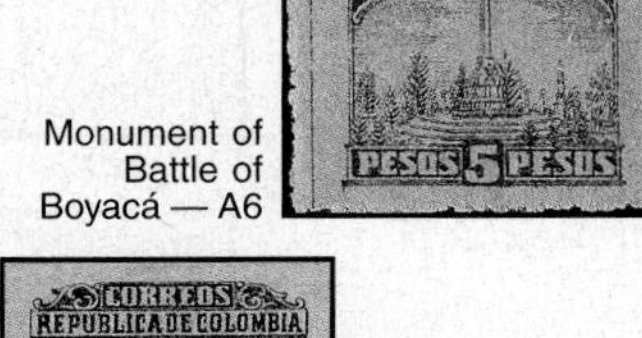

Monument of Battle of Boyacá — A6

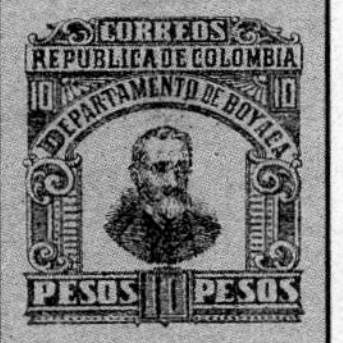

President José Manuel Marroquin — A7

1903 **Litho.** ***Imperf.***

4 A2 10c dark gray .60 .60
5 A3 20c red brown .70 .70
6 A5 1p red 6.50 6.50
a. 1p claret 7.50 7.50
8 A6 5p black, *rose* 2.50 2.50
a. 5p black, *buff* 24.00 24.00
9 A7 10p black, *buff* 2.50 2.50
a. 10p black, *rose* 24.00 24.00
b. As "a,"tête bêche pair 50.00
Nos. 4-9 (5) 12.80 12.80

Perf. 12

10 A2 10c dark gray .70 .70
11 A3 20c red brown .80 .80
12 A4 50c green .70 .70
13 A4 50c dull blue 5.00 5.00
14 A5 1p red .70 .70
a. 1p claret 6.00 6.00
16 A6 5p black, *rose* 22.00 22.00
a. 5p black, *buff* 19.00 19.00
17 A7 10p black, *buff* 2.25 2.25
a. 10p black, *rose* 22.00 22.00
b. Tête bêche pair 24.00 24.00
Nos. 10-17 (7) 32.15 32.15

Statue of Bolívar — A8

1904

18 A8 10c orange .50 .50
a. Imperf., pair 7.50 7.50

CAUCA

Stamps of these designs were issued by a provincial post between 1879(?) and 1890.

Stamps of this design are believed to be of private origin and without official sanction.

Items inscribed "No hay estampillas" (No stamps available) and others inscribed "Manuel E. Jiménez" are considered by specialists to be receipt labels, not postage stamps.

CUNDINAMARCA

kün-di-nə-'mär-kə

Originally a State, now a Department of the Republic of Colombia.
(See Antioquia.)

Coat of Arms
A1 A2

1870 **Unwmk.** **Litho.** ***Imperf.***

1 A1 5c blue 10.50 10.50
2 A2 10c red 32.50 32.50

The counterfeits, or reprints, show traces of the cuts made to deface the dies.

A3

A4

A5

A6

1877-82

3 A3 10c red ('82) 7.00 7.00
a. Laid paper ('77) 8.00 8.00
4 A4 20c green ('82) 15.00 15.00
a. Laid paper ('77) 24.00 24.00
7 A5 50c purple ('82) 16.00 16.00
8 A6 1p brown ('82) 24.00 24.00
Nos. 3-8 (4) 62.00 62.00

A7

Redrawn

1884

10 A7 5c blue 1.60 1.60
11 A7 5c blue (redrawn) 1.60 1.60
a. Tête bêche pair 160.00 160.00

The redrawn stamp has no period after "COLOMBIA."

A8

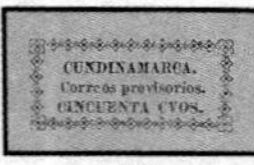
A9

A10

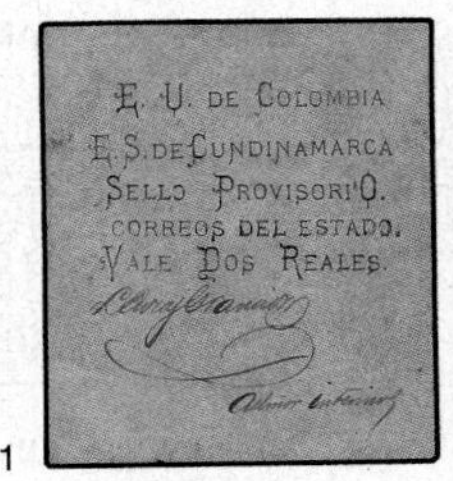
A11

1883 **Typeset**

13 A8 10c black, *yellow* 30.00 30.00
14 A9 50c black, *rose* 30.00 30.00
15 A10 1p black, *brown* 75.00 75.00
16 A11 2r black, *green* *2,200.*

Typeset varieties exist: 4 of the 10c, 2 each of 50c and 1p.

Some experts doubt that No. 16 was issued. The variety without signature and watermarked "flowers" is believed to be a proof. Forgeries exist.

A12

1886 **Litho.**

17 A12 5c blue 1.60 1.60
18 A12 10c red 10.00 10.00
19 A12 10c red, *lilac* 5.50 5.50
20 A12 20c green 8.50 8.50
a. 20c yellow green 10.00 10.00
21 A12 50c purple 11.00 11.00
22 A12 1p orange brown 11.50 11.50
Nos. 17-22 (6) 48.10 48.10

Nos. 17 to 22 have been reprinted. The colors are aniline and differ from those of the original stamps. The impression is coarse and blurred.

A13

A14

A15

A16

A17

A18

A19

A20

A21

1904 ***Perf. 10½, 12***

23 A13 1c orange .50 .50
24 A14 2c gray blue .50 .50
25 A15 3c rose .70 .70
26 A15 5c olive grn .70 .70
27 A16 10c pale brn .70 .70
28 A17 15c pink .70 .70
29 A18 20c blue, *grn* .70 .70
30 A18 20c blue 1.25 1.25
31 A19 40c blue 1.25 1.25
32 A19 40c blue, *buff* 42.50 42.50
33 A20 50c red vio 1.25 1.25
34 A21 1p gray grn 1.25 1.25
Nos. 23-34 (12) 52.00 52.00

Imperf

23a A13 1c orange 1.50 1.50
24a A14 2c blue 1.50 1.50
b. 2c slate 13.00 13.00
25a A15 3c rose 1.75 1.75
26a A15 5c olive green 3.25 3.25
27a A16 10c pale brown 4.00 4.00
28a A17 15c pink 1.00 1.00
29a A18 20c blue, *green* 4.00 4.00
30a A18 20c blue 4.00 4.00
31a A19 40c blue 1.25 1.25
32a A19 40c blue, *buff* 42.50 42.50
33a A20 50c red violet 1.40 1.40
34a A21 1p gray green 1.40 1.40
Nos. 23a-34a (12) 67.55 67.55

REGISTRATION STAMPS

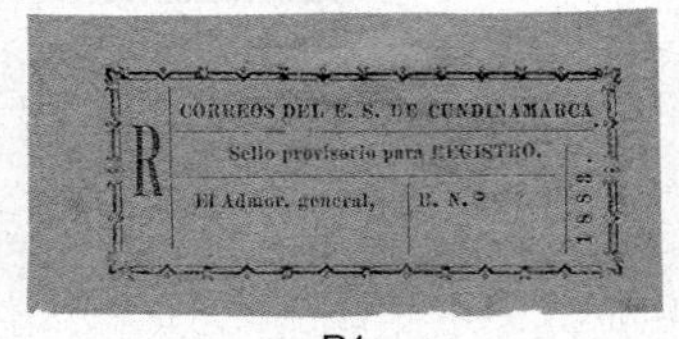
R1

1883 **Unwmk.** ***Imperf.***

F1 R1 black, *orange* 35.00 35.00

R2

1904 ***Perf. 12***

F2 R2 10c bister 1.75 1.75
a. Imperf. 7.50 7.50

INSURED LETTER STAMP

IL1

1883 ***Imperf.***

Thin Paper with Vertical Mesh

G1 IL1 20c blk, *emerald grn* 160.00 240.00

Magdalena

Items inscribed "No hay estampillas" (No stamps available) are considered by specialists to be not postage stamps but receipt labels.

Panama

Issues of Panama as a state and later Department of Colombia are listed with the Republic of Panama issues (Nos. 1-30).

SANTANDER

săn-ˌtän-'deˌəˌr

Originally a State, now a Department of the Republic of Colombia.
(See Antioquia.)

Coat of Arms
A1 A2

1884 **Unwmk.** **Litho.** ***Imperf.***

1 A1 1c blue .60 .60
a. 1c gray blue 1.00 1.00
2 A2 5c red 1.00 1.00
3 A2 10c bluish purple 3.75 3.75
a. Tête bêche pair —
Nos. 1-3 (3) 5.35 5.35

No. 2 exists unofficially perforated 14.

A3

1886 ***Imperf.***

4 A3 1c blue 1.75 1.75
5 A3 5c red .60 .60
6 A3 10c red violet 1.00 1.00
a. 10c deep violet 1.00 1.00
b. Inscribed "CINCO CENTAVOS" 52.50 52.50
Nos. 4-6 (3) 3.35 3.35

The numerals in the upper corners are omitted on No. 5, while on No. 6 there are no numerals in the side panels. No. 6 exists unofficially perforated 12.

A4

1887

7 A4 1c blue .50 .50
a. 1c ultramarine 3.50 3.50
8 A4 5c red 3.50 3.50
9 A4 10c violet 11.00 11.00
Nos. 7-9 (3) 15.00 15.00

A5

A6

A7

1889 ***Perf. 11½ and 13½***

10 A5 1c blue .70 .70
11 A6 5c red 2.50 2.50
12 A7 10c purple .90 .90
a. Imperf., pair 40.00 *40.00*
Nos. 10-12 (3) 4.10 4.10

A8

1892 ***Perf. 13½***

13 A8 5c red, *rose buff* 2.00 2.00

A9

1895-96

14	A9	5c brown	1.40	1.40
15	A9	5c yel grn ('96)	1.40	1.40

A10

A11

A12

1899 ***Perf. 10***

16	A10	1c black, *green*	.70	.70
17	A11	5c black, *pink*	.75	.75

Perf. 13½

18	A12	10c blue	1.50	1.50
a.		Perf. 12	2.00	2.00
		Nos. 16-18 (3)	2.95	2.95

A13

1903 ***Imperf.***

19	A13	50c red	1.20	1.20
a.		50c rose	1.20	1.20
b.		"SANTENDER"	5.00	5.00
c.		"Corrcos"	5.00	5.00
d.		"Corceos"	5.00	5.00
e.		Tête bêche pair	10.00	10.00
f.		Pair, one without overprint	5.50	5.50

The overprint "Correos de Departmento Bucaramanga" on the 50c red revenue stamp has been proved to be a cancellation.

A14

A15

Arms
A16

Locomotive
A17

A18

A19

A20

1904 ***Imperf.***

22	A14	5c dark green	.50	.50
a.		5c yellow green	.80	.80
24	A15	10c rose	.25	.25
25	A16	20c brown violet	.50	.50
26	A17	50c yellow	.70	.70
27	A18	1p black	.50	.50
28	A19	5p dark blue	.70	.70
29	A20	10p carmine	.80	.80
		Nos. 22-29 (7)	3.95	3.95

1905

30	A14	5c pale blue	1.20	1.20
31	A15	10c red brown	1.20	1.20
32	A16	20c yellow green	1.20	1.20
33	A17	50c red violet	1.20	1.20
34	A18	1p dark blue	2.25	2.25
35	A19	5p pink	1.20	1.20
36	A20	10p red	3.25	3.25
		Nos. 30-36 (7)	11.50	11.50

A21

1907 ***Imperf.***

37	A21	½c on 50c rose	1.60	*3.25*

City of Cucuta

Stamps of these and similar designs on white and yellow paper, with and without surcharges of ½c, 1c or 2c, are believed to have been produced without government authorization.

TOLIMA

tə-lē-mə

Originally a State, now a Department of the Republic of Colombia. (See Antioquia.)

A1

1870 Unwmk. Typeset *Imperf.*

White Wove Paper

1	A1	5c black	125.00	125.00
2	A1	10c black	150.00	150.00
a.		Vert. se-tenant pair	*1,500.*	*1,500.*

Printed from two settings. Setting I, ten types of 5c. Setting II, six types of 5c and four types of 10c. No. 2a is contained in a unique strip of 3.

Blue Laid Batonné Paper

3	A1	5c black	*950.00*	

Buff Laid Batonné Paper

4	A1	5c black	300.00	200.00

Blue Wove Paper

5	A1	5c black	140.00	90.00

Blue Vertically Laid Paper

6	A1	5c black	225.00	140.00
a.		Paper with ruled blue vertical lines		

Blue Horizontally Laid Paper

7	A1	5c black	200.00	150.00

Blue Quadrille Paper

8	A1	5c black	300.00	160.00

Ten varieties each of Nos. 3-5 and 7; 20 varieties each of Nos. 6 and 8.

Official imitations were made in 1886 from new settings of the type. There are only 2 varieties of each value. They are printed on blue and white paper, wove, batonné, laid, etc.

A2

A3

A4

A5

Yellowish White Wove Paper

1871 Litho. *Imperf.*

9	A2	5c deep brown	4.50	4.50
a.		5c red brown	4.50	4.50
b.		Value reads "CINGO"	80.00	80.00
10	A3	10c blue	12.50	12.50
11	A4	50c green	16.00	16.00
12	A5	1p carmine	26.00	26.00
		Nos. 9-12 (4)	59.00	59.00

The 5p stamps, type A2, are bogus varieties made from an altered die of the 5c.

The 10c, 50c and 1 peso stamps have been reprinted on bluish white wove paper. They are from new plates and most copies show traces of fine lines with which the dies had been defaced. Reprints of the 5c have a large cross at the top. The 10c on laid batonné paper is known only as a reprint.

A6

A7

A8

A9

1879

Grayish or White Wove Paper

14	A6	5c yellow brown	.90	.90
a.		5c purple brown	.90	.90
15	A7	10c blue	1.00	1.00
16	A8	50c green, *bluish*	1.00	1.00
a.		White paper	3.25	3.25
17	A9	1p vermilion	4.50	4.50
a.		1p carmine rose	18.00	18.00
		Nos. 14-17 (4)	7.40	7.40

A10

1883 ***Imperf.***

18	A6	5c orange	.90	.90
19	A7	10c vermilion	1.90	1.90
20	A10	20c violet	3.00	3.00
		Nos. 18-20 (3)	5.80	5.80

Coat of Arms — A12

1884 ***Imperf.***

23	A12	1c gray	.50	.50
24	A12	2c rose lilac	.50	.50
a.		2c slate	.50	.50
25	A12	2½c dull orange	.50	.50
26	A12	5c brown	.50	.50
27	A12	10c blue	.70	.70
a.		10c slate	.50	.50
28	A12	20c lemon	.70	.70
a.		Laid paper	10.00	10.00
29	A12	25c black	.60	.60
30	A12	50c green	.60	.60
31	A12	1p vermilion	.80	.80
32	A12	2p violet	1.20	1.20
a.		Value omitted	60.00	60.00
33	A12	5p yellow	.80	.80
34	A12	10p lilac rose	2.25	2.25
a.		Laid paper	60.00	60.00
b.		10p gray	*350.00*	
		Nos. 23-34 (12)	9.65	9.65

A13

A14

Condor with Long Wings Touching Flagstaffs
A15 A16

1886 Litho. *Perf. 10½, 11*

White Paper

36	A13	5c brown	2.75	2.75
a.		5c yellow brown	2.75	2.75
b.		Imperf., pair	35.00	
37	A14	10c blue	7.50	7.50
a.		Imperf., pair	35.00	
38	A15	50c green	6.50	6.50
a.		Imperf., pair	35.00	
39	A16	1p vermilion	5.50	5.50
a.		Imperf., pair	52.50	
		Nos. 36-39 (4)	22.25	22.25

No. 38 has been reprinted in pale gray green, perforated 10½, and No. 39 in bright vermilion, perforated 11½. The impressions show many signs of wear.

Lilac Tinted Paper

36c	A13	5c orange brown	25.00	25.00
37b	A14	10c blue	25.00	25.00
38b	A15	50c green	19.00	19.00
39b	A16	1p vermilion	17.00	17.00
		Nos. 36c-39b (4)	86.00	86.00

Items similar to A15 and A16 but with condor with long wings and upper flagstaffs omitted are forgeries.

A17

A18

Condor with Short Wings
A19 A20

1886 White Paper *Perf. 12*

44	A19	1c gray	12.50	12.50
45	A17	2c rose lilac	13.00	13.00
46	A18	2½c dull org	37.50	37.50
47	A19	5c brown	17.00	16.00
48	A20	10c blue	16.00	16.00
49	A20	20c lemon	13.00	13.00
a.		Tête bêche pair	550.00	550.00
50	A20	25c black	12.50	12.50
51	A20	50c green	7.50	7.50
52	A20	1p vermilion	10.00	8.50
53	A20	2p violet	14.50	14.50
b.		Tête bêche pair	375.00	375.00
54	A20	5p orange	26.00	26.00
55	A20	10p lilac rose	15.00	15.00
		Nos. 44-55 (12)	194.50	192.00

Imperf., Pairs

44a	A19	1c	35.00
47a	A19	5c	57.50
48a	A20	10c	57.50
52a	A20	1p	42.50
53a	A20	2p	52.50
54a	A20	5p	80.00
55a	A20	10p	35.00

A23

1888 ***Perf. 10½***

62	A23	5c red	.50	.50
63	A23	10c green	.60	.60
64	A23	50c blue	1.50	1.50
65	A23	1p red brown	3.75	3.75
		Nos. 62-65 (4)	6.35	6.35

For overprint see Colombia No. L14.

1895 ***Perf. 12, 13½***

66	A23	1c blue, *rose*	.50	.50
67	A23	2c grn, *lt grn*	.50	.50
68	A23	5c red	.50	.50
a.		Vert. pair, imperf. btwn.	25.00	
69	A23	10c green	1.00	1.00
70	A23	20c blue, *yellow*	.60	.60
71	A23	1p brown	4.50	4.50
		Nos. 66-71 (6)	7.60	7.60

Imperf., Pairs

62a	A23	5c	17.00	
63a	A23	10c	24.00	
64a	A23	50c	29.00	29.00
65a	A23	1p	42.50	
66a	A23	1c	42.50	
67a	A23	2c	42.50	
70a	A23	20c	47.50	

"No Hay Estampillas"

Items inscribed "No hay estampillas" (No stamps available) are considered by specialists to be not postage stamps but receipt labels.

"Honda Issue"

This item seems to be of private origin.

A24

A25

A26

A27

A28

A29

A30

A31

Sewing Machine or Regular Perf. 12

1903-04 **Litho.**

79	A24	4c black, *green*	.50	.50
80	A25	10c dull blue	.50	.50
81	A26	20c orange	1.00	1.00
82	A27	50c black, *rose*	1.00	1.00
a.		50c black, *buff*	1.00	1.00
84	A28	1p brown	1.00	1.00
85	A29	2p gray	.50	.50
86	A30	5p red	.50	.50
a.		Tête bêche pair	16.00	*24.00*
87	A31	10p black, *blue*	.50	.50
a.		10p black, *light green*	.50	.50
b.		10p black, *grn*, glazed	7.50	7.50
		Nos. 79-87 (8)	5.50	5.50

Imperf

79a	A24	4c black, *green*	.50	.50
80a	A25	10c dull blue	.50	.50
81a	A26	20c orange	2.50	2.50
82b	A27	50c black, *rose*	3.50	3.50
c.		50c black, *buff*	3.50	3.50
84a	A28	1p brown	.50	.50
85a	A29	2p gray	.50	.50
86b	A30	5p red	.50	.50
c.		Tête bêche pair	24.00	*32.50*
87c	A31	10p black, *blue*	5.00	5.00
d.		Tête bêche pair		
e.		10p black, *light green*	7.50	7.50
f.		10p black, *green*, glazed	37.50	37.50
		Nos. 79a-87c (8)	13.50	13.50

COMORO ISLANDS

'kä-mə-,rō 'ī-ləndz

LOCATION — In Mozambique Channel between Madagascar and Mozambique
GOVT. — Republic
AREA — 838 sq. mi.
POP. — 562,723 (1999 est.)
CAPITAL — Moroni

The Comoro Archipelago consists of the islands of Mayotte, Anjouan, Grand Comoro (Grande Comore) and Moheli, which issued their own stamps as French protectorates or colonies from 1887-1914. The archipelago was attached to Madagascar from 1914 to 1946, when it became a separate French territory. In July 1975, Anjouan, Grand Comoro and Moheli united to declare independence as the State of Comoro. Mayotte remained French.

100 Centimes = 1 Franc

Catalogue values for all unused stamps in this country are for Never Hinged items.

Anjouan Bay — A2

Comoro Woman Grinding Grain — A3

Moroni Mosque on Grand Comoro A4

1950 **Unwmk.** **Engr.** ***Perf. 13***

30	A2	10c blue	.30	.50
31	A2	50c green	.30	.50
32	A2	1fr dk ol brn	.40	.50
33	A3	2fr brt grn	.75	.50
34	A3	5fr purple	1.10	.75
35	A3	6fr vio brn	1.25	1.10
36	A4	7fr red	1.10	.75
37	A4	10fr dk grn	1.25	1.00
38	A4	11fr dp ultra	1.50	1.25
		Nos. 30-38 (9)	7.95	6.85

Imperforates

Most Comoro Islands stamps exist imperforate in issued and trial colors, and also in small presentation sheets in issued colors.

Common Design Types pictured following the introduction.

Military Medal Issue

Common Design Type

1952 **Engraved and Typographed**

39	CD101 15fr multi	45.00	37.50

Mosque of Ouani, Anjouan — A5

Coelacanth A6

1952-54 **Engr.**

40	A5	15fr dark brown	1.75	1.50
41	A5	20fr red brown	3.75	3.25
42	A6	40fr aqua & indigo ('54)	23.50	17.00
		Nos. 40-42 (3)	29.00	21.75

FIDES Issue

Common Design Type

Design: 9fr, Women at water pump.

1956 **Unwmk.** ***Perf. 13x12½***

43	CD103 9fr dp vio	2.25	1.60

Human Rights Issue

Common Design Type

1958 **Engr.** ***Perf. 13***

44	CD105 20fr ol grn & dk bl	9.00	9.00

Flower Issue

Common Design Type

1959 **Photo.** ***Perf. 12½x12***

45	CD104 10fr Colvillea	5.25	4.25

View of Dzaoudzi and Radio Symbol A8

Comoro radio station: 25fr, Radio tower and radio waves over Islands.

1960, Dec. 23 **Engr.** ***Perf. 13***

46	A8	20fr maroon, vio bl & grn	1.50	1.10
47	A8	25fr ultra, brn & grn	1.75	.90

Harpa Conoidalis — A9

Sea Shells: 50c, Cypraecassis rufa. 2fr, Murex ramosus. 5fr, Turbo marmoratus. 20fr, Pterocera scorpio. 25fr, Charonia tritonis.

1962, Jan. 13 **Photo.**

Shells in Natural Colors

48	A9	50c lilac & brn	1.00	1.00
49	A9	1fr yel & red	1.00	1.00
50	A9	2fr pale grn & pink	2.40	2.40
51	A9	5fr yel & grn	2.75	2.75
52	A9	20fr salmon & brn	10.00	10.00
53	A9	25fr bister & pink	14.00	14.00
		Nos. 48-53,C5-C6 (8)	69.65	62.65

Wheat Emblem and Globe A10

1963, Mar. 21 **Engr.** ***Perf. 13***

54	A10	20fr choc & dk grn	4.75	4.00

FAO "Freedom from Hunger" campaign.

Red Cross Centenary Issue

Common Design Type

1963, Sept. 2 **Unwmk.** ***Perf. 13***

55	CD113 50fr emer, gray & car	7.50	6.00

Human Rights Issue

Common Design Type

1963, Dec. 10 **Engr.**

56	CD117 15fr dk red & yel grn	7.50	6.00

Tobacco Pouch — A13

Designs: 4fr, Censer. 10fr, Carved lamp.

1963, Dec. 27 ***Perf. 13***

Size: 22x36mm

57	A13	3fr multi	.75	.75
58	A13	4fr org, dp cl & sl grn	1.00	1.00
59	A13	10fr org brn, dk red brn & grn	2.00	2.00
		Nos. 57-59,C8-C9 (5)	16.25	11.25

Philatec Issue

Common Design Type

1964, Mar. 31

60	CD118 50fr dk bl, red & grn	4.00	3.50

Grand Comoro Canoe — A14

Design: 30fr, Boutre felucca.

Size: 22x37mm

1964, Aug. 7 **Photo.** ***Perf. 13x12½***

61	A14	15fr multi	2.75	2.25
62	A14	30fr lt grn & multi	5.00	4.00
		Nos. 61-62,C10-C11 (4)	18.00	10.10

Spiny Lobster — A15

Designs: 12fr, Hammerhead shark, horiz. 20fr, Turtle, horiz. 25fr, Merou fish.

1965, Dec. 20 **Engr.** ***Perf. 13***

63	A15	1fr grn, lil & ocher	1.25	.75
64	A15	12fr org red, slate & gray	2.75	1.60
65	A15	20fr org, red & bl grn	4.00	1.75
66	A15	25fr bl grn, dk brn & red	7.00	3.25
		Nos. 63-66 (4)	15.00	7.35

Hotel Itsandra, Moroni A16

Design: 15fr, Lake Salé, Grand Comoro.

1966, Dec. 19 Photo. *Perf. 12½x13*

67	A16	15fr multi	1.10	.70
68	A16	25fr multi	1.25	.70
		Nos. 67-68,C18-C19 (4)	14.35	8.50

Comoro Sunbird A17

Birds: 10fr, Malachite kingfisher. 15fr, Rothschild's fody. 30fr, Cuckoo-roller.

1967, June 20 Photo. *Perf. 12½x13*
Size: 36x23mm

69	A17	2fr ocher & multi	2.50	1.50
70	A17	10fr lil & multi	4.25	2.00
71	A17	15fr yel grn & multi	6.25	3.00
72	A17	30fr pink & multi	13.00	6.50
		Nos. 69-72,C20-C21 (6)	48.50	27.50

For surcharge see No. 133.

WHO Anniversary Issue
Common Design Type

1968, May 4 Engr. *Perf. 13*

73	CD126	40fr grn, vio & dp car	2.40	1.75

Surgeonfish A19

Design: 25fr, Imperial angelfish.

1968, Aug. 1 Engr. *Perf. 13*
Size: 36x22mm

74	A19	20fr vio bl, yel & red brn	3.25	3.25
75	A19	25fr Prus bl, dk bl & org	4.00	4.00
		Nos. 74-75,C23-C24 (4)	24.00	15.75

For surcharge & overprint see Nos. C52, C74.

Human Rights Year Issue
Common Design Type

1968, Aug. 10 Engr. *Perf. 13*

76	CD127	60fr brn, grn & org	3.25	3.25

Msoila Prayer Rug and Praying Man — A20

Each stamp shows a different prayer position.

1969, Feb. 27 Engr. *Perf. 13*

77	A20	20fr bl grn, rose red & pur	1.10	.75
78	A20	30fr pur, rose red & bl grn	1.25	1.10
79	A20	45fr rose red, pur & bl grn	2.25	1.40
		Nos. 77-79 (3)	4.60	3.25

Vanilla Flower A21

Design: 15fr, Flower of ylang-ylang tree. 25fr, Poinsettia (country name at upper left).

1969-70 Photo. *Perf. 12½x13*
Size: 36x23mm

80	A21	10fr multi	1.00	.50
81	A21	15fr multi	1.40	.70
82	A21	25fr multi ('70)	3.25	1.50
		Nos. 80-82,C26-C28 (6)	21.65	13.45

Issued: Nos. 80-81, 3/20. No. 82, 3/5.

ILO Issue
Common Design Type

1969, Nov. 24 Engr. *Perf. 13*

83	CD131	5fr org, emerald & gray	1.25	.75

UPU Headquarters Issue
Common Design Type

1970, May 20 Engr. *Perf. 13*

84	CD133	65fr pur, bl grn & red brn	5.50	2.00

Chiromani Costume, Anjouan — A22

25fr, Bouiboui costume, Grand Comoro.

1970, Oct. 30 Photo. *Perf. 12½x13*

85	A22	20fr grn, yel & red	1.60	.80
86	A22	25fr brn, yel & dk bl	1.90	1.10

Friday Mosque — A23

1970, Dec. 18 Engr. *Perf. 13*

87	A23	5fr rose car, grn & grnsh bl	.75	.75
88	A23	10fr dp lil, grn & vio	1.00	.75
89	A23	40fr cop red, grn & dp brn	1.75	1.40
		Nos. 87-89 (3)	3.50	2.90

Great White Egret — A24

Birds: 10fr, Comoro pigeon. 15fr, Green-backed heron. 25fr, Comoro blue pigeon. 35fr, Humbolt's flycatcher. 40fr, Allen's gallinule.

1971, Mar. 12 Photo. *Perf. 12½x13*

90	A24	5fr multi	1.50	.80
91	A24	10fr yel & multi	2.00	.80
92	A24	15fr bl & multi	3.25	1.75
93	A24	25fr org & multi	4.75	2.00
94	A24	35fr yel grn & multi	6.50	2.50
95	A24	40fr gray & multi	8.00	3.25
		Nos. 90-95 (6)	26.00	11.10

For overprint see No. 145.

Pyrostegia Venusta — A25

Flowers: 3fr, Dogbane, horiz. 20fr, Frangipani.

Size: 22x36mm, 36x22mm

1971, July 19 Photo. *Perf. 13*

96	A25	1fr ver & grn	.95	.85
97	A25	3fr yel, grn & red	1.40	1.00
98	A25	20fr ver & grn	3.50	2.50
		Nos. 96-98,C37-C38 (5)	17.35	11.50

For surcharges see Nos. 131-132, C75, C83.

Lithograph Cone A26

Sea Shells: 10fr, Pacific lettered cone. 20fr, Aulicus cone. 35fr, Polita nerita. 60fr, Snake-head cowrie.

1971, Oct. 4

99	A26	5fr lt ultra & multi	1.25	1.00
100	A26	10fr multi	1.75	1.40
101	A26	20fr vio & multi	3.75	2.25
102	A26	35fr lt bl & multi	7.25	2.75
103	A26	60fr lt vio & multi	9.50	3.50
		Nos. 99-103 (5)	23.50	10.90

For surcharge see No. 150.

De Gaulle Issue
Common Design Type

Designs: 20fr, Gen. de Gaulle, 1940. 35fr, Pres. de Gaulle, 1970.

1971, Nov. 9 Engr. *Perf. 13*

104	CD134	20fr dk car & blk	4.00	2.50
105	CD134	35fr dk car & blk	5.00	3.25

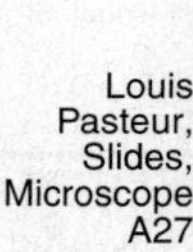

Louis Pasteur, Slides, Microscope A27

1972, Aug. 2

106	A27	65fr indigo, org, & ol brn	5.50	4.75

Sesquicentennial of the birth of Louis Pasteur (1822-1895), chemist.

Type of Air Post Issue 1971

Designs: 10fr, View of Goulaivoini. 20fr, Bay, Mitsamiouli. 35fr, Gate and fountain, Foumbouni. 50fr, View of Moroni.

1973, June 28 Photo. *Perf. 13*

107	AP10	10fr bl & multi	1.00	.30
108	AP10	20fr grn & multi	1.50	.75
109	AP10	35fr bl & multi	2.50	1.25
110	AP10	50fr bl & multi	2.75	1.75
		Nos. 107-110,C53 (5)	17.25	10.55

For overprint see No. 143.

Bank of Madagascar and Comoros — A28

Buildings in Moroni: 15fr, Post and Telecommunications Administration. 20fr, Prefecture.

1973, July 10 Photo. *Perf. 13x12½*

111	A28	5fr multi	.65	.55
112	A28	15fr multi	.90	.80
113	A28	20fr multi	1.25	1.00
		Nos. 111-113 (3)	2.80	2.35

For surcharge see No. 134.

Salimata Hamissi Mosque A29

20fr, Zaouiyat Chaduli Mosque, vert.

Perf. 12½x13, 13x12½

1973, Oct. 20 Photo.

114	A29	20fr multi	1.25	.95
115	A29	35fr multi	2.10	1.25

For surcharges see Nos. 135, 138.

Cheikh Mausoleum A30

Design: 50fr, Mausoleum of President Said Mohamed Cheikh (different view).

1974, Mar. 16 Engr. *Perf. 13*

116	A30	35fr grn, ol brn & blk	1.60	1.10
117	A30	50fr grn, ol brn & blk	2.50	1.25

For surcharge see No. 140.

Koran Stand, Anjouan A31

Designs: 15fr, Carved combs, vert. 20fr, 3-legged table, vert. 75fr, Sugar press.

1974, May 10 Photo. *Perf. 12½x13*

118	A31	15fr emer & multi	1.25	.60
119	A31	20fr grn & multi	1.40	.65
120	A31	35fr multi	2.25	1.10
121	A31	75fr multi	4.50	2.00
		Nos. 118-121 (4)	9.40	4.35

For overprints and surcharge see Nos. 137, 141, 149.

UPU Emblem, Symbolic Postmark A32

1974, Oct. 9 Engr. *Perf. 13x12½*

122	A32	30fr multi	2.00	1.75

Centenary of Universal Postal Union.
For surcharge see No. 155.

Bracelet A33

1975, Feb. 28 Engr. *Perf. 13*

123	A33	20fr shown	1.10	.95
124	A33	35fr Diadem	1.90	1.25
125	A33	120fr Saber	5.00	3.25
126	A33	135fr Dagger	7.00	4.00
		Nos. 123-126 (4)	15.00	9.45

For surcharges see Nos. 136, 142, 151, 154.

Mohani Village, Moheli — A34

50fr, Djoezi Village, Moheli. 55fr, Chirazi tombs.

1975, May 26 Photo. *Perf. 13*

127	A34 30fr vio bl & multi		2.00	1.00
128	A34 50fr Prus bl & multi		3.25	1.50
129	A34 55fr grn & multi		3.50	2.50
	Nos. 127-129 (3)		8.75	5.00

For overprints and surcharge see Nos. 139, 146, 148.

Scuba Diver Photographing Coelacanth — A35

1975, June 27 Engr. *Perf. 13*

130	A35 50fr multi	8.25	5.75

1975 coelacanth expedition.
For overprint see No. 147.

STATE OF COMORO

In 1978 the islands' name became the Federal and Islamic Republic of the Comoros.

Issues of 1971-75 Srchd. and Ovptd. with Bars and: "ETAT COMORIEN" in Black, Silver or Red

Tambourine Player — A36

No. 153, Women dancers & tambourine players.

Printing & Perforations as Before, Photogravure (A36)

1975 ***Perf. 13 (A36)***

131	A25	5fr on 1fr	*.40*	*.25*
132	A25	5fr on 3fr	*.40*	*.25*
133	A17	10fr on 2fr	*1.25*	*.50*
134	A28	15fr on 20fr (R)	*.80*	*.25*
135	A29	15fr on 20fr (S)	*.80*	*.25*
136	A33	15fr on 20fr	*.80*	*.25*
137	A31	20fr	*1.00*	*.25*
138	A29	25fr on 35fr	*1.00*	*.25*
139	A34	30fr	*1.00*	*.60*
140	A30	30fr on 35fr	*1.00*	*.30*
141	A31	30fr on 35fr	*1.00*	*.30*
142	A33	30fr on 35fr	*1.00*	*.60*
143	AP10	35fr	*1.25*	*.75*
144	SP2	35fr on 35fr + 10fr	*1.25*	*.75*
145	A24	40fr	*2.75*	*1.50*
146	A34	50fr	*1.90*	*1.90*
147	A35	50fr	*2.50*	*1.25*
148	A34	50fr on 55fr (S)	*1.90*	*.95*
149	A31	75fr	*2.00*	*.55*
150	A26	75fr on 60fr (S)	*4.00*	*2.00*
151	A33	100fr on 120fr	*2.50*	*.90*
152	A36	100fr bl & multi	*3.25*	*1.75*
153	A36	100fr on 150fr (S)	*2.50*	*.90*
154	A33	200fr on 135fr	*6.00*	*2.40*
155	A32	500fr on 30fr	*12.00*	*6.75*
		Nos. 131-155 (25)	*54.25*	*26.40*

Nos. 152-153 exist without overprint or surcharge. Value, each $90.
No. 155 exists with red surcharge. Value $12.

Litho. & Embossed "Gold Foil" Stamps
These stamps generally are of a different design format than the rest of the issue. Since there is a commemorative inscription tieing them to the issue a separate illustration is not being shown.

Apollo-Soyuz — A37

Spacecraft and astronauts: 10fr, Soyuz lift-off, Alexei A. Leonov and Valeri N. Kubasov, vert. 30fr, Apollo lift-off, Thomas P. Stafford, Vance D. Brand, Donald K. Slayton, vert. 50fr, Meeting in space. 100fr, Chairman Brezhnev, President Ford talking with astronauts and cosmonauts. 200fr, Spacecraft preparing to dock. 400f, Return to Earth. 500fr, Spacecraft, mission emblems. 1500fr, Apollo-Soyuz crew. No. 164, Preparing to dock, diff.

1975, Dec. 15 Litho. *Perf. 13½*

156	A37	10fr multicolored	.40	.25
157	A37	30fr multicolored	.50	.25
158	A37	50fr multicolored	.70	.55
159	A37	100fr multicolored	1.00	.60
160	A37	200fr multicolored	2.00	1.25
161	A37	400fr multicolored	4.00	2.50
		Nos. 156-161 (6)	8.60	5.40

Litho. & Embossed

Size: 45x45mm

162	A37	1500fr gold & multi	17.50	—

Souvenir Sheets

Litho.

163	A37	500fr multicolored	4.50	1.75

Litho. & Embossed

164	A37	1500fr gold & multi	17.50	—

Nos. 159-164 are airmail. No. 163 contains one 64x44mm stamp. No. 164 contains one 45x45mm stamp.
No. 162 exists in a souvenir sheet of 1. Value $50.
For overprints see Nos. 477-478.

A38

American Revolution, Bicent. — A39

Designs: 15fr, Lewis and Clark, Blackfoot Indian. 25fr, John C. Fremont, Kit Carson, Indian dancer. 35fr, Daniel Boone, Buffalo Bill Cody, wagon train. 40fr, Richard E. Egan, Johnny Frey, Pony Express. 75fr, Henry Wells, William G. Fargo, stagecoach. 400fr, Frontiersman, Indian. 500fr, Leland Stanford, Thomas C. Dunant, transcontinental railroad. 1000fr, George Washington, winter at Valley Forge. 1500fr, John Paul Jones, ship.

1976, Jan. 15 Litho.

165	A38	15fr multicolored	.25	.25
166	A38	25fr multicolored	.45	.25
167	A38	35fr multicolored	.75	.35
168	A38	40fr multicolored	.85	.45
169	A38	75fr multicolored	1.50	.60
170	A38	500fr multicolored	6.25	2.50
		Nos. 165-170 (6)	10.05	4.40

Litho. & Embossed

171	A39	1000fr gold & multi	13.50	—

Souvenir Sheets

Litho.

172	A38	400fr multicolored	5.50	1.75

Litho. & Embossed

173	A39	1500fr gold & multi	16.50	—

Nos. 170-173 are airmail. See Nos. 230, 232 and note after No. 479.
No. 171 exists in a souvenir sheet of 1. Value $55.

1976 Winter Olympics, Innsbruck — A40

5fr, Women's figure skating. 30fr, Slalom skiing. 35fr, Speed skating. 50fr, Downhill skiing. 200fr, Ski jumping. 400fr, Cross country skiing. No. 180, 1000fr, Downhill skier, hockey.
500fr, Hockey. No. 182, 1000fr, Olympic Rings.

1976, Mar. 30 Litho.

174	A40	5fr multicolored	.25	.25
175	A40	30fr multicolored	.25	.25
176	A40	35fr multicolored	.50	.25
177	A40	50fr multicolored	.65	.50
178	A40	200fr multicolored	2.10	1.00
179	A40	400fr multicolored	4.50	1.25
		Nos. 174-179 (6)	8.25	3.50

Litho. & Embossed

Size: 56x35mm

180	A40	1000fr multicolored	*13.00*	—

Souvenir Sheets

Litho.

181	A40	500fr multicolored	7.00	1.75

Litho. & Embossed

182	A40	1000fr multicolored	*11.00*	—

Nos. 178-182 are airmail. Nos. 181-182 contain one 58x35mm stamp. For overprint see No. 471.
No. 162 exists in a souvenir sheet of 1. Value $45.

1976 Summer Olympics, Montreal — A41

20fr, Runner, Athens, 1896. 25fr, Sprints. 40fr, High jump, Paris, 1900. 75fr, High jump. 100fr, Women stretching, St. Louis, 1904. 500fr, Uneven parallel bars.
400fr, Olympic Stadium, Montreal.

1976, Mar. 30 Litho.

183	A41	20fr multicolored	.25	.25
184	A41	25fr multicolored	.35	.25
185	A41	40fr multicolored	.50	.25
186	A41	75fr multicolored	1.00	.45
187	A41	100fr multicolored	1.10	.50
188	A41	500fr multicolored	6.00	1.75
		Nos. 183-188 (6)	9.20	3.45

Souvenir Sheet

189	A41	400fr multicolored	5.00	1.25

Nos. 187-189 are airmail.
For overprint see No. 476.

Fairy Tales — A42

15fr, Hansel & Gretel. 30fr, Alice in Wonderland. 35fr, Pinocchio. 40fr, Good Little Henry. 50fr, Peter and the Wolf. 400fr, Thousand and One Nights.

1976, June 28

190	A42	15fr multicolored	.25	.25
191	A42	30fr multicolored	.50	.25
192	A42	35fr multicolored	.65	.25
193	A42	40fr multicolored	.65	.25
194	A42	50fr multicolored	1.00	.25
195	A42	400fr multicolored	6.50	2.00
		Nos. 190-195 (6)	9.55	3.25

No. 195 is airmail. Nos. 190-191, 193, 195 are vert.

Invention of Telephone, Cent. — A43

Designs: 10fr, A. G. Bell, 1st telephone. 25fr, Charles Bourseul, Paris-London phone service, 1891. 75fr, Philipp Reis, telephone operators. 100fr, Earth to Moon to Earth communications. 200fr, Satellite. 400fr, Ship-to-Satellite communications. No. 201, Satellite in orbit, antenna. No. 203, Global communications.

1976, July 1

196	A43	10fr multicolored	.25	.25
197	A43	25fr multicolored	.35	.25
198	A43	75fr multicolored	1.00	.30
199	A43	100fr multicolored	1.40	.50
200	A43	200fr multicolored	2.25	.90
201	A43	500fr multicolored	5.50	1.75
		Nos. 196-201 (6)	10.75	3.95

Souvenir Sheets

202	A43	400fr multicolored	7.00	1.75
203	A43	500fr multicolored	7.00	1.75

Nos. 199-203 are airmail. Nos. 202-203 contain a 73x44mm stamp. For overprint see No. 472.

Comoro Flag, Map and Government Buildings — A44

1976, Nov. 18 Litho. *Perf. 13½*

204	A44 30fr multi	.75	.30
205	A44 50fr multi	1.50	.30

1st anniversary of independence.
For overprints and surcharges see Nos. 353-372.

Viking Probe to Mars — A45

Designs: 5fr, Nicolaus Copernicus, rocket launch. 10fr, Albert Einstein, Carl Sagan, Thomas Young, horiz. 25fr, Viking probe orbiting Mars. 35fr, Discovery of America by Vikings, horiz. 100fr, Flag, Viking landing on Mars. 500fr, Viking emblem, surface of Mars, horiz. 400fr, Viking probe. No. 212, Wagon train, frontiersman, rocket launch. No. 214, Viking on Martian surface, robotic shovel.

1976, Nov. 23

206	A45	5fr multicolored	.30	.25
207	A45	10fr multicolored	.30	.25
208	A45	25fr multicolored	.40	.25
209	A45	35fr multicolored	.40	.25
210	A45	100fr multicolored	1.40	.40
211	A45	500fr multicolored	8.00	1.50
		Nos. 206-211 (6)	10.80	2.90

Litho. & Embossed
Size: 57x39mm

212 A45 1500fr gold & multi *14.00* —

Souvenir Sheets
Litho.

213 A45 400fr multicolored *5.00* 1.50

Litho. & Embossed

214 A45 1500fr gold & multi *15.00* —

American Revolution, bicentennial. Nos. 211-214 are airmail. No. 213 contains one 60x42mm stamp.

No. 212 exists in a souvenir sheet of 1. Value $50.

UN Postal Administration, 25th Anniv. — A46

Designs: 15fr, UN #24, irrigating field. 30fr, UN #43, doctor, nurse. 50fr, UN #162, mother holding child. 75fr, UN #42, communications satellite in orbit. 200fr, UN #32, Concorde, Zeppelin. 400fr, UN #18, cargo plane. 500fr, People passing letters around globe.

1976, Nov. 25 **Litho.**

215 A46 15fr multicolored .25 .25
216 A46 30fr multicolored .30 .25
217 A46 50fr multicolored .60 .30
218 A46 75fr multicolored .80 .30
219 A46 200fr multicolored 2.50 1.00
220 A46 400fr multicolored 5.00 2.00
Nos. 215-220 (6) 9.45 4.10

Souvenir Sheet

221 A46 500fr multicolored *5.00* 2.00

Nos. 219-221 are airmail. No. 221 contains one 57x40mm stamp. For overprints see Nos. 282-284, 473.

Nos. 215-220 exist as souvenir sheets of one. Value, set, $45.

Comoro Flag, UN Headquarters and Emblem — A47

1976, Nov. 25

222 A47 40fr multicolored 1.40 .30
223 A47 50fr multicolored 1.90 .40

1st anniv. of UN membership.

Type of 1976 and

US Bicentennial — A48

Civil War Battles: 10fr, Fort Sumter, Lincoln. 30fr, Bull Run, Gen. P.G.T. Beauregard, vert. 50fr, Antietam, Gen. Joseph E. Johnston. 100fr, Gettysburg, Gen. Meade. 200fr, Chattanooga, Gen. Sherman, vert. 400fr, Appomattox, Gen. Pickett. 500fr, Surrender at Appomattox, Generals Lee and Grant. 1000fr, Lincoln, battlefield. No. 230, Pres. Kennedy, lunar lander.

1976, Dec. 30 **Litho.**

224 A48 10fr multicolored .25 .25
225 A48 30fr multicolored .30 .25
226 A48 50fr multicolored .65 .25
227 A48 100fr multicolored 1.10 .45
228 A48 200fr multicolored 2.50 .80
229 A48 400fr multicolored 5.00 1.50
Nos. 224-229 (6) 9.80 3.50

Litho. & Embossed
Size: 61x51mm

230 A39 1500fr gold & multi *17.00* —

Souvenir Sheets
Litho.

231 A48 500fr multicolored *6.50* 1.75

Litho. & Embossed

232 A39 1000fr gold & multi *9.50* —

American Revolution bicentennial. Nos. 227-232 are airmail. No. 231 contains one 60x42mm stamp.

No. 224-229 exist as souvenir sheets of one. Value, set, $32.50.

No. 230 exists in a souvenir sheet of one. Value $50.

Endangered Species — A49

15fr, Andean condor, vert. 20fr, Australian tiger cat. 35fr, Leopard, vert. 40fr, White rhinoceros. 75fr, Nyala, vert. 400fr, Orangutan.
500fr, Lemur, vert.

1976, Dec. 30 **Litho.**

233 A49 15fr multicolored .30 .25
234 A49 20fr multicolored .65 .25
235 A49 35fr multicolored 1.00 .25
236 A49 40fr multicolored 1.25 .45
237 A49 75fr multicolored 3.00 .55
238 A49 400fr multicolored 8.00 1.50
Nos. 233-238 (6) 14.20 3.25

Souvenir Sheet

239 A49 500fr multicolored 7.00 1.75

Nos. 238-239 airmail. No. 239 contains one 40x58mm stamp.

See note after No. 479.

Endangered Species — A50

10fr, Wolf. 30fr, Aye-aye. 40fr, Cephalopus zebra. 50fr, Giant tortoise. 200fr, Ocelot. 400fr, Penguin.
500fr, Sumatran tiger.

1977, Apr. 14

240 A50 10fr multicolored .25 .25
241 A50 30fr multicolored .45 .25
242 A50 40fr multicolored .90 .30
243 A50 50fr multicolored 1.00 .30
244 A50 200fr multicolored 3.00 .75
245 A50 400fr multicolored 6.50 1.50
Nos. 240-245 (6) 12.10 3.35

Souvenir Sheet

246 A50 500fr multicolored 8.00 1.50

Nos. 244-246 airmail. No. 246 contains one 58x40mm stamp.

Giffard Airship, 1851 and Paris-St. Germain Train, 1837, France — A51

Airships & Locomotives: 25fr, Santos-Dumont's airship, 1906, Brazilian Tander 120FIN, Brazil. 50fr, Astra, 1914, Trans-Siberian Express, 1905, Russia. 75fr, R.34, 1919, Southern Belle, 1910, Great Britain. 200fr, Navy airship, Pacific Class locomotive, 1930, US. No. 252, Hindenburg, Rheingold Express, 1933, Germany. No. 253, Graf-Zeppelin, 1928, Nord-Express Type 231, 1925, Germany.

1977, Apr. 14

247 A51 20fr multicolored .30 .25
248 A51 25fr multicolored .30 .25
249 A51 50fr multicolored .75 .25
250 A51 75fr multicolored 1.10 .25
251 A51 200fr multicolored 2.75 .60
252 A51 500fr multicolored 6.25 1.60
Nos. 247-252 (6) 11.45 3.20

Souvenir Sheet

253 A51 500fr multi, horiz. 6.00 2.00

Nos. 251-253 are airmail. No. 253 contains one 58x39mm stamp.

Nobel Prize, 75th Anniv. — A52

Nobel Prize winners: 30fr, Medicine. 40fr, Physics. 50fr, Literature. 100fr, Physics. 200fr, Chemistry. 400fr, Peace.
500fr, Nobel medal.

1977, July 7

254 A52 30fr multicolored .75 .25
255 A52 40fr multicolored .75 .25
256 A52 50fr multicolored 1.25 .25
257 A52 100fr multicolored 3.25 .25
258 A52 200fr multicolored 5.50 .75
259 A52 400fr multicolored 12.50 1.25
Nos. 254-259 (6) 24.00 3.00

Souvenir Sheet

260 A52 500fr multicolored 5.50 1.75

Nos. 258-260 are airmail.
See note after No. 479.

Peter Paul Rubens, 400th Birth Anniv. — A53

Portraits: 20fr, Portrait of the Artist's Daughter, Clara. 25fr, Suzanne Fourment. 50fr, Toilet of Venus, (detail). 75fr, Ceres (detail). 200fr, Young Woman with Blonde Braided Hair. No. 266, Helene Fourment in her Wedding Dress. No. 267, Self-portrait.

1977, July 7

261 A53 20fr multicolored .25 .25
262 A53 25fr multicolored .30 .25
263 A53 50fr multicolored .65 .25
264 A53 75fr multicolored 1.10 .30
265 A53 200fr multicolored 2.50 .60
266 A53 500fr multicolored 6.25 1.50
Nos. 261-266 (6) 11.05 3.15

Souvenir Sheet

267 A53 500fr multicolored 5.50 1.75

Nos. 265-267 are airmail.
See note after No. 479.

Fish A54

30fr, Swordfish. 40fr, Gaterin. 50fr, Sea scorpion. 100fr, Chaetodon lunula. 200fr, Amphiprion. 400fr, Tetrodon.
500fr, Coelacanth.

1977, Nov. 21

268 A54 30fr multicolored .50 .25
269 A54 40fr multicolored 1.00 .25
270 A54 50fr multicolored 1.75 .25
271 A54 100fr multicolored 3.25 .45
272 A54 200fr multicolored 4.00 .75
273 A54 400fr multicolored 7.50 1.50
Nos. 268-273 (6) 18.00 3.45

Souvenir Sheet

274 A54 500fr multicolored 8.00 2.00

Nos. 272-274 airmail. No. 274 contains one 52x47mm stamp.

Space Exploration — A55

30fr, Jupiter lander. 50fr, Voyager probe, Uranus, vert. 75fr, Pioneer probe, Venus. 100fr, Space shuttle, vert. 200fr, Viking III, Mars. 400fr, Apollo-Soyuz, vert.
500fr, Allegory of the Sun.

1977, Nov. 21

275 A55 30fr multicolored .30 .25
276 A55 50fr multicolored .60 .25
277 A55 75fr multicolored 1.00 .25
278 A55 100fr multicolored 1.10 .40
279 A55 200fr multicolored 2.50 .60
280 A55 400fr multicolored 5.00 1.25
Nos. 275-280 (6) 10.50 3.00

Souvenir Sheet

281 A55 500fr multicolored 5.00 1.75

Nos. 279-281 airmail. No. 281 contains one 52x42mm stamp.

No. 219 Overprinted in One Line in Gold, Silver or Red "Paris-New-York - 22 Nov. 1977"

1977, Nov. 22

282 A46 200fr multicolored 6.00 2.75
283 A46 200fr multicolored (S) 30.00 —
284 A46 200fr multicolored (R) 10.00 —
Nos. 282-284 (3) 46.00 2.75

Birds — A56

15fr, Porphyrula alleni. 20fr, M. superciliosus. 35fr, Alcedo vintsioides johannae. 40fr, Terpsiphone. 75fr, Nectarinia comorensis. 400fr, Egretta alba.
500fr, Foudia eminentissima, horiz.

1978, Feb. 6

285 A56 15fr multicolored .35 .25
286 A56 20fr multicolored .50 .25
287 A56 35fr multicolored .70 .30
288 A56 40fr multicolored 1.00 .40
289 A56 75fr multicolored 2.00 .50
290 A56 400fr multicolored 8.00 2.25
Nos. 285-290 (6) 12.55 3.95

Souvenir Sheet

291 A56 500fr multicolored 6.00 1.75

Nos. 290-291 are airmail. For overprint and surcharges see Nos. 444-448.

World Cup Soccer Championships, Argentina — A57

Designs: 30fr, Greece, 5th. cent. B.C. 50fr, Brittany, 19th cent. 75fr, London, 14th cent. 100fr, Italy, 18th cent. 200fr, England, 19th cent. 400fr, English Cup match, 1891. 500fr,

English Cup final, 1962. No. 298, Player, satellite. No. 300, Players.

1978, Feb. 6

292	A57	30fr multicolored	.30	.25
293	A57	50fr multicolored	.60	.25
294	A57	75fr multicolored	.75	.30
295	A57	100fr multicolored	1.10	.40
296	A57	200fr multicolored	2.50	.60
297	A57	400fr multicolored	5.00	1.25
		Nos. 292-297 (6)	10.25	3.05

Litho. & Embossed

Size: 60x42mm

298	A57	1000fr gold & multi	11.00	—

Souvenir Sheets

Litho.

299	A57	500fr multicolored	6.00	1.75

Litho. & Embossed

300	A57	1000fr gold & multi	9.00	4.00

Nos. 296-300 are airmail. No. 300 contains one 60x42mm stamp.

No. 298 exists in a souvenir sheet of 1. Value $50.

For overprints and surcharges see Nos. 402-408, 449-453.

Composers — A58

30fr, J.S. Bach. 40fr, W.A. Mozart. 50fr, Berlioz. 100fr, Verdi. 200fr, Tchaikovsky. 400fr, George Gershwin.

500fr, Beethoven.

1978, Apr. 5 **Litho.**

301	A58	30fr multicolored	.90	.25
302	A58	40fr multicolored	1.10	.25
303	A58	50fr multicolored	1.50	.30
304	A58	100fr multicolored	3.00	.30
305	A58	200fr multicolored	4.50	.60
306	A58	400fr multicolored	9.00	1.25
		Nos. 301-306 (6)	20.00	2.95

Souvenir Sheet

307	A58	500fr multicolored	9.00	1.75

Nos. 305-307 are airmail. For overprints and surcharges see Nos. 454-458.

Albrecht Durer, 450th Death Anniv. — A59

Portraits: 20fr, Oswolt Krel. 25fr, Elspeth Tucher. 50fr, Hieronymus Holzschuher. 75fr, Young Woman. 200fr, Emperor Maximilian I. No. 313, Young Woman, (detail). No. 314, Self-portrait.

1978, Apr. 5

308	A59	20fr multicolored	.25	.25
309	A59	25fr multicolored	.30	.25
310	A59	50fr multicolored	.65	.30
311	A59	75fr multicolored	1.00	.30
312	A59	200fr multicolored	2.50	.60
313	A59	500fr multicolored	6.00	1.60
		Nos. 308-313 (6)	10.70	3.30

Souvenir Sheet

314	A59	500fr multicolored	5.50	1.75

Nos. 312-314 airmail. No. 314 contains one 42x52mm stamp. See note after No. 479.

Issues Not Valid for Postage

The government changed in May 1978. A number of sets that had not been issued seem to have been invalid for postage until they were overprinted with the new country name. These are a set of 9 for the 25th anniv. of Elizabeth's coronation, a set of 7 for butterflies, a set of 6 for the 10th Intl. Communications Year, a set of 7 for the history of aviation, a set of 9 for Rubens, and a set of 9 for Durer.

These sets, unoverprinted, exist both mint and cancelled to order. They are no scarcer than the previous listed issues.

See note after No. 479.

Islamic Republic

Nos. 204-205 Surcharged and Overprinted with 3 Lines and: "République / Fédérale / et Islamique / des Comores"

1978, July 24 **Litho.** ***Perf. 13½***

353	A44	30fr multi	1.75	—
354	A44	40fr on 30fr multi	1.75	—
355	A44	50fr multi	1.75	—
356	A44	100fr on 50fr multi	1.75	—
		Nos. 353-356	1.50	

Nos. 353 and 355 were also overprinted to commemorate World Cup Soccer winner; Albrecht Dürer; Railroad anniversary; Voyager I and II; 1980 Olympic Games; World Cup Soccer, Espana '82.

Nos. 353, 355 Overprinted

1978, July 25 **Litho.** ***Perf. 13½***

357	A44	30fr multi	*8.50*	—
358	A44	50fr multi	*12.50*	—

Coronation of Queen Elizabeth II, 25th anniv.

Nos. 353, 355 Overprinted

1978, July 26 **Litho.** ***Perf. 13½***

359	A44	30fr multi	*6.00*	—
360	A44	50fr multi	*9.00*	—

Birth of Capt. James Cook, 250th anniv.

Nos. 353, 355 Overprinted

1978, July 31 **Litho.** ***Perf. 13½***

365	A44	30fr multi	*6.00*	—
366	A44	50fr multi	*10.00*	—

Intl. Civil Aviation Organization.

Nos. 353, 355 Overprinted

1978, Aug. 3 **Litho.** ***Perf. 13½***

371	A44	30fr multi	*7.00*	—
372	A44	50fr multi	*8.00*	—

Intl. Year of the Child (in 1979).

Europe-Africa A66

Various satellites or spacecraft.

1978, Dec. 16

386	A66	10fr multicolored	.25	.25
387	A66	25fr multicolored	.25	.25
388	A66	35fr multicolored	.30	.25
389	A66	50fr multicolored	.55	.25
390	A66	100fr multicolored	1.00	.60
391	A66	500fr multicolored	5.00	1.25
		Nos. 386-391 (6)	7.35	2.85

Souvenir Sheet

392	A66	500fr multicolored	5.50	1.75

Nos. 390-392 airmail. No. 392 contains one 61x40mm stamp.

Sir Rowland Hill — A67

20fr, Saxony #1. 30fr, Netherlands #1. 40fr, Great Britain #2. 75fr, US #2. 200fr, France #33. 400fr, Basel #3L1. 1500fr, British Guiana #13.

500fr, Moheli, Mayotte, Anjouan, Grand Comoro #1. No. 401, 1500fr, Hill, Mauritius #3.

1978, Dec. 16

393	A67	20fr multi	.25	.25
394	A67	30fr multi	.30	.25
395	A67	40fr multi	.60	.25
396	A67	75fr multi	.75	.30
397	A67	200fr multi	2.10	.60
398	A67	400fr multi	4.50	1.25
		Nos. 393-398 (6)	8.50	2.90

Litho. & Embossed

Size: 39x58mm

399	A67	1500fr multi	13.00	—

Souvenir Sheets

Litho.

400	A67	500fr multi	5.50	1.75

Litho. & Embossed

401	A67	1500fr multi	13.00	—

Nos. 397-401 are airmail. No. 400 contains one 57x49mm stamp. No. 401 contains one 58x39mm stamp.

No. 399 exists in a souvenir sheet of 1. Value $35.

Nos. 292-297, 299 Ovptd. in Black & Silver

1978, Dec. 16

402	A57	30fr multicolored	.30	.25
403	A57	50fr multicolored	.60	.25
404	A57	75fr multicolored	.90	.25
405	A57	100fr multicolored	1.10	.45
406	A57	200fr multicolored	2.25	.60
407	A57	400fr multicolored	4.75	1.25
		Nos. 402-407 (6)	9.90	3.05

Souvenir Sheet

408	A57	500fr multicolored	5.50	1.25

Nos. 406-407 are airmail.

Exists with Country name in red on silver. Value approx. triple those of overprints in black.

Galileo and Voyager I — A68

Exploration of Solar System: 30fr, Kepler and Voyager II. 40fr, Copernicus and Voyager I, 100fr, Huygens and Voyager II. 200fr, William Herschel and Voyager II. 400fr, Urbain Leverrier and Voyager II. 500fr, Voyagers I and II, symbolic solar system.

1979, Feb. 19 **Litho.** ***Perf. 13***

409	A68	20fr multi	.25	.25
410	A68	30fr multi	.30	.25
411	A68	40fr multi	.50	.25
412	A68	100fr multi	1.10	.25
413	A68	200fr multi	1.90	.50
414	A68	400fr multi	4.00	1.00
		Nos. 409-414 (6)	8.05	2.50

Souvenir Sheet

415	A68	500fr multi	5.00	1.50

Nos. 413-415 airmail.

Philidor, Anderssen, Steinitz and King — A69

100fr, Chess pieces and board, Venetian chess player. 500fr, Chess Grand Masters Alekhine, Spassky, Fischer, and bishop.

1979, Feb. 19

416	A69	40fr multi	.50	.25
417	A69	100fr multi	1.00	.25
418	A69	500fr multi	5.00	1.50
		Nos. 416-418 (3)	6.50	2.00

Chess Grand Masters. No. 418 airmail.

Nos. 416-418 exist as souvenir sheets of one. Value, set, $30.

Nos. 419-425 are reserved for Summer Olympics set of 6 with one souvenir sheet, released Mar. 28, 1979. Values: set, unused $7; set, used $3; souvenir sheet, unused $6; souvenir sheet, used $3.

Charaxes Defulvata — A71

Fauna: 50fr, Leptosomus discolor. 75fr, Bee eater.

1979, Apr. 10 **Litho.** ***Perf. 12½***

426	A71	30fr multi	2.00	.30
427	A71	50fr multi	5.00	1.00
428	A71	75fr multi	7.00	2.00
		Nos. 426-428 (3)	14.00	3.30

Otto Lilienthal and Glider — A72

History of Aviation: No. 430, Wright brothers and Flyer A. No. 431, Louis Bleriot and Bleriot XI. 100fr, Claude Dornier and Dornier-Wal hydrofoil. 200fr, Charles Lindbergh and Spirit of St. Louis.

1979, May 2 *Perf. 13*

Black Overprint and Surcharge

429 A72 30fr multi .50 .50
430 A72 50fr multi .80 .80
431 A72 50fr on 75fr multi .80 .80
432 A72 100fr multi 1.60 1.60
433 A72 200fr multi 2.50 2.50
Nos. 429-433 (5) 6.20 6.20

No. 433 airmail.
For unoverprinted stamps see note after No. 314.

Papilio Dardanus Cenea A73

Butterflies: 15fr, Papilio dardanus. 30fr, Chrysiridia croesus. 50fr, Precis octavia. 75fr, Bunaea alcinoe.

1979, May 2

Black Overprint and Surcharge

434 A73 5fr on 20fr multi .25 .25
435 A73 15fr multi .35 .25
436 A73 30fr multi .70 .45
437 A73 50fr multi 1.40 .95
438 A73 75fr multi 2.25 1.50
Nos. 434-438 (5) 4.95 3.40

For unoverprinted stamps see note after No. 314.

Man Reading Proclamation — A74

No. 439, Coronation coach. No. 440, Drummer. No. 441, With crown, orb, scepter. No. 443, St. Edward's Crown.

1979, May 2 **Litho.** *Perf. 13½*

Black Surcharge and Overprint

439 A74 5fr on 25fr multi .25 .25
440 A74 10fr multi .30 .30
441 A74 50fr on 40fr multi .70 .70
442 A74 50fr on 200fr shown 1.10 1.10
443 A74 100fr multi 1.40 1.40
Nos. 439-443 (5) 3.75 3.75

No. 442 is airmail.
For unoverprinted stamps see note after No. 314.

Nos. 285-289 (Birds) Overprinted or Surcharged like A72-A74

1979, May 2 **Litho.** *Perf. 13*

444 A56 15fr multi .25 .30
445 A56 30fr on 35fr multi .60 .70
446 A56 50fr on 20fr multi 1.10 1.25
447 A56 50fr on 40fr multi 1.10 1.25
448 A56 200fr on 75fr multi 3.50 4.00
Nos. 444-448 (5) 6.55 7.50

Nos. 292-296 (Soccer) Overprinted or Surcharged like A72-A74

1979, May 2 **Litho.** *Perf. 13*

449 A57 1fr on 100fr multi .25 .25
450 A57 2fr on 75fr multi .25 .25
451 A57 3fr on 30fr multi .25 .25
452 A57 50fr multi .90 .55
453 A57 200fr multi 2.25 2.25
Nos. 449-453 (5) 3.90 3.55

No. 453 airmail.

Nos. 301-305 (Composers) Overprinted or Surcharged like A72-A74

1979, May 2 *Perf. 13½*

454 A58 5fr on 100fr multi .25 .25
455 A58 30fr multi 1.25 1.25
456 A58 40fr multi 1.75 1.75
457 A58 50fr multi 2.25 2.25
458 A58 50fr on 200fr multi 3.50 3.50
Nos. 454-458 (5) 9.00 9.00

No. 458 airmail.

Intl. Year of the Child — A75

Intl. Year of the Child emblem and: 20fr, Astronaut on moon, child in astronaut costume. 30fr, Luger, child with snowboard. 40fr, Woman from Dürer painting, child practicing Chinese calligraphy. 100fr, Steam locomotive, child with toy train. 200fr, Adults and children playing soccer. 400fr, Olympic rower, child in rowboat.

500fr, Karl Benz, boy in toy car, horiz.

No. 465A, Louis Blériot, child with remote-control airplane, horiz.

No. 465B, Capt. James Cook, child with teddy bear and toy gun, horiz.

1979, May 30 **Litho.** *Perf. 13½*

459 A75 20fr multi .25 .25
460 A75 30fr multi .30 .25
461 A75 40fr multi .40 .25
462 A75 100fr multi 1.00 .35
463 A75 200fr multi 2.00 .50
464 A75 400fr multi 4.00 1.10
Nos. 459-464 (6) 7.95 2.70

Souvenir Sheet

465 A75 500fr multi 5.75 2.75

Litho. & Embossed

Size: 51x42mm

465A A75 1500fr gold & multi 13.50 —

Souvenir Sheet

Perf. 13¼

465B A75 1500fr gold & multi 13.50 —

Nos. 463-465A are airmail. Nos. 465 and 465B each contain one 51x42mm stamp.

Litchi Nuts — A76

1979, June 15 **Litho.** *Perf. 12½*

466 A76 60fr shown 1.00 .30
467 A76 70fr Papayas 1.25 .45
468 A76 100fr Avocados 1.40 .55
469 A76 125fr Bananas 1.90 .90
Nos. 466-469 (4) 5.55 2.20

For surcharges see Nos. 515, 533.

Basketball Players — A77

1979, Aug. 28 **Litho.** *Perf. 13*

470 A77 200fr multi 2.50 1.40

Indian Ocean Olympics.

Nos. 176, 198, 218, 187, 159-160 and Type A78 Overprinted in Black

Nimbus Weather Satellite — A78

No. 475, Apollo-Soyuz. No. 479, Molniya.

Printing & Perfs. as Before, Litho. (A78)

1979, Sept. 15 *Perf. 13 (A78)*

471 A40 35fr multi .70 .70
472 A43 75fr multi 1.50 1.50
473 A46 75fr multi 1.50 1.50
474 A78 75fr multi 1.50 1.50
475 A78 100fr multi 2.10 2.10
476 A41 100fr multi 2.10 2.10
477 A37 100fr multi 2.10 2.10
478 A37 200fr multi 4.25 4.25
479 A78 200fr multi 4.25 4.25
Nos. 471-479 (9) 20.00 20.00

Nos. 476-479 airmail.
For type A78 see note after No. 314.

Nos. 166-167, 169, 235-236, 257, 262, 309, 311, the unissued Rubens set (4 values) and Durer set (5 values) exist with this overprint, supposedly also issued Sept. 15. Value, set of 18 $12.

Dugout on Beach A80

Anjouan Puppet — A81

1980, Jan. 4 **Litho.** *Perf. 13*

498 A80 60fr multi 1.00 .25
499 A81 100fr multi 1.50 .45

For surcharge see No. 534.

Sultan Said Ali — A82

1980, Feb. 20 *Perf. 12½x13*

500 A82 40fr shown .75 .25
501 A82 60fr Sultan Ahmed 1.00 .25

Sherlock Holmes, Doyle — A83

1980, Feb. 25 *Perf. 12½*

502 A83 200fr multi 4.75 1.75

Sir Arthur Conan Doyle (1859-1930), writer.
For surcharge see No. 513.

Grand Mosque, Holy Ka'aba, Mecca — A84

1980, Mar. 12 *Perf. 13x12½*

503 A84 75fr multi 1.00 .40

Hegira, 1350th anniv.
For surcharge see No. 514.

Year of the Holy City of Jerusalem A85

1980, Mar. 12 *Perf. 13x13½*

504 A85 60fr multi 1.00 .40

Kepler, Copernicus and Pluto — A86

1980, Apr. 30 **Litho.** *Perf. 12½*

505 A86 400fr multi 4.50 2.25

Discovery of Pluto, 50th anniversary.
For surcharge see No. 531.

Muscle System, Avicenna — A87

1980, Apr. 30 **Engr.** *Perf. 13*

506 A87 60fr multi 1.00 .40

Avicenna, Arab physician, birth millennium.

Soccer Players — A88

World Cup Soccer 1982; Various soccer scenes. 60fr, 150fr, 500fr, vert.

1981, Feb. 20 **Litho.** ***Perf. 12½***
507 A88 60fr multi .65 .25
508 A88 75fr multi .75 .25
509 A88 90fr multi 1.25 .25
510 A88 100fr multi 1.10 .45
511 A88 150fr multi 1.90 .60
Nos. 507-511 (5) 5.65 1.80

Souvenir Sheet

512 A88 500fr multi 5.00 1.50

For overprints & surcharge see Nos. 532, 555-560.

Nos. 502-503, 469 Surcharged

and

Merops Superciliosus A89

Red, Black or Blue Surcharge

Perf. 12½, 13x12½ (No. 514)

1981, Feb. **Litho.**
513 A83 15fr on 200fr multi .50 .50
514 A84 20fr on 75fr multi .50 .50
515 A76 40fr on 125fr multi (Bk) 1.50 1.50
516 A89 60fr on 75fr multi (Bl) 3.00 3.00
Nos. 513-516 (4) 5.50 5.50

A90

Space Exploration: 50fr, Apollo program, vert. 75fr, 100fr, 500fr, Columbia space shuttle.

1981, July 13 **Litho.** ***Perf. 14***
517 A90 50fr multi .60 .25
518 A90 75fr multi .75 .25
519 A90 100fr multi 1.25 .30
520 A90 450fr multi 6.00 1.50
Nos. 517-520 (4) 8.60 2.30

Souvenir Sheet

521 A90 500fr multi 4.00 1.50

For overprints and surcharges see Nos. 599, 804F.

Prince Charles and Lady Diana, Buckingham Palace — A91

200fr, Highwood House. 450fr, Carnarvon Castle.

1981, Sept. 1 **Litho.** ***Perf. 14½***
522 A91 125fr shown .90 .30
523 A91 200fr multicolored 1.35 .60
524 A91 450fr multicolored 3.00 1.25
a. Souvenir sheet of 3 6.50 2.00
Nos. 522-524 (3) 5.25 2.15

Royal wedding. No. 524a contains Nos. 522-524 in changed colors.
For overprints see Nos. 551-553.

Official Stamp Flag Type

1981, Oct. **Litho.** ***Perf. 13***
526 O1 5fr multi .25 .25
527 O1 15fr multi .25 .25
528 O1 25fr multi .30 .25
529 O1 35fr multi .40 .25
530 O1 75fr multi .75 .35
Nos. 526-530 (5) 1.95 1.35

Nos. 505, 509, 468, 499 Surcharged

No. 531

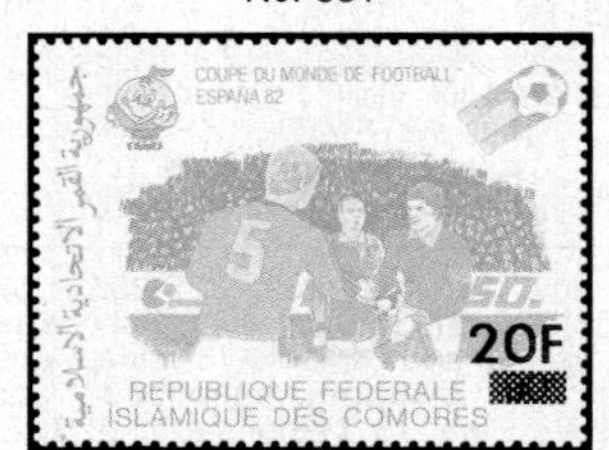

No. 532

No. 533

No. 534

1981, Nov. **Litho.** ***Perf. 12½***
531 A86 5fr on 400fr multi .40 .40
532 A88 20fr on 90fr multi .80 .80
533 A76 45fr on 100fr multi 2.00 .25
534 A81 45fr on 100fr multi 2.00 .25
Nos. 531-534 (4) 5.20 1.70

75th Anniv. of Grand Prix — A92

Winners and their Cars: 20fr, Mercedes, 1914. 50fr, Delage, 1925. 75fr, Rudi Caracciola, 1926. 90fr, Stirling Moss, 1955. 150fr, Maserati, 1957.
500fr, Changing wheels, vert.

1981, Dec. 28 **Litho.** ***Perf. 12½***
535 A92 20fr multicolored .25 .25
536 A92 50fr multicolored .50 .25
537 A92 75fr multicolored .70 .25
538 A92 90fr multicolored .90 .35
539 A92 150fr multicolored 1.30 .45
Nos. 535-539 (5) 3.65 1.55

Souvenir Sheet

Perf. 13

540 A92 500fr multicolored 6.00 1.75

For overprint see No. 600.

Scouting Year — A93

1982, Jan. 5 ***Perf. 12½***
541 A93 50fr Climbing rocks .60 .25
542 A93 75fr Boating .85 .25
543 A93 250fr Sailing 3.00 .90
544 A93 350fr Sailing, diff. 3.75 1.10
Nos. 541-544 (4) 8.20 2.50

Souvenir Sheet

Perf. 13

545 A93 500fr Baden-Powell 6.50 1.75

For overprint see No. 601.

21st Birthday of Princess of Wales — A94

Various portraits of Princess Diana.

1982, July 1 **Litho.** ***Perf. 14***
546 A94 200fr multi 2.00 .60
547 A94 300fr multi 3.25 .90

Souvenir Sheet

548 A94 500fr multi 5.00 1.50

Johannes von Goethe (1749-1832) A95

1982, July
549 A95 75fr multi .75 .25
550 A95 350fr multi 3.75 .90

Nos. 522-524a Overprinted in Blue

1982, July 31 ***Perf. 14½***
551 A91 125fr multi 1.25 .60
552 A91 200fr multi 2.00 .90
553 A91 450fr multi 3.75 2.00
a. Souvenir sheet of 3 7.50 7.50
Nos. 551-553 (3) 7.00 3.50

Birth of Prince William of Wales, June 21.

Nos. 507-512 Overprinted with Finalists and Score in Red

1982, Sept. 20 **Litho.** ***Perf. 12½***
555 A88 60fr multi .65 .25
556 A88 75fr multi .75 .35
557 A88 90fr multi 1.00 .45
558 A88 100fr multi 1.10 .45
559 A88 150fr multi 1.40 .60
Nos. 555-559 (5) 4.90 2.10

Souvenir Sheet

560 A88 500fr multi 5.00 1.50

Italy's victory in 1982 World Cup.

Paintings by Norman Rockwell A96

1982, Oct. 11 **Litho.** ***Perf. 14***
561 A96 60fr 1931 .65 .25
562 A96 75fr 1925 .70 .25
563 A96 100fr 1922 1.25 .25
564 A96 150fr 1919 1.40 .55
565 A96 200fr 1924 2.00 .60
566 A96 300fr 1918 3.50 1.00
Nos. 561-566 (6) 9.50 2.90

Sultans of Anjouan — A97

30fr, Said Mohamed Sidi, vert. 60fr, Ahmed Abdallah, vert. 75fr, Salim. 300fr, Sidi, Abdallah.

1982, Dec. ***Perf. 12½x13, 13x12½***
567 A97 30fr multicolored .40 .25
568 A97 60fr multicolored .75 .25
569 A97 75fr multicolored 1.00 .25
570 A97 300fr multicolored 3.50 1.40
Nos. 567-570 (4) 5.65 2.15

Landscapes — A98

1983, Sept. 30 **Litho.** ***Perf. 13***
571 A98 60fr D'Ziani Lake .75 .30
572 A98 100fr Sunset 1.25 .45
573 A98 175fr Anjouan, vert. 2.00 .75

574 A98 360fr Itsandra 4.00 1.25
575 A98 400fr Anjouan, diff. 5.00 1.60
Nos. 571-575 (5) 13.00 4.35

For surcharge see No. 815S.

Woman from Moheli A99

1983, Oct. 17 Litho. ***Perf. 12½x13***
576 A99 30fr shown .45 .25
577 A99 45fr Woman, diff. .65 .25
578 A99 50fr Man from Mayotte .70 .25
Nos. 576-578 (3) 1.80 .75

Horses — A100

1983, Nov. 30 Litho. ***Perf. 13***
579 A100 75fr Arabian .60 .25
580 A100 100fr Anglo-Arabian .90 .30
581 A100 125fr Lippizaner 1.10 .40
582 A100 150fr Tennessee 1.35 .50
583 A100 200fr Appaloosa 1.75 .70
584 A100 300fr Pure English 2.75 1.00
585 A100 400fr Clydesdale 3.50 1.25
586 A100 500fr Andalusian 4.50 1.50
Nos. 579-586 (8) 16.45 5.90

Double Portrait, by Raphael A101

200fr, Girl, fresco detail. 300fr, St. George Killing Dragon. 400fr, Balthazar Castiglione.

1983, Dec. 30 Litho. ***Perf. 13***
587 A101 100fr shown 1.10 .45
588 A101 200fr multicolored 2.25 .80
589 A101 300fr multicolored 2.75 .90
590 A101 400fr multicolored 5.00 1.25
Nos. 587-590 (4) 11.10 3.40

For surcharges see Nos. 703, 800E, 815M.

Ships and Automobiles — A102

No. 591, William Fawcett. No. 592, De Dion, 1885. No. 593, Lightning. No. 594, Benz Victoria, 1893. No. 595, Rapido. No. 596, Columbia Electric, 1901. No. 597, Sindia. No. 598, Fiat, 1902.

1984, Oct. 9 Litho. ***Perf. 12½***
591 A102 100fr multi 1.10 .30
592 A102 100fr multi 1.35 .30
593 A102 150fr multi 1.70 .45
594 A102 150fr multi 2.00 .60
595 A102 200fr multi 2.25 .75
596 A102 200fr multi 2.75 .75
597 A102 350fr multi 4.00 1.00
598 A102 350fr multi 4.50 1.10
Nos. 591-598 (8) 19.65 5.25

For surcharge see No. 812Q.

Nos. 521, 540, 545, C126, C131 Ovptd. in Black, Blue, Red or Gold

No. 599

No. 600

No. 601

No. 603

No. 599, '85 / HAMBOURG (Bk). No. 600, TSUKUBA EXPO '85 (Bl). No. 601, ARGENTINA '85/BUENOS AIRES (R). No. 602, Rome, ITALIA '85 emblem (R). No. 603, OLYMPHILEX/ '85 / LAUSANNE (G).

1985, Mar. 11 ***Perf. 14, 13***

Souvenir Sheets

599 A90 500fr multi 5.00 5.00
600 A92 500fr multi 5.00 5.00
601 A93 500fr multi 5.00 5.00
602 AP31 500fr multi 5.00 5.00
603 AP32 500fr multi 5.00 5.00
Nos. 599-603 (5) 25.00 25.00

Nos. 602-603 airmail.

Victor Hugo (1802-1885), Author, Pantheon, Paris — A103

Anniversaries and events: 200fr, IYY, Jules Verne (1828-1905), author. 300fr, IYY, Mark Twain (1835-1910), author. 450fr, Queen Mother, 85th birthday, vert. 500fr, Statue of Liberty, cent., vert.

1985, May 27 Litho. ***Perf. 13***
604 A103 100fr multi 1.10 .30
605 A103 200fr multi 2.00 .60
606 A103 300fr multi 3.00 .90
607 A103 450fr multi 4.50 1.25
608 A103 500fr multi 5.50 1.50
Nos. 604-608 (5) 16.10 4.55

For surcharges see Nos. 704, 800A.

Sea Shells — A104

75fr, Lambis chiragra. 125fr, Strombe lentifinosum. 200fr, Tonna gala. 300fr, Cymbium glans. 450fr, Lambis crocata.

1985, Oct. 23 ***Perf. 14***
609 A104 75fr multicolored 1.10 .25
610 A104 125fr multicolored 1.50 .35
611 A104 200fr multicolored 2.40 .60
612 A104 300fr multicolored 3.75 .90
613 A104 450fr multicolored 5.75 1.40
Nos. 609-613 (5) 14.50 3.50

Comoros Admission to UN, 10th Anniv. — A105

1985, Nov. 12 Litho. ***Perf. 13x12½***
614 A105 5fr multi .25 .25
615 A105 30fr multi .25 .25
616 A105 75fr multi .80 .25
617 A105 125fr multi 1.25 .50
618 A105 400fr multi 4.25 1.50
Nos. 614-618 (5) 6.80 2.75

For surcharge see No. 800F.

Moroni Rotary Club, 20th Anniv. — A106

1985, Nov. 30 ***Perf. 13***
619 A106 25fr multi .40 .25
620 A106 75fr multi .90 .40
621 A106 125fr multi 1.10 .45
622 A106 500fr multi 4.00 2.00
Nos. 619-622 (4) 6.40 3.10

Mushrooms — A107

75fr, Boletus edulis. 125fr, Sarcoscypha coccinea. 200fr, Hypholoma fasciculare. 350fr, Astraeus hygrometricus. 500fr, Armillariella mellea.

1985, Dec. 24 ***Perf. 13½***
623 A107 75fr multicolored 1.00 .30
624 A107 125fr multicolored 1.20 .45
625 A107 200fr multicolored 2.25 .60
626 A107 350fr multicolored 4.00 .90
627 A107 500fr multicolored 5.50 1.50
Nos. 623-627 (5) 13.95 3.75

For surcharge see No. 815R.

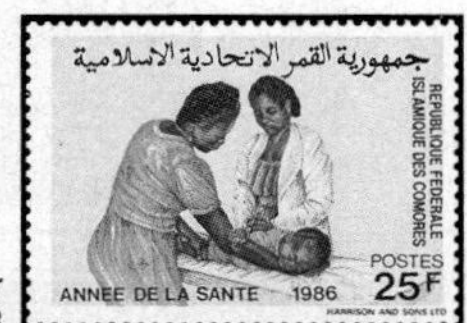

Health Year A108

25fr, Pediatric examination. 100fr, Weighing child. 200fr, Immunization.

1986, Oct. 2 Litho. ***Perf. 15x14½***
628 A108 25fr multicolored .25 .25
629 A108 100fr multicolored 1.20 .60
630 A108 200fr multicolored 2.25 1.25
Nos. 628-630 (3) 3.70 2.10

For surcharge see No. 705.

Musical Instruments A109

1986, Dec. 24 Litho. ***Perf. 13***
631 A109 75fr Ndzoumara .80 .40
632 A109 125fr Ndzedze 1.10 .60
633 A109 210fr Gaboussi 1.90 .90
634 A109 500fr Ngoma 5.50 1.75
Nos. 631-634 (4) 9.30 3.65

For surcharges see Nos. 796P, 796T, 800L, 815A.

Role of Women in National Development — A110

75fr, Working fields. 125fr, Harvesting crops, vert. 1000fr, Basketweaving.

1987, Mar. 7 Litho. ***Perf. 13***
635 A110 75fr multi .50 .30
636 A110 125fr multi 1.00 .50
637 A110 1000fr multi 9.50 3.50
Nos. 635-637 (3) 11.00 4.30

Service Organizations — A111

Emblems and activities: 75fr, Nos. 642, Kiwanis or 643c, Rotary Intl. for child survival. 125fr, Nos. 641, Kiwanis or 643b, Lions Intl. for aid to the handicapped. 210fr, No. 643a, Kiwanis helping poor and homeless children.

1988 Litho. *Perf. 13½*

638 A111 75fr dk bl, lt bl & multi .65 .30
639 A111 125fr dk brn, lt brn & multi 1.25 .45
640 A111 210fr org, yel & multi 1.90 .75
641 A111 425fr red, pink & multi 4.00 1.75
642 A111 500fr bl, yel & multi 5.50 2.00
643 Strip of 3 11.50 6.00
a. A111 210fr grn, lt grn & multi 2.10 .75
b. A111 425fr pur, pink & multi 4.50 1.75
c. A111 500fr red, orange & multi 6.00 2.00
Nos. 638-643 (6) 24.80 11.25

For surcharges see Nos. 654-656, 815B, 815W.

A112

1988 Olympics, Calgary and Seoul — A113

75fr, Women's figure skating. 100fr, Running. 125fr, Women's speed skating. 150fr, Equestrian. 350fr, Two-man luge. 400fr, Biathlon. 500fr, Pole vault. 600fr, Soccer.
No. 652, Women's downhill skiing, satellite. No. 653, Track, satellite.

1988 Litho. *Perf. 13½*

644 A112 75fr multicolored .65 .25
645 A112 100fr multicolored 1.00 .30
646 A112 125fr multicolored 1.00 .40
647 A112 150fr multicolored 1.50 .50
648 A112 350fr multicolored 3.25 .90
649 A112 400fr multicolored 4.00 1.40
650 A112 500fr multicolored 4.00 1.25
651 A112 600fr multicolored 6.00 1.50
Nos. 644-651 (8) 21.40 6.50

Souvenir Sheets

652 A113 750fr multicolored 7.75 1.50
653 A113 750fr multicolored 7.75 1.50

Nos. 649 and 651-653 are airmail.
For surcharges see Nos. 800C, 800M, 815V.

No. 643 and Service Organization Types Surcharged

No. 655, like #643b. No. 656, like #643c.

1988, July 18 Litho. *Perf. 13½*

654 Strip of 3 4.75 5.00
a. A111 75fr on 210fr #643a .65 .45
b. A111 200fr on 425fr #643b 1.75 .90
c. A111 300fr on 500fr #643c 2.75 1.25
655 A111 125fr on 425fr pur, lt pur & multi, blk letters .90 .60
656 A111 400fr on 500fr car, pink & multi 3.25 2.00
Nos. 654-656 (3) 8.90 7.60

Nos. 655-656 not issued without surcharge.

Discovery of America, 500th Anniv. (in 1992) — A114

Designs: 75fr, Christopher Columbus, *Santa Maria.* 125fr, Martin Alonzo Pinzon (c. 1441-1493), *Pinta.* 150fr, Vicente Yanez Pinzon (c. 1460-1523), *Nina.* 250fr, Search for Cipango, legendary rich islands off the coast of Asia. 375fr, *Santa Maria* shipwrecked. 450fr, Preparing for 4th voyage. 750fr, Samana Cay landing.

1988, Apr. 18 Litho. *Perf. 13½*

657 A114 75fr multi .65 .25
658 A114 125fr multi 1.10 .30
659 A114 150fr multi 1.50 .45
660 A114 250fr multi 2.10 .75
661 A114 375fr multi 3.75 1.00
662 A114 450fr multi 4.50 1.25
Nos. 657-662 (6) 13.60 4.00

Souvenir Sheet

663 A114 750fr multi, horiz. 7.75 1.50

Nos. 661-663 airmail. No. 663 contains one 42x30mm stamp.
For surcharges see Nos. 702, 815D.

1992 Summer Olympics, Barcelona A115

1988, Apr. 18

664 A115 75fr Discus, vert. .60 .25
665 A115 100fr shown .90 .30
666 A115 125fr Cycling 1.25 .35
667 A115 150fr Wrestling 1.50 .50
668 A115 375fr Basketball, vert. 3.75 1.00
669 A115 600fr Tennis, vert. 6.00 1.25
Nos. 664-669 (6) 14.00 3.65

Souvenir Sheet

670 A115 750fr Marathon, vert. 7.75 1.50

Nos. 668-670 are airmail.

Famous Men — A116

Rotary Intl. — A117

150fr, Yuri Gagarin (1934-68), USSR, cosmonaut. 300fr, Jean-Henri Dunant, Red Cross founder. 400fr, Roger Clemens, baseball player. 500fr, Garry Kasparov, USSR, 1985 world chess champion. 600fr, Paul Harris, US, Rotary founder. 750fr, Neil Armstrong walking on the Moon, John F. Kennedy. No. 678, The Thinker by Rodin, Rotary Intl. emblem.

1988, Dec. 6 Litho. *Perf. 13½*

671 A116 150fr multi 1.75 .50
672 A116 300fr multi 1.75 .50
673 A116 400fr multi 1.75 .50
674 A116 500fr multi 1.75 .50
675 A116 600fr multi 1.75 .50
a. Souv. sheet of 5, #671-675 + label 10.00 —
Nos. 665-669 (5) 18.40 3.50

Litho. & Embossed

676 A117 1500fr gold & multi 15.00 —

Souvenir Sheets

Litho.

677 A116 750fr multi 7.75 1.50

Litho. & Embossed

678 A117 1500fr gold & multi 15.00 —

Intl. Red Cross, 125th anniv. (300fr), Rotary Intl. (600fr, Nos. 676, 678). Nos. 674-678 are airmail.
Nos. 672-673 exist in souv. sheets of 1.
No. 676 exists in a souvenir sheet of 1. Value $42.50.

Inventors and Sportsmen A118

Portraits and modes of transportation: Designs: 75fr, Alain Prost, F-1 MacLaren-Honda. 125fr, George Stephenson and locomotive *Borsig of 1935.* 500fr, Ettore Bugatti (1881-1947), 1939 Bugatti Aravis Type 57. 600fr, Rudolf Diesel (1858-1913) and V200 BB diesel-electric locomotive. 750fr, Dennis Conner, captain of the *Stars and Stripes,* winner of the 1987 America's Cup. No. 684, Michael Fay, patron of the *New Zealand,* an entry in the America's Cup. No. 685, Enzo Ferrari and 1989 Ferrari Formula 1, horiz.

1988, Dec. 27 Litho. *Perf. 13½*

679 A118 75fr multi .75 .45
680 A118 125fr multi 1.25 .25
681 A118 500fr multi 5.00 1.25
682 A118 600fr multi 6.00 1.25
683 A118 750fr multi 7.00 1.25
684 A118 1000fr multi 10.00 1.25
Nos. 679-684 (6) 30.00 5.70

Souvenir Sheet

685 A118 1000fr multi 10.00 1.50

Nos. 683-685 are airmail.
Nos. 679-684 exist in souv. sheets of 1.

Scouts, Butterflies and Birds — A119

Scouts involved in various activities and species: 50fr, Gathering specimens, *Papilio nireus aristophontes oberthur* female. 75fr, Studying specimen and male. 150fr, Cooking out, *Charaxes fulvescens separanus poulton.* 375fr, Picking mushrooms, *Lonchura cucullatus.* 450fr, Examining specimen, *Charaxes castor comoranus rothschild.* 500fr, Identifying specimen, *Zosterops maderaspatana.* 750fr, Studying specimens, *Foudia omissa* and *Charaxes paradoxa lathy* female. No. 692, Photographing specimen, *Junonia rhadama.* No. 694, Examining specimen, *Agapornis cana cana.*

1989 Litho.

686 A119 50fr multi .50 .25
687 A119 75fr multi .60 .25
688 A119 150fr multi 1.40 .30
689 A119 375fr multi 4.00 .75
690 A119 450fr multi 4.75 1.00
691 A119 500fr multi 5.75 1.25
Nos. 686-691 (6) 17.00 3.80

Litho. & Embossed

692 A119 1500fr gold & multi 16.00 —

Souvenir Sheets

Litho.

693 A119 750fr multi 10.00 1.50

Litho. & Embossed

694 A119 1500fr gold & multi 13.00 —

Nos. 690-694 are airmail. Issue dates: Nos. 692, 694, May 15; others, Mar. 15.
No. 692 exists in a souvenir sheet of 1. Value $42.50.
For surcharges see Nos. 800D, 815T.

Gold Medalists of the 1988 Summer Olympics A120

Communication satellites, various equestrians and their mounts: 75fr, Nicole Uphoff, West Germany, individual dressage, and Aussat K3. 150fr, Pierre Durand, France, individual jumping, and Brazilsat. 375fr, Janos Martinek, Hungary, individual modern pentathlon, and ECS 4. 600fr, Mark Todd, New Zealand, individual three-day event, and Olympus. 750fr, Team jumping, West Germany, and satellite. No. 699, Pierre Durand, France, individual show jumping. No. 701, Nicole Uphoff, West Germany, individual dressage.

1989, Apr. 10 Litho. *Perf. 13½*

695 A120 75fr multi .65 .25
696 A120 150fr multi 1.25 .35
697 A120 375fr multi 3.00 .75
698 A120 600fr multi 5.00 1.25
Nos. 695-698 (4) 9.90 2.60

Litho. & Embossed

699 A120 1500fr gold & multi 16.00 —

Souvenir Sheets

Litho.

700 A120 750fr multi 6.75 1.50

Litho. & Embossed

701 A120 1500fr gold & multi 13.00 —

No. 701 contains one 39x38mm stamp. Nos. 698-701 are airmail.
No. 699 exists in a souvenir sheet of 1. Value $45.
For surcharges see Nos. 796Q, 804I.

Nos. 660, 588, 605 and 630 Surcharged

1989 Litho. *Perfs. as Before*

702 A114 25fr on 250fr #660 .40 .25
703 A101 150fr on 200fr #588 1.50 .50
704 A103 150fr on 200fr #605 1.50 .50
705 A108 150fr on 200fr #630 1.50 .50
Nos. 702-705 (4) 4.90 1.75

1992 Summer Olympics, Barcelona A121

1989, Apr. 26 Litho. *Perf. 13½*

706 A121 75fr Running .65 .25
707 A121 150fr Soccer 1.25 .40
708 A121 300fr Tennis 2.50 .60
709 A121 375fr Baseball 3.25 .80
710 A121 500fr Pommel horse 4.00 1.00
711 A121 600fr Table tennis 5.00 1.25
Nos. 706-711 (6) 16.65 4.30

Souvenir Sheet

712 A121 750fr Equestrian 6.75 1.50

Nos. 710-712 are airmail.
For surcharges see Nos. 796J, 796K, 800J, 812R.

Dr. Joseph-Ignace Guillotin (1738-1814) — A122

French Revolution, Bicent.: 150fr, French artillery, Gen. Francois-Christophe Kellermann (1735-1820). 375fr, Royalist insurgents & leader, Jean Cottereau (1757-94). 600fr, King Louis XVI (1774-92), troops. 1000fr, Storming of the Bastille & Jacques Necker, statesman (1732-1804). No. 717, Lafayette, Mounier, Sieyes & Declaration of the Rights of Man and Citizen. No. 719, Robespierre & St. Just before the Convention on 9 Thermidor.

1989, Oct. 25 Litho. *Perf. 13½*

713 A122 75fr multicolored .70 .25
714 A122 150fr multicolored 1.25 .35
715 A122 375fr multicolored 3.00 .60
716 A122 600fr multicolored 5.00 1.25
Nos. 713-716 (4) 9.95 2.45

Litho. & Embossed

717 A122 1500fr gold & multi 13.00 —

Souvenir Sheets
Litho.

718 A122 1000fr multicolored 8.50 1.75

Litho. & Embossed

719 A122 1500fr gold & multi 13.00

Philexfrance 1989. No. 716-719 are airmail.
No. 714 incorrectly inscribed "Francois-Etienne."
Nos. 713-716 exist in souvenir sheets of 1.
No. 717 exists in a souvenir sheet of 1. Value $22.
For surcharges see Nos. 796B, 800W, 804J.

Airport Pavilion A124

Designs: 10fr, 25fr, Airport pavilion. 50fr, 75fr, 150fr, Federal Assembly.

1990, Apr. 1 Litho. *Perf. 13*

722 A124 5fr brn, org & brt red .25 .25
723 A124 10fr brn, org & brt bl .25 .25
724 A124 25fr brn, org & brt grn .25 .25
725 A124 50fr blk & brt red .45 .25
726 A124 75fr blk & brt bl .75 .30
727 A124 150fr blk & grn 1.40 .60
Nos. 722-727 (6) 3.35 1.90

World Cup Soccer Championships, Italy — A125

Players from: 50fr, Brazil. 75fr, England. 100fr, Federal Republic of Germany. 150fr, Belgium. 375fr, Italy. 600fr, Argentina. 750fr, Argentina and Italy.

1990 Litho. *Perf. 13½*

728 A125 50fr multicolored .45 .25
729 A125 75fr multicolored .65 .30
730 A125 100fr multicolored .80 .35
731 A125 150fr multicolored 1.10 .45
732 A125 375fr multicolored 3.00 1.00
733 A125 600fr multicolored 5.00 1.25
Nos. 728-733 (6) 11.00 3.60

Litho. & Embossed

734 A125 1500fr gold & multi 13.00 5.00

Souvenir Sheets
Litho.

735 A125 750fr multicolored 6.75 1.50

Litho. & Embossed

736 A125 1500fr gold & multi 13.00 —

Nos. 732-736 are airmail.
Nos. 728-733 exist in a souvenir sheet of 6. Value, $12.50.
No. 734 exists in a souvenir sheet of 1. Value $22.50.
For surcharges see Nos. 796L, 796O, 804K.

Telecom '91 A125a

75fr, Emblem, vert.

1990, Oct. 29 Litho. *Perf. 13½*

736A A125a 75fr multi 1.00 .60
736B A125a 150fr shown 2.00 1.25

Nos. 736A-736B exist imperf.

A126

Designs: 75fr, Hubble Space Telescope placed in orbit. 150fr, Pope John Paul II, Pres. Gorbachev meet Dec. 3, 1989. 200fr, Kevin Mitchell, San Francisco Giants, Natl. League Most Valuable Player, 1989. 250fr, De Gaulle, France, and Adenauer, West Germany, meet in Sept. 1962. 300fr, Cassini probe to Titan, 2002. 375fr, Bullet train and Concorde, France. 450fr, Garry Kasparov, World Chess Champion. 500fr, Paul Harris (1868-1947), founder of Rotary Intl.

1990, Nov. 26 Litho. *Perf. 13½*

737 A126 75fr sil & multi .75 .25
738 A126 150fr sil & multi 1.50 .40
739 A126 200fr sil & multi 2.00 .40
740 A126 250fr sil & multi 2.50 .40
741 A126 300fr sil & multi 3.00 .50
742 A126 375fr sil & multi 3.75 .65
743 A126 450fr sil & multi 4.50 1.00
744 A126 500fr sil & multi 5.25 .75
Nos. 737-744 (8) 23.25 4.35

Nos. 743-744 are airmail.
No. 737-744 exist in souv. sheets of 1. Value, set of 8 $50.
For surcharges see Nos. 796A, 796R, 800I, 804A, 804L, 815E, 815U.

A127

Winter Olympics participants: 75fr, Edi Reinalter, Switzerland, slalom, 1948. 100fr, Canadian hockey team, 1924. 375fr, Gratia Van der Oye, women's slalom, Holland, 1936. 600fr, Heikki Hasu, Finland, combined cross country and ski jumping, 1948. 750fr, Helene Engelman & Alfred Berger, Austria, pairs figure skating, 1924. No. 751, Speed skater, horiz. No. 751A, Luge, horiz.

1990, Dec. 10

746 A127 75fr multicolored .60 .25
747 A127 100fr multicolored .75 .30
748 A127 375fr multicolored 3.50 1.00
749 A127 600fr multicolored 6.00 1.25
Nos. 746-749 (4) 10.85 2.80

Souvenir Sheet

750 A127 750fr multicolored 7.00 1.50

Litho. & Embossed

751 A127 1500fr gold & multi 16.00 —

Souvenir Sheet

751A A127 1500fr gold & multi 15.00 —

1992 Winter Olympics, Albertville. Nos. 748-751A are airmail. No. 750 contains one 36x41mm stamp.
No. 751 exists in a souvenir sheet of 1. Value $22.
For surcharges see Nos. 796M, 800K, 804M, 812S.

A128

Ground station, Moroni Volo-Volo.

1991, May 17 Litho. *Perf. 13½*

752 A128 75fr multicolored 1.00 .25
753 A128 150fr multicolored 1.60 .45
754 A128 225fr multicolored 2.40 .75
755 A128 300fr multicolored 3.50 1.00
756 A128 500fr multicolored 5.50 1.25
Nos. 752-756 (5) 14.00 3.70

For surcharge see 815N.

Indian Ocean Conference — A129

1991, June 17

757 A129 75fr multicolored .50 .25
758 A129 150fr multicolored 1.40 .75
759 A129 225fr multicolored 2.00 1.00
Nos. 757-759 (3) 3.90 2.00

World War II, 50th Anniv. A130

Actors, Films: 150fr, Errol Flynn, Objective Burma. 300fr, Henry Fonda, The Longest Day. 450fr, Humphrey Bogart, Sahara.

1991, Aug. 5

760 A130 150fr sil & multi 1.75 .45
761 A130 300fr sil & multi 3.25 .75
762 A130 450fr sil & multi 5.00 .90
Nos. 760-762 (3) 10.00 2.10

No. 762 is airmail. Nos. 760-762 exist in souvenir sheets of 1. Value, set of 3 $15.
For surcharges see Nos. 796D, 800H, 804B, 804G.

A131

Charles de Gaulle A132

De Gaulle and: 125fr, Battle of Koufra. 375fr, Battle of Britain. 500fr, Battle of Monte Cassino. 1000fr, Airplanes. 1500fr, De Gaulle at podium.

1991, Aug. 5 Litho. *Perf. 13½*

763 A131 125fr multi 1.50 .30
764 A131 375fr multi 3.00 .75
765 A131 500fr multi 5.00 .90
Nos. 763-765 (3) 9.50 1.95

Souvenir Sheet

766 A131 1000fr multi 12.00 2.00

Litho. & Embossed

767 A132 1500fr gold & multi 16.00 —

Nos. 765-767 are airmail. No. 767 exists in souvenir sheet of 1. Value $20.
For surcharges see Nos. 796G, 804N, 816I.

Anniversaries and Events — A133

Designs: 100fr, Satellite Columbus in polar orbit. 150fr, Gandhi. 250fr, Jean-Henri Dunant. 300fr, Wolfgang Amadeus Mozart. 375fr, Brandenburg Gate. 400fr, Konrad Adenauer. 450fr, Elvis Presley. 500fr, Ferdinand von Zeppelin.

1991, Nov. 18 Litho. *Perf. 13½*

768 A133 100fr multicolored 1.25 .30
769 A133 150fr multicolored 1.60 .35
770 A133 250fr multicolored 2.50 .60
771 A133 300fr multicolored 3.00 .60
772 A133 375fr multicolored 4.25 .90
773 A133 400fr multicolored 5.00 .90
774 A133 450fr multicolored 5.50 1.00
a. Souv. sheet, #771, 774 — —
775 A133 500fr multicolored 5.50 1.00
a. Souv. sheet, #772-773, 775 — —
Nos. 768-775 (8) 28.60 5.65

Nobel Peace Prize, 90th anniv. (No. 770). Mozart, bicent. of death (No. 771). Brandenburg Gate, bicent. (No. 772). Konrad Adenauer, 25th anniv. of death (No. 773). Elvis Presley, 15th anniv. of death (in 1992) (No. 774). Count Zeppelin, 75th anniv. of death (in 1992) (No. 775).
Nos. 774-775 are airmail. Nos. 768-775 exist in souvenir sheets of 1. Value, set $50.
For surcharges see Nos. 796F, 796H, 800G, 804C, 804O, 815F, 815O, 816J.

Mushrooms — A134

75fr, Cepe comestible. 150fr, Geastre en etoile. 600fr, Pezize ecarlate.

1992, Mar. 23 Litho. *Perf. 13½*

776 A134 75fr multicolored .80 .40
777 A134 150fr multicolored 1.50 .60
778 A134 600fr multicolored 6.00 1.50
Nos. 776-778 (3) 8.30 2.50

No. 778 is airmail. Nos. 776-778 exist imperf. and in souvenir sheets of one. Values, imperf set $12; set of souvenir sheets $10.

Shells A135

125fr, Conus textile. 150fr, Cypraecassis rufa. 500fr, Leporicypraea mappa.
750fr, Nautilus pompilius.

1992, Mar. 23

779 A135 125fr multicolored 1.60 .50
780 A135 150fr multicolored 1.75 .65
781 A135 500fr multicolored 6.00 1.90
Nos. 779-781 (3) 9.35 3.05

Souvenir Sheet

782 A135 750fr multicolored 10.50 2.00

Nos. 781-782 are airmail. Nos. 779-781 exist imperf. and in souvenir sheets of one. Values, imperf set $15; set of souvenir sheets $12. No. 782 exists imperf. Value, $12.
For surcharges see Nos. 800N, 816K.

Space Programs A136

Designs: 75fr, Mercury rocket, chimpanzee Ham, US. 125fr, Mars Observer, US. No. 785, Veronica rocket, cat Felix, France. No. 786, Mars rover, US, Mars car, USSR. 500fr, Phobos project, USSR. 600fr, Sputnik II, dog Laika, USSR. 1000fr, Viking, US, vert.

1992, Mar. 30 Litho. *Perf. 13½*

783	A136	75fr multicolored	1.25	.25
784	A136	125fr multicolored	1.75	.30
785	A136	150fr multicolored	2.25	.70
786	A136	150fr multicolored	2.10	.70
787	A136	500fr multicolored	6.50	1.25
a.		Souv. sheet, #784, 786-787	20.00	—
788	A136	600fr multicolored	7.75	1.40
a.		Souv. sheet, #783, 785, 788	20.00	—
		Nos. 783-788 (6)	21.60	4.60

Souvenir Sheet

789	A136	1000fr multicolored	13.00	2.25

Nos. 787-789 are airmail. Nos. 783-788 exist imperf. and in souvenir sheets of one. Values: imperf set, $32.50; set of souvenir sheets, $25. No. 789 contains one 30x42mm stamp.

For surcharges see Nos. 800O, 804Q.

Voyages of Discovery A137

Designs: 75fr, Space shuttle Endeavour, sailing ship Endeavour, Capt. Cook. 100fr, Satellite, sailing ship Golden Hinde, Sir Francis Drake. 150fr, ISO observation satellite, sailing ship Susan Constant, John Smith. 225fr, Probe B, sailing ship Discovery, Robert F. Scott. 375fr, Magellan probe over Venus, sailing ship, Ferdinand Magellan. 500fr, Newton probe, sailing ship Sao Gabriel, Vasco da Gama.

1000fr, Hermes-Columbus space shuttle, Columbus and his fleet.

1992, May 28 Litho. *Perf. 13½*

790	A137	75fr multicolored	1.25	.25
791	A137	100fr multicolored	1.40	.30
792	A137	150fr multicolored	2.25	.45
793	A137	225fr multicolored	2.75	.75
794	A137	375fr multicolored	5.25	1.00
795	A137	500fr multicolored	6.00	1.25
a.		Souvenir sheet of 6, #790-795	15.00	7.00
		Nos. 790-795 (6)	18.90	4.00

Souvenir Sheet

796	A137	1000fr multicolored	13.00	2.25

Nos. 794-796 are airmail. Nos. 790-795 exist imperf. in souvenir sheets of one. Values: imperf sets $35; set of souvenir sheets $45.

For surcharges see Nos. 796E, 800P, 804P.

Various Stamps Surcharged

a — (Obliterator of dots)

Methods and Perfs as Before

1992-95

796A	A126	10fr on 300fr #741	—	
796B	A122	15fr on 375fr #715	—	
796C	AP41	25fr on 210fr #C164	—	
796D	A130	25fr on 300fr #761	—	
796E	A137	25fr on 375fr #794	—	
796F	A133	35fr on 400fr #773	—	
796G	A131	50fr on 375fr #764	—	
796H	A133	50fr on 375fr #772	—	
796I	AP34	50fr on 475fr #C138	—	
796J	A121	75fr on 300fr #708	—	—
796K	A121	75fr on 375fr #709	—	
796L	A125	75fr on 375fr #732	—	
796M	A127	75fr on 375fr #748	—	
796N	AP42	75fr on 600fr #C170	—	
796O	A125	100fr on 375fr #732	—	
796P	A109	150fr on 210fr #633	—	
796Q	A120	150fr on 375fr #697	—	—
796R	A126	150fr on 375fr #742	—	
796S	AP40	150fr on 450fr #C162	—	
796T	A109	150fr on 500fr #634	—	
796U	AP42	150fr on 500fr #C169	—	

No. 796J exists with quadruple surcharge.

No. 796Q exists with inverted surcharge and with double surcharge, one inverted.

Organization of African Unity, 30th Anniv. — A138

1993, Feb. 15 Litho. *Perf. 13½x13*

797	A138	25fr blue & multi	.25	.25
798	A138	50fr pink & multi	.50	.25

Perf. 12

799	A138	75fr green & multi	1.40	.45
800	A138	150fr vermilion & multi	2.25	1.00
		Nos. 797-800 (4)	4.40	1.95

Various Stamps Surcharged

b — (Bar obliterator)

Methods and Perfs as Before

1992-95

800A	A103	50fr on 450fr #607	—	
x.		Zero in surcharge thin at top and bottom	—	
800B	AP47	75fr on 800fr #C192	—	
800C	A112	100fr on 350fr #648	—	—
800D	A119	100fr on 375fr #689	—	
g.		Zero in surcharge thin at top and bottom	—	
y.		150fr on 375fr #689 (error)	—	
800E	A101	100fr on 400fr #590	—	—
800F	A105	100fr on 400fr #618	—	
h.		Zero in surcharge thin at top and bottom	—	
800G	A133	100fr on 400fr #773	—	
i.		Zero in surcharge thin at top and bottom	—	
800H	A130	125fr on 450fr #762	—	
800I	A126	150fr on 250fr #740	—	—
800J	A121	150fr on 375fr #709	—	
z.		Zero in surcharge thin at top and bottom	—	
800K	A127	150fr on 375fr #748	—	
a.		Zero in surcharge thin at top and bottom	—	
800L	A109	150fr on 500fr #634	—	—
k.		Zero in surcharge thin at top and bottom	—	
800M	A112	150fr on 500fr #650	—	
b.		Zero in surcharge thin at top and bottom	—	
800N	A135	150fr on 500fr #781	—	—
800O	A136	150fr on 500fr #787	—	
800P	A137	150fr on 500fr #795	—	
c.		Zero in surcharge thin at top and bottom	—	
800Q	AP41	150fr on 500fr #C165	—	
d.		Zero in surcharge thin at top and bottom	—	
800R	AP44	150fr on 500fr #C177	—	
l.		Zero in surcharge thin at top and bottom	—	
m.		Denomination above obliterator	—	
n.		As "l," denomination above obliterator	—	
800S	AP45	150fr on 500fr #C181	—	
e.		Zero in surcharge thin at top and bottom	—	
800T	AP42	150fr on 500fr #C185	—	
o.		Zero in surcharge thin at top and bottom	—	
800U	AP47	150fr on 500fr #C191	—	
800V	AP50	150fr on 500fr #C212	—	
p.		Zero in surcharge thin at top and bottom	—	
800W	A122	150fr on 600fr #716	—	

Surcharge on No. 800W is sideways reading top to bottom. Nos. 800B and 800F exist with inverted surcharge, Nos. 800F, 800R, 800W, and perhaps other values exist with misplaced surcharge.

No. 800F exists with zeros in surcharge in different sizes.

1994 World Cup Soccer Championships, U.S. — A139

1993, May 12 Litho. *Perf. 13x12½*

801	A139	25fr red & multi	.25	.25
802	A139	75fr brown & multi	.65	.30
803	A139	100fr blue & multi	1.40	.40
804	A139	150fr green & multi	1.60	.60
		Nos. 801-804 (4)	3.90	1.55

Various Stamps Surcharged Type "b" in Black or Red

Methods and Perfs as Before

1992-95

804A	A126	200fr on 300fr #741	—	
s.		Zero in surcharge thin at top and bottom	—	
804B	A130	200fr on 300fr #761	—	
804C	A133	200fr on 300fr #771	—	
w.		Zero in surcharge thin at top and bottom	—	—
804D	AP45	200fr on 300fr #C180	—	
x.		Zero in surcharge thin at top and bottom	—	
804E	AP47	200fr on 300fr #C190	—	
t.		Zero in surcharge thin at top and bottom	—	
804F	A90	200fr on 450fr #520	—	
u.		Overprint right side up	—	
y.		Overprint right side up, zero in surcharge thin at top and bottom	—	
804G	A130	200fr on 450fr #762	—	
a.		Zero in surcharge thin at top and bottom	—	
b.		As "a," two obliterators	—	
804H	AP40	200fr on 450fr #C162	—	
c.		Zero in surcharge thin at top and bottom	—	
804I	A120	225fr on 375fr #697	—	
804J	A122	225fr on 375fr #715	—	
804K	A125	225fr on 375fr #732	—	
804L	A126	225fr on 375fr #742	—	
804M	A127	225fr on 375fr #748	—	
v.		"f" in surcharge omitted	—	
804N	A127	225fr on 375fr #764	—	
804O	A133	225fr on 375fr #772	—	
804P	A137	225fr on 375fr #794	—	
804Q	A136	225fr on 500fr #787	—	

Red Surcharge

804R	AP40	200fr on 300fr #C161	—	

Surcharge on No. 804F is inverted.

No. 804D exists with "020fr" surcharge. Nos. 804D and 804F exists with zeroes in surcharge in different sizes.

Intl. Telecommunications Day — A140

1993, May 17

805	A140	50fr red & multi	.30	.25
806	A140	75fr blue & multi	.50	.30
807	A140	100fr green & multi	.90	.40
808	A140	150fr black & multi	1.25	.60
		Nos. 805-808 (4)	2.95	1.55

Miniature Sheet

Prehistoric Animals — A141

Designs: a, 75fr, Edaphosaurus. b, 75fr, Moschops. c, 75fr, Sauroctonus. d, 75fr, Ornitholestes. e, 75fr, Kentrosaurus. f, 75fr, Compsognathus. g, 75fr, Styracosaurus. h, 75fr, Acanthopholis. i, 150fr, Edmontonia. j, 150fr, Struthiomimus. k, 450fr, Dromiceiomimus. l, 450fr, Iguanodon. m, 150fr, Diatryma. n, 150fr, Uintatherium. o, 525fr, Synthetoceras. p, 525fr, Euryapteryx.

1200fr, Tyrannosaurus rex.

1994, Apr. 5 Litho. *Perf. 13½*

809	A141	Sheet of 16, #a.-p.	17.50	9.00

Souvenir Sheet

810	A141	1200fr multicolored	11.50	3.00

No. 810 is airmail and contains one 42x60mm stamp.

Miniature Sheets

Flora — A142

No. 811a: 75fr, Hibiscus syriacus. b, 75fr, Anacardier. c, 75fr, Suillus lutens. d, 150fr, Pyrostegia venusta. e, 150fr, Manioc. f, 150fr, Lycogala epidendron. g, 525fr, Allamanda cathartica. h, 525fr, Cacao. i, 525fr, Clathrus ruber.

Butterflies, insects: No. 812a, 75fr, Colotis zoe. b, 150fr, Acherontia atropos. c, 450fr, Danaus chrysippus. d, 75fr, Charaxes comoranus. e, 150fr, Euchloron megaera. f,

450fr, Papilio phorbanta. g, 75fr, Hypurgus ova. h, 150fr, Onthophagus catta. i, 450fr, Echinosoma bolivari.

1994, May 24 Litho. *Perf. 13½*

811 A142 Sheet of 9 16.00 5.50
j. Souvenir sheet of 3, #811a, 811d, 811g *16.00 5.00*
k. Souvenir sheet of 3, #811b, 811e, 811h *16.00 5.00*
l. Souvenir sheet of 3, #811c, 811f, 811i *16.00 5.00*
812 A142 Sheet of 9, #a.-i. 15.00 5.00
j. Souv. sheet of 3, #812a-812c *16.00 5.00*
k. Souv. sheet of 3, #812d-812f *16.00 5.00*
l. Souv. sheet of 3, #812g-812i *16.00 5.00*

For surcharges see No. 826F.

Independence, 20th Anniv. — A142a

Designs: 100fr, 200fr, 300fr, Maps of Grand Comoro, Moheli, Mayotte and Anjouan.

1995 (?) Litho. *Perf. 13x12¾*

812M A142a 100fr multi
812N A142a 200fr multi — —
812O A142a 300fr multi

For surcharge see No. 826M.

Various Stamps Surcharged in Gold

c — (Wide numerals, obliterator of small sqares in grid)

Methods and Perfs as Before

1996, Dec.

812P AP40 200fr on 300fr #C161 —
812Q A102 200fr on 350fr #598 —
812R A121 200fr on 375fr #709 —
v. "2" same size as "0" —
812S A127 200fr on 375fr #748 —
812T AP31 200fr on 400fr #C125 — —
812U AP44 200fr on 500fr #C177 —

Size of numerals and obliteration grids varies.

A143

Diana, Princess of Wales (1961-97): Various portraits.

1997, Dec. 15 Litho. *Perf. 14*

813 A143 150fr Sheet of 12, #a.-l. 10.00 4.00
814 A143 375fr Sheet of 6, #a.-f. 12.00 5.00

Souvenir Sheet

815 A143 1000fr multicolored 5.50 2.25

Various Stamps Surcharged Type "c" in Black

Methods and Perfs as Before

1996, Dec.

815A A109 200fr on 210fr #633 —
815B A111 200fr on 210fr #640 —
815C AP41 200fr on 210fr #C164 — —
815D A114 200fr on 250fr #660 —
815E A126 200fr on 250fr #740 —
815F A133 200fr on 250fr #770 —
815G AP30 200fr on 250fr #C116 — —
815H AP38 200fr on 250fr #C151 —
815I AP38 200fr on 250fr #C152 —
x. Pair, #815H-815I + label —
815J AP42 200fr on 250fr #C168 —
815K AP42 200fr on 250fr #C184 —
815L AP28 200fr on 260fr #C110 — —
815M A101 200fr on 300fr #589 —
y. With gold obliterator over old value — —
815N A128 200fr on 300fr #755 —
815O A133 200fr on 300fr #771 —
815P AP31 200fr on 300fr #C124 —
815Q AP37 200fr on 300fr #C150 —
815R A107 200fr on 350fr #626 —
815S A98 200fr on 360fr #574 —
815T A119 200fr on 375fr #689 —
815U A126 200fr on 375fr #742 —
815V A112 200fr on 400fr #649 —
815W A111 200fr on 425fr #641 —

Size of surcharge numerals and obliteration grid varies. Black surcharge on No. 815My is misplaced. No. 815Q exists with misplaced surcharge that is faintly tripled, a surcharge with thinner zeroes, and a pair containing No. C150 next to No. 815Q with misplaced surcharge that is faintly tripled and has thinner zeroes. No. 815W exists with an inverted surcharge and with a double surcharge, one inverted.

Mother Teresa (1910-97) — A144

1997, Dec. 15 Litho. *Perf. 14*

816 A144 200fr multicolored 1.50 1.00

No. 816 was issued in sheets of 9.

Aromatic Plants — A144a

Designs: 25fr, 50fr, 1000fr, Piper nigrum. 100fr, 125fr, 200fr, Cinnamomum ceylanicum. 300fr, Syzigium aromaticum. 500fr, Myristica fragrans.

1997, Dec. 15 Litho. *Perf. 14*

816A A144a 25fr multi —
816B A144a 50fr multi —
816C A144a 100fr multi —
816D A144a 125fr multi —
816E A144a 200fr multi —
816F A144a 300fr multi —
816G A144a 500fr multi —
816H A144a 1000fr multi —

Various Stamps Surcharged Type "c" in Black

Methods and Perfs as Before

1996, Dec.

816I A131 200fr on 500fr #765 — —
816J A133 200fr on 500fr #775 — —
816K A135 200fr on 500fr #781 — —
816L AP42 200fr on 500fr #C169 — —
816M AP42 200fr on 500fr #C185 — —
816N AP42 200fr on 600fr #C170 — —
816O AP42 200fr on 600fr #C186 — —

Size of surcharge and obliteration grid varies.

Vertical Pairs from No. B4 Surcharged with Silver Bar to Obliterate Surtax

Methods and Perfs as before.

1996, Dec.

816P Surcharged pair of #B4a, B4e —
t. SP3 200fr on 200fr+10fr Galileo —
u. SP3 200fr on 200fr+10fr Planet A & 3 stars —
816Q Surcharged pair of #B4b, B4f —
v. SP3 200fr on 200fr+10fr Copernicus —
w. SP3 200fr on 200fr+10fr ICE —
816R Surcharged pair of #B4c, B4g —
x. SP3 200fr on 200fr+10fr Kepler —
y. SP3 200fr on 200fr+10fr Planet A & 5 stars —
816S Surcharged pair of #B4d, B4h —
z. SP3 200fr on 200fr+10fr Halley —
aa. SP3 200fr on 200fr+10fr Vega —

A full sheet of Nos. 816P-816S is not known to exist.

Cats A145

Designs, vert: 75fr, Silver banded. 150fr, Lac de Van. No. 819, 200fr, European short hair. No. 820, 200fr, Somali. No. 821, 375fr, Japanese bobtail. No. 822, 375fr, Egyptian mau.

No. 823, each 375fr: a, Poupée de chiffon. b, Maine coon. c, Norwegian forest cat. d, Persian. e, Droop-eared. f, Marbled American short hair.

No. 824, each 375fr: a, Manx. b, Cashmere. c, British shorthair. d, Cornish rex. e, American curl. f, Ocicat.

No. 825, 1500fr, Silver-chocolate Somali. No. 826, 1500fr, Chocolate Persian, vert.

1998, June 3 Litho. *Perf. 14*

817-822 A145 Set of 6 7.50 7.50

Sheets of 6

823-824 A145 Set of 2 24.00 24.00

Souvenir Sheets

825-826 A145 Set of 2 15.00 6.00

No. C215D Surcharged Type "c" in Red or Black

Methods and Perfs as Before

1997 (?)

826A AP52a 100fr on 225fr — —
826B AP52a 200fr on 225fr — —
826C AP52a 200fr on 225fr (Bk) —
826D AP52a 500fr on 225fr —
826E AP52a 600fr on 225fr —

Size of surcharge numerals varies. No. 826B exists with inverted surcharge, No. 826C exists with double surcharge.

No. 811 Surcharged on Six Stamps

d — (Obliterator of Triangles and Wavy Lines)

Methods and Perfs as Before

1998 (?)

826F Sheet of 9 —
g. A142 200fr on 150fr Pyrostegia venusta —
h. A142 200fr on 150fr Manioc —
i. A142 200fr on 150fr Lycogala epidendron —
j. A142 200fr on 525fr Allamanda cathartica —
k. A142 200fr on 525fr Cacao —
l. A142 200fr on 525fr Clathrus ruber —

The three 75fr stamps on the sheet received no surcharge.

No. 812O Surcharged

e — (Obliterator of Bars, Dots, and Semicircles)

Methods and Perfs as Before

1998 (?)

826M A142a 100fr on 300fr —

Size of surcharge numerals varies.

Marine Life A146

No. 827, each 150fr: a, Pomacanthus imperator. b, Cephalopholis miniata. c, Diver. d, Nautilus pompilius. e, Sphyraena barracuda. f, Manta birostris. g, Lutjanus sebae. h, Chaetodonplus duboulayi. i, Amphiprion bicinctus.

No. 828, vert , each 150fr: a, Istiophorus platypterus. b, Sterna fuscata. c, Larus pipixcan. d, Hippocampus kuda. e, Amphiprion ocellaris (2 fish). f, Octopus vulgaris. g, Chaetodon striatus. h, Actini aquina. i, Acanthurus leucosternon.

No. 829: a, Diomedea exulans. b, Delphinus delphis. c, Sailboat. d, Sphyrna zygaena. e, Loligo forbesi. f, Galeocerdo cuvieri. g, Pomacanthus imperator, diff. h, Amphiprion ocellaris (1 fish). i, Forcipiger flavissimus. j, Electrophorus electricus. k, Dermochelys coriaoea. l, Asterias rubens.

No. 830, 1500fr, Mastigias papua, vert. No. 831, 1500fr, Sepia officinalis. No. 832, 1500fr, Zancius canescens.

1998, Aug. 10 Litho. *Perf. 14*

Sheets of 9 or 12

827-828 A146 Set of 2 13.00 13.00
829 A146 200fr #a.-l. 12.00 12.00

Souvenir Sheets

830-832 A146 Set of 3 22.50 22.50

Nos. 830-832 each contain one 51x38mm or 38x51mm stamp.

Betty Boop — A146a

No. 832A: b, Wearing hula skirt, dancing. c, With dog, wearing blue dress, in pink heart. d, Wearing polka dot dress. e, In bathtub. f, Face in red heart. g, Holding top hat. h, With flamingos. i, With dog, Wearing red dress, blue ribbon. j, Wearing hula skirt, on surf board.

1125fr, With fishing pole.

1998 Litho. *Perf. 13¼*

832A A146a 300fr Sheet of 9, #b-j 14.00 14.00

Souvenir Sheet

832K A146a 1125fr multi 6.00 6.00

No. 832A contains nine 35x41mm stamps.

Popeye — A146b

No. 832L: m, Wimpy. n, Popeye, Olive Oyl, ship's wheel. o, Swee'Pea. p, Head of Popeye. q, Popeye. r, Head of Olive Oyl. s, Jeep. t, Olive Oyl. u, Brutus.

No. 832V, 1125fr, Popeye with spinach can. No. 832W, 1125fr, Like #832Ln, horiz.

1998

832L A146b 450fr Sheet of 9, #m-u 20.00 20.00

Souvenir Sheets

832V-832W A146b Set of 2 11.50 11.50

No. 832L contains nine 35x51mm stamps, No. 832W contains one 60x50mm stamp.

Coelacanth — A147

World Wildlife Fund: a, Swimming right, colored background. b, Swimming right, white background. c, In net. d, Swimming left.

No. 833E: f, Like #833a. g, Like #833d. h, Like #833c. i, Like #833b.

1998

833 A147 200fr Strip of 4, #a-d 11.50 11.50

833E A147 375fr Sheet of 4, #f-i 5.00 5.00

No. 833 was issued in sheets of 3 vertical strips.

No. 833E exists imperf. Value $45.

I Love Lucy — A147a

No. 833F, vert. — Lucy: g, With black ribbon in hair. h, Wearing burlap sack. i, With trapeze in mouth. j, With one arm raised. k, On telephone. l, Wearing red and white apron. m, Wearing bright green dress. n, Wearing blue dress. o, With fishing gear.

1125fr, With Ricky, with fishing gear.

1998 Litho. *Perf. 13¼*

833F A147a 250fr Sheet of 9, #g-o 13.00 13.00

Souvenir Sheet

833P A147a 1125fr multi 7.00 7.00

No. 833F contains nine 35x51mm stamps.

Diana, Princess of Wales (1961-97) A148

Nos. 834-835, 835J, Various portraits.

No. 836, 1125fr, Wearing scarf, green dress. No. 837, 1125fr, Wearing black and white hat and outfit.

1998 Litho. *Perf. 13½*

Sheets of 9

834 A148 250fr #a.-i. 11.50 11.50
835 A148 350fr #a.-i. 14.50 14.50
835J A148 450fr #k.-s. 18.00 18.00

Souvenir Sheets

836-837 A148 Set of 2 10.00 10.00

Nos. 835, 835J contain 42x51mm stamps. Nos. 836-837 each contain one 42x60mm stamp.

Entertainers A149

No. 838: Various portraits of Grace Kelly (Princess Grace of Monaco) (1929-92).

No. 839: Various portraits of Frank Sinatra (1915-98).

1998 Sheets of 9

838 A149 300fr #a.-i. 13.00 13.00
839 A149 500fr #a.-i. 21.00 21.00

Classic Automobiles — A150

No. 840, each 150fr: a, 1936 Jaguar SS. b, 1939 Lincoln Continental. c, 1903 Mercedes. d, 1936 MG-TA. e, 1946 Oldsmobile Custom Cruiser 98. f, 1933 Pontiac. g, 1940 Rolls-Royce Silver Ghost 40/50. h, 1950 Studebaker Starlight Coupe. i, 1932 Ford V8.

No. 841, each 150fr: a, 1927 Alfa Romeo RLSS. b, 1933 DuPont Model G. c, Bentley Speed Six. d, 1932 Cadillac 355. e, 1955 Corvette. f, 1934 Chrysler Airflow. g, Buick Coupe deVille. h, Model T Ford. i, 1920 Duesenberg Model A.

No. 842, 1500fr, Rolls-Royce Phantom II Continental. No. 843, 1500fr, 1927 Daimler Double Six.

1998, Oct. 29 Litho. *Perf. 14*

Sheets of 9

840-841 A150 Set of 2 13.00 13.00

Souvenir Sheets

842-843 A150 Set of 2 17.00 17.00

Birds — A151

No. 844, 75fr, Macareux moine. No. 845, 75fr, Calliste à tête verte. No. 846, 150fr, Soutmanga de la reine Christine. No. 847, 150fr, Rale d'eau. No. 848, 200fr, Lophophore replendissant. No. 849, 200fr, Francolin noir. No. 850, 375fr, Mesia â oreillonis argentes. No. 851, 375fr, Mérion splendide.

No. 852: a, Canard plongeur austral. b, Garrot a ceil d'or. c, Harle huppé. d, Canard colvert. e, Canard branchu. f, Sarcelle elegante.

No. 853: a, Emérillon. b, Nyctale de tengmalm. c, Aigle royal d, Kétoupa malais. e, Caracara. f, Chouette à lunettes

No. 854, Jacana du mexique. No. 855, Toucan de cuvier.

1999, Jan. 23 Litho. *Perf. 14*

844-851 A151 Set of 8 8.50 8.50

Sheets of 6, #a-f

852-853 A151 375fr Set of 2 22.50 22.50

Souvenir Sheets

854-855 A151 1500fr Set of 2 16.00 16.00

Fauna A152

No. 856, vert, each 150fr: a, Giraffa camalopardalis. b, Macaca fusata. c, Loxodonta africana. d, Ovis dalli. e, Phoenicopterus ruber. f, Orcinus orca. g, Ursus horribilis. h, Lemur catta.

No. 857, vert, each 150fr: a, Pongo pygmaeus. b, Ceratotherium simum. c, Ailuropoda melanoleuca. d, Tursiops truncartus. e, Felis caracel. f, Eudyptes chrysocome. g, Bison bison. h, Panthera uncia.

No. 858, vert, each 150fr: a, Phascolarctos cinereus. b, Ammotragus levia. c, Hippopatamus amphibius. d, Saimiri boliviensis. e, Acinonyx jubatus. f, Gorilla gorilla. g, Branta sandvicensis. h, Thalarctos maritimus.

No. 859, each 150fr: a, Panthera tigris. b, Phoca groenlandica. c, Acipenser sturio. d, Lepidochelys kempii. e, Ailuropoda melanoleuca. f, Isurus oxyrinchus. g, Chelydra serpentina. h, Eretmochelys imbricata.

Each 1500fr: No. 860: Pan troglodytes, vert. No. 861, Panthera tigris altaica, vert. No. 862, Oryx gazella, vert. No. 863, Hippotigris zebra. No. 864, Diceros bicornis. No. 865, Panthera leo. No. 866, Amazona viridgenalis. No. 867, Pygoscelis papua, vert.

1999, Jan. 25 Sheets of 8

856-859 A152 Set of 4 25.00 25.00

Souvenir Sheets

860-867 A152 Set of 8 65.00 65.00

Fish A153

No. 868, 75fr, Pomacantus imperator. No. 869, 75fr, Heniochus intermedium. No. 870, 150fr, Mirolaprichthys. No. 871, 150fr, Pomacanthus paru. No. 872, 375fr, Ostzacion tuberculatus. No. 873, 375fr, Colisa calia.

No. 874, each 150fr: a, Coris aygula. b, Chromis caeruleys. c, Euxiphipops navarchus. d, Pseudobalistes fuscus. e, Zebrasoma flavescens. f, Mycteroperca urba. g, Epinephelus flavocaeruleus. h, Equetus lanceolatus. i, Acanthurus leucostemon.

No. 875, each 150fr: a, Chaetodon tinkeri. b, Ostzaciidae. c, Seatophagus argus. d, Adioryx coruscus. e, Pygoplites diacanthus. f, Paracanthurus hepatus. g, Chaetodon plebius. h, Lythrypnus dalli. i, Myrichthys oculatus.

Each 1500fr: No. 876, Amphiprion percula. No. 877, Cymnothorne undulatus.

1998, Oct.-Nov. Litho. *Perf. 14*

868-873 A153 Set of 6 7.00 7.00

Sheets of 9

874-875 A153 Set of 2 14.00 14.00

Souvenir Sheets

876-877 A153 Set of 2 16.00 16.00

Marine Life — A154

No. 878, 75fr, Tubastrea aurea. No. 879, 75fr, Condylachtis gigantea. No. 880, 150fr, Paracanthurus hepatus. No. 881, 150fr, Balistoides conspicillum. No. 882, 200fr, Diodon holocanthus. No. 883, 200fr, Sebastes rubrivintus. No. 884, 375fr, Trygonorhina fasciata. No. 885, 375fr, Phocoenoides dalli.

No. 886, each 150fr: a, Epinephelus guttatus. b, Diademichthys lineatus. c, Plotosus lineatus. d, Rhinomuraena quaesita. e, Zanclus cornutus. f, Persephona punctata. g, Murex pecten. h, Tetrosomus gibbosus.

No. 887, each 150fr: a, Lythrypnus dalli. b, Premnas biaculeatus. c, Pseudanthias tuka. d, Capros aper. e, Balistoides conspicillum. f, Oreaster reticulatus. g, Octopus joubini. h, Fasciolaris tulipa.

Each 1500fr: No. 888, S. picturatus. No. 889, Megaptera novaeangliae.

1999

878-885 A154 Set of 8 8.50 8.50

Sheets of 8

886-887 A154 Set of 2 15.00 15.00

Souvenir Sheets

888-889 A154 Set of 2 19.00 19.00

Prehistoric Animals — A155

No. 890, each 150fr: a, Meganeura. b, Archaeopteryx. c, Peteinosaurus. d, Eudimorphodon. e, Brachiosaurus. f, Gallimimus. g, Tarbosaurus. h, Parasaurolophus. i, Sauropelta. j, Herrarasaurus. k, Stegosaurus. l, Lambeosaurus.

No. 891, each 150fr: a, Ramphorhinchus. b, Quetzalcoatlus. c, Pterodactylus. d, Pteranodon. e, Dimorphodon. f. Camarasaurus. g, Tenontosaurus. h, Protoceratops. i, Coelurosaurus. j, Mixosaurus. k, Ceresiosaurus. l, Sharovipteryx.

Each 1500fr: No. 892, Ceratosaurus. No. 893, Mesosaurus. No. 894, Megazostrodon. No. 895, Diatryma.

1999 Sheets of 12

890-891 A155 Set of 2 19.00 19.00

Souvenir Sheets

892-895 A155 Set of 4 32.50 32.50

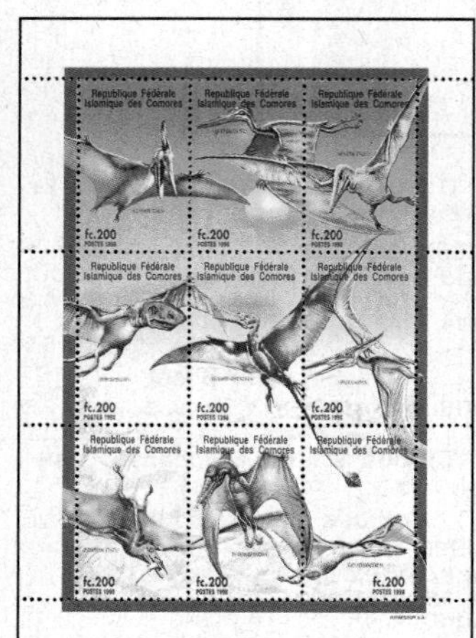

Prehistoric Animals, Lemurs and Butterflies — A156

Prehistoric animals — No. 895A — Prehistoric sea creatures: b, Eurhinodelphis. c, Stenopterygius. d, Ichthyosaurus. e, Pakicetus. f, Xenacanthus. g, Zygorhiza. h, Basilosaurus. i, Mesosaurus. j, Cetotherium. No. 896: a, Elasmosaurus (b). b, Quetzalcoatl (c). c, Mesadactylus (b). d, Dimorphodon (e). e, Rhamphorhynchus (c, d, f, i). f, Pteranodon (c, i). g, Pterodactylus (h). h, Eudimorphodon (i). i, Ornithodesmus (g, h).

Lemurs — No. 897: a, Haplorhinien primitif. b, Aye aye (c, e, f). c, Lemur vari. d, Indri. e, Makis varis (f, i). f, Potto. g, Lemur catta. h, Lemur macaos. i, Microcebe souris.

Butterflies — No. 898: a, Charaxes nobilis. b, Charaxes eupale. c, Charaxes brutus. d, Lobobunea turlini. e, Papilio nobilis. f, Athletes gigas. g, Papilio antimachus. h, Epiphora albida. i, Papilio zalmoxis.

1998 Sheets of 9 ***Perf. 13¼x13½***

895A A156 150fr #b-j 6.50 6.50
896 A156 200fr #a.-i. 9.75 9.75
897 A156 250fr #a.-i. 12.00 12.00
898 A156 300fr #a.-i. 14.50 14.50

See Nos. 928-933.

A157

Endangered Species — A157a

Designs: 75fr, Galago crassicaudatus. 150fr, Vulpes vulpes. 200fr, Anomalurus pusillus. 375fr, Loxodonta africana, vert.

Primates, vert: Nos. 903a-903c, Various views of Pan troglodytes. Nos. 903d-903f, Various views of gorilla gorilla. Nos. 903g-903i, Various views of pongo pygmaeus.

No. 904, each 375fr: a, Tragelaphus strepsiceros. b, Capra hircus. c, Egretta alba. d, Tockus flavirostris.

No. 905, each 375fr: a, Ursus maritimus. b, Megaptera novaeangliae. c, Phoca vitulina. d, Aptenodytes forsteri.

No. 906, each 375fr: a, Pelecanus occidentalis. b, Orcinus orca. c, Delphinus delphis. d, Iguana iguana.

No. 907: a, Panthera tigris altaica. b, Camelus bactrianus. c, Canus lupus. d, Cuon alpinus. e, Rangifer tarandus dawsoni. f, Gulo gulo.

Each 1500fr: No. 908, Loxodonta africana, vert. No. 909, Ursus thibetanus.

Perf. 14, 14½x14 (#904-906)

1999, Jan. 25 Litho.

899-902 A157 Set of 4 4.50 4.50
903 A157 150fr Sheet of 9, #a.-i. 8.00 8.00

Sheets of 4

904-906 A157a Set of 3 24.00 24.00

Sheet of 6

907 A157 375fr #a.-f. 12.00 12.00

Souvenir Sheets

908-909 A157 Set of 2 16.00 16.00

Mushrooms
A158 A159

No. 910, 75fr, Russula xerampelina. No. 911, 75fr, Catathelasma imperiale. No. 912, 150fr, Cortinarius violaceus. No. 913, 150fr, Cortinarius camphoratus. No. 914, 200fr, Rozites caperata. No. 915, 200fr, Coprinus picaceus. No. 916, 375fr, Coprinus cromatus. No. 917, 375fr, Russula cavipes.

No. 918, each 150fr: a, Boletus edulis. b, Suillus grevillei. c, Boletinus cavipes. d, Morchella esculenta. e, Morchella conica. f, Clitocybe dealbata. g, Hygrocybe nigrescens. h, Clitocybe geotropa. i, Lepiota cristata.

No. 919, each 150fr: a, Amanita citrina. b, Amanita phalloides. c, Cortinarius praestans. d, Phallus impudicus. e, Cortinarius bicolor. f, Cortinarius renidens. g, Lactarius torminosus. h, Boletus satanas. i, Cystolepiota bucknalii.

No. 920, each 375fr: a, Amanita muscaria. b, Coprinus comatus. c, Clitocybe odora. d, Cantharellus cibarius. e, Mycena epipterygia. f, Marasmius oreades.

No. 921, each 375fr: a, Boletus edulis. b, Laccaria laccata. c, Agaricus campestris. d, Hypholoma fasciculare. e, Lepiota procera. f, Russula aurata.

Each 1500fr: No. 922, Ramaria aurea, horiz. No. 923, Panellus serotinus. No. 924, Macrolepiota procera. No. 925, Amanita muscaria. No. 926, Hebeloma crustuliniforme. No. 927, Lepiota molybdites.

1999 Litho. ***Perf. 14***

910-917 A158 Set of 8 8.50 8.50

Sheets of 9

918-919 A158 Set of 2 14.00 14.00

Sheets of 6

920-921 A159 Set of 2 24.00 24.00

Souvenir Sheets

922-925 A158 Set of 4 32.50 32.50
926-927 A159 Set of 2 16.00 16.00

Raptors — A160

No. 927A — Birds: b, Souimanga royal. c, Martin-pecheur huppe. d, Pie-grieche. e, Barbican a tete roughe. f, Beau-marquet. g, Rollier a poitrine lilas. h, Pintade vulturine. i, Grenadier. j, Outarde korhaon.

No. 928: a, Sparrow hawk. b, Red-tailed buzzard. c, Dark kite. d, African fish eagle. e, Bald eagle. f, Fawn-colored vulture. g, Peregrine falcon. h, Osprey. i, Harpie eagle.

Dinosaurs — No. 929: a, Dilophosaurus. b, Megalosaurus. c, Ceratosaurus. d, Coelophysis. e, Tyrannosaurus. f, Deinonychus. g, Allosaurus. h, Stegosaurus. i, Albertosaurus.

Gems — No. 930: a, Ruby. b, Liroconite. c, Emerald. d, Euclase. e, Diamond. f, Chrysoberyl. g, Plancheite. h, Kasolite. i, Indigolite.

Meteorites — No. 931: a, Martian. b, Antarctic. c, C2 Chondrite. d, Archondrite. e, Octaedrite moyenne. f, Iron. g, Tektite. h, Chondrite olivine. i, Iron, diff.

Mushrooms — No. 932: a, Paxillus atrotomentosus. b, Craterellus cornucopioides. c, Boletus satanas. d, Clavaria truncata. e, Phallus impudicus. f, Scleroderma aurantiacum. g, Amanita citrina. h, Catathe lasma. i, Inocybe fastigiata.

1125fr, Wulfenite.

1998 Sheets of 9 ***Perf. 13¼x13½***

927A A160 175fr #b-j 10.00 10.00
928 A160 200fr #a.-i. 11.00 11.00
929 A160 250fr #a.-i. 11.50 11.50
930 A160 375fr #a.-i. 15.00 15.00
931 A160 400fr #a.-i. 16.00 16.00
932 A160 400fr #a.-i. 16.00 16.00

Souvenir Sheet

933 A160 1125fr multicolored 4.50 4.50

No. 933 contains one 36x51mm stamp.

Captions on Nos. 928e and 928h are transposed.

See Nos. 896-898.

"Illegal" Stamps

Comoro Islands postal officials have declared as "illegal" the following items:

Muhammad Ali, sheet of nine 300fr stamps (previously No. 934);

Muhammad Ali, 1125fr souvenir sheet (previously No. 935);

Babe Ruth, sheet of nine 375fr stamps;

Babe Ruth, two 1125fr souvenir sheets;

Ocean Life, sheet of nine stamps with values of 100, 150, 250, 300, 350, 400, 450, and 500fr;

Horses, sheet of nine stamps with values of 100, 150, 250, 300, 350, 400, 450, and 500fr;

Pandas, sheet of nine stamps with values of 100, 150, 250, 300, 350, 400, 450, and 500fr;

Flora and Fauna: 25fr Harpe costata, 25fr Hibiscus, 50fr Volute lapponica, 50fr Tournesol de Comoros, 100fr Ghetonia mydas, 125fr Octopus vulgaris, 150fr Ylang ylang, 300fr Coelacanth, 300fr Tellina variegata.

Famous People: 250fr, Willy Messerschmitt, Messerschmitt BF-109G-6/R6. 300fr, Louis Pasteur, rabies vaccine administered to Joseph Meister. 350fr, Dr. Albert Schweitzer. 400fr, Ferdinand von Zeppelin, flying Zeppelin. 475fr, Henri Dunant, Nobel Prize. 500fr, Albert Einstein, Gravity Probe B. 550fr, Ayrton Senna, race car. 600fr, Pope John Paul II. 750fr, Iranian Pres. Mohammad Khatami, Pope John Paul II. 800fr, Crew of Apollo 11. 1125fr souvenir sheet, Lindbergh, Spirit of St. Louis.

Submarines — A161

No. 934: a, USS Salt Lake City, US. b, Le Terrible, France. c, Amethyste, France.

1999 Litho. ***Perf. 13¼***

934 A161 150fr Sheet of 3, #a-c 3.00 3.00

Automobiles — A161a

No. 935: a, Cadillac Eldorado, Cadillac Series 62, US. b, Aston Martin DB2 IV Mark III, Austin Healey. c, Alfa Romeo Superlegera, Alfa Romeo Giuletta.

1125fr, Aston Martin DB5.

1999

935 A161a 200fr Sheet of 3, #a-c 3.00 3.00

Souvenir Sheet

935D A161a 1125fr multi 5.50 5.50

No. 935D contains one 51x30mm stamp.

Motorcycles — A162

No. 935E: f, Honda NR. g, Christian Leliard and motorcycle. h, Joe S. Wright and motorcycle.

1999

935E A162 250fr Sheet of 3, #f-h 4.00 4.00

Helicopters — A162a

No. 936: a, Westland Wessex. b, MIL MI-8. c, Sikorsky 5-76 Spirit.

1999

936 A162a 300fr Sheet of 3, #a-c 4.50 4.50

Dogs and Sleds — A163

No. 937: a, Alaskan malamute, US. b, Greenlandic. c, Siberian husky.

1999

937 A163 400fr Sheet of 3, #a-c 6.00 6.00

Airplanes A164

No. 938: a, Tupolev Tu-160. b, Lockheed F-117A. c, Rafale C.01.

No. 939: a, Ilyshin Il-76. b, Boeing E-3. c, Concorde.

1125fr, Concorde, diff.

1999 Litho. ***Perf. 13¼***

Sheets of 3

938 A164 375fr #a.-c. 5.00 5.00
939 A164 450fr #a.-c. 6.50 6.50

Souvenir Sheet

940 A164 1125fr mulicolored 6.75 6.75

No. 940 contains one 50x30mm stamp.

Trains A165

No. 941: a, Series E. b, Series 9100. c, Kitson-Still I-C-I.

No. 942: a, HST 125. b, TGV. c, RTG.

1125fr, Sereis DD40AX.

1999 Litho. ***Perf. 13¼***

Sheets of 3

941 A165 400fr #a.-c. 6.50 6.50
942 A165 500fr #a.-c. 8.00 8.00

Souvenir Sheet

943 A165 1125fr mulicolored 6.00 6.00

No. 943 contains one 50x30mm stamp.

Space Achievements — A166

No. 944: a, Shuttles Discovery, Buran. b, Ariane V. c, John Glenn, Saturn V.

No. 945: a, Valentina Tereshkova, Soyuz 4. b, Dogs Laika, Bielka. c, Yuri Gagarin, Vostok 1.

1125fr, Space Shuttle Discovery, John Glenn.

1999 Litho. *Perf. 13¼*

Sheets of 3

944 A166	500fr #a.-c.		7.00	7.00
945 A166	600fr #a.-c.		9.00	9.00

Souvenir Sheet

946 A166	1125fr multi		6.00	6.00

No. 946 contains one 51x30mm stamp.

Teams in 1998 World Cup Soccer Tournament — A167

Players in 1998 World Cup Soccer Tournament — A168

No. 947, 150fr: a, Italy. b, Chile, c, Cameroun. d, Austria. e, Netherlands. f, Belgium. g, South Korea. h, Mexico.

No. 948, 250fr: a, Brazil. b, Scotland. c, Morocco. d, Norway. e, Spain. f, Nigeria. g, Paraguay. h, Bulgaria.

No. 949, 300fr: a, France. b, South Africa. c, Saudi Arabia. d, Denmark. e, Germany. f, United States. g, Yugoslavia. h, Iran.

No. 950, 500fr: a, England. b, Colombia. c, Romania. d, Tunisia. e, Argentina. f, Croatia. g, Jamaica. h, Japan.

No. 951, 350fr: a, Desailly, French flag. b, Ronaldo, Brazilian flag. c, Suker, Croatian flag. d, Kluivert, Netherlands flag. e, French players, World Cup trophy. f, Brazilian player (yellow and green shirt). g, Croatian player (checked shirt). h, Netherlands player (orange shirt).

1998 Litho. *Perf. 13x13½*

Sheets of 8, #a-h

947-950 A167	Set of 4		40.00	40.00
951 A168	multi		12.00	12.00

Trucks — A169

No. 952: a, Truck with ornamentation over cab. b, Blue truck. c, Green truck. d, Yellow truck.

1999 Litho. *Perf. 13¼*

952 A169	350fr Sheet of 4, #a-d		10.00	10.00

Automobile Racing, Chess, Tennis and Table Tennis, Fishing and Diving — A170

No. 953, 250fr — Automobile racing: a, Giuseppe Farina and Alfa 1500. b, Juan Fangio and Mercedes 2.5L. c, Jack Brabham and Cooper Climax 2.5L. d, Jim Clark and Lotus Climax 1.5L.

No. 954, 300fr — Chess players: a, Garry Kasparov. b, Akiba Rubinstein. c, Max Euwe. d, Mikhail Botvinnik.

No. 955, 375fr — Fishing and diving: a, Shark fishing. b, Sport fishing. c, Diver, back half of shark. d, Diver, front half of shark.

No. 956, 500fr — Chess players: a, Bent Larsen. b, José Raúl Capablanca. c, Boris Spassky. d, Bobby Fischer.

No. 957, 600fr — Tennis and table tennis: a, Female tennis player. b, Male table tennis player. c, Female table tennis player. d, Male tennis player.

No. 958, 1125fr — Chess players: a, Samuel Reshevsky. b, Vassili Smyslov.

No. 959, 1125fr — Fishing and diving: a, Sport fishing, diff. b, Divers and marine life.

No. 960, 1125fr — Tennis and table tennis: a, Male table tennis player, diff. b, Women tennis players.

1999 *Perf. 13¼*

Sheets of 4, #a-d

953-957 A170	Set of 5		47.50	47.50

Souvenir Sheets of 2, #a-b

958-960 A170	Set of 3		16.00	16.00

Nos. 816E, 816G Surcharged

Methods and Perfs. As Before

2001, June 16

963 A144a	100fr on 500fr multi		—	—
964 A144a	125fr on 200fr multi		—	—

Traditional Costumes A171

Designs: 125fr, Woman. No. 966, 150fr, No. 969, 300fr, Woman, diff. No. 967, 150fr, No. 968, 300fr, Man.

2002, Apr. 8 Litho. *Perf. 13¼x13*

965-969 A171	Set of 5		*8.50*	*8.50*

Flowers — A172

Designs: 50fr, Cananga odorata. 600fr, Vanilla planifolia.

2003, Oct. 9

970-971 A172	Set of 2		*5.25*	*5.25*

Marine Mammals A173

Designs: 75fr, Peponocephala electra. 1000fr, Megaptera novaeangliae.

2003, Oct. 9 *Perf. 13x13¼*

972-973 A173	Set of 2		*9.00*	*9.00*

Wood Handicrafts A174

Designs: 100fr, Carved door. 300fr, Candleholder.

2003, Oct. 9 *Perf. 13¼x13*

974-975 A174	Set of 2		*3.25*	*3.25*

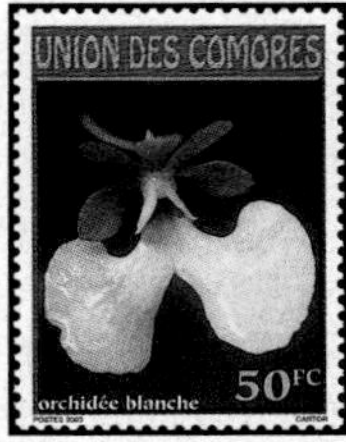

Orchids — A175

Orchid color: 50fr, White. 75fr, Yellow. 100fr, Mauve. 600fr, Red.

2003, Oct. 9

976-979 A175	Set of 4		*6.50*	*6.50*

Diplomatic Relations Between Comoro Islands and People's Republic of China, 30th Anniv. — A176

No. 980: a, 125fr, Chinese President Hu Jintao and Comoro Islands President Azali Assoumani, country flags. b, 125fr, Coelacanth, Worldwide Fund for Nature emblem, country arms. c, 300fr, Comoros Islands Broadcasting Center, country arms. d, 600fr, Comoros Islands People's Palace, country flags.

2006, Jan. 1 Litho. *Perf. 12*

980 A176	Block of 4, #a-d		5.75	5.75

Comoro Islands postal officials have declared as "illegal" the following items:

Impressionist Paintings, sheet of five 500fr stamps.

Paintings in the Louvre, six different sheets of two 500fr stamps.

American Actors and Actresses, four different sheets of four 350fr stamps.

European Astronauts, three souvenir sheets of one 500fr stamp.

Disneyland, 50th anniv., souvenir sheet of one 500fr stamp.

Léopold Sédar Senghor (1906-2001), First President of Senegal — A177

Perf. 13x13¼, 13¼x13

2007, June 1 Litho.

980E A177	125fr pur & blk		—	
981 A177	125fr grn & multi		.70	.70
982 A177	125fr yel & multi, vert.		.70	.70
983 A177	300fr grn & blk		1.75	1.75
983A A177	300fr blue & multi		—	
984 A177	300fr red vio & blk, vert.		1.75	1.75
985 A177	350fr pur & multi, vert.		2.00	2.00
986 A177	500fr brn & blk, vert.		2.75	2.75
	Nos. 981-983, 984-986 (6)		9.65	9.65

Dated 2006.

Medicinal Plants — A178

Designs: 75fr, Cymbopogon citratus. 125fr, Ocimum suave. 150fr, Aloe molucaca. 250fr, Like 75fr. 300fr, Like 150fr. 500fr, Like 125fr.

2007, June 1 *Perf. 13¼x13*

987-992 A178	Set of 6		7.75	7.75

A179

Transportation and Space — A180

No. 993 — Military aircraft and flags: a, 125fr, B-24 Liberator, U.S. flag. b, 150fr, Mitsubishi G4-M3, Japanese flag. c, 225fr, Petlyakov Pe-2, Russian flag. d, 300fr, Savoia-Marchetti SM-79, Italian flag. e, 400fr, Nakajima Ki84, Japanese flag. f, 1000fr, Dornier Do-335, German flag.

3000fr, Mitsubishi A6M5, Japanese flag.

2008, Oct. 1 *Perf. 13x13¼*

993 A179	Sheet of 6, #a-f		12.50	12.50

Souvenir Sheet

Perf. 13¼ Syncopated

994 A180	3000fr multi		17.00	17.00

Medical Vehicles

No. 995 — Red Cross flag and: a, 125fr, English ambulance. b, 150fr, ASLAV-A, Australia. c, 225fr, Red Cross vehicle, U.S. d, 300fr, Devon Air Ambulance helicopter, United Kingdom. e, 400fr, USNS Mercy. f, 1000fr, Medical worker on motorcycle, Hong Kong.

3000fr, M1133 Medical evacuation vehicle, U.S.

2008, Oct. 1 *Perf. 13x13¼*

995 A179	Sheet of 6, #a-f		12.50	12.50

Souvenir Sheet

Perf. 13¼ Syncopated

996 A180	3000fr multi		17.00	17.00

Submarines

No. 997: a, 125fr, Nautilus, 1800. b, 150fr, Brandtaucher, 1850. c, 225fr, Pioneer, 1861. d, 300fr, Flach, 1866. e, 400fr, Ictineo I 1858. f, 1000fr, Resurgam, 1878.

3000fr, Turtle, 1776.

2008, Oct. 1 *Perf. 13x13¼*

997 A179	Sheet of 6, #a-f		12.50	12.50

Souvenir Sheet

Perf. 13¼ Syncopated

998 A180	3000fr multi		17.00	17.00

U.S. High Speed Trains

No. 999 — Acela Express and U.S. landmarks: a, 125fr, Hollywood sign. b, 150fr, Golden Gate Bridge. c, 225fr, World Trade

Center. d, 300fr, Statue of Liberty. e, 400fr, San Francisco skyline. f, 1000fr, White House.
3000fr, U.S. Capitol.

2008, Oct. 1 ***Perf. 13x13¼***
999 A179 Sheet of 6, #a-f 12.50 12.50

Souvenir Sheet

Perf. 13¼ Syncopated

1000 A180 3000fr multi 17.00 17.00

Chinese High Speed Trains

No. 1001 — Maglev, flag of People's Republic of China, and Chinese landmarks: a, 200fr, Xian. b, 250fr, Tea house. c, 350fr, Pudong. d, 450fr, Great Wall of China. e, 500fr, Potala Palace. f, 1000fr, Gate of Heavenly Peace.
3000fr, Great Wall of China, diff.

2008, Oct. 1 ***Perf. 13x13¼***
1001 A179 Sheet of 6, #a-f 15.50 15.50

Souvenir Sheet

Perf. 13¼ Syncopated

1002 A180 3000fr multi 17.00 17.00

Japanese High Speed Trains

No. 1003 — Shinkansen, Japanese flag, and Japanese landmarks: a, 200fr, Amanohashidate. b, 250fr, Itsukushima Shrine. c, 350fr, Umeda Sky Building, Osaka. d, 450fr, Buildings in Shiodome. e, 500fr, Temple in Kyoto. f, 1000fr, Himeji Castle.
3000fr, Minato Mirai 21.

2008, Oct. 1 ***Perf. 13x13¼***
1003 A179 Sheet of 6, #a-f 15.50 15.50

Souvenir Sheet

Perf. 13¼ Syncopated

1004 A180 3000fr multi 17.00 17.00

Automobiles

No. 1005: a, 200fr, 1886 Daimler. b, 250fr,1906 Renault GP. c, 350fr, 1923 Ford Model T. d, 450fr, 1954 Mercedes Benz 300 SL. e, 500fr, 1988 Ferrari Testarossa. f, 1000fr, 2007 Bugatti Veyron.
3000fr, 2007 Lamborghini Murcielago LP640 Versace.

2008, Oct. 1 ***Perf. 13x13¼***
1005 A179 Sheet of 6, #a-f 15.50 15.50

Souvenir Sheet

Perf. 13¼ Syncopated

1006 A180 3000fr multi 17.00 17.00

Airplanes and Airports

No. 1007 — Airplane at airport and flag: a, 200fr, Changri Airport, Singapore flag. b, 250fr, John F. Kennedy Airport, New York, and U.S. flag. c, 350fr, Frankfort Airport, German flag. d, 450fr, Narita Airport, Tokyo, Japanese flag. e, 500fr, Beijing Airport, flag of People's Republic of China. f, 1000fr, Schiphol Airport, Amsterdam, Netherlands flag.
3000fr, 2007 Heathrow Airport, London, British flag.

2008, Oct. 1 ***Perf. 13x13¼***
1007 A179 Sheet of 6, #a-f 15.50 15.50

Souvenir Sheet

Perf. 13¼ Syncopated

1008 A180 3000fr multi 17.00 17.00

Mars Probes

No. 1009 — Mars and: a, 200fr, Spirit. b, 250fr, Mars Polar. c, 350fr, Viking. d, 450fr, Mars Climate. e, 500fr, Phoenix. f, 1000fr, Sojourner.
3000fr, Mariner 3.

2008, Oct. 1 ***Perf. 13x13¼***
1009 A179 Sheet of 6, #a-f 15.50 15.50

Souvenir Sheet

Perf. 13¼ Syncopated

1010 A180 3000fr multi 17.00 17.00

Ocean Liners

No. 1011: a, 200fr, Titanic. b, 250fr, Golden Princess. c, 350fr, Mauretania. d, 450fr, MS Queen Victoria. e, 500fr, Queen Elizabeth 2. f, 1000fr, Queen Mary 2.
3000fr, Pacific Princess.

2008, Oct. 1 ***Perf. 13x13¼***
1011 A179 Sheet of 6, #a-f 15.50 15.50

Souvenir Sheet

Perf. 13¼ Syncopated

1012 A180 3000fr multi 17.00 17.00

Postal Vehicles

No. 1013: a, 125fr, English postal van, carrier pigeon with letter, British flag. b, 150fr, Swiss postal bus, Horn, Swiss flag. c, 225fr, Spanish postal truck, posthorn, Spanish flag. d, 300fr, Swedish postal truck, carrier pigeon with letter, Swedish flag. e, 400fr, Israeli postal van, carrier pigeon with letter, Israeli flag. f, 1000fr, German postal buses, post horn, German flag.
3000fr, Hungarian postal van, posthorn, Hungarian flag.

2009, Jan. 5 ***Perf. 13x13¼***
1013 A179 Sheet of 6, #a-f 12.50 12.50

Souvenir Sheet

Perf. 13¼ Syncopated

1014 A180 3000fr multi 16.50 16.50

Dated 2008.

Subway Trains

No. 1015: a, 125fr, Beijing train and system map, Forbidden City, flag of People's Republic of China. b, 150fr, London train and system map, Big Ben, British flag. c, 225fr, Paris train and system map, Eiffel Tower, French flag. d, 300fr, Tokyo train and system map, Tokyo Tower, Japanese flag. e, 400fr, New York train and system map, Statue of Liberty, U.S. flag. f, 1000fr, Moscow train and system map, Red Square, Russian flag.
3000fr, Madrid train and system map, Statue of Bear and Tree, Spanish flag.

2009, Jan. 5 ***Perf. 13x13¼***
1015 A179 Sheet of 6, #a-f 12.50 12.50

Souvenir Sheet

Perf. 13¼ Syncopated

1016 A180 3000fr multi 16.50 16.50

Dated 2008.

German High Speed Trains

No. 1017 — ICE, flag of Germany and: a, 125fr, Cologne Cathedral. b, 150fr, Neuschwanstein Castle. c, 225fr, Göltsch Viaduct. d, 300fr, Kaiser Wilhelm Memorial Church, Berlin. e, 400fr, Brandenburg Gate. f, 1000fr, Eltz Castle.
3000fr, Brandenburg Gate, diff.

2009, Jan. 5 ***Perf. 13x13¼***
1017 A179 Sheet of 6, #a-f 12.50 12.50

Souvenir Sheet

Perf. 13¼ Syncopated

1018 A180 3000fr multi 16.50 16.50

Dated 2008.

French High Speed Trains

No. 1019 — TGV, flag of France and: a, 125fr, Notre Dame Cathedral, Paris. b, 150fr, Louvre Museum. c, 225fr, Hôtel de Ville, Paris. d, 300fr, Eiffel Tower. e, 400fr, Moulin Rouge. f, 1000fr, Arc de Triomphe.
3000fr, Eiffel Tower, diff.

2009, Jan. 5 ***Perf. 13x13¼***
1019 A179 Sheet of 6, #a-f 12.50 12.50

Souvenir Sheet

Perf. 13¼ Syncopated

1020 A180 3000fr multi 16.50 16.50

Dated 2008.

Fire Trucks

No. 1021: a, 125fr, Zuk, Poland. b, 150fr, Isuzu Forward, Japan. c, 225fr, Pegaso 7217, Spain. d, 300fr, A LF 16/12, Germany. e, 400fr, WPFD Engine 3, U.S. f, 1000fr, Scientific Support Truck, United Kingdom.
3000fr, Palm Beach fire truck, U.S.

2009, Jan. 5 ***Perf. 13x13¼***
1021 A179 Sheet of 6, #a-f 12.50 12.50

Souvenir Sheet

Perf. 13¼ Syncopated

1022 A180 3000fr multi 16.50 16.50

Dated 2008.

Sailing Ships and Lighthouses

No. 1023 — Various lighthouses and: a, 125fr, Lettie G, 1893. b, 150fr, Maple Leaf, 1904. c, 225fr, Etoile, 1930. d, 300fr, Brigantine St. Lawrence, 1952. e, 400fr, Cuauhtemoc, 1982. f, 1000fr, Royal clipper, 2001.
3000fr, Belle Poule, 1834.

2009, Jan. 5 ***Perf. 13x13¼***
1023 A179 Sheet of 6, #a-f 12.50 12.50

Souvenir Sheet

Perf. 13¼ Syncopated

1024 A180 3000fr multi 16.50 16.50

Dated 2008.

Airplanes

No. 1025: a, 125fr, Airbus A380. b, 150fr, Concorde F-BTSD. c, 225fr, Concorde G-BOAC. d, 300fr, Airbus A380, diff. e, 400fr, Airbus A380, diff. f, 1000fr, Concorde F-BVFC.
3000fr, Concorde F-BTSD, diff.

2009, Jan. 5 ***Perf. 13x13¼***
1025 A179 Sheet of 6, #a-f 12.50 12.50

Souvenir Sheet

Perf. 13¼ Syncopated

1026 A180 3000fr multi 16.50 16.50

Dated 2008.

Antique Automobiles

No. 1027: a, 200fr, 1893 Duryea. b, 250fr, 1897 Oldsmobile. c, 350fr, 1896 Ford. d, 450fr, 1903 Vauxhall. e, 500fr, 1886 Daimler Maybach. f, 1000fr, 1906 Haynes.
3000fr, 1904 Mercedes Simplex.

2009, Jan. 5 ***Perf. 13x13¼***
1027 A179 Sheet of 6, #a-f 15.00 15.00

Souvenir Sheet

Perf. 13¼ Syncopated

1028 A180 3000fr multi 16.50 16.50

Dated 2008.

Combat Vehicles

No. 1029: a, 200fr, Jino Motors truck, South Korea. b, 250fr, PTU, Singapore. c, 350fr, BRDM, Russia. d, 450fr, KRAZ AVC-30, Ukraine. e, 500fr, Avalanche truck, Russia. f, 1000fr, Fahd 240/30, Egypt.
3000fr, 1904 Humber Flying Pig MK2, FV1611, Great Britain.

2009, Jan. 5 ***Perf. 13x13¼***
1029 A179 Sheet of 6, #a-f 15.00 15.00

Souvenir Sheet

Perf. 13¼ Syncopated

1030 A180 3000fr multi 16.50 16.50

Dated 2008.

Motorcycles and Their Inventors

No. 1031: a, 200fr, 1885 Daimler, Karl Benz. b, 250fr, 1901 NSU, Christian Schmidt. c, 350fr, 1920 Excelsior 20R, William G. Henderson. d, 450fr, 1914 Indian V-Twin, Oscar Hedstrom. e, 500fr, 1927 Böhmerland, Albin Hugo Liebisch. f, 1000fr, 1923 BMW R32, Max Friz.
3000fr, 1905 Scott, Alfred Angus Scott.

2009, Jan. 5 ***Perf. 13x13¼***
1031 A179 Sheet of 6, #a-f 15.00 15.00

Souvenir Sheet

Perf. 13¼ Syncopated

1032 A180 3000fr multi 16.50 16.50

Dated 2008.

A181

Birds and Lighthouses, Famous People — A182

No. 1033: a, 125fr, Alopochen aegyptiacus, El Montaza Lighthouse, Egypt. b, 150fr, Larus dominicanus, Agulhas Lighthouse, South Africa. c, 225fr, Gavia stellata, Europa Point Lighthouse, Gibraltar. d, 300fr, Oceanites oceanicus, Ilha do Goa Lighthouse, Mozambique. e, 400fr, Thalassarche cauta, Walvis Bay Lighthouse, Namibia. f, 1000fr, Pelecanus rufescens, Bwene Lighhouse, Tanzania.
3000fr, Phaethon aethereus, Lagos Lighthouse, Nigeria.

2009, Jan. 7 ***Perf. 13x13¼***
1033 A181 Sheet of 6, #a-f 12.50 12.50

Souvenir Sheet

Perf. 13¼ Syncopated

1034 A182 3000fr multi 16.50 16.50

Dated 2008.

Scouting Centenary (in 2007)

No. 1035 — Robert Baden-Powell, Scouting emblem and: a, 125fr, Two Scouts saluting. b, 150fr, Two Scouts reading map. c, 225fr, Two Scouts standing with book. d, 300fr, Three Scouts looking at plant. e, 400fr, Two Scouts standing. f, 1000fr, Scouts and tent.
3000fr, Scouts practicing first aid.

2009, Jan. 7 ***Perf. 13x13¼***
1035 A181 Sheet of 6, #a-f 12.50 12.50

Souvenir Sheet

Perf. 13¼ Syncopated

1036 A182 3000fr multi 16.50 16.50

Dated 2008.

Medical Pioneers

No. 1037: a, 125fr, Sir Humphry Davy. b, 150fr, Robert Koch. c, 225fr, Emil Adolf von Behring. d, 300fr, Louis Pasteur. e, 400fr, Sir Frederick Banting. f, 1000fr, Sir Alexander Fleming.
3000fr, Jean Henri Dunant.

2009, Jan. 7 ***Perf. 13x13¼***
1037 A181 Sheet of 6, #a-f 12.50 12.50

Souvenir Sheet

Perf. 13¼ Syncopated

1038 A182 3000fr multi 16.50 16.50

Dated 2008.

Classical Composers

No. 1039: a, 125fr, Joseph Haydn. b, 150fr, Louis Hector Berlioz. c, 225fr, Franz Schubert. d, 300fr, Ludwig van Beethoven. e, 400fr, Franz Liszt. f, 1000fr, Johannes Brahms.
3000fr, Wolfgang Amadeus Mozart.

2009, Jan. 7 ***Perf. 13x13¼***
1039 A181 Sheet of 6, #a-f 12.50 12.50

Souvenir Sheet

Perf. 13¼ Syncopated

1040 A182 3000fr multi 16.50 16.50

Dated 2008.

Ornithologists

No. 1041: a, 125fr, John James Audubon and Corvus cristatus. b, 150fr, John Gould and Trogon ambiguus. c, 225fr, Audubon and Columba migratoria. d, 300fr, Gould and Tanager darwinii. e, 400fr, Audubon and Corvus corax. f, 1000fr, Gould and Astrapia nigra.
3000fr, Gould, Audubon, two birds.

2009, Jan. 7 ***Perf. 13x13¼***
1041 A181 Sheet of 6, #a-f 12.50 12.50

Souvenir Sheet

Perf. 13¼ Syncopated

1042 A182 3000fr multi 16.50 16.50

Dated 2008.

Paleontologists

No. 1043: a, 125fr, Barnum Brown and Archaeopteryx. b, 150fr, Thomas Condon and Gallimimus. c, 225fr, Robert Broom and Irritator. d, 300fr, William Buckland and Dimorphodon. e, 400fr, Edward Drinker Cope and Parasaurolophus. f, 1000fr, Edwin H. Colbert and Allosaurus.
3000fr, Roy Chapman Andrews and fossil dinosaur egg.

2009, Jan. 7 ***Perf. 13x13¼***
1043 A181 Sheet of 6, #a-f 12.50 12.50

Souvenir Sheet

Perf. 13¼ Syncopated

1044 A182 3000fr multi 16.50 16.50

Dated 2008.

Humanists

No. 1045: a, 125fr, Miriam Makeba and Nelson Mandela. b, 150fr, Mahatma Gandhi. c, 225fr, Mother Teresa. d, 300fr, Yassir Arafat. e, 400fr, Shirin Ebadi. f, 1000fr, Mohammed El-Baradei.
3000fr, Dr. Martin Luther King, Jr.

2009, Jan. 7 ***Perf. 13x13¼***
1045 A181 Sheet of 6, #a-f 12.50 12.50

Souvenir Sheet

Perf. 13¼ Syncopated

1046 A182 3000fr multi 16.50 16.50

Dated 2008.

Aviators

No. 1047: a, 125fr, Edward Rickenbacker. b, 150fr, Jimmy Doolittle. c, 225fr, Beryl Markham. d, 300fr, Elinor Smith. e, 400fr, Antoine de Saint-Exupéry. f, 1000fr, Charles Lindbergh.
3000fr, Wiley Post.

2009, Jan. 7 ***Perf. 13x13¼***
1047 A181 Sheet of 6, #a-f 12.50 12.50

Souvenir Sheet

Perf. 13¼ Syncopated

1048 A182 3000fr multi 16.50 16.50

Dated 2008.

Astronauts and Cosmonauts

No. 1049: a, 125fr, Yuri Gagarin and Vostok 1. b, 150fr, Neil Armstrong and Apollo 11. c, 225fr, Alan Shepard, Jr. and Apollo 14. d, 300fr, Valentina Tereshkova and Vostok 6. e, 400fr, Pavel Popovich and Soyuz 14. f, 1000fr, John Glenn and Mercury 6.
3000fr, Yang Liwei and Shenzhou 5.

2009, Jan. 7 ***Perf. 13x13¼***
1049 A181 Sheet of 6, #a-f 12.50 12.50

Souvenir Sheet

Perf. 13¼ Syncopated

1050 A182 3000fr multi 16.50 16.50

Dated 2008.

Mineralogists

No. 1051: a, 200fr, Ignacy Domeyko and sulfur. b, 250fr, James Dwight Dana and barite. c, 350fr, William Niven and rhodochrosite. d, 450fr, George Kunz and legrandite. e, 500fr, Waldemar Brogger and pyrite. f, 1000fr, Otto von Abich and rutile.
3000fr, Max von Laue and calcite.

2009, Jan. 7 ***Perf. 13x13¼***
1051 A181 Sheet of 6, #a-f 15.00 15.00

Souvenir Sheet

Perf. 13¼ Syncopated

1052 A182 3000fr multi 16.50 16.50

Dated 2008.

Entomologists

No. 1053: a, 200fr, Nathan Banks and Nymphalis antiopa. b, 250fr, Louis Agassiz and Apatura ilia. c, 350fr, Henry Walter Bates and Gonepterix rhamni. d, 450fr, Per Olof Christopher Aurivillus and Biston betularius. e, 500fr, John Henry Comstock and Parnassius apollo. f, 1000fr, Jean Henri Fabre and Acronicta aceris.
3000fr, William Kirby and Acherontia atropos.

2009, Jan. 7 ***Perf. 13x13¼***
1053 A181 Sheet of 6, #a-f 15.00 15.00

Souvenir Sheet

Perf. 13¼ Syncopated

1054 A182 3000fr multi 16.50 16.50

Dated 2008.

Mycologists

No. 1055: a, 200fr, Charles Horton Peck and Chroogomphus vinicolor. b, 250fr, Michel Adanson and Macrolepiota procera. c, 350fr, Miles Joseph Berkeley and Paxillus involutus. d, 450fr, Andrea Cesalpino and Tricholoma flavovirens. e, 500fr, Eduard Fischer and Phallus impudicus. f, 1000fr, Charles Edwin Bessey and Armillariella mellea.
3000fr, Peter Adolph Karsten and Marasmius oreades.

2009, Jan. 7 ***Perf. 13x13¼***
1055 A181 Sheet of 6, #a-f 15.00 15.00

Souvenir Sheet

Perf. 13¼ Syncopated

1056 A182 3000fr multi 16.50 16.50

Dated 2008.

Explorers

No. 1057: a, 200fr, Ferdinand Magellan. b, 250fr, Vasco da Gama. c, 350fr, Christopher Columbus. d, 450fr, James Cook. e, 500fr, Marco Polo. f, 1000fr, Amerigo Vespucci.
3000fr, Columbus, diff.

2009, Jan. 7 ***Perf. 13x13¼***
1057 A181 Sheet of 6, #a-f 15.00 15.00

Souvenir Sheet

Perf. 13¼ Syncopated

1058 A182 3000fr multi 16.50 16.50

Dated 2008.

David Livingstone

No. 1059 — Livingstone, map of Africa, and: a, 200fr, Livingstone with compass. b, 250fr, Lion attacking man. c, 350fr, Livingstone with rifle. d, 450fr, Men reading newspapers, African man and boy. e, 500fr, Livingstone with daughter. f, 1000fr, Livingstone reading book to Africans.
3000fr, Meeting Henry M. Stanley.

2009, Jan. 7 ***Perf. 13x13¼***
1059 A181 Sheet of 6, #a-f 15.00 15.00

Souvenir Sheet

Perf. 13¼ Syncopated

1060 A182 3000fr multi 16.50 16.50

Dated 2008.

Nobel Peace Prize Recipients

No. 1061: a, 200fr, Jane Addams, 1931, and peace marchers. b, 250fr, Nelson Mandela, 1993, and globe. c, 350fr, Kofi Annan, 2001, United Nations emblem and dove. d, 450fr, Mother Teresa, 1979, and children. e, 500fr, Aung San Suu Kyi, 1991, Burmese children. f, 1000fr, Wangari Muta Maathai, 2004, globe and dove.
3000fr, Dr. Albert Schweitzer, 1952, map of Africa, Red Cross, hands.

2009, Jan. 7 ***Perf. 13x13¼***
1061 A181 Sheet of 6, #a-f 15.00 15.00

Souvenir Sheet

Perf. 13¼ Syncopated

1062 A182 3000fr multi 16.50 16.50

Dated 2008.

World Chess Champions

No. 1063: a, 200fr, Boris Spassky. b, 250fr, Bobby Fischer. c, 350fr, Anatoly Karpov. d, 450fr, Garry Kasparaov. e, 500fr, Vladimir Kramnik. f, 1000fr, Viswanathan Anand.
3000fr, Tigran Petrosian.

2009, Jan. 7 ***Perf. 13x13¼***
1063 A181 Sheet of 6, #a-f 15.00 15.00

Souvenir Sheet

Perf. 13¼ Syncopated

1064 A182 3000fr multi 16.50 16.50

Dated 2008.

Vincent Van Gogh

No. 1065 — Self-portraits and: a, 200fr, Vincent's Bedroom in Arles. b, 250fr, Olive Trees and the Alpilles in the Background. c, 350fr, Wheat Field with Cypresses. d, 450fr, The Night Café in the Place Lamartine in Arles. e, 500fr, The Red Vineyard. f, 1000fr, Starry Night.
3000fr, Starry Night over the Rhone.

2009, Jan. 7 ***Perf. 13x13¼***
1065 A181 Sheet of 6, #a-f 15.00 15.00

Souvenir Sheet

Perf. 13¼ Syncopated

1066 A182 3000fr multi 16.50 16.50

Dated 2008.

70th Birthday of Romy Schneider

No. 1067 — Schneider and scenes from her films: a, 200fr, Le Trio Infernal, 1974. b, 250fr, Adorable Sinner, 1959. c, 350fr, Ludwig, 1972. d, 450fr, Sissi: The Young Empress, 1956. e, 500fr, César and Rosalie, 1972. f, 1000fr, Max and the Junkmen, 1971.
3000fr, Christine, 1958.

2009, Jan. 7 ***Perf. 13x13¼***
1067 A181 Sheet of 6, #a-f 15.00 15.00

Souvenir Sheet

Perf. 13¼ Syncopated

1068 A182 3000fr multi 16.50 16.50

Dated 2008.

A183

Mushrooms and Fauna — A184

No. 1069 — Mushrooms: a, 125fr, Amanita caesarea. b, 150fr, Amanita pantherina. c, 225fr, Pleurotus eryngii. d, 300fr, Amanita rubescens. e, 400fr, Boletus edulis. f, 1000fr, Pluteus leoninus.
3000fr, Amanita phalloides.

2009, Mar. 2 ***Perf. 13x13¼***
1069 A183 Sheet of 6, #a-f 11.50 11.50

Souvenir Sheet

Perf. 13¼ Syncopated

1070 A184 3000fr multi 15.50 15.50

Camels

No. 1071: a, 125fr, Camelus dromedarius. b, 150fr, Camelus bactrianus. c, 225fr, Camelus bactrianus, diff. d, 300fr, Camelus dromedarius, diff. e, 400fr, Camelus dromedarius, diff. f, 1000fr, Camelus bactrianus, diff.
3000fr, Two Camelus bactrianus.

2009, Mar. 2 ***Perf. 13x13¼***
1071 A183 Sheet of 6, #a-f 11.50 11.50

Souvenir Sheet

Perf. 13¼ Syncopated

1072 A184 3000fr multi 15.50 15.50

Gorillas

No. 1073: a, 125fr, Gorilla gorilla gorilla. b, 150fr, Gorilla gorilla. c, 225fr, Gorilla beringei graueri. d, 300fr, Gorilla beringei beringei. e, 400fr, Gorilla beringei. f, 1000fr, Gorilla gorilla diehli.
3000fr, Gorilla gorilla, diff.

2009, Mar. 2 ***Perf. 13x13¼***
1073 A183 Sheet of 6, #a-f 11.50 11.50

Souvenir Sheet

Perf. 13¼ Syncopated

1074 A184 3000fr multi 15.50 15.50

Dogs

No. 1075: a, 125fr, Aidi. b, 150fr, Africanis. c, 225fr, Sloughi. d, 300fr, Basenji. e, 400fr, Boerboel. f, 1000fr, Azawakh.
3000fr, Rhodesian ridgeback.

2009, Mar. 2 ***Perf. 13x13¼***
1075 A183 Sheet of 6, #a-f 11.50 11.50

Souvenir Sheet

Perf. 13¼ Syncopated

1076 A184 3000fr multi 15.50 15.50

Beetles

No. 1077: a, 125fr, Trachelophorus giraffa. b, 150fr, Cicindela campestris. c, 225fr, Leptinotarsa decemlineata (light blue frame). d, 300fr, Gelastorcoris oculatus (light blue frame). e, 400fr, Scarites guineensis. f, 1000fr, Goliathus albosignatus.
3000fr, Staphylinus olens.

2009, Mar. 2 ***Perf. 13x13¼***
1077 A183 Sheet of 6, #a-f 11.50 11.50

Souvenir Sheet

Perf. 13¼ Syncopated

1078 A184 3000fr multi 15.50 15.50

Bees and Wasps

No. 1079: a, 125fr, Chrysis ignita. b, 150fr, Megarhyssa macrurus. c, 225fr, Leptinotarsa decemlineata (yellowish green frame). d, 300fr, Gelastorcoris oculatus (yellowish green frame). e, 400fr, Parazumia symmorpha. f, 1000fr, Pteromalus puparum.
3000fr, Sphex ichneumoneus.

2009, Mar. 2 ***Perf. 13x13¼***
1079 A183 Sheet of 6, #a-f 11.50 11.50

Souvenir Sheet

Perf. 13¼ Syncopated

1080 A184 3000fr multi 15.50 15.50

Fish

No. 1081: a, 125fr, Latimeria chalumnae. b, 150fr, Synanceia verrucosa. c, 225fr, Scorpaena scrofa. d, 300fr, Periophthalmus argentilineatus. e, 400fr, Lophius americanus. f, 1000fr, Pristis microdon.
3000fr, Narcine brasiliensis.

2009, Mar. 2 ***Perf. 13x13¼***
1081 A183 Sheet of 6, #a-f 11.50 11.50

Souvenir Sheet

Perf. 13¼ Syncopated

1082 A184 3000fr multi 15.50 15.50

Shells and Lighthouses

No. 1083: a, 125fr, Pleurotomaria fricana and Hood Point Lighthouse. b, 150fr, Patella ferruginea and Swakopmund Lighthouse. c, 225fr, Tectus pyramis and Cape Columbine Lighthouse. d, 300fr, Monodonta turbinata and Seal Point Lighthouse. e, 400fr, Mesalia opalina and Moroni Lighthouse. f, 1000fr, Cypraea diliculum and Cape Agulhas Lighthouse.
3000fr, Ranella olearia and Umhlanga Rocks Lighthouse.

2009, Mar. 2 ***Perf. 13x13¼***
1083 A183 Sheet of 6, #a-f 11.50 11.50

Souvenir Sheet

Perf. 13¼ Syncopated

1084 A184 3000fr multi 15.50 15.50

Cats

No. 1085: a, 200fr, Sokoke. b, 250fr, Abyssinian. c, 350fr, Egyptian Mau. d, 450fr, Sokoke, diff. e, 500fr, Abyssinian, diff. f, 1000fr, Egyptian Mau, diff.
3000fr, Felis nigripes.

2009, Mar. 2 ***Perf. 13x13¼***
1085 A183 Sheet of 6, #a-f 14.50 14.50

Souvenir Sheet

Perf. 13¼ Syncopated

1086 A184 3000fr multi 15.50 15.50

Owls

No. 1087: a, 200fr, Otus pembaensis. b, 250fr, Ptilopsis granti. c, 350fr, Tyto alba. d, 450fr, Asio otus. e, 500fr, Strix woodfordii. f, 1000fr, Tyto soumagnei.
3000fr, Bubo africanus.

2009, Mar. 2 ***Perf. 13x13¼***
1087 A183 Sheet of 6, #a-f 14.50 14.50

Souvenir Sheet

Perf. 13¼ Syncopated

1088 A184 3000fr multi 15.50 15.50

Kingfishers

No. 1089: a, 200fr, Megaceryle maxima. b, 250fr, Alcedo atthis. c, 350fr, Halcyon senegalensis. d, 450fr, Ipsidina picta. e, 500fr, Todiramphus chloris. f, 1000fr, Alcedo cristata.
3000fr, Halcyon malimbica.

2009, Mar. 2 ***Perf. 13x13¼***
1089 A183 Sheet of 6, #a-f 14.50 14.50

Souvenir Sheet

Perf. 13¼ Syncopated

1090 A184 3000fr multi 15.50 15.50

Butterflies

No. 1091: a, 200fr, Crenis pechuelli. b, 250fr, Charaxes zingha. c, 350fr, Taenaris catops turdula. d, 450fr, Danaus chrysippus alcippus. e, 500fr, Anaea cyanae. f, 1000fr, Epiphile orea negrina.
3000fr, Cithaeria aurora.

2009, Mar. 2 ***Perf. 13x13¼***
1091 A183 Sheet of 6, #a-f 14.50 14.50

Souvenir Sheet

Perf. 13¼ Syncopated

1092 A184 3000fr multi 15.50 15.50

Dolphins

No. 1093: a, 200fr, Stenella coeruleoalba. b, 250fr, Stenella attenuata. c, 350fr, Sousa

plumbea. d, 450fr, Stenella longirostris. e, 500fr, Tursiops truncatus. f, 1000fr, Lissodelphis peronii.
3000fr, Lagenorhynchus cruciger.

2009, Mar. 2 ***Perf. 13x13¼***
1093 A183 Sheet of 6, #a-f 14.50 14.50

Souvenir Sheet
Perf. 13¼ Syncopated
1094 A184 3000fr multi 15.50 15.50

Frogs

No. 1095: a, 200fr, Xenopos laevis. b, 250fr, Astyloternus robustus. c, 350fr, Mantella aurantiaca. d, 450fr, Rana goliath. e, 500fr, Pyxicephalus adspersus. f, 1000fr, Breviceps mossambicus.
3000fr, Phrynomantis bifasciatus.

2009, Mar. 2 ***Perf. 13x13¼***
1095 A183 Sheet of 6, #a-f 14.50 14.50

Souvenir Sheet
Perf. 13¼ Syncopated
1096 A184 3000fr multi 15.50 15.50

Prehistoric Animals

No. 1097: a, 200fr, Heterodontosaurus. b, 250fr, Malawisaurus. c, 350fr, Carnotaurus. d, 450fr, Rhamphorhynchus. e, 500fr, Ouranosaurus. f, 1000fr, Herrerasaurus.
3000fr, Abrictosaurus.

2009, Mar. 2 ***Perf. 13x13¼***
1097 A183 Sheet of 6, #a-f 14.50 14.50

Souvenir Sheet
Perf. 13¼ Syncopated
1098 A184 3000fr multi 15.50 15.50

SEMI-POSTAL STAMPS

Anti-Malaria Issue
Common Design Type
Perf. 12½x12

1962, Apr. 7 **Engr.** **Unwmk.**
B1 CD108 25fr + 5fr brt pink 3.50 3.50

WHO drive to eradicate malaria.

Nurse Feeding Infant — SP1

1967, July 3 **Engr.** ***Perf. 13***
B2 SP1 25fr + 5fr multi 3.25 3.25

For the Red Cross.

Mother and Child — SP2

1974, Aug. 10 **Engr.** ***Perf. 13***
B3 SP2 35fr + 10fr red & dk brn 2.75 2.75

For the Red Cross.
For surcharge see No. 144.

Space Achievements SP3

World Philatelic Programs emblems (stamp collecting or Halley's Comet) and astronomer or satellite: a, Galileo. b, Copernicus. c, Kepler. d, Halley. e, *Planet A,* Japan, and 3 stars. f, *ICE,* US. g, *Planet A,* 5 stars. h, *Vega,* USSR.

Miniature Sheet

1988 **Litho.** ***Perf. 13½***
B4 Sheet of 8 15.00 15.00
a.-h. SP3 200fr +10fr multi 1.50 1.50

See No. C193.
For surcharges see Nos. 816P-816S.

AIR POST STAMPS

Comoro Village — AP1

Comoro Men and Moroni Mosque — AP2

Design: 200fr, Mosque of Ouani, Anjouan.

1950-54 **Unwmk.** **Engr.** ***Perf. 13***
C1 AP1 50fr grn & red brn 3.75 1.20
C2 AP2 100fr dk brn & red 5.75 1.50
C3 AP1 200fr dk grn, rose brn & pur ('54) 22.00 8.00
Nos. C1-C3 (3) 31.50 10.70

Liberation Issue
Common Design Type

1954, June 6
C4 CD102 15fr sepia & red 32.50 19.00

Madrepora Fructicosa AP3

100fr, Coral, shells and sea anemones.

1962, Jan. 13 **Photo.** ***Perf. 12½x13***
C5 AP3 100fr multi 13.50 13.50
C6 AP3 500fr multi 25.00 18.00

Telstar Issue
Common Design Type

1962, Dec. 5 **Engr.** ***Perf. 13***
C7 CD111 25fr dp vio, dl pur & red lil 4.50 2.75

Type of Regular Issue
Unwmk.

1963, Dec. 27 **Engr.** ***Perf. 13***
Size: 26½x48mm
C8 A13 65fr Baskets 4.25 3.00
C9 A13 200fr Pendant 8.25 4.50

Boat Type of Regular Issue

1964, Aug. 7 **Photo.** ***Perf. 13***
Size: 27x48mm
C10 A14 50fr Mayotte pirogue 4.00 1.60
C11 A14 85fr Schooner 6.25 2.25

Olympic Torch and Boxers — AP4

1964, Oct. 10 **Engr.** ***Perf. 13***
C12 AP4 100fr red brn, dk brn & gray grn 6.50 6.50

18th Olympic Games, Tokyo, Oct. 10-25.

Order of Star of Grand Comoro — AP5

1964, Dec. 10 **Photo.** ***Perf. 13***
C13 AP5 500fr multi 17.50 15.00

ITU Issue
Common Design Type

1965, May 17 **Engr.** ***Perf. 13***
C14 CD120 50fr gray, grnsh bl & ol 18.00 9.00

French Satellite A-1 Issue
Common Design Type

Designs: 25fr, Diamant rocket and launching installations. 30fr, A-1 satellite.

1966, Jan. 17 **Engr.** ***Perf. 13***
C15 CD121 25fr dk pur & ultra 3.75 3.75
C16 CD121 30fr dk pur & ultra 5.00 5.00
a. Strip of 2, #C15-C16 + label 9.00 9.00

French Satellite D-1 Issue
Common Design Type

1966, May 16 **Engr.** ***Perf. 13***
C17 CD122 30fr dk grn, org & brn 4.00 4.00

Old Gun Battery, Dzaoudzi — AP6

200fr, Ksar Castle, Mutsamudu, vert.

1966, Dec. 19 **Photo.** ***Perf. 13***
C18 AP6 50fr multi 4.25 2.10
C19 AP6 200fr multi 7.75 5.00

Bird Type of Regular Issue

Birds: 75fr, Madagascar paradise flycatchers. 100fr, Blue-cheeked bee eaters.

1967, June 20 **Photo.** ***Perf. 13***
Size: 27x48mm
C20 A17 75fr yel grn & multi 10.00 6.50
C21 A17 100fr lt bl & multi 12.50 8.00

Woman Skier — AP7

1968, Apr. 29 **Engr.** ***Perf. 13***
C22 AP7 70fr brt grn, lt bl & choc 4.75 3.75

10th Winter Olympic Games, Grenoble, France, Feb. 6-18, 1968.

Fish Type of Regular Issue

50fr, Moorish idol. 90fr, Diagramma lineatus.

1968, Aug. 1 **Engr.** ***Perf. 13***
Size: 47½x27mm
C23 A19 50fr plum blk & yel 7.50 3.75
C24 A19 90fr brt grn, yel & gray grn 9.25 4.75

For surcharge & overprint see Nos. C52, C74.

Swimmer, Butterfly Stroke — AP8

1969, Jan. 27 **Photo.** ***Perf. 12½***
C25 AP8 65fr ver, grnsh bl & blk 5.25 3.50

19th Olympic Games, Mexico City, 10/12-27.

Flower Type of Regular Issue

50fr, Heliconia sp. 85fr, Tuberose. 200fr, Orchid (angraecum eburneum).

1969, Mar. 20 **Photo.** ***Perf. 13***
Size: 27x48mm
C26 A21 50fr multi, vert. 3.50 2.75
C27 A21 85fr multi, vert. 4.25 3.50
C28 A21 200fr multi, vert. 8.25 4.50
Nos. C26-C28 (3) 16.00 10.75

Concorde Issue
Common Design Type

1969, Apr. 17 **Engr.**
C29 CD129 100fr pur & brn org 18.00 12.00

View of EXPO, Globe and Moon — AP9

90fr, Geisha, map of Japan & EXPO emblem.

1970, Sept. 13 **Photo.** ***Perf. 13***
C30 AP9 60fr slate & multi 4.50 2.40
C31 AP9 90fr multi 5.50 3.25

EXPO '70 International Exposition, Osaka, Japan, Mar. 15-Sept. 13.

Sunset over Mutsamudu — AP10

Map of Archipelago — AP11

Designs: 20fr, Sada Village, Mayotte. 65fr, Old Iconi Palace, Grand Comoro. 85fr, Nioumatchoua Island, Moheli.

1971, May 3 Photo. *Perf. 13*
C32 AP10 15fr dk bl & multi 1.20 .65
C33 AP10 20fr multi 1.75 .80
C34 AP10 65fr grn & multi 3.75 1.60
C35 AP10 85fr bl & multi 5.50 2.50

Engr.
C36 AP11 100fr brn red, grn & vio bl 7.50 5.50
Nos. C32-C36 (5) 19.70 11.05

See Nos. 107-110, C45-C49, C53, C62-C64. For overprints & surcharges see Nos. 143, C69, C71, C73, C76-C77, C79-C80, C82, C84.

Flower Type of Regular Issue

Flowers: 60fr, Hibiscus schizopetalus. 85fr, Acalypha sanderii.

1971, July 19 Photo. *Perf. 13*
Size: 27x48mm
C37 A25 60fr grn, ver & yel 5.00 2.40
C38 A25 85fr grn, red & yel 6.50 4.75

For surcharge see No. C75.

Mural, Moroni Airport — AP12

Designs: 85fr, Mural in Arrival Hall, Moroni Airport. 100fr, View of Moroni Airport.

1972, Mar. 30 Photo. *Perf. 13*
C39 AP12 65fr gray & multi 2.00 .85
C40 AP12 85fr gray & multi 2.25 1.20

Engr.
C41 AP12 100fr brn, bl & slate grn 4.00 2.10
Nos. C39-C41 (3) 8.25 4.15

New airport in Moroni.

Eiffel Tower and Moroni Telephone Exchange — AP13

75fr, Frenchman and Comoro Islander talking on telephone, radio tower and beacons.

1972, Apr. 24
C42 AP13 35fr dl red & gray 1.25 .85
C43 AP13 75fr dk car, vio & bl 2.25 .95

First radio-telephone connection between France and Comoro Islands.

Underwater Spear-fishing — AP14

1972, July 5 Engr. *Perf. 13*
C44 AP14 70fr vio bl, brt grn & mar 8.75 5.50

For surcharge see No. C78.

Types of 1971

Designs: 20fr, Cape Sima. 35fr, Bambao Palace. 40fr, Domoni Palace. 60fr, Gomajou Peninsula. 100fr, Map of Anjouan Island.

1972, Nov. 15 Photo.
C45 AP10 20fr brn & multi .90 .65
C46 AP10 35fr dk grn & multi 1.20 .80
C47 AP10 40fr bl & multi 1.75 .95
C48 AP10 60fr grnsh blk & multi 2.50 1.60

Engr.
C49 AP11 100fr mar, bl & sl grn 13.50 7.25
Nos. C45-C49 (5) 19.85 11.25

Pres. Said Mohamed Cheikh (1904-70) AP15

1973, Mar. 16 Photo. *Perf. 13*
C50 AP15 20fr multi 1.25 .80
C51 AP15 35fr multi 1.60 1.00

For overprints see Nos. C70, C72.

No. C24 Surcharged

1973, Apr. 30 Engr. *Perf. 13*
C52 A19 120fr on 90fr multi 13.00 7.25

Intl. Commission for Coelacanth Studies.

Map of Grand Comoro AP16

1973, June 28 Engr. *Perf. 13*
C53 AP16 135fr vio, bl & dk brn 9.50 6.50

See Nos. C65, C68. For surcharges see Nos. C90-C92.

Karthala Volcano AP17

1973, July 16 Photo. *Perf. 13x12½*
C54 AP17 120fr multi 7.50 5.50

Eruption of Karthala, Sept. 1972.
For surcharge see No. C89.

Armauer G. Hansen — AP18

Design: 150fr, Nicolaus Copernicus (1473-1543), Polish astronomer.

1973, Sept. 5 Engr. *Perf. 13*
C55 AP18 100fr brn, dk bl & sl grn 7.00 3.50
C56 AP18 150fr grnsh bl, vio bl & choc 8.00 5.25

Cent. of the discovery of the Hansen bacillus, the cause of leprosy.
For overprint & surcharge see Nos. C81, C93.

Pablo Picasso (1881-1973) — AP19

1973, Sept. 30 Photo.
C57 AP19 200fr blk & multi 12.00 9.75

Souvenir Sheet
C58 AP19 100fr blk & multi 16.00 14.50

For overprint see No. C87.

Order of the Star of Anjouan — AP20

1974, Jan. 7 Photo. *Perf. 13*
C59 AP20 500fr brn, bl & gold 13.00 9.50

For overprint see No. C95.

Said Omar ben Soumeth — AP21

135fr, Grand Mufti Said Omar, horiz.

1974, Jan. 31 *Perf. 13x13½, 13½x13*
C60 AP21 135fr blk & multi 4.50 2.75
C61 AP21 200fr blk & multi 5.50 3.50

For overprint & surcharge see Nos. C85, C88.

Types of 1971-73

Designs (Views on Mayotte): 20fr, Moya Beach. 35fr, Chiconi. 90fr, Port Mamutzu. 120fr, Map of Mayotte.

1974, Aug. 31 Photo. *Perf. 13*
C62 AP10 20fr bl & multi 1.20 .95
C63 AP10 35fr grn & multi 2.50 2.00
C64 AP10 90fr multi 6.25 3.50

Engr.
C65 AP16 120fr ultra & grn 9.00 5.50
Nos. C62-C65 (4) 18.95 11.95

Jet Take-off — AP22

1975, Jan. 10 Engr. *Perf. 13*
C66 AP22 135fr multi 7.25 4.75

First direct route Moroni-Hahaya-Paris.
For surcharge see No. C86.

Rotary Emblem, Meeting House, Map — AP23

1975, Feb. 23 Photo. *Perf. 13*
C67 AP23 250fr multi 10.50 7.25

Rotary Intl., 70th anniv., Moroni Rotary Club, 10th anniv.
For surcharge see No. C94.

Map Type of 1973

Design: 230fr, Map of Moheli, horiz.

1975, May 26 Engr. *Perf. 13*
C68 AP16 230fr ocher, ol grn & bl 11.00 8.00

STATE OF COMORO

Issues of 1968-75 Surcharged and Overprinted in Black, Silver, Red or Orange

1975 Printing & Perfs. as Before
C69 AP10 10fr on 20fr #C62 *.60 .25*
C70 AP15 20fr (S) *1.00 .25*
C71 AP10 30fr on 35fr (R) #C63 *1.00 .25*
C72 AP15 35fr (S) *1.25 .75*
C73 AP10 40fr (O) *1.50 .75*
C74 A19 50fr *2.50 1.25*
C75 A25 75fr on 60fr *2.00 1.10*
C76 AP10 75fr on 60fr *2.00 1.10*

C77 AP10 75fr on 65fr (O) *2.00 1.10*
C78 AP14 75fr on 70fr *2.50 1.25*
C79 AP11 100fr #C36 *4.00 2.00*
C80 AP11 100fr #C49 *4.00 2.00*
C81 AP18 100fr *4.00 2.00*
C82 AP10 100fr on 85fr (O) *2.50 1.50*
C83 A25 100fr on 85fr *2.50 1.50*
C84 AP10 100fr on 90fr *2.50 1.50*
C85 AP21 100fr on 135fr (S) *2.50 1.50*
C86 AP22 100fr on 135fr *3.00 2.00*
C87 AP19 200fr (S) *8.00 4.00*
C88 AP21 200fr (S) *6.00 3.50*
C89 AP17 200fr on 120fr *8.00 4.00*
C90 AP16 200fr on 120fr *6.00 3.50*
C91 AP16 200fr on 135fr *6.00 3.50*
C92 AP16 200fr on 230fr *6.00 3.50*
C93 AP18 400fr on 150fr *10.00 5.25*
C94 AP23 400fr on 250fr *10.00 5.25*
C95 AP20 500fr *12.00 7.25*
Nos. C69-C95 (27) 113.35 61.80

See postage section for airmail stamps that are part of joint postage/airmail sets.

Rotary Emblem, Landscape AP26

1979, July 31 Litho. *Perf. 13x12½*
C107 AP26 400fr multi 7.00 3.00

Rotary International.

IYC Emblem, Mother and Child — AP27

1979, July 31 *Perf. 13x13½*
C108 AP27 250fr multi 3.50 3.50

Intl. Year of the Child. See No. CB1. For surcharges see Nos. C121, C202.

Dimadjou Dispensary, Map of Southern Africa, Emblem AP28

260fr, Globe, Concorde, emblem.

1980, Feb. 23 Litho. *Perf. 12½*
C109 AP28 100fr shown 1.25 .40
C110 AP28 260fr multicolored 3.00 1.00

Rotary International, 75th anniv. and Moroni Rotary Club, 15th anniv. (100fr).
For surcharges see Nos. 815L, C119-C120.

First Transatlantic Flight, 50th Anniversary — AP29

1980, May 30 Litho. *Perf. 13*
C111 AP29 200fr multi 3.50 1.75

No. C111 Surcharged in Blue

1981, Feb. Litho. *Perf. 13*
C112 AP29 30fr on 200fr multi 1.00 .35

The Dove and the Rainbow, by Picasso — AP30

Picasso Birth Centenary: 70fr, Still Life on a Sideboard. 150fr, Studio with Plaster Head. 250fr, Bowl and Pot, vert. 500fr, The Red Tablecloth.

1981, June 30 Litho. *Perf. 12½*
C113 AP30 40fr multi .55 .25
C114 AP30 70fr multi .95 .25
C115 AP30 150fr multi 1.90 .50
C116 AP30 250fr multi 3.25 .70
C117 AP30 500fr multi 6.25 1.50
Nos. C113-C117 (5) 12.90 3.20

For surcharges see Nos. 815G, C118.

Nos. C114, C109-C110, CB1 Srchd.

1981, Nov. Litho. *Perf. 12½, 13*
C118 AP30 10fr on 70fr multi .40 .40
C119 AP28 10fr on 100fr multi .80 .80
C120 AP28 50fr on 260fr multi 2.00 .25
C121 AP27 50fr on 200fr+30fr multi 2.00 .25
Nos. C118-C121 (4) 5.20 1.70

Manned Flight Bicentenary — AP31

Balloons: 100fr, Montgolfiere, 1783. 200fr, Lunardi, 1784. 300fr, Blanchard and Jeffries, 1785. 400fr, Giffard, 1852, horiz.
500fr, Paris Siege. 1870.

1983, Apr. 20 Litho. *Perf. 13*
C122 AP31 100fr multicolored 1.00 .30
C123 AP31 200fr multicolored 1.90 .50
C124 AP31 300fr multicolored 3.25 .90
C125 AP31 400fr multicolored 4.50 1.25
Nos. C122-C125 (4) 10.65 2.95

Souvenir Sheet

C126 AP31 500fr multicolored 5.50 1.50

For overprints and surcharges see Nos. 602, 812T, 815P.

Pre-Olympic Year Sailing — AP32

150fr, Type 470, pink and yellow sail. 200fr, Flying Dutchman. 300fr, Type 470, white sails. 400fr, Finn.
500fr, Soling.

1983, June 30 Litho. *Perf. 13*
C127 AP32 150fr multi 1.50 .40
C128 AP32 200fr multi 2.25 .50
C129 AP32 300fr multi 3.25 .90
C130 AP32 400fr multi 4.75 1.00
Nos. C127-C130 (4) 11.75 2.80

Souvenir Sheet

C131 AP32 500fr multi 5.50 1.50

For overprint and surcharge see Nos. 603, C206.

1984 Summer Olympics — AP33

60fr, Basketball, 2 players. 100fr, Basketball, 6 players. 165fr, Basketball, 4 players. 175fr, Baseball catcher, horiz. 200fr, Baseball, horiz.
500fr, Basketball, diff.

1984, July 10 Litho. *Perf. 13*
C132 AP33 60fr multicolored .50 .25
C133 AP33 100fr multicolored .90 .40
C134 AP33 165fr multicolored 1.50 .65
C135 AP33 175fr multicolored 1.60 .65
C136 AP33 200fr shown 1.90 .80
Nos. C132-C136 (5) 6.40 2.75

Souvenir Sheet

C137 AP33 500fr multicolored 8.00 1.50

Nos. C132-C134 vert.

Development Conference AP34

475fr, Tools for development.

1984, July 2 Litho. *Perf. 13*
C138 AP34 475fr multi 5.50 2.00

For surcharge see No. 796I.

Audubon Bicentenary — AP35

100fr, Hirundo rustica, vert. 125fr, Icterus galbula, vert. 150fr, Buteo lineatus. 500fr, Sphyropicus varius.

1985, Jan. 15 Litho. *Perf. 13*
C139 AP35 100fr multicolored 1.25 .40
C140 AP35 125fr multicolored 1.50 .50
C141 AP35 150fr multicolored 2.00 .60
C142 AP35 500fr multicolored 5.25 2.00
Nos. C139-C142 (4) 10.00 3.50

Moroni Port Missile Defense — AP36

No. C146, Ngome Ntsoudjini Scout troop.

1985, May 20 Litho. *Perf. 13x12½*
C145 AP36 200fr multi 3.00 1.25
C146 AP36 200fr multi 3.00 1.25
a. Pair, #C145-C146 + label 6.00 6.00

PHILEXAFRICA '85, Lome.
For surcharges see Nos. C207-C208.

Natl. Flag, Sun, Outline Map of Islands — AP37

1985, July 6
C147 AP37 10fr multi .30 .25
C148 AP37 15fr multi .30 .25
C149 AP37 125fr multi 2.25 .60
C150 AP37 300fr multi 5.50 1.50
Nos. C147-C150 (4) 8.35 2.60

Natl. independence, 10th anniv.
For surcharge see No. 815Q.

Runners — AP38

1985, Nov. 12
C151 AP38 250fr shown 2.75 1.75
C152 AP38 250fr Mining 2.75 1.75
a. Pair, #C151-C152 + label 6.00 6.00

PHILEXAFRICA '85, Lome, Togo, 11/16-24.
For surcharges see Nos. 815H-815I, C204-C205.

Air Transport Union, UTA, 50th Anniv. — AP39

25fr, F-AOUL seaplane. 75fr, Camel driver, DC-8. 100fr, Noratlas and Heron DC-4s. 125fr, UTA cargo plane. 1000fr, Aircraft, 1935-1985.

1985, Dec. 30 Litho. *Perf. 13*
C153 AP39 25fr multi .25 .25
C154 AP39 75fr multi .75 .30
C155 AP39 100fr multi 1.10 .40
a. Souv. sheet of 3, #C153-C155, perf. 12½ 3.50 2.25
C156 AP39 125fr multi 1.40 .60

Size: 40x52mm

Perf. 12½x13

C157 AP39 1000fr multi 12.00 6.00
a. Souv. sheet of 2, #C156-C157, perf. 12½ 13.00 8.00
Nos. C153-C157 (5) 15.50 7.55

Halley's Comet — AP40

Comets, astronomers and probes: 125fr, Edmond Halley, Giotto probe. 150fr, Giacobini-Zinner, 1959. 225fr, Encke, 1961. 300fr, Bradfield, 1980. 450fr, Planet A probe.

1986, Mar. 7 ***Perf. 13***

C158 AP40 125fr multi 1.25 .45
C159 AP40 150fr multi 1.50 .50
C160 AP40 225fr multi 2.50 .90
C161 AP40 300fr multi 3.00 1.25
C162 AP40 450fr multi 5.00 1.75
Nos. C158-C162 (5) 13.25 4.85

For surcharges see Nos. 796S, 804H, 804R, 812P.

1986 World Cup Soccer Championships, Mexico — AP41

Various soccer plays.

1986, June 11 **Litho.** ***Perf. 13***

C163 AP41 125fr multi 1.25 .45
C164 AP41 210fr multi 2.25 .80
C165 AP41 500fr multi 5.50 2.00
C166 AP41 600fr multi 6.00 2.25
Nos. C163-C166 (4) 15.00 5.50

For surcharges see Nos. 796C, 800Q, 815C.

Tennis at the 1988 Summer Olympics — AP42

Various players.

1987, Jan. 28 **Litho.** ***Perf. 13½***

C167 AP42 150fr multi 1.75 .45
C168 AP42 250fr multi 3.00 .75
C169 AP42 500fr multi 5.50 1.50
C170 AP42 600fr multi 6.75 1.75
Nos. C167-C170 (4) 17.00 4.45

For overprints and surcharges see Nos. 796N, 796U, 815J, 816L, 816N, C183-C186, C203.

World Wildlife Fund — AP43

Various pictures of the mongoose lemur.

1987, Feb. 18 ***Perf. 13***

C171 AP43 75fr multi, vert. 2.00 .50
C172 AP43 100fr multi 3.00 .75
C173 AP43 125fr multi 5.00 1.00
C174 AP43 150fr multi 6.00 1.25
Nos. C171-C174 (4) 16.00 3.50

1988 Winter Olympics, Calgary AP44

150fr, Slalom. 225fr, Ski jumping. 500fr, Women's giant slalom. 600fr, Luge.

1987, Apr. 10 **Litho.** ***Perf. 13½***

C175 AP44 150fr multi 1.25 .45
C176 AP44 225fr multi 2.25 .75
C177 AP44 500fr multi 5.50 1.60
C178 AP44 600fr multi 6.00 2.25
Nos. C175-C178 (4) 15.00 5.05

For surcharges see Nos. 800R, 812U.

AP45

Aviation History AP46

Designs: 200fr, Inventors Didier Daurat and Raymond Vanier with 1935 Air Blue F-ANR1. 300fr, Farman biplane, 1st scheduled airmail delivery, Paris-LeMans-St. Nazaire, Aug. 17, 1918. 500fr, Bleriot aircraft, 1st scheduled airmail delivery, Villacoublay-Vendome-Poitiers-Pauillac, Oct. 15, 1913. 1000fr, Henri Pequet and his aircraft, Feb. 18, 1911.

1987, Dec. 29 **Litho.** ***Perf. 13***

C179 AP45 200fr multi 2.00 .65
C180 AP45 300fr multi 3.00 1.00
C181 AP45 500fr multi 5.00 1.60

Perf. 12½x13

C182 AP46 1000fr multi 10.00 2.25
Nos. C179-C182 (4) 20.00 5.50

Airmail history exposition, Allahabad.
For surcharges see Nos. 800S, 804D.

Nos. C167-C170 Ovptd. in Red for 1988 Olympic Tennis Champions

Overprint includes name of athlete and "Medaille d'or / Seoul" or "Medaille / d'argent / Seoul."

1988, Nov. **Litho.** ***Perf. 13½***

C183 AP42 150fr "Miloslav Mecir / (Tchec.)" 1.25 .75
C184 AP42 250fr "Tim Mayotte / (U.S.A.)" 1.90 1.40
C185 AP42 500fr "Steffi Graf / (R.F.A.)" 5.00 2.75
C186 AP42 600fr "Gabriela Sabatini / (Argentine)" 6.00 3.75
Nos. C183-C186 (4) 14.15 8.65

For surcharges see Nos. 800T, 815K, 816M, 816O.

Early Aviators and Aircraft — AP47

100fr, Alberto Santos-Dumont (1873-1932), & *Bagatelle,* 1st documented power flight in Europe, Oct. 23, 1906. 150fr, Wright Brothers & *Flyer A.* 200fr, Louis Bleriot (1872-1936) & *Bleriot XI,* 1st crossing of the English Channel in a heavier-than-air craft, July 25, 1909. 300fr, Henri Farman (1874-1958) & Voisin biplane, 1st fixed-route 1-kilometer circular flight, Jan. 13, 1908. 500fr, Gabriel (1880-1973) & Charles (1882-1912) Voisin, established 1st biplane factory (1908), & Voisin biplane. 800fr, Roland Garros (1888-1918), 1st trans-Mediterranean flight, Sept. 23, 1913.

1988, Dec. 7 **Litho.** ***Perf. 13***

C187 AP47 100fr pur .90 .45
C188 AP47 150fr brt lil rose 1.60 .60
C189 AP47 200fr blk 2.00 .90
C190 AP47 300fr dark yel org 3.00 .90
C191 AP47 500fr dark blue 5.00 1.50
C192 AP47 800fr lt olive grn 7.50 3.00
Nos. C187-C192 (6) 20.00 7.35

For surcharges see Nos. 800B, 800U, 804E, C209.

Souvenir Sheet

Space Achievements — AP48

Design: World Philatelic Programs stamp collecting emblem, Soviet satellite and Edmond Halley.

1988 **Litho.** ***Perf. 13½***

C193 AP48 750fr multi 8.00 1.50

Nos. C108, C168, C151-C152, C128, C145-C146 and C189 Surcharged

1989 **Litho.** ***Perfs. as Before***

C202 AP27 5fr on 250fr #C108 .25 .25
C203 AP42 25fr on 250fr #C168 .25 .25
C204 AP38 50fr on 250fr #C151 .50 .25
C205 AP38 50fr on 250fr #C152 .50 .25
a. Pair, #C204-C205 + label 1.25 1.25
C206 AP32 150fr on 200fr #C128 1.40 .60
C207 AP36 150fr on 200fr #C145 1.40 .60
C208 AP36 150fr on 200fr #C146 1.40 .60
a. Pair, #C207-C208 + label 6.00 6.00
C209 AP47 150fr on 200fr #C189 1.40 .60
Nos. C202-C209 (8) 7.10 3.40

World Cup Soccer, Championships, Italy — AP50

Various soccer plays and map of Italy.

1990, June **Litho.** ***Perf. 13***

C210 AP50 75fr multicolored .60 .30
C211 AP50 150fr multicolored 1.40 .60
C212 AP50 500fr multicolored 4.25 1.90
C213 AP50 1000fr multicolored 8.75 4.00
Nos. C210-C213 (4) 15.00 6.80

For surcharge see No. 800V.

Souvenir Sheet

Garry Kasparov, Anatoly Karpov, Russian Chess Champions — AP51

Litho. & Embossed

1991, Aug. 5 ***Perf. 13½***

C214 AP51 1500fr gold & multi 12.00 —

World Chess Championships.

1992 Summer Olympics, Barcelona AP52

Litho. & Embossed

1992, July 28 ***Perf. 13½***

C215 AP52 1500fr gold & multi 26.50 12.00

Sculpted Table — AP52a

1994 (?) **Litho.** ***Perf. 13¼x13½***

Background Color

C215A AP52a 15fr blue — 5.00
C215B AP52a 75fr green — —
C215C AP52a 100fr pink — —
C215D AP52a 225fr orange — —

For surcharges see Nos. 826A-826E.

Sea Turtles AP53

1995 **Litho.** ***Perf. 13½x13¼***

Frame Color

C216 AP53 10fr blue 15.00 15.00
C217 AP53 25fr pink — —
C218 AP53 30fr green 25.00 25.00
C219 AP53 50fr lilac 50.00 50.00

No. C215A Surcharged in Blue Violet

Perf. 13¼x13½

2001, June 16 **Litho.**
C220 AP52a 300fr on 15fr — —

AIR POST SEMI-POSTAL STAMP

Type of Air Post 1979

Design: IYC emblem, mother and son.

1979, July 31 **Photo.** ***Perf. 13½x13***
CB1 AP27 200fr + 30fr multi 3.50 3.50

International Year of the Child.
For surcharge see No. C121.

POSTAGE DUE STAMPS

Anjouan Mosque — D1

1950 **Unwmk.** **Engr.** ***Perf. 14x13***
J1 D1 50c deep green 1.20 .95
J2 D1 1fr black brown 1.20 1.00

Coelacanth — D2

1954
J3 D2 5fr dk brown & green 1.10 1.00
J4 D2 10fr gray & red brown 1.50 1.50
J5 D2 20fr indigo & blue 2.75 2.50
Nos. J3-J5 (3) 5.35 5.00

Hibiscus D3

2fr, Pineapple, vert. 5fr, White butterfly. 10fr, Chameleon. 15fr, Blooming banana, vert. 20fr, Orchids. 30fr, Allamanda cathartica. 40fr, Cashews, vert. 50fr, Custard apple, vert. 100fr, Breadfruit. 200fr, Vanilla. 500fr, Ylang ylang.

1977, Nov. 19 **Litho.** ***Perf. 13½***
J6 D3 1fr shown .35 .25
J7 D3 2fr multicolored .35 .25
J8 D3 5fr multicolored .35 .25
J9 D3 10fr multicolored .35 .25
J10 D3 15fr multicolored .35 .25
J11 D3 20fr multicolored .35 .25
J12 D3 30fr multicolored .50 .25
J13 D3 40fr multicolored .95 .25
J14 D3 50fr multicolored 1.10 .25
J15 D3 100fr multicolored 2.10 .75
J16 D3 200fr multicolored 4.50 .95
J17 D3 500fr multicolored 10.75 1.50
Nos. J6-J17 (12) 22.00 5.45

OFFICIAL STAMPS

Comoro Flag — O1

Perf. 13x12½

1979-85 **Litho.** **Unwmk.**
O1 O1 5fr multi .25 .25
O2 O1 10fr multi .25 .25
O3 O1 20fr multi .25 .25
O4 O1 30fr multi .50 .25
O5 O1 40fr multi .65 .25
O6 O1 60fr multi ('80) .60 .25
O7 O1 75fr multi ('85) .40 .25
O8 O1 100fr multi 1.25 .60
Nos. O1-O8 (8) 4.15 2.35

See Nos. 526-530.

Pres. Said Mohamed Cheikh (1904-1970) — O2

1980-85
O9 O2 100fr multi 1.00 .40
O10 O2 125fr multi ('85) 2.00 1.50
O11 O2 400fr multi 3.00 1.25
Nos. O9-O11 (3) 6.00 3.15

CONGO, DEMOCRATIC REPUBLIC

ˌde-mə-ˈkra-tik ri-ˈpə-blik of ˈkäŋ-ˌgō

LOCATION — Central Africa
GOVT. — Republic
AREA — 895,348 sq. mi. (estimated)
POP. — 22,480,000 (est. 1971)
CAPITAL — Kinshasa (Leopoldville)

Congo was an independent state, founded by Leopold II of Belgium, until 1908 when it was annexed to Belgium as a colony. Congo became an independent republic in 1960. The name was changed to Republic of Zaire, Oct. 28, 1971. In 1998 some issues again used the name Congo Democratic Republic. See Zaire in Vol. 6 for later issues.

100 Centimes = 1 Franc
100 Sengi = 1 Li-Kuta,
100 Ma-Kuta = 1 Zaire (1967)

Catalogue values for all unused stamps in this country are for Never Hinged items.

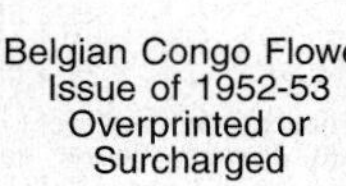

Belgian Congo Flower Issue of 1952-53 Overprinted or Surcharged

Perf. 11½

1960, June 30 **Photo.** **Unwmk.**

Flowers in Natural Colors

Size: 21x25½mm

Granite Paper

323 A86 10c dp plum & ocher .25 .25
324 A86 10c on 15c red & yel grn .25 .25
325 A86 20c grn & gray .25 .25
326 A86 40c grn & sal .25 .25
327 A86 50c on 60c bl grn & pink .25 .25
328 A86 50c on 75c dp plum & gray .25 .25
329 A86 1fr car & yel .30 .25
330 A86 1.50fr vio & ap grn .30 .25
331 A86 2fr ol grn & buff .30 .25
332 A86 3fr ol grn & pink .45 .25
333 A86 4fr choc & lil 1.50 1.00
334 A86 5fr dp plum & lt bl grn .55 .25
335 A86 6.50fr dk car & lil .70 .25
336 A86 8fr grn & lt yel .80 .30
337 A86 10fr dp plum & pale ol 1.50 .30
338 A86 20fr vio bl & dl sal 3.50 .80

Nos. 324, 327-328 exist without "CONGO" overprint but with surcharge, also without surcharge but with "CONGO." Inverted and double overprints exist. Values from $10 to $50 each.

Belgian Congo Flower Issue of 1952-53 Overprinted or Surcharged

Size: 22x32mm

339 A86 50fr dp plum & gray bl 19.00 6.00
340 A86 100fr grn & buff 45.00 10.00
Nos. 323-340 (18) 75.40 21.40

Belgian Congo Nos. 306-317, Ovptd. or Srchd. in Red, Blue, Black or Brown

341 A92 10c bl & brn (R) .25 .25
342 A93 20c red org & sl (Bl) .25 .25
343 A92 40c brn & bl (Bk) .25 .25
344 A93 50c brt ultra, red & sep (R) .25 .25
345 A92 1fr brn, grn & blk (Br) .25 .25
346 A93 1.50fr blk & org yel (R) .25 .25
347 A92 2fr crim, blk & brn (Bl) .45 .25
348 A93 3.50fr on 3fr blk, gray & lil rose (Bk) .65 .25
349 A92 5fr brn, dk brn & brt grn (Br) .85 .25
350 A93 6.50fr bl, brn & org yel (R) 1.00 .25
a. Black overprint 1.10 .60
351 A92 8fr org brn, ol bis & lil (Br) 1.25 .30
352 A93 10fr multi (R) 1.50 .40
Nos. 341-352 (12) 7.20 3.20

Inverted and double overprints exist. Values from $15 to $20 each.

Belgian Congo No. 318 Overprinted

1960
353 A94 50c gldn brn, ocher & red brn 1.00 .90

Belgian Congo Nos. 321-322 Overprinted and Surcharged

Inscription in French

354 A95 3.50fr on 3fr gray & org red .85 .50

Inscription in Flemish

355 A95 3.50fr on 3fr gray & org red .85 .50
Nos. 353-355 (3) 2.70 1.90

Nos. 353-355 are known with inverted double and triple overprints. Value, each $11. Overprints in other colors are proofs.

Nos. 354-355 exist with surcharge omitted. Value, set $165.

Map of Congo — A93a

1960 **Photo.** ***Perf. 11½***
356 A93a 20c brown .25 .25
357 A93a 50c rose red .25 .25
358 A93a 1fr green .25 .25
359 A93a 1.50fr red brn .25 .25
360 A93a 2fr rose car .25 .25
361 A93a 3.50fr lilac .25 .25
362 A93a 5fr brt bl .25 .25
363 A93a 6.50fr gray .25 .25
364 A93a 10fr orange .30 .25
365 A93a 20fr ultra .70 .25
Nos. 356-365 (10) 3.00 2.50

Congo's Independence.

Nos. 356-365 exist imperf. Value, set unused $25.

For overprints see Nos. 371-380.

Flag, People and Broken Chain — A94

1961, Jan. 4 **Unwmk.** ***Perf. 11½***

Flag in Blue and Yellow

366 A94 2fr rose vio .25 .25
367 A94 3.50fr vermilion .25 .25
368 A94 6.50fr yel brn .25 .25
369 A94 10fr brt grn .35 .25
370 A94 20fr car rose .50 .30
Nos. 366-370 (5) 1.60 1.30

Signing of the Independence Agreement by Belgium, Jan. 4, 1959.

Nos. 356-365 Overprinted in Blue, Black or Red

1961
371 A93a 20c brn (Bl) 1.60 1.60
372 A93a 50c rose red (Bk) 1.60 1.60
373 A93a 1fr grn (R) 1.60 1.60
374 A93a 1.50fr red brn (Bl) 1.60 1.60
375 A93a 2fr rose car (Bk) 1.60 1.60
376 A93a 3.50fr lil (Bl) 1.60 1.60
377 A93a 5fr brt bl (R) 1.60 1.60
378 A93a 6.50fr gray (R) 1.60 1.60
379 A93a 10fr org (Bk) 1.60 1.60
380 A93a 20fr ultra (R) 1.60 1.60
Nos. 371-380 (10) 16.00 16.00

Coquilhatville Conf., Apr.-May, 1961.

Nos. 371-380 exist with inverted overprints. Value $15 each.

Pres. Joseph Kasavubu — A95

Kasavubu and Map of Congo — A96

10fr-100fr, Kasavubu in uniform and map.

Perf. 11½

1961, June 30 Unwmk. Photo.

Portrait and Inscription in Dark Brown

No.	Type	Value	Color	Unused	Used
381	A95	10c	yellow	.25	.25
382	A95	20c	dp rose	.25	.25
383	A95	40c	bl grn	.25	.25
384	A95	50c	salmon	.25	.25
385	A95	1fr	lilac	.25	.25
386	A95	1.50fr	lt brn	.25	.25
387	A95	2fr	brt grn	.25	.25
388	A96	3.50fr	rose pink	.25	.25
389	A96	5fr	gray	*6.50*	.25
390	A96	6.50fr	ultra	1.00	.25
391	A96	8fr	olive	1.00	.25
392	A95	10fr	lt vio	2.25	.80
393	A95	20fr	orange	2.25	.25
394	A95	50fr	lt bl	3.75	.35
395	A95	100fr	apple green	6.25	.55
			Nos. 381-395 (15)	25.00	4.70

First anniversary of independence.
Exists imperf. Value, set $70.

Nos. 381-387, 389 and 392 Overprinted

No. 396

No. 403

1961

Portrait and Inscription in Dark Brown

No.	Type	Value	Color	Unused	Used
396	A95	10c	yellow	.25	.25
397	A95	20c	dp rose	.25	.25
398	A95	40c	bl grn	.25	.25
399	A95	50c	salmon	.55	.35
400	A95	1fr	lilac	.55	.35
401	A95	1.50fr	lt brn	1.50	1.00
402	A95	2fr	brt grn	1.50	1.00
403	A96	5fr	gray	1.50	1.00
404	A95	10fr	lt vio	1.50	1.00
			Nos. 396-404 (9)	7.85	5.45

Congolese parliament re-opening, 7/1961.
Nos. 396-404 exist with inverted overprints. Value $9 each.

Dag Hammarskjold and Map of Africa with Congo — A97

1962, Jan. 20 Photo. *Perf. 11½*

Gray Background

No.	Type	Value	Color	Unused	Used
405	A97	10c	dk brn	.25	.25
406	A97	20c	Prus bl	.25	.25
407	A97	30c	brown	.25	.25
408	A97	40c	dk bl	.25	.25
409	A97	50c	brn red	.25	.25
410	A97	3fr	ol grn	*4.50*	*1.25*
411	A97	6.50fr	dk vio	1.25	.30
412	A97	8fr	red brn	1.50	.45
			Nos. 405-412 (8)	8.50	3.25

Souvenir Sheets

Imperf

No.	Type	Value	Color	Unused	Used
413	A97	25fr	blk brn	8.00	8.00
a.			Overprint in green	4.00	4.00
b.			Overprint in blue	50.00	

Dag Hammarskjold, Sec. Gen. of the UN, 1953-61.

Nos. 405-412 exist imperf. Value, set unused $12.

No 413a is overprinted "30 Juin 1962" on stamp and "2eme Anniversaire de l'Independance" on sheet margin. Issued June 30, 1962.

For overprints see Nos. 417-424.

Malaria Eradication Emblem and Mosquito — A98

1962, June 15 Granite Paper

No.	Type	Value	Color	Unused	Used
414	A98	1.50fr	yel, blk & dk red	.25	.25
415	A98	2fr	yel grn, brn & bl grn	.25	.25
416	A98	6.50fr	ultra, blk & mar	.25	.25
			Nos. 414-416 (3)	.75	.75

WHO drive to eradicate malaria.
Nos. 414-416 exist imperf. Value, set unused $2.

Nos. 405-412 Overprinted in Blue, Purple, Black or Carmine

1962, Oct. 15 Gray Background

No.	Type	Value	Color	Unused	Used
417	A97	10c	dk brn (Bl)	.25	.25
418	A97	20c	Prus bl (P)	.25	.25
419	A97	30c	brn (Bk)	.25	.25
420	A97	40c	dk bl (C)	.25	.25
421	A97	50c	brn red (Bl)	*2.50*	*1.00*
422	A97	3fr	ol grn (P)	.25	.25
423	A97	6.50fr	dk vio (Bk)	.25	.25
424	A97	8fr	red brn (C)	.40	.25
			Nos. 417-424 (8)	4.40	2.75

Reorganization of Adoula administration.
Inverted overprints exist. Value, $10 each.

Canceled to Order

Starting in 1963, values in the used column are for "canceled to order" stamps. Postally used examples sell for much more.

A99

1963, Jan. 28 Engr. *Perf. 10½x13*

No.	Type	Value	Color	Unused	Used
425	A99	2fr	dull purple	*1.25*	.75
426	A99	4fr	red	.25	.25
427	A99	7fr	dark blue	.25	.25
428	A99	20fr	slate green	.40	.25
			Nos. 425-428 (4)	2.15	*1.50*

Congo's 1st participation at the UPU Cong., New Delhi, Mar. 1963.

Nos. 425-428 exist imperf. Value, set unused $30.

An imperf sheet containing No. 428 in brown exists. Value $35.

For overprints see Nos. 468-471.

Shoebill — A100

Birds: 10c, Pelicans. 20c, Crested guinea fowl, horiz. 30c, Openbill. 40c, White-bellied storks, horiz. 2fr, Marabou. 3fr, Greater flamingos, horiz. 4fr, Congolese peacock. 5fr, Hartlaub ducks, horiz. 6fr, Secretary bird. 7fr, Black-casqued hornbill, horiz. 8fr, Sacred ibis and nest. 10fr, Crowned crane, horiz. 20fr, Saddle-bill stork, horiz.

1963 Unwmk. Photo. *Perf. 11½*

No.	Type	Value	Color	Unused	Used
429	A100	10c	pink, ultra & ocher	.25	.25
430	A100	20c	rose red, bl & blk	.25	.25
431	A100	30c	grn, ocher & blk	.25	.25
432	A100	40c	gray, org & blk	.25	.25
433	A100	1fr	brn, emer & gray	.25	.25
434	A100	2fr	gray, red & ind	*3.25*	.60
435	A100	3fr	ol grn, blk & rose	.25	.25
436	A100	4fr	car rose, vio bl & grn	.25	.25
437	A100	5fr	lake, lt bl & blk	.45	.25
438	A100	6fr	pur, yel & blk	*3.50*	.60
439	A100	7fr	bl grn, blk & ind	.55	.25
440	A100	8fr	yel, org & blk	.65	.25
441	A100	10fr	bl, blk & rose	.65	.25
442	A100	20fr	cit, red & blk	1.20	.25
			Nos. 429-442 (14)	12.00	4.20

Nos. 429-442 exist imperf. Value, set unused $60.

Nos. 436 and 438 exist in imperf sheets of one. Value, each $45.

Cinchona Ledgeriana — A101

Red Cross Nurse A102

10c, 30c, 5fr, Strophanthus sarmentosus.

Perf. 12½x13½, 13½x12½

1963, May 25 Engr. Unwmk.

Cross in Red

No.	Type	Value	Color	Unused	Used
443	A101	10c	vio & dl grn	.25	.25
444	A101	20c	magenta & bl	.25	.25
445	A101	30c	grn & org	.25	.25
446	A101	40c	bl & vio	.25	.25
447	A101	5fr	ol & rose claret	.25	.25
448	A101	7fr	org & blk	.25	.25
449	A102	9fr	gray olive & red	.25	.25
450	A102	20fr	purple & red	*2.50*	.75
			Nos. 443-450 (8)	4.25	2.50

International Red Cross centenary.

Nos. 443-450 exist imperf. Value, set unused $35.

A souvenir sheet of three contains imperf. 5fr, 7fr, and 20fr stamps similar to Nos. 447, 448 and 450, but in changed colors. Size: 109x75mm. Value $55.

Men Joining Hands and Map of Congo A103

1963, June 29 Photo. *Perf. 11½*

No.	Type	Value	Color	Unused	Used
451	A103	4fr	multi	1.00	.25
452	A103	5fr	multi	.25	.25
453	A103	9fr	multi	.25	.25
454	A103	12fr	multi	.25	.25
			Nos. 451-454 (4)	1.75	1.00

Issued to celebrate national reconciliation.

Nos. 451-454 exist imperf. Value, set unused $12.50.

Bulldozer and Kabambare Sewer, Leopoldville — A104

Designs: 30c, 5fr, 12fr, Excavator and blueprint. 50c, 9fr, Building Ituri road.

1963, July 1 Engr. Unwmk.

No.	Type	Value	Color	Unused	Used
455	A104	20c	multi	.25	.25
456	A104	30c	multi	.25	.25
457	A104	50c	multi	.25	.25
458	A104	3fr	multi	1.10	.25
459	A104	5fr	multi	.25	.25
460	A104	9fr	multi	.25	.25
461	A104	12fr	multi	.25	.25
			Nos. 455-461 (7)	2.60	1.75

Issued to publicize aid to Congo by the European Economic Community.

Nos. 455-461 exist imperf. Value, set unused $40.

Leopoldville Airport N'Djili — A105

5fr, 7fr, 50fr, Tail assembly and airport.

1963, Nov. 30 Photo. *Perf. 11½*

No.	Type	Value	Color	Unused	Used
462	A105	2fr	gray, yel & red brn	.25	.25
463	A105	5fr	mag, vio & yel	.25	.25
464	A105	6fr	bl, yel & dk brn	1.75	.25
465	A105	7fr	multi	.25	.25
466	A105	30fr	lil, yel & ol	.40	.25
467	A105	50fr	multi	.60	.25
			Nos. 462-467 (6)	3.50	1.50

Issued to publicize Air Congo.

Nos. 462-467 exist imperf. Value, set unused $30.

For surcharge see No. 606.

Nos. 425-428 Overprinted with Silver Frame on Three Sides and Black Inscription

Engraved and Typographed

1963, Dec. 10 *Perf. 10½x13*

No.	Type	Value	Color	Unused	Used
468	A99	2fr	dull purple	.25	.25
469	A99	4fr	red	.25	.25
470	A99	7fr	dark blue	.25	.25
471	A99	20fr	slate green	.35	.25
			Nos. 468-471 (4)	1.10	1.00

Universal Declaration of Human Rights, 15th anniv.

Nos. 468-471 exist with side date panels transposed ("1963" at left, "1948" at right). Value, each $55. Nos. 468-471 exist imperf. Value, set $30.

Laboratory Technician and Atomic Emblem A106

1.50fr, 60fr, University. 8fr, 75fr, First African nuclear reactor. 25fr, 100fr, University and crest.

1964, Feb. 1 Photo. *Perf. 14x12½*

No.	Type	Value	Color	Unused	Used
472	A106	50c	multi	.25	.25
473	A106	1.50fr	multi	.25	.25
474	A106	8fr	multi	*2.75*	*2.50*
475	A106	25fr	multi	.25	.25
476	A106	30fr	multi	.30	.25
477	A106	60fr	multi	.50	.30
478	A106	75fr	multi	.60	.50
479	A106	100fr	multi	1.00	.80
a.			Souv. sheet of 3	6.50	6.50
			Nos. 472-479 (8)	5.90	5.10

Lovanium University, Leopoldville, 10th anniv.

No. 479a contains 3 imperf. multicolored stamps: 20fr, design as 50c; 30fr, as 8fr; 100fr.

Nos. 472-479 exist imperf. Value, set unused $30.

Belgian Congo Issues of 1952-59 Overprinted and Surcharged in Black on Metallic Panels

Nos. 480 and 482

Nos. 481 and 483

1964 *Perf. 11½*

480 A93 1fr on 20c red org & sl (#307) .25 .25
481 A86 2fr on 1.50fr (#273) *11.00* *3.75*
482 A93 5fr on 6.50fr (#315) .25 .25
483 A86 8fr on 6.50fr (#278) 1.10 .35

Republic Issues of 1960-61 Surcharged in Black on Overprinted Metallic Rectangles or Ovals

Nos. 487-488

Nos. 489-489a

Nos. 490-491

484 A86 1fr on 6.50fr (#335) .25 .25
485 A93 1fr on 20c (#342) .25 .25
486 A86 2fr on 1.50fr (#330) .25 .25
487 A95 3fr on 20c (#382) .45 .25
488 A95 4fr on 40c (#383) .55 .25
489 A93 5fr on 6.50fr ("Congo" red) (#350) .90 .25
a. "Congo" black .90 .25
490 A93a 6fr on 6.50fr (#363) .90 .30
491 A93a 7fr on 20c (#356) .90 .35
Nos. 480-491 (12) 17.05 6.75

Pole Vault A107

7fr, 20fr, Javelin, vert. 8fr, 100fr, Hurdling.

Perf. 11½

1964, July 13 **Unwmk.** **Photo.**

Granite Paper

492 A107 5fr gray, dk brn & car .25 .25
493 A107 7fr rose, vio & emer .95 .35
494 A107 8fr org, yel, red brn & vio bl .25 .25
495 A107 10fr bl, vio brn & mag .25 .25
496 A107 20fr gray grn, red brn & ver .25 .25
497 A107 100fr lil, dk brn & grn .95 .25
a. Souv. sheet of 3 10.00 10.00
Nos. 492-497 (6) 2.90 1.60

18th Olympic Games, Tokyo, Oct. 10-25. No. 497a contains 3 imperf. stamps (20fr orange & dark brown, pole vault; 30fr citron and dark brown, hurdling; 100fr dull green and dark brown, javelin). Sheet issued Sept. 10.

Nos. 492-497 exist imperf. Value, set unused $75.

National Palace, Leopoldville — A108

1964, Sept. 15 **Granite Paper**

498 A108 50c lil rose & bl .25 .25
499 A108 1fr bl & lil rose .25 .25
500 A108 2fr brn red & vio .25 .25
501 A108 3fr emer & red .25 .25
502 A108 4fr org & vio bl .25 .25
503 A108 5fr gray vio & emer .25 .25
504 A108 6fr sep & org .25 .25
505 A108 7fr gray ol & red brn .25 .25
506 A108 8fr rose red & vio bl *1.50* .30
507 A108 9fr vio bl & rose red .25 .25
508 A108 10fr brn ol & grn .25 .25
509 A108 20fr bl & brn org .25 .25
510 A108 30fr dk car rose & grn .25 .25
511 A108 40fr ultra & dk car rose .35 .25
512 A108 50fr brn org & grn .40 .25
513 A108 100fr slate & ver .75 .25
Nos. 498-513 (16) 6.00 4.05

Nos. 498-513 exist imperf. Value, set unused $25.

For overprints and surcharges see Nos. 574-577, 593-598, 609-615, 670-671, 673-674, 676-677, 680, 684-687.

Pres. John F. Kennedy (1917-63) A109

1964, Dec. 8 **Photo.** *Perf. 13½*

514 A109 5fr dk bl & blk .25 .25
515 A109 6fr rose claret & blk .25 .25
516 A109 9fr brn & blk .25 .25
517 A109 30fr pur & blk .50 .25
518 A109 40fr dl grn & blk *2.75* .80
519 A109 60fr red brn & blk 1.00 .30
Nos. 514-519 (6) 5.00 2.10

Souvenir Sheet

520 A109 150fr blk & mar 6.50 6.50

Nos. 514-519 exist imperf. Value, set unused $90. No. 520 exists imperf. Value, unused $90.

Rocket and Unisphere — A110

Engraved and Typographed

1965, Mar. 1 **Unwmk.** *Perf. 12*

521 A110 50c lil & blk .25 .25
522 A110 1.50fr bl & lil .25 .25
523 A110 2fr red brn & brt grn .25 .25
524 A110 10fr brt grn & dk red .70 .50
525 A110 18fr vio bl & brn .25 .25
526 A110 27fr rose red & grn .30 .25
527 A110 40fr gray & org .35 .25
Nos. 521-527 (7) 2.35 2.00

New York World's Fair, 1964-65.

Nos. 521-527 exist imperf. Value, set unused $20.

Basketball A111

6fr, 40fr, Soccer, horiz. 15fr, 60fr, Volleyball.

1965, Apr. **Photo.** *Perf. 13½*

528 A111 5fr blk, grnsh bl & ocher .25 .25
529 A111 6fr blk, bl gray & crim .25 .25
530 A111 15fr blk, org & yel grn .25 .25
531 A111 24fr blk, rose lil & brt grn .40 .25
532 A111 40fr blk, brt grn & ultra *1.60* .40
533 A111 60fr blk, bl & red lil .50 .25
Nos. 528-533 (6) 3.25 1.65

First African Games, Leopoldville, Mar. 31-Apr. 7, 1965.

Nos. 528-533 exist imperf. Value, set unused $17.50.

For surcharges see Nos. 604-605.

Earth and Satellites A112

Designs: 9fr, 15fr, 20fr, 40fr, Satellites at left, globe at right.

Perf. 14x14½

1965, June 28 **Photo.** **Unwmk.**

534 A112 6fr blk, sal & vio .25 .25
535 A112 9fr blk, lt grn & gray .25 .25
536 A112 12fr org, gray & blk .25 .25
537 A112 15fr grn, ultra & blk .25 .25
538 A112 18fr blk, lt grn & gray 1.20 .25
539 A112 20fr blk, sal & vio .25 .25
540 A112 30fr grn, ultra & blk .25 .25
541 A112 40fr org, gray & blk .35 .25
Nos. 534-541 (8) 3.05 2.00

Cent. of the ITU.

Nos. 534-541 exist imperf. Value, set unused $47.50.

Congolese Paratrooper and Parachutes A113

1965, July 5 *Perf. 13x14*

542 A113 5fr brt bl & brn .25 .25
543 A113 6fr org & brn .25 .25
544 A113 7fr br grn & brn .30 .25
545 A113 9fr brt pink & brn .25 .25
546 A113 18fr lem & brn .25 .25
Nos. 542-546 (5) 1.30 1.25

Fifth anniversary of independence.

Nos. 542-546 exist imperf. Value, set unused $17.50.

Matadi Harbor and ICY Emblem — A114

ICY Emblem and: 8fr, 25fr, Katanga mines. 9fr, 60fr, Tshopo Dam, Stanleyville.

1965, Oct. 25 **Photo.** *Perf. 13x14*

547 A114 6fr ultra, blk & yel .25 .25
548 A114 8fr org red, blk & bl .25 .25
549 A114 9fr bl grn, blk & brn org .25 .25
550 A114 12fr car rose, blk & gray .75 .30
551 A114 25fr ol, blk & rose red .25 .25
552 A114 60fr gray, blk & org .50 .25
Nos. 547-552 (6) 2.25 1.55

International Cooperation Year, 1965.

Nos. 547-552 exist imperf. Value, set unused $20.

For overprints and surcharges see Nos. 559-560, 607-608.

Soldiers Giving First Aid — A115

The Army Serving the Country: 7fr, Bridge building. 9fr, Feeding child. 19fr, Maintenance of telegraph lines. 20fr, House building. 30fr, Soldier and flag. (19fr, 20fr, 30fr, vert.)

Perf. 12½x13, 13x12½

1965, Nov. 17

553 A115 5fr sal, brn & red .25 .25
554 A115 7fr yel & grn .25 .25
555 A115 9fr ol & brn .25 .25
556 A115 19fr brt grn & brn .80 .45
557 A115 20fr lt bl & brn .25 .25
558 A115 30fr multi .40 .25
Nos. 553-558 (6) 2.20 1.70

See Nos. 582-586.

Nos. 553-558 exist imperf. Value, set unused $17.50.

For surcharges see Nos. 602, 678-679, 683.

Nos. 551-552 Overprinted on Metallic Strip

1966, Mar. 23 **Photo.** *Perf. 13x14*

559 A114 25fr ol & blk 1.40 .55
560 A114 60fr gray & blk 1.40 .65

6th World Meteorological Day.

Nos. 559-560 exist with inverted overprint and black missing. Value, each $15.

Woman's Head and Goat — A116

10fr, Sculptured heads. 12fr, Sitting figure and two heads, vert. 53fr, Figure with earrings and kneeling woman with bowl, vert.

Perf. 11½x13, 13x11½

1966, Apr. 23 **Litho.** **Unwmk.**

561 A116 10fr red, blk & gray .25 .25
562 A116 12fr grn, blk & bl .25 .25
563 A116 15fr dp bl, blk & lil .30 .25
564 A116 53fr dp rose, blk & vio bl 1.30 1.00
Nos. 561-564 (4) 2.10 1.75

Intl. Negro Arts Festival, Dakar, Senegal, Apr. 1-24.

Nos. 561-564 exist imperf. Value, set unused $15.

Pres. Joseph Desiré Mobutu and Fishing Industry A117

Pres. Mobutu and: 4fr, Pyrethrum harvest. 6fr, Building industry. 8fr, Winnowing rice. 10fr, Cotton harvest. 12fr, Banana harvest. 15fr, Coffee harvest. 24fr, Pineapple harvest. No. 573a, Pres. Mobutu without cap, and men rolling up sleeves.

1966, May 1 **Photo.** *Perf. 11½*

565 A117 2fr dk brn & dk bl .25 .25
566 A117 4fr dk brn & org .25 .25
567 A117 6fr dk brn & ol .50 .25

568 A117 8fr dk brn & brt grnsh bl .25 .25
569 A117 10fr dk brn & brn red .25 .25
570 A117 12fr dk brn & vio .25 .25
571 A117 15fr dk brn & lt ol grn .25 .25
572 A117 24fr dk brn & lil rose .25 .25
Nos. 565-572 (8) 2.25 2.00

Souvenir Sheet

Perf. 11x11½

573 Sheet of 4 2.00 1.50
a. A117 15fr red, black & ultra .50 .35

Lt. Gen. Joseph Desiré Mobutu, Pres. of Congo, and publicizing the "Back to Work" campaign.

Nos. 565-572 exist imperf. Value, set unused $15. No. 573 exists imperf. Value, unused $15.

For surcharges see Nos. 601, 603, 616, 619-624, 672, 675, 681-682.

Nos. 510-513 Overprinted

1966, June 13 ***Perf. 11½***
574 A108 30fr dk car rose & grn 1.10 1.10
575 A108 40fr ultra & dk car rose 1.20 1.20
576 A108 50fr brn org & grn 1.40 1.40
577 A108 100fr slate & ver 1.40 1.40
Nos. 574-577 (4) 5.10 5.10

Inauguration of WHO Headquarters, Geneva.

Nos. 574-577 exist with inverted overprint. Value, set $25.

Soccer Player — A118

30fr, 2 soccer players. 50fr, 3 soccer players. 60fr, Jules Rimet Cup, soccer ball & globe.

1966, July 25 **Photo.** ***Perf. 14***
578 A118 10fr ocher, vio & grn .25 .25
579 A118 30fr brt rose lil, vio & ap grn .45 .25
580 A118 50fr ap grn, Prus bl & tan 1.50 1.00
581 A118 60fr brt grn, dk brn & gold 1.50 .50
Nos. 578-581 (4) 3.70 2.00

World Cup Soccer Championship, Wembley, England, July 11-30.

Nos. 578-581 exist imperf. Value, set unused $20.

For overprints see Nos. 587-590.

Army Type of 1965

The Army Serving the Country: 2fr, Soldiers giving first aid. 6fr, Feeding child. 10fr, House building, vert. 18fr, Bridge building. 24fr, Soldier and flag, vert.

1966, Aug. 8 ***Perf. 12½x13, 13x12½***
582 A115 2fr sal pink, grn blue & red .25 .25
583 A115 6fr ultra red brn .25 .25
584 A115 10fr yel grn & red brn .50 .30
585 A115 18fr car rose & vio .25 .25
586 A115 24fr multi .25 .25
Nos. 582-586 (5) 1.50 1.30

Nos. 582-586 exist imperf. Value, set unused $10.

Nos. 578-581 Overprinted in Black, Carmine or Green

1966, Nov. 14 **Photo.** ***Perf. 14***
587 A118 10fr pair, B and C .75 .75
588 A118 30fr pair, B and G 2.25 2.00
589 A118 50fr pair, B and C 3.50 3.00
590 A118 60fr pair, B and C 4.50 4.00
Nos. 587-590 (4) 11.00 9.75

England's victory in the World Soccer Cup Championship.

The two colors of the overprint alternate in the sheets.

Nos. 587-590 exist with inverted overprint. Value, set $75.

Souvenir Sheets

Pres. John F. Kennedy — A119

1966, Dec. 28 **Engr.** ***Perf. 13***
591 A119 150fr brown 22.50 17.50
592 A119 150fr slate 22.50 17.50

Issued in memory of Pres. John F. Kennedy.

No. 591 has slate green, No. 592 deep orange marginal design.

Two imperf. sheets exist: 150fr brown with violet blue margin and 150fr slate with lilac margin. Size: 65x76mm. Values, $20 each.

Perforated sheets exist in imperf. colors. Value, set $200.

Nos. 498-503 Surcharged in Black, Red or Maroon and

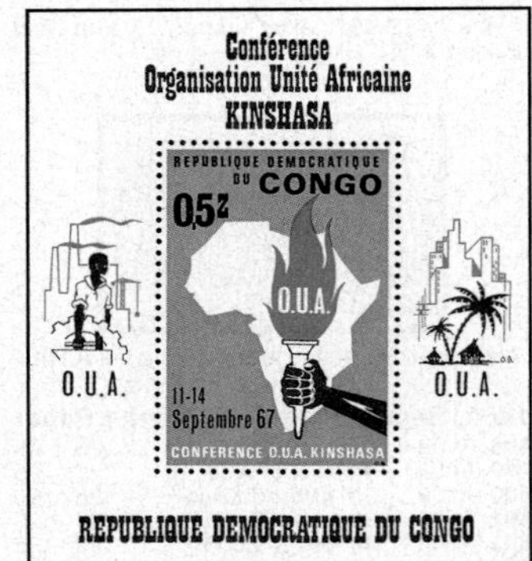

Map of Africa, Torch — A120

1967, Sept. 11 **Photo.** ***Perf. 11½***
593 A108 1k on 2fr .25 .25
a. Inverted overprint 5.00
594 A108 3k on 5fr .25 .25
595 A108 5k on 4fr .35 .25
596 A108 6.60k on 1fr (R) .50 .25
a. Inverted overprint 5.00
597 A108 9.60k on 50c .70 .30
a. Inverted overprint 5.00
598 A108 9.80k on 3fr (M) .75 .50
Nos. 593-598 (6) 2.80 1.80

Souvenir Sheet

599 A120 50k grnsh bl, blk & red 2.75 2.75

Fourth meeting of the Org. for African Unity, Kinshasa (Leopoldville), Sept. 9-11.

No. 599 exists imperf. Value, unused $17.50.

No. 599 in other colors was not a postal issue.

Souvenir Sheet

Horn Blower and EXPO Emblem — A121

1967, Sept. 28 **Engr.** ***Perf. 11½***
600 A121 50k dk brn 3.50 3.50

EXPO '67, International Exhibition, Montreal, Apr. 28-Oct. 27, 1967.

No. 600 exists imperf. Value, unused $20.

Nos. 565-566 and 582 Overprinted and Surcharged on Metallic Panel in Magenta or Brown

No. 601

No. 602

Perf. 11½, 12½x13
1967, Oct. 9 **Photo.**
601 A117 4k on 2fr (M) .25 .25
602 A115 5k on 2fr (B) .45 .25
603 A117 21k on 4fr (M) 1.40 .75
Nos. 601-603 (3) 2.10 1.25

Promulgation of the Constitution, June 4, 1967.

Nos. 528 and 530 Surcharged and Overprinted

1967, Oct. 16 **Photo.** ***Perf. 13½***
604 A111 1k on 5fr multi .35 .25
605 A111 9.60k on 15fr multi .75 .65

First Congolese Games, Kinshasa, June 25-July 2, 1967.

Nos. 604-605 exist with red overprint. Value, set $25.

No. 465 Surcharged and Overprinted

1967, Oct. 16 ***Perf. 11½***
606 A105 9.60k on 7fr multi 1.10 .25

1st flight of the BAC 111 in the service of Air Congo, May 14, 1967.

Nos. 547 and 549 Surcharged in Red or Black

1968, Feb. 10 **Photo.** ***Perf. 13x14***
607 A114 1k on 6fr (R) .35 .25
608 A114 9k on 9fr (B) .90 .65

Intl. Children's Day. The surcharge is on a rectangle printed in metallic ink.

Nos. 498, 504 and 501 Surcharged in Blue or Red

1968, Feb. 10 ***Perf. 11½***
609 A108 5k on 50c lil rose & bl (Bl) .45 .25
610 A108 10k on 6fr sepia & org (R) .60 .50
611 A108 15k on 3fr emer & red (R) .80 .80
Nos. 609-611 (3) 1.85 1.55

International Tourist Year. The surcharge is on a rectangle printed in metallic ink.

Nos. 500, 498 and 502 Surcharged in Black, Violet Blue or Gold

No. 612

No. 613

No. 614

No. 615

1968, July Photo. *Perf. 11½*

612 A108 1k on 2fr .30 .25
613 A108 2k on 50c (VBl) .45 .25
614 A108 2k on 50c (G) .45 .25
615 A108 9.60k on 4fr 2.00 1.10
Nos. 612-615 (4) 3.20 1.85

The surcharge on No. 612 consists of a black rectangle and new denomination in upper right corner; the surcharge on No. 613 has a violet blue rectangle with denomination printed in white on it; on No. 614 the rectangle is gold and the denomination black; on No. 615 the rectangle is black and the denomination white.

Nos. 612-615 exist with inverted surcharge. Value, set $7.50.

No. 565 Surcharged in White on Black Rectangle

1968, Oct. Photo. *Perf. 11½*

616 A117 10k on 2fr dk brn & dk bl .70 .25

Leopard A122

1968, Nov. 5 Litho. *Perf. 10½*

617 A122 2k brt grnsh bl & blk .30 .25
618 A122 9.60k red & blk 1.50 .25

Nos. 617-618 exist imperf. Value, set unused $20.

Nos. 617-618 exist with inverted surcharge. Values: No. 617, $300; No. 618, $140.

Mobutu Type of 1966 Surcharged

1968, Dec. 20 Photo. *Perf. 11½*

619 A117 15s on 2fr sep & brt bl .25 .25
620 A117 1k on 6fr sep & brn .25 .25
621 A117 3k on 10fr sep & emer .25 .25
622 A117 5k on 12fr sep & org .30 .25
623 A117 20k on 15fr sep & brt grn 1.00 .50
624 A117 50k on 24fr sep & brt lil 2.75 1.25
Nos. 619-624 (6) 4.80 2.75

Nos. 619-624 exist imperf. Value, set $15.

Human Rights Flame — A123

1968, Dec. 30 *Perf. 12½x13*

625 A123 2k lt ultra & brt grn .25 .25
626 A123 9.60k grn & dp car .75 .30
627 A123 10k brt lil & brn .75 .35
628 A123 40k org brn & pur 2.50 1.25
Nos. 625-628 (4) 4.25 2.15

International Human Rights Year.

Nos. 625-628 exist imperf. Value, set unused $15.

Type of 1968 Overprinted in Gold

1969, Jan. 27 Photo. *Perf. 12½x13*

629 A123 2k ap grn & red brn .25 .25
630 A123 9.60k rose & emer .75 .30
631 A123 10k gray & ultra .75 .35
632 A123 40k grnsh bl & pur 2.50 1.25
Nos. 629-632 (4) 4.25 2.15

4th summit meeting of OCAM (Organisation Communitee Afrique et Malgache), Kinshasa, Jan. 27.

Nos. 629-632 exist imperf. Value, set unused $15.

Kinshasa Fair Emblem and Cotton Boll — A124

Fair Emblem and: 6k, Copper. 9.60k, Coffee. 9.80k, Diamond. 11.60k, Oil palm fruits.

1969, May 2 Photo. *Perf. 12½x13*

633 A124 2k brt pur, gold & red lil .25 .25
634 A124 6k grn, gold & bl grn .95 .40
635 A124 9.60k brn, gold & lt brn 1.25 .40
636 A124 9.80k ultra & gold 1.40 .60
637 A124 11.60k hn brn, gold & brn 1.60 .80
Nos. 633-637 (5) 5.45 2.45

Kinshasa Fair, Limete, June 30-July 21.

Nos. 633-637 exist imperf. Value, set unused $25.

Fair Entrance, Emblem — A125

Fair Emblem and: 3k, Gecomin Mining Co. Pavilion. 10k, Administration Building. 25k, Pavilion of the Organization for African Unity.

1969, June 30 Photo. *Perf. 11½*
Granite Paper

638 A125 2k brt rose lil & gold .25 .25
639 A125 3k blue & gold .25 .25
640 A125 10k lt ol grn & gold .75 .40
641 A125 25k copper red & gold 1.75 1.00
Nos. 638-641 (4) 3.00 1.90

Kinshasa Fair, Limete, June 30-July 21.

Nos. 638-641 exist imperf. Value, set unused $15.

Congo Arms — A126

Pres. Mobutu — A127

1969, July-Sept. Litho. *Perf. 14*

642 A126 10s org & blk .25 .25
643 A126 15s ultra & blk .25 .25
644 A126 30s brt grn & blk .25 .25
645 A126 60s brt rose lil & blk .25 .25
646 A126 90s dp bister & blk .25 .25

Perf. 13

647 A127 1k sky bl & multi .25 .25
648 A127 2k org & multi .25 .25
649 A127 3k multi .30 .25
650 A127 5k brt rose & multi .40 .25
651 A127 6k ultra & multi .40 .25
652 A127 9.60k multi .75 .40
653 A127 10k lt lil & multi 1.00 .50
654 A127 20k yel & multi 1.75 1.00
655 A127 50k multi 5.00 2.50
656 A127 100k fawn & multi 10.00 6.00
Nos. 642-656 (15) 21.35 12.90

Nos. 642-656 exist imperf. Value, set unused $25.

Well Driller, by Oscar Bonnevalle — A128

Paintings: 4k, Preparation of cocoa, by Jean Van Noten. 8k, Dock workers, by Constantin Meunier. 10k, Poultry shop, by Henri Evenepoel. 15k, Steel industry, by Constantin Meunier.

Perf. 13x14, 14x13 (8k)
1969, Dec. 15 Litho.
Size: 41x41mm

657 A128 3k multi .25 .25
658 A128 4k multi .25 .25

Size: 28x41mm

659 A128 8k multi .45 .30

Size: 41x41mm

660 A128 10k multi .65 .40
661 A128 15k multi 1.40 .50
Nos. 657-661 (5) 3.00 1.70

50th anniv. of the ILO.

Nos. 657-661 exist imperf. Value, set unused $15.

Souvenir Sheet

Adoration of the Kings, by Rubens — A129

1969, Dec. Engr. *Perf. 13*

662 A129 50k red lilac 5.50 5.50

Issued for Christmas 1969.

No. 662 exists imperf. Value, unused $15.

Pres. Mobutu, Map and Flag of Congo A130

1970, June 30 Litho. *Perf. 13½x13*

663 A130 10s multi .25 .25
664 A130 90s pur & multi .25 .25
665 A130 1k brn & multi .25 .25
666 A130 2k multi .25 .25
667 A130 7k multi .35 .25
668 A130 10k multi .55 .25
669 A130 20k multi 1.10 .50
Nos. 663-669 (7) 3.00 2.00

10th anniversary of independence.

Nos. 663-669 exist imperf. Value, set unused $12.

Issues of 1964-1966 Surcharged

Perf. 11½, 12½x13, 13x12½
1970, Sept. 24 Photo.

670 A108 10s on 1fr (#499) .25 .25
671 A108 20s on 2fr (#500) .25 .25
672 A117 20s on 2fr (#565) .80 .45
673 A108 30s on 3fr (#501) .25 .25
674 A108 40s on 4fr (#502) .25 .25
675 A117 40s on 4fr (#566) .80 .45
676 A108 60s on 7fr (#505) 2.60 1.60
677 A108 90s on 9fr (#507) 2.60 1.60
678 A115 90s on 9fr (#555) .55 .40
679 A115 1k on 7fr (#554) .55 .40
680 A108 1k on 6fr (#504) .45 .25
681 A117 1k on 12fr (#570) 2.50 1.60
682 A117 2k on 24fr (#572) 1.10 .50
683 A115 2k on 24fr (#586) 1.10 .50
684 A108 3k on 30fr (#510) 2.00 1.10
685 A108 4k on 40fr (#511) .45 .25
686 A108 5k on 50fr (#512) 7.50 4.25
687 A108 10k on 100fr (#513) 2.00 1.10
Nos. 670-687 (18) 26.00 15.45

Telecommunications Building, Geneva — A131

Designs: 2k, 6.60k, UPU Headquarters, Bern. 9.80k, 10k, 11k, UN Headquarters, NY.

1970, Oct. 24 Photo. *Perf. 11½*

688 A131 1k pink & grn .25 .25
689 A131 2k org & grn .25 .25
690 A131 6.60k grnsh bl & rose car .40 .25
691 A131 9.60k yel & vio bl .50 .35
692 A131 9.80k lt ultra & brn .50 .35
693 A131 10k lt pur & brn .50 .35
694 A131 11k rose & brn .70 .45
Nos. 688-694 (7) 3.10 2.25

ITU; new UPU Headquarters, Bern; 25th anniv. of the UN.

Nos. 688-694 exist imperf. Value, set unused $35.

Pres. Mobutu, Congolese Flag and Arch — A132

1970, Nov. 24 Litho. *Perf. 13*

695 A132 2k yel & multi .25 .25
696 A132 10k bl & multi 1.00 .50
697 A132 20k red & multi 2.75 1.75
Nos. 695-697 (3) 4.00 2.50

Fifth anniversary of new government.

Nos. 695-697 exist imperf. Value, set unused $6.

Stamps of design A132 denominated 1k, 6k, and 11k were printed but not issued. Value, set $125.

Apollo 11 in Flight A133

Designs: 2k, Astronaut and spacecraft on moon. 7k, Pres. Mobutu decorating astronauts' wives. 10k, Pres. Mobutu with Neil A. Armstrong, Col. Edwin E. Aldrin, Jr. and Lt.

Col. Michael Collins. 30k, Armstrong, Aldrin and Collins in space suits.

1970, Dec. 24 *Perf. 13x13½*

698	A133	1k bl & blk	.30	.25
699	A133	2k brt pur & blk	.50	.25
700	A133	7k dl org & blk	1.50	.85
701	A133	10k rose red & blk	2.00	1.25
702	A133	30k grn & blk	5.50	3.50
		Nos. 698-702 (5)	9.80	6.10

Visit of US Apollo 11 astronauts and their wives to Kinshasa.

Nos. 698-702 exist imperf. Value, set unused $30.

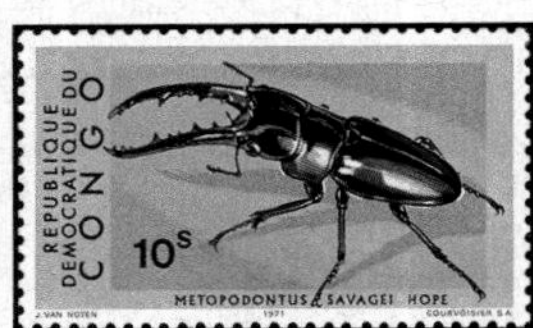

Metopodontus Savagei — A134

Designs: Various insects of Congo.

1971, Jan. 25 **Photo.** *Perf. 11½*

703	A134	10s dl rose & multi	.75	.30
704	A134	50s gray & multi	.75	.30
705	A134	90s multi	.75	.30
706	A134	1k citron & multi	.75	.30
707	A134	2k gray grn & multi	.75	.30
708	A134	3k lt vio & multi	1.75	.60
709	A134	5k bl & multi	5.00	2.00
710	A134	10k multi	7.00	2.50
711	A134	30k grn & multi	16.00	6.75
712	A134	40k ocher & multi	25.00	10.00
		Nos. 703-712 (10)	58.50	23.35

Nos. 703-712 exist imperf. Value, set unused $65.

Colotis Protomedia — A135

Various butterflies and moths of Congo.

1971, Feb. 24

713	A135	10s lt ultra & multi	.75	.35
714	A135	20s choc & multi	.75	.35
715	A135	70s dp org & multi	.75	.35
716	A135	1k vio bl & multi	.75	.35
717	A135	3k multi	1.75	.60
718	A135	5k dk grn & multi	4.75	1.50
719	A135	10k multi	6.25	2.00
720	A135	15k emer & multi	11.00	3.50
721	A135	25k yel & multi	17.50	4.50
722	A135	40k multi	24.00	11.00
		Nos. 713-722 (10)	68.25	24.50

Nos. 713-722 exist imperf. Value, set unused $75.

UN Emblem, Racial Unity — A136

1971, Mar. 21 **Photo.** *Perf. 11½*

723	A136	1k lt grn & multi	.25	.25
724	A136	4k gray & multi	.25	.25
725	A136	5k lt lil & multi	.40	.25
726	A136	10k lt bl & multi	.75	.35
		Nos. 723-726 (4)	1.65	1.10

Intl. year against racial discrimination.

Nos. 723-726 exist imperf. Value, set unused $10.

Hypericum Bequaertii A137

Flowers: 4k, Dissotis brazzae. 20k, Begonia wollastonii. 25k, Cassia alata.

1971, May 24 **Litho.** *Perf. 14*

727	A137	1k multi	1.00	.25
728	A137	4k multi	1.75	.45
729	A137	20k multi	9.25	2.50
730	A137	25k multi	12.00	3.25
		Nos. 727-730 (4)	24.00	6.45

Nos. 727-730 exist imperf. Value, set unused $30.

Obelisk at N'sele, Pres. Mobutu A138

1971, May 20 **Photo.** *Perf. 11½*

731	A138	4k gold & multi	.60	.25

Fourth anniversary of the People's Revolutionary Movement.

No. 731 exists imperf. Value, unused $10.

Radar Station A139

Designs: 1k, Waves. 6k, Map of Africa with telecommunications network.

1971, June 25 **Photo.** *Perf. 11½*

732	A139	1k rose & multi	.25	.25
733	A139	3k yel & multi	.55	.35
734	A139	6k lt bl & multi	1.40	1.00
		Nos. 732-734 (3)	2.20	1.60

3rd World Telecommunications Day, May 17 (1k); opening of satellite telecommunications ground station, Kinshasa, June 30 (3k); Pan-African telecommunication system (6k).

Nos. 732-734 exist imperf. Value, set unused $15.

Grass Monkeys A140

Designs: 20s, Moustached monkeys, vert. 70s, De Brazza's monkeys. 1k, Yellow baboons. 3k, Pygmy chimpanzee, vert. 5k, Mangabeys, vert. 10k, Owlfaced monkeys. 15k, Diana monkeys. 25k, Black-and-white colobus, vert. 40k, L'Hoest's monkeys, vert.

1971, Aug.

735	A140	10s vio & multi	.75	.35
736	A140	20s lt bl & multi	.75	.35
737	A140	70s ocher & multi	1.25	.45
738	A140	1k gray & multi	1.25	.45
739	A140	3k rose & multi	2.00	1.00
740	A140	5k brn & multi	4.50	2.50
741	A140	10k multi	8.75	4.75
742	A140	15k multi	14.00	6.50
743	A140	25k brt bl & multi	23.50	11.00
744	A140	40k red & multi	32.50	16.00
		Nos. 735-744 (10)	89.25	43.35

Nos. 735-744 exist imperf. Value, set unused $120.

Hotel Inter-Continental, Kinshasa — A141

1971, Oct. 2 **Photo.** *Perf. 13*

745	A141	2k silver & multi	.25	.25
746	A141	12k gold & multi	.55	.25

Nos. 745-746 exist imperf. Value, set unused $6.

Man Reading A142

Designs: 2.50k, Open book and abacus. 7k, Five letters surrounding symbolic head.

1971, Oct. 24

747	A142	50s multi	.25	.25
748	A142	2.50k multi	.25	.25
749	A142	7k multi	1.25	.75
		Nos. 747-749 (3)	1.75	1.25

Fight against illiteracy.

Nos. 747-749 exist imperf. Value, set unused $10.

Succeeding issues are listed in Vol. 6 under Zaire. Beginning in 1998, Zaire reverted to using the Congo name, at least temporarily. Until the situation is resolved, the current stamps inscribed "Congo" will be listed under Zaire.

SEMI-POSTAL STAMPS

Women Carrying Food, Wheat Emblem, and Tractor SP22

1963, Mar. 21 **Photo.** *Perf. 14x13*

B48	SP22	5fr + 2fr multi	.25	.25
B49	SP22	9fr + 4fr multi	.45	.25
B50	SP22	12fr+ 6fr multi	.50	.25
B51	SP22	20fr+ 10fr multi	2.25	1.75
		Nos. B48-B51 (4)	3.45	2.50

FAO "Freedom from Hunger" campaign.

Nos. B48-B51 exist imperf. Value, set unused $30.

No. B51 exists in an imperf sheet of one, in light and dark violet. Value $30.

CONGO, PEOPLE'S REPUBLIC

'pē-pəls ri-'pə-blik of 'käŋ-ˌgō

(ex-French)

LOCATION — West Africa at equator
GOVT. — Republic
AREA — 132,046 sq. mi.
POP. — 2,716,814 (1999 est.)
CAPITAL — Brazzaville

The former French colony of Middle Congo became a member state of the French Community on November 28, 1958, and achieved independence on August 15, 1960. For some years before 1958, the colony was joined with three other French territories to form French Equatorial Africa. Issues of Middle Congo (1907-1933) are listed under that heading.

100 Centimes = 1 Franc

Catalogue values for all unused stamps in this country are for Never Hinged items.

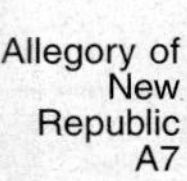

Allegory of New Republic A7

1959 Unwmk. Engr. *Perf. 13*
89 A7 25fr brn, dp clar, org & ol .75 .25

1st anniv. of the proclamation of the Republic.

Imperforates
Most stamps of the Republic of the Congo exist imperforate in issued and trial colors, and also in small presentation sheets in issued colors.

Common Design Types pictured following the introduction.

C.C.T.A. Issue
Common Design Type

1960 Unwmk. *Perf. 13*
90 CD106 50fr dl grn & plum 1.00 1.00

President Fulbert Youlou — A8

1960
91 A8 15fr grn, blk & car .35 .35
92 A8 85fr indigo & car 2.00 .45

Flag, Map and UN Emblem — A9

1961, Mar. 11 *Perf. 13*
Flag in Green, Yellow & Red
93 A9 5fr vio brn & dk bl .25 .25
94 A9 20fr org & dk bl .45 .25
95 A9 100fr grn & dk bl 2.00 .80
Nos. 93-95 (3) 2.70 1.30

Congo's admission to United Nations.

Rainbow Runner A10

Fish: 50c, 3fr, Rainbow runner. 1fr, 2fr, Sloan's viperfish. 5fr, Hatchet fish. 10fr, A deep-sea fish.

1961, Nov. 28 Engr.
96 A10 50c brn, ol grn & sal .30 .25
97 A10 1fr bl grn & sepia .30 .25
98 A10 2fr ultra, sep & dk grn .30 .25
99 A10 3fr dk bl, grn & salmon .45 .30
100 A10 5fr red brn, grn & blk .70 .30
101 A10 10fr blue & red brn 1.40 .45
Nos. 96-101 (6) 3.45 1.80

Brazzaville Market — A11

1962, Mar. 23 Unwmk. *Perf. 13*
102 A11 20fr blk, red & grn .90 .25

Abidjan Games Issue
Common Design Type

20fr, Boxing. 50fr, Running, finish line.

1962, July 21 Photo. *Perf. 12½x12*
103 CD109 20fr car, brt pink, brn & blk .45 .25
104 CD109 50fr car, brt pink, brn & blk .90 .30
Nos. 103-104,C7 (3) 3.85 1.80

African-Malgache Union Issue
Common Design Type

1962, Sept. 8
105 CD110 30fr multicolored 1.50 .50

Waves Around Globe A11a

Design: 100fr, Orbit patterns around globe.

1963, Sept. 19 *Perf. 12½*
106 A11a 25fr org, grn & ultra .75 .30
107 A11a 100fr lt red brn, bl & plum 1.75 .90

Issued to publicize space communications.

King Makoko's Collar — A12

Unwmk.
1963, Oct. 21 Engr. *Perf. 13*
108 A12 10fr shown .45 .25
109 A12 15fr Kebekebe mask .60 .25

UNESCO Emblem, Scales and Tree A12a

1963, Dec. 10 Unwmk. *Perf. 13*
110 A12a 25fr grn, dk bl & brn .90 .30

15th anniv. of the Universal Declaration of Human Rights.

Barograph and WMO Emblem A12b

1964, Mar. 23 Engr.
111 A12b 50fr grn, red brn & ultra 1.50 .60

Fourth World Meteorological Day.

Mechanic with Machine — A13

1964, Apr. 8
112 A13 20fr grnsh bl, mag & dk brn .90 .30

Training of technicians.

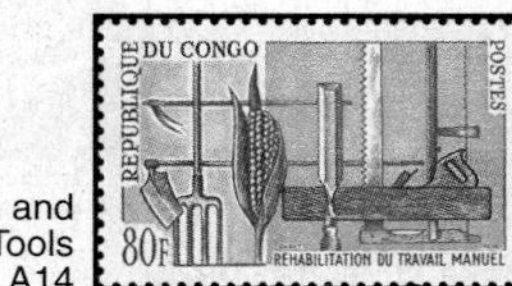

Corn and Tools A14

1964, Apr. 24 Unwmk. *Perf. 13*
113 A14 80fr brn, grn & brn car 1.60 .60

Importance of manual labor.

Diaboua Ballet A15

Kébékébé Dance — A16

1964, May 8 Engr.
114 A15 30fr multicolored 1.25 .30
115 A16 60fr multicolored 2.25 .65

Carved Figure — A17

1964, May 22
116 A17 50fr brn red & sepia 1.50 .55

Classroom A18

1964, May 26
117 A18 25fr dk brn, red & blue .90 .30

Issued to publicize education.

Type of Air Post Issue, 1963, Inscribed

1964, Aug. 15 Photo. *Perf. 13x12*
118 AP5 20fr lt bl, red, ocher, dk brn & grn .80 .25

1st anniv. of the revolution and Natl. Feast Day, Aug. 15.

Fire Squid A19

15fr, Johnson's deep-sea angler (fish).

1964, Oct. 20 Engr. *Perf. 13*
119 A19 2fr ver, lt grn & brn .80 .50
120 A19 15fr vio, lt ol grn & dp cl 2.75 1.50

Cooperation Issue
Common Design Type

1964, Nov. 7 Unwmk. *Perf. 13*
121 CD119 25fr car, brt grn & dk brn .90 .35

Communications Emblems — A20

1965, Jan. 1 Litho. *Perf. 12½x13*
122 A20 25fr ol, red brn & blk .90 .25

Issued to commemorate the establishment of the national postal administration.

Sitatunga — A21

Dancer on Stilts — A22

Design: 20fr, Elephant, horiz.

1965, Mar. 15 Engr. *Perf. 13*
123 A21 15fr redsh brn, dl grn & bl 1.00 .40
124 A21 20fr blk, dp bl & sl grn 1.00 .40
125 A22 85fr lil & multi 3.50 1.50
Nos. 123-125 (3) 5.50 2.30

Pres. Alphonse Massamba-Debat
A23

1965-66 Photo. *Perf. 12x12½*

126 A23 20fr dk brn, grn & yel .40 .25
127 A23 25fr brn, bl grn, emer & blk ('66) .40 .25
128 A23 30fr brn, bl grn, org & blk ('66) .70 .25
Nos. 126-128 (3) 1.50 .75

Soccer Player
A24

Designs: 25fr, Games' emblem (map of Africa and runners). 50fr, Field ball player. 85fr, Runner. 100fr, Bicyclist.

1965, July 17 Photo. *Perf. 12½*

Size: 28x28mm

129 A24 25fr blk, red, yel & grn .50 .30

Size: 34x34mm

130 A24 40fr yel grn & multi .70 .45
131 A24 50fr red & multi .70 .45
132 A24 85fr blk & multi 1.25 .65
133 A24 100fr yel & multi 1.75 .75
a. Min. sheet of 5, #129-133 7.50 7.50
Nos. 129-133 (5) 4.90 2.60

1st African Games, Brazzaville, July 18-25.

Arms of Congo — A25

1965, Nov. 15 Litho. *Perf. 12½x13*

134 A25 20fr multicolored .90 .25

Cooperative Village
A26

30fr, Gymnastic drill team with streamers.

1966, Feb. 18 *Perf. 12½x13*

135 A26 25fr multicolored .90 .25
136 A26 30fr multicolored .90 .30

Sculptured Mask — A27

Designs: 30fr, Weaver, painting. 85fr, String instrument, painting, horiz.

Perf. 13x12½, 12½x13

1966, Apr. 9 Photo.

137 A27 30fr multicolored .70 .30
138 A27 85fr multicolored 1.90 .70
139 A27 90fr multicolored 2.25 1.00
Nos. 137-139 (3) 4.85 2.00

Intl. Negro Arts Festival, Dakar, Senegal, 4/1-24.

Men and Clocks
A28

1966, Apr. 15 *Perf. 12½x12*

140 A28 70fr pale brn, ocher & dk brn 1.60 .50

Introduction of the shorter work day (less lunch time, earlier quitting time).

WHO Headquarters, Geneva — A29

1966, May 3 Photo. *Perf. 12½x13*

141 A29 50fr org yel, vio & bl 1.50 .50

Inauguration of the WHO Headquarters, Geneva.

Church of St. Peter Claver — A30

1966, June 15 Photo. *Perf. 13x12½*

142 A30 70fr multicolored 1.50 .40

Women's Basketball — A31

Sport: 1fr, Women's volleyball, horiz. 3fr, Women's field ball, horiz. 5fr, Athletes of various races. 10fr, Torch bearer. 15fr, Soccer and gold medal of First African Games.

1966, July 15 Engr. *Perf. 13*

143 A31 1fr ultra, choc & ol .25 .25
144 A31 2fr choc, grn & bl .25 .25
145 A31 3fr dk grn, dk car & choc .25 .25
146 A31 5fr slate, emer & choc .30 .25
147 A31 10fr dl bl, dk grn & vio .55 .25
148 A31 15fr vio, car & choc .75 .30
Nos. 143-148 (6) 2.35 1.55

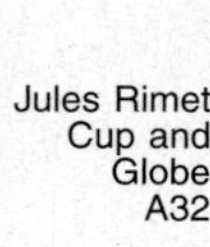

Jules Rimet Cup and Globe
A32

1966, July 15 Photo. *Perf. 12½x12*

149 A32 30fr brt red, gold, blk & bl 1.25 .45

8th World Soccer Cup Championship, Wembley, England, July 11-30.

Savorgnan de Brazza School
A33

1966, Sept. 15 Photo. *Perf. 12½x12*

150 A33 30fr dk pur, grn, yel & blk 1.00 .25

Pointe-Noire Railroad Station — A34

1966, Oct. 15 Engr. *Perf. 13*

151 A34 60fr grn, red & brn 1.50 .60

Student with Microscope — A35

1966, Nov. 28 Engr. *Perf. 13*

152 A35 90fr brn, grn & ind 1.50 .70

20th anniv. of UNESCO.

Balumbu Mask — A36

Masks: 10fr, Kuyu. 15fr, Bakwélé. 20fr, Batéké.

1966, Dec. 12 Engr. *Perf. 13*

153 A36 5fr car rose & dk brn .45 .25
154 A36 10fr Prus bl & brn .50 .25
155 A36 15fr sep, dl org & dk bl .60 .25
156 A36 20fr dp bl & multi .80 .25
Nos. 153-156 (4) 2.35 1.00

Order of the Revolution and Map — A37

Learning the Alphabet
A38

Design: 45fr, Harvesting and loading sugar cane, and sugar mill.

Perf. 12x12½, 12½x12

1967, Mar. 15 Photo.

157 A37 20fr org & multi .80 .30
158 A38 25fr blk, ocher & dk car .80 .35
159 A38 45fr blk, yel grn & lt bl 1.50 .30
Nos. 157-159 (3) 3.10 .95

Issued to honor the members of the Order of the Revolution (20fr); to publicize the literacy campaign (25fr); to publicize, sugar production (45fr).

Mahatma Gandhi — A39

1967, Apr. 21 Engr. *Perf. 13*

160 A39 90fr blue & black 2.25 .75

Issued in memory of Mohandas K. Gandhi (1869-1948), Hindu nationalist leader.

"Elegant Lady" — A40

Dolls: 10fr, Fruit vendor 25fr, Woman pounding saka-saka. 30fr, Mother and child.

1967, June Photo. *Perf. 13x12½*

161 A40 5fr gold & multi .25 .25
162 A40 10fr yel grn & multi .45 .25
163 A40 25fr lt ultra & multi .50 .25
164 A40 30fr multicolored .60 .25
Nos. 161-164 (4) 1.80 1.00

ITY Emblem, Village and Waterfall
A41

1967, July 5 Engr. *Perf. 13*

165 A41 60fr rose cl, org & ol grn 1.10 .40

Issued for International Tourist Year, 1967.

Europafrica Issue

Symbols of Cooperation — A42

1967, July 20 Photo. *Perf. 12x12½*

166 A42 50fr multicolored 1.00 .30

Arms of Brazzaville — A43

1967, Aug. 15 Litho. *Perf. 12½x13*

167 A43 30fr yel & multi .90 .35

Fourth anniversary of the revolution.

UN Emblem, Dove and People — A44

1967, Oct. 24 Photo. *Perf. 13x12½*
168 A44 90fr bl, dk brn, red brn & yel 1.75 .60

Issued for United Nations Day, Oct. 24.

Boy and UNICEF Emblem — A45

1967, Dec. 11 Engr. *Perf. 13*
169 A45 90fr mar, blk & ultra 1.75 .60

21st anniv. of UNICEF.

Albert Luthuli, Dove and Globe A46

1968, Jan. 29 Engr. *Perf. 13*
170 A46 30fr brt grn & ol bis 1.00 .35

Albert Luthuli (1899-1967) of South Africa, winner of 1960 Nobel Peace Prize.

Arms of Pointe Noire — A47

1968, Feb. 20 Litho. *Perf. 12½x13*
171 A47 10fr brt pink & multi .90 .30

Motherhood — A48

1968, May 25 Engr. *Perf. 13*
172 A48 15fr dk car rose, sky bl & blk .90 .30

Issued for Mother's Day.

Mayombe Viaduct — A49

1968, June 24
173 A49 45fr mar, slate grn & bl 2.00 .45

A50

5fr, Daimler, 1889. 20fr, Berliet, 1897. 60fr, Peugeot, 1898. 80fr, Renault, 1900. 85fr, Fiat, 1902.

1968, July 29 Photo. *Perf. 13x12½*
174 A50 5fr multi .45 .25
175 A50 20fr multi .90 .30
176 A50 60fr multi 1.75 .40
177 A50 80fr multi 2.75 .70
178 A50 85fr multi 3.25 .90
Nos. 174-178,C67-C68 (7) 17.85 6.05

Tanker, Refinery and Map of Area Served — A50a

1968, July 30 *Perf. 12½*
179 A50a 30fr multicolored .90 .30

Issued to commemorate the opening of the Port Gentil (Gabon) Refinery, June 12, 1968.

WHO Emblem and Tree of Life — A51

1968, Nov. 28 Engr. *Perf. 13*
180 A51 25fr dk grn, red & dp lil .90 .30

20th anniv. of WHO.

Development Bank Issue
Common Design Type

1969, Sept. 10 Engr. *Perf. 13*
181 CD130 25fr car rose, grn & ocher .50 .25
182 CD130 30fr bl, grn & ocher .50 .25

Bicycle A52

Bicycles & Motorcycles: 75fr, Hirondelle. 80fr, Folding bicycle. 85fr, Peugeot. 100fr, Excelsior Manxman. 150fr, Norton. 200fr, Brough Superior "Old Bill." 300fr, Matchless and N.L.G.-J.A.P.S.

1969, Oct. 6 Engr. *Perf. 13*
183 A52 50fr multicolored 1.25 .30
184 A52 75fr multicolored 1.50 .30
185 A52 80fr multicolored 1.75 .40
186 A52 85fr multicolored 2.00 .50
187 A52 100fr multicolored 3.00 .85
188 A52 150fr multicolored 4.00 1.00
189 A52 200fr multicolored 5.25 1.75
190 A52 300fr multicolored 9.50 2.75
Nos. 183-190 (8) 28.25 7.85

Mayombe Train and Tourist Year Emblem — A53

40fr, Train and Mbamba Tunnel, vert.

Perf. 13x12½, 12½x13
1969, Oct. 20 Photo.
191 A53 40fr multicolored 2.40 .40
192 A53 60fr multicolored 4.00 .65

Issued for African Tourist Year.

Loutete Cement Works A54

Loutete Cement Works: 15fr, Mixing tower, vert. 25fr, Cable transport, vert. 30fr, General view of plant.

1969, Dec. 10 Engr. *Perf. 13*
193 A54 10fr dk gray, rose cl & dk ol .25 .25
194 A54 15fr Prus bl, red brn & pur .50 .25
195 A54 25fr mar, brn & Prus bl .60 .25
196 A54 30fr vio brn, ultra & blk .70 .25
a. Min. sheet of 4, #193-196 2.75 2.75
Nos. 193-196 (4) 2.05 1.00

ASECNA Issue
Common Design Type

1969, Dec. 12
197 CD132 100fr dull brown 2.00 .40

Pineapple Harvest and ILO Emblem A55

30fr, Worker at lathe and ILO emblem.

1969, Dec. 20 Engr. *Perf. 13*
198 A55 25fr bl, olive & brn .60 .25
199 A55 30fr rose red, choc & slate .85 .35

50th anniv. of the ILO.

SOTEXCO Textile Plant, Kinsoundi A56

20fr, Women in spinnery. 25fr, Hand-printing textiles. 30fr, Checking woven cloth.

1970, Jan. 20
200 A56 15fr grn, blk & lil .45 .25
201 A56 20fr plum, car & sl grn .45 .25
202 A56 25fr bl, slate & brn .60 .25
203 A56 30fr gray, car rose & brn .60 .25
Nos. 200-203 (4) 2.10 1.00

Hotel Cosmos, Brazzaville A57

1970, Jan. 30
204 A57 90fr slate grn, bl & red brn 1.40 .50

The status of the three sets for Kennedy, etc., Summer Olympics, and Baroque paintings is not certain.

Linzolo Church — A58

Diosso Gorge A59

Design: 90fr, Foulakari waterfall.

1970 Engr. *Perf. 13*
205 A58 25fr multicolored .80 .25
206 A59 70fr multicolored 1.50 .30
207 A59 90fr multicolored 2.25 .40
Nos. 205-207 (3) 4.55 .95

Issue dates: 25fr, Feb. 10; others, Feb. 25.

Volvaria Esculenta — A60

Mushrooms: 10fr, Termitomyces entolomoides. 15fr, Termitomyces microcarpus. 25fr, Termitomyces aurantiacus. 30fr, Termitomyces mammiformis. 50fr, Tremella fuciformis.

1970, Mar. 31 Photo. *Perf. 13*
208 A60 5fr multicolored 3.00 .50
209 A60 10fr multicolored 4.50 .75
210 A60 15fr multicolored 6.50 1.00
211 A60 25fr multicolored 12.50 2.00
212 A60 30fr multicolored 17.50 3.00
213 A60 50fr multicolored 35.00 5.00
Nos. 208-213 (6) 79.00 12.25

Laying Coaxial Cable A61

Design: 30fr, Full view of rail car; 3 cable layers on railway roadbed.

1970, Apr. 30 Engr. *Perf. 13*
214 A61 25fr dk brn & multi 1.00 .30
215 A61 30fr brn & multi 1.25 .60

Issued to publicize the laying of the coaxial cable linking Brazzaville and Pointe Noire.
For surcharges see Nos. 263-264.

UPU Headquarters Issue
Common Design Type

1970, May 20
216 CD133 30fr dk pur, gray & mag 1.00 .25

Mother Feeding Child — A62

Design: 90fr, Mother nursing infant.

1970, May 30 Photo.
217 A62 85fr vio bl & multi 1.00 .30
218 A62 90fr lil & multi 1.10 .40

Issued for Mother's Day.

Dag Hammarskjold, UN Emblem — A63

UN Emblem and: No. 220, Trygve Lie, horiz. No. 221, U Thant, horiz.

1970, June 20 Engr. *Perf. 13*
219 A63 100fr scar, dk red & dk pur 1.40 .80
220 A63 100fr dk red, ultra & ind 1.40 .80

221 A63 100fr grn, emer & dk red 1.40 .80
a. Souv. sheet of 3, #219-221 5.50 5.50
Nos. 219-221 (3) 4.20 2.40

25th anniv. of the UN and to honor its Secretaries General.

Brillantaisia Vogeliana A64

Sternotomis Variabilis — A65

Plants and Beetles: 2fr, Plectranthus decurrens. 3fr, Myrianthemum mirabile. 5fr, Conarus griffonianus. 15fr, Chelorrhina polyphemus. 20fr, Metopodontus savagei.

Perf. 12½x12, 12x12½

1970, June 30 **Photo.**
222 A64 1fr dk grn & multi .70 .25
223 A64 2fr multicolored .70 .25
224 A64 3fr indigo & multi .70 .25
225 A64 5fr lemon & multi 1.40 .25
226 A65 10fr lilac & multi 2.25 .40
227 A65 15fr orange & multi 3.25 .40
228 A65 20fr multicolored 3.25 .60
Nos. 222-228 (7) 12.25 2.40

For surcharge see No. 288.

Stegosaurus — A66

Prehistoric Fauna: 20fr, Dinotherium, vert. 60fr, Brachiosaurus, vert. 80fr, Arsinoitherium.

1970, July 20
229 A66 15fr dl grn, ocher & red brn 1.75 .30
230 A66 20fr lt bl & multi 3.50 .65
231 A66 60fr lt bl & multi 6.25 .95
232 A66 80fr lt bl & multi 8.00 1.75
Nos. 229-232 (4) 19.50 3.65

Mikado 141, 1932 A67

Locomotives: 60fr, Steam locomotive 130+032, 1947. 75fr, Alsthom BB 1100, 1962. 85fr, Diesel BB BB 302, 1969.

1970, Aug. 20 **Engr.** ***Perf. 13***
233 A67 40fr mag, bl grn & blk 2.75 .80
234 A67 60fr blk, bl & grn 3.25 .90
235 A67 75fr red, bl & blk 4.50 1.25
236 A67 85fr car, sl grn & ocher 7.50 1.75
Nos. 233-236 (4) 18.00 4.70

Cogniauxia Padolaena — A68

Tropical Flowers: 2fr, Celosia cristata. 5fr, Plumeria acutifolia. 10fr, Bauhinia variegata. 15fr, Poinsettia. 20fr, Thunbergia grandiflora.

1971, Feb. 10 **Photo.** ***Perf. 12x12½***
237 A68 1fr lil & multi .25 .25
238 A68 2fr yel & multi .25 .25
239 A68 5fr ultra & multi .25 .25
240 A68 10fr yel & multi 1.10 .25
241 A68 15fr multicolored 1.60 .30
242 A68 20fr dk red & multi 2.75 .40
Nos. 237-242 (6) 6.20 1.70

Green Night Adder — A69

Reptiles: 10fr, African Egg-eating snake, horiz. 15fr, Flap-necked chameleon. 20fr, Nile crocodile, horiz. 25fr, Rock python, horiz. 30fr, Gaboon viper. 40fr, Brown house snake, horiz. 45fr, Jameson's mamba.

Perf. 12x12½, 12½x12

1971, June 26 **Photo.**
243 A69 5fr multicolored .40 .25
244 A69 10fr multicolored .40 .25
245 A69 15fr multicolored 1.40 .25
246 A69 20fr red & multi 2.25 .25
247 A69 25fr grn & multi 3.00 .35
248 A69 30fr multicolored 3.75 .75
249 A69 40fr bis & multi 4.25 .95
250 A69 45fr multicolored 5.75 1.00
Nos. 243-250 (8) 21.20 4.05

Pseudimbrasia Deyrollei — A70

Caterpillars: 15fr, Bunaea alcinoe, vert. 20fr, Epiphora vacuna ploetzi. 25fr, Imbrasia eblis. 30fr, Imbrasia dione, vert. 40fr, Holocera angulata.

1971, July 3 ***Perf. 13***
251 A70 10fr ver, blk & grn 1.00 .25
252 A70 15fr multicolored 1.50 .30
253 A70 20fr yel grn, blk & ocher 2.25 .40
254 A70 25fr multicolored 3.50 .60
255 A70 30fr red, blk & yel 5.00 .90
256 A70 40fr bl, blk & org 6.75 1.25
Nos. 251-256 (6) 20.00 3.70

Boy Scout — A70a

Scouts, Lord Baden-Powell — A70b

Designs: c, Scout facing left. d, Scout facing forward. e, Lord Baden-Powell.

Embossed on Metallic Foil

1971, July 14 ***Die Cut Perf. 10½***
256A A70a 90fr Block of 4, #b.-e, silver 12.00 12.00
256F A70b 1000fr gold 30.00 30.00

No. 256F is airmail.

Cymothoe Sangaris A71

Butterflies and Moths: 40fr, Papilio dardanus, vert. 75fr, Iolaus timon. 90fr, Papilio phorcas, vert. 100fr, Euchloron megaera.

1971, Oct. 15 ***Perf. 12½x12, 12x12½***
257 A71 30fr yel & multi 1.75 .40
258 A71 40fr grn & multi 3.25 .65
259 A71 75fr multicolored 5.25 1.25
260 A71 90fr multicolored 7.00 1.90
261 A71 100fr ultra & multi 9.50 2.50
Nos. 257-261 (5) 26.75 6.70

Black and White Men Working Together — A72

1971, Oct. 30 ***Perf. 13x12½***
262 A72 50fr org & multi 1.75 .50

Intl. Year Against Racial Discrimination.

Nos. 214-215 Surcharged

1971, Nov. 18 **Engr.** ***Perf. 13***
263 A61 30fr on 25fr multicolored .65 .30
264 A61 40fr on 30fr multicolored .95 .35

Inauguration of cable service between Brazzaville and Pointe Noire. Words of surcharge arranged differently on No. 264.

Map of Congo — A73

1971, Dec. 31 **Photo.** ***Perf. 12½x13***
265 A73 30fr bl & multi .35 .25
266 A73 40fr yel grn & multi .45 .25
267 A73 100fr gray & multi 1.10 .40
Nos. 265-267 (3) 1.90 .90

"Labor, Democracy, Peace."

Lion — A74

2fr, African elephants. 3fr, Leopard. 4fr, Hippopotamus. 5fr, Gorilla, vert. 20fr, Potto. 30fr, De Brazza's monkey. 40fr, Pygmy chimpanzee, vert.

1972, Jan. 31 **Engr.** ***Perf. 13***
268 A74 1fr grn & multi .35 .25
269 A74 2fr dk red & multi .50 .25
270 A74 3fr red brn & multi .80 .25
271 A74 4fr vio & multi 1.00 .25
272 A74 5fr brn & multi 1.10 .25
273 A74 20fr org & multi 2.75 .35
274 A74 30fr ocher & multi 3.50 .45
275 A74 40fr Prus bl & multi 5.25 .75
Nos. 268-275 (8) 15.25 2.80

WHO, 25th Anniv. — A75

Perf. 12½x13, 13x12½

1973, June 30 **Typo.**
276 A75 40fr WHO Emblem .65 .25
277 A75 50fr WHO emblem, horiz. .95 .25

Kronenbourg Brewery — A76

Brewery Trademark and: 40fr, Laboratory. 75fr, Vats and controls. 85fr, Automatic control room. 100fr, Pressure room. 250fr, Bottling plant.

1973, July 15 **Engr.** ***Perf. 13***
278 A76 30fr red & multi .50 .25
279 A76 40fr red & multi .60 .25
280 A76 75fr red & multi 1.20 .30
281 A76 85fr red & multi 1.75 .40
282 A76 100fr red & multi 1.90 .55
283 A76 250fr red & multi 3.75 1.00
Nos. 278-283 (6) 9.70 2.75

Kronenbourg Brewery, Brazzaville.

Golwe Locomotive, 1935 — A77

Locomotives: 40fr, Diesel, 1935. 75fr, Diesel Whithcomb, 1946. 85fr, Diesel CC200.

1973, Aug. 1 **Engr.** ***Perf. 13***
284 A77 30fr indigo & multi 2.00 .50
285 A77 40fr vio bl & multi 3.00 .85
286 A77 75fr multicolored 4.25 1.50
287 A77 85fr multicolored 5.50 2.75
Nos. 284-287 (4) 14.75 5.60

No. 225 Srchd. and Ovptd. in Ultramarine

1973, Aug. 16 **Photo.** ***Perf. 12½x12***
288 A64 100fr on 5fr multicolored 1.75 .60

African solidarity in drought emergency.

African Postal Union Issue
Common Design Type

1973, Sept. 12 **Engr.** ***Perf. 13***
289 CD137 100fr bl grn, vio & brn 1.60 .50

Bees, Beehive, Honeycomb
A78

1973, Dec. 10 Engr. *Perf. 13*
290 A78 30fr sl grn, dk red & bl 1.10 .25
291 A78 40fr sl bl, sl grn & lt grn 1.50 .25

"Work and economy."

Family, UN and FAO Emblems
A79

40fr, Grain, emblems. 100fr, Grain, emblems, vert.

1973, Dec. 10
292 A79 30fr dk car & dk brn .50 .25
293 A79 40fr dk grn, yel & ind .60 .25
294 A79 100fr grn, brn & org 1.40 .40
Nos. 292-294 (3) 2.50 .90

World Food Program, 10th anniversary.

Amilcar Cabral, Cattle and Child — A80

1974, July 15 Engr. *Perf. 13*
295 A80 100fr multicolored 1.60 .60

First death anniversary of Amilcar Cabral (1924-1973), leader of anti-Portuguese guerrilla activity in Portuguese Guinea.

Félix Eboué, Cross of Lorraine
A81

1974, Aug. 31 Litho. *Perf. 13*
296 A81 30fr bl & multi .80 .30
297 A81 40fr brt pink & multi 1.60 .60

Félix A. Eboué (1884-1944), Governor of Chad, first colonial governor to join Free French in WWII, 30th death anniversary.

Pineapples
A82

1974, Nov. 12
298 A82 30fr shown .60 .30
299 A82 30fr Bananas .70 .30
300 A82 30fr Safous .70 .30
301 A82 40fr Avocados 1.25 .30
302 A82 40fr Mangos 1.25 .30
303 A82 40fr Papaya 1.25 .30
304 A82 40fr Orange 1.25 .30
Nos. 298-304 (7) 7.00 2.10

Charles de Gaulle and Conference Building — A83

1974, Nov. 25 Engr. *Perf. 13*
305 A83 100fr multicolored 5.00 1.90

Brazzaville Conference, 25th anniversary.

George Stephenson and Various Locomotives — A84

1974, Dec. 15
306 A84 75fr slate grn & ol 4.00 1.00

George Stephenson (1781-1848), English inventor and railroad founder.

UDEAC Issue

Presidents and Flags of Cameroun, CAR, Congo, Gabon and Meeting Center — A84a

1974, Dec. 8 Photo. *Perf. 13*
307 A84a 40fr gold & multi .65 .25

See note after Cameroun No. 595.
See No. C195.

Irish Setter
A85

1974, Dec. 15 Photo. *Perf. 13x13½*
308 A85 30fr shown 1.25 .30
309 A85 40fr Borzoi 1.50 .30
310 A85 75fr Pointer 3.25 .75
311 A85 100fr Great Dane 4.50 .80
Nos. 308-311 (4) 10.50 2.15

1974, Dec. 15

Designs: Cats.

312 A85 30fr Havana chestnut 1.25 .30
313 A85 40fr Red Persian 1.50 .30
314 A85 75fr Blue British 3.50 .75
315 A85 100fr African serval 5.00 .80
Nos. 312-315 (4) 11.25 2.15

Labor Party Flags and People
A86

40fr, Hands holding flowers and tools.

1974, Dec. 31 Engr. *Perf. 13x12½*
316 A86 30fr red & multi .65 .25
317 A86 40fr red & multi .95 .25

5th anniversary of Congolese Labor Party and of introduction of red flag.

Symbols of Development — A87

U Thant and UN Headquarters — A88

Paul G. Hoffman and UN Emblem
A89

Perf. 13x12½, 12½x13
1975, Feb. 28 Litho.
318 A87 40fr multicolored .90 .35
319 A88 50fr light blue & multi .90 .35
320 A89 50fr yellow & multi .90 .35
Nos. 318-320 (3) 2.70 1.05

National economic development.

Map of China and Mao Tse-tung — A90

1975, Mar. 9 Engr. *Perf. 13*
321 A90 75fr multicolored 5.50 1.50

25th anniv. of the PRC.

Woman Breaking Bonds, Women's Activities, Map of Congo
A91

1975, June 20 Litho. *Perf. 12½*
322 A91 40fr gold & multi .80 .35

Revolutionary Union of Congolese Women, URFC, 10th anniversary.

CARA Soccer Team — A92

Design: 40fr, Team captain and manager receiving trophy, vert.

1975, July 15 Litho. *Perf. 12½*
323 A92 30fr multicolored .65 .25
324 A92 40fr multicolored .95 .25

CARA team, winners of African Soccer Cup 1974.

Citroen, 1935 — A93

Designs: Early autombiles.

1975, July 17 *Perf. 12*
325 A93 30fr shown 1.10 .40
326 A93 40fr Alfa Romeo, 1911 1.35 .40
327 A93 50fr Rolls Royce, 1926 1.75 .55
328 A93 75fr Duryea, 1893 3.50 .70
Nos. 325-328 (4) 7.70 2.05

Tipoye Transport — A94

1975, Aug. 5
329 A94 30fr shown .90 .40
330 A94 40fr Dugout canoe 1.00 .65

Traditional means of transportation.

Raising Red Flag — A95

1975, Aug. 15
331 A95 30fr shown .80 .25
332 A95 40fr National Conference .80 .25

2nd anniv. of installation of popular power (30fr) and 3rd anniv. of Natl. Conf. (40fr).

Line Fishing — A96

Traditional Fishing: 30fr, Trap fishing, horiz. 60fr, Spear fishing. 90fr, Net fishing, horiz.

1975, Aug. 31 Litho. *Perf. 12*

333 A96 30fr multicolored .80 .25
334 A96 40fr multicolored .80 .30
335 A96 60fr multicolored 1.25 .50
336 A96 90fr multicolored 2.50 1.00
Nos. 333-336 (4) 5.35 2.05

Woman Pounding "Foufou" — A97

Household Tasks: No. 338, Woman chopping wood. 40fr, Woman preparing manioc, horiz.

1975, Sept. 5

337 A97 30fr multicolored .60 .25
338 A97 30fr multicolored .60 .25
339 A97 40fr multicolored .90 .25
Nos. 337-339 (3) 2.10 .75

Musical Instruments A98

1975, Sept. 20 *Perf. 12½*

340 A98 30fr Esanga .75 .25
341 A98 40fr Kalakwa 1.25 .25
342 A98 60fr Likembe 1.50 .30
343 A98 75fr Ngongui 2.00 .40
Nos. 340-343 (4) 5.50 1.20

Dzeke (Congolese) Shell Money — A99

Ancient Money: No. 346, like No. 344. Nos. 345, 347, Okengo, Congolese, iron bar. 40fr, Gallic coin, c. 60 B.C. 50fr, Roman denarius, 37 B.C. 60fr, Danubian coin, 2nd cent. B.C. 85fr, Greek stater, 4th cent. B.C.

1975-76 Engr. *Perf. 13*

344 A99 30fr red & multi .60 .25
345 A99 30fr vio & multi .60 .25
346 A99 35fr ol & multi .90 .25
347 A99 35fr dk car rose & multi .90 .25
348 A99 40fr Prus bl & brn .90 .25
349 A99 50fr Prus bl & ol 1.00 .30
350 A99 60fr dk grn & brn 1.25 .35
351 A99 85fr mag & sl grn 2.10 .45
Nos. 344-351 (8) 8.25 2.35

Nos. 346-347 inscribed "1976" and issued Mar. 1976; others issued Oct. 5, 1975.

Moschops — A100

Pre-historic Animals: 70fr, Tyrannosaurus. 95fr, Cryptocleidus. 100fr, Stegosaurus.

1975, Oct. 15 Litho. *Perf. 13*

352 A100 55fr multicolored 2.25 .30
353 A100 75fr multicolored 3.25 .35
354 A100 95fr multicolored 5.75 .75
355 A100 100fr multicolored 8.00 1.25
Nos. 352-355 (4) 19.25 2.65

Albert Schweitzer (1875-1965), Medical Missionary — A101

1975, Oct. 15 Engr.

356 A101 75fr ol, brn & red 1.50 .40

Alexander Fleming A102

Designs: No. 358, André Marie Ampère. No. 359, Clement Ader.

1975, Nov. 15 Engr. *Perf. 13*

357 A102 60fr brn, grn & blk 1.60 .45
358 A102 95fr blk, red & grn 2.50 .65
359 A102 95fr red, blue & indigo 2.50 .65
Nos. 357-359 (3) 6.60 1.75

Fleming (1881-1955), developer of penicillin; Ampère (1775-1836), physicist; Ader (1841-1925), aviation pioneer.

UN Emblem "ONU" and "30" — A103

1975, Dec. 20 Engr. *Perf. 13*

360 A103 95fr car, ultra & grn 1.60 .50

United Nations, 30th anniversary.

Women's Broken Chain — A104

Design: 60fr, Equality between man and woman, globe, IWY emblem.

1975, Dec. 20 Litho. *Perf. 12½*

361 A104 35fr mag, ocher & gray .90 .25
362 A104 60fr ultra, brn & blk 1.75 .50

International Women's Year, 1975.

Pres. Marien Ngouabi, Flag and Workers — A105

Echo of the P.C.T. A106

1975, Dec. 31 *Perf. 12½x12, 13x12½*

363 A105 30fr multicolored .55 .25
364 A106 35fr multicolored .65 .25

6th anniversary of the Congolese Labor Party (P.C.T.). See No. C215.

A.G. Bell and 1876 Telephone A107

1976, Apr. 25 Litho. *Perf. 12½x13*

365 A107 35fr yel, brn & org brn .65 .25

Cent. of 1st telephone call by Alexander Graham Bell, Mar. 10, 1876. See No. C229.

Women Selling Fruit and Vegetables A108

1976, Sept. 19 Litho. *Perf. 12½x13*

366 A108 35fr shown .50 .25
367 A108 60fr Market scene 1.20 .30

Congolese Coiffure — A109

Designs: Various women's hair styles.

1976, Oct. 10 Litho. *Perf. 13*

368 A109 35fr multicolored .55 .25
369 A109 60fr multicolored .90 .25
370 A109 95fr multicolored 1.40 .35
371 A109 100fr multicolored 1.60 .40
Nos. 368-371 (4) 4.45 1.25

Pole Vault, Map of Central Africa A110

95fr, Long jump and map of Central Africa.

1976, Oct. 25 *Perf. 12½*

372 A110 60fr yel & multi .70 .25
373 A110 95fr yel & multi 1.25 .40
Nos. 372-373,C230-C231 (4) 6.45 2.50

Gold medalists, 1st Central African Games, Yaoundé, July 27-30, 1975.

Antelope A111

1976, Oct. 27 Litho. *Perf. 12½*
Size: 36x36mm

374 A111 5fr shown .55 .25
375 A111 10fr Buffalos .65 .25
376 A111 15fr Hippopotamus 1.00 .30
377 A111 20fr Wart hog 2.00 .35
378 A111 25fr Elephants 2.25 .40
Nos. 374-378 (5) 6.45 1.55

1976, Dec. 8 Size: 26x36mm

Birds — 5fr, Saddle-bill storks. 10fr, Malachite kingfisher. 20fr, Crowned cranes.

379 A111 5fr multicolored 1.25 .25

Size: 36x36mm

380 A111 10fr multicolored 1.50 .25
381 A111 20fr multicolored 2.40 .60
Nos. 379-381 (3) 5.15 1.10

Bicycling, Map of Participants A112

1976, Dec. 21 Photo. *Perf. 12½x13*

382 A112 35fr shown .35 .25
383 A112 60fr Fieldball .60 .25
384 A112 80fr Running 1.00 .35
385 A112 95fr Soccer 1.25 .40
Nos. 382-385 (4) 3.20 1.25

First Central African Games, Libreville, Gabon, June-July 1976.

Heliotrope A113

Flowers: 5fr, Water lilies. 15fr, Bird-of-paradise flower.

1976, Dec. 23 Photo. *Perf. 12½x13*

386 A113 5fr multicolored .30 .25
387 A113 10fr multicolored .40 .25
388 A113 15fr multicolored .70 .25
Nos. 386-388 (3) 1.40 .75

Torch and Olive Branches A114

1976, Dec. 25 Litho. *Perf. 12½x13*

389 A114 35fr multicolored .90 .25

National Pioneer Movement.

The Spirit of '76 — A115

125fr, Pulling down George III statue. 150fr, Battle of Princeton. 175fr, Generals of Revolutionary War. 200fr, Burgoyne's surrender at Saratoga. 500fr, Battle of Lexington.

1976, Dec. 29 Litho. *Perf. 14*

390	A115	100fr multicolored	1.00	.25
391	A115	125fr multicolored	1.10	.35
392	A115	150fr multicolored	1.60	.40
393	A115	175fr multicolored	2.00	.50
394	A115	200fr multicolored	2.25	.60
		Nos. 390-394 (5)	7.95	2.10

Souvenir Sheet

395	A115	500fr multicolored	5.75	1.50

American Bicentennial.

Dugout Canoe Race A116

Design: 60fr, 2-man dugout canoes.

1977, Mar. 27 Litho. *Perf. 13x13½*

396	A116	35fr multicolored	.60	.25
397	A116	60fr multicolored	1.00	.35

Dugout canoe races on Congo River.

Lilan Goua A117

Fresh-water Fish: 15fr, Liko ko. 25fr, Liyan ga. 35fr, Mbessi. 60fr, Mongandza.

1977, June 15 Litho. *Perf. 12½*

398	A117	10fr multicolored	.75	.25
399	A117	15fr multicolored	.90	.25
400	A117	25fr multicolored	1.25	.25
401	A117	35fr multicolored	2.00	.30
402	A117	60fr multicolored	3.50	.45
		Nos. 398-402 (5)	8.40	1.50

Traditional Headdress — A118

1977, June 30 Litho. *Perf. 12½*

403	A118	35fr shown	.45	.30
404	A118	60fr Leopard cap	.90	.35

See Nos. C234-C235.

Bondjo Wrestling A119

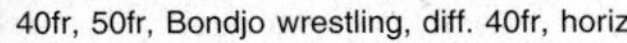

40fr, 50fr, Bondjo wrestling, diff. 40fr, horiz.

1977, July 15

405	A119	25fr multicolored	.50	.25
406	A119	40fr multicolored	.60	.25
407	A119	50fr multicolored	.70	.30
		Nos. 405-407 (3)	1.80	.80

"Schwaben" LZ 10, 1911 — A120

Zeppelins: 60fr, "Viktoria Luise." LZ 11, 1913. 100fr, LZ 120. 200fr, LZ 127. 300fr, "Graf Zeppelin II" LZ 130.

1977, Aug. 5 Litho. *Perf. 11*

408	A120	40fr multicolored	.50	.25
409	A120	60fr multicolored	.75	.25
410	A120	100fr multicolored	1.25	.30
411	A120	200fr multicolored	2.50	.60
412	A120	300fr multicolored	4.00	.95
		Nos. 408-412 (5)	9.00	2.35

History of the Zeppelin. Exist imperf. See No. C236.

Coat of Arms and Rising Sun A121

1977, Aug. 15

413	A121	40fr multicolored	.90	.25

14th anniversary of the revolution.

Victor Hugo and The Hunchback of Notre Dame — A122

Designs (Hugo and): 60fr, Les Miserables. 100fr, Les Travailleurs de la Mer (octopus).

1977, Aug. 20 Engr. *Perf. 13*

414	A122	35fr multicolored	.75	.30
415	A122	60fr multicolored	1.00	.30
416	A122	100fr multicolored	1.90	.45
		Nos. 414-416 (3)	3.65	1.05

Victor Hugo (1802-1885), French novelist.

Mao Tse-tung A123

Lithographed; Gold Embossed

1977, Sept. 9 *Perf. 12x12½*

417	A123	400fr red & gold	16.00	8.00

Chairman Mao Tse-tung (1893-1976), Chinese Communist leader, 1st death anniv.

Peter Paul Rubens A124

1977, Sept. 20 Gold Embossed

418	A124	600fr gold & lt bl	10.00	6.00

Peter Paul Rubens (1577-1640), painter.

Child Leading Blind Woman Across Street A125

1977, Oct. 22 Litho. *Perf. 12½x13*

419	A125	35fr multicolored	1.00	.25

World Health Day: To see is life.

Paul Kamba and Records A126

1977, Oct. 29

420	A126	100fr multicolored	1.60	.50

Paul Kamba (1912-1950), musician.

Trajan Vuia and Flying Machine — A127

Designs: 75fr, Louis Bleriot and plane. 100fr, Roland Garros and plane. 200fr, Charles Lindbergh and Spirit of St. Louis. 300fr, Tupolev Tu-144. 500fr, Lindbergh and Spirit of St. Louis over ship in Atlantic.

1977, Nov. 18 Litho. *Perf. 14*

421	A127	60fr multicolored	.60	.25
422	A127	75fr multicolored	.90	.25
423	A127	100fr multicolored	1.10	.30
424	A127	200fr multicolored	2.25	.50
425	A127	300fr multicolored	3.25	.70
		Nos. 421-425 (5)	8.10	2.00

Souvenir Sheet

426	A127	500fr multicolored	5.75	1.25

History of aviation.

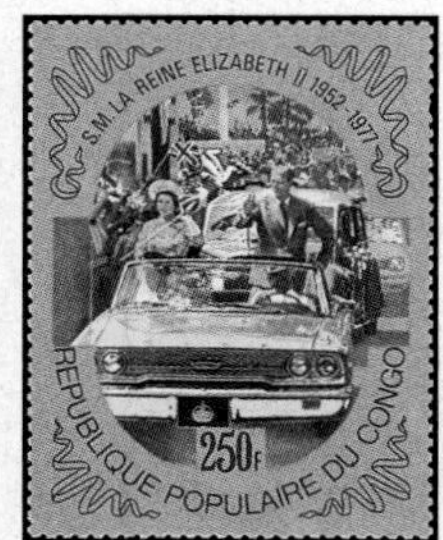

Elizabeth II and Prince Philip A128

Design: 300fr, Elizabeth II wearing Crown.

1977, Dec. 21

427	A128	250fr multicolored	2.25	.65
428	A128	300fr multicolored	2.75	.70

Reign of Queen Elizabeth II, 25th anniv. See No. C239. For overprints see Nos. 468-469, C244.

King Baudouin A129

Design: No. 430, Charles de Gaulle.

1977, Dec. 21

429	A129	200fr multicolored	2.25	.65
430	A129	200fr multicolored	2.25	.65

King Baudouin of Belgium and Charles de Gaulle, president of France.

Ambete Sculpture A130

Congolese art: 85fr, Babembe sculpture.

1978, Feb. 18 Engr. *Perf. 13*

431	A130	35fr lt brn & multi	.65	.25
432	A130	85fr lt grn & multi	1.50	.45

St. Simon, by Rubens A131

Rubens Paintings: 140fr, Duke of Lerma. 200fr, Madonna and Saints. 300fr, Rubens and his Wife Helena Fourment. 500fr, Farm at Laeken.

1978, Mar. 7 Litho. *Perf. 13½x14*

433	A131	60fr gold & multi	.60	.25
434	A131	140fr gold & multi	1.50	.30
435	A131	200fr gold & multi	2.25	.45
436	A131	300fr gold & multi	3.50	.65
		Nos. 433-436 (4)	7.85	1.65

Souvenir Sheet

437	A131	500fr gold & multi	6.00	1.40

Peter Paul Rubens, 400th birth anniv.

Pres. Ngouabi and Microphones — A132

60fr, Ngouabi at his desk, horiz. 100fr, Portrait.

Perf. 12½x13, 13x12½

1978, Mar. 18 **Litho.**

438 A132 35fr multicolored .45 .25
439 A132 60fr multicolored .50 .25
440 A132 100fr multicolored .90 .40
Nos. 438-440 (3) 1.85 .90

Pres. Marien Ngouabi, 1st death anniv.

Ferenc Puskas and Argentina '78 Emblem — A133

Players and Emblem: 75fr, Giacinto Facchetti. 100fr, Bobby Moore. 200fr, Raymond Kopa. 300fr, Pele. 500fr, Franz Beckenbauer.

1978, Apr. 4 ***Perf. 14x13½***

441 A133 60fr multicolored .60 .25
442 A133 75fr multicolored .70 .25
443 A133 100fr multicolored 1.10 .25
444 A133 200fr multicolored 2.25 .55
445 A133 300fr multicolored 3.25 .75
Nos. 441-445 (5) 7.90 2.05

Souvenir Sheet

446 A133 500fr multicolored 6.25 1.25

11th World Cup Soccer Championship, Argentina, June 1-25.
For overprints see Nos. 481-486.

Pearl S. Buck and Chinese Women — A134

Nobel Prize winners: 75fr, Fridtjof Nansen, refugees and Nansen passport. 100fr, Henri Bergson, book and flame. 200fr, Alexander Fleming and Petri dish. 300fr, Gerhart Hauptmann and book. 500fr, Henri Dunant and Red Cross Station.

1978, Apr. 29

447 A134 60fr multicolored .60 .25
448 A134 75fr multicolored .70 .25
449 A134 100fr multicolored 1.10 .30
450 A134 200fr multicolored 2.00 .50
451 A134 300fr multicolored 2.75 .60
Nos. 447-451 (5) 7.15 1.90

Souvenir Sheet

452 A134 500fr multicolored 6.00 1.40

African Buffalos A135

Endangered animals and Wildlife Fund Emblem: 35fr, Okapi, vert. 85fr, Rhinoceros. 150fr, Chimpanzee, vert. 200fr, Hippopotamus. 300fr, Buffon's kob, vert.

1978 ***Perf. 14½***

453 A135 35fr multicolored 1.25 .45
454 A135 60fr multicolored 1.75 .55
455 A135 85fr multicolored 4.25 .85
456 A135 150fr multicolored 6.00 1.25
457 A135 200fr multicolored 8.00 1.75
458 A135 300fr multicolored 15.00 2.50
Nos. 453-458 (6) 36.25 7.35

Issue dates: 35fr, Aug. 11; others, July 11.

Emblem, Young People, Gun and Fist — A136

1978, July 28 ***Perf. 12½***

459 A136 35fr multicolored .80 .30

11th World Youth Festival, Havana, 7/28-8/5.

Pyramids and Camels — A137

Seven Wonders of the Ancient World: 50fr, Hanging Gardens of Babylon. 60fr, Statue of Zeus, Olympia. 95fr, Colossus of Rhodes. 125fr, Mausoleum of Halicarnassus. 150fr, Temple of Artemis, Ephesus. 200fr, Lighthouse, Alexandria. 300fr, Map of Eastern Mediterranean showing locations. 50fr, 60fr, 95fr, 125fr, 200fr, vertical.

1978, Aug. 12 **Litho.** ***Perf. 14***

460 A137 35fr multicolored .50 .25
461 A137 50fr multicolored .60 .25
462 A137 60fr multicolored .75 .25
463 A137 95fr multicolored 1.00 .30
464 A137 125fr multicolored 1.25 .45
465 A137 150fr multicolored 1.75 .55
466 A137 200fr multicolored 2.25 .75
467 A137 300fr multicolored 3.25 1.00
Nos. 460-467 (8) 11.35 3.80

Nos. 427-428 Overprinted in Silver

No. 468

No. 469

1978, Sept. **Litho.** ***Perf. 14***

468 A128 250fr multicolored 2.25 .90
469 A128 300fr multicolored 2.75 1.25

25th anniversary of coronation of Queen Elizabeth II. See No. C244.

Kwame Nkrumah and Map of Africa — A138

1978, Sept. 23 **Litho.** ***Perf. 13x12½***

470 A138 60fr multicolored .80 .40

Nkrumah (1909-72), Pres. of Ghana.

Wild Boar Hunt — A139

Local hunting and fishing: 50fr, Fish smoking. 60fr, Hunter with spears and dog, vert.

1978 **Litho.** ***Perf. 12***

471 A139 35fr multicolored 2.00 .25
472 A139 50fr multicolored .80 .25
473 A139 60fr multicolored 2.75 .25
Nos. 471-473 (3) 5.55 .75

Issue dates: 35fr, 60fr, Oct. 5; 50fr, Oct. 10.

View of Kalchreut, by Dürer — A140

Paintings by Dürer: 150fr, Elspeth Tucher, vert. 250fr, "The Great Piece of Turf," vert. 350fr, Self-portrait, vert.

1978, Nov. 23 **Litho.** ***Perf. 14***

474 A140 65fr multicolored .60 .25
475 A140 150fr multicolored 1.40 .35
476 A140 250fr multicolored 2.25 .65
477 A140 350fr multicolored 3.50 .90
Nos. 474-477 (4) 7.75 2.15

Albrecht Dürer (1471-1528), German painter.

Basketmaker A141

Productive Labor: 90fr, Woodcarver. 140fr, Women hoeing field.

1978, Nov. 18 **Litho.** ***Perf. 12½***

Size: 25x36mm

478 A141 85fr multicolored .90 .40
479 A141 90fr multicolored 1.00 .40

Size: 27x48mm

Perf. 12

480 A141 140fr multicolored 1.50 .65
Nos. 478-480 (3) 3.40 1.45

Nos. 441-446 Overprinted in Silver

a

b

c

d

e

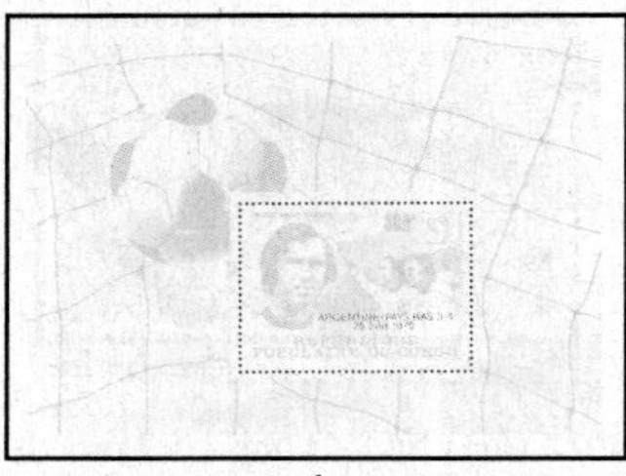

f

1978, Nov. ***Perf. 14x13½***

481 A133 (a) 60fr multicolored .65 .25
482 A133 (b) 75fr multicolored .75 .35
483 A133 (c) 100fr multicolored 1.05 .45
484 A133 (d) 200fr multicolored 2.10 .65
485 A133 (e) 300fr multicolored 3.00 1.00
Nos. 481-485 (5) 7.55 2.70

Souvenir Sheet

486 A133 (f) 500fr multicolored 6.00 2.40

Winners, World Soccer Cup Championships 1962-1978.

Heart and Charts A142

1978, Dec. 16 Engr. *Perf. 13*

487 A142 100fr multicolored 1.60 .50

Fight against hypertension.

Party Emblem and Road — A143

1978, Dec. 31 Litho. *Perf. 12½x12*

488 A143 60fr multicolored .75 .25

Congolese Labor Party, 9th anniversary.

Capt. Cook, Polynesians and House — A144

Capt. James Cook (1728-1779): 150fr, Island scene. 250fr, Polynesian longboats. 350fr, Capt. Cook's ships off Hawaii.

1979, Jan. 16 *Perf. 14½*

489 A144 65fr multicolored .70 .25
490 A144 150fr multicolored 1.75 .35
491 A144 250fr multicolored 2.75 .60
492 A144 350fr multicolored 3.50 1.00
Nos. 489-492 (4) 8.70 2.20

Pres. Marien Ngouabi — A145

1979, Mar. 18 Litho. *Perf. 12*

493 A145 35fr multicolored .35 .25
494 A145 60fr multicolored .50 .25

Assassination of President Ngouabi, 2nd anniv.

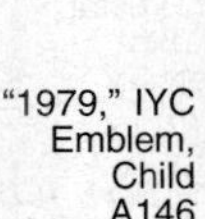

"1979," IYC Emblem, Child A146

A146a

1979, Apr. 30 Litho. *Perf. 12½x13*

495 A146 45fr multicolored .45 .25
496 A146 75fr multicolored .90 .35

Souvenir Sheet

Perf. 14½

496A A146a 250fr multicolored 2.75 1.00

International Year of the Child. Issued: 45fr, 75fr, Apr. 30; 250fr, Sept. 5.

Pottery Vases and Solanum — A147

Design: 150fr, Mail runner, Concorde, train, UPU emblem, envelope.

1979, June 8 Litho. *Perf. 13*

497 A147 60fr multicolored 1.75 .60

Engr.

498 A147 150fr multicolored 3.50 1.25

Philexafrique II, Libreville, Gabon, June 8-17. Nos. 497, 498 each printed in sheets of 10 with 5 labels showing exhibition emblem.

Rowland Hill, Diesel Locomotive, Germany No. 78 — A148

Designs (Rowland Hill and): 100fr, Old steam locomotive and France No. B10. 200fr, Diesel locomotive and US No. 245. 300fr, Steam locomotive and England-Australia First Aerialpost vignette, 1919. 500fr, Electric train, Concorde and Middle Congo No. 75.

1979, June 30 *Perf. 14*

499 A148 65fr multicolored .60 .25
500 A148 100fr multicolored 1.00 .25
501 A148 200fr multicolored 2.25 .50
502 A148 300fr multicolored 3.00 .75
Nos. 499-502 (4) 6.85 1.75

Souvenir Sheet

503 A148 500fr multicolored 5.75 1.25

Sir Rowland Hill (1795-1879), originator of penny postage.

Salvador Allende, Flags, Demonstrators — A149

1979, July 21 Litho. *Perf. 12½*

504 A149 100fr multicolored 1.60 .50

Salvador Allende, president of Chile.

Old Man Telling Stories — A150

1979, July 28

505 A150 45fr multicolored .80 .25

Story telling as education.

Handball Players A151

75fr, Players and ball. 250fr, Pres. Ngouabi, cup on map of Africa, player.

1979, July 31 Litho. *Perf. 12½*

Size: 40x30mm, 30x40mm

506 A151 45fr multi .60 .25
507 A151 75fr multi, vert. 1.00 .25

Size: 22x40mm

Perf. 12x12½

508 A151 250fr multicolored 2.75 1.00

Marien Ngouabi Handball Cup.

Map and Flag of Congo — A152

1979, Aug. 15

509 A152 50fr multicolored .80 .25

16th anniversary of revolution.

Souvenir Sheet

Virgin and Child, by Dürer — A153

1979, Aug. 13 *Perf. 13½*

510 A153 500fr red brn & lt grn 6.50 2.50

Albrecht Dürer (1471-1528), German engraver and painter.

Bach and Contemporary Instruments — A155

No. 512, Albert Einstein, astronauts on moon.

1979, Sept. 10 *Perf. 13½*

511 A155 200fr multicolored 2.25 .75
512 A155 200fr multicolored 2.25 .75

Yoro Fishing Port A156

1979, Sept. 26 Litho. *Perf. 12½*

513 A156 45fr shown .65 .25
514 A156 75fr Port at night .95 .35

Mukukulu Dam — A157

1979, Oct. 5 *Perf. 12½x12*

515 A157 20fr multicolored .60 .25
516 A157 45fr multicolored 1.10 .30

Emblem, Control Tower, Jets A158

1979, Dec. 12 Litho. *Perf. 12½*

517 A158 100fr multicolored 1.60 .50

ASECNA (Air Safety Board), 20th anniv.

Congolese Labor Party, 10th Anniversary A159

1979, Dec. 31

518 A159 45fr multicolored .80 .25

Post Office, 15th Anniv. — A160

1980, Mar. 30 Litho. *Perf. 12½*

519 A160 45fr multicolored .60 .25
520 A160 95fr multicolored 1.10 .30

Visit of Pope John Paul II — A161

1980, May 5

521 A161 100fr multicolored 3.50 1.00

Rotary International, 75th Anniversary — A162

1980, May 10 Litho. ***Perf. 12½***
522 A162 150fr multicolored 1.50 .50

Pointe Noire Foundry A163

1980, June 18 Litho. ***Perf. 12½***
523 A163 30fr shown .30 .25
524 A163 35fr Different view .50 .25

Claude Chappe, Tower — A164

1980, June 21 Litho. ***Perf. 12½***
525 A164 200fr multicolored 2.50 1.00

Claude Chappe (1763-1805), French engineer.

Mossaka Harbor — A165

1980, June 23
532 A165 45fr shown .60 .25
533 A165 90fr Different view 1.10 .25

Papilio Dardanus (Front and Back) — A167

15fr, Kalima aethiops. 20fr, Papilio demodocus. 60fr, Euphaedra. 90fr, Hypolimnas misippus.
300fr, Charaxes smaragdalis.

1980, July 12 Litho. ***Perf. 12½***
534 A167 5fr shown .60 .30
a. Perf. 12½x13 1.60 1.60
535 A167 15fr multicolored 1.40 .30
a. Perf. 12½x13 2.00 2.00
536 A167 20fr multicolored 1.40 .40
a. Perf. 12½x13 2.40 2.40
537 A167 60fr multicolored 3.25 .75
538 A167 90fr multicolored 6.50 1.00
Nos. 534-538 (5) 13.15 2.75

Souvenir Sheet

539 A167 300fr multicolored 12.00 17.00

July 31st Hospital — A168

1980, July 31
540 A168 45fr multicolored .80 .25

Human Rights Emblem, People — A169

500fr, Man breaking chain.

1980, Aug. 2
541 A169 350fr shown 2.75 1.00
542 A169 500fr multicolored 4.50 1.50

Human Rights Convention, 32nd anniv.

Citizens and Congolese Arms A170

95fr, Dove on flag, fists, vert. 150fr, Dove holding Congolese arms.

1980, Aug. 15 ***Perf. 12½***
543 A170 75fr shown .70 .30
544 A170 95fr multicolored .90 .30
545 A170 150fr multicolored 1.50 .60
Nos. 543-545 (3) 3.10 1.20

August 13-15th Revolution, 17th anniv.

Coffee and Cocoa Trees on Map of Congo — A171

Coffee and Cocoa Day: 95fr, Branches, map of Congo.

1980, Aug. 18 ***Perf. 13½x13***
546 A171 45fr multicolored .60 .25
547 A171 95fr multicolored 1.10 .40

Logging A172

1980, Aug. 28
548 A172 70fr shown .80 .30
549 A172 75fr Wood transport .80 .30

Pres. Neto of Angola, 1st Death Anniv. — A173

1980, Sept. 11
550 A173 100fr multicolored .90 .30

Lark — A174

Designs: Birds.

1980, Sept. 17
551 A174 45fr multi, horiz. .90 .30
552 A174 75fr multi, horiz. 1.10 .30
553 A174 90fr multi, horiz. 1.40 .35
554 A174 150fr multicolored 2.25 .50
555 A174 200fr multicolored 3.00 1.00
556 A174 250fr multicolored 3.50 1.25
a Souv. sheet of 6, #551-556 22.50 17.50
Nos. 551-556 (6) 12.15 3.70

World Tourism Conference, Manila, Sept. 27 — A175

1980, Sept. 27 Litho. ***Perf. 13½x13***
557 A175 100fr multicolored 1.00 .35

First Day of School Term — A176

1980, Oct. 2 Photo. ***Perf. 13***
558 A176 50fr multicolored .70 .25

First House in Brazzaville — A177

Brazzaville Centenary: 65fr, First native village. 75fr, Old Town Hall, 1912. 150fr, View from bank of Bacongo, 1912. 200fr, Meeting of explorer Savorgnan de Brazza and chief Makoko, 1880.

1980, Oct. 3 Litho. ***Perf. 12½***
559 A177 45fr multicolored .50 .25
560 A177 65fr multicolored .70 .30
561 A177 75fr multicolored 1.00 .40
562 A177 150fr multicolored 1.75 .65
563 A177 200fr multicolored 2.25 1.00
Nos. 559-563 (5) 6.20 2.60

Boys on Bank of Congo River — A178

1980, Oct. 30
564 A178 80fr shown .85 .25
565 A178 150fr Djoue Bridge 1.90 .40

Revolutionary Stadium and Athletes — A179

1980, Nov. 20 ***Perf. 13x12½***
566 A179 60fr multicolored .80 .25

Rebuilt Railroad Bridge over Congo River A180

1980, Nov. 29 ***Perf. 13x13½***
567 A180 75fr multicolored .90 .30

Mangoes, Loudima Fruit Packing Station A181

1980, Dec. 2 ***Perf. 13***
568 A181 10fr shown .25 .25
569 A181 25fr Oranges .50 .25
570 A181 40fr Citrons .60 .25
571 A181 85fr Mandarins 1.10 .30
Nos. 568-571 (4) 2.45 1.05

African Postal Union, 5th Anniversary A182

1980, Dec. 24 ***Perf. 13½***
572 A182 100fr multicolored .90 .30

Moungouni Earth Satellite Station A183

1980, Dec. 30 ***Perf. 12½***
573 A183 75fr multicolored .80 .25

Hertzian Wave Communication, Brazzaville — A184

1980, Dec. 30 ***Perf. 12½x12***

574 A184 150fr multicolored 1.60 .40

1980 African Handball Champion Team — A185

100fr, Receiving cup, vert.

Perf. 12½x13, 13x12½

1981, Jan. 26 **Litho.**

575 A185 100fr multicolored 1.25 .35
576 A185 150fr shown 1.50 .60

Pres. Denis Sassou-Nguesso — A186

1981, Feb. 5 **Litho.** ***Perf. 12½***

577 A186 45fr multicolored .45 .25
578 A186 75fr multicolored .60 .25
579 A186 100fr multicolored .90 .25
Nos. 577-579 (3) 1.95 .75

Luna 17, 1970. — A187

Space Conquest: 150fr, Space shuttle in orbit. 200fr, Shuttle, space station. 300fr, Shuttle, landing field. 500fr, Shuttle lift-off.

1981, May 4 **Litho.** ***Perf. 14x13½***

580 A187 100fr multicolored 1.00 .25
581 A187 150fr multicolored 1.40 .40
582 A187 200fr multicolored 2.00 .55
583 A187 300fr multicolored 2.75 .80
Nos. 580-583 (4) 7.15 2.00

Souvenir Sheet

584 A187 500fr multicolored 5.00 1.40

For overprint see No. 725.

Fight Against Apartheid — A188

1981, May 5 **Litho.** ***Perf. 12½***

585 A188 100fr deep blue .90 .25

Twin Palm Tree of Louingui — A189

1981, May 22 ***Perf. 12x12½***

586 A189 75fr multicolored 1.00 .25

13th World Telecommunications Day — A190

1981, June 6 ***Perf. 12½***

587 A190 120fr multicolored 1.50 .50

Rubber Extraction — A191

1981, June 27 ***Perf. 13***

588 A191 50fr shown .60 .25
589 A191 70fr Sap draining .90 .30

Intl. Year of the Disabled A192

1981, June 29 **Engr.**

590 A192 45fr multicolored .60 .25

See No. B7.

Bird Trap — A194

Designs: Animal traps. 10fr vert.

1981, July

596 A194 5fr multicolored .90 .25
597 A194 10fr multicolored .90 .25
598 A194 15fr multicolored 1.40 .25
599 A194 20fr multicolored 1.40 .25
600 A194 30fr multicolored 2.00 .25
601 A194 35fr multicolored 2.00 .30
Nos. 596-601 (6) 8.60 1.55

Mausoleum of King Maloango — A195

150fr, Mausoleum, portrait.

1981, July 4 **Litho.** ***Perf. 12½***

602 A195 75fr shown .70 .25
603 A195 150fr multicolored 1.25 .40

Prince Charles and Lady Diana, Coach A196

Royal wedding: Couple and coaches.

1981, Sept. 1 **Litho.** ***Perf. 14½***

604 A196 100fr multicolored 1.00 .25
605 A196 200fr multicolored 2.00 .55
606 A196 300fr multicolored 3.25 .80
Nos. 604-606 (3) 6.25 1.60

Souvenir Sheet

607 A196 400fr multicolored 4.00 1.10

World Food Day — A197

1981, Oct. 16 **Litho.** ***Perf. 13½x13***

608 A197 150fr multicolored 1.75 .55

12th World UPU Day A198

1981, Oct. 24 **Engr.** ***Perf. 13x12½***

609 A198 90fr multicolored 1.00 .25

Royal Guard A199

1981, Oct. 31 **Litho.** ***Perf. 12½x13***

610 A199 45fr multicolored .90 .25

Eradication of Manioc Beetle — A200

1981, Nov. 18 **Litho.** ***Perf. 12½***

611 A200 75fr multicolored 1.20 .25

Natl. Red Cross — A201

10fr, Bandaging patient. 35fr, Treating child. 60fr, Drawing well water.

1981, Nov. 18 ***Perf. 13***

612 A201 10fr multicolored .30 .25
613 A201 35fr multicolored .50 .25
614 A201 60fr multicolored .80 .25
Nos. 612-614 (3) 1.60 .75

Giant Baobab ("Tree of Savorgnan de Brazza") A202

1981, Dec. 19 **Litho.** ***Perf. 13***

615 A202 45fr multicolored 1.00 .25
616 A202 75fr multicolored 1.40 .30

Fetish Figure — A203

Designs: Various carved figures.

1981, Dec. 19 ***Perf. 12½***

617 A203 15fr multicolored .30 .25
a. Perf. 12½x13 .30 .25
618 A203 25fr multicolored .40 .25
a. Perf. 12½x13 .40 .25
619 A203 45fr multicolored .50 .25
620 A203 50fr multicolored .60 .25
a. Perf. 12½x13 .60 .35
621 A203 60fr multicolored .70 .25
Nos. 617-621 (5) 2.50 1.25

Caves of Bangou A204

1981, Dec. 29 ***Perf. 13x13½***

622 A204 20fr multicolored .45 .25
623 A204 25fr multicolored .45 .25

King Makoko and His Queen, Ivory Sculptures by R. Engongodzo — A205

25fr, Woman, facing right, vert. 35fr, Woman, facing left, vert.

Perf. 13½x13, 13x13½

1982, Feb. 27 **Litho.**

624 A205 25fr multicolored .35 .25
625 A205 35fr multicolored .45 .25
626 A205 100fr shown 1.00 .30
Nos. 624-626 (3) 1.80 .80

George Stephenson (1781-1848) and Inter City 125, Gt. Britain — A206

Locomotives: 150fr, Sinkansen Bullet Train, Japan. 200fr, Advanced Passenger Train, Gt. Britain. 300fr, TGV-001, France.

1982, Mar. 2 **Litho.** ***Perf. 12½***

627 A206 100fr multicolored 1.00 .25
628 A206 150fr multicolored 1.60 .40
629 A206 200fr multicolored 2.25 .55
630 A206 300fr multicolored 3.25 .80
Nos. 627-630 (4) 8.10 2.00

Scouting Year A207

100fr, Looking through binoculars. 150fr, Reading map. 200fr, Helping woman. 300fr, Crossing rope bridge. 500fr, Hiking, horiz.

1982, Apr. 13 **Litho.** ***Perf. 13***

631 A207 100fr multicolored 1.25 .25
632 A207 150fr multicolored 1.50 .40
633 A207 200fr multicolored 2.25 .55
634 A207 300fr multicolored 3.25 .80
Nos. 631-634 (4) 8.25 2.00

Souvenir Sheet

635 A207 500fr multicolored 5.00 1.75

For overprint see No. 726.

Franklin Roosevelt A208

1982, June 12 **Litho.** ***Perf. 13***

636 A208 150fr shown 1.75 .60
637 A208 250fr Washington 2.75 .85
638 A208 350fr Goethe 3.75 1.10
Nos. 636-638 (3) 8.25 2.55

21st Birthday of Princess Diana, July 1 — A209

1982, June 12 ***Perf. 14***

639 A209 200fr Candles 2.00 .55
640 A209 300fr "21" 2.75 .80

Souvenir Sheet

641 A209 500fr Diana 5.00 1.40

5-Year Plan, 1982-1986 A210

60fr, Road construction. 100fr, Communications, vert. 125fr, Operating room equipment, vert. 150fr, Hydroelectric power, vert.

Perf. 13x12½, 12½x13

1982, June 19

642 A210 60fr multicolored .80 .25
643 A210 100fr multicolored 1.25 .30
644 A210 125fr multicolored 1.60 .35
645 A210 150fr multicolored 1.75 .40
Nos. 642-645 (4) 5.40 1.30

ITU Plenipotentiary Conference, Nairobi — A211

1982, June 26 ***Perf. 13***

646 A211 300fr multicolored 3.00 .90

Nos. 604-607 Overprinted in Blue

1982, July 30 ***Perf. 14½***

647 A196 100fr multicolored .90 .30
648 A196 200fr multicolored 1.75 .60
649 A196 300fr multicolored 2.75 1.00
Nos. 647-649 (3) 5.40 1.90

Souvenir Sheet

650 A196 400fr multicolored 3.50 2.50

Birth of Prince William of Wales, June 21.

Nutrition Campaign A212

1982, July 24 **Litho.** ***Perf. 12½***

651 A212 100fr multicolored 1.40 .25

WHO African Headquarters, Brazzaville — A213

1982, July 24 **Litho.** ***Perf. 12½***

652 A213 125fr multicolored 1.60 .45

TB Bacillus Centenary — A214

1982, Aug. 7 ***Perf. 12½x12***

653 A214 250fr Koch, bacillus 3.25 1.10

Pres. Sassou-Nguesso and 1980 Simba Prize — A215

1982, Oct. 20 **Litho.** ***Perf. 13***

654 A215 100fr multicolored .90 .30

Turtles — A216

Various turtles and tortoises.

1982, Dec. 1

655 A216 30fr multicolored .90 .25
656 A216 45fr multicolored 1.50 .30
657 A216 55fr multicolored 1.60 .40
Nos. 655-657 (3) 4.00 .95

Boy Gathering Coconuts — A217

1982, Dec. 11

658 A217 100fr multicolored 1.40 .30

Nest in Tree Trunk — A218

75fr, Nests in palm tree. 100fr, Woven nest on thorn branch.

1982, Dec. 29 ***Perf. 12½***

659 A218 40fr shown 1.00 .25
660 A218 75fr multicolored 1.60 .25
661 A218 100fr multicolored 2.50 .40
Nos. 659-661 (3) 5.10 .90

Hertzian Wave Communication Network — A219

1982, Dec. 30 ***Perf. 13x12½***

662 A219 45fr multicolored .45 .25
663 A219 60fr multicolored .50 .25
664 A219 95fr multicolored .90 .30
Nos. 662-664 (3) 1.85 .80

30th Anniv. of Customs Cooperation Council — A220

1983, Jan. 26 **Litho.** ***Perf. 12½x13***

665 A220 100fr Headquarters .90 .30

Mausoleum of Pres. Marien Ngouabi — A221

1983, Feb. 8 ***Perf. 13***

666 A221 60fr multicolored .50 .25
667 A221 80fr multicolored .80 .25

Ironsmiths — A222

1983 ***Perf. 12½***

668 A222 45fr shown .80 .25
669 A222 150fr Weaver, vert. 1.50 .50

Issue dates: 45fr, Mar. 5; 150fr, Feb. 24.

Carved Chess Pieces, by R. Engongonzo — A223

Various pieces.

1983, Feb. 26 ***Perf. 13***

670 A223 40fr multicolored .40 .25
671 A223 60fr multicolored 1.00 .25
672 A223 95fr multicolored 2.00 .50
Nos. 670-672 (3) 3.40 1.00

Easter 1983 A224

Raphael drawings: 200fr, Transfiguration study. 300fr, Deposition from Cross, horiz. 400fr, Christ in Glory.

1983, Apr. 20 **Litho.** ***Perf. 13***

673 A224 200fr multicolored 2.00 .50
674 A224 300fr multicolored 3.25 .65
675 A224 400fr multicolored 4.50 .85
Nos. 673-675 (3) 9.75 2.00

Seashells A225

1983 **Litho.** ***Perf. 15x14***

675A A225 25fr multicolored *150.00 65.00*
676 A225 35fr multicolored 1.40 .30
677 A225 65fr multicolored 1.75 .35

Dated 1982.

A226

Various traditional combs.

1983, May ***Perf. 14***

678 A226 30fr multicolored .35 .25
679 A226 70fr multicolored .90 .25
680 A226 85fr multicolored 1.00 .25
Nos. 678-680 (3) 2.25 .75

A227

Litho & Engr.

1983, Aug. 10 ***Perf. 12½x13***

681 A227 60fr multicolored .65 .25
682 A227 100fr multicolored .95 .30

20th anniv. of revolution.

Centenary of the Arrival of Christian Missionaries — A228

Churches and Clergymen: 150fr, A. Carrie, Church of the Sacred Heart, Loango, vert. 250fr, Msgr. Augouard; St. Louis, Liranga; St. Joseph, Linzolo.

1983, Aug. 23 ***Perf. 12½***

683 A228 150fr multicolored 1.60 .40
684 A228 250fr multicolored 2.75 .70

Local Flowers — A229

5fr, Liana thunderaie, vert. 15fr, Bougainvillea. 20fr, Anthurium, vert. 45fr, Allamanda. 75fr, Hibiscus, vert.

1984, Jan. 20 **Litho.** ***Perf. 12½***

685 A229 5fr multicolored .25 .25
686 A229 15fr multicolored .35 .25
687 A229 20fr multicolored .50 .25
688 A229 45fr multicolored 1.00 .25
689 A229 75fr multicolored 1.40 .30
Nos. 685-689 (5) 3.50 1.30

35th Anniv. of World Peace Council A230

1984, Mar. 31 **Litho.** ***Perf. 13x12½***

690 A230 50fr multicolored .45 .25
691 A230 100fr multicolored .90 .30

Anti-Nuclear Arms Campaign A231

1984, May 31 **Litho.** ***Perf. 12x12½***

692 A231 200fr Explosion, victims 2.00 .50

Agriculture Day A232

10fr, Rice. 15fr, Pineapples. 60fr, Manioc, vert. 100fr, Palm tree, map, vert.

Perf. 13x13½, 13½x13

1984, June 30 **Litho.**

693 A232 10fr multicolored .25 .25
694 A232 15fr multicolored .25 .25
695 A232 60fr multicolored .60 .25
696 A232 100fr multicolored 1.10 .35
Nos. 693-696 (4) 2.20 1.10

Congress Palace — A233

1984, July 27 ***Perf. 13***

697 A233 60fr multicolored .60 .25
698 A233 100fr multicolored 1.00 .30

Chinese-Congolese cooperation.

CFCO-Congo Railways, 50th Anniv. — A234

10fr, Loulombo Station. 25fr, Les Bandas Chinese Labor Camp. 125fr, "50". 200fr, Administration building.

1984, July 30 ***Perf. 13½***

699 A234 10fr multicolored .35 .25
700 A234 25fr multicolored .60 .25
701 A234 125fr multicolored 2.75 .70
702 A234 200fr multicolored 6.25 1.00
Nos. 699-702 (4) 9.95 2.20

Locomotives — A235

Ships on the Congo River — A236

No. 703, CC 203. No. 704, Tugboat. No. 705, BB 103. No. 706, Pusher tugboat. No. 707, BB-BB 301. No. 708, Dredger. No. 709, BB 420 L'Eclair. No. 710, Cargo ship.

1984, Aug. 24 ***Perf. 12½***

703 A235 100fr multi 1.10 .35
704 A236 100fr multi 1.10 .35
705 A235 150fr multi 1.60 .50
706 A236 150fr multi 1.60 .50
707 A235 300fr multi 3.25 1.10
708 A236 300fr multi 3.25 1.10
709 A235 500fr multi 5.25 1.75
710 A236 500fr multi 5.25 1.75
Nos. 703-710 (8) 22.40 7.40

World Fisheries Year A237

5fr, Basket of fish. 20fr, Net fishermen in boat. 25fr, School of fish. 40fr, Net fisherman. 55fr, Trawler

1984, Oct. 16 ***Perf. 13½***

711 A237 5fr multicolored .50 .25
712 A237 20fr multicolored .80 .25
713 A237 25fr multicolored .80 .25
714 A237 40fr multicolored 1.25 .30
715 A237 55fr multicolored 2.25 .35
Nos. 711-715 (5) 5.60 1.40

Anti-polio Campaign A238

250fr, Disabled men, hand. 300fr, Target, disabled women, horiz.

1984, Oct. 30

716 A238 250fr multicolored 2.75 .90
717 A238 300fr multicolored 3.25 1.00

M'Bamou Palace Hotel, Brazzaville A239

1984, Dec. 15 ***Perf. 14½***

718 A239 60fr multicolored .50 .25
719 A239 100fr multicolored 1.00 .30

Fauna A240

1984, Dec. ***Perf. 15x14½***

720 A240 30fr Pangolin 5.00 .75
721 A240 70fr Bat 6.25 1.50
722 A240 85fr Civet cat 8.00 2.00
Nos. 720-722 (3) 19.25 4.25

Stamps are dated "1983".

Congo River Logging A241

60fr, Log raft, crew hut. 100fr, Tugboat pushing logs.

1984, Dec. ***Perf. 13½x13***

723 A241 60fr multicolored .60 .25
724 A241 100fr multicolored 1.25 .35

Nos. 584, 635 Ovptd. in Black or Green

Souvenir Sheets

TSUKUBA EXPO '85

ITALIA '85 emblem, ROME

1985, Mar. 8 *Perf. 14x13½, 13*

725 A187 500fr multi 5.75 4.50
726 A207 500fr multi 5.75 4.50

See Nos. C336-C337.

Zonocerus Variegatus — A242

1985, Mar. 15 *Perf. 13*

727 A242 125fr multicolored 1.75 .35

Burial of a Teke Chief — A243

1985, Apr. 30 *Perf. 12½*

728 A243 225fr multicolored 2.25 .75

Edible Fruit A244

5fr, Trichoscypha acuminata, vert. 10fr, Aframomum africanum. 125fr, Gambeya lacuurtiana. 150fr, Landolphia jumelei.

Perf. 13½, 13 (#732A), 13½x13¼ (#732B)

1985, June 15

729 A244 5fr multicolored .25 .25
730 A244 10fr multicolored .25 .25
730A A244 90fr like #730
731 A244 125fr multicolored 1.40 .40
732 A244 150fr multicolored 1.75 .55
732A A244 205fr like #731
732B A244 300fr Like #732 — —

Sizes: No. 729, 22x36mm, Nos. 731, 732A, 36x22mm.

Nos. 730A, 732A, 732B inscribed "Congo" only.

For overprints, see Nos. 1155, 1170, 1183-1185.

Compare type A244 with type A352.

Lions Club Intl., 30th Anniv. — A245

250fr, Flag, District 403B.

1985, June 25 *Perf. 12½*

733 A245 250fr multicolored 2.75 .70

Russian Soldier, Kremlin, Fall of Berlin A246

1985, July 27 *Perf. 12*

734 A246 60fr multicolored .80 .25

Defeat of Nazi Germany, end of World War II, 40th anniv.

Lady Olave Baden-Powell, Girl Guides Founder — A247

Anniversaries and events: 150fr, Girl Guides, 75th anniv. 250fr, Jacob Grimm, fabulist; Sleeping Beauty. 350fr, Johann Sebastian Bach, composer; European Music Year, St. Thomas Church organ, Leipzig. 450fr, Queen Mother, 85th birthday, vert. 500fr, Statue of Liberty, cent., vert.

1985, Aug. 26 *Perf. 13*

735 A247 150fr multicolored 1.60 .50
736 A247 250fr multicolored 2.25 .90
737 A247 350fr multicolored 3.00 1.25
738 A247 450fr multicolored 3.75 1.60
739 A247 500fr multicolored 5.00 2.00
Nos. 735-739 (5) 15.60 6.25

PHILEXAFRICA '85, Lome, Togo, Nov. 16-24 — A248

No. 741, Airport, postal van.

1985, Oct. 10 *Perf. 13x12½*

740 A248 250fr shown 2.75 1.00
741 A248 250fr multicolored 2.75 1.00
a. Pair, #740-741 + label 6.50 6.50

REPUBLIQUE POPULAIRE DU CONGO

150F

Cortinarius

Mushrooms — A249

100fr, Coprinus, vert. 150fr, Cortinarius. 200fr, Armillariella mellea. 300fr, Dictyophora. 400fr, Crucibulum vulgare.

1985, Dec. 14 Litho. *Perf. 13*

742 A249 100fr multicolored 1.25 .35
743 A249 150fr multicolored 2.00 .50
744 A249 200fr multicolored 2.75 .85
745 A249 300fr multicolored 3.50 1.25
746 A249 400fr multicolored 5.50 1.50
Nos. 742-746 (5) 15.00 4.45

Arbor Day — A250

60fr, Planting sapling. 200fr, Map, lifecycle diagram.

1986, Mar. 6 *Perf. 13½*

747 A250 60fr multicolored .45 .25
748 A250 200fr multicolored 1.90 .90

Children's Hoop Races — A251

1986, Apr. 30 *Perf. 12½*

749 A251 5fr Two boys .35 .25
750 A251 10fr One boy .35 .25
751 A251 60fr Three boys, horiz. .90 .25
a. Souvenir sheet of 3, #749-751 2.00 1.75
Nos. 749-751 (3) 1.60 .75

Intl. Environment Day — A252

60fr, Garbage disposal. 125fr, Dumping garbage.

1986, June 5 Litho. *Perf. 13½*

752 A252 60fr multicolored .70 .25
753 A252 125fr multicolored 1.30 .45

A253

Traditional Modes of Transporting Goods: 5fr, Basket on head, child in sling carrier. 10fr, Child in carrier on hip, large basket strapped to forehead. 60fr, Man carrying load on shoulder.

1986, July 15 Litho. *Perf. 13x12½*

754 A253 5fr multicolored .30 .25
755 A253 10fr multicolored .30 .25
756 A253 60fr multicolored .80 .40
Nos. 754-756 (3) 1.40 .90

Mission of the Sisters of St. Joseph of Cluny, Cent. A254

1986, Aug. 19 Litho. *Perf. 12½x13*

757 A254 230fr multicolored 2.75 1.25

A255

1986, Aug. 30 Litho. *Perf. 13½*

758 A255 40fr multicolored .45 .25
759 A255 60fr multicolored .55 .25
760 A255 100fr multicolored 1.00 .35
Nos. 758-760 (3) 2.00 .85

UNESCO intl. communications development program.

Intl. Peace Year — A256

1986, Sept. 15 Litho. *Perf. 13½*

761 A256 100fr multicolored 1.00 .30

World Food Day A257

75fr, Food staples. 120fr, Mother feeding child.

1986, Oct. 16

762 A257 75fr multicolored .80 .25
763 A257 120fr multicolored 1.25 .40

UN Child Survival Campaign A258

Mothers, children and pinwheels in various designs.

1986, Oct. 27

764 A258 15fr multi, vert. .25 .25
765 A258 30fr multicolored .25 .25
766 A258 70fr multi, vert. .70 .30
Nos. 764-766 (3) 1.20 .80

A258a

1986, Dec. 5 Litho. *Perf. 12x12½*

766A A258a 100fr multicolored 1.50 .35

27th Soviet Communist Party congress.

A259

1987, Feb. 10 Litho. *Perf. 13½*

767 A259 30fr multicolored .25 .25
768 A259 45fr multicolored .45 .25
769 A259 75fr multicolored .70 .25
770 A259 120fr multicolored 1.10 .35
Nos. 767-770 (4) 2.50 1.10

Election of President Sassou-Nguesso, head of the Organization of African States.

Traditional Wedding A260

1987, Feb. 18 Litho. *Perf. 12½x13*

771 A260 5fr multicolored .25 .25
772 A260 15fr multicolored .25 .25
773 A260 20fr multicolored .25 .25
Nos. 771-773 (3) .75 .75

The Blue Lake — A261

1987, July 16 *Perf. 12½*

774 A261 5fr multicolored .25 .25
775 A261 15fr multicolored .25 .25
776 A261 75fr multicolored 1.00 .30
777 A261 120fr multicolored 1.25 .40
Nos. 774-777 (4) 2.75 1.20

Pres. Marien Ngouabi — A262

1987, July 16 *Perf. 13*

778 A262 75fr multicolored .75 .30
779 A262 120fr multicolored 1.25 .40

Tenth death anniv.

Congress of African Scientists — A263

1987, Sept. 10 *Perf. 13x12½*

780 A263 15fr multicolored .25 .25
781 A263 90fr multicolored .70 .30
782 A263 230fr multicolored 2.00 .80
Nos. 780-782 (3) 2.95 1.35

4th African Games, Nairobi — A264

1987, Oct. 30 *Perf. 12½*

783 A264 75fr multicolored .75 .40
784 A264 120fr multicolored 1.25 .60

Raoul Follereau (1903-1977), Philanthropist — A265

1987, Oct. 20 *Perf. 13½*

785 A265 120fr multicolored 1.50 .60

Cure leprosy.

FAO, 40th Anniv. — A266

1987, Nov. 17 *Perf. 12½*

786 A266 300fr multicolored 2.75 1.10

Anti-Apartheid Campaign A267

Nelson Mandela A268

Perf. 13½x15, 14½x15

1987, Sept. 21 Litho.

787 A267 60fr multicolored .60 .25
788 A268 240fr multicolored 2.40 .75

Natl. UNICEF Vaccination Campaign A269

30fr, Inoculating adults, horiz. 500fr, Inoculating children, horiz.

Perf. 13½x14½, 14½x13½

1987, Sept. 28

789 A269 30fr multicolored .25 .25
790 A269 45fr shown .50 .25
791 A269 500fr multicolored 5.25 2.00
Nos. 789-791 (3) 6.00 2.50

No. 791 is airmail.

Africa Fund — A270

1987, Sept. 28 *Perf. 13½x15*

792 A270 25fr multicolored .30 .25
793 A270 50fr multicolored .65 .25
794 A270 70fr multicolored .80 .25
Nos. 792-794 (3) 1.75 .75

Self-sufficiency in Food Production by the Year 2000 — A271

1987, Nov. 20 Litho. *Perf. 13½*

795 A271 20fr multicolored .30 .25
796 A271 55fr multicolored .65 .25
797 A271 100fr multicolored 1.20 .35
Nos. 795-797 (3) 2.15 .85

Simon Kimbangu (b. 1887), Founder of the Church of Christ on Earth — A272

75fr, Kimbangu, vert. 120fr, Kimbangu, parrot, vert. 240fr, Kimbanguist Church, Nkamba.

1987, Nov. 28 *Perf. 12½*

798 A272 75fr multicolored .70 .30
799 A272 120fr multicolored 1.10 .40
800 A272 240fr multicolored 2.75 1.00
a. Souvenir sheet of 3, #798-800 5.75 5.00
Nos. 798-800 (3) 4.55 1.70

October Revolution, Russia, 70th Anniv. — A273

Lenin inspecting revolutionary troops, Red Square, from an unspecified painting.

1988, Feb. 19 Litho. *Perf. 12½x12*

801 A273 75fr multicolored 2.10 .60
802 A273 120fr multicolored 3.00 1.00

African Writers Opposing Apartheid — A274

1988, Apr. 6 Litho. *Perf. 13½*

803 A274 15fr multicolored .30 .25
804 A274 60fr multicolored .55 .25
805 A274 75fr multicolored .90 .30
Nos. 803-805 (3) 1.75 .80

For overprint see No. 1157.

Intl. Fund for Agricultural Development (IFAD), 10th Anniv. — A275

1988, Apr. 30

806 A275 240fr multicolored 2.25 .85

Invention of the Telegraph by Samuel Morse, 150th Anniv. (in 1987) — A276

1988, Apr. 28

807 A276 90fr Morse, vert. .90 .30
808 A276 120fr shown 1.10 .40

A277

5fr, Eucalyptus trees, Brazzaville. 10fr, Stop cutting down trees.

1988, Sept. 20 Litho. *Perf. 13½*

809 A277 5fr multicolored .40 .25
810 A277 10fr multicolored .60 .25

Fight against desertification.

A278

Campaigns: No. 812, Return to the Land Campaign (farming). 120fr, Self-sufficiency in food production.

1988, Aug. 12 Litho. *Perf. 13½*

811 A278 75fr shown .80 .30
812 A278 75fr multicolored .80 .30
813 A278 120fr multicolored .95 .40
Nos. 811-813 (3) 2.55 1.00

Congo Revolution, 25th anniv.

Yoro Fishing Village A279

1988, Sept. 1

814 A279 35fr shown .45 .25
815 A279 40fr Liberty Place .45 .25

Intl. Day for the Fight Against AIDS A280

75fr, Emblem. 180fr, Modified UN emblem, campaign emblem.

1988, Dec. 1 Litho. *Perf. 13½*

816 A280 60fr shown .45 .25
817 A280 75fr multicolored .70 .25
818 A280 180fr multicolored 1.75 .60
Nos. 816-818 (3) 2.90 1.10

Natl. Committee for the Fight Against AIDS and Evangelical Anglican Church of Congo anti-AIDS campaign.

February 5 Movement, 10th Anniv. A281

75fr, Rally. 120fr, Pres. Sassou-Nguesso, natl. achievements.

1989, Apr. 21 Litho. *Perf. 13½*

819 A281 75fr multicolored .75 .30
820 A281 120fr multicolored 1.00 .40

UN Declaration of Human Rights, 40th Anniv. (in 1988) A282

1989, May 19 *Perf. 13*

821 A282 120fr multicolored .90 .40
822 A282 350fr multicolored 2.75 1.20

Marien Nguabi, Founder of Congo Labor Party A282a

1989, July 31 Litho. *Perf. 12½x13*

822A A282a 240fr red & yellow 2.25 .75

Red Cross and Red Crescent Societies, 125th Annivs. A283

120fr, Dunant, emblem, Congo Red Cross.

1989, Sept. 19 Litho. *Perf. 13*

823 A283 75fr shown 1.20 .40
824 A283 120fr multicolored 1.40 .65

No. 824 is airmail.

Organization of African Unity, 25th Anniv. — A284

1989, Oct. 19 Litho. *Perf. 12½*

825 A284 120fr multicolored 1.10 .40

African Development Bank, 25th Anniv. — A285

1989, Dec. 22 Litho. *Perf. 12½x13*

826 A285 75fr multicolored .80 .35
827 A285 120fr multicolored 1.10 .40

WHO, 40th Anniv. (in 1988) A286

75fr, Blood donation, vert.

1989, Dec. 28 Litho. *Perf. 12½*

828 A286 60fr shown .75 .35
829 A286 75fr multicolored .90 .50

See Nos. 846-847 for overprints.

Congo Labor Party (PCT), 20th Anniv. — A287

1989, Dec. 22 Litho. *Perf. 13x12½*

830 A287 75fr multicolored .75 .35
831 A287 120fr multicolored 1.10 .40

Cacti A288

35fr, Opuntia phaeacantha discata. 40fr, Opuntia ficus indica. 60fr, Opuntia erinacea. 75fr, Opuntia rufida. 120fr, Opuntia leptocaulis.
220fr, Opuntia compresa.

Perf. 12½x13, 13x12½

1989, Nov. 22

832 A288 35fr multicolored .40 .25
833 A288 40fr multicolored .55 .25
834 A288 60fr multicolored 1.00 .25
835 A288 75fr multicolored 1.40 .30
836 A288 120fr multicolored 1.90 .45
Nos. 832-836 (5) 5.25 1.50

Souvenir Sheet

Perf. 12½

837 A288 220fr multicolored 5.00 2.10

Nos. 832-833, 835 and 837 vert. No. 837 contains one 32x40mm stamp.

1992 Winter Olympics, Albertville A289

1989, Dec. 22 *Perf. 12½*

838 A289 75fr Ice dancing .60 .25
839 A289 80fr Nordic skiing .60 .30
840 A289 100fr Speed skating .90 .35
841 A289 120fr Luge 1.10 .45
842 A289 200fr Alpine skiing 1.75 .70
843 A289 240fr Ice hockey 2.25 .85
844 A289 400fr Ski jumping 3.25 1.40
Nos. 838-844 (7) 10.45 4.30

Souvenir Sheet

Perf. 13

845 A289 500fr Bobsled 4.50 2.40

No. 845 contains one 32x40mm stamp.

Nos. 828-829 Ovptd. in 3 or 5 Lines

1989, Dec. 28 *Perf. 12½*

846 A286 60fr multicolored .80 .45
847 A286 75fr multicolored .95 .60

Health care for everyone.

Intl. Literacy Year — A290

1990, June 26 Litho. *Perf. 13½*

848 A290 75fr bl, blk & yel .90 .35

Birds A291

Designs: 25fr, Tourterelle des bois. 50fr, Fauvette pitchou, vert. 70fr, Faucon crecerelle, vert. 150fr, Perroquet gris, vert.

1990, July 10

849 A291 25fr multicolored .40 .25
850 A291 50fr multicolored .75 .30
851 A291 70fr multicolored 1.25 .55
852 A291 150fr multicolored 2.50 1.25
Nos. 849-852 (4) 4.90 2.35

Dance Masks — A292

1990, July 24 *Perf. 13*

853 A292 120fr Mondo 1.10 .40
854 A292 360fr Bapunu 3.50 1.25
855 A292 400fr Kwele 4.00 1.50
Nos. 853-855 (3) 8.60 3.15

For overprints see Nos. 1172, 1173.

Flowering Plants — A293

30fr, Tournesol (sunflower). 45fr, Cassia alata, horiz. 75fr, Oeillette (opium poppy). 90fr, Acalypha sanderil.

1990, Sept. 15 Litho. *Perf. 12½*

856 A293 30fr multicolored .30 .25
857 A293 45fr multicolored .50 .25
858 A293 75fr multicolored .75 .25
859 A293 90fr multicolored 1.10 .35
Nos. 856-859 (4) 2.65 1.10

1992 Summer Olympics, Barcelona — A294

100fr, Street scene, vert. 200fr, Sailing, diff. 240fr, Marketplace. 350fr, Harbor. 500fr, Monument, vert.
750fr, Cathedral, vert.

1990, June 28 Litho. *Perf. 13½*

860 A294 100fr multicolored .70 .30
861 A294 150fr shown .95 .35
862 A294 200fr multicolored 1.20 .40
863 A294 240fr multicolored 1.50 .55
864 A294 350fr multicolored 2.40 .75
865 A294 500fr multicolored 3.25 .90
Nos. 860-865 (6) 10.00 3.25

Souvenir Sheet

866 A294 750fr multicolored 5.50 3.50

Nos. 864-865 airmail. Nos. 860-865 exist in miniature sheets of 1.

Royal Necklaces A295

1990, Aug. 18 Litho. *Perf. 13½*

867 A295 75fr shown .75 .35
868 A295 100fr Necklace, diff. 1.00 .60

Boy Scouts Observing Nature A296

Scout: 35fr, Photographing butterfly, Euphaedra eusimoides. 40fr, Picking mushrooms, Armillaria mellea. 75fr, Drawing butterfly, Palla decius. 80fr, Using magnifying glass, Kallima ansorgei. 500fr, Using microscope, Cortinarius speciocissimus. 600fr, Feeding butterfly, Graphium illyris. No. 874B, Photographing butterfly, Berberia plistonax, horiz. 750fr, Photographing mushrooms, Volvariella bombycina. No. 875A, Examining mushrooms, Coprinus domesticus.

1991, June 8 Litho. *Perf. 13½*

869 A296 35fr multicolored .50 .25
870 A296 40fr multicolored .60 .25
871 A296 75fr multicolored .80 .25
872 A296 80fr multicolored 1.00 .25
873 A296 500fr multicolored 4.50 1.25

874 A296 600fr multicolored 4.50 1.25
a. Min. sheet of 4, #869, 871-872, 874 8.50 3.75
Nos. 869-874 (6) 11.90 3.50

Litho. & Embossed

874B A296 1500fr gold & multi *32.50* —

Souvenir Sheets
Litho.

875 A296 750fr multicolored 5.25 2.25

Litho. & Embossed

875A A296 1500fr gold & multi 14.00 —

Nos. 869-874 exist in souvenir sheets of 1. Nos. 873-875 are airmail.

Medicinal Plants — A297

Designs: 15fr, Ocimum viride. 20fr, Kalanchoe pinnata, vert. 30fr, Euphorbia hirta. 60fr, Catharanthus roseus, vert. 75fr, Bidens pilosa, vert. 100fr, Brillantaisia patula, vert. 120fr, Cassia occidentalis, vert.

1991, Jan. 30 Litho. *Perf. 11½*
876 A297 15fr multicolored .30 .25
877 A297 20fr multicolored .30 .25
878 A297 30fr multicolored .30 .25
879 A297 60fr multicolored .60 .25
880 A297 75fr multicolored .80 .35
881 A297 100fr multicolored 1.20 .55
882 A297 120fr multicolored 1.25 .75
Nos. 876-882 (7) 4.75 2.65

Mushrooms A298

30fr, Amanita rubescens. 45fr, Catathelasma imperiale. 75fr, Amanita caesarea. 90fr, Boletus regius. 120fr, Pluteus cervinus. 150fr, Boletus chrysenteron. 200fr, Agaricus arvensis.
350fr, Boletus versipellis, horiz.

1991, Mar. 25 Litho. *Perf. 13*
883 A298 30fr multi .35 .25
883A A298 45fr multi .50 .25
883B A298 75fr multi .90 .25
883C A298 90fr multi 1.10 .25
883D A298 120fr multi 1.35 .40
883E A298 150fr multi 1.75 .60
883F A298 200fr multi 2.50 .75
Nos. 883-883F (7) 8.45 2.75

Souvenir Sheet
Perf. 12½

883G A298 350fr multi 8.00 3.00

No. 883G contains one 40x32mm stamp.

Trains — A298a

Designs: 60fr, Dr-16, Finland. 75fr, TGV, France. 120fr, S350, Italy. 200fr, DE24000, Turkey. 250fr, DE1024, Germany
350fr, ETR450, Italy.

1991, Apr. 10 Litho. *Perf. 12½x12¼*
883H A298a 60fr multi .65 .25
883I A298a 75fr multi .70 .30
883J A298a 120fr multi 1.25 .45
883K A298a 200fr multi 2.25 .75
883L A298a 250fr multi 3.25 1.00
Nos. 883H-883L (5) 8.10 2.75

Souvenir Sheet
Perf. 12½

883M A298a 350fr multi 6.00 1.50

Dated 1990.

African Tourism Year — A299

1991, Apr. 15 Litho. *Perf. 13½*
884 A299 75fr shown .80 .35
885 A299 120fr Zebra, map 1.20 .60

Allegory of New Republic — A300

1991, May 13 Litho. *Perf. 13*
888 A300 15fr blue .25 .25
889 A300 30fr brt grn .25 .25
890 A300 60fr org yel .40 .25
891 A300 75fr brt pink .55 .30
892 A300 120fr dk brown 1.00 .45
Nos. 888-892 (5) 2.45 1.50

Trans-Siberian Railroad, Cent. — A301

1991, June 6 Litho. *Perf. 13*
899 A301 120fr Map 1.35 .50
900 A301 240fr Map, train 2.75 1.20

Telecom 91 — A302

1991, June 29 Litho. *Perf. 13*
901 A302 75fr multicolored .75 .30
902 A302 120fr multi, vert. 1.25 .60

6th World Forum and Exposition on Telecommunications, Geneva, Switzerland.

Insects — A303

1991, July 2 *Perf. 12½*
903 A303 75fr Peanut beetle 1.00 .25
904 A303 120fr Centaur, horiz. 1.40 .45
905 A303 200fr Coffee beetle 2.25 .75
906 A303 300fr Goliath beetle 3.50 1.50
Nos. 903-906 (4) 8.15 2.95

Water conservation A304

1991, July 16 Litho. *Perf. 12½*
907 A304 75fr multicolored .90 .35

Amnesty Intl., 30th Anniv. A305

Designs: 40fr, Candle, sun, vert. 75fr, "30," broken chains, vert.

1991, Aug. 13 *Perf. 13½*
908 A305 40fr multicolored .35 .25
909 A305 75fr multicolored .60 .25
910 A305 80fr multicolored .70 .35
Nos. 908-910 (3) 1.65 .85

Congo Postage Stamps, Cent. — A306

75fr, Similar to French Congo #1. 120fr, Similar to French Congo #35. 240fr, Similar to Congo Republic #89. 500fr, Similar to French Congo #1, 35 and Congo Republic #89.

Litho. & Engr.

1991, Aug. *Perf. 13x13½*
911 A306 75fr beige & dk grn .80 .30
912 A306 120fr beige, dk grn & brn 1.10 .45
913 A306 240fr multicolored 2.25 1.10
914 A306 500fr multicolored 4.50 2.00
a. Strip of 4, #911-914 10.00 9.00
Nos. 911-914 (4) 8.65 3.85

Ducks A307

75fr, Anas acuta. 120fr, Somateria mollissima, vert. 200fr, Anas clypeata, vert. 240fr, Anas platyrhynchos.

1991, Aug. 8 Litho. *Perf. 12½*
915 A307 75fr multicolored 1.25 .30
916 A307 120fr multicolored 1.50 .45
917 A307 200fr multicolored 2.00 .75
918 A307 240fr multicolored 3.50 1.00
Nos. 915-918 (4) 8.25 2.50

Automobiles and Space — A308

Designs: 35fr, Ferrari 512S by Pininfarina. 40fr, Vincenzo Lancia, Lancia Stratos by Bertone. 75fr, Maybach Zeppelin type 12, Wilhelm Maybach. 80fr, Mars Observer, 1992. 500fr, Magellan probe surveying Venus. 600fr, Magnification of Sun, Ulysses probe. 750fr, Crew of Apollo 11.

1991, Aug. 23 Litho. *Perf. 13½*
919 A308 35fr multicolored .30 .25
920 A308 40fr multicolored .30 .25
921 A308 75fr multicolored .60 .30
922 A308 80fr multicolored .65 .30
923 A308 500fr multicolored 4.25 2.25
924 A308 600fr multicolored 5.00 2.50
Nos. 919-924 (6) 11.10 5.85

Souvenir Sheet

925 A308 750fr multicolored 6.50 3.50

Nos. 923-925 are airmail. No. 925 contains one 60x42mm stamp. Nos. 919-921 exist in souvenir sheets of 1.

Butterflies A309

75fr, Petit bleu. 120fr, Charaxe. 240fr, Papillon feuille, vert. 300fr, Papillon de l'oranger, vert.

1991, Aug. 31 *Perf. 11½*
926 A309 75fr multi 1.20 .30
927 A309 120fr multi 1.50 .50
928 A309 240fr multi 2.10 .80
929 A309 300fr multi 3.75 1.00
Nos. 926-929 (4) 8.55 2.60

For overprints see Nos. 1156, 1165.

Celebrities and Organizations — A310

Designs: 100fr, Bo Jackson, baseball and football player. 150fr, Nick Faldo, golfer. 200fr, Rickey Henderson, Barry Bonds, baseball players. 240fr, Garry Kasparov, World Chess Champion. 300fr, Starving child, Lions and Rotary Clubs emblems. 350fr, Wolfgang Amadeus Mozart. 400fr, De Gaulle, Churchill. 500fr, Jean-Henri Dunant, founder of Red Cross. 750fr, De Gaulle, vert.

1991, Sept. 2 *Perf. 13½*
930 A310 100fr multicolored 1.00 .40
931 A310 150fr multicolored 1.40 .60
932 A310 200fr multicolored 2.00 .80
933 A310 240fr multicolored 2.75 .95
934 A310 300fr multicolored 3.00 1.25
935 A310 350fr multicolored 3.75 1.40
936 A310 400fr multicolored 4.50 1.60
937 A310 500fr multicolored 5.00 2.00
Nos. 930-937 (8) 23.40 9.00

Souvenir Sheet

938 A310 750fr multicolored 8.00 3.50

Nos. 936-938 are airmail. No. 938 contains one 35x50mm stamp.
For overprint, see No. 1199.

Gen. Charles de Gaulle in Africa — A311

120fr, De Gaulle, Free French flag, vert. 240fr, De Gaulle, Appeal of Brazzaville, 1940.

1991, Sept. 2 *Perf. 13½x13, 13x13½*
939 A311 75fr multicolored .90 .40
940 A311 120fr multicolored 1.25 .60
941 A311 240fr multicolored 2.40 1.20
Nos. 939-941 (3) 4.55 2.20

A312

Paintings — A313

1991, Oct. 12 *Perf. 11½*

942 A312 75fr multicolored .75 .35
943 A313 120fr multicolored 1.10 .45

Discovery of America, 500th Anniv. (in 1992) — A314

20fr, Portrait of Christopher Columbus by Sebastian Del Pombo. 35fr, Portrait of Columbus. 40fr, Portrait of Columbus facing right. 55fr, Santa Maria. 75fr, Nina. 150fr, Pinta. 200fr, Arms & signature of Columbus.

1991, May 30 *Perf. 13*

944 A314 20fr multicolored .40 .25
945 A314 35fr multicolored .40 .25
946 A314 40fr multicolored .50 .35
947 A314 55fr multicolored .65 .35
948 A314 75fr multicolored .95 .35
949 A314 150fr multicolored 1.75 .85
950 A314 200fr multicolored 2.25 1.00
Nos. 944-950 (7) 6.90 3.40

Primates A315

30fr, Cercopithecus diana. 45fr, Pan troglodytes. 60fr, Theropithecus gelada. 75fr, Papio hamadryas. 90fr, Macaca nemestrina. 120fr, Gorilla gorilla. 240fr, Mandrillus sphinx.
250fr, Gorilla gorilla.

1991, Dec. 13 **Litho.** *Perf. 13*

951 A315 30fr multicolored .35 .25
952 A315 45fr multicolored .45 .25
953 A315 60fr multicolored .85 .25
954 A315 75fr multicolored 1.00 .35
955 A315 90fr multicolored 1.20 .50
956 A315 120fr multicolored 1.60 .50
957 A315 240fr multicolored 3.50 .75
Nos. 951-957 (7) 8.95 2.85

Souvenir Sheet

958 A315 250fr multicolored 4.25 1.50

Nos. 953-958 are vert.

Anniversaries and Events A316

Designs: 50fr, Launching of Sputnik II with dog, Laika, 1957. 75fr, Mahatma Gandhi and Martin Luther King, Jr. 1964. 120fr, Launching of Meteosat and ERS-1 over Europe and Africa. 240fr, Maybach Zeppelin automobile and Ferdinand von Zeppelin, 75th death anniversary. 300fr, Konrad Adenauer, 25th death anniversary and opening of the Brandenburg Gate, 1989. 500fr, Pope John Paul II's visit to Africa. 600fr, Elvis Presley, American entertainer.

1992, Feb. 4 **Litho.** *Perf. 13½*

959 A316 50fr multicolored .75 .25
960 A316 75fr multicolored .75 .25
961 A316 120fr multicolored 1.25 .45
962 A316 240fr multicolored 2.75 .85
963 A316 300fr multicolored 2.50 .80
964 A316 500fr multicolored 5.25 1.40
a. Souvenir sheet of 3, #960, 963-964 11.50 5.75
Nos. 959-964 (6) 13.25 4.00

Souvenir Sheet

965 A316 600fr multicolored 6.00 2.40

Nos. 959-964 exist in souvenir sheets of 1.
Nos. 962, 964-965 are airmail.
For Overprint, see No. 1166.

Explorers A317

Genoa '92: 75fr, Juan de la Cosa, nautical chart. 95fr, Martin Alonso Pinzon, astrolabe. 120fr, Alonso de Ojeda, hour glass. 200fr, Vicente Yanez Pinzon, sun dial. 250fr, Bartholomew Columbus, quadrant.
400fr, Columbus, flag, horiz.

1992, Oct. 21 **Litho.** *Perf. 13*

966 A317 75fr multicolored .90 .30
967 A317 95fr multicolored 1.10 .30
968 A317 120fr multicolored 1.75 .30
969 A317 200fr multicolored 2.50 .40
970 A317 250fr multicolored 3.50 .50
Nos. 966-970 (5) 9.75 1.80

Souvenir Sheet

971 A317 400fr multi 12.50 12.50

Birds — A318

Designs: 60fr, Sagittarius serpentarius. 75fr, Ephippiorhynchus senegalensis. 120fr, Bugeranus carunculatus. 200fr, Ardea melanocephala. 250fr, Phoenicopterus ruber roseus.
400fr, Balearica regulorum.

1992, Oct. 21

972 A318 60fr multicolored .70 .25
973 A318 75fr multicolored .80 .25
974 A318 120fr multicolored 1.10 .30
975 A318 200fr multicolored 2.00 .40
976 A318 250fr multicolored 2.75 .50
Nos. 972-976 (5) 7.35 1.70

Souvenir Sheet

977 A318 400fr multicolored 4.00 1.00

For overprint, see No. 1191.

Wild Cats — A319

45fr, Panthera leo. 60fr, Panthera tigris. 75fr, Lynx lynx. 95fr, Caracal caracal. 250fr, Leopardus pardalis.
500fr, Acinonyx jubatus.

1992, Nov. 21 **Litho.** *Perf. 13*

978 A319 45fr multicolored .50 .50
979 A319 60fr multicolored .60 .60
980 A319 75fr multicolored .70 .70
981 A319 95fr multicolored .80 .80
982 A319 250fr multicolored 2.25 2.25
Nos. 978-982 (5) 4.85 4.85

Souvenir Sheet

983 A319 400fr multicolored 4.50 1.75

No. 983 contains one 32x40mm stamp.

1992 Winter Olympics, Albertville — A320

Gold medalists: 150fr, N. Mishkutyonok, A. Dmitriev, pairs figure skating, Unified team. 200fr, I. Appelt, H. Winkler, G. Haldacher, T. Schroll, 4-man bobsled, Austria. 500fr, Gunda Niemann, speed skating, Germany. 600fr, Bjorn Daehlie, cross-country skiing, Norway. 750fr, Alberto Tomba, giant slalom, Italy.

1992, Dec. 21 **Litho.** *Perf. 13½*

984 A320 150fr multicolored 1.25 .40
985 A320 200fr multicolored 1.75 .50
986 A320 500fr multicolored 4.00 1.10
987 A320 600fr multicolored 6.00 1.00
Nos. 984-987 (4) 13.00 3.00

Souvenir Sheet

988 A320 750fr multicolored 7.00 2.00

Nos. 986-988 are airmail. No. 988 contains one 35x50mm stamp. Name on No. 987 spelled incorrectly.

1992 Summer Olympics, Barcelona A321

Barcelona landmarks, Olympic event: 75fr, Steeple of La Sagrada Familia, baseball. 100fr, The Muse, Palace of Music, running. 150fr, Cupola interior, long jump. 200fr, St. Paul Hospital, pole vault. 400fr, Sculpture, by Miro, shot put. 500fr, Galley, Maritime Museum, table tennis. 750fr, La Sagrada Familia, tennis.

1992, Dec. 21

989 A321 75fr multicolored .80 .25
990 A321 100fr multicolored 1.00 .30
991 A321 150fr multicolored 1.25 .40
992 A321 200fr multicolored 2.00 .65
993 A321 400fr multicolored 3.50 .65
994 A321 500fr multicolored 4.50 1.00
Nos. 989-994 (6) 13.05 3.25

Souvenir Sheet

995 A321 750fr multicolored 7.00 1.50

Nos. 993-995 are airmail.

Christmas A321a

Paintings: 95fr, The Madonna of the Grand Duke, by Raphael. 120fr, Virgin and Child, by Francesco Mazzo. 200fr, The Madonna with a Book, by Botticelli. 250fr, The Madonna Carondelet, by Fra Bartolommeo. 400fr, Madonna and Child, by Raphael.

1992, Dec. 20 **Litho.** *Perf. 12½*

995A A321a 95fr multicolored 1.25 .30
995B A321a 120fr multicolored — —
995C A321a 200fr multicolored 2.75 .75
995D A321a 250fr multicolored 3.25 1.25
Nos. 995A-995D (4) 7.25 2.30

Souvenir Sheet

995E A321a 400fr multicolored 4.50 1.90

Nos. 995A-995E were not available until late 1993.
For overprint, see No. 1192.

Birds of Prey — A322

1993, Jan. 15 **Litho.** *Perf. 12½x13*

996 A322 45fr Charognard .65 .25
997 A322 75fr Vulture 2.00 .30
998 A322 120fr Eagle 2.50 .65
Nos. 996-998 (3) 5.15 1.20

A323

Traditional ceramics: 45fr, Liloko. 75fr, Mbeya. 120fr, Jug with ladles, Mbeya.

1993, Dec. 21 **Litho.** *Perf. 13½*

999 A323 45fr multicolored .60 .30
1000 A323 75fr multicolored 1.20 .50
1001 A323 120fr multicolored 1.75 .85
Nos. 999-1001 (3) 3.55 1.65

1994 World Cup Soccer Championships, United States — A324

Design: 75fr, Player stretching to kick ball. 95fr, Goalie diving to stop ball. 120fr, Player stretching to kick ball. 200fr, Player kicking. 250fr, Goalie catching ball. 400fr, Players competing for ball.

1993, Jan. 15 **Litho.** *Perf. 12¾*

1002 A324 75fr multi 1.40 .80
1003 A324 95fr multi 1.45 1.10
1004 A324 120fr multi 2.40 1.40
1005 A324 200fr multi 3.50 2.10
1006 A324 250fr multi 4.00 2.75
Nos. 1002-1006 (5) 12.75 8.15

Souvenir Sheet
Perf. 12½

1007 A324 400fr multi 6.00 4.00

No. 1007 contains one 40x32mm stamp.

Wild Animals A325

Designs: 60fr, Damaliscus lunatus. 75fr, Gazella granti. 95fr, Equus quagga. 120fr, Panthera pardus. 200fr, Syncerus caffer. 250fr, Hippopotamus ampibius. 300fr, Necrosyrtes monachu. 350fr, Panthera leo.

1993, Feb. 20 Litho. *Perf. 13*

1008	A325	60fr	multicolored	.75	.25
1009	A325	75fr	multicolored	1.25	.25
1010	A325	95fr	multicolored	1.40	.30
1011	A325	120fr	multicolored	1.90	.30
1012	A325	200fr	multicolored	3.25	.40
1013	A325	250fr	multicolored	4.00	.40
1014	A325	300fr	multicolored	4.75	.40
1015	A325	350fr	multicolored	5.50	.75
a.			Sheet of 8, #1008-1015	20.00	20.00
			Nos. 1008-1015 (8)	22.80	3.05

No. 1015a is a continuous design.

Wild Flowers — A326

Designs: 75fr, Hibiscus schizopetalus. 95fr, Pentas lanceolata. 120fr, Ricinus communis. 200fr, Delonix regia. 250fr, Stapelia gigantea.

1993, May 20 Litho. *Perf. 12½*

1016	A326	75fr	multicolored	.85	.30
1017	A326	95fr	multicolored	1.10	.40
1018	A326	120fr	multicolored	2.25	.50
1019	A326	200fr	multicolored	3.75	1.00
1020	A326	250fr	multicolored	4.50	1.60
			Nos. 1016-1020 (5)	12.45	3.80

Deep Sea Submersibles A327

75fr, Transport PC-1202. 95fr, J. Sea Link 1. 120fr, Nemo. 200fr, Robot. 250fr, Alvin.
400fr, Star III.

1993, June 25

1021	A327	75fr	multi	1.10	.50
1022	A327	95fr	multi	1.40	.75
1023	A327	120fr	multi	1.75	1.00
1024	A327	200fr	multi	2.75	1.50
1025	A327	250fr	multi	3.25	2.00
			Nos. 1021-1025 (5)	10.25	5.75

Souvenir Sheet

1026	A327	400fr	multi	7.00	4.00

No. 1026 contains one 32x40mm stamp.

1996 Summer Olympic Games, Atlanta A329

Designs: 50fr, Equestrian. 75fr, Cycling. 120fr, Sailing. 240fr, shown. 300fr, Hurdles. 500fr, Women's basketball. No. 1036, Running.

1993, Apr. 26 Litho. *Perf. 13½*

1030-1035	A329	Set of 6	15.00	4.00
1035a		Sheet of 6, #1030-1035	17.50	6.00

Souvenir Sheet

1036	A329	750fr	multicolored	6.50	1.50

Nos. 1030-1036 exist imperf. Nos. 1030-1035 exist in souvenir sheets of 1.

Brasiliana '93 — A330

Birds: 75fr, Vidua whydah. 95fr, Vidua regia. 120fr, Steganura paradisea. 200fr, Vidua macroura. 250fr, Anthreptes platura.
400fr, Coliuspasser macrourus, horiz.

1993, July 15 Litho. *Perf. 12x12½*

1037-1041	A330	Set of 5	11.00	11.00

Souvenir Sheet

1042	A330	400fr	multicolored	10.00	10.00

Prehistoric Animals — A331

75fr, Ichthyostega. 95fr, Archaeopteryx. 120fr, Brachiosaurus. 200fr, Tyrannosaurus. 250fr, Pteranodon, vert.
400fr, Brontosaurus.

1993, Aug. 20 Litho. *Perf. 13*

1043	A331	75fr	multicolored	1.00	1.00
1044	A331	95fr	multicolored	1.25	1.25
1045	A331	120fr	multicolored	1.60	1.60
1046	A331	200fr	multicolored	2.50	2.50
1047	A331	250fr	multicolored	3.50	3.50
			Nos. 1043-1047 (5)	9.85	9.85

Souvenir Sheet

1048	A331	400fr	multicolored	6.50	6.50

No. 1048 contains one 32x40mm stamp.

Powered Flight, 90th Anniv. — A332

Designs: 75fr, Wilbur Wright, Model B airplane, vert. 95fr, Orville Wright and Model B biplane, vert. 120fr, First flight by Orville Wright. 200fr, Flight at Kitty Hawk. 250fr, Wright Brothers and airplane.

Perf. 12¼x12½, 12½x12¼

1993, Dec. 17 Litho.

1049	A332	75fr	multi	.65	.65
1050	A332	95fr	multi	.85	.85
1051	A332	120fr	multi	.95	.95
1052	A332	200fr	multi	1.75	1.75
1053	A332	250fr	multi	2.25	2.25
			Nos. 1049-1053 (5)	6.45	6.45

Evolution of the Elephant A333

25fr, Palaeomastodon. 45fr, Mammut. 50fr, Amebelodon. 75fr, Platybelodon. 120fr, Mammuthus.

1994, June 20 Litho. *Perf. 12½*

1054	A333	25fr	multicolored	.75	.30
1055	A333	45fr	multicolored	1.25	.50
1056	A333	50fr	multicolored	1.45	.50
1057	A333	75fr	multicolored	2.25	.80
1058	A333	120fr	multicolored	3.50	1.40
			Nos. 1054-1058 (5)	9.20	3.50

Protection of Nature — A335

Designs: 50fr, Choeropsis liberiensis. 90fr, Hyemoschus aquaticus. 205fr, Taurotragus euryceros, vert. 300fr, Redunca redunca, vert.

1994, Aug. 27 Litho. *Perf. 12½*

1063	A335	50fr	multicolored	.50	.35
1064	A335	90fr	multicolored	.80	.35
1065	A335	205fr	multicolored	1.90	1.10
1066	A335	300fr	multicolored	2.75	1.60
			Nos. 1063-1066 (4)	5.95	3.40

For overprint see No. 1167.

Seaplanes — A336

Designs: 30fr, Cant Z-505, Italy. 45fr, Martin Mariner PBM-3, US. No. 1069, E-59, Russia. No. 1070, Short Sunderland, Great Britain. No. 1071, Martin Mars XPB2M-1, US.
400fr, Boeing 314, US.

1994, Sept. 2 Litho. *Perf. 12½*

1067	A336	30fr	multicolored	.40	.25
1068	A336	45fr	multicolored	.50	.25
1069	A336	90fr	multicolored	1.00	.40
1070	A336	90fr	multicolored	1.00	.40
1071	A336	90fr	multicolored	1.00	.40
			Nos. 1067-1071 (5)	3.90	1.70

Souvenir Sheet

1071A	A336	400fr	multicolored	5.00	2.50

No. 1071A contains one 40x32mm stamp.

Intl. Year of the Family — A337

205fr, African map, child. 300fr, Family, native huts.

1995, Jan. 28 Litho. *Perf. 12½*

1072	A337	90fr	shown	.75	.40
1073	A337	205fr	multicolored	1.60	1.00
1074	A337	300fr	multicolored	2.50	1.50
			Nos. 1072-1074 (3)	4.85	2.90

For overprint see No. 1168.

Insects — A338

1994, July 24 Litho. *Perf. 12½*

1075	A338	90fr	Tarantula	1.90	.40
1076	A338	205fr	Spider	4.50	1.10
1077	A338	240fr	Ladybug	5.00	1.25
			Nos. 1075-1077 (3)	11.40	2.75

Souvenir Sheet

1078	A338	400fr	Bee	4.75	2.00

Costumes — A338a

1995 Litho. *Perf. 12¾x12½*

1078A	A338a	90fr	M'Bochi	1.00	.60
1078B	A338a	205fr	Téké	1.70	.90
1078C	A338a	500fr	Loango	3.75	1.50
			Nos. 1078A-1078C (3)	6.45	3.00

Rotary Intl., 90th Anniv. A339

Designs: 90fr, Polio victim. No. 1080, Playing ball with children. No. 1081, Children with food. 300fr, Delivering polio vaccine.
1500fr, Paul Harris, Rotary emblem.

1996, Feb. 6 Litho. *Perf. 14*

1079	A339	90fr	multicolored	.60	.25
1080	A339	205fr	multicolored	1.25	.50
1081	A339	205fr	multicolored	1.25	.50
1082	A339	300fr	multicolored	1.60	.60
			Nos. 1079-1082 (4)	4.70	1.85

Souvenir Sheet

1083	A339	1500fr	multicolored	5.00	3.25

For overprint, see Mo. 1201.

18th World Scout Jamboree, The Netherlands — A340

Designs: No. 1084, Handshake. No. 1085, Scout helping another with arm sling. 205fr, Saving life in water. 300fr, Lord Baden-Powell.
1000fr, Scout salute.

1996, Feb. 6 Litho. *Perf. 14*

1084	A340	90fr	multicolored	.40	.25
1085	A340	90fr	multicolored	.40	.25
1086	A340	205fr	multicolored	1.00	.40
1087	A340	300fr	multicolored	1.40	.50
			Nos. 1084-1087 (4)	3.20	1.40

Souvenir Sheet

1088	A340	1000fr	multicolored	3.50	2.10

1998 World Cup Soccer Tournament A340a

Various players. Denominations: 90fr, 150fr, 205fr, 300fr, 400fr, 500fr.
No. 1088G, 100fr, Player's legs.

1996 Litho. *Perf. 12¾*

1088A-1088F	A340a	Set of 6	5.00	5.00

Souvenir Sheet

Perf. 13¼x13

1088G	A340a	1000fr	multi	3.00	3.00

No. 1088G contains one 40x31mm stamp.

Antique Automobiles — A341

90fr, 1936 Armstrong Siddeley Twelve. 150fr, 1935 Aston Martin Mark II. 205fr, 1938 Morris 8. 300fr, 1955-62 MG Series MGA. 400fr, 1932 SS1. 500fr, 1938 Alvis 25 SB.

1996, Apr. 30 Litho. *Perf. 12½x12*

1089	A341	90fr multicolored	.40	.25
1090	A341	150fr multicolored	.65	.40
1091	A341	205fr multicolored	.85	.50
1092	A341	300fr multicolored	1.25	.75
1093	A341	400fr multicolored	1.75	1.00
1094	A341	500fr multicolored	2.10	1.25
		Nos. 1089-1094 (6)	7.00	4.15

Domestic Cats — A342

90fr, Persian. 150fr, Siamese. 205fr, Norwegian forest. 300fr, Exotic shorthair. 400fr, Maine coon. 500fr, Red abyssinian.
1000fr, Turkish Angora.

1996, Mar. 10 *Perf. 13x12½*

1095	A342	90fr multicolored	.40	.25
1096	A342	150fr multicolored	.65	.40
1097	A342	205fr multicolored	.90	.50
1098	A342	300fr multicolored	1.35	.75
1099	A342	400fr multicolored	1.75	1.00
1100	A342	500fr multicolored	2.25	1.25
		Nos. 1095-1100 (6)	7.30	4.15

Souvenir Sheet

1101	A342	1000fr multicolored	3.00	2.50

No. 1101 contains one 32x40mm stamp.

1996 Summer Olympic Games, Atlanta A343

90fr, Fencing, vert. 150fr, Archery, vert. 205fr, Basketball, vert. 300fr, Baseball, vert. 400fr, Volleyball. 500fr, 2-man kayak.
1000fr, Judo, vert.

1996 *Perf. 13x12½, 12½x13*

1102	A343	90fr multi	.40	.25
1103	A343	150fr multi	.65	.40
1104	A343	205fr multi	.95	.55
1105	A343	300fr multi	1.40	.80
1106	A343	400fr multi	2.00	1.10
1107	A343	500fr multi	2.10	1.25
		Nos. 1102-1107 (6)	7.50	4.35

Souvenir Sheet

1108	A343	1000fr multi	4.75	2.50

No. 1108 contains one 32x40mm stamp.

Flowers — A344

Designs: 90fr, Nerium oleander. 150fr, Eucaliptus globulus. 205fr, Centaurea cyanus. 300fr, Coffea arabica. 400fr, Hibiscus sabdariffa. 500fr, Cassia angustifolia.

1996, May 10 *Perf. 12½*

1109	A344	90fr multicolored	.35	.25
1110	A344	150fr multicolored	.60	.40
1111	A344	205fr multicolored	.80	.55
1112	A344	300fr multicolored	1.10	.80
1113	A344	400fr multicolored	1.50	1.10
1114	A344	500fr multicolored	1.75	1.25
		Nos. 1109-1114 (6)	6.10	4.35

Mother Carrying Baby — A345

1996 Litho. *Perf. 13*

1115	A345	40fr blue	*4.00*
1116	A345	50fr violet brown	*5.00*
1117	A345	90fr orange	*9.00*
1118	A345	100fr green blue	*10.00*
1119	A345	115fr gray	*11.00*
1120	A345	205fr brown	*20.00*
		Nos. 1115-1120 (6)	*59.00*

It has been stated that this set was not issued.

See Nos. 1145-1150.
For overprints, see Nos. 1159, 1185A, 1236-1236A.

A346

1996, Aug. 31 Litho. *Perf. 13½*

1121	A346	90fr orange & multi	.50	.30
1122	A346	205fr green & multi	1.25	.75

Investiture of Pres. Pascal Lissouba, 4th anniv.

Owls — A347

1996, Mar. 29 *Perf. 14½*

1123	A347	90fr Tyto alba	.70	.25
1124	A347	205fr Bubo poensis	1.50	.50
1125	A347	300fr Scotopelia peli	2.40	.90
1126	A347	500fr Asio capensis	3.50	1.50
		Nos. 1123-1126 (4)	8.10	3.15

Military Aircraft — A348

Designs: 90fr, Vought-Sikorsky Vindicator SB2U-1. 150fr, Grumman Wildcat F4F-3. 205fr, North American SNJ-2. 300fr, Brewster Bermuda. 400fr, Blackburn Skua 1. 500fr, Mitsubishi Type 98-1.
1000fr, P-40 Warhawk (Flying Tigers).

1996, June 24 Litho. *Perf. 12½x12*

1127	A348	90fr multicolored	.35	.25
1128	A348	150fr multicolored	.60	.30
1129	A348	205fr multicolored	.80	.50
1130	A348	300fr multicolored	1.20	.75
1131	A348	400fr multicolored	1.60	1.00
1132	A348	500fr multicolored	2.00	1.25
		Nos. 1127-1132 (6)	6.55	4.05

Souvenir Sheet
Perf. 13

1133	A348	1000fr multicolored	4.00	2.50

No. 1133 contains one 32x40mm stamp.

Aquatic Flowers — A348a

Design: 90fr, Cyrtosperma senegalense; 205fr, Pistia stratioque.

1996, July 3 Litho. *Perf. 14x14¼*

1133A	A348a	90fr multi	.70	.50
1133B	A348a	205fr multi	1.50	1.25

Crocodilians A348b

205fr, Nile crocodile. 255fr, Gavial. 300fr, Caiman.

1996, July 16 Litho. *Perf. 14*

1133C	A348b	205fr multi	1.25	.90
1133D	A348b	255fr multi	1.60	1.00
1133E	A348b	300fr multi	1.90	1.00
		Nos. 1133C-1133E (3)	4.75	2.90

Volleyball, Cent. — A348c

Motion Pictures, Cent. — A348d

World Tourism Organization, 25th Anniv. — A348e

UNICEF, 50th Anniv. — A348f

Food and Agriculture Organization, 50th Anniv. — A348g

United Nations, 50th Anniv. — A348h

1996 Litho. *Perf. 12½*

1133F	A348c	90fr multi	—	—
1133G	A348d	90fr multi	—	—
1133H	A348e	205fr multi	—	—
1133I	A348f	300fr multi	—	—
1133J	A348g	300fr multi	—	—
1133K	A348h	300fr multi	—	—

Arctocebus Calabarensis A349

a, 90fr, With young. b, 205fr, Touching leaf. c, 300fr, Climbing to left. d, 255fr, Walking on branch.

1998, June 3 Litho. *Perf. 14*

1134	A349	Strip of 4, #a.-d.	5.00	5.00

No. 1134 issued in sheets of 12 stamps.
World Wildlife Fund.

Endangered Species — A350

No. 1135, Kabus defassa, vert. No. 1136, Caphalophus sylvicutor. 205fr, Potamochoerus porcus. 300fr, Tragelaplus spekei.

1996 Litho. *Perf. 14*

1135	A350	90fr multi	.55	.25
1136	A350	90fr multi, vert.	.55	.25
1137	A350	205fr multi, vert.	1.10	.45
1138	A350	300fr multi	1.60	.65
		Nos. 1135-1138 (4)	3.80	1.60

Diana, Princess of Wales (1961-97) — A351

Nos. 1139-1141: Various portraits with white rose.
Diana, rose, famous people in sheet margin: 750fr, Henry Kissinger, vert. No. 1143, Mother Teresa, vert. No. 1144, Hillary Clinton, vert.

1998, Aug. 31 Litho. *Perf. 14*
Sheets of 6

1139	A351	205fr #a.-f.	5.50	2.00
1140	A351	255fr #a.-f., vert.	7.00	2.75
1141	A351	300fr #a.-f., vert.	8.00	3.00

Souvenir Sheets

1142	A351	750fr multicolored	3.00	3.00
1143-1144	A351	1000fr each	5.00	5.00

Stamps of Type A345 inscribed only "Congo" ovptd.

1998 Litho. *Perf. 13*

1145 A345 40fr blue *12.50 8.00*
1146 A345 50fr violet brown *18.00 8.00*
1147 A345 90fr orange *18.00 8.00*
1148 A345 100fr green blue *18.00 8.00*
1149 A345 115fr gray *20.00 8.00*
1150 A345 205fr brown *25.00 8.00*
Nos. 1145-1150 (6) *48.00*

A352

Designs: 90fr, Aframomum africanum. 205fr, Gambeya lacuurtiana (37x24mm). 300fr, Landolphia jumeli.

Perf. 13½x13¼, 13 (#1152)

1998 Litho.

1151 A352 90fr multi *10.00*
1152 A352 205fr multi — *10.00*
1153 A352 300fr multi *10.00*
Nos. 1151-1153 (3) *30.00*

No. 1153 has denomination in yellow.

No. 732A Overprinted

No. 929 Overprinted

1998 Litho. *Perf. 13*

1155 A244 205fr multi — —
1156 A309 300fr multi — —

An additional stamp was issued in this set. The editors would like to examine them.

Nos. 732B, 804, 854, 855, 929, 963, 1066, 1074, 1118, 1133D and 1133J Overprinted Like

Perfs. as before, Perf. 14 (#1164), Perf. 13½x13¼ (#1170)

Methods as before, Litho. (#1164, 1170)

1998

1157 A274 60fr multi (#804)
1159 A345 100fr green blue (#1118)
1164 A348b 255fr multi (#1133D)
1165 A309 300fr multi (#929)
1166 A316 300fr multi (#963) —
1167 A335 300fr multi (#1066)
a. Overprint reading horizontally
1168 A337 300fr multi (#1074)
1169 A348g 300fr multi (#1133J) — —
1170 A244 300fr multi (#732B) — —
a. Overprint reading horizontally — —
1172 A292 360fr multi (#854) — —
a. Inverted overprint — —
1173 A292 400fr multi (#855) — —

Numbers have been reserved for additional overprinted stamps. Overprint reads horizontally on Nos. 1157, 1159, 1166, 1169, 1172 and 1173, vertically reading down on Nos. 1164, 1167, 1168 and 1170, and vertically reading up on No. 1165. No. 1170 has white denomination.

1998 World Cup Soccer Championships, France — A358

Designs: 90fr, Netherlands, 4th place. 205fr, Croatia, bronze medal. 300fr, Brazil, silver medal. 500fr, France, gold medal.

1998, Nov. 16 Litho. *Perf. 13x13¼*

1175-1178 A358 Set of 4 12.00 5.00

Masks — A359

90fr, Kwele wood mask. 150fr, Kwele wood mask. No. 1181, Teke/Tsangui wood mask. No. 1182, Kuyu wood mask.

Perf. 13¼x13½

1998, Nov. 20 Litho.

1179 A359 90fr multicolored .90 .40
1180 A359 150fr multicolored 1.20 .70
1181 A359 205fr multicolored 1.20 1.00
1182 A359 205fr multicolored 1.20 1.00
Nos. 1179-1182 (4) 4.50 3.10

No. 732B Overprinted

Type I — Unserifed Upper and Lower Case Letters, 7x3mm

Type II — Serifed Upper and Lower Case Letters, 12x3mm

Type III — Upper Case Letters, 9x2mm

Methods and Perfs as Before

1999 ?

1183 A244 300fr multi (I) — —
1184 A244 300fr multi (II) — —
1185 A244 300fr multi (III) — —

Nos. 1118, 1119 Overprinted Like No. 1149 But With Wider "G" In Overprint

Method and Perf. As Before

1999 ?

1185A A345 100fr green blue —
1185B A345 115fr gray —

Nos. 934, 975, 995B, 1082, 1133I, C342-C343 Overprinted Like No. 1157

Methods as Before, Litho. (#1204)

1999 ? *Perf. as Before, 12½ (#1204)*

1187 AP120 200fr multi (#C342) — —
1188 AP120 200fr multi (#C343) — —
a. Horiz. pair, #1187-1188, + central label — —
1191 A318 200fr multi (#975) — —
1192 A321a 200fr multi (#995C) — —
1199 A310 300fr multi (#934) — —
1201 A339 300fr multi (#1082) — —
1204 A348f 300fr multi (#1133I) — —

Overprint reads horizontally on No. 1204, horizontally and inverted on Nos. 1187-1188, vertically reading down on Nos. 1191 and 1199, and vertically reading up on Nos. 1192 and 1201.

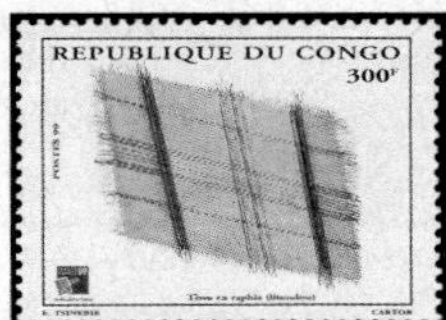

PhilexFrance 99 — A360

Design: 205fr, Raffia cloth with tassels. 300fr, Woven raffia cloth.

1999, July 2 Litho. *Perf. 13x13¼*

1211 A360 205fr multi 2.00 1.00
1212 A360 300fr multi 2.50 1.50

First French Postage Stamp, 150th Anniv. A361

Litho. With Hologram

1999 *Perf. 13x13¼*

1213 A361 300fr multi 2.50 2.50

Central African Economic and Monetary Community Week — A363

Designs: 90fr, Map and flags. 205fr, Map and circle of flags.

1999 Litho. *Perf. 14½*

1227 A363 90fr multi — *5.00*
1228 A363 205fr multi — —

Additional stamps may exist in this set. The editors would like to examine any examples.

Third Pan-African Music Festival — A364

Designs: 120fr, Emblem. 270fr, Map of Africa with drummers.

2001, Aug. 4 Litho. *Perf. 13½x13*

1229-1230 A364 Set of 2 3.25 3.25

Independence, 40th Anniv. — A365

Designs: 90fr, Dove, vine, map, hands, people. 205fr, Tools, clasped and opened hands, map.

2001, Nov. 15 Litho. *Perf. 13¼x13*

1231-1232 A365 Set of 2 *30.00* —

Birds — A366

Designs: 90fr, Egretta garzetta. No. 1234, Ardea cenerea. No. 1234A, Egretta garzetta (white bird). 205fr, Ardea purpurea. No. 1235, Ciconia nigra. No. 1235A, Ciconia ciconia.

2001 *Perf. 13¼*

1233 A366 90fr multi — —
1234 A366 120fr multi — —
1234A A366 120fr multi — —
1234B A366 205fr multi — —
1235 A366 270fr multi — —
1235A A366 270fr multi — —

Type of A345 Inscribed "REPUBLIQUE DU CONGO" Overprinted "LEGAL" Like No. 1145

2001 ? Litho. *Perf. 13*

1236 A345 90fr blue — —
1236A A345 205fr green blue —

Fruit — A367

Designs: 40fr, Mbila esobe, horiz. 50fr, Ikami, horiz. 70fr, Tsiat. 80fr, Bamou, horiz. 120fr, Malombo, horiz. 270fr, Ntondolo. 380fr, Tsia. 1500fr, Ntondolo.

2002, June 25 Litho. *Perf. 13½*

1237 A367 40fr multi — —
1238 A367 50fr multi — —
1239 A367 70fr multi — —
1240 A367 80fr multi — —
1241 A367 120fr multi — —
1242 A367 270fr multi — —
1242A A367 380fr multi — —
1242B A367 1500fr multi — —

Birds — A368

Designs: 40fr, Calao (hornbill). 80fr, Cigogne blanche (white stork). 120fr, Grue cendrée (gray crane). 270fr, Marabout.

2002, July 23 *Perf. 13½x13*

1243-1246 A368 Set of 4 — —

Elephants A369

Designs; 120fr, Mammoth. 270fr, Elephant on savannah, horiz. 350fr, Elephant, horiz. 500fr, Forest elephant near lake.

Perf. 13¼x13, 13x13¼

2003, June 20

1247-1250 A369 Set of 4 — —

Flowers — A370

Designs: 120fr, Muflier (antirrhinum). 270fr, Pivoine (peony). 400fr, Petunia. 600fr, Mauve (mallow), horiz.

2003, July 6

1251-1254 A370 Set of 4 8.00 8.00

Moringa Olifera — A371

Highlighted portion: 30fr, Bark. 70fr, Root. 90fr, Leaves. 115fr, Seeds and open pod. 120fr, Flowers. 360fr, Pod.

2005, Feb. 3 Litho. ***Perf. 13¼x13***

1255-1260 A371 Set of 6 5.00 5.00

Dated 2004.

Fruits — A372

Designs: 120fr, Custard apple. 200fr, Tangerine. 270fr, Guava. 360fr, Grapefruit.

2005, July 13 Litho. ***Perf. 13½***

1261-1264 A372 Set of 4 7.25 7.25

Albert Einstein (1879-1955), Physicist — A373

2005, Aug. 17 Litho. ***Perf. 13¼x13***

1265 A373 400fr multi 4.25 4.25

A374

Brazzaville, 125th Anniv. — A375

2005, Oct. 3 ***Perf. 13¼x13***

1266 A374 120fr multi 1.10 1.10

Perf. 13½x13¼

1267 A375 360fr multi 3.25 3.25

Pope Benedict XVI A376

Pope Benedict XVI: 360fr, Waving. 500fr, Holding crucifix.

2005, Nov. 28 ***Perf. 13¼x13½***

1268-1269 A376 Set of 2 4.25 3.75

Coat of Arms — A377

Colors: 30fr, Dark brown. 40fr, Red. 50fr, Bister brown. 60fr, Dark green.

2006, Jan. 4 Litho. ***Perf. 13½***

1270-1273 A377 Set of 4 — —

Denis Sassou-Nguesso, President of African Union — A378

2006, Mar. 14 Litho. ***Perf. 13x13¼***

1274 A378 500fr multi 2.40 2.40

Léopold Sédar Senghor (1906-2001), First President of Senegal — A379

2006, May 15

1275 A379 360fr multi 1.75 1.75

Animals — A380

Designs: 40fr, Crocodile. 50fr, Pangolin, horiz. 60fr, Lizard, horiz. 120fr, Cat, horiz.

2006 Litho. ***Perf. 13¼x13, 13x13¼***

1276-1279 A380 Set of 4 5.00 2.50

World Religion Day A381

2007 ***Perf. 13½x13***

1280 A381 120fr multi 1.20 1.00

Opening of Pierre Savorgnan de Brazza Memorial, Brazzaville A382

Memorial and: 120fr, Statue. 500fr, Photo of Savorgnan de Brazza. 1000fr, Statue, diff.

2008 ***Perf. 13¼***

1281-1283 A382 Set of 3 7.00 7.00

Centenary Emblem — A382a

Old Church — A382b

Vehicle on Dirt Road — A382c

2009 Litho. ***Perf. 13x13¼***

1283A A382a 90fr multi — —
1283B A382b 360fr multi — —
1283C A382b 395fr multi — —
1283D A382c 1500fr multi — —

Protestant Evangelization in Congo, cent.

A383

Pan-African Postal Union, 30th Anniv. — A384

2010 Litho. ***Perf. 13½x13¼***

1284 A383 120fr multi 1.00 1.00
1285 A384 360fr multi 3.00 3.00

50th Anniv. Emblem A385

President and Flag of Republic of Congo A386

President and Flag of People's Republic of Congo A387

President Denis Sassou-Nguesso and Flag of Republic of Congo — A388

President: No. 1287, Abbé Fulbert Youlou (1917-72). No. 1288, Alphonse Massamba-Débat (1921-77). No. 1288A, Marien Ngouabi (1938-77). No. 1289, Joachim Yhombi-Opango. No. 1290, Denis Sassou-Nguesso. No. 1291, Pascal Lissouba.

2010 Litho. ***Perf. 13½***

1286 A385 120fr multi — —
1287 A386 270fr multi — —
1288 A386 270fr multi — —
1288A A387 270fr multi — —
1289 A387 270fr multi — —
1290 A387 270fr multi — —
1291 A386 270fr multi — —

1292 A388 270fr multi — —
a. Souvenir sheet of 8, #1286-1288, 1288A, 1289-1292 — —

Republic of Congo, 50th anniv. Additional stamps may exist in this set. The editors would like to examine any examples.

15th Francophonie Summit, Dakar — A389

Designs: 120fr, Building, Pres. Denis Sassou-Nguesso. 360fr, Conferees on sofa.

2014 Litho. *Perf. 13¼x13*
1293 A389 120fr multi — —
1294 A389 360fr multi — —

Miniature Sheet

Diplomatic Relations Between Congo Republic and People's Republic of China, 50th Anniv. — A390

No. 1295: a, 120fr, Congolese and Chinese masks. b, 120fr, Gorilla and Giant panda. c, 240fr, Building, flags of Congo Republic and People's Republic of China. d, 240fr, Congo Republic #698, building, sculpture with Chinese inscription. e, 360fr, Meeting of Chinese Chairman Mao Zedong and Congo Republic President. f, 500fr, Meeting of Chinese President Xi Jinping and Congolese Pres. Denis Sassou-Nguesso, building, and flags of Congo Republic and People's Republic of China.

2014, Feb. 22 Litho. *Perf. 12*
1295 A390 Sheet of 6, #a-f — —

11th African Games, Brazzaville — A391

2015 Litho. *Perf. 13¼x13*
1296 A391 200fr multi — —

SEMI-POSTAL STAMPS

Anti-Malaria Issue
Common Design Type

1962, Apr. 7 Engr. *Perf. 12½x12*
B3 CD108 25fr + 5fr bister 1.40 1.00

Freedom from Hunger Issue
Common Design Type

1963, Mar. 21 Unwmk. *Perf. 13*
B4 CD112 25fr + 5fr vio bl, bl grn & brn 1.40 1.00

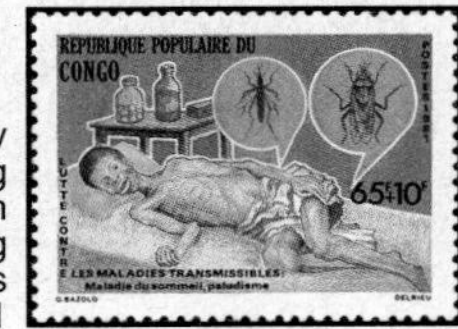

Boy Suffering from Sleeping Sickness SP1

Fight Against Communicable Diseases; 40fr+5fr, Examination, treatment, vert.

1981, June 6 Litho. *Perf. 13*
B5 SP1 40fr + 5fr multi .60 .25
B6 SP1 65fr + 10fr multi 1.00 .30

IYD Type of 1981

1981, June 29 *Perf. 12½*
B7 A192 75fr + 5fr multi .90 .35

AIR POST STAMPS

Olympic Games Issue
French Equatorial Africa No. C37 Surcharged in Red Like Chad No. C1

1960 Unwmk. Engr. *Perf. 13*
C1 AP8 250fr on 500fr grnsh blk, blk & sl 8.00 8.00

17th Olympic Games, Rome, 8/25-9/11.

Helicrysum Mechowiam — AP1

Flowers: 200fr, Cogniauxia podolaena. 500fr, Thesium tencio.

1961, Sept. 28 Engr. *Perf. 13*
C2 AP1 100fr grn, lil & yel 2.90 1.60
C3 AP1 200fr bl grn, yel & brn 4.75 2.40
C4 AP1 500fr brn red, yel & sl grn 14.50 6.00
Nos. C2-C4 (3) 22.15 10.00

Air Afrique Issue
Common Design Type

1961, Nov. 25 Unwmk. *Perf. 13*
C5 CD107 50fr lil rose, sl grn & grn 1.75 .90

Loading Timber, Pointe-Noire Harbor — AP2

1962, June 8 Photo. *Perf. 12½x12*
C6 AP2 50fr multicolored 1.50 .90

Opening of the Intl. Fair and Exhib., Pointe-Noire, June 8-11.

Abidjan Games — AP3

1962, July 21 *Perf. 12x12½*
C7 AP3 100fr Basketball 2.50 1.25

Costus Spectabilis AP4

Design: 250fr, Mountain acanthus.

1963 Unwmk. *Perf. 13*
C8 AP4 100fr multicolored 4.00 1.75
C9 AP4 250fr multicolored 8.00 3.25

Issued: 100fr, 8/9; 250fr, 11/4.

Brazzaville City Hall and Pres. Fulbert Youlou — AP4a

1963, Aug. Photo. *Perf. 13x12*
C10 AP4a 100fr multicolored 150.00 125.00

African Postal Union Issue
Common Design Type

1963, Sept. 8 *Perf. 12½*
C13 CD114 85fr pur, ocher & red 1.40 .75

Air Afrique Issue, 1963
Common Design Type

Perf. 13x12

1963, Nov. 19 Unwmk. Photo.
C14 CD115 50fr multicolored 1.60 .60

Liberty Place, Brazzaville — AP5

1963, Nov. 28
C15 AP5 25fr multicolored 1.00 .40

See No. 118.

Europafrica Issue
Common Design Type

1963, Nov. 30 *Perf. 12x13*
C16 CD116 50fr gray, yel & dk brn 1.60 1.00

Timber Industry — AP6

1964, May 12 Engr. *Perf. 13*
C17 AP6 100fr grn, brn red & blk 2.50 1.10

Chiefs of State Issue

Map and Presidents of Chad, Congo, Gabon and CAR AP6a

1964, June 23 Photo. *Perf. 12½*
C18 AP6a 100fr multicolored 1.60 1.00

See note after Central African Republic No. C19.

Europafrica Issue

Sunburst, Wheat, Cogwheel and Globe — AP7

1964, July 20 *Perf. 12x13*
C19 AP7 50fr yel, Prus bl & mar 1.60 .75

See note after Cameroun No. 402.

Hammer Thrower, Olympic Flame and Stadium — AP8

50fr, 100fr, vert.

1964, July 30 Engr. *Perf. 13*
C20 AP8 25fr shown .40 .30
C21 AP8 50fr Weight lifter .75 .60
C22 AP8 100fr Volleyball 1.60 1.10
C23 AP8 200fr High jump 3.00 2.25
a. Min. sheet of 4, #C20-C23 7.25 7.25
Nos. C20-C23 (4) 5.75 4.25

18th Olympic Games, Tokyo, 10/10-25/64.

Communications Symbols — AP8a

1964, Nov. 2 Litho. ***Perf. 12½x13***

C24 AP8a 25fr dl rose & dk brn .90 .45

See note after Chad No. C19.

Town Hall, Brazzaville — AP9

1965, Jan. 30 Photo. ***Perf. 12½***

C25 AP9 100fr multicolored 1.20 .75

Coupling Hooks — AP10

1965, Feb. 27 Photo. ***Perf. 13x12***

C26 AP10 50fr multicolored 1.40 .75

Economic Europe-Africa Association.

Breguet Dial Telegraph, ITU Emblem and Telstar — AP11

1965, May 17 Engr. ***Perf. 13***

C27 AP11 100fr dk bl, ocher & brn 2.25 .75

Cent. of the ITU.

Pope John XXIII (1881-1963), St. Peter's Cathedral — AP12

Perf. 12½x13

1965, June 26 Photo. Unwmk.

C28 AP12 100fr gldn brn & multi 1.50 .75

Pres. John F. Kennedy — AP13

Portraits: 25fr on 50fr, Patrice Lumumba, premier of Congo Republic (ex-Belgian). 50fr, Sir Winston Churchill. 80fr, Barthélémy Boganda, premier of Central African Republic.

1965, June ***Perf. 12½***

C29 AP13 25fr on 50fr dk brn & red .50 .40
 a. Surcharge omitted 35.00 35.00
C30 AP13 50fr dk brn & yel grn 1.00 1.00
C31 AP13 80fr dk brn & bl 1.75 1.50
C32 AP13 100fr dk brn & org yel 2.60 2.25
 a. Min. sheet of 4, #C29-C32 6.25 6.25
 Nos. C29-C32 (4) 5.85 5.15

A second miniature sheet contains one each of Nos. C29a, C30-C32. Value, $50.

Issued: 25fr, 80fr, 6/25; 50fr, 100fr, No. C32a, 6/26.

Log Rolling — AP14

1965, Aug. 14 Engr. ***Perf. 13***

C33 AP14 50fr grn, brn & red brn 1.60 .75

Issued to publicize national unity.

World Map and Symbols of Agriculture and Industry — AP15

1965, Oct. 18 Engr. ***Perf. 13***

C34 AP15 50fr dk bl, blk, brn & org 1.40 .90

International Cooperation Year, 1965.

Abraham Lincoln — AP16

1965, Dec. 15 Photo. ***Perf. 13***

C35 AP16 90fr pink & multi 1.40 .60

Centenary of death of Abraham Lincoln.

Charles de Gaulle, Torch and Map of Africa — AP17

1966, Feb. 28 Engr. ***Perf. 13***

C36 AP17 500fr dk red, dk grn & dk red brn 30.00 26.00

22nd anniv. of the Brazzaville Conf.

D-1 Satellite over Brazzaville Space Tracking Station — AP18

1966, May 15 Engr. ***Perf. 13***

C37 AP18 150fr blk, dl red & bl grn 2.25 1.25

Grain, Atom Symbol and Map of Africa and Europe — AP19

1966, July 20 Photo. ***Perf. 12x13***

C38 AP19 50fr multicolored 1.10 .75

See note after Gabon No. C46.

Pres. Massamba-Debat and President's Palace — AP20

3rd anniv. of the Revolution: 30fr, Robespierre and storming of the Bastille. 50fr, Lenin and storming of the Winter Palace.

1966, Aug. 15 Photo. ***Perf. 12x12½***

C39 AP20 25fr multicolored .45 .30
C40 AP20 30fr multicolored .65 .30
C41 AP20 50fr multicolored 1.60 .50
 a. Souv. sheet of 3, #C39-C41 2.25 2.25
 Nos. C39-C41 (3) 2.70 1.10

Air Afrique Issue, 1966

Common Design Type

1966, Aug. 31 Photo. ***Perf. 13***

C42 CD123 30fr lilac, lemon & blk 1.00 .25

Dr. Albert Schweitzer — AP21

1966, Sept. 4 Photo. ***Perf. 12½***

C43 AP21 100fr red, blk, bl & lil 2.25 1.25

Issued to honor Dr. Albert Schweitzer (1875-1965), medical missionary.

Crab, Microscope and Pagoda — AP22

1966, Dec. 26 Photo. ***Perf. 13***

C44 AP22 100fr multicolored 1.75 1.00

9th Intl. Anticancer Cong., Tokyo. 10/23-29.

AP23

Birds: 50fr, Social Weaver. 75fr, European Bee-eater. 100fr, Lilac-breasted roller. 150fr, Regal sunbird. 200fr, Crowned cranes. 250fr, Secretary bird. 300fr, Knysna touraco.

1967 Photo. ***Perf. 13***

C45 AP23 50fr multicolored 1.60 .75
C46 AP23 75fr multicolored 3.25 1.00
C47 AP23 100fr multicolored 3.25 1.00
C48 AP23 150fr multicolored 4.25 2.25
C49 AP23 200fr multicolored 7.50 2.50
C50 AP23 250fr multicolored 9.50 3.00
C51 AP23 300fr multicolored 13.50 5.00
 Nos. C45-C51 (7) 42.85 15.50

Issued: Nos. C45-C47, 2/13; others, 6/20.

Shackled Hands AP24

1967, May 24 Photo. ***Perf. 12½x13***

C52 AP24 500fr multicolored 8.00 3.00

Issued for African Liberation Day.

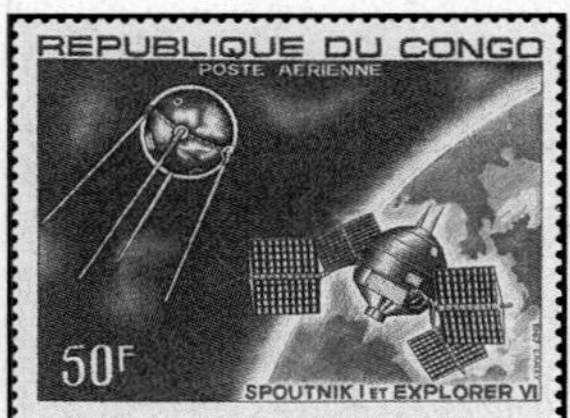

Sputnik 1, Explorer 6 and Earth — AP25

Space Craft: 75fr, Ranger 6, Lunik 2 and moon. 100fr, Mars 1, Mariner 4 and Mars. 200fr, Gemini, Vostok and earth.

1967, Aug. 1 Engr. *Perf. 13*

C53 AP25 50fr multicolored	.60	.30
C54 AP25 75fr multicolored	1.10	.35
C55 AP25 100fr multicolored	1.60	.60
C56 AP25 200fr multicolored	2.75	1.50
Nos. C53-C56 (4)	6.05	2.75

Space explorations.

African Postal Union Issue, 1967

Common Design Type

1967, Sept. 9 Engr. *Perf. 13*

C57 CD124 100fr ver, ol & emer 1.60 .60

Boy Scouts, Tents and Jamboree Emblem — AP26

Design: 70c, Borah Peak, Idaho; tents, Scout sign and Jamboree emblem.

1967, Sept. 29

C58 AP26 50fr multicolored	.80	.30
C59 AP26 70fr multicolored	1.20	.50

12th Boy Scout World Jamboree, Farragut State Park, ID, Aug. 1-9.

Sikorsky S-43 and Map of Africa — AP27

1967, Oct. 2 Photo. *Perf. 13*

C60 AP27 30fr multicolored .90 .30

30th anniv. of the 1st airmail connection by Aeromaritime Lines from Casablanca to Pointe-Noire.

Men of Four Races Dancing on Globe — AP28

1968, Feb 8 Engr. *Perf. 13*

C61 AP28 70fr dk brn, ultra & emer 1.50 .60

Friendship among peoples.

The Oath of the Horatii, by Jacques Louis David — AP29

Paintings: 25fr, On the Barricades, by Delacroix. No. C63, Grandfather and Grandson, by Ghirlandajo, vert. No. C64, The Demolition of the Bastille, by Hubert Robert. 200fr, Negro Woman Arranging Peonies, by Jean F. Bazille.

1968 Photo. *Perf. 12x12½, 12½x12*

C62 AP29 25fr multicolored	1.75	.35
C63 AP29 30fr multicolored	.90	.30
C64 AP29 30fr multicolored	1.75	.50
C65 AP29 100fr multicolored	2.25	.90
C66 AP29 200fr multicolored	5.00	1.75
Nos. C62-C66 (5)	11.65	3.80

Issue dates: Nos. C62, C64, Aug. 15. Nos. C63, C65-C66, Mar. 20.

See Nos. C78-C81, C111-C115.

Early Automobile Type

1968, July 29 Photo. *Perf. 13x12½*

C67 A50 150fr Ford, 1915	3.50	1.75
C68 A50 200fr Citroen, 1922	5.25	1.75

Europafrica Issue

Square Knot — AP30

1968, July 20 Photo. *Perf. 13*

C69 AP30 50fr multicolored 1.50 .50

5th anniv. of the economic agreement between the European Economic Community and the African and Malgache Union.

Martin Luther King, Jr. — AP31

1968, Aug. 5 *Perf. 12½*

C70 AP31 50fr lt grn, Prus grn & blk 1.60 .40

Robert F. Kennedy — AP32

1968, Sept. 30 Photo. *Perf. 13x12½*

C71 AP32 50fr dp car, ap grn & blk .85 .40

Running — AP33

Olympic Rings and: 20fr, Soccer, vert. 60fr, Boxing, vert. 85fr, High jump.

1968, Dec. 27 Engr. *Perf. 13*

C72 AP33 5fr emer, brt bl & choc	.25	.25
C73 AP33 20fr dk bl, brn & dk grn	.45	.25
C74 AP33 60fr mar, brt grn & choc	.90	.60
C75 AP33 85fr blk, car rose & choc	1.75	.85
Nos. C72-C75 (4)	3.35	1.95

19th Olympic Games, Mexico City, 10/12-27.

PHILEXAFRIQUE Issue

G. De Gueidan, by Nicolas de Largillière AP34

1968, Dec. 30 Photo. *Perf. 12½*

C76 AP34 100fr pink & multi 2.75 1.75

Issued to publicize PHILEXAFRIQUE, Philatelic Exhibition, in Abidjan, Feb. 14-23. Printed with alternating pink label.

See Nos. C89-C93.

2nd PHILEXAFRIQUE Issue

Common Design Type

Design: 50fr, Middle Congo No. 72 and Pointe-Noire harbor.

1969, Feb. 14 Engr. *Perf. 13*

C77 CD128 50fr car rose, sl grn & bis brn 2.00 1.75

Painting Type of 1968

Paintings: 25fr, Battle of Rivoli, by Carle Vernet. 50fr, Battle of Marengo, by Jacques Augustin Pajou. 75fr, Battle of Friedland, by Horace Vernet. 100fr, Battle of Jena, by Charles Thevenin.

1969, May 20 Photo. *Perf. 12x12½*

C78 AP29 25fr vio bl & multi	1.25	.45
C79 AP29 50fr cop red & multi	1.75	.80
C80 AP29 75fr grn & multi	3.00	1.10
C81 AP29 100fr brn & multi	5.00	1.40
Nos. C78-C81 (4)	11.00	3.75

Bicentenary of birth of Napoleon I.

Ernesto Ché Guevara — AP35

1969, June 10 Photo. *Perf. 12½*

C82 AP35 90fr brn, org & blk 1.30 .50

Issued in memory of Ernesto Ché Guevara (1928-1967), Cuban revolutionist.

Doll, Train and Space Toy — AP36

1969, June 20 Engr. *Perf. 13*

C83 AP36 100fr mag, org & gray 1.75 .75

International Toy Fair, Nuremberg, Germany.

Europafrica Issue

Ribbon Tied Around Bar — AP37

1969, Aug. 5 Photo. *Perf. 13x12*

C84 AP37 50fr bl grn, lil & blk .90 .35

See note after Chad No. C11.

Souvenir Sheet

Armstrong, Aldrin and Collins — AP38

Design: No. C85b, Blast-off from Moon.

Embossed on Gold Foil

1969, Sept. 15 *Imperf.*

C85 AP38 1000fr #a-b 30.00 27.50

See note after Algeria No. 427. No. C85 contains one each of Nos. C85a and C85b with simulated perforations.

Painter, Poto-Poto School — AP39

150fr, Sculpture lesson (man, infant and sculpture). 200fr, Potter working on vase.

1970, Feb. 20 Engr. *Perf. 13*

C86 AP39 100fr multicolored	2.25	.60
C87 AP39 150fr multicolored	3.00	.95
C88 AP39 200fr multicolored	3.75	1.75
Nos. C86-C88 (3)	9.00	3.30

Painting Type (Philexafrique)

Paintings: 150fr, Child with Cherries, by John Russell. 200fr, Erasmus, by Hans Holbein the Younger. 250fr, "Silence" (head), by Bernardino Luini. 300fr, Scene from the Massacre of Scio, by Delacroix. 500fr, The Capture of Constantinople by the Crusaders, by Delacroix.

1970 Photo. *Perf. 12½*

C89 AP34 150fr lil & multi	4.50	1.50
C90 AP34 200fr multicolored	5.75	1.75
C91 AP34 250fr brn & multi	6.25	2.25
C92 AP34 300fr multicolored	8.00	3.25
C93 AP34 500fr brn & multi	13.50	4.50
Nos. C89-C93 (5)	38.00	13.25

Aurichalcite — AP40

1970, Mar. 20
C94 AP40 100fr shown 5.25 1.75
C95 AP40 150fr Dioptase 8.00 2.50

Lenin — AP41

1970, June 25 Photo. *Perf. 12½*
C96 AP41 45fr shown 1.00 .35
C97 AP41 75fr Lenin, seated 1.75 .50

Centenary of the birth of Lenin (1870-1924), Russian communist leader.

Karl Marx — AP42

Design: No. C99, Friedrich Engels.

1970, July 10 Engr. *Perf. 13*
C98 AP42 50fr emer, dk brn & dk red 1.40 .35
C99 AP42 50fr ultra, dk brn & dk red 1.40 .35

Karl Marx (1818-1883) and Friedrich Engels (1820-1895), German socialist writers.

Otto Lilienthal's Glider, 1891 — AP43

Designs: 50fr, "Spirit of St. Louis," Lindbergh's first transatlantic solo flight, 1927. 70fr, Sputnik 1, first satellite in space. 90fr, First man on the moon, Apollo 11, 1969.

1970, Sept. 5 Engr. *Perf. 13*
C100 AP43 45fr dp car, bl & ol bis 1.00 .30
C101 AP43 50fr emer, sl grn & brn 1.00 .35
C102 AP43 70fr brt bl, ol bis & dp car 1.25 .50
C103 AP43 90fr brn, bl & ol gray 1.90 .75
Nos. C100-C103 (4) 5.15 1.90

Forerunners of space exploration.

Saint on Horseback AP44

Designs from Stained Glass Windows, Brazzaville Cathedral: 150fr, Saint with staff. 250fr, The Elevation of the Host, from rose window.

1970, Dec. 10 Photo. *Perf. 12½*
C104 AP44 100fr multicolored 1.25 .50
C105 AP44 150fr multicolored 1.75 .85
C106 AP44 250fr multicolored 3.00 1.75
a. Souv. sheet of 3, #C104-C106 6.75 6.75
Nos. C104-C106 (3) 6.00 3.10

Christmas 1970.

Marilyn Monroe and NYC — AP45

Portraits: 150fr, Martine Carol and Paris. 200fr, Erich von Stroheim and Vienna. 250fr, Sergei Eisenstein and Moscow.

1971, Mar. 16 Engr. *Perf. 13*
C107 AP45 100fr brt grn, red brn & ultra 7.00 .50
C108 AP45 150fr brn, brt lil & ultra 7.00 .75
C109 AP45 200fr choc & ultra 7.00 1.10
C110 AP45 250fr brt grn, brn vio & ultra 7.00 1.25
Nos. C107-C110 (4) 28.00 3.60

History of motion pictures.

Painting Type of 1968

Paintings: 100fr, Christ Carrying Cross, by Paolo Veronese. 150fr, Christ on the Cross, Burgundian School, 1500, vert. 200fr, Descent from the Cross, by Rogier van der Weyden. 250fr, Christ Laid in the Tomb, Flemish School, 1500, vert. 500fr, Resurrection, by Hans Memling, vert.

1971, Apr. 26 Photo. *Perf. 13*
C111 AP29 100fr green & multi 1.75 .75
C112 AP29 150fr green & multi 2.75 .90
C113 AP29 200fr green & multi 4.00 1.10
C114 AP29 250fr green & multi 4.50 1.60
C115 AP29 500fr green & multi 10.00 3.00
Nos. C111-C115 (5) 23.00 7.35

Easter 1971.

Map of Africa and Telecommunications System — AP46

1971, June 18 Photo. *Perf. 12½*
C116 AP46 70fr bl, gray & dk brn .80 .30
C117 AP46 85fr bl, lil rose & dk brn 1.25 .35
C118 AP46 90fr grn, yel & dk brn 1.60 .70
Nos. C116-C118 (3) 3.65 1.35

Pan-African telecommunications system.

Globe and Waves — AP47

1971, June 19
C119 AP47 65fr lt bl & multi .80 .30

3rd World Telecommunications Day.

Japanese Mask and Play — AP48

Design: 150fr, Japanese and African women, symbolic leaves.

1971, June 28 Engr. *Perf. 13*
C120 AP48 75fr lil, blk & mag 1.00 .70
C121 AP48 150fr dk brn, brn red & red lil 1.60 1.10

PHILATOKYO '71 International Stamp Exhibition, Tokyo, Apr. 20-30.

Olympic Torch and Rings — AP49

350fr, Olympic rings and various sports.

1971, July 20 Engr. *Perf. 13*
C122 AP49 150fr multi 1.90 .95
C123 AP49 350fr multi, horiz. 4.50 2.50

Pre-Olympic Year, 1971.

Scout Emblem, Japanese Dragon and African Carved Canoe — AP50

Designs (Boy Scout Emblem and): 90fr, Japanese mask and African boy, vert. 100fr, Japanese woman and African drummer, vert. 250fr, Congolese mask.

1971, Aug. 25
C124 AP50 85fr multicolored 1.10 .30
C125 AP50 90fr multicolored 1.25 .35
C126 AP50 100fr multicolored 1.60 .45
C127 AP50 250fr multicolored 3.25 .90
Nos. C124-C127 (4) 7.20 2.00

13th Boy Scout World Jamboree, Asagiri Plain, Japan, Aug. 2-10.

Olympic Rings and Running — AP51

Designs (Olympic Rings and): 85fr, Hurdles. 90fr, Weight lifting, boxing, discus, running, javelin. 100fr, Wrestling. 150fr, Boxing.

1971, Sept. 30
C128 AP51 75fr plum, bl & dk brn .75 .35
C129 AP51 85fr scar, sl & dk brn .85 .35
C130 AP51 90fr vio bl & dk brn 1.10 .60
C131 AP51 100fr brn & slate 1.40 .60
C132 AP51 150fr grn, red & dk brn 2.40 1.00
Nos. C128-C132 (5) 6.50 2.90

75th anniv. of the 1st modern Olympic Games.

Congo No. C36 and de Gaulle — AP52

Design: No. C135, Charles de Gaulle.

1971, Nov. 9
C133 AP52 500fr slate grn & multi 18.00 15.00

Pres. Marien Ngouabi's Tribute to de Gaulle — AP53

Lithographed; Gold Embossed
Perf. 12½
C134 AP53 1000fr gold, grn & red 27.50 20.00
C135 AP53 1000fr gold, grn & red 27.50 20.00
a. Pair, #C134-C135 55.00 55.00

Charles de Gaulle (1890-1970), president of France.

African Postal Union Issue, 1971
Common Design Type

Design: 100fr, Allegory of Congo Republic (woman) and UAMPT Building, Brazzaville.

1971, Nov. 13 Photo. *Perf. 13x13½*
C136 CD135 100fr bl & multi 1.60 .75

Flag of Congo Republic and "Revolution" — AP54

1971, Nov. 30
C137 AP54 100fr red & multi 1.75 .60

8th anniversary of revolution.

Workers and Flag — AP55

40fr, Flag of Congo Republic and sun.

1971, Dec. 31 Photo. *Perf. 13x12½*

C138 AP55 30fr multicolored .75 .30
C139 AP55 40fr red & multi 1.50 .50

2nd anniv. of founding of Congolese Labor Party (No. C138), and adoption of red flag (No. C139).

Book Year Emblem — AP56

1972, June 3 Litho. *Perf. 12½*

C140 AP56 50fr red, grn & yel 1.00 .40

International Book Year 1972.

Congolese Soccer Team — AP57

No. C142, Captain of winning team and cup, vert.

1973, Feb. 22 Photo. *Perf. 13*

C141 AP57 100fr ultra, red & blk 1.50 .75
C142 AP57 100fr red, yel & blk 1.50 .75

Girl Holding Bird, Environment Emblem — AP58

1973, Mar. 5 Engr.

C143 AP58 85fr org, slate grn & bl 1.75 .90

UN Conference on Human Environment, Stockholm, Sweden, June 5-16, 1972.

Miles Davis AP59

Designs: 140fr, Ella Fitzgerald. 160fr, Count Basie. 175fr, John Coltrane.

1973, Mar. 5 Photo. *Perf. 13x13½*

C144 AP59 125fr multicolored 3.50 .95
C145 AP59 140fr multicolored 3.50 1.00
C146 AP59 160fr multicolored 4.50 1.50
C147 AP59 175fr multicolored 4.50 1.50
Nos. C144-C147 (4) 16.00 4.95

Black American jazz musicians.

Olympic Rings, Hurdling — AP60

150fr, Pole vault, vert. 250fr, Wrestling.

1973, Mar. 15 Engr. *Perf. 13*

C148 AP60 100fr shown 1.10 .60
C149 AP60 150fr multi 1.75 .90
C150 AP60 250fr multi 2.75 1.50
Nos. C148-C150 (3) 5.60 3.00

20th Olympic Games, Munich, 8/26-9/11/72.

Refinery and Storage Tanks, Djéno — AP61

Designs: 230fr, Off-shore drilling platform, vert. 240fr, Workers assembling drill, vert. 260fr, Off-shore drilling installation.

1973, Mar. 20

C151 AP61 180fr red, bl & indigo 3.25 1.50
C152 AP61 230fr red, bl & blk 4.00 1.50
C153 AP61 240fr red, ind & brn 4.50 1.60
C154 AP61 260fr red, bl & blk 7.25 2.25
Nos. C151-C154 (4) 19.00 6.85

Oil installations, Pointe-Noire.

Astronauts, Landing Module and Lunar Rover on Moon — AP62

1973, Mar. 31

C155 AP62 250fr multicolored 4.00 1.75

Apollo 17 US moon mission, 12/7-19/72.

ITU Emblem, Symbols of Communications AP63

1973, May 24 Engr. *Perf. 13*

C156 AP63 120fr multicolored 2.25 .90

5th International Telecommunications Day.

White Horse, by Delacroix — AP64

Designs: Paintings by Eugene Delacroix.

1973, June 30 Photo. *Perf. 13*

C157 AP64 150fr shown 2.25 1.50
C158 AP64 250fr Lion sleeping 5.00 2.40
C159 AP64 300fr Lion and tiger 5.25 2.50
Nos. C157-C159 (3) 12.50 6.40

See Nos. C169-C171.

Copernicus and Heliocentric System — AP65

1973, June 30 Engr.

C160 AP65 50fr multicolored 1.00 .45

500th anniversary of the birth of Nicolaus Copernicus (1473-1543), Polish astronomer.

Plane, Ship, Rocket, Village, Sun and Clouds — AP66

1973, July

C161 AP66 50fr red & multi 1.60 .60

Cent. of intl. meteorological cooperation.

Pres. Marien Ngouabi — AP67

1973, Aug. 12 Photo. *Perf. 13*

C162 AP67 30fr multicolored .35 .25
C163 AP67 40fr aqua & multi .45 .25
C164 AP67 75fr red & multi 1.00 .35
Nos. C162-C164 (3) 1.80 .85

10th anniversary of independence.

Stamps, Album, African Woman AP68

No. C167, Stamps in shape of map of Congo, album, globe. No. C168, Like 30fr.

1973, Aug. 12

C165 AP68 30fr pur & multi 1.90 .30
C166 AP68 40fr multicolored .25 .25
C167 AP68 100fr dk brn & multi 3.75 .80
C168 AP68 100fr ocher & multi .90 .40
Nos. C165-C168 (4) 6.80 1.75

Nos. C165, C168 for the 10th anniv. of the revolution, Nos. C166-C167 the Intl. Philatelic Exhib., Brazzaville.

Painting Type of 1973 Inscribed "EUROPAFRIQUE"

Details from "Earth and Paradise," by Jan Brueghel, the Elder: No. C169, Spotted hyena. No. C170, Leopard and lion. No. C171, Elephant and creatures.

1973, Oct. 10 Photo. *Perf. 13*

C169 AP64 100fr multi 3.00 1.50
C170 AP64 100fr multi 3.00 1.50
C171 AP64 100fr multi 3.00 1.50
Nos. C169-C171 (3) 9.00 4.50

US and Russian Spacecraft Docking — AP69

Design: 80fr, US and USSR spacecraft docked in space and emblems of 1975 joint space mission.

1973, Oct. 15 Engr. *Perf. 13*

C172 AP69 40fr bl, red & brn .50 .35
C173 AP69 80fr red, grn & bl 1.10 .50

Planned joint US and Soviet space missions.
For overprint see No. C251.

UPU Monument, Satellites, Big Dipper — AP70

1973, Nov. 20 Engr. *Perf. 13*

C174 AP70 80fr vio bl & lt bl 1.60 .50

Universal Postal Union Day.

Astronauts Working in Space — AP71

40fr, Spacecraft & Skylab docking in space.

1973, Nov. 30

C175 AP71 30fr ultra, sl grn & choc .65 .25
C176 AP71 40fr mag, org & sl grn .95 .25

Skylab, first space laboratory.

Goalkeeper, Soccer — AP72

Design: 100fr, Soccer player kicking ball.

1973, Dec. 20

C177 AP72 40fr sl grn, sepia & brn .75 .25
C178 AP72 100fr pur, red & slate grn 1.90 .75

World Soccer Cup, Munich, 1974.

John F. Kennedy (1917-1963) AP73

1973, Dec. 20 Photo. *Perf. 12½*

C179 AP73 150fr ultra, gold & blk 1.75 .90

Runners — AP74

1973, Dec. 20 Engr. *Perf. 13*

C180 AP74 40fr sl grn, red & brn .60 .25
C181 AP74 100fr red, sl grn, & brn 1.75 .75

2nd African Games, Lagos, Nigeria.

Flag over Map of Congo — AP75

1973, Dec. 31 Photo.

C182 AP75 40fr dp grn & multi .80 .25

4th anniversary of Congolese Labor Party and of the Congo Red Flag.

Soccer and Games Emblem — AP76

1974, June 20 Photo. *Perf. 13*

C183 AP76 250fr multicolored 3.75 1.90

World Cup Soccer Championship, Munich, June 13-July 7.

Astronauts Yuri A. Gagarin and Alan B. Shepard — AP77

Designs: 30fr, Space, globe, Russian and American flags with names of astronauts who perished in space. 100fr, Alexei Leonov and Neil A. Armstrong in space and on moon.

1974, June 30 Engr. *Perf. 13*

C184 AP77 30fr red, ultra & brn .45 .25
C185 AP77 40fr red, bl & brn .70 .25
C186 AP77 100fr car, grn & brn 1.60 .90
Nos. C184-C186 (3) 2.75 1.40

For overprint see No. C254.

Soccer Game Superimposed on Ball — AP78

1974, July 31 Photo. *Perf. 13*

C187 AP78 250fr multicolored 3.50 1.75

Germany's victory in World Cup Soccer Championship.

Link-up Emblem, Stages of Link-up — AP79

300fr, Spacecraft docking over globe.

1974, Aug. 8 Engr. *Perf. 13*

C188 AP79 200fr pur, bl & red 2.25 1.10
C189 AP79 300fr multi, horiz. 3.50 1.50

Russo-American space cooperation.
For overprint see No. C255.

Symbols of Communications, UPU Emblem — AP80

1974, Aug. 10

C190 AP80 500fr blk & red 6.75 3.00

Centenary of Universal Postal Union.
For surcharge see No. C194.

Lenin and Pendulum Trace Pattern — AP81

1974, Sept. 16 Engr. *Perf. 13*

C191 AP81 150fr multicolored 2.10 1.10

Lenin (1870-1924).

Churchill and Order of the Garter AP82

Marconi and Wireless Telegraph AP83

1974, Oct. 1 Litho. *Perf. 13*

C192 AP82 200fr lt grn & multi 2.50 1.25
C193 AP83 200fr lt ultra & multi 2.50 1.25

No. C190 Srchd. in Violet Blue with New Value, 2 Bars and "9 OCTOBER 1974"

1974, Oct. 9

C194 AP80 300fr on 500fr multi 4.25 2.75

Universal Postal Union Day.

UDEAC Issue

Presidents and Flags of Cameroun, CAR, Gabon and Congo — AP83a

1974, Dec. 8 Photo. *Perf. 13*

C195 AP83a 100fr gold & multi 1.60 .50

See note after Cameroun No. 595.

Regatta at Argenteuil, by Monet — AP84

Impressionist Paintings: 40fr, Seated Dancer, by Degas. 50fr, Girl on Swing, by Renoir. 75fr, Girl with Straw Hat, by Renoir. All vertical.

1974, Dec. 15

C196 AP84 30fr gold & multi 1.50 .35
C197 AP84 40fr gold & multi 2.00 .35
C198 AP84 50fr gold & multi 2.75 .50
C199 AP84 75fr gold & multi 3.25 .80
Nos. C196-C199 (4) 9.50 2.00

National Fair AP85

1974, Dec. 20

C200 AP85 30fr multicolored 1.05 .35

National Fair, Aug. 24-Sept. 8.

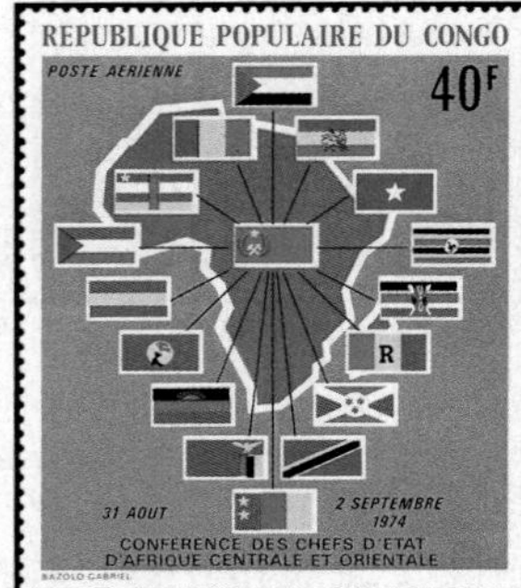

Flags of Participating Nations, Map of Africa — AP86

1974, Dec. 20 *Perf. 13*

C201 AP86 40fr ultra & multi .80 .45

Conference of Chiefs of State of Central and East Africa, Brazzaville, Aug. 31-Sept. 2.

"Five Weeks in a Balloon," by Jules Verne AP87

Design: 50fr, "Around the World in 80 Days," by Jules Verne.

1975, June 30 Litho. *Perf. 12½*

C202 AP87 40fr multicolored 1.40 .50
C203 AP87 50fr multicolored 1.75 1.00

Jules Verne (1828-1905), French science fiction writer, 70th death anniversary.

Paris-Brussels Train, 1890 — AP88

Design: 75fr, Santa Fe, 1880.

1975, June 30

C204 AP88 50fr ocher & multi 2.00 .75
C205 AP88 75fr lt bl & multi 4.25 .90

Soyuz and Apollo-Soyuz Emblem — AP89

Design: 100fr, Apollo and emblem.

1975, July 20 Litho. *Perf. 12½*

C206 AP89 95fr org, blk & mag 1.25 .50
C207 AP89 100fr vio, bl & blk 1.40 .60

Apollo Soyuz space test project (Russo-American space cooperation), launching July 15; link-up, July 17.
For overprints see Nos. C252-C253.

Bicycling and Montreal Olympic Emblem — AP90

Designs (Montreal Olympic Emblem and): 40fr, Boxing, vert. 50fr, Basketball, vert. 95fr, High jump. 100fr, Javelin. 150fr, Running.

Perf. 12½x13, 13x12½

1975, Oct. 30 **Photo.**

C208	AP90	40fr multicolored	.50	.25
C209	AP90	50fr red & multi	.60	.25
C210	AP90	85fr bl & multi	1.00	.35
C211	AP90	95fr org & multi	1.10	.45
C212	AP90	100fr multicolored	1.40	.50
C213	AP90	150fr multicolored	1.75	.80
	Nos. C208-C213 (6)		6.35	2.60

Pre-Olympic Year 1975.

Map of Africa, Sports and Flags — AP91

1975, Dec. 20 **Litho.** ***Perf. 12½***

C214 AP91 30fr multicolored .80 .35

1st African Games, Brazzaville, 10th anniv.

Workers and Flag — AP92

1975, Dec. 31 **Litho.** ***Perf. 12½***

C215 AP92 60fr multicolored 1.10 .25

Congolese Labor Party (P.C.T.), 6th anniv.

Alphonse Fondere — AP93

Historic Ships: 5fr, like 30fr. 10fr, 40fr, Hamburg, 1839. 15fr, 50fr, Gomer, 1831. 20fr, 60fr, Great Eastern, 1858. 95fr, J.M. White II, 1878.

1976 **Engr.** ***Perf. 13***

C216	AP93	5fr multicolored	.25	.25
C217	AP93	10fr multicolored	.25	.25
C218	AP93	15fr multicolored	.30	.25
C219	AP93	20fr multicolored	.50	.25
C220	AP93	30fr multicolored	.75	.25
C221	AP93	40fr multicolored	1.00	.35
C222	AP93	50fr multicolored	1.25	.50
C223	AP93	60fr multicolored	1.75	.60
C224	AP93	95fr multicolored	2.50	1.00
	Nos. C216-C224 (9)		8.55	3.70

Issued: Nos. C216-C219, May; Nos. C220-C224, Mar. 7.

Europafrica Issue

Peasant Family, by Louis Le Nain — AP94

Paintings: 80fr, Boy with Top, by Jean B. Chardin. 95fr, Venus and Aeneas, by Nicolas Poussin. 100fr, The Rape of the Sabine Women, by Jacques Louis David.

1976, Mar. 20 **Litho.** ***Perf. 12½***

C225	AP94	60fr gold & multi	1.25	.45
C226	AP94	80fr gold & multi	1.40	.70
C227	AP94	95fr gold & multi	1.90	.70
C228	AP94	100fr gold & multi	2.10	.85
	Nos. C225-C228 (4)		6.65	2.70

Nos. C225-C228 printed in sheets of 8 stamps and horizontal gutter with commemorative inscription.

Telephone Type of 1976

1976, Apr. 25 **Litho.** ***Perf. 12½x13***

C229 A107 60fr pink, mar & crim .90 .30

Sports Type of 1976

Designs: 150fr, Runner and map of Central Africa. 200fr, Discus and map.

1976, Oct. 25 ***Perf. 12½***

C230 A110 150fr multicolored 1.75 .75
C231 A110 200fr multicolored 2.75 1.10

Map of Africa, Flag and OAU Headquarters AP95

1976, Dec. 16 **Typo.** ***Perf. 13x14***

C232 AP95 60fr multicolored .90 .35

13th anniv. of the Organization for African Unity.

Europafrica Issue

Map of Europe and Africa — AP96

1977, June 28 **Litho.** ***Perf. 13***

C233 AP96 75fr multicolored 1.00 .45

Headdress Type of 1977

1977, June 30 ***Perf. 12½***

250fr, Two straw caps. 300fr, Beaded cap.

C234 A118 250fr multicolored 2.75 1.50
C235 A118 300fr multicolored 3.00 1.75

Zeppelin Type of 1977
Souvenir Sheet

Design: 500fr, LZ 127 over US Capitol.

1977, Aug. 5 **Litho.** ***Perf. 11***

C236 A120 500fr multicolored 6.75 2.00

No. C236 exists imperf.

Checkerboard AP97

1977, Aug. 20 **Engr.** ***Perf. 13***

C237 AP97 60fr red & blk .90 .35

Lomé Convention on General Agreement on Tariffs and Trade (GATT).

Newton, Intelsat Satellite and Classical "Planets" — AP98

1977, Aug. 25

C238 AP98 140fr multicolored 2.00 .90

Isaac Newton (1642-1727), natural philosopher and mathematician.

Elizabeth II Type of 1977
Souvenir Sheet

Design: 500fr, Royal family on balcony.

1977, Dec. 21 **Litho.** ***Perf. 14***

C239 A128 500fr multicolored 5.75 1.75

For overprint see No. C244.

Mallard AP99

Birds: 75fr, Purple heron, vert. 150fr, Reed warbler, vert. 240fr, Hoopoe, vert.

1978, May 22 ***Perf. 13x12½, 12½x13***

C240	AP99	65fr multicolored	1.40	.50
C241	AP99	75fr multicolored	1.40	.50
C242	AP99	150fr multicolored	3.50	1.00
C243	AP99	240fr multicolored	5.50	1.75
	Nos. C240-C243 (4)		11.80	3.75

No. C239 Overprinted in Silver: "ANNIVERSAIRE DU / COURONNEMENT / 1953-1978"

1978, Sept. **Litho.** ***Perf. 14***
Souvenir Sheet

C244 A128 500fr multicolored 4.50 3.00

25th anniv. of coronation of Elizabeth II.

Philexafrique II-Essen Issue
Common Design Types

No. C245, Leopard and Congo No. C243. No. C246, Eagle and Wurttemberg No. 1.

1978, Nov. 1 **Litho.** ***Perf. 12½***

C245	CD138	100fr multicolored	2.00	1.10
C246	CD139	100fr multicolored	2.00	1.10
a.		Pair, #C245-C246	7.00	7.00

Map of Africa, Satellites AP100

1978, Nov. 25 **Engr.** ***Perf. 13***

C247 AP100 100fr multicolored 1.60 .50

Pan-African Telecommunications Network, PANAFTEL.

Map of Africa and People — AP101

1979, Aug. 2 **Litho.** ***Perf. 12½***

C248 AP101 45fr multicolored .50 .25
C249 AP101 75fr multicolored .85 .40

5th Conference of Panafrican Youth Movement, Brazzaville, Aug. 2-7.

Abala Peasant Woman AP102

1979, Aug. 20

C250 AP102 150fr multicolored 1.75 .90

Nos. C173, C206-C207, C186, C189 Overprinted

No. C251

No. C252

Perf. 13, 12½

1979, Nov. 5 **Engr., Litho.**

C251	AP69	80fr multicolored	1.00	.90
C252	AP89	95fr multicolored	1.10	1.00
C253	AP89	100fr multicolored	1.10	1.00
C254	AP77	100fr multicolored	1.10	1.00
C255	AP79	300fr multicolored	3.00	2.75
	Nos. C251-C255 (5)		7.30	6.65

Apollo 11 moon landing, 10th anniversary.

Runner, Olympic Rings — AP103

Pre-Olympic Year: 100fr, Boxing. 200fr, Fencing. 300fr, Soccer. 500fr, Moscow '80 emblem.

1979 Litho. *Perf. 13½*

C256	AP103 65fr multi	.60	.25
C257	AP103 100fr multi	.95	.25
C258	AP103 200fr multi, vert.	1.90	.50
C259	AP103 300fr multi	2.75	.75
C260	AP103 500fr multi, vert.	4.75	1.25
	Nos. C256-C260 (5)	10.95	3.00

Cross-Country Skiing — AP104

Lake Placid '80 Emblem and: 60fr, Slalom. 200fr, Ski jump, 350fr, Downhill skiing, horiz. 500fr, Woman skier.

1979, Dec *Perf. 14½*

Size: 24x42mm, 42x24mm

C261	AP104 40fr multicolored	.45	.25
C262	AP104 60fr multicolored	.60	.25
C263	AP104 200fr multicolored	1.90	.45
C264	AP104 350fr multicolored	3.50	.90

Size: 31½x46½mm

Perf. 14

C265	AP104 500fr multicolored	4.50	1.40
	Nos. C261-C265 (5)	10.95	3.25

13th Winter Olympic Games, Lake Placid, NY, Feb. 12-24, 1980.

Nos. C261-C265 Overprinted in Black

40fr, Zimiatov. 60fr, Moser-Proell. 200fr, Tomanen. 350fr, Stock. 500fr, Stenmark-Wenzel.

1980, Apr. 28

C266	AP104 40fr multi	.45	.25
C267	AP104 60fr multi	.60	.25
C268	AP104 200fr multi	1.90	.75
C269	AP104 350fr multi	3.50	1.25
C270	AP104 500fr multi	4.75	1.90
	Nos. C266-C270 (5)	11.20	4.40

Long Jump, Olympic Rings — AP105

1980, May 2 Litho. *Perf. 14½*

C271	AP105 75fr multi, vert.	.90	.25
C272	AP105 150fr multi	1.40	.30
C273	AP105 250fr multi, vert.	2.25	.50
C274	AP105 350fr multi, vert.	3.25	.70
	Nos. C271-C274 (4)	7.80	1.75

Souvenir Sheet

C275	AP105 500fr multi	5.00	1.60

22nd Summer Olympic Games, Moscow, July 19-Aug. 3.

For overprints see Nos. C292-C296.

Stadium, Mascot, Madrid Club Emblem — AP106

Stadium, Mascot and Club Emblem: 75fr, Zaragoza. 100fr, Madrid Athletic Club. 150fr, Valencia. 175fr, Spain. 250fr, Barcelona.

1980, June 23 Litho. *Perf. 14x13½*

C276	AP106 60fr multicolored	.60	.25
C277	AP106 75fr multicolored	.60	.25
C278	AP106 100fr multicolored	1.00	.25
C279	AP106 150fr multicolored	1.40	.35
C280	AP106 175fr multicolored	1.60	.50
	Nos. C276-C280 (5)	5.20	1.60

Souvenir Sheet

C281	AP106 250fr multicolored	2.75	1.25

World Soccer Cup 1982.

For overprints see Nos. C298-C303.

Adoration of the Shepherds — AP107

Rembrandt Paintings: 100fr, The Burial. 200fr, Christ at Emmaus. 300fr, Annunciation, vert. 500fr, Crucifixion, vert.

1980, July 4 *Perf. 12½*

C282	AP107 65fr multicolored	.55	.30
C283	AP107 100fr multicolored	.85	.50
C284	AP107 200fr multicolored	1.75	.60
C285	AP107 300fr multicolored	2.50	.85
C286	AP107 500fr multicolored	4.50	1.50
	Nos. C282-C286 (5)	10.15	3.75

Albert Camus (1913-1960), Writer — AP108

Design: 150fr, Jacques Offenbach (1819-1880), composer, vert.

1980, July 5 Engr. *Perf. 13*

C287	AP108 100fr multicolored	1.25	.50
C288	AP108 150fr multicolored	2.25	1.25

Raffia Dancing Skirts — AP109

Traditional Dancing Costumes: 300fr, Tam-tam dancers, vert. 350fr, Masks.

1980, Aug. 6 Litho. *Perf. 13½*

C289	AP109 250fr multicolored	2.75	.95
C290	AP109 300fr multicolored	3.25	1.50
C291	AP109 350fr multicolored	4.00	1.90
	Nos. C289-C291 (3)	10.00	4.35

Nos. C271-C275 Overprinted

75fr, Dombrowki (RDA), 150fr, Saneiev (URSS), 250fr, Simeoni (IT), 350fr, Thompson (GB)

1980, Nov. 14 Litho. *Perf. 14½*

C292	AP105 75fr multicolored	.70	.30
C293	AP105 150fr multicolored	1.40	.60
C294	AP105 250fr multicolored	2.25	.90
C295	AP105 350fr multicolored	3.25	1.50
	Nos. C292-C295 (4)	7.60	3.30

Souvenir Sheet

C296	AP105 500fr multicolored	5.00	4.00

The Studio by Picasso — AP109a

150fr, Landscape. 200fr, Cannes Studio. 300fr, Still Life. 500fr, Still Life, diff.

1981, July 4 *Perf. 12½*

C296A	AP109a 100fr shown	1.10	.50
C296B	AP109a 150fr multi	1.60	.75
C296C	AP109a 200fr multi	2.10	1.00
C296D	AP109a 300fr multi	3.75	1.50
C296E	AP109a 500fr multi	6.25	2.50
	Nos. C296A-C296E (5)	14.80	6.25

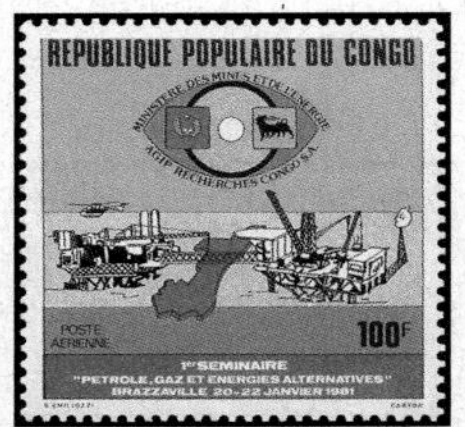

1st Seminar on Petroleum, Gas and Energy Alternatives, Brazzaville AP109b

45fr, Emblem, oil platform, other energy sources. 100fr, Emblem, map, oil platforms. 150fr, Map, other energy sources. 200fr, Maps of Africa, Congo, oil worker.

1981 Litho. *Perf. 12½*

C296F	AP109b 45fr multi	20.00	13.00
C296G	AP109b 75fr multi	32.50	19.00
C296H	AP109b 100fr multi	45.00	27.50
C296I	AP109b 150fr multi	65.00	40.00
C296J	AP109b 200fr multi	90.00	50.00
	Nos. C296F-C296J (5)	252.50	149.50

1350th Anniv. of Mohamed's Death at Medina — AP110

400fr, Medina Mosque minaret.

1982, July 17 Litho. *Perf. 13*

C297	AP110 400fr multi	3.75	1.75

Nos. C276-C281 Overprinted in Black on Silver

No. C298

No. C299

No. C300

No. C301

No. C302

1982, Oct. 7 Litho. *Perf. 14x13½*

C298	AP106 60fr multicolored	.55	.25
C299	AP106 75fr multicolored	.65	.30
C300	AP106 100fr multicolored	1.00	.45
C301	AP106 150fr multicolored	1.60	.60
C302	AP106 175fr multicolored	1.75	.60
	Nos. C298-C302 (5)	5.55	2.20

Souvenir Sheet

C303	AP106 250fr multicolored	2.50	1.90

50th Anniv. of Amelia Earhart's Transatlantic Flight — AP111

1982, Dec. 4 Engr. *Perf. 13*

C304	AP111 150fr multicolored	1.75	.75

Wind Surfing AP112

Various wind surfing scenes, 1984 Olympic Games, 100fr, 300fr, 400fr vert.

1983, June 4 **Litho.** ***Perf. 13***

C305 AP112 100fr multicolored .90 .25
C306 AP112 200fr multicolored 1.75 .50
C307 AP112 300fr multicolored 2.75 .70
C308 AP112 400fr multicolored 3.50 1.00
Nos. C305-C308 (4) 8.90 2.45

Souvenir Sheet

C309 AP112 500fr multicolored 5.00 2.50

For overprint see No. C336.

Manned Flight Bicentenary AP113

Various balloons: 100fr, Montgolfiere, 1783. 200fr, Flesselles, 1784. 300fr, Auguste Piccard, 1931. 400fr, Don Piccard.
500fr, Mail transport balloon, 1870.

1983, June 7

C310 AP113 100fr multicolored 1.10 .25
C311 AP113 200fr multicolored 2.10 .40
C312 AP113 300fr multicolored 3.00 .60
C313 AP113 400fr multicolored 4.50 .90
Nos. C310-C313 (4) 10.70 2.15

Souvenir Sheet

C314 AP113 500fr multicolored 5.75 1.60

For overprint see No. C337.

Christmas 1983 AP114

Various Virgin and Child Paintings by Botticelli.

1984, Jan. 21 **Litho.** ***Perf. 13***

C315 AP114 150fr multicolored 1.25 .50
C316 AP114 350fr multicolored 3.00 1.10
C317 AP114 500fr multicolored 4.50 1.50
Nos. C315-C317 (3) 8.75 3.10

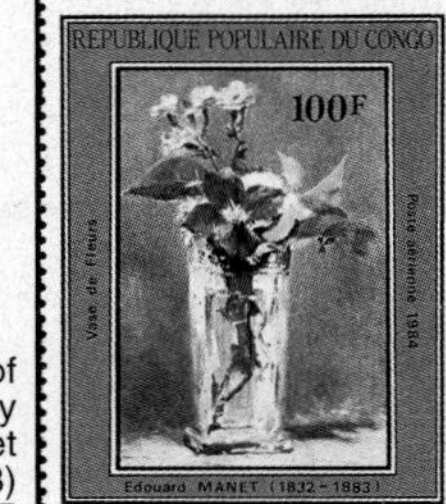

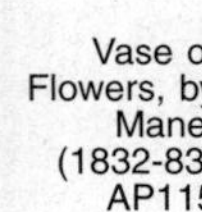
Vase of Flowers, by Manet (1832-83) AP115

Paintings: 200fr, Small Holy Family, by Raphael. 300fr, La Belle Jardiniere, by Raphael. 400fr, Virgin of Loretto, by Raphael. 500fr, Portrait of Richard Wagner (1813-83), by Giuseppe Tivoli.

1984, Feb. 24 **Litho.** ***Perf. 13***

C318 AP115 100fr multicolored .90 .30
C319 AP115 200fr multicolored 1.90 .70
C320 AP115 300fr multicolored 2.75 1.00
C321 AP115 400fr multicolored 3.75 1.40
C322 AP115 500fr multicolored 5.00 1.50
Nos. C318-C322 (5) 14.30 4.90

1984 Summer Olympics — AP116

1984, Mar. 31 ***Perf. 13***

C323 AP116 45fr Judo, vert. .45 .25
C324 AP116 75fr Judo, diff. .70 .25
C325 AP116 150fr Wrestling 1.40 .50
C326 AP116 175fr Fencing 1.60 .60
C327 AP116 350fr Fencing, diff. 3.25 1.10
Nos. C323-C327 (5) 7.40 2.70

Souvenir Sheet

C328 AP116 500fr Boxing 5.00 2.50

1984 Summer Olympic Gold Medalists — AP117

Sailing/yachting: 100fr, Stephan Van Den Berg, Netherlands, Windglider Class. 150fr, US, Soling Class. 200fr, Spain, 470 Class. 500fr, US, Flying Dutchman Class.

1984, Dec. 18 **Litho.** ***Perf. 13***

C329 AP117 100fr multi, vert. 1.00 .45
C330 AP117 150fr multi 1.40 .65
C331 AP117 200fr multi 2.00 .90
C332 AP117 500fr multi, vert. 4.50 2.25
Nos. C329-C332 (4) 8.90 4.25

Virgin and Child, by Giovanni Bellini (c. 1430-1516) — AP118

Religious paintings: 100fr, Holy Family, by Andrea del Sarto (1486-1530). 400fr, Virgin with Angels, by Cimabue (c. 1240-1302).

1985, Feb. 12 **Litho.** ***Perf. 13***

C333 AP118 100fr multi, vert. .80 .45
C334 AP118 200fr multi 1.60 .90
C335 AP118 400fr multi, vert. 3.00 1.75
Nos. C333-C335 (3) 5.40 3.10

Christmas 1984.

Nos. C309, C314 Ovptd. with Exhibition in Blue or Green

Overprint's are: No. C336, OLYMPHILEX '85 / LAUSANNE (B). No. C337, MOPHILA '85 / HAM - BURG (G).

1985, Mar. 8 ***Perf. 13***

Souvenir Sheets

C336 AP112 500fr multicolored 5.00 4.00
C337 AP113 500fr multicolored 5.00 4.00

Audubon Birth Bicentenary — AP119

Illustrations of North American bird species by Audubon: 100fr, Passiformes fringillidae, vert. 150fr, Eudocimus ruber, vert. 200fr, Buteo jamaicensis. 350fr, Camptorhynchus labradorius.

1985, Apr. 11 ***Perf. 13½***

C338 AP119 100fr multicolored 1.00 .45
C339 AP119 150fr multicolored 1.50 .65
C340 AP119 200fr multicolored 1.90 .90
C341 AP119 350fr multicolored 3.75 1.50
Nos. C338-C341 (4) 8.15 3.50

PHILEXAFRICA '85, Lome — AP120

Youths in public service activities: No. C342, Community health care. No. C343, Agriculture.

1985, May 20 ***Perf. 13***

C342 AP120 200fr multicolored 2.50 1.50
C343 AP120 200fr multicolored 2.50 1.50
a. Pair, #C342-C343 + label 6.00 6.00

For overprints see Nos. 1187-1188.

Admission to UN, 25th Anniv. — AP121

1985, Aug. 13

C344 AP121 190fr multicolored 1.75 .75

Rainbow, emblem AP122

1985, Oct. 25 ***Perf. 12½***

C345 AP122 180fr multicolored 1.60 .65

UN, 40th Anniv.

Christmas — AP123

Paintings: 100fr, The Virgin and the Infant Jesus, by David. 200fr, Adoration of the Magi, by Hieronymus Bosch (1450-1516). 400fr, Virgin and Child, by Van Dyck.

1985, Dec. 20 **Litho.** ***Perf. 13***

C346 AP123 100fr multicolored .90 .35
C347 AP123 200fr multicolored 1.90 .75
C348 AP123 400fr multicolored 3.50 1.75
Nos. C346-C348 (3) 6.30 2.85

Nos. C346-C347 vert.

Halley's Comet — AP124

125fr, Halley, comet. 150fr, West's Comet, 1976. 225fr, Ikeya Seki's Comet, 1965. 300fr, Trajectory diagram. 350fr, Comet, Vega probe.

1986, Feb. 17

C349 AP124 125fr multicolored 1.00 .50
C350 AP124 150fr multicolored 1.25 .60
C351 AP124 225fr multicolored 1.75 .90
C352 AP124 300fr multicolored 2.25 1.25
C353 AP124 350fr multicolored 2.75 1.50
Nos. C349-C353 (5) 9.00 4.75

Nos. C350-C351 vert.

Cosmos-Frantel Hotel — AP125

1986, May 1 ***Perf. 13½***

C354 AP125 250fr multicolored 2.50 .90

1986 World Cup Soccer Championships, Mexico — AP126

Various soccer plays.

1986, July 22 **Litho.** ***Perf. 13***

C355 AP126 150fr multicolored 1.25 .60
C356 AP126 250fr multicolored 2.00 1.00
C357 AP126 440fr multicolored 3.75 1.75
C358 AP126 600fr multicolored 6.50 2.50
Nos. C355-C358 (4) 13.50 5.85

Air Africa, 25th Anniv. — AP127

1986, Nov. 29 Litho. *Perf. 13½*

C359 AP127 200fr multicolored 2.00 .75

1988 Winter Pre-Olympics, Calgary — AP128

150fr, Downhill skiing. 250fr, Bobsled. 440fr, Women's cross-country skiing. 600fr, Ski jumping.

1986, Dec. 15 *Perf. 13*

C360 AP128 150fr multicolored 1.25 .60
C361 AP128 250fr multicolored 2.25 .95
C362 AP128 440fr multicolored 4.00 1.50
C363 AP128 600fr multicolored 5.75 2.40
Nos. C360-C363 (4) 13.25 5.45

Nos. C361-C362 vert.

Christmas AP129

Paintings by Rogier van der Weyden (c.1399-1464): 250fr, Virgin and Child. 440fr, The Nativity. 500fr, Virgin with Carnation.

1986, Dec. 23 *Perf. 13½*

C364 AP129 250fr multicolored 2.25 1.00
C365 AP129 440fr multicolored 4.25 1.75
C366 AP129 500fr multicolored 4.50 2.10
Nos. C364-C366 (3) 11.00 4.85

Crocodiles, World Wildlife Fund — AP130

75fr, Osteolaemus tetraspis. 100fr, Crocodylus cataphractus. 125fr, Osteolaemus tetraspis, diff. 150fr, Crocodylus cataphractus, diff.

1987, Jan. 22 *Perf. 13*

C367 AP130 75fr multicolored 2.25 1.10
C368 AP130 100fr multicolored 2.75 1.25
C369 AP130 125fr multicolored 3.50 1.75
C370 AP130 150fr multicolored 4.00 3.00
Nos. C367-C370 (4) 12.50 7.10

1988 Summer Olympics, Seoul — AP131

1987, July 11 Litho. *Perf. 13*

C371 AP131 100fr Backstroke .90 .35
C372 AP131 200fr Freestyle 1.75 .75
C373 AP131 300fr Breaststroke 2.75 1.10
C374 AP131 400fr Butterfly 3.50 1.40
Nos. C371-C374 (4) 8.90 3.60

Souvenir Sheet

C375 AP131 750fr Start of event 6.75 3.50

Launch of Sputnik, First Artificial Satellite, 30th Anniv. — AP132

1987, June 5 *Perf. 12½x12*

C376 AP132 60fr multicolored .50 .25
C377 AP132 240fr multicolored 2.25 1.10

Butterflies — AP133

75fr, Precis epicleli. 120fr, Deilephila nerii. 450fr, Euryphene senegalensis. 550fr, Precis almanta.

1987, Sept. 4 *Perf. 12½*

C378 AP133 75fr multicolored 1.20 .30
C379 AP133 120fr multicolored 2.00 .45
C380 AP133 450fr multicolored 6.00 1.75
C381 AP133 550fr multicolored 8.00 2.40
Nos. C378-C381 (4) 17.20 4.90

Coubertin, Eternal Flame and Greece No. 125 — AP134

Cameo portrait, athletes and stamps: 120fr, Runners, France No. 198. 350fr, Congo Republic No. C22, hurdler. 600fr, High jump, Congo Republic No. C75.

1987, Nov. 4

C382 AP134 75fr shown .80 .30
C383 AP134 120fr multicolored 1.10 .45
C384 AP134 350fr multicolored 3.50 1.25
C385 AP134 600fr multicolored 5.25 2.10
Nos. C382-C385 (4) 10.65 4.10

Pierre de Coubertin (1863-1937), promulgator of the modern Olympics.

Arrival of Schweitzer in Lambarene, 75th Anniv. — AP135

1988, Apr. 17 Litho. *Perf. 12½*

C386 AP135 240fr multicolored 2.75 1.25

Dr. Albert Schweitzer (1875-1965), Nobel Peace Prize winner of 1952, founded Lambarene Hospital, Gabon, in 1913.

1988 Summer Olympics, Seoul — AP136

Pentathlon: 75fr, Swimming. 170fr, Cross-country running, vert. 200fr, Shooting. 600fr, Equestrian. 700fr, Fencing.

1988, June 10 Litho. *Perf. 13*

C387 AP136 75fr multicolored .70 .25
C388 AP136 170fr multicolored 1.60 .60
C389 AP136 200fr multicolored 1.75 .70
C390 AP136 600fr multicolored 5.00 2.00
Nos. C387-C390 (4) 9.05 3.55

Souvenir Sheet

C391 AP136 750fr multicolored 7.00 3.75

Elimination Matches, 1990 World Cup Soccer Championships — AP137

Various athletes and cities in Italy.

1989, June 15 Litho. *Perf. 13*

C392 AP137 75fr Bari .60 .30
C393 AP137 120fr Rome 1.00 .45
C394 AP137 500fr Florence 4.75 1.90
C395 AP137 550fr Naples 5.25 2.00
Nos. C392-C395 (4) 11.60 4.65

PHILEXFRANCE '89 — AP138

Paintings: 300fr, Storming of the Bastille, July 14, 1789, from a gouache by J.P. Houel. 400fr, Eiffel Tower, by G. Seurat.

1989, June 22

C396 AP138 300fr multicolored 2.75 1.10
C397 AP138 400fr multicolored 3.75 1.50

French revolution, bicent. (300fr); Eiffel Tower, cent. (400fr).

First Moon Landing, 20th Anniv. AP139

Man's first step on the Moon: No. C398, Astronaut on ladder. No. C399, Conducting experiments on the Moon's surface.

1989, June 22

C398 AP139 400fr multicolored 3.75 1.50
C399 AP139 400fr multicolored 3.75 1.50

World Cup Soccer Championships, Italy — AP140

Various soccer plays and architecture.

1990, June 8 Litho. *Perf. 13*

C400 AP140 120fr multicolored 1.00 .50
C401 AP140 240fr multicolored 2.10 .95
C402 AP140 500fr multicolored 4.25 2.00
C403 AP140 600fr multicolored 5.25 2.40
Nos. C400-C403 (4) 12.60 5.85

Pan African Postal Union, 10th Anniv. AP141

1991, Jan. 10 Litho. *Perf. 13½*

C404 AP141 60fr shown .55 .25
C405 AP141 120fr Emblem 1.00 .50

1992 Winter Olympics, Albertville AP142

120fr, Ice hockey. 300fr, Speed skating. 1500fr, Slalom skiing.

1991, June 8 Litho. *Perf. 13½*

C406 AP142 120fr multi 1.40 .60
C407 AP142 300fr multi 3.00 1.50

Litho. & Embossed

C408 AP142 1500fr multi 7.50 7.50

Numbers have been reserved for souvenir sheets in this set.

1992 Summer Olympics, Barcelona AP143

No. C411, Equestrian. No. C412, Long jump.

Litho. & Embossed

1992, Dec. 21 *Perf. 13½*

No.	Type	Description	Unused	Used
C411	AP143	1500fr gold & multi	16.00	16.00

Souvenir Sheet

No.	Type	Description	Unused	Used
C412	AP143	1500fr gold & multi	21.00	21.00

Anniversaries AP144

Designs: 90fr, Victor Schoelcher, missionary, death cent. 205fr, Martin Luther King, civil rights reformer, 25th death anniv. 300fr, Claude Chappe (1763-1805), bicent. of visual telegraph.

1993 **Litho.** *Perf. 14*

No.	Type	Description	Unused	Used
C413	AP144	90fr multicolored	*1.00*	*.50*
C414	AP144	205fr multicolored	*2.50*	*1.25*
C415	AP144	300fr multicolored	*3.50*	*1.75*
		Nos. C413-C415 (3)	*7.00*	*3.50*

1994 Winter Olympics, Lillehammer AP145

400fr, Ice dancing. 600fr, Ice hockey. 750fr, Downhill skiing.

1993, Apr. 26 **Litho.** *Perf. 13*

No.	Type	Description	Unused	Used
C416	AP145	400fr multicolored	*4.00*	*1.40*
C417	AP145	600fr multicolored	*7.50*	*1.75*

Souvenir Sheet

No.	Type	Description	Unused	Used
C418	AP145	750fr multicolored	*8.00*	*4.00*

Nos. C416-C417 exist in imperf. souvenir sheets of 1. Nos. C416-C418 exist imperf.

AIR POST SEMI-POSTAL STAMPS

Hathor Pillar — SPAP1

Unwmk.

1964, Mar. 9 **Engr.** *Perf. 13*

No.	Type	Description	Unused	Used
CB1	SPAP1	10fr + 5fr vio & chnt	.90	.50
CB2	SPAP1	25fr + 5fr org brn & slate grn	1.10	.70
CB3	SPAP1	50fr + 5fr slate grn & brn red	2.25	1.60
		Nos. CB1-CB3 (3)	4.25	2.80

UNESCO world campaign to save historic monuments in Nubia.

POSTAGE DUE STAMPS

Messenger — D6

MH. 1521 Broussard Plane — D7

Early Transportation: 1fr, Litter. 2fr, Canoe. 5fr, Bicyclist. 10fr, Steam locomotive. 25fr, Seaplane.

Unwmk.

1961, Dec. 4 **Engr.** *Perf. 11*

No.	Type	Description	Unused	Used
J34	D6	50c ultra, ol bis & red	.25	.25
a.		Pair, #J34, J40	.25	
J35	D6	1fr red brn, red & grn	.25	.25
a.		Pair, #J35, J41	.30	
J36	D6	2fr grn, ultra & brn	.25	.25
a.		Pair, #J36, J42	.40	
J37	D6	5fr pur & gray brn	.25	.25
a.		Pair, #J37, J43	.50	
J38	D6	10fr bl, grn & chocolate	.70	.70
a.		Pair, #J38, J44	1.40	1.40
J39	D6	25fr bl, dk grn & dk brn	1.60	1.60
a.		Pair, #J39, J45	3.25	

Modern transportation: 1fr, Land Rover. 2fr, River boat transporting barge. 5fr, Trailer-truck. 10fr, Diesel locomotive. 25fr, Boeing 707 jet plane.

No.	Type	Description	Unused	Used
J40	D7	50c ultra, olive bis & red	.25	.25
J41	D7	1fr red & grn	.25	.25
J42	D7	2fr ultra, grn & brn	.25	.25
J43	D7	5fr pur & gray brn	.25	.25
J44	D7	10fr dk grn & chocolate	.70	.70
J45	D7	25fr bl, dk grn & sepia	1.60	1.60
		Nos. J34-J45 (12)	6.60	6.60

Pairs printed tête bêche, se-tenant at the base.

Flowers — D8

Flowers: 2fr, Phaeomeria magnifica. 5fr, Millettia laurentii. 10fr, Tuberose. 15fr, Pyrostegia venusta. 20fr, Hibiscus.

1971, Mar. 25 **Photo.** *Perf. 12x12½*

No.	Type	Description	Unused	Used
J46	D8	1fr multi	.35	.35
J47	D8	2fr multi	.45	.45
J48	D8	5fr pink & multi	.55	.55
J49	D8	10fr dk grn & multi	.70	.70
J50	D8	15fr multi	1.10	1.10
J51	D8	20fr multi	1.40	1.40
		Nos. J46-J51 (6)	4.55	4.55

Flowers and Fruit — D9

5fr, Passiflora quadrangulares. 10fr, Cannaceae, vert. 15fr, Ananas comosus, vert.

1986, June 5 **Litho.** *Perf. 13*

No.	Type	Description	Unused	Used
J52	D9	5fr multicolored	.25	.25
J53	D9	10fr multicolored	.45	.45
J54	D9	15fr multicolored	.55	.55
		Nos. J52-J54 (3)	1.25	1.25

OFFICIAL STAMPS

Coat of Arms — O1

Perf. 14x13

1968-70 **Unwmk.** **Typo.**

No.	Type	Description	Unused	Used
O1	O1	1fr multi ('70)	.25	.25
O2	O1	2fr multi ('70)	.25	.25
O3	O1	5fr multi ('70)	.25	.25
O4	O1	10fr multi ('70)	.25	.25
O5	O1	25fr emer & multi	.45	.25
O6	O1	30fr red & multi	.60	.25
O7	O1	50fr multi ('70)	1.10	.50
O8	O1	85fr multi ('70)	2.25	.90
O9	O1	100fr multi ('70)	2.75	1.10
O10	O1	200fr multi ('70)	3.75	2.00
		Nos. O1-O10 (10)	11.90	6.00

COOK ISLANDS

'kuk 'ī-ləndz

(Rarotonga)

LOCATION — South Pacific Ocean, northeast of New Zealand
GOVT. — Internal self-government, linked to New Zealand
AREA — 91 sq. mi.
POP. — 19,103 (1996)
CAPITAL — Avarua

Fifteen islands in Northern and Southern groups extend over 850,000 square miles of ocean.

Separate stamp issues used by Aitutaki (1903-32 and 1972 onward) and Penrhyn Islands (1902-32 and 1973 onward). Niue is included geographically, but administered separately. It continues to issue separate stamps.

12 Pence = 1 Shilling
20 Shillings = 1 Pound
100 Cents = 1 Dollar (1967)

Catalogue values for unused stamps in this country are for Never Hinged items, beginning with Scott 127 in the regular postage section, Scott B1 in the semi-postal section, Scott C1 in the air post section, Scott CB1 in the air post semi-postal section and Scott O16 in the official section.

For more detailed listings for classic issues of Cook Islands, see the Scott *Classic Specialized Catalogue of Stamps and Covers 1840-1940.*

Watermarks

Wmk. 61 — Single-lined N Z and Star Close Together

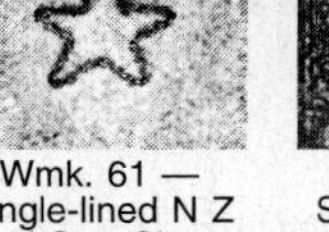

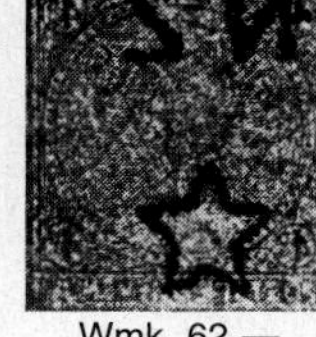

Wmk. 62 — Single-lined N Z and Star Wide Apart

Wmk. 253 — Multiple N Z and Star

A1

1892 **Unwmk.** **Typo.** *Perf. 12½*

Toned Paper

No.	Type	Description	Unused	Used
1	A1	1p black	35.00	30.00
2	A1	1½p violet	50.00	45.00
a.		Imperf, pair	*19,000.*	
3	A1	2½p blue	47.50	45.00
4	A1	10p carmine	160.00	150.00
		Nos. 1-4 (4)	292.50	270.00

White Paper

No.	Type	Description	Unused	Used
5	A1	1p black	35.00	30.00
a.		Vert. pair, imperf. between	*11,000.*	
6	A1	1½p violet	50.00	45.00
7	A1	2½p blue	47.50	45.00
8	A1	10p carmine	160.00	150.00
		Nos. 5-8 (4)	292.50	270.00

Nos. 1-8 were printed in sheets of 60 (6x10), from a setting of six slightly different cliches.

Queen Makea Takau — A2

1893-94 **Wmk. 62** *Perf. 12x11½*

No.	Type	Description	Unused	Used
9	A2	1p brown	50.00	*55.00*
10	A2	1p blue ('94)	13.00	2.50
11	A2	1½p brt violet	19.00	8.50
12	A2	2½p rose	55.00	27.50
13	A2	5p olive gray	24.00	16.00
14	A2	10p green	85.00	57.50
		Nos. 9-14 (6)	246.00	*167.00*

Torea — A3

1898-1900 *Perf. 11*

No.	Type	Description	Unused	Used
15	A3	½p blue ('00)	6.50	*15.00*
a.		"d" omitted at upper right	*1,750.*	
16	A2	1p brown	32.50	21.00
17	A2	1p blue	6.00	5.50
18	A2	1½p violet	19.00	7.50
19	A3	2p chocolate ('00)	15.00	8.50
20	A2	2½p car rose ('00)	25.00	15.00
21	A2	5p olive gray	30.00	21.00
22	A3	6p red violet ('00)	24.00	*29.00*
23	A2	10p green	26.00	*57.50*
24	A3	1sh car rose ('00)	57.50	57.50
		Nos. 15-24 (10)	241.50	*237.50*

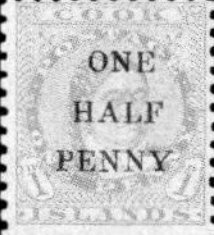

No. 17 Surcharged in Black

1899

No.	Type	Description	Unused	Used
25	A2	½p on 1p blue	40.00	*50.00*
a.		Double surcharge	1,000.	*1,200.*
b.		Inverted surcharge	1,200.	1,100.

No. 16 Overprinted in Black

1901

26 A2 1p brown 210.00 160.00
a. Inverted overprint 2,400. 1,900.
c. Double overprint 1,900. 1,900.

Some single stamps were overprinted by favor. Other varieties could exist.
Forgeries exist.

Types of 1893-98

1902 Unwmk.

27 A3 ½p green 10.00 10.00
a. Vert. pair, imperf. horiz. *1,400.*
28 A2 1p rose 16.00 *11.00*
29 A2 2½p dull blue 15.00 *25.00*
Nos. 27-29 (3) 41.00 *46.00*

1902 Wmk. 61 *Perf. 11*

30 A3 ½p green 4.25 *3.75*
31 A2 1p rose 4.75 *3.50*
32 A2 1½p brt violet 4.75 *10.00*
33 A3 2p chocolate 11.00 *12.00*
a. Figures of value omitted *2,750. 3,600.*
b. Perf. 11x14 *2,600.*
34 A2 2½p dull blue 4.50 *8.25*
35 A2 5p olive gray 42.50 *57.50*
36 A3 6p purple 37.50 *32.50*
37 A2 10p blue green 55.00 *120.00*
38 A3 1sh car rose 55.00 *82.50*
a. Perf. 11x14 *3,000.*
Nos. 30-38 (9) 219.25 *330.00*

1909-19 *Perf. 14, 14x14½, 14½x14*

39 A3 ½p green, perf 14½x14 ('11) 13.00 *9.50*
a. ½p dp grn, perf 14 ('15) 42.50 *17.50*
b. As "a," wmk upright 14.00 *22.50*
40 A2 1p red, wmk. sideways ('09) 15.00 5.00
41 A2 1½p purple, perf 14x15 ('16) 21.00 4.75
42 A3 2p dp brown ('19) 6.00 *57.50*
43 A2 10p dp green ('18) 40.00 *110.00*
44 A3 1sh car rose ('19) 32.50 *110.00*
Nos. 39-44 (6) 127.50 *296.75*

Nos. 39-40 are on both ordinary and chalky paper; Nos. 41-44 on chalky paper.

New Zealand Stamps of 1909-19 Surcharged in Dark Blue or Red

1919 Typo. *Perf. 14x15*

48 A43 ½p yel green (R) .45 *1.25*
a. Pair, one without surcharge
49 A42 1p carmine 1.25 *5.00*
50 A47 1½p brown org (R) .60 *.90*
51 A43 2p yellow (R) 1.75 *2.00*
52 A43 3p chocolate 3.25 *15.00*

Engr. *Perf. 14x14½*

53 A44 2½p dull blue (R) 2.75 2.50
54 A45 3p violet brown 3.50 *4.00*
55 A45 4p purple 2.25 *4.25*
56 A44 4½p dark green 2.25 *9.50*
57 A45 6p car rose 2.00 *5.50*
58 A44 7½p red brown, perf 14x13½ 2.10 *6.50*
59 A45 9p ol green (R) 3.00 *17.50*
60 A45 1sh carmine 3.25 *30.00*
Nos. 48-60 (13) 28.40 *103.90*

The Polynesian surcharge restates the denomination of the basic stamp.

Landing of Capt. Cook
A4

Avarua Waterfront
A5

Capt. James Cook — A6

Palm — A7

Houses at Arorangi — A8

Avarua Harbor — A9

1920 Unwmk. Engr. *Perf. 14*

61 A4 ½p green & black 4.75 *30.00*
62 A5 1p car & black 5.50 *30.00*
a. Center inverted *875.00*
63 A6 1½p blue & black 10.00 10.00
64 A7 3p red brn & blk 2.50 *6.50*
65 A8 6p org & red brn 4.75 *10.00*
66 A9 1sh vio & black 9.00 *20.00*
a. Center inverted *875.00*
Nos. 61-66 (6) 36.50 *106.50*

The stamps overprinted or inscribed "Rarotonga" were used throughout the Cook Islands.
For surcharges see Nos. 72, 73, 78, 79.

New Zealand Postal-Fiscal Stamps of 1906-13 Overprinted in Red or Dark Blue — a

Perf. 14, 14½, 14x14½

1921 Typo. Wmk. 61

67 PF1 2sh blue (R) 32.50 *65.00*
68 PF1 2sh6p brown 22.50 *60.00*
69 PF1 5sh green (R) 32.50 *77.50*
70 PF1 10sh claret 90.00 *140.00*
71 PF2 £1 rose 150.00 *260.00*
Nos. 67-71 (5) 327.50 *602.50*

Types of 1920 Issue

1924-26 Engr. *Perf. 14*

72 A4 ½p yel grn & black 5.25 10.00
73 A5 1p carmine & black 7.00 2.50

Issued: ½p, May 13, 1926; 1p, Nov. 10, 1924.

New Zealand Stamps of 1926 Overprinted in Red

1926-28 Typo. *Perf. 14, 14½x14*

74 A56 2sh blue ('27) 19.00 *47.50*
a. 2sh dark blue 12.00 *47.50*
75 A56 3sh violet ('28) 19.00 *50.00*

Rarotongan Chief (Te Po) — A10

Avarua Harbor — A11

1927, Oct. 15 Engr. *Perf. 14*

76 A10 2½p dk bl & red brn 12.00 *37.50*
77 A11 4p dull vio & bl grn 19.00 *17.50*

No. 63 Surcharged in Red

1931 Unwmk.

78 A6 2p on 1½p blue & blk 11.00 4.75

Same Surcharge on Type of 1920

Wmk. 61

79 A6 2p on 1½p blue & blk 5.50 *13.00*

No. 79 was not issued without surcharge.

New Zealand Postal-Fiscal Stamps of 1931-32 Overprinted Type "a" in Blue or Red

1931, Nov. 12 Typo.

80 PF5 2sh6p dp brown (Bl) 16.00 *26.00*
81 PF5 5sh green (R) 27.50 *65.00*
82 PF5 10sh dk car (Bl) 45.00 *110.00*
83 PF5 £1 pink (Bl) ('32) 125.00 *200.00*
Nos. 80-83 (4) 213.50 *401.00*

See Nos. 103-108, 124A-126C.

Landing of Capt. Cook — A12

Capt. James Cook — A13

Double Canoe — A14

Islanders Unloading Ship — A15

View of Avarua Harbor — A16

R.M.S. Monowai — A17

King George V — A18

Unwmk.

1932, Mar. 16 Engr. *Perf. 13*

Center in Black

84 A12 ½p deep green 4.00 *19.00*
a. Perf. 14 32.50 *105.00*
85 A13 1p brown lake 10.00 5.25
a. Center inverted *9,500. 9,500.*
b. Perf. 14 17.50 *32.50*
86 A14 2p brown 3.50 *8.75*
b. Perf. 14 10.00 *24.00*
87 A15 2½p dark ultra 27.50 *70.00*
b. Perf. 14 20.00 *65.00*

Perf. 14

88 A16 4p ultra 12.00 *65.00*
a. Perf. 13 32.50 *75.00*
b. Perf. 14x13 35.00 *130.00*
89 A17 6p orange 5.00 *17.50*
a. Perf. 13 30.00 *57.50*
90 A18 1sh deep violet 24.00 *26.00*
Nos. 84-90 (7) 86.00 *211.50*

Nos. 84 to 90 were available for postage in Aitutaki, Penrhyn and Rarotonga and replaced the special issues for those islands.
Inverted centers of the ½p (value $1,000), 1p (value $550), and 2p (value $3,500) are from printers waste.

1933-36 Wmk. 61 *Perf. 14*

91 A12 ½p dp grn & blk 1.20 *5.25*
92 A13 1p dk car & black ('35) 1.50 *2.40*
93 A14 2p brn & blk ('36) 1.75 .60
94 A15 2½p dk ultra & blk 1.75 *2.50*
95 A16 4p blue & black 1.75 .60
96 A17 6p org & blk ('36) 2.00 *2.50*
97 A18 1sh dp vio & black ('36) 27.50 *42.50*
Nos. 91-97 (7) 37.45 *56.35*

See Nos. 116-121.

Silver Jubilee Issue

Types of 1932 Overprinted in Black or Red

1935, May 7

98 A13 1p dk car & brn red .65 *1.50*
99 A15 2½p dk ultra & bl (R) 2.00 *3.50*
100 A17 6p dull org & green 7.00 *7.00*
Nos. 98-100 (3) 9.65 *12.00*
Set, never hinged 16.00

The vertical spacing of the overprint is wider on No. 100.

New Zealand Stamps of 1926 Overprinted in Black — b

1936, July 15 Typo. *Perf. 14*

101 A56 2sh blue 15.00 *50.00*
102 A56 3sh violet 16.00 *80.00*

1931-35 New Zealand Postal-Fiscal Stamps Ovptd. Type "b" in Black or Red

1932-36

103 PF5 2sh6p brown ('36) 50.00 *110.00*
104 PF5 5sh grn (R) ('36) 52.50 *130.00*
105 PF5 10sh dk car ('36) 92.50 *250.00*
106 PF5 £1 pink ('36) 125.00 *275.00*
107 PF5 £3 lt grn (R) 500.00 *900.00*
108 PF5 £5 dk blue (R) 250.00 *400.00*
Nos. 103-108 (6) 1,070. *2,065.*

Issue dates: Mar. 1932, July 15, 1936.

New Zealand Stamps of 1937 Overprinted in Black

Perf. 14x13½

1937, June 1 Engr. Wmk. 253

109 A78 1p rose carmine .25 .25
110 A78 2½p dark blue .25 .25
111 A78 6p vermilion .35 .30
Nos. 109-111 (3) .85 .80
Set, never hinged 2.25

King George VI
A19

Village and Palms
A20

Coastal Scene with Canoe — A21

1938, May 2 Wmk. 61 *Perf. 14*

112 A19 1sh dp violet & blk 6.00 *12.00*
113 A20 2sh dk red brn & blk 13.50 15.00
114 A21 3sh yel green & blue 37.50 *42.50*
Nos. 112-114 (3) 57.00 69.50
Set, never hinged 90.00

See Nos. 122-124.

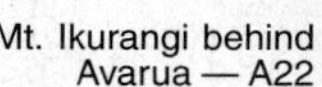

Mt. Ikurangi behind Avarua — A22

Perf. 13½x14

1940, Sept. 2 Engr. Wmk. 253
115 A22 3p on 1½p violet & blk .80 .70

Issued only with surcharge. Stamps without surcharge are from the printer's archives. Value $275.
See Niue No. 76.

Types of 1932-38

1944-46 Engr. *Perf. 14*
116 A12 ½p dk ol grn & blk ('45) 1.00 *4.50*
117 A13 1p dk car & blk ('45) 1.25 1.25
118 A14 2p brn & blk ('46) 1.50 *7.00*
119 A15 2½p dk bl & blk ('45) .60 *2.00*
120 A16 4p blue & black 3.00 *15.00*
121 A17 6p org & black 1.75 *2.50*
122 A19 1sh dp vio & blk 2.00 *3.50*
123 A20 2sh dk red brn & blk 25.00 *55.00*
124 A21 3sh yel green & blue ('45) 26.00 *35.00*
Nos. 116-124 (9) 62.10 125.75
Set, never hinged 100.00

New Zealand Nos. AR76, AR78, AR86 and Type of 1931 Postal-Fiscal Stamps Overprinted Type "b" in Black or Red

1943-50 Wmk. 253 Typo. *Perf. 14*
124A PF5 2sh6p brn ('51) 30.00 *45.00*
125 PF5 5sh green (R) 11.50 *37.50*
126 PF5 10sh dp pink ('51) 50.00 *100.00*
126A PF5 £1 pink ('54) 45.00 *110.00*
126B PF5 £3 lt grn (R) ('53) 42.50 *175.00*
126C PF5 £5 dk bl (R) ('54) 200.00 *400.00*
Nos. 124A-126C (6) 379.00 *867.50*
Set, never hinged 575.00

Values for Nos. 124A-126C are for the second printing with watermarks inverted.
For surcharges see Nos. 192-194.

Catalogue values for unused stamps in this section, from this point to the end of the section, are for Never Hinged items.

Peace Issue
New Zealand Nos. 248, 250, 254 and 255 Overprinted in Black or Blue

c

d

Perf. 13x13½, 13½x13

1946, June 1 Engr.
127 A94 (c) 1p emerald .30 .25
128 A96 (d) 2p rose vio (Bl) .35 .35
129 A100(c) 6p org red & red brn .80 .70
130 A101(c) 8p brn lake & blk (Bl) .55 .55
Nos. 127-130 (4) 2.00 1.85

Ngatangiia Channel, Rarotonga A23

Capt. James Cook Statue and Map of Cook Islands — A24

Designs: 1p, Cook and map of Hervey Isls. 2p, Rev. John Williams, his ship Messenger of Peace, and map of Rarotonga. 3p, Aitutaki map and palms. 5p, Mail plane landing at Rarotonga airport. 6p, Tongareva (Penrhyn) scene. 8p, Islander's house, Rarotonga. 2sh, Thatched house, mat weaver. 3sh, Steamer Matua offshore.

Perf. 13½x13, 13x13½

1949, Aug.1 Engr. Wmk. 253
131 A23 ½p brown & violet .25 *1.25*
132 A23 1p green & orange 3.00 3.00
133 A23 2p carmine & brn 1.75 3.00
134 A23 3p ultra & green 4.50 *1.75*
135 A23 5p purple & grn 5.00 1.25
136 A23 6p car rose & blk 5.25 2.25
137 A23 8p orange & olive .65 *2.25*
138 A24 1sh chocolate & bl 3.50 3.00
139 A24 2sh rose car & brn 5.00 *11.00*
140 A24 3sh bl grn & lt ultra 17.50 *27.50*
Nos. 131-140 (10) 46.40 *56.25*

For surcharge see No. 147.

Coronation Issue
Type of New Zealand

1953, May 25 Photo. *Perf. 14x14½*
145 A113 3p brown 1.25 1.25
146 A114 6p slate black 1.40 1.40

No. 135 Surcharged in Black

1960, Apr. 1 Engr. *Perf. 13½x13*
147 A23 1sh6p on 5p purple & grn .70 .55

Tiare Maori — A25

Fishing God — A26

Frangipani — A26a

Fairy Tern — A26b

Hibiscus — A26c

Bonito — A26d

Oranges — A26e

Queen Elizabeth II — A27

Island Scene A28

Administration building, Mangaia — A28a

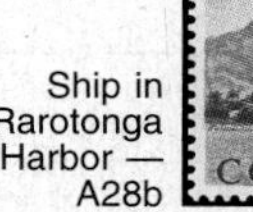
Ship in Rarotonga Harbor — A28b

Perf. 13½x13, 13x13½
Litho.; Engr.; (1sh6p)

1963, June 4
148 A25 1p multicolored .60 *.70*
149 A26 2p multicolored .25 *.65*
150 A26a 3p multicolored .55 *.55*
151 A26b 5p multicolored 6.25 2.00
152 A26c 6p multicolored .80 .60
153 A26d 8p blue & dark blue 3.50 1.40
154 A26e 1sh orange & green .80 .75
155 A27 1sh6p violet 2.25 2.00
156 A28 2sh gray & brown 1.60 1.25
157 A28a 3sh emer & black 1.60 1.90
158 A28b 5sh ultra & brown 13.00 5.25
Nos. 148-158 (11) 31.20 17.05

For overprints and surcharges see Nos. 167-169, 179-181, 183-184, 186-190.

Solar Eclipse and Palm Tree — A29

1965, May 31 Litho. *Perf. 13x13½*
159 A29 6p black, lt blue & yel .30 .30

Observation of the solar eclipse on Manuae Island, May 30, 1965. Exists imperf.
For surcharge see No. 185.

Flag of New Zealand and Map of Cook Islands A30

Designs: 10p, London Missionary Society Church and graveyard. 1sh, Reading of Proclamation of Cession, Oct. 8, 1900, and Queen Elizabeth II. 1sh9p, Nikao School and flag of New Zealand.

Perf. 13½x13

1965, Sept. 16 Litho. Wmk. 253
160 A30 4p blue & red .25 .25
161 A30 10p multicolored .25 .25
162 A30 1sh multicolored .25 .25
163 A30 1sh9p multicolored .45 .45
Nos. 160-163 (4) 1.20 1.20

Establishment of internal self-government.
For surcharges see Nos. 182, 191.

Nos. 160-162 and 156-158 Overprinted in Red

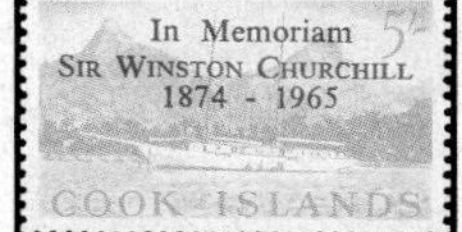

1966, Jan. 24 Litho. Wmk. 253
164 A30 4p blue & red 1.10 .30
165 A30 10p multicolored 2.00 .50
a. Inverted overprint *275.00*
166 A30 1sh multicolored 2.00 .85
a. Inverted overprint *200.00*
167 A28 2sh gray & brown 2.00 1.25
168 A28 3sh emer & black 2.00 1.25
169 A28 5sh ultra & brown 2.25 1.75
Nos. 164-169 (6) 11.35 5.90

Statesman and WWII leader.
Lower case "l" instead of "1" in "1874" in overprint exists on all. Value set, $70.

Adoration of the Wise Men, by Fra Angelico — A31

Paintings: 2p, Nativity, by Hans Memling, vert. 4p, Adoration of the Wise Men, by Velazquez. 10p, Adoration of the Wise Men, by Hieronymus Bosch. 1sh6p, Adoration of the Shepherds, by Jose Ribera, vert.

Perf. 13x14½, 14½x13

1966, Nov. 28 Photo. Unwmk.
170 A31 1p multicolored .25 .25
171 A31 2p multicolored .25 .25
172 A31 4p multicolored .25 .25
173 A31 10p multicolored .30 .30
174 A31 1sh6p multicolored .40 .40
Nos. 170-174 (5) 1.45 1.45

Christmas. Issued in sheets of 6 with ornamental gold border.

Perf. 13x12, 12x13

170a A31 1p .50 *.85*
171a A31 2p 16.00 *14.00*
172a A31 4p 1.25 *1.25*
173a A31 10p 2.75 *6.00*
174a A31 1sh6p 42.50 8.50
Nos. 170a-174a (5) 63.00 *30.60*

Tennis and Queen Elizabeth A32

Sport: 1p, Women's basketball and Games' emblem. 4p, Boxing and team emblem. 7p, Soccer and Queen Elizabeth II.

1967, Jan. 12 *Perf. 13½*
175 A32 ½p brt olive & multi .25 .25
176 A32 1p brt blue & multi .25 .25
177 A32 4p purple & multi .25 .25
178 A32 7p red & multi .25 .25
Nos. 175-178,C10-C11 (6) 1.50 1.50

Second South Pacific Games, Noumea, New Caledonia, Dec. 8-18, 1966.

Nos. 148-155, 157-161 Surcharged with New Value or Black or Red

Pair (#181b), with Type I on left (#181) and Type II on right (#181a)

1967
179 A25 1c on 1p .35 *1.75*
180 A26 2c on 2p .25 .25
181 A25 2½c on 3p (I) .25 .25
a. Type II .25 .25
b. Pair, #181 and #181a .35 .45
182 A30 3c on 4p .25 .25
183 A26 4c on 5p 7.25 .40
184 A25 5c on 6p .25 .25
185 A29 5c on 6p 4.00 1.25
186 A26 7c on 8p .25 .25
187 A25 10c on 1sh .25 .25
188 A27 15c on 1sh6p (R) 1.60 1.10
189 A28 30c on 3sh (R) 22.50 7.00
190 A28 50c on 5sh (R) 3.25 2.00
191 A30 $1 on 10p (R) 14.50 5.50
Nos. 179-191 (13) 54.95 20.50

Issued: 2c, 2½c, 3c, 5c, 7c, 10c, 4/3; others 5/4.

No. 191 is surcharged "10/ $1.00" and 3 bars over old value.

Numerous varieties of surcharge include wrong-font "c," thin numerals, etc.

Nos. 126A, 126B and 126C Surcharged in Red

Wmk. 253

1967, June 6 Typo. *Perf. 14*

192	PF5	$2 on £1 pink	70.00	*100.00*
193	PF5	$6 on £3 lt green	175.00	*200.00*
194	PF5	$10 on £5 dk blue	200.00	*225.00*
		Nos. 192-194 (3)	445.00	525.00

Frequently found with stained gum.

Stamp of 1892, Village and Queen Victoria A33

Designs: 3c (4p), PO, Rarotonga, and Elizabeth II. 8c (10p), View of Avarua, Rarotonga, and 10p stamp of 1892. 18c (1sh9p), Map of Cook Islands, DC-3, S.S. Moana Roa and Capt. Cook.

Perf. 13½

1967, July 3 Photo. Unwmk.

195	A33	1c (1p) multi	.25	.25
196	A33	3c (4p) multi	.25	.25
197	A33	8c (10p) multi	.30	.30
198	A33	18c (1sh9p) multi	1.10	.80
a.		Souvenir sheet of 4, #195-198	2.75	2.75
		Nos. 195-198 (4)	1.90	1.60

75th anniv. of the 1st Cook Islands stamps. Issued in sheets of 8 stamps and 1 label with inscription in yellow margin.

Hibiscus — A34

Elizabeth II A35

Elizabeth II and Flowers — A36

Flowers: 1c, Rose of Sharon. 2c, 15c, Frangipani. 2½c, Butterfly pea. 3c, Suva queen and Queen Elizabeth II. 4c, Water lily. 5c, Bauhania. 6c, Yellow hibiscus. 8c, Alamanda and Queen Elizabeth II. 9c, Stephanotis. 10c, Flaymboyant poinciana. 20c, Thunbergia. 25c, Canna lily and Queen Elizabeth II. 30c, Poinsettia. 50c, Gardenia.

The $4 exists with "FOUR DOLLARS" in two widths: type 1, 32½mm; type 2, 33½mm.

1967-69 Photo. *Perf. 14x13½*

199	A34	½c gold & multi	.30	.25
200	A34	1c gold & multi	.30	.25
201	A34	2c gold & multi	.30	.25
202	A34	2½c gold & multi	.55	.25
203	A34	3c gold & multi	.60	.25
204	A34	4c *Walter Lily*	.90	*1.25*
205	A34	4c *Water Lily*	2.25	2.00
206	A34	5c gold & multi	.40	.25
207	A34	6c gold & multi	.45	.25
208	A34	8c gold & multi	.45	.25
209	A34	9c gold & multi	.45	.25
210	A34	10c gold & multi	.45	.25
211	A34	15c gold & multi	.45	.25
212	A34	20c gold & multi	5.00	1.50
213	A34	25c gold & multi	.90	.45
214	A34	30c gold & multi	.75	.55
215	A34	50c gold & multi	1.10	.55
216	A35	$1 gold & multi	2.40	.60
217	A35	$2 gold & multi	5.50	.90
218	A36	$4 multi, type 2 ('68)	2.25	*4.00*
a.		Type 1	40.00	*55.00*
219	A36	$6 multi ('68)	2.25	*5.00*
219A	A36	$8 multi ('69)	6.25	*12.00*
220	A36	$10 multi ('68)	4.25	*11.00*
		Nos. 199-220 (23)	38.50	42.55

Nos. 199-220 (except No. 204) were reprinted in 1970/71 with the fluorescent printing described below. Value, set: unused $60; used $40.

For surcharges see Nos. 290-291, 305-309, B1-B13, B17-B18, B20. For overprints see Nos. 277-283, 302-304, 315, 351-356, O1-O15.

Fluorescence

Since 1968 a number of stamps have been issued with a "fluorescent security underprinting" in a multiple coat of arms pattern. Some issues have this underprint, some do not.

Stamps issued both with and without the underprint are Nos. 199-203, 205-220, 283, 290-291.

From Nos. 292-296 onward, all stamps have this underprint unless otherwise noted.

Ia Orana Maria, by Gauguin A37

Gauguin Paintings: 3c, Riders on the Beach. 5c, Still Life with Flowers. 8c, Whispered Words. 15c, Maternity. 22c, Why Are You Angry?

1967, Oct. 23 Photo. *Perf. 13½*

221	A37	1c gold & multi	.25	.25
222	A37	3c gold & multi	.25	.25
223	A37	5c gold & multi	.25	.25
224	A37	8c gold & multi	.25	.25
225	A37	15c gold & multi	.30	.25
226	A37	22c gold & multi	.40	.40
a.		Souvenir sheet of 6, #221-226	2.75	2.75
		Nos. 221-226 (6)	1.70	1.65

Nos. 221-226 are printed in sheets of 6 (3x2).

For surcharge see No. B3.

Holy Family by Rubens — A38

Paintings: 3c, Adoration of the Magi, by Albrecht Durer. 4c, The Lucca Madonna, by Jan Van Eyck. 8c, Adoration of the Shepherds, by Jacopo da Bassano. 15c, Nativity, by El Greco. 25c, Madonna and Child, by Antonio Allegri da Correggio.

1967, Dec. 4 *Perf. 12x13*

227	A38	1c gold & multi	.25	.25
228	A38	3c gold & multi	.25	.25
229	A38	4c gold & multi	.25	.25
230	A38	8c gold & multi	.25	.25
231	A38	15c gold & multi	.25	.25
232	A38	25c gold & multi	.30	.30
		Nos. 227-232 (6)	1.55	1.55

Christmas.

Capt. Cook and Matavai Bay, Tahiti, by Sydney Parkinson A39

1c, Ships off Huahine Island, Tahiti, by John & James Clevely. 2c, town & harbor of Kamchatka, by John Webber, & Queen Elizabeth II. 4c, "The Ice Islands" (Antarctica), by William Hodges.

1968, Sept. 12 Photo. *Perf. 13*

233	A39	½c gold & multi	.25	.25
234	A39	1c gold & multi	.25	.25
235	A39	2c gold & multi	.25	.25
236	A39	4c gold & multi	.25	.25
		Nos. 233-236,C12-C15 (8)	3.20	3.20

Bicent. of Capt. Cook's 1st voyage of discovery. Printed in sheets of 10 stamps and 2 labels (3x4). Labels show portraits of Elizabeth II and Cook.

Gymnast A40

1968, Oct. 21

237	A40	1c Sailing	.25	.25
238	A40	5c shown	.25	.25
239	A40	15c High jump	.25	.25
240	A40	20c Woman diver	.30	.25
241	A40	30c Bicyclist	.55	.25
242	A40	50c Woman hurdler	.45	.30
		Nos. 237-242 (6)	2.05	1.55

19th Olympic Games, Mexico City, Oct. 12-27. Printed in sheets of 10 stamps and 2 labels (3x4).

Virgin and Child, by Titian — A41

Paintings: 4c, Holy Family, by Raphael. 10c, Madonna of the Rosary, by Murillo. 20c, Adoration of the Magi, by Memling. 30c, Adoration of the Magi, by Ghirlandajo.

1968, Dec. 2 Photo. *Perf. 13*

243	A41	1c gold & multi	.25	.25
244	A41	4c gold & multi	.25	.25
245	A41	10c gold & multi	.25	.25
246	A41	20c gold & multi	.25	.25
247	A41	30c gold & multi	.30	.30
a.		Souv. sheet, #243-247 + label	1.75	1.75
		Nos. 243-247 (5)	1.30	1.30

Issued in sheets of 6 (2x3).

Training on Ropeway A42

Designs: ½c, Boy Scouts cooking over campfire. 5c, Training with signal flags, and Queen Elizabeth II. 10c, Planting a tree. 20c, Erecting a hut. 30c, Lord Baden-Powell, lake and mountains (visit to Rarotonga in 1935).

1969, Feb. 6 Photo. *Perf. 13½*

248	A42	½c multicolored	.25	.25
249	A42	1c multicolored	.25	.25
250	A42	5c multicolored	.25	.25
251	A42	10c multicolored	.25	.25
252	A42	20c multicolored	.25	.25
253	A42	30c multicolored	.35	.35
		Nos. 248-253 (6)	1.60	1.60

5th Natl. Boy Scout Jamboree, Christchurch, New Zealand, Jan. 2-12.

Issued in sheets of 10 stamps and 2 labels (4x3).

A43

No. 254a, Soccer. No. 254b, Pole vault. No. 255a, Weight lifting. No. 255b, Basketball, Elizabeth II. No. 256a, Long jump. No. 256b, Tennis. No. 257a, Running. No. 257b, Javelin, Elizabeth II. No. 258a, Boxing. No. 258b, Golf.

Perf. 13½x13

1969, July 7 Photo. Unwmk.

254	A43	½c Pair, #a.-b.	.40	.40
255	A43	1c Pair, #a.-b.	.40	.40
256	A43	4c Pair, #a.-b.	1.20	1.20
257	A43	10c Pair, #a.-b.	1.60	1.60
258	A43	15c Pair, #a.-b.	3.00	3.00
c.		Souv. sheet, #254-258 + 2 labels	7.75	7.50
		Nos. 254-258 (5)	6.60	6.60

3rd South Pacifc Games, Port Moresby, Papua and New Guinea, Aug. 13-23.

Issued in sheets of 10.

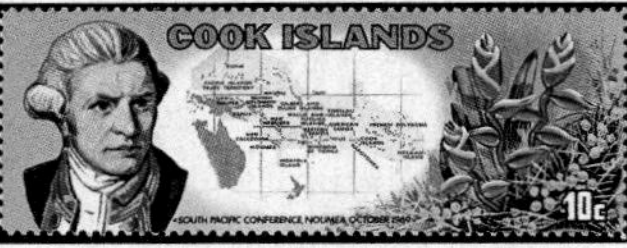

Map of Cook Islands and Capt. Cook — A44

Map of Cook Islands and: 5c, Premier Albert Henry of Cook Islands. 25c, Coat of arms of New Zealand. 30c, Queen Elizabeth II.

1969, Oct. 8 Photo. *Perf. 13*

264	A44	5c red & multi	.35	.35
265	A44	10c lemon & multi	1.00	.50
266	A44	25c green & multi	.50	.50
267	A44	30c blue & multi	.50	.50
		Nos. 264-267 (4)	2.35	1.85

South Pacific Conf., Noumea, Oct. 1969.

Madonna and Child, by Filippo Lippi A45

Paintings: 4c, Holy Family, by Baccio della Porta. 10c, Madonna and Child, by Anton Raphael Mengs. 20c, Madonna and Child, by Le Maitre de Flemalle. 30c, Madonna and Child by Correggio.

1969, Nov. 21 Photo. *Perf. 13½*

268	A45	1c buff & multi	.25	.25
269	A45	4c buff & multi	.25	.25
270	A45	10c buff & multi	.25	.25
271	A45	20c buff & multi	.25	.25
272	A45	30c buff & multi	.25	.25
a.		Souv. sheet, #268-272 + label	1.50	1.50
		Nos. 268-272 (5)	1.25	1.25

Issued in sheets of 8 stamps, one label with portrait of Queen Elizabeth II.

Resurrection of Christ, by Raphael — A46

The Resurrection of Christ by: 8c, Dirk Bouts. 20c, Albert Altdorfer. 25c, Murillo.

1970, Mar. 12 Photo. *Perf. 13½*
Size: 25½x56mm

273 A46 4c gold & multi .25 .25
274 A46 8c gold & multi .25 .25
275 A46 20c gold & multi .25 .25
276 A46 25c gold & multi .25 .25
a. Souv. sheet, #273-276 + 2 labels 1.40 1.40
Nos. 273-276 (4) 1.00 1.00

Easter 1970.
Printed in sheets of 8 stamps and a label (3x3) showing portrait of Queen Elizabeth II and name of painting and painter.
See Nos. 316-318.

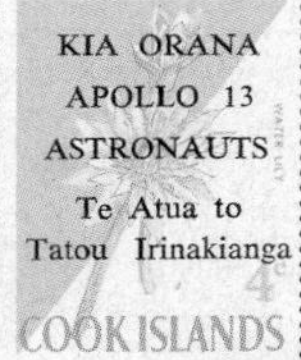

Nos. 205, 208, 211-212, 214, 217 Overprinted

1970, Apr. *Perf. 14x13½*

277 A34 4c gold & multi .30 .30
278 A34 8c gold & multi .30 .30
279 A34 15c gold & multi .30 .30
280 A34 20c gold & multi .40 .40
281 A34 30c gold & multi .30 .30
282 A35 $2 gold & multi 1.25 1.25

No. 218 Overprinted

283 A36 $4 gold & multi 2.50 2.50
Nos. 277-283 (7) 5.35 5.35

Splashdown of Apollo 13 west of Rarotonga, Apr. 17, 1970.
Issued: Nos. 277-282, 4/17; $4, 4/30.
Values for No. 283 is for stamps with fluorescence.
Stamps without fluorescence: Value, mint $32.50, used $50.

Queen Elizabeth II, Prince Philip, Princess Anne and Prince Charles — A47

Design: 30c, Wedgwood bust of Capt. Cook and "Endeavour." $1, Royal visit commemorative coin, obverse and reverse.

1970, June 12 Photo. *Perf. 13½*

284 A47 5c gold & multi .90 .30
285 A47 30c gold & multi 2.25 1.50
286 A47 $1 gold & multi 3.00 3.00
a. Souv. sheet, #284-286 + label 9.75 9.75
Nos. 284-286 (3) 6.15 4.80

Visit of the British royal family.

Nos. 284-286 Overprinted in Silver or Black: "Fifth Anniversary Self-Government August 1970"

1970, Aug. 27 Photo. *Perf. 13½*

287 A47 5c gold & multi (S) .60 .25
288 A47 30c gold & multi 1.10 .50
289 A47 $1 gold & multi 1.50 1.25
Nos. 287-289 (3) 3.20 2.00

5th anniv. of self-government. The overprint on No. 287 is arranged in one line around 3 sides of the design; the overprint on Nos. 288-289 is in 3 horizontal lines.

Nos. 219A-220 Surcharged

1970, Nov. 11 Photo. *Perf. 14x13½*

290 A36 $4 on $8 multi *3.50 3.50*
291 A36 $4 on $10 multi *2.50 2.50*

In each sheet of 15, 3 stamps have 2 surcharged bars instead of one.
Nos. 290-291 without fluorescence: Value, mint $70, used $85.

Nativity A48

Illuminations from 14th Century Robert de Lisle Psalter: 4c, Angel and shepherds. 10c, The Circumcision. 20c, The Adoration of the Kings. 30c, The Presentation at the Temple.

1970, Nov. 30 Photo. *Perf. 13½*

292 A48 1c gold & multi .25 .25
293 A48 4c gold & multi .25 .25
294 A48 10c gold & multi .25 .25
295 A48 20c gold & multi .25 .25
296 A48 30c gold & multi .25 .25
a. Souv. sheet, #292-296 + label 1.50 1.50
Nos. 292-296 (5) 1.25 1.25

Christmas.
Issued in sheets of 5 stamps and a label (3x2) showing portrait of Queen Elizabeth II and source of design.

Nos. 214-215 Overprinted

1971

296B A34 30c +20c multi .40 .60
296C A34 50c +20c multi 1.25 *2.00*

Issued: 30c, 2/25; 50c, 3/8.
Nos. 296B-296C were issued to prepay regular postage plus the fee of a private carrier who had contracted to deliver mail within the United Kingdom during a postal strike. The strike ended on March 8, and these stamps were withdrawn March 12.

Queen Elizabeth II and Prince Philip — A49

Designs: 4c, Royal family at Balmoral. 10c, Prince Philip sailing. 15c, Prince Philip as polo player. 25c, Prince Philip and royal yacht.

1971, Mar. 11 Litho. *Perf. 13½*

297 A49 1c brt blue & multi .25 .25
298 A49 4c brt blue & multi .30 .30
299 A49 10c brt blue & multi .85 .85
300 A49 15c brt blue & multi 1.00 1.00
301 A49 25c brt blue & multi 1.60 1.60
a. Souv. sheet, #297-301 + 2 labels 5.50 5.50
Nos. 297-301 (5) 4.00 4.00

Visit of Prince Philip, Duke of Edinburgh to Rarotonga, Feb. 27, 1971. Printed in sheets of 10 stamps and 2 labels showing Queen Elizabeth II commemorative coin and a portrait of Prince Philip.

Nos. 210, 213-214 Overprinted

1971, Sept. 8 Photo. *Perf. 14x13½*

302 A34 10c gold & multi .50 .50
303 A34 25c gold & multi .50 .50
304 A34 30c gold & multi .50 .50
Nos. 302-304 (3) 1.50 1.50

4th South Pacific Games, Papeete, French Polynesia, Sept. 8-19. See Nos. B8-B13

Nos. 202, 205, 208-209 and 211 Surcharged with New Value and Three Bars

1971, Oct. 20

305 A34 10c on 2½c multi .25 .25
306 A34 10c on 4c multi .25 .25
307 A34 10c on 8c multi .25 .25
308 A34 10c on 9c multi .25 .25
309 A34 10c on 15c multi .25 .25
Nos. 305-309 (5) 1.25 1.25

Madonna and Child, by Bellini — A50

Christmas: Paintings of the Madonna and Child, by Giovanni Bellini.

1971, Nov. 30 *Perf. 13½*

310 A50 1c gold & multi .25 .25
311 A50 4c gold & multi .25 .25
312 A50 10c gold & multi .30 .30
313 A50 20c gold & multi .40 .30
314 A50 30c gold & multi .55 .40
a. Souv. sheet, #310-314 + label 2.25 2.25
Nos. 310-314 (5) 1.75 1.50

See No. B14.

No. 216 Overprinted: "SOUTH PACIFIC / COMMISSION / FEB. 1947-1972"

1972, Feb. 17 Photo. *Perf. 14x13½*

315 A35 $1 gold & multi .80 .80

South Pacific Commission, 25th anniv.

Easter Type of 1970

Illuminations from 14th century Robert de Lisle Psalter: 5c, St. John. 10c, Christ crucified. 30c, Virgin Mary.

1972, Mar. 6 Photo. *Perf. 13½*
Size: 21x68mm

316 A46 5c gold & multi .25 .25
317 A46 10c gold & multi .25 .25
318 A46 30c gold & multi .30 .30
a. Souvenir sheet of 3, #316-318 1.00 1.00
Nos. 316-318 (3) .80 .80

Printed in sheets of 12.
For surcharges see Nos. B15-B16, B19.

Rocket over Moon — A51

No. 319a, Shown. No. 319b, Earth over moon. No. 320a, Landing module and astronaut. No. 320b, Astronaut collecting moon rocks. No. 321a, Earth and rocket over moon. No. 321b, Lunar rover and astronaut. No. 322a, Helicopter over raft in Pacific. No. 322b, Capsule and parachutes.

1972, Apr. 17

319 A51 5c Pair, #a.-b. .25 .25
320 A51 10c Pair, #a.-b. .50 .50
321 A51 25c Pair, #a.-b. 1.40 1.40
322 A51 30c Pair, #a.-b. 1.60 1.60
c. Souvenir sheet of 8 6.00 6.00
Nos. 319-322 (4) 3.75 3.75

Apollo moon explorations.
No. 322c contains Nos. 319-322 arranged in 2 blocks of 4 divided by a map showing splashdown area of Apollo X, XII and XIII.
For surcharges see Nos. B21-B24.

High Jump, Olympic Rings — A52

1972, June 26

327 A52 10c shown .30 .30
328 A52 25c Running .55 .55
329 A52 30c Boxing .55 .55
a. Souv. sheet, #327-329 + label 2.00 2.00
Nos. 327-329 (3) 1.40 1.40

20th Olympic Games, Munich, Aug. 26-Sept. 10. Sheets of 8 stamps and label.
See No. B29.

Rest on Flight to Egypt, by Caravaggio — A53

Paintings: 5c, Virgin of the Swallows, by Guercino. 10c, Virgin with Green Cushion, by Andrea Solario. 20c, Virgin and Child, by Lorenzo di Credi. 30c, Virgin and Child, by Giovanni Bellini.

1972, Oct. 11 Photo. *Perf. 13½*

330 A53 1c gold & multi .25 .25
331 A53 5c gold & multi .35 .25
332 A53 10c gold & multi .45 .25
333 A53 20c gold & multi .55 .30
334 A53 30c gold & multi .90 .40
a. Souv. sheet, #330-334 + label 4.00 4.00
Nos. 330-334 (5) 2.50 1.45

Christmas. See No. B30.

Princess Elizabeth and Prince Philip — A54

Designs: 5c, Wedding ceremony, Westminster Abbey. 15c, Bridal portrait. 30c, Official wedding picture of royal family.

1972, Nov. 20 **Size: 29x40mm**

335	A54	5c silver & multi	.25	.25
336	A54	10c silver & multi	.35	.35

Size: 40x40mm

337	A54	15c silver & multi	.40	.40

Size: 66x40mm

338	A54	30c silver & multi	.55	.55
		Nos. 335-338 (4)	1.55	1.55

25th anniversary of the marriage of Queen Elizabeth II and Prince Philip.

Nos. 335-337 printed in sheets of 8 stamps and one label; No. 338 in sheets of 6.

1c Coin with Queen Elizabeth II and Taro Leaf A55

Queen Elizabeth II Coins: 2c, Pineapples. 5c, Hibiscus. 10c, Oranges. 20c, Fairy terns. 50c, Bonito. $1, Tangaroa, Polynesian god of creation, vert.

1973, Mar. 15 Photo. *Perf. 13x13½*

Size: 37x24mm

339	A55	1c dp car, blk & gold	.25	.25
340	A55	2c blue, blk & gold	.25	.25
341	A55	5c green, blk & gold	.25	.25

Size: 46x30mm

342	A55	10c vio, blue, blk & sil	.25	.25
343	A55	20c dk green, blk & sil	.35	.35
344	A55	50c dp car, black & sil	.60	.60

Size: 32x54½mm

345	A55	$1 blue, blk & silver	.80	.80
		Nos. 339-345 (7)	2.75	2.75

Coinage commemorating silver wedding anniversary of Queen Elizabeth II.

Printed in sheets of 20 stamps and label showing Westminster Abbey.

"Noli me Tangere," by Titian — A56

Paintings: 10c, Descent from the Cross, by Rubens. 30c, The Lamentation of Christ, by Dürer.

1973, Apr. 9

346	A56	5c gold & multi	.25	.25
347	A56	10c gold & multi	.30	.30
348	A56	30c gold & multi	.35	.35
a.		Souvenir sheet of 3, #346-348	1.00	1.00
		Nos. 346-348 (3)	.90	.90

Easter. Printed in sheets of 15 stamps and one label.

See Nos. 378-380, B31-B33, B39-B41.

Queen Elizabeth II in Coronation Regalia — A57

1973, June 1 Photo. *Perf. 14x13½*

349	A57	10c gold & multi	.75	.75

Souvenir Sheet

Perf. 13½x14½

350	A57	50c gold & multi	3.00	3.00

20th anniv. of the coronation of Queen Elizabeth II. No. 349 printed in sheets of 5 stamps and one label.

Nos. 206, 208, 210, 212-214 Overprinted

1973, July 25 Photo. *Perf. 14x13½*

351	A34	5c gold & multi	.25	.25
352	A34	8c gold & multi	.25	.25
353	A34	10c gold & multi	.25	.25
354	A34	20c gold & multi	.25	.25
355	A34	25c gold & multi	.25	.25
356	A34	30c gold & multi	.25	.25
		Nos. 351-356 (6)	1.50	1.50

Nuclear Test Ban Treaty, 10th anniv. and as protest against French nuclear testing on Mururoa atoll.

Tipairua — A58

Historic South Pacific sailing vessels.

1973, Sept. 17 Photo. *Perf. 13½x13*

357	A58	½c shown	.25	.25
358	A58	1c Wa'a Kaulua	.25	.25
359	A58	1½c Tainui	.25	.25
360	A58	5c War canoe	.40	.25
361	A58	10c Pahi	.50	.35
362	A58	15c Amatasi	.85	.85
363	A58	25c Vaka	1.25	1.25
		Nos. 357-363 (7)	3.75	3.45

Annunciation A59

Designs from 15th Century Prayer Book: 5c, The Visitation. 10c, Adoration of the Shepherds. 20c, Adoration of the Kings. 30c, Slaughter of the Innocents.

1973, Oct. 30 Photo. *Perf. 13x13½*

364	A59	1c multicolored	.25	.25
365	A59	5c multicolored	.25	.25
366	A59	10c multicolored	.25	.25
367	A59	20c multicolored	.25	.25
368	A59	30c multicolored	.25	.25
a.		Souv. sheet, #364-368 + label	.90	.90
		Nos. 364-368 (5)	1.25	1.25

Christmas. See Nos. B34-B38.

Princess Anne — A60

30c, Mark Phillips. 50c, Princess and Mark Phillips.

1973, Nov. 14 Photo. *Perf. 14*

369	A60	25c shown	.25	.25
370	A60	30c multicolored	.30	.25
371	A60	50c multicolored	.35	.35
a.		Souv. sheet, #369-371 + label	1.00	1.00
		Nos. 369-371 (3)	.90	.85

Wedding of Princess Anne and Capt. Mark Phillips.

Running and Games Emblem A61

1c, Diving. 3c, Boxing. 10c, Weight lifting. 30c, Bicycling. 50c, Discobolus.

1974, Jan. 24 Photo. *Perf. 14*

372	A61	1c multi, vert.	.25	.25
373	A61	3c multi, vert.	.25	.25
374	A61	5c multi	.25	.25
375	A61	10c multi	.25	.25
376	A61	30c multi	.50	.50
		Nos. 372-376 (5)	1.50	1.50

Souvenir Sheet

377	A61	50c multi, vert.	1.25	1.25

10th British Commonwealth Games, Christchurch, New Zealand, Jan. 24-Feb. 2. No. 377 contains one stamp 35x45mm.

Easter Type of 1973 Dated "1974"

Paintings: 5c, Jesus Carrying Cross, by Raphael. 10c, Jesus in the Arms of God, by El Greco. 30c, Descent from the Cross, by Caravaggio.

1974, Mar. 25 *Perf. 13½x13*

378	A56	5c gold & multi	.25	.25
379	A56	10c gold & multi	.25	.25
380	A56	30c gold & multi	.30	.30
a.		Souvenir sheet of 3, #378-380	1.25	1.25
		Nos. 378-380 (3)	.80	.80

Easter. See Nos. B39-B41.

Phallicium Glaucum A62

Queen Elizabeth II — A63

Queen and Shells — A64

Cook Islands sea shells: 1c, Vasum turbinellus. 1½c, Corculum cardissa. 2c, Terebellum terebellum. 3c, Aulica vespertilio. 4c, Strombus gibberulus. 5c, Cymatium pileare. 6c, Cyprae caputserpentis. 8c, Bursa granularis. 10c, Tenebra muscaria. 15c, Mitra mitra. 20c, Natica alapillonis roding. 25c, Gloripallium pallium. 30c, Conus miles. 50c, Conus textile. 60c, Oliva sericea roding.

The designs of the 2c, 5c, 10c, 30c include portrait of Queen Elizabeth II.

1974-75 Photo. *Perf. 13½*

381	A62	½c shown	.30	.30
382	A62	1c multicolored	.30	.30
383	A62	1½c multicolored	.30	.30
384	A62	2c multicolored	.30	.30
385	A62	3c multicolored	.40	.30
386	A62	4c multicolored	.45	.30
387	A62	5c multicolored	.50	.30
388	A62	6c multicolored	.50	.30
389	A62	8c multicolored	.60	*1.50*
390	A62	10c multicolored	.60	.40
391	A62	15c multicolored	.65	.30
392	A62	20c multicolored	.90	.30
393	A62	25c multicolored	.95	*2.00*
394	A62	30c multicolored	1.00	.40
395	A62	50c multicolored	7.00	3.25
396	A62	60c multicolored	7.50	3.25
397	A63	$1 shown	2.50	*3.50*
398	A63	$2 multi ('75)	2.50	*2.75*

Perf. 14x13½

399	A64	$4 multi ('75)	3.50	5.50
400	A64	$6 multi ('75)	11.00	5.50
401	A64	$8 multi ('75)	12.50	9.00
402	A64	$10 multi ('75)	18.00	6.50
		Nos. 381-402 (22)	72.25	46.55

Issued: 50c, 60c, $1, 8/26; $2, 1/27; $4, 3/17; $6, 4/29; $8, 5/30; $10, 6/30; others, 5/17.

For surcharges & overprints see Nos. 488-498, 526-528, 991, O16-O26, O30-O31.

Soccer Player and Map of Oceania A65

50c, Munich stadium & map of Oceania. $1, Soccer player, Munich stadium & World Cup.

1974, July 5 Photo. *Perf. 13½*

Size: 31x29mm

403	A65	25c multicolored	.30	.30
404	A65	50c multicolored	.40	.40

Size: 68x28½mm

405	A65	$1 multicolored	.75	.75
a.		Souvenir sheet of 3, #403-405	1.50	1.50
		Nos. 403-405 (3)	1.45	1.45

World Cup Soccer Championship, Munich, June 13-July 7. Nos. 403-405 printed in sheets of 8 and commemorative label.

$2.50 Capt. Cook Silver Coin — A66

Commemorative Silver Coins: $7.50, $7.50 coin with Queen Elizabeth II on obverse; Capt. Cook, map of Islands and "Resolution" on reverse. $2.50 coin shows "Resolution," "Adventure" and globe on reverse.

1974, July 22 Photo. *Perf. 14*

406	A66	$2.50 sil, vio & blk	10.00	6.75
407	A66	$7.50 grn, sil & blk	20.00	15.00
a.		Souvenir sheet of 2, #406-407	37.50	37.50

Bicentenary of Capt. Cook's 2nd voyage of discovery. Nos. 406-407 printed in sheets of 5 and commemorative label.

Cook Islands Nos. 1, 49, 62, 66, 77 — A67

Stamps of Cook Islands: 25c, DC-3 over old Rarotonga landing strip, and No. 19. 30c, Rarotonga Post Office, UPU emblem and No. 65. 50c, UPU emblem and Nos. 1, 19, 49, 62, 65-66 and 77.

1974, Sept. 16 Photo. *Perf. 13½x14*

408 A67 10c gold & multi .25 .25
409 A67 25c gold & multi .35 .35
410 A67 30c gold & multi .40 .40
411 A67 50c gold & multi .75 .75
a. Souv. sheet, #408-411, perf. 13½ 1.60 1.60
Nos. 408-411 (4) 1.75 1.75

Cent. of UPU. Nos. 408-411 printed in sheets of 8 and commemorative label.

Virgin and Child, with St. John, by Raphael — A68

Paintings: 5c, Holy Family, by Andrea del Sarto. 10c, Nativity, by Correggio. 20c, Holy Family, by Rembrandt. 30c, Nativity, by Van der Weyden.

1974, Oct. 15 Photo. *Perf. 13½*

412 A68 1c multicolored .25 .25
413 A68 5c multicolored .25 .25
414 A68 10c multicolored .25 .25
415 A68 20c multicolored .40 .40
416 A68 30c multicolored .55 .55
a. Souv. sheet, #412-416 + label 1.75 1.75
Nos. 412-416 (5) 1.70 1.70

Christmas 1974. Nos. 412-416 printed in sheets of 15 and one label showing Queen Elizabeth II.

See Nos. B42-B46.

Churchill and Blenheim Palace A69

Sir Winston Churchill (1874-1965) and: 10c, Parliament. 25c, Chartwell. 30c, Buckingham Palace. 50c, St. Paul's Cathedral.

1974, Nov. 20 Photo. *Perf. 14*

417 A69 5c violet & multi .25 .25
418 A69 10c maroon & multi .25 .25
419 A69 25c dk blue & multi .30 .30
420 A69 30c brown & multi .40 .40
421 A69 50c multicolored .75 .75
a. Souv. sheet, #417-421 + label 2.25 2.25
Nos. 417-421 (5) 1.95 1.95

Nos. 417-421 printed in sheets of 5 stamps and one label showing $100 commemorative gold coin.

Vasco Nunez de Balboa — A70

5c, Ferdinand Magellan & route around South America. 10c, Juan Sebastian de Elcano & ship. 25c, Andres de Urdaneta & ship. 25c, Miguel Lopez de Legaspi & ship.

1975, Feb. 3 *Perf. 13½*

422 A70 1c multicolored .25 .25
423 A70 5c multicolored .65 .25
424 A70 10c multicolored 1.25 .30
425 A70 25c multicolored 2.00 .90
426 A70 30c multicolored 2.25 1.00
Nos. 422-426 (5) 6.40 2.70

16th century explorers of the Pacific Ocean.

Apollo and Apollo-Soyuz Emblem — A71

Apollo-Soyuz Emblem &: No. 427b, Soyuz. No. 428a, Aleksei A. Leonov & Valery N. Kubasov. No. 428b, Donald K. Slayton, Vance D. Brand & Thomas P. Stafford. No. 429a, Cosmonaut inside Soyuz capsule. No. 429b, American astronauts inside Apollo capsule.

1975, July 15 Photo. *Perf. 13½*

427 A71 25c Pair, #a.-b. .80 .80
428 A71 30c Pair, #a.-b. .90 .90
429 A71 50c Pair, #a.-b. 1.25 1.25
c. Souvenir sheet of 6, #427-429 2.75 2.75
Nos. 427-429 (3) 2.95 2.95

Apollo Soyuz space test project (Russo-American space cooperation), launching July 15; link-up, July 17. Printed sheets of 18 stamps and 2 labels showing flags.

$100 Gold Commemorative Coin — A72

1975, Aug. 8 Photo. *Perf. 13½x13*

433 A72 $2 gold & dp violet 3.50 3.25

Bicentenary of the completion of Capt. Cook's second voyage of discovery.

Cook Islands' Flag, Map of Islands and New Zealand A73

Prime Minister Sir Albert Henry — A74

Design: 25c, View of Rarotonga and flag.

1975, Aug. 8 *Perf. 13½x13, 13x13½*

434 A73 5c gold & multi .40 .25
435 A74 10c gold & multi .50 .25
436 A73 25c gold & multi 1.25 .50
Nos. 434-436 (3) 2.15 1.00

Tenth anniversary of self-government.

Virgin and Child, 15th Century, Flemish — A75

Paintings: 10c, Madonna in the Field, by Raphael. 15c, Holy Family, by Raphael. 20c, Adoration of the Shepherds, by J. B. Mayno. 35c, Annunciation, by Murillo.

1975, Dec. 1 Photo. *Perf. 13½*

437 A75 6c gold & multi .25 .25
438 A75 10c gold & multi .25 .25
439 A75 15c gold & multi .30 .30
440 A75 20c gold & multi .30 .30
441 A75 35c gold & multi .45 .45
a. Souv. sheet, #437-441 + label 1.60 1.60
Nos. 437-441 (5) 1.55 1.55

Christmas. See Nos. B47-B51.

Descent from the Cross, by Raphael A76

Paintings: 15c, Pieta, by Veronese. 35c, Pieta, by El Greco.

1976, Mar. 29 Photo. *Perf. 13½*

442 A76 7c gold & multi .25 .25
443 A76 15c gold & multi .50 .50
444 A76 35c gold & multi .80 .80
a. Souvenir sheet of 3, #442-444 1.75 1.75
Nos. 442-444 (3) 1.55 1.55

Easter. Nos. 442-444 printed in sheets of 20 with label showing Queen Elizabeth II.

See Nos. B52-B54.

Benjamin Franklin and "Resolution" — A77

Designs: $2, Capt. James Cook and "Resolution." $3, Cook, "Resolution" and Franklin.

1976, May 29 Photo. *Perf. 13½*

445 A77 $1 gold & multi 3.75 2.50
446 A77 $2 gold & multi 7.75 5.50

Souvenir Sheet

Perf. 13

447 A77 $3 gold & multi 11.50 6.50

American Bicentennial. No. 447 contains one stamp 73x31mm. Nos. 445-446 printed in sheets of 5 and corner label with Franklin's request to assist Capt. Cook.

For overprint see No. O29.

Nos. 445-447 Overprinted "Royal Visit July 1976"

1976, July 6 Photo. *Perf. 13½*

448 A77 $1 gold & multi 2.25 1.75
449 A77 $2 gold & multi 6.00 5.25

Souvenir Sheet

Perf. 13

450 A77 $3 gold & multi 7.50 6.75

Visit of Queen Elizabeth II and Prince Philip to the United States.

High Hurdles — A78

15c, Field hockey. 30c, Fencing. 35c, Soccer.

1976, July 22 *Perf. 13½*

451 A78 7c Pair, #a.-b. .40 .40
452 A78 15c Pair, #a.-b. .50 .50
453 A78 30c Pair, #a.-b. .90 .90
454 A78 35c Pair, #a.-b. 1.10 1.10
c. Souvenir sheet of 8, #451-454 3.50 3.50
Nos. 451-454 (4) 2.90 2.90

21st Olympic Games, Montreal, Canada, 7/17-8/1. Printed in sheets of 10 stamps + 2 labels.

The Visitation — A80

Designs: 10c, Virgin and Child. 15c, Adoration of the Shepherds. 20c, Adoration of the Kings. 35c, Holy Family. After painted Renaissance altar sculptures.

1976, Oct. 12 Photo. *Perf. 14x13½*

459 A80 6c gold & multi .25 .25
460 A80 10c gold & multi .25 .25
461 A80 15c gold & multi .25 .25
462 A80 20c gold & multi .25 .25
463 A80 35c gold & multi .25 .25
a. Souv. sheet, #459-463 + label 1.25 1.25
Nos. 459-463 (5) 1.25 1.25

Christmas. Nos. 459-463 printed in sheets of 20 with label showing Queen Elizabeth II.

See Nos. B55-B59.

$5 Silver Coin, 1976 — A81

1976, Nov. 15 Photo. *Perf. 13½*

464 A81 $1 multicolored 2.00 1.50

National Wildlife and Conservation Day. Issued in sheets of 5 stamps and commemorative label.

See Nos. 502, 536.

A82

No. 465a, Crown. No. 465b, Elizabeth II in Coronation Vestments. No. 466a, Westminster Abbey. No. 466b, Coach in procession. No. 467a, Queen and Prince Philip after coronation. No. 467b, Investiture of Sir Albert Henry, Premier of Cook Islands, 1974.

1977, Feb. 7 Photo. *Perf. 13½x13*

465 A82 25c Pair, #a.-b. .40 .40
466 A82 50c Pair, #a.-b. .75 .75
467 A82 $1 Pair, #a.-b. 1.25 1.25
c. Souv. sheet, #465-467, perf. 13 2.75 2.75
Nos. 465-467 (3) 2.40 2.40

Reign of Queen Elizabeth II, 25th anniv. Printed in sheets of 8.

For overprints see No. O27.

Crucifixion, by Rubens — A83

Paintings by Rubens: 15c, Christ Between the Thieves. 35c, Descent from the Cross.

1977, Mar. 28 Photo. *Perf. 14x13½*

471	A83	7c gold & multi	.40	.40
472	A83	15c gold & multi	.50	.50
473	A83	35c gold & multi	1.00	1.00
a.		Souv. sheet, #471-473, perf 13	2.00	2.00
		Nos. 471-473 (3)	1.90	1.90

Easter 1977, and 400th birth anniv. of Peter Paul Rubens (1577-1640), Flemish painter. Nos. 471-473 printed in sheets of 24 stamps and corner label with portrait of Queen Elizabeth II and description.
See Nos. B60-B62.

Virgin and Child, by Memling — A84

Virgin and Child by: 10c, Hans Memling. 15c, Geertgen Tot Sin Jans. 20c, Carlo Crivelli. 35c, School of Henry Blex.

1977, Oct. 3 Photo. *Perf. 13½*

474	A84	6c gold & multi	.25	.25
475	A84	10c gold & multi	.25	.25
476	A84	15c gold & multi	.25	.25
477	A84	20c gold & multi	.35	.35
478	A84	35c gold & multi	.55	.55
a.		Souv. sheet, #474-478 + label	1.60	1.60
		Nos. 474-478 (5)	1.65	1.65

Christmas. Nos. 474-478 printed in sheets of 24 and label. See Nos. B63-B67.

$5-silver Coin, 1977 — A85

1977, Nov. 15 Photo. *Perf. 13½*

479	A85	$1 silver & multi	2.00	.95

National Wildlife Conservation Day. No. 479 issued in sheets of 5 and one label.

Capt. Cook, by Nathaniel Dance and "Resolution" — A86

$1, "Capt. Cook Landing at Owyhee" and Capt. Cook. $2, Cook Islands $200 commemorative coin, 1978, and Cook Monument, Hawaii, 1825.

1978, Jan. 20 Litho. *Perf. 13½*

480	A86	50c gold & multi	.80	.80
481	A86	$1 gold & multi	1.25	1.25
482	A86	$2 gold & multi	2.50	2.50
a.		Souvenir sheet of 3, #480-482	4.75	4.75
		Nos. 480-482 (3)	4.55	4.55

Bicentennial of Capt. Cook's arrival in Hawaii.
Nos. 480-482 issued in sheets of 5 with corner label showing ship off Hawaiian coast.
For overprints see Nos. 499-501a.

Pieta, by Rogier van der Weyden A87

Paintings, National Gallery, London: 35c, Burial of Jesus, by Michelangelo. 75c, Jesus at Emmaus, by Caravaggio.

1978, Mar. 20 Photo. *Perf. 13½x13*

483	A87	15c gold & multi	.30	.30
484	A87	35c gold & multi	.50	.50
485	A87	75c gold & multi	.75	.75
a.		Souv. sheet, #483-485 + label	1.25	1.25
		Nos. 483-485 (3)	1.55	1.55

Easter. Nos. 483-485 printed in sheets of 5 and corner label showing National Gallery.
See Nos. B68-B70.

Souvenir Sheets

Coronation of Queen Elizabeth II, 25th anniv. — A88

1978, June 6 Photo. *Perf. 13*

486	A88	Sheet of 4 + 2 labels	1.30	1.30
a.		50c Queen Elizabeth II	.30	.30
b.		50c Lion of England	.30	.30
c.		50c Imperial State Crown	.30	.30
d.		50c Tangaroa figure	.30	.30
487	A88	Sheet of 4 + label	1.55	1.30
a.		70c like 486a	.30	.30
b.		70c Scepter with Cross	.30	.30
c.		70c St. Edward's Crown	.30	.30
d.		70c Rarotongan staff god	.30	.30
e.		Souv. sheet of 8, #486a-487d + label	2.50	2.50

Coronation of Queen Elizabeth II, 25th anniv.

Nos. 381, 383, 388-389, 393-396 Srchd. in Silver, Black or Gold

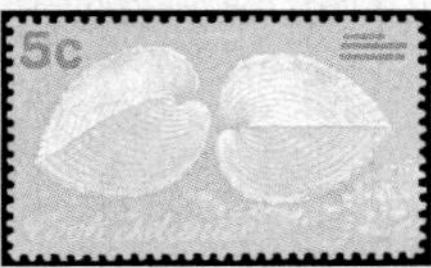

1978, Nov. 10 Photo. *Perf. 13½*

488	A62	5c on 1½c multi (S)	.25	.25
489	A62	7c on ½c multi	.25	.25
490	A62	10c on 6c multi (G)	.40	.40
491	A62	10c on 8c multi (G)	.40	.40
492	A62	15c on ½c multi	.65	.60
493	A62	15c on 25c multi (S)	.65	.60
494	A62	15c on 30c multi	.65	.60
495	A62	15c on 50c multi (S)	.65	.60
496	A62	15c on 60c multi (G)	.65	.60
497	A62	17c on ½c multi	.80	.80
498	A62	17c on 50c multi (S)	.80	.80
		Nos. 488-498 (11)	6.15	5.90

See Nos. 526-528.

Nos. 480-482a Overprinted in Black on Silver Panel

1978, Nov. 13 Litho. *Perf. 13½*

499	A86	50c gold & multi	1.00	1.00
500	A86	$1 gold & multi	1.50	1.50
501	A86	$2 gold & multi	2.25	2.25
a.		Souvenir sheet of 3, #499-501	15.00	15.00
		Nos. 499-501 (3)	4.75	4.75

250th anniv. of Capt. Cook's birth. Similar overprint in 4 lines was applied to labels. Label of No. 501a overprinted only with dates 1728, 1978.

Coin Type of 1976

$1, $5 Silver coin, 1978 (Polynesian warbler).

1978, Nov. 15 Photo. *Perf. 13½*

502	A81	$1 multicolored	1.60	1.60

National Wildlife and Conservation Day. Sheets of 24 containing 4 panes of 6.

A89

Virgin and Child by: 15c, Rogier van der Weyden. 17c, Carlo Crivelli. 35c, Murillo.

1978, Dec. 8 Photo. *Perf. 13*

503	A89	15c multicolored	.35	.35
504	A89	17c multicolored	.45	.45
505	A89	35c multicolored	.75	.75
a.		Souvenir sheet of 3, #503-505	1.60	1.60
		Nos. 503-505 (3)	1.55	1.55

Christmas. See Nos. B71-B73.

A90

Descent from the Cross, by Gaspar de Crayer (Details): 10c, Pieta. 12c, St. John. 15c, Mary Magdalene. 20c, Cherubs.

1979, Apr. 5 Photo. *Perf. 13*

506	A90	10c multicolored	.25	.25
507	A90	12c multicolored	.25	.25
508	A90	15c multicolored	.25	.25
509	A90	20c multicolored	.50	.50
		Nos. 506-509 (4)	1.25	1.25

Easter. See No. B74.

A91

20c, Capt. Cook, by John Weber. 30c, Resolution, by Henry Roberts. 35c, Endeavour. 50c, Death of Capt. Cook, by George Carter.

1979, July 23 Photo. *Perf. 14x13½*

510	A91	20c multicolored	.40	.40
511	A91	30c multicolored	.55	.55
512	A91	35c multicolored	.65	.65
513	A91	50c multicolored	.80	.80
a.		Souvenir sheet of 4	2.50	2.50
		Nos. 510-513 (4)	2.40	2.40

Capt. Cook (1728-1779), explorer. No. 513a contains 4 stamps similar to Nos. 510-513 with black frames.

Sir Rowland Hill, Originator of Penny Postage — A92

No. 514a, Postrider. No. 514b, Stagecoach. No. 514c, Automobile. No. 514d, Streamlined train. No. 515a, Cap-Horniers, sailing ship. No. 515b, River steamer. No. 515c, Liner Deutschland. No. 515d, Liner United States. No. 516a, Balloon Neptune. No. 516b, Junkers F13. No. 516c, Graf Zeppelin. No. 516d, Concorde.

1979, Sept. 10 *Perf. 14½*

514	A92	30c Block of 4, #a.-d.	1.00	1.00
515	A92	35c Block of 4, #a.-d.	1.10	1.10
516	A92	50c Block of 4, #a.-d.	1.60	1.60
e.		Souv. sheet of 12, #514-516	4.00	4.00
		Nos. 514-516 (3)	3.70	3.70

Nos. 381, 383, 396 Srchd. in Gold or Silver

1979, Sept. 12 Photo. *Perf. 13½*

526	A62	6c on ½c multi	.25	.25
527	A62	10c on 1½c multi (S)	.25	.25
528	A62	15c on 60c multi	.25	.25
		Nos. 526-528 (3)	.75	.75

Nos. 526-528 have 3 thick bars of equal length over old value.

Girl and Baby, IYC Emblem — A93

IYC Emblem and: 50c, Boy playing tree drum. 65c, Children dancing.

1979, Oct. 10 *Perf. 13*

529	A93	30c multicolored	.25	.25
530	A93	50c multicolored	.35	.35
531	A93	65c multicolored	.45	.45
		Nos. 529-531 (3)	1.05	1.05

See No. B75.

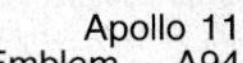
Apollo 11 Emblem — A94

50c, Apollo 11 crew, lunar map. 60c, Astronaut walking on moon. 65c, Splashdown.

1979, Nov. 7 *Perf. 14*

532	A94	30c multicolored	.30	.30
533	A94	50c multicolored	.50	.50
534	A94	60c multicolored	.60	.60
535	A94	65c multicolored	.70	.70
a.		Souv. sheet, #532-535, perf. 13	2.50	2.50
		Nos. 532-535 (4)	2.10	2.10

Apollo 11 moon landing, 10th anniv.

Coin Type of 1976

$1, $5 Silver coin, 1979 (Rarotonga fruit dove).

Perf. 13½x14½

1979, Nov. 15 Photo.

536 A81 $1 multicolored 1.75 1.75

National Wildlife and Conservation Day.

Christmas Tree Ornaments — A95

Christmas (Flowers and): 10c, Star. 12c, Bells and candle. 15c, Ancestral statue.

1979, Dec. 14 ***Perf. 14***

537 A95 6c multicolored .25 .25
538 A95 10c multicolored .25 .25
539 A95 12c multicolored .25 .25
540 A95 15c multicolored .25 .25
Nos. 537-540,B76-B79 (8) 2.00 2.00

See also Nos. C16-C19, CB1-CB4.

A96

Bible illustrations by Gustave Dore, 1833-1883: No. 541a, Flagellation. No. 541b, Jesus Wearing Crown of Thorns. No. 542a, Jesus Mocked. No. 542b, Jesus Falls. No. 543a, The Crucifixion. No. 543b, Descent from the Cross.

1980, Mar. 31 Photo. ***Perf. 13***

541 A96 20c Pair, #a.-b. .50 .50
542 A96 30c Pair, #a.-b. .70 .70
543 A96 35c Pair, #a.-b. .80 .80
Nos. 541-543 (3) 2.00 2.00

Easter. See Nos. 553, B80-B83.

Doves with Olive Branch, Rotary Emblem A97

1980, May 27 Photo. ***Perf. 14***

547 A97 30c shown .35 .35
548 A97 35c Flowers .40 .40
549 A97 50c Flags, globe .55 .55
Nos. 547-549 (3) 1.30 1.30

Rotary Intl., 75th anniv. See No. B87

Easter Type of 1980 and

New Zealand No. 1 — A98

No. 550a, Postrider. No. 550b, Coach. No. 550c, Automobile. No. 550d, Train.

New Zealand #2 and: No. 551a, Sailing ship. No. 551b, River steamer. No. 551c, Transatlantic liner (facing left). No. 551d, Transatlantic liner (facing right).

New Zealand #3 and: No. 552a, 1870-71 mail balloon. No. 552b, 1919 plane. No. 552c, Graf Zeppelin. No. 552d, Concorde.

1980, Aug. 22 Photo. ***Perf. 14***

550 A98 30c Block of 4, #a.-d. 1.25 1.00
551 A98 35c Block of 4, #a.-d. 1.60 1.25
552 A98 50c Block of 4, #a.-d. 2.25 1.40
e. Souvenir sheet of 12 6.25 5.50
Nos. 550-552 (3) 5.10 3.65

Souvenir Sheet

Perf. 13

553 A96 Sheet of 6, #541-543 2.50 1.50

ZEAPEX '80, New Zealand Intl. Stamp Exhib., Auckland, Aug. 23-31. No. 552e contains four each of Nos. 550-552 arranged horizontally (4x3). No. 553 has black on gold overprint: "ZEAPEX / '80 / Auckland / +10c" in margin.

Queen Mother Elizabeth, 80th Birthday — A99

1980, Sept. 22 Photo. ***Perf. 13***

554 A99 50c multicolored .75 .75

Souvenir Sheet

555 A99 $2 multicolored 1.50 1.50

No. 554 issued in sheets of 9 (3x3).

Johannes Kepler, Spacecraft — A100

Designs: Nos. 556a, 559a, Kepler, spacecraft (diff.). No. 556b, Kepler, Apollo Command Module, moon. No. 559b, Kepler, lunar rover, astronaut on moon. Nos. 557a-558b, Jules Verne, various scenes from From Earth to Moon, vert.

1980, Nov. 7 Photo. ***Perf. 13***

556 A100 12c Pair, #a-b 1.00 1.00
557 A100 20c Pair, #a-b 1.00 1.00
558 A100 30c Pair, #a-b 1.10 1.10
c. Souvenir sheet, #557-558 2.25 2.25
559 A100 50c Pair, #a-b 2.00 2.00
c. Souv. sheet, #556, 559 3.00 3.00
Nos. 556-559 (4) 5.10 5.10

Death anniversaries of Johannes Kepler, German astronomer and Jules Verne, French science fiction writer.

Burning Bush Coral — A101

Daisy Coral — A102

Nos. 564a, 570a, 576a, Siphonogorgia. Nos. 564b, 570b, 576b, Pavona practorta. Nos. 564c, 570c, 576c, Stylaster echinatus. Nos. 564d, 570d, 576d, Tubastraea. Nos. 565a, 571a, 577a, Millepora alcicornis. Nos. 565b, 571b, 577b, Junceella gemmaea. Nos. 565c, 571c, 577c, Fungia fungites. Nos. 565d, 571d, 577d, Heliofungia actiniformis. Nos. 566a, 572a, 578a, Distichopora violacea. Nos. 566b, 572b, 578b, Stylaster. Nos. 566c, 572c, 578c, Gonipora. Nos. 566d, 572d, 578d, Caulastraea echinulata. Nos. 567a, 573a, 579a, Ptilosarcus gurneyi. Nos. 567b, 573b, 579b, Stylophora pistillata. Nos. 567c, 573c, 579c, Melithaea squamata. Nos. 567d, 573d, 579d, Porites andrewsi. Nos. 568a, 574a, 580a, Lobophyllia bemprichii. Nos. 568b, 574b, 580b, Palauastrea ramosa. Nos. 568c, 574c, 580c, Bellonella indica. Nos. 568d, 574d, 580d, Pectinia alcicornis. Nos. 569a, 575a, 581a, Sarcophyton digitatum. Nos. 569b, 575b, 581b, Melithaea albitincta. Nos. 569c, 575c, 581c, Plerogyra sinuosa. Nos. 569d, 575d, 581d, Dendrophyllia gracilis.

1980-82 ***Perf. 13½x13***

Strips of 4 (#564-575) or Blocks of 4 (#576-581)

564 A101 1c #a.-d. .60 .60
565 A101 3c #a.-d. .65 .65
566 A101 4c #a.-d. .70 .70
567 A101 5c #a.-d. .75 .75
568 A101 6c #a.-d. .80 .80
569 A101 8c #a.-d. .85 .85
570 A101 10c #a.-d. .90 .90
571 A101 12c #a.-d. 1.00 1.00
572 A101 15c #a.-d. 1.10 1.10
573 A101 20c #a.-d. 1.25 1.25
574 A101 25c #a.-d. 1.40 1.40
575 A101 30c #a.-d. 1.75 1.75
576 A101 35c #a.-d. 1.90 1.90
577 A101 50c #a.-d. 2.50 2.50
578 A101 60c #a.-d. 2.75 2.75
579 A101 70c #a.-d. 7.00 7.00
580 A101 80c #a.-d. 7.50 7.50
581 A101 $1 #a.-d. 8.00 8.00

Perf. 14x13½

582 A102 $2 like #566c 8.00 3.25
583 A102 $3 like #565d 10.00 3.25
584 A102 $4 like #567b 4.00 *10.00*
585 A102 $6 like #564c 6.00 *15.00*
586 A102 $10 like #569b 22.50 *27.50*
Nos. 564-586 (23) 91.90 100.40

Issued: 1-8c, 11/21/80; 10-30c, 12/19/80; 35-60c, 3/16/81; 70c, 80c, 4/13/81; $1, 5/20/81; $2, $3, 11/27/81; $4, $6, 1/11/82; $10, 3/5/82.

For surcharges see Nos. 710-714, 716, 738, 740, 811-815, 953-954, 956-957, 959, 961-962, 964, 978-979, 984-986, B109-B111, O50-O53. For overprints see Nos. 992, 1049.

Annunciation, 13th Century Prayerbook Illustration — A102a

1980, Dec. 1 Photo. ***Perf. 14***

652 A102a 15c shown .25 .25
653 A102a 30c Visitation .30 .30
654 A102a 40c Nativity .40 .40
655 A102a 50c Epiphany .50 .50
a. Souvenir sheet of 4, #652-655 1.35 1.35
Nos. 652-655 (4) 1.45 1.45

Christmas. See Nos. B88-B91.

Crucifixion, 12th Cent. Prayerbook Illustration — A103

1981, Apr. 10 ***Perf. 14***

656 A103 15c shown .25 .25
657 A103 25c Placing in Tomb .35 .35
658 A103 40c Marys at the Tomb .50 .50
Nos. 656-658 (3) 1.10 1.10

Easter. See Nos. B92-B95.

Prince Charles and Lady Diana — A104

1981, July 29 Photo. ***Perf. 14***

659 A104 $1 Charles .50 .50
660 A104 $2 shown 1.25 1.25
a. Souv. sheet of 2, #659-660 2.00 2.00

Royal Wedding. Issued in sheets of 4. For overprints and surcharges see Nos. 679-680, 715, 835, 980-981, B97-B98.

Soccer Players — A105

Designs: Various soccer players.

1981, Oct 20 Photo. ***Perf. 14***

661 A105 20c Pair, #a.-b. .80 .80
662 A105 30c Pair, #a.-b. 1.00 1.00
663 A105 35c Pair, #a.-b. 1.40 1.40
664 A105 50c Pair, #a.-b. 1.75 1.75
Nos. 661-664 (4) 4.95 4.95

ESPANA '82 World Cup Soccer Championships. See No. B96.

Virgin and Child, by Rubens — A107

Christmas: Rubens Paintings: 15c, Coronation of St. Catherine. 40c, Adoration of the Shepherds. 50c, Adoration of the Kings.

1981, Dec. 14 Photo. ***Perf. 14x13½***

669 A107 8c shown .45 .25
670 A107 15c multicolored .55 .25
671 A107 40c multicolored 1.00 1.00
672 A107 50c multicolored 1.25 1.25
Nos. 669-672 (4) 3.25 2.75

Souvenir Sheets

1982, Jan. 18

673 A107 75c +5c like #669 .85 .85
674 A107 75c +5c like #670 .85 .85
675 A107 75c +5c like #671 .85 .85
676 A107 75c +5c like #672 .85 .85

Surtax was for school children. See No. B99.

21st Birthday of Princess Diana — A108

No. 677a, 21st Birthday. No. 677b, 1 July 1982. No. 678a, Wedding portrait. No. 678b, 1 July 1982. No. 678cd, $1.25, No. 678ce, $2.50, both inscribed "21st Birthday / 1 July 1982."

1982, June 21 Photo. ***Perf. 14***

677 A108 $1.25 Pair, #a.-b. 3.50 3.50
678 A108 $2.50 Pair, #a.-b. 4.00 4.00
c. Souv. sheet of 2, #d.-e. 6.25 6.25

Issued in sheets of 4.

See Nos. 681-682. For surcharges and overprints see Nos. 739-740, 833-834, 982.

Nos. 659-660a Overprinted

No. 680cd, $1; No. 680ce, $2, both inscribed "21 JUNE 1982 ROYAL BIRTH."

1982, July 12

679 A104 $1 Pair, #a.-b. 1.75 1.75
680 A104 $2 Pair, #a.-b. 4.00 4.00
c. Souv. sheet of 2, #d.-e. 4.25 4.25

Issued in sheets of 4.
For surcharges see Nos. 987-988.

Design A108 Inscribed

No. 682cd, $1.25; No. 682ce, $2.50, both inscribed "Royal Birth / June 1982."

1982, Aug. 3

681 A108 $1.25 Pair, #a.-b. 2.50 2.50
682 A108 $2.50 Pair, #a.-b. 5.00 5.00
c. Souv. sheet of 2, #d.-e. 5.50 5.50

Issued in sheets of 4.

Serenade, by Norman Rockwell (1894-1978) A109

10c, The Hikers. 20c, The Doctor and the Doll. 30c, Home From Camp.

1982, Sept. 10 Photo. *Perf. 14*

683 A109 5c shown .25 .25
684 A109 10c multicolored .25 .25
685 A109 20c multicolored .25 .25
686 A109 30c multicolored .25 .25
Nos. 683-686 (4) 1.00 1.00

Christmas A110

Princess Diana Holding Prince William. Various Details from Virgin with Garlands, by Rubens.

1982, Nov. 30 Photo. *Perf. 14*

687 A110 35c multicolored 1.40 .75
688 A110 48c multicolored 2.00 1.50
689 A110 60c multicolored 2.25 1.75
690 A110 $1.70 multicolored 3.00 *5.00*
Nos. 687-690 (4) 8.65 9.00

Souvenir Sheets

Perf. 13½

691 Sheet of 4 6.50 6.50
a. A110 60c like 35c 1.50 1.50
b. A110 60c like 48c 1.50 1.50
c. A110 60c like #689 1.50 1.50
d. A110 60c like $1.70 1.50 1.50
692 A110 75c + 5c like 35c 1.75 1.75
693 A110 75c + 5c like 48c 1.75 1.75
694 A110 75c + 5c like 60c 1.75 1.75
695 A110 75c + 5c like $1.70 1.75 1.75

No. 691 contains 4 stamps (27x32mm, showing only painting details) plus 2 labels showing Diana and William. Nos. 692-695 show Diana and William (27x39mm), multicolored margins show painting details. Surtax was for child welfare.

Commonwealth Day — A111

No. 696a, Tangaroa statue. No. 696b, Rarotonga oranges. No. 696c, Rarotonga Airport. No. 696d, Prime Minister Thomas Davis.

1983, Mar. 14 Photo. *Perf. 14*

696 A111 60c Block of 4, #a.-d. 2.75 2.75

For overprints see No. O46.

Scouting Year — A112

36c, Camping. 48c, Rope swing. 60c, Tree planting.

1983, Apr. 5 Photo. *Perf. 13x13½*

700 A112 12c Pair, #a.-b. .90 .90
701 A112 36c Pair, #a.-b. 1.25 1.25
702 A112 48c Pair, #a.-b. 1.75 1.75
703 A112 60c Pair, #a.-b. 2.75 2.75
Nos. 700-703 (4) 6.65 6.65

Souvenir Sheet of 8

704 #a.-d. 7.00 7.00

No. 704 contains one each of Nos. 700-703 with 2c surtax.

Nos. 700-704 Overprinted

1983, July 4 Photo. *Perf. 13x13½*

705 A112 12c Pair, #a.-b. 1.25 1.25
706 A112 36c Pair, #a.-b. 1.75 1.75
707 A112 48c Pair, #a.-b. 2.25 2.25
708 A112 60c Pair, #a.-b. 3.00 3.00
Nos. 705-708 (4) 8.25 8.25

Souvenir Sheet of 8

709 A112 #a.-d. 6.50 6.50

Nos. 569, 572, 574-575, 579, 587, 660 Surcharged in Black or Gold

No. 710a

No. 712a

No. 715

No. 716

Perf. 13½x13, 14x13½, 14

1983, Aug. 12 Photo.

Strips of 4, #a.-d. (#710-713) or Block of 4, #a.-d. (#714)

710 A101 18c on 8c #569 2.75 2.75
711 A101 36c on 15c #572 4.25 4.25
712 A101 36c on 30c #575 4.50 4.50
713 A101 48c on 25c #574 6.00 6.00
714 A101 72c on 70c #579 10.00 10.00
715 A104 96c on $2 #660 (G) 7.50 5.00
716 A102 $5.60 on $6 #585 (G) 20.00 18.00
Nos. 710-716 (7) 55.00 50.50

A114

A115

1983, Sept. 9 *Perf. 14*

732 Pair 1.00 1.00
a. A114 6c Gt. Britain .50 .50
b. A115 6c Cook Islds. Group Federal flag .50 .50
733 Pair 1.25 1.25
a. A114 12c Raratonga ensign .60 .60
b. A115 12c New Zealand .60 .60
734 Pair 1.50 1.50
a. A114 15c Cook Islds, 1973-79 .70 .70
b. A115 15c Cook Islds, 1983 .70 .70
c. Souvenir sheet of 6, #732-734 2.00 2.00
735 Pair 1.50 1.50
a. A114 20c like #732a .70 .70
b. A115 20c like #732b .70 .70
736 Pair 1.60 1.60
a. A114 30c like #733a .75 .75
b. A115 30c like #733b .75 .75
737 Pair 1.75 1.75
a. A114 35c like #734a .85 .85
b. A115 35c like #734b .85 .85
c. Souvenir sheet of 6, #735-737 3.50 3.50
Nos. 732-737 (6) 8.60 8.60

Nos. 732-737 have different background landscapes; Nos. 735-737 airmail with silver background. Nos. 734c, 737c perf. 13½.

Nos. 576, 586, 678 Surcharged in Black or Gold

Perf. 13½x13, 14x13½, 14

1983, Aug. 30 Photo.

Block of 4, #a.-d.

738 A101 36c on 35c #576 4.25 4.25

Pair, #a.-b. (#739)

739 A108 96c on $2.50 #678 (G) 5.50 5.50
740 A102 $5.60 on $10 #586 (G) 20.00 18.00
Nos. 738-740 (3) 29.75 27.75

Satellite Earth Station — A116

Designs: Various satellites in orbit.

1983, Oct. 10 Litho. *Perf. 13½*

744 A116 36c multicolored .75 .75
745 A116 48c multicolored 1.00 1.00
746 A116 60c multicolored 1.25 1.25
747 A116 96c multicolored 1.75 1.75
Nos. 744-747 (4) 4.75 4.75

Souvenir Sheet

748 A116 $2 multicolored 3.50 3.50

World Communications Year.

Christmas A117

Raphael Paintings: 12c, La Belle Jardiniere. 18c, Madonna and Child with Five Saints. 36c, Madonna and Child with Saint John. 48c, Madonna of the Fish. 60c, Madonna of the Baldacchino.

1983 Photo. *Perf. 14*

749 A117 12c multicolored .75 .75
750 A117 18c multicolored 1.00 1.00
751 A117 36c multicolored 1.50 1.50
752 A117 48c multicolored 1.90 1.90
753 A117 60c multicolored 2.50 2.50
Nos. 749-753 (5) 7.65 7.65

Souvenir Sheets

Perf. 13½

754 Sheet of 5 3.00 3.00
a. A117 12c + 3c like #749 .25 .25
b. A117 18c + 3c like #750 .25 .25
c. A117 36c + 3c like #751 .50 .50
d. A117 48c + 3c like #752 .65 .65
e. A117 60c + 3c like #753 .85 .85
755 A117 85c + 5c like #749 1.20 1.20
756 A117 85c + 5c like #750 1.20 1.20
757 A117 85c + 5c like #751 1.20 1.20
758 A117 85c + 5c like #752 1.20 1.20
759 A117 85c + 5c like #753 1.20 1.20

Nos. 749-753 issued in sheets of 5 + label. Surtax was for children's charities.

Issued: Nos. 749-754, Nov. 14; others, Dec. 9.

Manned Flight Bicent. — A118

Various balloons: 36c, 1st manned flight, 1783. 48c, Ascent of Adorne, Strasbourg, 1784. 60c, 1785. 72c, Man on horse, 1785. 96c, Godard's aerial acrobatics, 1850.
$2.50, Blanchard & Jefferies, 1785.

1984, Jan. 16 Photo. *Perf. 13*

760	A118 36c multicolored	.70	.70
761	A118 48c multicolored	.85	.85
762	A118 60c multicolored	.95	.95
763	A118 72c multicolored	1.10	1.10
764	A118 96c multicolored	1.25	1.25
	Nos. 760-764 (5)	4.85	4.85

Souvenir Sheets

765	A118 $2.50 multicolored	3.25	3.25
766	Sheet of 5	4.75	4.75
a.	A118 36c + 5c like 36c	.60	.60
b.	A118 48c + 5c like 48c	.70	.70
c.	A118 60c + 5c like 60c	1.05	1.05
d.	A118 72c + 5c like 72c	1.20	1.20
e.	A118 96c + 5c like 96c	1.60	1.60

No. 765 contains 1 stamp 30x48mm, perf. 13½.

Save the Whales Campaign A119

10c, Cuvier's beaked whale. 18c, Risso's dolphin. 20c, True's beaked whale. 24c, Long-finned pilot whale. 30c, Narwhal. 36c, Beluga whale. 42c, Common dolphin. 48c, Commerson's dolphin. 60c, Bottle-nosed dolphin. 72c, Sowerby's whale. 96c, Common porpoise. $2, Boutu.

1984, Feb. 10 Photo. *Perf. 13*

767	A119 10c multicolored	.55	.55
768	A119 18c multicolored	.75	.75
769	A119 20c multicolored	.85	.85
770	A119 24c multicolored	.90	.90
771	A119 30c multicolored	1.00	1.00
772	A119 36c multicolored	1.25	1.25
773	A119 42c multicolored	1.50	1.50
774	A119 48c multicolored	1.60	1.60
775	A119 60c multicolored	1.75	1.75
776	A119 72c multicolored	2.25	2.25
777	A119 96c multicolored	2.50	2.50
778	A119 $2 multicolored	3.50	3.50
	Nos. 767-778 (12)	18.40	18.40

1984 Summer Olympics A120

Posters of Various Summer Olympics: 18c, Athens, 1896. 24c, Paris, 1900. 36c, St. Louis, 1904. 48c, London, 1948. 60c, Tokyo, 1964. 72c, Berlin, 1936. 96c, Rome, 1960. $1.20, Los Angeles, 1932.
72c, 96c, $1.20 airmail.

1984, Mar. 8 Photo. *Perf. 13½*

779	A120 18c multicolored	.45	.45
780	A120 24c multicolored	.50	.55
781	A120 36c multicolored	.60	.60
782	A120 48c multicolored	.70	.70
783	A120 60c multicolored	.80	.80
784	A120 72c multicolored	.90	.90
785	A120 96c multicolored	1.00	1.00
786	A120 $1.20 multicolored	1.25	1.25
	Nos. 779-786 (8)	6.20	6.25

For overprints see Nos. 826-828.

Coral — A121

and

Nos. 582-586 Surcharged

1c, Siphonogorgia. 2c, Millepora alcicornis. 3c, Distichopora violacea. 5c, Ptilosarcus gurneyi. 10c, Lobophyllia bemprichii. 12c, Sarcophyton digitatum. 14c, Pavona praetorta. 18c, Junceela gemmacea. 20c, Stylaster. 24c, Stylophora pistillata. 30c, Palauastrea ramosa. 36c, Melithaea albitincta. 40c, Stylaster echinatus. 42c, Fungia fungites. 48c, Gonipora. 50c, Melithaea squamata. 52c, Bellonella indica. 55c, Plerogyra sinuosa. 60c, Tubastraea. 70c, Heliofungia actinformis. 85c, Caulastraea echinulata. 96c, Porites andrewsi. $1.10, Pectinia alcicornis. $1.20, Dendrophyllia gracilis.

1984 *Perf. 13½x13*

787	A121 1c multi	.25	*.50*
788	A121 2c multi	.25	.25
789	A121 3c multi	.30	.30
790	A121 5c multi	.30	.30
791	A121 10c multi	.30	.30
792	A121 12c multi	.30	.30
793	A121 14c multi	.40	.30
794	A121 18c multi	.55	.35
795	A121 20c multi	.65	.35
796	A121 24c multi	.75	.35
797	A121 30c multi	.90	.35
798	A121 36c multi	1.00	.40
799	A121 40c multi	1.10	.40
800	A121 42c multi	1.25	.40
801	A121 48c multi	1.25	.40
802	A121 50c multi	1.25	.40
803	A121 52c multi	1.30	.40
804	A121 55c multi	1.40	.60
805	A121 60c multi	1.50	.60
806	A121 70c multi	2.00	.60
807	A121 85c multi	2.00	1.25
808	A121 96c multi	2.00	1.50
809	A121 $1.10 multi	2.00	1.75
810	A121 $1.20 multi	2.50	2.50

Perf. 14x13½

Size: 59½x38½mm

811	A102 $3.60 on $2 #582	5.75	5.75
812	A102 $4.20 on $3 #583	6.25	6.25
813	A102 $5 on $4 #584	6.50	6.50
814	A102 $7.20 on $6 #585	9.00	9.00
815	A102 $9.60 on $10 #586	11.00	11.00
	Nos. 787-815 (29)	64.00	53.35

Issued: Nos. 787-801, 3/23; Nos. 802-810, 5/15; Nos. 811-813, 6/28; No. 814, 7/20; No. 815, 8/10.
For surcharges & overprints see Nos. 948-952, 955, 958, 960, 963, 965-967, B105-B108, O32-O45.

Nos. 784-786 Overprinted With Winners

No. 826

No. 827

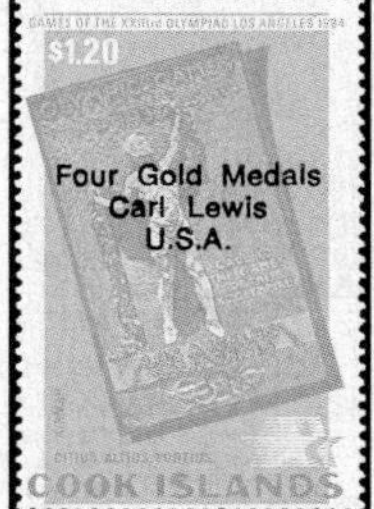

No. 828

1984, Aug. 24 Photo. *Perf. 13½*

826	A120 72c multicolored	.75	.75
827	A120 96c multicolored	1.10	1.10
828	A120 $1.20 multicolored	1.75	1.75
	Nos. 826-828 (3)	3.60	3.60

1984 Summer Olympics. Nos. 826-828 airmail.

AUSIPEX '84 — A123

36c, Captain Cook's cottage. 48c, The Endeavour. 60c, Cook's landing. $2, Portrait, by John Webber.

1984, Sept. 20

829	A123 36c multicolored	1.75	1.50
830	A123 48c multicolored	2.50	2.50
831	A123 60c multicolored	2.60	2.75
832	A123 $2 multicolored	3.00	3.00
a.	Souv. sheet, #829-832, 90c ea	8.50	8.50
b.	Sheet of 4, STAMPEX '86 emblem	8.00	8.00
	Nos. 829-832 (4)	9.85	9.75

No. 832b issued Aug. 4, 1986, for STAMPEX '86, Adelaide, Aug. 4-10; margin ovptd. with exhibition emblem, stamp picturing James Cook ovptd. with gold circle and black "Stampex 86 / Adelaide."

Nos. 677-678 Ovptd. & Surcharged in Gold

No. 659 Ovptd. & Surcharged in Silver

1984, Oct. 15 Photo. *Perf. 14*

833	A108 $1.25 Pair, #a.-b.	1.75	1.75
834	A108 $2.50 Pair, #a.-b.	4.50	4.50
835	A104 $3 on $1 No. 659	3.25	3.25
	Nos. 833-835 (3)	9.50	9.50

Nos. 833-835 printed in sheets of 4 stamps.

A124

Christmas (Paintings): 36c, Virgin on Throne with Child, by Giovanni Bellini (c. 1430-1516). 48c, Virgin and Child, 15th century, artistunknown. 60c, Virgin and Child with Saints, by Alvise Vivarini (c. 1446-1505). 96c, Virgin and Child with Angels, by Hans Memling (c. 1435-1494). $1.20, Adoration of the Magi, by Giovanni Tiepolo (1696-1770).

1984

838	A124 36c multicolored	1.25	.85
839	A124 48c multicolored	1.50	.95
840	A124 60c multicolored	2.00	2.00
841	A124 96c multicolored	2.50	2.50
842	A124 $1.20 multicolored	3.00	3.00
	Nos. 838-842 (5)	10.25	9.30

Souvenir Sheets

Perf. 13½

843	Sheet of 5	4.25	4.25
a.	A124 36c +5c like #838	.50	.50
b.	A124 48c +5c like #839	.65	.65
c.	A124 60c +5c like #840	.75	.75
d.	A124 96c +5c like #841	1.10	1.10
e.	A124 $1.20 +5c like #842	1.25	1.25
844	A124 95c + 5c like #838	1.25	1.25
845	A124 95c + 5c like #839	1.25	1.25
846	A124 95c + 5c like #840	1.25	1.25
847	A124 95c + 5c like #841	1.25	1.25
848	A124 95c + 5c like #842	1.25	1.25

Surtax of No. 843 for children's organizations, of Nos. 844-848 for youth education.
Issued: Nos. 838-843, 11/21; Nos. 844-848, 12/10.

A125

Illustrations of North American bird species by artist, naturalist John J. Audubon: 30c, Downy woodpecker. 55c, Black-throated blue warbler. 65c, Yellow-throated warbler. 75c, Chestnut-sided warbler. 95c, Dickcissel. $1.15, White-crowned sparrow.
$1.30, Red-cockaded woodpecker. $2.80, Seaside sparrow. $5.30, Zenaida dove.

1985, Apr. 23 *Perf. 13x13½*

849	A125 30c multicolored	1.25	1.25
850	A125 55c multicolored	2.00	2.00
851	A125 65c multicolored	2.25	2.25
852	A125 75c multicolored	2.50	2.50
853	A125 95c multicolored	2.75	2.75
854	A125 $1.15 multicolored	3.00	3.00
	Nos. 849-854 (6)	13.75	13.75

Souvenir Sheets

855	A125 $1.30 multicolored	2.00	2.00
856	A125 $2.80 multicolored	3.50	3.50
857	A125 $5.30 multicolored	7.50	7.50

Audubon birth bicentenary.

Locomotives — A126

20c, Kingston Flyer, New Zealand. 55c, Class 640, Italy. 65c, Gotthard, Switzerland. 75c, Union Pacific 6900, US. 95c, Super Continental, Canada. $1.15, TGV, France. $2.20, Flying Scotsman, U.K. $3.40, Orient Express, Europe.

1985, May 14 Litho. *Perf. 14x13½*

858	A126 20c multicolored	.25	.25
859	A126 55c multicolored	.35	.35
860	A126 65c multicolored	.45	.45
861	A126 75c multicolored	.50	.50
862	A126 95c multicolored	.60	.60
863	A126 $1.15 multicolored	.65	.65
864	A126 $2.20 multicolored	1.00	1.00
865	A126 $3.40 multicolored	1.25	1.25
	Nos. 858-865 (8)	5.05	5.05

Intl. Youth Year — A127

Paintings: 55c, Helena Fourment, by Rubens. 65c, Vigee-Lebrun and Daughter, by Elizabeth Vigee-Lebrun (1755-1842). 75c, On the Terrace, by Renoir. $1.30, Young Mother Sewing, by Mary Cassatt (1845-1926).

1985, June 6 Photo. *Perf. 13x13½*

866	A127 55c multicolored	2.75	2.75
867	A127 65c multicolored	3.25	3.25
868	A127 75c multicolored	3.75	3.75
869	A127 $1.30 multicolored	6.00	6.00
	Nos. 866-869 (4)	15.75	15.75

Souvenir Sheet

870	Sheet of 4	8.75	8.75
a.	A127 55c + 10c like #866	1.25	1.25
b.	A127 65c + 10c like #867	1.50	1.50
c.	A127 75c + 10c like #868	2.00	2.00
d.	A127 $1.30 + 10c like #869	3.25	3.25

Surtax for youth organizations.

Queen Mother, 85th Birthday A128

Portraits: 65c, Lady Elizabeth, 1908, by Mable Hankey. 75c, Duchess of York, 1923, by Savely Sorine. $1.15, Duchess of York, 1925, by Philip De Laszlo. $2.80, $5.30, Queen Elizabeth, 1938, by Sir Gerald Kelly.

1985, June 28

871	A128 65c multi	.55	.55
872	A128 75c multi	.65	.65
873	A128 $1.15 multi	1.00	1.00
874	A128 $2.80 multi	1.50	1.50
874A	Sheet of 4 ('86)	6.00	6.00
b.-e.	A128 55c, like #871-874	1.40	1.40
	Nos. 871-874A (5)	9.70	9.70

Souvenir Sheet

875	A128 $5.30 multi	4.50	4.50

Nos. 871-874 printed in sheets of four.
No. 874A issued 8/4/86, for 86th birthday.
For surcharges see Nos. B114, B116, B122, B134, B140.

A129

Portraits of prime ministers: 30c, Albert Henry, 1965-78. 50c, Sir Thomas Davis, 1978-83. 65c, Geoffrey Henry, 1983.

1985, July 29

876	A129 30c multicolored	1.00	1.00
877	A129 50c multicolored	1.50	1.50
878	A129 65c multicolored	2.00	2.00
	Nos. 876-878 (3)	4.50	4.50

Souvenir Sheet

879	Sheet of 3	3.75	3.75
a.	A129 55c like #876	1.20	1.20
b.	A129 55c like #877	1.20	1.20
c.	A129 55c like #878	1.20	1.20

Self-government, 20th anniv.

A130

1985, July 29 *Perf. 14*

880	A130 55c Golf	4.00	4.00
881	A130 65c Rugby	4.25	4.25
882	A130 75c Tennis	5.25	5.25
	Nos. 880-882 (3)	13.50	13.50

Souvenir Sheet

883	Sheet of 3	11.50	11.50
a.	A130 55c + 10c like #880	3.25	3.25
b.	A130 65c + 10c like #881	3.25	3.25
c.	A130 75c + 10c like #882	3.25	3.25

South Pacific Mini Games, Rarotonga, July 31-Aug. 10. Surtax for the benefit of the Mini Games.

A131

Seahorse & conf. emblems: 55c, South Pacific Bureau for Economic Cooperation. 65c, No. 887b, South Pacific Forum. 75c, No. 887c, Pacific Islands Conf.

1985, July 29 *Perf. 14*

884	A131 55c blk, scar & gold	1.25	1.25
885	A131 65c blk, vio & gold	1.40	1.40
886	A131 75c blk, brt grn & gold	1.50	1.50
	Nos. 884-886 (3)	4.15	4.15

Souvenir Sheet

887	50c Sheet of 3, #a.-c.	2.50	2.50

Pacific islands conf., Rarotonga, 7/30-8/10.

A132

Virgin and Child paintings by Botticelli: 55c, Madonna of the Magnificent. 65c, Madonna with Pomegranate. 75c, Madonna with Child & Six Angels. 95c, Madonna & Child with St. John.

1985

888	A132 55c multicolored	1.60	1.60
889	A132 65c multicolored	2.10	2.10
890	A132 75c multicolored	2.50	2.60
891	A132 95c multicolored	3.25	3.25
	Nos. 888-891 (4)	9.45	9.55

Souvenir Sheets

Perf. 13½

892	A132 $2.75 Sheet of 4	6.00	6.00
a.	A132 50c like #888	1.25	1.25
b.	A132 50c like #889	1.25	1.25
c.	A132 50c like #890	1.25	1.25
d.	A132 50c like #891	1.25	1.25

Imperf

893	A132 $1.20 like #888	1.75	1.75
894	A132 $1.45 like #889	2.00	2.00
895	A132 $2.20 like #890	3.25	3.25
896	A132 $2.75 like #891	3.50	3.50

Christmas. Issue dates: Nos. 888-892, Nov. 18; Nos. 893-896, Dec. 9.

Halley's Comet — A133

Paintings: 55c, No. 902a, The Eve of the Deluge, by John Martin (1789-1854). 65c, No. 902b, Lot and His Daughters, by Lucas van Leyden (1494-1533). 75c, No. 902c, Auspicious Comet, 1587, anonymous. $1.25, No. 902d, Events Following Charles I, by Herman Saftleven (1609-1658). $2, No. 902e, Ossian Receiving Napoleonic Officers, by Anne Louis Girodet-Trioson (1764-1824). $4, Halley's Comet over the Thames, 1759, by Samuel Scott (1702-1772).

1986, Mar. 13 Photo. *Perf. 14*

897	A133 55c multicolored	1.25	1.25
898	A133 65c multicolored	1.50	1.50
899	A133 75c multicolored	1.75	1.75
900	A133 $1.25 multicolored	2.25	2.25
901	A133 $2 multicolored	3.50	3.50
	Nos. 897-901 (5)	10.25	10.25

Souvenir Sheets

Perf. 13½

902	Sheet of 5 + label	6.00	6.00
a.-e.	A133 70c, each single	1.10	1.10
903	A133 $4 multicolored	7.50	7.50

For surcharges see Nos. B113, B115, B117, B123, B129.

Elizabeth II, 60th Birthday — A134

Various portraits.

1986, Apr. 21 *Perf. 13x13½*

904	A134 95c multi	1.10	1.10
905	A134 $1.25 multi	1.25	1.25
906	A134 $1.50 multi	1.60	1.60
	Nos. 904-906 (3)	3.95	3.95

Souvenir Sheets

907	A134 $1.10 like #904	2.00	2.00
908	A134 $1.95 like #905	3.50	3.50
909	A134 $2.45 like #906	4.75	5.75

For surcharges see Nos. 972-974, B118, B124, B127, B136-B137, B139.

AMERIPEX '86 — A135

Designs: $1, US No. 1, The Resolution, Rarotonga. $1.50, Downtown Chicago. $2, No. 398, Benjamin Franklin, The Resolution.

1986, May 21 Photo. *Perf. 14*

910	A135 $1 multi	3.50	3.50
911	A135 $1.50 multi	5.25	5.25
912	A135 $2 multi	6.75	6.75
	Nos. 910-912 (3)	15.50	15.50

For surcharges see Nos. B119, B128, B130.

Statue of Liberty, Cent. — A136

1986, July 4

913	A136 $1 Head	1.00	1.00
914	A136 $1.25 Torch	1.25	1.25
915	A136 $2.75 Liberty Is.	2.75	2.75
	Nos. 913-915 (3)	5.00	5.00

For surcharges see Nos. B120, B125, B132.

Wedding of Prince Andrew and Sarah Ferguson — A137

1986, July 23

916	A137 $1 Sarah Ferguson	.80	.80
917	A137 $2 Prince Andrew	1.60	1.60

Size: 60x33½mm

Perf. 13½x13

918	A137 $3 Couple	2.40	2.40
	Nos. 916-918 (3)	4.80	4.80

Nos. 916-918 each printed in sheets of 4.
For surch. see Nos. 975-977, B121, B131, B135.

Christmas A138

Paintings by Rubens: 55c, No. 922a, The Holy Family. $1.30, $6.40, No. 922b, Virgin with Garland. $2.75, No. 922c, Adoration of Magi.

1986, Nov. 17 Litho. *Perf. 13½*

919	A138 55c multi	1.40	1.40
920	A138 $1.30 multi	3.25	3.25
921	A138 $2.75 multi	6.50	6.50
	Nos. 919-921 (3)	11.15	11.15

Souvenir Sheets

922	Sheet of 3	14.00	14.00
a.-c.	A138 $2.40, any single	4.50	4.50
923	A138 $6.40 multi	15.00	15.00

No. 922 contains 3 stamps 38½x49mm.
For surcharges see Nos. B100-B104, B112, B126, B133, B138, B141A.

Stamps of 1980-84 Surcharged in Black

Strips of 4, #a.-d. (#953, 954, 956, 957) or

Blocks of 4, #a.-d. (#959, 961, 962, 964)

1987, Feb. Litho. *Perfs. as before*

948	A121 5c on 1c #787	.25	.25
949	A121 5c on 2c #788	.25	.25
950	A121 5c on 3c #789	.25	.25
951	A121 5c on 12c #792	.25	.25
952	A121 5c on 14c #793	.25	.25
953	A101 10c on 15c #572	.55	.55

954 A101 10c on 25c #574 .55 .55
955 A121 18c on 24c #796 .25 .25
956 A101 18c on 12c #571 1.10 1.10
957 A101 18c on 20c #573 1.10 1.10
958 A121 55c on 52c #803 .90 .90
959 A101 55c on 35c #576 3.25 3.25
960 A121 65c on 42c #800 1.00 1.00
961 A101 65c on 50c #577 4.50 4.50
962 A101 65c on 60c #578 4.50 4.50
963 A121 75c on 48c #801 1.25 1.25
964 A101 75c on 70c #579 4.50 4.50
965 A121 95c on 96c #808 1.50 1.50
966 A121 95c on $1.10 #809 1.50 1.50
967 A121 95c on $1.20 #810 1.50 1.50

Stamps of 1981-86 Surcharged in Black (A102), Black and Gold (#968-970, A137) or Gold (#971, A134, A104, A108)

968 A123 $1.30 on 36c #829 1.90 1.90
969 A123 $1.30 on 48c #830 1.90 1.90
970 A123 $1.30 on 60c #831 1.90 1.90
971 A123 $1.30 on $2 #832 1.90 1.90
972 A134 $2.80 on 95c #904 4.25 4.25
973 A134 $2.80 on $1.25 #905 4.25 4.25
974 A134 $2.80 on $1.50 #906 4.25 4.25
975 A137 $2.80 on $1 #916 4.25 4.25
976 A137 $2.80 on $2 #917 4.25 4.25
977 A137 $2.80 on $3 #918 4.25 4.25
978 A102 $6.40 on $4 #584 7.50 7.50
979 A102 $7.20 on $6 #585 8.50 8.50
980 A104 $9.40 on $1 #659 11.00 11.00
981 A104 $9.40 on $2 #660 11.00 11.00

Pair, #a.-b.

982 A108 $9.40 on $2.50 #678 22.00 22.00
Nos. 948-982 (35) 122.30 122.30

Issued: 5c, Nos. 955, 958, 960, 963, 95c, $6.40, $7.20, 2/10; 10c, Nos. 956-957, 959, 961-962, 964, 2/11; $12.30, $2.80, $9.40, 2/12.

For surcharge see No. B111.

Stamps of 1980-82 Surcharged in Black (A102) or Gold (A104)

No. 984

No. 989

Perfs. as before

1987, June 17 **Photo.**

984 A102 $2.80 on $2 #582 2.75 2.75
985 A102 $5 on $3 #583 4.75 4.75
986 A102 $9.40 on $10 #586 8.50 8.50

Pairs, #a.-b.

987 A104 $9.40 on $1 #679 17.00 17.00
988 A104 $9.40 on $2 #680 17.00 17.00
Nos. 984-988 (5) 50.00 50.00

Souvenir Sheet

989 A104 $9.20 on #680c 15.00 15.00

Nos. 399 and 584 Ovptd. in Black on Gold Bar

1987, Nov. 20 **Photo.** ***Perf. 14x13½***

991 A64 $4 on #399 4.00 4.00
992 A102 $4 on #584 4.00 4.00

Christmas — A139

The Holy Family, religious paintings by Rembrandt in European museums: $1.25, No. 996a, The Louvre, Paris. $1.50, No. 996b, $6, The Holy Family with Angels, The Hermitage, Leningrad. $1.95, No. 996c, The Alte Pinakothek, Munich.

1987, Dec. 7 **Photo.** ***Perf. 13½***

993 A139 $1.25 multi 2.50 2.50
994 A139 $1.50 multi 3.50 3.50
995 A139 $1.95 multi 4.50 4.50
Nos. 993-995 (3) 10.50 10.50

Souvenir Sheets

996 Sheet of 3 8.50 8.50
a.-c. A139 $1.15 any single 2.50 2.50

Perf. 13x13½

997 A139 $6 multi 11.00 11.00

Size of Nos. 996a-996c: 49½x38½mm. No. 997 contains 1 stamp 39½x31½mm.

1988 Summer Olympics, Seoul A140

Designs: a, Cook Islands commemorative silver coin (obverse and reverse) issued on Aug. 20, 1987, for the '88 Summer Games. b, Seoul Olympic Park, torch and emblem. c, Steffi Graf, women's tennis champion, and '88 gold medal.

1988, Apr. 26 **Photo.** ***Perf. 13½x14***

998 Strip of 3 15.00 15.00
a.-c. A140 $1.50 multicolored 5.00 5.00

Souvenir Sheet

Perf. 13½

999 A140 $10 multi 15.00 15.00

Participation of national athletes in the Olympics for the first time, introduction of tennis as an Olympic gold-medal event.

No. 999 contains one stamp 114x47mm combining the designs of Nos. 998a-998c.

Nos. 998-999 Overprinted

a-c

d

1988, Oct. 12 **Photo.** ***Perf. 13½x14***

1000 Strip of 3 12.00 12.00
a.-c. A140 $1.50 multicolored 4.00 4.00

Souvenir Sheet

Perf. 13½

1001 A140(d) $10 on No. 999 16.00 16.00

Christmas A141

Paintings by Albrecht Durer: 70c, Virgin and Child. 85c, Virgin and Child, diff. 95c, Virgin and Child, diff. $1.25, Virgin and Child, diff. $6.40, The Nativity.

1988, Nov. 11 ***Perf. 13½***

1002 A141 70c multi 2.75 2.75
1003 A141 85c multi 3.25 3.25
1004 A141 95c multi 3.75 3.75
1005 A141 $1.25 multi 5.00 5.00
Nos. 1002-1005 (4) 14.75 14.75

Souvenir Sheet

1006 A141 $6.40 multi 12.00 12.00

No. 1006 contains one stamp 45x60mm.

Scene and Left Half of Mission Emblem A142

1st Moon Landing, 20th Anniv. — A144

No. 1007a, Launch vehicle in space. No. 1007b, *Eagle* landing on Moon. No. 1008a, Astronaut descending ladder. No. 1008b, Astronaut on Moon. No. 1009a, Seismic experiment. No. 1009b, Solar wind experiment. No. 1010a, Liftoff from Moon. No. 1010b, Splashdown and recovery.

The "b" stamps have the right half of the emblem.

1989, July 14 **Photo.** ***Perf. 13***

1007 A142 40c Pair, #a.-b. 3.00 3.00
1008 A142 55c Pair, #a.-b. 4.50 4.50
1009 A142 65c Pair, #a.-b. 5.00 5.00
1010 A142 75c Pair, #a.-b. 5.50 5.50
Nos. 1007-1010 (4) 18.00 18.00

Souvenir Sheet

1011 A144 $4.20 Armstrong and Aldrin 8.75 8.75

Printed with continuous designs.

World Wildlife Fund A145

Endangered bird species: 15c, $1, Pomarea dimidiata. 20c, $1.25, Pomarea dimidiata (two). 65c, $1.50, Ptilinopus rarotongensis (two). 70c, $1.75, Ptilinopus rarotongensis.

1989, Oct. 4 **Photo.** ***Perf. 13½x13***

1016 A145 15c multicolored 1.40 1.40
1017 A145 20c multicolored 2.00 2.00
1018 A145 65c multicolored 5.50 5.50
1019 A145 70c multicolored 6.25 6.25
Nos. 1016-1019 (4) 15.15 15.15

Souvenir Sheets

Without WWF Emblem

Perf. 13½

1020 A145 $1 like 15c 2.75 2.75
1021 A145 $1.25 like 20c 3.25 3.25
1022 A145 $1.50 like 65c 3.75 3.75
1023 A145 $1.75 like 70c 4.25 4.25

World Wildlife Fund. Nos. 1020-1023 are airmail and contain one 52x34mm stamp; decorative margins continue the designs.

For overprints see Nos. C24-C27.

Christmas — A146

Details of *Adoration of the Magi*, by Rubens: 70c, Witnesses. 85c, Madonna. 95c, Christ child. $1.50, Attendant. $6.40, Entire painting.

1989, Nov. 24 **Photo.** ***Perf. 13½x13***

1024 A146 70c multicolored 1.60 1.60
1025 A146 85c multicolored 1.75 1.75
1026 A146 95c multicolored 2.10 2.10
1027 A146 $1.50 multicolored 3.25 3.25
Nos. 1024-1027 (4) 8.70 8.70

Souvenir Sheet

Perf. 13½

1028 A146 $6.40 multicolored 15.00 15.00

No. 1028 contains one 45x60mm stamp.

Religious History A147

70c, John Williams, LMS Mission Church. 85c, Bernardine Castanie, Roman Catholic Church. 95c, Osborne J.P. Widstoe, Church of Jesus Christ of Latter Day Saints. $1.60, J.E. Caldwell, Seventh Day Adventist Church.

1990, Feb. 19 **Photo.** ***Perf. 13½x13***

1029 A147 70c multicolored 1.00 1.00
1030 A147 85c multicolored 1.20 1.20
1031 A147 95c multicolored 1.40 1.40
1032 A147 $1.60 multicolored 2.40 2.40
Nos. 1029-1032 (4) 6.00 6.00

Souvenir Sheet

Perf. 13½

1033 Sheet of 4 7.00 7.00
a. A147 90c like 70c 1.50 1.50
b. A147 90c like 85c 1.50 1.50
c. A147 90c like 95c 1.50 1.50
d. A147 90c like $1.60 1.50 1.50

No. 1033 contains 4 36x36mm stamps.

Penny Black, 150th Anniv. — A148

Paintings: 85c, No. 1038a, *Woman Writing a Letter,* by Gerard Terborch (1617-1681). $1.15, No. 1038b, *Portrait of George Gisze,* by Hans Holbein the Younger. $1.55, No. 1038c, *Portrait of Mrs. John Douglas,* by Thomas Gainsborough. $1.85, No. 1038d, *Portrait of a Gentleman,* by Albrecht Durer.

1990, May 2 Photo. *Perf. 13½*

1034 A148 85c multicolored 1.40 1.40
1035 A148 $1.15 multicolored 2.00 2.00
1036 A148 $1.55 multicolored 2.60 2.60
1037 A148 $1.85 multicolored 3.25 3.25
Nos. 1034-1037 (4) 9.25 9.25

Souvenir Sheet

1038 Sheet of 4 13.00 13.00
a.-d. A148 $1.05 any single 3.00 3.00

The margin of No. 1038 pictures the Stamp World '90 emblem and Great Britain #1-2.

1992 Olympics A149

Designs: a. Summer Games, Barcelona (runners). b. Eternal flame, commemorative coin obverse (Queen Elizabeth II) and reverse (athletes). c. Winter Games, Albertville (skier).

1990, June 15 Photo. *Perf. 14*

1039 Strip of 3 18.00 18.00
a.-c. A149 $1.85 any single 6.00 6.00

Queen Mother, 90th Birthday A150

1990, July 20 Photo. *Perf. 13½*

1040 A150 $1.85 multicolored 6.50 6.50

Souvenir Sheet

1041 A150 $6.40 multicolored 13.00 13.00

Christmas A151

Paintings: 70c, Adoration of the Magi by Memling. 85c, The Holy Family by Lotto. 95c, Madonna and Child with Saints John and Catherine by Titian. $1.50, The Holy Family by Titian. $6.40, Madonna and Child Enthroned, Surrounded by Saints by Vivarini.

1990, Nov. 29 Litho. *Perf. 14*

1042 A151 70c multicolored 1.75 1.75
1043 A151 85c multicolored 2.40 2.40
1044 A151 95c multicolored 2.50 2.50
1045 A151 $1.50 multicolored 3.75 3.75
Nos. 1042-1045 (4) 10.40 10.40

Souvenir Sheet

1046 A151 $6.40 multicolored 15.00 15.00

For overprints and surcharges see Nos. 1251, 1254, 1257-1258.

Souvenir Sheet

1992 Olympic Games — A152

1991, Feb. 12 *Perf. 13½*

1047 A152 $6.40 multicolored 15.00 15.00

Discovery of America 500th Anniv. (in 1992) — A153

1991, Feb. 14 Photo. *Perf. 13½x13*

1048 A153 $1 multicolored 4.25 4.25

No. 586 Ovptd. "65th BIRTHDAY" in Gold

1991, Apr. 22 Litho. *Perf. 14x13½*

1049 A102 $10 multicolored 18.00 18.00

Christmas A154

Paintings: 70c, Adoration of the Child, by Delle Notti (Gerrit van Honthorst). 85c, Birth of the Virgin, by Murillo. $1.15, Adoration of the Shepherds, by Rembrandt. $1.50, Adoration of the Shepherds, by Le Nain. $6.40, Madonna and Child, by Fra Filippo Lippi, vert.

1991, Nov. 12 Litho. *Perf. 14*

1050 A154 70c multicolored 1.00 1.00
1051 A154 85c multicolored 3.00 3.00
1052 A154 $1.15 multicolored 4.25 4.25
1053 A154 $1.50 multicolored 5.75 5.75
Nos. 1050-1053 (4) 14.00 14.00

Souvenir Sheet

1054 A154 $6.40 multicolored 15.00 15.00

For overprints and surcharges see Nos. 1252-1253, 1255-1256.

Marine Life — A155

A155a

5c, Red-breasted maori wrasse. 10c, Blue sea star. 15c, Black & gold angelfish. 20c, Spotted pebble crab. 25c, Black-tipped cod. 30c, Spanish dancer. 50c, Royal angelfish. 80c, Squirrel fish. 85c, Red pencil sea urchin. 90c, Red-spot rainbow fish. $1, Black-lined maori wrasse. $2, Longnose butterflyfish. $3, Red-spot rainbow fish. $5, Blue sea star. $7, Royal angelfish. $10, Spotted pebble crab. $15, Red pencil sea urchin.

1992-94 Litho. *Perf. 14½x13½*

1058 A155 5c multi .40 .40
1059 A155 10c multi .40 .40
1062 A155 15c multi .40 .40
1064 A155 20c multi .50 .50
1065 A155 25c multi .55 .55
1066 A155 30c multi .65 .65
1071 A155 50c multi 1.10 1.10
1076 A155 80c multi 1.75 1.75
1077 A155 85c multi 1.75 1.75
1078 A155 90c multi 1.75 1.75
1080 A155 $1 multi 2.00 2.00
1081 A155 $2 multi 3.75 3.75
1082 A155a $3 multi 4.50 4.50
1083 A155a $5 multi 8.00 8.00
1085 A155a $7 multi 12.00 12.00
1087 A155a $10 multi 17.00 17.00
1089 A155a $15 multi 25.00 25.00
Nos. 1058-1089 (17) 81.50 81.50

Issued: 85c, 90c, $1, $2, 3/23/92; $3, $5, 10/25/93; $7, 12/6/93; $10, 1/31/94; $15, 9/9/94; others, 1/22/92.

See Nos. 1154-1176 for stamps with buff border. For overprints see Nos. O54-O68.

Endangered Wildlife — A156

$1.15 each: No. 1095, Tiger. No. 1096, Asiatic elephant. No. 1097, Grizzly bear. No. 1098, Black rhinoceros. No. 1099, Chimpanzee. No. 1100, Asian bighorn. No. 1101, Heavisides dolphin. No. 1102, Eagle owl. No. 1103, Bee hummingbird. No. 1104, Felisconcolor cougar. No. 1105, European otter. No. 1106, Red kangaroo.

1992 Litho. *Perf. 14*

1095-1106 A156 Set of 12 20.00 20.00

Issued: No. 1095, 4/6; No. 1096, 4/7; No. 1097, 4/8; No. 1098, 4/9; No. 1099, 4/10; No. 1100, 4/11; No. 1101, 7/13; No. 1102, 7/14; No. 1103, 7/15; No. 1104, 7/16; No. 1105, 7/17; No. 1106, 7/18.

See Nos. 1119-1124, 1134-1138.

For surcharges see Nos. 1239-1250.

Discovery of America, 500th Anniv. — A157

1992, May 22 Litho. *Perf. 14x14½*

1107 A157 $6 multicolored 9.00 9.00

Souvenir Sheet

Perf. 15x14

1107A A157 $10 Coming ashore 10.50 10.50

Issued: No. 1107, 5/22. No. 1107A, 9/21.

No. 1107A contains one 40x30mm stamp.

1992 Summer Olympics, Barcelona — A158

Designs: No. 1108a, $50 coin, soccer players. b, Flags of Spain, Cook Islands, Barcelona medal. c, $10 coin, basketball players. No. 1109a, Runners. b, $10, $50 coins. c, Cyclists. $6.40, Javelin.

1992, July 24 Litho. *Perf. 13*

1108 A158 $1.75 Strip of 3, #a.-c. 9.00 9.00
1109 A158 $2.25 Strip of 3, #a.-c. 11.00 11.00

Souvenir Sheet

1110 A158 $6.40 multicolored 19.00 19.00

6th Festival of Pacific Arts, Rarotonga A159

80c, UNESCO poster. 85c, $1, $1.75, Different carvings of Rarotongan fertility god, Tangaroa.

1992, Oct. 16 Litho. *Perf. 15x14*

1111 A159 80c multicolored 1.75 1.75
1112 A159 85c multicolored 2.00 2.00
1113 A159 $1 multicolored 2.40 2.40
1114 A159 $1.75 multicolored 3.75 3.75
Nos. 1111-1114 (4) 9.90 9.90

For overprints see Nos. 1231-1234.

Overprinted in Black

1992, Oct. 16

1115 A159 80c on #1111 2.10 2.10
1116 A159 85c on #1112 2.50 2.50
1117 A159 $1 on #1113 2.50 2.50
1118 A159 $1.75 on #1114 4.75 4.75
Nos. 1115-1118 (4) 11.85 11.85

Endangered Wildlife Type of 1992

No. 1119, Jackass penguin. No. 1120, Asian lion. No. 1121, Peregrine falcon. No. 1122, Persian fallow deer. No. 1123, Key deer. No. 1124, Alpine ibex.

1992 Litho. *Perf. 14*

1119 A156 $1.15 multicolored 1.75 1.75
1120 A156 $1.15 multicolored 1.75 1.75
1121 A156 $1.15 multicolored 1.75 1.75
1122 A156 $1.15 multicolored 1.75 1.75
1123 A156 $1.15 multicolored 1.75 1.75
1124 A156 $1.15 multicolored 1.75 1.75
Nos. 1119-1124 (6) 10.50 10.50

Issued: No. 1119, 11/2; No. 1120, 11/3; No. 1121, 11/4; No. 1122, 11/5; No. 1123, 11/6; No. 1124, 11/7.

Christmas A160

Paintings by El Parmigianino: 70c, Worship of Shepherds. 85c, $6.40, Virgin with Long Neck. $1.15, Virgin with Rose. $1.90, St. Margaret's Virgin.

1992, Nov. 20 Litho. *Perf. 13½*

1125 A160 70c multicolored 1.00 1.00
1126 A160 85c multicolored 1.60 1.60
1127 A160 $1.15 multicolored 2.10 2.10
1128 A160 $1.90 multicolored 3.75 3.75
Nos. 1125-1128 (4) 8.45 8.45

Souvenir Sheet

1129 A160 $6.40 multicolored 12.50 12.50

No. 1129 contains one 36x47mm stamp.

Queen Elizabeth II's Accession to the Throne, 40th Anniv. — A161

Various portraits of Queen Elizabeth II.

1992, Dec. 10 Litho. *Perf. 14*

1130 A161 80c multicolored 1.25 1.25
1131 A161 $1.15 multicolored 2.00 2.00
1132 A161 $1.50 multicolored 3.25 3.25
1133 A161 $1.95 multicolored 4.50 4.50
Nos. 1130-1133 (4) 11.00 11.00

Endangered Wildlife Type of 1992

No. 1134, English mandrill. No. 1135, Gorilla. No. 1136, Vanessa atlanta. No. 1137, Sichuan takin. No. 1138, Ring tailed lemur.

1993 Litho. *Perf. 14*

1134 A156 $1.15 multicolored 2.00 2.00
1135 A156 $1.15 multicolored 2.00 2.00
1136 A156 $1.15 multicolored 2.00 2.00
1137 A156 $1.15 multicolored 2.00 2.00
1138 A156 $1.15 multicolored 2.00 2.00
Nos. 1134-1138 (5) 10.00 10.00

Issued: No. 1134, 2/1; No. 1135, 2/2; No. 1136, 2/3; No. 1137, 2/4; No. 1138, 2/5.

Coronation of Queen Elizabeth II, 40th Anniv. — A162

Designs: $1, Coronation ceremony. $2, Coronation portrait. $3, Queen, family on balcony, Buckingham Palace.

1993, June 2 Litho. *Perf. 14*

1139 A162 $1 multicolored 2.25 2.25
1140 A162 $2 multicolored 4.75 4.75
1141 A162 $3 multicolored 7.00 7.00
Nos. 1139-1141 (3) 14.00 14.00

Christmas A163

Paintings: 70c, Virgin with Child, by Filippo Lippi. 85c, Bargellini Madonna, by Lodovico Carracci. $1.15, Virgin of the Curtain, by Raphael. $2.50, Holy Family, by Il Bronzino. $4, Saint Zachary Virgin, by Il Parmigianino.

1993, Nov. 8 Litho. *Perf. 14*

1142 A163 70c multicolored 1.00 1.00
1143 A163 85c multicolored 1.40 1.40
1144 A163 $1.15 multicolored 1.75 1.75
1145 A163 $2.50 multicolored 3.50 3.50

Size: 32x47mm

Perf. 13½

1146 A163 $4.00 multicolored 6.25 6.25
Nos. 1142-1146 (5) 13.90 13.90

1994 Winter Olympics, Lillehammer — A164

1994, Feb. 11 Litho. *Perf. 13½x14*

1147 A164 $5 multicolored 10.00 10.00

1994 World Cup Soccer Championships, US — A165

1994, June 17 Litho. *Perf. 14*

1148 A165 $4.50 multicolored 8.00 8.00

First Manned Moon Landing, 25th Anniv. — A166

Apollo 11 emblem and: No. 1149a, First step onto Moon, US flag. No. 1149b, Astronaut carrying experiment packs on Moon. No. 1150a, Astronaut, US flag. No. 1150b, Flag, reflection shown in astronaut's visor.

1994, July 20

1149 A166 $2.25 Pair, #a.-b. + label 9.00 9.00
1150 A166 $2.25 Pair, #a.-b. + label 9.00 9.00

Living Reef Type of 1992

1994, Oct. 24 Litho. *Perf. 14½x13½*

Size: 41x31mm

Buff & Multicolored

1154 A155 5c like #1058 .50 .50
1158 A155 15c like #1062 .50 .50
1160 A155 20c like #1064 .60 .60
1161 A155 25c like #1065 .65 .65
1162 A155 30c like #1066 .75 .75
1167 A155 50c like #1071 1.40 1.40
1172 A155 80c like #1076 2.25 2.25
1173 A155 85c like #1077 2.40 2.40
1174 A155 90c like #1078 2.50 2.50
1176 A155 $1 like #1080 2.75 2.75
Nos. 1154-1176 (10) 14.30 14.30

Nos. 1158 and 1161 Surcharged

Method and Perf. As Before

1998 ?

1177 A155 10c on 15c #1158 — —
1178 A155 20c on 25c #1161 —

The year of issue of Nos. 1177-1178 is unknown. A damaged example of No. 1178 exists uncanceled on cover.

Miniature Sheet

The Return of Tommy Tricker — A167

Scenes from film: a, Three people in canoe. b, Traditional dancers. c, Couple walking on beach. d, Aerial view of island. e, Girls performing hand gestures. f, Girls walking along sand bar.

1994, Nov. 23 Litho. *Perf. 14*

1191 A167 85c Sheet of 6, #a.-f. 9.50 9.50

See No. 1213.

Christmas — A168

Paintings: No. 1192a, The Virgin and Child, by Morales. b, Adoration of Kings, by Gerard David. c, Adoration of Kings, by Vinc Foppa. d, The Madonna & Child with St. Joseph & Infant Baptist, by Baroccio.

No. 1193a, Madonna with Iris, in style of Durer. b, Adoration of Shepherds, by Le Nain. c, The Virgin and Child, by follower of Leonardo. d, The Mystic Nativity, by Botticelli.

1994, Nov. 30 Litho. *Perf. 14*

1192 A168 85c Block of 4, #a.-d. 6.75 6.75
1193 A168 $1 Block of 4, #a.-d. 7.75 7.75

Robert Louis Stevenson (1850-94), Writer — A169

Adventure scenes from books: a, "Treasure Island." b, "David Balfour." c, "Dr. Jekyll and Mr. Hyde." d, "Kidnapped."

1994, Dec. 12 *Perf. 14x15*

1194 A169 $1.50 Block of 4, #a.-d. 14.00 14.00

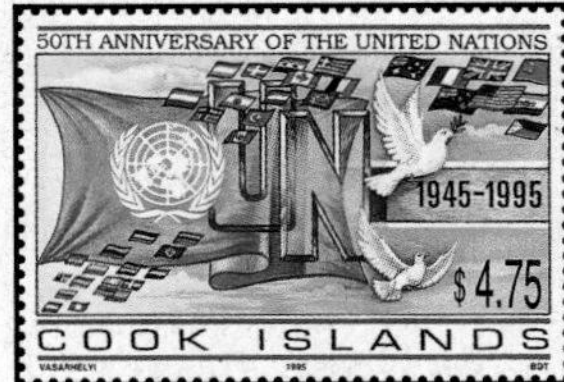

UN, 50th Anniv. — A170

$4.50, FAO, 50th anniv.

1995 Litho. *Perf. 13x13½*

1195 A170 $4.75 multicolored 6.25 6.25

Perf. 13½

1196 A170 $4.50 multicolored 6.75 6.75

Each issued in sheets of 4.
Issued: $4.75, 7/17; $4.50, 10/12.

Queen Mother, 95th Birthday — A172

1995, Aug. 31

1197 A172 $5 multicolored 12.00 12.00

End of World War II, 50th Anniv. — A173

Designs: a, German surrender, Rheims. b, Japanese surrender, Tokyo Bay.

1995, Sept. 4 *Perf. 13*

1198 A173 $3.50 Pair, #a.-b. 22.00 22.00

No. 1198 was issued in sheets of 4 stamps.

Year of the Sea Turtle A174

Designs: 85c, Green turtle in water. $1, Hawksbill turtle in water. $1.75, Green turtle nesting. $2.25, Hawksbill turtle hatchlings leaving nest.

1995, Nov. 20 Litho. *Perf. 14*

1199 A174 85c multicolored 2.00 2.00
1200 A174 $1 multicolored 2.75 2.75
1201 A174 $1.75 multicolored 4.25 4.25
1202 A174 $2.25 multicolored 5.75 5.75
Nos. 1199-1202 (4) 14.75 14.75

1996 Summer Olympics, Atlanta A175

1996, Jan. 12 Litho. *Perf. 14*

1203 A175 85c Discus 1.40 1.40
1204 A175 $1 Torch bearer 1.75 1.75
1205 A175 $1.50 Sprinting 2.60 2.60
1206 A175 $1.85 Gymnastics 3.50 3.50
1207 A175 $2.10 Archery 4.00 4.00
1208 A175 $2.50 Javelin 4.50 4.50
Nos. 1203-1208 (6) 17.75 17.75

Queen Elizabeth II, 70th Birthday — A176

Designs: $1.90, No. 1212a, In blue hat, coat. $2.25, No. 1212b, Wearing tiara. $2.75, No. 1212c, In robes of Order of the Garter.

1996, June 21 Litho. *Perf. 14*

1209 A176 $1.90 multicolored 3.00 3.00
1210 A176 $2.25 multicolored 4.00 4.00
1211 A176 $2.75 multicolored 4.50 4.50
Nos. 1209-1211 (3) 11.50 11.50

Sheet of 3

1212 A176 $2.50 #a.-c. + label 14.00 14.00

Nos. 1209-1211 were issued in sheets of 4.

"The Return of Tommy Tricker" Type of 1994

No. 1213a-1213f, like #1191a-1191f.

1997, Aug. 28 Litho. *Perf. 14*

1213 A167 90c Sheet of 6, #a.-f. 9.50 9.50

Nos. 1213a-1213f Overprinted in Silver

a

b

1997, Sept. 12 Litho. *Perf. 14*

1214 A167 90c Sheet 6, #a.-f. 9.00 9.00

Nos. 1214a, 1214d-1214e are overprinted type "a"; Nos. 1214b-1214c, 1214f type "b."

Butterflies A177

5c, Lampides boeticus (female). 10c, Vanessa atalanta. 15c, Lampides boeticus (male). 20c, Papilio godeffroyi. 25c, Danaus hamata. 30c, Xois sesara. 50c, Vagrans egista. 70c, Parthenos sylvia. 80c, Hyblaea sanguinea. 85c, Melanitis leda. 90c, Ascalapha odorata. $1, Precis villida. $1.50, Parthenos sylvia. $2, Lampides boeticus. $3, Precis villida. $4, Melanitis leda. $5, Vagrans egista. $7, Hyblaea sanguinea. $10, Vanessa atalanta. $15, Papilio godeffroyi.

1997-98 Litho. *Perf. 13*

1215	A177	5c multi	.25	.25
1216	A177	10c multi	.25	.25
1217	A177	15c multi	.25	.25
1218	A177	20c multi	.30	.30
1219	A177	25c multi	.35	.35
1220	A177	30c multi	.35	.35
1221	A177	50c multi	.55	.55
1222	A177	70c multi	.80	.80
1223	A177	80c multi	.95	.95
1224	A177	85c multi	.95	.95
1225	A177	90c multi	1.00	1.00
1226	A177	$1 multi	1.10	1.10

Perf. 13½

Size: 41x25mm

1226A	A177	$1.50 multi	1.60	1.60
1226B	A177	$2 multi	2.25	2.25
1226C	A177	$3 multi	3.25	3.25
1226D	A177	$4 multi	4.75	4.75
1226E	A177	$5 multi	5.50	5.50
1226F	A177	$7 multi	8.50	8.50
1226G	A177	$10 multi	11.50	11.50
1226H	A177	$15 multi	15.00	15.00
	Nos. 1215-1226H (20)		59.45	59.45

Issued: 5c, 10c, 15c, 20c, 25c, 30c, 50c, 70c, 10/22/97; 80c, 85c, 90c, $1, 11/12/97; $1.50, $2, $3, 3/11/98; $4, $5, 6/19/98; $7, $10, 9/18/98; $15, 11/13/98.

For surcharges, see Nos. 1259-1264.

Queen Elizabeth II and Prince Philip, 50th Wedding Anniv. A178

1997, Nov. 20 *Perf. 14*

1227 A178 $2 multicolored 3.00 3.00

Souvenir Sheet

1228 A178 $5 like #1227, close-up 9.00 9.00

No. 1228 is a continuous design.

Diana, Princess of Wales (1961-97) — A179

1998, Mar. 18 Litho. *Perf. 14*

1229 A179 $1.15 shown 1.50 1.50

Souvenir Sheet

1230 A179 $3.50 like #1229 5.25 5.25

No. 1229 was issued in sheets of 5 + label. See No. B142.

Nos. 1111-1114 Ovptd.

Printing Methods and Perfs as before

1999, Dec. 31

1231	A159	80c on #1111	1.25	1.25
1232	A159	85c on #1112	1.25	1.25
1233	A159	$1 on #1113	1.50	1.50
1234	A159	$1.75 on #1114	2.50	2.50
	Nos. 1231-1234 (4)		6.50	6.50

Queen Mother, 100th Birthday — A180

No. 1235: a, As child. b, As young woman. c, Wearing green hat. d, Wearing tiara.

2000, Oct. 20 Litho. *Perf. 14*

1235 A180 $4.50 Sheet of 4, #a-d 18.00 18.00

Souvenir Sheet

1236 A180 $6 Wearing blue hat 5.50 5.50

2000 Summer Olympics, Sydney — A181

No. 1237: a, Ancient runner. b, Track and field. c, Ancient archery. d, Archery.

2000, Nov. 14

1237 A181 $1.75 Sheet of 4, #a-d 9.00 9.00

Souvenir Sheet

1238 A181 $3.90 Torch bearer 4.50 4.50

Nos. 1095-1106 Surcharged in Gold

2001, Apr. 30 Litho. *Perf. 14*

1239	A156	80c on $1.15 #1101	1.25	1.25
1240	A156	80c on $1.15 #1102	1.25	1.25
1241	A156	80c on $1.15 #1103	1.25	1.25
1242	A156	80c on $1.15 #1104	1.25	1.25
1243	A156	80c on $1.15 #1105	1.25	1.25
1244	A156	80c on $1.15 #1106	1.25	1.25
1245	A156	90c on $1.15 #1095	1.25	1.25
1246	A156	90c on $1.15 #1096	1.25	1.25
1247	A156	90c on $1.15 #1097	1.25	1.25
1248	A156	90c on $1.15 #1098	1.25	1.25
1249	A156	90c on $1.15 #1099	1.25	1.25
1250	A156	90c on $1.15 #1100	1.25	1.25
	Nos. 1239-1250 (12)		15.00	15.00

Nos. 1042-1045, 1050-1053 Surcharged or Overprinted in Black or Gold

2002, Nov. 11 Litho. *Perf. 14*

1251	A151	20c on 70c #1042	.25	.25
1252	A154	20c on 70c #1050	.25	.25
1253	A154	80c on $1.15 #1052 (G)	1.50	1.50
1254	A151	85c #1043	1.60	1.60
1255	A154	85c #1051	1.60	1.60
1256	A154	90c on $1.50 #1053	1.75	1.75
1257	A151	95c #1044	1.90	1.90
1258	A151	$1 on $1.50 #1045	2.25	2.25
	Nos. 1251-1258 (8)		11.10	11.10

Nos. 1226A-1226F Surcharged

Nos. 1260-1264

Methods and Perfs As Before

2003, June 30

1259	A177	20c on $1.50 #1226A	.30	.30
1260	A177	80c on $2 #1226B	1.00	1.00
1261	A177	85c on $3 #1226C	1.25	1.25
1262	A177	85c on $4 #1226D	1.25	1.25
1263	A177	90c on $5 #1226E	1.50	1.50
1264	A177	90c on $7 #1226F	1.50	1.50
	Nos. 1259-1264 (6)		6.80	6.80

Obliterator on Nos. 1260-1264 is a Moai head.

United We Stand — A182

2003, Sept. 30 Litho. *Perf. 14*

1265 A182 90c multi 3.00 3.00

Printed in sheets of 4.

2004 Summer Olympics, Athens A183

Designs: 40c, Poster for 1992 Barcelona Olympics. 60c, Pancration, horiz. $1, Cycling, horiz. $2, Gold medal, 1936 Berlin Olympics.

2004, Sept. 29 Litho. *Perf. 14¼*

1266-1269 A183 Set of 4 6.50 6.50

For overprints, see Nos. 1275-1278.

Worldwide Fund for Nature (WWF) — A184

Birds of Suwarrow National Park: 80c, Cook Islands reed warblers. 90c, Mangaia kingfishers. $1.15, Rarotonga starlings. $1.95, Atiu swiftlets.

2005, June 13 Litho. *Perf. 14*

1270-1273 A184 Set of 4 6.50 6.50

Each stamp printed in sheets of 4.

Pope John Paul II (1920-2005) A185

2005, Nov. 11

1274 A185 $1.35 multi		2.75	2.75

Printed in sheets of 5 + label.

Sheets of Nos. 1266-1269 Overprinted in Gold

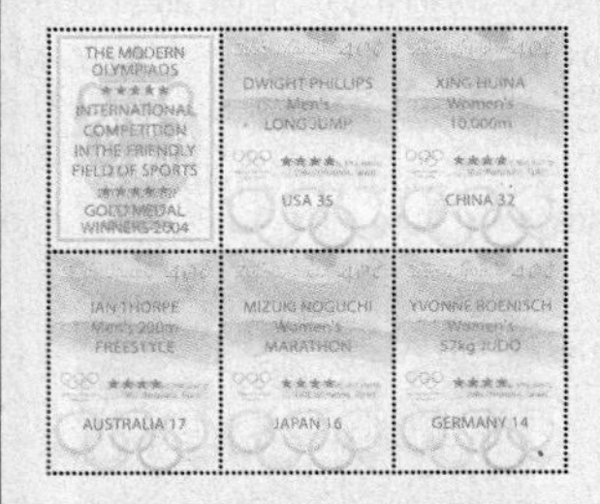

Overprints on Nos. 1276, 1277 and 1278: a, "DWIGHT PHILLIPS / Men's / LONG JUMP / **** / USA 35." b, "XING HUINA / Women's / 10,000m / **** / CHINA 32." c, "IAN THORPE / Men's 200m / FREESTYLE / **** / AUSTRALIA 17." d, "MIZUKI NOGUCHI / Women's / MARATHON / **** / JAPAN 16." e, "YVONNE BOENISCH / Women's / 57kg JUDO / **** / GERMANY 14."

Methods and Perfs. As Before

2005, Nov. 29

1275 A183 40c Sheet of 5, #a-e, + label (#1266)		—	—
1276 A183 60c Sheet of 5, #a-e, + label (#1267)		—	—
1277 A183 $1 Sheet of 5, #a-e, + label (#1268)		—	—
1278 A183 $2 Sheet of 5, #a-e, + label (#1269)		—	—

A186

A187

A188

Designs: 5c, Black-lined Maori wrasse. 10c, Blue lorikeets. 20c, Daisy coral. 30c, Ocean sunfish. 40c, Female Lampides boeticus butterfly. 50c, Rarotonga starlings.

No. 1285: a, Mangaia kingfishers. b, Cook Islands reef warblers. c, Rarotonga starlings, diff. d, Matiu swiftlets.

No. 1286: a, Male Lampides boeticus. b, Vagrans egista. c, Melantis leda. d, Female Lampides boeticus, diff.

No. 1287: a, Daisy coral, diff. b, Hydroid coral. c, Sea star. d, Smooth sea star.

No. 1288: a, Black-tipped cod. b, Red spot rainbow fish. c, Black-lined Maori wrasse, diff. d, Fish (incorrectly identified as Smooth sea star).

No. 1289: a, Three Ocean sunfish, Latin name at LL. b, Three Ocean sunfish, large clump of seaweed, Latin name at LR. c, Two Ocean sunfish, diver. d, Three Ocean sunfish, small clump of seaweed at top, Latin name at LR.

No. 1290: a, Blue lorikeets on palm branch. b, Blue lorikeets in tree hollow. c, Blue lorikeets and white flowers. d, Blue lorikeets and pink flowers.

No. 1291 — Queen Elizabeth II and: a, Hawksbill turtle. b, Leatherback turtle. c, Green turtle. d, Olive ridley turtle.

No. 1292 — Queen Elizabeth II and: a, Sowerby's whales. b, Cuvier's beaked whales. c, Bottle-nosed dolphin. d, Commerson's dolphins.

$7.50, Queen Elizabeth II, fish and marine life. $10, Queen Elizabeth II, butterflies and flowers. $15, Queen Elizabeth II and birds.

Illustrations A187 and A188 reduced.

2007 Litho. *Perf. 13¼*

1279	A186	5c multi	.25	.25
1280	A186	10c multi	.25	.25
1281	A186	20c multi	.30	.30
1282	A186	30c multi	.45	.45
1283	A186	40c multi	.60	.60
1284	A186	50c multi	.75	.75

Size: 48x27mm

Perf. 14x14¾

1285	Block of 4	4.75	4.75
a.-d.	A186 80c Any single	1.10	1.10
1286	Block of 4	5.25	5.25
a.-d.	A186 90c Any single	1.25	1.25
1287	Block of 4	5.75	5.75
a.-d.	A186 $1 Any single	1.40	1.40
1288	Block of 4	6.50	6.50
a.-d.	A186 $1.10 Any single	1.60	1.60
1289	Block of 4	7.00	7.00
a.-d.	A186 $1.20 Any single	1.75	1.75
1290	Block of 4	11.50	11.50
a.-d.	A186 $2 Any single	2.75	2.75

Perf. 13¾

1291	Block of 4	19.00	19.00
a.-d.	A187 $3 Any single	4.75	4.75
1292	Block of 4	31.00	31.00
a.-d.	A187 $5 Any single	7.75	7.75

Perf. 13¼

1293	A188	$7.50 multi	12.00	12.00
1294	A188	$10 multi	15.50	15.50
1295	A188	$15 multi	24.00	24.00
		Nos. 1279-1295 (17)	144.85	144.85

Issued: Nos. 1279-1290, 3/20; No. 1291, 10/10; No. 1292, 11/13; Nos. 1293-1295, 12/10.

Miniature Sheet

2008 Summer Olympics, Beijing — A189

No. 1296: a, 40c, Weight lifting. b, 60c, High jump. c, $1, Swimming. d, $1.50, Running.

2008, July 28 Litho. *Perf. 14¾x14*

1296 A189 Sheet of 4, #a-d		5.25	5.25

Pacific Mini-Games, Rarotonga A190

Designs: 20c, Shot put and discus. 80c, High jump. 90c, Weight lifting. $3, Running.

2009, Sept. 21 Litho. *Perf. 13¾*

1297-1300 A190 Set of 4		7.25	7.25
1300a Souvenir sheet, #1297-1300		7.25	7.25

Nos. 1297-1300 Ovptd. in Gold with Names of Winners

Overprint text: 20c, Daniel Kilama / New Caledonia / Men's Discus Throw / 27th Sept. 2009. 80c, Johanna Sui / Tahiti / Women's High Jump / 24th Sept. 2009. 90c, Yukio Peter / Nauru / 84kg Clean & Jerk / 1st Oct. 2009. $3, Niko Verekauta / Fiji / Men's 100 metres / 24th Sept. 2009.

2009, Oct. 21 Litho. *Perf. 13¾*

1301-1304 A190 Set of 4		7.25	7.25
1304a Souvenir sheet, #1301-1304		7.25	7.25

Flowers — A191

Designs: 10c, Catharanthus roseus. 20c, Ixora casei. 30c, Hibiscus rosa-sinensis cultivar. 40c, Heliconia psittacorum. 50c, Hibiscus schizopetalus, vert. 70c, Alpinia purpurata, vert. 80c, Bougainvillea spectabilis. 90c, Hibiscus rosa-sinensis. $1, Nymphaea capensis. $1.10, Euphorbia pulcherrima. $1.20, Impatiens walleriana. $2, Anthurium andraeanum. $3, Chrysanthemum cultivar. $4, Acalypha pendula, vert. $5, Heliconia rostrata, vert. $7.50, Tagetes patular cultivar. $10, Phalaenopsis cultivar. $20, Catharanthus roseus, diff.

2010, Sept. 10 Litho. *Perf. 13¾*

Sizes: 60x37mm, 37x60mm

1305	A191	10c multi	.25	.25
1306	A191	20c multi	.30	.30
1307	A191	30c multi	.45	.45
1308	A191	40c multi	.60	.60
1309	A191	50c multi	.75	.75
1310	A191	70c multi	1.00	1.00
1311	A191	80c multi	1.25	1.25
1312	A191	90c multi	1.40	1.40
1313	A191	$1 multi	1.50	1.50
1314	A191	$1.10 multi	1.60	1.60
1315	A191	$1.20 multi	1.75	1.75
1316	A191	$2 multi	3.00	3.00
1317	A191	$3 multi	4.50	4.50
1318	A191	$4 multi	5.75	5.75
1319	A191	$5 multi	7.25	7.25
1320	A191	$7.50 multi	11.00	11.00
1321	A191	$10 multi	14.50	14.50
1322	A191	$20 multi	29.00	29.00
		Nos. 1305-1322 (18)	85.85	85.85

See Nos. 1328-1337, 1388-1389.
For overprints see Nos. O70-O117.

ANZAC Day A192

Designs: 80c, Girl Guides in parade. 90c, Boy Scouts in parade. $1.10, Monument, vert. $1.20, Cook Islands flag, vert.

No. 1327: a, Church interior. b, Church exterior.

Perf. 14¾x14¼, 14¼x14¾

2010, Sept. 14

1323-1326 A192 Set of 4		6.00	6.00

Souvenir Sheet

1327 A192 $3 Sheet of 2, #a-b		9.00	9.00

For overprints, see Nos. 1391-1400.

Flower Type of 2010 in Smaller Sizes

Designs as before.

2010, Oct. 27 Litho. *Perf. 14*

Sizes: 42x28mm, 28x42mm

1328	A191	10c multi	.25	.25
1329	A191	20c multi	.30	.30
1330	A191	30c multi	.50	.50
1331	A191	50c multi	.80	.80
1332	A191	80c multi	1.25	1.25
1333	A191	90c multi	1.50	1.50
1334	A191	$1 multi	1.60	1.60
1335	A191	$1.10 multi	1.75	1.75
1336	A191	$1.20 multi	1.90	1.90
1337	A191	$2 multi	3.25	3.25
		Nos. 1328-1337 (10)	13.10	13.10

For surcharges, see Nos. 1437-1445.

Expo 2010, Shanghai A193

Designs: 80c, Anthurium flower. 90c, Angelfish. $1.10, Fish near ocean floor. $1.20, Coconuts.

$6, Palm tree and ocean, vert.

2010, Oct. 27 *Perf. 14¾x14¼*

1338-1341 A193 Set of 4		6.50	6.50

Souvenir Sheet

Perf. 14¼

1342 A193 $6 multi		9.75	9.75

No. 1342 contains one 38x50mm stamp.

Miniature Sheet

Aerial Views of Islands — A194

No. 1343: a, 10c, Aitutaki. b, 10c, Penrhyn. c, 20c, Palmerston. d, 20c, Mitiaro. e, 30c, Rarotonga. f, 30c, Takutea. g, 50c, Atiu. h, 70c, Suwarrow. i, 80c, Pukapuka. j, 80c, Nassau. k, 90c, Mangaia. l, 90c, Manihiki. m, 90c, Manuae. n, $1.10, Rakahanga. o, $1.20, Mauke.

2010, Nov. 8 *Perf. 14*

1343 A194 Sheet of 15, #a-o		14.00	14.00

Service of Queen Elizabeth II and Prince Philip — A195

Designs: 80c, Queen Elizabeth II. 90c, Queen and Prince Philip. $1, Queen and Prince Philip, diff. $1.10, Queen and Prince Philip, diff. $1.20, Queen and Prince Philip, diff. $1.50, Prince Philip.

$6.60, Queen and Prince Philip, diff.

2010, Dec. 6 Litho. *Perf. 13¼*

1344-1349 A195 Set of 6		9.75	9.75
1349a Sheet of 6, #1344-1349, + 3 labels		9.75	9.75

Souvenir Sheet

1350 A195 $6.60 multi		10.00	10.00

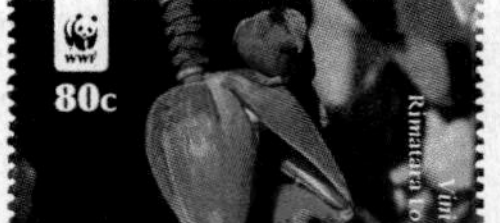

Worldwide Fund for Nature (WWF) — A196

Rimatara lorikeet: 80c, Pair on flower. 90c, In flight. $2.40, On branch. $3.60, Trio at nest.

2010, Dec. 9 Litho. *Perf. 14*

1351-1354 A196 Set of 4 11.50 11.50

A197

Engagement of Prince William and Catherine Middleton — A198

Designs: Nos. 1355, 1358a, 1360, Middleton. Nos. 1356, 1358b, 1361, Prince in military uniform.

No. 1357: a, Prince in military uniform. b, Prince playing polo. c, Middleton, fence. d, Prince, man and woman in background. e, Middleton, woman in background. f, Couple, Prince at left. g, Middleton with black hat. h, Prince. i, Couple, Middleton at left. j, Hands of couple, engagement ring.

$8.10, Couple, Prince in uniform at left.

2011, Jan. 14 *Perf. 14*

1355 A197 $2.40 multi 3.75 3.75
1356 A197 $3.60 multi 5.50 5.50

Miniature Sheets

1357 A198 10c Sheet of 10, #a-j 1.60 1.60

Perf. 13¾x13½

1358 A197 Sheet of 2, #a-b 9.25 9.25

Souvenir Sheets

Perf. 14¼

1359 A197 $8.10 multi 12.50 12.50
1360 A197 $11 multi 17.00 17.00
1361 A197 $11 multi 17.00 17.00
Nos. 1359-1361 (3) 46.50 46.50

No. 1358 contains two 28x44mm stamps. Nos. 1359-1361 each contain one 38x50mm stamp.

Peonies — A199

No. 1362: a, 80c, Pink peonies (30x40mm). b, 90c, Purple peony (30x30mm). c, $1.10, Peach peonies (30x30mm). d, $1.20, Pink peony (30x30mm).

$8.10, Red peony.

2011, Apr. 8 Litho. *Perf. 14¾*

1362 A199 Sheet of 4, #a-d 6.25 6.25

Souvenir Sheet

1363 A199 $8.10 multi 13.00 13.00

No. 1363 contains one 70x60mm stamp.

Wedding of Prince William and Catherine Middleton A200

Designs: 20c, Couple, Prince at right. 30c, Westminster Abbey. 80c, Couple, Prince at left.

2011, Apr. 29 *Perf. 13¼*

1364-1366 A200 Set of 3 2.10 2.10
1366a Souvenir sheet of 3, #1364-1366 2.10 2.10

Rarotonga Tourism — A201

Designs: 10c, Whale breaching ocean's surface near boat. 20c, Palm trees, boat. 30c, Starfish. 50c, Palm trees near ocean. 70c, Crab. 80c, Cook Islands flag on boat. 90c, Airplane, windsurfer. $1, Trees near beach. $1.10, Cliffs, airplane. $1.20, Palm trees near beach. $1.50, Goat. $2, Chicken. $3, Island and beach. $4, Fish. $5, Aerial view of Rarotonga. cruise ship.

2011, July 22 Litho. *Perf. 14*

1367 A201 10c multi .25 .25
1368 A201 20c multi .35 .35
1369 A201 30c multi .50 .50
1370 A201 50c multi .85 .85
1371 A201 70c multi 1.25 1.25
1372 A201 80c multi 1.40 1.40
1373 A201 90c multi 1.50 1.50
1374 A201 $1 multi 1.75 1.75
1375 A201 $1.10 multi 1.90 1.90
1376 A201 $1.20 multi 2.00 2.00
1377 A201 $1.50 multi 2.50 2.50
1378 A201 $2 multi 3.50 3.50
1379 A201 $3 multi 5.00 5.00
1380 A201 $4 multi 6.75 6.75
1381 A201 $5 multi 8.50 8.50
a. Sheet of 15, #1367-1381 38.00 38.00
Nos. 1367-1381 (15) 38.00 38.00

National Environment Service A202

Designs: 80c, Bristle-thighed curlew. 90c, Fiddler crab. $1.10, Taro plant and flower. $1.20, Wetlands flora.

2011, Oct. 21 *Perf. 13¾*

1382-1385 A202 Set of 4 6.50 6.50

Nos. 1382-1385 each were printed in sheets of 4.

Souvenir Sheets

Stamps at Work — A203

No. 1386: a, $1.10, Quick response code. b, $5, Emblem for Wetlands for Healthy Islands.

No. 1387: a, $1.10, Quick response code, text and website address. b, $5, Damage from 2011 Japan tsunami.

2011, Oct. 21 *Perf. 15x14¼*

Sheets of 2, #a-b

1386-1387 A203 Set of 2 19.50 19.50

Twenty percent of the sales of No. 1387 were donated to Japan tsunami relief efforts.

Flowers Type of 2010 With Head of Queen Elizabeth II Added at Lower Right

Designs: $26.90, Plumeria rubra. $31.10, Hypolimnas bolina.

2011, Oct. 25 *Perf. 14¼x15*

Size: 44x29mm

1388 A191 $26.90 multi 42.50 42.50
1389 A191 $31.10 multi 50.00 50.00

Christmas A204

No. 1390: a, Five gold rings. b, Six geese a laying. c, Seven swans a swimming. d, Eight maids a milking.

2011, Dec. 23 Litho. *Perf. 13¼*

1390 Horiz. strip of 4 13.00 13.00
a. A204 $1.10 multi 1.75 1.75
b. A204 $1.20 multi 1.90 1.90
c. A204 $2.10 multi 3.50 3.50
d. A204 $3.60 multi 5.75 5.75
e. Souvenir sheet of 4, #1390a-1390d 13.00 13.00

Nos. 1323-1327 Overprinted in Gold or Silver

Methods and Perfs As Before

2012, Jan. 10

1391 A192 80c On No. 1323 (G) 1.40 1.40
1392 A192 80c On No. 1323 (S) 1.40 1.40
1393 A192 90c On No. 1324 (G) 1.50 1.50
1394 A192 90c On No. 1324 (S) 1.50 1.50
1395 A192 $1.10 On No. 1325 (G) 1.90 1.90
1396 A192 $1.10 On No. 1325 (S) 1.90 1.90
1397 A192 $1.20 On No. 1326 (G) 2.00 2.00
1398 A192 $1.20 On No. 1326 (S) 2.00 2.00
Nos. 1391-1398 (8) 13.60 13.60

Souvenir Sheets of 2, #a-b

1399 A192 $3 On No. 1327 (G) 10.00 10.00
1400 A192 $3 On No. 1327 (S) 10.00 10.00

Overprint reads up on Nos. 1395-1398.

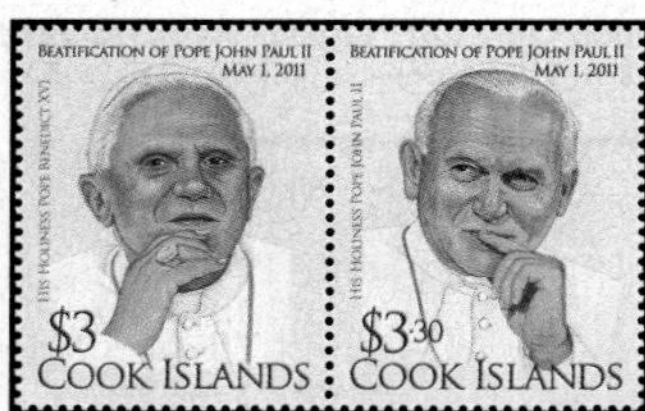

Beatification of Pope John Paul II — A205

No. 1401: a, $3, Pope Benedict XVI. b, $3.30, Pope John Paul II.

2012, Jan. 10 Litho. *Perf. 13¾*

1401 A205 Horiz. pair, #a-b 10.50 10.50

No. 1401 was printed in sheets containing two pairs.

Reign of Queen Elizabeth II, 60th Anniv. — A206

Queen Elizabeth II: 80c, Wearing tiara. 90c, Wearing red hat. $1, Wearing tiara, diff. $1.10, Wearing gray hat. $1.20, With dog. $1.50, Wearing aquamarine dress.

$6.60, Wearing aquamarine dress, diff.

2012, Feb. 6 *Perf. 13¼*

1402-1407 A206 Set of 6 11.00 11.00
1407a Souvenir sheet of 6, #1402-1407, + 3 labels 11.00 11.00

Souvenir Sheet

1408 A206 $6.60 multi 11.00 11.00

Worldwide Fund for Nature (WWF) — A207

Designs: 90c, Partula assimilis. $1.20, Libera fratercula. $1.50, Lamprocystis globosa. $2.70, Sinployea peasei.

2012, Apr. 11 *Perf. 14*

1409-1412 A207 Set of 4 10.00 10.00
1412a Sheet of 16, 4 each #1409-1412 40.00 40.00

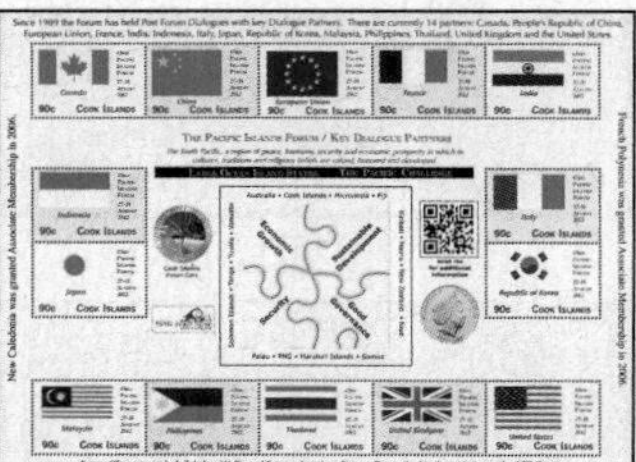

2012 Summer Olympics, London — A208

Designs: 80c, Swimming. 90c, Map of South Pacific, Great Britain and Ireland. $2, Sailing.

2012, June 22 *Perf. 13¾*

1413-1415 A208 Set of 3 6.00 6.00
1415a Souvenir sheet of 3, #1413-1415 6.00 6.00
1415b Souvenir sheet of 6, 2 each #1413-1415 12.00 12.00

Miniature Sheets

43rd Pacific Islands Forum, Rarotonga — A209

No. 1416 — Flag of: a, Canada. b, People's Republic of China. c, European Union. d, France. e, India. f, Indonesia. g, Italy. h, Japan. i, Republic of Korea. j, Malaysia. k, Philippines. l, Thailand. m, United Kingdom. n, United States.

No. 1417 — Flag of: a, Australia. b, Cook Islands. c, Fiji. d, Kiribati. e, Micronesia. f, Nauru. g, New Zealand. h, Niue. i, Palau. j, Papua New Guinea. k, Marshall Islands. l, Samoa. m, Solomon Islands. n, Tonga. o, Tuvalu. p, Vanuatu.

2012, Aug. 22 ***Perf. 14***

1416 A209 90c Sheet of 14, #a-n 21.00 21.00
1417 A209 90c Sheet of 16, #a-p 24.00 24.00

Adoration of the Magi, by Giotto di Bondone A210

Entry into Jerusalem, by Giotto A211

Lamentation, by Giotto — A212

Kiss of Judas, by Giotto A213

Life of Mary Magdalene - Raising of Lazarus, by Giotto A214

Death of Mary, by Giotto A215

Perf. 14¾x14¼

2012, Nov. 16 **Litho.**

Stamps With White Frames

1418	Horiz. pair	2.80	2.80
a.	A210 80c multi	1.40	1.40
b.	A211 80c multi	1.40	1.40
1419	Horiz. pair	3.00	3.00
a.	A212 90c multi	1.50	1.50
b.	A213 90c multi	1.50	1.50
1420	Horiz. pair	10.00	10.00
a.	A214 $3 multi	5.00	5.00
b.	A215 $3 multi	5.00	5.00
	Nos. 1418-1420 (3)	15.80	15.80

Miniature Sheet
Stamps Without White Frame

1421	Sheet of 6	16.00	16.00
a.	A210 80c multi	1.40	1.40
b.	A211 80c multi	1.40	1.40
c.	A212 90c multi	1.50	1.50
d.	A213 90c multi	1.50	1.50
e.	A214 $3 multi	5.00	5.00
f.	A215 $3 multi	5.00	5.00

Christmas.

Miniature Sheets

A215a

43rd Pacific Islands Forum, Rarotonga — A215b

No. 1422G: i, Woman with Cook Islands sash with Minister of Education Teina Bishop, New Zealand Prime Minister John Key and John Carter, New Zealand High Commissioner to the Cook Islands. j, Canoe with sails. k, Women from Aitutaki holding a quilted bedspread. l, Leaders of Pacific islands seated in row. m, President of French Polynesia Oscar Temaru and Cook Islands Prime Minister Henry Puna in front of airplane. n, Australian Prime Minister Julia Gillard. o, Canoe on shore.

No. 1422H: p, Pres. Temaru, Prime Minister Puna, Cook Islands Deputy Prime Minister Tom Marsters and entourage walking away from airplane. q, Prime Minister Puna departing airplane, two women. r, U.S. airplane. s, People leaving Royal New Zealand Air Force airplane. t, Crowds near entrance to Aitutaki Airport. u, U.S. Secretary of State Hillary Clinton with Cook Island Minister of Finance Mark Brown. v, Aitutaki dancers performing for leaders.

2012, Nov. 30 **Litho.** ***Perf. 14***

1421G A215a 80c Sheet of 7, #i-o, + label 9.50 9.50
1421H A215b 90c Sheet of 7, #p-v, + label 10.50 10.50

A216

Personalizable Stamps — A217

2012, Dec. 21 **Litho.** ***Perf. 14x14¾***

1422 A216 $4 multi 6.75 6.75
1423 A217 $4 multi 6.75 6.75

Items Commemorating British Coronations — A218

Coronation of Queen Elizabeth II, 60th Anniv. — A219

Various items commemorating the coronation of: 80c, Queen Victoria. 90c, King Edward VII. $1.10, King George V. $1.20, Seed packet for Coronation mixture of sweet pea seeds. $3.60, Illustration from *The Coronation Cut-Out Story Book.*
$3.90, Queen Elizabeth II.

2013, Feb. 6 **Litho.** ***Perf. 14***

1424-1428 A218 Set of 5 12.50 12.50

Souvenir Sheet
Perf. 15x14

1429 A219 $3.90 multi 6.50 6.50

Nos. 1424-1428 each were printed isn sheets of 8 + central label.

A220

A221

A222

A223

A224

Cook Islands Marine Park A225

2013, Feb. 20 **Litho.** ***Perf. 14***

1430	A220 80c multi	1.40	1.40
1431	A221 80c multi	1.40	1.40
1432	A222 80c multi	1.40	1.40
1433	A223 90c multi	1.50	1.50
1434	A224 90c multi	1.50	1.50
1435	A225 90c multi	1.50	1.50
	Nos. 1430-1435 (6)	8.70	8.70

New Year 2013 (Year of the Snake) A226

No. 1436 — Snake with background color of: a, Green. b, Red.

Perf. 14¾x14¼

2013, Feb. 21 **Litho.**

1436 A226 $1.20 pair, #a-b 4.00 4.00

Printed in sheets containing 2 each of Nos. 1436a-1436b.

Nos. 1328, 1330-1337 Surcharged in Gold

Methods and Perfs. As Before

2013, Apr. 9

1437	A191 20c on 10c #1328	.35	.35
1438	A191 20c on 30c #1330	.35	.35
1439	A191 20c on 50c #1331	.35	.35
1440	A191 20c on 80c #1332	.35	.35
1441	A191 20c on 90c #1333	.35	.35
1442	A191 20c on $1 #1334	.35	.35
1443	A191 20c on $1.10 #1335	.35	.35
1444	A191 20c on $1.20 #1336	.35	.35
1445	A191 20c on $2 #1337	.35	.35
	Nos. 1437-1445 (9)	3.15	3.15

Ships — A227

No. 1446, 20c: a, Ndrua. b, Hamatafua.
No. 1447, 50c: a, Single-masted Vaa Kalua. b, Double-masted Vaa Kalua.
No. 1448, 60c: a, Vaka Motu. b, Toniaki.
No. 1449, 80c: a, Vaka. b, Pahi.
No. 1450, 90c: a, Vaka, diff. b, Pahi, diff.
No. 1451, $2.30: a, Vaka Motu, diff. b, Tipaerua.
No. 1452, $4.50: a, Pahi, diff. b, Waka Tou. c, Tipaerua, diff.

2013, May 24 Litho. *Perf. 14¾x14¼*
Horiz. Pairs, #a-b

1446-1451	A227	Set of 6	17.00	17.00

Souvenir Sheet

1452	A227	$4.50 Sheet of 3, #a-c	22.00	22.00

Animals — A228

Designs: No. 1453, $1.50, American bison. No. 1454, $1.50, Gazella dama. No. 1455, $1.50, Phascolarctos cinereus. No. 1456, $1.50, Eurasian lynx. No. 1457, $1.50, Loxodonta africana. No. 1458, $1.50, Grus americana.

2013, May 31 Litho. *Perf. 14x14¾*

1453-1458	A228	Set of 6	14.50	14.50

Miniature Sheet

Duchess of Cambridge — A229

No. 1459 — Duchess of Cambridge: a, Wearing pink dress (40x52mm). b, Wearing dark blue jacket and black hat (40x26mm). c, Wearing yellow jacket and hat, meeting with group of dignitaries (40x26mm). d, Wearing white dress and hat, reviewing Scout troop (40x26mm). e, Wearing light blue dress (40x52mm). f, Wearing polka dot dress (40x52mm). g, Wearing wedding gown, kissing Duke of Cambridge (40x26mm).

2013, Aug. 1 Litho. *Perf. 13¼*

1459	A229	$1 Sheet of 7, #a-g	11.50	11.50

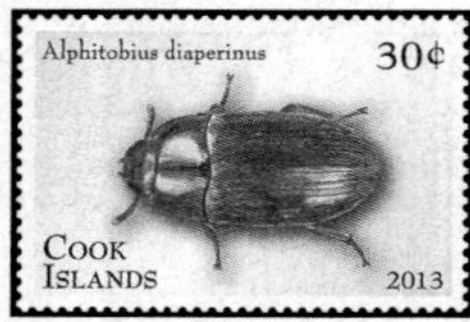

Insects and Spiders A230

Designs: 30c, Alphitobius diaperinus. 50c, Leptocoris rufomarginatus. 70c, Nabis capsiformis. $1, Polistes jokahamae. $1.30, Agrius convulvi. $1.50, Harmonia octomaculata. $1.70, Cosmopolites sordidus. $3.80, Graeffea crouanii. $4.10, Leptoglossus australis. $5.30, Nezara viridula. $6.50, Neoscona theisi. $8.50, Tholumis tillarga.

2013, Sept. 2 Litho. *Perf. 14*
Stamps With White Frames

1460	A230	30c multi	.50	.50
1461	A230	50c multi	.85	.85
1462	A230	70c multi	1.25	1.25
1463	A230	$1 multi	1.60	1.60
1464	A230	$1.30 multi	2.10	2.10
1465	A230	$1.50 multi	2.50	2.50
1466	A230	$1.70 multi	2.75	2.75
1467	A230	$3.80 multi	6.25	6.25
1468	A230	$4.10 multi	6.75	6.75
1469	A230	$5.30 multi	8.75	8.75
1470	A230	$6.50 multi	10.50	10.50
1471	A230	$8.50 multi	14.00	14.00
		Nos. 1460-1471 (12)	57.80	57.80

Miniature Sheet
Stamp Without White Frame

1472	Sheet of 12	58.00	58.00
a.	A230 30c multi	.50	.50
b.	A230 50c multi	.85	.85
c.	A230 70c multi	1.25	1.25
d.	A230 $1 multi	1.60	1.60
e.	A230 $1.30 multi	2.10	2.10
f.	A230 $1.50 multi	2.50	2.50
g.	A230 $1.70 multi	2.75	2.75
h.	A230 $3.80 multi	6.25	6.25
i.	A230 $4.10 multi	6.75	6.75
j.	A230 $5.30 multi	8.75	8.75
k.	A230 $6.50 multi	10.50	10.50
l.	A230 $8.50 multi	14.00	14.00

See Nos. 1491-1503.

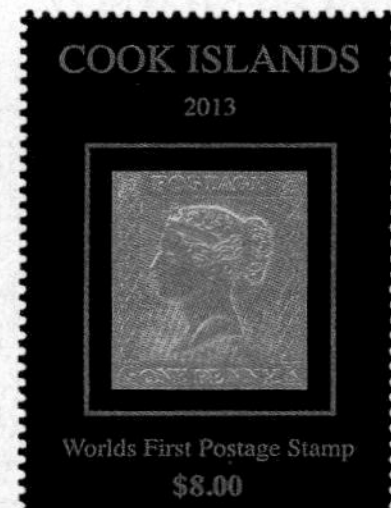

Great Britain No. 1 — A231

Litho. & Embossed With Foil Application

2013, Sept. 18 *Perf. 13x13¼*

1473	A231	$8 blk & gold	13.50	13.50

Souvenir Sheets

2013 China International Collection Exposition, Beijing — A232

No. 1474 — Stamps inscribed "Cook Islands": a, $1, Painting by Paul Gauguin. b, $3, Beijing Exhibition Center.

No. 1475 — Stamps inscribed "Rarotonga / Cook Islands": a, $1, Painting by Paul Gauguin, diff. b, $3, Beijing Exhibition Center.

2013, Sept. 26 Litho. *Perf. 12*

1474	A232	Sheet of 2, #a-b	6.75	6.75
1475	A232	Sheet of 2, #a-b	6.75	6.75

Pres. John F. Kennedy (1917-63) A233

Designs: $2.40, Pres. Kennedy. $3.10, Pres. Kennedy and quote,

2013, Nov. 8 Litho. *Perf. 14¼*

1476-1477	A233	Set of 2	9.00	9.00

Christmas — A234

Paintings by: $1, Gerard van Honthorst. $1.30, Michelangelo Merisi da Caravaggio. No. 1480, $1.50, Rembrandt.

No. 1481: a, $1.50, Bernardo Daddi. b, $1.70, Pieter Aertsen. c, $4.50, Lorenzo Lotto.

2013, Nov. 18 Litho. *Perf. 13¼*

1478-1480	A234	Set of 3	6.25	6.25

Souvenir Sheet

1481	A234	Sheet of 3, #a-c	13.00	13.00

Highland Paradise Scenes — A235

Various scenes from Highland Paradise tourist educational show.

2014, Jan. 3 Litho. *Perf. 13¼*

1482	A235	10c multi	.25	.25
1483	A235	20c multi	.35	.35
1484	A235	30c multi	.50	.50
1485	A235	50c multi	.85	.85
1486	A235	60c multi	1.00	1.00
1487	A235	$1 multi	1.60	1.60
1488	A235	$1.30 multi	2.10	2.10
1489	A235	$1.50 multi	2.50	2.50
1490	A235	$1.70 multi	2.75	2.75
		Nos. 1482-1490 (9)	11.90	11.90

Dated "2013."

Insects and Spiders Type of 2013

Designs: 10c, Teleogryllus oceanicus. 40c, Euconocephalus roberti. $1, Apis mellifera. $2.10, Crocidolomia pavonana. $2.50, Junonia villida. $3, Aedes polynesiensis. $3.50, Homalodisca coagulata. $4.50, Lygus flavoscutellatus. $5.50, Euploea lewinii perryi. $6.70, Hypolimnas bolina. $7, Porcellio laevis. $10.10, Vagrans egista bodenia.

2014, Jan. 6 Litho. *Perf. 14*
Stamps With White Frames

1491	A230	10c multi	.25	.25
1492	A230	40c multi	.65	.65
1493	A230	$1 multi	1.60	1.60
1494	A230	$2.10 multi	3.50	3.50
1495	A230	$2.50 multi	4.00	4.00
1496	A230	$3 multi	5.00	5.00
1497	A230	$3.50 multi	5.75	5.75
1498	A230	$4.50 multi	7.25	7.25
1499	A230	$5.50 multi	9.00	9.00
1500	A230	$6.70 multi	11.00	11.00
1501	A230	$7 multi	11.50	11.50
1502	A230	$10.10 multi	16.50	16.50
		Nos. 1491-1502 (12)	76.00	76.00

Miniature Sheet
Stamp Without White Frame

1503	Sheet of 12	76.00	76.00
a.	A230 10c multi	.25	.25
b.	A230 40c multi	.65	.65
c.	A230 $1 multi	1.60	1.60
d.	A230 $2.10 multi	3.50	3.50
e.	A230 $2.50 multi	4.00	4.00
f.	A230 $3 multi	5.00	5.00
g.	A230 $3.50 multi	5.75	5.75
h.	A230 $4.50 multi	7.25	7.25
i.	A230 $5.50 multi	9.00	9.00
j.	A230 $6.70 multi	11.00	11.00
k.	A230 $7 multi	11.50	11.50
l.	A230 $10.10 multi	16.50	16.50

Souvenir Sheet

New Year 2014 (Year of the Horse) — A236

No. 1504 — Horse, with denomination color of: a, Red. b, White.

2014, Jan. 8 Litho. *Perf. 13¼*

1504	A236	$3 Sheet of 2, #a-b	9.75	9.75

Souvenir Sheet

Christening of Prince George of Cambridge — A237

No. 1505 — Prince George being held by: a, $4, Duchess of Cambridge. b, $5, Duke of Cambridge.

2014, Jan. 14 Litho. *Perf. 14*

1505	A237	Sheet of 2, #a-b	14.50	14.50

Easter — A238

No. 1506 — Religious painting by: a, 50c, Il Moro. b, $1, Tintoretto. c, $1.30, Giovanni Bellini. d, $1.50, Raphael (Sanzio). e, $1.70, William Blake.

$9.50, Painting by Hans Memling.

2014, Apr. 9 Litho. *Perf. 13¼*

1506	A238	Sheet of 5, #a-e, + label	10.50	10.50

Souvenir Sheet

1507	A238	$9.50 multi	16.50	16.50

Small Island Developing States — A239

No. 1508: a, Tropical cyclone. b, Rising sea levels at Rarotonga. c, Pacific Small Island Developing States emblem. d, Map of Cook Islands. e, "Island Voices Global Choices" emblem. f, Fishing boats. g, Sailboat. h, Cruise liner. i, Kayak. j, Wind surfing. k, Nurse shark. l, Barracuda. m, Triggerfish. n, Pilot whale. o, Manta ray. p, Flag of Cook Islands.

No. 1509: a, Like #1508a. b, Like #1508p. c, Like #1508b. d, Like #1508c. e, Like #1508d. f, Like #1508e.

No. 1510: a, Like #1508f. b, Like #1508p. c, Like #1508g. d, Like #1508h. e, Like #1508i. f, Like #1508j.

No. 1511: a, Like #1508k. b, Like #1508p. c, Like #1508l. d, Like #1508m. e, Like #1508n. f, Like #1508o.

2014, May 9 Litho. *Perf. 13¼*

1508 Block of 18, #1508a-1508o, 3 #1508p 15.50 15.50
a.-p. A239 50c Any single .85 .85

Miniature Sheets

1509 Sheet of 6 21.00 21.00
a.-f. A239 $2 Any single 3.50 3.50
1510 Sheet of 6 25.50 25.50
a.-f. A239 $2.40 Any single 4.25 4.25
1511 Sheet of 6 27.00 27.00
a.-f. A239 $2.60 Any single 4.50 4.50
Nos. 1509-1511 (3) 73.50 73.50

No. 1508 was printed in sheets containing 3 blocks of 18. The frame on each stamp in the sheet, depicting a map of the Pacific Ocean, differs.

Souvenir Sheet

Nelson Mandela (1918-2013), President of South Africa — A240

No. 1512 — Mandela with: a, $2.50, Child. b, $4.50, U. S. Pres. Bill Clinton.

2014, May 13 Litho. *Perf. 14*

1512 A240 Sheet of 2, #a-b 12.00 12.00

Tourism — A241

No. 1513, 30c: a, Relaxing. b, Shopping. c, Dancing. d, Dining.

No. 1514, 50c: a, Church service. b, Scootering. c, Hiking. d, Snorkeling.

No. 1515, $1: a, Kayaking. b, Swimming. c, Scuba diving. d, Fishing.

No. 1516, $1.70: a, Vaka sailing. b, Windsurfing. c, Kitesurfing. d, Paddleboarding.

No. 1517, $3.80: a, Whale watching, b, Sightseeing. c, Glass bottom boat. d, Birdwatching.

No. 1518, $4.10: a, Rugby. b, Beach volleyball. c, Golfing. d, Bike riding.

2014, June 23 Litho. *Perf. 14¼x14*

Blocks of 4, #a-d

1513-1518 A241 Set of 6 80.00 80.00

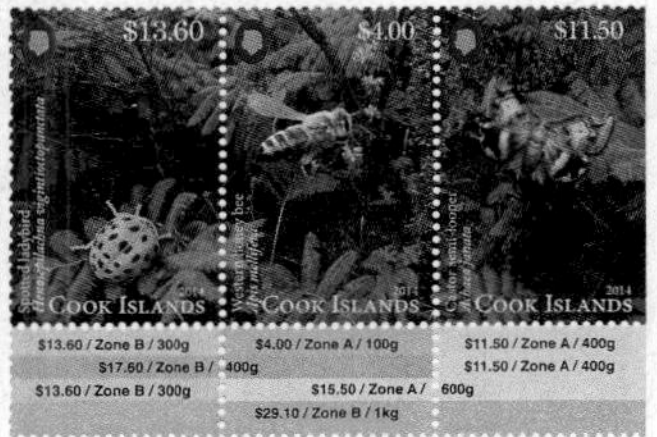

Insects — A242

No. 1519: a, $4, Western honey bee. b, $11.50, Castor semi-looper moth. c, $13.60, Spotted ladybird.

2014, Sept. 12 Litho. *Perf. 13¼*

1519 A242 Horiz. strip of 3, #a-c, + 3 labels 46.00 46.00

Worldwide Fund for Nature (WWF) A243

Various depictions of spotless crake: Nos. 1520, 1524a, $1. Nos. 1521, 1524b, $1.30. Nos. 1522, 1524c, $1.50. Nos. 1523, 1524d, $1.70

$7.50, Spotless crake, diff.

Perf. 14¾x14¼

2014, Nov. 28 Litho.

Stamps With White Frame

1520-1523 A243 Set of 4 8.75 8.75

Stamps Without White Frame

1524 A243 Strip of 4, #a-d 8.75 8.75

Souvenir Sheet

1525 A243 $7.50 multi 12.00 12.00

For surcharges, see Nos. 1571-1576.

Souvenir Sheet

Christmas — A244

No. 1526 — Religious paintings by: a, Giotto di Bondone. b, Jan Gossaert. c, Caravaggio.

Perf. 14¾x14¼

2014, Dec. 12 Litho.

1526 A244 $1.50 Sheet of 3, #a-c 7.00 7.00

Souvenir Sheet

New Year 2015 (Year of the Sheep) — A245

No. 1527: a, $3.80, Red ram. b, $4.10, Blue ram.

2015, Jan. 5 Litho. *Perf. 13¼*

1527 A245 Sheet of 2, #a-b 11.50 11.50

Miniature Sheet

Easter — A246

No. 1528 — Religious paintings by: a, Matthias Grünewald. b, Peter Paul Rubens. c, Jean Jouvenet. d, Giampietrino.

2015, Mar. 31 Litho. *Perf. 14*

1528 A246 $2 Sheet of 4, #a-d 12.50 12.50

Souvenir Sheet

Birth of Princess Charlotte of Cambridge — A247

No. 1529: a, Duchess of Cambridge holding Princess Charlotte. b, Duke of Cambridge holding Prince George.

Perf. 14¾x14¼

2015, June 23 Litho.

1529 A247 $4.50 Sheet of 2, #a-b 12.00 12.00

Magna Carta, 800th Anniv. A248

Quotations starting with: $1, "To no one will we deny or delay. . ." $1.30, "No free man shall be seized. . ." $1.50, "Given by our hand in the meadow. . ." $1.70, "To no one will we deny or delay. . .," diff.

2015, July 15 Litho. *Perf. 14¼x14¾*

1530-1533 A248 Set of 4 7.25 7.25

A249

Self-Government, 50th Anniv. — A250

No. 1535 — Cook Islands stamps: a, #162. b, #164. c, #195. d, #233. e, #253. f, #288. g, #301. h, #322. i, #357. j, #409.

No. 1536 — Cook Islands stamps: a, #435. b, #464. c, #479. d, #502. e, #531. f, #549. g, #660. h, #685. i, #696a. j, #760. k, #877. l, #B100. m, #B113. n, #998a. o, #1010b.

No. 1537 — Cook Islands stamps: a, #1029. b, #1048. c, #1111. d, #1140. e, #1191b. f, #1198b. g, #1204. h, #1214a. i, #O68. j, #1234. k, #1238. l, #1241. m, #1258. n, #1265. o, #1269.

No. 1538 — Cook Islands stamps: a, #1271. b, #1291a. c, #1296c. d, #1299. e, #1343a. f, #1383. g, #1422Hq. h, #1434. i, #1482. j, #1534.

2015, Aug. 5 Litho. *Perf. 14*

1534 A249 $1 multi 1.25 1.25

Miniature Sheets

Perf. 13¾

1535 Sheet of 10 1.25 1.25
a.-j. A250 10c Any single .25 .25
1536 Sheet of 15 6.00 6.00
a.-o. A250 30c Any single .40 .40
1537 Sheet of 15 7.50 7.50
a.-o. A250 40c Any single .50 .50
1538 Sheet of 10 6.50 6.50
a.-j. A250 50c Any single .65 .65
Nos. 1535-1538 (4) 21.25 21.25

New Year 2016 (Year of the Monkey) A251

Designs: $2.60: Adult and juvenile monkeys, leaves. $3, Juvenile monkey on back of adult.

No. 1541: a, $3.80, Like $2.60. b, $4.10, Like $3.

2015, Sept. 25 Litho. *Perf. 13¼*

1539-1540 A251 Set of 2 7.25 7.25

Self-Adhesive

1541 A251 Sheet of 2, #a-b 10.50 10.50

No. 1541 contains two 51x51mm diamond-shaped stamps.

Miniature Sheet

Queen Elizabeth II, Longest-Reigning British Monarch — A252

No. 1542 — Various photographs of Queen Elizabeth II: a, $1.30. b, $1.50. c, $1.70. d, $2.

2015, Nov. 20 Litho. *Perf. 14*

1542 A252 Sheet of 4, #a-d 8.75 8.75

Souvenir Sheet

Christmas — A253

No. 1543 — Details from Nativity, by Antoniazzo Romano: a, Joseph and saint. b, Infant Jesus and animals. c, Virgin Mary and saint.

2015, Dec. 9 Litho. *Perf. 13¼*

1543 A253 $1 Sheet of 3, #a-c 4.00 4.00

A254

A255

Night Skies — A256

Various depictions of night sky, as shown.

Perf. 14¾x14¼

2015, Dec. 29 Litho.

1544	A254	30c Block of 4, #a-d	1.60	1.60
1545	A255	$1 Block of 4, #a-d	5.50	5.50
1546	A256	$1.30 Block of 4, #a-d	7.00	7.00
		Nos. 1544-1546 (3)	14.10	14.10

Worldwide Fund for Nature (WWF) A257

Various depictions of Reef manta ray: Nos. 1547, 1551a, $1. Nos. 1548, 1551b, $1.50. Nos. 1549, 1551c, $1.70. Nos. 1550, 1551d, $2.

2016, Feb. 15 Litho. *Perf. 14¾x14*

Stamps With White Frames

1547-1550	A257	Set of 4	8.25	8.25

Stamps Without White Frames

1551	A257	Horiz. strip of 4, #a-d	8.25	8.25

No. 1551 printed in sheets containing two strips.

Souvenir Sheet

Queen Elizabeth II, 90th Birthday — A258

No. 1552 — Queen Elizabeth II: a, Holding parasol. b, Wearing coat.

2016, May 10 Litho. *Perf. 13¼*

1552	A258	$3 Sheet of 2, #a-b	8.25	8.25

Marae Moana Marine Park — A259

Designs: 30c, Sperm whales. 80c, Melon-headed whales. $1, Emblem of Marae Moana Marine Park. $1.10, Spinner dolphin. $1.30, Spotted dolphins. $1.50, Whale shark. $1.70, Tiger shark. $2, Staghorn coral. $2.40, Yellow scroll coral. $2.50, Black saddled coral groupers. $2.60, Green turtles. $3, Bristle-thighed curlews.

2016, May 27 Litho. *Perf. 14¼x14¾*

1553	A259	30c multi	.40	.40
1554	A259	80c multi	1.10	1.10
1555	A259	$1 multi	1.40	1.40
1556	A259	$1.10 multi	1.50	1.50
1557	A259	$1.30 multi	1.75	1.75
1558	A259	$1.50 multi	2.10	2.10
1559	A259	$1.70 multi	2.40	2.40
1560	A259	$2 multi	2.75	2.75
1561	A259	$2.40 multi	3.25	3.25
1562	A259	$2.50 multi	3.50	3.50
1563	A259	$2.60 multi	3.50	3.50
1564	A259	$3 multi	4.25	4.25
		Nos. 1553-1564 (12)	27.90	27.90

New Year 2017 (Year of the Rooster) A260

Designs: $2.30, Red rooster. $4.50, Turquoise blue rooster.

2016, Aug. 10 Litho. *Perf. 13¼*

1565-1566	A260	Set of 2	10.00	10.00
1566a		Souvenir sheet of 2, #1565-1566	10.00	10.00

2016 Summer Olympics, Rio de Janeiro A261

No. 1567: a, Sailing. b, Canoeing slalom. c, Weight lifting. d, Swimming. e, Track and field.

2016, Sept. 6 Litho. *Perf. 13¾*

1567		Horiz. strip of 5	15.00	15.00
a.-e.		A261 $2 Any single	3.00	3.00

A262

Christmas A263

No. 1568: a, Stained-glass window depicting Holy Family. b, Five-sectioned stained-glass window.

No. 1569: a, Stained-glass window depicting Holy Family, diff. b, Two-sectioned stained-glass window.

2016, Dec. 19 Litho. *Perf. 13¼*

1568	A262	50c Vert. pair, #a-b	1.40	1.40
1569	A263	$1 Vert. pair, #a-b	2.75	2.75

Miniature Sheet

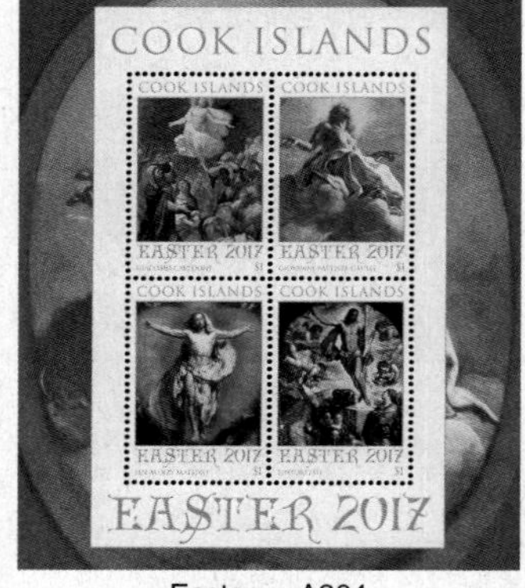

Easter — A264

No. 1570 — Paintings of the Resurrection of Jesus by: a, Giacomo Cavedone. b, Giovanni Battista Gaulli. c, Jan Alojzy Matejko. d, Tintoretto.

2017, Apr. 12 Litho. *Perf. 13*

1570	A264	$1Sheet of 4, #a-d	5.50	5.50

Nos. 1521-1523 Surcharged

Methods and Perfs. As Before

2017, June 9

1571	A243	50c on $1.30 #1521	.75	.75
1572	A243	50c on $1.50 #1522	.75	.75
1573	A243	50c on $1.70 #1523	.75	.75
1574	A243	$1 on $1.30 #1521	1.50	1.50
1575	A243	$1 on $1.50 #1522	1.50	1.50
1576	A243	$1 on $1.70 #1523	1.50	1.50
		Nos. 1571-1576 (6)	6.75	6.75

Miniature Sheet

Pres. John F. Kennedy (1917-63) — A265

No. 1577: a, $1, Alan Shepard, Jr. (1923-98), astronaut, and Friedship 7 space capsule. b, $1, Pres. Kennedy looking in window of Friendship 7. c, $2.50, Pres. Kennedy signing Nuclear Test Ban Treaty. d, $2.50, Nuclear weapon test Bravo on Bikini Atoll.

2017, July 3 Litho. *Perf. 13*

1577	A265	Sheet of 4, #a-d	10.50	10.50

Miniature Sheet

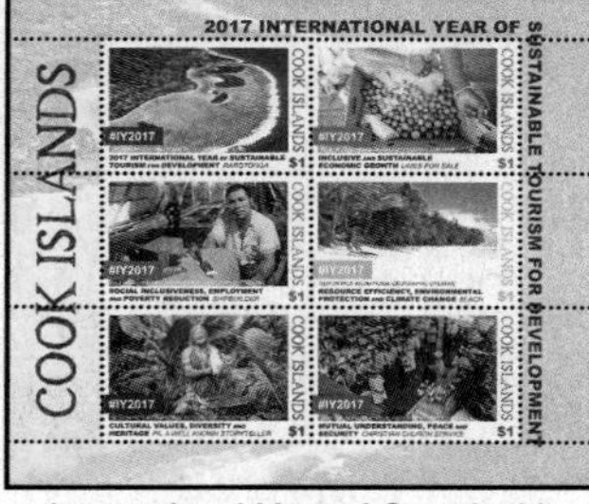

International Year of Sustainable Tourism for Development — A266

No. 1578: a, Aerial view of Rarotonga. b, Limes for sale. c, Shipbuilder. d, Beach. e, Pa, a well-known storyteller. f, Christian church service.

2017, July 14 Litho. *Perf. 13*

1578	A266	$1 Sheet of 6, #a-f	9.00	9.00

Miniature Sheet

Reign of Queen Elizabeth II, 65th Anniv. — A267

No. 1579 — Queen Elizabeth II wearing: a, Turquoise blue hat. b, White hat with gray fringe and flower. c, White hat, Queen waving. d, Tiara.

2017, July 17 Litho. *Perf. 13*

1579	A267	$2.50 Sheet of 4, #a-d	15.00	15.00

Winning Photographs in Cook Islands News Memories of Summer Photography Contest — A268

Photograph: $1.60, Woman casting fishing net, by Pua Tua (third place). $2.40, Child splashing water, by Raita Rongo (second place). $4.80, Child in sprinkler stream, by Rongo (first place).

2017, Aug. 28 Litho. *Perf. 13*

1580-1582	A268	Set of 3	12.50	12.50

Worldwide Fund for Nature (WWF) A269

Various depictions of bristle-thighed curlew: Nos. 1583, 1587a, $1. Nos. 1584, 1587b, $1.60. Nos. 1585, 1587c, $1.70. Nos. 1586, 1587d, $2.40.

2017, Oct. 31 Litho. *Perf. 13x13¼*

Stamps With White Frame

1583-1586 A269 Set of 4 9.25 9.25

Stamps Without White Frame

1587 A269 Strip of 4, #a-d 9.25 9.25

No. 1587 was printed in sheets containing two strips. For surcharges, see Nos. 1690-1692.

New Year 2018 (Year of the Dog) — A270

Dog: $3, Standing. $3.80, Prone.

2017, Nov. 1 Litho. *Perf. 13¼*

1588-1589 A270 Set of 2 9.50 9.50

1589a Souvenir sheet of 2, #1588-1589 9.50 9.50

Christmas — A271

No. 1590, $1: a, Beach sandals. b, Star and bow.

No. 1591, $2.40: a, Christmas ornament on palm tree. b, Church.

2017, Dec. 5 Litho. *Perf. 12½*

Horiz. pairs, #a-b

1590-1591 A271 Set of 2 9.75 9.75

Miniature Sheet

Easter — A272

No. 1592: a, $1, Church. b. $1, Cross. c, $2.40, Flowers. d, $2.40, Easter eggs, shell and flower.

2018, Mar. 19 Litho. *Perf. 13*

1592 A272 Sheet of 4, #a-d 10.00 10.00

Souvenir Sheet

Dutchess of Cambridge at Commonwealth Fashion Exchange, London — A273

2018, Apr. 10 Litho. *Perf. 13*

1593 A273 $5 multi 7.00 7.00

2018 Birdpex Philatelic Exhibition, Mondorf-les-Bains, Luxembourg — A274

No. 1594: a, Short-tailed shearwater. b, Tropical shearwater.

2018, May 4 Litho. *Perf. 13½x13*

1594 A274 Horiz. pair 8.25 8.25

a. $1 multi 1.40 1.40

b. $4.80 multi 6.75 6.75

For surcharges, see No. 1632.

Souvenir Sheet

Birth of Prince Louis of Cambridge — A275

No. 1595: a, Prince George of Cambridge. b, Duke and Duchess of Cambridge holding Prince Louis. c, Princess Charlotte of Cambridge.

2018, May 21 Litho. *Perf. 13*

1595 A275 $2.40 Sheet of 3, #a-c 10.00 10.00

Wedding of Prince Harry and Meghan Markle — A276

No. 1596 — Bride and groom: a, On church steps. b, Kissing.

$8, Bride and groom in carriage.

2018, Aug. 2 Litho. *Perf. 13*

1596 A276 $4.80 Sheet of 2, #a-b 12.50 12.50

Souvenir Sheet

1597 A276 $8 multi 10.50 10.50

New Year 2019 (Year of the Pig) — A277

Pig facing: $3, Left. $3.80, Right.

2018, Dec. 10 Litho. *Perf. 13½*

1598-1599 A277 Set of 2 9.25 9.25

Miniature Sheets

Christmas — A278

No. 1600 — Details of religious paintings by: a, Raphael. b, Rogier van der Weyden. c, Bartolomeo Montagna. d, Carlo Crivelli. e, Guido Reni. f, Antonello da Messina.

No. 1601 — Details of religious paintings by: a, Raphael. b, Gerard David. c, Montagna. d, Peter Paul Rubens. e, Hans Memling. f, Sandro Botticelli.

2018, Dec. 14 Litho. *Perf. 13*

1600 A278 50c Sheet of 6, #a-f 4.00 4.00

1601 A278 $1 Sheet of 6, #a-f 8.00 8.00

Birds A279

Stamps inscribed "Cook Islands": Nos. 1602, 1614a, 20c, Swamp harrier. Nos. 1603, 1614b, 30c, Bateleur eagle. Nos. 1604, 1614c, 40c, Eurasian pygmy owls. Nos. 1605, 1614d, 50c, Madagascar harrier hawk. Nos. 1606, 1614e, $1, Barn owl. Nos. 1607, 1614f, $2, Japanese sparrowhawk. Nos. 1608, 1614g, $2.40, Hooded vultures. Nos. 1609, 1614h, $2.60, Booted eagle and chick. Nos. 1610, 1614i, $4.50, Whistling kite. Nos. 1611, 1614j, $5, Letter-winged kites. Nos. 1612, 1614k, $7.50, Egyptian vulture and eggs. Nos. 1613, 1614l, $10, Barking owls.

Stamps inscribed "Rarotonga Cook Islands": Nos. 1615, 1627a, 20c, Pale chanting goshawk. Nos. 1616, 1627b, 30c, Great horned owl. Nos. 1617, 1627c, 40c, Eurasian eagle owl. Nos. 1618, 1627d, 50c, Costa Rican pygmy owl. Nos. 1619, 1627e, $1, Jackal buzzard. Nos. 1620, 1627f, $2, Northern harrier. Nos. 1621, 1627g, $2.40, Eastern marsh harrier. Nos. 1622, 1627h, $2.60, Long-winged harrier. Nos. 1623, 1627i, $4.50, Asian barred owlet. Nos. 1624, 1627j, $5, Crested eagles. Nos. 1625, 1627k, $7.50, Lesser spotted eagle. Nos. 1626, 1627l, $10, White-browed hawk owl.

2018, Dec. 20 Litho. *Perf. 13*

Stamps Inscribed "Cook Islands"

Stamps With White Frames

1602 A279 20c multi .25 .25

1603 A279 30c multi .40 .40

1604 A279 40c multi .55 .55

1605 A279 50c multi .65 .65

1606 A279 $1 multi 1.40 1.40

1607 A279 $2 multi 2.75 2.75

a. Souvenir sheet of 6, #1602-1607 6.00 6.00

1608 A279 $2.40 multi 3.25 3.25

1609 A279 $2.60 multi 3.50 3.50

1610 A279 $4.50 multi 6.00 6.00

1611 A279 $5 multi 6.75 6.75

1612 A279 $7.50 multi 10.00 10.00

1613 A279 $10 multi 13.50 13.50

a. Souvenir sheet of 6, #1608-1613 43.00 43.00

Nos. 1602-1613 (12) 49.00 49.00

Stamps Without White Frames

1614 A279 Sheet of 12, #a-l 49.00 49.00

Stamps Inscribed "Rarotonga Cook Islands"

Stamps With White Frames

1615 A279 20c multi .25 .25

1616 A279 30c multi .40 .40

1617 A279 40c multi .55 .55

1618 A279 50c multi .65 .65

1619 A279 $1 multi 1.40 1.40

1620 A279 $2 multi 2.75 2.75

a. Souvenir sheet of 6, #1615-1620 6.00 6.00

1621 A279 $2.40 multi 3.25 3.25

1622 A279 $2.60 multi 3.50 3.50

1623 A279 $4.50 multi 6.00 6.00

1624 A279 $5 multi 6.75 6.75

1625 A279 $7.50 multi 10.00 10.00

1626 A279 $10 multi 13.50 13.50

a. Souvenir sheet of 6, #1621-1626 43.00 43.00

Nos. 1615-1626 (12) 49.00 49.00

Stamps Without White Frames

1627 A279 Sheet of 12, #a-l 49.00 49.00

Nos. 1607a, 1613a, 1620a and 1626a have stamps with white frames on one or two sides. See Nos. 1640-1649, 1650-1659, 1670-1674, 1675-1679.

Suwarrow Atoll National Park — A280

No. 1628: a, Frigatebird and Red-footed booby. b, Masked boobies. c, Two people conducting seabird survey. d, Four people conducting seabird study. e, Coconut crab. f, Brown booby juvenile.

$4.50, Frigatebird chick in nest.

2019, May 30 Litho. *Perf. 13*

1628 A280 50c Sheet of 6, #a-f 4.00 4.00

Souvenir Sheet

Perf. 13¼x13

1629 A280 $4.50 multi 6.00 6.00

No. 1629 contains one 48x40mm stamp.

Islands — A281

No. 1630: a, Oahu, Hawaii. b, Fiji. c, Vavau, Tonga. d, Samoa. e, Easter Island. f, Rarotonga, Cook Islands.

$10, Mitre Peak and Milford Sound, South Island, New Zealand.

2019, June 11 Litho. *Perf. 13*

1630 A281 $1 Sheet of 6, #a-f 8.00 8.00

Souvenir Sheet

Perf. 13¼x13

1631 A281 $10 multi 13.50 13.50

No. 1631 contains one 48x40mm stamp.

No. 1594 Surcharged

Methods and Perfs. As Before

2019, June 19

1632 A274 Horiz. pair 1.40 1.40
a. 50c on $1 #1594a .70 .70
b. 50c on $4.80 #1594b .70 .70

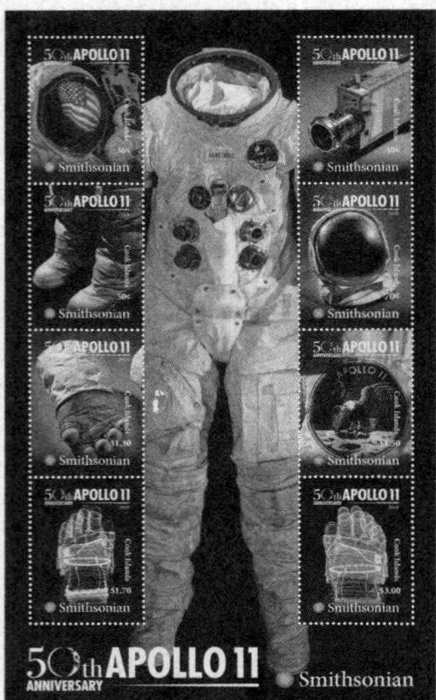

Flight of Apollo 11, 50th Anniv. — A282

No. 1633: a, 30c, Reflections of U.S. flag in visors of astronaut's helmets. b, 40c, Video camera. c, 50c, Astronaut's boots. d, 70c, Astronaut's helmets. e, $1.30, Astronaut's glove. f, $1.50, Apollo 11 mission patch on space suit. g, $1.70, Wiring in left hand glove. h, $3, Wiring in right hand glove.

No. 1634, horiz.: a, $1.10, Camera. b, $2.60, Astronaut near Lunar Module on Moon, shadow of astronaut. c, $5, Astronaut's footprint on Moon.

No. 1635: a, $1, Lunar Module leaving Moon. b, $2, Astronaut in Command Module. c, $2.50, Soldiers in life raft approaching Command Module in ocean. d, $4, Astronaut's mobile quarantine facility.

2019, June 19 Litho. ***Perf. 13¼x13***

1633 A282 Sheet of 8, #a-h 12.50 12.50

Perf. 13x13¼

1634 A282 Sheet of 3, #a-c 12.00 12.00

Perf. 13

1635 A282 Sheet of 4, #a-d 13.00 13.00
Nos. 1633-1635 (3) 37.50 37.50

No. 1635 contains four 40x40mm stamps.

New Year 2020 (Year of the Rat) — A283

Stamps inscribed "Cook Islands" — Rat with front legs at: $3, Left. $3.80. Right.

Stamps inscribed "Rarotonga": $3, Rats and jar. $3.80, Three rats.

2019, Oct. 11 Litho. ***Perf. 13¼***

Stamps Inscribed "Cook Islands"

1636-1637 A283 Set of 2 8.75 8.75

Stamps Inscribed "Rarotonga"

1638-1639 A283 Set of 2 8.75 8.75

Birds Type of 2018

Stamps inscribed "Cook Islands": Nos. 1640, 1644a, $2.50, White-backed vulture. Nos. 1641, 1644b, $20.60, Red-backed hawk. Nos. 1642, 1644c, $25, Galapagos hawk and juveniles. Nos. 1643, 1644d, $30, Wedge-tailed eagle.

Stamps inscribed "Rarotonga Cook Islands": Nos. 1645, 1649a, $2.50, Levant sparrowhawk. Nos. 1646, 1649b, $3, Zone-tailed hawk. Nos. 1647, 1649c, $4, Roadside hawk. Nos. 1648, 1649d, $6, Harris's hawk.

2019, Nov. 15 Litho. ***Perf. 13***

Stamps Inscribed "Cook Islands"

Stamps With White Frames

1640 A279 $2.50 multi 3.25 3.25
1641 A279 $20.60 multi 27.00 27.00
1642 A279 $25 multi 32.50 32.50
1643 A279 $30 multi 39.00 39.00
Nos. 1640-1643 (4) 101.75 101.75

Stamps Without White Frames

Stamp Size: 48x40mm

Perf. 13¼x13

1644 A279 Block or vert. strip of 4, #a-d 102.00 102.00
e. Souvenir sheet of 4, #1644a-1644d 102.00 102.00

Stamps Inscribed "Rarotonga Cook Islands"

Stamps With White Frames

Perf. 13

1645 A279 $2.50 multi 3.25 3.25
1646 A279 $3 multi 4.00 4.00
1647 A279 $4 multi 5.25 5.25
1648 A279 $6 multi 8.00 8.00
Nos. 1645-1648 (4) 20.50 20.50

Stamps Without White Frames

Stamp Size: 48x40mm

Perf. 13¼x13

1649 A279 Block or vert. strip of 4, #a-d 20.50 20.50
e. Souvenir sheet of 4, #1649a-1649d 20.50 20.50

Stamps from Nos. 1644e and 1649e have white frames on two sides.

Birds Type of 2018

Stamps inscribed "Cook Islands": Nos. 1650, 1654a, $5.50, Military macaw. Nos. 1651, 1654b, $6.70, Blue-and-yellow macaw. Nos. 1652, 1654c, $22.40, Red-and-green macaw. Nos. 1653, 1654d, $29.90, Red-fronted macaw.

Stamps inscribed "Rarotonga Cook Islands": Nos. 1655, 1659a, $5.50, Long-tailed sylph, vert. Nos. 1656, 1659b, $6.70, Violet-crowned woodnymph, vert. Nos. 1657, 1659c, $22.40, Sword-billed hummingbird, vert. Nos. 1658, 1659d, $22.90, Green hermit, vert.

2019, Nov. 20 Litho. ***Perf. 13***

Stamps Inscribed "Cook Islands"

Stamps With White Frames

1650 A279 $5.50 multi 7.25 7.25
1651 A279 $6.70 multi 8.75 8.75
1652 A279 $22.40 multi 29.00 29.00
1653 A279 $29.90 multi 39.00 39.00
Nos. 1650-1653 (4) 84.00 84.00

Stamps Without White Frames

Stamp Size: 48x40mm

Perf. 13¼x13

1654 A279 Block or vert. strip of 4, #a-d 84.00 84.00
e. Souvenir sheet of 4, #1654a-1654d 84.00 84.00

Stamps Inscribed "Rarotonga Cook Islands"

Stamps With White Frames

Perf. 13

1655 A279 $5.50 multi 7.25 7.25
1656 A279 $6.70 multi 8.75 8.75
1657 A279 $22.40 multi 29.00 29.00
1658 A279 $22.90 multi 30.00 30.00
Nos. 1655-1658 (4) 75.00 75.00

Stamps Without White Frames

Stamp Size: 48x40mm

Perf. 13x13¼

1659 A279 Block or vert. strip of 4, #a-d 75.00 75.00
e. Souvenir sheet of 4, #1659a-1659d 75.00 75.00

Stamps from Nos. 1654e and 1659e have white frames on two sides.

SEMI-POSTAL STAMPS

Catalogue values for unused stamps in this section are for Never Hinged items.

Nos. 203-204, 223, 210, 213, 215-216 Surcharged

No. B1

No. B3

No. B7

Perf. 14x13½, 13½

1968, Feb. 12 Photo.

B1 A34 3c + 1c multi .25 .25
B2 A34 4c + 1c multi .25 .25
B3 A37 5c + 2c multi .25 .25
B4 A34 10c + 2c multi .25 .25
B5 A34 25c + 5c multi .30 .30
B6 A34 50c + 10c multi .60 .60
B7 A35 $1 + 10c multi 1.00 1.00
Nos. B1-B7 (7) 2.90 2.90

Surtax for the victims of hurricane of Dec. 15-18, 1967. The surcharge on No. B3 is printed on a silver rectangle. The surcharge on No. B7 is in smaller type with serifs, measuring 7½mm in depth.

Nos. 210, 213-214 Surcharged in Ultramarine

1971, Sept. 8 Photo. ***Perf. 14x13½***

B8 A34 10c + 1c multi .25 .25
B9 A34 10c + 3c multi .25 .25
B10 A34 25c + 1c multi .40 .40
B11 A34 25c + 3c multi .40 .40
B12 A34 30c + 1c multi .50 .50
B13 A34 30c + 3c multi .50 .50
Nos. B8-B13 (6) 2.30 2.30

4th South Pacific Games, Papeete, French Polynesia, Sept. 8-19.

Christmas Type of Regular Issue

Souvenir Sheet

50c+5c, Holy Family in a Garland of Flowers, by Jan Brueghel and Pieter van Avont.

1971, Nov. 30 Photo. ***Perf. 13½***

B14 A50 50c + 5c gold & multi 1.10 1.10

No. B14 contains one stamp 45x40mm.

Nos. 316-318, 211, 213 and 215 Surcharged in Red or Black

a

b

1972, Mar. 30 Photo. ***Perf. 13½***

B15 A46(a) 5c + 2c multi (R) .25 .25
B16 A46(a) 10c + 2c multi (R) .25 .25
B17 A34(b) 15c + 5c multi .25 .25
B18 A34(b) 25c + 5c multi .40 .40
B19 A46(a) 30c + 5c multi (R) .50 .50
B20 A34(b) 50c + 10c multi .60 .60
Nos. B15-B20 (6) 2.25 2.25

Surtax for victims of hurricane of Mar. 22-26.

Nos. 319-322c with Surcharge Similar to Type "a"

1972, May 24 Photo. ***Perf. 13½***

B21 A51 5c + 2c, pair, #a.-b. .35 .35
B22 A51 10c + 2c, pair, #a.-b. .45 .45
B23 A51 25c + 2c, pair, #a.-b. .55 .55
B24 A51 30c + 2c, pair, #a.-b. .65 .65
c. Souvenir sheet of 8 3.50 3.50
Nos. B21-B24 (4) 2.00 2.00

Surtax for victims of hurricane of Mar. 22-26. Stamps of No. B24c each surcharged 3c.

Olympic Type of Regular Issue

Souvenir Sheet

50c+5c, Pierre de Coubertin, Olympic rings.

1972, June 26

B29 A52 50c + 5c multi 2.00 2.00

Christmas Type of Regular Issue

Souvenir Sheet

Design: 50c+5c, Nativity, by Correggio.

1972, Oct. 11 Photo. ***Perf. 13½***

B30 A53 50c + 5c multi 1.50 1.25

No. B30 contains one stamp 30x40mm.

Easter Type of Regular Issue

Souvenir Sheets

1973, Apr. 30 Photo. ***Perf. 13½x14***

B31 A56 50c + 5c like #346 .50 .50
B32 A56 50c + 5c like #347 .50 .50
B33 A56 50c + 5c like #348 .50 .50
Nos. B31-B33 (3) 1.50 1.50

Surtax was for school children.

Christmas Type of Regular Issue

Souvenir Sheets

1973, Dec. 3 Photo. ***Perf. 13x13½***

B34 A59 50c + 5c like #364 .35 .35
B35 A59 50c + 5c like #365 .35 .35
B36 A59 50c + 5c like #366 .35 .35
B37 A59 50c + 5c like #367 .35 .35
B38 A59 50c + 5c like #368 .35 .35
Nos. B34-B38 (5) 1.75 1.75

Surtax was for school children.

Easter Type of 1973

Dated "1974"

Souvenir Sheets

1974, Apr. 22 ***Perf. 13½x14***

B39 A56 50c + 5c like #378 .50 .50
B40 A56 50c + 5c like #379 .50 .50
B41 A56 50c + 5c like #380 .50 .50
Nos. B39-B41 (3) 1.50 1.50

Christmas Type of 1974

Souvenir Sheets

1974 Photo. ***Perf. 13½x13***

B42 A68 50c + 5c like #412 .35 .35
B43 A68 50c + 5c like #413 .35 .35
B44 A68 50c + 5c like #414 .35 .35

B45 A68 50c + 5c like #415 .35 .35
B46 A68 50c + 5c like #416 .35 .35
Nos. B42-B46 (5) 1.75 1.75

Christmas Type of 1975
Souvenir Sheets

1975, Dec. 1 *Perf. 13½*
B47 A75 75c + 5c like #437 .50 .50
B48 A75 75c + 5c like #438 .50 .50
B49 A75 75c + 5c like #439 .50 .50
B50 A75 75c + 5c like #440 .50 .50
B51 A75 75c + 5c like #441 .50 .50
Nos. B47-B51 (5) 2.50 2.50

Size of stamps: 23x40mm.

Easter Type of 1976
Souvenir Sheets

1976, May 3 Photo. *Perf. 13½*
B52 A76 60c + 5c like #442 .55 .55
B53 A76 60c + 5c like #443 .55 .55
B54 A76 60c + 5c like #444 .55 .55
Nos. B52-B54 (3) 1.65 1.65

Size of stamps: 36x36mm.

Christmas Type of 1976
Souvenir Sheets

1976, Nov. 2 Photo. *Perf. 14x13½*
B55 A80 75c + 5c like #459 .50 .50
B56 A80 75c + 5c like #460 .50 .50
B57 A80 75c + 5c like #461 .50 .50
B58 A80 75c + 5c like #462 .50 .50
B59 A80 75c + 5c like #463 .50 .50
Nos. B55-B59 (5) 2.50 2.50

Easter Type of 1977
Souvenir Sheets

1977, Apr. 18 Photo. *Perf. 13½x14*
B60 A83 60c + 5c like #471 .60 .60
B61 A83 60c + 5c like #472 .60 .60
B62 A83 60c + 5c like #473 .60 .60
Nos. B60-B62 (3) 1.80 1.80

Size of stamps: 30x42mm.

Christmas Type of 1977
Souvenir Sheets

1977, Oct. 31 Photo. *Perf. 14x13½*
B63 A84 75c + 5c like #474 .45 .45
B64 A84 75c + 5c like #475 .45 .45
B65 A84 75c + 5c like #476 .45 .45
B66 A84 75c + 5c like #477 .45 .45
B67 A84 75c + 5c like #478 .45 .45
Nos. B63-B67 (5) 2.25 2.25

Easter Type of 1978
Souvenir Sheets

1978, Apr. 10 Photo. *Perf. 14x13½*
B68 A87 60c + 5c like #483 .45 .45
B69 A87 60c + 5c like #484 .45 .45
B70 A87 60c + 5c like #485 .45 .45
Nos. B68-B70 (3) 1.35 1.35

Christmas Type of 1978
Souvenir Sheets

1979, Jan. 12 Photo. *Perf. 13*
B71 A89 75c + 5c like #503 .45 .45
B72 A89 75c + 5c like #504 .45 .45
B73 A89 75c + 5c like #505 .45 .45
Nos. B71-B73 (3) 1.35 1.35

Easter Type of 1979
Souvenir Sheet

1979, Apr. 5 Photo. *Perf. 13*
B74 Sheet of 4 1.00 1.00
a. A90 10c + 2c like #506 .25 .25
b. A90 12c + 2c like #507 .25 .25
c. A90 15c + 2c like #508 .25 .25
d. A90 20c + 2c like #509 .25 .25

IYC Type of 1979
Souvenir Sheet

1979, Oct. 10
B75 Sheet of 3 1.40 1.40
a. A93 30c + 5c like #529 .30 .30
b. A93 50c + 5c like #530 .40 .40
c. A93 65c + 5c like #531 .50 .50

Christmas Type of 1979

1980, Jan. 15 Photo. *Perf. 14*
B76 A95 6c + 2c like #537 .25 .25
B77 A95 10c + 2c like #538 .25 .25
B78 A95 12c + 2c like #539 .25 .25
B79 A95 15c + 2c like #540 .25 .25
Nos. B76-B79 (4) 1.00 1.00

Easter Type of 1980
Souvenir Sheets

1980, Mar. 31 Photo. *Perf. 13*
B80 A96 Sheet of 6, #a.-f. 1.40 1.40

No. B80 contains Nos. 541-543, each stamp with 2c surcharge.

1980, Apr. 23 **Souvenir Sheets**
B81 A96 75c + 5c like #541a .50 .50
B82 A96 75c + 5c like #541b .50 .50
B83 A96 75c + 5c like #542a .50 .50
B84 A96 75c + 5c like #542b .50 .50
B85 A96 75c + 5c like #543a .50 .50
B86 A96 75c + 5c like #543b .50 .50
Nos. B81-B86 (6) 3.00 3.00

Surtax was for school children.

Rotary Type of 1980
Souvenir Sheet

1980, May 27 Photo. *Perf. 14*
B87 Sheet of 3 1.50 1.50
a. A97 30c + 3c like #547 .35 .35
b. A97 35c + 3c like #548 .45 .45
c. A97 50c + 3c like #549 .60 .60

Christmas Type of 1980
Souvenir Sheets

1981, Jan. 9 Photo. *Imperf.*
B88 A102a 75c + 5c like #652 .50 .50
B89 A102a 75c + 5c like #653 .50 .50
B90 A102a 75c + 5c like #654 .50 .50
B91 A102a 75c + 5c like #655 .50 .50
Nos. B88-B91 (4) 2.00 2.00

Easter Type of 1981
Souvenir Sheets

1981, Apr. 10 Photo. *Perf. 13½*
B92 Sheet of 3 1.20 1.20
a. A103 15c + 2c like #656 .25 .25
b. A103 25c + 2c like #657 .30 .30
c. A103 40c + 2c like #658 .50 .50

1981, Apr. 28 *Imperf.*
B93 A103 75c + 5c like #656 .65 .65
B94 A103 75c + 5c like #657 .65 .65
B95 A103 75c + 5c like #658 .65 .65
Nos. B93-B95 (3) 1.95 1.95

Surtax was for school children.

Espana '82 Soccer Type
Souvenir Sheet

1981 Photo. *Perf. 13½*
B96 A105 Sheet of 8, #a.-h. 6.50 6.50

No. B96 contains Nos. 661-664, each stamp with 3c surcharge.

Royal Wedding Type of 1981
Nos. 659-660a Surcharged in Black

1981, Nov. 10 Photo. *Perf. 14*
B97 A104 $1 + 5c multi .75 *1.50*
B98 A104 $2 + 5c multi 1.50 *2.50*
a. Souvenir sheet of 2 3.50 *4.00*

Intl. Year of the Disabled. No. B98a contains Nos. B97-B98 each with 10c surtax, which was for benefit of the disabled; black overprint in margin.

Christmas Type of 1981
Souvenir Sheet

1981, Dec. 14 Photo. *Perf. 13½*
B99 Sheet of 4 2.75 2.75
a. A107 8c + 3c like #669 .25 .25
b. A107 15c + 3c like #670 .35 .35
c. A107 40c + 3c like #671 .75 .75
d. A107 50c + 3c like #672 1.00 1.00

Surtax was for school children.

Nos. 919-923 Surcharged in Silver

No. B100

No. B104

1986, Nov. 21 Litho. *Perf. 13½*
B100 A138 55c + 10c multi 2.50 2.50
B101 A138 $1.30 + 10c multi 5.25 5.25
B102 A138 $2.75 + 10c multi 10.00 10.00
Nos. B100-B102 (3) 17.75 17.75

Souvenir Sheets

B103 Sheet of 3 16.00 16.00
a.-c. A138 $2.40 + 10c on Nos. 922a-922c, any single 5.25 5.25
B104 A138 $6.40 + 50c multi 16.00 16.00

No. B103 ovptd. in margin "VISIT TO SOUTH PACIFIC / OF POPE JOHN PAUL II" and "FIRST PAPAL VISIT / NOVEMBER 21-24 1986."

For surcharges see Nos. B112, B141.

Stamps of 1982 and 1987 Surcharged in Sans-serif Capitals

No. B109

Perfs. as before
1987, June 30 **Photo.**
Surcharged +25c
B105 A121 55c on #958 1.10 1.10
B106 A121 65c on #960 1.25 1.25
B107 A121 75c on #963 1.40 1.40
B108 A121 95c on #965 1.60 1.60

Surcharged +50c
B109 A101 $2.80 on #582 4.50 4.50
B110 A101 $5 on #583 7.75 7.75
B111 A102 $6.40 on #978 9.50 9.50
Nos. B105-B111 (7) 27.10 27.10

Stamps of 1985-86 Surcharged in Silver or Black

1987, June 30 *Perfs. as before*
Surcharged +50c
B112 A138 55c on #B100 1.40 1.40
B113 A133 55c on #897 (B) 1.40 1.40
B114 A128 65c on #871 1.50 1.50
B115 A133 65c on #898 1.50 1.50
B116 A128 75c on #872 1.60 1.60
B117 A133 75c on #899 1.60 1.60
B118 A134 95c on #908 (B) 1.90 1.90
B119 A135 $1 on #910 2.10 2.10
B120 A136 $1 on #913 2.10 2.10
B121 A137 $1 on #916 2.10 2.10
B122 A128 $1.15 on #873 2.25 2.25
B123 A133 $1.25 on #900 2.25 2.25
B124 A134 $1.25 on #905 2.25 2.25
B125 A136 $1.25 on #914 (B) 2.25 2.25
B126 A138 $1.30 on #920 2.50 2.50
B127 A134 $1.50 on #906 (B) 2.50 2.50
B128 A135 $1.50 on #911 (B) 2.50 2.50
B129 A133 $2 on #901 (B) 3.25 3.25
B130 A135 $2 on #912 (B) 3.25 3.25
B131 A137 $2 on #917 3.25 3.25
B132 A136 $2.75 on #915 4.50 4.50
B133 A138 $2.75 on #921 4.50 4.50
B134 A128 $2.80 on #874 4.50 4.50
B135 A137 $3 on #918 4.75 4.75
Nos. B112-B135 (24) 61.70 61.70

Souvenir Sheets
B136 A134 $1.10 on #907 (B) 2.00 2.00
B137 A134 $1.95 on #908 3.00 3.00
B138 A138 $2.40 on #922 11.00 11.00
B139 A134 $2.45 on #909 (B) 3.75 3.75
B140 A128 $5.30 on #875 7.25 7.25
B141 A138 $6.40 on #B104 8.50 8.50
B141A A138 $6.40 on #923 —
Nos. B136-B141 (6) 35.50 35.50

Issued: Nos. B118, B121, B124, B127, B131, B135-B137, B139-B140, 7/31; others 6/30.

No. 1230 Surcharged in Silver
Souvenir Sheet

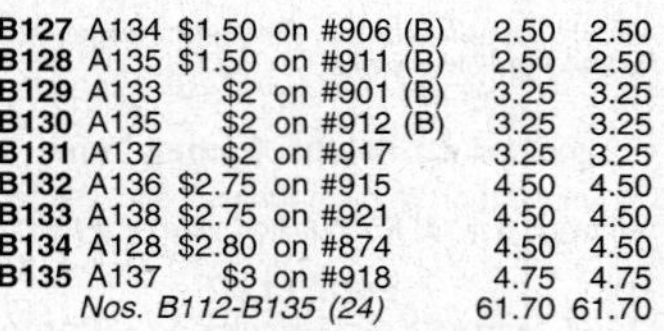

1998, Nov. 20 Litho. *Perf. 14*
B142 A179 $3.50 +$1 multi 4.75 4.75

AIR POST STAMPS

Catalogue values for unused stamps in this section are for Never Hinged items.

Stamps of 1936-63 Overprinted and Surcharged

Perf. 13x13½, 13½x13
Litho., Engr.
1966, Apr. 22 **Wmk. 253**
C1 A25 6p on #152 .70 .25
C2 A26 7p on 8p #153 1.00 .25
C3 A25 10p on 3p #150 .65 .35
C4 A25 1sh on #154 .70 .45
C5 A27 1sh6p on #155 1.25 1.25
C6 A28 2sh3p on 3sh #157 1.00 1.00
C7 A28 5sh on #158 1.60 1.75
C8 A28 10sh on 2sh #156 2.00 *8.00*

No. 106 Overprinted

Perf. 14
Typo.
C9 PF5 £1 pink 12.00 *16.00*
a. Airplane missing *37.50* *50.00*
Nos. C1-C9 (9) 20.90 29.30

No. C9a occurs on all stamps from the right vertical column of the sheet due to a lack of airplane symbols. The size and position of the airplane symbol varies in relation to "Airmail" on the other stamps. The surcharges are printed on silver ovals.

2nd South Pacific Games Type

Sport: 10p, Women runners and Games' emblem. 2sh3p, Runner and team emblem.

Perf. 13½

1967, Jan. 12 Unwmk. Photo.
C10 A32 10p org & multi .25 .25
C11 A32 2sh3p multi .25 .25

Capt. Cook Type of Regular Issue

6c, The "Resolution" and "Discovery" Beating Through the Ice, by Webber. 10c, The Island of Otaheite, by Hodges, and Queen Elizabeth II. 15c, View of Karakakooa (Kealakekua), Hawaii, by Webber. 25c, The Landing at Middleburg, Tonga, by Hodges, & Captain Cook. (All horiz.)

1968, Sept. 12 Photo. *Perf. 13*
C12 A39 6c gold & multi .35 .35
C13 A39 10c gold & multi .40 .40
C14 A39 15c gold & multi .45 .45
C15 A39 25c gold & multi 1.00 1.00
Nos. C12-C15 (4) 2.20 2.20

See note after No. 236.

Christmas Type of 1979

1979, Dec. 14 Photo. *Perf. 14*
C16 A95 20c like #537 .25 .25
C17 A95 25c like #538 .25 .25
C18 A95 30c like #539 .30 .30
C19 A95 35c like #540 .40 .40
Nos. C16-C19 (4) 1.20 1.20

Franklin D. Roosevelt — AP1

80c, Benjamin Franklin. $1.40, George Washington, by Gilbert Stuart.

1982, Sept. 30 Photo. *Perf. 14*
C20 AP1 60c multicolored .80 .80
C21 AP1 80c multicolored 1.00 1.00
C22 AP1 $1.40 multicolored 1.75 1.75
a. Souvenir sheet of 3 4.00 4.00
Nos. C20-C22 (3) 3.55 3.55

No. C22a contains Nos. C20-C22, perf. 13½ with portraits in square frames.

No. C22 Overprinted in Gold and Black

1983, Aug. 12 Photo. *Perf. 14*
C23 AP1 96c on $1.40 multi 1.60 1.60

Endangered Bird Species Type

Souvenir Sheets

Nos. 1020-1023 Overprinted

1990, Dec. 5 Litho. *Perf. 13½*
C24 A145 $1 Flycatcher 3.50 3.50
C25 A145 $1.25 Flycatchers 4.25 4.25
C26 A145 $1.50 Fruit dove 5.50 5.50
C27 A145 $1.75 Fruit doves 6.25 6.25
Nos. C24-C27 (4) 19.50 19.50

Birdpex '90, 20th Intl. Ornithological Cong., New Zealand.

AIR POST SEMI-POSTAL STAMPS

Catalogue values for unused stamps in this section are for Never Hinged items.

Christmas Type of 1979

1980, Jan. 15 Photo. *Perf. 14*
CB1 A95 20c + 4c like #C16 .25 .25
CB2 A95 25c + 4c like #C17 .30 .30
CB3 A95 30c + 4c like #C18 .35 .35
CB4 A95 35c + 4c like #C19 .40 .40
Nos. CB1-CB4 (4) 1.30 1.30

OFFICIAL STAMPS

Flower Issue of 1967-69 Overprinted or Surcharged in Black on Silver

1975 Photo. Unwmk. *Perf. 14x13½*
O1 A34 1c multi (#200) .25
O2 A34 2c multi (#201) .25
O3 A34 3c multi (#203) .25
O4 A34 4c multi (#205) .25
O5 A34 5c on 2½c multi (#202) .25
O6 A34 8c multi (#208) .30
O7 A34 10c on 6c multi (#207) .30
O8 A34 18c on 20c multi (#212) .35
O9 A34 25c on 9c multi (#209) .55
O10 A34 30c on 15c multi (#211) .65
O11 A34 50c multi (#215) .70
O12 A35 $1 multi (#216) 1.30
O13 A35 $2 multi (#217) 2.00
O14 A36 $4 multi (#218) 3.75
O15 A36 $6 multi (#219) 4.50
Nos. O1-O15 (15) 15.65

No. O1-O15 were not sold to the public unused. Arrangement of surcharge varies on different denominations.

Silver panel on Nos. O14-O15 measures 26½x6mm and is rounded at both ends.

Issue dates: 1c-$2, Mar. 17, $4-$6, May 19.

Catalogue values for unused stamps in this section, from this point to the end of the section, are for Never Hinged items.

Nos. 381-382, 389, 393-396, 467, 446 Ovptd. or Srchd. in Silver or Black

No. O16

No. O18

No. O27

Photo., Litho.

1978, Oct. 19 *Perf. 13½*
O16 A62 1c multi (S) .85 .25
O17 A62 2c on ½c multi .85 .25
O18 A62 5c on ½c multi .95 .25
O19 A62 10c on 8c multi (S) 1.10 .25
O20 A62 15c on 50c multi (S) 1.25 .25
O21 A62 18c on 60c multi (S) 1.25 .25
O22 A62 25c multicolored 1.60 .25
O23 A62 30c multi (S) 1.60 .30
O24 A62 35c on 60c multi (S) 1.60 .35
O25 A62 50c multi (S) 2.10 .50
O26 A62 60c multi (S) 2.40 .60
O27 A82 $1 Pair, #a.-b. (S) 10.00 2.00
O29 A77 $2 multicolored 7.25 2.25
O30 A64 $4 multi ('79) 13.50 3.50
O31 A64 $6 multi ('79) 13.50 5.50
Nos. O16-O31 (15) 59.80 16.75

Diagonal overprints on No. O27. Overprint on No. O29-O31: 19x4mm.

Nos. 790-791, 795, 797, 799, 805, 807, 809-810 Ovptd. or Srchd. in Silver

1985, July 10 Photo. *Perf. 13½x13*
O32 A121 5c multi .55 .55
O33 A121 10c multi .55 .55
O34 A121 20c multi .65 .65
O35 A121 30c multi .65 .65
O36 A121 40c multi .65 .65
O37 A121 55c on 85c multi .80 .80
O38 A121 60c multi .80 .80
O39 A121 $1.10 multi 1.60 1.25
O40 A121 $2 on $1.20 multi 3.25 2.50
Nos. O32-O40 (9) 9.50 8.40

Nos. 792-794, 802, 806, 696 and 583-586 Ovptd. or Srchd. in Silver, Gold (75c) or Black and Silver ($5, $18)

No. O41

No. O53

1986-90 Photo. *Perfs. as Before*
O41 A121 12c multi 5.00 5.00
O42 A121 14c multi 5.00 5.00
O43 A121 18c multi 5.00 5.00
O44 A121 50c multi 6.25 6.25
O45 A121 70c multi 6.75 6.75
O46 A111 75c on 60c, #a.-d. 13.50 13.50
O50 A102 $5 on $3 multi 17.00 17.00
O51 A102 $9 on $4 multi 9.00 9.00
O52 A102 $14 on $6 multi 14.00 14.00
O53 A102 $18 on $10 multi 20.00 20.00
Nos. O41-O53 (10) 101.50 101.50

Issued: $9, 5/30/89; $14, 7/12/89; $18, 6/4/90; others 5/5/86.

Nos. 1058-1059, 1062, 1064-1066, 1071, 1076-1078, 1080-1083, 1085, 1087 Ovptd. in Silver

1995-98 Litho. *Perf. 14½x13½*
O54 A155 5c multicolored .40 .40
O55 A155 10c multicolored .40 .40
O56 A155 15c multicolored .50 .50
O57 A155 20c multicolored .55 .55
O58 A155 25c multicolored .60 .60
O59 A155 30c multicolored .65 .65
O60 A155 50c multicolored .80 .80
O61 A155 80c multicolored 1.30 1.30
O62 A155 85c multicolored 1.30 1.30
O63 A155 90c multicolored 1.30 1.30
O64 A155 $1 multicolored 1.50 1.50
O65 A155 $2 multicolored 2.40 2.40
O66 A155a $3 multicolored 3.75 3.75
O67 A155a $5 multicolored 4.75 4.75
O68 A155a $7 multicolored 6.75 6.75
O69 A155a $10 multi 8.50 8.50
Nos. O54-O69 (16) 35.45 35.45

Overprint on Nos. O66-O69 has larger, sans serif letters.

Nos. O66-O69 were not sold unused to local customers.

Issued: 5c-90c, 2/24/95; $1-$2, 5/15/95; $3-$7, 7/17/98, $10, 11/12/98.

Nos. 1305-1322 Overprinted in Gold

2010, Oct. 12 Litho. *Perf. 13¾*
Sizes: 60x37mm, 37x60mm
O70 A191 10c multi .25 .25
O71 A191 20c multi .30 .30
O72 A191 30c multi .50 .50
O73 A191 40c multi .65 .65
O74 A191 50c multi .80 .80
O75 A191 70c multi 1.10 1.10
O76 A191 80c multi 1.25 1.25
O77 A191 90c multi 1.50 1.50
O78 A191 $1 multi 1.60 1.60
O79 A191 $1.10 multi 1.75 1.75
O80 A191 $1.20 multi 1.90 1.90
O81 A191 $2 multi 3.25 3.25
O82 A191 $3 multi 4.75 4.75
O83 A191 $4 multi 6.50 6.50
O84 A191 $5 multi 8.00 8.00
Size: 60x37mm
O85 A191 $7.50 multi 12.00 12.00
O86 A191 $10 multi 16.00 16.00
O87 A191 $20 multi 32.00 32.00
Nos. O70-O87 (18) 94.10 94.10

Overprint reads up on vertical stamps.

Nos. 1305-1309 Overprinted in Metallic Green Like No. O70

2010, Oct. 12 Litho. *Perf. 13¾*
Sizes: 60x37mm, 37x60mm
O88 A191 10c multi .25 .25
O89 A191 20c multi .30 .30
O90 A191 30c multi .50 .50
O91 A191 40c multi .65 .65
O92 A191 50c multi .80 .80
O93 A191 70c multi 1.10 1.10
O94 A191 80c multi 1.25 1.25
O95 A191 90c multi 1.50 1.50
O96 A191 $1 multi 1.60 1.60
O97 A191 $1.10 multi 1.75 1.75
O98 A191 $1.20 multi 1.90 1.90
O99 A191 $2 multi 3.25 3.25
O100 A191 $3 multi 4.75 4.75
O101 A191 $4 multi 6.50 6.50
O102 A191 $5 multi 8.00 8.00
Nos. O88-O102 (15) 34.10 34.10

Overprint reads up on vertical stamps.

Nos. 1305-1309 Overprinted in Metallic Red Like No. O70

2010, Oct. 12 Litho. *Perf. 13¾*
Sizes: 60x37mm, 37x60mm
O103 A191 10c multi .25 .25
O104 A191 20c multi .30 .30
O105 A191 30c multi .50 .50
O106 A191 40c multi .65 .65
O107 A191 50c multi .80 .80
O108 A191 70c multi 1.10 1.10

O109 A191 80c multi 1.25 1.25
O110 A191 90c multi 1.50 1.50
O111 A191 $1 multi 1.60 1.60
O112 A191 $1.10 multi 1.75 1.75
O113 A191 $1.20 multi 1.90 1.90
O114 A191 $2 multi 3.25 3.25
O115 A191 $3 multi 4.75 4.75
O116 A191 $4 multi 6.50 6.50
O117 A191 $5 multi 8.00 8.00
Nos. O103-O117 (15) 34.10 34.10

Overprint reads up on vertical stamps.

CORFU

kor-'fü

LOCATION — An island in the Ionian Sea opposite the Greek-Albanian border
GOVT. — A department of Greece
AREA — 245 sq. mi.
POP. — 114,620 (1938)
CAPITAL — Corfu

In 1922 Italy occupied Corfu (Kerkyra) during a controversy with Greece over the assassination of an Italian official in Epirus. Italy again occupied Corfu in 1941-43.

100 Centesimi = 1 Lira
100 Lepta = 1 Drachma

Watermark

Wmk. 140 — Crown

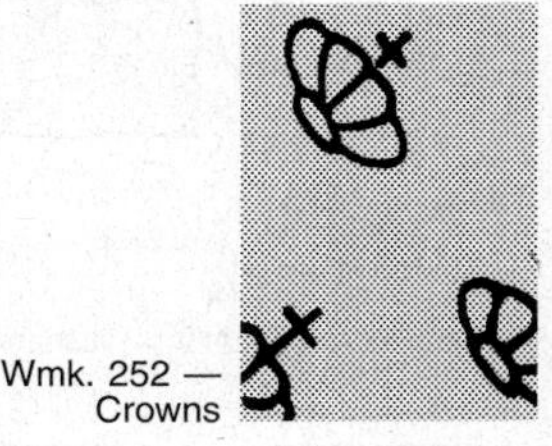

Wmk. 252 — Crowns

ISSUED UNDER ITALIAN OCCUPATION

Italian Stamps of 1901-23 Overprinted

1923, Sept. 20 Wmk. 140 *Perf. 14*
N1 A48 5c green 6.25 *11.50*
N2 A48 10c claret 6.25 *11.50*
N3 A48 15c slate 6.25 *11.50*
N4 A50 20c brown orange 6.25 *11.50*
N5 A49 30c orange brown 6.25 *11.50*
N6 A49 50c violet 6.25 *11.50*
N7 A49 60c blue 6.25 *11.50*
a. Vert. pair, one without overprint *1,500.*
N8 A46 1 l brown & green 6.25 *11.50*
Nos. N1-N8 (8) 50.00 *92.00*
Set, never hinged 115.00

Italian Stamps of 1901-23 Surcharged

1923, Sept. 24
N9 A48 25 l on 10c claret 60.00 45.00
N10 A49 60 l on 25c blue 10.00
N11 A49 70 l on 30c org brn 10.00
N12 A49 1.20d on 50c violet 25.00 *45.00*
N13 A46 2.40d on 1 l brn & grn 25.00 *45.00*
N14 A46 4.75d on 2 l grn & org 15.00
Nos. N9-N14 (6) 145.00
Set, never hinged 267.00

Nos. N10, N11, N14 were not placed in use.

Issue for Corfu and Paxos

Nos. N15-N34, NC1-NC12, NJ1-NJ11 and NRA1-NRA3 have been extensively counterfeited, some with forged cancellations.

Stamps of Greece, 1937-38, Overprinted in Black

Perf. 12x13½, 12½x12, 13½x12
1941, June 5 Wmk. 252
N15 A69 5 l brn red & blue 5.75 3.75
a. Inverted overprint *60.00 47.50*
b. Double overprint *80.00 110.00*
N16 A70 10 l bl & brn red (On 397) 1.90 *2.75*
N17 A70 10 l bl & brn red (On 413) 1,550. 1,350.
N18 A71 20 l black & grn 2.75 *3.75*
a. Inverted overprint *80.00 47.50*
N19 A72 40 l green & blk 3.25 *4.25*
a. Inverted overprint *80.00 47.50*
b. Double overprint *80.00 110.00*
N20 A73 50 l brown & blk 1.90 *2.75*
a. Inverted overprint *55.00 47.50*
N21 A74 80 l ind & yel brn 3.75 *5.00*
N22 A67 1d green 14.50 14.50
N23 A84 1.50d green 14.50 14.50
N24 A75 2d ultra 7.75 *11.00*
N25 A67 3d red brown 7.75 11.00
N26 A76 5d red 7.75 *11.00*
N27 A77 6d olive brown 7.75 *11.00*
N28 A78 7d dark brown 12.00 *12.00*
N29 A67 8d deep blue 24.50 24.50
N30 A79 10d red brown 725.00 375.00
N31 A80 15d green 28.00 28.00
N32 A81 25d dark blue 28.00 28.00
N33 A84 30d org brn 115.00 100.00
N34 A67 100d carmine lake 375.00 350.00
Nos. N15-N34 (20) 2,937. 2,363.
Set, never hinged 3,900.

AIR POST STAMPS

Greece Nos. C37 and C26-C35, Overprinted Like Nos. N15-N34
Perf. 12½x13, 13x12½, 13½x12½
1941, June 5 Unwmk.
NC1 D3 50 l dk brown 11.00 7.75
NC2 AP16 1d red 750.00 275.00
NC3 AP17 2d gray blue 11.00 7.75
NC4 AP18 5d violet 13.50 13.00
NC5 AP19 7d deep ultra 17.50 13.00
NC6 AP20 10d bister brn (On C26) 950.00 400.00
NC7 AP20 10d brown org (On C35) 62.50 50.00
NC8 AP21 25d rose 135.00 60.00
NC9 AP22 30d dk grn 145.00 90.00
NC10 AP23 50d violet 145.00 90.00
a. Double overprint *550.00*
NC11 AP24 100d brown *1,300. 650.00*

On No. C36
Serrate Roulette 13½
NC12 D3 50 l vio brn 90.00 23.00
a. On No. C36a *350.00*
Nos. NC1-NC12 (12) *3,631. 1,680.*
Set, never hinged 5,500.

POSTAGE DUE STAMPS

Postage Due Stamps of Greece, 1913-35 Overprinted Like #N15-N34
1941, June 5 Unwmk.
Serrate Roulette 13½
NJ1 D3 10 l carmine 4.50 *5.00*
NJ2 D3 25 l ultra 4.50 *5.00*
NJ3 D3 80 l lilac brown *1,150. 450.00*
Perf. 12½x13, 13½x12½
NJ4 D3 1d lt bl (On J80) *1,600. 900.00*
NJ5 D3 2d light red 8.50 *14.00*
NJ6 D3 5d gray 22.50 *24.00*
NJ7 D3 10d gray green 22.50 *24.00*
NJ8 D3 15d red brown 22.50 *24.00*
NJ9 D3 25d light red 22.50 *24.00*
NJ10 D3 50d orange 22.50 *24.00*
NJ11 D3 100d slate green 600.00 450.00
Nos. NJ1-NJ11 (11) 3,480. 1,944.
Set, never hinged 5,000.

POSTAL TAX STAMPS

Greece Nos. RA61-RA63 Overprinted Like Nos. N15-N34 Wmk., Unwmk.
1941, June 5 *Perf. 13½*
NRA1 PT7 10 l brt rose, *pale rose* 3.25 *4.50*
NRA2 PT7 50 l gray grn, *pale green* 5.50 *7.00*
NRA3 PT7 1d dull blue, *lt blue* 37.50 *45.00*
Nos. NRA1-NRA3 (3) 46.25 *56.50*
Set, never hinged 67.50

Stamps overprinted "CORFU" were replaced by Italian stamps overprinted "Isole Jonie." See Ionian Islands.

COSTA RICA

ˌkōs-tə-ˈrē-kə

LOCATION — Central America between Nicaragua and Panama
GOVT. — Republic
AREA — 19,730 sq. mi.
POP. — 3,674,490 (1999 est.)
CAPITAL — San Jose

8 Reales = 100 Centavos = 1 Peso
100 Centimos = 1 Colon (1900)

Catalogue values for unused stamps in this country are for Never Hinged items, beginning with Scott 238 in the regular postage section, Scott C117 in the air post section, Scott CE1 in the air post special delivery section, Scott E1 in the special delivery section, and Scott RA1 in the postal tax section.

Watermarks

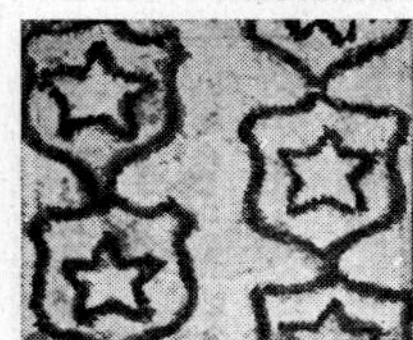

Wmk. 215 — Small Star in Shield, Multiple

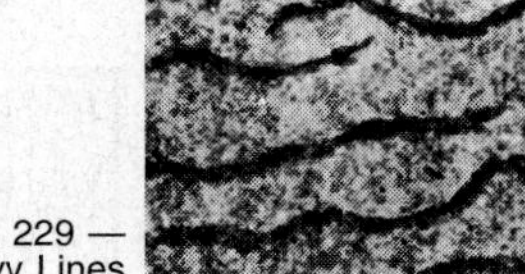

Wmk. 229 — Wavy Lines

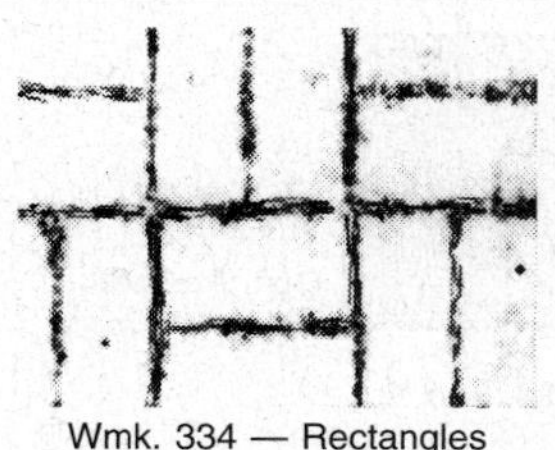

Wmk. 334 — Rectangles

Values for unused stamps are for examples with original gum as defined in the catalogue introduction. Very fine examples of Nos. 1-22 will have perforations just clear of the design on one or more sides due to the placement of the stamps on the plates and to imperfect perforating methods.

Coat of Arms — A1

1863 Unwmk. Engr. *Perf. 12*
1 A1 ½r blue .50 *1.10*
a. ½r light blue .50 *1.10*
b. Pair, imperf. horiz. *6,000.*
2 A1 2r scarlet 1.75 *2.25*
3 A1 4r green 16.00 *16.00*
4 A1 1p orange 42.50 *42.50*
Nos. 1-4 (4) 60.75 61.85

The ½r was printed from two plates. The second is in light blue with little or no sky over the mountains.

Imperforate stamps of Nos. 1-2 are corner stamps from poorly perforated sheets.

Nos. 1-3 Surcharged in Red or Black

a

b

c

d

e

1881-82 Red or Black Surcharge
7 A1(a) 1c on ½r ('82) 3.00 *6.00*
a. On No. 1a 15.00 —
8 A1(b) 1c on ½r ('82) 18.00 *30.00*
9 A1(c) 2c on ½r, #1a 3.00 2.75
a. On No. 1 8.00 —
12 A1(c) 5c on ½r 15.00
13 A1(d) 5c on ½r ('82) 65.00
14 A1(d) 10c on 2r (Bk) ('82) 72.50 —
15 A1(e) 20c on 4r ('82) 300.00 —

Overprints with different fonts and "OFICIAL" were never placed in use, and are said to have been surcharged to a dealer's order. The ½r surcharged "DOS CTS" is not a postage stamp. It probably is an essay.

Postally used examples of Nos. 7-15 are rare. Nos. 13-15 exist with a favor cancel having a hyphen between "San" and "Jose." Values are same as unused. Fake cancellations exist.

Counterfeits exist of surcharges on Nos. 7-15.

Gen. Prospero Fernández — A6

1883, Jan. 1

No.	Type	Description	Unused	Used
16	A6	1c green	3.00	1.50
17	A6	2c carmine	3.25	1.50
18	A6	5c blue violet	32.50	2.00
19	A6	10c orange	150.00	12.00
20	A6	40c blue	3.00	*3.00*
		Nos. 16-20 (5)	191.75	20.00

Unused examples of 40c usually lack gum.
For overprints see Nos. O1-O20, O24, Guanacaste 1-38, 44.

President Bernardo Soto Alfaro — A7

1887

No.	Type	Description	Unused	Used
21	A7	5c blue violet	7.00	.50
22	A7	10c orange	4.00	3.00

Unused examples of 5c usually lack gum.
For overprints see Nos. O22-O23, Guanacaste 42-43, 45.

A8

A9

1889 **Black Overprint**

No.	Type	Description	Unused	Used
23	A8	1c rose	5.00	3.00
24	A9	5c brown	7.00	3.00

Vertical and inverted overprints are fakes.
For overprints see Guanacaste Nos. 47-54.

President Soto Alfaro
A10 A11

A12

A13

A14 A15

A16

A17

A18

A19

1889 ***Perf. 14-16 & Compound***

No.	Type	Description	Unused	Used
25	A10	1c brown	.35	*.45*
a.		Horiz. pair, imperf. vert	*150.00*	
b.		Imperf. pair	*150.00*	
c.		Horiz. or vert. pair, imperf. btwn.	*150.00*	
26	A11	2c dark green	.35	*.45*
a.		Imperf., pair	50.00	
b.		Vert. pair, imperf. horiz.	125.00	
c.		Horiz. pair, imperf. btwn.	125.00	
27	A12	5c orange	.45	.35
a.		Imperf., pair		*750.00*
b.		Horiz. pair, imperf. btwn.	*350.00*	
28	A13	10c red brown	.40	.35
a.		Vert. or horiz. pair, imperf. btwn.	*150.00*	*500.00*
29	A14	20c yellow green	.30	*.35*
a.		Vert. pair, imperf. horiz.	200.00	
b.		Horizontal pair, imperf. btwn.	*150.00*	
30	A15	50c rose red	1.00	
		Telegram cancel		.75
31	A16	1p blue	1.25	
		Telegram cancel		.75
32	A17	2p dull violet	6.00	
a.		2p slate	6.00	10.00
		Telegram cancel		4.00
33	A18	5p olive green	25.00	
		Telegram cancel		10.00
34	A19	10p black	100.00	
		Telegram cancel		45.00
		Nos. 25-34 (10)	135.10	1.95

Nos. 30-34 normally were used on telegrams and most examples were removed from the forms and sold by the government.

Most unused examples of No. 34 have no gum or only part gum. These sell for somewhat less.

For overprints see Nos. O25-O30, Guanacaste 55-67.

Arms of Costa Rica
A20 A21

A22

A23

A24

A25

A26

A27

A28

A29

1892 ***Perf. 12-15 & Compound***

No.	Type	Description	Unused	Used
35	A20	1c grnsh blue	.30	*.40*
36	A21	2c yellow	.30	*.40*
37	A22	5c red lilac	.30	.25
a.		5c violet	60.00	.30
38	A23	10c lt green	.80	.35
a.		Horiz. pair, imperf. btwn.	—	*100.00*
39	A24	20c scarlet	12.00	.25
a.		Horiz. pair, imperf. btwn.	—	*100.00*
40	A25	50c gray blue	4.00	*4.25*
41	A26	1p green, *yel*	1.25	1.00
42	A27	2p brown red, *lilac*	3.00	1.00
a.		2p rose red, *pale lil*	12.00	1.00
43	A28	5p dk blue, *blue*	2.00	1.00
44	A29	10p brown, *pale buff*	35.00	5.00
a.		10p brown, *yellow*	8.00	
		Nos. 35-44 (10)	58.95	13.90

Imperfs. of Nos. 35-44 are proofs.
For overprints see Nos. O31-O36.

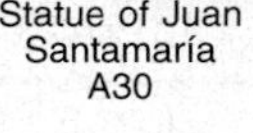
Statue of Juan Santamaría
A30

Juan Mora Fernández
A31

View of Port Limón — A32

Braulio Carrillo ("Branlio" on stamp) — A33

National Theater — A34

José M. Castro — A35

Birris Bridge — A36

Juan Rafael Mora — A37

Jesús Jiménez — A38

Coat of Arms — A39

1901, Jan. ***Perf. 12-15½***

No.	Type	Description	Unused	Used
45	A30	1c green & blk	3.25	.30
a.		Horiz. pair, imperf. btwn.	*150.00*	
46	A31	2c ver & blk	1.25	.30
47	A32	5c gray blue & blk	3.25	.30
a.		Vert. pair, imperf. btwn.	—	*300.00*
48	A33	10c ocher & blk	3.25	.35
49	A34	20c lake & blk	22.50	.25
a.		Vert. pair, imperf. btwn.	*1,000.*	
50	A35	50c dull lil & dk bl	5.50	1.00
51	A36	1col ol bis & blk	110.00	3.50
52	A37	2col car rose & dk grn	16.00	3.00
53	A38	5col brown & blk	75.00	3.50
54	A39	10col yel grn & brn red	29.00	3.00
		Nos. 45-54 (10)	269.00	15.50

The 2c exists with center inverted. Value $77,500.

Nos. 45-57 in other colors are private reprints made in 1948. They have little value.

For surcharge and overprints see Nos. 58, 78, O37-O44.

Remainders

In 1914 the government sold a large quantity of stamps at very much less than face value. The lot included most regular issues from 1901 to 1911 inclusive, postage due stamps of 1903 and Official stamps of 1901-03. These stamps were canceled with groups of thin parallel bars. The higher valued used stamps, such as Nos. 64, 65-68a, sell for much less than the values quoted, which are for stamps with regular postal cancellations. A few sell for much higher prices.

José M. Cañas — A40

Julián Volio — A41

Eusebio Figueroa Oreamuno — A42

1903 ***Perf. 13½, 14, 15***

No.	Type	Description	Unused	Used
55	A40	4c red vio & blk	2.00	.70
56	A41	6c olive grn & blk	7.25	4.00
57	A42	25c gray lil & brn	16.00	.30
		Nos. 55-57 (3)	25.25	5.00

See note on private reprints following No. 54.
For overprints see Nos. 81, O45-O47.

No. 49 Surcharged in Black:

1905

No.	Type	Description	Unused	Used
58	A34	1c on 20c lake & blk	.60	.60
a.		Inverted surcharge	10.00	10.00
b.		Diagonal surcharge	.60	.60

Examples surcharged in other colors are proofs.

Statue of Juan Santamaria
A43

Juan Mora Fernández
A44

José M. Cañas
A45

Mauro Fernández
A46

Braulio Carrillo — A47

Julián Volio — A48

Eusebio Figueroa Oreamuno A49

José M. Castro A50

Jesús Jiménez — A51

Juan Rafael Mora — A52

Perf. 11x14, 14 (1c, 5c, 10c, 25c)

1907 **Unwmk.**

59 A43 1c red brn & ind 8.00 .40
a. Perf. 11x14 60.00 3.00
b. Imperf pair 20.00 —
60 A44 2c yel grn & blk 3.00 .30
a. Perf. 14 3.00 .30
b. Imperf pair 15.00 —
61 A45 4c car & indigo 12.00 2.50
a. Perf. 14 500.00 45.00
b. Imperf pair 15.00 —
62 A46 5c yel & dull bl 3.00 .30
a. Perf. 11x14 60.00 1.00
b. Imperf pair 15.00 —
63 A47 10c blue & blk 10.00 .50
a. Perf. 11x14 20.00 1.00
b. Imperf pair 30.00 —
64 A48 20c olive grn & blk 25.00 6.00
a. Perf. 14 25.00 6.00
Remainder cancel 2.00
b. Imperf pair —
65 A49 25c gray lil & blk 3.00 3.00
Remainder cancel 1.00
a. Perf. 11x14 150.00 50.00
b. Imperf pair —
66 A50 50c red lil & blue 75.00 25.00
Remainder cancel 2.00
a. Perf. 14 175.00 50.00
Remainder cancel 5.00
b. Imperf pair 100.00
67 A51 1col brown & blk 25.00 20.00
Remainder cancel 2.00
a. Perf. 14 25.00 20.00
Remainder cancel 2.00
b. Imperf pair —
68 A52 2col claret & grn 160.00 100.00
Remainder cancel 3.00
a. Perf. 14 300.00 150.00
b. Imperf pair 200.00
Nos. 59-68 (10) 324.00 158.00

The remainder cancel value applies to both perforations.

The imperforate varieties of the above set are valued without gum. Ungummed stamps were probably placed on the market in London, while gummed stamps appear to have been sent to Costa Rica and accepted for postal use. There is a small premium for gummed stamps.

The 1c, 2c, 5c, 20c, 50c, 1 col and 2 col exist with center inverted. Value, set $62,500.

Nos. 59-68 exist with papermaker's watermark.

No. 65b with brown vignette is a proof. Value, pair $40. The actual No. 65b (black vignette) is worth much more.

For overprints see Nos. 77, 79-80, 82-84, O48-O55, O60-O64.

Statue of Juan Santamaria A53

Juan Mora Fernández A54

José M. Cañas A55

Mauro Fernández A56

Braulio Carrillo — A57

Julián Volio — A58

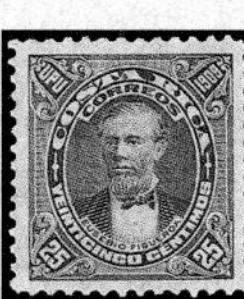
Eusebio Figueroa Oreamuno A59

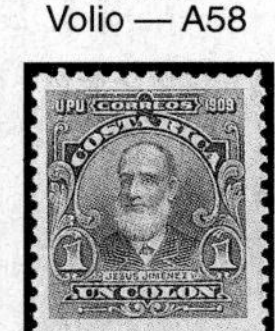
Jesús Jiménez A60

1910 ***Perf. 12***

69 A53 1c brown .25 .25
70 A54 2c dp green .30 .25
71 A55 4c scarlet .35 .35
72 A56 5c orange 1.00 .25
73 A57 10c deep blue .40 .25
74 A58 20c olive grn .50 .35
75 A59 25c dp violet 17.00 1.50
76 A60 1col dk brown .50 .50
Nos. 69-76 (8) 20.30 3.70

For overprints and surcharge see Nos. 111C-111J, B1, C2, O56-O59.

No. 60a Overprinted in Red

1911 ***Perf. 14***

77 A44 2c yel grn & blk 3.00 1.10
a. Inverted overprint 6.00 5.00
b. Double overprint, both inverted 45.00

Stamps of 1901-07 Overprinted in Red or Black

78 A30 1c grn & blk (R) 4.00 1.00
a. Black overprint 35.00 18.00
b. Inverted overprint
79 A43 1c red brn & ind (Bk) 1.25 .40
a. Inverted overprint 4.50 3.50
b. Double overprint 5.50 5.00
80 A44 2c yel grn & blk (Bk) 1.00 .40
a. Inverted overprint 3.75 3.50
b. Dbl. ovpt., one as on No. 77 40.00 27.50
c. Double overprint, one inverted 15.00 15.00
d. Pair, one stamp No. 77 25.00 25.00
e. Perf. 11x14 30.00 *1.00*

No. 55 Overprinted in Black

81 A40 4c red vio & blk 1.50 .65

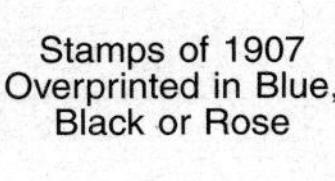

Stamps of 1907 Overprinted in Blue, Black or Rose

Perf. 14, 11x14 (#83, 84)

82 A46 5c yel & bl (Bl) 3.00 .30
a. "Habilitada" 3.25 2.50
b. "2911" 5.50 3.25
c. Roman "I" in "1911" 4.00 2.50
d. Double overprint 5.50 5.00
e. Inverted overprint 6.00 3.75
f. Black overprint *250.00* 2.00
g. Triple overprint 6.00
h. Vert. pair, imperf. horiz. *100.00*
83 A47 10c blue & blk (Bk) 5.00 1.40
a. As #83, Roman "I" in "1911" 7.00 5.00
c. As #83, double overprint 20.00 11.50
d. Perf. 14 45.00 5.25
84 A47 10c blue & blk (R) 15.00 13.50
a. Roman "I" in "1911" *100.00* *100.00*
c. Perf. 14 *100.00* *100.00*
Nos. 77-84 (8) 33.75 18.75

Many counterfeits of overprint exist.

Telegraph Stamps Surcharged in Rose, Blue or Black

A61

A62

A63

1911 ***Perf. 12***

86 A61 1c on 10c bl (R) .50 .30
a. "Coereos" 7.75 6.00
b. Inverted surcharge
87 A61 1c on 10c bl (Bk) *210.00* *87.50*
88 A61 1c on 25c vio (Bk) .50 .30
a. "Coereos" 8.75 6.00
b. Pair, one without surcharge 20.00
c. Double surcharge 9.00
e. Double surch., one inverted 12.50
89 A61 1c on 50c red brn (Bl) .55 .40
a. Inverted surcharge 5.50 5.00
b. Double surcharge 4.50
90 A61 1c on 1col brn (R) .55 .40
91 A61 1c on 5col red (Bl) 1.00 .55
92 A61 1c on 10col dk brn (R) 1.50 .70

Perf. 14

93 A62 2c on 5c brn org (Bk) 3.50 1.90
a. Inverted surcharge *9.00* *3.75*
b. "Correos" inverted *17.50*
c. Double surcharge 9.00

Perf. 14x11

94 A62 2c on 10c bl (R) 100.00 100.00
a. Perf. 14 *350.00* *350.00*
b. "Correos" inverted 2,000.
c. As "b," perf. 14
95 A62 2c on 50c cl (Bk) 1.00 .55
a. Inverted surcharge 4.50 3.25
b. Double surcharge 12.50
c. Perf. 14 45.00 20.00
96 A62 2c on 1col brn (Bk) 1.25 .70
a. Inverted surcharge 12.50
b. Double surcharge 16.00
c. Perf. 14 2.00 .80
97 A62 2c on 2col car (Bk) 1.25 .60
a. Inverted surcharge 8.00 5.00
b. "Correos" inverted 10.00 5.50
c. Double surcharge
d. Perf. 14 27.50 16.00
98 A62 2c on 5col grn (Bk) 1.00 .70
a. Inverted surcharge 10.00 7.00
b. "Correos" inverted *16.00* *4.25*
c. Perf. 14 6.00 3.00
99 A62 2c on 10col mar (Bk) 1.50 .70
a. "Correos" inverted *400.00*
b. Perf. 14 6.00 3.00

Perf. 12

100 A63 5c on 5c org (Bl) .40 .30
a. Double surcharge 27.50 16.00
b. Inverted surcharge 27.50 9.50
c. Pair, one without surcharge 16.00

Counterfeits exist of Nos. 87, 94 and all minor varieties. Genuine used examples of No. 94 are rare and have a cancel only used on registered mail. Genuine "Coereos" errors do not exist on No. 87. Used examples of No. 94 with target cancels are counterfeits. No. 94c is unique. All examples of Nos. 94b and 94c have stains and are valued thus.

Nos. 93-99 exist with papermaker's watermark.

Coffee Plantation — A64

1921, June 17 **Litho.** ***Perf. 11½***

103 A64 5c bl & blk 3.00 3.00
a. Tête bêche pair 15.00 6.50
b. Imperf., pair *60.00*
c. As "a," imperf. *200.00*

Centenary of coffee raising in Costa Rica.

No. 103 exists on pink surfaced paper. Value: single, $200; tete-beche pair, $2,000.

Liberty with Torch of Freedom — A65

1921 **Typo.** ***Perf. 11***

104 A65 5c violet 1.00 .40
a. Imperf, pair *100.00*

Cent. of Central American independence.

Beware of trimmed singles that look like No. 104a.

For overprint see No. 111.

Juan Mora and Julio Acosta — A66

1921, Sept. 15 ***Perf. 11½***

105 A66 2c orange & blk 2.00 2.00
106 A66 3c green & blk 2.00 2.00
107 A66 6c scarlet & blk 3.75 3.75
108 A66 15c dk blue & blk 8.00 8.00
109 A66 30c orange brn & blk 10.00 10.00
Nos. 105-109 (5) 25.75 25.75

Centenary of Central American independence. Issue requested by Costa Rican Philatelic Society. Authorized by decree calling for 2,000 of 30c and 5,000 each of other values. Nos. 105-109 imperf were not regularly issued. Inverted centers exist of both perf and imperf. They are rare. Used values are for Independence commemorative cancel.

Each sheet of 20 (4x5) contains 5 tête-bêche pairs. Value, set of 5 pairs $75.

Simón Bolívar — A67

1921 **Engr.** ***Perf. 12***

110 A67 15c deep violet .75 .30

For overprint see No. 111H. For surcharge see No. 148.

No. 104 Overprinted

1922 ***Perf. 11***

111 A65 5c violet .75 .40
a. Inverted overprint 10.00
b. Double overprint 15.00

Stamps of 1910-1921 Overprinted in Blue, Red, Black or Gold

1922 ***Perf. 12***

111C A53 1c brown (Bl) .30 .25
111D A54 2c deep green (R) .40 .25
111E A55 4c scarlet .30 .25
111F A56 5c orange 3.00 .40

111G A57 10c deep blue (R) .75 .40
111H A67 15c deep violet (G) 8.00 3.00
Nos. 111C-111H (6) 12.75 4.55

Inverted overprints occur on all values. Value, set $20. Counterfeits predominate.

No. 72 Overprinted

1923

111J A56 5c orange 3.00 .75
k. "VD." for "UD." 75.00 75.00

Jesús Jiménez — A68

1923, June 18 Litho. *Perf. 11½*

112 A68 2c brown .40 .40
113 A68 4c green .40 .40
114 A68 5c blue .60 .40
115 A68 20c carmine .85 .50
116 A68 1col violet 1.10 1.25
Nos. 112-116 (5) 3.35 2.95

Pres. Jesús Jiménez (1823-98).

Nos. 112-116, imperf, were not regularly issued. Value, set $4.

For overprints see Nos. O65-O69.

National Monument A70

Harvesting Coffee — A71

Banana Growing — A73

General Post Office A74

Columbus Soliciting Aid of Isabella A75

Christopher Columbus A76

Columbus at Cariari A77

Map of Costa Rica — A78

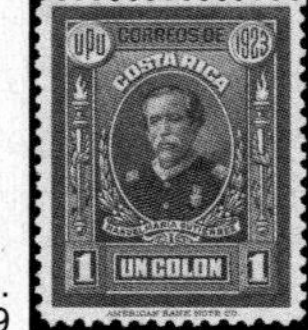

Manuel M. Gutiérrez — A79

1923-26 Engr. *Perf. 12*

117 A70 1c violet .25 .25
118 A71 2c yellow .50 .25
119 A73 4c deep green .75 .30
120 A74 5c light blue 1.50 .25
121 A74 5c yellow grn ('26) .50 .25
122 A75 10c red brown 3.00 .25
123 A75 10c car rose ('26) .50 .25
124 A76 12c carmine rose 10.00 6.00
125 A77 20c deep blue 10.00 .75
126 A78 40c orange 11.00 6.00
127 A79 1col olive green 2.40 1.00
Nos. 117-127 (11) 40.40 15.55

See Nos. 151-156. For surcharges & overprints see Nos. 136-140, 147, 189, 218, C2.

Rodrigo Arias Maldonado — A80

1924 *Perf. 12½*

128 A80 2c dark green .30 .30
a. Perf. 14 .50 .30

See No. 162.

Map of Guanacaste A81

Mission at Nicoya A82

1924 Litho. *Perf. 12*

129 A81 1c carmine rose .30 .25
130 A81 2c violet .40 .25
131 A81 5c green .40 .25
132 A81 10c orange 2.25 .50
133 A82 15c light blue 1.00 .50
134 A82 20c gray black 2.00 1.00
135 A82 25c light brown 3.00 1.50
Nos. 129-135 (7) 9.35 4.25

Centenary of annexation of Province of Guanacaste to Costa Rica.

Exist imperf. Value, set, $50.

Stamps of 1923 Surcharged

a

b

1925

136 A74(a) 3c on 5c lt blue .30 .25
137 A75(a) 6c on 10c red brn .40 .25
138 A78(a) 30c on 40c orange 1.50 .40
139 A79(b) 45c on 1col ol grn 1.75 .50
a. Double surcharge 250.00
Nos. 136-139 (4) 3.95 1.40

No. 124 Surcharged

1926

140 A76 10c on 12c car rose 1.50 .30

College of San Luis, Cartago A83

Chapui Asylum, San José — A84

Normal School, Heredia A85

Ruins of Ujarrás A86

1926 Unwmk. Engr. *Perf. 12½*

143 A83 3c ultra .55 .25
144 A84 6c dark brown .55 .25
145 A85 30c deep orange 3.00 .40
146 A86 45c black violet 5.00 1.60
Nos. 143-146 (4) 9.10 2.50

For surcharges see Nos. 190-190D, 217.

No. 124 Surcharged in Black

1928, Jan. 7 *Perf. 12*

147 A76 10c on 12c car rose 4.75 4.75

Issued in honor of Col. Charles A. Lindbergh during his Good Will Tour of Central America.

The surcharge was privately reprinted using an original die. Reprints can be distinguished by distinct dots under the "10s." All errors and inverted surcharges are reprints.

No. 110 Surcharged

1928

148 A67 5(c) on 15c dp violet .30 .30
a. Inverted surcharge 35.00

Type I — A88

Type II

Type III

Type IV

Type V

Surcharge Typo. (I-V) & Litho. (V)

1929 *Perf. 12½*

149 A88 5c on 2col car (I) .50 .25
a.-d. Types II-V .60 .25
e. Type V (litho.) 3.00 3.00

Telegraph Stamp Surcharged for Postage as in 1929, Surcharge Lithographed

1929

150 A88 13c on 40c deep grn .35 .25
a. Inverted surcharge 2.00 2.00

Excellent counterfeits exist of No. 150a.

Types of 1923-26 Issues Dated "1929"

Imprint of Waterlow & Sons

1930 Size: 26x21½mm *Perf. 12½*

151 A70 1c dark violet .70 .25
155 A74 5c green .70 .25
156 A75 10c carmine rose .70 .25
Nos. 151-156 (3) 2.10 .75

Juan Rafael Mora — A89

1931, Jan. 29

157 A89 13c carmine rose 2.50 .25

For surcharge see No. 209.

Seal of Costa Rica Philatelic Society ("Octubre 12 de 1932") — A90

1932, Oct. 12 *Perf. 12*

158 A90 3c orange .25 .25
159 A90 5c dark green .40 .25
160 A90 10c carmine rose .50 .25
161 A90 20c dark blue .85 .40
Nos. 158-161 (4) 2.00 1.15

Phil. Exhib., Oct. 12, 1932. See Nos. 179-183.

Maldonado Type of 1924

1934, Aug. 11 *Perf. 12½*

162 A80 3c dark green 1.00 .25

Red Cross Nurse — A91

1935, May 31 *Perf. 12*
163 A91 10c rose carmine 6.00 .25

50th anniv. of the founding of the Costa Rican Red Cross Society.

Air View of Cartago A92

Miraculous Statuette and View of Cathedral A93

Vision of 1635 — A94

1935, Aug. 1 *Perf. 12½*
164 A92 5c green .25 .25
165 A93 10c carmine .25 .25
166 A92 30c orange .25 .25
167 A94 45c dark violet 1.50 .55
168 A93 50c blue black 1.50 1.00
Nos. 164-168 (5) 3.75 2.30

Tercentenary of the Patron Saint, Our Lady of the Angels, of Costa Rica.

Map of Cocos Island A95

1936, Jan. 29 *Perf. 14, 11½ (25c)*
169 A95 4c ocher .50 .25
170 A95 8c dark violet .65 .25
171 A95 25c orange .80 .25
172 A95 35c brown vio .95 .25
173 A95 40c brown 1.25 .40
174 A95 50c yellow 1.50 .60
175 A95 2col yellow grn 11.00 10.00
176 A95 5col green 30.00 25.00
Nos. 169-176 (8) 46.65 37.00

Exist imperf. Value, set, $50.
For surcharges see Nos. 196-200, C55-C56.

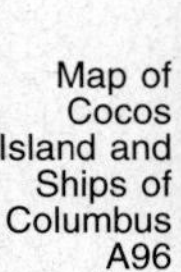

Map of Cocos Island and Ships of Columbus A96

1936, Dec. 5 *Perf. 12*
177 A96 5c green .40 .25
178 A96 10c carmine rose .55 .25

For overprints see Nos. 247, O80-O81.

Seal of Costa Rica Philatelic Society ("Diciembre 1937") — A97

1937, Dec. 15
179 A97 2c dark brown .45 .25
180 A97 3c black .45 .25
181 A97 5c green .45 .25
182 A97 10c orange red .45 .25
Nos. 179-182 (4) 1.80 1.00

Souvenir Sheet

Imperf

183 Sheet of 4 6.50 4.00
a. A97 2c dark brown .25 .25
b. A97 3c black .25 .25
c. A97 5c green .25 .25
d. A97 10c orange red .25 .25

Phil. Exhib., Dec. 1937.

Purple Guaria Orchid, National Flower — A98

Tuna — A99

Native with Donkey Carrying Bananas A101

3c, Cacao pod. 10c, Coffee harvesting.

1937-38 **Wmk. 229** *Perf. 12½*
184 A98 1c green & vio ('38) .90 .25
185 A98 3c chocolate ('38) .90 .25

Unwmk. *Perf. 12*
186 A99 2c olive gray .65 .25
187 A101 5c dark green .90 .25
188 A101 10c carmine rose 1.50 .25
Nos. 184-188 (5) 4.85 1.25

National Exposition.

No. 125 Overprinted in Black

1938, Sept. 23 **Unwmk.** *Perf. 12*
189 A77 20c deep blue 7.50 .30

No. 146 Surcharged in Red

a

b

c

d

e

1940 *Perf. 12½*
190 A86(a) 15c on 45c blk vio .60 .30
190A A86(b) 15c on 45c blk vio .60 .30
190B A86(c) 15c on 45c blk vio .60 .30
190C A86(d) 15c on 45c blk vio .60 .30
190D A86(e) 15c on 45c blk vio .60 .30
Nos. 190-190D (5) 3.00 1.50

No. 190D exists with inverted surcharge. Value, $5.

Allegory A103

Black Overprint

1940, Dec. 2 **Engr.** *Perf. 12*
191 A103 5c green .35 .25
192 A103 10c rose carmine .75 .25
193 A103 20c deep blue 2.00 .75
194 A103 40c brown 8.00 2.25
195 A103 55c orange yellow 22.50 9.50
Nos. 191-195 (5) 33.60 13.00

Pan-American Health Day. See Nos. C46-C54.
Exist without overprint.

Stamps of 1936 Srchd. in Black

1941 *Perf. 14, 11½*
196 A95 15c on 25c orange .75 .75
197 A95 15c on 35c brn vio .75 .75
198 A95 15c on 40c brown .75 .75
199 A95 15c on 2col yel grn .75 .75
200 A95 15c on 5col green 2.00 2.00
Nos. 196-200 (5) 5.00 5.00

Nos. 196-200 exist with surcharge inverted. Value, set of 5, $20.

National Stadium A104

Engr.; Flags Typo. in Natl. Colors

1941, May 8 *Perf. 12½*
201 A104 5c green .70 .25
a. Flags omitted 250.00
202 A104 10c orange .55 .30
203 A104 15c car rose .80 .40
204 A104 25c dk blue .85 .55
205 A104 40c chestnut 3.25 1.40
206 A104 50c purple 4.25 2.00
207 A104 75c red orange 6.75 5.75
208 A104 1col dk carmine 13.00 10.50
Nos. 201-208 (8) 30.15 21.15

Caribbean and Central American Soccer Championship. See Nos. C57-C66, C121-C123.

No. 157 Surcharged in Black

1941, July 26 *Perf. 12*
209 A89 5c on 13c car rose .25 .25

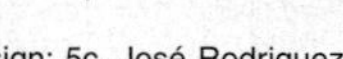

Cleto González Viquez — A105

Design: 5c, José Rodriguez.

1941-45 **Engr.** *Perf. 12½*
210 A105 3c dp orange .25 .25
210A A105 3c dp plum ('43) .25 .25
210B A105 3c carmine ('45) .25 .25
211 A105 5c dp violet .25 .25
211A A105 5c brown blk ('43) .25 .25
Nos. 210-211A (5) 1.25 1.25

See No. 256.

Old University of Costa Rica A106

New National University A107

1941, Aug. 26 *Perf. 12*
212 A106 5c green .40 .25
213 A107 10c yellow org .40 .25
214 A106 15c lilac rose .75 .25
215 A107 25c dull blue 1.00 .35
216 A106 50c fawn 7.50 2.25
Nos. 212-216 (5) 10.05 3.35

National University, founded in 1940. See Nos. C74-C80.

Nos. 144, 189 Srchd. in Black or Red

1942, April *Perf. 12½, 12*
217 A84 5c on 6c dk brn 1.00 .25
218 A77 15c on 20c dp bl (R) 6.00 .25

Nos. 217-218 exist with inverted surcharge. Value, each $10.

Torch of Freedom, "Victory" and Flags of American Nations — A108

1942, Sept. 25 *Perf. 12*
219 A108 5c rose .30 .25
220 A108 5c yellow grn .30 .25
221 A108 5c purple .30 .25
222 A108 5c dp blue .30 .25
223 A108 5c red orange .30 .25
Nos. 219-223 (5) 1.50 1.25

For overprints see Nos. 238-241.

Juan Mora Fernández — A109

Designs: 2c, Bruno Carranza. 3c, Tomas Guardia. 5c, Manuel Aguilar. 15c, Francisco Morazan. 25c, Jose M. Alfaro. 50c, Francisco M. Oreamuno. 1col, Jose M. Castro. 2col, Juan Rafael Mora.

1943-47 **Engr.**
224 A109 1c red lilac .25 .25
225 A109 2c black .25 .25
226 A109 3c deep blue .25 .25
227 A109 5c brt blue grn .25 .25
a. 5c bright green ('47) .25 .25
228 A109 15c scarlet .25 .25
229 A109 25c brt ultra 1.00 .25
230 A109 50c dp violet 3.00 .45
231 A109 1col black brown 4.00 2.00
232 A109 2col deep orange 5.00 3.00
Nos. 224-232 (9) 14.25 6.95

See Nos. 344-368, C81-C91A, C124-C127, C154-C158, C179-C181, C768-C772, C790-C794, C854-C858. For surcharges see Nos. C154-C158, C182, C184-C185.

View of San Ramón A118

1944, Jan. 19
233 A118 5c dark green .25 .25
234 A118 10c orange .25 .25
235 A118 15c rose pink .30 .25
236 A118 40c gray black 1.25 .80
237 A118 50c deep blue 2.40 1.60
Nos. 233-237 (5) 4.45 3.15

100th anniv. of the founding of the City of San Ramón. See Nos. C94-C102.

Catalogue values for unused stamps in this section, from this point to the end of the section, are for Never Hinged items.

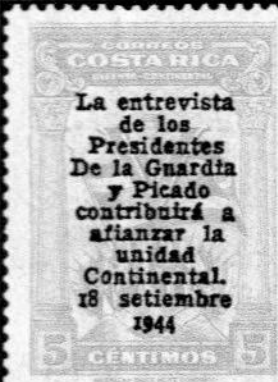

Nos. 220-223 Overprinted in Red or Black

1944, Sept. 18
238 A108 5c yel green .45 .25
239 A108 5c purple (R) .45 .25
240 A108 5c dp blue (R) .45 .25
241 A108 5c red orange .45 .25
Nos. 238-241 (4) 1.80 1.00

Amicable settlement of a boundary dispute with Panama. This overprint also exists on No. 219.

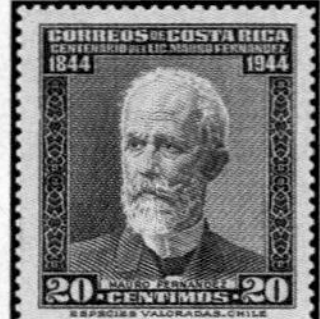

Mauro Fernández (1844-1905), Statesman — A119

Unwmk.
1945, July 21 **Engr.** ***Perf. 14***
242 A119 20c deep green .55 .25

For surcharge see No. 246.

Coffee Harvesting — A120

1945, Oct. 9 ***Perf. 12***
243 A120 5c dk green & blk .45 .25
244 A120 10c orange & blk .45 .25
245 A120 20c car rose & blk 1.00 .25
Nos. 243-245 (3) 1.90 .75

No. 242 Surcharged in Red Brown

1946 **Unwmk.** ***Perf. 14***
246 A119 15c on 20c dp green .55 .25

Exists with inverted surcharge. Value, $6.

No. O80 Overprinted in Red

1947, Mar. 19 ***Perf. 12***
247 A96 5c green .55 .25

Exist with inverted overprint. Value, $10.

Cervantes — A121

Wmk. 215
1947, Nov. 10 **Engr.** ***Perf. 14***
249 A121 30c deep blue .65 .25
250 A121 55c deep carmine 1.10 .40

Miguel de Cervantes Saavedra, novelist, playwright & poet, 400th birth anniv.

A122

1947, Aug. 26 **Unwmk.** ***Perf. 12***
251 A122 5c brt green .35 .25
252 A122 10c car rose .35 .25
253 A122 15c ultra .35 .25
254 A122 25c orange red .50 .25
255 A122 50c lilac .80 .30
Nos. 251-255,C160-C167 (13) 10.40 6.30

Franklin D. Roosevelt. For surcharges see Nos. C224-C226.

Small Portrait Type of 1941

Design: 3c, Bishop Bernardo A. Thiel.

1948 ***Perf. 12½***
256 A105 3c deep ultra .35 .25

Old University of Costa Rica A123

Black Surcharge

1953, June 25 **Litho.** ***Perf. 12***
257 A123 5c on 10c green .60 .25

Inverted and double overprints exist. Exists without overprint. Value, $35.

Revenue Stamp Surcharged in Red or Blue — A124

1955-56 **Unwmk.** **Engr.** ***Perf. 12***
258 A124 5c on 2c emerald .45 .25
259 A124 15c on 2c emer (Bl) .45 .25
260 A124 15c on 2c emer ('56) .45 .25
Nos. 258-260,C341-C344 (7) 4.20 2.10

For surcharges see Nos. C341-C344, C431-C433.

Justo A. Facio — A125

1960, Apr. 20 **Photo.** ***Perf. 13½***
261 A125 10c brown red .65 .25

Centenary of the birth (in 1859) of Prof. Justo A. Facio. Exists imperf. Value, $35.

Nos. RA12-RA15 Surcharged in Red

1963, Mar.
262 PT3 10c on 5c dk car .65 .25
263 PT3 10c on 5c sepia .65 .25
264 PT3 10c on 5c dull grn .65 .25
265 PT3 10c on 5c blue .65 .25
Nos. 262-265 (4) 2.60 1.00

Anglo-Costa Rican Bank — A126

1963 **Unwmk.** ***Perf. 13½***
266 A126 10c gray .60 .25

Centenary of the Anglo-Costa Rican Bank.

Arms of San José — A127

Coats of Arms: 35c, Cartago. 50c, Heredia. 55c, Alajuela. 65c, Guanacaste. 1col, Puntarenas. 2col, Limon.

1969, Sept. 14 **Litho.** ***Perf. 14x13½***
267 A127 15c multicolored .35 .25
268 A127 35c multicolored .35 .25
269 A127 50c gray & multi .35 .25
270 A127 55c buff & multi .35 .25
271 A127 65c multicolored .90 .25
272 A127 1col pink & multi 3.25 .40
273 A127 2col multicolored 4.50 .60
Nos. 267-273 (7) 10.05 2.25

Alberto M. Brenes Mora — A128

1976, Mar. 1 **Litho.** ***Perf. 10½***
274 A128 1col violet blue .75 .25
Nos. 274,C653-C657 (6) 10.70 4.40

Prof. Alberto Manuel Brenes Mora, botanist, birth centenary.

Map of Costa Rica, Reader with Book — A129

1978, July 17 **Litho.** ***Perf. 13½***
275 A129 50c multicolored .65 .25

National five-year literacy plan.

World Communications Year — A130

1983, May 17 **Litho.** ***Perf. 13x13½***
276 A130 10c multicolored .55 .25
277 A130 50c multicolored .45 .25
278 A130 10col multicolored 1.90 .30
Nos. 276-278 (3) 2.90 .80

A131

1983, May 30 **Litho.** ***Perf. 10½***
279 A131 20col black 2.60 .55

1st World Cong. of Human Rights, 1982.

UPU Membership Centenary — A132

3col, #17, UPU monument. 10col, #20, San Jose post office.

1983, June 30 **Litho.** ***Perf. 16***
280 A132 3col multi 1.40 .25
281 A132 10col multi 2.75 .50

French Alliance Centenary — A133

Scene in San Jose, by Christina Fournier.

1983, July 21 **Litho.** ***Perf. 11***
282 A133 12col multicolored 2.25 .55

Christmas 1983 — A134

Nativity tableau in continuous design.

1983, Dec. 5 Litho. *Perf. 13½*

283 1.50col multi .35 .25
284 1.50col multi .35 .25
285 1.50col multi .35 .25
a. A134 Strip of 3, #283-285 2.40 2.40

Costa Rican Gardens Association.

Fishery Development Administration A135

1983, Dec. 19 Litho. *Perf. 13½*

286 A135 8.50col multi 1.00 .30

Local Birds — A136

10c, Quetzal. 50c, Cyanerpes cyaneus. 1col, Turdus grayi. 1.50col, Momotus momota. 3col, Colibri thalassinus. 10col, Notiochelindon cyanoleuca.

1984, Jan. 9 Litho. *Perf. 13½*

287 A136 10c multicolored 1.00 .25
288 A136 50c multicolored 1.20 .25
289 A136 1col multicolored 1.20 .25
290 A136 1.50col multicolored 1.20 .25
291 A136 3col multicolored 2.60 .25
292 A136 10col multicolored 8.50 .30
Nos. 287-292 (6) 15.70 1.55

Dated 1983. 10c, 1.50col, 3col vert.

José Joaquin Mora, Hero of 1856 Independence Campaign — A137

Paintings, Juan Santamaria Museum, San José: 1.50col, Pancha Carrasco. 3 col, Death of Juan Santamaria, horiz. 8.50col, Juan Rafael Mora Porras.

1984, Apr. 10 Litho. *Perf. 10½*

293 A137 50c multi .40 .25
294 A137 1.50col multi .40 .25
295 A137 3col multi .40 .25
296 A137 8.50col multi 2.50 .55
Nos. 293-296 (4) 3.70 1.30

For surcharge see No. 440.

Jesus Bonilla Chavarria, Composer A138

Musicians and Composers: 5col, Benjamin Gutierrez (b. 1937). 12col, Pilar Jimenez (1835-1922). 13col, Jose Daniel Zuniga Zeledon (1889-1981).

1984, May 30 Litho. *Perf. 13½*

297 A138 3.50col black & lil .40 .25
298 A138 5col black & pink .50 .25
299 A138 12col black & grn 1.40 .80
300 A138 13col black & yel 1.75 .90
Nos. 297-300 (4) 4.05 2.20

Figurines, Jade Museum — A139

1984, June 27 Litho. *Perf. 13½*

301 A139 4col Man (pendant) 1.40 .25
302 A139 7col Seated man 2.75 .50
303 A139 10col Dish, horiz. 3.50 .70
Nos. 301-303 (3) 7.65 1.45

1984 Summer Olympics A140

1984, July 27

304 A140 1col Basketball .25 .25
305 A140 8col Swimming .75 .25
306 A140 11col Bicycling 1.10 .40
307 A140 14col Running 1.50 .65
308 A140 20col Boxing 1.90 1.25
309 A140 30col Soccer 3.00 1.40
Nos. 304-309 (6) 8.50 4.20

Public Street Lighting Centenary A141

6col, Street scene by Luis Chacon.

1984, Aug. 9 Litho. *Perf. 10½*

310 A141 6col multi .85 .40

10th Natl. Stamp Exhibition, Sept. 10-16 — A142

No. 311, Natl. monument. No. 312, Juan Mora Fernandez monument.

1984, Sept. 10 Litho. *Perf. 10½*

311 A142 10col multicolored 1.20 .55
312 A142 10col multicolored 1.20 .55
a. Min. sheet, 2 each #311-312 16.00 10.00

Natl. Arms — A143

1984, Oct. 29 Engr. *Perf. 14x13½*

313 A143 100col dk green 8.50 3.75
314 A143 100col yel org 8.50 3.75

Detail from Sistine Virgin by Raphael — A144

1984, Dec. 7 Litho. *Perf. 10½*

315 3col multicolored .25 .25
316 3col multicolored .25 .25
a. A144 Pair, #315-316 2.50 2.00

20th Intl. Bicycle Race, Costa Rica — A146

1984, Dec. 19 Litho. *Perf. 13½*

317 A146 6col multi .90 .30

Intl. Youth Year A147

11col, IYY emblem, #C476.

1985, Jan. 31 *Perf. 10½*

322 A147 11col multi 1.75 .55

Scouting Movement, 75th anniv.

Labor Monument, San Jose — A148

Natl. values: 11col, Freedom of speech-wooden hand printing press. 13col, Neutrality-dove, natl. flag, outline map.

1985, Feb. 28

323 A148 6col shown .90 .30
324 A148 11col bl, blk & yel 1.40 .50
325 A148 13col multi 1.60 .55

Size: 68x38mm

326 A148 30col Nos. 323-325 4.50 1.10
Nos. 323-326 (4) 8.40 2.45

Natl. Red Cross Cent., UN 40th Anniv. A149

1985, May 3 *Perf. 10½*

327 A149 3col No. 163, horiz. 2.75 1.00
328 A149 5col No. C120 2.75 1.50

Club Emblem A150

1st Club Pres., Ricardo Saprissa Ayma A151

Design: No. 330, Hands holding soccer ball.

1985, July 16 *Perf. 10½*

329 A150 3col multi 1.20 .25
330 A150 3col multi 1.20 .25
a. Pair, #329-330 2.50 1.00
331 A151 6col multi 2.25 .30
Nos. 329-331 (3) 4.65 .80

Saprissa Soccer Club, 50th Anniv.

Orchids — A152

No. 332, Brassia arcuigera. No. 333, Encyclia peraltensis. No. 334, Maxillaria especie. No. 335, Oncidium turialbae. No. 336, Trichopilia marginata. No. 337, Stanhopea ecornuta.

1985, Dec. 3

332 A152 6col multicolored 8.25 1.20
333 A152 6col multicolored 8.25 1.20
334 A152 6col multicolored 8.25 1.20
a. Strip of 3, #332-334 25.00 15.00
335 A152 13col multicolored 7.25 2.00
336 A152 13col multicolored 7.25 2.00
337 A152 13col multicolored 7.25 2.00
a. Strip of 3, #335-337 25.00 15.00
Nos. 332-337 (6) 46.50 9.60

11th Natl. Philatelic Exposition A153

1985, Dec. 3 Litho. *Perf. 13½*

338 A153 20col No. C41 1.75 .55

Christmas 1985 — A153a

1985, Dec. 12 Litho. *Perf. 10½*

338A A153a 3col multi .65 .25

Compulsory Education, Cent. A154

Designs: 3col, Primary school, horiz. 30col, Mauro Fernandez Acuna, founder.

1986, Feb. 28 *Perf. 13½*

339 A154 3col pale yel & brn .35 .25
340 A154 30col pale pink & brn 2.25 .90

Agriculture Students — A155

No. 341, Students on farm. No. 342, IDB emblem. No. 343, Capo Bianco fisherman.

1986, Mar. 21 *Perf. 10½*

341 10col multi 1.50 .25
342 10col multi 1.50 .25
343 10col multi 1.50 .25
a. A155 Strip of 3, #341-343 5.50 5.50
Nos. 341-343 (3) 4.50 .75

Inter-American Development Bank Annual Governors' Assembly, San Jose.

Presidents Type of 1943

Designs: Nos. 344, 349, 354, 359, 364, Francisco J. Orlich Bolmarcich, 1962-66.
Nos. 345, 350, 355, 360, 365, Jose Joaquin Trejos Fernandez, 1966-70.
Nos. 346, 351, 356, 361, 366, Daniel Oduber Quiros, 1974-78.
Nos. 347, 352, 357, 362, 367, Rodrigo Carazo Odio, 1978-82.
Nos. 348, 353, 358, 363, 368, Luis Alberto Monge Alvarez, 1982-86.

1986, May 12 Litho. *Perf. 10½*

344 A109 3col turq blue .50 .25
345 A109 3col turq blue .50 .25
346 A109 3col turq blue .50 .25
347 A109 3col turq blue .50 .25
348 A109 3col turq blue .50 .25
a. Strip of 5, #344-348 *3.50 3.00*
349 A109 6col yel brn .75 .25
350 A109 6col yel brn .75 .25
351 A109 6col yel brn .75 .25
352 A109 6col yel brn .75 .25
353 A109 6col yel brn .75 .25
a. Strip of 5, #349-353 8.00 8.00
354 A109 10col brn org 1.20 .30
355 A109 10col brn org 1.20 .30
356 A109 10col brn org 1.20 .30
357 A109 10col brn org 1.20 .30
358 A109 10col brn org 1.20 .30
a. Strip of 5, #354-358 13.00 12.00
359 A109 11col slate gray 1.50 .40
360 A109 11col slate gray 1.50 .40
361 A109 11col slate gray 1.50 .40
362 A109 11col slate gray 1.50 .40
363 A109 11col slate gray 1.50 .40
a. Strip of 5, #359-363 16.00 15.00
364 A109 13col olive 1.75 .45
365 A109 13col olive 1.75 .45
366 A109 13col olive 1.75 .45
367 A109 13col olive 1.75 .45
368 A109 13col olive 1.75 .45
a. Strip of 5, #364-368 22.50 17.50
Nos. 344-368 (25) 28.50 8.25
Nos. 348a-368a 39.00

1986 World Cup Soccer Championships, Mexico — A156

No. 369, Players. No. 370, Character trademark, vert. No. 373, Players, diff.

1986, May 30 Litho. *Perf. 13½*

369 A156 1col multi .40 .25
370 A156 1col multi .40 .25
371 A156 4col as No. 370 2.00 .25
372 A156 6col as No. 369 2.75 .25
373 A156 11col multi 5.50 .50
Nos. 369-373 (5) 11.05 1.50

A second printing of No. 370 differs in paper and shade from the first printing, but the most obvious difference is in the absence of the initials "LIL" by the left foot of the soccer player. Unused stamps are rare. Value for used, $10.

Intl. Peace Year — A157

Peace in many languages: a, "Hoa binh," etc. b, "Vrede," etc. c, "Pace," etc.

1986, July 31 Litho. *Perf. 10½*

374 Strip of 3 7.75 1.25
a.-c. A157 5col, any single 1.50 .25

A158

Gold Museum, Central Bank of Costa Rica — A158a

Designs: Various undescribed works of Pre-Columbian art.

1986, Sept. 19 *Perf. 10½*

375 A158 Strip of 5 21.00 5.00
a.-e. 6col any single 2.50 .75
376 A158a Strip of 5 15.00 4.00
a.-e. 13col any single 1.25 1.25

Exist perf 13½, value $17.50 for the two strips of 5 unused

A159

Fauna and Flora — A160

2col, Centurio senex. 3col, Glossophaga soricina. 4col, Ectophylla alba. 5col, Ectophylla alba, diff. 6col, Agalychnis callidryas. 10col, Dendrobates pumilio. 11col, Hyla ebraccata. 20col, Phyllobates lugubris. 50col, Agalychnis callidryas, diff.

1986, Dec. 16 Litho. *Perf. 13x13½*

377 A159 2col multicolored .75 .75
378 A159 3col multicolored 1.40 1.00
379 A159 4col multicolored 1.75 1.00
380 A159 5col multicolored 2.50 1.00
381 A159 6col multicolored 3.00 1.00
382 A159 10col multicolored 4.25 1.00
383 A159 11col multicolored 4.75 1.75
384 A159 20col multicolored 7.50 3.00
Nos. 377-384 (8) 25.90 10.50

Souvenir Sheet

Perf. 12½x12

385 A160 50col multicolored *87.50 60.00*

Natl. Science and Technology Day — A161

Mural (detail), by Francisco Amighetti, Clorito Picado Social Security Clinic.

1987, July 31 Litho. *Perf. 10½*

386 A161 8col multi *6.25* .25

Natl. Museum, Cent. A162

Artifacts: No. 387a, Dowel-shaped figure of a man. No. 387b, Ape-like carved stone figurine. No. 387c, Polished stone ritual figure. No. 387d, Carved granite capital. No. 387e, Two-legged pot. No. 388a, Bowl. No. 388b, Sculpture. No. 388c, Water jar.

1987, Aug. 7

387 Strip of 5 17.50 2.40
a.-e. A162 8col any single, vert. .40 .25
388 Strip of 3 17.50 2.75
a.-c. A162 15col any single .65 .25
Nos. 387-388 (2) 35.00 5.15

Horse-drawn Wagon — A163

No. 390, Street in old San Jose. No. 391, Provincial coat of arms.

1987, Oct. 26

389 A163 20col shown 1.25 .50
390 A163 20col multicolored 1.25 .50
a. Pair, #389-390 2.75 2.00
391 A163 20col multicolored 1.25 .50
Nos. 389-391 (3) 3.75 1.50

City of San Jose, 250th anniv. Rotary Club, 60th anniv.

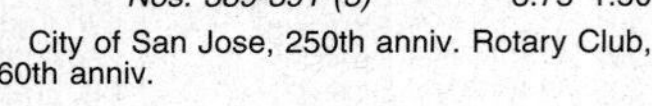

Columbus Day A164

1987, Oct. 26 *Perf. 10½*

392 A164 30col Map, 16th cent. 3.25 .65

Day of the Race; 495th anniv. of Columbus's departure from Palos, Spain, on first journey to the New World.

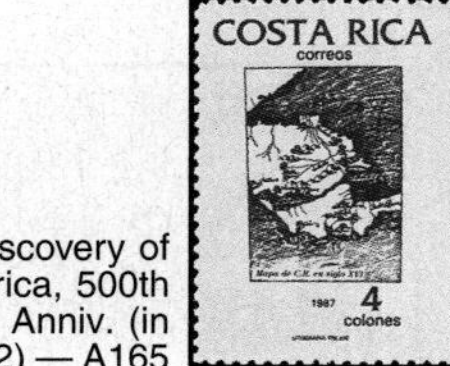

Discovery of America, 500th Anniv. (in 1992) — A165

Maps of Honduras, Nicaragua, Costa Rica and Panama, believed to be Asia by Columbus: No. 393, Costa Rica, 16th cent. No. 394, Map of "Asia" by Bartholomeu Columbus (1461-1514).

1987, Nov. 20 Litho. *Perf. 13½*

393 A165 4col yel & dk red brn .25 .25
394 A165 4col yel & dk red brn .25 .25
a. Pair, #393-394 4.00 4.00

Pres. Oscar Arias, 1987 Nobel Peace Prize Winner — A166

1987, Dec. 2 *Perf. 10½*

395 A166 10col multi *3.25* .30

Two Houses, a Watercolor by Fausto Pacheco (1899-1966) A167

1987, Dec. 22 Litho. *Perf. 10½*

396 A167 1col multi .80 .30

Intl. Year of Shelter for the Homeless.

17th General Conference for the Preservation of Natural Resources A168

No. 397, Green turtle. No. 398, Emblem, golden toad. No. 399, Blue butterfly.

1988, Feb. 1 Litho. *Perf. 13½*

397 A168 5col multi .90 .25
398 A168 5col multi .90 .25
399 A168 5col multi .90 .25
a. A168 Strip of 3, #397-399 3.25 2.50

Intl. Red Cross and Red Crescent Organizations, 125th Annivs. — A169

1988, Apr. 18 Litho. *Perf. 10½*

400 A169 30col lt blue & dark red 1.60 .65

North and South Campaign A170

18col, Adult education. 20col, Cultural radio programs.

1988, June 6 Photo. *Perf. 11½*

Granite Paper

401 A170 18col multi 2.60 1.20
402 A170 20col multi 2.60 1.20

Cultural cooperation with Liechtenstein. See Liechtenstein Nos. 886-887. For overprint see No. C921.

A171

1988, June 27 Litho. *Perf. 10½*

403 A171 3col dk blue, dark red & yel 1.25 .25

Anglo-Costa Rican Bank, 125th anniv.

A172

No. 404, Character trademark. No. 405, Games emblem.

1988, Sept. 16 Litho. ***Perf. 13½***
404 A172 25col multicolored .95 .50
405 A172 25col multicolored .95 .50
a. Pair, #404-405 6.00 5.00

1988 Summer Olympics, Seoul.

Girls' High School, Cent. A173

10col, Student, courtyard.

1988, Oct. 17 Litho. ***Perf. 10½***
406 A173 10col cream, brown 1.25 .25

A174

1988, Nov. 18
407 A174 10col gray, greenish bl & red brn .65 .25

Educator Omar Dengo (1888-1928) and the Teachers' College, Heredia.

A175

Indian glass-bead and lion-tooth necklace.

1988, Nov. 28 ***Perf. 13½***
408 A175 4col multi 1.25 .25

Discovery of America, 500th anniv. (in 1992).

A176

1988, Dec. 26 Litho. ***Perf. 10½***
409 A176 2col Observation tower .90 .30

Natl. Meteorological Institute, cent. For surcharge see No. 439.

A177

Indigenous flora: 5col, Eschweilera costarricensis. 10col, Heliconia wagneriana. 15col, Heliconia lophocarpa. 20col, Aechmea magdalenae. 25col, Psammisia ramiflora. 30col, Passiflora vitifolia.

1989, Feb. 28
410 A177 5col multicolored .60 .25
411 A177 10col multicolored 1.10 .25
412 A177 15col multicolored 1.50 .25
413 A177 20col multicolored 1.75 .25
414 A177 25col multicolored 2.00 .25
415 A177 30col multicolored 2.50 .25
Nos. 410-415 (6) 9.45 1.50

Nation at Arms — A178

1989, July 1 Litho. ***Perf. 10½***
416 A178 30col multi 1.60 .70

French Revolution, bicent.

Sugar Mill — A179

1989, Aug. 28 Litho. ***Perf. 13½***
417 A179 10col multi .90 .60

Grecia County, 151st anniv.
For overprints see Nos. RA106-RA109.

America Issue — A180

UPAE emblem and pre-Columbian stone carvings: 50col, Three-footed bench for grinding corn. 100col, Sphere.

Litho. & Engr.
Perf. 12½x12

1989, Oct. 12 **Wmk. 334**
418 A180 50col multi 2.50 1.75
419 A180 100col multi 5.50 3.25

For overprint see No. C916.

Orchid — A181

Perf. 10½

1989, Oct. 23 Litho. Unwmk.
420 A181 10col multi *6.25* 1.00

"100 Years of Democracy" summit of Presidents.

Map, H.F. Pittier, Emblem — A182

Perf. 13½

1989, Nov. 27 Litho. Unwmk.
421 A182 18col multi 1.00 .40

Natl. Geographic Institute, cent.
For surcharge see No. 452.

America Issue — A183

Pre-Columbian gold frog figurine and facing portraits of Ferdinand V and Isabella I on gold coin struck by Spain from 1476 to 1516.

1989, Dec. 4 ***Perf. 10½***
422 A183 4col multicolored 1.25 .25

Discovery of America, 500th anniv. (in 1992).

Natl. Theater, Cent. A184

Perf. 10½

1990, Feb. 27 Litho. Unwmk.
423 A184 5col *Coffee Allegory* 1.00 .30

World Cup Soccer Championships, Italy — A185

1990, June 1 Litho. ***Perf. 10½***
424 A185 5col multicolored .65 .25

Univ. of Costa Rica, 50th Anniv. A187

1990, Aug. 24 Litho. ***Perf. 10½***
426 A187 18col multicolored 1.25 .25

Education, Democracy, Peace — A188

Litho. & Engr.

1990, Oct. 31 ***Perf. 12½***
427 A188 100col shown 4.50 2.25
428 A188 200col Flag as map 9.00 3.50
429 A188 500col National arms 24.00 9.00
Nos. 427-429 (3) 37.50 14.75

"Invisible" security printing is sometimes visible.
For overprints see Nos. 448, C920. For surcharges see Nos. 546-548, 553.

Hospitals — A190

No. 431, St. Vincent de Paul Hospital, Heredia. No. 432, Natl. Psychiatric hospital.

1990, Dec. 18 Engr. ***Perf. 13x12½***
431 A190 50col multicolored 2.75 .70
432 A190 100col multicolored 4.75 1.00

America Issue — A191

No. 433, Ara macao. No. 434, Ara ambigua. No. 435, Cassia grandis. No. 436, Tabebuia ochracea.

1990, Dec. 21 Litho. ***Perf. 10½***
433 A191 18col multi 1.00 .40
434 A191 18col multi 1.00 .40
a. Pair, #433-434 9.00 7.50
435 A191 24col multi 1.90 1.90
436 A191 24col multi 1.90 1.90
a. Pair, #435-436 9.00 7.50
Nos. 433-436 (4) 5.80 4.60

Costa Rica-Panama Border Treaty, 50th Anniv. — A192

Designs: a, Flags, national arms. b, Presidents. c, Map.

1991, May 24 Litho. ***Perf. 10½***
437 Strip of 3 4.50 2.50
a.-c. A192 10col Any single 1.00 .60

No. 437 was issued in a sheet of five strips. Value $20.

Discovery of America, 500th Anniv. (in 1992) — A193

1991, Oct. 11 Litho. ***Perf. 13½***
438 A193 4col multicolored .95 .25

No. 409 Surcharged

No. 296 Surcharged

1991, Oct. 21 Litho. ***Perf. 10½***
439 A176 1col on 2col #409 .65 .25
440 A137 3col on 8.50col #296 .65 .25

Former Presidents, Supreme Court of Justice — A194

Designs: a, Benito Serrano Jimenez. b, Luis Davila Solera. c, Fernando Baudrit Solera. d, Alejandro Alvarado Garcia.

Perf. 14½x13½

1992, Feb. 28 **Litho.**
441 A194 5col Strip of 4, #a.-d. 4.50 2.00

A sheet exists containing an unissued 5th stamp. Value, sheet $500.

DINADECO, Natl. Directorate of Community Development, 25th Anniv. A195

1992, Apr. 28 **Litho.** *Perf. 10½*
442 A195 15col multicolored 3.25 .60

Compare with No. C505.

A196

1992, May 26 **Litho.** *Perf. 13½*
443 A196 15col lake & black 1.50 .35

Dr. Solon Nunez Frutos, public health pioneer.

Solar Eclipse — A197

a, Total eclipse. b, Post Office Bldg. during eclipse. c, Partial eclipse.

1992, July 17 **Litho.** *Perf. 13*
444 A197 45col Strip of 3, #a.-c. 11.00 6.00

A198

1992, Aug. 14 **Litho.** *Perf. 13½*
445 A198 35col multicolored 2.25 .60

Interamerican Institute for Agricultural Cooperation, 50th anniv.

A199

1992, Nov. 5 **Litho.** *Perf. 10½*
446 A199 2col Waterfall 1.10 .40
447 A199 15col Coastline 1.60 .60

Cocos Island, 450th anniv. of discovery.

No. 427 Overprinted

Litho. & Engr.

1992, Nov. 27 *Perf. 12½*
448 A188 100col black & blue *5.00 2.50*

America Issue A200

15col, Anolis townsendi. 35col, Pinaroloxias inornata.

1992, Dec. 15 **Litho.** *Perf. 10½*
449 A200 15col multi *3.50* .30
450 A200 35col multi *5.50* .50

Natl. Theater A201

Detail from painting "Allegory of Fine Arts," by Roberto Fontana.

1993, Jan. 29 **Litho.** *Perf. 10½*
451 A201 20col multicolored 1.00 .60

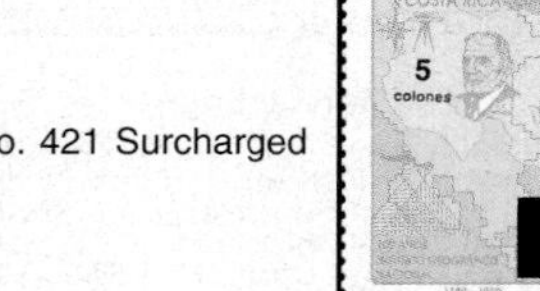
No. 421 Surcharged

1993, Mar. 26 **Litho.** *Perf. 13½*
452 A182 5col on 18col multi .75 .25

50,000 stamps originally were overprinted with a tiny block and four thin bars over the value, but this was considered unacceptable. So these stamps plus 1,550,000 unoverprinted stamps were overprinted with the large black square and surcharge, as shown.

Protection of the Dolphin A202

10col, Delphinus delphis. 20col, Stenella coeruleoalbus.

1993, May 17 **Litho.** *Perf. 10½*
453 A202 10col multicolored 2.50 1.25
454 A202 20col multicolored 4.50 1.25

Costa Rican Civil Service, 40th Anniv. — A203

1993, May 28 **Litho.** *Perf. 13½*
455 A203 5col multicolored .70 .25

Costa Rican Chamber of Industries, 50th Anniv. A204

1993, July 15 *Perf. 10½*
456 A204 45col multicolored 2.00 .90

School of Communication Sciences, University of Costa Rica, 25th Anniv. — A205

1993, Aug. 19 **Litho.** *Perf. 13½*
457 A205 20col black, blue & red 1.25 .50

Protection of the Tropical Rain Forest — A206

2col, Passiflora vitifolia. 35col, Gurania megistantha.

1993, Aug. 27 *Perf. 10½*
458 A206 2col multi 1.75 .40
459 A206 35col multi 2.75 .80

Social Guarantees and Labor Code, 50th Anniv. A207

1993, Sept. 14 **Litho.** *Perf. 10½*
460 A207 20col multicolored .75 .50

A208

1993, Oct. 25 **Litho.** *Perf. 13½*
461 A208 45col multicolored 1.25 .70

Intl. Assoc. of Professional Custom-House Agents, 15th Congress.

A209

1993, Nov. 26 *Perf. 10½*
462 A209 20col multicolored 1.10 .30

Miguel Angel Castro Carazo (1893-1960), educator and humanitarian.
For surcharge see No. 481.

Law School of Costa Rica, 150th Anniv. — A211

1993, Dec. 23 **Litho.** *Perf. 10½*
464 A211 20col multicolored .85 .40

Natl. Theater — A212

1994, Mar. 18 **Litho.** *Perf. 13*
465 A212 20col multi .85 .40

Marine Life — A213

5col, Cyphoma gibbosum. 10col, Ophioderma rubicundum. 15col, Myripristis jacobus. 20col, Holocanthus passer. 35col, Paranthias furcifer. 45col, Tubastraea coccinea. 50col, Acanthaster planci. 55col, Ocypode. 70col, Arothron meleagris. 100col, Thalassoma lucasanum.

Litho. & Embossed

1994, Apr. 29 *Perf. 12½x12*

466	A213	5col	multicolored	.45	.25
467	A213	10col	multicolored	.85	.25
468	A213	15col	multicolored	1.40	.30
469	A213	20col	multicolored	1.75	.35
470	A213	35col	multicolored	3.00	.55
471	A213	45col	multicolored	3.75	.75
472	A213	50col	multicolored	4.50	.85
473	A213	55col	multicolored	5.00	.95
474	A213	70col	multicolored	6.00	1.25
	Nos. 466-474 (9)			26.70	5.50

Souvenir Sheet

Perf. 13

475 A213 100col multicolored 11.00 8.00

America Issue A214

Illustrations from 19th century Book of Figueroa: a, Man on horseback. b, Back of ox carrying bundles.

1994, Dec. 19 Litho. *Perf. 10½*

476 A214 20col Pair, #a.-b. + label 10.00 6.00

No. 476 is a continuous design.

Rotary Intl., 90th Anniv. — A215

1995, Mar. Litho. *Perf. 13½*

477 A215 20col multicolored 1.10 .50

Antonio Jose de Sucre (1795-1830) — A216

Design: 30col, Jose Marti (1853-95).

1995, June Litho. *Perf. 10½*

478 A216 10col multicolored .40 .25
479 A216 30col multicolored 1.00 .75

Guanacaste Institute, 50th Anniv. — A217

1995, July 24 *Perf. 13½*

480 A217 50col ol grn, blk & cream 1.40 1.00

No. 462 Surcharged in Blue or Black

1995, Sept. 11 Litho. *Perf. 10½*

481 A209 5col on 20col multi .60 .25

UN, 50th Anniv. — A218

1995, Oct. 24 Litho. *Perf. 10½*

482 A218 5col multicolored .65 .25

13th Natl. Philatelic Expo — A219

Paintings by Lola Fernández: No. 483, Noviembre. No. 484, Enero.

1995, Dec. 1

483 A219 50col multicolored 1.75 1.50
484 A219 50col multicolored 1.75 1.50
a. Pair, Nos. 483-484 13.00 12.00

America Issue A220

30col, Jabiru mycteria. No. 486, View of coast. No. 487, River, trees. 50col, Atta cephalotes.

1995, Dec. 25 Litho. *Rouletted 13½*

485 A220 30col multicolored 1.50 .80
486 A220 40col multicolored 1.50 1.25
487 A220 40col multicolored 1.50 1.25
a. Pair, #486-487 4.50 3.50
488 A220 50col multicolored 2.50 1.50
a. Souvenir sheet, #485-488 12.00 8.00
Nos. 485-488 (4) 7.00 4.80

Seaport City of Limón A221

Designs: a, Early picture of steam train. b, Photo of ship in port, 1922. c, Aerial view of seaport, 1995. d, Painting of fruit seller, by Diego Villalobos. e, Drawing of Calipso singers, by Jorge Esquivel.

1996, Jan. 31 Litho. *Perf. 10½*

489 Strip of 5 7.00 5.00
a.-e. A221 30col Any single 1.00 .60

Jerusalem, 3000th Anniv. — A222

1996, May 17 Litho. *Perf. 13½*

490 A222 30col multicolored 1.00 .75

1996 Summer Olympic Games, Atlanta A223

Olympic swimmers, coaches from Costa Rica: a, F. Rivas, M.M. Paris. b, S. Poll, R. Yglesias. c, C. Poll, A. Cruz.

1996, July 18 Litho. *Perf. 10½*

491 Strip of 3 4.25 3.50
a.-c. A223 5col Any single 1.25 .75

No. 491 is a continuous design.

A224

First lady, presidents: a, Juana del Castillo. b, Juan Mora Fernández. c, J.M. Castro Madriz. d, Pacífica Fernández.

1996, Sept. 13 Litho. *Perf. 10½*

492 Block of 4, #a.-d. 4.00 3.00
a.-d. A224 30col Any single 1.00 .60

Independence, 175th anniv. No. 492 was issued in sheets of 16 stamps.

A225

1996, Oct. 4 Litho. *Perf. 13½*

493 A225 15col multicolored .65 .25

Aqueducts and sewage systems, 35th anniv. Exists imperf.

A226

America issue (Paintings): No. 494, Black from Lemon, by Manuel da la Cruz González. No. 495, Peasant Women, by Gonzalo Morales Alvarado, vert.

1996, Dec. 16 *Perf. 10½*

494 A226 45col multicolored 2.75 1.00
495 A226 45col multicolored 2.75 1.00

A227

Entrance of the Saints at San Ramón, parade of people: a, Building with palm trees on top. b, Church on hill. c, Tree, holy family.

1997, Aug. 14 Litho. *Perf. 13½*

496 A227 30col Strip of 3 5.50 3.00
a.-c. A227 30col Any single 1.60 .60

Costa Rican traditions.

School of Fine Arts, Cent. A228

1997, Sept. 24 *Perf. 10½*

497 A228 50col multicolored 1.50 .70

Radio Netherlands, 50th Anniv. — A229

1997, Sept. 26 *Perf. 13½*

498 A229 45col multicolored 1.25 .65

Exists imperf.

14th Natl. Philatelic Exhibition A230

1997, Oct. 9 *Perf. 10½*

499 A230 30col Postmen 1.25 .50

America Issue.

Church of the Immaculate Conception, Heredia, Bicent. — A231

1997, Nov. 10 Litho. *Perf. 10½*

502 A231 50col multicolored 1.50 1.00

Second Republic, 50th Anniv. — A232

Former Pres. José Figueres demolishing wall of Fort Bellavista: 10col, 45col, Complete photo. 30col, Detail of Figueres' head. 50col, Hammer head hitting wall.

Litho. & Engr.

1998, Mar. 30 *Perf. 12½*

503 A232 10col multicolored .65 .40
504 A232 30col multicolored 1.00 .50
505 A232 45col multicolored 1.50 .60
506 A232 50col multicolored 1.75 .75
a. Souvenir sheet of 2, #504, 506 7.50 3.50

Natl. University, 25th Anniv. — A233

1998, July 27 Litho. *Perf. 10½*

507 A233 50col multicolored 2.75 1.25

Butterflies A234

10col, Caligo memnon. 15col, Morpho peleides. 20col, Papilio thoas. 30col, Siproeta stelenes. 35col, Ascia monuste. 40col, Parides iphidamas. 45col, Smyrna blonfildia. 50col, Callicore pitheas. 55col, Historis odius. 60col, Danaus plexippus.

1998, July 16

508 A234 10col multicolored .80 .30
509 A234 15col multicolored 1.25 .40
510 A234 20col multicolored 1.75 .60
511 A234 30col multicolored 2.50 .90
512 A234 35col multicolored 3.00 1.10
513 A234 40col multicolored 3.25 1.25
514 A234 45col multicolored 3.50 1.40
515 A234 50col multicolored 4.00 1.50
516 A234 55col multicolored 4.50 1.75
517 A234 60col multicolored 5.50 1.90
Nos. 508-517 (10) 30.05 11.10

1998 World Cup Soccer Championships, France — A235

1998, Feb. 27 Litho. *Perf. 10½*
518 A235 50col multicolored 1.50 1.00

A236

1998, Nov. 30 Litho. *Perf. 13½*
519 A236 50col brn, yel brn & lt yel 2.25 .80

Carmen Lyra (1888-1949), author.

Gandhi (1869-1948) — A237

1998, Dec. 11 Litho. *Perf. 13½*
520 A237 50col multicolored 2.75 1.40

Intl. Union for the Conservation of Nature, 50th Anniv. A238

Turtles: a, Rhinoclemmys pulcherrima. b, Trachemys scripta. c, Chelydra serpentina.

1998, Dec. 1
521 A238 Strip of 3 14.00 11.00
a. A238 70col multi 4.50 3.50
b. A238 60col multi 4.50 3.00
c. A238 70col multi 4.50 3.50

Mushrooms A239

No. 522: a, Morchella esculenta. b, Boletus edulis.

1999, July 2 Litho. *Perf. 10½*
522 Pair 5.00 4.50
a.-b. A239 50col Either single 2.25 2.25

SOS Children's Villages, 50th Anniv. — A240

1999, June Litho. *Perf. 10½*
523 A240 50col multicolored 2.75 .90

Costa Rican Institute of Electricity, 50th Anniv. A241

1999, Sept. 21 Litho. *Perf. 13¼*
524 A241 75col multi 1.00 .60

A242

1999, Oct. 7 Engr. *Perf. 13¾x14*
525 A242 300col violet 3.25 3.00

Archbishop Víctor M. Sanabria (1899-1952). See No. 538.

Intl. Year of Older Persons — A243

1999, Oct. 29 Litho. *Perf. 13¼*
526 A243 50col multi 1.00 .65

Supreme Election Tribunal, 50th Anniv. A244

1999, Nov. 5 *Perf. 10½*
527 A244 70col multi 2.00 .80

UPU, 125th Anniv. — A245

1999, Dec. 1 *Perf. 13¼*
528 A245 75col multi 1.10 .75

Carmen Granados (1915-99), Humorist — A246

1999, Dec. 1
529 A246 50col multi 1.10 .75

America Issue, A New Millennium Without Arms — A247

70col, Male face, both hands.

1999, Dec. 1
530 A247 50col shown 1.00 .50
531 A247 70col multicolored 1.25 .70

PhilexFrance '99 — A248

No. 533, Flower, Eiffel Tower.

1999, Dec. 1
532 A248 300col shown 5.00 3.50
533 A248 300col multi 5.00 3.50

Natl. Bank, 50th Anniv. — A249

No. 534 — Pre-Columbian artifacts: a, Jaguar. b, Scorpion. c, Bat. d, Crab. e, Beast with horns.

No. 535 — Obverse and reverse of coins: a, Gold, from 1825. b, Gold, from 1850. c, Silver one-eighth peso. d, Gold 20-peso. e, 1935 1-colon.

2000, Jan. 28 Litho. *Perf. 13¼*
534 Vert. strip of 5 9.50 7.00
a.-e. A249 60col Any single 1.25 1.00
535 Vert. strip of 5 22.50 12.50
a.-e. A249 90col Any single 3.00 1.50

Nos. 534-535 were printed in sheets of three strips. Value, set of two sheets $100.

2000 Summer Olympics, Sydney — A250

No. 536, 60col: a, Taekwando. b, Cycling. c, Swimming. d, Soccer.

No. 537, 70col: a, Running. b, Boxing. c, Men's rings. d, Tennis.

2000, Aug. 31 Blocks of 4, #a-d
536-537 A250 Set of 2 11.00 10.00

There were two printings of Nos. 536-537. In the first printing, colors are paler, and the green Olympic ring is misregistered on Nos. 536a-536d. In the second, colors are more intense, and the green ring is properly registered. Values the same.

Famous Person Type of 1999

Pres. Rafael A. Calderón Guardia (1900-70).

2000, Sept. 14 Engr. *Perf. 12½*
538 A242 100col deep blue 3.50 .50
a. Perf 13¾x14 5.00 1.50

Paintings by Max Jiménez — A251

No. 539: a, Fishermen in Cojimar. b, Adamant.

2000, Nov. Litho. *Perf. 10½*
539 Horiz. pair 4.50 2.50
a.-b. A251 50col Either single 1.00 .50

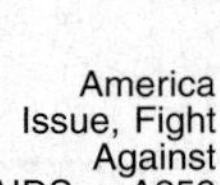

America Issue, Fight Against AIDS — A252

Designs: 60col, Stylized people. 90col, Stylized person.

2000, Dec. *Perf. 13¼*
540-541 A252 Set of 2 3.00 2.00

Christmas — A253

2000, Dec.
542 A253 100col multi 1.75 1.25

America Issue — UNESCO World Heritage A254

Birds form Cocos Island Natl. Park: 95col, Coccyzus ferrugineus. 115col, Pinaroloxias inornata.

2001, Apr. 5 Litho. *Perf. 10½*
543-544 A254 Set of 2 6.50 4.00

Costa Rica — Netherlands Diplomatic Relations, 150th Anniv. — A255

2001, July 20
545 A255 65col multi 2.00 .75

No. 429 Surcharged

2001 Method and Perf. As Before
546 A188 65col on 500col multi 1.25 .75
547 A188 80col on 500col multi 2.25 1.00
548 A188 95col on 500col multi 3.00 1.10
Nos. 546-548 (3) 6.50 2.85

Issued: No. 546, 8/24. Nos. 547-548, 9/7.

Third Hispanic-Costa Rican Exposition — A256

Orchids: a, Guaria turrialba. b, Tricopilia.

2001, Oct. 5 Litho. *Perf. 13¼*
549 A256 65col Horiz. pair, #a-b 5.50 4.00

Campaign Against Child Labor — A257

2001, Nov. 15 ***Perf. 13¼***
550 A257 100col multi 2.00 1.25

Pres. Tomás Guardia (1832-82) and Locomotive — A258

2001, Nov. 21
551 A258 65col multi 3.25 .80

A second printing of No. 551 was issued in 2002. It features a lighter beige and has yellow gum. This printing of 500 sheets of 15 stamps was made to complete the contract. Value, unused $25.

Costa Rican Team for 2002 World Cup Soccer Championships, Japan and Korea — A259

2002, Mar. 15 ***Perf. 10½***
552 A259 65col multi 2.25 .80

No. 428 Surcharged in Red

Litho. & Engr.

2002, Jan. 24 ***Perf. 12½***
553 A188 65col on 200col multi 1.25 .75

America Issue — Youth, Education and Literacy — A260

Designs: 65col, Children and globe. 100col, Blind person reading Braille.

Litho. & Embossed

2002, Mar. ***Perf. 10½***
554-555 A260 Set of 2 3.25 2.00

Taiwan Friendship Bridge A261

2002, Apr. 3 **Litho.**
556 A261 95col multi 2.40 1.00

16th Rio Group Congress A262

2002, Apr. 10
557 A262 65col blue & green 1.25 .75

Pan-American Health Organization, Cent. — A263

No. 558: a, People (red denomination at UR). b, Emblem. c, Mother and child (black denomination at LR). d, Child and man (red denomination at LR).
50col, Emblem.

2002, July 5
558 A263 10col Block of 4, #a-d 2.25 1.40
559 A263 50col multi 1.50 1.00

In Remembrance of Sept. 11, 2001 Terrorist Attacks — A264

Litho. & Embossed

2002, Sept. 11
560 A264 110col multi 4.25 2.00

Marine Life of Uvita Island A265

Designs: No. 561, 75col, Gorgona flabellum. No. 562, 75col, Ulva lactuca. No. 563, 75col, Cittarium pica. No. 564, 75col, Liriope tetraphyla.

Litho & Embossed

2002, Sept. 25
561-564 A265 Set of 4 7.00 6.50

Space Exploration — A266

No. 565: a, Dr. Franklin Chang-Diaz, astronaut, and space shuttle. b, Phanaeus changdiazi and satellite.

Litho. & Embossed

2003, June 15 ***Perf. 10½***
565 A266 115col Horiz. pair, #a-b 7.00 7.00

No. 565 was printed in sheets of 5 pairs. Value, $37.50.

Coco Island National Park — A267

No. 566: a, Denomination at UR. b, Denomination at UL.

2003, Aug. 1
566 A267 75col Horiz. pair, #a-b 4.00 4.00

No. 566 was printed in sheets of 5 pairs. Value, $27.50.

America Issue - Fish — A268

No. 567: a, Archocentrus sajica. b, Astatheros diquis.

2003
567 A268 110col Horiz. pair, #a-b 6.00 5.50

Scenes from Cocorí, by Joaquín Gutiérrez — A269

No. 568: a, Boy, turtle, monkey and bird. b, Boy looking at reflection in water. c, Toucan in tree, boy and monkey on ground. d, Sailor, girl and boy. e, Boy, bird on branch. f, Jaguar, turtle armadillo, monkey, boy and father. g, Boy and monkey pushing turtle. h, Monkey with open arms, turtle, boy. i, Mother and boy. j, Mother, boy, rose bush. k, Boy, father playing musical instrument (80x150mm).

Litho. & Embossed

2003, Sept. 3 ***Perf. 10½***
568 A269 Sheet of 11 17.00 17.00
a.-j. 25col Any single .80 .60
k. 225col multi 5.00 5.00

National Anthem, Cent. — A270

No. 569: a, Lyricist José Maria Zeledón (24x35mm). b, Flag, text of anthem (49x35mm).

2003, Sept. 10 **Litho.**
569 A270 75col Horiz. pair, #a-b 4.50 4.25

No. 569 was printed in sheets of 5 pairs. Value, $24.

Election of Pope John Paul II, 25th Anniv. — A271

2003, Oct. 16 **Litho.** ***Perf. 13¼x13½***
570 A271 130col multi 3.25 3.00

Charles Lindbergh's Flight to Costa Rica, 75th Anniv. — A272

Litho. & Embossed

2003, Dec. 16 ***Perf. 13½x13¼***
571 A272 110col multi 2.40 2.25

Guayabo de Turrialba Archaeological Monument — A273

2003, Dec. 18
572 A273 110col multi 2.40 2.25

America Issue A274

Flora: No. 573, 75col, Ceiba pentandra. No. 574, 75col, Tetranema floribundum. 90col, Ceiba pentandra, diff. 110col, Tetranema gamboanum.

2004, Mar. 23 **Litho.** ***Perf. 10½***
573-576 A274 Set of 4 7.00 6.50

Volcanoes A275

Designs: 85col, Arenal. 120col, Irazú. 140col, Poás.

2004-05 ***Perf. 10½***
577-579 A275 Set of 3 7.00 7.00
577a Perf. 13¼ ('05) 1.75 1.75
578a Perf. 13¼ ('05) 3.00 3.00
579a Perf. 13¼ ('05) 3.25 3.25

Issued: Nos. 577-579, 6/24/04; 577a, 578a, 579a, 2005.
Nos. 577a, 578a and 579a have printer's inscription "LIL S.A."

2004 Summer Olympics, Athens A276

No. 580 — Various athletes in: a, Blue. b, Yellow orange. c, Green. d, Red.

2004, July 15
580 Horiz. strip of 4 11.00 11.00
a.-d. A276 120col Any single 2.50 2.50

A277

Design: Dr. Miguel Angel Rodríguez, Organization of American States President.

2004, Sept. 15
581 A277 120col multi 2.40 2.25

FIFA (Fédération Internationale de Football Association), Cent. — A278

No. 582: a, Emblem (34x34mm). b, Soccer player and field (39x34mm).

2004, Feb. 15 Litho. *Perf. 10½*
582 A278 140col Horiz. pair, #a-b 9.50 9.00

No. 582 was printed in sheets of 5 pairs. Value, $54.

Rotary International, Cent. — A279

No. 583: a, Emblem and frog. b, Centenary emblem. c, Emblem and butterfly.

2005, Feb. 23
583 Horiz. strip of 3 9.00 8.25
a.-c. A279 140col Any single 2.50 2.50

Souvenir Sheet

Popes — A280

No. 584: a, Pope John Paul II (1920-2005). b, Pope Benedict XVI.

2005, Aug. 22
584 A280 140col Sheet of 4, 2 each #a-b 11.00 11.00
a.-b. A281 95col Either single 5.00 5.00

An imperf. sheet lacking postal validity exists. Value, $150.

Intl. Year of Physics — A281

No. 585: a, Albert Einstein (1879-1955). b, Max Planck (1858-1947).

2005, June 7
585 Horiz. pair 4.50 4.25
a.-b. A281 95col Either single 2.00 2.00

No. 585 was printed in sheets of five pairs. Value, $25.

Flora and Fauna in National Parks — A282

No. 586: a, Passiflora vitifolia. b, Dryas iulia moderata. c, Potos flavus.

2005, Oct. 11 Litho. *Perf. 10½*
586 Strip of 3 5.25 5.00
a.-c. A282 85col Any single 1.50 1.50

America Issue, Fight Against Poverty — A283

No. 587: a, Child at computer. b, Man sawing wood. c, Medical worker.

2005, Oct. 19
587 Strip of 3 7.75 7.25
a.-c. A283 120col Any single 2.25 2.25

Intl. Year of Sports and Physical Education A284

2005, Dec. 6
588 A284 85col multi 2.00 1.90

Cartago Sport Club, Cent. — A285

2006, Mar. 20
589 A285 85col multi 2.00 2.00

No. 589 was printed in sheets of 5. Value, $12.

Miniature Sheet

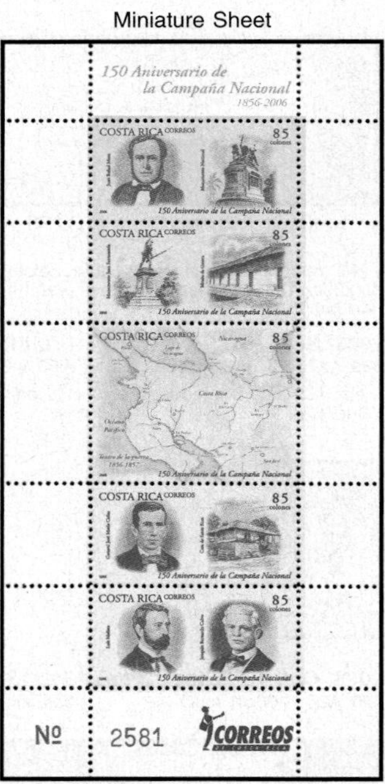

National Campaign Against Nicaraguan Pres. William Walker, 150th Anniv. — A286

No. 590: a, Juan Rafael Mora, National Monument. b, Juan Santamaría Monument, barracks. c, Map (50x40mm). d, Gen. José María Cañas, Santa Rosa House. e, Luis Molina, Joaquín Bernardo Calvo.

2006, Apr. 7
590 A286 85col Sheet of 5, #a-e 9.50 9.50

2006 World Cup Soccer Championships, Germany — A287

2006, May 15
591 A287 120col multi 3.00 2.75

No. 591 was printed in sheets of 9 + 6 tabs. Value, $27.50.

America Issue, Energy Conservation — A288

2006, July 31 Litho. *Perf. 10½*
592 A288 155col multi + label 3.50 3.25

Miniature Sheet

Birds and Marine Life of Cocos Island — A289

No. 593: a, Sula sula. b, Mycteroperca olfax. c, Zanclus cornutis. d, Eretmochely imbricaas. e, Tursiops truncatus. f, Myripristis berndti. g, Dendroica petechia aureola. h, Carcharhinus limbatus. i, Anous stolidus. j, Acarus rubroviolaceus.

2006, Aug. 25 Litho. *Perf. 10½*
593 A289 180col Sheet of 10, #a-j 47.50 47.50

Pres. José Figueres Ferrer (1906-90) — A290

2006, Sept. 25 *Perf. 10½*
594 A290 115col gray & multi 3.25 3.00

Souvenir Sheet

Imperf

595 A290 1000col tan & multi 30.00 30.00

No. 594 was printed in sheets of 6 + 3 labels. Value, $20.

Fruits A291

No. 596: a, Hymenaea courbaril. b, Bixa orellana. c, Garcinia intermedia.

2006, Oct. 12 *Perf. 10½*
596 Strip of 3 12.50 12.00
a.-c. A291 155col Any single 4.00 4.00

National Symbols — A292

No. 597: a, Flag. b, Coat of arms.

2006, Nov. 27
597 A292 155col Pair, #a-b 6.50 6.00

Printed in sheets containing two pairs. Value, $12.50.

Pres. Francisco J. Orlich (1907-69) — A293

2007, Mar. 7
598 A293 115col multi 3.00 3.00

No. 598 was printed in sheets of 6 + central label. Value, $20.

Orchids — A294

No. 599: a, Guarianthe skinneri (pink flowers). b, Galeandra arundinis. c, Encyclia ossenbachiana. d, Dracula inexperata. e, Guarianthe skinneri (white flowers). f, Kefersteinia retanae. g, Coryanthes kaiseriana. h, Psychopsis krameriana. i, Chondroscaphe yamilethae. j, Cattleya dowiana.
1000col, Brassia suavissima.

2007, Mar. 19 Litho. *Perf. 10½*
599 A294 180col Sheet of 10, #a-j 30.00 30.00

Souvenir Sheet

Imperf

600 A294 1000col multi 40.00 40.00

No. 599 contains ten 45x37mm stamps. No. 600 has simulated perforations.

Salesian Order in Costa Rica, Cent. — A295

2007, Apr. 30 *Perf. 10½*
601 A295 110col multi 3.25 3.25

Miniature Sheet

Pre-Columbian Art — A296

No. 602: a, Frog-shaped gold pendant (25x45mm). b, Bird-shaped jadeite pendant (25x45mm). c, Stone metate, horiz. (50x30mm). d, Ceramic censer with alligator (25x45mm). e, Stone figure of warrior (25x45mm).

2007, May 4

602 A296 155col Sheet of 5, #a-e 16.00 16.00

America Issue, Education For All — A297

No. 603: a, 115col, Teacher and students. b, 155col, Family around fire.

2007, June 8

603 A297 Horiz. pair 7.50 7.25

Plasma Technology — A298

No. 604: a, Astronaut and spacecraft's robot arm. b, Plasma containment vessel.

2007, July 6

604 A298 240col Horiz. pair, #a-b 10.00 9.50

Nos. 604a and 604b were printed in sheets of containing two of each stamp. Value, $20.

Guanacaste Musical Instruments — A299

Designs: No. 605, 115col, Marimba. No. 606, 115col, Quijongo, vert. (30x50mm).

2007, July 25

605-606 A299 Set of 2 5.00 4.50

Nos. 605-606 were printed in sheets containing two of each stamp + label. Value, $10.

Virgin of the Angels Icon, 225th Anniv. as Patron of Cartago — A300

No. 607 — Icon with denomination at: a, LR. b, LL.
1000col, Interior of Cartago Basilica, vert.

2007, July 27

607 A300 115col Horiz. pair, #a-b 5.00 4.50

No. 607 was printed in sheets of 3 pairs + 1 label. Value, $15.

Souvenir Sheet

608 A300 1000col multi 30.00 30.00

No. 608 contains one 75x115mm stamp.

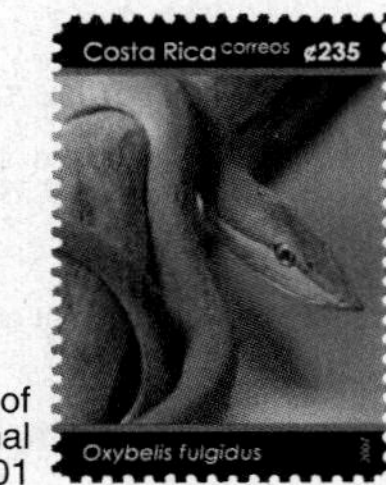

Fauna of National Parks — A301

No. 609: a, Oxybelis fulgidus. b, Stagmomantis sp. c, Heliodoxa jacula. d, Pulsatrix perspicillata.

2007, Aug. 17 Litho. *Perf. 10½*

609 Horiz. strip of 4 19.00 19.00
a.-d. A301 235col Any single 4.50 4.50

No. 609 was printed in sheets of two strips of 4. Value, $36.

2007 Special Olympics, Shanghai — A302

No. 610: a, Cycling. b, Swimming. c, Running.

2007, Sept. 10

610 Horiz. strip of 3 15.00 14.00
a.-c. A302 240col Any single 3.50 3.50

Accounts of My Aunt Panchita, Children's Book by Carmen Lyra — A303

No. 611, vert. — Text: a, Por qué Tío Conejo tiene las orejas tan largas. b, La Mica. c, Uvieta. d, Tío Conejo y los caites de su abuela.
1000col, De como Tío Conejo salió de un apuro.

2007, Oct. 18

611 A303 100col Sheet of 4, #a-d 9.00 8.00

Souvenir Sheet

612 A303 1000col multi 30.00 30.00

No. 611 contains four 37x50mm stamps.

Ox Cart Heritage — A304

No. 613: a, Man with oxen. b, Decorated wheel.

2007, Nov. 23

613 A304 180col Vert. pair, #a-b, + central label 7.50 7.50

Nos. 613a and 613b were printed in sheets of containing two of each stamp. Value, $15.

Esquipulas II Central American Peace Accords, 20th Anniv. — A305

No. 614 — Nobel Peace medal of Pres. Oscar Arias Sánchez: a, Reverse (three men). b, Obverse (Alfred Nobel).

2007, Dec. 10

614 A305 135col Horiz. pair, #a-b 6.00 6.00

No. 614 was printed in sheets of 4 pairs. Value, $24.

Dr. Fernando Centeno Güell (1907-93), Poet and Educator — A306

2008, Feb. 14

615 A306 115col multi 2.50 2.25

No. 615 was printed in sheets of 6. Value, $15.

Churches — A307

No. 616: a, Our Lord of Agony Chapel, Guanacaste. b, San Francisco Church, San José. c, Our Lady of Sorrow Church, San José. d, Santa Ana Church, San José. e, Our Lady of Carmel Cathedral, Puntarenas. f, San Bartolomé Apóstol Church, Heredia.
1000col, Our Lady of Mercy Parish Church, San José.

2008, Mar. 17

616 A307 230col Sheet of 6, #a-f 27.50 27.50

Souvenir Sheet

617 A307 1000col multi 70.00 40.00

No. 616 contains six 40x40mm stamps.

Souvenir Sheet

Women's Superior College, 120th Anniv. — A308

2008, Mar. 31

618 A308 1000col multi 30.00 30.00

Miniature Sheet

Marine Mammals — A309

No. 619: a, Megaptera novaengliae, side view. b, Sotalia guianensis. c, Stenella attenuata. d, Megaptera novaengliae flukes.

2008, June 16 Litho. *Perf. 10½*

619 A309 240col Sheet of 4, #a-d 20.00 20.00

Intl. Year of Planet Earth — A310

No. 620: a, San Vicente Cataracts. b, Santa Elena Peninsula.

2008, July 1

620 Pair 7.50 7.00
a.-b. A310 175col Either single 3.50 3.50

Nos. 620a and 620b were printed in sheets of containing two of each stamp. Value, $15.

Miniature Sheet

Art — A311

No. 621: a, La Ultima Escena, by Rudy Espinoza. b, Mujer que Avanza, sculpture by Crisanto Badilla. c, Transitoriedad del Hombre, by Miguel Hernández. d, Arquetipo, by Lola Fernández.

2008, July 3

621 A311 240col Sheet of 4, #a-d 20.00 19.00

Miniature Sheet

Ministry of Labor and Social Security, 80th Anniv. — A312

No. 622 — Details from mural "The Second Republic," by Luccio Ranucci: a, Man with hat, striped pole. b, Woman with basket of fruit. c, Man and woman embracing. d, Man carrying sack on head.

2008, Aug. 28 Litho. *Perf. 10½*

622 A312 240col Sheet of 4, #a-d 20.00 19.00

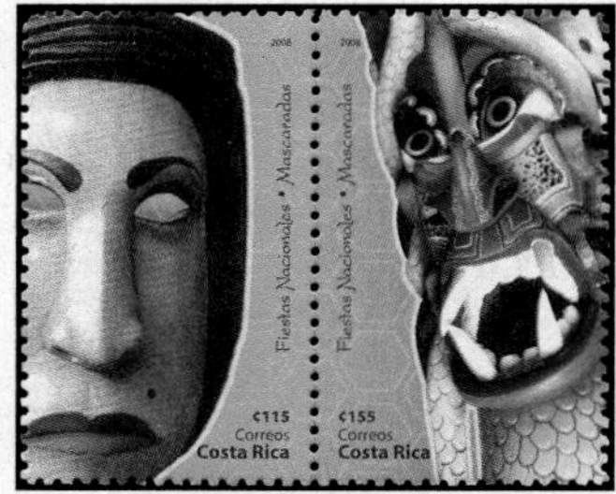

Masks — A313

No. 623 — Masks with background colors of: a, 115col, Brown orange. b, 155col, Green.

2008, Oct. 31

623 A313 Horiz. pair, #a-b 6.00 5.50

Nos. 623a and 623b were printed in sheets of containing two of each stamp. Value, $12.

Hogar Crea Drug Rehabilitation Centers in Costa Rica, 25th Anniv. — A314

2009, Feb. 25 Litho. *Perf. 10½*

624 A314 160col multi 3.25 3.25

No. 624 was issued in sheets of 6. Value, $16.

Carlos Luis Fallas (1906-66), Author — A315

2009, Apr. 30 Litho. *Perf. 10½*

625 A315 150col multi 2.25 2.00

No. 625 was issued in sheets of 6. Value, $13.

Miniature Sheet

Children's Literature — A316

No. 626: a, Tolo, the Giant North Wind (kite), by Adela Ferreto de Saénz. b, The Ship of the Stars (ship and boy), by Alfredo Cardona Peña. c, Old Stories (rabbit and gourds), by María Leal de Noguera. d, Paul's Music (boy holding box), by Lara Ríos.

2009, May 27

626 A316 65col Sheet of 4, #a-d 6.00 5.00

Alberto Martén, Economist, Solidarity Movement Founder — A317

2009, June 19

627 A317 135col multi 2.75 2.75

Miniature Sheet

Costa Rican Electrical Institute (ICE), 60th Anniv. — A318

No. 628: a, People and ICE building. b, Construction workers in tunnel. c, Lineman on ladder. d, Computers and satellite dishes. e, Houses and windmills. f, Hand planting seedling, girl.

2009, June 30

628 A318 340col Sheet of 6, #a-f 32.50 32.50

Diplomatic Relations Between Costa Rica and Switzerland — A319

2009, July 8

629 A319 225col multi 4.50 4.25

Miniature Sheet

National Parks — A320

No. 630: a, Arenal Volcano. b, Celeste River. c, Cerro Chirripó. d, Cocos Island. e, Monteverde. f, Poás Volcano. g, Tortuguero.

2009, Aug. 24

630 A320 240col Sheet of 7, #a-g 9.50 9.25

America Issue, Traditional Games — A321

No. 631: a, Marbles. b, Kite flying.

2009, Sept. 9 Litho. *Perf. 10½*

631 Horiz. pair 2.50 2.00
a.-b. A321 135col Either single .75 .75

Intl. Holocaust Remembrance Day — A322

2010, Jan. 27 *Perf. 13¼*

632 A322 500col gray & black 4.00 4.00

No. 632 was printed in sheets of four with labels at left, bottom and right. Value, $30.

Miniature Sheet

Locomotives — A323

No. 633: a, Steam locomotive, 1889. b, Electric Series AEG locomotive, 1926. c, Yellow and white Apolo Series Diesel-electric locomotive, 1990. d, Blue, white and red Diesel-electric locomotive, 1979-80.

2010, May 4 Litho. *Perf. 10½*
633 A323 200col Sheet of 4, #a-d 5.00 5.00

America Issue, National Symbols — A324

2010, June 24

634		Horiz. pair	6.50	6.50
a.	A324 280col Turdus grayi		2.00	2.00
b.	A324 340col Odocoileus virginianus		3.00	3.00

No. 634 was printed in sheets containing two pairs. Value, $15.

Miniature Sheet

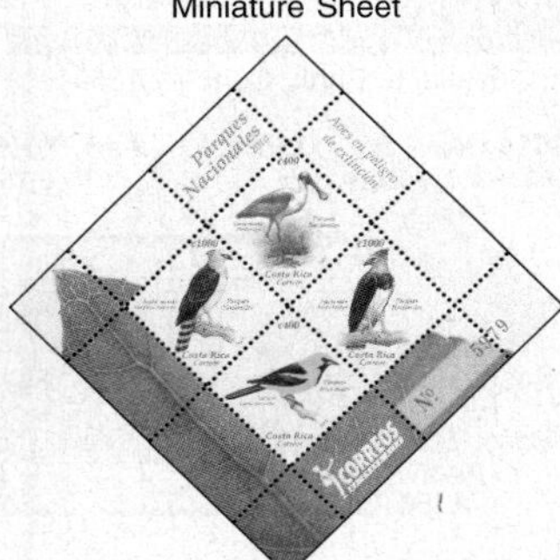

Endangered Birds — A325

No. 635: a, 400col, Platalea ajaja. b, 400col, Icterus mesomelas. c, 1000col, Morphnus guianensis. d, 1000col, Harpia harpyja.

2010, June 24 Litho. *Perf. 10½*
635 A325 Sheet of 4, #a-d 16.00 15.00

University Anniversaries — A326

No. 636: a, Mural by Eduardo Torijano at University of Costa Rica. b, Monument to Disarmament, Work and Peace by Thelvia Marin at Univeristy for Peace.

2010, Aug. 26
636 A326 500col Pair, #a-b 6.00 5.50

University of Costa Rica, 70th anniv., University for Peace, 30th anniv.

Miniature Sheet

Details of Sculptures by Jiménez Deredia — A327

No. 637: a, 225col, Pareja. b, 225col, Ricordo Profondo. c, 395col, Continuación. d, 395col, Génesi Ricordo Profondo. Names of sculptures are in sheet margin above stamps.

Perf. 10½ on 2 or 3 Sides

2011, Feb. 23
637 A327 Sheet of 4, #a-d, + label 7.50 6.50

Souvenir Sheet

Opening of New National Stadium — A328

No. 638 — National Stadium built in: a, 1924. b, 2011.

2011, Mar. 26 *Perf. 10½*
638 A328 1000col Sheet of 2, #a-b 11.00 10.00

Pres. Laura Chinchilla A329

2011, May 9 *Perf. 10½ Vert.*
639 A329 340col multi 2.25 2.00

No. 639 was printed in sheets of 2 + 2 labels. Value, $8.

Souvenir Sheet

Cartoons by Costa Rican Artists — A330

No. 640 — Cartoons by: a, 500col, Francisco "Paco" Hernández (1885-1961) and Noé Solano (1889-1971). b, 1000col, Hugo Diaz "Lalo" (1930-2001) and Jorge Chavarria "Kokin" (1932-94).

2011, June 15 *Perf. 10½*
640 A330 Sheet of 2, #a-b 9.00 8.50

Miniature Sheet

Athletes — A331

No. 641: a, 200col, Hanna Gabriel, boxer. b, 200col, Nery Brenes, sprinter. c, 330col, Bryan Ruiz, soccer player. d, 330col, Andrey Amador, cyclist.

2011, July 14
641 A331 Sheet of 4, #a-d 7.00 6.00

Rights of the Child — A332

No. 642 — Banner inscribed: a, Participación. b, No Discriminación. c, Educación.

2011, Aug. 12

642		Horiz. strip of 3	7.25	6.50
a.	A332 225col multi		1.25	1.10
b.	A332 340col multi		2.00	1.75
c.	A332 600col multi		3.25	3.00

Miniature Sheet

Flora and Fauna of Monteverde Children's Forest — A333

No. 643: a, 500col, Forest and lake. b, 500col, Lithobates vibicarius. c, 1000col, Lepanthes ciliisepala. d, 1000col, Leopardus wiedii.

2011, Aug. 24 *Perf. 10½ on 3 Sides*
643 A333 Sheet of 4, #a-d, + 2 labels 17.00 17.00

Tricolín, Comic Strip by Carlos Figueroa — A334

No. 644: a, Tricolín, Tricolína and Costa Rican flag. b, Tricolín and Tricolína donating money for Red Cross. c, Tricolín and Pepín planting flower. d, Tricolín, Tricolína, and Pepín.

2011, Sept. 9 *Die Cut Perf. 12x11½*
Self-Adhesive

644		Block or horiz. strip of 4	16.00	13.00
a.	A334 300col multi		3.50	3.50
b.	A334 320col multi		3.50	3.50
c.	A334 350col multi		3.75	3.75
d.	A334 395col multi		4.00	4.00

Mailboxes — A335

No. 645: a, Black mailbox. b, Blue mailbox.

2011, Oct. 10 *Perf. 10½*
645 A335 400col Pair, #a-b 5.50 5.00

America issue. No. 645 was printed in sheets containing two pairs. Value, $11.

Souvenir Sheet

Scouting in Costa Rica, Cent. — A336

No. 646 — Boy Scouts and Girl Guides: a, Near tents. b, Around campfire.

2011, Oct. 28
646 A336 340col Sheet of 2, #a-b 3.75 3.50

Souvenir Sheet

National Museum, 125th Anniv. — A337

No. 647: a, Grinding stone, butterfly at right. b, Butterfly at left, Pre-Columbian stone sphere.

2012, May 4
647 A337 395col Sheet of 2, #a-b 4.25 4.00

Bank of Costa Rica, 135th Anniv. A338

2012, June 7
648 A338 275col multi 1.75 1.50

No. 648 was printed in sheets of 2. Value, $3.50.

Souvenir Sheet

2012 Summer Olympics, London — A339

No. 649: a, 365col, Runner. b. 435col, Taekwondo.

2012, June 25
649 A339 Sheet of 2, #a-b 4.50 4.25

Souvenir Sheet

Intl. Year of Cooperatives — A340

No. 650: a, 275col, People holding rainbow and trees. b, 395col, People wrapping ribbons around sphere.

2012, July 6
650 A340 Sheet of 2, #a-b 3.75 3.50

Manuel Antonio National Park — A341

2012, Aug. 24 ***Perf. 10½ Horiz.***

Booklet Stamp

651 A341 545col multi 3.25 3.00
a. Booklet pane of 3 15.00 —
Complete booklet, #651a 20.00

Souvenir Sheet

America Issue — A342

No. 652: a, 385col, Legend of La Segua. b, 485col, Legend of the Cart Without Oxen.

2012, Oct. 9 ***Perf. 10½***
652 A342 Sheet of 2, #a-b 4.75 4.50

Souvenir Sheet

First Costa Rican Postage Stamps, 150th Anniv. — A343

No. 653: a, Costa Rica #1. b, Costa Rica #2.

Litho. & Embossed With Foil Application

2013, Apr. 17
653 A343 1000col Sheet of 2, #a-b 10.00 10.00

Souvenir Sheet

Bancrédito Commercial Bank, 95th Anniv. — A344

2013, May 15 **Litho.**
654 A344 400col multi 2.25 2.10

"Costa Rica, Land of Immigrants" A345

2013, June 20
655 A345 500col multi 2.75 2.75

No. 655 was printed in sheets of 2. Value, $6.

Souvenir Sheet

Braulio Carrillo National Park — A346

2013, Aug. 23 **Litho.** ***Perf.***
656 A346 1500col multi 8.00 7.50

Jorge Manuel Dengo (1918-2012), Vice-President — A347

2013, Sept. 18 **Litho.** ***Perf. 10½***
657 A347 500col multi 2.75 2.75

No. 657 was printed in sheets of 2. Value, $6.

Campaign Against Discrimination A348

2013, Oct. 9 **Litho.** ***Perf. 10½***
658 A348 300col multi 1.75 1.75

America issue. No. 658 was printed in sheets of 2 + central label. Value, $4.

Souvenir Sheet

Pres. Juan Rafael Mora Porras (1814-60) — A349

2014, Feb. 7 **Litho.** ***Perf. 10½***
659 A349 360col multi 2.25 2.00

America issue.

Souvenir Sheet

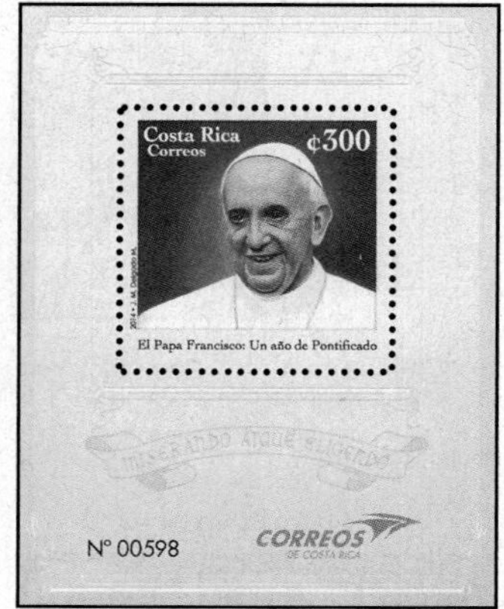

Election of Pope Francis, 1st Anniv. — A350

2014, Mar. 19 **Litho.** ***Perf. 10½***
660 A350 300col multi 2.25 2.25

Souvenir Sheet

2014 World Cup Soccer Championships, Brazil — A351

No. 661: a, 500col, 2014 World Cup mascot. b, 710col, World Cup.

2014, Apr. 24 **Litho.** ***Perf. 10½***
661 A351 Sheet of 2, #a-b 6.50 6.00

Souvenir Sheet

Endangered Cats in Corcovado National Park — A352

No. 662: a, 690col, Puma yagouaroundi. 1220col, Panthera onca.

2014, Aug. 22 **Litho.** ***Perf. 13***
662 A352 Sheet of 2, #a-b 10.00 9.50

Souvenir Sheet

National Bank, Cent. — A353

2014, Nov. 3 **Litho.** ***Perf. 10½***
663 A353 500col multi 2.75 2.75

Vuelta de Costa Rica Bicycle Race, 50th Anniv. A354

2014, Dec. 11 **Litho.** ***Perf. 13¼***
664 A354 500col multi 2.75 2.50

No. 664 was printed in sheets of 2. Value, $6.

Souvenir Sheet

Forensic Medicine in Costa Rica, 50th Anniv. — A355

2015, Jan. 30 Litho. *Perf. 10½*
665 A355 360col multi 2.25 2.00

Costa Rica Chamber of Commerce, Cent. — A356

2015, Mar. 4 Litho. *Perf. 10½*
666 A356 500col multi 2.90 2.75

No. 666 was printed in sheets of 2. Value, $5.75.

Souvenir Sheet

El Buen Pastor Episcopal Church, San José, 150th Anniv. — A357

2015, Apr. 23 Litho. *Imperf.*
667 A357 1000col multi 5.25 5.00

No. 667 has simulated perforations.

Souvenir Sheet

Education and Training For All — A358

No. 668 — Adult students with denomination in: a, Orange yellow. b, Blue.

2015, May 7 Litho. *Perf. 10½*
668 A358 690col Sheet of 2, #a-b 7.25 6.75

National Apprentice Institute, 50th anniv.; Normal School, cent.

Fire Departments in Costa Rica, 150th Anniv. — A359

No. 669: a, Fire fighters spraying water on fire. b, Fire fighters, truck and children.

2015, July 16 Litho. *Perf. 14*
669 A359 1500col Sheet of 2, #a-b 15.00 15.00

Nelson Mandela (1918-2013), President of South Africa — A360

2015, July 18 Litho. *Perf. 10½*
Booklet Stamp
670 A360 1220col multi 6.50 6.00
a. Booklet pane of 3 18.00 —
Complete booklet, #670a 19.00

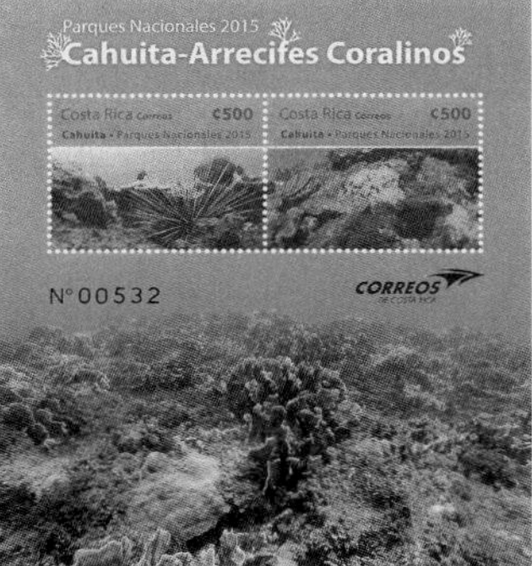

Coral Reefs of Cahuita National Park — A361

No. 671: a, Coral and sea urchin. b, Coral. 1000col, Coral, diff.

2015, Aug. 24 Litho. *Perf. 13x13¼*
671 A361 500col Sheet of 2, #a-b 3.75 3.50

Souvenir Sheet

672 A361 1000col multi 6.75 6.50

Campaign Against Human Trafficking A362

2015, Oct. 9 Litho. *Perf. 10½*
673 A362 500col black & blue 2.75 2.50

America Issue. No. 673 was printed in sheets of 2. Value, $5.25.

Coope Ande Credit Union, 50th Anniv. — A363

2015, Nov. 4 Litho. *Perf. 10½*
674 A363 600col multi 3.50 3.50

No. 674 was printed in sheets of 2. Value, $7.50.

Souvenir Sheet

Francisca Carrasco (1816-90), First Woman in Costa Rican Military — A364

Litho., Sheet Margin Litho. With Foil Application

2016, Apr. 4 *Perf. 10½*
675 A364 2060col multi 10.50 10.00

Souvenir Sheet

Pres. José Joaquín Trejos Fernández (1916-2010) — A365

2016, Apr. 18 Litho. *Perf. 10½*
676 A365 1950col multi 9.75 9.50

Souvenir Sheet

Archaeological Sites — A366

Diquís Culture Stone Spheres: No. 677: a, Stone sphere. b, Stone sphere and triangular ramp of stones at archaeological dig site.

Litho. & Thermography

2016, June 23 *Perf. 13¼x13½*
677 A366 650col Sheet of 2, #a-b 7.50 7.00

Souvenir Sheet

2016 Summer Olympics, Rio de Janeiro — A367

No. 678: a, 600col, Fencing. b, 1400col, Mountain biking.

2016, July 15 Litho. *Perf. 10½*
678 A367 Sheet of 2, #a-b 10.50 10.00

Dermochelys Coriacea — A368

No. 679 — Turtle facing: a, 1370col, Right. b, 2100col, Left.
1100col, Turtle facing forward.

Litho. & Embossed

2016, Aug. 24 *Perf. 13½x13¼*
679 A368 Sheet of 2, #a-b 5.00 5.00

Souvenir Sheet

680 A368 1100col multi 40.00 40.00

Fauna of Marino Las Baulas National Park.

Souvenir Sheet

Writers — A369

No. 681: a, 420col, Aquileo J. Echeverría (1866-1909). b, 650col, Yolanda Oreamuno (1916-56).

2016, Oct. 10 **Litho.** ***Perf. 10½***
681 A369 Sheet of 2, #a-b 5.75 5.25

Maternity, Sculpture by Francisco Zuñiga — A370

2016, Nov. 1 **Litho.** ***Perf. 10½***
682 A370 600col multi 3.25 3.00

Social Security Fund, 75th anniv. No. 682 was printed in sheets of 2. Value, $6.50.

Souvenir Sheet

University of Costa Rica Nursing School, Cent. — A371

2017, Mar. 1 **Litho.** ***Perf. 10½***
683 A371 2100col multi 10.50 10.00

Souvenir Sheet

International Women's Day — A372

No. 684: a, 550col, Shirley Cruz, soccer player. b, 600col, Christiana Figueres, diplomat. c, 600col, Sandra Cauffman, electrical engineer, physicist and NASA official.

2017, Mar. 8 **Litho.** ***Perf. 10½***
684 A372 Sheet of 3, #a-c 10.50 9.50

Souvenir Sheet

Panal, by Rafael "Felo" García — A373

2017, Apr. 7 **Litho.** ***Perf. 10½***
685 A373 2060col multi 10.50 10.00

National Directorate of Community Development, 50th anniv.

Souvenir Sheet

Guarianthe Skinneri and Great Wall of China — A374

2017, June 30 **Litho.** ***Perf. 10½***
686 A374 1400col multi 5.25 5.00

Diplomatic relations between Costa Rica and People's Republic of China.

Miniature Sheet

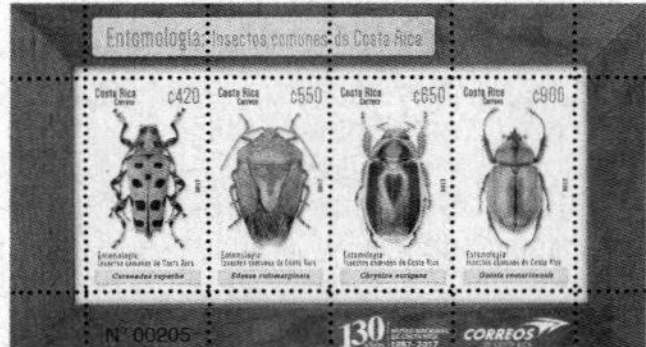

Insects — A375

No. 687: a, 420col, Carneades superba. b, 550col, Edessa rufomarginata. c, 650col, Chrysina aurigans, d, 900col, Golofa costaricensis.

2017, July 20 **Litho.** ***Perf. 10½***
687 A375 Sheet of 4, #a-d 9.75 8.75

National Museum of Costa Rica, 130th anniv.

Craugastor Escoces — A376

2017, Aug. 24 **Litho.** ***Perf. 10½***
688 A376 1100col multi 5.25 5.00

Juan Castro Blanco National Park. No. 688 was printed in sheets of 2. Value, $10.75.

Miniature Sheet

Independence, 200th Anniv. (in 2021) — A377

No. 689 — Costa Rican: a, 650col, Flag. b, 800col, Coat of arms. c, 900col, National anthem.

2017, Sept. 14 **Litho.** ***Perf. 13¼***
689 A377 Sheet of 6, 2 each #689a-689c, + 3 labels 22.50 22.50

America Issue — A378

No. 690 — San Juan-La Selva Biological Corridor: a, 420col, Parrot (30x40mm). b, 650col, Pond and forest (50x40mm).

2017, Sept. 27 **Litho.** ***Perf. 14***
690 A378 Horiz. pair, #a-b 3.75 3.75

Main Post Office, San José, Cent. — A379

No. 691: a, 1100col, Entrance. b, 1400col, Corner of building.
2100col, Arch decoration.

Litho. & Embossed

2017, Oct. 9 ***Perf. 10½***
691 A379 Sheet of 2, #a-b 12.00 11.00

Souvenir Sheet

692 A379 2100col multi 10.00 9.50

National Association of Educators, 75th Anniv. — A380

2017, Oct. 24 **Litho.** ***Perf. 13¼***
693 A380 600col multi 3.00 2.75

Souvenir Sheet

Fountain at University of Costa Rica — A381

2018, Mar. 5 **Litho.** ***Perf. 10½***
694 A381 2165col multi 10.50 10.00

Economic Sciences Faculty, 75th anniv., School of Collective Communication Sciences, 50th anniv.

Souvenir Sheet

Writers — A382

No. 695: a, 630col, Fabián Dobles (1918-97). b, 685col, Joaquín Gutiérrez (1918-2000).

2018, Apr. 4 **Litho.** ***Perf. 10½***
695 A382 Sheet of 2, #a-b 7.00 6.50

Miniature Sheet

Composers — A383

No. 696: a, 630col, Guadalupe Urbina. b, 630col, Fidel Gamboa (1961-2011). c, 685col, José Campany (1961-2001). d, 685col, Amelia Barquero.

2018, May 31 **Litho.** ***Perf. 10½***
696 A383 Sheet of 4, #a-d 13.50 12.50

Souvenir Sheet

2018 World Cup Soccer Championships, Russia — A384

No. 697: a, World Cup. b, Mascot Zabivaka.

2018, June 12 **Litho.** ***Perf. 13¾***
697 A384 1155col Sheet of 2, #a-b 11.00 10.50

Souvenir Sheet

Social Guarantees, 75th Anniv. — A385

2018, July 2 **Litho.** ***Perf. 10½***
698 A385 2890col multi 12.50 12.00

Nasua Narica — A386

2018, Aug. 24 **Litho.** ***Perf. 10½***
699 A386 580col multi 2.75 2.10

Carara National Park. No. 699 was printed in sheets of 2.

Souvenir Sheet

José María Castro Madriz (1818-92), First President of Costa Rica — A387

2018, Aug. 31 Litho. ***Perf. 10½***
700 A387 1155col multi 5.25 4.50

Miniature Sheet

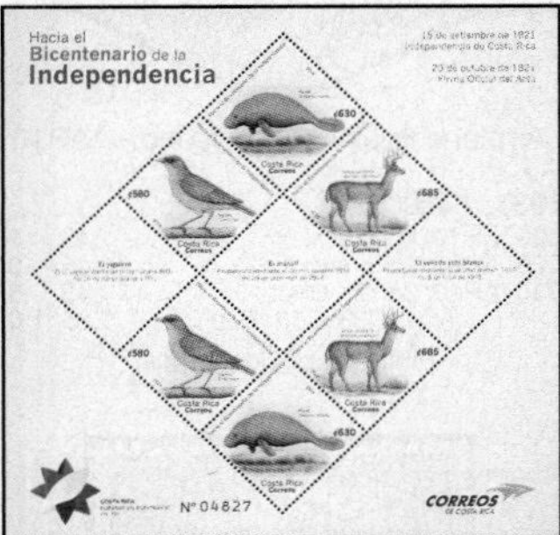

Independence, 200th Anniv. (in 2021) — A388

No. 701: a, 580col, Turdus craye. b, 630col, Trichechus manatus. c, 685col, Odocoileus virginianus.

Litho. & Embossed

2018, Sept. 13 ***Perf. 13¼***
701 A388 Sheet of 6, 2 each #701a-701c, + 3 labels 17.50 16.00

See No. 711.

America Issue — A389

No. 702: a, 445col, Chicken. b, 840col, Horse.

2018, Oct. 9 Litho. ***Perf. 10½***
702 A389 Horiz. pair, #a-b 6.00 5.50

Souvenir Sheet

Mauro Fernández Acuña (1843-1905), Politician — A390

2018, Dec. 19 Litho. ***Perf. 10½***
703 A390 2205col multi 9.50 9.00

Souvenir Sheet

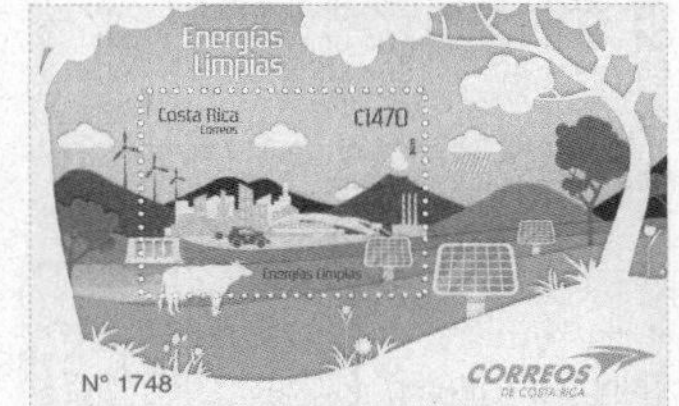

Clean Energy — A391

2019, Mar. 29 Litho. ***Perf. 10½***
704 A391 1470col multi 6.50 6.00

Souvenir Sheet

Pres. Jesús Jiménez (1823-97), Valeriano Fernández (1831-1925), Philosopher, and Caridad Salazar (1869-1948), Children's Writer — A392

2019, Apr. 22 Litho. ***Perf. 10½***
705 A392 2165col multi 9.50 9.00

Declaration of free and compulsory primary education, 150th anniv.

Souvenir Sheet

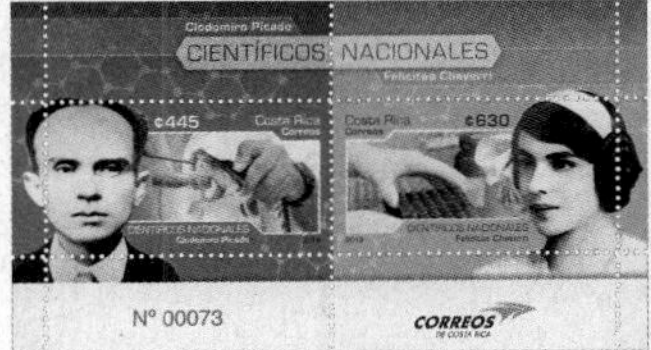

Scientists — A393

No. 706: a, 445col, Clodomiro Picado (1887-1944), developer of antivenins. b, 630col, Felícitas Chaverri (1886-1934), head of Department of Drugs and Narcotics.

2019, May 16 Litho. ***Perf. 10½***
706 A393 Sheet of 2, #a-b 5.75 5.25

Souvenir Sheet

Cities — A394

No. 707: a, 685col, Orosí. b, 845col, Santo Domingo.

2019, May 24 Litho. ***Perf. 10½***
707 A394 Sheet of 2, #a-b 7.75 7.25

Chirripó National Park — A395

No. 708: a, 580col, Slug. b, 685col, Stenostylus sp.
1440col, Crestones rock formation.

2019, Aug. 23 Litho. ***Perf. 13x13¼***
708 A395 Sheet of 2, #a-b 6.50 6.00

Souvenir Sheet

709 A395 1440col multi 7.25 7.00

Souvenir Sheet

Traditional Foods — A396

No. 710: a, 445col, Ceviche. b, 945col, Rice and beans.

2019, Aug. 30 Litho. ***Perf. 10½***
710 A396 Sheet of 2, #a-b 7.50 7.00

America issue.

Independence Type of 2018

Miniature Sheet

No. 711: a, 630col, Diquis stone spheres. b, 685col, National Theater. c, 840col, Crestones of Cerro Chirripó.

2019, Sept. 12 Litho. ***Perf. 13¼***
711 A388 Sheet of 6, 2 each #711a-711c, + 3 labels 22.50 20.00

Souvenir Sheet

Writers — A397

No. 712: a, 630col, Eunice Odio (1919-74), poet. b, 840col, Carmen Naranjo (1928-2012), writer.

2019, Oct. 9 Litho. ***Perf. 10½***
712 A397 Sheet of 2, #a-b 7.50 7.00

Souvenir Sheet

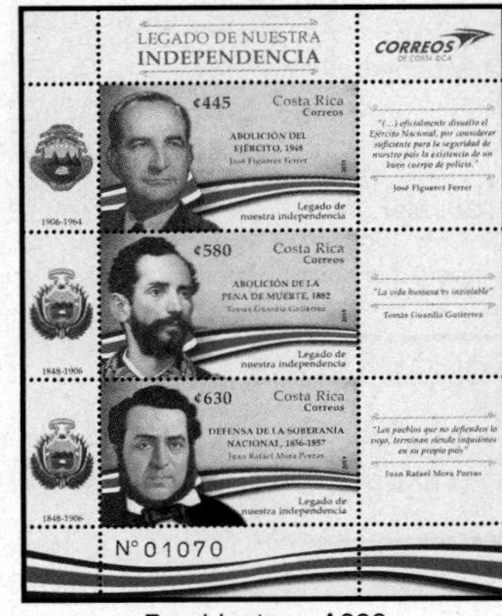

Presidents — A398

No. 713: a, 445col, Pres. José Figueres Ferrer (1906-90), abolisher of National Army. b, 580col, Pres. Tomás Guardia Gutiérrez (1831-82), abolisher of death penalty. c, 630col, Pres. Juan Rafael Mora Porres (1814-60), leader of national forces in 1856 Filibuster War.

2019, Oct. 29 Litho. ***Perf. 13¼***
713 A398 Sheet of 3, #a-c 8.75 8.00

American Convention on Human Rights (Pact of San José), 50th Anniv. — A399

No. 714: a, 685col, Gavel (26x36mm). b, 945col, Inter-American Court of Human Rights, San José (51x36mm).

2019, Nov. 22 Litho. ***Perf. 10½***
714 A399 Horiz. pair, #a-b 8.00 7.50

Souvenir Sheet

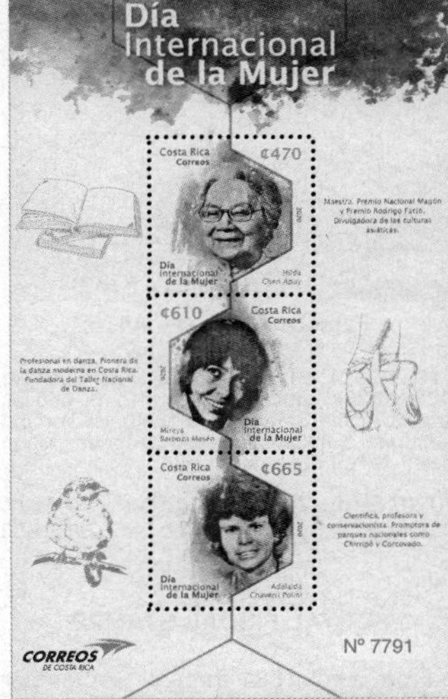

International Women's Day — A400

No. 715: a, 470col, Hilda Chen Apuy (1923-2017), co-founder of University of Costa Rica School of Anthropology. b, 610col, Mireya Barboza Mesén (1935-2000), ballerina and choreographer. c, 665col, Adelaida Chaverri Polini (1947-2003), ecologist.

2020, Mar. 9 Litho. ***Perf. 10½***
715 A400 Sheet of 3, #a-c 6.00 6.00

Souvenir Sheet

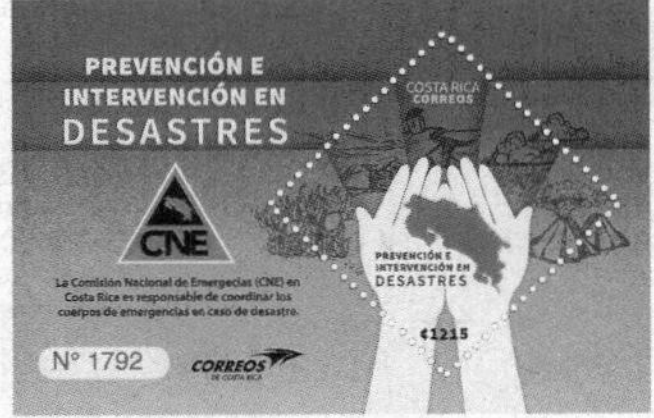

National Commission on Emergencies — A401

2020, Apr. 24 Litho. ***Perf. 10½***
716 A401 1215col multi 4.25 4.25

Souvenir Sheet

Musicians — A402

No. 717: a, 720col, María Mayela Padilla, singer and songwriter. b, 885col, Marta Fonseca and Bernal Villegas, rock musicians. c, 1215col, Walter "Gavitt" Ferguson, calypso singer and songwriter.

2020, May 29 Litho. *Perf. 10½*
717 A402 Sheet of 3, #a-c 10.00 10.00

Turrialba Volcano National Park — A404

2020, Aug. 24 Litho. *Perf. 10½*
719 A404 720col multi 2.50 2.50

Souvenir Sheet

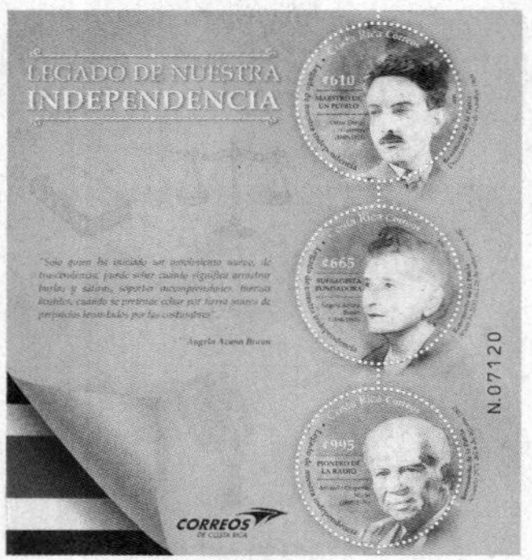

Famous People — A405

No. 720: a, 610col, Omar Dengo Guerrero (1888-1928), educator and writer. b, 665col, Angela Acuña Braun (1888-1983), lawyer and suffragist. c, 995col, Amando Céspedes Marín (1888-1976), radio newscaster.

2020, Sept. 24 Litho. *Perf.*
720 A405 Sheet of 3, #a-c 7.50 7.50

POSTAL-FISCAL STAMPS

From April 1884 through September 1889 revenue stamps were permitted for postal use, when post offices exhausted supplies of regular postage stamps.

Used values are for stamps with postal cancels.

PF1

1884 Engr. *Perf. 12*
AR1 PF1 1c rose .50 *5.00*
AR2 PF1 2c light blue *20.00* 5.00

PF2

1888
AR3 PF2 5c brown .50 *3.00*
AR4 PF2 10c blue *.25* 3.00

Nos. AR2-AR4 are normally found without gum.

SEMI-POSTAL STAMPS

No. 72 Surcharged in Red

1922 Unwmk. *Perf. 12*
B1 A56 5c + 5c orange 1.00 .40

Issued for the benefit of the Costa Rican Red Cross Society. In 1928, owing to a temporary shortage of the ordinary 5c stamp, No. B1 was placed on sale as a regular 5c stamp, the surtax being disregarded.

Discus Thrower SP1

Trophy SP2

Parthenon SP3

1924 Litho. *Imperf.*
B2 SP1 5c dark green 1.60 *2.00*
B3 SP2 10c carmine 1.60 *2.00*
B4 SP3 20c dark blue 20.00 *20.00*
a. Tête bêche pair 60.00 *60.00*

Perf. 12
B5 SP1 5c dark green 1.60 *2.25*
B6 SP2 10c carmine 1.60 *2.25*
B7 SP3 20c dark blue 3.50 *4.00*
a. Tête bêche pair 16.00 *20.00*
Nos. B2-B7 (6) 29.90 *32.50*

These stamps were sold at a premium of 10c each, to help defray the expenses of athletic games held at San José in Dec. 1924.

AIR POST STAMPS

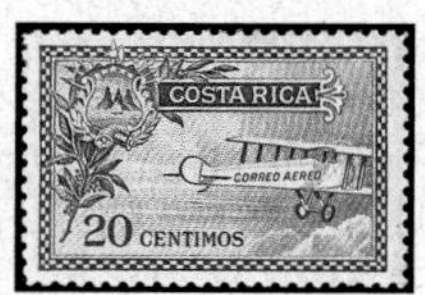

Airplane AP1

Perf. 12½
1926, June 4 Unwmk. Engr.
C1 AP1 20c ultramarine 3.00 .65

No. 123 Overprinted

1930, Mar. 14 *Perf. 12*
C2 A75 10c carmine rose 2.00 .25

Inverted or double overprints are fakes.

AP3

1930-32 *Perf. 12½*
C3 AP3 5c on 10c dk brn ('32) .40 .25
C4 AP3 20c on 50c ultra .50 .25
C5 AP3 40c on 50c ultra .60 .25
Nos. C3-C5 (3) 1.50 .75

Almost all inverted or double surcharges of Nos. C3-C5 are fakes.

Telegraph Stamp Overprinted

1930, Mar. 19
C6 AP3 1col orange 2.00 .50

No. O79 Surcharged in Red

1930, Mar. 11
C7 O7 8c on 1col lilac & blk .80 .65
C8 O7 20c on 1col lilac & blk 1.25 .70
C9 O7 40c on 1col lilac & blk 2.40 1.50
C10 O7 1col on 1col lilac & blk 3.50 2.00
Nos. C7-C10 (4) 7.95 4.85

AP6

Red Surcharge on Revenue Stamps

1931-32 *Perf. 12*
C11 AP6 2col on 2col gray grn 35.00 35.00
C12 AP6 3col on 5col lil brn 35.00 35.00
C13 AP6 5col on 10col gray blk 35.00 35.00
Nos. C11-C13 (3) 105.00 105.00

There were two printings of this issue which were practically identical in the colors of the stamps and the surcharges.

Nos. C11 and C13 have the date "1929" on the stamp, No. C12 has "1930."

AP7

Black Overprint on Telegraph Stamp

1932, Mar. 8 *Perf. 12½*
C14 AP7 40c green 3.00 .30
a. Inverted overprint 35.00 27.50

Unofficial "proofs," inverts and double overprints were made from a defaced plate.

Mail Plane about to Land AP8

Allegory of Flight AP9

1934, Mar. 14 *Perf. 12*
C15 AP8 5c green .25 .25
C16 AP8 10c carmine rose .25 .25
C17 AP8 15c chocolate .40 .25
C18 AP8 20c deep blue .40 .25
C19 AP8 25c deep orange .55 .25
C20 AP8 40c olive blk 1.75 .25
C21 AP8 50c gray blk .85 .25
C22 AP8 60c orange yel 1.50 .25
C23 AP8 75c dull violet 2.75 .50
C24 AP9 1col deep rose 1.50 .25
C25 AP9 2col lt blue 7.50 .95
C26 AP9 5col black 7.50 4.75
C27 AP9 10col red brown 10.00 8.00
Nos. C15-C27 (13) 35.20 16.45

Nos. C15-C27 with holes punched through were for use of government officials.

See Nos. C216-C219. For overprints see Nos. C67-C73, C92-C93, C103-C116, CO1-CO13.

Airplane over Poás Volcano — AP10

1937, Feb. 10
C28 AP10 1c black .45 .35
C29 AP10 2c brown .45 .35
C30 AP10 3c dk violet .45 .35
Nos. C28-C30 (3) 1.35 1.05

First Fair of Costa Rica.

Puntarenas — AP11

Perf. 12, 12½
1937, Dec. 15 Unwmk.
C31 AP11 2c black gray .25 .25
C32 AP11 5c green .30 .25
C33 AP11 20c deep blue .30 .25
C34 AP11 1.40col olive brn 2.50 2.50
Nos. C31-C34 (4) 3.35 3.25

National Bank AP12

1938, Jan. 11 Wmk. 229 *Perf. 12½*
C35 AP12 1c purple .25 .25
C36 AP12 3c red orange .25 .25
C37 AP12 10c carmine rose .30 .25
C38 AP12 75c brown 2.50 2.00
Nos. C35-C38 (4) 3.30 2.75

Nos. C31-C38 for the Natl. Products Exposition held at San José, Dec. 1937.

Airport Administration Building, La Sabana — AP13

1940, May 2 Engr. Unwmk.
C39 AP13 5c green .60 .25
C40 AP13 10c rose pink .60 .25
C41 AP13 25c lt blue .80 .25
C42 AP13 35c red brown .80 .25
C43 AP13 60c red org 1.25 .40
C44 AP13 85c violet 3.00 1.00
C45 AP13 2.35col turq grn 13.00 5.50
Nos. C39-C45 (7) 20.05 7.90

Opening of the Intl. Airport at La Sabana.

Duran Sanatorium AP14

Overprinted in Black

1940, Dec. 2 *Perf. 12*

C46 AP14 10c scarlet .25 .25
C47 AP14 15c purple .25 .25
C48 AP14 25c lt blue .50 .40
C49 AP14 35c bister brn .70 .65
C50 AP14 60c pck green 1.00 .95
C51 AP14 75c olive 2.75 2.50
C52 AP14 1.35col red org 8.75 8.00
C53 AP14 5col sepia 45.00 40.00
C54 AP14 10col red lilac 140.00 100.00
Nos. C46-C54 (9) 199.20 153.00

Pan-American Health Day. Nos. C46-C54 exist without overprint. Value, set $5,000.

No. 174 Surcharged in Black or Blue

1940, Dec. 17 *Perf. 14*

C55 A95 15c on 50c yel (Bk) 1.00 1.00
C56 A95 30c on 50c yel (Bl) 1.00 1.00

Pan-American Aviation Day, proclaimed by President F. D. Roosevelt.

The 15c surcharge exists normal and inverted on No. 171, Value, normal $50. Inverted surcharge is worth more.

International Soccer Game at National Stadium — AP15

1941, May 8 *Perf. 12*

C57 AP15 15c red .80 .25
C58 AP15 30c dp ultra .90 .25
C59 AP15 40c red brn .95 .35
C60 AP15 50c purple 1.40 .80
C61 AP15 60c brt green 1.60 .90
C62 AP15 75c yel org 2.75 1.40
C63 AP15 1col dull vio 4.75 4.50
C64 AP15 1.40col rose 9.50 8.75
C65 AP15 2col blue grn 20.00 17.50
C66 AP15 5col black 52.50 37.50
Nos. C57-C66 (10) 95.15 72.20

Caribbean and Central American Soccer Championship. See Nos. C121-C123. For surcharges see Nos. C145-C147.

Air Post Stamps of 1934 Overprinted or Surcharged in Black

1941, June 2

C67 AP8 5c on 20c dp bl .25 .25
C68 AP8 15c on 20c dp bl .25 .25
C69 AP8 40c on 75c dl vio .35 .25
C70 AP9 65c on 1col dp rose .65 .50
C71 AP9 1.40col on 2col lt bl 3.25 3.25
C72 AP9 5col black 12.00 12.00
C73 AP9 10col red brn 14.50 12.50
Nos. C67-C73 (7) 31.25 29.00

Issued in commemoration of the settlement of the Costa Rica-Panama border dispute.

Nos. C67-C73 are found with hyphen omitted in overprint.

Nos. C67-C69 exist with inverted overprint. Value, each, $35.

University Types of 1941

1941, Aug. 26 *Perf. 12*

C74 A107 15c salmon .25 .25
C75 A106 30c lt blue .30 .25
C76 A107 40c orange .40 .30
C77 A106 60c turq green .50 .40
C78 A107 1col violet 1.90 1.90
C79 A106 2col black 4.75 4.75
C80 A107 5col sepia 16.00 16.00
Nos. C74-C80 (7) 24.10 23.85

Portrait Type of 1943-47

Designs: 40c, Manuel Aguilar. No. C83, Francisco Morazan. No. C83A, Jose R. De Gallegos. 50c, Jose M. Alfaro. 60c, Francisco M. Oreamuno. 65c, Jose M. Castro. 85c, Juan Rafael Mora. 1col, Jose M. Montealegre. 1.05col, Braulio Carrillo. 1.15col, Jesus Jimenez. 1.40col, Bruno Carranza. 2col, Tomas Guardia.

1943-45 **Engr.**

C81 A109 10c rose pink .25 .25
C82 A109 40c blue .30 .25
C82A A109 40c car rose .30 .25
C83 A109 45c magenta .50 .30
C83A A109 45c black .25 .25
C84 A109 50c turq grn 1.75 .25
C84A A109 50c red org .40 .25
C85 A109 60c brt ultra .65 .25
C85A A109 60c brt green .25 .25
C86 A109 65c scarlet .95 .30
C86A A109 65c brt ultra .30 .25
C87 A109 85c dp org 1.25 .50
C87A A109 85c dull pur 1.60 .65
C88 A109 1col black 1.60 .50
C88A A109 1col scarlet .65 .40
C88B A109 1.05col bis brn .90 .55
C89 A109 1.15col red brn 2.10 1.75
C89A A109 1.15col green 3.00 1.25
C90 A109 1.40col dp vio 3.25 2.40
C90A A109 1.40col org yel 1.75 1.60
C91 A109 2col black 5.25 1.25
C91A A109 2col olive grn 1.60 .50
Nos. C81-C91A (22) 28.85 14.20

Issued: Nos. C82A, C83A, C84A, C85A, C86A, C87A, C88A, C88B, C89A, C90A, C91A, 1945.

See Nos. C124-C127, C179-C181. For surcharges see Nos. C154-C158, C182, C184-C185.

Nos. C26-C27 Ovptd. in Red or Blue

1943, Sept. 16

C92 AP9 5col black (R) 4.50 3.00
C93 AP9 10col red brown (Bl) 5.25 3.25

Mercury and Plane AP31

1944, Jan. 19

C94 AP31 10c red org .25 .25
C95 AP31 15c dk car .25 .25
C96 AP31 40c brt ultra .40 .25
C97 AP31 45c dp red lil .40 .30
C98 AP31 60c turq grn .55 .40
C99 AP31 1col dk red brn 1.60 .80
C100 AP31 1.40col gray blk 8.75 5.25
C101 AP31 5col violet 24.00 16.00
C102 AP31 10col black 70.00 62.50
Nos. C94-C102 (9) 106.20 86.00

City of San Ramón founding, 100th anniv.

No. CO10 With Additional Overprint in Black

1944, Nov. 22

C103 AP9 1col deep rose 2.00 .95
a. Blue overprint 150.00 100.00

Nos. CO1-CO13 Overprinted in Carmine or Black

1945, Jan. 12 **Unwmk.** *Perf. 12*

C104 AP8 5c green .60 .50
C105 AP8 10c car rose (Bk) .60 .55
C106 AP8 15c chocolate .60 .55
C107 AP8 20c deep blue .50 .40
C108 AP8 25c dp org (Bk) .60 .60
C109 AP8 40c olive blk .35 .35
C110 AP8 50c gray blk .60 .60
C111 AP8 60c org yel (Bk) .90 .35
C112 AP8 75c dull violet .75 .50
C113 AP9 1col dp rose (Bk) .75 .35
C114 AP9 2col light blue 8.00 4.50
C115 AP9 5col black 8.00 5.50
C116 AP9 10col red brn (Bk) 11.00 8.25
Nos. C104-C116 (13) 33.25 23.00

No. C104 exists with the overprint inverted. No. C104 with the overprint in black is probably a trial color. Value, $200.

Catalogue values for unused stamps in this section, from this point to the end of the section, are for Never Hinged items.

AP32

Telegraph Stamps Overprinted in Black or Carmine

1945, Feb. 28 **Unwmk.** *Perf. 12½*

C117 AP32 40c green (C) .80 .25
C118 AP32 50c ultra (C) .40 .25
C119 AP32 1col orange (Bk) 3.00 .40
Nos. C117-C119 (3) 4.20 .90

No. C117 exists with inverted overprint. Value, $15.

Florence Nightingale and Edith Cavell AP33

1945 **Engr.**

C120 AP33 1col black & car 1.25 .50

Costa Rican Red Cross Soc., 60th anniv

For surcharge see No. C183.

Soccer Type of 1941 Inscribed: "Febrero 1946"

1946, May 13 *Perf. 12*

C121 AP15 25c green 1.60 .65
C122 AP15 30c dull yellow 2.25 .65
C123 AP15 55c deep blue 2.50 .65
Nos. C121-C123 (3) 6.35 1.95

Portrait Type of 1943-47

Designs: 25c, Aniceto Esquivel. 30c, Vicente Herrera. 55c, Prospero Fernandez. 75c, Bernardo Soto.

1946, May 12

C124 A109 25c blue .30 .25
C125 A109 30c red brown .30 .25
C126 A109 55c plum .60 .30
C127 A109 75c blue green 1.25 .40
Nos. C124-C127 (4) 2.45 1.20

Hospital of St. John of God AP38

1946, June 24 **Unwmk.** *Perf. 12½*
Center in Black

C128 AP38 5c yellow grn .40 .25
C129 AP38 10c dk brown .50 .25
C130 AP38 15c carmine .50 .25
C131 AP38 25c dk blue .50 .25
C132 AP38 30c dp orange .95 .25
C133 AP38 40c olive grn .50 .25
C134 AP38 50c violet .95 .25
C135 AP38 60c dk sl grn 2.00 .55
C136 AP38 75c brown 1.50 .40
a. Horiz. pair, imperf. btwn. 100.00
C137 AP38 1col blue 2.00 .35
C138 AP38 2col brn org 2.50 .80
C139 AP38 3col dk vio brn 5.00 2.00
C140 AP38 5col yellow 7.00 2.40
Nos. C128-C140 (13) 24.30 8.25

Nos. C128, C129, C131, C132, C134, C135 and C140 exist imperf.

Rafael Iglesias — AP39

3col, Ascensión Esquivel. 5col, Cleto González Víquez. 10col, Ricardo Jiménez Oreamuno.

1947, Jan. 15 **Wmk. 215** *Perf. 14*
Center in Black

C141 AP39 2col blue 2.00 1.25
C142 AP39 3col dp car 2.75 1.60
C143 AP39 5col dk green 4.75 2.00
C144 AP39 10col orange 7.25 5.25
Nos. C141-C144 (4) 16.75 10.10

Nos. C141-C144 also exist in a souvenir sheet of 4. Value, $600. The sheet in sepia is a proof and worth less.

Nos. C121-C123 Surcharged in Black

1947, May 5 **Unwmk.** *Perf. 12*

C145 AP15 15c on 25c green 1.20 .80
C146 AP15 15c on 30c dull yel 1.20 .80
C147 AP15 15c on 55c dp blue 1.20 .80
Nos. C145-C147 (3) 3.60 2.40

Nos. C145-C147 exist with inverted surcharge.

Columbus in Cariari AP43

1947, May 18 **Engr.** *Perf. 12½*
Center in Black

C148 AP43 25c green .35 .25
C149 AP43 30c dp ultra .45 .25
C150 AP43 40c red orange .60 .25
C151 AP43 45c violet .75 .30
C152 AP43 50c brt carmine .85 .25
C153 AP43 65c brown org 2.50 .95
Nos. C148-C153 (6) 5.50 2.25

For surcharges see Nos. C178, C220-C223.

Nos. C84A, C85A, C127, C88A-C88B Surcharged in Black or Red

1947, June 3 *Perf. 12*

C154 A109 15c on 50c red org .60 .30
C155 A109 15c on 60c brt grn (R) .60 .30
C156 A109 15c on 75c bl grn (R) .60 .30
C157 A109 15c on 1col scar .80 .50

No.	Type	Description	Unused	Used
C158	A109	15c on 1.05col bis brn	.60	.30
		Nos. C154-C158 (5)	3.20	1.70

No. C155 is known with black surcharge. Value, $10. No. C156 with inverted surcharge. Value, $10.

Early Steam Locomotive — AP44

1947, Nov. 10 ***Perf. 12½***

No.	Type	Description	Unused	Used
C159	AP44	35c bl grn & blk	2.50	.55

Electric railroad to the Pacific coast, 50th anniv.

Roosevelt Type of Regular Issue

1947, Aug. 26 ***Perf. 12***

No.	Type	Description	Unused	Used
C160	A122	15c green	.35	.25
C161	A122	30c car rose	.35	.25
C162	A122	45c red brown	.35	.25
C163	A122	65c orange yel	.35	.25
C164	A122	75c blue	.40	.25
C165	A122	1col olive grn	.75	.35
C166	A122	2col black	2.00	1.00
C167	A122	5col scarlet	3.50	2.40
		Nos. C160-C167 (8)	8.05	5.00

For surcharges see Nos. C224-C226.

National Theater AP46

Rafael Iglesias AP47

1948, Jan. 26 ***Perf. 12½***

Center in Black

No.	Type	Description	Unused	Used
C168	AP46	15c brt ultra	.25	.25
C169	AP46	20c red	.25	.25
C170	AP47	35c dk green	.40	.25
C171	AP46	45c purple	.50	.25
C172	AP46	50c carmine	.50	.25
C173	AP46	75c red violet	1.10	.80
C174	AP46	1col olive	2.00	1.10
C175	AP46	2col red brn	3.25	1.60
C176	AP47	5col org yel	5.25	4.00
C177	AP47	10col brt blue	12.00	8.00
		Nos. C168-C177 (10)	25.50	16.75

50th anniversary of National Theater.

No. C150 Surcharged in Carmine

1948, Apr. 21

No.	Type	Description	Unused	Used
C178	AP43	35c on 40c	1.25	.50

Exists with surcharge inverted.

Portrait Type of 1943-47

5c, Salvador Lara. 15c, Carlos Duran.

1948 **Engr.** ***Perf. 12***

No.	Type	Description	Unused	Used
C179	A109	5c sepia	.55	.25
C180	A109	10c olive brown	.55	.25
C181	A109	15c violet	.55	.25
		Nos. C179-C181 (3)	1.65	.75

Nos. C88B, C120, C89A and C90A Surcharged in Carmine or Black

Perf. 12½, 12

1949, Aug. 28 **Unwmk.**

No.	Type	Description	Unused	Used
C182	A109	35c on 1.05col bis brn	.40	.25
C183	AP33	50c on 1col blk & car	.70	.45
a.		2nd & 3rd lines both read "125 Aniversario"	6.00	3.00
C184	A109	55c on 1.15col grn	1.10	.70
C185	A109	55c on 1.40col org yel (Bk)	1.10	.60
		Nos. C182-C185 (4)	3.30	2.00

125th anniv. of the annexation of the province of Guanacaste.

Overprint differs on No. C183, with "Guanacaste" in capitals, and lower case "a" in "Anexión."

The variety "l" for "i" in "Anexion" is found on Nos. C182, C184 and C185.

Symbols of UPU AP48

1950, Jan. 11 **Photo.** ***Perf. 11½***

No.	Type	Description	Unused	Used
C186	AP48	15c lilac rose	.35	.25
C187	AP48	25c chalky blue	.55	.40
C188	AP48	1col gray green	.85	.55
		Nos. C186-C188 (3)	1.75	1.20

75th anniv. of the UPU.

Battle of El Tejar, Cartago AP49

Occupation of Limón — AP50

25c, Lucha ranch. 35c, Trenches of San Isidro Battalion. 55c, 75c, Observation post. 80c, 1col, Dr. Carlos Luis Valverde.

Inscribed: "Guerra de Liberacion Nacional 1948"

Engraved; Center Photogravure

1950, July 20 ***Perf. 12½***

Center in Black

No.	Type	Description	Unused	Used
C189	AP49	15c brt car	.25	.25
C190	AP50	20c dull green	.25	.25
C191	AP49	25c dull blue	.35	.25
C192	AP49	35c chestnut	.50	.25
C193	AP49	55c lilac	.85	.25
C194	AP49	75c red org	1.50	.30
C195	AP50	80c gray	1.50	.50
C196	AP50	1col org yel	2.00	.55
		Nos. C189-C196 (8)	7.20	2.60

2nd anniv. of the War for Natl. Liberation.

Bull (Cattle Raising) — AP51

1c, 10c, 2col, Bull. 2c, 30c, 3col, Tuna fishing. 3c, 65c, Pineapple. 5c, 50c, 5col, Bananas. 45c, 80c, 10col, Coffee picker.

Inscribed: "Feria Nacional Agricola Ganadera e Industrial Cartago 1950"

1950, July 27 **Center in Black**

No.	Type	Description	Unused	Used
C197	AP51	1c brt green	.70	.25
C198	AP51	2c brt blue	.70	.25
C199	AP51	3c chocolate	.80	.25
C200	AP51	5c dp ultra	.80	.25
C201	AP51	10c green	.80	.25
C202	AP51	30c purple	.80	.25
C203	AP51	45c vermilion	.90	.25
C204	AP51	50c blue gray	1.00	.25
C205	AP51	65c dk blue	1.00	.25
C206	AP51	80c dp rose	2.75	.65
C207	AP51	2col org yel	4.75	1.60
C208	AP51	3col blue	8.50	4.00
C209	AP51	5col carmine	12.00	6.50
C210	AP51	10col dp claret	12.00	6.50
		Nos. C197-C210 (14)	47.50	21.50

National Agricultural, Livestock and Industrial Fair, Cartago, 1950.

For surcharge see No. RA1.

Queen Isabella I and Caravels of Columbus AP52

Unwmk.

1952, Mar. 4 **Engr.** ***Perf. 13***

No.	Type	Description	Unused	Used
C211	AP52	15c carmine	.30	.25
C212	AP52	20c orange	.60	.25
C213	AP52	25c ultra	.85	.25
C214	AP52	55c dp green	3.00	.25
C215	AP52	2col violet	5.75	.50
		Nos. C211-C215 (5)	10.50	1.50

Birth of Queen Isabella I of Spain, 500th anniv.

Mail Plane Type of 1934

1952-53 ***Perf. 12***

No.	Type	Description	Unused	Used
C216	AP8	5c blue	.50	.25
C217	AP8	10c green	.50	.25
C218	AP8	15c car rose ('53)	.75	.25
C219	AP8	35c purple	1.75	.25
		Nos. C216-C219 (4)	3.50	1.00

Nos. C216-C217 were reprinted in 1953 in different shades. Values the same.

Nos. C149-C151, C153 Surcharged in Red: "HABILITADO PARA CINCO CENTIMOS 1953"

1953, Apr. 24 ***Perf. 12½***

Center in Black

No.	Type	Description	Unused	Used
C220	AP43	5c on 30c dp ultra	2.50	1.50
C221	AP43	5c on 40c red org	.50	.30
C222	AP43	5c on 45c vio	.50	.30
C223	AP43	5c on 65c brn org	.50	.30
		Nos. C220-C223 (4)	4.00	2.40

Nos. C161-C163 Surcharged in Black

1953, Apr. 11 ***Perf. 12***

No.	Type	Description	Unused	Used
C224	A122	15c on 30c car rose	.55	.25
C225	A122	15c on 45c red brn	.55	.25
C226	A122	15c on 65c org yel	.55	.25
		Nos. C224-C226 (3)	1.65	.75

Refinery of Vegetable Oils and Fats — AP53

Industries: 10c, Pottery. 15c, Sugar. 20c, Soap. 25c, Lumber. 30c, Matches. 35c, Textiles. 40c, Leather. 45c, Tobacco. 50c, Preserving. 55c, Canning. 60c, General. 65c, Metals. 75c, Pharmaceuticals. 80c, Pharmaceuticals. 1col, Paper. 2col, Rubber. 3col, Airplane maintenance. 5col, Marble. 10col, Beer.

Engraved; Center Photogravure

1954-59 **Unwmk.** ***Perf. 13x12½***

Center in Black

No.	Type	Description	Unused	Used
C227	AP53	5c red	.25	.25
C228	AP53	10c dk blue	.25	.25
C229	AP53	15c green	.25	.25
C230	AP53	20c violet	.25	.25
C231	AP53	25c magenta	.30	.25
C232	AP53	30c purple	.70	.40
C233	AP53	35c red vio	.45	.25
C234	AP53	40c black	.70	.30
C235	AP53	45c dk green	1.50	.40
C236	AP53	50c vio brown	.85	.25
C237	AP53	55c yellow	.70	.25
C238	AP53	60c brown	1.75	.65
C239	AP53	65c carmine	2.00	.95
C240	AP53	75c violet	2.75	.80
C240A	AP53	80c pur & gray	1.50	.80
C241	AP53	1col blue	.85	.40
a.		Imperf., pair	200.00	
C242	AP53	2col rose pink	2.75	1.25
C243	AP53	3col ol grn	3.75	2.00
C244	AP53	5col black	5.75	1.60
C245	AP53	10col yellow	16.00	9.50
		Nos. C227-C245 (20)	43.30	21.05

Issued: 30c, 35c, 60c, 65c, 75c, 2col, 3col, Oct. 20; 80c, Oct. 2, 1959; others, Sept. 1.

See Nos. C252-C255. For surcharges and overprint, see Nos. C314-C315, C334-C336, RA2, RA11.

Globe, Rotary Emblem — AP54

25c, Hand protecting boy. 40c, 2col, Hospital. 45c, Globe & palm leaves. 60c, Lighthouse.

1956, Feb. 7 **Engr.** ***Perf. 12***

No.	Type	Description	Unused	Used
C246	AP54	10c green	.30	.25
C247	AP54	25c dk blue	.30	.25
C248	AP54	40c dk brown	.70	.40
C249	AP54	45c brt red	.45	.25
C250	AP54	60c dk red vio	.70	.30
C251	AP54	2col yel org	2.00	.65
		Nos. C246-C251 (6)	4.45	2.10

50th anniv. of Rotary Intl. (in 1955).

Industries Type of 1954

Designs as in 1954.

Engraved; Center Photogravure

1956, Feb. 17 ***Perf. 12***

Center in Black

No.	Type	Description	Unused	Used
C252	AP53	5c ultra	.40	.25
C253	AP53	10c violet blue	.60	.25
C254	AP53	15c orange yel	.75	.25
C255	AP53	75c red orange	1.25	.30
		Nos. C252-C255 (4)	3.00	1.05

Map of Costa Rica — AP55

10c, Map of Guanacaste. 15c, Inn. 20c, House of Santa Rosa. 25c, Gen. Jose Manuel Quiros. 30c, Old Presidential Palace. 35c, Joaquin Bernardo Calvo. 40c, Luis Molina. 45c, Gen. Jose Joaquin Mora. 50c, Gen. Jose Maria Canas. 55c, Juan Santamaria monument. 60c, National monument. 65c, Antonio Vallerriestra. 70c, Ramon Castilla y Marquesado. 75c, San Carlos fortress. 80c, Francisco Maria Oreamuno. 1col, Pres. Juan Rafael Mora.

1957, June 21 **Engr.** ***Perf. 13½x13***

No.	Type	Description	Unused	Used
C256	AP55	5c lt blue	.30	.25
C257	AP55	10c green	.35	.25
C258	AP55	15c dp orange	.35	.25
C259	AP55	20c lt brown	.35	.25
C260	AP55	25c vio blue	.45	.25
C261	AP55	30c violet	.60	.25
C262	AP55	35c car rose	.65	.25
C263	AP55	40c slate	.65	.25
C264	AP55	45c rose red	.75	.25
C265	AP55	50c ultra	.80	.25
C266	AP55	55c ocher	1.40	.25
C267	AP55	60c brt car	1.25	.30
C268	AP55	65c carmine	1.40	.30
C269	AP55	70c orange yel	1.60	.30
C270	AP55	75c emerald	1.60	.30
C271	AP55	80c dk brown	2.10	.40
C272	AP55	1col black	2.40	.40
		Nos. C256-C272 (17)	17.00	4.75

Centenary of War of 1856-57.

Cleto Gonzalez Viquez — AP56

Highway and Gonzalez Viquez AP57

Designs: 10c, Ricardo Jimenez Oreamuno. 20c, Puntarenas wharf and Jimenez. 35c, Post and Telegraph Bldg. and Jimenez. 55c, Pipeline and Gonzalez Viquez. 80c, National Library and Gonzalez Viquez. 1col, Electric train and Jimenez. 2col, Gonzales and Jimenez.

1959, Nov. 23 Engr. *Perf. 13½*
C274 AP56 5c car & ultra .30 .25
C275 AP56 10c red & gray .30 .25

Perf. 13½x13
C276 AP57 15c dk bl grn & blk .30 .25
C277 AP57 20c car & brn .60 .25
C278 AP57 35c rose lil & bl .30 .25
C279 AP57 55c olive & vio .60 .25
C280 AP57 80c ultra .75 .35
C281 AP57 1col orange & mar 1.25 .50
C282 AP57 2col gray & mar 2.75 1.60
Nos. C274-C282 (9) 7.15 3.95

For surcharge and overprint see Nos. C337, C339.

Soccer AP58

Designs: Various soccer scenes.

Perf. 13½
1960, Mar. 7 Unwmk. Photo.
C283 AP58 10c black .35 .30
C284 AP58 25c ultra .35 .30
C285 AP58 35c red orange .35 .30
C286 AP58 50c red brown .50 .30
C287 AP58 85c Prus green 1.50 .90
C288 AP58 5col dp claret 3.50 2.50
Nos. C283-C288 (6) 6.55 4.60

Souvenir Sheet
Imperf
C289 AP58 2col blue 6.75 6.50

3rd Pan-American Soccer Games, San José, Mar. 1960.
Nos. C283-C288 exist imperf. Value, pair $150.

WRY Uprooted Oak Emblem — AP59

1960, Apr. 7 Unwmk. *Perf. 11½*
Granite Paper
C290 AP59 35c vio bl, blk & yel .35 .25
C291 AP59 85c black & brt pink 1.00 .55

Refugee Year, July 1, 1959-June 30, 1960.

Banner and "OEA" — AP60

35c, "OEA" in oval. 55c, Clasped hands. 2col, "OEA" & map of Americas. 5col, Flags forming bird. 10col, Map of Costa Rica, flags & "OEA."

1960, Aug. 15 Litho. *Perf. 10*
C292 AP60 25c black & multi .25 .25
a. Multi, impression sideways 60.00
C293 AP60 35c multicolored .35 .30
a. Pair, imperf. between 60.00
C294 AP60 55c multicolored .55 .40
C295 AP60 5col multicolored 3.50 2.75
C296 AP60 10col black & multi 5.50 4.50
Nos. C292-C296 (5) 10.15 8.20

Souvenir Sheet
Imperf
C297 AP60 2col multicolored 3.00 2.75

Pan-American Conf., San Jose, Aug. 15.

St. Louisa de Marillac and Orphanage — AP61

St. Vincent de Paul — AP62

25c, St. Vincent & old seminary. 50c, St. Louisa & sickroom. 1col, St. Vincent & new seminary.

1960, Oct. 26 Engr. *Perf. 14x13½*
C298 AP61 10c green .35 .25
C299 AP61 25c carmine .35 .25
C300 AP61 50c dk blue .35 .25
C301 AP61 1col brown org .75 .30
C302 AP62 5col brown 4.00 1.75
Nos. C298-C302 (5) 5.80 2.80

St. Vincent (1581?-1660) and St. Louisa (1591-1660). Nos. C298-C302 exist imperf.

Runner AP63

Sports: 2c, Woman swimmer. 3c, Bicyclist. 4c, Weight lifter. 5c, Woman tennis player. 10c, Boxers. 25c, Soccer player. 85c, Basketball player. 1col, Baseball batter. 5col, Romulus and Remus statue. 10col, Pistol marksman.

Perf. 13½x14
1960, Dec. 14 Photo. Unwmk.
Designs in Black
C303 AP63 1c brt yellow .25 .25
C304 AP63 2c lt ultra .25 .25
C305 AP63 3c dp rose .25 .25
C306 AP63 4c yellow .25 .25
C307 AP63 5c brt yel grn .25 .25
C308 AP63 10c pink .25 .25
C309 AP63 25c lt bl grn .25 .25
C310 AP63 85c lilac 1.50 .80
C311 AP63 1col gray 1.75 1.00
C312 AP63 10col lt violet 12.00 8.00
Nos. C303-C312 (10) 17.00 11.55

Souvenir Sheets
Perf. 14x13½
C313 AP63 5col multi 6.25 6.00

17th Olympic Games, Rome, 8/25-9/11.
Nos. C303-C313 exist imperf.

No. C255 Srchd. and Ovptd. in Blue or Ultramarine

Engraved and Photogravure
1961, Apr. 21 *Perf. 12*
Center in Black
C314 AP53 25c on 75c red org (Bl) .40 .25
C315 AP53 75c red orange (U) .85 .25

15th Amateur Baseball Championships.

Alberto Brenes C. — AP64

No. C317, Manuel Aguilar. No. C318, Agustin Gutierrez L. No. C319, Vicente Herrera.

1961, June 12 Photo. *Perf. 12*
C316 AP64 10c deep claret .55 .25
C317 AP64 10c blue .55 .25
C318 AP64 25c bright violet .55 .25
C319 AP64 25c gray .55 .25
Nos. C316-C319 (4) 2.20 1.00

First Continental Congress of Lawyers, San José, June 11-15. Exist imperf.
See Nos. C330-C333.

Miguel Obregon — AP65

1961, July 19 Litho. *Perf. 13½*
C320 AP65 10c Prussian green .65 .25

Birth centenary of Prof. Miguel Obregon L. Exists imperf. Value $50.

UN Food and Agriculture Organization AP66

UN day (UN Organizations): 20c, WHO. 25c, ILO. 30, ITU. 35c, World Meteorological Organization. 45c, UNESCO. 85c, ICAO. 5col, "United Nations" holding the world. 10col, Int. Bank for Reconstruction and Development.

Perf. 11½
1961, Oct. 24 Unwmk. Engr.
C321 AP66 10c lt green .25 .25
C322 AP66 20c orange .25 .25
C323 AP66 25c Prus grn .25 .25
C324 AP66 30c dk blue .25 .25
C325 AP66 35c carmine rose 1.10 .25
C326 AP66 45c violet .35 .25
C327 AP66 85c blue .80 .55
C328 AP66 10col dk sl grn 6.25 4.50
Nos. C321-C328 (8) 9.50 6.55

Souvenir Sheet
Imperf
C329 AP66 5col ultra 4.75 4.50

For overprint see No. C338.

Portrait Type of 1961

No. C330, Dr. José Maria Soto Alfaro. No. C331, Dr. Elias Rojas Roman. No. C332, Dr. Andres Saenz Llorente. No. C333, Dr. Juan José Ulloa Giralt.

1961 Photo. *Perf. 13½*
C330 AP64 10c blue green .35 .25
C331 AP64 10c violet .35 .25
C332 AP64 25c dark gray .75 .25
C333 AP64 25c deep claret .75 .25
Nos. C330-C333 (4) 2.20 1.00

9th Congress of Physicians of Central America and Panama.

Nos. C229, C236 and C280 Surcharged in Black, Orange or Red

No. C334

No. C334A

Engraved; Center Photogravure
1962 *Perf. 13x12½, 13½x13*
C334 AP53 10c ("10") on 15c .35 .25
C334A AP53 10c ("¢0.10") on 15c (R) .35 .25
C335 AP53 25c on 15c .35 .25
C336 AP53 35c on 50c (O) .50 .25

Engr.
C337 AP57 85c on 80c (R) 1.50 .80
Nos. C334-C337 (5) 3.05 1.80

No. C336 exists with double surcharge. Value, $35.

Nos. C324 and C282 Overprinted in Red

1962, Sept. 12 *Perf. 11½, 13½x13*
C338 AP66 30c dark blue .75 .40
C339 AP57 2col gray & mar 1.90 1.25

2nd Central American Phil. Convention.

Revenue Stamp Surcharged in Red

1962 Engr. *Perf. 12*
C341 A124 25c on 2c emer .45 .25
C342 A124 35c on 2c emer .45 .25
C343 A124 45c on 2c emer .70 .30
C344 A124 85c on 2c emer 1.25 .55
Nos. C341-C344 (4) 2.85 1.35

Arms and Malaria Eradication Emblem AP67

1963, Feb. 14 Photo. *Perf. 11½*
C345 AP67 25c brt rose .30 .25
C346 AP67 35c brown org .30 .25
C347 AP67 45c ultra .40 .25
C348 AP67 85c blue grn .90 .50
C349 AP67 1col dk blue 1.50 .65
Nos. C345-C349 (5) 3.40 1.90

WHO drive to eradicate malaria.

Central American Tapir — AP68

Designs: 5c, Paca. 25c, Jaguar. 30c, Ocelot. 35c, Whitetail deer. 40c, Manatee. 85c, White-throated capuchin monkey. 5col, White-lipped peccary.

Perf. 13½

1963, May **Unwmk.** **Photo.**

C354	AP68	5c yel ol & brn	.25	.25
C355	AP68	10c orange & sl	.30	.25
C356	AP68	25c blue & yel	.50	.35
C357	AP68	30c lt yel grn & brn	.70	.40
C358	AP68	35c bis & red brn	1.25	.40
C359	AP68	40c emer & sl bl	1.50	.55
C360	AP68	85c green & blk	4.50	.55
C361	AP68	5col gray grn & choc	12.50	4.00
		Nos. C354-C361 (8)	21.50	6.75

See Nos. C367-C370.

Stamp of 1863 and Packet "Monarch" — AP69

Issue of 1863 and: 2col, Recaredo Bonilla Carrillo, Postmaster, 1862-63. 3col, Burros, overland mail transport, 1839. 10col, Burro railway car.

1963, June 26 **Litho.**

C362	AP69	25c dl rose & chlky bl	.25	.25
C363	AP69	2col gray bl & org	1.75	1.25
C364	AP69	3col bister & emer	3.25	2.00
C365	AP69	10col dl grn & ocher	11.00	6.00
		Nos. C362-C365 (4)	16.25	9.50

Centenary of Costa Rica's stamps.

No. C362 is inscribed "William Le Lacheur," the builder and captain of the "Monarch."

Souvenir Sheets

Stamps of 1863 and San José Postmark — AP70

Perf. 13½, Imperf.

1963, June 26 **Unwmk.**

C366	AP70	5col bl, red, grn & org	5.50	5.50

Cent. of Costa Rica's stamps.

In 1968 examples of No. C366 were overprinted "2-4 Agosto 1968" and "III Exposicion Filatelica Nacional / 'Costa Rica 68'". Value, $10.50.

Animal Type of 1963 Surcharged in Red

No. C367, Little anteater. No. C368, Gray fox. No. C369, Armadillo. No. C370, Great anteater.

1963, Sept. 14 **Photo.** ***Perf. 13½***

C367	AP68	10c on 1c brt grn & org brn	1.20	.30
C368	AP68	25c on 2c org yel & ol grn	1.20	.30
C369	AP68	35c on 3c bluish grn & brn	1.60	.30
C370	AP68	85c on 4c dp rose & dk brn	3.00	.65
		Nos. C367-C370 (4)	7.00	1.55

Examples of No. C370 exist without surcharge. Value, $1,000, less than 10 exist.

Pres. Kennedy — AP71

Portraits — Presidents: 25c, Francisco J. Orlich, Costa Rica. 30c, Julio A. Rivera, El Salvador. 35c, Miguel Ydigoras F., Guatemala. 85c, Dr. Ramon Villeda M., Honduras. 1col, Luis A. Somoza, Nicaragua. 3col, Roberto F. Chiari, Panama.

1963, Dec. 7 **Unwmk.** ***Perf. 14***

Portraits in Black Brown

C371	AP71	25c violet brn	.35	.25
C372	AP71	30c brt lil rose	.35	.25
C373	AP71	35c ocher	.35	.25
C374	AP71	85c gray blue	.60	.25
C375	AP71	1col orange brn	.65	.30
C376	AP71	3col lt ol grn	2.90	1.60
C377	AP71	5col gray	3.75	2.25
		Nos. C371-C377 (7)	8.95	5.15

Meeting of Central American Presidents with Pres. John F. Kennedy, San José, Mar. 18-20, 1963.

Ancestral Figure — AP72

Ancient Art: 5c, Dog, horiz. 10c, Ornamental stool, horiz. 25c, Male figure. 30c, Ceremonial dancer. 35c, Ceramic vase. 50c, Frog. 55c, Bell. 75c, Six-limbed figure. 85c, Seated man. 90c, Bird-shaped jug. 1col, Twin human beaker, horiz. 2col, Alligator, horiz. 3col, Twin-tailed lizard. 5col, Figure under arch. 10col, Polished stone figure.

1963-64 **Photo.** ***Perf. 12***

C378	AP72	5c lt yel grn & Prus grn	.25	.25
C379	AP72	10c buff & dk grn	.25	.25
C380	AP72	25c rose & dk brn	.25	.25
C381	AP72	30c ocher & Prus grn ('64)	.25	.25
C382	AP72	35c sal & sl grn	.25	.25
C383	AP72	45c lt bl & dk brn	.25	.25
C384	AP72	50c dl bl & dk brn	.45	.25
C385	AP72	55c yel grn & dk brn	.60	.25
C386	AP72	75c ocher & dk red brn	.60	.25
C387	AP72	85c yel & red brn	1.50	1.40
C388	AP72	90c cit & red brn ('64)	1.90	1.75
C389	AP72	1col lt bl & dk brn ('64)	1.25	.30
C390	AP72	2col buff & dk grn ('64)	2.00	.65
C391	AP72	3col yel grn & dk brn ('64)	6.00	.95
C392	AP72	5col cit & sep ('64)	6.00	5.25
C393	AP72	10col rose lil & sl grn	10.00	8.75
		Nos. C378-C393 (16)	31.80	21.30

For surcharges and overprint see Nos. C395, C397-C398, C400, C426-C428.

Flags of Central American States — AP73

1964, Mar. 11 ***Perf. 14***

C394	AP73	30c bl, gray, red & blk	1.25	.35

Central American Independence issue. For surcharge see No. C396.

Nos. C381, C394 and C387 Surcharged

1964, Oct. ***Perf. 12, 14***

C395	AP72	5c on 30c	.75	.25
C396	AP73	15c on 30c	.75	.25
C397	AP72	15c on 85c	.75	.25
		Nos. C395-C397 (3)	2.25	.75

No. C388 Surcharged in Black

1964, Nov. 22 ***Perf. 12***

C398	AP72	15c on 90c cit & red brn	.75	.25

Paris Postal Conference.

Alfredo Gonzalez F. — AP74

1965, June **Photo.** ***Perf. 12***

C399	AP74	35c dk blue green	3.50	.25

50th anniv. of the National Bank and honoring Alfredo Gonzalez Flores (1877-1962), 1st governor of the bank.

No. C390 Overprinted in Black

1965, Aug. 14 **Unwmk.** ***Perf. 12***

C400	AP72	2col buff & dk grn	1.50	.80

75th anniv. of Chapui Asylum, San José.

Girl, FAO Emblem and Hands Holding Grain — AP75

FAO Emblem and: 15c, Map of Costa Rica and silos, horiz. 50c, World population chart and children. 1col, Plane over map of Costa Rica, horiz.

1965, Oct. 25 **Litho.** ***Perf. 14***

C401	AP75	15c lt brn & blk	.40	.25
C402	AP75	35c black & yel	.40	.25
C403	AP75	50c ultra & dk grn	.40	.25
C404	AP75	1col grn, blk & sil	1.00	.25
		Nos. C401-C404 (4)	2.20	1.00

FAO "Freedom from Hunger" campaign.

Church of Nicoya — AP76

5c, Leonidas Briceno B. 15c, Scroll dated "25 de Julio de 1964." 35c, Map of Guanacaste and Nicoya peninsula. 50c, Dancing couple. 1col, Map showing local products.

1965, Dec. 20 ***Perf. 13½x14***

C405	AP76	5c red brn & blk	.50	.25
C406	AP76	10c blue & gray	.50	.25
C407	AP76	15c bis & slate	.50	.25
C408	AP76	35c blue & slate	.50	.25
C409	AP76	50c gray & vio bl	.75	.25
C410	AP76	1col buff & slate	1.50	.40
		Nos. C405-C410 (6)	4.25	1.65

Acquisition of the Nicoya territory.

Runner and Olympic Rings — AP77

Olympic Rings and Emblem: 10c, Bicyclists. 40c, Judo. 65c, Basketball. 80c, Soccer. 1col, Hands holding torches, and Mt. Fuji.

1965, Dec. 23 ***Perf. 13x13½***

C411	AP77	5c bister & multi	.35	.25
C412	AP77	10c lt lil & multi	.35	.25
C413	AP77	40c multicolored	.35	.25
C414	AP77	65c lemon & multi	.35	.25
C415	AP77	80c tan & multi	.65	.25
C416	AP77	1col multicolored	1.00	.30
	a.	Souvenir sheet of 2	6.50	3.00
		Nos. C411-C416 (6)	3.05	1.55

18th Olympic Games, Tokyo, Oct. 10-25, 1964. No. C416a contains two 1col stamps, one like No. C416, the other with gray background replacing yellow orange.

No. C416a was issued both perf and imperf. Same values.

Nos. C411-C416 exist imperf.

Pres. Kennedy Speaking in San José Cathedral — AP78

Designs: 45c, Friendship 7 capsule circling globe, and Kennedy, horiz. 85c, Kennedy and John, Jr. 1col, Curtis-Lee Mansion and flame from Kennedy grave, Arlington, Va.

Perf. 13½x13, 13x13½

1965, Dec. 23 Litho. Unwmk.

C417 AP78 45c brt bl & lil .30 .25
C418 AP78 55c org & brt bl .40 .25
C419 AP78 85c gray, dk brn & red brn .85 .40
C420 AP78 1col multicolored 1.00 .50
a. Souvenir sheet of 2 1.50 1.25
Nos. C417-C420 (4) 2.55 1.40

President John F. Kennedy (1917-63). No. C420a contains two 1col stamps, one like No. C420, the other with green background replacing dark blue. Exists with light blue background instead of green; value $150.

No. C420a was issued both perf and imperf. Same values.

Nos. C417-C420 exist imperf.

For surcharges see Nos. C429-C430.

Firemen with Hoses — AP79

Designs: 5c, Fire engine "Knox," horiz. 10c, 1866 fire pump. 35c, Fireman's badge. 50c, Emblem and flags of Confederation of Central American Fire Brigades.

1966, Mar. 12 Litho. *Perf. 11*

C421 AP79 5c black & red .60 .25
C422 AP79 10c bister & red .90 .25
C423 AP79 15c blk, red brn & red 1.20 .25
C424 AP79 35c black & yel 2.40 .25
C425 AP79 50c dk blue & red 4.75 .50
Nos. C421-C425 (5) 9.85 1.50

Centenary of San José Fire Brigade.

Nos. C381, C383, C386 and C418-C419 Surcharged

a

b

1966, Dec. Photo. *Perf. 12*

C426 AP72(a) 15c on 30c .35 .25
C427 AP72(a) 15c on 45c .35 .25
C428 AP72(a) 35c on 75c .35 .25

Litho. *Perf. 13x13½*

C429 AP78(a) 35c on 55c .35 .25
C430 AP78(b) 50c on 85c 1.25 .25
Nos. C426-C430 (5) 2.65 1.25

Central Bank of Costa Rica — AP80

1967, Mar. 1 Litho. *Perf. 11*

C434 AP80 5c brt green .60 .25
C435 AP80 15c brown .60 .25
C436 AP80 35c scarlet .60 .25
Nos. C434-C436 (3) 1.80 .75

Power Lines — AP81

Telecommunications Building, San Pedro — AP82

Electrification Program: 15c, Telephone Central. 25c, La Garita Dam. 35c, Rio Mache Reservoir. 50c, Cachi Dam.

1967, Apr. 24 Litho. *Perf. 11*

C437 AP81 5c dark gray .45 .25
C438 AP82 10c brt rose .45 .25
C439 AP81 15c brown org .45 .25
C440 AP82 25c brt ultra .45 .25
C441 AP82 35c brt green .55 .25
C442 AP82 50c red brown .65 .30
Nos. C437-C442 (6) 3.00 1.55

Chondrorhyncha Aromatica — AP83

Orchids: 10c, Miltonia endresii. 15c, Stanhopea cirrhata. 25c, Trichopilia suavis. 35c, Odontoglossum schlieperianum. 50c, Cattleya skinneri. 1col, Cattleya dowiana. 2col, Odontoglossum chiriquense.

1967, June 15 Engr. *Perf. 13x13½*
Orchids in Natural Colors

C443 AP83 5c multicolored .25 .25
C444 AP83 10c olive & multi .40 .30
C445 AP83 15c multicolored .55 .30
C446 AP83 25c multicolored .95 .30
C447 AP83 35c dull vio & multi 1.25 .30
C448 AP83 50c brown & multi 1.60 .30
C449 AP83 1col vio & multi 3.50 .80
C450 AP83 2col dk ol bis & multi 6.50 1.50
Nos. C443-C450 (8) 15.00 4.05

Issued for the University Library.

Institute Emblem — AP84

1967, Oct. 6 Litho. *Perf. 13x13½*

C451 AP84 50c vio bl, lt bl & bl .65 .25

Inter-American Agriculture Institute, 25th anniv.

Church of Solitude — AP85

Costa Rican Churches: 10c, Basilica of Santo Domingo, Heredia. 15c, Cathedral of Tilaran. 25c, Cathedral of Alajuela. 30c, Mercy Church. 35c, Basilica of Our Lady of Angels. 40c, Church of St. Raphael, Heredia. 45c, Ujarras ruins. 50c, Ruins of parish church, Cartago. 55c, Cathedral of San José. 65c, Parish church, Puntarenas. 75c, Church of Orosi. 80c, Cathedral of St. Isidro, the General. 85c, St. Ramon Church. 90c, Church of the Abandoned. 1col, Coronado Church. 2col, Church of St. Teresita. 3col, Parish Church, Heredia. 5col, Carmelite Church. 10col, Limon Cathedral.

1967, Dec. 15 Engr. *Perf. 12½*

C452 AP85 5c green .25 .25
C453 AP85 10c blue .25 .25
C454 AP85 15c lilac .25 .25
C455 AP85 25c dull yel .25 .25
C456 AP85 30c orange brn .25 .25
C457 AP85 35c lt blue .25 .25
C458 AP85 40c dp orange .30 .25
C459 AP85 45c dl bl grn .30 .25
C460 AP85 50c olive .40 .25
C461 AP85 55c brown .40 .25
C462 AP85 65c car rose .65 .25
C463 AP85 75c sepia .70 .30
C464 AP85 80c yellow 1.40 .45
C465 AP85 85c violet blk 1.60 .45
C466 AP85 90c emerald 1.60 .65
C467 AP85 1col slate 1.25 .35
C468 AP85 2col brt green 5.50 1.75
C469 AP85 3col orange 7.25 3.00
C470 AP85 5col vio blue 8.00 3.00
C471 AP85 10col carmine 9.75 4.50
Nos. C452-C471 (20) 40.60 17.20

Nos. C452 and C454 exist imperf; Nos. C455 and C470 exist imperf horiz.

See Nos. C561-C576.

LACSA Emblem — AP86

45c, LACSA emblem, jet, horiz. 50c, Decorated wheel, anniversary emblem.

Perf. 13x13½, 13½x13

1967, Dec. 12 Litho. & Engr.

C472 AP86 40c ultra, grnsh bl & gold .40 .25
C473 AP86 45c blk, pale grn, ultra & gold .50 .25
C474 AP86 50c blue & multi .75 .25
Nos. C472-C474 (3) 1.65 .75

20th anniv. (in 1966) of Lineas Aereas Costaricenses, LACSA, Costa Rican Airlines.

Scout Directing Traffic — AP87

Designs: 25c, Campfire under tree. 35c, Flag of Costa Rica, Scout flag and emblem. 50c, Encampment, horiz. 65c, Photograph of first Scout troop, horiz.

1968, Mar. 15 *Perf. 13*

C475 AP87 15c lt bl, blk & lt brn .35 .25
C476 AP87 25c lt ultra, vio bl & org .35 .25
C477 AP87 35c blue & multi .60 .25
C478 AP87 50c multicolored .90 .30
C479 AP87 65c sal, dk bl & brn 1.50 .40
Nos. C475-C479 (5) 3.70 1.45

Costa Rican Boy Scouts, 50th anniversary.

Runner — AP88

Sports: 40c, Women's running. 55c, Boxing. 65c, Bicycling. 75c, Weight lifting. 1col, High diving. 3col, Rifle shooting.

1969, Jan. 17 Litho. *Perf. 10x11*

C481 AP88 30c multi .30 .25
C482 AP88 40c multi .30 .25
C483 AP88 55c multi .30 .25
C484 AP88 65c lil & multi .40 .25
C485 AP88 75c multi .40 .25
C486 AP88 1col multi .55 .25
C487 AP88 3col multi 2.10 .95
Nos. C481-C487 (7) 4.35 2.45

19th Olympic Games, Mexico City, 10/12-27.

Philatelic Exhibition Emblem — AP89

1969, June 5 Litho. *Perf. 11x10*

C488 AP89 35c multicolored .35 .25
C489 AP89 40c pink & multi .35 .25
C490 AP89 50c lt blue & multi .35 .25
C491 AP89 2col multicolored 1.60 .55
Nos. C488-C491 (4) 2.65 1.30

4th Natl. Philatelic Exhib., San José, 6/5-8.

ILO Emblem AP90

1969, Oct. 29 Litho. *Perf. 10*

C492 AP90 35c bl grn & blk .55 .25
C493 AP90 50c scarlet & blk .55 .25

50th anniv. of the ILO.

Soccer — AP91

Designs: 65c, Soccer ball, map of North and Central America. 85c, Soccer player. 1col, Two players in action.

1969, Nov. 23 Litho. *Perf. 11x10*

C494 AP91 65c gray & multi .50 .25
C495 AP91 75c multicolored .50 .25
C496 AP91 85c multicolored .65 .30
C497 AP91 1col pink & multi .90 .40
Nos. C494-C497 (4) 2.55 1.20

Issued to publicize the 4th Soccer Championships (CONCACAF), Nov. 23-Dec. 7.

Stylized Crab — AP92

1970, May 14 Litho. *Perf. 12½*

C498 AP92 10c blk & lil rose .30 .25
C499 AP92 15c blk & yel .30 .25
C500 AP92 50c blk & brn org .30 .25
C501 AP92 1.10col blk & emer 1.50 .25
Nos. C498-C501 (4) 2.40 1.00

10th Inter-American Cancer Cong., 5/22-29.

Revenue Stamps (Basic Type of A124) Surcharged

1967, Jan. Engr. *Perf. 12*

C431 A124 15c on 5c blue .35 .25
C432 A124 35c on 10c claret .50 .25
C433 A124 50c on 20c rose red .85 .25
Nos. C431-C433 (3) 1.70 .75

Costa Rica No. 124, Magnifying Glass and Stamps — AP93

2col, Father, son with stamps, album.

1970, Sept. 14 Litho. *Perf. 11*
C502 AP93 1col ultra, brn & car rose 1.10 .25
C503 AP93 2col blk, pink & ultra 1.40 .55

The 5th National Philatelic Exhibition.

EXPO Emblem and Costa Rican Cart — AP94

EXPO Emblem and: 10c, Japanese floral arrangement, vert. 35c, Pavilion and Tower of the Sun. 40c, Japanese tea ceremony. 45c, Woman picking coffee, vert. 55c, Earth seen from moon, vert.

1970, Oct. 22 Litho. *Perf. 13x13½*
C504 AP94 10c multicolored .30 .25
C505 AP94 15c green & multi .30 .25
C506 AP94 35c blue & multi .65 .25
C507 AP94 40c gray & multi .75 .25
C508 AP94 45c multicolored .95 .25
C509 AP94 55c black & multi 2.50 .30
Nos. C504-C509 (6) 5.45 1.55

EXPO '70 International Exhibition, Osaka, Japan, Mar. 15-Sept. 13.

Escazu Valley, by Margarita Bertheau — AP95

Paintings: 25c, "Irazu," by Rafael A. Garcia, vert. 80c, Shore landscape, by Teodorico Quiros. 1col, "The Other Face," by Cesar Valverde. 2.50col, Mother and Child, by Luis Daell, vert.

1970, Nov. 4 Litho. *Perf. 12½*
C510 AP95 25c multi .90 .30
C511 AP95 45c multi .90 .30
C512 AP95 80c multi 1.40 .55
C513 AP95 1col multi 1.40 .65
C514 AP95 2.50col multi 2.75 2.00
Nos. C510-C514 (5) 7.35 3.80

Arms of Costa Rica, 1964 — AP96

Various Coats of Arms, dated: 10c, Nov. 27, 1906. 15c, Sept. 29, 1848. 25c, Apr. 21, 1840. 35c, Nov. 22, 1824. 50c, Nov. 2, 1824. 1col, Mar. 6, 1824. 2col, May 10, 1823.

1971, Feb. 10 Litho. *Perf. 14x13½*
C515 AP96 5c buff & multi .55 .25
C516 AP96 10c multi .55 .25
C517 AP96 15c yel & multi .65 .25
C518 AP96 25c pink & multi .65 .25
C519 AP96 35c multi .85 .25
C520 AP96 50c rose & multi .95 .25
C521 AP96 1col beige & multi 1.25 .40
C522 AP96 2col multi 1.75 .80
Nos. C515-C522 (8) 7.20 2.70

National Theater AP97

1971, Apr. 14 Litho. *Perf. 11*
C523 AP97 2col plum .65 .30

Organization of American States meeting.

José Matias Delgado, Manuel José Arce AP98

Flag of Costa Rica — AP99

Independence Leaders: 10c, Miguel Larreinaga and Manuel Antonio de la Cerda, Nicaragua. 15c, José Cecilio del Valle, Dionisio de Herrera, Honduras. 35c, Pablo Alvarado and Florencio del Castillo, Costa Rica. 50c, Antonio Larrazabal and Pedro Molina, Guatemala. 2col, Costa Rica coat of arms.

1971, Sept. 14 *Perf. 13*
C524 AP98 5c multi .30 .25
C525 AP98 10c multi .30 .25
C526 AP98 15c gray, brn & blk .30 .25
C527 AP98 35c multi .30 .25
C528 AP98 50c multi .30 .25
C529 AP99 1col multi .30 .25
C530 AP99 2col multi 1.50 .40
Nos. C524-C530 (7) 3.30 1.90

Central American independence, sesqui.

Soccer Federation Emblem — AP100

1971, Dec. 6
C531 AP100 50c multi .55 .25
C532 AP100 60c multi .55 .25

50th anniv. of Soccer Federation of Costa Rica.

Children of the World — AP101

1972, Jan. 11 *Perf. 12½*
C533 AP101 50c multi .45 .25
C534 AP101 1.10col red & multi .55 .25

25th anniv. (in 1971) of UNICEF.

Tree of Guanacaste AP102

Designs: 40c, Hermitage, Liberia. 55c, Petroglyphs, Rincón Brujo. 60c, Painted head, sculpture from Curubandé, vert.

1972, Feb. 28 *Perf. 11*
C535 AP102 20c brn, ol & brt grn .65 .25
C536 AP102 40c brn & ol .65 .25
C537 AP102 55c blk & brn .65 .25
C538 AP102 60c blk, buff & ver .65 .25
Nos. C535-C538 (4) 2.60 1.00

Bicentenary of the founding of the city of Liberia, Guanacaste.

Farm and Family — AP103

Designs: 45c, Cattle, dairy products and meat, horiz. 50c, Kneeling figure with plant. 10col, Farmer and map of Americas.

1972, June 30 Litho. *Perf. 12½*
C539 AP103 20c multi .40 .25
C540 AP103 45c multi .40 .25
C541 AP103 50c dp yel, grn & blk .40 .25
C542 AP103 10col brn, org & blk 3.25 1.75
Nos. C539-C542 (4) 4.45 2.50

30th anniversary of the Inter-American Institute of Agricultural Sciences.

Inter-American Exhibitions AP104

1972, Aug. 26 Litho. *Perf. 13*
C543 AP104 50c orange & brn .35 .25
C544 AP104 2col blue & vio .65 .30

4th Interamerican Philatelic Exhibition, EXFILBRA, Rio de Janeiro, Aug. 26-Sept. 2.

First Book Printed in Costa Rica — AP105

Intl. Book Year: 50c, 5col, Natl. Library, horiz.

1972, Dec. 7 Litho. *Perf. 12½*
C545 AP105 20c brt blue .55 .25
C546 AP105 50c gold & multi .55 .25
C547 AP105 75c multicolored .55 .25
C548 AP105 5col multicolored 2.50 .95
Nos. C545-C548 (4) 4.15 1.70

No. C545 exists on thin dull paper with shiny gum. Values: unused $20, used $10.

Road to Irazú Volcano AP106

15c, Coco-Culebra Bay. 40c, Manuel Antonio Beach. 45c, Tourist Office emblem. 50c, Lindora Lake. 60c, San Jose P.O., vert.

1972-73 *Perf. 11x11½, 11½x11*
C549 AP106 5c like 20c .45 .25
C550 AP106 15c multi .45 .25
C551 AP106 20c shown .45 .25
C552 AP106 25c like 15c .45 .25
C553 AP106 40c multi .45 .25
C554 AP106 45c multi .45 .25
C555 AP106 50c multi .45 .25
C556 AP106 60c multi .45 .25
C557 AP106 80c like 40c .65 .25
C558 AP106 90c like 45c .65 .25
C559 AP106 1col like 50c .65 .25
C560 AP106 2col like 60c 1.25 .50
Nos. C549-C560 (12) 6.80 3.25

Tourism year of the Americas.
Issued: 20c, 25c, 80c, 90c, 1col, 2col, 12/26; others, 3/21/73.
No. C555 exists with inverted center, used only. Value $10,000.

Church Type of 1967

Designs as before.

1973, July 16 Engr. *Perf. 12½*
C561 AP85 5c slate grn .35 .25
C562 AP85 10c olive .35 .25
C563 AP85 15c orange .35 .25
C564 AP85 25c brown .35 .25
C565 AP85 30c rose claret .35 .25
C566 AP85 35c violet .35 .25
C567 AP85 40c brt green .35 .25
C568 AP85 45c dull yellow .35 .25
C569 AP85 50c rose magenta .35 .25
C570 AP85 55c blue .35 .25
C571 AP85 65c black .50 .25
C572 AP85 75c rose red .65 .25
C573 AP85 80c yellow grn .75 .25
C574 AP85 85c lilac .90 .25
C575 AP85 90c brt pink 1.00 .25
C576 AP85 1col dark blue 1.25 .25
Nos. C561-C576 (16) 8.55 4.00

Human Rights Flame — AP107

1973, Dec. 10 Photo. *Perf. 10½*
C577 AP107 50c black & red .65 .25

25th anniversary of the Universal Declaration of Human Rights.

OAS Emblem — AP108

1973, Dec. 17 Litho. *Perf. 10½*
C578 AP108 20c dk bl & dp car .65 .25

25th anniv. of the OAS.

Joaquin Vargas Calvo — AP109

No. C580, Alejandro Monestel. No. C581, Julio Mata. No. C582, Julio Fonseca. No. C583, Rafael A. Chaves. No. C584, Manuel M. Gutierrez.

1974, Jan. 14
C579 AP109 20c shown .50 .25
C580 AP109 20c multicolored .50 .25
C581 AP109 20c multicolored .50 .25
C582 AP109 60c multicolored .50 .25
C583 AP109 2col multicolored 1.25 .30
C584 AP109 5col multicolored 2.75 1.25
Nos. C579-C584 (6) 6.00 2.55

Costa Rican composers honored by the National Symphony Orchestra.

Revenue Stamps Overprinted in Black — AP110

1974, Apr. 5 Engr. *Perf. 12*

C585 AP110 50c brown .35 .25
C586 AP110 1col violet .40 .25
C587 AP110 2col orange 1.00 .40
C588 AP110 5col olive 2.25 1.75
Nos. C585-C588 (4) 4.00 2.65

Telephone Building, San Pedro — AP111

Designs: 65c, Rio Macho Control, horiz. 85c, Turbines, Rio Macho Center. 1.25col, Cachi Dam and reservoir, horiz. 2col, I.C.E. Headquarters.

1974, July 30 Litho. *Perf. 10½*

C589 AP111 50c gold & multi .30 .25
C590 AP111 65c gold & multi .30 .25
C591 AP111 85c gold & multi .40 .25
C592 AP111 1.25col gold & multi .65 .25
C593 AP111 2col gold & multi 1.25 .40
Nos. C589-C593 (5) 2.90 1.40

25th anniversary of Costa Rican Electrical Institute (I.C.E.).

EXFILMEX 74 Emblem AP112

1974, Aug. 22 *Perf. 13*

C594 AP112 65c green .30 .25
C595 AP112 3col lilac rose 1.10 .40

5th Inter-American Philatelic Exhibition, EXFILMEX-74 UPU, Mexico City, Oct. 26-Nov. 3.

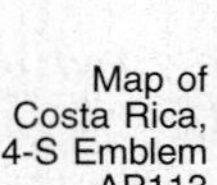

Map of Costa Rica, 4-S Emblem AP113

50c, Young harvesters and 4-S emblem.

1974, Oct. 7 Litho. *Perf. 12x11*

C596 AP113 20c brt green .65 .25
C597 AP113 50c multicolored .65 .25

25th anniversary of 4-S Clubs of Costa Rica (similar to US 4-H Clubs).

Roberto Brenes Mesen — AP114

Designs: 85c, "Love and Death," manuscript. 5col, Hands of writer, horiz.

1974, Oct. 14 Litho. *Perf. 10½*

C598 AP114 20c black & brn .35 .25
C599 AP114 85c black & red .35 .25
C600 AP114 5col black & red brn 2.00 .90
Nos. C598-C600 (3) 2.70 1.40

Mesen, educator & writer, birth centenary.

"Life Insurance" AP115

Designs: 20c, Ricardo Jiménez Oreamuno and Tomás Soley Güell, horiz. 50c, Harvest Insurance (hand holding shovel), horiz. 85c, Maritime insurance (hand holding paper boat). 1.25col, INS emblem. 2col, Workers rehabilitation (arm with crutch). 2.50col, Workers' Compensation (hand holding wrench). 20col, Fire insurance (hands protecting house).

1974, Oct. 30 *Perf. 14*

C601 AP115 20c multi .35 .25
C602 AP115 50c multi .35 .25
C603 AP115 65c multi .35 .25
C604 AP115 85c multi .35 .25
C605 AP115 1.25col multi .40 .25
C606 AP115 2col multi .70 .25
C607 AP115 2.50col multi .85 .40
C608 AP115 20col multi 5.50 4.50
Nos. C601-C608 (8) 8.85 6.40

Costa Rican Insurance Institute (Instituto Nacional de Seguros, INS), 50th anniversary.
For surcharges see Nos. C721-C722.

WPY Emblem — AP116

1974, Nov. 13 Litho. *Perf. 11x11½*

C609 AP116 2col vio bl & red .85 .25

World Population Year.

Oscar J. Pinto F. — AP117

Designs: 50c, Alberto Montes de Oca D., champion sharpshooter. 1col, Eduardo Garnier, sports promoter. O. J. Pinto, introducer of soccer.

1974, Dec. 2 *Perf. 13*

C610 AP117 20c gray & dk bl .35 .25
C611 AP117 50c gray & dk bl .35 .25
C612 AP117 1col gray & dk bl 1.00 .25
Nos. C610-C612 (3) 1.70 .75

First Central American Olympic Games, held in Guatemala, 1973.

Mormodes Buccinator AP118

Masdevallia Ephippium AP119

Orchids: No. C614, Gongora claviodora. No. C616, Encyclia spondiadum. No. C617, Lycaste skinneri alba. No. C618, Peristeria elata. No. C619, Miltonia roezelii. No. C620, Brassavola digbyana. No. C621, Epidendrum mirabile. No. C622, Barkeria lindleyana. No. C623, Cattleya skinneri. No. C624, Sobralia macrantha. No. C625, Lycaste cruenta. No. C626, Oncidium obryzatum. No. C627, Gongora armeniaca. No. C628, Sievekingia suavis. No. C629, Hexisea imbricata. No. C630, Warcewiczella discolor. No. C631, Oncidium kramerianum. No. C632, Cattleya dowiana.

1975, Mar. 7 Litho. *Perf. 10½, 13½*

C613 AP118 25c shown 1.25 .25
C614 AP118 25c multi 1.25 .25
C615 AP119 25c shown 1.25 .25
C616 AP119 25c multi 1.25 .25
a. Block of 4, #C613-C616 5.25 2.50
b. As "a," perf. 10½ 3.50 2.50
C617 AP118 65c multi 3.25 .25
C618 AP118 65c multi 3.25 .25
C619 AP119 65c multi 3.25 .25
C620 AP119 65c multi 3.25 .25
a. Block of 4, #C617-C620, perf. 13½ 13.00 4.50
b. As "a," perf. 10½ 20.00 4.50
C621 AP118 80c multi 4.50 .30
C622 AP118 80c multi 4.50 .30
C623 AP119 80c multi 4.50 .30
C624 AP119 80c multi 4.50 .30
a. Block of 4, #C621-C624 18.00 5.00
b. As "a," perf. 10½ 32.50 5.00
C625 AP118 1.40col multi 5.50 .40
C626 AP118 1.40col multi 5.50 .40
C627 AP119 1.40col multi 5.50 .40
C628 AP119 1.40col multi 5.50 .40
a. Block of 4, #C625-C628 22.50 9.00
b. As "a," perf. 10½ 17.50 9.00

Perf. 13½

C629 AP118 1.75col multi 3.25 .40
C630 AP118 2.15col multi 3.25 .55
C631 AP119 2.50col multi 5.50 1.10
C632 AP119 3.25col multi 6.50 1.40
Nos. C613-C632 (20) 76.50 8.25

5th National Orchid Exhibition.

Nos. C613-C628 were printed in both perforations on two different papers: dull finish and shiny. Nos. C629-C632 were printed on shiny paper.

Most examples of Nos. C617-C620, perf 10½, were surcharged.

For overprints and surcharges see Nos. C715-C720, C723-C728.

Radio Club Emblem AP120

Members' Flags and Emblem — AP121

Design: 2col, Federation emblem.

1975, Apr. 16 Litho. *Perf. 13½*

C633 AP120 1col blk & red lil .85 .25
C634 AP121 1.10col multi 1.00 .25
C635 AP120 2col black & bl 1.50 .25
Nos. C633-C635 (3) 3.35 .75

16th Central American Radio Amateurs' Convention, San José, May 2-4.

Nicoya Beach AP122

Designs: 75c, Driving cattle. 1col, Colonial Church, Nicoya. 3col, Savannah riders, vert.

1975, Aug. 1 Litho. *Perf. 13½*

C636 AP122 25c gray & multi .35 .25
C637 AP122 75c gray & multi .35 .25
C638 AP122 1col gray & multi .50 .25
C639 AP122 3col gray & multi 1.50 .85
Nos. C636-C639 (4) 2.70 1.60

Sesqui. of annexation of Nicoya District.

Costa Rica #158 AP123

Designs (Type A90 of 1932): No. C641, #159. No. C642, #160. No. C643, #161.

1975, Aug. 14 Litho. *Perf. 12*

C640 AP123 2.20col blk & org 1.00 .35
C641 AP123 2.20col blk & dk grn 1.00 .35
C642 AP123 2.20col blk & car rose 1.00 .35
C643 AP123 2.20col blk & dk bl 1.00 .35
a. Block of 4, #C640-C643 7.00 7.00

6th Natl. Phil. Exhib., San José, Aug. 14-17.
For surcharges see Nos. C885-C892.

IWY Emblem AP124

1975, Oct. 9 Litho. *Perf. 10½*

C644 AP124 40c vio bl & red .40 .25
C645 AP124 1.25col blk & ultra .75 .25

International Women's Year 1975.

UN Emblem AP125

UN, 30th Anniv.: 60c, UN General Assembly, horiz. 1.20col, UN Headquarters, NY.

1975, Oct. 24 *Perf. 12*

C646 AP125 10c bl & blk .35 .25
C647 AP125 60c multi .35 .25
C648 AP125 1.20col multi .95 .25
Nos. C646-C648 (3) 1.65 .75

The Visitation, by Jorge Gallardo AP126

Paintings by Jorge Gallardo: 1col, Nativity and Star. 5col, St. Joseph in his Workshop, Virgin and Child.

1975, Nov. 3 *Perf. 10½*

C649 AP126 50c multi .35 .25
C650 AP126 1col multi .60 .25
C651 AP126 5col multi 2.25 .70
Nos. C649-C651 (3) 3.20 1.20

Christmas 1975.

"20-30" Club Emblem — AP127

1976, Jan. 16 Litho. *Perf. 12*

C652 AP127 1col multi .65 .25

"20-30" Club of Costa Rica, 20th anniv.

Quercus Brenessi Trel — AP128

Plants: 30c, Maxillaria albertii schecht. 55c, Calathea brenesii standl. 2col, Brenesia costaricensis schlecht. 10col, Philodendron brenesii standl.

1976, Mar. 1 ***Perf. 10½***

C653	AP128	5c multi	.60	.25
C654	AP128	30c multi	.60	.25
C655	AP128	55c multi	.85	.25
C656	AP128	2col tan & multi	1.40	.40
C657	AP128	10col multi	6.50	3.00
		Nos. C653-C657 (5)	9.95	4.15

Prof. Alberto Manuel Brenes Mora, botanist, birth centenary.

"Literary Development" AP129

Designs: 1.10col, Man holding book, stylized. 5col, Costa Rican flag emanating from book, horiz.

1976, Apr. 9 **Litho.** ***Perf. 16***

C658	AP129	15c multi	.35	.25
C659	AP129	1.10col multi	.35	.25
C660	AP129	5col multi	1.50	.80
		Nos. C658-C660 (3)	2.20	1.30

Publishing in Costa Rica.
Nos. C658-C660 exist imperf.

Postrider, 1839 — AP130

Costa Rica No. 13, Post Office AP131

Designs: 65c, Costa Rica No. 14 and Post Office. 85c, Costa Rica No. 15 and Post Office. 2col, UPU Monument, Bern, vert.

1976, May 24 ***Perf. 10½***

C661	AP130	20c apple grn & blk	.50	.25
C662	AP131	50c bister & multi	.50	.25
C663	AP131	65c multi	.50	.25
C664	AP131	85c multi	.50	.25
C665	AP130	2col blk & lt bl	1.25	.50
		Nos. C661-C665 (5)	3.25	1.50

Cent. of UPU (in 1974).
Nos. C662-C664 exist without the surcharges on reproductions of Nos. 13-15.

Telephones, 1876 and 1976 — AP132

Designs: 2col, Wall telephone. 5col, Alexander Graham Bell.

1976, June 28

C666	AP132	1.60col lt bl & blk	.50	.25
C667	AP132	2col multicolored	.65	.25
C668	AP132	5col yellow & blk	1.50	.95
		Nos. C666-C668 (3)	2.65	1.45

Centenary of first telephone call by Alexander Graham Bell, Mar. 10, 1876.

Inverted Center Stamp of 1901 and Association Emblems — AP133

Design: 5col, 1901 stamp between Costa Rican Philatelic Society and Interamerican Philatelic Federation emblems.

1976, Nov. 11 **Litho.** ***Perf. 10½***

C669	AP133	50c multi	.35	.25
C670	AP133	1col multi	.35	.25
C671	AP133	2col multi	1.25	.25
		Nos. C669-C671 (3)	1.95	.75

Souvenir Sheet

Perf. 12

C672	AP133	5col multi	5.50	2.50

7th Natl. Phil. Exhib. and 9th Plenary Assembly of the Interamerican Phil. Fed. (FIAF), San José, Nov. 1976.
No. C670 exists in colors of No. C671.
No. C671 exists on thin dull paper, with bright gum. Value, mint, $25.
No. C672 was issued both perf and imperf. Same values.

"Seeing Eye" and Map of Costa Rica AP134

Amadeo Quiros Blanco — AP135

1976, Nov. 22 ***Perf. 16***

C673	AP134	35c black & blue	.40	.25
C674	AP135	2col multicolored	.85	.40

General Audit Office, 25th anniversary.

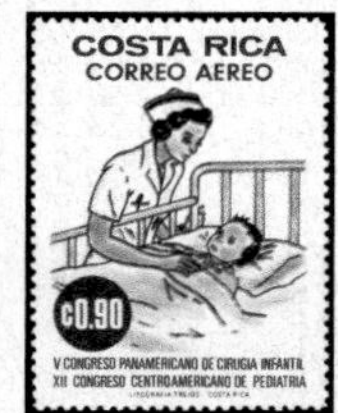

Nurse Attending Child — AP136

1.10col, National Children's Hospital, horiz.

1976, Nov. 29

C675	AP136	90c multi	.40	.25
C676	AP136	1.10col multi	.75	.25

5th Panamerican Congress of Pediatric Surgery and 12th Congress of Pediatrics.

LACSA Circling Globe — AP137

Designs: 1.20col, Route map. 3col, LACSA emblem and Costa Rican flag.

1976, Dec. 1 ***Perf. 10½***

C677	AP137	1col multi	.35	.25
C678	AP137	1.20col multi	.55	.25
C679	AP137	3col multi	1.50	.70
		Nos. C677-C679 (3)	2.40	1.20

Costa Rican Air Lines (LACSA), 30th anniversary.

Boston Tea Party AP138

US Bicent.: 5col, Declaration of Independence. 10col, Ringing Liberty Bell to announce Independence, vert.

1976, Dec. 24

C680	AP138	2.20col multi	.45	.30
C681	AP138	5col multi	1.25	.70
C682	AP138	10col multi	2.00	1.40
		Nos. C680-C682 (3)	3.70	2.40

Tree of Guanacaste AP139

Felipe J. Alvarado AP140

Designs (Rotary Emblem and): 60c, Dr. Paul Blanco Cervantes Hospital, horiz. 3col, Map of Costa Rica, horiz. 10col, Paul Harris.

1977, Mar. 31 **Litho.** ***Perf. 16***

C683	AP139	40c multi	.35	.25
C684	AP140	50c multi	.35	.25
C685	AP139	60c multi	.35	.25
C686	AP139	3col multi	1.25	.65
C687	AP140	10col multi	3.75	2.50
		Nos. C683-C687 (5)	6.05	3.90

Rotary Club of San José, 50th anniversary.

Boruca Cloth AP141

Design: 1.50col, Painted wood ornament.

1977, Feb. 22

C688	AP141	75c multi	.35	.25
C689	AP141	1.50col multi	.75	.25

Natl. Artisan & Small Industry Program.

Juana Pereira — AP142

Designs: 1col, First Church of Our Lady of the Angels, horiz. 1.10col, Our Lady of the Angels (gold sculpture). 1.25col, Crown of Our Lady of the Angels.

1977, June 6 **Litho.** ***Perf. 10½***

C690	AP142	50c multi	.35	.25
C691	AP142	1col multi	.35	.25
C692	AP142	1.10col multi	.35	.25
C693	AP142	1.25col multi	1.00	.25
		Nos. C690-C693 (4)	2.05	1.00

50th anniv. of the coronation of Our Lady of the Angels, patron saint of Costa Rica.

Alonso de Anguciana de Gamboa — AP143

Designs: 75c, Church of Esparza. 1col, Statue of Our Lady of Candlemas. 2col, Statue of Diego de Artieda y Chirino.

1977, July 4 **Litho.** ***Perf. 10½***

C694	AP143	35c multi	.35	.25
C695	AP143	75c multi	.35	.25
C696	AP143	1col multi	.50	.25
C697	AP143	2col multi	1.25	.40
		Nos. C694-C697 (4)	2.45	1.15

400th anniv. of the founding of Esparza.
For surcharge see No. C883.

CARE Emblem and Child — AP144

1col, CARE emblem and soybeans, horiz.

1977, Sept. 14 **Litho.** ***Perf. 16***

C698	AP144	80c multi	.40	.25
C699	AP144	1col multi	.75	.25

20th anniversary of CARE (relief organization) in Costa Rica.

Institute's Emblem — AP145

First Map of Americas, 1540 — AP146

1977, Oct. 21 **Litho.** ***Perf. 16***

C700	AP145	50c blk & multi	.65	.25
C701	AP146	1.40col blk & multi	1.25	.40

Hispanic Cultural Institute of Costa Rica, 25th anniversary.

Mercy Church, by Ricardo Ulloa B. — AP147

Paintings: 1col, Christ, by Floria Pinto de Herrero. 5col, St. Francis and the Birds, by Louisa Gonzalez Y Saenz.

1977, Nov. 9 **Litho.** ***Perf. 10½***

C702	AP147	50c multi	.50	.25
C703	AP147	1col multi	.50	.25
C704	AP147	5col multi	2.25	.70
		Nos. C702-C704 (3)	3.25	1.20

Health Ministry Emblem — AP148

1977, Nov. 16 *Perf. 16*
C705 AP148 1.40col multi .65 .25

Creation of Ministry of Health.

Picnic — AP149

Designs: 50c, Weaver. 2col, Beach scene. 5col, Fruit and vegetable market. 10col, Swans on lake.

1978, Mar. 21 **Litho.** *Perf. 10½*
C706 AP149 50c blk & multi .30 .25
C707 AP149 1col blk & multi .45 .25
C708 AP149 2col blk & multi 1.25 .25
C709 AP149 5col blk & multi 2.25 .85
C710 AP149 10col blk & multi 3.00 1.90
Nos. C706-C710 (5) 7.25 3.50

Conf. of Latin American Tourist Organizations.

San Martin — AP150

1978, Aug. 7 **Litho.** *Perf. 10½*
C711 AP150 5col multi 1.50 .80

Gen. José de San Martin (1778-1850), soldier and statesman, fought for South American independence.

Geographical Institute Emblem — AP151

1978, Aug. 28 **Litho.** *Perf. 12½*
C712 AP151 5col multi 1.50 .65

Pan-American Geography and History Institute, 50th anniversary. Exists imperf.

University Federation Emblem — AP152

1978, Sept. 18 *Perf. 11*
C713 AP152 80c ultra .65 .25

Central American University Federation, 30th anniversary.

Emblems — AP153

1978, Oct. 24 *Perf. 16*
C714 AP153 2col aqua, blk & gold .80 .40

6th Interamerican Philatelic Exhibition, Argentina 78, Buenos Aires, Oct. 1978.

Nos. C629-C631 Overprinted

1978, Nov. 1 **Litho.** *Perf. 13½*
C715 AP118 1.75col multi .65 .30
C716 AP118 2.15col multi .85 .40
C717 AP119 2.50col multi 1.40 .55
Nos. C715-C717 (3) 2.90 1.25

1st Pan Am flight in Costa Rica, 50th anniv.

Nos. C629-C631 Overprinted: "50 Aniversario de la / visita de Lindbergh a / Costa Rica 1928-1978"

1978, Nov. 1
C718 AP118 1.75col multi 1.50 .30
C719 AP118 2.15col multi 1.75 .40
C720 AP119 2.50col multi 2.25 .50
Nos. C718-C720 (3) 5.50 1.20

50th anniversary of Lindbergh's visit.

Nos. C603 and C607 Surcharged

1978, Nov. 8 *Perf. 14*
C721 AP115 50c on 65c multi .35 .25
C722 AP115 2col on 2.50col multi .95 .25

Asilo Carlos Maria Ulloa, birth centenary.

No. C617-C620, C630-C631 Surcharged

Perf. 10½, 13½

1978, Nov. 13 **Litho.**
C723 AP118 50c on 65c .75 .60
C724 AP118 50c on 65c .75 .60
C725 AP119 50c on 65c .75 .60
C726 AP119 50c on 65c .75 .60
a. Block of 4, #C723-C726 3.50 3.50
C727 AP118 1.20col on 2.15col 1.40 .55
C728 AP119 2col on 2.50col 1.40 .55
Nos. C723-C728 (6) 5.80 3.50

Nos. C723-C726, perf. 13½, value *$20*, unused, *$10*, used, each. No. C726a, unused, *$400.*

Star over Map of Costa Rica — AP154

1978, Nov. 13 *Perf. 10½*
C729 AP154 50c blue & blk .35 .25
C730 AP154 1col rose lil & blk .35 .25
C731 AP154 5col orange & blk 1.50 .65
a. Strip of 3, #C729-C731 2.75 2.00

Christmas 1978. Nos. C729-C731 printed in sheets of 100 and se-tenant in sheet of 15 (3x5). Value, se-tenant sheet, $20.

"Flying Men," Chorotega AP155

Designs: 1.20col, Oviedo giving his History of Indies to Duke of Calabria, horiz. 10col, Lord of Oviedo's coat of arms.

1978, Nov. 20 *Perf. 11½*
C732 AP155 85c multi .35 .25
C733 AP155 1.20col blk & lt bl .35 .25
C734 AP155 10col multi 2.50 2.00
Nos. C732-C734 (3) 3.20 2.50

500th birth anniv. of Gonzalo Fernandez de Oviedo, 1st chronicler of Spanish Indies.

Msgr. Domingo Rivas AP156

San José Cathedral AP157

1978, Dec. 6 *Perf. 16, 13½ (20col)*
C735 AP156 1col black & indigo .35 .25
C736 AP157 20col multicolored 4.25 3.50

Centenary of the Cathedral of San José.

View of Coco Island AP158

Designs: 2.10, 3, 5 col, various views of Coco Island. 10col, Installation of memorial plaque, people and flag. 5, 10col vert.

1979, Apr. 30 **Litho.** *Perf. 10½*
C737 AP158 90c multi .45 .25
C738 AP158 2.10col multi .85 .40
C739 AP158 3col multi 1.40 .55
C740 AP158 5col multi 2.00 1.00
C741 AP158 10col multi 4.00 2.25
a. Souv. sheet, #C737-C741 13.00 12.00
Nos. C737-C741 (5) 8.70 4.45

Visit of Pres. Rodrigo Carazo Odio to Coco Island, June 24, 1978, in the interest of national defense.

No. C741a exists imperf. Value $750.

Shrimp AP159

Designs: 85c, Mahogany snapper. 1.80col, Corvina. 3col, Crayfish. 10col, Tuna.

1979, May 14 **Litho.** *Perf. 13½*
C742 AP159 60c multi .55 .25
C743 AP159 85c multi .55 .25
C744 AP159 1.80col multi 1.00 .25
C745 AP159 3col multi 1.50 .55
C746 AP159 10col multi 5.50 3.50
Nos. C742-C746 (5) 9.10 4.80

Marine life protection.

Hungry Nestlings, IYC Emblem — AP160

1979, May 24 *Perf. 11*
C747 AP160 1col multi 1.00 .25
C748 AP160 2col multi 1.90 .50
C749 AP160 20col multi 12.50 5.50
Nos. C747-C749 (3) 15.40 6.25

International Year of the Child.

Microwave Transmitters, Mt. Irazu — AP161

Design: 1col, Arenal Dam, horiz.

1979, June 28 **Litho.** *Perf. 14*
C750 AP161 1col multi .35 .25
C751 AP161 5col multi 1.50 .70

Costa Rican Electricity Institute, 30th anniversary.

Costa Rica No. 1 and Rowland Hill AP162

Design: 10col, Penny Black and Hill.

1979, July 16 *Perf. 13*
C752 AP162 5col lil rose & bl gray 1.25 .55
C753 AP162 10col dl bl & blk 2.75 1.25

Sir Rowland Hill (1795-1879), originator of penny postage.

Poverty, by Juan Ramon Bonilla AP163

National Sculpture Contest: 60c, Hope, by Hernan Gonzalez. 2.10col, Cattle, by Victor M. Bermudez, horiz. 5col, Bust of Clorito Picado, by Juan Rafael Chacon. 20col, Mother and Child, by Francisco Zuniga.

1979, July 16 Litho. *Perf. 12*

C754	AP163	60c	multi	.30	.25
C755	AP163	1col	multi	.35	.25
C756	AP163	2.10col	multi	.70	.25
C757	AP163	5col	multi	2.00	1.10
C758	AP163	20col	multi	6.00	2.50
	Nos. C754-C758 (5)			9.35	4.35

Danaus Plexippus — AP164

Butterflies: 1col, Phoebis philea. 1.80col, Rothschildia. 2.10col, Prepona omphale. 2.60col, Marpesia marcella. 4.05col, Morpho cypris.

1979, Aug. 31 Litho. *Perf. 13½*

C759	AP164	60c	multi	3.00	.40
C760	AP164	1col	multi	5.00	.40
C761	AP164	1.80col	multi	7.00	.65
C762	AP164	2.10col	multi	10.00	1.25
C763	AP164	2.60col	multi	10.00	2.50
C764	AP164	4.05col	multi	20.00	3.50
	Nos. C759-C764 (6)			55.00	8.70

SOS Emblem, Houses AP165

Children's Drawings: 5col, 5.50col, Landscapes, diff.

1979, Sept. 18

C765	AP165	2.50col	multi	1.00	.40
C766	AP165	5col	multi	2.25	.60
C767	AP165	5.50col	multi	2.75	.90
	Nos. C765-C767 (3)			6.00	1.90

SOS Children's Villages, 30th anniversary.

President Type of 1943

Presidents of Costa Rica: 60c, Rafael Yglesias C. 85c, Ascension Esquivel Ibarra. 1col, Cleto Gonzalez Viquez. 2col, Ricardo Jimenez Oreamuno.

1979, Oct. 8 Litho. *Perf. 13½*

C768	A109	10c	dk blue	.35	.25
C769	A109	60c	dull purple	.35	.25
C770	A109	85c	red orange	.35	.25
C771	A109	1col	red orange	.45	.25
C772	A109	2col	brown	1.00	.40
a.	Strip of 5, #C768-C772			3.00	1.50
	Nos. C768-C772 (5)			2.50	1.40

Printed in sheets of 100 and se-tenant in sheets of 25 (5x5).

See Nos. C790-C794.

Holy Family, Creche — AP167

1979, Nov. 16 Litho. *Perf. 12½*

C773	AP167	1col	multi	.35	.25
C774	AP167	1.60col	multi	1.00	.25

Christmas 1979.

Reforestation AP168

1980, Jan. 14 Litho. *Perf. 11*

C775	AP168	1col	multi	.35	.25
C776	AP168	3.40col	multi	1.00	.50

Anatomy Lesson, by Rembrandt AP169

1980, Feb. 7 Litho. *Perf. 10½*

C777	AP169	10col	multi	4.25	1.75

Legal medicine teaching in Costa Rica, 50th anniversary.

Rotary Intl., 75th Anniv. — AP170

1980, Feb. 26 *Perf. 16*

C778	AP170	2.10col	multi	.45	.25
C779	AP170	5col	multi	1.40	.65

14th Intl. Symposium on Remote Sensing of the Environment, San José, Apr. 23-30 — AP171

Designs: 2.10col, Puerto Limon. 5col, Gulf of Nicoya, satellite photo.

1980, Mar. 10 Litho. *Perf. 12½*

C780	AP171	2.10col	multi	.45	.25
C781	AP171	5col	multi	1.40	.65

Exist imperf.

Soccer, Moscow '80 Emblem — AP172

3col, Bicycling. 4.05col, Baseball. 20col, Swimming.

1980, Apr. 16 Litho. *Perf. 10½*

C782	AP172	1col	shown	.50	.25
C783	AP172	3col	multi	8.25	.75
C784	AP172	4.05col	multi	8.25	1.00
C785	AP172	20col	multi	8.25	5.00
	Nos. C782-C785 (4)			25.25	7.00

22nd Summer Olympic Games, Moscow, July 19-Aug. 3.

Poas Volcano AP173

2.50col, Cahuita Beach.

1980, May 14 Litho. *Perf. 10½*

C786	AP173	1col	shown	.35	.25
C787	AP173	2.50col	multi	.95	.40

National Parks Service, 10th anniversary.

José Maria Zeledon Brenes, Score — AP174

Design: 10col, Manuel Maria Gutierrez.

1980, June 25 Litho. *Perf. 12½*

C788	AP174	1col	multi	.35	.25
C789	AP174	10col	multi	2.00	1.40

National anthem composed by Brenes (words) and Gutierrez (music). Nos. C788-C789 exist imperf.

President Type of 1943

1col, Alfredo Gonzalez F. 1.60col, Federico Tinoco G. 1.80col, Francisco Aguilar B. 2.10col, Julio Acosta G. 3col, Leon Cortes C.

1980, Aug. 14 Litho. *Perf. 11*

C790	A109	1col	dk red	.35	.25
C791	A109	1.60col	slate bl	.55	.25
C792	A109	1.80col	brown	.55	.25
C793	A109	2.10col	dull green	.75	.25
C794	A109	3col	dark purple	1.25	.50
	Nos. C790-C794 (5)			3.45	1.50

8th Natl. Phil. Exhib. — AP175

1980, Sept. 11 *Perf. 13½*

C795	AP175	5col	multi	.80	.60
C796	AP175	20col	multi	3.50	2.75

Fruits — AP176

60c, Cacao. 1col, Coffee. 2.10col, Bananas. 3.40col, Flowers. 5col, Sugar cane.

1980, Sept. 24 *Perf. 10½*

C797	AP176	10c	shown	.30	.25
C798	AP176	60c	multi	.55	.25
C799	AP176	1col	multi	.85	.25
C800	AP176	2.10col	multi	1.75	.25
C801	AP176	3.40col	multi	2.25	.50
C802	AP176	5col	multi	2.75	.95
	Nos. C797-C802 (6)			8.45	2.45

Giant Tree, by Jorge Carvajal — AP177

Paintings: 2.10col, Secret Look, by Rolando Cubero. 2.45col, Consuelo, by Fernando Carballo. 3col, Volcano, by Lola Fernandez. 4.05col, attending Mass, by Francisco Amighetti.

1980, Oct. 22 Litho. *Perf. 10½*

C803	AP177	1col	multi	.45	.25
C804	AP177	2.10col	multi	.65	.25

Size: 28x30mm

C805	AP177	2.45col	multi	.80	.30

Size: 22x36mm

C806	AP177	3col	multi	.90	.40
C807	AP177	4.05col	multi	1.40	.50
	Nos. C803-C807 (5)			4.20	1.70

Virgin and Child, by Raphael AP178

Christmas 1980: 10col, Virgin and Child and St. John, by Raphael.

1980, Nov. 11 *Perf. 13½*

C808	AP178	1col	multi	.50	.30
C809	AP178	10col	multi	2.75	1.75

Juan Santamaria International Airport AP179

1col, Caldera Harbor. 2.10col, Rio Frio Railroad Bridge. 2.60col, Highway to Colon. 5col, Huetar post office.

1980, Dec. 11 Litho. *Perf. 10½*

Sizes: 30x30mm, 31x25mm (1.30col), 25x32mm (2.60col)

C810	AP179	1col	multi	.35	.25
C811	AP179	1.30col	shown	.50	.25
C812	AP179	2.10col	multi	1.00	.40
C813	AP179	2.60col	multi	1.00	.40
C814	AP179	5col	multi	1.60	.80
	Nos. C810-C814 (5)			4.45	2.10

Paying your taxes means progress.

For surcharge see No. C884.

Repertorio Americano Cover, J. Garcia Monge and Signature — AP180

1981, Jan. 2 Litho. *Perf. 10½*

C815	AP180	1.60col	multi	.45	.25
C816	AP180	3col	multi	.95	.40

Birth centenary of J. Garcia Monge, founder of Repertorio Americano journal.

Arms of Aserri (Site of Cornea Bank) — AP181

1981, Jan. 28 Litho. *Perf. 13½*

C817	AP181	1col	shown	.35	.25
C818	AP181	1.80col	Eye	1.00	.25
C819	AP181	5col	Rojas	3.00	.80
	Nos. C817-C819 (3)			4.35	1.30

Establishment of human cornea bank, founded by Abelardo Rojas.

Harpia Harpyja — AP182

2.50col, Ara macao. 3col, Felis concolor. 5.50col, Ateles geoffrovi.

1980, Dec. 23 *Perf. 11*

C820	AP182	2.10col	shown	1.60	.40
C821	AP182	2.50col	multi	2.10	.55
C822	AP182	3col	multi	2.75	.65
C823	AP182	5.50col	multi	6.50	1.10
	Nos. C820-C823 (4)			12.95	2.70

Medical and Surgical Clinic AP183

1981, Apr. 8 Litho. *Perf. 10½*
C824 AP183 5c multi .35 .25
C825 AP183 10c multi .35 .25
C826 AP183 50c multi .35 .25
C827 AP183 1.30col multi .55 .25
C828 AP183 3.40col multi .75 .50
C829 AP183 4.05col multi, vert. 1.25 .55
Nos. C824-C829 (6) 3.60 2.05

University of Costa Rica, 40th anniversary.

Mail Transport by Horse — AP184

2.10col, Train, 1857. 10col, Mail carriers, 1858.

1981, May 6 Litho. *Perf. 10½*
C830 AP184 1col shown .35 .25
C831 AP184 2.10col multi .65 .25
C832 AP184 10col multi 3.25 1.60
Nos. C830-C832 (3) 4.25 2.10

Heinrich von Stephan (1831-97), UPU founder.

13th World Telecommunications Day — AP185

1981, May 18 *Perf. 11*
C833 AP185 5col multi 3.00 .60
C834 AP185 25col multi 8.00 4.00

Bishop Bernardo Thiel — AP186

1981, June 8 Litho. *Perf. 10½*
C835 Strip of 5, stained glass windows 4.50 4.00
a. AP186 1col Sts. Peter & Paul .30 .30
b. AP186 1col St. Vincent de Paul .30 .30
c. AP186 1col Death of St. Joseph .30 .30
d. AP186 1col Archangel Michael .30 .30
e. AP186 1col Holy Family .30 .30
C836 AP186 2col shown 1.25 .40

Consecration of Bernardo Augusto Thiel as Bishop of San Jose.

Juan Santamaria AP187

2.40col, Alajuela Cathedral, horiz.

1981, June 26 *Perf. 13½*
C837 AP187 1col shown .35 .25
C838 AP187 2.45col multi .90 .40

Alajuela province.

Potters — AP188

1.60col, Bricklayers. 1.80col, Farmers. 2.50col, Fishermen. 3col, Nurse, patient. 5col, Children, traffic policeman.

1981, July 10 Litho. *Perf. 10½*
C839 AP188 15c shown .35 .25
C840 AP188 1.60col multi .35 .25
C841 AP188 1.80col multi .35 .25
C842 AP188 2.50col multi .35 .25
C843 AP188 3col multi .85 .25
C844 AP188 5col multi 1.25 .25
Nos. C839-C844 (6) 3.50 1.50

Model of New Natl. Archives AP189

Natl. Archives Centenary: 1.40col, Leon Fernandez Bonilla, founder, vert. 2col, Arms, vert. 3col, St. Thomas University, former headquarters.

1981, Aug. 24 Litho. *Perf. 13½*
C845 AP189 1.40col multi .45 .25
C846 AP189 2col multi .75 .25
C847 AP189 3col multi .95 .50
C848 AP189 3.50col multi 1.00 .60
Nos. C845-C848 (4) 3.15 1.60

Men Reaching for Sun, Map AP190

1col, Man in wheelchair, stairs, vert. 2.60col, Man reaching for scale, vert.

1981, Sept. 9 Litho. *Perf. 11*
C849 AP190 1col multi .35 .25
C850 AP190 2.60col multi .85 .25
C851 AP190 10col shown 4.00 .80
Nos. C849-C851 (3) 5.20 1.30

Intl. Year of the Disabled.

World Food Day — AP191

1981, Oct. 16 Litho. *Perf. 10½*
C852 AP191 5col multi .60 .25
C853 AP191 10col multi 1.10 .55

President Type of 1943

1col, Rafael A. Calderon Guardia, 1940. 2col, Teodoro Picado Michalski, 1944. 3col, José Figueres Ferrer, 1953. 5col, Otilio Ulate Blanco, 1949. 10col, Mario Echandi Jimenez, 1958.

1981, Dec. 7 Litho. *Perf. 13½*
C854 A109 1col pink .60 .55
C855 A109 2col orange .60 .55
C856 A109 3col green .75 .55
C857 A109 5col dk bl 1.50 .90
C858 A109 10col blue 3.00 2.00
Nos. C854-C858 (5) 6.45 4.55

Bar Assoc. of Costa Rica Centenary (1981) AP192

1col, Emblem, horiz. 2col, E. Figueroa, 1st president. 20col, Bar building, horiz.

1982, Mar. 22 Litho. *Perf. 13½*
C859 AP192 1col multi .35 .25
C860 AP192 2col multi .35 .25
C861 AP192 20col multi 3.00 1.40
Nos. C859-C861 (3) 3.70 1.90

National Progress AP193

95c, Housing. 1.15col, Agricultural fair. 1.45col, Education. 1.65col, Drinkable water. 1.80col, Rural medical care. 2.10col, Recreational areas. 2.35col, Natl. Theater Square. 2.60col, Communications. 3col, Electric railroad. 4.05col, Irrigation.

1982 *Perf. 10½*
C862 AP193 95c multi .45 .35
C863 AP193 1.15col multi .45 .35
C864 AP193 1.45col multi .45 .35
C865 AP193 1.65col multi .45 .35
C866 AP193 1.80col multi .45 .35
C867 AP193 2.10col multi .45 .35
C868 AP193 2.35col multi .70 .55
C869 AP193 2.60col multi 1.10 .75
C870 AP193 3col multi 1.50 1.00
C871 AP193 4.05col multi 1.75 1.25
Nos. C862-C871 (10) 7.75 5.65

Issue dates: 1.80col, 2.10col, 2.60col, 3col, 4.05col, May 5; others, June 16.

City of Alajuela Bicentenary AP194

Designs: 5col, Central Park Fountain. 10col, Juan Santamaria Historical and Cultural Museum, horiz. 15col, Church of Christ of Esquipulas. 20col, Monsignor Esteban Lorenzo de Tristan, 25col, Father Juan Manuel Lopez del Corral.

1982, Aug. 9
C872 AP194 5col multi .60 .30
C873 AP194 10col multi 1.25 .55
C874 AP194 15col multi 1.90 1.25
C875 AP194 20col multi 2.50 1.25
C876 AP194 25col multi 3.50 1.60
Nos. C872-C876 (5) 9.75 4.95

Perez Zeledon County, 50th Anniv. (1981) — AP195

Designs: 10c, Saint's Stone. 50c, Monument to Mothers. 1col, Pedro Perez Zeledon. 1.25col, St. Isidore Labrador Church. 3.50col, Municipal Building, horiz. 4.25col, Arms.

1982, Aug. 30
C877 AP195 10c multi .45 .30
C878 AP195 50c multi .45 .30
C879 AP195 1col multi .45 .30
C880 AP195 1.25col multi .45 .30
C881 AP195 3.50col multi .75 .30
C882 AP195 4.25col multi 1.10 .30
Nos. C877-C882 (6) 3.65 1.80

Nos. C695 and C813 Surcharged

No. C883

No. C884

1982, Oct. 28 Litho. *Perf. 10½*
C883 AP143 3col on 75c multi .50 .25
C884 AP179 5col on 2.60col multi .95 .25

Nos. C640-C643 Surcharged and Overprinted

1982, Oct. 28 *Perf. 12*
C885 AP123 8.40col on #C640 .70 .40
C886 AP123 8.40col on #C641 .70 .40
C887 AP123 8.40col on #C642 .70 .40
C888 AP123 8.40col on #C643 .70 .40
C889 AP123 9.70col on #C640 .90 .55
C890 AP123 9.70col on #C641 .90 .55
C891 AP123 9.70col on #C642 .90 .55
C892 AP123 9.70col on #C643 .90 .55
Nos. C885-C892 (8) 6.40 3.80

9th Natl. Stamp Exhibition.

TB Bacillus Centenary AP196

1.50col, Koch. 3col, Koch, slide. 3.30col, Health Ministry.

1982, Nov. 19 *Perf. 13½*
C893 AP196 1.50col multi .35 .25
C894 AP196 3col multi .65 .25
C895 AP196 3.30col multi .65 .25
Nos. C893-C895 (3) 1.65 .75

Pan-American Blood Donors' Society, 7th Cong. — AP197

30col, Natl. Blood Assoc. emblem. 50col, Cong. emblem.

1982, Nov. 25 *Perf. 11*
C896 AP197 30col multi 2.25 1.40
C897 AP197 50col multi 3.50 2.00

AP198

8.40col, Emblem, horiz. 9.70col, Emblem, diff. 11.70col, Handshake, horiz. 13.05col, Emblem, diff., horiz.

1982, Dec. 13 Litho. *Perf. 10½*

C898	AP198	8.40col multi	.70	.25
C899	AP198	9.70col multi	1.00	.40
C900	AP198	11.70col multi	1.00	.40
C901	AP198	13.05col multi	1.25	.50
	Nos. C898-C901 (4)		3.95	1.55

Inter-Governmental Migration Committee, 30th anniv.

AP199

4.80col, St. Francis of Assisi, by El Greco. 7.40col, Portrait, diff.

1983, Jan. 3 *Perf. 16*

C902	AP199	4.80col multi	.65	.25
C903	AP199	7.40col multi	1.20	.25

For surcharges see Nos. C908-C911.

Visit of Pope John Paul II — AP200

1983, Mar. 1 Litho. *Perf. 10½*

C904	AP200	5col multi	3.00	.25
C905	AP200	10col multi	3.00	.50
C906	AP200	15col multi	6.50	.75
	Nos. C904-C906 (3)		12.50	1.50

Bolivar, by Francisco Zuniga Chavarria — AP201

1983, July 22 Litho. *Perf. 16*

C907	AP201	10col multi	1.25	.25

Nos. C902-C903 Surcharged

1983, Sept. 23 Litho. *Perf. 16*

C908	AP199	10c on 4.80col	.55	.25
C909	AP199	50c on 4.80col	.55	.25
C910	AP199	1.50col on 7.40col	.55	.25
C911	AP199	3col on 7.40col	.55	.25
	Nos. C908-C911 (4)		2.20	1.00

LACSA Costa Rica Airlines, 40th Anniv. — AP202

Various childrens' drawings: 1col, Adriana E. Hidalgo. 7col, Osvaldo A.G. Vega. 16col, David V. Rodriguez.

1986, Dec. 12 Litho. *Perf. 13½*

C912	AP202	1col multi	*.90*	.25
C913	AP202	7col multi	*6.00*	.30
C914	AP202	16col multi	*14.00*	.75
	Nos. C912-C914 (3)		*20.90*	1.30

Nos. C912-C913 exist perf 11. Unused examples are rare. Value used, $5 each.

Roman Macaya Lahmann, Aviation Pioneer AP203

1988, Sept. 26 Litho. *Perf. 10½*

C915	AP203	10col multi	.75	.25

No. 418 Overprinted

1990, Nov. 5

C916	A180	50col multicolored	4.25	2.00

Bagging Coffee Beans — AP204

Perf. 10½

1990, Nov. 16 Litho. Unwmk.

C917	AP204	50col multicolored	3.25	.80

AP205

1990, Dec. 6

C918	AP205	50col blue & black	3.75	.80

First postage stamps, 150th anniv.

National Theater — AP206

Banana Picker, 1897, by Alleardo Villa.

1991, Mar. 25 Litho. *Perf. 10½*

C919	AP206	30col multicolored	2.25	.80

No. 428 Overprinted

Litho. & Engr.

1991, Sept. 13 *Perf. 12½*

C920	A188	200col	8.75	2.00

12th Natl. Philatelic Exposition.

No. 402 Overprinted

1991, Oct. 11 Litho. *Perf. 11½*

Granite Paper

C921	A170	20col multicolored	5.00	2.00

Basketball, cent.

Social Security Administration, 50th Anniv. AP207

1991, Nov. 1 Litho. *Perf. 13½*

C922	AP207	15col multicolored	3.25	1.00

La Poesia by Vespasiano Bignami — AP208

1992, Jan. 24 Litho. *Perf. 10½*

C923	AP208	35col multicolored	5.25	2.00

National Theater.

Discovery of America, 500th Anniv. AP209

No. C924 — Columbus' ships: a, Nina. b, Santa Maria. c, Pinta.

1992, Oct. 8 Litho. *Perf. 13½*

C924		Strip of 3	6.00	6.00
a.-c.		A209 45col Any single	1.50	1.50

Intl. Arts Festival — AP210

1993, Mar. 15 Litho. *Perf. 13½*

C925	AP210	45col multicolored	2.00	1.00

Telecommunications Institute, 30th Anniv. — AP211

1993, Nov. 25 Litho. *Perf. 13½*

C926	AP211	45col multicolored	1.45	.70

Ministry of the Interior, 150th Anniv. AP212

1994, Mar. 8 Litho. *Perf. 10½*

C927	AP212	45col multicolored	1.45	.70

Intl. Year of the Family — AP213

1994, May 5 Litho. *Perf. 10½*

C928	AP213	45col multicolored	2.75	1.30

LACSA, 50th Anniv. AP214

5col, Douglas DC-3. 10col, Curtiss C-46. 20col, Beechcraft. 30col, DC-6B. 35col, BAC 1-11. 40col, Convair CV 440. 45col, Electra L-188. 50col, Boeing 727-200. 55col, Douglas DC-8. 60col, Airbus A320.

1996, Mar. 29 Litho. *Perf. 10½*

C929	AP214	5col multi	.30	.25
C930	AP214	10col multi	.30	.25
C931	AP214	20col multi	.45	.40
C932	AP214	30col multi	.80	.65
C933	AP214	35col multi	.85	.70
C934	AP214	40col multi	1.10	.90
C935	AP214	45col multi	1.10	.95
C936	AP214	50col multi	1.25	1.00
C937	AP214	55col multi	1.50	1.25
C938	AP214	60col multi	1.75	1.40
	Nos. C929-C938 (10)		9.40	7.75

No. C932 Surcharged

2001, Oct. 5 Litho. *Perf. 10½*

C939	AP214	5col on 30col multi	.75	.40

10th Intl. Art Festival — AP215

2006, Mar. 17 Litho. *Perf. 10½*

C940	AP215	120col multi	2.25	2.00

AIR POST SPECIAL DELIVERY STAMPS

Catalogue values for unused stamps in this section are for Never Hinged items.

UPU Headquarters and Monument, Bern — APSD1

Perf. 10x11

1970, May 20 Litho. Unwmk.

CE1 APSD1 35c multi 1.00 .25
CE2 APSD1 60c multi 1.00 .25

Opening of the UPU Headquarters in Bern. The red and black label attached to the 60c is inscribed "EXPRES." Values are for stamps with label attached.

Stamps with labels removed were used for regular airmail.

AIR POST OFFICIAL STAMPS

Air Post Stamps of 1934 Ovptd. in Red

1934 Unwmk. *Perf. 12*

CO1 AP8 5c green .25 .25
CO2 AP8 10c car rose .25 .25
CO3 AP8 15c chocolate .50 .50
CO4 AP8 20c deep blue .80 .80
CO5 AP8 25c deep org .80 .80
CO6 AP8 40c olive blk .80 .80
CO7 AP8 50c gray blk .80 .80
CO8 AP8 60c org yel .95 .95
CO9 AP8 75c dull vio .95 .95
CO10 AP9 1col deep rose 1.75 1.75
CO11 AP9 2col light blue 5.00 5.00
CO12 AP9 5col black 8.50 8.50
CO13 AP9 10col red brown 12.50 12.50
Nos. CO1-CO13 (13) 33.85 33.85

For overprints see Nos. C103-C116.

SPECIAL DELIVERY STAMPS

Catalogue values for unused stamps in this section are for Never Hinged items.

Winged Letter SD1

Unwmk.

1972, Mar. 20 Litho. *Perf. 11*

E1 SD1 75c brown & red .40 .30
E2 SD1 1.50col blue & red .80 .40

1973 *Perf. 11x12*

E3 SD1 75c green & red .55 .30

1973, Nov. 5 Litho. *Perf. 12*

E4 SD1 75c lilac & orange 1.75 .75

Exists perf 11x11½.

Concorde SD2

1976, May 17 Litho. *Perf. 16*

E5 SD2 1col vermilion & multi 1.00 .75

SD3

1979, June 15 Litho. *Perf. 12½*

E6 SD3 2col multi 1.10 .50

SD4

1980, Dec. 18 Litho. *Perf. 12½*

E7 SD4 2col multi 1.00 .50

1982, Dec. 20 Litho. *Perf. 11*

E8 SD4 4col multi 1.40 .40

POSTAGE DUE STAMPS

D1

1903 Unwmk. Engr. *Perf. 14*

Numerals in Black

J1 D1 5c slate blue 6.75 1.25
J2 D1 10c brown orange 6.75 1.25
J3 D1 15c yellow green 3.50 1.75
J4 D1 20c carmine 4.75 1.75
J5 D1 25c slate gray 4.75 2.40
J6 D1 30c brown 6.00 2.50
J7 D1 40c olive bister 6.75 2.50
J8 D1 50c red violet 6.75 2.50
Nos. J1-J8 (8) 46.00 15.90

D2

1915 Litho. *Perf. 12*

J9 D2 2c orange 1.25 .55
J10 D2 4c dark blue 1.25 .55
J11 D2 8c gray green 1.25 .55
J12 D2 10c violet 1.25 .55
J13 D2 20c brown 1.25 .55
Nos. J9-J13 (5) 6.25 2.75

OFFICIAL STAMPS

Values for unused stamps are for examples with original gum as defined in the catalogue introduction. Examples without gum have probably been used and are so regarded.

Very fine examples of Nos. O1-O24 will have perforations just clear of the design on one or more sides.

Nos. O1-O55, to about 1915, normally were not canceled when affixed to official mail. Occasionally they were canceled in a foreign country of destination. Used values are for favor-canceled stamps or for stamps without gum.

Regular Issues Overprinted

Overprinted in Red, Black, Blue or Green

1883-85 Unwmk. *Perf. 12*

O1 A6 1c green (R) 2.00 1.10
O2 A6 1c green (Bk) 4.00 1.10
O3 A6 2c carmine (Bk) 4.00 1.40
O4 A6 2c carmine (Bl) 2.40 1.60
O5 A6 5c blue vio (R) 7.00 3.00
O6 A6 10c orange (G) 10.00 4.00
O7 A6 40c blue (R) 10.00 4.00
Nos. O1-O7 (7) 39.40 16.20

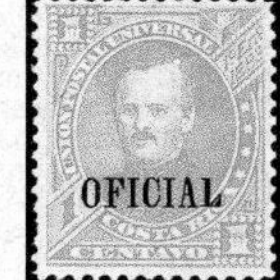

Overprinted

1886

O8 A6 1c green (Bk) 3.50 1.10
O9 A6 2c carmine (Bk) 3.50 1.60
O10 A6 5c blue vio (R) 24.00 11.00
O11 A6 10c orange (Bk) 24.00 11.00
Nos. O8-O11 (4) 55.00 24.70

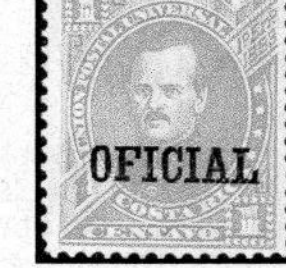

Overprinted

O12 A6 1c green (Bk) 3.50 1.00
O13 A6 2c carmine (Bk) 3.50 1.40
O14 A6 5c blue vio (R) 24.00 11.00
O15 A6 10c orange (Bk) 24.00 11.00
Nos. O12-O15 (4) 55.00 24.40

Nos. O8-O11 and O12-O15 exist se-tenant in vertical pairs.

Overprinted in Black

O16 A6 5c blue vio 60.00 60.00
O17 A6 10c orange — 275.00

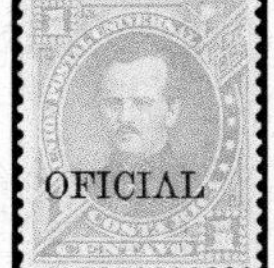

Overprinted

1887

O18 A6 1c green 1.25 .55
O19 A6 2c carmine 1.25 .50
O21 A6 10c orange 37.50 24.00
c. Double overprint 42.50
O22 A7 5c blue vio 12.00 3.50
O23 A7 10c orange .90 .50
c. Double overprint 27.50
O24 A6 40c blue 1.25 .50
Nos. O18-O24 (6) 54.15 29.55

Overprinted "OFICAL"

O18a A6 1c green
O19a A6 2c carmine 25.00 14.50
O22a A7 5c blue violet 25.00
O23a A7 10c orange 25.00 3.50
O24a A6 40c blue 25.00 17.00
Nos. O18a-O24a (5) 100.00

Dangerous counterfeits exist of Nos. O18a-O24a.

Without Period

O18b A6 1c green 25.00 15.00
O19b A6 2c carmine 25.00 15.00
O22b A7 5c blue violet 25.00 15.00
O23b A7 10c orange 25.00 15.00
Nos. O18b-O23b (4) 100.00 60.00

Nos. O18b-O23b are from a separate plate without periods. No. O23 exists without period (position 32). These must be collected in pairs.

Issues of 1889-1901 Overprinted

1889 *Perf. 14, 15*

O25 A10 1c brown .25 .25
O26 A11 2c dk green .25 .25
O27 A12 5c orange .25 .25
O28 A13 10c red brown .25 .25
O29 A14 20c yellow grn .40 .25
O30 A15 50c rose red 1.40 1.40
Nos. O25-O30 (6) 2.80 2.65

1892

O31 A20 1c grnsh blue .25 .25
O32 A21 2c yellow .25 .25
O33 A22 5c violet .25 .25
O34 A23 10c lt green 4.00 1.60
O35 A24 20c scarlet .25 .25
O36 A25 50c gray blue 1.00 .55
Nos. O31-O36 (6) 6.00 3.15

1901-02

O37 A30 1c green & blk .40 .40
O38 A31 2c ver & blk .40 .40
O39 A32 5c gray bl & blk .40 .40
O40 A33 10c ocher & blk .80 .80
O41 A34 20c lake & blk 1.25 1.25
O42 A35 50c lilac & dk bl 10.00 4.00
O43 A36 1col ol bis & blk 17.50 10.00
Nos. O37-O43 (7) 30.75 17.25

No. 46 Overprinted in Green

1903

O44 A31 2c ver & blk 3.00 3.00
b. "PROVISIORO" 10.00 10.00
d. Inverted overprint 10.00 10.00
f. As "b," inverted 15.00 10.00

Counterfeit overprints exist.

Regular Issue of 1903 Overprinted Like Nos. O25-O43

1903 *Perf. 14, 12½x14*

O45 A40 4c red vio & blk 1.40 1.40
O46 A41 6c ol grn & blk 1.75 1.75
O47 A42 25c gray lil & brn 9.50 6.00
Nos. O45-O47 (3) 12.65 9.15

Counterfeit overprints exist.

Regular Issue of 1907 Overprinted

1908 *Perf. 14*

O48 A43 1c red brn & ind .25 .25
O49 A44 2c yel grn & blk .25 .25
O50 A45 4c car & ind .25 .25
O51 A46 5c yel & dull bl .25 .25
O52 A47 10c blue & blk .80 .80
O53 A49 25c gray lil & blk .30 .25
O54 A50 50c red lil & bl .55 .55
O55 A51 1col brown & blk 1.25 1.25
Nos. O48-O55 (8) 3.90 3.85

Various varieties of the overprint and basic stamps exist.

Imperf examples of Nos. O48, O49, O53 were found in 1970.

Regular Issue of 1910 Overprinted in Black

1917
O56 A56 5c orange .40 .40
a. Inverted overprint 6.00 3.50
O57 A57 10c deep blue .25 .25
a. Inverted overprint 3.50 3.50

No. 74 Surcharged

1920 Red Surcharge *Perf. 12*
O58 A58 15c on 20c olive grn .55 .55

Nos. 72, 61, 59, 65-67 Surcharged or Overprinted

1921 Black Surcharge *Perf. 12*
O59 A56 10c on 5c orange .65 .50
a. "10 CTS." inverted 17.50

Perf. 14
O60 A45 4c car & indigo .55 .55
a. "1291" for "1921" 12.00
O61 A43 6c on 1c red brn & ind .70 .70
O62 A49 20c on 25c gray lil & blk .70 .70

Overprinted like No. O60
O63 A50 50c red lil & bl 5.00 2.00
O64 A51 1col brown & blk 7.00 4.00
Nos. O59-O64 (6) 14.60 8.45

Nos. O60 to O64 exist with date and new values inverted. These may be printer's waste but probably were deliberately made.

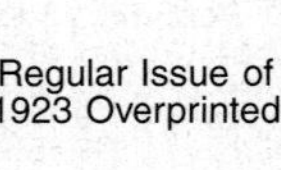
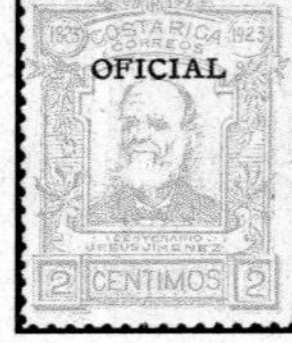
Regular Issue of 1923 Overprinted

1923 *Perf. 11½*
O65 A68 2c brown .25 .25
O66 A68 4c green .25 .25
O67 A68 5c blue .40 .40
O68 A68 20c carmine .25 .25
O69 A68 1col violet .50 .50
Nos. O65-O69 (5) 1.65 1.65

Nos. O65 to O69 exist imperforate but were not regularly issued in that condition. Value, set: $5.

O7

1926 Unwmk. Engr. *Perf. 12½*
O70 O7 2c ultra & blk .25 .25
O71 O7 3c mag & blk .25 .25
O72 O7 4c lt bl & blk .25 .25
O73 O7 5c grn & blk .25 .25
O74 O7 6c ocher & blk .25 .25
O75 O7 10c rose red & blk .25 .25
O76 O7 20c ol grn & blk .25 .25
O77 O7 30c red org & blk .25 .25
O78 O7 45c brown & blk .25 .25
O79 O7 1col lilac & blk .50 .50
Nos. O70-O79 (10) 2.75 2.75

See Nos. O82-O94. For surcharges see Nos. C7-C10.

Regular Issue of 1936 Overprinted in Black

1936 Unwmk. *Perf. 12*
O80 A96 5c green .25 .25
O81 A96 10c carmine rose .25 .25

Type of 1926

1937 *Perf. 12½*
O82 O7 2c vio & blk .25 .25
O83 O7 3c bis brn & blk .25 .25
O84 O7 4c rose car & blk .25 .25
O85 O7 5c ol grn & blk .25
O86 O7 8c blk brn & blk .25
O87 O7 10c rose lake & blk .25
O88 O7 20c ind & blk .25 .25
O89 O7 40c red org & blk .25 .25
O90 O7 55c dk vio & blk .25
O91 O7 1col brn vio & blk .30 .30
O92 O7 2col gray bl & blk .70 .70
O93 O7 5col dl yel & blk 3.00 3.00
O94 O7 10col blue & blk 55.00 20.00
Nos. O82-O94 (13) 61.25 25.25

Nine stamps of this series exist with perforated star (2c, 3c, 4c, 20c, 40c, 1col, 2col, 5col, 10col). These were issued to officials for postal purposes. Unpunched stamps were sold to collectors but had no franking power. Values for unused are for unpunched. Value, punched set of 9: $25.

POSTAL TAX STAMPS

The 1927 postal tax stamps covered the 10c per book charge for books sent by mail. The stamps were sold at the post office and applied to any package containing books.

Regular Stamps and Revenue Stamps Overprinted in Black

Nos. RA1B-RA1D Overprinted

1927, Mar. 17
RA1A A75 10c car rose *35.00* 5.00
RA1B 50c brown (overprinted on revenue stamp) *50.00* 10.00
RA1C A79 1col olive green *50.00* 10.00
RA1D 2col blue green (overprinted on revenue stamp) *750.00* 500.00
Nos. RA1A-RA1D (4) *885.00* 525.00

No. 124 Surcharged in Black

1927, Dec. 23
RA1E A76 10c on 12c carmine rose 25.00 5.00

Catalogue values for unused stamps in this section, from this point to the end of the section, are for Never Hinged items.

Most postal tax issues were to benefit the Children's Village and were obligatory on all mail during Dec.

No. C198 Surcharged in Red

Engraved; Center Photogravure
1958 Unwmk. *Perf. 12½*
RA1 AP51 5c on 2c brt bl & blk .55 .25

Type of 1954 Surcharged in Green

Design: Like No. C228, pottery.

RA2 AP53 5c on 10c dk bl & blk .75 .25
a. Inverted surcharge 8.50

Father Edward J. Flanagan — PT1

Paintings: No. RA4, Boy by El Greco. No. RA5, Boy by Jose Ribera. No. RA6, Girl by Amadeo Modigliani.

Perf. 13½
1959, Nov. 25 Unwmk. Photo.
RA3 PT1 5c green .90 .25
RA4 PT1 5c dl gray vio .90 .25
RA5 PT1 5c olive .90 .25
RA6 PT1 5c lilac rose .90 .25
Nos. RA3-RA6 (4) 3.60 1.00

Nos. RA3-RA6 exist imperf.

Father Peralta — PT2

Designs: No. RA8, Girl by Renoir. No. RA9, Boys with cups by Velazquez. No. RA10, Singing children, sculpture by F. Zuñiga.

1960 Litho. *Perf. 14*
RA7 PT2 5c chocolate .90 .25
RA8 PT2 5c dp org .90 .25
RA9 PT2 5c plum .90 .25
RA10 PT2 5c grysh bl .90 .25
Nos. RA7-RA10 (4) 3.60 1.00

Nos. RA7-RA10 exist imperf.

No. C229 Surcharged in Black

Engraved; Center Photogravure
1961 *Perf. 13x12½*
RA11 AP53 5c on 15c grn & blk .65 .25

Nicolas, Son of Rubens — PT3

Designs: No. RA13, Madonna by Bellini. RA14, Angel playing stringed instrument by Melozzo. RA15, Msgr. Rubén Odio H.

1962 Photo. *Perf. 13½*
RA12 PT3 5c dark carmine .95 .25
RA13 PT3 5c sepia .95 .25
RA14 PT3 5c dull green .95 .25
RA15 PT3 5c blue .95 .25
Nos. RA12-RA15 (4) 3.80 1.00

For surcharges see Nos. 262-265.

Type of 1962, Inscribed "1963"

Designs as before.

1963 Photo. *Perf. 13½*
RA16 PT3 5c sepia (RA12) .70 .25
RA17 PT3 5c ultra (RA13) .70 .25
RA18 PT3 5c dk car (RA14) .70 .25
RA19 PT3 5c black (RA15) .70 .25
Nos. RA16-RA19 (4) 2.80 1.00

Boys in Workshop — PT4

Designs: No. RA21, Two playing boys. No. RA22, Teacher and children. No. RA23, Priest with boys.

1964 Litho. *Perf. 12½*
RA20 PT4 5c bright green .65 .25
RA21 PT4 5c rose lilac .65 .25
RA22 PT4 5c blue .65 .25
RA23 PT4 5c brown .65 .25
Nos. RA20-RA23 (4) 2.60 1.00

Brother Casiano de Madrid — PT5

Designs: No. RA25, National Children's Hospital. No. RA26, Poinsettia. No. RA27, Santa Claus with children (diamond).

1965, Dec. 10 Litho. *Perf. 10*
RA24 PT5 5c red brown .55 .25
RA25 PT5 5c green .55 .25
RA26 PT5 5c red .55 .25
RA27 PT5 5c ultra .55 .25
Nos. RA24-RA27 (4) 2.20 1.00

Christmas Ornaments — PT6

1966 Litho. *Perf. 11*
RA28 PT6 5c shown .55 .25
RA29 PT6 5c Angel .55 .25
RA30 PT6 5c Church .55 .25
RA31 PT6 5c Reindeer .55 .25
Nos. RA28-RA31 (4) 2.20 1.00

General Post Office, San José — PT7

1967, Mar. Litho. *Perf. 11*
RA32 PT7 10c blue .65 .25

No. RA32 was issued as a postal tax stamp to be used by organizations normally allowed free postage. On Dec. 15, 1972, it was authorized for use as an ordinary postage stamp.

Madonna and Child — PT8

1967 **Litho.** ***Perf. 11***

RA33 PT8 5c olive green .55 .25
RA34 PT8 5c dp lil rose .55 .25
RA35 PT8 5c brt blue .55 .25
RA36 PT8 5c grnsh blue .55 .25
Nos. RA33-RA36 (4) 2.20 1.00

Star of Bethlehem, Mother and Child — PT9

1968, Dec. **Litho.** ***Perf. 12½***

RA37 PT9 5c gray .55 .25
RA38 PT9 5c rose red .55 .25
RA39 PT9 5c dk rose brn .55 .25
RA40 PT9 5c bister brn .55 .25
Nos. RA37-RA40 (4) 2.20 1.00

Madonna and Child — PT10

1969, Dec. **Litho.** ***Perf. 12½***

RA41 PT10 5c dk blue .55 .25
RA42 PT10 5c orange .55 .25
RA43 PT10 5c brown red .55 .25
RA44 PT10 5c blue green .55 .25
Nos. RA41-RA44 (4) 2.20 1.00

Christ Child, Star — PT11

1970, Dec. **Litho.** ***Perf. 12½***

RA45 PT11 5c brt purple .60 .25
RA46 PT11 5c lilac rose .60 .25
RA47 PT11 5c olive .60 .25
RA48 PT11 5c ocher .60 .25
Nos. RA45-RA48 (4) 2.40 1.00

Christ Child and "PAX" — PT12

1971, Nov. 29

RA49 PT12 10c dk blue .55 .25
RA50 PT12 10c orange .55 .25
RA51 PT12 10c brown .55 .25
RA52 PT12 10c green .55 .25
Nos. RA49-RA52 (4) 2.20 1.00

Madonna and Child — PT13

1972, Nov. 30 ***Perf. 11x11½***

RA53 PT13 10c dk blue .55 .25
RA54 PT13 10c brt red .55 .25
RA55 PT13 10c lilac .55 .25
RA56 PT13 10c green .55 .25
Nos. RA53-RA56 (4) 2.20 1.00

Madonna and Child — PT14

1973, Nov. 30 **Litho.** ***Perf. 12½***

RA57 PT14 10c purple .55 .25
RA58 PT14 10c car rose .55 .25
RA59 PT14 10c gray .55 .25
RA60 PT14 10c orange brn .55 .25
Nos. RA57-RA60 (4) 2.20 1.00

Boys Eating Cake, by Murillo — PT15

Paintings: No. RA62, Virgin and Child, with St. John, by Raphael. No. RA63, Maternity, by Juan R. Bonilla. No. RA64, Praying Child, by Reynolds.

1974, Nov. 25 ***Perf. 13***

RA61 PT15 10c brt pink .55 .25
RA62 PT15 10c rose lilac .55 .25
RA63 PT15 10c dk gray .55 .25
RA64 PT15 10c violet bl .55 .25
Nos. RA61-RA64 (4) 2.20 1.00

See No. RA110.

"Happy Dreams," by Sonia Romero — PT16

Paintings: No. RA66, Virgin with Carnation, by Leonardo da Vinci. No. RA67, Children with Tortoise, by Francisco Amighetti. No. RA68, Boy with Pigeon, by Picasso.

1975, Nov. 25 **Litho.** ***Perf. 10½***

RA65 PT16 10c gray .70 .30
RA66 PT16 10c red lilac .70 .30
RA67 PT16 10c orange brown .70 .30
RA68 PT16 10c brt blue .70 .30
Nos. RA65-RA68 (4) 2.80 1.20

Virgin and Child, by Hans Memling — PT17

Paintings: No. RA70, Girl with Sombrero, by Auguste Renoir. No. RA71, Meditation (boy), by Floria Pinto de Herrero. No. RA72, Gaston de Mezerville (boy), by Lolita Zeller de Peralta.

1976, Nov. 24 **Litho.** ***Perf. 10½***

RA69 PT17 10c rose lilac .55 .25
RA70 PT17 10c rose carmine .55 .25
RA71 PT17 10c gray .55 .25
RA72 PT17 10c violet blue .55 .25
Nos. RA69-RA72 (4) 2.20 1.00

Boy's Head, by Amparo Cruz — PT18

Paintings: No. RA74, Girl's head, by Rubens. No. RA75, Girl and infant, by Cristina Fournier. No. RA76, Mariano Goya, by Goya.

1977, Nov. **Litho.** ***Perf. 10½***

RA73 PT18 10c gray olive .55 .25
RA74 PT18 10c rose red .55 .25
RA75 PT18 10c brt ultra .55 .25
RA76 PT18 10c brt rose lil .55 .25
Nos. RA73-RA76 (4) 2.20 1.00

Boy with Kite — PT19

Designs: Nos. RA78-RA79, Girl flying kite.

1978, Nov. 20 **Litho.** ***Perf. 12½***

RA77 PT19 10c magenta .55 .25
RA78 PT19 10c slate .55 .25
RA79 PT19 10c lilac .55 .25
RA80 PT19 10c violet blue .55 .25
Nos. RA77-RA80 (4) 2.20 1.00

Boy Leaning on Tree — PT20

1979, Nov. 19 **Litho.** ***Perf. 12½***

RA81 PT20 10c blue .55 .25
RA82 PT20 10c orange .55 .25
RA83 PT20 10c magenta .55 .25
RA84 PT20 10c green .55 .25
Nos. RA81-RA84 (4) 2.20 1.00

Boy on Swing — PT21

1980, Nov. 18 **Litho.** ***Perf. 12½***

RA85 PT21 10c brt blue .55 .25
RA86 PT21 10c brt yellow .55 .25
RA87 PT21 10c crimson rose .55 .25
RA88 PT21 10c brt green .55 .25
Nos. RA85-RA88 (4) 2.20 1.00

Boy Riding Toy Car — PT22

1981, Nov. 19 **Litho.** ***Perf. 11***

RA89 PT22 10c blue .55 .25
RA90 PT22 10c green .55 .25
RA91 PT22 10c red .55 .25
RA92 PT22 10c orange .55 .25
Nos. RA89-RA92 (4) 2.20 1.00

Youth Running Machine — PT23

1982, Nov. 19 **Litho.** ***Perf. 10½***

RA93 PT23 10c red .55 .25
RA94 PT23 10c gray .55 .25
RA95 PT23 10c purple .55 .25
RA96 PT23 10c grnsh blue .55 .25
Nos. RA93-RA96 (4) 2.20 1.00

Youths Working on Wheelchair — PT24

1983, Nov. 24 **Litho.** ***Perf. 16***

RA97 PT24 10c red .55 .25
RA98 PT24 10c orange .55 .25
RA99 PT24 10c ultra .55 .25
RA100 PT24 10c green .55 .25
Nos. RA97-RA100 (4) 2.20 1.00

Christmas 1983.

Girl on Bicycle — PT25

1984, Nov. 20 **Litho.** ***Perf. 10½***

RA101 PT25 10c violet .95 .30

Christmas 1984.

Taking a Child in Out of the Cold — PT26

1985, Dec. 1 **Litho.** ***Perf. 13***

RA102 PT26 10c dull brown .95 .30

Christmas 1985.

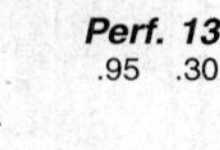

Depressed Child — PT27

1986, Dec. 1 **Litho.** ***Perf. 10½***

RA103 PT27 10c lemon .95 .30

Christmas stamps, 25th anniv.; Christmas 1986.

Christmas — PT28

1987, Dec. 1 **Litho.** ***Perf. 10½***

RA104 PT28 10c dk ol bis & brt bl .85 .30

No postal tax stamp was issued for 1988.

Teaching Children — PT29

1989, Dec. 1 **Litho.** ***Perf. 13½***

RA105 PT29 1col blue, blk & brt apple grn .85 .30

Christmas 1989.

No. 417 Ovptd. in Red, Blue, Green, or Orange

1990, Nov. 16 Litho. *Perf. 13½*

RA106 A179 10col multi (R) 2.75 .25

RA107 A179 10col multi (Bl) 2.75 .25

RA108 A179 10col multi (G) 2.75 .25

RA109 A179 10col multi (O) 2.75 .25

Nos. RA106-RA109 (4) 11.00 1.00

No. RA109 exists with a silver overprint.

Art Type of 1974

Design: 10col, Praying Child, by Reynolds.

1991, Nov. 18 Litho. *Perf. 10½*

RA110 PT15 10col dark ultra 1.40 .35

Christmas — PT30

Boy in workshop.

1992, Dec. 1 Litho. *Perf. 10½*

RA111 PT30 10col red .85 .30

Christmas PT31

1993, Nov. 17

RA112 PT31 10col multicolored 1.25 .30

Christmas PT32

1994, Nov. 23 Litho. *Perf. 10½*

RA113 PT32 11col lilac & slate 1.25 .30

No. RA113 exists imperf.

Christmas — PT33

Painting of mother and child, by Claudio Carazo.

1995, Dec. 1 *Perf. 13½*

RA114 PT33 12col multicolored .95 .30

a. Miniature sheet, #RA114 + 5 labels 3.50 3.25

No. RA114a contains 4 progressive proofs of No. RA114 + one label of text and sold for 112col.

Sculpture — PT34

1996, Dec. 1 Litho. *Perf. 10½*

RA115 PT34 14col multi .85 .30

Christmas — PT35

Bust of Antonio Obando Chan, by Olger Villegas Cruz.

1997, Dec. 1

RA116 PT35 15col multicolored .75 .30

Christmas PT36

No. RA117: a, Flower. b, Flower up close, one in background. c, Berries on branch.

1998 Litho. *Perf. 13½*

RA117 Strip of 3 2.50 1.60

a.-c. PT36 16col Any single .65 .40

Children's Village PT37

1999, Dec. 1 Litho. *Perf. 13¼*

RA118 PT37 17col multi .75 .30

Child — PT38

Color: a, Green. b, Red. c, Blue. d, Brown.

2000, Dec. 1 Litho. *Perf. 10½*

RA119 Horiz. strip of 4 9.50 4.00

a.-d. PT38 20col Any single 1.50 .65

Child Examining Stamp — PT39

Panel color: a, Purple. b, Green. c, Red. d, Orange.

2001, Dec. 1 Litho. *Perf. 10½*

RA120 Horiz. strip of 4 3.25 1.65

a.-d. PT39 21col Any single .65 .35

Child — PT40

Panel color: a, Purple. b, Blue. c, Orange. d, Green.

2002 Litho. *Perf. 10½*

RA121 Horiz strip of 4 3.00 2.50

a.-d. PT40 22col Any single .55 .45

Child Pointing at Star — PT41

No. RA122 — Background color: a, Purple. b, Green. c, Red. d, Yellow orange.

2003, Dec. 1 Litho. *Perf. 13½x13¼*

RA122 Horiz. strip of 4 2.75 2.00

a.-d. PT41 23col Any single .60 .40

Three Magi — PT42

No. RA123 — Magi in: a, Lemon. b, Green. c, Purple. d, Red violet.

2004 Litho. *Perf. 13¼*

RA123 Horiz. strip of 4 3.50 2.50

a.-d. PT42 25col Any single .65 .50

Children — PT43

No. RA124 — Denomination color: a, White. b, Buff. c, Dull orange. d, Red.

2005, Dec. 1 Litho. *Perf. 10½*

RA124 Horiz. strip of 4 3.50 2.50

a.-d. PT43 28col Any single .65 .50

Surtax for Children's Village.

Child Reading PT44

No. RA125 — Frame color: a, Yellow bister. b, Dull brown. c, Olive green. d, Orange brown.

2006, Dec. 1 Litho. *Perf. 10½*

RA125 Horiz. strip of 4 4.50 3.50

a.-d. PT44 32col Any single .85 .65

Children's Art — PT45

No. RA126: a, Family and hearts. b, Children at school. c, Children on playground equipment. d, Boy on skateboard.

2007, Dec. 1 Litho. *Perf. 10½*

RA126 Horiz. strip of 4 4.00 3.00

a.-d. PT45 35col Any single .75 .60

Surtax for Children's Village.

Children's Art — PT46

No. RA127: a, Child flying kite, by Luis Paulino Murillo Méndez. b, Boy and jaguar, by David Malavassi Zúñiga. c, Bird and sailboat, by Valeria Vargas Arias. d, Child in water, by Dannia María Berrocal Fonseca.

2008, Dec. 1 Litho. *Perf. 13½*

RA127 Horiz. strip of 4 5.75 5.50

a.-d. PT46 40col Any single .90 .90

Surtax for Children's Village.

Miniature Sheet

Masquerade Costumes — PT47

No. RA128: a, Devil and man in purple hat. b, Bull and clown. c, Grim reaper. d, Stilt walker and tall woman.

2009, Dec. 1 Litho. *Perf. 10½*

RA128 PT47 45col Sheet of 4, #a-d 3.50 3.25

Surtax for Children's Village.

Children's Art — PT48

No. RA129: a, School, tree and sun (gray panels). b, Child in workshop (blue panels). c, Sun, hills, flora and fauna (pink panels). d, Sun, house on hill (yellow panels).

2010, Dec. 1

RA129 Horiz. strip of 4 3.00 2.75

a.-d. PT48 45col Any single .60 .40

Surtax for Children's Village.

Children's Art — PT49

No. RA130: a, Head (orange yellow panel). b, Children with banner (blue panel). c, Children in playground (yellow green panel). d, Various children (bright rose panel).

2011, Dec. 1

RA130 PT49 55col Block of 4, #a-d 4.25 3.25

Surtax for Children's Village.

Boy Holding Sun — PT50

No. RA131 — Background color: a, Light blue. b, Blue. c, Brown orange. d, Yellow bister.

2012, Dec. 1 Litho. *Perf. 10½*

RA131	Horiz. strip of 4	2.50	1.75
a.-d.	PT50 60col Any single	.45	.35

Surtax for Children's Village.

PT51

No. RA132: a, Forest (denomination in olive green). b, Arches in wall (denomination in orange). c, Rock formation (denomination in lilac). d, Toucan (denomination in blue).

2013, Dec. 2 Litho. *Perf. 10½*

RA132	PT51 60col Block of 4, #a-d	3.00	2.75

No. RA132 was printed in sheets of 20 (5 of each stamp) + 4 labels. Surtax for Children's Village.

Traditional Dishes — PT52

No. RA133: a, Gallo pinto. b, Olla de carne. c, Casado con pollo. d, Picadillo de Vainica.

2014, Dec. 1 Litho. *Perf. 13½x13*

RA133	Strip of 4	2.40	1.75
a.-d.	PT52 65col Any single	.45	.35

Surtax for Children's Village.

PT53

No. RA134: a, Our Lady of Consolation Church (pink panels). b, Welder (blue panels). c, Fountain and building, San Agustín Technical College (orange panels). d, Sculpure and building, San Agustín Technical College (green panels).

2015, Dec. 1 Litho. *Perf. 14*

RA134	PT53 65col Block or vert. strip of 4, #a-d	2.50	1.60

Surtax for Children's Village.

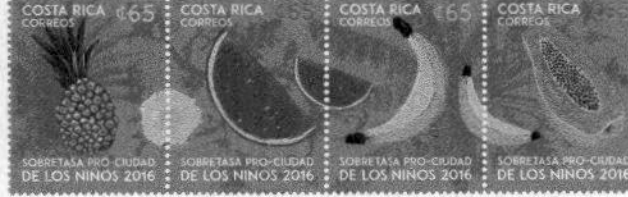
Fruit — PT54

No. RA135: a, Whole and cut pineapple. b, Cut pineapple and watermelon slices. c, Watermelon slice and bananas. d, Banana and papaya.

2016, Dec. 1 Litho. *Perf. 13¼*

RA135	PT54 65col Horiz. strip of 4, #a-d	2.25	1.50

Surtax for Children's Village.

Child's Drawing PT55

No. RA136 — Frame color: a, Orange red. b, Bright yellow green. c, Blue. d, Purple.

2017, Dec. 1 Litho. *Perf. 13*

RA136	Horiz. strip of 4	2.40	2.00
a.-d.	PT55 65col Any single	.40	.30

Surtax for Children's Village.

Old Motor Vehicles PT56

No. RA137: a, 1956 Willys Station Wagon. b, 1946 Chevrolet Pickup truck. c, 1933 Chrysler Convertible. d, 1927 Ford Model T.

2018, Dec. 1 Litho. *Perf. 13*

RA137	Horiz. strip of 4	2.50	1.00
a.-d.	PT56 70col Any single	.25	.25

Surtax for Children's Village.

Fish — PT57

No. RA138: a, Rhincodon typus. b, Sphyrna lewini. c, Mobula birostris. d, Pristis pristis.

2019, Dec. 2 Litho. *Perf. 10½*

RA138	Horiz. strip of 4	1.00	1.00
a.-d.	PT57 70col Any single	.25	.25

Surtax for Children's Village.

GUANACASTE

ˌgwä-nə-ˈkästā

(A province of Costa Rica)

LOCATION — Northwestern coast of Central America
AREA — 4,000 sq. mi. (approx.)
POP. — 69,531 (estimated)
CAPITAL — Liberia

Residents of Guanacaste were allowed to buy Costa Rican stamps, overprinted "Guanacaste," at a discount from face value because of the province's isolation and climate, which make it difficult to keep mint stamps. Use was restricted to the province.

Counterfeits of most Guanacaste overprints are plentiful.

For 5c stamps between Nos. 5-43, unused examples without gum sell for slightly more than the used value.

Very fine examples of Nos. 1-54 will have perforations just clear of the design on one or more sides.

Dangerous counterfeits exist of Nos. 1-63.

On Issue of 1883

16mm

1885 Unwmk. *Perf. 12*

Overprinted Horizontally in Black

1	A6	1c green	4.00	3.25
2	A6	2c carmine	4.00	3.25
a.		"Gnanacaste"	*250.00*	
3	A6	10c orange	35.00	21.00
a.		"Gnanacaste"	*500.00*	

Same Overprint in Red

4	A6	1c green	4.00	4.00
a.		"Gnanacaste"	*200.00*	
b.		Overprinted in black & red	*300.00*	
5	A6	5c blue violet	30.00	4.00
a.		"Gnanacaste"	*350.00*	
6	A6	40c blue	25.00	21.00

17½mm

Overprinted Horizontally in Black

7	A6	1c green	10.00	7.00
8	A6	2c carmine	10.00	7.00
9	A6	5c blue violet	60.00	20.00
10	A6	10c orange	75.00	35.00
11	A6	40c blue	75.00	60.00

Same Overprint in Red

12	A6	5c blue violet	*2,000.*	250.00
13	A6	40c blue	*2,000.*	

18½mm — c

Overprinted Horizontally in Black

14	A6	2c carmine	10.00	7.00
15	A6	10c orange	100.00	75.00

Same Overprint in Red

16	A6	1c green	7.00	7.00
a.		Double ovpt., one in blk	250.00	
17	A6	5c blue violet	45.00	15.00
18	A6	40c blue	75.00	75.00

Same Overprint, Vertically in Black

19	A6	1c green	*5,000.*	
20	A6	2c carmine	*4,250.*	
21	A6	5c blue violet	800.00	200.00
22	A6	10c orange	200.00	200.00

e

f

g

h

i

Overprinted Type e, Vertically

23	A6	1c green	3,000.	2,000.
24	A6	2c carmine	1,500.	300.00
25	A6	5c blue violet	400.00	75.00
26	A6	10c orange	75.00	75.00

Overprinted Type f, Vertically

27	A6	1c green	3,000.	2,000.
28	A6	2c carmine	1,000.	400.00
29	A6	5c blue violet	400.00	125.00
30	A6	10c orange	100.00	100.00

Overprinted Type g, Vertically

31	A6	1c green	3,000.	2,500.
32	A6	2c carmine	1,500.	1,000.
33	A6	5c blue violet	800.00	250.00
34	A6	10c orange	200.00	150.00

Overprinted Type h, Vertically

35	A6	1c green	3,000.	1,500.
36	A6	2c carmine	1,000.	300.00
37	A6	5c blue violet	600.00	75.00
38	A6	10c orange	100.00	60.00

Overprinted Type i, Vertically

39	A6	1c green	*500.00*
39A	A6	2c carmine	*300.00*
40	A6	5c blue violet	20.00
41	A6	10c orange	*250.00*

On Issues of 1883-87

Overprinted Horizontally in Black

1888-89

42	A7	5c blue violet	15.00	3.00

Overprinted Horizontally in Black

43	A7	5c blue violet	15.00	3.00

Overprinted Horizontally in Black

44	A6	2c carmine	4.00	4.00
45	A7	10c orange	4.00	4.00

Inverted overprints on Nos. 44-45 are fakes.

This overprint also exists on Costa Rica Nos. AR3 and AR4, which are normally found without gum. Value, $50 each. This overprint on Costa Rica No. AR1 is fake.

On Issue of 1889

Overprinted Like Nos. 7-13

1889 Horizontally

47	A8	2c blue	25.00

Vertically

48	A8	2c blue (c)	250.00
49	A8	2c blue (e)	100.00
51	A8	2c blue (f)	100.00
52	A8	2c blue (g)	350.00
54	A8	2c blue (h)	100.00

Nos. 47-54 are overprinted "Correos." Stamps without "Correos" are known postally used. Unused examples are valued the same as Nos. 47-54, unused. The 1c without "Correos" is known postally used. The 1c with "Correos" is counterfeit.

On Nos. 25-33 Overprinted Horizontally in Black

1889 *Perf. 14 and 15*

55	A10	1c brown	10.00	3.50
56	A11	2c dark green	4.50	1.50
57	A12	5c orange	6.75	2.10
58	A13	10c red brown	6.75	2.10
59	A14	20c yellow green	1.00	.70
60	A15	50c rose red	1.75	1.50
61	A16	1p blue	4.50	4.50
62	A17	2p violet	13.00	6.75
63	A18	5p olive green	60.00	37.50
		Nos. 55-63 (9)	108.25	60.15

Overprinted "GUAGACASTE"

60a	A15	50c rose red	*325.00*	*325.00*
61a	A16	1p blue	*325.00*	*325.00*
62a	A17	2p violet	*400.00*	*400.00*
63a	A18	5p olive green	*600.00*	*600.00*

Values for Nos. 60a-63a used are for examples with remainder cancels.

Overprinted Horizontally in Black

64	A10	1c brown	2.25	1.50
a.		Vert. pair, imperf. between		
65	A11	2c dark green	2.25	1.50
66	A12	5c orange	2.25	1.50
67	A13	10c red brown	2.25	1.50
		Nos. 64-67 (4)	9.00	6.00

CRETE

'krēt

LOCATION — An island in the Mediterranean Sea south of Greece
GOVT. — A department of Greece
AREA — 3,235 sq. mi.
POP. — 336,150 (1913)
CAPITAL — Canea

Formerly Crete was a province of Turkey. After an extended period of civil wars, France, Great Britain, Italy and Russia intervened and declaring Crete an autonomy, placed it under the administration of Prince George of Greece as High Commissioner. In October, 1908, the Cretan Assembly voted for union with Greece and in 1913 the union was formally effected.

40 Paras = 1 Piaster
4 Metallik = 1 Grosion (1899)
100 Lepta = 1 Drachma (1900)

Issued Under Joint Administration of France, Great Britain, Italy and Russia

British Sphere of Administration District of Heraklion (Candia)

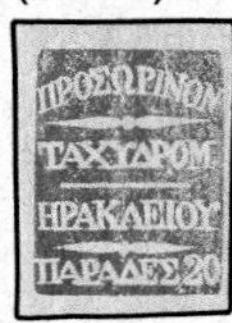

A1

Handstamped

1898 Unwmk. *Imperf.*

1	A1	20pa violet	425.00	230.00

A2

1898 Litho. *Perf. 11½*

2	A2	10pa blue	6.50	2.00
a.		Horiz. pair, imperf. btwn.	*210.00*	
b.		Imperf., pair	*230.00*	
c.		Horiz. pair, imperf. vert.	—	
3	A2	20pa green	6.50	2.00
a.		Imperf., pair	230.00	

1899

4	A2	10pa brown	6.50	2.00
a.		Horiz. pair, imperf. btwn.	*210.00*	
b.		Imperf., pair	*230.00*	
5	A2	20pa rose	6.50	2.00
a.		Imperf., pair	230.00	

Used values for Nos. 2-5 are for stamps canceled by the straight-line "Heraklion" town postmark. Stamps canceled with any other postmark used for postal duty are scarce and worth much more. Other cancellations, values from: Ag. Thomas, $65; Ag. Myron, $70; Arkanais, $90; Episkopi, $170; Kastelli, $175; Moirais, $175; Xarakas, $190; Chersonissos, $235; and Moxos.

Counterfeits exist of Nos. 1-5.

Russian Sphere of Administration District of Rethymnon

Coat of Arms

A3 A4

1899 Handstamped *Imperf.*

Laid paper

No Gum

10	A3	1m green	13.50	5.75
11	A3	2m black	11.50	4.50
12	A3	2m rose	345.00	230.00
13	A4	1m blue	115.00	75.00

Wove paper

10E	A3	1m green	13.00	5.00
11E	A3	2m black	13.00	5.00
12E	A3	2m rose	225.00	165.00
13E	A4	1m blue	115.00	65.00

Quadrille paper

10J	A3	1m green	375.00	—
11J	A3	2m black	375.00	80.00
12J	A3	2m rose	525.00	
13J	A4	1m violet		650.00

Nos. 10-13 normally have a circular control mark applied in violet or blue on blocks of four stamps. They also are known without this control mark (errors) and occasionally with the small round control marks of the next issue, in blue or violet (probably proofs). They are sometimes found with pin-perforations. Other varieties exist.

Counterfeits exist.

Poseidon's Trident — A5a

A5

1899 Litho. *Perf. 11½*

With Control Mark Overprinted in Violet

Without Stars at Sides

14	A5	1m orange	175.00	115.00
15	A5	2m orange	175.00	115.00
16	A5	1gr orange	175.00	115.00
17	A5	1m green	175.00	115.00
18	A5	2m green	175.00	115.00
19	A5	1gr green	175.00	115.00
20	A5	1m yellow	175.00	115.00
21	A5	2m yellow	175.00	115.00
22	A5	1gr yellow	175.00	115.00
23	A5	1m rose	175.00	115.00
24	A5	2m rose	175.00	115.00
25	A5	1gr rose	175.00	115.00
26	A5	1m violet	175.00	115.00
27	A5	2m violet	175.00	115.00
28	A5	1gr violet	175.00	115.00
29	A5	1m blue	175.00	115.00
30	A5	2m blue	175.00	115.00
31	A5	1gr blue	175.00	115.00
32	A5	1m black	1,320.	1,150.
33	A5	2m black	1,320.	1,150.
34	A5	1gr black	1,320.	1,150.

With Stars at Sides

35	A5a	1m blue	42.50	32.50
36	A5a	2m blue	15.00	12.50
37	A5a	1gr blue	13.50	9.00
38	A5a	1m rose	165.00	75.00
39	A5a	2m rose	15.00	12.50
40	A5a	1gr rose	13.50	8.75
41	A5a	1m green	42.50	32.50
42	A5a	2m green	15.00	12.50
43	A5a	1gr green	13.50	9.00
44	A5a	1m violet	42.50	32.50
45	A5a	2m violet	15.00	9.00
46	A5a	1gr violet	13.50	8.75
a.		Horiz. pair, imperf. btwn.	250.00	
b.		Vert. pair, imperf. horiz.	190.00	
		Nos. 35-46 (12)	406.50	254.50

Almost all of Nos. 14 to 46 may be found without control mark, with double control marks and in various colors.

Used values for Nos. 10-46 are for stamps with postmarks of Rethymnon. Thirteen other post offices existed, and stamps with postmarks other than Rethymnon are scarce and command significant premiums: Ag. Galini, $125; Amari, $90; Anogeia, $525; Garazo, $160; Damasta, $550; Kastelli, $125; Margaritais, $550; Melampes, $375; Pigi, $125; Roystika, $70; Xenia, $105; Spili, $105; Fodede, $550.

Counterfeits exist of Nos. 14-46.

Nos. 14-31 exist imperf. Value, unused pair each $1,150.

Issued by the Cretan Government

Hermes — A6

Hera — A7

Prince George of Greece — A8

1900, Mar. 1 Engr. *Perf. 14*

50	A6	1 l violet brown	.45	.45
51	A7	5 l green	1.80	.45
52	A8	10 l red	1.35	.45
53	A7	20 l carmine rose	5.00	2.25
		Nos. 50-53 (4)	8.60	3.60

See #64-71. For overprints and surcharges see #54-63, 72-73, 85, 88, 93, 97-99, 108, 111.

Overprinted

Red Overprint

54	A8	25 l blue	.80	1.25
55	A6	50 l lilac	2.00	1.35
56	A9	1d gray violet	11.50	13.50
57	A10	2d brown	35.00	35.00
58	A11	5d green & blk	185.00	200.00
		Nos. 54-58 (5)	234.30	251.10

Black Overprint

59	A8	25 l blue	1.75	.75
60	A6	50 l lilac	1.75	1.75
61	A9	1d gray violet	9.00	7.00
a.		Inverted overprint	*350.00*	*350.00*
62	A10	2d brown	32.50	17.00
63	A11	5d green & blk	100.00	115.00
		Nos. 59-63 (5)	145.00	141.50

Talos — A9

Minos — A10

St. George and the Dragon — A11

1901 Without Overprint

64	A6	1 l bister	1.00	1.15
65	A7	20 l orange	3.00	1.15
66	A8	25 l blue	8.75	.90
67	A6	50 l lilac	37.50	27.50
68	A6	50 l ultra	13.50	13.00
69	A9	1d gray violet	40.00	28.00
70	A10	2d brown	13.00	11.50
71	A11	5d green & blk	17.50	13.00
		Nos. 64-71 (8)	134.25	96.20

No. 64 is a revenue stamp that was used for postage for short periods in 1901 and 1904.

Types A6 to A8 in olive yellow, and types A9 to A11 in olive yellow and black are revenue stamps.

See note following No. 53.

Surcharges with the year "1922" on designs A6, A8, A9, A11, A13, A15-A23 and D1 are listed under Greece.

No. 66 Overprinted in Black

1901

72	A8	25 l blue	22.50	.75
a.		First letter of ovpt. invtd.	475.00	300.00
b.		Inverted overprint	700.00	350.00
c.		"S" of "PROSORINON" omitted	200.00	80.00

No. 65 Surcharged in Black

1904, Dec.

73	A7	5 l on 20 l orange	2.25	.75
a.		Without "5" at right	*150.00*	*150.00*

Mycenaean Seal — A12

Britomartis (Cortyna Coin) — A13

Prince George — A14

Kydon and Dog (Cydonia Coin) — A15

Triton (Itanos Coin) — A16

Ariadne (Knossos Coin) — A17

Zeus as Bull Abducting Europa (Cortyna Coin) A18

Palace of Minos Ruins, Knossos A19

Arkadi Monastery and Mt. Ida — A20

1905, Feb. 15

74	A12	2 l dull violet	1.25	.35
75	A13	5 l yellow grn	1.50	.35
76	A14	10 l red	1.50	.75
77	A15	20 l blue grn	5.50	1.00
78	A16	25 l ultra	7.00	1.00
79	A17	50 l yellow brn	7.50	3.25
80	A18	1d rose car & dp brn	75.00	65.00
81	A19	3d orange & blk	50.00	40.00
82	A20	5d ol grn & blk	25.00	25.00
		Nos. 74-82 (9)	174.25	136.70

For overprints see Nos. 86-87, 89, 91-92, 94-95, 104, 106, 109-110, 112-113, 115-120.

The so-called revolutionary stamps of 1905 were issued for sale to collectors and, so far as can be ascertained, were of no postal value.

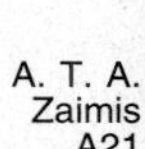

A. T. A. Zaimis A21

Prince George Landing at Suda A22

1907, Aug. 28

83	A21	25 l blue & blk	36.00	.90
84	A22	1d green & blk	9.00	7.00

Administration under a High Commissioner. For overprints see Nos. 90, 105, 107.

Stamps of 1900-1907 Overprinted in Black

1908, Sept. 21

85	A6	1 l violet brn	.60	.45
a.		Inverted overprint	—	
86	A12	2 l dull violet	.60	.45
a.		Pair, one without ovpt.	—	
87	A13	5 l yellow grn	.60	.45
88	A8	10 l red	1.25	.90
a.		Pair, one without ovpt.	—	
89	A15	20 l blue grn	3.25	1.15
90	A21	25 l blue & blk	9.00	2.75
91	A17	50 l yellow brn	12.50	4.50
a.		Inverted overprint	—	
92	A18	1d rose car & dp brn	97.50	70.00
93	A10	2d brown	11.50	9.00
94	A19	3d orange & blk	47.50	40.00
95	A20	5d ol grn & blk	37.50	32.50
		Nos. 85-95 (11)	221.80	162.15
		Set, never hinged	400.00	

This overprint exists inverted and double, as well as with incorrect, reversed, misplaced and omitted letters. Similar errors are found on the Postage Due and Official stamps with this overprint.

Hermes by Praxiteles — A23

1908

96	A23	10 l brown red	2.75	.80
a.		Pair, one without overprint	150.00	150.00

Nos. 96 and 114 were not regularly issued without overprint.

For overprints see Nos. 103, 114.

Genuine examples of No. 96 with overprint inverted or doubled are not known to exist.

No. 53 Surcharged

1909

97	A7	5 l on 20 l car rose	230.00	*250.00*

Forgeries exist of No. 97.

On No. 65

98	A7	5 l on 20 l orange	1.30	1.15
a.		Inverted surcharge	150.00	150.00
b.		Double surcharge	120.00	120.00

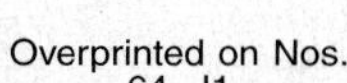

Overprinted on Nos. 64, J1

99	A6	1 l bister	3.50	3.50
100	D1	1 l red	1.30	1.30

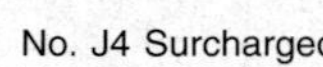

No. J4 Surcharged

101	D1	2 l on 20 l red	1.25	1.25
b.		Inverted surcharge	75.00	
c.		Second letter of surcharge "D" instead of "P"	50.00	50.00

No. J4 Surcharged

102	D1	2 l on 20 l red	1.25	1.25
a.		Double overprint	*125.00*	*125.00*

Overprinted in Black

a

b

c

103	A23(a)	10 l brown red	3.00	1.15
a.		Inverted overprint	110.00	
104	A15(a)	20 l blue grn	4.00	1.15
105	A21(c)	25 l blue & blk	5.50	2.00
106	A17(a)	50 l yellow brn	7.75	4.25
107	A22(b)	1d green & blk	12.50	7.25
108	A10(a)	2d brown	12.50	10.50
109	A19(b)	3d org & blk	127.50	115.00
110	A20(b)	5d ol grn & blk	52.50	52.50
		Nos. 103-110 (8)	225.25	193.80

Stamps of 1900-08 Overprinted in Red or Black

1909-10

111	A6	1 l violet brown	.35	.25
112	A12	2 l dull violet	.35	.25
113	A13	5 l yellow green	.35	.25
114	A23	10 l brown red (Bk)	.60	.60
115	A15	20 l blue green	2.00	.75
116	A16	25 l ultra	2.50	.80
117	A17	50 l yellow brn	7.00	2.25
118	A18	1d rose car & dp brn (Bk)	100.00	100.00
119	A19	3d orange & blk	85.00	85.00
120	A20	5d ol grn & blk	55.00	55.00
		Nos. 111-120 (10)	253.15	245.15

POSTAGE DUE STAMPS

D1

1901 Unwmk. Litho. *Perf. 14*

J1	D1	1 l red	.30	.30
J2	D1	5 l red	.50	.30
J3	D1	10 l red	.75	.45
J4	D1	20 l red	1.00	*.50*
J5	D1	40 l red	11.50	11.50
J6	D1	50 l red	11.50	11.50
J7	D1	1d red	22.50	22.50
J8	D1	2d red	14.50	12.50
		Nos. J1-J8 (8)	62.55	59.55
		Set, never hinged	115.00	

For overprints and surcharges see Nos. 100-102, J9-J26.

Surcharged in Black

1901

J9	D1	1d on 1d red	11.50	10.00

Overprinted in Black

1908

J10	D1	1 l red	.35	.35
J11	D1	5 l red	.60	.60
J12	D1	10 l red	.60	.60
J13	D1	20 l red	2.00	2.00
J14	D1	40 l red	8.50	7.50
J15	D1	50 l red	11.00	9.00
J16	D1	1d red	475.00	475.00
a.		Pair, one without ovpt.	—	
J17	D1	1d on 1d red	11.50	10.00
J18	D1	2d red	19.00	10.00
		Nos. J10-J18 (9)	528.55	515.05

Nos. J10-J18 exist with inverted overprint. See note after No. 95.

Counterfeits of No. J16 exist.

Overprinted in Black

1910

J19	D1	1 l red	.45	.30
J20	D1	5 l red	1.00	.35
J21	D1	10 l red	1.00	.35
J22	D1	20 l red	3.25	1.75
J23	D1	40 l red	11.00	6.00
J24	D1	50 l red	16.50	12.00
J25	D1	1d red	27.50	27.50
J26	D1	2d red	27.50	27.50
		Nos. J19-J26 (8)	88.20	75.75

OFFICIAL STAMPS

O1

O2

Unwmk.

1908, Jan. 14 Litho. *Perf. 14*

O1 O1 10 l dull claret 18.00 1.50
O2 O2 30 l blue 37.50 1.50

Nos. O1-O2 exist imperf.

Nos. O1-O2 Overprinted

O3 O1 10 l dull claret 13.00 1.20
a. Inverted overprint 115.00 115.00
O4 O2 30 l blue 27.50 1.30
a. Inverted overprint 200.00 200.00

See note after No. 95.

Nos. O1-O2 Overprinted

1910

O5 O1 10 l dull claret 2.25 1.30
O6 O2 30 l blue 2.25 1.30

Nos. O5-O6 remained in use until 1922, nine years after union with Greece.

CROATIA

krō-'ā-sh,ē,-ə

LOCATION — Southeastern Europe
GOVT. — Independent state
AREA — 44,453 sq. mi.
POP. — 7,000,000 (approx.)
CAPITAL — Zagreb

The Independent Croatian State of 1941-45 became part of the Yugoslav Federation in 1945.

Croatia declared its independence in 1991.

100 Paras = 1 Dinar
100 Banica = 1 Kuna

Catalogue values for unused stamps in this country are for Never Hinged items, beginning with Scott 1 in the regular postage section, Scott B1 in the semi-postal section, Scott C1 in the airmail section and Scott RA1 in the postal tax section.

Watermark

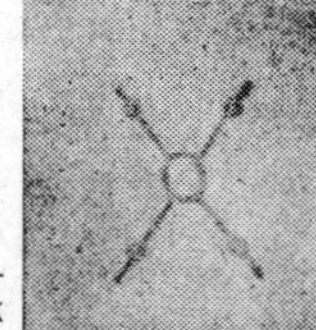

Wmk. 278 — Network Connecting Circles

Yugoslavia Nos. 143 to 148B Overprinted in Black

Perf. 12½

1941, Apr. 12 Unwmk. Typo.

1 A16 50p orange 4.50 3.75
a. Inverted overprint 225.00
2 A16 1d yellow grn 5.25 3.75
a. Double overprint 110.00
3 A16 1.50d red 6.00 2.25
a. Double overprint 110.00
4 A16 2d deep magenta 6.75 3.75
5 A16 3d dull red brn 11.00 6.75
a. Double overprint 110.00
6 A16 4d ultra 15.00 7.50
7 A16 5d dark blue 18.50 8.25
8 A16 5.50d dk violet brn 22.50 9.00
a. Double overprint 110.00
Nos. 1-8 (8) 89.50 45.00

Counterfeit overprints exist of Nos. 1-8, especially the inverted and double overprint varieties.

Yugoslavia Nos. 142 to 154 Overprinted in Black

1941, Apr. 21

9 A16 25p black .75 .50
a. Inverted overprint 75.00
b. Double overprint 75.00
10 A16 50p orange .75 .50
a. Inverted overprint 75.00
11 A16 1d yellow grn .75 .50
a. Inverted overprint —
12 A16 1.50d red .80 .50
a. Double overprint 150.00
13 A16 2d deep magenta .80 .50
14 A16 3d dull red brn 1.10 .95
15 A16 4d ultra 1.50 1.40
16 A16 5d dark blue 1.90 1.40
a. Double overprint 200.00
17 A16 5.50d dk violet brn 2.25 1.40
a. Inverted overprint 375.00
b. Double overprint 200.00
18 A16 6d slate blue 3.00 2.25
19 A16 8d sepia 3.75 2.25
20 A16 12d brt violet 4.50 3.00
a. Inverted overprint 375.00
21 A16 16d dull violet 5.25 4.50
a. Double overprint 200.00
22 A16 20d blue 6.75 5.25
23 A16 30d bright pink 12.00 10.00
Nos. 9-23 (15) 45.85 34.90

The overprint exists double, both inverted, on Nos. 16, 18 and 19.

Yugoslavia Nos. 147, 148 Surcharged in Black

1941, May 16

24 A16 1d on 3d dull red brn .40 .40
a. Inverted overprint 75.00
b. Double overprint 75.00
25 A16 2d on 4d ultra .40 .40
a. Inverted overprint 75.00
b. Double overprint 75.00

Postage Due Stamps of Yugoslavia, Nos. J28, J30 to J32, Overprinted in Black

1941, May 17

26 D4 50p violet .50 .45
27 D4 2d deep blue 1.35 1.25
28 D4 5d orange 1.90 1.40
29 D4 10d chocolate 2.25 1.60
Nos. 26-29 (4) 6.00 4.70

Counterfeit cancellations exist for Nos. 1-29 on cover.

Imperforates

Nearly all Croatian stamps, from No. 30 through 80, B3 through B76, J6 through J25, O1 through O24 and RA1 through RA7 exist imperforate, imperforate vertically, and imperforate horizontally. These are primarily from the special Ministerial Albums issued by the State Printing Office.

Ozalj Castle — A1

Designs: 50b, City of Jajce. 75b, Old Warasdin. 1k, Velebit Mountains. 1.50k, Zelanjak. 2k, Zagreb Cathedral. 3k, Osjek Cathedral. 4k, Drina River. No. 38, Konjic. No. 39, Zemun. 6k, Dubrovnik. 7k, Save River. 8k, Sarajevo. 10k, Plitvice. 12k, Klis Fortress, Split. 20k, Hvar. 30k, Syrmia. 50k, Senj. 100k, Banjaluka (without "F.I.").

Perf. 11¼.

1941-43 Unwmk. Photo.

Ordinary Paper

30 A1 25b henna .25 .25
31 A1 50b slate blue .25 .25
32 A1 75b dk olive grn .25 .25
33 A1 1k Pruss grn .25 .25
34 A1 1.50k deep green .25 .25
35 A1 2k carmine lake .25 .25
36 A1 3k brown red .25 .25
37 A1 4k deep ultra .25 .25
38 A1 5k black 2.00 1.15
39 A1 5k blue .25 .25
40 A1 6k lt olive brn .25 .25
41 A1 7k orange red .30 .25
42 A1 8k chestnut .40 .30
43 A1 10k dark plum .90 .45
44 A1 12k olive brown 1.50 .50
45 A1 20k golden brown 1.10 .40
46 A1 30k black brown 1.50 .50
47 A1 50k dk slate green 3.75 1.50
48 A1 100k violet 5.25 3.50
Nos. 30-48 (19) 19.20 *11.05*

Nos. 30-48 exist with a variety of perforations, including 11¼x10¾ and 12. Examples of Nos. 30, 36 and 48 exist with a special printer's mark in the design. Two varieties of printer's mark are known for No. 30, one for the first printing, and one for the second. Usually one stamp per pane has the printer's mark.

Nos. 31, 35 and 43 exist on thin to pelure paper, as does No. 32, though the latter was not issued to the public. Shades of all values exist.

For overprints and surcharge see Nos. 49-51, 53.

Tête bêche Pairs

30a A1 25b 1.75 *2.75*
31a A1 50b 2.00 *3.50*
33a A1 1k 2.50 *4.00*
34a A1 1.50k 2.75 *5.00*
35a A1 2k 3.00 *6.00*
37a A1 4k 3.95 *6.50*
38a A1 5k 7.00 *7.50*
40a A1 6k 4.00 *7.00*
41a A1 7k 4.50 *7.25*
42a A1 8k 5.00 *8.00*
43a A1 10k 5.50 *9.50*
45a A1 20k 6.50 *10.00*
46a A1 30k 7.25 *11.00*
47a A1 50k 13.00 *13.00*
Nos. 30a-47a (14) 68.70 *101.00*

Types of 1941 Overprinted in Brown or Green

1942, Apr. 9

49 A1 2k dark brown .60 .40
50 A1 5k dark carmine .90 .85
51 A1 10k dark blue green (G) 1.50 1.25
Nos. 49-51 (3) 3.00 *2.50*

First anniversary of Croatian independence.

The overprint exists double on No. 50.

Tête bêche pairs of Nos. 49-51 are from Ministerial Albums.

Banjaluka ("F.I." at upper right) — A20

1942, June 13

52 A20 100k violet 4.25 4.25

Banjaluka Philatelic Exhibition.

No. 52 exists in se-tenant pair with No. 48. Value unused, $300.

No. 52 exists with a special printer's mark in the design. The mark typically appears on one stamp in a given pane.

No. 35 Surcharged in Red Brown with New Value and Bar

1942, June 23

53 A1 25b on 2k carmine lake .55 .55
a. Tête bêche pair 3.25 3.25

No. 53 exists with double surcharge. It is not scarce.

Trakoscan Castle — A21

Design: 12.50k, Citadel of Veliki Tabor.

1943, Mar. 28 Pelure Paper

54 A21 3.50k brown carmine .75 .55
55 A21 12.50k violet black 1.00 .85

Nos. 54 was reissued in 1944 on ordinary paper, perf 12. Value the same for both varieties. No. 55 also exists on ordinary paper. It is scarce.

Catherine Zrinski — A23

2k, Fran Krsto Frankopan. 3.50k, Peter Zrinski.

Various Frames

1943, June 7 Engr. *Perf. 12¼x12½*

56 A23 1k dark blue .40 .40
57 A23 2k dark olive green .40 .40
58 A23 3.50k dark red .50 *.55*
Nos. 56-58 (3) 1.30 *1.35*

Many perforation varieties of this issue exist, including 12x12½, 12½x13, 12½, 13, 12½x14, 13x12½, and 14x12½.

Rudjer Boscovich — A26

1943, Dec. 13 *Perf. 11*

59 A26 3.50k copper red .50 .40
60 A26 12.50k dk violet brn .65 .50

Rugjer Boscovich (1711-1787). Mathematician and physicist.

No. 60 exists with a special printer's mark in the design. The mark typically appears on one stamp in a given pane.

Ante Pavelich — A27

1943-44 Litho. *Perf. 12½, 14*

61 A27 25b orange ver .30 .25
62 A27 50b Prus blue .30 .25
63 A27 75b olive green .30 .25
64 A27 1k lt green .30 .25
65 A27 1.50k dull gray vio .30 .25
66 A27 2k rose lake .30 .25
67 A27 3k rose brown .30 .25
68 A27 3.50k bright blue .30 .25
a. 3.50k dark blue, perf. 11½ 4.00 *4.75*
69 A27 4k brt red violet .30 .25
70 A27 5k ultra .30 .25
71 A27 8k orange brn .35 .25
72 A27 9k rose pink .35 .25
73 A27 10k violet brn .40 .25
74 A27 12k dk olive bis .45 .25
75 A27 12.50k gray black .55 .25
76 A27 18k dull brown .70 .30
77 A27 32k dark brown .75 .30
78 A27 50k grnsh blue 1.50 .50

79 A27 70k orange 1.90 .90
80 A27 100k violet 3.00 1.50
Nos. 61-80 (20) 12.95 7.25

Nos. 61, 63, 70, and 77 measure 20½x26mm. Nos. 62, 64-69, 71-76, and 78-80 measure 22x27½mm.

Nos. 61, 63, 67, 70, 71 and 72 are perf 12½. Nos. 62, 64-66, 68, 69, 73 and 75-80 are perf 14. No. 74 exists either perf 12½ or 14.

No. 80 exists with a special printer's mark in the design. The mark typically appears on one stamp in a given pane.

Issue dates: 2k, 1943; No. 68a, June 13, 1943, Pavelich's Saint's Day; others, 1944.

"Labor Day 1945" — A28

1945 Photo. *Perf. 11½*
81 A28 3.50k red brown .85 *1.60*

No. 81 exists imperforate. Value, never hinged $900.

From 1951 to 1972 44 labels were circulated by a Croatian Government in Exile. These had no postal value.

GOVT. — Independent state
AREA — 21,823 sq. mi.
POP. — 4,676,865 (1999 est.)
CAPITAL — Zagreb

Croatia declared its independence from Yugoslavia in 1991.

100 Paras = 1 Dinar (1991)
100 Lipa = 1 Kuna (1994)

Nos. RA20, RA20a Srchd. in Black and Gold

1991, Nov. 21 Litho. *Perf. 14*
100 PT10 4d on 1.20d #RA20 .70 .70
a. Perf. 11x10½ .50 .50
b. Perf. 11 7.50 7.50

A35

1991, Dec. 10 *Perf. 12*
101 A35 30d multicolored 2.00 2.00

Declaration of independence, 10/8/91.

Christmas — A36

Creche figures of the Holy Family from Kosljun Monastery.

1991, Dec. 11 *Perf. 12*
102 A36 4d multicolored .80 .80

No. RA21 Surcharged in Black and Gold

1992, Jan. 3 *Perf. 10½x11*
103 PT11 20d on 1.70d #RA21 5.75 5.75

Croatian Arms — A37

1992, Jan. 15 *Perf. 11x10½*
104 A37 10d multicolored .60 .60
a. Perf. 14 .40 .40

See No. RA22.

1992 Winter Olympics, Albertville A38

1992, Feb. 4 *Perf. 11x10½*
105 A38 30d multicolored *1.50 1.50*

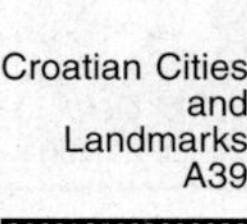

Croatian Cities and Landmarks A39

A39a

Designs: 6d, Knin. 7d, Eltz Castle, Vukovar. 20d, Church, Ilok. 30d, Starcevic Street, Gospic. 45d, Rector's Palace, Dubrovnik. 50d, St. Jakov's Cathedral, Sibenik. 100d, Vinkovci. 200d, Pazin, vert. No. 115, Beli Manastir. 500d, Slavonski Brod. 1000d, Varazdin. 2000d, Karlovac. 5000d, Zadar, vert. 10,000d, Vis.

1992-94 *Perf. 14*
107 A39 6d multi *.25 .25*
108 A39 7d multi *.25 .25*
109 A39 20d multi *.35 .35*
a. Perf. 11x10½ *1.00 1.00*
110 A39 30d multi *.90 .90*
111 A39 45d multi *.90 .90*
112 A39 50d multi *.90 .90*
113 A39a 100d multi *.65 .65*
114 A39a 200d multi *.35 .35*
115 A39 300d multi *2.00 2.00*
117 A39a 500d multi *1.90 1.90*
118 A39a 1000d multi *1.00 .70*
119 A39a 2000d multi *2.00 1.50*
120 A39a 5000d multi *3.00 2.50*
121 A39a 10,000d multi *5.50 5.00*
Nos. 107-121 (14) 19.95 18.15

Issued: 6d, 4/18; 7d, 4/8; No. 109, 2/28; No. 109a, 9/9; 30d, 5/21; 45d, 4/14; 50d, 4/28; 115, 6/26; 100d, 12/14; 500d, 2/9/93; 1000d, 3/16/93; 200d, 4/9/93; 2000d, 5/20/93; 5000d, 9/24/93; 10,000d, 2/22/94.

See Nos. 355-356, 437A, 456.

Statue of King Tomislav — A40

1992, May 5 Engr. *Perf. 12½ Horiz.*
Coil Stamp
124 A40 10d dark green .40 .40

Railroad Station, Zagreb, Cent. — A41

1992, June 30 Litho. *Perf. 14*
125 A41 30d multicolored .40 .30

Matica, Society of Knowledge and Literacy, 150th Anniv. — A42

1992, July 8
126 A42 20d red, gold & black .35 .30

Bishop Josip Juraj Strossmayer, Founder — A43

1992, July 9
127 A43 30d multicolored .40 .40

Croatian Academy of Arts and Sciences, 125th anniv., in 1991.

1992 Summer Olympics, Barcelona A44

Design: 105d, Abstract design.

1992, July 25
128 A44 40d shown .30 .30
129 A44 105d multicolored 1.25 1.25

Flowers A45

Designs: 30d, Edraianthus pumilio. 85d, Degenia velebitica, vert.

1992, July 28
130 A45 30d multicolored .35 .35
131 A45 85d multicolored .90 .90

Wildlife — A46

40d, Monticola solitarius. 75d, Elaphe situla.

1992, July 31
132 A46 40d multicolored .45 .45
133 A46 75d multicolored .85 .85

Discovery of America, 500th Anniv. — A47

Europa: 30d, 60d, Sailing ship. 75d, 130d, Indian in Chicago, by Ivan Mestrovic (1883-1962).

1992, Sep. 4 Litho. *Perf. 14*
134 A47 30d multicolored *.55 .55*
135 A47 60d multicolored *1.15 1.15*
136 A47 75d red & black *1.30 1.30*
137 A47 130d red, blk & gold *2.00 2.00*
Nos. 134-137 (4) 5.00 5.00

Issued: 30d, 75d, July 31; others, Sept. 4.

A48

1992, Oct. 2
138 A48 40d reddish org & blue .35 .35
139 A48 130d pale blue & pur 1.00 1.00

Declaration of Croatian Literary Language, 25th Anniv. (No. 138). Spelling reform by Dr. Ivan Broz, cent. (No. 139).

City of Samobor, 750th Anniv. — A49

1992, Oct. 16
140 A49 90d multicolored .65 .40

Gift of the St. Juraj Church by Archbishop Mucimir, 1100th Anniv. — A50

1992, Oct. 30
141 A50 60d multicolored .40 .30

Reign of King Bela IV, 750th Anniv. — A51

1992, Nov. 16 Litho. *Perf. 14*
142 A51 180d multicolored .85 .85

Christmas A52

1992, Dec. 7
143 A52 80d multicolored .40 .35

Blaz Lorkovic (1839-1892), Scientist — A53

1992, Dec. 21
144 A53 250d multicolored .90 .90

Kolo Literature Review, 150th Anniv. — A54

1992, Dec. 22
145 A54 300d multicolored 1.10 1.10

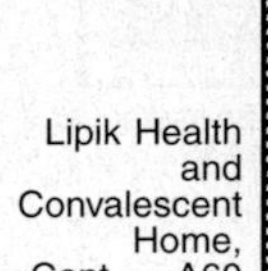
Ivan Bunic-Vucic (1592-1658) A55

1992, Dec. 29
146 A55 350d multicolored 1.10 1.10

800th Anniv. of Krapina — A55a

1993, Jan. 15
146A A55a 300d multicolored .70 .70

Nikola Tesla (1856-1943), Physicist A56

1993, Jan. 30
147 A56 250d multicolored .70 .70

Self-Portrait, by Ferdo Quiquerez (1845-1893) A57

1993, Feb. 10
148 A57 100d multicolored .40 .40

Wildlife — A58

500d, Cervus elaphus. 550d, Haliaeetus albicilla.

1993, Feb. 23 Litho. *Perf. 14*
149 A58 500d multi 1.00 1.00
150 A58 550d multi 1.00 1.00

Self-Portrait, by Zlatko Sulentic (1893-1971) A59

1993, Mar. 17
151 A59 350d multicolored .55 .55

Lipik Health and Convalescent Home, Cent. — A60

1993, Apr. 22 Litho. *Perf. 14*
152 A60 400d multicolored .55 .55

Ivan Goran Kovacic (1913-1943), Author — A61

1993, Apr. 24
153 A61 200d multicolored .35 .35

59th PEN Congress, Dubrovnik A62

1993, Apr. 24
154 A62 800d multicolored 1.25 1.25

Ivan Kukuljevic (1816-89), Politician, Historian, Writer — A63

1993, May 2 Litho. *Perf. 14*
155 A63 500d multicolored .65 .65

Croatian Natl. Theatre, Split, Cent. — A64

1993, May 6 Litho. *Perf. 14*
156 A64 600d multicolored .75 .75

Pag, 500th Anniv. — A65

1993, May 18
157 A65 800d multicolored .75 .75

Croatian Membership in United Nations, 1st Anniv. — A66

1993, May 22
158 A66 500d multicolored .60 .60

Europa A67

Contemporary paintings by: 700d, Ivo Dulcic (1916-75). 1000d, Miljenko Stancic (1926-77). 1100d, Ljubo Ivancic (b. 1925).

1993, June 5
159 A67 700d multicolored *.75 .75*
160 A67 1000d multicolored *1.50 1.50*
161 A67 1100d multicolored *2.25 2.25*
a. Min. sheet, 2 each #159-161 *9.00 9.00*
Nos. 159-161 (3) 4.50 4.50

Intl. Art Biennial, Venice — A68

Works of art by: 250d, Milivoj Bijelic. 600d, Ivo Dekovic. 1000d, Zeljko Kipke.

1993, June 10 Litho. *Perf. 14*
162 A68 250d multicolored .30 .30
a. Souvenir sheet of 4 1.00 1.00
163 A68 600d multicolored .85 .85
a. Souvenir sheet of 4 3.00 3.00
164 A68 1000d multicolored 1.20 1.20
a. Souvenir sheet of 4 4.00 4.00
Nos. 162-164 (3) 2.35 2.35

1993 Mediterranean Games — A69

1993, June 15 Litho. *Perf. 14*
165 A69 700d multicolored .65 .65

Adolf Waldinger (1843-1904), Painter — A70

1993, June 16
166 A70 300d multicolored .35 .35

Famous Croatian Battles A71

800d, Krbavskom, 1493. 1300d, Sisak, 1593.

1993, July 6 Litho. *Perf. 14*
167 A71 800d multi .65 .65
168 A71 1300d multi 1.10 1.10

Miroslav Krleza (1893-1981), Writer — A72

1993, July 7
169 A72 400d multicolored .40 .40

Croatian Membership in UPU, 1st Anniv. — A73

1993, July 20 Litho. *Perf. 14*
170 A73 1800d multicolored 1.25 .80

Vlaho Paljetak (1893-1944), Composer A74

1993, Aug. 7
171 A74 500d multicolored .45 .45

Stamp Day — A75

1993, Sept. 9 Litho. *Perf. 14*
172 A75 600d multicolored .50 .50

Map of Istria, 1620 — A76

1993, Sept. 20
173 A76 2200d multicolored 1.20 1.20

Incorporation of Istria, Rijeka and Zadar into Croatia, 50th anniv.

Tadija Smiciklas (1843-1914), Historian — A77

1993, Oct. 1
174 A77 800d black, gold & red .60 .60

Archaelogical Museum, Split, Cent. — A78

1993, Oct. 27
175 A78 1000d multicolored .60 .60

A79

1993, Nov. 17 Litho. *Perf. 14*
176 A79 3000d multicolored 1.50 1.50

Uprising of 13th Pioneer Battalion, Villefranche-de-Rouergue, France, 50th anniv.

A80

Josip Eugen Tomic (1843-1906), writer.

1993, Nov. 18
177 A80 900d multicolored .50 .50

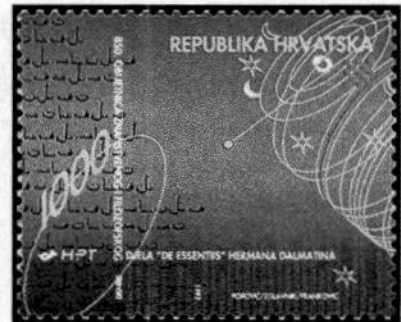

Publication of De Essentiis, by Hermana Dalmatin, 850th Anniv. — A81

1993, Nov. 30
178 A81 1000d multicolored .50 .50

Christmas A82

Paintings: 1000d, Christmas at the Front, by Miroslav Sutej. 4000d, Birth of Christ, 15th cent. fresco, Marienkirch of Dvigrad.

1993, Dec. 3
179 A82 1000d multicolored 1.00 1.00
180 A82 4000d multicolored 2.00 2.00

Nos. 179-180 are known with gold omitted. Values: No. 179, $90 mint; No. 180, $175 mint.

Organized Skiing in Croatia, Cent. — A83

1993, Dec. 15
181 A83 1000d multicolored .80 .80

Croatian Natl. Guard, 125th Anniv. A84

1993, Dec. 22
182 A84 1100d multicolored .80 .80

Printers of Senj, 500th Anniv. — A85

1994, Jan. 29
183 A85 2200d multicolored 1.10 .80

1994 Winter Olympics, Lillehammer A86

1994, Feb. 12
184 A86 4000d multicolored 1.90 1.60

Dinosaurs from Western Istria — A87

a, 2400d, Iguanodons. b, 4000d, Map, skeleton.

1994, Mar. 7
185 A87 Pair, #a.-b. 3.25 3.25

Nos. 185a-185b are a continuous design.

Zora Dalmatinska Magazine, 150th Anniv. — A88

1994, Mar. 15
186 A88 800d multicolored .50 .35

Croatian University, Zagreb, 325th Anniv. — A89

Design: 2200d, University building, Emperor Leopold I's seal, vice-chancellor's chain.

1994, Apr. 19 Litho. *Perf. 14*
187 A89 2200d multicolored 1.10 .75

Protect the Environment A90

1994, Apr. 22 Litho. *Perf. 14*
188 A90 3800d Canis lupus 2.00 1.75

ILO, 75th Anniv. — A91

1994, May 2
189 A91 1000d multicolored .60 .40

A92

Europa — A93

European inventions, discoveries: 3800d, Faust Vrancic (1551-1617), parachute. 4000d, Slavoljub Penkala (1871-1922), fountain pen.

1994, May 16
190 A92 3800d multicolored *2.25 2.00*
191 A93 4000d multicolored *2.75 2.00*

Flowers — A94

2.40k, Iris croatica. 4k, Colchicum visianii.

1994, June 3
192 A94 2.40k multicolored 1.00 .60
193 A94 4k multicolored 1.60 1.25

A95

Drazen Petrovic (1964-93), basketball player.

1994, June 7
194 A95 1k multicolored .75 .75

Tourism in Croatia, 150th Anniv. — A96

Designs: 80 l, Plitvice Lakes Natl. Park. 1k, Waterfalls, Krka River. 1.10k, Kornati Islands Natl. Park. 2.20k, Kopacki Trscak nature reserve. 2.40k Sailboats, Opatijska Riviera resort. 3.80k, Brijuni islands. 4k, Trakoscan castle, Zagorje.

1994, June 15 Litho. *Perf. 14*
196 A96 80 l multicolored .45 .25
197 A96 1k multicolored .50 .30
198 A96 1.10k multicolored .55 .35
199 A96 2.20k multicolored 1.25 .40
200 A96 2.40k multicolored 1.40 .60
201 A96 3.80k multicolored 2.10 .75
202 A96 4k multicolored 2.40 1.00
a. Min. sheet of 7, #196-202 + 2 labels 8.50 8.00
Nos. 196-202 (7) 8.65 3.65

Croatian Musicians A97

Designs: 1k, Kresimir Baranovic (1894-1975), composer, vert. 2.20k, Vatroslav Lisinski (1819-54), composer, vert. 2.40k, Pauline song-book (1644), harpist.

1994, June 20
211 A97 1k multicolored .50 .35
212 A97 2.20k multicolored 1.10 .75
213 A97 2.40k multicolored 1.25 .85
Nos. 211-213 (3) 2.85 1.95

Croatian Fraternal Union, Cent. — A98

1994, Aug. 15 Litho. *Perf. 14*
214 A98 2.20k multicolored 1.25 1.25

Intl. Year of the Family — A99

1994, Aug. 31
215 A99 80 l multicolored .50 .50

A100

1994, Sept. 10
216 A100 1k multicolored .60 .60

Intl. Olympic Committee, cent.

Visit of Pope John Paul II — A101

1994, Sept. 10
217 A101 1k multicolored .75 .75

No. 217 printed with se-tenant label.

Antoine de Saint-Exupery (1900-44), Aviator, Author A102

1994, Sept. 20
218 A102 3.80k multicolored 1.90 1.40

13th Intl. Congress on Early Christian Archeology A103

1994, Sept. 23
219 A103 4k multicolored 2.00 1.40

No. 219 printed with se-tenant label.

Modern Croatian Paintings A104

Designs: 2.40k, Still Life with Fruits and Basket, by Marino Tartaglia, 1926. 3.80k, In the Park, by Milan Steiner, c. 1918. 4k, Self-portrait, by Vilko Gecan, 1929.

1994, Oct. 12
220 A104 2.40k multicolored 1.00 .75
221 A104 3.80k multicolored 1.60 1.25
222 A104 4k multicolored 1.75 1.25
Nos. 220-222 (3) 4.35 3.25

Ivan Belostenec (1594-1675), Writer & Lexicographer A105

1994, Nov. 9
223 A105 2.20k multicolored 1.10 .90

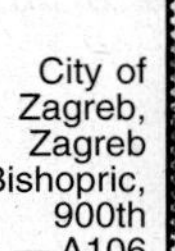

City of Zagreb, Zagreb Bishopric, 900th Anniv. — A106

Designs: No. 224a, 1k, Zagreb exchange building, designed by V. Kovacic, S. Penkala's airplane, Cibona office tower, designed by Hrzic, Pitesa and Serbetic. b, 1k, Maxi Cat, by Zlatko Grgic, Zagreb School of Animated Film. c, 1k, St. Mark's Church, Gradec; photo of gas lantern, by Toso Dabac. d, 4k, Late Gothic bishop's staff, Valvasor's view of Zagreb.
13.50k, Zagreb street scene, Penkala's airplane, vert.

1994, Nov. 16
224 A106 Strip of 4, #a.-d. 3.00 3.00

Souvenir Sheet

225 A106 13.50k multicolored 5.00 5.00

No. 224 is a continuous design. No. 225 contains one 24x48mm stamp.

Christmas A107

Design: 1k, Epiphany, by unknown sculptor.

1994, Dec. 1 Litho. *Perf. 14*
226 A107 1k multicolored .60 .50

Virgin Mary's Sanctuary, Loreto, 700th Anniv. — A108

Design: 4k, The Moving of the Holy House, by Giovanni Battista Tiepolo.

1994, Dec. 10
227 A108 4k multicolored 2.00 1.50

Necktie in Croatia — A109

Tie designs: 1.10k, Businessman's, 1995. 3.80k, English Dandy, 1810. 4k, Croatian soldier, 1630.

1995, Jan. 19 Litho. *Perf. 14*
228 A109 1.10k multicolored .60 .45
229 A109 3.80k multicolored 1.90 1.50
230 A109 4k multicolored 2.00 1.90
a. Souvenir sheet of 3, #228-230 4.75 4.75
Nos. 228-230 (3) 4.50 3.85

Croatian Monasteries — A110

1k, Jesuit Monastery, Zagreb, 350th anniv. 2.40k, Franciscan Monastery, Visovac, 550th anniv.

1995, Feb. 16
231 A110 1k multicolored .50 .30
232 A110 2.40k multicolored 1.25 .95

Hunting Dogs — A111

Designs: 2.20k, Istrian short-haired. 2.40k, Posavinian. 3.80k, Istrian wire-haired.

1995, Mar. 9 Litho. *Perf. 14*
233 A111 2.20k multicolored 1.00 .75
234 A111 2.40k multicolored 1.25 .80
235 A111 3.80k multicolored 1.75 1.40
Nos. 233-235 (3) 4.00 2.95

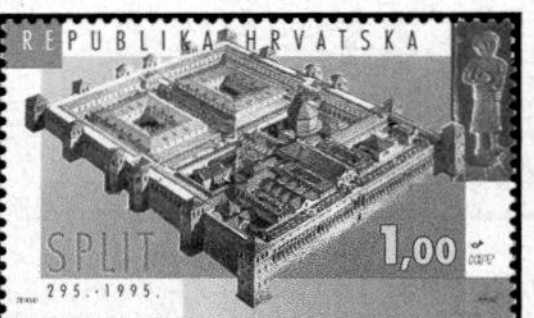
Town of Split, 1700th Anniv. — A112

No. 236: a, 1k, Drawing of reconstruction of Diocletian's Palace. b, 2.20k, "Split Harbour," by Emanuel Vidovic, 1937. c, 4k, Modern view of town, bust of Marko Marulic by Ivan Mestrovic.
13.40k, Buildings, vert.

1995, Apr. 20 Litho. *Perf. 14*
236 A112 Strip of 3, #a.-c. 4.00 4.00

Souvenir Sheet

237 A112 13.40k multicolored 6.25 6.25

No. 237 contains one 24x48mm stamp.

World Team Handball Championships, Iceland — A113

1995, May 4
238 A113 4k multicolored 2.00 1.25

Peace & Freedom A114

Europa: 2.40k, Clearing storm clouds. 4k, Hands of angel, by Francisco Robba.

1995, May 9
239 A114 2.40k multicolored *1.75 1.25*
240 A114 4k multicolored *2.25 1.60*

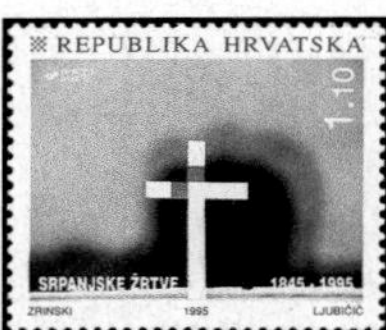
Anti-Austria Demonstrations, 150th Anniv. — A115

1995, May 15
241 A115 1.10k multicolored .65 .45
242 A115 3.80k multicolored 1.25 1.10

Croatian surrender to British forces at Bleiburg, 50th anniv. (No. 242).

Independence Day — A116

1995, May 30 Litho. *Perf. 14*
243 A116 1.10k multicolored .75 .40

Croatian Sculptures at Venice Biennial, 1995 — A117

2.20k, Installation (a part), by Martina Kramer. 2.40k, Paracelsus Paraduchamps, by Mirko Zrinscak, vert. 4k, Shadows, by Goran Petercol.

1995, June 8 Litho. *Perf. 14*
244 A117 2.20k multicolored 1.00 .65
245 A117 2.40k multicolored 1.10 .75
246 A117 4k multicolored 1.90 1.75
Nos. 244-246 (3) 4.00 3.15

St. Anthony of Padua (1195-1231) — A118

1995, June 13
247 A118 1k multicolored .45 .30

Marine Life — A119

2.40k, Caretta caretta. 4k, Tursiops truncatus.

1995, June 29 Litho. *Perf. 14*
248 A119 2.40k multi 1.00 .90
249 A119 4k multi 1.75 1.50

Liberation of the City of Knin — A120

1995, Aug. 5 Litho. *Perf. 14*
250 A120 1.30k multicolored .75 .60

Krka River Hydroelectric Power Plant, Cent. — A121

1995, Aug. 28

251 A121 3.60k multicolored 1.45 1.00

Stamp Day — A122

1995, Sept. 9 Litho. *Perf. 14*

252 A122 1.30k multicolored .70 .70

Franz von Suppe (1819-95), Composer A123

1995, Sept. 15

253 A123 6.50k multicolored 3.00 2.00

See Austria Nos. 1686-1687.

Liberation of Petrinja from Turkish Rule, 400th Anniv. — A124

1995, Sept. 21

254 A124 2.20k multicolored 1.10 .90

Croatian Music — A125

Composers, conductors: 1.20k, Ivo Tijardovic (1895-1976). 1.40k, Lovro Von Matacic (1899-1985). 6.50k, Jakov Gotovac (1895-1982).

1995, Sept. 23

255 A125 1.20k multicolored .55 .55
256 A125 1.40k multicolored .65 .60
257 A125 6.50k multicolored 3.25 2.50
Nos. 255-257 (3) 4.45 3.65

Herman Bollé (1845-1926), Architect — A126

2.40k, Izidor Krsnjavi (1845-1927), painter. 3.60k, Croatian National Theatre, cent.

1995, Oct. 14 Litho. *Perf. 14*

258 A126 1.80k multicolored .80 .50
259 A126 2.40k multicolored 1.00 .70
260 A126 3.60k multicolored 1.75 1.25
Nos. 258-260 (3) 3.55 2.45

Croatian Towns — A127

1995, Oct. 20

261 A127 1k Bjelovar .45 .45
262 A127 1.30k Osijek, vert. .55 .55
263 A127 1.40k Cakovec, vert. .60 .60
264 A127 2.20k Rovinj 1.10 1.10
265 A127 2.40k Korcula 1.25 1.25
266 A127 3.60k Zupanja 1.60 1.60
Nos. 261-266 (6) 5.55 5.55

See No. 448.

UN, FAO, 50th Anniv. — A128

No. 268, "5, 0" in form of cracker, FAO.

1995, Oct. 24

267 A128 3.60k multicolored 1.40 1.00
268 A128 3.60k multicolored 1.60 1.00
a. Pair, #267-268 3.25 3.25

Croatian Scientists — A129

1k, Spiro Brusina (1845-1908). 2.20k, Bogoslav Sulek (1816-95). 6.50k, Front of European language dictionary, published by Faust Vrancic (1551-1617).

1995, Oct. 30

269 A129 1k multicolored .65 .30
270 A129 2.20k multicolored 1.00 .65
271 A129 6.50k multicolored 3.00 2.25
Nos. 269-271 (3) 4.65 3.20

Institute for Blind Children, Cent. — A130

1995, Nov. 23 Litho. *Perf. 14*

272 A130 1.20k multicolored 1.00 1.00

Christmas A131

1995, Dec. 1

273 A131 1.30k multicolored .65 .45

Maroc Polo's Return from China, 700th Anniv. A132

1995, Dec. 7

274 A132 3.60k multicolored 1.75 1.50

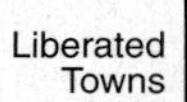

Liberated Towns A133

20 l, Hrvatska Kostajnica. 30 l, Slunj. 50 l, Gracac. 1.20k, Drnis, vert. 6.50k, Glina. 10k, Obrovac, vert.

1995, Dec. 16

275 A133 20 l multi .25 .25
276 A133 30 l multi .25 .25
277 A133 50 l multi .35 .35
278 A133 1.20k multi .70 .70
279 A133 6.50k multi 3.25 3.25
280 A133 10k multi 4.50 4.50
Nos. 275-280 (6) 9.30 9.30

Incunabula A134

Designs: 1.40k, Lectionary of Bernardin of Split. 3.60k, Spovid Opcena (General Confession).

1995, Dec. 28

281 A134 1.40k multicolored .75 .40
282 A134 3.60k multicolored 1.75 1.25

Spirituality of the Croats — A135

Designs: No. 283, Mosaic of St. Marko Krizevcanin (1589-1619), Catholic martyr. No. 284, Veneration of Miraculous Crucifix, St. Guido's Church, Rijeka, 700th anniv. No. 285, Ivan Merz (1896-1928), Catholic educator.

1996, Jan. 18 Litho. *Perf. 14*

283 A135 1.30k multicolored .60 .50
284 A135 1.30k multicolored .60 .50
285 A135 1.30k multicolored .60 .50
a. Strip of 3, Nos. 283-285 2.00 2.00

Political Anniversaries A136

1.20k, Rakovica Uprising by Eugen Kvaternik, 125th anniv., horiz. 1.40k, Ante Starcevic (1823-96). 2.20k, Constitution of Neutral Peasant Republic of Croatia, 75th anniv., Stjepan Radic (1871-1928). 3.60k, Labin Republic, 75th anniv.

1996, Feb. 28

286 A136 1.20k multicolored .60 .50
287 A136 1.40k multicolored .70 .60
288 A136 2.20k multicolored .95 .80
289 A136 3.60k multicolored 1.75 1.40
Nos. 286-289 (4) 4.00 3.30

Institute for Pharmacognosy, University of Zagreb, Cent. — A137

1996, Mar. 23 Litho. *Perf. 14*

290 A137 6.50k multicolored 3.00 2.00

Croatian Music — A138

a, Vinko Jelíc (1596-1636), composer. b, First performance of opera "Love and Music." c, Josip Stolcer Slavenski (1896-1955), composer. d, "Lijepa Nasa," Croatian national anthem, 150th anniv.

1996, Mar. 28

291 A138 2.20k Strip of 4, #a.-d. 3.75 3.75

Famous Women Writers — A139

(Europa): 2.20k, Cvijeta Zuzoric (b. 1551 or 1552). 3.60k, Ivana Brlic Mazuranic (1874-1938).

1996, Apr. 11 Litho. *Perf. 14*

292 A139 2.20k multicolored 1.60 1.60
293 A139 3.60k multicolored 2.25 2.25

A140

The Zrinskis and The Frankopans: 1.30k, Nikola Subic Zrinski of Sziget (1508-56). 1.40k, Nikola Zrinski (1620-64). 2.20k, Petar Zrinski (1621-71). 2.40k, Katarina Zrinski (1625-73). 3.60k, Fran Krsto Frankopan (1643-71).

1996, Apr. 30

294 A140 1.30k multicolored .55 .55
295 A140 1.40k multicolored .60 .60
296 A140 2.20k multicolored 1.00 1.00
297 A140 2.40k multicolored 1.10 1.10
298 A140 3.60k multicolored 1.40 1.40
a. Sheet of 5, #294-298 5.00 5.00
Nos. 294-298 (5) 4.65 4.65

Natl. Guard, 5th Anniv. — A141

1996, May 28 Litho. *Perf. 14*

299 A141 1.30k multicolored .65 .65

Flowers — A142

Designs: 2.40k, Campanula istriaca. 3.60k, Centaurea ragusina.

1996, June 5

300 A142 2.40k multicolored 1.00 1.00
301 A142 3.60k multicolored 1.60 1.60

England '96, European Soccer Championship A143

1996, June 8

302 A143 2.20k red & black 1.10 .90

Father Ferdinand Konscak's Expedition to Lower California, 250th Anniv. — A144

1996, June 10

303 A144 2.40k multicolored 1.10 1.00

1996 Summer Olympics, Atlanta A145

1996, July 4

304 A145 3.60k multicolored 1.75 1.25

A146

1996, July 4

305 A146 1.40k multicolored .65 .60

Josip Fon, founder of Croatian Sokol Gymnastics Society, 150th birth anniv.

A147

1996, Sept. 9 **Litho.** ***Perf. 14***

306 A147 1.30k multicolored .65 .40

Croatian postage stamps, 5th anniv.

1st Written Reference, Zumberak Region, 700th Anniv. — A148

1996, Sept. 14

307 A148 2.20k multicolored 1.00 1.00

A149

1996, Sept. 19

308 A149 1.30k multicolored .60 .60

First written record of fishing in Croatia, 1000th anniv.

A150

Events of the early Middle Ages: 1.20k, Vekenega's Book of Gospels, 900th anniv. 1.40k, Visit by Saxon Benedictine abbot Gottschalk (805-870), to Duke Trpimir's court, 1150th anniv.

1996, Sept. 19

309 A150 1.20k multicolored .55 .50
310 A150 1.40k multicolored .65 .55

Scientists A151

Designs: a, Gjuro Pilar (1846-93), geologist. b, Frane Bulic (1846-1934), archeologist. c, Ante Sercer (1896-1968), otolaryngologist.

1996, Oct. 4 **Litho.** ***Perf. 14***

311 A151 2.40k Strip of 3, #a.-c. 3.25 3.25

Beginning of Higher Education in Croatia, 600th Anniv. — A152

Oldest preserved Croatian text written in Latin script, "Order and Law" of Dominican nuns, Zadar.

1996, Oct. 16 ***Perf. 13½***

312 A152 1.40k multicolored .70 .50

Paintings — A153

Designs: 1.30k, Rain, by Menci Clement Crncic (1865-1930). 1.40k, The Peljesac-Korcula Channel, by Mato Celestin Medovic (1857-1919). 3.60k, Pink Dream, by Vlaho Bukovac (1855-1922).

1996, Nov. 7 **Litho.** ***Perf. 14***

313 A153 1.30k multicolored .60 .60
314 A153 1.40k multicolored .70 .70
315 A153 3.60k multicolored 1.75 1.75
Nos. 313-315 (3) 3.05 3.05

UNICEF, 50th Anniv. — A154

1996, Nov. 15

316 A154 3.60k multicolored 1.60 1.25

City of Osijek, 800th Anniv. — A155

Views of city: No. 317, River bank, church, coat of arms. No. 318, Boats in water, view looking down covered walkway through building.

1996, Dec. 2 **Litho.** ***Perf. 14***

317 A155 2.20k multicolored 1.00 .75
318 A155 2.20k multicolored 1.00 .75
a. Pair, #317-318 2.25 2.25

Christmas — A156

1996, Dec. 3

319 A156 1.30k multicolored .70 .50

First Croatian Savings Bank, Zagreb, 150th Anniv. — A157

Design: 3.60k, Publishing of "The Bases of Corn Trade," by Josip Sipus, bicent.

1996, Dec. 14

320 A157 2.40k multicolored 1.00 .80
321 A157 3.60k multicolored 1.75 1.25

Motion Pictures, Cent. — A158

Designs: a, Shooting of film, "Vatroslav Lisinski," Oktavijan Miletic, cameraman, director. b, Characters from animated series, "Professor Baltazar." c, Mirjana Bohanec, Relja Basic in "Who Sings Means No Harm."

1997, Jan. 16 **Litho.** ***Perf. 14***

322 A158 1.40k Strip of 3, #a.-c. 2.00 2.00

Great Europeans A159

Designs: 2.20k, Miguel de Cervantes (1547-1676), author. 3.60k, Johannes Gutenberg (1397-1468), printer, horiz.

1997, Feb. 7

323 A159 2.20k multicolored .90 .65
324 A159 3.60k multicolored 1.50 1.10

Legends A160

Europa: 1.30k, Home Genies, from story, "Stribor's Forest." 3.60k, "Vili Joze," by Vladimir Nazor, vert.

1997, Mar. 6 **Litho.** ***Perf. 14***

325 A160 1.30k multicolored *1.10 1.10*
326 A160 3.60k multicolored *2.75 2.75*

Fauna of Croatia — A161

1997, Apr. 22 **Litho.** ***Perf. 14***

327 A161 1.40k Pinna nobilis .60 .60
328 A161 2.40k Radziella styx 1.00 1.00
329 A161 3.60k Tonna galea 1.60 1.60
Nos. 327-329 (3) 3.20 3.20

Admission of Croatia to UN, 5th Anniv. A162

6.50k, Pres. Franjo Tudjman.

1997, May 22 **Litho.** ***Perf. 14***

330 A162 6.50k multi 3.00 3.00

First Croatian Esperantist Conference, 90th Anniv. A163

Ludwig Lazarus Zamenhof, conf. logo.

1997, May 31

331 A163 1.20k multicolored .70 .70

Congress of Intl. Amateur Rugby Federation, Dubrovnik A164

1997, June 6

332 A164 2.20k multicolored 1.10 .80

Siege of Vukovar, Serbo-Croatian War, 1991 — A165

Painting by Zlatko Kauzlaric Atac.

1997, June 8 **Litho.** ***Perf. 14***
333 A165 6.50k multicolored 3.00 3.00

Croatian Kings — A166

1.30k, King Peter Svacic, 900th death anniv. 2.40k, King Stephen Drzislav, 1000th death anniv.

1997, July 3
334 A166 1.30k multicolored .60 .60
335 A166 2.40k multicolored 1.25 1.25

16th Century Courier from Dubrovnik A167

1997, Sept. 9 **Litho.** ***Perf. 14***
336 A167 2.30k multicolored 1.10 .90

Stamp Day.

Croatian Olympic Medals — A168

Designs: 1k, Tennis, bronze, Barcelona, 1992. 1.20k, Basketball, silver, Barcelona 1992. 1.40k, Water polo, silver, Atlanta, 1996. 2.20k, Handball, gold, Atlanta, 1996.

1997, Sept. 10
337 A168 1k multicolored .40 .40
338 A168 1.20k multicolored .50 .50

Size: 27x31mm

339 A168 1.40k multicolored .75 .75
340 A168 2.20k multicolored 1.00 1.00
Nos. 337-340 (4) 2.65 2.65

Defense of Sibenik — A169

Designs: No. 341, Fort, airplanes. No. 342, Turkish cavalry, fort.

1997, Sept. 18
341 A169 1.30k multicolored .50 .50
342 A169 1.30k multicolored .50 .50
a. Pair, #341-342 1.25 1.25

Serbo-Croatian War, 1991 (No. 341). War with the Turks, 350th anniv. (No. 342).

Anniversaries A170

No. 343: a, Frane Petríc (1529-97), philosopher. b, Vicko Lovrin, 16th century painter. c, Frano Krsiníc (1897-1982), sculptor. d, Dubravko Dujsin (1894-1947), actor.

1997, Oct. 17 **Litho.** ***Perf. 14***
343 A170 1.40k Strip of 4, #a.-d. 2.75 2.75

A171

A172

1997, Oct. 23
344 A171 2.20k multicolored 1.00 .70
345 A172 3.60k multicolored 1.50 1.00

Use of Croatian language in parliament, 150th anniv. (No. 344).
Croatian Grammar School, Zadar, cent. (No. 345).

Palaeontological Finds in Croatia — A173

Designs: 1.40k, Gomphotherium angustidens. 2.40k, Viviparus novskaensis.

1997, Nov. 6
346 A173 1.40k multicolored .60 .60
347 A173 2.40k multicolored 1.10 1.10

Modern Art A174

Paintings: 1.30k, Painter in the Pond, by Nikola Masic (1852-1902). 2.20k, Angelus, by Emanuel Vidovic (1870-1953). 3.60k, Tree in the Snow, by Slava Raskaj (1877-1906).

1997, Nov. 14
348 A174 1.30k multicolored .60 .45
349 A174 2.20k multicolored .90 .55
350 A174 3.60k multicolored 1.75 1.25
Nos. 348-350 (3) 3.25 2.25

Contemporary Christmas Painting, by Ivan Antolcic — A175

"Birth of Jesus," by Isidor Krsnjavi A176

1997, Nov. 28 **Litho.** ***Perf. 13½***
351 A175 1.30k multicolored .50 .40

Perf. 14

352 A176 3.60k multicolored 1.60 1.10

Croatian Literature — A177

1997, Dec. 18 ***Perf. 14***
353 A177 1k shown .55 .40
354 A177 1.20k Book, words .60 .40

Printing of the translation of "Electra," by Dominko Zlataric, 400th anniv. (No. 353). Publication of "The Best of Folk Speech and the Illyric or Croatian Language," by Filip Grabovac, 250th anniv. (No. 354).

Cities and Landmarks Type of 1992

1997 **Litho.** ***Perf. 14***
355 A39 5 l Ilok .25 .25
356 A39 10 l Dubrovnik .25 .25

Events and Festivals — A178

Europa: 1.45k, Varazdin Baroque Evenings, musical notes. 4k, Dubrovnik Summer Festival.

1998, Jan. 23 ***Perf. 13½***
357 A178 1.45k multicolored *1.00 1.00*
358 A178 4k multicolored *2.50 2.50*

1998 Winter Olympic Games, Nagano — A179

1998, Feb. 7 ***Perf. 14***
359 A179 2.45k multicolored 1.10 .75

Croatian Events of 1848 — A180

a, 1.60k, Flag, battle near Moor. b, 4k, Portrait of Ban Josip Jelacic. c, 1.60k, Croatian Assembly.

1998, Mar. 25 **Litho.** ***Perf. 14***
360 A180 Strip of 3, #a.-c. 3.25 3.25

No. 360b is 21x32mm.

Ante Topic Mimara (1898-1987), Art Collector, Painter A181

1998, Apr. 7 **Litho.** ***Perf. 14***
361 A181 2.65k multicolored 1.25 .90

A182

Mushrooms: a, 1.30k, Amanita caesarea. b, 7.20k, Morchella conica. c, 1.30k, Lactarius deliciosus.

1998, Apr. 22
362 A182 Strip of 3, #a.-c. 4.50 4.50

A183

1998, May 8
363 A183 1.50k multicolored .65 .65

Archbishop Alojzije Stepinac (1898-1960).

27th European Regional Conference of Interpol, Dubrovnik A184

1998, May 13
364 A184 2.45k multicolored 1.10 .90

Souvenir Sheet

Expo '98, Lisbon — A185

14.85k, Fishing boat, Falkusa.

1998, June 3 **Litho.** ***Perf. 14***
365 A185 14.85k multi 6.25 6.25

1998 World Cup Soccer Championships, France — A186

1998, June 10
366 A186 4k multicolored 2.00 1.50

Writers A187

1.20k, Juraj Barakovic (1548-1628). 1.50k, Milan Begovic (1876-1948). 1.60k, Mate Balota (Mijo Mirkovic, 1898-1963). 2.45k, Antun Gustav Matos (1873-1914). 2.65k, Matija Antun Relkovic (1732-98). 4.00k, Antun Branko Simic (1898-1925).

1998, June 13 **Litho.** ***Perf. 14***

367	A187	1.20k multicolored	.60	.50
368	A187	1.50k multicolored	.70	.60
369	A187	1.60k multicolored	.75	.70
370	A187	2.45k multicolored	1.00	.90
371	A187	2.65k multicolored	1.10	1.00
372	A187	4k multicolored	1.75	1.60
		Nos. 367-372 (6)	5.90	5.30

19th Conference of the Countries of the Danube Region, Osijek — A188

1998, June 15
373 A188 1.80k multicolored .75 .65

Stjepan Betlheim (1898-1970), Psychiatrist A189

1998, July 22
374 A189 1.50k multicolored .65 .50

Souvenir Sheet

Croatian Soccer Team, Bronze Medalists at 1998 World Cup Soccer Championships, France — A190

Portions of team picture, denomination: a, red, LL. b, yellow, CR (player in yellow & blue shirt). c, yellow, CL. d, yellow, LR.

1998, July 24
375 A190 4k Sheet of 4, #a.-d. 7.25 7.25

Croatian Ships — A191

1.20k, Serilia Liburnica. 1.50k, Condura Croatica. 1.60k, Dubrovnik carrack. 1.80k, Bracera. 2.45k, Ship from the Neretva. 2.65k, Bark. 4k, Training ship, "Villa Velebita." 7.20k, Passenger ship, "Amorella." 20k, Missile gun boat, "Kralj Petar Kresimir IV."

1998, Aug. 27 **Litho.** ***Perf. 14***

376	A191	1.20k multi	.70	.70
376A	A191	1.50k multi	.80	.80
376B	A191	1.60k multi	.85	.85
376C	A191	1.80k multi	.90	.90
376D	A191	2.45k multi	1.30	1.30
376E	A191	2.65k multi	1.50	1.50
376F	A191	4k multi	2.00	2.00
376G	A191	7.20k multi	3.50	3.50
376H	A191	20k multi	9.25	9.25
i.		Sheet of 9, #376-376H + 3 labels	20.00	20.00
		Nos. 376-376H (9)	20.80	20.80

Stamp Day — A192

1998, Sept. 9
377 A192 1.50k multicolored .65 .50

Bishopric of Sibenik, 700th Anniv. — A193

1998, Sept. 29 **Litho.** ***Perf. 14***
378 A193 4k multicolored 1.60 1.60

Pope John Paul II, Second Visit to Croatia A194

1998, Oct. 2
379 A194 1.50k multicolored .90 .90

History of Public Transportation A195

Designs: a, 1.50k, Horse tram. b, 1.50k, First automobile in Zagreb, 1901. c, 7.20k, Zagreb funicular. d, 1.50k, Karlovac-Rijeka Railway Line, 1873. e, 1.50k, New Highway, Zagreb-Rijeka.

1998, Oct. 23 **Litho.** ***Perf. 14***
380 A195 Strip of 5, #a.-e. 6.00 6.00

No. 380c is 20x24mm.

Christmas — A196

Adoration of the Shepherds, by Juraj Julije Klovic (1498-1578).

1998, Nov. 21 ***Perf. 14x13***
381 A196 1.50k multicolored .80 .75

See Vatican City No. 1088.

Father Luka Ibrisimovic (1620-98) A197

1998, Nov. 30 **Litho.** ***Perf. 14***
382 A197 1.90k multicolored .90 .75

Universal Declaration of Human Rights, 50th Anniv. — A198

1998, Dec. 10
383 A198 5k multicolored 2.00 2.00

Modern Art A199

Paintings: 1.90k, Paromlin Road, by Josip Vanista. 2.20k, Cypresses, by Frano Simunovic, vert. 5k, Koma, by Dalibor Martinis, vert.

1998, Dec. 15

384	A199	1.90k multicolored	.90	.90
385	A199	2.20k multicolored	1.00	1.00
386	A199	5k multicolored	2.10	2.10
		Nos. 384-386 (3)	4.00	4.00

Zagreb Intl. Trade Fair — A200

1999, Jan. 21 **Litho.** ***Perf. 14***
387 A200 1.80k multicolored .90 .80

Cardinal Juraj Haulik (1788-1869), Archbishop of Zagreb — A201

Photo. & Engr.

1999, Jan. 28 ***Perf. 11½***
388 A201 5k multicolored 2.10 2.10

See Slovakia 321.

National Parks — A202

Europa: 1.80k, Mljet Island. 5k, Lonja Field.

1999, Mar. 12 **Litho.** ***Perf. 14***

389	A202	1.80k multicolored	*2.00*	*2.00*
390	A202	5k multicolored	*3.50*	*3.50*

Vipera Ursinii — A203

World Wildlife Fund: a, One coiled in grass and rock. b, Two. c, Head. d, One coiled on rock.

1999, Apr. 27 **Litho.** ***Perf. 14***
391 A203 2.20k Strip of 4, #a.-d. 4.25 4.25

Council of Europe, 50th Anniv. — A204

1999, May 5
392 A204 2.80k multicolored 1.25 1.25

19th Convention of the Foundation of European Carnival Cities, Dubrovnik — A205

1999, May 8
393 A205 2.30k multicolored 1.10 1.10

Croatian Coins — A206

Designs: a, 2.30k, Obv., rev. of 1849 kreutzer. b, 5k, One kuna.

1999, May 30 **Litho.** ***Perf. 14***
394 A206 Pair, #a.-b. 3.25 3.25

Minting of Jelacic kreutzer, 150th anniv. (No. 394a). Croatian kuna, 5th anniv. (No. 394b).

Famous Croats — A207

1.80k, Vladimir Nazor (1876-1949), poet. 2.30k, Ferdo Livadic (1799-1879), composer. 2.50k, Ivan Rendic (1849-1932), sculptor. 2.80k, Milan Lenuci (1849-1924), architect. 3.50k, Vjekoslav Klaic (1849-1929), historian, muscician. 4k, Emilij Laszowski (1868-1949), historian. 5k, Antun Kanizlic (1699-1777), poet, missionary.

1999, June 18

395	A207	1.80k multicolored	.65	.65
396	A207	2.30k multicolored	.95	.90
397	A207	2.50k multicolored	1.25	1.10
398	A207	2.80k multicolored	1.30	1.30
399	A207	3.50k multicolored	1.40	1.40
400	A207	4k multicolored	1.60	1.60
401	A207	5k multicolored	2.10	2.10
		Nos. 395-401 (7)	9.25	9.05

Euphrasian Basilica, Porec — A208

1999, June 25

402 A208 4k multicolored 1.75 1.75

2nd World Military Games, Zagreb A209

1999, Aug. 7 Litho. ***Perf. 14***

403 A209 2.30k multicolored 1.10 .90

Discovery of Early Krapina Man, Cent. — A210

Designs: a, 1.80k, Bones, rendition of Krapina man. b, 4k, Ancient bones, paleontologist Dragutin Gorjanovic-Kramberger.

1999, Aug. 23

404 A210 Pair, #a.-b. 3.00 3.00

Stamp Day and UPU, 125th Anniv. — A211

1999, Sept. 9 Litho. ***Perf. 14***

405 A211 2.30k multicolored 1.10 1.00

Paulist Order in Lepoglava, 600th Anniv. — A212

a, Lace, Jesus Expelling the Money Changers from Temple, by Ivan Ranger, altar angel from St. Mary's Church, Lepoglava. b, St. Mary's Church facade, altar angel. c, St. Elizabeth, lace.

1999, Sept. 11 Litho.

406 A212 5k Strip of 3, #a.-c. 6.50 6.50

150th Anniv. of "Jelacic March" by Johann Strauss the Elder — A213

1999, Sept. 16 Litho.

407 A213 3.50k multicolored 1.75 1.75

World Ozone Layer Protection Day A214

1999, Sept. 16 Litho.

408 A214 5k multicolored 2.10 2.10

Grammar School Anniversaries A215

2.30k, Pazin, cent. 3.50k, Pozega, 300th anniv.

1999, Oct. 15 Litho. ***Perf. 14***

409 A215 2.30k multi 1.00 .90

410 A215 3.50k multi 1.50 1.25

Andrija Hebrang (1899-1949), Politician — A216

1999, Oct. 21

411 A216 1.80k multicolored .80 .80

Our Lady of the Rose Garden, by Blaz Jurjev Trogiranin A217

1999, Oct. 28

412 A217 5k multicolored 2.00 2.00

Christmas, opening of exhibition of Croatian religious art and artifacts, Vatican City.

Christmas — A218

1999, Nov. 24 Litho. ***Perf. 14***

413 A218 2.30k multicolored 1.10 1.10

Modern Art A219

Designs: 2.30k, Winter Landscape, by Gabrijel Jurkic (1886-1974). 3.50k, Klek, by Oton Postruznik (1900-78). 5k, Stone Table, by Ignjat Job (1895-1936), vert.

1999, Dec. 15

414 A219 2.30k multicolored 1.10 1.10

415 A219 3.50k multicolored 1.40 1.40

416 A219 5k multicolored 2.00 2.00

Nos. 414-416 (3) 4.50 4.50

Pres. Franjo Tudjman (1922-99) — A220

1999, Dec. 16 Vignette Color

417 A220 2.30k black 1.10 1.00

418 A220 5k blue 2.50 2.00

Millennium A221

2000, Jan. 1 Litho. ***Perf. 14***

419 A221 2.30k multi 2.75 2.25

Valentine's Day — A222

2000, Feb. 1

420 A222 2.30k multi 2.00 1.60

Split Grammar School, 300th Anniv. — A223

2000, Mar. 25 Litho. ***Perf. 14***

421 A223 2.80k multi 1.25 1.10

Croatian Writers' Assoc., 100th Anniv. — A224

2000, Apr. 22 Litho. ***Perf. 14***

422 A224 2.30k black & red 2.75 2.75

A225

A226

A227

A228

A229

(1.80k) Lo Schiavone (Andrija Medulic, c. 1500-63), painter; (2.30k) Matija Petar Katancic (1750-1825), writer; (2.80k) Marija Ruzicka-Strozzi (1850-1937), actress; (3.50k) Marko Marulic (1450-1524), writer; (5k) Blaz Jurjev Trogiranin (c. 1390-1450), painter.

2000, Apr. 22

423 A225 1.80k multi .65 .65

424 A226 2.30k multi .95 .95

425 A227 2.80k multi 1.10 1.10

426 A228 3.50k multi 1.40 1.40

427 A229 5k multi 1.90 1.90

Nos. 423-427 (5) 6.00 6.00

Europa, 2000

Common Design Type and

A230

2000, May 9

428 A230 2.30k multi *2.00 2.00*

429 CD17 5k multi *4.25 4.25*

Independence Day — A231

2000, May 30 Litho. ***Perf. 14***

430 A231 2.30k multi 1.50 1.50

Souvenir Sheet

Expo 2000, Hanover — A232

2000, June 1

431 A232 14.40k multi 6.25 6.25

Flora — A233

No. 432: a, 3.50k, Micromeria croatica. b, 5k, Geranium dalmaticum.

2000, June 5

432 A233 Pair, #a-b 4.00 4.00

c. Booklet pane of 10 #432a 15.00

Booklet, #432c 16.00

d. Booklet pane of 10 #432b 20.00

Booklet, #432d 21.00

Kastav Statute, 600th Anniv. — A234

2000, June 6
433 A234 1.80k multi .85 .85

World Mathematics Year — A235

2000, June 15
434 A235 3.50k multi 1.60 1.60

Ivan Ranger (1700-53), Artist — A236

2000, June 19
435 A236 1.80k multi .85 .85

Souvenir Sheet

Baska Stone Tablet, 900th Anniv. — A237

2000, June 24
436 A237 16.70k multi 7.25 7.25

Archdeacon Toma of Split (1200-68) A238

2000, July 10
437 A238 3.50k multi 1.60 1.60

Type of 1992-94 Redrawn

2000, Aug. 1 Litho. *Perf. 14*
437A A39a 3.50k Vis 1.60 1.60

No. 437A has "HP" and post horn in LR corner.

Stamp Day — A239

No. 438: a, 2.30k, Austria #5. b, 2.30k, Automatic mail sorting equipment.

2000, Sept. 9 Litho. *Perf. 14*
438 A239 Pair, #a-b 2.25 2.25

First stamps used in Croatia, 150th anniv. (No. 438a).

2000 Summer Olympics, Sydney A240

2000, Sept. 15
439 A240 5k multicolored 3.00 3.00

Altarpiece, Church of the Blessed Virgin Mary, Ostarije A241

2000, Nov. 23
440 A241 2.30k multi 1.10 1.10
a. Booklet pane of 10 11.00
Booklet, #440a 11.50

Modern Art A242

Designs: 1.80k, Korcula, by Vladimir Varlaj. 2.30k, Brusnik, by Duro Tiljak. 5k, Boats, by Ante Kastelacic.

2000, Dec. 1
441-443 A242 Set of 3 4.00 4.00

See Nos. 471-473, 505-507.

Start of New Millennium A243

2001, Jan. 1 Litho. *Perf. 14*
444 A243 2.30k multi 1.75 1.75

Souvenir Sheet

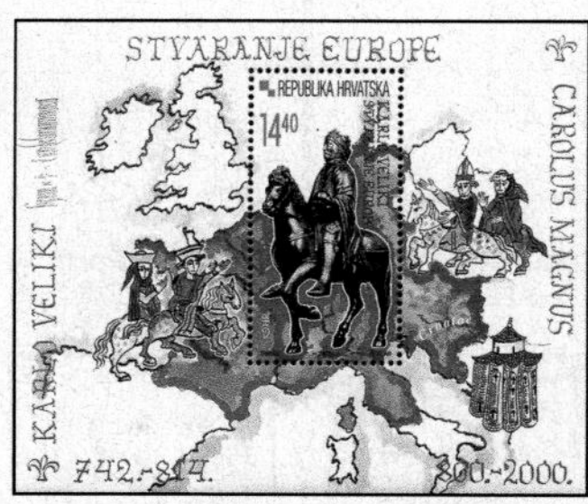
Equestrian Statue of Charlemagne — A244

2001, Jan. 19
445 A244 14.40k multi 6.25 6.25

Crowning of Charlemagne as Emperor of the Romans, 1200th anniv. (in 2000).

Dzore Drzic (1461-1501), Writer — A245

2001, Mar. 15 Litho. *Perf. 14*
446 A245 2.80k multi 1.40 1.40

Comic Strip "Black Rider," by Andrija Maurovic (1901-81) A246

2001, Mar. 29
447 A246 5k multi 2.25 2.25

Makarska A247

2001, Mar. 30
448 A247 2.30k multi 1.00 1.00
a. Perf. 14 syncopated 1.00 1.00

Issued: No. 448a, 6/2/06.

Janica Kostelic, Skier — A248

2001, Apr. 19 Litho. *Perf. 14*
449 A248 2.80k multi 2.40 2.00

Kastel Stafilic Olive Trees, 1500th Anniv. — A249

2001, Apr. 20
450 A249 1.80k multi .85 .85

Europa — A250

No. 451: a, 3.50k, Denomination at R. b, 5k, Denomination at L.

2001, May 9
451 A250 Horiz. pair, #a-b 3.50 3.50

World No Smoking Day — A251

2001, May 31
452 A251 2.50k multi 1.10 1.10

Butterflies A252

Designs: 2.50k, Parnassius apollo. 2.80k, Maculinea teleius. 5k, Coenonympha oedippus.

2001, June 5
453-455 A252 Set of 3 4.75 4.75

Type of 1992 Redrawn

2.80k, Eltz Castle, Vukovar.

2001, June 21 Litho. *Perf. 14*
456 A39 2.80k multi 1.25 1.25
a. Perf. 14 syncopated 1.10 1.10

No. 456 has "1991-2001" inscription, and "HP" and post horn at LL.
Issued: No. 456a, 6/19/06.

Souvenir Sheet

Trsteno Arboretum — A253

2001, July 12 Litho. *Perf. 14*
457 A253 14.40k multi 6.50 6.50

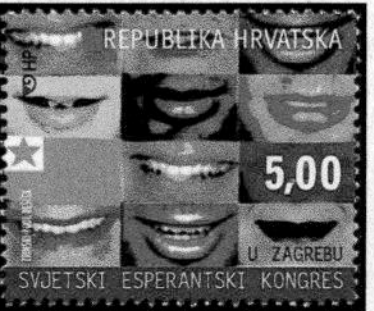
World Esperanto Congress, Zagreb — A254

2001, July 21
458 A254 5k multi 2.40 2.40

Refugee Organizations, 50th Annivs. A255

Designs: 1.80k, UN High Commissioner for Refugees. 5k, Intl. Organization for Migration.

2001, July 28
459-460 A255 Set of 2 3.25 3.25

Victory of Goran Ivanisevic at Wimbledon A256

2001, Aug. 31
461 A256 2.50k multi 2.50 2.25

Printed in sheets of 9 + label.

Stamp Day — A257

2001, Sept. 9
462 A257 2.50k multi .90 .90

Printed in sheets of 16 + 4 labels.

Native Dog Breeds A258

Designs: 1.80k, Croatian sheepdog. 5k, Dalmatian.

2001, Oct. 4
463-464 A258 Set of 2 3.25 3.25

Independence, 10th Anniv. — A259

2001, Oct. 8
465 A259 2.30k multi 1.10 1.10

Printed in sheets of 25 + 5 labels.

Year of Dialogue Among Civilizations — A260

2001, Oct. 9
466 A260 5k multi 4.00 4.00

Fortresses — A261

Designs: 1.80k, Klis, 16th cent. 2.50k, Ston, 14th-15th cents. 3.50k, Sisak, 16th cent.

2001, Oct. 26 Litho. ***Perf. 14***
467-469 A261 Set of 3 3.50 3.50

See Nos. 499-501, 525-527, 565-567, 594-596, 630-632.

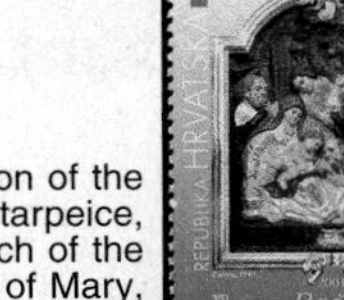
Adoration of the Magi Altarpeice, Church of the Visitation of Mary, Cucerje — A262

2001, Nov. 22 Litho. ***Perf. 14***
470 A262 2.30k multi 1.10 1.00
a. Booklet pane of 10 11.00 11.00
Complete booklet, #470a 11.00

Modern Art Type of 2000

Designs: No. 471, 2.50k, Maternité du Port-Royal, by Leo Junek. No. 472, 2.50k, Amphitheater Ruins, by Vjekoslav Parac. 5k, Nude with a Baroque Figure, by Slavko Sohaj, vert.

2001, Dec. 1
471-473 A242 Set of 3 4.75 4.75

Croatian Nobel Laureates — A263

Laureates: 2.80k, Lavoslav (Leopold) Ruzicka, Chemistry, 1939. 3.50k, Vladimir Prelog, Chemistry, 1975. 5k, Ivo Andric, Literature, 1961.

2001, Dec. 5
474-476 A263 Set of 3 5.50 5.50

Famous Croats and Events A264

Designs: 1.80k, Ivan Gucetic (1451-1502), writer. 2.30k, Dobrisa Cesaric (1902-80), writer. 2.50k, Publishing of Juraj Rattkay's *History of Croatian Rulers,* 350th anniv. 2.80k, Franjo Vranjanin Laurana (c. 1420-1502), sculptor. 3.50k, Beatification of Bishop Augustin Kazotic (c. 1260-1323), 300th anniv. 5k, Matko Laginja (1852-1930), politician and writer.

2002, Jan. 24 Litho. ***Perf. 14***
477-482 A264 Set of 6 8.00 8.00

2002 Winter Olympics, Salt Lake City — A265

2002, Feb. 8
483 A265 5k multi 2.40 2.40

Croatian Chamber of Economy, 150th Anniv. — A266

2002, Feb. 16
484 A266 2.50k multi 1.25 1.25

Souvenir Sheet

Trpimir's Deed of Gift, 1150th Anniv. — A267

2002, Mar. 4
485 A267 14.40k multi 6.50 6.50

Franjo Cardinal Kuharic (1919-2002) A268

2002, Mar. 25
486 A268 2.30k multi .90 .90

Divan, by Vlaho Bukovac — A269

Litho. & Engr.
2002, Apr. 23 ***Perf. 11¾***
487 A269 5k multi 2.40 2.40

See Czech Republic No. 3169.

Royal Borough of Krizevci, 750th Anniv. — A270

2002, Apr. 24 Litho. ***Perf. 14***
488 A270 1.80k multi .85 .85

Varazdin Post Office, Cent. — A271

2002, Apr. 26
489 A271 2.30k multi 1.10 1.10

Europa — A272

Clown color: a, 3.50k, Orange. b, 5k, Blue.

2002, May 9 Litho. ***Perf. 14***
490 A272 Horiz. pair, #a-b *4.25 4.25*

2002 World Cup Soccer Championships, Japan and Korea — A273

Stylized players facing: a, 3.50k, Left. b, 5k, Right.

2002, May 15
491 A273 Horiz. pair, #a-b 4.00 4.00

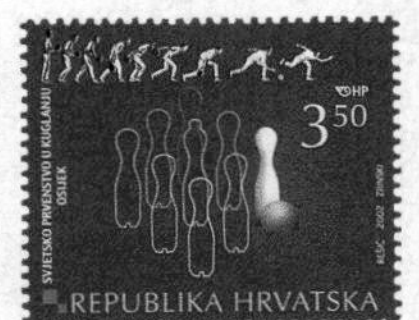
World Bowling Championships, Osijek — A274

2002, May 18
492 A274 3.50k multi 1.60 1.60

Oak Trees — A275

Designs: 1.80k, Quercus rober. 2.50k, Quercus petraea. 2.80k, Quercus ilex.

2002, June 5
493-495 A275 Set of 3 3.25 3.25
493a Booklet pane of 10 6.00 —
Complete booklet, #493a 6.25
494a Booklet pane of 10 12.00 —
Complete booklet, #494a 12.50
495a Booklet pane of 10 14.75 —
Complete booklet, #495a 15.25

15th World Animated Films Festival, Zagreb — A276

2002, June 18
496 A276 5k multi 2.40 2.40

Lace — A277

Lace from: 3.50k, Pag Island, Croatia. 5k, Liedekerke, Belgium.

2002, July 13 Photo. ***Perf. 11½***
497-498 A277 Set of 2 4.00 4.00

See Belgium Nos. 1927-1928.

Fortresses Type of 2001

Designs: No. 499, 2.50k, Nehaj, 16th cent. No. 500, 2.50k, Skocibuha, 16th cent. 5k, Veliki Tabor, 16th cent.

2002, Sept. 20 Litho. ***Perf. 14***
499-501 A261 Set of 3 4.50 4.50

Old Slavonic Academy, Krk, Cent. — A278

2002, Oct. 3 Litho. & Embossed
502 A278 4k red & black 1.75 1.75

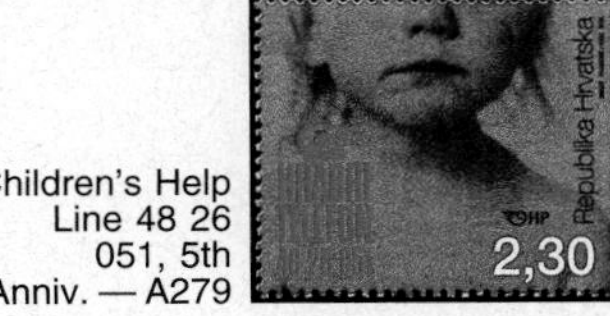
Children's Help Line 48 26 051, 5th Anniv. — A279

2002, Oct. 15 Litho.
503 A279 2.30k multi 1.10 1.10

Christmas A280

2002, Nov. 21
504 A280 2.30k multi 1.25 1.25
a. Booklet pane of 10 12.50 —
Complete booklet, #504a 13.00

Modern Art Type of 2002

Designs: No. 505, 2.50k, Flowers on the Window, by Antun Motika (1902-92), vert. No. 506, 2.50k, The Girl in the Boat, by Milivoj Uzelac (1897-1977), vert. 5k, On the Drava River, by Krsto Hegedusic (1901-75).

2002, Dec. 2 Litho. ***Perf. 14***
505-507 A242 Set of 3 4.75 4.75

Zagreb Bishopric, 150th Anniv. — A281

2002, Dec. 11
508 A281 2.80k multi 1.40 1.40

Printed in sheets of 19 + label.

Pavao Ritter Vitezovic (1652-1713), Writer — A282

2002, Dec. 13
509 A282 2.30k multi 1.10 1.10

Pacta Conventa, 900th Anniv. — A283

2002, Dec. 14
510 A283 3.50k multi 1.60 1.60

Fairies From Stories by Ivana Brlic Mazuranic — A284

No. 511: a, 2.30k, Kosjenka, fairy character from *Regoc.* b, 2.80k, Tintilinic, fairy character from *Suma Striborova.*

2003, Jan. 15
511 A284 Horiz. pair, #a-b 2.40 2.40

St. Valentine's Day — A285

Litho. With Foil Application

2003, Feb. 1
512 A285 2.30k multi 1.10 1.10

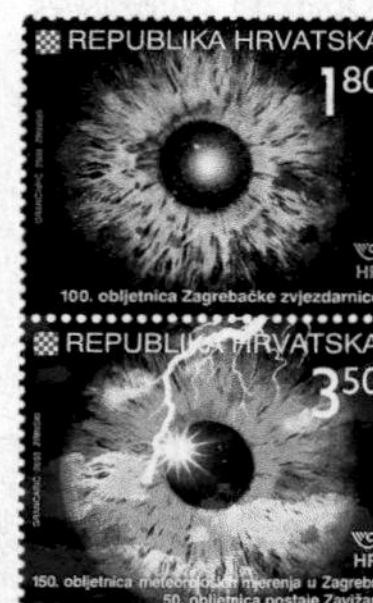

Astronomy and Meteorology A286

No. 513: a, 1.80k, Zagreb Astronomical Observatory, cent. b, 3.50k, Meteorological measurements in Zagreb, 150th anniv.; Meteorological station on Zavizan, 50th anniv.

2003, Feb. 17 **Litho.**
513 A286 Pair, #a-b 2.25 2.25

Souvenir Sheet

Croatia, 2003 World Handball Champions — A287

No. 514: a, Five team members, one wearing red shirt. b, Eight team members, one with arm extended. c, Six team members. d, Four team members, one wearing blue shirt.

2003, Feb. 20
514 A287 4k Sheet of 4, #a-d 7.00 7.00

Paulist High School, Lepoglava, 500th Anniv. — A288

2003, Mar. 1
515 A288 5k multi 2.40 2.40

Missal of Hrvoje Vukcic Hrvatinic, 600th Anniv. — A289

2003, Mar. 25
516 A289 5k multi 2.40 2.40

Land Mine Danger A290

2003, Apr. 8
517 A290 2.30k multi 1.10 1.10

Alpine Skiing World Cup Victories of Janica and Ivica Kostelic A291

No. 518: a, Janica. b, Ivica.

2003, Apr. 16
518 A291 3.50k Pair, #a-b 5.00 5.00

Printed in sheets containing 4 vertical pairs and 2 labels.

Christian Institutions in Rome Founded by Croatian Roman Brotherhood of St. Jerome, 550th Anniv. — A292

2003, Apr. 22
519 A292 2.80k multi 1.25 1.25

Famous Croatians A293

Designs: 1.80k, Antun Soljan (1932-93), writer. 2.30k, Hanibal Lucic (1485-1553), writer. 5k, Federiko Benkovic (1667-1753), painter.

2003, Apr. 22
520-522 A293 Set of 3 4.25 4.25

Poster for Performance of Marya Delvard, by Tomislav Krizman, 1907 — A294

Poster for Performance of "The Firebird," by Boris Bucan, 1983 — A295

2003, May 9 **Litho.** ***Perf. 14***
523 A294 3.50k multi *1.50 1.50*
524 A295 5k multi *2.25 2.25*

Europa.

Fortresses Type of 2001

Designs; 1.80k, Kostajnica, 15th-18th cent. 2.80k, Slavonski Brod, 18th cent. 5k, Minceta Tower, 15th cent., vert.

2003, May 13
525-527 A261 Set of 3 4.25 4.25

Visit of Pope John Paul II — A296

2003, June 2
528 A296 2.30k multi 1.75 1.75

Rodents A297

Designs: 2.30k, Sciuris vulgaris. 2.80k, Glis glis. 3.50k, Castor fiber.

2003, June 5
529-531 A297 Set of 3 4.00 4.00
531a Booklet pane, 6 #529, 2 each #530-531 13.00 —
Complete booklet, #531a 13.00

Souvenir Sheet

Robe of King Ladislaus, 11th Cent. — A298

2003, June 13
532 A298 10k multi 4.25 4.25

Stamp Day — A299

2003, Sept. 9 **Litho.** ***Perf. 14***
533 A299 2.30k multi 1.10 1.10

Souvenir Sheet

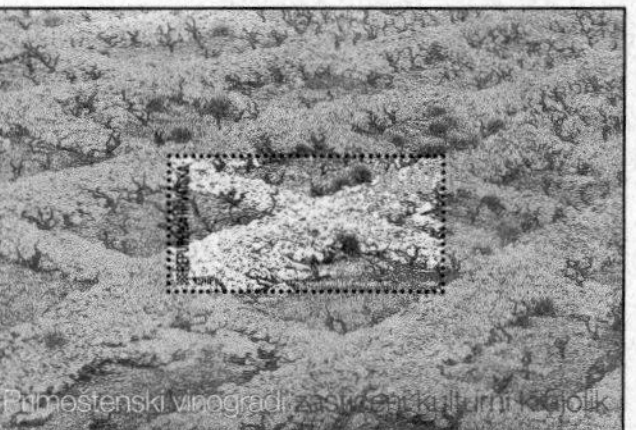

Primosten Vineyards — A300

Litho. with Foil Application

2003, Sept. 19
534 A300 10k multi 4.75 4.75

Ursuline Sisters in Croatia, 300th Anniv. — A301

2003, Oct. 20 **Litho.**
535 A301 2.50k multi 1.10 1.10

Christmas A302

2003, Nov. 20 **Litho.** ***Perf. 14***
536 A302 2.30k multi 1.00 1.00

Self-Adhesive

Serpentine Die Cut 5¼

537 A302 2.30k multi 1.00 1.00

Modern Art A304

Designs: 1.80k, Flower Girl II, by Slavko Kopac, vert. No. 539, 3.50k, Dry Stone Wall 5-71, by Oton Gliha. No. 540, 3.50k, Pont des Arts, by Josip Racic.

2003, Nov. 21 ***Perf. 14***
538-540 A304 Set of 3 4.00 4.00

See Nos. 568-570, 604-606, 636-638, 668-670, 712-714, 749-751.

18th World Women's Handball Championships — A305

2003, Dec. 1
541 A305 5k multi 2.25 2.25

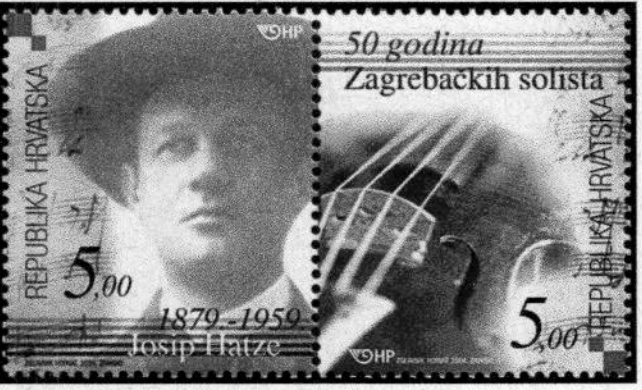

Musicians — A306

No. 542: a, Josip Hatze (1879-1959), composer. b, Zagreb Soloists, 50th anniv.

2004, Jan. 5 **Litho.** ***Perf. 14***
542 A306 5k Horiz. pair, #a-b 4.50 4.50

Hval's Manuscript, 600th Anniv. — A307

2004, Jan. 22
543 A307 2.30k multi 1.40 1.40

European Boxing Championships, Pula — A308

2004, Feb. 19 **Litho.** ***Perf. 14***
544 A308 2.80k multi 1.25 1.25

Worldwide Fund for Nature (WWF) — A309

Ardea purpurea: a, In grass. b, Standing with head extended. c, With young. d, In flight.

2004, Mar. 22
545 Strip or block of 4 8.50 8.50
a.-d. A309 5k Any single 1.75 1.75

Famous Croats — A310

Designs: 2.30k, Ivan Lucic (1604-79), historian. No. 547, 3.50k, Antun Vrancic (1504-75), archbishop, writer. No. 548, 3.50k, St. Jerome, sculpture by Andrija Alesi (c. 1425-1504). 10k, Printing of Croatian grammar book, by Bartol Kasic (1575-1650), 400th anniv.

2004, Apr. 22
546-549 A310 Set of 4 8.25 8.25

Souvenir Sheet

Risnjak National Park — A311

2004, Apr. 22
550 A311 10k multi 5.25 5.25

Martyrdom of St. Domnio, 1700th Anniv. — A312

2004, May 7
551 A312 3.50k multi 1.75 1.75

Europa A313

Designs: No. 552, 3.50k, Summer vacation items. No. 553, 3.50k, Winter vacation items.

2004, May 9
552-553 A313 Set of 2 *3.00 3.00*

FIFA (Fédération Internationale de Football Association), Cent. A314

2004, May 21 **Litho.** ***Perf. 14***
554 A314 2.50k multi 1.25 1.25

Medicinal Herbs — A315

Designs: 2.30k, Rosa canina. 2.80k, Viola odorata. 3.50k, Mentha piperita.

2004, June 5
555-557 A315 Set of 3 4.00 4.00
555a Booklet pane of 10 10.00 —
Complete booklet, #555a 10.50
556a Booklet pane of 10 12.50 —
Complete booklet, #556a 13.00
557a Booklet pane of 10 16.50 —
Complete booklet, #557a 17.50

Nos. 555-557 are impregnated with a floral scent.

Intl. Marionette Union Congress, Intl. Puppetry Art Festival, Rijeka A316

2004, June 6
558 A316 3.50k multi 1.75 1.75

European Soccer Championships, Portugal — A317

2004, June 12
559 A317 3.50k multi 1.75 1.75

Values are for stamps with surrounding selvage.

Restoration of Old Bridge, Mostar, Bosnia & Herzegovina A318

2004, July 23 **Litho.** ***Perf. 14***
560 A318 3.50k multi 1.75 1.75

2004 Summer Olympics, Athens — A319

2004, Aug. 13
561 A319 3.50k multi 1.75 1.75

Virovitica A320

2004, Aug. 16
562 A320 5k multi 2.40 2.40
a. Perf. 14 syncopated — —

Issued: No. 562a, 12/7/07. For surcharge see No. 779.

Zagreb Post Office, Cent. A321

2004, Sept. 9
563 A321 2.30k multi 1.00 1.00

Printed in sheets of 16 + 4 labels.

Father Andrija Kacic Miosic (1704-60), Poet — A322

2004, Sept. 15
564 A322 2.80k multi 1.25 1.25

Fortresses Type of 2001

Designs: No. 565, 3.50k, Dubovac, 15th-19th cent. No. 566, 3.50k, Gripe, 17th cent. No. 567, 3.50k, Valpovo, 15th-18th cent.

2004, Sept. 29
565-567 A261 Set of 3 4.75 4.75

Modern Art Type of 2003

Designs: No. 568, 2.30k, Self-portrait, by Miroslav Kraljevic, vert. No. 569, 2.30k, Noon in Supetar, by Jerolim Mise, vert. No. 570, 2.30k, Stari Grad, by Juraj Plancic, vert.

2004, Nov. 15 **Litho.** ***Perf. 14***
568-570 A304 Set of 3 3.25 3.25

Christmas A323

2004, Nov. 25
571 A323 2.30k multi 1.10 1.10

Antun and Stjepan Radic and Plowman — A324

2004, Dec. 22 **Litho.** ***Perf. 14***
572 A324 7.20k multi 3.25 3.25

Croatian People's Peasant Party, Cent.

Fairy Tale Characters — A325

No. 573: a, Mermaid Halugica. b, Dwarf Pedalj Muza Lakat Brade.

2005, Jan. 14
573 A325 5k Horiz. pair, #a-b 4.50 4.50

World Conference on the Information Society, Tunis — A326

2005, Feb. 10

574 A326 2.80k multi 1.40 1.40

Values are for stamps with surrounding selvage.

Souvenir Sheet

Bust of Livia Drusilla — A327

2005, Feb. 24

575 A327 10k multi 5.00 5.00

Souvenir Sheet

Expo 2005, Aichi, Japan — A328

2005, Mar. 25 ***Perf.***

576 A328 10k multi 5.00 5.00

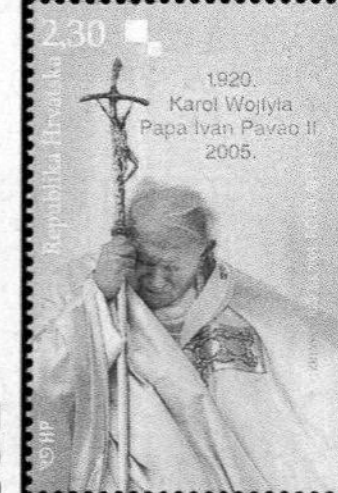

Pope John Paul II (1920-2005) A329

2005, Apr. 8 ***Perf. 14***

577 A329 2.30k multi 1.25 1.25

World Music Days, Zagreb A330

Stjepan Sulek (1914-86), Composer A331

2005, Apr. 15

578 A330 2.30k multi 1.10 1.10
579 A331 2.30k multi 1.10 1.10

Insects — A332

Designs: 1.80k, Coccinella septempunctata. 2.30k, Rosalia alpina. 3.50k, Lucanus cervus.

2005, Apr. 22

580-582 A332 Set of 3 3.75 3.75

Liberation of Western Slavonia, 10th Anniv. A333

2005, May 1

583 A333 1.80k multi .95 .95

Dr. Josip Buturac (1905-93), Historian — A334

2005, May 6

584 A334 2.80k multi 1.25 1.25

Europa — A335

No. 585: a, Loaf of bread. b, Glass of wine.

2005, May 9

585 A335 3.50k Horiz. pair, #a-b *3.50 3.50*

Coast of Hvar Island — A336

No. 586: a, Rock at L, tree tops at bottom. b, Tree tops at LL. c, Rock at R. d, Canoe, rock at R. e, Small rock in center. f, Rocks at UL, trees. g, Rocks at R, trees. h, Tree tops at LL corner, rock at UR corner. i, Rocks at UL and LL corners. j, Rocks at LL.

2005, May 24 **Litho.** ***Perf. 14***

586 A336 Booklet pane of 10 13.00 —
a.-e. 1.80k Any single .90 .90
f.-j. 3.50k Any single 1.40 1.40
Complete booklet, #586 14.00

Kresimir Cosic (1948-95), Basketball Player — A337

2005, May 25

587 A337 3.50k multi 1.50 1.50

Printed in sheets of 9 + 1 label.

Krapanj Island Sponge and Coral Diving — A338

2005, June 2 **Litho.**

588 A338 3.50k multi 1.75 1.75

Portions of the design were applied by a thermographic process producing a shiny, raised effect.

Emperor Constantine's Bath, Varazdinske Toplice A339

2005, June 20 ***Perf. 14***

589 A339 1.80k multi 1.00 1.00

Intl. Fire Brigade Olympics, Varazdin — A340

2005, July 15

590 A340 2.30k multi 1.25 1.25

Printed in sheets of 8 + 2 labels.

European Philatelic Cooperation, 50th Anniv. (in 2006) A341

Designs: 7.20k, Vignette of #134. 8k, Stylized gull.

2005, Sept. 8

591-592 A341 Set of 2 *7.00 7.00*
592a Souvenir sheet, #591-592 *60.00 60.00*

Europa stamps, 50th anniv. (in 2006).

Telegraph A342

2005, Sept. 9

593 A342 2.30k multi 1.25 1.25

First overhead telegraph lines in Croatia, 155th anniv., Stamp Day.

Fortresses Type of 2001

Designs: 1k, Ilok, 14th-15th cents. 2.30k, Motovun, 13th-15th cents., vert. 3.50k, St. Nicholas, 16th cent.

2005, Sept. 15

594-596 A261 Set of 3 3.50 3.50

Famous People — A343

Designs: 1k, Adam Baltazar Krcelic (1715-78), historian. No. 598, 2.30k, Dragutin Tadijanovic (b. 1905), poet. No. 599, 2.30k, Tin Ujevic (1891-1955), poet. 2.80k, Madonna and Child, by Juraj Culinovic (c.1433-1504).

2005, Nov. 4

597-600 A343 Set of 4 4.00 4.00

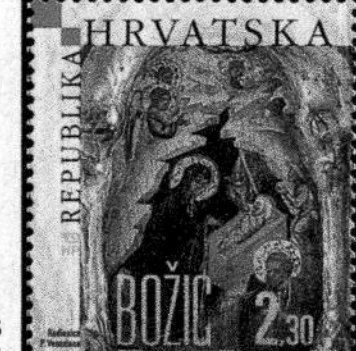

Clock Tower, Rijeka — A344

2005, Nov. 10 **Litho.** ***Perf. 14***

601 A344 3.50k multi 1.75 1.75
a. Perf. 14 syncopated 1.75 1.75

Issued: No. 601a, 6/12/06. For surcharge see No. 778.

Christmas A345

2005, Nov. 22 ***Perf. 14***

602 A345 2.30k multi 1.25 1.25

Booklet Stamp
Self-Adhesive
Serpentine Die Cut 5¼

603 A345 2.30k multi 1.25 1.25
a. Booklet pane of 10 12.50 12.50
Complete booklet, #603a 12.50 12.50

Modern Art Type of 2003

Designs: 1.80k, Zadar, by Edo Murtic. 5k, Meander, by Julije Knifer. 10k, Drawing, by Miroslav Sutej, vert.

2005, Dec. 1 ***Perf. 14***

604-606 A304 Set of 3 8.75 8.75

Davis Cup and Members of Croatian Tennis Team — A346

2005, Dec. 22 **Litho.** ***Perf. 14***

607 A346 5k multi 2.75 2.75

Croatia, winners of 2005 Davis Cup. Printed in sheets of 9 + label.

Composers A347

Designs: 1.80k, Boris Papandopulo (1906-91). 2.30k, Milo Cipra (1906-85). 2.80k, Ivan Brkanovic (1906-87).

2006, Jan. 17

608-610 A347 Set of 3 3.50 3.50

2006 Winter Olympics, Turin — A348

2006, Feb. 10

611 A348 3.50k multi 1.90 1.90

Rembrandt (1606-69), Painter A349

2006, Mar. 7
612 A349 5k multi 2.75 2.75

Famous Men — A350

Designs: No. 613, 1k, Andrija Ljudevit Adamic (1766-1828), merchant. No. 614, 1k, Josip Kozarac (1858-1906), writer. 5k, Vanja Radaus (1906-75), sculptor. 7.20k, Ljubo Karaman (1886-1971), art historian.

2006, Mar. 21 ***Perf. 14 Syncopated***
613-616 A350 Set of 4 7.25 7.25

European Track and Field Championships, Göteborg, Sweden — A351

2006, Apr. 4
617 A351 2.30k multi 1.25 1.25

2006 World Cup Soccer Championships, Germany A352

2006, Apr. 4
618 A352 2.80k multi 1.25 1.25

Flag and Crowd — A353

No. 619 — Location and placement of denomination: a, At left, with denomination above crowd. b, At right, with top of numerals over red in flag. c, At left, with top of "8" and "0" above white in flag. d, At left, with serif of "1" above red in flag. e, At left, with entire denomination above red in flag. f, At right, with parts of "5" and "0" above red in flag. g, At right, with entire denomination above red in flag. h, At right, with entire denomination above white in flag. i, At left, with entire denomination above red in flag. j, At right, with denomination above crowd.

2006, Apr. 25
619 A353 Booklet pane of 10 16.00 —
a.-e. 1.80k Any single 1.00 1.00
f.-j. 3.50k Any single 2.10 2.10
Complete booklet, #619 17.00

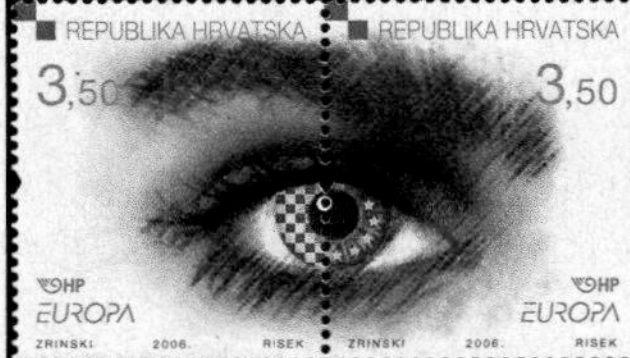
Europa — A354

No. 620: a, Denomination at left. b, Denomination at right.

2006, May 9
620 A354 3.50k Horiz. pair, #a-b 3.50 3.50

Worldwide Fund for Nature (WWF) A355

No. 621 — Various views of Sterna albifrons with denomination in: a, Gray. b, Dull green. c, Yellow orange. d, Red.

2006, May 23
621 Strip of 4 10.00 10.00
a.-d. A355 5k Any single 2.40 2.40

Croatian Automobile Club, Cent. — A356

Perf. 13¾x14 Syncopated
2006, June 4
622 A356 5k multi 2.75 2.75

Aquatic Flowers A357

Designs: 2.30k, Nymphaea alba. 2.80k, Nuphar lutea. 3.50k, Menyanthes trifoliata.

2006, June 5 ***Perf. 14 Syncopated***
623-625 A357 Set of 3 4.50 4.50
623a Booklet pane of 10 12.50 12.50
Complete booklet, #623a 12.50
624a Booklet pane of 10 14.00 14.00
Complete booklet, #624a 14.00
625a Booklet pane of 10 18.00 18.00
Complete booklet, #625a 18.00

Nikola Tesla (1856-1943), Inventor — A358

Perf. 14x13½ Syncopated
2006, July 10 **Litho.**
626 A358 3.50k multi 1.75 1.75

Bjelovar, 250th Anniv. A359

Perf. 14 Syncopated
2006, Aug. 22 **Litho.**
627 A359 2.80k multi 1.50 1.50

Stamp Day — A360

2006, Sept. 9 **Litho. & Embossed**
628 A360 2.30k multi 1.25 1.25

Jewish Community of Zagreb, 200th Anniv. — A361

Perf. 14¼x13¾ Syncopated
2006, Sept. 15 **Litho.**
629 A361 5k multi 2.75 2.75

Fortresses Type of 2001

Designs: No. 630, 1k, St. Mary of Mercy Church, Vrboska, 16th cent. No. 631, 1k, Church of the Holy Spirit, Sudurad, Sipan, 16th cent. 7.20k, Frankapan Citadel, Ogulin, 16th cent.

Perf. 13¾x14¼ Syncopated
2006, Sept. 21
630-632 A261 Set of 3 4.75 4.75

White Cane Safety Day — A362

Perf. 14 Syncopated
2006, Oct. 15 **Litho. & Embossed**
633 A362 1.80k black & red 1.00 1.00

Christmas A363

Perf. 14¼ Syncopated
2006, Nov. 27 **Litho.**
634 A363 2.30k multi 1.25 1.25

Booklet Stamp
Self-Adhesive
Serpentine Die Cut 5¼

635 A363 2.30k multi 1.25 1.25
a. Booklet pane of 10 12.50
Complete booklet, #635a 12.50

Modern Art Type of 2003

Designs: 1k, Still Life, by Vladimir Becic. 1.80k, Composition Tyma 3, by Ivan Picelj. 10k, Self-portrait as Hunter, by Nasta Rojc, vert.

2006, Dec. 1 ***Perf. 14 Syncopated***
636-638 A304 Set of 3 6.00 6.00

Classical Gymnasium, Zagreb, 400th Anniv. — A364

Perf. 14 Syncopated
2007, Jan. 9 **Litho.**
639 A364 5k multi 2.40 2.40

Fairy Tale Characters — A365

No. 640: a, Monster Orko. b, Devil Macic.

2007, Jan. 18
640 A365 2.30k Horiz. pair, #a-b 2.50 2.50

National and University Library, Zagreb, 400th Anniv. A366

2007, Feb. 22
641 A366 5k multi 2.50 2.50

Crustaceans A367

Designs: 1.80k, Palinurus elephas. 2.30k, Nephrops norvegicus. 2.80k, Astacus astacus.

2007, Mar. 15
642 A367 1.80k multi .85 .85
a. Booklet pane of 10 8.50 —
Complete booklet, #642a 8.50
643 A367 2.30k multi 1.05 1.05
a. Booklet pane of 10 10.50 —
Complete booklet, #643a 10.50
644 A367 2.80k multi 1.35 1.35
a. Booklet pane of 10 13.50 —
Complete booklet, #644a 13.50
Nos. 642-644 (3) 3.25 3.25

Native Breeds of Farm Animals A368

Designs: 2.80k, Istrian ox. 3.50k, Posavina horse. 5k, Dalmatian donkey.

2007, Mar. 20
645-647 A368 Set of 3 5.75 5.75

Europa — A369

No. 648: a, Scouting emblem and dove. b, Scout neckerchief.

2007, Apr. 16
648 A369 3.50k Horiz. pair, #a-b 3.25 3.25

Scouting, cent.

Scientists — A370

Designs: 5k, Andrija Mohorovicic (1857-1936), seismologist. 7.20k, Duro Baglivi (1668-1707), physician.

Perf. 14x13½ Syncopated
2007, Apr. 23
649-650 A370 Set of 2 6.00 6.00

Souvenir Sheet

World Championship Victory of Croatian Water Polo Team — A371

No. 651: a, Man with red shirt at right, denomination at UL. b, Man with red shirt at LR, denomination at UR. c, Man with red shirt at left, denomination at UR.

Litho. With Foil Application
2007, May 3 ***Perf. 14¼ Syncopated***
651 A371 5k Sheet of 3, #a-c 7.75 7.75

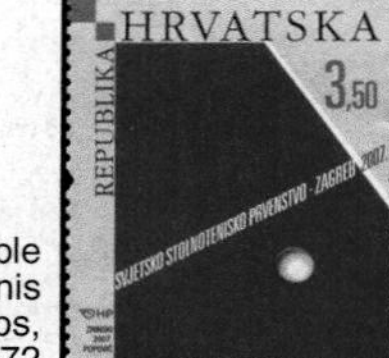
World Table Tennis Championships, Zagreb — A372

Perf. 14 Syncopated
2007, May 21 Litho. & Embossed
652 A372 3.50k multi 1.75 1.75

Starting with No. 652 some stamps have an imprinted wing-shaped tagging design that looks like a watermark.

Diplomatic Relations Between Croatia and People's Republic of China, 15th Anniv. — A373

No. 653: a, "China" in Glagolithic letters. b, "Croatia" in Chinese characters.

2007, May 30 Litho. ***Perf. 12***
653 A373 5k Horiz. pair, #a-b 5.00 5.00

Zagreb City Museum, Cent. — A374

2007, May 31 ***Perf. 14 Syncopated***
654 A374 2.30k multi 1.10 1.10

Souvenir Sheet

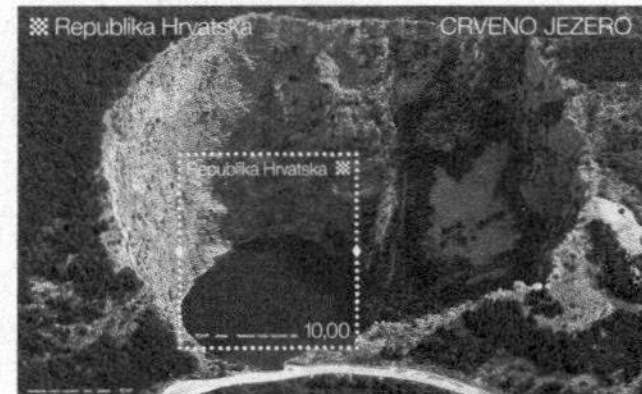
Red Lake — A375

2007, June 8
655 A375 10k multi 4.50 4.50

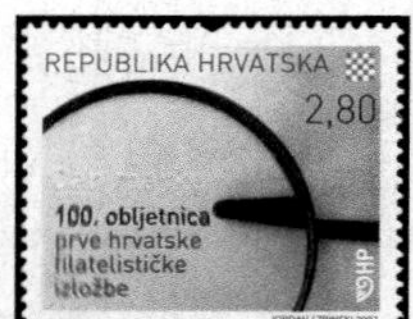
First Croatian Philatelic Exhibition, Cent. — A376

Perf. 14 Syncopated
2007, Sept. 9 Litho. & Embossed
656 A376 2.80k multi 1.25 1.25

Stamp Day.

Lighthouses — A377

Designs: No. 657, 5k, St. John on the Sea Lighthouse. No. 658, 5k, Porer Lighthouse. No. 659, 5k, Savudrija Lighthouse.

Perf. 13¾x14¼ Syncopated
2007, Sept. 14 Litho.
657-659 A377 Set of 3 7.00 7.00

Veprinac Statute, 500th Anniv. — A378

Perf. 14¼x13¾ Syncopated
2007, Oct. 2
660 A378 2.70k multi 1.25 1.25

City Views — A379

Designs: 1.80k, Omis. 2.30k, Koprivnica, horiz. 2.80k, Krk.

2007, Oct. 30 ***Perf. 14 Syncopated***
661 A379 1.80k multi .85 .85
a. Perf. 14 ('10) .70 .70
662 A379 2.30k multi 1.00 1.00
663 A379 2.80k multi 1.30 1.30
Nos. 661-663 (3) 3.15 3.15

For surcharge see No. 777.

Blanka Vlasic, 2007 World Women's High Jump Champion A380

2007, Nov. 8
664 A380 2.30k multi 1.25 1.25

Christmas A381

Perf. 14¼ Syncopated
2007, Nov. 15 Litho.
665 A381 2.30k multi 1.25 1.25

Booklet Stamp
Self-Adhesive
Serpentine Die Cut 5¼
666 A381 2.30k multi 1.25 1.25
a. Booklet pane of 10 12.50
Complete booklet, #666a 12.50

Marija Juric Zagorka (1873-1957), Writer — A382

Perf. 14¼x13¾ Syncopated
2007, Nov. 16
667 A382 7.20k multi 3.25 3.25

Modern Art Type of 2003

Designs: 2.80k, Area by the Sava River, by Branko Senoa. No. 669, 5k, Pegasus's Garden, by Ferdinand Kulmer. No. 670, 5k, Bridgeport, by Ivan Benkovic.

Perf. 14 Syncopated
2007, Dec. 1 Litho.
668-670 A304 Set of 3 5.75 5.75

New Year 2008 — A383

2007, Dec. 5
671 A383 1.80k multi .80 .80

Composers A384

Designs: No. 672, 2.30k, Igor Kuljeric (1938-2006). No. 673, 2.30k, Krsto Odak (1888-1965).

2008, Jan. 22
672-673 A384 Set of 2 2.25 2.25

Publication of *Arithmetika Horvatszka*, by Mijo Silobod Bolsic, 250th Anniv. — A385

Perf. 13¾x14 Syncopated
2008, Jan. 25
674 A385 3.50k multi 1.75 1.75

Steam Locomotives — A386

Designs: No. 675, 5k, MAV 601/JZ 32. No. 676, 5k, MAV 651/JZ 31.

2008, Feb. 15
675-676 A386 Set of 2 4.50 4.50

Nos. 675-676 were printed in sheets of 6 containing three of each stamp.

St. Nicholas Church, Cavtat A387

Perf. 14 Syncopated
2008, Mar. 8 Litho.
677 A387 7.20k multi 3.25 3.25

For surcharge see No. 780.

2008 Summer Olympics, Beijing A388

2008, Mar. 11
678 A388 5k multi 2.00 2.00

Printed in sheets of 9 + label.

Flowers — A389

Designs: 1.80k, Helleborus niger. 2.80k, Onosma stellulata. 3.50k, Lonicera glutinosa.

2008, Mar. 20

679	A389 1.80k multi	.95	.95
a.	Booklet pane of 10	9.50	—
	Complete booklet, #679a	9.50	
680	A389 2.80k multi	1.50	1.50
a.	Booklet pane of 10	15.00	—
	Complete booklet, #680a	15.00	
681	A389 3.50k multi	1.75	1.75
a.	Booklet pane of 10	17.50	—
	Complete booklet, #681a	17.50	
	Nos. 679-681 (3)	4.20	4.20

Famous Writers — A390

Designs: 2.30k, Petar Zoranic (1508-c. 1569), novelist. 2.80k, Silvije Strahimir Kranjcevic (1865-1908), poet. 7.20k, Marin Drzic (1508-67), dramatist.

Perf. 14 Syncopated

2008, Apr. 22 **Litho.**

682-684	A390 Set of 3	5.75	5.75

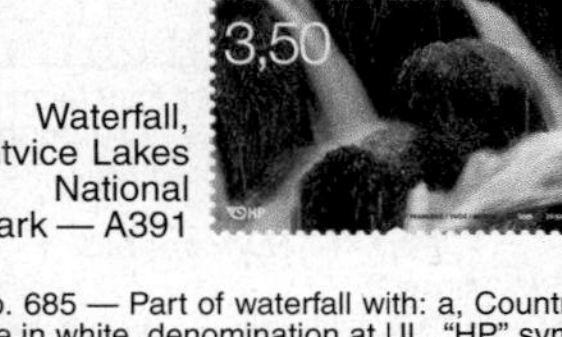

Waterfall, Plitvice Lakes National Park — A391

No. 685 — Part of waterfall with: a, Country name in white, denomination at UL, "HP" symbol in white at LL. b, Country name in white, denomination at UR, "HP" symbol in white at LL, green foliage at UL. c, Country name in black, denomination at UR. d, Country name in white, denomination at UR, "HP" symbol in black at LL. e, Country name in white, denomination at UR, "HP" symbol in white at LL, green foliage at UR. f, Country name in white, denomination in black at LR, "HP" symbol in black at LL, rock with foliage in center. g, Country name in white, denomination in black at LR, "HP" symbol in black at LL, all rocks covered by spray. h, Country name in black, denomination at LR. i, Country name in white, denomination in white at LR. j, Country name in white, denomination in black at LR, "HP" symbol in white at LL.

Perf. 14 Syncopated

2008, Apr. 25 **Litho.**

685	Booklet pane of 10	17.50	—
a.-j.	A391 3.50k Any single	1.75	1.75
	Complete booklet, #685	17.50	

2008 Volkswagen Beetle — A392

2008, May 8

686	A392 2.30k multi + label	1.10	1.10

Europa A393

Designs: 3.50k, Insured envelope with wax seal. 5k, Airmail envelope.

2008, May 9 **Litho.**

687	A393 3.50k multi	1.60	1.60

Litho. & Embossed

688	A393 5k multi	2.40	2.40

Portions of the design of No. 687 were applied using a thermographic process producing a shiny raised effect.

UEFA Euro 2008 Soccer Championships, Austria and Switzerland — A394

2008, May 14 Litho. ***Perf. 14x13½***

689	A394 3.50k multi	1.50	1.50

Values are for stamps with surrounding selvage. Printed in sheets of 9 + label.

Adris Group — A395

2008, May 16 ***Perf. 14 Syncopated***

690	A395 2.30k multi + label	1.10	1.10

Souvenir Sheet

Ivan Vucetic (1858-1925), Fingerprint Classifier — A396

2008, Apr. 20

691	A396 10k multi	5.00	5.00

Souvenir Sheet

Expo Zaragoza 2008 — A397

Litho. With Foil Application

2008, June 16

692	A397 10k multi	4.50	4.50

Souvenir Sheet

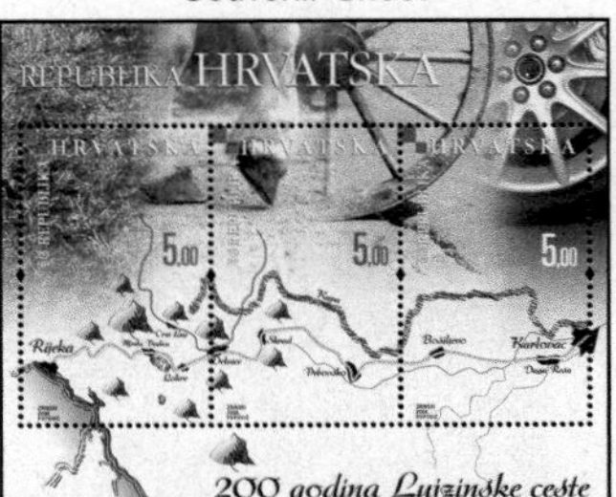

Lujzinske Road, 200th Anniv. — A398

No. 693 — Parts of map of Lujzinske Road with denomination in: a, Red. b, Green. c, White.

Perf. 14x13½ Syncopated

2008, June 17 **Litho.**

693	A398 5k Sheet of 3, #a-c	7.00	7.00

Western Union — A399

2008, July 11 ***Perf. 14 Syncopated***

694	A399 3.50k multi + label	1.50	1.50

Postal Workers' Games — A400

Litho. With Foil Application

2008, Sept. 9 ***Perf. 14 Syncopated***

695	A400 2.80k multi	1.30	1.30

Stamp Day.

Lighthouses A401

Designs: No. 696, 5k, Pinida Lighthouse. No. 697, 5k, Vnetak Lighthouse. No. 698, 5k, Zaglav Lighthouse.

Perf. 14¼x13¾ Syncopated

2008, Sept. 12 **Litho.**

696-698	A401 Set of 3	7.00	7.00

Order of St. Clare, Split, 700th Anniv. — A402

2008, Sept. 16

699	A402 2.80k multi	1.25	1.25

Details From Native Costumes A403

Costume from: 10 l, Sunja. 20 l, Bistra. 50 l, Bizovac. 1k, Ravni Kotari. 10k, Pag.

2008, Sept. 30 ***Perf. 14 Syncopated***

700-704	A403 Set of 5	6.00	6.00
701a	Perf. 14 ('10)	.25	.25
702a	Perf. 14 ('13)		—
703a	Perf. 14 ('10)	.35	.35
704a	Sheet of 5, #700-704 + label	6.00	6.00
704b	Perf. 14 ('14)	—	—

European Healthy Cities Movement, 20th Anniv. — A404

2008, Oct. 17 ***Perf. 14¼ Syncopated***

705	A404 2.80k multi + label	1.25	1.25

Collegium Ragusinum, Dubrovnik, 350th Anniv. — A405

Perf. 14¼x13¾ Syncopated

2008, Nov. 7 **Litho. & Embossed**

706	A405 7.20k multi	3.00	3.00

Intl. Amateur Radio Union Region 1 Conference, Cavtat — A406

Perf. 13¾x14¼ Syncopated

2008, Nov. 14 **Litho.**

707	A406 3.50k multi	1.50	1.50

The Book on the Art of Trading, by Benedikt Kotruljevic, 550th Anniv. of Publication A407

Perf. 14¼x13¾ Syncopated

2008, Oct. 22 **Litho.**

708	A407 2.80k multi	1.25	1.25

New Year's Day — A408

Perf. 14 Syncopated

2008, Nov. 21 **Litho.**

709	A408 1.80k multi	.75	.75

Christmas A409

2008, Nov. 27 ***Perf. 14 Syncopated***

710	A409 2.80k multi	1.50	1.50

Booklet Stamp
Self-Adhesive

711 A409 2.80k multi 1.00 1.00
a. Booklet pane of 10 10.00
Complete booklet, #711a 10.00

Modern Art Type of 2003

Designs: 1.65k, Two Trees at the Foot of a Hill, by Oskar Herman. 1.80k, Carousel, by Nevenka Djordjevic. 6.50k, Still Life, by Ivo Rezek.

Perf. 14 Syncopated
2008, Dec. 1 **Litho.**
712-714 A304 Set of 3 4.50 4.50

Zora Choral Society, 150th Anniv. — A410

Perf. 14x13¾ Syncopated
2008, Dec. 5
715 A410 1.65k multi .75 .75

Ivan Mestrovic (1883-1962), Sculptor — A411

Perf. 14 Syncopated
2008, Dec. 15 **Litho.**
716 A411 5k multi 2.10 2.10

21st Men's World Handball Championships — A412

Perf. 13¾x14¼ Syncopated
2009, Jan. 16 **Litho. & Embossed**
717 A412 3.50k multi 1.50 1.50

Printed in sheets of 9 + label

Bruno Bjelinski (1909-92), Composer A413

Josip Andreis (1909-82), Musicologist A414

Perf. 14¼x13¾ Syncopated
2009, Jan. 21 **Litho.**
718 A413 1.80k multi .75 .75
719 A414 3.50k multi 1.50 1.50

Street and Bridge, Sisak — A415

2009, Jan. 22 ***Perf. 14 Syncopated***
720 A415 8k multi 3.50 3.50

Remains of St. Tryphon in Kotor, 1200th Anniv. — A416

No. 721 — St. Tryphon: a, Drawing. b, Sculpture from altarpiece, Kotor Cathedral.

2009, Feb. 3 ***Perf. 14¼ Syncopated***
721 A416 3.50k Horiz. pair, #a-b 2.75 2.75

Fairy Tale Characters — A417

No. 722: a, Svarozic. b, Bjesomar.

2009, Feb. 27
722 A417 1.65k Horiz. pair, #a-b 1.50 1.50

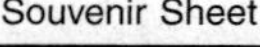
Souvenir Sheet

Protection of Polar Regions and Glaciers — A418

No. 723: a, Sun over glacier. b, Intl. Polar Year emblem and glacier.

2009, Mar. 27 **Litho. & Embossed**
723 A418 5k Sheet of 2, #a-b 3.75 3.75

Easter A419

Perf. 14 Syncopated
2009, Mar. 30 **Litho.**
724 A419 3.50k multi 1.60 1.60

Entry Into NATO A420

2009, Apr. 4
725 A420 8k multi 3.00 3.00

Juraj Sizgoric (1445-c. 1509), Poet — A421

Juraj Habdelic (1609-78), Writer — A422

Ljudevit Gaj (1809-72), Writer, Illyrian Movement Leader — A423

Petar Segedin (1909-98), Writer — A424

Perf. 14¼x13¾ Syncopated
2009, Apr. 22
726 A421 3.50k multi 1.25 1.25
727 A422 3.50k multi 1.25 1.25
728 A423 5k multi 1.90 1.90
729 A424 5k multi 1.90 1.90
Nos. 726-729 (4) 6.30 6.30

Europa — A425

No. 730 — Image of space from Hubble Space Telescope with red diamond at: a, Left. b, Right.

Perf. 14x13½ Syncopated
2009, May 9 **Litho.**
730 A425 8k Horiz. pair, #a-b 6.00 6.00

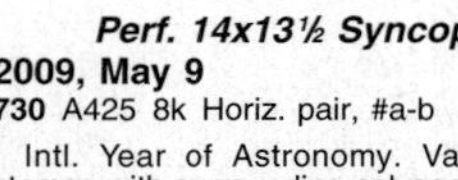
Intl. Year of Astronomy. Values are for stamps with surrounding selvage.

Franciscans in Cakovec, 350th Anniv. — A426

2009, May 20 ***Perf. 14 Syncopated***
731 A426 3.50k multi 1.40 1.40

Souvenir Sheet

King Andrew's Charter Proclaiming Varazdin as Free Royal Borough, 800th Anniv. — A427

Perf. 14 Syncopated
2009, June 9 **Litho.**
732 A427 15k multi 6.00 6.00

Souvenir Sheet

St. John, Sculpture by Ivan Duknovic (c. 1440-1509) — A428

2009, June 23 ***Perf. 14***
733 A428 10k multi 4.75 4.75

Zagreb Jazz Quartet, 50th Anniv. A429

2009, June 29
734 A429 10.70k multi 5.00 5.00

Fish — A430

Designs: 3.50k, Acipenser naccarii. No. 736, 5k, Knipowitschia mrakovcici. No. 737, 5k, Ballerus sapa.

2009, Sept. 1 Litho. *Perf. 14*

735 A430 3.50k multi 1.75 1.75
a. Booklet pane of 10 17.50 —
Complete booklet, #735a 17.50
736 A430 5k multi 2.50 2.50
a. Booklet pane of 10 25.00 —
Complete booklet, #736a 25.00
737 A430 5k multi 2.50 2.50
a. Booklet pane of 10 25.00 —
Complete booklet, #737a 25.00
Nos. 735-737 (3) 6.75 6.75

Stamp Day — A431

2009, Sept. 9

738 A431 3.50k multi 1.50 1.50

Croatian Post Inc., 10th Anniv.

Lighthouses A432

Designs: No. 739, 3.50k, Gruica Lighthouse. No. 740, 3.50k, Strazica Lighthouse. 8k, Voscica Lighthouse.

2009, Sept. 11

739-741 A432 Set of 3 5.75 5.75

Franciscan Order, 800th Anniv. — A433

2009, Sept. 17 Litho. *Perf. 14*

742 A433 3.50k multi 1.60 1.60

Souvenir Sheet

Stone Buildings — A434

No. 743 — Stone building in: a, Pazin, Croatia. b, Kopriva na Krasu, Slovenia.

2009, Sept. 25

743 A434 8k Sheet of 2, #a-b 7.50 7.50

See Slovenia No. 812.

St. Martin's Hermit Chapel, Podsused, 800th Anniv. A435

2009, Oct. 29

744 A435 3.50k multi 1.60 1.60

National Folk Dance Ensemble, 60th Anniv. A436

2009, Nov. 11

745 A436 3.50k multi 1.60 1.60

Rights of the Child A437

2009, Nov. 20

746 A437 3.50k multi 1.30 1.30

Declaration of the Rights of the Child, 50th anniv.; UN Convention on the Rights of the Child, 20th anniv.

New Year's Day — A438

2009, Nov. 24 Litho. *Perf. 14*

747 A438 3.50k multi 1.50 1.50

Serpentine Die Cut 5¼

Booklet Stamp

Self-Adhesive

748 A438 3.50k multi 1.50 1.50
a. Booklet pane of 10 15.00
Complete booklet, #748a 15.00

Modern Art Type of 2003

Designs: No. 749, 1.80k, Gray Sail, by Zlatko Prica. No. 750, 1.80k, A Bosom Full of Wind, by Nives Kavuric Kurtovic, vert. No. 751, 1.80k, Flora, by Ordan Petlevski.

2009, Dec. 1 Litho. *Perf. 14*

749-751 A304 Set of 3 2.00 2.00

A439

Christmas A440

2009, Dec. 4 Litho. *Perf. 14*

752 A439 3.50k multi 1.50 1.50
753 A440 8k multi 3.25 3.25

Serpentine Die Cut 5¼

Booklet Stamp

Self-Adhesive

754 A439 3.50k multi 1.50 1.50
a. Booklet pane of 10 15.00
Complete booklet, #754a 15.00

Statute of Lastovo, 700th Anniv. — A441

2010, Jan. 8 Litho. *Perf. 14*

755 A441 3.50k multi 1.60 1.60

2010 Winter Olympics, Vancouver A442

2010, Feb. 12 *Perf. 14¼x14*

756 A442 3.50k multi 1.60 1.60

Souvenir Sheet

Peonies — A443

No. 757: a, Paeonia mascula. b, Paeonia officinalis.

2010, Mar. 8 Litho. *Perf. 14*

757 A443 3k Sheet of 2, #a-b 3.00 3.00

Embroidery A444

Embroidery from: 1.60k, Primorje. 3.10k, Medimurje. 4.60k, Posavina. 7.10k, Draganic.

2010, Mar. 15

758-761 A444 Set of 4 7.75 7.75
761a Sheet of 4, #758-761 7.75 7.75

For surcharge, see No. 1140.

Fruit A445

Designs: 1k, Fragaria vesca. No. 763, Vitis vinifera. No. 764, Ribes uva-crispa.

2010, Mar. 16 Litho. & Embossed

762 A445 1k multi .45 .45
a. Booklet pane of 10 4.50 —
Complete booklet, #762a 4.50
763 A445 4k multi 1.75 1.75
a. Booklet pane of 10 17.50 —
Complete booklet, #763a 17.50
764 A445 4k multi 1.75 1.75
a. Booklet pane of 10 17.50 —
Complete booklet, #764a 17.50
Nos. 762-764 (3) 3.95 3.95

Easter A446

2010, Mar. 19 Litho. *Perf. 14*

765 A446 3.10k multi 1.40 1.40

Establishment of Bjelovar-Krizevci Diocese — A447

2010, Mar. 19

766 A447 6.50k multi 2.75 2.75

Printed in sheets of 8 + 2 labels.

Steam Locomotives — A448

No. 767: a, Series MAV 326/JZ 125. b, Series SüdB 18.

2010, Mar. 29

767 Vert. pair + central label 6.75 6.75
a.-b. A448 7.10k Either single 3.25 3.25

Capuchin Order in Croatia, 400th Anniv. — A449

2010, Apr. 15

768 A449 6.10k multi 2.75 2.75

Famous Men — A450

Designs: 1.60k, Grgo Gamulin (1910-97), art historian. 3.10k, Janko Polic Kamov (1886-1910), writer. 4.50k, Ivan Matetic Ronjgov (1880-1960), composer. 6.10k, Marko Antun de Dominis (1560-1624), archbishop and physicist.

2010, Apr. 22

769-772 A450 Set of 4 7.00 7.00

Souvenir Sheet

Expo 2010, Shanghai — A451

2010, Apr. 29

773 A451 10k multi 4.50 4.50

Europa — A452

No. 774 — Children's book and: a, Fairy on branch, fairy with horn. b, Fairy looking at butterfly, fairy on flower.

Litho. With Foil Application

2010, May 7 ***Perf. 14***

774 A452 7.10k Horiz. pair, #a-b 6.25 6.25

Souvenir Sheet

Lubenice — A453

2010, May 21 **Litho.**

775 A453 10k multi 4.75 4.75

2010 World Cup Soccer Championships, South Africa — A454

2010, June 11

776 A454 4.50k multi 2.25 2.25

Printed in sheets of 9 + label.

Nos. 562a, 601, 661a and 677 Surcharged

Methods and Perfs. As Before

2010

777 A379 1.60k on 1.80k #661a .65 .65
778 A344 3.10k on 3.50k #601 1.25 1.25
779 A320 4.50k on 5k #562a 2.10 2.10
780 A367 7.10k on 7.20k #677 3.25 3.25
Nos. 777-780 (4) 7.25 7.25

Issued: Nos. 777-778, 5/17; Nos. 779-780, 7/19.

Lighthouses A455

Designs: No. 781, 3.10k, Vir Lighthouse. No. 782, 3.10k, Veli Rat Lighthouse. No. 783, 3.10k, Tajer Lighthouse.

2010, Sept. 7 **Litho.** ***Perf. 14***

781-783 A455 Set of 3 4.50 4.50

Souvenir Sheet

Minerals — A456

No. 784: a, Calcite from Brac. b, Agate from Lepoglava.

Litho. & Embossed (#784a), Litho.

2010, Oct. 15

784 A456 3.10k Sheet of 2, #a-b 3.00 3.00

Souvenir Sheet

Dubrovnik Tramway, Cent. — A457

2010, Nov. 22 **Litho.** ***Perf. 14***

785 A457 15k multi 7.00 7.00

Adoration of the Shepherds, by Josip Biffel — A458

2010, Nov. 25

786 A458 3.10k multi 1.50 1.50

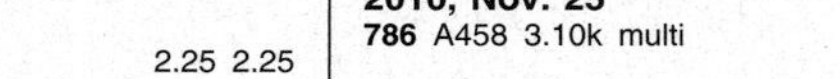

Booklet Stamp
Self-Adhesive

Serpentine Die Cut 5¼

787 A458 3.10k multi 1.50 1.50
a. Booklet pane of 10 15.00
Complete booklet, #787a 15.00

Christmas.

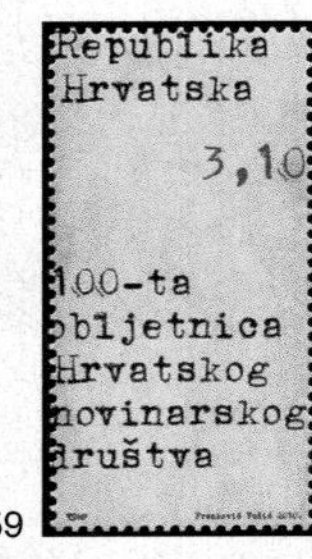

A459

2010, Dec. 1 **Litho.** ***Perf. 14***

788 A459 3.10k multi 1.40 1.40

Croatian Journalist Society, cent.

New Year 2011 — A460

2010, Dec. 6

789 A460 1.60k multi .75 .75

Intl. Children's Festival, Sibenik — A461

2011, Feb. 14 **Litho.** ***Perf. 14***

790 A461 1.60k multi .85 .85

Fauna — A462

Designs: 1.60k, Ursus arctos. 3.10k, Falco eleonorae. 4.60k, Monachus monachus.

2011, Mar. 15

791 A462 1.60k multi .80 .80
a. Booklet pane of 10 8.00 —
Complete booklet, #791a 8.00
792 A462 3.10k multi 1.60 1.60
a. Booklet pane of 10 16.00 —
Complete booklet, #792a 16.00
793 A462 4.60k multi 2.40 2.40
a. Booklet pane of 10 24.00 —
Complete booklet, #793a 24.00
Nos. 791-793 (3) 4.80 4.80

Stations of the Cross — A463

No. 794 — Station: a, 1. b, 2. c, 3. d, 4. e, 5. f, 6. g, 7. h, 8. i, 9. j, 10. k, 11. l, 12. m, 13. n, 14.

2011, Mar. 23

794 Booklet pane of 14 24.50 —
a.-n. A463 3.10k Any single 1.75 1.75
Complete booklet, #794 24.50

Visit to Croatia of Pope Benedict XVI — A464

2011, Apr. 4 **Litho.**

795 A464 3.10k multi 1.75 1.75

Souvenir Sheet

Wreck of the Elhawi Star, Rijeka Harbor — A465

2011, Apr. 14 ***Perf. 14***

796 A465 10k multi 5.00 5.00

Souvenir Sheet

New Tendencies Art Exhibit, 50th Anniv. — A466

2011, Apr. 15

797 A466 10k black & silver 5.00 5.00

Famous People — A467

Designs: No. 798, 1.60k, Jagoda Truhelka (1864-1957), writer. No. 799, 1.60k, August Harambasic (1861-1911), poet and politician. No. 800, 1.60k, Grigor Vitez (1911-66), writer.

2011, Apr. 22

798-800 A467 Set of 3 2.25 2.25

Croatian Academy of Sciences and Arts, 150th Anniv. — A468

2011, Apr. 29

801 A468 9.50k multi 4.50 4.50

Europa — A469

No. 802 — Paintings: a, Beech, by Josip Zanki. b, Forest Scene with Spider's Web, by Lovro Artukovic.

2011, May 5

802 A469 7.10k Horiz. pair, #a-b 6.25 6.25

Intl. Year of Forests.

Castles and Palaces A470

Arms and: No. 803, 3.10k, Pejacevic Castle, Nasice. No. 804, 3.10k, Hilleprand-Mailáth Castle, Donji Miholjac. No. 805, 4.60k, Hilleprand-Prandau Normann-Ehrenfels Castle, Valpovo. No. 806, 4.60k, Palace of Prince Eugene of Savoy, Bilje.

2011, June 16 **Litho.** ***Perf. 14***

803-806 A470 Set of 4 7.00 7.00
806a Sheet of 8, 2 each #803-806, + 8 labels 15.00 15.00

Nos. 803-806 each were printed in sheets of 9 + label. See Nos. 876-879, 956-959.

Independence, 20th Anniv. — A471

2011, June 24

807 A471 3.10k multi 1.50 1.50

Printed in sheets of 25 + 5 labels.

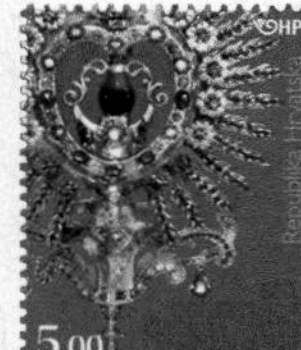

Eucharistic Miracle of Ludbreg, 600th Anniv. — A472

2011, Sept. 1

808 A472 5k multi 2.50 2.50

Quick Response Code — A473

2011, Sept. 9

809 A473 3.10k brown & black 1.60 1.60

Stamp Day.

Rudjer Boskovich (1711-87), Astronomer, and Dome of St. Peter's Basilica — A474

2011, Sept. 13

810 A474 7.10k multi 3.75 3.75

See Vatican City No. 1482.

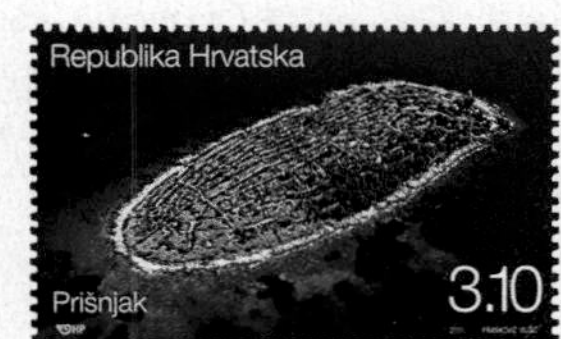

Lighthouses — A475

Designs: No. 811, 3.10k, Prisnjak Lighthouse. No. 812, 3.10k, Mulo Lighthouse. 7.10k, Blitvenica Lighthouse.

2011, Oct. 18

811-813 A475 Set of 3 6.50 6.50

Institute of Art History, Zagreb, 50th Anniv. — A476

2011, Oct. 28

814 A476 4.60k multi 2.50 2.50

The Birth of Jesus, Fresco by Zeljko Hegedusic and Eugen Kokot — A477

2011, Nov. 3

815 A477 3.10k multi 1.75 1.75

Serpentine Die Cut 5¼

Booklet Stamp
Self-Adhesive

816 A477 3.10k multi 1.75 1.75
a. Booklet pane of 10 17.50
Complete booklet, #816a 17.50

Christmas.

Siege of Vukovar, 20th Anniv. A478

2011, Nov. 18 ***Perf. 14***

817 A478 3.10k multi 1.75 1.75

Ivica Kostelic, 2011 World Cup Skiing Overall Champion A479

2011, Nov. 23

818 A479 7.10k multi 3.50 3.50

Printed in sheets of 9 + label.

New Year 2012 A480

Litho. With Foil Application

2011, Nov. 24

819 A480 3.10k multi 1.60 1.60

Art A481

Designs: 3.10k, Space-B, by Ante Kuduz. 4.50k, Woman with Cat, by Marijan Trepse, vert. 9.50k, Lovers, by Anka Krizmanic.

2011, Dec. 1 **Litho.** ***Perf. 14***

820-822 A481 Set of 3 8.00 8.00

Vasa Posta Foundation A482

2011, Dec. 5

823 A482 3.10k multi 1.60 1.60

Printed in sheets of 8 + label.

New Year 2012 (Year of the Dragon) A483

2012, Jan. 4

824 A483 1.60k ol brn & blk .90 .90

St. Valentine's Day — A484

2012, Feb. 1 ***Perf. 14x13¾***

825 A484 3.10k multi + 2 labels 2.25 2.25
a. Booklet pane of 4 + 8 labels 9.00 —
Complete booklet, #825a 9.00

No. 825 was printed in sheets of 4 stamps + 8 labels. These sheets were affixed inside booklet covers, and booklet panes have folds along the left margin and throuch the center row of perforations.

Cats — A485

No. 826: a, 1.60k, Ragdoll cat and bird. b, 1.60k, Domestic cat and ball. c, 3.10k, Siamese cat and sock. d, 3.10k, Persian cat and mouse.

2012, Feb. 21 ***Perf. 14***

826 A485 Block of 4, #a-d 4.50 4.50

Flowers A486

Designs: 1.60k, Galanthus nivalis. 3.10k, Primula vulgaris. 4.60k, Crocus vernus.

2012, Mar. 15

827 A486 1.60k multi .80 .80
a. Booklet pane of 10 8.00 —
Complete booklet, #827a 8.00
828 A486 3.10k multi 1.50 1.50
a. Booklet pane of 10 15.00 —
Complete booklet, #828a 15.00
829 A486 4.60k multi 2.25 2.25
a. Booklet pane of 10 22.50 —
Complete booklet, #829a 22.50
Nos. 827-829 (3) 4.55 4.55

Easter A487

2012, Mar. 16

830 A487 3.10k multi 1.50 1.50
a. Booklet pane of 4 6.00 —
Complete booklet, #830a 6.00

Famous People A488

Designs: No. 831, 1.60k, Bishop Juraj Dobrila (1812-82). No. 832, 1.60k, Vesna Parun (1922-2010), poet. No. 833, 1.60k, Dragojla Jarnevic (1812-75), poet.

2012, Apr. 19

831-833 A488 Set of 3 2.25 2.25

Statute of Split, 700th Anniv. A489

2012, Apr. 25
834 A489 3.10k multi 1.50 1.50

No. 834 was printed in sheets of 10 + 2 labels.

Paklenica National Park — A490

Apoxyomenos Statue Found in the Adriatic Sea — A491

2012, May 9
835 A490 7.10k multi 3.50 3.50
836 A491 7.10k multi 3.50 3.50

Europa.

Croatian Chess Federation, Cent. A492

2012, May 12
837 A492 4.60k multi 2.25 2.25

No. 837 was printed in sheets of 9 + label.

Lighthouses — A493

Designs: 3.10k, St. Peter's Lighthouse. No. 839, 7.10k, St. Nicholas's Lighthouse. No. 840, 7.10k, Pokonji Dol Lighthouse.

2012, May 31
838-840 A493 Set of 3 8.25 8.25

Croatian Soccer Team's Participation in 2012 European Soccer Championships A494

2012, June 8
841 A494 4.60k multi 2.00 2.00

Printed in sheets of 9 + label.

UNESCO Intangible Cultural Heritage of Croatia A495

Designs: 1.60k, Festival of St. Blaise (Festa Sv. Vlaha). 3.10k, Lacemaking, Hvar. 4.60k, Gingerbread heart, butterfly and cross. 7.10k, Carved wooden bird toy.

2012, June 12
842-845 A495 Set of 4 6.50 6.50
845a Souvenir sheet of 4, #842-845 + 5 labels 6.50 6.50

Miniature Sheet

Seafood Dishes — A496

No. 846: a, Rakovica (spider crab). b, Kamenice (oysters). c, Hobotnica (octopi). d, Orada (gilthead sea bream).

2012, July 2 ***Serpentine Die Cut 5¼***
Self-Adhesive

846 A496 4.60k Sheet of 4, #a-d, + 4 etiquettes 7.50 7.50

2012 Summer Olympics, London — A497

2012, July 23 ***Perf. 14***
847 A497 3.10k multi 1.25 1.25

Printed in sheets of 9 + label.

A498

A499

A500

Hemaris Croatica — A501

2012, Sept. 18
848 Strip of 4 7.00 7.00
a. A498 4.60k multi 1.75 1.75
b. A499 4.60k multi 1.75 1.75
c. A500 4.60k multi 1.75 1.75
d. A501 4.60k multi 1.75 1.75

Worldwide Fund for Nature (WWF).

Theater in Hvar, 400th Anniv. — A502

2012, Sept. 25
849 A502 1.60k multi .65 .65

Locomotives — A503

No. 850: a, MAV 424/JDZ/JZ 11. b, SüdB 29/JDZ 124.

2012, Oct. 1
850 Vert. pair + 2 central labels 5.50 5.50
a.-b. A503 7.10k Either single 2.75 2.75

First locomotives on Zidani Most-Sisak line, 150th anniv.

Souvenir Sheet

Diplomatic Relations Between Croatia and San Marino, 20th Anniv. — A504

No. 851 —Traditional costumes with denomination at: a, LR. b, LL.

2012, Oct. 16
851 A504 7.10k Sheet of 2, #a-b 5.50 5.50

See San Marino No. 1874.

Euroherc Insurance Company, 20th Anniv. — A505

2012, Oct. 19
852 A505 3.10k multi + label 1.25 1.25

Souvenir Sheet

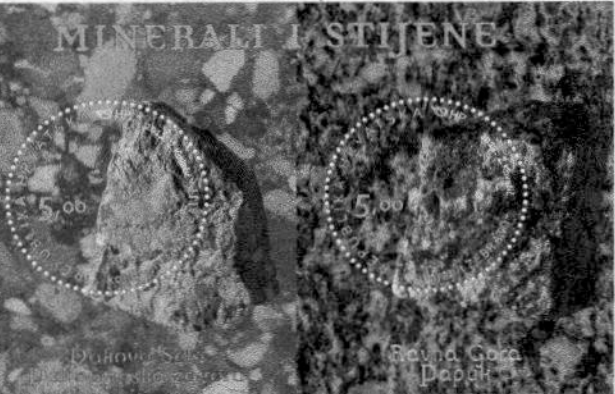

Rocks and Minerals — A506

No. 853: a, Roselite. b, Zebrato granite.

Litho. & Embossed With Foil Application

2012, Oct. 24 ***Perf.***
853 A506 5k Sheet of 2, #a-b 4.00 4.00

Intl. Day of the Romani Language — A507

2012, Nov. 5 **Litho.** ***Perf. 14***
854 A507 3.10k multi 1.25 1.25

Krapina Neanderthal Man Museum A508

Designs: 1.60k. Timeline and statues of hominids. 3.10k, Diorama of Neanderthals in cave.

2012, Nov. 7
855-856 A508 Set of 2 1.90 1.90

Christmas A509

Litho. With Foil Application

2012, Nov. 15 ***Perf. 14***
857 A509 3.10k multi 1.25 1.25

Booklet Stamp
Self-Adhesive
Serpentine Die Cut 5¼

858 A509 3.10k multi 1.25 1.25
a. Booklet pane of 10 12.50
Complete booklet, #858a 12.50

Greek Catholic Church in Croatia, 400th Anniv. — A510

2012, Nov. 27 Litho. *Perf. 14*
859 A510 3.10k multi 1.25 1.25

New Year 2013 — A511

Litho. With Foil Application

2012, Dec. 4
860 A511 3.10k multi 1.25 1.25

Dogs — A512

No. 861: a, German shepherd with bone. b, Yorkshire terrier with sausages. c, Golden retriever with newspaper. d, Bichon frisé in basket.

2013, Feb. 21 Litho.
861 A512 3.10k Block or vert. strip of 4, #a-d 4.25 4.25

Easter A513

2013, Mar. 11
862 A513 3.10k multi 1.10 1.10

Amphibians A514

Designs: 1.60k, Bombina bombina. 3.10k, Salamandra salamandra. 4.60k, Proteus anguinus.

2013, Apr. 8
863 A514 1.60k multi .55 .55
a. Booklet pane of 10 5.50 —
Complete booklet, #863a 5.50
864 A514 3.10k multi 1.10 1.10
a. Booklet pane of 10 11.00 —
Complete booklet, #864a 11.00
865 A514 4.60k multi 1.60 1.60
a. Booklet pane of 10 16.00 —
Complete booklet, #865a 16.00
Nos. 863-865 (3) 3.25 3.25

Famous People A515

Designs: No. 866, 1.20k, Stjepan Gradic (1613-83), diplomat. No. 867, 1.20k, Antonija Krasnik (1874-1956), decorative artist. No. 868, 5.80k, Ranko Marinkovic (1913-2001), writer. No. 869, 5.80k, Milka Trnina (1863-1941), opera singer.

2013, Apr. 16
866-869 A515 Set of 4 5.00 5.00

Souvenir Sheet

Bridges — A516

No. 870: a, Railway Bridge, Zagreb (49x24mm). b, Old Bridge, Tounj (36x30mm).

2013, Apr. 29
870 A516 7.10k Sheet of 2, #a-b 5.00 5.00

Europa — A517

Postal vehicles: No. 871, 7.10k, Moped. No. 872, 7.10k, Van.

2013, May 9
871-872 A517 Set of 2 5.25 5.25

A518

Admission of Croatia to European Union — A519

2013, July 1
873 A518 3.10k multi 1.10 1.10

Souvenir Sheet

874 A519 20k multi 7.00 7.00

No. 873 was printed in sheets of 25 stamps + 5 labels.

Pula Film Festival, 60th Anniv. A520

2013, July 2
875 A520 3.10k multi 1.10 1.10

Castles and Palaces Type of 2011

Arms and: No. 876, 1.60k, Odescalchi Castle, Ilok. No. 877, 1.60k, Eltz Castle, Vukovar. No. 878, 1.60k, Pejacevic Castle, Virovitica. No. 879, 1.60k, Turkovic Castle, Kutjevo.

2013, July 18
876-879 A470 Set of 4 2.25 2.25
879a Souvenir sheet of 8, 2 each #876-879, + 8 labels 4.50 4.50

Mushrooms A521

No. 880: a, Macrolepiota procera. b, Boletus regius. c, Tuber magnatum, Tuber melanosporum.

2013, Sept. 3 *Perf. 14*
880 Horiz. strip of 3 5.25 5.25
a.-c. A521 4.60k Any single 1.75 1.75

Lapitch, the Little Shoemaker A522

2013, Sept. 4
881 A522 3.10k multi 1.10 1.10

Publishing of Lapitch, the Little Shoemaker, children's book by Ivana Brlic Mazuranic, cent.

Souvenir Sheet

Portrait of Count Teodor Pejacevic (1855-1928), by Vlaho Bukovac — A523

2013, Sept. 18
882 A523 11k multi 4.00 4.00

Diplomatic relations between Croatia and the Sovereign Military Order of Malta, 20th anniv.

Lighthouses — A524

Designs: 4.60k, Plocica Lighthouse. 5.80k, Stoncica Lighthouse. 7.60k, Sucuraj Lighthouse.

2013, Sept. 26 *Perf. 14*
883-885 A524 Set of 3 6.50 6.50

Salesians in Croatia, Cent. — A525

2013, Oct. 1 Litho. *Perf. 14*
886 A525 1.20k multi .45 .45

Gas Lighting System in Zagreb, 150th Anniv. — A526

2013, Oct. 3 Litho. *Perf. 14*
887 A526 7.60k multi 2.75 2.75

No. 887 was printed in sheets of 8 + label.

Souvenir Sheet

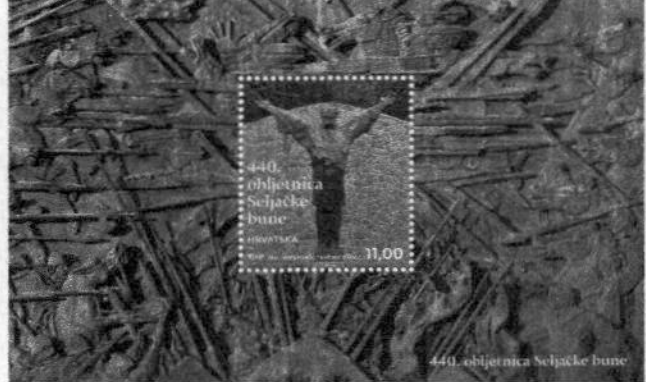
Peasant's Revolt, 440th Anniv. — A527

2013, Oct. 11 Litho. *Perf. 14*
888 A527 11k multi 4.00 4.00

Mirko (1871-1913) and Stevo (1875-1936) Seljan, Explorers, Map of Guayra Falls, South America — A528

2013, Oct. 15 Litho. *Perf. 14*
889 A528 7.60k multi 2.75 2.75

Faros Swimming Marathon — A529

2013, Nov. 5 Litho. *Perf. 14*
890 A529 7.60k multi 2.75 2.75

No. 890 was printed in sheets of 9 + label.

Christmas A530

Litho. With Foil Application

2013, Nov. 27 ***Perf. 14***
891 A530 3.10k multi 1.10 1.10

Litho.

Booklet Stamp Self-Adhesive

Serpentine Die Cut 5¼

892 A530 3.10k multi 1.10 1.10
a. Booklet pane of 10 11.00
Complete booklet, #892a 11.00

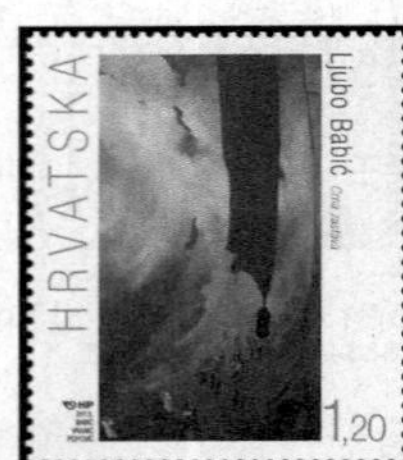

Art — A531

Designs: 1.20k, Black Flag, by Ljubo Babic. 3.10k, Sappho, by Bela Cikos Sesija. 5.80k, PAFAMA, by Josip Seissel.

2013, Dec. 3 **Litho.** ***Perf. 14***
893-895 A531 Set of 3 3.75 3.75

New Year 2014 A532

Litho. With Foil Application

2013, Dec. 5 ***Perf. 14***
896 A532 3.10k multi 1.10 1.10

2014 Winter Olympics, Sochi, Russia A533

2014, Feb. 7 **Litho.** ***Perf. 14***
897 A533 3.10k multi 1.10 1.10

No. 897 was printed in sheets of 9 + label.

Pets — A534

No. 898: a, Chinchilla eating apple slice. b, Guinea pig eating biscuit. c, Rabbit in top hat. d, Hamster with carrot.

2014, Feb. 21 **Litho.** ***Perf. 14***
898 A534 3.10k Block of 4, #a.-d. 4.50 4.50

Temple of Augustus, Pula — A535

2014, Mar. 3 **Litho.** ***Perf. 14***
899 A535 2.80k multi 1.00 1.00

Souvenir Sheet

University of Zagreb Faculty of Science Botanical Garden, 125th Anniv. — A536

2014, Apr. 1 **Litho.** ***Perf. 14***
900 A536 11k multi 4.00 4.00

Dalmatian Braided Bread — A537

2014, Apr. 2 **Litho.** ***Perf. 14***
901 A537 3.10k multi 1.10 1.10

Easter.

Miniature Sheet

Marine Life — A538

No. 902: a, Ornate wrasse (Vladika arbanaska). b, Golden sponge (Promjenjiva sumporaca). c, European fan worm (Kozasti perjanicar). d, mediterranean violet aeolid (Ljubicasta flabelina).

Serpentine Die Cut 5¼

2014, Apr. 9 **Litho.**

Self-Adhesive

902 A538 Sheet of 4 + 4 etiquettes 8.50
a.-d. 5.80k Any single 2.10 2.10

Orchids A539

Designs: No. 903, Ophrys dinarica. No. 904, Serapias istriaca. 3.10k, Ophrys libunica.

2014, Apr. 11 **Litho.** ***Perf. 14***
903 A539 2.80k multi 1.00 1.00
a. Booklet pane of 10 10.00
Complete booklet, #903a 10.00
904 A539 2.80k multi 1.00 1.00
a. Booklet pane of 10 10.00
Complete booklet, #904a 10.00
905 A539 3.10 multi 1.10 1.10
a. Booklet pane of 10 11.00
Complete booklet, #905a 11.00

Famous People A540

Designs: 1.20k, Ivan Bjelovucic (1889-1949), first man to fly over Alps. 2.80k, Ivan Gundulic (1589-1638), writer. 3.10k, Ivan Mazuranic (1814-90), poet. 7.60k, Dora Pejacevic (1885-1923), composer.

2014, Apr. 18 **Litho.** ***Perf. 14***
906-909 A540 Set of 4 5.50 5.50

Canonization of Popes John Paul II and John XXIII — A541

No. 910—Arms and portrait of: a, Pope John Paul II. b, Pope John XXIII.

2014, Apr. 25 **Litho.** ***Perf. 14***
910 A541 7.60k Pair, #a.-b. 5.75 5.75

Europa A542

Musical instruments:3.10k, Lijerica. 7.60k, Sopile.

2014, May 9 **Litho.** ***Perf. 14***
911-912 A542 Set of 2 4.00 4.00

Lighthouses — A543

Designs: 2.80k, Palagruza Lighthouse. No. 914, 5.80k, Struga Lighthouse. No. 915, 5.80k, Susac Lighthouse.

2014, May 30 **Litho.** ***Perf. 14***
913-915 A543 Set of 3 5.25 5.25

Villa Angiolina, Opatija, 170th Anniv. A544

2014, June 11 **Litho.** ***Perf. 14***
916 A544 2.80k multi 1.00 1.00

No. 916 was printed in sheets of 8 + central label.

2014 World Cup Soccer Championships, Brazil — A545

2014, June 12 **Litho.** ***Perf. 14***
917 A545 7.60k multi 2.75 2.75

No. 917 was printed in sheets of 9 + label.

Volunteer Fire Departments in Croatia, 150th Anniv. — A546

2014, June 17 **Litho.** ***Perf. 14***
918 A546 5k multi 1.90 1.90

No. 918 was printed in sheets of 8 + 2 labels.

Prelog, 750th Anniv. — A547

2014, Sept. 23 **Litho.** ***Perf. 14***
919 A547 3.10k multi 1.10 1.10

Souvenir Sheet

Carved Wooden Doorway of Split Cathedral, 800th Anniv. — A548

2014, Sept. 23 **Litho.** ***Perf. 14***
920 A548 11k multi 3.75 3.75

Statute of the Town and Island of Korcula, 800th Anniv. — A549

2014, Sept. 26 **Litho.** ***Perf. 14***
921 A549 2.80k multi .95 .95

St. Nicholas Benedictine Monastery, Trogir, 950th Anniv. — A550

2014, Sept. 30 **Litho.** ***Perf. 14***
922 A550 2.80k multi .95 .95

Locomotives — A551

No. 923: a, KkStB 229/JDZ/JZ 116. b, MAV 375/JDZ/HDZ/JZ 51.

2014, Oct. 1 **Litho.** ***Perf. 14***
923 Vert. pair + 2 central labels 3.50 3.50
a.-b. A551 5k Either single 1.75 1.75

Monument in Mirogoj Cemetery, Zagreb A552

2014, Oct. 14 **Litho.** ***Perf. 14***
924 A552 7.60k multi 2.50 2.50

World War I, cent.

Details from Traditional Costumes — A553

Detail from costume from: 3.10k, Slavonia. 5.80k, Vrlika. 7.60k, Gorski Kotar. 11k, Lovas.

2014, Oct. 20 **Litho.** ***Perf. 14***
925 A553 3.10k multi 1.00 1.00
926 A553 5.80k multi 1.90 1.90
927 A553 7.60k multi 2.50 2.50
928 A553 11k multi 3.75 3.75
a. Souvenir sheet of 4, #925-928 9.25 9.25
Nos. 925-928 (4) 9.15 9.15

See Nos. 1023-1026, 1076-1079.

Souvenir Sheet

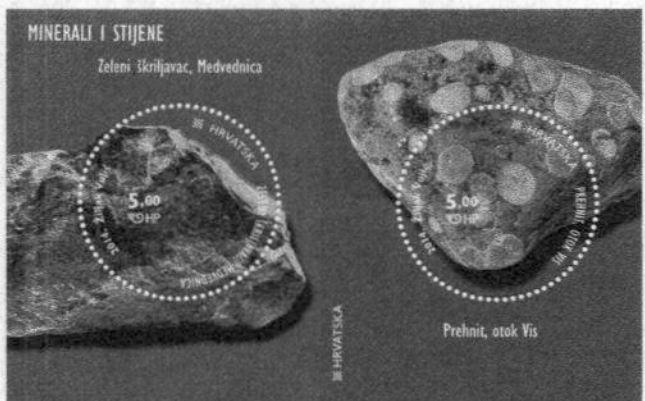

Rocks and Minerals — A554

No. 929: a, Green schist (green background). b, Prehnite (blue background).

Litho. & Embossed

2014, Oct. 24 ***Perf.***
929 A554 5k Sheet of 2, #a-b 3.25 3.25

Souvenir Sheet

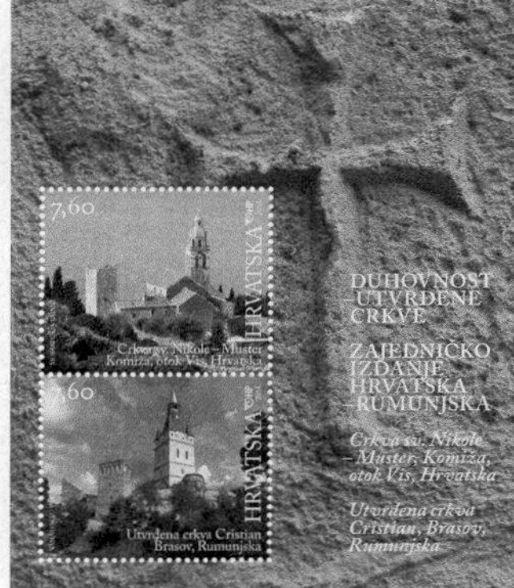

Fortified Churches — A555

No. 930: a, St. Nicholas Church, Komiza. b, Evangelical Church, Cristian, Romania.

2014, Nov. 14 **Litho.** ***Perf. 14***
930 A555 7.60k Sheet of 2, #a-b 5.00 5.00

See Romania Nos. 5625-5626.

Requisition, by Ivan Generalic (1914-92) — A556

2014, Nov. 17 **Litho.** ***Perf. 14***
931 A556 3.10k multi 1.00 1.00

Christmas — A557

Litho. With Foil Application

2014, Nov. 27 ***Perf. 14***
932 A557 3.10k multi 1.00 1.00

Booklet Stamp
Self-Adhesive

Serpentine Die Cut 5¼

933 A557 3.10k multi 1.00 1.00
a. Booklet pane of 10 10.00
Complete booklet, #933a 10.00

Royal University Library and Land Archives A558

Designs: No. 934, 4.60k, Building exterior. No. 935, 4.60k, Reading room. No. 936, 4.60k, Table lamps, vert.

2014, Dec. 1 **Litho.** ***Perf. 14***
934-936 A558 Set of 3 4.50 4.50

New Year 2015 — A559

2014, Dec. 4 **Litho.** ***Perf. 14***
937 A559 3.10k multi 1.00 1.00

St. Valentine's Day — A560

2015, Feb. 4 **Litho.** ***Perf. 14***
938 A560 6.50k multi 1.90 1.90

Values are for stamps with surrounding selvage.

112 Emergency Services Day — A561

2015, Feb. 11 **Litho.** ***Perf. 14***
939 A561 6.50k brt orange & blk 1.90 1.90

Pet Birds — A562

No. 940: a, Canary wearing horned helmet. b, Budgerigar wearing captain's hat. c, Zebra finch with didgeridoo. d, Sulphur-crested cockatoo wearing leather jacket.

2015, Feb. 19 **Litho.** ***Perf. 14***
940 A562 3.10k Block of 4, #a-d 3.75 3.75

Rotary International District 1913, 110th Anniv. — A563

2015, Feb. 23 **Litho.** ***Perf. 14***
941 A563 3.10k multi .90 .90

Easter — A564

Litho. With Foil Application

2015, Mar. 16 ***Perf. 14***
942 A564 3.10k multi .90 .90

Croatian Paralympic Committee, 50th Anniv. — A565

2015, Mar. 23 **Litho.** ***Perf. 14***
943 A565 5k multi 1.50 1.50

No. 943 was printed in sheets of 9 + label.

Lace — A566

No. 944: a, Colors of Croatian flag, lace from Lepoglav. b, Colors of Spanish flag, lace from Seville.

2015, Mar. 31 **Litho.** ***Perf. 14***
944 A566 7.60k Pair, #a-b 4.50 4.50

See Spain No. 4037.

Wildlife — A567

Designs: 2.80k, Capreolus capreolus. 4.60k, Vulpes vulpes. 6.50k, Sus scrofa.

2015, Apr. 15 **Litho.** ***Perf. 14***
945 A567 2.80k multi .85 .85
a. Booklet pane of 10 8.50 —
Complete booklet, #945a 8.50
946 A567 4.60k multi 1.40 1.40
a. Booklet pane of 10 14.00 —
Complete booklet, #946a 14.00
947 A567 6.50k multi 2.00 2.00
a. Booklet pane of 10 20.00 —
Complete booklet, #947a 20.00
Nos. 945-947 (3) 4.25 4.25

Famous People — A568

Designs: No. 948, 3.10k, Ivan Supek (1915-2007), scientist and writer. No. 949, 3.10k, Luka Sorkocevic (1734-89), composer. No. 950, 3.10k, Josip Juraj Strossmayer (1815-1905), bishop and politician.

2015, Apr. 21 **Litho.** ***Perf. 14***
948-950 A568 Set of 3 2.75 2.75

No. 949, a stamp that does not show an image of Sorkocevic, was designed, printed and sent to post offices after the original stamp, which showed a picture of Thomas Jefferson instead of Sorkocevic, was printed and distributed to post offices. The stamp with Jefferson's image was recalled from all post offices prior to the April 21 day of issue, but 22 examples of it were, nonetheless, sold at a post office before that day.

1000th Stamp Design of Croatia Post — A569

2015, Apr. 27 Litho. *Perf. 14*
951 A569 3.10k multi .95 .95

Souvenir Sheet

Bridges — A570

No. 952: a, Modrus 1 Bridge. b, Krka River Bridge.

2015, Apr. 29 Litho. *Perf. 14*
952 A570 7.60k Sheet of 2, #a-b 4.50 4.50

Europa A571

Toys: 4.60k, To Tak wood pieces and connectors. 7.60k, Porcelain doll.

2015, May 7 Litho. *Perf. 14*
953-954 A571 Set of 2 3.75 3.75

International Telecommunications Union, 150th Anniv. — A572

2015, May 15 Litho. *Perf. 14*
955 A572 10k multi 3.00 3.00

Castles and Palaces Type of 2011

Designs: No. 956, 4.60k, Jankovic Castle, Daruvar. No. 957, 4.60k, Markovic-Kulmer Castle, Cernik. No. 958, 4.60k, Erdödy-Rubido Castle, Gornja Rijeka. No. 959, 4.60k, Old Town, Durdevac.

2015, May 20 Litho. *Perf. 14*
956-959 A470 Set of 4 5.50 5.50
959a Souvenir sheet of 8, 2 each #956-959, + 8 labels 11.00 11.00

Lighthouses — A573

Designs: 2.80k, Daksa Lighthouse. 3.10k, Glavat Lighthouse. 4.60k, Grebeni Lighthouse. 6.50k, Sveti Andrija Lighthouse.

2015, June 10 Litho. *Perf. 14*
960-963 A573 Set of 4 5.00 5.00

Bracera — A574

2015, July 9 Litho. *Perf. 14*
964 A574 5.80k multi 1.75 1.75

A575

UNESCO Intangible Cultural Heritage — A576

Designs: No. 965, 3.10k, Zvoncari (carnival procession of bell ringers from Kastav). No. 966, 3.10k, Becarac (musician with stringed instrument). No. 967, 3.10k, Klapsko Pjevanje (a capella singers). No. 968, 3.10k, Sinjska Alka (horseman at Alka Chivalric Tournament, Sinj).

11k, Alka Chivalric Tournament, 300th anniv.

2015, July 27 Litho. *Perf. 14*
965-968 A575 Set of 4 3.75 3.75
968a Souvenir sheet of 4, #965-968, + 5 labels 3.75 3.75

Souvenir Sheet
Litho., Sheet Margin Litho. With Foil Application

969 A576 11k multi 3.25 3.25

Victory and Homeland Thanksgiving Day — A577

2015, Aug. 3 Litho. *Perf. 14*
970 A577 3.10k multi .90 .90

2015 Men's European Basketball Cahmpionships, Zagreb — A578

2015, Sept. 4 Litho. *Perf. 14*
971 A578 5k multi 1.50 1.50

No. 971 was printed in sheets of 8 + label.

Traffic Safety — A579

2015, Sept. 7 Litho. *Perf. 14*
972 A579 3.10k multi .95 .95

Christmas A580

2015, Nov. 25 Litho. *Perf. 14*
973 A580 3.10k multi .90 .90

Booklet Stamp
Self-Adhesive
Serpentine Die Cut 5¼

974 A580 3.10k multi .90 .90
a. Booklet pane of 10 9.00
Complete booklet, #974a 9.00

Sculpture A581

Designs: 1.20k, Metal Sculpture XX, by Dusan Dzamonja. 3.10k, Dunja I, by Kosta Angeli Radovani. 4.60k, The Bull, by Vojin Bakic.

2015, Dec. 1 Litho. *Perf. 14*
975-977 A581 Set of 3 2.50 2.50

Advertising Slogan for Mercedes-Benz Automobiles — A582

2016, Feb. 2 Litho. *Perf. 14*
978 A582 4.60k lt bl + label 1.40 1.40

St. Blaise, by Carmelo Reggio — A583

2016, Feb. 3 Litho. *Perf. 14*
979 A583 3.10k multi .90 .90

St. Blaise (d. 316), patron saint of Dubrovnik.

Pet Fish — A584

No. 980: a, Angelfish and baby carriage. b, Goldfish, hat, gold and miner's pan. c, Guppy, rainbow, airplane. d, Siamese fighting fish, castle, shield and lance.

2016, Feb. 22 Litho. *Perf. 14*
980 A584 3.10k Block of 4, #a-d 3.50 3.50

Easter A585

2016, Mar. 8 Litho. *Perf. 14*
981 A585 3.10k multi .95 .95

Herbs — A586

Designs: 2.80k, Rosmarinus officinalis. 3.10k, Lavandula angustifolia. 4.60k, Helichrysum italicum.

2016, Mar. 21 Litho. *Perf. 14*
982 A586 2.80k multi .85 .85
a. Booklet pane of 10 8.50 —
Complete booklet, #982a 8.50
983 A586 3.10k multi .95 .95
a. Booklet pane of 10 9.50 —
Complete booklet, #983a 9.50
984 A586 4.60k multi 1.40 1.40
a. Booklet pane of 10 14.00 —
Complete booklet, #984a 14.00
Nos. 982-984 (3) 3.20 3.20

Nos. 982-984 are impregnated with the scent of the depicted plant.

Famous People — A587

Designs: No. 985, 3.10k, Sidonija Erdödy Rubido (1819-84), opera singer. No. 986, 3.10k, Slavko Kolar (1891-1963), writer. No. 987, 3.10k, Mia Corak Slavenska (1916-2002), ballerina. No. 988, 3.10k, Mirko Bogovic (1816-93), poet.

2016, Apr. 20 Litho. *Perf. 14*
985-988 A587 Set of 4 3.75 3.75

Radio Announcer and Cameraman — A588

2016, Apr. 26 **Litho.** ***Perf. 14***
989 A588 3.10k multi + label .95 .95

Croatian radio broadcasting 90th anniv.; Croatian television broadcasting, 60th anniv.

Islamic Center, Zagreb — A589

2016, Apr. 27 **Litho.** ***Perf. 14***
990 A589 3.10k multi .95 .95

Islam in Croatia, cent.

Croatian Inventors and Their Inventions A590

Designs: 5k, Giovanni Biagio Luppis (1813-75) and torpedo. 6.50k, Eduard Slavoljub Penkala (1871-1922) and mechanical pencil, vert.

2016, Apr. 27 **Litho.** ***Perf. 14***
991-992 A590 Set of 2 3.50 3.50

A591

Europa A592

2016, May 9 **Litho.** ***Perf. 14***
993 A591 4.60k multi 1.40 1.40
994 A592 7.60k multi 2.25 2.25

Think Green Issue.

Dominican Order, 800th Anniv. — A593

2016, May 24 **Litho.** ***Perf. 14***
995 A593 3.10k multi .95 .95

Greetings to the Sun, by Nikola Basic — A594

Sea Organ, by Basic A595

2016, June 1 **Litho.** ***Perf. 14***
996 A594 2.80k multi .85 .85
997 A595 4.60k multi 1.40 1.40

Monuments in Zadar.

Declaration of Statehood, 25th Anniv. — A596

2016, June 23 **Litho.** ***Perf. 14***
998 A596 3.10k multi .95 .95

No. 998 was printed in sheets of 26 + 4 labels.

2016 European University Games, Zagreb and Rijeka — A597

2016 European Junior Synchronized Swimming and Diving Championships, Rijeka — A598

2016, June 28 **Litho.** ***Perf. 14***
999 A597 3.10k multi .95 .95
1000 A598 3.10k multi .95 .95

Nos. 999-1000 were each printed in sheets of 9 + label.

Ocellated Wrasse — A599

2016, July 7 **Litho.** ***Perf. 14***
1001 A599 5.80k multi 1.75 1.75

Souvenir Sheet

Battle of Lissa (Vis), 150th Anniv. — A600

2016, July 18 **Litho.** ***Perf. 14***
1002 A600 7.60k multi 2.25 2.25

See Slovenia No. 1188.

2016 Summer Olympics, Rio de Janeiro — A601

2016, Aug. 3 **Litho.** ***Perf. 14***
1003 A601 4.60k multi 1.40 1.40

No. 1003 was printed in sheets of 8 + label.

Souvenir Sheet

Battle of Szigetvár, 450th Anniv. — A602

No. 1004: a, 4.50k, Szigetvár coat of arms. b, 6.50k, Zrinski's Charge from the Szigetvár Fortress, by Bertalan Székely.

2016, Sept. 5 **Litho.** ***Perf. 14***
1004 A602 Sheet of 2, #a-b 3.25 3.25

See Hungary No. 4402.

Resumption of Croatian Postage Stamps, 25th Anniv. — A603

Litho. & Embossed With Hologram Affixed

2016, Sept. 9 ***Perf. 14***
1005 A603 11k multi 3.25 3.25

St. James Cathedral, Sibenik A604

2016, Sept. 15 **Litho.** ***Perf. 14***
1006 A604 3.10k multi .95 .95

Sibenik, 950th anniv.

Campaign Against Hate Speech A605

2016, Sept. 21 **Litho.** ***Perf. 14***
1007 A605 3.10k multi .95 .95

Locomotives — A606

No. 1008: a, Steam locomotive model 207. b, Steam locomotive JDZ/HDZ/JZ 83-106.

2016, Oct. 1 **Litho.** ***Perf. 14***
1008 Vert. pair + 2 central labels 6.00 6.00
a.-b. A606 9.50k Either single 3.00 3.00

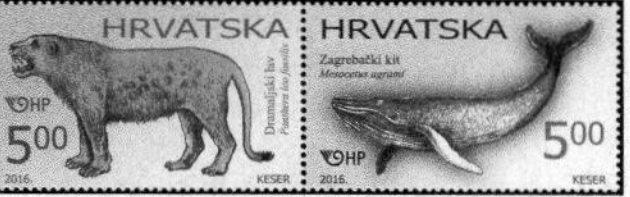

Depictions of Fossilized Animals — A607

No. 1009: a, Panthera leo fossils (Lion of Dramalj). b, Mesocetus agrami (Whale of Zagreb).

2016, Oct. 12 **Litho.** ***Perf. 14***
1009 A607 5k Pair, #a-b 3.00 3.00

Souvenir Sheet

Minerals — A608

No. 1010: a, 4.50k, Sea salt crystals (35mm diameter). b, 6.50k, Rhyolite (30x36mm).

Perf. (4.50k), Perf. 14 (6.50k)

2016, Oct. 24 **Litho. & Embossed**
1010 A608 Sheet of 2, #a-b 3.25 3.25

Canonization of St. Teresa of Calcutta (Mother Teresa) — A609

2016, Nov. 15 **Litho.** ***Perf. 14***
1011 A609 7.60k multi 2.25 2.25

Adoration of the Magi, by an Italo-Cretan Master — A610

2016, Nov. 24 **Litho.** ***Perf. 14***
1012 A610 3.10k multi .90 .90

Booklet Stamp Self-Adhesive

Serpentine Die Cut 5¼

1013	A610 3.10k multi	.90	.90
a.	Booklet pane of 10	9.00	
	Complete booklet, #1013a	9.00	

Christmas.

Adris Foundation — A611

2016, Nov. 28 Litho. *Perf. 14*

1014	A611 3.10k multi + label	.90	.90

No. 1014 was printed in sheets of 10 + 10 labels.

Viktor Kovacic (1874-1924), Architect — A612

Designs: 2.80k, Furniture in room of Kovacic's apartment. 4.60k, Decorative detail by Kovacic, vert. 7.60k, Stock Exchange Palace (Croatian National Bank), Zagreb, vert.

2016, Dec. 1 Litho. *Perf. 14*

1015-1017	A612 Set of 3	4.25	4.25

Souvenir Sheet

Statue of Ban Josip Jelacic, Zagreb, 150th Anniv. — A613

2016, Dec. 5 Litho. *Perf. 14*

1018	A613 15k multi	4.25	4.25

Black Luca, Hrvatko and Emblem of Croatian National Bank — A614

2016, Dec. 9 Litho. *Perf. 14*

1019	A614 3.10k multi + label	.85	.85

No. 1019 was printed in sheets of 10 + 10 labels.

A615

A616

A617

Gyps Fulvus — A618

2017, Jan. 23 Litho. *Perf. 14*

1020	Strip of 4	5.75	5.75
a.	A615 4.60k multi	1.40	1.40
b.	A616 4.60k multi	1.40	1.40
c.	A617 4.60k multi	1.40	1.40
d.	A618 4.60k multi	1.40	1.40

Worldwide Fund for Nature (WWF).

St. Valentine's Day — A619

2017, Feb. 3 Litho. *Perf. 14x13¾*

1021	A619 3.10k multi	.90	.90

Values are for stamps with surrounding selvage.

Reptiles — A620

No. 1022: a, Iguana on hammock. b, Milk snake and striped socks. c, Veiled chameleon and package. d, Musk turtle and diving board.

2017, Feb. 20 Litho. *Perf. 14*

1022	A620 3.10k Block or vert. strip of 4, #a-d	3.75	3.75

Details From Traditional Costumes Type of 2014

Designs: 3k, Pin on dress from Zlarin. 4.60k, Embroidery from Podravina. 5k, Embroidery from Konavle. 6.50k, Pleated skirt from Istria.

2017, Mar. 14 Litho. *Perf. 14*

1023	A553 3k multi	.90	.90
1024	A553 4.60k multi	1.40	1.40
1025	A553 5k multi	1.50	1.50
1026	A553 6.50k multi	1.90	1.90
a.	Souvenir sheet of 4, #1023-1026	5.75	5.75
	Nos. 1023-1026 (4)	5.70	5.70

World Poetry Day — A622

2017, Mar. 21 Litho. *Perf. 14*

1027	A622 2.80k multi + label	.80	.80

Bats — A623

Designs: 2.80k, Rhinolophus blasii. 3.10k, Plecotus kolombatovici. 6.50k, Myotis emarginatus.

2017, Mar. 21 Litho. *Perf. 14*

1028	A623 2.80k multi	.80	.80
a.	Booklet pane of 10	8.00	—
	Complete booklet, #1028a	8.00	
1029	A623 3.10k multi	.90	.90
a.	Booklet pane of 10	9.00	—
	Complete booklet, #1029a	9.00	
1030	A623 6.50k multi	1.90	1.90
a.	Booklet pane of 10	19.00	—
	Complete booklet, #1030a	19.00	
	Nos. 1028-1030 (3)	3.60	3.60

Easter Breakfast A624

2017, Apr. 3 Litho. *Perf. 14*

1031	A624 3.10k multi	.90	.90

Famous People — A625

Designs: No. 1032, 3.10k, Zinka Kunc Milanov (1906-89), opera singer. No. 1033, 3.10k, Frano Supilo (1870-1917), journalist and politician. No. 1034, 3.10k, Faust Vrancic (1551-1617), writer and lexicographer.

2017, Apr. 18 Litho. *Perf. 14*

1032-1034	A625 Set of 3	2.75	2.75

Souvenir Sheet

Bridges — A626

No. 1035: a, Kosinj Bridge over Lika River. b, Limska Draga Highway Viaduct.

2017, Apr. 27 Litho. *Perf. 14*

1035	A626 7.60k Sheet of 2, #a-b	4.50	4.50

Europa A627

Designs: No. 1036, 7.60k, Veliki Tabor Castle. No. 1037, 7.60k, Trakoscan Castle.

2017, May 9 Litho. *Perf. 14*

1036-1037	A627 Set of 2	4.75	4.75

Souvenir Sheet

Holy Roman Empress Maria Theresa (1717-80) — A628

2017, May 13 Litho. *Perf. 14*

1038	A628 15k multi	4.50	4.50

See Austria No. 2677, Hungary No. 4433, Slovenia No. 1219, Ukraine No. 1093.

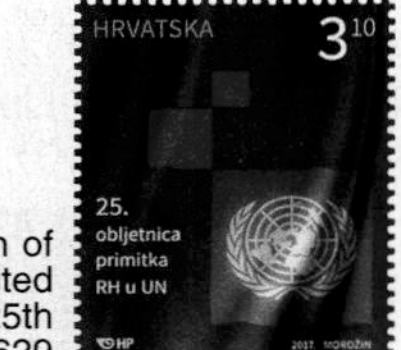

Admission of Croatia to United Nations, 25th Anniv. — A629

2017, May 22 Litho. *Perf. 14*

1039	A629 3.10k multi	.95	.95

Lions Clubs International, Cent. — A630

2017, June 7 Litho. *Perf. 14*

1040	A630 3.10k multi	.95	.95

Aerial Views of Zagreb Tourist Attractions A631

Designs: 2.80k, Dolac Market. 5.80k, St. Mark's Church.

2017, June 8 Litho. *Perf. 14*

1041-1042	A631 Set of 2	2.75	2.75

Olive Grove, Lun
A632

2017, July 10 Litho. *Perf. 14*
1043 A632 5.80k multi 1.90 1.90

First Croatian Movie, *Brcko u Zagreb*, Cent. — A633

2017, Aug. 28 Litho. *Perf. 14*
1044 A633 7.60k multi 2.50 2.50

Anemone Coronaria and Iris Croatica Prodán
A634

2017, Sept. 4 Litho. *Perf. 14*
1045 A634 7.60k multi 2.40 2.40

Diplomatic relations between Croatia and Israel, 20th anniv. See Israel No. 2150.

Autism Awareness
A635

2017, Sept. 18 Litho. *Perf. 14*
1046 A635 3.10k multi 1.00 1.00

Matija Vlacic Ilirik (1520-75), Lutheran Theologian
A636

2017, Oct. 4 Litho. *Perf. 14*
1047 A636 3.10k multi 1.00 1.00

Protestant Reformation, 500th anniv.

7th Guards Brigade, 25th Anniv. — A637

2017, Oct. 18 Litho. *Perf. 14*
1048 A637 7.60k multi 2.40 2.40

Wax Figure of Jesus, Blessed Virgin Mary Church, Lepoglava — A638

Litho. With Foil Application

2017, Nov. 23 *Perf. 14*
1049 A638 3.10k gold & multi 1.00 1.00

Booklet Stamp
Self-Adhesive

Serpentine Die Cut 5¼

1050 A638 3.10k gold & multi 1.00 1.00
a. Booklet pane of 10 10.00
Complete booklet, #1050a 10.00

Christmas.

Golden Spin of Zagreb International Ice Skating Competition, 50th Anniv. — A639

2017, Nov. 27 Litho. *Perf. 14*
1051 A639 3.10k multi 1.00 1.00

No. 1051 was printed in sheets of 9 + label.

Paintings
A640

Designs: No. 1052, 3.10k, By the Red Light, by Robert Auer (1873-1952). No. 1053, 3.10k, Bora, by Ferdo Kovacevic (1870-1927). No. 1054, 3.10k, Astronomer, by Ivan Tisov (1870-1928).

2017, Dec. 1 Litho. *Perf. 14*
1052-1054 A640 Set of 3 3.00 3.00

University of Zagreb Faculty of Medicine, Cent. — A641

2017, Dec. 4 Litho. *Perf. 14*
1055 A641 3.10k multi 1.00 1.00

2018 Winter Olympics, PyeongChang, South Korea — A642

2018, Feb. 7 Litho. *Perf. 14*
1056 A642 5.80k multi 1.90 1.90

Cats — A643

No. 1057 — Envelopes and: a, Russian Blue cat (Ruska Plava). b, Birman cat (Sveta Birma). c, Maine Coon cat. d, Himalayan cat (Himalajska).

2018, Feb. 22 Litho. *Perf. 14*
1057 A643 3.10k Block of 4, #a-d 4.00 4.00

Descent from the Cross, by Mile Skracic — A644

2018, Mar. 15 Litho. *Perf. 14*
1058 A644 3.10k multi 1.10 1.10

Easter.

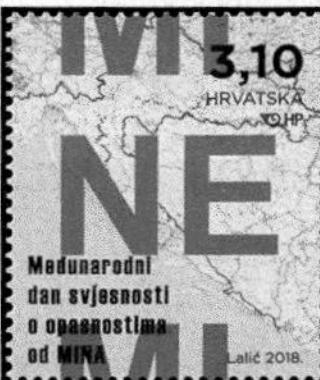

Fruit and Nuts — A645

Designs: No. 1059, Cornus mas. No. 1060, Castanea sativa. No. 1061, Vaccinium myrtillus.

2018, Mar. 21 Litho. *Perf. 14*
1059 A645 3.10k multi 1.10 1.10
a. Booklet pane of 10 11.00 —
Complete booklet, #1059a 11.00
1060 A645 3.10k multi 1.10 1.10
a. Booklet pane of 10 11.00 —
Complete booklet, #1060a 11.00
1061 A645 3.10k multi 1.10 1.10
a. Booklet pane of 10 11.00 —
Complete booklet, #1061a 11.00
Nos. 1059-1061 (3) 3.30 3.30

International Landmine Awareness Day — A646

2018, Apr. 4 Litho. *Perf. 14*
1062 A646 3.10k multi 1.00 1.00

Protected Food Products
A647

Designs: No. 1063, 3.10k, Dalmatian prosciutto (Dalmatinski prsut). No. 1064, 3.10k, Cres extra virgin olive oil (Cres ekstra djevicansko maslinovo ulje). No. 1065, 3.10k, Neretva Valley tangerines (Neretvanska mandarina).

2018, Apr. 12 Litho. *Perf. 14*
1063-1065 A647 Set of 3 3.00 3.00

Famous People — A648

Designs: No. 1066, 3.10k, Marin Getaldic (1568-1626), mathematician. No. 1067, 3.10k, Nives Kavuric-Kurtovic (1938-2016), painter. No. 1068, 3.10k, Petar Preradovic (1818-72), poet.

2018, Apr. 19 Litho. *Perf. 14*
1066-1068 A648 Set of 3 3.00 3.00

Europa
A649

Designs: No. 1069, 3.10k, Stone bridge, Novigrad na Dobri. No. 1070, 3.10k, Dr. Franjo Tudman Bridge, Dubrovnik.

2018, May 2 Litho. *Perf. 14*
1069-1070 A649 Set of 2 2.00 2.00

Professor Balthazar Animated Television Series, 50th Anniv. — A650

2018, May 3 Litho. *Perf. 14*
1071 A650 3.10k multi 1.00 1.00

Father Bernardin Sokol (1888-1944), Professor of Music — A651

2018, May 15 Litho. *Perf. 14*
1072 A651 3.10k multi 1.00 1.00

Church of St. Nicholas, Varazdin — A652

Stilt Walker at Spancirfest, Varazdin — A653

2018, June 4 Litho. *Perf. 14*
1073 A652 3.10k multi 1.00 1.00
1074 A653 3.10k multi 1.00 1.00

2018 World Cup Soccer Championships, Russia — A654

2018, June 14 Litho. *Perf. 14*
1075 A654 6.50k multi 2.10 2.10

No. 1075 was printed in sheets of 9 + label.

Details From Traditional Costumes Type of 2014

Designs: 1k, Embrodery from Sestine. 3.10k, Floral silk scarf designs from Slavonia. 8.60k, Woman's dress from Susak. 15k, Beaded headpiece from Bratina.

2018, June 28 Litho. *Perf. 14*
1076 A553 1k multi .30 .30
1077 A553 3.10k multi .95 .95
1078 A553 8.60k multi 2.75 2.75
1079 A553 15k multi 4.75 4.75
a. Souvenir sheet of 4, #1076-1079 8.75 8.75
Nos. 1076-1079 (4) 8.75 8.75

Compare No. 1077 with No. 925.

Arsen 2, Record Album by Arsen Dedic (1938-2015) A655

Jubilarni Koncert, Record Album by Ivo Robic (1923-2000) A656

Mimo Teku Rijeke, Record Album by Vice Vukov (1936-2008) A657

Serpentine Die Cut 11½
2018, July 4 Litho.
Self-Adhesive
1080 A655 7.60k multi 2.40 2.40
1081 A656 7.60k multi 2.40 2.40
1082 A657 7.60k multi 2.40 2.40
Nos. 1080-1082 (3) 7.20 7.20

Stone House — A658

2018, July 10 Litho. *Perf. 14*
1083 A658 7.60k multi 2.40 2.40

Souvenir Sheet

Second-Place Finish of Croatian 2018 World Cup Soccer Team — A659

No. 1084 — Photograph of team wearing medals with 2018 World Cup emblem at: a, LL. b, LR.

2018, Aug. 31 Litho. *Perf. 14*
1084 A659 6k Sheet of 2, #a-b 3.75 3.75

Stamp Day — A660

2018, Sept. 6 Litho. *Perf. 14*
1085 A660 3.10k lilac & multi 1.00 1.00

Souvenir Sheet

1086 Sheet of 4, #1085, 1086a-1086c 8.00 8.00
a. A660 1.50k red vio & multi .45 .45
b. A660 8.60k light blue & multi 2.75 2.75
c. A660 11.50k gray green & multi 3.75 3.75

First stamps of Croatia-Slavonia, cent.

Forest Protection A661

2018, Sept. 17 Litho. *Perf. 14*
1087 A661 3.10k multi 1.00 1.00

Locomotives — A662

No. 1088: a, Steam locomotive No. 7. b, DEV-1 Diesel-electric.

2018, Oct. 5 Litho. *Perf. 14*
1088 Vert. pair + 2 central labels 4.80 4.80
a.-b. A662 7.60k Either single 2.40 2.40

Souvenir Sheet

Minerals and Rocks — A663

No. 1089: a, Quartz (red line). b, Augite diabase conglomerate rock (blue line).

2018, Oct. 24 Litho. *Perf. 14*
1089 A663 5k Sheet of 2, #a-b 3.25 3.25

Emblem of Tigers Brigade of 1st Guards — A664

2018, Nov. 5 Litho. *Perf. 14*
1090 A664 7.60k multi 2.40 2.40

No. 1090 was printed in sheets of 6 + label.

Souvenir Sheet

Lipizzan Horses — A665

2018, Nov. 7 Litho. *Perf. 14*
1091 A665 15k multi 4.75 4.75

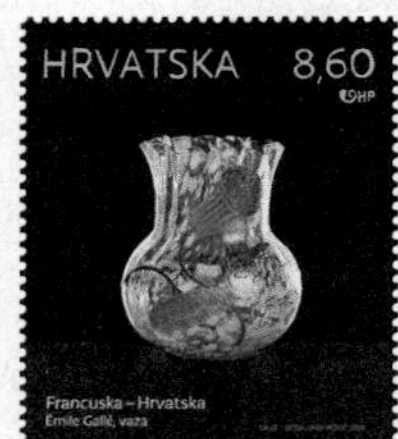

Vase by Emile Gallé (1846-1904) A666

Vase by Antonija Krasnik (1874-1956) A667

Litho. With Foil Application
2018, Nov. 8 *Perf. 14*
1092 A666 8.60k multi 2.75 2.75
1093 A667 8.60k multi 2.75 2.75

See France Nos. 5544-5545.

Christmas A668

2018, Nov. 26 Litho. *Perf. 14*
1094 A668 3.10k multi .95 .95

Booklet Stamp
Self-Adhesive
Serpentine Die Cut 5¼

1095 A668 3.10k multi .95 .95
a. Booklet pane of 10 9.50
Complete booklet, #1095a 9.50

Architecture and Designs by Vjenceslav Richter (1917-2002) — A669

Designs: No. 1096, 3.10k, Yugoslavian Pavilion for 1958 World's Fair, Brussels. No. 1097, 3.10k, Sinusoids II sculpture, vert. No. 1098, 3.10k, Plywood and wrought iron chair, vert.

2018, Nov. 29 Litho. *Perf. 14*
1096-1098 A669 Set of 3 3.00 3.00

Souvenir Sheet

Forts — A670

No. 1099: a, Fort Santiago, Manila, Philippines. b, St. Michael's Fortress, Sibenik, Croatia.

2018, Dec. 5 Litho. *Perf. 14*
1099 A670 6.50k Sheet of 2, #a-b 4.00 4.00

Diplomatic relations between Croatia and Philippines, 25th anniversary. See Philippines No. 3794.

20th Century Necklace A671

2019, Jan. 23 Litho. *Perf. 14*
1100 A671 3.10k multi .95 .95

Ethnographic Museum, Zagreb, cent.

Dogs — A672

No. 1101: a, St. Bernard. b, Pug. c, Siberian husky. d, Cavalier King Charles spaniel.

2019, Feb. 20 Litho. *Perf. 14*
1101 A672 3.10k Block or vert. strip of 4, #a-d 3.75 3.75

Rotary International in Croatia, 90th Anniv. — A673

2019, Mar. 6 Litho. *Perf. 14*

1102 A673 3.10k multi .95 .95

Emblem of 1st Croatian Guards Brigade — A674

Emblem of 2nd Croatian Guards Brigade "Thunders" A675

Emblem of 3rd Croatian Guards Brigade "Martens" — A676

Emblem of 4th Croatian Guards Brigade "Spiders" — A677

2019, Mar. 11 Litho. *Perf. 14*

1103 A674 8.60k multi 2.60 2.60
1104 A675 8.60k multi 2.60 2.60
1105 A676 8.60k multi 2.60 2.60
1106 A677 8.60k multi 2.60 2.60
Nos. 1103-1106 (4) 10.40 10.40

Nos. 1103-1106 were each printed in sheets of 6 + central label.

Apis Mellifera Carnica A678

Designs: No. 1107, Worker bee (radilica). No. 1108, Drone bee (trut). 6.50k, Queen bee (matica).

2019, Mar. 21 Litho. *Perf. 14*

1107 A678 3.10k multi .95 .95
a. Booklet pane of 10 9.50 —
Complete booklet, #1107a 9.50
1108 A678 3.10k multi .95 .95
a. Booklet pane of 10 9.50 —
Complete booklet, #1108a 9.50
1109 A678 6.50k multi 2.00 2.00
a. Booklet pane of 10 20.00 —
Complete booklet, #1109a 20.00
Nos. 1107-1109 (3) 3.90 3.90

Luka Modric, Soccer Player — A679

2019, Mar. 25 Litho. *Perf. 14*

1110 A679 10k multi 3.00 3.00

No. 1110 was printed in sheets of 9 + label.

Souvenir Sheet

2018 Davis Cup Championship of Croatian Tennis Team — A680

No. 1111 — Team members and Davis Cup with demonination at: a, UL. b, UR.

2019, Mar. 28 Litho. *Perf. 14*

1111 A680 Sheet of 2 4.00 4.00
a.-b. 6.50k Either single 2.00 2.00

Croatian Membership in North Atlantic Treaty Organization, 10th Anniv. — A681

2019, Apr. 1 Litho. *Perf. 14*

1112 A681 3.10k sil & multi .95 .95

Easter — A682

2019, Apr. 4 Litho. *Perf. 14*

1113 A682 3.10k multi .95 .95

Famous People A683

Designs: No. 1114, 3.10k, Vatroslav Lisinski (1819-54), composer. No. 1115, 3.10k, Andela Horvat (1911-85), art historian. No. 1116, 3.10k, Jure Kastelan (1919-90), poet.

2019, Apr. 16 Litho. *Perf. 14*

1114-1116 A683 Set of 3 3.00 3.00

Souvenir Sheet

Bridges — A684

No. 1117: a, Old Bridge, Sisak (43x30mm). b, Jezerane Viaduct (30x36mm).

2019, Apr. 24 Litho. *Perf. 14*

1117 A684 Sheet of 2 4.00 4.00
a.-b. 6.50k Either single 2.00 2.00

Europa — A685

Birds: No. 1118, 8.60k, Lastavica bregunica (sand martins). No. 1119, 8.60k, Galeb klaukavac (yellow-legged gulls).

2019, May 9 Litho. *Perf. 14*

1118-1119 A685 Set of 2 5.25 5.25

Castles — A686

Designs: No. 1120, 3.10k, Luznica Castle. No. 1121, 3.10k, Janusevec Castle. No. 1122, 3.10k, Orsic Castle. No. 1123, 3.10k, Lovrecina Castle.

2019, May 20 Litho. *Perf. 14*

1120-1123 A686 Set of 4 3.75 3.75
1123a Souvenir sheet of 8, 2 each #1120-1123, + 8 central labels 7.50 7.50

Kuna Currency, 25th Anniv. — A687

2019, May 30 Litho. *Perf. 14*

1124 A687 3.10k multi .95 .95

No. 1124 was printed in sheets of 25 + 5 labels.

Icons of the Virgin Mary — A688

Marian Shrines — A689

Designs: Nos. 1125, 1129, Statue of the Mother of God, Marian Bistrica. Nos. 1126, 1130, Painting of Our Lady of Vocin. Nos. 1127, 1131, Shrine, Marian Bistrica. Nos. 1128, 1132, Church of the Visitation of the Blessed Virgin Mary, Vocin.

2019, June 4 Litho. *Perf. 14*

1125 A688 3.10k multi .95 .95
1126 A688 3.10k multi .95 .95
1127 A689 8.60k multi 2.60 2.60
1128 A689 8.60k multi 2.60 2.60
Nos. 1125-1128 (4) 7.10 7.10

Booklet Stamps
Self-Adhesive

Serpentine Die Cut 11

1129 A688 3.10k multi .95 .95
1130 A688 3.10k multi .95 .95
1131 A689 8.60k multi 2.60 2.60
a. Booklet pane of 10, 5 each #1129, 1131 18.00
1132 A689 8.60k multi 2.60 2.60
a. Booklet pane of 10, 5 each #1130, 1132 18.00
Nos. 1129-1132 (4) 7.10 7.10

Nos. 1125-1128 were each printed in sheets of 8 + central label.

Small Waterfalls — A690

Lake Kozjac Waterfall — A691

Great Cascades — A692

Great Waterfall in Winter — A693

2019, June 10 Litho. *Perf. 14*

1133 A690 3.10k multi .95 .95
a. Booklet pane of 1 .95 —
1134 A691 3.10k multi .95 .95
a. Booklet pane of 1 .95 —
1135 A692 8.60k multi 2.60 2.60
a. Booklet pane of 1 2.60 —
1136 A693 8.60k multi 2.60 2.60
a. Booklet pane of 1 2.60 —
Complete booklet, #1133a, 1134a, 1135a, 1136a 7.25
b. Souvenir sheet of 4, #1133-1136 7.25 7.25
Nos. 1133-1136 (4) 7.10 7.10

Plitvice Lakes waterfalls.

Children's Folk Costumes From Susak — A694

2019, July 8 Litho. *Perf. 14*

1137 A694 8.60k multi 2.60 2.60

National Parks and Flora A695

Designs: No. 1138, 8.60k, Northern Velebit National Park, Croatia, and Dianthus velebiticus. No. 1139, 8.60k, Seoraksan National Park, South Korea, and Pinus pumila.

2019, Aug. 29 Litho. *Perf. 14*

1138-1139 A695 Set of 2 5.25 5.25

See South Korea No. 2558.

No. 758 Surcharged

Methods and Perfs. As Before

2019, Sept. 2

1140 A444 3.60k on 1.60k #758 1.10 1.10

Health Through Sport — A696

2019, Sept. 18 Litho. *Perf. 14*

1141 A696 3.10k multi .95 .95

Miniature Sheet

Emblems of Special Police Units — A697

No. 1142: a, ATJ Lucko. b, Alfe. c, Ajkule. d, Bak. e, Ban. f, Barun. g, Batt. h, Delta. i, Grof. j, Grom. k, Jastrebovi. l, Omege. m, Orao. n, Osa. p, Ris. q, Poskoci. r, Roda. s, Simini Andeli Pakla. t, Tigrovi. u, Trenk. v, Prvi Hrvatski Redarstvenik.

2019, Sept. 27 Litho. *Perf. 14*

1142 A697 Sheet of 21 + 4 labels 23.50 23.50

a.-u. 3.60k Any single 1.10 1.10

Zagreb Fair, 110th Anniv. — A698

2019, Oct. 28 Litho. *Perf. 14*

1143 A698 A multi + label .95 .95

No. 1143 sold for 3.10k on day of issue.

University of Zagreb, 350th Anniv. — A699

2019, Oct. 30 Litho. *Perf. 14*

1144 A699 3.60k multi 1.10 1.10

University of Zagreb Faculty of Veterinary Medicine, Cent. — A700

2019, Nov. 13 Litho. *Perf. 14*

1145 A700 3.60k multi 1.10 1.10

Father Antun Cvek (1934-2019), Founder of Bishop Josip Lang Foundation A701

2019, Nov. 18 Litho. *Perf. 14*

1146 A701 A multi .95 .95

No. 1146 sold for 3.10k on day of issue and was printed in sheets of 9 + label.

Christmas — A702

Litho. With Foil Application

2019, Nov. 22 *Perf. 14*

1147 A702 A multi .95 .95

Booklet Stamp
Self-Adhesive

Serpentine Die Cut 5¼

1148 A702 A multi .95 .95

a. Booklet pane of 10 9.50

Complete booklet, #1148a 9.50

Nos. 1147-1148 each sold for 3.10k on day of issue.

Paintings A703

Designs: No. 1149, 3.10k, Landscape, by Hugo Conrad von Hötzendorf (1807-69). No. 1150, 3.10k, Return of the Fishermen, by Jozo Kljakovic (1889-1969). No. 1151, 3.10k, Portrait of a Girl, by Vjekoslav Karas (1821-58), vert.

2019, Nov. 25 Litho. *Perf. 14*

1149-1151 A703 Set of 3 2.75 2.75

Zagreb Polytechnic School, Cent. — A704

2019, Nov. 28 Litho. *Perf. 14*

1152 A704 3.10k multi .95 .95

Sveti Duh Clinical Hospital, Zagreb, 215th Anniv. — A705

2019, Dec. 23 Litho. *Perf. 14*

1153 A705 3.10k multi .95 .95

Croatian Presidency of the Council of the European Union — A706

2020, Jan. 2 Litho. *Perf. 14*

1154 A706 8.60k multi 2.60 2.60

No. 1154 was printed in sheets of 25 + 5 labels.

Rijeka, Croatia, 2020 European Capital of Culture A707

Galway, Ireland, 2020 European Capital of Culture A708

2020, Jan. 23 Litho. *Perf. 14*

1155 A707 8.60k multi 2.60 2.60

1156 A708 8.60k multi 2.60 2.60

See Ireland Nos. 2265-2266.

Kopacki Rit Nature Park — A709

Blue Cave — A710

Lake Mir and Telascica Bay — A711

2020, Jan. 28 Litho. *Perf. 14*

1157 A709 A multi .95 .95

1158 A710 B multi 2.60 2.60

1159 A711 C multi 2.60 2.60

Nos. 1157-1159 (3) 6.15 6.15

Coil Stamps
Self-Adhesive

Serpentine Die Cut 11

1160 A709 A multi .95 .95

1161 A710 B multi 2.60 2.60

1162 A711 C multi 2.60 2.60

Nos. 1160-1162 (3) 6.15 6.15

Nos. 1159 and 1162 are airmail. On day of issue, Nos. 1157 and 1160 each sold for 3.10k, and Nos. 1158-1159, 1161-1162 each sold for 8.60k.

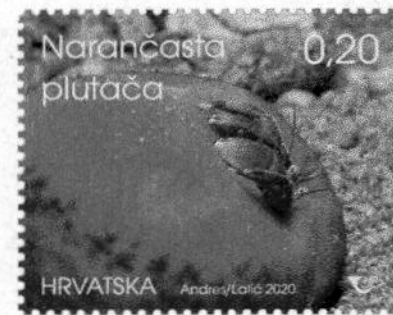

Suberites Domuncula A712

Eunicella Cavolini — A713

Hacelia Attenuata — A714

2020, Feb. 14 Litho. *Perf. 14*

1163 A712 20 l multi .25 .25

1164 A713 50 l multi .25 .25

1165 A714 10k multi 3.00 3.00

Nos. 1163-1165 (3) 3.50 3.50

Small Animals — A715

No. 1166: a, Shetland pony. b, Croatian dwarf chickens. c, African pygmy hedgehog. d, Vietnamese pot-bellied pig.

2020, Feb. 20 Litho. *Perf. 14*

1166 A715 3.10k Block or vert. strip of 4, #a-d 3.75 3.75

Emblem of 9th Croatian Guards Brigade "Wolves" — A716

Emblem of 5th Croatian Guards Brigade "Falcons" — A717

Emblem of 84th Croatian Guards Battalion "Termites" — A718

Emblem of 81st Croatian Guards Battalion "Godfathers" A719

2020, Mar. 11 Litho. *Perf. 14*

1167 A716 8.60k multi	2.50	2.50
1168 A717 8.60k multi	2.50	2.50
1169 A718 8.60k multi	2.50	2.50
1170 A719 8.60k multi	2.50	2.50
Nos. 1167-1170 (4)	10.00	10.00

Nos. 1167-1170 were each printed in sheets of 6 + central label.

Flowers — A720

Designs: No. 1171, Genista bolopetala. No. 1172, Moebringia tommasinii. 6.50k, Fritillaria meleagris.

2020, Mar. 20 Litho. *Perf. 14*

1171 A720 3.10k multi	.90	.90
a. Booklet pane of 10	9.00	—
Complete booklet, #1171a	9.00	
1172 A720 3.10k multi	.90	.90
a. Booklet pane of 10	9.00	—
Complete booklet, #1172a	9.00	
1173 A720 6.50k multi	1.90	1.90
a. Booklet pane of 10	19.00	—
Complete booklet, #1173a	19.00	
Nos. 1171-1173 (3)	3.70	3.70

Easter — A721

2020, Mar. 26 Litho. *Perf. 14*

1174 A721 3.10k multi .90 .90

Bicyclist — A722

2020, Mar. 27 Litho. *Perf. 14*

1175 A722 A multi + label .90 .90

Campaign against global warming. No. 1175 sold for 3.10k on day of issue.

Protected Croatian Food Products A723

Designs: No. 1176, 6.50k, Ogulinsko Kiselo Zelje (Ogulin sauerkraut). No. 1177, 6.50k, Licki Krumpir (Lika potatoes). No. 1178, 6.50k, Baranjski Kulen (Baranja sausage).

2020, Apr. 14 Litho. *Perf. 14*

1176-1178 A723 Set of 3 5.75 5.75

Famous People — A724

Designs: No. 1179, A, Ivan Krstitelj Rabjanin (1470-1540), cannon and bell founder. No. 1180, A, Count Janko Draskovic (1770-1856), politician and writer. No. 1181, A, Lelja Dobronic (1920-2006), art historian.

2020, Apr. 22 Litho. *Perf. 14*

1179-1181 A724 Set of 3 2.75 2.75

Nos. 1179-1181 each sold for 3.10k on day of issue.

Europa — A725

No. 1182 — 19th century lithograph of St. Francis Chapel on Velebit Mountain: a, Mail coach. b, Chapel.

2020, May 8 Litho. *Perf. 14*

1182 A725 8.60k Horiz. pair, #a-b 5.00 5.00

Novigrad, 800th Anniv. — A726

2020, May 20 Litho. *Perf. 14*

1183 A726 3.10k multi .90 .90

St. Jerome (c. 347-420), Patron Saint of Dalmatia — A727

2020, May 27 Litho. *Perf. 14*

1184 A727 10k multi 3.00 3.00

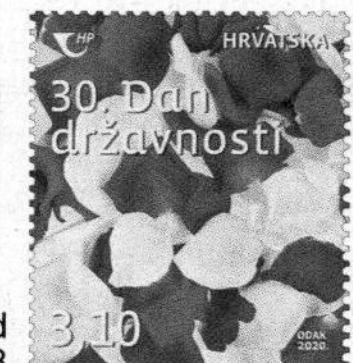

30th Statehood Day — A728

2020, May 28 Litho. *Perf. 14*

1185 A728 3.10k multi .90 .90

No. 1185 was printed in sheets of 25 + 5 labels.

A729

Balbi's Arch, Rovinj — A730

Rovinj
8,60 HRVATSKA

A731

St. Euphemia's Church, Rovinj — A732

2020 Litho. *Perf. 14*

1186 A729 3.10k multi	.95	.95
1187 A730 3.10k multi	.95	.95
1188 A731 8.0k multi	2.60	2.60
1189 A732 8.0k multi	2.60	2.60
Nos. 1186-1189 (4)	7.10	7.10

Issued: Nos. 1186, 1188, 6/4; Nos. 1187, 1189, 6/25.

Canonization of St. Nicholas Tavelic (c. 1340-91), 50th Anniv. — A733

2020, June 19 Litho. *Perf. 14*

1190 A733 3.10k multi .95 .95

Rab Cake — A734

2020, July 13 Litho. *Perf. 14*

1191 A734 8.60k multi 2.75 2.75

Operations Lightning and Storm, 25th Anniv. — A735

2020, Aug. 3 Litho. *Perf. 14*

1192 A735 3.10k multi 1.00 1.00

No. 1192 was printed in sheets of 25 + 5 labels.

Archaeological Museum, Split, 200th Anniv. — A736

2020, Aug. 17 Litho. *Perf. 14*

1193 A736 A multi 1.00 1.00

No. 1193 sold for 3.10k on day of issue.

Drone, Airplane, Train, Ship, Van and QR Code — A737

Serpentine Die Cut 11½

2020, Sept. 9 **Litho.**

Self-Adhesive

1194 A737 50k multi 15.50 15.50

Cryptocurrency stamp for Stamp Day. No. 1194 is on a credit-card piece of plastic and was sold in a protective cover.

Oliver Dragojevic (1947-2018), Singer — A738

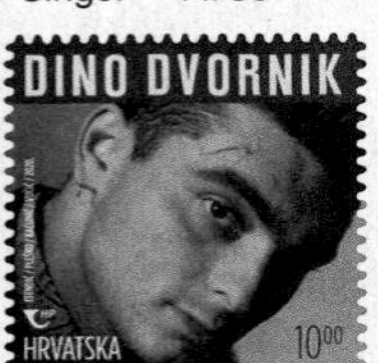

Dino Dvornik (1964-2008), Singer — A739

Toma Bebic (1935-90), Singer — A740

Serpentine Die Cut 11½

2020, Sept. 28 **Litho.**

Self-Adhesive

1195 A738 10k multi 3.25 3.25
1196 A739 10k black 3.25 3.25
1197 A740 10k multi 3.25 3.25
Nos. 1195-1197 (3) 9.75 9.75

Locomotives — A741

No. 1198: a, Locomotive JZ 642. b, Locomotive JZ 661.

2020, Oct. 5 **Litho.** ***Perf. 14***

1198 A741 6.50k Pair, #a-b 4.00 4.00

No. 1198 was printed in sheet containing 3 each of Nos. 1198a-1198b.

National Theater Building, Zagreb, 125th Anniv. A742

2020, Oct. 14 **Litho.** ***Perf. 14***

1199 A742 3.30k multi 1.00 1.00

Souvenir Sheet

Rocks — A743

No. 1200: a, Hraschina meteorite, denomination at UL. b, Lithothamnium limestone, denomination at UR.

2020, Oct. 22 **Litho.** ***Perf. 14***

1200 A743 5k Sheet of 2, #a-b 3.25 3.25

SEMI-POSTAL STAMPS

Catalogue values for unused stamps in this section are for Never Hinged items.

Types of Yugoslavia, 1941, Overprinted in Gold "NEZAVISNA / DRZAVA / HRVATSKA"

Perf. 11½

1941, May 10 **Unwmk.** **Engr.**

B1 SP80 1.50d + 1.50d bl blk 22.50 22.50
B2 SP81 4d + 3d choc 22.50 22.50

Panes of 16 stamps and 9 labels.

This overprint exists on Yugoslavia No. B124. Value $2,500.

In 1941, 5,000 sets of Yugoslavia Nos. 142-154 were overprinted "NEZAVISNA DRZAVA HRVATSKA 10. IV. 1941" and with a small shield in red or blue. Sold for double face value. Value: set, $550.

Costume of Sinj, Dalmatia — SP1

Designs (Costumes): 2k+2k, Travnik, Bosnia. 4k+4k, Turopolje, Croatia.

1941, Oct. 12 **Photo.** ***Perf. 10½x10***

B3 SP1 1.50k + 1.50k Prus bl & red 1.00 1.00
B4 SP1 2k + 2k ol brn & red 1.25 1.25
B5 SP1 4k + 4k brn lake & red 2.25 2.25
Nos. B3-B5 (3) 4.50 4.50

The surtax aided the Croatian Red Cross.

Nos. B3-B5 were issued in panes of 20 stamps and 5 labels.

Nos. B3-B5 exist with a special printer's mark in the design. The printer's mark appears on one stamp in one pane of the four in the printed sheet. Value, $35 each.

Soldiers with Arms of the Axis States — SP4

1941, Dec. 3 ***Perf. 11***

B6 SP4 4k + 2k blue 3.75 *4.00*

The surtax was used for Croatian Volunteers in the East.

Issued in panes of 100 stamps.

Model Plane — SP5

Model Plane — SP6

Designs: 3k+3k, Boy with model plane. 4k+4k, Model seaplane in flight.

1942, Mar. 25

B7 SP5 2k + 2k sepia 1.90 1.90
B8 SP6 2.50k + 2.50k dl grn 1.90 1.90
B9 SP5 3k + 3k brn car 1.90 1.90
B10 SP6 4k + 4k dp bl 1.90 1.90
Nos. B7-B10 (4) 7.60 7.60

Nos. B7-B10 were issued both in panes of 25 and in panes of 24 plus label.

Nos. B7-B10 exist with a special printer's mark in the design. The mark appears on one stamp in every pane. Value, $10

Values for used souvenir sheets are for those with special philatelic cancels. Faked postal cancellations on souvenir sheets are common, especially using cancellers stolen after WWII. Genuine postal cancellations are the exception and sell for much more. Expertization is recommended.

Souvenir Sheets

Perf. 11

B11 Sheet of 2 45.00 45.00
a. SP5 2k+8k brown carmine 15.00 15.00
b. SP5 3k+12k deep blue 15.00 15.00

Imperf

B12 Sheet of 2 45.00 45.00
a. SP5 2k+8k deep blue 15.00 15.00
b. SP5 3k+12k brown carmine 15.00 15.00

The sheets measure 125x110mm.

Aviation Exposition of Zagreb. The surtax aided society of Croatian Wings (Hrvatska Krila).

Nos. B11-B12 exist with colors of stamps and inscriptions transposed, with missing colors and with one stamp missing.

Nos. B11-B12 exist with a special printer's mark in the design. The mark typically appears on one stamp in a given pane.

Boy Trumpeters SP10

Triumphal Arch — SP11

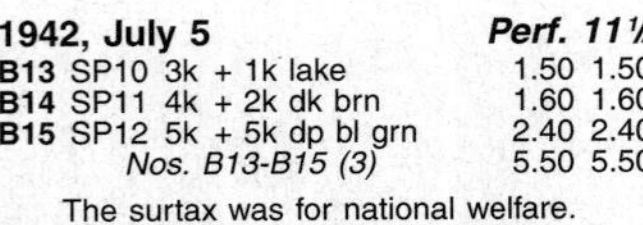

Mother and Child — SP12

1942, July 5 ***Perf. 11½***

B13 SP10 3k + 1k lake 1.50 1.50
B14 SP11 4k + 2k dk brn 1.60 1.60
B15 SP12 5k + 5k dp bl grn 2.40 2.40
Nos. B13-B15 (3) 5.50 5.50

The surtax was for national welfare.

Issued in panes of 25.

Nos. B13-B15 exist with a special printer's mark in the design. The printer's mark appears on one stamp in one pane of the four in the printed sheet. Value, $40 each.

Matthew Gubec SP13

Ante Starcevich SP14

SP15

1942, Nov. 22 ***Perf. 14½***

B16 SP13 3k + 6k dark red 1.00 1.00
B17 SP14 4k + 7k sepia 1.00 1.00

Souvenir Sheets

Perf. 12, Imperf.

B18 SP15 5k + 20k dull blue 24.00 24.00

Heroes of Senj, May 9, 1937. Nos. B16-B17 were printed in panes of 16 + 9 labels, each bearing a hero's name. The surtax aided the Natl. Youth Soc.

Sestine Peasant — SP16

Designs: 3k+1k, Slavonian peasant. 4k+2k, Bosnian peasant. 10k+5k, Dalmatian peasant. 13k+6k, Sestine peasant.

1942, Oct. 4 ***Perf. 11½***

B20 SP16 1.50k + 50b org brn & red 1.40 1.40
B21 SP16 3k + 1k dl pur & red 1.40 1.40
B22 SP16 4k + 2k dp bl & red 2.10 2.10
B23 SP16 10k + 5k dk ol bis & red 3.00 3.00
B24 SP16 13k + 6k rose lake & red 5.50 5.50
Nos. B20-B24 (5) 13.40 13.40

The surtax aided the Croatian Red Cross.

Issued in panes of 24 stamps plus label.

Croatian Labor Corpsman — SP20

Designs: 3k+3k, Corpsman with wheelbarrow. 7k+4k, Corpsman plowing.

1943, Jan. 17 Wmk. 278 *Perf. 11*

B25 SP20 2k + 1k ol gray & sepia 4.75 *5.00*
B26 SP20 3k + 3k brn & sepia 4.75 *5.00*
B27 SP20 7k + 4k gray bl & sepia 4.75 *5.00*
Nos. B25-B27 (3) 14.25 *15.00*

The surtax aided the State Labor Service (Drzavna Radna Sluzba). Issued in panes of 9.

Arms of Zagreb and "Golden Bull" — SP23

1943, Mar. 21 Unwmk.

B28 SP23 3.50k (+ 6.50k) ultra 4.50 *4.75*

700th anniversary of Zagreb's "Golden Bull," a Magna Carta of civic rights and privileges granted to the city in 1242 by King Bela because the Croats annihilated Tartar hordes at Grobnik.

Issued in panes of 8 with marginal inscriptions.

Ante Pavelich — SP24

1943, Apr. 10 *Perf. 13¾x14*

B29 SP24 5k + 3k copper red .60 .60
a. Sheetlet of 16 #B29 + 9 labels 12.00 12.00
B30 SP24 7k + 5k dark green .60 .60
a. Sheetlet of 16 #B30 + 9 labels 12.00 12.00

Surtax aided the National Youth Society.

Nos. B29-B30 were issued in panes of 100 stamps. Nos. B29a and B30a were issued Apr. 12 and are perf 14½.

Souvenir Sheets

1943, May 17 *Perf. 12, Imperf.*

B31 SP24 12k + 8k dp ultra 30.00 30.00

Sailor at Sea of Azov — SP26

Designs: 2k+1k, Flier at Sevastopol and Rzhev. 3.50k+1.50k, Infantrymen at Stalingrad. 9k+4.50k, Panzer Division at Don River.

1943, July 1 *Perf. 11*

B33 SP26 1k + 50b grn .40 .25
B34 SP26 2k + 1k dk red .40 .25
B35 SP26 3.50k + 1.50k dk bl .40 .25
B36 SP26 9k + 4.50k chestnut .40 .25
Nos. B33-B36 (4) 1.60 1.00

Souvenir Sheets

Perf. 11, Imperf.

B37 Sheet of 4 7.50 7.50
a. SP26 1k+50b dark blue 1.40 *1.40*
b. SP26 2k+1k green 1.40 *1.40*
c. SP26 3.50k+1.50k dk red brown 1.40 *1.40*
d. SP26 9k+4.50k bluish black 1.40 *1.40*

Surtax aided the National Youth Society. Issued to honor the Croatian Legion which fought with the Germans in Russia. The surtax aided the Legion.

Issued in panes of 100.

St. Mary's Church and Cistercian Cloister, Zagreb, in 1650 SP31

1943, Sept. 12 Engr. *Perf. 14½*

B39 SP31 18k + 9k dl gray vio 5.25 5.25

Souvenir Sheet

Perf. 12½

B40 SP31 18k + 9k blk brn 13.00 13.00

Croatian Phil. Soc. Exhibition at Zagreb.

No. B39 issued in pane of 40.

Nos. B39-B40 exist with a special printer's mark in the design. The printer's mark appears on one stamp in the pane for No. 39, value $30; the mark appears on one souvenir sheet of the six in the printed sheet for No. B40, value $52.50.

No. B39 Ovptd. in Red

1943, Sept. 12

B41 SP31 18k + 9k dl gray vio 12.00 *14.00*

Return to Croatia of the Dalmatian and Croatian coasts.

The overprint exists inverted, double, and double, one inverted.

No. B41 exists with a special printer's mark in the design. The mark typically appears on one stamp in a given pane.

Mother and Children — SP33

Nurse and Patient — SP34

1943, Oct. 3 Litho. *Perf. 11*

Cross in Red

B42 SP33 1k + 50b bl grn .75 .75
B43 SP33 2k + 1k bril car .75 .75
B44 SP33 3.50k + 1.50k brt bl .75 .75
B45 SP34 8k + 3k red brn .90 .90
B46 SP34 9k + 4k yel grn 1.00 1.00
B47 SP33 10k + 5k dp vio 1.00 1.00
B48 SP34 12k + 6k brt ultra 1.25 1.25
B49 SP33 12.50k + 6k dk brn 1.75 1.75
B50 SP34 18k + 8k brn org 2.00 2.00
B51 SP34 32k + 12k dk gray 3.25 3.25
Nos. B42-B51 (10) 13.40 13.40

The surtax aided the Croatian Red Cross. Issued in panes of 100.

Post Horn and Arms — SP35

Carrier Pigeon and Plane — SP36

Mercury — SP37

Winged Wheel — SP38

1944, Feb. 3

B52 SP35 7k + 3.50k ol bis & red .90 .90
a. Double impression of red —
B53 SP36 16k + 8k bl & dk bl .90 .90
B54 SP37 24k + 12k red & rose red .90 .90
B55 SP38 32k + 16k gray & red .90 .90
Nos. B52-B55 (4) 3.60 3.60

The surtax benefited communications and railway employees. Panes of 9.

St. Sebastian — SP39

War Invalids SP40

Statue of Ancient Croatian King — SP41

Death of King Peter Svacic, 1097 — SP42

1944, Feb. 15

B56 SP39 7k + 3.50k org red & rose car 1.00 1.00
B57 SP40 16k + 8k yel grn & dk grn 1.00 1.00
B58 SP41 24k + 12k yel brn & red 1.00 1.00
B59 SP42 32k + 16k bl & dk bl 1.00 1.00
Nos. B56-B59 (4) 4.00 4.00

The surtax aided wounded war victims.

Issued in panes of eight stamps, with marginal inscriptions and a central label picturing St. Sebastian.

Black Legion in Combat — SP43

Guarding the Drina — SP44

Jure Francetic — SP45

1944, May 22 Photo. *Imperf.*

B60 SP43 3.50k + 1.50k brn red .25 .25
B61 SP44 12.50k + 6.50k slate bl .25 .25
B62 SP45 18k + 9k olive brn .25 .25
Nos. B60-B62 (3) .75 .75

Third anniversary of Croatian independence.

The surtax aided the National Youth Society. Panes of 20.

Perf. 14½

B63 SP45 12.50k + 287.50k int blk 12.00 *14.50*

Issued to commemorate Jure Francetic. Issued in pane of 30.

Labor Corpsmen Marching SP46

Corpsman Digging SP47

Designs: 18k+9k, Officer instructing corpsman. 32k+16k, Pavelich reviewing Labor Corps. Panes of 8 plus label.

Perf. 11½, 12½, 14½

1944, Aug. 20 Engr.

B65 SP46 3.50k + 1k dk red .50 .50
B66 SP47 12.50k + 6k sepia .50 .50
B67 SP47 18k + 9k dk bl .50 .50
B68 SP47 32k + 16k gray grn .50 .50
Nos. B65-B68 (4) 2.00 2.00

Nos. B68 exists only perf 12½, while B65-B67 exist perf 11½, 12½ or 14½. Values are for copies perf 11½ or 12½. Values Nos. B65-B67 perf 14½, $5 each unused or used.

Souvenir Sheet

Perf. 12½

B69 SP47 32k + 16k dk brn, *cr* 4.50 *5.00*

The surtax aided the State Labor Service (Drzavna Radna Sluzba).

Palm Leaf — SP51

1944, Nov. 12 Litho. *Perf. 11*

B70 SP51 2k + 1k dl grn & red .45 .45
B71 SP51 3.50k + 1.50k car lake & red .45 .45
B72 SP51 12.50k + 6k ind & red .45 .45
Nos. B70-B72 (3) 1.35 1.35

The surtax aided the Croatian Red Cross. Panes of 16.

Men of Storm Division — SP52

70k+70k, Soldiers of Storm Division in action. 100k+100k, Storm Division emblem.

1944 Unwmk. Litho. *Perf. 11*

No.	Design	Description	Unused	Used
B73	SP52	50k + 50k brick red	175.00	*190.00*
B74	SP52	70k + 70k sepia	175.00	*190.00*
B75	SP52	100k + 100k chlky, pale & dp bl	175.00	*190.00*
		Nos. B73-B75 (3)	525.00	*570.00*

Nos. B73-B75 issued in panes of 20.

Souvenir Sheet

No.		Description	Unused	Used
B76		Sheet of 3	1,650.	1,650.
a.		SP52 50k + 50k brick red	400.	400.
b.		SP52 70k + 70k sepia	400.	400.
c.		SP52 100k + 100k chalky, pale & deep blue	400.	400.

Nos. B76a to B76c are inscribed "O. A." in brick red at right below design. The sheet measures 216x132mm. The surtax aided the First Croatian Storm Division. Counterfeits are plentiful.

Postman SP55

Telephone Line Repairman SP56

24k+12k, Switchboard operator. 50k+25k, 100k+50k, Postman delivering parcel.

1945 Photo.

No.	Design	Description	Unused	Used
B77	SP55	3.50k + 1.50k sl gray	.40	.40
B78	SP56	12.50k + 6k brn car	.40	.40
B79	SP56	24k + 12k dk grn	.40	.40
B80	SP56	50k + 25k brn vio	.40	.40
		Nos. B77-B80 (4)	1.60	1.60

Souvenir Sheet

No.	Design	Description	Unused	Used
B81	SP56	100k + 50k dp brn	11.00	11.00

The surtax on #B77-B81 aided employees of the P.T.T. Panes of 8.

Famous Croatians SP60

No. B100, Ban Josip Jelacic (1801-59). No. B101, Dr. Ante Starcevic (1823-96). 7d + 3d, Stjepan Radic (1871-1928).

1992 Litho. *Perf. 11x10½*

No.	Design	Description	Unused	Used
B100	SP60	4d +2d multi	.65	.65
B101	SP60	4d +2d multi	.65	.65

Perf. 14

No.	Design	Description	Unused	Used
B102	SP60	7d +3d multi	.65	.65
		Nos. B100-B102 (3)	1.95	1.95

Issued: No. B100, 2/1; No. B101, 3/4; No. B102, 4/2.

The surcharge on Nos. B100-B102 was initially an obligatory tax on all internal and overseas mail. From May 15, 1992, these stamps were valid for postage at their 6d or 10d face values.

AIR POST STAMPS

Catalogue values for unused stamps in this section are for Never Hinged items.

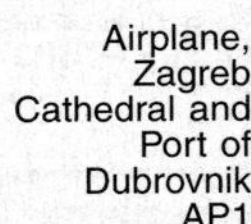

Airplane, Zagreb Cathedral and Port of Dubrovnik AP1

Airplane Over Ruins of Diocletian's Palace, Split — AP2

Coat of Arms, Airplane, Zagreb Cathedral and Pula Amphitheatre AP3

Paper Airplane Made From Picture of Osijek Cathedral AP4

1991-92 Litho. *Perf. 11x10½*

No.	Design	Description	Unused	Used
C1	AP1	1d multicolored	*.50*	.50
a.		Perf. 14	.50	.50
C2	AP2	2d multicolored	*1.50*	.50
a.		Perf. 14	.50	.50
C3	AP3	3d multicolored	*.50*	.50
C4	AP4	4d multicolored	*.50*	.50
		Nos. C1-C4 (4)	*3.00*	2.00

Issued: No. C1, 9/9/91; No. C1a, 6/24/92; No. C2, 10/9/91; No. C2a, 1992; No. C3, 11/20/91; No. C4, 2/14/92.

Miniature Sheet

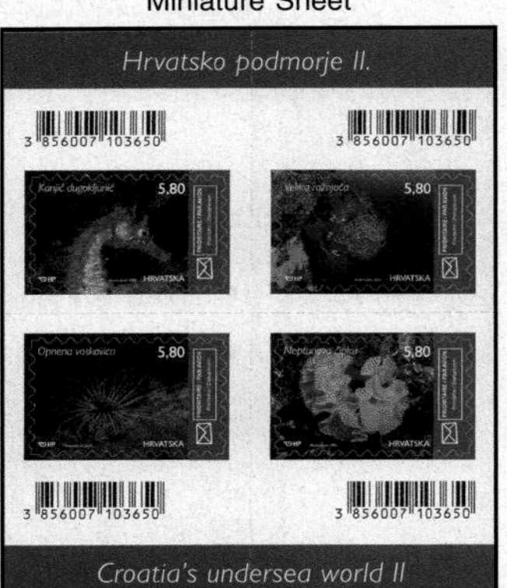

Marine Life — AP5

No. C5: a, Long-snouted seahorse (konjic dugokljunic). b, Violescent sea-whip (velika roznjaca). c, Cylinder anemone (opnena voskovica). d, Neptune's lace (neptunova cipka).

Serpentine Die Cut 5½x5¼

2015, June 15 Litho.

Self-Adhesive

No.	Design	Description	Unused	Used
C5	AP5	Sheet of 4	7.00	
a.-d.		5.80k Any single	1.75	1.75

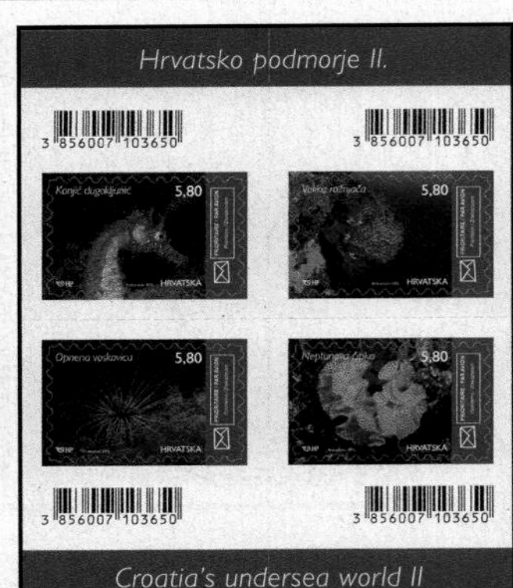

Marine Life — AP5

No.C6: a, Crv cjevas (Bispira volutacornis). b, Pjegavi jezinac (Sphaerechinus granularis). c, Pjegavi straznjoskrznjak (Peltodoris atromaculata). d, Murina (Muraena helena).

Serpentine Die Cut 5½x5¼

2019, May 15 Litho.

Self-Adhesive

No.	Design	Description	Unused	Used
C6	AP5	Sheet of 4	10.50	
a.-d.		8.60k Any single	2.60	2.60

POSTAGE DUE STAMPS

Yugoslavia Nos. J28-J32 Overprinted in Black

1941, Apr. 26 Unwmk. *Perf. 12½*

No.	Design	Description	Unused	Used
J1	D4	50p violet	.40	*.65*
a.		Double overprint	150.00	
b.		50p rose violet	9.00	*18.00*
c.		As "b," double overprint		200.00
J2	D4	1d deep magenta	.40	*.65*
a.		Inverted overprint	200.00	
b.		Double overprint		*300.00*
J3	D4	2d deep blue	10.00	*20.00*
a.		Double overprint	300.00	
J4	D4	5d orange	1.25	*2.00*
a.		Double overprint	300.00	
J5	D4	10d chocolate	6.00	*12.00*
		Nos. J1-J5 (5)	18.05	*35.30*
		Set, never hinged	40.00	

Counterfeit overprints exist, particularly of Nos. J3 and J5.

D1

1941, Sept. 12 Litho. *Perf. 11*

No.	Design	Description	Unused	Used
J6	D1	50b carmine lake	.25	*.50*
J7	D1	1k carmine lake	.25	*.50*
J8	D1	2k carmine lake	.30	*.70*
J9	D1	5k carmine lake	.50	*1.00*
J10	D1	10k carmine lake	.75	*1.40*
		Nos. J6-J10 (5)	2.05	*4.10*
		Set, never hinged	5.00	

D2

1943 *Perf. 11½, 12x12½, 12½*

Size: 24x24mm

No.	Design	Description	Unused	Used
J11	D2	50b lt blue & gray	.25	*.25*
J12	D2	1k lt blue & gray	.25	*.25*
J13	D2	2k lt blue & gray	.25	*.25*
J14	D2	4k lt blue & gray	.25	*.35*
J15	D2	5k lt blue & gray	.25	*.40*
J16	D2	6k lt blue & gray	.25	*.45*
J17	D2	10k blue & indigo	.25	*.40*
J18	D2	15k blue & indigo	.25	*1.10*
J19	D2	20k blue & indigo	.65	*1.60*
		Nos. J11-J19 (9)	2.65	*5.05*
		Set, never hinged	5.00	

1942, July 30 *Perf. 10½, 11½*

Size: 25x24¼mm

No.	Design	Description	Unused	Used
J20	D2	50b lt blue & gray	.25	*.40*
J21	D2	1k lt blue & gray	.25	*.50*
J22	D2	2k lt blue & gray	.25	*.50*
J23	D2	5k lt blue & gray	.25	*.50*
J24	D2	10k lt blue & blue	.65	*1.10*
J25	D2	20k lt blue & blue	.90	*1.60*
		Nos. J20-J25 (6)	2.55	*4.60*
		Set, never hinged	6.00	

Nos. J21-J25 exist both perf 10½ and 11½. No. J20 exists only perf 11½.

OFFICIAL STAMPS

Croatian Coat of Arms
O1 O2

1942-43 Unwmk. Litho.

Ordinary Paper

Perf. 11½

No.	Design	Description	Unused	Used
O1	O1	25b rose lake	.25	.25
O2	O1	50b slate blk	.25	.25
O3	O1	75b gray grn	.25	.25
O4	O1	1k orange brn	.25	.25
O5	O1	2k turq blue	1.10	*1.10*
O6	O1	3k vermilion	.25	.25
O7	O1	4k brown vio	.25	.25
O8	O1	5k ultra, *thin paper*	.25	*.40*
O9	O1	6k brt violet	.25	.25
O10	O1	10k lt green	.25	*.30*
O11	O1	12k brown rose	.25	*.35*
O12	O1	20k dark blue	.25	*.40*
O13	O2	30k brn vio & gray	.25	*.40*
O14	O2	40k vio blk & gray	.30	*.50*
O15	O2	50k brn lake & gray	.65	*1.00*
O16	O2	100k black & pink	.65	*1.00*
		Nos. O1-O16 (16)	5.70	*7.20*
		Set, never hinged	8.00	

Perf. 10½

No.	Design	Description	Unused	Used
O1a	O1	25b rose lake	.25	.25
O2a	O1	50b slate blk	.25	.25
O3a	O1	75b gray grn	.25	.25
O4a	O1	1k orange brn	.25	.25
O5a	O1	2k turq blue	1.10	*2.00*
O6a	O1	3k vermilion	.25	.25
O7a	O1	4k brown vio	.25	.25
O8a	O1	5k ultra	.95	*1.75*
O9a	O1	6k brt violet	1.40	*2.50*
O10a	O1	10k lt green	.25	.25
O11a	O1	12k brown rose	1.25	*2.25*
O12a	O1	20k dark blue	1.25	*2.25*
O13a	O2	30k brn vio & gray	.25	*.40*
O14a	O2	40k vio blk & gray	.30	*.50*
O15a	O2	50k brn lake & gray	.65	*1.00*
O16a	O2	100k black & pink	.65	*1.00*
		Nos. O1a-O16a (16)	9.55	*15.40*
		Set, never hinged	15.00	

1943-44 Thin Paper *Perf. 11½*

No.	Design	Description	Unused	Used
O17	O1	25b claret	.25	.25
O18	O1	50b gray	.25	.25
O19	O1	75b dull green	.25	.25
O20	O1	1k orange brn	.25	.25
O21	O1	2k slate blue	.25	.25
O22	O1	3.50k car rose	.25	.25
a.		Ordinary paper	3.00	*3.00*
O23	O1	6k brt red vio	.25	.25
O24	O1	12.50k deep orange	.25	.25
a.		Ordinary paper	2.00	*2.00*
		Set, never hinged	1.50	

POSTAL TAX STAMPS

Catalogue values for unused stamps in this section are for Never Hinged items.

Nurse and Soldier — PT1

Unwmk.

1942, Oct. 4 Litho. *Perf. 11*

RA1 PT1 1k olive grn & red .85 .80

The tax aided the Croatian Red Cross. Issued in sheets of 24 plus label.

No. RA1 can be found with a red cross printed on the nurse's hat. The original design included this element, but it was removed from the final approved design. Early printings of No. RA1, probably trial printings, included the red cross.

Wounded Soldier — PT2

1943, Oct. 3

RA2 PT2 2k blue & red .70 .70

The tax aided the Croatian Red Cross.

Ruins — PT3

Wounded Soldier — PT4

1944, Jan. 1 Photo. *Perf. 12*

RA3 PT3 1k dk slate green .25 .25
RA4 PT4 2k carmine lake .30 .30
RA5 PT4 5k black .35 .35
RA6 PT4 10k deep blue .55 .40
RA7 PT4 20k brown 1.10 .90
Nos. RA3-RA7 (5) 2.55 2.20

Interior of Zagreb Cathedral PT10

1991, Apr. 1 Litho. *Perf. 14*

RA20 PT10 1.20d black & gold .65 .55
a. Perf. 11x10½ .85 .80
b. Perf. 11 15.00 12.00
c. Imperf .90 .90

Worker's Fund. Required on mail during April 1991.

For surcharges see Nos. 100, 100a.

Shrine of the Virgin, 700th Anniv. PT11

1991, May 16 *Perf. 10½x11*

RA21 PT11 1.70d multicolored .80 .65
a. Imperf 1.25 1.10

Workers' Fund. Required on mail May 16-31.

Croatian Arms Type of 1992

1991, July 1 *Perf. 11x10½*

RA22 A37 2.20d multicolored .80 .70
a. Imperf 1.25 1.00

Required on mail during July.

Members of Parliament PT12

1991, Aug. 1 *Perf. 11x10½*

RA23 PT12 2.20d multicolored .80 .70
a. Imperf 1.25 1.00

Worker's Fund. Required on mail during Aug.

Red Cross and Tuberculosis PT13

1991, Sept 14 *Perf. 11*

RA24 PT13 2.20d blue & red .50 .45

Required on mail Sept. 14-21.

Re-erection of Ban Josip Jelacic Equestrian Statue, Zagreb PT14

1991, Nov. 1 *Perf. 11x10½*

RA25 PT14 2.20d multicolored .80 .70
a. Imperf. 1.25 1.00

Worker's Fund. Required on mail during Nov.

New Constitution PT15

1991, Dec. 2 Litho. *Perf. 10¾x10½*

Language of Inscription

RA26 PT15 2.20d English *3.25 3.00*
RA27 PT15 2.20d Croatian *1.15 1.00*
RA28 PT15 2.20d French *3.25 3.00*
RA29 PT15 2.20d German *3.25 3.00*
RA30 PT15 2.20d Russian *3.25 3.00*
RA31 PT15 2.20d Spanish *3.25 3.00*
a. Vert. strip, #RA26-RA31 *35.00 35.00*
Nos. RA26-RA31 (6) 17.40 16.00

Nos RA26-RA31 were printed in sheet containing 15 of No. RA27, 2 each of the other stamps and five labels. Obligatory on mail Dec. 2-31.

Sheet exists imperf. Value $225.

"VUKOVAR" with Barbed Wire — PT16

1992, Jan. 1 Litho. *Perf. 11x10½*

RA32 PT16 2.20d black & brown 1.15 .90
a. Imperf. 1.60 1.40

Vukovar Refugee's Fund. Required on mail during Jan.

Red Cross PT17

Red Cross and Solidarity PT18

1992 *Perf. 11*

RA33 PT17 3d red & black .50 .50
RA34 PT18 3d red & black .30 .30

Issued: No. RA33, May 8. No. RA34, June 1.

No. RA33 was required on mail May 8-15; No. RA34, June 1-7.

Madonna of Bistrica — PT19

1992, Aug. 1 Litho. *Perf. 14*

RA35 PT19 5d blue & gold .45 .40

Required on mail, Aug. 1-8.

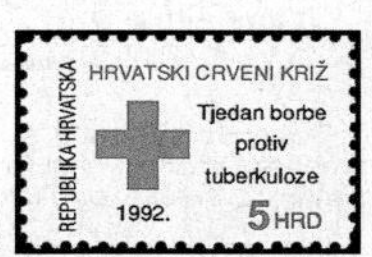

Red Cross — PT20

1992, Sept. 21 Litho. *Perf. 11*

RA36 PT20 5d black & red .50 .30

Required on mail Sept. 14-21.

St. George Slaying Dragon PT21

1992, Nov. 4 *Perf. 14*

RA37 PT21 15d multicolored .50 .30

Cancer Research League. Required on mail Nov. 4-11.

See No. RA43.

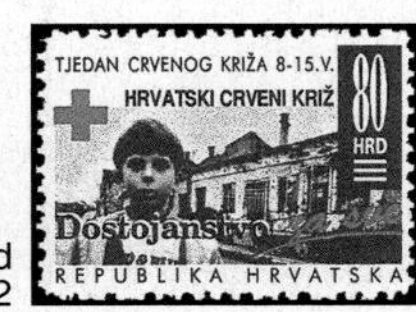

Red Cross — PT22

1993, May 8 Litho. *Rough Perf. 11*

RA38 PT22 80d black & red .50 .30

Required on mail May 8-15.

Red Cross and Solidarity PT23

1993, June 1

RA39 PT23 100d black & red .50 .30

Required on mail June 1-7.

Cardinal Stepinac (1898-1960) PT24

1993, July 15 Litho. *Perf. 14*

RA40 PT24 150d multicolored .50 .30

Required on mail July 15-22.

Zrinski-Frankopan Foundation — PT25

Design: 200d, Gen. Peter Zrinski (1621-1671), Politician and Fran Krsto Frankopan, Count of Tersat (1643-1671), Poet.

1993, Aug. 12 Litho. *Perf. 14*

RA41 PT25 200d gray & blue .50 .30

Required on mail Aug. 12-19.

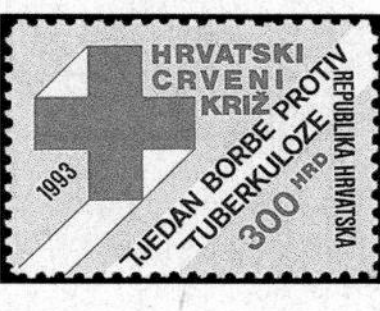

Red Cross Campaign Against Tuberculosis PT26

1993, Sept. 14 Litho. *Perf. 11*

RA42 PT26 300d gray, red & black .50 .45

Required on mail Sept. 14-21.

St. George Slaying Dragon Type of 1992

1993, Oct. 11 Litho. *Perf. 14*

RA43 PT21 400d multicolored .45 .40

Cancer Research League. Required on mail Oct. 11-31.

Save the Children of Croatia PT27

1993, Nov. 1 *Perf. 13½x14*

RA44 PT27 400d multicolored .50 .45

Required on mail Nov. 1-30.

Croatian Red Cross — PT28

1994, May 5 Litho. *Perf. 11*

RA45 PT28 500d multicolored .50 .45

Required on mail May 8-15.

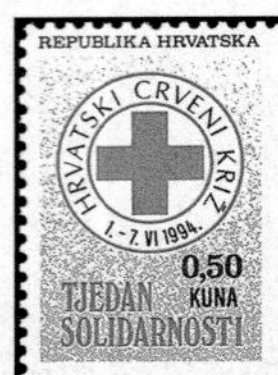

Red Cross Solidarity — PT29

1994, May 5 **Litho.** ***Perf. 11***

RA46 PT29 50 l multicolored .50 .45

Required on mail June 1-7.

Ludberg Church — PT30

1994, July 15 ***Perf. 14***

RA47 PT30 50 l multicolored .50 .30

Required on mail July 15-22.

Save the Children of Croatia — PT31

1994, Aug. 16 **Litho.** ***Perf. 14***

RA48 PT31 50 l multicolored .50 .30

Required on mail Aug. 16-29.

St. George Slaying Dragon — PT32

1994, Sept. 1

RA49 PT32 50 l multicolored .50 .30

Cancer Research League. Required on mail Sept. 1-8.

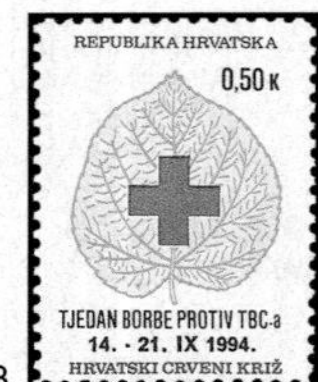

PT33

1994, Sept. 14 ***Perf. 11***

RA50 PT33 50 l blk, grn & red .50 .30

Red Cross Campaign against Tuberculosis. Required on mail Sept. 14-21.

PT34

1994, Oct. 15 **Litho.** ***Perf. 14***

RA51 PT34 50 l multicolored .50 .35

Town of Slavonski Brod, 750th anniv.

Homage to Olympia, by Ivan Lackovic PT35

Intl. Olympic Committee, Cent. — PT36

Designs: a, Tennis. b, Soccer. c, Basketball. d, Team handball. e, Canoeing, kayaking. f, Water polo. g, Track and field. h, Gymnastics.

1994, Nov. 2 **Litho.** ***Perf. 14***

RA52 PT35 50 l Pair, #a.-b. 1.40 1.25

RA53 PT36 50 l Sheet of 8, #a.-h. 5.75 5.75

RA54 PT36 50 l Sheet of 8, #a.-h. 5.75 5.75

Nos. RA52b, RA53a, RA53d-RA53e, RA53h, RA54b-RA54c, RA54f-RA54g have IOC centennial emblem. Others have emblem of Croatian Olympic Committee.

Required on mail Nov. 2-15.

Natl. Olympic Committee PT37

Designs: a, Rowing. b, Pétanque. c, Monument to Drazen Petrovic, Olympic Park, Lausanne. d, Tennis. e, Basketball.

1995, Apr. 17 **Litho.** ***Perf. 14***

RA55 PT37 50 l Strip of 5, #a.-e. 2.00 2.00

Required on mail Apr. 17-30.

Red Cross Stamps — PT38

1995, May 8 ***Perf. 11***

RA56 PT38 50 l multicolored .50 .30

Required on mail May 8-15.

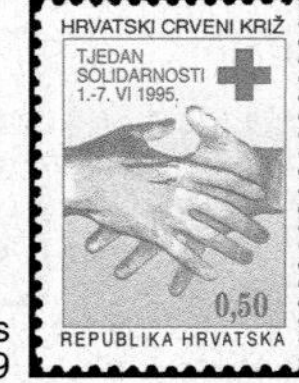

Red Cross Stamps — PT39

1995, June 1

RA57 PT39 50 l multicolored .50 .30

Required on mail June 1-7.

Sts. Peter and Paul Cathedral, Osijek — PT40

1995, July 17 ***Perf. 14***

RA58 PT40 65 l multicolored .50 .40

Required on mail July 17-30.

Holy Mother of Freedom PT41

Design: No. RA59, Like No. RA60, but with black surcharge on white panel. #RA60, Croatian Pieta, by Ivan Lackovic. #RA61, Gedenkstatte Church Project.

1995, Aug. 14 **Litho.** ***Perf. 14***

RA59 PT41 65 l on 50 l multi 2.50 2.50

RA60 PT41 65 l multicolored .55 .50

RA61 PT41 65 l multicolored .55 .50

Nos. RA59-RA61 (3) 3.60 3.50

No. RA59 not issued without surcharge. Examples without surcharge are printer's waste. Required on mail Aug. 14-27.

Red Cross and Tuberculosis — PT42

1995, Sept. 14 **Litho.** ***Perf. 11***

RA62 PT42 65 l multicolored .50 .40

Required on mail Sept. 14-21.

Save the Croatian Children — PT43

1995, Oct. 16 ***Perf. 14***

RA63 PT43 65 l multicolored .50 .40

Required on mail Oct. 16-29.

PT44

Performance scene: a, Woman seated at top of steps. b, Gathering of people. c, People, large statue in background.

1995, Oct. 16

RA64 PT44 65 l Strip of 3, #a.-c. 1.50 1.50

Croatian Natl. Theater, Zagreb, cent. No. RA64 has continuous design. Required on mail 10/16-29.

Fight Against Drugs — PT45

1995, Nov. 6 **Litho.** ***Perf. 14***

RA65 PT45 65 l multicolored .50 .35

Required on mail Nov. 20-30.

PT46

1995, Nov. 20 **Litho.** ***Perf. 14x13¾***

RA66 PT46 65 l multicolored .50 .35

Croatian Anti-Cancer League. Required on mail Nov. 20-30.

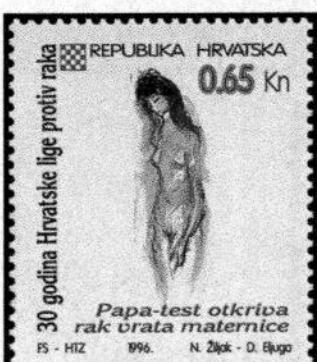

PT47

1996, Feb. 15 **Litho.** ***Perf. 14x13½***

RA67 PT47 65 l multicolored .50 .35

Croatian Anti-Cancer League. Required on mail Feb. 15-28.

PT48

1996, Mar. 18 **Litho.** ***Perf. 14***

RA68 PT48 65 l multicolored .50 .35

Sanctuary of the Virgin Mary of Bistrica. Required on mail Mar. 18-31.

Croatian Olympic Committee PT49

1996, Apr. 17 **Litho.** ***Perf. 14***

RA69 PT49 65 l multi .60 .35

No. RA69 exists imperf. and in booklets, which were not placed on sale. Required on mail Apr. 17-30.

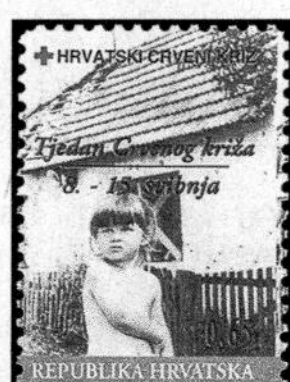

Red Cross — PT50

1996, May 8 **Litho.** ***Perf. 11***

RA70 PT50 65 l multicolored .50 .35

Required on mail May 8-15.

Red Cross Solidarity Week — PT51

1996, June 6 Litho. *Perf. 11*
RA71 PT51 65 l multicolored .50 .35

Required on mail June 1-7.

Croatian Children — PT52

1996, June 14 Litho. *Perf. 14x13½*
RA72 PT52 65 l multicolored .50 .35

Required on mail 6/14-27.

PT53

1996, July 3 Litho. *Perf. 14*
RA73 PT53 65 l multicolored .50 .35

Osijek, 800th anniv. Required on mail July 3-16.

PT54

1996, July 17 Litho. *Perf. 14*
RA74 PT54 65 l multicolored .50 .35

Renovation of Dakovo Cathedral. Required on mail July 17-30.

Split, 1700th Anniv. — PT55

1996, Aug. 1 Litho. *Perf. 14*
RA75 PT55 65 l multicolored .50 .35

Required on mail Aug. 1-14.

Aid to Vukovar — PT56

1996, Aug. 16 Litho. *Perf. 14x13½*
RA76 PT56 65 l multicolored .50 .35

Required on mail 8/16-29.

Fight Against Drugs — PT57

1996, Sept. 1 Litho. *Perf. 14*
RA77 PT57 65 l multicolored .55 .35

Required on mail Sept. 1-12.

PT58

1996, Sept. 14 Litho. *Perf. 11*
RA78 PT58 65 l multicolored .50 .35

Red Cross Tuberculosis Week. Required on mail Sept. 14-21.

PT59

1996, Oct. 10 Litho. *Perf. 14*
RA79 PT59 65 l multicolored .55 .35

Isolation of insulin, 75th anniv. Required on mail Oct. 10-17.

PT60

1996, Nov. 11 Litho. *Perf. 14*
RA80 PT60 65 l multicolored .50 .35

Remete pilgrimage. Required on mail Nov. 11-24.

PT61

1997, Jan. 6 Litho. *Perf. 14*
RA81 PT61 65 l multicolored .50 .35

Antun Mihanovic (1796-1861), natl. anthem lyricist. Required on mail Jan. 6-26.

House of Dr. Ante Starcevic PT62

1997, Jan. 27 Litho. *Perf. 14*
RA82 PT62 65 l multicolored .50 .35

Required on mail Jan. 27-Feb. 14.

PT63

1997, Feb. 15 Litho. *Perf. 14*
RA83 PT63 65 l multicolored .50 .35

Croatian Anti-Cancer League. Required on mail Feb. 15-28.

Red Cross — PT64

1997, May 8 Litho. *Perf. 10½x11*
RA84 PT64 65 l multicolored .50 .35
a. Perf 10½ .50 .35
b. Perf 11 *35.00*

Required on mail May 8-15.

Numerous charity stamps were issued between 1997 and 2001, but their use on mail was not obligatory.

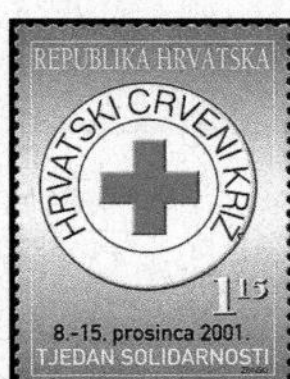

Red Cross Solidarity Week — PT65

2001, Dec. 8 Litho. *Perf. 14*
RA85 PT65 1.15k red & black 1.25 1.00

Obligatory on mail Dec. 8-15.

Red Cross Week — PT66

2002, May 8
RA86 PT66 1.15k multi 1.25 1.10

Obligatory on mail May 8-15.

Red Cross Anti-Tuberculosis Week — PT67

2002, Sept. 14
RA87 PT67 1.15k multi 1.25 1.00

Obligatory on mail Sept. 14-21.

Red Cross Solidarity Week — PT68

2002, Dec. 8
RA88 PT68 1.15k multi 1.25 1.00

Obligatory on mail Dec. 8-15.

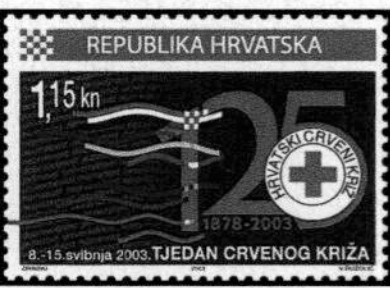

Red Cross Week — PT69

2003, May 8
RA89 PT69 1.15k multi 1.25 1.10

Obligatory on mail May 8-15.

Red Cross Anti-Tuberculosis Week — PT70

2003, Sept. 14
RA90 PT70 1.15k multi 1.25 1.10

Obligatory on mail Sept. 14-21.

Red Cross Solidarity Week — PT71

2003, Dec. 8
RA91 PT71 1.15k multi 1.25 1.10

Obligatory on mail Dec. 8-15.

Red Cross Week — PT72

2004, May 8
RA92 PT72 1.15k multi 1.25 1.10

Obligatory on mail May 8-15.

Red Cross Anti-Tuberculosis Week — PT73

2004, Sept. 14
RA93 PT73 1.15k multi .50 .50

Obligatory on mail Sept. 14-21.

Red Cross Solidarity Week — PT74

2004, Dec. 8
RA94 PT74 1.15k multi .50 .50
Obligatory on mail Dec. 8-15.

Red Cross Week — PT75

2005, May 8 Litho. *Perf. 14*
RA95 PT75 1.15k multi .60 .60
Obligatory on mail May 8-15.

Red Cross Anti-Tuberculosis Week — PT76

2005, Sept. 14
RA96 PT76 1.15k multi .50 .50
Obligatory on mail Sept. 14-21.

Red Cross Solidarity Week — PT77

2005, Dec. 8
RA97 PT77 1.15k multi .50 .50
Obligatory on mail Dec. 8-15.

Red Cross Week — PT78

2006, May 8 Litho. *Perf. 14*
RA98 PT78 1.15k multi 1.25 1.25
Obligatory on mail May 8-15.

Red Cross Anti-Tuberculosis Week — PT79

2006, Sept. 14
RA99 PT79 1.15k multi 1.25 1.25
Obligatory on mail Sept. 14-21.

Red Cross Solidarity Week — PT80

2006, Dec. 8
RA100 PT80 1.15k multi 1.25 1.25
Obligatory on mail Dec. 8-15.

Red Cross Week — PT81

2007, May 8 Litho. *Perf. 14¼*
RA101 PT81 1.15k multi — —
Obligatory on mail May 8-15.

Red Cross Anti-Tuberculosis Week — PT82

2007, Sept. 14 Litho. *Perf. 14¼*
RA102 PT82 1.15k multi — —
Obligatory on mail Sept. 14-21.

Red Cross Solidarity Week — PT83

2007, Dec. 8 Litho. *Perf. 14¼*
RA103 PT83 1.15k multi — —
Obligatory on mail Dec. 8-15.

Red Cross Week — PT84

2008, May 8 Litho. *Perf. 14¼*
RA104 PT84 1.15k multi — —
Obligatory on mail May 8-15.

Red Cross Anti-Tuberculosis Week — PT85

2008, Sept. 14 Litho. *Perf. 14¼*
RA105 PT85 1.15k multi .45 .45
Obligatory on mail Sept. 14-21.

Red Cross Solidarity Week — PT86

2008, Dec. 8 Litho. *Perf. 14¼*
RA106 PT86 1.15k multi — —
Obligatory on mail Dec. 8-15.

Red Cross Week — PT87

2009, May 8 Litho. *Perf. 14¼*
RA107 PT87 1.75k multi — —
Obligatory on mail May 8-15.

Red Cross Anti-Tuberculosis Week — PT88

2009, Sept. 14 Litho. *Perf. 14¼*
RA108 PT88 1.75k multi — —
Obligatory on mail Sept. 14-21.

Red Cross Solidarity Week — PT89

2009, Dec. 8 Litho. *Perf. 14¼*
RA109 PT89 1.75k multi — —
Obligatory on mail Dec. 8-15.

Red Cross Week — PT90

2010, May 8 Litho. *Perf. 14¼*
RA110 PT90 1.55k on 1.75k multi — —
Obligatory on mail May 8-15. No. RA110 was not issued without surcharge.

Red Cross Anti-Tuberculosis Week — PT91

2010, Sept. 14 Litho. *Perf. 14¼*
RA111 PT91 1.55k multi — —
Obligatory on mail Sept. 14-21.

Red Cross Solidarity Week — PT92

2010, Dec. 8 Litho. *Perf. 14¼*
RA112 PT92 1.55k multi — —
Obligatory on mail Dec. 8-15.

Red Cross Week — PT93

2011, May 8 Litho. *Perf. 14¼*
RA113 PT93 1.55k multi — —
Obligatory on mail May 8-15.

Red Cross Anti-Tuberculosis Week — PT94

2011, Sept. 14 Litho. *Perf. 14¼*
RA114 PT94 1.55k multi — —
Obligatory on mail Sept. 14-21.

Red Cross Solidarity Week — PT95

2011, Dec. 8 Litho. *Perf. 14¼*
RA115 PT95 1.55k multi — —
Obligatory on mail Dec. 8-15.

Red Cross Week — PT96

2012, May 8 Litho. *Perf. 14¼*
RA116 PT96 1.55k multi — —
Obligatory on mail May 8-15.

Red Cross Anti-Tuberculosis Week — PT97

2012, Sept. 14 Litho. *Perf. 14¼*
RA117 PT97 1.55k multi — —
Obligatory on mail Sept. 14-21.

Red Cross Solidarity Week — PT98

2012, Dec. 8 Litho. ***Perf. 14¼***
RA118 PT98 1.55k multi — —
Obligatory on mail Dec. 8-15.

Red Cross Week — PT99

2013, May 8 Litho. ***Perf. 14¼***
RA119 PT99 1.55k multi — —
Obligatory on mail May 8-15.

Red Cross Anti-Tuberculosis Week — PT100

2013, Sept. 14 Litho. ***Perf. 14¼***
RA120 PT100 1.55k multi — —
Obligatory on mail Sept. 14-21.

Red Cross Solidarity Week PT101

2013, Dec. 8 Litho. ***Perf. 14¼***
RA121 PT101 1.55k multi — —
Obligatory on mail Dec. 8-15.

Red Cross Week — PT102

2014, May 8 Litho. ***Perf. 14***
RA122 PT102 1.55k multi — —
Obligatory on mail May 8-15.

Red Cross Anti-Tuberculosis Week — PT103

2014, Sept. 14 Litho. ***Perf. 14***
RA123 PT103 1.55k multi —
Obligatory on mail Sept. 14-21.

Red Cross Anti-Tuberculosis Week — PT106

2015, Sept. 14 Litho. ***Perf. 14***
RA126 PT106 1.55k multi — —
Obligatory on mail Sept. 14-21.

Red Cross Solidarity Week — PT107

2015, Dec. 8 Litho. ***Perf. 14***
RA127 PT107 1.55k multi — —
Obligatory on mail Dec. 8-15.

Red Cross Week — PT108

2016, May 8 Litho. ***Perf. 14***
RA128 PT108 1.55k multi — —
20th National Youth Competition. Obligatory on mail May 8-15.

Red Cross Anti-Tuberculosis Week — PT109

2016, Sept. 14 Litho. ***Perf. 14***
RA129 PT109 1.55k multi — —
Obligatory on mail Sept. 14-21.

Red Cross Solidarity Week — PT110

2016, Dec. 8 Litho. ***Perf. 14***
RA130 PT110 1.55k multi — —
Obligatory on mail Dec. 8-15.

Red Cross Week — PT111

2017, May 8 Litho. ***Perf. 14***
RA131 PT111 1.55k multi — —
Obligatory on mail May 8-15.

Red Cross Anti-Tuberculosis Week — PT112

2017, Aug. 1 Litho. ***Perf. 14***
RA132 PT112 1.55k multi — —
Obligatory on mail Aug. 1-8.

Red Cross Week PT114

2018, May 8 Litho. ***Perf. 14***
RA134 PT114 1.55k multi — —
Croatian Red Cross, 140th anniv. Obligatory on mail May 8-15.

Red Cross Solidarity Week PT116

2018, Dec. 8 Litho. ***Perf. 14***
RA136 PT116 1.55k multi — —
Obligatory on mail Dec. 8-15.

Red Cross Week — PT117

2019, May 8 Litho. ***Perf. 14***
RA137 PT117 1.55k multi — —
Obligatory on mail May 8-15.

CUBA

'kyü-bə

LOCATION — The largest island of the West Indies; south of Florida
GOVT. — Former Spanish possession
AREA — 44,206 sq. mi.
POP. — 11,096,395 (1999 est.)
CAPITAL — Havana

Formerly a Spanish possession, Cuba made several unsuccessful attempts to gain her freedom, which finally led to the intervention of the US in 1898. In that year under the Treaty of Paris, Spain relinquished the island to the US in trust for its inhabitants.

In 1902 a republic was established and the Cuban Congress took over the government from the military authorities.

8 Reales Plata = 1 Peso
100 Centesimos = 1 Escudo or Peseta (1867)
1000 Milesimas = 100 Centavos = 1 Peso

Catalogue values for unused stamps in this country are for Never Hinged items, beginning with Scott 402 in the regular postage section, Scott B3 in the semi-postal section, Scott C38 in the airpost section, Scott CB1 in the airpost semi-postal section, Scott E13 in the special delivery section, and Scott RA1 in the postal tax section.

Pen cancellations are common on the earlier stamps of Cuba. Stamps so canceled sell for very much less than those with postmark cancellations.

Watermarks

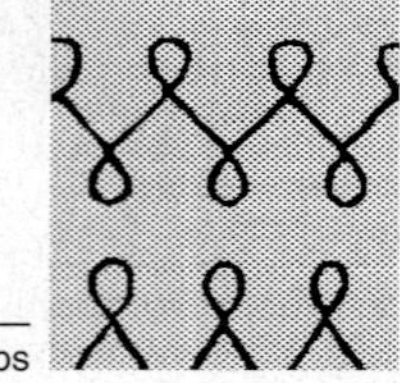
Wmk. 104 — Loops

Loops from different rows may or may not be directly opposite each other.

Wmk. 105 — Crossed Lines

Wmk. 106 — Star

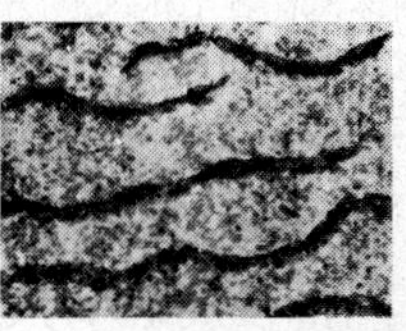
Wmk. 229 — Wavy Lines

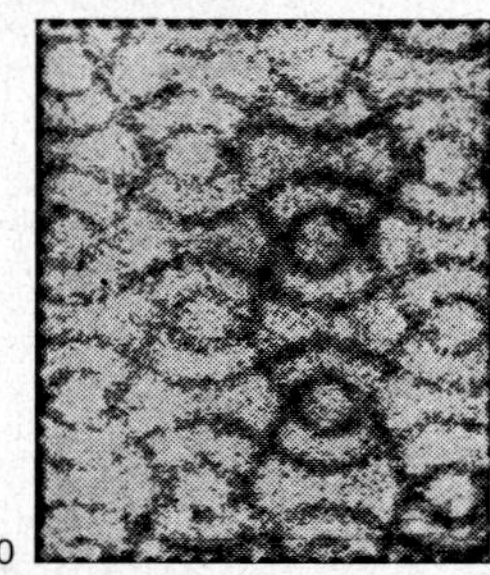
Wmk. 320

Wmk. 321 — "R de C"

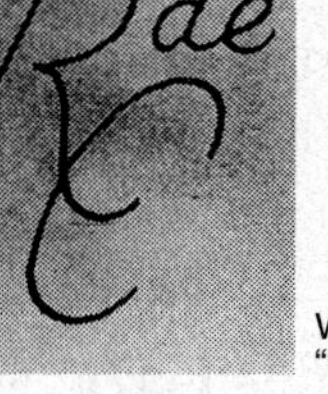
Wmk. 376 — "R de C"

Issued under Spanish Dominion

Used also in Puerto Rico: Nos. 1-3, 9-14, 17-21, 32-34, 35A-37, 39-41, 43-45, 47-49, 51-53, 55-57.

Used also in the Philippines: Nos. 2-3.

Identifiable cancellations of those countries will increase the value of the stamps.

Queen Isabella II — A1

Blue Paper

1855 Typo. Wmk. 104 *Imperf.*

1	A1	½r p blue green	100.00	7.50
a.		½r p blackish green	150.00	30.00
2	A1	1r p gray green	100.00	6.50
3	A1	2r p carmine	750.00	15.00
4	A1	2r p orange red	1,500.	20.00
a.		2r p vermilion	1,600.	22.00
		Nos. 1-4 (4)	2,450.	49.00

See Nos. 9-14. For surcharges see Nos. 5-8, 15.

Counterfeit surcharges are plentiful.

Nos. 3-4 Surcharged

1855-56

5	A1	¼r p on 2r p car	1,200.	300.00
a.		Without fraction bar	*3,000.*	2,000.
6	A1	¼r p on 2r p org red	*4,000.*	800.00
a.		Without fraction bar	—	*3,000.*

Surcharged

7	A1	¼r p on 2r p car	1,000.	250.00
a.		Without fraction bar	*2,500.*	1,500
8	A1	¼r p on 2r p org red	1,600.	500.00
a.		Without fraction bar	—	—

The "Y ¼" surcharge met the "Ynterior" rate for delivery within the city of Havana.

Rough Yellowish Paper

1856 Wmk. 105

9	A1	½r p yellow grn	10.00	2.00
10	A1	1r p green	1,250.	30.00
a.		1r p emerald	*1,750.*	100.00
11	A1	2r p orange red	700.00	40.00

White Smooth Paper

1857 Unwmk.

12	A1	½r p blue	5.00	1.00
13	A1	1r p gray green	5.00	1.00
a.		1r p pale yellow green	5.00	3.25
14	A1	2r p dull rose	25.00	5.00
		Nos. 12-14 (3)	35.00	7.00

Surcharged

1860

15	A1	¼r p on 2r p dl rose	300.00	100.00
a.		1 of ¼ inverted	500.00	200.00
		On cover		1,500.
b.		"Y ⅓" instead of "1 ¼"		—

Queen Isabella II
A2 A3

1862-64 *Imperf.*

16	A2	¼r p black	25.00	*60.00*
17	A3	¼r p blk, *buff* ('64)	250.00	*60.00*
18	A3	½r p green ('64)	5.00	1.00
19	A3	½r p grn, *pale rose* ('64)	15.00	3.00
20	A3	1r p bl, *sal* ('64)	6.00	2.00
a.		Diagonal half used as ½r p on cover		300.00
21	A3	2r p ver, *buff* ('64)	24.00	8.00
a.		2r p red, *buff*	35.00	15.00
		Nos. 16-21 (6)	325.00	134.00

No. 17 Overprinted in Black

1866

22	A3	¼r p black, *buff*	85.00	*120.00*

Exists with handstamped "1866."

A5

1866

23	A5	5c dull violet	50.00	60.00
24	A5	10c blue	6.00	1.10
25	A5	20c green	4.00	1.10
a.		Diag. half used as 10c on cover		—
26	A5	40c rose	50.00	60.00
		Nos. 23-26 (4)	110.00	122.20

For the Type A5 20c in dull lilac, see Spain No. 87.

Stamps Dated "1867"

1867 *Perf. 14*

27	A5	5c dull violet	40.00	35.00
28	A5	10c blue	35.00	4.00
a.		Imperf., pair	110.00	*6.50*
b.		Diagonal half used as 5c on cover		300.00
29	A5	20c green	30.00	5.00
a.		Imperf., pair	110.00	75.00
b.		Diag. half used as 10c on cover		325.00
30	A5	40c rose	20.00	30.00
		Nos. 27-30 (4)	125.00	74.00

A6

1868 Stamps Dated "1868"

31	A6	5c dull violet	30.00	20.00
32	A6	10c blue	5.00	2.00
a.		Diagonal half used as 5c on cover		250.00
33	A6	20c green	10.00	4.00
a.		Diag. half used as 10c on cover		275.00
34	A6	40c rose	25.00	15.00
a.		Diag. half used as 20c on cover		175.00
		Nos. 31-34 (4)	70.00	41.00

Nos. 31-34 Overprinted in Black

1868

35	A6	5c dull violet	75.00	32.50
35A	A6	10c blue	75.00	32.50
36	A6	20c green	75.00	32.50
37	A6	40c rose	75.00	32.50
		Nos. 35-37 (4)	300.00	130.00

1869 Stamps Dated "1869"

38	A6	5c rose	50.00	40.00
39	A6	10c red brown	5.00	2.00
a.		Diagonal half used as 5c on cover		140.00
40	A6	20c orange	10.00	3.00
41	A6	40c dull violet	40.00	30.00
		Nos. 38-41 (4)	105.00	75.00

Nos. 38-41 Ovptd. Like Nos. 35-37

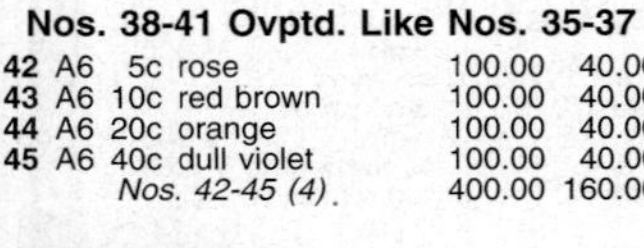

42 A6 5c rose 100.00 40.00
43 A6 10c red brown 100.00 40.00
44 A6 20c orange 100.00 40.00
45 A6 40c dull violet 100.00 40.00
Nos. 42-45 (4) 400.00 160.00

"Espana" — A8

1870 ***Perf. 14***

46 A8 5c blue 250.00 125.00
47 A8 10c green 5.00 2.00
a. Diagonal half used as 5c on cover 250.00
48 A8 20c red brown 4.00 3.00
a. Diag. half used as 10c on cover 300.00
49 A8 40c rose 300.00 100.00

"Espana" — A9

1871

50 A9 12c red lilac 25.00 12.00
a. Imperf., pair 100.00 —
51 A9 25c ultra 3.00 1.00
a. Imperf., pair 50.00 —
b. Diagonal half used as 12c on cover 125.00
52 A9 50c gray green 4.00 2.00
a. Imperf., pair 75.00 —
b. Diagonal half used as 25c on cover 250.00
53 A9 1p yel brown 40.00 15.00
a. Imperf., pair 125.00 —
Nos. 50-53 (4) 72.00 30.00

King Amadeo — A10

1873 ***Perf. 14***

54 A10 12½c dark green 40.00 30.00
55 A10 25c gray 3.00 1.00
a. Diagonal half used as 12½c on cover 120.00
b. 25c lilac 10.00 4.00
c. As "b," half used as 12½c on cover 150.00
d. As "b," imperf., pair 50.00 —
56 A10 50c brown 3.00 1.00
a. Imperf., pair 75.00 —
b. Half used as 25c on cover 200.00
57 A10 1p red brown 450.00 75.00
a. Diagonal half used as 50c on cover 750.00

"España" — A11

1874

58 A11 12½c brown 30.00 25.00
a. Half used as 5c on cover 500.00
59 A11 25c ultra 1.00 .60
a. Diagonal half used as 12½c on cover 100.00
60 A11 50c dp violet 2.00 5.00
a. Diagonal half used as 25c on cover 200.00
b. "1374" instead of "1874" — —
61 A11 50c gray 5.00 2.00
a. Diagonal half used as 25c on cover 175.00
62 A11 1p carmine 350.00 400.00
a. Imperf., pair 700.00 *250.00*
Nos. 58-62 (5) 388.00 432.60

Examples of Nos. 61, 63-65, 67-87 with fine impressions in slightly different colors are proofs.

Coat of Arms — A12

1875

63 A12 12½c lt violet 1.50 2.00
a. Imperf., pair 100.00
64 A12 25c ultra 1.25 1.60
a. Imperf., pair 100.00 —
b. Diagonal half used as 12½c on cover 100.00
65 A12 50c blue green 1.00 2.00
a. Imperf., pair 100.00
b. Diag. half used as 25c on cover *80.00*
66 A12 1p brown 15.00 10.00
b. Diag. half used as 50c on cover 135.00
Nos. 63-66 (4) 18.75 15.60

King Alfonso XII — A13

1876

67 A13 12½c green 3.00 6.00
a. 12½c emerald green 3.75 6.00
68 A13 25c gray 4.00 3.00
a. Diagonal half used as 12½c on cover 100.00
b. 25c pale violet 4.50 3.25
d. 25c bluish gray 4.50 3.25
69 A13 50c ultra 3.00 6.00
a. Imperf., pair 75.00 *16.00*
b. Diag. half used as 25c on cover 100.00
70 A13 1p black 15.00 25.00
a. Imperf., pair 40.00 *40.00*
b. Diag. half used as 50c on cover 125.00
Nos. 67-70 (4) 25.00 40.00

King Alfonso XII — A14

1877

71 A14 10c lt green 40.00 —
72 A14 12½c gray 6.00 12.50
a. Imperf., pair 100.00 —
b. Diagonal half used on cover 300.00
73 A14 25c dk green 1.00 .50
a. Imperf., pair 100.00 —
b. Diagonal half used as 12½c on cover 75.00
74 A14 50c black 1.00 1.50
a. Imperf., pair 100.00 —
b. Half used as 25c on cover 100.00
75 A14 1p brown 30.00 25.00
Nos. 71-75 (5) 78.00

No. 71 was not placed in use.

1878 **Stamps Dated "1878"**

76 A14 5c blue 1.00 2.00
77 A14 10c black 100.00
78 A14 12½c brown bis 6.00 10.00
a. 12½c olive brown 6.00 10.00
c. Diagonal half used on cover 200.00
d. As "a," diagonal half used on cover 200.00
79 A14 25c yel green 1.00 2.00
b. No. 79, diagonal half used as 12½c on cover 100.00
c. 25c deep green 1.00 2.00
80 A14 50c dk blue grn 1.00 2.00
b. Diagonal half used as 25c on cover 100.00
81 A14 1p carmine 25.00 15.00
b. 1p rose 16.00 *500.00*
c. Diagonal half used as 50c on cover *900.00*
Nos. 76-81 (6) 134.00 31.00

No. 77 was not placed in use.

Imperf., Pairs

76a A14 5c blue 100.00
77a A14 10c black 400.00
78b A14 12½c brown bister 100.00
79a A14 25c deep green 100.00
80a A14 50c dk blue green 200.00
81a A14 1p carmine 150.00

1879 **Stamps Dated "1879"**

82 A14 5c slate black 1.00 3.00
83 A14 10c orange 200.00 *75.00*
84 A14 12½c rose 1.00 3.00
85 A14 25c ultra 1.00 2.00
a. Diagonal half used as 12½c on cover 100.00
b. Imperf., pair 75.00
86 A14 50c gray 1.00 1.00
a. Diag. half used as 25c on cover 100.00
87 A14 1p olive bister 25.00 30.00
Nos. 82-87 (6) 229.00 114.00

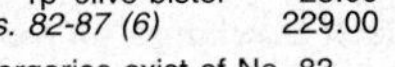

Forgeries exist of No. 83.

A15

1880

88 A15 5c green 1.00 2.00
89 A15 10c lake 125.00 —
a. Double impression of frame and lettering 200.00
90 A15 12½c gray 1.00 .50
91 A15 25c gray blue 1.00 .50
a. Diagonal half used as 12½c on cover 100.00
92 A15 50c brown 1.00 .50
a. Diagonal half used as 25c on cover 100.00
93 A15 1p yellow brn 8.00 5.00
a. Diagonal half used as 50c on cover 400.00
Nos. 88-93 (6) 137.00 8.50

No. 89 was not placed in use. Forged cancels exist.

A16

1881

94 A16 1c green 1.00 .50
95 A16 2c lake 50.00
96 A16 2½c olive bister 1.00 .50
97 A16 5c gray blue .50 .25
98 A16 10c yellow brown .50 .25
a. Diagonal half used as 5c on cover 100.00
99 A16 20c dark brown 6.00 10.00
Nos. 94-99 (6) 59.00 11.50

No. 95 was not placed in use.

A17

1882

100 A17 1c green .75 .50
a. Diag. half used as ½c on cover 150.00
101 A17 2c lake 5.00 3.00
a. Diag. half used as 1c on cover 100.00
102 A17 2½c dk brown 10.00 5.00
103 A17 5c gray blue 8.00 .50
a. Diag. half used as 2½c on cover 100.00
104 A17 10c olive bister .75 .50
a. Diag. half used as 5c on cover 100.00
105 A17 20c red brown 130.00 50.00
a. Diag. half used as 10c on cover 500.00
Nos. 100-105 (6) 154.50 59.50

See Nos. 121-131. For surcharges see Nos. 106-120.

Issue of 1882 Surcharged or Overprinted in Black, Blue or Red

a

b

c

d

e

1883 **Type "a"**

106 A17 5 on 5c (R) 3.00 2.00
a. Triple surcharge
b. Double surcharge 25.00 25.00
c. Inverted surcharge 30.00 30.00
d. Without "5" in surcharge 20.00 20.00
e. Dbl. surch., types "a" & "d" 75.00 —
107 A17 10 on 10c (Bl) 3.50 2.50
a. Inverted surcharge 75.00
b. Double surcharge 30.00 30.00
108 A17 20 on 20c 45.00 75.00
a. "10" instead of "20" 75.00 *75.00*
b. Double surcharge 75.00
c. As "a," inverted surcharge *90.00* *90.00*

Type "b"

109 A17 5 on 5c (R) 3.00 2.00
a. Inverted surcharge 30.00 30.00
b. Double surcharge 25.00 25.00
110 A17 10 on 10c (Bl) 10.00 12.00
a. Inverted surcharge 35.00 35.00
b. Double surcharge 35.00 35.00
111 A17 20 on 20c 120.00 150.00
a. Double surcharge
b. Dbl. surch., types "b" & "c"

Type "c"

112 A17 5 on 5c (R) 2.50 2.00
a. Inverted surcharge 35.00 35.00
b. Dbl. surch., types "c" & "d" —
c. Dbl. surch., types "c" & "a"
113 A17 10 on 10c (Bl) 10.00 12.00
a. Inverted surcharge 40.00 40.00
b. Double surcharge 40.00 40.00
114 A17 20 on 20c 60.00 100.00
a. "10" instead of "20" 100.00 120.00
b. Double surcharge 100.00 120.00
c. Dbl. surch., types "a" & "c" 100.00 120.00

Type "d"

115 A17 5 on 5c (R) 3.00 2.00
a. Inverted surcharge 35.00 35.00
b. Double surcharge 30.00 30.00
116 A17 10 on 10c (Bl) 4.00 3.00
a. Inverted surcharge 40.00 40.00
b. Double surcharge 40.00 40.00
c. Dbl. surch., types "d" & "c"
117 A17 20 on 20c 85.00 100.00
a. Dbl. surch., types "a" & "d" — —

Type "e"

118 A17 5c gray blue (R) 4.00 3.00
a. Double overprint 40.00 40.00
119 A17 10c olive bis (Bl) 12.00 15.00
a. Double overprint 40.00 40.00
120 A17 20c red brown 250.00 300.00
a. Double overprint 300.00 300.00
Nos. 106-120 (15) 615.00 780.50

Handstamped overprints and surcharges are counterfeits.

Numerous other varieties exist.

Type of 1882

Original 1st retouch 2nd retouch

The differences between the stamps of 1882 and the various retouches are as follows:

Original state: The medallion is surrounded by a heavy line of color of nearly even thickness, touching the horizontal line below the word "Cuba" (or "Filipinas," "Puerto Rico," as the case may be); the opening in the hair above the temple is narrow and pointed.

1st retouch: The line around the medallion is thin, except at the upper right, and does not touch the horizontal line above it; the opening in the hair is slightly wider and a trifle rounded; the lock of hair above the forehead is shaped like a broad "V" and ends in a point; there is a faint white line below it, which is not found on the stamps in the original state. Owing to wear of the plate the shape of the lock of hair and the width of the white line below it vary.

2nd retouch: The opening in the hair forms a semi-circle; the lock above the forehead is nearly straight, having only a slight wave, and the white line is much broader than before.

1883-86

121 A17 1c grn, 2nd retouch 150.00 40.00
122 A17 2½c olive bister .50 .30
124 A17 2½c violet 1.00 .40
a. 2½c red lilac ('85) 1.00 .40
b. 2½c ultramarine 125.00 150.00
125 A17 5c gray bl, 1st retouch 100.00 .50
a. Diag. half used as 2½c on cover 75.00
126 A17 5c gray bl, 2nd retouch 120.00 2.00
a. Diag. half used as 2½c on cover 125.00
127 A17 10c brn, 1st retouch 3.00 1.00
a. Diagonal half used as 5c on cover 75.00
c. Imperf, pair 300.00 —
128 A17 20c olive bister 15.00 10.00
Nos. 121-128 (7) 389.50 54.20

1888

129 A17 2½c red brown 1.75 .85
130 A17 10c blue 1.50 1.00
a. Diagonal half used as 5c on cover 175.00
131 A17 20c brnsh gray 15.00 10.00
Nos. 129-131 (3) 18.25 11.85

King Alfonso XIII — A18

1890-97

132 A18 1c gray brown 20.00 6.50
133 A18 1c ol gray ('91) 10.00 4.00
134 A18 1c ultra ('94) 5.00 .50
135 A18 1c dk vio ('96) 1.50 .50
136 A18 2c slate blue 10.00 3.00
137 A18 2c lilac brn ('91) 2.00 .75
138 A18 2c rose ('94) 35.00 5.00
139 A18 2c claret ('96) 9.00 5.00
140 A18 2½c emerald 12.50 5.00
141 A18 2½c salmon ('91) 60.00 5.00
142 A18 2½c lilac ('94) 4.00 3.00
143 A18 2½c rose ('96) 4.00 6.00
144 A18 5c olive gray 1.00 .75
b. Diagonal half used as 2½c on cover 500.00
145 A18 5c emerald ('91) 1.00 .50
b. Diagonal half used as 2½c on cover 500.00
146 A18 5c sl blue ('96) .75 1.00
b. Diagonal half used as 2½c on cover 600.00
147 A18 10c brown violet 6.00 1.00
b. Diagonal half used as 5c on cover 500.00
148 A18 10c claret ('91) 2.50 .50
b. Diagonal half used as 5c on cover 400.00
149 A18 10c emerald ('96) 1.00 1.50
150 A18 20c dk violet 2.00 1.00
151 A18 20c ultra ('91) 25.00 8.00
152 A18 20c red brn ('94) 20.00 30.00
153 A18 20c violet ('96) 15.00 10.00
b. Diagonal half used as 10c on cover 600.00
154 A18 40c orange brn ('97) 40.00 35.00
155 A18 80c lilac brn ('97) 80.00 70.00
Nos. 132-155 (24) 367.25 203.50

Imperf., Pairs

134a A18 1c ultramarine 100.00
135a A18 1c dark violet 100.00
138a A18 2c rose 100.00
139a A18 2c claret 100.00
142a A18 2½c lilac 100.00
143a A18 2½c rose 100.00
145a A18 5c emerald 100.00
146a A18 5c slate blue 100.00
148a A18 10c claret 100.00
149a A18 10c emerald 100.00
152a A18 20c red brown 135.00
153a A18 20c violet 125.00
154a A18 40c orange brown 115.00
155a A18 80c red brown 175.00

King Alfonso XIII — A19

1898

156 A19 1m orange brn .75 1.00
157 A19 2m orange brn .30 1.00
158 A19 3m orange brn .30 1.00
159 A19 4m orange brn 6.00 12.00
160 A19 5m orange brn .30 1.00
161 A19 1c black vio .30 1.00
162 A19 2c dk blue grn .30 1.00
163 A19 3c dk brown .30 1.00
164 A19 4c orange 16.00 12.00
165 A19 5c car rose 1.25 .50
166 A19 6c dk blue .50 1.50
167 A19 8c gray brown 2.00 4.00
168 A19 10c vermilion 1.30 .75
169 A19 15c slate green 6.00 10.00
170 A19 20c maroon 4.00 1.00
171 A19 40c dark lilac 5.00 8.00
172 A19 60c black 10.00 20.00
173 A19 80c red brown 20.00 25.00
174 A19 1p yel green 20.00 25.00
175 A19 2p slate blue 35.00 40.00
Nos. 156-175 (20) 129.60 166.75

Nos. 156-160 were issued for use on newspapers.

Nos. 156-175 exist imperf. Value, unused pairs, $7,500. Only one set of pairs is currently known.

For surcharges see Nos. 176-189C, 196-200.

Issued under Administration of the United States

Puerto Principe Issue

Issues of Cuba of 1898 and 1896 Surcharged

a

b

Black Surcharge on Nos. 156-158, 160

Types a, c, d, e, f, g and h are 17½mm high, the others are 19½mm high.

1898-99

176 A19 (a) 1c on 1m org brn 100.00 60.00
177 A19 (b) 1c on 1m org brn 600.00 115.00
a. Broken figure "1" 3,000. 275.00
b. Inverted surcharge 500.00
d. As "a," inverted 1,500.

c

d

178 A19 (c) 2c on 2m org brn 65.00 62.50
a. Inverted surcharge 500.00 100.00
179 A19 (d) 2c on 2m org brn 82.50 77.50
a. Inverted surcharge — 500.00

k

l

179B A19 (k) 3c on 1m org brn 300. 175.
c. Double surcharge — 3,000.

An unused example is known with "cents" omitted.

179D A19 (l) 3c on 1m org brn 1,350. 675.00

e

f

179F A19 (e) 3c on 2m org brn 1,500.

Value is for examples with minor faults.

179G A19 (f) 3c on 2m org brn — 2,000.

Value is for examples with minor faults.

180 A19 (e) 3c on 3m org brn 150. 100.
a. Inverted surcharge 375.
181 A19 (f) 3c on 3m org brn 600. 400.
a. Inverted surcharge 750.

g

h

i

j

182 A19 (g) 5c on 1m org brn 1,000. 165.
a. Inverted surcharge — 1,000.
183 A19 (h) 5c on 1m org brn 1,500. 1,000.
a. Inverted surcharge — 1,500.
184 A19 (g) 5c on 2m org brn 1,000. 275.
185 A19 (h) 5c on 2m org brn 1,500. 600.
186 A19 (g) 5c on 3m org brn 1,500. 350.
a. Inverted surcharge 1,200. 700.
187 A19 (h) 5c on 3m org brn — 1,000.
a. Inverted surcharge — 1,000.
188 A19 (g) 5c on 5m org brn 145. 230.
a. Inverted surcharge — 750.
b. Double surcharge — —
189 A19 (h) 5c on 5m org brn 3,000. 425.
a. Inverted surcharge 3,000. 900.
b. Double surcharge — —

The 2nd printing of Nos. 188-189 has shiny ink. Values are for the 1st printing.

189C A19 (i) 5c on 5m org brn 7,500.

No. 191

Black Surcharge on No. P25

190 N2 (g) 5c on ½m bl grn 375. 115.
a. Inverted surcharge 1,000. 210.
b. Pair, one without surcharge 500.

Value for 190b is for pair with unsurcharged stamp at right. Also exists with unsurcharged stamp at left.

191 N2 (h) 5c on ½m bl grn 1,000. 275.
a. Inverted surcharge 1,000.
192 N2 (i) 5c on ½m bl grn 3,000. 100.
a. Dbl. surch., one diagonal 3,500. —
193 N2 (j) 5c on ½m bl grn 900. 500.

Red Surcharge on No. 161

196 A19 (k) 3c on 1c blk vio 150. 125.
a. Inverted surcharge 500.
197 A19 (l) 3c on 1c blk vio 250. 200.
a. Inverted surcharge 1,500.
198 A19 (i) 5c on 1c blk vio 92.50 72.50
a. Inverted surcharge 500.
b. Surcharge vert. reading up —
c. Double surcharge 600. 2,750.
d. Double invtd. surch. — —

Value for No. 198b is for surcharge reading up. One example is known with surcharge reading down.

199 A19 (j) 5c on 1c blk vio 150. 115.
a. Inverted surcharge 3,000.
b. Vertical surcharge — —
c. Double surcharge 3,000. 3,000.

m

200 A19 (m) 10c on 1c blk vio 62.50 92.50
a. Broken figure "1" 160.00 225.00

Black Surcharge on Nos. P26-P30

201 N2 (k) 3c on 1m bl grn 350. 350.
a. Inverted surcharge 450.
b. "EENTS" 600. 450.
c. As "b", inverted 850.
202 N2 (l) 3c on 1m bl grn 1,000. 400.
a. Inverted surcharge 850.
203 N2 (k) 3c on 2m bl grn 1,650. 400.
a. "EENTS" 1,650. 500.
b. Inverted surcharge 1,500.
c. As "a," inverted 2,750.
204 N2 (l) 3c on 2m bl grn 2,750. 600.
a. Inverted surcharge 1,500.
205 N2 (k) 3c on 3m bl grn 900. 400.
a. Inverted surcharge 750.
b. "EENTS" 1,250. 450.
c. As "b," inverted 2,750.
206 N2 (l) 3c on 3m bl grn 1,500. 550.
a. Inverted surcharge 1,000.
211 N2 (i) 5c on 1m bl grn 1,800.
a. "EENTS" — 3,000.
212 N2 (j) 5c on 1m bl grn — 2,250.
213 N2 (i) 5c on 2m bl grn 3,000. 1,800.
a. "EENTS" 3,000. 3,000.
214 N2 (j) 5c on 2m bl grn 3,250. 1,750.
215 N2 (i) 5c on 3m bl grn 550.
a. "EENTS" 1,000.
216 N2 (j) 5c on 3m bl grn 3,000. 1,000.
217 N2 (i) 5c on 4m bl grn 3,000. 900.
a. "EENTS" 3,000. 1,500.
b. Inverted surcharge 2,000.
c. As "a," inverted 3,000.
218 N2 (j) 5c on 4m bl grn 3,000. 1,500.
a. Inverted surcharge 2,000.
219 N2 (i) 5c on 8m bl grn 2,500. 1,250.
a. Inverted surcharge 1,500.
b. "EENTS" 3,000. 2,750.
c. As "b," inverted 2,500.
220 N2 (j) 5c on 8m bl grn 2,000.
a. Inverted surcharge 2,500.

Beware of forgeries of the Puerto Principe issue. Obtaining expert opinions is recommended.

United States Stamps Nos. 279, 267, 267b, 279Bf, 279Bh, 268, 281, 282C and 283 Surcharged in Black

1899 **Wmk. 191** ***Perf. 12***

221 A87 1c on 1c yel grn 4.50 .40
Never hinged 11.50

No.	Type	Description	Unused	Used
222	A88	2c on 2c reddish car, III	10.00	.75
		Never hinged	25.00	
b.		2c on 2c vermilion, type III	10.00	.75
222A	A88	2c on 2c reddish car, IV	6.00	.40
		Never hinged	15.00	
c.		2c on 2c vermilion, IV	6.00	.40
d.		As No. 222A, inverted surcharge	*5,500.*	*4,000.*
223	A88	2½c on 2c reddish car, III	6.00	.80
		Never hinged	15.00	
b.		2½c on 2c vermilion, III	6.00	.80
223A	A88	2½c on 2c reddish car, IV	3.50	.50
		Never hinged	8.75	
c.		2½c on 2c vermilion, IV	3.50	.50
224	A89	3c on 3c purple	12.00	1.75
		Never hinged	30.00	
a.		Period between "B" and "A"	40.00	35.00
225	A91	5c on 5c blue	12.50	2.00
		Never hinged	30.00	
226	A94	10c on 10c brn, I	25.00	6.00
		Never hinged	70.00	
b.		"CUBA" omitted	*7,000.*	*4,000.*
226A	A94	10c on 10c brn, II	*6,000.*	
		Nos. 221-226 (8)	79.50	12.60

The 2½c was sold and used as a 2c stamp. Excellent counterfeits of this and the preceding issue exist, especially inverted and double surcharges.

Issues of the Republic under US Military Rule

Statue of Columbus A20

Royal Palms A21

"Cuba" — A22

Ocean Liner — A23

Cane Field — A24

1899 Wmk. US-C (191C) *Perf. 12*

No.	Type	Description	Unused	Used
227	A20	1c yellow green	3.50	.25
		Never hinged	8.75	
228	A21	2c carmine	3.50	.25
		Never hinged	8.75	
a.		scarlet	3.50	.25
b.		Booklet pane of 6	*5,500.*	
229	A22	3c purple	3.50	.30
		Never hinged	8.75	
230	A23	5c blue	4.50	.30
		Never hinged	11.00	
231	A24	10c brown	11.00	.80
		Never hinged	27.50	
		Nos. 227-231 (5)	26.00	1.90

No. 228b was issued by the Republic.

See Nos. 233-237. For surcharge see No. 232.

Issues of the Republic

No. 229 Surcharged in Carmine

1902, Sept. 30

No.	Type	Description	Unused	Used
232	A22	1c on 3c purple	2.75	.75
		Never hinged	4.00	
a.		Inverted surcharge	150.00	150.00
b.		Surcharge sideways (numeral horizontal)	300.00	300.00
c.		Double surcharge	200.00	200.00

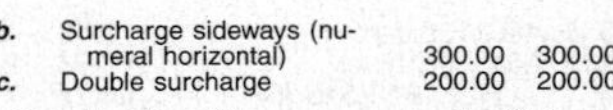

Counterfeits of the errors are plentiful.

Re-engraved

The re-engraved stamps of 1905-07 may be distinguished from the issue of 1899 as follows:

ORIGINAL RE-ENGRAVED

1c — The ends of the label inscribed "Centavo" are rounded instead of square.

2c — The foliate ornaments, inside the oval disks bearing the numerals of value, have been removed.

5c — Two lines forming a right angle have been added in the upper corners of the label bearing the word "Cuba."

10c — A small ball has been added to each of the square ends of the label bearing the word "Cuba."

1905 Unwmk. *Perf. 12*

No.	Type	Description	Unused	Used
233	A20	1c green	2.00	1.50
		Never hinged	4.00	
234	A21	2c rose	1.75	1.10
		Never hinged	3.75	
a.		Booklet pane of 6	175.00	75.00
236	A23	5c blue	42.50	8.00
		Never hinged	70.00	
237	A24	10c brown	3.50	.80
		Never hinged	6.00	
		Nos. 233-237 (4)	49.75	11.40

Maj. Gen. Antonio Maceo — A26

1907

No.	Type	Description	Unused	Used
238	A26	50c gray bl & blk	1.75	.80
		Never hinged	3.25	

See No. 245.

Bartolomé Masó A27

Máximo Gómez A28

Julio Sanguily A29

Ignacio Agramonte A30

Calixto García A31

José M. Rodriquez y Rodriquez (Mayia) A32

Carlos Roloff — A33

1910, Feb. 1

No.	Type	Description	Unused	Used
239	A27	1c grn & vio	1.00	.30
a.		Center inverted	350.00	200.00
240	A28	2c car & grn	2.50	.30
a.		Center inverted	575.00	425.00
b.		Center omitted	1,500.	
241	A29	3c vio & bl	2.50	.30
242	A30	5c bl & grn	24.00	4.75
243	A31	8c ol & vio	2.00	.30
244	A32	10c brn & bl	12.50	2.50
a.		Center inverted	925.00	
245	A26	50c vio & blk	2.50	*3.00*
246	A33	1p slate & blk	10.00	5.00
		Nos. 239-246 (8)	57.00	16.45
		Set, never hinged	72.50	

1911-13

No.	Type	Description	Unused	Used
247	A27	1c green	1.00	.25
248	A28	2c car rose	1.35	.25
a.		Booklet pane of 6 ('13)	200.00	100.00
250	A30	5c ultra	3.75	.35
251	A31	8c ol grn & blk	2.40	.90
252	A33	1p black	9.50	4.00
		Nos. 247-252 (5)	18.00	5.75
		Set, never hinged	25.00	

Map of Cuba — A34

1914-15

No.	Type	Description	Unused	Used
253	A34	1c green	.80	.25
a.		Booklet pane of 6	150.00	75.00
254	A34	2c car rose	.95	.25
a.		Booklet pane of 6	150.00	75.00
255	A34	2c red ('15)	1.50	.25
a.		Booklet pane of 6	150.00	75.00
256	A34	3c violet	4.75	.35
257	A34	5c blue	6.50	.35
258	A34	8c ol grn	5.25	3.00
259	A34	10c brown	9.50	3.00
260	A34	10c ol grn ('15)	11.50	3.00
261	A34	50c orange	70.00	20.00
262	A34	1p gray	100.00	24.00
		Nos. 253-262 (10)	210.75	54.45
		Set, never hinged	325.00	

Complete set of eight 1914 stamps, imperf. pairs, value $1,000.

Nos. 253, 254, 256 and E5 exist with "1917 GOB./CONSTITUCIONAL/CAMAGUEY" overprint. These were not authorized.

Gertrudis Gómez de Avellaneda, Cuban Poetess (1814-73) A34a

1914

No.	Type	Description	Unused	Used
263	A34a	5c blue	18.00	7.00

José Martí A35

Máximo Gómez A36

José de la Luz Caballero A37

Calixto García A38

Ignacio Agramonte A39

Tomás Estrada Palma A40

José A. Saco — A41

Antonio Maceo — A42

Carlos Manuel de Céspedes — A43

1917-18 Unwmk. *Perf. 12*

No.	Type	Description	Unused	Used
264	A35	1c bl grn	1.00	.25
a.		Booklet pane of 6	75.00	50.00
b.		Booklet pane of 30	350.00	
265	A36	2c rose	1.05	.25
a.		Booklet pane of 6	75.00	50.00
b.		Booklet pane of 30	300.00	

266 A36 2c lt red ('18) .85 .25
a. Booklet pane of 6 75.00 50.00
267 A37 3c violet 1.10 .25
a. Imperf. pair 275.00
b. Booklet pane of 6 75.00 50.00
268 A38 5c dp bl 1.05 .25
269 A39 8c red brn 5.50 .25
270 A40 10c yel brn 3.25 .25
271 A41 20c gray grn 18.50 1.60
272 A42 50c dl rose 18.50 .70
273 A43 1p black 19.00 .70
Nos. 264-273 (10) 69.80 4.75
Set, never hinged 110.00

1925-28 Wmk. 106 *Perf. 12*

274 A35 1c bl grn 1.10 .25
a. Booklet pane of 6 350.00
b. Booklet pane of 30 *750.00*
275 A36 2c brt rose 1.20 .25
a. Booklet pane of 6 125.00
b. Booklet pane of 30 350.00
276 A38 5c dp bl 2.50 .25
277 A39 8c red brn ('28) 5.75 .65
278 A40 10c yel brn ('27) 7.00 .70
279 A41 20c olive grn 11.00 1.10
Nos. 274-279 (6) 28.55 3.20
Set, never hinged 50.00

1926 *Imperf.*

280 A35 1c blue green 2.50 .80
281 A36 2c brt rose 1.60 .70
282 A38 5c deep blue 2.50 .80
Nos. 280-282 (3) 6.60 2.30
Set, never hinged 10.00

See Nos. 304-310. For overprint and surcharge see Nos. 317-318, 644.

Arms of Republic A44

1927, May 20 Unwmk. *Perf. 12*

283 A44 25c violet 18.50 5.00
Never hinged 30.00

25th anniversary of the Republic.
For surcharges see Nos. 355, C3.

Tomás Estrada Palma A45

Designs: 2c, Gen. Gerardo Machado. 5c, Morro Castle. 8c, Havana Railway Station. 10c, Presidential Palace. 13c, Tobacco Plantation. 20c, Treasury Building. 30c, Sugar Mill. 50c, Havana Cathedral. 1p, Galician Clubhouse, Havana.

1928, Jan. 2 Wmk. 106

284 A45 1c deep green 1.75 .30
285 A45 2c brt rose 2.00 .30
286 A45 5c deep blue 2.50 .50
287 A45 8c lt red brn 3.75 1.75
288 A45 10c bister brn 2.50 .80
289 A45 13c orange 3.50 1.50
290 A45 20c olive grn 2.50 1.00
291 A45 30c dk violet 6.50 1.75
292 A45 50c carmine rose 10.00 3.25
293 A45 1p gray black 16.00 6.25
Nos. 284-293 (10) 51.00 17.40
Set, never hinged 67.50

Sixth Pan-American Conference.

Capitol, Havana A55

1929, May 18

294 A55 1c green 1.75 .35
295 A55 2c carmine rose 1.75 .30
296 A55 5c blue 2.40 .40
297 A55 10c bister brn 2.75 .50
298 A55 20c violet 4.50 2.75
Nos. 294-298 (5) 13.15 4.30
Set, never hinged 21.00

Opening of the Capitol, Havana.

Hurdler — A56

1930, Mar. 15 Engr.

299 A56 1c green 5.00 1.75
300 A56 2c carmine 3.50 1.50
301 A56 5c deep blue 3.50 2.00
302 A56 10c bister brn 5.50 2.50
303 A56 20c violet 18.00 3.25
Nos. 299-303 (5) 35.50 11.00
Set, never hinged 50.00

2nd Central American Athletic Games.

Types of 1917 Portrait Issue
Flat Plate Printing

1930-45 Wmk. 106 Engr. *Perf. 10*

304 A35 1c blue green .80 .25
a. Booklet pane of 6 50.00
b. Booklet pane of 30 —
305 A36 2c brt rose 75.00 —
a. Booklet pane of 6 1,500.
305B A37 3c dk rose vio ('42) 4.00 .75
c. Booklet pane of 6 125.00 —
306 A38 5c dk blue 2.75 .25
306A A39 8c red brn ('45) 2.75 .25
307 A40 10c brown 2.75 .25
a. 10c yellow brown ('35) 3.50 .75
307B A41 20c olive grn ('41) 4.75 .75
Nos. 304-307B (7) 92.80 2.50

Nos. 305 and 305B were printed for booklet panes and all examples have straight edges.
For surcharge see No. 644.

Rotary Press Printing

308 A35 1c blue grn 2.75 .25
a. Booklet pane of 50 *3,000.*
309 A36 2c brt rose 2.75 .25
a. Booklet pane of 50 *3,000.*
310 A37 3c violet 3.75 .75
a. 3c dull violet ('38) 3.75 .75
b. 3c rose violet ('41) 3.75 .75
c. Booklet pane of 50 3,000.
Nos. 308-310 (3) 9.25 1.25

Flat plate stamps measure 18½x21½mm; rotary press, 19x22mm.

The Mangos of Baragua — A57
War Memorial — A61

Battle of Mal Tiempo A58

Battle of Coliseo A59

Maceo, Gómez and Zayas A60

Wmk. 229

1933, Apr. 23 Photo. *Perf. 12½*

312 A57 3c dk brown 3.50 1.50
313 A58 5c dk blue 4.50 1.25
314 A59 10c emerald 5.50 1.50
315 A60 13c red 3.50 1.60
316 A61 20c black 7.75 2.00
Nos. 312-316 (5) 24.75 7.85
Set, never hinged 35.00

War of Independence and dedication of the "Soldado Invasor" (the American Army that came to the aid of the revolution against Spain) monument.

Types of 1917 Issues with Carmine or Black Overprint Reading Up or Down

Rotary Press Printing

Wmk. 106

1933, Dec. 23 Engr. *Perf. 10*

317 A35 1c blue green (C) 1.00 .25

With Additional Surcharge of New Value and Bars

318 A37 2c on 3c vio (Bk) 1.60 .30

Establishment of a revolutionary junta.
Catalogue values for Nos. 317-318 unused are for examples with overprint reading up. Values for overprint reading down: $4, unused; 75¢ used.

Dr. Carlos J. Finlay — A62

1934, Dec. 3 Engr. *Perf. 10*

319 A62 2c dark carmine 3.00 1.60
320 A62 5c dark blue 3.50 2.00
Set, never hinged 9.50

Cent. of the birth of Dr. Carlos J. Finlay (1833-1915), physician-biologist who found that a mosquito transmitted yellow fever.

Pres. José Miguel Gómez — A63

Gómez Monument A64

1936, May *Perf. 10*

322 A63 1c green 2.75 .40
323 A64 2c carmine 4.50 .75
Set, never hinged 10.00

Unveiling of a monument to Gen. José Miguel Gómez, ex-president.

Matanzas Issue

Map of Cuba A65

2c, Map of Free Zone. 4c, S. S. "Rex" in Matanzas Bay. 5c, Ships in Matanzas Bay. 8c, Caves of Bellamar. 10c, Valley of Yumuri. 20c, Yumuri River. 50c, Ships Leaving Port.

Wmk. 229

1936, May 5 Photo. *Perf. 12½*

324 A65 1c blue green .45 .25
325 A65 2c red .70 .25
326 A65 4c claret 1.20 .25
327 A65 5c ultra 1.75 .25
328 A65 8c orange brn 3.00 .70
329 A65 10c emerald 3.25 .70
330 A65 20c brown 6.25 2.50
331 A65 50c slate 11.50 3.50
Nos. 324-331,C18-C21,CE1,E8 (14) 73.75 30.80
Set, never hinged 92.50

Exist imperf. Value 20% more.

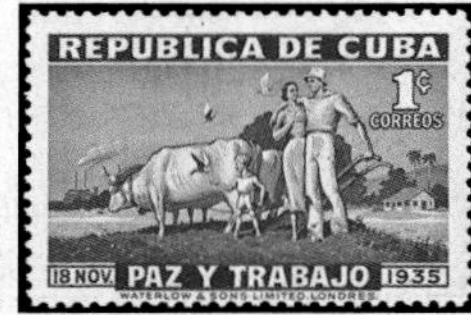

"Peace and Work" A73

Máximo Gómez Monument — A74

Torch — A75

"Independence" — A76

"Messenger of Peace" — A77

1936, Nov. 18 *Perf. 12½*

332 A73 1c emerald .75 .25
333 A74 2c crimson 1.00 .30
334 A75 4c maroon 1.20 .30
335 A76 5c ultra 7.25 .55
336 A77 8c dk green 9.00 2.00
Nos. 332-336,C22-C23,E9 (8) 36.45 7.75
Set, never hinged 52.50

Maj. Gen. Máximo Gómez, birth centenary.
Issued both perf and imperf. Values for imperfs are approx. 400% higher.

Sugar Cane — A78

Primitive Sugar Mill — A79

Modern Sugar Mill — A80

Wmk. 106

1937, Oct. 2 **Engr.** ***Perf. 10***

337 A78 1c yellow green 1.50 .40
338 A79 2c red 1.50 .25
339 A80 5c bright blue 1.50 .40
Nos. 337-339 (3) 4.50 1.05
Set, never hinged 7.50

Cuban sugar cane industry, 400th anniv.

Argentine Emblem — A81

Mountain Scene (Bolivia) — A82

Arms of Brazil — A83

Canadian Scene — A84

Camilo Henriquez (Chile) A85

Gen, Francisco de Paula Santander (Colombia) A86

Natl. Monument (Costa Rica) — A87

Autograph of José Marti (Cuba) — A88

Columbus Lighthouse (Dominican Rep.) — A89

Juan Montalvo (Ecuador) — A90

Abraham Lincoln (US) A91

Quetzal and Scroll (Guatemala) A92

Arms of Haiti A93

Francisco Morazán (Honduras) A94

Fleet of Columbus — A95

Wmk. 106

1937, Oct. 13 **Engr.** ***Perf. 10***

340 A81 1c deep green 2.50 2.50
341 A82 1c green 2.00 2.00
342 A83 2c carmine 1.50 1.50
343 A84 2c carmine 1.50 1.50
344 A85 3c violet 1.75 1.75
345 A86 3c violet 1.75 1.75
346 A87 4c bister brown 3.75 3.75
347 A88 4c bister brown 3.75 3.75
348 A89 5c blue 6.50 4.00
349 A90 5c blue 6.50 3.75
350 A91 8c citron 3.75 3.75
351 A92 8c citron 3.25 3.25
352 A93 10c maroon 2.50 2.50
353 A94 10c maroon 2.50 2.50
354 A95 25c rose lilac 26.00 8.00
Nos. 340-354,C24-C29,E10-E11 (23) 137.25 95.50
Set, never hinged 190.00

Nos. 340-354 were sold by the Cuban PO for 3 days, Oct. 13-15, during which no other stamps were sold. They were postally valid for the full face value. Proceeds from their three-day sale above 30,000 pesos were paid by the Cuban POD to the Assoc. of American Writers and Artists. Remainders were overprinted "SVP" (Without Postal Value).

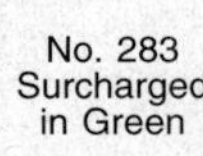

No. 283 Surcharged in Green

1937, Nov. 19 **Unwmk.** ***Perf. 12***

355 A44 10c on 25c violet 13.50 3.50
Never hinged 19.50

Centenary of Cuban railroads.

Ciboney Indian and Cigar — A96

Cigar and Globe — A97

Tobacco Plant and Cigars — A98

1939, Aug. 28 **Wmk. 106** ***Perf. 10***

356 A96 1c yellow green .75 .25
357 A97 2c red 1.00 .25
358 A98 5c brt ultra 1.25 .30
Nos. 356-358 (3) 3.00 .80
Set, never hinged 4.75

General Calixto García
A99 A100

1939, Nov. 6 ***Perf. 10, Imperf.***

359 A99 2c dark red 1.00 .25
360 A100 5c deep blue 1.50 .40
Set, never hinged 3.75

Birth centenary of General Garcia.

Values are for perf examples. Value of imperfs approx. 20% higher.

Gonzalo de Quesada — A101

1940, Apr. 30 **Engr.** ***Perf. 10***

361 A101 2c rose red 2.40 .50
Never hinged 3.50

Pan American Union, 50th anniversary.

Rotary Club Emblem, Cuban Flag and Tobacco Plant — A102

1940, May 18 **Wmk. 106** ***Perf. 10***

362 A102 2c rose red 3.00 .75
Never hinged 4.50

Rotary Intl. Convention held at Havana.

Lions Emblem, Cuban Flag and Royal Palms — A103

1940, July 23

363 A103 2c orange vermilion 5.50 1.00
Never hinged 8.50

Lions International Convention, Havana.

Dr. Nicolás J. Gutiérrez A104

1940, Oct. 28

364 A104 2c orange ver 1.90 .30
365 A104 5c blue 2.00 .30
a. Sheet of four, imperf., unwmkd. 4.50 3.00
Never hinged 7.00
b. As "a," black overprint ('51) 11.00 4.75
Never hinged 17.00
Set, never hinged 5.50

100th anniv. of the publication of the 1st Cuban Medical Review, "El Repertorio Medico Habanero."

No. 365a contains 2 each of Nos. 364-365 imperf. and sold for 25c.

For overprint see No. C43A.

In 1951 No. 365a was overprinted in black: "50 Aniversario Descubrimiento Agente Transmisor de la Flebre Amarilla por el Dr. Carlos J. Finlay Honor a los Martires de la Ciencia 1901 1951." The overprint is illustrated over No. C43A, but does not include the plane and "Correo Aereo."

Major General Guillermo Moncada — A105

Moncada Riding into Battle A106

1941, June 25

366 A105 3c dk brown, *buff* 3.50 1.25
367 A106 5c bright blue 3.50 1.25
Set, never hinged 10.00

Maj. Gen. Guillermo Moncada (1841-96).

Globe Showing Western Hemisphere A107

Maceo, Bolívar, Juárez, Lincoln and Arms of Cuba A108

"Labor: Wealth of America" — A109

Tree of Fraternity, Havana A110

Statue of Liberty — A111

Perf. 10, Imperf.

1942, Feb. 23 **Wmk. 106**

368 A107 1c emerald .75 .25
369 A108 3c orange brown 1.00 .25
370 A109 5c blue 2.00 .75
371 A110 10c red violet 2.50 .75
372 A111 13c red 2.50 .65
Nos. 368-372 (5) 8.75 2.65
Set, never hinged 11.00

Spirit of Democracy in the Americas.

The imperforate varieties are without gum. Value, set mint $10, used $5.

Ignacio Agramonte Loynaz — A112

Rescue of Sanguily by Agramonte A113

1942, Apr. 10 ***Perf. 10***

373	A112 3c bister brn	3.50	1.00
374	A113 5c brt blue, *bluish*	3.75	1.25
	Set, never hinged	11.00	

100th anniv. of the birth of Ignacio Agramonte Loynaz, patriot.

"Unmask the Fifth Columnists" — A114

"Be Careful, The Fifth Column is Spying on You" — A115

"Destroy it. The Fifth Column is like a Serpent" — A116

"Fulfill your Patriotic Duty by Destroying the Fifth Column" — A117

"Don't be Afraid of the Fifth Column. Attack it" — A118

1943, July 5

375	A114 1c dk blue grn	1.25	.30
376	A115 3c red	1.75	.30
377	A116 5c brt blue	1.90	.45
378	A117 10c brown	4.25	1.90
379	A118 13c dull rose vio	4.00	1.75
	Nos. 375-379 (5)	13.15	4.70
	Set, never hinged	19.00	

General Eloy Alfaro and Flags of Cuba and Ecuador A119

1943, Sept. 20

380	A119 3c green	2.50	.30
	Never hinged	3.00	

General Eloy Alfaro of Ecuador, 100th birth anniv.

Retirement Security A120

1943, Nov. 8 **Wmk. 106** ***Perf. 10***

381	A120 1c yellow green	1.20	.30
382	A120 3c vermilion	1.20	.30
383	A120 5c bright blue	1.60	.40

1944, Mar. 18

384	A120 1c bright yel grn	1.60	.40
385	A120 3c salmon	2.00	.40
386	A120 5c light blue	3.75	1.20
	Nos. 381-386 (6)	11.35	3.00
	Set, never hinged	17.00	

Half the proceeds from the sale of Nos. 381-386 were used for the Communications Ministry Employees' Retirement Fund.

Portrait of Columbus — A121

Bartolomé de Las Casas — A122

First Statue of Columbus at Cárdenas — A123

Discovery of Tobacco A124

Columbus Sights Land A125

1944, May 19

387	A121 1c dk yellow grn	2.75	.40
a.	Pair, imperf horiz.		175.00
388	A122 3c brown	2.50	.25
389	A123 5c brt blue	3.00	.75
390	A124 10c dark violet	3.75	.75
391	A125 13c dark red	4.00	1.25
	Nos. 387-391,C36-C37 (7)	21.40	4.55
	Set, never hinged	32.50	

450th anniv. of the discovery of America.

Major General Carlos Roloff — A126

1944, Aug. 21

392	A126 3c violet	2.00	.30
	Never hinged	3.00	

Maj. Gen. Carlos Roloff, 100th birth anniv.

Americas Map and 1st Brazilian Postage Stamps — A127

1944, Dec. 20 **Engr.**

393	A127 3c brown orange	2.25	.50
	Never hinged	3.25	

Cent. of the 1st postage stamps of the Americas, issued by Brazil in 1843.

Seal of the Society — A128

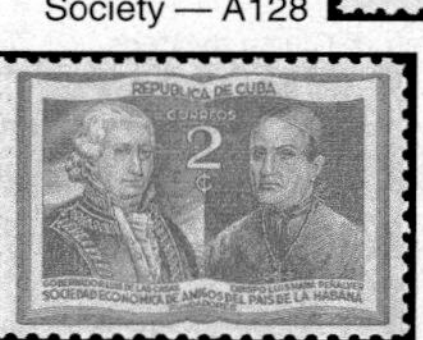

Luis de las Casas and Luis Maria Penalyer A129

1945, Oct. 5 **Wmk. 106** ***Perf. 10***

394	A128 1c yellow green	1.75	.25
395	A129 2c scarlet	1.60	.25
	Set, never hinged	5.00	

Sesquicentenary of the founding of the Economic Society of Friends of the Country.

Aged Couple A130

1945, Dec. 27

396	A130 1c dk yellow grn	.50	.25
397	A130 2c scarlet	.70	.25
398	A130 5c cobalt blue	1.20	.25

1946, Mar. 26

399	A130 1c brt yellow grn	1.00	.25
400	A130 2c salmon pink	.95	.25
401	A130 5c light blue	2.25	.25
	Nos. 396-401 (6)	6.60	1.50
	Set, never hinged	9.50	

See note after No. 386.

Catalogue values for unused stamps in this section, from this point to the end of the section, are for Never Hinged items.

Gabriel de la Concepcion Valdés Plácido A131

1946, Feb. 5

402	A131 2c scarlet	2.00	.30

Cent. of the death of the poet Gabriel de la Concepcion Valdés.

Manuel Marquez Sterling — A132

1946, Apr. 30

403	A132 2c scarlet	4.00	.50

Founding of the Manuel Marquez Sterling Professional School of Journalism, 3th anniv.

Globe and Cross — A133

1946, July 4 **Engr.**

404	A133 2c scarlet, *pink*	2.40	.25

80th anniv. of the Intl. Red Cross.

Cow and Milkmaid — A134

1947, Feb. 20 **Wmk. 106** ***Perf. 10***

405	A134 2c scarlet	3.50	.40

1947 National Livestock Exposition.

Franklin D. Roosevelt — A135

1947, Apr. 12
406 A135 2c vermilion 3.00 .40

2nd anniv. of the death of Franklin D. Roosevelt.

Antonio Oms Sarret and Aged Couple A136

1947, Oct. 20
407 A136 1c dp yellow grn 1.40 .30
408 A136 2c scarlet 1.20 .30
409 A136 5c lt blue 2.25 .55
Nos. 407-409 (3) 4.85 1.15

See note after No. 386.

Marta Abreu Arenabio de Estevez — A137

"Charity" — A138

Marta Abreu Monument, Santa Clara A139

"Patriotism" A140

1947, Nov. 29
410 A137 1c dp yellow grn 2.25 .40
411 A138 2c scarlet 2.00 .30
412 A139 5c brt blue 2.50 .40
413 A140 10c dk violet 4.25 .90
Nos. 410-413 (4) 11.00 2.00

Birth cent. of Marta Abreu Arenabio de Estevez, philanthropist and humanitarian.

Armauer Hansen A141

1948, Apr. 9
414 A141 2c rose carmine 3.50 .40

International Leprosy Congress, Havana.

Mother and Child A142

1948, Oct. 15 **Engr.**
415 A142 1c yellow grn 1.40 .25
416 A142 2c scarlet 1.25 .25
417 A142 5c brt blue 2.40 .40
Nos. 415-417 (3) 5.05 .90

See note after No. 386.

Death of José Martí — A143

Martí Rowing to Shore — A144

1948, Nov. 10 **Wmk. 106** ***Perf. 10***
418 A143 2c scarlet 1.60 .25
419 A144 5c brt blue 2.50 .45

50th anniversary of the death of José Martí, patriot (in 1945).

Tobacco Picking — A145

Liberty Carrying Flag and Cigars — A146

Cigar and Arms of Cuba — A147

1948, Dec. 6 **Size: 22½x26mm**
420 A145 1c green 1.50 .25
421 A146 2c rose car 1.40 .30
422 A147 5c brt blue 2.75 .30
Nos. 420-422 (3) 5.65 .85

Cuba's tobacco industry. See Nos. 445-447. For overprints and surcharge see Nos. 448-451, 512.

Equestrian Statue of Gen. Antonio Maceo — A148

Sword Salute to Maceo A149

Designs: 2c, Portrait of Maceo. 5c, Mausoleum, El Cacahual. 10c, East to West invasion. 20c, Battle of Peralejo. 50c, Declaration of Baragua. 1p, Death of Maceo at San Pedro.

1948, Dec. 15 **Wmk. 229** ***Perf. 12½***
423 A148 1c blue green 1.75 .25
424 A148 2c red 1.60 .25
425 A148 5c blue 2.40 .25
426 A149 8c black & brown 1.60 .45
427 A149 10c brown & bl grn 1.25 .35
428 A149 20c blue & car 3.75 1.40
429 A149 50c car & ultra 6.00 4.00
430 A149 1p black & violet 12.00 6.00
Nos. 423-430 (8) 30.35 12.95

Birth cent. (in 1945) of Maceo.

Symbol of Pharmacy A150

1948, Dec. 28 ***Perf. 10***
431 A150 2c rose carmine 3.50 .40

1st Pan-American Congress of Pharmacy, Havana, Dec. 1948.

Morro Lighthouse — A151

1949, Jan. 17 **Wmk. 229** ***Perf. 12½***
432 A151 2c carmine 3.25 .40

Centenary (in 1944) of the erection of the Morro Lighthouse.

Jagua Castle, Cienfuegos A152

1949, Jan. 27 **Wmk. 106** ***Perf. 10***
433 A152 1c yellow green 2.00 .30
434 A152 2c rose red 3.00 1.00

200th anniv. of the construction of Jagua Castle and the cent. of the publication of the 1st newspaper in Cienfuegos.

Manuel Sanguily y Garritt — A153

1949, Mar. 31
435 A153 2c rose red 1.40 .30
436 A153 5c blue 2.00 .30

Manuel Sanguily y Garritt (1848-1925), cabinet member, editor, author.

Map of Isle of Pines — A154

1949, Apr. 26
437 A154 5c blue 4.00 .70

20th anniv. of the recognition of Cuban ownership of the Isle of Pines.

Ismael Cespedes — A155

1949, Sept. 28
438 A155 1c yellow green 1.75 .30
439 A155 2c scarlet 1.25 .30
440 A155 5c brt blue 1.75 .30
Nos. 438-440 (3) 4.75 .90

See note after No. 386.

Gen. Enrique Collazo — A156

1950, Feb. 28 **Engr.** ***Perf. 10***
441 A156 2c scarlet 1.60 .25
442 A156 5c brt blue 2.00 .45

Centenary (in 1948) of the birth of General Enrique Collazo.

Enrique José Varona — A157

1950, Feb. 28
443 A157 2c scarlet 1.40 .25
444 A157 5c brt blue 2.00 .25

Centenary of the birth of Enrique José Varona, writer and patriot.

Tobacco Types of 1948

1950, June 20 **Re-engraved**
Size: 21x25mm
445 A145 1c green 1.25 .30
446 A146 2c rose red 1.25 .30
447 A147 5c blue 2.00 .30
Nos. 445-447 (3) 4.50 .90

The re-engraved stamps show slight differences in many minor details.

For overprints and surcharge see Nos. 448-451, 512.

No. 446 Overprinted in Black

1950, Apr. 27
448 A146 2c rose red 2.50 .30

Natl. Bank of Cuba opening, Apr. 27, 1950.

Re-engraved Tobacco Types of 1950 Overprinted in Carmine

1950, May 18

449 A145 1c yellow green 1.00 .30
450 A146 2c lilac rose 1.10 .30
451 A147 5c light blue 1.30 .30
Nos. 449-451 (3) 3.40 .90

75th anniv. (in 1949) of the UPU.
No. 451 exists with surcharge inverted.

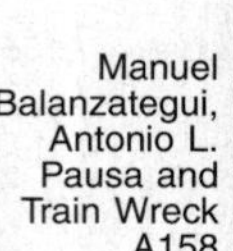

Manuel Balanzategui, Antonio L. Pausa and Train Wreck A158

1950, Sept. 21 **Engr.**

452 A158 1c yellow grn 1.40 .70
453 A158 2c scarlet 1.40 .70
454 A158 5c brt blue 4.00 .70
Nos. 452-454 (3) 6.80 2.10

Fernando Figueredo — A159

1951, Mar. 17 **Wmk. 106** ***Perf. 10***

455 A159 1c green 1.10 .25
456 A159 2c scarlet 1.25 .25
457 A159 5c brt blue 1.40 .25
Nos. 455-457 (3) 3.75 .75

Three-fourths of the proceeds from the sale of these stamps were used for the Communication Ministry Employees' Retirement Fund.

See Nos. 474, C51-C56, E15. For surcharges see Nos. 474, C51-C56, E15.

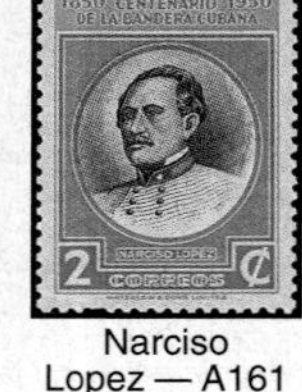

Miguel Teurbe Tolón and Flag — A160

Narciso Lopez — A161

Emilia Teurbe Tolón Sewing Flag — A162

Cuban Flag — A163

Engraved and Lithographed

1951, July 3 **Wmk. 229** ***Perf. 13***

458 A160 1c Prus grn, ultra & red 1.50 .30
459 A161 2c red & gray blk 1.40 .30
460 A162 5c ultra & red 1.60 .65
461 A163 10c rose vio, bl & red 3.50 1.00
Nos. 458-461,C41-C43,E13 (8) 24.25 8.40

Centenary of adoption of Cuba's flag.

Clara Louise Maass and Hospitals A164

Hospitals: Lutheran Memorial, Newark, N.J. and Las Animas, Havana.

Wmk. 106

1951, Aug. 24 **Engr.** ***Perf. 10***

462 A164 2c scarlet 2.00 .50

75th anniv. of the birth of Clara Louise Maass, (1876-1901), American nurse and martyr in yellow fever fight.

Airmail Type and

José Raul Capablanca — A165

Capablanca Club, Havana A166

Wmk. 229

1951, Nov. 1 **Photo.** ***Perf. 13***

463 A165 1c blue grn & org 3.75 .65
464 AP27 2c rose car & dk brn 3.50 .90
465 A166 5c black & dp ultra 12.00 1.90
Nos. 463-465,C44-C46,E14 (7) 75.25 18.10

Jose Raul Capablanca, World Chess titlist (1921). Value imperf., set of 7 pairs, $1,500.

Antonio Guiteras Holmes — A167

Guiteras Preparing Social Legislation A168

Fort of the Morrillo A169

Wmk. 106

1951, Oct. 22 **Engr.** ***Perf. 10***

466 A167 1c yellow green 1.50 .25
467 A168 2c rose carmine 2.25 .50
468 A169 5c deep blue 2.50 .50
Nos. 466-468,C47-C49 (6) 18.25 4.95

16th anniv. of the Action of the Morrillo and to honor Antonio Guiteras Holmes, who was killed there.

Souvenir sheets containing stamps similar to Nos. 466-468, but in different colors, are listed as Nos. C49a-C49b.

Poinsettia — A170

1951, Dec. 1 **Engr. and Typo.**

469 A170 1c green & car 5.25 1.00
470 A170 2c rose car & grn 3.75 .60

See Nos. 498-499.

Maj. Gen. José Maceo — A171

1952, Feb. 6 **Engr.**

471 A171 2c yellow brown 2.50 .25
472 A171 5c indigo 2.50 .25

Birth centenary of Maceo.

Isabella I — A172

1952, Feb. 22

473 A172 2c bright red 2.75 .50

500th anniv. of the birth of Queen Isabella I of Spain.

Souvenir sheets containing 2c stamps of type A172 are listed as Nos. C50a-C50b.

Type of 1951 Surcharged in Green

1952, Mar. 18

474 A159 10c on 2c yel brn 2.25 2.25

Receipt of Autonomy A173

Designs: 2c, Tomas Estrada Palma and Luis Estevez Romero. 5c, Barnet, Finlay, Guiteras and Nuñez. 8c, Capitol. 20c, Map, Central Highway. 50c, Sugar Mill.

Centers in Black

Wmk. 106

1952, May 27 **Engr.** ***Perf. 12½***

475 A173 1c dk green 2.75 .25
476 A173 2c dk carmine 1.60 .25
477 A173 5c dk blue 1.25 .25
478 A173 8c dk brown car 2.00 .25
479 A173 20c dk olive grn 2.40 .40
480 A173 50c dp orange 6.00 1.40
Nos. 475-480,C57-C60,E16 (11) 29.35 8.05

50th anniv. of the Republic of Cuba.

Hands Holding Coffee Beans A174

Designs: 2c, Map and man picking coffee beans. 5c, Farmer with pan of beans.

1952, Aug. 22 **Wmk. 229** ***Perf. 13½***

481 A174 1c green 2.00 .25
482 A174 2c rose red 1.00 .25
483 A174 5c dk vio bl & aqua 2.50 .40
Nos. 481-483 (3) 5.50 .90

Bicentenary of coffee cultivation.

Col. Charles Hernandez y Sandrino — A175

1952, Oct. 7 **Wmk. 106** ***Perf. 10***

484 A175 1c yellow grn 3.50 .30
485 A175 2c scarlet 5.00 .30
486 A175 5c blue 4.50 .30
487 A175 8c black 4.50 .45
488 A175 10c brown red 5.50 .45
489 A175 20c brown 9.00 3.75
Nos. 484-489,C63-C72,E17 (17) 85.35 25.20

See note after No. 457.

Alonso Alvarez de la Campa — A176

Portraits: 2c, Carlos A. Latorre. 3c, Anacleto Bermudez. 5c, Eladio G. Toledo. 8c, Angel Laborde. 10c, Jose M. Medina. 13c, Pascual Rodriguez. 20c, Carlos Verdugo.

Frame Engraved; Center in Black

1952, Nov. 27

490 A176 1c green 1.25 .25
491 A176 2c carmine 2.50 .25
492 A176 3c purple 1.75 .25
493 A176 5c blue 1.75 .60
494 A176 8c bister brn 2.25 .50
495 A176 10c orange brn 2.10 .50
496 A176 13c lilac rose 3.50 .75
497 A176 20c olive grn 4.75 1.25
Nos. 490-497,C73-C74 (10) 26.85 6.15

Execution of 8 medical students, 81st anniv.

Christmas Type of 1951

Centers: Tree.

Frame Engr.; Center Typo.

1952, Dec. 1 **Dated "1952-1953"**

498 A170 1c yel grn & car 7.50 1.90
499 A170 3c vio & dk grn 7.50 1.50

Birthplace of José Martí — A177

Marti at St. Lazarus Quarry — A178

No. 501, Court martial. No. 502, Martiano house, Havana. No. 504, El Abra ranch, Isle of Pines. No. 505, Symbols, "Marti the Poet." No. 506, Marti and Bolivar statue, Caracas. No. 507, At desk in New York. No. 508, House where revolutionary party was formed. No. 509, 1st issue of "Patria."

1953 **Engr.** ***Perf. 10***

500 A177 1c dk grn & red brn 1.75 .25
501 A177 1c dk grn & red brn 1.40 .25
502 A177 3c purple & brn 2.00 .25
503 A178 3c purple & brn 2.00 .25
504 A177 5c dp bl & dk brn 1.25 .25
505 A178 5c ultra & brn 1.75 .25
506 A178 10c red brn & blk .80 .40
507 A178 10c dk brn & blk 2.00 .40
508 A178 13c dk ol grn & dk brn 2.00 .80
509 A177 13c dk ol grn & brn 2.50 1.00
Nos. 500-509,C79-C89 (21) 28.55 12.90

Centenary of birth of José Marti.

Rafael Montoro Valdez — A179

1953, Mar. 5

510 A179 3c dark violet 3.00 .40

Rafael Montoro Valdez, statesman, birth cent.

Francisco Carrera Justiz — A180

1953, Mar. 9

511 A180 3c rose red 3.25 .50

Francisco Carrera Justiz, educator, statesman.

No. 446 Surcharged with New Value

1953, June 16

512 A146 3c on 2c rose red 1.50 .25

Board of Accounts Bldg., Havana — A181

1953, Nov. 3 **Engr.**

513 A181 3c blue 1.35 .45
Nos. 513,C90-C91 (3) 6.65 2.25

1st Intl. Cong. of Boards of Accounts, Havana, Nov. 2-9.

Miguel Coyula Llaguno — A182

Communications Assoc. Flag — A183

Antonio Ginard Rojas — A183b

Designs: 3c, 8c, Enrique Calleja Hensell.

1954 **Dated 1953**

514 A182 1c green .30 .25
515 A182 3c rose red .50 .25
516 A183 5c blue 1.25 .25
517 A182 8c brn car 1.50 .50
518 A183b 10c brown 2.50 1.25
Nos. 514-518,C92-C95,E19 (10) 24.80 9.25

Nos. 515 and 517 show the same portrait, but inscriptions are arranged differently.

See note after No. 457.

Carlos J. Finlay — A184

Maximo Gomez — A184a

Portraits: 1c, José Marti. 3c, José de la Luz Caballero. 4c, Miguel Aldama. 5c, Calixto Garcia. 8c, Ignacio Agramonte. 10c, Tomas Estrada Palma. 14c, Serafin Sanchez. 20c, José Antonio Saco. 50c, Antonio Maceo. 1p, Carlos Manuel de Cespedes.

1954-56 **Wmk. 106** ***Perf. 10***

519 A184 1c green .75 .25
520 A184a 2c rose car 1.00 .25
521 A184 3c violet 1.00 .25
521A A184 4c red lil ('56) .75 .25
522 A184a 5c slate bl .75 .25
523 A184a 8c car lake 1.40 .35
524 A184 10c sepia 1.40 .35
525 A184 13c org red .75 .35
525A A184a 14c gray ('56) 1.25 .35
526 A184 20c olive 2.25 .35
527 A184a 50c org yel 2.40 .45
528 A184a 1p orange 2.75 1.00
Nos. 519-528 (12) 16.45 4.45

See Nos. 674-680. For surcharges see Nos. 636, 641-643.

Maj. Gen. José M. Rodriguez — A185

Design: 5c, Gen. Rodriguez on horseback.

1954, June 8 **Engr.** ***Perf. 12½***

Center in Dark Brown

529 A185 2c dark carmine 1.50 .25
530 A185 5c deep blue 2.40 .40

Cent. of the birth of Maj. Gen. José Maria Rodriguez (in 1851).

Gen. Batísta Sanatorium — A186

1954, Sept. 21 **Wmk. 106** ***Perf. 10***

531 A186 3c deep blue 3.00 .25

See No. C107.

Santa Claus — A187

1954, Dec. 15

532 A187 2c dk grn & car 5.25 1.25
533 A187 4c car & dk grn 5.25 1.25

Christmas 1954.

Maria Luisa Dolz — A188

1954, Dec. 23

534 A188 4c deep blue 2.75 .40

Cent. of the birth of Maria Luisa Dolz, educator and defender of women's rights. See No. C108.

Cuban Flag and Scouts Saluting A189

1954, Dec. 27 ***Perf. 12½***

535 A189 4c dark green 3.25 .35

Issued to publicize the national patrol encampment of the Boy Scouts of Cuba.

Rotary Emblem and Paul P. Harris — A190

1955, Feb. 23 **Engr.** **Wmk. 106**

536 A190 4c blue & dk blue 2.25 .25

Rotary International, 50th anniversary. See No. C109.

Maj. Gen. Francisco Carrillo — A191

Portrait: 5c, Gen. Carrillo standing.

1955, Mar. 8 ***Perf. 10***

537 A191 2c brt red & dk bl 1.25 .25
538 A191 5c dk bl & dk brn 1.50 .30

Cent. of the birth of Maj. Gen. Francisco Carrillo (1851-1926).

Stamp of 1885 and Convent of San Francisco — A192

Designs (including 1855 stamp): 4c, Volanta carriage. 10c, Havana, 19th century. 14c, Captain general's residence.

1955, Apr. ***Perf. 12½***

539 A192 2c lil rose & dk grnsh bl 2.00 .25
540 A192 4c ocher & dk grn 2.00 .30
541 A192 10c ultra & dk red 2.00 .75
542 A192 14c grn & dp org 3.00 .75
Nos. 539-542,C110-C113 (8) 21.50 4.40

Cent. of Cuba's 1st postage stamps.

Maj. Gen. Mario G. Menocal A193

Gen. Emilio Nuñez A194

Portraits: 10c, J. G. Gomez. 14c, A. Sanchez de Bustamente.

1955, June 22

543 A193 2c dark green 1.25 .25
544 A194 4c lilac rose 1.25 .25
545 A193 10c deep blue 1.50 .40
546 A194 14c gray violet 3.00 .90
Nos. 543-546,C114-C116,E20 (8) 25.75 7.40

See note after No. 457.

Turkey — A195

1955, Dec. 15 **Engr.**

547 A195 2c slate grn & dk car 3.75 1.50
548 A195 4c rose lake & brt grn 4.25 1.50

Christmas 1955.

Gen. Emilio Nuñez — A196

1955, Dec. 27

549 A196 4c claret 1.60 .45
Nos. 549,C127-C128 (3) 6.20 1.75

Cent. of the birth of Gen. Emilio Nunez, Cuban revolutionary hero.

Francisco Cajigal de la Vega (1695-1777) A197

1956, Mar. 27 ***Perf. 12½***

552 A197 4c rose brn & slate bl 3.75 .55

Cuban post bicent. See No. C129.

Julian del Casal — A198

Portraits: 4c, Luisa Perez de Zambrana. 10c, Juan Clemente Zenea. 14c, José Joaquin Palma.

1956, May 2 **Portraits in Black**

553 A198 2c green .50 .25
554 A198 4c rose lilac 1.50 .25
555 A198 10c blue 1.90 .25
556 A198 14c violet 3.25 .25
Nos. 553-556,C131-C133,E21 (8) 16.50 4.25

See note after No. 457.

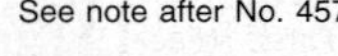

Victor Muñoz — A199

1956, May 13

557 A199 4c brown & green 1.50 .55

Victor Munoz (1873-1922), founder of Mother's Day in Cuba. See No. C134.

Masonic Temple, Havana — A200

1956, June 5

558 A200 4c blue 2.25 .55

See No. C135.

Virgin of Charity, El Cobre — A201

1956, Sept. 8 ***Perf. 12½***

559 A201 4c brt blue & yel 3.00 .30

Issued in honor of Our Lady of Charity of Cobre, patroness of Cuba. See No. C149.

"The Cry of Yara" — A202

1956, Oct. 10
560 A202 4c dk grn & brn 2.25 .30

Cuba's independence from Spain.

Raimundo G. Menocal A203

1956, Dec. 3 Wmk. 106 ***Perf. 12½***
561 A203 4c dark brown 2.00 .30

Cent. of the birth of Prof. Raimundo G. Menocal, physician.

The Three Wise Men — A204

1956, Dec. 1
562 A204 2c red & slate grn 5.00 1.10
563 A204 4c slate grn & red 5.00 1.10

Christmas 1956.

Martin Morua Delgado — A205

1957, Jan. 30
564 A205 4c dark green 2.00 .30

Delgado, patriot, birth cent.

Boy Scouts at Campfire — A206

1957, Feb. 22 Wmk. 106 ***Perf. 12½***
565 A206 4c slate grn & red 2.00 .40

Cent. of the birth of Lord Baden-Powell, founder of the Boy Scouts. See No. C152.

"The Blind," by M. Vega A207

Paintings: 4c, "The Art Critics" by M. Melero. 10c, "Volanta in Storm" by A. Menocal. 14c, "The Convalescent" by L. Romañach.

1957, Mar. Engr. ***Perf. 12½***

Side and Lower Inscriptions in Dark Brown

566 A207 2c olive green .50 .25
567 A207 4c orange red 1.40 .30
568 A207 10c olive green 1.60 .50
569 A207 14c ultra 2.00 .55
Nos. 566-569,C153-C155,E22 (8) 14.60 4.30

See note after No. 457.

Emblem of Philatelic Club of Cuba — A208

1957, Apr. 24
570 A208 4c ocher, blue & red 2.50 .30

Issued for Stamp Day, Apr. 24, and the National Philatelic Exhibition. See No. C156.

Juan F. Steegers — A209

1957, Apr. 30
571 A209 4c blue 2.00 .30

Juan Francisco Steegers y Perera (1856-1921), dactyloscopy pioneer. See No. C157.

Victoria Bru Sanchez — A210

1957, June 3 Wmk. 106 ***Perf. 12½***
572 A210 4c indigo 3.25 .30

Joaquin de Aguero in Battle of Jucaral — A211

1957, July 4
573 A211 4c dark green 2.50 .30

Issued to honor Joaquin de Aguero, Cuban freedom fighter and patriot. See No. C162.

Boy, Dogs and Cat — A212

1957, July 17
574 A212 4c Prus green 1.75 .55

Mrs. Jeanette Ryder, founder of the Humane Society of Cuba. See Nos. C163-C163a.

Col. Rafael Manduley del Rio — A213

1957, July 31
575 A213 4c Prus green 4.00 1.50

Issued to honor Col. Manduley del Rio, patriot, on the cent. of his birth (in 1856).

Palace of Justice A214

1957, Sept. 2 Engr. ***Perf. 12½***
576 A214 4c blue gray 2.00 .40

Opening of the new Palace of Justice in Havana. See No. C165.

Generals of the Liberation — A215

1957, Sept. 26
577 A215 4c dl grn & red brn 1.25 .30
578 A215 4c dl bl & red brn 1.25 .30
579 A215 4c rose & brown 1.25 .30
580 A215 4c org yel & brn 1.25 .30
581 A215 4c lt violet & brn 1.25 .30
Nos. 577-581 (5) 6.25 1.50

Generals of the army of liberation.

1st Publication Printed in Cuba — A216

1957, Oct. 18 Wmk. 106 ***Perf. 12½***
582 A216 4c slate blue 2.50 .40
Nos. 582,C167-C168 (3) 7.75 1.15

José Marti National Library.

Patio — A217

1957, Nov. 19
583 A217 4c red brn & grn 1.50 .40
Nos. 583,C173-C174 (3) 6.50 1.40

Cent. of the 1st Cuban Normal School.

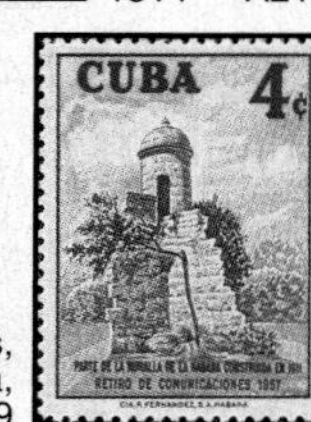

Trinidad, Founded 1514 — A218

Fortifications, Havana, 1611 — A219

Views: 10c, Padre Pico street, Santiago de Cuba. 14c, Church of Our Lady, Camaguey.

1957, Dec. 17 Engr. ***Perf. 12½***
584 A218 2c brown & indigo .50 .25
585 A219 4c slate grn & brn 1.10 .25
586 A219 10c sepia & red 1.20 .30
587 A219 14c green & dk red 1.00 .25
Nos. 584-587,C175-C177,E23 (8) 11.05 3.50

See note after No. 457.

Nativity — A220

1957, Dec. 20
588 A220 2c multicolored 2.50 1.00
589 A220 4c multicolored 3.50 1.00

Christmas 1957.

Dayton Hedges and Ariguanabo Textile Factory A221

1958, Jan. 30 Wmk. 106 ***Perf. 12½***
590 A221 4c blue 2.00 .70

Issued to honor Dayton Hedges, founder of Cuba's textile industry. See No. C178.

Dr. Francisco Dominguez Roldan — A222

1958, Feb. 21
591 A222 4c green 2.75 .30

Roldan (1864-1942), who introduced radiotherapy and physiotherapy to Cuba.

José Ignacio Rivero y Alonso — A223

1958, Apr. 1
592 A223 4c lt olive green 2.40 .70

José Ignacio Rivero y Alonso, editor of Diario de la Marina, 1919-44. See No. C179.

Map of Cuba and Mail Route, 1756 A224

1958, Apr. 24 ***Perf. 12½***
593 A224 4c dk grn, aqua & buff 2.50 .30

Issued for Stamp Day, Apr. 24 and the National Philatelic Exhibition. See No. C180.

Maj. Gen. José Miguel Gomez — A225

1958, June 6 Wmk. 106 Perf. 12½

594 A225 4c slate 1.90 .40

Maj. Gen. José Miguel Gomez, President of Cuba, 1909-13. See No. C181.

Nicolas Ruiz Espadero — A226

Musicians: 4c, Ignacio Cervantes. 10c, José White. 14c, Brindis de Salas.

1958, June 27 Perf. 12½

Indigo Emblem

595 A226 2c brown .60 .25
596 A226 4c dark gray 1.20 .25
597 A226 10c olive green 2.00 .25
598 A226 14c red 2.00 .25

Green Emblem

Physicians: 2c, Tomas Romay Chacon. 4c, Angel Arturo Aballi. 10c, Fernando Gonzalez del Valle. 14c, Vicente Antonio de Castro.

599 A226 2c brown 1.10 .25
600 A226 4c gray 1.10 .25
601 A226 10c dark carmine 1.40 .25
602 A226 14c dark blue 2.00 .25

Red Emblem

Lawyers: 2c, Jose Maria Garcia Montes. 4c, Jose A. Gonzalez Lanuza. 10c, Juan B. Hernandez Barreiro. 14c, Pedro Gonzalez Llorente.

603 A226 2c sepia .50 .25
604 A226 4c gray .80 .25
605 A226 10c olive grn 1.00 .25
606 A226 14c slate blue 1.10 .25
Nos. 595-606 (12) 14.80 3.00

For surcharges see Nos. 629-631.

Carlos de la Torre — A227

1958, Aug. 29 Engr. Wmk. 321

607 A227 4c violet blue 2.00 .40
Nos. 607,C182-C184 (4) 17.50 5.50

Dr. Carlos de la Torre y Huerta (1858-1950), naturalist. For surcharge see No. 632.

Poey's "Memorias" Title Page — A228

Felipe Poey — A229

1958, Sept. 26 Wmk. 106

608 A228 2c black & lt violet 3.00 .25
609 A229 4c brown black 3.25 .25
Nos. 608-609,C185-C191,E26-E27 (11) 87.50 18.80

Felipe Poey (1799-1891), naturalist.

Theodore Roosevelt — A230

1958, Oct. 27 Perf. 12½

610 A230 4c gray green 2.00 .40

Theodore Roosevelt, birth cent. See No. C192.

Cattleyopsis Lindenii Orchid — A231

4c, Oncidium Guibertianum Orchid.

Engraved and Photogravure

1958, Dec. 16 Wmk. 321 Perf. 12½

611 A231 2c multicolored 2.90 1.25
612 A231 4c multicolored 3.75 1.25

Christmas. For surcharge see No. 633.

Revolutionary Government

Flag and Revolutionary A232

Engr. & Typo.

1959, Jan. 28 Wmk. 321

613 A232 2c car rose & gray .75 .30

Day of Liberation, Jan. 1, 1959.

Gen. Adolfo Flor Crombet (1848-95) — A233

1959, Mar. 18 Engr. Wmk. 106

614 A233 4c slate green 2.00 .40

For surcharge see No. 634.

Maria Teresa Garcia Montes — A234

1959, Nov. 11 Perf. 12½

615 A234 4c brown 1.10 .40

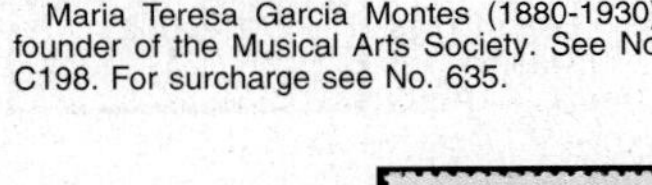

Maria Teresa Garcia Montes (1880-1930), founder of the Musical Arts Society. See No. C198. For surcharge see No. 635.

Carlos Manuel de Cespedes — A235

Presidents: No. 617, Salvador Cisneros Betancourt. No. 618, Manuel de Jesus Calvar. No. 619, Bartolomé Maso. No. 620, Juan B. Spotorno. No. 621, Tomas Estrada Palma. No. 622, Francisco Javier de Céspedes. No. 623, Vicente Garcia.

1959, Oct. 10 Wmk. 106 Perf. 12½

616 A235 2c slate blue .55 .25
617 A235 2c green .55 .25
618 A235 2c deep violet .55 .25
619 A235 2c orange brown .55 .25
620 A235 4c dark carmine .70 .25
621 A235 4c deep brown .70 .25
622 A235 4c dark gray .70 .25
623 A235 4c dark violet .70 .25
Nos. 616-623 (8) 5.00 2.00

Issued to honor former Cuban presidents.

No. B3 Surcharged in Red

1960

624 SP2 2c on 2c + 1c car & ultra 1.25 .25

See No. C199.

Rebel Attack on Moncada Barracks A236

Designs: 2c, Rebels disembarking from "Granma." 10c, Battle of the Uvero. 12c, Map of Cuba and rebel ("The Invasion").

1960, Jan. 28 Wmk. 320

625 A236 1c gray ol, bl & ver .25 .25
626 A236 2c bl, gray ol & brn .60 .25
627 A236 10c bl, gray ol & red 1.75 .65
628 A236 12c brt bl, brn & grn 2.40 .30
Nos. 625-628,C200-C202 (7) 12.10 3.80

First anniversary of revolution.

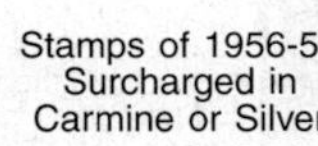

Stamps of 1956-59 Surcharged in Carmine or Silver

1960, Feb. 3

629 A226 1c on 4c dk gray & ind .50 .25
630 A226 1c on 4c gray & grn .50 .25
631 A226 1c on 4c gray & red .50 .25
632 A227 1c on 4c violet bl .50 .25
633 A231 1c on 4c multi (S) 1.00 .50
634 A233 1c on 4c slate grn .50 .25
635 A234 1c on 4c brown .50 .25
636 A184a 2c on 14c gray 1.25 .25
Nos. 629-636,C203-C204 (10) 9.60 3.55

Tomas Estrada Palma Statue, Havana — A237

Statues: 2c, Mambi Victorioso (Battle of San Juan Hill), Santiago de Cuba. 10c, Marta Abreo de Estevez. 12c, Ignacio Agramonte, Camaguey.

Wmk. 321

1960, Mar. 28 Engr. Perf. 12½

637 A237 1c brn & dk bl .25 .25
638 A237 2c green & red .30 .25
639 A237 10c choc & red .90 .25
640 A237 12c gray ol & vio 1.25 .45
Nos. 637-640,C206-C208 (7) 7.40 2.95

See note after No. 386.

Nos. 521A, 522 and 525 Surcharged in Violet Blue, Red or Black

1960 Wmk. 106 Perf. 10

641 A184 2c on 4c red lil (VB) .80 .40
642 A184a 2c on 5c sl bl (R) 1.00 .40
643 A184 2c on 13c org red 1.00 .40

No. 307B Surcharged in Black

644 A41 10c on 20c ol grn 1.25 .50
Nos. 641-644 (4) 4.05 1.70

17th Olympic Games, Rome, Aug. 25-Sept. 11 — A238

Wmk. 321

1960, Sept. 22 Engr. Perf. 12½

645 A238 1c Sailboats .45 .25
646 A238 2c Marksman .55 .25
Nos. 645-646,C212-C213 (4) 3.30 1.25

For souvenir sheet see No. C213a.

Camilo Cienfuegos and View of Escolar A239

1960, Oct. 27 Litho. Unwmk.

647 A239 2c brn, bl, grn & red 2.00 .25

1st anniv. of the death of Camilo Cienfuegos, revolutionary hero.

Morning Glory A240

Tobacco and Christmas Hymn A241

1960 Litho. Perf. 12½

648 A240 1c red .75 .75
649 A241 1c Tobacco 1.50 1.50
650 A241 1c Mariposa 1.50 1.50
651 A241 1c Guaiacum 1.50 1.50
652 A241 1c Coffee 1.50 1.50
a. Block of 4, #649-652 7.00
653 A240 2c ultra 1.00 1.00
654 A241 2c Tobacco 3.00 3.00
655 A241 2c Mariposa 3.00 3.00
656 A241 2c Guaiacum 3.00 3.00
657 A241 2c Coffee 3.00 3.00
a. Block of 4, #654-657 14.00
658 A240 10c ocher 4.00 2.50
659 A241 10c Tobacco 6.00 6.00
660 A241 10c Mariposa 6.00 6.00
661 A241 10c Guaiacum 6.00 6.00
662 A241 10c Coffee 6.00 6.00
a. Block of 4, #659-662 30.00
Nos. 648-662 (15) 47.75 46.25

Issued for Christmas 1960.

Nos. 648-662 were printed in three sheets of 25. Nine stamps of type A240 form a center cross, stamps of type A241 form a block of four in each corner with the musical bars joined in an oval around the floral designs.

"Public Capital for Economic Benefit" — A242

Designs: 2c, Chart and symbols of agriculture and industry. 6c, Cogwheels.

Perf. 11½

1961, Jan. 10 Unwmk. Photo.

No.	Type	Description	Unused	Used
663	A242	1c yel, blk & org	.40	.25
664	A242	2c bl, blk & red	.40	.25
665	A242	6c yel, red org & blk	1.40	.25
		Nos. 663-665,C215-C218 (7)	10.45	2.90

Issued to publicize the conference of underdeveloped countries, Havana.

Jesus Menéndez and Sugar Cane — A243

1961, Jan. 22 Litho. *Perf. 12½*

No.	Type	Description	Unused	Used
666	A243	2c dk grn & brn	1.50	.35

Jesus Menéndez, leader in sugar industry.

Overprinted in Red

1961, May 2

No.	Type	Description	Unused	Used
667	A243	2c dk grn & brn	1.50	.35

Issued for May Day, 1961.

Dove and UN Emblem — A244

1961, Apr. 12 Litho. *Perf. 12½*

No.	Type	Description	Unused	Used
668	A244	2c red brn & yel grn	.40	.25
669	A244	10c emer & rose lil	1.10	.45
a.		Souv. sheet, #668-669, imperf.	3.25	3.25
		Nos. 668-669,C222-C223 (4)	3.50	1.45

15th anniv. (in 1960) of the UN.

Stamp Day A245

Stamp Day: 1c, Revolutionary 10c stamp of 1874, 1868 "cancel." 2c, #238, 1902 "cancel." 10c, #613, 1959 "cancel."

1961, Apr. 24 Unwmk.

No.	Type	Description	Unused	Used
670	A245	1c dull rose & dk grn	.35	.25
671	A245	2c salmon & dk grn	.40	.25
672	A245	10c pale grn, car rose & blk	1.50	.40
		Nos. 670-672 (3)	2.25	.90

For overprint see No. 681.

Hand Releasing Dove — A246

1961, July 26 *Perf. 12½*

No.	Type	Description	Unused	Used
673	A246	2c blk, red, yel & gray	1.50	.25

26th of July (1953) movement, Castro's revolt against Fulgencio Batista.

Burelage on back consisting of wavy lines and diagonal rows of "CUBA CORREOS" in pale salmon.

Portrait Type of 1954

Designs: Same as before. On the 2c, "1833" is replaced by "?."

Wmk. 321 (Nos. 674, 676); Unwmkd.
Perf. 12½ (Nos. 674, 676); Rouletted

1961-69 Engr.

No.	Type	Description	Unused	Used
674	A184	1c brown red	.50	.25
675	A184	1c lt blue ('69)	.30	.25
676	A184a	2c slate green	.50	.25
677	A184a	2c yel grn ('69)	.30	.25
678	A184	3c org ('64)	1.50	.25
679	A184	13c brn ('64)	1.50	.30
680	A184	20c lilac ('69)	1.75	.25
		Nos. 674-680 (7)	6.35	1.80

Issued: Nos. 674, 676, 8/1; Nos. 678-679, 12/764; others, 9/69.

For Nos. 675, 677-680, see embargo note following No. 702.

No. 672 Ovptd. in Red

Perf. 12½

1961, Oct. 7 Litho. Unwmk.

No.	Type	Description	Unused	Used
681	A245	10c pale grn, car rose & blk	2.00	.45

1st Official Phil. Exhib., Havana, Oct. 7-17.

Education Year — A247

Designs: One letter (per stamp) of "CUBA," book and various quotations by Jose Marti about the virtues of literacy.

1961, Nov. 22

No.	Type	Description	Unused	Used
682	A247	1c pale grn, red & blk	.25	.25
683	A247	2c blue, red & blk	.25	.25
684	A247	10c vio, red & blk	1.00	.25
685	A247	12c org, red & blk	2.00	.75
		Nos. 682-685 (4)	3.50	1.50

A248

Christmas A249

No. 686, Polymita flammulata. No. 687, Polymita fulminata. No. 688, Polymita nigrofasciata. No. 689, Polymita fuscolimbata. No. 690, Polymita roseolimbata. No. 691, Tiaris canorus. No. 692, Ara tricolor. No. 693, Priotelus temnurus. No. 694, Mellisuga helenae. No. 695, Campephilus principalis. No. 696, Othreis toddi. No. 697, Uranidia boisduvalii. No. 698, Phoebis avellaneda. No. 699, Phaloe cubana. No. 700, Papilio gundlachianus.

1c, Snails. 2c, Birds, vert. 10c, Butterflies.

1961, Dec. 1

No.	Type	Description	Unused	Used
686	A248	1c multicolored	.50	.25
687	A249	1c multicolored	.50	.25
688	A249	1c multicolored	.50	.25
689	A249	1c multicolored	.50	.25
690	A249	1c multicolored	.50	.25
a.		Block of 5 + label, Nos. 686-690	2.50	1.50
691	A248	2c multicolored	2.00	.50
692	A249	2c multicolored	2.00	.50
693	A249	2c multicolored	2.00	.50
694	A249	2c multicolored	2.00	.50
695	A249	2c multicolored	2.00	.50
a.		Block of 5 + label, Nos. 691-695	12.50	4.00
696	A248	10c multicolored	3.00	1.00
697	A249	10c multicolored	3.00	1.00
698	A249	10c multicolored	3.00	1.00
699	A249	10c multicolored	3.00	1.00
700	A249	10c multicolored	3.00	1.00
a.		Block of 5 + label, Nos. 696-700	15.00	7.50
		Nos. 686-700 (15)	27.50	8.75

Stamps of the same denomination printed se-tenant in sheets of 20 stamps plus 5 labels picturing bells and star. Stamps of Type A249 are arranged in blocks of 4; Type A248 stamps and labels form a cross in sheet.

See Nos. 760-774, 912-926, 1025-1039, 1179-1193, 1303-1317, 1464-1478, 1572-1586.

3rd Anniv. of the Revolution A250

1962, Jan. 3

No.	Type	Description	Unused	Used
701	A250	1c multi	.85	.35
702	A250	2c multi	1.75	.45

See Nos. C226-C228.

Cuban goods have been embargoed by the United States since a Feb. 7, 1962 proclamation by President Kennedy, but according to the Office of Foreign Assets Control of the Treasury Department, used Cuban stamps can be imported and sold without limitation, and unused stamps may be imported for personal use, but not resold.

Natl. Militia A251

Silhouettes of militiamen and women and their peace-time occupations: 1c, Farmer. 2c, Welder. 3c, Seamstress.

1962, Feb. 26

No.	Type	Description	Unused	Used
703	A251	1c blue grn & blk	.40	.25
704	A251	2c deep blue & blk	.60	.35
705	A251	10c brt org & blk	2.50	.55
		Nos. 703-705 (3)	3.50	1.15

Bay of Pigs Invasion, 1st Anniv. — A252

1962, Apr. 17

No.	Type	Description	Unused	Used
706	A252	2c multi	.75	.25
707	A252	3c multi	.75	.25
708	A252	10c multi	6.00	.50
		Nos. 706-708 (3)	7.50	1.00

1st West Indies Packet A253

1962, Apr. 24

No.	Type	Description	Unused	Used
709	A253	10c red & gray	3.25	.90

Stamp Day. See No. E32.

Intl. Labor Day — A254

1962, May 1

No.	Type	Description	Unused	Used
710	A254	2c ocher & blk	.35	.25
711	A254	3c ver & blk	.75	.25
712	A254	10c greenish blue & blk	2.00	.70
		Nos. 710-712 (3)	3.10	1.20

Natl. Sports Institute (INDER) Emblem and Athletes — A255

No. 713, Judo. No. 714, Discus. No. 715, Gymnastics. No. 716, Wrestling. No. 717, Weight lifting. No. 718, Roller skating. No. 719, Equestrian. No. 720, Archery. No. 721, Bicycling. No. 722, Bowling. No. 723, Power boating. No. 724, One-man kayak. No. 725, Swimming. No. 726, Sculling. No. 727, Yachting. No. 728, Soccer. No. 729, Volleyball. No. 730, Baseball. No. 731, Basketball. No. 732, Tennis. No. 733, Boxing. No. 734, Underwater fishing. No. 735, Model-plane flying. No. 736, Pistol shooting. No. 737, Water polo. No. 738, Paddleball. No. 739, Fencing. No. 740, Sports Palace. No. 741, Chess. No. 742, Jai alai.

1962, July 25 Wmk. 321

No.	Type	Description	Unused	Used
713	A255	1c multi	.35	.25
714	A255	1c multi	.35	.25
715	A255	1c multi	.35	.25
716	A255	1c multi	.35	.25
717	A255	1c multi	.35	.25
718	A255	2c multi	.35	.25
719	A255	2c multi	.35	.25
720	A255	2c multi	.35	.25
721	A255	2c multi	.35	.25
722	A255	2c multi	.35	.25
723	A255	3c multi	1.00	.25
724	A255	3c multi	1.00	.25
725	A255	3c multi	1.00	.25
726	A255	3c multi	1.00	.25
727	A255	3c multi	1.00	.25
728	A255	9c multi	.90	.35
729	A255	9c multi	.90	.35
730	A255	9c multi	.90	.35
731	A255	9c multi	.90	.35
732	A255	9c multi	.90	.35
733	A255	10c multi	.90	.35
734	A255	10c multi	.90	.35
735	A255	10c multi	.90	.35
736	A255	10c multi	.90	.35
737	A255	10c multi	.90	.35
738	A255	13c multi	1.00	.50
739	A255	13c multi	1.00	.50
740	A255	13c multi	1.00	.50
741	A255	13c multi	1.00	.50
742	A255	13c multi	1.00	.50
		Nos. 713-742 (30)	22.50	9.75

Stamps of the same denomination printed se-tenant in sheets of 25. Various combinations possible.

9th Anniv. of the Revolution A256

Attack on Moncada Barracks: Abel Santamaria and: 2c, Barracks under siege. 3c, Children at Moncada School.

1962, July 26

No.	Type	Description	Unused	Used
743	A256	2c brn car & dark ultra	.75	.35
744	A256	3c dark ultra & brn car	1.15	.55

8th World Youth Festival for Peace and Friendship, Helsinki, July 28-Aug. 6 — A257

1962, July 28

No.	Type	Description	Unused	Used
745	A257	2c Dove, emblem	1.25	.25
746	A257	3c Hand grip, emblem	1.75	.50
a.		Min. sheet of 2, Nos. 745-746, imperf.	6.75	6.75

A258

1962, Aug. 27

No.	Type	Description	Unused	Used
747	A258	1c Boxing	.25	.25
748	A258	2c Tennis	.25	.25
749	A258	3c Baseball	.25	.25
750	A258	13c Fencing	2.10	.90
		Nos. 747-750 (4)	2.85	1.65

9th Central American and Caribbean Games, Kingston, Jamaica, Aug. 11-25.

A259

First Natl. Congress of the Federation of Cuban Women — A260

1962, Oct. 1

No.	Type	Description	Unused	Used
751	A259	9c rose, blk & grn	.75	.25
752	A260	13c blk, grn & lt blue	1.90	.65

Latin American University Games — A261

1962, Oct. 13 **Wmk. 106**

No.	Type	Description	Unused	Used
753	A261	1c Running	.40	.25
754	A261	2c Baseball	.60	.25
755	A261	3c Basketball	.85	.25
756	A261	13c World map	1.75	.55
		Nos. 753-756 (4)	3.60	1.30

World Health Organization Campaign to Eradicate Malaria — A262

Designs: 1c, Magnified specimen of the parasitic protozoa, microscope. 2c, Swamp and mosquito. 3c, Chemist's structural formulas for quinine, cinchona plant.

1962, Dec. 14

No.	Type	Description	Unused	Used
757	A262	1c multi	.35	.25
758	A262	2c multi	.35	.25
759	A262	3c multi	1.25	.45
		Nos. 757-759 (3)	1.95	.95

Christmas Type of 1961

No. 760, Epicrates angulifer. No. 761, Cricosaurus typica. No. 762, Anolis equestris. No. 763, Tropidophis wrighti. No. 764, Cyclura macleayi. No. 765, Cubispa turquino. No. 766, Chrysis superba. No. 767, Essostruta roberto. No. 768, Hortensia conciliata. No. 769, Lachnopus argus. No. 770, Monophyllus cubanus. No. 771, Capromys pilorides. No. 772, Capromys pre-hensilis. No. 773, Solenodon cubensis. No. 774, Capromys pilorides (Blanca).

2c, Reptiles. 3c, Insects, vert. 10c, Rodents.

1962, Dec. 21 **Unwmk.**

No.	Type	Description	Unused	Used
760	A248	2c multi	.65	.25
761	A249	2c multi	.65	.25
762	A249	2c multi	.65	.25
763	A249	2c multi	.65	.25
764	A249	2c multi	.65	.25
a.		Block of 5 + label, Nos. 760-764	3.50	1.50
765	A248	3c multi	1.00	.60
766	A249	3c multi	1.00	.60
767	A249	3c multi	1.00	.60
768	A249	3c multi	1.00	.60
769	A249	3c multi	1.00	.60
a.		Block of 5 + label, Nos. 765-769	5.50	4.50
770	A248	10c multi	4.00	1.25
771	A249	10c multi	4.00	1.25
772	A249	10c multi	4.00	1.25
773	A249	10c multi	4.00	1.25
774	A249	10c multi	4.00	1.25
a.		Block of 5 + label, Nos. 770-774	21.00	9.00
		Nos. 760-774 (15)	28.25	10.50

Christmas 1962. See note after No. 700.

Around 1962 a 1ctv. label picturing Fidel Castro was used as a voluntary contribution stamp. It is not inscribed "Correos" and was not valid for postage.

Soviet Space Flights — A263

Spacecraft and cosmonauts: 1c, Vostok 1, Yuri A. Gagarin, Apr. 12, 1961. 2c, Vostok 2, Gherman S. Titov, Aug. 6-7, 1961. 3c, Vostok 3, Andrian G. Nikolaev, Aug. 11-15, 1962, and Vostok 4, Pavel R. Popovich, Aug. 12-15, 1962. 9c, Vostok 5, Valery F. Bykovsky, June 14-19, 1963. 13c, Vostok 6, Valentina V. Tereshkova, June 16-19, 1963.

1963-64 **Wmk. 321**

No.	Type	Description	Unused	Used
775	A263	1c ultra, red & yel	.35	.25
776	A263	2c grn, yel & rose lake	.65	.25
777	A263	3c yel, vio & ver	.65	.25
778	A263	9c red, dark vio & yel	1.25	.45
779	A263	13c dark blue green, dull red brown & yel	3.25	.70
		Nos. 775-779 (5)	6.15	1.90

Issued: 1c, 2c, 3c, 2/26/63; others, 8/15/64.

Attack of the Presidential Palace, 6th Anniv. — A264

9c, Guerillas attacking palace. 13c, Four student leaders. 30c, Jose A. Echeverria, Menelao Mora.

1963, Mar. 13

No.	Type	Description	Unused	Used
780	A264	9c dark red & blk	1.10	.25
781	A264	13c chalky blue & sep	1.30	.45
782	A264	30c org & grn	3.50	1.00
		Nos. 780-782 (3)	5.90	1.70

4th Pan American Games, Sao Paulo, Brazil, Apr. 20-May 5 — A265

1963, Apr. 20

No.	Type	Description	Unused	Used
783	A265	1c Baseball	1.25	.35
784	A265	13c Boxing	3.25	.65

Stamp Day A266

3c, Mask mailbox, 19th cent. 10c, Mask mailbox at the Plaza de la Catedral, Havana.

1963, Apr. 25

No.	Type	Description	Unused	Used
785	A266	3c black & dark org	1.00	.25
786	A266	10c black & pur	2.50	.50

See Nos. 828-829, 956-957 and 1102-1103.

Labor Day — A267

1963, May 1

No.	Type	Description	Unused	Used
787	A267	3c shown	.50	.25
788	A267	13c Four workers	1.75	.60

Intl. Children's Week, June 1-7 — A268

1963, June 1

No.	Type	Description	Unused	Used
789	A268	3c blue blk & bister brn	.50	.25
790	A268	30c blue blk & red	2.75	.80

Ritual Effigy — A269

Taino Civilization artifacts: 3c, Wood-carved throne, horiz. 9c, Stone-carved figurine.

1963, June 29

No.	Type	Description	Unused	Used
791	A269	2c org & red brn	.75	.25
792	A269	3c ultra & red brn	.90	.25
793	A269	9c rose & gray	1.60	.45
		Nos. 791-793 (3)	3.25	.95

Montane Anthropology Museum, 60th anniv.

Broken Chains at Moncada A270

2c, Attack on the Presidential Palace. 3c, The insurrection. 7c, Strike of April 9. 9c, Triumph of the revolution. 10c, Agricultural reform and nationalization of industry. 13c, Bay of Pigs victory.

1963, July 26

No.	Type	Description	Unused	Used
794	A270	1c pink & blk	.25	.25
795	A270	2c lt blue & vio brn	.30	.25
796	A270	3c lt vio & brn	.35	.25
797	A270	7c apple green & rose	.40	.25
798	A270	9c olive bister & rose vio	.95	.40
799	A270	10c beige & sage grn	2.25	.60
800	A270	13c pale org & slate blue	3.00	1.20
		Nos. 794-800 (7)	7.50	3.20

Indigenous Fruit — A271

1963, Aug. 19

No.	Type	Description	Unused	Used
801	A271	1c Star apple	.25	.25
802	A271	2c Cherimoya	.25	.25
803	A271	3c Cashew nut	.45	.25
804	A271	10c Custard apple	2.00	.60
805	A271	13c Mangoes	2.25	1.50
		Nos. 801-805 (5)	5.20	2.85

Geometric Shapes A272

View of a Town — A273

Designs: No. 806, Circle, triangle, square, vert. No. 807, Roof, window, vert. No. 808, View of a town. No. 809, View of a town in blue. No. 810, View of a town in olive bister and red. No. 811, Circle, triangle, vert. No. 812, House, roof and doorway, vert. No. 813, House, girders.

1963, Sept. 29 **Unwmk.**

No.	Type	Description	Unused	Used
806	A272	3c multi	.50	.25
807	A272	3c multi	.50	.25
808	A273	3c multi	.50	.25
809	A273	3c multi	.50	.25
810	A273	13c multi	1.50	.55
811	A272	13c multi	1.50	.55
812	A272	13c multi	1.50	.55
813	A272	13c multi	1.50	.55
		Nos. 806-813 (8)	8.00	3.20

7th Intl. Congress of the Intl. Union of Architects.

Ernest Hemingway (1899-1961), American Author — A274

Hemingway and: 3c, The Old Man and the Sea. 9c, For Whom the Bell Tolls. 13c, Hemingway Museum (former residence), San Francisco de Paula, near Havana.

1963, Dec. 5 **Wmk. 321**

No.	Type	Description	Unused	Used
814	A274	3c brn & lt blue	.75	.25
815	A274	9c sage grn & pink	1.75	.25
816	A274	13c blk & yel grn	3.00	.60
		Nos. 814-816 (3)	5.50	1.10

Natl. Museum, 50th Anniv. — A275

Works of art: 2c, El Zapateo (Dance), by Victor P. Landaluze. 3c, Abduction of the Mulatto Women, by Carlos Enriquez, vert. 9c, Greek Panathean amphora, vert. 13c, My Beloved (bust of a young woman), by Jean Antoine Houdon, vert.

1964, Mar. 19 **Unwmk.**

817 A275 2c multi .35 .25
818 A275 3c multi .75 .25
819 A275 9c multi 1.10 .40
820 A275 13c multi 2.10 .65
Nos. 817-820 (4) 4.30 1.55

General Strike on Apr. 9, 6th Anniv. — A276

Rebel leaders: 2c, Bernardo Juan Borrell. 3c, Marcelo Salado. 10c, Oscar Lucero. 13c, Sergio Gonzalez.

1964, Apr. 9

821 A276 2c blk, yel grn & dull org .40 .25
822 A276 3c blk, red & dull org .70 .25
823 A276 10c blk, pur & beige 1.25 .30
824 A276 13c blk, brt blue & beige 2.50 .60
Nos. 821-824 (4) 4.85 1.40

Bay of Pigs Invasion, 3rd Anniv. A277

Designs: 3c, Fish in net. 10c, Victory Monument. 13c, Fallen eagle, vert.

1964, Apr. 17

825 A277 3c multi .35 .25
826 A277 10c multi .70 .35
827 A277 13c multi 2.25 .70
Nos. 825-827 (3) 3.30 1.30

Stamp Day Type of 1963

3c, Vicente Mora Pera, 1st postal director. 13c, Unissued provisional stamp, 1871.

1964, Apr. 24

828 A266 3c ocher & dull lil .60 .25
829 A266 13c dull vio & lt olive grn 2.75 .50

Labor Day — A278

1964, May 1

830 A278 3c Industry .40 .25
831 A278 13c Agriculture 1.60 .55

Diplomatic Relations with China — A279

Designs: 1c, China Monument, Havana. 2c, Cuban and Chinese farmers. 3c, Natl. flags.

1964, May 15

832 A279 1c multi .35 .25
833 A279 2c org brn, blk & apple grn .70 .25
834 A279 3c multi 1.40 .25
Nos. 832-834 (3) 2.45 .75

15th UPU Congress, Vienna, May-June A280

13c, Hemispheres on world map. 30c, Heinrich von Stephan. 50c, UPU Monument, Bern.

1964, May 29

835 A280 13c multicolored .85 .30
836 A280 30c multicolored 1.90 .80
837 A280 50c multicolored 4.00 1.40
Nos. 835-837 (3) 6.75 2.50

Development of Natl. Industry A281

1964, June 16

838 A281 1c Fish .40 .25
839 A281 2c Cow .60 .25
840 A281 13c Chickens 2.75 .50
Nos. 838-840 (3) 3.75 1.00

Merchant Fleet — A282

1964, June 30

841 A282 1c Rio Jibacoa .25 .25
842 A282 2c Camilo Cienfuegos .50 .25
843 A282 3c Sierra Maestra .75 .25
844 A282 9c Bahia de Siguanea 1.50 .50
845 A282 10c Oriente 4.00 1.00
Nos. 841-845 (5) 7.00 2.25

Unification of Viet Nam — A283

Designs: 2c, Vietnamese guerrilla, American soldier. 3c, Northerner and southerner shaking hands over map of united Viet Nam. 10c, Ox-drawn plow, machinised harvester. 13c, Natl. flags and profiles of Cuban and Vietnamese farmers.

1964, July 20

846 A283 2c multi .30 .25
847 A283 3c multi .45 .25
848 A283 10c multi 1.00 .25
849 A283 13c multi 2.75 .60
Nos. 846-849 (4) 4.50 1.35

11th Anniv. of the Revolution — A284

Designs: 3c, Raul Gomez Garcia and poem. 13c, Cover of La Historia Me Absolvera, by Fidel Castro.

1964, July 25

850 A284 3c red, tan & blk .75 .25
851 A284 13c multi 3.00 .60

1964 Summer Olympics, Tokyo, Oct. 10-25 — A285

1c, Gymnastics. 2c, Rowing. 3c, Boxing. 7c, Running, horiz. 10c, Fencing, horiz. 13c, Foil, cleats, oar, boxing glove, sun, horiz.

1964, Oct. 10 **Wmk. 376** ***Perf. 10***

852 A285 1c multi .30 .25
853 A285 2c multi .30 .25
854 A285 3c multi .30 .25
855 A285 7c multi .70 .25
856 A285 10c multi 1.50 .55
857 A285 13c multi 2.50 .85
Nos. 852-857 (6) 5.60 2.40

Satellite and Globe A286

Satellite and Partial Globe A287

No. C31 and Partial Globe A288

Various satellites and rockets.

1964, Oct. 15

858 A286 1c shown .25 .25
859 A287 1c shown .25 .25
860 A287 1c Globe LL .25 .25
861 A287 1c Globe UR .25 .25
862 A287 1c Globe UL .25 .25
a. Block of 5 + label, Nos. 858-862 1.00 1.00
863 A286 2c Spacecraft and globe .55 .25
864 A287 2c Globe LR .55 .25
865 A287 2c Globe LL .55 .25
866 A287 2c Globe UR .55 .25
867 A287 2c Globe UL .55 .25
a. Block of 5 + label, Nos. 863-867 3.00 1.50
868 A286 3c Satellite and globe .75 .35
869 A287 3c Globe LR .75 .35
870 A287 3c Globe LL .75 .35
871 A287 3c Globe UR .75 .35
872 A287 3c Globe UL .75 .35
a. Block of 5 + label, Nos. 868-872 4.00 2.50
873 A286 9c Satellite and globe, diff 1.75 .70
874 A287 9c Globe LR 1.75 .70
875 A287 9c Globe LL 1.75 .70
876 A287 9c Globe UR 1.75 .70
877 A287 9c Globe UL 1.75 .70
a. Block of 5 + label, Nos. 873-877 11.00 5.00
878 A286 13c Satellite and globe, diff. 2.40 1.75
879 A287 13c Globe LR 2.40 1.75
880 A287 13c Globe LL 2.40 1.75
881 A287 13c Globe UR 2.40 1.75
882 A287 13c Globe UL 2.40 1.75
a. Block of 5 + label, Nos. 878-882 16.00 10.00
883 A288 50c blk & lt grn 4.00 2.50
a. Souvenir sheet of one, Wmk. 321 15.00 12.50
Nos. 858-883 (26) 32.50 19.00

Experimental Cuban postal rocket flight, 25th anniv. Stamps of the same denomination printed se-tenant in sheets of 20 stamps and 5 inscribed labels. Stamps of Type A287 arranged in blocks of 4 with a complete globe in center of block; Type A286 stamps and labels form a cross in center of sheet. Inscribed "1939-Cohete Postal Cubano-1964."

No. 883a contains one 46x28mm stamp.

Type of A288 Ovptd. in Silver

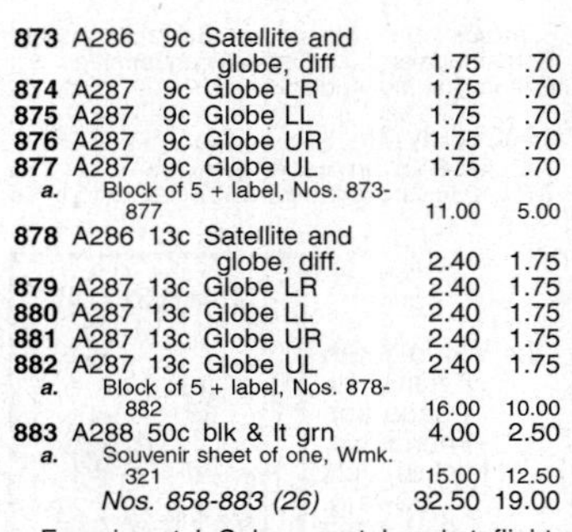

1964, Oct. 17 **Unwmk.**

884 A288 50c dk red brn & lt grn 5.00 1.50

No. 884 not issued without overprint.

40th Death Anniv. of Lenin — A289

Designs: 13c, Lenin Mausoleum, horiz. 30c, Lenin, star, hammer and sickle.

1964, Nov. 7 **Wmk. 376**

885 A289 3c org & blk .65 .25
886 A289 13c pur, pink & blk 1.10 .35
887 A289 30c blue & blk 2.25 .90
Nos. 885-887 (3) 4.00 1.50

Havana Zoo — A290

1c, Leopard, horiz. 2c, Elephant. 3c, Fallow deer. 4c, Kangaroo, horiz. 5c, Lions, horiz. 6c, Eland, horiz. 7c, Zebra, horiz. 8c, Hyena, horiz. 9c, Tiger, horiz. 10c, Guanaco, horiz. 13c, Chimpanzees, horiz. 20c, Peccary, horiz. 30c, Raccoon. 40c, Hippopotamus, horiz. 50c, Tapir, horiz. 60c, Dromedary. 70c, Bison, horiz. 80c, Black bear. 90c, Water buffalo, horiz. 1p, Deer in nature park, horiz.

1964, Nov. 25

888 A290 1c multi .30 .25
889 A290 2c multi .30 .25
890 A290 3c multi .30 .25
891 A290 4c multi .30 .25
892 A290 5c multi .40 .25
893 A290 6c multi .50 .25
894 A290 7c multi .50 .25
895 A290 8c multi .75 .25
896 A290 9c multi .75 .25
897 A290 10c multi .80 .25
898 A290 13c multi .90 .25
899 A290 20c multi 1.10 .25
900 A290 30c multi 1.60 .60
901 A290 40c multi 2.75 1.00

902 A290 50c multi 3.00 1.40
903 A290 60c multi 4.50 1.90
904 A290 70c multi 4.75 1.90
905 A290 80c multi 5.00 2.40
906 A290 90c multi 5.50 3.00

Size: 47x32mm

907 A290 1p multi 9.25 3.00
Nos. 888-907 (20) 43.25 18.20

Heroes of the 1895 War of Independence — A291

1964, Dec. 7

908 A291 1c Jose Marti .25 .25
909 A291 2c Antonio Maceo .40 .25
910 A291 3c Maximo Gomez .60 .35
911 A291 13c Calixto Garcia 1.75 .70
Nos. 908-911 (4) 3.00 1.55

Christmas Type of 1961

No. 912, Dwarf cup coral. No. 913, Eusmilia fastigiata. No. 914, Acropora palmata. No. 915, Acropora profilera. No. 916, Diploria labyrinthiformis. No. 917, Condylactis gigantea. No. 918, Physalia physalis. No. 919, Aurelia aurita. No. 920, Linuche unguiculata. No. 921, Cassiopea frondosa. No. 922, Neocrinus blakei. No. 923, Eucidaris tribuloidas. No. 924, Tripneutes. No. 925, Ophiocoma echinata. No. 926, Oreaster celiculatus.

2c, Coral. 3c, Jellyfish. 10c, Starfish, sea-urchins.

1964, Dec. 18

912 A248 2c multi .80 .30
913 A249 2c multi .80 .30
914 A249 2c multi .80 .30
915 A249 2c multi .80 .30
916 A249 2c multi .80 .30
a. Block of 5 + label, Nos. 912-916 4.50 2.00
917 A248 3c multi 1.25 .50
918 A249 3c multi 1.25 .50
919 A249 3c multi 1.25 .50
920 A249 3c multi 1.25 .50
921 A249 3c multi 1.25 .50
a. Block of 5 + label, Nos. 917-921 7.50 3.00
922 A248 10c multi 2.00 1.00
923 A249 10c multi 2.00 1.00
924 A249 10c multi 2.00 1.00
925 A249 10c multi 2.00 1.00
926 A249 10c multi 2.00 1.00
a. Block of 5 + label, Nos. 922-926 12.50 7.00
Nos. 912-926 (15) 20.25 9.00

Christmas 1964. See note after No. 700.

Dr. Tomas Romay (1764-1849), Physician and Scientist — A292

Romay Monument — A293

Designs: 2c, First vaccination against smallpox. 3c, Portrait and treatise on vaccination.

1964, Dec. 21

927 A292 1c blk & olive brn .50 .25
928 A292 2c blk & tan .50 .25
929 A293 3c olive & dk red brn .75 .25
930 A293 10c bister & blk 2.10 .40
Nos. 927-930 (4) 3.85 1.15

Second Declaration of Havana A294

Map of Latin America and ripples or map of Cuba and peasant breaking shackles under text from the Declaration of Havana: No. 931a, 932a "Visperas de su muerte..." No. 931b, 932b, "Un continente, que juntos suponen representos..." No. 931c, 932c, "Y no se ocultaran ni el gobierna..." No. 931d, 932d, "Millones de mulatos latinamericanos que saben..." No. 931e, "A labran la tierra en condiciones..."

1964, Dec. 23

931 Strip of 5 5.00 3.50
a.-e. A294 3c any single .75 .40
932 Strip of 5 15.00 12.50
a.-e. A294 13c any single 1.75 1.50

Nos. 931-932 printed in sheets of 25 (5x5).

Dioramas in New Cuban Postal Museum — A295

1965, Jan. 4

Yellow & Black Border

933 A295 13c Maritime Post 2.50 .85
934 A295 30c Insurrection Post 2.50 1.25

Souvenir Sheet

Imperf

935 Sheet of 2 8.50 7.50
a. A295 13c like #933, blue & blk border 1.00 1.00
b. A295 30c like #934, blue & blk border 3.00 3.00
Nos. 933-935 (3) 13.50 9.60

Stamps in No. 935 have simulated perforations; buff margin is inscribed "PRECIO 50c" LR.

Fishing Fleet — A296

1965, May 1

936 A296 1c Schooner .25 .25
937 A296 2c Omicron .40 .25
938 A296 3c Victoria .60 .25
939 A296 9c Cardenas .90 .60
940 A296 10c Sigma 2.10 .40
941 A296 13c Lambda 3.25 .90
Nos. 936-941 (6) 7.50 2.65

Intl. Women's Day — A297

1965, Mar. 8

942 A297 3c Lidia Doce 1.10 .30
943 A297 13c Clara Zetkin 1.60 .60

Technical Revolution — A298

Designs: 3c, Jose Antonio Echeverria University School. 13c, Stylized symbols of science and research, molecular structure and satellite dish.

1965, Mar. 31

944 A298 3c tan, blk & dark red brn .50 .25
945 A298 13c multi 2.50 .75

Cosmonauts, Rocket — A299

30c, Cosmonauts Pavel I. Balyayev, Aleksei A. Leonov taking first space walk.

1965, Apr. 2

946 A299 30c dark blue, blk & brn 2.50 .70
947 A299 50c brt pink & blue blk 4.50 1.40

Flight of Voskhod 2, the first man to walk in space, Mar. 17.

Abstract Wood Carving by Eugenio Rodriguez A300

Paintings in the Natl. Museum, Havana: 3c, Garden with Sunflowers, by Victor Manuel. 10c, Abstract, by Wilfredo Lam, horiz. 13c, Children, by Enrique Ponce, horiz.

1965, Apr. 12

948 A300 2c multi .35 .25

Size: 35x46mm

949 A300 3c multi .55 .25

Size: 46x35mm

950 A300 10c multi 1.50 .45

Size: 43x37mm

951 A300 13c multi 2.50 .80
Nos. 948-951 (4) 4.90 1.75

Abraham Lincoln — A301

Designs: 1c, Log cabin, birth site, horiz. 2c, Memorial, Washington, DC, horiz. 3c, Monument, Washington, DC. 13c, Portrait, quote.

1965, Apr. 15

952 A301 1c yel bister, red brn & gray .25 .25
953 A301 2c lt blue & dark blue .45 .25
954 A301 3c red org, blk & blue blk 1.25 .35
955 A301 13c org, blk & blue blk 2.50 .60
Nos. 952-955 (4) 4.45 1.45

Stamp Day Type of 1963

Stamp Day 1965: 3c, 18th Cent. postmarks and packet. 13c, No. C16 and airplanes over capital.

1965, Apr. 24

956 A266 3c sep & dark org 3.00 .25
957 A266 13c brt blue, sal rose & blk 2.75 .60

Intl. Quiet Sun Year — A302

1c, Sun, Earth's magnetic pole, horiz. 2c, Sun Year emblem. 3c, Earth's magnetic field, horiz. 6c, Atmospheric currents, horiz. 30c, Solar rays on planet surface. 50c, Effect on satellite orbits, horiz.

1965, May 10

958 A302 1c multicolored .30 .25
959 A302 2c multicolored .35 .25
960 A302 3c multicolored .60 .25
961 A302 6c multicolored .70 .25
962 A302 30c multicolored 2.25 .55
963 A302 50c multicolored 3.00 1.25
a. Souv. sheet of one, imperf. 7.00 7.00
b. As "a," changed colors 10.00 10.00
Nos. 958-963 (6) 7.20 2.80

Stamps in Nos. 963a-963b have simulated perforations.

Stamp in No. 963b is blue blk, Prus blue, org yel & red. Issued Oct. 10 for the Philatelic Space Exhibition, Havana, Oct. 10-17.

Intl. Telecommunications Union, Cent. — A303

1c, Station, horiz. 2c, Satellite. 3c, Telstar, horiz. 10c, Telstar, receiving station. 30c, ITU emblem, horiz.

1965, May 17

964 A303 1c gold & multi .25 .25
965 A303 2c multi .25 .25
966 A303 3c multi .45 .25
967 A303 10c multi 1.25 .25
968 A303 30c multi 3.00 .90
Nos. 964-968 (5) 5.20 1.90

9th Communist World Youth and Students Congress — A304

13c, Flags of Cuba and Algeria, emblem. 30c, Flags, guerrillas.

1965, June 10

969 A304 13c multi 1.60 .50
970 A304 30c multi 2.50 .75

Matias Perez, Cuban Aeronautics Pioneer — A305

1965, June 23

No.	Type	Description		
971	A305	3c pink & blk	1.75	.95
972	A305	13c dull vio & blk, diff.	2.75	.95

Flowers and Maps of Their Locations A306

1c, Rosa canina, Europe. 2c, Chrysanthemum hortorum, Asia. 3c, Strelitzia reginae, Africa. 4c, Dahlia pinnata, No. America. 5c, Cattleya labiata, So. America. 13c, Grevillea banksii, Oceania. 30c, Brunfelsia nitida, Cuba.

1965, July 20

No.	Type	Description		
973	A306	1c multicolored	.25	.25
974	A306	2c multicolored	.30	.25
975	A306	3c multicolored	.30	.30
976	A306	4c multicolored	.30	.25
977	A306	5c multicolored	1.60	.25
978	A306	13c multicolored	3.25	.95
979	A306	30c multicolored	4.75	1.60
		Nos. 973-979 (7)	10.75	3.85

1st Natl. Games — A307

1965, July 25

No.	Type	Description		
980	A307	1c Swimming	.25	.25
981	A307	2c Basketball	.35	.25
982	A307	3c Gymnastics	.70	.25
983	A307	30c Hurdling	2.50	.70
		Nos. 980-983 (4)	3.80	1.45

Revolution Museum Opening A308

1c, Anti-tank guns. 2c, Tanks. 3c, Bazookas. 10c, Uniform, guerillas. 13c, Compass, yacht Granma.

1965, July 26

No.	Type	Description		
984	A308	1c multi	.25	.25
985	A308	2c multi	.25	.25
986	A308	3c multi	.25	.25
987	A308	10c multi	.75	.25
988	A308	13c multi	2.10	.45
		Nos. 984-988 (5)	3.60	1.45

A309

1c, Finlay's signature. 2c, Anopheles mosquito. 3c, Portrait. 7c, Microscope. 9c, Dr. Claudio Delgado. 10c, Monument. 13c, Discussing theory with doctors.

1965, Aug. 20

No.	Type	Description		
989	A309	1c multicolored	.25	.25
990	A309	2c multicolored	.25	.25
991	A309	3c multicolored	.35	.25
992	A309	7c multicolored	.45	.25
993	A309	9c multicolored	.75	.25
994	A309	10c multicolored	1.90	.30
995	A309	13c multicolored	2.75	.65
		Nos. 989-995 (7)	6.70	2.20

Carlos J. Finlay (1833-1915), discovered transmission of yellow fever via aedes aegypti (not anopheles) mosquito. Nos. 990-995 vert.

Butterflies A310

No. 996, Dismorphia cubana. No. 997, Anetia numidia briarea. No. 998, Carathis gortynoides. No. 999, Hymenitis cubana. No. 1000, Eubaphe heros. No. 1001, Lycorea ceres demeter. No. 1002, Eubaphe disparitis. No. 1003, Siderone nemesis. No. 1004, Syntomidopsis variegata. No. 1005, Ctenuchidia virgo. No. 1006, Prepona antimache crossina. No. 1007, Sylepta reginalis. No. 1008, Chlosyne perezi perezi. No. 1009, Anaea clytemnestra iphigenia. No. 1010, Anetia cubana.

1965, Sept. 22 **Unwmk.**

No.	Type	Description		
996	A310	2c multicolored	.50	.25
997	A310	2c multicolored	.50	.25
998	A310	2c multicolored	.50	.25
999	A310	2c multicolored	.50	.25
1000	A310	2c multicolored	.50	.25
a.		Strip of 5, Nos. 996-1000	3.75	2.50
1001	A310	3c multicolored	.75	.25
1002	A310	3c multicolored	.75	.25
1003	A310	3c multicolored	.75	.25
1004	A310	3c multicolored	.75	.25
1005	A310	3c multicolored	.75	.25
a.		Strip of 5, Nos. 1001-1005	5.00	3.25
1006	A310	13c multicolored	2.50	.80
1007	A310	13c multicolored	2.50	.80
1008	A310	13c multicolored	2.50	.80
1009	A310	13c multicolored	2.50	.80
1010	A310	13c multicolored	2.50	.80
a.		Strip of 5, Nos. 1006-1010	15.00	7.50
		Nos. 996-1010 (15)	18.75	6.50

Cuban Mint, 50th Anniv. A311

Coins (obverse and reverse): No. 1011, 20 centavos, 1962. No. 1012, 1 peso, 1934. No. 1013, 40 centavos, 1962. No. 1014, 1 peso, 1915. No. 1015, Marti peso, 1953. No. 1016, 20 pesos, 1915.

1965, Oct. 13

No.	Type	Description		
1011	A311	1c multicolored	.30	.25
1012	A311	2c multi	.30	.25
1013	A311	3c multi	.30	.25
1014	A311	8c multi	.80	.25
1015	A311	10c multi	1.90	.40
1016	A311	13c multi	2.75	.50
		Nos. 1011-1016 (6)	6.35	1.90

Tropical Fruit — A312

1965, Nov. 15 ***Perf. 12½***

No.	Type	Description		
1017	A312	1c Oranges	.25	.25
1018	A312	2c Custard apples	.25	.25
1019	A312	3c Papayas	.25	.25
1020	A312	4c Bananas	.35	.25
1021	A312	10c Avocado	.60	.25
1022	A312	13c Pineapple	.95	.70
1023	A312	20c Guavas	2.50	.70
1024	A312	50c Marmalade plums	5.50	1.25
		Nos. 1017-1024 (8)	10.65	3.90

Christmas Type of 1961

Birds: No. 1025, Icterus galbula. No. 1026, Passerina ciris. No. 1027, Setophaga ruticillar. No. 1028, Dendroica tusca. No. 1029, Pheucticus ludovicianus. No. 1030, Pyranga olivacea. No. 1031, Dendroica dominica. No. 1032, Vermivora pinus. No. 1033, Protonotaria citrea. No. 1034, Wilsonia citrina. No. 1035, Passerina cyanea. No. 1036, Anas discors. No. 1037, Aix sponsa. No. 1038, Spatula clypeata. No. 1039, Nycticorax hoactli.

1965, Dec. 1

No.	Type	Description		
1025	A248	3c multicolored	1.50	1.25
1026	A249	3c multicolored	1.50	1.25
1027	A249	3c multicolored	1.50	1.25
1028	A249	3c multicolored	1.50	1.25
1029	A249	3c multicolored	1.50	1.25
a.		Block of 5 + label, Nos. 1025-1029	9.00	7.25
1030	A248	5c multicolored	1.60	1.60
1031	A249	5c multicolored	1.60	1.60
1032	A249	5c multicolored	1.60	1.60
1033	A249	5c multicolored	1.60	1.60
1034	A249	5c multicolored	1.60	1.60
a.		Block of 5 + label, Nos. 1030-1034	10.00	10.00
1035	A248	13c multicolored	3.50	2.75
1036	A249	13c multicolored	3.50	2.75
1037	A249	13c multicolored	3.50	2.75
1038	A249	13c multicolored	3.50	2.75
1039	A249	13c multicolored	3.50	2.75
a.		Block of 5 + label, Nos. 1035-1039	21.00	20.00
		Nos. 1025-1039 (15)	33.00	28.00

Christmas 1965. See note after No. 700.

Intl. Athletic Competition, Havana, 7th Anniv. — A313

1965, Dec. 11 **Wmk. 376** ***Perf. 10***

No.	Type	Description		
1040	A313	1c Hurdling	.25	.25
1041	A313	2c Discus	.25	.25
1042	A313	3c Shot put	.55	.25
1043	A313	7c Javelin	.60	.25
1044	A313	9c High jump	.75	.35
1045	A313	10c Hammer throw	1.60	.60
1046	A313	13c Running	2.00	.90
		Nos. 1040-1046 (7)	6.00	2.85

Fish in the Natl. Aquarium — A314

1c, Echeneis naucrates. 2c, Katsuwonus pelamis. 3c, Abudefduf saxatilis. 4c, Istiophorus. 5c, Epinephelus striatus. 10c, Lutianus analis. 13c, Ocyurus chrysurus. 30c, Holocentrus ascensionis.

1965, Dec. 5 **Unwmk.** ***Perf. 12½***

No.	Type	Description		
1047	A314	1c multicolored	.25	.25
1048	A314	2c multicolored	.25	.25
1049	A314	3c multicolored	.55	.25
1050	A314	4c multicolored	.75	.25
1051	A314	5c multicolored	.75	.25
1052	A314	10c multicolored	1.00	.30
1053	A314	13c multicolored	3.25	.80
1054	A314	30c multicolored	5.00	1.25
		Nos. 1047-1054 (8)	11.80	3.60

Andre Voisin (d. 1964), French Naturalist — A315

13c, Portrait, flags, microscope, plant.

1965, Dec. 21 **Wmk. 376**

No.	Type	Description		
1055	A315	3c shown	1.00	.25
1056	A315	13c multicolored	2.00	.55

Transportation — A316

1c, Skoda bus, Czechoslovakia. 2c, Ikarus bus, Hungary. 3c, Leyland bus, G.B. 4c, TEM-4 locomotive, USSR. 7c, BB-69.000 locomotive, France. 10c, Remolcador tugboat, DDR. 13c, 15 de Marzo freighter, Spain. 20c, Ilyushin 18 jet, USSR.

1965, Dec. 30

No.	Type	Description		
1057	A316	1c multicolored	.25	.25
1058	A316	2c multicolored	.25	.25
1059	A316	3c multicolored	.25	.25
1060	A316	4c multicolored	3.00	.70
1061	A316	7c multicolored	3.00	.70
1062	A316	10c multicolored	1.25	.35
1063	A316	13c multicolored	2.00	.60
1064	A316	20c multicolored	3.00	1.00
		Nos. 1057-1064 (8)	13.00	4.10

A317

7th Anniv. of the Revolution A318

1c, Guerrillas. 2c, Commander and tank. 3c, Sailor, patrol boat. 10c, Jet aircraft. 13c, Rocket.

1966, Jan. 2

No.	Type	Description		
1065	A317	1c multi	.40	.25
1066	A317	2c multi	.40	.25
1067	A317	3c multi	.90	.25
1068	A318	10c multi	1.90	.45
1069	A318	13c multi	2.40	.70
		Nos. 1065-1069 (5)	6.00	1.90

Conference of Asian, African and South American Countries, Havana — A319

1966, Jan. 3

No.	Type	Description		
1070	A319	2c Emblem at R	.25	.25
1071	A319	3c Emblem at L	.40	.25
1072	A319	13c Emblem at center	2.00	.50
		Nos. 1070-1072 (3)	2.65	1.00

Guardalabarca Beach — A320

2c, Gran Piedra mountain. 3c, Guama Village. 13c, Soroa waterfall, vert.

1966, Feb. 10

No.	Type	Description		
1073	A320	1c shown	.30	.25
1074	A320	2c multi	.30	.25
1075	A320	3c multi	.90	.25
1076	A320	13c multi	2.50	.60
		Nos. 1073-1076 (4)	4.00	1.35

11th Medical and 7th Natl. Dental Congresses — A321

1966, Feb. 28 **Wmk. 376**

1077	A321	3c multi	.60	.25
1078	A321	13c multi, diff.	2.50	.65

Folk Art A322

1c, Afro-cuban ritual puppet. 2c, Sombreros. 3c, Ceramic vase. 7c, Lanterns, lamp. 9c, Table lamp. 10c, Shark, wood sculpture. 13c, Snail-shell necklace, earrings.

1966, Feb. 28 **Unwmk.**

1079	A322	1c multicolored	.25	.25
1080	A322	2c multicolored	.25	.25
1081	A322	3c multicolored	.25	.25
1082	A322	7c multicolored	.25	.25
1083	A322	9c multicolored	.80	.25
1084	A322	10c multicolored	1.20	.30
1085	A322	13c multicolored	2.40	.60
		Nos. 1079-1085 (7)	5.40	2.15

Nos. 1079-1083 vert.

Chelsea College, by Canaletto — A323

Ceramics and paintings in the National Museum: 1c, Ming vase. 3c, Portrait of a Lady, by Goya. 13c, Portrait of Fayum, encaustic painting. Nos. 1086, 1088-1089 vert.

1966, Mar. 31 **Wmk. 376**

1086	A323	1c multi	.25	.25
1087	A323	2c multi	.30	.25
1088	A323	3c multi	.75	.25
1089	A323	13c multi	2.90	.70
		Nos. 1086-1089 (4)	4.20	1.45

First Man in Space, 5th Anniv. A324

Designs: 1c, Konstantin Eduardovich Tsiolkovsky (1857-1935), Soviet rocket and space sciences pioneer. 2c, Cosmonauts in training, vert. 3c, Yuri Gagarin, rocket, Earth. 7c, Cosmonauts Nikolaev and Popovich, vert. 9c, Tereshkova and Bykovsky. 10c, Komarov, Feoktistov and Yegorov. 13c, Leonov taking first space walk.

1966, Apr. 12

1090	A324	1c multi	.25	.25
1091	A324	2c multi	.25	.25
1092	A324	3c multi	.35	.25
1093	A324	7c multi	.60	.25
1094	A324	9c multi	.85	.25
1095	A324	10c multi	1.10	.30
1096	A324	13c multi	2.25	.55
		Nos. 1090-1096 (7)	5.65	2.10

Bay of Pigs Invasion, 5th Anniv. A325

2c, Tank. 3c, Burning ship, plane crash. 9c, Tank in ditch. 10c, Soldier, gunners. 13c, Operations map.

1966, Apr. 17

1097	A325	2c multi	.25	.25
1098	A325	3c multi	.95	.25
1099	A325	9c multi	.40	.25
1100	A325	10c multi	1.50	.25
1101	A325	13c multi	2.75	.50
		Nos. 1097-1101 (5)	5.85	1.50

Stamp Day Type of 1963

Designs: 3c, Cuban Postal Museum interior. 13c, No. 613 and stamp collector.

1966, Apr. 24

1102	A266	3c sage grn & sal rose	1.00	.25
1103	A266	13c brn, sal rose & blk	3.00	.80

Stamp Day 1966. 1st Anniv. of the Cuban Postal Museum (No. 1102); 1st anniv. of the Cuban Philatelic Federation (No. 1103).

Flowers and Symbols of Industry — A326

2c, Anvil. 3c, Machete. 10c, Hammer. 13c, Hemisphere, gearwheel.

1966, May 1

1104	A326	2c multi	.25	.25
1105	A326	3c multi	.30	.25
1106	A326	10c multi	.70	.25
1107	A326	13c multi	1.75	.90
		Nos. 1104-1107 (4)	3.00	1.65

Labor Day.

Opening of the World Health Organization Headquarters, Geneva — A327

Views of WHO headquarters and emblem or emblem on flag.

1966, May 3

1108	A327	2c blk & yel org	.25	.25
1109	A327	3c blk, lt blue & yel org	.75	.25
1110	A327	13c blk, lt blue & yel org	2.10	.55
		Nos. 1108-1110 (3)	3.10	1.05

A328

1966, June 11

1111	A328	1c Running, vert.	.25	.25
1112	A328	2c Rifle shooting	.30	.25
1113	A328	3c Baseball, vert.	.40	.25
1114	A328	7c Volleyball, vert.	.45	.25
1115	A328	9c Soccer, vert.	.60	.25
1116	A328	10c Boxing, vert.	1.20	.25
1117	A328	13c Basketball, vert.	2.40	.55
		Nos. 1111-1117 (7)	5.60	2.05

10th Central American and Caribbean Games, Puerto Rico, June 11-25.

Progress in Education A329

Designs: 1c, Makarenko School, Playa de Tarara. 2c, Natl. Literacy Campaign Museum. 3c, Lantern, literacy campaign emblem for 1961. 10c, Frank Pais education team in the mountains. 13c, Farmer, factory worker.

1966, June 15

1118	A329	1c grn & blk	.25	.25
1119	A329	2c yel, olive bister & blk	.25	.25
1120	A329	3c brt blue, lt blue & blk	.30	.25
1121	A329	10c golden brn, brn & blk	.90	.25
1122	A329	13c multi	2.40	.45
		Nos. 1118-1122 (5)	4.10	1.45

1st Graduating class of Makarenko School (1c), 5th anniv. of the Natl. Literacy Campaign (3c), 4th anniv. of agricultural and industrial trade education (13c).

12th Congress of the Cuban Labor Organization — A330

1966, Aug. 12

1123	A330	3c multi	1.00	.25

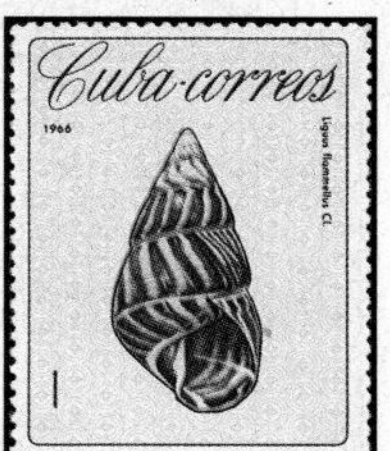

Sea Shells — A331

1c, Liguus flammellus. 2c, Cypraea zebra. 3c, Strombus pugilis. 7c, Aequipecten muscosu. 9c, Liguus fasciatus crenatus. 10c, Charonia variegata. 13c, Liguus fasciatus archeri.

1966, Aug. 25 **Unwmk.**

1124	A331	1c multicolored	.35	.25
1125	A331	2c multicolored	.45	.25
1126	A331	3c multicolored	.70	.25
1127	A331	7c multicolored	.80	.25
1128	A331	9c multicolored	.90	.25
1129	A331	10c multicolored	1.75	.40
1130	A331	13c multicolored	3.50	.80
		Nos. 1124-1130 (7)	8.45	2.45

Breeding Messenger Pigeons — A332

2c, Timer. 3c, Coops. 7c, Breeder tending coops. 9c, Pigeons in yard. 10c, Two men, message. 13c, Baracoa to Havana championship flight, July 26, 1959.

1966, Sept. 18 **Wmk. 376**

1131	A332	1c shown	.40	.25
1132	A332	2c multicolored	.40	.25
1133	A332	3c multicolored	.40	.25
1134	A332	7c multicolored	.80	.25
1135	A332	9c multicolored	.80	.35
1136	A332	10c multicolored	2.50	.50

Size: 47x32mm

1137	A332	13c multicolored	3.75	.90
		Nos. 1131-1137 (7)	9.05	2.75

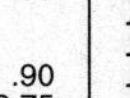

Provincial and Natl. Coats of Arms, Map of Cuba — A333

1966, Oct. 10

1138	A333	1c Pinar del Rio	.25	.25
1139	A333	2c Havana	.30	.25
1140	A333	3c Matanzas	.30	.25
1141	A333	4c Las Villas	.40	.25
1142	A333	5c Camaguey	.60	.25
1143	A333	9c Oriente	1.25	.50

Size: 30x48mm

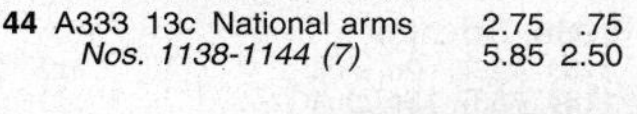

1144	A333	13c National arms	2.75	.75
		Nos. 1138-1144 (7)	5.85	2.50

17th World Chess Olympiad, Havana — A334

1c, Pawn. 2c, Rook. 3c, Knight. 9c, Bishop. 10c, Queen, games, horiz. 13c, King and emblem, horiz.

30c, Capablanca Vs. Lasker, 1914, horiz.

1966, Oct. 18

1145	A334	1c multicolored	.30	.25
1146	A334	2c multicolored	.30	.25
1147	A334	3c multicolored	.50	.25
1148	A334	9c multicolored	1.00	.25
1149	A334	10c multicolored	2.40	.25
1150	A334	13c multicolored	3.25	.60
		Nos. 1145-1150 (6)	7.75	1.85

Souvenir Sheet

Imperf

1151	A334	30c multicolored	12.00	12.00

No. 1151 contains one 49½x31mm stamp.

Cuban-Soviet Diplomatic Relations — A335

2c, Lenin Hospital. 3c, Oil tanker, world map. 10c, Workers, gearwheels. 13c, Agriculture.

1966, Nov. 7

1152	A335	2c multicolored	.25	.25
1153	A335	3c multicolored	.35	.25
1154	A335	10c multicolored	1.10	.25
1155	A335	13c multicolored	2.25	.70
		Nos. 1152-1155 (4)	3.95	1.45

2nd Song Festival A336

Cuban composers and their compositions: 1c, Amadeo Roldan. 2c, Eduardo Sanchez de Fuentes. 3c, Moises Simons. 7c, Jorge Anckermann. 9c, Alejandro G. Caturla. 10c, Eliseo Grenet. 13c, Ernesto Lecuona.

1966, Nov. 18

1156	A336	1c multicolored	.25	.25
1157	A336	2c multicolored	.30	.25
1158	A336	3c multicolored	.30	.25
1159	A336	7c multicolored	.80	.25
1160	A336	9c multicolored	.80	.25
1161	A336	10c multicolored	2.75	.50
1162	A336	13c multicolored	3.50	1.00
		Nos. 1156-1162 (7)	8.70	2.75

Viet Nam War — A337

Flag of Viet Nam and: 2c, US aircraft discharging bombs, dead cattle. 3c, Gas mask and victims. 13c, US bombs, women and children.

1966, Nov. 23

1163	A337	2c multi	.40	.25
1164	A337	3c multi	.60	.25
1165	A337	13c multi	2.00	.60
		Nos. 1163-1165 (3)	3.00	1.10

10th Anniv. of Successful Revolution Campaigns — A338

Revolution leaders, scenes of the insurrection: 1c, Antonio Fernandez. 2c, Candido Gonzalez. 3c, Jose Tey. 7c, Tony Aloma. 9c, Otto Parellada. 10c, Juan Manuel Marquez. 13c, Frank Pais.

1966, Nov. 30

1166	A338	1c multicolored	.25	.25
1167	A338	2c multicolored	.25	.25
1168	A338	3c multicolored	.25	.25
1169	A338	7c multicolored	.30	.25
1170	A338	9c multicolored	.60	.25
1171	A338	10c multicolored	2.00	.50
1172	A338	13c multicolored	1.90	.80
		Nos. 1166-1172 (7)	5.55	2.55

Intl. Leisure Time and Recreation Seminar — A339

9c, World map, stopwatch, eye. 13c, Earth, clock, emblem.

1966, Dec. 2

1173	A339	3c shown	.25	.25
1174	A339	9c multicolored	1.40	.25
1175	A339	13c multicolored	2.00	.75
		Nos. 1173-1175 (3)	3.65	1.25

1st Natl. Telecommunications Forum — A340

1966, Dec. 12

1176	A340	3c shown	.75	.25
1177	A340	10c Satellite in orbit	3.50	.25
1178	A340	13c Shell, satellite	4.75	.70
a.		Souv. sheet of 3, #1176-1178, imperf	14.00	14.00
		Nos. 1176-1178 (3)	9.00	1.20

No. 1178a sold for 30c.

Christmas Type of 1961

No. 1179, Cypripedium eurylochus. No. 1180, Cattleya speciosissima. No. 1181, Cattleya mendelii majestica. No. 1182, Cattleya trianae amesiana. No. 1183, Cattleya labiata macfarlanei. No. 1184, Cypripedium morganiae burfordense. No. 1185, Cattleya Countess of Derby. No. 1186, Cypripedium hookerae volunteanum. No. 1187, Cattleya warscewiczii reginae burfordense. No. 1188, Cypripedium stonei cannartae. No. 1189, Cattleya mendelii Duchess of Montrose. No. 1190, Oncidium macranthum. No. 1191, Cypripedium stonei platytoenium. No. 1192, Cattleya dowiana aurea. No. 1193, Laelia anceps.

1966, Dec. 20 **Unwmk.**

1179	A248	1c multicolored	.75	.25
1180	A249	1c multicolored	.75	.25
1181	A249	1c multicolored	.75	.25
1182	A249	1c multicolored	.75	.25
1183	A249	1c multicolored	.75	.25
a.		Block of 5 + label, #1179-1183	5.50	5.50
1184	A248	3c multicolored	1.25	.25
1185	A249	3c multicolored	1.25	.25
1186	A249	3c multicolored	1.25	.25
1187	A249	3c multicolored	1.25	.25
1188	A249	3c multicolored	1.25	.25
a.		Block of 5 + label, #1184-1188	9.00	9.00
1189	A248	13c multicolored	4.00	.50
1190	A249	13c multicolored	4.00	.50
1191	A249	13c multicolored	4.00	.50
1192	A249	13c multicolored	4.00	.50
1193	A249	13c multicolored	4.00	.50
a.		Block of 5 + label, #1189-1193	27.50	27.50
		Nos. 1179-1193 (15)	30.00	5.00

Christmas 1966. See note after No. 700.

8th Anniv. of the Revolution — A341

No. 1194, Liberation, 1959. No. 1195, Agrarian Reform, 1960. No. 1196, Education, 1961. No. 1197, Agriculture, 1965. No. 1198, Rodin's Thinker, Planning, 1962. No. 1199, Organization, 1963. No. 1200, Economy, 1964. No. 1201, Solidarity, 1966.

1967, Jan. 2

1194	A341	3c multicolored	.30	.25
1195	A341	3c multicolored	.30	.25
1196	A341	3c multicolored	.30	.25
1197	A341	3c multicolored	.30	.25
a.		Strip of 4, Nos. 1194-1197	2.40	2.40
1198	A341	13c multicolored	1.90	.45
1199	A341	13c multicolored	1.90	.45
1200	A341	13c multicolored	1.90	.45
1201	A341	13c multicolored	1.90	.45
a.		Strip of 4, Nos. 1198-1201	15.00	15.00
		Nos. 1194-1201 (8)	8.80	2.80

Nos. 1198-1201 vert.

Spring, by Jorge Arche — A342

Paintings in the Natl. Museum: 1c, Coffee Machine, by Angel Acosta Leon, vert. 2c, Country People, by Eduardo Abela, vert. 13c, Still-life, by Amelia Pelaez, vert. 30c, Landscape, by Gonzalo Escalante.

1967, Feb. 27

1202	A342	1c multi	.45	.25
1203	A342	2c multi	.75	.25
1204	A342	3c multi	1.00	.30
1205	A342	13c multi	2.25	1.00
1206	A342	30c multi	6.00	2.00
		Nos. 1202-1206 (5)	10.45	3.80

Natl. Events, Mar. 13, 1957 A343

3c, Attack on Presidential Palace. 13c, Landing of Corynthia. 30c, Cienfuegos revolt.

1967, Mar. 13 **Wmk. 376**

1207	A343	3c multicolored	.25	.25

Size: 41x28mm

1208	A343	13c multicolored	2.50	.70
1209	A343	30c multicolored	2.40	.80
		Nos. 1207-1209 (3)	5.15	1.75

Evolution of Man — A344

Prehistoric men: 2c, Australopithecus. 3c, Pithecanthropus erectus. 4c, Sinanthropus pekinensis. 5c, Neanderthal man. 13c, Cro-magnon man carving tusk. 20c, Cro-magnon man painting petroglyph.

1967, Mar. 31 **Unwmk.**

1210	A344	1c multi	.30	.25
1211	A344	2c multi	.50	.25
1212	A344	3c multi	.50	.25
1213	A344	4c multi	.75	.40
1214	A344	5c multi	1.10	.50
1215	A344	13c multi	3.75	.85
1216	A344	20c multi	7.50	1.40
		Nos. 1210-1216 (7)	14.40	3.90

Stamp Day A345

Carriages.

1967, Apr. 24

1217	A345	3c Victoria	.35	.25
1218	A345	9c Volante	2.00	.45
1219	A345	13c Quitrin	3.00	.80
		Nos. 1217-1219 (3)	5.35	1.50

EXPO '67, Montreal, Apr. 28-Oct. 27 — A346

1c, Cuban pavilion. 2c, Space exploration. 3c, Petroglyph, hieroglyph. 13c, Agriculture, computer technology. 20c, Athletes.

1967, Apr. 28

1220	A346	1c multicolored	.40	.25
1221	A346	2c multicolored	.40	.25
1222	A346	3c multicolored	.50	.25
1223	A346	13c multicolored	2.90	.70
1224	A346	20c multicolored	3.25	.80
		Nos. 1220-1224 (5)	7.45	2.25

Botanical Gardens, Sequicentennial A347

Flowering plants: 1c, Eugenia malaccencis. 2c, Jacaranda filicifolia. 3c, Coroupita guianensis. 4c, Spathodea campanulata. 5c, Cassia fistula. 13c, Plumieria alba. 20c, Erythrina poeppigiana.

1967, May 30

1225	A347	1c multicolored	.25	.25
1226	A347	2c multicolored	.25	.25
1227	A347	3c multicolored	.45	.25
1228	A347	4c multicolored	.45	.25
1229	A347	5c multicolored	.90	.25
1230	A347	13c multicolored	2.25	.55
1231	A347	20c multicolored	4.00	.65
		Nos. 1225-1231 (7)	8.55	2.45

Natl. Ballet — A348

1967, June 15

1232	A348	1c Giselle	.35	.25
1233	A348	2c Swan Lake	.35	.25
1234	A348	3c Don Quixote	.50	.25
1235	A348	4c Calaucan	1.00	.25
1236	A348	13c Swan Lake	2.75	.70
1237	A348	20c Nutcracker	4.00	1.25
		Nos. 1232-1237 (6)	8.95	2.95

Intl. Ballet Festival, Havana.

5th Pan American Games, Winnipeg, Canada, July 22-Aug. 7 — A349

1c, Baseball, horiz. 2c, Swimming, horiz. 3c, Basketball. 4c, Gymnastic rings. 5c, Water polo. 13c, Weight lifting, horiz. 20c, Javelin.

1967, July 22

1238	A349	1c multi	.25	.25
1239	A349	2c multi	.30	.25
1240	A349	3c multi	.45	.25
1241	A349	4c multi	.70	.25
1242	A349	5c multi	.80	.25
1243	A349	13c multi	2.25	.45
1244	A349	20c multi	3.25	.80
		Nos. 1238-1244 (7)	8.00	2.50

1st Conference of Latin American Solidarity Organization (OLAS) — A350

Portrait of representative, map of South American homeland: No. 1245, Camilo Torres, Colombia. No. 1246, Luis de la Puente Uceda,

Peru. No. 1247, Luis A. Turcios Lima, Guatemala. No. 1248, Fabricio Ojeda, Venezuela.

1967, July 28 Wmk. 376

1245	A350	13c pale grn, blk & red	1.60	.60
1246	A350	13c lil, blk & red	1.60	.60
1247	A350	13c dark chalky blue, blk & red	1.60	.60
1248	A350	13c golden brn, blk & red	1.60	.60
		Nos. 1245-1248 (4)	6.40	2.40

Portrait of Sonny Rollins, by Alan Davie — A351

Bathers, by Gustave Singier A352

Modern Art: No. 1250, Twelve Selenites, by Felix Labisse. No. 1251, Night of the Drinker, by Friedensreich Hundertwasser. No. 1252, Figure, by Mariano. No. 1253, All-Souls, by Wilfredo Lam. No. 1254, Darkness and Cracks, by Antonio Tapies. No. 1256, Torso of a Muse, by Jean Arp. No. 1257, Figure, by M.W. Svanberg. No. 1258, Oppenheimer's Information, by Erro. No. 1259, Where Cardinals Are Born, by Max Ernst. No. 1260, Havana Landscape, by Portocarrero. No. 1261, EG 12, by Victor Vasarely. No. 1262, Frisco, by Alexander Calder. No. 1263, The Man with the Pipe, by Picasso. No. 1264, Abstract Composition, by Sergei Poliakoff. No. 1265, Painting, by Bram van Velde. No. 1266, Sower of Fires, by R. Matta. No. 1267, The Art of Living, by Rene Magritte. No. 1268, Poem, by Joan Miro. No. 1269, Young Tigers, by Jean Messagier. No. 1270, Painting, by M. Vieira da Silva. No. 1271, Live Cobra, by Pierre Alechinsky. No. 1272, Stalingrad, by Asger Jorn. 30c, Warriors, by Edouard Pignon. 50c, Cloister, a mural at the exhibition representing the Salon de Mayo pictures.

1967, July 29 Unwmk.

1249	A351	1c shown	.75	.25
1250	A351	1c multi	.75	.25
1251	A351	1c multi	.75	.25
1252	A351	1c multi	.75	.25
1253	A351	1c multi	.75	.25
a.		Strip of 5, Nos. 1249-1253	5.00	5.00

Sizes: 36½x54mm, 36½x53mm, 36½x45mm, 36½x41mm

1254	A352	2c multi	.75	.25
1255	A352	2c shown	.75	.25
1256	A352	2c multi	.75	.25
1257	A352	2c multi	.75	.25
1258	A352	2c multi	.75	.25
a.		Strip of 5, Nos. 1254-1258	5.00	5.00

Sizes: 36½x54mm, 36½x40mm, 36½x42mm, 36½x49mm

1259	A352	3c multi	1.40	.30
1260	A352	3c multi	1.40	.30
1261	A352	3c multi	1.40	.30
1262	A352	3c multi	1.40	.30
1263	A352	3c multi	1.40	.30
a.		Strip of 5, Nos. 1259-1263	8.00	8.00

Sizes: 35x15mm, 35x67mm, 35x46½mm, 35x55mm

1264	A352	4c multi	1.60	1.00
1265	A352	4c multi	1.60	1.00
1266	A352	4c multi	1.60	1.00
1267	A352	4c multi	1.60	1.00
1268	A352	4c multi	1.60	1.00
a.		Strip of 5, Nos. 1264-1268	10.00	10.00

Sizes: 49x32mm, 49x35mm, 49x46mm

1269	A351	13c multi	4.25	3.00
1270	A351	13c multi	4.25	3.00
1271	A351	13c multi	4.25	3.00
1272	A351	13c multi	4.25	3.00
a.		Strip of 4, Nos. 1269-1272	20.00	20.00

Size: 54x32mm

1273	A351	30c multi	17.50	11.00
		Nos. 1249-1273 (25)	57.00	32.00

Souvenir Sheet

Imperf

1274	A351	50c multi	18.00	12.50

Salon de Mayo Art Exhibition, Havana. No. 1274 contains one 88x45mm stamp with simulated perforations. Issued Oct. 7.

World Underwater Fishing Championships — A353

1967, Sept. 5

1275	A353	1c Green moray	.25	.25
1276	A353	2c Octopus	.25	.25
1277	A353	3c Great barracuda	.25	.25
1278	A353	4c Blue shark	.75	.25
1279	A353	5c Spotted jewfish	1.25	.25
1280	A353	13c Sting ray	2.50	.75
1281	A353	20c Green turtle	4.75	1.00
		Nos. 1275-1281 (7)	10.00	3.00

Soviet Space Program A354

1967, Oct. 4 Wmk. 376

1282	A354	1c Sputnik 1	.25	.25
1283	A354	2c Lunik 3	.25	.25
1284	A354	3c Venusik	.25	.25
1285	A354	4c Cosmos	.40	.25
1286	A354	5c Mars 1	.65	.25
1287	A354	9c Electron 1 & 2	.75	.25
1288	A354	10c Luna 9	1.10	.45
1289	A354	13c Luna 10	2.25	.60
a.		Souv. sheet of 8, #1282-1289, imperf.	12.00	12.00
		Nos. 1282-1289 (8)	5.90	2.55

Stamps in No. 1289a have simulated perfs.

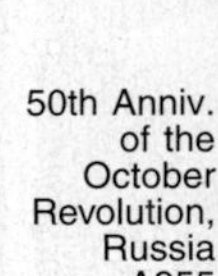

50th Anniv. of the October Revolution, Russia A355

Paintings: 1c, Storming the Winter Palace, by Sokolov-Skalia and Miasnikov. 2c, Lenin Addressing Congress, by W.A. Serov. 3c, Lenin, by H.D. Nalbandian. 4c, Lenin Explaining Electrification Map, by L.A. Schmatko. 5c, Dawn of the Five-Year Plan, by J.D. Romas. 13c, Kusnetzkroi Steel Furnace No. 1, by P. Kotov. 30c, Victory, by A. Krivonogov.

1967, Nov. 7 Unwmk.

1290	A355	1c 64x36mm	.25	.25
1291	A355	2c 48x36mm	.25	.25
1292	A355	3c 35x37mm	.35	.25
1293	A355	4c 48x36mm	.40	.25
1294	A355	5c 50x36mm	2.40	.50
1295	A355	13c 36x50mm	2.25	.50
1296	A355	30c 50x36mm	3.00	.85
		Nos. 1290-1296 (7)	8.90	2.85

Castle of the Royal Forces, Havana — A356

Historic architecture: 2c, Iznaga Tower, Trinidad, vert. 3c, Castle of Our Lady of the Angels, Cienfuegos. 4c, St. Francis de Paula Church, Havana. 13c, St. Francis Convent, Havana. 30c, Castle del Morro, Santiago de Cuba.

1967, Nov. 7 Wmk. 376

Sizes: 26x47mm (1c), 41x29mm (3c, 4c), 38½x31mm (13c)

1297	A356	1c multi	.25	.25
1298	A356	2c multi	.25	.25
1299	A356	3c multi	.65	.25
1300	A356	4c multi	.65	.25
1301	A356	13c multi	3.25	.50
1302	A356	30c multi	5.00	1.00
		Nos. 1297-1302 (6)	10.05	2.50

Christmas Type of 1961

Birds: No. 1303, Struthia camelus australis. No. 1304, Chysolophus pictus. No. 1305, Ciconia ciconia ciconia. No. 1306, Balearica pavonina. No. 1307, Dromiceius novaehollandiae. No. 1308, Anodorhynchus hyacinthus. No. 1309, Psittacus erithacus. No. 1310, Domicella garrula. No. 1311, Ramphastos sulfuratus. No. 1312, Kakatoe galerita galerita. No. 1313, Phoenicopterus ruber. No. 1314, Pelecanus erythrorhynchos. No. 1315, Alopochen aegyptiacus. No. 1316, Dendronessa galericulata. No. 1317, Chenopsis atrata.

1967, Dec. 20

1303	A248	1c multicolored	1.25	.60
1304	A249	1c multicolored	1.25	.60
1305	A249	1c multicolored	1.25	.60
1306	A249	1c multicolored	1.25	.60
1307	A249	1c multicolored	1.25	.60
a.		Block of 5 + label, Nos. 1303-1307	9.00	9.00
1308	A248	3c multicolored	2.00	1.00
1309	A249	3c multicolored	2.00	1.00
1310	A249	3c multicolored	2.00	1.00
1311	A249	3c multicolored	2.00	1.00
1312	A249	3c multicolored	2.00	1.00
a.		Block of 5 + label, Nos. 1308-1312	14.00	14.00
1313	A248	13c multicolored	3.75	1.75
1314	A249	13c multicolored	3.75	1.75
1315	A249	13c multicolored	3.75	1.75
1316	A249	13c multicolored	3.75	1.75
1317	A249	13c multicolored	3.75	1.75
a.		Block of 5 + label, Nos. 1313-1317	25.00	25.00
		Nos. 1303-1317 (15)	35.00	16.75

Christmas 1967. See note after No. 700.

Ernesto "Che" Guevara (1928-1967), Revolution Leader — A356a

1968, Jan. 3

1318	A356a	13c blk, dark red & buff	7.50	1.00

Cultural Congress, Havana — A357

Abstract designs: No. 1319, Independence fostering culture. No. 1320, Integral formation of man. No. 1321, Responsibility of intellectuals. No. 1322, Relationship between culture and the mass media. No. 1323, The arts versus science and technology.

1968, Jan. 4

1319	A357	3c multi, vert.	.25	.25
1320	A357	3c multi, vert.	.25	.25
1321	A357	13c multi, vert.	1.50	.40
1322	A357	13c multi, vert.	1.60	.50
1323	A357	30c multi	2.40	1.00
		Nos. 1319-1323 (5)	6.00	2.40

Canaries and Breeding Cycles A358

1968, Apr. 13

1324	A358	1c F.C.C. 4016	.25	.25
1325	A358	2c A.C.C. 774	.25	.25
1326	A358	3c A.C.C. 122	.30	.25
1327	A358	4c F.C.C. 4477	.30	.25
1328	A358	5c A.C.C 117	.65	.25
1329	A358	13c A.N.R. 1175	3.00	.55
1330	A358	20c A.C.C. 777	4.00	.70
		Nos. 1324-1330 (7)	8.75	2.50

Stamp Day A359

Paintings: 13c, The Village Postman, by J. Harris. 30c, The Philatelist, by G. Sciltian.

1968, Apr. 24 Unwmk.

1331	A359	13c multi	1.75	.50
1332	A359	30c multi	2.75	.70

World Health Organization, 20th Anniv. — A360

13c, Nurse, mother, child. 30c, Surgeons.

1968, May 10 Wmk. 376

1333	A360	13c multi	2.00	.75
1334	A360	30c multi	2.50	.90

Intl. Children's Day — A361

1968, June 1

1335	A361	3c multi	1.00	.25

Seville Camaguey Flight, 35th Anniv. — A362

13c, Plane Four Winds. 30c, Capt. Barberan, Lt. Collar, pilots.

1968, June 20

1336 A362 13c multi 2.25 .45
1337 A362 30c multi 2.75 .60

Natl. Food Production — A363

1c, Yellow tuna, can. 2c, Cow, dairy products. 3c, Rooster, eggs. 13c, Rum, sugar cane. 20c, Crayfish, box.

1968, June 29

1338 A363 1c multi .25 .25
1339 A363 2c multi .25 .25
1340 A363 3c multi .50 .25
1341 A363 13c multi 3.00 .50
1342 A363 20c multi 3.25 .70
Nos. 1338-1342 (5) 7.25 1.95

Attack of Moncada Barracks, 15th Anniv. A364

3c, Siboney farmhouse. 13c, Assault route, Santiago de Cuba. 30c, Students, school.

1968, July 26
Size: 43x29mm (13c)

1343 A364 3c multi .50 .25
1344 A364 13c multi 2.50 .75
1345 A364 30c multi 4.00 1.00
Nos. 1343-1345 (3) 7.00 2.00

Committee for the Defense of the Revolution, 8th Anniv. — A365

1968, Sept. 28

1346 A365 3c multi 2.00 .25

Guerilla Day A366

Che Guevara and: 1c, Rifleman and "En Cualquier Lugar..." 3c, Machine gunners and "Crear tres muchos Viet Nam." 9c, Silhouette of battalion and "Este Tipo De Lucha..." 10c, Guerillas cheering and "Hoy aquilatamos..." 13c, Map of Caribbean, So. America and "Hasta La Victoria Siempre."

1968, Oct. 8

1347 A366 1c gold, brt blue grn & blk .25 .25
1348 A366 3c gold, org brn blk .25 .25
1349 A366 9c multi .60 .25
1350 A366 10c gold, lt olive grn & blk 1.40 .25
1351 A366 13c gold, red org & blk 2.50 .70
Nos. 1347-1351 (5) 5.00 1.70

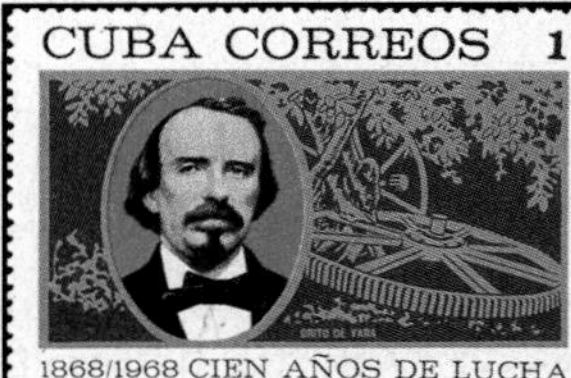

Cuban War of Independence, Cent. — A367

Independence fighters and scenes: No. 1352, C.M. de Cespedes, broken wheel. No. 1353, E. Betances, horsemen, flag. No. 1354, I. Agramonte, Clavellinas Monument. No. 1355, A. Maceo, Baragua Protest. No. 1356, J. Marti, horsemen. No. 1357, M. Gomez, The Invasion. No. 1358, J.A. Mella, declaration. No. 1359, A. Guiteras, El Morrillo monument. No. 1360, A. Santamaria, attack on Moncada Barracks. No. 1361, F. Pais memorial. No. 1362, J. Echeverria, student protest. No. 1363, C. Cienfuegos, insurrection. No. 1364, Che Guevara, 1st Declaration of Havana.

1968, Oct. 10 **Unwmk.**

1352 A367 1c multicolored .30 .25
1353 A367 1c multicolored .30 .25
1354 A367 1c multicolored .30 .25
1355 A367 1c multicolored .30 .25
1356 A367 1c multicolored .30 .25
a. Strip of 5, Nos. 1352-1356 2.25 2.25
1357 A367 3c multicolored .30 .25
1358 A367 3c multicolored .30 .25
1359 A367 3c multicolored .30 .25
1360 A367 3c multicolored .30 .25
1361 A367 3c multicolored .30 .25
a. Strip of 5, Nos. 1357-1361 2.25 2.25
1362 A367 9c multicolored 1.50 .25
1363 A367 13c multicolored 3.25 .75
1364 A367 30c multicolored 3.75 1.25
Nos. 1352-1364 (13) 11.50 4.75

Souvenir Sheet

The Burning of Bayamo, by J.E. Hernandez Giro — A368

1968, Oct. 18 ***Imperf.***

1365 A368 50c multi 12.50 12.50

Natl. Philatelic Exhibition, independence cent. Stamp in No. 1365 has simulated perforations.

19th Summer Olympics, Mexico City, Oct. 12-27 — A369

1c, Parade of athletes. 2c, Women's basketball, vert. 3c, Hammer throw, vert. 4c, Boxing. 5c, Water polo. 13c, Pistol shooting. 30c, Mexican flag, calendar stone.
50c, Running.

1968, Oct. 21 ***Perf. 12½***

1366 A369 1c multicolored .25 .25
1367 A369 2c multicolored .25 .25
1368 A369 3c multicolored .25 .25
1369 A369 4c multicolored .25 .25
1370 A369 5c multicolored .45 .25
1371 A369 13c multicolored 2.50 .55

Size: 32x50mm

1372 A369 30c multicolored 3.75 .80
Nos. 1366-1372 (7) 7.70 2.60

Souvenir Sheet
Imperf

1373 A369 50c multicolored 10.00 4.00

Stamp in No. 1373 has simulated perforations.

Civilian Activities of the Armed Forces A370

3c, Crop dusting. 9c, Che Guevara's Brigade. 10c, Road building. 13c, Plowing, harvesting.

1968, Dec. 2 **Wmk. 376** ***Perf. 12½***

1374 A370 3c multicolored .25 .25
1375 A370 9c multicolored .60 .25
1376 A370 10c multicolored 1.00 .25
1377 A370 13c multicolored 2.10 .70
Nos. 1374-1377 (4) 3.95 1.45

San Alejandro School of Painting, Sesquicentennial — A371

Paintings: 1c, Manrique de Lara's Family, by Jean Baptiste Vermay, vert. 2c, Seascape, by Leopoldo Romanach. 3c, Wild Cane, by Antonio Rodriguez, vert. 4c, Self-portrait, by Miguel Melero, vert. 5c, The Lottery List, by Jose Joaquin Tejada. 13c, Portrait of Nina, by Armando B. Menocal, vert. 30c, Landscape, by Esteban B. Chartrand. 50c, Siesta, by Guillermo Collazo.

1968, Dec. 30 **Unwmk.**
Sizes: 38x48mm (1c, 3c), 39x50mm (4c, 13c), 53x36mm (30c)

1378 A371 1c multi .25 .25
1379 A371 2c multi .25 .25
1380 A371 3c multi .30 .25
1381 A371 4c multi .30 .25
1382 A371 5c multi 1.25 .40
1383 A371 13c multi 3.50 .70
1384 A371 30c multi 5.00 1.10
Nos. 1378-1384 (7) 10.85 3.20

Souvenir Sheet
Imperf

1385 A371 50c multi 9.00 3.50

No. 1385 contains one 52x41½mm stamp that has simulated perforations.

10th Anniv. of the Revolution A372

1969, Jan. 3 **Wmk. 376** ***Perf. 12½***

1386 A372 13c multi 2.00 .60

Villaclarenos Rebellion, Cent. — A373

3c, Gutierrez and Sanchez.

1969, Feb. 6

1387 A373 3c multi 1.10 .25

Women's Day — A374

Design: Mariana Grajales, rose and statue.

1969, Mar. 8

1388 A374 3c multi 1.00 .25

Cuban Pioneers and Young Communists Unions — A375

3c, Pioneers. 13c, Young Communists.

1969, Apr. 4

1389 A375 3c multi .40 .25
1390 A375 13c multi 2.00 .80

Guaimaro Assembly, Cent. — A376

1969, Apr. 10

1391 A376 3c dark brn 1.10 .25

The Postman, by Jean C. Cazin A377

Paintings: 30c, Portrait of a Young Man, by George Romney.

1969, Apr. 24 **Unwmk.**

1392 A377 13c multi 2.25 .75

Size: 35½x43½mm

1393 A377 30c multi 3.75 1.25

Stamp Day.

Agrarian Reform, 10th Anniv. A378

1969, May 17 **Wmk. 376**

1394 A378 13c multi 2.50 .70

Marine Life A379

1c, Petrochirus bahamensis. 2c, Stenopus hispidus. 3c, Panulirus argus. 4c, Callinectes sapidus. 5c, Gecarcinus ruricola. 13c, Macrobrachium carcinus. 30c, Carpilius coralinus.

1969, May 20 **Unwmk.**

1395 A379 1c multicolored .25 .25
1396 A379 2c multicolored .40 .25
1397 A379 3c multicolored .40 .25
1398 A379 4c multicolored .50 .25
1399 A379 5c multicolored .50 .25
1400 A379 13c multicolored 3.25 .45
1401 A379 30c multicolored 5.00 .80
Nos. 1395-1401 (7) 10.30 2.50

Intl. Labor Organization, 50th Anniv. — A380

13c, Blacksmith breaking chains.

1969, June 6 **Wmk. 376**

1402 A380 3c shown .40 .25
1403 A380 13c multi 2.10 .70

Paintings in the Natl. Museum — A381

Designs: 1c, Flowers, by Raul Milian, vert. 2c, Annunciation, by Antonia Eiriz. 3c, Factory, by Marcelo Pogolotti, vert. 4c, Territorial Waters, by Luis Martinez Pedro, vert. 5c, Miss Sarah Gale, by John Hoppner, vert. 13c, Two Women Wearing Mantilla, by Ignacio Zuloaga. 30c, Virgin and Child, by Francisco de Zurbaran.

1969, June 15 **Unwmk.**

1404 A381 1c 39x59mm .25 .25
1405 A381 2c 49x40mm .25 .25
1406 A381 3c 39½x49mm .45 .25
1407 A381 4c 39½x43mm .30 .25
1408 A381 5c 39½x45½mm .30 .25
1409 A381 13c 38x41½mm 2.10 .70
1410 A381 30c 39x45mm 3.25 .90
Nos. 1404-1410 (7) 6.90 2.85

Broadcasting Institute — A382

13c, Hemispheres, tower. 1p, Waves on graph.

1969, July 5 **Wmk. 376**

1411 A382 3c shown .40 .25
1412 A382 13c multicolored 2.00 .75
1413 A382 1p multicolored 4.50 1.75
Nos. 1411-1413 (3) 6.90 2.75

Fish A383

1c, Apogon maculatus. 2c, Bodianus rufus. 3c, Microspathodon chrysurus. 4c, Gramma loreto. 5c, Chromis marginatus. 13c, Myripristis jacobus. 30c, Nomeus gronovii, vert.

1969, July 20 **Unwmk.**

1414 A383 1c multicolored .25 .25
1415 A383 2c multicolored .25 .25
1416 A383 3c multicolored .35 .25
1417 A383 4c multicolored .40 .25
1418 A383 5c multicolored .50 .25
1419 A383 13c multicolored 2.75 .55
1420 A383 30c multicolored 4.50 .90
Nos. 1414-1420 (7) 9.00 2.70

Natl. Film Industry, 10th Anniv. — A384

1969, Aug. 5 **Wmk. 376**

1421 A384 1c Poster .25 .25
1422 A384 3c Documentaries .25 .25
1423 A384 13c Cartoons 2.50 .60
1424 A384 30c Entertainers 3.50 .70
Nos. 1421-1424 (4) 6.50 1.80

Napoleon in Milan, by Andrea Appiani — A385

Paintings in the Napoleon Museum, Havana: 2c, Hortensia de Beauharnais, by Francois Gerard. 3c, Napoleon as First Consul, by J.B. Regnault. 4c, Elisa Bonaparte, by Robert Lefevre. 5c, Napoleon Planning Coronation Ceremony, by J.G. Vibert, horiz. 13c, Napoleon as Cuirassier Corporal, by Jean Meissonier. 30c, Napoleon Bonaparte, by LeFevre.

1969, Aug. 20 **Unwmk.**

1425 A385 1c 46x56mm .25 .25
1426 A385 2c 41½x55mm .25 .25
1427 A385 3c 45½x56mm .25 .25
1428 A385 4c 43x62½mm .45 .25
1429 A385 5c 63x47½mm .70 .30
1430 A385 13c 43x62½mm 3.25 .70
1431 A385 30c 45x59½mm 4.25 .90
Nos. 1425-1431 (7) 9.40 2.90

See Nos. 2448-2453.

Cuba's Victory at the 17th World Amateur Baseball Championships, Santo Domingo — A386

1969, Sept. 11

1432 A386 13c multi 2.50 .60

No. 1432 printed se-tenant with inscribed label listing finalists.

Alexander von Humboldt (1769-1859), German Naturalist — A387

1969, Sept. 14

1433 A387 3c Surinam eel .25 .25
1434 A387 13c Night ape 2.25 .75
1435 A387 30c Condors 4.00 .85
Nos. 1433-1435 (3) 6.50 1.85

World Fencing Championships, Havana — A388

Designs: 1c, Ancient Egyptians in combat. 2c, Roman gladiators. 2c, Viking and Norman. 4c, Medieval tournament. 5c, French musketeers. 13c, Japanese samurai. 30c, Mounted Cubans, War of Independence. 50c, Modern fencers.

1969, Oct. 2

1436 A388 1c multi .25 .25
1437 A388 2c multi .25 .25
1438 A388 3c multi .25 .25
1439 A388 4c multi .40 .25
1440 A388 5c multi .60 .25
1441 A388 13c multi 2.75 .45
1442 A388 30c multi 4.25 .80
Nos. 1436-1442 (7) 8.75 2.50

Souvenir Sheet

Imperf

1443 A388 50c multi 12.00 12.00

Stamp in No. 1443 has simulated perforations.

Natl. Revolutionary Militia, 10th Anniv. — A389

1969, Oct. 26 **Wmk. 376**

1444 A389 3c multi 1.10 .25

Disappearance of Maj. Camilo Cienfuegos, 10th Anniv. — A390

1969, Oct. 28

1445 A390 13c multi 2.00 .60

Agriculture — A391

No. 1446, Strawberries, grapes. No. 1447, Onions, asparagus. No. 1448, Rice. No. 1449, Banana. No. 1450, Pineapple, vert. No. 1451, Tobacco, vert. No. 1452, Citrus fruits, vert. No. 1453, Coffee, vert. No. 1454, Rabbits, vert. No. 1455, Pigs, vert. No. 1456, Sugar cane. No. 1457, Bull.

1969, Nov. 2 **Unwmk.**

1446 A391 1c multicolored .25 .25
1447 A391 1c multicolored .25 .25
1448 A391 1c multicolored .25 .25
1449 A391 1c multicolored .25 .25
a. Strip of 4, #1446-1449 1.25 1.25
1450 A391 3c multicolored .50 .50
1451 A391 3c multicolored .50 .50
1452 A391 3c multicolored .50 .50
1453 A391 3c multicolored .50 .50
1454 A391 3c multicolored .50 .50
a. Strip of 5, #1450-1454 3.00 3.00
1455 A391 10c multicolored .50 .25
1456 A391 13c multicolored 2.75 .60
1457 A391 30c multicolored 4.00 .85
Nos. 1446-1457 (12) 10.75 5.20

Sporting Events — A392

1c, 2nd Natl. Games. 2c, 11th Anniv. Games. 3c, Barrientos Commemorative, vert. 10c, 2nd Olympic Trials, vert. 13c, 6th Socialist Bicycle Race, vert. 30c, 6th Capablanca Memorial Chess Championships, vert.

1969, Nov. 15

1458 A392 1c multicolored .25 .25
1459 A392 2c multicolored .25 .25
1460 A392 3c multicolored .25 .25
1461 A392 10c multicolored .30 .25
1462 A392 13c multicolored 2.75 .80
1463 A392 30c multicolored 3.75 1.25
Nos. 1458-1463 (6) 7.55 3.05

Christmas Type of 1961

Flowering plants: No. 1464, Plumbago capensis. No. 1465, Petrea volubilis. No. 1466, Clitoria ternatea. No. 1467, Duranta repens. No. 1468, Ruellia tuberosa. No. 1469, Turnera ulmifolia. No. 1470, Thevetia peruviana. No. 1471, Hibiscus elatus. No. 1472, Allamanda cathartica. No. 1473, Cosmos sulphureus. No. 1474, Delonix regia. No. 1475, Neriun oleander. No. 1476, Cordia sebestena. No. 1477, Lochnera rosea. No. 1478, Jatropha integerrima.

1969, Dec. 1

1464 A248 1c multicolored .40 .25
1465 A249 1c multicolored .40 .25
1466 A249 1c multicolored .40 .25
1467 A249 1c multicolored .40 .25
1468 A249 1c multicolored .40 .25
a. Block of 5 + label, Nos. 1464-1468 3.00 3.00
1469 A248 3c multicolored 1.00 .25
1470 A249 3c multicolored 1.00 .25
1471 A249 3c multicolored 1.00 .25
1472 A249 3c multicolored 1.00 .25
1473 A249 3c multicolored 1.00 .25
a. Block of 5 + label, Nos. 1469-1473 7.50 7.50
1474 A248 13c multicolored 2.25 1.00
1475 A249 13c multicolored 2.25 1.00

1476 A249 13c multicolored 2.25 1.00
1477 A249 13c multicolored 2.25 1.00
1478 A249 13c multicolored 2.25 1.00
a. Block of 5 + label, Nos. 1474-1478 15.00 15.00
Nos. 1464-1478 (15) 18.25 7.50

Christmas 1969. See note after No. 700.

Zapata Swamp Fauna — A393

1c, Trelanorhynus variabilis. 2c, Hyla insulsa. 3c, Atractosteus tristoechus. 4c, Capromys nana. 5c, Crocodylus rhombifer. 13c, Amazona leucocephala. 30c, Agelaius phoeniceus assimilis.

1969, Dec. 15

1479 A393 1c multicolored .25 .25
1480 A393 2c multicolored .25 .25
1481 A393 3c multicolored .25 .25
1482 A393 4c multicolored .25 .25
1483 A393 5c mutlicolored .25 .25
1484 A393 13c multicolored 2.75 .55
1485 A393 30c multicolored 4.25 1.00
Nos. 1479-1485 (7) 8.25 2.80

Nos. 1482, 1484-1485 vert.

Tourism A394

1c, Jibacoa Beach. 3c, Trinidad City. 13c, Santiago de Cuba. 30c, Vinales Valley.

1970, Jan. 25 **Wmk. 376**

1486 A394 1c multi .25 .25
1487 A394 3c multi .25 .25
1488 A394 13c multi 3.50 1.00
1489 A394 30c multi 4.25 1.25
Nos. 1486-1489 (4) 8.25 2.75

Medicinal Plants — A395

1c, Guarea guara. 3c, Ocimum sanctum. 10c, Canella winterana. 13c, Bidens pilosa. 30c, Turnera ulmifolia. 50c, Picramnia pentandra.

1970, Feb. 10 **Unwmk.**

1490 A395 1c multi .25 .25
1491 A395 3c multi .25 .25
1492 A395 10c multi .45 .25
1493 A395 13c multi 2.25 .70
1494 A395 30c multi 2.75 .85
1495 A395 50c multi 4.00 1.00
Nos. 1490-1495 (6) 9.95 3.30

11th Central American and Caribbean Games, Panama, Feb. 28-Mar. 14 — A396

1970, Feb. 28 **Wmk. 376**

1496 A396 1c Weight lifting .25 .25
1497 A396 3c Boxing .25 .25
1498 A396 10c Gymnastics .25 .25
1499 A396 13c Running 2.40 .65
1500 A396 30c Fencing 3.25 .90
Nos. 1496-1500 (5) 6.40 2.30

Souvenir Sheet

Imperf

1501 A396 50c Baseball 12.00 6.00

No. 1501 contains one 50x37mm stamp that has simulated perforations.

EXPO '70, Osaka, Japan, Mar. 15-Sept. 13 — A397

1c, Enjoying life. 2c, Improving on nature, vert. 3c, Better living standard. 13c, Intl. cooperation, vert. 30c, Cuban pavilion.

1970, Mar. 15

1502 A397 1c multicolored .25 .25
1503 A397 2c multicolored .40 .25
1504 A397 3c multicolored .40 .25
1505 A397 13c multicolored 2.75 .50
1506 A397 30c multicolored 3.50 .75
Nos. 1502-1506 (5) 7.30 2.00

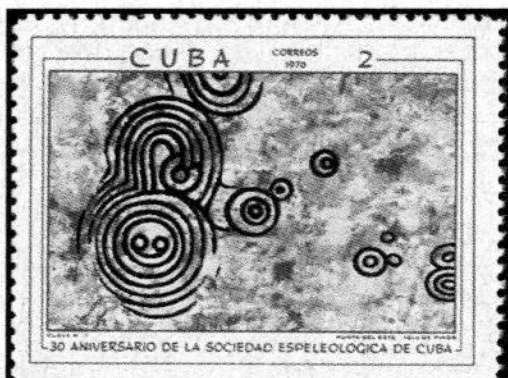

Speleological Soc., 30th Anniv. — A398

Petroglyphs in Cuban caves: 1c, Ambrosio Cave, Varadero Matanzas. 2c, Cave No. 1, Punta del Este, Isle of Pines. 3c, Pichardo Cave, Cubitas Camaguey Mountains. 4c, Ambrosio Cave, diff. 5c, Cave No. 1, diff. 13c, Garcia Ribiou Cave, Havana. 30c, Cave No. 2, Punta del Este.

1970, Mar. 28 **Unwmk.**

Sizes: 29x45mm (1c, 3c, 4c, 13c)

1507 A398 1c multi .25 .25
1508 A398 2c shown .25 .25
1509 A398 3c multi .25 .25
1510 A398 4c multi .25 .25
1511 A398 5c multi .25 .25
1512 A398 13c multi 2.25 .70
1513 A398 30c multi 4.25 .80
Nos. 1507-1513 (7) 7.75 2.75

Aviation Pioneers — A399

1970, Apr. 10

1514 A399 3c Jose D. Blino 1.00 .25
1515 A399 13c Adolfo Teodore 3.00 .65

Lenin Birth Centenary — A400

Paintings and quotes: 1c, Lenin in Kazan, by O. Vishniakov. 2c, Young Lenin, by V. Prager. 3c, Second Socialist Party Congress, by Y. Vinogradov. 4c, First Manifesto, by F. Golubkov. 5c, First Day of Soviet Power, by N. Babasiuk. 13c, Lenin in Smolny, by M. Sokolov. 30c, Autumn in Gorky, by A. Varlamov. 50c, Lenin at Gorky, by N. Baskakov.

1970, Apr. 22

Sizes: 67½x46mm (1c, 4c, 5c)

1516 A400 1c multi .25 .25
1517 A400 2c shown .25 .25
1518 A400 3c multi .25 .25
1519 A400 4c multi .25 .25
1520 A400 5c multi .25 .25
1521 A400 13c multi 2.75 .55
1522 A400 30c multi 3.25 .70
Nos. 1516-1522 (7) 7.25 2.50

Souvenir Sheet

Imperf

1523 A400 50c multi 13.00 6.50

No. 1523 contains one 48x46mm stamp that has simulated perforations.

Stamp Day — A401

13c, The Letter, by J. Arche. 30c, Portrait of A Cadet, Anonymous.

1970, Apr. 24

1524 A401 13c multicolored 2.50 .60

Size: 30x44mm

1525 A401 30c multicolored 3.00 .80

Da Vinci's Anatomical Drawing, Earth, Moon — A402

1970, May 17 **Wmk. 376**

1526 A402 30c multi 3.25 .60

World Telecommunications Day.

Ho Chi Minh (1890-1969), President of North Viet Nam — A403

No. 1527, Vietnamese fisherman. No. 1528, Two women. No. 1529, Plowing field. No. 1530, Teacher, students in air-raid shelter. No. 1531, Nine women in paddy. No. 1532, Camouflaged machine shop.

1970, May 19 **Unwmk.**

1527 A403 1c multicolored .25 .25

Size: 32x44mm

1528 A403 3c multicolored .50 .25
1529 A403 3c multicolored .50 .25

Size: 33x45mm

1530 A403 3c multicolored .50 .25
1531 A403 3c multicolored .50 .25

Size: 34x41½mm

1532 A403 3c multicolored .50 .25

Size: 34x39mm

1533 A403 13c shown 2.25 .70
Nos. 1527-1533 (7) 5.00 2.20

Cuban Cigar Industry A404

3c, Plantation, Eden cigar band. 13c, Factory, El Mambi band. 30c, Packing cigars, Lopez Hermanos band.

1970, July 5

1534 A404 3c multicolored .25 .25
1535 A404 13c multicolored 2.25 .70
1536 A404 30c multicolored 3.25 1.00
Nos. 1534-1536 (3) 5.75 1.95

Projected Sugar Production: Over 10 Million Tons — A405

1c, Cane-crushing. 2c, Sowing and crop dusting. 3c, Cutting sugar cane. 10c, Transporting cane. 13c, Modern cutting machine. 30c, Intl. Brigade, cane cutters, vert. 1p, Sugar warehouse.

1970, July 26

1537 A405 1c multicolored .25 .25
1538 A405 2c multicolored .25 .25
1539 A405 3c multicolored .25 .25
1540 A405 10c multicolored 4.25 .45
1541 A405 13c multicolored 1.50 .25
1542 A405 30c multicolored 2.00 .75
1543 A405 1p multicolored 4.00 2.00
Nos. 1537-1543 (7) 12.50 4.20

Pedro Figueredo (d. 1870), Composer — A406

Versions of the Natl. Anthem.

1970, Aug. 17

1544 A406 3c 1868 Version .30 .25
1545 A406 20c 1898 Version 2.00 .60

Women's Federation, 10th Anniv. — A407

1970, Aug. 23

1546 A407 3c multi 1.00 .50

Militia, by Servando C. Moreno — A408

Paintings in the Natl. Museum: 2c, Washerwomen, by Aristides Fernandez. 3c, Puerta del Sol, Madrid, by L. Paret Y Alcazar. 4c, Fishermen's Wives, by Joaquin Sorolla. 5c, Portrait of a Woman, by Thomas de Keyser. 13c, Mrs. Edward Foster, by Sir Thomas Lawrence. 30c, Tropical Gypsy, by Victor M. Garcia.

1970, Aug. 31

1547 A408 1c shown .25 .25

Size: 45x41mm

1548 A408 2c multi .25 .25
1549 A408 3c multi .25 .25

Size: 40x41mm

1550 A408 4c multi .25 .25

Size: 38x45½mm

1551 A408 5c multi .25 .25
1552 A408 13c multi 2.00 .50
1553 A408 30c multi 3.00 .80
Nos. 1547-1553 (7) 6.25 2.55

See Nos. 1640-1646, 1669-1675, 1773-1779.

Havana Declaration, 10th Anniv. — A409

1970, Sept. 2

1554 A409 3c Jose Marti Square .75 .25

Committee for the Defense of the Revolution, 10th Anniv. A410

1970, Sept. 28

1555 A410 3c multi .80 .25

39th Sugar Technician's Assoc. (ATAC) Conference — A411

1970, Oct. 11

1556 A411 30c multi 3.00 .70

Wildlife — A412

1c, Numida meleagris galeata. 2c, Dendrocygna arborea. 3c, Phasianus colchicus torquatus. 4c, Zenaida macroura macroura. 5c, Colinus virginianus cubanensis. 13c, Sus scrofa. 30c, Odocoileus virginianus.

1970, Oct. 20

1557 A412 1c multicolored .75 .25
1558 A412 2c multicolored 1.00 .25
1559 A412 3c multicolored 1.00 .25
1560 A412 4c multicolored 1.25 .25
1561 A412 5c multicolored 1.50 .25
1562 A412 13c multicolored 2.25 1.00
1563 A412 30c multicolored 4.25 1.50
Nos. 1557-1563 (7) 12.00 3.75

Black-magic Feast, by M. Puente — A413

Afro-Cuban folk paintings: 3c, Hat Dance, by V.P. Landaluze. 10c, Los Hoyos Conga Dance, by Domingo Ravenet. 13c, Climax of the Rumba, by Eduardo Abela.

1970, Nov. 5

Sizes: 36x48½mm (3c, 13c), 44½x44mm (10c)

1564 A413 1c shown .25 .25
1565 A413 3c multi .35 .25
1566 A413 10c multi .90 .45
1567 A413 13c multi 2.50 .70
Nos. 1564-1567 (4) 4.00 1.65

Road Safety Week A414

1970, Nov. 15

1568 A414 3c Zebra, road signs .90 .25
1569 A414 9c Prudence the Bear 1.30 .25

Intl. Education Year — A415

1970, Nov. 20

1570 A415 13c Abacus, "a" 2.00 .30
1571 A415 30c Cow, microscope 2.50 .70

Christmas Type of 1961

Birds: No. 1572, Dives atroviolaceus. No. 1573, Glaucidium siju siju. No. 1574, Todus multicolor. No. 1575, Xiphidiopicus percussus percussus. No. 1576, Ferminia cerverai. No. 1577, Teretistris fornsi. No. 1578, Myadestes elisabeth elisabeth. No. 1579, Polioptila lembeyei. No. 1580, Vireo gundlachii gundlachii. No. 1581, Teretistris fernandinae. No. 1582, Torreornis inexpectata inexpectata. No. 1583, Chondrohierax wilsonii. No. 1584, Accipiter gundlachi. No. 1585, Starnoenas cyanocephala. No. 1586, Aratinga euops.

1970, Dec. 1

1572 A248 1c multicolored .75 .25
1573 A249 1c multicolored .75 .25
1574 A249 1c multicolored .75 .25
1575 A249 1c multicolored .75 .25
1576 A249 1c multicolored .75 .25
a. Block of 5 + label, Nos. 1572-1576 5.00 5.00
1577 A248 3c multicolored 1.60 .35
1578 A249 3c multicolored 1.60 .35
1579 A249 3c multicolored 1.60 .35
1580 A249 3c multicolored 1.60 .35
1581 A249 3c multicolored 1.60 .35
a. Block of 5 + label, Nos. 1577-1581 10.00 10.00
1582 A248 13c multicolored 2.25 .75
1583 A249 13c multicolored 2.25 .75
1584 A249 13c multicolored 2.25 .75
1585 A249 13c multicolored 2.25 .75
1586 A249 13c multicolored 2.25 .75
a. Block of 5 + label, Nos. 1582-1586 15.00 15.00
Nos. 1572-1586 (15) 23.00 6.75

Christmas 1970. See note after No. 700.

Camilo Cienfuegos Military Academy — A416

1970, Dec. 2

1587 A416 3c multi .90 .25

7th Congress of the Intl. Organization of Journalists — A417

1971, Jan. 4

1588 A417 13c multi 2.10 .50

World Meteorology Day — A418

1c, Class, weather chart, computer, vert. 3c, Weather map. 8c, Equipment, vert.

Size: 39½x35½mm (3c)

1971, Feb. 16

1589 A418 1c multi .25 .25
1590 A418 3c multi .25 .25
1591 A418 8c multi 1.00 .25
1592 A418 30c shown 4.25 1.25
Nos. 1589-1592 (4) 5.75 2.00

6th Pan American Games, Cali, Colombia — A419

1c, Emblem, vert. 2c, Women's running, vert. 3c, Rifle shooting. 4c, Gymnastics, vert. 5c, Boxing, vert. 13c, Water polo. 30c, Baseball.

1971, Feb. 20

1593 A419 1c multicolored .25 .25
1594 A419 2c multicolored .25 .25
1595 A419 3c multicolored .25 .25
1596 A419 4c multicolored .25 .25
1597 A419 5c multicolored .25 .25
1598 A419 13c multicolored 2.25 .30
1599 A419 30c multicolored 2.75 .55
Nos. 1593-1599 (7) 6.25 2.10

Porcelain and Mosaics in the Metropolitan Museum, Havana — A420

Designs: 1c, Parisian vase, 19th cent. 3c, Mexican bowl, 17th cent. 10c, Parisian vase, diff. 13c, Colosseum, Italian mosaic, 19th cent. 20c, Mexican bowl, 17th cent. 30c, St. Peter's Square, Italian mosaic, 19th cent.

1971, Mar. 11

Sizes: 34½x53mm (1c, 10c), 46x53mm (3c), 42x48mm (20c)

1600 A420 1c multi .25 .25
1601 A420 3c multi .25 .25
1602 A420 10c multi .40 .25
1603 A420 13c shown 2.25 .25
1604 A420 20c multi 2.25 .55
1605 A420 30c multi 2.75 .65
Nos. 1600-1605 (6) 8.15 2.20

See Nos. 1699-1705.

Natl. Child Centers, 10th Anniv. — A421

1971, Apr. 10

1606 A421 3c multicolored .85 .25

Manned Space Flight 10th Anniv. — A422

Cosmonauts in training.

1971, Apr. 12

1607 A422 1c multi .25 .25
1608 A422 2c multi, diff. .25 .25
1609 A422 3c multi, diff. .25 .25
1610 A422 4c multi, diff. .25 .25
1611 A422 5c multi, diff. .25 .25
1612 A422 13c multi, diff. 2.25 .30
1613 A422 30c multi, diff. 3.00 .65
Nos. 1607-1613 (7) 6.50 2.20

Souvenir Sheet

Imperf

1614 A422 50c multi 8.00 8.00

Stamp in No. 1614 has simulated perf.

Bay of Pigs Invasion, 10th Anniv. A423

1971, Apr. 17

1615 A423 13c multi 3.00 .60

Stamp Day — A424

Packets: 13c, Jeune Richard attacking the Windsor Castle, 1807. 30c, Orinoco.

1971, Apr. 24

1616 A424 13c multi 3.25 .90
1617 A424 30c multi 4.50 1.00

Cuban Intl. Broadcast Service, 10th Anniv. — A425

1971, May 1 **Wmk. 376**

1618 A425 3c multi .25 .25
1619 A425 50c multi 4.00 .90

Orchids A426

1c, Cattleya skinnerii. 2c, Vanda hibrida. 3c, Cypripedium collossum. 4c, Cypripedium gloucophyllum. 5c, Vanda tricolor. 13c, Cypripedium mowgh. 30c, Cypripedium solum.

1971, May 15

1620 A426 1c multicolored .25 .25
1621 A426 2c multicolored .25 .25
1622 A426 3c multicolored .25 .25
1623 A426 4c multicolored .25 .25
1624 A426 5c multicolored .25 .25
1625 A426 13c multicolored 2.25 .45
1626 A426 30c multicolored 4.00 .85
Nos. 1620-1626 (7) 7.50 2.55

See Nos. 1677-1683 and 1780-1786.

Enrique Loynaz del Castillo (b. 1861), Composer — A427

3c, Portrait, Invasion Hymn.

1971, June 5 **Wmk. 376**

1627 A427 3c multicolored .90 .25

Bee Keeping — A428

1971, June 20 **Unwmk.**

1628 A428 1c Egg, larvae, pupa .25 .25
1629 A428 3c Worker .25 .25
1630 A428 9c Drone .50 .25
1631 A428 13c Defense of hive 2.50 .30
1632 A428 30c Queen 3.50 .80
Nos. 1628-1632 (5) 7.00 1.85

Children's Drawings — A429

1c, Sailboat. 3c, The Little Train. 9c, Sugar Cane Cutter. 10c, Return of the Fishermen. 13c, The Zoo. 20c, House and Garden. 30c, Landscape.

1971, Aug. 30 **Size: 45x39mm**

1633 A429 1c multi .25 .25
1634 A429 3c multi .85 .25

Sizes: 45½x35½mm (9c, 13c), 47x37½mm (10c)

1635 A429 9c multi .25 .25
1636 A429 10c multi .40 .25
1637 A429 13c multi 1.60 .30

Size: 47x42mm

1638 A429 20c multi 2.50 .55

Size: 31½x50mm

1639 A429 30c multi 2.75 .85
Nos. 1633-1639 (7) 8.60 2.70

Art Type of 1970

Paintings in the Natl. Museum: 1c, St. Catherine of Alexandria, by F. Zurburan. 2c, The Cart, by Federico Americo. 3c, St. Christopher and Child, by J. Bassano. 4c, Little Devil, by Rene Portocarrero. 5c, Portrait of a Woman, by Nicolas Maes. 13c, Phoenix, by Raul Martinez. 30c, Sir William Pitt, by Thomas Gainsborough.

1971, Sept. 20

1640 A408 1c 31x55mm .25 .25
1641 A408 2c 48x37mm .25 .25
1642 A408 3c 31x55mm .25 .25
1643 A408 4c 37x48mm .25 .25
1644 A408 5c 37x48mm .35 .25
1645 A408 13c 39x48½mm 2.25 .45
1646 A408 30c 39x48½mm 3.00 .75
Nos. 1640-1646 (7) 6.60 2.45

Sport Fishing — A431

1c, Albula vulpes. 2c, Seriola species. 3c, Micropterus salmoides. 4c, Coryphaena hippurus. 5c, Megalops atlantica. 13c, Acanthocybium solandri. 30c, Makaira ampla.

1971, Oct. 30

1647 A431 1c multicolored .25 .25
1648 A431 2c multicolored .25 .25
1649 A431 3c multicolored .25 .25
1650 A431 4c multicolored .25 .25
1651 A431 5c multicolored .30 .25
1652 A431 13c multicolored 2.00 .55
1653 A431 30c multicolored 3.25 .95
Nos. 1647-1653 (7) 6.55 2.75

19th World Amateur Baseball Championships — A432

1971, Nov. 22 **Wmk. 376**

1654 A432 3c shown .25 .25
1655 A432 1p Globe as baseball 6.00 1.40

Execution of Medical Students, Cent. A433

Paintings: 3c, Dr. Fermin Valdez Dominguez, anonymous. 13c, Execution of the Medical Students, by M. Mesa. 30c, Capt. Federico Capdevila, anonymous.

1971, Nov. 27 **Unwmk.**

Size: 61½x46mm (13c)

1656 A433 3c multi .35 .25
1657 A433 13c multi 1.90 .40
1658 A433 30c multi 2.75 .55
Nos. 1656-1658 (3) 5.00 1.20

Spindalis Zena Pretrei — A434

Birds: 1c, Falco sparverius sparverioides vigors. 2c, Glaucidium siju siju. 3c, Priotelus temnurus temnurus. 4c, Saurothera merlini merlini. 5c, Nesoceleus fernandinae. 30c, Mimocichla plumbea rubripes. 50c, Chlorostilbon ricordii ricordii and Archilochus colubris. Nos. 1659-1663 vert.

1971, Dec. 10

1659 A434 1c multi .40 .25
1660 A434 2c multi .40 .25
1661 A434 3c multi .50 .25
1662 A434 4c multi .60 .25
1663 A434 5c multi .75 .25
1664 A434 13c shown 1.40 .55
1665 A434 30c multi 2.75 1.00

Size: 55½x29mm

1666 A434 50c multi 5.00 1.75
Nos. 1659-1666 (8) 11.80 4.55

Death centenary of Ramon de la Sagra, naturalist.

Cuba's Victory at the World Amateur Baseball Championships — A435

1971, Dec. 8 **Wmk. 376**

1667 A435 13c multi 1.50 .60

UNICEF, 25th Anniv. A436

1971, Dec. 11

1668 A436 13c multi 2.00 .70

Art Type of 1970

Paintings in the Natl. Museum: 1c, Arrival of an Ambassador, by Vittore Carpaccio. 2c, Senora Malpica, by G. Collazo. 3c, La Chorrera Tower, by Esteban Chartrand. 4c, Creole Landscape, by Carlos Enriquez. 5c, Sir William Lemon, by George Romney. 13c, Landscape, by Henry Cleenewerk. 30c, Valencia Beach, by Joaquin Sorolla y Bastida.

1972, Jan. 25 **Unwmk.**

1669 A408 1c 50x33mm .25 .25
1670 A408 2c 27½x52mm .25 .25
1671 A408 3c 50x33mm .25 .25
1672 A408 4c 35x43mm .25 .25
1673 A408 5c 35x43mm .25 .25
1674 A408 13c 43x33mm 2.00 .40
1675 A408 30c 43x33mm 3.50 .95
Nos. 1669-1675 (7) 6.75 2.60

Academy of Sciences, 10th Anniv. — A437

13c, Capitol Type of 1929.

1972, Feb. 20 **Wmk. 376**

1676 A437 13c multi 1.90 .50

Orchid Type of 1971

1c, Brasso cattleya sindorossiana. 2c, Cypripedium doraeus. 3c, Cypripedium exul. 4c, Cypripedium rosy dawn. 5c, Cypripedium champolliom. 13c, Cypripedium bucolique. 30c, Cypripedium sullanum.

1972, Feb. 25 **Unwmk.**

1677 A426 1c multicolored .25 .25
1678 A426 2c multicolored .25 .25
1679 A426 3c multicolored .25 .25
1680 A426 4c multicolored .25 .25
1681 A426 5c multicolored .25 .25
1682 A426 13c multicolored 2.25 .65
1683 A426 30c multicolored 3.00 .80
Nos. 1677-1683 (7) 6.50 2.70

Eduardo Agramonte (1849-1872), Revolutionary, Physician — A438

3c, Portrait by F. Martinez.

1972, Mar. 8

1684 A438 3c multi .75 .25

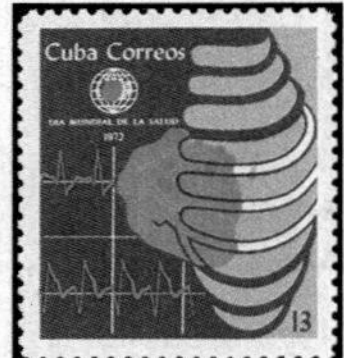

World Health Day — A439

1972, Apr. 7 **Wmk. 376**

1685 A439 13c multicolored 1.90 .50

Soviet Space Program — A440

1c, Sputnik 1. 2c, Vostok 1. 3c, Valentina Tereshkova. 4c, Alexei Leonov. 5c, Lunokhod 1, moon vehicle. 13c, Linking Soyuz capsules. 30c, Victims of Soyuz 11 accident.

1972, Apr. 12 **Unwmk.**

1686 A440 1c multicolored .25 .25
1687 A440 2c multicolored .25 .25
1688 A440 3c multicolored .25 .25
1689 A440 4c multicolored .25 .25
1690 A440 5c multicolored .25 .25
1691 A440 13c multicolored 2.10 .40
1692 A440 30c multicolored 2.50 .70
Nos. 1686-1692 (7) 5.85 2.35

Stamp Day — A441

Designs: 13c, Postmaster-Gen. Vicente Mora Pera, by Ramon Loy. 30c, Soldier's Letter, Cuba to Venezuela, 1897.

1972, Apr. 24

1693 A441 13c shown 1.50 .50

Size: 48x39mm

1694 A441 30c multicolored 2.50 .55

Labor Day — A442

1972, May 1 **Wmk. 376**

1695 A442 3c multicolored .90 .25

Jose Marti, Ho Chi Minh — A443

3rd Conference Against War in Indo-China, May 19 — A444

30c, Roses, conference emblem.

1972, May 19

1696 A443 3c shown .40 .25
1697 A444 13c shown 1.60 .40
1698 A443 30c multicolored 2.00 .55
Nos. 1696-1698 (3) 4.00 1.20

Metropolitan Museum Type of 1971

Portraits: 1c, Salvador del Muro, by J. Del Rio. 2c, Luis de las Casas, by Del Rio. 3c, Cristopher Columbus, anonymous. 4c, Tomas Gamba, by V. Escobar. 5c, Maria Galarraga, by Escobar. 13c, Isabel II, by Federico Madrazo. 30c, Carlos III, by Miguel Melero.

1972, May 25 **Unwmk.**

Size: 34x43½mm

1699 A420 1c multi .25 .25
1700 A420 2c multi .25 .25
1701 A420 3c multi .25 .25
1702 A420 4c multi .30 .25
1703 A420 5c multi .30 .25

Size: 34x51½mm

1704 A420 13c multi 1.75 .40
1705 A420 30c multi 2.50 .70
Nos. 1699-1705 (7) 5.60 2.35

Children's Songs Competition, Natl. Library A445

1972, June 5 **Wmk. 376**

1706 A445 3c multi .80 .25

Thoroughbred Horses — A446

1972, June 30 **Unwmk.**

1707 A446 1c Tarpan .25 .25
1708 A446 2c Kertag .25 .25
1709 A446 3c Creole .25 .25
1710 A446 4c Andalusian .25 .25
1711 A446 5c Arabian .25 .25
1712 A446 13c Quarter horse 3.00 .55
1713 A446 30c Pursang 3.50 .80
Nos. 1707-1713 (7) 7.75 2.60

Frank Pais (d. 1957), Educator, Revolutionary — A447

1972, July 26 **Wmk. 376**

1714 A447 13c blk & red 1.50 .50

1972 Summer Olympics, Munich, Aug. 26-Sept. 10 — A448

1c, Athlete, emblems, vert. 2c, "M," boxing. 3c, "U," weight lifting. 4c, "N," fencing. 5c, "I," rifle shooting. 13c, "C," running. 30c, "H," basketball.
50c, Gymnastics.

1972, Aug. 26 **Unwmk.**

1715 A448 1c multicolored .25 .25
1716 A448 2c multicolored .25 .25
1717 A448 3c multicolored .25 .25
1718 A448 4c multicolored .25 .25
1719 A448 5c multicolored .25 .25
1720 A448 13c multicolored 1.75 .35
1721 A448 30c multicolored 2.25 .65
Nos. 1715-1721 (7) 5.25 2.25

Souvenir Sheet

Imperf

1722 A448 50c multicolored 6.00 1.90

Stamp in No. 1722 has simulated perforations.

Intl. Hydrological Decade — A449

Landscapes: 1c, Tree Trunks, by Domingo Ramos. 3c, Cyclone, by Tiburcio Lorenzo. 8c, Vinales, by Ramos. 30c, Forest and Brook, by Antonio R. Morey, vert.

1972, Sept. 20

1723 A449 1c multi .25 .25
1724 A449 3c multi .25 .25
1725 A449 8c multi .80 .25
1726 A449 30c multi 2.60 .50
Nos. 1723-1726 (4) 3.90 1.25

Butterflies from the Gundlach Collection — A450

1c, Papilio thoas oviedo. 2c, Papilio devilliers. 3c, Papilio polixenes polixenes. 4c, Papilio androgeus epidaurus. 5c, Papilio cayguanabus. 13c, Papilio andraemon hernandezi. 30c, Papilio celadon.

1972, Sept. 25

1727 A450 1c multicolored .25 .25
1728 A450 2c multicolored .25 .25
1729 A450 3c multicolored .25 .25
1730 A450 4c multicolored .25 .25
1731 A450 5c multicolored .30 .25
1732 A450 13c multicolored 3.50 .85
1733 A450 30c multicolored 4.75 1.10
Nos. 1727-1733 (7) 9.55 3.20

A451

Miguel de Cervantes Saavedra (1547-1616), Spanish Author — A452

Paintings by A. Fernandez: 3c, In La Mancha, vert. 13c, Battle with Wine Skins. 30c, Don Quixote de La Mancha, vert. 50c, Scene from Don Quixote, by Jose Moreno Carbonero.

1972, Sept. 29

Size: 34½x46mm (3c, 30c)

1734 A451 3c multi .25 .25
1735 A451 13c shown 2.10 .50
1736 A451 30c multi 2.25 .55
Nos. 1734-1736 (3) 4.60 1.30

Souvenir Sheet

Perf. 12½ on 3 Sides

1737 A452 50c shown 5.25 3.75

Guerrilla Day, 5th Anniv. — A453

3c, Ernesto "Che" Guevara. 13c, Tamara "Tania" Bunke. 30c, Guido "Inti" Peredo.

1972, Oct. 8

1738 A453 3c multicolored .25 .25
1739 A453 13c multicolored 2.25 .50
1740 A453 30c multicolored 2.40 .60
Nos. 1738-1740 (3) 4.90 1.35

Traditional Musical Instruments A454

3c, Abwe (rattles). 13c, Bonko enchemiya (drum). 30c, Iya (drum).

1972, Oct. 25

1741 A454 3c multi .25 .25
1742 A454 13c multi 2.25 .45
1743 A454 30c multi 2.25 .55
Nos. 1741-1743 (3) 4.75 1.25

MATEX '72, 3rd Natl. Philatelic Exhibition, Matanzas — A455

1972, Nov. 18 **Wmk. 376**

1744 A455 13c No. 467 2.50 .45
1745 A455 30c No. C49 3.25 .55

Nos. 1744-1745 printed se-tenant with insribed labels picturing Type A232, emblem of the Cuban Philatelic Federation.

Historic Ships A456

1c, Viking long boat, 6th-9th cent. 2c, Caravel, 15th cent., vert. 3c, Galleass, 16th cent. 4c, Galleon, 17th cent., vert. 5c, Clipper, 19th cent. 13c, Steam packet, 19th cent. 30c, Atomic icebreaker Lenin.

1972, Nov. 30 **Unwmk.**

1746 A456 1c multicolored .25 .25
1747 A456 2c multicolored .25 .25
1748 A456 3c multicolored .25 .25
1749 A456 4c multicolored .30 .25
1750 A456 5c multicolored .35 .25
1751 A456 13c multicolored 2.10 .75

Size: 52½x29mm.

1752 A456 30c multicolored 4.25 1.25
Nos. 1746-1752 (7) 7.75 3.25

UNESCO Save Venice Campaign — A457

3c, Lion of St. Mark. 13c, Bridge of Sighs, vert. 30c, St. Mark's Cathedral.

1972, Dec. 8

1753	A457	3c multicolored	.25	.25
1754	A457	13c multicolored	1.75	.45
1755	A457	30c multicolored	2.25	.85
		Nos. 1753-1755 (3)	4.25	1.55

Cuba, World Amateur Baseball Champion in 1972 — A458

1972, Dec. 15

1756	A458	3c Umpire	1.25	.30

Sport Events, 1972 — A459

1972, Dec. 22

1757	A459	1c shown	.25	.25
1758	A458	2c Pole vault	.25	.25
1759	A458	3c like No. 1756	.25	.25
1760	A458	4c Wrestling	.25	.25
1761	A458	5c Fencing	.25	.25
1762	A458	13c Boxing	1.60	.55
1763	A458	30c Marlin	2.25	.80
		Nos. 1757-1763 (7)	5.10	2.60

Barrientos Memorial Athletics Championships, 11th Amateur Baseball Championships, Cerro Pelado Intl. Tournament, Central American and Caribbean Fencing Tournament, Giraldo Cordova Tournament, Ernest Hemingway Natl. Fishing Contest.

No. 1759 inscribed "XI serie nacional de beisbol aficionado."

Medals Won by Cubans at the 1972 Summer Olympics, Munich A460

1c, Bronze, Women's 100-meter. 2c, Bronze, women's relay. 3c, Gold, 54kg boxing. 4c, Silver, 81kg boxing. 5c, Bronze, 51kg boxing. 13c, Gold, 87kg boxing. 30c, Gold, silver cup, heavyweight boxing. 50c, Bronze, basketball.

1973, Jan. 28

1764	A460	1c multi	.25	.25
1765	A460	2c multi	.25	.25
1766	A460	3c multi	.25	.25
1767	A460	4c multi	.25	.25
1768	A460	5c multi	.25	.25
1769	A460	13c multi	1.75	.60
1770	A460	30c multi	2.25	.90
		Nos. 1764-1770 (7)	5.25	2.75

Souvenir Sheet

Imperf

1771	A460	50c multi	6.25	2.25

Stamp in No. 1771 has simulated perforations.

Portrait by A.M. Esquivel — A461

1973, Feb. 10

1772	A461	13c multi	2.00	.45

Gertrudis Gomez de Avellaneda (1814-1873), poet.

Art Type of 1970

Paintings in the Natl. Museum: 1c, Bathers in the Lagoon, by C. Enriquez. 2c, Still-life, by W.C. Heda. 3c, Gallantry, by P. Landaluze. 4c, Return in the Late Afternoon, by C. Troyon. 5c, Elizabetta Mascagni, by F.X. Fabre. 13c, The Picador, by De Lucas Padilla, horiz. 30c, In the Garden, by Arburu Morell.

1973, Feb. 28

Sizes: 36x46mm, 46x36mm

1773	A408	1c multi	.25	.25
1774	A408	2c multi	.25	.25
1775	A408	3c multi	.25	.25
1776	A408	4c multi	.25	.25
1777	A408	5c multi	.25	.25
1778	A408	13c multi	1.75	.55
1779	A408	30c multi	2.50	.80
		Nos. 1773-1779 (7)	5.50	2.60

Orchid Type of 1971

1c, Dendrobium hybrid. 2c, Cypripedium exul. 3c, Vanda miss. joaquin rose marie. 4c, Phalaenopsis schilleriana. 5c, Vanda gilbert tribulet. 13c, Dendrobium hybrid, diff. 30c, Arachnis catherine.

1973, Mar. 26

1780	A426	1c multicolored	.25	.25
1781	A426	2c multicolored	.25	.25
1782	A426	3c multicolored	.25	.25
1783	A426	4c multicolored	.30	.25
1784	A426	5c multicolored	.35	.25
1785	A426	13c multicolored	2.50	.55
1786	A426	30c multicolored	3.25	.80
		Nos. 1780-1786 (7)	7.15	2.60

A462

1973, Apr. 7 **Wmk. 376**

1787	A462	10c multi, *buff*	1.10	.30

World Health Day. World Health Organization, 25th anniv.

Anti-Polio Campaign — A463

1973, Apr. 9 **Unwmk.**

1788	A463	3c multi	.75	.25

Soviet Space Program — A464

1c, Soyuz rocket launch, vert. 2c, Luna 1, Moon. 3c, Luna 16 taking-off from Moon, vert. 4c, Venera 7. 5c, Molniya 1, vert. 13c, Mars 3. 30c, Radar observation ship, Yuri Gagarin.

1973, Apr. 12

1789	A464	1c multicolored	.25	.25
1790	A464	2c multicolored	.25	.25
1791	A464	3c multicolored	.25	.25
1792	A464	4c multicolored	.25	.25
1793	A464	5c multicolored	.25	.25
1794	A464	13c multicolored	1.25	.70
1795	A464	30c multicolored	3.50	.85
		Nos. 1789-1795 (7)	6.00	2.80

Stamp Day A465

Postmarks: 13c, Santiago de Cuba, 1760. 30c, Havana, 1760.

1973, Apr. 24

1796	A465	13c multi	2.00	.50
1797	A465	30c multi	2.10	.60

See Nos. 1888-1891.

Portrait by A. Espinosa A466

1973, May 11

1798	A466	13c multi	1.50	.45

Maj.-Gen. Ignacio Agramonte (1841-1873).

Birthplace, Torun, and Inventions — A467

Copernicus Monument, Warsaw — A468

13c, Copernicus, spacecraft. 30c, Manuscript, Frombork Tower.

1973, May 25

1799	A467	3c shown	.25	.25
1800	A467	13c multicolored	1.75	.45
1801	A467	30c multicolored	3.00	.60
		Nos. 1799-1801 (3)	5.00	1.30

Souvenir Sheet

Perf. 12½ on 3 Sides

1802	A468	50c shown	6.25	2.25

500th anniversary of the birth of Nicolaus Copernicus (1473-1543), Polish astronomer.

Improvement of School Education — A469

1973, June 12 **Wmk. 376**

1803	A469	13c multi	1.25	.25

Cattle — A470

1973, June 28 **Unwmk.**

1804	A470	1c Jersey	.25	.25
1805	A470	2c Charolaise	.25	.25
1806	A470	3c Creole	.25	.25
1807	A470	4c Swiss	.25	.25
1808	A470	5c Holstein	.25	.25
1809	A470	13c Santa Gertrudis	1.50	.40
1810	A470	30c Brahman	3.00	.75
		Nos. 1804-1810 (7)	5.75	2.40

A471

1973, July 10 **Wmk. 376**

1811	A471	13c multi	1.40	.30

10th Communist Festival of Youths and Students, East Berlin.

A472

3c, Siboney Farm, Santiago de Cuba. 13c, Moncada Barracks. 30c, Revolution Plaza, Havana.

1973, July 26 **Unwmk.**

1812	A472	3c multicolored	.35	.25
1813	A472	13c multicolored	1.40	.30
1814	A472	30c multicolored	2.25	.45
		Nos. 1812-1814 (3)	4.00	1.00

20th anniv. of the Revolution.

10th Anniv. of the Revolutionary Navy — A473

3c, Midshipman, missile frigate.

1973, Aug. 3 **Wmk. 376**

1815	A473	3c multicolored	1.00	.30

Interior, by Manuel Vicens A474

Paintings in the Natl. Museum: 1c, Amalia of Saxony, by J.K. Rossler. 3c, Margarita of Austria, by J. Pantoja de la Cruz. 4c, City Hall Official, anonymous. 5c, View of Santiago de Cuba, by Hernandez Giro. 13c, The Catalan, by J.J. Tejada. 30c, Alley in Guayo, by Tejada.

1973, Aug. 30 **Unwmk.**
Sizes: 26½x41mm (1c, 3c), 28½x39mm (4c, 13c, 30c)

1816 A474 1c multi .25 .25
1817 A474 2c multi .25 .25
1818 A474 3c multi .25 .25
1819 A474 4c multi .25 .25
1820 A474 5c multi .25 .25
1821 A474 13c multi 1.90 .60
1822 A474 30c multi 2.25 .70
Nos. 1816-1822 (7) 5.40 2.55

WMO Emblem, Paintings by J. Madrazo A475

1973, Sept. 4
1823 A475 8c Spring 1.00 .25
1824 A475 8c Summer 1.00 .25
1825 A475 8c Fall 1.00 .25
1826 A475 8c Winter 1.00 .25
Nos. 1823-1826 (4) 4.00 1.00

World Meteorogogical Organization, cent. Nos. 1823-1826 printed se-tenant in strips of 4; frame reversed on 2nd and 4th stamp in strip.

A476

27th World and 1st Pan American Weight Lifting Championships: Various weightlifting positions.

1973, Sept. 12
1827 A476 1c multi, diff. .25 .25
1828 A476 2c shown .25 .25
1829 A476 3c multi, diff. .25 .25
1830 A476 4c multi, diff. .25 .25
1831 A476 5c multi, diff. .25 .25
1832 A476 13c multi, diff. 1.25 .45
1833 A476 30c multi, diff. 2.25 .75
Nos. 1827-1833 (7) 4.75 2.45

A477

Flowering plants: 1c, Erythrina standleyana. 2c, Lantana camara. 3c, Canavalia maritima. 4c, Dichromena colorata. 5c, Borrichia arborescens. 13c, Anguria pedata. 30c, Cordia sebestena.

1973, Sept. 28
1834 A477 1c multicolored .25 .25
1835 A477 2c multicolored .25 .25
1836 A477 3c multicolored .25 .25
1837 A477 4c multicolored .25 .25
1838 A477 5c multicolored .25 .25
1839 A477 13c multicolored 2.10 .65
1840 A477 30c multicolored 3.00 .90
Nos. 1835-1840 (6) 6.10 2.55

8th World Trade Union Congress, Varna, Bulgaria — A478

1973, Oct. 5 **Wmk. 376**
1841 A478 13c multi 1.40 .35

Cuban Natl. Ballet, 25th Anniv. — A479

1973, Oct. 28 **Unwmk.**
1842 A479 13c gold & brt ultra 2.00 .40

Sea Shells — A480

1c, Liguus fasciatus fasciatus. 2c, Liguus fasciatus guitarti. 3c, Liguus fasciatus whartoni. 4c, Liguus fasciatus angelae. 5c, Liguus fasciatus trinidadense. 13c, Liguus blainianus. 30c, Liguus vittatus.

1973, Oct. 29
1843 A480 1c multicolored .25 .25
1844 A480 2c multicolored .25 .25
1845 A480 3c multicolored .25 .25
1846 A480 4c multicolored .25 .25
1847 A480 5c multicolored .25 .25
1848 A480 13c multicolored 2.60 .70
1849 A480 30c multicolored 3.50 .85
Nos. 1843-1849 (7) 7.35 2.80

Maps of Cuba A481

1c, Juan de la Cosa, 1502. 3c, Ortelius, 1572. 13c, Bellini, 1762. 40c, 1973.

1973, Oct. 29
1850 A481 1c multi .25 .25
1851 A481 3c multi .25 .25
1852 A481 13c multi 2.00 .25
1853 A481 40c multi 2.25 .80
Nos. 1850-1853 (4) 4.75 1.55

15th Anniversary of the Revolution — A482

1974, Jan. 2
1854 A482 1c No. 625 .25 .25
1855 A482 3c No. 626 .25 .25
1856 A482 13c No. C200 1.75 .55
1857 A482 40c No. C201 3.50 .80
Nos. 1854-1857 (4) 5.75 1.85

Woman, by F. Ponce de Leon — A483

Portraits in the Camaguey Museum: 3c, Mexican Girls, by J. Arche. 8c, Young Woman, by A. Menocal. 10c, Mulatto Woman Drinking from Coconut, by L. Romanach. 13c, Head of an Old Man, by J. Arburu.

1974, Jan. 10
1858 A483 1c multi .25 .25
1859 A483 3c multi .25 .25
1860 A483 8c multi .35 .25
1861 A483 10c multi 1.25 .25
1862 A483 13c multi 1.75 .40
Nos. 1858-1862 (5) 3.85 1.40

Amilcar Cabral — A484

1974, Jan. 20
1863 A484 13c multi 1.30 .25

Amilcar Cabral, Guinea-Bissau freedom fighter, 1st death anniv.

Lenin, by I.V. Kosmin — A485

1974, Jan. 21
1864 A485 30c multi 2.75 .55

50th death anniv. of Lenin.

12th Central American and Caribbean Games, Santo Domingo — A486

1974, Feb. 8
1865 A486 1c Emblem .25 .25
1866 A486 2c Javelin .25 .25
1867 A486 3c Boxing .25 .25
1868 A486 4c Baseball, horiz. .25 .25
1869 A486 13c Basketball, horiz. 1.50 .25
1870 A486 30c Volleyball, horiz. 2.00 .70
Nos. 1865-1870 (6) 4.50 1.95

Portrait by F. Martinez — A487

1974, Feb. 27
1871 A487 13c multi 1.25 .25

Carlos M. de Cespedes (d. 1874), patriot.

Portrait of a Man, by J.B. Vermay — A488

Paintings in the Natl. Museum: 2c, The Wet Nurse, by C.A. Van Loo. 3c, Cattle in River, by R. Morey. 4c, Village, by Morey. 13c, Faun and Bacchus, by Rubens. 30c, Young Woman Playing Cards, by R. Madrazo.

1974, Mar. 7
1872 A488 1c shown .25 .25
1873 A488 2c multi .25 .25
1874 A488 3c multi .25 .25
1875 A488 4c multi .25 .25
1876 A488 13c multi 1.25 .25
1877 A488 30c multi 2.00 .55
Nos. 1872-1877 (6) 4.25 1.80

Council for Mutual Economic Assistance (COMECON), 25th Anniv. — A489

30c, Comecon building, Moscow.

1974, Mar. 15
1878 A489 30c multicolored 2.00 .70

Visit of Leonid I. Brezhnev to Cuba, Jan. 28-Feb. 3 — A490

13c, Jose Marti, Lenin, flags. 30c, Brezhnev, Fidel Castro.

1974, Mar. 28
1879 A490 13c multicolored 2.00 .30
1880 A490 30c multicolored 2.10 .55
Nos. 1879-1880 (2) 4.10 .85

Science Fiction A491

Paintings by A. Sokolov: 1c, Martian Crater. 2c, Fiery Labyrinth. 3c, Amber Wave. 4c, Flight Through Space. 13c, Planet in Nebula. 30c, World of Two Suns.

1974, Apr. 12

1881	A491	1c multi	.25	.25
1882	A491	2c multi	.25	.25
1883	A491	3c multi	.25	.25
1884	A491	4c multi	.25	.25
1885	A491	13c multi	1.60	.25
1886	A491	30c multi	2.75	.60
		Nos. 1881-1886 (6)	5.35	1.85

Cosmonauts Day.

UPU, Cent. A492

1974, Apr. 15

1887	A492	30c Letter, 1874	2.50	.60

Stamp Day Type of 1973

Postmarks.

1974, Apr. 24

1888	A465	1c Havana	.25	.25
1889	A465	3c Matanzas	.30	.25
1890	A465	13c Trinidad	1.40	.25
1891	A465	20c Guana Vacoa	2.00	.35
		Nos. 1888-1891 (4)	3.95	1.10

18th Sports Congress of Friendly Armies — A493

1974, May 5 **Wmk. 376**

1892	A493	3c multi	.80	.25

Felipe Poey (1799-1891), Naturalist — A494

1c, Eumaeus atala atala. 2c, Pineria terebra. 3c, Chaetodon sedentarius. 4c, Eurema dina dina. 13c, Hemitrochus fuscolabiata. 30c, Eupomacentrus partitus. 50c, Apogon binotatus.

1c, 4c, Butterflies. 2c, 13c, Sea shells. 3c, 30c, 50c, Fish.

1974, May 26 ***Perf. 12½x12***

1893	A494	1c multicolored	.25	.25
1894	A494	2c multicolored	.25	.25
1895	A494	3c multicolored	.25	.25
1896	A494	4c multicolored	.60	.25
1897	A494	13c multicolored	2.25	.45
1898	A494	30c multicolored	3.00	.55
		Nos. 1893-1898 (6)	6.60	2.00

Souvenir Sheet

Imperf

1899	A494	50c multicolored	7.00	2.50

Stamp in No. 1899 has simulated perforations.

Havana Philharmonic Orchestra, 50th Anniv. — A495

1c, Antonio Mompo, cello. 3c, Cesar Perez Sentenat, piano. 5c, Pedro Mercado, trumpet. 10c, Pedro Sanjuan, Havana Philharmonic emblem. 13c, Roberto Ondina, flute.

1974, June 8 ***Perf. 12½***

1900	A495	1c multi	.25	.25
1901	A495	3c multi	.25	.25
1902	A495	5c multi	.25	.25
1903	A495	10c multi	1.40	.25
1904	A495	13c multi	1.60	.25
		Nos. 1900-1904 (5)	3.75	1.25

Garden Flowers — A496

1c, Heliconia humilis. 2c, Anthurium andraeanum. 3c, Canna generalis. 4c, Alpinia purpurata. 13c, Gladiolus grandiflorus. 30c, Amomum capitatum.

1974, June 12

1905	A496	1c multicolored	.25	.25
1906	A496	2c multicolored	.25	.25
1907	A496	3c multicolored	.25	.25
1908	A496	4c multicolored	.25	.25
1909	A496	13c multicolored	1.50	.25
1910	A496	30c multicolored	4.25	.60
		Nos. 1905-1910 (6)	6.75	1.85

A497

World Amateur Boxing Championships: Emblem and various boxers.

Perf. 12x12½

1974, Aug. 24 **Litho.** **Unwmk.**

1911	A497	1c multi	.25	.25
1912	A497	3c multi	.35	.25
1913	A497	13c multi	1.50	.25
		Nos. 1911-1913 (3)	2.10	.75

Extinct Birds — A498

1c, Dodo. 3c, Ara de Cuba (parrot). 8c, Passenger pigeon. 10c, Moa. 13c, Great auk.

1974, Aug. 28 ***Perf. 13***

1914	A498	1c multi	.40	.25
1915	A498	3c multi	.40	.25
1916	A498	8c multi	.85	.25
1917	A498	10c multi	2.75	.55
1918	A498	13c multi	3.50	.80
		Nos. 1914-1918 (5)	7.90	2.10

Pres. Salvador Allende of Chile (d. 1973) A499

1974, Sept. 11

1919	A499	13c multi	1.60	.45

Wildflowers A500

1c, Suriana maritima. 3c, Cassia ligustrina. 8c, Flaveria linearis. 10c, Stachytarpheta jamaicensis. 13c, Bacopa monnieri.

1974, Sept. 14 ***Perf. 13x12½***

1920	A500	1c multi	.25	.25
1921	A500	3c multi	.25	.25
1922	A500	8c multi	.30	.25
1923	A500	10c multi	2.10	.25
1924	A500	13c multi	3.25	.85
		Nos. 1920-1924 (5)	6.15	1.85

Model Aircraft — A501

3c, Sky diving. 8c, Glider. 10c, Crop dusting. 13c, Commercial aviation.

1974, Sept. 22 ***Perf. 12½***

1925	A501	1c shown	.25	.25
1926	A501	3c multi	.25	.25
1927	A501	8c multi	.45	.25
1928	A501	10c multi	1.10	.25
1929	A501	13c multi	2.00	.25
		Nos. 1925-1929 (5)	4.05	1.25

Civil Aeronautic Institute, 10th anniv. Nos. 1927-1929 horiz.

History of Cuban Baseball — A502

1c, Indians playing ball. 3c, 1st Official game, 1874. 8c, Emilio Sabourin. 10c, Umpire, players, 1974. 13c, Latin-American Stadium, Havana.

1974, Oct. 3 ***Perf. 13***

1930	A502	1c multicolored	.25	.25
1931	A502	3c multicolored	.25	.25
1932	A502	8c multicolored	.40	.25
1933	A502	10c multicolored	1.20	.25
1934	A502	13c multicolored	1.90	.25
		Nos. 1930-1934 (5)	4.00	1.25

Nos. 1930-1932 vert.

Mambi 10c Stamp (Revolutionary Junta Issue), Cent. — A503

1974, Oct. 10

1935	A503	13c multi	1.25	.25

16th Conference of Customs Organizations of Socialist Countries — A504

30c, Comecon Building, Moscow.

1974, Oct. 15

1936	A504	30c multicolored	1.90	.55

Disappearance of Major Camilo Cienfuegos, 15th Anniv. — A505

Wmk. 376

1974, Oct. 28 **Litho.** ***Perf. 13***

1937	A505	3c multi	1.00	.25

8th World Mining Conference — A506

1974, Nov. 3

1938	A506	13c multi	2.00	.25

Petroleum Institute, 15th Anniv. — A507

1974, Nov. 20

1939	A507	3c multi	.70	.25

Intersputnik Earth Station Opening — A508

13c, Satellite, satellite dish. 1p, Satellite, flags.

1974, Nov. 30 **Unwmk.**

1940	A508	3c shown	.25	.25
1941	A508	13c multicolored	1.25	.25
1942	A508	1p multicolored	2.75	1.10
		Nos. 1940-1942 (3)	4.25	1.60

Philatelic Federation, 10th Anniv. — A509

1974, Nov. 30 ***Perf. 12½x13***
1943 A509 30c multi 2.40 .45

Souvenir Sheet

Mercury — A510

1974, Dec. 6 ***Imperf.***
1944 A510 50c multi 6.00 1.25

4th Natl. Phil. Exhib., Havana.

1st World Peace Congress, 25th Anniv. — A511

30c, *F. Joliot-Curie,* by Picasso.

1974, Dec. 16 **Wmk. 376** ***Perf. 13***
1945 A511 30c red, blk & buff 3.00 .45

Ruben Martinez Villena (b. 1899), Revolutionary — A512

1974, Dec. 20 **Unwmk.**
1946 A512 3c red org & yel 1.25 .25

Souvenir Sheet

Cuban Victories, 1st Amateur Boxing Championships — A513

1975, Jan. 6 **Litho.** ***Imperf.***
1947 A513 50c Trophy 6.25 1.25

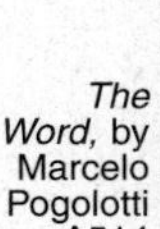

The Word, by Marcelo Pogolotti A514

Paintings in the Natl. Museum: 2c, *The Silk-Cotton Tree,* by Henry Cleenewerk. 3c, *Landscape,* by Guillermo Collazo. 5c, *Still-life,* by Francisco Peralta. 13c, *Maria Wilson,* by Federico Martinez, vert. 30c, *The Couple,* by Mariano Fortuny.

1975, Jan. 20 ***Perf. 13***

1948	A514	1c multi	.25	.25
1949	A514	2c multi	.25	.25
1950	A514	3c multi	.25	.25
1951	A514	5c multi	.25	.25
1952	A514	13c multi	1.40	.25
1953	A514	30c multi	2.50	.45
		Nos. 1948-1953 (6)	4.90	1.70

Intl. Women's Year A515

1975, Feb. 6
1954 A515 13c multi 1.10 .25

Fishing Industry A516

Various fish and fishing vessels: 1c, Long-finned tuna. 2c, Tuna. 3c, Mediterranean grouper. 8c, Hake. 13c, Prawn. 30c, Lobster.

1975, Feb. 22

1955	A516	1c multicolored	.25	.25
1956	A516	2c multicolored	.25	.25
1957	A516	3c multicolored	.25	.25
1958	A516	8c multicolored	.25	.25
1959	A516	13c multicolored	.85	.70
1960	A516	30c multicolored	3.00	.70
		Nos. 1955-1960 (6)	4.85	2.40

Minerals — A517

1975, Mar. 15 **Litho.** ***Perf. 13x12½***

1961	A517	3c Nickel	.40	.25
1962	A517	13c Copper	1.60	.25
1963	A517	30c Chromium	3.00	.45
		Nos. 1961-1963 (3)	5.00	.95

Cosmonaut's Day — A518

1c, Cosmodrome. 2c, Probe, vert. 3c, Eclipse. 5c, Threshold to Space. 13c, Midday on Mars. 30c, Cosmonaut's view of Earth.

1975, Apr. 12 ***Perf. 13x12½, 12½x13***

1964	A518	1c multicolored	.25	.25
1965	A518	2c multicolored	.25	.25
1966	A518	3c multicolored	.25	.25
1967	A518	5c multicolored	.30	.25
1968	A518	13c multicolored	1.40	.25
1969	A518	30c multicolored	2.25	.45
		Nos. 1964-1969 (6)	4.70	1.70

The future of space.

Stamp Day A519

Various covers.

1975, Apr. 24 ***Perf. 13***

1970	A519	3c multi	.25	.25
1971	A519	13c multi	1.40	.25
1972	A519	30c multi	2.10	.40
		Nos. 1970-1972 (3)	3.75	.90

Victory Over Fascism, 30th Anniv. — A520

Design: Raising red flag over Reichstag, Berlin.

1975, May 9 ***Perf. 13x12½***
1973 A520 30c multi 2.00 .40

A521

Works in the Decorative Art Museum — A522

1c, Sevres porcelain vase, vert. 2c, Meissen porcelain statue *Shepherdess and Dancers,* vert. 3c, Chinese porcelain dish *Lady with Parasol.* 5c, Chinese screen detail *The Phoenix,* vert. 13c, *Allegory of Music,* by Francois Boucher (1703-70), vert. 30c, *Portrait of a Lady,* by L. Tocque, vert. 50c, *The Swing,* by Hubert Robert (1733-1808).

1975, May 10 ***Perf. 12½x13, 13x12½***

1974	A521	1c multi	.25	.25
1975	A521	2c multi	.25	.25
1976	A521	3c shown	.25	.25
1977	A521	5c multi	.45	.25
1978	A521	13c multi	1.40	.25
1979	A521	30c multi	1.90	.40
		Nos. 1974-1979 (6)	4.50	1.65

Souvenir Sheet

Perf. 13x12½ on 3 Sides

1980 A522 50c shown 5.25 1.25

No. 1980 contains one 25x39mm stamp.

Intl. Children's Day — A523

Wmk. 376

1975, May 31 **Litho.** ***Perf. 13***
1981 A523 3c multi .50 .25

Indigenous Birds — A524

Designs: 1c, Vireo gundlachi. 2c, Gymnoglaux lawrenci. 3c, Aratingo eoups. 5c, Staroenas cyanocephala. 13c, Chondrohierax wilsoni. 30c, Cyanolimnas cerverai.

1975, June 18 **Unwmk.**

1982	A524	1c multicolored	.25	.25
1983	A524	2c multicolored	.25	.25
1984	A524	3c multicolored	.25	.25
1985	A524	5c multicolored	.40	.25
1986	A524	13c multicolored	1.75	.40
1987	A524	30c multicolored	2.50	.70
		Nos. 1982-1987 (6)	5.40	2.10

See Nos. 2121-2125, 2180-2182, C276-C276.

Scientific Investigation Center, 10th Anniv. — A525

1975, July 1 ***Perf. 12½***
1988 A525 13c multi 1.40 .25

Irrigation and Drainage Commission, 25th Anniv. — A526

1975, Aug. 2 ***Perf. 13***
1989 A526 13c multi 1.40 .25

Afforestation A527

Designs: 1c, Cedrela mexicana. 3c, Swietenia mahagoni. 5c, Calophyllum brasiliense. 13c, Hibiscus tiliaceus. 30c, Pinus caribaea.

1975, Aug. 20

1990 A527 1c multicolored .25 .25
1991 A527 3c multicolored .40 .25
1992 A527 5c multicolored .40 .25
1993 A527 13c multicolored 1.25 .25
1994 A527 30c multicolored 1.90 .40
Nos. 1990-1994 (5) 4.20 1.40

Cuban Women's Federation, 15th Anniv. — A528

1975, Aug. 23

1995 A528 3c multi .75 .25

Intl. Conference on the Independence of Puerto Rico — A529

1975, Sept. 5 **Litho.**

1996 A529 13c multi 1.10 .25

A530

7th Pan American Games, Mexico: Aztec calendar stone and various athletes.

1975, Sept. 20 ***Perf. 12½x13***

1997 A530 1c Baseball .25 .25
1998 A530 3c Boxing .25 .25
1999 A530 5c Basketball .25 .25
2000 A530 13c High jump 1.50 .30
2001 A530 30c Weight lifting 2.00 .30
Nos. 1997-2001 (5) 4.25 1.35

Souvenir Sheet

Imperf

2002 A530 50c Stone, emblem 5.00 1.25

A531

1975, Sept. 28 ***Perf. 12½x13***

2003 A531 3c multi .75 .25

Revolutionary Defense Committees (CDR), 15th anniv.

Friendship Among the Peoples Institute, 15th Anniv. A532

1975, Oct. 8 ***Perf. 12½x13***

2004 A532 3c multi .50 .25

Natl. Bank, 25th Anniv. A533

Designs: 1-peso coins and banknotes identified by serial numbers.

1975, Oct. 13 ***Perf. 13x12½***

2005 A533 13c Coin, 1915 1.10 .25
2006 A533 13c C882736A, 1934 1.10 .25
2007 A533 13c A000387A, 1946 1.10 .25
2008 A533 13c 933906, 1964 1.10 .25
2009 A533 13c K000000, 1976 1.10 .25
a. Strip of 5, Nos. 2005-2009 6.75 6.75
Nos. 2005-2009 (5) 5.50 1.25

Locomotives — A534

1c, La Junta, 1837. 3c, Steam engine 2-8-0 No. 12. 5c, Diesel TEM 4 No. 51010. 13c, Diesel DVM 9I-7 55. 30c, Diesel M 62K No. 61601.

1975, Oct. 28 **Unwmk.** ***Perf. 12½***

2010 A534 1c multicolored .25 .25
2011 A534 3c multicolored .30 .25
2012 A534 5c multicolored .30 .25
2013 A534 13c multicolored 3.00 .25
2014 A534 30c multicolored 3.50 .45
Nos. 2010-2014 (5) 7.35 1.45

Railway history.

Development of the Textile Industry — A535

13c, Bobbins, flag, loom operator.

1975, Nov. 10 ***Perf. 13x12½***

2015 A535 13c multi 1.20 .25

Veterinary Medicine — A536

Parasites and host species: 1c, Haemonchus, lamb. 2c, Ancylostoma caninum, dog. 3c, Dispharynx nasuta, rooster. 5c, Gasterophilus intestinalis, horse. 13c, Ascaris lumbricoides, pig. 30c, Boophilus microplus, bull.

1975, Nov. 25 **Litho.** ***Perf. 13***

2016 A536 1c multicolored .25 .25
2017 A536 2c multicolored .25 .25
2018 A536 3c multicolored .25 .25
2019 A536 5c multicolored .25 .25
2020 A536 13c multicolored 1.40 .25
2021 A536 30c multicolored 2.50 .40
Nos. 2016-2021 (6) 4.90 1.65

Manuel Ascunce Domenech Educational Detachment A537

1975, Nov. 27 **Litho.**

2022 A537 3c multi .40 .25

Development of Agriculture and Irrigation — A538

1975, Dec. 15 **Litho.** ***Perf. 13x12½***

2023 A538 13c Irrigation 1.25 .25

1st Communist Party Congress — A539

3c, "1," revolutionaries, vert. 30c, Party leaders.

1975, Dec. 17 ***Perf. 12½x13, 13x12½***

2024 A539 3c multi .25 .25
2025 A539 13c shown 1.10 .25
2026 A539 30c multi 1.50 .30
Nos. 2024-2026 (3) 2.85 .80

8th Latin-American Obstetrics and Gynecology Congress — A540

1976, Jan. 24 ***Perf. 13***

2027 A540 3c multi .60 .25

Paintings in Natl. Museums — A541

Designs: 1c, *Seated Woman,* by Victor Manuel, vert. 2c, *Garden,* by Santiago Rusinol. 3c, *Guadalquivir River,* by Manuel Barron y Carrillo. 5c, *Self-portrait,* by Jan Havicksz Steen, vert. 13c, *Portrait of a Woman,* by Louis Michel Van Loo, vert. 30c, *La Chula,* by Jose Arburu Morell, vert.

Sizes: 29x40mm (1c, 5c, 13c), 40x29mm (2c), 44x27mm (3c), 27x44mm (30c)

Perf. 13, 12½ (3c, 30c)

1976, Jan. 30

2028 A541 1c multi .25 .25
2029 A541 2c multi .25 .25
2030 A541 3c multi .25 .25
2031 A541 5c multi .25 .25
2032 A541 13c multi 1.40 .25
2033 A541 30c multi 2.25 .50
Nos. 2028-2033 (6) 4.65 1.75

10th Cong. of Ministers from Socialist Communications Organizations, Feb. 12, Havana — A542

1976, Feb. 12 **Litho.** ***Perf. 13***

2034 A542 13c multi 1.40 .25

Hunting Dogs A543

1c, American foxhound. 2c, Labrador retriever. 3c, Borzoi. 5c, Irish setter. 13c, Pointer. 30c, Cocker spaniel.

1976, Feb. 20

2035 A543 1c multi .25 .25
2036 A543 2c multi .25 .25
2037 A543 3c multi .25 .25
2038 A543 5c multi .25 .25
2039 A543 13c multi 1.50 .30
2040 A543 30c multi 2.50 .40
Nos. 2035-2040 (6) 5.00 1.70

Socialist Constitution — A544

13c, Natl. flag, arms, anthem.

1976, Feb. 24 ***Perf. 12½***

2041 A544 13c multi 1.40 .25

Chess Champions — A545

Designs: 1c, Ruy Lopez Segura and chessboard. 2c, Francois Philidor and frontispiece of his book, *Analysis of the Game of Chess.* 3c, Wilhelm Steinitz and knight. 13c, Emanuel Lasker and king. 30c, Jose Raul Capablanca learning to play chess as a small boy.

1976, Mar. 15 ***Perf. 13x12½***

2042 A545 1c multi .25 .25
2043 A545 2c multi .25 .25
2044 A545 3c multi .25 .25
2045 A545 13c multi 1.75 .25
2046 A545 30c multi 1.90 .55
Nos. 2042-2046 (5) 4.40 1.55

Havana Radio Intl. Broadcasts, 15th Anniv. — A546

1976, Mar. 26
2047 A546 50c multi 2.00 .70

World Health Day — A547

1976, Apr. 7
2048 A547 30c multi 1.50 .45

Child Care Centers, 15th Anniv. — A548

1976, Apr. 10 ***Perf. 12½x13***
2049 A548 3c multi .60 .25

1st Manned Space Flight, 15th Anniv. A549

1c, Gagarin, lift-off. 2c, V. Tesreshkova, rockets. 3c, A. Leonov's space walk, vert. 5c, Spacecraft, vert. 13c, Spacecraft, diff., vert. 30c, Space link-up.

1976, Apr. 12 ***Perf. 13***
2050 A549 1c multicolored .25 .25
2051 A549 2c multicolored .25 .25
2052 A549 3c multicolored .25 .25
2053 A549 5c multicolored .40 .25
2054 A549 13c multicolored 1.10 .25
2055 A549 30c multicolored 1.75 .35
Nos. 2050-2055 (6) 4.00 1.60

Bay of Pigs Invasion, 15th Anniv. — A550

13c, Bomber, pilot. 30c, Soldiers exulting, vert.

1976, Apr. 17 ***Perf. 13x12½, 12½x13***
2056 A550 3c shown .25 .25
2057 A550 13c multi .95 .25
2058 A550 30c multi 1.75 .45
Nos. 2056-2058 (3) 2.95 .95

Natl. Militia, 17th anniv. (3c); Air Force, 15th anniv. (13c); proclamation of the socialist revolution, 15th anniv. (30c).

Nat. Assoc. of Small Farmers (ANAP), 15th Anniv. — A551

1976, May 17 ***Perf. 13x12½***
2059 A551 3c multi .55 .25

1976 Summer Olympics, Montreal — A552

1c, Volleyball. 2c, Basketball. 3c, Long jump. 4c, Boxing. 5c, Weight lifting. 13c, Judo. 30c, Swimming.
50c, Character trademark (beaver).

1976, May 25 ***Perf. 12½x13***
2060 A552 1c multi .25 .25
2061 A552 2c multi .25 .25
2062 A552 3c multi .25 .25
2063 A552 4c multi .25 .25
2064 A552 5c multi .25 .25
2065 A552 13c multi 1.10 .25
2066 A552 30c multi 1.50 .45
Nos. 2060-2066 (7) 3.85 1.95

Souvenir Sheet
Imperf
2067 A552 50c multi 4.25 1.25

See Nos. 2106, 2112.

Modern Secondary Schools — A553

1976, June 12 **Litho.** ***Perf. 13***
2068 A553 3c red, pale grn & blk .55 .25

Indigenous Birds — A554

Designs: 1c, Teretistris fornsi. 2c, Glaucidium siju. 3c, Nesoceleus fernandinae. 5c, Todus mutlicolor. 13c, Accipiter gundlachi. 30c, Priotelus temnurus.

1976, June 15 ***Perf. 13x12½***
2069 A554 1c multicolored .30 .25
2070 A554 2c multicolored .30 .25
2071 A554 3c multicolored .40 .25
2072 A554 5c multicolored .70 .25
2073 A554 13c multicolored 1.40 .25
2074 A554 30c multicolored 3.25 .80
Nos. 2069-2074 (6) 6.35 2.05

EXPO '76, USSR A555

Designs: 1c, Anatomical scanning device. 3c, Child, doe. 10c, Cosmonauts. 30c, Tupolev supersonic jet.

1976, July 5 ***Perf. 12½x13, 13x12½***
2075 A555 1c multicolored .25 .25
2076 A555 3c multicolored .25 .25
2077 A555 10c multicolored .45 .25
2078 A555 30c multicolored 2.40 .55
Nos. 2075-2078 (4) 3.35 1.30

Public health and industrial safety (1c), environmental protection (3c), space exploration (10c) and modern transportation (30c). Nos. 2075-2077 vert.

Death Cent. of "El Inglesito" A556

1976, Aug. 4 ***Perf. 13***
2079 A556 13c Henry M. Reeve .70 .25

Portrait of G. Collazo, by Jean Dabour — A557

Paintings by Collazo: 2c, *The Art Lovers,* horiz. 3c, *The Patio.* 5c, *Coconut Tree.* 13c, *New York Studio,* horiz. 30c, *R. Emelina Collazo.*

Sizes: 33x44mm, 44x33mm (2c), 31x46mm (5c, 30c), 46x31mm (13c)

Perf. 13, 12½x13 (5c, 30c), 13x12½ (13c)

1976, Sept. 2
2080 A557 1c multi .25 .25
2081 A557 2c multi .25 .25
2082 A557 3c multi .25 .25
2083 A557 5c multi .25 .25
2084 A557 13c multi .60 .25
2085 A557 30c multi 1.90 .50
Nos. 2080-2085 (6) 3.50 1.75

Camilo Cienfuegos Military Schools, 10th Anniv. — A558

1976, Sept. 23 ***Perf. 13***
2086 A558 3c multi .40 .25

Development of the Merchant Marine — A559

Various cargo and passenger ships.

1976, Oct. 2 ***Perf. 12½***
2087 A559 1c multi .30 .25
2088 A559 2c multi .30 .25
2089 A559 3c multi .30 .25
2090 A559 5c multi .40 .25
2091 A559 13c multi 1.25 .45
2092 A559 30c multi 2.60 .80
Nos. 2087-2092 (6) 5.15 2.25

8th Intl. Health Film Festival of Socialist Countries, Havana — A560

1976, Oct. 4 ***Perf. 13x12½***
2093 A560 3c multi .40 .25

5th Intl. Ballet Festival, Havana A561

Scenes from ballets: 1c, *Apollo.* 2c, *The River and the Forest,* vert. 3c, *Giselle.* 5c, *Oedipus Rex,* vert. 13c, *Carmen,* vert. 30c, *Vital Song,* vert.

1976, Nov. 6 ***Perf. 13***
2094 A561 1c multicolored .25 .25
2095 A561 2c multicolored .25 .25
2096 A561 3c multicolored .25 .25
2097 A561 5c multicolored .25 .25
2098 A561 13c multicolored 1.00 .25
2099 A561 30c multicolored 2.00 .35
Nos. 2094-2099 (6) 4.00 1.60

3rd Military Games A562

1976, Nov. 25 ***Perf. 13***
2100 A562 3c multi .50 .25

Granma Landings, 20th Anniv. — A563

1976, Dec. 2 ***Perf. 13x12½***
2101 A563 1c Landing craft .25 .25
2102 A563 3c Landing force .25 .25
2103 A563 13c Castro, soldiers 1.00 .25
2104 A563 30c Globe, rifles 1.50 .55
Nos. 2101-2104 (4) 3.00 1.30

Souvenir Sheet

Cuban Landscape, by F. Cadava — A564

1976, Dec. 8 ***Perf. 13x13½***
2105 A564 50c multi 5.25 3.50

CIENFUEGOS '76, 5th natl. phil. exhib.

Summer Olympics Type of 1976 and

Victory of Cuban Athletes at the Montreal Games — A565

1c, Volleyball. 2c, Hurdles. 3c, Running (starting blocks). 8c, Boxing. 13c, Running (finish line). 30c, Judo.

1976, Dec. 10 ***Perf. 12½x13***

2106 A565 1c multicolored .25 .25
2107 A565 2c multicolored .25 .25
2108 A565 3c multicolored .25 .25
2109 A565 8c multicolored .25 .25
2110 A565 13c multicolored .85 .25
2111 A565 30c multicolored 1.50 .45
Nos. 2106-2111 (6) 3.35 1.70

Souvenir Sheet

Imperf

2112 A552 50c like No. 2063 5.25 4.00

Paintings in the Natl. Museum A566

1c, *Golden Cross Inn,* by S. Scott. 3c, *Portrait of a Man,* by J.C. Verspronck, vert. 5c, *Venetian Landscape,* by Francesco Guardi. 10c, *Valley Corner,* by H. Cleenewerck, vert. 13c, *F. Xaviera Paula,* anonymous, vert. 30c, *F. de Medici,* by C. Allori, vert.

Perf. 13, 12½x13 (3c, 10c, 30c), 12½ (13c)

1977, Jan. 18

Sizes: 40x29mm, 27x42mm (3c, 10c, 30c), 27x43½mm (13c)

2113 A566 1c multi .25 .25
2114 A566 3c multi .25 .25
2115 A566 5c multi .25 .25
2116 A566 10c multi .55 .25
2117 A566 13c multi .80 .25
2118 A566 30c multi 1.90 .40
Nos. 2113-2118 (6) 4.00 1.65

Rural Transport A567

1977, Feb. 15 ***Perf. 13***

2119 A567 3c multi .80 .25

Constitution of Popular Government — A568

1976, Dec. 1 ***Perf. 13x12½***

2120 A568 13c multi .70 .25

Bird Type of 1975

Designs: 1c, Xiphidiopicus percussus. 4c, Tiaris canora. 10c, Dives atroviolaceus. 13c, Ferminia cerverai. 30c, Mellisuga helenae.

1977, Feb. 25 ***Perf. 13***

2121 A524 1c multicolored .40 .25
2122 A524 4c multicolored .45 .25
2123 A524 10c multicolored 1.00 .25
2124 A524 13c multicolored 1.50 .30
2125 A524 30c multicolored 3.00 .75
Nos. 2121-2125 (5) 6.35 1.80

Lenin Park Aquarium, Havana — A569

Designs: 1c, Chichlasoma meeki. 3c, Barbus tetrazona tetrazona. 5c, Cyprinus carpio. 10c, Betta splendens. 13c, Pterophyllum scalare, vert. 30c, Hemigrammus caudovittatus.

1977, Mar. 15

2126 A569 1c multicolored .25 .25
2127 A569 3c multicolored .25 .25
2128 A569 5c multicolored .25 .25
2129 A569 10c multicolored .30 .25
2130 A569 13c multicolored 1.10 .25
2131 A569 30c multicolored 2.40 .50
Nos. 2126-2131 (6) 4.55 1.75

Sputnik (1st Artificial Satellite), 20th Anniv. — A570

1c, DDR #370, *Sputnik.* 3c, Hungary #1216, *Luna 16.* 5c, North Korea #134, *Cosmos.* 10c, Poland #822, *Sputnik 3.* 13c, Yugoslavia #870, Earth, Moon. 30c, Cuba #866, Earth, Moon. 50c, Russia #2021, *Sputnik.*

1977, Apr. 12 ***Perf. 13x12½***

2132 A570 1c multi .25 .25
2133 A570 3c multi .25 .25
2134 A570 5c multi .25 .25
2135 A570 10c multi .35 .25
2136 A570 13c multi 1.00 .25
2137 A570 30c multi 1.90 .40
Nos. 2132-2137 (6) 4.00 1.65

Souvenir Sheet

Imperf

2138 A570 50c multi 4.25 1.25

No. 2138 has simulated perfs.

Antonio Maria Romeu (1876-1955), Composer — A571

1977, May 10 **Litho.** ***Perf. 13***

2139 A571 3c multi .40 .25

See No. C251.

Flowering Plants — A572

Designs: 1c, Hibiscus rosa sinensis. 2c, Nerium oleander. 5c, Allamanda cathartica. 10c, Pelargonium zonale.

1977, May 31

2140 A572 1c multicolored .25 .25
2141 A572 2c multicolored .25 .25
2142 A572 5c multicolored .25 .25
2143 A572 10c multicolored .40 .25
Nos. 2140-2143 (4) 1.15 1.00

Dr. Juan Tomas Roig (b. 1877), botanist. See Nos. C252-C254.

Fire Prevention Week — A573

2c, Horse-drawn fire pump, diff. 6c, Early motorized vehicle. 10c, Modern truck. 13c, Turntable-ladder truck. 30c, Crane vehicle.

1977, June 20

2144 A573 1c shown .25 .25
2145 A573 2c multicolored .25 .25
2146 A573 6c multicolored .25 .25
2147 A573 10c multicolored .50 .25
2148 A573 13c multicolored .90 .25
2149 A573 30c multicolored 1.90 .40
Nos. 2144-2149 (6) 4.05 1.65

Natl. Decorations (Ribbons and Medals of Honor) — A574

1977, July 26 ***Perf. 12x12½***

2150 A574 1c shown .25 .25
2151 A574 3c multi, diff. .25 .25

See Nos. C255-C256.

Paintings by Jorge Arche — A575

1c, *Portrait of Mary.* 3c, *Jose Marti.* 5c, *Portrait of Aristides.* 10c, *Bathers.*

Perf. 13x12½, 12½x13 (10c), 13 (5c)

1977, Aug. 25

Sizes: 26x38mm, 29x40mm (5c), 38x26mm (10c)

2152 A575 1c multicolored .25 .25
2153 A575 3c multicolored .25 .25
2154 A575 5c multicolored .25 .25
2155 A575 10c multicolored .50 .25
Nos. 2152-2155 (4) 1.25 1.00

Nos. 2152-2154 vert. See Nos. C257-C259.

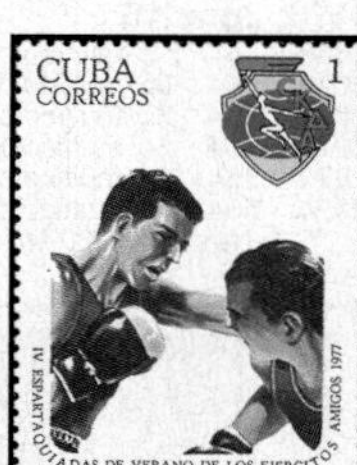

4th Military Spartakiad (Summer Sports) — A576

1977, Sept. 10 ***Perf. 13***

2156 A576 1c Boxing .25 .25
2157 A576 3c Volleyball .25 .25
2158 A576 5c Parachuting .25 .25
2159 A576 10c Running .35 .25
Nos. 2156-2159 (4) 1.10 1.00

See Nos. C260-C261.

Intl. Airmail Service, 50th Anniv. A577

Designs: 1c, Biplane and No. C62. 2c, Three-engine plane and Cuba-Key West 1st flight cancel, Oct. 28, 1927. 5c, Flying boat and intl. airmail service 1st flight cachet. 10c, DC-3 aircraft and Havana-Madrid cachet, Apr. 26, 1948.

1977, Oct. 27 **Litho.** ***Perf. 12x12½***

2160 A577 1c multi .25 .25
2161 A577 2c multi .25 .25
2162 A577 5c multi .25 .25
2163 A577 10c multi .50 .25
Nos. 2160-2163 (4) 1.25 1.00

See Nos. C263-C264.

October Revolution, Russia, 60th Anniv. — A578

3c, Cruiser *Aurora.* 13c, Lenin, Flags. 30c, Hammer, sickle, symbols of agriculture, technology.

1977, Nov. 7 ***Perf. 13x12½***

2164 A578 3c multicolored .25 .25
2165 A578 13c multicolored .40 .25
2166 A578 30c multicolored 1.40 .40
Nos. 2164-2166 (3) 2.05 .90

Felines, Havana Zoo — A579

1977, Nov. 24 **Litho.** ***Perf. 13***

2167 A579 1c Cat .25 .25
2168 A579 2c Black panther .25 .25
2169 A579 8c Puma .25 .25
2170 A579 10c Leopard 1.00 .25
Nos. 2167-2170 (4) 1.75 1.00

See Nos. C266-C267.

Martyrs of the Revolution, 20th Death Annivs. — A580

3c, Cienfuegos Uprising. 20c, Siege on the Presidential Palace.

1977, Dec. 2 ***Perf. 12½x12***

2171 A580 3c multicolored .25 .25
2172 A580 20c multicolored 1.00 .25

See No. C268.

Intl. Measurement System — A581

1977, Dec. 9

2173 A581 3c multicolored .40 .25

Havana University, 250th Anniv. — A582

1978, Jan. 5 ***Perf. 13x12½***

2174 A582 3c multicolored .25 .25

See Nos. C270-C271.

Landscape with Figures, by J. Pilliment — A583

Paintings in the Natl. Museum of Art: 1c, *Seated Woman,* by R. Madrazo, vert. 4c, *Girl,* by J. Sorolla, vert. 10c, *The Cow,* by E. Abela.

Perf. 12x12½, 13 (4c, 6c, 10c)

1978, Feb. 20

Sizes: 27x42mm, 29x40mm (4c), 40x29mm (6c, 10c)

2175 A583 1c multi .25 .25
2176 A583 4c multi .25 .25
2177 A583 6c shown .25 .25
2178 A583 10c multi .55 .25
Nos. 2175-2178 (4) 1.30 1.00

See Nos. C273-C274.

Frontier Troops, 15th Anniv. — A584

1978, Mar. 5 ***Perf. 13***

2179 A584 13c multi 1.40 .25

Bird Type of 1975

Birds: 1c, Myadestes elisabeth. 4c, Palioptila lembeyei. 10c, Teretistris fernandinae.

Perf. 13, 12½x12 (4c)

1978, Mar. 10 **Size: 42x27mm**

2180 A524 1c multicolored .40 .25
2181 A524 4c multicolored .50 .25
2182 A524 10c multicolored 1.25 .25
Nos. 2180-2182 (3) 2.15 .75

Name of bird inscribed below vignette. See Nos. C275-C276.

Cosmonaut's Day — A585

1978, Apr. 12 ***Perf. 13***

2183 A585 1c Intercosmos, vert. .25 .25
2184 A585 2c Luna 24 .25 .25
2185 A585 5c Venera 9, vert. .35 .25
2186 A585 10c Cosmos .35 .25
Nos. 2183-2186 (4) 1.20 1.00

See Nos. C278-C279.

9th World Trade Unions Congress, Prague — A586

1978, Apr. 16

2187 A586 30c ver, deep brn & blk 1.00 .45

Cactus Flowers — A587

Designs: 1c, Melocactus guitarti. 4c, Leptocereus wrightii. 6c, Opuntia militaris. 10c, Cylindropuntia hystrix.

1978, May 15 ***Perf. 12½x13 (1c), 13***

2188 A587 1c multicolored .25 .25
2189 A587 4c multicolored .25 .25
2190 A587 6c multicolored .25 .25
2191 A587 10c multicolored .65 .25
Nos. 2188-2191 (4) 1.40 1.00

Natl. Botanical Gardens. See Nos. C281-C282.

Lenin Park Aquarium, Havana — A588

Designs: 1c, Barbus arulios. 4c, Hiphessobrycon flammeus. 6c, Poecilia reticulata. 10c, Colis lalia.

1978, June 15 ***Perf. 13***

2192 A588 1c multicolored .25 .25
2193 A588 4c multicolored .25 .25
2194 A588 6c multicolored .25 .25
2195 A588 10c multicolored .55 .25
Nos. 2192-2195 (4) 1.30 1.00

See Nos. C286-C287.

MEDELLIN '78, 13th Central American and Caribbean Games — A589

1978, July 1

2196 A589 1c Basketball .25 .25
2197 A589 3c Boxing .25 .25
2198 A589 5c Weight lifting .25 .25
2199 A589 10c Fencing, horiz. .45 .25
Nos. 2196-2199 (4) 1.20 1.00

See Nos. C288-C289.

Attack on Moncada Barracks, 25th Anniv. — A590

1978, July 26

2200 A590 3c multi .30 .25

See Nos. C290-C291.

World Youth and Students Festival, Havana A591

Natl. flags and views of host cities.

1978, July 28

2201 A591 3c Prague, 1947 .30 .25
2202 A591 3c Budapest, 1949 .30 .25
2203 A591 3c Berlin, 1951 .30 .25
2204 A591 3c Bucharest, 1953 .30 .25
2205 A591 3c Warsaw, 1955 .30 .25
a. Strip of 5, Nos. 2201-2205 1.60 1.60
Nos. 2201-2205 (5) 1.50 1.25

See Nos. C292-C297.

Young Workers' Army, 5th Anniv. — A592

1978, Aug. 3

2206 A592 3c multi .30 .25

Tuna Industry A593

1c, Tuna boat. 2c, Processing ship. 5c, Shrimp boat. 10c, Inshore stern trawler.

1978, Aug. 30 ***Perf. 12½x12***

2207 A593 1c multicolored .25 .25
2208 A593 2c multicolored .25 .25
2209 A593 5c multicolored .25 .25
2210 A593 10c multicolored .35 .25
Nos. 2207-2210 (4) 1.10 1.00

See Nos. C298-C299.

Paintings by Amelia Pelaez del Casal (1896-1968) — A594

1c, *The White Mantle.* 3c, *Still-life with Flowers,* vert. 6c, *Women,* vert. 10c, *Fish,* vert.

Perf. 13x12½, 13 (3c, 6c), 12½x13

1978, Sept. 15

2211 A594 1c multicolored .25 .25
2212 A594 3c multicolored .25 .25
2213 A594 6c multicolored .25 .25
2214 A594 10c multicolored .45 .25
Nos. 2211-2214 (4) 1.20 1.00

See Nos. C301-C303.

African Fauna, Havana Zoo A595

1978, Oct. 20 ***Perf. 13***

2215 A595 1c Rhinoceros .25 .25
2216 A595 4c Okapi, vert. .25 .25
2217 A595 6c Mandrill .25 .25
2218 A595 10c Giraffe, vert. .65 .25
Nos. 2215-2218 (4) 1.40 1.00

See Nos. C307-C308.

Natl. Ballet, 30th Anniv. — A596

3c, *Grande Pas de Quatre.*

1978, Oct. 28 ***Perf. 13x12½***

2219 A596 3c multicolored .35 .25

See Nos. C309-C310.

A597

Flowers of the Pacific: Various species.

1978, Nov. 30 **Litho.** ***Perf. 13***

2220 A597 1c multi .25 .25
2221 A597 4c multi .25 .25
2222 A597 6c multi .25 .25
2223 A597 10c multi .50 .25
Nos. 2220-2223 (4) 1.25 1.00

See Nos. C311-C312.

A598

3c, Castro, soldier. 13c, Industry. 1p, Flag, globe, flame.

1979, Jan. 1 ***Perf. 12½x13 (3c), 13***

2224 A598 3c multicolored .25 .25
2225 A598 13c multicolored .50 .25
2226 A598 1p multicolored 3.00 1.50
Nos. 2224-2226 (3) 3.75 2.00

Triumph of the Revolution, 20th anniv.

Doves and Pigeons A599

Designs: 1c, Starnoenas cyanocephala. 3c, Geotrygon chysia. 7c, Geotrygon caniceps. 8c, Geotrygon montana. 13c, Columba leucocephala. 30c, Columba inornata.

1979, Jan. 30 *Perf. 13*

2227	A599	1c	multicolored	.35	.25
2228	A599	3c	multicolored	.45	.25
2229	A599	7c	multicolored	.50	.25
2230	A599	8c	multicolored	.60	.25
2231	A599	13c	multicolored	1.00	.25
2232	A599	30c	multicolored	2.10	.80
	Nos. 2227-2232 (6)			5.00	2.05

Paintings in the Natl. Museum of Art A600

Designs: 1c, *Genre Scene,* by David Teniers. 3c, *Arrival of Spanish Troops,* by J. Louis Meissonier. 6c, *A Joyful Gathering,* by Sir David Wilkie. 10c, *A Robbery,* by E. De Lucas Padilla. 13c, *Tea Time,* by R. Madrazo, vert. 30c, *Peasants in Front of a Tavern,* by Adriaen van Ostade.

1979, Feb. 20

2233	A600	1c	multi	.25	.25
2234	A600	3c	multi	.25	.25
2235	A600	6c	multi	.35	.25
2236	A600	10c	multi	.50	.25
2237	A600	13c	multi	.90	.25
2238	A600	30c	multi	1.75	.30
	Nos. 2233-2238 (6)			4.00	1.55

See Nos. 2262-2267, C317.

Marine Flora — A601

Designs: 3c, Nymphaea capensis. 10c, Nymphaea ampla. 13c, Nymphaea coerulea. 30c, Nymphaea rubra.

1979, Mar. 20

2239	A601	3c	multicolored	.25	.25
2240	A601	10c	multicolored	.40	.25
2241	A601	13c	multicolored	.65	.25
2242	A601	30c	multicolored	1.50	.40
	Nos. 2239-2242 (4)			2.80	1.15

All are incorrectly inscribed "Nymphaca."

Cuban Film Industry, 20th Anniv. — A602

1979, Mar. 24

2243	A602	3c	multicolored	.25	.25

Cosmonaut's Day — A603

1979, Apr. 12

2244	A603	1c	Rocket launch	.25	.25
2245	A603	4c	Soyuz	.25	.25
2246	A603	6c	Salyut	.25	.25
2247	A603	10c	Link-up	.40	.25
2248	A603	13c	Soyuz, Salyut	.75	.25
2249	A603	30c	Parachute landing	1.40	.25
	Nos. 2244-2249 (6)			3.30	1.50

See No. C315.

6th Summit Meeting of Non-Aligned Countries — A604

3c, Understanding, cooperation. 13c, Fight colonialism. 30c, New world economic order.

1979, Apr. 17

2250	A604	3c	multicolored	.25	.25
2251	A604	13c	multicolored	.50	.25
2252	A604	30c	multicolored	1.40	.40
	Nos. 2250-2252 (3)			2.15	.90

House of the Americas Museum, 20th Anniv. — A605

13c, Cuna Indian tapestry.

1979, Apr. 28 *Perf. 13x12½*

2253	A605	13c	multicolored	.50	.25

Agrarian Reform, 20th Anniv. — A606

1979, May 17 *Perf. 12½x12*

2254	A606	3c	multicolored	.40	.25

Souvenir Sheet

The Party, by Jules Pascin — A607

1979, May 18 *Perf. 13*

2255	A607	50c	multi	3.50	1.25

PHILASERDICA '79 phil. exhib., Sofia.

Nocturnal Butterflies — A608

Designs: 1c, Eulepidotis rectimargo. 4c, Othreis materna. 6c, Noropsis hieroglyphica. 10c, Heterochroma. 13c, Melanchroia regnatrix. 30c, Attera gemmata.

1979, May 25

2256	A608	1c	multicolored	.25	.25
2257	A608	4c	multicolored	.25	.25
2258	A608	6c	multicolored	.40	.25
2259	A608	10c	multicolored	.40	.25
2260	A608	13c	multicolored	.80	.25
2261	A608	30c	multicolored	2.00	.45
	Nos. 2256-2261 (6)			4.10	1.70

Art Type of 1979

Paintings by Victor Manuel Garcia (d. 1969): 1c, *Main Avenue, Paris.* 3c, *Portrait of Enmita.* 6c, *San Juan River, Matanzas.* 10c, *Woman Carrying Hay.* 13c, *Still-life with Vase.* 30c, *Street at Night.* Nos. 2262-2267 vert.

1979, June 15

2262	A600	1c	multi	.25	.25
2263	A600	3c	multi	.25	.25
2264	A600	6c	multi	.25	.25
2265	A600	10c	multi	.30	.25
2266	A600	13c	multi	.40	.25
2267	A600	30c	multi	1.50	.45
	Nos. 2262-2267 (6)			2.95	1.70

See No. C317.

World Peace Council, 30th Anniv. A609

1979, June 29 *Perf. 12½x13*

2268	A609	30c	multi	1.10	.35

1980 Summer Olympics, Moscow — A610

1c, Wrestling. 4c, Boxing. 6c, Women's volleyball. 10c, Shooting. 13c, Weight lifting. 30c, High jump.

1979, July 30 *Perf. 13x12½*

2269	A610	1c	multicolored	.25	.25
2270	A610	4c	multicolored	.25	.25
2271	A610	6c	multicolored	.25	.25
2272	A610	10c	multicolored	.30	.25
2273	A610	13c	multicolored	.50	.25
2274	A610	30c	multicolored	1.25	.30
	Nos. 2269-2274 (6)			2.80	1.55

Roses — A611

Designs: 1c, Rosa eglanteria. 2c, Rosa centifolia anemonoides. 3c, Rosa indica vulgaris. 5c, Rosa eglanteria punicea. 10c, Rosa sulfurea. 13c, Rosa muscosa alba. 20c, Rosa gallica purpurea velutina.

1979, Aug. 20 *Perf. 13*

2275	A611	1c	multicolored	.25	.25
2276	A611	2c	multicolored	.25	.25
2277	A611	3c	multicolored	.25	.25
2278	A611	5c	multicolored	.25	.25
2279	A611	10c	multicolored	.30	.25
2280	A611	13c	multicolored	.50	.25
2281	A611	20c	multicolored	1.00	.25
	Nos. 2275-2281 (7)			2.80	1.75

A612

1979, Aug. 30

2282	A612	13c	multicolored	.50	.25

Council for Mutual Economic Assistance, 30th anniv.

Cubana Airlines, 50th Anniv. A613

Various aircraft.

1979, Oct. 8

2283	A613	1c	Ford trimotor	.25	.25
2284	A613	2c	Sikorsky S-38	.25	.25
2285	A613	3c	Douglas DC-3	.25	.25
2286	A613	4c	Brittania	.25	.25
2287	A613	13c	Ilyushin IL-14	.75	.25
2288	A613	40c	Tupolev TU-104	2.10	.40
	Nos. 2283-2288 (6)			3.85	1.65

Disappearance of Camilo Cienfuegos, 20th Anniv. — A614

1979, Oct. 28

2289	A614	3c	multi	.30	.25

Reinoso, Sugar Cane and Blossom A615

1979, Nov. 12

2290	A615	13c	multi	.65	.25

Sugar Cane Research Institute, 15th anniv., and sesquicentennial of the birth of Alvaro Reinoso.

Zoo Animals A616

1979, Nov. 15

2291 A616 1c Chimpanzees .25 .25
2292 A616 2c Leopards .25 .25
2293 A616 3c Deer .25 .25
2294 A616 4c Lion cubs .25 .25
2295 A616 5c Bear cubs .25 .25
2296 A616 13c Squirrels .50 .25
2297 A616 30c Pandas 1.25 .30
2298 A616 50c Tiger cubs 1.75 .50
Nos. 2291-2298 (8) 4.75 2.30

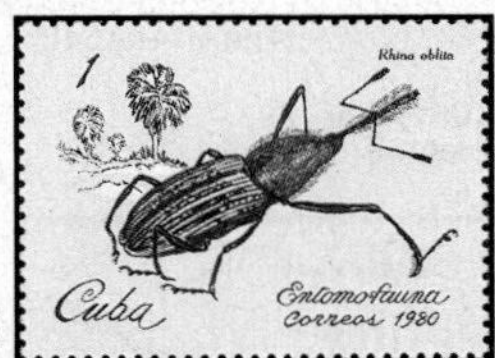

Insects A617

Designs: 1c, Rhina oblita. 5c, Odontocera josemartii, vert. 6c, Pinthocoelium columbinum. 10c, Calasoma splendida, vert. 13c, Homophileurus cubanus, vert. 30c, Heterops dimidiata, vert.

1980, Jan. 25

2299 A617 1c multicolored .25 .25
2300 A617 5c multicolored .25 .25
2301 A617 6c multicolored .25 .25
2302 A617 10c multicolored .40 .25
2303 A617 13c multicolored .70 .25
2304 A617 30c multicolored 1.50 .70
Nos. 2299-2304 (6) 3.35 1.95

1980 Summer Olympics, Moscow — A618

1980, Feb. 20 ***Perf. 12½***

2305 A618 1c Weight lifting .25 .25
2306 A618 2c Shooting .25 .25
2307 A618 5c Javelin .30 .25
2308 A618 6c Wrestling .30 .25
2309 A618 8c Judo .30 .25
2310 A618 10c Running .45 .25
2311 A618 13c Boxing .75 .25
2312 A618 30c Women's volley-ball 1.60 .60
Nos. 2305-2312 (8) 4.20 2.35

Souvenir Sheet

Imperf

2313 A618 50c Mischa character 3.00 2.25

No. 2313 contains one 32x40mm stamp.

Paintings in the Natl. Museum A619

Designs: 1c, *The Oak Trees,* by Henry Joseph Harpignies, vert. 4c, *Family Reunion,* by Willem van Mieris. 6c, *Domestic Fowl,* by Melchior De Hondecoeter, vert. 9c, *Innocence,* by William A. Bougereau, vert. 13c, *Venetian Scene II,* by Michele Marieschi. 30c, *Spanish Peasant Woman,* by Joaquin Dominguez Bequer, vert.

Sizes: 29x40mm, 40x29mm (4c), 28x42mm (9c, 30c), 38x26mm (13c)

Perf. 12½, 13 (9c, 30c), 12½x13 (13c)

1980, Mar. 11

2314 A619 1c multi .25 .25
2315 A619 4c multi .25 .25
2316 A619 6c multi .25 .25
2317 A619 9c multi .50 .25
2318 A619 13c multi .75 .25
2319 A619 30c multi 1.50 .65
Nos. 2314-2319 (6) 3.50 1.90

Souvenir Sheet

LONDON '80 — A620

50c, *Malvern Hall,* by John Constable.

1980, Apr. 1 ***Perf. 13***

2320 A620 50c multi 3.00 2.25

Intercosmos Program — A621

1c, Emblem, flags. 4c, Astrophysics. 6c, Satellite communications. 10c, Meteorology. 13c, Biology and medicine. 30c, Surveying satellite.

1980, Apr. 12

2321 A621 1c multicolored .25 .25
2322 A621 4c multicolored .25 .25
2323 A621 6c multicolored .25 .25
2324 A621 10c multicolored .45 .25
2325 A621 13c multicolored .60 .25
2326 A621 30c multicolored 1.90 .65
Nos. 2321-2326 (6) 3.70 1.90

Cuban Postage Stamps, 125th Anniv. — A622

30c, Nos. 1, 7 and 613.

1980, Apr. 24 ***Perf. 12½***

2327 A622 30c multi 1.25 .45

Orchids — A623

Designs: 1c, Bletia purpurea. 4c, Oncidium leiboldii. 6c, Epidendrum cochieatum. 10c, Cattleyopsis lindenii. 13c, Encyclia fucata. 30c, Encyclia phoenicea.

1980, May 20 ***Perf. 13***

2328 A623 1c multicolored .25 .25
2329 A623 4c multicolored .25 .25
2330 A623 6c multicolored .25 .25
2331 A623 10c multicolored .50 .25
2332 A623 13c multicolored .90 .25
2333 A623 30c multicolored 1.90 .60
Nos. 2328-2333 (6) 4.05 1.85

Marine Mammals — A624

Designs: 1c, Tursiops truncatus. 3c, Megaptera novaeangliae, vert. 13c, Ziphius cavirostris. 30c, Monachus tropicalis.

1980, June 20

2334 A624 1c multicolored .30 .25
2335 A624 3c multicolored .30 .25
2336 A624 13c multicolored 1.00 .25
2337 A624 30c multicolored 2.50 .50
Nos. 2334-2337 (4) 4.10 1.25

Urban Reform Campaign, 20th Anniv. — A625

Nationalization of Foreign Industry, 20th Anniv. — A626

1980, July 26 ***Perf. 13x12½, 12½x13***

2338 A625 3c multi .25 .25
2339 A626 13c multi .35 .25

Moncada Program.

Colonial Copperware A627

3c, Wine pitcher, 19th cent. 13c, Oil jar, 18th cent. 30c, Lidded pitcher, 19th cent.

Perf. 12½, 12½x13 (13c)

1980, July 29

Sizes: 27x43½mm, 38x26mm (13c)

2340 A627 3c multicolored .25 .25
2341 A627 13c multicolored .65 .25
2342 A627 30c multicolored 1.25 .30
Nos. 2340-2342 (3) 2.15 .80

Cuban Women's Federation, 20th Anniv. — A628

1980, Aug. 23 ***Perf. 13***

2343 A628 3c multi .40 .25

Souvenir Sheet

ESPAMER '80, Madrid — A629

Design: *Clotilde Passing Through the Country Garden,* by Joaquin Sorolla y Bastida.

1980, Aug. 29

2344 A629 50c multi 3.00 2.25

Postage stamps of Spain, 130th anniv.

1st Havana Declaration, 20th Anniv. — A630

1980, Sept. 2

2345 A630 13c multi .50 .25

Construction of Naval Vessels in Cuba, 360th Anniv. — A631

Ships under construction: 1c, *Our Lady of Atocha,* galleon, 1620. 3c, *El Rayo,* warship, 1749. 7c, *Santisima Trinidad,* 1769. 10c, *Santisima Trinidad,* diff., 1805, vert. 13c, Steamships *Congreso* and *Colon,* 1851. 30c, Cardenas and Chullima shipyards.

1980, Sept. 15

2346 A631 1c multi .25 .25
2347 A631 3c multi .25 .25
2348 A631 7c multi .25 .25
2349 A631 10c multi .50 .25
2350 A631 13c multi .90 .25
2351 A631 30c multi 1.50 .60
Nos. 2346-2351 (6) 3.65 1.85

A633

1980, Sept. 26 ***Perf. 13***

2354 A633 13c multi .60 .25

Fidel Castro's 1st speech before the UN General Assembly, 20th anniv.

A634

1980, Sept. 28 ***Perf. 13x12½***

2355 A634 3c multi .30 .25

Revolutionary defense committees, 20th anniv.

Souvenir Sheet

ESSEN '80, 49th Intl. Philatelic Federation Congress — A635

Painting: *Portrait of a Lady,* by Ludger Tom Ring The Younger.

1980, Oct. 2 **Litho.** ***Perf. 13***
2356 A635 50c multi 3.00 2.25

Early Locomotives — A636

1c, Josefa. 2c, Chaparra Sugar Co. No. 22. 7c, Steam storage locomotive. 10c, 2-4-2 locomotive. 13c, 2-4-0 locomotive. 30c, Oil combustion engine, 1909.

1980, Oct. 15

2357 A636 1c multicolored .25 .25
2358 A636 2c multicolored .25 .25
2359 A636 7c multicolored .25 .25
2360 A636 10c multicolored .60 .25
2361 A636 13c multicolored 1.25 .25
2362 A636 30c multicolored 2.40 .60
Nos. 2357-2362 (6) 5.00 1.85

Lighthouses A637

3c, Roncali, San Antonio. 13c, Jagua, Cienfuegos. 30c, Maisi Point, Guantanamo.

1980, Oct. 30

2363 A637 3c multicolored .25 .45
2364 A637 13c multicolored .70 .45
2365 A637 30c multicolored 1.60 .45
Nos. 2363-2365 (3) 2.55 1.35

See Nos. 2440-2442, 2553-2555, 2614-2616.

Victory of Cuban Athletes at the 1980 Summer Olympics, Moscow — A638

1980, Nov. 10 **Litho.** ***Perf. 12½x12***

2366 A638 13c Bronze medals .50 .25
2367 A638 30c Silver medals 1.10 .25
2368 A638 50c Gold medals 2.25 .55
Nos. 2366-2368 (3) 3.85 1.05

Nos. 2366-2368 each printed se-tenant with label containing statistical data.

Wildflowers A639

Designs: 1c, Pancratium arenicolum. 4c, Urechites lutea. 6c, Solanum elaegnifolium. 10c, Hamelia patens. 13c, Morinda royoc. 30c, Centrosema virginianum.

1980, Nov. 20 ***Perf. 13***

2369 A639 1c multicolored .25 .25
2370 A639 4c multicolored .25 .25
2371 A639 6c multicolored .30 .25
2372 A639 10c multicolored .50 .25
2373 A639 13c multicolored .95 .25
2374 A639 30c multicolored 2.25 .40
Nos. 2369-2374 (6) 4.50 1.65

Souvenir Sheet

7th Natl. Stamp Exhibition — A640

1980, Nov. 22

2375 A640 50c Mail train 3.50 2.25

2nd Communist Party Congress A641

13c, Industry, communication. 30c, Athletics, elderly, education.

1980, Dec. 17

2376 A641 3c shown .25 .25
2377 A641 13c multicolored .40 .25
2378 A641 30c multicolored 1.00 .25
Nos. 2376-2378 (3) 1.65 .75

Paintings in the Natl. Museum of Art A642

Designs: 1c, *Lady Mayo,* by Anton Van Dyck, vert. 6c, *The Spinner,* by Giovanni Battista Piazzetta, vert. 10c, *Daniel Collyer,* by Francis Cotes, vert. 13c, *Gardens, Palma de Mallorca,* by Santiago Rusinol Prats. 20c, *Landscape with Roadway and Houses,* by Frederick Waters Watts. 50c, *Landscape with Sheep,* by Jean-Francois Millet.

1981, Jan. 20

2379 A642 1c multi .25 .25
2380 A642 6c multi .25 .25
2381 A642 10c multi .50 .25
2382 A642 13c multi .55 .25
2383 A642 20c multi .90 .30
2384 A642 50c multi 1.90 .60
Nos. 2379-2384 (6) 4.35 1.90

See Nos. 2510-2515.

Pelagic Fish A643

Designs: 1c, Isurus oxyrhynchus. 3c, Lampris regius. 10c, Istiophorus platypterus. 13c, Mola mola, vert. 30c, Coruphaena hippurus. 50c, Tetrapturus albidus.

1981, Feb. 25

2385 A643 1c multicolored .25 .25
2386 A643 3c multicolored .25 .25
2387 A643 10c multicolored .45 .25
2388 A643 13c multicolored 1.60 .25
2389 A643 30c multicolored 1.00 .40
2390 A643 50c multicolored 1.75 .95
Nos. 2385-2390 (6) 5.30 2.35

1982 World Cup Soccer Championships, Spain — A644

Globe and various soccer players.

1981, Mar. 20 ***Perf. 12½***

2391 A644 1c multi .25 .25
2392 A644 2c multi .25 .25
2393 A644 3c multi .25 .25
2394 A644 10c multi, vert. .45 .25
2395 A644 13c multi, vert. .50 .25
2396 A644 50c multi 2.00 .65
Nos. 2391-2396 (6) 3.70 1.90

Souvenir Sheet

Perf. 13

2397 A644 1p Soccer ball, flag 4.50 2.00

No. 2397 contains one 40x32mm stamp.

Opening of the 1st Kindergarten, 20th Anniv. — A645

1981, Apr. 10 ***Perf. 13***

2398 A645 3c multi .50 .25

1st Man in Space, 20th Anniv. A646

Designs: 1c, Jules Verne, Russian scientist Konstantin E. Tsiolkovski, and Sergei P. Korolev, designer of the 1st Soviet spacecraft, vert. 2c, Yuri Gagarin, 1st man in space. 3c, Valentina Tereshkova, 1st woman in space, and *Vostok 6.* 5c, Aleksei A. Leonov, 1st man to walk in space. 13c, Konstantin Feoktistov, Boris Yegorov and Vladimir Komarov, *Voskhod 1* crew, 1st 3-man orbital flight. 30c, Valeri Ryumin and Leonid Popov, set a space endurance record. 50c, Arnaldo Tamayo Mendez, 1st Cuban cosmonaut, and Soviet cosmonaut Yuri Romanenko on joint space flight, vert.

1981, Apr. 12 ***Perf. 12½***

2399 A646 1c multi .25 .25
2400 A646 2c multi .25 .25
2401 A646 3c multi .25 .25
2402 A646 5c multi .25 .25
2403 A646 13c multi .45 .25
2404 A646 30c multi .90 .35
2405 A646 50c multi 2.00 .60
Nos. 2399-2405 (7) 4.35 2.20

A647

Designs: 3c, Rocket, aircraft. 13c, Hand raising gun.

1981, Apr. 19 **Litho.** ***Perf. 13***

2406 A647 3c multi, vert. .25 .25
2407 A647 13c multi, vert. .40 .25
2408 A647 30c multi .85 .60
Nos. 2406-2408 (3) 1.50 1.10

Creation of armed forces (DAAFAR) (3c), Bay of Pigs Invasion, 20th Anniv. (13c), Proclamation of the socialist revolution (30c).

Attack on Goicuria Barracks, 25th Anniv. — A648

1981, Apr. 29

2409 A648 3c multi .30 .25

Natl. Assoc. of Small Farmers (ANAP), 20th Anniv. A649

1981, May 17

2410 A649 3c multi .45 .25

Souvenir Sheet

WIPA '81 — A650

1981, May 22 **Litho.**

2411 A650 50c Austria No. 643 3.00 1.50

Fighting Cocks A651

1981, May 25 ***Perf. 12½x13, 13x12½***

2412 A651 1c Canelo, vert. .25 .25
2413 A651 3c Cenizo .25 .25
2414 A651 7c Blanco, vert. .25 .25
2415 A651 13c Pinto, vert. .50 .25
2416 A651 30c Giro 1.40 .35
2417 A651 50c Jabao, vert. 2.25 .60
Nos. 2412-2417 (6) 4.90 1.95

Ministry of the Interior, 20th Anniv. — A652

1981, June 6 ***Perf. 13***

2418 A652 13c multi .40 .25

Souvenir Sheet

Mother and Child, by Zlatka Dabova — A653

1981, June 14

2419 A653 50c gold, sil & blk 2.25 1.10

Bulgaria, 1300th anniv. BULGARIA '81 phil. exhib.

Horse-drawn Carriages — A654

1981, June 25

2420 A654 1c Streetcar .25 .25
2421 A654 4c Bus .25 .25
2422 A654 9c Breake .25 .25
2423 A654 13c Landau .40 .25
2424 A654 30c Phaeton 1.25 .45
2425 A654 50c Funeral coach 2.25 .75
Nos. 2420-2425 (6) 4.65 2.20

House in the Country, by Mario Caridad — A655

1981, July 15 ***Perf. 12½***

2426 A655 30c multi 1.25 .30

Intl. Year of the Disabled.

Sandinistas, 25th Anniv. — A656

1981, July 23 ***Perf. 13***

2427 A656 13c multi .75 .25

State Institutions, 20th Annivs. — A657

1981, July 26 ***Perf. 12½***

2428 A657 3c multi .25 .25
2429 A657 13c multi, diff. .45 .25
2430 A657 30c multi, diff. 1.25 .25
Nos. 2428-2430 (3) 1.95 .75

Institute for Sports, Physical Education and Recreation (3c); Radio Havana (13c); and Ministry of Foreign Trade (MINCEX) (30c).

Carlos J. Finlay and Cent. of His Theory of Biological Vectors — A658

1981, Aug. 14 ***Perf. 13***

2431 A658 13c multi 1.00 .25

Nonaligned Countries Movement, 20th Anniv. — A659

1981, Sept. 1

2432 A659 50c multi 1.75 .80

Horses — A660

Nos. 2433-2437 vert.

1981, Sept. 15 ***Perf. 13***

Size: 29x40mm

2433 A660 1c multi .25 .25
2434 A660 3c multi, diff. .25 .25
2435 A660 8c multi, diff. .25 .25
2436 A660 13c multi, diff. .35 .25
2437 A660 30c multi, diff. 1.10 .45

Size: 68x27mm

Perf. 12½

2438 A660 50c Herd 2.00 .75
Nos. 2433-2438 (6) 4.20 2.20

Souvenir Sheet

Idyll in a Tea House, by Kitagawa Utamaro — A661

1981, Oct. 9 ***Perf. 13***

2439 A661 50c multi 2.75 1.25

PHILATOKYO '81.

Lighthouse Type of 1980

1981, Oct. 15 **Litho.**

2440 A637 3c North Rock .25 .25
2441 A637 13c Lucrecia Point .50 .25
2442 A637 40c East Guano 2.10 .50
Nos. 2440-2442 (3) 2.85 1.00

Jose Marti Natl. Library, 80th Anniv. — A662

Sugar mills, lithographs from *Los Ingenios,* by Eduardo Laplante (b. 1818): 3c, Flor de Cuba, 1838. 13c, El Progreso, 1845. 30c, Santa Teresa, 1847.

1981, Oct. 18 ***Perf. 12½x12***

2443 A662 3c multi .25 .25
2444 A662 13c multi .30 .25
2445 A662 30c multi 1.10 .55
Nos. 2443-2445 (3) 1.65 1.05

Pablo Picasso (b. 1881) and No. 1263 A663

1981, Oct. 25 ***Perf. 12½x13***

2446 A663 30c multi 1.25 .40

Souvenir Sheet

ESPAMER '81, Buenos Aires — A664

1981, Nov. 13 ***Perf. 13***

2447 A664 1p Packet 5.00 4.50

Art Type of 1969

Paintings in the Napoleon Museum: 1c, *Napoleon in Coronation Costume,* anonymous. 3c, *Napoleon with Landscape in the Background,* by Jean Horace Vernet. 10c, *Bonaparte in Egypt,* by Edouard Detaille. 13c, *Napoleon on Horseback,* by Hippolyte Bellange. 30c, *Napoleon in Normandy,* by Bellange. 50c, *Death of Napoleon,* anonymous.

1981, Dec. 1 ***Perf. 12½***

Sizes: 42x58mm, 58x42mm (3c, 13c, 30c, 50c)

2448 A385 1c multi .25 .25
2449 A385 3c multi, horiz. .25 .25
2450 A385 10c multi .40 .25
2451 A385 13c multi, horiz. .40 .25
2452 A385 30c multi, horiz. 1.25 .40
2453 A385 50c multi, horiz. 2.10 .70
Nos. 2448-2453 (6) 4.65 2.10

Napoleon Museum, 20th anniv.

25th Annivs. A665

3c, Revolutionaries, vert. 20c, Marksman. 1p, Yacht *Granma.*

1981, Dec. 2 ***Perf. 13***

2454 A665 3c multi .25 .25
2455 A665 20c multi .45 .25
2456 A665 1p multi 4.75 1.40
Nos. 2454-2456 (3) 5.45 1.90

November 30th insurrection (3c); creation of the revolutionary armed forces (20c); and disembarking of revolutionary forces (1p).

Fauna — A666

1981, Dec. 14 **Litho.** ***Perf. 12½x12***

2457 A666 1c Hummingbird .60 .25
2458 A666 2c Parakeet .95 .25
2459 A666 5c Hutia .25 .25
2460 A666 20c Almiqui .65 .25
2461 A666 35c Manatee 1.00 .25
2462 A666 40c Crocodile 1.00 .55
Nos. 2457-2462 (6) 4.45 1.80

Fernando Ortiz, Folklorist, Birth Cent. A667

3c, Portrait by Jorge Arche y Silva. 10c, Hanging idol. 30c, Arara drum. 50c, Chango statue.

1981, Dec. 20 ***Perf. 12½x13***

2463 A667 3c multi .25 .25
2464 A667 10c multi .40 .25
2465 A667 30c multi 1.40 .45
2466 A667 50c multi 2.10 .70
Nos. 2463-2466 (4) 4.15 1.65

Literacy Campaign, 20th Anniv. — A668

No. 2467, Conrado Benitez. No. 2468, Manuel Asunce.

1981, Dec. 25 ***Perf. 12½x12***

2467 A668 5c multi .30 .25
2468 A668 5c multi .30 .25
a. Pair, #2467-2468 .75 .25
Nos. 2467-2468 (2) .60 .50

A669

1982 World Cup Soccer Championships, Spain — A670

Various athletes.

1982, Jan. 15 ***Perf. 13***

No.	Type	Value	Description	Unused	Used
2469	A669	1c	multi, vert.	.25	.25
2470	A669	2c	multi, vert.	.25	.25
2471	A669	5c	multi, vert.	.25	.25
2472	A669	10c	multi, vert.	.30	.25
2473	A669	20c	shown	.75	.25
2474	A669	40c	multi	1.40	.50
2475	A669	50c	multi, vert.	1.75	.70
			Nos. 2469-2475 (7)	4.95	2.45

Souvenir Sheet

No.	Type	Value	Description	Unused	Used
2476	A670	1p	shown	5.00	2.50

No. 2476 contains one 32x40mm stamp.

10th World Trade Unions Congress, Havana — A671

30c, Lazaro Pena, delegate.

1982, Feb. 10 **Litho.**

No.	Type	Value	Description	Unused	Used
2477	A671	30c	multi	1.00	.40

Butterflies — A672

Designs: 1c, Euptoieta hegesia. 4c, Metamorpha stelenes insularis. 5c, Heliconius charithonius ramsdeni. 20c, Phoebis avellaneda. 30c, Hamadryas ferox diasia. 60c, Marpesia eleuchea.

1982, Feb. 25 ***Perf. 12½***

No.	Type	Value	Description	Unused	Used
2478	A672	1c	multicolored	.25	.25
2479	A672	4c	multicolored	.25	.25
2480	A672	5c	multicolored	.25	.25
2481	A672	20c	multicolored	1.40	.30
2482	A672	30c	multicolored	2.25	.55
2483	A672	50c	multicolored	4.00	.95
			Nos. 2478-2483 (6)	8.40	2.55

Exports — A673

3c, Sugar (processing plant). 4c, Lobster (fishing boat). 6c, Canned fruits. 7c, Agricultural machinery. 8c, Nickel (passenger jet, industrial complex, car). 9c, Rum. 10c, Coffee. 30c, Fresh fruit. 50c, Tobacco. 1p, Cement. Nos. 2489-2493 vert.

1982, Feb. 26 ***Perf. 12x12½, 12½x12***

No.	Type	Value	Description	Unused	Used
2484	A673	3c	lt grn	.25	.25
2485	A673	4c	car rose	.25	.25
2486	A673	6c	dull blue	.25	.25
2487	A673	7c	brt org	.40	.25
2488	A673	8c	brt vio	.40	.25
2489	A673	9c	slate	.40	.25
2490	A673	10c	dull red brn	.50	.25
2491	A673	30c	bister	.75	.25
2492	A673	50c	orange	2.10	.40
2493	A673	1p	olive bister	4.00	1.25
			Nos. 2484-2493 (10)	9.30	3.65

Tulips A674

1982, Mar. 30 ***Perf. 12½x13***

No.	Type	Value	Description	Unused	Used
2494	A674	1c	Greenland	.25	.25
2495	A674	3c	Mariette	.25	.25
2496	A674	8c	Ringo	.25	.25
2497	A674	20c	La Tulipe Noire	.80	.25
2498	A674	30c	Jewel of Spring	1.40	.25
2499	A674	50c	Orange Parrot	1.90	.60
			Nos. 2494-2499 (6)	4.85	1.85

Communist Youth Organization, 20th Anniv. — A675

1982, Apr. 4 ***Perf. 13***

No.	Type	Value	Description	Unused	Used
2500	A675	5c	multi	2.75	1.00

2nd UN Congress on the Peaceful Use of Outer Space — A676

1c, Gorizont. 3c, Meteor. 6c, Salyut-Soyuz link-up. 20c, Lunokhod moon vehicle. 30c, Venera with heat shield. 50c, Intelsat-4a.

1982, Apr. 12

No.	Type	Value	Description	Unused	Used
2501	A676	1c	multicolored	.25	.25
2502	A676	3c	multicolored	.25	.25
2503	A676	6c	multicolored	.25	.25
2504	A676	20c	multicolored	.50	.25
2505	A676	30c	multicolored	1.35	.30
2506	A676	50c	multicolored	1.90	.60
			Nos. 2501-2506 (6)	4.50	1.90

Cover A677

1982, Apr. 24 ***Perf. 12½x12***

No.	Type	Value	Description	Unused	Used
2507	A677	20c	Havana-Veracruz	.75	.25
2508	A677	30c	Havana-Tampico	1.25	.25

Stamp Day. English post office, 1842-1877 (20c); and French post office, 1862-1877 (30c).

Broadcasting and Television Institute (ICRT), 20th Anniv. — A678

1982, May 24 ***Perf. 12x12½***

No.	Type	Value	Description	Unused	Used
2509	A678	30c	multi	1.00	.25

Art Type of 1981 With Larger Type

Paintings in the Natl. Museum of Art: 1c, *Portrait of a Youth* (girl), by Jean B. Greuze, vert. 3c, *Procession in Brittany,* by Jules Breton. 9c, *Landscape,* by Jean Piliment. 20c, *Late Afternoon,* by William A. Bouguereau, vert. 30c, *Tiger,* by Ferdinand V.E. Delacroix. 40c, *The Chair,* by Wilfredo Lam, vert.

Perf. 13, 13x12½ (3c), 12x12½ (20c, 40c), 12½x12 (30c)

1982, May 31 **Litho.**

No.	Type	Value	Description	Unused	Used
2510	A642	1c	29x40mm	.25	.25
2511	A642	3c	46x36mm	.25	.25
2512	A642	9c	40x29mm	.25	.25
2513	A642	20c	27x42mm	.65	.25
2514	A642	30c	42x27mm	1.10	.40
2515	A642	40c	27x42mm	1.75	.40
			Nos. 2510-2515 (6)	4.25	1.80

Souvenir Sheet

PHILEXFRANCE '82 — A679

1p, Steamship Louisiana at St. Nazaire.

1982, June 7 ***Perf. 13***

No.	Type	Value	Description	Unused	Used
2516	A679	1p	multicolored	5.00	2.50

DEPORFILEX '82 — A680

1982, June 10 ***Perf. 13x12½***

No.	Type	Value	Description	Unused	Used
2517	A680	20c	Hurdler, No. 300	1.50	.25

Reptiles A681

Designs: 1c, Pseudemys decussata. 2c, Tropidophis pardalis. 3c, Crocodylus rhombifer. 20c, Cyclura nubila. 30c, Anolis allisonis. 50c, Alsophis cantherigerus.

1982, June 15 ***Perf. 13***

No.	Type	Value	Description	Unused	Used
2518	A681	1c	multicolored	.25	.25
2519	A681	2c	multicolored	.25	.25
2520	A681	3c	multicolored	.25	.25
2521	A681	20c	multicolored	.85	.25
2522	A681	30c	multicolored	1.25	.30
2523	A681	50c	multicolored	2.40	.50
			Nos. 2518-2523 (6)	5.25	1.80

George Dimitrov (1882-1949), Bulgarian Prime Minister — A682

1982, June 18

No.	Type	Value	Description	Unused	Used
2524	A682	30c	multi	1.00	.25

Koch, Bacillus A683

1982, July 18

No.	Type	Value	Description	Unused	Used
2525	A683	20c	multi	1.25	.25

Discovery of the tubercle bacillus by Dr. Robert Koch, cent.

14th Central American and Caribbean Games — A684

1982, Aug. 1

No.	Type	Value	Description	Unused	Used
2526	A684	1c	Baseball	.25	.25
2527	A684	2c	Boxing	.25	.25
2528	A684	10c	Water polo	.35	.25
2529	A684	20c	Javelin	.80	.30
2530	A684	35c	Weight lifting	1.25	.50
2531	A684	50c	Volleyball	2.00	.55
			Nos. 2526-2531 (6)	4.90	2.10

Hydraulic Development Plan, 20th Anniv. — A685

5c, Fruit, *Eichornia crassipes,* ship. 20c, Arid soil, *Nymphaea alba,* irrigation & reservoir systems.

1982, Aug. 9

No.	Type	Value	Description	Unused	Used
2532	A685	5c	multi	.40	.25
2533	A685	20c	multi	1.00	.25

Souvenir Sheet

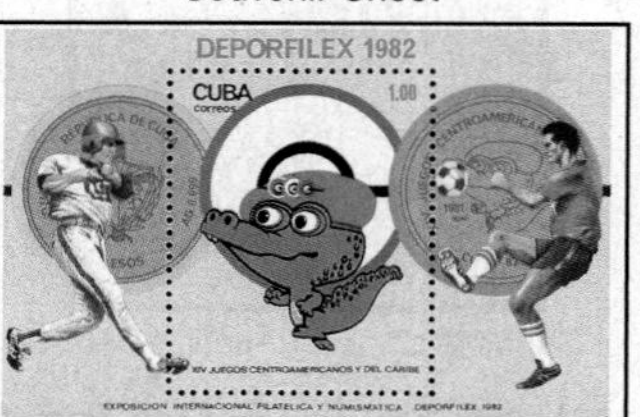

DEPORFILEX '82, Intl. Stamp and Coin Exhibition — A686

1p, Cuco, character trademark.

1982, Aug. 10 **Litho.**

No.	Type	Value	Description	Unused	Used
2534	A686	1p	multi	4.75	2.25

14th Central American and Caribbean Games.

Namibia Day — A687

1982, Aug. 26

2535 A687 50c multi 1.75 .75

1982 World Cup Soccer Championships, Spain — A688

Various athletes.

1982, Aug. 30

2536 A688 5c multi .25 .25
2537 A688 20c multi .75 .30
2538 A688 30c multi 1.10 .40
2539 A688 50c multi 1.90 .80
Nos. 2536-2539 (4) 4.00 1.75

Also exist in miniature sheets of 16 + 9 labels containing 4 each Nos. 2536-2539 in blocks of 4. Value $30.

Natl. Folklore Ensemble, 20th Anniv. — A689

Paintings by V.P. Landaluze.

1982, Sept. 10

2540 A689 20c *Little Devil*, vert. .90 .25
2541 A689 30c *Day of Kings* 1.10 .45

Prehistoric Fauna — A690

Designs: 1c, Ornimegalonyx oteroi, vert. 5c, Crocodylus rhombifer. 7c, Aquila borrasi, vert. 20c, Geocapromys colombianus. 35c, Megalocnus rodens, vert. 50c, Nesophontes micrus.

1982, Sept. 15 **Litho.**

2542 A690 1c multicolored .65 .25
2543 A690 5c multicolored .25 .25
2544 A690 7c multicolored 2.50 .40
2545 A690 20c multicolored .65 .25
2546 A690 35c multicolored 1.00 .50
2547 A690 50c multicolored 1.40 .75
Nos. 2542-2547 (6) 6.45 2.40

15th Death Anniv. of Che Guevara — A691

1982, Oct. 8 ***Perf. 13x12½***

2548 A691 20c multi 1.25 .40

Discovery of America, 490th Anniv. — A692

1982, Oct. 12 ***Perf. 13***

2549 A692 5c shown 1.10 .25
2550 A692 20c *Santa Maria*, vert. 1.25 .40
2551 A692 35c *Pinta*, vert. 1.90 .90
2552 A692 50c *Nina*, vert. 2.40 1.10
Nos. 2549-2552 (4) 6.65 2.65

Lighthouse Type of 1980

5c, Jutias Caye. 20c, Paredon Grande Caye. 30c, Morro Santiago de Cuba.

1982, Oct. 25

2553 A637 5c multicolored 1.00 .25
2554 A637 20c multicolored 2.75 .25
2555 A637 30c multicolored 3.75 .45
Nos. 2553-2555 (3) 7.50 .95

George Washington, 250th Birth Anniv. — A693

Designs: Quotations and anonymous oil paintings, 18th-19th cent.

1982, Oct. 29 ***Perf. 12x12½***

2556 A693 5c multi .25 .25
2557 A693 20c multi, diff. .75 .25

Souvenir Sheet

8th Natl. Philatelic Exposition, Ciego de Avila — A694

1p, Paddle steamer *Almendares.*

1982, Nov. 13

2558 A694 1p multi 5.00 2.50

8th Congress of the Cuban Philatelic Federation, Nov. 13-22.

Lenin Park, 10th Anniv. A695

1982, Dec. 28

2559 A695 5c multi *16.00 16.00*

Chess Champion Jose Raul Capablanca and King — A696

1982, Dec. 29

2560 A696 5c shown .25 .25
2561 A696 20c Rook 1.10 .25
2562 A696 30c Knight 1.40 .50
2563 A696 50c Queen 2.25 .80
a. Bklt. pane of 4, Nos. 2560-2563 25.00 25.00
Nos. 2560-2563 (4) 5.00 1.80

Exist in sheets of 4+2 labels picturing chessmen.

USSR, 60th Anniv. — A697

1982, Dec. 30 ***Perf. 13x12½***

2564 A697 30c multi 1.25 .25

World Communications Year — A698

1983, Jan. 24 **Litho.** ***Perf. 13***

2565 A698 20c multi .75 .25

No. 507 and Birthplace — A699

1983, Jan. 28 ***Perf. 13x12½***

2566 A699 5c multi .30 .25

Jose Marti (b. 1853), writer, revolution leader.

1984 Summer Olympics, Los Angeles A700

1983, Jan. 31 ***Perf. 13***

2567 A700 1c Javelin .25 .25
2568 A700 5c Volleyball .25 .25
2569 A700 6c Basketball .25 .25
2570 A700 20c Weight lifting .80 .25
2571 A700 30c Wrestling 1.10 .40
2572 A700 50c Boxing 1.75 .60
a. Block of 6, #2567-2572 17.50 17.50
With tabs 23.00 23.00
Nos. 2567-2572 (6) 4.40 2.00

Souvenir Sheet

Perf. 13½x13

2573 A700 1p Judo 5.25 4.50

No. 2573 contains one 32x40mm stamp.

Radio Rebelde, 25th Anniv. — A701

1983, Feb. 24 ***Perf. 13***

2574 A701 20c multi .70 .25

Karl Marx, Death Cent. A702

1983, Mar. 14

2575 A702 30c multi 1.00 .40

1st Manned Balloon Flight, Bicent. — A703

Various balloons.

1983, Mar. 30

2576 A703 1c multi .25 .25
2577 A703 3c multi .25 .25
2578 A703 5c multi .25 .25
2579 A703 7c multi .35 .25
2580 A703 30c multi 2.10 .70
2581 A703 50c multi 2.10 .70
a. Strip of 6 10.00 10.00
With tabs 14.00 14.00
Nos. 2576-2581 (6) 5.30 2.40

Souvenir Sheet

2582 A703 1p Jose D. Blino 4.50 2.00

No. 2582 contains one 32x40mm stamp.

Cosmonauts' Day — A704

1c, *Vostok 1.* 4c, Satellite *Frances D1.* 5c, *Mars 2.* 20c, *Soyuz.* 30c, Meteorological satellite. 50c, Intercosmos satellite.

1983, Apr. 12 **Litho.**

2583	A704	1c	multicolored	.25	.25
2584	A704	4c	multicolored	.25	.25
2585	A704	5c	multicolored	.25	.25
2586	A704	20c	multicolored	.75	.25
2587	A704	30c	multicolored	1.10	.50
2588	A704	50c	multicolored	1.75	.70
			Nos. 2583-2588 (6)	4.35	2.20

Stamp Day A705

20c, Havana-Key West cover. 30c, Spain-Havana cover.

1983, Apr. 24

2589	A705	20c	multicolored	.75	.30
2590	A705	30c	multicolored	1.25	.30

1st Intl. airmail services.

Souvenir Sheet

TEMBAL '83, Basel — A706

1983, May 21 ***Perf. 13½x13***

2591	A706	1p	Weasel	5.25	4.50

Simon Bolivar, Liberator of South America A707

5c, Jose Rafael de las Heras. 20c, Bolivar.

1983, July 24 ***Perf. 12½x13***

2592	A707	5c	multicolored	.25	.25
2593	A707	20c	multicolored	.60	.25

Attack of Moncada Barracks, 30th Anniv. — A708

Designs: 5c, Jose Marti, Moncada barracks. 20c, Abel Santamaria, Jose Luis Tasende and Boris Luis Santa Coloma, martyrs, vert. 30c, *History Will Absolve Me,* declaration of Fidel Castro, vert.

1983, July 26 ***Perf. 13***

2594	A708	5c	multi	.25	.25
2595	A708	20c	multi	.65	.25
2596	A708	30c	multi	.85	.50
			Nos. 2594-2596 (3)	1.75	1.00

Souvenir Sheet

Alberto Santos-Dumont (1873-1932) — A709

1983, July 29 ***Perf. 13x13½***

2597	A709	1p	Dumont's aircraft	5.25	4.50

BRASILIANA '83, Rio; 140th anniv. of 1st stamp issued in the Americas.

9th Pan American Games, Caracas — A710

1983, Aug. 14 ***Perf. 13x12½***

2598	A710	1c	Weight lifting	.25	.25
2599	A710	2c	Volleyball	.25	.25
2600	A710	3c	Baseball	.25	.25
2601	A710	20c	High jump	.75	.25
2602	A710	30c	Basketball	1.00	.50
2603	A710	50c	Boxing	1.75	.70
			Nos. 2598-2603 (6)	4.25	2.20

Port, by Claude Joseph Vernet — A711

1983, Sept. 5

2604	A711	30c	multi	1.50	.55

French alliance, cent.

Pres. Salvador Allende of Chile (d. 1973) — A712

1983, Sept. 12

2605	A712	20c	multi	.70	.25

1st Congress of Farmers at Arms, 25th Anniv. — A713

1983, Sept. 21 ***Perf. 12½x12***

2606	A713	5c	multi	.25	.25

Raphael, 500th Birth Anniv. — A714

1c, *Girl with Veil.* 2c, *The Cardinal.* 5c, *Francesco M. Della Rovere.* 20c, *Portrait of a Youth.* 30c, *Magdalena Doni.* 50c, *La Fornarina.*

1983, Sept. 30 **Litho.** ***Perf. 13***

2607	A714	1c	multi	.25	.25
2608	A714	2c	multi	.25	.25
2609	A714	5c	multi	.25	.25
2610	A714	20c	multi	.75	.25
2611	A714	30c	multi	1.10	.40
2612	A714	50c	multi	1.75	.65
			Nos. 2607-2612 (6)	4.35	2.05

State Quality Seal A715

1983, Oct. 14

2613	A715	5c	multi	.60	.25

Lighthouse Type of 1980

1983, Oct. 20

2614	A637	5c	Carapachibey	.25	.25
2615	A637	20c	Cadiz Bay	.80	.30
2616	A637	30c	Gobernadora Point	2.00	.80
			Nos. 2614-2616 (3)	3.05	1.35

Turtles A716

Designs: 1c, Eretmochelys imbricata. 2c, Lepidochelys kempi. 5c, Chrysemys decussata. 20c, Caretta caretta. 30c, Chelonia mydas. 50c, Dermochelys coriacea.

1983, Nov. 15

2617	A716	1c	multicolored	.25	.25
2618	A716	2c	multicolored	.25	.25
2619	A716	5c	multicolored	.25	.25
2620	A716	20c	multicolored	.80	.25
2621	A716	30c	multicolored	1.40	.25
2622	A716	50c	multicolored	2.75	.75
			Nos. 2617-2622 (6)	5.70	2.00

World Communications Year — A717

1c, Bell's Gallow Frame, telephone. 5c, Telegram, airmail. 10c, Satellite, satellite dish. 20c, Television, radio. 30c, 24th Communications conference.

1983, Nov. 23

2623	A717	1c	multicolored	.25	.25
2624	A717	5c	multicolored	.25	.25
2625	A717	10c	multicolored	.45	.25
2626	A717	20c	multicolored	.75	.25
2627	A717	30c	multicolored	1.10	.40
			Nos. 2623-2627 (5)	2.80	1.40

Nos. 319 and 990 A718

1983, Dec. 3 ***Perf. 13x12½***

2628	A718	20c	multi	.70	.25

See note after No. 320.

Flowers, Birds — A719

Designs: No. 2629, Opuntia dillenii. No. 2630, Euphorbia podocarpifolia. No. 2631, Dinema cubincola. No. 2632, Guaiacum officinale. No. 2633, Magnolia cubensis. No. 2634, Jatropha angustifolia. No. 2635, Cochlospermum vitifolium. No. 2636, Tabebuia lepidota. No. 2637, Kalmiella ericoides. No. 2638, Jatropha integerrima. No. 2639, Melocactus actinacanthus. No. 2640, Cordia sebestana. No. 2641, Tabernae - montana apoda. No. 2642, Lantana camara. No. 2643, Cordia gerascanthus. No. 2644, Tiaris canora. No. 2645, Phaethon lepturus. No. 2646, Myadestes elisabeth. No. 2647, Saurothera merlini. No. 2648, Polioptila lembeyei. No. 2649, Mellisuga helenae. No. 2650, Mimus polyglottos. No. 2651, Todus multicolor. No. 2652, Amazona leucocephala. No. 2653, Ferminia cerverai. No. 2654, Pelecanus occidentalis. No. 2655, Melanerpes superciliaris. No. 2656, Mimocichla plumbea. No. 2657, Aratinga euops. No. 2658, Sturnella magna.

No. 2658B, Hedychium coronarium. No. 2658C, Priotelus temnurus.

1983, Dec. 20 ***Perf. 13***

2629	A719	5c	multicolored	.55	.25
2630	A719	5c	multicolored	.55	.25
2631	A719	5c	multicolored	.55	.25
2632	A719	5c	multicolored	.55	.25
2633	A719	5c	multicolored	.55	.25
a.			Strip of 5, Nos. 2629-2633	4.50	4.50
2634	A719	5c	multicolored	.55	.25
2635	A719	5c	multicolored	.55	.25
2636	A719	5c	multicolored	.55	.25
2637	A719	5c	multicolored	.55	.25
2638	A719	5c	multicolored	.55	.25
2639	A719	5c	multicolored	.55	.25
2640	A719	5c	multicolored	.55	.25
2641	A719	5c	multicolored	.55	.25
2642	A719	5c	multicolored	.55	.25
2643	A719	5c	multicolored	.55	.25
a.			Block of 10, Nos. 2634-2643	9.00	9.00
2644	A719	5c	multicolored	.55	.25
2645	A719	5c	multicolored	.55	.25
2646	A719	5c	multicolored	.55	.25
2647	A719	5c	multicolored	.55	.25

No.	Type	Description	Unused	Used
2648	A719	5c multicolored	.55	.25
a.		Strip of 5, Nos. 2644-2648	4.50	4.50
2649	A719	5c multicolored	.55	.25
2650	A719	5c multicolored	.55	.25
2651	A719	5c multicolored	.55	.25
2652	A719	5c multicolored	.55	.25
2653	A719	5c multicolored	.55	.25
2654	A719	5c multicolored	.55	.25
2655	A719	5c multicolored	.55	.25
2656	A719	5c multicolored	.55	.25
2657	A719	5c multicolored	.55	.25
2658	A719	5c multicolored	.55	.25
a.		Block of 10, Nos. 2649-2658	9.00	9.00
		Nos. 2629-2658 (30)	16.50	7.50

Souvenir Sheets

No.	Type	Description	Unused	Used
2658B	A719	100c multicolored	5.25	4.50
2658C	A719	100c multicolored	5.25	4.50

Flowers — A720

1983, Dec. 30 ***Perf. 12½***

No.	Type	Description	Unused	Used
2659	A720	60c Tobacco	1.75	.55
2660	A720	70c Lily	2.25	.60
2661	A720	80c Mariposa	2.50	.70
2662	A720	90c Orchid	3.50	1.00
		Nos. 2659-2662 (4)	10.00	2.85

25th Anniv. of the Revolution — A721

20c, Flags, Santa Clara Railway tracks.

1983, Dec. 31 **Litho.** ***Perf. 13***

No.	Type	Description	Unused	Used
2663	A721	5c shown	.25	.25
2664	A721	20c multicolored	2.25	1.00

25th Anniv. of the Revolution — A722

No. 2665, Guevara, Castro. No. 2666, Star. No. 2667, PCC emblem, workers.

1984, Jan. 8

No.	Type	Description	Unused	Used
2665	A722	20c multi	.55	.25
2666	A722	20c multi	.55	.25
2667	A722	20c multi	1.35	.80
a.		Strip of 3, #2665-2667	2.60	1.50
		Nos. 2665-2667 (3)	2.45	1.30

Lenin, 60th Death Anniv. A723

30p, Spasski Tower, Russia Nos. 295, 265.

1984, Jan. 21 ***Perf. 12½x12***

No.	Type	Description	Unused	Used
2668	A723	30p multi	1.25	.25

Cuban Labor Union, 45th Anniv. A724

1984, Jan. 28 ***Perf. 13***

No.	Type	Description	Unused	Used
2669	A724	5c multi	.25	.25

Butterflies — A725

Designs: 1c, Ixias balice. 2c, Phoebis avellaneda. 3c, Anthocaris sara. 5c, Victorina. 20c, Heliconius cydno cydnides. 30c, Parides gundlachianus calzadillae. 50c, Catagramma sorana.

1984, Jan. 31 ***Perf. 13x12½***

No.	Type	Description	Unused	Used
2670	A725	1c multicolored	.25	.25
2671	A725	2c multicolored	.25	.25
2672	A725	3c multicolored	.25	.25
2673	A725	5c multicolored	.25	.25
2674	A725	20c multicolored	.80	.25
2675	A725	30c multicolored	1.40	.65
2676	A725	50c multicolored	2.40	.95
		Nos. 2670-2676 (7)	5.60	2.85

Marine Mammals — A726

Designs: 1c, Grampus griseus, vert. 2c, Delphinus delphis, vert. 5c, Physeter catodon. 6c, Stenella plagiodon, vert. 10c, Pseudorca crassidens. 30c, Tursiops truncatus, vert. 50, Megaptera novaeangliae.

1984, Feb. 15 ***Perf. 12x12½, 12½x12***

No.	Type	Description	Unused	Used
2677	A726	1c multicolored	.25	.25
2678	A726	2c multicolored	.25	.25
2679	A726	5c multicolored	.25	.25
2680	A726	6c multicolored	.25	.25
2681	A726	10c multicolored	.70	.25
2682	A726	30c multicolored	1.60	.40
2683	A726	50c multicolored	2.75	.70
		Nos. 2677-2683 (7)	6.05	2.35

Augusto C. Sandino (1893-1934), Nicaraguan Revolutionary — A727

1984, Feb. 21 ***Perf. 13***

No.	Type	Description	Unused	Used
2684	A727	20c multicolored	.70	.25

Red Cross in Cuba, 75th Anniv. — A728

1984, Mar. 10

No.	Type	Description	Unused	Used
2685	A728	30c Flag, No. 404	1.25	.35

Cuban Film Industry, 25th Anniv. A729

1984, Mar. 24

No.	Type	Description	Unused	Used
2686	A729	20c multi	.85	.30

Caribbean Flowers — A730

Designs: 1c, Brownea grandiceps. 2c, Couroupita guianensis. 5c, Triplaris surinamensis. 20c, Amherstia nobilis. 30c, Plumieria alba. 50c, Delonix regia.

1984, Mar. 29

No.	Type	Description	Unused	Used
2687	A730	1c multicolored	.25	.25
2688	A730	2c multicolored	.25	.25
2689	A730	5c multicolored	.25	.25
2690	A730	20c multicolored	.80	.30
2691	A730	30c multicolored	1.10	.50
2692	A730	50c multicolored	2.00	.90
		Nos. 2687-2692 (6)	4.65	2.45

Cosmonauts' Day — A731

2c, *Electron 1*, 1964. 3c, *Electron 2*, 1964. 5c, *Intercosmos 1*, 1969. 10c, *Mars 5*, 1974. 30c, *Soyuz*, 1969. 50c, USSR-Bulgaria space flight, 1979.
1p, *Luna 1*, 1959.

1984, Apr. 12

No.	Type	Description	Unused	Used
2693	A731	2c multi	.25	.25
2694	A731	3c multi	.25	.25
2695	A731	5c multi	.25	.25
2696	A731	10c multi	.30	.25
2697	A731	30c multi	.90	.50
2698	A731	50c multi	1.90	.90
		Nos. 2693-2698 (6)	3.85	2.40

Souvenir Sheet

Perf. 12½

No.	Type	Description	Unused	Used
2699	A731	1p multi	4.00	2.00

No. 2699 contains one 32x40mm stamp.

Mothers' Day — A732

1984, Apr. 19 ***Perf. 13***

No.	Type	Description	Unused	Used
2700	A732	20c Red roses	.85	.30
2701	A732	20c Pink roses	.85	.30

Stamp Day — A733

Designs: Mural, by R. Rodriguez Radillo (details): 20c, Mexican runner. 30c, Egyptian boatman.

1984, Apr. 24 ***Perf. 13x12½***

No.	Type	Description	Unused	Used
2702	A733	20c multicolored	.90	.30
2703	A733	30c multicolored	1.10	.50

See Nos. 2787-2788, 2860-2861, 3025-3026, 3122-3123, 3213-3214.

Souvenir Sheet

ESPANA '84, Madrid — A734

1984, Apr. 27 ***Perf. 13x13½***

No.	Type	Description	Unused	Used
2704	A734	1p Clipper ship	5.00	4.00

Women's Basketball, 1984 Summer Olympics A735

1984, May 5 ***Perf. 13***

No.	Type	Description	Unused	Used
2705	A735	20c multi	1.25	.35

Agrarian Reform Act, 25th Anniv. — A736

1984, May 17 ***Perf. 13½x13***

No.	Type	Description	Unused	Used
2706	A736	5c multi	.40	.25

Banco Popular de Ahorro, 1st Anniv. — A737

1984, May 18 ***Perf. 13***

No.	Type	Description	Unused	Used
2707	A737	5c multi	.40	.25

Early Locomotives — A738

1984, June 11 ***Perf. 12½x12***

No.	Type	Description	Unused	Used
2708	A738	1c multi	.25	.25
2709	A738	4c multi, diff.	.25	.25
2710	A738	5c multi, diff.	.25	.25
2711	A738	10c multi, diff.	.50	.25
2712	A738	30c multi, diff.	1.50	.40
2713	A738	50c multi, diff.	2.25	.80
		Nos. 2708-2713 (6)	5.00	2.20

Souvenir Sheet

19th UPU Congress, HAMBURG '84 — A739

1984, June 19 ***Perf. 13x13½***
2714 A739 1p Nos. 73, 232 5.25 4.25

Intl. Olympic Committee, 90th Anniv. — A740

30c, Coubertin, torch-bearer.

1984, June 23 ***Perf. 13***
2715 A740 30c multi 1.40 .50

Children's Day A741

1984, July 15 ***Perf. 12½x13***
2716 A741 5c multi .25 .25

1984 Summer Olympics, Los Angeles A742

1984, July 28 ***Perf. 13***
2717 A742 1c Wrestling .25 .25
2718 A742 3c Discus .25 .25
2719 A742 5c Volleyball .25 .25
2720 A742 20c Boxing .80 .30
2721 A742 30c Basketball 1.10 .50
2722 A742 50c Weight lifting 2.00 .90
Nos. 2717-2722 (6) 4.65 2.45

Souvenir Sheet

Perf. 12½

2723 A742 1p Baseball 5.00 4.00

No. 2723 contains one 32x40mm stamp.

Emilio Roig de Leuchsenring (1889-1964), Historian A743

1984, Aug. 8 ***Perf. 13***
2724 A743 5c multi .25 .25

Friendship Games, Aug. 18-26, Havana — A744

3c, Volleyball. 5c, Women's volleyball. 8c, Water polo. 30c, Boxing.

1984, Aug. 18
2725 A744 3c multicolored .25 .25
2726 A744 5c multicolored .35 .25
2727 A744 8c multicolored .35 .25
2728 A744 30c multicolored 1.00 .35
Nos. 2725-2728 (4) 1.95 1.10

Cattle Breeding A745

1984, Sept. 20
2729 A745 2c Artificial pastures .25 .25
2730 A745 3c Cuban carib .25 .25
2731 A745 5c Charolaise, vert. .25 .25
2732 A745 30c Cuban cebu, vert. 1.25 .40
2733 A745 50c White-udder 2.25 .75
Nos. 2729-2733 (5) 4.25 1.90

Souvenir Sheet

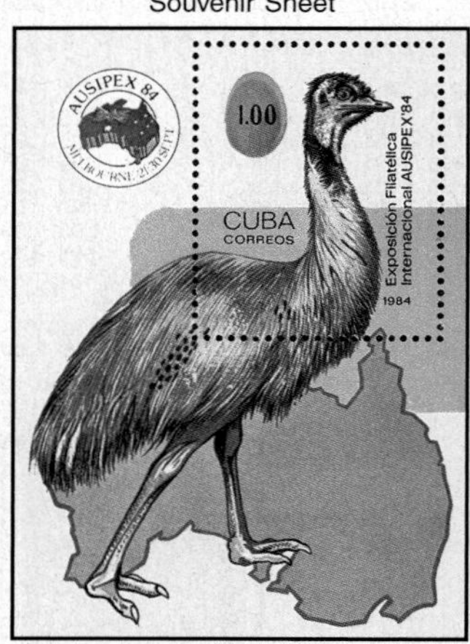

AUSIPEX '84, Sept. 21-30, Melbourne — A746

1984, Sept. 21 ***Perf. 12½***
2734 A746 1p Emu 5.25 5.00

Fauna — A747

Designs: 1c, Polymita. 2c, Solenodon cubanus. 3c, Alsophis cantherigerus. 4c, Osteopilus septentrionalis. 5c, Mellisuga helenae. 10c, Capromys melanurus. 30c, Todus multicolor. 50c, Parrots (cotorra).

1984, Oct. 10 ***Perf. 13***
2735 A747 1c multicolored .25 .25
2736 A747 2c multicolored .25 .25
2737 A747 3c multicolored .25 .25
2738 A747 4c multicolored .25 .25
2739 A747 5c multicolored .35 .25
2740 A747 10c multicolored .25 .25
2741 A747 30c multicolored 1.75 .95
2742 A747 50c multicolored 2.75 1.25
Nos. 2735-2742 (8) 6.10 3.70

ESPAMER '85, Havana — A748

Columbus Day: a, Ferdinand, Isabella. b, Departure from Palos. c, *Nina, Pinta, Santa Maria.* d, Landing in America.

1984, Oct. 12
2743 Sheet of 4 + 2 labels 5.00 2.50
a. A748 5c multicolored .25 .25
b. A748 20c multicolored 1.50 .70
c. A748 30c multicolored 2.25 1.10
d. A748 50c multicolored 1.00 .50

Souvenir Sheet

9th Natl. Phil. Exhibition, Oct. 20-28, Santiago de Cuba — A749

1984, Oct. 20 ***Perf. 12½***
2744 A749 1p multicolored 5.25 4.00

Natl. Revolutionary Militia, 25th Anniv. — A750

1984, Oct. 26 ***Perf. 12½x13***
2745 A750 5c multi .30 .25

Disappearance of Camilo Cienfuegos, 25th Anniv. — A751

1984, Oct. 28 ***Perf. 13x12½***
2746 A751 5c multi .40 .25

UN Child Survival Campaign A752

1984, Nov. 11 ***Perf. 13***
2747 A752 5c Breast-feeding .45 .25

Classic Automobiles — A753

1c, 1909 Morgan. 2c, 1922 Austin. 5c, 1903 De Dion-Bouton. 20c, 1908 Ford Model T. 30c, 1885 Benz. 50c, 1910 Benz.

1984, Nov. 25
2748 A753 1c multi .25 .25
2749 A753 2c multi .25 .25
2750 A753 5c multi .25 .25
2751 A753 20c multi .90 .25
2752 A753 30c multi 1.40 .35
2753 A753 50c multi 2.50 .70
Nos. 2748-2753 (6) 5.55 2.05

Postal Museum, 20th Anniv. — A754

1985, Jan. 2 ***Perf. 13x12½***
2754 A754 20c multi .75 .25

Portrait of Celia Sanchez, by E. Escobedo A755

1985, Jan. 11 ***Perf. 13***
2755 A755 5c multi .40 .25

Celia Sanchez (1920-1980), party leader.

PORTO '85, Intl. Pigeon Exhibition — A756

1985, Jan. 23
2756 A756 20c multi .85 .25

1986 World Cup Soccer Championships, Mexico — A757

Athletes and Flags of previous host nations: 1c, Chile, 1962. 2c, Great Britain, 1966. 3c, Mexico, 1970. 4c, Federal Republic of Germany, 1974. 5c, Argentina, 1978. 30c, Spain, 1982. 50c, Sweden, 1958.

1p, Mexico, 1986.

1985, Jan. 25
2757 A757 1c multi .25 .25
2758 A757 2c multi .25 .25
2759 A757 3c multi .25 .25
2760 A757 4c multi .25 .25
2761 A757 5c multi .25 .25

2762 A757 30c multi 1.40 .50
2763 A757 50c multi 2.10 .65
Nos. 2757-2763 (7) 4.75 2.40

Souvenir Sheet

Perf. 12½

2764 A757 1p multi 4.25 3.75

No. 2764 contains one 40x32mm stamp.

Baconao Natl. Park — A758

Dinosaurs.

1985, Feb. 14 ***Perf. 13x12½***

2765 A758 1c Pteranodon .30 .25
2766 A758 2c Brontosaurus .30 .25
2767 A758 4c Iguanodontus .30 .25
2768 A758 5c Estegosaurus .30 .25
2769 A758 8c Monoclonius .50 .25
2770 A758 30c Corythosaurus 1.50 .50
2771 A758 50c Tyrannosaurus 2.75 .70
Nos. 2765-2771 (7) 5.95 2.45

13th Congress of the Postal Unions of the Americas, Havana — A759

Design: Uruguay #196, congress emblem and Argentina #287.

1985, Mar. 11 ***Perf. 12½x12***

2772 A759 20c multi 2.00 .70

ESPAMER '85 — A760

Indian activities: 1c, Playing ball. 2c, Medicine man preparing calumet and other ritual items. 5c, Net and spear fishing. 20c, Potter. 30c, Hunting. 50c, Hollowing-out canoe, decorating paddle. 1p, Cooking.

1985, Mar. 19 ***Perf. 12½x13***

2773 A760 1c multi .25 .25
2774 A760 2c multi .25 .25
2775 A760 5c multi .40 .25
2776 A760 20c multi .40 .25
2777 A760 30c multi .65 .40
2778 A760 50c multi 2.75 .80
Nos. 2773-2778 (6) 4.70 2.20

Souvenir Sheet

Perf. 12½

2779 A760 1p multi 5.25 5.00

No. 2779 contains one 32x40mm stamp.
An imperf. souvenir sheet exists containing Nos. 2773-2779. Value $40.

Cosmonauts' Day — A761

Designs: 2c, Spacecraft orbiting Moon. 3c, Two spacecraft. 10c, Space walkers linked. 13c, Space walkers welding. 20c, *Vostok 2.* 50c, *Lunokhod 1* moon vehicle.

1985, Apr. 12 ***Perf. 13x12½***

2780 A761 2c multi .25 .25
2781 A761 3c multi .25 .25
2782 A761 10c multi .45 .25
2783 A761 13c multi .60 .25
2784 A761 20c multi .70 .25
2785 A761 50c multi 2.25 .70
Nos. 2780-2785 (6) 4.50 1.95

12th Youth and Students Festival, Moscow A762

1985, Apr. 19 ***Perf. 13***

2786 A762 30c Lenin Mausoleum 1.00 .50

Stamp Day Type of 1984

Mural, by R. Rodriguez Radillo (1967), details: 20c, Roman charioteer (courier of *Cursus Publicus*). 35c, Medieval nobleman, monks (monastic messenger mail).

1985, Apr. 24 ***Perf. 13x12½***

2787 A733 20c multi .80 .25
2788 A733 35c multi 1.10 .40

Mothers' Day — A763

1985, May 2 ***Perf. 13***

2789 A763 1c Peonies .25 .25
2790 A763 4c Carnations .25 .25
2791 A763 5c Dahlias .25 .25
2792 A763 13c Roses .45 .25
2793 A763 20c Roses, diff. .75 .25
2794 A763 50c Tulips 2.00 .55
Nos. 2789-2794 (6) 3.95 1.80

50th Death Anniv. of Antonio Guiteras and Carlos Aponte, Revolutionaries — A764

1985, May 9 ***Perf. 12½x12***

2795 A764 5c multi .25 .25

End of WWII, 40th Anniv. A765

20c, Soviet memorial, Berlin-Treptow. 30c, Dove.

1985, May 10

2796 A765 5c shown .25 .25
2797 A765 20c multicolored .65 .30
2798 A765 30c multicolored 1.10 .55
Nos. 2796-2798 (3) 2.00 1.10

Souvenir Sheet

ARGENTINA '85, Buenos Aires — A766

1985, June 5 ***Perf. 13½x13***

2799 A766 1p *Vulture gryphus* 5.25 5.00

Motorcycle, Cent. — A767

2c, 1885 Daimler. 5c, 1910 Kaiser Tricycle. 10c, 1925 Fanomobile. 30c, 1926 Mars A20. 50c, 1936 Simson BSW.

1985, June 28 ***Perf. 13***

2800 A767 2c multi .25 .25
2801 A767 5c multi .25 .25
2802 A767 10c multi .50 .25
2803 A767 30c multi 1.25 .30
2804 A767 50c multi 2.25 .70
Nos. 2800-2804 (5) 4.50 1.75

Development of Health Care Since the Revolution — A768

1985, July 18 ***Perf. 12½x12***

2805 A768 5c Hospitals .25 .25

Federation of Cuban Women (FMC), 25th Anniv. — A769

1985, Aug. 23

2806 A769 5c multi .25 .25

No. 2806 printed se-tenant with label picturing federation emblem.

Universiade Games, Japan — A770

1985, Aug. 27 ***Perf. 13***

2807 A770 50c multi 1.75 .55

1st Havana Declaration, 25th Anniv. — A771

5c, Jose Marti statue, revolutionaries.

1985, Sept. 2

2808 A771 5c multicolored .50 .25

Souvenir Sheet

ITALIA '85 — A772

1985, Sept. 25 ***Perf. 12½***

2809 A772 1p Roman galley 5.25 4.25

Revolutionary Defense Committees (CDR), 25th Anniv. — A773

1985, Sept. 28 ***Perf. 13***

2810 A773 5c multicolored .25 .25

Aquarium Fish — A774

Designs: 1c, Centropyge argi. 3c, Holacanthus tricolor. 5c, Chaetodon capistratus. 10c, Chaetodon sedentarius. 20c, Chaetodon ocellatus. 50c, Holacanthus ciliaris.

1985, Sept. 30 **Litho.**

2811 A774 1c multicolored .25 .25
2812 A774 3c multicolored .25 .25
2813 A774 5c multicolored .25 .25
2814 A774 10c multicolored .35 .25
2815 A774 20c multicolored .80 .50
2816 A774 50c multicolored 2.10 1.60
Nos. 2811-2816 (6) 4.00 3.10

Communist Party Central Committee, 20th Anniv. — A775

1985, Oct. 1

2817 A775 5c multicolored .40 .25

Souvenir Sheet

EXFILNA '85 — A776

1p, Spain No. C45, Cuba No. 387.

1985, Oct. 18
2818 A776 1p multicolored 5.25 4.25

UN, 40th Anniv. — A777

1985, Oct. 24
2819 A777 20c multicolored .65 .25

Sites on the UNESCO World Heritage List — A778

Designs: 2c, Plaza Vieja, 16th cent. 5c, Royal Army Castle, c. 1558. 20c, Havana Cathedral, c. 1748. 30c, Captains-General Palace (Havana City Museum), 1776. 50c, The Temple, 1827.

1985, Nov. 25

2820	A778	2c multi	.25	.25
2821	A778	5c multi	.25	.25
2822	A778	20c multi	.70	.25
2823	A778	30c multi	1.10	.45
2824	A778	50c multi	1.90	.60
		Nos. 2820-2824 (5)	4.20	1.80

1986 World Cup Soccer Championships, Mexico — A779

Various athletes.

1986, Jan. 20

2825	A779	1c multi	.25	.25
2826	A779	4c multi	.25	.25
2827	A779	5c multi	.25	.25
2828	A779	10c multi	.30	.25
2829	A779	30c multi	1.00	.30
2830	A779	50c multi	1.50	.55
		Nos. 2825-2830 (6)	3.55	1.85

Souvenir Sheet
Perf. 13½x13

2831 A779 1p multi 4.50 4.25

No. 2831 contains one 32x40mm stamp. No. 2831 exists imperf. Value $125.

3rd Communist Party Congress, Havana — A780

20c, Party and natl. flags, emblem.

1986, Feb. 4 ***Perf. 13***
2832 A780 5c shown .25 .25
2833 A780 20c multicolored 1.25 .25

Natl. Sports Institute (INDER), 25th Anniv. A781

1986, Feb. 23
2834 A781 5c multicolored .30 .25

A782

1986, Feb. 23
2835 A782 5c multicolored .30 .25

Ministry of Domestic Trade, 25th anniv.

A783

Exotic flowers in the Botanical Gardens: 1c, Tecomaria capensis. 3c, Michelia champaca. 5c, Thunbergia grandiflora. 8c, Dendrobium phalaenopsis. 30c, Allamanda violacea. 50c, Rhodactus bleo.

1986, Feb. 25 ***Perf. 12½x12***

2836	A783	1c multicolored	.25	.25
2837	A783	3c multicolored	.25	.25
2838	A783	5c multicolored	.25	.25
2839	A783	8c multicolored	.30	.25
2840	A783	30c multicolored	1.00	.25
2841	A783	50c multicolored	1.60	.40
		Nos. 2836-2841 (6)	3.65	1.65

Gundlach and Birds — A784

Designs: 1c, Agelaius assimilis. 3c, Dendroica pityophila. 7c, Myiarchus sagrae. 9c, Dendroica petechia gundlachi. 30c, Geotrygon caniceps. 50c, Colaptes auratus chrysocaulosus.

1986, Mar. 14 **Litho.** ***Perf. 13½x13***

2842	A784	1c multicolored	.25	.25
2843	A784	3c multicolored	.25	.25
2844	A784	7c multicolored	.30	.25
2845	A784	9c multicolored	.50	.30
2846	A784	30c multicolored	2.00	1.00
2847	A784	50c multicolored	3.25	1.60
		Nos. 2842-2847 (6)	6.55	3.65

Juan Cristobal Gundlach (d. 1896), ornithologist.

Pioneers Youth Organization, 25th Anniv. — A785

1986, Apr. 3 ***Perf. 13***
2848 A785 5c Induction .30 .25

150th Birth Anniv. of Maximo Gomez — A786

1986, Apr. 4
2849 A786 20c multicolored .70 .25

A787

1986, Apr. 10 ***Perf. 12½***
2850 A787 5c multicolored .40 .25

Kindergartens, 25th anniv.

A788

1st Man in Space, 25th Anniv.: 1c, *Vostok* and rocket designer Sergei Korolev. 2c, Yuri Gagarin, *Vostok 1.* 5c, Valentina Tereshkova, *Vostok 6.* 20c, *Salyut-Soyuz* space link. 30c, Capsule landing. 50c, *Soyuz* rocket launch. 1p, Konstantin Tsiolkovski (1857-1935), rocket scientist.

1986, Apr. 12 ***Perf. 13x13½***

2851	A788	1c multi	.25	.25
2852	A788	2c multi	.25	.25
2853	A788	5c multi	.25	.25
2854	A788	20c multi	.60	.25
2855	A788	30c multi	.75	.25
2856	A788	50c multi	1.50	.55
		Nos. 2851-2856 (6)	3.60	1.80

Souvenir Sheet
Perf. 12½

2857 A788 1p multi 4.50 4.00

No. 2857 contains one 32x40mm stamp.

Natl. Flag and No. 2407 A789

20c, Banners, natl. crest.

1986, Apr. 19 ***Perf. 13***
2858 A789 5c shown .25 .25
2859 A789 20c multicolored .75 .25

Bay of Pigs invasion, 25th anniv. (5c); Proclamation of Socialist Revolution, 25th anniv. (20c).

Stamp Day Type of 1984

Mural, by R. Rodriguez Radillo (1967), details: 20c, Mail coach, 18th-19th cent. 30c, Pony Express.

1986, Apr. 24 ***Perf. 13x12½***
2860 A733 20c multi .75 .25
2861 A733 30c multi 1.00 .25

Radio Havana, 25th Anniv. — A790

1986, May 1
2862 A790 5c multicolored .40 .25

EXPO '86, Vancouver — A791

Locomotives: 1c, *Stourbridge Lion,* 1829, US. 4c, Stephenson's *Rocket,* 1829, GB. 5c, 1st Russian locomotive, 1845. 8c, Seguin's locomotive, 1830, France. 30c, 1st Canadian locomotive, 1836. 50c, Urban locomotive, Belgian Grand Central Rlwy., 1872. 1p, US locomotive pulling Cuban sugar train, 1837.

1986, May 2 **Litho.** ***Perf. 12½x12***

2863	A791	1c multi	.25	.25
2864	A791	4c multi	.25	.25
2865	A791	5c multi	.25	.25
2866	A791	8c multi	.25	.25
2867	A791	30c multi	.80	.30
2868	A791	50c multi	2.10	.55
		Nos. 2863-2868 (6)	3.90	1.85

Souvenir Sheet
Perf. 13x13½

2869 A791 1p multi 5.25 5.00

No. 2869 contains one 40x32mm stamp.

Assoc. of Small Farmers, (ANAP), 25th Anniv. — A792

1986, May 17 ***Perf. 13***
2870 A792 5c multicolored .40 .25

Intl. Peace Year A793

1986, June 2
2871 A793 30c multicolored 1.00 .25

Ministry of the Interior (MININT), 25th Anniv. — A794

1986, June 6

2872 A794 5c multicolored .40 .25

Martin Luther King, Jr. A795

1986, June 27 ***Perf. 13½x13***

2873 A795 20c multicolored .90 .25

Bonifacio Byrne (d. 1936), Poet A796

1986, July 5 ***Perf. 13***

2874 A796 5c multicolored .30 .25

Cuban Union of Writers and Artists (UNEAC), 25th Anniv. — A797

1986, July 10 ***Perf. 13x12½***

2875 A797 5c multi .45 .25

Sandinista Movement in Nicaragua (FSLN), 25th Anniv. — A798

Augusto Cesar Sandino and Carlos Fonseca.

1986, July 23 ***Perf. 13x12***

2876 A798 20c multi .65 .25

Ministry of Transportation, 25th Anniv. — A799

1986, Aug. 1 ***Perf. 13***

2877 A799 5c multicolored .40 .25

7th University Games of Central America and the Caribbean A800

1986, Aug. 9

2878 A800 20c multicolored .80 .25

Souvenir Sheet

STOCKHOLMIA '86 — A801

Designs: a, 2c Mambi Revolutionary stamp of 1897. b, Sweden Type A7, cancellation.

1986, Aug. 28 ***Perf. 12½***

2879 A801 Sheet of 2 4.50 3.75
a.-b. 50c multi

Nonaligned Countries Movement, 25th Anniv. — A802

1986, Sept. 1 ***Perf. 13½x13***

2880 A802 50c multi 1.75 .45

Orchids — A803

Designs: 1c, Cattleya hardyana. 4c, Brassolaelio cattleya. 5c, Phalaenopsis marget moses. 10c, Laelio cattleya prism palette. 30c, Phalaenopsis violacea. 50c, Disa uniflora.

1986, Sept. 15 ***Perf. 12½***

2881	A803	1c multicolored	.25	.25
2882	A803	4c multicolored	.25	.25
2883	A803	5c multicolored	.25	.25
2884	A803	10c multicolored	.30	.25
2885	A803	30c multicolored	1.25	.30
2886	A803	50c multicolored	1.75	.50
		Nos. 2881-2886 (6)	4.05	1.80

Latin American History — A804

Pre-Columbian artifacts: No. 2887, Mayan dwelling and votive jade sculpture. No. 2888, Inca vase and Tiahuanacu sun gate (Bolivia). No. 2889, Spain No. C47, discovery of America 500th anniv. emblem, scroll. No. 2890, Diaguitan duck-shaped pitcher and Pucara de Quitor ruins (Chile). No. 2891, San Agustin Archaeological Park megaliths and Quimbayan sculpture (Colombia). No. 2892, Moler grinding stone and Chorotega ceramic figurine. No. 2893, Tabaco idol and Indian dwelling (Cuba). No. 2894, Spain No. C38. No. 2895, Taino dwelling and chair (Dominica). No. 2896, Tolita statue and Ingapirca Castle ruins. No. 2897, Maya vase and Tikal Temple (Guatemala). No. 2898, Copan ruins and Maya idol. No. 2899, Spain No. C37. No. 2900, Chichen Itza Temple and Zapotecan urn (Mexico). No. 2901, Punta de Zapote megaliths and Ometepe ceramic figurine. No. 2902, Tonosi lidded ceramic bowl and Barriles monoliths. No. 2903, Ruins at Machu-Picchu and Inca statue (Peru). No. 2904, Spain No. C49. No. 2905, Teepees and triangular sculpture (Puerto Rico). No. 2906, Fertility statue from Santa Ana and Santo Domingo Cave.

1986, Oct. 12 ***Perf. 13***

2887	A804	1c multi	.25	.25
2888	A804	1c multi	.25	.25
2889	A804	1c multi	.25	.25
2890	A804	1c multi	.25	.25
2891	A804	1c multi	.25	.25
a.		Strip of 5, Nos. 2887-2891	3.50	3.50
2892	A804	5c multi	.25	.25
2893	A804	5c multi	.25	.25
2894	A804	5c multi	.25	.25
2895	A804	5c multi	.25	.25
2896	A804	5c multi	.25	.25
a.		Strip of 5, Nos. 2892-2896	3.50	3.50
2897	A804	10c multi	.25	.25
2898	A804	10c multi	.25	.25
2899	A804	10c multi	.25	.25
2900	A804	10c multi	.25	.25
2901	A804	10c multi	.25	.25
a.		Strip of 5, Nos. 2897-2901	4.00	4.00
2902	A804	20c multi	.65	.30
2903	A804	20c multi	.65	.30
2904	A804	20c multi	.65	.30
2905	A804	20c multi	.65	.30
2906	A804	20c multi	.65	.30
a.		Strip of 5, Nos. 2902-2906	9.75	9.75
		Nos. 2887-2906 (20)	7.00	5.25

Discovery of America, 500th anniv. (in 1992). See Nos. 2966-2985, 3065-3084, 3253-3272, 3463-3466.

Intl. Brigades, Spain, 50th Anniv. — A805

1986, Oct. 14 ***Perf. 12½x12***

2907 A805 30c multicolored .85 .35

Paintings in the Natl. Museum A806

Designs: 2c, *Two Children,* by Gutierrez de la Vega, vert. 4c, *Sed,* by Jean-Georges Vibert. 6c, *Virgin and Child,* by Niccolo Abbate, vert. 10c, *Bullfight,* by Eugenio de Lucas Velazquez. 30c, *The Five Senses,* anonymous. 50c, *Arrival at Thomops Castle,* by Jean Louis Ernest.

1986, Nov. 5 ***Perf. 13***

2908	A806	2c multi	.25	.25
2909	A806	4c multi	.25	.25
2910	A806	6c multi	.25	.25
2911	A806	10c multi	.30	.25
2912	A806	30c multi	.60	.30
2913	A806	50c multi	1.25	.55
		Nos. 2908-2913 (6)	2.90	1.85

Anniversaries — A807

1986, Dec. 2 **Litho.** ***Perf. 12½***

2914 A807 5c *Granma* .40 .25

Size: 26x38mm

2915 A807 20c Soldier, rifle, flag 1.00 .25

Granma Landings, 30th anniv. (5c); Revolutionary Armed Forces, 30th anniv. (20c).

Scholarship Program, 25th Anniv. — A808

1986, Dec. 22 ***Perf. 13***

2916 A808 5c Guevara, students .30 .25

Natl. Literacy Campaign, 25th Anniv. — A809

5c, Marti, man learning to write.

1986, Dec. 25 ***Perf. 13x12½***

2917 A809 5c multicolored .40 .25

Siege of La Plata, 30th Anniv. A810

5c, Map, revolutionaries.

1987, Jan. 17 ***Perf. 12½x12***

2918 A810 5c multicolored .30 .25

Paintings in the Natl. Museum A811

3c, *Gypsy,* by Joaquin Sorolla. 5c, *Sir Walter Scott,* by Sir John W. Gordon. 10c, *Farm Meadows,* by Alfred de Breanski. 20c, *Still-life,* by Isaac van Duynen. 30c, *Landscape with Figures,* by Francesco Zuccarelli. 40c, *The Failure* (defeated bullfighter), by Ignacio Zuloaga.

1987, Feb. 5 ***Perf. 13***

2919	A811	3c multi, vert.	.25	.25
2920	A811	5c multi, vert.	.25	.25
2921	A811	10c multi	.30	.25
2922	A811	20c multi	.75	.25
2923	A811	30c multi	.80	.30
2924	A811	40c multi, vert.	1.25	.50
		Nos. 2919-2924 (6)	3.60	1.80

Siege of the Presidential Palace, 30th Anniv. — A812

5c, Palace, van, Echeverra.

1987, Mar. 13 ***Perf. 12½x12***

2925 A812 5c multicolored .30 .25

Lazarus Ludwig Zamenhof and Russia Type A77 — A813

1987, Mar. 16 ***Perf. 13½x13***
2926 A813 30c multicolored 3.50 .60

Esperanto, cent.

Souvenir Sheet

EXFILNA '87, 10th Natl. Stamp Exposition, Holguin — A814

1987, Mar. 28 ***Perf. 13x13½***
2927 A814 1p Nos. 552, C129 4.50 3.75

25th Anniv. and 5th Cong. of the Youth Communist League (U.J.C.) — A815

1987, Apr. 4 ***Perf. 13***
2928 A815 5c multicolored .75 .25

Intercosmos, 20th Anniv. — A816

3c, Intercosmos 1. 5c, Intercosmos 2. 10c, TD. 20c, Cosmos 93. 30c, Prognoz. 50c, Vostok 3.
1p, Rocket, Vostok 3.

1987, Apr. 12 **Litho.** ***Perf. 12½x12***

2929	A816	3c multicolored	.25	.25
2930	A816	5c multicolored	.25	.25
2931	A816	10c multicolored	.30	.25
2932	A816	20c multicolored	.65	.25
2933	A816	30c multicolored	1.00	.30
2934	A816	50c multicolored	1.50	.55
		Nos. 2929-2934 (6)	3.95	1.85

Souvenir Sheet
Perf. 13½x13

2935 A816 1p multi 4.50 2.25

No. 2935 contains one 32x40mm stamp.

Stamp Day A817

Stamped covers and canceled stamps: 30c, Havana, 1890. 50c, Santiago de Cuba, 1869.

1987, Apr. 24 ***Perf. 13***

2936	A817	30c multi	1.10	.30
2937	A817	50c multi	1.90	.60

Mothers' Day — A818

Various dahlias and roses.

1987, May 2

2938	A818	3c multi	.25	.25
2939	A818	5c multi	.25	.25
2940	A818	10c multi	.25	.25
2941	A818	13c multi	.30	.25
2942	A818	30c multi	.70	.25
2943	A818	50c multi	1.25	.50
		Nos. 2938-2943 (6)	3.00	1.75

Bone-lengthening Procedure (Femur in Frame) — A819

1987, May 4
2944 A819 5c multi .30 .25

ORTOPEDIA '87, medical congress for orthopedists from Spanish and Portuguese-speaking countries, Havana.

Cuban Broadcasting and Television Institute, 25th Anniv. — A820

1987, May 24 ***Perf. 13***
2945 A820 5c multi .30 .25

Battle of Uvero, 30th Anniv. A821

Views of monument, Sierra Maestra Mts.

1987, May 28 ***Perf. 13½x13***
2946 A821 5c multicolored .30 .25

CAPEX '87 — A822

Natl. flags, stamps and 19th cent. mail carriers pictured on cigarette cards: 3c, Messenger, llamas and Bolivia Type A9. 5c, Early p.o., automobile and France Type A17. 10c, Messengers riding elephants and Thailand Type A2. 20c, Messenger riding camel and stamp of Egypt, 1879. 30c, Mail troika and stamp of Russia. 50c, Post rider and stamp of Indo-China. 1p, Post rider and Mambi Revolutionary stamp.

1987, June 6 ***Perf. 12½x13***

2947	A822	3c multi	.25	.25
2948	A822	5c multi	.25	.25
2949	A822	10c multi	.25	.25
2950	A822	20c multi	.50	.25
2951	A822	30c multi	.70	.25
2952	A822	50c multi	1.25	.50
		Nos. 2947-2952 (6)	3.20	1.75

Souvenir Sheet
Perf. 13½x13

2953 A822 1p multi 4.50 2.25

No. 2953 contains one 32x40mm stamp.

Dinosaur Exhibits, Bacanao Natl. Park A823

1987, June 25 ***Perf. 13***

2954	A823	3c multi	.25	.25
2955	A823	5c multi	.25	.25
2956	A823	10c multi	.30	.25
2957	A823	20c multi	.80	.25
2958	A823	35c multi	1.00	.30
2959	A823	40c multi	1.10	.40
		Nos. 2954-2959 (6)	3.70	1.70

Frank Pais (d. 1957), Teacher and Student Leader — A824

5c, Pais, Rafael Maria Mendive University.

1987, July 30 ***Perf. 12½x12***
2960 A824 5c multicolored .30 .25

10th Pan American Games, Indianapolis — A825

1987, Aug. 8
2961 A825 50c multicolored 1.75 .45

Printed se-tenant with inscribed label picturing the 1991 Havana Games character trademark.

Siege of Cienfuegos, 30th Anniv. — A826

1987, Sept. 5 ***Perf. 13***
2962 A826 5c Memorial .30 .25

Souvenir Sheet

HAFNIA '87, Denmark — A827

1p, Danish mailman, 1887, Type A6.

1987, Sept. 16 ***Perf. 13½x13***
2963 A827 1p multi 4.50 3.50

Souvenir Sheet

ESPAMER '87, La Coruna, Oct. 2-12 — A828

1p, La Coruna Port, 1525.

1987, Oct. 2
2964 A828 1p multi 4.50 4.00

20th Heroic Guerrillas Day — A829

1987, Oct. 8 ***Perf. 12½x12***
2965 A829 50c Coins, #1364 1.25 .55

Latin American History Type of 1986

Indians and birds: No. 2966, Tehuelche Indian of Argentina, *Habia rubica.* No. 2967, *Ramphastos cuvieri,* Tibirica Indian of Brazil. No. 2968, Spain #C31 & discovery of America 500th anniv. emblem. No. 2969, *Vultur gryphus,* Lautaro Indian of Chile. No. 2970, Calarca Indian of Colombia, *Opisthocomus hoazin.* No. 2971, *Priotelus temnurus,* Hatuey Indian of Cuba. No. 2972, *Columbigallina passerina,* Enriquillo Indian of the Dominican Republic. No. 2973, Spain #427. #2974, *Semnornis ramphastinus,* Ruminahui Indian of Ecuador. No. 2975, *Pharomachrus mocinno,* Tecum Uman Indian of Guatemala. No. 2976, Anacaona Indian of Haiti, *Aramus guarauna.* No. 2977, Lempira Indian of Honduras, *Diglossa baritula.* #2978, Spain #C42. No. 2979, *Onychorhinchus mexicanus,* Cuauhtemoc Indian of Mexico. No. 2980, *Setofaga picta,* Nicarao Indian of Nicaragua. No. 2981, *Rupicola peruviana,* Atahualpa Indian of Peru. No. 2982, Atlacatl Indian of El Salvador, *Bluteo jamaicensis.* #2983, Spain #432. No. 2984, Abayuba Indian of Uruguay, *Phytotoma rutila.* No. 2985, Guaycaypuro Indian of Venezuela, *Ara arauna.*

1987, Oct. 12 ***Perf. 13***

2966	A804	1c multi	.25	.25
2967	A804	1c multi	.25	.25
2968	A804	1c multi	.25	.25
2969	A804	1c multi	.25	.25
2970	A804	1c multi	.25	.25
a.		Strip of 5, Nos. 2966-2970	1.00	1.00
2971	A804	5c multi	.25	.25
2972	A804	5c multi	.25	.25
2973	A804	5c multi	.25	.25
2974	A804	5c multi	.25	.25
2975	A804	5c multi	.25	.25
a.		Strip of 5, Nos. 2971-2975	1.25	1.25
2976	A804	10c multi	.35	.25
2977	A804	10c multi	.35	.25
2978	A804	10c multi	.35	.25
2979	A804	10c multi	.35	.25
2980	A804	10c multi	.35	.25
a.		Strip of 5, Nos. 2976-2980	1.90	1.90
2981	A804	20c multi	.50	.40
2982	A804	20c multi	.50	.40
2983	A804	20c multi	.50	.40
2984	A804	20c multi	.50	.40

2985 A804 20c multi .50 .40
a. Strip of 5, Nos. 2981-2985 2.75 2.75
Nos. 2966-2985 (20) 6.75 5.75

Discovery of America, 500th anniv. (in 1992).

October Revolution, Russia, 70th Anniv. — A830

30c, Soviet spacecraft, Russia No. 379.

1987, Nov. 7 ***Perf. 12½x12***
2986 A830 30c multi 1.00 .25

Cuban Railway, 150th Anniv. — A831

Stamps on stamps.

1987, Nov. 19 ***Perf. 13x12½***
2987 A831 3c No. 453 .25 .25
2988 A831 5c No. 1061 .25 .25
2989 A831 10c No. 2010 .25 .25
2990 A831 20c No. 2011 .45 .25
2991 A831 35c No. 2360 .85 .30
2992 A831 40c No. 2361 .90 .40
Nos. 2987-2992 (6) 2.95 1.70

Souvenir Sheet
Perf. 13x13½

2993 A831 1p No. 355 4.75 2.25

No. 2993 contains 40x32mm one stamp.
An imperf. sheet containing Nos. 2987-2992 exists, inscribed to promote the 17th Pan American Railway Congress. Value, $7.

San Alejandro Art School, 170th Anniv. — A832

Paintings: 1c, *Landscape,* by Domingo Ramos. 2c, *Portrait of Rodriguez Morey,* by Eugenio Gonzalez Olivera. 3c, *Landscape with Malangas and Palm Trees,* by Valentin Sanz Carta. 5c, *Wagons,* by Eduardo Morales. 10c, *Portrait of Elena Herrera,* by Armando Menocal, vert. 30c, *Rape of Dejanira,* by Miguel Melero, vert. 50c, *The Card Player,* by Leopoldo Romanach.

1988, Jan. 12 ***Perf. 13x12½, 12½x13***
2994 A832 1c multi .25 .25
2995 A832 2c multi .25 .25
2995A A832 3c multi .25 .25
2996 A832 5c multi .25 .25
2997 A832 10c multi .30 .25
2998 A832 30c multi .85 .25
2999 A832 50c multi 1.50 .50
Nos. 2994-2999 (7) 3.65 2.00

Poisonous Mushrooms A833

Designs: 1c, Boletus satanas. 2c, Amanita citrina. 3c, Tylopilus felleus. 5c, Paxillus involutus. 10c, Inocybe patouillardii. 30c, Amanita muscaria. 50c, Hypholoma fasciculare.

1988, Feb. 15 ***Perf. 13***
3000 A833 1c multicolored .25 .25
3001 A833 2c multicolored .25 .25
3002 A833 3c multicolored .25 .25
3003 A833 5c multicolored .25 .25
3004 A833 10c multicolored .55 .25
3005 A833 30c multicolored 1.50 .55
3006 A833 50c multicolored 2.40 1.00
Nos. 3000-3006 (7) 5.45 2.80

Radio Rebelde, 30th Anniv. — A834

1988, Feb. 24 ***Perf. 12½x12***
3007 A834 5c multi .30 .25

Monuments A835

No. 3008, Mario Munoz, Santiago de Cuba. No. 3009, Frank Pais Memorial, eternal flame.

1988 **Litho.** ***Perf. 13***
3008 A835 5c multi .45 .25
3009 A835 5c multi .45 .25

Battle fronts, 30th annivs. Issue dates: No. 3008, Mar. 5. No. 3009, Mar. 11.

Mothers' Day — A836

1988, Mar. 30
3010 A836 1c Red roses .25 .25
3011 A836 2c Pale pink peonies .25 .25
3012 A836 3c Daisies .25 .25
3013 A836 5c Dahlias .25 .25
3014 A836 13c White roses .30 .25
3015 A836 35c Carnations .90 .25
3016 A836 40c Pink roses 1.10 .30
Nos. 3010-3016 (7) 3.30 1.80

Cosmonauts' Day — A837

2c, Gorizont. 3c, Mir-Kvant space link. 4c, Signo 3. 5c, Mars, space probe. 10c, Phobos. 30c, Vega. 50c, Spacecraft.
1p, Spacecraft, diff.

1988, Apr. 12
3017 A837 2c multicolored .25 .25
3018 A837 3c multicolored .25 .25
3019 A837 4c multicolored .25 .25
3020 A837 5c multicolored .25 .25
3021 A837 10c multicolored .25 .25
3022 A837 30c multicolored .50 .25
3023 A837 50c multicolored 1.10 .50
Nos. 3017-3023 (7) 2.85 2.00

Souvenir Sheet
Perf. 13½x13

3024 A837 1p multicolored 4.50 2.00

No. 3024 contains one 32x40mm stamp.

Stamp Day Type of 1984

Mural, by R. Rodriguez Radillo (1967) details: 30c, Mail coach, telegraph operator. 50c, Passenger pigeon.

1988, Apr. 24 ***Perf. 13x12½***
3025 A733 30c multi 1.10 .40
3026 A733 50c multi 1.90 .50

Institute for Research on Sugar Cane and Byproducts (ICIDCA), 25th Anniv. — A838

1988, May 23 ***Perf. 12½x12***
3027 A838 5c multi .40 .25

Cubana Airlines Transatlantic Flights — A839

1988, May 25
3028 A839 2c Madrid, 1948 .25 .25
3029 A839 4c Prague, 1961 .25 .25
3030 A839 5c Berlin, 1972 .25 .25
3031 A839 10c Luanda, 1975 .25 .25
3032 A839 30c Paris, 1983 .90 .25
3033 A839 50c Moscow, 1987 1.60 .50
Nos. 3028-3033 (6) 3.50 1.75

Souvenir Sheet

FINLANDIA '88 — A840

1p, Steam packet Furst Menschikoff.

1988, June 1 ***Perf. 12½***
3034 A840 1p multicolored 4.50 2.00

Postal Union of the Americas and Spain (UPAE) Conference on Stamps of the Americas, Havana — A841

1988, June 20 ***Perf. 12½x12***
3035 A841 20c multi .75 .35

Beetles A842

Designs: 1c, Megasoma elephas fabricus. 3c, Platycoelia flavoscutellata ohaus, vert.. 4c, Plusiotis argenteola bates. 5c, Heterosternus oberthuri ohaus. 10c, Odontotaenius zodiacus truqui. 35c, Chrysophora chrysochlora latreille, vert.. 40c, Phanaeus leander waterhouse.

1988, June 30 ***Perf. 13***
3036 A842 1c multicolored .25 .25
3037 A842 3c multicolored .25 .25
3038 A842 4c multicolored .25 .25
3039 A842 5c multicolored .25 .25
3040 A842 10c multicolored .30 .25
3041 A842 35c multicolored 1.00 .30
3042 A842 40c multicolored 1.25 .50
Nos. 3036-3042 (7) 3.55 2.05

Jose Raul Capablanca (1888-1942), Chess Champion — A843

30c, Chessmen, vert. 40c, J. Corzo, Capablanca. 50c, Lasker, Capablanca. 1p, Winning configuration, 1921, vert. 3p, Portrait by E. Valderrama, vert. 5p, Chessmen, Capablanca.

1988, July 15 ***Perf. 12½x13, 13x12½***
3043 A843 30c multicolored .80 .35
3044 A843 40c multicolored 1.00 .35
3045 A843 50c multicolored 1.25 .45
3046 A843 1p multicolored 3.00 1.10
3047 A843 3p multicolored 8.50 3.00
3048 A843 5p multicolored 16.00 5.25
Nos. 3043-3048 (6) 30.55 10.50

Souvenir Sheets

3049 Sheet of 2 2.50 1.25
a. A843 30c No. 464, vert. 1.00 .60
b. like No. 3043, size: 32x40mm 1.00 .60
3050 Sheet of 2 3.00 1.50
a. A843 40c No. 465 1.25 .60
b. like No. 3044, size: 40x32mm 1.25 .60
3051 Sheet of 2 4.25 2.10
a. A843 50c No. C44 1.75 1.00
b. like No. 3045, size: 40x32mm 1.75 1.00
3052 Sheet of 2 7.75 4.00
a. A843 1p No. 464, vert. 3.25 1.75
b. like No. 3046, size: 32x40mm 3.25 1.75
3053 Sheet of 2 22.50 11.50
a. A843 3p No. C46, vert. 9.50 4.75
b. like No. 3047, size: 32x40mm 9.50 4.75
3054 Sheet of 2 40.00 20.00
a. A843 5p No. C45, vert. 18.00 9.00
b. like No. 3048, size: 32x40mm 18.00 9.00
Nos. 3049-3054 (6) 80.00 40.35

Attack on Moncada Barracks, 35th Anniv. A844

1988, July 26 ***Perf. 13***
3055 A844 5c blk, yel ocher & red .30 .25

Souvenir Sheet

PRAGA '88 — A845

1p, Czechoslovakia #45.

1988, Aug. 26 ***Perf. 12½***
3056 A845 1p multicolored 4.50 2.00

Czechoslovakian postage stamps, 70th anniv.

Revolutionary Invasion Force, 30th Anniv. — A846

1988, Aug. 31 *Perf. 12½x12*
3057 A846 5c multicolored .45 .25

World Marxist Review, 30th Anniv. A847

1988, Sept. 1 *Perf. 13*
3058 A847 30c multi 1.25 .35

Locomotives — A848

20c, Stephenson's Rocket, 1837. 30c, Miller, US, 1839. 50c, La Junta. 1p, J.G. Brill trolley, US, 1922. 2p, TEM 4K, USSR, c. 1960. 5p, CAP 9 electric, c. 1988.

1988, Sept. 19 *Perf. 12½x13*
3059 A848 20c multicolored .50 .25
3060 A848 30c multicolored .95 .45
3061 A848 50c multicolored 2.00 .90
3062 A848 1p multicolored 3.75 1.25
3063 A848 2p multicolored 7.50 3.00
3064 A848 5p multicolored 16.00 8.25
Nos. 3059-3064 (6) 30.70 14.10

Latin American History Type of 1986

Natl. arms & patriots: No. 3065, San Martin, Argentina. No. 3066, M.A. Padilla, Bolivia. No. 3067, #390 & discovery of America 500th anniv. emblem. No. 3068, Tiradentes, Brazil. No. 3069, O'Higgins, Chile. No. 3070, A. Narino, Colombia. No. 3071, Marti, Cuba. No. 3072, #391 & emblem. No. 3073, Duarte, Dominican Republic. No. 3074, Sucre, Ecuador. No. 3075, M.J. Arce, El Salvador. No. 3076, Dessalines, Haiti. No. 3077, #C36 & emblem. No. 3078, Hidalgo, Mexico. No. 3079, J.D. Estrada, Nicaragua. No. 3080, Diaz, Paraguay. No. 3081, F. Bolognesi, Peru. No. 3082, #C37 & emblem. No. 3083, Artigas, Uruguay. No. 3084, Bolivar, Venezuela.

1988, Oct. 12 *Perf. 13*
3065 A804 1c multi .25 .25
3066 A804 1c multi .25 .25
3067 A804 1c multi .25 .25
3068 A804 1c multi .25 .25
3069 A804 1c multi .25 .25
a. Strip of 5, Nos. 3065-3069 1.00 1.00
3070 A804 5c multi .25 .25
3071 A804 5c multi .25 .25
3072 A804 5c multi .25 .25
3073 A804 5c multi .25 .25
3074 A804 5c multi .25 .25
a. Strip of 5, Nos. 3070-3074 1.00 1.00
3075 A804 10c multi .25 .25
3076 A804 10c multi .25 .25
3077 A804 10c multi .25 .25
3078 A804 10c multi .25 .25
3079 A804 10c multi .25 .25
a. Strip of 5, Nos. 3075-3079 1.50 1.50
3080 A804 20c multi .40 .25
3081 A804 20c multi .40 .25
3082 A804 20c multi .40 .25
3083 A804 20c multi .40 .25
3084 A804 20c multi .40 .25
a. Strip of 5, Nos. 3080-3084 2.50 2.50
b. Sheet of 20, Nos. 3065-3084 7.50 7.50
Nos. 3065-3084 (20) 5.75 5.00

Discovery of America, 500th anniv. (in 1992).

Havana Museum, 20th Anniv. — A849

Design: Captain-General's Palace and Maces of Municipal Havana.

1988, Oct. 16 Litho. *Perf. 12½x12*
3085 A849 5c multi + label .50 .25

Anniversaries — A850

No. 3086, Swan Lake. No. 3087, Theater in 1838 and 1988.

1988, Oct. 28 *Perf. 13*
3086 A850 5c multicolored .45 .25
3087 A850 5c multicolored .45 .25
a. Pair, Nos. 3086-3087 1.00 .85

Natl. Ballet, 40th anniv. (No. 3086); Grand Theater of Havana, 150th anniv. (No. 3087).

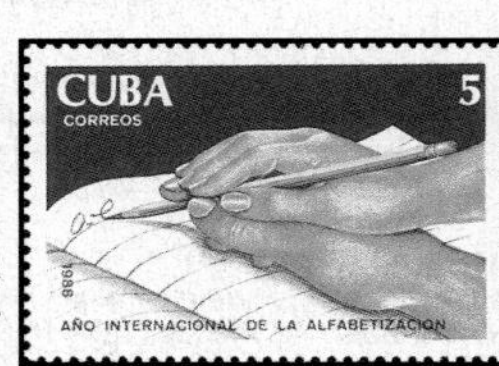

Intl. Literacy Year A851

1988, Dec. 5
3088 A851 5c multicolored .30 .25

UN Declaration of Human Rights, 40th Anniv. — A851a

1988, Dec. 10
3088A A851a 30c multi 1.25 .35

Battle of Santa Clara, 30th Anniv. — A852

30c, Monument, Che Guevara Plaza.

1988, Dec. 28 *Perf. 13x12½*
3089 A852 30c multicolored 1.25 .35

30th Anniv. of the Revolution — A853

1989, Jan. 1 *Perf. 13*
3090 A853 5c multi .25 .25
3091 A853 20c multi .65 .25
3092 A853 30c multi .85 .25
3093 A853 50c multi 1.75 .50
Nos. 3090-3093 (4) 3.50 1.25

Edible Mushrooms — A854

Designs: 2c, Pleurotus levis. 3c, Pleurotus floridanus. 5c, Amanita caesarea. 10c, Lentinus cubensis. 40c, Pleurotus ostreatus (brown). 50c, Pleurotus ostreatus (yellow)

1989, Jan. 10
3094 A854 2c multicolored .25 .25
3095 A854 3c multicolored .25 .25
3096 A854 5c multicolored .25 .25
3097 A854 10c multicolored .50 .25
3098 A854 40c multicolored 2.00 .40
3099 A854 50c multicolored 2.25 .50
Nos. 3094-3099 (6) 5.50 1.90

2c, 3c, 5c, 40c, 50c, vert.

Souvenir Sheet

INDIA '89 — A855

1p, Indian River Post, 1858.

1989, Jan. 20
3100 A855 1p multicolored 4.50 2.00

Central Organization of Cuban Trade Unions (CTC), 50th Anniv. — A856

5c, No. 2477, CTC emblem.

1989, Jan. 28 *Perf. 12½*
3101 A856 5c multicolored .30 .25

Butterflies A857

Designs: 1c, Metamorpho dido. 3c, Callithea saphhira. 5c, Papilio zagreus. 10c, Mynes sestia. 30c, Papilio dardanus. 50c, Catagranma sorana.

1989, Feb. 15
3102 A857 1c multicolored .25 .25
3103 A857 3c multicolored .25 .25
3104 A857 5c multicolored .25 .25
3105 A857 10c multicolored .30 .25
3106 A857 30c multicolored 1.40 .30
3107 A857 50c multicolored 2.50 .65
Nos. 3102-3107 (6) 4.95 1.95

1990 World Cup Soccer Championships, Italy — A858

Various athletes.

1989, Mar. 15 *Perf. 13*
3108 A858 1c multi .25 .25
3109 A858 3c multi, diff. .25 .25
3110 A858 5c multi, diff. .25 .25
3111 A858 10c multi, diff. .25 .25
3112 A858 30c multi, diff. 1.00 .25
3113 A858 50c multi, diff. 1.40 .40
Nos. 3108-3113 (6) 3.40 1.65

Souvenir Sheet

Perf. 12½

3114 A858 1p multi, diff., horiz. 4.50 2.00

No. 3114 contains one 40x32mm stamp.

Natl. Revolutionary Police (PNR), 30th Anniv. — A859

1989, Mar. 23 *Perf. 13*
3115 A859 5c multicolored .30 .25

Cosmonauts' Day — A860

Spacecraft and rocket mail covers: 1c, *Zodiac* and cover, Australia 1934. 3c, Lighthouse and cover, India, 1934. 5c, Cover, England, 1934. 10c, *Icarus* and cover, The Netherlands, 1935. 40c, *La Douce France* and cover, France, 1935. 50c, Rocket mail cover, Cuba, 1939.

1989, Apr. 12
3116 A860 1c multi .25 .25
3117 A860 3c multi .25 .25
3118 A860 5c multi .25 .25
3119 A860 10c multi .25 .25
3120 A860 40c multi 1.10 .40
3121 A860 50c multi 1.40 .55
Nos. 3116-3121 (6) 3.50 1.95

Stamp Day Type of 1984

Details of mural by R. Rodriguez Radillo (1967): 30c, Mail coach, Satellite dish. 50c, Galleon, longboats, train, passenger pigeon, horses.

1989, Apr. 24 Litho. *Perf. 13x12½*
3122 A733 30c multi .65 .30
3123 A733 50c multi 3.00 2.00

Casa de Las Americas, 30th Anniv. A861

1989, Apr. 28 *Perf. 12½x13*
3124 A861 5c multi .30 .25

Souvenir Sheet

BULGARIA '89 — A862

1989, May 1 ***Perf. 12½***
3125 A862 1p Bulgaria No. 346 4.50 2.25

58th FIP Congress and 101st anniv. of Bulgarian Railways.

Cuban Postal Code A863

1989, May 5 ***Perf. 13***
3126 A863 5c multi .30 .25

Mothers' Day — A864

Perfume bottles and flowers: 1c, Habano, tobacco. 3c, Violeta, violets. 5c, Mariposa, mariposa. 13c, Coral Negro, roses. 30c, Ala Alonso, jasmine. 50c, D'Man, lemon blossoms.

1989, May 10

3127	A864 1c multi	.25	.25
3128	A864 3c multi	.25	.25
3129	A864 5c multi	.25	.25
3130	A864 13c multi	.35	.25
3131	A864 30c multi	.90	.30
3132	A864 50c multi	1.60	.70
	Nos. 3127-3132 (6)	3.60	2.00

Agrarian Reform Law, 30th Anniv. — A865

1989, May 17 ***Perf. 12x12½***
3133 A865 5c multi .30 .25

Council for Mutual Economic Assistance (CAME), 40th Anniv. A866

1989, June 1 Litho. ***Perf. 12½x13***
3134 A866 30c multi 1.25 .25

13th World Communist Youth and Student Festival, Pyongyang — A867

1989, July 1 Litho. ***Perf. 12½***
3135 A867 30c multi 1.25 .25

Souvenir Sheet

Rouget de Lisle Singing La Marseillaise, by Pils — A868

1989, July 7 ***Perf. 13***
3136 A868 1p multi 4.50 2.00

PHILEXFRANCE '89, French revolution bicent. and Cuban revolution 30th anniv.

BRASILIANA '89 — A869

Exotic birds: 1c, Ramphastos toco. 3c, Agamia agami. 5c, Eudocimus ruber. 10c, Psophia leucoptera. 35c, Harpia harpyja. 50c, Cephalopterus ornatus.

1989, July 28 Litho. ***Perf. 12½***

3137	A869 1c multicolored	.25	.25
3138	A869 3c multicolored	.25	.25
3139	A869 5c multicolored	.25	.25
3140	A869 10c multicolored	.30	.25
3141	A869 35c multicolored	1.25	.50
3142	A869 50c multicolored	1.75	.70
	Nos. 3137-3142 (6)	4.05	2.20

Warships A870

1989, Sept. 29 Litho. ***Perf. 12½***

3143	A870 1c *El Fenix*	.25	.25
3144	A870 3c *Triunfo*	.25	.25
3145	A870 5c *El Rayo*	.25	.25
3146	A870 10c *San Carlos*	.25	.25
3147	A870 30c *San Jose*	1.00	.40
3148	A870 50c *San Genaro*	1.50	.70
	Nos. 3143-3148 (6)	3.50	2.10

America Issue — A871

UPAE emblem and pre-Columbian art: 5p, Stone carving, Indians in dugout canoe. 20p, Petroglyph, Indian drawing on stone wall.

1989, Oct. 12 ***Perf. 12½x12***
3149 A871 5c multi .35 .25
3150 A871 20c multi .85 .40

Latin American History — A872

Writers and orchids: No. 3151, Domingo Sarmiento (1811-1888), Argentine educator, and *Govenia utriculata.* No. 3152, Joaquim Maria Machado de Assis (1839-1908), Brazilian novelist, and *Laelia grandis.* No. 3153, Salvador No. 69 and discovery of America anniv. emblem. No. 3154, Jorge Isaacs (1837-1895), Colombian novelist, and *Cattleya trianae.* No. 3155, Alejo Carpentier, Cuban writer, and *Cochleanthes discolor.* No. 3156, Pablo Neruda (1904-1973), Chilean poet, and *Oxalis adenophylla.* No. 3157, Pedro Urena, Dominican writer, and *Epidendrum fragrans.* No. 3158, Salvador No. 86 and anniv. emblem. No. 3159, Juan Montalvo (1832-1889), Ecuadorian satirist, and *Miltonia vexillaria.* No. 3160, Miguel Asturias (1899-1974), Guatemalan writer awarded the 1966 Lenin Peace Prize and 1967 Nobel Prize for literature, and *Odontoglossum rossii.* No. 3161, Jose C. del Valle, Honduran writer, and *Laelia anceps.* No. 3162, Alfonso Reyes (1889-1959), Mexican poet, and *Laelia anceps alba.* No. 3163, Salvador No. 87 and anniv. emblem. No. 3164, Ruben Dario (1867-1917), Nicaraguan poet, and *Brassavola acaulis.* No. 3165, Belisario Porras (1856-1942), president of Panama, and *Pescatorea celina.* No. 3166, Ricardo Palma (1833-1919), Peruvian writer, and *Coryanthes leucocorys.* No. 3167, Eugenio Maria de Hostos (1839-1903), Puerto Rican writer, and *Guzmania berteroniana.* No. 3168, Salvador No. 88 and anniv. emblem. No. 3169, Jose E. Rodo (1872-1917), Uruguayan philosopher, essayist, and *Cypella hebertii.* No. 3170, Romulo Gallegos, Venezuelan writer, and *Cattleya mossiae.*

1989, Oct. 27 Litho. ***Perf. 13***

3151	A872 1c multicolored	.25	.25
3152	A872 1c multicolored	.25	.25
3153	A872 1c multicolored	.25	.25
3154	A872 1c multicolored	.25	.25
3155	A872 1c multicolored	.25	.25
a.	Strip of 5, Nos. 3151-3155	1.00	1.00
3156	A872 5c multicolored	.25	.25
3157	A872 5c multicolored	.25	.25
3158	A872 5c multicolored	.25	.25
3159	A872 5c multicolored	.25	.25
3160	A872 5c multicolored	.25	.25
a.	Strip of 5, Nos. 3156-3160	1.00	1.00
3161	A872 10c multicolored	.35	.25
3162	A872 10c multicolored	.35	.25
3163	A872 10c multicolored	.35	.25
3164	A872 10c multicolored	.35	.25
3165	A872 10c multicolored	.35	.25
a.	Strip of 5, Nos. 3161-3165	2.00	2.00
3166	A872 20c multicolored	.55	.25
3167	A872 20c multicolored	.55	.25
3168	A872 20c multicolored	.55	.25
3169	A872 20c multicolored	.55	.25
3170	A872 20c multicolored	.55	.25
a.	Strip of 5, Nos. 3166-3170	3.00	3.00
b.	Sheet of 20, #3151-3170	8.00	8.00
	Nos. 3151-3170 (20)	7.00	5.00

Discovery of America 500th anniv. (in 1992).

Disappearance of Camilo Cienfuegos, 30th Anniv. — A873

1989, Oct. 28
3171 A873 5c multicolored .40 .25

Founding of the City of Trinidad, 475th Anniv. A874

1989, Nov. 6 ***Perf. 12½x13***
3172 A874 5c multicolored .40 .25

Paintings in the Natl. Museum — A875

Designs: 1c, *Familiar Scene,* by Antoine Faivre. 2c, *Flowers,* by Emile Jean Horace Vernet (1789-1863). 5c, *The Judgement of Paris,* by Charles Le Brun (1619-1690). 20c, *Outskirts of Nice,* by Eugene Louis Boudin (1824-1898). 30c, *Portrait of Sarah Bernhardt,* by G.J.V. Clairin. 50c, *Fishermen in Port,* by C.J. Vernet.

Perf. 12½, 12½x13 (30p)
1989, Nov. 20 Litho.
Size of 30p: 36x46mm

3173	A875 1c multicolored	.25	.25
3174	A875 2c multicolored	.25	.25
3175	A875 5c multicolored	.25	.25
3176	A875 20c multicolored	.75	.25
3177	A875 30c multicolored	1.00	.25
3178	A875 50c multicolored	2.00	.55
	Nos. 3173-3178 (6)	4.50	1.80

11th Pan-American Games, Havana, 1991 — A876

1989, Dec. 15 Litho. ***Perf. 12½***

3179	A876 5c Cycling	.25	.25
3180	A876 5c Fencing	.25	.25
3181	A876 5c Water polo	.25	.25
3182	A876 5c Shooting	.25	.25
3183	A876 5c Archery	.25	.25
3184	A876 20c Tennis, vert.	.65	.25
3185	A876 30c Swimming, vert.	1.00	.25
3186	A876 35c Diving, vert.	1.35	.30
3187	A876 40c Field hockey	1.40	.30
3188	A876 50c Basketball, vert.	2.10	.65
	Nos. 3179-3188 (10)	7.75	3.00

Jose Marti's *Golden Age,* Cent. — A877

1989, Dec. 20 ***Perf. 13***
3189 A877 5c scar, lt blue & blk .45 .25

Cuban Postal Museum, 25th Anniv. — A878

1990, Jan. 2 *Perf. 13x12½*
3190 A878 5c *Almendares* .25 .25
3191 A878 30c Mail train 1.50 .75

Speleological Soc., 50th Anniv. — A879

1990, Jan. 15 *Perf. 12½*
3192 A879 30c multicolored 1.50 .35

1990 World Cup Soccer Championships, Italy — A880

Various Italian architecture and athletes: No. 3193a, Dribbling (in red and blue). No. 3193b, Heading (in red and green). No. 3193c, Kicking (in green). 10c, Goalie catching ball. 30c, Dribbling, diff. 50c, Kicking, diff. 1p, Goalie catching ball, diff.

1990, Jan. 30 **Litho.** *Perf. 12½*
3193 Strip of 3 .50 .25
a.-c. A880 5c any single .25 .25
3194 A880 10c multicolored .25 .25
3195 A880 30c multicolored 1.25 .30
3196 A880 50c multicolored 2.00 .55
a. Sheet of 6, #3193a-3193c, 3194-3196 + 3 labels 4.25 2.10
Nos. 3193-3196 (4) 4.00 1.35

Souvenir Sheet

3197 A880 1p multicolored 4.50 1.75

No. 3193 has a continuous design picturing The Colosseum.

1992 Summer Olympics, Barcelona — A881

1c, Baseball. 4c, Running. 5c, Basketball. 10c, Women's volleyball. 30c, Wrestling. 50c, Boxing.
1p, High jump.

1990, Feb. 20 **Litho.** *Perf. 12½*
3198 A881 1c multicolored .25 .25
3199 A881 4c multicolored .25 .25
3200 A881 5c multicolored .25 .25
3201 A881 10c multicolored .45 .25
3202 A881 30c multicolored 1.20 .30
3203 A881 50c multicolored 2.10 .65
Nos. 3198-3203 (6) 4.50 1.95

Souvenir Sheet

3204 A881 1p multicolored 4.50 2.00

Nos. 3198-3201 and 3203 are vert.
No. 3204 contains one 40x32mm stamp.

75th Universal Esperanto Congress — A882

1990, Mar. 7
3205 A882 30c Tower of Babel 1.25 .35

No. 3205 printed se-tenant with inscribed label publicizing the congress.

Souvenir Sheet

1992 Winter Olympics, Albertville — A883

1990, Mar. 30 **Litho.** *Perf. 13*
3206 A883 1p multicolored 4.50 2.25

Cosmonauts' Day — A884

Spacecraft and rocket mail covers: 1c, Austria, 1932. 2c, Germany, 1933. 3c, Netherlands, 1934. 10c, Belgium, 1935. 30c, Yugoslavia, 1935. 50c, United States, 1936.

1990, Apr. 12 *Perf. 12½*
3207 A884 1c multicolored .25 .25
3208 A884 2c multicolored .25 .25
3209 A884 3c multicolored .25 .25
3210 A884 10c multicolored .25 .25
3211 A884 30c multicolored 1.10 .25
3212 A884 50c multicolored 2.00 .55
Nos. 3207-3212 (6) 4.10 1.80

Stamp Day Type of 1984

Details of mural by R. Rodriguez Radillo (1967): 30c, Train station. 50c, Jet aircraft in flight.

1990, Apr. 24 *Perf. 13x12½*
3213 A733 30c multicolored 2.25 .75
3214 A733 50c multicolored 1.25 .45

Labor Day, Cent. A885

1990, Apr. 30 *Perf. 13*
3215 A885 5c multicolored .45 .25

Souvenir Sheet

Great Britain No. 1 on Cover — A886

1990, May 3
3216 A886 1p multicolored 4.50 2.00

Stamp World London '90, Penny Black 150th anniv.

Penny Black, 150th Anniv. A887

Portraits of Sir Rowland Hill and stamps of Great Britain: 2c, No. 1. 3c, No. 2. 5c, Type A5. 10c, No. 5. 30c, First day postmark. 50c, 5 #1 on Mulready envelope.

1990, May 6 **Litho.** *Perf. 12½x12*
3217 A887 2c multicolored .25 .25
3218 A887 3c multicolored .25 .25
3219 A887 5c multicolored .25 .25
3220 A887 10c multicolored .25 .25
3221 A887 30c multicolored 1.25 .25
3222 A887 50c multicolored 2.25 .60
Nos. 3217-3222 (6) 4.50 1.85

Celia Sanchez Manduley (1920-1980) — A888

1990, May 9 *Perf. 12½x13*
3223 A888 5c multicolored .50 .25

Ho Chi Minh (1890-1969), Vietnamese Communist Party Leader — A889

1990, May 19 *Perf. 12½*
3224 A889 50c multicolored 1.90 .45

Oceanography Institute, 25th Anniv. — A890

Designs: 5c, Specimen analysis and *Lachnolaimus maximus.* 30c, Research ship, fish, coral reef. 50c, Specimen collection and *Panullrus argus.*

1990, June 18 **Litho.** *Perf. 12½*
3225 A890 5c multicolored .25 .25
3226 A890 30c multicolored 1.10 .30
3227 A890 50c multicolored 1.75 .50
Nos. 3225-3227 (3) 3.10 1.05

5th Latin American Botanical Conference A891

Designs: 3c, Banara minutiflora. 5c, Oplonia nannophylla. 10c, Jacquinia brunnescens. 30c, Rondeletia brachycarpa. 50c, Rondeletia odorata.

1990, June 25 **Litho.** *Perf. 12½*
3228 A891 3c multicolored .25 .25
3229 A891 5c multicolored .25 .25
3230 A891 10c multicolored .30 .25
3231 A891 30c multicolored 1.00 .25
3232 A891 50c multicolored 1.50 .60
Nos. 3228-3232 (5) 3.30 1.60

Tourism A892

1990, June 30
3233 A892 5c Wind surfing .25 .25
3234 A892 10c Spear fishing .35 .25
3235 A892 30c Deep sea fishing 1.00 .25
3236 A892 40c Hunting 1.60 .55
Nos. 3233-3236 (4) 3.20 1.30

Nos. 3233, 3236 vert.

Art Treasures A893

5c, "La Flauta Del Dios Pan." 20c, "Un Pastor." 50c, "Ganimedes." 1p, "Venus Anadiomena."

1990, July 20
3237 A893 5c multicolored .25 .25
3238 A893 20c multicolored .60 .25
3239 A893 50c multicolored 1.60 .40
3240 A893 1p multicolored 2.75 .85
a. Sheet of 4, #3237-3240 6.50 6.50
Nos. 3237-3240 (4) 5.20 1.75

Birds A894

Designs: 2c, Podiceps cristatus. 3c, Gallirallus australis. 5c, Nestor notabilis. 10c, Xenicus longipes. 30c, Cracticus torquatus. 50c, Prosthemadera novaeseelandiae.
1p, Kiwi.

1990, Aug. 24 **Litho.** *Perf. 13*
3241 A894 2c multicolored .25 .25
3242 A894 3c multicolored .25 .25
3243 A894 5c multicolored .25 .25
3244 A894 10c multicolored .50 .25
3245 A894 30c multicolored 1.10 .35
3246 A894 50c multicolored 1.90 .65
Nos. 3241-3246 (6) 4.25 2.00

Souvenir Sheet

3247 A894 1p multicolored 4.50 2.25

New Zealand '90. No. 3247 contains one 39x31mm stamp.

8th UN Congress on Crime Prevention A895

1990, Aug. 27 **Litho.** *Perf. 12½*
3248 A895 50c blue, silver & red 2.25 .45

Discovery of America, 500th Anniv. (in 1992) — A896

1990, Oct. 12 Litho. *Perf. 12½*

3249	A896	5c Ship, shore		.40	.25
3250	A896	20c Columbus, village		1.00	.35

Cuban Television, 40th Anniv. — A897

1990, Oct. 12 Litho. *Perf. 13*

3251	A897	5c multicolored	.45	.25

Nationalization of Railroads, 30th Anniv. — A898

1990, Oct. 13 *Perf. 13x12½*

3252	A898	50c multicolored	2.50	.75

Latin American History Type of 1986

Latin American stamps or flags and costumes: No. 3253, Argentina. No. 3254, Bolivia. No. 3255, Argentina No. 91. No. 3256, Colombia. No. 3257, Costa Rica. No. 3258, Cuba. No. 3259, Chile. No. 3260, Dominican Republic No. 110. No. 3261, Ecuador. No. 3262, El Salvador. No. 3263, Guatemala. No. 3264, Mexico. No. 3265, Puerto Rico No. 133. No. 3266, Nicaragua. No. 3267, Panama. No. 3268, Paraguay. No. 3269, Peru. No. 3270, El Salvador No. 103. No. 3271, Puerto Rico. No. 3272, Venezuela.

1990, Oct. 27 *Perf. 12½*

3253	A804	1c multicolored	.25	.25
3254	A804	1c multicolored	.25	.25
3255	A804	1c multicolored	.25	.25
3256	A804	1c multicolored	.25	.25
3257	A804	1c multicolored	.25	.25
a.		Strip of 5, Nos. 3253-3257	1.00	1.00
3258	A804	5c multicolored	.25	.25
3259	A804	5c multicolored	.25	.25
3260	A804	5c multicolored	.25	.25
3261	A804	5c multicolored	.25	.25
3262	A804	5c multicolored	.25	.25
a.		Strip of 5, Nos. 3258-3262	1.00	1.00
3263	A804	10c multicolored	.30	.25
3264	A804	10c multicolored	.30	.25
3265	A804	10c multicolored	.30	.25
3266	A804	10c multicolored	.30	.25
3267	A804	10c multicolored	.30	.25
a.		Strip of 5, Nos. 3263-3267	1.50	1.50
3268	A804	20c multicolored	.75	.25
3269	A804	20c multicolored	.75	.25
3270	A804	20c multicolored	.75	.25
3271	A804	20c multicolored	.75	.25
3272	A804	20c multicolored	.75	.25
a.		Strip of 5, Nos. 3268-3272	4.50	4.50
b.		Sheet of 20, #3253-3272	5.00	5.00
		Nos. 3253-3272 (20)	7.75	5.00

Discovery of America, 500th anniv. (in 1992).

11th Jai Alai World Championships A899

1990, Nov. 14 Litho. *Perf. 12½*

3273	A899	30c multicolored	1.40	.40

No. 3273 printed with se-tenant label.

11th Pan American Games, Havana — A900

No. 3274, Judo. No. 3275, Sailing. No. 3276, Kayak. No. 3277, Rowing. No. 3278, Equestrian. No. 3279, Table tennis. No. 3280, Men's gymnastics, vert. No. 3281, Baseball, vert. No. 3282, Team handball, vert. No. 3283, Soccer, vert.

1990, Nov. 15 Litho. *Perf. 12½*

3274	A900	5c multicolored	.25	.25
3275	A900	5c multicolored	.25	.25
3276	A900	5c multicolored	.25	.25
3277	A900	5c multicolored	.25	.25
3278	A900	5c multicolored	.25	.25
3279	A900	10c multicolored	.30	.25
3280	A900	20c multicolored	.60	.25
3281	A900	30c multicolored	.90	.25
3282	A900	35c multicolored	1.10	.35
3283	A900	50c multicolored	1.60	.70
		Nos. 3274-3283 (10)	5.75	3.05

See Nos. 3311-3320.

A901

1990, Nov. 20 Litho. *Perf. 13*

3284	A901	5c Boxing	.25	.25
3285	A901	30c Baseball	1.10	.25
3286	A901	50c Volleyball	1.90	.50
		Nos. 3284-3286 (3)	3.25	1.00

16th Central American and Caribbean Games, Mexico.

Butterflies A902

Designs: 2c, Chioides marmorosa. 3c, Composia fidelissima. 5c, Danaus plexippus. 10c, Hypolimnas misippus. 30c, Hypna iphigenia. 50c, Hemiargus ammon

1991, Jan. 25 Litho. *Perf. 12½*

3287	A902	2c multicolored	.25	.25
3288	A902	3c multicolored	.25	.25
3289	A902	5c multicolored	.35	.25
3290	A902	10c multicolored	.45	.25
3291	A902	30c multicolored	1.25	.25
3292	A902	50c multicolored	2.10	.50
		Nos. 3287-3292 (6)	4.65	1.75

Jose Luis Guerra Aguiar (1914-1990), Director of Postal Museum — A903

1991, Feb. 17 Litho. *Perf. 12½*

3293	A903	5c multicolored	.45	.25

A904

1991, Feb. 20

3294	A904	1c Long jump	.25	.25
3295	A904	2c Javelin	.25	.25
3296	A904	3c Field hockey	.25	.25
3297	A904	5c Weight lifting	.25	.25
3298	A904	40c Cycling	1.25	.35
3299	A904	50c Gymnastics	1.75	.50
		Nos. 3294-3299 (6)	4.00	1.85

Souvenir Sheet

3300	A904	1p Torchbearer	3.50	1.75

1992 Summer Olympics, Barcelona.

A905

1st Man in Space, 30th anniv.: 5c, Yuri Gagarin. No. 3302, Cosmonaut Y. Romanenko. No. 3303, Cosmonaut A. Tamayo Mendez. No. 3304, Mir space station. No. 3305, Mir space station, docked Soyuz, earth. 50c, Soviet space shuttle Buran.

1991, Apr. 12 Litho. *Perf. 13*

3301	A905	5c multicolored	.25	.25
3302	A905	10c multicolored	.25	.25
3303	A905	10c multicolored	.25	.25
a.		Pair, #3302-3303	.40	.25
3304	A905	30c multicolored	1.00	.25
3305	A905	30c multicolored	1.00	.25
a.		Pair, #3304-3305	2.00	1.00
3306	A905	50c multicolored	1.60	.50
a.		Sheet of 6, #3301-3306	4.50	—
		Nos. 3301-3306 (6)	4.35	1.75

Proclamation of the Socialist Revolution, 30th Anniv. — A906

Design: 50c, Ship, jet on fire.

1991, Apr. 19 *Perf. 12½*

3307	A906	5c multicolored	.25	.25
3308	A906	50c multicolored	1.90	.80

Bay of Pigs invasion, 30th anniv., No. 3308.

Stamp Day A907

Details from mural by R. Rodriguez Radillo: 30c, Rocket lift-off. 50c, Dish antenna, horiz.

1991, Apr. 24 *Perf. 12½x13, 13x12½*

3309	A907	30c multicolored	1.25	.30
3310	A907	50c multicolored	1.90	.40

11th Pan American Games Type of 1990

1991, May 15 Litho. *Perf. 12½*

3311	A900	5c Volleyball	.25	.25
3312	A900	5c Rhythmic gymnastics	.25	.25
3313	A900	5c Synchronized swimming	.25	.25
3314	A900	5c Weight lifting	.25	.25
3315	A900	5c Baseball	.25	.25
3316	A900	10c Bowling	.25	.25
3317	A900	20c Boxing	.55	.25
3318	A900	30c Running	.85	.25
3319	A900	35c Wrestling	1.10	.30
3320	A900	50c Karate	1.50	.50
		Nos. 3311-3320 (10)	5.50	2.80

Nos. 3311-3315 & 3317 are vert.

Airships A908

Designs: 5c, First ellipsoidal, 1784, J.B.M. Meusnier. 10c, First with steam engine, 1852, H. Giffard. 20c, First with gas engine, 1872, P. Haenlein. 30c, First with gasoline engine, 1896, H. Wolfert. 50c, First rigid aluminum, 1897, D. Schwarz. 1p, LZ-129 Hindenburg, 1936, F. von Zeppelin.

1991, July 1 Litho. *Perf. 13*

3321	A908	5c multicolored	.25	.25
3322	A908	10c multicolored	.35	.25
3323	A908	20c multicolored	.70	.30
3324	A908	30c multicolored	.90	.50
3325	A908	50c multicolored	1.60	.95
3326	A908	1p multicolored	3.25	1.60
		Nos. 3321-3326 (6)	7.05	3.85

Espamer '91, Buenos Aires, Argentina.

Simon Bolivar A909

1991, June 22 Litho. *Perf. 12½x13*

3327	A909	50c multicolored	2.00	.60

Amphictyonic Cong. of Panama, 165th anniv.

Birds
A910

Designs: 45c, Melanerpes superciliaris. 50c, Myadestes elisabeth. 2p, Priotelus temnurus. 4p, Tiaris canora. 5p, Campephilus principalis. 10p, Amazona leucocephala, horiz. 16.45p, Mellisuga helenae, horiz.

1991, July 15 ***Perf. 12½x13, 13x12½***

3328	A910	45c	multicolored	1.25	.40
3329	A910	50c	multicolored	1.50	.50
3330	A910	2p	multicolored	5.25	2.00
3331	A910	4p	multicolored	10.00	3.50
3332	A910	5p	multicolored	12.50	4.25
3333	A910	10p	multicolored	25.00	6.50
3334	A910	16.45p	multicolored	40.00	13.00
			Nos. 3328-3334 (7)	95.50	30.15

Tourism — A911

Designs: No. 3335, Varadero Beach, vert. No. 3336, Cayo Largo, vert. No. 3337, Artillerymen at fortress San Carlos de la Cabana. No. 3338, Tres Reyes del Morro Castle.

1991, July 30

3335	A911	20c	multicolored	.60	.25
3336	A911	20c	multicolored	.60	.25
3337	A911	30c	multicolored	1.00	.30
3338	A911	30c	multicolored	1.00	.30
			Nos. 3335-3338 (4)	3.20	1.10

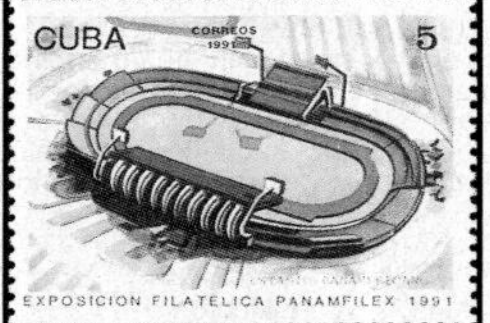

Panamfilex '91 — A912

11th Pan American Games venues: 5c, Pan American Stadium. 20c, Swimming venue. 30c, Multisports center. 50c, Velodrome. 1p, Havana City Coliseum and Sports Center.

1991, Aug. 4 **Litho.** ***Perf. 12½***

3339	A912	5c	multicolored	.25	.25
3340	A912	20c	multicolored	.60	.30
3341	A912	30c	multicolored	.80	.50
3342	A912	50c	multicolored	1.50	.90
			Nos. 3339-3342 (4)	3.15	1.95

Souvenir Sheet

3343	A912	1p	multicolored	3.50	1.75

No. 3343 contains one 40x32mm stamp.

Paintings
A913

5c, Kataoka Dengoemon Takafusa, by Utagawa Kuniyoshi. 10c, Evening Walk, by Hosoda Eishi. 20c, Courtesans, by Torii Kiyonaga. 30c, Conversation, by Utamaro. 50c, Bridge at Inari-bashi, by Hiroshige. 1p, On the Terrace, by Kiyonaga.

1991, Sept. 9 **Litho.** ***Perf. 12½x13***

3344	A913	5c	multicolored	.25	.25
3345	A913	10c	multicolored	.35	.25
3346	A913	20c	multicolored	.70	.30
3347	A913	30c	multicolored	.90	.40
3348	A913	50c	multicolored	1.60	.75
3349	A913	1p	multicolored	3.25	1.75
			Nos. 3344-3349 (6)	7.05	3.70

Phila Nippon '91, Tokyo.

Souvenir Sheet

1992 Winter Olympics, Albertville — A914

1991, Sept. 25 **Litho.** ***Perf. 12½***

3350	A914	1p	multicolored	3.50	1.75

Cuban Communist Party, 4th Congress
A915

1991, Oct. 10

3351	A915	5c	shown	.25	.25
3352	A915	50c	Congress symbol	1.75	.50

Discovery of America, 500th Anniv. (in 1992) — A916

Designs: 5c, Columbus, Vicente and Martin Pinzon. 20c, Santa Maria, Nina and Pinta.

1991, Oct. 12

3353	A916	5c	multicolored	.25	.25
3354	A916	20c	multicolored	1.25	.25

Jose Marti
A917

1991, Oct. 15 ***Perf. 13x12½***

3355	A917	50c	multicolored	2.00	.40

Publication of "Simple Verses," cent.

Latin American History
A918

Stamps or musicians and instruments: No. 3356, Julian Aguirre, Argentina, charango. No. 3357, Eduardo Caba, Bolivia, antara. No. 3358, Chile #2. No. 3359, Heitor Villalobos, Brazil, resonator trumpet. No. 3360, Guillermo Uribe-Holguin, Colombia, drum. No. 3361, Miguel Failde, Cuba, claves. No. 3362, Enrique Soro, Chile, drum. No. 3363, Chile #57. No. 3364, Segundo L. Moreno, Ecuador, xylophone. No. 3365, Ricardo Castillo, Guatemala, marimba. No. 3366, Carlos Chavez, Mexico, guitar. No. 3367, Luis A. Delgadillo, Nicaragua, maracas. No. 3368, Chile #69. No. 3369, Alfredo De Saint-Malo, Panama, mejorana. No. 3370, Jose Asuncion Flores, Paraguay, harp. No. 3371, Daniel Alomia, Peru, flute. No. 3372, Juan Morell y Campos, Puerto Rico, cuatro. No. 3373, Chile #72. No. 3374, Eduardo Farini, Uruguay, drums. No. 3375, Juan V. Lecuna, Venezuela, cuatro, diff.

1991, Oct. 27 ***Perf. 13***

3356	A918	1c	multicolored	.25	.25
3357	A918	1c	multicolored	.25	.25
3358	A918	1c	multicolored	.25	.25
3359	A918	1c	multicolored	.25	.25
3360	A918	1c	multicolored	.25	.25
a.			Strip of 5, #3356-3360	1.00	1.00
3361	A918	5c	multicolored	.25	.25
3362	A918	5c	multicolored	.25	.25
3363	A918	5c	multicolored	.25	.25
3364	A918	5c	multicolored	.25	.25
3365	A918	5c	multicolored	.25	.25
a.			Strip of 5, #3361-3365	1.00	1.00
3366	A918	10c	multicolored	.40	.25
3367	A918	10c	multicolored	.40	.25
3368	A918	10c	multicolored	.40	.25
3369	A918	10c	multicolored	.40	.25
3370	A918	10c	multicolored	.40	.25
a.			Strip of 5, #3366-3370	2.00	2.00
3371	A918	20c	multicolored	.70	.25
3372	A918	20c	multicolored	.70	.25
3373	A918	20c	multicolored	.70	.25
3374	A918	20c	multicolored	.70	.25
3375	A918	20c	multicolored	.70	.25
a.			Strip of 5, #3371-3375	4.00	4.00
b.			Sheet of 20, #3356-3375	8.00	—
			Nos. 3356-3375 (20)	8.00	5.00

Discovery of America, 500th anniv. in 1992 (Nos. 3358, 3363, 3368, 3373).

Jose Marti Pioneers Organization, 1st Congress
A919

1991, Oct. 29

3376	A919	5c	multicolored	.40	.25

Toussaint L'Ouverture (1743-1803) — A920

1991, Nov. 20 ***Perf. 12½x13***

3377	A920	50c	multicolored	2.00	.40

Haitian Revolution, Bicent.

Cuban Revolutionary Armed Forces, 35th Anniv. — A921

Design: 50c, Landing of the Granma expedition, 35th anniv., vert.

Perf. 12½x12, 12x12½

1991, Dec. 2 **Litho.**

3378	A921	5c	multicolored	.25	.25
3379	A921	50c	multicolored	1.40	.40

Gen. Ignacio Agramonte (1841-1873), Revolutionary Hero — A922

1991, Dec. 23 **Litho.** ***Perf. 12½x13***

3380	A922	5c	multicolored	.40	.25

Souvenir Sheet

1992 Winter Olympics, Albertville — A923

1992, Jan. 15 ***Perf. 13***

3381	A923	1p	multicolored	3.00	1.75

1992 Summer Olympics, Barcelona — A924

1992, Jan. 20 **Litho.** ***Perf. 13x12½***

3382	A924	3c	Table tennis	.25	.25
3383	A924	5c	Handball	.25	.25
3384	A924	10c	Shooting	.30	.25
3385	A924	20c	Long jump, vert.	.45	.25
3386	A924	35c	Judo	1.00	.40
3387	A924	50c	Fencing	1.40	.40
			Nos. 3382-3387 (6)	3.65	1.80

Souvenir Sheet

Perf. 12½

3388	A924	100c	Rhythmic gymnastics, vert.	2.90	1.75

No. 3388 contains one 32x40mm stamp.

Environmental Protection A925

5c, Terraced hillsides. 20c, Save the whales. 35c, Ozone hole over Antarctica. 40c, Nuclear disarmament.

1992, Feb. 10 *Perf. 13*

3389 A925 5c multicolored .25 .25
3390 A925 20c multicolored .50 .25
3391 A925 35c multicolored 1.00 .40
3392 A925 40c multicolored 1.10 .40
Nos. 3389-3392 (4) 2.85 1.30

Dogs A926

5c, Boxer. 10c, Great dane. 20c, German shepherd. 30c, Various breeds. 35c, Doberman pinscher. 40c, Fox terrier. 50c, Poodle.

1p, Bichon frise, vert.

1992, Mar. 10 Litho. *Perf. 13x12½*

3393 A926 5c multi .25 .25
3394 A926 10c multi .25 .25
3395 A926 20c multi .50 .25
3396 A926 30c multi .95 .25
3397 A926 35c multi .95 .30
3398 A926 40c multi 1.20 .40
3399 A926 50c multi 1.50 .50
Nos. 3393-3399 (7) 5.60 2.20

Souvenir Sheet

Perf. 12½

3400 A926 1p multi 3.00 2.00

No. 3400 contains one 32x40mm stamp.
Nos. 3401-3404 will not be assigned.

Union of Young Communists, 30th Anniv. — A928

1992, Apr. 4 Litho. *Perf. 13*

3405 A928 5c multicolored .35 .25

Cuban Revolutionary Party, Cent. — A929

1992, Apr. 10 *Perf. 13x12½*

3406 A929 5c multicolored .25 .25
3407 A929 50c multicolored 1.40 .50

Discovery of America, 500th Anniv. — A930

5c, Landing at Bariay. 20c, Landing at San Salvador.

1992, Apr. 14 *Perf. 12½*

3408 A930 5c multi .25 .25
3409 A930 20c multi .60 .25

Granada '92 Philatelic Exhibition — A931

Views of the Alhambra, Granada: 5c, With Sierra Nevada mountains beyond. 10c, Arches at sunset. 20c, Interior architecture. 30c, Patio, fountain of lions. 35c, Bedroom. 50c, View of Albaicin.

1992, Apr. 17 *Perf. 13*

3410 A931 5c multicolored .25 .25
3411 A931 10c multicolored .25 .25
3412 A931 20c multicolored .60 .25
3413 A931 30c multicolored 1.00 .25
3414 A931 35c multicolored 1.10 .40
3415 A931 50c multicolored 1.60 .50
Nos. 3410-3415 (6) 4.80 1.90

La Bodeguita Del Medio Restaurant, 50th Anniv. — A932

1992, Apr. 26

3416 A932 50c multicolored 1.50 .50

Fish A933

Designs: 5c, Holacanthus isabelita. 10c, Equetus lanceolatus. 20c, Acanthurus coeruleus. 30c, Abudefduf saxatilis. 50c, Microspathodon chrysurus.

1992, May 15 Litho. *Perf. 12½*

3417 A933 5c multicolored .25 .25
3418 A933 10c multicolored .25 .25
3419 A933 20c multicolored .60 .25
3420 A933 30c multicolored 1.00 .25
3421 A933 50c multicolored 1.60 .50
Nos. 3417-3421 (5) 3.70 1.50

Orchids — A934

1992, June 20 Litho. *Perf. 12½*

3422 A934 3c Cattleya hibrida .25 .25
3423 A934 5c Phalaenopsis .25 .25
3424 A934 10c Cattleyopsis lindenii .25 .25
3425 A934 30c Bletia purpurea .90 .25
3426 A934 35c Oncidium luridum 1.00 .30
3427 A934 40c Vanda hibrida 1.25 .40
Nos. 3422-3427 (6) 3.90 1.70

Soroa Orchid Garden, 40th anniv.

Mellisuga Helenae — A935

1992, July 7 *Perf. 13*

3428 A935 5c Sitting on nest .40 .25
3429 A935 10c Wings extended .50 .30
3430 A935 20c Sitting on branch 1.10 .40
3431 A935 30c In flight 1.75 .60
Nos. 3428-3431 (4) 3.75 1.55

World Wildlife Fund.
Nos. 3428-3431 exist imperf.

Tourism A936

10c, Guardalavaca Beach. 20c, Bucanero Hotel. 30c, Sailing ship, Havana. 50c, Varadero Beach.

1992, July 15 Litho. *Perf. 12½*

3432 A936 10c multicolored .35 .25
3433 A936 20c multicolored .60 .25
3434 A936 30c multicolored 1.10 .40
3435 A936 50c multicolored 1.40 .50
Nos. 3432-3435 (4) 3.45 1.40

Souvenir Sheet

Expo '92, Seville — A937

1992, July 27 Litho. *Perf. 13*

3436 A937 1.50p multicolored 4.50 2.25

1992 Summer Olympics, Barcelona A938

Athlete, sport: 5c, Eligio (Kid Chocolate) Sardinas, boxing. 35c, Ramon Fonst, fencing. 40c, Sergio Martinez, cycling. 50c, Martin Dihigo, baseball.

1992, July 20 Litho. *Perf. 12½x13*

3437 A938 5c multicolored .25 .25
3438 A938 35c multicolored 1.00 .30
3439 A938 40c multicolored 1.10 .40
3440 A938 50c multicolored 1.50 .60
Nos. 3437-3440 (4) 3.85 1.55

Olymphilex '92.

Discovery of America, 500th Anniv. — A939

5c, Alvarez Cabral. 10c, Alonso Pinzon. 20c, Alonso de Ojeda. 30c, Amerigo Vespucci. 35c, Prince Henry the Navigator. 40c, Bartolomeu Dias. 1p, Columbus' fleet.

1992, Sept. 18 Litho. *Perf. 12½*

3441 A939 5c multicolored .25 .25
3442 A939 10c multicolored .30 .25
3443 A939 20c multicolored .60 .25
3444 A939 30c multicolored 1.00 .30
3445 A939 35c multicolored 1.10 .30
3446 A939 40c multicolored 1.25 .40
Nos. 3441-3446 (6) 4.50 1.75

Souvenir Sheet

Perf. 13

3447 A939 1p multi, vert. 3.00 1.60

Genoa '92. No. 3447 contains one 32x40mm stamp.

Nos. 3442 and 3444 exist imperf. Value, each $12.

1992 Summer Olympics Medal Winners, Barcelona — A940

Medals and participants in events: No. 3448, Bronze, 4x100-meter relay, women's high jump, and women's 800-meter. No. 3449, Gold, high jump, women's discus. No. 3450, Silver, 4x400-meter relay, bronze, discus. No. 3451, Gold and silver, boxing. No. 3452, Gold, baseball. No. 3453, Gold, women's volleyball. No. 3454, Gold, silver, and bronze, judo. No. 3455, Gold and bronze, Greco-Roman and freestyle wrestling. No. 3456, Silver and bronze, fencing, silver, weight lifting.

1992, Sept. 24 Litho. *Perf. 13*

3448 A940 5c multicolored .25 .25
3449 A940 5c multicolored .25 .25
3450 A940 5c multicolored .25 .25
3451 A940 20c multicolored .55 .25
3452 A940 20c multicolored .55 .25
3453 A940 20c multicolored .55 .25
3454 A940 50c multicolored 1.50 .50
3455 A940 50c multicolored 1.50 .50
3456 A940 50c multicolored 1.50 .50
Nos. 3448-3456 (9) 6.90 3.00

6th World Track and Field Cup, Havana A941

1992, Sept. 24 Litho. *Perf. 13*

3457 A941 5c High jump .25 .25
3458 A941 20c Javelin .60 .25
3459 A941 30c Hammer throw .90 .25
3460 A941 40c Long jump, vert. 1.25 .40
3461 A941 50c Hurdles, vert. 1.50 .50
Nos. 3457-3461 (5) 4.50 1.65

Souvenir Sheet

3462 A941 1p Women's relay 3.00 1.75

No. 3462 contains one 40x32mm stamp.

Latin American History Type of 1986

Discovery of America: No. 3463a, Columbus, Queen Isabella. b, Columbus at Rabida Monastery. c, Columbus, pointing up, outlining his plan. d, Columbus, with scroll, before Salamanca Council. e, Departure of Columbus' fleet from Palos.

No. 3464a, Three ships stopping at Canary Islands. b, Columbus speaking to crew. c, Land sighted, Oct. 12, 1492. d, Columbus landing in New World. e, Meeting natives.

No. 3465a, Grounding of Santa Maria at Hispanola. b, Arrival of Nina at Palos. c, Columbus welcomed in Barcelona. d, Columbus describes his voyage to Ferdinand and Isabella. e, Departure of fleet from Cadiz on second voyage.

No. 3466a, King and Queen welcome Columbus. b, Fleet on Columbus' third voyage. c, Columbus deported from Hispanola to Spain as prisoner. d, Columbus on ship, fourth voyage. e, Death of Columbus, May 20, 1506 in Valladolid.

1992, Oct. 3 *Perf. 13*

3463 A804 1c Strip of 5, #a.-e. .65 .30
3464 A804 5c Strip of 5, #a.-e. .65 .30
3465 A804 10c Strip of 5, #a.-e. 1.25 .75
3466 A804 20c Strip of 5, #a.-e. 4.00 1.50
a. Sheet of 20, #3463-3466 20.00 20.00
Nos. 3463-3466 (4) 6.55 2.85

Jose Maria Chacon y Calvo (1892-1969), Historian A942

1992, Oct. 29 *Perf. 13*

3467 A942 30c multicolored .90 .40

Churches A943

Designs: 5c, Basilica of Nuestra Senora de la Caridad del Cobre. 20c, Santa Maria del Rosario Church. 30c, Espiritu Santo Church. 50c, Santo Angel Custodio Church.

1992, Nov. 10 **Litho.** *Perf. 12½*

3468 A943 5c multicolored .25 .25
3469 A943 20c multicolored .60 .25
3470 A943 30c multicolored .90 .25
3471 A943 50c multicolored 1.50 .30
Nos. 3468-3471 (4) 3.25 1.05

Development of the Diesel Engine — A944

1993, Jan. 20 **Litho.** *Perf. 12½*

3472 A944 5c Truck .25 .25
3473 A944 10c Automobile .25 .25
3474 A944 30c Tugboat .55 .40
3475 A944 40c Locomotive 2.00 1.00
3476 A944 50c Tractor 1.00 .65
Nos. 3472-3476 (5) 4.05 2.55

Souvenir Sheet

3477 A944 1p Rudolf Diesel 3.00 1.75

No. 3477 contains one 40x32mm stamp. Rudolf Diesel, 80th anniv. of death (No. 3477).

Davis Cup Tennis Competition — A945

Various tennis players in action.

Perf. 12x12½, 12½x12

1993, Feb. 10 **Litho.**

3478 A945 5c multi, vert. .25 .25
3479 A945 20c multi, vert. .60 .25
3480 A945 30c multi, vert. .90 .40
3481 A945 35c multicolored 1.00 .50
3482 A945 40c multicolored 1.25 .60
Nos. 3478-3482 (5) 4.00 2.00

Souvenir Sheet

Perf. 12½

3483 A945 1p multicolored 2.75 1.25

No. 3483 contains one 40x32mm stamp.

Scientists A946

Designs: 3c, Pierre-Paul-Emile Roux (1853-1933), bacteriologist. 5c, Carlos J. Finlay (1833-1915), suggested mosquito as carrier of yellow fever. 10c, Ivan Petrovich Pavlov (1849-1936), physiologist, investigated conditioned reflexes. 20c, Louis Pasteur, chemist, developer of pasteurization. 30c, Santiago Ramon y Cajal (1852-1934), histologist, isolated the neuron. 35c, Sigmund Freud, psychoanalyst. 40c, Wilhelm Conrad Roentgen, physicist, discoverer of x-ray. 50c, Joseph Lister, surgeon, introduced principle of antisepsis. 1p, Robert Koch, bacteriologist, developer of tuberculin, vert.

1993, Mar. 3 **Litho.** *Perf. 12½*

3484 A946 3c multicolored .25 .25
3485 A946 5c multicolored .25 .25
3486 A946 10c multicolored .25 .25
3487 A946 20c multicolored .55 .25
3488 A946 30c multicolored .80 .40
3489 A946 35c multicolored .90 .50
3490 A946 40c multicolored 1.10 .60
3491 A946 50c multicolored 1.25 .65
Nos. 3484-3491 (8) 5.35 3.15

Souvenir Sheet

3492 A946 1p multicolored 2.75 1.40

Most issues between Nos. 3493-3650 exist imperforate.

Bicycles — A947

Bicycles designed by: 3c, Leonardo da Vinci, 15th cent. 5c, Karl Von Drais de Sauerbrun, 1813. 10c, Ernest Michaux, 1856. 20c, James Starley, 1869. 30c, Harry Lawson, 1879. 35c, Guaso (Cuba), 1992.

1993, Apr. 14 *Perf. 13*

3493 A947 3c multicolored .25 .25
3494 A947 5c multicolored .25 .25
3495 A947 10c multicolored .30 .25
3496 A947 20c multicolored .60 .25
3497 A947 30c multicolored .90 .40
3498 A947 35c multicolored 1.00 .50
Nos. 3493-3498 (6) 3.30 1.90

Cuban Natl. Museum, 80th Anniv. A948

Paintings by Joaquin Sorolla y Bastida (1863-1923): 3c, Child Eating Watermelon, 1920, vert. 5c, Valencian Fisherwomen, 1909. 10c, Regattas. 20c, Contadina, 1889. 40c, Summer, 1904. 50c, Boats on the Ocean, 1908.

1993, May 29 **Litho.** *Perf. 13x12½*

3499 A948 3c multicolored .25 .25

Perf. 12½x13

3500 A948 5c multicolored .30 .25
3501 A948 10c multicolored .35 .25
3502 A948 20c multicolored .65 .25
3503 A948 40c multicolored 1.25 .60
3504 A948 50c multicolored 1.75 .65
Nos. 3499-3504 (6) 4.55 2.25

Water Birds A949

Designs: 3c, Jacana spinosa. 5c, Ardea herodias, vert. 10c, Himantopus mexicanus. 20c, Nycticorax nycticorax. 30c, Grus canadensis, vert. 50c, Aramus guarauna.

Perf. 12½, 13x12½ (5, 30c)

1993, June 15

3505 A949 3c multicolored .25 .25
3506 A949 5c multicolored .25 .25
3507 A949 10c multicolored .40 .25
3508 A949 20c multicolored .80 .25
3509 A949 30c multicolored 1.10 .40
3510 A949 50c multicolored 2.25 .65
Nos. 3505-3510 (6) 5.05 2.05

Brasiliana '93. Nos. 3506, 3510 are 27x44mm.

Anniversaries — A950

No. 3511, Jose Marti, Moncada Barracks. No. 3512, "History Will Absolve Me," declaration of Fidel Castro, Marti. No. 3513, Jose Marti, Rafael M. Mendive, vert. No. 3514, Carlos Manuel de Cespedes, gear wheels.

1993, July 26 **Litho.** *Perf. 13*

3511 A950 5c multicolored .25 .25
3512 A950 5c multicolored .25 .25
3513 A950 5c multicolored .25 .25
3514 A950 5c multicolored .25 .25
Nos. 3511-3514 (4) 1.00 1.00

Attack on Moncada Barracks, 40th anniv. (No. 3511). Declaration of Fidel Castro, 40th anniv. (No. 3512). Birth of Jose Marti, 140th anniv. (No. 3513). Declaration of the Ten Years' War, 125th anniv. (No. 3514).

Flowers from Cienfuegos Botanical Gardens A951

Designs: 3c, Sedum allantoides. 5c, Heliconia caribaea. 10c, Anthurium andraeanum. 20c, Pseudobombax ellipticum. 35c, Ixora coccinea. 50c, Callistemon specious.

1993, Aug. 20

3515 A951 3c multicolored .25 .25
3516 A951 5c multicolored .25 .25
3517 A951 10c multicolored .35 .25
3518 A951 20c multicolored .70 .25
3519 A951 35c multicolored 1.10 .50
3520 A951 50c multicolored 1.90 .65
Nos. 3515-3520 (6) 4.55 2.15

Bangkok '93, Intl. Philatelic Exhibition A952

Butterflies: 3c, Battus devillievs. 5c, Anteos maerula. 20c, Ascia monuste evonima. 30c, Junonia coenia. 35c, Anartia jatrophae guantanamo. 50c, Hypolimnas misippus.

1993, Sept. 10 **Litho.** *Perf. 13*

3521 A952 3c multicolored .25 .25
3522 A952 5c multicolored .25 .25
3523 A952 20c multicolored .70 .25
3524 A952 30c multicolored 1.00 .40
3525 A952 35c multicolored 1.10 .40
3526 A952 50c multicolored 1.60 .65
Nos. 3521-3526 (6) 4.90 2.20

Endangered Species A953

5c, Phoenicopterus ruber. 50c, Ajaia ajaja.

1993, Oct. 12 **Litho.** *Perf. 13*

3527 A953 5c multicolored .25 .25
3528 A953 50c multicolored 1.75 .65

Latin American Revolutionaries A954

Flags, map and: No. 3529, Simon Bolivar. No. 3530, Jose Marti. No. 3531, Benito Juarez, Mexican President. No. 3532, Ernesto "Che" Guevara.

1993, Oct. 27 **Litho.** *Perf. 13*

3529 A954 50c multicolored 1.40 .65
3530 A954 50c multicolored 1.40 .65
3531 A954 50c multicolored 1.40 .65
3532 A954 50c multicolored 1.40 .65
a. Block of 4, #3529-3532 7.25 3.50
Nos. 3529-3532 (4) 5.60 2.60

17th Central American and Caribbean Games, Ponce, Puerto Rico — A955

1993, Nov. 10 **Litho.** *Perf. 12½*

3533 A955 5c Swimming .25 .25
3534 A955 10c Pole vault .25 .25
3535 A955 20c Boxing .70 .25
3536 A955 35c Gymnastics, vert. 1.10 .40
3537 A955 50c Baseball, vert. 1.60 .65
Nos. 3533-3537 (5) 3.90 1.80

Souvenir Sheet

3538 A955 1p Basketball 3.75 1.75

No. 3538 contains one 40x32mm stamp.

Mariana Grajales (1808-93), Patriot — A956

1993, Nov. 27 *Perf. 13*

3539 A956 5p multicolored .50 .25

Peter I. Tchaikovsky (1840-93), Composer A957

1993, Nov. 30

3540 A957 5c Portrait .25 .25
3541 A957 20c Swan Lake Ballet .65 .25
3542 A957 30c Statue .90 .40
3543 A957 50c Museum, horiz. 1.25 .65
Nos. 3540-3543 (4) 3.05 1.55

A958

1994, Jan. 1 **Litho.** *Perf. 13*

3544 A958 5c multicolored .30 .25

35th anniv. of the Revolution.

A959

Various soccer players.

1994, Jan. 1

3545 A959 5c multicolored .25 .25
3546 A959 20c multicolored .60 .25
3547 A959 30c multicolored .85 .40
3548 A959 35c multicolored .95 .40
3549 A959 40c multicolored 1.25 .50
3550 A959 50c multicolored 1.40 .65
Nos. 3545-3550 (6) 5.30 2.45

Souvenir Sheet

3551 A959 1p multicolored 3.00 1.50

1994 World Cup Soccer Championships, US. No. 3551 contains one 40x31mm stamp.

Cats A960

1994, Feb. 15 **Litho.** *Perf. 12½*

3552 A960 5c Blue Persian .25 .25
3553 A960 10c Havana .25 .25
3554 A960 20c Maine coon .70 .25
3555 A960 30c Blue British shorthair 1.00 .40
3556 A960 35c Bicolor Persian 1.10 .40
3557 A960 50c Gold chinchilla 1.60 .65
Nos. 3552-3557 (6) 4.90 2.20

Souvenir Sheet

Perf. 13

3558 A960 1p Abyssinian, vert. 3.50 2.00

No. 3558 contains one 30x38mm stamp.

Medicinal Plants — A961

Designs: 5c, Salvia officinalis. 10c, Aloe barbadensis. 20c, Helianthus annuus. 30c, Matricaria chamomilla. 40c, Calendula officinalis. 50c, Tilia platyphyllos.

1994, Mar. 30 **Litho.** *Perf. 12½*

3559 A961 5c multicolored .25 .25
3560 A961 10c multicolored .25 .25
3561 A961 20c multicolored .65 .25
3562 A961 30c multicolored .90 .40
3563 A961 40c multicolored 1.25 .50
3564 A961 50c multicolored 1.50 .65
Nos. 3559-3564 (6) 4.80 2.30

Carriages — A962

Designs: 5c, Public coach, 1860. 10c, Coach of Ferdinand VII, Maria Louisa. 30c, Louis XV-style coach. 35c, Elizabeth II gala day's coach. 40c, Catalina II's summer coach. 50c, Volanta habanera.

1994, Apr. 20 *Perf. 12½x12*

3565 A962 5c multicolored .25 .25
3566 A962 10c multicolored .25 .25
3567 A962 30c multicolored 1.00 .40
3568 A962 35c multicolored 1.10 .40
3569 A962 40c multicolored 1.25 .50
3570 A962 50c multicolored 1.50 .65
Nos. 3565-3570 (6) 5.35 2.45

No. 3570 is 68x37mm.

Aquaculture — A963

Designs: 5c, Crassostrea rhizophorae. 20c, Cardisoma guanhumi. 30c, Tilapia melanopleura. 35c, Hippospongia lachne. 40c, Panulirus argus. 50c, Cyprinus carpio.

1994, May 10 **Litho.** *Perf. 12½*

3571 A963 5c multicolored .35 .25
3572 A963 20c multicolored .60 .25
3573 A963 30c multicolored .85 .40
3574 A963 35c multicolored 1.00 .40
3575 A963 40c multicolored 1.25 .50
3576 A963 50c multicolored 1.50 .65
Nos. 3571-3576 (6) 5.55 2.45

Intl. Olympic Committee, Cent. — A964

1994, June 23 **Litho.** *Perf. 12½*

3577 A964 5c Flag, runners .25 .25
3578 A964 30c Flag, world map 1.10 .40
3579 A964 50c Flag, Olympic flame 1.90 .65
Nos. 3577-3579 (3) 3.25 1.30

Scientists A965

Designs: 5c, Michael Faraday (1791-1867), physicist. 10c, Marie Curie (1867-1934), physical chemist. 20c, Pierre Curie (1859-1906), chemist. 30c, Albert Einstein (1879-1955), physicist, mathematician. 40c, Max Planck (1858-1947), theoretical physicist. 50c, Otto Hahn (1879-1968), physical chemist.

1994, July 20 **Litho.** *Perf. 12½*

3580 A965 5c multicolored .25 .25
3581 A965 10c multicolored .25 .25
3582 A965 20c multicolored .45 .25
3583 A965 30c multicolored .75 .40
3584 A965 40c multicolored 1.00 .50
3585 A965 50c multicolored 1.25 .65
Nos. 3580-3585 (6) 3.95 2.30

Cactus Flowers A966

Designs: 5c, Opuntia dillenii. 10c, Opuntia millspaughii, vert. 30c, Leptocereus santamarinae. 35c, Pereskia marcanoi. 40c, Dendrocereus nudiflorus, vert. 50c, Pilocereus robinii.

1994, Aug. 15 **Litho.** *Perf. 12½*

3586 A966 5c multicolored .25 .25
3587 A966 10c multicolored .25 .25
3588 A966 30c multicolored .75 .40
3589 A966 35c multicolored .80 .40
3590 A966 40c multicolored 1.00 .50
3591 A966 50c multicolored 1.25 .65
Nos. 3586-3591 (6) 4.30 2.45

Souvenir Sheet

2nd Spanish-Cuban Philatelic Exhibition, Havana — A967

Design: 1p, Cuban postal rocket, #C31.

1994, Sept. 18

3592 A967 1p multicolored 2.50 1.50

Experimental postal rocket flight, 55th anniv.

Dogs A968

5c, Rough collie. 20c, American cocker spaniel. 30c, Dalmatian. 40c, Afghan hound. 50c, English cocker spaniel.

1994, Sept. 20

3593 A968 5c multicolored .25 .25
3594 A968 20c multicolored .50 .25
3595 A968 30c multicolored .75 .40
3596 A968 40c multicolored 1.00 .50
3597 A968 50c multicolored 1.25 .65
Nos. 3593-3597 (5) 3.75 2.05

Cayo Largo Island A969

Fauna: 15c, Carpilius corallinus. 65c, Cyclura nubila, vert. 75c, Pelecanus occidentalis. 1p, Chelonia mydas.

1994, Sept. 30 **Litho.** *Perf. 12½*

3598 A969 15c multicolored .30 .25
3599 A969 65c multicolored 1.50 .90
3600 A969 75c multicolored 1.75 1.00
3601 A969 1p multicolored 2.50 1.25
Nos. 3598-3601 (4) 6.05 3.40

A970

1994, Oct. 28

3602 A970 15c multicolored .50 .25

Camilo Cienfuegos Gorriaran, revolutionary, 35th anniv. of disappearance.

A971

Fauna of the Caribbean: 10c, Epinephelus flavolimbatus, horiz. No. 3604, Phoenicopterus ruber. No. 3605, Aetobatus narinari. No. 3606, Istiophorus platypterus, horiz. No. 3607, Tursiops truncatus, horiz. No. 3608, Pelecanus occidentalis.

1994, Oct. 30

3603 A971 10c multicolored .30 .25
3604 A971 15c multicolored .30 .25
3605 A971 15c multicolored .30 .25
3606 A971 15c multicolored .30 .25
3607 A971 65c multicolored 1.60 .90
3608 A971 65c multicolored 1.60 .90
Nos. 3603-3608 (6) 4.40 2.80

ICAO, 50th Anniv. A972

1994, Nov. 9

3609 A972 65c multicolored 1.50 .90

Zoological Garden, Havana, 55th Anniv. — A973

15c, Bronze monument. 65c, Ara chloroptera. 75c, Carduelis carduelis.

1994, Nov. 14 Litho. *Perf. 13*

3610	A973 15c multicolored	.25	.25
3611	A973 65c multicolored	1.60	.90
3612	A973 75c multicolored	1.90	1.00
	Nos. 3610-3612 (3)	3.75	2.15

Cuban Philatelic Federation, 30th Anniv. — A974

1994, Nov. 20

3613	A974 15c multicolored	.50	.25

America Issue — A975

Postal transportation: 15c, 18th Cent. Spanish galleon, maritime postal service, vert. 65c, 19th Cent. postal rider, insurgent postal service.

1994, Dec. 12

3614	A975 15c multicolored	.25	.25
3615	A975 65c multicolored	1.75	.90

Postal Museum, 30th Anniv. — A976

1995, Jan. 2

3616	A976 15c multicolored	.50	.25

Lizards — A977

Designs: 15c, Anolis baracoae. 65c, Sphaerodactylus ramsdeni. 75c, Leiocephalus raviceps. 85c, Sphaerodactylus ruibali. 90c, Anolis ophiolepis. 1p, Sphaerodactylus armasi.

1994, Nov. 30 Litho. *Perf. 12½*

3617	A977 15c multicolored	.30	.25
3618	A977 65c multicolored	1.60	.90
3619	A977 75c multicolored	1.75	1.00
3620	A977 85c multicolored	2.00	1.25
3621	A977 90c multicolored	2.25	1.25
3622	A977 1p multicolored	2.50	1.40
	Nos. 3617-3622 (6)	10.40	6.05

Cuban War of Independence, Cent. — A978

1995, Feb. 24 Litho. *Perf. 12½*

3623	A978 15c Jose Marti, flag	.50	.25

Pan American Games, Mar del Plata, Argentina — A979

1995, Mar. 11 Litho. *Perf. 13*

3624	A979 10c Boxing, vert.	.25	.25
3625	A979 15c Weight lifting, vert.	.25	.25
3626	A979 65c Volleyball, vert.	1.25	.80
3627	A979 75c Wrestling	1.40	1.00
3628	A979 85c Baseball	1.60	1.00
3629	A979 90c High jump	1.75	1.10
	Nos. 3624-3629 (6)	6.50	4.40

National Aquarium, 35th Anniv. — A980

Fish: 10c, Holacanthus cillaris. 15c, Hypoplectrus guttavarius. 65c, Anisotremus virginicus. 75c, Amblycirrhitus pinos. 85c, Pomaacanthus paru. 90c, Acanthurus coeruleus.

1995, Apr. 28 Litho. *Perf. 13*

3630	A980 10c multicolored	.25	.25
3631	A980 15c multicolored	.30	.25
3632	A980 65c multicolored	1.25	.70
3633	A980 75c multicolored	1.50	.80
3634	A980 85c multicolored	1.75	1.10
3635	A980 90c multicolored	2.00	1.10
	Nos. 3630-3635 (6)	7.05	4.20

FAO, 50th Anniv. A981

1995, Apr. 7 Litho. *Perf. 13*

3636	A981 75c multicolored	1.40	1.00

First Cuban Postage Stamp, 140th Anniv. — A982

65c, Ornamental letter drop, envelope.

1995, Apr. 24 Litho. *Perf. 12½*

3637	A982 15c blk & blue grn	.30	.25
3638	A982 65c multicolored	1.40	.75

Jose Marti, Death Cent. A983

Designs: 15c, Marti killed in combat, signature, portrait. 65c, Landing of Marti, Cuban patriots on Playitas beach. 75c, Montecristi Manifesto signed in Domincan Republic, Marti. 85c, Meeting of Marti, Maceo, Gomez at La Mejorana Farm. 90c, Marti's mausoleum, Santiago, Cuba, vert.

1995, May 19 *Perf. 12½x13, 13x12½*

3639	A983 15c multicolored	.25	.25
3640	A983 65c multicolored	1.25	.80
3641	A983 75c multicolored	1.40	1.00
3642	A983 85c multicolored	1.75	1.00
3643	A983 90c multicolored	1.75	1.10
	Nos. 3639-3643 (5)	6.40	4.15

Antonio Maceo (1845-96), Revolutionary — A984

1995, June 14 Litho. *Perf. 12½*

3644	A984 15c multicolored	.90	.25

Butterflies — A985

Designs: 10c, Dione vanillae. 15c, Eunica tatila. 65c, Melete salacia. 75c, Greta cubana. 85c, Eurema daira. 90c, Phoebis sennae.

1995, June 20 *Perf. 12½x13*

3645	A985 10c multicolored	.25	.25
3646	A985 15c multicolored	.25	.25
3647	A985 65c multicolored	1.25	.80
3648	A985 75c multicolored	1.40	1.00
3649	A985 85c multicolored	1.75	1.00
3650	A985 90c multicolored	1.75	1.10
	Nos. 3645-3650 (6)	6.65	4.40

World War II Combat Planes — A986

Designs: 10c, Supermarine "Spitfire," Great Britain. 15c, IL-2, Russia. 65c, Curtiss P-40, US. 75c, Messerschmitt Bf-109, Germany. 85c, Morane-Sauinier 406, France.

1995, July 30 Litho. *Perf. 12½*

3651	A986 10c multicolored	.30	.25
3652	A986 15c multicolored	.30	.25
3653	A986 65c multicolored	1.40	.80
3654	A986 75c multicolored	1.60	1.00
3655	A986 85c multicolored	1.90	1.00
	Nos. 3651-3655 (5)	5.50	3.30

A987

1995, Aug. 6 Litho. *Perf. 12½*

3656	A987 15c multicolored	.40	.25

Ernesto Lecuona, composer, pianist, birth cent.

A988

Color of Horse or Horses

1995, Aug. 10

3657	A988 10c golden brn, white	.25	.25
3658	A988 15c white, horiz.	.25	.25
3659	A988 65c dk brn, white	1.40	.80
3660	A988 75c red brown	1.60	1.00
3661	A988 85c tan	1.75	1.00
3662	A988 90c white	2.00	1.10
	Nos. 3657-3662 (6)	7.25	4.40

Singapore '95.

Souvenir Sheet

Beijing Intl. Stamp & Coin Expo '95 — A989

1995, Aug. 28 *Perf. 13*

3663	A989 50c multicolored	1.25	.75

1996 Summer Olympics, Atlanta — A990

10c, Wrestling. 15c, Weight lifting. 65c, Women's volleyball. 75c, Women's athletics. 85c, Baseball. 90c, Women's judo.
1p, Boxing.

1995, Sept. 25 Litho. *Perf. 13*

3664	A990 10c multicolored	.25	.25
3665	A990 15c multicolored	.25	.25
3666	A990 65c multicolored	1.25	.80
3667	A990 75c multicolored	1.50	1.00
3668	A990 85c multicolored	1.60	1.00
3669	A990 90c multicolored	1.75	1.10
	Nos. 3664-3669 (6)	6.60	4.40

Souvenir Sheet

3670	A990 1p multicolored	2.50	1.50

No. 3670 contains one 30x36mm stamp.

Cuban Sugar Industry, 400th Anniv. A991

Paintings from "Los Ingenios," by Edouard Laplante, 1852: 15c, Steam train, sugar factory. 65c, Sugar factory, tower, bridge.

1995, Oct. 3

3671 A991 15c multicolored 1.00 .35
3672 A991 65c multicolored .60 .70

UN, 50th Anniv. A992

1995, Oct. 24 Litho. *Perf. 13*

3673 A992 65c multicolored 1.25 .80

Zoological Gardens, Havana — A993

Designs: 10c, Panthera leo, vert. 15c, Equus grevyi. 65c, Pongo pygmaeus, vert. 75c, Elephas maximus. 85c, Sciurus vulgaris. 90c, Procyon lotor.

1995, Oct. 30 Litho. *Perf. 13*

3674 A993 10c multicolored .25 .25
3675 A993 15c multicolored .30 .25
3676 A993 65c multicolored 1.25 .80
3677 A993 75c multicolored 1.50 1.00
3678 A993 85c multicolored 1.75 1.00
3679 A993 90c multicolored 2.00 1.10
Nos. 3674-3679 (6) 7.05 4.40

UNESCO, 50th Anniv. — A994

UNESCO World Culture and National Heritage sites: 65c, Santa Clara de Asis Convent. 75c, San Francisco de Asis Minor Basilica.

1995, Nov. 4

3680 A994 65c multicolored 1.20 .80
3681 A994 75c multicolored 1.40 1.00

Orchids — A995

Designs: 5c, Epidendrum porpax. 10c, Cyrtopodium punctatum. 15c, Polyrrhiza lindeni. 40c, Bletia patula. 45c, Galeandra beyrichii. 50c, Vanilla dilloniana. 65c, Macradenia lutescens. 75c, Oncidium luridum. 85c, Ionopsis utricularioides.

1995, Nov. 10 *Perf. 12½*

3681A A995 5c multicolored .25 .25
3681B A995 10c multicolored .30 .25
3681C A995 15c multicolored .40 .25
3682 A995 40c multicolored .80 .55
3683 A995 45c multicolored .90 .55
3684 A995 50c multicolored 1.00 .65
3685 A995 65c multicolored 1.25 .80
3686 A995 75c multicolored 1.40 1.00
3687 A995 85c multicolored 1.60 1.00
Nos. 3681A-3687 (9) 7.90 5.30

Issued: 40c-85c, 11/10/95; 5c-15c, 6/28/96.

Motion Pictures, Cent. — A996

1995, Dec. 7 *Perf. 13*

3688 A996 15c Lumiere Brothers .30 .25
3689 A996 15c Marilyn Monroe .30 .25
3690 A996 15c Marlene Dietrich .30 .25
3691 A996 15c Vittorio DeSica .30 .25
3692 A996 15c Charlie Chaplin .30 .25
3693 A996 15c Greta Garbo .30 .25
3694 A996 65c Humphrey Bogart 1.40 .80
3695 A996 75c Montaner 1.60 1.00
3696 A996 85c Cantinflas 1.90 1.00
a. Sheet of 9, #3688-3696 17.50 —
Nos. 3688-3696 (9) 6.70 4.30

Souvenir Sheet

4th Cuban-Spanish Philatelic Exhibition, Havana — A997

1995, Dec. 11 Litho. *Perf. 13*

3697 A997 1p multicolored 2.50 1.50

America Issue — A998

15c, Centurus superciliaris. 65c, Todus multicolor.

1995, Dec. 12

3698 A998 15c multicolored .35 .25
3699 A998 65c multicolored 1.40 .80

Generals Who Died in 1895 War — A999

Designs: No. 3700, Alfonso Goulet Goulet, Francisco Adolfo Crombet Ballon. No. 3701, Jesus Calvar O, Jose Guillermo Moncada, Tomas Jordan. No. 3702, Francisco Borrero Lavadi, Francisco Inchaustegui Cabrera.

1995, Dec. 20 *Perf. 12½*

3700 A999 15c multicolored .50 .25
3701 A999 15c multicolored .50 .25
3702 A999 15c multicolored .50 .25
a. Strip of 3, #3700-3702 1.75 1.50
Nos. 3700-3702 (3) 1.50 .75

See Nos. 3758-3760.

Island of Coco Cay, Jardines del Rey A1000

Bird, scenic view: 10c, Sterna antillarum, aerial view of island. 15c, Eudocimus albus, people on beach. 45c, Spindalis zena, couple on steps of resort complex. 50c, Turdus plumbeus, resort. 65c, Mimus polyglottos, resort. 75c, Phoenicopterus ruber, couple in pool at resort.

1995, Dec. 23

3703 A1000 10c multicolored .25 .25
3704 A1000 15c multicolored .30 .25
3705 A1000 45c multicolored 1.00 .55
3706 A1000 50c multicolored 1.10 .60
3707 A1000 65c multicolored 1.40 .80
3708 A1000 75c multicolored 1.60 1.00
Nos. 3703-3708 (6) 5.65 3.45

Patriots — A1001

Designs: 15c, Carlos M. de Céspedes (1819-74). 65c, José Marti (1853-95). 75c, Antonio Maceo (1845-96). 1.05p, Ignacio Agramonte (1841-73). 2.05p, Máximo Gómez (1836-1905). 3p, Calixto Garcia (1839-98).

1996, Jan. 10

3709 A1001 15c green .25 .25
3710 A1001 65c blue 1.10 .80
3711 A1001 75c carmine 1.25 1.00
3712 A1001 1.05p lilac 1.90 1.40
3713 A1001 2.05p brown 4.00 2.50
3714 A1001 3p light brown 5.50 3.75
Nos. 3709-3714 (6) 14.00 9.70

See Nos. 3755-3757.

Organization of Solidarity of the Peoples of Africa, Asia and Latin America (OSPAAAL), 30th Anniv. — A1002

1996, Jan. 14

3715 A1002 65c multicolored 1.40 .75

Scientists — A1003

10c, Leonardo da Vinci (1452-1519). 15c, Mikhail V. Lomonosov (1711-65), atmospheric scientist. 65c, James Watt (1736-1819), engineer, inventor. 75c, Guglielmo Marconi (1874-1937), physicist. 85c, Charles R. Darwin (1809-82), naturalist.

1996, Jan. 30 Litho. *Perf. 12½*

3716 A1003 10c multicolored .25 .25
3717 A1003 15c multicolored .30 .25
3718 A1003 65c multicolored 1.25 .80
3719 A1003 75c multicolored 1.50 1.00
3720 A1003 85c multicolored 1.75 1.00
Nos. 3716-3720 (5) 5.05 3.30

1996 Summer Olympics, Atlanta — A1004

1996, Feb. 15 Litho. *Perf. 12½*

3721 A1004 10c Athletics, vert. .25 .25
3722 A1004 15c Weight lifting, vert. .30 .25
3723 A1004 65c Judo, vert. 1.25 .80
3724 A1004 75c Wrestling 1.50 1.00
3725 A1004 85c Boxing 1.75 1.00
Nos. 3721-3725 (5) 5.05 3.30

Souvenir Sheet

3726 A1004 1p Baseball, vert. 2.00 1.50

No. 3726 contains one 40x32mm stamp.

Espamer '96, Aviation and Space, Philatelic Exhibition, Seville — A1005

1996, Mar. 4

3727 A1005 15c C-4 Autogiro .25 .25
3728 A1005 65c CASA C-352 1.25 .80
3729 A1005 75c Alcotan C-201 1.60 1.00
3730 A1005 85c CASA C-212 1.75 1.00
Nos. 3727-3730 (4) 4.85 3.05

Juan C. Gundlach (1810-1896), Ornithologist — A1006

Birds: 10c, Ceryle alcyon. 15c, Setophaga ruticilla. 65c, Geothlypis trichas. 75c, Passerina ciris. 85c, Bombycilla cedrorum.
1p, Vireo gundlachi.

1996, Mar. 15 *Perf. 12½*

3731 A1006 10c multicolored .30 .25
3732 A1006 15c multicolored .30 .25
3733 A1006 65c multicolored 1.40 .80
3734 A1006 75c multicolored 1.60 1.00
3735 A1006 85c multicolored 1.90 1.00
Nos. 3731-3735 (5) 5.50 3.30

Souvenir Sheet

3736 A1006 1p multicolored 3.00 1.90

No. 3736 contains one 40x32mm stamp.

Souvenir Sheet

ESPAMER '96, Stamp Exhibition of America and Europe, Seville — A1007

1996, Mar. 14 Litho. *Perf. 12½*

3737 A1007 1p multicolored 3.00 1.50

First Man in Space, 35th Anniv. — A1008

Designs: 15c, Yuri A. Gagarin (1934-68). 65c, Spaceship, map showing orbital route.

1996, Apr. 12 Litho. *Perf. 12½*

3738	A1008	15c multi	.35	.25
3739	A1008	65c multi, horiz.	1.25	.80

Bay of Pigs Invasion, 35th Anniv. — A1009

1996, Apr. 19

3740	A1009	15c shown	.35	.25
3741	A1009	65c Natl. flags	1.25	.80

Cuban Sailing Ships A1010

Designs: 10c, Bahama. 15c, Santísima Trinidad. 65c, Principe de Asturias. 75c, San Pedro de Alcántara. 85c, Santa Ana.
1p, San Genaro.

1996, May 8 Litho. *Perf. 12½*

3742	A1010	10c multicolored	.25	.25
3743	A1010	15c multicolored	.30	.25
3744	A1010	65c multicolored	1.40	.80
3745	A1010	75c multicolored	1.60	1.00
3746	A1010	85c multicolored	1.75	1.00
		Nos. 3742-3746 (5)	5.30	3.30

Souvenir Sheet

3747	A1010	1p multicolored	2.00	1.00

CAPEX '96. No. 3747 contains one 40x32mm stamp.

Fauna of the Caribbean A1011

Designs: 10c, Todus multicolor. No. 3749, Eulampis jugularis. No. 3750, Aix sponsa. No. 3751, Chaetodon ocellatus. No. 3752, Papilio cresphontes. No. 3753, Hypoplectrus indigo.

1996, June 18 Litho. *Perf. 12½*

3748	A1011	10c multicolored	.30	.25
3749	A1011	15c multicolored	.30	.25
3750	A1011	15c multicolored	.30	.25
3751	A1011	15c multicolored	.30	.25
3752	A1011	65c multicolored	1.40	.80
3753	A1011	65c multicolored	1.40	.80
		Nos. 3748-3753 (6)	4.00	2.60

Jose M. Maceo Grajales (1849-96), Revolutionary War Leader — A1012

1996, July 5

3754	A1012	15c multicolored	.50	.25

Patriot Type of 1996

Designs: 10c. Serafin Sánchez. 85c, Juan Gualberto Gomez. 90c, Quintin Bandera.

1996, July 10

3755	A1001	10c orange	.25	.25
3756	A1001	85c olive	1.75	1.00
3757	A1001	90c olive brown	2.00	1.10
		Nos. 3755-3757 (3)	4.00	2.35

Generals Who Died in 1895 War Type of 1995

No. 3758, Esteban Tamayo (1843-96), Angel Guerra (1842-96). No. 3759, Juan Fernández Ruz (1821-96), José Maria Aguirre (1843-96), Serafin Sánchez (1846-96). No. 3760, Juan Bruno Zayas (1867-96), Pedro Vargas Sotomayor (1868-96).

1996, July 30

3758	A999	15c multicolored	.35	.25
3759	A999	15c multicolored	.35	.25
3760	A999	15c multicolored	.35	.25
a.		Strip of 3, #3758-3760	1.70	.90
		Nos. 3758-3760 (3)	1.05	.75

Santiago de Cuba — A1013

Flower, scenic view: 15c, Jacaranda arborea, beach. 65c, Begonia bissei, Fort San Pedro de la Roca. 75c, Byrsonima crassifolia, palm trees, mountains, vert. 85c, Pereskia zinniiflora, church, vert.

Perf. 13x12½, 12½x13

1996, Sept. 27 Litho.

3761	A1013	15c multicolored	.30	.25
3762	A1013	65c multicolored	1.25	.65
3763	A1013	75c multicolored	1.50	.75
3764	A1013	85c multicolored	1.60	.85
		Nos. 3761-3764 (4)	4.65	2.50

Steam Locomotives — A1014

Designs: 10c, Baldwin 0-4-2, 1878. 15c, American 2-6-0, 1904. 65c, Baldwin 4-6-0, 1906. 75c, Rogers 2-4-4, 1914. 90c, Baldwin 2-8-0, 1920.

1996, Sept. 30 *Perf. 12½*

3765	A1014	10c multicolored	.30	.25
3766	A1014	15c multicolored	.30	.25
3767	A1014	65c multicolored	1.40	.80
3768	A1014	75c multicolored	1.60	.90
3769	A1014	90c multicolored	1.75	1.00
		Nos. 3765-3769 (5)	5.35	3.20

Traditional Costumes A1015

America Issue: 15c, Free black couple, 19th cent. 65c, Guayabera couple, 20th cent.

1996, Oct. 12 Litho. *Perf. 12½*

3770	A1015	15c multicolored	.35	.25
3771	A1015	65c multicolored	1.25	.80

UNICEF, 50th Anniv. — A1016

1996, Nov. 8 Litho. *Perf. 12½*

3772	A1016	15c multicolored	.50	.25

World Chess Championship Won by José Raúl Capablanca, 75th Anniv. — A1017

Designs: 15c, Portrait, chess board. 65c, Portrait, seated at chess board. 75c, Rook with top shaped as world, portrait. 85c, Playing chess as a child. 90c, In championship match, 1921.

1996, Nov. 30 Litho. *Perf. 12½*

3773	A1017	15c multicolored	.30	.25
3774	A1017	65c multicolored	1.25	.80
3775	A1017	75c multicolored	1.50	1.00
3776	A1017	85c multicolored	1.75	1.00
3777	A1017	90c multicolored	1.90	1.10
		Nos. 3773-3777 (5)	6.70	4.15

Revolutionary Armed Forces and Return of Castro from Mexico, 40th Anniv. — A1018

1996, Dec. 2

3778	A1018	15c Yacht Granma	.25	.25
3779	A1018	65c Armed forces	1.25	1.00

Maj. Gen. Antonio Maceo (1845-96) — A1019

Designs: 10c, Monument, Santiago, vert. No. 3781, Portrait, vert. No. 3782, Monument, Duaba. 65c, Detail of painting showing Maceo dying from combat wounds. 75c, Maceo, young man and monument, San Pedro.

1996, Dec. 7

3780	A1019	10c multicolored	.25	.25
3781	A1019	15c multicolored	.30	.25
3782	A1019	15c multicolored	.30	.25
3783	A1019	65c multicolored	1.40	1.10
3784	A1019	75c multicolored	1.60	1.40
		Nos. 3780-3784 (5)	3.85	3.25

Medals Won at 1996 Summer Olympic Games, Atlanta — A1020

Medal, sport: No. 3785a, Gold, judo. b, Bronze, wrestling.
No. 3786: a, Gold, weight lifting. b, Gold, wrestling. c, Silver, fencing. d, Silver, swimming.
No. 3787: a, Gold, women's volleyball. b, Gold, boxing. c, Silver, women's running. d, Gold, baseball.

1996, Dec. 10

3785	A1020	10c Pair, #a-b + 4 labels	.50	.25
3786	A1020	15c Block, #a-d + 2 labels	1.25	.65
3787	A1020	65c Block, #a-d + 2 labels	5.00	2.50
		Nos. 3785-3787 (3)	6.75	3.40

New Year 1996 (Year of the Rat) — A1021

1996, Dec. 28 Litho. *Perf. 12½*

3788	A1021	15c multicolored	.50	.25

Espamer '98 — A1022

Locomotives: 15c, Minho Douro 0-6-0, Portugal. No. 3790, Vulcan Iron Works 0-4-0, Brazil. No. 3791, Baldwin 2-6-0, Dominican Republic. No. 3792, American Locomotive Co. 2-6-4, Panama. No. 3793, Baldwin 0-4-0, Puerto Rico. No. 3794, Slaughter, Gruning Co. 0-4-0, Spain. No. 3795, Yorkshire Engine Co. 4-4-0, Argentina. No. 3796, 2-6-0 Paraguay. No. 3797, H.K. Porter Co. 2-8-2, Chile. No. 3798, 2-6-0, Mexico.
1p, Baldwin 0-4-2 (1884), Cuba.

1996, Dec. 30

3789	A1022	15c multicolored	.30	.25
3790	A1022	65c multicolored	1.40	.70
3791	A1022	65c multicolored	1.40	.70
3792	A1022	65c multicolored	1.40	.70
3793	A1022	65c multicolored	1.40	.70
3794	A1022	65c multicolored	1.40	.70
3795	A1022	75c multicolored	1.50	.80
3796	A1022	75c multicolored	1.50	.80
3797	A1022	75c multicolored	1.50	.80
3798	A1022	75c multicolored	1.50	.80
		Nos. 3789-3798 (10)	13.30	6.95

Souvenir Sheet

3799	A1022	1p multicolored	3.00	1.75

No. 3799 contains one 36x28mm.

Hong Kong '97, Intl. Philatelic Exhibition — A1023

Cats: 10c, Brown-point Siamese, vert. No. 3801, Japanese bobtail. No. 3802, Burmese, vert. No. 3803, Singapore. No. 3804, Korat. 1p, Blue-point Siamese.

1997, Jan. 15 Litho. *Perf. 12½*

3800	A1023	10c multicolored	.25	.25
3801	A1023	15c multicolored	.30	.25
3802	A1023	15c multicolored	.30	.25
3803	A1023	65c multicolored	1.50	1.00
3804	A1023	75c multicolored	1.90	1.10
		Nos. 3800-3804 (5)	4.25	2.85

Souvenir Sheet

3805	A1023	1p multicolored	3.00	2.00

No. 3805 contains one 40x31mm stamp.

Motion Pictures, Cent. A1024

Film scenes from: 15c, "El Romance del Palmar," directed by Ramón Peón. 65c, "Memorias del Subdesarrollo," directed by Tomás Gutiérrez Alea, vert.

1997, Jan. 24 Litho. *Perf. 13*

3806	A1024	15c multicolored	.30	.25
3807	A1024	65c multicolored	1.60	1.00

Zoo Animals A1025

Designs: 10c, Camelus dromedarius. No. 3809, Ailuropada melanoleuca. No. 3810, Cerothoterium simun. 75c, Pongo pygmaeus. 90c, Bison bonasus.

1997, Feb. 20 Litho. *Perf. 12½*

3808	A1025	10c multicolored	.25	.25
3809	A1025	15c multicolored	.30	.25
3810	A1025	15c multicolored	.30	.25
3811	A1025	75c multicolored	1.75	1.00
3812	A1025	90c multicolored	2.00	1.10
		Nos. 3808-3812 (5)	4.60	2.85

New Year 1997 (Year of the Ox) — A1026

1997, Feb. 22

3813	A1026	15c multicolored	.50	.25

Attack on the Presidential Palace, 40th Anniv. — A1027

15c, Menelao Mora Morales.

1997, Mar. 13 Litho. *Perf. 12½*

3814	A1027	15c multicolored	.60	.25

1998 World Cup Soccer Championships, France — A1028

Action scenes: 10c, Three players. No. 3816, Player in green, player in blue & yellow. No. 3817, Player in yellow & black, player in green. 65c, Player in yellow & blue, player in blue and red. 75c, Player in red & blue, player in yellow & black.
1p, Player down.

1997, Mar. 25

3815	A1028	10c multicolored	.25	.25
3816	A1028	15c multicolored	.30	.25
3817	A1028	15c multicolored	.30	.25
3818	A1028	65c multicolored	1.25	1.00
3819	A1028	75c multicolored	1.75	1.25
		Nos. 3815-3819 (5)	3.85	3.00

Souvenir Sheet

3820	A1028	1p multicolored	2.40	1.25

No. 3820 contains one 40x31mm stamp.

Young Communist League (UJC), 35th Anniv. — A1029

1997, Apr. 4

3821	A1029	15c multicolored	.75	.25

Paddle Steamer Caledonia — A1030

Stamp Day: 15c, Maritime Postal Service, 170th anniv. 65c, Air Postal Service, 70th anniv.

1997, Apr. 24 Litho. *Perf. 12½*

3822	A1030	15c multicolored	.40	.25
3823	A1030	65c multicolored	1.60	.95

Death of Generals in War of 1895, 102nd Anniv. — A1031

No. 3824, Adolfo de Castillo, Enrique del Junco Cruz-Muñoz. No. 3825, Alberto Rodríguez Acosta, Mariano Sánchez Vaillant.

1997, May 18 Litho. *Perf. 12½*

3824		15c multicolored	.30	.25
3825		15c multicolored	.30	.25
a.	A1031	Pair, #3824-3825	.65	.30

Gen. Gregorio Luperon, Death Cent. — A1032

1997, May 20

3826	A1032	65c multicolored	1.50	1.00

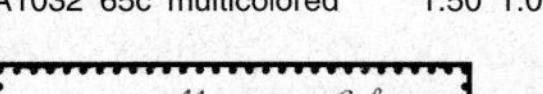

Butterflies — A1033

Designs: 10c, Eurema nicippe. No. 3828, Eurema dina. No. 3829, Colobura dirce clementi. 65c, Vanesa atalanta. 85c, Kricogonia castalia.

1997, May 20

3827	A1033	10c multicolored	.25	.25
3828	A1033	15c multicolored	.30	.25
3829	A1033	15c multicolored	.30	.25
3830	A1033	65c multicolored	1.50	.90
3831	A1033	85c multicolored	1.75	1.00
		Nos. 3827-3831 (5)	4.10	2.65

Cuban Assoc. of the UN, 50th Anniv. A1034

1997, May 31

3832	A1034	65c multicolored	1.60	.95

Chinese In Cuba, 150th Anniv. — A1035

1997, May 29 *Perf. 13*

3833	A1035	15c multicolored	1.40	.50

14th World Festival of Youth and Students A1036

Designs: 10c, Dove holding olive twig, rainbow. No. 3835, Children playing on playground equipment, vert. No. 3836, Monument with arms extended. 65c, Maj. Ernesto "Che" Guevara, revolutionary hero. 75c, Monument, diff.

1997, July 28 Litho. *Perf. 12½*

3834	A1036	10c multicolored	.25	.25
3835	A1036	15c multicolored	.30	.25
3836	A1036	15c multicolored	.30	.25
3837	A1036	65c multicolored	1.50	.95
3838	A1036	75c multicolored	1.75	1.00
		Nos. 3834-3838 (5)	4.10	2.70

Frank País (1934-57), Revolutionary Hero — A1037

1997, July 30

3839	A1037	15c multicolored	.50	.25

Seven Wonders of the Ancient World A1038

Designs: 10c, Lighthouse of Alexandria. No. 3841, Pyramids of Egypt. No. 3842, Gardens of Semiramis at Babylon. No. 3843, Colossus at Rhodes. No. 3844, Mausoleum of Halicarnassus. No. 3845, Statue of Zeus at Olympia. 75c, Temple of Artemis at Ephesus.

1997, July 30

3840	A1038	10c multicolored	.25	.25
3841	A1038	15c multicolored	.30	.25
3842	A1038	15c multicolored	.30	.25
3843	A1038	15c multicolored	.30	.25
3844	A1038	65c multicolored	1.25	.95
3845	A1038	65c multicolored	1.25	.95
3846	A1038	75c multicolored	1.50	1.00
		Nos. 3840-3846 (7)	5.15	3.90

Independence of India, 50th Anniv. — A1039

15c, Mahatma Gandhi.

1997, Aug. 15

3847	A1039	15c multicolored	.50	.25

Caribbean Birds — A1040

No. 3848, Sicalis flaveola. No. 3849, Eubucco bourcierii. No. 3850, Trogon curucui. No. 3851, Amazona leucocephala. No. 3852, Amazona ochrocephala. No. 3853, Hylocharis eliciae. No. 3854, Carduelis carduelis.

1997, Aug. 15

3848	A1040	15c multicolored	.30	.25
3849	A1040	15c multicolored	.30	.25
3850	A1040	15c multicolored	.30	.25
3851	A1040	15c multicolored	.30	.25
3852	A1040	65c multicolored	1.40	1.00
3853	A1040	65c multicolored	1.40	1.00
3854	A1040	75c multicolored	1.60	1.10
		Nos. 3848-3854 (7)	5.60	4.10

Famous Composers — A1041

10c, Liszt. No. 3856, Chopin. No. 3857, Bach. No. 3858, Beethoven. 65c, Ignacio Cervantes (1847-1905). 75c, Mozart.

1997, Sept. 15 Litho. *Perf. 12½*

3855 A1041 10c multicolored .30 .25
3856 A1041 15c multicolored .30 .25
3857 A1041 15c multicolored .30 .25
3858 A1041 15c multicolored .30 .25
3859 A1041 65c multicolored 1.40 .95
3860 A1041 75c multicolored 1.60 1.00
Nos. 3855-3860 (6) 4.20 2.95

Tourism in Pinar del Rio — A1042

Bird, scene: 10c, Myadestes elisabeth, Viñales Valley. 15c, Corvus nasicus, Jutia Key. 65c, Dendroica pityophila, Soroa Falls. 75c, Tyrannus cubensis, San Juan River.

1997, Sept. 27 Litho.

3861 A1042 10c multi .40 .25
3862 A1042 15c multi .40 .25
3863 A1042 65c multi, vert. 1.60 .95
3864 A1042 75c multi, vert. 1.75 1.00
Nos. 3861-3864 (4) 4.15 2.45

Caribbean Flowers — A1043

Designs: No. 3865, Hibiscus elatus (majagua). No. 3866, Cordia sebestena (vomitel). No. 3867, Bidens pilosa (romerillo). No. 3868, Catharanthus roseus (vicaria). 65c, Reullia tuberosa (salta perico). 75c, Turnera ulmifolia (marilope).

1997, Sept. 30

3865 A1043 15c multicolored .40 .25
3866 A1043 15c multicolored .40 .25
3867 A1043 15c multicolored .40 .25
3868 A1043 15c multicolored .40 .25
3869 A1043 65c multicolored 1.60 .95
3870 A1043 75c multicolored 1.75 .95
Nos. 3865-3870 (6) 4.95 2.90

Eastern University, 50th Anniv. — A1044

1997, Oct. 1 *Perf. 13*

3871 A1044 15c multicolored .70 .25

Che Guevara (1928-67), 5th Cuban Communist Party Congress A1045

No. 3872, Flags. No. 3873, Text, Guevara. No. 3874, Portrait of Guevara.

1997, Oct. 8

3872 A1045 15c multi .40 .25
3873 A1045 15c multi 1.60 .95
3874 A1045 75c multi 1.75 .95
Nos. 3872-3874 (3) 3.75 2.15

America Issue — A1046

15c, 19th cent. postman. 65c, 20th cent. postman.

1997, Oct. 12 Litho. *Perf. 13*

3875 A1046 15c multi .50 .25
3876 A1046 65c multi 1.40 .85

Hominids — A1047

Designs: 10c, Australopithecus. No. 3878, Pithecanthropus (Java man). No. 3879, Sinanthropus (Peking man). No. 3880, Neanderthal. 65c, Cro-magnon man. 75c, Oberkassel man.

1997, Oct. 30 *Perf. 12½*

3877 A1047 10c multicolored .30 .25
3878 A1047 15c multicolored .30 .25
3879 A1047 15c multicolored .30 .25
3880 A1047 15c multicolored .30 .25
3881 A1047 65c multicolored 1.25 .95
3882 A1047 75c multicolored 1.50 .95
Nos. 3877-3882 (6) 3.95 2.90

October Revolution, 80th Anniv. — A1048

1997, Nov. 7 *Perf. 12½*

3884 A1048 75c multicolored 1.50 1.00

Cuban Railroad, 160th Anniv. — A1049

10c, John Bull, 1830, UK. No. 3886, Old Ironsides, Baldwin, 1832, US. No. 3887, Baldwin Pacific Type 4-6-2, 1910-13, US. 65c, TE.M4:1 diesel electric, 1970, USSR. 75c, TE.114-K, diesel electric, 1975, USSR.

1997, Nov. 19 Litho. *Perf. 12½*

3885 A1049 10c multicolored .25 .25
3886 A1049 15c multicolored .30 .25
3887 A1049 15c multicolored .30 .25
3888 A1049 65c multicolored 1.60 .95
3889 A1049 75c multicolored 1.75 .95
Nos. 3885-3889 (5) 4.20 2.65

UN Conference on Commerce and Employment, Havana, 50th Anniv. — A1050

1997, Nov. 21

3890 A1050 65c multicolored 1.40 .95

Victor Manuel Garcia, Painter, Birth Cent. A1051

1997, Dec. 29 Litho. *Perf. 12½*

3891 A1051 15c #1553, Garcia .55 .25

Visit of Pope John Paul II A1052

Pope John Paul II, different coats of arms, and: 65c, Havana Cathedral. 75c, Basilica of Our Lady of Charity, Cobre, vert.

No. 3894, vert: a, Pope John Paul II greeting Fidel Castro. b, Pope waving.

1998, Jan. 18 Litho. *Perf. 12½*

3892 A1052 65c multicolored 1.40 .95
3893 A1052 75c multicolored 1.60 .95

Souvenir Sheet of 2

3894 A1052 50c #a.-b. 2.00 1.50

Nos. 3894a-3894b are 32x40mm.

Assassination of Jesus Menendez, 50th Anniv. — A1053

1998, Jan. 22

3895 A1053 15c multicolored .55 .25

1998 World Cup Soccer Championships, France — A1054

Various soccer plays: 10c, 2 players. No. 3897, Player in black & yellow. No. 3898, Player on ground, 1 in striped shirt. No. 3899, 3 players, 2 in striped shirts. No. 3900, 3 players, 2 in blue shirts.

1p, Player with #11 on sleeve.

1998, Feb. 10 Litho. *Perf. 12½*

3896 A1054 10c multi, vert. .30 .25
3897 A1054 15c multi, vert. .40 .25
3898 A1054 15c multi, vert. .40 .25
3899 A1054 65c multi 1.50 1.00
3900 A1054 65c multi 1.50 1.00
Nos. 3896-3900 (5) 4.10 2.75

Souvenir Sheet

Perf. 13

3901 A1054 1p multicolored 2.25 1.50

No. 3901 contains one 40x32mm stamp.

Capt. Isabel Rubio Diaz, Medical Aide During Revolution, Death Cent. — A1055

1998, Feb. 15 *Perf. 13*

3902 A1055 15c multicolored .65 .25

Brig. Gen. Vidal Ducasse Reeve (1852-98) A1056

1998, Feb. 19 *Perf. 12½*

3903 A1056 15c multicolored .65 .25

No. 3903 inscribed "Revee."

"Radio Rebelde," 40th Anniv. — A1057

1998, Feb. 23

3904 A1057 15c multicolored .65 .25

Fire Engines A1058

Designs: 10c, 1901 Shand Mason & Co., London. No. 3906, 1905 Horse-drawn municipal fire wagon, Havana. No. 3907, 1921 American-La France Fire Engine Co. 65c, 1952 Chevrolet 6400, US. 75c, 1956 American-La France Foamite Co., US.

1998, Mar. 10

3905 A1058 10c multicolored .30 .25
3906 A1058 15c multicolored .35 .25
3907 A1058 15c multicolored .35 .25
3908 A1058 65c multicolored 1.40 .90
3909 A1058 75c multicolored 1.60 .90
Nos. 3905-3909 (5) 4.00 2.55

Protest of Baragua, 120th Anniv. — A1059

1998, Mar. 15

3910 A1059 15c multicolored .65 .25

Victory at Cuito Cuanavale, Angola, 10th Anniv. — A1060

1998, Mar. 23 **Litho.** ***Perf. 12½***
3911 A1060 15c multicolored .65 .25

New Year 1998 (Year of the Tiger) — A1061

1998, Mar. 30
3912 A1061 15c multicolored .65 .25

Dogs — A1062

1998, Apr. 15 **Litho.** ***Perf. 12½***
3913 A1062 10c Chihuahua .40 .25
3914 A1062 15c Beagle .45 .25
3915 A1062 15c Xoloitzcuintle .45 .25
3916 A1062 65c German pointer 1.50 1.00
3917 A1062 75c Chow chow 1.75 1.25
Nos. 3913-3917 (5) 4.55 3.00

Evolution of the Chimpanzee A1063

Pan troglodytes and: 10c, Proconsul. No. 3919, Cranium. No. 3920, Right hand and foot. 65c, New-born chimpanzee. 75c, Map of Africa showing chimpanzee's range.

1998, May 15 **Litho.** ***Perf. 12½***
3918 A1063 10c multicolored .35 .25
3919 A1063 15c multicolored .35 .25
3920 A1063 15c multicolored .35 .25
3921 A1063 65c multicolored 1.50 1.25
3922 A1063 75c multicolored 1.60 1.25
Nos. 3918-3922 (5) 4.15 3.25

Lisbon '98, World Stamp Exhibition — A1064

Deep sea fish: No. 3923, Raja batis. No. 3924, Eurypharynx pelecanoides. 65c, Caulophryne. 75c, Chauliodus sloani.

1998, May 22 **Litho.** ***Perf. 12½***
3923 A1064 15c multicolored .30 .25
3924 A1064 15c multicolored .30 .25
3925 A1064 65c multicolored 1.25 1.10
3926 A1064 75c multicolored 1.50 1.25
Nos. 3923-3926 (4) 3.35 2.85

Souvenir Sheet

Juvalux '98, World Stamp Exhibition for Youth Philately and Postal History, Luxembourg — A1065

1p, Postman on bicycle.

1998, May 20 **Litho.** ***Perf. 12½***
3927 A1065 1p multi 2.00 1.50

Federico Garcia Lorca (1898-1936), Poet — A1066

1998, June 2
3928 A1066 75c multicolored 2.00 1.25

Intl. Year of the Oceans A1067

No. 3929, Canarreos flower coral, coral crab, small fish. No. 3030, French angel fish, brain coral, gorgonia.

1998, June 5
3929 A1067 65c multicolored 1.50 1.00
3930 A1067 65c multicolored 1.50 1.00
a. Pair, #3929-3930 3.50 1.75

Diana, Princess of Wales (1961-97) A1068

Various portraits, color of clothes: No. 3931, Pale yellow and pink. No. 3932, Black and white. No. 3933, Multicolored print. No. 3934, Red. No. 3935, Pink and black plaid. 65c, White. 75c, Blue.

1998, June 30 **Litho.** ***Perf. 13***
3931 A1068 10c multicolored .30 .25
3932 A1068 10c multicolored .30 .25
3933 A1068 10c multicolored .30 .25
3934 A1068 15c multicolored .40 .25
3935 A1068 15c multicolored .40 .25
3936 A1068 65c multicolored 1.90 1.10
3937 A1068 75c multicolored 2.10 1.25
a. Sheet of 7, #3931-3937 + tabs 12.50 —
Nos. 3931-3937 (7) 5.70 3.60

Expo 2000, Hanover A1069

No. 3938, Mascot, "Twipsy." No. 3939, Mascot in London, 1851. No. 3940, Mascot in Brussels, 1958. No. 3941, German flag, map of Germany. 65c, Mascot in Paris, 1889. 75c, Mascot on top of world, fireworks.

1998, July 31 ***Perf. 12½***
3938 A1069 15c multi, vert. .40 .25
3939 A1069 15c multi .40 .25
3940 A1069 15c multi .40 .25
3941 A1069 15c multi .40 .25
3942 A1069 65c multi, vert. 1.40 1.00
3943 A1069 75c multi 1.60 1.25
Nos. 3938-3943 (6) 4.60 3.25

Maracaibo '98, 18th Central America and Caribbean Games — A1070

1998, Aug. 8
3944 A1070 15c multicolored .50 .25

Attack on Moncada Barracks, 45th Anniv. — A1071

Designs: 15c, Siboney farmhouse, Abel Santamaría. 65c, Barracks, José Marti.

1998, July 26 **Litho.** ***Perf. 13***
3945 A1071 15c multicolored .40 .25
3946 A1071 65c multicolored 1.60 .95

Democratic Republic of Korea, 50th Anniv. — A1072

75c, Kim Il Sung (1912-94).

1998, Sept. 8 **Litho.** ***Perf. 13***
3947 A1072 75c multi 1.75 1.10

Japanese Immigration to Cuba, Cent. — A1073

1998, Sept. 9 **Litho.** ***Perf. 13***
3948 A1073 75c multicolored 1.75 1.10

Orchids A1074

10c, Coelogyne flaccida. No. 3950, Dendrobium fimbriatum. No. 3951, Arunding graminifolia. No. 3952, Bletia patula. No. 3953, Phaius tankervilliaea.

1998, Sept. 10
3949 A1074 10c multicolored .30 .25
3950 A1074 15c multicolored .40 .25
3951 A1074 15c multicolored .40 .25
3952 A1074 65c multicolored 1.50 .75
3953 A1074 65c multicolored 1.50 .75
Nos. 3949-3953 (5) 4.10 2.25

5th Congress of the Revolution Defense Committees A1075

1998, Sept. 25 **Litho.** ***Perf. 13***
3954 A1075 15c multicolored .45 .25

World Tourism Day — A1076

Holguin Province, reptiles: 10c, Looking through gateway, city of Gibara, anolis equestris, vert. 15c, Mayabe Valley, anolis vermiculatus, vert. 65c, Guardalavaca Beach, anolis allisoni. 75c, Mayari pine forest, anolis mestrei.

1998, Sept. 27
3955 A1076 10c multicolored .30 .25
3956 A1076 15c multicolored .50 .25
3957 A1076 65c multicolored 1.50 .75
3958 A1076 75c multicolored 1.75 1.00
Nos. 3955-3958 (4) 4.05 2.25

Women Who Aided Cuban Revolutionary Movements A1077

America Issue: 65c, Bernarda Toro Pelegrin (1852-1911). 75c, Maria Magdalena Cabrales Isaac (1842-1905).

1998, Oct. 12
3959 A1077 65c multicolored 1.40 .75
3960 A1077 75c multicolored 1.60 .85

World Wildlife Fund Protected Fauna — A1078

Arantinga Euops: 10c, Two on tree branch. 15c, One looking out of nest. 65c, One on tree branch. 75c, One up close.

1998, Oct. 21

3961 A1078 10c multicolored .40 .25
3962 A1078 15c multicolored .55 .25
3963 A1078 65c multicolored 2.50 .90
3964 A1078 75c multicolored 2.90 1.00
a. Strip of 4, #3961-3964 9.00 —
Nos. 3961-3964 (4) 6.35 2.40

Cuban Natl. Ballet, 50th Anniv. — A1079

1998, Oct. 28

3965 A1079 15c Swan Lake .50 .25
3966 A1079 65c Giselle 1.40 .95

Massacre of O'Farrill and Goicuria, 40th Anniv. — A1080

Rogelio Perea, Angel Ameijeiras, Pedro Gutiérrez.

1998, Nov. 8

3967 A1080 15c multicolored .45 .25

Battle of Guisa, 40th Anniv. A1081

Design: Capt. Braulio Coroneaux, tank.

1998, Nov. 30 Litho. *Perf. 12½*

3968 A1081 15c multicolored .45 .25

A1082

1998, Dec. 10 Litho. *Perf. 12½*

3969 A1082 65c multicolored 1.50 .95

Universal Declaration of Human Rights, 50th anniv.

A1083

Calixto Garcia Iñiguez (1839-98), revolutionary Major General.

1998, Dec. 11 *Perf. 13*

3970 A1083 65c multicolored 1.50 .95

Padre Félix Varela (1788-1853) — A1084

1998, Dec. 16

3971 A1084 75c multicolored 1.90 1.10

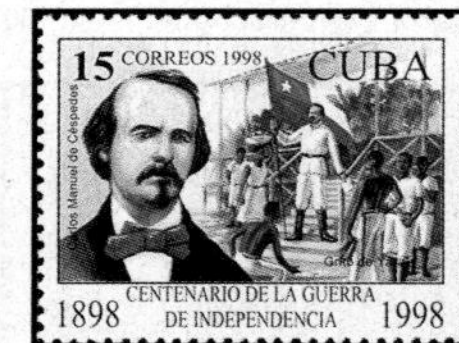

War for Independence, Cent. — A1085

War heroes, historical scene: No. 3972, Carlos Manuel de Céspedes. No. 3973, Ignacio Agramonte. No. 3974, Máximo Gómez. No. 3975, José Maceo. No. 3976, Salvador Cisneros. No. 3977, Calixto Garcia. No. 3978, Adolfo Flor. No. 3979, Serafin Sánchez. 65c, José Marti. 75c, Antonio Maceo.

1998, Dec. 25 Litho. *Perf. 12½*

3972 A1085 15c multicolored .30 .25
3973 A1085 15c multicolored .30 .25
3974 A1085 15c multicolored .30 .25
3975 A1085 15c multicolored .30 .25
3976 A1085 15c multicolored .30 .25
3977 A1085 15c multicolored .30 .25
3978 A1085 15c multicolored .30 .25
3979 A1085 15c multicolored .30 .25
3980 A1085 65c multicolored 1.40 .75
3981 A1085 75c multicolored 1.75 1.00
a. Sheet of 10, #3972-3981 + 3 labels 10.00 10.00
Nos. 3972-3981 (10) 5.55 3.75

No. 3981a was initially issued with "como ellos" in the label inscription instead of "como nosotros." The error was caught quickly, and the sheet was reissued Jan. 5, 1999. Very few error sheets exist in collector hands. Value $1,100.

Battle for Palma Soriano, 40th Anniv. A1086

1998, Dec. 27 Litho. *Perf. 13*

3982 A1086 15c multicolored .45 .25

Cuban Revolution, 40th Anniv. — A1087

a, Boat, soldiers in water. b, Fidel Castro with soldier. c, Castro giving speech, pigeons.

1999, Jan. 1

3983 A1087 65c Strip of 3, #a.-c. 4.00 2.40

Natl. Revolutionary Police, 40th Anniv. — A1088

1999, Jan. 5

3984 A1088 15c multicolored .60 .25

Cuban Workers' Trade Union Organization, 60th Anniv. — A1089

1999, Jan. 28 Litho. *Perf. 12½*

3985 A1089 15c multicolored .45 .25

New Year 1999 (Year of the Rabbit) — A1090

1999, Feb. 5 *Perf. 13*

3986 A1090 75c multicolored 2.60 1.25

Lenin (1870-1924) — A1091

1999, Feb. 21 Litho. *Perf. 12½*

3987 A1091 75c multicolored 1.75 1.10

Dinosaurs — A1092

1999, Mar. 10

3988 A1092 10c Ornithosuchus .30 .25
3989 A1092 15c Saltopus .50 .25
3990 A1092 15c Bactrosaurus .50 .25
3991 A1092 65c Protosuchus 1.50 .95
3992 A1092 75c Mussaurus 1.75 1.10
Nos. 3988-3992 (5) 4.55 2.80

Cuban Musicians — A1093

No. 3993, Dámaso Pérez Prado. No. 3994, Benny Moré. No. 3995, Chano Pozo. No. 3996, Miguelito Valdés. No. 3997, Bola de Nieve. No. 3998, Rita Montaner.

1999, Mar. 22 *Perf. 13*

3993 A1093 5c multi .25 .25
3994 A1093 15c multi .40 .25
3995 A1093 15c multi .40 .25
3996 A1093 35c multi .90 .50
3997 A1093 65c multi 1.50 .95
3998 A1093 75c multi 1.75 1.10
Nos. 3993-3998 (6) 5.20 3.30

Simón Bolivar's Visit to Cuba, Bicent. A1094

1999, Mar. 25

3999 A1094 65c Portrait 1.50 .95
4000 A1094 65c Monument 1.50 .95
a. Pair, #3999-4000 3.50 2.00

State Security Organization, 40th Anniv. — A1095

1999, Mar. 26 Litho. *Perf. 12½*

4001 A1095 65c multicolored 1.90 .95

Souvenir Sheet

China '99 World Philatelic Exhibition — A1096

1999, Apr. 10 Litho. *Perf. 12½*

4002 A1096 1p Giant panda 2.75 1.50

Stamp Day A1097

1999, Apr. 24

4003 A1097 15c Postal rocket .50 .25
4004 A1097 65c Post rider 1.50 .80

Test of Cuban Postal Rocket, 60th anniv. Insurgent Postal Service, 130th anniv.

Casa de las Américas, 40th Anniv. — A1098

1999, Apr. 24

4005	A1098 65c multicolored		2.00	.80

Souvenir Sheet

IBRA '99, World Philatelic Exhibition, Nuremberg — A1099

1999, Apr. 27

4006	A1099 1p Train		3.00	1.50

Agrarian Reform Law, 40th Anniv. A1100

1999, May 17

4007	A1100 65c multicolored		1.50	.80

Felipe Poey, Scientist, Birth Bicent. A1101

Fish: 5c, Gramma loreto Poey. 15c, Liopropoma rubre Poey. No. 4010, Hypoplectrus gummigutta. No. 4011, Stegastes dorsopunicans.

1p, Portrait of Poey, hypoplectrus guttavarius.

1999, May 26 Litho. *Perf. 12½*

4008	A1101	5c multicolored	.25	.25
4009	A1101	15c multicolored	.40	.25
4010	A1101	65c multicolored	1.90	.80
4011	A1101	65c multicolored	1.90	.80
	Nos. 4008-4011 (4)		4.45	2.10

Souvenir Sheet

Perf. 13¼x13

4012	A1101	1p multicolored	3.00	1.00

No. 4012 contains one 32x40mm stamp.

Souvenir Sheet

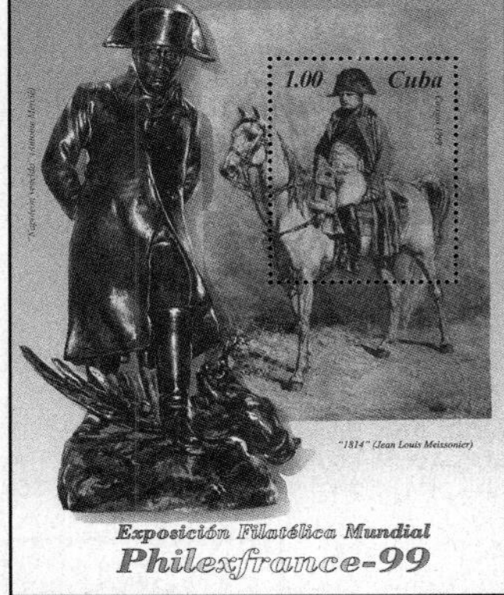

Philexfrance '99, World Philatelic Exhibition — A1102

Sculpture in sheet margin: "1814," by Jean Louis Meissonier (1815-1891).

1999, June 2 *Perf. 13*

4013	A1102 1p multicolored		3.00	1.50

1999 Pan-American Games, Winnipeg — A1103

1999, June 25 Litho. *Perf. 13*

4014	A1103	15c Baseball	.40	.25
4015	A1103	65c Volleyball, vert	1.50	.80
4016	A1103	75c Boxing	1.75	.90
	Nos. 4014-4016 (3)		3.65	1.95

People's Republic of China, 50th Anniv. A1104

5c, Victory at Wioming, by Gao Hong. 15c, Nanchang Insurrection, by Cai Lang. 40c, Red Army Crossing a Swamp, by Gao Quan. 65c, Occupation of the Presidential Palace, by Cheng Yifei and Wei Jingshan. 75c, Proclamation of the People's Republic of China, by Dong Xiwen.

1999, Aug. 21 Litho. *Perf. 12¾*

4017	A1104	5c multicolored	.25	.25
4018	A1104	15c multicolored	.40	.25
4019	A1104	40c multicolored	1.00	.70
4020	A1104	65c multicolored	1.40	1.00
4021	A1104	75c multicolored	1.60	1.25
	Nos. 4017-4021 (5)		4.65	3.45

China 1999 World Philatelic Exhibition, Beijing — A1105

No. 4022, Morning Glories, by Qi Baishi. No. 4023, Three Galloping Horses, by Xu Beihong. No. 4024, Hunan Woman, by Fu Baoshi. No. 4025, Birthplace of Luxun, by Wu Guanzhong. No. 4026, Horse Riders, by Huangzhou. 40c, Pine Tree, by He Xiangning. 65c, Sleep, by Jin Shangyi. 75c, Poetic Scene in Xun Yang, by Chen Yifei.

1999, Aug. 22 Litho. *Perf. 13*

4022	A1105	5c multicolored	.25	.25
4023	A1105	5c multicolored	.25	.25
4024	A1105	15c multicolored	.35	.25
4025	A1105	15c multicolored	.35	.25
4026	A1105	15c multicolored	.35	.25
4027	A1105	40c multicolored	1.00	.70
4028	A1105	65c multicolored	1.40	1.10
4029	A1105	75c multicolored	1.60	1.25
a.	Sheet of 8, #4022-4029 + label		8.50	8.50
	Nos. 4022-4029 (8)		5.55	4.30

UPU, 125th Anniv. A1106

1999, Sept. 16 Litho. *Perf. 12¾*

4030	A1106 75c multicolored		1.00	.75

World Tourism Day A1107

Butterflies and Havana tourist sites: 10c, Antia numidia, Morro Castle. 15c, Papilio polyxenes, Havana Cathedral. 65c, Dryas julia, Convent of San Francisco. 75c, Eueides cleobaea, Capitol.

1999, Sept. 27 *Perf. 12½x12¾*

4031	A1107	10c multicolored	.25	.25
4032	A1107	15c multicolored	.60	.25
4033	A1107	65c multicolored	2.00	1.00
4034	A1107	75c multicolored	2.50	1.10
	Nos. 4031-4034 (4)		5.35	2.60

Expo 2000, Hanover, Germany A1108

5c, World map, Expo 2000 emblem. No. 4036, "Twipsy" mascot, vert. No. 4037, "Twipsy" and 1876 Philadelphia Exposition. No. 4038, "Twipsy" and 1970 Osaka Exposition. 65c, "Twipsy" and 2000 Exposition. 75c, "Twipsy" and 1967 Montreal Exposition.

1999, Oct. 1 *Perf. 12¾*

4035	A1108	5c multicolored	.25	.25
4036	A1108	15c multicolored	.35	.25
4037	A1108	15c multicolored	.35	.25
4038	A1108	15c multicolored	.35	.25
4039	A1108	65c multicolored	1.60	1.00
4040	A1108	75c multicolored	2.00	1.10
	Nos. 4035-4040 (6)		4.90	3.10

Cubana Airlines, 70th Anniv. — A1109

1999, Oct. 8 *Perf. 12½x12¼*

4041	A1109	15c Fokker	.35	.25
4042	A1109	15c DC-10	.35	.25
4043	A1109	65c A-320	1.60	1.00
4044	A1109	75c DC-3	2.00	1.10
	Nos. 4041-4044 (4)		4.30	2.60

America Issue, A New Millennium Without Arms — A1110

15c, Pigeon, mushroom cloud. 65c, Dove, globe.

1999, Oct. 12 *Perf. 12¾*

4045	A1110	15c multi	.40	.25
4046	A1110	65c multi	1.25	1.10

National Instiutions, 40th Anniv. — A1111

15c, MINFAR. 65c, Natl. Revolutionary Militia.

1999, Oct. 16 *Perf. 12¾*

4047	A1111	15c multi	.35	.25
4048	A1111	65c multi	1.00	.75

Disappearance of Camilo Cienfuegos, 40th Anniv. — A1112

1999, Oct. 28 Litho. *Perf. 12¾*

4049	A1112 15c multicolored		1.00	.25

Souvenir Sheet

12th Congress of Cuban Philatelic Federation — A1113

1999, Dec. 11 *Perf. 13*

4050	A1113 1p multicolored		2.00	1.25

Ernest Hemingway (1899-1961), Writer — A1114

1999, Dec. 15 *Perf. 12½x12¼*

4051	A1114 65c multicolored		1.75	1.00

9th Summit of Ibero-American Heads of State and Government, Havana — A1115

Designs: 65c, Plaza Vieja. 75c, Plaza of St. Francis of Assisi.
1p, Plaza de Armas.

1999, Nov. 5 Litho. ***Perf. 12¾x12½***

4052 A1115 65c multi .90 .75
4053 A1115 75c multi 1.10 1.00

Souvenir Sheet

Perf. 13

4054 A1115 1p multi 1.50 1.25

No. 4054 contains one 40x31mm stamp.

Rubén Martínez Villena (1899-1934), Revolutionary — A1116

1999, Dec. 20 ***Perf. 12½x12¾***

4055 A1116 15c multi .40 .25

Dr. Tomás Romay Chacón (1764-1849) A1117

1999, Dec. 21 ***Perf. 13***

4056 A1117 65c multi 1.00 .90

New Year 2000 (Year of the Dragon) — A1118

2000, Jan. 10 ***Perf. 12½***

4057 A1118 15c multi .75 .25

Folklore A1119

Paintings depicting Cuban folklore by Concepción Ferrant (1882-1968): 10c, Rumba Caliente. 15c, Cachumba. 65c, En Casa de un Babalao. 75c, Tata Cuñengue.

2000, Jan. 26 ***Perf. 12½x12¾***

4058 A1119 10c multi .25 .25
4059 A1119 15c multi .35 .30
4060 A1119 65c multi 1.40 1.00
4061 A1119 75c multi 1.60 1.10
Nos. 4058-4061 (4) 3.60 2.65

Butterflies — A1120

10c, Helcyra superba. No. 4063, Pantaporia punctata. No. 4064, Neptis themis. 65c, Curetis acuta. 75c, Chrysozephyrus ataxus.

2000, Feb. 25 ***Perf. 12¾***

4062 A1120 10c multi .30 .25
4063 A1120 15c multi .40 .30
4064 A1120 15c multi .40 .30
4065 A1120 65c multi 1.40 1.25
4066 A1120 75c multi 1.60 1.40
Nos. 4062-4066 (5) 4.10 3.50

Bangkok 2000 Stamp Exhibition.

Group of 77 South Summit, Havana — A1121

2000, Apr. 7 Litho. ***Perf. 13x12½***

4067 A1121 75c multi 2.00 1.25

Lenin, 130th Anniv. of Birth — A1122

2000, Apr. 22 ***Perf. 12¾***

4068 A1122 75c multi 1.90 1.25

Che Guevara in Congo, 35th Anniv. A1123

2000, Apr. 24

4069 A1123 65c multi 1.75 1.10

Stamp Day — A1124

Designs: 65c, Cuba #2, building. 90c, Airplane, cover, Jaime González, pilot of first experimental airmail flight in Cuba.

2000, Apr. 24

4070 A1124 65c multi 1.50 1.10
4071 A1124 90c multi 2.00 1.50

Capt. San Luis (Eliseo Reyes), Military Hero (1940-67) A1125

2000, Apr. 27

4072 A1125 65c multi 1.60 1.00

The Stamp Show 2000, London A1126

Locomotives: 5c, 1882 Baldwin 0-6-0. 10c, 1895 Baldwin 2-8-0. 15c, 1912 Baldwin 2-8-0. 65c, 1919 Alco 2-8-0. 75c, 1925 Alco 2-8-2.
1p, 1920 Henschel 2-6-0.

2000, May 5 ***Perf. 12¾***

4073 A1126 5c multi .25 .25
4074 A1126 10c multi .30 .25
4075 A1126 15c multi .40 .30
4076 A1126 65c multi 1.60 1.10
4077 A1126 75c multi 1.90 1.25
Nos. 4073-4077 (5) 4.45 3.15

Souvenir Sheet

Perf. 13

4078 A1126 1p multi 3.00 1.50

No. 4078 contains one 40x32mm stamp.

WIPA 2000 Philatelic Exhibition, Vienna — A1127

Airships of: 10c, Henri Giffard, 1852. 15c, Albert and Gaston Tissandier, 1883, vert. 50c, Charles Renard and Arthur Krebs, 1884. 65c, Pierre and Paul Lebaudy, 1903. 75c, August von Perseval, 1906.
1p, Ferdinand von Zeppelin.

Perf. 12½x12¼, 12¼x12½

2000, May 18

4079 A1127 10c multi .35 .25
4080 A1127 15c multi .50 .30
4081 A1127 50c multi 1.40 .90
4082 A1127 65c multi 1.90 1.10
4083 A1127 75c multi 2.10 1.25
Nos. 4079-4083 (5) 6.25 3.80

Souvenir Sheet

Perf. 12½

4084 A1127 1p multi 3.00 1.50

No. 4084 contains one 40x32mm stamp.

Second World Meeting of Friendship and Solidarity With Cuba — A1128

2000, June 23 Litho. ***Perf. 12¾***

4085 A1128 65c multi 1.50 1.10

José de la Luz y Caballero (1800-62), Educator — A1129

2000, July 11 ***Perf. 12½x12¼***

4086 A1129 65c multi 1.50 1.10

Amadeo Roldan (1900-39), Violinist — A1130

2000, July 12 ***Perf. 12¾***

4087 A1130 65c multi 1.50 1.10

La Edad de Oro, by José Marti — A1131

5c, Bebé y El Señor Don Pomposo. 10c, La Muñeca Negra. 15c, Nene Traviesa. 50c, Los Dos Ruiseñores. 65c, Frontispiece of La Edad de Oro. 75c, El Camarón Encantado.

2000, July 20

4088-4093 A1131 Set of 6 5.00 4.25
4093a Sheet of 6, #4088-4093 7.00 7.00

Latin American Association for Integration — A1132

2000, Aug. 12

4094 A1132 65c multi 1.50 1.25

Souvenir Sheet

Olymphilex 2000, Sydney — A1133

2000, Aug. 17 *Perf. 13*
4095 A1133 1p multi 2.25 1.10

2000 Summer Olympics, Sydney A1134

Designs: 5c, Runners. 15c, Soccer. 65c, Baseball. 75c, Cycling.

2000, Aug. 20 *Perf. 12¾*
4096-4099 A1134 Set of 4 4.00 4.00

Dr. Pedro Kouri Esmeja (1900-64) A1135

2000, Aug. 21 **Litho.**
4100 A1135 65c multi 1.50 1.25

Federation of Cuban Women, 40th Anniv. — A1136

2000, Aug. 23
4101 A1136 15c multi .40 .30

España 2000 Intl. Philatelic Exhibition — A1137

Designs: 10c, 1851 Havana-Bilbao stampless cover, ship. No. 4103, 15c, Spain #1, Cibeles Fountain, Madrid. No. 4104, 15c, 1850 Zaragoza-Cadiz cover, Palacio de Cristal, Madrid. 65c, Spain #1-5, Palacio de Comunicaciones, Madrid. 75c, Cuba #1, Centro Gallego, Havana.

2000, Sept. 7 *Perf. 12¾x12½*
4102-4106 A1137 Set of 5 4.00 3.00
4106a Sheet of 5, #4102-4106 + label 4.75 4.75

Souvenir Sheet
Perf. 12½

4107 A1137 100c Queen Isabella II, vert. 3.00 2.25

No. 4107 contains one 32x40mm stamp.

Beaches — A1138

No. 4108, Coconuts Bay, PRC. No. 4109, Varadero Beach, Cuba.

2000, Sept. 26 *Perf. 12½x12¼*
4108-4109 A1138 15c Set of 2 .60 .60
4109a Pair, #4108-4109 .80 .80

See People's Republic of China No. 3052.

World Tourism Day A1139

Marine Life: 10c, Eretmochelys imbricata, vert. 15c, Epinephelus striatus, vert. 65c, Pomacanthus paru. 75c, Anisotremus surinamensis.

Perf. 12½x12¾, 12¾x12½
2000, Sept. 27
4110-4113 A1139 Set of 4 3.50 2.00

Committees of Defense of the Revolution, 40th Anniv. — A1140

2000, Sept. 28 *Perf. 12¾*
4114 A1140 15c multi .60 .30

America Issue — AIDS Prevention A1141

Ribbon, heart-shaped map and: 15c, Family. 65c, Couple.

2000, Oct. 12
4115-4116 A1141 Set of 2 2.00 1.25

Cuban Military in Angola, 25th Anniv. — A1142

2000, Nov. 7
4117 A1142 75c multi 1.90 1.40

Visit by Alexander von Humboldt, Bicent. — A1143

Humboldt and: 15c, House in Trinidad. 65c, House in Havana, Political Essay on the Island of Cuba.

2000, Dec. 19 **Litho.** *Perf. 12¾*
4118-4119 A1143 Set of 2 2.00 1.25

20th Pan-American Railway Congress A1144

2000, Sept. 18 **Litho.** *Perf. 12¾*
4120 A1144 65c multi 1.50 1.25

Millennium — A1145

Snails: a, Polymita versicolor. b, Polymita picta iolimbata. c, Polymita picta roseolimbata. d, Polymita picta picta. e, Polymita picta nigrolimbata.

2000, Dec. 20
4121 A1145 65c Block of 5, #a-e, + label 7.00 4.00

New Year 2001 (Year of the Snake) — A1146

2001, Jan. 10
4122 A1146 15c multi .75 .25

Hong Kong 2001 Stamp Exhibition — A1147

Birds: 5c, Aix galericulata. 10c, Chrysolophus pictus. 15c, Ardea cinerea. 65c, Gallus gallus. 75c, Streptotelia decaocto. 1p, Grus grus.

2001, Jan. 25 *Perf. 12¾*
4123-4127 A1147 Set of 5 4.25 3.25

Souvenir Sheet
Perf. 12½

4128 A1147 1p multi 3.00 1.25

No. 4128 contains one 32x40mm stamp.

National Institute for Sport Physical Education and Recreation, 40th Anniv. — A1148

2001, Feb. 23 *Perf. 12½x12¼*
4129 A1148 65c multi 1.60 .80

UN High Commissioner for Refugees, 50th Anniv. — A1149

2001, Mar. 15 *Perf. 12¾x12½*
4130 A1149 65c multi 1.50 .75

Antique Locomotives — A1150

Locomotives from, 10c, 1863. 15c, 1876. 40c, 1885. 65c, 1914. 75c, 1932.

2001, Mar. 20 ***Perf. 12½x12¼***
4131-4135 A1150 Set of 5 4.75 2.40

105th Interparliamentary Union Congress, Havana — A1151

2001, Mar. 30 ***Perf. 12¾***
4136 A1151 65c multi 1.75 .80

Bay of Pigs Invasion, 40th Anniv. — A1152

2001, Apr. 19 ***Perf. 12¾x12½***
4137 A1152 65c multi 1.50 .75

Cats and Dogs A1153

Designs: 10c, Cats, emblem of Cat Aficionados Association. No. 4139, 15c, Dogs, Cats, emblem of Aniplant. No. 4140, 15c, Dogs, emblem of Cynological Federation of Cuba. 65c, Dogs, emblem of Sporting Dog Federation of Cuba. 75c, Dogs, cats.

2001, Apr. 25 ***Perf. 12½x12¾***
4138-4142 A1153 Set of 5 4.00 2.00

Radio Havana, 40th Anniv. — A1154

2001, May 1 ***Perf. 12½x12¼***
4143 A1154 65c multi 1.50 .75

Tourism Convention — A1155

2001, May 7 ***Perf. 12¾x12½***
4144 A1155 65c multi 1.50 .75

Belgica 2001 Intl. Stamp Exhibition, Brussels A1156

Designs: 5c, St. Michel Cathedral. 10c, Sablon Church, horiz. 15c, Royal Residence, horiz. 65c, Sacred Heart Basilica, horiz. 75c, Atomium.
1p, Royal Palace.

2001, May 10 ***Perf. 12¾***
4145-4149 A1156 Set of 5 4.00 2.00

Souvenir Sheet

Perf. 12½

4150 A1156 100c multi 2.40 1.25

No. 4150 contains one 32x40mm stamp.

Interior Ministry, 40th Anniv. A1157

2001, June 6 ***Perf. 12¾***
4151 A1157 65c multi 1.75 .80

Phila Nippon '01, Japan A1158

Japanese trains: 5c., JR 500. 10c, JR 700. 15c, MAX 1. 65c, MAX 2. 75c, 300.

2001, June 20 **Litho.** ***Perf. 12¾***
4152-4156 A1158 Set of 5 3.75 1.50

Souvenir Sheet

Perf. 12½

4157 A1158 100c Zero 2.40 1.25

No. 4157 contains one 40x32mm stamp.

Republic of San Marino, 1700th Anniv. — A1159

2001, July 20 **Litho.** ***Perf. 12½x12¼***
4158 A1159 75c multi 1.75 .75

Aquaculture — A1160

Designs: 5c, Tinca tinca. 10c, Rana temporaria. 15c, Cardisoma guanhumi. 65c, Mytilus edulis. 75c, Tilapia mariae.
1p, Potamobius pallipes.

2001, Sept. 17 ***Perf. 12¾***
4159-4163 A1160 Set of 5 3.75 1.50

Souvenir Sheet

Perf. 12½

4164 A1160 1p multi 2.40 1.25

No. 4164 contains one 40x32mm stamp.

Recovery of Raw Materials, 40th Anniv. — A1161

2001, Sept. 21 ***Perf. 12¾x12½***
4165 A1161 65c multi 1.60 .75

Tourism — A1162

Designs: 10c, Valle de Viñales. 15c, Trinidad. 65c, Sirena Beach, Cayo Largo del Sur. 75c, Morro Castle, Havana.

2001, Sept. 27
4166-4169 A1162 Set of 4 3.75 1.75

Year of Dialogue Among Civilizations A1163

2001, Oct. 9 ***Perf. 12¾***
4170 A1163 65c multi 2.00 .75

America Issue — UNESCO World Heritage A1164

Flora and fauna from Desembarco del Granma Natl. Park: 15c, Tetramicra malpighiarum. 65c, Liggus vittatus.

2001, Oct. 12 ***Perf. 12½x12¾***
4171-4172 A1164 Set of 2 1.75 .85

José Marti National Library, Cent. A1165

2001, Oct. 18 ***Perf. 12¾***
4173 A1165 15c multi .45 .25

Cuban Airliner Explosion Near Barbados, 25th Anniv. — A1166

Various details of painting.

2001, Oct. 22

4174	Horiz. strip of 5	3.25	1.60
a.	A1166 5c shown	.25	.25
b.	A1166 10c multi	.25	.25
c.	A1166 15c multi	.35	.25
d.	A1166 50c multi	1.10	.55
e.	A1166 65c multi	1.40	.90

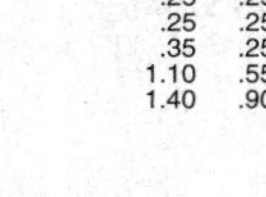

Eduardo R. Chibas, Communist Leader, Cent. of Birth — A1167

2001, Nov. 27 **Litho.** ***Perf. 13***
4175 A1167 65c multi 1.60 .80

Napoleonic Museum, 40th Anniv. — A1168

Equestrian statues of Napoleon and map of battle of: No. 4176, 10c, Eylau. No. 4177, 10c, Marengo. 65c, Waterloo. 75c, Aboukir.

2001, Dec. 1 ***Perf. 12¾x12½***
4176-4179 A1168 Set of 4 3.75 1.75

Pablo de la Torriente Brau (1901-36), Writer — A1169

2001, Dec. 12 ***Perf. 12¾***
4180 A1169 75c multi 1.75 .80

Cuban Federation of Pigeon Fanciers, 4th Congress A1170

Pigeons: No. 4181, 65c, Empedrado oscura 2021-61-ME. No. 4182, 65c, Empedrado claro 2241-55-ME. No. 4183, 65c, Mosaico 1561-66-HM. No. 4184, 65c, Mosaico, 3013-67-HM. No. 4185, 65c Bronceado, 338-59-HE.

2001, Dec. 14 ***Perf. 12½***
4181-4185 A1170 Set of 5 7.00 3.50

Film Stars Who Never Won Academy Awards
A1171

Designs: 5c, Tyrone Power. No. 4187, 10c, Ava Gardner. No. 4188, 10c, Steve McQueen. No. 4189, 15c, Rita Hayworth. No. 4190, 15c, Marilyn Monroe. No. 4191, 15c, James Dean. No. 4192, 65c, Rock Hudson. No. 4193, 65c, Natalie Wood. 75c, Richard Burton.

2001, Dec. 20

4186-4194 A1171 Set of 9 6.75 3.50
a. Sheet of 9, #4186-4194 8.00 8.00

New Year 2002 (Year of the Horse) — A1172

2002, Jan. 21 Litho. ***Perf. 12½x12¾***

4195 A1172 15c multi .75 .30

Cigar Production — A1173

Cigars and: 5c, Hat, Cuba No. 358, tobacco leaf. 10c, Clock, cigar cylinder. 15c, Map of Cuba, Simon Bolivar. 65c, Cuba Nos. 356, 357, map, cigar smoker. 75c, Flag, tobacco field, man.

1p, Fidel Castro, map, star.

2002, Feb. 15 ***Perf. 12¾***

4196-4200 A1173 Set of 5 3.75 2.00

Souvenir Sheet

Perf. 1313¼

4201 A1173 1p multi 2.50 1.25

Fourth Havana Festival, Cohiba brand, 36th anniv. No. 4201 contains one 40x32mm stamp.

Second UPAEP Information Workshop — A1174

2002, Feb. 21 ***Perf. 12½x12¼***

4202 A1174 65c multi 1.50 .75

Explorers
A1175

Explorers: 5c, Reading map. 15c, Tying knots. 50c, Starting campfire for cooking. 65c, Starting fire. 75c, Using orientation techniques.

2002, Mar. 20 ***Perf. 12½***

4203-4207 A1175 Set of 5 5.00 2.50
a. Sheet of 5, #4203-4207, + label 7.00 7.00

Union of Young Communists, 40th Anniv. — A1176

2002, Apr. 4 ***Perf. 12½x12¼***

4208 A1176 15c multi .45 .25

ExpoVid 2002 Wine Event — A1177

Designs: 15c, Cigar smokers, wine bottles and glasses, map of wine producing areas. 65c, Wine glass and barrels. 75c, Wine glass and vineyard.

2002, June 5 ***Perf. 12¾x12½***

4209-4211 A1177 Set of 3 3.50 1.75

2002 World Cup Soccer Championships, Japan and Korea — A1178

Player and flag from: No. 4212, 15c, South Korea. No. 4213, 15c, France. No. 4214, 15c, Germany. No. 4215, 15c, Brazil. No. 4216, 15c, Spain. 65c, Argentina. 75c, Italy. 85c, Japan.

2002, Apr. 21 Litho. ***Perf. 12½***

4212-4219 A1178 Set of 8 6.50 3.25
4219a Sheet, #4212-4219 9.50 9.50

Souvenir Sheet

Hispano-Cubano Philatelic Exposition — A1179

2002, Apr. 27 ***Perf. 13***

4220 A1179 1p multi 2.25 1.10

Juan Tomas Roig, Botanist, 125th Anniv. of Birth
A1180

Designs: 5c, Bust of Roig, experimental agronomic station, Santiago de las Vegas. 10c, Bust and house of Roig. 15c, Roig, laboratory glassware and Nicotiana tabacum. 50c, Building, Allophyllum roiggi, and sculpture of Roig. 65c, Roig, laboratory glassware and botanical dictionary.

2002, May 10 ***Perf. 12½x12¾***

4221-4225 A1180 Set of 5 3.25 1.50
4225a Sheet, #4221-4225, + label 5.25 5.25

Medi Cuba Suiza — A1181

2002, June 18 ***Perf. 12¾x12½***

4226 A1181 75c multi 1.60 .80

Mushrooms
A1182

Designs: 5c, Amanita junquillea. 15c, Lepiota puellaris. 45c, Cortinarius cumatilis. 65c, Pholliota adiposa. 75c, Coprinus comatus.

2002, June 20 ***Perf. 12¾***

4227-4231 A1182 Set of 5 4.50 2.25
4231a Sheet, #4227-4231, + label 8.00 8.00

Nicolás Guillén (1902-89), Poet — A1183

2002, July 10 ***Perf. 12¾x12½***

4232 A1183 65c multi 1.75 .90

Dockers, By Marcelo Pogolotti (1902-88)
A1184

2002, July 12 ***Perf. 12¾***

4233 A1184 15c multi .50 .30

Agostinho Neto (1922-79), Pres. of Angola — A1185

2002, Sept. 17 ***Perf. 12¾x12½***

4234 A1185 65c multi 1.75 .90

España 2002 Youth Philatelic Exposition, Salamanca — A1186

Birds: 5c, Calidris minutilla. 10c, Tringa melanoleucas. 15c, Charadius semipalmatus. 65c, Plurialis squatarola. 75c, Arenaria interpres.

1p, Porzana carolina.

2002, Sept. 20 ***Perf. 12½x12¼***

4235-4239 A1186 Set of 5 4.50 2.25
4239a Sheet, #4235-4239, + label 6.00 6.00

Souvenir Sheet

Perf. 13

4240 A1186 1p multi 2.50 1.25

No. 4240 contains one 40x31mm stamp.

Third Intl. Meeting of War Correspondents — A1187

2002, Oct. 7 ***Perf. 12¾***

4241 A1187 65c multi 1.75 .90

Ernesto "Che" Guevara (1928-67), Revolutionary Leader — A1188

Various depictions of Guevara: 5c, 10c, 15c, 50c, 65c, 75c.

2002, Oct. 8 **Litho.**

4242-4247 A1188 Set of 6 5.25 2.75
4247a Sheet, #4242-4247 45.00 45.00

America Issue — Youth, Education and Literacy — A1189

Designs: 15c, Emblem of Literacy Army, man with book, teacher with student. 65c, Building, flag, children at computer.

2002, Oct. 12 ***Perf. 12½x12¼***

4248-4249 A1189 Set of 2 2.00 1.00

Old Automobiles — A1190

Designs: No. 4250, 5c, 1956 Pontiac Catalina. No. 4251, 5c, 1957 Mercury Monterrey. 15c, 1959 Cadillac Fleetwood. 65c, Hudson Hornet. 75c, 1957 Chevrolet Bel Air. 85c, 1957 Mercedes-Benz 190SL.

2002, Oct. 19 ***Perf. 12¾***
4250-4255 A1190 Set of 6 6.00 3.50
a. Sheet, #4250-4255, + 6 labels 17.00 17.00

15th Intercontinental Baseball Cup — A1191

Baseball players: 5c, G. Mesa. 15c, A. Pacheco. 50c, O. Linares. 65c, O. Kindelan. 75c, L. Ulacia.

2002, Nov. 1
4256-4260 A1191 Set of 5 5.00 3.00
4260a Sheet of 5, #4256-4260 + 4 labels 17.00 17.00

20th Havana Intl. Fair — A1192

2002, Nov. 3
4261 A1192 65c multi 1.75 .90

Railroads, 165th Anniv. — A1193

Designs: 5c, Rocket. 15c, Miller. 50c, Vulcan. 65c, Consolidation. 75c, Mikado.

2002, Nov. 12 ***Perf. 12½x12¼***
4262-4266 A1193 Set of 5 6.50 3.00
4266a Sheet, #4262-4266, + label 17.00 17.00

Camagüey Ballet, 35th Anniv. — A1194

Designs: 65c, Twelve dancers. 75c, Two dancers.

2002, Dec. 1 ***Perf. 12¾***
4267-4268 A1194 Set of 2 3.25 2.00

Pan-American Health Organization, Cent. — A1195

2002, Dec. 2
4269 A1195 65c multi 1.50 .90

Paintings of Wilfredo Lam (1902-82) A1196

Designs: 15c, Emi Cosinca, 1950. 45c, Yo Soy, 1949. 65c, Retrado de H.H., 1941-42. 75c, Mujer Sentada, 1951.

2002, Dec. 8 ***Perf. 12¾***
4270-4273 A1196 Set of 4 4.50 3.00
4273a Sheet, #4270-4273, + 4 labels 16.00 16.00

Dulce M. Loynaz (1902-97), Writer A1197

Perf. 12½x12¾

2002, Dec. 19 **Litho.**
4274 A1197 65c multi 1.50 .90

Souvenir Sheet

Tursiops Truncatus — A1198

2002, Dec. 20 ***Perf. 12½***
4275 A1198 1p multi 3.00 1.50

Fifth National Philatelic Competition.

Prehistoric and Modern-Day Animals — A1199

Designs: 5c, Megaloceros, Cervus elaphus. 10c, Theropithecus, Papio anubis. 15c, Coelodonta, Diceros bicornis. 45c, Canis dirus, Canis lupus. 65c, Ursus spelaeus, Ursus arctos. 75c, Smilodon, Panthera leo. 1p, Mammuthus primigenius.

2002, Dec. 27 ***Perf. 12½x12¼***
4276-4281 A1199 Set of 6 5.00 2.00

Souvenir Sheet

Perf. 13

4282 A1199 1p multi 2.75 1.10

No. 4282 contains one 40x32mm stamp.

New Year 2003 (Year of the Ram) A1200

Ram with background in: No. 4283, 15c, Green. No. 4284, 15c, Red.

2003, Jan. 6 ***Perf. 12½***
4283-4284 A1200 Set of 2 1.75 .80

San Alejandro Academy for Arts, 185th Anniv. — A1201

Paintings by: 5c, Amelia Pelaez. 15c, René Portocarrero. 65c, Mario Carreña, horiz. 75c, Servando Cabrera.

2003, Jan. 12 ***Perf. 12¾***
4285-4288 A1201 Set of 4 3.75 2.00

José Martí (1853-95), Patriot — A1202

Designs: 15c, Birthplace. No. 4290, 65c, Martí and text. No. 4291, 65c, Martí, sky and text, horiz. 75c, Portrait.
1p, Martí, horiz.

2003, Jan. 28 ***Perf. 12¾***
4289-4292 A1202 Set of 4 4.25 2.50

Souvenir Sheet

Perf. 12½

4293 A1202 1p multi 2.50 1.40

No. 4293 contains one 40x32mm stamp.

Arrival of Europeans at Havana, 510th Anniv. — A1203

Various Cuban stamps and: No. 4294, 15c, Woman with Cigar boxes, map of Cuba (diamond-shaped). No. 4295, 15c, Men at table holding cigars and drinks (diamond-shaped). 50c, Tobacco farmer, field, hands rolling cigar. 65c, Building, Trinidad. 75c, Cigar, building, palm tree, people in room.
1p, Indian lighting cigar, vert.

2003, Feb. 6 ***Perf. 12½***
4294-4298 A1203 Set of 5 4.50 2.50

Souvenir Sheet

4299 A1203 1p multi 2.50 1.40

No. 4299 contains one 32x40mm stamp.

Radio Rebelde, 45th Anniv. A1204

2003, Feb. 13 ***Perf. 12¾***
4300 A1204 65c multi 1.50 .85

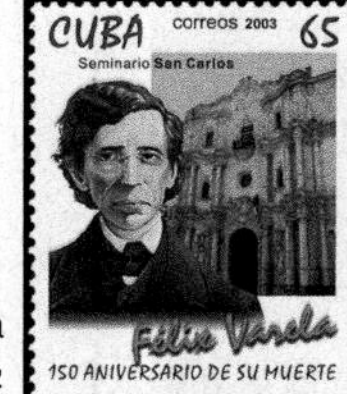

Félix Varela (1788-1853), Priest — A1205

2003, Feb. 25 ***Perf. 12½***
4301 A1205 65c multi 1.50 .85

Military Units, 45th Anniv. — A1206

Designs: No. 4302, 15c, 2nd Frank Pais Front. No. 4303, 15c, 3rd Mario Muñoz Front.

2003 ***Perf. 12¾***
4302-4303 A1206 Set of 2 1.10 .55

Issued: No. 4302, 3/5; No. 4303, 3/11.

16th World Sexology Congress A1207

2003, Mar. 11
4304 A1207 65c multi 1.50 .85

Transportation and Shipping — A1208

Designs: 5c, Container ship. 10c, Truck. 15c, Train. 65c, Airplane and delivery van. 75c, Airplane and delivery van, diff.

2003, Apr. 10 ***Perf. 12½***
4305-4309 A1208 Set of 5 3.75 2.00

Flora & Fauna — A1209

Designs: 5c, Nymphaea ampla, Lepisosteus tristoechus. 10c, Magnolia grandiflora, Spindalis zena pretrei. 15c, Lillium candidum, Polymita picta. 65c, Strelitzia regiae, Solenodon cubanus. 75c, Hibiscus rosasinensis, Mellisuga helenae.

2003, May 15
4310-4314 A1209 Set of 5 4.00 2.00

Pan American Games, Santo Domingo, Dominican Republic A1210

Designs: 5c, Kayaking. 15c, Judo. 50c, Track. 65c, Volleyball.

2003, June 27 ***Perf. 12½x12¾***
4315-4318 A1210 Set of 4 3.00 1.50

Attack on Moncada Barracks, 50th Anniv. — A1211

Designs: 15c, Men and barracks. 65c, Fidel Castro, text.

2003, July 26 ***Perf. 12¾***
4319-4320 A1211 Set of 2 1.75 .75

Railroads A1212

Designs: 5c, Three-wheeled handcar, 1930-35. 10c, Crane, 1920. 15c, B-B 120/120 E locomotive, 1925. 65c, DVM-9 Ganz Mavag locomotive, 1969. 75c, 2-6-0 locomotive, 1905.

2003, Aug. 7
4321-4325 A1212 Set of 5 4.00 2.00

UN Conference to Combat Desertification — A1213

2003, Aug. 25 ***Perf. 12½x12¼***
4326 A1213 65c multi 2.75 .85

Expo Bangkok A1214

Wildlife: 5c, Nyctea scandiaca. 10c, Fratercula arctica. 15c, Sula bassana. 65c, Ursus maritimus. 75c, Alopex lagopus.
1p, Pagolphilus groenlandicus.

2003, Aug. 28 ***Perf. 12¾***
4327-4331 A1214 Set of 5 4.00 2.00

Souvenir Sheet

Perf. 12½

4332 A1214 1p multi 2.75 1.40

No. 4332 contains one 32x40mm stamp.

Butterflies and Flowers — A1215

Designs: 5c, Dione juno, Gardenia jasminoides. 15c, Apatura ilia, Chrysanthemus sinence. 65c, Inachis io, Hibiscus rosasinensis. 75c, Marpesia iole, Althaea rosea.
1p, Danaus plexippus, Zantedeschia aethiopica, vert.

2003, Sept. 11 **Litho.** ***Perf. 12½***
4333-4336 A1215 Set of 4 3.75 2.00

Souvenir Sheet

4337 A1215 1p multi 2.75 1.40

No. 4337 contains one 32x40mm stamp.

Ecotourism — A1216

Bird and location: 10c, Aratinga eops, Baracoa. 15c, Xiphidiopicus percussus, Valle de los Ingenios. 65c, Tiaris canora, Sierra Maestra. 75c, Priotelus temnurus, Granma.

2003, Sept. 27 ***Perf. 12¾x12½***
4338-4341 A1216 Set of 4 2.75 1.75

Worldwide Fund for Nature (WWF) — A1217

Crocodylus rhombifer: No. 4342, 15c, Eggs and hatchling. No. 4343, 15c, Adult at water's edge. 65c, Capturing prey. 75c, With open mouth.

2003, Sept. 30 **Litho.** ***Perf. 12¾***
4342-4345 A1217 Set of 4 4.00 2.00
4345a Sheet, 4 each #4342-4345 27.50 27.50

America Issue — Flora and Fauna — A1218

Designs: 15c, Xiphidiopicus percussus. 65c, Encyclia phoenicea.

2003, Oct. 12
4346-4347 A1218 Set of 2 1.75 .85

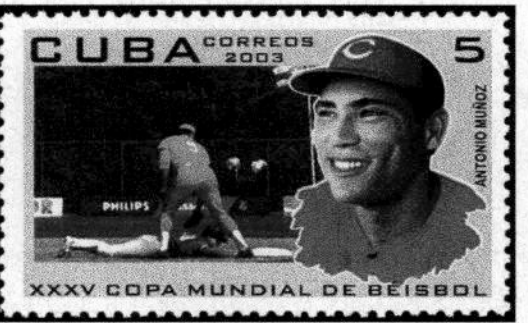

35th Baseball World Cup — A1219

Cuban players: 5c, Antonio Muñoz. 10c, Lourdes Gourriel. No. 4350, 15c, Jorge L. Valdes. No. 4351, 15c, Lazaro Vargas. 65c, Lazaro Valle. 75c, Javier Mendez.
1p, Players celebrating, vert.

2003, Oct. 17 ***Perf. 12½x12¼***
4348-4353 A1219 Set of 6 4.50 2.25

Souvenir Sheet

Perf. 12½

4354 A1219 1p multi 2.75 1.40

No. 4354 contains one 32x40mm stamp.

Ballet — A1220

Designs: No. 4355, 65c, National Ballet of Cuba, 55th anniv. No. 4356, 65c, Alicia Alonso as Giselle, 60th anniv., vert.

Perf. 12¾x12½, 12½x12¾

2003, Oct. 28
4355-4356 A1220 Set of 2 3.00 1.50

Powered Flight, Cent. — A1221

Emblem and: 5c, Wright Brothers. 15c, Pitcairn PA-5. 65c, Stearman C-3MB. 75c, Douglas M-2.

2003, Dec. 17 ***Perf. 12½x12¼***
4357-4360 A1221 Set of 4 4.00 2.00

Cuban Revolution, 45th Anniv. — A1222

2004, Jan. 1 ***Perf. 12¾***
4361 A1222 65c multi 2.00 1.00

Expocuba, 15th Anniv. — A1223

2004, Jan. 4 ***Perf. 12½x12¼***
4362 A1223 65c multi 1.50 .85

2004 Summer Olympics, Athens — A1224

Sports: 10c, Baseball. 15c (No. 4363A), Track. 65c, Boxing. 75c, Equestrian.

2004, Jan. 6 **Litho.**
4363-4365 A1224 Set of 4 3.75 1.90

New Year 2004 (Year of the Monkey) A1225

Monkey with denomination in: No. 4366, 15c, Blue. No. 4367, 15c, Orange.

2004, Jan. 9 ***Perf. 12¾***
4366-4367 A1225 Set of 2 1.00 .50

Julio A. Mella (1903-29), Communist Leader A1226

2004, Jan. 10
4368 A1226 65c multi 1.50 1.10

José Martí (1853-95) — A1227

Designs: No. 4369, 5c, Martí in 1862, Colegio San Pablo, Prado No. 88. No. 4370, 5c, Martí's father, Mariano, Tapineria No. 16, Valencia. No. 4371, 5c, Martí's mother, Leonor Pérez, birthplace, Paula No. 41. No. 4372, 10c, Martí's high school, 1862, Martí, Fermín Valdés Domínguez, 1869. No. 4373, 10c, Martí in 1869, Havana Royal Jail. No. 4374, 15c, Martí in 1870, El Abra farm, Isle of Pines. No. 4375, 15c, Martí in 1870, Martí Forge. No. 4376, 15c, Martí and son, José Francisco, 1879, Guanabacoa Lyceum. 65c, Martí and son, 1879, Mercaderes Law Offices. 75c, Martí in 1895, La Jatía farm, Oriente.

2004, Jan. 28 ***Perf. 12½x12¼***
4369-4378 A1227 Set of 10 4.75 2.75

See Nos. 4525-4535, 4570-4578, 4691-4700, 4800-4807.

Town of Santa María de Puerto del Principe, 490th Anniv. — A1228

2004, Feb. 2 ***Perf. 12¾x12½***
4379 A1228 15c multi .50 .25

Trolleys A1229

Designs: 5c, Santiago. 10c, Havana. 15c, Camagüey. 65c, Matanzas. 75c, Camagüey, diff.
1p, Havana, diff.

2004, Feb. 20 ***Perf. 12¾***
4380-4384 A1229 Set of 5 3.75 1.90

Souvenir Sheet
Perf. 12½

4385 A1229 1p multi 2.50 1.25

No. 4385 contains one 40x32mm stamp.

Souvenir Sheet

Cuba — Mexico Binational Philatelic Exhibition — A1230

2004, Feb. 25 ***Perf. 12½***
4386 A1230 1p multi 2.50 1.25

EGREM Recording Co., 40th Anniv. — A1231

Recording artists: 10c, Cascarita, Julio Cuevas. 15c, Carlos Puebla. 65c, Benny Moré. 75c, Compay Segundo.

2004, Mar. 24 ***Perf. 12¾***
4387-4390 A1231 Set of 4 3.50 1.75

España 2004 Intl. Philatelic Exhibition — A1232

Dogs: 5c, Spanish pointer. 10c, Spanish hound. 15c, Mallorquin bulldog. 65c, Catalan sheepdog. 75c, Pyrenean mastiff.
1p, Spanish mastiff.

2004, Mar. 24 ***Perf. 12½x12¼***
4391-4395 A1232 Set of 5 4.75 2.25

Souvenir Sheet
Perf. 12½

4396 A1232 1p multi 3.25 1.50

No. 4396 contains one 40x32mm stamp.

National Police, 45th Anniv. — A1233

2004, Mar. 26 ***Perf. 12½x12¼***
4397 A1233 15c multi + label .60 .25

Souvenir Sheet

Second Cuban Sports Olympiad — A1234

2004, Apr. 18 ***Perf. 12½***
4398 A1234 1p multi 2.50 1.25

Nature and Man Foundation, 10th Anniv. — A1235

2004, May 16 Litho. ***Perf. 12¼x12½***
4399 A1235 65c multi 1.50 .75

FIFA (Fédération Internationale de Football Association), Cent. — A1236

FIFA emblem and various players: 10c, 15c, 65c, 75c.

2004, May 21 ***Perf. 12¾***
4400-4403 A1236 Set of 4 3.50 1.75

Pets A1237

Designs: 5c, Parakeets. 10c, Fish. 15c, Dogs. 65c, Cats. 75c, Finches.
1p, Horse, horiz.

2004, June 25 ***Perf. 12½x12¾***
4404-4408 A1237 Set of 5 3.75 1.90

Souvenir Sheet
Perf. 12½

4409 A1237 1p multi 2.50 1.25

No. 4409 contains one 40x32mm stamp.

Intl. Chess Federation, 80th Anniv. — A1238

Chess players: 15c, Maria Teresa Mora. 65c, José Raúl Capablanca, horiz. 75c, Ernesto "Che" Guevara.

2004, July 20 ***Perf. 12¾***
4410-4412 A1238 Set of 3 3.50 1.75

Minerals — A1239

Designs: 5c, Corundum. 10c, Thenardite. 15c, Uraninite. 65c, Realgar. 75c, Fluorite.
1p, Copper.

2004, July 30 ***Perf. 13***
4413-4417 A1239 Set of 5 3.50 1.75

Souvenir Sheet
Perf. 12½

4418 A1239 1p multi 2.50 1.25

No. 4418 contains one 40x32mm stamp.

Convention Hall, 25th Anniv. — A1240

2004, Sept. 3 ***Perf. 12¾***
4419 A1240 65c multi 1.50 1.25

Cuban Aviation, 75th Anniv. — A1241

Designs: 15c, Lockheed Constellation. 65c, IL-62M. 75c, Airbus 330.

2004, Oct. 8 ***Perf. 12½x12¼***
4420-4422 A1241 Set of 3 3.50 1.75

America Issue — A1242

Map of Cuba and: 15c, Bird over islands. 65c, Fish and marine life.

2004, Oct. 12
4423-4424 A1242 Set of 2 1.75 .90

Marine Mammals — A1243

Designs: 5c, Delphinus delphis. 10c, Lagenorhynchus obliquidens. 15c, Stenella attenuata. 65c, Grampus griseus. 75c, Tursiops truncatus.
1p, Orcinus orca.

2004, Oct. 20 ***Perf. 12½x12¼***
4425-4429 A1243 Set of 5 3.50 1.75

Souvenir Sheet
Perf. 13

4430 A1243 1p multi 2.50 1.25

No. 4430 contains one 40x32mm stamp.

Disappearance of Camilo Cienfuegos, 45th Anniv. A1244

2004, Oct. 28 ***Perf. 12¾***
4431 A1244 65c multi 1.50 .75

Railroad Stations, Cent. — A1245

Designs: 15c, Agramonte Station, 1906 ALCO No. 48 4-6-0. 65c, Aguacate Station, 1907 BLW No. 57 4-6-0. 75c, Guira de Melina Station, 1903 ALCO No. 7 4-4-0.

2004, Nov. 10 ***Perf. 13***
4432-4434 A1245 Set of 3 3.50 1.75

Souvenir Sheet

13th Philatelic Congress, Havana — A1245a

2004, Nov. 20 Litho. *Perf. 12½*
4434A A1245a 1p multi 2.25 2.25

Founding of San Cristóbal de la Habana, 485th Anniv. A1246

Designs: 15c, Temple. 65c, Painting showing priest in red vestments at base of tree. 75c, Paintig showing group of men at base of tree.

Perf. 12½x12¾
2004, Nov. 30 Litho.
4435-4437 A1246 Set of 3 3.00 1.50

Latin American Parliament Foundation, 40th Anniv. — A1246a

2004, Nov. 30 Litho. *Perf. 12¾*
4437A A1246a 65c multi 1.40 .70

Ministry of Foreign Affairs, 45th Anniv. — A1247

2004, Dec. 23 *Perf. 12½x12¼*
4438 A1247 65c multi 1.40 .70

Alejo Carpentier (1904-80), Writer — A1248

2004, Dec. 26 *Perf. 12¾*
4439 A1248 65c multi 1.40 .70

First Baseball Game in Cuba, 130th Anniv. — A1249

Baseball players: 5c, Rey Vicente Anglada. 10c, Braudilio Vinent. 15c, Rogelio Garcia. 65c, Luis G. Casanova. 75c, Victor Mesa.
1p, Martin Dihigo, vert.

2004, Dec. 27 *Perf. 12½x12¼*
4440-4444 A1249 Set of 5 4.00 2.00

Souvenir Sheet
Perf. 12½

4445 A1249 1p multi 2.25 1.10

No. 4445 contains one 32x40mm stamp.

Jose L. Guerra Aguiar Cuban Postal Museum, 40th Anniv. — A1250

Designs: 15c, Plaza Mayor, Trinidad and 1855 Trinidad to Barcelona cover. 65c, Charity Sanctuary, El Cobre and 1861 El Cobre to Santiago de Cuba cover. 85c, Matanzas Cathedral, Matanzas and 1848 Mantanzas to Havana cover.

2005, Jan. 2 *Perf. 12¾x12½*
4446-4448 A1250 Set of 3 3.50 1.75

New Year 2005 (Year of the Rooster) A1251

Designs: No. 4449, 15c, Rooster in air. No. 4450, 15c, Rooster on ground.

2005, Jan. 4 *Perf. 12¼x12½*
4449-4450 A1251 Set of 2 .60 .30

Ministry of Information Technology and Communications, 5th Anniv. — A1252

2005, Jan. 12 *Perf. 12½x12¼*
4451 A1252 65c multi 1.40 .70

Dinosaurs — A1253

Designs: 5c, Carnotaurus. 10c, Oviraptor. 30c, Parasaurolophus. 65c, Sauropelta. 90c, Iguanodon.
1p, Velociraptor.

2005, Jan. 20 Litho. *Perf. 12½x12¼*
4452-4456 A1253 Set of 5 4.25 2.10

Souvenir Sheet
Perf. 13

4457 A1253 1p multi 2.25 1.10

No. 4457 contains one 40x32mm stamp.

Miguel de Cervantes and Title Page of *Don Quixote* — A1254

2005, Jan. 24 *Perf. 12¾x12½*
4458 A1254 65c multi 1.40 .70

Publication of *Don Quixote*, 400th anniv.

Bridges A1255

Designs: 10c, Bacunayagua Bridge. 15c, La Concordia Bridge. 50c, El Triunfo Bridge. 65c, Yayabo Bridge. 75c, Canimar Bridge.
1p, Plaza Bridge.

2005, Feb. 5 *Perf. 13x12¾*
4459-4463 A1255 Set of 5 4.75 2.40

Souvenir Sheet
Perf. 13

4464 A1255 1p multi 2.25 1.10

No. 4464 contains one 40x32mm stamp.

Cuban Telecommunications Enterprise, 10th Anniv. — A1256

2005, Feb. 24 *Perf. 12½x12¾*
4465 A1256 90c multi 1.90 .95

Parrots — A1257

Designs: 5c, Amazona ochrocephala, Amazona leucocephala. 10c, Agapornis personata, Agapornis fischeri. 15c, Cacatua galerita, Cacatua leadbeateri. 65c, Psittacula krameri, Psittacula himalayana, vert. 1.05p, Aratinga guarouba, Aratinga euops.
1p, Ara macao, Ara araruana, Anodorhynchus hyacythus.

Perf. 12½x12¼, 12¼x12½
2005, Feb. 23 Litho.
4466-4470 A1257 Set of 5 4.25 2.10

Souvenir Sheet
Perf. 13

4471 A1257 1p multi 2.25 1.10

No. 4471 contain one 32x40mm stamp.

Cats A1258

Various cats: 5c, 10c, 40c, 65c, 75c. 10c is vert.

2005, Mar. 15 *Perf. 12¾*
4472-4476 A1258 Set of 5 4.25 2.10

Perf. 13

4477 A1258 1p Two cats, vert. 2.25 1.10

No. 4477 contains one 32x40mm stamp.

Cuba — Canada Diplomatic Relations, 60th Anniv. — A1259

2005, Mar. 20 *Perf. 12¾x12½*
4478 A1259 65c multi 1.75 .70

Wildlife — A1260

2005, Mar. 21 *Perf. 12½x12¼*

4479	A1260	15c Manatee	.30	.25
4480	A1260	65c Parrot	1.40	.70
4481	A1260	75c Crocodile	1.50	.75
4482	A1260	90c Hummingbird	1.75	.90
		Nos. 4479-4482 (4)	4.95	2.60

World Water Day — A1261

2005, Mar. 22 *Perf. 13*
4483 A1261 90c multi 1.90 .95

Boats — A1262

Designs: 10c, Fishing boat, fish. 20c, Schooner, fish. 30c, Bonito boat, bonito. 45c, Shrimp boat, shrimp. 90c, Lobster boat, lobster.
1p, Cargo ship, horiz.

2005, Apr. 15 *Perf. 12½*
4484-4488 A1262 Set of 5 4.25 2.10

Souvenir Sheet

4489 A1262 1p multi 2.25 1.10

First Cuban Postage Stamps, 150th Anniv. — A1263

Designs: 15c, St. Francis of Assisi Convent, Cuba #1. 65c, Morro Lighthouse, Cuba #2. 75c, Colonial Post Office, Cuba #3.

2005, Apr. 24 *Perf. 12¾x12½*
4490-4492 A1263 Set of 3 3.50 1.75

Social Security For All — A1264

2005, May 5 **Litho.**
4493 A1264 65c multi 1.40 .70

Major General Máximo Gómez (1836-1905) — A1265

2005, June 17 *Perf. 12½*
4494 A1265 1.05p multi 2.25 1.10

Souvenir Sheet

Santiago de Cuba, 490th Anniv. — A1266

2005, July 4 *Perf. 13*
4495 A1266 1p multi 2.25 1.10

16th World Youth and Student Festival, Venezuela — A1267

2005, July 29 *Perf. 12¾x12½*
4496 A1267 65c multi 1.40 .70

Dances A1268

Parrot and: No. 4497, 65c, Samba dancers and Brazilian flag. No. 4498, 65c, Son dancers, Cuban flag.

2005, Aug. 15 *Perf. 12¾*
4497-4498 A1268 Set of 2 2.75 1.50

See Brazil Nos. 2967-2968.

Cuban — Soviet Space Flight, 25th Anniv. — A1269

No. 4499: a, Cosmonaut Arnaldo Tamayo Mendez. b, Cosmonaut Yuri Romanenko.

2005, Sept. 18 *Perf. 12½*
4499 A1269 90c Horiz. pair, #a-b 4.00 2.00

Albert Einstein's Visit to Cuba, 75th Anniv. — A1270

Designs: 65c, Caricature of Einstein. 75c, Equation for energy, Einstein writing.

2005, Sept. 21
4500-4501 A1270 Set of 2 4.50 2.00

Locomotives — A1271

Designs: 5c, DSB B40, 1869. 10c, Great Northern, 1902. No. 4504, 15c, Minaret, 1929. No. 4505, 15c, C. F. White, 1885. 2.05p, Western Pacific FP7A 805D.
1p, 14th No. 4 Krauss & Co., 1884.

2005, May 10 **Litho.** *Perf. 12¾*
4502-4506 A1271 Set of 5 5.50 2.75

Souvenir Sheet

Perf. 13

4507 A1271 1p multi 2.25 1.10

No. 4507 contains one 40x32mm stamp.

Zoo Animals A1272

Designs: 10c, Loxodonta africana. 15c, Acunonyx jubatus, horiz. 50c, Synceros caffer, horiz. 65c, Giraffa camelopardalis. 75c, Panthera leo.
1p, Equus burchelli, horiz.

2005, July 21 *Perf. 12¾*
4508-4512 A1272 Set of 5 4.75 2.40

Souvenir Sheet

Perf. 13

4513 A1272 1p multi 2.25 1.10

No. 4513 contains one 40x32mm stamp.

Santiago de Cuba, 490th Anniv. — A1273

2005, Sept. 22 *Perf. 12¾x12½*
4514 A1273 75c multi 2.00 1.00

Revolutionary Defense Committees, 45th Anniv. — A1274

2005, Sept. 28 *Perf. 12½x12¼*
4515 A1274 50c multi 1.10 .55

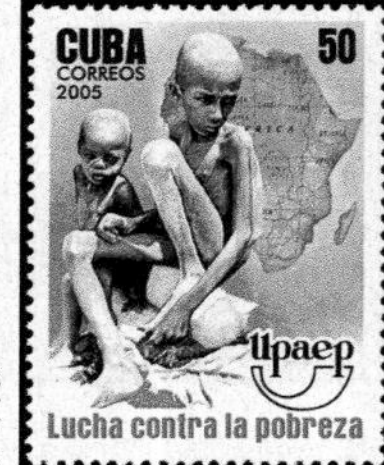
Diplomatic Relations Between Cuba and People's Republic of China, 45th Anniv. — A1275

No. 4516: a, Chinese General Secretary Hu Jintao and Cuban Pres. Fidel Castro. b, Great Wall of China and Morro Castle, Havana.

2005, Sept. 28 *Perf. 13x13¼*
4516 A1275 15c Horiz. pair, #a-b 1.00 .50

America Issue, Fight Against Poverty A1276

Designs: 50c, Starving children, map of Africa. 75c, Woman and child, map of South America.

2005, Oct. 12 *Perf. 12¾*
4517-4518 A1276 Set of 2 2.75 1.40

Horses A1277

Breeds: 10c, Gelderlander. 20c, Arabian. 30c, Quarterhorse. 65c, Wild horses. 75c, Lipizzaner.
100c, Holsteiner, vert.

2005, Oct. 21 *Perf. 12¾*
4519-4523 A1277 Set of 5 4.25 2.10

Souvenir Sheet

Perf. 12¾x12½

4524 A1277 100c multi 2.25 1.10

No. 4524 contains one 32x40mm stamp.

José Martí Type of 2004

Martí and: No. 4525, 5c, Central University, Madrid, 1871. No. 4526, 5c, Zaragoza University, 1871. No. 4527, 5c, F. Valdés Dominguez, Teatro Principal, Zaragoza, 1872. No. 4528, 10c, Victor Hugo House, Paris, 1872. No. 4529, 10c, Moneda No. 12, Mexico City, 1875. No. 4530, 15c, Normal School, Guatemala City, 1876. No. 4531, 15c, San Ildefonso No. 40, Mexico City, 1894. No. 4532, 15c, Plaza de Guardiola, Mexico City, 1894. 65c, Plaza Bolívar, Caracas, 1885. 75c, Santa María College, Caracas, 1893.
1p, Martínez Ibor Tobacco Factory, Tampa, 1892.

2005, Oct. 20 *Perf. 12½x12¼*
4525-4534 A1227 Set of 10 4.75 2.40

Souvenir Sheet

Perf. 13

4535 A1227 1p multi 2.25 1.10

No. 4535 contains one 40x32mm stamp.

World Summit on the Information Society, Tunis — A1278

2005, Nov. 16 ***Perf. 12½x12¼***
4536 A1278 75c multi 1.60 .80

Establishment of Local Delivery of Mail in Havana, 150th Anniv. — A1279

Designs 15c, Cuba #7, cover to Havana. 65c, Cuba #16, Colonial Havana mailbox.

2005, Nov. 19 ***Perf. 12¾x12½***
4537-4538 A1279 Set of 2 1.60 .80

Cuban Men Convicted of Terrorism Imprisoned In the United States A1280

2005, Nov. 25 ***Perf. 12½x12¾***
4539 A1280 65c multi 2.50 1.00

Europa Stamps, 50th Anniv. (in 2006) A1281

Designs: 1.30p, Spain #1126, Castilla de la Fuerza, Havana. 2.05p, Spain #1010, Santisima Church, Trinidad, Cuba. 2.55p, Spain #1526, Morro Castle, Santiago de Cuba. 3.90p, Spain #1263, San Cristóbal Cathedral, Havana.

2005, Nov. 30 ***Perf. 12½***
4540-4543 A1281 Set of 4 20.00 10.00
4543a Souvenir sheet, #4540-4543 20.00 20.00

Nos. 4540-4543, 4543a exist imperf. Values, same.

Jewelry A1282

Jewelry by: 5c, Antonio Barcala. 10c, Raúl Valladares. 45c, Carlos de la Torre. 65c, J. Carlo Rafart. 75c, Osvaldo Castilla.
1p, 19th cent. jewelry in Gold Museum.

2005, Dec. 1 ***Perf. 12¾***
4544-4548 A1282 Set of 5 4.25 2.10

Souvenir Sheet
Perf. 12½

4549 A1282 1p multi 2.25 1.10

No. 4549 contains one 32x40mm stamp.

Friendship Among the Peoples Institute, 45th Anniv. — A1283

2005, Dec. 14 ***Perf. 12¾x12½***
4550 A1283 1.05p multi 2.25 1.10

Snails and Mushrooms A1284

Designs: 10c, Clathrus cancellatus. 20c, Polymita genus picta. 30c, Lepiota puellaris. 65c, Polymita genus muscarum. 75c, Clitocybe infundibuliformis.
1p, Polymita genus versicolor, horiz.

2005, Dec. 15 ***Perf. 12¾***
4551-4555 A1284 Set of 5 4.25 2.10

Souvenir Sheet
Perf. 13

4556 A1284 1p multi 2.25 1.10

No. 4556 contains one 40x32mm stamp.

Hotel Inglaterra, 130th Anniv. — A1285

2005, Dec. 23 ***Perf. 12¾x12½***
4557 A1285 65c multi 1.25 .70

New Year 2006 (Year of the Dog) — A1286

Designs: No. 4558, 15c, Shih tzu. No. 4559, 15c, Pug.

2006, Jan. 4 ***Perf. 12¼x12½***
4558-4559 A1286 Set of 2 1.00 .30

Organization of Solidarity of the People of Asia, Africa and Latin America, 40th Anniv. A1287

2006, Jan. 16 ***Perf. 12¾***
4560 A1287 65c multi 1.40 .70

Establishment of Cuban Postal Service, 250th Anniv. — A1288

Stampless cover and: 75c, Horse and rider. 2.05p, Ship.

2006, Mar. 1 ***Perf. 12½x12¼***
4561-4562 A1288 Set of 2 6.00 3.00

OPEC Intl. Development Fund, 30th Anniv. — A1289

2006, Mar. 23 **Litho.**
4563 A1289 75c multi 1.60 .80

Souvenir Sheet

Havana '06 Intl. Philatelic Exhibition — A1290

2006, Mar. 25 ***Perf. 12½***
4564 A1290 1p multi 2.25 1.10

Pope John Paul II (1920-2005) — A1291

Designs: 65c, Pope, Mass in Santa Clara. 75c, Mass in Camagüey (44x27mm). 90c, Mass in Santiago de Cuba (44x27mm). 1.05p, Pope, Mass in Havana.

2006, Apr. 2 ***Perf. 12½x12¼***
4565-4568 A1291 Set of 4 7.25 3.75

Bay of Pigs Invasion, 45th Anniv. — A1292

2006, Apr. 17 ***Perf. 12¼x12½***
4569 A1292 65c multi 1.40 .70

José Martí Type of 2004

Martí and: No. 4570, Madame Griffou's Hotel, New York, 1890. No. 4571, Gonzalo de Quesada, 116 West 64th Street, New York, 1893. No. 4572, Son, José Francisco, 324 Classon Ave., New York, 1885. No. 4573, Masonic Temple, New York, 1888.
No. 4574: a, Cajobabo beach, Gomez monument. b, Martí monument, monument at Dos Ríos.
Martí and: 75c, Hardman Hall, New York, 1891. 85c, Office, 120 Front Street, New York, 1891. 90c, María Mantilla, Bath Beach, Long Island.
1p, Home of Teodoro Pérez, Cayo Hueso, 1893.

2006, May 19 **Litho.** ***Perf. 12½x12¼***
4570 A1227 5c multi .25 .25
4571 A1227 5c multi .25 .25
4572 A1227 10c multi .25 .25
4573 A1227 10c multi .25 .25
4574 A1227 15c Horiz. pair, #a-b .65 .65
4575 A1227 75c multi 1.60 1.60
4576 A1227 85c multi 1.90 1.90
4577 A1227 90c multi 1.90 1.90
Nos. 4570-4577 (8) 7.05 7.05

Souvenir Sheet
Perf. 13

4578 A1227 1p multi 2.25 2.25

No. 4578 contains one 40x32mm stamp.

Prehistoric Animals — A1293

Designs: 5c, Dsungaripetrus, Yangchuanosaurus. 10c, Pterodactylus, Sprinosaurus. 30c, Pteranodon, Pachycephalosaurus. 35c, Scaphognathus, Muttaburrasaurus. 65c, Quetzalcoatlus, Stegosaurus. 1.05p, Sordes, Saichania.
1p, Stenonychosaurus, vert.

2006, May 24 ***Perf. 12½x12¼***
4579-4584 A1293 Set of 6 5.50 5.50

Souvenir Sheet
Perf. 12½

4585 A1293 1p multi 2.25 2.25

No. 4585 contains one 32x40mm stamp.

Ministry of the Interior, 45th Anniv. — A1294

2006, June 6 ***Perf. 12½x12¼***
4586 A1294 75c multi 1.60 1.60

Fowl — A1295

Designs: 5c, Chickens. No. 4588, 15c, Turkeys. No. 4589, 15c, Guinea fowl. 45c, Geese. 50c, Pheasants. 75c, Peafowl.
1p, Ducks.

2006, June 15 ***Perf. 12½x12¼***
4587-4592 A1295 Set of 6 4.50 4.50

Souvenir Sheet
Perf. 13

4593 A1295 1p multi 2.25 2.25

No. 4593 contains one 40x32mm stamp.

Cerro Pelado Declaration, 40th Anniv. — A1296

Designs: 65c, Ship, man and crowd. 75c, People in cargo hoist. 85c, Men assisting woman down ship's stairs, flags of Cuba and Puerto Rico.

2006, June 25 ***Perf. 12½x12¾***
4594-4596 A1296 Set of 3 4.75 4.75

2006 World Cup Soccer Championships, Germany — A1296a

Various Cuban soccer players: 15c, 45c, 65c, 75c.

2006, June **Litho.** ***Perf. 12¾***
4596A-4596D A1296a Set of 4 4.00 4.00

Genetic Engineering and Biotechnology Center, 20th Anniv. — A1297

2006, July 1 ***Perf. 12½x12¼***
4597 A1297 65c multi 1.40 1.40

Comic Strips by Virgilio Martinez — A1298

Designs: 15c, Pucho y Sus Perrerias. 65c, Cucho.

2006, July 16 ***Perf. 12¾x12¼***
4598-4599 A1298 Set of 2 1.75 1.75

Airplanes — A1299

Designs: 10c, Granville GeeBee R2. No. 4601, 15c, Bücker Jungmann. No. 4602, 15c, Comte AC-4 Gentleman. 50c, Mustang TF-51. 75c, Supermarine Spitfire. 85c, Lavochkin La-9.
1p, Bücker Jungmeister.

2006, July 20 ***Perf. 12¾***
4600-4605 A1299 Set of 6 5.50 5.50

Souvenir Sheet
Imperf

4606 A1299 1p multi 2.25 2.25

No. 4606 contains one 36x28mm stamp.

Dogs — A1300

Designs: 5c, Bulldog. 10c, American cocker spaniel. 15c, Shar-pei. 20c, Airedale terrier. 35c, Pomeranian. 2.05p, Dalmatian.
1p, Whippet, vert.

2006, Aug. 18 ***Perf. 12½x12¼***
4607-4612 A1300 Set of 6 6.25 6.25

Souvenir Sheet
Perf. 13

4613 A1300 1p multi 2.25 2.25

Recovery of Raw Materials, 45th Anniv. — A1301

Designs: 15c, Ernesto "Che" Guevara. 65c, Cuban and recovery program flags.

2006, Aug. 24 ***Perf. 12¾***
4614-4615 A1301 Set of 2 1.75 1.75

14th Congress of Non-Aligned Countries, Havana A1302

2006, Sept. 10
4616 A1302 65c multi 1.40 1.40

Pedro Santacilia, Benito Juárez and Mexico House, Havana — A1303

2006, Sept. 15 ***Perf. 12½x12¼***
4617 A1303 65c multi 1.40 1.40

Benito Juárez (1806-72), President of Mexico.

Souvenir Sheet

7th Hispano-Cuban Philatelic Exposition — A1304

No. 4618: a, Statue, arms of Cuba, denomination at LR. b, Statue, arms of Spain, denomination at LL.

2006, Sept. 20 ***Imperf.***
4618 A1304 50c Sheet of 2, #a-b 2.25 2.25

España 06 World Philatelic Exposition, Malaga, Spain — A1305

Designs: 5c, Rio Hanabanilla. 10c, Laguna Bacanao. 15c, Sierra de la Gran Piedra. 20c, Valle de los Ingenios. 50c, Laguna del Tesoro. 75c, Sierra Maestra.
1p, Valle de Viñales.

2006, Sept. 20 ***Perf. 12¾***
4619-4624 A1305 Set of 6 3.75 3.75

Souvenir Sheet
Perf. 13

4625 A1305 1p multi 2.25 2.25

No. 4625 contains one 40x32mm stamp.

America Issue, Energy Conservation — A1306

Equipment for harnessing energy source: No. 4626, 65c, Petroleum. No. 4627, 65c, Water. No. 4628, 65c, Solar. No. 4629, 65c, Wind.

2006, Oct. 12 ***Perf. 12¾***
4626-4629 A1306 Set of 4 5.50 5.50

Saiz Brothers Association, 20th Anniv. A1307

2006, Oct. 18
4630 A1307 75c multi 1.60 1.60

20th Intl. Ballet Festival, Havana A1308

Dancers: 75c, Alicia Alonso and Igor Youskévitch. 85c, Alonso.

2006, Oct. 28 ***Perf. 12¼x12½***
4631-4632 A1308 Set of 2 3.50 3.50

A1309

Belgica '06 Intl. Youth Philately Exposition, Belgium — A1310

Trains: 5c, Rocket and Intercity Diesel-electric. 10c, Turbine locomotive, Diesel-electric locomotive. 15c, Shinkasen and City of Los Angeles. 65c, Steam locomotive, Diesel locomotive. 75c, TEE Diesel-electric, TGV electric. 85c, Brisbane electric monorail, Wuppertal monorail.
No. 4639: a, Steam locomotive. b, Diesel locomotive.

2006, Nov. 2 ***Perf. 12¾***
4633-4638 A1309 Set of 6 5.50 5.50

Souvenir Sheet
Perf. 12½

4639 A1310 50c Sheet of 2, #a-b 2.25 2.25

TeleFood Emblem — A1311

2006, Nov. 11 ***Perf. 12¾***
4640 A1311 75c multi 1.60 1.60

Animals Serving Man — A1312

Designs: 5c, Equus caballus, Greek horse-drawn chariot. 15c, Camelus dromedarius, Ibn Battuta on camel. 30c, Capra aegagrus, Roman musician. 40c, Lama lama, Peruvian pre-Columbian ceramic llama. 50c, Felis catus, painting by Kuniyoshi Utagawa. 1.05p, Elephas maximus, elephant with Indian caparison.
1p, Canis familiaris, Grecian with dog.

2006, Oct. 1 Litho. ***Perf. 12½x12¼***
4641-4646 A1312 Set of 6 5.50 5.50

Souvenir Sheet

Perf. 12½

4647 A1312 1p multi 2.25 2.25

No. 4647 contains one 40x32mm stamp.

Fire Fighting and Rescue Equipment — A1313

Designs: 5c, 1899 Horse-drawn ambulance, Brazil, and megaphone. 10c, Fireman's hat, and 1898 Merryweather fire truck, England. 20c, 1910 Laurin & Klement fire truck, Bohemia, and fire hydrant. 30c, 1939 American La France ladder truck, US, and badge. 45c, 1925 Leyland Motors pumper motorcycle, United Kingdom, and portable hose and tank. 90c, Brussels fire badge and 1930 Magirus ladder truck, Germany.

1p, Fireman spraying water, vert.

2006, Nov. 13 ***Perf. 12¾***
4648-4653 A1313 Set of 6 4.50 4.50

Souvenir Sheet

Perf. 12½

4654 A1313 1p multi 2.25 2.25

No. 4654 contains one 32x40mm stamp.

Santiago Rebellion, 50th Anniv. — A1314

2006, Nov. 30 ***Perf. 12½x12¼***
4655 A1314 65c multi 1.40 1.40

Governmental Reorganization, 30th Anniv. — A1315

2006, Dec. 2
4656 A1315 75c multi 1.60 1.60

Granma Landings, 50th Anniv. — A1316

Revolutionary Armed Forces, 50th Anniv. — A1317

2006, Dec. 2 ***Perf. 13***
4657 A1316 65c multi 1.40 1.40
4658 A1317 65c multi 1.40 1.40

General Antonio Maceo Grajales (1845-96) — A1317a

2006, Dec. 7 Litho. ***Perf. 12½x12¼***
4658A A1317a 1.05p multi 2.10 2.10

Intl. Film and Television School, 20th Anniv. — A1318

2006, Dec. 15 ***Perf. 12¾***
4659 A1318 75c multi 1.60 1.60

Martí Forge Museum, 55th Anniv. — A1319

2006, Dec. 15 ***Perf. 12½x12¼***
4660 A1319 90c multi 1.90 1.90

Literacy Campaign, 45th Anniv. A1320

2006, Dec. 19 ***Perf. 12¾***
4661 A1320 65c multi 1.40 1.40

Major General Ignacio Agramonte y Loinaz (1841-73) — A1321

2006, Dec. 23 ***Perf. 12½x12¼***
4662 A1321 65c multi 1.40 1.40

Special Education, 45th Anniv. — A1322

2007, Jan. 4 ***Perf. 12¾***
4663 A1322 85c multi 1.75 1.75

Francesa Pharmacy, 125th Anniv. A1323

2007, Jan. 18 Litho.
4664 A1323 65c multi 1.40 1.40

Electric Trains A1324

Designs: 5c, First American electric locomotive, 1895. 10c, Locomotive, Netherlands. 15c, Interurban train, Australia. 65c, High-speed train, Italy. 85c, Helensburgh-Bridgeton train, Great Britain. 1.05p, Lyon-St. Etienne interurban train, France.

1p, High-speed train, Germany.

2007, Jan. 18 ***Perf. 12¾***
4665-4670 A1324 Set of 6 6.00 6.00

Souvenir Sheet

Imperf

4671 A1324 1p multi 2.25 2.25

No. 4671 contains one 40x32mm stamp with simulated perforations.

12th Intl. Information Fair and Convention — A1325

2007, Feb. 12 ***Perf. 12½x12¼***
4672 A1325 75c multi 1.60 1.60

Cats A1326

Designs: 10c, Two cats. No. 4674, 15c, Kitten with paw raised. No. 4675, 15c, Cat. 50c, Cat and telephone. 75c, Cat with ball. 90c, Cat, diff.

1p, Cat, diff.

2007, Feb. 14 ***Perf. 12¾***
4673-4678 A1326 Set of 6 5.50 5.50

Souvenir Sheet

Imperf

4679 A1326 1p multi 2.25 2.25

No. 4679 contains one 40x32mm stamp with simulated perforations.

Fifth Congress of Cuban Pigeon Fanciers Federation — A1327

2007, Feb. 24 ***Perf. 12¾***
4680 A1327 75c multi 1.60 1.60

Souvenir Sheet

Patria Newspaper, 115th Anniv. — A1328

Imperf. With Simulated Perforations

2007, Mar. 14
4681 A1328 1p multi 2.25 2.25

Animals in National Zoo — A1329

Designs: 5c, Ara ararauana. 10c, Tsetudo elephantopus. 15c, Balearica regulorum. 20c, Procyon lotor. 45c, Panthera pardus. 2.05p, Pongo pygmaeus.

1p, Giraffa camelopardalis, vert.

2007, Mar. 31 ***Perf. 12½x12¼***
4682-4687 A1329 Set of 6 6.50 6.50

Souvenir Sheet

Imperf

4688 A1329 1p multi 2.25 2.25

No. 4688 contains one 32x40mm stamp with simulated perforations.

Raúl Roa García (1907-82), Foreign Minister A1330

2007, Apr. 18 ***Perf. 12¾***
4689 A1330 65c multi 1.40 1.40

Union of Young Communists, 45th Anniv. — A1331

2007, Apr. 4 ***Perf. 12½x12¼***
4690 A1331 75c multi 1.60 1.60

José Martí Type of 2004

Martí and: No. 4691, 5c, Cuban High School, Tampa, 1892. No. 4692, 5c, Casa de los Pedrosa, Tampa, 1892. No. 4693, 10c, Hotel Duval, Cayo Hueso, 1891. No. 4694, 10c, Hotel Cherokee, Tampa, 1891. No. 4695, 15c, Cayo Hueso Committee, 1891 (68x28mm). No. 4696, 15c, F. Valdés Domínguez, Gato Brothers Cigar Factory, Cayo Hueso, 1894. 35c, Club San Carlos, Cayo Hueso, 1893. 40c, Hotel Myrtle Bank, Kingston, 1892. 50c, Gen. Francisco Gómez Toro, Friends of the Country Society Building, Santo Domingo, 1894. 65c, Máximo Gómez, Gómez's house, Montecristi.

2007, Apr. 10 ***Perf. 12½x12¼***
4691-4700 A1227 Set of 10 5.50 5.50

World Food Program Children's Art Exhibition, 10th Anniv. — A1332

2007, May 3 Litho. *Perf. 12¾*
4701 A1332 65c multi 1.40 1.40

Folklore Union — A1333

2007, May 7 *Perf. 12¼x12½*
4702 A1333 75c multi 1.60 1.60

Islands and Wildlife — A1334

Designs: 5c, Cayo Guillermo, pelican. No. 4704, 15c, Cayo Las Brujas, sea gull. No. 4705, 15c, Cayo Levisa, conches. 20c, Cayo Santa Maria, iguana. 50c, Cayo Ensenachos, plover. 85c, Cayo Largo, Carey turtle.
1p, Cayo Coco, flamingos.

2007, May 8 *Perf. 12½x12¼*
4703-4708 A1334 Set of 6 4.25 4.25

Souvenir Sheet
Imperf

4709 A1334 1p multi 2.25 2.25

No. 4709 contains one 40x32mm stamp.

Singers and Songwriters A1335

Designs: 5c, Benny Moré. 10c, Ignacio Piñeiro. 30c, Arsenio Rodríguez. 35c, Miguelito Cuní. 65c, Pio Leyva. 75c, Ibrahim Ferrer.
1p, Miguel Matamoros.

2007, May 10 *Perf. 12¾*
4710-4715 A1335 Set of 6 4.75 4.75

Souvenir Sheet
Imperf

4716 A1335 1p multi 2.25 2.25

No. 4716 contains one 32x40mm stamp with simulated perforations.

Souvenir Sheet

Martí Studies Youth Seminary, 35th Anniv. — A1336

2007, May 19 *Imperf.*
4717 A1336 1p multi 2.25 2.25

Cuban Radio and Television Institute, 45th Anniv. — A1337

2007, May 24 *Perf. 12½x12¼*
4718 A1337 3p multi 6.50 6.50

Integral Development Group of the Capital, 20th Anniv. — A1338

2007, May 25 Litho.
4719 A1338 65c multi 1.40 1.40

Cuban Admission to the United Nations, 60th Anniv. A1339

2007, May 29 *Perf. 12¾*
4720 A1339 65c multi 1.40 1.40

2007 Pan American Games, Rio de Janeiro — A1340

Designs: No. 4721, 15c, Fencing. No. 4722, 15c, Boxing. 20c, Wrestling. 45c, Running. 65c, Gymnastics. 75c, Cycling.
1p, Games emblem, vert.

2007, June 20 *Perf. 12¾*
4721-4726 A1340 Set of 6 5.00 5.00

Souvenir Sheet
Imperf

4727 A1340 1p multi 2.25 2.25

No. 4727 contains one 32x40mm stamp.

Third Technological Transfer and Intl. Trade Workshop — A1341

2007, July 3 *Perf. 12½x12¼*
4728 A1341 65c multi 1.40 1.40

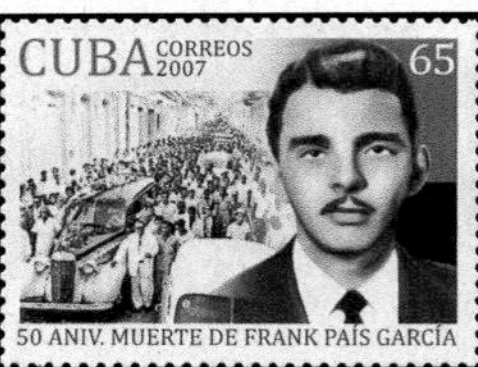

Frank País (1934-57), Revolutionary Hero — A1342

2007, July 30 *Perf. 12¾*
4729 A1342 65c multi 1.40 1.40

Radio Cubana, 85th Anniv. A1343

2007, Aug. 22 *Perf. 12¾*
4730 A1343 65c multi 1.40 1.40

Seven Wonders of the Modern World A1344

Designs: 10c, Great Wall of China. 15c, Petra, Jordan. 20c, Christ the Redeemer Statue, Brazil. 40c, Machu Picchu, Peru. 65c, Chichén Itzá Pyramids, Mexico. 75c, Roman Colosseum. 85c, Taj Mahal, India.

2007, Aug. 16 Litho. *Perf. 12¾*
4731-4737 A1344 Set of 7 6.25 6.25

Transportation — A1345

Designs: 10c, Cocotaxis (40x29mm). 15c, Lada 2105 taxi (40x29mm). 30c, Girón VI bus (40x29mm). 40c, Bus trailer on truck (44x27mm). 75c, DAF articulated bus (44x27mm). 85c, Yutong bus (44x27mm).
1p, La Gaviota train.

Perf. 12¾, 12½x12¼ (#4741-4743)
2007, Sept. 3
4738-4743 A1345 Set of 6 5.25 5.25

Souvenir Sheet
Imperf

4744 A1345 1p multi 2.00 2.00

No. 4744 contains one 40x32mm stamp with simulated perforations.

Central Youth Club, 20th Anniv. — A1346

2007, Sept. 8 *Perf. 12¼x12½*
4745 A1346 65c multi 1.40 1.40

Cubans Convicted of Espionage by United States A1347

Designs: No. 4746, 65c, Raised hand with "Cuban Five" emblem. No. 4747, 65c, Fernando González Liort. No. 4748, 65c, Gerardo Hernández Nordelo. No. 4749, 65c, Antonio Guerrero Rodriguez. No. 4750, 65c, Ramón Labañino Salazar. No. 4751, 65c, René González Schwerert.

2007, Sept. 12 *Perf. 12¾*
4746-4751 A1347 Set of 6 8.00 8.00

Tree Planting Campaign — A1348

2007, Oct. 24 *Perf. 12½x12¼*
4752 A1348 65c multi 1.40 1.40

International Design Conference — A1350

Rose Varieties A1349

Designs: 5c, Pink Parfait. No. 4754, 15c, Alison Wheatcroft. No. 4755, 15c, Prima Ballerina. 45c, Fragrant Cloud. 50c, Blue Moon. 75c, Grandmère Jenny.
1p, Rosa highdownensis.

2007, Oct. 25 *Perf. 12¾*
4753-4758 A1349 Set of 6 4.25 4.25

Souvenir Sheet
Imperf

4759 A1349 1p multi 2.00 2.00

No. 4759 contains one 40x32mm stamp with simulated perforations.

Designs: 75c, Electronic machine. 85c, Caricatures.

2007, Oct. 26 *Perf. 12½x12¼*
4760-4761 A1350 Set of 2 3.25 3.25

Souvenir Sheet

International Air Mail Service From Cuba, 80th Anniv. — A1351

2007, Oct. 27 ***Imperf.***

4762 A1351 1p multi 2.00 2.00

Seventh Natl. Philatelic Championship. No. 4762 has simulated perforations.

Protected Animals — A1352

Designs: 5c, Eretmochelys imbricata. 10c, Trichechus manatus. 20c, Mesocapromys sanfelipensis. 30c, Mesocapromys nanus. 45c, Epinephelus itajara. 85c, Balistes vetula. 1p, Chelonia mydas.

2007, Nov. 15 ***Perf. 12½x12¼***

4763-4768 A1352 Set of 6 4.00 4.00

Souvenir Sheet

Imperf

4769 A1352 1p multi 2.00 2.00

No. 4769 contains one 40x32mm stamp with simulated perforations.

Cuban UNESCO Commission, 60th Anniv. — A1353

2007, Nov. 17 ***Perf. 12½x12¼***

4770 A1353 65c multi 1.40 1.40

Cuban Railroads, 170th Anniv. — A1354

2007, Nov. 19 ***Perf. 12¾***

4771 A1354 3p multi 6.00 6.00

Camagüey Ballet, 40th Anniv. — A1355

2007, Dec. 1 **Litho.**

4772 A1355 75c multi 1.50 1.50

Infomed Health Network, 15th Anniv. — A1356

2007, Dec. 15

4773 A1356 65c green & black 1.40 1.40

Federation of University Students, 85th Anniv. — A1357

2007, Dec. 20

4774 A1357 65c multi 1.40 1.40

Seven Marvels of Cuban Civil Engineering — A1358

Designs: 5c, White Aqueduct, Havana. 10c, Sewer system, Havana. 20c, Central Highway, Santiago. 30c La Bahia Tunnel, Havana. 85c, Bacunayagua Bridge, Matanzas. 90c, La Farola Viaduct, Guantánamo.
1p, FOSCA Building, Havana.

2007, Dec. 31 ***Perf. 12¾***

4775-4780 A1358 Set of 6 5.00 5.00

Souvenir Sheet

Imperf

4781 A1358 1p multi 2.00 2.00

No. 4781 contains one 40x32mm stamp with simulated perforations.

World Ozone Layer Protection Day, 20th Anniv. — A1359

2007 ***Perf. 12¾***

4782 A1359 65c multi 1.40 1.40

Tourism — A1360

No. 4783, 75c — El Yunque, Baracoa and: a, Atlantea perezi. b, Polymita picta.

No. 4784, 75c — Alexander von Humboldt National Park and: a, Eleutherodactylus iberia. b, Solenodon cubanus.

2007 **Litho.** **Horiz. Pairs, #a-b**

4783-4784 A1360 Set of 2 6.00 6.00

Miniature Sheet

America Issue, Education For All — A1361

No. 4785: a, Teacher and children, children in uniforms, girl at computer. b, Students at table. c, Students, flag, marchers. d, Artist, people sitting in front of building, man at computer.

2007

4785 A1361 75c Sheet of 4, #a-d 6.00 6.00

Ernesto "Che" Guevara (1928-67) — A1362

Designs: 65c, Guevara sitting with other men. 75c, Monument to Guevara, La Higuera, Bolivia. 85c, Guevara and text. 90c, Guevara and marchers.

2007 ***Perf. 12½x12¼***

4786-4789 A1362 Set of 4 6.50 6.50

4789a Miniature sheet, #4786-4789 6.50 6.50

Historic Central City of Cienfuegos — A1363

Buildings: 15c, City Hall. 65c, San Lorenzo and Santo Tomás College. 75c, Tomás Terry Theater. 85c, Ferrer Palace.
1p, Gazebo, José Martí Park.

2007 **Litho.** ***Perf. 12¾***

4790-4793 A1363 Set of 4 5.00 5.00

Souvenir Sheet

Imperf

4794 A1363 1p multi 2.00 2.00

No. 4794 contains one 40x32mm stamp with simulated perforations.

University of Havana, 280th Anniv. — A1364

2008, Jan. 5 **Litho.** ***Perf. 12½x12¼***

4795 A1364 65c multi 1.40 1.40

2008 Summer Olympics, Beijing — A1365

Designs: 15c, Baseball. 45c, Swimming. 65c, Discus. 75c, Volleyball.

2008, Jan. 18 ***Perf. 12¾***

4796-4799 A1365 Set of 4 4.00 4.00

José Martí Type of 2004

Designs: No. 4800, 15c, Martí at Twilight Park, New York, 1892, vert. No. 4801, 15c, Martí with members of Cuban Revolutionary Party, 1892, vert. 30c, Martí, and family of Carmen Miyares, Sandy Hill, New York, 1893, vert. 40c, Mausoleum, Santa Ifigenia, vert. 45c, Martí, tomb of Félix Varela, San Agustín. 50c, Martí, Dellundé House, Cabo Haitiano. 65c, Hanábana Memorial, Matanzas. 85c, Cover from 1889 in Postal Museum.

2008, Jan. 28

4800-4807 A1227 Set of 8 7.00 7.00

Subway Trains and Stations — A1366

Trains and stations in: No. 4808, 15c, New York. No. 4809, 15c, Paris. 30c, Caracas. 65c, Madrid. 75c, Mexico City. 1.05p, Tokyo.

No. 4814: a, 1866 London Underground train. b, Modern London Underground train, Westminster station emblem.

2008, Feb. 15 ***Perf. 12½x12¼***

4808-4813 A1366 Set of 6 6.25 6.25

Souvenir Sheet

Imperf

4814 A1366 50c Sheet of 2, #a-b 2.00 2.00

No. 4814 contains two 39x24mm stamps with simulated perforations.

Radio Rebelde, 50th Anniv. A1367

2008, Feb. 24 ***Perf. 12¾***

4815 A1367 75c multi 1.50 1.50

Frontier Guards, 45th Anniv. A1368

2008, Mar. 3

4816 A1368 65c multi 1.40 1.40

Dr. Mario Muñoz Monroy Third Guerrilla Front, 50th Anniv. — A1369

2008, Mar. 6 Litho. *Perf. 12¾*
4817 A1369 75c multi 1.50 1.50

Aquaculture — A1370

Designs: No. 4817A, Cyprinus carpio. No. 4817B, Hypophthalmicthys molitrix. 45c, Aristychthys nobilis. 65c, Penaeus vannamei. 75c, Ctenopharyngodon idella. 85c, Clarias gariepinus.
1p, Oreochromis aurea.

2008, Apr. 8 *Perf. 12½x12¼*

4817A	A1370 15c multi	.30	.30
4817B	A1370 15c multi	.30	.30
4817C	A1370 45c multi	.90	.90
4818	A1370 65c multi	1.30	1.30
4819	A1370 75c multi	1.50	1.50
4820	A1370 85c multi	1.75	1.75
	Nos. 4817A-4820 (6)	6.05	6.05

Souvenir Sheet
Imperf

4821 A1370 1p multi 2.00 2.00

No. 4821 contains one 31x28mm stamp.

Souvenir Sheet

Cuban Postal Stationery, 130th Anniv. — A1371

2008, Apr. 24 *Imperf.*
4822 A1371 1p multi 2.00 2.00

Bohemia Magazine, Cent. — A1372

2008, May 10 *Perf. 12¾*
4823 A1372 65c multi 1.40 1.40

Second Frank Pais Front, 50th Anniv. — A1373

2008, Mar. 11 Litho. *Perf. 12¾*
4824 A1373 65c multi 1.40 1.40

Birds — A1374

Designs: 5c, Cartacuba (Cuban tody). 10c, Ruiseñor (nightingale). 15c, Carpintero verde (green woodpecker). 50c, Tocororo (Cuban trogon). 65c, Catey (parakeet), horiz. 75c, Cabrerito de la Ciénaga (Zapata sparrow), horiz. 90c, Zunzuncito (hummingbird), horiz. 1.05p, Juan Chiví (Cuban vireo), horiz.

2008, May 22
4825-4832 A1374 Set of 8 8.50 8.50

"Wings of Liberty" Symposium, Cuban National Museum of Natural History.

Visit of Indonesian Pres. Sukarno, 48th Anniv. — A1375

Sukarno and: No. 4833, 65c, Fidel Castro (shown). No. 4834, 65c, Ernesto "Che" Guevara.

2008 Litho. *Perf. 12½x12¼*
4833-4834 A1375 Set of 2 2.60 2.60

Flora and Fauna at Ramsar Sites in Cuba and Iran — A1376

No. 4835: a, Cyanolimnas cerverai and Nymphaea ampla, Ciénaga de Zapata, Cuba. b, Nelumbo nucifera and Porphyrio porphyrio, Anzali, Iran.

2008, Oct. 16 Litho. *Perf. 12½x12¼*
4835 Horiz. pair with central label 3.00 3.00
a.-b. A1376 75c Either single 1.50 1.50

See Iran No. 3003.

Cuban Literature, 400th Anniv. — A1377

Designs: 15c, Emblem written backward on torn page. 75c, Snails. 2.05p, White star in red triangle.

2008, Oct. 20 *Perf. 12¼x12½*
4836-4838 A1377 Set of 3 6.00 6.00

National Ballet, 60th Anniv. A1378

Designs: 10c, Dancers in Swan Lake (El Lago de los Cisnes). 15c, Dancers in Giselle. 50c, Dancers in Coppélia, horiz. 65c, Dancer in Romeo and Juliet, horiz. 75c, Dancers in The Nutcracker (Cascanueces), horiz. 85c, Scenery for Sleeping Beauty (La Bella Durmiente del Bosque), horiz.
1p, Ballerina at Intl. Ballet Festival, Havana.

2008, Oct. 28 *Perf. 12¾*
4839-4844 A1378 Set of 6 6.00 6.00

Souvenir Sheet
Imperf

4845 A1378 1p multi 2.00 2.00

No. 4845 has simulated perforations.

Vilma Espín Guillois (1930-2007), Wife of Pres. Raúl Castro — A1379

2008 *Perf. 12¾*
4846 A1379 65c multi 1.40 1.40

Joséito Fernández (1908-79), Singer A1380

2008
4847 A1380 65c multi 1.40 1.40

Dr. Carlos J. Finlay (1833-1915), Yellow Fever Researcher A1381

2008
4848 A1381 65c multi 1.40 1.40

José Raúl Capablanca (1888-1942), World Chess Champion — A1382

Designs: 1.05p, Capablanca playing chess. 2.05p, Capablanca seated, vert.

2008 *Perf. 12½x12¼, 12¼x12½*
4849-4850 A1382 Set of 2 6.25 6.25

Dogs — A1383

Designs: 10c, Neapolitan mastiff. 15c, Golden retriever. 40c, Rottweiler. 65c, Shetland sheepdog. 85c, Chow chow. 90c, Boxer.
1p, Chihuahua.

2008 *Perf. 12¾*
4851-4856 A1383 Set of 6 6.25 6.25

Souvenir Sheet
Imperf

4857 A1383 1p multi 2.00 2.00

Owls and Butterflies A1384

Designs: No. 4858, 15c, Tyto alba, Lycaena dispar. No. 4859, 15c, Bubo bubo, Lolana iolas. 45c, Strix nebulosa, Vanessa cardui. 65c, Strix aluco, Colias erate. 75c, Asio otus, Aporia crataegi. 85c, Strix uralensis, Colias hecla.
1p, Anthocharis damone butterfly, horiz.

2008 *Perf. 12¾*
4858-4863 A1384 Set of 6 6.00 6.00

Souvenir Sheet
Imperf

4864 A1384 1p multi 2.00 2.00

No. 4864 contains one 40x32mm stamp. EFIRO 2008 Intl. Philatelic Exhibition, Romania (No. 4864).

Animals in National Zoo — A1385

Designs: 5c, Panthera leo. 10c, Ailurus fulgens. 15c, Cacatua galerita. 30c, Crocodylus rhombifer. 40c, Phoenicopterus ruber. 2.05p, Equus burchelli.
1p, Loxodonta africana.

2008 *Perf. 12½x12¼*
4865-4870 A1385 Set of 6 6.25 6.25

Souvenir Sheet
Imperf

4871 A1385 1p multi 2.00 2.00

No. 4871 contains one 40x32mm stamp with simulated perforations.

Ernesto "Che" Guevara (1928-67), Revolutionary Leader — A1386

Designs: 65c, Guevara as infant with mother, birthplace in Rosario, Argentina. 75c, Guevara as boy, childhood home, Villa Nydia. 85c, Guevara as young man, Guevara on bicycle. 1.05p, Guevara on raft, Guevara with cigar.

2008 ***Perf. 12¾***
4872-4875 A1386 Set of 4 6.75 6.75
4875a Souvenir sheet, #4872-4875 6.75 6.75

America Issue, National Holidays — A1387

Designs: 15c, Starting Day of the War of Independence. 65c, Liberation Day. 75c, Labor Day. 2.05p, National Rebellion Day.

2008 **Litho.** ***Perf. 12½x12¼***
4876-4879 A1387 Set of 4 7.25 7.25
4879a Souvenir sheet of 4, #4876-4879 7.25 7.25

Tourism A1388

Buildings in: No. 4880, 15c, Havana. No. 4881, 15c, Trinidad. 30c, Sancti Spiritus. 65c, Camagüey. 75c, Bayamo. 85c, Santiago de Cuba.
1p, Baracoa.

2008 ***Perf. 12¼x12½***
4880-4885 A1388 Set of 6 5.75 5.75

Souvenir Sheet
Imperf

4886 A1388 1p multi 2.00 2.00

No. 4886 contains one 32x40mm stamp with simulated perforations.

Gran Caribe Hotels, 50th Anniv. A1389

Designs: 5c, Hotel Habana Riviera. 10c, Hotel Habana Libre, vert. 15c, Hotel Deauville, vert. 50c, Hotel Victoria, vert. 65c, Hotel Presidente.
1p, Hotel Sevilla, vert.

2008 ***Perf. 12¾***
4887-4891 A1389 Set of 5 3.00 3.00

Souvenir Sheet
Imperf

4892 A1389 1p multi 2.00 2.00

No. 4892 contains one 32x40mm stamp with simulated perforations.

Carlos de la Torre y la Huerta (1858-1950), Naturalist — A1390

De la Torre y la Huerta and: 5c, Hand holding shells. 15c, Polymita picta nigrolimbata, light blue background. 50c, Polymita picta nigrolimbata, pink background. 65c, Polymita picta iolimbata. 75c, Polymita picta nigrolimbata, light green background. 90c, Polymita picta fuscolimbata.
1p, Liguus fasciatus.

2008 ***Perf. 12½x12¼***
4893-4898 A1390 Set of 6 6.00 6.00

Souvenir Sheet
Imperf

4899 A1390 1p multi 2.00 2.00

No. 4899 contains one 40x32mm stamp with simulated perforations.

Paleolithic Man and Animals — A1391

Designs: 10c, Australopithecus afarensis and Megatherium. 15c, Australopithecus africanus and Toxodon. 50c, Australopithecus robustus and Bison. 65c, Homo habilis and Hippidion. 75c, Homo erectus and Megantereon. 90c, Neanderthal man and Mammoths.
1p, Coelodonts.

2008 ***Perf. 12¾***
4900-4905 A1391 Set of 6 6.25 6.25

Souvenir Sheet
Imperf

4906 A1391 1p multi 2.00 2.00

No. 4906 contains one 45x34mm stamp with simulated perforations.

A1392

Transportation — A1392a

Designs: 15c, 1802 steam carriage of Richard Trevithick. 30c, 1829 steam carriage of Sir Goldsworthy Gurney. 40c, 1832 steam carriage of William Church. 65c, 1858 steam carriage of Thomas Rickett. 75c, 1890 Motorwagen of Karl Benz. 85c, 1836 steam omnibus of Walter Hancock.
1p, 1958 Panhard-Levassor automobile.

2008 ***Perf. 12½x12¼***
4907-4912 A1392 Set of 6 6.25 6.25

Souvenir Sheet
Imperf

4913 A1392a 1p multi 2.00 2.00

No. 4913 has simulated perforations.

Matanzas, 315th Anniv. — A1393

Designs: 15c, Building arches, Plaza de la Vigía. 40c, Palacio Junco Provincial Museum. 50c, Fire house. 75c, Palace of Justice. 85c, Sauto Theater. 90c, Palace of Government.
1p, Unknown Soldier's Monument, vert.

2008 ***Perf. 12½x12¼***
4914-4919 A1393 Set of 6 7.25 7.25

Souvenir Sheet
Imperf

4920 A1393 1p multi 2.00 2.00

No. 4920 has simulated perforations.

Triumph of the Cuban Revolution, 50th Anniv. — A1394

No. 4921, 15c: a, Liberation Day (man with wide-brimmed hat at left). b, Liberation Day (tank at left). c, Arrival of Fidel Castro in Havana. d, First march. e, Fidel Castro, Revolutionary Government Prime Minister, addressing crowd. f, Camilo Cienfuegos dissolves Bureau for the Repression of Communist Activities. g, Granting of Cuban citizenship to Ernesto "Che" Guevara. h, Fidel Castro's first visit to Venezuela. i, Creation of the P.N.R. (National Revolutionary Police). j, Creation of State Security organizations. k, Creation of T.G.F. (Border Guard). l, Agrarian Reform Law. m, Takeover of Cuban telephone system. n, Creation of the F.M.C. (Federation of Cuban Women). o, Creation of the C.D.R. (Committees for the Defense of the Revolution). p, Start of literacy campaign. q, Creation of I.N.D.E.R. (Institute of Sports, Physical Education and Recreation). r, Radio across Cuba. s, Designation of Guevara as Industry Minister. t, Creation of Union of Young Communists. u, Creation of the Civil Defense. v, Creation of the National Civil Defense Committee. w, First sugar harvest. x, Guevara speaks at the United Nations.

No. 4922, 15c: a, Constitution of the Central Committee of the Cuban Communist Party. b, Day of the Heroic Guerrilla. c, Free distribution of Guevara's diary. d, First National Education and Cultural Congress. e, First Congress of the P.C.C. (Cuban Communist Party). f, First Rural Education Congress. g, Establishment in Cuba of Intl. Children's Day. h, Vaccinations in Cuba, 205th anniv. i, Creation of M.I.N.A.Z. (Cuban Ministry of Sugar). j, Creation of I.N.P. (National Fishing Institute). k, Development of fishing industry. l, 11th World Youth and Student Festival. m, Cuban cosmonaut. n, Day of Cuban Science (building at right). o, Day of Cuban Science (building at left). p, Family doctors and nurses. q, Elimination of apartheid, 15th anniv. r, Beginning of Battle of Ideas. s, Social security. t, Creation of the E.I.E.D. u, National culture (ballet dancer at left). v, National culture (guitarists at right). w, Battle of Ideas program (classroom at right). x, Battle of Ideas program (people waving flags at right).

No. 4923, 1p, Cuban flags. No. 4924, 1p, Revolution Plaza, Havana.

2009, Jan. 1 **Litho.** ***Perf. 12¾***
Sheets of 24, #a-x
4921-4922 A1394 Set of 2 14.50 14.50

Souvenir Sheets
Imperf

4923-4924 A1394 Set of 2 4.00 4.00

Nos. 4923-4924 have simulated perforations.

Ernesto "Che" Guevara and Cuban Flag — A1394a

2009 **Litho.** ***Perf. 12¾***
4924A A1394a 75c multi 1.50 1.50

Cuban Revolution, 50th anniv. See Russia No. 7124.

Second World Baseball Classic A1395

Designs: 5c, Batter swinging at ball. 10c, Play at home plate. 15c, Fielder stretching to catch ball. 45c, Pitcher in wind-up. 65c, Runner sliding into base. 75c, Runner and fielder watching ball.
1p, Cuban team.

2009, Jan. 27 ***Perf. 12¾***
4925-4930 A1395 Set of 6 4.50 4.50

Souvenir Sheet
Imperf

4931 A1395 1p multi 2.00 2.00

No. 4931 has simulated perforations.

Souvenir Sheet

Cuban Workers' Union, 70th Anniv. — A1396

2009, Jan. 29 ***Imperf.***
4932 A1396 1p multi 2.00 2.00

No. 4932 has simulated perforations.

Santa María del Puerto de Príncipe, 495th Anniv. A1397

2009, Feb. 2 ***Perf. 12¾***
4933 A1397 90c multi 1.90 1.90

Souvenir Sheet

13th Intl. Information Fair and Convention, Havana — A1398

2009, Feb. 9 ***Imperf.***
4934 A1398 1p multi 2.00 2.00

No. 4934 has simulated perforations.

Charles Darwin (1809-92), Naturalist A1398a

Designs: 10c, Darwin and his birthplace, Shrewsbury, England. 65c, HMS Beagle and map of its expedition. 75c, Publication of *On the Origin of Species.* 85c, Darwin and his notes.

Perf. 12½x12¼

2009, Feb. 12 **Litho.**

4934A-4934D A1398a Set of 4 4.75 4.75

Art — A1399

Designs: 15c, Coloritmo, by Alejandro Otero. 30c, Atmósfera Cromoplástica IV, by Luis Tomasello. 40c, Autopista del Sur, by León Ferrari. 65c, Tridim-L, by Victor Vasarely. 75c, Untitled work, by Jesús Soto. 85c, Untitled work, by Julio Le Parc.

1p, Physicromie 105, by Carlos Cruz Diez, horiz.

2009, Feb. 25 ***Perf. 12¾***

4935-4940 A1399 Set of 6 6.25 6.25

Souvenir Sheet

Imperf

4941 A1399 1p multi 2.00 2.00

No. 4941 has simulated perforations.

High Speed Trains A1400

Designs: No. 4942, 15c, Acela Express, US. No. 4943, 15c, AVE, Spain. 30c, ATP Eurostar, Great Britain. 65c, ICE, Germany. 75c, ICN, Switzerland. 1.05p, TGV, France.

No. 4948: a, Shinkansen Model 500, Japan. b, Shinkansen Model 700, Japan.

2009, Feb. 27 ***Perf. 12½x12¼***

4942-4947 A1400 Set of 6 6.25 6.25

Souvenir Sheet

Imperf

4948 A1400 50c Sheet of 2, #a-b 2.00 2.00

No. 4948 has simulated perforations.

Cuban Arts and Cinematographic Industry Institute, 50th Anniv. — A1401

Designs: No. 4949, 10c, Actress from *La Bella del Alhambra.* No. 4950, 10c, Actress from *Reina y Rey.* No. 4951, 15c, Character from animated film *Elpidio Valdés.* No. 4952, 15c, Actresses from *Lucía.* 45c, Actor from *Primera Carga al Machete.* 65c, Actor from *El Hombre de Maisinicú.* 75c, Actor and actress from *Clandestinos.* 90c, Actress from *Retrato de Teresa.* 1.05p, Santiago Alvarez, ICAIC reporter.

1p, Scene from *Fresa y Chocolate.*

2009, Mar. 24 ***Perf. 12½x12¼***

4949-4957 A1401 Set of 9 8.75 8.75

Souvenir Sheet

Imperf

4958 A1401 1p multi 2.00 2.00

No. 4958 has simulated perforations.

State Security Organizations, 50th Anniv. — A1402

2009, Mar. 26 ***Perf. 12¼x12½***

4959 A1402 65c multi 1.40 1.40

Motorcycles — A1403

Designs: 10c, Cagiva Mito N1. 15c, Honda CBR 900. 50c, Hyosung-GT 8. 65c, Kawasaki ZX-7R 750cc. 75c, Gussi MGS. 90c, Ducati Monster 900.

1p, Hyosung-GT 125-R-LD, vert.

2009, Apr. 8 ***Perf. 12¾***

4960-4965 A1403 Set of 6 6.25 6.25

Souvenir Sheet

Imperf

4966 A1403 1p multi 2.00 2.00

China 2009 World Philatelic Exhibition, Luoyang. No. 4966 has simulated perforations.

Cats A1404

Designs: 10c, Cat and kittens. 15c, Kittens and baseball. 40c, Two cats clawing fabric. 65c, Two cats on tile floor. 75c, Cat. 1.05p, Cat eating food.

1p, Two cats on roof, vert.

2009, Apr. 12 ***Perf. 12¾***

4967-4972 A1404 Set of 6 6.25 6.25

Souvenir Sheet

Imperf

4973 A1404 1p multi 2.00 2.00

No. 4973 has simulated perforations.

Tourism A1405

Art from hotels and restaurants: No. 4974, 10c, Stained-glass window, by René Portocarrero, Bodeguita del Medio Restaurant. No. 4975, Detail from mural, by Amelia Peláez, Hotel Habana Libre Tryp. 45c, Painting by Domingo Ramos, Hotel Nacional de Cuba, horiz. 65c, Detail from mural, by Mariano Rodríguez, Hotel Bello Caribe, horiz. 75c, Detail from mural, by Raúl Martínez, Hotel Bella Caribe, horiz. 85c, Mural, by Manuel A. Sosabravo, Hotel Habana Libre Tryp, horiz.

1p, Mural by various artists, Hotel Inglaterra, horiz.

2009, Apr. 21 ***Perf. 12¾***

4974-4979 A1405 Set of 6 6.00 6.00

Souvenir Sheet

Imperf

4980 A1405 1p multi 2.00 2.00

No. 4980 has simulated perforations.

Haydee Santamaría Cuadrado (1922-80), Founder of Casa de las Americas — A1406

2009, Apr. 28 ***Perf. 12¾***

4981 A1406 3p multi 6.00 6.00

World Heritage Sites A1407

Designs: 15c, Havana. 45c, Cienfuegos. 50c, Trinidad. 1.05p, Camagüey.

2009, May 8 **Litho.**

4982-4985 A1407 Set of 4 4.50 4.50

4985a Souvenir sheet, #4982-4985 4.50 4.50

Parrots A1408

Designs: 5c, Guacamayo sereno. 10c, Guacamayo azul-dorado. 15c, Guacamayo de hombro rojo. No. 4989, 20c, Guacamayo cuellodorado. No. 4990, Guacamayo de Jacinto. 65c, Guacamayo escarlata. 75c, Guacamayo frente rojo. 90c, Guacamayo militar.

2009, May 16

4986-4993 A1408 Set of 8 6.00 6.00

Institute of Design, 25th Anniv. — A1409

2009, May 28 ***Perf. 12½x12¼***

4994 A1409 65c multi 1.40 1.40

Souvenir Sheet

Ernesto Guevara Central Palace of Pioneers, 30th Anniv. — A1410

2009, June 1 ***Imperf.***

4995 A1410 1p multi 2.00 2.00

No. 4995 has simulated perforations.

National Revolutionary Police, 50th Anniv. — A1411

2009, June 6 ***Perf. 12½x12¼***

4996 A1411 1.05p multi 2.10 2.10

FORDES Gallery, 5th Anniv. — A1412

2009, June 14

4997 A1412 75c multi 1.50 1.50

Zoo Animals A1413

Designs: 5c, Ceratotherium simum. 10c, Syncerus caffer caffer. 15c, Acinonyx jubatus, vert. 30c, Papio hamadryas, vert. 40c, Struthio camelus, vert. 2.05p, Lycaon pictus, vert.

1p, Hippopotamus amphibius.

2009, June 20 ***Perf. 12¾***

4998-5003 A1413 Set of 6 6.25 6.25

Souvenir Sheet

Imperf

5004 A1413 1p multi 2.00 2.00

No. 5004 contains one 47x30mm stamp with simulated perforations.

Cuban Cuisine — A1414

Designs: 40c, Arroz con pollo a la chorrera (chicken with rice). 45c, Plátano maduro frito (fried plantains). 50c, Frijoles negros dormidos (black beans with onion).

2009, June 29 ***Perf. 12½x12¼***

5005-5007 A1414 Set of 3 2.75 2.75

Diplomatic Relations Between Cuba and Sri Lanka, 50th Anniv. — A1415

2009, July 29 ***Perf. 12¼x12½***

5008 A1415 1.05p multi 2.10 2.10

Peace and National Sovereignty Movement, 60th Anniv. — A1416

2009, Aug. 4 ***Perf. 12¾***
5009 A1416 65c multi 1.40 1.40

Los Malagones Peasant Militia, 50th Anniv. — A1417

2009, Aug. 31 ***Perf. 12¼x12½***
5010 A1417 90c multi 1.90 1.90

Havana Convention Center, 30th Anniv. — A1418

2009, Sept. 3 ***Perf. 12¾***
5011 A1418 50c multi 1.00 1.00

Tourism A1419

Birds: 15c, Coloptes fernandinae. 40c, Torreonis inexpectata. 50c, Ferminia cerverai. 65c, Agelaius assimilis. 75c, Mellisuga helenae. 90c, todus multicolor.
1p, Aratinga euops.

2009, Sept. 14 ***Perf. 12¾***
5012-5017 A1419 Set of 6 6.75 6.75

Souvenir Sheet
Imperf

5018 A1419 1p multi 2.00 2.00

No. 5018 has simulated perforations.

People's Republic of China, 60th Anniv. A1420

2009, Sept. 28 **Litho.** ***Perf. 12¾***
5019 A1420 85c multi 1.75 1.75

Cubana Airlines, 80th Anniv. — A1421

Designs: 5c, Ford Trimotor. 15c, Sikorsky S-38B. 45c, DC-3. 50c, DC-4. 65c, IL-62M. 75c, IL-96 300.
1p, Tu-204.

2009, Oct. 8 ***Perf. 12½x12¼***
5020-5025 A1421 Set of 6 5.25 5.25

Souvenir Sheet
Imperf

5026 A1421 1p multi 2.00 2.00

No. 5026 has simulated perforations.

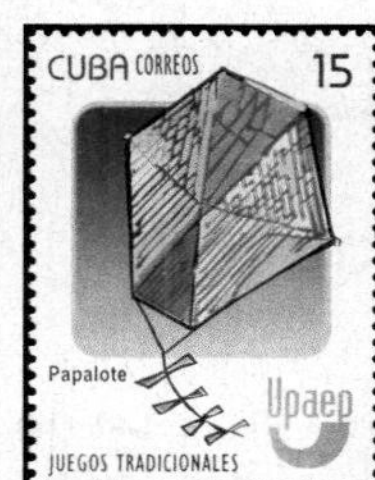

America Issue, Traditional Games A1422

Designs: 15c, Kite. 65c, Top. 75c, Dominos. 2.05p, Jacks.

2009, Oct. 12 ***Perf. 12¾***
5027-5030 A1422 Set of 4 7.25 7.25
5030a Souvenir sheet, #5027-5030 7.25 7.25

Souvenir Sheet

First Rocket Mail Flight in Cuba, 70th Anniv. — A1423

2009, Oct. 15 ***Imperf.***
5031 A1423 1p multi 2.00 2.00

Ministry of the Revolutionary Armed Forces, 50th Anniv. — A1424

2009, Oct. 16 ***Perf. 12¾***
5032 A1424 75c multi 1.50 1.50

Disappearance of Camilo Cienfuegos, 50th Anniv. — A1425

2009, Oct. 28 ***Perf. 12½x12¼***
5033 A1425 65c multi 1.40 1.40

Rights of the Child Convention, 20th Anniv. A1426

2009, Nov. 20 ***Perf. 12¾***
5034 A1426 1.05p multi 2.10 2.10

Cuban Federation of Sport Fishing, 30th Anniv. — A1427

Designs: 15c, Fisherman pulling fish into boat. 30c, Fisherman in water holding rod and fish. 45c, Sailfish and boat. No. 5038, 65c, Fisherman in water holding rod and fish, horiz. 75c, Fish on line, two fishermen in boat, horiz. 85c, Fishermen on sea wall, horiz.
No,. 5041, 65c, Tilapia, horiz

Perf. 12¼x12½, 12½x12¼
2009, Nov. 21
5035-5040 A1427 Set of 6 6.50 6.50

Souvenir Sheet
Imperf

5041 A1427 65c multi 1.40 1.40

No. 5041 has simulated perforations.

Ministry of Foreign Relations, 50th Anniv. — A1428

2009, Dec. 23 ***Perf. 12½x12¼***
5042 A1428 1.05p multi 2.10 2.10

Peony A1429

2009 ***Perf. 13¼x13½***
5043 A1429 30c multi .60 .60

Printed in sheets of 4.

José L. Guerra Aguiar Cuban Postal Museum, 45th Anniv. — A1430

2010, Jan. 2 ***Perf. 12½x12¼***
5044 A1430 65c multi 1.40 1.40

A1431

A1432

A1433

New Year 2010 (Year of the Tiger) A1434

2010, Jan. 5 ***Perf. 12¾***
5045 A1431 15c multi .30 .30
5046 A1432 15c multi .30 .30
5047 A1433 15c multi .30 .30
5048 A1434 15c multi .30 .30
a. Souvenir sheet, #5045-5048 1.25 1.25
Nos. 5045-5048 (4) 1.20 1.20

January 1960 Speech of Fidel Castro, 50th Anniv. — A1435

2010, Jan. 15 ***Perf. 12½x12¼***
5049 A1435 65c multi 1.40 1.40

Diplomatic Relations Between Cuba and Indonesia, 50th Anniv. — A1436

2010, Jan. 22
5050 A1436 85c multi 1.75 1.75

Association of Rebel Youth, 50th Anniv. — A1437

2010, Jan. 28
5051 A1437 3p multi 6.00 6.00

Trains
A1438

Designs: 5c, Fidel Castro leaving train. 10c, DF7G-C locomotive. 15c, Tank car. 65c, Flat car carrying shipping containers. 75c, Box cars. 1.05p, DF7K-C locomotive.
1p, Locomotive at end of track, vert.

2010, Jan. 29 ***Perf. 12¾***
5052-5057 A1438 Set of 6 5.50 5.50

Souvenir Sheet
Imperf

5058 A1438 1p multi 2.00 2.00

Diplomatic Relations Between Cuba and India, 50th Anniv. — A1439

2010, Feb. 10 ***Perf. 12¾***
5059 A1439 85c multi 1.75 1.75

National Aquarium, 50th Anniv. — A1440

Designs: 10c, Bispira brunnea. No. 5061, 15c, Hypoplectrus gummigutta. No. 5062, 15c, Holocanthus ciliaris. 50c, Seal. 75c, Epinephelus guttatus. 85c, Tursiops truncatus.
1p, Acanthurus coeruleus.

2010, Feb. 12 ***Perf. 12¾***
5060-5065 A1440 Set of 6 5.00 5.00

Souvenir Sheet
Imperf

5066 A1440 1p multi 2.00 2.00
No. 5066 has simulated perforations.

A1441

La Colmenita Youth Theater Company, 20th Anniv. — A1442

2010, Feb. 14 ***Perf. 12¾***
5067 A1441 50c multi 1.00 1.00
5068 A1442 50c multi 1.00 1.00

Underwater Photography — A1443

Designs: 10c, Fish and coral. 15c, Coral and starfish. 45c, Crab and sea anemone. 50c, Sponges and feather duster worms. 75c, Sea cucumber and coral. 85c, Sea horse and diver photographing tube worm.
1p, Fish and diver.

2010, Feb. 20 ***Perf. 12½x12¼***
5069-5074 A1443 Set of 6 5.75 5.75

Souvenir Sheet
Imperf

5075 A1443 1p multi 2.00 2.00

Central Planning, 50th Anniv. — A1444

2010, Mar. 11 ***Perf. 12½x12¼***
5076 A1444 75c multi 1.50 1.50

Dogs and Art — A1445

Designs: 10c, Peruvian hairless dog, Mochica figurine of dog, Peru. 15c, Bichon Frise, pitcher depicting hunter and dogs. 40c, Neapolitan mastiff, Roman mosaic of hunter and dog. 65c, Chihuahua, figurine of dog, map of Colima, Mexico. 75c, Pug, Chinese painting of hunters and dog. 90c, King Charles spaniel, The Birth of Louis XIII, by Peter Paul Rubens.
1p, Pharaoh hound, Egyptian painting from tomb of Ipy.

2010, Mar. 12 ***Perf. 12¾***
5077-5082 A1445 Set of 6 6.00 6.00

Souvenir Sheet
Imperf

5083 A1445 1p multi 2.00 2.00
No. 5083 has simulated perforations.

Diplomatic Relations Between Cuba and Canada, 65th Anniv. — A1446

2010, Mar. 16 ***Perf. 12¾***
5084 A1446 65c multi 1.40 1.40

Bilateral Relations Between Cuba and Namibia, 20th Anniv. A1447

2010, Mar. 24 **Litho.**
5085 A1447 85c multi 1.75 1.75

2010 World Cup Soccer Championships, South Africa — A1448

Flags of competing nations, various soccer players and list of teams in: 15c, Groups A and B. 45c, Groups C and D. 65c, Groups E and F. 75c, Groups G and H.

2010, Mar. 24
5086-5089 A1448 Set of 4 4.00 4.00

Congress of the Young Communist's League — A1449

2010, Apr. 2
5090 A1449 65c multi 1.40 1.40

National Symphonic Orchestra, 50th Anniv. — A1450

Designs: 15c, Amadeo Roldán (1900-39), composer. 30c, Gonzalo Roig (1890-1970), composer. 40c, Enrique González Mántici (1912-74), composer. 75c, Manuel Duchesne Cuzán, General director of National Symphonic Orchestra.

2010, Apr. 11 ***Perf. 12½x12¼***
5091-5094 A1450 Set of 4 3.25 3.25

Diplomatic Relations Between Cuba and Cambodia, 50th Anniv. — A1451

2010, Apr. 15
5095 A1451 85c multi 1.75 1.75

Cuban National Chorus, 50th Anniv. — A1452

2010, Apr. 17 **Litho.**
5096 A1452 90c multi 1.90 1.90

First Cuban Computer, 40th Anniv. — A1453

2010, Apr. 18 ***Perf. 12¾***
5097 A1453 75c multi 1.50 1.50

First Cuban Stamps, 155th Anniv. — A1454

Designs: 75c, Matanzas mail box, 1859, bicyclist in front of building. 85c, Cuba #147, account book of first postal administrator, 1765.

2010, Apr. 24 ***Perf. 12½x12¼***
5098-5099 A1454 Set of 2 3.25 3.25

Tourism
A1455

Designs: 15c, Santiago de Cuba. 20c, Guantánamo. 35c, Holguín. 65c, Camagüey. 75c, Granma. 90c, Las Tunas.
1p, Santiago de Cuba, diff.

2010, May 4 ***Perf. 12¼x12½***
5100-5105 A1455 Set of 6 6.00 6.00

Souvenir Sheet
Imperf

5106 A1455 1p multi 2.00 2.00

ICAIC Latin American Newsreels, 50th Anniv. — A1456

2010, June 1 ***Perf. 12¾***
5107 A1456 75c multi 1.50 1.50

Flora and Fauna A1457

Designs: 15c, Dellia sp. 35c, Bietia purpurea. 40c, Anolis equestris. 65c, Broughtonia orgiesiana. 75c, Priotrochatella stellata. 85c, Todus multicolor, vert.
1p, Pinus caribaea.

Perf. 12½x12¼, 12¼x12½

2010, June 11

5108-5113 A1457 Set of 6 6.50 6.50

Souvenir Sheet

Imperf

5114 A1457 1p multi 2.00 2.00

Expo 2010, Shanghai — A1458

Map of China, aviation posters and aircraft: 5c, Savoia-Marchetti 55X. 10c, Farman 60 Goliath. 15c, Fokker VII. 45c, Koolhoven F.K. 50. 65c, Junkers 52/3M. 85c, Latécoère 28. 1p, Handley Page 42E.

2010, Apr. 26 Litho. ***Perf. 12½x12¼***

5115-5120 A1458 Set of 6 4.50 4.50

Souvenir Sheet

Imperf

5121 A1458 1p multi 2.00 2.00

No. 5121 has simulated perforations.

Writings of José Martí — A1459

Designs: No. 5122, 15c, *La Patria Libre,* white warbler, flag similar to Chile's. No. 5123, 15c, *La Nacion,* great antshrike, flag of Argentina. No. 5124, 15c, *Revista Universal,* king vulture, flag of Mexico. No. 5125, 15c, Proclamation of President of Paraguay, plantcutter, flag of Paraguay. No. 5126, 15c, *Patria,* hummingbird, flag of Cuba. No. 5127, 15c, Montecristi Manifesto, woodpecker, flag similar to Dominican Republic's. No. 5128, 15c, *La República Española y la Revolucion Cubana,* house sparrow and flag similar to Spain's, vert. No. 5129, 15c, *Mis Hijos* (translation of Victor Hugo's *Mes Fils*), long-tailed tit, flag of France, vert. No. 5130, 15c, *Guatemala,* quetzal, flag of Guatemala, vert. 65c, Pamphlet for International Monetary Conference, crested gallito, flag of Uruguay, vert. 75c, *Revista Venezolana,* troupial, flag of Venezuela, vert. 90c, Books of poetry, quill pen and inkwell, vert.

Perf. 12½x12¼, 12¼x12½

2010, May 19

5122-5133 A1459 Set of 12 7.50 7.50

Birds Endemic to Various Countries — A1460

Designs: 5c, Eumomota superciliosa, Nicaragua. 10c, Priotelus temnurus, Cuba. 15c, Amazona imperialis, Dominica. No. 5137, 20c, Amazona guildingii, St. Vincent and the Grenadines. No. 5138, 20c, Fregata magnificens, Antigua and Barbuda. 65c, Vultur gryphus, Bolivia. 75c, Icterus icterus, Venezuela, vert. 90c, Turdus rufiventris, Brazil, vert.

2010, May 26 ***Perf. 12¾***

5134-5141 A1460 Set of 8 6.00 6.00

Ernest Hemingway Intl. Fishing Tournament, 60th Anniv. — A1461

Emblem and: No. 5142, 65c, Fishing boat, rod and reel. No. 5143, 65c, Ernest Hemingway. No. 5144, 65c, Swordfish. No. 5145, 65c Trophy.

2010, May 29 ***Perf. 12¼x12½***

5142-5145 A1461 Set of 4 5.25 5.25

Dr. Enrique Hart Ramírez (1900-89), Judge — A1462

2010, June 1 ***Perf. 12¾***

5146 A1462 65c multi 1.40 1.40

Diplomatic Relations Between Cuba and North Korea, 50th Anniv. — A1463

2010, Aug. 29 **Litho.**

5147 A1463 85c multi 1.75 1.75

La Caridad Theater, Santa Clara, 125th Anniv. A1464

Designs: 15c, Theater in 1885. 30c, Theater in 2010. 75c, Theater interior. 90c, Marta Abreu de Estévez (1845-1909), philanthropist, vert.

2010, Sept. 8

5148-5151 A1464 Set of 4 4.25 4.25

Architectural Arches of Havana — A1465

Designs: 15c, Elliptical arch. 65c, Mixtilinear arch. 75c, Polylobular arch.

2010, Sept. 9 ***Perf. 12½x12¼***

5152-5154 A1465 Set of 3 3.25 3.25

Lighthouses A1466

Maps and: No. 5155, 15c, Cayo Jutía Lighthouse, Pinar del Rio. No. 5156, 15c, Cayo Cruz del Padre Lighthouse, Matanzas. No. 5157, 15c, Cayo Lucrecia Lighthouse, Holguin. 2.05p, Morro Lighthouse, Santiago de Cuba.

2010, Sept. 15 ***Perf. 12¼x12½***

5155-5158 A1466 Set of 4 5.00 5.00

5158a Souvenir sheet, #5155-5158 5.00 5.00

Electric Automobiles — A1467

Designs: 5c, 1893 Jeantaud and Raffard. 10c, 1903 American Pope-Tribune. 15c, 1903 STAE. 20c, Matra Zoom. 45c, Zilent. 75c, Jeep Treo.
1p, Aptera, vert.

2010, Sept. 20 ***Perf. 12¾***

5159-5164 A1467 Set of 6 3.50 3.50

Souvenir Sheet

Imperf

5165 A1467 1p multi 2.00 2.00

Portugal 2010 Intl. Philatelic Exhibition. No. 5165 has simulated perforations.

Tourism — A1468

Designs: 20c, Papilio androgeus epidaurus, Viñales National Park. 50c, Mesocapromys nanus, Ciénaga de Zapata National Park. 75c, Trichechus manatus manatus, Alejandro de Humboldt National Park. 90c, Amazona leucocephala, Desembarco del Granma National Park.

2010, Sept. 27 ***Perf. 12½x12¼***

5166-5169 A1468 Set of 4 4.75 4.75

Diplomatic Relations Between Cuba and People's Republic of China, 50th Anniv. — A1469

Designs: No. 5170, 15c, Chinese Army, flag of People's Republic of China. No. 5171, 15c, Chinese landscape, arms of People's Republic of China. No. 5172, 85c, Cuban soldiers, horses and boat, flag of Cuba. No. 5173, 85c, Cuban landscape, arms of Cuba.

2010, Sept. 28

5170-5173 A1469 Set of 4 4.00 4.00

America Issue, National Symbols A1470

Designs: No. 5174, 65c, School children, Cuban flag and coat of arms, bust of José Marti. No. 5175, 65c, Cuban coat of arms. No. 5176, 65c, Cuban flag. No. 5177, 65c, Cuban national anthem.

2010, Oct. 12 Litho. ***Perf. 12¾***

5174-5177 A1470 Set of 4 5.25 5.25

World Statistics Day — A1471

2010 ***Perf. 12½x12¼***

5178 A1471 65c multi 1.40 1.40

Cuban Television, 60th Anniv. A1472

2010, Oct. 24 ***Perf. 12¾***

5179 A1472 1.05p multi 2.10 2.10

22nd Intl. Ballet Festival, Havana — A1473

2010, Oct. 28 ***Perf. 12¼x12½***

5180 A1473 65c multi 1.40 1.40

Souvenir Sheet

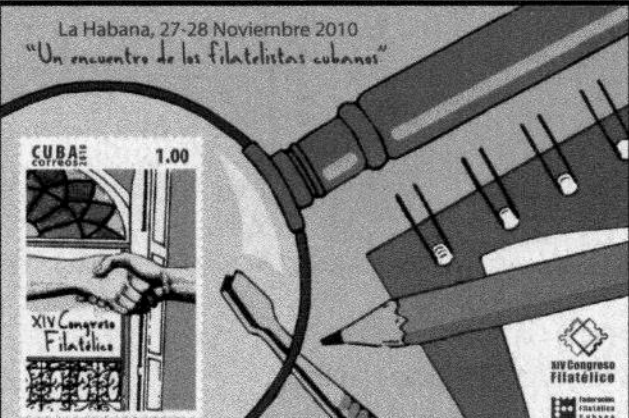

14th Philatelic Congress, Havana — A1474

2010 ***Imperf.***

5181 A1474 1p multi 2.00 2.00

Diplomatic Relations Between Cuba and Viet Nam. 50th Anniv. — A1475

2010, Dec. 2 ***Perf. 12¼x12½***
5182 A1475 85c multi 1.75 1.75

Diplomatic Relations Between Cuba and Russia, 50th Anniv. — A1476

2010, Dec. 2 ***Perf. 12¾***
5183 A1476 75c multi 1.50 1.50

Diplomatic Relations Between Cuba and Bulgaria, 50th Anniv. — A1477

No. 5184: a, Alexander Nevsky Cathedral, Sofia, Bulgaria, flag of Bulgaria. b, Flag of Cuba, Havana Cathedral.

2010, Dec. 10 ***Perf. 12½x12¼***
5184 A1477 75c Horiz. pair, #a-b 3.00 3.00

Dora Alonso (1910-2001), Writer — A1478

2010, Dec. 22 ***Perf. 12¾***
5185 A1478 75c multi 1.50 1.50

Diplomatic Relations Between Cuba and Mongolia, 50th Anniv. — A1479

2010 ***Perf. 12¼x12½***
5186 A1479 85c multi 1.75 1.75

José Lezama Lima (1910-76), Writer — A1480

2010, Dec. 19 Litho. ***Perf. 12¾***
5187 A1480 65c multi 1.40 1.40

Souvenir Sheet

14th Intl. Information Convention and Fair, Havana — A1481

2011, Feb. 7 Litho. ***Imperf.***
5188 A1481 1p multi 2.00 2.00

Airplanes and Female Aviators — A1482

Designs: 10c, Bleriot, Matilde Moisant (1878-1964). 15c, Stinson "American Girl," Ruth Elder (1902-77). 20c, Lockheed Vega, Ruth Rowland (1901-60). 50c, Golden Eagle, Bobbi Trout (1906-2003). 65c, Seversky Executive, Jacqueline Cochran (1906-80). 90c, Lockheed Electra, Amelia Earhart (1897-1937).

1p, Curtiss Robin, Berta Moraleda, first Cuban aviatrix.

2011, Feb. 12 ***Perf. 12½x12¼***
5189-5194 A1482 Set of 6 5.00 5.00

Souvenir Sheet

Imperf

5195 A1482 1p multi 2.00 2.00

Indipex 2011 Intl. Philatelic Exhibition, New Delhi.

New Year 2011 (Year of the Rabbit) A1483

Rabbit and background color of: No. 5196, 15c, Green. No. 5197, 15c, Red.

2011, Feb. 15 ***Perf. 12¾***
5196-5197 A1483 Set of 2 .60 .60

Postal Union of the Americas, Spain and Portugal (UPAEP), Cent. — A1484

2011, Feb. 17
5198 A1484 65c multi 1.40 1.40

Central Army, 50th Anniv. — A1485

2011, Apr. 4 Litho. ***Perf. 12½x12¼***
5199 A1485 65c multi 1.40 1.40

Eastern Army, 50th Anniv. — A1486

2011, Apr. 21 Litho. ***Perf. 12½x12¼***
5200 A1486 65c multi 1.40 1.40

Earth Day A1487

Designs: 65c, Cart. 90c, Fountain.

2011, Apr. 22 ***Perf. 12¾***
5201-5202 A1487 Set of 2 3.25 3.25

Radio Havana, 50th Anniv. — A1488

2011, May 1 ***Perf. 12½x12¼***
5203 A1488 2.05p multi 4.25 4.25

Flora and Fauna A1489

Designs: 15c, Anolis vermiculata, Nymphaea. 35c, Apis mellifera, Bidens alba. 40c, Lycorea ceres demeter, Euphorbia helenae. 65c, Osteopilus septentrionalis, Plumeria obtusa. 75c, Ardea alba, Avicennia germinanas. 85c, Liguus fasciatus, Catopsis sp.

1p, Crocodylus rhombifer, Coccoloba uvifera, vert.

2011, June 6 ***Perf. 12¾***
5204-5209 A1489 Set of 6 6.50 6.50

Souvenir Sheet

Imperf

5210 A1489 1p multi 2.00 2.00

Ministry of the Interior, 50th Anniv. — A1490

2011, June 8 ***Perf. 12½x12¼***
5211 A1490 90c multi 1.90 1.90

Western Army, 50th Anniv. A1491

2011, June 14 ***Perf. 12¾***
5212 A1491 75c multi 1.50 1.50

Dances A1492

Designs: No. 5213, 10c, Danzón. No. 5214, 10c, Mambo. 45c, Son. 65c, Rumba. 75c, Cha cha cha. 85c, Salsa.

No. 5219: a, Female Carnaval dancer. b, Male Carnaval dancer.

2011, June 29 ***Perf. 12¼x12½***
5213-5218 A1492 Set of 6 6.00 6.00

Souvenir Sheet

Imperf

5219 A1492 50c Sheet of 2, #a-b 2.00 2.00

Diplomatic Relations Between Cuba and the Philippines, 65th Anniv. A1493

2011, July 1 ***Perf. 12¾***
5220 A1493 85c multi 1.75 1.75

Locomotives — A1494

Designs: 5c, Best Friend of Charleston, 1830. 10c, Lafayette, 1837. 15c, Robert Stephenson Patentee, 1830. 65c, Thomas Ellis St. David, 1848. 75c, Stephenson long-boiler, 1848. 90c, 4-2-2 Stirling single-wheeler No. 1, 1870.

1p, Shinkansen, 1964.

2011, July 28 ***Perf. 12½x12¼***
5221-5226 A1494 Set of 6 5.25 5.25

Souvenir Sheet

Imperf

5227 A1494 1p multi 2.00 2.00

Japan 2011 Intl. Philatelic Exhibition, Yokohama.

Baracoa, 500th Anniv. — A1495

2011, Aug. 15 ***Perf. 12½x12¼***
5228 A1495 3p multi 6.00 6.00

Non-Aligned Countries Movement, 50th Anniv. — A1496

2011, Sept. 6 ***Perf. 12¾***
5229 A1496 65c multi 1.40 1.40

Birds Endemic to Various Countries — A1497

Designs: 5c, Ramphastos sulfuratus, Belize. 10c, Melanerpes portoricensis, Puerto Rico. 15c, Icterus nigrogularis, Curaçao. 30c, Eumomota superciliosa, El Salvador. 50c, Vanellus chilensis lampronotus, Uruguay, vert. 65c, Pharomachrus mocinno, Guatemala, vert. 75c, Pelecanus occidentalis, St. Kitts and Nevis, vert. 85c, Orthorhycus cristatus, St. Eustatius, Caribbenan Netherlands, vert.

Perf. 12½x12¼, 12¼x12½

2011, Sept. 19
5230-5237 A1497 Set of 8 6.75 6.75

America Issue — A1498

Designs: No. 5238, 65c, Blue mailbox, denomination in pale orange. No. 5239, 65c, Blue green mailbox, denomination in pale rose. No. 5240, 65c, Three mailboxes, denomination in light blue. No. 5241, 65c, Blue green mailbox, denomination in lilac.

2011, Oct. 12 ***Perf. 12¾***
5238-5241 A1498 Set of 4 5.25 5.25

Animals — A1499

Designs: 5c, Ursus maritimus, map of Arctic region. 10c, Cervus elaphus canadensis, map of North America. 15c, Lama glama, map of South America. 50c, Canis lupus, map of Europe. 65c, Pongo pygmaeus, map of East Asia. 85c, Phascolarctos cinereus, map of Australia.

1p, Panthera leo, map of Africa.

2011, Oct. 18 ***Perf. 12½x12¼***
5242-5247 A1499 Set of 6 4.75 4.75

Souvenir Sheet

Imperf

5248 A1499 1p multi 2.00 2.00

Coral and Fish — A1500

Corals: 10c, Scolymia cubensis. 15c, Mussa angulosa. 20c, Manicina areolata. 30c, Mycetophyllia lamarckiana. 50c, Acropora prolifera. 65c, Tubastraea coccinea.

1p, Stylaster roseus.

2011, Oct. 18 ***Perf. 12½x12¼***
5249-5254 A1500 Set of 6 4.00 4.00

Souvenir Sheet

Imperf

5255 A1500 1p multi 2.00 2.00

Revista Pionero, 50th Anniv. — A1501

2011, Nov. 25 ***Perf. 12½x12¼***
5256 A1501 1.05p multi 2.10 2.10

Havana Tourist Attractions A1502

Designs: 5c, La Giraldilla, Castillo de la Fuerza. 10c, El Templete Monument. 15c, Plaza de la Catedra. 20c, Bacardi Building. 65c, Grand Theater of Havana. 75c, National Capitol (now Cuban Academy of Sciences).

1p, Morro Castle.

2011, Dec. 12 ***Perf. 12¼x12½***
5257-5262 A1502 Set of 6 4.00 4.00

Souvenir Sheet

Imperf

5263 A1502 1p multi 2.00 2.00

Birds and Protected Habitats A1503

Designs: 5c, Contopus caribaeus, Hanabanilla Nature Preserve. 10c, Saurothera merlini, Caguanes National Park. 20c, Spindalis zena, Topes de Collantes Nature Preserve. 45c, Otus lawrencii, Jobo Rosado Protected Area. 65c, Teretistris fernandinae, Alturas de Banao Ecological Reserve. 85c, Priotelus temnurus, El Nicho Nature Preserve.

1p, Grus canadensis, Caguanes National Park.

2011, Dec. 13 ***Perf. 12¼x12½***
5264-5269 A1503 Set of 6 4.75 4.75

Souvenir Sheet

Imperf

5270 A1503 1p multi 2.00 2.00

Stage Debut of Ballerina Alicia Alonso, 80th Anniv. — A1504

No. 5271 — Alonso with feet: a, Not visible. b, Visible.

2011, Dec. 29 ***Perf. 12¼x12½***
5271 A1504 65c Horiz. pair, #a-b 2.60 2.60

African National Congress, Cent. — A1505

2012, Jan. 8 ***Perf. 12¾***
5272 A1505 85c multi 1.75 1.75

Artemisa Province, 1st Anniv. A1506

2012, Jan. 9
5273 A1506 65c multi 1.40 1.40

Electrical Workers Day A1507

2012, Jan. 14
5274 A1507 75c multi 1.50 1.50

Communication Workers Day — A1508

2012, Feb. 24 ***Perf. 12½x12¼***
5275 A1508 65c multi 1.40 1.40

Woman at a Window, by René Portocarrero (1912-85) A1509

2012, Feb. 24 ***Perf. 12¾***
5276 A1509 1.05p multi 2.10 2.10

Diplomatic Relations Between Ukraine and Cuba, 20th Anniv. — A1510

2012, Mar. 12 ***Perf. 12½x12¼***
5277 A1510 75c multi 1.50 1.50

Alejandro Robaina and His Automobile — A1511

No. 5278 — Tobacco field and: a, Robaina (1919-2010), farmer of cigar tobacco. b, Automobile.

2012, Mar. 20 ***Perf. 12¾***
5278 A1511 65c Horiz. pair, #a-b 2.60 2.60

Diplomatic Relations Between Azerbaijan and Cuba, 20th Anniv. — A1512

2012, Apr. 16 **Litho.**
5279 A1512 75c multi 1.50 1.50

Diplomatic Relations Between Belarus and Cuba, 20th Anniv. — A1513

2012, Apr. 16 ***Perf. 12½x12¼***
5280 A1513 75c multi 1.50 1.50

A1514

Design: Capt. Orlando Pantoja Tamayo (1933-67), Capt. Eliseo Reyes Rodriguez (1940-67), First Lt. Antonio Briones Montoto (1939-67), Guerrillas in Intl. Conflicts.

2012, Apr. 25 Litho. ***Perf. 12½x12¼***
5281 A1514 65c multi 1.40 1.40

Afro-Cuban Dances — A1515

Designs: 15c, Elegbá. 20c, Ogún. 30c, Shangó. 50c, Oyá. 65c, Yemayá. 75c, Obatalá.
1p, Oghún.

2012, May 7 Litho. ***Perf. 12¼x12½***
5282-5287 A1515 Set of 6 5.25 5.25

Souvenir Sheet
Imperf

5288 A1515 1p multi 2.00 2.00

No. 5288 has simulated perforations.

Butterflies — A1516

Designs: 5c, Phoebis avellaneda. 10c, Parides gundiachianus. 15c, Greta cubana. 35c, Eurytides celadon. 40c, Anartia chrysopelea. 65c, Dismorphia cubana. 75c, Calisto israel. 85c, Libytheana motya.

2012, May 22 Litho. ***Perf. 12¾***
5289-5296 A1516 Set of 8 6.75 6.75

Cuban Institute of Radio and Television, 50th Anniv. — A1517

2012, May 24 Litho. ***Perf. 12¾***
5297 A1517 90c multi 1.90 1.90

Visit of Pope Benedict XVI to Cuba — A1518

2012, June 6 Litho. ***Perf. 12¼x12½***
5298 A1518 75c multi 1.50 1.50

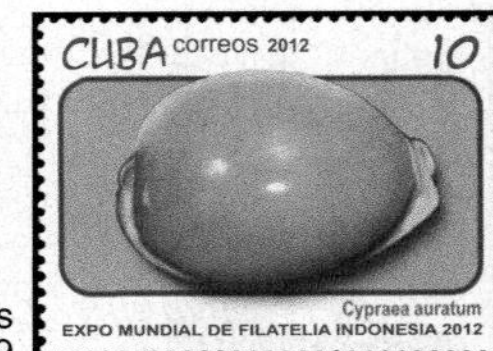
Shells A1519

Designs: 10c, Cypraea auratum. 30c, Strombus pugilis. 45c, Voluta fulgetrum. 65c, Architectonica maximum. 75c, Murex beaui. 85c, Spondylus aurantium.
1p, Epitonium pretiosum, vert.

2012, June 6 Litho. ***Perf. 12¾***
5299-5304 A1519 Set of 6 6.25 6.25

Souvenir Sheet
Imperf

5305 A1519 1p multi 2.00 2.00

No. 5305 has simulated perforations.

Paulina Alvarez (1912-65), Singer — A1520

2012, June 13 Litho. ***Perf. 12¾***
5306 A1520 1.05p multi 2.10 2.10

2012 Summer Olympics, London A1521

Cuban Olympic gold medal winning athletes: 10c, Orlando Martinez. 15c, Téofilo Stevenson. 20c, Alberto Juantorena. 50c, María Caridad Colón. 65c, Driulys González. 90c, Mireya Luis.
1p, Javier Sotomayor, horiz.

2012, July 5 Litho. ***Perf. 12¾***
5307-5312 A1521 Set of 6 5.00 5.00

Souvenir Sheet
Imperf

5313 A1521 1p multi 2.00 2.00

No. 5313 has simulated perforations.

Diplomatic Relations Between Cuba and Timor, 10th Anniv. — A1522

2012, July 18 Litho. ***Perf. 12½x12¼***
5314 A1522 75c multi 1.50 1.50

Civil Defense, 50th Anniv. — A1523

2012, July 20 Litho. ***Perf. 12½x12¼***
5315 A1523 65c multi 1.40 1.40

Cienfuegos Military Insurrection, 55th Anniv. — A1524

2012, Sept. 5 Litho. ***Perf. 12¼x12½***
5316 A1524 65c multi 1.40 1.40

2012 National Census — A1525

2012, Sept. 6 Litho. ***Perf. 12½x12¼***
5317 A1525 65c multi 1.40 1.40

National Lyric Theater, 50th Anniv. — A1526

Perf. 12¼x12½

2012, Sept. 14 Litho.
5318 A1526 65c multi 1.40 1.40

Diplomatic Relations Between Cuba and Kiribati, Tonga, Cook Islands, Nauru, Solomon Islands and Fiji, 10th Anniv. — A1527

Perf. 12¼x12½

2012, Sept. 26 Litho.
5319 A1527 75c multi 1.50 1.50

Diplomatic Relations Between Cuba and France, 110th Anniv. — A1528

2012, Oct. 3 Litho. ***Perf. 12¼x12½***
5320 A1528 75c multi 1.50 1.50

Diplomatic Relations Between Cuba and Switzerland, 110th Anniv. — A1529

2012, Oct. 3 Litho. ***Perf. 12¼x12½***
5321 A1529 75c multi 1.50 1.50

Myths and Legends A1530

Designs: No. 5322, 65c, La Gaviota del Rio San Juan (The Gull of San Juan River). No. 5323, 65c, El Güije. No. 5324, 65c, La Giraldilla statue, La Macorina driving car. No. 5325, 65c, La Tatagua y las Matas de Guao.

2012, Oct. 12 Litho. ***Perf. 12¾***
5322-5325 A1530 Set of 4 5.25 5.25

America Issue.

Miner's Day — A1531

2012, Oct. 24 Litho. ***Perf. 12½x12¼***
5326 A1531 65c multi 1.40 1.40

Cirilo Villaverde (1812-94), Writer — A1532

2012, Oct. 27 Litho. ***Perf. 12½x12¼***
5327 A1532 75c multi 1.50 1.50

First Cuban Expedition to Antarctica, 30th Anniv. — A1533

2012, Nov. 7 Litho. ***Perf. 12¾***
5328 A1533 75c multi 1.50 1.50

Road Safety Campaign — A1534

Designs: 65c, Children's drawing of girl and traffic light. 90c, Children, car, traffic signs.

2012, Nov. 20 Litho. *Perf. 12¾*
5329-5330 A1534 Set of 2 3.25 3.25

Ameijeiras Brothers Hospital, Havana, 30th Anniv. — A1535

2012, Nov. 26 Litho. *Perf. 12¾*
5331 A1535 65c multi 1.40 1.40

Flora and Fauna A1536

Designs: 5c, Ardilla (squirrel). 10c, Bala de Cañón (cannonball tree flower). 15c, Flor de loto (lotus flower). 65c, Pavo real (peacock), vert. 75c, Polimita (snail), vert. 90c, Orquídea (orchid), vert.
1p, Zorzal real (red-legged thrush), vert.

Perf. 12½x12¼, 12¼x12½
2012, Nov. 29 Litho.
5332-5337 A1536 Set of 6 5.25 5.25

Souvenir Sheet
Imperf

5338 A1536 1p multi 2.00 2.00
Second Cuban Philatelic Cup.

Camagüey Ballet, 50th Anniv. — A1537

Designs: 75c, Fernando Alonso (1914-2013), ballet director, and dancers. 85c, Dancers in *Don Quixote.*

2012, Dec. 1 Litho. *Perf. 12¾*
5339-5340 A1537 Set of 2 3.25 3.25

Diplomatic Relations Between Cuba and Jamaica, Trinidad & Tobago, Barbados and Guyana, 40th Anniv. — A1538

2012, Dec. 6 Litho. *Perf. 12¾*
5341 A1538 65c multi 1.40 1.40

Program For Combatting Diabetic Foot Ulcers, 5th Anniv. — A1539

Designs: 65c, Person's feet. 75c, Boxes and vial of Heberprot-P.

2012, Dec. 14 Litho. *Perf. 12¾*
5342-5343 A1539 Set of 2 3.00 3.00

Orchids A1540

Various orchids: 5c, 10c, 15c, 65c, 75c, 90c.
1p, Orchid, diff.

2013, Jan. 15 Litho. *Perf. 12¾*
5344-5349 A1540 Set of 6 5.25 5.25

Souvenir Sheet
Imperf

5350 A1540 1p multi 2.00 2.00
No. 5350 has simulated perforations.

Finland-Cuba Friendship Association, 50th Anniv. — A1541

2013, Jan. 17 Litho. *Perf. 12¾*
5351 A1541 75c multi 1.50 1.50

Bust of José Martí, by Alberto Lescay Menencio A1542

2013, Jan. 19 Litho. *Perf. 12¾*
5352 A1542 3p multi 6.00 6.00
Martí (1853-95), national hero.

National Museum, Cent. — A1543

Paintings: 5c, Torre de Babel (Tower of Babel), by School of Marten van Valckenborgh. 10c, Paisaje (Landscape), by Thomas Creswick. 50c, Saludos al Mar Caribe (Salute to the Caribbean Sea), by Mario Carreño. 65c, Jarrón con Flores (Vase with Flowers), by Amelia Peláez. 75c, Gallo Amarillo (Yellow Rooster), by Mariano Rodríguez. 85c, La Alicantina (Woman from Alicante), by Hermenegildo Anglada.
1p, Homenaje a la Soledad (Homage to Solitude), by Servando Cabrera Moreno.

2013, Jan. 25 Litho. *Perf. 12¾*
5353-5358 A1543 Set of 6 6.00 6.00

Souvenir Sheet
Imperf

5359 A1543 1p multi 2.00 2.00
No. 5359 has simulated perforations.

Items Connected to José Martí (1853-95), National Hero — A1544

Designs: 10c, Braid of Martí's hair from childhood, drawing of woman sewing. 15c, Shackle, drawing of men trying to remove leg shackles. 20c, Rostrum from San Carlos Club, Tampa, Florida. 30c, Mambisa badge with flag design. 35c, Colt revolvers. 40c, Pen, drawing of Martí writing.

2013, Jan. 28 Litho. *Perf. 12¾*
5360-5365 A1544 Set of 6 3.00 3.00

Chamber of Commerce, 50th Anniv. — A1545

2013, Feb. 1 Litho. *Perf. 12¾*
5366 A1545 90c multi 1.90 1.90

Customs Department, 50th Anniv. — A1546

2013, Feb. 5 Litho. *Perf. 12¾*
5367 A1546 1.05p multi 2.10 2.10

Third World Baseball Classic — A1547

No. 5368, 15c — Baseball and: a, Cuban uniform shirt., flags of Japan, People's Republic of China, Cuba and Brazil. b, Pitcher for Cuban team, trophy.

No. 5369, 65c — Baseball and: a, Player with glove, trophy. b, Flags of United States, Mexico, Italy and Canada, baseball glove.

No. 5370, 75c — Baseball and: a, Batter, trophy. b, Flags of Venezuela, Puerto Rico, Dominican Republic and Spain, batting helmet.

No. 5371, 85c — Baseball and: a, Catcher's mask, flags of South Korea, Netherlands, Australia and Republic of China. b, Catcher, trophy.

2013, Mar. 2 Litho. *Perf. 12½x12¼*
Horiz. Pairs, #a-b
5368-5371 A1547 Set of 4 9.75 9.75

José Raúl Capablanca (1888-1942), World Chess Champion — A1548

Capablanca and chess position in match between Capablanca and: 15c, Ossip Bernstein, 1911. 65c, Rudolf Spielmann, 1927. 75c, Mikhail Botvinnik, 1936. 85c, Jens Enevoldsen, 1939.

2013, Mar. 8 Litho. *Perf. 12½x12¼*
5372-5375 A1548 Set of 4 5.00 5.00

Pets A1549

Designs: 5c, Pigeon. 15c, Parrot, vert. 50c, Dog. 65c, Turtle. 75c, Cat. 85c, Rabbit.
1p, Horse.

Perf. 12½x12¼, 12¼x12½
2013, Mar. 12 Litho.
5376-5381 A1549 Set of 6 6.00 6.00

Souvenir Sheet
Imperf

5382 A1549 1p multi 2.00 2.00
No. 5382 has simulated perforations.

Souvenir Sheet

Informática 2013 International Convention and Fair — A1550

2013, Mar. 18 Litho. *Imperf.*
5383 A1550 1p multi 2.00 2.00

Prehistoric Animals — A1551

Designs: 5c, Cricosaurus. 15c, Pterosaurus, vert. 50c, Caribemys. 65c, Gallardosaurus. 75c, Camarasaurus. 85c, Ichthyosaurus.
1p, Vinialesaurus.

Perf. 12½x12¼, 12¼x12½
2013, Apr. 3 Litho.
5384-5389 A1551 Set of 6 6.00 6.00

Souvenir Sheet
Imperf

5390 A1551 1p multi 2.00 2.00
No. 5390 has simulated perforations.

Sauto Theater, 150th Anniv. A1552

2013, Apr. 6 Litho. *Perf. 12¾*
5391 A1552 65c multi 1.40 1.40

Australia 2013 Intl. Philatelic Exhibition, Melbourne — A1553

No. 5392, 15c: a, Parrot. b, Lyrebird.
No. 5393, 45c: a, Garfish. b, Platypus.
No. 5394, 85c: a, Hutia. b, Koala.
1p, Kangaroo and crocodile, horiz.

2013, Apr. 10 Litho. *Perf. 12¼x12½*
Horiz. Pairs, #a-b

5392-5394 A1553 Set of 3 6.00 6.00

Souvenir Sheet
Imperf

5395 A1553 1p multi 2.00 2.00

No. 5392 has simulated perforations.

Labor Day — A1554

2013, May 1 Litho. *Perf. 12¾*
5396 A1554 65c multi 1.40 1.40

Visit of Dr. Alexander Fleming to Cuba, 60th Anniv. — A1555

2013, May 12 Litho. *Perf. 12½x12¼*
5397 A1555 65c multi 1.40 1.40

First Flight From Key West to Havana, by Domingo Rosillo del Toro, Cent. — A1556

2013, May 17 Litho. *Perf. 12½x12¼*
5398 A1556 2.05p multi 4.25 4.25

Souvenir Sheet

National Ballet of Cubaa, 65th Anniv. — A1557

2013, May 20 Litho. *Imperf.*
5399 A1557 1p multi 2.00 2.00

No. 5399 has simulated perforations.

Butterflies — A1558

Designs: 5c, Papilio caiguanabus. 10c, Proteides maysi. 15c, Allosmaitia coelebs. 40c, Anetia cubana. 65c, Kricogonia cabrerai. 75c, Papilio oxynius. 85c, Atlantea perezi. 90c, Eurema lucina.

2013, May 22 Litho. *Perf. 12¾*
5400-5407 A1558 Set of 8 7.75 7.75

Compare with Type A1608.

Ministry of Construction, 50th Anniv. — A1559

2013, May 23 Litho. *Perf. 12¾*
5408 A1559 90c multi 1.90 1.90

Debut of Alicia Alonso in Ballet *Giselle,* 70th Anniv. — A1560

Paintings of Alonso by: 5c, Servando Cabrera Moreno. 15c, Lorenzo Homar. 20c, Carlos Guzmán. 65c, Alicia Leal. 75c, Francisco Rodón (48x31mm). 90c, Agostino Brotto (48x31mm).
1p, Photograph of Alonso and other dancers, vert.

Perf. 12¾, 12½x12¾ (75p, 90p)
2013, June 5 Litho.
5409-5414 A1560 Set of 6 5.50 5.50

Souvenir Sheet
Imperf

5415 A1560 1p multi 2.00 2.00

No. 5415 contains one 31x48mm stamp with simulated perforations.

Eighth Federation of University Students Congress — A1561

2013, June 12 Litho. *Perf. 12¾*
5416 A1561 65c multi 1.40 1.40

Souvenir Sheet

Seventh International Forum on Industrial Design, Havana — A1562

2013, June 18 Litho. *Imperf.*
5417 A1562 1p multi 2.00 2.00

No. 5417 has simulated perforations.

Ernesto "Che" Guevara (1928-67), Guerrilla Leader A1563

2013, June 28 Litho. *Perf. 12¾*
5418 A1563 65c multi 1.40 1.40

Birds A1564

Designs: 10c, Lophura diardi. 35c, Polyplectron bicalcaratum. 40c, Grus japonensis, vert. 50c, Pica sericea. 65c, Phasianus versicolor. 75c, Falco cherrug, vert.
1p, Pavo cristatus, vert.

Perf. 12½x12¼, 12¼x12½
2013, July 17 Litho.
5419-5424 A1564 Set of 6 5.50 5.50

Souvenir Sheet
Imperf

5425 A1564 1p multi 2.00 2.00

Thailand 2013 International Philatelic Exhibition, Bangkok. No. 5425 has simulated perforations.

Simón Bolívar (1783-1830), Liberator of South America — A1565

Designs: No. 5426, 65c, Paintings of Bolívar. No. 5427, 65c, Bolívar House, Havana, vert.

Perf. 12½x12¼, 12¼x12½
2013, July 24 Litho.
5426-5427 A1565 Set of 2 2.60 2.60

Bolívar House, 20th anniv. as museum.

Dr. Mario Muñoz Monroy (1912-53), Revolutionist A1566

2013, July 26 Litho. *Perf. 12¾*
5428 A1566 75c multi 1.50 1.50

Assault on the Moncada and Carlos M. De Céspedes Barracks, 60th Anniv. — A1567

Designs: 45c, Moncada Barracks. 75c, Barracks, diff.

2013, July 26 Litho. *Perf. 12¾*
5429-5430 A1567 Set of 2 2.40 2.40

Angerona Coffee Plantation, 200th Anniv. — A1568

2013, Aug. 12 Litho. *Perf. 12¾*
5431 A1568 1.05p multi 2.10 2.10

El Brinco Cave A1569

2013, Sept. 6 Litho. *Perf. 12½x12¼*
5432 A1569 75c multi 1.50 1.50

22nd Congress of the Postal Union of Spain, Portugal and the Americas, Havana — A1570

Designs: 65p, Quill pen writing on computer screen. 1p, UPAEP emblem.

2013, Sept. 9 Litho. *Perf. 12¾*
5433 A1570 65c multi 1.40 1.40

Souvenir Sheet
Imperf

5434 A1570 1p multi 2.00 2.00

No. 5434 contains one 40x32mm stamp.

Armed Peasants Congress, 55th Anniv. — A1571

2013, Sept. 21 Litho. *Perf. 12¾*
5435 A1571 85c multi 1.75 1.75

8th Congress of the Committee for the Defense of the Revolution — A1572

2013, Sept. 28 Litho. *Perf. 12¾*
5436 A1572 65c multi 1.40 1.40

Matanzas, 320th Anniv. — A1573

2013, Oct. 12 Litho. *Perf. 12¾*
5437 A1573 65c multi 1.40 1.40

Campaign Against Discrimination — A1574

Campaign against: No. 5438, 65c, Child abuse. No. 5439, 65c, Homophobia. No. 5440, 65c, Racial discrimination. No. 5441, 65c, Disability discrimination.

2013, Oct. 12 Litho. *Perf. 12¾*
5438-5441 A1574 Set of 4 5.25 5.25

America Issue.

North Korean National Holiday, 65th Anniv. — A1575

2013, Oct. 16 Litho. *Perf. 12¼x12½*
5442 A1575 85c multi 1.75 1.75

Brasiliana 2013 International Philatelic Exhibition, Rio de Janeiro — A1576

No. 5443, 15c: a, Cuica player. b, Tres player.
No. 5444, 40c: a, Woman of Candomblé religion. b, Woman of Cuban Santería religion.
No. 5445, 90c: a, Samba dancer. b, Rumba dancer.
1p, Statue of Jesus Christ, Havana.

2013, Oct. 16 Litho. *Perf. 12¼x12½*
Horiz. Pairs, #a-b
5443-5445 A1576 Set of 3 6.00 6.00

Souvenir Sheet
Imperf
5446 A1576 1p multi 2.00 2.00

No. 5446 has simulated perforations.

Tenth National Championship of Philately — A1577

Famous people: 15c, Mario Benedetti (1920-2009), writer. 20c, Alexander von Humboldt (1769-1859), geographer and naturalist. 45c, Nat King Cole (1919-65), singer. 65c, Juan Manuel Fangio (1911-95), race car driver. 75c, Antonio Gades (1936-2004), flamenco dancer. 85c, María Félix (1914-2002), actress.
1p, Ernest Hemingway (1899-1961), writer.

2013, Oct. 22 Litho. *Perf. 12½x12¼*
5447-5452 A1577 Set of 6 6.25 6.25

Souvenir Sheet
Imperf
5453 A1577 1p multi 2.00 2.00

No. 5453 has simulated perforations.

Bayamo, 500th Anniv. — A1578

Designs: 50c, Church steeple. 65c, Carlos M. Céspedes Barracks and flagpole, horiz.

2013, Nov. 5 Litho. *Perf. 12¾*
5454-5455 A1578 Set of 2 2.40 2.40

Arab House, Havana, 30th Anniv. — A1579

Designs: 75c, Bottle from Syria, 19th cent. 85c, Doorway.

2013, Nov. 13 Litho. *Perf. 12¾*
5456-5457 A1579 Set of 2 3.25 3.25

National Museum of Dance, Havana — A1580

Perf. 12¼x12½
2013, Nov. 25 Litho.
5458 A1580 75c multi 1.50 1.50

Cuban Revolutionary Fighters Association, 20th Anniv. — A1581

2013, Dec. 6 Litho. *Perf. 12¾*
5459 A1581 1.05p multi 2.10 2.10

General Prosecutor's Office, 40th Anniv. — A1582

2013, Dec. 23 Litho. *Perf. 12¾*
5460 A1582 65c multi 1.40 1.40

Colonel Juan Delgado González (1868-98) — A1583

Perf. 12½x12¼
2013, Dec. 27 Litho.
5461 A1583 90c multi 1.90 1.90

Triumph of Cuban Revolutionists, 55th Anniv. — A1584

2013, Dec. 30 Litho. *Perf. 12¾*
5462 A1584 65c multi 1.40 1.40

Santísima Trinidad, 500th Anniv. — A1585

Designs: 40c, Trinidad Church. 85c, Manaca-Iznaga Tower, locomotive.

2014, Jan. 12 Litho. *Perf. 12¼x12½*
5463-5464 A1585 Set of 2 2.50 2.50

Consecration of the Greek Orthodox Cathedral of St. Nicholas, 10th Anniv. — A1586

Designs: 90c, Cathedral, Archbishop Bartholomew of Constantinople, Fidel Castro. 1p, St. Nicholas, vert.

2014, Jan. 25 Litho. *Perf. 12½x12¼*
5465 A1586 90c multi 1.90 1.90

Souvenir Sheet
Imperf
5466 A1586 1p multi 2.00 2.00

No. 5466 has simulated perforations.

2014 World Cup Soccer Championships, Brazil — A1587

Designs: 35c, Soccer player. 65c, Maracana Stadium, Rio de Janeiro. 75c, Mascot. 85c, Player making bicycle kick.

2014, Feb. 1 Litho. *Perf. 12¼x12½*
5467-5470 A1587 Set of 4 5.25 5.25

Santa María del Puerto Príncipe (Camagüey), 500th Anniv. — A1588

Famous people from Camagüey: 5c, Enrique José Varona (1848-1933), writer. 10c, Gertrudis Gómez de Avellaneda (1814-73), writer. 15c, Vicentina de la Torre (1926-95), dancer. 65c, Fidelio Ponce de León (1895-1949), painter. 75c, Rafael Fortún (1919-82), sprinter. 85c, Jorge González Allué (1910-2001), composer.
1p, Plaza del Carmen, vert.

2014, Feb. 2 Litho. *Perf. 12¾*
5471-5476 A1588 Set of 6 5.25 5.25

Souvenir Sheet
Imperf
5477 A1588 1p multi 2.00 2.00

No. 5477 has simulated perforations.

Diplomatic Relations Between Cuba and Haiti, 110th Anniv. — A1589

2014, Feb. 3 Litho. *Perf. 12¾*
5478 A1589 3p multi 6.00 6.00

Fans A1590

Woman holding fan and fan from: 5c, 1860. 10c, 1860, diff. 15c, 1920. 45c, 1795-1800. 65c, 1850. 75c, 1717.

Perf. 12½x12¼

2014, Feb. 14 **Litho.**
5479-5484 A1590 Set of 6 4.50 4.50

20th Congress of Worker's Central Union — A1591

Perf. 12½x12¼

2014, Feb. 21 **Litho.**
5485 A1591 75c multi 1.50 1.50

Community of Latin American States Summit, Havana — A1592

Perf. 12¼x12½

2014, Feb. 24 **Litho.**
5486 A1592 75c multi 1.50 1.50

9th Congress of Federation of Cuban Women — A1593

2014, Mar. 5 Litho. ***Perf. 12¼x12½***
5487 A1593 65c multi 1.40 1.40

Hugo Chávez (1954-2013), President of Venezuela — A1594

Chávez: 65c, Saluting. 75c, With hand over heart. 85c, With arm raised.

2014, Mar. 5 Litho. ***Perf. 12½x12¼***
5488-5490 A1594 Set of 3 4.50 4.50

Alejandro Robaina Pereda (1919-2010), Tobacco Grower — A1595

Cigar box and: 10c, Hand holding tobacco seedling, classification of tobacco leaves. 15c, Tobacco growers in field. 30c, Tobacco leaves and equipment for cigar making. 65c, Cigars with Robaina band. 75c, Cigar humidor, lit match. 85c, Cigar box art for Vegas Robaina cigars.
1p, Robaina, vert.

Perf. 12½x12¼

2014, Mar. 20 **Litho.**
5491-5496 A1595 Set of 6 5.75 5.75

Souvenir Sheet

Imperf

5497 A1595 1p multi 2.00 2.00

No. 5497 has simulated perforations.

Gertrudis Gomez de Avellaneda (1814-73), Writer — A1596

Perf. 12¼x12½

2014, Mar. 22 **Litho.**
5498 A1596 1.05p multi 2.10 2.10

Operation Transbordo, 50th Anniv. — A1597

Designs: 45c, Alberto Delgado Delgado (1932-64), undercover agent. 65c, Boat.

2014, Mar. 26 Litho. ***Perf. 12¾***
5499-5500 A1597 Set of 2 2.25 2.25

Diplomatic Relations Between Antigua and Barbuda and Cuba, 20th Anniv. — A1598

2014, Apr. 4 Litho. ***Perf. 12¾***
5501 A1598 65c multi 1.40 1.40

National Revolutionary Police, 55th Anniv. — A1599

2014, Apr. 19 Litho. ***Perf. 12¾***
5502 A1599 90c multi 1.90 1.90

Ministry of Science, Technology and the Environment, 20th Anniv. — A1600

2014, Apr. 21 Litho. ***Perf. 12½x12¼***
5503 A1600 90c multi 1.90 1.90

Flags of South Africa and Cuba, Nelson Mandela (1918-2013), President of South Africa — A1601

2014, Apr. 28 Litho. ***Perf. 12¾***
5504 A1601 85c multi 1.75 1.75

Diplomatic relations between South Africa and Cuba, end of apartheid in South Africa, 20th anniv.

Labor Day — A1602

2014, May 1 Litho. ***Perf. 12¼x12½***
5505 A1602 65c multi 1.40 1.40

Ernesto "Che" Guevara (1928-67), Minister of Industry, and Metallurgical Industries — A1603

Guevara, photographs of industry, plants or finished products and emblem of: 10c, Planta Mecanica. 45c, Profix. 75c, CIME. 85c, Inpud. 90c, Taino.

2014, May 2 Litho. ***Perf. 12½x12¼***
5506-5510 A1603 Set of 5 6.25 6.25

State Council Historical Affairs Office, 50th Anniv. — A1604

2014, May 9 Litho. ***Perf. 12½x12¼***
5511 A1604 75c multi 1.50 1.50

Bejucal, 300th Anniv. — A1605

2014, May 10 Litho. ***Perf. 12¼x12½***
5512 A1605 65c multi 1.40 1.40

St. Francis of Assisi Basilica and Convent Museum, 20th Anniv. — A1606

2014, May 16 Litho. ***Perf. 12½x12¼***
5513 A1606 90c multi 1.90 1.90

First Agrarian Reform Law, 55th Anniv. — A1607

2014, May 17 Litho. ***Perf. 12½x12¼***
5514 A1607 65c multi 1.40 1.40

Butterflies — A1608

Designs: 5c, Eurema amelia. 10c, Astraptes cassander. 15c, Panoquina corrupta. 20c, Chioides marmorosa. 40c, Eunica heraclitus. 50c, Parachoranthus magdalia. 65c, Holguinia holguin. 75c, Eantis munroei. 90c, Oarisma nanus.

2014, May 22 Litho. ***Perf. 12¾***
5515-5523 A1608 Set of 9 7.50 7.50

Compare with Type A1558.

Diplomatic Relations Between Cuba and Congo Republic, 50th Anniv. — A1609

2014, May 23 Litho. ***Perf. 12¼x12½***
5524 A1609 85c multi 1.75 1.75

National Museum of Natural History, 50th Anniv. — A1610

2014, May 26 Litho. *Perf. 12½x12¼*
5525 A1610 75c multi 1.50 1.50

Souvenir Sheet

Hotel Cubanacan Comodoro — A1611

2014, May 31 Litho. *Imperf.*
5526 A1611 1p multi 2.00 2.00

Third Cuba Philately Cup.

Sancti Spiritus, 500th Anniv. — A1612

Designs: 65c, Rio Yayabo Bridge. 75c, Parroquial Mayor Church, vert.

Perf. 12½x12¼, 12¼x12½
2014, June 4 Litho.
5527-5528 A1612 Set of 2 3.00 3.00

Diplomatic Relations Between Nigeria and Cuba, 40th Anniv. — A1613

2014, July 1 Litho. *Perf. 12¼x12½*
5529 A1613 85c multi 1.75 1.75

Office of the Comptroller General, 5th Anniv. — A1614

2014, Aug. 1 Litho. *Perf. 12½x12¼*
5530 A1614 90c multi 1.90 1.90

Spanish Heritage Festival, 25th Anniv. — A1615

2014, Aug. 5 Litho. *Perf. 12½x12¼*
5531 A1615 65c multi 1.40 1.40

Show Jumping Horses — A1616

Designs: 15c, Golden Horse. 20c, Captain VZ. 30c, Fairmont R.E. 65c, Gigaa VDP. 75c, Google. 85c, Goldmann Jr.
1p, Fumuto and rider.

Perf. 12½x12¼
2014, Aug. 16 Litho.
5532-5537 A1616 Set of 6 6.00 6.00

Size: 83x83mm
Imperf

5538 A1616 1p multi 2.00 2.00

No. 5538 has simulated perforations.

African Animals and Map of Africa — A1617

2014, Sept. 2 Litho. *Perf. 12½x12¼*
5539 A1617 85c multi 1.75 1.75

Diplomatic relations between Cuba and Burundi, Cameroun, Gabon, Senegal, Uganda, Liberia and Madagascar, 40th anniv.

Latin American Parliament, 50th Anniv. — A1618

2014, Sept. 5 Litho. *Perf. 12½x12¼*
5540 A1618 65c multi 1.40 1.40

Diplomatic Relations Between Benin and Cuba, 40th Anniv. — A1619

2014, Sept. 12 Litho. *Perf. 12¾*
5541 A1619 85c multi 1.75 1.75

Guitars — A1620

Perf. 12¼x12½
2014, Sept. 25 Litho.
5542 A1620 65c multi 1.40 1.40

75th birthday of Leo Brouwer, guitarist and composer.

People's Republic of China, 65th Anniv. — A1621

Perf. 12½x12¼
2014, Sept. 29 Litho.
5543 A1621 85c multi 1.75 1.75

Lighthouses A1622

Designs: 15c, Morro Castle Lighthouse, Havana. 35c, Cayo Jutías Lighthouse, Pinar del Rio. 75c, Cayo Cruz del Padre Lighthouse, Matanzas. 85c, Morro Lighthouse, Santiago.

2014, Oct. 5 Litho. *Perf. 12¼x12½*
5544-5547 A1622 Set of 4 4.25 4.25

Philakorea 2014 Intl. Stamp Exhibition, Seoul — A1623

Dogs: 10c, Poodle (caniche). 20c, Yorkshire terrier. 30c, Schnauzer. 40c, Beagle. 65c, German shepherd (pastor aleman). 75c, Golden retriever.
1p, Collie (pastor escocés de pelo largo).

Perf. 12½x12¼
2014, June 15 Litho.
5548-5553 A1623 Set of 6 5.00 5.00

Souvenir Sheet
Imperf

5554 A1623 1p multi 2.00 2.00

No. 5554 contains one 43x33mm stamp with simulated perforations.

Malaysia 2014 Intl. Stamp Exhibition, Kuala Lumpur — A1624

Cats: 10c, Shorthaired cat (pelos cortos). 20c, Persian cat (Persas). 40c, Balinese cat (Balineses). 65c. Bengal cat (Bengalies). 75c, Siamese cat (Siameses), horiz. 85c, Semi-longhaired cat (pelos semi-largos).
1p, Cuban blue cat (azules cubanos).

Perf. 12¼x12½, 12½x12¼
2014, July 30 Litho.
5555-5560 A1624 Set of 6 6.00 6.00

Souvenir Sheet
Imperf

5561 A1624 1p multi 2.00 2.00

No. 5554 has simulated perforations.

Trains A1625

Designs: 5c, Talgo AVE series 100. 15c, Alstom FGC series 113. 50c, Siemens AVE series 103. 65c, Talgo AVE series 130. 75c, CRH380A. 85c, JR-Maglev MLX01.
1p, Cabina AVE series 102.

Perf. 12½x12¼
2014, Sept. 15 Litho.
5562-5567 A1625 Set of 6 6.00 6.00

Souvenir Sheet
Imperf

5568 A1625 1p multi 2.00 2.00

No. 5568 contains one 61x26mm trapezoidal stamp with simulated perforations.

Marine Life A1626

Designs: 5c, Volvarina moresi. 10c, Sepia officinalis. 30c, Amblyrhynchus cristatus. 65c, Physeter macrocephalus, vert. 75c, Aptenodytes patagonicus, vert. 85c, Eretmochelys imbricata, vert.
1p, Pomacanthus arcuatus, vert.

2014, Oct. 4 Litho. *Perf. 12¾*
5569-5574 A1626 Set of 6 5.50 5.50

Souvenir Sheet
Imperf

5575 A1626 1p multi 2.00 2.00

No. 5575 has simulated perforations.

Famous Men — A1626a

Designs: No. 5575A, 65c, José Martí (1853-95), writer. No. 5575B, 65c, Antonio Maceo Grajales (1845-96), military leader. No. 5575C, 65c, Ignacio Agramonte y Loynaz

(1841-73), revolutionist. No. 5575D, 65c, Carlos Manuel de Céspedes (1819-74), declarer of Cuban independence.

2014, Oct. 12 Litho. *Perf. 12¾*
5575A-5575D A1626a Set of 4 5.25 5.25

America Issue.

Airplanes of Cubana Arilines — A1627

Designs: 15c, Curtiss Robin. 20c, Bristol Britannia. 45c, Lockheed 10 Electra. 75c, Antonov 158.

2014, Oct. 22 Litho. *Perf. 12½x12¼*
5576-5579 A1627 Set of 4 3.25 3.25

Independence of Malawi, Tanzania and Zambia, 50th Anniv. — A1628

2014, Oct. 24 Litho. *Perf. 12¼x12½*
5580 A1628 85c multi 1.75 1.75

National Road Safety Day A1629

Children's drawings: 15c, Taxi and signs. 20c, Children in crosswalk. 40c, Tractor and cow on road. 50c, Car, sign and traffic light. 65c, Child chasing ball in street. 75c, Railroad crossing.
1p, Policeman, crosswalk, traffic light.

2014, Nov. 17 Litho. *Perf. 12¾*
5581-5586 A1629 Set of 6 5.50 5.50

Souvenir Sheet

Imperf

5587 A1629 1p multi 2.00 2.00

No. 5587 has simulated perforations.

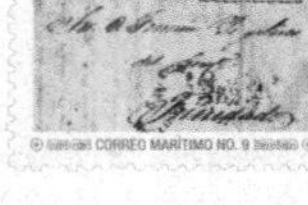

Cuban Philatelic Treasures A1630

Designs: 10c, Stampless cover, ship. 20c, Cover with three stamps, mask. 30c, Havana local post cover with two stamps, watchtower, horiz. 65c, Cover with Mambí insurrection stamps, mounted soldier with Cuban flag. 75c, Cover with Puerto Principe surcharges, tower. 85c, Experimental rocket mail cover, rocket.
1p, Statue and birds, horiz.

Perf. 12¼x12½, 12½x12¼

2014, Nov. 20 Litho.
5588-5593 A1630 Set of 6 5.75 5.75

Souvenir Sheet

Imperf

5594 A1630 1p multi 2.00 2.00

No. 5554 contains one 44x31mm stamp with simulated perforations.

Diplomatic Relations Between Cuba and the Bahamas, 40th Anniv. — A1631

Perf. 12½x12¼

2014, Nov. 28 Litho.
5595 A1631 3p multi 6.00 6.00

José Antonio Echeverria City University, 50th Anniv. — A1632

2014, Dec. 2 Litho. *Perf. 12½x12¼*
5596 A1632 65c multi 1.40 1.40

2014 Diabetes Congress, Varadero Beach — A1633

Designs: 65c, Infected foot, bottle of medicine and surgeon's saw. 75c, People pulling on fabric covering over feet.

Perf. 12½x12¼

2014, Dec. 10 Litho.
5597-5598 A1633 Set of 2 3.00 3.00

Protected Flora and Fauna — A1634

Designs: 5c, Todus multicolor. 10c, Peireskia cubensis. 15c, Eretmochelys imbricata. 75c, Tetramicra eulophiae. 85c, Starnoenas cyanocephala. 90c, Bonnetia cubensis.
1p, Colaptes fernandinae, vert.

2014, Dec. 15 Litho. *Perf. 12¾*
5599-5604 A1634 Set of 6 5.75 5.75

Souvenir Sheet

Imperf

5605 A1634 1p multi 2.00 2.00

No. 5605 has simulated perforations.

Tomás Romay Chacón (1764-1849), Physician — A1635

Perf. 12½x12¼

2014, Dec. 21 Litho.
5606 A1635 65c multi 1.40 1.40

José Luis Guerra Aguiar Postal Museum, 50th Anniv. — A1636

Designs: 5c, 1826 stampless cover from Santiago de Cuba to Puerto Principe. 10c, 1883 cover with stamps depicting King Alfonso XII. 15c, Handstamp and free frank covers of General Máximo Gómez Báez. 20c, Cuba #238, printing stone for stamp similar to #238. 65c, Handstamp, cover with Cuba #C324-C325. 75c, Children looking at museum exhibit, magnifying glass and album pages.
1p, Cover with Cuba #935a-935b.

2015 Jan. 9 Litho. *Perf. 12½x12¼*
5607-5612 A1636 Set of 6 4.00 4.00

Souvenir Sheet

Imperf

5613 A1636 1p multi 2.00 2.00

No. 5613 contains one 44x33mm stamp with simulated perforations.

National Organization of Collective Law Offices, 50th Anniv. — A1637

2015, Jan. 22 Litho. *Perf. 12½x12¼*
5614 A1637 65c multi 1.40 1.40

Fish — A1638

Inscriptions: 5c, Siamese fighting fish (Luchador de Siam). 15c, Clown loach (Locha payaso), horiz. 45c, Pearl gourami (Gurami perla), horiz. 65c, Butterfly cichlid (Ciclido mariposa), horiz. 75c, Mollies (Pez molly), horiz. 90c, Goldfish, horiz.
1p, Angelfish (Escalar).

Perf. 12¼x12½, 12½x12¼

2015, Jan. 20 Litho.
5615-5620 A1638 Set of 6 6.00 6.00

Souvenir Sheet

Imperf

5621 A1638 1p multi 2.00 2.00

No. 5621 contains one 29x45mm stamp with simulated perforations.

Dogs A1639

Designs: 15c, Cocker spaniels. 30c, Golden retrievers. 40c, Border collies. 65c, Alaskan malamutes. 75c, Labrador retrievers. 85c, St. Bernards.
1p, German shepherds, vert.

2015, Jan. 20 Litho. *Perf. 12½x12¼*
5622-5627 A1639 Set of 6 6.25 6.25

Souvenir Sheet

Imperf

5628 A1639 1p multi 2.00 2.00

No. 5628 has simulated perforations.

Faustino Pérez Hernández (1920-92), Central Committee Member, Zaza Dam — A1640

Perf. 12½x12¼

2015, Feb. 15 Litho.
5629 A1640 1.05p multi 2.10 2.10

Ballet "Dioné," 75th Anniv. — A1641

Designs: 75c, Composer Eduardo Sánchez de Fuentes (1874-1944) and scene from ballet. 90c, Dancers Alicia and Fernando Alonso.

2015, Mar. 4 Litho. *Perf. 12½x12¼*
5630-5631 A1641 Set of 2 3.50 3.50

Ballet Performances of Anna Pavlova in Cuba, Cent. — A1642

Perf. 12¼x12½

2015, Mar. 18 Litho.
5632 A1642 65c multi 1.40 1.40

Manuel López Portilla (1940-60), State Security Agent — A1643

Perf. 12¼x12½

2015, Mar. 26 Litho.
5633 A1643 65c multi 1.40 1.40

Explosion of Ship "La Coubre" in Havana Harbor, 55th Anniv. — A1644

2015, Apr. 1 Litho. *Perf. 12½x12¼*
5634 A1644 3p multi 6.00 6.00

Railway Cars — A1645

Designs: 10c, Tanker cars. 20c, Flat cars. 50c, Lumber cars. 65c, Cars carrying intermodal containers. 75c, Coal cars. 85c, Automobile carrier.
1p, Poultry car.

2015, Mar. 4 Litho. *Perf. 12½x12¼*
5635-5640 A1645 Set of 6 6.25 6.25

Souvenir Sheet

Imperf

5641 A1645 1p multi 2.00 2.00

No. 5641 contains one 45x30mm stamp with simulated perforations.

Endangered Birds — A1646

Birds and maps of their range: 5c, Passerina ciris. 15c, Chiroxiphia caudata, vert. 20c, Amadina fasciata. 75c, Carduelis carduelis, vert. 85c, Chloebia gouldiae, vert. 90c, Leionthrix argentauris.
1p, Ferminia cerverai, vert.

Perf. 12½x12¼, 12¼x12½
2015, Apr. 10 Litho.
5642-5647 A1646 Set of 6 6.00 6.00

Souvenir Sheet

Imperf

5648 A1646 1p multi 2.00 2.00

No. 5648 has simulated perforations.

Landing of José Martí and General Máximo Gómez Báez at Playita, 120th Anniv. — A1647

No. 5649 — Playita and: a, 65c, Martí. b, 75c, Gómez.

2015, Apr. 11 Litho. *Perf. 12¼x12½*
5649 A1647 Horiz. pair, #a-b 3.00 3.00

Raúl Ferrer (1915-93), Poet and Educator — A1648

2015, Apr. 17 Litho. *Perf. 12¾*
5650 A1648 75c multi 1.50 1.50

Use of First Stamps in Cuba, 160th Anniv. — A1649

No. 5651: a, 10c, Havana postal badge, mailman and mailboxes. b, 30c, Padlock and key, horse-drawn postal wagons. c, 65c, Post office scale, postal workers sorting mail. d, 75c, Title of Postal Administration, post office.

2015, Apr. 24 Litho. *Perf. 12½x12¼*
5651 A1649 Block of 4, #a-d 3.75 3.75

Labor Day — A1650

2015, May 1 Litho. *Perf. 12¼x12½*
5652 A1650 75c multi 1.50 1.50

Diplomatic Relations Between Cuba and Russia, 55th Anniv. — A1651

2015, May 8 Litho. *Perf. 12¼x12½*
5653 A1651 85c multi 1.75 1.75

Havana Explosion and Fire of 1890, 125th Anniv. — A1652

Firefighter killed in explosion and horse-drawn: 5c, Cervantes pumper. 10c, Colón pumper. 15c, Fire wagon. 40c, Ambulance. 65c, Gámiz pumper. 75c, Cuba pumper.
1p, Megaphone and monument plaque listing the victims, vert.

2015, May 15 Litho. *Perf. 12¾*
5654-5659 A1652 Set of 6 4.25 4.25

Souvenir Sheet

Imperf

5660 A1652 1p multi 2.00 2.00

No. 5660 has simulated perforations.

Ferry "Pinero" — A1653

2015, May 16 Litho. *Perf. 12½x12¼*
5661 A1653 75c multi 1.50 1.50

Arrival of Fidel Castro and other Moncada Barracks attackers at Batabanó, 60th anniv.

International Telecommunication Union, 150th Anniv. — A1654

2015, May 17 Litho. *Perf. 12¼x12½*
5662 A1654 65c multi 1.40 1.40

Elisio Reyes (1940-67), Guerrilla Fighter — A1655

2015, May 23 Litho. *Perf. 12½x12¼*
5663 A1655 65c multi 1.40 1.40

Wild Cats A1656

Designs: 15c, Panthera onca, Olmec ceremonial hatchet. 35c, Puma concolor, gorget. 50c, Panthera tigris, carving of tiger. 65c, Panthera leo, Thracian grave decoration. 75c, Acinonyx jubatus, decorated Egyptian knife. 85c, Panthera pardus, Nigerian bronze plaque.
1p, Felis silvestris catus, Japanese drawing of cat.

2015, Apr. 15 Litho. *Perf. 12½x12¼*
5664-5669 A1656 Set of 6 6.50 6.50

Souvenir Sheet

Imperf

5670 A1656 1p multi 2.00 2.00

No. 5670 has simulated perforations.

Prehistoric Fauna — A1657

Designs: 10c, Carcharodon megalodon. 35c, Metaxytherium. 50c, Ptychodus. 65c, Aetomylaeus cubensis. 75c, Physetérid. 85c, Orycterocetus.
1p, Aspidorhynchus.

2015, May 6 Litho. *Perf. 12½x12¼*
5671-5676 A1657 Set of 6 6.50 6.50

Souvenir Sheet

Imperf

5677 A1657 1p multi 2.00 2.00

No. 5677 has simulated perforations.

Santiago de Cuba, 500th Anniv. — A1658

Designs: 5c, Lieutenant General Maceo Grajales, painting by Luis Desangles. 10c, Monument to Frank Pais. 15c, Fidel Castro at Mausoleum of José Martí. 30c, San Pedro de la Roca Castle. 75c, La Isabelica coffee plantation building, horiz. 85c, Tumba Francesa dancers and musicians, horiz.
1p, City Hall.

2015, May 20 Litho. *Perf. 12¾*
5678-5683 A1658 Set of 6 4.50 4.50

Souvenir Sheet

Imperf

5684 A1658 1p multi 2.00 2.00

No. 5684 has simulated perforations.

National Flowers of Central and South American Countries A1659

Flowers: 5c, Dahlia (Mexico). 15c, Golden trumpet (Brazil). 20c, Mayflower orchid (Venezuela). 30c, Ceibo (Argentina, Uruguay). 40c, Virgin orchid (Honduras). 65c, Rose (Ecuador). 75c, Copihue (Chile). 90c, White ginger (Cuba).

2015, May 26 Litho. *Perf. 12¼x12½*
5685-5692 A1659 Set of 8 7.00 7.00

Watercraft — A1660

Designs: 5c, SC CL Globe, China. 20c, Paraw, Philippines. 50c, Paddlewheeler Junco, Viet Nam. 65c, Kettuvallam, India. 75c, Dhoni, Maldive Islands, vert. 85c, Junk, China, vert.
1p, Turtle ship, Korea, vert.

Perf. 12½x12¼, 12¼x12½
2015, June 1 Litho.
5693-5698 A1660 Set of 6 6.00 6.00

Souvenir Sheet

Imperf

5699 A1660 1p multi 2.00 2.00

Singapore 2015 Intl. Philatelic Exhibition. No. 5699 contains one 32x48mm stamp with simulated perforations.

San Juan de los Remedios, 500th Anniv. — A1661

Designs: 65c, Buildings of San Juan de los Remedios. 75c, Alejandro García Caturla (1906-40), composer.

Perf. 12½x12¼

2015, June 24 **Litho.**
5700-5701 A1661 Set of 2 3.00 3.00

National Office of Tax Administration, 20th Anniv. — A1662

Perf. 12¼x12½

2015, June 28 **Litho.**
5702 A1662 65c multi 1.40 1.40

History of the Telephone A1663

Designs: 10c, 19th cent. desk telephone. 20c, 20th cent. wall telephone. 30c, 19th cent. desk telephone, diff. 50c, 20th cent. desk telephone. 65c, 20th cent. desk telephones, diff. 75c, 20th cent. two desk telphones.
1p, 20th cent. public pay telephone.

2015, July 14 **Litho.** ***Perf. 12¾***
5703-5708 A1663 Set of 6 5.00 5.00

Souvenir Sheet

Imperf

5709 A1663 1p multi 2.00 2.00

No. 5709 has simulated perforations.

Mariana Grajales Coello (1808-93), Mother of Generals José and Antonio Maceo Grajales A1664

Designs: 65c, Mariana Grajales Coello and Cuban flag. 75c, Monument.

2015, July 24 **Litho.** ***Perf. 12¼x12½***
5710-5711 A1664 Set of 2 3.00 3.00

Alicia Alonso National School of Ballet, 65th Anniv. — A1665

2015, Aug. 5 **Litho.** ***Perf. 12½x12¼***
5712 A1665 65c multi 1.40 1.40

Cuban Court of International Commercial Arbitration, 50th Anniv. — A1666

Perf. 12¼x12½

2015, Sept. 16 **Litho.**
5713 A1666 3p multi 6.00 6.00

Committee for the Defense of the Revolution, 55th Anniv. — A1667

Perf. 12½x12¼

2015, Sept. 21 **Litho.**
5714 A1667 65c multi 1.40 1.40

Campaign Against Human Trafficking A1668

Campaign against: No. 5715, 65c, Sexual exploitation (Explotación sexual). No. 5716, 65c, Forced labor (Trabajo forzado). No. 5717, 65c, Organ extraction (Extracción de órganos). No. 5718, 65c, Servitude (Servidumbre).

2015, Oct. 12 **Litho.** ***Perf. 12¼x12½***
5715-5718 A1668 Set of 4 5.25 5.25

America Issue.

Paintings and Artifacts Connected to José Martí — A1669

Designs: 5c, Martí on horseback, spurs from Battle of Dos Ríos. 10c, House of General Máximo Gómez, Montecristi, and inkstand. 15c, Martí leading cavalrymen, Winchester rifle. 20c, Martí in rowboat, oarlocks. 30c, Martí reading *Patria* newpaper, plaque from Patria building. 40c, Martí addressing crowd, pulpit. 75c, María García Granados (1860-78), love interest of Martí and subject of Martí poem, cushion. 85c, Martí writing, desk and chair.

2015, Oct. 15 **Litho.** ***Perf. 12¼x12½***
5719-5726 A1669 Set of 8 5.75 5.75

Cuban Television, 65th Anniv. — A1670

2015, Oct. 24 **Litho.** ***Perf. 12¾***
5727 A1670 75c multi 1.50 1.50
a. Dated "2015" — —

No. 5727 has "201" date at lower right.

Cuban Wushu and Qigong School, 20th Anniv. — A1671

2015, Oct. 26 **Litho.** ***Perf. 12½x12¼***
5728 A1671 85c multi 1.75 1.75

Visit of Pope Francis — A1672

Perf. 12½x12¼

2015, Nov. 11 **Litho.**
5729 A1672 75c multi 1.50 1.50

11th National Stamp Championships — A1673

Designs: 10c, Marlon Brando (1924-2004), actor, Academy Award. 15c, Mother Teresa (St. Teresa of Calcutta) (1910-97), crucifix. 20c, Babe Ruth (1895-1948), baseball player, baseball. 65c, Charles A. Lindbergh (1902-74), aviator, Spirit of St. Louis. 75c, Gabriel García Márquez (1927-2014), writer, book, eyeglasses and butterflies. 85c, Diego Rivera (1886-1957), painter, detail of "The Uprising."
1p, Diego A. Maradona, soccer player, World Cup trophy.

Perf. 12½x12¼

2015, Nov. 20 **Litho.**
5730-5735 A1673 Set of 6 5.50 5.50

Souvenir Sheet

Imperf

5736 A1673 1p multi 2.00 2.00

No. 5736 has simulated perforations.

Nico López (1932-56), Revolutionary — A1674

2015, Dec. 2 **Litho.** ***Perf. 12½x12¼***
5737 A1674 65c multi 1.40 1.40

Communist Party Schools, 55th anniv.

Souvenir Sheet

Alicia Alonso, Ballet Dancer — A1675

2016, Jan. 1 **Litho.** ***Imperf.***
5738 A1675 1p multi 2.00 2.00

Reopening of Alicia Alonso Grand Theater, Havana.

Conrado Benítez (1942-61), Revolutionary Martyr — A1676

2016, Jan. 5 **Litho.** ***Perf. 12¾***
5739 A1676 90c multi 1.90 1.90

Research Center for Animal Breeding of Tropical Livestock, 45th Anniv. — A1677

Designs: 65c, Research center, livestock. 75c, Researchers and livestock.

2016, Jan. 8 **Litho.** ***Perf. 12½x12¼***
5740-5741 A1677 Set of 2 3.00 3.00

Mayabeque Province, 5th Anniv. — A1678

2016, Jan. 9 **Litho.** ***Perf. 12¼x12½***
5742 A1678 90c multi 1.90 1.90

Francisco de Albear Fernández y de Lara (1816-87), Civil Engineer — A1679

2016, Jan. 11 Litho. ***Perf. 12½x12¼***
5743 A1679 1.05p multi 2.10 2.10

Waterbirds — A1680

Designs: 10c, Alcedo atthis. 15c, Phaethon rubricauda. 45c, Branta canadensis. 75c, Threskiornis aethiopicus. 85c, Anas platyrhynchos. 90c, Branta canadensis, vert.
1p, Fratercula arctica, vert.

Perf. 12½x12¼, 12¼x12½
2016, Jan. 15 Litho.
5744-5749 A1680 Set of 6 6.50 6.50

Souvenir Sheet
Imperf

5750 A1680 1p multi 2.00 2.00

No. 5750 contains one 30x36mm stamp with simulated perforations. Bird name inscription on No. 5749 is incorrect.

General Calixto García University Hospital, Havana, 120th Anniv. — A1681

2016, Jan. 23 Litho. ***Perf. 12¼x12½***
5751 A1681 65c multi 1.40 1.40

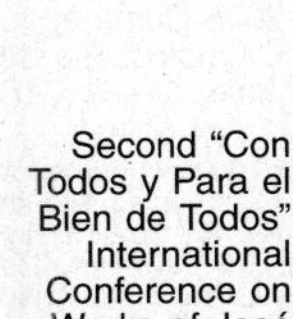

Second "Con Todos y Para el Bien de Todos" International Conference on Works of José Martí, Havana — A1682

2016, Jan. 25 Litho. ***Perf. 12¼x12½***
5752 A1682 2.05p multi 4.25 4.25

Dinosaurs — A1683

Designs: 5c, Cryolophosaurus. 20c, Amargasaurus. 65c, Camarasaurus. 75c, Pachyrhinosaurus. 85c, Baryonyx. 90c, Allosaurus.
1p, Gorgosaurus.

2016, Jan. 31 Litho. ***Perf. 12½x12¼***
5753-5758 A1683 Set of 6 7.00 7.00

Souvenir Sheet
Imperf

5759 A1683 1p multi 2.00 2.00

No. 5759 has simulated perforations.

Classic Automobiles — A1684

Designs: 5c, 1932 Duesenberg SJ Dual-cowl Phaeton. 15c, 1936 Bugatti Type 57SC Atlantic. 50c, 1931 Lincoln Model K. 65c, 1936 Mercedes-Benz 540 K. 75c, 1934 Chevrolet Master Sport Coupe. 85c, 1934 Ford Deluxe Roadster.
1p, 1938 Volkswagen Type 1.

Perf. 12½x12¼
2016, Feb. 20 Litho.
5760-5765 A1684 Set of 6 6.00 6.00

Souvenir Sheet
Imperf

5766 A1684 1p multi 2.00 2.00

No. 5766 has simulated perforations.

Ministry of Industry, 55th Anniv. — A1685

Perf. 12¼x12½
2016, Feb. 22 Litho.
5767 A1685 3p multi 6.00 6.00

Restoration of Teatro Martí, Havana — A1686

Designs: 45c, Building exterior. 50c, Stage. 65c, Seats and ceiling.

2016, Feb. 24 Litho. ***Perf. 12¾***
5768-5770 A1686 Set of 3 3.25 3.25

Establishment of Cuban Postal Service, 260th Anniv. — A1687

Designs: 10c, Mail ship and captain, 1777. 40c, Postman, horse and carriage, 1902. 65c, Special delivery postman on motorcycle, 1950. 85c, Postman on bicycle, 2013.
1p, Postman on horse.

2016, Mar. 1 Litho. ***Perf. 12¾***
5771-5774 A1687 Set of 4 4.00 4.00

Souvenir Sheet
Imperf

5775 A1687 1p multi 2.00 2.00

No. 5775 has simulated perforations.

Fe del Valle Ramos (1917-61), Department Store Worker Killed in Arson Fire — A1688

2016, Mar. 8 Litho. ***Perf. 12¾***
5776 A1688 65c multi 1.40 1.40

Fauna — A1689

Designs: No. 5777, 90c, Buteo regalis, Bison bison. No. 5778, 90c, Ramphastos toco, Leopardus pardalis. No. 5779, 90c, Oncorhynchus mykiss. No. 5780, 90c, Trichechus manatus, Atractosteus tristoechus.

Perf. 12¼x12½
2016, Mar. 10 Litho.
5777-5780 A1689 Set of 4 7.25 7.25

Souvenir Sheet

16th Informática Intl. Convention and Fair — A1690

2016, Mar. 14 Litho. ***Imperf.***
5781 A1690 1p multi 2.00 2.00

Central Army, 55th Anniv. — A1691

2016, Apr. 4 Litho. ***Perf. 12¼x12½***
5782 A1691 65c multi 1.40 1.40

Sculptures by José Villa Soberón — A1692

Designs: 10c, Caballero de París. 35c, Tin Tan. 40c, Gabriel García Márquez. 75c, John Lennon. 85c, Benny Moré. 90c, Antonio Gades.
1p, Ernest Hemingway, vert.

2016, Apr. 5 Litho. ***Perf. 12½x12¼***
5783-5788 A1692 Set of 6 6.75 6.75

Souvenir Sheet
Imperf

5789 A1692 1p multi 2.00 2.00

2016 Copa Cuba National Stamp Exhibition. No. 5789 has simulated perforations.

Trains A1693

Designs: 10c, Liverpool & Manchester Railway train, 1830. 20c, American express train, 1885. 35c, Orient Express, 1883. 75c, Trans-Siberian train, 1883. 85c, Blue Train, 1903. 90c, Union Pacific train.
1p, Shinkansen Sereis 700 train.

2016, Apr. 5 Litho. ***Perf. 12½x12¼***
5790-5795 A1693 Set of 6 6.50 6.50

Souvenir Sheet
Imperf

5796 A1693 1p multi 2.00 2.00

No. 5796 has simulated perforations.

Eastern Army, 55th Anniv. — A1694

2016, Apr. 21 Litho. ***Perf. 12½x12¼***
5797 A1694 65c multi 1.40 1.40

Labor Day — A1695

2016, Apr. 29 Litho. ***Perf. 12¼x12½***
5798 A1695 75c multi 1.50 1.50

National Association of Small Farmers, 55th Anniv. — A1696

2016, May 17 Litho. ***Perf. 12¼x12½***
5799 A1696 85c multi 1.75 1.75

Musical Instruments — A1697

Designs: 5c, Laúd. 15c, Corneta China. 35c, Catá. 75c, Chequeré. 85c, Iyá.

2016, May 18 Litho. ***Perf. 12½x12¼***
5800-5804 A1697 Set of 5 4.50 4.50

Enrique José Varona (1848-1933), Writer — A1698

2016, May 19 Litho. ***Perf. 12½x12¼***
5805 A1698 75c multi 1.50 1.50

Cuban Academy of Language, 90th anniv.

Extinct and Endangered Hutias — A1699

Designs: 5c, Mesocapromys sanfelipensis. 15c, Mesocapromys nanus. 35c, Mesocapromys angelcabrerai. 45c, Mesocapromys auritus. 75c, Mysateles melanurus. 85c, Mysateles prehensilis.
1p, Capromys pilorides.

2016, May 23 Litho. ***Perf. 12¼x12½***
5806-5811 A1699 Set of 6 5.25 5.25

Souvenir Sheet

Imperf

5812 A1699 1p multi 2.00 2.00

No. 5812 has simulated perforations.

National Flowers of North and South American Countries — A1700

Designs: 5c, Maga, Puerto Rico. 15c, Bougainvillea (bugambilia), Canada. 20c, Romerillo, St. Lucia. 30c, Plumeria (sacuanjoche), Nicaragua. 40c, Soufriere tree flower, St. Vincent and the Grenadines. 65c, Poinciana (framboyán), Haiti and St. Kitts and Nevis, vert. 75c, Dagger's log, Antigua and Barbuda, vert. 90c, Kantuta, Bolivia, vert.

2016, May 26 Litho. ***Perf. 12¾***
5813-5820 A1700 Set of 8 7.00 7.00

Victims of Terrorism — A1701

Designs: 65c, Airplane, boat, people walking on street. 75c, Newspaper headline, people looking at wall of photographs.

2016, June 3 Litho. ***Perf. 12½x12¼***
5821-5822 A1701 Set of 2 3.00 3.00

Ministry of the Interior, 55th Anniv. A1702

2016, June 5 Litho. ***Perf. 12¾***
5823 A1702 90c multi 1.90 1.90

Western Army, 55th Anniv. — A1703

Perf. 12½x12¼

2016, June 14 Litho.
5824 A1703 65c multi 1.40 1.40

Center for Genetic Engineering and Biotechnology, 30th Anniv. — A1704

2016, July 1 Litho. ***Perf. 12¾***
5825 A1704 90c multi 1.90 1.90

Cuban Amateur Radio Federation, 50th Anniv. — A1705

2016, July 15 Litho. ***Perf. 12¼x12½***
5826 A1705 1.05p multi 2.10 2.10

Miguel de Cervantes (c. 1547-1616), Writer — A1706

William Shakespeare (1564-1616), Writer — A1707

No. 5827: a, Don Quixote and windmill. b, Cervantes and quotation.
No. 5828: a, Roses and dagger. b, Shakespeare and quotation.

2016, Apr. 23 Litho. ***Perf. 12½x12¼***
5827 A1706 65c Horiz. pair, #a-b 2.60 2.60
5828 A1707 75c Horiz. pair, #a-b 3.00 3.00

Ships A1708

Designs: 15c, López Mena, Argentina and Uruguay. 30c, Beringov Proliv, Russia. 50c, Tûranor PlanetSolar, Switzerland. 65c, Horizon Ferry, Singapore. 75c, Adastra, Hong Kong. 85c, Madame Gu, Netherlands.
1p, Siem Moxie, Norway, vert.

2016, May 28 Litho. ***Perf. 12½x12¼***
5829-5834 A1708 Set of 6 6.50 6.50

Souvenir Sheet

Imperf

5835 A1708 1p multi 2.00 2.00

No. 5835 contains one 33x49mm stamp with simulated perforations.

Ministry of Transportation, 55th Anniv. — A1709

2016, Aug. 3 Litho. ***Perf. 12½x12¼***
5836 A1709 3p multi 6.00 6.00

Desembarco del Granma National Park — A1710

Designs: 65c, Cabo Cruz Lighthouse, Thalasseus maximus. 75c, Terrace system, Plumeria sp. 85c, Coccothrinax saxicola, Polymita venusta. 90c, Hoyo de Morlotte, Liguus vittatus.

2016, Aug. 13 Litho. ***Perf. 12¾***
5837-5840 A1710 Set of 4 6.50 6.50

2016 Summer Olympics, Rio de Janeiro — A1711

Designs: 10c, Boxing. 20c, Rowing. 30c, Volleyball, vert. 65c, Wrestling, vert. 75c, Judo. 85c, Taekwondo.
1p, Running, vert.

Perf. 12½x12¼, 12¼x12½

2016, Aug. 21 Litho.
5841-5846 A1711 Set of 6 5.75 5.75

Souvenir Sheet

Imperf

5847 A1711 1p multi 2.00 2.00

No. 5835 has simulated perforations.

Mella Theater, Havana, 55th Anniv. — A1712

Perf. 12¼x12½

2016, Sept. 10 Litho.
5848 A1712 1.05p multi 2.10 2.10

University Student Federation's Relief Performance for Alicia Alonso, 60th Anniv. — A1713

2016, Sept. 15 Litho. ***Perf. 12¾***
5849 A1713 90c multi 1.90 1.90

Caricatos Talent Agency, 16th Anniv. — A1714

Designs: 65c, Enrique Almirante (1930-2007), actor. 90c, Raúl Pomares (1934-2015), actor and director.

2016, Sept. 24 Litho. ***Perf. 12¾***
5850-5851 A1714 Set of 2 3.25 3.25

Copextel, 25th Anniv. — A1715

2016, Oct. 6 Litho. ***Perf. 12¾***
5852 A1715 75c multi 1.50 1.50

2016 Summer Olympics, Rio de Janeiro — A1716

Designs: No. 5853, 65c, 90-day journey of Olympic torch from Mt. Olympus to Rio de Janeiro. No. 5854, 65c, Rio de Janeiro, first South American host city of Olympics. No. 5855, 65c, Golf returns as Olympic sport. No. 5856, 65c, Rugby returns as an Olympic sport.

2016, Oct. 12 Litho. ***Perf. 12¼x12½***
5853-5856 A1716 Set of 4 5.25 5.25

Asociación Hermanos Saíz (Hip-Hop and Rap Music Promotional Organization), 30th Anniv. — A1717

2016, Oct. 18 Litho. ***Perf. 12¼x12½***
5857 A1717 75c multi 1.50 1.50

Alicia Alonso International Festival of Ballet, Havana, 25th Anniv. — A1718

Designs: 15c, Dido Abandonada. 35c, Ad Libitum. 40c, La Diva. 65c, Elegía por un Joven. 75c, Tula, horiz. 85c, Cascanueces, horiz.
1p, Carmen, horiz.

Perf. 12¼x12½, 12½x12¼

2016, Oct. 28 **Litho.**

5858-5863 A1718 Set of 6 6.50 6.50

Souvenir Sheet

Imperf

5864 A1718 1p multi 2.00 2.00

No. 5864 has simulated perforations.

Fire Brigades in Cuba, 320th Anniv. — A1719

Designs: 5c, Fire fighters and horse-drawn wagon, 1898. 10c, Havana fire fighters, 1920. 15c, DGPCI fire fighters, 1985. 40c, Fire fighters with hose, 2016. 65c, Fire fighter on rope, 2016. 85c, Fire fighter with rescue dog, 2016.
1p, Fire fighter Enriqueta Reyes, 1957, vert.

Perf. 12½x12¼

2016, Nov. 13 **Litho.**

5865-5870 A1719 Set of 6 4.50 4.50

Souvenir Sheet

Imperf

5871 A1719 1p multi 2.00 2.00

No. 5871 contains one 33x44mm stamp with simulated perforations.

Road Safety Day A1720

Designs: 10c, Surveyors. 15c, Bus at bus stop. 45c, Car testing. 75c, Motorcyclist and bicylist. 85c, Person being put in ambulance.

Perf. 12½x12¼

2016, Nov. 16 **Litho.**

5872-5876 A1720 Set of 5 4.75 4.75

Return of Fidel Castro to Cuba on the Granma, 60th Anniv. — A1721

Designs: 65c, Granma and map of voyage. 75c, Cuban revolutionary soldier.

Perf. 12½x12¼

2016, Nov. 25 **Litho.**

5877-5878 A1721 Set of 2 3.00 3.00

Lt. General José Antonio de la Caridad Maceo y Grajales (1845-96) A1722

Maceo: 50c, On horse. 65c, On rearing horse.

2016, Dec. 7 **Litho.** ***Perf. 12¾***

5879-5880 A1722 Set of 2 3.00 3.00

Flora and Fauna of Pico Turquino National Park — A1723

Designs: 40c, Anetia briarea numidia. 65c, Lepanthes turquinoensis. 75c, Spindalis zena. 85c, Cysticopsis.

Perf. 12¼x12½

2016, Dec. 15 **Litho.**

5881-5884 A1723 Set of 4 5.50 5.50

Declaration of Melena del Sur as First Cuban Municipality Free of Illiteracy, 55th Anniv. — A1724

Perf. 12¼x12½

2016, Dec. 22 **Litho.**

5885 A1724 65c multi 1.40 1.40

Gibara, 200th Anniv. — A1725

Designs: 75c, Calixto García Park. 85c, Gibara Bay.

2017, Jan. 17 **Litho.** ***Perf. 12½x12¼***

5886-5887 A1725 Set of 2 3.25 3.25

Special Education in Cuba, 55th Anniv. — A1726

2017, Jan. 18 **Litho.** ***Perf. 12½x12¼***

5888 A1726 1.05p multi 2.10 2.10

Cuban Theater Day — A1727

Designs: 10c, *Aire Frío,* play by Virgilio Piñera. 15c, National Folklore Group. 35c, Raquel Revuelta in *Madre Coraje*. 40c, National Lyrical Theater production of *The Magic Flute.* 50c, Roberto Blanco, vert. 75c, Vicente Revuelta in *Galileo Galilei*, vert.
1p, Villanueva Theater events

Perf. 12½x12¼, 12¼x12½

2017, Jan. 22 **Litho.**

5889-5894 A1727 Set of 6 4.50 4.50

Souvenir Sheet

Imperf

5895 A1727 1p multi 2.00 2.00

No. 5895 contains one 49x33mm stamp with simulated perforations.

Cuban Coast Guard Boat A1728

2017, Feb. 8 **Litho.** ***Perf. 12½x12¼***

5896 A1728 3p multi 6.00 6.00

Shipbuilding Slips at Boca de Jaruco, 500th Anniv. — A1729

2017, Mar. 8 **Litho.** ***Perf. 12½x12¼***

5897 A1729 65c multi 1.40 1.40

Birds of Guanahacabibes Peninsula Reserve, 30th Anniv. — A1730

Designs: 65c, Elanoides forficatus, Roncali Lighthouse, map. 75c, Ictinia mississippiensis. 85c, Pandion haliaetus. 90c, Falco peregrinus.

2017, Mar. 16 **Litho.** ***Perf. 12¾***

5898-5901 A1730 Set of 4 6.50 6.50

Cuban Oil Union, 25th Anniv. A1731

Perf. 12½x12¼

2017, Mar. 25 **Litho.**

5902 A1731 85c multi 1.75 1.75

Birds and Lighthouses A1732

Designs: No. 5903, 90c, Buteogallus gundlachii, Columbus Lighthouse, Cayo Sabinal, Cuba. No. 5904, 90c, Athene cunicularia arubensis, California Lighthouse, Aruba. No. 5905, 90c, Calliphlox evelynae, Hope Town Lighthouse, Elbow Cay, Bahamas. No. 5906, 90c, Aratinga acuticaudata neoxena, Punta Zaragoza Lighthouse, Isla Margarita, Venezuela.

2017, Apr. 1 **Litho.** ***Perf. 12¼x12½***

5903-5906 A1732 Set of 4 7.25 7.25

Young Communist League, 55th Anniv. — A1733

2017, Apr. 3 **Litho.** ***Perf. 12½x12¼***

5907 A1733 65c multi 1.40 1.40

José Martí Program, 20th Anniv. — A1734

2017, Apr. 6 **Litho.** ***Perf. 12¾***

5908 A1734 90c multi 1.90 1.90

Antes del Alba Ballet, 70th Anniv. — A1735

Various sketches for costumes for ballet by Carlos Enríquez: 10c, 15c, 30c, 50c, 75c, 90c.
1p, Ballerina in costume.

2017, Apr. 20 **Litho.** ***Perf. 12¾***

5909-5914 A1735 Set of 6 5.50 5.50

Souvenir Sheet

Imperf

5915 A1735 1p multi 2.00 2.00

No. 5915 has simulated perforations.

Gran Teatro de La Habana Alicia Alonso, 180th Anniv. A1736

Designs: 10c, Illustration of theater in 19th century. 15c, Stage, 1856. 40c, Theater, 1953. 65c, García Lorca Hall, 2016. 75c, Stage, 2016. 85c, Ceiling, lamp and balconies, 2016.
1p, Illustration of coach outside of theater.

2017, Apr. 22 Litho. *Perf. 12¾*
5916-5921 A1736 Set of 6 6.00 6.00

Souvenir Sheet
Imperf

5922 A1736 1p multi 2.00 2.00

No. 5922 has simulated perforations.

Birds of Prey — A1737

Designs: 10c, Falco sparverius. 35c, Falco columbarius. 65c, Buteogallus anthracinus. 75c, Rostrhamus sociabilis. 85c, Buteo platypterus. 90c, Glaucidium siju.
1p, Athene cunicularia.

2017, Jan. 16 Litho. *Perf. 12¾*
5923-5928 A1737 Set of 6 7.25 7.25

Souvenir Sheet
Imperf

5929 A1737 1p multi 2.00 2.00

No. 5929 has simulated perforations.

Bees A1738

Designs: 5c, Apis mellifera sentellata. 20c, Apis cerana. 65c, Apis mellifera ligustica. 75c, Apis mellifera carnica. 85c, Apis mellifera lamarckii. 90c, Megachile centuncularis.
1p, Apis mellifera mellifera.

2017, Feb. 11 Litho. *Perf. 12¾*
5930-5935 A1738 Set of 6 7.00 7.00

Souvenir Sheet
Imperf

5936 A1738 1p multi 2.00 2.00

No. 5936 has simulated perforations.

Technology — A1739

Designs: 40c, Software and video games. 45c, Digital television. 65c, Wi-fi. 75c, Internet.

Perf. 12½x12¼
2017, Mar. 15 Litho.
5937-5940 A1739 Set of 4 4.50 4.50

National Flowers — A1740

Flower and map of: 5c, Peristeria elata, Panama. 15c, Guarianthe skinneri, Costa Rica. 20c, Rose, United States. 30c, Guaiacum officinale, Jamaica, vert. 40c, Pereskia quisqueyana, Dominican Republic. 65c, Warszewiczia coccinea, Trinidad & Tobago. 75c, Ixora coccinea, Surinam. 90c, Prosthechea cochleata, Belize, vert.

Perf. 12½x12¼, 12¼x12½
2017, May 26 Litho.
5941-5948 A1740 Set of 8 7.00 7.00

Admission of Cuba to the United Nations, 70th Anniv. — A1741

2017, May 29 Litho. *Perf. 12¼x12½*
5949 A1741 85c multi 1.75 1.75

Ministry of the Interior Fighters Who Died in Bolivia With Ernesto "Che" Guevara in 1968 — A1742

2017, June 5 Litho. *Perf. 12¾*
5950 A1742 75c multi 1.50 1.50

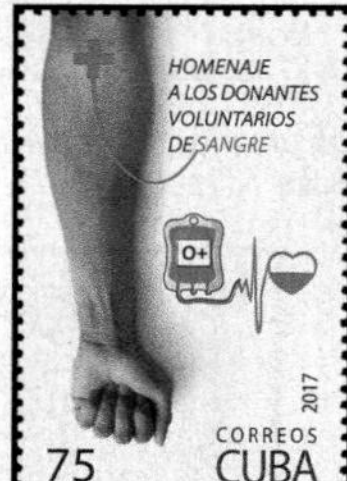

Blood Donation A1743

2017, June 8 Litho. *Perf. 12¼x12½*
5951 A1743 75c multi 1.50 1.50

Artistic Agency of Performing Arts (ACTUAR), 38th Anniv. — A1744

Designs: 65c, Alden Knight, actor. 85c, Rosita Fornes, actress.

2017, July 3 Litho. *Perf. 12¾*
5952-5953 A1744 Set of 2 3.00 3.00

World Environment Day — A1745

Designs: 10c, Sea turtles on beach, Guanahacabibes Peninsula Biosphere Reserve. 15c, Hutia, Sierra del Rosario Biosphere Reserve, horiz. 20c, Cuban crocodile, Ciénaga de Zapata Biosphere Reserve, horiz. 35c, Flamingos, Buenavista Biosphere Reserve, horiz. 85c, Cuban tody, Baconao Biosphere Reserve. 90c, Cuban land snail, Cuchillas del Toa Biosphere Reserve, horiz.
1p, Coral reef, Guanahacabibes Peninsula Biosphere Reserve.

Perf. 12¼x12½, 12½x12¼
2017, July 5 Litho.
5954-5959 A1745 Set of 6 5.25 5.25

Souvenir Sheet
Imperf

5960 A1745 1p multi 2.00 2.00

No. 5960 has simulated perforations.

Helicopters — A1746

Designs: 10c, Eurocopter HH-65 Dolphin. 15c, Westland WS-61 Sea King. 30c, MBB/Kawasaki BK117. 75c, Sikorsky S-92. 85c, Kamov Ka-32A11BC. 90c, Agusta Westland CH-149 Cormorant.
1p, Mil Mi-17.

2017, July 15 Litho. *Perf. 12½x12¼*
5961-5966 A1746 Set of 6 6.25 6.25

Souvenir Sheet
Imperf

5967 A1746 1p multi 2.00 2.00

No. 5967 has simulated perforations.

Cintio Vitier (1921-2009), Poet — A1747

2017, July 19 Litho. *Perf. 12¾*
5968 A1747 65c multi 1.40 1.40

Center for José Martí Studies, 40th anniv.

Course of Study for Childhood Nursing, 130th Anniv. — A1748

Designs: 50c, Nurse examining woman. 75c, Nurse treating child.

2017, July 28 Litho. *Perf. 12½x12¼*
5969-5970 A1748 Set of 2 2.50 2.50

Civil Defense, 55th Anniv. — A1749

2017, July 31 Litho. *Perf. 12½x12¼*
5971 A1749 75c multi 1.50 1.50

Continuous Broadcasting of Radio Cubana, 95th Anniv. — A1750

Perf. 12½x12¼
2017, Aug. 15 Litho.
5972 A1750 75c multi 1.50 1.50

Cuban National Commission of UNESCO, 70th Anniv. — A1751

No. 5973 — Buildings and: a, Woman. b, Man playing drum.

Perf. 12¼x12½
2017, Aug. 29 Litho.
5973 A1751 75c Vert. pair, #a-b 3.00 3.00

September 5, 1957 Cienfuegos Uprising, 60th Anniv. — A1752

Buildings and: 65c, Man waving flag. 75c, Men with rifles.

2017, Sept. 5 Litho. *Perf. 12½x12¼*
5974-5975 A1752 Set of 2 3.00 3.00

Youth Electronics and Computing Club, 30th Anniv. — A1753

2017, Sept. 7 Litho. *Perf. 12½x12¼*
5976 A1753 75c multi 1.50 1.50

First Protest Song Festival, 50th Anniv. — A1754

2017, Sept. 8 Litho. *Perf. 12¼x12½*
5977 A1754 65c multi 1.40 1.40

Miniature Sheet

Capture and Execution of Ernesto "Che" Guevara (1928-67), 50th Anniv. — A1755

No. 5978: a, Guevara and cover of his Bolivian Diary. b, Map and Guevara holding rifle. c, Guevara and other guerrilla fighters. d, Monument to Guevara, La Higuera, Bolivia.

2017, Oct. 8 Litho. ***Perf. 12½x12¼***
5978 A1755 85c Sheet of 4, #a-d 7.00 7.00

University of Oriente, 70th Anniv. — A1756

2017, Oct. 10 Litho. ***Perf. 12½x12¼***
5979 A1756 65c multi 1.40 1.40

National Pharmaceutical Association, 110th Anniv. — A1757

2017, Oct. 10 Litho. ***Perf. 12¼x12½***
5980 A1757 90c multi 1.90 1.90

America Issue — A1758

Tourist attractions: No. 5981, 65c, Valle de Viñales. No. 5982, 65c, Ciudad Trinidad. No. 5983, 65c, Ciénaga de Zapata. No. 5984, 65c, Playa Santa Lucía.

2017, Oct. 12 Litho. ***Perf. 12½x12¼***
5981-5984 A1758 Set of 4 5.25 5.25

Beaches A1759

Designs: 5c, Playa Sirena. 20c, Playa Santa Lucía, horiz. 40c, Playa Pilar, horiz. 45c, Playa Varadero, horiz. 75c, Playa Ensenachos. 85c, Playa Ancón, horiz.
1p, Playa Guardalavaca.

Perf. 12¼x12½, 12½x12¼
2017, Oct. 24 Litho.
5985-5990 A1759 Set of 6 5.50 5.50

Souvenir Sheet

Imperf

5991 A1759 1p multi 2.00 2.00

No. 5991 contains one 42x29mm stamp that has simulated perforations.

Tropical Food Research Institute, 50th Anniv. — A1760

2017, Oct. 27 Litho. ***Perf. 12½x12¼***
5992 A1760 65c multi 1.40 1.40

Brasiliana 2017 International Philatelic Exhibition, Brasilia, Brazil — A1761

Birds: 5c, Cardenilla dominica (red-cowled cardinal). 15c, Guaruba guarouba, vert. 45c, Tangara cyanoventris. 75c, Ramphodon naevius. 85c, Cotinga maculata, vert. 90c, Antilophia bokermanni.
1p, Anodorhynchus leari.

Perf. 12½x12¼, 12¼x12½
2017, Nov. 1 Litho.
5993-5998 A1761 Set of 6 6.50 6.50

Souvenir Sheet

Imperf

5999 A1761 1p multi 2.00 2.00

No. 5999 has simulated perforations.

Ignacio Agramonte Loynaz University of Camagüey, 50th Anniv. — A1762

2017, Nov. 6 Litho. ***Perf. 12¼x12½***
6000 A1762 90c multi 1.90 1.90

October Revolution, Cent. — A1763

Designs: 75c, Lenin Memorial, Lenin Hill, Havana. 85c, Sculpture of Worker and Kolkhoz Woman, Moscow.

2017, Nov. 7 Litho. ***Perf. 12¼x12½***
6001-6002 A1763 Set of 2 3.25 3.25

Endangered Animals — A1764

Designs: 15c, Polar bear. 30c, Orangutan. 50c, Sperm whale. 75c, Bengal tiger. 85c, African elephants. 90c, Kangaroos.
1p, Cuban solenodon.

Perf. 12½x12¼
2017, Nov. 15 Litho.
6003-6008 A1764 Set of 6 7.00 7.00

Souvenir Sheet

Imperf

6009 A1764 1p multi 2.00 2.00

No. 6009 contains one 45x29mm stamp that has simulated perforations.

José María Pérez Capote (1911-57), Executed Labor Leader — A1765

Perf. 12½x12¼
2017, Nov. 20 Litho.
6010 A1765 85c multi 1.75 1.75

First Railway In Cuba, 180th Anniv. — A1766

Perf. 12½x12¼
2017, Nov. 20 Litho.
6011 A1766 90c multi 1.90 1.90

Marta Abreu Cental University, Las Villas, 65th Anniv. — A1767

Perf. 12½x12¼
2017, Nov. 30 Litho.
6012 A1767 65c multi 1.40 1.40

National Union of Culture Workers, 40th Anniv. — A1768

Perf. 12½x12¼
2017, Dec. 14 Litho.
6013 A1768 75c multi 1.50 1.50

Reactivation of Camilo Cienfuegos Oil Refinery, 10th Anniv. — A1769

Cienfuegos and various oil tankers and smokestacks: 15c, 35c, 50c, 85c.

Perf. 12¼x12½
2017, Dec. 21 Litho.
6014-6017 A1769 Set of 4 3.75 3.75

Life of José Martí (1853-95), National Hero — A1770

Martí: 10c, With his sisters, 1864. 15c, With teacher at school, 1868. 20c, Holding manuscript, 1875. 45c, With his family, 1879. 65c, At home, 1890. 75c, As delegate of Cuban Revolutionary Party, 1892.

2018, Jan. 27 Litho. ***Perf. 12½x12¼***
6018-6023 A1770 Set of 6 4.75 4/75

Cuban Chamber of Commerce, 55th Anniv. — A1771

2018, Feb. 1 Litho. ***Perf. 12½x12¼***
6024 A1771 65c multi 1.40 1.40

Pedro Felipe Figueredo Cisneros (1818-70), composer of Cuban National Anthem — A1772

Perf. 12½x12¼
2018, Feb. 18 Litho.
6025 A1772 75c multi 1.50 1.50

Endangered Birds — A1773

Designs: 10c, Branta ruficollis. 30c, Amazona oratrix. 65c, Porphyrio martello. 75c, Harpyhailaetus coronatus. 85c, Rhynochetos jubatus. 90c, Crax rubra.
1p, Tyrannus cubensis.

Perf. 12½x12¼
2018, Feb. 20 Litho.
6026-6031 A1773 Set of 6 7.25 7.25

Souvenir Sheet

Imperf

6032 A1773 1p multi 2.00 2.00

No. 6032 has simulated perforations.

Specialized Communications of the Revolutionary Armed Forces, 60th Anniv — A1774

2018, Feb. 21 Litho. *Perf. 12¾*
6033 A1774 65c multi 1.40 1.40

2018 World Cup Soccer Championships, Russia — A1775

Soccer player and flags of competing countries in: 10c, Group A. 15c, Group E. 35c, Group B. 50c, Group F. 65c, Group C. 75c, Group G. 85c, Group D. 90c, Group H.
1p, Mascot of 2018 World Cup.

2018, Mar. 5 Litho. *Perf. 12½x12¼*
6034-6041 A1775 Set of 8 8.50 8.50

Souvenir Sheet

Imperf

6042 A1775 1p multi 2.00 2.00

No. 6042 contains one 48x32mm stamp with simulated perforations.

Che Guevara International Pedagogical Detachment, 40th Anniv. — A1776

2018, Mar. 8 Litho. *Perf. 12½x12¼*
6043 A1776 90c multi 1.90 1.90

Cuban Military Mission to Ethiopia, 40th Anniv. — A1777

2018, Mar. 9 Litho. *Perf. 12¼x12½*
6044 A1777 85c multi 1.75 1.75

Marius Petipa (1818-1910), Ballet Dancer and Choreographer A1778

Designs: 85c, Petipa. 90c, Alicia Alonso in *Don Quixote.*

Perf. 12¼x12½

2018, Mar. 11 Litho.
6045-6046 A1778 Set of 2 3.50 3.50

Baraguá Protest, 140th Anniv. — A1779

Perf. 12¼x12½

2018, Mar. 15 Litho.
6047 A1779 65c multi 1.40 1.40

Labor Day — A1780

2018, Apr. 20 Litho. *Perf. 12¼x12½*
6048 A1780 65c multi 1.40 1.40

Transportation for Tourists — A1781

Designs: 10c, Motorcycle. 15c, 1950's convertible. 40c, Bicycle. 65c, Double-decker bus. 75c, Catamaran. 85c, Recreational vehicle.

2018, Apr. 30 Litho. *Perf. 12½x12¼*
6049-6054 A1781 Set of 6 6.00 6.00

Segundo Cabo Palace, Havana — A1782

2018, May 9 Litho. *Perf. 12¼x12½*
6055 A1782 75c multi 1.50 1.50

Cuban Day Against Homophobia and Transphobia — A1783

2018, May 10 Litho. *Perf. 12½x12¼*
6056 A1783 75c multi 1.50 1.50

Marine Life A1784

Designs: 10c, Abyssobrotula galatheae. 20c, Anoplogaster cornuta. 45c, Oxynotus caribbaeus. 75c, Mithrax spinosissimus. 90c, Scarus coeruleus. 1.05p, Megalops atlanticus.
1p, Mulloidichthys martinicus.

2018, May 15 Litho. *Perf. 12½x12¼*
6057-6062 A1784 Set of 6 7.00 7.00

Souvenir Sheet

Imperf

6063 A1784 1p multi 2.00 2.00

No. 6063 has simulated perforations.

Flora of Western Hemisphere Nations — A1785

Designs: 10c, Passiflora edulis, Paraguay. 15c, Tabebuia chrysotricha, Brazil, vert. 20c, Yucca elephantipes, El Salvador. 30c, Cantua buxifolia, Peru, vert. 40c, Victoria amazonica, Guyana. 65c, Acer saccharum leaf, Canada, vert. 75c, Lycaste skinneri, Guatemala. 90c, Cattleya trianae, Colombia, vert.

Perf. 12½x12¼, 12¼x12½

2018, May 26 Litho.
6064-6071 A1785 Set of 8 7.00 7.00

Miniature Sheet

Ernesto "Che" Guevara (1928-67), Guerilla Leader and Finance Minister — A1786

No. 6072 — Guevara: a, With cinder block and handcart. b, With podium. c, Playing chess. d, With cameras.

Perf. 12½x12¼

2018, June 14 Litho.
6072 A1786 90c Sheet of 4, #a-d 7.25 7.25

Health and Medicine Achievements — A1787

Designs: 40c, Dr. Carlos M. Ramírez Corría (1903-77), neurosurgeon. 50c, Cuban Institute of Ocular Microsurgery, 30th anniv. 65c, First international medical mission by Cubans, 55th anniv. 75c, Cuban Pediatrics Society, 90th anniv.

2018, July 4 Litho. *Perf. 12½x12¼*
6073-6076 A1787 Set of 4 4.75 4.75

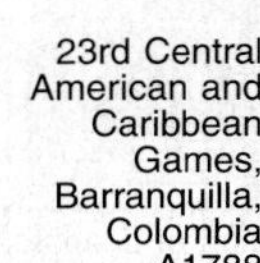

23rd Central American and Caribbean Games, Barranquilla, Colombia A1788

Cuban athletes: 65c, Raúl Cascaret (1962-95), wrestler. 75c, Basketball players in 1982 Cuba vs. Puerto Rico game. 85c, Player on National baseball team. 90c, Teofilo Stevenson (1952-2012), boxer.

2018, July 13 Litho. *Perf. 12¼x12½*
6077-6080 A1788 Set of 4 6.50 6.50

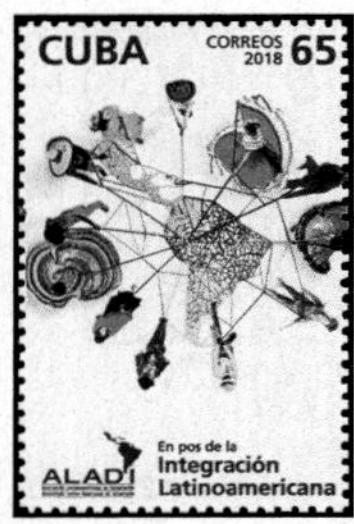

Latin American Integration Association A1789

2018, July 23 Litho. *Perf. 12¼x12½*
6081 A1789 65c multi 1.40 1.40

Horses — A1790

Designs: 10c, Percheron horse. 40c, Argentine polo ponies. 45c, Appaloosa horse. 75c, Trakehner horse. 85c, Lippizaner horses. 90c, Mustangs.
1p, Przewalski's horse.

Perf. 12½x12¼

2018, Aug. 30 Litho.
6082-6087 A1790 Set of 6 7.00 7.00

Souvenir Sheet

Imperf

6088 A1790 1p multi 2.00 2.00

2018 Thailand World Stamp Exhibition, Bangkok. No. 6088 has simulated perforations.

First World Championship of Cuban Women's Volleyball Team, 40th Anniv. — A1791

No. 6089: a, Team photograph. b, Player hitting ball over net.

2018, Sept. 6 Litho. *Perf. 12½x12¼*
6089 A1791 65c Horiz. pair, #a-b 2.60 2.60

Cuban Criminal Forensics, 55th Anniv. — A1792

2018, Sept. 7 Litho. *Perf. 12½x12¼*
6090 A1792 65c multi 1.40 1.40

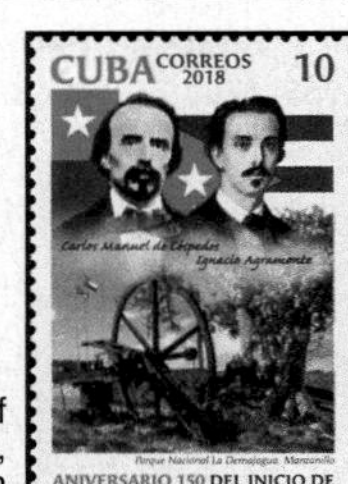

Cuban War of Independence, 150th Anniv. — A1793

Flag of Cuba and: 10c, Carlos Manuel de Céspedes (1819-74), Ignacio Agramonte (1841-73), revolution heroes, La Demajagua National Park. 15c, Mariana Grajales (1808-93), mother of Lieutenant General Antonio Maceo (1845-96) and Major General José Maceo (1849-96), Mangos de Baraguá Monument. 30c, José Martí (1853-95), national hero, Major General Máximo Gómez (1836-1905), General Calixto García (1839-98), Monument to the Invading Soldier, Mantua. 45c, Julio Antonio Mella (1903-29), founder of Cuban Communist Party, Rubén Martínez Villena (1899-1934), revolutionary leader, Antonio Guiteras (1906-35), politician, University of Havana. 65c, Aracelio Iglesias (1901-48), union leader, Jesús Menéndez (1911-48), union leader, Lázaro Peña (1911-74), labor leader, Society of Cigar Rollers Building, Havana. 75c, Abel Santamaría (1927-53), Frank País (1934-57), and José A. Echeverría (1932-57), leaders of revolution against Fulgencio Batista, Moncada Barracks, Santiago de Cuba. 85c, Ernesto "Che" Guevara (1928-67), guerilla leader, Celia Sánchez (1920-80), revolution leader, Camilo Cienfuegos (1932-59), revolution leader, Rebel Army General Command Headquarters, La Plata. 90c, Pres. Fidel Castro (1926-2016), José Martí Monument, Revolution Square, Havana.

2018, Oct. 10 Litho. *Perf. 12¼x12½*
6091-6098 A1793 Set of 8 8.50 8.50

Domesticated Animals — A1794

No. 6099, 65c: a, Horses and donkey. b, Cows.
No. 6100, 65c: a, Chickens. b, Bee.

2018, Oct. 12 Litho. *Perf. 12½x12¼*
Horiz. pairs, #a-b
6099-6100 A1794 Set of 2 5.25 5.25

America issue.

Cuban National Ballet, 70th Anniv. — A1795

Designs: 30c, Alicia Alonso and Igor Youskevitch in *The Nutcracker.* 35c, Dancers in *Tribute to José White.* 50c, Dancers in *Rítmicas.* 65c, Dancers in *Despertar (The Awakening).* 75c, Dancers in *Tarde in la Siesta (Late in the Afternoon).* 90c, Dancers in *Swan Lake.*
1p, Dancer in *La Avanzada.*

2018, Oct. 28 Litho. *Perf. 12¼x12½*
6101-6106 A1795 Set of 6 7.00 7.00

Souvenir Sheet

Imperf

6107 A1795 1p multi 2.00 2.00

No. 6107 has simulated perforations.

Birds — A1796

Designs: 10c, Colaptes fernandinae. 30c, Teretistris fernandinae, horiz. 65c, Icterus melanopsis, horiz. 75c, Caprimulgus cubanensis. 85c, Dives atroviolaceus. 90c, Gymnoglaux lawrencii, horiz.
1p, Buteogallus gundlachii.

2018, Nov. 3 Litho. *Perf. 12¾*
6108-6113 A1796 Set of 6 7.25 7.25

Souvenir Sheet

Imperf

6114 A1796 1p multi 2.00 2.00

15th Philatelic Congress. No. 6114 has simulated perforations.

Restoration of Arango y Parreño House, Havana — A1797

2018, Nov. 8 Litho. *Perf. 12¼x12½*
6115 A1797 65c multi 1.40 1.40

Palacio de Marqués de Arcos, Havana — A1798

2018, Nov. 8 Litho. *Perf. 12¼x12½*
6116 A1798 75c multi 1.50 1.50

José Raúl Capablanca (1888-1942), World Chess Champion — A1799

Capablanca: No. 6117, 1.05p, With chessboard and clock. No. 6118, 1.05p, Playing many opponents simultaneously. No. 6119, 1.05p, Playing chess, vert.

2018, Nov. 19 Litho. *Perf. 12¾*
6117-6119 A1799 Set of 3 6.50 6.50

Association of Combatants of the Cuban Revolution, 25th Anniv. — A1800

2018, Dec. 7 Litho. *Perf. 12½x12¼*
6120 A1800 65c multi 1.40 1.40

Major General Ignacio Agramonte (1841-73) A1801

Perf. 12¼x12½
2018, Dec. 23 Litho.
6121 A1801 65c multi 1.40 1.40

Office of the Attorney General, 45th anniv.

Battle of Santa Clara, 60th Anniv. A1802

Perf. 12½x12¼
2018, Dec. 30 Litho.
6122 A1802 75c multi 1.50 1.50

National Revolutionary Police Force, 60th Anniv. — A1803

2019, Jan. 5 Litho. *Perf. 12¼x12½*
6123 A1803 2.05p multi 4.25 4.25

Worker's Central Union of Cuba, 60th Anniv. — A1804

2019, Jan. 28 Litho. *Perf. 12¼x12½*
6124 A1804 75c multi 1.50 1.50

Souvenir Sheet

Statue of José Martí, by Anna Hyatt Huntington — A1805

2019, Jan. 28 Litho. *Imperf.*
6125 A1805 1p multi 2.00 2.00

Fourth International Congress for World Equilibrium, Havana. No. 6125 has simulated perforations.

Tenth Congress of the Federation of Cuban Women, Havana — A1806

Flag of Cuba, sword and: 5c, Ana Betancourt (1832-1901), Candelario Figueredo (1852-1914), patriots. 10c, Bernarda del Toro (1852-1911), wife of Major General Máximo Gómez, María Cabrales (1842-1905), wife of Lieutenant General Antonio Maceo. 20c, Rosa Castellanos (1834-1907), nurse, Adela Azcuy (1861-1914), nurse and poet. 30c, Lidia Doce (1916-58), Clodomira Acosta (1936-58), members of Cuban Rebel Army. 75c, Haydée Santamaría (1922-80), Melba Hernández (1921-2014), politicians. 85c, Celia Sánchez (1920-80), politician, Vilma Espín (1930-2007), Federation founder.

2019, Mar. 4 Litho. *Perf. 12½x12¼*
6126-6131 A1806 Set of 6 4.50 4.50

Souvenir Sheet

Santiago Alvarez (1919-98), Documentary Filmmaker — A1807

2019, Mar. 18 Litho. *Imperf.*
6132 A1807 1p multi 2.00 2.00

No. 6132 has simulated perforations.

Souvenir Sheet

Alejandro Robaina (1919-2010), Tobacco Grower — A1808

2019, Mar. 20 Litho. *Imperf.*
6133 A1808 1p multi 2.00 2.00

No. 6133 has simulated perforations.

Cuban Institute of Cinematographic Art and Industry, 60th Anniv. — A1809

Movie posters and scenes: 5c, *The Adventures of Juan Quin Quin,* directed by Julio García Espinosa (1926-2016). 10c, *Historias de la Revolución,* directed by Tomás Gutiérrez Alea (1928-96). 20c, *The Last Supper,* directed by Gutiérrez Alea. 75c, *Vampires in Havana,* directed by Juan Padrón. 85c, *José Martí: el Ojo de Canario,* directed by Fernando Pérez. 90c, *Conducta,* directed by Ernesto Daranas Serrano.

Perf. 12½x12¼

2019, Mar. 24 **Litho.**
6134-6139 A1809 Set of 6 5.75 5.75

State Security and Intelligence Organizations, 60th Anniv. — A1810

Perf. 12¼x12½

2019, Mar. 26 **Litho.**
6140 A1810 65c multi 1.40 1.40

Recording Artists — A1811

Designs: 30c, Rafael Somavilla (1927-80), orchestra leader. 35c, César Portillo de la Luz (1922-2013), musician. 65c, Celina González (1929-2015), singer. 75c, Juan Formell (1942-2014), musician.

Perf. 12½x12¼

2019, Mar. 31 **Litho.**
6141-6144 A1811 Set of 4 4.25 4.25

EGREM (national recording label), 55th anniv.

Verde Olivo Magazine, 60th Anniv. — A1812

2019, Apr. 9 **Litho.** ***Perf. 12¼x12½***
6145 A1812 85c multi 1.75 1.75

Forest Rangers, 60th Anniv. — A1813

2019, Apr. 10 **Litho.** ***Perf. 12¼x12½***
6146 A1813 75c multi 1.50 1.50

Cienfuegos, 200th Anniv. — A1814

No. 6147: a, 40c, La India Guanaroca, sculpture by Rita Longa, flamingos on Guanaroca Lake. b, 45c, Fortress of Nuesta Señora de los Angeles de Jagua, flag of Cienfuegos. c, 65c, Turnera ulmifolia, Old Town Hall. d, 75c, Founding of Fernandina de Jagua Colony, Now Cienfuegos, by Juan Roldán and Eduardo Carbonell.

1p, Coat of arms of Cienfuegos, Statue of José Martí.

2019, Apr. 22 **Litho.** ***Perf. 12½x12¼***
6147 A1814 Block of 4, #a-d 4.50 4.50

Souvenir Sheet

Imperf

6148 A1814 1p multi 2.00 2.00

No. 6148 has simulated perforations.

Carlos Manuel de Céspedes del Castillo (1819-74), National Hero, and Birthplace Museum, Bayamo — A1815

2019, Apr. 18 **Litho.** ***Perf. 12½x12¼***
6149 A1815 85c multi 1.75 1.75

Aboriginal Cultural Heritage — A1816

Designs: 5c, Yagua fiber sieve, woman making basket. 10c, Stone sculpture, traditional houses. 20c, Sandstone sculpture, traditional medicine. 30c, Fertility idol, farmers. 85c, Cassava tuber, food preparation. 90c, Tobacco implements, aborigines and modern people smoking.

1p, Dancers and musicians.

2019, Apr. 24 **Litho.** ***Perf. 12½x12¼***
6150-6155 A1816 Set of 6 5.00 5.00

Souvenir Sheet

Imperf

6156 A1816 1p multi 2.00 2.00

No. 6156 has simulated perforations.

Labor Day — A1817

2019, Apr. 26 **Litho.** ***Perf. 12¼x12½***
6157 A1817 65c red & black 1.40 1.40

Expocuba, 30th Anniv. — A1818

2019, Apr. 29 **Litho.** ***Perf. 12½x12¼***
6158 A1818 85c multi 1.75 1.75

Martí Forest, Ariguanabo, 25th Anniv. — A1819

Quotations by José Martí and: 10c, Ceiba pentandra. 15c, Mangifera indica. 30c, Guibourtia hymenifolia. 35c, Pinus cubensis. 75c, Talipariti elatum. 85c, Calycophyllum candidissimum.

1p, Monument to Simón Bolívar and José Martí.

2019, May 19 **Litho.** ***Perf. 12½x12¼***
6159-6164 A1819 Set of 6 5.00 5.00

Souvenir Sheet

Imperf

6165 A1819 1p multi 2.00 2.00

No. 6165 has simulated perforations.

SEMI-POSTAL STAMPS

Common Design Types pictured following the introduction.

Curie Issue

Common Design Type

Wmk. 106

1938, Nov. 23 **Engr.** ***Perf. 10***
B1 CD80 2c + 1c salmon 6.00 1.60
B2 CD80 5c + 1c deep ultra 6.00 1.75
Set, never hinged 18.00

40th anniv. of the discovery of radium by Pierre and Marie Curie. Surtax for the benefit of the Intl. Union for the Control of Cancer.

Catalogue values for unused stamps in this section, from this point to the end of the section, are for Never Hinged items.

Revolutionary Government

"Agriculture" Supporting "Industry" SP2

Engr., Center Typo.

1959, May 7 **Wmk. 321** ***Perf. 12½***
B3 SP2 2c + 1c car & ultra 1.50 .30

Agricultural reforms. See No. CB1. For surcharges see Nos. 624, C199.

Nurse — SP3

Wmk. 229

1959, Sept. 22 **Photo.** ***Perf. 12½***
B4 SP3 2c + 1c crimson rose 1.40 .75

Exists imperf, value about double.

AIR POST STAMPS

Seaplane over Havana Harbor AP1

Wmk. 106

1927, Nov. 1 **Engr.** ***Perf. 12***
C1 AP1 5c dark blue 7.75 .75
Never hinged 12.50

For overprint see No. C30.

Type of 1927 Issue Overprinted

1928, Feb. 8
C2 AP1 5c carmine rose 6.00 1.60
Never hinged 8.75

No. 283 Surcharged in Red

1930, Oct. 27 **Unwmk.**
C3 A44 10c on 25c violet 5.75 1.60
Never hinged 8.50

Airplane and Coast of Cuba — AP3

For Foreign Postage

1931, Feb. 26 **Wmk. 106** ***Perf. 10***
C4 AP3 5c green .50 .25
C5 AP3 10c dk blue 1.25 .25
C6 AP3 15c rose 5.00 .75
C7 AP3 20c brown 1.90 .25
C8 AP3 30c dk violet 4.00 .50
C9 AP3 40c dp orange 4.75 .50
C10 AP3 50c olive grn 6.50 .75
C11 AP3 1p black 13.00 2.00
Nos. C4-C11 (8) 36.90 5.25
Set, never hinged 55.00

See No. C40. For surcharges see Nos. C16-C17, C203, C225.

Airplane AP4

For Domestic Postage

1931-46

C12 AP4 5c rose vio ('32) 1.00 .25
a. 5c brown violet ('36) 1.00 .25
C13 AP4 10c gray blk 2.00 .25
C14 AP4 20c car rose 5.00 1.00
C14A AP4 20c rose pink ('46) 4.00 .25
C15 AP4 50c dark blue 5.50 1.00
Nos. C12-C15 (5) 17.50 2.75
Set, never hinged 27.50

See #C130. For overprints see #C31, E29-E30.

Type of 1931 Surcharged in Black

1935, Apr. 24 ***Perf. 10***
C16 AP3 10c + 10c red 15.00 14.00
Never hinged 20.00
a. Double surcharge 160.00

Imperf

C17 AP3 10c + 10c red 40.00 40.00
Never hinged 55.00 55.00

Matanzas Issue

Air View of Matanzas AP5

10c, Airship "Macon." 20c, Airplane "The Four Winds." 50c, Air View of Fort San Severino.

Wmk. 229

1936, May 5 Photo. ***Perf. 12½***
C18 AP5 5c violet 2.90 1.00
C19 AP5 10c yellow orange 3.00 1.40
C20 AP5 20c green 7.75 3.00
C21 AP5 50c greenish slate 19.00 10.00
Nos. C18-C21 (4) 32.65 15.40
Set, never hinged 42.50

Exist imperf. Value 20% more.

"Lightning" AP9

Allegory of Flight AP10

1936, Nov. 18
C22 AP9 5c violet 3.00 1.10
a. Imperf., pair 100.00
C23 AP10 10c orange brown 5.25 1.25
a. Imperf., pair 100.00
Set, never hinged 12.00

Major Gen. Maximo Gomez, birth cent.

Flat Arch (Panama) — AP11

Carlos Antonio López (Paraguay) — AP12

Inca Gate, Cuzco (Peru) — AP13

Atlacatl (Salvador) AP14

José Enrique Rodó (Uruguay) AP15

Simón Bolívar (Venezuela) AP16

Wmk. 106

1937, Oct. 13 Engr. ***Perf. 10***
C24 AP11 5c red 7.75 6.00
C25 AP12 5c red 8.50 6.00
C26 AP13 10c blue 9.50 6.75
C27 AP14 10c blue 9.50 6.75
C28 AP15 20c green 8.00 5.00
C29 AP16 20c green 8.00 5.00
Nos. C24-C29 (6) 51.25 35.50
Set, never hinged 70.00

See note after No. 354.

Type of 1927 Ovptd. in Black

1938, May **Wmk. 106**
C30 AP1 5c dark orange 7.25 3.75
Never hinged 9.50

1st airplane flight from Key West to Havana, made by Domingo Rosillo, 1913.

Type of 1931-32 Overprinted

1939, Oct. 15
C31 AP4 10c emerald 13.50 7.75
Never hinged 26.00

Issued in connection with an experimental postal rocket flight held at Havana.

Sir Rowland Hill, Map of Cuba and First Stamps of Britain, Spanish Cuba and Republic of Cuba — AP17

1940, Nov. 28 Engr. Wmk. 106
C32 AP17 10c brown 5.50 1.50
Never hinged 8.00

Souvenir Sheet

Unwmk. ***Imperf.***
C33 Sheet of 4 27.50 20.00
Never hinged 37.50
a. AP17 10c light brown 5.50 4.50
Never hinged 8.00

Cent. of the 1st postage stamp.

Sheet sold for 60c.

No. C33 exists with each of the four stamps overprinted in black: "Exposicion de las ACNU/24 de Octubre de 1951/Dia de las Naciones" and "Historia de la Aviacion" in lower margin. Value, $80.

For overprints see Nos. C39, C211.

Poet José Heredia and Palms AP18

Heredia and Niagara Falls — AP19

1940, Dec. 30 Wmk. 106
C34 AP18 5c emerald 3.25 1.00
C35 AP19 10c greenish slate 4.75 1.60
Set, never hinged 11.00

Death cent. of José Maria Heredia y Campuzano (1803-39), poet and patriot.

First Cuban Land Sighted by Columbus AP20

Columbus Lighthouse AP21

1944, May 19
C36 AP20 5c olive green 2.40 .40
C37 AP21 10c slate black 3.00 .75

450th anniv. of the discovery of America.

Catalogue values for unused stamps in this section, from this point to the end of the section, are for Never Hinged items.

Conference of La Mejorana (Maceo, Gomez and Marti) AP22

1948, May 21 Wmk. 229 ***Perf. 12½***
C38 AP22 8c org yel & blk 3.75 .80

50th anniv. of the start of the War of 1895.

Souvenir Sheet

No. C33 Overprinted in Ultramarine

1948, May 21 Unwmk. ***Imperf.***
C39 AP17 Sheet of 4 25.00 9.50

The overprint is applied in the center of the sheet, so that a part of the overprint falls on each stamp.

American Air Mail Soc. Convention, Havana, May 21 to 23, 1948. The sheets sold for 60c each.

Type of 1931

1948, June 15 Wmk. 106 ***Perf. 10***
C40 AP3 8c orange brown 2.75 .80

Narciso Lopez Landing at Cárdenas AP23

Flag on Cuban Fort — AP24

Flag on Morro Castle, Havana — AP25

Engraved and Lithographed

1951, July 3 Wmk. 229 ***Perf. 13***
C41 AP23 5c ol grn, ultra & red 2.75 1.25
C42 AP24 8c red brn, bl & red 2.75 1.25
C43 AP25 25c gray blk, bl & red 5.00 1.40
Nos. C41-C43 (3) 10.50 3.90

Centenary of adoption of Cuba's flag.

Souvenir Sheet

No. 365a Overprinted in Green

1951, Aug. 24 Unwmk. ***Imperf.***
C43A Sheet of 4 19.00 9.00

50th anniv. of the discovery of the cause of yellow fever by Dr. Carlos J. Finlay, and to honor the martyrs of science.

Postage Type and

Resignation Play of Dr. Lasker AP26

Capablanca Making "The Exact Play" — AP27

Wmk. 229

1951, Nov. 1 Photo. ***Perf. 13***
C44 AP26 5c shown 8.00 2.90
C45 AP27 8c shown 12.00 2.75
C46 A165 25c Capablanca 18.00 3.25
Nos. C44-C46 (3) 38.00 8.90

30th anniv. of the winning of the World Chess title by José Raul Capablanca.

Morrillo Types of Regular Issue
Wmk. 106

1951, Nov. 22 Engr. *Perf. 10*

C47	A167	5c violet	2.50	.70
C48	A168	8c deep green	2.50	1.00
C49	A169	25c dark brown	7.00	2.00
a.		Souv. sheet of 6, black brown, perf. 13	72.50	35.00
b.		Souv. sheet of 6, green, imperf.	225.00	125.00
		Nos. C47-C49 (3)	12.00	3.70

Nos. C49a and C49b contain one each of the 1c, 2c and 5c of types A167-A169 and of the 5c, 8c and 25c airmail stamps of types A167-A169. Sheets are unwatermarked and measure 124x133mm.

Isabella Type of Regular Issue, 1952

1952, Feb. 22

C50	A172	25c purple	4.50	.75
a.		Souv. sheet of 2, perf. 11	35.00	35.00
b.		Souv. sheet of 2, imperf.	25.00	25.00

Nos. C50a and C50b contain one each of a 2c of type A172 and a 25c air-mail stamp of type A172. In No. C50a, the 2c and marginal inscriptions are brown carmine; the 25c, dark blue. In No. C50b, the 2c and marginal inscriptions are dark blue; the 25c, brown carmine. Sheets measure 108x18mm.

Type of Regular Issue of 1951 Surcharged in Various Colors

1952, Mar. 18

Color: Yellow Brown

C51	A159	5c on 2c	3.50	.30
C52	A159	8c on 2c (C)	2.60	.30
C53	A159	10c on 2c (Bl)	2.00	.30
C54	A159	25c on 2c (V)	3.75	1.10
C55	A159	50c on 2c (C)	8.00	5.00
C56	A159	1p on 2c (Bl)	10.00	7.50
		Nos. C51-C56 (6)	29.85	14.50

Country School AP32

Entrance, University of Havana — AP33

10c, Presidential Mansion. 25c, Banknote.

Wmk. 106

1952, May 27 Engr. *Perf. 12½*

Centers Various Shades of Green

C57	AP32	5c dark purple	2.10	.25
C58	AP33	8c dark red	2.00	.50
C59	AP32	10c deep blue	2.50	.75
C60	AP32	25c dark violet brn	2.75	1.25
		Nos. C57-C60 (4)	9.35	2.75

Foundation of the Republic of Cuba, 50th anniv.

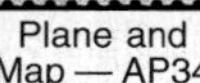

Plane and Map — AP34

Agustín Parlá — AP35

1952, July 22 Engr. *Perf. 10*

C61	AP34	8c black	2.50	.55
a.		Souv. sheet, 8c deep blue	18.00	10.00
b.		Souv. sheet, 8c deep green	18.00	10.00
C62	AP35	25c ultra	3.25	.75
a.		Souv. sheet, 25c deep blue	18.00	10.00
b.		Souv. sheet, 25c deep green	18.00	10.00

30th anniv. of the Key West-Mariel flight of Agustin Parla.

The four souvenir sheets are perf. 11.

Col. Charles Hernandez y Sandrino — AP36

1952, Oct. 7

C63	AP36	5c orange	1.00	.30
C64	AP36	8c brt yel grn	1.00	.30
C65	AP36	10c dk brown	1.60	.75
C66	AP36	15c dk Prus grn	1.90	.80
C67	AP36	20c aqua	2.50	1.00
C68	AP36	25c crimson	2.10	1.00
C69	AP36	30c dk vio bl	5.25	2.50
C70	AP36	45c rose lilac	9.25	3.50
C71	AP36	50c indigo	5.75	2.50
C72	AP36	1p bister	18.00	5.00
		Nos. C63-C72 (10)	48.35	17.65

Three-fourths of the proceeds from the sale were used for the Communications Ministry Employees' Retirement Fund.

Entrance, University of Havana — AP37

F. V. Dominguez, M. Estebanez and F. Capdevila — AP38

Engr.; Center Typo.

1952, Nov. 27

C73	AP37	5c indigo & dk blue	2.25	.40
C74	AP38	25c org & dk grn	4.75	1.40

Execution of 8 medical students, 81st anniv.

AP39

Lockheed Constellation Airliners — AP40

1953, May 22 Engr.

C75	AP39	8c orange brn	1.75	.25
C76	AP39	15c scarlet	3.25	.70

Typographed and Engraved

C77	AP40	2p dp green & dk brn	42.50	10.00
C78	AP40	5p blue & dk brn	82.50	17.50
		Nos. C75-C78 (4)	130.00	28.45

See Nos. C120-C121. For surcharge, see No. C224.

Page of Manifesto of Montecristi — AP42

House of Maximo Gomez AP43

No. C79, Marti in Kingston, Jamaica, No. C80, With Workers in Tampa, Florida. No. C83, Marti addressing liberating army. No. C84, Portrait. No. C85, Dos Rios obelisk. No. C86, Marti's first tomb. No. C87, Present tomb. No. C88, Monument in Havana. No. C89, Martian forge.

1953 Engr. *Perf. 10*

C79	AP42	5c dk car & blk	.30	.25
C80	AP42	5c dk car & blk	.30	.25
C81	AP43	8c dk green & blk	.75	.25
C82	AP42	8c dk green & blk	.75	.25
C83	AP43	10c dk blue & dk car	1.00	.75
C84	AP42	10c dk blue & dk car	.75	.75
C85	AP42	15c violet & gray	1.25	.90
C86	AP42	15c violet & gray	.90	.90
C87	AP42	25c brown & car	1.50	1.25
C88	AP42	25c brown & car	1.60	1.25
C89	AP43	50c yellow & bl	2.00	2.00
		Nos. C79-C89 (11)	11.10	8.80

Cent. of the birth of José Marti.

Board of Accounts Building — AP44

25c, Plane above Board of Accounts Bldg.

1953, Nov. 3

C90	AP44	8c rose carmine	2.40	.70
C91	AP44	25c dk gray grn	2.90	1.10

1st Intl. Cong. of Boards of Account, Havana, Nov. 2-9, 1953.

Miguel Coyula Llaguno AP45

Antonio Ginard Rojas AP46

Communications Association Flag — AP46a

Designs: 10c, Gregorio Hernandez Saez.

1954

C92	AP45	5c dark blue	.65	.25
C93	AP46	8c red violet	1.60	.40
C94	AP46	10c orange	2.00	.50
C95	AP46a	1p black	9.50	4.50
		Nos. C92-C95 (4)	13.75	5.65

See note after No. C72.

Alvaro Reinoso — AP47

Plane and Harvesters Cutting Cane AP48

Designs in Lower Triangle: 5c, Four-engine Plane and Cane Field. 10c, Tractor pulling loaded wagons. 15c, Train of sugar cane. 20c, Modern mill. 25c, Evaporators. 30, Sacks of sugar. 40c, Loading sugar on ship. 45c, Ox cart. 50c, Primitive sugar mill.

1954, Apr. 27 Engr.

C96	AP47	5c yellow green	1.50	.30
C97	AP48	8c brown	1.50	.50
C98	AP48	10c dark green	1.50	.50
C99	AP48	15c henna brn	3.00	.50
C100	AP48	20c blue	1.50	.30
C101	AP48	25c scarlet	1.15	.30
C102	AP48	30c lilac rose	2.75	.95
C103	AP48	40c deep blue	6.25	1.25
C104	AP48	45c violet	5.00	2.50
C105	AP48	50c brt blue	5.00	1.60
C106	AP47	1p dk gray blue	13.50	3.25
		Nos. C96-C106 (11)	42.65	11.95

For surcharges see Nos. C204.

Sanatorium Type of Regular Issue

1954, Sept. 21 Wmk. 106 *Perf. 10*

C107	A186	9c deep green	2.75	.65

Dolz Type of Regular Issue, 1954

1954, Dec. 23

C108	A188	12c carmine	4.50	.70

Rotary Type of Regular Issue, 1955

1955, Feb. 23

C109	A190	12c carmine	2.25	.65

Stamps of 1855 and 1905, Palace of Fine Arts AP52

Designs (including 2 stamps): 12c, Plaza de la Fraternidad. 24c, View of Havana. 30c, Plaza de la Republica.

1955, Apr. 24 *Perf. 12½*

C110	AP52	8c dk grnsh bl & grn	2.00	.35
C111	AP52	12c dk ol grn & red	2.75	.35
C112	AP52	24c dk red & ultra	3.50	.75
C113	AP52	30c dp org & brn	4.25	.90
		Nos. C110-C113 (4)	12.50	2.35

Cent. of Cuba's 1st postage stamps.

Mariel Bay — AP53

Views: 12c, Varadero beach. 1p, Vinales valley.

1955, June 22 Wmk. 106

C114	AP53	8c dk car & dk grn	1.25	1.25
C115	AP53	12c dk ocher & brt bl	7.00	1.60
C116	AP53	1p dk grn & ocher	7.50	2.00
		Nos. C114-C116 (3)	15.75	4.85

See note after No. C72.

Map of Crocier's 1914 Flight — AP54

Design: 30c, Crocier in plane.

1955, July 4 *Perf. 10*

C117	AP54	12c red & dk grn	2.50	.25
C118	AP54	30c dk grn & mag	2.75	.65

35th anniv. of the death of Jaime Gonzalez Crocier, aviation pioneer.

Cuban Museum, Tampa, Fla. — AP55

1955, July 1 Engr. *Perf. 12½*

C119	AP55	12c red & dk brn	3.25	.65

Cent. of Tampa's incorporation as a town.

Lockheed Type of 1953
Typographed and Engraved

1955, Sept. 21 Wmk. 106

C120	AP40 2p bl & ol grn	40.00	6.50
C121	AP40 5p dp rose & ol grn	70.00	15.00

Wright Brothers' Plane and Stamps AP56

Designs: 12c, Spirit of St. Louis. 24c, Graf Zeppelin. 30c, Constellation passenger plane. 50c, Convair jet fighter.

Engraved and Photogravure

1955, Nov. 12 Wmk. 106 *Perf. 12½*

Inscription and Plane in Black

C122	AP56 8c car & bl	3.00	.50
C123	AP56 12c yel grn & car	3.00	.90
C124	AP56 24c vio & car	3.75	1.50
C125	AP56 30c bl & red org	3.50	1.50
C126	AP56 50c ol grn & red org	5.00	2.50
a.	Souvenir sheet of 5	60.00	26.00
	Nos. C122-C126 (5)	18.25	6.90

International Centenary Philatelic Exhibition in Havana, Nov. 12-19, 1955.

No. C126a is printed on thick paper and measures 140x178mm. It contains one each of Nos. C122-C126 with the background of each stamp printed in a different color from the perforated stamps.

"Three Friends" and Gen. Emilio Nuñez AP57

Design: 12c, Landing on the Cuban Coast.

1955, Dec. 27 Engr. Unwmk.

C127	AP57 8c ultra & dk car	2.10	.55
C128	AP57 12c grn & dk red brn	2.50	.75

Gen. Emilio Nuñez, Cuban revolutionary hero, birth cent.

Post Type of Regular Issue, 1956

Bishop P. A. Morell de Santa Cruz (1694-1768).

1956, Mar. 27 Wmk. 106

C129	A197 12c dk brn & grn	3.25	.55

Plane Type of 1931-46

1956 Engr. *Perf. 10*

C130	AP4 50c greenish blue	5.00	1.00

Portrait Type of Regular Issue, 1956

Portraits: 8c, Gen. Julio Sanguily. 12c, Gen. José Maria Aguirre. 30c, Col. Ernesto Fonts Sterling.

1956, May 2 *Perf. 12½*

Portraits in Black

C131	A198 8c brown	1.25	.25
C132	A198 12c dull yellow	1.60	.75
C133	A198 30c indigo	3.00	1.25
	Nos. C131-C133 (3)	5.85	2.25

See note after No. C72.

Mother and Child — AP60

1956, May 13 Wmk. 106 *Perf. 12½*

C134	AP60 12c ultra & red	2.00	.40

Issued in honor of Mother's Day 1956.

Masonic Temple Havana — AP61

1956, June 5

C135	AP61 12c olive green	1.75	.55

Pigeon AP62

Gundlach Hawk — AP63

Birds: 8c, Wood duck. 19c, Herring gulls. 24c, White pelicans. 29c, Common merganser. 30c, Quail. 50c, Herons (great white, great blue and Wurdemann's). 1p, Northern caracara. 2p, Middle American jacana. 5p, Ivory-billed woodpecker.

1956

C136	AP62 8c blue	8.50	.25
C137	AP62 12c gray blue	5.25	.25
C138	AP63 14c green	2.25	.25
C139	AP63 19c redsh brn	2.75	.55
C140	AP63 24c lilac rose	2.25	.55
C141	AP62 29c green	2.25	.55
C142	AP62 30c dk olive bis	1.90	.80
C143	AP63 50c slate blk	3.25	1.10
C144	AP63 1p dk car rose	11.00	3.00
C145	AP62 2p rose violet	10.00	4.25
C146	AP63 5p brt red	23.50	8.75
	Nos. C136-C146 (11)	72.90	20.30

See Nos. C205, C235-C237. For surcharges and overprints, see Nos. C147, C151, C197, C209-C210

Type of 1956 Surcharged

Design: 24c, White pelicans.

1956, July 13

C147	AP63 8c on 24c deep org	2.00	.70

Opening of the new building of the Cuba Philatelic Club, Havana, July 14, 1956.

Hubert de Blanck — AP64

1956, July 6

C148	AP64 12c ultra	2.60	.40

Hubert de Blanck (1856-1932), composer.

Church of Our Lady of Charity — AP65

1956, Sept. 8

C149	AP65 12c grn & car	2.75	.55
a.	Souvenir sheet of 2, imperf.	18.00	9.50

Issued in honor of Our Lady of Charity of Cobre, patroness of Cuba.

No. C149a contains one each of Nos. 559 and C149. No. C149a exists with yellow of No. 559 omitted.

Benjamin Franklin AP66

1956, Oct. 5 Engr. *Perf. 12½*

C150	AP66 12c red brown	3.25	.55

Type of 1956 Surcharged in Blue

Design: 2p, Middle American jacana.

1956, Oct. 26 Wmk. 106

C151	AP62 12c on 2p dark gray	1.60	.95

Issued in honor of the 12th Inter-American Press Association Conference, Havana.

Lord Baden-Powell AP67

1957, Feb. 22

C152	AP67 12c slate	2.75	.70

Centenary of the birth of Lord Baden-Powell, founder of the Boy Scouts.

Hanabanilla Waterfall AP68

12c, Sierra de Cubitas. 30c, Puerto Boniato.

1957, Mar. 29

C153	AP68 8c blue & red	1.10	.25
C154	AP68 12c green & red	2.00	.50
C155	AP68 30c ol grn & dk pur	3.00	.70
	Nos. C153-C155 (3)	6.10	1.45

See note after No. 457.

Philatelic Club, Havana — AP69

1957, Apr. 24 Wmk. 106 *Perf. 12½*

C156	AP69 12c yel, grn & brn	3.00	.40

Stamp Day, and the Natl. Phil. Exhib.

Fingerprint — AP70

1957, Apr. 30

C157	AP70 12c claret brown	3.00	.40

Birth cent. (in 1856) of Juan Francisco Steegers y Perera, dactyloscopy pioneer.

Baseball Player — AP71

1957, May 17 Wmk. 106 *Perf. 12½*

C158	AP71 8c shown	2.50	.40
C159	AP71 12c Ballerina	2.75	.50
C160	AP71 24c Girl diver	3.50	.75
C161	AP71 30c Boxers	3.75	.75
	Nos. C158-C161 (4)	12.50	2.40

Issued to honor young Cuban athletes.

Joaquin de Aguero — AP72

1957, July 4

C162	AP72 12c indigo	3.00	.40

Issued to honor Joaquin de Aguero, Cuban freedom fighter and patriot.

Jeanette Ryder — AP73

1957, July 17

C163	AP73 12c dk red brn	1.50	.55
a.	Pair, #574, C163	4.80	2.00

Mrs. Jeanette Ryder, founder of the Humane Society of Cuba.

José M. de Heredia y Girard — AP74

1957, Aug. 16 Engr. Wmk. 106

C164	AP74 8c dk blue vio	3.00	.30

José Maria de Heredia y Girard (1842-1905), Cuban born French poet.

Justice Type of Regular Issue, 1957

1957, Sept. 2 *Perf. 12½*
C165 A214 12c green 2.75 .50

John Robert Gregg — AP75

1957, Oct. 1
C166 AP75 12c dark green 2.50 .70

90th anniv. of the birth of John Robert Gregg, inventor of the Gregg shorthand system.

D. Figarola Caneda — AP76

José Marti National Library AP77

1957, Oct. 18 Wmk. 106 *Perf. 12½*
C167 AP76 8c ultra 3.00 .25
C168 AP77 12c chocolate 2.25 .50

José Marti National Library.

Map of Cuba and UN Emblem AP78

1957, Oct. 24
C169 AP78 8c dk green & brn 2.00 .25
C170 AP78 12c car rose & grn 1.60 .55
C171 AP78 30c ind & brt pink 2.50 1.25
Nos. C169-C171 (3) 6.10 2.05

Issued for United Nations Day, 1957.

Map of Cuba and Florida AP79

1957, Oct. 28
C172 AP79 12c dk red brn & bl 3.50 .80

30th anniv. of airmail service from Key West to Havana.

Type of Regular Issue, 1957 and

Stairway and Bell Tower AP80

Design: 12c, Facade of Normal School.

1957, Nov. 19 Engr. *Perf. 12½*
C173 A217 12c indigo & ocher 1.75 .40
C174 AP80 30c dk car & gray 3.25 .60

View Types of Regular Issue, 1957

Views: 8c, El Viso Fort, El Caney. 12c, Sancti Spiritus Church. 30c, Concordia Bridge, Matanzas.

1957, Dec. 17 *Perf. 12½*
C175 A218 8c dk gray & red 1.00 .30
C176 A219 12c brown & gray 1.75 .40
C177 A218 30c red brn & bl gray 2.00 .75
Nos. C175-C177 (3) 4.75 1.45

See note after No. C72.

Hedges Types of Regular Issue, 1958

8c, Dayton Hedges & Matanzas rayon factory.

1958, Jan. 30 Wmk. 106 *Perf. 12½*
C178 A221 8c green 2.25 .80

Diario de la Marina Building — AP81

1958, Apr. 1
C179 AP81 29c black 4.25 1.10

Jose Ignacio Rivero y Alonso, editor of the newspaper, Diario de la Marina.

Map Showing Sea Mail Route, 1765 AP82

1958, Apr. 24 Wmk. 106 *Perf. 12½*
C180 AP82 29c dk bl aqua & buff 3.50 1.25

Issued for Stamp Day, Apr. 24, and the National Philatelic Exhibition.

Gen. Gomez in Battle — AP83

1958, June 6 **Engr.**
C181 AP83 12c slate green 2.00 .55

Issued in honor of Maj. Gen. José Miguel Gomez, President of Cuba, 1909-13.

Snail (Polymita Picta) — AP84

12c, Megalocnus Rodens. 30c, Ammonite.

1958, Aug. 29 Wmk. 321 *Perf. 12½*
C182 AP84 8c gray, red & yel 4.00 1.25
C183 AP84 12c brn, *yel grn* 5.50 1.75
C184 AP84 30c grn, *pink* 6.00 2.10
Nos. C182-C184 (3) 15.50 5.10

Centenary of the birth of Dr. Carlos de la Torre, naturalist.

Papilio Caiguanabus AP85

Cuban Sea Bass — AP86

12c, Teria gundlachia. 14c, Teria ebriola. 19c, Nathalis felicia. 29c, Butter Hamlet. 30c, Tattler.

1958, Sept. 26 Wmk. 106 *Perf. 12½*
C185 AP85 8c multicolored 3.75 .65
C186 AP85 12c emer, blk & org 4.00 .65
C187 AP85 14c multicolored 5.25 .90
C188 AP85 19c bl, blk & yel 4.75 1.25
C189 AP86 24c multicolored 5.50 1.25
C190 AP86 29c blk, brn & ultra 16.00 1.60
C191 AP86 30c blk, yel grn & sep 16.00 2.25
Nos. C185-C191 (7) 55.25 8.55

Felipe Poey (1799-1891), naturalist.

Battle of San Juan Hill, 1898 — AP87

Wmk. 106

1958, Oct. 27 Engr. *Perf. 12½*
C192 AP87 12c black brown 2.75 .50

Birth centenary of Theodore Roosevelt.

UNESCO Building, Paris — AP88

Design: 30c, "UNESCO" and map of Cuba.

1958, Nov. 7
C193 AP88 12c dk slate grn 2.00 .50
C194 AP88 30c dp ultra 2.00 1.00

UNESCO Headquarters in Paris opening, Nov. 3.

Revolutionary Government

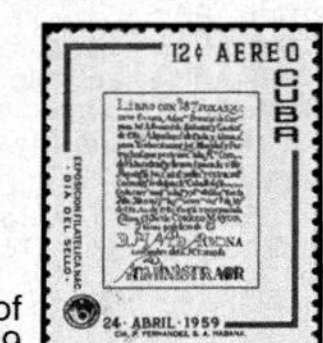

Postal Notice of 1765 — AP89

Design: 30c, Administrative postal book of St. Cristobal, Havana, 1765.

1959, Apr. 24 Wmk. 321 *Perf. 12½*
C195 AP89 12c Prus blue & sep 1.50 .40
C196 AP89 30c sepia & Prus bl 2.50 1.40

Issued for Stamp Day, Apr. 24, and the National Philatelic Exhibition.

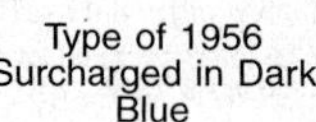

Type of 1956 Surcharged in Dark Blue

1959, Oct. 17 Wmk. 321 *Perf. 12½*
C197 AP63 12c on 1p emerald 2.75 1.50

Issued to publicize the meeting of the American Soc. of Travel Agents, Oct. 17-23.

Musical Arts Building — AP90

Wmk. 106

1959, Nov. 11 Engr. *Perf. 12½*
C198 AP90 12c yellow green 3.00 .90

40th anniversary of the Musical Arts Society.

No. CB1 Surcharged in Red

Engr. & Typo.

1960 Wmk. 321 *Perf. 12½*
C199 SPAP1 12c on 12 + 3c car & grn 2.25 .75

Type of Regular Issue, 1960

8c, Battle of Santa Clara. 12c, Rebel forces entering Havana. 29c, Bank-note changing hands ("Clandestine activities in the cities").

Wmk. 320

1960, Jan. 28 Engr. *Perf. 12½*
C200 A236 8c bl, gray ol & sal 1.60 .50
C201 A236 12c gray ol & ocher 2.50 .60
C202 A236 29c gray & car 3.00 1.25
Nos. C200-C202 (3) 7.10 2.35

Nos. C9 and C104 Srchd. in Red

1960, Feb. 3 **Wmk. 106**
C203 AP3 12c on 40c dp org 2.10 .65
C204 AP48 12c on 45c vio 2.25 .65

Pigeon Type of 1956

1960, Feb. 12 **Wmk. 321**
C205 AP62 12c brt blue grn 2.00 .55

Statue Type of Regular Issue, 1960.

Statues: 8c, José Marti, Matanzas. 12c, Heroes of the Cacarajicara, Pinar del Rio. 30c, Cosme de la Torriente, Isle of Pines, horiz.

1960, Mar. 28 *Perf. 12½*
C206 A237 8c gray & car .70 .25
C207 A237 12c blue & car 1.25 .25
C208 A237 30c violet & brn 2.75 1.25
Nos. C206-C208 (3) 4.70 1.75

See note after No. 386.

Type of 1956 and No. C33 Overprinted in Dark Blue

1960, Apr. 24 Wmk. 321 *Perf. 12½*
C209 AP62 8c orange yel .65 .40
C210 AP62 12c cerise 1.75 .65

Souvenir Sheet

C211 AP17 Sheet of 4 35.00 35.00

Stamp Day, 4/24/60, and Natl. Phil. Exhib.
No. C211 has added marginal inscription in dark blue for cent. of the ¼r on 2r (No. 15).

Type of Olympic Games Issue, 1960

Wmk. 321

1960, Sept. 22 Engr. *Perf. 12½*
C212 A238 8c Boxer .80 .25
C213 A238 12c Runner 1.50 .50
a. Souvenir sheet of 4 5.50 5.50

17th Olympic Games, Rome, Aug. 25-Sept. 11. No. C213a contains one each imperf. of types of Nos. 645-646 and Nos. C212-C213 in dark blue.

No. C3 and Flight Symbols of 1930, 1960 — AP91

1960, Oct. 30 Litho. Unwmk.
C214 AP91 8c multicolored 3.00 2.00

30th anniv. of national air mail service.

Sword of Sheaf of Wheat — AP92

12c, Two workers, horiz. 30c, Three maps, horiz. 50c, Hand inscribed "Peace" in 5 languages.

1961, Jan. 10 Photo. *Perf. 11½*
Granite Paper
C215 AP92 8c multicolored .75 .25
C216 AP92 12c multicolored 2.00 .25
C217 AP92 30c black & red 2.50 .65
C218 AP92 50c blk, bl & red 3.00 1.00
Nos. C215-C218 (4) 8.25 2.15

Conf. of Underdeveloped Countries, Havana.

José Marti and "Declaration of Havana" — AP93

Background in Spanish, English or French.

1961, Jan. 28 Litho. *Perf. 12½*
C219 AP93 8c pale grn, blk & red 1.25 .85
C220 AP93 12c org yel, blk & pale vio 1.75 1.00
C221 AP93 30c pale bl, blk & pale brn 4.00 3.50
a. Souvenir sheet of 3 15.00 15.00
Nos. C219-C221 (3) 7.00 5.35

Declaration of Havana, Sept. 1, 1960.
Sheets of 25 are imprinted in margin "E" for Spanish, "I" for English or "F" for French.
No. C221a contains one each of Nos. C219-C221, imperf. The 8c has background in Spanish, the 12c in English and the 30e in French.

UN Type of 1961

1961, Apr. 12 Unwmk. *Perf. 12½*
C222 A244 8c dp car & yel .60 .25
C223 A244 12c brt ultra & org 1.40 .50
a. Souv. sheet of 2, #C222-C223, imperf. 4.00 4.00

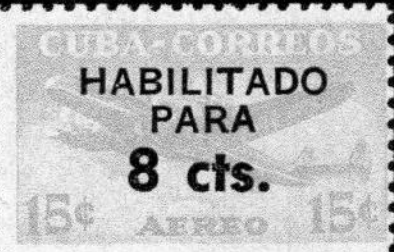

Nos. C76 and C7 Surcharged

Wmk. 106
1961, Oct. 1 Engr. *Perf. 10*
C224 AP39 8c on 15c No. C76 1.00 .40
C225 AP3 8c on 20c No. C7 1.00 .40

Revolution Anniv. Type of 1962
Perf. 12½
1962, Jan. 3 Litho. Unwmk.
C226 A250 8c multi 1.00 .30
C227 A250 12c multi 1.90 .55
C228 A250 30c multi 2.50 .90
Nos. C226-C228 (3) 5.40 1.75

1st Sugarcane Harvest in Socialist Cuba, 1st Anniv. — AP94

1962, Jan. 16
C229 AP94 8c salmon pink & dark brn 1.00 .25
C230 AP94 12c bluish lil & blk 2.50 .45

Cuban goods have been embargoed by the United States since a Feb. 7, 1962 proclamation by President Kennedy, but according to the Office of Foreign Assets Control of the Treasury Department, used Cuban stamps can be imported and sold without limitation, and unused stamps may be imported for personal use, but not resold.

Intl. Radio Service AP95

1962, Mar. 26 Wmk. 321
C231 AP95 8c multi 1.10 .25
C232 AP95 12c multi 2.10 .55
C233 AP95 30c multi 3.00 1.25
C234 AP95 1p multi 6.00 3.25
Nos. C231-C234 (4) 12.20 5.30

Bird Type of 1956

1962, July 20 Engr. Wmk. 321
C235 AP63 1p like #C144, royal blue 9.50 7.50
C236 AP62 2p like #C145, dark red 17.00 14.00
C237 AP63 5p like #C146, rose lake 22.50 17.50
Nos. C235-C237 (3) 49.00 39.00

PRAGA '62 — AP96

No. C238, Czechoslovakia No. 1080.

1962, Aug. 18 Litho.
C238 AP96 31c multi 3.50 1.50

Souvenir Sheet
Imperf
C239 AP96 31c like No. C238 17.50 12.00

No. C239 contains one 60x35½mm stamp.

Achievements of the Revolution — AP97

1c, Agrarian reform. 2c, Industrialization. 3c, Urban reform. 7c, Eradication of unemployment. 9c, Education. 10c, Public health. 13c, Excerpt from *La Historia Me Absolvera,* by Castro.

1966, July 26 Wmk. 376 *Perf. 12½*
C240 AP97 1c multi .25 .25
C241 AP97 2c multi .25 .25
C242 AP97 3c multi .50 .25
C243 AP97 7c multi .50 .25
C244 AP97 9c multi .95 .25
C245 AP97 10c multi 2.10 .25
C246 AP97 13c multi 2.75 .45
Nos. C240-C246 (7) 7.30 1.95

Camaguey-Seville Flight, 35th Anniv. — AP98

13c, Aircraft. 30c, Map, Lieut. Menendez Palaez.

1971, Jan. 12 Unwmk.
C247 AP98 13c multi 2.25 .25
C248 AP98 30c multi 3.25 .70

Havana-Santiago de Chile Direct Air Service, 1st Anniv. — AP99

1972, June 26 Wmk. 376
C249 AP99 25c multi 1.50 .75

6th Congress of Latin American and Caribbean Exporters of Sugar, Havana — AP100

Perf. 12½x12
1977, Feb. 28 Unwmk.
C250 AP100 13c multi .75 .25

Composer Type of 1977

13c, Jorge Ankerman and score.

1977, May 10 *Perf. 13*
C251 A571 13c multi 1.00 .25

Flower Type of 1977

Designs: 13c, Caesalpinia pulcherrima. 30c, .Catharanthus roseus.

1977, May 31
C252 A572 13c multicolored .80 .25
C253 A572 30c multicolored 1.60 .50

Souvenir Sheet
Perf. 13½x13
C254 A572 50c Juan Tomas Roig 4.00 .90

No. C254 contains one 32x40mm stamp.

Natl. Decorations Type of 1977

1977, July 26 *Perf. 12x12½*
C255 A574 13c multi, diff. .80 .25
C256 A574 30c multi, diff. 1.50 .45

Art Type of 1977

Paintings by Jorge Arche: 13c, *My Wife and I,* vert. 30c, *Domino Players.* 50c, *Self-portrait,* vert.

1977, Aug. 25 *Perf. 13x12½*
Size: 26x38mm
C257 A575 13c multi .60 .25
Size: 40x29mm
Perf. 13
C258 A575 30c multi 1.50 .40

Souvenir Sheet
Perf. 13½x13
C259 A575 50c multi 4.00 4.00

No. C259 contains one 32x40mm stamp.

Spartakiad Type of 1977

13c, Grenade-throwing. 30c, Rifle-shooting, horiz.

1977, Sept. 10 *Perf. 13*
C260 A576 13c multi .60 .25
C261 A576 30c multi 1.25 .40

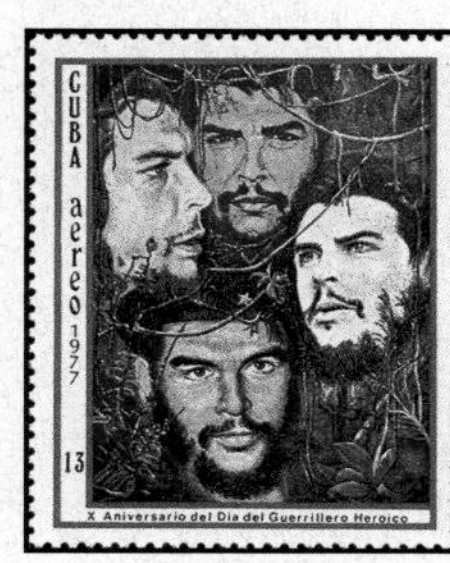

10th Heroic Guerrilla's Day AP101

13c, Guerrilla fighters.

1977, Oct. 8 *Perf. 12½x13*
C262 AP101 13c multi 2.75 .25

Airmail Service Type of 1977

13c, Havana-Mexico cachet. 30c, Havana-Prague cachet.

1977, Oct. 27 *Perf. 12x12½*
C263 A577 13c multi .85 .25
C264 A577 30c multi 1.50 .55

Souvenir Sheet

Adoration of the Magi, by Rubens — AP102

1977, Nov. 18 *Perf. 13*
C265 AP102 50c multi 4.00 4.00

Rubens' 400th birth anniv.

Havana Zoo Type of 1977

1977, Nov. 24
C266 A579 13c Tiger 1.25 .25
C267 A579 30c Lion 1.60 .55

Revolution Martyrs Type of 1977

1977, Dec. 2 *Perf. 12½x12*
C268 A580 13c *Corynthia* landing .75 .25

Pan American Health Organization (OPS), 75th Anniv. — AP103

1977, Dec. 2
C269 AP103 13c multi .75 .25

Havana University Type of 1978

13c, Crossed sabres, university. 30c, University, statue, crowd.

1978, Jan. 5 *Perf. 13x12½*
C270 A582 13c multi .75 .25
C271 A582 30c multi 1.10 .50

Portrait of Jose Marti (b. 1853), by A. Menocal AP104

1978, Jan. 28
C272 AP104 13c multi .80 .25

Art Type of 1978

Paintings in the Nat. Museum of Art: 13c, *El Guadalquivir,* by M. Barron. 30c, *Portrait of H.E. Ridley,* by J.J. Masqueries, vert.

1978, Feb. 20 *Perf. 12½x12, 13*
Sizes: 42x27mm, 29x40mm
C273 A583 13c multi .90 .25
C274 A583 30c multi 1.10 .40

Bird Type of 1975

Designs: 13c, Torreornis inexpectata, horiz. 30c, Ara tricolor.

1978, Mar. 10 *Perf. 12½x12, 13*
Size: 42x27mm, 27x42mm
C275 A524 13c multicolored 1.40 .50
C276 A524 30c multicolored 2.10 1.10

Baragua Protest, Cent. — AP105

13c, *Antonio Maceo,* by A. Melero.

1978, Mar. 15 *Perf. 13x13½*
C277 AP105 13c multi .70 .25

Cosmonaut's Day Type of 1978

1978, Apr. 12 *Perf. 13*
C278 A585 13c Venera 10 .70 .25
Size: 36x46mm
Perf. 12½x13
C279 A585 30c Lunokhod 2, vert. 1.25 .50

SOCFILEX '78, Budapest — AP106

30c, Parliament, Hungary No. 217.

1978, May 7 *Perf. 13x12½*
C280 AP106 30c multi 1.60 .55

Cactus Type of 1978

Designs: 13c, Rhodocactus cubensis. 30c, Harrisia taetra.

1978, May 15 *Perf. 13*
C281 A587 13c multicolored .80 .25
C282 A587 30c multicolored 1.75 .35

World Telecommunications Day — AP107

1978, May 17
C283 AP107 30c multi 2.00 .45

Organization of African Unity, 15th Anniv. — AP108

1978, May 25 *Perf. 13x12½*
C284 AP108 30c multi 1.20 .45

Souvenir Sheet

CAPEX '78, Toronto — AP109

50c, *Niven, Wales,* by G.H. Russell.

1978, June 9 *Perf. 13x13½*
C285 AP109 50c multi 3.50 2.25

Aquarium Type of 1978

Designs: 13c, Carassias auratus, vert. 30c, Symphysodon aequifasciata axelrodi.

1978, June 15 *Perf. 13*
C286 A588 13c multicolored 1.00 .25
C287 A588 30c multicolored 1.50 .50

MEDELLIN Games Type of 1978

1978, July 1
C288 A589 13c Volleyball .60 .25
C289 A589 30c Running 1.25 .45

Attack on Moncada Type of 1978

13c, Soldiers bearing rifles. 30c, Stylized dove, banners.

1978, July 26
C290 A590 13c multi .50 .25
C291 A590 30c multi 1.10 .35

Youth Festival Type of 1978

Natl. flags and views of host cities.

1978, July 28
C292 A591 13c Moscow, 1957 .70 .25
C293 A591 13c Vienna, 1959 .70 .25
C294 A591 13c Helsinki, 1962 .70 .25
C295 A591 13c Sofia, 1968 .70 .25
C296 A591 13c Berlin, 1973 .70 .25
a. Strip of 5, Nos. C292-C296 3.75 1.75
Nos. C292-C296 (5) 3.50 1.25
Size: 46x36mm
Perf. 13x12½
C297 A591 30c Havana, 1978 1.50 .35

Tuna Industry Type of 1978

1978, Aug. 30 *Perf. 12½x12*
C298 A593 13c Stern trawler .85 .25
C299 A593 30c Refrigerator ship 1.50 .60

Souvenir Sheet

PRAGA '78 — AP110

50c, *Marina,* by A. Brandeis.

1978, Sept. 8 *Perf. 13*
C300 AP110 50c multi 3.50 2.00

Art Type of 1978

Paintings by Amelia Pelaez del Casal (1896-1968): 13c, *Yellow Flowers,* vert. 30c, *Still-life in Blue,* vert. 50c, *Portrait of Amelia,* by L. Romanach, vert.

1978, Sept. 15 *Perf. 12x12½, 13*
C301 A594 13c multi .50 .25
C302 A594 30c multi 1.20 .45
Souvenir Sheet
Perf. 13½x13
C303 A594 50c multi 3.00 .90

No. C303 contains one 32x40mm stamp.

Socialist Communication Organizations Congress (OSS), 20th Anniv. — AP111

1978, Sept. 25 *Perf. 13*
C304 AP111 30c multi 2.50 .50

Souvenir Sheet

EXFILNA '78, 6th Natl. Philatelic Exposition — AP112

50c, 1st Postal Card, issued in 1878.

1978, Oct. 10 *Imperf.*
C305 AP112 50c multi 3.50 2.75

No. C305 has simulated perfs.

Intl. Anti-Apartheid Year — AP113

1978, Oct. 16 *Perf. 12½*
C306 AP113 13c multi 1.00 .75

Zoo Type of 1978

Designs: 13c, Acinonyx jubatos. 30c, Loxodonta africana, vert.

1978, Oct. 20 *Perf. 13*
C307 A595 13c multicolored .85 .25
C308 A595 30c multicolored 1.75 .65

Natl. Ballet Type of 1978

1978, Oct. 28 *Perf. 12½x13*
C309 A596 13c *Giselle,* vert. .85 .25
C310 A596 30c *Genesis,* vert. 1.60 .30

Pacific Flora Type of 1978

1978, Nov. 30 *Perf. 13*
C311 A597 13c multi, diff. .80 .25
C312 A597 30c multi, diff. 1.60 .30

25th Death Anniv. of Julius and Ethel Rosenberg, American Communists Executed for Espionage — AP114

1978, Dec. 20
C313 AP114 13c multi .65 .25

Julio A. Mella (d. 1929) AP115

1979, Jan. 10
C314 AP115 13c multi .65 .25

Cosmonaut's Day Type of 1979

1979, Apr. 12 *Perf. 13½x13*
Souvenir Sheet
C315 A603 50c Orbital complex 3.50 2.75

No. C315 contains one 32x40mm stamp.

Intl. Year of the Child — AP116

1979, June 1 *Perf. 13x12½*
C316 AP116 13c multi .90 .25

Art Type of 1979

50c, Portrait of Victor Emmanuel Garcia, by J. Arche, vert.

1979, June 15 *Perf. 13½x13*
C317 A600 50c multicolored 3.25 1.75

No. C317 contains one 32x40mm stamp.

CARIFESTA '79, Festival of Caribbean Peoples, Havana AP117

1979, July 16 *Perf. 12½x13*
C318 AP117 13c multi 1.50 .25

10th World Universiade Games, Mexico City — AP118

1979, Sept. 1 *Perf. 13x12½*
C319 AP118 13c grn, pale grn & gold .65 .25

6th Conference of Nonaligned Countries — AP119

50c, Convention Palace.

1979, Sept. 3
C320 AP119 50c multi 1.75 .90

Sir Rowland Hill (d. 1879), Originator of Penny Postage — AP120

1979, Sept. 4 *Perf. 13½x13*
C321 AP120 30c Hill, casket 1.40 .25

SOCFILEX '79, Bucharest — AP121

30c, Romania No. 683, flags.

1979, Oct. 25 *Perf. 12½*
C322 AP121 30c multi 1.40 .40

Intl. Radio Consultative Committee (CCIR), 50th Anniv. — AP122

30c, Ground receiving station.

1979, Nov. 30 *Perf. 12½x12*
C323 AP122 30c multi 1.50 .40

1st Soviet-Cuban Joint Space Flight — AP123

1980, Sept. 23 *Perf. 12½*
C324 AP123 13c multi .75 .25
C325 AP123 30c multi 1.75 .35

Capt. Mariano Barberan, Lt. Joaquin Collar, and Their Airplane Cuatro Vientos. — AP124

1993, June 11 **Litho.** *Perf. 13*
C326 AP124 30c multicolored 1.10 .45

1st Flight Seville-Camaguey, 60th anniv.

AIR POST SEMI-POSTAL STAMP

Catalogue values for unused stamps in this section are for Never Hinged items.

Farm Couple and Factory SPAP1

Engr. & Typo.
1959, May 7 **Wmk. 321** *Perf. 12½*
CB1 SPAP1 12c + 3c car & grn 2.00 .80

Agricultural reforms. See No. C199.

AIR POST SPECIAL DELIVERY STAMPS

Matanzas Issue

Matanzas Harbor APSD1

Wmk. 229
1936, May 5 **Photo.** *Perf. 12½*
CE1 ASPD1 15c light blue 5.00 3.50
Never hinged 8.00

Exists imperf. Value $6.50 unused, $4.50 used.

SPECIAL DELIVERY STAMPS

Issued under Administration of the United States

US No. E5 Surcharged in Red

1899 **Wmk. 191** *Perf. 12*
E1 SD3 10c blue 130. 100.
Never hinged 300.
a. No period after "CUBA" 575. 400.

Issue of the Republic under US Military Rule

Special Delivery Messenger SD2

Printed by the US Bureau of Engraving and Printing

1899 **Wmk. US-C (191C)**
Inscribed: "Immediata"
E2 SD2 10c orange 52.50 15.00
Never hinged 120.00

Issues of the Republic Inscribed: "Inmediata"

1902 *Perf. 12*
E3 SD2 10c orange 7.50 3.00

J. B. Zayas SD3

1910 **Unwmk.**
E4 SD3 10c orange & blue 30.00 10.00
Never hinged 50.00
a. Center inverted 1,250.

Airplane and Morro Castle SD4

1914, Feb. 24 *Perf. 12*
E5 SD4 10c dark blue 15.00 1.25

Exists imperf. Value, pair $500.

1927 **Wmk. Star (106)**
E6 SD4 10c deep blue 12.00 .50
Never hinged 18.00

1935 *Perf. 10*
E7 SD4 10c blue 12.00 .40
Never hinged 15.00

Matanzas Issue

Mercury SD5

Wmk. Wavy Lines (229)
1936, May 5 **Photo.** *Perf. 12½*
E8 SD5 10c deep claret 8.00 3.50
Never hinged 9.50

Exists imperf. Value $7.50 unused, $5 used.

"Triumph of the Revolution" — SD6

1936, Nov. 18
E9 SD6 10c red orange 9.00 2.00
Never hinged 12.00

Maj. Gen. Máximo Gómez (1836-1905).

Temple of Quetzalcoatl (Mexico) SD7

Ruben Dario (Nicaragua) SD8

Wmk. 106
1937, Oct. 13 **Engr.** *Perf. 10*
E10 SD7 10c deep orange 8.00 6.50
E11 SD8 10c deep orange 8.50 7.25
Set, never hinged 23.50

Issued for the benefit of the Association of American Writers and Artists. See note after No. 354.

Letter and Symbols of Transportation — SD9

1945, Oct. 30
E12 SD9 10c olive brown 2.75 .40
Never hinged 4.00

Catalogue values for unused stamps in this section, from this point to the end of the section, are for Never Hinged items.

Governor's Building, Cárdenas SD10

Engraved and Lithographed
1951, July 3 **Wmk. 229** *Perf. 13*
E13 SD10 10c henna brn, ultra & red 5.75 2.25

Cent. of the adoption of Cuba's flag.

Chess Type of Regular Issue, 1951
1951, Nov. 1 **Photo.**
E14 A166 10c dk grn & rose brn 18.00 5.75

Type of Regular Issue of 1951 Surcharged in Red Violet

Wmk. 106
1952, Mar. 18 **Engr.** *Perf. 10*
E15 A159 10c on 2c yel brn 6.00 2.00

Arms and Bars from National Hymn — SD12

1952, May 27 *Perf. 12½*
E16 SD12 10c dp org & bl 4.00 2.50

Republic of Cuba founding, 50th anniv.

Type of Air Post Stamps of 1952 Inscribed: "Entrega Especial"

1952, Oct. 7 *Perf. 10*
E17 AP36 10c pale olive grn 5.00 2.00

Three-fourths of the proceeds from the sale of No. E17 were used for the Communications Ministry Employees' Retirement Fund.

Roseate Tern — SD13

1953, July 28
E18 SD13 10c blue 4.00 1.10

Gregorio Hernandez Saez — SD14

1954, Feb. 23
E19 SD14 10c olive green 5.00 1.10

Felix Varela — SD15

1955, June 22 *Perf. 12½*
E20 SD15 10c brown car 3.00 .75

See note after No. E17.

Portrait Type of Regular Issue, 1956 Inscribed: "Entrega Especial"

Portrait: 10c, Jose Jacinto Milanes.

1956, May 2 **Wmk. 106**
E21 A198 10c dk car rose & blk 3.50 1.00

See note after No. E17.

Painting Type of Regular Issue, 1957 Inscribed: "Entrega Especial"

10c, "Yesterday" by E. Garcia Cabrera.

1957, Mar. 15 **Engr.** *Perf. 12½*
E22 A207 10c dk brn & turq bl 3.00 1.25

See note after No. E17.

View Type of Regular Issue, 1957 Inscribed: "Entrega Especial"

10c, Independence square, Pino del Rio.

1957, Dec. 17
E23 A218 10c dk pur & brn 2.50 1.00

See note after No. E17.

View in Havana and Messenger SD16

1958, Jan. 10 **Engr.**
E24 SD16 10c blue 2.75 .70
E25 SD16 20c green 3.25 .70

See Nos. E28, E31.

Fish Type of Regular Issue, 1958 Inscribed: "Entrega Especial"

Fish: 10c, Blackfish snapper. 20c, Mosquitofish.

1958, Sept. 26 **Wmk. 106** *Perf. 12½*
E26 AP86 10c blk, bl, pink & yel 9.00 1.75
E27 AP86 20c blk, ultra & pink 17.00 8.00

See note after No. C191.

Revolutionary Government Messenger Type of 1958

1960 **Wmk. 321** *Perf. 12½*
E28 SD16 10c brt vio 3.50 .80

Plane Type of Air Post Issue, of 1931-46, Srchd. in Black or Red

1960 **Wmk. 106** *Perf. 10*
E29 AP4 10c on 20c car rose 3.00 .50
E30 AP4 10c on 50c grnsh bl (R) 3.00 .50

Messenger Type of 1958

1961, June 28 **Wmk. 321** *Perf. 12½*
E31 SD16 10c orange 3.50 .80

West Indies Packet Type of 1962

Perf. 12½

1962, Apr. 24 **Litho.** **Unwmk.**
E32 A253 10c buff, dull ultra & brn 7.00 1.50

POSTAGE DUE STAMPS

Issued under Administration of the United States

Postage Due Stamps of the United States Nos. J38, J39, J41 and J42 Srchd. in Black Like Nos. 221-226A

1899 **Wmk. 191** *Perf. 12*
J1 D2 1c dp claret 45.00 5.25
Never hinged 110.00
J2 D2 2c dp claret 45.00 5.25
Never hinged 110.00
a. Inverted surcharge *4,000.*
J3 D2 5c dp claret 42.50 5.25
Never hinged 105.00
J4 D2 10c dp claret 25.00 2.50
Never hinged 60.00
Nos. J1-J4 (4) 157.50 18.25

Issues of the Republic

D1

1914 **Unwmk.** **Engr.** *Perf. 12*
J5 D1 1c carmine rose 8.00 1.25
J6 D1 2c carmine rose 9.00 1.25
J7 D1 5c carmine rose 10.00 2.50
Nos. J5-J7 (3) 27.00 5.00

1927-28
J8 D1 1c rose red 5.50 .90
J9 D1 2c rose red 8.50 .90
J10 D1 5c rose red 10.00 1.25
Nos. J8-J10 (3) 24.00 3.05

NEWSPAPER STAMPS

Issued under Spanish Dominion

N1

1888 **Unwmk.** **Typo.** *Perf. 14*
P1 N1 ½m black .25 *.25*
P2 N1 1m black .25 *.30*
P3 N1 2m black .25 *.30*
P4 N1 3m black 1.60 1.00
P5 N1 4m black 2.10 *2.00*
P6 N1 8m black 8.00 *8.50*
Nos. P1-P6 (6) 12.45 12.35

N2

1890
P7 N2 ½m red brown .55 *.65*
P8 N2 1m red brown .55 *.65*
P9 N2 2m red brown .90 *.95*
P10 N2 3m red brown 1.10 *1.10*
P11 N2 4m red brown 8.25 5.50
P12 N2 8m red brown 8.25 5.50
Nos. P7-P12 (6) 19.60 14.35

1892
P13 N2 ½m violet .25 *.30*
P14 N2 1m violet .25 *.30*
P15 N2 2m violet .25 *.30*
P16 N2 3m violet 1.10 .35
P17 N2 4m violet 4.25 1.90
P18 N2 8m violet 8.75 3.00
Nos. P13-P18 (6) 14.85 6.15

1894
P19 N2 ½m rose .25 *.30*
a. Imperf. pair 40.00 40.00
P20 N2 1m rose .50 .35
P21 N2 2m rose .55 .35
P22 N2 3m rose 2.10 1.40
P23 N2 4m rose 3.50 1.60
P24 N2 8m rose 6.00 4.00
Nos. P19-P24 (6) 12.90 8.00

1896
P25 N2 ½m blue green .25 *.30*
P26 N2 1m blue green .25 *.30*
P27 N2 2m blue green .25 *.30*
P28 N2 3m blue green 2.75 1.50
P29 N2 4m blue green 5.75 *7.00*
P30 N2 8m blue green 10.50 *10.00*
Nos. P25-P30 (6) 19.75 19.40

For surcharges see Nos. 190-193, 201-220.

POSTAL TAX STAMPS

Catalogue values for unused stamps in this section are for Never Hinged items.

Mother and Child — PT1

Wmk. Star. (106)

1938, Dec. 1 **Engr.** *Perf. 10*
RA1 PT1 1c bright green 2.50 .25

The tax benefited the National Council of Tuberculosis fund for children's hospitals. Obligatory on all mail during December and January. This note applies also to Nos. RA2-RA4, RA7-RA10, RA12-RA15, RA17-RA21.

Nurse with Child — PT2

1939, Dec. 1
RA2 PT2 1c orange vermilion 2.75 .25

"Health" Protecting Children — PT3

1940, Dec. 1
RA3 PT3 1c deep blue 2.50 .25

Mother and Child — PT4

1941, Dec. 1
RA4 PT4 1c olive bister 2.75 .25

Victory — PT5

1942-44
RA5 PT5 ½c orange 3.00 .25
RA6 PT5 ½c gray ('44) 2.75 .25

Issued: No. RA5, 7/1/42; No. RA6, 10/3/44.

Type of 1941 Overprinted in Black

1942, Dec. 1
RA7 PT4 1c salmon 2.25 .30
a. Inverted overprint 100.00 75.00

As PT3 — PT6

1943, Dec. 1
RA8 PT6 1c brown 2.25 .25

As PT4 — PT7

1949, Dec. 9
RA9 PT7 1c blue 1.50 .25

Type of 1949 Inscribed: "1950"

1950, Dec. 1 **Engr.**
RA10 PT7 1c rose red 2.50 .25

Proposed Communications Building — PT8

1951, June 5 Wmk. 106 *Perf. 10*

RA11 PT8 1c violet	1.75	.25

The tax was to help build a new Communications Building. This note applies also to Nos. RA16, RA34, RA43.

Woman Holding Child Aloft — PT9

1951, Dec. 1

RA12 PT9 1c violet blue	1.10	.25
RA13 PT9 1c brown carmine	1.10	.25
RA14 PT9 1c olive bister	1.10	.25
RA15 PT9 1c deep green	1.10	.25
Nos. RA12-RA15 (4)	4.40	1.00

Proposed Communications Building — PT10

1952, Feb. 8

RA16 PT10 1c slate blue	2.00	.25

See Nos. RA34, RA43.

Child — PT11

1952, Dec. 1

RA17 PT11 1c rose carmine	1.00	.25
RA18 PT11 1c yellow green	1.00	.25
RA19 PT11 1c blue	1.00	.25
RA20 PT11 1c orange	1.00	.25
Nos. RA17-RA20 (4)	4.00	1.00

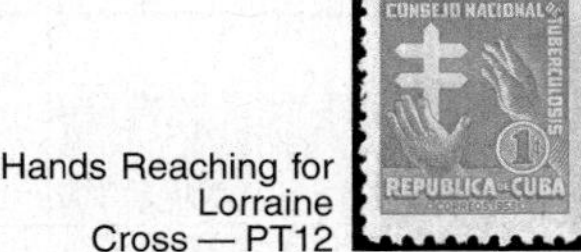
Hands Reaching for Lorraine Cross — PT12

1953, Dec. 1 *Perf. 9½*

RA21 PT12 1c rose carmine	1.75	.30

Child's Head, Lorraine Cross — PT13

1954, Nov. 1 *Perf. 9½x10*

RA22 PT13 1c rose red	.75	.30
RA23 PT13 1c violet	.75	.30
RA24 PT13 1c bright blue	.75	.30
RA25 PT13 1c emerald	.75	.30
Nos. RA22-RA25 (4)	3.00	1.20

The tax benefited the Natl. Council of Tuberculosis fund for children's hospitals. Obligatory on all mail during Nov., Dec., Jan. & Feb. This note also applies to Nos. RA26-RA33, RA35-RA42.

Rose and Watering Can — PT14

1955, Nov. 1

RA26 PT14 1c red orange	2.00	.30
RA27 PT14 1c red lilac	2.00	.30
RA28 PT14 1c bright blue	2.00	.30
RA29 PT14 1c orange yellow	2.00	.30
Nos. RA26-RA29 (4)	8.00	1.20

Child and Protective Hands — PT15

1956, Nov. 1

RA30 PT15 1c rose red	1.50	.30
RA31 PT15 1c yellow brown	1.50	.30
RA32 PT15 1c bright blue	1.50	.30
RA33 PT15 1c emerald	1.50	.30
Nos. RA30-RA33 (4)	6.00	1.20

Building Type of 1952

1957, Jan. 18 *Perf. 10*

RA34 PT10 1c rose red	1.75	.30

Mother and Child by Silvia Arrojo Fernandez — PT16

Wmk. 321

1957, Nov. 1 Engr. *Perf. 10*

RA35 PT16 1c dull rose	1.75	.30
RA36 PT16 1c bright blue	1.75	.30
RA37 PT16 1c gray	1.75	.30
RA38 PT16 1c emerald	1.75	.30
Nos. RA35-RA38 (4)	7.00	1.20

National Council of Tuberculosis — PT17

1958

RA39 PT17 1c rose red	1.50	.30
RA40 PT17 1c red brown	1.50	.30
RA41 PT17 1c gray	1.50	.30
RA42 PT17 1c emerald	1.50	.30
Nos. RA39-RA42 (4)	6.00	1.20

Building Type of 1952

1958 Wmk. 321

RA43 PT10 1c rose red	1.25	.30

CURACAO

'cər-ə-sau

LOCATION — North of Venezuela, east of Aruba in Caribbean Sea
AREA — 171 sq. mi.
POP. — 135,822 (2005)
CAPITAL — Willemstad

On Oct. 10, 2010, Curaçao, formerly part of Netherlands Antilles, became a constituent state within the Kingdom of the Netherlands. Stamps issued from 1873 to 1949 inscribed "Curaçao" were valid in all islands that comprised the Netherlands Antilles. These stamps are listed under "Netherlands Antilles."

100 Cents = 1 Gulden

Catalogue values for all unused stamps in this country are for Never Hinged items.

Map of Curaçao and West Indies, Arms and Flag A1

Perf. 13¾

2010, Oct. 10 Litho. Unwmk.

1 A1 111c multi	1.25	1.25

Souvenir Sheet

Touit Purpurata — A2

2010, Oct. 25 Litho. *Perf. 13¾*

2 A2 1500c multi	17.00	17.00

New Constitutional Status — A3

Designs: 1c, Sphere with colors of Curaçao flag, Diploria labyrinthiformis. 3c, Yellowtail snapper. 5c, Yellow goatfish. 30c, Blue hamlet. 63c, Rock beauty angelfish. 81c, Palometa jack. 112c, Spotfin butterflyfish. 166c, Cherubfish. 285c, Cocoa damselfish. 405c, Jewel damselfish. 630c, Schoolmaster snapper. Fish have colors of Curaçao flag.

2011, Jan. 11 *Perf. 13¼x12¾*

3 A3	1c multi	.25	.25
4 A3	3c multi	.25	.25
5 A3	5c multi	.25	.25
6 A3	30c multi	.35	.35
7 A3	63c multi	.70	.70
8 A3	81c multi	.90	.90
9 A3	112c multi	1.25	1.25
10 A3	166c multi	1.90	1.90
11 A3	285c multi	3.25	3.25
12 A3	405c multi	4.50	4.50
13 A3	630c multi	7.00	7.00
	Nos. 3-13 (11)	20.60	20.60

See Nos. 13A-13C, 215-216.

New Constitutional Status Type of 2011

Designs: 8c, Schoolmaster snapper. 115c, Spotfin butterflyfish. 171c, Cherubfish.

2012 Litho. *Perf. 13¼x12¾*

13A A3	8c multi	*20.00*	*20.00*
13B A3	115c multi	*20.00*	*20.00*
13C A3	171c multi	*20.00*	*20.00*

A4

Rabbit and: 112c, Big Wild Goose Pagoda, Xian, China. 145c, Great Wall of China, horiz. 166c, Temple of Heaven. 285c, Mountains near Li River, horiz. 405c, Paper lanterns.

Perf. 12¾x13¼, 13¼x12¾

2011, Feb. 11 Litho.

14-18 A4 Set of 5	12.50	12.50

New Year 2011 (Year of the Rabbit).

A5

Musical instruments: 49c, Double bass. 63c, Steel pan drums. 82c, Accordion. 145c, Saxophone. 166c, Djembe. 236c, Piano. 285c, Trombone. 405c, Pan flute. 700c, Cymbals.

2011, Mar. 11 *Perf. 12¾x13¼*

19-27 A5 Set of 9	24.00	24.00

Banknotes A6

Designs: 63c, 1947 Curaçao 1-gulden note. 75c, 1970 Netherlands Antilles 2½-gulden note. 112c, 1958 Curaçao 5-gulden note. 175c, 1948 Curaçao 10-gulden note. 200c, 1970 Netherlands Antilles 1-gulden note. 250c, 1967 Netherlands Antilles 5-gulden note. 300c, 1979 Netherlands Antilles 25-gulden note. 350c, 1972 Netherlands Antilles 50-gulden note. 475c, 1967 Netherlands Antilles 250-gulden note. 500c, 1962 Netherlands Antilles 500-gulden note.

2011, Apr. 11 *Perf. 14*

28-37 A6 Set of 10	28.00	28.00

2011 Paper Money Fair, Maastricht, Netherlands.

Souvenir Sheet

Prehistoric Animals — A7

No. 38: a, 700c, Ankylosaurus. b, 800c, Spinosaurus. c, 1000c, Saurolophus.

2011, June 11 ***Perf. 13¼x12¾***
38 A7 Sheet of 3, #a-c 27.00 27.00

New Technologies A8

Designs: 275c, Social media. 375c, Fiber optics. 475c Blackberry PIN messaging. 625c, Cloud computing.

2011, July 11
39-42 A8 Set of 4 19.50 19.50

Souvenir Sheet

Preservation of Polar Regions and Glaciers — A9

No. 43 — Iceberg and: a, 112c, Emblem. b, 405c, Map of Antarctica.

2011, Aug. 11 ***Perf. 13½***
43 A9 Sheet of 2, #a-b 5.50 5.50

Foods — A10

Designs: 63c, Almond cake. 81c, Apple pie. 112c, Blueberry pancakes. 145c, Broken glass cake. 166c, Lemon cake. 172c, Funchi (polenta cake). 195c, Chocolate cake. 285c, Fruit cake. 405c, Cherry cheesecake. 630c, Pumpkin cake

2011, Sept. 11 ***Perf. 13¼x12¾***
44-53 A10 Set of 10 22.50 22.50

Christmas — A11

Evergreen branches, candle and: 63c, Christmas cake (Bolo di Pasku), candy cane and hard candies. 112c, Ayaka. 145c, New Year's cake (Pan dushi) and hard candies. 166c, Christmas ham (Ham di Pasku). 172c, Salmon (Salmou di bari). 250c, Nuts (Nechi). 405c, Pickled pork (Sult).

2011, Nov. 11 ***Perf. 12¾x13¼***
54-60 A11 Set of 7 13.50 13.50

Miniature Sheet

Vegetables — A12

No. 61: a, 150c, Pumpkin and squashes. b, 200c, Okra. c, 225c, Onions. d, 325c, Bell peppers. e, 500c, Corn. f, 750c, Tomatoes.

2011, Dec. 11
61 A12 Sheet of 6, #a-f 22.00 22.00

Fish — A13

Designs: 25c, Myripristis botche. 150c, Neoniphon opercularis. 225c, Sargocentron spiniferum. 325c, Anyperodon leucogrammicus. 475c, Cephalopholis sonnerati. 500c, Epinephelus caeruleopunctatus. 700c, Abudefduf vaigiensis.

2012, Jan. 12 ***Perf. 14***
62-68 A13 Set of 7 27.00 27.00

Nos. 62-68 were printed in sheets of 14 containing two of each stamp and a central label.

New Year 2012 (Year of the Dragon) A14

Designs: No. 69, 500c, Dragon. No. 70, 500c, Dragon facing left, horiz.
No. 71, 500c, Yin-yang, dragon, Chinese character.

Perf. 13½x14, 14x13½
2012, Feb. 13 **Litho. & Embossed**
69-70 A14 Set of 2 10.00 10.00

Souvenir Sheet

71 A14 500c multi 5.00 5.00

Miniature Sheet

Birds — A15

No. 72: a, 75c, Laughing gulls (24x27mm). b, 150c, Dunlins (36x27mm). c, 200c, Gannets (24x27mm). d, 225c, Frigatebirds (36x27mm). e, 300c, Snowy egret (24x27mm). f, 350c, Flamingos (36x27mm). g, 500c, Great blue heron (24x27mm). h, 700c, Pelican (36x27mm).

Perf. 13¼x13¾
2012, Mar. 12 **Litho.**
72 A15 Sheet of 8, #a-h 26.00 26.00

Miniature Sheet

Railways in Curacao — A16

No. 73: a, 200c, Dumping cars (40x21mm). b, 250c, Horse tram (30x39mm). c, 300c, Plymouth locomotive (30x42mm). d, 350c, Motor tram (40x18mm).

2012, Apr. 12 ***Perf. 14x13½***
73 A16 Sheet of 4, #a-d, + central label 12.50 12.50

Souvenir Sheet

June 6, 2012 Transit of Venus — A17

2012, May 21 ***Perf. 13¼***
74 A17 2500c multi 25.00 25.00

A18

Indonesia 2012 World Stamp Exhibition, Jakarta — A19

2012, June 18 ***Perf. 13½x13***
75 A18 10c multi .25 .25

Souvenir Sheet

Perf.

76 A19 200c multi 2.25 2.25

Fruit — A20

Designs: 275c, Watermelons. 375c, Pineapples. 475c, Bananas. 625c, Mangos.

2012, June 12 ***Perf. 13x13½***
77-80 A20 Set of 4 19.50 19.50

Miniature Sheet

Sports — A21

No. 81: a, 25c, Cycling. b, 50c, Swimming. c, 75c, Sailboarding. d, 100c, Soccer. e, 125c, Handball. f, 150c, Judo. g, 175c, Track. h, 200c, Baseball.

2012, July 12 ***Perf. 13¾***
81 A21 Sheet of 8, #a-h 10.00 10.00

Flora — A22

Designs: 75c, Datura metel. 100c, Opuntia wentiana. 150c, Caesalpina pulcherrima. 200c, Melocactus macracanthus. 250c, Crescentia cujete, horiz. 300c, Ritterocereus griseus, horiz. 350c, Calutropis procera, horiz. 450c, Zizyphus spina-cristi, horiz.

Perf. 13x13½, 13½x13
2012, Aug. 13
82-89 A22 Set of 8 21.00 21.00

Miniature Sheet

Tourist Attractions — A23

No. 90: a, Tafelberg. b, Penha. c, Brug di Ponton Koningin Emmabrug (Queen Emma Pontoon Bridge), Willemstad. d, Bark'i Fruta (fruit market). e, Kenepa Grandi Beach. f, Landhuis Zeelandia. g, Koningin Julianabrug (Queen Juliana Bridge). h, Houses along Berg Altena. i, Handelskade, Willemstad. j, Statuut-monument (Statute of Autonomy Monument).

2012, Sept. 27 ***Perf. 13½x13***
90 A23 171c Sheet of 10, #a-j 19.50 19.50

Christmas — A24

Designs: 64c, Angel. 115c, Madonna and Child. 171c, Shepherd and donkey. 190c, Star of Bethlehem. 293c, Three Kings.

2012, Nov. 12 ***Perf. 13x13¼***
91-95 A24 Set of 5 9.50 9.50

Souvenir Sheet

End of Mayan Calendar Cycle — A25

No. 96: a, 200c, Pyramid at Chichen Itza, Mexico. b, 400c, Mayan Calendar. c, 600c, Date of end of Mayan Calendar cycle (Dec. 21, 2012).

2012, Dec. 21 ***Perf.***
96 A25 Sheet of 3, #a-c 13.50 13.50

Faith — A26

Designs: 118c, Names of various deities. 175c, Words for "faith" in various languages. 200c, Candles. 250c, Statue of Buddha and prayer wheel. 300c, Cross and stained-glass window depicting saint. 350c, Star of David and Torah.

2013, Jan. 21 ***Perf. 13¼x12¾***

97	A26 118c multi	1.40	1.40
a.	Tete-beche pair	2.80	2.80
98	A26 175c multi	2.00	2.00
a.	Tete-beche pair	4.00	4.00
99	A26 200c multi	2.25	2.25
a.	Tete-beche pair	4.50	4.50
100	A26 250c multi	2.75	2.75
a.	Tete-beche pair	5.50	5.50
101	A26 300c multi	3.50	3.50
a.	Tete-beche pair	7.00	7.00
102	A26 350c multi	4.00	4.00
a.	Tete-beche pair	8.00	8.00
	Nos. 97-102 (6)	15.90	15.90

New Year 2013 (Year of the Snake) A27

Various snakes and flowers: 175c, 301c, 428c.
500c, Snake in tree.

2013, Feb. 22 ***Perf. 13¼x12¾***
103-105 A27 Set of 3 10.50 10.50

Souvenir Sheet

Perf. 14x13¼
106 A27 500c multi 5.00 5.00

No. 106 contains one 50x40mm stamp.

Abstract Art — A28

Various works of abstract art and silhouettes of people: 118c, 175c, 200c, 250c, 301c, 450c.
250c, 301c, 450c are vert.

Perf. 13¼x12¾, 12¾x13¼
2013, Mar. 13
107-112 A28 Set of 6 17.00 17.00

Suggestions for Environmentally Friendly Living — A29

Inscriptions: 65c, Saving energy using LED lights. 118c, Drive Green. 175c, Solar energy. 181c, Recycle. 301c, Wind energy. 350c, Rainwater. 428c, Plant trees and protect wetlands.

2013, Apr. 15 ***Perf. 13¼x12¾***
113-119 A29 Set of 7 18.00 18.00

Souvenir Sheet

Royal Transition in the Netherlands — A30

No. 120 — Silhouette of: a, New King Willem-Alexander. b, Abdicating Queen Beatrix.

Litho. with Foil Application
2013, Apr. 30 ***Perf. 13¾***
120 A30 1000c Sheet of 2, #a-b 22.50 22.50

Baseball A31

Designs: 65c, Batter hitting ball. 118c, Catcher. 175c, Pitcher. 181c, Team celebrating victory. 301c, Outfielder. 350c, Fielder tagging runner out at base. 428c, Baseball field.

2013, May 13 Litho. ***Perf. 13¼x12¾***
121-127 A31 Set of 7 16.00 16.00

Ocean Liner Freewinds A32

Freewinds and: 118c, Palm fronds. 175c, Birds.
250c, Bow of Freewinds, vert.

2013, June 1 Litho. ***Perf. 13½x13***
128-129 A32 Set of 2 3.25 3.25

Souvenir Sheet

Perf. 13x13½
130 A32 250c multi 3.00 3.00

Virtues — A33

Designs: 118c, Respect. 175c, Love. 250c, Hope. 301c, Forgiveness. 350c, Mercy. 428c, Peace.

2013, July 22 Litho. ***Perf. 12¾x13¼***
131-136 A33 Set of 6 18.00 18.00

Souvenir Sheet

Schottegat, Curaçao — A34

2013, Aug. 20 Litho. ***Perf. 13¾***
137 A34 1000c multi 11.50 11.50

See Malta No. 1491.

Miniature Sheet

Tourist Attractions — A35

No. 138: a, Den Dunki Bridge. b, Spaanse (Spanish) Water. c, Blue Room. d, Veeris Hill. e, Boca Tabla Natural Bridge. f, Playa Kanoa. g, Noordkant. h, Blow hole near Watamula. i, Hato Caves. j, Natural Swimming Pool.

Perf. 13¼x12¾
2013, Sept. 27 **Litho.**
138 A35 175c Sheet of 10, #a-j 19.50 19.50

Fairy Tales — A36

Designs: 100c, The Wolf and the Seven Goats. 145c, The Frog Prince. 190c, Little Red Riding Hood. 293c, Pinocchio, vert. 301c, Puss in Boots, vert. 428c, Jack and the Beanstalk, vert.

Perf. 13¼x12¾, 12¾x13¼
2013, Oct. 21 **Litho.**
139-144 A36 Set of 6 16.50 16.50

Christmas A37

Fireworks and: 65c, Building with wreath and decorations in fence. 118c, Building with wreaths on gate. 175c, Shop, other buildings, street lights, Christmas tree. 190c, Church tower, vert. 301c, Clock tower with bells, street light, vert.

Perf. 13¼x12¾, 12¾x13¼
2013, Nov. 13 **Litho.**
145-149 A37 Set of 5 9.50 9.50

Beetles A38

Designs: 65c, Chlorocala africana oertzeni. 118c, Stephanorrhina julia. 175c, Amaurodes passerinii nyanzanus. 181c, Cetonischema speciosa jouselini protaetia. 250c, Goliathus orientalis. 301c, Eudicella aethiopica. 428c, Ranzania bertoloni. 500c, Dicronorrhina layardi.

Perf. 13¾x12¾
2013, Dec. 13 **Litho.**
150-157 A38 Set of 8 22.50 22.50

A39

A40

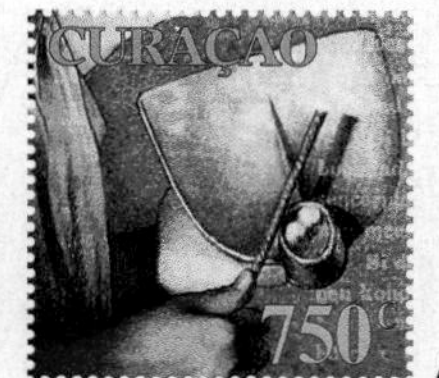
A41

Emancipation of Slaves in Kingdom of the Netherlands, 150th Anniv. — A42

2013 **Litho.**

158	Souvenir booklet	28.50	
a.	A39 500c multi, perf. 13¼	5.75	5.75
b.	A40 500c multi, perf.	5.75	5.75
c.	A41 750c multi, perf. 13¼	8.50	8.50
d.	A42 750c multi, perf. 13¼x14	8.50	8.50

Nos. 158a-158d were each printed in booklet panes of 1.

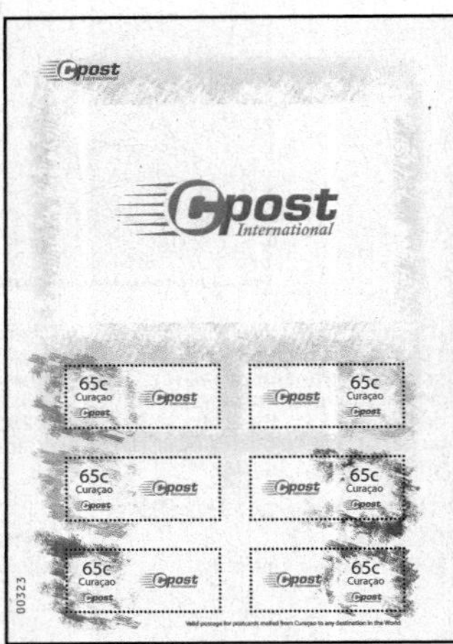

In 2014 Curacao began issuing personalizable stamps. Stamps were made available in sheets of 6 stamps. Numerous different frame designs, inscriptions, emblems and denominations have been reported.

Kingdom of the Netherlands, 200th Anniv. — A43

Designs: 150c, Crown and heraldic lion. 200c, Crown. 250c, Coat of arms. 300c, Post horn and motto, horiz. 350c, Heraldic lion and motto, horiz.

Perf. 12¾x13¼, 13¼x12¼

2014, Jan. 14 **Litho.**
159-163 A43 Set of 5 14.00 14.00

Miniature Sheet

New Year 2014 (Year of the Horse) — A44

No. 164 — Horse and: a, Men on boat (40x21mm). b, Building (30x42mm). c, Lanterns (30x39mm). d, Man carrying buckets (40x18mm).

2014, Jan. 31 **Litho.** ***Perf. 14x13¼***
164 A44 300c Sheet of 4, #a-d, + central label 13.50 13.50

Friendship — A45

Quote and heart with: 65c, Cake. 119c, Roses. 177c, Chocolate candies. 183c, Tedddy bear. 305c, Gemstone. 434c, Drink with fruit garnishes.

Perf. 12¾x13¼

2014, Feb. 14 **Litho.**
165-170 A45 Set of 6 14.50 14.50

Birds of Prey — A46

Designs: 100c, Haliaeetus leucocephalus. 200c, Spizaetus ornatus. 250c, Aquila chrysaetos. 300c, Geranoaetus melanoleucus. 350c, Falconidae polyborinae. 400c, Pandion haliaetus.

2014, Mar. 14 **Litho.** ***Perf. 13¼***
171-176 A46 Set of 6 18.00 18.00

Miniature Sheet

William Shakespeare (1564-1616), Writer — A47

No. 177 — Shakespeare, with denomination at: a, Lower right. b, Upper right. c, Bottom center above name. d, Lower left, next to country name.

2014, Apr. 23 **Litho.** ***Perf. 12¾x13¼***
177 A47 400c Sheet of 4, #a-d 18.00 18.00

Automobiles A48

Designs: 65c, 1964 Ford Mustang. 119c, 1965 Ford Mustang Fastback. 177c, 2014 Ford Mustang. 183c, 1958 Porsche 356A Speedster. 430c, 1964 Porsche 356C. 676c, 2014 Porsche 911 Targa.

2014, May 14 **Litho.** ***Perf. 13¼x12¾***
178-183 A48 Set of 6 18.50 18.50

Miniature Sheet

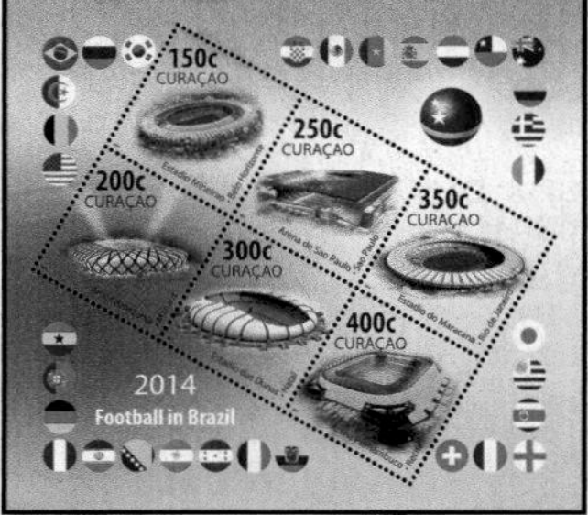

Stadiums of the 2014 World Cup Soccer Championships, Brazil — A49

No. 184: a, 150c, Estadio Mineirao, Belo Horizonte. b, 200c, Arena Amazonia, Manaus. c, 250c, Arena de Sao Paulo, Sao Paulo. d, 300c, Estadio das Dunas, Natal. e, 350c, Estadio do Maracana, Rio de Janeiro. f, 400c, Arena Pernambuco, Recife.

2014, June 12 **Litho.** ***Perf. 14x13¼***
184 A49 Sheet of 6, #a-f 18.50 18.50

Peace — A50

Designs: 65c, Dove and "Peace." 119c, Hebrew, Dutch, French and Latin words for "peace." 177c, Hindi, German, Danish and Italian words for "peace." 183c, Family, Papiamento word for "peace," Papiamento, English, Spanish and French words for "family." 305c, Arabic, Farsi, Russian and Spanish words for "peace." 434c, Chinese, Icelandic, Greek and Finnish words for "peace."

2014, July 28 **Litho.** ***Perf. 13¼x12¾***
185-190 A50 Set of 6 14.50 14.50

Miniature Sheet

PhilaKorea 2014 World Stamp Exhibition, Seoul — A51

No. 191 — Pinwheel and: a, Girl facing left. b, Dove. c, Rainbow. d, Boy facing right.

2014, Aug. 7 **Litho.** ***Perf. 12¾x13¼***
191 A51 400c Sheet of 4, #a-d 18.00 18.00

Fight Against Cancer — A52

Ribbons and various silhouettes of people: 86c, 119c, 177c, 183c, 285c, 750c.

Perf. 12¾x13¼

2014, Aug. 22 **Litho.**
192-197 A52 Set of 6 18.00 18.00

World Orchid Conference, South Africa — A53

Orchids: 119c, Angraecum stella-africae. 177c, Disa longicornu. 183c, Stenoglottis fimbriata. 305c, Ansellia africana. 382c, Calanthe sylvatica. 434c, Disa uniflora.

Perf. 12¾x13¼

2014, Sept. 10 **Litho.**
198-203 A53 Set of 6 18.00 18.00

Miniature Sheet

XCOR Space Expeditions — A54

No. 204: a, Space plane at space port. b, Space plane control panel. c, Space port. d, Stars, wing of space plane. e, Nose of space plane. f, XCOR Space Expeditions emblem. g, Earth's horizon as seen from space. h, Burning exhaust of test engine. i, Burning exhaust of space plane in flight. j, Earth, wing of space plane.

2014, Sept. 26 **Litho.** ***Perf. 14***
204 A54 177c Sheet of 10, #a-j 20.00 20.00

Caricatures of Marine Life — A55

Designs: 100c, Turtle, starfish, shell. 119c, Fish, oyster with pearl. 177c, Octopus, snail. 305c, Dolphin. 500c, Crab, sea urchin, shells, starfish.

2014, Oct. 14 **Litho.** ***Perf. 13x13½***
205-209 A55 Set of 5 13.50 13.50

Christmas A56

Christmas gifts and various children: 65c, 119c, 117c, 183c, 305c.

2014, Nov. 14 **Litho.** ***Perf. 13¼***
210-214 A56 Set of 5 9.50 9.50

New Constitutional Status Type of 2011

Designs: 2c, Cocoa damselfish. 4c, Jewel damselfish.

2014 **Litho.** ***Perf. 13¼x12¾***
215 A3 2c multi .25 .25
216 A3 4c multi .25 .25

Miniature Sheet

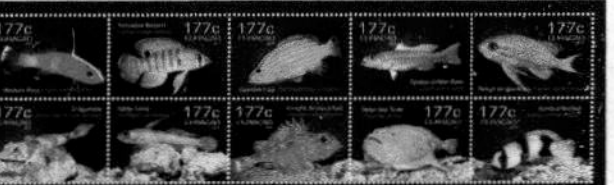

Fish — A57

No. 217: a, Bladefin bass. b, Yellowbar basslet. c, Spanish flag. d, Spottail golden bass. e, Rough-tongue bass. f, Dragonette. g, Saber goby. h, Longfin-scorpionfish. i, Deep sea toad. j, Banded basslet.

2014, Nov. 30 **Litho.** ***Perf. 14x13¾***
217 A57 177c Sheet of 10, #a-j 20.00 20.00

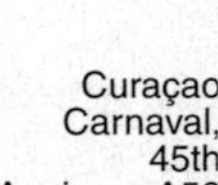

Curaçao Carnaval, 45th Anniv. — A58

Various costumed participants: 65c, 119c, 177c, 183c, 305c, 434c.

2015, Jan. 19 **Litho.** ***Perf. 13¼x13¾***
218-223 A58 Set of 6 14.50 14.50

New Year 2015 (Year of the Goat) — A59

Various goats: 177c, 183c, 305c, 535c.

2015, Feb. 19 **Litho.** ***Perf. 13½x14***
224-227 A59 Set of 4 13.50 13.50

Miniature Sheet

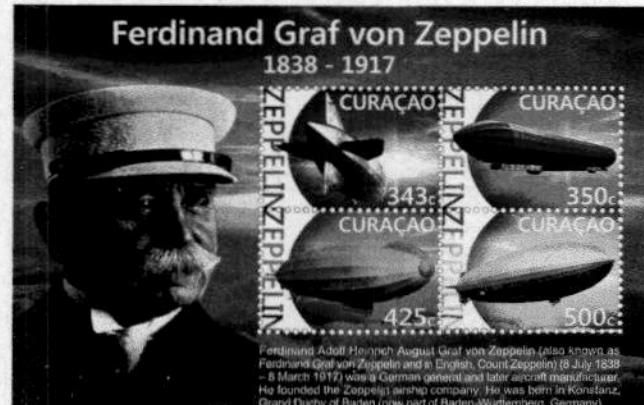

Zeppelins — A60

No. 228 — Various zeppelins with color of: a, 343c, Purple. b, 350c, Red. c, 425c, Green. d, 500c, Yellow.

2015, Mar. 19 Litho. ***Perf. 13x12¾***
228 A60 Sheet of 4, #a-d 18.00 18.00

Miniature Sheet

Travels of Pope Francis — A61

No. 229: a, Pope Francis, two women. b, Dove, Pope Francis, hands and camera. c, Back of head of Pope Francis. d, Pope Francis kissing child.

2015, Apr. 20 Litho. ***Perf. 13¼***
229 A61 400c Sheet of 4, #a-d 18.00 18.00

Mammals A62

Designs: 65c, Solenodontidae. 119c, Hutias. 177c, Odocoileus virginianus curassavicus. 183c, Sylvilagus floridanus. 430c, Tursiops truncatus. 676c, Leptonycteris curasoae.

2015, May 19 Litho. ***Perf. 13¾***
230-235 A62 Set of 6 18.50 18.50

Miniature Sheet

Space — A63

No. 236: a, 200c, Pluto and Charon. b, 250c, First man on the Moon, 1969. c, 400c, Mars Lander. d, 750c, Mars Rover Curiosity.

2015, June 29 Litho. ***Perf. 13¼***
236 A63 Sheet of 4, #a-d 18.00 18.00

Miniature Sheet

World War I, Cent. — A64

No. 237 — Poppy and: a, 250c, Soldiers. b, 350c, Soldier's helmet and gas mask. c, 450c, Airplane, airship and tank. d, 550c, Medal and cemetery.

2015, July 15 Litho. ***Perf. 13¾x13½***
237 A64 Sheet of 4, #a-d 18.00 18.00

A65

A66

A67

A68

A69

Self-Portraits of Vincent van Gogh (1853-90) and Places in Curaçao — A70

Perf. 13¼x12¾, 12¾x13¼
2015, July 29 Litho.

238	A65	119c multi	1.40	1.40
239	A66	177c multi	2.00	2.00
240	A67	183c multi	2.10	2.10
241	A68	285c multi	3.25	3.25
242	A69	305c multi	3.50	3.50
243	A70	434c multi	5.00	5.00
		Nos. 238-243 (6)	17.25	17.25

Miniature Sheet

Singapore 2015 World Stamp Exhibition — A71

No. 244: a, 325c, Merlion statue. b, 400c, Orchid. c, 425c, Singapore coat of arms. d, 500c, Flag of Singapore.

2015, Aug. 14 Litho. ***Perf. 12¾x13***
244 A71 Sheet of 4, #a-d 18.50 18.50

Miniature Sheet

Elvis Presley (1935-77) — A72

No. 245: a, 300c, Presley and RCA Victor emblem. b, 400c, Presley. c, 400c, Presley holding microphone and guitar, horiz. d, 500c, Presley playing guitar, horiz.

Perf. 13½x14, 14x13½
2015, Aug. 28 Litho.
245 A72 Sheet of 4, #a-d 18.00 18.00

Dogs — A73

Dogs of various breeds: 86c, 119c, 177c, 183c, 305c, 434c.

2015, Sept. 24 Litho. ***Perf. 13¾***
246-251 A73 Set of 6 14.50 14.50

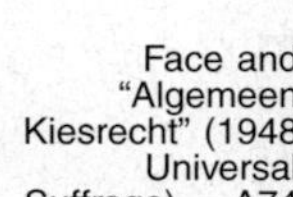

Face and "Algemeen Kiesrecht" (1948 Universal Suffrage) — A74

Face and "Eilandenregeling" (1951 Islands Regulation of the Netherlands Antilles) — A75

Face and "Statuut" (1954 Charter for the Kingdom of the Netherlands) A76

Face and "Van Eiland Naar Land" (2010 Dissolution of the Netherlands Antilles) — A77

2015, Oct. 8 Litho. ***Perf. 13¼***

252	A74	1.19g multi	1.40	1.40
253	A75	1.77g multi	2.00	2.00
254	A76	3.05g multi	3.50	3.50
255	A77	3.05g multi	3.50	3.50
		Nos. 252-255 (4)	10.40	10.40

Curaçao as constituent state within the Kingdom of the Netherlands, 5th anniv.

Youth Health — A78

Designs: 65c, Girl brushing teeth. 119c, Boy washing hands. 177c, Girl sitting on toilet. 305c, Child showering. 434c, Girl brushing hair.

2015, Oct. 29 Litho. ***Perf. 13¼x13***
256-260 A78 Set of 5 12.50 12.50

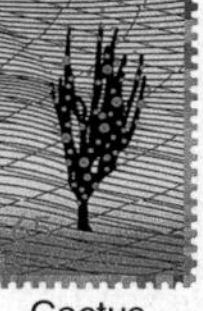

Cactus A79

Ship A80

Klein Curaçao Lighthouse A81

Santa Claus, Sleigh and Reindeer A82

Crane — A83

Queen Juliana Bridge — A84

2015, Nov. 26 Litho. ***Perf. 14x13½***

261	A79	65c multi	.75	.75
262	A80	86c multi	1.00	1.00
263	A81	119c multi	1.40	1.40
264	A82	177c multi	2.00	2.00
265	A83	183c multi	2.10	2.10
266	A84	305c multi	3.50	3.50
		Nos. 261-266 (6)	10.75	10.75

Christmas.

Repeating Numerals A85

Denomination color: 66c, Orange. 86c, Red. 121c, Purple. 179c, Deep green. 308c, Royal blue. 440c, Carmine red.

2016, Jan. 28 Litho. *Perf. 13¾*
267-272 A85 Set of 6 13.50 13.50

Miniature Sheet

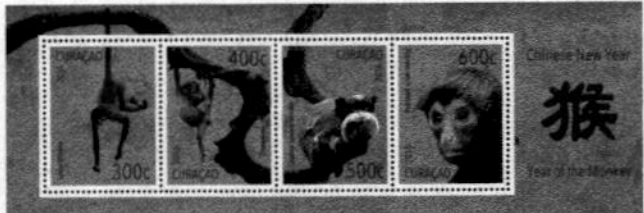

New Year 2016 (Year of the Monkey) — A86

No. 273: a, 300c, Spider monkey. b, 400c, Orangutan. c, 500c, Emperor tamarin monkey. d, 600c, Red-faced spider monkey.

2016, Feb. 8 Litho. *Perf. 14x13½*
273 A86 Sheet of 4, #a-d 20.00 20.00

Native Indian Drawings — A87

Various drawings: 93c, 121c, 156c, 185c, 285c, 684c.

Perf. 12¾x13¼
2016, Mar. 24 Litho.
274-279 A87 Set of 6 17.00 17.00

Ship Hulls — A88

Various details of ship hulls: 300c, 350c, 400c, 450c, 500c, 550c.

2016, Apr. 28 Litho. *Perf. 13¼x12¾*
280-285 A88 Set of 6 28.50 28.50

Bays — A89

Designs: 66c, Jan Kok Bay. 121c, Santa Martha Bay. 179c, Piscadera Bay. 308c, San Juan Bay. 440c, Spanish Water Bay, vert. 684c, Sint Joris Bay.

Perf. 14x13½, 13½x14
2016, Aug. 8 Litho.
286-291 A89 Set of 6 20.00 20.00

Parts of Nos. 286-291 are coated with a thick varnish containing grit.

Christmas — A90

Designs: 66c, Christmas tree. 121c, Candy canes. 179c, Bells. 308c, Christmas ornaments. 440c, Holly. 684c, Stars.

2016, Nov. 17 Litho. *Perf. 13½*
292-297 A90 Set of 6 20.00 20.00

Nerw Year 2017 (Year of the Rooster) — A91

Head of rooster with: 66c, Brown ochre feathers. 121c, Orange brown feathers. 179c, Black feathers.

No. 301: a, Head of rooster facing right. b, Entire rooster. c, Head of rooster facing left.

2017, Feb. 28 Litho. *Perf. 13¼*
298-300 A91 Set of 3 4.25 4.25

Souvenir Sheet

301 A91 500c Sheet of 3, #a-c 17.00 17.00

Miniature Sheet

King Willem-Alexander, 50th Birthday — A92

No. 302: a, 121c, King Willem-Alexander, Queen Máxima and daughters (42x32mm). b, 179c, King Willem-Alexander (42x49mm). c, 308c, King Willem-Alexander (86x30mm). d, 440c, Wedding photograph of King Willem-Alexander and Queen Máxima (58x62mm). e, 684c, King Willem-Alexander and Queen Máxima, diff. (60mm diameter)

2017, Apr. 27 Litho. *Perf. 14¼x14½*
302 A92 Sheet of 5, #a-e 19.50 19.50

Butterflies A93

Designs: 121c, Dryas iulia. 145c, Tropical checkered skipper. 179c, Junonia evarete. 211c, Danaus plexippus. 308c, Heliconius erato. 684c, Danaus eresimus.

2017, May 3 Litho. *Perf. 13¼x12¾*
303-308 A93 Set of 6 18.50 18.50

Curaçao in the 1950s — A94

Designs: 121c, Sailboat and buildings. 179c, Airport. 211c, Car, bridge and buildings. 308c, Ship and buildings. 440c, City street. 684c, Marketplace.

Perf. 13¼x12¾
2017, June 19 Litho.
309-314 A94 Set of 6 22.00 22.00

Writers — A95

Designs: 66c, Elis Juliana (1927-2013). 121c, Boeli van Leeuwen (1922-2007). 179c, May Henriquez (1915-99). 308c, Tip Marrug (1923-2006). 440c, Luis Daal (1919-97). 684c, Frank Martinus Arion (1936-2015).

2017, Sept. 22 Litho. *Perf. 13¼*
315-320 A95 Set of 6 20.00 20.00

Christmas A96

Various Nativity scenes: 121c, 179c, 308c, 440c, 684c.

Perf. 13¼x12¾
2017, Nov. 17 Litho.
321-325 A96 Set of 5 19.50 19.50

New Year 2018 (Year of the Dog) — A97

Dog and: 66c, Waterfront buildings. 122c, Bridge and ship, horiz. 180c, Cactus, horiz. 310c, House and windmill, horiz. 443c, Bone, tree and hills, horiz. 690c, Building.

Perf. 12¾x13¼, 13¼x12¾
2018, Feb. 16 Litho.
326-331 A97 Set of 6 20.50 20.50

Flowers — A98

Designs: 86c, West Indian jasmine. 122c, Passion flower. 180c, Rubber vine. 190c, Orange Geiger tree. 285c, Peacock flowers. 425c, White and yellow frangipani. 443c, Giant milkweed. 690c, Prickly pear.

2018, Apr. 18 Litho. *Perf. 14*
332-339 A98 Set of 8 27.00 27.00

Lighthouses A99

Designs: 66c, Feu de Marigot Lighthouse, St. Martin. 122c, Klein Curaçao Lighthouse, Curaçao. 180c, Noordpunt Lighthouse, Curaçao. 310c, Fort Orange Lighthouse, Bonaire. 443c, California Lighthouse, Aruba. 690c, Ceru Bentana Lighthouse, Bonaire, horiz.

Perf. 13¼x13¾, 13¾x13¼
2018, July 18 Litho.
340-345 A99 Set of 6 20.50 20.50

Cruise Ship Freewinds A100

Designs: 122c, Ship at dock. 180c, Ship at sea, vert.

300c, Bow of ship, vert.

Perf. 13¼x12¾, 12¾x13¼
2018, July 26 Litho.
346-347 A100 Set of 2 3.50 3.50

Souvenir Sheet

348 A100 300c multi 3.50 3.50

Christmas A101

Designs: 66c, Christmas tree in house. 122c, Houses with Christmas decorations. 180c, House with Christmas decorations, bright star in sky. 310c, Family watching fireworks display. 443c, Man playing guitar to woman and child, Christmas tree in house. 690c, Goats and cacti, bright star in sky.

Litho. With Glitter Affixed
2018, Nov. 1 *Perf. 13¼*
349-354 A101 Set of 6 20.50 20.50

Aspects of Life in Curaçao A102

Designs: 68c, House and iguana. 1, Woman in traditional costume. 160c, Goat and dog. 2, Buildings. 319c, Chair and lamp in room. 456c, Sandals on beach and catamaran.

2019, Jan. 21 Litho. *Perf. 13¼*
355-360 A102 Set of 6 15.00 15.00

On day of issue, No. 356 sold for 124c and No. 358 sold for 186c.

Miniature Sheet

New Year 2019 (Year of the Pig) — A103

No. 361 — Various depictions of pigs: a, 350c. b, 400c. c, 450c. d, 500c. e, 550c. f, 600c.

2019, Feb. 5 Litho. *Perf. 14x13¼*
361 A103 Sheet of 6, #a-f 32.00 32.00

Marine Life — A104

Designs: 68c, Pylopagurus discoidalis. 1, Linckia nodosa. 2, Entemnotrochus adansonianus. 319c, Ophiarachnella petersi. 456c, Mantellina translucens. 711c, Calliostoma rosewateri.

No. 368: a, Acanthodromia erinacea. b, Allodardanus bredini. c, Stenocionops spinosissimus. d, Myropsis quinquespinosa.

Perf. 13½x12¾

2019, Mar. 19 Litho.
362-367 A104 Set of 6 21.00 21.00

Souvenir Sheet

368 A104 300c Sheet of 4, #a-d 13.50 13.50

No. 363 sold for 124c and No. 364 sold for 186c on day of issue.

Musicians — A105

Designs: 68c, Janchi Bosklajon (1863-1936). 1, Nicolaas "Shon Cola" Susana (1916-2003). 160c, Edgar Palm (1905-98). 2, Wim Statius Muller (1930-2019). 319c, Clara Henriquez (1939-63). 711c, Julián B. Coco (1924-2013).

2019, Apr. 26 Litho. *Perf. 12¾x13¼*
369-374 A105 Set of 6 17.50 17.50

On day of issue, No. 370 sold for 124c, and No. 372 sold for 186c.

Souvenir Sheet

Worker's Revolt, 50th Anniv. — A106

2019, May 30 Litho. *Perf. 13¼x14*
375 A106 1000c multi 11.50 11.50

Souvenir Sheet

Flag Day, 35th Anniv. — A107

2019, July 2 Litho. *Perf. 14x13¼*
376 A107 1000c multi 11.50 11.50

Miniature Sheet

Modern Architecture — A108

No. 377 — Various buildings: a, 450c. b, 550c. c, 650c. d, 750c.

2019, July 26 Litho. *Perf. 13½*
377 A108 Sheet of 4, #a-d 27.00 27.00

Miniature Sheet

Musical Heritage — A109

No. 378: a, 200c, Wiri (40x30mm). b, 300c, Cylinder (40x30mm), c, 500c, Ka'i orgel at dance party (50x30mm). d, 800c, Horace J. Sprock (1866-1949), importer of ka'i orgel to Curaçao (50x30mm).

2019, Sept. 23 Litho. *Perf. 14x13¼*
378 A109 Sheet of 4, #a-d 20.00 20.00

Children — A110

Designs: 68c, Girl walking. 124c, Girl sitting. 186c, Boy crouching, horiz. 315c, Boy sitting. 319c, Girl on knees, horiz. 456c, Girl sitting, horiz.

Perf. 13¼x14, 14x13¼

2019, Oct. 19 Litho.
379-384 A110 Set of 6 16.50 16.50

Souvenir Sheet

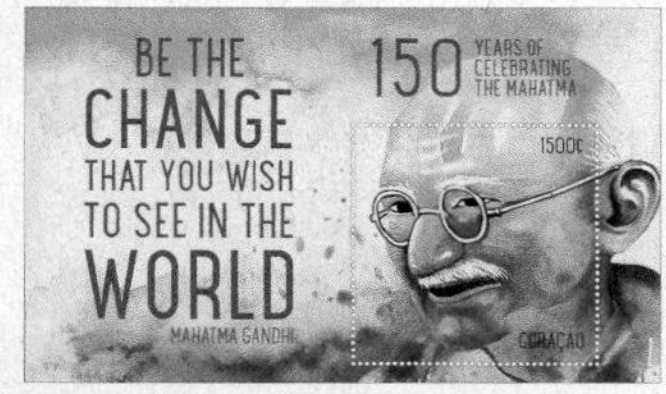

Mohandas K. Gandhi (1869-1948), Indian Nationalist Leader — A111

2019, Nov. 19 Litho. *Perf. 14x13¼*
385 A111 1500c multi 17.00 17.00

Biblical Figures — A112

Designs: 68c, Samson. 1, Moses, horiz. 2, Jesus, Simon and Andrew on boat, horiz. 315c, Daniel and lion. 319c, Jonah and whale. 711c, David and Goliath.

Perf. 12¾x13¼, 13¼x12¾

2019, Dec. 1 Litho.
386-391 A112 Set of 6 19.50 19.50

Christmas. On day of issue, No. 387 sold for 124c and No. 388 sold for 186c.

Miniature Sheet

KLM Royal Dutch Airlines, Cent. — A113

No. 392: a, 124c, DC-4 "Flying Dutchman" (30x21mm). b, 186c, Fokker F.XVIII "Snip and map" (40x21mm). c, 315c, DC-10 and flight map (30x42mm). d, 319c, Dr. Albert Plesman Airport, Curaçao (30x39mm). e, 456c, Lockheed-14 Super Electra (30x39mm). f, 747c, Boeing 747-400 (40x18mm).

2019, Dec. 19 Litho. *Perf. 14x13¼*
392 A113 Sheet of 6, #a-f, + label 24.00 24.00

New Year 2020 (Year of the Rat) — A114

Various rats: 70c, 1, 2, 331c, 474c, 739c.

Litho. With Foil Application

2020, Jan. 25 *Perf. 12¾x13¼*
393-398 A114 Set of 6 21.50 21.50

On day of issue, No. 394 sold for 127c and No. 395 sold for 192c,

50th Curaçao Carnival A115

Designs: 70c, Dancers. 1, Tumba Festival announcer. 2, Text and masks. 331c, Woman in costume. 474c, Woman wearing sash. 739c, Drummers.

2020, Feb. 20 Litho. *Perf. 13¼*
399-404 A115 Set of 6 21.50 21.50

On day of issue, No. 400 sold for 127c and No. 401 sold for 192c,

Souvenir Sheet

Margareth Abraham (1945-70), Flight Attendant Killed in Crash of ALM Flight 980 — A116

No. 405: a, 474c, Abraham seated in airplane. b, 739c, Abraham on stairway.

2020, May 2 Litho. *Perf. 14x13¼*
405 A116 Sheet of 2, #a-b 13.50 13.50

Souvenir Sheet

Front Line Workers in Coronavirus Pandemic — A117

No. 406 — Various front line workers with: a, Denomination in white. b, Country name in white. c, "Thank you" in white.

2020, June 18 Litho. *Perf. 13¼x14*
406 A117 600c Sheet of 3, #a-c 20.00 20.00

All proceeds of the sale of No. 406 were donated to Voedselbank Curaçao charity.

Sports — A118

Designs: 1, Soccer. 2, Baseball, 331c, Basketball. 335c, Cycling, horiz. 474c, Tennis. 739c, Sailing, horiz.

Perf. 13¼x14, 14x13¼

2020, Aug. 19 Litho.
407-412 A118 Set of 6 24.50 24.50

On day of issue, No. 407 sold for 127c and No. 408 sold for 192c,

Birds — A119

Designs: 70c, Blue-and-yellow macaw. 1, Green-headed tanager. 2, Masked trogon. 331c, Guianan toucan. 474c, Blue-crowned motmot. 739c, Toucan barbet.

2020, Sept. 20 Litho. *Perf. 11¼x12*
413-418 A119 Set of 6 21.50 21.50

Miniature Sheet

Presidents of the United States — A120

No. 419: a, 100c, George Washington (1732-99). b, 160c, Abraham Lincoln (1809-65). c, 320c, Franklin D. Roosevelt (1882-1945). d, 350c, John F. Kennedy (1917-63). e, Ronald Reagan (1911-2004). f, 440c, Barack Obama. g, 450c, Donald Trump.

2020, Oct. 6 Litho. *Perf. 13¾x13½*
419 A120 Sheet of 7, #a-g 25.00 25.00

Antique Automobiles A121

Designs: 70c, 1956 Ford Fairlane Sunliner. No. 421, 1, 1936 Buick Victoria Special. No. 422, 1, 1949 Packard Clipper. No. 423, 2, 1923 Ford Model T Touring Car. No. 424, 2, 1937 Ford Deluxe Convertible. 331c, 1956 Packard 400. 335c, 1948 Chevrolet Stylemaster. 474c, 1952 Dodge Coronet Gyro-matic. 739c, 1953 Chevrolet Bel Air.

2020, Oct. 31 Litho. ***Perf. 13¼x12¾***

420-428	A121	Set of 9	29.00	29.00

On day of issue, Nos. 421 and 422 each sold for 128c and Nos. 423 and 424 each sold for 193c.

SEMI-POSTAL STAMPS

Youth Care — SP1

Rabbit: 63c+26c, Writing molecular diagram on blackboard, molecular model. 112c+45c, With chemicals in test tubes and flasks. 166c+75c, Conducting experiment with plants and chemicals. 285c+125c, In rocket ship.

2011, Oct. 11 Litho. ***Perf. 12¾x13¼***

B1-B4	SP1	Set of 4	10.00	10.00

Intl. Year of Chemistry.

Intl. Year of Cooperatives SP2

Stylized people and: 64c+26c, Construction tools, bird. 190c+75c, Rowboat, fish. 293c+125c, Rowboat, house, flower, bird, fish.

2012, Oct. 9 ***Perf. 13¼x12¾***

B5-B7	SP2	Set of 3	8.75	8.75

SP3

SP4

SP5

Abolition of Slavery, 150th Anniv. — SP6

2013, July 1 Litho. ***Perf. 13¼x12¾***

B8	SP3	65c +25c multi	1.00	1.00
B9	SP4	118c +45c multi	1.90	1.90
B10	SP5	175c +75c multi	2.75	2.75
B11	SP6	301c +125c multi	4.75	4.75
		Nos. B8-B11 (4)	10.40	10.40

Wladimir "Coco" Balantien, Holder of New Record for Home Runs in a Japanese Baseball Season — SP7

2013, Dec. 2 Litho. ***Perf. 12¾x13¼***

B12	SP7	118c +100c multi	2.50	2.50

Pronunciation Symbols

ə .... banana, collide, abut

ˈə, ˌə .... humdrum, abut

ə .... immediately preceding \l\, \n\, \m\, \ŋ\, as in battle, mitten, eaten, and sometimes open \ˈō-p^{ə}m\, lock and key \-^{ə}ŋ-\; immediately following \l\, \m\, \r\, as often in French table, prisme, titre

ər .... further, merger, bird

ˈər- / ˈə-r .... as in two different pronunciations of hurry \ˈhər-ē, ˈhə-rē\

a .... mat, map, mad, gag, snap, patch

ā .... day, fade, date, aorta, drape, cape

ä .... bother, cot, and, with most American speakers, father, cart

ȧ .... father as pronounced by speakers who do not rhyme it with *bother*; French patte

au̇ .... now, loud, out

b .... baby, rib

ch .... chin, nature \ˈnā-chər\

d .... did, adder

e .... bet, bed, peck

ˈē, ˌē .... beat, nosebleed, evenly, easy

ē .... easy, mealy

f .... fifty, cuff

g .... go, big, gift

h .... hat, ahead

hw .... whale as pronounced by those who do not have the same pronunciation for both *whale* and *wail*

i .... tip, banish, active

ī .... site, side, buy, tripe

j .... job, gem, edge, join, judge

k .... kin, cook, ache

k̲ .... German ich, Buch; one pronunciation of loch

l .... lily, pool

m .... murmur, dim, nymph

n .... no, own

^{n} .... indicates that a preceding vowel or diphthong is pronounced with the nasal passages open, as in French *un bon vin blanc* \œ^{n} -bō^{n} -va^{n} -blä^{n}\

ŋ .... sing \ˈsiŋ\, singer \ˈsiŋ-ər\, finger \ˈfiŋ-gər\, ink \ˈiŋk \

ō .... bone, know, beau

ȯ .... saw, all, gnaw, caught

œ .... French boeuf, German Hölle

œ̄ .... French feu, German Höhle

ȯi .... coin, destroy

p .... pepper, lip

r .... red, car, rarity

s .... source, less

sh .... as in shy, mission, machine, special (actually, this is a single sound, not two); with a hyphen between, two sounds as in *grasshopper* \ˈgras-ˌhä-pər\

t .... tie, attack, late, later, latter

th .... as in thin, ether (actually, this is a single sound, not two); with a hyphen between, two sounds as in *knighthood* \ˈnīt-ˌhu̇d\

th̲ .... then, either, this (actually, this is a single sound, not two)

ü .... rule, youth, union \ˈyün-yən\, few \ˈfyü\

u̇ .... pull, wood, book, curable \ˈkyu̇r-ə-bəl\, fury \ˈfyu̇r-ē\

ue .... German füllen, hübsch

u̅e̅ .... French rue, German fühlen

v .... vivid, give

w .... we, away

y .... yard, young, cue \ˈkyü\, mute \ˈmyüt\, union \ˈyün-yən\

^{y} .... indicates that during the articulation of the sound represented by the preceding character the front of the tongue has substantially the position it has for the articulation of the first sound of *yard*, as in French *digne* \dēn^{y}\

z .... zone, raise

zh .... as in vision, azure \ˈa-zhər\ (actually, this is a single sound, not two); with a hyphen between, two sounds as in *hogshead* \ˈhȯgz-ˌhed, ˈhägz-\

\ .... slant line used in pairs to mark the beginning and end of a transcription: \ˈpen\

ˈ .... mark preceding a syllable with primary (strongest) stress: \ˈpen-mən-ˌship\

ˌ .... mark preceding a syllable with secondary (medium) stress: \ˈpen-mən-ˌship\

\- .... mark of syllable division

( ) .... indicate that what is symbolized between is present in some utterances but not in others: *factory* \ˈfak-t(ə-)rē\

÷ .... indicates that many regard as unacceptable the pronunciation variant immediately following: *cupola* \ˈkyü-pə-lə, ÷-ˌlō\

INDEX AND IDENTIFIER

All page numbers shown are those in this Volume 2A.

Postage stamps that do not have English words on them are shown in the Scott Stamp Illustrated Identifier. To purchase it visit AmosAdvantage.com or call Amos Media at 800-572-6885.

INDEX TO ADVERTISERS 2022 VOLUME 2 A

2022
VOLUME 2A
DEALER DIRECTORY
YELLOW PAGE LISTINGS

This section of your Scott Catalogue contains advertisements to help you conveniently find what you need, when you need it...!

Aerophilately

HENRY GITNER PHILATELISTS, INC.
PO Box 3077-S
Middletown, NY 10940
PH: 845-343-5151
PH: 800-947-8267
FAX: 845-343-0068
hgitner@hgitner.com
www.hgitner.com

Appraisals

DR. ROBERT FRIEDMAN & SONS STAMP & COIN BUYING CENTER
2029 W. 75th St.
Woodridge, IL 60517
PH: 800-588-8100
FAX: 630-985-1588
stampcollections@drbobstamps.com
www.drbobfriedmanstamps.com

Asia

KELLEHER & ROGERS LTD.
22 Shelter Rock Lane, Unit #53
Danbury, CT 06810
PH: 203-830-2500
Toll Free: 800-212-2830
info@kelleherauctions.com
www.kelleherauctions.com

Auctions

DUTCH COUNTRY AUCTIONS
The Stamp Center
4115 Concord Pike
Wilmington, DE 19803
PH: 302-478-8740
FAX: 302-478-8779
auctions@dutchcountryauctions.com
www.dutchcountryauctions.com

KELLEHER & ROGERS LTD.
22 Shelter Rock Lane, Unit #53
Danbury, CT 06810
PH: 203-830-2500
Toll Free: 800-212-2830
info@kelleherauctions.com
www.kelleherauctions.com

OAKWOOD AUCTIONS
18 Ringwood Dr., Unit #1
Stouffville, ON L4A 8C1
Canada
PH: 905-591-7600
info@oakwoodauctions.com
www.oakwoodauctions.com

British Commonwealth

COLLECTORS EXCHANGE ORLANDO STAMP SHOP
1814A Edgewater Drive
Orlando, FL 32804
PH: 407-620-0908
PH: 407-947-8603
FAX: 407-730-2131
jlatter@cfl.rr.com
www.OrlandoStampShop.com

ARON R. HALBERSTAM PHILATELISTS, LTD.
PO Box 150168
Van Brunt Station
Brooklyn, NY 11215-0168
PH: 718-788-3978
arh@arhstamps.com
www.arhstamps.com

ROY'S STAMPS
PO Box 28001
600 Ontario Street
St. Catharines, ON
CANADA L2N 7P8
Phone: 905-934-8377
Email: roystamp@cogeco.ca
www.roysstamps.com

British Commonwealth

THE STAMP ACT
PO Box 1136
Belmont, CA 94002
PH: 650-703-2342
thestampact@sbcglobal.net

WORLDSTAMPS/ FRANK GEIGER PHILATELISTS
PO Box 4743
Pinehurst, NC 28374
PH: 910-295-2048
Frank@WorldStamps.com
www.WorldStamps.com

Buying

DR. ROBERT FRIEDMAN & SONS STAMP & COIN BUYING CENTER
2029 W. 75th St.
Woodridge, IL 60517
PH: 800-588-8100
FAX: 630-985-1588
stampcollections@drbobstamps.com
www.drbobfriedmanstamps.com

Canada

CANADA STAMP FINDER
PO Box 92591
Brampton, ON L6W 4R1
PH: 514-238-5751
Toll Free in North America:
877-412-3106
FAX: 323-315-2635
canadastampfinder@gmail.com
www.canadastampfinder.com

ROY'S STAMPS
PO Box 28001
600 Ontario Street
St. Catharines, ON
CANADA L2N 7P8
Phone: 905-934-8377
Email: roystamp@cogeco.ca
www.roysstamps.com

WORLDSTAMPS/ FRANK GEIGER PHILATELISTS
PO Box 4743
Pinehurst, NC 28374
PH: 910-295-2048
Frank@WorldStamps.com
www.WorldStamps.com

China

KELLEHER & ROGERS LTD.
22 Shelter Rock Lane, Unit #53
Danbury, CT 06810
PH: 203-830-2500
Toll Free: 800-212-2830
info@kelleherauctions.com
www.kelleherauctions.com

THE STAMP ACT
PO Box 1136
Belmont, CA 94002
PH: 650-703-2342
thestampact@sbcglobal.net

Collections

DR. ROBERT FRIEDMAN & SONS STAMP & COIN BUYING CENTER
2029 W. 75th St.
Woodridge, IL 60517
PH: 800-588-8100
FAX: 630-985-1588
stampcollections@drbobstamps.com
www.drbobfriedmanstamps.com

Czechoslovakia

WORLDSTAMPS/ FRANK GEIGER PHILATELISTS
PO Box 4743
Pinehurst, NC 28374
PH: 910-295-2048
Frank@WorldStamps.com
www.WorldStamps.com

Ducks

MICHAEL JAFFE
PO Box 61484
Vancouver, WA 98666
PH: 360-695-6161
PH: 800-782-6770
FAX: 360-695-1616
mjaffe@brookmanstamps.com
www.brookmanstamps.com

Europe-Western

WORLDSTAMPS/ FRANK GEIGER PHILATELISTS
PO Box 4743
Pinehurst, NC 28374
PH: 910-295-2048
Frank@WorldStamps.com
www.WorldStamps.com

Falkland Islands

WORLDSTAMPS/ FRANK GEIGER PHILATELISTS
PO Box 4743
Pinehurst, NC 28374
PH: 910-295-2048
Frank@WorldStamps.com
www.WorldStamps.com

France & Colonies

E. JOSEPH McCONNELL, INC.
PO Box 683
Monroe, NY 10949
PH: 845-783-9791
FAX: 845-782-0347
ejstamps@gmail.com
www.EJMcConnell.com

WORLDSTAMPS/ FRANK GEIGER PHILATELISTS
PO Box 4743
Pinehurst, NC 28374
PH: 910-295-2048
Frank@WorldStamps.com
www.WorldStamps.com

French S. Antarctic

E. JOSEPH McCONNELL, INC.
PO Box 683
Monroe, NY 10949
PH: 845-783-9791
FAX: 845-782-0347
ejstamps@gmail.com
www.EJMcConnell.com

WORLDSTAMPS/ FRANK GEIGER PHILATELISTS
PO Box 4743
Pinehurst, NC 28374
PH: 910-295-2048
Frank@WorldStamps.com
www.WorldStamps.com

British Commonwealth

Japan

KELLEHER & ROGERS LTD.
22 Shelter Rock Lane, Unit #53
Danbury, CT 06810
PH: 203-830-2500
Toll Free: 800-212-2830
info@kelleherauctions.com
www.kelleherauctions.com

Korea

KELLEHER & ROGERS LTD.
22 Shelter Rock Lane, Unit #53
Danbury, CT 06810
PH: 203-830-2500
Toll Free: 800-212-2830
info@kelleherauctions.com
www.kelleherauctions.com

Manchukuo

KELLEHER & ROGERS LTD.
22 Shelter Rock Lane, Unit #53
Danbury, CT 06810
PH: 203-830-2500
Toll Free: 800-212-2830
info@kelleherauctions.com
www.kelleherauctions.com

Middle East - Arab

KELLEHER & ROGERS LTD.
22 Shelter Rock Lane, Unit #53
Danbury, CT 06810
PH: 203-830-2500
Toll Free: 800-212-2830
info@kelleherauctions.com
www.kelleherauctions.com

New Issues

DAVIDSON'S STAMP SERVICE
Personalized Service since 1970
PO Box 36355
Indianapolis, IN 46236-0355
PH: 317-826-2620
ed-davidson@earthlink.net
www.newstampissues.com

Proofs & Essays

HENRY GITNER PHILATELISTS, INC.
PO Box 3077-S
Middletown, NY 10940
PH: 845-343-5151
PH: 800-947-8267
FAX: 845-343-0068
hgitner@hgitner.com
www.hgitner.com

Stamp Stores

Delaware

DUTCH COUNTRY AUCTIONS
The Stamp Center
4115 Concord Pike
Wilmington, DE 19803
PH: 302-478-8740
FAX: 302-478-8779
auctions@dutchcountryauctions.com
www.dutchcountryauctions.com

Florida

DR. ROBERT FRIEDMAN & SONS STAMP & COIN BUYING CENTER
PH: 800-588-8100
FAX: 630-985-1588
stampcollections@drbobstamps.com
www.drbobfriedmanstamps.com

Stamp Stores

Illinois

DR. ROBERT FRIEDMAN & SONS STAMP & COIN BUYING CENTER
2029 W. 75th St.
Woodridge, IL 60517
PH: 800-588-8100
FAX: 630-985-1588
stampcollections@drbobstamps.com
www.drbobfriedmanstamps.com

New Jersey

BERGEN STAMPS & COLLECTIBLES
306 Queen Anne Rd.
Teaneck, NJ 07666
PH: 201-836-8987
bergenstamps@gmail.com

TRENTON STAMP & COIN
Thomas DeLuca
Store: Forest Glen Plaza
1804 Highway #33
Hamilton Square, NJ 08690
Mail: PO Box 8574
Trenton, NJ 08650
PH: 609-584-8100
FAX: 609-587-8664
TOMD4TSC@aol.com
www.trentonstampandcoin.com

New York

CK STAMPS
42-14 Union St. # 2A
Flushing, NY 11355
PH: 917-667-6641
ckstampsllc@yahoo.com

Ohio

HILLTOP STAMP SERVICE
Richard A. Peterson
PO Box 626
Wooster, OH 44691
PH: 330-262-8907 (0)
PH: 330-201-1377 (H)
hilltopstamps@sssnet.com
www.hilltopstamps.com

Supplies

BROOKLYN GALLERY COIN & STAMP, INC.
8725 4th Ave.
Brooklyn, NY 11209
PH: 718-745-5701
FAX: 718-745-2775
info@brooklyngallery.com
www.brooklyngallery.com

Topicals

E. JOSEPH McCONNELL, INC.
PO Box 683
Monroe, NY 10949
PH: 845-783-9791
FAX: 845-782-0347
ejstamps@gmail.com
www.EJMcConnell.com

WORLDSTAMPS/ FRANK GEIGER PHILATELISTS
PO Box 4743
Pinehurst, NC 28374
PH: 910-295-2048
Frank@WorldStamps.com
www.WorldStamps.com

Topicals - Columbus

MR. COLUMBUS
PO Box 1492
Fennville, MI 49408
PH: 269-543-4755
David@MrColumbus1492.com
www.MrColumbus1492.com

Topicals - Miscellaneous

HENRY GITNER PHILATELISTS, INC.
PO Box 3077-S
Middletown, NY 10940
PH: 845-343-5151
PH: 800-947-8267
FAX: 845-343-0068
hgitner@hgitner.com
www.hgitner.com

United Nations

BRUCE M. MOYER
Box 12031
Charlotte, NC 28220
PH: 908-237-6967
moyer@unstamps.com
www.unstamps.com

United States

ACS STAMP COMPANY
2914 W 135th Ave
Broomfield, Colorado 80020
303-841-8666
www.ACSStamp.com

BROOKMAN STAMP CO.
PO Box 90
Vancouver, WA 98666
PH: 360-695-1391
PH: 800-545-4871
FAX: 360-695-1616
info@brookmanstamps.com
www.brookmanstamps.com

U.S. Classics/Moderns

BARDO STAMPS
PO Box 7437
Buffalo Grove, IL 60089
PH: 847-634-2676
jfb7437@aol.com
www.bardostamps.com

U.S.-Collections Wanted

DUTCH COUNTRY AUCTIONS
The Stamp Center
4115 Concord Pike
Wilmington, DE 19803
PH: 302-478-8740
FAX: 302-478-8779
auctions@dutchcountryauctions.com
www.dutchcountryauctions.com

DR. ROBERT FRIEDMAN & SONS STAMP & COIN BUYING CENTER
2029 W. 75th St.
Woodridge, IL 60517
PH: 800-588-8100
FAX: 630-985-1588
stampcollections@drbobstamps.com
www.drbobfriedmanstamps.com

Wanted - Worldwide Collections

DUTCH COUNTRY AUCTIONS
The Stamp Center
4115 Concord Pike
Wilmington, DE 19803
PH: 302-478-8740
FAX: 302-478-8779
auctions@dutchcountryauctions.com
www.dutchcountryauctions.com

Websites

ACS STAMP COMPANY
2914 W 135th Ave
Broomfield, Colorado 80020
303-841-8666
www.ACSStamp.com

Wholesale

HENRY GITNER PHILATELISTS, INC.
PO Box 3077-S
Middletown, NY 10940
PH: 845-343-5151
PH: 800-947-8267
FAX: 845-343-0068
hgitner@hgitner.com
www.hgitner.com

Worldwide

KELLEHER & ROGERS LTD.
22 Shelter Rock Lane, Unit #53
Danbury, CT 06810
PH: 203-830-2500
Toll Free: 800-212-2830
info@kelleherauctions.com
www.kelleherauctions.com

GUILLERMO JALIL
Maipu 466, local 4
1006 Buenos Aires
Argentina
guillermo@jalilstamps.com
philatino@philatino.com
www.philatino.com (worldwide stamp auctions)
www.jalilstamps.com (direct sale, worldwide stamps)

Worldwide-Collections

DR. ROBERT FRIEDMAN & SONS STAMP & COIN BUYING CENTER
2029 W. 75th St.
Woodridge, IL 60517
PH: 800-588-8100
FAX: 630-985-1588
stampcollections@drbobstamps.com
www.drbobfriedmanstamps.com